DICCIONARIO
MANUAL
ESPAÑOL-INGLÉS
INGLÉS-ESPAÑOL

CONCISE
SPANISH-ENGLISH
ENGLISH-SPANISH
DICTIONARY

LAROUSSE

DICCIONARIO MANUAL

ESPAÑOL-INGLÉS
INGLÉS-ESPAÑOL

LAROUSSE

© **Larousse-Bordas, 1998**
© Larousse, 1993

2-03-420403-4 (hardcover edition)
2-03-420402-6 (paperback edition)
Distribución/Sales Larousse Kingfisher Chambers Inc., New York

Library of Congress Catalog Card Number
97-76154

ISBN 2-03-430500-0
Distribución/Sales Thomas Nelson & Sons Ltd, Surrey, England

LAROUSSE

CONCISE

SPANISH-ENGLISH

ENGLISH-SPANISH

DICTIONARY

LAROUSSE

Realizado por/Produced by
LAROUSSE
Idiomas • Language Reference

Dirección Editorial
General Editor

CATHERINE E. LOVE

Coordinación de la Obra
Coordinating Editors

JOAQUÍN BLASCO   ELVIRA DE MORAGAS   EDUARDO VALLEJO

Colaboradores
Editors

MONTSERRAT ALBERTE MONTSERRAT   TOM BARTLETT
JOSÉ Mª DÍAZ DE MENDÍVIL   CLAIRE EVANS CALDER
ELENA ESTREMERA PAÑOS   MARGARET JULL COSTA
ISABEL FERRER MARRADES   GILLA EVANS
CARMEN GONZÁLEZ BODEGUERO   WENDY LEE
ANNA JENÉ PALAT   HILARY MACARTNEY
SALUT LLONCH SOLER   HUGH O'DONNELL
JUDITH MEDALL CIRERA   KATHRYN PHILLIPS-MILES
VICTORIA ORDÓÑEZ DIVÍ   CLARE PLATER
MALIHE FORGHANI-NOWBARI   LEANE SHANKS
NÚRIA VILANOVA POUS   PATRICK WHITE

Informática Editorial
Data Management

GABINO ALONSO   CLAUDE NIMMO

Diseño
Design

FRÉDÉRIQUE LONGUÉPÉE

A NUESTROS LECTORES

El Diccionario MANUAL Larousse es la herramienta de trabajo ideal en una amplia gama de circunstancias, desde el aprendizaje de idiomas en la escuela y en casa hasta el uso diario en la oficina.

El MANUAL Español-Inglés Inglés-Español está pensado para responder rápida y eficazmente a los diferentes problemas que plantea la lectura del inglés actual y la redacción de trabajos escolares, cartas e informes.

Con sus más de 90.000 palabras y expresiones y por encima de las 120.000 traducciones, este diccionario permitirá al lector comprender con claridad un amplio espectro de textos literarios y periodísticos; entender documentos comerciales, folletos o manuales y realizar resúmenes y traducciones con rapidez y corrección.

De entre las características de esta obra, nueva en su totalidad, cabe destacar el tratamiento totalmente al día de siglas y abreviaturas, nombres propios, y términos comerciales e informáticos de uso frecuente.

A través de un tratamiento claro y detallado del vocabulario básico, de ejemplos de construcciones gramaticales y modismos, así como de los indicadores de sentido que guían hacia la traducción más adecuada, se permite al usuario escribir en inglés con precisión y seguridad.

Se ha puesto especial cuidado en la presentación de las entradas, tanto desde el punto de vista de su estructura como de la tipografía empleada. Para aquellos lectores que hayan superado el primer nivel de aprendizaje del inglés, pero no aspiren a alcanzar un grado de especialización en este lingua, el MANUAL es el diccionario ideal.

Le invitamos a que se ponga en contacto con nosotros si tiene cualquier observación o crítica que hacer; entre todos podemos hacer del MANUAL un diccionario aún mejor en el futuro.

EL EDITOR

TO OUR READERS

The Larousse CONCISE dictionary is the perfect companion for a wide variety of situations, from language learning at school and at home to everyday use in the office.

This Spanish dictionary is designed to provide fast and efficient solutions to the various problems encountered when reading present-day Spanish. It will also be an invaluable aid in preparing written work of all kinds, from schoolwork to letters and reports.

The CONCISE has over 90,000 references and 120,000 translations. It enables the user to read and enjoy a wide range of fiction and journalism, to understand trade literature, brochures and manuals, and to summarize and translate from Spanish quickly and accurately. This entirely new dictionary also features up-to-date coverage of common abbreviations and acronyms, proper names, business terms and computing vocabulary.

Writing Spanish accurately and confidently is no longer a problem thanks to the CONCISE's detailed coverage of essential vocabulary, and helpful sense-markers which guide the user to the most appropriate translation.

Careful thought has gone into the presentation of the entries, both in terms of layout and typography. For the user who has moved beyond beginners' level but is not intending to specialize in Spanish at an academic level, the CONCISE is the ideal reference work.

Send us your comments or queries - you will be helping us to make this dictionary an even better book in future.

THE PUBLISHER

ABBREVIATIONS _____ ABREVIATURAS

Grammatical, register
and regional labels

Etiquetas gramaticales,
estilísticas y dialectales

abbreviation	*abbr/abrev*	abreviatura
adjective	*adj*	adjetivo
adjective only used in feminine form	*adj f*	adjetivo femenino
adverb	*adv*	adverbio
American English	*Am*	inglés americano
Latin American Spanish	*Amer*	español latinoamericano
before noun	*antes de sust*	antes de sustantivo

indicates that the translation is always used attributively, i.e. directly before the noun which it modifies

indica que la traducción siempre se utiliza en inglés antepuesta al sustantivo al que modifica

article	*art*	artículo
Australian English	*Austr*	inglés australiano
auxiliary	*aux*	auxiliar
British English	*Br*	inglés británico
Canadian English	*Can*	inglés canadiense
compound	*comp*	sustantivo antepuesto a otro sustantivo con función de modificador

a noun used to modify another noun, e.g. gardening in gardening book or airforce in airforce base

p.ej. gardening en gardening book o airforce en airforce base

comparative	*compar*	comparativo
conjunction	*conj*	conjunción
continuous	*cont*	continuo
definite	*def*	determinado
demonstrative	*demos*	demostrativo
pejorative	*despec*	despectivo, peyorativo

implica un tono de desprecio o desaprobación, p.ej. villorrio, fregona, carca

dated	*desus*	desusado
especially	*esp*	especialmente

exclamation	*excl*	interjección
feminine noun	*f*	sustantivo femenino
informal	*fam*	familiar
figurative	*fig*	figurado
formal	*fml*	formal, culto
inseparable	*fus*	inseparable

*shows that a phrasal verb is "fused", i.e. inseparable, e.g. look after where the object can not come between the verb and the particle, e.g. I looked after him but not * I looked him after*

*indica que una locución verbal o "phrasal verb" (verbo + preposición o adverbio) es inseparable y el objeto no puede aparecer entre el verbo en sí y la partícula, p. ej. en look after se dice I looked after him no * I looked him after*

| generally, in most cases | *gen* | generalmente, en general |

identifies the most common translation of a word

suele indicar la traducción más común de una palabra

humorous	*hum*	humorístico
indefinite	*indef*	indeterminado
informal	*inf*	familiar
infinitive	*infin*	infinitivo
exclamation	*interj*	interjección
invariable	*inv*	invariable

applied to a noun to indicate that plural form same as singular, e.g. paréntesis m inv : los paréntesis, sheep pl inv : four sheep ; applied to a Spanish adjective to indicate that feminine and plural forms same as masculine, e.g. piloto adj inv : pisos piloto

indica que la forma plural de un sustantivo es igual a la del singular, p.ej. paréntesis m inv : los paréntesis, sheep pl inv : four sheep ; asimismo indica que un adjetivo español no varía ni en plural ni en femenino, p.ej. piloto adj inv : pisos piloto

| ironic | *iro/irón* | irónico |
| literal | *lit* | literal |

in conjunction with fig, shows that both a literal and figurative sense is being covered by the same translation

aparece sólo con la etiqueta fig e indica que la traducción abarca tanto el sentido literal como el figurado

phrase(s)	*loc*	locución, locuciones
adjectival phrase	*loc adj*	locución adjetiva
adverbial phrase	*loc adv*	locución adverbial
conjunctival phrase	*loc conj*	locución conjuntiva

| prepositional phrase | *loc prep* | locución preposicional |
| *adjectives, adverbs etc consisting of more than one word, e.g. a pesar de, a horcajadas, per cápita* | | *construcciones fijas de más de una palabra con función adjetiva, adverbial, etc; p.ej. a pesar de, a horcajadas, per cápita* |

masculine noun	*m*	sustantivo masculino
very informal	*mfam*	muy familiar
	m o f	sustantivo ambiguo
this label shows that the gender of the noun can be either masculine or feminine, e.g. azúcar m o f is sometimes masculine and sometimes feminine		*indica que el género del sustantivo es vacilante: a veces masculino, otras femenino; p. ej. azúcar m o f, a veces se usa "el azúcar", otras "la azúcar"*

| masculine or feminine noun | *m y f* | sustantivo masculino o femenino |
| *depending on gender, e.g. dentista m y f where you would say "un dentista" for a man and "una dentista" for a woman, camarero, -ra m y f where you would say "el camarero" for a man and "la camarera" for a woman, and gato, -ta m y f where you would say "el gato" for a male cat and "la gata" for a female cat* | | *según se refiera a un hombre o una mujer, p. ej. dentista m y f ("un dentista" o "una dentista"), camarero, -ra m y f ("el camarero" o "la camarera"), o a un animal macho o hembra, p. ej. gato, -ta m y f ("el gato" o "la gata")* |

noun	*n*	sustantivo
numeral	*num/núm*	número
oneself	*o.s.*	
pejorative	*pej*	peyorativo, despectivo
implies disapproval, e.g. bimbo, catty		

personal	*pers*	personal
phrase(s)	*phr*	locución, locuciones
plural	*pl*	plural
possessive	*poss/poses*	posesivo
past participle	*pp*	participio pasado
preposition	*prep*	preposición
pronoun	*pron*	pronombre
past tense	*pt*	pasado, pretérito
registered trademark	®	marca registrada
words considered to be trademarks have been designated in this dictionary by the symbol ®. However, neither the presence nor the absence of such designation should be regarded as affecting the legal status of any trademark.		*el símbolo ® indica que la palabra en cuestión se considera marca registrada. Hay que tener en cuenta, sin embargo, que ni la presencia ni la ausencia de dicho símbolo afectan a la situación legal de ninguna marca.*

relative	*relat*	relativo
someone, somebody	*sb*	
Scottish English	*Scot*	inglés escocés
separable	*sep*	separable

shows that a phrasal verb is separable, e.g. let in, help out where the object can come between the verb and the particle, I let her in, he helped me out

indica que una locución verbal o "phrasal verb" (verbo + preposición o adverbio) es separable y el objeto puede aparecer entre el verbo en sí y la partícula, p. ej. en let in, help out se dice I let her in, he helped me out

singular	*sg*	singular
slang	*sl*	argot
something	*sthg*	
subject	*subj/suj*	sujeto
superlative	*superl*	superlativo
uncountable noun	*U*	sustantivo "incontable"

i.e. an English noun which is never used in the plural or with "a"; used when the Spanish word is or can be a plural, e.g. infighting n (U) disputas fpl internas, balido m bleat, bleating (U)

esto es, sustantivo inglés que jamás se usa en plural o con el artículo "a"; utilizado cuando la palabra española es o puede ser plural, p. ej. infighting n (U) disputas fpl internas, balido m bleat, bleating (U)

usually	*usu*	normalmente
auxiliary verb	*vaux*	verbo auxiliar
verb	*vb/v*	verbo
intransitive verb	*vi*	verbo intransitivo
impersonal verb	*v impers*	verbo impersonal
always used with the subject "it"		*en inglés siempre con el sujeto "it"*
very informal	*v inf*	muy familiar
pronominal verb	*vpr*	verbo pronominal
transitive verb	*vt*	verbo transitivo
vulgar	*vulg*	vulgar
cultural equivalent	$\simeq$	equivalente cultural

| introduces a new part of speech within an entry | ◇ | introduce una nueva categoría gramatical dentro de una entrada |

| introduces a sub-entry, such as a plural form with its own specific meaning or a set phrase containing the headword (e.g. a phrasal verb or adverbial phrase) | ◆ | introduce una subentrada, como por ejemplo un plural que cambia de significado, un pronominal o una locución gramatical (adverbial, adjetiva, etc.) |

SPANISH VERBS

LOS VERBOS ESPAÑOLES

Spanish verbs have a number (from [4] to [81]) which refers to the conjugation table given at the back of the dictionary. This number is not repeated for reflexive verbs when these are sub-entries.

Los verbos españoles llevan un número (del [4] al [81]) que hace referencia a la tabla de conjugación que aparece al final de la obra. El número no se repite en los verbos pronominales cuando son subentradas.

SPANISH ALPHABETICAL ORDER _____

LA ORDENACIÓN ALFABÉTICA EN ESPAÑOL

As this dictionary follows international alphabetical order, the Spanish letter combinations ch and ll are **not** treated as separate letters. Thus entries with ch appear after cg and not at the end of c. Similarly, entries with ll appear after lk and not at the end of l. Note, however, that ñ <u>is</u> treated as a separate letter and follows n in alphabetical order.

En este diccionario se ha seguido la ordenación alfabética internacional ; por lo tanto, las consonantes ch y ll <u>no</u> se consideran letras aparte. Esto significa que las entradas con ch aparecerán después de cg y no al final de c ; del mismo modo las entradas con ll vendrán después de lk y no al final de l. Adviértase, sin embargo, que la letra ñ <u>sí</u> se considera letra aparte y sigue a la n en orden alfabético.

ENGLISH COMPOUNDS _____

LOS COMPUESTOS EN INGLÉS

A compound is a word or expression which has a single meaning but is made up of more than one word, e.g. **point of order**, **kiss of life**, **virtual reality**, **World Series** and **International Monetary Fund**. It is a feature of this dictionary that English compounds appear in the A-Z list in strict alphabetical order. The compound **blood pressure** will therefore come after **bloodless** which itself follows **blood group**.

En inglés se llama compuesto a una locución sustantiva de significado único pero formada por más de una palabra ; p.ej. **point of order**, **kiss of life**, **virtual reality**, **World Series** o **International Monetary Fund**. Uno de los rasgos distintivos de este diccionario es la inclusión de estos compuestos con entrada propia y en riguroso orden alfabético. De esta forma **blood pressure** vendrá después de **bloodless**, el cual sigue a **blood group**.

Administration, administrative	ADMIN	Administración
Aeronautics, aviation	AERON	Aeronáutica, aviación
Agriculture, farming	AGR	Agricultura
Anatomy	ANAT	Anatomía
Archeology	ARCHEOL	Arqueología
Architecture	ARCHIT/ARQUIT	Arquitectura
Astrology	ASTROL	Astrología
Astronomy	ASTRON	Astronomía
Automobile, cars	AUT(OM)	Automovilismo, coches
Biology	BIOL	Biología
Botany	BOT	Botánica
Chemistry	CHEM	Química
Cinema, film-making	CIN(EMA)	Cine
Commerce, business	COM(M)	Comercio, negocios
Computers, computer science	COMPUT	Informática
Construction, building	CONSTR	Construcción
Culinary, cooking	CULIN	Cocina
Sport	DEP	Deporte
Juridical, legal	DER	Derecho, jurídico
Ecology	ECOLOG	Ecología
Economics	ECON	Economía
School, education	EDUC	Educación
Electricity	ELEC(TR)	Electricidad
Electronics	ELECTRON/ELECTRÓN	Electrónica
Pharmacology, pharmaceuticals	FARM	Farmacología, farmacia
Railways	FERROC	Ferrocarril
Finance, financial	FIN	Finanzas
Physics	FÍS	Física
Photography	FOT	Fotografía
Soccer	FTBL	Fútbol
Geography, geographical	GEOGR	Geografía
Geology, geological	GEOL	Geología
Geometry	GEOM	Geometría
Grammar	GRAM(M)	Gramática
History	HIST	Historia
Industry	IND	Industria
Computers, computer science	INFORM	Informática
Juridical, legal	JUR	Derecho, jurídico
Linguistics	LING	Lingüística
Literature	LITER	Literatura
Mathematics	MAT(H)	Matemáticas
Mechanical Engineering	MEC	Mecánica
Medicine	MED	Medicina
Metallurgy	METAL	Metalurgia
Weather, meteorology, climatology	METEOR	Meteorología

Military, armed forces, armaments	MIL	Militar, fuerzas armadas, armamento
Mining	MIN	Minería
Mythology	MITOL	Mitología
Music	MUS/MÚS	Música
Mythology	MYTH	Mitología
Nautical, maritime	NAUT/NÁUT	Náutica, marítimo
Pharmacology, pharmaceutics	PHARM	Farmacología, farmacia
Photography	PHOT	Fotografía
Physics	PHYS	Física
Politics	POL(ÍT)	Política
Press, journalism	PRENS	Periodismo, prensa
Psychology, psychiatry	PSYCH/PSICOL	Psicología
Chemistry	QUÍM	Química
Railways	RAIL	Ferrocarril
Religion	RELIG	Religión
School, education	SCH	Educación
Sociology	SOCIOL	Sociología
Stock Exchange	ST EX	Bolsa
Bullfighting	TAUROM	Tauromaquia
Theatre	TEATR	Teatro
Technology, technical	TECH/TECN	Tecnología,técnico
Telecommunications	TELEC(OM)	Telecomunicaciones
Television	TV	Televisión
Printing, typography	TYPO	Imprenta
University	UNIV	Universidad
Veterinary science	VETER	Veterinaria
Zoology	ZOOL	Zoología

English Vowels
[ɪ] pit, big, rid
[e] pet, tend
[æ] pat, bag, mad
[ʌ] putt, cut
[ɒ] pot, log
[ʊ] put, full
[ə] mother, suppose

[iː] bean, weed
[ɑː] barn, car, laugh
[ɔː] born, lawn
[uː] loop, loose
[ɜː] burn, learn, bird

Vocales españolas
[i] piso, imagen
[e] tela, eso
[a] pata, amigo
[o] bola, otro
[u] luz, una

English Diphthongs
[eɪ] bay, late, great
[aɪ] buy, light, aisle
[ɔɪ] boy, foil
[əʊ] no, road, blow
[aʊ] now, shout, town
[ɪə] peer, fierce, idea
[eə] pair, bear, share
[ʊə] poor, sure, tour

Diptongos españoles
[ei] ley, peine
[ai] aire, caiga
[oi] soy, boina
[au] causa, aura
[eu] Europa, feudo

Semi-vowels
you, spaniel	[j]	hierba, miedo
wet, why, twin	[w]	agua, hueso

Semivocales

Consonants
pop, people	[p]	papá, campo
bottle, bib	[b]	vaca, bomba
	[ß]	curvo, caballo
train, tip	[t]	toro, pato
dog, did	[d]	donde, caldo
come, kitchen	[k]	que, cosa
gag, great	[g]	grande, guerra
	[ɣ]	aguijón, bulldog
chain, wretched	[ʧ]	ocho, chusma
jig, fridge	[dʒ]	
fib, physical	[f]	fui, afable
vine, livid	[v]	
think, fifth	[θ]	cera, paz
this, with	[ð]	cada, pardo
seal, peace	[s]	solo, paso

Consonantes

zip, hi**s**	[z]	
sheep, ma**ch**ine	[ʃ]	
u**s**ual, mea**s**ure	[ʒ]	
	[x]	**g**ema, **j**amón
how, per**h**aps	[h]	
metal, co**mb**	[m]	**m**adre, ca**m**a
night, di**nn**er	[n]	**n**o, pe**n**a
su**ng**, par**k**ing	[ŋ]	
	[ɲ]	ca**ñ**a
li**tt**le, he**lp**	[l]	a**l**a, **l**uz
right, ca**rr**y	[r]	ata**r**, pa**r**o
	[rr]	pe**rr**o, **r**osa
	[ʎ]	**ll**ave, co**ll**ar

The symbol ['] indicates that the following syllable carries primary stress and the symbol [ˌ] that the following syllable carries secondary stress.

The symbol [ʳ] in English phonetics indicates that the final "r" is pronounced only when followed by a word beginning with a vowel. Note that it is nearly always pronounced in American English.

Since Spanish pronunciation follows regular rules, phonetics are only provided in this dictionary for loan words from other languages, when these are difficult to pronounce. All one-word English headwords have phonetics. For English compound headwords, whether hyphenated or of two or more words, phonetics are given for any element which does not appear elsewhere in the dictionary as a headword in its own right.

Los símbolos ['] y [ˌ] indican que la sílaba siguiente lleva un acento primario o secundario respectivamente.

El símbolo [ʳ] en fonética inglesa indica que la "r" al final de palabra se pronuncia sólo cuando precede a una palabra que comienza por vocal. Adviértase que casi siempre se pronuncia en inglés americano.

Las palabras españolas no llevan transcripción fonética en este diccionario; sólo algunos préstamos lingüísticos procedentes de otras lenguas y de difícil pronunciación aparecen transcritos. Todas las entradas inglesas que constan de una palabra llevan transcripción fonética. En el caso de los compuestos ingleses (ya sea cuando lleven guiones o cuando no) se proporciona la transcripción fonética de todo aquel elemento que no aparezca en alguna otra parte del diccionario como entrada en sí misma.

a¹ (*pl* aes), **A** (*pl* Aes) *f* [letra] a, A.

a² *prep* (*a* + *el* = **al**) **-1.** [periodo de tiempo]: **a las pocas semanas** a few weeks later; **al mes de casados** a month after they were married; **al día siguiente** the following day. **-2.** [momento preciso] at; **a las siete** at seven o'clock; **a los 11 años** at the age of 11; **al caer la noche** at nightfall; **al oír la noticia se desmayó** on hearing the news, she fainted. **-3.** [frecuencia] per, every; **40 horas a la semana** 40 hours per ○ a week; **tres veces al día** three times a day. **-4.** [dirección] to; **voy a Sevilla** I'm going to Seville; **me voy al extranjero** I'm going abroad; **llegó a Barcelona/la fiesta** he arrived in Barcelona/at the party. **-5.** [posición]: **a la puerta** at the door; **está a la derecha/izquierda** it's on the right/left; **a orillas del mar** by the sea. **-6.** [distancia]: **está a más de cien kilómetros** it's more than a hundred kilometres away. **-7.** [con complemento indirecto] to; **dáselo a Juan** give it to Juan; **dile a Juan que venga** tell Juan to come. **-8.** [con complemento directo]: **quiere a sus hijos/su gato** she loves her children/her cat; **me cuidan como a un enfermo** they look after me as if I was ○ like an invalid. **-9.** [cantidad, medida, precio]: **a cientos/miles/docenas** by the hundred/thousand/dozen; **la leche se vende a litros** milk is sold by the litre ○ in litres; **¿a cuánto están las peras?** how much are the pears?; **tiene las peras a cien pesetas** she's selling pears for ○ at a hundred pesetas; **ganaron tres a cero** they won three nil. **-10.** [modo]: **lo hace a la antigua** he does it the old way; **a lo bestia** rudely; **a lo grande** in style; **a lo Mozart** after Mozart, in Mozart's style; **a escondidas** secretly. **-11.** [instrumento]: **escribir a máquina** to use a typewriter; **a lá-**piz in pencil; **a mano** by hand; **olla a presión** pressure cooker. **-12.** (*después de verbo y antes de infin*) [finalidad] to; **entró a pagar** he came in to pay; **aprender a nadar** to learn to swim. **-13.** (*después de sust y antes de infin*) [complemento de nombre]: **sueldo a convenir** salary to be agreed; **temas a tratar** matters to be discussed. **-14.** (*antes de infin*) [condición]: **a no ser por mí, hubieses fracasado** had it not been for me, you would have failed. **-15.** [en oraciones imperativas]: **¡a la cama!** go to bed!; **¡a callar todo el mundo!** quiet, everyone!; **¡a bailar!** let's dance! **-16.** (*antes de "por"*) [en busca de]: **ir a por pan** to go for bread. **-17.** [indica desafío]: **¿a que no lo haces?** I bet you won't do it!

AA ○ *mpl* (*abrev de* **Alcohólicos Anónimos**)
AA. ○ *fpl* (*abrev de* **Aerolíneas Argentinas**) AA.

AA EE *abrev de* **Ministerio de Asuntos Exteriores.**

ABA (*abrev de* **Agentes de Bolsa Asociados**) *mpl Spanish association of stockbrokers.*

ábaco *m* abacus.

abad, -desa *m y f* abbot (*f* abbess).

abadía *f* abbey.

abajo ○ *adv* **-1.** [posición - gen] below; [- en edificio] downstairs; **vive (en el piso de)** ~ she lives downstairs; **está aquí/allí** ~ it's down here/there; ~ **del todo** right at the bottom; **más** ~ further down. **-2.** [dirección] down; **ve** ~ [en edificio] go downstairs; **hacia/para** ~ down, downwards; **calle/escaleras** ~ down the street/stairs; **río** ~ downstream. **-3.** [en un texto] below.
○ *interj*: **¡**~ **...!** down with ...!; **¡**~ **la dictadura!** down with the dictatorship!
◆ **abajo de** *loc prep* less than.

◆ **de abajo** *loc adj* bottom; **el estante de ~** the bottom shelf.

abalanzarse [13] *vpr*: **~ sobre** to fall upon; **~ hacia** to rush towards.

abalear *vt Amer* to shoot.

abalorio *m* (*gen pl*) **-1.** [cuenta] glass bead. **-2.** [bisutería] trinket.

abanderado *m lit* & *fig* standard-bearer.

abandonado, -da *adj* **-1.** [desierto] deserted. **-2.** [desamparado] abandoned. **-3.** [descuidado - persona] unkempt; [- jardín, casa] neglected.

abandonar *vt* **-1.** [gen] to abandon; [lugar, profesión, cónyuge] to leave. **-2.** [desatender - obligaciones, estudios] to neglect.

◆ **abandonarse** *vpr* **-1.** [de aspecto] to neglect o.s., to let o.s. go. **-2.** [a una emoción]: **~se a** [desesperación, dolor] to succumb to; [vicio] to give o.s. over to.

abandono *m* **-1.** [acción - gen] abandonment; [- de lugar, profesión, cónyuge] leaving; [- de obligaciones, estudios] neglect. **-2.** [estado] state of abandon. **-3.** DEP: **ganar por ~** to win by default.

abanicar [10] *vt* to fan.

◆ **abanicarse** *vpr* to fan o.s.

abanico *m* **-1.** [para dar aire] fan. **-2.** *fig* [gama] range.

abaratar *vt* to reduce the price of.

◆ **abaratarse** *vpr* to go down in price, to become cheaper.

abarca *f* (*gen pl*) *type of sandal worn by country people.*

abarcar [10] *vt* **-1.** [incluir] to embrace, to cover; **quien mucho abarca poco aprieta** *proverb* don't bite off more than you can chew. **-2.** [ver] to be able to see, to have a view of.

abaritonado, -da *adj* baritone.

abarque *etc* → abarcar.

abarquillar *vt* [madera] to warp; [metal] to buckle; [cartón] to bend at the edges.

◆ **abarquillarse** *vpr* [madera] to warp; [metal] to buckle; [cartón] to curl up at the edges.

abarrotado, -da *adj*: **~ (de)** [teatro, autobús] packed (with); [desván, baúl] crammed (with).

abarrotar *vt*: **~ algo (de** O **con)** [teatro, autobús] to pack sthg (with); [desván, baúl] to cram sthg full (of).

abarrotería *f Amer* grocer's (store).

abarrotero, -ra *m y f Amer* grocer.

abarrotes *mpl Amer* groceries.

abastecer [30] *vt*: **~ algo/a alguien (de)** to supply sthg/sb (with).

◆ **abastecerse** *vpr*: **~se (de algo)** to stock up (on sthg).

abastecimiento *m* supply, supplying.

abasto *m*: **no dar ~ (a algo/para hacer algo)** to be unable to cope (with sthg/with doing sthg).

abate *m* ≃ abbé, *title given to French and Italian priests.*

abatible *adj* folding.

abatido, -da *adj* dejected.

abatir *vt* **-1.** [derribar - muro] to knock down; [- avión] to shoot down; [- árbol] to flatten. **-2.** [desanimar] to depress.

◆ **abatirse** *vpr*: **~se (sobre)** to swoop (down on).

abdicación *f* abdication.

abdicar [10] ◇ *vt*: **~ el trono (en alguien)** to abdicate the throne (in favour of sb). ◇ *vi* to abdicate; **~ de algo** *fig* to renounce sthg.

abdomen *m* abdomen.

abdominal *adj* abdominal.

◆ **abdominales** *mpl* sit-ups.

abecé *m lit* & *fig* ABC.

abecedario *m* **-1.** [alfabeto] alphabet. **-2.** [libro] spelling book.

abedul *m* birch (tree).

abeja *f* bee; **~ obrera** worker (bee); **~ reina** queen (bee).

abejorro *m* bumblebee.

aberración *f* perverse O evil thing.

aberrante *adj* perverse, evil.

abertura *f* opening.

abertzale [aßer'tʃale] *adj, m y f* Basque nationalist.

abeto *m* fir.

abierto, -ta ◇ *pp* → abrir. ◇ *adj* **-1.** [gen] open; **dejar el grifo ~** to leave the tap on; **estar ~ a** to be open to; **bien** O **muy ~** wide open. **-2.** *fig* [liberal] open-minded.

abigarrado, -da *adj* multi-coloured; *fig* motley.

abisal *adj* [fosa] very deep.

abismal *adj* vast, colossal.

abismar *vt* **-1.** [hundir] to engulf. **-2.** [abatir]: **~ a alguien en algo** to plunge sb into sthg.

◆ **abismarse** *vpr*: **~se en** [lectura] to be engrossed O absorbed in; [dolor] to be overwhelmed with.

abismo *m* **-1.** [profundidad] abyss; **estar al borde del ~** to be on the brink of ruin. **-2.** *fig* [diferencia] gulf.

Abiyán Abidjan.

abjurar [culto] ◇ *vt* to abjure. ◇ *vi*: **~ de algo** to abjure sthg.

ablandamiento *m* softening.

ablandar *vt* **-1.** [material] to soften. **-2.** *fig* [persona] to move; [actitud, rigor] to soften; [ira] to calm.

◆ **ablandarse** *vpr* **-1.** [material] to soften, to become softer. **-2.** *fig* [persona] to be moved; [actitud, rigor] to become softer; [ira] to cool off.

ablativo *m* ablative; ~ **absoluto** ablative absolute.

ablución *f* (*gen pl*) ablution.

ablusado, -da *adj* loose, baggy.

abnegación *f* abnegation, self-denial.

abnegarse [35] *vpr* to deny o.s.

abobado, -da *adj* **-1.** [estupefacto] blank, uncomprehending. **-2.** [estúpido] stupid.

abocado, -da *adj*: ~ **a** destined ○ doomed to.

abochornar *vt* to embarrass.

◆ **abochornarse** *vpr* to get embarrassed.

abofetear *vt* to slap.

abogacía *f* legal profession.

abogado, -da *m y f* **-1.** DER lawyer; ~ **defensor** counsel for the defence; ~ **del estado** public prosecutor; ~ **laboralista** labour lawyer; ~ **de oficio** legal aid lawyer. **-2.** *fig* [intercesor] intermediary; [defensor] advocate; ~ **del diablo** devil's advocate.

abogar [16] *vi* **-1.** DER to plead. **-2.** *fig* [defender]: ~ **por algo** to advocate sthg; ~ **por alguien** to stand up for sb.

abolengo *m* lineage; **de (rancio)** ~ of noble lineage.

abolición *f* abolition.

abolicionismo *m* abolitionism.

abolicionista *adj, m y f* abolitionist.

abolir [78] *vt* to abolish.

abolladura *f* dent.

abollar *vt* to dent.

◆ **abollarse** *vpr* to get dented.

abombado, -da *adj* buckled ○ bulging outwards.

abominable *adj* abominable.

abominación *f* abomination.

abominar ○ *vt* **-1.** [condenar] to condemn. **-2.** [detestar] to abhor, to abominate. ○ *vi*: ~ **de alguien/algo** [condenar] to condemn sb/sthg.

abonado, -da *m y f* [a telefónica, revista] subscriber; [al fútbol, teatro] season-ticket holder.

abonar *vt* **-1.** [pagar - factura etc] to pay; ~ **algo en la cuenta de alguien** to credit sb's account with sthg. **-2.** [tierra] to fertilize.

◆ **abonarse** *vpr*: ~**se (a)** [revista] to sub-

scribe (to); [fútbol, teatro] to buy a season ticket (for).

abonero, -ra *m y f Amer* hawker.

abono *m* **-1.** [pase] season ticket. **-2.** [fertilizante] fertilizer. **-3.** [pago] payment. **-4.** COM credit entry. **-5.** *Amer* [plazo] instalment; **pagar en ~s** to pay by instalments.

abordable *adj* [persona] approachable; [tema] that can be tackled; [tarea] manageable.

abordaje *m* NÁUT boarding.

abordar *vt* **-1.** [embarcación] to board. **-2.** *fig* [persona] to approach. **-3.** *fig* [tema, tarea] to tackle.

aborigen *adj* [indígena] indigenous; [de Australia] aboriginal.

◆ **aborígenes** *mpl y fpl* [población indígena] indigenous population (*sg*); [de Australia] aborigenes.

aborrecer [30] *vt* to abhor, to loathe.

aborrecible *adj* abhorrent, loathsome.

abortar ○ *vi* [MED - espontáneamente] to have a miscarriage, to miscarry; [- intencionadamente] to have an abortion. ○ *vt fig* [hacer fracasar] to foil.

abortista *adj, m y f* abortionist.

abortivo *m* abortifacient.

aborto *m* **-1.** [MED - espontáneo] miscarriage; [- intencionado] abortion. **-2.** *fam despec* [persona fea] freak.

abotargarse [16] *vpr* to swell (up).

abotonar *vt* to button up.

◆ **abotonarse** *vpr* to do one's buttons up; [abrigo, camisa] to button up.

abovedado, -da *adj* arched, vaulted.

abr. (*abrev de* **abril**) Apr.

abracadabra *m* abracadabra.

abrace *etc* → **abrazar**.

abrasador, -ra *adj* burning.

abrasar ○ *vt* **-1.** [quemar - casa, bosque] to burn down; [- persona, mano, garganta] to burn. **-2.** [desecar - suj: sol, calor, lejía] to scorch; [- suj: sed] to parch. ○ *vi* [café etc] to be burning ○ boiling hot.

◆ **abrasarse** *vpr* [casa, bosque] to burn down; [persona] to burn o.s.; [tierra, planta] to get scorched.

abrasivo, -va *adj* abrasive.

◆ **abrasivo** *m* abrasive.

abrazadera *f* TECN brace, bracket; [en carpintería] clamp.

abrazar [13] *vt* **-1.** [con los brazos] to hug, to embrace. **-2.** *fig* [doctrina] to embrace; [profesión] to go into.

◆ **abrazarse** *vpr* to hug ○ embrace (each other).

abrazo *m* embrace, hug; **un (fuerte)** ~ [en cartas] best wishes.

abrebotellas *m inv* bottle opener.

abrecartas *m inv* paper knife, letter opener.

abrelatas *m inv* tin opener *Br*, can opener *Am*.

abrevadero *m* [construido] drinking trough; [natural] watering place.

abrevar *vt* to water, to give water to.

abreviación *f* [de texto] abridgement; [de viaje, estancia] cutting short.

abreviado, -da *adj* [texto] abridged; [viaje, estancia] interrupted.

abreviar [8] ◇ *vt* [gen] to shorten; [texto] to abridge; [palabra] to abbreviate; [viaje, estancia] to cut short. ◇ *vi* [acelerar] to hurry up; **para** ~ [al hacer algo] to keep it quick; [al contar algo] to cut a long story short.

abreviatura *f* abbreviation.

abriboca *adj inv Amer* open-mouthed.

abridor *m* **-1.** [abrebotellas] (bottle) opener. **-2.** [abrelatas] (tin) opener *Br*, (can) opener *Am*.

abrigar [16] ◇ *vt* **-1.** [arropar - suj: persona] to wrap up; [- suj: ropa] to keep warm. **-2.** *fig* [albergar - esperanza] to cherish; [- sospechas, malas intenciones] to harbour.
◆ **abrigarse** *vpr* **-1.** [arroparse] to wrap up. **-2.** [resguardarse]: ~**se de** to shelter from.

abrigo *m* **-1.** [prenda] coat, overcoat. **-2.** [refugio] shelter; **al** ~ **de** [techumbre etc] under the shelter of; [peligro, ataque] safe from; [lluvia, viento] sheltered from; [ley] under the protection of.

abrigue *etc* → **abrigar**.

abril *m* April; **tiene 14** ~**es** he is 14 (years of age); *ver también* **septiembre**.

abrillantador *m* polish.

abrillantar *vt* to polish.

abrir ◇ *vt* **-1.** [gen] to open; [alas] to spread; [melón] to cut open. **-2.** [agua, gas] to turn on; [luz] to switch on. **-3.** [cerradura] to unlock, to open; [pestillo] to pull back; [grifo] to turn on; [cremallera] to undo. **-4.** [túnel] to dig; [canal, camino] to build; [agujero, surco] to make. **-5.** [apetito] to whet. **-6.** [encabezar - lista] to head; [- manifestación] to lead. ◇ *vi* [establecimiento] to open.
◆ **abrirse** *vpr* **-1.** [sincerarse]: ~**se a alguien** to open up to sb, to confide in sb. **-2.** [comunicarse]: ~**se (con)** to be more open (with). **-3.** [posibilidades] to open up. **-4.** [cielo] to clear. **-5.** *mfam* [irse] to clear off.

abrochar *vt* to do up; [cinturón] to fasten.
◆ **abrocharse** *vpr* to do up; [cinturón] to fasten; **¡abróchate!** [el abrigo] do your coat up!

abrogar [16] *vt* to abrogate, to repeal.

abroncar [10] *vt fam* **-1.** [reprender] to tick off, to tell off. **-2.** [abuchear] to boo.

abrótano *m* southernwood.

abrumador, -ra *adj* overwhelming.

abrumar *vt* [agobiar] to overwhelm.

abrupto, -ta *adj* [escarpado] sheer; [accidentado] rugged.

absceso *m* abscess.

abscisa *f* x-axis.

absentismo *m* **-1.** [de terrateniente] absentee landownership. **-2.** [de trabajador]: ~ **laboral** [justificado] absence from work; [injustificado] absenteeism.

ábside *m* apse.

absolución *f* **-1.** DER acquittal. **-2.** RELIG absolution.

absolutismo *m* absolutism.

absolutista *adj, m y f* absolutist.

absoluto, -ta *adj* [gen] absolute; [silencio, obediencia] total.
◆ **en absoluto** *loc adv* [en negativas] at all; [tras pregunta] not at all; **¿te gusta? — en** ~ do you like it? — not at all; **nada en** ~ nothing at all.

absolver [24] *vt*: ~ **a alguien (de algo)** DER to acquit sb (of sthg); RELIG to absolve sb (of sthg).

absorbente *adj* **-1.** [que empapa] absorbent. **-2.** [persona, carácter] domineering. **-3.** [actividad] absorbing.

absorber *vt* **-1.** [gen] to absorb. **-2.** [ocupar el tiempo de] to take up the time of. **-3.** [consumir, gastar] to soak up.

absorción *f* absorption.

absorto, -ta *adj*: ~ **(en)** absorbed o engrossed (in).

abstemio, -mia ◇ *adj* teetotal. ◇ *m y f* teetotaller.

abstención *f* abstention.

abstencionismo *m* abstentionism.

abstenerse [72] *vpr*: ~ **(de algo/de hacer algo)** to abstain (from sthg/from doing sthg).

abstinencia *f* abstinence.

abstracción *f* **-1.** [gen] abstraction. **-2.** [concentración] concentration.

abstracto, -ta *adj* abstract.
◆ **en abstracto** *loc adv* in the abstract.

abstraer [73] *vt* to consider separately, to detach.
◆ **abstraerse** *vpr*: ~**se (de)** to detach o.s. (from).

abstraído, **-da** *adj* lost in thought, engrossed.

abstuviera *etc* → **abstenerse**.

absuelto, **-ta** *pp* → **absolver**.

absuelva *etc* → **absolver**.

absurdo, **-da** *adj* absurd; **lo ~ sería que no lo hicieras** it would be absurd for you not to do it.

◆ **absurdo** *m*: **decir/hacer un ~** to say/do something ridiculous.

abubilla *f* hoopoe.

abuchear *vt* to boo.

abucheo *m* booing.

Abu Dhabi Abu Dhabi.

abuelo, **-la** *m y f* **-1.** [familiar] grandfather (*f* grandmother); **¡cuéntaselo a tu abuela!** *fam* pull the other one!; **éramos pocos y parió la abuela** *fam* that was all we needed; **no necesitar abuela** *fam* to be full of o.s. **-2.** [anciano] old person, old man (*f* old woman).

abuhardillado, **-da** *adj* attic (*antes de sust*).

abulia *f* apathy, lethargy.

abúlico, **-ca** ◇ *adj* apathetic, lethargic. ◇ *m y f* apathetic o lethargic person.

abultado, **-da** *adj* [paquete] bulky; [labios] thick.

abultar ◇ *vt* **-1.** [hinchar] to swell. **-2.** [suj: lente] to magnify. **-3.** [exagerar] to blow up. ◇ *vi* **-1.** [ser difícil de manejar] to be bulky. **-2.** [tener forma de bulto] to bulge.

abundancia *f* **-1.** [gran cantidad] abundance; **en ~** in abundance. **-2.** [riqueza] plenty, prosperity; **nadar** o **vivir en la ~** to be filthy rich.

abundante *adj* abundant.

abundar *vi* **-1.** [ser abundante] to abound; **abundaban los niños** there were hundreds of children there. **-2.** [estar de acuerdo]: **~ en** to agree completely with.

abundoso, **-sa** *adj Amer* abundant.

aburguesado, **-da** *adj* bourgeois.

aburguesarse *vpr* to adopt middle-class ways.

aburrido, **-da** ◇ *adj* **-1.** [harto, fastidiado] bored; **estar ~ de hacer algo** to be fed up with doing sthg. **-2.** [que aburre] boring. ◇ *m y f* bore.

aburrimiento *m* boredom.

aburrir *vt* to bore.

◆ **aburrirse** *vpr* to get bored; [estar aburrido] to be bored.

abusado, **-da** *adj Amer* astute, shrewd.

abusar *vi* **-1.** [excederse] to go too far; **~ de algo** to abuse sthg; **~ de alguien** to take

advantage of sb. **-2.** [forzar sexualmente]: **~ de alguien** to sexually abuse sb.

abusivo, **-va** *adj* [trato] very bad, appalling; [precio] extortionate.

abuso *m* **-1.** [uso excesivo]: **~ (de)** abuse (of); **~ de confianza** breach of confidence; **~s deshonestos** sexual abuse (*U*). **-2.** [escándalo] scandal, sin.

abusón, **-ona** ◇ *adj* self-seeking. ◇ *m y f* self-seeking person.

abyección *f culto* abjection.

abyecto, **-ta** *adj culto* vile, wretched.

a/c *abrev de* **a cuenta**.

a. C. (*abrev de* **antes de Cristo**) BC.

acá ◇ *adv* **-1.** [lugar] here; **de ~ para allá** back and forth; **más ~** closer; **¡ven ~!** come here! **-2.** [tiempo]: **de una semana ~** during the last week; **de un tiempo ~** recently. ◇ *pron* **-1.** [persona] he (*f* she). **-2.** [cosa] this one.

acabado, **-da** *adj* **-1.** [completo] perfect, consummate. **-2.** [fracasado] finished, ruined.

◆ **acabado** *m* [de producto] finish; [de piso] décor.

acabar ◇ *vt* **-1.** [concluir] to finish. **-2.** [consumir - provisiones, dinero] to use up; [- comida] to finish.

◇ *vi* **-1.** [gen] to finish, to end; **la espada acaba en punta** the sword ends in a point; **el asunto acabó mal** the affair finished o ended badly; **cuando acabes, avísame** tell me when you've finished; **~ de hacer algo** to finish doing sthg. **-2.** [haber hecho recientemente]: **~ de hacer algo** to have just done sthg; **acabo de llegar** I've just arrived. **-3.** [terminar por - persona]: **~ por hacer algo, ~ haciendo algo** to end up doing sthg. **-4.** [destruir]: **~ con** [gen] to destroy; [salud] to ruin; [paciencia] to exhaust; [violencia, crimen] to put an end to. **-5.** [matar]: **~ con alguien** to kill sb; *fig* to be the death of sb. **-6.** [volverse] to end up; **~ loco** to go mad. **-7.** (*en frase negativa*): **no acabo de entenderlo** I can't quite understand it; **no acaba de parecerme bien** I don't really think it's a very good idea. **-8.** *loc*: **de nunca ~** never-ending.

◆ **acabarse** *vpr* **-1.** [agotarse] to be used up, to be gone; **se nos ha acabado el petróleo** we're out of petrol; **se ha acabado la comida** there's no more food left, all the food has gone. **-2.** [concluir] to finish, to be over. **-3.** *loc*: **¡se acabó!** [¡basta ya!] that's enough!; [se terminó] that's it, then!

acabóse *m fam*: **¡es el ~!** it really is the limit!

acacia *f* acacia.

academia *f* **-1.** [colegio] school, academy. **-2.** [sociedad] academy.
◆ **Real Academia Española** *f institution that sets lexical and syntactical standards for Spanish.*

REAL ACADEMIA ESPAÑOLA:
This official institution, based in Spain but with counterparts in other Spanish-speaking countries, attempts to set lexical and syntactical standards for Spanish-speakers both in Spain and in Latin America. It publishes periodicals, grammars and a dictionary

academicismo *m* academicism.
académico, -ca ◇ *adj* academic. ◇ *m y f* academician.
acaecer *v impers culto* to take place, to occur.
acallar *vt* to silence.
acalorado, -da *adj* **-1.** [por cansancio] flushed (with effort). **-2.** [por calor] hot. **-3.** [apasionado - debate] heated; [- persona] hot under the collar; [- defensor] fervent.
acalorar *vt* **-1.** [dar calor] to (make) warm. **-2.** [excitar]: ~ **a alguien** to make sb hot under the collar.
◆ **acalorarse** *vpr* **-1.** [coger calor] to get hot. **-2.** [excitarse] to get aroused ○ excited.
acampada *f* **-1.** [acción] camping. **-2.** [lugar] camp site.
acampanado, -da *adj* flared.
acampar *vi* to camp.
acanalado, -da *adj* [columna] fluted; [tejido] ribbed; [hierro, uralita] corrugated.
acanalar *vt* **-1.** [terreno] to dig channels in. **-2.** [tejado] to corrugate.
acantilado *m* cliff.
acanto *m* acanthus.
acantonar *vt* to billet.
◆ **acantonarse** *vpr* to be billeted.
acaparador, -ra *adj* greedy.
acaparamiento *m* monopolization.
acaparar *vt* **-1.** [monopolizar] to monopolize; [mercado] to corner; **acaparaba las miradas de todos** all eyes were on her. **-2.** [guardarse] to hoard.
acápite *m Amer* paragraph.
acaramelado, -da *adj* **-1.** [con caramelo] covered in caramel. **-2.** *fig* [afectado] sickly sweet. **-3.** *fig* [cariñoso] starry-eyed.
acaramelar *vt* to cover in caramel.
◆ **acaramelarse** *vpr* to be starry-eyed.
acariciar [8] *vt* **-1.** [persona] to caress; [animal] to stroke. **-2.** *fig* [idea, proyecto] to cherish.
◆ **acariciarse** *vpr* to caress (each other).

acarrear *vt* **-1.** [transportar] to carry; [carbón] to haul. **-2.** *fig* [ocasionar] to bring, to give rise to.
acartonarse *vpr fam* to become wizened.
acaso *adv* perhaps; ¿~ **no lo sabías?** are you trying to tell me you didn't know?; **por si** ~ (just) in case.
◆ **si acaso** ◇ *loc adv* [en todo caso] if anything. ◇ *loc conj* [en caso de que] if.
acatamiento *m* respect, compliance.
acatar *vt* to respect, to comply with.
acatarrarse *vpr* to catch a cold.
acaudalado, -da *adj* well-to-do, wealthy.
acaudillar *vt* to lead.
acceder *vi* **-1.** [consentir]: ~ **(a algo/hacer algo)** to agree (to sthg/to do sthg). **-2.** [tener acceso]: ~ **a** to enter. **-3.** [alcanzar]: ~ **a** [trono] to accede to; [poder] to come to; [grado] to obtain.
accesible *adj* **-1.** [gen] accessible. **-2.** [persona] approachable.
accésit *m inv* runners-up prize, consolation prize.
acceso *m* **-1.** [entrada]: ~ **(a)** entrance (to). **-2.** [paso]: ~ **(a)** access (to). **-3.** [carretera] access road. **-4.** *fig* [ataque] fit; [de fiebre, gripe] bout.
accesorio, -ria *adj* incidental, of secondary importance.
◆ **accesorio** *m* (*gen pl*) accessory.
accidentado, -da ◇ *adj* **-1.** [vida] turbulent. **-2.** [viaje - en coche, tren, avión] bumpy; [- en barco] rough. **-3.** [terreno, camino] rough, rugged. ◇ *m y f* injured person, victim.
accidental *adj* **-1.** [no esencial] incidental, of secondary importance. **-2.** [imprevisto] accidental; [encuentro] chance.
accidentarse *vpr* to be involved in ○ have an accident.
accidente *m* **-1.** [desgracia] accident; ~ **de avión/coche** plane/car crash; ~ **laboral/mortal** industrial/fatal accident; ~ **de tráfico** road accident. **-2.** (*gen pl*) [del terreno] unevenness (*U*). **-3.** GRAM accidence.
acción *f* **-1.** [gen] action; **película de** ~ action film *Br* ○ movie *Am*. **-2.** [hecho] deed, act; ~ **de gracias** RELIG thanksgiving. FIN share; ~ **ordinaria/preferente** ordinary/preference share; **acciones en cartera** shares in portfolio.
accionamiento *m* activation.
accionar *vt* to activate.
accionariado *m* shareholders (*pl*).
accionista *m y f* shareholder.
Accra Accra.

acebo *m* **-1.** [hoja] holly. **-2.** [árbol] holly (bush).

acechanza *f* observation, surveillance.

acechar *vt* **-1.** [vigilar] to observe, to keep under surveillance; [suj: cazador] to stalk. **-2.** [amenazar] to be lying in wait for.

acecho *m* observation, surveillance; **estar al ~ de** to lie in wait for; *fig* to be on the lookout for.

acedera *f* sorrel.

acéfalo, -la *adj* [estado, organización] leaderless.

aceitar *vt* [motor] to lubricate; [comida] to pour oil onto.

aceite *m* oil; **~ de colza/girasol/oliva** rapeseed/sunflower/olive oil; **~ de ricino/de hígado de bacalao** castor/cod-liver oil.

aceitera *f* oil can.
◆ **aceiteras** *fpl* cruet (*sg*).

aceitoso, -sa *adj* oily.

aceituna *f* olive; **~ rellena** stuffed olive.

aceitunado, -da *adj* olive.

aceitunero, -ra *m y f* **-1.** [recogedor] olive picker. **-2.** [vendedor] olive merchant.

aceituno *m* olive tree.

aceleración *f* acceleration.

acelerado, -da *adj* rapid, quick; FÍS accelerated.

acelerador, -ra *adj* accelerating.
◆ **acelerador** *m* accelerator.

acelerar ◇ *vt* **-1.** [avivar] to speed up; TECN to accelerate. **-2.** [adelantar] to bring forward. ◇ *vi* to accelerate.
◆ **acelerarse** *vpr* to hurry up.

acelerón *m*: **dar un ~** AUTOM to put one's foot down.

acelga *f* chard.

acendrado, -da *adj* untarnished, pure.

acendrar *vt* **-1.** [metal] to purify. **-2.** *fig* [cualidad, sentimiento] to refine.

acento *m* **-1.** [gen] accent; **~ agudo/circunflejo/grave** acute/circumflex/grave accent; **~ ortográfico** (written) accent. **-2.** [intensidad] stress, accent.

acentuación *f* accentuation.

acentuado, -da *adj* **-1.** [con acento gráfico] stressed. **-2.** [marcado] marked, distinct.

acentuar [6] *vt* **-1.** [palabra, letra - al escribir] to accent, to put an accent on; [- al hablar] to stress. **-2.** *fig* [realzar] to accentuate. **-3.** *fig* [intensificar] to increase.
◆ **acentuarse** *vpr* [intensificarse] to deepen, to increase.

acepción *f* meaning, sense.

aceptable *adj* acceptable.

aceptación *f* **-1.** [aprobación] acceptance. **-2.** [éxito] success, popularity.

aceptar *vt* to accept.

acequia *f* irrigation channel.

acera *f* **-1.** [para peatones] pavement *Br*, sidewalk *Am*; **ser de la otra ~, ser de la ~ de enfrente** *fam despec* to be one of them, to be queer. **-2.** [lado de la calle] side of the street.

acerado, -da *adj* **-1.** [cortante] sharp. **-2.** [con acero] containing steel. **-3.** *fig* [fuerte, resistente] steely, tough. **-4.** [mordaz] cutting, biting.

acerar *vt* **-1.** [pavimentar] to pave. **-2.** [convertir en acero] to turn into steel. **-3.** [recubrir de acero] to steel.

acerbo, -ba *adj culto* **-1.** [áspero] bitter. **-2.** [mordaz] caustic, cutting.

acerca
◆ **acerca de** *loc adv* about.

acercamiento *m* [de personas, estados] rapprochement; [de suceso, fecha] approach.

acercar [10] *vt* to bring nearer ○ closer; **¡acércame el pan!** could you pass me the bread? ◆ **acercarse** *vpr* **-1.** [arrimarse - viniendo] to come closer; [- yendo] to go over. **-2.** [ir] to go; [venir] to come; [a casa de alguien] to come/go round. **-3.** [tiempo] to draw nearer, to approach.

acería *f* steelworks (*sg*).

acero *m* steel; **~ inoxidable** stainless steel.

acerque *etc* → **acercar**.

acérrimo, -ma *adj* [defensor] diehard (*antes de sust*); [enemigo] bitter.

acertado, -da *adj* **-1.** [con acierto - respuesta] correct; [- disparo] on target; [- comentario] appropriate. **-2.** [oportuno] good, clever.

acertante ◇ *adj* winning. ◇ *m y f* winner.

acertar [19] ◇ *vt* **-1.** [adivinar] to guess (correctly). **-2.** [el blanco] to hit. **-3.** [elegir bien] to choose well. ◇ *vi* **-1.** [atinar]: **~ (al hacer algo)** to be right (to do sthg). **-2.** [conseguir]: **~ a hacer algo** to manage to do sthg; **acertaba a pasar por allí** *fig* she happened to pass that way. **-3.** [hallar]: **~ con** to find.

acertijo *m* riddle.

acervo *m* [patrimonio] heritage.

acetato *m* acetate.

acético, -ca *adj* acetic.

acetileno *m* acetylene.

acetona *f* acetone.

achacar [10] *vt*: **~ algo a alguien/algo** to attribute sthg to sb/sthg.

achacoso, -sa *adj* **-1.** [persona] frail. **-2.** [cosa] faulty, defective.

achampañado, **-da** *adj* sparkling.

achantar *vt fam* to put the wind up.

◆ **achantarse** *vpr fam* to get the wind up.

achaparrado, **-da** *adj* squat.

achaque ◇ *v* → achacar. ◇ *m* ailment, complaint.

achatado, **-da** *adj* flattened.

achatar *vt* to flatten.

◆ **achatarse** *vpr* to level out.

achicar [10] *vt* **-1.** [tamaño] to make smaller. **-2.** [agua - de barco] to bale out; [- de mina] to drain. **-3.** *fig* [acobardar] to intimidate.

◆ **achicarse** *vpr* [acobardarse] to become intimidated.

achicharrar ◇ *vt* **-1.** [chamuscar] to burn. **-2.** *fig* [a preguntas] to plague, to overwhelm. ◇ *vi* [sol, calor] to be scorching.

◆ **achicharrarse** *vpr* **-1.** *fig* [de calor] to fry, to roast. **-2.** [chamuscarse] to burn.

achicoria *f* chicory.

achinado, **-da** *adj* **-1.** [ojos] slanting. **-2.** [persona] Chinese-looking. **-3.** *Amer* Indian-looking.

achique *etc* → achicar.

achispar *vt* to make tipsy.

◆ **achisparse** *vpr* to get tipsy.

achuchado, **-da** *adj fam* hard, tough.

achuchar *vt fam* **-1.** [abrazar] to hug. **-2.** *fig* [presionar] to be on at, to badger.

achuchón *m fam* **-1.** [abrazo] big hug. **-2.** [indisposición] mild illness; **le dio un** ∼ he took sick.

achunchar *vt Amer* [avergonzar] to shame.

◆ **achuncharse** *vpr* [avergonzarse] to be shamed.

achura *m Amer* [intestino] guts (*pl*).

achurar *vt Amer* **-1.** [acuchillar] to stab to death. **-2.** [animal] to disembowel.

aciago, **-ga** *adj culto* black, fateful.

acicalado, **-da** *adj* smart, neat and tidy.

acicalar *vt* [arreglar] to do up.

◆ **acicalarse** *vpr* to do o.s. up.

acicate *m* **-1.** [espuela] spur. **-2.** *fig* [estímulo] incentive.

acidez *f* **-1.** [cualidad] acidity. **-2.** MED: ∼ **(de estómago)** heartburn.

acid house ['aθid 'xaus] *m* acid house.

ácido, **-da** *adj* **-1.** QUÍM acidic. **-2.** [bebida, sabor, carácter] acid, sour.

◆ **ácido** *m* **-1.** QUÍM acid; ∼ **clorhídrico/desoxirribonucléico/ribonucleico/sulfúrico** hydrochloric / deoxyribonucleic / ribonucleic/sulphuric acid. **-2.** *fam* [droga] acid.

acierta *etc* → acertar.

acierto *m* **-1.** [a pregunta] correct answer. **-2.** [en quinielas] correct entry. **-3.** [habilidad, tino] good ◇ sound judgment. **-4.** [éxito] success.

ácimo = ázimo.

acimut (*pl* acimutes), **azimut** (*pl* azimutes) *m* azimuth.

aclamación *f* [ovación] acclamation, acclaim; **por** ∼ unanimously.

aclamar *vt* to acclaim.

aclaración *f* explanation.

aclarado *m* rinsing, rinse.

aclarar ◇ *vt* **-1.** [ropa] to rinse. **-2.** [explicar] to clarify, to explain. **-3.** ∼ **la voz** [carraspeando] to clear one's throat. **-4.** [lo oscuro] to make lighter. **-5.** [lo espeso - chocolate, sopa] to thin (down); [- bosque] to thin out. ◇ *v impers* **-1.** [amanecer] to get light. **-2.** [clarear, despejarse] to clear up.

◆ **aclararse** *vpr* **-1.** [entender] to understand. **-2.** [explicarse] to explain o.s. **-3.** [ver claro] to see clearly.

aclaratorio, **-ria** *adj* explanatory.

aclimatación *f* acclimatization.

aclimatar *vt* **-1.** [al clima]: ∼ **algo/a alguien (a)** to acclimatize sth/sb (to). **-2.** [a ambiente]: ∼ **algo/a alguien a algo** to get sth/sb used to sthg.

◆ **aclimatarse** *vpr* **-1.** [al clima]: ∼**se (a algo)** to acclimatize (to sthg). **-2.** [a ambiente] to settle in; ∼**se a algo** to get used to sthg.

acné *m* acne.

acobardar *vt* to frighten, to scare.

◆ **acobardarse** *vpr* to get frightened ◇ scared; ∼**se ante** to shrink back from.

acodado, **-da** *adj* **-1.** [persona] leaning (on one's elbows). **-2.** [cañería] elbowed.

acodarse *vpr*: ∼ **(en)** to lean (on).

acogedor, **-ra** *adj* [país, persona] friendly, welcoming; [casa, ambiente] cosy.

acoger [14] *vt* **-1.** [recibir] to welcome. **-2.** [dar refugio] to take in. **-3.** *fig* [idea, noticia etc] to receive.

◆ **acogerse a** *vpr* [inmunidad parlamentaria etc] to take refuge in; [ley] to have recourse to.

acogida *f* **-1.** [de persona] welcome, reception. **-2.** [de idea, película etc] reception.

acoja *etc* → acoger.

acojonante *adj vulg* **-1.** [impresionante] bloody incredible. **-2.** [que da miedo] shit scary.

acojonar *vulg* ◇ *vt* **-1.** [asustar] to scare

shitless. **-2.** [impresionar] to gobsmack. ◇ *vi*
[asustar] to be shit scary.
◆ **acojonarse** *vpr vulg* to be shit scared.
acolchado, -da *adj* padded.
acolchar *vt* to pad.
acólito *m* **-1.** [gen] acolyte. **-2.** [monaguillo]
altar boy.
acometer ◇ *vt* **-1.** [atacar] to attack; **le
acometió el sueño** he felt sleepy. **-2.** [em-
prender] to undertake. ◇ *vi* [embestir]: ~
contra to hurtle into.
acometida *f* **-1.** [ataque] attack, charge. **-2.**
[de luz, gas etc] (mains) connection.
acomodadizo, -za *adj* accommodating,
easy-going.
acomodado, -da *adj* **-1.** [rico] well-off,
well-to-do. **-2.** [instalado] ensconced.
acomodador, -ra *m y f* usher (*f* usherette).
acomodar *vt* **-1.** [instalar - persona] to seat,
to instal; [- cosa] to place. **-2.** [adaptar] to
fit.
◆ **acomodarse** *vpr* **-1.** [instalarse] to make
o.s. comfortable; ~**se en** to settle down in.
-2. [conformarse]: ~**se a** to adapt to.
acomodaticio, -cia *adj* [complaciente] accommodating, easy-going.
acomodo *m* [alojamiento] accommodation.
acompañamiento *m* **-1.** [comitiva - en en-
tierro] cortege; [- de rey] retinue. **-2.** CULIN &
MÚS accompaniment.
acompañante *m y f* companion.
acompañar ◇ *vt* **-1.** [ir con]: ~ **a alguien**
[gen] to go with O accompany sb; [a la puer-
ta] to show sb out; [a casa] to walk sb
home. **-2.** [estar con]: ~ **a alguien** to keep
sb company. **-3.** [compartir emociones con]:
~ **en algo a alguien** to be with sb in sthg.
-4. [adjuntar] to enclose. **-5.** MÚS to accompany. **-6.** [coexistir con] to accompany. **-7.**
CULIN: ~ **algo con algo** to serve sthg with
sthg.
◇ *vi* [hacer compañía] to provide company.
◆ **acompañarse** *vpr* MÚS: ~**se con** to accompany o.s. on.
acompasado, -da *adj* steady, rhythmic;
[pasos] measured.
acompasar *vt*: ~ **algo (a)** to synchronize
sthg (with).
acomplejado, -da ◇ *adj* inhibited, having
a complex. ◇ *m y f* inhibited person, person with a complex.
acomplejar *vt* to give a complex.
◆ **acomplejarse** *vpr* to develop a complex.
Aconcagua *m*: **el** ~ Aconcagua.
acondicionado, -da *adj* equipped; **estar
bien/mal** ~ to be in a fit/no fit state.

acondicionador *m* (air) conditioner.
acondicionamiento *m* conversion, up-
grading.
acondicionar *vt* **-1.** [reformar] to convert,
to upgrade. **-2.** [preparar] to prepare, to get
ready.
aconfesional *adj* with no official religion.
acongojar *vt* to distress, to cause anguish
to.
◆ **acongojarse** *vpr* to be distressed.
aconsejable *adj* advisable.
aconsejar *vt* **-1.** [dar consejos]: ~ **a alguien
(que haga algo)** to advise sb (to do sthg).
-2. [hacer aconsejable] to make advisable.
acontecer *v impers* to take place, to happen.
acontecimiento *m* event; **adelantarse** O
anticiparse a los ~**s** to jump the gun; [pre-
venir] to take preemptive measures.
acopiar [8] *vt* [juntar] to gather; [acaparar] to
buy up.
acopio *m* stock, store; **hacer** ~ **de** [existen-
cias, comestibles] to stock up on; [valor, pa-
ciencia] to summon up.
acoplable *adj*: ~ **(a)** attachable (to).
acoplamiento *m* [de piezas] attachment,
connection; [de módulo espacial] docking.
acoplar *vt* **-1.** [encajar] to attach, to fit together. **-2.** FERROC to couple. **-3.** *fig* [adaptar]
to adapt, to fit.
◆ **acoplarse** *vpr* **-1.** [adaptarse] to adjust to
each other; ~**se a** to adjust to. **-2.** [encajar]
to fit together; ~**se a algo** to fit sthg.
acoquinar *vt fam* to put the wind up.
◆ **acoquinarse** *vpr fam* to get the wind
up.
acorazado, -da *adj* armour-plated.
◆ **acorazado** *m* battleship.
acorazar [13] *vt* to armour-plate, to armour.
acordar [23] *vt*: ~ **algo/hacer algo** to agree
on sthg/to do sthg.
◆ **acordarse** *vpr*: ~**se (de algo/de hacer
algo)** to remember (sthg/to do sthg).
acorde ◇ *adj* **-1.** [conforme] in agreement.
-2. [en consonancia]: ~ **con** in keeping with.
◇ *m* MÚS chord.
acordeón *m* accordion.
acordeonista *m y f* accordionist.
acordonado, -da *adj* cordoned off.
acordonar *vt* **-1.** [atar] to do O lace up. **-2.**
[cercar] to cordon off.
acornear *vt* to gore.
acorralamiento *m* [de malhechor, animal de
caza] cornering.
acorralar *vt lit* & *fig* to corner.

acortar *vt* **-1.** [falda, pantalón etc] to take up; [cable] to shorten. **-2.** [tiempo] to cut short. **-3.** [extensión] to shorten.

◆ **acortarse** *vpr* [días] to get shorter; [reunión] to end early.

acosador, -ra *adj* relentless, persistent.

acosamiento *m* harassment.

acosar *vt* **-1.** [hostigar] to harass. **-2.** [perseguir] to pursue relentlessly.

acoso *m* **-1.** [hostigamiento] harassment; ~ **sexual** sexual harassment. **-2.** [persecución] relentless pursuit.

acostar [23] *vt* **-1.** [en la cama] to put to bed. **-2.** NÁUT to bring alongside.

◆ **acostarse** *vpr* **-1.** [irse a la cama] to go to bed. **-2.** [tumbarse] to lie down. **-3.** *fam* [tener relaciones sexuales]: ~**se con alguien** to sleep with sb.

acostumbrado, -da *adj* **-1.** [habitual] usual. **-2.** [habituado]: **estamos** ~**s** we're used to it; **estar** ~ **a** to be used to.

acostumbrar ◇ *vt* [habituar]: ~ **a alguien a algo/a hacer algo** to get sb used to sthg/to doing sthg. ◇ *vi* [soler]: ~ **a hacer algo** to be in the habit of doing sthg, usually to do sthg.

◆ **acostumbrarse** *vpr* [habituarse]: **terminé acostumbrándome** I got used to it eventually; ~**se a algo/a hacer algo** to get used to sthg/to doing sthg.

acotación *f* **-1.** [nota] note in the margin. **-2.** TEATR stage direction.

acotado, -da *adj* enclosed.

acotamiento *m* **-1.** [de terreno, campo] enclosing, demarcation. **-2.** *Amer* [arcén] hard shoulder.

acotar *vt* **-1.** [terreno, campo] to enclose, to demarcate; *fig* [tema etc] to delimit. **-2.** [texto] to write notes in the margin of.

acotejar *vt Amer* to arrange.

ácrata *adj, m y f* anarchist.

acre ◇ *adj* **-1.** [olor] acrid, pungent. **-2.** [sabor] bitter. **-3.** *fig* [brusco, desagradable] caustic. ◇ *m* acre.

acrecentar [19] *vt* to increase.

◆ **acrecentarse** *vpr* to increase.

acreditación *f* [credencial] credential.

acreditado, -da *adj* **-1.** [médico, abogado etc] distinguished; [marca] reputable. **-2.** [embajador, representante] accredited.

acreditar *vt* **-1.** [certificar] to certify; [autorizar] to authorize. **-2.** [confirmar] to confirm. **-3.** [dar fama] to be a credit to. **-4.** [embajador] to accredit. **-5.** FIN to credit.

acreedor, -ra ◇ *adj*: **hacerse** ~ **de algo** to earn sthg, to show o.s. to be worthy of sthg. ◇ *m y f* creditor.

acribillar *vt* **-1.** [agujerear] to perforate. **-2.** [herir]: ~ **(a)** to pepper ○ riddle (with); **me han acribillado los mosquitos** the mosquitoes have bitten me all over. **-3.** *fam fig* [molestar]: ~ **a alguien a preguntas** to pester sb with questions.

acrílico, -ca *adj* acrylic.

acrimonia = **acritud**.

acristalar *vt* to glaze.

acritud, acrimonia *f* **-1.** [de olor] acridity, pungency; [de sabor] bitterness. **-2.** *fig* [mordacidad] venom. **-3.** [desavenencia] acrimony.

acrobacia *f* **-1.** [en circo] acrobatics (*pl*). **-2.** [de avión] aerobatic manoeuvre.

acróbata *m y f* acrobat.

acrobático, -ca *adj* acrobatic.

acrónimo *m* acronym.

acrópolis *f inv* acropolis.

acta *f* (*el*) **-1.** [de junta, reunión] minutes (*pl*); **constar en** ~ to be recorded in the minutes; **levantar** ~ to take the minutes. **-2.** [de defunción etc] certificate; ~ **notarial** affidavit. **-3.** ~ **(de nombramiento)** certificate of appointment.

◆ **actas** *fpl* minutes.

actitud *f* **-1.** [disposición de ánimo] attitude. **-2.** [postura] posture, position.

activación *f* stimulation.

activar *vt* **-1.** [gen] to activate. **-2.** [explosivo] to detonate. **-3.** [estimular] to stimulate; [acelerar] to speed up.

actividad *f* activity; **desplegar una gran** ~ to be in a flurry of activity; **en** ~ active; ~**es extraescolares** extracurricular activities.

activismo *m* activism.

activista *m y f* activist.

activo, -va *adj* **-1.** [gen & GRAM] active. **-2.** [trabajador] hard-working. **-3.** [que trabaja] working; **en** ~ [en funciones] on active service. **-4.** [rápido] fast-acting.

◆ **activo** *m* FIN assets (*pl*); ~ **fijo/líquido/financiero** fixed/liquid/financial assets.

acto *m* **-1.** [acción] act; **hacer** ~ **de presencia** to show one's face; ~ **reflejo** reflex action; ~ **sexual** sexual act, sexual intercourse (*U*); ~ **de solidaridad** show of solidarity. **-2.** [ceremonia] ceremony. **-3.** TEATR act.

◆ **acto seguido** *loc adv* immediately after.

◆ **en el acto** *loc adv* on the spot, there and then; **"fotos de carnet en el ~"** "passport photos while you wait".

actor, -triz *m y f* actor (*f* actress).

actuación *f* **-1.** [conducta, proceder] conduct, behaviour. **-2.** [interpretación] performance. **-3.** DER proceedings (*pl*).

actual adj **-1.** [existente] present, current. **-2.** [de moda] modern, present-day. **-3.** [de actualidad] topical.

actualidad f **-1.** [momento presente] current situation; **de ~** [moderno] in fashion; [de interés actual] topical; **en la ~** at the present time, these days. **-2.** [vigencia] relevance to modern society. **-3.** [noticia] news (U); **ser ~** to be making the news.

actualización f updating; [de tecnología, industria] modernization.

actualizar [13] vt to update; [tecnología, industria] to modernize.

actualmente adv [hoy día] these days, nowadays; [en este momento] at the (present) moment.

actuar [6] vi **-1.** [gen] to act; **~ de** to act as. **-2.** DER to undertake proceedings.

actuario, -ria m y f **-1.** DER clerk of the court. **-2.** FIN: **~ de seguros** actuary.

acuarela f watercolour.

acuarelista m y f watercolourist.

acuario m aquarium.

◆ **Acuario** ◇ m [zodiaco] Aquarius; **ser Acuario** to be (an) Aquarius. ◇ m y f [persona] Aquarius.

acuartelamiento m **-1.** [acción] confinement to barracks. **-2.** [lugar] barracks (pl).

acuartelar vt **-1.** [alojar] to quarter. **-2.** [retener] to confine to barracks.

acuático, -ca adj aquatic.

acuchillar vt **-1.** [apuñalar] to stab. **-2.** [mueble, parquet] to grind down.

acuciante adj culto urgent, pressing.

acuciar [8] vt culto [suj: persona] to goad; [suj: necesidad, deseo] to press.

acuclillarse vpr to squat (down).

ACUDE (abrev de **Asociación de Consumidores y Usuarios de España**) f Spanish consumer association; ≃ CA Br, ≃ CAC Am.

acudir vi **-1.** [ir] to go; [venir] to come. **-2.** [recurrir]: **~ a** to go ○ turn to. **-3.** [presentarse]: **~ (a)** [escuela, iglesia] to attend; [cita, examen] to turn up (for); fig [memoria, mente] to come (to).

acueducto m aqueduct.

acuerda etc → **acordar**.

acuerdo m agreement; **de ~** all right, O.K.; **de ~ con** [conforme a] in accordance with; **estar de ~ (con alguien/en hacer algo)** to agree (with sb/to do sthg); **llegar a un ~, ponerse de ~** to reach agreement; **por común ~** by common consent; **~ marco** framework agreement.

acuesta etc → **acostar**.

acuicultivo m hydroponics (U).

acumulación f accumulation.

acumulador m accumulator.

acumular vt to accumulate.

◆ **acumularse** vpr to accumulate, to build up.

acunar vt to rock.

acuñar vt **-1.** [moneda] to mint. **-2.** [palabra] to coin.

acuoso, -sa adj **-1.** [gen] watery. **-2.** [jugoso] juicy.

acupuntor, -ra m y f acupuncturist.

acupuntura f acupuncture.

acurrucarse [10] vpr to crouch down; [por frío] to huddle up; [por miedo] to cower; [en sitio agradable] to curl up.

acusación f **-1.** [inculpación] charge. **-2.** [abogado]: **la ~** the prosecution.

acusado, -da ◇ adj [marcado] marked, distinct. ◇ m y f [procesado] accused, defendant.

acusador, -ra adj accusing.

acusar vt **-1.** [culpar] to accuse; JUR to charge; **~ a alguien de algo** [gen] to accuse sb of sthg; JUR to charge sb with sthg. **-2.** [mostrar] to show. **-3.** [padecer] to be susceptible to. **-4.** [recibo] to acknowledge.

◆ **acusarse** vpr **-1.** [mutuamente] to blame one another. **-2.** [uno mismo]: **~se de haber hecho algo** to confess to having done sthg.

acusativo m accusative.

acusatorio, -ria adj DER accusatory.

acuse

◆ **acuse de recibo** m acknowledgement of receipt.

acusica m y f fam telltale.

acústico, -ca adj acoustic.

◆ **acústica** f **-1.** [ciencia] acoustics (U). **-2.** [de local] acoustics (pl).

a.D. (abrev de **anno Domini**) AD.

ADA (abrev de **Asociación de Ayuda al Automovilista**) f Spanish motoring association; ≃ AA Br, ≃ AAA Am.

adagio m **-1.** [sentencia breve] adage. **-2.** MÚS adagio.

adalid m champion.

adaptación f **-1.** [aclimatación]: **~ (a)** adjustment (to). **-2.** [modificación] adaptation.

adaptado, -da adj: **~ (a)** suited (to).

adaptador, -ra m y f [persona] adapter.

◆ **adaptador** m ELECTR adapter.

adaptar vt **-1.** [acomodar, ajustar] to adjust. **-2.** [modificar] to adapt.

◆ **adaptarse** vpr: **~se (a)** to adjust (to).

Addis Abeba Addis Ababa.

adecentar vt to tidy up.

◆ **adecentarse** vpr to make o.s. decent.

ADECU (*abrev de* **Asociación para la Defensa de los Consumidores y Usuarios**) *f Spanish consumer association*, ≃ CA *Br*, ≃ CAC *Am*.

adecuado, -da *adj* appropriate, suitable.

adecuar [7] *vt* to adapt.

◆ **adecuarse a** *vpr* **-1.** [ser adecuado] to be appropriate for. **-2.** [adaptarse] to adjust to.

adefesio *m fam* **-1.** [persona fea] fright, sight. **-2.** [cosa fea] eyesore, monstrosity.

a. de JC., a.JC. (*abrev de* **antes de Jesucristo**) BC.

adelantado, -da *adj* advanced; **llevo el reloj** ~ my watch is fast; **por** ~ in advance.

adelantamiento *m* AUTOM overtaking.

adelantar ◇ *vt* **-1.** [dejar atrás] to overtake. **-2.** [mover hacia adelante] to move forward; [pie, reloj] to put forward. **-3.** [en el tiempo - trabajo, viaje] to bring forward; [- dinero] to pay in advance. **-4.** [conseguir]: **¿qué adelantas con eso?** what do you hope to gain ○ achieve by that? ◇ *vi* **-1.** [progresar] to make progress. **-2.** [reloj] to be fast.

◆ **adelantarse** *vpr* **-1.** [en el tiempo] to be early; [frío, verano] to arrive early; [reloj] to gain; ~**se a alguien** to beat sb to it. **-2.** [en el espacio] to go on ahead.

adelante ◇ *adv* forward, ahead; **(de ahora) en** ~ from now on, in future; **más** ~ [en el tiempo] later (on); [en el espacio] further on. ◇ *interj*: **¡~!** [¡siga!] go ahead!; [¡pase!] come in!

adelanto *m* advance; ~ **de dinero** advance.

adelfa *f* oleander.

adelgazamiento *m* slimming.

adelgazante *adj* slimming.

adelgazar [13] ◇ *vi* to lose weight, to slim. ◇ *vt* to lose.

ademán *m* [gesto - con manos etc] gesture; [- con cara] face, expression; **en** ~ **de** as if to.

◆ **ademanes** *mpl* [modales] manners.

además *adv* moreover, besides; [también] also; ~ **de** as well as, in addition to.

ADENA (*abrev de* **Asociación para la Defensa de la Naturaleza**) *f Spanish nature conservancy organization*, ≃ NCC *Br*.

adentrarse *vpr*: ~ **en** [jungla etc] to enter the heart of; [tema etc] to study in depth.

adentro *adv* inside; **tierra** ~ inland; **mar** ~ out to sea.

◆ **adentros** *mpl*: **para mis/tus** *etc* ~**s** to myself/yourself *etc*.

adepto, -ta ◇ *adj* [partidario] supporting; **ser** ~ **a** to be a follower of. ◇ *m y f*: ~ **(a)** follower (of).

aderezar [13] *vt* **-1.** [sazonar - ensalada] to dress; [- comida] to season. **-2.** [adornar] to deck out.

aderezo *m* **-1.** [aliño - de ensalada] dressing; [- de comida] seasoning. **-2.** [adorno] adornment.

adeudar *vt* **-1.** [deber] to owe. **-2.** COM to debit.

◆ **adeudarse** *vpr* to get into debt.

ADEVIDA (*abrev de* **Asociación en Defensa de la Vida Humana**) *f Spanish pro-life organization*, ≃ SPUC *Br*.

a.Dg. *abrev de* **a Dios gracias**.

adherencia *f* **-1.** [de sellos, pegatina] stickiness, adhesion; [de ruedas] roadholding. **-2.** [parte añadida] appendage.

adherente *adj* adhesive, sticky.

adherir [27] *vt* to stick.

◆ **adherirse** *vpr* **-1.** [pegarse] to stick. **-2.** [mostrarse de acuerdo]: ~**se a** to adhere to. **-3.** [afiliarse]: ~**se a** to join.

adhesión *f* [apoyo] support.

adhesivo, -va *adj* adhesive.

◆ **adhesivo** *m* **-1.** [pegatina] sticker. **-2.** [sustancia] adhesive.

adhiera *etc* → **adherir**.

adhiriera *etc* → **adherir**.

adicción *f*: ~ **(a)** addiction (to).

adición *f* addition.

adicional *adj* additional.

adicionar *vt* to add.

adicto, -ta ◇ *adj*: ~ **(a)** addicted (to). ◇ *m y f*: ~ **(a)** addict (of).

adiestramiento *m* training.

adiestrar *vt* to train; ~ **a alguien en algo/para hacer algo** to train sb in sthg/to do sthg.

adinerado, -da *adj* wealthy.

adiós ◇ *m* goodbye. ◇ *interj*: **¡~!** goodbye!; [al cruzarse con alguien] hello!

adiposidad *f* fattiness, adiposity.

adiposo, -sa *adj* fatty, adipose.

aditamento *m* **-1.** [complemento] accessory. **-2.** [cosa añadida] addition.

aditivo *m* additive.

adivinador, -ra *m y f* fortune-teller.

adivinanza *f* riddle.

adivinar *vt* **-1.** [predecir] to foretell; [el futuro] to tell. **-2.** [acertar] to guess (correctly). **-3.** [intuir] to suspect. **-4.** [vislumbrar] to spot, to make out.

◆ **adivinarse** *vpr* [vislumbrarse] to be visible.

adivino, -na *m y f* fortune-teller.

adjetivar *vt* GRAM to use adjectivally.

adjetivo, -va *adj* adjectival.

◆ **adjetivo** *m* adjective; ~ **calificativo/ demostrativo/numeral,** qualifying/demonstrative/quantitative adjective.

adjudicación *f* awarding.

adjudicar [10] *vt* [asignar] to award.

◆ **adjudicarse** *vpr* [apropiarse] to take for o.s.

adjuntar *vt* to enclose.

adjunto, -ta ◇ *adj* **-1.** [incluido] enclosed; ~ **le remito ...** please find enclosed .... **-2.** [auxiliar] assistant (*antes de sust*). ◇ *m y f* [auxiliar] assistant.

adminículo *m* gadget.

administración *f* **-1.** [suministro] supply; [de medicamento, justicia] administering. **-2.** [gestión] administration. **-3.** [gerentes] management; [oficina] manager's office.

◆ **Administración** *f* [gobierno] administration; **Administración local** local government; **Administración pública** civil service.

administrador, -ra *m y f* **-1.** [de empresa] manager. **-2.** [de bienes ajenos] administrator.

administrar *vt* **-1.** [gestionar - empresa, finca etc] to manage, to run; [- casa] to run. **-2.** [país] to run the affairs of. **-3.** [suministrar] to administer. **-4.** [racionar] to use sparingly.

◆ **administrarse** *vpr* [emplear dinero] to organize one's finances.

administrativo, -va ◇ *adj* administrative. ◇ *m y f* office clerk.

admirable *adj* admirable.

admiración *f* **-1.** [sentimiento] admiration. **-2.** [signo ortográfico] exclamation mark.

admirador, -ra *m y f* admirer.

admirar *vt* **-1.** [gen] to admire; **ser de ~** to be admirable. **-2.** [sorprender] to amaze.

◆ **admirarse** *vpr*: ~**se (de)** to be amazed (by).

admisible *adj* acceptable.

admisión *f* **-1.** [de persona] admission. **-2.** [de solicitudes etc] acceptance.

admitir *vt* **-1.** [acoger, reconocer] to admit; ~ **a alguien en** to admit sb to. **-2.** [aceptar] to accept. **-3.** [permitir, tolerar] to allow, to permit.

admón. (*abrev de* **administración**) admin.

admonición *f* warning.

ADN (*abrev de* **ácido desoxirribonucleico**) *m* DNA.

adobar *vt* to marinate.

adobe *m* adobe.

adobo *m* **-1.** [acción] marinating. **-2.** [salsa] marinade.

adocenado, -da *adj* mediocre, run-of-the-mill.

adocenarse *vpr* to lapse into mediocrity.

adoctrinar *vt* to instruct.

adolecer [30]

◆ **adolecer de** *vi* **-1.** [enfermedad] to suffer from. **-2.** [defecto] to be guilty of.

adolescencia *f* adolescence.

adolescente *adj, m y f* adolescent.

adonde *adv* where; **la ciudad ~ vamos** the city we are going to, the city where we are going.

adónde *adv* where.

adondequiera *adv* wherever.

adonis *m inv fig* Adonis, handsome young man.

adopción *f* [de hijo, propuesta] adoption; [de ley] passing.

adoptar *vt* [hijo, propuesta] to adopt; [ley] to pass.

adoptivo, -va *adj* [hijo, país] adopted; [padre] adoptive.

adoquín (*pl* **adoquines**) *m* cobblestone.

adoquinado, -da *adj* cobbled.

◆ **adoquinado** *m* **-1.** [suelo] cobbles (*pl*). **-2.** [acción] cobbling.

adoquinar *vt* to cobble.

adorable *adj* [persona] adorable; [ambiente, película] wonderful.

adoración *f* adoration; **sentir ~ por alguien** to worship sb.

adorar *vt* **-1.** [reverenciar] to worship. **-2.** [pirrarse por] to adore.

adormecer [30] *vt* **-1.** [producir sueño] to lull to sleep. **-2.** *fig* [aplacar] to calm. **-3.** [entumecer] to numb.

◆ **adormecerse** *vpr* to nod off, to drop off.

adormidera *f* poppy.

adormilarse *vpr* to doze.

adornar ◇ *vt* to decorate. ◇ *vi* to serve as decoration.

adorno *m* decoration; **de ~** [árbol, figura] decorative, ornamental; [person] serving no useful purpose.

adosado, -da *adj* [casa] semi-detached.

adosar *vt*: ~ **algo a algo** to push sthg up against sthg.

adquirir [22] *vt* **-1.** [comprar] to acquire, to purchase. **-2.** [conseguir - conocimientos, hábito, cultura] to acquire; [- éxito, popularidad] to achieve; [- enfermedad] to catch, to get.

adquisición *f* **-1.** [compra, cosa comprada] purchase; **ser una buena/mala ~** to be a good/bad buy. **-2.** [obtención] acquisition.

adquisitivo, -va *adj* purchasing (*antes de sust*).

adrede *adv* on purpose, deliberately.

adrenalina f adrenalin.

Adriático m: **el (mar)** ~ the Adriatic (Sea).

adscribir vt **-1.** [asignar] to assign. **-2.** [destinar] to appoint ◇ assign to.

◆ **adscribirse** vpr: ~**se (a)** [grupo, partido] to become a member (of); [ideología] to subscribe to.

adscrito, -ta ◇ pp → **adscribir.** ◇ adj assigned.

aduana f **-1.** [administración] customs (pl). **-2.** [oficina] customs (office). **-3.** [derechos] customs duty.

aducir [33] vt to adduce.

adueñarse

◆ **adueñarse de** vpr **-1.** [apoderarse] to take over, to take control of. **-2.** [dominar] to take hold of.

adujera etc → **aducir.**

adulación f flattery.

adulador, -ra ◇ adj flattering. ◇ m y f flatterer.

adular vt to flatter.

adulón, -ona m y f toady.

adulteración f adulteration.

adulterar vt **-1.** [alimento] to adulterate. **-2.** [falsear] to doctor, to distort.

adulterio m adultery.

adúltero, -ra ◇ adj adulterous. ◇ m y f adulterer (f adulteress).

adulto, -ta adj, m y f adult.

adusto, -ta adj dour.

aduzca etc → **aducir.**

advenedizo, -za adj, m y f parvenu (f parvenue).

advenimiento m advent; [al trono] accession.

adverbial adj adverbial.

adverbio m adverb; ~ **de cantidad/lugar/modo/tiempo** adverb of degree/place/manner/time.

adversario, -ria m y f adversary.

adversativo, -va adj adversative.

adversidad f adversity.

adverso, -sa adj adverse; [destino] unkind; [suerte] bad; [viento] unfavourable.

advertencia f warning; **servir de** ~ to serve as a warning.

advertir [27] vt **-1.** [notar] to notice. **-2.** [prevenir, avisar] to warn; **te advierto que no deberías hacerlo** I'd advise against you doing it; **te advierto que no me sorprende** mind you, it doesn't surprise me.

adviento m Advent.

advierta etc → **advertir.**

advirtiera etc → **advertir.**

adyacente adj adjacent.

AEE (abrev de **Agencia Espacial Europea**) f ESA.

Aenor (abrev de **Asociación Española para la Normalización y Racionalización**) f ≃ BSI Br, ≃ MBS Am.

Aeorma (abrev de **Asociación Española para la Ordenación del Medio Ambiente**) f Spanish association for the protection of the environment, ≃ EPA Am.

aeración f aeration.

aéreo, -a adj **-1.** [del aire] aerial. **-2.** AERON air (antes de sust).

aerobic [ae'roβik] m aerobics (U).

aerobio, -bia adj aerobic.

aeroclub (pl **aeroclubs**) m flying club.

aerodeslizador m hovercraft.

aerodinámico, -ca adj **-1.** FÍS aerodynamic. **-2.** [forma, línea] streamlined.

◆ **aerodinámica** f aerodynamics (U).

aeródromo m airfield, aerodrome.

aeroespacial adj aerospace (antes de sust).

aerofaro m beacon (at airport).

aerógrafo m airbrush.

aerolínea f airline.

aerolito m aerolite.

AEROMEXICO (abrev de **Aerovías de México, SA**) f Mexican state airline.

aeromodelismo m airplane modelling.

aeromoza f Amer air hostess.

aeronauta m y f aeronaut.

aeronáutico, -ca adj aeronautic.

◆ **aeronáutica** f aeronautics (U).

aeronaval adj air and sea (antes de sust).

aeronave f [gen] aircraft; [dirigible] airship.

aeroplano m aeroplane.

aeropuerto m airport.

aerosol m aerosol.

aerospacial = **aeroespacial.**

aerostático, -ca adj aerostatic.

aeróstato m hot-air balloon.

aerotaxi m light aircraft (for hire).

aerotransportado, -da adj airborne.

aerotrén m maglev.

AES (abrev de **acuerdo económico y social**) m agreement between Spanish government and trade unions on social and economic issues.

afabilidad f affability.

afable adj affable.

afamado, -da adj famous.

afán m **-1.** [esfuerzo] hard work (U). **-2.** [anhelo] urge.

afanador, -ra m y f Amer cleaner.

afanar vt fam [robar] to pinch, to swipe.

◆ **afanarse** vpr [esforzarse]: ~**se (por hacer**

algo) to do everything one can (to do sthg).

Afanías (*abrev de* **Asociación de Familias con Niños y Adultos Subnormales**) *f Spanish association for families of the mentally handicapped.*

afanoso, -sa *adj* **-1.** [trabajoso, penoso] hard, demanding. **-2.** [que se afana] keen, eager.

afasia *f* aphasia.

afear *vt* to make ugly, to scar.

afección *f* **-1.** MED complaint, disease. **-2.** [afecto] affection.

afectación *f* affectation.

afectado, -da ◇ *adj* **-1.** [gen] affected. **-2.** [afligido] upset, badly affected. ◇ *m y f* [víctima] victim.

afectar *vt* **-1.** [gen] to affect. **-2.** [afligir] to upset, to affect badly.

afectísimo, -ma *adj* [en cartas]: **suyo ~** yours faithfully.

afectivo, -va *adj* **-1.** [emocional] emotional. **-2.** [cariñoso] affectionate, loving. **-3.** [sensible] sensitive.

afecto *m* affection, fondness; **sentir ~ por alguien, tenerle ~ a alguien** to be fond of sb.

afectuoso, -sa *adj* affectionate, loving.

afeitado *m* **-1.** [del pelo] shave. **-2.** TAUROM *blunting of bull's horns for safety reasons.*

afeitar *f* **-1.** [pelo] to shave. **-2.** TAUROM *to blunt bull's horns for safety reasons.*

◆ **afeitarse** *vpr* to shave.

afeite *m* **-1.** [acicalamiento] toilet, washing and dressing. **-2.** [cosmético] make-up (U).

afelpado, -da *adj* plush.

◆ **afelpado** *m* rush mat.

afeminado, -da *adj* effeminate.

◆ **afeminado** *m* effeminate man.

afeminarse *vpr* to become effeminate.

aferrarse *vpr:* **~ a** *lit* & *fig* to cling to.

affaire [a'fer] *m* affair.

Afganistán Afghanistan.

afgano, -na *adj, m y f* Afghan.

AFI ◇ *m* (*abrev de* **alfabeto fonético internacional**) IPA. ◇ *f* (*abrev de* **Asociación Fonética Internacional**) International Phonetic Association.

afianzamiento *m* [en cargo, liderazgo] consolidation.

afianzar [13] *vt* **-1.** [teoría, diagnóstico etc] to reinforce. **-2.** [objeto] to secure.

◆ **afianzarse** *vpr* to steady o.s.; **~se en algo** [opinión etc] to become sure O convinced of sthg; [cargo, liderazgo] to consolidate sthg.

afiche *m Amer* poster.

afición *f* **-1.** [inclinación] fondness, liking; **por ~** as a hobby; **tener ~ a algo** to be keen on sthg. **-2.** [aficionados] fans (*pl*).

aficionado, -da ◇ *adj* **-1.** [interesado] keen; **ser ~ a algo** to be keen on sthg. **-2.** [amateur] amateur. ◇ *m y f* **-1.** [interesado] fan; **~ al cine** film fan. **-2.** [amateur] amateur.

aficionar *vt:* **~ a alguien a algo** to make sb keen on sthg.

◆ **aficionarse** *vpr:* **~se a algo** to become keen on sthg.

afijo, -ja *adj* affixed.

◆ **afijo** *m* affix.

afilado, -da *adj* **-1.** [fino] sharp; [dedos] pointed. **-2.** *fig* [hiriente, mordaz] cutting.

◆ **afilado** *m* sharpening.

afilador, -ra ◇ *adj* sharpening. ◇ *m y f* [persona] knifegrinder.

◆ **afiladora** *f* [objeto] grindstone, sharpener.

afilalápices *m inv* pencil sharpener.

afilar *vt* to sharpen.

◆ **afilarse** *vpr fig* to become pointed, to taper.

afiliación *f* **-1.** [acción] joining. **-2.** [efecto] membership.

afiliado, -da *m y f:* **~ (a)** member (of).

afiliarse [8] *vpr:* **~se a** to join, to become a member of.

afín *adj* **-1.** [semejante] similar, like. **-2.** [contiguo] neighbouring.

afinar *vt* **-1.** MUS [instrumento] to tune; **~ la voz** to sing in tune. **-2.** [perfeccionar, mejorar] to fine-tune. **-3.** [pulir] to refine.

afincar [10] *vi* to buy land.

◆ **afincarse** *vpr:* **~se en** to settle in.

afinidad *f* **-1.** [gen & QUÍM] affinity. **-2.** [parentesco]: **por ~** by marriage.

afinque *etc* → **afincar**.

afirmación *f* statement, assertion.

afirmar *vt* **-1.** [confirmar] to confirm. **-2.** [decir] to say, to declare. **-3.** [consolidar] to reaffirm. **-4.** CONSTR to reinforce.

◆ **afirmarse** *vpr* **-1.** [asegurarse] to be confirmed. **-2.** [ratificarse]: **~se en algo** to reaffirm sthg.

afirmativo, -va *adj* affirmative.

◆ **afirmativa** *f* affirmative.

aflicción *f* suffering, sorrow.

afligir [15] *vt* to afflict; [causar pena] to distress.

◆ **afligirse** *vpr* to be distressed.

aflojar ◇ *vt* **-1.** [destensar] to loosen; [cuerda] to slacken. **-2.** *fam* [dinero] to fork out. ◇ *vi* **-1.** [disminuir] to abate, to die down. **-2.** *fig* [ceder] to ease of.

◆ **aflojarse** *vpr* [gen] to come loose; [cuerda] to slacken.

aflorar *vi* **-1.** *fig* [surgir] to (come to the) surface, to show. **-2.** MIN to outcrop.

afluencia *f* stream, volume.

afluente *m* tributary.

afluir [51]

◆ **afluir a** *vi* **-1.** [gente] to flock to. **-2.** [río] to flow into. **-3.** [sangre, fluido] to flow to.

afluya *etc* → **afluir**.

afluyera *etc* → **afluir**.

afma. *abrev de* **afectísima**.

afmo. *abrev de* **afectísimo**.

afonía *f* loss of voice.

afónico, -ca *adj*: quedarse ~ to lose one's voice.

aforar *vt* TECN to gauge.

aforismo *m* aphorism.

aforo *m* [cabida] seating capacity.

afortunadamente *adv* fortunately.

afortunado, -da ◇ *adj* **-1.** [agraciado] lucky, fortunate. **-2.** [feliz, oportuno] happy, felicitous. ◇ *m y f* [gen] lucky person; [en lotería] lucky winner.

afrancesado, -da ◇ *adj* Frenchified. ◇ *m y f* HIST *supporter of the French during the Peninsular War*.

afrenta *f* **-1.** [vergüenza] disgrace. **-2.** [ofensa, agravio] affront.

África Africa.

africado, -da *adj* LING affricative.

africanismo *m* Africanism.

africano, -na *adj, m y f* African.

afro *adj inv* afro.

afroamericano, -na *adj* Afro-American.

afrodisíaco, -ca, afrodisiaco, -ca *adj* aphrodisiac.

◆ **afrodisíaco** *m* aphrodisiac.

afrontar *vt* **-1.** [hacer frente a] to face. **-2.** [carear] to bring face to face.

afrutado, -da *adj* fruity.

afuera *adv* outside; por (la parte de) ~ on the outside.

◆ **afueras** *fpl*: las ~s the outskirts.

afuerita *adv Amer fam* right outside.

afusilar *vt Amer fam* to shoot.

agachar *vt* to lower; [la cabeza] to bow.

◆ **agacharse** *vpr* [acuclillarse] to crouch down; [inclinar la cabeza] to stoop.

agalla *f* ZOOL gill.

◆ **agallas** *fpl fig* guts.

ágape *m culto* banquet, feast.

agarrada → **agarrado**.

agarradero *m* **-1.** [asa] hold. **-2.** *fam fig* [pretexto] pretext, excuse.

agarrado, -da *adj* **-1.** [asido]: ~ **(de)** gripped (by); ~s del brazo arm in arm; ~s de la mano hand in hand. **-2.** *fam* [tacaño] tight, stingy.

◆ **agarrado** *m fam* smooch.

◆ **agarrada** *f fam* row, bust-up.

agarrar ◇ *vt* **-1.** [asir] to grab. **-2.** [pillar -ladrón, enfermedad] to catch; ~la *fam fig* to get pissed. ◇ *vi* [tinte] to take; [planta] to take root.

◆ **agarrarse** *vpr* **-1.** [sujetarse] to hold on; ~se de O a algo to hold on to O clutch sthg. **-2.** [pegarse] to stick. **-3.** *fam fig* [pelearse] to scrap, to have a fight. **-4.** *fig* [pretextar]: ~se a algo to use sthg as an excuse.

agarrón *m* **-1.** [tirón] pull, tug. **-2.** *fam* [altercado] scrap, fight.

agarrotar *vt* [parte del cuerpo] to cut off the circulation in; [mente] to numb.

◆ **agarrotarse** *vpr* **-1.** [parte del cuerpo] to go numb. **-2.** [mecanismo] to seize up.

agasajar *vt* to lavish attention on, to treat like a king; ~ a alguien con algo to lavish sthg upon sb.

agasajo *m* lavish attention.

ágata *f* (*el*) agate.

agazaparse *vpr* **-1.** [para esconderse] to crouch. **-2.** [agacharse] to bend down.

agencia *f* **-1.** [empresa] agency; ~ de noticias O prensa news agency; ~ de aduanas customs agent's; ~ inmobiliaria estate agent's *Br*, real estate office *Am*; ~ matrimonial marriage bureau; ~ de publicidad advertising agency; ~ de viajes travel agency. **-2.** [sucursal] branch.

agenciar [8] *vt*: ~ algo a alguien to fix sb up with sthg.

◆ **agenciarse** *vpr* to get hold of, to fix o.s. up with.

agenda *f* **-1.** [de notas, fechas] diary; [de teléfonos, direcciones] book; ~ electrónica electronic pocket diary, digital organizer. **-2.** [de trabajo] agenda.

agente ◇ *m y f* [persona] agent; ~ de policía O de la autoridad policeman *Br* [policewoman); ~ de aduanas customs officer; ~ de cambio (y bolsa) stockbroker; ~ comercial broker; ~ secreto secret agent; ~s económicos ECON social partners. ◇ *m* **-1.** [causa activa] agent. **-2.** GRAM → **complemento**.

agigantar *vt* to blow up, to magnify.

ágil *adj* **-1.** [movimiento, persona] agile. **-2.** [estilo, lenguaje] fluent; [respuesta, mente] nimble, sharp.

agilidad *f* agility.

agilipollado, -da *adj vulg* dense.

agilizar [13] *vt* to speed up.

agio *m* ECON agio.

agiotaje *m* ECON agiotage, speculation.

agitación *f* -1. [movimiento - de botella etc] shaking; [- de líquido] stirring; [- de brazos] waving. -2. [intranquilidad] restlessness. -3. [jaleo] racket, commotion. -4. [conflicto] unrest.

agitador, -ra ◇ *adj* [viento] gusty. ◇ *m y f* agitator.

agitanado, -da *adj* gypsy-like.

agitar *vt* -1. [mover - botella etc] to shake; [- líquido] to stir; [- brazos] to wave. -2. [inquietar] to perturb, to worry. -3. [alterar, perturbar] to stir up.

◆ **agitarse** *vpr* [inquietarse] to get worried.

aglomeración *f* build-up; [de gente] crowd.

aglomerar *vt* to bring together.

◆ **aglomerarse** *vpr* to amass.

aglutinante *adj* -1. [adherente] agglutinant. -2. LING agglutinative.

aglutinar *vt* -1. [pegar] to agglutinate. -2. MED to bind. -3. *fig* [aunar, reunir - personas] to unite; [- ideas, esfuerzos] to pool.

agnóstico, -ca *adj, m y f* agnostic.

ago. (*abrev de* **agosto**) Aug.

agobiado, -da *adj*: ~ (de) [trabajo] snowed under (with); [problemas] weighed down (with).

agobiante *adj* [presión, trabajo, persona] overwhelming; [calor] oppressive.

agobiar [8] *vt* to overwhelm.

◆ **agobiarse** *vpr* to feel overwhelmed, to let things get one down.

agobio *m* -1. [físico] choking, suffocation. -2. [psíquico] pressure.

agolparse *vpr* -1. [gente] to crowd round; [sangre] to rush. -2. *fig* [problemas] to come to a head.

agonía *f* -1. [pena] agony. -2. [ansia] desperation. -3. [del moribundo] death throes (*pl*). -4. *fig* [decadencia] decline, dying days (*pl*).

agonizante *adj* dying.

agonizar [13] *vi* -1. [expirar] to be dying. -2. *fig* [extinguirse] to fizzle out. -3. *fig* [sufrir] to be in agony.

agorafobia *f* agoraphobia.

agorero, -ra *m y f* prophet of doom.

agosto *m* -1. [mes] August; *ver también* septiembre. -2. *fig* [cosecha] harvest (time). -3. *loc*: hacer su ~ to line one's pockets.

agotado, -da *adj* -1. [cansado]: ~ (de) exhausted (from). -2. [producto] out of stock, sold out. -3. [pila, batería] flat.

agotador, -ra *adj* exhausting.

agotamiento *m* -1. [cansancio] exhaustion. -2. [de producto] selling-out.

agotar *vt* [gen] to exhaust; [producto] to sell out of; [agua] to drain.

◆ **agotarse** *vpr* -1. [cansarse] to tire o.s. out. -2. [acabarse] to run out; [libro, disco, entradas] to be sold out; [pila, batería] to go flat.

agraciado, -da ◇ *adj* -1. [atractivo] attractive, fetching. -2. [afortunado]: ~ con algo lucky enough to win sthg. ◇ *m y f* [afortunado] lucky winner.

agraciar [8] *vt* -1. [embellecer] to make more attractive ○ fetching. -2. [conceder una gracia] to pardon. -3. *culto* [premiar] to reward.

agradable *adj* pleasant.

agradar ◇ *vi* to be pleasant. ◇ *vt* to please.

agradecer [30] *vt* -1. [suj: persona]: ~ algo a alguien [dar las gracias] to thank sb for sthg; [estar agradecido] to be grateful to sb for sthg. -2. [suj: cosas] to be thankful for.

◆ **agradecerse** *v impers* to be nice.

agradecido, -da *adj* grateful.

agradecimiento *m* gratitude.

agrado *m* -1. [gusto] pleasure; **ésto no es de mi ~** this is not to my liking. -2. [afabilidad] kindness.

agrandar *vt* to make bigger.

agrario, -ria *adj* [reforma] agrarian; [producto, política] agricultural.

agravación *f*, **agravamiento** *m* worsening, exacerbation.

agravante ◇ *adj* aggravating. ◇ *m o f* -1. [problema] additional problem. -2. DER aggravating circumstance.

agravar *vt* to aggravate; [impuestos etc] to increase (the burden of).

◆ **agravarse** *vpr* to get worse, to worsen.

agraviar [8] *vt* to offend.

agravio *m* -1. [ofensa] offence, insult. -2. [perjuicio] wrong.

agredido, -da *m y f* victim (*of an attack*).

agredir [78] *vt* to attack.

agregado, -da ◇ *adj* [añadido] added on. ◇ *m y f* -1. EDUC assistant teacher. -2. [de embajada] attaché; ~ **cultural** cultural attaché.

◆ **agregado** *m* -1. [añadido] addition. -2. ECON aggregate.

agregar [16] *vt*: ~ (algo a algo) to add (sthg to sthg).

◆ **agregarse** *vpr*: ~se a algo to join (sthg).

agresión *f* [ataque] act of aggression, attack.

agresividad *f* aggression.

agresivo, -va *adj lit* & *fig* aggressive.

agresor, -ra *m y f* attacker, assailant.

agreste *adj* **-1.** [abrupto, rocoso] rough, rugged. **-2.** [rural] country (*antes de sust*), rural. **-3.** *fig* [basto, rudo] coarse, uncouth.

agriar [9] *vt* **-1.** [vino, leche] to (turn) sour. **-2.** *fig* [carácter] to sour, to embitter.
◆ **agriarse** *vpr lit* & *fig* to turn sour.

agrícola *adj* agricultural; [pueblo] farming (*antes de sust*).

agricultor, -ra *m y f* farmer.

agricultura *f* agriculture; ~ extensiva/intensiva extensive/intensive farming.

agridulce *adj* bittersweet; CULIN sweet and sour.

agrietar *vt* **-1.** [muro, tierra] to crack. **-2.** [labios, manos] to chap.
◆ **agrietarse** *vpr* [la piel] to chap.

agrio, agria *adj* **-1.** [ácido] sour. **-2.** *fig* [áspero] acerbic, bitter.
◆ **agrios** *mpl* citrus fruits.

agriparse *vpr Amer* to catch the flu.

agro *m* farmland.

agronomía *f* agronomy.

agrónomo, -ma *m y f* agronomist.

agropecuario, -ria *adj* farming and livestock (*antes de sust*).

agrupación *f* **-1.** [asociación] group, association. **-2.** [agrupamiento] grouping.

agrupamiento *m* [concentración] grouping.

agrupar *vt* to group (together).
◆ **agruparse** *vpr* **-1.** [congregarse] to gather (round). **-2.** [unirse] to form a group.

agua *f* (*el*) water; ~ bendita/dulce/destilada/potable holy/fresh/distilled/drinking water; ~ mineral sin gas/con gas still/sparkling mineral water; claro como el ~ as clear as day; estar con el ~ al cuello to be up to one's neck (in it); hacer ~ NÁUT to leak; *fig* to go under; hacerse ~ en la boca to melt in one's mouth; quedar en ~ de borrajas to come to nothing; venir como ~ de mayo to be a godsend.
◆ **aguas** *fpl* **-1.** [manantial] waters, spring (*sg*); ~s termales thermal O hot springs. **-2.** [de río, mar] waters; ~s territoriales O jurisdiccionales territorial waters. **-3.** [de tejado] slope. **-4.** [de diamantes, telas] water (*U*). **-5.** *loc*: nadar entre dos ~s to sit on the fence; ha roto ~s her waters have broken.
◆ **agua de colonia** *f* eau de cologne.
◆ **agua oxigenada** *f* hydrogen peroxide.
◆ **aguas menores** *fpl* water (*U*), urine (*U*).
◆ **aguas residuales** *fpl* sewage (*U*).

aguacate *m* **-1.** [fruto] avocado (pear). **-2.** [árbol] avocado.

aguacero *m* shower.

aguachirle *f* dishwater (*U*), revolting drink.

aguado, -da *adj* **-1.** [con demasiada agua] watery; [diluido a propósito] watered-down. **-2.** *fig* [estropeado] ruined.
◆ **aguada** *f* ARTE gouache.

aguafiestas *m y f inv* spoilsport.

aguafuerte *m* etching.

aguaitada *f Amer fam* glance; echar una ~ a algo to have a look at sthg.

aguaitar *vt Amer fam* **-1.** [mirar] to look at. **-2.** [acechar] to spy on.

aguamarina *f* aquamarine.

aguamiel *m Amer* water mixed with honey or cane syrup.

aguanieve *f* sleet.

aguantar *vt* **-1.** [sostener] to hold. **-2.** [resistir - peso] to bear. **-3.** [tolerar, soportar] to bear, to stand; no sé cómo la aguantas I don't know how you put up with her. **-4.** [contener - risa] to contain; [- respiración] to hold. **-5.** [esperar - tiempo] to hold out for, to wait for.
◆ **aguantarse** *vpr* **-1.** [contenerse] to restrain o.s., to hold o.s. back. **-2.** [resignarse]: no quiere ~se he refuses to put up with it.

aguante *m* **-1.** [paciencia] self-restraint, tolerance. **-2.** [resistencia] strength; [de persona] stamina.

aguar [45] *vt* **-1.** [mezclar con agua] to water down. **-2.** *fig* [estropear] to spoil, to ruin.
◆ **aguarse** *vpr* to be spoiled.

aguardar *vt* to wait for, to await.

aguardiente *m* spirit, liquor.

aguarrás *m* turpentine.

aguatero *m Amer* water carrier.

aguce *etc* → aguzar.

agudeza *f* **-1.** [gen] sharpness. **-2.** [dicho ingenioso] witticism.

agudizar [13] *vt* **-1.** [afilar] to sharpen. **-2.** *fig* [acentuar] to exacerbate, to make worse.
◆ **agudizarse** *vpr* **-1.** [crisis] to get worse. **-2.** [ingenio] to get sharper.

agudo, -da *adj* **-1.** [gen] sharp; [crisis, problema, enfermedad] serious, acute. **-2.** *fig* [perspicaz] keen, sharp. **-3.** *fig* [ingenioso] witty. **-4.** GRAM oxytone. **-5.** MUS [nota, voz] high, high-pitched.

agüe *etc* → aguar.

agüero *m*: de buen/mal ~ that bodes well/ill.

aguerrido, -da *adj culto* **-1.** [valiente] battle-hardened. **-2.** *fig* [experimentado] veteran (*antes de sust*).

aguijar *vt* [caballo] to spur; [buey] to goad.

aguijón *m* **-1.** [de insecto] sting. **-2.** [de planta] thorn. **-3.** [de espada, palo] point; [de tenedor] prong. **-4.** *fig* [estímulo] spur, stimulus.

aguijonear *vt* **-1.** [espolear]: ~ **a alguien para que haga algo** to goad sb into doing sthg. **-2.** *fig* [estimular] to drive on.

águila *f* (*el*) **-1.** [ave] eagle. **-2.** *fig* [vivo, listo] sharp ○ perceptive person.

aguileño, -ña *adj* aquiline.

aguilucho *m* eaglet.

aguinaldo *m* Christmas box.

aguja *f* **-1.** [de coser, jeringuilla] needle; [de hacer punto] knitting needle; ~ **hipodérmica** hypodermic needle; **es como buscar una ~ en un pajar** it's like looking for a needle in a haystack. **-2.** [de reloj] hand; [de brújula] pointer; [de iglesia] spire. **-3.** FERROC point. **-4.** [de tocadiscos] stylus, needle.
◆ **agujas** *fpl* [de res] ribs.

agujerear *vt* to make a hole ○ holes in.

agujero *m* hole; ~ **negro** ASTRON black hole.

agujetas *fpl*: **tener** ~ to feel stiff.

agustino, -na *m y f* Augustinian.

aguzar [13] *vt* **-1.** [afilar] to sharpen. **-2.** *fig* [apetito] to whet; [ingenio] to sharpen.

ah *interj*: ¡~! [admiración] ooh!; [sorpresa] oh!; [pena] ah!

ahí *adv* there; **vino por** ~ he came that way; **la solución está** ~ that's where the solution lies; ¡~ **tienes!** here you are!, there you go!; **de** ~ **que** [por eso] and consequently, so; **está por** ~ [en lugar indefinido] he/she is around (somewhere); [en la calle] he/she is out; **por** ~, **por** ~ *fig* something like that; **por** ~ **va la cosa** you're not too far wrong.

ahijado, -da *m y f* **-1.** [de padrinos] godson (*f* goddaughter). **-2.** *fig* [protegido] protégé.

ahijar *vt* to adopt.

ahijuna, aijuna *interj Amer fam*: ¡~! wow!

ahínco *m* enthusiasm, devotion.

ahíto, -ta *adj* **-1.** *culto* [saciado]: **estar** ~ to be full. **-2.** *fig* [fastidiado]: ~ (**de**) fed up (with).

AHN (*abrev de* **Archivo Histórico Nacional**) *m Spanish national historical archive.*

ahogado, -da ◇ *adj* **-1.** [en el agua] drowned. **-2.** [falto de aliento - respiración] laboured; [- persona] out of breath; [- grito] muffled. **-3.** [estrecho] cramped. **-4.** *fig* [agobiado] overwhelmed, swamped. ◇ *m y f* drowned person.

ahogar [16] *vt* **-1.** [asfixiar - en el agua] to drown; [- cubriendo la boca y nariz] to smother, to suffocate. **-2.** [estrangular] to strangle. **-3.** [extinguir] to extinguish, to put out. **-4.** *fig* [dominar - levantamiento] to put down, to quell; [- pena] to hold back, to contain.
◆ **ahogarse** *vpr* **-1.** [en el agua] to drown. **-2.** [asfixiarse] to suffocate. **-3.** *fig* [de calor] to be stifled.

ahogo *m* **-1.** [asfixia] breathlessness, difficulty in breathing. **-2.** *fig* [angustia] anguish, distress. **-3.** *fig* [económico] financial difficulty.

ahogue *etc* → **ahogar.**

ahondar *vi* [profundizar] to go into detail; ~ **en** [penetrar] to penetrate deep into; [profundizar] to study in depth.

ahora ◇ *adv* **-1.** [en el presente] now; ~ **mismo** right now; **por** ~ for the time being. **-2.** [pronto] in a second ○ moment. ◇ *conj* **-1.** [ya ... ya]: ~ **habla,** ~ **canta** one minute she's talking, the next she's singing. **-2.** [pero] but, however; ~ **que** but, though; ~ **bien** but, however.

ahorcado, -da *m y f* hanged man (*f* hanged woman).

ahorcar [10] *vt* to hang.
◆ **ahorcarse** *vpr* to hang o.s.

ahorita, ahoritita *adv Amer fam* right now.

ahorque *etc* → **ahorcar.**

ahorrador, -ra ◇ *adj* thrifty, careful with money. ◇ *m y f* thrifty person.

ahorrar *vt* to save.
◆ **ahorrarse** *vpr*: ~**se algo** to save ○ spare o.s. sthg.

ahorro *m* **-1.** [gen] saving. **-2.** (*gen pl*) [cantidad ahorrada] savings (*pl*).

AHS (*abrev de* **Asociación de Hombres Separados**) *f Spanish association for men separated from their wives.*

ahuecar [10] ◇ *vt* **-1.** [poner hueco - manos] to cup; [- tronco] to hollow out. **-2.** [mullir - colchón] to plump up; [- tierra] to hoe. ◇ *vi fam* [irse] to clear off.
◆ **ahuecarse** *vpr fam fig* to puff up ○ swell with pride.

ahuevado, -da *adj Amer fam* [tonto] daft.

ahumado, -da *adj* smoked.
◆ **ahumado** *m* smoking.

ahumar *vt* **-1.** [jamón, pescado] to smoke. **-2.** [habitación etc] to fill with smoke.
◆ **ahumarse** *vpr* **-1.** [saber a humo] to acquire a smoky taste. **-2.** [ennegrecerse de humo] to become blackened with smoke.

ahuyentar *vt* **-1.** [espantar, asustar] to scare away. **-2.** *fig* [apartar] to drive away.

AID (*abrev de* **Asociación Internacional de Desarrollo**) *f* IDA.

AIEA (*abrev de* **Agencia Internacional de Energía Atómica**) *f* IAEA.

aijuna = **ahijuna**.

airado, -da *adj* angry.

airar *vt* to anger, to make angry.

◆ **airarse** *vpr* to get angry.

aire *m* **-1.** [fluido] air; **al ~ exposed; al ~ libre** in the open air; **cambiar de ~s** to have a change of scene; **dejar algo en el ~** to leave sthg up in the air; **estar en el ~** to be in the air; **saltar** ○ **volar por los ~s** to be blown sky high, to explode; **tomar el ~** to go for a breath of fresh air. **-2.** [viento] wind; [corriente] draught; **hoy hace (mucho) ~** it's (very) windy today. **-3.** *fig* [aspecto] air, appearance. **-4.** *fig* [parecido]: **tiene un ~ a su madre** she has something of her mother. **-5.** *fig* [gracia] grace, elegance. **-6.** *loc*: **a mi/tu** *etc* **~** my/your *etc* (own) way.

◆ **aires** *mpl* [vanidad] airs (and graces); **darse ~s** to put on airs.

◆ **aire (acondicionado)** *m* air-conditioning.

aireación *f* ventilation.

airear *vt* **-1.** [ventilar] to air. **-2.** *fig* [contar] to air (publicly).

◆ **airearse** *vpr* to get a breath of fresh air.

airoso, -sa *adj* **-1.** [garboso] graceful, elegant. **-2.** [triunfante]: **salir ~ de algo** to come out of sthg with flying colours.

aislacionismo *m* isolationism.

aislado, -da *adj* **-1.** [gen] isolated. **-2.** TECN insulated.

aislamiento *m* **-1.** [gen] isolation. **-2.** TECN insulation.

aislante *adj* insulating.

aislar *vt* **-1.** [gen] to isolate. **-2.** TECN to insulate.

AIT (*abrev de* **Asociación Internacional de Trabajadores**) *f* First International Working Men's Association.

aizkolari *m* competitor in the rural Basque sport of chopping felled tree-trunks.

ajá *interj* ¡~! [sorpresa] aha!; *fam* [aprobación] great!

Ajaccio [a'jaksio] Ajaccio.

ajar *vt* [flores] to wither, to cause to fade; [piel] to wrinkle; [colores] to make faded; [ropa] to wear out.

◆ **ajarse** *vpr* [flores] to fade, to wither; [piel] to wrinkle, to become wrinkled.

ajardinado, -da *adj* landscaped.

a.JC. = a. de JC.

ajedrecista *m y f* chess player.

ajedrez *m inv* chess.

ajenjo *m* **-1.** BOT wormwood, absinth. **-2.** [licor] absinth.

ajeno, -na *adj* **-1.** [de otro] of others; **jugar en campo ~** to play away from home. **-2.** [extraño]: **~ a** having nothing to do with; **~ a nuestra voluntad** beyond our control. **-3.** *fig* [libre]: **~ de** free from.

ajetreo *m* **-1.** [tarea] running around, hard work. **-2.** [animación] (hustle and) bustle.

ají *m Amer* chilli (pepper).

ajiaceite *m sauce made from garlic and olive oil.*

ajiaco *m Amer* [estofado] stew.

ajillo

◆ **al ajillo** *loc adj* CULIN *in a sauce made with oil, garlic and chilli.*

ajo *m* garlic; **~ blanco** CULIN cold garlic soup; **~ tierno** spring onion; **andar** ○ **estar en el ~** *fig* to be in on it.

ajuntarse *vpr fam* to live together.

ajustado, -da *adj* **-1.** [ceñido - ropa] tight-fitting; [- tuerca, pieza] tight; [- resultado, final] close. **-2.** [justo] correct, right; [precio] reasonable.

◆ **ajustado** *m* fitting.

ajustador, -ra ◇ *adj* adjusting. ◇ *m y f* typesetter.

ajustadores *mpl Amer* bra (*sg*).

ajustar *vt* **-1.** [arreglar] to adjust. **-2.** [apretar] to tighten. **-3.** [encajar - piezas de motor] to fit; [- puerta, ventana] to push to. **-4.** [pactar - matrimonio] to arrange; [- pleito] to settle; [- paz] to negotiate; [- precio] to fix, to agree.

◆ **ajustarse a** *vpr* **-1.** [adaptarse] to adapt to. **-2.** [conformarse] to fit in with.

ajuste *m* [de pieza] fitting; [de mecanismo] adjustment; [de salario] agreement; **~ de cuentas** *fig* settling of scores.

al → **a**.

ala *f* (*el*) **-1.** POLÍT & ZOOL wing; **ahuecar el ~** *fam* to clear off, to hop it; **cortar las ~s a alguien** to clip sb's wings. **-2.** [parte lateral - de tejado] **eaves** (*pl*); [- de sombrero] brim; [- de nariz] side; [- de mesa] leaf. **-3.** DEP winger, wing.

◆ **ala delta** *f* [aparato] hang glider.

alabanza *f* praise.

alabar *vt* to praise.

alabastro *m* alabaster.

alabear *vt* to warp.

◆ **alabearse** *vpr* to warp.

alacena *f* recess for storing food.

alacrán *m* [animal] scorpion.

alado, -da *adj* **-1.** [con alas] winged. **-2.** *fig* [ligero] swift, fleet.

ALALC (*abrev de* **Asociación Latinoamericana de Libre Comercio**) *f* LAFTA.

alambicado, -da *adj* elaborate, involved.

alambicar [10] *vt* **-1.** [destilar] to distil. **-2.** *fig* [complicar] to over-complicate.

alambique *m* still.

alambrada *f* wire-fence.

alambre *m* wire; ~ **de espino** O **púas** barbed wire.

alameda *f* **-1.** [sitio con álamos] poplar grove. **-2.** [paseo] tree-lined avenue.

álamo *m* poplar.

alano *m* [perro] mastiff.

alar *m* eaves (*pl*).

alarde *m*: ~ **(de)** show O display (of); **hacer** ~ **de algo** to show sthg off, to flaunt sthg.

alardear *vi*: ~ **de** to show off about.

alargador, -ra *adj* extension (*antes de sust*).

◆ **alargador** *m* extension lead.

alargamiento *m* extension, lengthening.

alargar [16] *vt* **-1.** [ropa etc] to lengthen. **-2.** [viaje, visita, plazo] to extend; [conversación] to spin out. **-3.** [pasar]: ~ **algo a alguien** to pass sthg (over) to sb.

◆ **alargarse** *vpr* **-1.** [hacerse más largo - días] to get longer; [- reunión] to be prolonged. **-2.** *fig* [hacerse muy largo] to go on for ages.

alarido *m* shriek, howl.

alarma *f* **-1.** [gen] alarm; **dar la** ~ to raise the alarm. **-2.** MIL call to arms.

alarmante *adj* alarming.

alarmar *vt* **-1.** [avisar] to alert. **-2.** *fig* [asustar] to alarm.

◆ **alarmarse** *vpr* [inquietarse] to be alarmed.

alarmista *m y f* alarmist.

Alaska Alaska.

alazán, -ana *adj* chestnut.

alba *f* (*el*) **-1.** [amanecer] dawn, daybreak; **al** ~ at dawn. **-2.** [vestidura] alb.

albacea *m y f* executor (*f* executrix).

albahaca *f* basil.

albaicín *m* *district of a town built on a hillside, esp that of Granada.*

albanés, -esa *adj, m y f* Albanian.

◆ **albanés** *m* [lengua] Albanian.

Albania Albania.

albañil *m* bricklayer.

albañilería *f* **-1.** [arte] bricklaying. **-2.** [obra] brickwork.

albarán *m* delivery note.

albaricoque *m* apricot.

albatros *m inv* albatross.

albedrío *m* [antojo, elección] fancy, whim; **a su** ~ as takes his/her fancy; **libre** ~ free will; **a su libre** ~ of his/her own free will.

alberca *f* **-1.** [depósito] water tank. **-2.** *Amer* [piscina] swimming pool.

albergar [16] *vt* **-1.** [personas] to accommodate, to put up. **-2.** [odio] to harbour; [esperanzas] to cherish.

◆ **albergarse** *vpr* to stay.

albergue *m* accommodation (*U*), lodgings (*pl*); [de montaña] shelter, refuge; ~ **de juventud** O **juvenil** youth hostel.

albino, -na *adj, m y f* albino.

albis

◆ **in albis** *loc adv*: **estar in** ~ to be in the dark; **quedarse in** ~ not to have a clue O the faintest idea.

albóndiga *f* meatball.

albor *m* **-1.** [blancura] whiteness. **-2.** [luz del alba] first light of day. **-3.** (*gen pl*) *fig* [principio] dawn, earliest days (*pl*).

alborada *f* **-1.** [amanecer] dawn, daybreak. **-2.** MÚS *popular song sung at dawn.* **-3.** MIL reveille.

alborear *v impers*: **empezaba a** ~ **dawn** was breaking.

albornoz *m* bathrobe.

alborotador, -ra ◇ *adj* rowdy. ◇ *m y f* troublemaker.

alborotar ◇ *vi* to be noisy O rowdy. ◇ *vt* **-1.** [perturbar] to disturb, to unsettle. **-2.** [amotinar] to stir up, to rouse. **-3.** [desordenar] to mess up.

◆ **alborotarse** *vpr* [perturbarse] to get worked up.

alboroto *m* **-1.** [ruido] din. **-2.** [jaleo] fuss, to-do. **-3.** [desorden] mess.

alborozar [13] *vt* to delight.

alborozo *m* delight, joy.

albricias *interj*: ¡~! great (news)!

albufera *f* lagoon.

álbum (*pl* **álbumes**) *m* album.

albúmina *f* albumin.

albuminoide *adj* albuminoid.

alcabala *f Amer* police checkpoint.

alcachofa *f* **-1.** BOT artichoke. **-2.** [pieza - de regadera] rose, sprinkler; [- de ducha] shower head.

alcahuete, -ta *m y f* **-1.** [mediador] go-between. **-2.** [chismoso] gossipmonger.

alcaide *m* prison governor.

alcalde, -desa *m y f* mayor (*f* mayoress).

alcaldía *f* **-1.** [cargo] mayoralty. **-2.** [lugar] mayor's office. **-3.** [jurisdicción] municipality.

álcali *m* alkali.

alcalino, -na *adj* alkaline.

alcaloide *m* alkaloid.

alcance *m* **-1.** [de arma, misil, emisora] range; **de corto/largo** ~ short-/long- range. **-2.** [de persona]: **a mi/a tu** *etc* ~ within my/your *etc* reach; **al** ~ **de la vista** within sight; **dar** ~ **a alguien** to catch up with sb; **fuera del** ~ **de** beyond the reach of. **-3.** [de reformas etc] scope, extent; **de** ~ important, far-reaching. **-4.** [talento]: **de pocos** ~**s** slow, dim-witted.

alcancía *f* money box.

alcanfor *m* camphor.

alcantarilla *f* sewer; [boca] drain.

alcantarillado *m* sewers (*pl*).

alcanzar [13] ◇ *vt* **-1.** [llegar a] to reach. **-2.** [igualarse con] to catch up with. **-3.** [agarrar] to take. **-4.** [entregar] to pass. **-5.** [suj: bala etc] to hit. **-6.** [lograr] to obtain. **-7.** [afectar] to affect. **-8.** [autobús, tren] to manage to catch. ◇ *vi* **-1.** [ser suficiente]: ~ **para algo/hacer algo** to be enough for sthg/to do sthg. **-2.** [poder]: ~ **a hacer algo** to be able to do sthg.

alcaparra *f* caper.

alcatraz *m* gannet.

alcaucil *m* *Amer* [alcachofa] artichoke.

alcayata *f* hook.

alcazaba *f* citadel.

alcázar *m* fortress.

alce ◇ *v* → **alzar.** ◇ *m* elk, moose.

alcista *adj* FIN bullish; [mercado] bull (*antes de sust*).

alcoba *f* bedroom.

alcohol *m* alcohol; ~ **etílico** QUÍM ethyl alcohol; ~ **de quemar** methylated spirits (*pl*).

alcoholemia *f* blood alcohol level.

alcohólico, -ca *adj, m y f* alcoholic.

alcoholímetro *m* **-1.** [para bebida] alcoholometer. **-2.** [para la sangre] Breathalyzer® *Br*, drunkometer *Am*.

alcoholismo *m* alcoholism.

alcoholizar [13] *vt* to turn into an alcoholic.

◆ **alcoholizarse** *vpr* to become an alcoholic.

alcohotest (*pl* **alcohotests**) *m* Breathalyzer® *Br*, drunkometer *Am*.

alcornoque *m* **-1.** [árbol] cork oak. **-2.** [madera] cork, corkwood. **-3.** *fig* [persona] idiot, fool.

alcotán *m* hobby (*bird*).

alcurnia *f* lineage, descent.

aldaba *f* **-1.** [llamador] doorknocker. **-2.** [pestillo] latch.

aldea *f* small village.

aldeano, -na *m y f* villager.

ale *interj*: ¡~! come on!

aleación *f* **-1.** [acción] alloying. **-2.** [producto] alloy.

alear *vt* to alloy.

aleatorio, -ria *adj* [número] random; [suceso] chance (*antes de sust*).

alebrestarse *vpr* *Amer* **-1.** [rebelarse] to rebel. **-2.** [ponerse nervioso] to get worked up.

aleccionador, -ra *adj* **-1.** [instructivo] instructive. **-2.** [ejemplar] exemplary.

aleccionar *vt* to instruct, to teach.

aledaño, -ña *adj* adjacent.

◆ **aledaños** *mpl* surrounding area (*sg*).

alegación *f* allegation.

alegar [16] *vt* [motivos, pruebas] to put forward; ~ **que** to claim (that).

alegato *m* **-1.** DER & *fig* plea. **-2.** [ataque] diatribe.

alegoría *f* allegory.

alegórico, -ca *adj* allegorical.

alegrar *vt* **-1.** [persona] to cheer up, to make happy; [fiesta] to liven up. **-2.** *fig* [habitación etc] to brighten up. **-3.** *fig* [emborrachar] to make tipsy.

◆ **alegrarse** *vpr* **-1.** [sentir alegría]: ~**se (de algo/por alguien)** to be pleased (about sthg/for sb). **-2.** *fig* [emborracharse] to get tipsy.

alegre *adj* **-1.** [contento] happy. **-2.** [que da alegría] cheerful, bright. **-3.** *fig* [arriesgado] happy-go-lucky. **-4.** *fam* [borracho] tipsy. **-5.** *fig* [deshonesto] loose.

alegría *f* **-1.** [gozo] happiness, joy. **-2.** [motivo de gozo] joy. **-3.** *fig* [irresponsabilidad] rashness, recklessness.

alegrón *m* *fam* pleasant surprise.

alegue *etc* → **alegar.**

alejamiento *m* **-1.** [lejanía] remoteness. **-2.** [distancia] distance. **-3.** [separación - de objetos etc] separation; [- entre personas] estrangement.

Alejandría Alexandria.

alejar *vt* **-1.** [poner más lejos] to move away. **-2.** *fig* [ahuyentar] to drive out.

◆ **alejarse** *vpr*: ~**se (de)** [ponerse más lejos] to go ○ move away (from); [retirarse] to leave.

alelado, -da *adj* stupid.

alelar *vt* to daze, to stupefy.

aleluya ◇ *m o f* hallelujah. ◇ *interj*: ¡~! Hallelujah!

alemán, -ana *adj, m y f* German.

◆ **alemán** *m* [lengua] German.

Alemania Germany.

alentador, -ra *adj* encouraging.

alentar [19] *vt* to encourage.

alergia *f lit* & *fig* allergy; **tener ~ a algo** to be allergic to sthg.

alérgico, -ca *adj lit* & *fig*: **~ (a)** allergic (to).

alero *m* **-1.** [del tejado] eaves (*pl*). **-2.** DEP winger, wing. **-3.** AUTOM wing. **-4.** *loc*: **estar en el ~** to be (hanging) in the balance.

alerón *m* aileron.

alerta ◇ *adj inv* & *adv* alert. ◇ *f* alert; **~ roja** red alert. ◇ *interj*: **¡~!** watch ○ look out!

alertar *vt* to alert.

aleta *f* **-1.** [de pez] fin. **-2.** [de buzo, foca] flipper. **-3.** [de coche] wing. **-4.** [de nariz] flared part.

aletargar [16] *vt* to make drowsy, to send to sleep.

◆ **aletargarse** *vpr* to become drowsy ○ sleepy.

aletear *vi* to flap ○ flutter its wings.

alevín *m* **-1.** [cría de pez] fry, young fish. **-2.** *fig* [persona] novice, beginner.

alevosía *f* **-1.** [traición] treachery. **-2.** [premeditación] premeditation.

alevoso, -sa *adj* **-1.** [traidor] treacherous. **-2.** [premeditado] premeditated.

alfa *f* (*el*) FÍS & MAT alpha; **~ y omega** beginning and end, alpha and omega.

alfabético, -ca *adj* alphabetical.

alfabetización *f* **-1.** [de personas - acción] teaching to read and write; [- estado] literacy. **-2.** [de palabras, letras] alphabetization.

alfabetizar [13] *vt* **-1.** [personas] to teach to read and write. **-2.** [palabras, letras] to put into alphabetical order.

alfabeto *m* alphabet; **~ Morse** Morse code.

alfalfa *f* alfalfa, lucerne.

alfanumérico, -ca *adj* INFORM alphanumeric.

alfaque *m* sandbank, bar.

alfarería *f* **-1.** [técnica] pottery. **-2.** [lugar] potter's, pottery shop.

alfarero, -ra *m y f* potter.

alféizar *m* window-sill.

alfeñique *m fam fig* [persona] weakling.

alférez *m* ≃ second lieutenant.

alfil *m* bishop.

alfiler *m* **-1.** [aguja] pin; **~ de gancho** *Amer* safety pin; **no cabe ni un ~** it's jam-packed; **prendido con ~es** *fig* sketchy. **-2.** [joya] brooch, pin; **~ de corbata** tie-pin.

alfiletero *m* pin box.

alfombra *f* carpet; [alfombrilla] rug.

alfombrar *vt* to carpet.

alfombrilla *f* **-1.** [alfombra pequeña] rug. **-2.** [felpudo] doormat. **-3.** [del baño] bathmat. **-4.** INFORM: **~ (del ratón)** mouse mat.

alforja *f* (*gen pl*) **-1.** [de persona] knapsack. **-2.** [de caballo] saddlebag.

alga *f* (*el*) [de mar] seaweed (*U*); [de río] algae (*pl*).

algarabía *f* **-1.** [habla confusa] gibberish. **-2.** [alboroto] racket.

algarada *f* racket, din.

algarroba *f* **-1.** [planta] vetch. **-2.** [fruto] carob ○ locust bean.

algarrobo *m* carob ○ locust tree.

algazara *f* racket, uproar.

álgebra *f* (*el*) algebra.

algebraico, -ca *adj* algebraic.

álgido, -da *adj* [culminante] critical.

algo ◇ *pron* **-1.** [alguna cosa] something; [en interrogativas] anything; **¿te pasa ~?** is anything the matter?; **~ es ~** something is better than nothing; **por ~ lo habrá dicho** he must have said it for a reason. **-2.** [cantidad pequeña] a bit, a little; **~ de** some, a little. **-3.** *fig* [cosa importante] something; **se cree que es ~** he thinks he's something (special).
◇ *adv* [un poco] rather, somewhat.

algodón *m* cotton; **~ (hidrófilo)** FARM cotton wool *Br*, absorbent cotton *Am*; **criado entre algodones** *fig* pampered.

algodonero, -ra *adj* cotton (*antes de sust*).

algoritmo *m* INFORM algorithm.

alguacil *m* **-1.** [del ayuntamiento] *mayor's assistant*. **-2.** [del juzgado] bailiff.

alguacilillo *m mounted official at bullfight*; *ver también* **tauromaquia**.

alguien *pron* **-1.** [alguna persona] someone, somebody; [en interrogativas] anyone, anybody; **¿hay ~ ahí?** is anyone there? **-2.** *fig* [persona de importancia] somebody; **se cree ~** she thinks she's somebody (special).

alguno, -na ◇ *adj* (*antes de sust masculino* **algún**) **-1.** [indeterminado] some; [en interrogativas] any; **¿tienes algún libro?** do you have any books?; **algún día** some ○ one day; **ha surgido algún (que otro) problema** the odd problem has come up. **-2.** (*después de sust*) [ninguno] any; **no tengo interés ~** I have no interest, I haven't any interest.
◇ *pron* **-1.** [persona] someone, somebody, (*pl*) some people; [en interrogativas] anyone, anybody; **¿conocisteis a ~s?** did you get to know any?; **~s de, ~s (de) entre** some ○ a few of. **-2.** [cosa] the odd one, (*pl*) some, (*pl*) a few; [en interrogativas] any; **me salió**

mal ~ I got the odd one wrong; ~ **de some** O a few of.

alhaja f -1. [joya] jewel. -2. [objeto de valor] treasure. -3. fig [persona] gem.

alhelí (pl alhelíes) m wallflower.

aliado, -da adj allied.

◆ **Aliados** mpl: los Aliados the Allies.

alianza f -1. [pacto, parentesco] alliance. -2. [anillo] wedding ring.

aliar [9] vt -1. [naciones] to ally. -2. [cualidades etc] to combine.

◆ **aliarse** vpr to form an alliance.

alias ◇ adv alias. ◇ m inv alias; [entre amigos] nickname.

alicaído, -da adj -1. [triste] depressed. -2. fig [débil] weak.

alicatado m tiling.

alicatar vt to tile.

alicates mpl pliers.

aliciente m -1. [incentivo] incentive. -2. [atractivo] attraction.

alícuota adj MAT aliquot.

alienación f -1. [gen] alienation. -2. [trastorno psíquico] derangement, madness.

alienante adj alienating.

alienar vt -1. [enajenar] to derange, to drive mad. -2. FILOSOFÍA to alienate.

alienígena m y f alien.

alienta etc → **alentar**.

aliento m -1. [respiración] breath; **cobrar** ~ to catch one's breath; **sin** ~ breathless. -2. fig [ánimo] strength.

aligerar vt -1. [peso] to lighten. -2. [ritmo] to speed up; [el paso] to quicken. -3. fig [aliviar] to relieve, to ease.

alijo m contraband (U); ~ **de drogas** consignment of drugs.

alimaña f pest (fox, weasel etc).

alimentación f -1. [acción] feeding. -2. [comida] food. -3. [régimen alimenticio] diet. -4. TECN feed, input.

alimentador, -ra adj TECN feeding.

◆ **alimentador** m TECN feed, feeder; ~ **de papel** INFORM paper feed.

alimentar ◇ vt [gen] to feed; [motor, coche] to fuel. ◇ vi [nutrir] to be nourishing.

◆ **alimentarse** vpr [comer]: ~se **de** to live on.

alimentario, -ria adj food (antes de sust).

alimenticio, -cia adj nourishing; **productos** ~s foodstuffs.

alimento m [gen] food; [valor nutritivo] nourishment.

alimón

◆ **al alimón** loc adv jointly, together.

alineación f -1. [en el espacio] alignment. -2. DEP line-up.

alineado, -da adj -1. [en el espacio] lined up. -2. DEP selected.

◆ **no alineado, -da** adj POLÍT non-aligned.

alineamiento m alignment.

◆ **no alineamiento** m POLÍT nonalignment.

alinear vt -1. [en el espacio] to line up. -2. DEP to select.

◆ **alinearse** vpr POLÍT to align.

aliñar vt [ensalada] to dress; [carne] to season.

aliño m [para ensalada] dressing; [para carne] seasoning.

alioli m garlic mayonnaise.

alirón interj: ¡~! hooray!

alisar vt to smooth (down).

alisio → **viento**.

aliso m alder.

alistamiento m enlistment.

alistarse vpr to enlist.

aliteración f alliteration.

aliviar [8] vt -1. [atenuar] to soothe. -2. [aligerar - persona] to relieve; [- carga] to lighten.

alivio m relief.

◆ **de alivio** loc adj [terrible] dreadful.

aljibe m -1. [de agua] cistern. -2. NÁUT tanker.

allá adv -1. [espacio] over there; ~ **abajo/ arriba** down/up there; **más** ~ further on; **más** ~ **de** beyond. -2. [tiempo]: **por los años cincuenta** back in the 50s; ~ **para el mes de agosto** around August some time. -3. loc: ~ **él/ella** etc that's his/her etc problem.

◆ **el más allá** m the great beyond.

allanamiento m forceful entry; ~ **de morada** breaking and entering.

allanar vt -1. [terreno] to flatten, to level. -2. fig [dificultad] to overcome. -3. [irrumpir en] to break into.

allegado, -da ◇ adj close. ◇ m y f -1. [familiar] relative. -2. [amigo] close friend.

allende adv beyond.

allí adv there; ~ **abajo/arriba** down/up there; ~ **mismo** right there; **está por** ~ it's around there somewhere.

alma f (el) -1. [gen] soul. -2. fig [catalizador - de negocio, equipo] backbone; **el** ~ **de la fiesta** the life and soul of the party. -3. [de bastón, ovillo] core. -4. loc: **se le cayó el** ~ **a los pies** his heart sank; **en el** ~ truly, from the bottom of one's heart; **ir con el** ~ **en pena, ser como un** ~ **en pena** to go about like a lost soul; **llegar al** ~ **a alguien** to touch sb's heart; **partir el ~ a alguien** to break sb's heart; **sentirlo en el ~** to be truly sorry; **ser un ~ de cántaro** to be thoughtless O uncaring.

almacén *m* warehouse.
◆ **(grandes) almacenes** *mpl* department store (*sg*).

almacenamiento *m* [gen & INFORM] storage.

almacenar *vt* **-1.** [gen & INFORM] to store. **-2.** [reunir] to collect.

almendra *f* almond.

almendrado, -da *adj* almond-shaped.
◆ **almendrado** *m* CULIN almond paste.

almendro *m* almond (tree).

almíbar *m* syrup.

almibarado, -da *adj* **-1.** [con almíbar] covered in syrup. **-2.** *fig* [afectado] syrupy, sugary.

almibarar *vt* to cover in syrup.

almidón *m* starch.

almidonado, -da *adj* starched.
◆ **almidonado** *m* starching.

almidonar *vt* to starch.

alminar *m* minaret.

almirantazgo *m* **-1.** [dignidad] admiralty. **-2.** [de la Armada] Admiralty.

almirante *m* admiral.

almirez *m* mortar.

almizcle *m* musk.

almizclero *m* musk deer.

almohada *f* pillow; **consultarlo con la ~** *fig* to sleep on it.

almohadilla *f* [gen, TECN & ZOOL] pad; [cojín] small cushion.

almohadillado, -da *adj* padded.

almohadón *m* cushion.

almoneda *f* **-1.** [venta] sale. **-2.** [subasta] auction.

almorávide *adj, m y f* Almoravid.

almorrana *f* (*gen pl*) piles (*pl*).

almorzar [37] ◇ *vt* **-1.** [al mediodía] to have for lunch. **-2.** [a media mañana] to have as a mid-morning snack. ◇ *vi* **-1.** [al mediodía] to have lunch. **-2.** [a mañana] to have a mid-morning snack.

almuerzo *m* **-1.** [al mediodía] lunch. **-2.** [a media mañana] mid-morning snack. **-3.** [desayuno] breakfast.

aló *interj Amer* [al teléfono] hello.

alocado, -da *m y f* crazy person.

alocución *f* address, speech.

alojamiento *m* accommodation; **dar ~ a** to put up.

alojar *vt* to put up.

◆ **alojarse** *vpr* **-1.** [hospedarse] to stay. **-2.** [introducirse] to lodge.

alondra *f* lark.

alopecia *f* alopecia.

alpaca *f* alpaca.

alpargata *f* (*gen pl*) espadrille.

Alpes *mpl*: **los ~** the Alps.

alpinismo *m* mountaineering.

alpinista *m y f* mountaineer.

alpino, -na *adj* Alpine.

alpiste *m* **-1.** [planta] canary grass. **-2.** [semilla] birdseed.

alquería *f* farmstead.

alquilar *vt* [casa, TV, oficina] to rent; [coche] to hire.
◆ **alquilarse** *vpr* [casa, TV, oficina] to be for rent; [coche] to be for hire; **"se alquila"** "to let".

alquiler *m* **-1.** [acción - de casa, TV, oficina] renting; [- de coche] hiring; **de ~** [casa] rented; [coche] hire (*antes de sust*); **tenemos pisos de ~** we have flats to let *Br*, we have apartments to rent *Am*. **-2.** [precio - de casa, oficina] rent; [- de televisión] rental; [- de coche] hire charge.

alquimia *f* alchemy.

alquimista *m y f* alchemist.

alquitrán *m* tar.

alquitranar *vt* to tar.

alrededor *adv* **-1.** [en torno] around; **mira a tu ~** look around you; **de ~** surrounding. **-2.** [aproximadamente]: **~ de** around, about.
◆ **alrededores** *mpl* surrounding area (*sg*).
◆ **alrededor de** *loc prep* around.

alta → **alto**.

altanería *f* haughtiness.

altanero, -ra *adj* haughty.

altar *m* altar; **~ mayor** high altar; **conducir** O **llevar al ~ a alguien** *fig* to lead sb down the aisle.

altavoz *m* [para anuncios] loudspeaker; [de tocadiscos] speaker.

alteración *f* **-1.** [cambio] alteration. **-2.** [excitación] agitation. **-3.** [alboroto] disturbance; **~ del orden público** breach of the peace.

alterar *vt* **-1.** [cambiar] to alter. **-2.** [perturbar - persona] to agitate, to fluster; [- orden público] to disrupt. **-3.** [estropear] to spoil; [leche] to turn.
◆ **alterarse** *vpr* **-1.** [perturbarse] to get agitated O flustered. **-2.** [estropearse] to spoil, to go off; [leche] to turn.

altercado *m* argument, row.

alternador *m* ELECTR alternator.

alternancia *f* alternation.

alternar ◇ *vt* to alternate. ◇ *vi* -1. [relacionarse]: ~ **(con)** to mix (with), to socialize (with). -2. [sucederse]: ~ **con** to alternate with.

◆ **alternarse** *vpr* -1. [en el tiempo] to take turns. -2. [en el espacio] to alternate.

alternativa → **alternativo**.

alternativamente *adv* [moverse] alternately.

alternativo, -va *adj* -1. [movimiento] alternating. -2. [posibilidad] alternative.

◆ **alternativa** *f* -1. [opción] alternative; **alternativa de poder** POLIT succession of power. -2. TAUROM *ceremony in which bullfighter shares the kill with his novice, accepting him as a professional*; **tomar la alternativa** to become a professional bullfighter.

alterne *m practice whereby women encourage people to drink in return for a commission*.

alterno, -na *adj* alternate; ELECTR alternating.

alteza *f fig* [de sentimientos] loftiness.

◆ **Alteza** *f* [tratamiento] Highness; **Su Alteza Real** His Royal Highness (*f* Her Royal Highness).

altibajos *mpl* -1. [del terreno] unevenness (*sg*). -2. *fig* [de vida etc] ups and downs.

altillo *m* -1. [armario] *small cupboard usually found above another cupboard*. -2. [cerro] hillock.

altímetro *m* altimeter.

altiplano *m* high plateau.

altísimo

◆ **Altísimo** *m*: **el Altísimo** the Most High.

altisonante *adj* high-sounding.

altitud *f* altitude.

altivez *f* haughtiness.

altivo, -va *adj* haughty.

alto, -ta *adj* -1. [gen] high; [persona, árbol, edificio] tall; [piso] top, upper. -2. [ruidoso] loud. -3. [avanzado] late; **a altas horas de la noche** late at night, in the small hours. -4. GEOGR upper, northern.

◆ **alto** ◇ *m* -1. [altura] height; **mide dos metros de** ~ [cosa] it's two metres high; [persona] he's two metres tall. -2. [interrupción] stop; **hacer un** ~ to make a stop. -3. [lugar elevado] height; **en lo** ~ **de** at the top of. -4. MÚS altos. -5. *loc*: **pasar por** ~ **algo** to pass over sthg; **por todo lo** ~ [lujoso] grand, luxurious; [a lo grande] in (great) style.

◇ *adv* -1. [arriba] high (up). -2. [hablar etc] loud.

◇ *interj*: ¡~! halt!, stop!

◆ **alta** *f* (*el*) -1. [del hospital] discharge; **dar de alta** ○ **el alta a alguien** to discharge sb (from hospital). -2. [documento] certificate

of discharge. -3. [en una asociación] membership; **darse de alta** to become a member.

altoparlante *m Amer* loudspeaker.

altozano *m* hillock.

altramuz *m* lupin.

altruismo *m* altruism.

altruista ◇ *adj* altruistic. ◇ *m y f* altruist.

altura *f* -1. [gen] height; [en el mar] depth; **volar a gran** ~ to fly at altitude; **tiene dos metros de** ~ [gen] it's two metres high; [persona] he's two metres tall; **Viella está a 1.000m de** ~ Viella is 1,000 metres above sea level. -2. [nivel] level; **está a la** ~ **del ayuntamiento** it's next to the town hall. -3. [latitud] latitude. -4. [valor] value; **a la** ~ **de** on a par with. -5. *fig* [de persona] stature. -6. *fig* [de sentimientos, espíritu] loftiness.

◆ **alturas** *fpl* [el cielo] Heaven (*sg*); **a estas** ~**s** *fig* this far on, this late.

alubia *f* bean.

alucinación *f* hallucination.

alucinado, -da *adj* -1. MED hallucinating. -2. *fam* [sorprendido] gobsmacked.

alucinante *adj* -1. MED hallucinatory. -2. *fam* [extraordinario] amazing.

alucinar ◇ *vi* -1. MED to hallucinate. -2. *fam* [equivocarse]: ¡**no alucines!** come off it! ◇ *vt fam fig* [seducir] to hypnotize, to captivate.

alucinógeno, -na *adj* hallucinogenic.

◆ **alucinógeno** *m* hallucinogen.

alud *m lit* & *fig* avalanche.

aludido, -da *m y f*: **el** ~ the aforesaid; **darse por** ~ [ofenderse] to take it personally; [reaccionar] to take the hint.

aludir *vi*: ~ **a** [sin mencionar] to allude to; [mencionando] to refer to.

alumbrado *m* lighting; ~ **público** street lighting.

alumbramiento *m* -1. [mediante luz] lighting. -2. [parto] delivery.

alumbrar ◇ *vt* -1. [iluminar] to light up. -2. [instruir] to enlighten. -3. [dar a luz] to give birth to. ◇ *vi* [iluminar] to give light.

aluminio *m* aluminium.

aluminosis *f inv* CONSTR *collapse of buildings as a result of inadequate building materials*.

alumnado *m* [de escuela] pupils (*pl*); [de universidad] students (*pl*).

alumno, -na *m y f* [de escuela, profesor particular] pupil; [de universidad] student.

alunizaje *m* landing on the moon.

alunizar [13] *vi* to land on the moon.

alusión f [sin mencionar] allusion; [mencionando] reference; **hacer ~ a** [sin mencionar] to allude to; [mencionando] to refer to.

alusivo, -va adj allusive.

aluvión m -1. [gen] flood. -2. GEOL alluvium.

alvéolo, alveolo m -1. [de panal] cell. -2. ANAT alveolus.

alza f (el) rise; **en ~** FIN rising; fig gaining in popularity; **jugar al ~** FIN to bull the market.

alzacuello m RELIG dog collar.

alzado, -da adj -1. [gen] raised. -2. [comerciante] fraudulent. -3. [precio] fixed.
◆ **alzado** m elevation.
◆ **alzada** f -1. [de caballo] height. -2. DER appeal.

alzamiento m uprising, revolt.

alzar [13] vt -1. [levantar] to lift, to raise; [voz] to raise; [vela] to hoist; [cuello de abrigo] to turn up; [mangas] to pull up. -2. [aumentar] to raise. -3. [construir] to erect. -4. [sublevar] to stir up, to raise.
◆ **alzarse** vpr -1. [levantarse] to rise. -2. [sublevarse] to rise up, to revolt. -3. [conseguir]: **~se con** [victoria] to win; [botín] to make off with; [premio] to carry off.

a.m. (abrev de **ante meridiem**) a.m.

ama → amo.

amabilidad f kindness; **¿tendría la ~ de ...?** would you be so kind as to ...?

amabilísimo, -ma superl → amable.

amable adj kind; **¿sería tan ~ de ...?** would you be so kind as to ...?

amado, -da m y f loved one.

amaestrado, -da adj [gen] trained; [en circo] performing.

amaestrar vt to train.

amagar [16] ◇ vt -1. [dar indicios de] to show signs of. -2. [mostrar intención] to threaten; **le amagó un golpe** he threatened to hit him. ◇ vi [tormenta] to be imminent, to threaten.

amago m -1. [indicio] sign, hint. -2. [amenaza] threat.

amague etc → amagar.

amainar ◇ vt NÁUT to take in. ◇ vi lit & fig to abate, to die down.

amalgama f QUÍM & fig amalgam.

amalgamar vt QUÍM & fig to amalgamate.

amamantar vt [animal] to suckle; [bebé] to breastfeed.

amancebamiento m living together, cohabitation.

amancebarse vpr to live together, to cohabit.

amanecer [30] ◇ m dawn. ◇ v impers: **amaneció a las siete** dawn broke at seven. ◇ vi [en un lugar] to see in the dawn.

amanerado, -da adj -1. [afeminado] effeminate. -2. [afectado] mannered, affected.

amaneramiento m -1. [afeminamiento] effeminacy. -2. [afectación] affectation.

amanerarse vpr -1. [afeminarse] to become effeminate. -2. [volverse afectado] to become affected.

amanita f amanita.

amansar vt -1. [animal] to tame. -2. fig [persona] to calm down. -3. fig [pasiones] to calm.
◆ **amansarse** vpr to calm down.

amante m y f -1. [querido] lover. -2. fig [aficionado]: **ser ~ de algo/hacer algo** to be keen on sthg/doing sthg; **los ~s del arte** art lovers.

amanuense m y f scribe.

amañar vt [falsear] to fix; [elecciones, resultado] to rig; [documento] to doctor.
◆ **amañarse** vpr: **amañárselas** to manage.

amaño m (gen pl) [treta] ruse, trick.

amapola f poppy.

amar [1] vt to love.

amaraje m [de hidroavión] landing at sea; [de vehículo espacial] splashdown.

amaranto m amaranth.

amarar vi [hidroavión] to land at sea; [vehículo espacial] to splash down.

amargado, -da ◇ adj [resentido] bitter. ◇ m y f bitter person.

amargar [16] vt to make bitter; fig to spoil, to ruin.
◆ **amargarse** vpr [suj: alimento, persona] to become bitter.

amargo, -ga adj lit & fig bitter.

amargor m [sabor] bitterness.

amargoso, -sa adj Amer bitter.

amargue etc → amargar.

amargura f [sentimiento] sorrow.

amariconado, -da adj fam despec poofy.
◆ **amariconado** m fam despec pansy.

amarillento, -ta adj yellowish.

amarillismo m PRENS sensationalism.

amarillo, -lla adj -1. [color] yellow. -2. PRENS sensationalist. -3. [sindicato] conservative.
◆ **amarillo** m [color] yellow.

amarilloso, -sa adj Amer yellowish.

amariposado, -da adj [afeminado] effeminate.

amarra f mooring rope ○ line; **largar** ○ **soltar ~s** to cast off.

◆ **amarras** *fpl* *fig* [contactos] connections, friends in high places.

amarrar *vt* **-1.** NÁUT to moor. **-2.** [atar] to tie (up); ~ **algo/a alguien a algo** to tie sthg/sb to sthg.

amarre *m* mooring.

amarrete *Amer* ◇ *adj* mean, tight. ◇ *m y f* mean person.

amartillar *vt* [arma] to cock.

amasar *vt* **-1.** [masa] to knead; [yeso] to mix. **-2.** *fam* *fig* [riquezas] to amass.

amasia *f Amer* mistress.

amasiato *m Amer* living in sin.

amasijo *m fam* *fig* [mezcla] hotchpotch.

amateur [ama'ter] (*pl* **amateurs**) *adj, m y f* amateur.

amateurismo [amate'rismo] *m* amateur nature.

amatista *f* amethyst.

amazacotado, -da *adj* **-1.** [comida] stodgy. **-2.** *fig* [pasajeros] packed, crammed.

amazona *f* **-1.** *fig* [jinete] horsewoman. **-2.** MITOL Amazon.

Amazonas *m*: **el** ~ the Amazon.

amazónico, -ca *adj* [gen] Amazon (*antes de sust*); [tribu, cultura] Amazonian.

ambages *mpl*: **sin** ~ without beating about the bush, in plain English.

ámbar *m* amber.

Amberes Antwerp.

ambición *f* ambition.

ambicionar *vt* to have as one's ambition.

ambicioso, -sa ◇ *adj* ambitious. ◇ *m y f* ambitious person.

ambidextro, -tra ◇ *adj* ambidextrous. ◇ *m y f* ambidextrous person.

ambientación *f* **-1.** CIN, LITER & TEATR setting. **-2.** RADIO sound effects (*pl*).

ambientador *m* air freshener.

ambiental *adj* **-1.** [físico, atmosférico] ambient. **-2.** ECOLOG environmental.

ambientar *vt* **-1.** CIN, LITER & TEATR to set. **-2.** [animar] to liven up.

◆ **ambientarse** *vpr* to settle down.

ambiente ◇ *adj* ambient. ◇ *m* **-1.** [aire] air, atmosphere. **-2.** [circunstancias] environment. **-3.** [ámbito] world, circles (*pl*). **-4.** [animación] life, atmosphere. **-5.** *Amer* [habitación] room.

ambigüedad *f* ambiguity.

ambiguo, -gua *adj* **-1.** [gen] ambiguous. **-2.** GRAM that may be either masculine or feminine.

ámbito *m* **-1.** [espacio, límites] confines (*pl*); **una ley de** ~ **provincial** an act which is provincial in its scope. **-2.** [ambiente] world, circles (*pl*).

ambivalencia *f* ambivalence.

ambivalente *adj* ambivalent.

ambos, -bas ◇ *adj pl* both. ◇ *pron pl* both (of them).

ambulancia *f* ambulance.

ambulante *adj* travelling; [biblioteca] mobile.

ambulatorio *m* state-run surgery O clinic.

ameba *f* amoeba.

amedrentar *vt* to scare, to frighten.

◆ **amedrentarse** *vpr* to get scared O frightened.

amén *adv* [en plegaria] amen; **en un decir** ~ *fig* in the twinkling of an eye; **decir** ~ **a** *fig* to accept unquestioningly.

◆ **amén de** *loc prep* **-1.** [además de] in addition to. **-2.** [excepto] except for, apart from.

amenaza *f* threat; ~ **de bomba** bomb scare; ~ **de muerte** death threat.

amenazar [13] *vt* to threaten; ~ **a alguien con hacerle algo** to threaten to do sthg to sb; ~ **a alguien con hacer algo** to threaten sb with doing sthg; ~ **a alguien con el despido/de muerte** to threaten to sack/kill sb.

amenidad *f* **-1.** [entretenimiento] entertaining qualities (*pl*). **-2.** [agrado] pleasantness.

amenizar [13] *vt fig* to liven up.

ameno, -na *adj* **-1.** [entretenido] entertaining. **-2.** [placentero] pleasant.

amenorrea *f* amenorrhea.

América America; ~ **del Sur** South America.

americana → americano.

americanismo *m* **-1.** [carácter] American character. **-2.** LING Americanism.

americanizar [13] *vt* to americanize.

◆ **americanizarse** *vpr* to become americanized.

americano, -na *adj, m y f* American.

◆ **americana** *f* [chaqueta] jacket.

amerindio, -dia *adj, m y f* American Indian, Amerindian.

ameritar *vt Amer* to deserve.

amerizaje *m* [de hidroavión] landing at sea; [de vehículo espacial] splashdown.

amerizar [13] *vi* [hidroavión] to land at sea; [vehículo espacial] to splash down.

ametralladora *f* machine gun.

ametrallar *vt* **-1.** [con ametralladora] to machinegun. **-2.** [con metralla] to shower with shrapnel.

amianto *m* asbestos.

amigable *adj* amicable.

amígdala f tonsil.

amigdalitis f inv tonsillitis.

amigo, -ga ◇ adj **-1.** [gen] friendly. **-2.** [aficionado]: ~ **de algo/hacer algo** keen on sthg/doing sthg; ~ **de la buena mesa** partial to good food. ◇ m y f **-1.** [persona] friend; **hacerse** ~ **de** to make friends with; **hacerse** ~**s** to become friends. **-2.** fam [compañero, novio] partner; [amante] lover. **-3.** [tratamiento] (my) friend; **Querido** ~ [en carta] Dear friend.

amigote, amiguete m fam pal, mate Br.

amiguismo m: **hay mucho** ~ there are always jobs for the boys.

amilanar vt [asustar] to terrify.

◆ **amilanarse** vpr [desanimarse] to be discouraged, to lose heart.

aminoácido m amino acid.

aminorar ◇ vt to reduce. ◇ vi to decrease, to diminish.

amistad f friendship; **hacer** ○ **trabar** ~ **(con)** to make friends (with).

◆ **amistades** fpl friends.

amistoso, -sa adj friendly.

amnesia f amnesia.

amnésico, -ca ◇ adj amnesic. ◇ m y f amnesiac.

amniótico, -ca adj amniotic.

amnistía f amnesty; ~ **fiscal** amnesty during which people guilty of tax evasion may pay what they owe without being prosecuted.

amnistiar [9] vt to grant amnesty to.

amo, ama m y f **-1.** [gen] owner. **-2.** [de criado, situación etc] master (f mistress); **ser el** ~ **del cotarro** fam to rule the roost.

◆ **ama de casa** f housewife.

◆ **ama de cría** f wet nurse.

◆ **ama de llaves** f housekeeper.

amodorrado, -da adj drowsy.

amodorrarse vpr to get drowsy.

amoldable adj adaptable; **ser** ~ **a** to be able to adapt to.

amoldar vt [adaptar]: ~ **(a)** to adapt (to).

◆ **amoldarse** vpr [adaptarse]: ~**se (a)** to adapt (to).

amonal m ammonal.

amonestación f **-1.** [reprimenda] reprimand. **-2.** DEP warning.

◆ **amonestaciones** fpl [para matrimonio] banns.

amonestar vt **-1.** [reprender] to reprimand. **-2.** DEP to warn. **-3.** [para matrimonio] to publish the banns of.

amoníaco, amoniaco m **-1.** [gas] ammonia. **-2.** [disolución] liquid ammonia.

amontonar vt **-1.** [apilar] to pile up. **-2.** [reunir] to accumulate.

◆ **amontonarse** vpr **-1.** [personas] to form a crowd. **-2.** [problemas, trabajo] to pile up; [ideas, solicitudes] to come thick and fast.

amor m love; ~ **libre/platónico** free/platonic love; **de mil** ~**es** with pleasure, gladly; **hacer el** ~ to make love; **por** ~ **al arte** for the love of it; **¡por el** ~ **de Dios!** for God's sake!

◆ **amor propio** m pride.

amoral adj amoral.

amoralidad f amorality.

amoratado, -da adj [de frío] blue; [por golpes] black and blue.

amoratar vt [suj: el frío] to turn blue; [suj: persona] to bruise.

◆ **amoratarse** vpr [por el frío] to turn blue; [por golpes] to turn black and blue.

amordazar [13] vt [persona] to gag; [perro] to muzzle.

amorfo, -fa adj **-1.** [sin forma] amorphous. **-2.** fig [persona] lacking in character.

amorío m fam [romance] fling.

amoroso, -sa adj [gen] loving; [carta, relación] love (antes de sust).

amortajar vt [difunto] to shroud.

amortiguación f **-1.** [de ruido] muffling; [de golpe] softening, cushioning. **-2.** AUTOM suspension, shock absorbers (pl).

amortiguador, -ra adj [de ruido] muffling; [de golpe] softening, cushioning.

◆ **amortiguador** m AUTOM shock absorber.

amortiguar [45] vt [ruido] to muffle; [golpe] to soften, to cushion.

◆ **amortiguarse** vpr [ruido] to die away; [golpe] to be cushioned.

amortizable adj ECON [bonos, acciones] redeemable.

amortización f ECON [de deuda, préstamo] amortization, paying-off; [de inversión, capital] recouping; [de bonos, acciones] redemption; [de bienes de equipo] depreciation.

amortizar [13] vt **-1.** [sacar provecho] to get one's money's worth out of. **-2.** [ECON deuda, préstamo] to amortize, to pay off; [- inversión, capital] to recoup; [- bonos, acciones] to redeem; [- bienes de equipo] to depreciate.

amoscarse [10] vpr fam to get in a huff.

amotinado, -da adj, m y f rebel, insurgent.

amotinamiento m rebellion, uprising; [de marineros] mutiny.

amotinar vt to incite to riot; [a marineros] to incite to mutiny.

◆ **amotinarse** *vpr* to riot; [marineros] to mutiny.

amovible *adj* **-1.** [pieza] detachable. **-2.** [cargo] revocable.

amparar *vt* **-1.** [proteger] to protect. **-2.** [dar cobijo a] to give shelter to, to take in.

◆ **ampararse** *vpr* **-1.** *fig* [apoyarse]: ~**se en** [ley] to have recourse to; [excusas] to draw on. **-2.** [cobijarse]: ~**se de** ○ **contra** to (take) shelter from.

amparo *m* [protección] protection; **al** ~ **de** [persona, caridad] with the help of; [ley] under the protection of.

amperaje *m* amperage.

amperímetro *m* ammeter.

amperio *m* amp, ampere.

ampliable *adj* **-1.** [gen] expandable. **-2.** FOT enlargeable. **-3.** [plazo] extendible.

ampliación *f* **-1.** [aumento] expansion; [de edificio, plazo] extension; ~ **de capital** ECON increase in capital. **-2.** FOT enlargement.

ampliadora *f* FOT enlarger.

ampliar [9] *vt* **-1.** [gen] to expand; [local] to add an extension to; [plazo] to extend. **-2.** FOT to enlarge, to blow up. **-3.** [estudios] to further, to continue.

amplificación *f* amplification.

amplificador, -ra *adj* amplifying.

◆ **amplificador** *m* ELECTRON amplifier.

amplificar [10] *vt* to amplify.

amplio, -plia *adj* **-1.** [sala etc] roomy, spacious; [avenida, gama] wide. **-2.** [ropa] loose. **-3.** [explicación etc] comprehensive; **en el sentido más** ~ **de la palabra** in the broadest sense of the word. **-4.** [mentalidad etc] broad.

amplitud *f* **-1.** [espaciosidad] roominess, spaciousness; [de avenida] wideness. **-2.** [de ropa] looseness. **-3.** *fig* [extensión] extent, comprehensiveness; ~ **de miras** broad-mindedness.

ampolla *f* **-1.** [en piel] blister. **-2.** [para inyecciones] ampoule. **-3.** [frasco] phial.

ampuloso, -sa *adj* pompous.

amputación *f* amputation.

amputar *vt* to amputate.

AMS (*abrev de* **Asociación de Mujeres Separadas**) *f Spanish association for women separated from their husbands.*

Amsterdam Amsterdam.

amueblado *m Amer* room hired for sex.

amueblar *vt* to furnish.

amuleto *m* amulet.

amurallado, -da *adj* walled.

amurallar *vt* to build a wall around.

anabolizante ◇ *adj* anabolic. ◇ *m* anabolic steroid.

anacarado, -da *adj* pearly.

anacardo *m* cashew.

anacoreta *m y f* anchorite, hermit.

anacrónico, -ca *adj* anachronistic.

anacronismo *m* anachronism.

ánade *m culto* duck.

anaerobio, -bia *adj* anaerobic.

anagrama *m* anagram.

anal *adj* ANAT anal.

anales *mpl lit & fig* annals.

analfabetismo *m* illiteracy.

analfabeto, -ta *adj, m y f* illiterate.

analgésico, -ca *adj* analgesic.

◆ **analgésico** *m* analgesic.

análisis *m inv* analysis; ~ **clínico** (clinical) test; ~ **gramatical** sentence analysis, parsing; ~ **de orina** urine analysis; ~ **de sangre** blood test.

analista *m y f* **-1.** [gen] analyst. **-2.** INFORM (computer) analyst; ~ **programador/de sistemas** programmer/systems analyst.

analítico, -ca *adj* analytical.

◆ **analítica** *f* MED clinical testing.

analizar [13] *vt* to analyse.

analogía *f* similarity; **por** ~ by analogy.

analógico, -ca *adj* **-1.** [análogo] analogous, similar. **-2.** INFORM & TECN analogue, analog. **-3.** → **reloj**.

análogo, -ga *adj*: ~ **(a)** analogous ○ similar (to).

ananá, ananás *m Amer* pineapple.

anaquel *m* shelf.

anaranjado, -da *adj* orange.

anarco *fam* ◇ *adj* anarchistic. ◇ *m y f* anarchist.

anarcosindicalismo *m* anarchosyndicalism.

anarcosindicalista *adj, m y f* anarchosyndicalist.

anarquía *f* **-1.** [falta de gobierno] anarchy. **-2.** [doctrina política] anarchism. **-3.** *fig* [desorden] chaos, anarchy.

anárquico, -ca *adj* anarchic.

anarquismo *m* anarchism.

anarquista *adj, m y f* anarchist.

anatema *m* [maldición] curse, anathema.

anatomía *f* anatomy.

anatómico, -ca *adj* **-1.** ANAT anatomical. **-2.** [asiento, calzado] orthopaedic.

anca *f (el)* haunch; ~**s de rana** frogs' legs.

ANCA (*abrev de* **Asociación Nacional de Controladores Aéreos**) *f Spanish association of air-traffic controllers.*

ANCABA (*abrev de* Asociación Nacional de Catedráticos de Bachillerato) *f Spanish association of secondary-school teachers.*

ancestral *adj* ancestral; [costumbre] age-old.

ancestro *m* ancestor.

ancho, -cha *adj* [gen] wide; [prenda] loose-fitting; **te va** o **está** ~ it's too big for you; **a mis/tus** *etc* **anchas** *fig* at ease; **quedarse tan** ~ not to care less; **lo dijo delante de todos y se quedó tan** ~ he said it in front of everyone, just like that.
◆ **ancho** *m* width; **a lo** ~ crosswise; **cinco metros de** ~ five metres wide; **a lo** ~ **de** across (the width of); ~ **de vía** gauge.

anchoa *f* anchovy (*salted*).

anchura *f* **-1.** [medida] width. **-2.** [de ropa] bagginess.

anciano, -na ◇ *adj* old. ◇ *m y f* old person, old man (*f* old woman).
◆ **anciano** *m* [de tribu] elder.

ancla *f* (*el*) anchor; **echar/levar** ~**s** to drop/weigh anchor.

anclar *vi* to anchor.

áncora *f* (*el*) anchor.

andadas *fpl*: **volver a las** ~ *fam fig* to return to one's evil ways.

andaderas *fpl* baby-walker (*sg*).

andador, -ra, andarín, -ina *adj* fond of walking.
◆ **andadores** *mpl* [para niño] harness (*sg*).

andadura *f* walking.

ándale, ándele *interj Amer fam*: ¡~! come on!

Andalucía Andalusia.

andalucismo *m* **-1.** [doctrina] *doctrine favouring Andalusian autonomy.* **-2.** [palabra] *Andalusian word or expression.*

andaluz, -za *adj, m y f* Andalusian.

andamiaje *m* scaffolding.

andamio *m* scaffold.

andanada *f* **-1.** MIL & *fig* broadside. **-2.** TAUROM *covered stand in a bullring.*

andando *interj*: ¡~! come on!, let's get a move on!

andante *adj* **-1.** [que anda] walking. **-2.** MÚS andante.

andanza *f* (*gen pl*) [aventura] adventure.

andar [52] ◇ *vi* **-1.** [caminar] to walk; [moverse] to move. **-2.** [funcionar] to work, to go; **el reloj no anda** the clock has stopped; **las cosas andan mal** things are going badly. **-3.** [estar] to be; ~ **preocupado** to be worried; ~ **mal de dinero** to be short of money; **creo que anda por el almacén** I think he's somewhere in the warehouse; ~ **tras algo/alguien** *fig* to be after sthg/sb. **-4.** (*antes de gerundio*): ~ **haciendo algo** to

be doing sthg; **anda echando broncas a todos** he's going round telling everybody off; **anda explicando sus aventuras** he's talking about his adventures. **-5.** [ocuparse]: ~ **en** [asuntos, líos] to be involved in; [papeleos, negocios] to be busy with. **-6.** [hurgar]: ~ **en** to rummage around in; ¿**has andado en mis papeles?** have you been fiddling with my papers? **-7.** (*antes de "a" y sust pl*) [expresa acción]: **en ese país andan a tiros** in that country they go round shooting one another. **-8.** [alcanzar, rondar]: ~ **por** to be about; **anda por los 60** he's about sixty. **-9.** *fam* [enredar]: ~ **con algo** to play with sthg. **-10.** *loc*: **quien mal anda mal acaba** everyone gets his just deserts.
◇ *vt* **-1.** [recorrer] to go, to travel. **-2.** *Amer* [llevar puesto] to wear.
◇ *m* gait, walk.
◆ **andarse** *vpr* [obrar]: ~**se con cuidado/ misterios** to be careful/secretive.
◆ **andares** *mpl* [de persona] gait (*sg*); **tener** ~**es de** to walk like.
◆ **anda** *interj*: ¡anda! [sorpresa, desilusión] oh!; [¡vamos!] come on!; [¡por favor!] go on!; ¡anda ya! [incredulidad] come off it!

andarín, -ina = andador.

andas *fpl*: **llevar a alguien en** ~ *fig* to be all over sb.

ándele = ándale.

andén *m* **-1.** FERROC platform. **-2.** *Amer* [bancal de tierra] terrace. **-3.** *Amer* [acera] pavement *Br*, sidewalk *Am*.

Andes *mpl*: **los** ~ the Andes.

andinismo *m Amer* mountaineering.

andinista *m y f Amer* mountaineer.

andino, -na *adj, m y f* Andean.

Andorra Andorra.

andorrano, -na *adj, m y f* Andorran.

andrajo *m* **-1.** [harapo] rag. **-2.** *fig & despec* [persona] good-for-nothing.

andrajoso, -sa ◇ *adj* ragged. ◇ *m y f* person dressed in rags.

andrógino, -na *adj* androgynous.
◆ **andrógino** *m* hermaphrodite.

androide ◇ *adj* [masculino] masculine. ◇ *m* [autómata] android.

andurriales *mpl* remote place (*sg*); ¿**qué haces por estos** ~? what are you doing as far off the beaten track as this?

anduviera *etc* → andar.

ANE (*abrev de* Asociación Numismática Española) *f Spanish numismatic association.*

anécdota *f* anecdote.

anecdotario *m* collection of anecdotes.

anecdótico, -ca *adj* **-1.** [con historietas] anecdotal. **-2.** [no esencial] incidental.

ANEF (*abrev de* **Asociación Nacional de Entrenadores de Fútbol**) *f Spanish football managers' association*.

anegar [16] *vt* **-1.** [inundar] to flood. **-2.** [ahogar - planta] to drown.

◆ **anegarse** *vpr* **-1.** [inundarse] to flood; **sus ojos se anegaron de lágrimas** tears welled up in his eyes. **-2.** [ahogarse] to drown.

anejo, -ja *adj*: ~ **(a)** [edificio] connected (to); [documento] attached (to).

◆ **anejo** *m* annexe.

anemia *f* anaemia.

anémico, -ca ◇ *adj* anaemic. ◇ *m y f* anaemia sufferer.

anémona *f* anemone.

anestesia *f* anaesthesia; ~ **general/local** general/local anaesthesia.

anestesiar [8] *vt* to anaesthetize, to place under anaesthetic.

anestésico, -ca *adj* anaesthetic.

◆ **anestésico** *m* anaesthetic.

anestesista *m y f* anaesthetist.

Aneto *m*: **el** ~ Aneto.

aneurisma *m* aneurysm.

anexar *vt* [documento] to attach.

anexión *f* annexation.

anexionar *vt* to annex.

anexionista *m y f* annexationist.

anexo, -xa *adj* [edificio] connected; [documento] attached.

◆ **anexo** *m* annexe.

anfeta *f fam* pep pill.

anfetamina *f* amphetamine.

anfibio, -bia *adj lit & fig* amphibious.

◆ **anfibio** *m* amphibian.

anfiteatro *m* [CIN & TEATR] circle. **-2.** [edificio] amphitheatre.

anfitrión, -ona ◇ *adj* host (*antes de sust*). ◇ *m y f* host (*f* hostess).

ánfora *f* (*el*) [cántaro] amphora.

ángel *m lit & fig* angel; ~ **custodio** O **de la guarda** guardian angel; **tener** ~ to have something special.

angelical *adj* angelic.

ángelus *m inv* RELIG angelus.

angina *f* (*gen pl*) [amigdalitis] sore throat; **tener** ~**s** to have a sore throat.

◆ **angina de pecho** *f* angina (pectoris).

anglicanismo *m* Anglicanism.

anglicano, -na *adj, m y f* Anglican.

anglicismo *m* anglicism.

angloamericano, -na *adj, m y f* Anglo-American.

anglófilo, -la *adj, m y f* anglophile.

anglófobo, -ba *adj, m y f* anglophobe.

anglófono, -na, **angloparlante** ◇ *adj* English-speaking, anglophone. ◇ *m y f* English speaker, anglophone.

anglosajón, -ona *adj, m y f* Anglo-Saxon.

Angola Angola.

angolano, -na *adj, m y f* Angolan.

angora *f* [de conejo] angora; [de cabra] mohair.

angosto, -ta *adj culto* narrow.

angostura *f* **-1.** [estrechez] narrowness. **-2.** [extracto] angostura.

anguila *f* eel; ~ **de mar** conger eel.

angula *f* elver.

angular *adj* angular.

◆ **gran angular** *m* FOT wide-angle lens.

ángulo *m* **-1.** [gen] angle; ~ **agudo/obtuso/recto** acute/obtuse/right angle; ~ **de mira** [para disparar] line of sight; ~ **de tiro** [para disparar] elevation. **-2.** [rincón] corner.

anguloso, -sa *adj* angular.

angustia *f* **-1.** [aflicción] anxiety. **-2.** PSICOL distress.

angustiar [8] *vt* to distress.

◆ **angustiarse** *vpr* [agobiarse]: ~**se (por)** to get worried (about).

angustioso, -sa *adj* [espera, momentos] anxious; [situación, noticia] distressing.

anhelante *adj*: ~ **(por algo/hacer algo)** longing (for sthg/to do sthg), desperate (for sthg/to do sthg).

anhelar *vt* to long O wish for; ~ **hacer algo** to long to do sthg.

anhelo *m* longing.

anhídrido *m* anhydride; ~ **carbónico** carbon dioxide.

anidar *vi* **-1.** [pájaro] to nest. **-2.** *fig* [sentimiento]: ~ **en** to find a place in.

ANIEL (*abrev de* **Asociación Nacional de Industrias de Electrónica**) *f Spanish electronics industry association*.

anilina *f* aniline.

anilla *f* ring.

◆ **anillas** *fpl* DEP rings.

anillo *m* **-1.** [gen & ASTRON] ring; ~ **de boda** wedding ring; **ir** O **venir como** ~ **al dedo** *fam* [persona] to be just the right person; [cosa] to be just what one needed; **no se me van a caer los** ~**s** *fam* it won't hurt me (to do it). **-2.** ZOOL annulus.

ánima *f* (*el*) soul; ~ **bendita** soul in Purgatory.

animación *f* **-1.** [alegría] liveliness. **-2.** [bullicio] hustle and bustle, activity. **-3.** CIN animation.

animado, **-da** *adj* **-1.** [con buen ánimo] cheerful. **-2.** [divertido] lively. **-3.** CIN animated.

animador, **-ra** *m y f* **-1.** [en espectáculo] compere. **-2.** [en fiesta de niños] children's entertainer. **-3.** [en béisbol etc] cheerleader.

animadversión *f* animosity.

animal ◇ *adj* **-1.** [reino, funciones] animal (*antes de sust*). **-2.** *fam* [persona - basto] rough; [- ignorante] ignorant. ◇ *m y f* [persona] *fam fig* animal, brute. ◇ *m* animal; ~ **doméstico** [de granja etc] domestic animal; [de compañía] pet.

animalada *f fam fig*: **decir/hacer una** ~ to say/do something mindless.

animalucho *m fig* & *despec* disgusting creature.

animar *vt* **-1.** [estimular] to encourage; ~ **a alguien a** ○ **para hacer algo** to encourage sb to do sthg. **-2.** [alegrar - persona] to cheer up. **-3.** [avivar - fuego, diálogo, fiesta] to liven up; [comercio] to stimulate.
◆ **animarse** *vpr* **-1.** [alegrarse - persona] to cheer up; [- fiesta etc] to liven up. **-2.** [decidir]: ~**se (a hacer algo)** to finally decide (to do sthg).

anímico, **-ca** *adj* mental.

ánimo ◇ *m* **-1.** [valor] courage. **-2.** [aliento] encouragement; **dar** ~**s a alguien** to encourage sb. **-3.** [intención]: **con/sin** ~ **de** with/without the intention of; **lo hice sin** ~ **de ofenderte** I didn't mean to offend you. **-4.** [humor] disposition. **-5.** [alma] mind. ◇ *interj* [para alentar]: ¡~! come on!

animosidad *f* animosity.

animoso, **-sa** *adj* [valiente] courageous; [decidido] undaunted.

aniñado, **-da** *adj* [comportamiento] childish; [voz, rostro] childlike.

aniquilación *f* annihilation.

aniquilar *vt* to annihilate, to wipe out.

anís (*pl* **anises**) *m* **-1.** [planta] anise. **-2.** [grano] aniseed. **-3.** [licor] anisette.

anisete *m* anisette.

aniversario *m* [gen] anniversary; [cumpleaños] birthday.

Ankara Ankara.

ano *m* anus.

anoche *adv* last night, yesterday evening; **antes de** ~ the night before last.

anochecer [30] ◇ *m* dusk, nightfall; **al** ~ at dusk. ◇ *v impers* to get dark. ◇ *vi*: ~ **en algún sitio** to be somewhere at nightfall.

anodino, **-na** *adj* **-1.** [sin gracia] dull, insipid. **-2.** [insustancial] lacking in substance.

ánodo *m* anode.

anomalía *f* anomaly.

anómalo, **-la** *adj* anomalous.

anonadado, **-da** *adj* **-1.** [sorprendido] astonished, bewildered. **-2.** [abatido] stunned.

anonadar *vt* **-1.** [sorprender] to astonish, to bewilder. **-2.** [abatir] to stun.
◆ **anonadarse** *vpr* **-1.** [sorprenderse] to be astonished ○ bewildered. **-2.** [abatirse] to be stunned.

anonimato *m* anonymity; **permanecer en el** ~ to remain nameless; **vivir en el** ~ to live out of the public eye.

anónimo, **-ma** *adj* anonymous.
◆ **anónimo** *m* anonymous letter.

anorak (*pl* **anoraks**) *m* anorak.

anorexia *f* anorexia.

anormal ◇ *adj* **-1.** [anómalo] abnormal. **-2.** *ofensivo* [subnormal] subnormal. ◇ *m y f ofensivo* subnormal person.

anormalidad *f* **-1.** [anomalía] abnormality. **-2.** [defecto físico o psíquico] handicap, disability.

anotación *f* [gen] note; [en registro] entry; ~ **contable** COM book entry.

anotar *vt* **-1.** [apuntar] to note down, to make a note of. **-2.** [tantear] to notch up.

anovulatorio, **-ria** *adj* anovulatory.
◆ **anovulatorio** *m* anovulant.

ANPE (*abrev de* **Asociación Nacional del Profesorado Estatal de EGB**) *f Spanish association of state primary-school teachers.*

anquilosamiento *m* **-1.** [estancamiento] stagnation. **-2.** MED paralysis.

anquilosarse *vpr* **-1.** [estancarse] to stagnate. **-2.** MED to become paralysed.

ánsar *m* [ave] goose.

ansia *f* (*el*) **-1.** [afán]: ~ **de** longing ○ yearning for. **-2.** [ansiedad] anxiousness; [angustia] anguish.
◆ **ansias** *fpl* [náuseas] sickness (*U*), nausea (*U*).

ansiar [9] *vt*: ~ **hacer algo** to long ○ be desperate to do sthg.

ansiedad *f* **-1.** [inquietud] anxiety; **con** ~ anxiously. **-2.** PSICOL nervous tension.

ansiolítico, **-ca** *adj* sedative.
◆ **ansiolítico** *m* sedative.

ansioso, **-sa** *adj* **-1.** [impaciente] impatient; **estar** ~ **por** ○ **de hacer algo** to be impatient to do sthg. **-2.** [angustiado] in anguish.

antagónico, **-ca** *adj* antagonistic.

antagonismo *m* antagonism.

antagonista *m y f* opponent.

antaño *adv* in days gone by.

antártico, **-ca** *adj* Antarctic.

◆ **Antártico** m: **el Antártico** the Antarctic; **el océano Glacial Antártico** the Antarctic Ocean.

Antártida f: **la** ~ the Antarctic.

ante¹ m **-1.** [piel] suede. **-2.** [animal] elk, moose.

ante² prep **-1.** [delante de, en presencia de] before. **-2.** [frente a · hecho, circunstancia] in the face of. **-3.** [respecto de] compared to; **su opinión prevaleció** ~ **la mía** his opinion prevailed over mine.

◆ **ante todo** loc adv **-1.** [sobre todo] above all. **-2.** [en primer lugar] first of all.

anteanoche adv the night before last.

anteayer adv the day before yesterday.

antebrazo m forearm.

antecámara f antechamber.

antecedente ◇ adj preceding, previous. ◇ m **-1.** [precedente] precedent. **-2.** GRAM & MAT antecedent.

◆ **antecedentes** mpl [de persona] record (sg); [de asunto] background (sg); **poner a alguien en** ~**s de** [informar] to fill sb in on; ~**s penales** criminal record (sg).

anteceder vt to come before, to precede.

antecesor, -ra m y f [predecesor] predecessor.

◆ **antecesores** mpl [antepasados] ancestors.

antedicho, -cha adj aforementioned.

antediluviano, -na adj lit & fig antediluvian.

antefirma f title of the signatory.

antelación f: **con** ~ in advance, beforehand; **con dos horas de** ~ two hours in advance.

antemano
◆ **de antemano** loc adv beforehand, in advance.

antemeridiano, -na adj morning (antes de sust).

antena f **-1.** RADIO & TV aerial, antenna; **estar/salir en** ~ to be/go on the air; ~ **colectiva** aerial shared by all the inhabitants of a block of flats; ~ **parabólica** satellite dish. **-2.** ZOOL antenna.

anteojeras fpl blinkers Br, blinders Am.

anteojos mpl desus o Amer [gafas] spectacles.

antepasado, -da m y f ancestor.

antepecho m [de puente] parapet; [de ventana] sill.

antepenúltimo, -ma adj, m y f last but two.

anteponer [65] vt: ~ **algo a algo** to put sthg before sthg.

◆ **anteponerse** vpr: ~**se a** to come before.

anteproyecto m draft; ~ **de ley** draft bill.

antepuesto, -ta pp → anteponer.

anterior adj **-1.** [previo]: ~ **(a)** previous (to). **-2.** [delantero] front (antes de sust).

anterioridad f: **con** ~ beforehand; **con** ~ **a** before, prior to.

anteriormente adv previously.

antes adv **-1.** [gen] before; **no importa si venís** ~ it doesn't matter if you come earlier; **ya no nado como** ~ I can't swim as I used to; **mucho/poco** ~ long/shortly before; **lo** ~ **posible** as soon as possible. **-2.** [primero] first; **esta señora está** ~ this lady is first. **-3.** [expresa preferencia]: ~ **... que** rather ... than; **prefiero la sierra** ~ **que el mar** I like the mountains better than the sea; **iría a la cárcel** ~ **que mentir** I'd rather go to prison than lie.

◆ **antes de** loc prep before; ~ **de hacer algo** before doing sthg.

◆ **antes (de) que** loc conj before; ~ **(de) que llegarais** before you arrived.

antesala f anteroom; **estar en la** ~ **de** fig to be on the verge of; **hacer** ~ [esperar] to wait.

antevíspera f day before yesterday.

antiabortista ◇ adj anti-abortion, pro-life. ◇ m y f anti-abortion o pro-life campaigner.

antiácido, -da adj antacid.

◆ **antiácido** m antacid.

antiadherente adj nonstick.

antiaéreo, -a adj anti-aircraft.

antiarrugas adj inv anti-wrinkle.

antibala, antibalas adj inv bullet-proof.

antibiótico, -ca adj antibiotic.

◆ **antibiótico** m antibiotic.

antichoc, antichoque adj shockproof.

anticiclón m anticyclone.

anticipación f earliness; **con** ~ in advance; **con un mes de** ~ a month in advance; **con** ~ **a** prior to.

anticipado, -da adj [elecciones] early; [pago] advance; **por** ~ in advance.

anticipar vt **-1.** [prever] to anticipate. **-2.** [adelantar] to bring forward. **-3.** [pago] to pay in advance. **-4.** [información]: **no te puedo** ~ **nada** I can't tell you anything just now.

◆ **anticiparse** vpr **-1.** [suceder antes] to arrive early; **se anticipó a su tiempo** he was ahead of his time. **-2.** [adelantarse]: ~**se a alguien** to beat sb to it.

anticipo m **-1.** [de dinero] advance. **-2.** [presagio] foretaste.

anticlerical adj anticlerical.

anticlericalismo m anticlericalism.

anticoagulante adj & m anticoagulant.

anticomunismo *m* anti-communism.
anticomunista *adj, m y f* anti-communist.
anticoncepción *f* contraception.
anticonceptivo, -va *adj* contraceptive.
◆ anticonceptivo *m* contraceptive.
anticonformismo *m* non-conformism.
anticongelante *adj & m* antifreeze.
anticonstitucional *adj* unconstitutional.
anticonstitucionalidad *f* unconstitutional nature.
anticorrosivo, -va *adj* anticorrosive.
◆ anticorrosivo *m* anticorrosive substance.
anticristo *m* Antichrist.
anticuado, -da *adj* old-fashioned.
anticuario, -ria *m y f* [comerciante] antique dealer; [experto] antiquarian.
◆ anticuario *m* [tienda] antique shop.
anticuerpo *m* antibody.
antidemocrático, -ca *adj* undemocratic.
antideportivo, -va *adj* unsporting, unsportsmanlike.
antidepresivo, -va *adj* antidepressant.
◆ antidepresivo *m* antidepressant (drug).
antideslizante *adj* anti-skid; [ruedas] non-skid.
antideslumbrante *adj* anti-dazzle.
antidisturbios *mpl* [policía] riot police.
antidopaje *m* doping tests (*pl*).
antidoping [anti'ðopin] *adj* doping (*antes de sust*).
antídoto *m* antidote.
antier *adv* Amer *fam* the day before yesterday.
antiestético, -ca *adj* unsightly.
antifascista *adj, m y f* anti-fascist.
antifaz *m* mask.
antigás *adj inv* gas (*antes de sust*).
antígeno *m* antigen.
antigripal ◇ *adj* designed to combat flu. ◇ *m* flu remedy.
antigualla *f despec* [cosa] museum piece; [persona] old fogey, old fossil.
antiguamente *adv* [hace mucho] long ago; [previamente] formerly.
Antigua y Barbuda Antigua and Barbuda.
antigubernamental *adj* anti-government.
antigüedad *f* -1. [gen] antiquity. -2. [veteranía] seniority.
◆ antigüedades *fpl* [objetos] antiques.
antiguo, -gua *adj* -1. [viejo] old; [inmemorial] ancient. -2. [anterior, previo] former. -3. [veterano] senior. -4. [pasado de moda] old-fashioned; a la antigua in an old-fashioned way.

◆ antiguos *mpl* HIST ancients.
antihéroe *m* antihero.
antihigiénico, -ca *adj* unhygienic.
antihistamínico, -ca *adj* antihistamine.
◆ antihistamínico *m* antihistamine.
antiinflacionista *adj* anti-inflationary.
antiinflamatorio *m* anti-inflammatory drug.
antílope *m* antelope.
antimateria *f* antimatter.
antimilitarismo *m* antimilitarism.
antimilitarista *adj, m y f* antimilitarist.
antimisil *m* antimissile.
antimonopolio *adj inv* ECON antitrust (*antes de sust*).
antinatural *adj* unnatural.
antiniebla *adj inv* → faro.
antioxidante ◇ *adj* anti-rust. ◇ *m* rust-proofing agent.
antipapa *m* antipope.
antiparasitario *m* -1. VETER flea collar. -2. TELECOM suppressor.
antiparras *fpl fam* specs.
antipatía *f* dislike; tener ~ a alguien to dislike sb.
antipático, -ca ◇ *adj* unpleasant. ◇ *m y f* unpleasant person.
antipirético, -ca *adj* antipyretic.
◆ antipirético *m* antipyretic.
antípodas *fpl*: las ~ the Antipodes.
antiquísimo, -ma ◇ *superl* → antiguo. ◇ *adj* ancient.
antirreflectante *adj* non-reflective.
antirreglamentario, -ria *adj* DEP illegal, against the rules.
antirrobo ◇ *adj inv* antitheft (*antes de sust*). ◇ *m* [en coche] antitheft device; [en edificio] burglar alarm.
antisemita ◇ *adj* anti-Semitic. ◇ *m y f* anti-Semite.
antiséptico, -ca *adj* antiseptic.
◆ antiséptico *m* antiseptic.
antisocial *adj* antisocial.
antiterrorismo *m* fight against terrorism.
antiterrorista *adj* anti-terrorist.
antítesis *f inv* antithesis.
antitetánico, -ca *adj* anti-tetanus (*antes de sust*).
antitético, -ca *adj culto* antithetical.
antivirus *m inv* -1. MED vaccine. -2. INFORM antivirus system.
antojadizo, -za *adj* capricious.
antojarse *vpr* -1. [capricho]: se le antojaron esos zapatos he fancied those shoes; se le ha antojado ir al cine he felt like going to

the cinema; **cuando se me antoje** when I feel like it. **-2.** [posibilidad]: **se me antoja que ...** I have a feeling that ....

antojitos *mpl Amer* snacks, tapas.

antojo *m* **-1.** [capricho] **whim**; [de embarazada] **craving**; **a mi/tu** *etc* ~ **my/your** *etc* (own) way; **tener un** ~ [embarazada] to have a craving. **-2.** [lunar] **birthmark**.

antología *f* **anthology**; **de** ~ **memorable**, **unforgettable**.

antológico, -ca *adj* **-1.** [recopilador] **anthological**. **-2.** [inolvidable] **memorable**, **unforgettable**.

antónimo *m* **antonym**.

antonomasia *f*: **por** ~ **par excellence**.

antorcha *f* **torch**.

antracita *f* **anthracite**.

ántrax *m inv* **anthrax**.

antro *m despec* **dive**, **dump**.

antropocentrismo *m* **anthropocentrism**.

antropofagia *f* **anthropophagy**, **cannibalism**.

antropófago, -ga ◇ *adj* **anthropophagous**. ◇ *m y f* **cannibal**.

antropología *f* **anthropology**.

antropólogo, -ga *m y f* **anthropologist**.

anual *adj* **annual**.

anualidad *f* **annuity**, **yearly payment**.

anuario *m* **yearbook**.

anudar *vt* to knot, to tie in a knot.

◆ **anudarse** *vpr* **-1.** [atarse] to get into a knot. **-2.** [entorpecerse]: **se le anudó la voz** he got a lump in his throat.

anuencia *f culto* **consent**, **approval**.

anulación *f* **-1.** [cancelación] **cancellation**; [de ley] **repeal**; [de matrimonio, contrato] **annulment**. **-2.** [DEP - de un partido] **calling-off**; [- de un gol] **disallowing**; [- de un resultado] **declaration as void**.

anular[1] ◇ *adj* [en forma de anillo] **annular**. ◇ *m* → **dedo**.

anular[2] *vt* **-1.** [cancelar - gen] to cancel; [- ley] to repeal; [- matrimonio, contrato] to annul. **-2.** [DEP - partido] to call off; [- gol] to disallow; [- resultado] to declare void. **-3.** [reprimir] to repress.

anunciación *f* **announcement**.

◆ **Anunciación** *f* RELIG **Annunciation**.

anunciante ◇ *adj* **advertising** (*antes de sust*). ◇ *m y f* **advertiser**.

anunciar [8] *vt* **-1.** [notificar] to announce. **-2.** [hacer publicidad de] to advertise. **-3.** [presagiar] to herald.

◆ **anunciarse** *vpr*: ~**se en** to advertise in, to put an advert in.

anuncio *m* **-1.** [notificación] **announcement**; [cartel, aviso] **notice**; [póster] **poster**. **-2.** ~ **(publicitario) advertisement**, **advert**; ~**s por palabras classified adverts**. **-3.** [presagio] **sign**, **herald**.

anverso *m* [de moneda] **head**, **obverse**; [de hoja] **front**.

anzuelo *m* **-1.** [para pescar] **(fish) hook**. **-2.** *fam* [señuelo] **bait**; **picar** O **morder el** ~ to take the bait.

añadido, -da *adj*: ~ **(a) added (to)**.

◆ **añadido** *m* **addition**.

añadidura *f* **addition**; **por** ~ **in addition**, **what is more**.

añadir *vt* to add.

añejo, -ja *adj* **-1.** [vino, licor] **mature**; [tocino] **cured**. **-2.** [costumbre] **age-old**.

añicos *mpl*: **hacer** O **hacerse** ~ to shatter.

añil *adj & m* [color] **indigo**.

año *m* **year**; **en el** ~ **1939** in 1939; **los** ~**s 30** the thirties; ~ **académico/escolar/fiscal academic/school/tax year**; ~ **bisiesto/solar leap/solar year**; ~ **nuevo New Year**; **¡Feliz Año Nuevo! Happy New Year!**; ~ **sabático sabbatical**; **el** ~ **de la nana** *fam* **the year dot**.

◆ **años** *mpl* [edad] **age** (*sg*); **¿cuántos** ~**s tienes?** — **tengo 17** ~**s how old are you?** — **I'm 17 (years old)**; **cumplir** ~**s to have one's birthday**; **cumplo** ~**s el 25 it's my birthday on the 25th**; **estar entrado** O **metido en** ~**s to be getting on**; **te has quitado** ~**s de encima** [rejuvenecer] **you look much younger**.

◆ **año luz** (*pl* **años luz**) *m* **light year**; **estar a** ~**s luz de** *fig* to be light years away from.

añoranza *f*: ~ **(de)** [gen] **nostalgia (for)**; [hogar, patria] **homesickness (for)**.

añorar *vt* to miss.

aorta *f* **aorta**.

aovado, -da *adj* **egg-shaped**.

aovar *vi* to lay eggs; [peces] to spawn.

ap. *abrev de* **aparte**.

AP (*abrev de* **Alianza Popular**) *m former name of PP, Spanish party to the right of the political spectrum*.

APA (*abrev de* **asociación de padres de alumnos**) *f Spanish association for parents of schoolchildren*, ≃ PTA.

apabullar *vt* to overwhelm.

◆ **apabullarse** *vpr* to be overwhelmed.

apacentar [19] *vt* to graze.

apache *adj, m y f* **Apache**.

apacible *adj* [gen] **mild**, **gentle**; [lugar, ambiente] **pleasant**.

apacienta *etc* → **apacentar**.

apaciguador, -ra *adj* calming.

apaciguar [45] *vt* **-1.** [tranquilizar] to calm down. **-2.** [aplacar - dolor etc] to soothe.

◆ **apaciguarse** *vpr* **-1.** [tranquilizarse] to calm down. **-2.** [aplacarse - dolor etc] to abate.

apadrinar *vt* **-1.** [niño] to act as a godparent to. **-2.** [artista] to sponsor.

apagado, -da *adj* **-1.** [luz, fuego] out; [aparato] off. **-2.** [color, persona] subdued. **-3.** [sonido] dull, muffled; [voz] low, quiet.

apagar [16] *vt* **-1.** [extinguir - fuego] to put out; [- luz] to put off; [- vela] to extinguish. **-2.** [desconectar] to turn ○ switch off; **apaga y vámonos** *fig* we have nothing more to talk about. **-3.** [aplacar - sed] to quench; [- dolor] to get rid of. **-4.** [rebajar - color] to soften; [- sonido] to muffle.

◆ **apagarse** *vpr* **-1.** [extinguirse - fuego, vela, luz] to go out; [- dolor, ilusión, rencor] to die down; [- sonido] to die away. **-2.** [morir] to pass away.

apagón *m* power cut.

apague *etc* → **apagar**.

apaisado, -da *adj* oblong.

apalabrar *vt* [concertar] to make a verbal agreement regarding; [contratar] to engage on the basis of a verbal agreement.

Apaches *mpl*: **los ~** the Appalachians.

apalancar [10] *vt* [para abrir] to lever open; [para mover] to lever.

◆ **apalancarse** *vpr mfam* [apoltronarse] to install o.s.

apalear *vt* to beat up.

apañado, -da *adj fam* [hábil, mañoso] clever, resourceful; **estar ~** *fig* to have had it.

apañar *vt fam* **-1.** [reparar] to mend. **-2.** [amañar] to fix, to arrange.

◆ **apañarse** *vpr fam* to cope, to manage; **apañárselas (para hacer algo)** to manage (to do sthg).

apaño *m fam* **-1.** [reparación] patch. **-2.** [chanchullo] fix, shady deal. **-3.** [acuerdo] compromise.

apapachado, -da *adj Amer* pampered, spoilt.

apapachador, -ra *adj Amer* comforting.

apapachar *vt Amer* to cuddle.

apapachos *mpl Amer* cuddles, caresses.

aparador *m* **-1.** [mueble] sideboard. **-2.** [escaparate] shop window.

aparato *m* **-1.** [máquina] machine; [de laboratorio] apparatus (*U*); [electrodoméstico] appliance. **-2.** [dispositivo] device. **-3.** [teléfono]: **¿quién está al ~?** who's speaking? **-4.** [avión] plane. **-5.** [MED - prótesis] aid; [- para

dientes] brace. **-6.** ANAT system. **-7.** POLÍT machinery. **-8.** [ostentación] pomp, ostentation.

aparatoso, -sa *adj* **-1.** [ostentoso] ostentatious, showy. **-2.** [espectacular] spectacular.

aparcamiento *m* **-1.** [acción] parking. **-2.** [parking] car park *Br*, parking lot *Am*; [hueco] parking place.

aparcar [10] ◇ *vt* **-1.** [estacionar] to park. **-2.** [posponer] to shelve. ◇ *vi* [estacionar] to park.

aparcero, -ra *m y f* sharecropper.

aparear *vt* [animales] to mate.

◆ **aparearse** *vpr* [animales] to mate.

aparecer [30] *vi* **-1.** [gen] to appear. **-2.** [acudir]: **~ por (un lugar)** to turn up at (a place). **-3.** [ser encontrado] to turn up.

◆ **aparecerse** *vpr* to appear.

aparecido, -da *m y f* ghost.

aparejado, -da *adj*: **llevar ~** [acarrear] to entail.

aparejador, -ra *m y f* quantity surveyor.

aparejar *vt* **-1.** [preparar] to get ready, to prepare. **-2.** [caballerías] to harness. **-3.** NÁUT to rig (out).

aparejo *m* **-1.** [de caballerías] harness. **-2.** MEC block and tackle. **-3.** NÁUT rigging.

◆ **aparejos** *mpl* equipment (*U*); [de pesca] tackle (*U*).

aparentar ◇ *vt* **-1.** [fingir] to feign. **-2.** [edad] to look. ◇ *vi* [presumir] to show off.

aparente *adj* **-1.** [falso, supuesto] apparent. **-2.** [visible] visible. **-3.** [llamativo] striking.

aparición *f* **-1.** [gen] appearance. **-2.** [de ser sobrenatural] apparition.

apariencia *f* **-1.** [aspecto] appearance; **en ~** apparently, outwardly; **guardar las ~s** to keep up appearances; **las ~s engañan** appearances can be deceptive. **-2.** [falsedad] illusion.

aparque *etc* → **aparcar**.

apartado, -da *adj* **-1.** [separado]: **~ de** away from. **-2.** [alejado] remote.

◆ **apartado** *m* [párrafo] paragraph; [sección] section.

◆ **apartado de correos** *m* PO Box.

apartamento *m* apartment.

apartar *vt* **-1.** [alejar] to move away; [quitar] to remove. **-2.** [separar] to separate. **-3.** [escoger] to take, to select.

◆ **apartarse** *vpr* **-1.** [hacerse a un lado] to move to one side, to move out of the way. **-2.** [separarse] to separate; **~se de** [gen] to move away from; [tema] to get away from; [mundo, sociedad] to cut o.s. off from.

aparte ◇ *adv* **-1.** [en otro lugar, a un lado] aside, to one side; **bromas ~** joking apart.

-2. [además] besides; ~ **de fea** ... besides being ugly .... **-3.** [por separado] separately. ◇ *adj inv* separate; **ser caso** ~ to be a different matter. ◇ *m* **-1.** [párrafo] new paragraph. **-2.** TEATR aside.
◆ **aparte de** *loc prep* [excepto] apart from, except from.

apartheid [apar'xeid] *m* apartheid.

apartotel, aparthotel *m* hotel apartments (*pl*).

apasionado, -da ◇ *adj* passionate. ◇ *m y f* lover, enthusiast.

apasionante *adj* fascinating.

apasionar *vt* to fascinate; **le apasiona la música** he's mad about music.
◆ **apasionarse** *vpr* to get excited; **~se por** O **con** to be mad about.

apatía *f* apathy.

apático, -ca ◇ *adj* apathetic. ◇ *m y f* apathetic person.

apátrida ◇ *adj* stateless. ◇ *m y f* stateless person.

apdo. *abrev de* **apartado**.

APE (*abrev de* **Asamblea Parlamentaria Europea**) *f* European Parliament.

apeadero *m* [de tren] halt.

apear *vt* **-1.** [bajar] to take down. **-2.** *fam* [disuadir]: ~ **alguien de** to talk sb out of.
◆ **apearse** *vpr* **-1.** [bajarse]: **~se (de)** [tren] to alight (from), to get off; [coche] to get out (of); [caballo] to dismount (from). **-2.** *fam* [disuadirse]: **~se de** to back down on.

apechugar [16] *vi*: ~ **con** to put up with, to live with.

apedrear ◇ *vt* [persona] to stone; [cosa] to throw stones at. ◇ *v impers* to hail.

apegarse [16] *vpr*: ~ **a** to become fond of O attached to.

apego *m* fondness, attachment; **tener/tomar** ~ **a** to be/become fond of.

apelación *f* appeal.

apelar *vi* **-1.** DER to (lodge an) appeal; ~ **ante/contra** to appeal to/against. **-2.** [recurrir]: ~ **a** [persona] to go to; [sentido común, bondad] to appeal to; [violencia] to resort to.

apelativo *m* name.

apellidar *vt* [dar por nombre] to name.
◆ **apellidarse** *vpr*: **se apellida Suárez** her surname is Suárez.

apellido *m* surname.

apelmazado, -da *adj* **-1.** [jersey] shrunk. **-2.** [arroz, bizcocho] stodgy.

apelmazar [13] *vt* **-1.** [jersey] to shrink. **-2.** [arroz, bizcocho] to make stodgy.
◆ **apelmazarse** *vpr* **-1.** [jersey] to shrink. **-2.** [arroz, bizcocho] to go stodgy.

apelotonar *vt* to bundle up.

◆ **apelotonarse** *vpr* [gente] to crowd together.

apenado, -da *adj Amer* ashamed.

apenar *vt* to sadden.
◆ **apenarse** *vpr* to be saddened.

apenas *adv* **-1.** [casi no] scarcely, hardly; ~ **me puedo mover** I can hardly move. **-2.** [tan sólo] only; ~ **hace dos minutos** only two minutes ago. **-3.** [tan pronto como] as soon as; ~ **llegó, sonó el teléfono** no sooner had he arrived than the phone rang.

apencar [10] *vi fam*: ~ **con** [trabajo] to take on; [responsabilidad] to shoulder; [consecuencias, dificultad] to live with.

apéndice *m* appendix.

apendicitis *f inv* appendicitis.

Apeninos *mpl*: **los** ~ the Appenines.

apenque *etc* → **apencar**.

apercibir *vt* **-1.** [darse cuenta de] to notice. **-2.** [amonestar] to reprimand, to give a warning to. **-3.** DER to issue with a warning.
◆ **apercibirse de** *vpr* to notice.

apergaminarse *vpr fam* to become wrinkled O wizened.

aperitivo *m* [bebida] aperitif; [comida] appetizer.

apero *m* (*gen pl*) tool; **~s de labranza** farming implements.

aperrearse *vpr fam* to refuse to change one's mind.

apertura *f* **-1.** [gen] opening; [de año académico, temporada] start. **-2.** [DEP - en rugby] kick-off; [- en ajedrez] opening (move). **-3.** POLÍT [liberalización] liberalization.

APERTURA:
'Apertura' is the name given in Spain to the period after 1970 when political changes were introduced by the Franco regime

aperturismo *m* progressive policies (*pl*).

aperturista *adj, m y f* progressive.

apesadumbrar *vt* to weigh down.
◆ **apesadumbrarse** *vpr* to be weighed down.

apestar ◇ *vi*: ~ **(a)** to stink (of). ◇ *vt* **-1.** [hacer que huela mal] to infest, to stink out. **-2.** [contagiar peste] to infect with the plague.

apestoso, -sa *adj* foul.

apetecer [30] ◇ *vi*: **¿te apetece un café?** do you fancy a coffee?; **me apetece salir** I feel like going out. ◇ *vt*: **tenían todo cuanto apetecían** they had everything they wanted.

apetecible *adj* [comida] appetizing, tempting; [vacaciones etc] desirable.

apetito *m* appetite; **abrir el** ~ to whet one's appetite; **perder el** ~ to lose one's appetite; **tener** ~ to be hungry.

apetitoso, -sa *adj* **-1.** [comida] appetizing. **-2.** [oferta, empleo] tempting.

API (*abrev de* **agente de la propiedad inmobiliaria**) *m* estate agent *Br*, real estate broker *Am*.

apiadar *vt* to earn the pity of.
◆ **apiadarse** *vpr* to show compassion; ~**se de** to take pity on.

ápice *m* **-1.** [pizca] iota; **ni un** ~ not a single bit; **no ceder un** ~ not to budge an inch. **-2.** [vértice - de montaña] peak; [- de hoja, lengua] tip; [- de edificio] top. **-3.** [punto culminante] peak, height.

apicultor, -ra *m y f* beekeeper.

apicultura *f* beekeeping.

apilar *vt* to pile up.
◆ **apilarse** *vpr* to pile up.

apiñado, -da *adj* [apretado] packed, crammed.

apiñar *vt* to pack ○ cram together.
◆ **apiñarse** *vpr* to crowd together; [para protegerse, por miedo] to huddle together.

apio *m* celery.

apisonadora *f* steamroller.

aplacar [10] *vt* to placate; [hambre] to satisfy; [sed] to quench.
◆ **aplacarse** *vpr* to calm down; [dolor] to abate.

aplace *etc* → **aplazar**.

aplanar *vt* to level.

aplaque *etc* → **aplazar**.

aplastante *adj fig* [apabullante] overwhelming, devastating.

aplastar *vt* **-1.** [por el peso] to flatten. **-2.** [derrotar] to crush.

aplatanado, -da *adj fam* listless.

aplatanar *vt fam* to make listless.
◆ **aplatanarse** *vpr fam* to become listless.

aplaudir *vt & vi* to applaud.

aplauso *m* **-1.** [ovación] round of applause; ~**s** applause (*U*). **-2.** *fig* [alabanza] applause.

aplazamiento *m* postponement.

aplazar [13] *vt* to postpone.

aplicación *f* **-1.** [gen & INFORM] application. **-2.** [decoración] appliqué.

aplicado, -da *adj* **-1.** [estudioso] diligent. **-2.** [ciencia] applied.

aplicar [10] *vt* [gen] to apply; [nombre, calificativo] to give.
◆ **aplicarse** *vpr* **-1.** [esmerarse]: ~**se (en**

algo) to apply o.s. (to sthg). **-2.** [concernir]: ~**se a** to apply to.

aplique *m* wall lamp.

aplomo *m* composure; **perder el** ~ to lose one's composure.

apocado, -da *adj* timid.

apocalipsis *m o f inv* calamity.
◆ **Apocalipsis** *m o f* Apocalypse.

apocalíptico, -ca *adj* apocalyptic.

apocamiento *m* timidity.

apocarse [10] *vpr* [intimidarse] to be frightened ○ scared; [humillarse] to humble o.s.

apocopar *vt* to apocopate.

apócope *f* apocopation.

apócrifo, -fa *adj* apocryphal.

apodar *vt* to nickname.
◆ **apodarse** *vpr* to be nicknamed.

apoderado, -da *m y f* **-1.** [representante] (official) representative. **-2.** TAUROM agent, manager.

apoderar *vt* [gen] to authorize, to empower; DER to grant power of attorney to.
◆ **apoderarse de** *vpr* **-1.** [adueñarse de] to seize. **-2.** *fig* [dominar] to take hold of, to grip.

apodo *m* nickname.

apogeo *m fig* height, apogee; **estar en (pleno)** ~ to be at its height.

apolillado, -da *adj* moth-eaten.

apolillar *vt* to eat holes in.
◆ **apolillarse** *vpr* to get moth-eaten.

apolítico, -ca *adj* apolitical.

apología *f* apology, eulogy; ~ **del terrorismo** defence of terrorism.

apoltronarse *vpr* **-1.** [apalancarse]: ~ **(en)** to become lazy ○ idle (in). **-2.** [acomodarse]: ~ **en** to lounge in.

apoplejía *f* apoplexy.

apoquinar *vt & vi fam* to fork out.

aporrear *vt* to bang.

aportación *f* **-1.** [proporcionamiento] provision. **-2.** [contribución] contribution; **hacer una** ~ to contribute.

aportar *vt* **-1.** [proporcionar] to provide. **-2.** [contribuir con] to contribute.

aposentar *vt* to put up, to lodge.
◆ **aposentarse** *vpr* to take up lodgings.

aposento *m* **-1.** [habitación] room; **retirarse a sus** ~**s** *desus o hum* to withdraw (to one's chamber). **-2.** [alojamiento] lodgings (*pl*).

aposición *f* apposition.

apósito *m* dressing.

aposta, apostas *adv* on purpose, intentionally.

apostante *m y f* person who places a bet.

apostar [23] ◇ vt -1. [jugarse] to bet. -2. [emplazar] to post. ◇ vi: ~ **(por)** to bet (on); **apuesto a que no viene** I bet he doesn't come.
◆ **apostarse** vpr -1. [jugarse] to bet; ~**se algo con alguien** to bet sb sthg. -2. [colocarse] to post o.s.

apostas = aposta.

apóstata m y f apostate.

apostilla f note.

apostillar vt to annotate.

apóstol m lit & fig apostle.

apostolado m -1. [de apóstol] apostolate. -2. [de ideales] mission.

apostólico, -ca adj apostolic.

apostolizar [13] vt to convert to Christianity.

apóstrofe m o f LITER apostrophe.

apóstrofo m GRAM apostrophe.

apostura f [garbo] dashing nature.

apoteósico, -ca adj tremendous.

apoteosis f inv [final] grand finale.

apoyacabezas m inv headrest.

apoyar vt -1. [inclinar] to lean, to rest. -2. fig [basar, respaldar] to support.
◆ **apoyarse** vpr -1. [sostenerse]: ~**se en** to lean on. -2. fig [basarse]: ~**se en** [suj: tesis, conclusiones] to be based on, to rest on; [suj: persona] to base one's arguments on. -3. [respaldarse] to support one another.

apoyo m lit & fig support.

APRA (abrev de **Alianza Popular Revolucionaria Americana**) f Peruvian political party to the centre-right of the political spectrum.

apreciable adj -1. [perceptible] appreciable, significant. -2. fig [estimable] worthy.

apreciación f [consideración] appreciation; [estimación] evaluation.

apreciar [8] vt -1. [valorar] to appreciate; [sopesar] to appraise, to evaluate. -2. [sentir afecto por] to think highly of. -3. [percibir] to tell, to make out. -4. [opinar]: ~ **que** to consider (that).

aprecio m esteem; **sentir** ~ **por alguien** to think highly of sb.

aprehender vt -1. [coger - persona] to apprehend; [- alijo, mercancía] to seize. -2. [comprender] to take in.

aprehensión f [de persona] arrest, capture; [de alijo, mercancía] seizure.

apremiante adj pressing, urgent.

apremiar [8] ◇ vt -1. [meter prisa]: ~ **a alguien para que haga algo** to urge sb to do sthg. -2. [obligar]: ~ **a alguien a hacer algo** to compel sb to do sthg. ◇ vi [ser urgente] to be pressing.

apremio m -1. [urgencia] urgency. -2. DER writ.

aprender ◇ vt -1. [estudiar] to learn. -2. [memorizar] to memorize. ◇ vi: ~ **(a hacer algo)** to learn (to do sthg); **¡para que aprendas!** that'll teach you!
◆ **aprenderse** vpr -1. [estudiar] to learn. -2. [memorizar] to memorize.

aprendiz, -za m y f -1. [ayudante] apprentice, trainee. -2. [novato] beginner.

aprendizaje m -1. [acción] learning. -2. [tiempo, situación] apprenticeship.

aprensión f: ~ **(por)** [miedo] apprehension (about); [escrúpulo] squeamishness (about).

aprensivo, -va adj -1. [miedoso] apprehensive. -2. [escrupuloso] squeamish. -3. [hipocondríaco] hypochondriac.

apresar vt [suj: animal] to catch; [suj: persona] to capture.

aprestar vt -1. [preparar] to prepare, to get ready. -2. [tela] to size.
◆ **aprestarse a** vpr: ~**se a hacer algo** to get ready to do sthg.

apresto m size.

apresurado, -da adj hasty, hurried.

apresuramiento m haste.

apresurar vt to hurry along, to speed up; ~ **a alguien para que haga algo** to try to make sb do sthg more quickly.
◆ **apresurarse** vpr to hurry; ~**se a hacer algo** to do sthg quickly.

apretado, -da adj -1. [gen] tight; [triunfo] narrow; [esprint] close; [caligrafía] cramped. -2. [apiñado] packed.

apretar [19] ◇ vt -1. [oprimir - botón, tecla] to press; [- gatillo] to pull, to squeeze; [- nudo, tuerca, cinturón] to tighten; **el zapato me aprieta** my shoe is pinching. -2. [estrechar] to squeeze; [abrazar] to hug. -3. [comprimir - ropa, objetos] to pack tight. -4. [juntar - dientes] to grit; [- labios] to press together. -5. fig [el paso, la marcha] to quicken. -6. fig [presionar] to press.
◇ vi [calor, lluvia] to get worse, to intensify; ~ **a correr** fam to run off.
◆ **apretarse** vpr [agolparse] to crowd together; [acercarse] to squeeze up.

apretón m [estrechamiento] squeeze; ~ **de manos** handshake.
◆ **apretones** mpl [aglomeración] crush (sg).

apretujar vt -1. [gen] to squash. -2. [hacer una bola con] to screw up.
◆ **apretujarse** vpr [en banco, autobús] to squeeze together; [por frío] to huddle up.

apretujón m fam [abrazo] bearhug.

aprieta etc → apretar.

aprieto *m fig* fix, difficult situation; **poner en un ~ a alguien** to put sb in a difficult position; **verse** ○ **estar en un ~** to be in a fix.

aprisa *adv* quickly.

aprisionar *vt* **-1.** [encarcelar] to imprison. **-2.** [inmovilizar - atando, con camisa de fuerza] to strap down; [- suj: viga etc] to trap.

aprobación *f* approval.

aprobado, -da *adj* [aceptado] approved.
◆ **aprobado** *m* EDUC pass.

aprobar [23] *vt* **-1.** [proyecto, moción, medida] to approve; [ley] to pass. **-2.** [comportamiento etc] to approve of. **-3.** [examen, asignatura] to pass.

apropiación *f* [robo] theft.

apropiado, -da *adj* suitable, appropriate.

apropiar [8] *vt*: **~ (a)** to adapt (to).
◆ **apropiarse de** *vpr lit & fig* to steal.

aprovechable *adj* usable.

aprovechado, -da ○ *adj* **-1.** [caradura]: **es muy ~** he's always sponging off other people. **-2.** [bien empleado - tiempo] well-spent; [- espacio] well-planned. **-3.** [aplicado] diligent. ○ *m y f* [caradura] sponger.

aprovechamiento *m* **-1.** [utilización] use. **-2.** [en el estudio] progress, improvement.

aprovechar ○ *vt* **-1.** [gen] to make the most of; [oferta, ocasión] to take advantage of; [conocimientos, experiencia] to use, to make use of; **~ que** ... to make the most of the fact that .... **-2.** [lo inservible] to put to good use. ○ *vi* **-1.** [ser provechoso] to be beneficial; **¡que aproveche!** enjoy your meal! **-2.** [mejorar] to make progress.
◆ **aprovecharse** *vpr*: **~se (de)** to take advantage (of).

aprovisionamiento *m* supplying.

aprovisionar *vt* to supply.

aproximación *f* **-1.** [acercamiento] approach. **-2.** [en cálculo] approximation. **-3.** [en lotería] *in lotteries, consolation prize given to numbers immediately before and after the winning number*. **-4.** *fig* [de países] rapprochement; [de puntos de vista] converging.

aproximadamente *adv* approximately.

aproximado, -da *adj* approximate.

aproximar *vt* to move closer.
◆ **aproximarse** *vpr* to come closer.

aprueba *etc* → **aprobar**.

aptitud *f* ability, aptitude; **tener ~ para algo** to have an aptitude for sthg.

apto, -ta *adj* **-1.** [adecuado, conveniente]: **~ (para)** suitable (for). **-2.** [capacitado - intelectualmente] capable, able; [- físicamente] fit. **-3.** CIN: **~/no ~ para menores** suitable/unsuitable for children.

apuesta ◇ *v* → **apostar**. ◇ *f* bet.

apuesto, -ta *adj* dashing.

apunar *vt Amer* to cause to have altitude sickness.
◆ **apunarse** *vpr Amer* to get altitude sickness.

apuntador, -ra *m y f* prompter.

apuntalamiento *m lit & fig* underpinning.

apuntalar *vt lit & fig* to underpin.

apuntar ◇ *vt* **-1.** [anotar] to make a note of, to note down; **~ a alguien** [en lista] to put sb down; **apúntamelo (en la cuenta)** put it on my account. **-2.** [dirigir - dedo] to point; [- arma] to aim; **~ alguien** [con el dedo] to point at sb; [con un arma] to aim at sb. **-3.** TEATR to prompt. **-4.** *fig* [sugerir] to hint at. **-5.** *fig* [indicar] to point out. ◇ *vi* **-1.** [vislumbrarse] to appear; [día] to break. **-2.** *fig* [indicar]: **~ a** to point to, to suggest.
◆ **apuntarse** *vpr* **-1.** [en lista] to put one's name down; [en curso] to enrol. **-2.** [participar]: **~se (a hacer algo)** to join in (doing sthg); **yo me apunto** I'm in.

apunte *m* **-1.** [nota] note. **-2.** [boceto] sketch. **-3.** COM entry. **-4.** TEATR prompt.
◆ **apuntes** *mpl* EDUC notes; **tomar ~s** to take notes.

apuñalar *vt* to stab.

apurado, -da *adj* **-1.** [necesitado] in need; **~ de** short of. **-2.** [avergonzado] embarrassed. **-3.** [difícil] awkward.

apurar *vt* **-1.** [agotar] to finish off; [existencias, la paciencia] to exhaust. **-2.** [meter prisa] to hurry. **-3.** [preocupar] to trouble. **-4.** [avergonzar] to embarrass. **-5.** [barba] to shave closely.
◆ **apurarse** *vpr* **-1.** [preocuparse]: **~se (por)** to worry (about). **-2.** [darse prisa] to hurry.

apuro *m* **-1.** [dificultad] fix, difficult situation; **estar en ~s** to be in a tight spot. **-2.** [penuria] hardship (*U*); **pasar ~s** to be hard up. **-3.** [vergüenza] embarrassment; **me da ~ (decírselo)** I'm embarrassed (to tell her).

aquaplaning [akwa'planin] *m* aquaplaning.

aquejado, -da *adj*: **~ de** suffering from.

aquejar *vt* to afflict; **le aquejan varias enfermedades** he suffers from a number of illnesses.

aquel, aquella (*pl* **aquellos, aquellas**) *adj demos* that, (*pl*) those.

aquél, aquélla (*pl* **aquéllos, aquéllas**) *pron demos* **-1.** [ése] that (one), (*pl*) those (ones); **este cuadro me gusta pero ~ del fondo no** I like this picture, but I don't like that one at the back; **~ fue mi último día en Londres** that was my last day in London. **-2.** [nombrado antes] the former; **tenía**

mos un coche y una moto, ésta estropeada y ~ sin gasolina we had a car and a motorbike, the former was out of petrol, the latter had broken down. **-3.** [con oraciones relativas] whoever, anyone who; ~ **que quiera hablar que levante la mano** whoever wishes ○ anyone wishing to speak should raise their hand; **aquéllos que ...** those who ....

aquelarre m coven.

aquella → aquel.

aquélla → aquél.

aquello pron demos (neutro) that; **no consiguió saber si** ~ **lo dijo en serio** he never found out whether she meant those words ○ that seriously; ~ **de su mujer es una mentira** all that about his wife is a lie.

aquellos, aquellas → aquel.

aquéllos, aquéllas → aquél.

aquí adv **-1.** [gen] here; ~ **abajo/arriba** down/up here; ~ **dentro/fuera** in/out here; ~ **mismo** right here; ~ **y allá** here and there; **de** ~ **para allá** [de un lado a otro] to and fro; **por** ~ over here. **-2.** [ahora] now; **de** ~ **a mañana** between now and tomorrow; **de** ~ **a poco** shortly, soon; **de** ~ **a un mes** a month from now, in a month. **-3.** [en tiempo pasado]: ~ **empezaron los problemas** that was when the problems started.

◆ **de aquí que** loc conj [por eso] hence, therefore.

aquiescencia f approval.

aquietar vt to calm down.

◆ **aquietarse** vpr to calm down.

aquilatar vt **-1.** [metales, joyas] to assay. **-2.** fig [examinar] to assess.

ara f (el) culto **-1.** [piedra] altar stone. **-2.** [altar] altar.

◆ **en aras de** loc prep culto for the sake of.

árabe ◇ adj Arab, Arabian. ◇ m y f [persona] Arab. ◇ m [lengua] Arabic.

arabesco m arabesque.

Arabia Saudí, Arabia Saudita Saudi Arabia.

arábigo, -ga adj **-1.** [de Arabia] Arab, Arabian. **-2.** [numeración] Arabic.

arácnido m arachnid.

arado m plough.

Aragón Aragon.

aragonés, -esa adj, m y f Aragonese.

Aral m: **el mar de** ~ the Aral Sea.

arameo m [lengua] Aramaic.

arancel m tariff.

arancelario, -ria adj tariff (antes de sust).

arándano m bilberry.

arandela f TECN washer.

araña f **-1.** [animal] spider; ~ **de mar** spider crab. **-2.** [lámpara] chandelier.

arañar vt **-1.** [gen] to scratch. **-2.** fig [reunir] to scrape together.

arañazo m scratch.

arar vt to plough.

arbitraje m **-1.** [DEP - en fútbol etc] refereeing; [- en tenis, críquet] umpiring. **-2.** DER arbitration.

arbitral adj DEP of the referee.

arbitrar ◇ vt **-1.** [DEP - en fútbol etc] to referee; [- en tenis, críquet] to umpire. **-2.** [medidas, recursos] to bring together. **-3.** DER to arbitrate. ◇ vi **-1.** [DEP - en fútbol etc] to referee; [- en tenis, críquet] to umpire. **-2.** DER to arbitrate.

arbitrariedad f **-1.** [cualidad] arbitrariness. **-2.** [acción] arbitrary action.

arbitrario, -ria adj arbitrary.

arbitrio m [decisión] judgment; **dejar algo al** ~ **de alguien** to leave sthg to sb's discretion; **libre** ~ free will.

◆ **arbitrios** mpl [impuestos] taxes.

árbitro m **-1.** [DEP - en fútbol etc] referee; [- en tenis, críquet] umpire. **-2.** DER arbitrator.

árbol m **-1.** BOT tree; ~ **de Navidad** Christmas tree. **-2.** TECN shaft; ~ **de levas** camshaft. **-3.** NÁUT mast.

◆ **árbol genealógico** m family tree.

arbolado, -da adj **-1.** [terreno] wooded; [calle] tree-lined. **-2.** [mar] tempestuous.

◆ **arbolado** m woodland (U).

arboladura f NÁUT masts and spars (pl).

arbolar vt **-1.** [barco] to mast. **-2.** [bandera] to raise, to hoist. **-3.** [mar] to whip up.

◆ **arbolarse** vpr to rear up.

arboleda f wood.

arbotante m flying buttress.

arbusto m bush, shrub.

arca f (el) **-1.** [arcón] chest. **-2.** [barco]: ~ **de Noé** Noah's Ark.

◆ **arcas** fpl coffers; ~**s públicas** Treasury (sg).

arcabuz m arquebus.

arcada f **-1.** (gen pl) [de estómago] retching (U); **me dieron** ~**s** I retched. **-2.** [ARQUIT - arcos] arcade; [- de puente] arch.

arcaico, -ca adj archaic.

arcaísmo m archaism.

arcángel m archangel.

arcano, -na adj arcane.

◆ **arcano** m **-1.** [carta] arcana. **-2.** [misterio] mystery.

arce m maple.

arcén m [de autopista] hard shoulder; [de carretera] verge.

archiconocido, -da *adj fam* very well-known.

archiduque, -quesa *m y f* archduke (*f* archduchess).

archimillonario, -ria *m y f* multimillionaire.

archipiélago *m* archipelago.

archisabido, -da *adj* very well-known.

archivador, -ra *m y f* archivist.

◆ **archivador** *m* filing cabinet.

archivar *vt* **-1.** [guardar - documento, fichero etc] to file. **-2.** *fig* [olvidar - suceso etc] to push to the back of one's mind.

archivo *m* **-1.** [lugar] archive; [documentos] archives (*pl*); **imágenes de** ~ TV library pictures. **-2.** [informe, ficha] file. **-3.** INFORM file; ~ **batch** batch file.

arcilla *f* clay.

arcipreste *m* archpriest.

arco *m* **-1.** GEOM arc. **-2.** ARQUIT arch; ~ **de herradura** horseshoe arch; ~ **triunfal** O **de triunfo** triumphal arch. **-3.** DEP, MIL & MÚS bow. **-4.** *Amer* DEP [portería] goal, goalmouth.

◆ **arco iris** *m* rainbow.

arcón *m* large chest.

arder *vi* to burn; [sin llama] to smoulder; ~ **de** *fig* to burn with; **está que arde** [persona] he's fuming; [reunión] it's getting pretty heated.

ardid *m* ruse, trick.

ardiente *adj* [gen] burning; [líquido] scalding; [admirador, defensor] ardent.

ardilla *f* squirrel.

ardite *m*: **no vale un** ~ *fam* it isn't worth a brass farthing.

ardor *m* **-1.** [calor] heat. **-2.** [quemazón] burning (sensation); ~ **de estómago** heartburn. **-3.** *fig* [entusiasmo] fervour.

arduo, -dua *adj* arduous.

ARE (*abrev de* **Asamblea de Regiones Europeas**) *f* AER.

área *f* (*el*) **-1.** [gen] area; ~ **metropolitana/ de servicio** metropolitan/service area; ~ **de libre cambio** ECON free exchange area. **-2.** [medida] = *100 square metres*, are. **-3.** DEP: ~ **(de castigo** O **penalti) (penalty)** area.

arena *f* **-1.** [de playa etc] sand; ~**s movedizas** quicksand (*U*). **-2.** [para luchar] arena. **-3.** TAUROM bullring.

arenal *m* sandy ground (*U*).

arenga *f* harangue.

arengar [16] *vt* to harangue.

arenilla *f* [polvo] dust.

◆ **arenillas** *fpl* MED kidney stones.

arenisca *f* sandstone.

arenoso, -sa *adj* sandy.

arenque *m* herring.

arete *m* earring.

argamasa *f* mortar.

Argel Algiers.

Argelia Algeria.

Argentina: (la) ~ Argentina.

argentinismo *m* *word peculiar to Argentinian Spanish*.

argentino, -na *adj, m y f* Argentinian.

argolla *f* **-1.** [aro] (large) ring. **-2.** *Amer* [alianza] wedding ring.

argonauta *m* Argonaut.

argot *m* **-1.** [popular] slang. **-2.** [técnico] jargon.

argucia *f* sophism.

argüir [44] ◇ *vt culto* **-1.** [argumentar] to argue. **-2.** [demostrar] to prove, to demonstrate. **-3.** [deducir] to deduce. ◇ *vi* [argumentar] to argue.

argumentación *f* line of argument.

argumentar *vt* **-1.** [teoría, opinión] to argue. **-2.** [razones, excusas] to allege.

argumento *m* **-1.** [razonamiento] argument. **-2.** [trama] plot.

arguya *etc* → **argüir**.

arguyera *etc* → **argüir**.

aria *f* MÚS aria.

aridez *f* [gen] dryness; [de zona, clima] aridity.

árido, -da *adj* [gen] dry; [zona, clima] arid.

◆ **áridos** *mpl* dry goods.

Aries ◇ *m* [zodiaco] Aries; **ser** ~ to be (an) Aries. ◇ *m y f* [persona] Aries.

ariete *m* **-1.** HIST & MIL battering ram. **-2.** DEP centre forward.

ario, -ria *adj, m y f* Aryan.

arisco, -ca *adj* surly.

arista *f* edge.

aristocracia *f* aristocracy.

aristócrata *m y f* aristocrat.

aristocrático, -ca *adj* aristocratic.

aristotélico, -ca *adj, m y f* Aristotelian.

aritmético, -ca *adj* arithmetic.

◆ **aritmética** *f* arithmetic.

arlequín *m* harlequin.

arma *f* (*el*) **-1.** [instrumento] arm, weapon; **presentar/rendir** ~**s** to present/surrender arms; ~ **biológica/nuclear/química** biological/nuclear/chemical weapon; ~ **blanca** blade, weapon with a sharp blade; ~ **de fuego** firearm; ~ **homicida** murder weapon. **-2.** *fig* [medio] weapon. **-3.** *loc*: **alzarse en** ~**s** to rise up; ~ **de dos filos** O **doble filo** double-edged sword; **ser de** ~**s tomar**

to be sb to be reckoned with, to be formidable.

◆ **armas** *fpl* [profesión] military career (*sg*).
armada → armado.
armadillo *m* armadillo.
armado, -da *adj* **-1.** [con armas] armed. **-2.** [con armazón] reinforced.
◆ **armada** *f* [marina] navy; [escuadra] fleet.
◆ **Armada** *f*: **la Armada Invencible** the Spanish Armada.
armador, -ra *m y f* shipowner.
armadura *f* **-1.** [de barco, tejado] framework; [de gafas] frame. **-2.** [de guerrero] armour.
armamentista, armamentístico, -ca *adj* arms (*antes de sust*).
armamento *m* **-1.** [armas] arms (*pl*). **-2.** [acción] armament, arming.
armañac *m* armagnac.
armar *vt* **-1.** [montar - mueble etc] to assemble; [- tienda] to pitch. **-2.** [ejército, personas] to arm. **-3.** [fusil, pistola] to load. **-4.** *fam fig* [provocar] to cause; **~la** *fam* to cause trouble.
◆ **armarse** *vpr* **-1.** [con armas] to arm o.s. **-2.** [prepararse]: **~se de** [valor, paciencia] to summon up. **-3.** *loc*: **se armó la gorda** ○ **la de San Quintín** ○ **la de Dios es Cristo** *fam* all hell broke loose.
armario *m* [para objetos] cupboard; [para ropa] wardrobe; **~ empotrado** fitted cupboard/wardrobe.
armatoste *m* [mueble, objeto] unwieldy object; [máquina] contraption.
armazón *f* [gen] framework, frame; [de avión, coche] chassis; [de edificio] skeleton.
Armenia Armenia.
armenio, -nia *adj, m y f* Armenian.
armería *f* **-1.** [museo] military ○ war museum. **-2.** [depósito] armoury. **-3.** [tienda] gunsmith's (shop). **-4.** [arte] gunsmith's craft.
armero *m* **-1.** [fabricante] gunsmith. **-2.** MIL armourer.
armiño *m* [piel] ermine; [animal] stoat.
armisticio *m* armistice.
armonía *f* harmony.
armónico, -ca *adj* harmonic.
◆ **armónico** *m* harmonic.
◆ **armónica** *f* harmonica.
armonio *m* harmonium.
armonioso, -sa *adj* harmonious.
armonizar [13] ◇ *vt* **-1.** [concordar] to match. **-2.** MUS to harmonize. ◇ *vi* [concordar]: **~ con** to match.
ARN (*abrev de* **ácido ribonucleico**) *m* RNA.

arnés *m* armour.
◆ **arneses** *mpl* [de animales] trappings, harness (*U*).
árnica *f* arnica.
aro *m* **-1.** [círculo] hoop; TECN ring; **los ~s olímpicos** the Olympic rings; **entrar** ○ **pasar por el ~** to knuckle under. **-2.** [servilletero] napkin ○ serviette ring. **-3.** [alianza] ring. **-4.** *Amer* [pendiente] earring.
aroma *m* aroma; [de vino] bouquet; CULIN flavouring.
aromático, -ca *adj* aromatic.
aromatizador *m* air freshener.
aromatizar [13] *vt* to perfume; CULIN to flavour.
arpa *f* (*el*) harp.
arpegio *m* arpeggio.
arpía *f* **-1.** MITOL harpy. **-2.** *fig* [mujer] old hag.
arpillera *f* sackcloth, hessian.
arpón *m* harpoon.
arponear *vt* to harpoon.
arquear *vt* [gen] to bend; [cejas, espalda, lomo] to arch.
◆ **arquearse** *vpr* to bend.
arqueo *m* **-1.** [curvamiento] bending; [de cejas, espalda, lomo] arching. **-2.** COM cashing up. **-3.** NAUT registered tonnage.
arqueología *f* archeology.
arqueológico, -ca *adj* archeological.
arqueólogo, -ga *m y f* archeologist.
arquero *m* **-1.** DEP & MIL archer. **-2.** [tesorero] treasurer. **-3.** DEP [portero] goalkeeper.
arquetipo *m* archetype.
arquitecto, -ta *m y f* architect.
arquitectónico, -ca *adj* architectural.
arquitectura *f* lit & *fig* architecture.
arquitrabe *m* architrave.
arquivolta *f* archivolt.
arrabal *m* [barrio pobre] slum (*on city outskirts*); [barrio periférico] outlying district.
arrabalero, -ra ◇ *adj* **-1.** [periférico] outlying. **-2.** [barriobajero] rough, coarse. ◇ *m y f* [barriobajero] rough ○ coarse person.
arracimarse *vpr* to cluster together.
arraigado, -da *adj* [costumbre, idea] deeply rooted; [persona] established.
arraigar [16] ◇ *vt* to establish. ◇ *vi* lit & *fig* to take root.
◆ **arraigarse** *vpr* [establecerse] to settle down.
arraigo *m* roots (*pl*); **tener mucho ~** to be deeply rooted.
arrancada *f* sudden start.
arrancar [10] ◇ *vt* **-1.** [desarraigar - árbol] to uproot; [- malas hierbas, flor] to pull up. **-2.**

[quitar, separar] to tear ◇ rip off; [cable, página, pelo] to tear out; [cartel, cortinas] to tear down; [muela] to pull out, to extract; [ojos] to gouge out. **-3.** [arrebatar]: ~ **algo a alguien** to grab ◇ snatch sthg from sb. **-4.** AUTOM & TECN to start up; INFORM to start up. **-5.** *fig* [obtener]: ~ **algo a alguien** [confesión, promesa, secreto] to extract sthg from sb; [sonrisa, dinero, ovación] to get sthg out of sb; [suspiro, carcajada] to bring sthg from sb. **-6.** *fig* [mover]: ~ **a alguien de un sitio** to shift sb from somewhere.
◇ *vi* **-1.** [partir] to set off. **-2.** [suj: máquina, coche] to start. **-3.** [provenir]: ~ **de** to stem from.
◆ **arrancarse** *vpr*: ~**se a hacer algo** to begin ◇ start to do sthg.

arranque *m* **-1.** [comienzo] start. **-2.** AUTOM starter motor. **-3.** *fig* [arrebato] fit.

arras *fpl* **-1.** [fianza] deposit (*sg*). **-2.** [en boda] *coins given by the bridegroom to the bride*.

arrasar *vt* to destroy, to devastate.

arrastrado, -da *adj fam* miserable, wretched.

arrastrar ◇ *vt* **-1.** [gen] to drag ◇ pull along; [pies] to drag; [carro, vagón] to pull; [suj: corriente, aire] to carry away. **-2.** *fig* [convencer] to win over, to sway; ~ **a alguien a algo/a hacer algo** to lead sb into sthg/to do sthg; **dejarse** ~ **por algo/alguien** to allow o.s. to be swayed by sthg/sb. **-3.** *fig* [producir] to bring. **-4.** *fig* [soportar - vida] to lead; [- deudas, penas] to have hanging over one.
◇ *vi* [rozar el suelo] to drag (along) the ground.
◆ **arrastrarse** *vpr* to crawl; *fig* to grovel.

arrastre *m* **-1.** [acarreo] dragging. **-2.** [pesca] trawling. **-3.** *loc*: **estar para el** ~ to have had it, to be done for.

arrayán *m* myrtle.

arre *interj*: ¡~! gee up!

arrear *vt* **-1.** [azuzar] to gee up. **-2.** *fam* [propinar] to give. **-3.** [poner arreos] to harness.

arrebatado, -da *adj* **-1.** [impetuoso] impulsive, impetuous. **-2.** [ruborizado] flushed. **-3.** [iracundo] enraged.

arrebatador, -ra *adj* captivating.

arrebatar *vt* **-1.** [arrancar]: ~ **algo a alguien** to snatch sthg from sb. **-2.** *fig* [cautivar] to captivate.
◆ **arrebatarse** *vpr* [enfurecerse] to get furious.

arrebato *m* **-1.** [arranque] fit, outburst; **un** ~ **de amor** a crush. **-2.** [furia] rage, fury.

arrebujar *vt* **-1.** [amontonar] to bundle (up). **-2.** [arropar] to wrap up (warmly).

◆ **arrebujarse** *vpr* [arroparse] to wrap o.s. up.

arrechar *vt Amer mfam* to make horny, to turn on.
◆ **arrecharse** *vpr Amer mfam* to get horny.

arrecho, -cha *adj Amer mfam* horny, randy.

arrechucho *m fam* funny turn.

arreciar [8] *vi* **-1.** [temporal etc] to get worse. **-2.** *fig* [críticas etc] to intensify.

arrecife *m* reef.

arredrarse *vpr*: ~ **ante** to be frightened of, to be intimidated by.

arreglado, -da *adj* **-1.** [reparado] fixed, repaired; [ropa] mended. **-2.** [ordenado] tidy. **-3.** [bien vestido] smart. **-4.** [solucionado] sorted out. **-5.** *fig* [precio] reasonable. **-6.** *loc*: **estamos** ~**s** we're really done for.

arreglar *vt* **-1.** [reparar] to fix, to repair; [ropa] to mend. **-2.** [ordenar] to tidy (up). **-3.** [solucionar] to sort out. **-4.** MÚS to arrange. **-5.** [acicalar] to smarten up; [cabello] to do. **-6.** [adornar - cuarto etc] to decorate, to fit out. **-7.** *fam* [escarmentar]: ¡**ya te arreglaré!** I'm going to sort you out!
◆ **arreglarse** *vpr* **-1.** [apañarse]: ~**se (con algo)** to make do (with sthg); **arreglárselas (para hacer algo)** to manage (to do sthg). **-2.** [acicalarse] to smarten up.

arreglista *m y f* MÚS (musical) arranger.

arreglo *m* **-1.** [reparación] mending, repair; [de ropa] mending. **-2.** [solución] settlement. **-3.** MÚS (musical) arrangement. **-4.** [acuerdo] agreement; **llegar a un** ~ to reach agreement; **con** ~ **a** in accordance with. **-5.** [decoración] decoration, doing up.

arrejuntar *vt fam* [cosas] to put together.
◆ **arrejuntarse** *vpr fam* [amantes] to shack up together.

arrellanarse *vpr* to settle back.

arremangado, -da *adj* rolled-up.

arremangar, remangar [16] *vt* to roll up.
◆ **arremangarse** *vpr* to roll up one's sleeves.

arremeter
◆ **arremeter contra** *vi* to attack.

arremetida *f* attack.

arremolinarse *vpr* **-1.** *fig* [personas]: ~ **alrededor de** to crowd around. **-2.** [agua, hojas] to swirl (about).

arrendador, -ra *m y f* lessor.

arrendamiento, arriendo *m* **-1.** [acción] renting, leasing. **-2.** [precio] rent, lease.

arrendar [19] *vt* **-1.** [dar en arriendo] to let, to lease. **-2.** [tomar en arriendo] to rent, to lease.

arrendatario, -ria ◇ *adj* leasing (*antes de sust*). ◇ *m y f* leaseholder, tenant.

arreos *mpl* harness (*U*).

arrepanchingarse [16] *vpr fam* to stretch out, to sprawl.

arrepentido, -da ◇ *adj* repentant. ◇ *m y f* -1. [gen] penitent. -2. POLIT *person who renounces terrorist activities.*

arrepentimiento *m* regret, repentance.

arrepentirse [27] *vpr* to repent; ~ **de algo/de haber hecho algo** to regret sthg/having done sthg.

arrestado, -da ◇ *adj* under arrest. ◇ *m y f* detainee, person under arrest.

arrestar *vt* to arrest.

arresto *m* [detención] arrest; ~ **domiciliario** house arrest.

◆ **arrestos** *mpl* courage (*U*).

arriar [9] *vt* to lower.

arriate *m* (flower) bed.

arriba ◇ *adv* -1. [posición - gen] above; [- en edificio] upstairs; **vive (en el piso de)** ~ she lives upstairs; **está aquí/allí** ~ it's up here/there; ~ **del todo** right at the top; **más** ~ further up. -2. [dirección] up; **ve** ~ [en edificio] go upstairs; **hacia/para** ~ up, upwards; **calle/escaleras** ~ up the street/stairs; **río** ~ upstream. -3. [en un texto] above; **el** ~ **mencionado** ... the above-mentioned .... -4. *loc*: **de** ~ **abajo** [cosa] from top to bottom; [persona] from head to toe ○ foot; **mirar a alguien de** ~ **abajo** [con desdén] to look sb up and down.
◇ *prep*: ~ **(de)** *Amer* [encima de] on top of.
◇ *interj*: ¡~ ...! up (with) ...!; ¡~ **los mineros!** up (with) the miners!; ¡~ **las manos!** hands up!

◆ **arriba de** *loc prep* more than.

◆ **de arriba** *loc adj* top; **el estante de** ~ the top shelf.

arribar *vi* to arrive; NÀUT to reach port.

arribeño, -ña *m y f Amer fam* highlander.

arribista *adj, m y f* arriviste.

arrienda *etc* → **arrendar**.

arriendo → **arrendamiento**.

arriero, -ra *m y f* muleteer.

arriesgado, -da *adj* -1. [peligroso] risky. -2. [osado] daring.

arriesgar [16] *vt* to risk; [hipótesis] to venture, to suggest.

◆ **arriesgarse** *vpr* to take risks/a risk.

arrimar *vt* -1. [acercar] to move ○ bring closer; ~ **algo a** [pared, mesa] to move sthg up against. -2. *fig* [arrinconar] to put away.

◆ **arrimarse** *vpr* -1. [acercarse] to come closer ○ nearer; **arrimaos que no cabemos** move up or we won't all fit in; ~**se a algo**

[acercándose] to move closer to sthg; [apoyándose] to lean on sthg. -2. *fig* [ampararse]: ~**se a alguien** to seek sb's protection.

arrinconado, -da *adj* -1. [en una esquina] in a corner. -2. [abandonado] discarded, forgotten.

arrinconar *vt* -1. [apartar] to put in a corner. -2. [abandonar] to discard, to put away. -3. *fig* [persona - dar de lado] to cold-shoulder; [- acorralar] to corner.

arritmia *f* arrythmia.

arrítmico, -ca *adj* arrythmic.

arroba *f* [peso] = *11.5 kg*; **por** ~**s** *fig* by the sackful.

arrobamiento *m* ecstasy, rapture.

arrobar *vt* to captivate.

◆ **arrobarse** *vpr* to go into raptures.

arrocero, -ra ◇ *adj* rice (*antes de sust*). ◇ *m y f* rice grower.

arrodillarse *vpr* to kneel down; *fig* to go down on one's knees, to grovel.

arrogancia *f* arrogance.

arrogante *adj* arrogant.

arrogarse [16] *vpr* to assume, to claim for o.s.

arrojado, -da *adj* bold, fearless.

arrojar *vt* -1. [lanzar] to throw; [con violencia] to hurl, to fling. -2. [despedir - humo] to send out; [- olor] to give off; [- lava] to spew out. -3. [echar]: ~ **a alguien de** to throw sb out of. -4. [resultado] to produce, to yield. -5. [vomitar] to throw up.

◆ **arrojarse** *vpr* to hurl o.s.

arrojo *m* courage, fearlessness.

arrollador, -ra *adj* [belleza, personalidad] dazzling.

arrollar *vt* -1. [enrollar] to roll (up). -2. [atropellar] to knock down, to run over. -3. [tirar - suj: agua, viento] to sweep away. -4. [vencer] to crush.

arropar *vt* -1. [con ropa] to wrap up; [en cama] to tuck up. -2. *fig* [proteger] to protect.

◆ **arroparse** *vpr* to wrap o.s. up.

arrostrar *vt* to face up to.

arroyo *m* -1. [riachuelo] stream. -2. [de la calle] gutter. -3. *loc*: **poner a alguien en el** ~ to throw sb out into the street; **sacar a alguien del** ~ to drag sb out of the gutter.

arroz *m* rice; ~ **blanco** boiled rice; ~ **integral** brown rice; ~ **con leche** rice pudding.

arrozal *m* paddy field.

arruga *f* -1. [en ropa, papel] crease. -2. [en piel] wrinkle, line.

arrugar [16] *vt* -1. [ropa, papel] to crease, to crumple. -2. [piel] to wrinkle.

◆ **arrugarse** *vpr* **-1.** [ropa] to get creased. **-2.** [piel] to get wrinkled. **-3.** *fam* [acobardarse]: ~**se ante** to shrink from.

arruinado, -da *adj* ruined.

arruinar *vt lit* & *fig* to ruin.

◆ **arruinarse** *vpr* to go bankrupt, to be ruined.

arrullar *vt* to lull to sleep.

◆ **arrullarse** *vpr* **-1.** [animales] to coo. **-2.** *fam fig* [personas] to whisper sweet nothings.

arrullo *m* **-1.** [de palomas] cooing. **-2.** [nana] lullaby. **-3.** *fig* [de agua, olas] murmur.

arrumaco *m* (U) *fam* lovey-dovey behaviour.

arrumar *vt Amer* to pile up.

arrumbar *vt* to put away.

arrume *m Amer* pile.

arsenal *m* **-1.** [de barcos] shipyard. **-2.** [de armas] arsenal. **-3.** [de cosas] array. **-4.** *fig* [de conocimientos] fount, store.

arsénico *m* arsenic.

art. (*abrev de* **artículo**) art.

arte *m o f* (*en sg gen m; en pl f*) **-1.** [gen] art; ~ **abstracto/figurativo** abstract/figurative art; ~ **dramático** drama. **-2.** [habilidad] artistry. **-3.** [astucia] artfulness, cunning; **malas** ~**s** trickery (U). **-4.** *loc*: **no tener** ~ **ni parte en** to have nothing whatsoever to do with; **como por** ~ **de birlibirloque** o **de encantamiento** o **de magia** as if by magic.

◆ **artes** *fpl* arts; ~**s gráficas/plásticas** graphic/plastic arts; ~**s liberales** liberal arts; ~**s marciales** martial arts; ~**s y oficios** ≃ technical college *Br*; **bellas** ~**s** fine arts.

artefacto *m* [aparato] device; [máquina] machine.

arteria *f lit* & *fig* artery.

arterial *adj* arterial.

arterioesclerosis, arteriosclerosis *f inv* arteriosclerosis.

artesa *f* trough.

artesanal *adj* [hecho a mano] handmade.

artesanía *f* craftsmanship; **de** ~ [producto] handmade.

artesano, -na *m y f* craftsman (*f* craftswoman).

artesonado *m* coffered ceiling.

ártico, -ca *adj* arctic.

◆ **Ártico** *m*: **el Ártico** the Arctic; **el océano Glacial Ártico** the Arctic Ocean.

articulación *f* **-1.** ANAT & TECN joint. **-2.** LING articulation. **-3.** [estructuración] coordination.

articulado, -da *adj* articulated.

articular *vt* **-1.** [palabras, piezas] to articulate. **-2.** [ley, contrato] to break down into separate articles. **-3.** [plan, proyecto] to coordinate.

articulista *m y f* journalist.

artículo *m* **-1.** [gen] article; ~ **definido** o **determinado** definite article; ~ **indefinido** o **indeterminado** indefinite article; ~ **básico** ECON basic product; ~ **de fondo** editorial, leader; ~ **de importación** import; ~ **líder** ECON product leader; ~ **de primera necesidad** basic commodity. **-2.** [de diccionario] entry.

◆ **artículo de fe** *m* RELIG article of faith; *fig* gospel (truth) (U).

artífice *m y f fig* architect.

artificial *adj* artificial.

artificiero *m* **-1.** [pirotécnico] explosives expert. **-2.** [desactivador] bomb disposal expert.

artificio *m* **-1.** [aparato] device. **-2.** *fig* [falsedad] artifice; [artimaña] trick.

artificioso, -sa *adj fig* [engañoso] deceptive.

artillería *f* artillery.

artillero *m* artilleryman.

artilugio *m* gadget, contrivance.

artimaña *f* (*gen pl*) trick, ruse.

artista *m y f* **-1.** [gen] artist. **-2.** [de espectáculos] artiste.

artístico, -ca *adj* artistic.

artritis *f inv* arthritis.

artrosis *f inv* arthrosis.

arveja *f Amer* pea.

arz. (*abrev de* **arzobispo**) Arch.

arzobispo *m* archbishop.

as *m* **-1.** [carta, dado] ace. **-2.** [campeón]: **un** ~ **del volante** an ace driver; **ser un** ~ to be brilliant.

asa *f* (*el*) handle.

asado *m* roast.

asador *m* **-1.** [aparato] roaster. **-2.** [varilla] spit.

asaduras *fpl* offal (U); [de pollo, pavo] giblets.

asaetear *vt* [disparar a] to shoot arrows at; [matar] to kill with arrows.

asalariado, -da *m y f* wage earner.

asalariar [8] *vt* to take on.

asalmonado, -da *adj* salmon (pink).

asaltante *m y f* [agresor] attacker; [atracador] robber.

asaltar *vt* **-1.** [atacar] to attack; [castillo, ciudad etc] to storm. **-2.** [robar] to rob. **-3.** *fig* [suj: dudas etc] to assail. **-4.** [importunar] to plague.

asalto *m* **-1.** [ataque] attack; [de castillo, ciudad] storming. **-2.** [robo] robbery. **-3.** DEP round.

asamblea *f* assembly; POLÍT mass meeting.

asar *vt* **-1.** [alimentos - al horno] to roast; [- a la parrilla] to grill. **-2.** *fig* [importunar]: ~ **a alguien a preguntas** to plague sb with questions.

◆ **asarse** *vpr fig* to be boiling hot.

ascendencia *f* **-1.** [linaje] descent. **-2.** [extracción social] extraction. **-3.** *fig* [influencia] ascendancy.

ascendente ◇ *adj* rising. ◇ *m* ASTROL ascendant.

ascender [20] ◇ *vi* **-1.** [subir] to go up, to climb. **-2.** [aumentar, elevarse] to rise, to go up. **-3.** [en empleo, deportes]: ~ **(a)** to be promoted (to). **-4.** [totalizar - precio etc] ~ **a** to come ○ amount to. ◇ *vt*: ~ **a alguien (a)** to promote sb (to).

ascendiente ◇ *m y f* [antepasado] ancestor. ◇ *m* [influencia] influence.

ascensión *f* ascent.

◆ **Ascensión** *f* RELIG Ascension.

ascenso *m* **-1.** [en empleo, deportes] promotion. **-2.** [ascensión] ascent.

ascensor *m* lift *Br*, elevator *Am*.

ascensorista *m y f* lift attendant *Br*, elevator attendant *Am*.

ascético, -ca *adj* ascetic.

ascetismo *m* asceticism.

ASCII (*abrev de* **American Standard Code for Information Interchange**) *m* ASCII.

asco *m* [sensación] revulsion; **siento** ~ I feel sick; **¡qué ~ de tiempo!** what foul weather!; **me da** ~ I find it disgusting; **¡qué ~!** how disgusting ○ revolting!; **tener** ~ **a algo** to find sthg disgusting ○ revolting; **hacer** ~**s a** to turn one's nose up at; **estar hecho un** ~ *fam* [cosa] to be filthy; [persona] to be a real sight; **ser un** ~ *fam* to be the pits.

ascua *f* (*el*) ember; **arrimar uno el** ~ **a su sardina** to put o.s. first, to look after number one; **en** ○ **sobre** ~**s** on tenterhooks.

aseado, -da *adj* [limpio] clean; [arreglado] smart.

asear *vt* to clean.

◆ **asearse** *vpr* to get washed and dressed.

asechanza *f* snare.

asediar [8] *vt* to lay siege to; *fig* to pester, to badger.

asedio *m* siege; *fig* pestering, badgering.

asegurado, -da *m y f* policy-holder.

asegurador, -ra ◇ *adj* insurance (*antes de sust*). ◇ *m y f* insurer.

asegurar *vt* **-1.** [fijar] to secure. **-2.** [garantizar] to assure; **te lo aseguro** I assure you; ~

a alguien que ... to assure sb that .... **-3.** COM: ~ **(contra)** to insure (against); ~ **algo en** [cantidad] to insure sthg for.

◆ **asegurarse** *vpr* **-1.** [cerciorarse]: ~**se de que ...** to make sure that ...; **asegúrate de cerrar la puerta** make sure you close the door. **-2.** COM to insure o.s., to take out an insurance policy.

asemejar

◆ **asemejar a** *vi* to be similar to, to be like.

◆ **asemejarse** *vpr* to be similar ○ alike; ~**se a** to be similar to, to be like.

asentado, -da *adj fig* [establecido] settled, established.

asentamiento *m* **-1.** [aseguramiento] securing. **-2.** [campamento] settlement.

asentar [19] *vt* **-1.** [instalar - empresa, campamento] to set up; [comunidad, pueblo] to settle. **-2.** [asegurar] to secure; [cimientos] to lay.

◆ **asentarse** *vpr* **-1.** [instalarse] to settle down. **-2.** [sedimentarse] to settle.

asentimiento *m* approval, assent.

asentir [27] *vi* **-1.** [estar conforme]: ~ **(a)** to agree (to). **-2.** [afirmar con la cabeza] to nod.

aseo *m* **-1.** [limpieza - acción] cleaning; [- cualidad] cleanliness. **-2.** [habitación] bathroom.

◆ **aseos** *mpl* toilets *Br*, restroom (*sg*) *Am*.

asepsia *f* **-1.** MED asepsis. **-2.** *fig* [indiferencia] detachment.

aséptico, -ca *adj* **-1.** MED aseptic. **-2.** *fig* [indiferente] detached.

asequible *adj* **-1.** [accesible, comprensible] accessible. **-2.** [razonable - precio, producto] affordable.

aserción *f* assertion.

aserradero *m* sawmill.

aserrar [19] *vt* to saw.

aserto *m* assertion.

asesinar *vt* to murder; [rey, jefe de estado] to assassinate.

asesinato *m* murder; [de rey, jefe de estado] assassination.

asesino, -na ◇ *adj lit* & *fig* murderous. ◇ *m y f* murderer (*f* murderess); [de rey, jefe de estado] assassin; ~ **a sueldo** hired assassin; ~ **profesional** professional killer.

asesor, -ra *m y f* adviser; FIN consultant; ~ **fiscal** tax consultant.

asesoramiento *m* advice; FIN consultancy.

asesorar *vt* to advise; FIN to provide with consultancy services.

◆ **asesorarse** *vpr* to seek advice; ~**se de** to consult.

asesoría f **-1.** [oficio] consultancy. **-2.** [oficina] consultant's office.

asestar vt [golpe] to deal; [tiro] to fire.

aseveración f assertion.

aseverar vt to assert.

asexuado, -da adj asexual.

asexual adj asexual.

asfaltado m [acción] asphalting, surfacing; [asfalto] asphalt, (road) surface.

asfaltadora f (road) surfacer.

asfaltar vt to asphalt, to surface.

asfalto m asphalt.

asfixia f asphyxiation, suffocation.

asfixiante adj asphyxiating; fig [calor] stifling.

asfixiar [8] vt **-1.** [ahogar] to asphyxiate, to suffocate. **-2.** fig [agobiar] to overwhelm.
◆ **asfixiarse** vpr **-1.** [ahogarse] to asphyxiate, to suffocate. **-2.** fig [agobiarse] to be overwhelmed; [por calor] to be stifling.

asga etc → **asir**.

así ◇ adv [de este modo] in this way, like this; [de ese modo] in that way, like that; **era ~ de largo** it was this/that long; **~ es/era/fue como** ... that is how ...; **~ ~** [no muy bien] so so; **algo ~** [algo parecido] something like that; **algo ~ como** [algo igual a] something like; **~ es** [para asentir] that is correct, yes; **y ~ todos los días** and the same thing happens day after day; **~ como** [también] as well as, and also; [tal como] just as, exactly as. ◇ conj **-1.** [de modo que]: **~ (es) que** so. **-2.** [aunque] although. **-3.** [tan pronto como]: **~ que** as soon as. **-4.** Amer [aun si] even if. ◇ adj inv [como éste] like this; [como ése] like that.
◆ **así pues** loc adv so, therefore.
◆ **así y todo, aun así** loc adv even so.

Asia Asia.

asiático, -ca adj, m y f Asian, Asiatic.

asidero m **-1.** [agarradero] handle. **-2.** fig [apoyo] support.

asiduidad f frequency.

asiduo, -dua adj, m y f regular.

asienta etc **-1.** → **asentar**. **-2.** → **asentir**.

asiento m **-1.** [mueble, localidad] seat; **tomar ~** to sit down; **~ abatible** seat that can be tipped forward. **-2.** [base] bottom. **-3.** [excavación arqueológica] site. **-4.** COM entry; **~ contable** book entry.

asierra etc → **aserrar**.

asignable adj: **~ a** that can be given to.

asignación f **-1.** [atribución] allocation. **-2.** [sueldo] salary.

asignar vt **-1.** [atribuir]: **~ algo a alguien** to assign ○ allocate sthg to sb. **-2.** [destinar]: **~ a alguien a** to send sb to.

asignatura f EDUC subject; **~ pendiente** subject which a pupil has to resit; fig unresolved matter.

asilado, -da m y f person living in an old people's home, convalescent home etc; **~ político** political refugee.

asilar vt [huérfano, anciano] to put into a home; [refugiado político] to grant political asylum to.

asilo m **-1.** [hospicio] home; **~ de ancianos** old people's home. **-2.** fig [amparo] asylum; **~ político** political asylum. **-3.** [hospedaje] accommodation.

asimetría f asymmetry.

asimilación f **-1.** [gen & LING] assimilation. **-2.** [comparación] comparison. **-3.** [equiparación] granting of equal rights.

asimilar vt **-1.** [gen] to assimilate. **-2.** [comparar] to compare. **-3.** [equiparar] to grant equal rights to.
◆ **asimilarse** vpr LING to become assimilated.

asimismo adv [también] also, as well; (a principio de frase) likewise.

asintiera etc → **asentir**.

asir [53] vt to grasp, to take hold of.
◆ **asirse a** vpr lit & fig to cling to.

asisito adv Amer fam so so.

asistencia f **-1.** [presencia - acción] attendance; [- hecho] presence. **-2.** [ayuda] assistance; **~ letrada** ○ **jurídica** legal advice; **~ médica** medical attention; **~ pública** social security; **~ sanitaria** health care; **~ social** social work; **~ técnica** technical assistance. **-3.** [afluencia] audience. **-4.** DEP assist.

asistencial adj MED healthcare (antes de sust).

asistenta f cleaning lady.

asistente m y f **-1.** [ayudante] assistant, helper; **~ social** social worker. **-2.** [presente] person present; **los ~s** the audience (sg).

asistido, -da adj AUTOM power (antes de sust); INFORM computer-assisted.

asistir ◇ vt **-1.** [ayudar] to attend to. **-2.** [acompañar] to accompany. ◇ vi: **~ a** to attend, to go to.

asma f (el) asthma.

asmático, -ca adj, m y f asthmatic.

asno m lit & fig ass.

asociación f association; **~ de consumidores** consumer association; **~ de ideas** association of ideas; **~ de vecinos** residents' association.

asociado, -da ◇ *adj* **-1.** [relacionado] associated. **-2.** [miembro] associate. ◇ *m y f* **-1.**
[miembro] associate, partner. **-2.** EDUC associate lecturer.

asocial *adj* asocial.

asociar [8] *vt* **-1.** [relacionar] to associate.
-2. COM to take into partnership.
◆ **asociarse** *vpr* to form a partnership.

asociativo, -va *adj* associative.

asolar [23] *vt* to devastate.

asomar ◇ *vi* [gen] to peep up; [del interior
de algo] to peep out. ◇ *vt* to stick; ~ **la cabeza por la ventana** to stick one's head out
of the window.
◆ **asomarse a** *vpr* [ventana] to stick one's
head out of; [balcón] to come/go out onto.

asombrar *vt* [causar admiración] to amaze;
[causar sorpresa] to surprise.
◆ **asombrarse** *vpr*: ~**se (de)** [sentir admira-
ción] to be amazed (at); [sentir sorpresa] to
be surprised (at).

asombro *m* [admiración] amazement; [sor-
presa] surprise.

asombroso, -sa *adj* [sensacional] amazing;
[sorprendente] surprising.

asomo *m* [indicio] trace, hint; [de esperanza]
glimmer; **ni por** ~ not under any circumstances.

asonancia *f* assonance.

asonante *adj* assonant.

asorochar *Amer vt* to cause to have altitude sickness.
◆ **asorocharse** *vpr* to get altitude sickness.

aspa *f* (*el*) X-shaped cross; [de molino]
arms (*pl*).

aspaviento *m* (*gen pl*) furious gesticula-
tions (*pl*).

aspecto *m* **-1.** [apariencia] appearance; tener **buen/mal** ~ [persona] to look well/
awful; [cosa] to look nice/horrible. **-2.** [face-
ta] aspect; **bajo este** ~ from this angle; **en
todos los** ~**s** in every respect.

aspereza *f* roughness; *fig* sharpness, sourness; **limar** ~**s** to smooth things over.

áspero, -ra *adj* **-1.** [rugoso] rough. **-2.** [acre]
sour. **-3.** *fig* [desagradable] sharp, sour.

aspersión *f* [de jardín] sprinkling; [de culti-
vos] spraying.

aspersor *m* [para jardín] sprinkler; [para cul-
tivos] sprayer.

aspiración *f* **-1.** [gen & LING] aspiration. **-2.**
[de aire - por una persona] breathing in; [- por
una máquina] suction.

aspirador *m*, **aspiradora** *f* vacuum
cleaner.

aspirante ◇ *adj* [persona] aspiring. ◇ *m y f*:
~ **(a)** candidate (for); [en deportes, concursos]
contender (for).

aspirar ◇ *vt* **-1.** [aire - suj: persona] to
breathe in, to inhale; [- suj: máquina] to
suck in. **-2.** LING to aspirate. ◇ *vi*: ~ **a algo**
[ansiar] to aspire to sthg.

aspirina® *f* aspirin.

asquear *vt* to disgust, to make sick.

asquerosidad *f* disgusting ○ revolting
thing.

asqueroso, -sa *adj* disgusting, revolting.

Assuán Aswan.

asta *f* (*el*) **-1.** [de bandera] flagpole, mast; **a
media** ~ at half-mast. **-2.** [de lanza] shaft;
[de brocha] handle. **-3.** [de toro] horn.

astado *m* TAUROM bull.

asterisco *m* asterisk.

asteroide *m* asteroid.

astigmatismo *m* astigmatism.

astil *m* [de hacha, pico] haft; [de azada] handle.

astilla *f* splinter; **hacer** ~**s** *fig* to smash to
smithereens.

astillar *vt* to splinter; [tronco] to chop up.
◆ **astillarse** *vpr* to splinter.

astillero *m* shipyard.

astracán *m* astrakhan.

astracanada *f despec* farce.

astrágalo *m* **-1.** ANAT astragalus. **-2.** ARQUIT
astragal.

astral *adj* astral.

astringente *adj* astringent.

astro *m* ASTRON heavenly body; *fig* star.

astrofísica *f* astrophysics (*U*).

astrología *f* astrology.

astrólogo, -ga *m y f* astrologer.

astronauta *m y f* astronaut.

astronáutica *f* astronautics (*U*).

astronave *f* spacecraft, spaceship.

astronomía *f* astronomy.

astronómico, -ca *adj lit* & *fig* astronomical.

astrónomo, -ma *m y f* astronomer.

astroso, -sa *adj* [andrajoso] shabby, ragged.

astucia *f* **-1.** [picardía] cunning, astuteness.
-2. (*gen pl*) [treta] cunning trick.

asturiano, -na *adj, m y f* Asturian.

Asturias Asturias.

astuto, -ta *adj* [ladino, tramposo] cunning;
[sagaz, listo] astute.

asuela *etc* → asolar.

asueto *m* break, rest; **unos días de** ~ a
few days off.

asumir *vt* **-1.** [gen] to assume. **-2.** [aceptar] to accept.

asunceno, -na *adj* of or relating to Asunción.

asunción *f* assumption.

◆ **Asunción** *f*: la **Asunción** RELIG the Assumption.

Asunción GEOGR Asunción.

asunto *m* **-1.** [tema - general] subject; [- específico] matter; [- de obra, libro] theme; ~s **a tratar** agenda (*sg*). **-2.** [cuestión, problema] issue. **-3.** [negocio] affair, business (*U*); **no es ~ tuyo** it's none of your business. **-4.** *fam* [romance] affair.

◆ **asuntos** *mpl* POLÍT affairs; ~s **exteriores** foreign affairs.

asustadizo, -za *adj* easily frightened.

asustado, -da *adj* frightened, scared.

asustar *vt* to frighten, to scare.

◆ **asustarse** *vpr*: ~**se (de)** to be frightened ○ scared (of).

Atacama *m*: **el (desierto de)** ~ the Atacama (Desert).

atacante ◇ *adj* attacking. ◇ *m y f* [agresor] attacker. ◇ *m* DEP forward.

atacar [10] *vt* **-1.** [gen] to attack; **me ataca los nervios** *fig* it gets on my nerves. **-2.** [sobrevenir]: **le atacó la risa/fiebre** he had a fit of laughter/bout of fever. **-3.** *fig* [acometer] to set about.

atado *m* bundle.

atadura *f lit & fig* tie.

atajar ◇ *vi* [acortar]: ~ **(por)** to take a short cut (through). ◇ *vt* **-1.** [contener] to put a stop to; [hemorragia, inundación] to stem. **-2.** *fig* [interrumpir] to cut short.

atajo *m* **-1.** [camino corto, medio rápido] short cut; **coger** ○ **tomar un** ~ to take a short cut. **-2.** *despec* [panda] bunch.

atalaya *f* **-1.** [torre] watchtower. **-2.** [altura] vantage point.

atañer *vi* **-1.** [concernir]: ~ **a** to concern; **en lo que atañe a este asunto** as far as this subject is concerned. **-2.** [corresponder]: ~ **a** to be the responsibility of.

ataque ◇ *v* → **atacar**. ◇ *m* **-1.** [gen & DEP] attack. **-2.** *fig* [acceso] fit, bout; ~ **cardíaco** ○ **al corazón** heart attack.

atar *vt* **-1.** [unir] to tie (up). **-2.** *fig* [relacionar] to link together. **-3.** *fig* [constreñir] to tie down; ~ **corto a alguien** *fam* to keep a tight rein on sb.

◆ **atarse** *vpr* **-1.** [comprometerse] to tie o.s. up in knots. **-2.** [ceñirse]: ~**se a** to become tied to.

atarazana *f* shipyard.

atardecer [30] ◇ *m* dusk. ◇ *v impers* to get dark.

atareado, -da *adj* busy.

atascar [10] *vt* to block (up).

◆ **atascarse** *vpr* **-1.** [obstruirse] to get blocked up. **-2.** *fig* [detenerse] to get stuck; [al hablar] to dry up.

atasco *m* **-1.** [obstrucción] blockage. **-2.** AUTOM traffic jam. **-3.** [impedimento] hindrance, obstacle.

atasque *etc* → **atascar**.

ataúd *m* coffin.

ataviar [9] *vt* [cosa] to deck out; [persona] to dress up.

◆ **ataviarse** *vpr* to dress up.

atávico, -ca *adj* atavistic.

atavío *m* **-1.** [adorno] adornment. **-2.** [indumentaria] attire (*U*).

ate *m Amer* quince jelly.

ateísmo *m* atheism.

atemorizar [13] *vt* to frighten.

◆ **atemorizarse** *vpr* to get frightened.

Atenas Athens.

atenazar [13] *vt* **-1.** [sujetar] to clench. **-2.** *fig* [suj: dudas] to torment, to rack; [suj: miedo, nervios] to grip.

atención ◇ *f* **-1.** [interés] attention; **a la** ~ **de** for the attention of; **llamar la** ~ [atraer] to attract attention; **llamar la** ~ **a alguien** [amonestar] to tell sb off; **poner** ○ **prestar** ~ to pay attention; **en** ~ **a** [teniendo en cuenta] out of consideration for; [en honor a] in honour of. ◇ *interj*: ¡~! [en aeropuerto, conferencia] your attention please!

◆ **atenciones** *fpl* attentions, attentiveness (*U*).

atender [20] ◇ *vt* **-1.** [satisfacer - petición, ruego] to attend to; [- consejo, instrucciones] to heed; [- propuesta] to agree to. **-2.** [cuidar de - necesitados, invitados] to look after; [- enfermo] to care for; [- cliente] to serve; **¿le atienden?** are you being served? ◇ *vi* **-1.** [estar atento]: ~ **(a)** to pay attention (to). **-2.** [tener en cuenta]: **atendiendo a** taking into account, bearing in mind. **-3.** [responder]: ~ **por** to answer to the name of.

ateneo *m* athenaeum.

atenerse [72]

◆ **atenerse a** *vpr* **-1.** [promesa, orden] to stick to; [ley, normas] to observe, to abide by. **-2.** [consecuencias] to bear in mind.

ateniense *adj, m y f* Athenian.

atentado *m*: ~ **contra alguien** attempt on sb's life; ~ **contra algo** crime against sthg; ~ **terrorista** terrorist attack.

atentamente *adv* **-1.** [con atención, cortesía] attentively; **mire** ~ watch carefully. **-2.** [en cartas] Yours sincerely ○ faithfully.

atentar *vi*: ~ **contra (la vida de) alguien** to make an attempt on sb's life; ~ **contra algo** [principio etc] to be a crime against sthg.

atento, -ta *adj* **-1.** [pendiente] attentive; **estar** ~ **a** [explicación, programa, lección] to pay attention to; [ruido, sonido] to listen out for; [acontecimientos, cambios, avances] to keep up with. **-2.** [cortés] considerate, thoughtful.

atenuante *m* DER extenuating circumstance.

atenuar [6] *vt* [gen] to diminish; [dolor] to ease; [luz] to filter.

ateo, -a ◇ *adj* atheistic. ◇ *m y f* atheist.

aterciopelado, -da *adj* velvety.

aterido, -da *adj* freezing.

aterirse *vpr* to be freezing.

aterrador, -ra *adj* terrifying.

aterrar *vt* to terrify.

aterrizaje *m* landing; ~ **forzoso** emergency landing.

aterrizar [13] *vi* **-1.** [avión] to land. **-2.** *fig* [persona] to turn up.

aterrorizar [13] *vt* to terrify; [suj: agresor] to terrorize.

◆ **aterrorizarse** *vpr* to be terrified.

atesorar *vt* **-1.** [riquezas] to amass. **-2.** *fig* [virtudes] to be blessed with.

atestado *m* official report.

atestar *vt* **-1.** [llenar] to pack, to cram. **-2.** DER to testify to.

atestiguar [45] *vt* to testify to.

atezado, -da *adj* tanned.

atiborrar *vt* to stuff full.

◆ **atiborrarse** *vpr fam fig*: ~**se (de)** to stuff one's face (with).

atice *etc* → **atizar**.

ático *m* penthouse.

atienda *etc* → **atender**.

atildar *vt* [acicalar] to smarten up.

atinar *vi* [adivinar] to guess correctly; [dar en el blanco] to hit the target; ~ **a hacer algo** to succeed in doing sthg; ~ **con** to hit upon.

atingencia *f Amer* **-1.** [relación] connection. **-2.** [puntualización] observation, remark.

atípico, -ca *adj* atypical.

atiplado, -da *adj* shrill.

atisbar *vt* **-1.** [divisar, prever] to make out. **-2.** [acechar] to observe, to spy on.

atisbo *m* (*gen pl*) trace, hint; [de esperanza] glimmer.

atizador *m* poker.

atizar [13] *vt* **-1.** [fuego] to poke, to stir. **-2.**

fig [sospechas, discordias etc] to fan. **-3.** *fam* [puñetazo, patada] to land, to deal.

◆ **atizarse** *vpr fam* [comida, bebida] to guzzle.

atlante *m* ARQUIT atlas, telamon.

atlántico, -ca *adj* Atlantic.

◆ **Atlántico** *m*: **el (océano) Atlántico** the Atlantic (Ocean).

atlantismo *m* POLÍT *doctrine followed by NATO*.

atlas *m inv* atlas.

atleta *m y f* athlete.

atlético, -ca *adj* athletic.

atletismo *m* athletics (*U*).

atmósfera *f lit & fig* atmosphere.

atmosférico, -ca *adj* atmospheric.

atolladero *m* [apuro] fix, jam; **meter en/sacar de un** ~ **a alguien** to put sb in/get sb out of a tight spot.

atolón *m* atoll.

atolondrado, -da ◇ *adj* **-1.** [precipitado] hasty, disorganized. **-2.** [aturdido] bewildered. ◇ *m y f* [precipitado] hasty ○ disorganized person.

atolondramiento *m* **-1.** [precipitación] haste, disorganization. **-2.** [aturdimiento] bewilderment.

atómico, -ca *adj* atomic; [central, armas] nuclear.

atomizador *m* atomizer, spray.

atomizar [13] *vt fig* [fragmentar] to break down (into constituent parts).

átomo *m lit & fig* atom; ~ **gramo** gram atom.

atónito, -ta *adj* astonished, astounded.

átono, -na *adj* atonic.

atontado, -da *adj* **-1.** [aturdido] dazed. **-2.** [tonto] stupid.

atontar *vt* **-1.** [aturdir] to daze. **-2.** [alelar] to dull the mind of.

atormentar *vt* to torture; *fig* to torment.

atornillar *vt* to screw.

atorón *m Amer* traffic jam.

atorrante *Amer* ◇ *adj* lazy. ◇ *m y f* layabout.

atosigar [16] *vt fig* to harass.

atracadero *m* landing stage.

atracador, -ra *m y f* [de banco] armed robber; [en la calle] mugger.

atracar [10] ◇ *vi* NÁUT: ~ **(en)** to dock (at). ◇ *vt* [banco] to rob; [persona] to mug.

◆ **atracarse** *vpr*: ~**se de** to stuff o.s. with.

atracción *f* **-1.** [gen] attraction. **-2.** [atractivo] attractiveness, charm. **-3.** [espectáculo] act. **-4.** *fig* [centro de atención] centre of attention. **-5.** (*gen pl*) [diversión infantil] fairground attraction.

atraco *m* robbery; ~ **a mano armada** armed robbery.

atracón *m fam* feast; **darse un** ~ to stuff one's face.

atractivo, -va *adj* attractive.
◆ **atractivo** *m* [de persona] attractiveness, charm; [de cosa] attraction.

atraer [73] *vt* **-1.** [gen] to attract. **-2.** *fig* [ocasionar] to bring.

atragantarse *vpr*: ~ **(con)** to choke (on); **se me ha atragantado este libro/tipo** *fig* I can't stand that book/guy.

atraiga, atrajera *etc* → **atraer.**

atrancar [10] *vt* **-1.** [cerrar] to bar. **-2.** [obturar] to block.
◆ **atrancarse** *vpr* **-1.** [encerrarse] to lock o.s. in. **-2.** [atascarse] to get blocked. **-3.** *fig* [al hablar, escribir] to dry up.

atrapar *vt* **-1.** [agarrar, alcanzar] to catch. **-2.** *fam* [conseguir] to get o.s. **-3.** *fam* [engañar] to take in.

atraque *etc* → **atracar.**

atrás ◇ *adv* **-1.** [detrás - posición] behind, at the back; [- movimiento] backwards; **echarse para** ~ to move backwards; **quedarse** ~ *fig* to fall behind. **-2.** [antes] earlier, before. ◇ *interj*: ¡~! get back!

atrasado, -da *adj* **-1.** [en el tiempo] delayed; [reloj] slow; [pago] overdue, late; [número, copia] back (*antes de sust*). **-2.** [en evolución, capacidad] backward.

atrasar ◇ *vt* to put back. ◇ *vi* to be slow.
◆ **atrasarse** *vpr* **-1.** [demorarse] to be late. **-2.** [quedarse atrás] to fall behind.

atraso *m* **-1.** [del reloj] slowness. **-2.** [de evolución] backwardness.
◆ **atrasos** *mpl fam* arrears.

atravesar [19] *vt* **-1.** [interponer] to put across. **-2.** [cruzar] to cross. **-3.** [traspasar] to penetrate. **-4.** *fig* [vivir] to go through.
◆ **atravesarse** *vpr* [interponerse] to be in the way; **se me ha atravesado la vecina** *fig* I can't stand my neighbour.

atrayente *adj* attractive.

atrechar *vi Amer fam* to take a short cut.

atreverse *vpr*: ~ **(a hacer algo)** to dare (to do sthg); ~ **a algo** to be bold enough for sthg; ~ **con alguien** to take sb on.

atrevido, -da ◇ *adj* [osado] daring; [caradura] cheeky. ◇ *m y f* [osado] daring person; [caradura] cheeky person.

atrevimiento *m* **-1.** [osadía] daring. **-2.** [insolencia] cheek.

atrezo *m* props (*pl*).

atribución *f* **-1.** [imputación] attribution. **-2.** [competencia] responsibility, duty.

atribuir [51] *vt* [imputar]: ~ **algo a** to attribute sthg to.
◆ **atribuirse** *vpr* [méritos] to claim for o.s.; [poderes] to assume.

atribular *culto vt* to distress.
◆ **atribularse** *vpr* to be distressed.

atributo *m* attribute.

atril *m* [para libros] lectern; MÚS music stand.

atrincherarse *vpr* **-1.** MIL to entrench o.s. **-2.** *fig* [escudarse]: ~ **en** to hide behind.

atrio *m* **-1.** [pórtico] portico. **-2.** [claustro] cloister.

atrocidad *f* **-1.** [crueldad] atrocity. **-2.** *fig* [necedad] stupid thing.

atrofia *f* MED atrophy; *fig* deterioration.

atrofiar [8] *vt* MED to atrophy; *fig* to weaken.
◆ **atrofiarse** *vpr* MED to atrophy; *fig* to deteriorate.

atronador, -ra *adj* deafening.

atropellado, -da *adj* hasty.

atropellar *vt* **-1.** [suj: vehículo] to run over. **-2.** *fig* [suj: persona] to trample on.
◆ **atropellarse** *vpr* [al hablar] to trip over one's words.

atropello *m* **-1.** [por vehículo] running over. **-2.** *fig* [moral] abuse.

atroz *adj* atrocious; [dolor] awful.

ATS (*abrev de* **ayudante técnico sanitario**) *m y f qualified nurse.*

atte. *abrev de* **atentamente.**

atuendo *m* attire.

atufar ◇ *vi* to stink. ◇ *vt* [suj: olor, humo - persona] to overpower; [- lugar] to stink out.

atún *m* tuna.

aturdido, -da *adj* dazed.

aturdimiento *m* **-1.** [desconcierto] bewilderment, confusion. **-2.** [irreflexión] thoughtlessness.

aturdir *vt* [gen] to stun; [suj: alcohol] to fuddle; [suj: ruido, luz] to confuse, to bewilder.
◆ **aturdirse** *vpr* [gen] to be stunned; [por alcohol] to get fuddled; [con ruido, luz] to get confused.

aturrullar, aturullar *fam vt* to fluster.
◆ **aturrullarse, aturullarse** *vpr* to get flustered.

audacia *f* [intrepidez] daring.

audaz *adj* [intrépido] daring.

audible *adj* audible.

audición *f* **-1.** [gen] hearing. **-2.** MÚS & TEATR audition.

audiencia f -1. [público, recepción] audiencia; **dar** ~ to grant an audience. -2. [DER - juicio] hearing; [- tribunal, edificio] court; ~ **provincial** provincial court; ~ **pública** public hearing.

audífono m hearing aid.

audiómetro m audiometer.

audiovisual adj audiovisual.

auditar vt FIN to audit.

auditivo, -va adj ear (antes de sust).

auditor, -ra m y f FIN auditor.

auditoría f FIN -1. [profesión] auditing. -2. [despacho] auditing company. -3. [balance] audit; ~ **externa/interna** external/internal audit.

auditorio m -1. [público] audience. -2. [lugar] auditorium.

auge m [gen & ECON] boom; **estar en (pleno)** ~ to be booming.

augurar vt [suj: persona] to predict; [suj: suceso] to augur.

augurio m omen, sign.

augusto, -ta adj august.

aula f (el) [de escuela] classroom; [de universidad] lecture room; ~ **magna** great hall.

aullar vi to howl.

aullido m howl.

aumentar ◇ vt -1. [gen] to increase; [peso] to put on. -2. [en óptica] to magnify. -3. [sonido] to amplify. ◇ vi to increase; [precios] to rise.

aumentativo, -va adj augmentative.

◆ **aumentativo** m augmentative.

aumento m -1. [incremento] increase; [de sueldo, precios] rise; **ir en** ~ to be on the increase; ~ **lineal** across-the-board pay rise. -2. [en óptica] magnification.

aun ◇ adv even. ◇ conj: ~ **estando cansado, lo hizo** even though he was tired, he did it; **ni** ~ **puesta de puntillas logra ver** she can't see, even on tiptoe; ~ **cuando** even though.

aún adv [todavía] still; (en negativas) yet, still; **no ha llegado** ~ he hasn't arrived yet, he still hasn't arrived.

aunar vt to join, to pool.

◆ **aunarse** vpr [aliarse] to unite.

aunque conj -1. [a pesar de que] even though, although; [incluso si] even if. -2. [pero] although.

aúpa interj: ¡~! [¡levántate!] get up!; ¡~ **el Atleti!** up the Athletic!

◆ **de aúpa** loc adj fam: **un susto de** ~ a real fright.

au pair [o'per] f au pair.

aupar vt to help up; fig [animar] to cheer on.

◆ **auparse** vpr to climb up.

aura f (el) -1. [halo] aura. -2. [viento] gentle breeze.

áureo, -a adj golden.

aureola f -1. ASTRON & RELIG halo. -2. fig [fama] aura.

aurícula f auricle.

auricular ◇ adj auricular. ◇ m [de teléfono] receiver.

◆ **auriculares** mpl [cascos] headphones.

aurora f first light of dawn; **al despuntar** o **romper la** ~ at dawn; ~ **boreal** aurora borealis, northern lights (pl).

auscultar vt to sound with a stethoscope.

ausencia f absence; **brillar por su** ~ to be conspicuous by one's/its absence.

ausentarse vpr to go away.

ausente ◇ adj -1. [no presente] absent; **estará** ~ **todo el día** he'll be away all day. -2. [distraído] absent-minded. ◇ m y f -1. [no presente]: **hay varios** ~s there are a number of absentees; **criticó a los** ~s he criticized the people who weren't there. -2. DER missing person.

ausentismo m absenteeism.

auspiciar [8] vt [apoyar] to back.

auspicio m [protección] protection; **bajo los** ~s de under the auspices of.

◆ **auspicios** mpl [señales] omens.

austeridad f austerity.

austero, -ra adj -1. [gen] austere. -2. [moderado] sober.

austral ◇ adj southern. ◇ m [moneda] austral.

Australia Australia.

australiano, -na adj, m y f Australian.

Austria Austria.

austríaco, -ca adj, m y f Austrian.

autarquía f -1. POLÍT autarchy. -2. ECON autarky.

autárquico, -ca adj -1. POLÍT autarchical. -2. ECON autarkic.

autenticidad f authenticity.

auténtico, -ca adj [gen] genuine; [piel, joyas] genuine, real; **un** ~ **imbécil** a real idiot.

autentificar [10] vt to authenticate.

autismo m autism.

autista ◇ adj autistic. ◇ m y f autistic person.

auto m -1. fam [coche] car. -2. DER judicial decree; ~ **de procesamiento** indictment. -3. LITER (mystery) play.

◆ **autos** mpl DER case documents; **constar**

en ~s to be recorded in the case documents.
◆ **auto de fe** *m* auto-da-fé.
◆ **de autos** *loc adj* DER: **la noche de** ~s the night of the crime.
autoabastecimiento *m* self-sufficiency.
autoadhesivo, -va *adj* self-adhesive.
autoalimentación *f* INFORM automatic paper feed.
autobanco *m* *system of computerized banking that can be operated from one's car.*
autobiografía *f* autobiography.
autobiográfico, -ca *adj* autobiographical.
autobombo *m* *fam*: **darse** ~ to blow one's own trumpet.
autobús *m* bus.
autocar *m* coach.
autocartera *f* *shares in a company held by that same company.*
autocensura *f* self-censorship.
autocine *m* drive-in (cinema).
autoclave *m* autoclave, sterilizing unit.
autocomplacencia *f* self-satisfaction.
autocontrol *m* self-control.
autocracia *f* autocracy.
autocrítica *f* self-criticism.
autóctono, -na ◇ *adj* indigenous, native. ◇ *m y f* native.
autodefensa *f* self-defence.
autodestrucción *f* self-destruction.
autodeterminación *f* self-determination.
autodidacta ◇ *adj* self-taught. ◇ *m y f* self-taught person.
autodirigido, -da *adj* guided.
autodisciplina *f* self-discipline.
autódromo *m* motor racing circuit.
autoedición *f* INFORM desktop publishing.
autoencendido *m* AUTOM automatic ignition.
autoescuela *f* driving school.
autoestima *f* self-esteem.
autoestop, autostop *m* hitch-hiking; **hacer** ~ to hitch-hike.
autoestopista, autostopista *m y f* hitch-hiker.
autofinanciación *f* self-financing.
autogestión *f* self-management.
autogobierno *m* self-government, self-rule.
autógrafo *m* autograph.
autómata *m* *lit* & *fig* automaton.
automático, -ca *adj* automatic.
◆ **automático** *m* [botón] press-stud.
automatismo *m* automatism.
automatización *f* automation.

automatizar [13] *vt* to automate.
automedicarse [10] *vpr* to self-administer medicine.
automotor, -triz *adj* self-propelled.
automóvil *m* car *Br*, automobile *Am*.
automovilismo *m* motoring; DEP motor racing.
automovilista *m y f* motorist, driver.
automovilístico, -ca *adj* motor (*antes de sust*); DEP motor-racing (*antes de sust*).
autonomía *f* **-1.** [POLÍT - facultad] autonomy; [- territorio] autonomous region. **-2.** [de persona] independence. **-3.** [de vehículo] range; [de videocámara] recording time; ~ **de vuelo** range.
autonómico, -ca *adj* autonomous.
autonomismo *m* autonomy movement.
autonomista *adj, m y f* autonomist.
autónomo, -ma ◇ *adj* **-1.** POLÍT autonomous. **-2.** [trabajador] self-employed; [traductor, periodista] freelance. ◇ *m y f* self-employed person; [traductor, periodista] freelance.
autopista *f* motorway *Br*, freeway *Am*; ~ **de peaje** toll motorway *Br*, tollway *Am*.
autopropulsado, -da *adj* self-propelled.
autopropulsión *f* self-propulsion.
autopsia *f* autopsy, post-mortem.
autor, -ra *m y f* **-1.** LITER author. **-2.** [de crimen] perpetrator; ~ **material del hecho** DER actual perpetrator of the crime.
autoría *f* authorship; [de crimen] perpetration.
autoridad *f* **-1.** [gen] authority; **imponer su** ~ to impose one's authority. **-2.** [ley]: **la** ~ the authorities (*pl*).
autoritario, -ria *adj, m y f* authoritarian.
autoritarismo *m* authoritarianism.
autorización *f* authorization; **dar** ~ **a alguien (para hacer algo)** to authorize sb (to do sthg).
autorizado, -da *adj* **-1.** [permitido] authorized. **-2.** [digno de crédito] authoritative.
autorizar [13] *vt* **-1.** [dar permiso] to allow; [en situaciones oficiales] to authorize. **-2.** [capacitar] to allow, to entitle.
autorradio *m* car radio.
autorretrato *m* self-portrait.
autorreverse *m* [de casete] auto reverse.
autoservicio *m* **-1.** [tienda] self-service shop. **-2.** [restaurante] self-service restaurant.
autostop = autoestop.
autostopista = autoestopista.
autosuficiencia *f* self-sufficiency.
autosuficiente *adj* self-sufficient.

autosugestión *f* autosuggestion.

autovacuna *f* autoinoculation.

autovía *f* dual carriageway *Br*, state highway *Am*.

auxiliar [8] ◇ *adj* [gen & GRAM] auxiliary. ◇ *m y f* assistant; ~ **administrativo** office clerk; ~ **de vuelo** air steward (*f* air hostess ○ stewardess). ◇ *vt* to assist, to help.

auxilio *m* assistance, help; **pedir/prestar** ~ to call for/give help; **primeros** ~**s** first aid (*U*).

av., avda. (*abrev de* **avenida**) Ave.

aval *m* -1. [persona] guarantor. -2. [documento] guarantee, reference; ~ **bancario** banker's reference.

avalancha *f lit* & *fig* avalanche.

avalar *vt* to endorse, to guarantee.

avalista *m y f* guarantor.

avance ◇ *v* → **avanzar**. ◇ *m* -1. [gen] advance. -2. FIN [anticipo] advance payment. -3. [RADIO & TV - meteorológico etc] summary; [- de futura programación] preview; ~ **informativo** news (*U*) in brief.

avanzada → **avanzado**.

avanzadilla *f* MIL advance patrol.

avanzado, -da ◇ *adj* -1. [gen] advanced. -2. [progresista] progressive. ◇ *m y f* person ahead of his/her time.

◆ **avanzada** *f* MIL advance patrol.

avanzar [13] ◇ *vi* to advance. ◇ *vt* -1. [adelantar] to move forward. -2. [anticipar] to tell in advance.

avaricia *f* greed, avarice; **la** ~ **rompe el saco** greed doesn't pay; **ser feo/pesado con** ~ to be ugly/boring in the extreme.

avaricioso, -sa ◇ *adj* avaricious, miserly. ◇ *m y f* miser.

avariento, -ta ◇ *adj* avaricious, miserly. ◇ *m y f* miser.

avaro, -ra ◇ *adj* miserly, mean. ◇ *m y f* miser.

avasallador, -ra ◇ *adj* overwhelming. ◇ *m y f* slave driver.

avasallar *vt* -1. [arrollar] to overwhelm. -2. [someter] to subjugate.

avatar *m* (*gen pl*) vagary, sudden change; **los** ~**es de la vida** the ups and downs of life.

avda. = **av.**

ave *f* (*el*) -1. [gen] bird; ~ **del paraíso** bird of paradise; ~ **rapaz** ○ **de rapiña** bird of prey; **ser un** ~ **pasajera** ○ **de paso** *fig* to be a rolling stone. -2. *Amer* [pollo] chicken.

AVE (*abrev de* **de alta velocidad española**) *m Spanish high-speed train.*

avecinarse *vpr* to be on the way.

avefría *f* lapwing.

avejentar *culto vt* to age, to put years on.

◆ **avejentarse** *vpr* to age.

avellana *f* hazelnut.

avellano *m* hazel (tree).

avemaría *f* (*el*) [oración] Hail Mary.

avena *f* -1. [planta] oat. -2. [grano] oats (*pl*).

avenencia *f* [acuerdo] compromise.

avenida *f* avenue.

avenido, -da *adj*: **bien/mal** ~**s** on good/bad terms.

avenirse [75] *vpr* -1. [llevarse bien] to get on (well). -2. [ponerse de acuerdo] to come to an agreement; ~ **a algo/a hacer algo** to agree on sthg/to do sthg.

aventajado, -da *adj* [adelantado] outstanding.

aventajar *vt* [rebasar] to overtake; [estar por delante de] to be ahead of; ~ **a alguien en algo** to surpass sb in sthg.

aventar [19] *vt* -1. [abanicar] to fan. -2. [trigo] to winnow. -3. *Amer* [tirar] to throw.

aventura *f* -1. [gen] adventure; **correr** ~**s** to have adventures. -2. [relación amorosa] affair.

aventurado, -da *adj* risky.

aventurarse *vpr* to take a risk ○ risks; ~ **a hacer algo** to dare to do sthg.

aventurero, -ra ◇ *adj* adventurous. ◇ *m y f* adventurer (*f* adventuress).

avergonzar [38] *vt* -1. [deshonrar] to shame. -2. [abochornar] to embarrass.

◆ **avergonzarse** *vpr*: ~**se (de)** [por remordimiento] to be ashamed (of); [por timidez] to be embarrassed (about).

avería *f* [de máquina] fault; AUTOM breakdown.

averiado, -da *adj* [máquina] out of order; [coche] broken down.

averiar [9] *vt* to damage.

◆ **averiarse** *vpr* [máquina] to be out of order; AUTOM to break down.

averiguación *f* investigation; **hacer averiguaciones** to make inquiries.

averiguar [45] *vt* to find out.

aversión *f* aversion; **tener** ~ **a** to feel aversion towards.

avestruz *m* ostrich.

aviación *f* -1. [navegación] aviation. -2. [ejército] airforce.

Aviaco (*abrev de* **Aviación y Comercio, SA**) *f division of Spanish state airline, Iberia, mainly responsible for charter flights.*

aviador, -ra *m y f* aviator.

AVIANCA (*abrev de* **Aerovías Nacionales de Colombia**) *f Colombian state airline.*

aviar [9] *vt* **-1.** [maleta] to pack; [habitación] to tidy up. **-2.** [comida] to prepare.

Aviateca (*abrev de* **Aviación Guatemalteca**) *f Guatemalan state airline.*

avícola *adj* poultry (*antes de sust*).

avicultura *f* poultry farming.

avidez *f* eagerness.

ávido, -da *adj*: ~ **de** eager for.

avienta *etc* → **aventar**.

avieso, -sa *adj* **-1.** [torcido] twisted. **-2.** *fig* [malo] evil.

avinagrado, -da *adj lit & fig* sour.

avinagrarse *vpr* to go sour; *fig* to become sour.

avío *m* **-1.** [preparativo] preparation. **-2.** [víveres] provisions (*pl*).
◆ **avíos** *mpl fam* [equipo] things, kit (*U*).

avión *m* plane; **en** ~ by plane; **por** ~ [en un sobre] airmail; ~ **nodriza** supply plane; ~ **a reacción** jet.

avioneta *f* light aircraft.

avisar *vt* **-1.** [informar]: ~ **a alguien** to let sb know, to tell sb. **-2.** [advertir]: ~ **(de)** to warn (of). **-3.** [llamar] to call, to send for.

aviso *m* **-1.** [advertencia, amenaza] warning; **andar** ○ **estar sobre** ~ to be on the alert; **poner sobre** ~ **a alguien** to warn sb. **-2.** [notificación] notice; [en teatros, aeropuertos] call; **hasta nuevo** ~ until further notice; **sin previo** ~ without notice; ~ **de vencimiento** COM due-date reminder. **-3.** TAUROM *warning to matador not to delay the kill any longer.*

avispa *f* wasp.

avispado, -da *adj fam* sharp, quick-witted.

avispero *m* **-1.** [nido] wasp's nest. **-2.** *fam fig* [lío] mess; **meterse en un** ~ to get into a mess.

avistar *vt* to sight, to make out.

avitaminosis *f inv* vitamin deficiency.

avituallamiento *m* provisioning.

avituallar *vt* to provide with food.

avivar *vt* **-1.** [sentimiento] to rekindle. **-2.** [color] to brighten. **-3.** [fuego] to stoke up.

avizor → **ojo**.

avutarda *f* great bustard.

axial *adj* axial.

axila *f* armpit.

axioma *m* axiom.

ay (*pl* **ayes**) ◇ *m* groan. ◇ *interj*: ¡~! [dolor físico] ouch!; [sorpresa, pena] oh!; ¡~ **de tí si te cojo!** Heaven help you if I catch you!

aya → **ayo**.

ayatollah [ajato'la] *m* ayatollah.

ayer ◇ *adv* yesterday; *fig* in the past; ~ **(por la) noche** last night; ~ **por la mañana** yesterday morning. ◇ *m fig* yesteryear.

ayo, -ya *m y f* [tutor] tutor (*f* governess).

ayuda *f* help, assistance; ECON & POLÍT aid; **acudir en** ~ **de alguien** to go to sb's assistance; ~ **en carretera** breakdown service.

ayudante *adj, m y f* assistant.

ayudar *vt* to help; ~ **a alguien a hacer algo** to help sb (to) do sthg; **¿en qué puedo** ~**le?** how can I help you?
◆ **ayudarse** *vpr*: ~**se de** to make use of.

ayunar *vi* to fast.

ayunas *fpl*: **en** ~ [sin comer] without having eaten; *fig* [sin enterarse] in the dark.

ayuno *m* fast; **hacer** ~ to fast.

ayuntamiento *m* **-1.** [corporación] ≃ town council. **-2.** [edificio] town hall.

azabache *m* jet; **negro como el** ~ jet-black.

azada *f* hoe.

azafata *f*: ~ **(de vuelo)** air hostess *Br*, air stewardess; ~ **de exposiciones y congresos** hostess; ~ **de tierra** stewardess.

azafate *m Amer* [bandeja] tray.

azafrán *m* saffron.

azahar *m* [del naranjo] orange blossom; [del limonero] lemon blossom.

azalea *f* azalea.

azar *m* chance, fate; **al** ~ at random; **por (puro)** ~ by (pure) chance.

azaroso, -sa *adj* [vida, viaje] eventful.

ázimo, ácimo *adj* [pan] unleavened.

azimut = **acimut**.

azogue *m* mercury.

azor *m* goshawk.

azoramiento *m* embarrassment.

azorar *vt* to embarrass.
◆ **azorarse** *vpr* to be embarrassed.

Azores *fpl*: **las** ~ the Azores.

azotaina *f fam* slapping, smacking.

azotar *vt* **-1.** [suj: persona] to beat; [en el trasero] to smack, to slap; [con látigo] to whip. **-2.** *fig* [suj: calamidad] to devastate.

azote *m* **-1.** [golpe] blow; [en el trasero] smack, slap; [latigazo] lash. **-2.** *fig* [calamidad] scourge.

azotea *f* [de edificio] terraced roof; **estar mal de la** ~ *fam fig* to be funny in the head.

azteca ◇ *adj, m y f* Aztec. ◇ *m* [lengua] Aztec.

azúcar *m o f* sugar; ~ **blanquilla/moreno** refined/brown sugar; ~ **cande** ○ **candi** sugar candy; ~ **glass** ○ **de lustre** icing sugar.

azucarado, **-da** *adj* sweet, sugary.

azucarero, **-ra** *adj* sugar (*antes de sust*).
◆ **azucarero** *m* sugar bowl.
◆ **azucarera** *f* sugar factory.

azucarillo *m* **-1.** CULIN lemon candy. **-2.** [terrón] sugar lump.

azuce *etc* → **azuzar**.

azucena *f* white lily.

azufre *m* sulphur.

azul *adj & m* blue; ~ **celeste/marino/ eléctrico** sky/navy/electric blue; ~ **turquesa** turquoise.

azulado, **-da** *adj* bluish.

azulejo *m* (glazed) tile.

azulete *m* [para lavar] blue.

azulgrana *adj inv* DEP Barcelona football club (*antes de sust*).

azuzar [13] *vt* **-1.** [animal] to set on. **-2.** *fig* [persona] to egg on.

B

b, **B** *f* [letra] b, B.

baba *f* **-1.** [saliva - de niño] dribble; [- de adulto] spittle, saliva; [- de animal] foam. **-2.** [de caracol etc] slime. **-3.** *loc*: **se le cae la ~ con su hija** *fam* she drools over her daughter; **tener mala ~** *fam* to be bad-tempered.

babear *vi* [niño] to dribble; [adulto, animal] to slobber; *fig* to drool.

babel *m o f fam fig* bedlam.

babero *m* bib.

babi *m* child's overall.

babia *f*: **estar** ○ **quedarse en ~** to have one's head in the clouds.

babilla *f* stifle.

babilónico, **-ca** *adj* **-1.** HIST Babylonian. **-2.** [fastuoso] lavish.

bable *m* Asturian dialect.

babor *m* port; **a ~** to port.

babosada *f Amer fam* [disparate] daft thing, rubbish (*U*).

baboso, **-sa** ◇ *adj* **-1.** [niño] dribbly; [adulto, animal] slobbering. **-2.** *Amer fam* [tonto] daft, stupid. ◇ *m y f Amer fam* [tonto] twit, idiot.
◆ **babosa** *f* ZOOL slug.

babucha *f* slipper.

baca *f* roof ○ luggage rack.

bacaladero, **-ra** *adj* cod-fishing (*antes de sust*).
◆ **bacaladero** *m* cod-fishing boat.

bacalao *m* [fresco] cod; [salado] dried salted cod; ~ **a la vizcaína** CULIN Basque dish of salt cod cooked in a thick sauce of olive oil, onions, tomato and red peppers; ~ **al pil-pil** CULIN Basque dish of salt cod cooked slowly in an earthenware dish with olive oil and garlic; **partir** ○ **cortar el ~** *fam fig* to be the boss.

bacán *Amer* ◇ *adj* fine. ◇ *m* toff; **como un ~** like a real gentleman.

bacanal *f* orgy.

bacarrá, **bacará** *m* baccarat.

bache *m* **-1.** [en carretera] pothole. **-2.** *fig* [dificultades] bad patch. **-3.** [en un vuelo] air pocket.

bachiller *m y f person who has passed the "bachillerato".*

bachillerato *m Spanish two-year course of secondary studies for academically orientated 16-18-year-olds;* ~ **unificado polivalente** → BUP.

bacilo *m* bacillus; ~ **de Koch** tubercle bacillus.

bacilón = **vacilón**.

bacín *m* chamber pot.

bacinica *f Amer* chamber pot.

backgammon *m inv* backgammon.

backup [ba'kap] (*pl* **backups**) *m* INFORM backup.

bacon ['beikon] *m inv* bacon.

bacteria *f* germ; ~**s** bacteria.

bacteriano, **-na** *adj* bacterial.

bactericida *adj* bactericidal.

bacteriología *f* bacteriology.

bacteriológico, **-ca** *adj* [guerra] germ (*antes de sust*).

bacteriólogo, **-ga** *m y f* bacteriologist.

báculo *m* **-1.** [de obispo] crosier. **-2.** *fig* [sostén] support.

badajo *m* clapper (*of bell*).

badén *m* **-1.** [de carretera] ditch. **-2.** [cauce] channel.

bádminton *m inv* badminton.

bafle (*pl* **bafles**), **baffle** (*pl* **baffles**) *m* loudspeaker.

bagaje *m fig* background; ~ **cultural** cultural baggage.

bagatela *f* trifle.

Bagdad Baghdad.

Bahamas *fpl*: **las** ~ the Bahamas.

bahía *f* bay.

Baikal *m*: **el (lago)** ~ Lake Baikal.

bailaor, -ra *m y f* flamenco dancer.

bailar ◇ *vt* to dance; **que me quiten lo bailado** *fam* no one can take away the good times. ◇ *vi* **-1.** [danzar] to dance; **es otro que tal baila** *fam* he's just the same, he's no different. **-2.** [no encajar] to be loose; **los pies me bailan (en los zapatos)** my shoes are too big.

bailarín, -ina *m y f* dancer; [de ballet] ballet dancer.

baile *m* **-1.** [gen] dance; ~ **clásico** ballet. **-2.** [fiesta] ball. **-3.** COM: ~ **de cifras** number transposition.

◆ **baile de San Vito** *m* St Vitus' dance.

bailongo *m fam* bop.

bailotear *vi fam* to boogie, to bop.

bailoteo *m fam* bopping.

baja → **bajo**.

bajada *f* **-1.** [descenso] descent; ~ **de bandera** [de taxi] minimum fare. **-2.** [pendiente] (downward) slope. **-3.** [disminución] decrease, drop.

bajamar *f* low tide.

bajar ◇ *vt* **-1.** [poner abajo - libro, cuadro etc] to take/bring down; [- telón, ventanilla, mano] to lower. **-2.** [descender - montaña, escaleras] to go/come down. **-3.** [precios, inflación, hinchazón] to reduce; [música, volumen, radio] to turn down; [fiebre] to bring down. **-4.** [ojos, cabeza, voz] to lower. ◇ *vi* **-1.** [descender] to go/come down; ~ **por algo** to go/come down sthg; ~ **corriendo** to run down. **-2.** [disminuir] to fall, to drop; [fiebre, hinchazón] to go/come down; [Bolsa] to suffer a fall.

◆ **bajarse** *vpr*: ~**se (de)** [coche] to get out (of); [moto, tren, avión] to get off; [árbol, escalera, silla] to get/come down (from).

bajel *m culto* vessel, ship.

bajero, -ra *adj* lower.

bajeza *f* **-1.** [cualidad] baseness. **-2.** [acción] nasty deed.

bajial *m Amer* lowland.

bajío *m* sandbank.

bajista ◇ *adj* FIN bearish; [mercado] bear (*antes de sust*). ◇ *m y f* MÚS bassist.

bajo, -ja *adj* **-1.** [gen] low; [persona, estatura] short; [piso] ground floor (*antes de sust*); [planta] ground (*antes de sust*); [sonido] soft, faint. **-2.** [territorio, época] lower; **el ~ Amazonas** the lower Amazon. **-3.** [pobre] lower-class. **-4.** [vil] base.

◆ **bajo** ◇ *m* **-1.** (*gen pl*) [dobladillo] hem. **-2.** [piso] ground floor flat. **-3.** [MÚS - instrumento, cantante] bass; [- instrumentista] bassist. ◇ *adv* **-1.** [gen] low. **-2.** [hablar] quietly,

softly. ◇ *prep* **-1.** [gen] under. **-2.** [con temperaturas] below.

◆ **baja** *f* **-1.** [descenso] drop, fall; **jugar a la baja** FIN to bear the market. **-2.** [cese]: **dar de baja a alguien** [en una empresa] to lay sb off; [en un club, sindicato] to expel sb; **darse de baja (de)** [dimitir] to resign (from); [salirse] to drop out (of). **-3.** [por enfermedad - permiso] sick leave (*U*); [- documento] sick note, doctor's certificate; **estar/darse de baja** to be on/to take sick leave. **-4.** MIL loss, casualty.

◆ **bajos** *mpl* [planta] ground floor (*sg*).

bajón *m* slump; **dar un ~** to slump.

bajorrelieve *m* bas-relief.

bajura → **pesca**.

bala *f* **-1.** [proyectil] bullet. **-2.** [fardo] bale.

◆ **bala perdida** *m fam* ne'er-do-well.

balacear *vt Amer* [tirotear] to shoot.

balacera *f Amer* shootout.

balada *f* ballad.

baladí (*pl* **baladíes**) *adj* trivial.

baladronada *f* boast.

balance *m* **-1.** [COM - operación] balance; [- documento] balance sheet; ~ **consolidado** consolidated balance sheet. **-2.** [resultado] outcome; **hacer ~ (de)** to take stock (of).

balancear *vt* [cuna] to rock; [columpio] to swing.

◆ **balancearse** *vpr* [en cuna, mecedora] to rock; [en columpio] to swing; [barco] to roll.

balanceo *m* **-1.** [gen] swinging; [de cuna, mecedora] rocking; [de barco] roll. **-2.** *Amer* AUTOM wheel balance.

balancín *m* **-1.** [mecedora] rocking chair; [en el jardín] swing hammock. **-2.** [columpio] seesaw. **-3.** AUTOM rocker arm.

balandrista *m y f* yachtsman (*f* yachtswoman).

balandro *m* yacht.

balanza *f* **-1.** [báscula] scales (*pl*); ~ **de cocina** kitchen scales; ~ **de precisión** precision balance; **la ~ se inclinó a nuestro favor** the balance ○ scales tipped in our favour. **-2.** COM: ~ **comercial/de pagos** balance of trade/payments.

balar *vi* to bleat.

balarrasa *m* ne'er-do-well.

balaustrada *f* balustrade; [de escalera] banister.

balazo *m* [disparo] shot; [herida] bullet wound.

balbucear, balbucir [79] *vi & vt* to babble.

balbuceo *m* babbling.

balbucir = **balbucear**.

Balcanes *mpl*: **los ~** the Balkans.

balcánico, -ca *adj* Balkan.

balcón *m* **-1.** [terraza] balcony. **-2.** [mirador] vantage point.

balda *f* shelf.

baldado, -da *adj* **-1.** [tullido] crippled. **-2.** [exhausto] shattered.

balde *m* pail, bucket.
◆ **de balde** *loc adv* free (of charge); **estar de** ~ [sobrar] to be getting in the way.
◆ **en balde** *loc adv* in vain.

baldío, -día *adj* **-1.** [sin cultivar] uncultivated; [no cultivable] waste (*antes de sust*). **-2.** [inútil] fruitless.

baldón *m* insult.

baldosa *f* [en casa, edificio] floor tile; [en la acera] paving stone.

baldosín *m* tile.

balear ◇ *vt Amer* to shoot. ◇ *adj* Balearic. ◇ *m y f* native/inhabitant of the Balearic Islands.

Baleares *fpl*: **las (islas)** ~ the Balearic Islands.

baleárico, -ca *adj* Balearic.

baleo *m Amer* [disparo] shot.

balido *m* bleat, bleating (*U*).

balín *m* pellet.

balístico, -ca *adj* ballistic.
◆ **balística** *f* ballistics (*U*).

baliza *f* NÁUT marker buoy; AERON beacon.

ballena *f* **-1.** [animal] whale. **-2.** [varilla - de corsé] stay; [- de paraguas] spoke.

ballenato *m* whale calf.

ballenero, -ra *adj* whaling (*antes de sust*).
◆ **ballenero** *m* [barco] whaler, whaling ship.

ballesta *f* **-1.** HIST crossbow. **-2.** AUTOM (suspension) spring.

ballet [ba'le] (*pl* **ballets**) *m* ballet.

balneario *m* spa.

balompié *m* football.

balón *m* **-1.** [pelota] ball; **echar balones fuera** to evade the issue. **-2.** [recipiente] bag; ~ **de oxígeno** oxygen bag; *fig* shot in the arm. **-3.** [en tebeos] (speech) balloon.

baloncestista *m y f* basketball player.

baloncesto *m* basketball.

balonmano *m* handball.

balonvolea *m* volleyball.

balotaje *m* second round of voting.

balsa *f* **-1.** [embarcación] raft. **-2.** [estanque] pond, pool. **-3.** *loc*: **ser una ~ de aceite** [mar] to be as calm as a millpond; [reunión] to go smoothly.

balsámico, -ca *adj* balsamic.

bálsamo *m* **-1.** FARM balsam. **-2.** [alivio] balm.

Báltico *m*: **el (mar)** ~ the Baltic (Sea).

baluarte *m* **-1.** [fortificación] bulwark. **-2.** *fig* [bastión] bastion, stronghold.

bamba *f* bamba.

bambalina *f* backdrop; **entre** ~**s** *fig* backstage.

bambolear *vi* to shake.
◆ **bambolearse** *vpr* [gen] to sway; [mesa, silla] to wobble.

bambú (*pl* **bambúes** O **bambús**) *m* bamboo.

banal *adj* banal.

banalidad *f* banality.

banalizar [13] *vt* to trivialize.

banana *f Amer* banana.

bananero, -ra *adj* banana (*antes de sust*).
◆ **bananero** *m* [árbol] banana tree.

banano *m* banana tree.

banca *f* **-1.** [actividad] banking; ~ **electrónica** electronic banking. **-2.** [institución]: **la** ~ the banks (*pl*). **-3.** [en juegos] bank; **hacer saltar la** ~ to break the bank. **-4.** [asiento] bench.

bancario, -ria *adj* banking (*antes de sust*).

bancarrota *f* bankruptcy; **en** ~ bankrupt; **ir a la** ~ to go bankrupt.

banco *m* **-1.** [asiento] bench; [de iglesia] pew. **-2.** FIN bank; ~ **central/comercial/ emisor/industrial** central/commercial/ issuing/industrial bank. **-3.** [de peces] shoal. **-4.** [de ojos, semen etc] bank. **-5.** [de carpintero, artesano etc] workbench.
◆ **banco azul** *m* POLÍT ≃ front bench *Br*.
◆ **banco de arena** *m* sandbank.
◆ **banco de datos** *m* INFORM data bank.
◆ **banco de pruebas** *m* MEC test bench; *fig* testing ground.
◆ **Banco Mundial** *m*: **el Banco Mundial** the World Bank.

banda *f* **-1.** [cuadrilla] gang; ~ **armada** terrorist organization. **-2.** MÚS band. **-3.** [faja] sash. **-4.** [cinta] ribbon. **-5.** [franja] stripe. **-6.** RADIO waveband; ~ **de frecuencias** frequency (band). **-7.** [margen] side; [en billar] cushion; [en fútbol] touchline. **-8.** *loc*: **cerrarse en** ~ to dig one's heels in.
◆ **banda magnética** *f* magnetic strip.
◆ **banda sonora** *f* soundtrack.

bandada *f* [de aves] flock; [de peces] shoal.

bandazo *m* [del barco] lurch; **dar** ~**s** [barco, borracho] to lurch; *fig* [ir sin rumbo] to chop and change; **dar un** ~ [con el volante] to swerve violently.

bandear *vt* to buffet.
◆ **bandearse** *vpr* to look after o.s., to cope.

bandeja f tray; **servir** O **dar algo a alguien en** ~ fig to hand sthg to sb on a plate.

bandera f flag; **jurar** ~ to swear allegiance (to the flag); ~ **blanca** white flag.
◆ **de bandera** loc adj fam [magnífico] fantastic, terrific.

banderilla f **-1.** TAUROM banderilla, *barbed dart thrust into bull's back*; *ver también* **tauromaquia**. **-2.** [aperitivo] *savoury hors d'œuvre on a stick*.

banderillero, -ra m y f TAUROM banderillero, *bullfighter's assistant who sticks "banderillas" into the bull*; *ver también* **tauromaquia**.

banderín m **-1.** [bandera] pennant. **-2.** MIL pennant-bearer.

banderola f pennant.

bandido, -da m y f **-1.** [delincuente] bandit. **-2.** [granuja] rascal.

bando m **-1.** [facción] side; **pasarse al otro** ~ to change sides. **-2.** [edicto - de alcalde] edict.

bandolero, -ra m y f bandit.
◆ **bandolera** f [correa] bandoleer; **en bandolera** slung across one's chest.

bandurria f *small 12-stringed guitar*.

Bangkok Bangkok.

Bangladesh [baŋglɑ'deʃ] Bangladesh.

Bangui Bangui.

banjo ['banjo] m banjo.

Banjul Banjul.

banquero, -ra m y f banker.

banqueta f **-1.** [asiento] stool. **-2.** *Amer* [acera] pavement *Br*, sidewalk *Am*.

banquete m [comida] banquet; ~ **de boda** wedding breakfast; ~ **eucarístico** holy communion.

banquillo m **-1.** [asiento] low stool; ~ **de los acusados** DER dock. **-2.** DEP bench.

bañada f *Amer* [acción de bañarse] bath.

bañadera f *Amer* [bañera] bath.

bañador m [for women] swimsuit; [for men] swimming trunks (*pl*).

bañar vt **-1.** [asear] to bath; MED to bathe. **-2.** [sumergir] to soak, to submerge. **-3.** [revestir] to coat. **-4.** [suj: río] to flow through; [suj: mar] to wash the coast of. **-5.** [suj: sol, luz] to bathe.
◆ **bañarse** vpr **-1.** [en el baño] to have O take a bath. **-2.** [en playa, piscina] to go for a swim.

bañera f bathtub, bath.

bañista m y f bather.

baño m **-1.** [acción - en bañera] bath; [en playa, piscina] swim; **darse un** ~ [en bañera] to have O take a bath; [en playa, piscina] to go for a swim; ~ **de asiento** hip bath; ~ **de**

sol sunbathing (*U*); **dar un** ~ **a alguien** fig to knock the spots off sb. **-2.** [bañera] bathtub, bath. **-3.** [cuarto de aseo] bathroom. **-4.** [vahos] inhalation (*U*). **-5.** [capa] coat.
◆ **baños** mpl [balneario] spa (*sg*).
◆ **baño María** m bain Marie.

baptismo m baptism.

baptista adj, m y f Baptist.

baptisterio m baptistry.

baquelita f Bakelite®.

baqueta f **-1.** [de fusil] ramrod; **tratar** O **llevar a la** ~ fig to treat harshly. **-2.** MUS drumstick.

baquetear vi [equipaje etc] to bump up and down.

bar m bar.

barahúnda f racket, din.

baraja f pack (of cards); **jugar con dos** ~s fig to play a double game.

barajar vt **-1.** [cartas] to shuffle. **-2.** [considerar - nombres, posibilidades] to consider; [- datos, cifras] to marshal, to draw on.
◆ **barajarse** vpr [nombres, posibilidades] to be considered; [datos, cifras] to be drawn upon, to be marshalled.

baranda, barandilla f handrail.

baratija f trinket, knick-knack.

baratillo m **-1.** [género] junk. **-2.** [tienda] junkshop; [mercadillo] flea market.

barato, -ta adj cheap.
◆ **barato** adv cheap, cheaply; **de** ~ for free.

barba f beard; ~ **incipiente** stubble; **apurarse la** ~ to shave close; **dejarse** ~ to let one's beard grow; **por** ~ [cada uno] per head; **hacer algo en las** ~s **de alguien** O **en sus propias** ~s to do sthg under sb's nose; **reírse de alguien en sus propias** ~s to laugh in sb's face.
◆ **barbas** fpl [de pez] barbel (*sg*).

barbacoa f barbecue.

Barbados Barbados.

barbaridad f **-1.** [cualidad] cruelty; **¡qué** ~! how terrible! **-2.** [disparate] nonsense (*U*). **-3.** [montón]: **una** ~ **(de)** tons (of); **se gastó una** ~ she spent a fortune.

barbarie f **-1.** [crueldad - cualidad] cruelty, savagery; [- acción] atrocity. **-2.** [incultura] barbarism.

barbarismo m **-1.** [extranjerismo] foreign word. **-2.** [incorrección] substandard usage.

bárbaro, -ra ◇ adj **-1.** HIST barbarian. **-2.** [cruel] barbaric, cruel. **-3.** [bruto] uncouth, coarse. **-4.** fam [extraordinario] brilliant, great. ◇ m y f HIST barbarian.
◆ **bárbaro** adv fam [magníficamente]: **pasarlo** ~ to have a wild time.

barbecho *m* fallow (land); [retirada de tierras] land set aside.

barbería *f* barber's (shop).

barbero, -ra *m y f* barber.

barbilampiño, -ña *adj* smooth-faced, beardless.

◆ **barbilampiño** *m* beardless man.

barbilla *f* chin.

barbitúrico *m* barbiturate.

barbo *m* barbel; ~ **de mar** red mullet.

barbotar *vi & vt* to mutter.

barbudo, -da ◇ *adj* bearded. ◇ *m y f* bearded person.

barbullar *vi* to jabber.

barca *f* dinghy, small boat.

barcaza *f* lighter.

Barcelona Barcelona.

barcelonés, -esa ◇ *adj* of/relating to Barcelona. ◇ *m y f* native/inhabitant of Barcelona.

barco *m* [gen] boat; [de gran tamaño] ship; **en** ~ by boat; ~ **cisterna** tanker; ~ **de guerra** warship; ~ **mercante** cargo ship; ~ **de vapor** steamer, steamboat; ~ **de vela** sailing ship.

bardo *m* bard.

baremo *m* [escala] scale.

bario *m* barium.

barítono *m* baritone.

barlovento *m* windward.

barman (*pl* **barmans**) *m* barman.

Barna. *abrev de* **Barcelona.**

barniz *m* [para madera] varnish; [para loza, cerámica] glaze; ~ **para las uñas** nail varnish.

barnizar [13] *vt* [madera] to varnish; [loza, cerámica] to glaze.

barómetro *m* barometer.

barón, -onesa *m y f* baron (*f* baroness).

barquero, -ra *m y f* boatman (*f* boatwoman).

barquilla *f* [de globo] basket.

barquillo *m* CULIN cornet, cone.

barra *f* **-1.** [gen] bar; [de hielo] block; [para cortinas] rod; [en bicicleta] crossbar; **la** ~ [de tribunal] the bar; ~ **de labios** lipstick; ~ **de pan** baguette, French stick. **-2.** [de bar, café] bar (*counter*); ~ **americana** *bar where hostesses chat with clients*; ~ **libre** *unlimited drink for a fixed price*. **-3.** [para bailarines] barre. **-4.** [signo gráfico] slash, oblique stroke. **-5.** INFORM: ~ **de menús** menu bar; ~ **de herramientas** tool bar. **-6.** *loc*: **sin pararse en** ~**s** stopping at nothing.

barrabasada *f fam* mischief (*U*).

barraca *f* **-1.** [chabola] shack. **-2.** [caseta de feria] stall. **-3.** [en Valencia y Murcia] thatched farmhouse.

barracón *m* large hut.

barranco *m* **-1.** [precipicio] precipice. **-2.** [cauce] ravine.

barraquismo *m* shanty towns (*pl*).

barrena *f* drill; **entrar en** ~ AERON to go into a spin; *fig* [persona, gobierno] to totter.

barrenar *vt* **-1.** [taladrar] to drill. **-2.** [frustrar] to scupper.

barrendero, -ra *m y f* street sweeper.

barreno *m* **-1.** [instrumento] large drill. **-2.** [agujero - para explosiones] blast hole.

barreño *m* washing-up bowl.

barrer ◇ *vt* **-1.** [con escoba, reflectores] to sweep. **-2.** [suj: viento, olas] to sweep away. **-3.** *fam* [derrotar] to thrash, to annihilate. ◇ *vi*: ~ **con** [llevarse] to finish off, to make short work of; ~ **hacia** ○ **para adentro** *fig* to look after number one.

barrera *f* **-1.** [gen] barrier; FERROC crossing gate; [de campo, casa] fence; **poner** ~**s a algo** *fig* to hinder sthg; ~**s arancelarias** tariff barriers. **-2.** TAUROM *barrier around the edge of a bull ring.* **-3.** DEP wall.

◆ **barrera del sonido** *f* sound barrier.

barriada *f* neighbourhood, area.

barrica *f* keg.

barricada *f* barricade.

barrido *m* **-1.** [con escoba] sweep, sweeping (*U*); **dar un** ~ **(a algo)** to sweep (sthg); **servir** ○ **valer tanto para un** ~ **como para un fregado** [persona] to be a jack-of-all-trades. **-2.** TECN scan, scanning (*U*). **-3.** CIN pan, panning (*U*).

barriga *f* belly; **echar** ~ to get a paunch; **rascarse** ○ **tocarse la** ~ *fig* to twiddle one's thumbs, to laze around.

barrigazo *m fam*: **darse un** ~ to fall flat on one's face.

barrigón, -ona ◇ *adj* paunchy. ◇ *m y f* [persona] portly person.

◆ **barrigón** *m* [barriga] big belly.

barril *m* barrel; **de** ~ [bebida] draught.

barrilete *m* **-1.** [de revólver] chamber. **-2.** *Amer* [cometa] kite.

barrio *m* **-1.** [vecindario] area, neighborhood *Am*; ~ **comercial/periférico** shopping/outlying district; ~ **chino** red light district; ~ **latino** Latin Quarter; **mandar a alguien al otro** ~ *fam* to do sb in, to finish sb off. **-2.** *Amer* [arrabal] shanty town.

barriobajero, -ra *despec* ◇ *adj* low-life (*antes de sust*). ◇ *m y f* common person.

barrizal *m* mire.

barro *m* **-1.** [fango] mud. **-2.** [arcilla] clay.

-3. [grano] blackhead. **-4.** loc: **arrastrarse por el ~** to abase o.s.

barroco, -ca adj **-1.** ARTE baroque. **-2.** [recargado] ornate.
◆ **barroco** m ARTE baroque.

barroquismo m ARTE baroque style.

barrote m bar.

barruntar vt **-1.** [presentir] to suspect. **-2.** [ser indicio de] to suggest, to hint at.

barrunto m **-1.** [presentimiento] suspicion. **-2.** [indicio] sign, indication.

bartola
◆ **a la bartola** loc adv fam: **tumbarse a la ~** to lounge around.

bártulos mpl things, bits and pieces; **liar los ~** fam fig to pack one's bags.

barullo m fam **-1.** [ruido] din, racket; **armar ~** to raise hell. **-2.** [desorden] mess.

basa f ARQUIT base.

basalto m basalt.

basamento m ARQUIT base, plinth.

basar vt [fundamentar] to base.
◆ **basarse en** vpr {suj: teoría, obra etc} to be based on; [suj: persona] to base one's argument on.

basca f **-1.** fam [de amigos] pals (pl), mates (pl). **-2.** [náusea] nausea.

báscula f scales (pl); **~ de baño/de precisión** bathroom/precision scales.

basculador m dumper truck.

bascular vi to tilt.

base f **-1.** [gen, MAT & MIL] base; [de edificio] foundations (pl); **~ aérea** air base; **~ espacial** space station; **~ de lanzamiento** launch site; **~ de operaciones** operational base. **-2.** [fundamento, origen] basis; **sentar las ~s para** to lay the foundations of. **-3.** [de partido, sindicato]: **las ~s** the grass roots (pl), the rank and file; **~ de ~** grassroots (antes de sust). **-4.** loc: **a ~ de** by (means of); **me alimento a ~ de verduras** I live on vegetables; **a ~ de bien** extremely well.
◆ **base de datos** f INFORM database; **~ de datos documental/relacional** INFORM documentary/relational database.
◆ **base imponible** f taxable income.

BASIC, basic ['beisik] m INFORM BASIC.

básico, -ca adj basic; **lo ~ de** the basics of.

basílica f basilica.

basilisco m: **ponerse hecho un ~** fam fig to go mad, to fly into a rage.

basta interj: ¡~! that's enough!; ¡~ **de chistes/tonterías!** that's enough jokes/of this nonsense!

bastante ◇ adv **-1.** [suficientemente] enough; **es lo ~ lista para ...** she's smart enough to .... **-2.** [considerablemente - antes de adj o adv] quite, pretty; [- después de verbo] quite a lot; **me gustó ~** I quite enjoyed it, I enjoyed it quite a lot. ◇ adj **-1.** [suficiente] enough; **no tengo dinero ~** I haven't enough money. **-2.** [mucho]: **éramos ~s** there were quite a few of us; **tengo ~ frío** I'm quite o pretty cold.

bastar vi to be enough; **basta con que se lo digas** it's enough for you to tell her; **con ocho basta** eight will be enough.
◆ **bastarse** vpr to be self-sufficient.

bastardía f bastardy.

bastardilla → letra.

bastardo, -da ◇ adj **-1.** [hijo etc] bastard (antes de sust). **-2.** [animal] crossbred. **-3.** despec [innoble] mean, base. ◇ m y f bastard.

bastidor m **-1.** [armazón] frame. **-2.** AUTOM chassis. **-3.** NAUT screw propeller's frame.
◆ **bastidores** mpl TEATR wings; **entre ~es** fig behind the scenes.

bastión m lit & fig bastion.

basto, -ta adj coarse.
◆ **bastos** mpl [naipes] ≃ clubs.

bastón m **-1.** [para andar] walking stick. **-2.** [de mando] baton; **empuñar el ~** fig to take the helm. **-3.** [para esquiar] ski stick.

bastonazo m blow (with a stick).

basura f lit & fig rubbish Br, garbage Am; **tirar algo a la ~** to throw sthg away.

basurero m **-1.** [persona] dustman Br, garbage man Am. **-2.** [vertedero] rubbish dump.

bata f **-1.** [de casa] housecoat; [para baño, al levantarse] dressing gown. **-2.** [de trabajo] overall; [de médico] white coat; [de laboratorio] lab coat.

batacazo m bump, bang.

batalla f battle; **~ campal** pitched battle; **de ~** [de uso diario] everyday.

batallador, -ra adj battling (antes de sust).

batallar vi **-1.** [con armas] to fight. **-2.** fig [por una cosa] to battle.

batallón m **-1.** MIL batallion. **-2.** fig [grupo numeroso] crowd.

batata f sweet potato.

bate m DEP bat.

batea f Amer washing trough.

bateador, -ra m y f batsman (f batswoman).

batear ◇ vt to hit. ◇ vi to bat.

batería ◇ f **-1.** ELECTR & MIL battery; **~ solar** solar cell. **-2.** MÚS drums (pl). **-3.** TEATR floodlights (pl). **-4.** [conjunto] set; [de preguntas] barrage; **~ de cocina** pots (pl) and pans. **-5.** loc **aparcado en ~** parked at an angle to the pavement. ◇ m y f drummer.

batiborrillo, batiburrillo m jumble.

batido, -da *adj* **-1.** [nata] whipped; [claras] whisked. **-2.** [senda, camino] well-trodden.
◆ **batido** *m* **-1.** [acción de batir] beating. **-2.** [bebida] milkshake.
◆ **batida** *f* **-1.** [de caza] beat. **-2.** [de policía] combing, search.

batidor *m* **-1.** [aparato manual] whisk. **-2.** [en caza] beater. **-3.** MIL scout.

batidora *f* [eléctrica] mixer.

batiente *m* **-1.** [de puerta] jamb; [de ventana] frame. **-2.** [costa] shoreline.

batín *m* short dressing gown.

batir ◇ *vt* **-1.** [gen] to beat; [nata] to whip; [récord] to break. **-2.** [suj: olas, lluvia, viento] to beat against. **-3.** [derribar] to knock down. **-4.** [explorar - suj: policía etc] to comb, to search. ◇ *vi* [suj: sol, lluvia] to beat down.
◆ **batirse** *vpr* [luchar] to fight.

batiscafo *m* bathyscaphe.

batista *f* batiste, cambric.

baturro, -rra ◇ *adj* Aragonese. ◇ *m y f* Aragonese peasant.

batuta *f* baton; **llevar la** ~ *fig* to call the tune.

baúl *m* **-1.** [cofre] trunk. **-2.** *Amer* [maletero] boot *Br*, trunk *Am*.

bautismal *adj* baptismal.

bautismo *m* baptism.

bautista *m y f* RELIG Baptist.
◆ **Bautista** *m* RELIG: **el Bautista** John the Baptist.

bautizar [13] *vt* **-1.** RELIG to baptize, to christen. **-2.** *fig* [denominar, poner mote] to christen. **-3.** *fam fig* [aguar] to dilute.

bautizo *m* **-1.** RELIG baptism, christening. **-2.** [fiesta] christening party.

bauxita *f* bauxite.

bávaro, -ra *adj, m y f* Bavarian.

Baviera Bavaria.

baya *f* berry.

bayeta *f* **-1.** [tejido] flannel. **-2.** [para fregar] cloth; ~ **de gamuza** chamois.

bayo, -ya *adj* bay.

bayoneta *f* bayonet.

baza *f* **-1.** [en naipes] trick. **-2.** [ventaja] advantage. **-3.** *loc*: **meter** ~ **en algo** to butt in on sthg; **no pude meter** ~ **(en la conversación)** I couldn't get a word in edgeways.

bazar *m* bazaar.

bazo *m* ANAT spleen.

bazofia *f* **-1.** [comida] pigswill (*U*). **-2.** *fig* [libro, película etc] rubbish (*U*).

bazuca, bazooka *m* bazooka.

bearnesa → salsa.

beatería *f* devoutness.

beatificación *f* beatification.

beatificar [10] *vt* to beatify.

beatitud *f* beatitude.

beato, -ta ◇ *adj* **-1.** [beatificado] blessed. **-2.** [piadoso] devout. **-3.** *fig* [santurrón] sanctimonious. ◇ *m y f* **-1.** RELIG beatified person. **-2.** [piadoso] devout person. **-3.** *fig* [santurrón] sanctimonious person.

beba *f Amer fam* little girl.

bebe *m Amer fam* baby.

bebé *m* baby; ~ **probeta** test-tube baby.

bebedero *m* **-1.** [de jaula] water dish. **-2.** [abrevadero] drinking trough.

bebedizo *m* potion; [de amor] love potion.

bebedor, -ra *m y f* [borrachín] heavy drinker.

beber ◇ *vt* **-1.** [líquido] to drink. **-2.** *fig* [absorber - palabras, consejos] to lap up; [- sabiduría, información] to draw, to acquire. ◇ *vi* **-1.** [tomar líquido] to drink. **-2.** *fig* [emborracharse] to drink (heavily). **-3.** [brindar]: ~ **a** algo **por** to drink to.

bebida *f* drink; **darse** O **entregarse a la** ~ to take to the bottle.

bebido, -da *adj* drunk.

bebito, -ta *m y f Amer* little baby.

bebop, be-bop [bi'boß] *m* bebop.

beca *f* [del gobierno] grant; [de organización privada] scholarship; ~ **de investigación** research grant.

becar [10] *vt* [suj: gobierno] to award a grant to; [suj: organización privada] to award a scholarship to.

becario, -ria *m y f* [del gobierno] grant holder; [de organización privada] scholarship holder.

becerrada *f* bullfight with young bulls.

becerro, -rra *m y f* calf.

bechamel [betʃa'mel], **besamel** *f* béchamel sauce.

bedel *m* janitor.

beduino, -na *adj, m y f* Bedouin.

befa *f* jeer; **hacer** ~ **de** to jeer at.

begonia *f* begonia.

beige [beis] *adj inv & m inv* beige.

béisbol *m* baseball.

bel canto *m inv* bel canto.

beldad *f culto* fairness, beauty.

belén *m* **-1.** [de Navidad] crib, Nativity scene. **-2.** *fam* [desorden] bedlam (*U*). **-3.** (*gen pl*) *fig* [embrollo] mess (*U*).

Belén Bethlehem.

belfo, -fa *adj* thick-lipped.
◆ **belfo** *m* horse's lip.

belga *adj, m y f* Belgian.

Bélgica Belgium.
Belgrado Belgrade.
Belice Belize.
beliceño, -ña *adj, m y f* Belizean.
belicismo *m* warmongering.
belicista ◇ *adj* belligerent. ◇ *m y f* warmonger.
bélico, -ca *adj* [gen] war (*antes de sust*); [actitud] bellicose, warlike.
belicoso, -sa *adj* bellicose; *fig* aggressive.
beligerancia *f* belligerence.
beligerante *adj, m y f* belligerent.
bellaco, -ca *m y f* villain, scoundrel.
belladona *f* belladonna, deadly nightshade.
bellaquería *f* wickedness, roguery.
belleza *f* beauty.
bello, -lla *adj* beautiful.
bellota *f* acorn.
Belmopan Belmopan.
bemol ◇ *adj* flat. ◇ *m* MÚS flat; **doble ~** double flat; **tener (muchos) ~es** [ser difícil] to be tricky; [tener valor] to have guts; [ser un abuso] to be a bit rich O much.
benceno *m* benzene.
bencina *f* benzine.
bendecir [66] *vt* to bless.
bendición *f* blessing.
◆ **bendiciones** *fpl* [boda] wedding (*sg*).
bendiga, bendijera *etc* → **bendecir**.
bendito, -ta ◇ *adj* **-1.** [santo] holy; [alma] blessed; **¡~ sea Dios!** *fam fig* thank goodness! **-2.** [dichoso] lucky. **-3.** [para enfatizar] damned. ◇ *m y f* simple soul; **dormir como un ~** to sleep like a baby.
benedictino, -na *adj, m y f* Benedictine.
benefactor, -ra ◇ *adj* beneficent. ◇ *m y f* benefactor (*f* benefactress).
beneficencia *f* charity.
beneficiar [8] *vt* to benefit.
◆ **beneficiarse** *vpr* to benefit; **~se de algo** to do well out of sthg.
beneficiario, -ria *m y f* beneficiary; [de cheque] payee.
beneficio *m* **-1.** [bien] benefit; **a ~ de** [gala, concierto] in aid of; **en ~ de** for the good of; **en ~ de todos** in everyone's interest; **en ~ propio** for one's own good. **-2.** [ganancia] profit; **~ bruto/neto** gross/net profit.
beneficioso, -sa *adj*: **~ (para)** beneficial (to).
benéfico, -ca *adj* **-1.** [favorable] beneficial. **-2.** [rifa, función] charity (*antes de sust*); [organización] charitable.
Benelux (*abrev de* **België-Nederland-Luxembourg**) *m*: **el ~** Benelux.

benemérito, -ta *adj* worthy.
◆ **Benemérita** *f*: **la Benemérita** *another name for the "Guardia Civil"*.
beneplácito *m* consent.
benevolencia *f* benevolence.
benevolente, benévolo, -la *adj* benevolent.
bengala *f* **-1.** [para pedir ayuda, iluminar etc] flare. **-2.** [para fiestas etc] sparkler.
benigno, -na *adj* **-1.** [gen] benign. **-2.** [clima, temperatura] mild.
benjamín, -ina *m y f* youngest child.
benzol *m* benzol.
beodo, -da *adj, m y f* drunk.
beque *etc* → **becar**.
berberecho *m* cockle.
berenjena *f* aubergine *Br*, eggplant *Am*.
berenjenal *m fam* [enredo] mess; **meterse en un ~** to get o.s. into a right mess.
bergantín *m* brigantine.
beriberi *m* beriberi.
berilio *m* beryllium.
Berlín Berlin.
berlina *f* four-door saloon.
berlinés, -esa ◇ *adj* of/relating to Berlin. ◇ *m y f* Berliner.
bermejo, -ja *adj* reddish.
bermellón *adj inv & m* vermilion.
bermudas *fpl* Bermuda shorts.
Berna Berne.
bernés, -esa *adj* of/relating to Berne.
berrear *vi* **-1.** [animal] to bellow. **-2.** [persona] to howl.
berrido *m* **-1.** [del becerro] bellow, bellowing (*U*). **-2.** [de persona] howl, howling (*U*).
berrinche *m fam* tantrum; **coger** O **agarrarse un ~** to throw a tantrum.
berro *m* watercress.
bertsolari *m* in Basque culture, poet who extemporizes poems at gatherings and literary competitions.
berza *f* cabbage.
berzotas *m y f inv fam* thickhead.
besamel = **bechamel**.
besar *vt* to kiss.
◆ **besarse** *vpr* to kiss.
beso *m* kiss; **comerse a ~s a alguien** to smother sb with kisses.
bestia ◇ *adj* **-1.** [ignorante] thick, stupid. **-2.** [torpe] clumsy. **-3.** [maleducado] rude. ◇ *m y f* **-1.** [ignorante, torpe] brute. **-2.** [maleducado] rude person. ◇ *f* [animal] beast; **~ de carga** beast of burden.
bestial *adj* **-1.** [brutal] animal, brutal; [apetito] tremendous. **-2.** *fam* [formidable] terrific.

bestialidad f -1. [brutalidad] brutality. -2. *fam* [tontería] rubbish (U), nonsense (U). -3. *fam* [montón]: **una ~ de** tons (pl) O stacks (pl) of.

bestiario m LITER bestiary.

best-seller [bes'seler] (pl **best-sellers**) m best-seller.

besucón, -ona fam ◇ adj kissy. ◇ m y f kissy person.

besugo m -1. [animal] sea bream. -2. fam [persona] idiot.

besuquear fam vt to smother with kisses.
♦ **besuquearse** vpr fam to smooch.

beta adj beta (antes de sust).

bético, -ca adj -1. [andaluz] Andalusian. -2. DEP of or relating to Real Betis Football Club.

betún m -1. [para calzado] shoe polish. -2. QUÍM bitumen; **~ de Judea** asphalt.

bianual adj -1. [dos veces al año] biannual, twice-yearly. -2. [cada dos años] biennial.

biberón m (baby's) bottle; **dar el ~ a** to bottle-feed.

Biblia f Bible; **ser la ~ en verso** fig to be endless.

bíblico, -ca adj biblical.

bibliófilo, -la m y f -1. [coleccionista] book collector. -2. [lector] book lover.

bibliografía f bibliography.

bibliográfico, -ca adj bibliographic.

bibliógrafo, -fa m y f bibliographer.

bibliorato m Amer file.

biblioteca f -1. [gen] library; **~ ambulante/pública** mobile/public library. -2. [mueble] bookcase.

bibliotecario, -ria m y f librarian.

bicameral adj bicameral, two-chamber (antes de sust).

bicarbonato m -1. FARM bicarbonate of soda. -2. QUÍM bicarbonate.

bicentenario m bicentenary.

bíceps m inv biceps.

bicha f fam snake.

bicharraco m fam -1. [animal] disgusting creature. -2. [persona mala] nasty piece of work.

bicho m -1. [animal] beast, animal; [insecto] bug. -2. fam [persona mala]: **(mal) ~** nasty piece of work; **~ raro** weirdo; **todo ~ viviente** every Tom, Dick and Harry. -3. [pillo] little terror.

bici f fam bike.

bicicleta f bicycle.

biciclo m penny-farthing.

bicoca f fam [compra, alquiler] bargain; [trabajo] cushy number.

bicolor adj two-coloured.

bidé m bidet.

bidimensional adj two-dimensional.

bidón m drum (for oil etc); [lata] can, canister; [de plástico] (large) bottle.

biela f connecting rod.

bien ◇ adv -1. [como es debido, adecuado] well; **has hecho ~** you did the right thing; **habla inglés ~** he speaks English well; **cierra ~ la puerta** shut the door properly; **hiciste ~ en decírmelo** you were right to tell me. -2. [expresa opinión favorable]: **estar ~** [de aspecto] to be nice; [de salud] to be O feel well; [de calidad] to be good; [de comodidad] to be comfortable; **está ~ que te vayas, pero antes despídete** it's all right for you to go, but say goodbye first; **oler ~** to smell nice; **pasarlo ~** to have a good time; **sentar ~ a alguien** [ropa] to suit sb; [comida] to agree with sb; [comentario] to please sb. -3. [muy, bastante] very; **hoy me he levantado ~ temprano** I got up nice and early today; **quiero un vaso de agua ~ fría** I'd like a nice cold glass of water. -4. [vale, de acuerdo] all right, OK; **¿nos vamos? –** ~ shall we go? – all right O OK. -5. [de buena gana, fácilmente] quite happily; **ella ~ lo haría, pero no la dejan** she'd be happy to do it, but they won't let her. -6. loc: **¡~ por ...!** three cheers for ...!; **¡está ~!** [bueno, vale] all right then!; [es suficiente] that's enough!; **¡ya está ~!** that's enough!; **estar ~ con alguien** to be on good terms with sb; **¡muy ~!** very good!, excellent!; **¡pues (sí que) estamos ~!** that's all we needed!; **tener a ~ hacer algo** to be good enough to do sthg.
◇ adj inv [adinerado] well-to-do.
◇ conj: **~ ... ~** either ... or; **dáselo ~ a mi hermano, ~ a mi padre** either give it to my brother or my father.
◇ m good; **el ~ y el mal** good and evil; **hacer el ~** to do good (deeds); **por el ~ de** for the sake of; **lo hice por tu ~** I did it for your own good.
♦ **bienes** mpl -1. [patrimonio] property (U); **~es inmuebles** O **raíces** real estate (U); **~es gananciales** shared possessions; **~es muebles** personal property (U). -2. [productos] goods; **~es de consumo** consumer goods; **~es de equipo** capital goods; **~es de producción** industrial goods.
♦ **más bien** loc adv rather; **no estoy contento, más ~ estupefacto** I'm not so much happy as stunned.
♦ **no bien** loc adv no sooner, as soon as; **no ~ me había marchado cuando empezaron a ...** no sooner had I gone than they started ....
♦ **si bien** loc conj although, even though.

bienal ◇ *adj* biennial. ◇ *f* biennial exhibition.

bienaventurado, -da *m y f* RELIG blessed person.

bienaventuranza *f* **-1.** RELIG divine vision. **-2.** [felicidad] happiness.
◆ **bienaventuranzas** *fpl* RELIG Beatitudes.

bienestar *m* wellbeing.

bienhechor, -ra ◇ *adj* beneficial. ◇ *m y f* benefactor (*f* benefactress).

bienintencionado, -da *adj* well-intentioned.

bienio *m* **-1.** [período] two years (*pl*). **-2.** [aumento de sueldo] two-yearly increment.

bienvenido, -da ◇ *adj* welcome. ◇ *interj*: ¡~! welcome!
◆ **bienvenida** *f* welcome; **dar la bienvenida a alguien** to welcome sb.

bies *m inv* bias binding; **al ~** [costura] on the bias; [sombrero etc] at an angle.

bifásico, -ca *adj* two-phase (*antes de sust*).

bife *m Amer* steak.

bífido, -da *adj* forked.

bifocal *adj* bifocal.

biftec = **bistec**.

bifurcación *f* fork; TECN bifurcation.

bifurcarse [10] *vpr* to fork.

bigamia *f* bigamy.

bígamo, -ma ◇ *adj* bigamous. ◇ *m y f* bigamist.

bígaro *m* winkle.

big bang [biɣ baŋ] (*pl* **big bangs**) *m* big bang.

bigote *m* moustache; **de ~s** *fig* fantastic.

bigotudo, -da *adj* with a big moustache.

bigudí (*pl* **bigudís** O **bigudíes**) *m* curler.

bikini = **biquini**.

bilateral *adj* bilateral.

biliar *adj* bile (*antes de sust*).

bilingüe *adj* bilingual.

bilingüismo *m* bilingualism.

bilioso, -sa *adj* lit & *fig* bilious.

bilirrubina *f* bilirubin.

bilis *f inv lit* & *fig* bile; **tragar ~** *fig* to bite one's tongue.

billar *m* **-1.** [juego] billiards (*U*); **~ americano** ≃ pool; **~ romano** bar billiards. **-2.** [mesa] billiard table. **-3.** [sala] billiard hall.

billete *m* **-1.** [dinero] note *Br*, bill *Am*. **-2.** [de rifa, transporte etc] ticket; **"no hay ~s"** TEATR "sold out"; **~ de andén** platform ticket; **~ de ida y vuelta** return (ticket) *Br*, round-trip (ticket) *Am*; **~ kilométrico** *ticket to travel a set distance* **~ sencillo** single (ticket) *Br*, one-way (ticket) *Am*. **-3.** [de lotería] lottery ticket.

billetera *f*, **billetero** *m* wallet.

billón *núm* billion *Br*, trillion *Am*; *ver también* seis.

bimensual *adj* twice-monthly.

bimestral *adj* two-monthly.

bimestre *m* two months (*pl*).

bimotor ◇ *adj* twin-engine (*antes de sust*). ◇ *m* twin-engined plane.

binario, -ria *adj* [gen & INFORM] binary.

bingo *m* **-1.** [juego] bingo. **-2.** [sala] bingo hall. **-3.** [premio] (full) house.

binoculares *mpl* binoculars; TEATR opera glasses.

binóculo *m* pince-nez.

binomio *m* **-1.** MAT binomial. **-2.** *fig* [de personas] duo.

biodegradable *adj* biodegradable.

biofeedback [bio'fidbak] *m inv* PSICOL biofeedback.

biofísico, -ca *adj* biophysical.
◆ **biofísica** *f* biophysics (*U*).

biogenético, -ca *adj* genetic.
◆ **biogenética** *f* genetics (*U*).

biografía *f* biography.

biografiar [9] *vt* to write the biography of.

biográfico, -ca *adj* biographical.

biógrafo, -fa *m y f* [persona] biographer.
◆ **biógrafo** *m Amer* [cine] cinema.

bioingeniería *f* bioengineering.

biología *f* biology.

biológico, -ca *adj* biological.

biólogo, -ga *m y f* biologist.

biomasa *f* biomass.

biombo *m* (folding) screen.

biometría *f* biometry.

biónico, -ca *adj* bionic.

biopsia *f* biopsy.

bioquímico, -ca ◇ *adj* biochemical. ◇ *m y f* [persona] biochemist.
◆ **bioquímica** *f* [ciencia] biochemistry.

biorritmo *m* biorhythm.

biosfera *f* biosphere.

bioterapia *f* biotherapy.

biotipo *m* biotype.

bióxido *m* dioxide.

bipartidismo *m* two-party system.

bipartidista *adj* two-party (*antes de sust*).

bipartito, -ta *adj* bipartite.

bípedo, -da *adj* biped.

biplano *m* biplane.

biplaza ◇ *adj* two-seater (*antes de sust*). ◇ *m* two-seater.

bipolar *adj* bipolar.

biquini, bikini *m* [bañador] bikini.

birlar *vt fam* to pinch, to nick.

birlibirloque → **arte**.

Birmania Burma.

birmano, -na *adj, m y f* Burmese.

◆ **birmano** *m* [lengua] Burmese.

birome *m o f Amer* biro.

birra *f mfam* beer.

birreactor, -ra *adj* twin-jet (*antes de sust*).

◆ **birreactor** *m* twin-jet aircraft.

birrete *m* -**1.** [de clérigo] biretta. -**2.** [de catedrático] mortarboard. -**3.** [de abogados, jueces] *cap worn by judges and lawyers*.

birria *f fam* -**1.** [fealdad - persona] sight, fright; [- cosa] monstrosity. -**2.** [cosa sin valor] rubbish (*U*).

bis (*pl* bises) ◇ *adj inv*: **viven en el 150** ~ they live at 150a. ◇ *m* encore. ◇ *adv* MÚS [para repetir] bis.

bisabuelo, -la *m y f* great-grandfather (*f* great-grandmother); ~s great-grandparents.

bisagra *f* hinge.

bisbisar, bisbisear *vt fam* to mutter.

bisbiseo *m* muttering.

bisección *f* bisection.

bisectriz *f* bisector.

bisel *m* bevel.

biselado *m* bevelling.

biselar *vt* to bevel.

bisemanal *adj* twice-weekly.

bisexual *adj, m y f* bisexual.

bisiesto → **año**.

bisílabo, -ba *adj* two-syllabled.

bisnieto, -ta *m y f* great-grandchild, great-grandson (*f* great-granddaughter).

bisonte *m* bison.

bisoñé *m* toupée.

bisoño, -ña *m y f* novice.

Bissau Bissau.

bistec, biftec *m* steak; ~ **a la rusa** *fried cutlet of minced beef, chopped pork, ham and onion*.

bisturí (*pl* bisturíes) *m* scalpel.

bisutería *f* imitation jewellery.

bit [bit] (*pl* bits) *m* INFORM bit.

bitácora *f* binnacle.

bíter, bitter *m* bitters (*U*).

bituminoso, -sa *adj* bituminous.

bizantino, -na ◇ *adj* -**1.** HIST Byzantine. -**2.** [discusión, razonamiento] hair-splitting. ◇ *m y f* Byzantine.

bizarría *f* -**1.** [valor] bravery. -**2.** [generosidad] generosity.

bizarro, -rra *adj* -**1.** [valiente] brave, valiant. -**2.** [generoso] generous.

bizco, -ca ◇ *adj* cross-eyed. ◇ *m y f* cross-eyed person.

bizcocho *m* [de repostería] sponge.

bizquear *vi* to squint.

bizquera *f* squint.

blablablá *m fam* blah, blahblah.

blanco, -ca ◇ *adj* white. ◇ *m y f* [persona] white (person).

◆ **blanco** *m* -**1.** [color] white. -**2.** [diana] target; **dar en el** ~ DEP & MIL to hit the target; *fig* to hit the nail on the head. -**3.** *fig* [objetivo] target; [de miradas] object. -**4.** [espacio vacío] blank (space).

◆ **blanca** *f* MÚS minim; **estar O quedarse sin blanca** *fig* to be flat broke.

◆ **blanco del ojo** *m* white of the eye.

◆ **en blanco** *loc adv* -**1.** [gen] blank; **se quedó con la mente en** ~ his mind went blank. -**2.** [sin dormir]: **una noche en** ~ a sleepless night.

blancura *f* whiteness.

blancuzco, -ca *adj* off-white.

blandengue *adj lit & fig* weak.

blandir [78] *vt* to brandish.

blando, -da *adj* -**1.** [gen] soft; [carne] tender. -**2.** *fig* [persona - débil] weak; [- indulgente] lenient, soft.

blandura *f* -**1.** [gen] softness; [de carne] tenderness. -**2.** *fig* [debilidad] weakness; [indulgencia] leniency.

blanqueador, -ra ◇ *adj* whitening (*antes de sust*). ◇ *m y f* whitewasher.

blanquear *vt* -**1.** [ropa] to whiten; [con lejía] to bleach. -**2.** [con cal] to whitewash. -**3.** *fig* [dinero] to launder.

blanquecino, -na *adj* off-white.

blanqueo *m* -**1.** [de ropa] whitening; [con lejía] bleaching. -**2.** [encalado] whitewashing. -**3.** *fig* [de dinero] laundering.

blanquillo *m Amer* egg.

blasfemar *vi* -**1.** RELIG: ~ **(contra)** to blaspheme (against). -**2.** [maldecir] to swear, to curse.

blasfemia *f* -**1.** RELIG blasphemy. -**2.** [palabrota] curse. -**3.** *fig* [injuria]: **es una** ~ **hablar así de** ... it's sacrilege to talk like that about ....

blasfemo, -ma ◇ *adj* blasphemous. ◇ *m y f* blasphemer.

blasón *m* -**1.** [escudo] coat of arms. -**2.** *fig* [orgullo] honour, glory.

bledo *m*: **me importa un** ~ **(lo que diga)** *fam* I don't give a damn (about what he says).

blenorragia *f* gonorrhœa.

blindado, -da *adj* armour-plated; [coche] armoured.

blindaje *m* armour-plating; [de coche] armour.

blindar *vt* to armour-plate.

bloc [blok] (*pl* **blocs**) *m* pad; ~ **de dibujo** sketchpad.

blocar [10] *vt* DEP to block.

blonda *f* [para tartas etc] doily.

bloomers ['blumers], **blúmers** *mpl Amer* knickers.

bloque ◇ *v* → **blocar**. ◇ *m* **-1.** [gen & INFORM] block. **-2.** POLÍT bloc; **en ~ en masse**; [votación] block (*antes de sust*). **-3.** MEC cylinder block.

bloquear *vt* **-1.** [gen & DEP] to block. **-2.** [aislar - suj: ejército, barcos] to blockade; [- suj: nieve, inundación] to cut off. **-3.** FIN to freeze. **-4.** AUTOM to lock.

◆ **bloquearse** *vpr* [persona] to have a mental block.

bloqueo *m* **-1.** [gen & DEP] blocking; ~ **mental** mental block. **-2.** ECON & MIL blockade. **-3.** FIN freeze, freezing (*U*). **-4.** AUTOM locking.

blues [blus] *m inv* MÚS blues.

blúmers = **bloomers**.

blusa *f* blouse.

blusón *m* smock.

bluyín *m*, **bluyínes** *mpl Amer* jeans (*pl*).

BNG (*abrev de* **Bloque Nacionalista Gallego**) *m Galician nationalist party*.

boa ◇ *f* ZOOL boa; ~ **constrictor** boa constrictor. ◇ *m* [prenda] (feather) boa.

boato *m* show, ostentation.

bobada *f fam*: **decir ~s** to talk nonsense; **hacer ~s** to mess about.

bobalicón, -ona *fam* ◇ *adj* simple. ◇ *m y f* simpleton.

bóbilis

◆ **de bóbilis bóbilis** *loc adv fam* [de balde] for free, for nothing.

bobina *f* **-1.** [gen] reel; [en máquina de coser] bobbin. **-2.** ELECTR coil.

bobinar *vt* to wind.

bobo, -ba ◇ *adj* **-1.** [tonto] stupid, daft. **-2.** [ingenuo] naïve, simple. ◇ *m y f* **-1.** [tonto] fool, idiot. **-2.** [ingenuo] simpleton.

bobsleigh [boßs'leix] (*pl* **bobsleighs**) *m* bobsleigh.

boca *f* **-1.** [gen] mouth; ~ **arriba/abajo** face up/down; **abrir** ○ **hacer ~** to whet one's appetite; **andar** ○ **ir de ~ en ~** to be on everyone's lips; **a pedir de ~** perfectly; **cerrar la ~ a alguien** to make sb shut up; **se fue de la ~** he let the cat out of the bag; **me lo has quitado de la ~** you took the words right out of my mouth; **meterse en la ~ del lobo** to put one's head into the

lion's mouth; **no decir esta ~ es mía** not to open one's mouth; **por la ~ muere el pez** silence is golden; **quedarse con la ~ abierta** to be left speechless; **se me hace la ~ agua** it makes my mouth water; **tapar la ~ a alguien** to silence sb. **-2.** [entrada] opening; [- de cañón] muzzle; ~ **del estómago** pit of the stomach; ~ **de metro** tube ○ underground entrance *Br*, subway entrance *Am*; ~ **de riego** hydrant.

◆ **boca a boca** *m* mouth-to-mouth resuscitation.

◆ **a boca de jarro** *loc adv* point-blank.

bocacalle *f* [entrada] entrance (*to a street*); [calle] side street; **gire en la tercera ~** take the third turning.

bocadillo *m* **-1.** CULIN sandwich. **-2.** [en cómic] speech bubble, balloon.

bocado *m* **-1.** [comida] mouthful; **no probar ~** [por estar desganado] not to touch one's food; [no haber podido comer] not to have a bite (to eat). **-2.** [mordisco] bite.

◆ **bocado de Adán** *m* Adam's apple.

bocajarro

◆ **a bocajarro** *loc adv* point-blank; **se lo dije a ~** I told him to his face.

bocamanga *f* cuff.

bocanada *f* [de líquido] mouthful; [de humo] puff; [de viento] gust.

bocata *m fam* sarnie.

bocazas *m y f inv fam despec* big mouth, blabbermouth.

boceto *m* sketch, rough outline.

bocha *f* [bolo] bowl.

◆ **bochas** *fpl* [juego] bowls (*U*).

bochinche *m fam* commotion, uproar.

bochorno *m* **-1.** [calor] stifling ○ muggy heat. **-2.** [vergüenza] embarrassment.

bochornoso, -sa *adj* **-1.** [tiempo] stifling, muggy. **-2.** [vergonzoso] embarrassing.

bocina *f* **-1.** AUTOM & MÚS horn. **-2.** [megáfono] megaphone, loudhailer.

bocinazo *m* AUTOM hoot.

bocio *m* goitre.

bock (*pl* **bocks**) *m* stein.

boda *f* wedding; ~**s de diamante/oro/plata** diamond/golden/silver wedding (*sg*).

bodega *f* **-1.** [cava] wine cellar. **-2.** [tienda] wine shop; [bar] bar. **-3.** [en buque, avión] hold. **-4.** *Amer* [colmado] small grocery store. **-5.** *Amer* [almacén] store.

bodegón *m* **-1.** ARTE still life. **-2.** [taberna] tavern, inn.

bodeguero, -ra *m y f* [dueño] owner of a wine cellar; [encargado] cellarman.

bodrio *m fam despec* [gen] rubbish (*U*);

[comida] pigswill (*U*); ¡qué ~! what a load of rubbish!

body ['boði] (*pl* bodies) *m* body (*garment*).

BOE (*abrev de* **Boletín Oficial del Estado**) *m official Spanish gazette.*

bofetada *f* slap (in the face); **dar una ~ a alguien** to slap sb (in the face); **darse de ~s con algo** *fig* [no pegar] to clash with sthg.

bofetón *m* hard slap (in the face).

bofia *f fam*: **la ~** the cops (*pl*).

boga *f*: **estar en ~** to be in vogue.

bogar [16] *vi* **-1.** [remar] to row. **-2.** [navegar] to sail.

bogavante *m* lobster.

Bogotá Bogotá.

bogotano, -na *adj* of/relating to Bogotá.

bogue *etc* → **bogar.**

Bohemia Bohemia.

bohemio, -mia ◇ *adj* **-1.** [vida etc] bohemian. **-2.** [de Bohemia] Bohemian. ◇ *m y f* **-1.** [artista] bohemian. **-2.** [de Bohemia] Bohemian.
◆ **bohemia** *f*: **la bohemia** the bohemian lifestyle.

bohío *m Amer* hut.

boicot (*pl* boicots), **boycot** (*pl* boycots) *m* boycott.

boicotear, boycotear *vt* to boycott.

boicoteo, boycoteo *m* boycotting.

boina *f* beret.

boîte [bwat] (*pl* boîtes) *f* nightclub.

boj (*pl* bojes) *m* **-1.** [árbol] box. **-2.** [madera] boxwood.

bol (*pl* boles) *m* bowl.

bola *f* **-1.** [gen] ball; [canica] marble; **~ de cristal** crystal ball; **~ de nieve** snowball; **~s de naftalina** mothballs; **convertirse en una ~ de nieve** *fig* to snowball. **-2.** *fam* [mentira] fib. **-3.** *Amer* [rumor] rumour. **-4.** *loc*: **en ~s** *fam* starkers; **no rascar ~** *fam* to get everything wrong.

bolada *f Amer fam* opportunity.

bolchevique *adj, m y f* Bolshevik.

bolchevismo *m* Bolshevism.

bolea *f* DEP volley.

bolear *vt Amer* to shine, to polish.

bolera *f* bowling alley.

bolería *f Amer* shoeshine store.

bolero *m* **-1.** [baile y música] bolero. **-2.** *Amer* [limpiabotas] shoeshine.

boletería *f Amer* box office, ticket office.

boletero, -ra *m y f Amer* box office attendant.

boletín *m* journal, periodical; **~ de noticias** ○ **informativo** news bulletin; **~ meteoroló-**

gico weather forecast; **~ de prensa** press release; **~ de subscripción** subscription form.

boleto *m* **-1.** [de lotería, rifa] ticket; [de quinielas] coupon; **~ de apuestas** betting slip. **-2.** *Amer* [billete] ticket.

boli *m fam* Biro®.

boliche *m* **-1.** [en la petanca] jack. **-2.** [bolos] ten-pin bowling. **-3.** [bolera] bowling alley. **-4.** *Amer* [tienda] small grocery store.

bólido *m* racing car; **ir como un ~** *fig* to go like the clappers.

bolígrafo *m* ballpoint pen, Biro®.

bolillo *m* **-1.** [en costura] bobbin. **-2.** *Amer* [panecillo] bread roll.

bolitas *fpl Amer* marbles.

bolívar *m* bolivar.

Bolivia Bolivia.

boliviano, -na *adj, m y f* Bolivian.

bollería *f* **-1.** [tienda] cake shop. **-2.** [productos] cakes (*pl*).

bollo *m* **-1.** [para comer - de pan] (bread) roll; [- dulce] bun. **-2.** [abolladura] dent; [abultamiento] bump.

bolo *m* **-1.** DEP [pieza] skittle. **-2.** [actuación] show. **-3.** *Amer* [borracho] drunk.
◆ **bolos** *mpl* [deporte] skittles.

bolsa *f* **-1.** [gen] bag; **~ de agua caliente** hot-water bottle; **~ de aire** air pocket; **~ de basura** bin liner; **~ de deportes** holdall, sports bag; **~ de plástico** [en tiendas] carrier ○ plastic bag; **~ de viaje** travel bag. **-2.** FIN: **~ (de valores)** stock exchange, stock market; **la ~ ha subido/bajado** share prices have gone up/down; **jugar a la ~** to speculate on the stock market. **-3.** MIN pocket. **-4.** ANAT sac. **-5.** *Amer* [saco de dormir] sleeping bag.
◆ **bolsa de trabajo** *f* employment bureau, labour exchange.

bolsillo *m* pocket; **de ~** pocket (*antes de sust*); **lo pagué de mi ~** I paid for it out of my own pocket; **meterse** ○ **tener a alguien en el ~** to have sb eating out of one's hand; **rascarse el ~** *fam* to fork out.

bolso *m* bag; [de mujer] handbag.

boludo, -da *m y f Amer mfam* prat *Br*, jerk *Am*.

bomba ◇ *f* **-1.** [explosivo] bomb; **~ atómica** atom ○ nuclear bomb; **~ H** ○ **de hidrógeno** H ○ hydrogen bomb; **~ lacrimógena** tear gas grenade; **~ de mano** (hand) grenade; **~ de neutrones** neutron bomb; **~ de relojería** time bomb; **-2.** [máquina] pump; **~ de cobalto** MED cobalt bomb; **~ hidráulica** hydraulic pump. **-3.** *fig* [acontecimiento] bombshell; **caer como una ~** to be a

bombshell. -4. *Amer* [gasolinera] petrol station *Br*, gas station *Am*. **-5.** *loc*: **pasarlo ~** *fam* to have a great time. ◇ *adj inv fam* astounding.

bombachas *fpl Amer* knickers.

bombachos *mpl* baggy trousers.

bombardear *vt lit* & *fig* to bombard.

bombardeo *m* bombardment; **~ aéreo** air raid; **~ atómico** FÍS bombardment in a particle accelerator.

bombardero, -ra *adj* bombing (*antes de sust*).
◆ **bombardero** *m* [avión] bomber.

bombazo *m* **-1.** [explosión] explosion, blast. **-2.** *fig* [noticia] bombshell.

bombear *vt* [gen & DEP] to pump.

bombeo *m* **-1.** [de líquido] pumping. **-2.** [abombamiento] bulge.

bombero, -ra *m y f* **-1.** [de incendios] fireman (*f* firewoman). **-2.** *Amer* [de gasolinera] petrol-pump *Br* O gas-pump *Am* attendant.

bombilla *f* light bulb.

bombillo *m Amer* light bulb.

bombín *m* bowler (hat).

bombo *m* **-1.** MÚS bass drum; **estar con ~** *fam fig* to be in the family way. **-2.** *fam fig* [elogio] hype; **a ~ y platillo** with a lot of hype. **-3.** MEC drum.

bombón *m* **-1.** [golosina] chocolate. **-2.** *fam fig* [mujer] peach.

bombona *f* cylinder; **~ de butano** (butane) gas cylinder.

bonachón, -ona *fam* ◇ *adj* kindly. ◇ *m y f* kindly person.

bonaerense *adj* of/relating to Buenos Aires.

bonancible *adj* [tiempo] fair; [mar] calm.

bonanza *f* **-1.** [de tiempo] fair weather; [de mar] calm at sea. **-2.** *fig* [prosperidad] prosperity.

bondad *f* [cualidad] goodness; [inclinación] kindness; **tener la ~ de hacer algo** to be kind enough to do sthg.

bondadoso, -sa *adj* kind, good-natured.

bonete *m* [eclesiástico] biretta; [universitario] mortarboard.

bongo, bongó *m* bongo (drum).

boniato *m* sweet potato.

bonificación *f* **-1.** [descuento] discount. **-2.** [mejora] improvement.

bonificar [10] *vt* **-1.** [descontar] to give a discount of. **-2.** [mejorar] to improve.

bonito, -ta *adj* pretty; [bueno] nice.
◆ **bonito** *m* bonito (tuna).

bono *m* **-1.** [vale] voucher. **-2.** COM bond; **~ basura/de caja** junk/short-term bond; **~ del** Estado/del tesoro government/treasury bond.

bonobús *m* multiple-journey ticket.

bonoloto *m Spanish state-run lottery*.

BONOLOTO:
In this Spanish state-run lottery participants try to guess a combination of six numbers between one and forty-nine. It is drawn four times a week

bonsai *m* bonsai.

boñiga *f* cowpat.

boom *m* boom.

boquerón *m* (fresh) anchovy.

boquete *m* hole.

boquiabierto, -ta *adj* open-mouthed; *fig* astounded, speechless.

boquilla *f* **-1.** [para fumar] cigarette holder. **-2.** [de pipa, instrumento musical] mouthpiece. **-3.** [de tubo, aparato] nozzle.
◆ **de boquilla** *loc adv fam*: **ser todo de ~** to be all hot air.

borbónico, -ca *adj* Bourbon.

borbotear, borbotar *vi* to bubble.

borbotón *m*: **salir a borbotones** to gush out.

borda *f* NÁUT gunwale; **tirar** O **echar algo por la ~** *fig* to throw sthg overboard.
◆ **fuera borda** *m* [barco] outboard motorboat; [motor] outboard motor.

bordado, -da *adj* embroidered.
◆ **bordado** *m* embroidery.

bordadura *f* embroidery.

bordar *vt* **-1.** [coser] to embroider. **-2.** *fig* [hacer bien] to do excellently.

borde ◇ *m* [gen] edge; [de carretera] side; [del mar] shore, seaside; [de río] bank; [de vaso, botella] rim; **al ~ de** *fig* on the verge O brink of. ◇ *m y f mfam* [antipático] stroppy person. ◇ *adj mfam* [antipático] stroppy, miserable.

bordear *vt* **-1.** [estar alrededor de] to border; [moverse alrededor de] to skirt (round). **-2.** *fig* [rozar] to be close to.

bordillo *m* kerb.

bordo *m* NÁUT board, side.
◆ **a bordo** *loc adv* on board.

boreal *adj* northern.

borgoña *m* burgundy.

bórico *adj* boric.

borla *f* tassel; [pompón] pompom.

borne *m* terminal.

Borneo Borneo.

boro *m* boron.

borrachera f -1. [embriaguez] drunkenness (U). -2. fig [emoción] intoxication.

borrachín, -ina m y f fam boozer.

borracho, -cha ◇ adj -1. [ebrio] drunk. -2. fig [emocionado]: ~ de drunk ○ intoxicated with. ◇ m y f [persona] drunk.
◆ **borracho** m [bizcocho] sponge soaked in alcohol, ≃ rum baba.

borrador m -1. [escrito] rough draft. -2. [goma de borrar] rubber Br, eraser Am.

borraja f borage.

borrar vt -1. [hacer desaparecer - con goma] to rub out Br, to erase Am; [- en ordenador] to delete; [- en casete] to erase. -2. [tachar] to cross out; fig [de lista etc] to take off. -3. fig [olvidar] to erase.
◆ **borrarse** vpr -1. [desaparecer] to disappear. -2. fig [olvidarse] to be wiped away.

borrasca f thunderstorm.

borrascoso, -sa adj stormy.

borrego, -ga m y f -1. [animal] lamb. -2. fam despec [persona] cretin, moron.

borrico, -ca m y f donkey; fig ass.

borriquero → cardo.

borrón m blot; fig blemish; **hacer ~ y cuenta nueva** to wipe the slate clean.

borroso, -sa adj [foto. visión] blurred; [escritura, texto] smudgy.

Bosnia Herzegovina Bosnia Herzegovina.

bosnio, -nia adj, m y f Bosnian.

bosque m [pequeño] wood; [grande] forest.

bosquejar vt -1. [esbozar] to sketch (out). -2. fig [dar una idea de] to give a rough outline of.

bosquejo m -1. [esbozo] sketch. -2. fig [de idea, tema, situación] rough outline.

bossa-nova f bossa nova.

bostezar [13] vi to yawn.

bostezo m yawn.

bota f -1. [calzado] boot; ~s **camperas/de montar** cowboy/riding boots; ~s **de agua** ○ **de lluvia** wellingtons; ~s **de goma** gumboots; **morir con las ~s puestas** fam to die with one's boots on; **ponerse las ~s** fam [comiendo] to stuff one's face. -2. [de vino] small leather container in which wine is kept.

botadura f launching.

botafumeiro m censer.

botana f Amer snack, tapa.

botánico, -ca ◇ adj botanical. ◇ m y f [persona] botanist.
◆ **botánica** f [ciencia] botany.

botanista m y f botanist.

botar ◇ vt -1. NÁUT to launch. -2. fam [despedir] to throw ○ kick out. -3. [pelota] to bounce. -4. DEP [córner etc] to take. -5. Amer [tirar] to throw away. ◇ vi -1. [saltar] to jump; **está que bota** fam fig he/she is hopping mad. -2. [pelota] to bounce.

botarate m fam despec madcap.

botavara f boom.

bote m -1. [tarro] jar; ~ **de humo** smoke canister. -2. [lata] can. -3. [botella de plástico] bottle. -4. [barca] boat; ~ **salvavidas** lifeboat. -5. [propinas] tips (pl); **dar algo de ~** to give sthg as a tip. -6. [salto] jump; **dar ~s** [gen] to jump up and down; [en tren, coche] to bump up and down. -7. [de pelota] bounce; **dar ~s** to bounce. -8. loc: **chupar del ~** fam to feather one's nest; **tener en el ~ a alguien** fam to have sb eating out of one's hand.
◆ **a bote pronto** loc adv -1. DEP on the rebound. -2. fig [sin pensar] off the top of one's head.
◆ **de bote en bote** loc adv chock-a-block.

botella f bottle; ~ **de oxígeno** oxygen cylinder.

botellazo m blow with a bottle.

botellero m wine rack.

botellín m small bottle.

botica f desus pharmacy, chemist's (shop) Br.

boticario, -ria m y f desus pharmacist, chemist Br.

botijo m earthenware jug.

botillería f Amer liquor store.

botín m -1. [de guerra, atraco] plunder, loot. -2. [calzado] ankle boot.

botiquín m [caja] first-aid kit; [mueble] first-aid cupboard.

botón m button.
◆ **botones** m inv [de hotel] bellboy, bellhop Am; [de oficinas etc] errand boy.
◆ **botón de muestra** m sample.

botonadura f buttons (pl).

Botsuana Botswana.

botulismo m botulism.

bouillabaisse = bullabesa.

boulder m DEP bouldering.

bouquet = buqué.

bourbon ['burbon] m bourbon.

boutique [bu'tik] f boutique.

bóveda f ARQUIT vault.
◆ **bóveda celeste** f firmament.
◆ **bóveda craneal** f cranial vault.

bovino, -na adj bovine.
◆ **bovinos** mpl cattle (U).

box (pl boxes) m -1. [de caballo] stall. -2. [de coches] pit; **entrar en ~es** to make a pit stop. -3. Amer DEP [boxeo] boxing.

boxeador, -ra m y f boxer.

boxear *vi* to box.

boxeo *m* boxing.

bóxer (*pl* **bóxers**) *m* boxer.

boya *f* **-1.** [en el mar] buoy. **-2.** [de una red] float.

boyante *adj* **-1.** [feliz] happy. **-2.** [próspero - empresa, negocio] prosperous; [- economía, comercio] buoyant.

boycot *etc* = **boicot**.

boy scout [bois'kaut] *m* boy scout.

bozal *m* **-1.** [gen] muzzle. **-2.** *Amer* [cabestro] halter.

Br. *abrev de* **bachiller**.

bracear *vi* **-1.** [mover los brazos] to wave one's arms about. **-2.** [nadar] to swim.

bracero *m* day labourer.

braga *f* (*gen pl*) knickers (*pl*).

bragazas *m inv fam despec* henpecked man.

braguero *m* truss.

bragueta *f* flies (*pl*) *Br*, zipper *Am*.

braguetazo *m fam* marriage for money.

brahmán = **bramán**.

brahmanismo = **bramanismo**.

braille ['braile] *m* Braille.

brainstorming [breins'tormin] (*pl* **brainstormings**) *m* brainstorming session.

bramán, brahmán *m* Brahman.

bramanismo, brahmanismo *m* Brahmanism.

bramante *m* string.

bramar *vi* **-1.** [animal] to bellow. **-2.** [persona - de dolor] to groan; [- de ira] to roar.

bramido *m* **-1.** [de animal] bellow. **-2.** [de persona - de dolor] groan; [- de ira] roar.

brandy, brandi *m* brandy.

branquia *f* (*gen pl*) gill.

brasa *f* ember; **a la** ~ CULIN barbecued.

brasear *vt* to barbecue.

brasero *m* brazier.

brasier, brassier *m Amer* bra.

Brasil: (el) ~ Brazil.

brasileño, -ña *adj, m y f* Brazilian.

brasilero, -ra *adj, m y f Amer* Brazilian.

Brasilia Brasilia.

brassier = **brasier**.

Bratislava Bratislava.

bravata *f* (*gen pl*) **-1.** [amenaza] threat. **-2.** [fanfarronería] bravado (*U*).

braveza *f* bravery.

bravío, -a *adj* [salvaje] wild; [feroz] fierce.

bravo, -va *adj* **-1.** [valiente] brave. **-2.** [animal] wild. **-3.** [mar] rough.
◆ **bravo** ◇ *m* [aplauso] cheer. ◇ *interj*: ¡~! bravo!

◆ **por las bravas** *loc adv* by force.

bravucón, -ona *despec* ◇ *adj* swaggering. ◇ *m y f* braggart.

bravuconada *f despec* show of bravado.

bravuconear *vi despec* to brag.

bravuconería *f despec* bravado.

bravura *f* **-1.** [de persona] bravery. **-2.** [de animal] ferocity.

braza *f* **-1.** DEP breaststroke; **nadar a** ~ to swim breaststroke. **-2.** [medida] fathom.

brazada *f* stroke.

brazalete *m* **-1.** [en la muñeca] bracelet. **-2.** [en el brazo] armband.

brazo *m* **-1.** [gen & ANAT] arm; [de animal] foreleg; **cogidos del** ~ arm in arm; **en** ~s in one's arms; **luchar a** ~ **partido** [con empeño] to fight tooth and nail; **con los** ~s **abiertos** with open arms; **quedarse** ◇ **estarse con los** ~s **cruzados** [*fig*] to sit around doing nothing; **no dar su** ~ **a torcer** not to give an inch; **ser el** ~ **derecho de alguien** to be sb's right-hand man (*f* woman). **-2.** [de árbol, río, candelabro] branch; [de grúa] boom, jib. **-3.** *fig* [trabajador] hand.
◆ **brazo de gitano** *m* ≈ swiss roll.
◆ **brazo de mar** *m* GEOGR arm (*of the sea*).

Brazzaville [bratsa'ßil] Brazzaville.

brea *f* **-1.** [sustancia] tar. **-2.** [para barco] pitch.

brear *vt fam fig* [a palos] to bash in; [a preguntas] to bombard.

brebaje *m* concoction, foul drink.

brecha *f* **-1.** [abertura] hole, opening. **-2.** MIL breach. **-3.** *fig* [impresión] impression. **-4.** *loc*: **estar siempre en la** ~ [amigo etc] always to be there (when one is needed); [socio, empleado] to work tirelessly; [deportista, artista] always to be up there with the best.

brécol *m* broccoli.

brega *f* [lucha] struggle, fight.

bregar [16] *vi* **-1.** [luchar] to struggle. **-2.** [trabajar] to work hard. **-3.** [reñir] to quarrel.

breña *f* scrub.

brete *m* fix, difficulty; **estar en un** ~ to be in a fix; **poner a alguien en un** ~ to put sb in a difficult position.

breteles *mpl inv Amer* braces.

breva *f* **-1.** [fruta] early fig. **-2.** [cigarro] flat cigar. **-3.** *loc*: **¡no caerá esa** ~! *fam* some chance (of that happening)!

breve ◇ *adj* brief; **en** ~ [pronto] shortly; [en pocas palabras] in short. ◇ *f* MUS breve.

brevedad *f* shortness; **a** ◇ **con la mayor** ~ as soon as possible.

breviario *m* **-1.** RELIG breviary. **-2.** [compendio] compendium.

brezal *m* moorland (*U*), moors (*pl*).

brezo *m* heather.

bribón, -ona *m y f* scoundrel, rogue.

bricolaje, **bricolage** *m* D.I.Y., do-it-yourself.

brida *f* **-1.** [de caballo] bridle. **-2.** [de tubo] bracket, collar. **-3.** MED adhesion.

bridge *m* bridge.

Bridgetown [bridʒ'taun] Bridgetown.

brigada ◇ *m* MIL ≃ warrant officer. ◇ *f* **-1.** MIL brigade. **-2.** [equipo] squad, team; ~ **antidisturbios/antidroga** riot/drug squad.

brigadier *m* brigadier.

brillante ◇ *adj* **-1.** [reluciente - luz, astro] shining; [- metal, zapatos, pelo] shiny; [- ojos, sonrisa, diamante] sparkling. **-2.** [magnífico] brilliant. ◇ *m* diamond.

brillantez *f fig* brilliance.

brillantina *f* brilliantine, Brylcreem®.

brillar *vi lit & fig* to shine.

brillo *m* **-1.** [resplandor - de luz] brilliance; [- de estrellas] shining; [- de zapatos] shine; **sacar** ~ **a** to polish, to shine. **-2.** [lucimiento] splendour, brilliance.

brilloso, -sa *adj Amer* shining.

brincar [10] *vi* **-1.** [saltar] to skip (about); ~ **de alegría** to jump for joy. **-2.** *fig* [enfadarse]: **está que brinca** he's hopping mad.

brinco *m* jump; **en un** ~ *fig* in a second, quickly.

brindar ◇ *vi* to drink a toast; ~ **por algo/alguien** to drink to sthg/sb. ◇ *vt* to offer.
◆ **brindarse** *vpr*: **-se a hacer algo** to offer to do sthg.

brindis *m inv* toast.

brinque *etc* → **brincar**.

brío *m* [energía, decisión] spirit, verve.

brioso, -sa *adj* spirited, lively.

brisa *f* breeze.

británico, -ca ◇ *adj* British. ◇ *m y f* British person, Briton; **los ~s** the British.

brizna *f* **-1.** [filamento - de hierba] blade; [- de tabaco] strand. **-2.** *fig* [un poco] trace, bit.

broca *f* (drill) bit.

brocado *m* brocade.

brocal *m* curb, parapet.

brocha *f* brush; ~ **de afeitar** shaving brush.

brochazo *m* brushstroke.

broche *m* **-1.** [cierre] clasp, fastener. **-2.** [joya] brooch; ~ **de oro** *fig* final flourish.

brocheta *f* CULIN shish kebab; [aguja] skewer.

broma *f* [ocurrencia, chiste] joke; [jugarreta] prank, practical joke; **en** ~ as a joke; **gastar una** ~ **a alguien** to play a joke ○ prank on

sb; **tomar algo a** ~ not to take sthg seriously; ~ **de mal gusto** bad joke; ~ **pesada** nasty practical joke; **ni en** ~ *fig* no way, not on your life.

bromear *vi* to joke.

bromista ◇ *adj* fond of playing jokes. ◇ *m y f* joker.

bromo *m* bromine.

bromuro *m* bromide.

bronca → **bronco**.

bronce *m* **-1.** [aleación] bronze. **-2.** [estatua] bronze (statue).

bronceado, -da *adj* tanned.
◆ **bronceado** *m* tan.

bronceador, -ra *adj* tanning (*antes de sust*), suntan (*antes de sust*).
◆ **bronceador** *m* [loción] suntan lotion; [leche] suntan cream.

broncear *vt* to tan.
◆ **broncearse** *vpr* to get a tan.

bronco, -ca *adj* **-1.** [tosco] rough; [paisaje, peñascos] rugged. **-2.** [grave - voz] harsh; [- tos] throaty. **-3.** *fig* [brusco] gruff, surly.
◆ **bronca** *f* **-1.** [jaleo] row; **armar (una) bronca** to kick up a row; **buscar bronca** to look for trouble. **-2.** [regañina] scolding, telling-off; **echar una bronca a alguien** to give sb a row, to tell sb off. **-3.** *Amer* [enfado]: **me da** ~ it makes me mad.

bronquial *adj* bronchial.

bronquio *m* bronchial tube.

bronquitis *f inv* bronchitis.

broquel *m* **-1.** [escudo] small shield. **-2.** *fig* [amparo] shield.

brotar *vi* **-1.** [planta] to sprout, to bud. **-2.** [agua, sangre etc]: ~ **de** to well up out of. **-3.** *fig* [esperanza, sospechas, pasiones] to stir. **-4.** [en la piel]: **le brotó un sarpullido** he broke out in a rash.

brote *m* **-1.** [de planta] bud, shoot. **-2.** *fig* [inicios] sign, hint.

broza *f* **-1.** [maleza] brush, scrub. **-2.** *fig* [relleno] waffle.

bruces
◆ **de bruces** *loc adv* face down; **se cayó de** ~ he fell flat on his face.

bruja → **brujo**.

Brujas Bruges.

brujería *f* witchcraft, sorcery.

brujo, -ja *adj* [hechicero] enchanting.
◆ **brujo** *m* wizard, sorcerer.
◆ **bruja** ◇ *f* **-1.** [hechicera] witch, sorceress. **-2.** [mujer fea] hag. **-3.** [mujer mala] (old) witch. ◇ *adj inv Amer fam* [sin dinero] broke, skint.

brújula *f* compass.

bruma *f* [niebla] mist; [en el mar] sea mist.

brumoso, -sa *adj* misty.
bruñido *m* polishing.
bruñir *vt* to polish.
brusco, -ca *adj* **-1.** [repentino, imprevisto] sudden, abrupt. **-2.** [tosco, grosero] brusque.
Bruselas Brussels.
bruselense *adj* of/relating to Brussels.
brusquedad *f* **-1.** [imprevisión] suddenness, abruptness. **-2.** [grosería] brusqueness.
brut *m inv* brut.
brutal *adj* **-1.** [violento] brutal. **-2.** *fam* [extraordinario] tremendous.
brutalidad *f* **-1.** [cualidad] brutality. **-2.** [acción] brutal act.
bruto, -ta ◇ *adj* **-1.** [torpe] clumsy; [ignorante] thick, stupid; [maleducado] rude. **-2.** [sin tratar]: **en** ~ [diamante] uncut; [petróleo] crude. **-3.** [sueldo, peso etc] gross. ◇ *m y f* brute.
Bta. *abrev de* beata.
Bto. *abrev de* beato.
bubónica → peste.
bucal *adj* oral.
bucanero *m* buccaneer.
Bucarest Bucharest.
buceador, -ra *m y f* (underwater) diver.
bucear *vi* **-1.** [en agua] to dive, to swim underwater. **-2.** *fig* [investigar]: ~ **en** to delve into.
buceo *m* (underwater) diving.
buche *m* **-1.** [de ave] crop. **-2.** [de animal] maw. **-3.** *fam* [de persona] belly.
bucle *m* **-1.** [rizo] curl, ringlet. **-2.** AUTOM & INFORM loop.
bucólico, -ca *adj* **-1.** [campestre] country (*antes de sust*). **-2.** LITER bucolic.
Budapest Budapest.
budín *m* pudding.
budismo *m* Buddhism.
budista *adj, m y f* Buddhist.
buen → bueno.
buenamente *adv*: hice lo que ~ pude I did what I could, I did as much as I could.
buenas → bueno.
buenaventura *f* **-1.** [adivinación] fortune; leer la ~ a alguien to tell sb's fortune. **-2.** [suerte] good luck.
bueno, -na (*compar* mejor, *superl* el mejor, la mejor) *adj* (*antes de sust masculino:* **buen**) **-1.** [gen] good. **-2.** [bondadoso] kind, good; ser ~ con alguien to be good to sb. **-3.** [curado, sano] well, all right. **-4.** [apacible - tiempo, clima] nice, fine. **-5.** [aprovechable] all right; [comida] fresh. **-6.** [uso enfático]: ese buen hombre that good man; un buen día one fine day. **-7.** *loc*: de buen ver good-

looking, attractive; de buenas a primeras [de repente] all of a sudden; [a simple vista] at first sight, on the face of it; estar ~ *fam* [persona] to be a bit of all right, to be tasty; estar de buenas to be in a good mood; estaría ~ *irón* that would really cap it all; librarse de una buena to have a narrow escape; lo ~ es que ... the best thing about it is that ...; poner ~ a alguien *irón* to criticize sb harshly; por las buenas willingly.
◆ **bueno** ◇ *m* CIN: el ~ the goody. ◇ *adv* **-1.** [vale, de acuerdo] all right, O.K. **-2.** [pues] well. ◇ *interj* Amer [al teléfono]: ¡~! hello.
◆ **buenas** *interj*: ¡buenas! hello!
Buenos Aires Buenos Aires.
buey (*pl* bueyes) *m* ox.
bueyada *f* Amer drove of oxen.
búfalo *m* buffalo.
bufanda *f* scarf.
bufar *vi* **-1.** [toro, caballo] to snort. **-2.** *fig* [persona] to be furious.
bufé (*pl* bufés), **buffet** (*pl* buffets) *m* **-1.** [en restaurante] buffet. **-2.** [mueble] sideboard.
bufete *m* lawyer's practice.
buffer ['bafer] (*pl* buffers) *m* INFORM buffer.
buffet = bufé.
bufido *m* **-1.** [de toro, caballo] snort. **-2.** *fam* [de persona] fit of rage.
bufo, -fa *adj* [gen & MÚS] comic.
bufón *m* buffoon, jester.
bufonada *f fig* clowning around (*U*).
bug [buk] *m* INFORM bug.
buganvilla *f* bougainvillea.
buhardilla *f* **-1.** [habitación] attic. **-2.** [ventana] dormer (window).
búho *m* owl.
buhonero, -ra *m y f* hawker, pedlar.
buitre *m* lit & fig vulture.
bujía *f* AUTOM spark plug.
bula *f* [documento] (papal) bull.
bulbo *m* ANAT & BOT bulb; ~ raquídeo rachidian bulb.
buldog (*pl* buldogs), **bulldog** (*pl* bulldogs) [bul'dox] *m* bulldog.
buldozer (*pl* buldozers), **bulldozer** (*pl* bulldozers) [bul'doθer] *m* bulldozer.
bulerías *fpl* popular Andalusian song and dance.
bulevar (*pl* bulevares) *m* boulevard.
Bulgaria Bulgaria.
búlgaro, -ra *adj, m y f* Bulgarian.
◆ **búlgaro** *m* [lengua] Bulgarian.
bulimia *f* bulimia.
bulín *m* Amer bachelor flat.

bulla f racket, uproar; **armar** ~ to kick up a racket.

bullabesa, bouillabaisse [buja'ßes] f CULIN bouillabaisse.

bullanguero, -ra ◇ adj noisy, rowdy. ◇ m, f noisy ○ boisterous person.

bulldog = buldog.

bulldozer = buldozer.

bullicio m [de ciudad, mercado] hustle and bustle; [de multitud] hubbub.

bullicioso, -sa ◇ adj -1. [agitado - reunión, multitud] noisy; [- calle, mercado] busy, bustling. -2. [inquieto] rowdy, boisterous. ◇ m y f boisterous person.

bullir vi -1. [hervir] to boil; [burbujear] to bubble. -2. fig [multitud] to bustle; [ratas, hormigas etc] to swarm; [mar] to boil; ~ **de** to seethe with.
◆ **bullirse** vpr to budge, to move.

bulo m false rumour.

bulto m -1. [volumen] bulk, size; **a** ~ approximately, roughly; **hacer mucho** ~ to take up a lot of space; **de** ~ glaringly obvious; **escurrir el** ~ [trabajo] to shirk; [cuestión] to evade the issue. -2. [abombamiento - en rodilla, superficie etc] bump; [- en maleta, bolsillo etc] bulge. -3. [forma imprecisa] blurred shape. -4. [paquete] package; [maleta] item of luggage; [fardo] bundle; ~ **de mano** ○ item of hand luggage.

bumerán (pl **bumeráns**), **bumerang** (pl **bumerangs**) m boomerang.

bungalow [buŋga'lo] (pl **bungalows**) m bungalow.

búnquer (pl **búnquers**), **bunker** (pl **bunkers**) m -1. [refugio] bunker. -2. POLÍT reactionary forces (pl).

buñuelo m [CULIN - dulce] ≃ doughnut; [- de bacalao etc] ≃ dumpling; ~ **de viento** doughnut.

buñolería f stand or shop selling doughnuts.

BUP m academically orientated secondary-school course formerly taught in Spain, now known as the 'bachillerato'.

buque m ship; ~ **de carga** cargo ship; ~ **de guerra** warship; ~ **nodriza** supply ship; ~ **de pasajeros** passenger ship, liner; ~ **de vapor** steamer, steamship.

buqué, bouquet [bu'ke] m bouquet.

burbuja f bubble; **con** ~s fizzy; **hacer** ~s to bubble.

burbujear vi to bubble.

burbujeo m bubbling.

burdel m brothel.

burdeos ◇ adj inv maroon. ◇ m inv Bordeaux.

Burdeos Bordeaux.

burdo, -da adj [gen] crude; [tela] coarse.

burgués, -esa ◇ adj middle-class, bourgeois. ◇ m y f member of the middle class; HIST & POLÍT member of the bourgeoisie.

burguesía f middle class; HIST & POLÍT bourgeoisie; **alta** ~ upper middle class; HIST & POLÍT haute bourgeoisie.

burla f -1. [mofa] taunt; **hacer** ~ **de** to mock; ~s **aparte** joking aside. -2. [broma] joke. -3. [engaño] trick.
◆ **burlas** fpl ridicule (U), mockery (U).

burladero m TAUROM wooden board behind which bullfighter can hide from bull.

burlador m Casanova, Don Juan.

burlar vt [esquivar] to evade; [ley] to flout; **burla burlando** fig without anyone noticing.
◆ **burlarse de** vpr to mock, to make fun of.

burlesco, -ca adj [tono] jocular; LITER burlesque.

burlete m draught excluder.

burlón, -ona adj -1. [bromista] waggish, fond of telling jokes. -2. [sarcástico] mocking.

buró m -1. [escritorio] bureau, writing desk. -2. POLÍT executive committee. -3. Amer [mesa de noche] bedside table.

burocracia f bureaucracy.

burócrata m y f bureaucrat.

burocrático, -ca adj bureaucratic.

burocratizar [13] vt to bureaucratize.

burrada f -1. [acción, dicho]: **hacer** ~s to act stupidly; **decir** ~s to talk nonsense. -2. fam [cantidad]: **una** ~ **(de)** tons (pl) (of), masses (pl) (of).

burro, -rra ◇ adj [necio] stupid, dim. ◇ m y f -1. [animal] donkey; **apearse** ○ **bajarse del** ~ fam to back down; **no ver tres en un** ~ fam to be as blind as a bat. -2. fam [necio] ass, dimwit. -3. fam [trabajador]: ~ **(de carga)** workhorse.

bursátil adj stock-market (antes de sust).

bus (pl **buses**) m AUTOM & INFORM bus.

busca ◇ f search; **en** ~ **de** in search of; **la** ~ **de** the search for; **andar a la** ~ fig to find a way of getting by. ◇ m → **buscapersonas**.

buscador, -ra m y f hunter; ~ **de oro** gold prospector.

buscapersonas, busca m inv bleeper, pager.

buscapiés m inv firecracker, jumping jack.

buscapleitos m y f inv troubleseeker.

buscar [10] ◇ *vt* **-1.** [gen] to look for; [provecho, beneficio propio] to seek; **voy a ~ el periódico** I'm going for the paper ○ to get the paper; **ir a ~ a alguien** to pick sb up. **-2.** [en diccionario, índice, horario] to look up. **-3.** INFORM to search for. **-4.** *fam* [provocar] to push, to try the patience of. ◇ *vi* to look.
◆ **buscarse** *vpr* **-1.** [castigo etc]: **buscársela** to be asking for it. **-2.** [personal, aprendiz etc]: **"se busca camarero"** "waiter wanted".
buscavidas *m y f inv fam* **-1.** [ambicioso] go-getter. **-2.** [entrometido] nosy parker *Br.*
buscón, -ona *m y f* [estafador] swindler.
◆ **buscona** *f fam despec* [prostituta] whore.
buseta *f Amer* minibus.
busque *etc* → **buscar**.
búsqueda *f* search.
busto *m* **-1.** [pecho] chest; [de mujer] bust. **-2.** [escultura] bust.
butaca *f* **-1.** [mueble] armchair. **-2.** [localidad] seat.
butacón *m* large easy chair.
butano *m* butane (gas).
buten
◆ **de buten** *loc adj fam* wicked, terrific.
butifarra *f type of Catalan pork sausage.*
buzo *m* **-1.** [persona] diver. **-2.** *Amer* [chandal] tracksuit.
buzón *m* letter box; **echar algo al ~** to post sthg.
byte [bait] (*pl* **bytes**) *m* INFORM byte.

c, C *f* [letra] c, C.
c., c/ (*abrev de* **calle**) St.
c / **-1.** (*abrev de* **cuenta**) a/c. **-2.** = **c**.
cabal *adj* **-1.** [honrado] upright, honest. **-2.** [exacto] exact; [completo] complete; **a los nueve meses ~es** at exactly nine months.
◆ **cabales** *mpl*: **no estar en sus ~es** not to be in one's right mind.
cábala *f* **-1.** [doctrina] cabbala. **-2.** (*gen pl*) [conjeturas] guess; **hacer ~s** to speculate, to guess.
cabalgadura *f* mount.
cabalgar [16] *vi* to ride.

cabalgata *f* cavalcade, procession.
cabalístico, -ca *adj* **-1.** [de cábala] cabbalistic. **-2.** *fig* [oculto] mysterious.
◆ **cabalística** *f* cabbalism.
caballa *f* mackerel.
caballar *adj* equine, horse (*antes de sust*).
caballeresco, -ca *adj* **-1.** [persona, modales] chivalrous. **-2.** [literatura] chivalric.
caballería *f* **-1.** [animal] mount, horse. **-2.** [cuerpo militar] cavalry.
caballeriza *f* stable.
caballerizo *m* groom, stable lad.
caballero ◇ *adj* [cortés] gentlemanly. ◇ *m* **-1.** [gen] gentleman; [al dirigir la palabra] sir; **ser todo un ~** to be a real gentleman; **"caballeros"** [en aseos] "gents"; [en grandes almacenes] "menswear". **-2.** [miembro de una orden] knight; **~ andante** knight errant. **-3.** [noble] nobleman.
caballerosidad *f* chivalry.
caballeroso, -sa *adj* chivalrous.
caballete *m* **-1.** [de lienzo] easel. **-2.** [de mesa] trestle. **-3.** [de nariz] bridge. **-4.** [de tejado] ridge.
caballito *m* small horse, pony.
◆ **caballitos** *mpl* [de feria] merry-go-round (*sg*).
◆ **caballito de mar** *m* sea horse.
caballo *m* **-1.** [animal] horse; **montar a ~** to ride. **-2.** [pieza de ajedrez] knight. **-3.** [naipe] ≃ queen. **-4.** MEC: **~ (de fuerza ○ de vapor)** horsepower. **-5.** *mfam* [heroína] smack. **-6.** *loc:* **estar a ~ entre dos cosas** to be halfway between two things; **a ~ regalado no le mires el diente** ○ **el dentado** *proverb* don't look a gift horse in the mouth *proverb.*
◆ **caballo de batalla** *m* **-1.** [dificultad, escollo] bone of contention. **-2.** [objetivo, obsesión] hobbyhorse.
◆ **caballo marino** *m* sea horse.
cabaña *f* **-1.** [choza] hut, cabin. **-2.** [ganado] livestock (*U*).
cabaret (*pl* **cabarets**) *m* cabaret.
cabaretera *f* cabaret girl.
cabe *prep culto* near.
cabecear *vi* **-1.** [persona - negando] to shake one's head; [- afirmando] to nod one's head. **-2.** [caballo] to toss its head. **-3.** [dormir] to nod (off). **-4.** [en fútbol] to head the ball. **-5.** [balancearse - coche] to lurch; [- barco] to pitch.
cabecera *f* **-1.** [gen] head; [de cama] headboard. **-2.** [de texto] heading; [de periódico] headline. **-3.** [de río] headwaters (*pl*).
cabecilla *m y f* ringleader.
cabellera *f* long hair (*U*).

cabello *m* hair (U).
◆ **cabello de ángel** *m* CULIN pumpkin and syrup preserve.

cabelludo, -da *adj* hairy.

caber [54] *vi* -1. [gen] to fit; **no cabe nadie más** there's no room for anyone else; **no me cabe en el dedo** it won't fit my finger; ~ **por** to go through. -2. MAT: **nueve entre tres caben a tres** three into nine goes three (times). -3. [ser posible] to be possible; **cabe destacar que ...** it's worth pointing out that ...; **cabe preguntarse si ...** one might ask whether .... -4. *loc*: **dentro de lo que cabe** as far as possible; **no ~ en sí de gozo/celos** to be beside o.s. with joy/jealousy.

cabestrante, cabrestante *m* capstan.

cabestrillo
◆ **en cabestrillo** *loc adj* in a sling.

cabestro *m* -1. [cuerda] halter. -2. [animal] leading ox.

cabeza *f* -1. [gen] head; ~ **abajo** upside down; ~ **arriba** the right way up; **por ~** per head; **obrar con ~** to use one's head; **tirarse de ~ (a)** to dive (into); **venir a la ~** to come to mind; ~ **(lectora)** [gen] head; [de tocadiscos] pickup. -2. [pelo] hair. -3. [posición] front, head; **a la ○ en ~** [en competición etc] in front, in the lead; [en lista] at the top ○ head. -4. [ciudad] main town; ~ **de partido** ≃ county town. -5. *loc*: **alzar ○ levantar** ~ to get back on one's feet, to recover; **andar ○ estar mal de la** ~ to be funny in the head; **ir de** ~ to head straight for; **meterle algo en la** ~ **a alguien** to get sthg into sb's head; **se le ha metido en la** ~ **que ...** he has got it into his head that ...; **se me pasó por la** ~ it crossed my mind; **perder la** ~ to lose one's head; **romperse la** ~ to rack one's brains; **sentar la** ~ to settle down; **se le subió a la** ~ it went to his head; **traer de** ~ **a alguien** to drive sb mad.
◆ **cabeza de ajo** *f* head of garlic.
◆ **cabeza de chorlito** *m* scatterbrain.
◆ **cabeza de familia** *m* head of the family.
◆ **cabeza de lista** *m* POLIT *person who heads a party's list of candidates.*
◆ **cabeza de turco** *f* scapegoat.

cabezada *f* -1. [de sueño] nod, nodding (U); **dar ~s** to nod off; **echar ○ dar una ~** to have a nap. -2. [golpe] butt.

cabezal *m* -1. [de aparato] head. -2. [almohada] bolster.

cabezazo *m* -1. [golpe · que se da] head butt; [· que se recibe] blow ○ bump on the head. -2. DEP header.

cabezón, -ona ◇ *adj* -1. [de cabeza grande] with a big head. -2. [terco] pigheaded, stubborn. ◇ *m y f* [terco] pigheaded ○ stubborn person.

cabezonería *f fam* pigheadedness, stubbornness.

cabezota *fam* ◇ *adj* pigheaded. ◇ *m y f* pigheaded ○ stubborn person.

cabezudo, -da *fam* ◇ *adj* pigheaded, stubborn. ◇ *m y f* pigheaded ○ stubborn person.
◆ **cabezudo** *m* [en fiesta] *giant-headed carnival figure.*

cabida *f* capacity; **dar ~ a, tener ~ para** to hold, to have room for.

cabildo *m* -1. [municipio] ≃ district council. -2. [de eclesiásticos] chapter. -3. [sala] chapterhouse.

cabina *f* -1. [locutorio] booth, cabin; ~ **de proyección** projection room; ~ **telefónica** phone box *Br*, phone booth. -2. [de avión] cockpit; [de camión] cab. -3. [vestuario · en playa] bathing hut; [· en piscina] changing cubicle.

cabinera *f Amer* air hostess.

cabizbajo, -ja *adj* crestfallen, downcast.

cable *m* cable; **echar un ~** *fam fig* to help out, to lend a hand.

cableado, -da *adj* INFORM hardwired.
◆ **cableado** *m* INFORM hardwiring.

cablegrafiar [9] *vt* to cable.

cablegrama *m* cablegram, cable.

cablevisión *f* cable television.

cabo *m* -1. GEOGR cape. -2. NÁUT cable, rope. -3. MIL corporal; ~ **primero** *military rank between corporal and sergeant.* -4. [trozo] bit, piece; [trozo final] stub, stump; [de cuerda] end. -5. *loc*: **atar ~s** to put two and two together; **no dejar ningún ~ suelto** to tie up all the loose ends; **estar al ~ de la calle** to be well-informed; **llevar algo a ~** to carry sthg out.
◆ **cabo suelto** *m* loose end.
◆ **al cabo de** *loc prep* after.
◆ **de cabo a rabo** *loc adv* from beginning to end.

cabotaje *m* coastal shipping.

Cabo Verde Cape Verde.

cabra *f* -1. [animal] goat; ~ **montés** wild goat; **estar como una ~** *fam* to be off one's head; **la ~ siempre tira al monte** *proverb* you can't make a leopard change his spots. -2. [piel] goatskin.

cabrales *m inv Asturian cheese similar to Roquefort.*

cabré → **caber**.

cabrear vt mfam: ~ **a alguien** to get sb's goat, to annoy sb.
◆ **cabrearse** vpr mfam: **~se (con)** to get really narked Br ○ pissed Am (with).

cabreo m mfam rage, fit; **cogerse** ○ **coger un** ~ to get really narked Br ○ pissed Am .

cabrero, -ra m y f goatherd.

cabrestante = cabestrante.

cabría → caber.

cabrío → macho.

cabriola f prance; **hacer ~s** to prance about.

cabrita f Amer popcorn.

cabritilla f kid, kidskin.

cabrito m **-1.** [animal] kid (goat). **-2.** mfam [cabrón] bastard, bugger Br.

cabro, -bra m y f Amer fam kid.

cabrón, -ona vulg ◇ adj: **¡qué ~ eres!** you bastard! ◇ m y f bastard (f bitch).
◆ **cabrón** m **-1.** vulg [cornudo] cuckold. **-2.** [animal] billy goat.

cabronada f vulg: **hacerle una ~ a alguien** to be a bastard to sb.

cabronazo m vulg bastard.

cabuya f Amer rope.

caca f fam **-1.** [excremento] pooh; **hacer ~** to do a pooh. **-2.** [cosa sucia] nasty ○ dirty thing. **-3.** fig [desastre] crap (U).

cacahuate m Amer peanut.

cacahuete m **-1.** [fruto] peanut. **-2.** [planta] groundnut.

cacao m **-1.** [bebida] cocoa. **-2.** [semilla] cocoa bean. **-3.** [árbol] cacao. **-4.** fa.n [confusión] chaos, mess; [jaleo] fuss, rumpus; **~ mental** mental confusion.

cacarear ◇ vt fam **-1.** [jactarse de] to boast about. **-2.** [pregonar] to blab about. ◇ vi [gallo] to cluck, to cackle.

cacatúa f **-1.** [ave] cockatoo. **-2.** fam [mujer vieja] old bat.

cace etc → cazar.

cacería f hunt.

cacerola f pot, pan.

cacha f **-1.** fam [muslo] thigh. **-2.** [mango de cuchillo] handle; [- de pistola] butt.
◆ **cachas** m inv fam [hombre fuerte] he-man, strong man; **estar cachas** to be well-built.

cachalote m sperm whale.

cacharro m **-1.** [recipiente] pot; **fregar los ~s** to do the dishes. **-2.** fam [trasto] junk (U), rubbish (U). **-3.** [máquina] crock; [coche] banger.

cachaza f fam: **tener ~** to be cool.

cachear vt to frisk.

cachemir m, **cachemira** f cashmere.

cacheo m frisk, frisking (U).

cachet [ka'tʃe] m **-1.** [distinción] cachet. **-2.** [cotización de artista] fee.

cachetada f Amer fam smack.

cachete m **-1.** [moflete] chubby cheek. **-2.** [bofetada] slap.

cachetear vt to slap.

cachiporra f club, cudgel; [de policía] truncheon.

cachirulo m **-1.** [chisme] thingamajig. **-2.** [pañuelo] headscarf worn by men as part of traditional Aragonese costume.

cachivache m fam knick-knack.

cacho m **-1.** fam [pedazo] piece, bit. **-2.** Amer [asta] horn.

cachondearse vpr fam: ~ **(de)** to take the mickey (out of).

cachondeo m fam **-1.** [diversión] lark; **irse de ~** to go out on the town. **-2.** despec [cosa poco seria] joke; **tomarse algo a ~** to treat sthg as a joke.

cachondo, -da fam ◇ adj **-1.** [divertido] funny. **-2.** [salido] randy. ◇ m y f: ~ **(mental)** joker.

cachorro, -rra m y f [de perro] pup, puppy; [de gato] kitten; [de león, lobo, oso] cub.

cacique m **-1.** [persona influyente] cacique, local political boss. **-2.** despec & fig [déspota] despot. **-3.** [jefe indio] chief, cacique.

caciquil adj fig despotic.

caciquismo m caciquism.

caco m fam thief.

cacofonía f cacophony.

cacofónico, -ca adj cacophonous.

cacto, cactus (pl **cactus**) m cactus.

cacumen m **-1.** [ingenio] brains (pl), wits (pl). **-2.** fam [cabeza] nut, head.

CAD (abrev de **computer aided design**) m CAD.

cada adj inv **-1.** [gen] each; [con números, tiempo] every; ~ **dos meses** every two months; ~ **cosa a su tiempo** one thing at a time; ~ **cual** each one, everyone; ~ **uno de** each of. **-2.** [valor progresivo]: ~ **vez más** more and more; ~ **vez más largo** longer and longer; ~ **día más** more and more each day. **-3.** [valor enfático] such; **¡se pone ~ sombrero!** she wears such hats!

cadalso m scaffold.

cadáver m corpse, (dead) body; **antes pasarán por encima de mi ~** over my dead body.

cadavérico, -ca adj cadaverous; [pálido] deathly pale.

caddy = cadi.

cadena *f* **-1.** [gen] chain; **en ~** [accidente] multiple; **tirar de la ~** to pull the chain, to flush the toilet; **~ alimenticia** food chain; **~ de tiendas** chain of stores; **romper sus ~s** to break out of one's chains. **-2.** TV channel. **-3.** [RADIO - emisora] station; [- red de emisoras] network. **-4.** [de proceso industrial] line; **~ de montaje** assembly line. **-5.** [aparato de música] sound system. **-6.** GEOGR range. **-7.** *fig* [sujeción] chains (*pl*), bonds (*pl*).
♦ **cadenas** *fpl* AUTOM (tyre) chains.
♦ **cadena perpetua** *f* life imprisonment.

cadencia *f* **-1.** [ritmo] rhythm, cadence. **-2.** LITER & MÚS cadence.

cadencioso, -sa *adj* rhythmical.

cadeneta *f* chain stitch.

cadera *f* hip.

cadete *m* cadet.

cadi, caddy (*pl* **caddies**) *m* caddie.

cadmio *m* cadmium.

caducar [10] *vi* **-1.** [carnet, ley, pasaporte etc] to expire. **-2.** [medicamento] to pass its use-by date; [alimento] to pass its sell-by date.

caducidad *f* expiry.

caduco, -ca *adj* **-1.** [viejo] decrepit; [idea] outmoded. **-2.** [perecedero] transitory. **-3.** [desfasado] no longer valid. **-4.** BOT deciduous.

caduque *etc* → **caducar**.

caer [55] *vi* **-1.** [gen] to fall; [diente, pelo] to fall out; **dejar ~ algo** to drop sthg; **~ bajo** to sink (very) low; **estar al ~** to be about to arrive. **-2.** [al perder equilibrio] to fall over ○ down; **~ de un tejado/caballo** to fall from a roof/horse. **-3.** *fig* [abalanzarse]: **~ sobre** to ○ descend upon. **-4.** *fig* [aparecer]: **dejarse ~ por casa de alguien** to drop by sb's house. **-5.** *fig* [sentar]: **~ bien/mal a alguien** [comentario, noticia etc] to go down well/badly (with sb). **-6.** *fig* [mostrarse]: **me cae bien/mal** I like/don't like him. **-7.** *fig* [estar situado]: **cae cerca de aquí** it's not far from here. **-8.** *fig* [recordar]: **~ (en algo)** to be able to remember (sthg); **no caigo** I can't remember.
♦ **caer en** *vi* **-1.** [entender] to get, to understand; [solución] to hit upon. **-2.** [coincidir - fecha] to fall on; **cae en domingo** it falls on a Sunday. **-3.** [incurrir] to fall into.
♦ **caerse** *vpr* **-1.** [persona] to fall over ○ down; **~se de** to fall from; **~se de ingenuo/listo** *fig* to be incredibly naive/clever. **-2.** [objetos] to drop, to fall. **-3.** [desprenderse - diente, pelo etc] to fall out; [- botón] to fall off; [- cuadro] to fall down. **-4.** [falda, pantalones etc] to fall down; **se te**

caen los pantalones your trousers are falling down.

café (*pl* **cafés**) ◇ *m* **-1.** [gen] coffee; **~ solo/con leche** black/white coffee; **~ instantáneo** ○ **soluble** instant coffee; **~ americano** large weak black coffee; **~ expreso** expresso; **~ irlandés** Irish coffee; **~ molido** ground coffee. **-2.** [establecimiento] cafe. ◇ *adj inv* [color] coffee-coloured.

cafeína *f* caffeine.

cafetal *m* coffee plantation.

cafetera → **cafetero**.

cafetería *f* cafe.

cafetero, -ra ◇ *adj* **-1.** [de café] coffee (*antes de sust*); [país] coffee-producing. **-2.** [bebedor de café] fond of coffee. ◇ *m y f* **-1.** [cultivador] coffee grower. **-2.** [comerciante] coffee merchant.
♦ **cafetera** *f* **-1.** [gen] coffee pot. **-2.** [en bares] expresso machine; [eléctrica] percolator, coffee machine. **-3.** *fam* [aparato viejo] old crock.

cafeto *m* coffee bush.

cafiche *m* *Amer fam* pimp.

cafre ◇ *adj* brutish. ◇ *m y f* brute.

cagado, -da *m y f* *vulg* [cobarde] yellow-belly, chicken.
♦ **cagada** *f* *vulg* **-1.** [equivocación] cock-up. **-2.** [excremento] shit.

cagar [16] *vulg* ◇ *vi* [defecar] to shit, to crap. ◇ *vt* [estropear] to bugger up; **~la** *fig* to cock it up.
♦ **cagarse** *vpr* *vulg lit* & *fig* to shit o.s.

Cagliari Cagliari.

cagón, -ona *adj* *vulg* **-1.** [que caga] shitty. **-2.** [miedica] chicken, cowardly.

cague *etc* → **cagar**.

cagueta *vulg* ◇ *adj* chicken, cowardly. ◇ *m y f* coward, chicken.

caído, -da *adj* **-1.** [árbol, hoja] fallen. **-2.** [decaído] low.
♦ **caída** *f* **-1.** [gen] fall, falling (*U*); [de diente, pelo] loss. **-2.** [de paro, precios, terreno]: **caída (de)** drop (in). **-3.** [de falda, vestido etc] drape. **-4.** *loc*: **a la caída del sol** at sunset; **a la caída de la tarde** at nightfall.
♦ **caídos** *mpl*: **los ~s** the fallen.
♦ **caída de ojos** *f* droop of one's eyelids.

caiga *etc* → **caer**.

caimán *m* **-1.** [animal] alligator, cayman. **-2.** *fig* [persona] sly fox.

Cairo → **El Cairo**.

caja *f* **-1.** [gen] box; [para transporte, embalaje] crate; **una ~ de cervezas** a crate of beer; **~ torácica** thorax. **-2.** [de reloj] case; [de engranajes etc] housing; **~ de cambios** gearbox. **-3.** [ataúd] coffin. **-4.** [de dinero] cash

box; ~ **fuerte** O **de caudales** safe, strongbox. **-5.** [en tienda, supermercado] till; [en banco] **cashier's desk. -6.** [banco]: ~ **(de ahorros)** savings bank. **-7.** [hueco - de escalera] well; [- de chimenea, ascensor] shaft. **-8.** IMPRENTA case. **-9.** [de instrumento musical] body. **-10.** COM [cuenta contable] cash account.
◆ **caja de música** f music box.
◆ **caja de reclutamiento, caja de reclutas** f recruiting office.
◆ **caja negra** f black box.
◆ **caja registradora** f cash register.

cajero, -ra m y f [en tienda] cashier; [en banco] teller.
◆ **cajero** m: ~ **(automático)** cash machine, cash dispenser.

cajetilla f **-1.** [de cigarrillos] packet. **-2.** [de cerillas] box. **-3.** Amer [petimetre] fop, dandy.

cajón m **-1.** [de mueble] drawer. **-2.** [recipiente] crate, case. **-3.** loc: **eso es de** ~ fam that goes without saying.
◆ **cajón de sastre** m muddle, jumble.

cajuela f Amer boot Br, trunk Am.

cal f lime; ~ **viva** quicklime; **cerrar a** ~ **y canto** to shut tight O firmly; **dar una de** ~ **y otra de arena** to be inconsistent.

cala f **-1.** [bahía pequeña] cove. **-2.** [del barco] hold. **-3.** [de fruta] sample slice. **-4.** BOT arum lily. **-5.** fam [dinero] peseta.

calabacín m courgette Br, zucchini Am.

calabaza f pumpkin, gourd; **dar** ~**s a alguien** fam [a pretendiente] to turn sb down; [en exámenes] to fail sb.

calabobos m inv drizzle.

calabozo m cell.

calada → calado.

caladero m fishing grounds (pl).

calado, -da adj soaked.
◆ **calado** m **-1.** NÁUT draught. **-2.** AUTOM stalling. **-3.** [bordado] openwork.
◆ **calada** f **-1.** [inmersión] soaking. **-2.** [de cigarrillo] drag; **dar una calada** to take a drag.

calafatear vt to caulk.

calamar m squid.

calambre m **-1.** [descarga eléctrica] (electric) shock. **-2.** [contracción muscular] cramp (U).

calamidad f calamity; **pasar** ~**es** to suffer great hardship; **ser una** ~ fig to be a dead loss.

calamitoso, -sa adj calamitous.

calandria f **-1.** [pájaro] calandra lark. **-2.** [para papel y telas] calender.

calaña f despec: **de esa** ~ of that ilk.

calar ◇ vt **-1.** [empapar] to soak. **-2.** fig [persona] to see through. **-3.** [gorro, sombre-

ro] to jam on. **-4.** [tela] to do openwork embroidery on. **-5.** [fruta] to cut a sample of. **-6.** [perforar] to perforate, to pierce. ◇ vi **-1.** NÁUT to draw. **-2.** fig [penetrar]: ~ **en** to have an impact on.
◆ **calarse** vpr **-1.** [empaparse] to get soaked. **-2.** [motor] to stall.

calato, -ta adj Amer [desnudo] naked.

calavera ◇ f [cráneo] skull. ◇ m fig madcap, crazy person.
◆ **calaveras** fpl Amer AUTOM rear lights.

calcado, -da adj traced; **ser** ~ **a alguien** to be the spitting image of sb.

calcañal m heel.

calcar [10] vt **-1.** [dibujo] to trace. **-2.** [imitar] to copy.

calcáreo, -a adj calcareous.

calce ◇ v → calzar. ◇ m **-1.** [cuña] wedge. **-2.** Amer DER footnote.

calceta f stocking; **hacer** ~ to knit.

calcetín m sock.

calcificarse [10] vpr to calcify.

calcinación f burning.

calcinar vt **-1.** [quemar] to burn, to char. **-2.** TECN to calcine.

calcio m calcium.

calco m **-1.** [reproducción] tracing. **-2.** fig [imitación] carbon copy. **-3.** LING calque, loan translation.

calcografía f chalcography.

calcomanía f transfer.

calculador, -ra adj lit & fig calculating.
◆ **calculadora** f calculator; **calculadora de bolsillo** pocket calculator.

calcular vt **-1.** [cantidades] to calculate. **-2.** [suponer] to reckon; **le calculo sesenta años** I reckon he's about sixty.

cálculo m **-1.** [operación] calculation; ~ **mental** mental arithmetic (U). **-2.** [ciencia] calculus; ~ **diferencial/infinitesimal/integral** differential/infinitesimal/integral calculus. **-3.** [evaluación] estimate; ~ **de probabilidades** probability theory. **-4.** MED stone, calculus.

caldas fpl hot springs.

caldear vt **-1.** [calentar] to heat (up). **-2.** fig [excitar] to warm up, to liven up.

caldera f **-1.** [recipiente] cauldron. **-2.** [máquina] boiler; ~ **de vapor** steam boiler.

calderero, -ra m y f boilermaker.

caldereta f [de pescado] fish stew; [de carne] meat stew.

calderilla f small change, coppers (pl) Br.

caldero m cauldron.

calderón m MÚS pause.

caldillo m stock.

caldo *m* **-1.** [sopa] broth. **-2.** [caldillo] stock. **-3.** [vino] wine. **-4.** [aceite] oil.
◆ **caldo de cultivo** *m* **-1.** BIOL culture medium. **-2.** *fig* [condición idónea] breeding ground.

caldoso, -sa *adj* watery.

calé *adj, m y f* gypsy.

calefacción *f* heating; ~ **central** central heating.

calefactor *m* heater.

caleidoscopio = **calidoscopio**.

calendario *m* calendar; ~ **escolar/laboral** school/working year.

calentador *m* **-1.** [aparato] heater. **-2.** [prenda] legwarmer.

calentamiento *m* **-1.** [subida de temperatura de] heating. **-2.** [ejercicios] warm-up.

calentar [19] ◇ *vt* **-1.** [subir la temperatura de] to heat (up), to warm (up). **-2.** *fig* [animar] to liven up. **-3.** *fig* [pegar] to hit, to strike. **-4.** *mfam fig* [sexualmente] to turn on. ◇ *vi* [entrenarse] to warm up.
◆ **calentarse** *vpr* **-1.** [por calor - suj: persona] to warm o.s., to get warm; [- suj: cosa] to heat up. **-2.** *mfam fig* [sexualmente] to get randy *Br* ○ horny.

calentón, -ona *m y f mfam* randy *Br* ○ horny person.

calentura *f* **-1.** [fiebre] fever, temperature. **-2.** [herida] cold sore.

calenturiento, -ta *adj* **-1.** [con fiebre] feverish. **-2.** *fig* [incontrolado] wild; [sexualmente] filthy.

calesa *f* calash.

calesitas *fpl Amer* merry-go-round (*sg*).

calibrado *m*, **calibración** *f* **-1.** [gen] calibration. **-2.** [de arma] boring.

calibrador *m* callipers (*pl*).

calibrar *vt* **-1.** [medir] to calibrate, to gauge. **-2.** [dar calibre a - arma] to bore. **-3.** *fig* [juzgar] to gauge.

calibre *m* **-1.** [diámetro - de pistola] calibre; [- de alambre] gauge; [- de tubo] bore. **-2.** [instrumento] gauge. **-3.** *fig* [tamaño] size. **-4.** *fig* [importancia] importance, significance.

calidad *f* **-1.** [gen] quality; **de** ~ quality (*antes de sust*); ~ **de vida** quality of life. **-2.** [clase] class. **-3.** [condición]: **en** ~ **de** in one's capacity as.

cálido, -da *adj* warm.

calidoscopio, caleidoscopio *m* kaleidoscope.

calienta → **calentar**.

calientapiés *m inv* foot warmer.

calientaplatos *m inv* hotplate.

caliente ◇ *v* → **calentar**. ◇ *adj* **-1.** [gen] hot; [templado] warm; **en** ~ *fig* in the heat of the moment. **-2.** *fig* [acalorado] heated. **-3.** *mfam* [excitado] randy *Br*, horny.

califa *m* caliph.

califato *m* caliphate.

calificación *f* **-1.** [atributo] quality. **-2.** EDUC mark.

calificado, -da *adj* **-1.** [importante] eminent. **-2.** [apto] qualified.

calificar [10] *vt* **-1.** [denominar]: ~ **a alguien de algo** to call sb sthg, to describe sb as sthg. **-2.** EDUC to mark. **-3.** GRAM to qualify.

calificativo, -va *adj* qualifying.
◆ **calificativo** *m* epithet.

caligrafía *f* **-1.** [arte] calligraphy. **-2.** [rasgos] handwriting.

calígrafo, -fa *m y f* calligrapher.

calina *f* haze, mist.

calipso *m* calypso.

cáliz *m* **-1.** RELIG chalice. **-2.** ANAT & BOT calyx.

calizo, -za *adj* chalky.
◆ **caliza** *f* limestone.

callado, -da *adj* quiet, silent.

callampa *f Amer* [seta] mushroom.

callandito *adv fam* on the quiet.

callar ◇ *vi* **-1.** [no hablar] to keep quiet, to be silent; **quien calla otorga** silence signifies consent. **-2.** [dejar de hablar] to be quiet, to stop talking. ◇ *vt* **-1.** [ocultar] to keep quiet about; [secreto] to keep. **-2.** [acallar] to silence.
◆ **callarse** *vpr* **-1.** [no hablar] to keep quiet, to be silent. **-2.** [dejar de hablar] to be quiet, to stop talking; **¡cállate!** shut up! **-3.** [ocultar] to keep quiet about; [secreto] to keep.

calle *f* **-1.** [vía de circulación] street, road; ~ **arriba/abajo** up/down the street; ~ **de dirección única** one-way street; ~ **peatonal** pedestrian precinct. **-2.** DEP lane. **-3.** *Amer* [callejón] cul-de-sac. **-4.** *loc*: **dejar a alguien en la** ~ to put sb out of a job; **echar a alguien a la** ~ [de un trabajo] to sack sb; [de un lugar público] to kick ○ throw sb out; **echarse a la** ~ [manifestarse] to take to the streets; **hacer la** ~ to walk the streets; **llevarse a alguien de** ~ to win sb over; **traer** ○ **llevar a uno por la** ~ **de la amargura** to drive sb mad.

callejear *vi* to wander the streets.

callejero, -ra *adj* **-1.** [gen] street (*antes de sust*); [perro] stray. **-2.** [persona] fond of being out and about.
◆ **callejero** *m* [guía] street map.

callejón *m* alley; ~ **sin salida** cul-de-sac; *fig* blind alley, impasse.

callejuela *f* backstreet, side street.

callista *m y f* chiropodist.

callo *m* -1. [dureza] callus; [en el pie] corn; **dar el ~** *fam fig* to slog. -2. *fam fig* [persona fea] sight, fright.

◆ **callos** *mpl* CULIN tripe (*U*); **~ a la madrileña** *tripe cooked with ham, smoked pork sausage, onion and peppers.*

callosidad *f* callus, hard skin (*U*).

calloso, -sa *adj* calloused.

calma *f* -1. [sin ruido o movimiento] calm; **en ~** calm; **~ chicha** dead calm. -2. [sosiego] tranquility; **perder la ~** to lose one's composure; **tómatelo con ~** take it easy. -3. [apatía] sluggishness, indifference.

calmante ◇ *adj* sedative, soothing. ◇ *m* sedative.

calmar *vt* -1. [mitigar] to relieve. -2. [tranquilizar] to calm, to soothe.

◆ **calmarse** *vpr* to calm down; [dolor, tempestad] to abate.

calmoso, -sa *adj* calm.

caló *m* gypsy dialect.

calor *m* -1. [gen] heat; [tibieza] warmth; **entrar en ~** [gen] to get warm; [público, deportista] to warm up; **hacer ~** to be warm o hot; **tener ~** to be warm o hot; **~ animal** body heat; **~ específico** FÍS specific heat. -2. *fig* [afecto, entusiasmo] warmth; **al ~ de** under the wing of.

caloría *f* calorie.

calórico, -ca *adj* caloric.

calorífero, -ra *adj* [que da calor] heat-producing.

calorífico, -ca *adj* calorific.

calostro *m* colostrum.

calote *m* *Amer* swindle.

calque *etc* → **calcar**.

calumnia *f* [oral] slander; [escrita] libel.

calumniar *vt* [oralmente] to slander; [por escrito] to libel.

calumnioso, -sa *adj* [de palabra] slanderous; [por escrito] libellous.

caluroso, -sa *adj* -1. [gen] hot; [templado] warm. -2. *fig* [afectuoso] warm.

calva → **calvo**.

calvados *m inv* Calvados.

calvario *m* -1. [vía crucis] Calvary, stations (*pl*) of the Cross. -2. *fig* [sufrimiento] ordeal.

calvicie *f* baldness.

calvinista *adj* Calvinist.

calvo, -va ◇ *adj* bald; **ni tanto ni tan ~** neither one extreme nor the other. ◇ *m y f* bald person.

◆ **calva** *f* -1. [en la cabeza] bald patch. -2. [en tejido, terreno] bare patch.

calza *f* -1. [cuña] wedge, block. -2. *desus* [media] stocking. -3. *Amer* [empaste] filling (*in tooth*).

calzado, -da *adj* -1. [con zapatos] shod. -2. [ave] feather-legged.

◆ **calzado** *m* footwear.

◆ **calzada** *f* road (surface).

calzar [13] *vt* -1. [poner calzado] to put on. -2. [proveer de calzado] to provide shoes for. -3. [llevar un calzado] to wear; **¿qué número calza?** what size do you take? -4. [poner cuña a] to wedge, to block. -5. *Amer* [empastar] to fill (*a tooth*).

◆ **calzarse** *vpr* to put on.

calzo *m* [cuña] wedge.

calzón *m* (*gen pl*) -1. *desus* [pantalón] trousers (*pl*). -2. *Amer* [bragas] knickers (*pl*).

calzonazos *m inv* *fam* henpecked husband.

calzoncillo *m* (*gen pl*) underpants (*pl*).

CAM (*abrev de* **computer aided manufacturing**) *f* CAM.

cama *f* bed; **estar en** o **guardar ~** to be confined to bed; **hacer la ~** to make the bed; **~ individual/de matrimonio** single/double bed; **~ de agua** water bed; **~ nido** pull-out bed (*under other bed*); **~ turca** divan bed; **hacerle** o **ponerle la ~ a alguien** *fig* to plot against sb.

camada *f* litter.

camafeo *m* cameo.

camaleón *m* *lit & fig* chameleon.

camaleónico, -ca *adj* *fig* fickle.

cámara ◇ *f* -1. [gen & TECN] chamber; **~ alta/baja** upper/lower house; **~ de aire/gas** air/gas chamber; **~ de Comercio** Chamber of Commerce; **~ de compensación** clearing house; **~ frigorífica** cold-storage room; **~ mortuoria** funeral chamber. -2. CIN, FOT & TV camera; **a ~ lenta** *lit & fig* in slow motion; **~ oscura** camera obscura. -3. [de balón, neumático] inner tube. -4. [habitáculo] cabin. ◇ *m y f* [persona] cameraman (*f* camerawoman).

◆ **de cámara** *loc adj* MÚS chamber (*antes de sust*).

camarada *m y f* -1. POLÍT comrade. -2. [compañero] colleague.

camaradería *f* camaraderie.

camarero, -ra *m y f* -1. [de restaurante] waiter (*f* waitress); [de hotel] steward (*f* chambermaid). -2. [de rey etc] chamberlain (*f* lady-in-waiting).

◆ **camarera** *f* *Amer* [azafata] air hostess.

camarilla *f* clique; POLÍT lobby, pressure group.

camarón m shrimp.

camarote m cabin.

camastro m ramshackle bed.

cambalache m fam **-1.** [trueque] swap. **-2.** Amer [tienda] junk shop.

cambiante adj changeable.

cambiar [8] ◇ vt **-1.** [gen] to change; ~ libras por pesetas to change pounds into pesetas. **-2.** [canjear]: ~ **algo (por)** to exchange sthg (for). ◇ vi **-1.** [gen] to change; ~ **de** [gen] to change; [casa] to move; ~ **de trabajo** to move jobs. **-2.** AUTOM [de marchas] to change gear.

◆ **cambiarse** vpr: ~**se (de)** [ropa] to change; [casa] to move; ~**se de vestido** to change one's dress.

cambiazo m fam **-1.** [cambio grande] radical change. **-2.** [sustitución] switch (in order to steal bag etc); **dar el** ~ fig to do a switch.

cambio m **-1.** [gen] change; **a las primeras de** ~ at the first opportunity. **-2.** [trueque] exchange; **a** ~ **(de)** in exchange O return (for). **-3.** [FIN - de acciones] price; [- de divisas] exchange rate; **"cambio"** "bureau de change"; ~ **base** base rate. **-4.** AUTOM: ~ **automático** automatic transmission; ~ **de marchas** O **velocidades** gear change.

◆ **cambio de rasante** m brow of a hill.

◆ **libre cambio** m **-1.** ECON [librecambismo] free trade. **-2.** FIN [de divisas] floating exchange rates (pl).

◆ **en cambio** loc adv **-1.** [por otra parte] on the other hand, however. **-2.** [en su lugar] instead.

cambista m y f money changer.

Camboya Cambodia.

camboyano, -na adj, m y f Cambodian.

cambujo, -ja adj Amer [oscuro] dark.

cambur m Amer **-1.** [empleo] job. **-2.** [empleado] clerk. **-3.** [plátano] banana.

camelar vt fam **-1.** [seducir, engañar] to butter up, to win over. **-2.** [enamorar] to flirt with.

camelia f camellia.

camello, -lla m y f [animal] camel.

◆ **camello** m fam [traficante] drug pusher O dealer.

camellón m Amer central reservation.

camelo m fam **-1.** [engaño] humbug (U). **-2.** [noticia falsa] hoax.

camembert ['kamember] m camembert.

camerino m dressing room.

Camerún Cameroon.

camerunés, -esa ◇ adj of/relating to Cameroon. ◇ m y f native/inhabitant of Cameroon.

camilla ◇ f [gen] stretcher; [de psiquiatra, dentista] couch. ◇ adj → **mesa**.

camillero, -ra m y f stretcher-bearer.

caminante m y f walker.

caminar ◇ vi **-1.** [a pie] to walk. **-2.** fig [ir]: ~ **(hacia)** to head (for). ◇ vt [una distancia] to travel, to cover.

caminata f long walk.

camino m **-1.** [sendero] path, track; [carretera] road; ~ **de herradura** bridle path; **abrir** ~ **a** to clear the way for; **abrirse** ~ to get on O ahead; **ir cada cual por su** ~ to each go his/her own way. **-2.** [ruta] way; **a medio** ~ halfway; **estar a medio** ~ to be halfway there; **quedarse a medio** ~ to stop halfway through; ~ **de** on the way to; **en el** O **de** ~ on the way. **-3.** [viaje] journey; **ponerse en** ~ to set off. **-4.** fig [medio] way.

◆ **camino de Santiago** m **-1.** ASTRON the Milky Way. **-2.** RELIG Way of St. James, pilgrimage route to Santiago de Compostela.

◆ **camino trillado** m fig well-trodden path.

camión m **-1.** [de mercancías] lorry Br, truck Am; ~ **cisterna** tanker; ~ **de la mudanza** removal van. **-2.** Amer [autobús] bus.

camionero, -ra m y f lorry driver Br, trucker Am.

camioneta f van.

camisa f **-1.** [prenda] shirt. **-2.** TECN lining. **-3.** ZOOL slough, skin. **-4.** BOT skin. **-5.** loc: **jugarse hasta la** ~ to stake one's shirt; **meterse en** ~ **de once varas** to complicate matters unnecessarily; **mudar** O **cambiar de** ~ to change sides; **no le llega la** ~ **al cuerpo** she's scared stiff.

◆ **camisa de fuerza** f straitjacket.

camisería f [tienda] shirt shop, outfitter's.

camisero, -ra ◇ adj shirt (antes de sust). ◇ m y f **-1.** [que confecciona] shirtmaker. **-2.** [que vende] outfitter.

camiseta f **-1.** [ropa interior] vest. **-2.** [de verano] T-shirt. **-3.** [DEP - de tirantes] vest; [- de mangas] shirt.

camisola f **-1.** [prenda interior] camisole. **-2.** Amer DEP sports shirt.

camisón m nightdress.

camomila f camomile.

camorra f trouble; **buscar** ~ to look for trouble.

camorrista ◇ adj belligerent, quarrelsome. ◇ m y f troublemaker.

camp [kam] adj inv camp.

campal → **batalla**.

campamento m camp.

campana *f* bell; ~ **de buzo** O **de salvamento** diving bell; ~ **extractora de humos** extractor hood; **echar las** ~**s al vuelo** *fam* to jump for joy; **oír** ~**s y no saber dónde** not to know what one is talking about.

campanada *f* **-1.** [de campana] peal. **-2.** [de reloj] stroke. **-3.** *fig* [suceso] sensation.

campanario *m* belfry, bell tower.

campanilla *f* **-1.** [de la puerta] (small) bell; [con mango] handbell. **-2.** ANAT uvula. **-3.** [flor] campanula, bellflower.

campanilleo *m* tinkling (*U*).

campante *adj fam*: **estar** O **quedarse tan** ~ to remain quite unruffled.

campaña *f* **-1.** [gen] campaign; **hacer** ~ **(de/contra)** to campaign (for/against); **de** ~ MIL field (*antes de sust*). **-2.** [campo llano] open countryside.

campechanía *f* geniality, good-natured character.

campechano, **-na** *adj fam* genial, good-natured.

campeón, **-ona** *m y f* champion.

campeonato *m* championship; **de** ~ *fig* terrific, great.

campero, **-ra** *adj* country (*antes de sust*); [al aire libre] open-air.

◆ **campero** *m Amer* jeep.

◆ **campera** *f* **-1.** [bota] ≃ cowboy boot. **-2.** *Amer* [chaqueta] short leather jacket.

campesinado *m* peasants (*pl*), peasantry.

campesino, **-na** ◇ *adj* country (*antes de sust*), rural. ◇ *m y f* farmer; [muy pobre] peasant.

campestre *adj* country (*antes de sust*).

campiña *f* countryside.

camping ['kampin] (*pl* **campings**) *m* **-1.** [actividad] camping; **ir de** ~ to go camping. **-2.** [terreno] campsite.

campista *m y f* camper.

campito *m Amer* property, estate.

campo *m* **-1.** [gen & INFORM] field; ~ **de aviación** airfield; ~ **de batalla** battlefield; ~ **magnético** magnetic field; ~ **de tiro** firing range; **dejar el** ~ **libre** *fig* to leave the field open. **-2.** [campiña] country, countryside; ~ **abierto** open countryside; **a** ~ **traviesa** cross country. **-3.** [DEP - de fútbol] pitch; [- de tenis] court; [- de golf] course; **jugar en** ~ **propio** to play at home.

◆ **campo de concentración** *m* concentration camp.

◆ **campo de trabajo** *m* [de vacaciones] work camp; [para prisioneros] labour camp.

◆ **campo visual** *m* field of vision.

camposanto *m* cemetery.

Campsa (*abrev de* **Compañía Arrendataria del Monopolio de Petróleos, SA**) *f Spanish state petroleum company.*

campus *m inv* campus.

camuflaje *m* camouflage.

camuflar *vt* to camouflage.

can *m* hound, dog.

cana → **cano**.

Canadá: **(el)** ~ Canada.

canadiense *adj*, *m y f* Canadian.

canal ◇ *m* **-1.** [cauce artificial] canal. **-2.** GEOGR [estrecho] channel, strait. **-3.** RADIO & TV channel. **-4.** ANAT canal, duct. **-5.** [de agua, gas] conduit, pipe. **-6.** *fig* [medio, vía] channel; ~ **de comercialización** ECON distribution channel. **-7.** [res] carcass; **abrir en** ~ to slit open; *fig* to tear apart. ◇ *m o f* [de un tejado] (valley) gutter.

canalé *m* ribbed knitwear.

canalización *f* **-1.** [encauzamiento] piping. **-2.** (*gen pl*) [cañería] pipes (*pl*). **-3.** *fig* [orientación] channelling.

canalizar [13] *vt* **-1.** [territorio] to canalize; [agua] to channel. **-2.** [cauce] to deepen the course of. **-3.** *fig* [orientar] to channel.

canalla *m y f* swine, dog.

canallada *f* [acto] dirty trick.

canalón *m* **-1.** [de tejado] gutter; [en la pared] drainpipe. **-2.** CULIN = **canelón**.

canapé *m* **-1.** CULIN canapé. **-2.** [sofá] sofa, couch.

Canarias *fpl*: **las (islas)** ~ the Canary Islands, the Canaries.

canario, **-ria** ◇ *adj* of the Canary Isles. ◇ *m y f* [persona] Canary Islander.

◆ **canario** *m* [pájaro] canary.

canasta *f* **-1.** [gen & DEP] basket. **-2.** [juego de naipes] canasta.

canastilla *f* **-1.** [cesto pequeño] basket. **-2.** [de bebé] layette.

canasto *m* large basket.

◆ **canastos** *interj*: **¡**~**!** [expresa enfado] for Heaven's sake!; [expresa sorpresa] good heavens!

Canberra Canberra.

cancán *m* [baile] cancan.

cancela *f* wrought-iron gate.

cancelación *f* cancellation.

cancelar *vt* **-1.** [anular] to cancel. **-2.** [deuda] to pay, to settle.

cáncer *m* MED & *fig* cancer.

◆ **Cáncer** ◇ *m* [zodiaco] Cancer; **ser** ~ to be (a) Cancer. ◇ *m y f* [persona] Cancer, Cancerian.

cancerbero *m* DEP goalkeeper.

cancerígeno, **-na** *adj* carcinogenic.

cancerología f oncology.

cancerológico, -ca adj oncological.

cancerólogo, -ga m y f cancer specialist, oncologist.

canceroso, -sa ◇ adj [úlcera, tejido] cancerous; [enfermo] suffering from cancer. ◇ m y f [enfermo] cancer patient.

canciller m **-1.** [de gobierno, embajada] chancellor. **-2.** [de asuntos exteriores] foreign minister.

cancillería f **-1.** [de gobierno] chancellorship. **-2.** [de embajada] chancellery. **-3.** [de asuntos exteriores] foreign ministry.

canción f song; ~ de cuna lullaby; la misma ~ fig the same old story.

cancionero m songbook.

candado m padlock.

candela f **-1.** [vela] candle. **-2.** fam fig [lumbre] light. **-3.** Amer fire.

candelabro m candelabra.

candelero m candlestick; **estar en el ~** fig to be in the limelight.

candente adj **-1.** [incandescente] red-hot. **-2.** fig [actual] burning (antes de sust).

Candia Canea.

candidato, -ta m y f candidate.

candidatura f **-1.** [para un cargo] candidacy; **presentar uno su ~ (a)** to put o.s. forward as a candidate (for). **-2.** [lista] list of candidates.

candidez f ingenuousness.

cándido, -da adj ingenuous, simple.

candil m **-1.** [lámpara] oil lamp. **-2.** Amer [araña] chandelier.

candilejas fpl footlights.

candor m ingenuousness, simplicity.

candoroso, -sa adj ingenuous, simple.

caneca f Amer rubbish bin Br, trashcan Am.

canelo, -la adj **-1.** [caballo, perro] cinnamon-coloured. **-2.** fam fig [inocentón] gullible.
◆ **canela** f cinnamon; **ser canela fina** fig to be sheer class.

canelón, canalón m CULIN cannelloni (pl).

canesú (pl **canesúes** ○ **canesús**) m **-1.** [de vestido] bodice. **-2.** [de blusa] yoke.

cangrejo m crab; ~ de río crayfish.

canguelo m fam: **le entró ~** she got the wind up.

canguro ◇ m [animal] kangaroo. ◇ m y f fam [persona] babysitter; **hacer de ~** to babysit.

caníbal ◇ adj cannibalistic. ◇ m y f cannibal.

canibalismo m cannibalism.

canica f [pieza] marble.
◆ **canicas** fpl [juego] marbles.

caniche m poodle.

canícula f dog ○ hottest days (pl).

canijo, -ja ◇ adj sickly. ◇ m y f sickly person.

canilla f **-1.** [espinilla] shinbone. **-2.** [bobina] bobbin. **-3.** Amer [grifo] tap. **-4.** Amer [pierna] leg.

canillita m Amer newspaper seller.

canino, -na adj canine.
◆ **canino** m [diente] canine (tooth).

canje m exchange.

canjeable adj exchangeable.

canjear vt to exchange.

cannabis m inv cannabis.

cano, -na adj grey.
◆ **cana** f grey hair; **echar una cana al aire** fig to let one's hair down.

canoa f canoe.

canódromo m greyhound track.

canon m **-1.** [norma] canon. **-2.** [modelo] ideal. **-3.** [impuesto] tax. **-4.** MÚS canon.
◆ **cánones** mpl DER canon law (U).

canónico, -ca adj canonical; [derecho] canon (antes de sust).

canónigo m canon.

canonizar [13] vt to canonize.

canoso, -sa adj grey; [persona] grey-haired.

cansado, -da adj **-1.** [gen] tired; ~ de algo/de hacer algo tired of sthg/of doing sthg. **-2.** [pesado, cargante] tiring.

cansador, -ra adj Amer boring.

cansancio m tiredness.

cansar ◇ vt to tire (out). ◇ vi to be tiring.
◆ **cansarse** vpr: **~se (de)** lit & fig to get tired (of).

cansino, -na adj lethargic.

Cantabria Cantabria.

Cantábrica → cordillera.

Cantábrico m: **el (mar) ~** the Cantabrian Sea.

cántabro, -bra adj, m y f Cantabrian.

cantaleta f Amer nagging.

cantamañanas m y f inv unreliable person.

cantante ◇ adj singing. ◇ m y f singer.

cantaor, -ra m y f flamenco singer.

cantar ◇ vt **-1.** [canción] to sing. **-2.** [bingo, línea, el gordo] to call (out). ◇ vi **-1.** [persona, ave] to sing; [gallo] to crow; [insecto] to chirp. **-2.** fam fig [confesar] to talk. **-3.** fam fig [apestar] to whiff, to pong. **-4.** fam fig [desentonar] to stick out like a sore thumb. **-5.** fig [alabar]: ~ **a** to sing the praises of. ◇ m LITER poem; **eso es otro ~** that's another story.

cántara f large pitcher.

cántaro m large pitcher; **a ~s** in torrents; **llover a ~s** to rain cats and dogs.

cantata f cantata.

cantautor, -ra m y f singer-songwriter.

cante m: **~ (jondo** ○ **hondo)** flamenco singing; **dar el ~** fam to call attention to o.s.

cantegril m Amer shanty town.

cantera f -1. [de piedra] quarry. -2. fig [de profesionales] young blood (U).

cantero m Amer flowerbed.

cántico m canticle.

cantidad ◇ f -1. [medida] quantity. -2. [abundancia] abundance, large number; **en ~** in abundance; **~ de** lots of. -3. [número] number. -4. [suma de dinero] sum (of money). ◇ adv fam really; **me gusta ~** I don't half like it.

cantiga, cántiga f ballad.

cantilena, cantinela f: **la misma ~** fig the same old story.

cantimplora f water bottle.

cantina f [de soldados] mess; [en fábrica] canteen; [en estación de tren] buffet.

cantinela = cantilena.

cantinero, -ra m y f canteen manager (f canteen manageress).

canto m -1. [acción, arte] singing. -2. [canción] song; **~ del cisne** swansong; **~ de sirena** wheedling. -3. fig [alabanza] hymn. -4. [lado, borde] edge; **de ~** edgeways; **darse con un ~ en los dientes** to consider o.s. lucky; **por el ~ de un duro** by a hair's breadth. -5. [de cuchillo] blunt edge. -6. [guijarro] pebble; **~ rodado** [pequeño] pebble; [grande] boulder.

cantón m [territorio] canton.

cantor, -ra ◇ adj singing (antes de sust). ◇ m y f singer.

cantoral m choir book.

canturrear vt & vi fam to sing softly.

canutas fpl fam: **pasarlas ~** to have a rough time.

canutillo m glass tube.

canuto m -1. [tubo] tube. -2. fam [porro] joint.

caña f -1. BOT cane; **~ de azúcar** sugarcane. -2. [de río, de estanque] reed. -3. [tuétano] bone marrow. -4. [de la bota, del calcetín] leg. -5. [de cerveza] small glass of beer. -6. loc: **darle** ○ **meterle ~ a algo** fam to get a move on with sthg.

◆ **caña de pescar** f fishing rod.

cañabrava f Amer kind of cane.

cañada f gorge, ravine.

cáñamo m hemp.

cañamón m hempseed.

cañaveral m reedbed.

cañería f pipe.

cañizo m wattle.

caño m [de fuente] jet.

cañón m -1. [arma] gun; HIST cannon. -2. [de fusil] barrel; [de chimenea] flue; [de órgano] pipe. -3. GEOGR canyon. -4. loc: **estar ~** fam to be gorgeous.

cañonazo m -1. [disparo de cañón] gunshot. -2. [en fútbol] powerful shot.

cañonear vt to shell.

cañonera f gunboat.

caoba f mahogany.

caos m inv chaos.

caótico, -ca adj chaotic.

cap. (abrev de **capítulo**) ch.

CAP (abrev de **Certificado de Aptitud Pedagógica**) m Spanish teaching certificate needed to teach in secondary education.

capa f -1. [manto] cloak, cape; **andar de ~ caída** to be in a bad way; **de ~ y espada** cloak and dagger; **defender a ~ y espada** to defend tooth and nail; **hacer de su ~ un sayo** to do as one pleases. -2. [baño - de barniz, pintura] coat; [- de chocolate etc] coating. -3. [estrato] layer; GEOL stratum, layer; **~ atmosférica** atmosphere; **~ de ozono** ozone layer; **~ terrestre** earth's surface. -4. [grupo social] stratum, class. -5. TAUROM cape; ver también **tauromaquia**.

capacho m wicker basket.

capacidad f -1. [gen] capacity; **con ~ para 500 personas** with a capacity of 500. -2. [aptitud] ability; **no tener ~ para algo/para hacer algo** to be no good at sthg/at doing sthg.

◆ **capacidad adquisitiva** f purchasing power.

capacitación f training.

capacitar vt: **~ a alguien para algo** [habilitar] to qualify sb for sthg; [formar] to train sb for sthg.

capar vt to castrate.

caparazón m lit & fig shell.

capataz m y f foreman (f forewoman).

capaz adj -1. [gen] capable; **~ de algo/de hacer algo** capable of sthg/of doing something. -2. DER competent. -3. [espacioso]: **muy/poco ~** with a large/small capacity; **~ para** with room for.

capazo m large wicker basket.

capcioso, -sa adj [pregunta] trick (antes de sust).

CAPE (*abrev de* **Comisión Autónoma de Puertos Españoles**) *f Spanish ports authority.*

capea *f* TAUROM *bullfight with young bulls.*

capear *vt fig* [eludir] to get out of.

capellán *m* chaplain.

caperuza *f* **-1.** [gorro] hood. **-2.** [capuchón] top, cap.

capicúa ◇ *adj inv* reversible. ◇ *m inv* reversible number.

capilar ◇ *adj* **-1.** [del cabello] hair (*antes de sust*). **-2.** ANAT & FÍS capillary. ◇ *m* ANAT capillary.

capilaridad *f* FÍS capillarity, capillary action.

capilla *f* chapel; ~ **ardiente** funeral chapel; **estar en** ~ *fig* [condenado a muerte] to be awaiting execution; *fam* [en ascuas] to be on tenterhooks.

capirotazo *m* flick.

capirote *m* **-1.** [gorro] hood. **-2.** → **tonto.**

cápita
◆ **per cápita** *loc adj* per capita.

capital ◇ *adj* **-1.** [importante] supreme. **-2.** [principal] main. ◇ *m* ECON capital; ~ **circulante/fijo/social** working/fixed/share capital; ~ **escriturado** declared capital, capital stock; ~ **líquido** liquid assets (*pl*); ~ **bajo riesgo** sum at risk; ~ **de riesgo** venture capital. ◇ *f* [ciudad] capital.

capitalidad *f* capital status.

capitalismo *m* capitalism.

capitalista *adj, m y f* capitalist.

capitalización *f* capitalization.

capitalizar [13] *vt* **-1.** ECON to capitalize. **-2.** *fig* [sacar provecho] to capitalize on.

capitán, -ana *m y f* captain; ~ **general** MIL ≃ field marshal *Br*, general of the army *Am*.
◆ **capitana** *f* NÁUT flagship.

capitanear *vt* **-1.** DEP & MIL to captain. **-2.** [dirigir] to head, to lead.

capitanía *f* MIL **-1.** [empleo] captaincy. **-2.** [oficina] military headquarters; ~ **general** Captaincy General.

capitel *m* capital.

capitolio *m* **-1.** [edificio] capitol. **-2.** [acrópolis] acropolis.

capitoste *m y f despec* big wheel, big boss.

capitulación *f* capitulation, surrender.
◆ **capitulaciones matrimoniales** *fpl* marriage settlement (*sg*).

capitular *vi* to capitulate, to surrender.

capítulo *m* **-1.** [sección, división] chapter. **-2.** *fig* [tema] subject: **ser** ~ **aparte** to be another matter (altogether).

capó, capot [ka'po] *m* bonnet *Br*, hood *Am*.

capón *m* **-1.** [animal] capon. **-2.** [golpe] rap on the head.

caporal *m* MIL ≃ corporal.

capot = **capó.**

capota *f* hood *Br*, top *Am*.

capotazo *m* TAUROM *pass with the cape.*

capote *m* **-1.** [capa] cape with sleeves; [militar] greatcoat. **-2.** TAUROM cape. **-3.** *loc:* **echar un** ~ **a alguien** to give sb a (helping) hand.

capricho *m* whim, caprice; **darse un** ~ to treat o.s.

caprichoso, -sa *adj* capricious.

Capricornio ◇ *m* [zodiaco] Capricorn; **ser** ~ to be (a) Capricorn. ◇ *m y f* [persona] Capricorn.

cápsula *f* **-1.** [gen & ANAT] capsule. **-2.** [tapón] cap.

captar *vt* **-1.** [atraer - simpatía] to win; [- interés] to gain, to capture. **-2.** [entender] to grasp. **-3.** [sintonizar] to pick up, to receive.
◆ **captarse** *vpr* [atraer] to win, to attract.

captura *f* capture.

capturar *vt* to capture.

capucha *f* hood.

capuchino, -na *adj* Capuchin.
◆ **capuchino** *m* **-1.** [fraile] Capuchin. **-2.** [café] cappuccino.

capuchón *m* cap, top.

capullo, -lla *vulg* ◇ *adj* bloody stupid. ◇ *m y f* [persona] prat.
◆ **capullo** *m* **-1.** [de flor] bud. **-2.** [de gusano] cocoon. **-3.** *fam* [prepucio] foreskin.

caqui, kaki ◇ *adj inv* [color] khaki. ◇ *m* **-1.** BOT kaki. **-2.** [color] khaki.

cara *f* **-1.** [rostro, aspecto] face; **a** ~ **descubierta** openly; ~ **a** [frente a] facing; ~ **a** ~ face to face; **de** ~ [sol, viento] in one's face; **poner** ~ **de tonto** to put a stupid face; **tener buena/mala** ~ [persona] to look well/awful; **tener** ~ **de enfadado** to look angry; **tiene** ~ **de ponerse a llover** it looks as if it's going to rain. **-2.** [lado] side; GEOM face. **-3.** [de moneda] heads (*U*); ~ **o cruz** heads or tails; **echar algo a** ~ **o cruz** to toss (a coin) for sthg. **-4.** *fam* [osadía] cheek; **tener (mucha)** ~, **tener la** ~ **muy dura** to have a cheek. **-5.** [parte frontal] front. **-6.** *loc:* **se le cayó la** ~ **de vergüenza** she blushed with shame; **cruzar la** ~ **a alguien** to slap sb in the face; **dar la** ~ **por alguien** to make excuses for sb; **de** ~ **a** with a view to; **decir algo a alguien en** ○ **a la** ~ to say sthg to sb's face; **echar en** ~ **algo a alguien** to reproach sb for sthg; **hacer** ~ **a** to stand up to; **por su linda ~, por su ~ bonita** because his/her face fits; **romper** ○ **partir la ~ a alguien** to smash sb's face in; **tener dos ~s** to be two-faced; **verse las ~s** [pelearse] to have it out; [enfrentarse] to fight it out.

carabela f caravel.

carabina f -1. [arma] carbine, rifle. -2. fam fig [mujer] chaperone.

carabinero m -1. [en España] customs policeman. -2. [en Italia] carabiniere. -3. Am [policía] policeman.

Caracas Caracas.

caracol m -1. [animal] snail. -2. [concha] shell. -3. [del oído] cochlea. -4. [rizo] curl.
◆ **caracoles** interj desus fam: ¡~es! good grief!

caracola f conch.

caracolada f CULIN stew made with snails.

caracolear vi [caballo] to prance about.

carácter (pl **caracteres**) m character; **tener buen/mal ~** to be good-natured/bad-tempered; **una reunión de ~ privado/oficial** a private/official meeting; **caracteres de imprenta** typeface (sg).

característico, -ca adj characteristic.
◆ **característica** f characteristic.

caracterización f -1. [gen] characterization. -2. [maquillaje] make-up.

caracterizar [13] vt -1. [definir] to characterize. -2. [representar] to portray. -3. [maquillar] to make up.
◆ **caracterizarse por** vpr to be characterized by.

caradura fam ○ adj cheeky. ○ m y f cheeky person.

carajillo m coffee with a dash of liqueur.

carajo mfam ○ m: **me importa un ~** I couldn't give a monkey's; **irse al ~** to go down the tubes; **¡vete al ~!** go to hell! ○ interj: ¡~! damn it!

caramba interj: ¡~! [sorpresa] good heavens!; [enfado] for heaven's sake!

carámbano m icicle.

carambola f cannon (in billiards); **por ~** by a fluke.
◆ **carambolas** interj Amer: ¡~s! good heavens!

caramelo m -1. [golosina] sweet. -2. [azúcar fundido] caramel; **de ~** fig great.

carantoñas fpl: **hacer ~ a alguien** to butter sb up.

caraota f Amer bean.

caraqueño, -ña ○ adj of/relating to Caracas. ○ m y f native/inhabitant of Caracas.

cárate = **kárate**.

carátula f -1. [de libro] front cover; [de disco] sleeve. -2. [máscara] mask.

caravana f -1. [gen] caravan. -2. [de coches] tailback.
◆ **caravanas** fpl Amer [pendientes] earrings.

caravaning [kara'ßanin] m caravanning.

caray interj: ¡~! [sorpresa] good heavens!; [enfado] damn it!

carbón m -1. [para quemar] coal; **negro como el ~** [negro] black as coal; [bronceado] brown as a berry; **~ de leña** ○ **vegetal** charcoal; **~ mineral** ○ **de piedra** coal. -2. [para dibujar] charcoal.

carbonato, -da adj carbonated.

carbonato m carbonate.

carboncillo m charcoal.

carbonero, -ra ○ adj coal (antes de sust). ○ m y f [persona] coal merchant.
◆ **carbonera** f -1. [lugar] coal bunker. -2. [de leña] charcoal stack.

carbónico, -ca adj carbonic.

carbonilla f -1. [ceniza] cinder. -2. [carbón pequeño] small coal.

carbonizar [13] vt to char, to carbonize; **morir carbonizado** to burn to death.
◆ **carbonizarse** vpr to carbonize.

carbono m carbon; **~ 14** carbon 14.

carburador m carburettor.

carburante m fuel.

carburar ○ vt to carburate. ○ vi fam to function.

carburo m carbide.

carca fam despec ○ adj old-fashioned. ○ m y f old fogey.

carcaj (pl **carcajes**) m quiver.

carcajada f guffaw; **reír a ~s** to roar with laughter.

carcajearse vpr to roar with laughter.

carcamal m y f fam despec old crock.

cárcel f prison; **meter a alguien en la ~** to put sb in prison; **~ de alta seguridad** top security prison.

carcelario, -ria adj prison (antes de sust).

carcelero, -ra m y f warder, jailer.

carcinoma m carcinoma, cancerous tumour.

carcoma f -1. [insecto] woodworm. -2. [polvo] wood dust.

carcomer vt lit & fig to eat away at.
◆ **carcomerse** vpr fig [consumirse] to be eaten up ○ consumed.

carcomido, -da adj [madera] wormeaten.

cardado m -1. [de lana] carding. -2. [del pelo] backcombing.

cardán m cardan joint.

cardar vt -1. [lana] to card. -2. [pelo] to backcomb.

cardenal *m* **-1.** RELIG cardinal. **-2.** [hematoma] bruise.
cardenalicio, -cia *adj* cardinal's (*antes de sust*).
cárdeno, -na *adj* purple.
◆ **cárdeno** *m* [color] purple.
cardiaco, -ca, cardíaco, -ca *adj* cardiac, heart (*antes de sust*).
cárdigan, cardigán *m* cardigan.
cardinal *adj* cardinal.
cardiograma *m* electrocardiogram.
cardiología *f* cardiology.
cardiólogo, -ga *m y f* cardiologist.
cardiopatía *f* heart condition.
cardiovascular *adj* cardiovascular.
cardo *m* **-1.** [planta] thistle; ~ **borriquero** cotton thistle. **-2.** *fam fig* [persona] prickly customer.
carear *vt* DER to bring face to face.
carecer [30] *vi:* ~ **de algo** to lack sthg.
carencia *f* [ausencia] lack; [defecto] deficiency.
carente *adj:* ~ **de** lacking (in).
careo *m* DER confrontation.
carero, -ra *adj fam* pricey.
carestía *f* **-1.** [escasez] scarcity, shortage. **-2.** [encarecimiento]: **la** ~ **de la vida** the high cost of living.
careta *f* **-1.** [máscara] mask; ~ **antigás** gas mask. **-2.** *fig* [engaño] front.
carey *m* **-1.** [tortuga] sea turtle. **-2.** [material] tortoiseshell.
carga *f* **-1.** [acción] loading. **-2.** [cargamento - de avión, barco] cargo; [- de tren] freight. **-3.** [peso] load. **-4.** *fig* [sufrimiento] burden. **-5.** [ataque, explosivo] charge; ~ **de profundidad** depth charge; **volver a la** ~ *fig* to persist. **-6.** [de batería, condensador] charge. **-7.** [para mechero, bolígrafo] refill. **-8.** *fig* [componente] charge. **-9.** [impuesto] tax; ~**s sociales** social security contributions.
cargado, -da *adj* **-1.** [abarrotado]: ~ **(de)** loaded (with); **estar** ~ **de** *fam* to have loads of. **-2.** [arma] loaded. **-3.** [bebida] strong. **-4.** [bochornoso - habitación] stuffy; [- tiempo] sultry, close; [- cielo] overcast.
cargador *m* **-1.** [de arma] chamber. **-2.** [persona] loader; ~ **de muelle** docker, stevedore. **-3.** ELECTR charger.
cargamento *m* cargo.
cargante *adj fam fig* annoying.
cargar [16] ◇ *vt* **-1.** [gen] to load; [pluma, mechero] to refill. **-2.** [peso encima] to throw over one's shoulder. **-3.** ELECTR to charge. **-4.** *fig* [responsabilidad, tarea] to give,

to lay upon. **-5.** *fam fig* [molestar] to annoy. **-6.** [producir pesadez - suj: humo] to make stuffy; [- suj: comida] to bloat. **-7.** [gravar]: ~ **un impuesto a algo/alguien** to tax sthg/sb. **-8.** [importe, factura, deuda]: ~ **algo (a)** to charge sthg (to). ◇ *vi* **-1.** [recaer]: ~ **sobre alguien** to fall on sb. **-2.** [atacar]: ~ **(contra)** to charge.
◆ **cargar con** *vi* **-1.** [paquete etc] to carry away. **-2.** *fig* [coste, responsabilidad] to bear; [consecuencias] to accept; [culpa] to get.
◆ **cargarse** *vpr* **-1.** *fam* [romper] to break. **-2.** *fam* [suspender] to fail. **-3.** *fam* [matar - persona] to bump off; [- animal] to kill. **-4.** [por el humo] to get stuffy. **-5.** [colmarse]: ~**se de** to be loaded down with. **-6.** *loc:* ¡**te la vas a** ~! *fam* you're in for it!
cargo *m* **-1.** [gen, ECON & DER] charge; **con** ~ **a** charged to; **correr a** ~ **de** to be borne by; **estar a** ~ **de algo, tener algo a** ~ **de uno** to be in charge of sthg; **hacerse** ~ **de** [asumir el control de] to take charge of; [ocuparse de] to take care of; [comprender] to understand; **tener** ~ **de conciencia** to feel pangs of conscience, to feel remorse. **-2.** [empleo] post, position; **alto** ~ high-ranking official.
cargosear *vt Amer* to annoy, to pester.
cargoso, -sa *adj Amer* annoying.
carguero *m* cargo boat.
cariacontecido, -da *adj* crestfallen.
cariado, -da *adj* decayed.
cariar [8] *vt* to decay.
◆ **cariarse** *vpr* to decay.
cariátide *f* caryatid.
Caribe *m:* **el (mar)** ~ the Caribbean (Sea).
caribeño, -ña ◇ *adj* Caribbean. ◇ *m y f* native/inhabitant of the Caribbean Islands.
caricatura *f* caricature.
caricaturesco, -ca *adj* caricature (*antes de sust*).
caricaturista *m y f* caricaturist.
caricaturizar [13] *vt* to caricature.
caricia *f* caress; [a perro, gato etc] stroke.
caridad *f* charity.
caries *f inv* tooth decay.
carillón *m* carillon.
cariñena *m* wine from Cariñena, in the province of Zaragoza.
cariño *m* **-1.** [afecto] affection; **tomar** ~ **a** to grow fond of. **-2.** [cuidado] loving care. **-3.** [apelativo] love.
cariñoso, -sa *adj* affectionate.
carioca ◇ *adj* of/relating to Rio de Janeiro. ◇ *m y f* native/inhabitant of Rio de Janeiro.
carisma *m* charisma.
carismático, -ca *adj* charismatic.

Cáritas *f charitable organization run by the Catholic Church.*

caritativo, -va *adj* charitable.

cariz *m* look, appearance; **tomar mal/buen** ~ to take a turn for the worse/better.

carlinga *f* [AERON - para piloto] cockpit; [- para pasajeros] cabin.

carlista *adj, m y f* Carlist.

carmelita *adj, m y f* Carmelite.

carmesí (*pl* **carmesíes**) *adj & m* crimson.

carmín ◇ *adj* [color] carmine. ◇ *m* **-1.** [color] carmine. **-2.** [lápiz de labios] lipstick.

carnada *f* lit & fig bait.

carnal *adj* **-1.** [de la carne] carnal. **-2.** [parientes] first (*antes de sust*).

carnaval *m* carnival.

carnavalada *f fam* farce.

carnavalesco, -ca *adj* carnival (*antes de sust*).

carnaza *f* lit & fig bait.

carne *f* **-1.** [de persona, fruta] flesh; **en ~ viva** raw; **entrado** O **metido en ~s** plump; **ser de ~ y hueso** fig to be human. **-2.** [alimento] meat; ~ **de cerdo** pork; ~ **de cordero** lamb; ~ **picada** mince; ~ **de ternera** veal; ~ **de vaca** beef; **poner toda la ~ en el asador** fig to go for broke.
◆ **carne de cañón** *f* cannon fodder.
◆ **carne de gallina** *f* gooseflesh.

carné (*pl* **carnés**), **carnet** (*pl* **carnets**) *m* **-1.** [documento] card; ~ **de conducir** driving licence; ~ **de identidad** identity card. **-2.** [agenda] notebook.

carnear *vt Amer* to slaughter, to butcher.

carnet = carné.

carnicería *f* **-1.** [tienda] butcher's. **-2.** fig [destrozo] butchery (*U*). **-3.** fig [masacre] carnage (*U*).

carnicero, -ra ◇ *adj* [animal] carnivorous. ◇ *m y f* lit & fig [persona] butcher.
◆ **carnicero** *m* ZOOL carnivore.

cárnico, -ca *adj* meat (*antes de sust*).

carnívoro, -ra *adj* carnivorous.
◆ **carnívoro** *m* carnivore.

carnosidad *f* **-1.** [de una herida] proud flesh (*U*). **-2.** [gordura] fleshy part.

carnoso, -sa *adj* fleshy; [labios] full.

caro, -ra *adj* **-1.** [precio] expensive. **-2.** culto [querido] cherished, fond.
◆ **caro** *adv*: **costar** ~ to be expensive; **vender** ~ **algo** to sell sthg at a high price; fig not to give sthg up easily; **pagar** ~ **algo** fig to pay dearly for sthg.

carolingio, -gia *adj, m y f* Carolingian.

carota *m y f fam* cheeky so-and-so.

carótida *adj & f* carotid.

carozo *m Amer* stone (*of fruit*).

carpa *f* **-1.** [pez] carp. **-2.** [de circo] big top; [para fiestas etc] marquee.

carpanta *f fam* ravenous hunger.

Cárpatos *mpl*: **los** ~ the Carpathians.

carpeta *f* file, folder.

carpetazo *m*: **dar** ~ **a algo** to shelve sthg.

carpetovetónico, -ca *adj* deeply Spanish.

carpintería *f* **-1.** [arte] carpentry; [de puertas y ventanas] joinery. **-2.** [taller] carpenter's/joiner's shop.

carpintero, -ra *m y f* carpenter; [de puertas y ventanas] joiner.

carraca *f* **-1.** [instrumento] rattle. **-2.** fig [cosa vieja] old crock.

carrara *m* Carrara marble.

carraspear *vi* **-1.** [hablar ronco] to speak with a hoarse voice. **-2.** [toser] to clear one's throat.

carraspera *f* hoarseness.

carrera *f* **-1.** [acción de correr] run, running (*U*). **-2.** DEP & fig race; ~ **armamentística** O **de armamentos** arms race; ~ **contra reloj** race against the clock; ~ **de coches** motor race; ~ **de obstáculos** steeplechase. **-3.** [trayecto] route. **-4.** [de taxi] ride. **-5.** [estudios] university course; **hacer la** ~ **de derecho** to study law (at university). **-6.** [profesión] career; **hacer** ~ [triunfar] to succeed (in life). **-7.** [en medias] ladder. **-8.** [calle] *name of certain Spanish streets*; **hacer la** ~ [prostituirse] to walk the streets.

carrerilla *f*: **coger** O **tomar** ~ to take a run-up.
◆ **de carrerilla** *loc adv* by heart.

carreta *f* cart.

carrete *m* **-1.** [de hilo] bobbin, reel; [de alambre] coil. **-2.** FOT roll (of film). **-3.** [para pescar] reel. **-4.** [de máquina de escribir] spool. **-5.** *loc*: **dar** ~ **a alguien** to draw sb out.

carretera *f* road; ~ **de circunvalación** ring road; ~ **comarcal** ≈ B road *Br*; ~ **de cuota** *Amer* toll road; ~ **nacional** ≈ A road *Br*, state highway *Am*.

carretero, -ra *m y f* [conductor] carter; **fumar como un** ~ fig to smoke like a chimney.
◆ **carretero** *m Amer* [carretera] road.

carretilla *f* wheelbarrow.

carricoche *m* old car.

carril *m* **-1.** [de carretera] lane; ~ **de aceleración** fast lane; ~ **bus** bus lane. **-2.** [de vía de tren] rail. **-3.** [de ruedas] rut.

carrillo *m* cheek; **comer a dos ~s** fig to cram one's face with food.

carro m **-1.** [vehículo] cart; ~ **de combate** MIL tank; **¡para el ~!** [espera un momento] hang on a minute! **-2.** [de máquina de escribir] carriage. **-3.** Amer [coche] car; ~ **comedor** dining car; ~ **dormitorio** sleeper.

carrocería f bodywork Br, body.

carromato m **-1.** [carro] wagon. **-2.** [coche viejo] old car.

carroña f carrion.

carroza ◇ f [coche] carriage. ◇ m y f fam [viejo] old fogey.

carruaje m carriage.

carrusel m **-1.** [tiovivo] carousel, merry-go-round. **-2.** [de caballos] mounted patrol.

carta f **-1.** [escrito] letter; **echar una ~** to post a letter; ~ **certificada/urgente** registered/express letter; ~ **de recomendación** reference (letter). **-2.** [naipe] (playing) card; **echar las ~s a alguien** to tell sb's fortune (with cards). **-3.** [menú] menu; ~ **de vinos** wine list. **-4.** [mapa] map; NÁUT chart; ~ **astral** star chart. **-5.** [documento] charter; ~ **de crédito** COM letter of credit; ~ **de naturaleza** naturalization papers (pl); ~ **de pago** COM receipt; ~ **de trabajo** work permit; ~ **verde** green card; ~**s credenciales** letters of credence. **-6.** loc: **a ~ cabal** through and through; **jugarse la última ~** to play one's last card; **jugarse todo a una ~** to put all one's eggs in one basket; **no saber a qué ~ quedarse** to be unsure; **poner las ~s boca arriba** o **sobre la mesa** to put one's cards on the table; **tomar ~s en un asunto** to intervene in a matter.
◆ **carta blanca** f carte blanche.
◆ **carta de ajuste** f test card.

cartabón m set square.

cartapacio m **-1.** [carpeta] folder. **-2.** [cuaderno] note book.

cartearse vpr to correspond.

cartel m **-1.** [anuncio] poster; **"prohibido fijar ~es"** "billposters will be prosecuted". **-2.** fig [fama]: **de ~** famous, star (antes de sust); **tener ~** to be all the rage.

cártel m cartel.

cartelero, -ra adj popular, big-name.
◆ **cartelera** f **-1.** [tablón] hoarding, billboard. **-2.** PRENS entertainments page; **estar en ~** to be showing; **lleva un año en ~** it's been running for a year.

cartelista m y f poster artist.

carteo m correspondence.

cárter m AUTOM housing.

cartera f **-1.** [para dinero] wallet. **-2.** [para documentos] briefcase; [sin asa] portfolio; [de colegial] satchel; **tener algo en ~** fig to have sthg in the pipeline. **-3.** COM, FIN & POLÍT

portfolio; ~ **de pedidos** [pedidos pendientes] orders (pl) in hand; [pedidos atrasados] backlog; ~ **de valores** portfolio. **-4.** Amer [bolso] bag.

carterista m y f pickpocket.

cartero, -ra m y f postman (f postwoman).

cartesiano, -na adj, m y f FILOSOFÍA Cartesian.

cartilaginoso, -sa adj cartilaginous.

cartílago m cartilage.

cartilla f **-1.** [documento] book; ~ **(de ahorros)** savings book; ~ **militar** booklet to say one has completed one's military service; ~ **de parado** ≃ UB40 Br, registration card issued to the unemployed; ~ **de la seguridad social** social security card. **-2.** [para aprender a leer] primer. **-3.** loc: **leerle la ~ a alguien** to read sb the riot act; **no saberse la ~** not to have a clue.

cartografía f cartography.

cartógrafo, -fa m y f cartographer.

cartomancia f cartomancy.

cartón m **-1.** [material] cardboard; ~ **piedra** papier mâché. **-2.** [de cigarrillos] carton.

cartoné
◆ **en cartoné** loc adv bound in boards.

cartuchera f cartridge belt.

cartucho m **-1.** [de arma] cartridge; **quemar el último ~** fig to play one's last card. **-2.** [envoltorio - de monedas] roll; [- de avellanas etc] paper cone.

cartujo, -ja adj Carthusian.
◆ **cartujo** m **-1.** [religioso] Carthusian. **-2.** fig [persona retraída] hermit.
◆ **cartuja** f charterhouse.

cartulina f card.

casa f **-1.** [edificio] house; ~ **adosada** semi-detached house; ~ **de campo** country house; ~ **unifamiliar** house (usually detached) on an estate; **se le cae la ~ encima** [se deprime] it's the end of the world for him; **echar** o **tirar la ~ por la ventana** to spare no expense; **empezar la ~ por el tejado** to put the cart before the horse; **ser de andar por ~** [sencillo] to be simple o basic; **en ~ del herrero cuchillo de palo** proverb the shoemaker's wife is always worst shod. **-2.** [hogar] home; **en ~** at home; **ir a ~** to go home; **pásate por mi ~** come round to my place. **-3.** [familia] family. **-4.** [linaje] house. **-5.** [empresa] company; ~ **de empeño** o **préstamo** pawnshop; ~ **de citas** brothel; ~ **discográfica** record company; ~ **de huéspedes** guesthouse. **-6.** [organismo]: ~ **Consistorial** town hall; ~ **de socorro** first-aid post.

Casablanca Casablanca.

casaca f frock coat.

casación f annulment.

casadero, -ra adj marriageable.

casado, -da ◇ adj: ~ **(con)** married (to). ◇ m y f married man (f married woman); **los recién** ~s the newly-weds.

casamentero, -ra ◇ adj matchmaking. ◇ m y f matchmaker.

casamiento m wedding, marriage.

casanova m Casanova.

casar ◇ vt **-1.** [en matrimonio] to marry. **-2.** [unir] to fit together. ◇ vi to match.
◆ **casarse** vpr: ~**se (con)** to get married (to); ~**se por la iglesia/lo civil** to have a church/civil wedding; **no** ~**se con nadie** fig to be totally impartial.

cascabel m (small) bell; **poner el** ~ **al gato** fig to dare to go ahead.

cascada f [de agua] waterfall; **en** ~ one after another.

cascado, -da adj **-1.** fam [estropeado] bust; [persona, ropa] worn-out. **-2.** [ronco] rasping.

cascanueces m inv nutcracker.

cascar [10] ◇ vt **-1.** [romper] to crack. **-2.** fam [dañar] to damage, to harm; ~**la** fig to kick the bucket. **-3.** fam [la voz] to make hoarse. **-4.** fam [pegar] to thump. ◇ vi fam [hablar] to witter on.
◆ **cascarse** vpr [romperse] to crack.

cáscara f **-1.** [de almendra, huevo etc] shell. **-2.** [de limón, naranja] skin, peel.

cascarilla f husk.

cascarón m eggshell; **salir del** ~ fig to leave the nest.

cascarrabias m y f inv grouch, misery guts (sg).

casco m **-1.** [para la cabeza] helmet; [de motorista] crash helmet. **-2.** [de barco] hull. **-3.** [de ciudad]: ~ **antiguo** old (part of) town; ~ **urbano** city centre. **-4.** [de caballo] hoof. **-5.** [envase] empty bottle. **-6.** [pedazo] fragment, piece.
◆ **cascos** mpl fam [cabeza] nut (sg); **calentarse** ○ **romperse los** ~s to rack one's brains; **ser alegre** ○ **ligero de** ~s to be scatterbrained.

cascote m piece of rubble.

caserío m **-1.** [pueblecito] hamlet. **-2.** [casa de campo] country house.

casero, -ra ◇ adj **-1.** [de casa - comida] home-made; [- trabajos] domestic; [- reunión, velada] at home; [de la familia] family (antes de sust). **-2.** [hogareño] home-loving. ◇ m y f **-1.** [propietario] landlord (f landlady). **-2.** [encargado] house agent.

caserón m large, rambling house.

caseta f **-1.** [casa pequeña] hut. **-2.** [en la playa] bathing hut. **-3.** [de feria] stall, booth. **-4.** [para perro] kennel.

casete, cassette [ka'sete] ◇ f [cinta] cassette. ◇ m [magnetófono] cassette recorder.

casi adv almost; ~ **me muero** I almost ○ nearly died; ~ **no dormí** I hardly slept at all; ~, ~ almost, just about; ~ **nunca** hardly ever.

casilla f **-1.** [taquilla] box office. **-2.** [de caja, armario] compartment; [para cartas] pigeonhole; ~ **de correos** Amer Post Office Box. **-3.** [en un impreso] box. **-4.** [de ajedrez etc] square. **-5.** loc: **sacar a alguien de sus** ~s to drive sb mad; **salir** ○ **salirse de sus** ~s to fly off the handle.

casillero m **-1.** [mueble] set of pigeonholes. **-2.** [casilla] pigeonhole.

casino m **-1.** [para jugar] casino. **-2.** [asociación] (social) club.

casis [ka'sis] m inv **-1.** [arbusto] blackcurrant bush. **-2.** [fruto] blackcurrant. **-3.** [licor] cassis.

caso m **-1.** [gen, DER & GRAM] case; **el** ~ **es que** the fact is (that); **en el mejor/peor de los** ~s at best/worst; ~ **de conciencia** matter of conscience; ~ **de fuerza mayor** force (U) of circumstance. **-2.** [ocasión] occasion; **en** ~ **de** in the event of; **en** ~ **de que** if; **(en)** ~ **de que venga** should she come; **en cualquier** ~ **todo** ~ in any event ○ case. **-3.** loc: **hacer** ~ **a** to pay attention to; **hacer omiso de** to ignore; **ir al** ~ to get to the point; **no hacer** ○ **venir al** ~ to be irrelevant; **ser un** ~ fam to be a case, to be a right one; **ser un** ~ **perdido** to be a lost cause.

caspa f dandruff.

Caspio m: **el (mar)** ~ the Caspian Sea.

cáspita interj: ¡~! desus [sorpresa] my word!; [enfado] dash it!

casque etc → **cascar**.

casquete m [gorro] skullcap.
◆ **casquete esférico** m segment of a sphere.
◆ **casquete polar** m polar cap.

casquillo m **-1.** [de bala] case. **-2.** [de lámpara] socket, lampholder.

casquivano, -na adj fam harebrained.

cassette = **casete**.

casta f **-1.** [linaje] stock, lineage. **-2.** [especie, calidad] breed. **-3.** [en la India] caste.

castaña → **castaño**.

castañazo m fam bash.

castañetear ◇ vt [chasquear] to click. ◇ vi [dientes] to chatter.

castañeteo *m* **-1.** [de castañuelas] clacking. **-2.** [de dientes] chattering.

castaño, -ña *adj* [color] chestnut.

◆ **castaño** *m* **-1.** [çolor] chestnut; **pasar de ~ oscuro** *fig* to be beyond a joke. **-2.** [árbol] chestnut (tree); **~ de Indias** horse-chestnut (tree). **-3.** [madera] chestnut.

◆ **castaña** *f* **-1.** [fruto] chestnut; **sacarle a alguien las castañas del fuego** *fam* to get sb out of trouble. **-2.** *fam* [golpe] thump. **-3.** *fam* [borrachera]: **agarrarse una castaña** to get legless.

castañuela *f* castanet.

castellanizar [13] *vt* to hispanicize.

castellano, -na *adj, m y f* Castilian.

◆ **castellano** *m* [lengua] (Castilian) Spanish.

castellano-leonés, -esa *adj, m y f* Castilian-Leonese.

casticismo *m* purism.

castidad *f* chastity.

castigador, -ra *fam* ◇ *adj* seductive. ◇ *m y f* ladykiller (*f* man-eater).

castigar [16] *vt* **-1.** [imponer castigo] to punish. **-2.** DEP to penalize. **-3.** [maltratar] to damage. **-4.** *fig* [enamorar] to seduce.

castigo *m* **-1.** [sanción] punishment; **~ ejemplar** exemplary punishment. **-2.** [sufrimiento] suffering (*U*); [daño] damage (*U*). **-3.** DEP penalty.

Castilla-La Mancha Castile and La Mancha.

Castilla-León Castile and León.

castillo *m* **-1.** [edificio] castle; **~s en el aire** ○ **de naipes** *fig* castles in the air. **-2.** NÁUT: **~ de popa** quarterdeck; **~ de proa** forecastle.

castizo, -za *adj* pure; [autor] purist.

casto, -ta *adj* chaste.

castor *m* beaver.

castración *f* castration.

castrar *vt* **-1.** [animal, persona] to castrate; [gato] to doctor. **-2.** *fig* [debilitar] to sap, to impair.

castrense *adj* military.

castrista *adj, m y f* Castroist.

casual *adj* chance, accidental.

casualidad *f* coincidence; **dio la ~ de que ...** it so happened that ...; **por ~** by chance; **¡qué ~!** what a coincidence!

casualmente *adv* by chance.

casuístico, -ca *adj* casuistic.

◆ **casuística** *f* casuistry.

casulla *f* chasuble.

cata *f* tasting.

catabolismo *m* catabolism.

cataclismo *m* cataclysm.

catacumbas *fpl* catacombs.

catador, -ra *m y f* taster.

catadura *f* *fig* look, appearance.

catafalco *m* catafalque.

catalán, -ana *adj, m y f* Catalan, Catalonian.

◆ **catalán** *m* [lengua] Catalan.

catalanismo *m* **-1.** [palabra] Catalanism. **-2.** POLÍT Catalan nationalism.

catalejo *m* telescope.

catalepsia *f* catalepsy.

catalítico, -ca *adj* QUÍM catalytic.

catalizador, -ra *adj* **-1.** QUÍM catalytic. **-2.** *fig* [impulsor] catalysing (*antes de sust*).

◆ **catalizador** *m* **-1.** QUÍM & *fig* catalyst. **-2.** AUTOM catalytic converter.

catalizar [13] *vt* **-1.** QUÍM to catalyse. **-2.** *fig* [impulsar] to provoke.

catalogación *f* cataloguing.

catalogar [16] *vt* **-1.** [en catálogo] to catalogue. **-2.** [clasificar]: **~ a alguien (de)** to class sb (as).

catálogo *m* catalogue.

Cataluña Catalonia.

catamarán *m* catamaran.

cataplasma *f* **-1.** MED poultice. **-2.** *fam fig* [pesado] bore.

catapulta *f* catapult.

catapultar *vt* to catapult.

catar *vt* to taste.

catarata *f* **-1.** [de agua] waterfall; **(~s del)** Iguazú the Iguaçu Falls; **(~s del)** Niágara the Niagara Falls. **-2.** (*gen pl*) MED cataract.

catarro *m* cold.

catarsis *f inv* [purificación] catharsis.

catártico, -ca *adj* cathartic.

catastro *m* land registry.

catástrofe *f* catastrophe; [accidente de avión, tren etc] disaster.

catastrófico, -ca *adj* catastrophic.

catastrofismo *m* [pesimismo] scaremongering, alarmism.

catastrofista *adj, m y f* alarmist.

catavino *m* wine taster.

catch [katʃ] *m* DEP all-in wrestling.

cátcher ['katʃer] (*pl* **catchers**) *m* DEP catcher.

catchup ['ketʃup], **ketchup** *m inv* ketchup.

cate *m fam* fail.

catear *vt fam* to fail.

catecismo *m* catechism.

cátedra *f* **-1.** [cargo - en universidad] chair; [- en instituto] post of head of department.

-2. [departamento] department. **-3.** *loc:* poner O sentar ~ to lay down the law.

catedral *f* cathedral.

catedralicio, -cia *adj* cathedral (*antes de sust*).

catedrático, -ca *m y f* [de universidad] professor; [de instituto] head of department.

categoría *f* **-1.** [gen] category. **-2.** [posición social] standing; **de** ~ important. **-3.** [calidad] quality; **de (primera)** ~ first-class.

categórico, -ca *adj* categorical.

catequesis *f inv* catechesis.

catequizar [13] *vt* **-1.** [enseñar religión] to instruct in the Christian doctrine. **-2.** *fig* [adoctrinar] to convert.

caterva *f* host, multitude.

cateto, -ta *despec* ◇ *adj* uncultured, uncouth. ◇ *m y f* country bumpkin.
◆ **cateto** *m* GEOM cathetus.

catire, -ra *adj* Amer blond.

cátodo *m* cathode.

catolicismo *m* Catholicism.

católico, -ca ◇ *adj* Catholic; **no estar muy** ~ *fam fig* to be under the weather. ◇ *m y f* Catholic.

catón *m* **-1.** [libro] primer. **-2.** *fig* [persona severa] severe person.

catorce *núm* fourteen; *ver también* **seis**.

catorceavo, -va, catorzavo, -va *núm* fourteenth; **la catorceava parte** a fourteenth.

catre *m* [cama] camp bed; **irse al** ~ *fam* to hit the sack.

catrín, -trina *m y f* Amer fam toff.

caucásico, -ca *adj, m y f* Caucasian.

Caucaso *m:* **el** ~ the Caucasus.

cauce *m* **-1.** AGR & *fig* channel. **-2.** [de río] river-bed; **volver a su** ~ to return to normal.

caucho *m* **-1.** [sustancia] rubber; ~ **vulcanizado** vulcanized rubber. **-2.** [planta] rubber tree.

caudal *m* **-1.** [cantidad de agua] flow, volume. **-2.** [capital, abundancia] wealth.

caudaloso, -sa *adj* **-1.** [río] with a large flow. **-2.** [persona] wealthy, rich.

caudillaje *m* leadership.

caudillo *m* [en la guerra] leader, head.
◆ **Caudillo** *m:* **el Caudillo** HIST title used to refer to Franco.

causa *f* **-1.** [origen, ideal] cause. **-2.** [razón] reason; **a** ~ **de** because of. **-3.** DER case.

causal *adj* causal.

causalidad *f* causality.

causante ◇ *adj:* **la razón** ~ the cause. ◇ *m y f* cause.

causar *vt* [gen] to cause; [impresión] to make; [placer] to give.

causticidad *f lit* & *fig* causticity.

cáustico, -ca *adj lit* & *fig* caustic.

cautela *f* caution, cautiousness; **con** ~ cautiously.

cauteloso, -sa ◇ *adj* cautious, careful. ◇ *m y f* cautious person.

cauterizar [13] *vt* to cauterize.

cautivador, -ra ◇ *adj* captivating, enchanting. ◇ *m y f* charmer.

cautivar *vt* **-1.** [apresar] to capture. **-2.** [seducir] to captivate, to enchant.

cautiverio *m,* **cautividad** *f* captivity; **vivir en** ~ to live in captivity.

cautivo, -va *adj, m y f* captive.

cauto, -ta *adj* cautious, careful.

cava ◇ *m* [bebida] *Spanish champagne-type wine.* ◇ *f* **-1.** [bodega] wine cellar. **-2.** [excavación] digging.

cavar *vt* & *vi* [gen] to dig; [con azada] to hoe.

caverna *f* cave; [más grande] cavern.

cavernícola *m y f* caveman (*f* cavewoman).

cavernoso, -sa *adj* cavernous; [voz, tos] hollow.

caviar (*pl* caviares) *m* caviar.

cavidad *f* cavity; [formada con las manos] cup.

cavilación *f* deep thought, pondering.

cavilar *vi* to think deeply, to ponder.

caviloso, -sa *adj* thoughtful, pensive.

cayado *m* **-1.** [de pastor] crook. **-2.** [de obispo] crozier.

Cayena Cayenne.

cayera *etc* → **caer**.

caza ◇ *f* **-1.** [acción de cazar] hunting; **dar** ~ **a** to hunt down; **salir** O **ir de** ~ to go hunting; ~ **de brujas** *fig* witch-hunt. **-2.** [animales, carne] game; ~ **mayor/menor** big/small game. ◇ *m* fighter (plane).

cazabombardero *m* fighter-bomber.

cazador, -ra ◇ *adj* hunting. ◇ *m y f* [persona] hunter; ~ **furtivo** poacher.
◆ **cazadora** *f* [prenda] bomber jacket.

cazadotes *m inv* fortune hunter.

cazalla *f* [bebida] aniseed-flavoured spirit.

cazar [13] *vt* **-1.** [animales etc] to hunt. **-2.** *fig* [pillar, atrapar] to catch; [en matrimonio] to trap.

cazo *m* saucepan.

cazoleta *f* **-1.** [recipiente] pot. **-2.** [de pipa] bowl.

cazuela *f* **-1.** [recipiente] pot; [de barro] earthenware pot; [para el horno] casserole (dish). **-2.** [guiso] casserole, stew; **a la ~** casseroled.

cazurro, -rra ◇ *adj* [bruto] stupid. ◇ *m y f* [bruto] idiot, fool.

CBS (*abrev de* **Columbia Broadcasting System**) *f* CBS.

c/c (*abrev de* **cuenta corriente**) a/c.

CC *m* **-1.** *abrev de* **código civil. -2.** *abrev de* **código de circulación. -3.** (*abrev de* **cuerpo consular**) *consular staff.*

CCA ◇ *m* (*abrev de* **Consejo de Cooperación Aduanera**) CCC. ◇ *f* (*abrev de* **Compañía Cubana de Aviación**) CCA.

CCEI (*abrev de* **Conferencia de Cooperación Económica Internacional**) *f* CIEC.

CC OO (*abrev de* **Comisiones Obreras**) *fpl Spanish communist-inspired trade union.*

CC-RTV (*abrev de* **Corporación Catalana de Radio y Televisión**) *f independent Catalan broadcasting company.*

CD *m* **-1.** (*abrev de* **club deportivo**) sports club; [en fútbol] FC. **-2.** (*abrev de* **cuerpo diplomático**) CD. **-3.** (*abrev de* **compact disc**) CD.

CDC (*abrev de* **Convergència Democràtica de Catalunya**) *m Catalan political party to the centre-right of the political spectrum.*

CDN (*abrev de* **Centro Dramático Nacional**) *m Spanish national theatre.*

CDS (*abrev de* **Centro Democrático y Social**) *m Spanish political party at the centre of the political spectrum.*

ce *f*: **~ por be** *fig* in great detail.

CE ◇ *m* (*abrev de* **Consejo de Europa**) CE. ◇ *f* **-1.** (*abrev de* **Comunidad Europea**) EC. **-2.** (*abrev de* **constitución española**) *Spanish Constitution.*

CEA *f* **-1.** (*abrev de* **Compañía Ecuatoriana de Aviación**) CEA. **-2.** (*abrev de* **Confederación Europea de Agricultura**) ECA.

CEAPA (*abrev de* **Confederación Española de Asociaciones de Padres de Alumnos**) *f confederation of Spanish parent-teacher associations.*

CEAR (*abrev de* **Comisión Española de Ayuda al Refugiado**) *f charitable organization that helps refugees in Spain.*

cebada *f* barley.

cebador *m* **-1.** [de fluorescente] ballast. **-2.** [de pólvora] primer.

cebar *vt* **-1.** [sobrealimentar] to fatten (up). **-2.** [máquina, arma] to prime. **-3.** [anzuelo] to bait.

◆ **cebarse en** *vpr* to take it out on.

cebo *m* **-1.** [para cazar] bait. **-2.** [para alimentar] feed, food. **-3.** *fig* [para atraer] incentive.

cebolla *f* onion.

cebolleta *f* **-1.** BOT spring onion. **-2.** [en vinagre] pickled onion; [muy pequeña] silverskin onion.

cebollino *m* **-1.** BOT chive; [cebolleta] spring onion. **-2.** *fam* [necio] idiot.

cebón, -ona ◇ *adj* fattened. ◇ *m* pig.

cebra *f* zebra.

cebú (*pl* **cebúes**) *m* zebu.

ceca *f* mint.

◆ **Ceca** *f*: **ir de la Ceca a la Meca** *fig* to go here, there and everywhere.

CECA (*abrev de* **Comunidad Europea del Carbón y del Acero**) *f* ECSC.

cecear *vi* to lisp.

ceceo *m* lisp.

cecina *f* dried, salted meat.

CECU (*abrev de* **Confederación Estatal de Consumidores y Usuarios**) *f Spanish consumer association,* ≃ CA *Br.*

CEDA (*abrev de* **Confederación Española de Derechas Autónomas**) *f Spanish extreme right-wing Catholic political party.*

cedazo *m* sieve.

ceder ◇ *vt* **-1.** [traspasar, transferir] to hand over. **-2.** [conceder] to give up. ◇ *vi* **-1.** [venirse abajo] to give way. **-2.** [destensarse] to give, to become loose. **-3.** [disminuir] to abate. **-4.** [rendirse] to give up; **~ a** to give in to; **~ en** to give up on.

CEDES (*abrev de* **Centro de Debates y Estudios Sindicales**) *m centre for debating and studying trade-union issues.*

CEDI (*abrev de* **Centro Europeo de Documentación e Información**) *m European Documentation and Information Centre.*

cedilla *f* cedilla.

cedro *m* cedar.

cédula *f* document; **~ de citación** summons (*sg*); **~ de habitabilidad** *certificate stating that a place is habitable;* **~ hipotecaria** mortgage bond; **~ (de identidad)** *Amer* identity card; **~ de vecindad** identity card.

CEE (*abrev de* **Comunidad Económica Europea**) *f* EEC.

cefalea *f* headache, cephalalgia (MED).

cefalópodo *m* cephalopod.

cegador, -ra *adj* blinding.

cegar [35] ◇ *vt* **-1.** [gen] to blind. **-2.** [tapar - ventana] to block off; [- tubo] to block up. ◇ *vi* to be blinding.

◆ **cegarse** *vpr lit & fig* to be blinded.

cegato, -ta ◇ *adj* short-sighted. ◇ *m y f fam* short-sighted person.

cegesimal *adj* of or relating to cgs units.

cegué *etc* → **cegar.**

ceguera *m lit & fig* blindness.

CEH (*abrev de* **Centro de Estudios Hispánicos**) *m* centre for Hispanic studies.

CEI (*abrev de* **Confederación de Estados Independientes**) *f* CIS.

Ceilán Ceylon.

ceja *f* **-1.** ANAT eyebrow; **quemarse las ~s** *fam* to burn the midnight oil; **se le metió entre ~ y ~** *fam* he got it into his head; **tener a alguien entre ~ y ~** *fam* not to be able to stand the sight of sb. **-2.** [borde] border, edging. **-3.** [MÚS - puente] bridge; [- cejilla] capo.

cejar *vi*: **~ en** to give up on.

cejijunto, -ta *adj* **-1.** [persona] bushy-eyebrowed. **-2.** [gesto] frowning.

cejilla *f* MÚS capo.

celada *f* [trampa] trick, trap.

celador, -ra *m y f* [de colegio, hospital] watchman; [de prisión] warder; [de museo] attendant.

Celam (*abrev de* **Consejo Episcopal Latinoamericano**) *m* Latin-American episcopal council.

celda *f* cell; **~ de castigo** solitary confinement cell.

celdilla *f* cell.

celebérrimo, -ma *adj* extremely famous.

celebración *f* **-1.** [festejo] celebration. **-2.** [realización] holding.

celebrar *vt* **-1.** [festejar] to celebrate. **-2.** [llevar a cabo] to hold; [oficio religioso] to celebrate. **-3.** [alegrarse de] to be delighted with. **-4.** [alabar] to praise, to applaud.

◆ **celebrarse** *vpr* **-1.** [festejarse] to be celebrated; **esa fiesta se celebra el 24 de Julio** that festivity falls on 24th July. **-2.** [llevarse a cabo] to take place, to be held.

célebre *adj* famous, celebrated.

celebridad *f* **-1.** [fama] fame. **-2.** [persona famosa] celebrity.

celeridad *f* speed.

celeste *adj* **-1.** [del cielo] celestial, heavenly. **-2.** → **azul**.

celestial *adj* celestial, heavenly.

celestina *f* lovers' go-between.

celibato *m* celibacy.

célibe *adj, m y f* celibate.

celo *m* **-1.** [esmero] zeal, keenness. **-2.** [devoción] devotion. **-3.** [de animal] heat; **en ~** on heat, in season. **-4.** [cinta adhesiva] Sellotape®.

◆ **celos** *mpl* jealousy (*U*); **dar ~s a alguien** to make sb jealous; **tener ~s de alguien** to be jealous of sb.

celofán *m* cellophane.

celosía *f* lattice window, jalousie.

celoso, -sa ◇ *adj* **-1.** [con celos] jealous. **-2.** [cumplidor] keen, eager. ◇ *m y f* [con celos] jealous person.

celta ◇ *adj* Celtic. ◇ *m y f* [persona] Celt. ◇ *m* [lengua] Celtic.

celtíbero, -ra, celtibero, -ra *adj, m y f* Celtiberian.

céltico, -ca *adj* Celtic.

célula *f* cell.

◆ **célula fotoeléctrica** *f* photoelectric cell, electric eye.

◆ **célula fotovoltaica** *f* photovoltaic cell.

celular *adj* cellular, cell (*antes de sust*).

celulitis *f inv* cellulitis.

celuloide *m* **-1.** QUÍM celluloid. **-2.** [película] film.

celulosa *f* cellulose.

CEM (*abrev de* **Centro de Estudios para la Mujer**) *m* centre for women's studies.

cementerio *m* **-1.** [de muertos] cemetery, graveyard. **-2.** [de cosas inutilizables] dump; **~ de automóviles** ○ **coches** scrapyard; **~ nuclear** ○ **radioactivo** nuclear dumping ground.

cemento *m* [gen] cement; [hormigón] concrete; **~ armado** reinforced concrete.

CEMT (*abrev de* **Conferencia Europea de Ministros de Transportes**) *f* European Conference of Transport Ministers.

cena *f* dinner, evening meal; **dar una ~** to give a dinner party; **~ de despedida** farewell dinner.

◆ **Última Cena** *f*: **la Última Cena** the Last Supper.

cenáculo *m* culto & fig [círculo] circle.

cenador *m* arbour, bower.

cenagal *m* bog, marsh.

cenagoso, -sa *adj* muddy, boggy.

cenar ◇ *vt* to have for dinner. ◇ *vi* to have dinner.

cencerro *m* cowbell; **estar como un ~** *fam* fig to be as mad as a hatter.

cenefa *f* border.

cenetista ◇ *adj* of or relating to the CNT. ◇ *m y f* member of the CNT.

cenicero *m* ashtray.

ceniciento, -ta *adj* ashen, ash-grey.

◆ **cenicienta** *f* fig Cinderella.

CENIDE (*abrev de* **Centro Nacional de Investigaciones para el Desarrollo de la Educación**) *m* Spanish educational development research centre.

cenit = **zenit**.

cenital *adj* midday (*antes de sust*).

cenizo, -za *adj* ashen, ash-grey.

◆ **cenizo** *m* **-1.** [mala suerte] bad luck. **-2.** [gafe] jinx.

◆ **ceniza** *f* ash.

◆ **cenizas** *fpl* [de cadáver] ashes.

censar *vt* to take a census of.

censo *m* **-1.** [padrón] census; ~ **electoral** electoral roll. **-2.** [tributo] tax. **-3.** DER lease.

CENSOLAR (*abrev de* **Centro de Estudios de la Energía Solar**) *m Spanish solar energy research centre.*

censor, -ra *m y f* **-1.** [funcionario] censor. **-2.** [crítico] critic.

◆ **censor de cuentas** *m* ECON auditor.

censura *f* **-1.** [prohibición] censorship. **-2.** [organismo] censors (*pl*). **-3.** [reprobación] censure, severe criticism.

censurable *adj* censurable.

censurar *vt* **-1.** [prohibir] to censor. **-2.** [reprobar] to criticize severely, to censure.

centauro *m* centaur.

centavo, -va *núm* hundredth; **la centava parte** a hundredth.

◆ **centavo** *m* [moneda - en países anglosajones] cent; [- en países latinoamericanos] centavo; **sin un** ~ penniless.

centella *f* **-1.** [rayo] flash. **-2.** [chispa] spark. **-3.** *fig* [cosa, persona]: **es una** ~ he's like lightning; **rápido como una** ~ quick as a flash.

centellear *vi* to sparkle; [estrella] to twinkle.

centelleo *m* sparkle, sparkling (*U*); [de estrella] twinkle, twinkling (*U*).

centena *f* hundred; **una** ~ **de** a hundred.

centenar *m* hundred; **un** ~ **de** a hundred; **a** ~**es** by the hundred.

centenario, -ria *adj* [persona] in one's hundreds; [cifra] three-figure (*antes de sust*).

◆ **centenario** *m* centenary; **quinto** ~ five hundredth anniversary.

centeno *m* rye.

centésimo, -ma *núm* hundredth.

centígrado, -da *adj* Centigrade.

◆ **centígrado** *m* Centigrade.

centigramo *m* centigram.

centilitro *m* centilitre.

centímetro *m* **-1.** [medida] centimetre. **-2.** [cinta] measuring tape.

céntimo *m* [moneda] cent; **estar sin un** ~ *fig* to be flat broke.

centinela *m* sentry.

centollo *m* spider crab.

centrado, -da *adj* **-1.** [basado]: ~ **en** based on. **-2.** [equilibrado] stable, steady. **-3.** [rueda, cuadro etc] centred.

central ◇ *adj* central. ◇ *m* DEP central defender. ◇ *f* **-1.** [oficina] headquarters, head office; [de correos, comunicaciones] main office; ~ **telefónica** telephone exchange. **-2.** [de energía] power station; ~ **eólica** wind farm; ~ **hidroeléctrica** O **hidráulica** hydroelectric power station; ~ **nuclear** nuclear power station; ~ **térmica** thermal power station.

centralismo *m* centralism.

centralista *adj, m y f* centralist.

centralita *f* switchboard.

centralización *f* centralization.

centralizar [13] *vt* to centralize.

centrar *vt* **-1.** [gen & DEP] to centre. **-2.** [arma] to aim. **-3.** [persona] to steady, to make stable. **-4.** [atención, interés] to be the centre of.

◆ **centrarse** *vpr* **-1.** [concentrarse]: ~**se en** to concentrate O focus on. **-2.** [equilibrarse] to find one's feet.

céntrico, -ca *adj* central.

centrifugadora *f* **-1.** [máquina centrífuga] centrifuge. **-2.** [para secar ropa] spindryer.

centrifugar [16] *vt* **-1.** TECN to centrifuge. **-2.** [ropa] to spin-dry.

centrífugo, -ga *adj* centrifugal.

centrípeto, -ta *adj* centripetal.

centrista ◇ *adj* centre (*antes de sust*). ◇ *m y f* centrist.

centro *m* **-1.** [gen] centre; **ser de** ~ POLÍT to be at the centre of the political spectrum; ~ **docente** O **de enseñanza** educational institution; ~ **nervioso/óptico** nerve/optic centre; ~ **de cálculo** computer centre; ~ **de desintoxicación** detoxification centre; ~ **de planificación familiar** family planning clinic; ~ **social** community centre. **-2.** [de ciudad] town centre; **me voy al** ~ I'm going to town.

◆ **centro comercial** *m* shopping centre.

◆ **centro de atracción** *m* centre of attraction.

◆ **centro de gravedad** *m* centre of gravity.

◆ **centro de mesa** *m* centrepiece.

centrocampista *m y f* DEP midfielder.

centuplicar [10] *vt* to increase a hundredfold.

centuria *f* century.

ceñido, -da *adj* tight.

ceñidor *m* belt.

ceñir [26] *vt* **-1.** [apretar] to be tight on. **-2.** [abrazar] to embrace. **-3.** *fig* [amoldar]: ~ **a** to keep O restrict to.

◆ **ceñirse** *vpr* **-1.** [apretarse] to tighten. **-2.** [limitarse]: ~**se a** to keep O stick to.

ceño *m* frown, scowl; **fruncir el** ~ to frown, to knit one's brow.

CEOE (*abrev de* **Confederación Española de Organizaciones Empresariales**) *f* ≃ CBI *Br*.

CEOTMA (*abrev de* **Centro de Estudios de Ordenación del Territorio y Medio Ambiente**) *m Spanish government body for the regulation of town planning and environmental pollution*.

cepa *f lit* & *fig* stock; **de pura** ~ [auténtico] real, genuine; [pura sangre] thoroughbred.

CEPA (*abrev de* **Colectivo de Educación Permanente de Adultos**) *m Spanish continuing adult education group*.

CEPAL (*abrev de* **Comisión Económica para América Latina**) *f* ECLAC.

cepillado *m* -**1.** [gen] brush, brushing (*U*). -**2.** [de madera] planing.

cepillar *vt* -**1.** [gen] to brush. -**2.** [madera] to plane. -**3.** *fam* [birlar] to pinch. -**4.** *fam* [adular] to butter up, to flatter.

◆ **cepillarse** *vpr* -**1.** [gen] to brush. -**2.** *fam* [comida, trabajo etc] to polish off. -**3.** *fam* [suspender] to fail. -**4.** *mfam* [matar] to bump off. -**5.** *vulg* [fornicar] to screw.

cepillo *m* -**1.** [para limpiar] brush; ~ **de dientes** toothbrush. -**2.** [de carpintero] plane. -**3.** [de donativos] collection box, poor box.

cepo *m* -**1.** [para cazar] trap. -**2.** [para vehículos] wheel clamp. -**3.** [para sujetar] clamp. -**4.** [para presos] stocks (*pl*).

ceporro *m fam* idiot, blockhead.

CEPSA (*abrev de* **Compañía Española de Petróleos, SA**) *f Spanish petroleum company*.

CEPYME (*abrev de* **Confederación Española de la Pequeña y Mediana Empresa**) *f Spanish confederation of SME's*.

cera *f* [gen] wax; [de abeja] beeswax; ~ **depilatoria** hair-removing wax.

cerámica *f* -**1.** [arte] ceramics (*U*), pottery. -**2.** [objeto] piece of pottery.

ceramista *m y f* potter.

cerbatana *f* blowpipe.

cerca ◇ *f* -**1.** [valla] fence. -**2.** [muro] wall. ◇ *adv* near, close; **por aquí** ~ nearby; **de** ~ [examinar etc] closely; [afectar, vivir] deeply.

◆ **cerca de** *loc prep* -**1.** [en el espacio] near, close to. -**2.** [aproximadamente] nearly, about.

cercado *m* -**1.** [valla] fence. -**2.** [lugar] enclosure.

cercanía *f* [cualidad] nearness, closeness.

◆ **cercanías** *fpl* [lugar] outskirts, suburbs.

cercano, -na *adj* -**1.** [pueblo, lugar] nearby. -**2.** [tiempo] near. -**3.** [pariente, fuente de información]: ~ **(a)** close (to).

cercar [10] *vt* -**1.** [vallar] to fence (off). -**2.** [rodear, acorralar] to surround.

cercenar *vt culto* -**1.** [extremidad] to amputate. -**2.** [restringir] to cut back, to curtail.

cerciorar *vt* to assure; ~**se (de)** to make sure (of).

cerco *m* -**1.** [gen] circle, ring. -**2.** [de puerta, ventana] frame. -**3.** [de astro] halo. -**4.** [asedio] siege; **poner** ~ **a** to lay siege to.

cerda → **cerdo**.

cerdada *f fam* dirty trick.

Cerdeña Sardinia.

cerdo, -da *m y f* -**1.** [animal] pig (*f* sow). -**2.** *fam fig* [persona] pig, swine.

◆ **cerdo** *m* [carne] pork.

◆ **cerda** *f* [pelo - de cerdo, jabalí] bristle; [- de caballo] horsehair.

cereal *m* cereal; ~**es** (breakfast) cereal (*U*).

cerebral *adj* -**1.** [del cerebro] brain (*antes de sust*), cerebral. -**2.** [racional] cerebral.

cerebro *m* -**1.** [gen] brain. -**2.** *fig* [cabecilla] brains (*sg*). -**3.** *fig* [inteligencia] brains (*pl*).

◆ **cerebro electrónico** *m* electronic brain.

ceremonia *f* ceremony.

ceremonial *adj* & *m* ceremonial.

ceremonioso, -sa *adj* ceremonious.

céreo, -a *adj* wax (*antes de sust*).

cereza *f* cherry.

cerezo *m* -**1.** [árbol] cherry tree. -**2.** [madera] cherry (wood).

cerilla *f* match.

cerillo *m Amer* match.

cerner [20], **cernir** *vt* [cribar] to sieve, to sift.

◆ **cernerse** *vpr* -**1.** [ave, avión] to hover. -**2.** *fig* [amenaza, peligro] to loom.

cernícalo *m* -**1.** [ave] kestrel. -**2.** *fam* [bruto] brute.

cernir = **cerner**.

cero ◇ *adj inv* zero. ◇ *m* -**1.** [signo] nought, zero; [en fútbol] nil; [en tenis] love. -**2.** [cantidad] nothing. -**3.** FÍS & METEOR zero; ~ **absoluto** absolute zero. -**4.** *loc*: **ser un** ~ **a la izquierda** *fam* [un inútil] to be useless; [un don nadie] to be a nobody; **partir de** ~ to start from scratch; *ver también* **seis**.

cerque *etc* → **cercar**.

cerquillo *m Amer* fringe.

cerrado, -da *adj* -**1.** [al exterior] closed, shut; [con llave, pestillo etc] locked. -**2.** [tiempo, cielo] overcast; [noche] dark. -**3.** [mentalidad, sociedad]: ~ **(a)** closed (to). -**4.** [rodeado] surrounded; [por montañas] walled in. -**5.** [circuito] closed. -**6.** [curva] sharp, tight.

-7. [vocal] close. **-8.** [acento, deje] broad, thick.

cerradura f lock.

cerrajería f **-1.** [oficio] locksmithery. **-2.** [local] locksmith's (shop).

cerrajero, -ra m y f locksmith.

cerrar ◇ vt **-1.** [gen] to close; [puerta, cajón, boca] to shut, to close; [puños] to clench; [con llave, pestillo etc] to lock. **-2.** [tienda, negocio - definitivamente] to close down. **-3.** [apagar] to turn off. **-4.** [bloquear - suj: accidente, inundación etc] to block; [- suj: policía etc] to close off. **-5.** [tapar - agujero, hueco] to fill, to block (up); [- bote] to put the lid ○ top on. **-6.** [cercar] to fence (off), to enclose. **-7.** [cicatrizar] to heal, to close up. **-8.** [ir último en] to bring up the rear of. ◇ vi to close, to shut; [con llave, pestillo etc] to lock up.

◆ **cerrarse** vpr **-1.** [al exterior] to close, to shut. **-2.** [incomunicarse] to clam up; ~**se a** to close one's mind to. **-3.** [herida] to heal, to close up. **-4.** [acto, debate, discusión etc] to (come to a) close.

cerrazón f fig [obstinación] stubbornness, obstinacy.

cerril adj **-1.** [animal] wild. **-2.** fam fig [obstinado] stubborn, obstinate; [tosco, grosero] ignorant, rude.

cerro m hill; **irse por los ~s de Úbeda** to stray from the point.

cerrojazo m **-1.** [cierre brusco] slamming. **-2.** fig [interrupción] sudden interruption.

cerrojo m bolt; **echar el ~** to bolt the door.

certamen m competition, contest.

certero, -ra adj **-1.** [tiro] accurate. **-2.** [opinión, respuesta etc] correct.

certeza f certainty; **tener la ~ de que** to be certain (that).

certidumbre f certainty.

certificación f **-1.** [hecho] certification. **-2.** [documento] certificate.

certificado, -da adj [gen] certified; [carta, paquete] registered.

◆ **certificado** m certificate; ~ **de calidad** quality guarantee; ~ **de depósito** BANCA certificate of deposit; ~ **médico** medical certificate; ~ **de origen** COM certificate of origin.

certificar [10] vt **-1.** [constatar] to certify. **-2.** fig [sospechas, inocencia] to confirm. **-3.** [en correos] to register.

cerumen m earwax.

cerval adj: **miedo ~** terror.

cervantino, -na adj Cervantine.

cervatillo m (small) fawn.

cervato m fawn.

cervecería f **-1.** [fábrica] brewery. **-2.** [bar] bar.

cervecero, -ra ◇ adj beer (antes de sust). ◇ m y f [que hace cerveza] brewer.

cerveza f beer; ~ **de barril** draught beer; ~ **negra** stout; ~ **rubia** lager.

cervical ◇ adj cervical, neck (antes de sust). ◇ f (gen pl) back of the neck.

cerviz f ANAT nape, back of the neck.

cesante ◇ adj **-1.** [destituido] sacked; [ministro] removed from office. **-2.** Amer [parado] unemployed. ◇ m y f sacked person; [ministro] person removed from office.

cesantear vt Amer to make redundant.

cesantía f **-1.** [destitución] sacking; [de ministro] removal from office. **-2.** Amer [desempleo] unemployment.

cesar ◇ vt [destituir] to sack; [ministro] to remove from office. ◇ vi **-1.** [parar]: ~ **(de hacer algo)** to stop ○ cease (doing sthg); **sin ~** non-stop, incessantly. **-2.** [dimitir]: ~ **(de ○ en)** to resign (from).

cesárea f caesarean (section).

cese m **-1.** [detención, paro] stopping, ceasing. **-2.** [destitución] sacking; [de ministro] removal from office.

Cesedén (abrev de **Centro Superior de Estudios de la Defensa Nacional**) m Spanish national defence studies centre.

Cesid (abrev de **Centro Superior de Investigación de la Defensa**) m Spanish military intelligence and espionage service.

cesio m caesium.

cesión f cession, transfer; ~ **de bienes** surrender of property.

CESL (abrev de **Confederación Europea de Sindicatos Libres**) f ECFTU.

césped m **-1.** [hierba] lawn, grass (U). **-2.** DEP field, pitch.

cesta f basket.

◆ **cesta de la compra** f fig cost of living.

cestería f **-1.** [oficio] basketmaking. **-2.** [tienda] basket shop.

cesto m **-1.** [cesta] (large) basket. **-2.** DEP basket.

cetáceos mpl cetaceans.

cetrería f falconry.

cetrino, -na adj culto sallow.

cetro m **-1.** [vara] sceptre. **-2.** fig [reinado] reign. **-3.** fig [superioridad]: **ostentar el ~ de** to hold the crown of.

CEU (abrev de **Centro de Estudios Universitarios**) m private secondary school and university in Spain.

Ceuta Ceuta.

ceutí (*pl* **ceutíes**) *adj* of/relating to Ceuta.

cf., **cfr.** (*abrev de* **confróntese**) cf.

CFI (*abrev de* **Corporación Financiera Internacional**) *f* IFC.

cfr. = cf.

cg (*abrev de* **centigramo**) cg.

cgo. *abrev de* **cargo.**

CGPJ (*abrev de* **Consejo General del Poder Judicial**) *m* governing body of the Spanish judiciary, elected by the Spanish parliament.

ch, **Ch** *f* ch, Ch.

ch/ *abrev de* **cheque.**

CH (*abrev de* **Confederación Helvética**) *f* CH.

chabacanada *f* vulgar thing.

chabacanería *f* **-1.** [acción, comentario]: **lo que hizo/dijo fue una ~** what he did/said was vulgar. **-2.** [cualidad] vulgarity.

chabacano, **-na** *adj* vulgar.
◆ **chabacano** *m Amer* apricot.

chabola *f* shack; **barrios de ~s** shanty town (*sg*).

chabolismo *m* shanty towns (*pl*).

chabolista *m y f* shanty town dweller.

chacal *m* jackal.

chacarero, **-ra** *m y f Amer* farmer.

chacha *f* maid.

chachachá *m* cha-cha.

cháchara *f fam* chatter, nattering; **estar de ~** to have a natter.

chachi *adj inv fam* cool, neat *Am*.

chacina *f* cured ○ prepared pork.

chacolí (*pl* **chacolís**) *m* light wine from the Basque Country.

chacota *f*: **tomar algo a ~** to take sthg as a joke.

chacra *f Amer* farm.

Chad *m*: **el ~** Chad.

chafar *vt* **-1.** [aplastar] to flatten. **-2.** [arrugar] to crease. **-3.** *fig* [estropear] to spoil, to ruin. **-4.** *fig* [abatir] to depress.
◆ **chafarse** *vpr* [estropearse] to be ruined.

chaflán *m* **-1.** [de edificio] corner. **-2.** GEOM bevel.

chagra *Amer* ○ *m y f* peasant, person from the country. ○ *f* farm.

chal *m* shawl.

chalado, **-da** *fam* ○ *adj* crazy, mad; **estar ~ por algo/alguien** *fig* to be crazy about sthg/sb. ○ *m y f* nutter.

chaladura *f fam* **-1.** [locura] craziness, madness. **-2.** [enamoramiento] crazy infatuation.

chalán, **-ana** *m y f fig & despec* shark, wheeler-dealer.

chalana *f* NÁUT barge.

chalar *vt* to drive round the bend.

chalé (*pl* **chalés**), **chalet** (*pl* **chalets**) *m* [gen] detached house (with garden); [en el campo] cottage; [de alta montaña] chalet; **~ adosado** semi-detached house.

chaleco *m* waistcoat, vest *Am*; [de punto] tank-top; **~ antibalas** bullet-proof vest; **~ salvavidas** life jacket.

chalet = **chalé.**

chalupa *f* NÁUT small boat.

chamaco, **-ca** *m y f Amer fam* nipper, lad (*f* lass).

chamán *m* shaman.

chamarileo *m* dealing in second-hand goods.

chamarra *f* sheepskin jacket.

chambelán *m* chamberlain.

chambergo *m* wide-brimmed hat with a bell-shaped top.

chamiza *f* **-1.** [hierba] thatch. **-2.** [leña] brushwood.

chamizo *m* **-1.** [leña] half-burnt wood (*U*). **-2.** [casa] thatched hut. **-3.** *fam despec* [lugar] hovel, dive.

champa *f Amer* **-1.** [tienda de campaña] tent. **-2.** [cobertizo] shed.

champán, **champaña** *m* champagne.

champiñón *m* mushroom.

champú (*pl* **champús** ○ **champúes**) *m* shampoo.

chamuscar [10] *vt* to scorch; [cabello, barba, tela] to singe.
◆ **chamuscarse** *vpr* [cabello, barba, tela] to get singed.

chamusquina *f* scorch, scorching (*U*); **me huele a ~** *fam fig* it smells a bit fishy to me.

chance *f Amer* opportunity.

chanchada *f Amer* dirty trick.

chancho *m Amer* pig.

chanchullero, **-ra** *fam* ○ *adj* crooked, dodgy. ○ *m y f* trickster, crook.

chanchullo *m fam* fiddle, racket.

chancla *f* **-1.** *despec* [calzado viejo] old shoe. **-2.** [chancleta] low sandal; [para la playa] flip-flop.

chancleta *f* low sandal; [para la playa] flip-flop.

chanclo *m* **-1.** [de madera] clog. **-2.** [de plástico] galosh.

chándal (*pl* **chandals**), **chandal** (*pl* **chandals**) *m* tracksuit.

changarro *m Amer* small shop.

changurro *m typical Basque dish of dressed crab.*

chanquete *m tiny transparent fish eaten in Málaga.*

chantaje *m* blackmail; **hacer ~ a** to blackmail.

chantajear *vt* to blackmail.

chantajista *m y f* blackmailer.

chantillí, chantilly *m* whipped cream.

chanza *f* joke.

chao *interj fam*: ¡~! bye!, see you!

chapa *f* -1. [lámina - de metal] sheet, plate; [- de madera] board; **de tres ~s** three-ply. -2. [tapón] top, cap. -3. [insignia] badge. -4. [ficha de guardarropa] metal token ○ disc. -5. *Amer* [cerradura] lock.

◆ **chapas** *fpl* [juego] *children's game played with bottle tops.*

chapado, -da *adj* [con metal] plated; [con madera] veneered; **~ a la antigua** *fig* stuck in the past, old-fashioned.

◆ **chapado** *m* [metal] plate; [madera] veneer.

chapar *vt* [con metal] to plate; [con madera] to veneer.

chaparro, -rra ◇ *adj* short and squat. ◇ *m y f* [persona] short, squat person.

◆ **chaparro** *m* BOT dwarf oak.

chaparrón *m* downpour; *fam fig* [gran cantidad] torrent.

chapear *vt* -1. [con metal] to plate; [con madera] to veneer. -2. *Amer* [escardar] to clear with a machete.

chapela *f* beret.

chapista *m y f* AUTOM panel beater.

chapopote *m Amer* bitumen, pitch.

chapotear *vi* to splash about.

chapucear *vt* to botch (up).

chapucería *f* botch (job).

chapucero, -ra ◇ *adj* [trabajo] shoddy, sloppy; [persona] bungling. ◇ *m y f* bungler.

chapulín *m Amer* grasshopper.

chapurrear, chapurrar *vt* to speak badly.

chapurreo *m* jabbering.

chapuza *f* -1. [trabajo mal hecho] botch (job). -2. [trabajo ocasional] odd job.

chapuzón *m* dip; **darse un ~** to go for a dip.

chaqué (*pl* **chaqués**) *m* morning coat.

chaqueta *f* jacket; [de punto] cardigan; **cambiarse de ~** *fig* to change sides.

chaqueteo *m* changing sides.

chaquetero, -ra *adj, m y f* turncoat.

chaquetilla *f* short jacket.

chaquetón *m* long jacket.

charada *f* *newspaper puzzle in which a word must be guessed, with its meaning and certain syllables given as clues.*

charanga *f* -1. [banda] brass band. -2. *fam* [fiesta] party.

charca *f* pool, pond.

charco *m* puddle; **cruzar el ~** *fig* to cross the pond ○ Atlantic.

charcutería *f* -1. [tienda] *shop selling cold cooked meats and cheeses*, ≃ delicatessen. -2. [productos] cold cuts (*pl*) and cheese.

charcutero, -ra *m y f* owner of "charcutería".

charla *f* -1. [conversación] chat. -2. [conferencia] talk.

charlar *vi* to chat.

charlatán, -ana ◇ *adj* talkative. ◇ *m y f* -1. [hablador] chatterbox. -2. [mentiroso] trickster, charlatan. -3. [vendedor] travelling salesman (*f* travelling saleswoman).

charlatanería *f* -1. [locuacidad] talkativeness. -2. [palabrería] spiel.

charlestón *m* charleston.

charlotada *f* -1. [payasada] clowning around (*U*). -2. TAUROM slapstick bull-fight.

charlotear *vi* to chat.

charloteo *m* chat, chatting (*U*).

charnego, -ga *m y f pejorative term referring to immigrant to Catalonia from another part of Spain.*

charol *m* -1. [piel] patent leather. -2. [barniz] shiny varnish. -3. *Amer* [bandeja] tray.

charola *f Amer* tray.

charretera *f* epaulette.

charro, -rra ◇ *adj* -1. [salmantino] Salamancan. -2. *fig* [recargado] gaudy, showy. ◇ *m y f* Salamancan.

charrúa *Amer adj inv* & *m y f inv* Uruguayan.

chárter ◇ *adj inv* charter (*antes de sust*). ◇ *m* charter plane.

chasca *f Amer* mop of·hair.

chascar [10] ◇ *vt* -1. [lengua] to click. -2. [dedos] to snap. ◇ *vi* -1. [madera] to crack. -2. [lengua] to click.

chascarrillo *m fam* funny story.

chasco *m* -1. [decepción] disappointment; **llevarse un ~** to be disappointed. -2. [burla] trick; **dar un ~ a alguien** to play a trick on sb.

chasis *m inv* -1. AUTOM chassis. -2. FOT plateholder. -3. *fam* [esqueleto] body.

chasque *etc* → chascar.

chasquear ◇ *vt* -1. [látigo] to crack. -2. [la lengua] to click. -3. *fig* [engañar] to play a trick on. ◇ *vi* [madera] to crack.

chasquido *m* [de látigo, madera, hueso] crack; [de lengua, arma] click; [de dedos] snap.

chasquillas *fpl Amer* fringe (*sg*) *Br*, bangs *Am*.

chatarra *f* **-1.** [metal] scrap (metal). **-2.** [objetos, piezas] junk. **-3.** *fam despec* [joyas] cheap and nasty jewellery; [condecoraciones] brass, medals (*pl*). **-4.** *fam* [monedas] small change.

chatarrería *f* scrapyard.

chatarrero, -ra *m y f* scrap (metal) dealer.

chatear *vi* to go out drinking.

chateo *m* pub crawl, pub crawling (*U*); **ir de ~** to go out drinking.

chato, -ta ◇ *adj* **-1.** [nariz] snub; [persona] snub-nosed. **-2.** [aplanado] flat. ◇ *m y f* **-1.** [persona] snub-nosed person. **-2.** *fam* [apelativo] love, dear.
◆ **chato** *m* [de vino] small glass of wine.

chau, chaucito *interj Amer fam*: ¡~! see you later!

chaucha *f Amer* **-1.** [moneda] coin of little value. **-2.** [haba] early bean. **-3.** [patata] early potato.

chauvinismo = chovinismo.

chauvinista = chovinista.

chaval, -la *m y f fam* kid, lad (*f* lass).

chavalería *f fam* kids (*pl*).

chavalo, -la *m y f Amer fam* lad (*f* lass).

chaveta *f* **-1.** [clavija] cotter pin. **-2.** *fam* [cabeza] nut, head; **perder la ~** to go off one's rocker. **-3.** *Amer* [navaja] penknife.

chavo *m fam* **-1.** [dinero]: **no tener un ~** to be penniless. **-2.** *Amer* [hombre] guy, bloke.

che, ché *interj*: ¡~! hey!

checo, -ca *adj, m y f* Czech.
◆ **checo** *m* [lengua] Czech.

checoslovaco, -ca *adj, m y f* Czechoslovak, Czechoslovakian.

Checoslovaquia Czechoslovakia.

chef [ʃef] (*pl* chefs) *m* chef.

cheli *m fam* modern Spanish slang used by young people.

chelín, schilling ['ʃilin] *m* shilling.

chelo, -la *adj Amer* blond (*f* blonde).

chepa *f fam* hump.

cheposo, -sa ◇ *adj* hunchbacked. ◇ *m y f* hunchback.

cheque *m* cheque *Br*, check *Am*; **extender un ~** to make out a cheque; **~ en blanco/sin fondos** blank/bad cheque; **~ cruzado** O **barrado** crossed cheque; **~ (de) gasolina** petrol voucher; **~ nominativo** cheque in favour of a specific person; **~ al portador** cheque payable to the bearer; **~ de viaje** traveller's cheque.

chequear *.vt* **-1.** MED: **~ a alguien** to ex-

amine sb, to give sb a checkup. **-2.** [comprobar] to check.

chequeo *m* **-1.** MED. checkup. **-2.** [comprobación] check, checking (*U*).

chequera *f* chequebook *Br*, checkbook *Am*.

chévere *adj Amer fam* great, fantastic.

cheviot (*pl* cheviots) *m* cheviot.

chic *adj inv* chic.

chica *f* **-1.** [joven] girl. **-2.** [tratamiento] darling. **-3.** [criada] maid.
◆ **chica de alterne** *f* girl who works in bars encouraging customers to drink in return for a commission.

chicano, -na *adj, m y f* Chicano, Mexican-American.
◆ **chicano** *m* [lengua] Chicano.

chicarrón, -ona *m y f* strapping lad (*f* strapping lass).

chicha *f* **-1.** *fam* [para comer] meat. **-2.** *fam* [de persona] flesh. **-3.** *loc*: **no ser ni ~ ni limonada** O **limoná** not to be one thing or the other.

chícharo *m Amer* pea.

chicharra *f* **-1.** ZOOL cicada. **-2.** *Amer* [timbre] electric buzzer.

chicharro *m* **-1.** [alimento] pork crackling. **-2.** [pez] horse mackerel.

chicharrón *m* [frito] pork crackling.
◆ **chicharrones** *mpl* [embutido] cold processed meat made from pork.

chiche *Amer* ◇ *m* [adorno] adornment. ◇ *f mfam* [pecho de mujer] tit.

chichón *m* bump.

chichonera *f* helmet.

chicle *m* chewing gum.

chiclé, chicler *m* AUTOM jet.

chico, -ca *adj* [pequeño] small.
◆ **chico** *m* **-1.** [joven] boy. **-2.** [tratamiento] sonny, mate. **-3.** [recadero] messenger, office-boy.

chicote *m Amer* whip.

chifla *f* **-1.** [silbido] whistle. **-2.** [burla] mockery.

chiflado, -da *fam* ◇ *adj* crazy, mad. ◇ *m y f* nutter.

chifladura *f* **-1.** [locura] madness. **-2.** [pasión] craze, craziness (*U*).

chiflar ◇ *vt fam* [encantar]: **me chiflan las patatas fritas** I'm mad about chips. ◇ *vi* [silbar] to whistle.

chiflido *m Amer* whistling.

chigüín *m Amer* kid, nipper.

chihuahua *m* chihuahua.

chiíta *adj, m y f* Shi'ite.

chilaba *f* jellaba.

chile *m* chilli; **~ con carne** chilli con carne.

Chile Chile.

chileno, -na *adj, m y f* Chilean.

chilindrón *m* CULIN *seasoning made of tomatoes and peppers.*

chillar ◇ *vi* **-1.** [gritar - personas] to scream, to yell; [aves, monos] to screech; [cerdo] to squeal; [ratón] to squeak. **-2.** [chirriar] to screech; [puerta, madera] to creak; [bisagras] to squeak. ◇ *vt fam* [reñir] to yell at.

chillido *m* [de persona] scream, yell; [de ave, mono] screech; [de cerdo] squeal; [de ratón] squeak.

chillón, -ona ◇ *adj* **-1.** [voz] piercing. **-2.** [persona] noisy, screeching. **-3.** [color] loud, gaudy. ◇ *m y f* noisy person.

chilpayate, -ta *m y f Amer* kid.

chimenea *f* **-1.** [hogar] fireplace. **-2.** [tubo] chimney.

chimpancé *m* chimpanzee.

china → chino.

China: (la) ~ China.

chinchar *vt fam* to pester, to bug.

◆ **chincharse** *vpr fam* to get cross; **ahora te chinchas** now you can lump it.

chinche ◇ *adj fam fig* [persona] annoying. ◇ *f* [insecto] bedbug. ◇ *m y f fam fig* [persona] pest, pain.

chincheta *f* drawing pin *Br*, thumbtack *Am.*

chinchilla *f* chinchilla.

chinchín *m* **-1.** [ruido] noise of a brass band. **-2.** [brindis] toast; ¡~! cheers!; **hacer ~ por alguien** to toast sb.

chinchón *m strong aniseed liquor.*

chinchorro *m Amer* **-1.** [red] net. **-2.** [hamaca] hammock.

chinchoso, -sa ◇ *adj* annoying. ◇ *m y f* pest, pain.

chinero *m* china ◇ glass cabinet.

chingado, -da *adj* **-1.** *fam* [enfadado] cheesed off. **-2.** *mfam* [estropeado] buggered. **-3.** *Amer vulg* [jodido] fucking.

◆ **chingada** *f Amer vulg:* ¡vete a la chingada! fuck off!

chingar [16] ◇ *vt* **-1.** *fam* [molestar] to cheese off. **-2.** *mfam* [estropear] to bugger up. **-3.** *Amer vulg* [fornicar con] to fuck. ◇ *vi vulg* [fornicar] to screw, to fuck.

◆ **chingarse** *vpr mfam* [beberse] to knock back.

chinita *f Amer* **-1.** [criada] maid. **-2.** [animal] ladybird.

chino, -na *adj, m y f* Chinese; **engañar a alguien como a un** ~ *fig* to take sb for a ride; **trabajar como un** ~ *fig* to slave away.

◆ **chino** *m* **-1.** [lengua] Chinese. **-2.** [instrumento] sieve.

china *f* **-1.** [piedra] small stone, pebble; **tocarle a uno la china** to have bad luck. **-2.** *fam* [droga] deal, *small amount of hash.* **-3.** *Amer* [india] Indian woman. **-4.** *Amer* [criada] maid.

◆ **chinos** *mpl* [juego] *game in which each player must guess the number of coins or pebbles in the other's hand.*

chip (*pl* chips) *m* INFORM chip.

chipé, chipén *adj inv fam* brilliant, terrific; **ser de** ~ to be brilliant ◇ terrific.

chipirón *m* baby squid.

Chipre Cyprus.

chipriota *adj, m y f* Cypriot.

chiquero *m* TAUROM bull-pen.

chiquillada *f* childish thing.

chiquillería *f* kids (*pl*).

chiquillo, -lla *m y f* kid.

chiquitín, -ina ◇ *adj* tiny. ◇ *m y f* tiny tot.

chiquito, -ta *adj* tiny; **no andarse con chiquitas** *fig* not to mess about.

◆ **chiquito** *m* [de vino] small glass of wine.

chiribita *f* [chispa] spark.

◆ **chiribitas** *fpl fam* [en los ojos] spots in front of one's eyes.

chirigota *f fam* joke.

chirimbolo *m fam* thingamajig, whatsit.

chirimía *f* shawm.

chirimoya *f* custard apple.

chiringuito *m fam* **-1.** [bar] refreshment stall. **-2.** [negocio]: **montarse un** ~ to set up a little business.

chiripa *f fam fig* fluke; **de** ◇ **por** ~ by luck.

chirivía *f* BOT parsnip.

chirla *f* small clam.

chirona *f fam* clink, slammer; **en** ~ in the clink.

chirriar [9] *vi* [gen] to screech; [puerta, madera] to creak; [bisagra, muelles] to squeak.

chirrido *m* [gen] screech; [de puerta, madera] creak; [de bisagra, muelles] squeak.

chis = chist.

chisme *m* **-1.** [cotilleo] rumour, piece of gossip. **-2.** *fam* [cosa] thingamajig, thingy.

chismorrear *vi* to spread rumours, to gossip.

chismorreo *m* gossip.

chismoso, -sa ◇ *adj* gossipy. ◇ *m y f* gossip, scandalmonger.

chispa *f* **-1.** [de fuego, electricidad] spark; **echar** ~s *fam* to be hopping mad. **-2.** [de lluvia] spot (of rain). **-3.** *fig* [pizca] bit. **-4.** *fig* [agudeza] sparkle.

chispazo *m lit & fig* spark.

chispeante *adj* **-1.** [que chispea] that gives off sparks. **-2.** *fig* [conversación, discurso, mirada] sparkling.

chispear ◇ *vi* **-1.** [chisporrotear] to spark. **-2.** [relucir] to sparkle. ◇ *v impers* [llover] to spit (with rain).

chisporrotear *vi* [fuego, leña] to crackle; [aceite] to splutter; [comida] to sizzle.

chisporroteo *m* [de fuego, leña] crackling; [de aceite] spluttering; [de comida] sizzling.

chisquero *m* (cigarette) lighter.

chist, chis *interj* ¡~! ssh!

chistar *vi*: **me fui sin ~** I left without a word.

chiste *m* joke; **contar ~s** to tell jokes; **~ verde** dirty joke.

chistera *f* [sombrero] top hat.

chistorra *f type of cured pork sausage typical of Aragon and Navarre.*

chistoso, -sa ◇ *adj* funny. ◇ *m y f* amusing ○ funny person.

chistu *m* Basque flute.

chistulari *m y f "chistu" player.*

chita
◆ **a la chita callando** *loc adv fam* quietly, on the quiet.

chitón *interj* ¡~! quiet!

chivar *vt fam* to whisper, to tell secretly.
◆ **chivarse** *vpr fam*: **~se (de/a)** [niños] to split (on/to); [delincuentes] to grass (on/to).

chivatazo *m fam* tip-off; **dar el ~** to grass.

chivato, -ta *m y f fam* [delator] grass, informer; [acusica] telltale.
◆ **chivato** *m* **-1.** [luz] warning light; [alarma] alarm bell. **-2.** *Amer fam* [pez gordo] big cheese.

chivo, -va *m y f* kid, young goat; **ser el ~ expiatorio** *fig* to be the scapegoat.

choc (*pl* **chocs**), **choque, shock** [tʃok] *m* shock.

chocante *adj* startling.

chocar [10] ◇ *vi* **-1.** [colisionar]: **~ (contra)** to crash (into), to collide (with). **-2.** *fig* [enfrentarse] to clash. ◇ *vt* **-1.** [manos] to shake; **¡chócala!** put it there! **-2.** [copas, vasos] to clink. **-3.** *fig* [sorprender] to startle.

chochear *vi* **-1.** [viejo] to be senile. **-2.** *fam fig* [de cariño]: **~ por alguien** to dote on sb.

chochez *f* **-1.** [vejez] senility. **-2.** [dicho, hecho]: **decir/hacer chocheces** to say/do senile things.

chocho, -cha *adj* **-1.** [viejo] senile. **-2.** *fam fig* [encariñado] soft, doting.
◆ **chocho** *m* **-1.** *vulg* [órgano] cunt. **-2.** *fam* [altramuz] lupin.

choclo *m Amer* corn *Br*, maize *Am*.

choclón *m Amer fam* crowd.

chocolate *m* **-1.** [para comer, beber] chocolate; **~ (a la taza)** thick drinking chocolate; **~ blanco** white chocolate; **~ con leche** milk chocolate. **-2.** *fam* [para fumar] hash.

chocolatera → **chocolatero.**

chocolatería *f* **-1.** [fábrica] chocolate factory. **-2.** [establecimiento] *café where drinking chocolate is served.*

chocolatero, -ra *m y f* **-1.** [aficionado al chocolate] chocoholic, person fond of chocolate. **-2.** [oficio] chocolate maker ○ seller.

chocolatina *f* chocolate bar.

chófer (*pl* **chóferes**) *m y f* chauffeur.

chollo *m fam* [producto, compra] bargain; [trabajo, situación] cushy number.

chomba, chompa *f Amer* sweater, jumper.

chompipe *m Amer species of turkey.*

chonchón *m Amer* lamp.

chongo *m Amer* [moño] bun.

chopera *f* poplar grove.

chopito *m* baby squid in batter.

chopo *m* poplar.

choque ◇ *v* → **chocar.** ◇ *m* **-1.** [impacto] impact; [de coche, avión etc] crash. **-2.** *fig* [enfrentamiento] clash. **-3.** = **choc.**

choriceo *m fam* [robo] robbery; [timo] rip-off.

chorizar [13] *vt fam* to nick, to pinch.

chorizo *m* **-1.** [embutido] *highly seasoned pork sausage.* **-2.** *fam* [ladrón] thief.

chorlito *m* **-1.** ZOOL plover. **-2.** → **cabeza.**

choro *m Amer* mussel.

chorra *mfam* ◇ *m y f* [tonto] wally, idiot; **hacer el ~** to muck about. ◇ *f* [suerte] luck.

chorrada *f mfam* rubbish (*U*); **decir ~s** to talk rubbish.

chorrear ◇ *vi* **-1.** [gotear - gota a gota] to drip; [- en un hilo] to trickle. **-2.** [brotar] to spurt (out), to gush (out). ◇ *vt* [suj: jersey etc] to drip; [suj: persona] to drip with.

chorreo *m* **-1.** [goteo - gota a gota] dripping; [- en un hilo] trickling. **-2.** [brote] spurting, gushing.

chorreras *fpl* frill (*sg*).

chorro *m* **-1.** [de líquido - borbotón] jet, spurt; [- hilo] trickle; **salir a ~s** to spurt ○ gush out. **-2.** *fig* [de luz, gente etc] stream; **tiene un ~ de dinero** she has loads of money. **-3.** *loc*: **como los ~s del oro** as clean as a new pin.

chotearse *vpr fam*: **~ (de)** to make fun (of).

choteo *m fam* joking, kidding; **tomar algo a ~** to take sthg as a joke.

chotis *m inv dance typical of Madrid.*

choto, -ta *m y f* **-1.** [cabrito] kid, young goat. **-2.** [ternero] calf.

chovinismo, chauvinismo [tʃoßi'nismo] *m* chauvinism.

chovinista, chauvinista [tʃoßi'nista] ◇ *adj* chauvinistic. ◇ *m y f* chauvinist.

choza *f* hut.

christmas = **crismas**.

chubasco *m* shower.

chubasquero *m* raincoat, mac.

chúcaro, -ra *adj Amer fam* wild.

chuchería *f* **-1.** [golosina] sweet. **-2.** [objeto] trinket.

chucho *m fam* mutt, dog.

chueco, -ca *adj Amer* twisted.

chufa *f* **-1.** [planta] chufa. **-2.** [tubérculo] tiger nut.

chulada *f* **-1.** [bravuconada] swaggering (*U*). **-2.** *fam* [cosa bonita] delight, gorgeous thing.

chulapo, -pa, chulapón, -ona *m y f* HIST lower-class native of Madrid.

chulear *fam* ◇ *vt:* ~ **a una mujer** to live off a woman. ◇ *vi* [fanfarronear]: ~ **(de)** to be cocky (about).

chulería *f* **-1.** [valentonería] cockiness. **-2.** [salero] charm, winning ways (*pl*).

chuleta ◇ *f* **-1.** [de carne] chop. **-2.** [en exámenes] crib note. ◇ *m y f fam* [chulo] cocky person. ◇ *adj fam* [chulo] cocky.

chulo, -la ◇ *adj* **-1.** [descarado] cocky; **ponerse** ~ to get cocky. **-2.** *fam* [bonito] lovely. ◇ *m y f* **-1.** [descarado] cocky person. **-2.** [madrileño] working-class native of Madrid.
◆ **chulo** *m* [proxeneta] pimp.

chumba → **higuera**.

chumbera *f* prickly pear.

chumbo → **higo**.

chuminada *f fam* silly thing.

chungo, -ga *adj fam* [persona] horrible, nasty; [cosa] lousy.
◆ **chunga** *f fam:* **tomarse algo a chunga** to take sthg as a joke.

chupa *f fam* coat.

chupachup® (*pl* **chupachups**) *m* lollipop.

chupado, -da *adj* **-1.** [delgado] skinny. **-2.** *fam* [fácil]: **estar** ~ to be dead easy ○ a piece of cake.
◆ **chupada** *f* [gen] suck; [fumando] puff, drag.

chupar *vt* **-1.** [succionar] to suck; [fumando] to puff at. **-2.** [absorber] to soak up. **-3.** [quitar]: ~**le algo a alguien** to milk sb for sthg.

◆ **chuparse** *vpr* **-1.** [adelgazar] to get thinner. **-2.** *fam* [aguantar] to put up with. **-3.** *loc:* **¡chúpate esa!** take that!

chupatintas *m y f inv despec* pen-pusher.

chupe *m Amer* stew.

chupete *m* dummy *Br*, pacifier *Am*.

chupetear *vt* to suck on ○ away at.

chupi *adj fam* great, brill.

chupinazo *m* **-1.** [cañonazo] cannon shot. **-2.** [en fútbol] hard kick.

chupón, -ona *m y f fam* [gorrón] sponger, cadger.
◆ **chupón** *m Amer* [chupete] dummy *Br*, pacifier *Am*.

chupóptero, -ra *m y f fam* parasite.

churrería *f shop selling "churros".*

churrero, -ra *m y f "churros" seller.*

churrete *m* blob; [de grasa] stain.

churrigueresco, -ca *adj* churrigueresque.

churro *m* **-1.** [para comer] *dough formed into sticks or rings and fried in oil.* **-2.** *fam* [fracaso] botch. **-3.** *fam* [suerte] fluke, stroke of luck.

churrusco *m* piece of burnt toast.

churumbel *m fam* kid.

chusco, -ca *adj fam* funny.
◆ **chusco** *m fam* crust of stale bread.

chusma *f* rabble, mob.

chut (*pl* **chuts**) *m* kick.

chutar *vi* **-1.** [lanzar] to shoot. **-2.** *fam* [funcionar] to work; **esto va que chuta** it's going very well.
◆ **chutarse** *vpr mfam* to shoot up.

chute *m mfam* fix.

chuzo *m:* **llover a** ~**s, caer** ~**s de punta** *fig* to rain cats and dogs.

CI (*abrev de* **coeficiente de inteligencia**) *m* IQ.

cía., Cía. (*abrev de* **compañía**) Co.

cianuro *m* cyanide.

ciático, -ca *adj* sciatic.
◆ **ciática** *f* sciatica.

cibercafé *m* cybercafe.

ciberespacio *m* cyberspace.

cibernético, -ca *adj* cybernetic.
◆ **cibernética** *f* cybernetics (*U*).

CIC *m* **-1.** (*abrev de* **Código de Derecho Canónico**) canon law code. **-2.** (*abrev de* **Consejo Interamericano Cultural**) inter-American cultural council.

cicatería *f* stinginess, meanness.

cicatero, -ra ◇ *adj* stingy, mean. ◇ *m y f* skinflint, miser.

cicatriz *f lit & fig* scar.

cicatrización *f* scarring.

cicatrizante ◇ *adj* healing. ◇ *m* healing substance.

cicatrizar [13] ◇ *vi* to form a scar, to heal (up). ◇ *vt fig* to heal.

cicerón *m* eloquent speaker.

cicerone *m y f* guide.

cíclico, -ca *adj* cyclical.

ciclismo *m* cycling.

ciclista ◇ *adj* cycling (*antes de sust*). ◇ *m y f* cyclist.

ciclo *m* **-1.** [gen] cycle. **-2.** [de conferencias, actos] series.

ciclocrós *m* cyclo-cross.

ciclomotor *m* moped.

ciclón *m* cyclone.

cíclope *m* Cyclops.

ciclópeo, -a *adj culto* & *fig* [enorme] colossal, massive.

ciclostil, ciclostilo *m* cyclostyle.

CICR (*abrev de* **Comité Internacional de la Cruz Roja**) *m* IRCC.

cicuta *f* hemlock.

CIDEM (*abrev de* **Consejo Interamericano de Música**) *m inter-American music association*.

CIE (*abrev de* **Centro Internacional de la Infancia**) *m* ICC.

CIEA (*abrev de* **Centro Internacional de Estudios Agrícolas**) *m international agricultural studies centre*.

ciega → cegar.

ciego, -ga ◇ *adj* **-1.** [gen] blind; **a ciegas** *lit* & *fig* blindly. **-2.** *fig* [enloquecido]: ~ **(de)** blinded (by). **-3.** [pozo, tubería] blocked (up). **-4.** *mfam* [drogado] stoned. ◇ *m y f* [invidente] blind person; **los** ~**s** the blind; **hacerse el** ~ to turn a blind eye.
◆ **ciego** *m* **-1.** ANAT caecum. **-2.** *mfam* [de droga] trip.

ciegue → cegar.

cielo *m* **-1.** [gen] sky; **a** ~ **abierto** [gen] in the open; MIN opencast. **-2.** RELIG heaven. **-3.** *fig* [Dios]: **el** ~ the Good Lord. **-4.** [nombre cariñoso] my love, my dear. **-5.** [parte superior] roof; ~ **del paladar** roof of the mouth; ~ **raso** ceiling. **-6.** *loc*: **me viene bajado del** ~ it's a godsend (to me); **como llovido del** ~ [inesperadamente] out of the blue; [oportunamente] at just the right moment; **estar en el séptimo** ~ to be in seventh heaven; **se le juntó el** ~ **con la tierra** he lost his nerve; **mover** ~ **y tierra** to move heaven and earth; **ser un** ~ to be an angel; **ver el** ~ **abierto** to see one's way out.
◆ **cielos** *interj*: ¡~! good heavens!

ciempiés *m inv* centipede.

cien = ciento.

ciénaga *f* marsh, bog.

ciencia *f* **-1.** [gen] science; ~**s económicas** economics (*U*); ~**s exactas** exact ◇ pure sciences; ~**s naturales/sociales** natural/social sciences; ~**s ocultas** occult sciences. **-2.** *fig* [habilidad] learning, knowledge; ~ **infusa** *fig* intuitive knowledge.
◆ **ciencias** *fpl* EDUC science (*U*).
◆ **ciencia ficción** *f* science fiction.
◆ **a ciencia cierta** *loc adv* for certain.

cieno *m* mud, sludge.

cientificismo *m* over-emphasis on scientific ideas.

científico, -ca ◇ *adj* scientific. ◇ *m y f* scientist.

cientista *m y f*: ~ **social** *Amer* sociologist.

ciento, cien *núm* a ◇ one hundred; ~ **cincuenta** a ◇ one hundred and fifty; **cien mil** a ◇ one hundred thousand; ~**s de** hundreds of; **por** ~ per cent; ~ **por** ~, **cien por cien** a hundred per cent; **darle** ~ **y raya a uno** to run rings around sb; **eran** ~ **y la madre** everybody and his dog was there; *ver también* **seis**.

cierna *etc* → cerner.

cierne
◆ **en ciernes** *loc adv*: **estar en** ~**s** to be in its infancy; **una campeona en** ~**s** a budding champion.

cierre *m* **-1.** [gen] closing, shutting; [de fábrica] shutdown; RADIO & TV closedown; ~ **centralizado** AUTOM central locking; ~ **patronal** lockout. **-2.** [mecanismo] fastener; ~ **metálico** [de tienda etc] metal shutter; ~ **relámpago** *Amer* zip.

cierto, -ta *adj* **-1.** [verdadero] true; **estar en lo** ~ to be right; **lo** ~ **es que** ... the fact is that .... **-2.** [seguro] certain, definite. **-3.** [algún] certain; ~ **hombre** a certain man; **en cierta ocasión** once, on one occasion.
◆ **cierto** *adv* right, certainly.
◆ **por cierto** *loc adv* by the way.

ciervo, -va *m y f* deer, stag (*f* hind).

cierzo *m* north wind.

CIF (*abrev de* **código de identificación fiscal**) *m tax code*.

cifra *f* **-1.** [gen] figure; ~ **de negocios** ECON turnover. **-2.** [clave]: **en** ~ in code.

cifrado, -da *adj* coded, in code.

cifrar *vt* **-1.** [codificar] to code. **-2.** *fig* [centrar] to concentrate, to centre.
◆ **cifrarse en** *vpr* to come to, to amount to.

cigala *f* Dublin Bay prawn.

cigarra *f* cicada.

cigarrero, -ra *m y f* [persona] cigar maker.
◆ **cigarrera** *f* [caja] cigar case.

cigarrillo *m* cigarette.

cigarro *m* **-1.** [habano] cigar. **-2.** [cigarrillo] cigarette.

cigüeña *f* stork.

cigüeñal *m* crankshaft.

cilantro *m* coriander.

CILCE (*abrev de* **Centro Internacional de Lengua y Cultura Españolas**) *m* *international centre for Spanish language and culture.*

CILEH (*abrev de* **Centro de Investigaciones Literarias Españolas e Hispanoamericanas**) *m* *Spanish and Latin American literary research centre.*

cilicio *m* hair shirt.

cilindrada *f* cylinder capacity.

cilíndrico, -ca *adj* cylindrical.

cilindro *m* [gen] cylinder; [de imprenta] roller.

CIM (*abrev de* **Centro de Instrucción de Marinería**) *m* *Spanish naval training centre.*

cima *f* **-1.** [punta - de montaña] peak, summit; [- de árbol] top. **-2.** *fig* [apogeo] peak, high point.

CIMA (*abrev de* **Comisión Interministerial de Medio Ambiente**) *f interministerial commission for the environment.*

cimarrón, -ona *m y f Amer* runaway slave.

címbalo *m* (*gen pl*) cymbal.

cimbreante *adj* swaying.

cimbrear *vt* **-1.** [vara] to waggle. **-2.** [caderas] to sway.

CIME (*abrev de* **Comité Intergubernamental para la Migración Europea**) *m* ICEM.

cimentación *f* **-1.** [acción] laying of the foundations. **-2.** [cimientos] foundations (*pl*).

cimentar [19] *vt* **-1.** [edificio] to lay the foundations of; [ciudad] to found, to build. **-2.** *fig* [idea, paz, fama] to cement, to consolidate.

cimero, -ra *adj* **-1.** [alto] topmost. **-2.** *fig* [sobresaliente] foremost, most outstanding.

cimienta *etc* → **cimentar.**

cimiento *m* (*gen pl*) **-1.** CONSTR foundation; **echar los ~s** *lit & fig* to lay the foundations. **-2.** *fig* [base] basis.

cimitarra *f* scimitar.

cinabrio *m* cinnabar.

cinc, zinc *m* zinc.

cincel *m* chisel.

cincelar *vt* to chisel.

cincha *f* girth.

cincho *m* **-1.** [cinturón] belt. **-2.** [aro de hierro] hoop.

cinco *núm* five; **¡choca esos ~!** *fig* put it there!; *ver también* **seis.**

cincuenta *núm* fifty; **los (años)** ~ the fifties; *ver también* **seis.**

cincuentenario *m* fiftieth anniversary.

cincuentón, -ona *m y f* fifty-year-old.

cine *m* cinema; **hacer** ~ to make films; ~ **de estreno/de verano** first-run/open-air cinema; ~ **mudo** silent films (*pl*); ~ **sonoro** talking pictures (*pl*), talkies (*pl*).

◆ **cine fórum** *m* *film with discussion group.*

cineasta *m y f* film maker ○ director.

cineclub *m* **-1.** [asociación] film society. **-2.** [sala] club cinema.

cinéfilo, -la *m y f* film buff.

cinegético, -ca *adj* hunting (*antes de sust*).

◆ **cinegética** *f* hunting.

cinemascope *m* cinemascope.

cinemateca *f* film library.

cinemática *f* kinematics (U).

cinematografía *f* cinematography, filmmaking.

cinematográfico, -ca *adj* film (*antes de sust*).

cinematógrafo *m* **-1.** [aparato] film projector. **-2.** [local] cinema.

cinerama *m* cinerama.

cinético, -ca *adj* kinetic.

◆ **cinética** *f* kinetics (U).

cíngaro, -ra, zíngaro, -ra *adj, m y f* Tzigane.

cínico, -ca ◇ *adj* cynical. ◇ *m y f* cynic.

cinismo *m* cynicism.

cinta *f* **-1.** [tira - de plástico, papel] strip, band; [- de tela] ribbon; ~ **adhesiva** ○ **autoadhesiva** adhesive ○ sticky tape; ~ **aislante** ○ **aisladora** insulating tape; ~ **de impresora** printer ribbon; ~ **métrica** tape measure; ~ **perforada** punched tape. **-2.** [de imagen, sonido, ordenadores] tape; ~ **digital/magnética** digital/magnetic tape; ~ **magnetofónica** recording tape; ~ **de vídeo** videotape. **-3.** [mecanismo] belt; ~ **transportadora** conveyor belt. **-4.** [película] film.

cinto *m* belt.

cintura *f* waist; **meter en** ~ to bring under control.

cinturilla *f* waistband.

cinturón *m* **-1.** [cinto] belt; ~ **negro** DEP black belt; **apretarse el** ~ to tighten one's belt. **-2.** AUTOM ring road. **-3.** [cordón] cordon.

◆ **cinturón de seguridad** *m* seat ○ safety belt.

ciña, ciñera *etc* → **ceñir.**

CIO (*abrev de* **Comité Internacional Olímpico**) *m* IOC.

CIOA (*abrev de* **Comisión Internacional para la Ordenación Alimentaria**) *f international committee for the regulation of food standards.*

cipote[1] ◇ *adj fam* thick. ◇ *m vulg* prick, cock.

cipote[2], **-ta** *m y f Amer* lad (*f* lass).

ciprés *m* cypress.

CIR (*abrev de* **Centro de Instrucción de Reclutas**) *m Spanish training centre for new army recruits.*

circense *adj* circus (*antes de sust*).

circo *m* **-1.** [gen] circus. **-2.** GEOGR cirque, corrie.

circuito *m* **-1.** DEP & ELECTRÓN circuit; ~ **impreso/integrado** printed/integrated circuit; ~ **cerrado** closed circuit; **corto** ~ short-circuit. **-2.** [contorno] belt. **-3.** [viaje] tour.

circulación *f* **-1.** [gen] circulation; ~ **fiduciaria** ○ **monetaria** paper currency. **-2.** [tráfico] traffic. **-3.** [conducción] driving.

circular ◇ *adj & f* circular. ◇ *vi* **-1.** [pasar]: ~ **(por)** [líquido] to flow ○ circulate (through); [persona] to move ○ walk (around); [vehículos] to drive (along); **este autobús no circula hoy** this bus doesn't run today. **-2.** [de mano en mano] to circulate; [moneda] to be in circulation. **-3.** [difundirse] to go round.

circulatorio, -ria *adj* circulatory.

círculo *m lit & fig* circle.
◆ **círculos** *mpl* [medios] circles.
◆ **círculo polar** *m* polar circle; **el** ~ **polar ártico/antártico** the Arctic/Antarctic Circle.
◆ **círculo vicioso** *m* vicious circle.

circumpolar *adj* circumpolar.

circuncidar *vt* to circumcise.

circuncisión *f* circumcision.

circundante *adj* surrounding.

circundar *vt* to surround.

circunferencia *f* circumference.

circunflejo → **acento**.

circunlocución *f* circumlocution.

circunloquio *m* circumlocution.

circunnavegar [16] *vt* to circumnavigate, to sail round.

circunscribir *vt* **-1.** [limitar] to restrict, to confine. **-2.** GEOM to circumscribe.
◆ **circunscribirse** *a vpr* to confine o.s. to.

circunscripción *f* **-1.** [limitación] limitation. **-2.** [distrito] district; MIL division; POLÍT constituency.

circunscrito, -ta ◇ *pp* → **circunscribir**. ◇ *adj* restricted, limited.

circunspección *f culto* **-1.** [comedimiento] circumspection. **-2.** [seriedad] **graveness, seriousness.**

circunspecto, -ta *adj culto* **-1.** [comedido] circumspect. **-2.** [serio] grave, serious.

circunstancia *f* circumstance; **en estas** ~**s under the circumstances;** ~ **atenuante/agravante/eximente** DER extenuating/aggravating/exonerating circumstance.

circunstancial *adj* **-1.** [accidental] chance (*antes de sust*). **-2.** GRAM → **complemento**.

circunvalación *f* [acción] going round.

circunvalar *vt* to go round.

cirílico, -ca *adj* Cyrillic.

cirio *m* (wax) candle; ~ **pascual** paschal candle; **montar un** ~ to make a row.

cirrosis *f inv* cirrhosis.

ciruela *f* plum; ~ **claudia** greengage; ~ **pasa** prune.

ciruelo *m* plum tree.

cirugía *f* surgery; ~ **estética** ○ **plástica** cosmetic ○ plastic surgery.

cirujano, -na *m y f* surgeon.

cisco *m* **-1.** [carbón] slack; **hecho** ~ *fig* shattered. **-2.** *fam* [alboroto] row, rumpus.

CISL (*abrev de* **Confederación Internacional de Sindicatos Libres**) *f* ICFTU.

cisma *m* **-1.** [separación] schism. **-2.** [discordia] split.

cismático, -ca *adj, m y f* schismatic.

cisne *m* swan.

cisterciense *adj, m y f* Cistercian.

cisterna *f* **-1.** [de retrete] cistern. **-2.** [aljibe, tanque] tank.

cistitis *f inv* cystitis.

cita *f* **-1.** [entrevista] appointment; [de novios] date; **darse** ~ to meet; **tener una** ~ to have an appointment. **-2.** [referencia] quotation.

citación *f* DER summons (*sg*).

citar *vt* **-1.** [convocar] to make an appointment with. **-2.** [aludir] to mention; [textualmente] to quote. **-3.** DER to summons.
◆ **citarse** *vpr*: ~**se (con alguien)** to arrange to meet (sb).

cítara *f* zither.

citología *f* **-1.** [análisis ginecológico] smear test. **-2.** BIOL cytology.

citoplasma *m* cytoplasm.

cítrico, -ca *adj* citric.
◆ **cítricos** *mpl* citrus fruits.

CiU (*abrev de* **Convergència i Unió**) *f* Catalan coalition party to the centre-right of the political spectrum.

ciudad *f* **-1.** [localidad] city; [pequeña] town; ~ **dormitorio/satélite** commuter/satellite town; ~ **jardín** garden city. **-2.** [instalaciones] complex; ~ **sanitaria** hospital complex; ~ **universitaria** university campus.

◆ **Ciudad eterna** f: la Ciudad eterna the Eternal City.

◆ **Ciudad santa** f: la Ciudad santa the Holy City.

ciudadanía f **-1.** [nacionalidad] citizenship. **-2.** [población] public, citizens (pl).

ciudadano, -na ◇ adj city (antes de sust); [orgullo, deberes etc] civic. ◇ m y f citizen; **el ~ de a pie** the man in the street.

Ciudad del Cabo Cape Town.

Ciudad del Vaticano Vatican City.

Ciudad de México Mexico City.

ciudadela f citadel, fortress.

cívico, -ca adj civic; [conducta] public-spirited.

civil ◇ adj lit & fig civil. ◇ m **-1.** [no militar] civilian. **-2.** fam [Guardia Civil] member of "Guardia Civil".

civilización f civilization.

civilizado, -da adj civilized.

civilizar [13] vt to civilize.

◆ **civilizarse** vpr to become civilized.

civismo m **-1.** [urbanidad] community spirit. **-2.** [cortesía] civility, politeness.

cizalla f **-1.** [herramienta] shears (pl), metal cutters (pl). **-2.** [recortes] metal cuttings (pl).

cizaña f BOT darnel; **meter** O **sembrar ~** to sow discord; **separar la ~ del buen grano** to separate the wheat from the chaff.

CJM (abrev de **código de justicia militar**) m Spanish code of military justice.

cl (abrev de **centilitro**) cl.

clamar ◇ vt **-1.** [expresar] to exclaim. **-2.** [exigir] to cry out for. ◇ vi **-1.** [implorar] to appeal. **-2.** [protestar] to cry out.

clamor m clamour.

clamoroso, -sa adj **-1.** [rotundo] resounding. **-2.** [vociferante] loud, clamorous.

clan m **-1.** [tribu, familia] clan. **-2.** [banda] faction.

clandestinidad f secrecy; **en la ~** underground.

clandestino, -na adj clandestine; POL underground.

claque f claque.

claqué m tap dancing.

claqueta f clapperboard.

clara → claro.

claraboya f skylight.

clarear ◇ vt to light up. ◇ v impers **-1.** [amanecer]: **empezaba a ~** dawn was break-

ing. **-2.** [despejarse] to clear up, to brighten up.

◆ **clarearse** vpr [transparentarse] to be see-through.

clarete → vino.

claridad f **-1.** [transparencia] clearness, clarity. **-2.** [luz] light. **-3.** [franqueza] candidness; **ser de una ~ meridiana** to be crystal clear. **-4.** [lucidez] clarity.

clarificación f clarification.

clarificador, -ra adj clarifying.

clarificar [10] vt **-1.** [gen] to clarify; [misterio] to clear up. **-2.** [purificar] to refine.

clarín ◇ m [instrumento] bugle. ◇ m y f [persona] bugler.

clarinete ◇ m [instrumento] clarinet. ◇ m y f [persona] clarinettist.

clarinetista m y f clarinettist.

clarividencia f farsightedness, perception.

clarividente ◇ adj farsighted, perceptive. ◇ m y f perceptive person.

claro, -ra adj **-1.** [gen] clear; **~ está que ...** of course ...; **dejar algo ~** to make sthg clear; **a las claras** clearly; **pasar una noche en ~** to spend a sleepless night; **poner algo en ~** to get sthg clear, to clear sthg up; **sacar algo en ~ (de)** to make sthg out (from). **-2.** [luminoso] bright. **-3.** [color] light. **-4.** [diluido - té, café] weak; [- salsa] thin. **-5.** [poco tupido] thin, sparse.

◆ **claro** ◇ m **-1.** [en bosque] clearing; [en multitud] space, gap. **-2.** METEOR bright spell. **-3.** [en pintura] highlight. ◇ adv clearly. ◇ interj: ¡~! of course!

◆ **clara** f **-1.** [de huevo] white. **-2.** [bebida] shandy. **-3.** [calvicie] bald patch.

◆ **claro de luna** m moonlight.

claroscuro m chiaroscuro.

clase f **-1.** [gen] class; **~ alta/media** upper/middle class; **~ obrera** O **trabajadora** working class; **~ preferente/turista** club/tourist class; **~ salón** Amer FERROC first class; **primera ~** first class; **~s pasivas** pensioners. **-2.** [tipo] sort, kind; **toda ~ de** all sorts O kinds of. **-3.** [EDUC - asignatura, alumnos] class; [- aula] classroom; **dar ~s** [en un colegio] to teach; [en una universidad] to lecture; **~s particulares** private classes O lessons; **~s de recuperación** extra lessons for pupils who have failed their exams.

clasicismo m **-1.** ARTE & LITER classicism. **-2.** [tradicionalismo] classical nature.

clásico, -ca ◇ adj **-1.** [de la Antigüedad] classical. **-2.** [ejemplar, prototípico] classic. **-3.** [peinado, estilo, música etc] classical. **-4.** [habitual] customary. **-5.** [peculiar]: **~ de** typical of. ◇ m y f [persona] classic.

◆ **clásicas** fpl [estudios] classics.

clasificación f classification; DEP (league) table.

clasificador, -ra adj classifying.
◆ **clasificador** m [mueble] filing cabinet.
◆ **clasificadora** f [máquina] sorter.

clasificar [10] vt to classify.
◆ **clasificarse** vpr **-1.** [ganar acceso]: ~se (para) to qualify (for); DEP to get through (to). **-2.** [llegar]: se clasificó en segundo lugar she came second.

clasismo m class discrimination.

clasista ◇ adj class-conscious; despec snobbish. ◇ m y f class-conscious person; despec snob.

claudia → ciruela.

claudicación f withdrawal.

claudicar [10] vi **-1.** [ceder] to give in. **-2.** [renunciar]: ~ de to renounce.

claustro m **-1.** ARQUIT & RELIG cloister. **-2.** [de universidad] senate.
◆ **claustro materno** m womb.

claustrofobia f claustrophobia.

cláusula f clause.

clausura f **-1.** [acto solemne] closing ceremony. **-2.** [cierre] closing down. **-3.** [aislamiento] enclosed life, enclosure.

clausurar vt **-1.** [acto] to close, to conclude. **-2.** [local] to close down.

clavadista m y f Amer diver.

clavado, -da adj **-1.** [con clavos] nailed. **-2.** [en punto - hora] on the dot. **-3.** [a la medida] just right. **-4.** [parecido] almost identical; ser ~ a alguien to be the spitting image of sb. **-5.** [fijo] fixed.
◆ **clavada** f mfam [estafa] rip-off.

clavar vt **-1.** [clavo, estaca etc] to drive; [cuchillo] to thrust; [chincheta, alfiler] to stick. **-2.** [cartel, placa etc] to nail, to fix. **-3.** fig [mirada, atención] to fix, to rivet; ~ los ojos en to stare at. **-4.** mfam [estafar] to sting, to rip off; me han clavado mil pesetas they stung me for a thousand pesetas.
◆ **clavarse** vpr [hincarse]: me clavé un cristal en el pie I got a splinter of glass in my foot.

clave ◇ adj inv key. ◇ m MÚS harpsichord. ◇ f **-1.** [código] code; en ~ in code. **-2.** fig [solución] key. **-3.** MÚS clef. **-4.** INFORM key; ~ de acceso access key.

clavecín m spinet.

clavel m carnation.

claveteado m studding.

clavetear vt **-1.** [adornar con clavos] to stud (with nails). **-2.** [poner clavos] to nail roughly.

clavicémbalo m harpsichord.

clavicordio m clavichord.

clavícula f collar bone.

clavija f **-1.** ELECTR & TECN pin; [de auriculares, teléfono] jack. **-2.** MÚS peg; apretar las ~s a alguien to put the screws on sb.

clavo m **-1.** [pieza metálica] nail; agarrarse a un ~ ardiendo to clutch at straws; estaré allí como un ~ I'll be there on the dot; dar en el ~ to hit the nail on the head; remachar el ~ to make matters worse. **-2.** BOT & CULIN clove. **-3.** MED [para huesos] pin.

claxon (pl cláxones) m horn; tocar el ~ to sound the horn.

clemencia f mercy, clemency.

clemente adj **-1.** [persona] merciful, clement. **-2.** fig [invierno etc] mild.

clementina f clementine.

cleptomanía f kleptomania.

cleptómano, -na m y f kleptomaniac.

clerecía f **-1.** [clero] clergy. **-2.** [oficio] priesthood.

clerical ◇ adj clerical. ◇ m y f clericalist.

clérigo m [católico] priest; [anglicano] clergyman.

clero m clergy.

cliché, clisé m **-1.** FOT negative. **-2.** IMPRENTA plate. **-3.** fig [tópico] cliché.

cliente, -ta m y f [de tienda, bar] customer; [de banco, abogado] client; [de hotel] guest.

clientela f [de tienda, garaje] customers (pl); [de banco, abogado etc] clients (pl); [de hotel] guests (pl); [de bar, restaurante] clientele.

clima m lit & fig climate; ~ mediterráneo/tropical Mediterranean/tropical climate.

climaterio m climacteric.

climático, -ca adj climatic.

climatización f air conditioning.

climatizado, -da adj air-conditioned.

climatizar [13] vt to air-condition.

climatología f **-1.** [tiempo] weather. **-2.** [ciencia] climatology.

climatológico, -ca adj climatological.

clímax m inv climax.

clínico, -ca adj clinical.
◆ **clínico** m doctor.
◆ **clínica** f clinic.

clip m **-1.** [para papel] paper clip. **-2.** [para el pelo] hairclip. **-3.** [videoclip] (video) clip.

clíper m clipper.

clisé = cliché.

clítoris m inv clitoris.

cloaca f sewer.

clon m clone.

clonar vt to clone.

clónico, -ca adj clonic.

cloquear vi to cluck.

cloración f chlorination.

clorato m chlorate.

clorhídrico → ácido.

clórico, -ca adj chloric.

cloro m chlorine.

clorofila f chlorophyll.

cloroformo m chloroform.

cloruro m chloride; ~ **de cal** bleaching powder; ~ **de sodio** ○ **sódico** sodium chloride.

clown m clown.

club (pl **clubs** ○ **clubes**) m club; ~ **de fans** fan club; ~ **náutico** yacht club.

clueca adj broody.

cm (abrev de **centímetro**) cm.

CMRE (abrev de **Consejo de Municipios y Regiones de Europa**) m CEMR.

CMT (abrev de **Confederación Mundial del Trabajo**) f WCL.

CNA (abrev de **Comité Nacional de Árbitros**) m Spanish referees' committee.

CNAE (abrev de **Censo Nacional de Actividades Económicas**) m Spanish census of economic activities.

CNAG (abrev de **Confederación Nacional de Agricultores y Ganaderos**) f Spanish national farmers' confederation.

CNT (abrev de **Confederación Nacional del Trabajo**) f Spanish anarchist trade union federation created in 1911.

CNUMAD (abrev de **Conferencia de las Naciones Unidas sobre el Medio Ambiente y el Desarrollo**) f UNCED.

Co. (abrev de **compañía**) Co.

coacción f coercion.

coaccionar vt to coerce.

coactivo, -va adj coercive.

coadjutor, -ra ◇ adj coadjutant. ◇ m y f coadjutor.

coagulación f clotting, coagulation.

coagulante ◇ adj clotting. ◇ m clotting agent.

coagular vt [gen] to coagulate; [sangre] to clot; [leche] to curdle.

◆ **coagularse** vpr [gen] to coagulate; [sangre] to clot; [leche] to curdle.

coágulo m clot.

coalición f coalition.

coaligar = **coligar**.

coartada f alibi.

coartar vt to limit, to restrict.

coaseguro m COM coinsurance.

coautor, -ra m y f coauthor.

coaxial adj coaxial.

coba f fam [halago] flattery; **dar** ~ **a alguien** [hacer la pelota] to suck up ○ crawl to sb; [aplacar] to soft-soap sb.

cobalto m cobalt.

cobarde ◇ adj cowardly. ◇ m y f coward.

cobardía f cowardice.

cobaya m o f guinea pig.

cobertizo m **-1.** [tejado adosado] lean-to. **-2.** [barracón] shed.

cobertura f **-1.** [gen] cover. **-2.** [de un edificio] covering. **-3.** PRENS: ~ **informativa** news coverage.

cobija f Amer blanket.

cobijar vt **-1.** [albergar] to house. **-2.** [proteger] to shelter.

◆ **cobijarse** vpr to take shelter.

cobijo m shelter; **dar** ~ **a alguien** to give shelter to sb, to take sb in.

cobista m y f fam creep.

COBOL (pl **COBOLS**) m INFORM COBOL.

cobra f cobra.

cobrador, -ra m y f [del autobús] conductor (f conductress); [de deudas, recibos] collector.

cobrar ◇ vt **-1.** [COM - dinero] to charge; [- cheque] to cash; [- deuda] to collect; **cantidades por** ~ amounts due; **¿me cobra, por favor?** how much do I owe you? **-2.** [en el trabajo] to earn, to be paid. **-3.** [adquirir - importancia] to get, to acquire; ~ **fama** to become famous. **-4.** [sentir - cariño, afecto] to start to feel; ~ **le afecto a alguien** to take a liking to sb. ◇ vi **-1.** [en el trabajo] to get paid. **-2.** fam [recibir una paliza] to catch it; **¡vas a** ~**!** you'll be in for it!

◆ **cobrarse** vpr: **el accidente se cobró nueve vidas** nine people were killed in the crash.

cobre m copper; **no tener un** ~ Amer to be flat broke.

cobrizo, -za adj **-1.** [color, piel] copper (antes de sust). **-2.** [de cobre - metal] containing copper.

cobro m [de talón] cashing; [de pago] collection; ~ **revertido** reverse charge.

coca f **-1.** [planta] coca. **-2.** fam [cocaína] coke.

cocaína f cocaine.

cocainómano, -na m y f cocaine addict.

cocción f [gen] cooking; [en agua] boiling; [en horno] baking.

cóccix, coxis m inv coccyx.

cocear vi to kick.

cocer [41] vt **-1.** [gen] to cook; [hervir] to boil; [en horno] to bake. **-2.** [cerámica, ladrillos] to fire.

◆ **cocerse** vpr **-1.** [gen] to cook; [hervir] to

boil; [en horno] to bake. **-2.** *fig* [plan] to be afoot.

cochambre *f fam* [suciedad] filth; [basura] rubbish.

cochambroso, -sa *adj fam* filthy.

cochayuyo *m Amer* seaweed.

coche *m* **-1.** [automóvil] car, automobile *Am;* ~ **de bomberos** fire engine; ~ **de carreras** racing car; ~ **celular** police van; ~ **deportivo** sports car; ~ **familiar** estate car; ~ **grúa** breakdown van ○ lorry *Br* ○ truck *Am;* ~ **patrulla** patrol car. **-2.** [de tren] coach, carriage; ~ **cama** sleeping car, sleeper; ~ **restaurante** restaurant ○ dining car. **-3.** [de caballos] carriage. **-4.** *loc*: **ir en el** ~ **de San Fernando** *fam* to go on foot.
◆ **coche bomba** *m* car bomb.

cochera *f* [para coches] garage; [de autobuses, tranvías] depot.

cochero *m* coachman.

cochinada *f fam fig* [guarrería] dirty ○ filthy thing; [grosería] obscenity, dirty word; [mala jugada] dirty trick.

cochinilla *f* **-1.** [crustáceo] woodlouse. **-2.** [insecto] cochineal.

cochinillo *m* sucking pig.

cochino, -na ◇ *adj* **-1.** [persona] filthy. **-2.** [tiempo, dinero] lousy. ◇ *m y f* [animal - macho] pig; [- hembra] sow.

cocido *m* stew; ~ **madrileño** CULIN *stew made with chickpeas, bacon, meat and root vegetables, typical of Madrid.*

cociente *m* quotient.

cocina *f* **-1.** [habitación] kitchen. **-2.** [electrodoméstico] cooker, stove; ~ **eléctrica/de gas** electric/gas cooker. **-3.** [arte] cooking; ~ **española** Spanish cuisine ○ cooking; **libro/clase de** ~ cookery book/class.

cocinar *vt & vi* to cook.

cocinero, -ra *m y f* cook.

cocker *m* cocker spaniel.

coco *m* **-1.** [árbol] coconut palm; [fruto] coconut. **-2.** *fam* [cabeza] nut, head; **comerse el** ~ to worry (one's head); **comer el** ~ **a alguien** [convencer] to brainwash sb. **-3.** *fam* [fantasma] bogeyman. **-4.** BOT [bacteria] coccus.

cococha *f* barbel.

cocodrilo *m* crocodile.

cocotero *m* coconut palm.

cóctel, coctel *m* **-1.** [bebida, comida] cocktail. **-2.** [reunión] cocktail party.
◆ **cóctel molotov** *m* Molotov cocktail.

coctelera *f* cocktail shaker.

cód. *abrev de* **código.**

coda *f* coda.

codazo *m* nudge, jab (*with one's elbow*); **abrirse paso a** ~**s** to elbow one's way through.

codearse *vpr*: ~ **(con)** to rub shoulders (with).

codeína *f* codeine.

codera *f* elbow patch.

códice *m* codex.

codicia *f* **-1.** [de riqueza] greed. **-2.** *fig* [de aprender, saber]: ~ **(de)** thirst (for).

codiciar [8] *vt* to covet.

codicioso, -sa *adj* greedy.

codificación *f* **-1.** [de norma, ley] codification. **-2.** [de mensaje en clave] encoding. **-3.** INFORM coding.

codificador, -ra ◇ *adj* codifying. ◇ *m y f* INFORM [profesional] encoder.
◆ **codificador** *m* [aparato] encoder.

codificar [10] *vt* **-1.** [ley] to codify. **-2.** [un mensaje] to encode. **-3.** INFORM to code.

código *m* [gen & INFORM] code; ~ **postal/territorial** post/area code; ~ **mercantil** ○ **de comercio** commercial law; ~ **de barras/de señales** bar/signal code; ~ **de circulación** highway code; ~ **civil/penal** civil/penal code; ~ **ASCII** ASCII code; ~ **máquina** machine code; ~ **Morse** Morse code.

codillo *m* **-1.** [en un cuadrúpedo] upper foreleg. **-2.** [de jamón] shoulder. **-3.** [de un tubo] elbow, bend.

codirector, -ra *m y f* co-director.

codo *m* **-1.** [en brazo, tubería] elbow; **estaba de** ~**s sobre la mesa** she was leaning (with her elbows) on the table. **-2.** [medida] cubit. **-3.** *loc*: ~ **con** ~, ~ **a** ~ side by side; **empinar el** ~ *fam* to booze; **hablar por los** ~**s** *fam* to talk nineteen to the dozen, to be a chatterbox.

codorniz *f* quail.

COE (*abrev de* **Comité Olímpico Español**) *m* SOC.

coedición *f* coedition.

coeditar *vt* to coedit.

coeficiente *m* **-1.** [gen] coefficient; ~ **de caja** BANCA cash ratio; ~ **intelectual** ○ **de inteligencia** intelligence quotient, I.Q. **-2.** [índice] rate.

coercer [11] *vt* to restrict, to constrain.

coerción *f* coercion.

coercitivo, -va *adj* coercive.

coerza *etc* → **coercer.**

coetáneo, -a *adj, m y f* contemporary.

coexistencia *f* coexistence; ~ **pacífica** peaceful coexistence.

coexistente *adj* coexisting.

coexistir *vi* to coexist.

cofia *f* [de enfermera, camarera] cap; [de monja] coif.

cofrade *m y f* **-1.** [de cofradía religiosa] brother (*f* sister). **-2.** [de cofradía no religiosa] member.

cofradía *f* **-1.** [religiosa] brotherhood (*f* sisterhood). **-2.** [no religiosa] guild.

cofre *m* **-1.** [arca] chest, trunk. **-2.** [para joyas] jewel box.

coger [14] ◇ *vt* **-1.** [asir, agarrar] to take; ~ a alguien de ○ por la mano to take sb by the hand. **-2.** [atrapar - ladrón, pez, pájaro] to catch. **-3.** [alcanzar - persona, vehículo] to catch up with. **-4.** [recoger - frutos, flores] to pick. **-5.** [quedarse con - propina, empleo, piso] to take. **-6.** [contratar - personal] to take on. **-7.** [quitar]: ~ algo (a alguien) to take sthg (from sb). **-8.** [tren, autobús] to take, to catch; no me gusta ~ el avión I don't like flying. **-9.** [contraer - gripe, resfriado] to catch, to get; ~ una borrachera to get drunk. **-10.** [sentir - manía, odio, afecto] to start to feel; ~ cariño/miedo a to become fond/scared of. **-11.** [suj: coche] to knock over, to run over; [suj: toro] to gore. **-12.** [oír] to catch; [entender] to get; no cogió el chiste he didn't get the joke. **-13.** [sorprender, encontrar]: ~ a alguien haciendo algo to catch sb doing sthg. **-14.** [sintonizar - canal, emisora] to get, to receive. **-15.** [abarcar - espacio] to cover, to take up. **-16.** *Amer vulg* [fornicar] to screw.
◇ *vi* **-1.** [situarse] to be; coge muy cerca de aquí it's not very far from here. **-2.** [dirigirse]: ~ a la derecha/la izquierda to turn right/left. **-3.** *loc*: cogió y se fue he upped and went; de pronto cogió y me insultó he turned round and insulted me.
◆ **cogerse** *vpr* **-1.** [agarrarse]: ~se de ○ a algo to cling to ○ clutch sthg. **-2.** [pillarse]: ~se los dedos/la falda en la puerta to catch one's fingers/skirt in the door.

cogestión *f* copartnership.

cogida *f* **-1.** [de torero] goring. **-2.** [de frutos] picking.

cognac = **coñá.**

cogollo *m* **-1.** [de lechuga] heart. **-2.** [brote - de árbol, planta] shoot.

cogorza *f fam*: agarrarse una ~ to get smashed, to get blind drunk.

cogotazo *m* rabbit punch.

cogote *m* nape, back of the neck.

cogulla *f* RELIG habit.

cohabitación *f* cohabitation.

cohabitar *vi* to cohabit, to live together.

cohecho *m* bribery.

coherencia *f* **-1.** [de razonamiento] coherence. **-2.** FÍS cohesion.

coherente *adj* coherent.

cohesión *f* cohesion.

cohesivo, -va *adj* cohesive.

cohete *m* rocket.

cohibición *f* inhibition.

cohibido, -da *adj* inhibited.

cohibir *vt* to inhibit.
◆ **cohibirse** *vpr* to become inhibited.

cohorte *f* cohort.

COI (*abrev de* **Comité Olímpico Internacional**) *m* IOC.

coima *f Amer fam* bribe.

Coimbra Coimbra.

coincidencia *f* coincidence.

coincidir *vi* **-1.** [superficies, versiones, gustos] to coincide. **-2.** [personas - encontrarse] to meet; [- estar de acuerdo] to agree.

coito *m* (sexual) intercourse.

coja → coger.

cojear *vi* **-1.** [persona] to limp. **-2.** [mueble] to wobble. **-3.** *fig* [adolecer] to falter, to flounder.

cojera *f* [acción] limp; [estado] lameness.

cojín *m* cushion.

cojinete *m* [en eje] bearing; [en un riel de ferrocarril] chair.

cojo, -ja ◇ *v* → coger. ◇ *adj* **-1.** [persona] lame. **-2.** [mueble] wobbly. **-3.** *fig* [razonamiento, frase] faulty. ◇ *m y f* cripple; no ser ~ ni manco *fig* to know a thing or two.

cojón *m* (*gen pl*) *vulg* ball; ¡ahora lo vas a hacer por cojones! you bloody well are going to do it!; tener cojones to have balls ○ guts.
◆ **cojones** *interj vulg*: ¡cojones! [enfado] for fuck's sake!

cojonudo, -da *adj vulg* bloody brilliant.

cojudear *vt Amer fam* **-1.** [hacer tonterías] to piss about, to muck about. **-2.** [engañar] to trick.

cojudez *f Amer mfam* rubbish, stupidity.

cojudo, -da *adj Amer mfam* bloody stupid.

col *f* cabbage; ~ de Bruselas Brussels sprout; ~ lombarda red cabbage.

cola *f* **-1.** [de animal, avión] tail. **-2.** [de vestido de novia] train. **-3.** [fila] queue *Br*, line *Am*; hacer ~ to queue (up) *Br*, to stand in line *Am*; ~ de impresión INFORM printout queue. **-4.** [pegamento] glue. **-5.** [de clase, lista] bottom; [de desfile] end. **-6.** [bebida] cola. **-7.** [peinado]: ~ (de caballo) pony tail. **-8.** *fam* [pene] willy. **-9.** *loc*: no pegan ni con ~ *fam* they don't match at all; tener ○ traer

~ to have serious consequences ◇ repercussions.

colaboración f **-1.** [gen] collaboration. **-2.** [de prensa] contribution, article.

colaboracionismo m collaborationism.

colaboracionista ◇ adj collaborationist. ◇ m y f collaborator.

colaborador, -ra ◇ adj cooperative. ◇ m y f **-1.** [gen] collaborator. **-2.** [de prensa] contributor, writer.

colaborar vi **-1.** [ayudar] to collaborate. **-2.** [en prensa]: **~ en** O **con** to write for, to work for. **-3.** [contribuir] to contribute.

colación f **-1.** [para comer] snack. **-2.** loc: **sacar** O **traer algo a ~** [tema] to bring sthg up.

coladero m fam easy way through.

colado, -da adj **-1.** [líquido] strained. **-2.** [enamorado]: **estar ~ por alguien** fam to have a crush on sb.
◆ **colada** f [ropa] laundry; **hacer la ~** to do the washing.

colador m [para líquidos] strainer, sieve; [para verdura] colander.

colágeno m collagen.

colapsar ◇ vt to bring to a halt, to stop. ◇ vi to come O grind to a halt.

colapso m **-1.** MED collapse, breakdown. **-2.** [de actividad] stoppage; [de tráfico] traffic jam, hold-up.

colar [23] ◇ vt **-1.** [verdura, té] to strain; [café] to filter. **-2.** [dinero falso] to pass off as genuine; [mentira] to slip through. **-3.** [por un sitio estrecho] to slip, to squeeze. ◇ vi [pasar por bueno]: **esto no colará** this won't wash.
◆ **colarse** vpr **-1.** [líquido]: **~ por** to seep through. **-2.** [persona] to slip, to sneak; [en una cola] to jump the queue Br O line Am; **~se en una fiesta** to gatecrash a party. **-3.** fam [por error] to slip up. **-4.** loc fam: **~se por alguien** to fall for sb.

colateral adj **-1.** [lateral] on either side. **-2.** [pariente] collateral.

colcha f bedspread.

colchón m **-1.** [de cama] mattress; **~ inflable** air bed. **-2.** INFORM buffer.

colchonero, -ra ◇ m y f upholsterer, mattress-maker. ◇ adj DEP of or relating to the Atlético de Madrid Football Club.

colchoneta f [para playa] beach mat; [en gimnasio] mat.

cole m fam school.

colear vi **-1.** [animal] to wag its tail. **-2.** fig [asunto, problema] to drag on.

colección f lit & fig collection.

coleccionable ◇ adj collectable. ◇ m special supplement in serialized form.

coleccionar vt to collect.

coleccionista m y f collector.

colecta f collection.

colectividad f community.

colectivismo m collectivism.

colectivización f collectivization.

colectivizar [13] vt to collectivize.

colectivo, -va adj collective.
◆ **colectivo** m group.

colector, -ra ◇ adj collecting. ◇ m y f [persona] collector.
◆ **colector** m **-1.** [sumidero] sewer; **~ de basuras** chute. **-2.** MEC [de motor] manifold. **-3.** [de transistor] collector.

colega m y f **-1.** [compañero profesional] colleague. **-2.** [homólogo] counterpart, opposite number. **-3.** fam [amigo] mate.

colegiado, -da adj who belongs to a professional association.
◆ **colegiado** m DEP referee.

colegial, -la m y f schoolboy (f schoolgirl).
◆ **colegial** adj school (antes de sust).

colegiarse [8] vpr to become a member of a professional association.

colegiata f collegiate church.

colegio m **-1.** [escuela] school; **~ de pago** fee-paying O private school. **-2.** [de profesionales]: **~ (profesional)** professional association.
◆ **colegio electoral** m [lugar] polling station; [votantes] ward.
◆ **colegio mayor** m hall of residence.

colegir [42]
◆ **colegir de** vi to infer from, to gather from.
◆ **colegirse de** vpr to be inferred from.

colegislador, -ra adj [asamblea] joint legislative.

coleópteros mpl coleoptera.

cólera ◇ m MED cholera. ◇ f [ira] anger, rage; **montar en ~** to get angry, to lose one's temper.

colérico, -ca adj **-1.** [carácter] bad-tempered. **-2.** MED cholera (antes de sust).

colesterol m cholesterol.

coleta f pigtail; **cortarse la ~** to call it a day, to retire.

coletazo m flick O swish of the tail; **está dando (los últimos) ~s** it's in its death throes.

coletilla f postscript.

colgado, -da adj **-1.** [cuadro, jamón etc]: **~ (de)** hanging (from). **-2.** [teléfono] on the hook. **-3.** fam fig [abandonado]: **dejar ~ a al-**

guien to leave sb in the lurch. **-4.** *fam* [enganchado]: **quedarse ~ (con)** to get hooked (on).

colgador *m* hanger, coathanger.

colgajo *m* **-1.** [de ropa] hanging piece of material. **-2.** [de piel] flap.

colgante ◇ *adj* hanging. ◇ *m* pendant.

colgar [39] ◇ *vt* **-1.** [suspender, ahorcar] to hang; **~ el teléfono** to hang up. **-2.** [imputar]: **~ algo a alguien** to blame sthg on sb. **-3.** [suspender en los estudios] to fail. **-4.** [abandonar] to give up. ◇ *vi* **-1.** [pender]: **~ (de)** to hang (from). **-2.** [hablando por teléfono] to hang up, to put the phone down.
◆ **colgarse** *vpr*: **~se (de)** [gen] to hang (from); [ahorcarse] to hang o.s. (from).

colibrí *m* hummingbird.

cólico *m* stomach ache; **~ hepático** biliary colic; **~ nefrítico** O **renal** renal colic.

coliflor *f* cauliflower.

coligar, coaligar [16] *vt* to ally, to unite.
◆ **coligarse** *vpr* to unite, to join together.

colige, coligió *etc* → **colegir**.

coligue *etc* → **coligar**.

colija *etc* → **colegir**.

colilla *f* (cigarette) butt O stub.

colimba *f Amer fam* military service.

colina *f* hill.

colindante *adj* neighbouring, adjacent.

colindar *vi* to be adjacent, to adjoin.

colirio *m* eyewash, eyedrops (*pl*).

coliseo *m* coliseum.

colisión *f* [de automóviles] collision, crash; [de ideas, intereses] clash.

colisionar *vi* **-1.** [coche]: **~ (contra)** to collide (with), to crash (into). **-2.** *fig* [ideas] to clash.

colista *m y f* [en liga de fútbol etc] bottom team; [en carreras] tailender.

colitis *f inv* stomach infection.

collado *m* [colina] hill.

collage *m* collage.

collar *m* **-1.** [de personas] necklace. **-2.** [para animales] collar. **-3.** [abrazadera] collar, ring.

collarín *m* surgical collar.

collera *f Amer* cufflink.

colmado, -da *adj*: **~ (de)** full to the brim (with).
◆ **colmado** *m* grocer's (shop).

colmar *vt* **-1.** [recipiente] to fill (to the brim). **-2.** *fig* [aspiración, deseo] to fulfil; **~ a alguien de regalos/elogios** to shower gifts/praise on sb.

colmena *f* beehive.

colmenar *m* apiary.

colmillo *m* **-1.** [de persona] canine, eyetooth. **-2.** [de perro] fang; [de elefante] tusk. **-3.** *loc*: **enseñar los ~s** to show one's teeth.

colmo *m* height; **para ~ de desgracias** to crown it all; **es el ~ de la locura** it's sheer madness; **¡eso es el ~!** *fam* that's the last straw!

colocación *f* **-1.** [acción] placing, positioning; [situación] place, position. **-2.** [empleo] position, job.

colocado, -da *adj* **-1.** [gen] placed; **estar muy bien ~** to have a very good job. **-2.** *fam* [borracho] legless; [drogado] high, stoned.

colocar [10] *vt* **-1.** [en su sitio] to place, to put. **-2.** [en una posición]: **~ los brazos en alto** to raise one's arms. **-3.** [en un empleo] to find a job for. **-4.** [casar] to marry off. **-5.** [invertir] to place, to invest.
◆ **colocarse** *vpr* **-1.** [en un trabajo] to get a job. **-2.** *fam* [emborracharse] to get legless; [drogarse] to get high O stoned.

colofón *m* **-1.** [remate, fin] climax, culmination. **-2.** [de libro] colophon.

coloide *adj* colloid.

Colombia Colombia.

colombianismo *m* Colombian expression.

colombiano, -na *adj, m y f* Colombian.

colombino, -na *adj* Columbian, of Christopher Columbus.

Colombo Colombo.

colombofilia *f* pigeon-fancying.

colon *m* colon.

colón *m* colon (*unit of currency in Costa Rica and El Salvador*).

colonia *f* **-1.** [gen] colony. **-2.** [de niños]: **~ (de verano)** (summer) camp; **ir de ~s** to go to summer camp. **-3.** [perfume] eau de cologne. **-4.** *Amer* [barrio] district; **~ proletaria** shanty town, slum area.

Colonia Cologne.

colonial *adj* colonial.

colonialismo *m* colonialism.

colonialista *adj, m y f* colonialist.

colonización *f* colonization.

colonizador, -ra ◇ *adj* colonizing. ◇ *m y f* colonizer, colonist.

colonizar [13] *vt* to colonize.

colono *m* settler, colonist.

coloque *etc* → **colocar**.

coloquial *adj* colloquial.

coloquio *m* **-1.** [conversación] conversation. **-2.** [debate] discussion, debate.

color *m* **-1.** [gen] colour; **~ rojo** red; **~ azul** blue; **~ local** local colour; **de ~** [persona] coloured; **en ~** [foto, televisor] colour; **~ pri-**

mario primary colour; **~es complementarios** complementary colours. **-2.** *fig* [aspecto] tone. **-3.** [en los naipes] suit. **-4.** *loc*: **dar ~ a algo** to colour sthg in; *fig* to brighten ○ liven sthg up; **no hay ~** it's no contest; **sacarle** ○ **salirle a alguien los ~es (a la cara)** to make sb blush; **ver las cosas de ~ de rosa** to see things through rose-coloured ○ rose-tinted spectacles.

colorado, -da *adj* [color] red; **ponerse ~** to blush, to go red.
◆ **colorado** *m* [color] red.

Colorado *m*: **el (río) ~** the Colorado (river).

colorante *m* colouring.

colorear *vt* to colour (in).

colorete *m* rouge, blusher.

colorido *m* colours (*pl*).

colorín *m* (*gen pl*) bright colour; **~ colorado, este cuento se ha acabado** and they all lived happily ever after.

colorista *adj* colouristic.

colosal *adj* **-1.** [estatura, tamaño] colossal. **-2.** [extraordinario] great, enormous.

coloso *m* **-1.** [estatua] colossus. **-2.** *fig* [cosa, persona] giant.

colt® *m* Colt®.

columna *f* **-1.** [gen] column; **quinta ~** fifth column. **-2.** *fig* [pilar] pillar.
◆ **columna vertebral** *f* spinal column.

columnata *f* colonnade.

columnista *m y f* columnist.

columpiar [8] *vt* to swing.
◆ **columpiarse** *vpr* to swing.

columpio *m* swing.

colza *f* BOT rape.

coma ◇ *m* MED coma; **en ~** in a coma. ◇ *f* **-1.** GRAM comma. **-2.** MAT ≃ decimal point.

comadre *f* [mujer chismosa] gossip, gossipmonger; [vecina] neighbour.

comadrear *vi* to gossip.

comadreja *f* weasel.

comadreo *m* gossip.

comadrona *f* midwife.

comandancia *f* **-1.** [rango] command. **-2.** [edificio] command headquarters.

comandante *m* [MIL - rango] major; [- de un puesto] commander, commandant; **~ en jefe** commander-in-chief.

comandar *vt* MIL to command.

comando *m* MIL commando; **~ terrorista** terrorist unit.

comarca *f* region, area.

comarcal *adj* district (*antes de sust*), local.

comatoso, -sa *adj* comatose.

comba *f* **-1.** [juego] skipping; **jugar a la ~** to skip. **-2.** [cuerda] skipping rope.

combado, -da *adj* curved.

combadura *f* [de alambre, barra] bend; [de pared] bulge; [de viga] sag.

combar *vt* to bend.
◆ **combarse** *vpr* [gen] to bend; [madera] to warp; [pared] to bulge.

combate *m* [gen] fight; [batalla] battle; **dejar a alguien fuera de ~** [en boxeo] to knock sb out; *fig* to put sb out of the running.

combatiente *m y f* combatant, fighter.

combatir ◇ *vi*: **~ (contra)** to fight (against). ◇ *vt* to combat, to fight.

combatividad *f* fighting spirit.

combativo, -va *adj* aggressive, combative.

combi *m* [frigorífico] fridge-freezer.

combinación *f* **-1.** [gen] combination. **-2.** [de bebidas] cocktail. **-3.** QUÍM compound. **-4.** [prenda] slip. **-5.** [plan] scheme. **-6.** [de medios de transporte] connections (*pl*).

combinado *m* **-1.** [bebida] cocktail. **-2.** DEP combined team. **-3.** *Amer* [radiograma] radiogram.

combinar *vt* **-1.** [gen] to combine. **-2.** [bebidas] to mix. **-3.** [colores] to match. **-4.** [planificar] to arrange, to organize.

combinatoria *f* MAT combinatorial analysis.

combustible ◇ *adj* combustible. ◇ *m* fuel.

combustión *f* combustion.

comecocos *m inv fam* **-1.** [para convencer]: **este panfleto es un ~** this pamphlet is designed to brainwash you. **-2.** [cosa difícil de comprender] mind-bending problem ○ puzzle *etc*.

COMECON (*abrev de* **Council for Mutual Economic Assistance**) *m* COMECON.

comedero *m* trough.

comedia *f* comedy; *fig* [engaño] farce; **~ musical** musical (comedy).

comediante, -ta *m y f* actor (*f* actress); *fig* [farsante] fraud.

comedido, -da *adj* moderate, restrained.

comedimiento *m* moderation, restraint.

comediógrafo, -fa *m y f* playwright, dramatist.

comedirse [26] *vpr* to be restrained.

comedor *m* **-1.** [habitación - de casa] dining room; [- de fábrica] canteen. **-2.** [muebles] dining-room suite.

comendadora *f* mother superior.

comensal *m y f* fellow diner.

comentar *vt* [opinar sobre] to comment on; [hablar de] to discuss.

comentario *m* **-1.** [observación] comment, remark. **-2.** [crítica] commentary.
◆ **comentarios** *mpl* [murmuraciones] gossip (*U*).

comentarista *m y f* commentator.

comenzar [34] ◇ *vt* to start, to begin; ~ **a hacer algo** to start doing ○ to do sthg; ~ **diciendo que ...** to start ○ begin by saying that .... ◇ *vi* to start, to begin.

comer ◇ *vi* [ingerir alimentos - gen] to eat; [- al mediodía] to have lunch. ◇ *vt* **-1.** [alimentos] to eat. **-2.** [colores] to fade. **-3.** [en juegos de tablero] to take, to capture. **-4.** *fig* [consumir] to eat up. **-5.** *loc*: **sin ~lo ni beberlo** through no fault of one's own.
◆ **comerse** *vpr* **-1.** [alimentos] to eat. **-2.** [desgastar - recursos] to eat up; [- metal] to corrode. **-3.** [en los juegos de tablero] to take, to capture. **-4.** *fig* [palabras] to swallow. **-5.** *Amer vulg* [fornicar]: ~**se a** to fuck.

comercial *adj* commercial.

comercialización *f* marketing.

comercializar [13] *vt* to market.

comerciante *m y f* tradesman (*f* tradeswoman); [tendero] shopkeeper.

comerciar [8] *vi* to trade, to do business.

comercio *m* **-1.** [de productos] trade; ~ **exterior/interior** foreign/domestic trade; ~ **justo** fair trade; **libre** ~ free trade. **-2.** [actividad] business, commerce. **-3.** [tienda] shop.

comestible *adj* edible, eatable.
◆ **comestibles** *mpl* [gen] food (*U*); [en una tienda] groceries.

cometa ◇ *m* ASTRON comet. ◇ *f* kite.

cometer *vt* [crimen] to commit; [error] to make.

cometido *m* **-1.** [objetivo] mission, task. **-2.** [deber] duty.

comezón *f* **-1.** [picor] itch, itching (*U*). **-2.** *fig* [remordimiento] twinge; [deseo] urge, itch.

cómic (*pl* **cómics**), **comic** (*pl* **comics**) *m* (adult) comic.

comicidad *f* humorousness.

comicios *mpl* elections.

cómico, -ca ◇ *adj* **-1.** [de la comedia] comedy (*antes de sust*), comic. **-2.** [gracioso] comic, comical. ◇ *m y f* [actor de teatro] actor (*f* actress); [humorista] comedian (*f* comedienne), comic.

comida ◇ *v* → **comedirse**. ◇ *f* **-1.** [alimento] food (*U*). **-2.** [almuerzo, cena etc] meal. **-3.** [al mediodía] lunch.

comidiera *etc* → **comedirse**.

comidilla *f fam*: **ser la ~ del pueblo** to be the talk of the town.

comidió → **comedirse**.

comience *etc* → **comenzar**.

comienzo *m* start, beginning; **a ~s de los años 50** in the early 1950s; **dar ~** to start, to begin.

comillas *fpl* inverted commas, quotation marks; **entre ~** in inverted commas.

comilón, -ona *fam* ◇ *adj* greedy. ◇ *m y f* [persona] greedy pig, glutton.
◆ **comilona** *f fam* [festín] blow-out.

comino *m* [planta] cumin, cummin; **me importa un ~** I don't give a damn; **no valer un ~** not to be worth tuppence.

COMINTERN (*abrev de* **Internacional Comunista**) *f* COMINTERN, the Third International.

comisaría *f* police station, precinct *Am*.

comisario, -ria *m y f* **-1.** **(de policía)** police superintendent. **-2.** [delegado] commissioner; ~ **político** political commissar.

comisión *f* **-1.** [de un delito] perpetration. **-2.** COM commission; **(trabajar) a** ~ (to work) on a commission basis; ~ **fija** ECON flat fee. **-3.** [delegación] commission, committee; ~ **investigadora** committee of inquiry; ~ **parlamentaria** parliamentary committee; ~ **permanente** standing commission; ~ **de servicio** special assignment.

comisionado, -da *m y f* committee member.

comisionar *vt* to commission.

comisionista *m y f* commission agent.

comisura *f* corner (*of mouth, eyes*).

comité *m* committee; ~ **ejecutivo** executive committee; ~ **de empresa** works council.

comitiva *f* retinue.

como ◇ *adv* **-1.** (*comparativo*): **tan ... ~ ...** as ... as ...; **es (tan) negro ~ el carbón** it's as black as coal; **ser ~ algo** to be like sthg; **vive ~ un rey** he lives like a king; **lo que dijo fue ~ para ruborizarse** his words were enough to make you blush. **-2.** [de la manera que] as; **lo he hecho ~ es debido** I did it as ○ the way it should be done; **me encanta ~ bailas** I love the way you dance. **-3.** [según] as; ~ **te decía ayer ...** as I was telling you yesterday .... **-4.** [en calidad de] as; **trabaja ~ bombero** he works as a fireman; **dieron el dinero ~ anticipo** they gave the money as an advance. **-5.** [aproximadamente] about; **me quedan ~ mil pesetas** I've got about a thousand pesetas left; **estamos ~ a mitad de camino** we're about half-way there; **tiene un sabor ~ a naranja** it tastes a bit like an orange.
◇ *conj* **-1.** [ya que] as, since; ~ **no llegabas, nos fuimos** as ○ since you didn't arrive, we left. **-2.** [si] if; ~ **no me hagas caso, lo**

pasarás mal if you don't listen to me, there will be trouble. **-3.** [que] that; **después de tantas veces ~ te lo he explicado** after all the times (that) I've explained it to you.

◆ **como que** *loc conj* **-1.** [que] that; **le pareció ~ que lloraban** it seemed to him (that) they were crying. **-2.** [expresa causa]: **pareces cansado — ~ que he trabajado toda la noche** you seem tired — well, I've been up all night working. **-3.** [expresa incredulidad]: **~ que te voy a creer a ti que eres un mentiroso** as if I'd believe a liar like you!

◆ **como quiera** *loc adv* [de cualquier modo] anyway, anyhow.

◆ **como quiera que** *loc conj* **-1.** [de cualquier modo que] whichever way, however; **~ quiera que sea** whatever the case may be. **-2.** [dado que] since, given that.

◆ **como si** *loc conj* as if.

cómo ◇ *adv* **-1.** [de qué modo, por qué motivo] how; **¿~ lo has hecho?** how did you do it?; **¿~ son?** what are they like?; **no sé ~ has podido decir eso** I don't know how you could say that; **¿~ que no la has visto nunca?** what do you mean you've never seen her?; **¿a ~ están los tomates?** how much are the tomatoes?; **¿~?** *fam* [¿qué dices?] sorry?, what?; **¿~ es eso?** *fam* [¿por qué?] how come? **-2.** [exclamativo] how; **¡~ pasan los años!** how time flies!; **¡~ no!** of course!; **está lloviendo, ¡y ~!** it isn't half raining! ◇ *m*: **el ~ y el porqué** the whys and wherefores.

cómoda *f* chest of drawers.

comodidad *f* comfort, convenience (U); **para su ~** for your convenience.

◆ **comodidades** *fpl* comforts.

comodín *m* **-1.** [naipe] joker. **-2.** *fig* [cosa] multi-purpose gadget; [persona] jack-of-all-trades.

cómodo, -da *adj* **-1.** [gen] comfortable. **-2.** [útil] convenient. **-3.** [oportuno, fácil] easy.

comodón, -ona ◇ *adj* [amante de la comodidad] comfort-loving; [vago] laid-back; **no seas ~** don't be lazy. ◇ *m y f* [amante de la comodidad] comfort-lover; [vago] laid-back person.

comodoro *m* commodore.

comoquiera *adv*: **~ que** [de cualquier manera que] whichever way, however; [dado que] since, seeing as.

compa *m y f Amer fam* mate, buddy.

compacidad *f* compactness.

compact *m* compact disc player.

compactación *f* INFORM compression; **~ de ficheros** zipping.

compactar *vt* to compress.

compact disk, compact disc *m* compact disc.

compacto, -ta *adj* compact.

compactoteca *f* compact disc library.

compadecer [30] *vt* to pity, to feel sorry for.

◆ **compadecerse de** *vpr* to pity, to feel sorry for.

compadre *m fam* [amigo] friend, mate.

compadrear *vi Amer* to brag, to boast.

compadreo *m fam* [amistad] friendship.

compaginación *f* **-1.** [combinación] reconciling. **-2.** [en imprenta] page make-up.

compaginar *vt* **-1.** [combinar] to reconcile. **-2.** [en imprenta] to make up.

◆ **compaginarse** *vpr*: **~se con** to square with, to go together with.

compañerismo *m* comradeship.

compañero, -ra *m y f* **-1.** [pareja, acompañante] companion. **-2.** [colega] colleague; **~ de clase** classmate; **~ de piso** flatmate. **-3.** [par]: **el ~ de este guante** the other glove of this pair.

compañía *f* company; **en ~ de** accompanied by, in the company of; **hacer ~ a alguien** to keep sb company.

comparación *f* comparison; **en ~ con** in comparison with, compared to.

comparado, -da *adj* comparative.

comparar *vt*: **~ algo (con)** to compare sthg (to).

comparativo, -va *adj* comparative.

◆ **comparativo** *m* GRAM comparative.

comparecencia *f* appearance.

comparecer [30] *vi* to appear.

comparsa ◇ *f* **-1.** TEATR extras (*pl*). **-2.** [en carnaval] *group of people at carnival in same costume and with masks.* ◇ *m y f* **-1.** TEATR extra. **-2.** *fig* [en carreras, competiciones] also-ran; [en organizaciones, empresas] nobody.

compartimentar *vt* to compartmentalize.

compartimento, compartimiento *m* compartment; **~ estanco** watertight compartment.

compartir *vt* **-1.** [ganancias] to share (out). **-2.** [piso, ideas] to share.

compás *m* **-1.** [instrumento] pair of compasses. **-2.** NÁUT [brújula] compass. **-3.** [MÚS - período] bar; [- ritmo] rhythm, beat; **al ~ (de la música)** in time (with the music); **llevar el ~** to keep time; **perder el ~** to lose the beat.

◆ **compás de espera** *m* pause, interlude.

compasión *f* compassion, pity.

compasivo, **-va** *adj* compassionate, sympathetic.

compatibilidad *f* [gen & INFORM] compatibility.

compatibilizar [13] *vt* to make compatible.

compatible *adj* [gen & INFORM] compatible.

compatriota *m y f* compatriot, fellow countryman (*f* fellow countrywoman).

compeler *vt* to compel, to force.

compendiar [8] *vt* [cualidades, características] to summarize; [libro, historia] to abridge.

compendio *m* **-1.** [libro] compendium. **-2.** *fig* [síntesis] epitome, essence.

compenetración *f* mutual understanding.

compenetrarse *vpr* to understand each other.

compensación *f* **-1.** [gen] compensation; **en ~ (por)** in return (for). **-2.** BANCA compensation; **~ bancaria** bank clearing.

compensar *vt* **-1.** [valer la pena] to make up for; **no me compensa (perder tanto tiempo)** it's not worth my while (wasting all that time). **-2.** [indemnizar]: **~ a alguien (de o por)** to compensate sb (for).

competencia *f* **-1.** [entre personas, empresas] competition; **~ desleal** ECON unfair competition, dumping. **-2.** [incumbencia] field, province. **-3.** [aptitud, atribuciones] competence.

competente *adj* competent; **~ en materia de** responsible for.

competer
◆ **competer a** *vi* [gen] to be up to, to be the responsibility of; [una autoridad] to come under the jurisdiction of.

competición *f* competition.

competidor, **-ra** ◇ *adj* rival, competing. ◇ *m y f* competitor.

competir [26] *vi*: **~ (con/por)** to compete (with/for).

competitividad *f* competitiveness.

competitivo, **-va** *adj* competitive.

compilación *f* [acción] compiling; [colección] compilation.

compilador, **-ra** ◇ *adj* compiling (*antes de sust*). ◇ *m y f* [persona] compiler.
◆ **compilador** *m* INFORM compiler.

compilar *vt* [gen & INFORM] to compile.

compinche *m y f fam* crony.

compita, **compitiera** *etc* → **competir**.

complacencia *f* pleasure, satisfaction.

complacer [29] *vt* to please.

complaciente *adj* **-1.** [amable] obliging, helpful. **-2.** [indulgente] indulgent.

complejidad *f* complexity.

complejo, **-ja** *adj* complex.
◆ **complejo** *m* complex; **~ de Edipo/de inferioridad/de superioridad** Oedipus/inferiority/superiority complex; **~ industrial** industrial park.

complementar *vt* to complement.
◆ **complementarse** *vpr* to complement each other.

complementario, **-ria** *adj* complementary.

complemento *m* **-1.** [añadido] complement. **-2.** GRAM object, complement; **~ agente** agent; **~ circunstancial** adjunct; **~ directo/indirecto** direct/indirect object.

completar *vt* to complete.
◆ **completarse** *vpr* to be completed.

completo, **-ta** *adj* **-1.** [entero, perfecto] complete; **por ~** completely; **un deportista muy ~** an all-round sportsman. **-2.** [lleno] full.

complexión *f* build.

complicación *f* **-1.** [gen] complication. **-2.** [complejidad] complexity.

complicado, **-da** *adj* **-1.** [difícil] complicated. **-2.** [implicado]: **~ (en)** involved (in).

complicar [10] *vt* **-1.** [dificultar] to complicate. **-2.** [comprometer]: **~ a alguien (en)** to involve sb (in).
◆ **complicarse** *vpr* [problema] to become complicated; [enfermedad] to get worse.

cómplice *m y f* accomplice.

complicidad *f* complicity.

complot, **compló** *m* plot, conspiracy.

componenda *f* shady deal.

componente ◇ *adj* component, constituent. ◇ *m* **-1.** [gen & ELECTR] component. **-2.** [persona] member.

componer [65] *vt* **-1.** [formar un todo, ser parte de] to make up. **-2.** [música, versos] to compose. **-3.** [arreglar - algo roto] to repair. **-4.** [adornar - cosa] to deck out, to adorn; [- persona] to dress up. **-5.** [texto - en imprenta] to set, to compose.
◆ **componerse** *vpr* **-1.** [estar formado]: **~se de** to be made up of, to consist of. **-2.** [engalanarse] to dress up. **-3.** *loc*: **allá se las compongan** that's their problem; **componérselas (para hacer algo)** to manage (to do sthg).

comportamiento *m* behaviour.

comportar *vt* to involve, to entail.
◆ **comportarse** *vpr* to behave.

composición *f* composition; **hacer o hacerse una ~ de lugar** to size up the situation.

compositor, **-ra** *m y f* composer.

compostelano, **-na** *adj* of/relating to Santiago de Compostela.

compostura f **-1.** [reparación] repair. **-2.** [de persona, rostro] composure. **-3.** [en comportamiento] restraint; **guardar la** ~ to show restraint.

compota f CULIN compote, stewed fruit (U).

compra f purchase; **ir de** ~**s** to go shopping; **ir a** ○ **hacer la** ~ to do the shopping; ~ **a plazos** hire purchase.

comprador, -ra ◇ adj buying, purchasing. ◇ m y f [gen] buyer, purchaser; [en una tienda] shopper, customer.

comprar vt **-1.** [adquirir] to buy, to purchase. **-2.** [sobornar] to buy (off), to bribe.

compraventa f buying and selling, trading.

comprender vt **-1.** [incluir] to include, to comprise. **-2.** [entender] to understand.
◆ **comprenderse** vpr [personas] to understand each other.

comprensible adj understandable, comprehensible.

comprensión f understanding.

comprensivo, -va adj understanding.

compresa f **-1.** [para menstruación] sanitary towel Br, sanitary napkin Am. **-2.** [para herida] compress.

compresión f compression.

compresor, -ra adj compressing.
◆ **compresor** m compressor.

comprimido, -da adj compressed.
◆ **comprimido** m pill, tablet.

comprimir vt to compress.

comprobación f checking.

comprobante m [documento] supporting document, proof; [recibo] receipt.

comprobar [23] vt [averiguar] to check; [demostrar] to prove.

comprometedor, -ra adj compromising.

comprometer vt **-1.** [poner en peligro - éxito etc] to jeopardize; [- persona] to compromise. **-2.** [avergonzar] to embarrass. **-3.** [hacer responsable]: ~ **a alguien (a hacer algo)** to oblige ○ compel sb (to do sthg).
◆ **comprometerse** vpr **-1.** [hacerse responsable]: ~**se (a hacer algo)** to commit o.s. (to doing sthg). **-2.** [ideológicamente, moralmente]: ~**se (en algo)** to become involved (in sthg).

comprometido, -da adj **-1.** [con una idea] committed. **-2.** [difícil] compromising, awkward.

compromisario m delegate, representative (in an election).

compromiso m **-1.** [obligación] commitment; [acuerdo] agreement. **-2.** [cita] engage-

ment; ~ **matrimonial** engagement. **-3.** [dificultad] compromising ○ difficult situation.

compuerta f sluice, floodgate.

compuesto, -ta ◇ pp → **componer**. ◇ adj **-1.** [formado]: ~ **de** composed of, made up of. **-2.** [palabra] compound (antes de sust). **-3.** [arreglado - persona] dressed up.
◆ **compuesto** m GRAM & QUÍM compound.

compulsar vt to check against the original.

compulsivo, -va adj compulsive, urgent.

compungido, -da adj contrite, remorseful.

compusiera etc → **componer**.

computable adj computable.

computador m, **computadora** f computer.

computar vt **-1.** [calcular] to compute, to calculate. **-2.** [considerar] to count, to regard as valid.

computarizar [13] vt to computerize.

cómputo m calculation.

comulgar [16] vi **-1.** RELIG to take communion. **-2.** fig [estar de acuerdo]: ~ **con algo** to share sthg.

común adj **-1.** [gen] common; **por lo** ~ generally; **poco** ~ unusual. **-2.** [compartido - amigo, interés] mutual; [- bienes, pastos] communal; **tener algo en** ~ to have sthg in common; **hacer algo en** ~ to do sthg together. **-3.** [ordinario - vino etc] ordinary, average.

comuna f commune.

comunal adj communal.

comunicación f **-1.** [gen] communication; **ponerse en** ~ **con alguien** to get in touch with sb; **medios de** ~ **de masas** mass media. **-2.** [escrito oficial] communiqué; [informe] report.
◆ **comunicaciones** fpl communications.

comunicado, -da adj: **bien** ~ [lugar] well-served, with good connections.
◆ **comunicado** m announcement, statement; ~ **a la prensa** press release.

comunicante ◇ adj communicating. ◇ m y f informant.

comunicar [10] ◇ vt **-1.** [transmitir - sentimientos, ideas] to convey; [- movimiento, virus] to transmit. **-2.** [información]: ~ **algo a alguien** to inform sb of sthg, to tell sb sthg. ◇ vi **-1.** [hablar - gen] to communicate; [- al teléfono] to get through; [escribir] to get in touch. **-2.** [dos lugares]: ~ **con algo** to connect with sthg, to join sthg. **-3.** [el teléfono] to be engaged Br, to be busy Am; **está comunicando** the line's engaged.
◆ **comunicarse** vpr **-1.** [hablarse] to com-

municate (with each other). **-2.** [dos lugares] to be connected. **-3.** [propagarse] to spread.

comunicativo, -va *adj* communicative, open.

comunidad *f* **-1.** [gen] community; ~ **autónoma** autonomous region; ~ **de propietarios** residents' association; **Comunidad Económica Europea** European Economic Community. **-2.** [estado de lo común - espiritual etc] communion; ~ **de bienes** co-ownership (*between spouses*).

COMUNIDAD AUTÓNOMA:

This regional division of the Spanish state, provided for in the Spanish Constitution (1978), consists either of a single province or a group of neighbouring provinces. The 'Comunidades Autónomas' have their own administrative bodies, such as a parliament, a cabinet etc

comunión *f lit* & *fig* communion.

comunismo *m* communism.

comunista *adj, m y f* communist.

comunitario, -ria *adj* **-1.** [de la comunidad] community (*antes de sust*). **-2.** [de la CEE] Community (*antes de sust*), of the European Community.

con *prep* **-1.** [gen] with; ¿~ **quién vas?** who are you going with?; **lo ha conseguido** ~ **su esfuerzo** he has achieved it through his own efforts; **una cartera** ~ **varios documentos** a briefcase containing several documents; ~ **el tiempo lo olvidé** in time I forgot it. **-2.** [a pesar de] in spite of; ~ **todo** despite everything; ~ **lo estudioso que es, le suspendieron** for all his hard work, they still failed him. **-3.** [hacia]: **para** ~ towards; **es amable para** ~ **todos** she is friendly towards ○ with everyone. **-4.** (+ *infin*) [para introducir una condición] by (+ *gerund*); ~ **hacerlo así** by doing it this way; ~ **salir a las diez es suficiente** if we leave at ten, we'll have plenty of time. **-5.** [a condición de que]: ~ **(tal) que** (+ *subjuntivo*) as long as; ~ **que llegue a tiempo me conformo** I don't mind as long as he arrives on time. **-6.** [para expresar queja o decepción]: **mira que perder** ¡~ **lo bien que jugaste!** it's bad luck you lost, you played really well!

conato *m* attempt; ~ **de robo** attempted robbery; **un** ~ **de incendio** the beginnings of a fire.

concadenar = concatenar.

concatenación *f* succession.

concatenar, concadenar *vt* to link together.

concavidad *f* **-1.** [cualidad] concavity. **-2.** [lugar] hollow.

cóncavo, -va *adj* concave.

concebir [26] ◇ *vt* [plan, hijo] to conceive; [imaginar] to imagine. ◇ *vi* to conceive.

conceder *vt* **-1.** [dar] to grant; [premio] to award. **-2.** [asentir] to admit, to concede.

concejal, -la *m y f* (town) councillor.

concejalía *f* seat on the town council.

concejo *m* (town) council.

concelebrar *vt* to concelebrate.

concentración *f* **-1.** [gen] concentration. **-2.** [de gente] gathering; ~ **parcelaria** ECON land consolidation. **-3.** DEP training camp.

concentrado *m* concentrate.

concentrar *vt* **-1.** [gen] to concentrate. **-2.** [reunir - gente] to bring together; [- tropas] to assemble.

◆ **concentrarse** *vpr* to concentrate.

concéntrico, -ca *adj* concentric.

concepción *f* conception.

concepto *m* **-1.** [idea] concept. **-2.** [opinión] opinion. **-3.** [motivo]: **bajo ningún** ~ under no circumstances; **en** ~ **de** by way of, as. **-4.** [de una cuenta] heading, item.

conceptual *adj* conceptual.

conceptualismo *m* conceptualism.

conceptualista ◇ *adj* conceptualistic. ◇ *m y f* conceptualist.

conceptuar [6] *vt* to consider, to judge.

concerniente *adj*: ~ **a** concerning, regarding.

concernir [21] *v impers* to concern; **en lo que concierne a** as regards; **por lo que a mí me concierne** as far as I'm concerned.

concertación *f* settlement.

concertar [19] ◇ *vt* [precio] to agree on; [cita] to arrange; [pacto] to reach. ◇ *vi* [concordar]: ~ **(con)** to tally (with), to fit in (with).

concertina *f* concertina.

concertino *m* first violin.

concertista *m y f* soloist.

concesión *f* **-1.** [de préstamo etc] granting; [de premio] awarding. **-2.** COM & *fig* concession.

concesionario, -ria ◇ *adj* concessionary. ◇ *m y f* [persona con derecho exclusivo de venta] licensed dealer; [titular de una concesión] concessionaire, licensee.

concha *f* **-1.** [de los animales] shell. **-2.** [material] tortoiseshell. **-3.** *Amer vulg* [coño] cunt.

◆ **concha de su madre** *m y f Amer vulg* bastard.

conchabarse *vpr fam*: ~ **(contra)** to gang up (on).

conchudo, -da *adj Amer vulg* bloody stupid.

conciba, concibiera *etc* → concebir.

conciencia, consciencia *f* **-1.** [conocimiento] consciousness, awareness; **tener/tomar ~ de** to be/become aware of. **-2.** [moral, integridad] conscience; **a ~** conscientiously; **me remuerde la ~** I have a guilty conscience.

concienciar [8] *vt* to make aware.
◆ **concienciarse** *vpr* to become aware.

concienzudo, -da *adj* conscientious.

concierna *etc* → concernir.

concierta *etc* → concertar.

concierto *m* **-1.** [actuación] concert. **-2.** [composición] concerto. **-3.** [acuerdo] agreement. **-4.** [orden] order.

conciliación *f* [en un litigio] reconciliation; [en un conflicto laboral] conciliation.

conciliar [8] ◇ *adj* conciliar. ◇ *vt* to reconcile; **~ el sueño** to get to sleep.

concilio *m* council; **~ ecuménico** ecumenical council.

concisión *f* conciseness.

conciso, -sa *adj* concise.

concitar *vt* to stir up, to arouse.

conciudadano, -na *m y f* fellow citizen.

cónclave, conclave *m* conclave.

concluir [51] ◇ *vt* to conclude; **~ haciendo** O **por hacer algo** to end up doing sthg. ◇ *vi* to (come to an) end.

conclusión *f* conclusion; **llegar a una ~** to come to O to reach a conclusion; **en ~** in conclusion.

concluyente *adj* conclusive.

concomerse *vpr*: **~ de** [envidia] to be green with; [arrepentimiento] to be consumed with; [impaciencia] to be itching with.

concomitancia *f* concomitance.

concomitante *adj* concomitant.

concordancia *f* [gen & GRAM] agreement.

concordar [23] ◇ *vt* to reconcile. ◇ *vi* **-1.** [estar de acuerdo]: **~ (con)** to agree O tally (with). **-2.** GRAM: **~ (con)** to agree (with).

concordato *m* concordat.

concordia *f* harmony.

concreción *f* **-1.** [acción y efecto] precision. **-2.** [de partículas] concretion.

concretar *vt* **-1.** [precisar] to specify, to state exactly. **-2.** [reducir a lo esencial] to summarize.
◆ **concretarse** *vpr* **-1.** [limitarse]: **~se a hacer algo** to confine O limit o.s. to doing sthg. **-2.** [materializarse] to take shape.

concreto, -ta *adj* specific, particular; **en ~** [en resumen] in short; [específicamente] specifically; **nada en ~** nothing definite.
◆ **concreto armado** *m Amer* concrete.

concubina *f* concubine.

concubinato *m* concubinage.

concuerda → concordar.

conculcar [10] *vt* to infringe, to break.

concuñado, -da *m y f* [hermano del cuñado] brother or sister of one's brother-in-law or sister-in-law; [cónyuge del cuñado] spouse of one's brother-in-law or sister-in-law.

concupiscencia *f* concupiscence, lustfulness.

concurrencia *f* **-1.** [asistencia] attendance; [espectadores] crowd, audience. **-2.** [de sucesos] concurrence. **-3.** COM competition; **no ~** DER non-competition clause.

concurrente ◇ *adj* concurrent. ◇ *m y f* person present.

concurrido, -da *adj* [bar, calle] crowded, busy; [espectáculo] well-attended.

concurrir *vi* **-1.** [reunirse]: **~ a algo** to go to sthg, to attend sthg. **-2.** [influir]: **~ (a)** to contribute (to). **-3.** [participar]: **~ a** [concurso] to take part in, to compete in; [examen] to sit *Br*, to take.

concursante *m y f* [en concurso] competitor, contestant; [en oposiciones] candidate.

concursar *vi* [competir] to compete, to participate; [en oposiciones] to be a candidate.

concurso *m* **-1.** [prueba - literaria, deportiva] competition; [- de televisión] game show; **~ de belleza** beauty contest. **-2.** [para una obra] tender; **salir a ~** to be put out to tender. **-3.** [ayuda] cooperation.

condado *m* [territorio] county.

condal *adj*: **la Ciudad ~** Barcelona.

conde, -desa *m y f* count (*f* countess).

CONDECA *(abrev de* **Consejo de Defensa Centroamericana**) *m Central American defence council.*

condecoración *f* **-1.** [insignia] medal. **-2.** [acto] decoration.

condecorar *vt* to decorate.

condena *f* sentence; **cumplir ~** to serve a sentence.

condenable *adj* condemnable.

condenado, -da ◇ *adj* **-1.** [a una pena] convicted, sentenced; [a un sufrimiento] condemned. **-2.** *fam* [maldito] damned, wretched. ◇ *m y f* convicted person; [a muerte] condemned person; **trabajar como un ~** to work like a slave.

condenar *vt* **-1.** [declarar culpable] to convict. **-2.** [castigar]: **~ a alguien a algo** to sentence sb to sthg. **-3.** [predestinar]: **estar con-**

denado a to be doomed to. **-4.** [recriminar] to condemn.

◆ **condenarse** *vpr* to be damned.

condensación *f* condensation.

condensado, -da *adj* condensed.

condensador, -ra *adj* condensing.

◆ **condensador** *m* condenser.

condensar *vt lit* & *fig* to condense.

condescendencia *f* [benevolencia] graciousness, kindness; [altivez] condescension.

condescender [20] *vi*: ~ **a** [con amabilidad] to consent to, to accede to; [con desprecio] to deign to, to condescend to.

condescendiente *adj* obliging.

condestable *m* HIST constable.

condición *f* **-1.** [gen] condition; **condiciones de un contrato** terms of a contract; **a** O **con la** ~ **de que alguien haga algo** on condition that sb does sthg; **con una sola** ~ on one condition; **sin condiciones** unconditional. **-2.** [naturaleza] nature. **-3.** [clase social] social class; **de** ~ **humilde** of humble circumstances.

◆ **condiciones** *fpl* **-1.** [aptitud] talent (*U*), ability (*U*). **-2.** [circunstancias] conditions; **condiciones atmosféricas/de vida** weather/living conditions. **-3.** [estado] condition (*U*); **estar en condiciones de** O **para hacer algo** [físicamente] to be in a fit state to do sthg; [por la situación] to be in a position to do sthg; **no estar en condiciones** [carne, pescado] to be off.

condicionado, -da *adj* conditioned.

condicional *adj* & *m* conditional.

condicionamiento *m* conditioning.

condicionante *m* determinant.

condicionar *vt*: ~ **algo a algo** to make sthg dependent on sthg.

condimentación *f* seasoning.

condimentar *vt* to season.

condimento *m* seasoning (*U*).

condiscípulo, -la *m y f* schoolmate.

condolencia *f* condolence.

condolerse [24] *vpr*: ~ (**de**) to feel pity (for).

condominio *m* [de un territorio] condominium; [de una cosa] joint ownership.

condón *m* condom.

condonar *vt* **-1.** [deuda, pena] to remit. **-2.** [violencia, terrorismo] to condone.

cóndor *m* condor.

conducción *f* **-1.** [de vehículo] driving. **-2.** [por tubería] piping; [por cable] wiring. **-3.** [conducto - de agua, gas] pipe; [- de electricidad] cable. **-4.** *fig* [dirección] management, running.

conducir [33] ◇ *vt* **-1.** [vehículo] to drive. **-2.** [dirigir - empresa] to manage, to run; [- ejército] to lead; [- asunto] to handle. **-3.** [una persona a un lugar] to lead. **-4.** [por tubería, cable - calor] to conduct; [- líquido] to convey; [- electricidad] to carry. ◇ *vi* **-1.** [en vehículo] to drive. **-2.** [a sitio, situación]: ~ **a** to lead to.

◆ **conducirse** *vpr* to behave.

conducta *f* behaviour, conduct.

conductismo *m* PSICOL behaviourism.

conductividad *f* FÍS conductivity.

conducto *m* **-1.** [de fluido] pipe. **-2.** *fig* [vía] channel; **por** ~ **de** through. **-3.** ANAT duct.

conductor, -ra ◇ *adj* FÍS conductive. ◇ *m y f* **-1.** [de vehículo] driver. **-2.** FÍS conductor.

conduela *etc* → **condolerse**.

conectado, -da *adj* **-1.** ELECTR: ~ (**a**) connected (to). **-2.** INFORM on-line.

conectar ◇ *vt*: ~ **algo** (**a** O **con**) to connect sthg (to O up to). ◇ *vi*: ~ **con** RADIO & TV to go over to; [persona] to contact.

conejera *f* [madriguera] (rabbit) warren; [conejar] rabbit hutch.

conejillo

◆ **conejillo de Indias** *m* guinea pig.

conejo, -ja *m y f* rabbit (*f* doe); ~ **a la cazadora** CULIN *rabbit cooked in olive oil with chopped onion, garlic and parsley.*

conexión *f* **-1.** [gen] connection. **-2.** RADIO & TV link-up; ~ **vía satélite** satellite link.

◆ **conexiones** *fpl* [influencia] connections.

conexo, -xa *adj* related, connected.

confabulación *f* conspiracy.

confabular

◆ **confabularse** *vpr*: ~**se** (**para**) to plot O conspire (to).

confección *f* **-1.** [de ropa] tailoring, dressmaking; **de** ~ off-the-peg. **-2.** [de comida] preparation, making; [de lista] drawing up.

confeccionar *vt* **-1.** [ropa] to make (up); [lista] to draw up. **-2.** [plato] to prepare; [bebida] to mix.

confederación *f* confederation.

confederado, -da *adj* confederate.

◆ **confederado** *m* HIST Confederate.

confederarse *vpr* to confederate, to form a confederation.

conferencia *f* **-1.** [charla] lecture; **dar una** ~ to give a talk O lecture; ~ **de prensa** press conference. **-2.** [reunión] conference. **-3.** [por teléfono] (long-distance) call.

conferenciante *m y f* lecturer.

conferenciar [8] *vi* to have a discussion.

conferir [27] *vt* **-1.** ~ **algo a alguien** [honor, dignidad] to confer O bestow sthg upon sb;

[responsabilidades] to give sthg to sb. **-2.** [cualidad] to give.

confesar [19] *vt* [gen] to confess; [debilidad] to admit.

◆ **confesarse** *vpr* RELIG: ~ **(de algo)** to confess (sthg).

confesión *f* **-1.** [gen] confession. **-2.** [credo] religion, (religious) persuasion.

confesional *adj* denominational; **estado ~** *country with an official state religion.*

confesionario *m* confessional.

confeso, -sa *adj* self-confessed.

confesor *m* confessor.

confeti *mpl* confetti (*U*).

confiado, -da *adj* [seguro] confident; [crédulo] trusting.

confianza *f* **-1.** [seguridad]: ~ **(en)** confidence (in); ~ **en uno mismo** self-confidence. **-2.** [fe] trust; **de ~** trustworthy. **-3.** [familiaridad] familiarity; **tengo mucha ~ con él** I am very close to him; **amigo de ~** close ○ intimate friend; **en ~** in confidence.

confiar [9] *vt* **-1.** [secreto] to confide. **-2.** [responsabilidad, persona, asunto]: ~ **algo a alguien** to entrust sthg to sb.

◆ **confiar en** *vi* **-1.** [tener fe] to trust in. **-2.** [suponer]: ~ **en que** to be confident that.

◆ **confiarse** *vpr* **-1.** [despreocuparse] to be too sure (of o.s.), to be overconfident. **-2.** [sincerarse]: ~**se a** to confide in.

confidencia *f* confidence, secret.

confidencial *adj* confidential.

confidente *m y f* **-1.** [amigo] confidant (*f* confidante). **-2.** [soplón] informer.

confiera *etc* → **conferir**.

confiesa *etc* → **confesar**.

configuración *f* **-1.** [gen & INFORM] configuration. **-2.** [del terreno] lie; [de la costa] outline, shape; [de ciudad] layout.

configurar *vt* **-1.** [formar] to shape, to form. **-2.** INFORM to configure.

confín *m* (*gen pl*) **-1.** [límite] border, boundary. **-2.** [extremo - del reino, universo] outer reaches (*pl*); **en los confines de** on the very edge of.

confinamiento *m* **-1.** [de un detenido]: ~ **(en)** confinement (to). **-2.** [de un desterrado]: ~ **(en)** banishment (to).

confinar *vt* **-1.** [detener]: ~ **(en)** to confine (to). **-2.** [desterrar]: ~ **(en)** to banish (to).

confiriera *etc* → **conferir**.

confirmación *f* [gen & RELIG] confirmation.

confirmar *vt* to confirm.

confiscar [10] *vt* to confiscate.

confitado, -da *adj* candied; **frutas confitadas** crystallized fruit.

confitar *vt* to candy.

confite *m* sweet *Br*, candy *Am*.

confitería *f* **-1.** [tienda] sweetshop, confectioner's. **-2.** *Amer* [café] cafe.

confitero, -ra *m y f* confectioner.

confitura *f* preserve, jam.

conflagración *f* conflict, war.

conflictividad *f* conflict; ~ **laboral** industrial unrest.

conflictivo, -va *adj* [asunto] controversial; [situación] troubled; [trabajador] difficult.

conflicto *m* [gen] conflict; [de intereses, opiniones] clash; ~ **laboral** industrial dispute.

confluencia *f* confluence; **la ~ de las dos calles** the place where the two roads meet.

confluir [51] *vi* **-1.** [corriente, cauce]: ~ **(en)** to converge ○ meet (at). **-2.** [personas]: ~ **(en)** to come together ○ to gather (in).

conformar *vt* [configurar] to shape.

◆ **conformarse con** *vpr* [suerte, destino] to resign o.s. to; [apañárselas con] to make do with; [contentarse con] to settle for.

conforme ◇ *adj* **-1.** [acorde]: ~ **a** in accordance with. **-2.** [de acuerdo]: ~ **(con)** in agreement (with). **-3.** [contento]: ~ **(con)** happy (with). ◇ *adv* **-1.** [gen] as; ~ **envejecía** as he got older; **te lo cuento ~ lo vi** I'm telling you exactly what I saw. **-2.** [en cuanto] as soon as; ~ **amanezca, iré** I'll leave as soon as it gets light; ~ **a** in accordance ○ keeping with.

conformidad *f* [aprobación]: ~ **(con)** approval (of); **dar uno su ~** to give one's consent.

conformismo *m* conformity.

conformista *adj, m y f* conformist.

confort (*pl* **conforts**) *m* comfort; **"todo ~"** "all mod cons".

confortable *adj* comfortable.

confortar *vt* to console, to comfort.

confraternidad *f* brotherhood.

confraternizar [13] *vi* to get along (like brothers).

confrontación *f* **-1.** [enfrentamiento] confrontation. **-2.** [comparación] comparison.

confrontar *vt* **-1.** [enfrentar] to confront. **-2.** [comparar] to compare.

confucianismo, confucionismo *m* Confucianism.

confundir *vt* **-1.** [trastocar]: ~ **una cosa con otra** to mistake one thing for another; ~ **dos cosas** to get two things mixed up. **-2.** [liar] to confuse. **-3.** [mezclar] to mix up. **-4.** [abrumar] to embarrass, to overwhelm.

◆ **confundirse** *vpr* **-1.** [equivocarse] to make a mistake; **~se de piso** to get the wrong flat; **se ha confundido** [al teléfono] you've got the wrong number. **-2.** [liarse] to get confused; **me confundo con tanta información** I get confused by all that information. **-3.** [mezclarse - colores, siluetas]: **~se (en)** to merge (into); [- personas]: **~se entre la gente** to lose o.s. in the crowd.

confusión *f* **-1.** [gen] confusion. **-2.** [error] mix-up; **ha habido una ~** there has been a bit of a mix-up.

confusionismo *m* confusion.

confuso, -sa *adj* **-1.** [incomprensible - estilo, explicación] obscure. **-2.** [poco claro - rumor] muffled; [- clamor, griterío] confused; [- contorno, forma] blurred. **-3.** [turbado] confused, bewildered.

conga *f* conga.

congelación *f* **-1.** [de alimentos] freezing. **-2.** ECON [de precios, salarios] freeze.

congelador *m* freezer.

congelados *mpl* frozen foods.

congelar *vt* [gen & ECON] to freeze.

◆ **congelarse** *vpr* to freeze.

congénere *m y f* kind ○ sort (*of person*).

congeniar [8] *vi*: **~ (con)** to get on (with).

congénito, -ta *adj* [enfermedad] congenital; [talento] innate.

congestión *f* congestion.

congestionar *vt* to block.

◆ **congestionarse** *vpr* **-1.** AUTOM & MED to become congested. **-2.** [cara - de rabia etc] to flush, to turn purple.

conglomerado *m* **-1.** GEOL & TECN conglomerate. **-2.** *fig* [mezcla] combination.

conglomerar *vt* **-1.** TECN to conglomerate. **-2.** *fig* [intereses etc] to unite.

Congo *m*: **el ~** (the) Congo.

congoja *f* anguish.

congoleño, -ña *adj, m y f* Congolese.

congraciarse [8] *vpr*: **~ con alguien** to win sb over.

congratular *vt*: **~ a alguien (por)** to congratulate sb (on).

◆ **congratularse** *vpr*: **~ (por)** to be pleased (about).

congregación *f* congregation.

congregar [16] *vt* to assemble, to bring together.

congresista *m y f* **-1.** [en un congreso] delegate. **-2.** [político] congressman (*f* congresswoman).

congreso *m* **-1.** [de una especialidad] congress. **-2.** [asamblea nacional]: **~ de diputados** [en España] *lower house of Spanish Parliament*, ≃ House of Commons *Br*, ≃ House

of Representatives *Am*; **el Congreso** [en Estados Unidos] Congress. **-3.** [edificio] parliament building.

congrio *m* conger eel.

congruente *adj* consistent, congruous.

cónico, -ca *adj* conical.

conífera *f* conifer.

conjetura *f* conjecture; **hacer ~s, hacerse una ~** to conjecture.

conjeturar *vt* to conjecture about, to make predictions about.

conjugación *f* **-1.** GRAM conjugation. **-2.** [de opiniones] combination; [de esfuerzos, ideas] pooling.

conjugar [16] *vt* **-1.** GRAM to conjugate. **-2.** [opiniones] to bring together, to combine; [esfuerzos, ideas] to pool.

conjunción *f* **-1.** ASTRON & GRAM conjunction. **-2.** [de hechos, esfuerzos] combination.

conjuntado, -da *adj* coordinated.

conjuntar *vt* to coordinate.

conjuntiva → **conjuntivo.**

conjuntivitis *f inv* conjunctivitis.

conjuntivo, -va *adj* conjunctive.

◆ **conjuntiva** *f* ANAT conjunctiva.

conjunto, -ta *adj* [gen] joint; [hechos, acontecimientos] combined.

◆ **conjunto** *m* **-1.** [gen] set, collection; **un ~ de circunstancias** a number of reasons; **~ urbanístico** housing estate. **-2.** [de ropa] outfit. **-3.** [MUS - de rock] group, band; [- de música clásica] ensemble. **-4.** [totalidad] whole; **en ~** overall, as a whole. **-5.** MAT set.

conjura *f* conspiracy, plot.

conjurar ◇ *vi* [conspirar] to conspire, to plot. ◇ *vt* **-1.** [exorcizar] to exorcize. **-2.** [evitar - un peligro] to ward off, to avert.

conjuro *m* spell, incantation.

conllevar *vt* **-1.** [implicar] to involve, to entail. **-2.** [soportar] to bear.

conmemoración *f* commemoration; **en ~ de** in commemoration of.

conmemorar *vt* to commemorate.

conmemorativo, -va *adj* commemorative.

conmensurable *adj* measurable.

conmigo *pron pers* with me; **~ mismo/misma** with myself.

conminación *f* threat.

conminar *vt*: **~ a alguien (con hacer algo)** to threaten sb (with doing sthg).

conmiseración *f* compassion, pity.

conmoción *f* **-1.** [física o psíquica] shock; **~ cerebral** concussion. **-2.** *fig* [trastorno, disturbio] upheaval.

conmocionar *vt* **-1.** [psíquicamente] to shock, to stun. **-2.** [físicamente] to concuss.

conmovedor, -ra *adj* moving, touching.

conmover [24] *vt* **-1.** [emocionar] to move, to touch. **-2.** [sacudir] to shake.

◆ **conmoverse** *vpr* **-1.** [emocionarse] to be moved, to be touched. **-2.** [sacudirse] to be shaken.

conmutación *f* DER commutation.

conmutador *m* **-1.** ELECTR switch. **-2.** *Amer* [centralita] switchboard.

conmutar *vt* to commute.

connivencia *f*: **en ~** in collusion.

connotación *f* connotation; **una ~ irónica** a hint of irony.

connotar *vt* to suggest, to have connotations of.

cono *m* cone.

conocedor, -ra *m y f*: **~ (de)** [gen] expert (on); [de vinos] connoisseur (of).

conocer [31] *vt* **-1.** [gen] to know; **darse a ~** to make o.s. known; **~ bien un tema** to know a lot about a subject; **~ alguien de vista** to know sb by sight; **~ a alguien de oídas** to have heard of sb. **-2.** [descubrir - lugar, país] to get to know. **-3.** [a una persona - por primera vez] to meet. **-4.** [reconocer]: **~ a alguien (por algo)** to recognize sb (by sthg).

◆ **conocerse** ◇ *vpr* **-1.** [a uno mismo] to know o.s. **-2.** [dos o más personas - por primera vez] to meet, to get to know each other; [- desde hace tiempo] to know each other. ◇ *v impers* [parecer]: **se conoce que ...** apparently ....

conocido, -da ◇ *adj* well-known. ◇ *m y f* acquaintance.

conocimiento *m* **-1.** [gen] knowledge; **hablar/actuar con ~ de causa** to know what one is talking about/doing. **-2.** MED [sentido] consciousness; **perder/recobrar el conocimiento** to lose/regain consciousness.

◆ **conocimientos** *mpl* knowledge (U); **tener muchos ~s** to be very knowledgeable.

conozca *etc* → **conocer**.

conque *conj* so; **¿~ te has cansado?** so you're tired, are you?

conquista *f* **-1.** [de tierras, persona] conquest. **-2.** *fig* [de libertad, derecho] winning.

conquistador, -ra ◇ *adj* [seductor] seductive. ◇ *m y f* **-1.** [de tierras] conqueror. **-2.** HIST conquistador. **-3.** *fig* [persona seductora] Casanova, womanizer (*f* man-eater).

conquistar *vt* **-1.** [tierras] to conquer. **-2.** *fig* [libertad, derechos, simpatía] to win. **-3.** *fig* [seducir] to win the heart of.

consabido, -da *adj* [conocido] well-known; [habitual] usual.

consagración *f* **-1.** RELIG consecration. **-2.** [dedicación] dedication. **-3.** [reconocimiento] recognition.

consagrado, -da *adj* **-1.** RELIG consecrated. **-2.** [dedicado] dedicated. **-3.** [reconocido] recognized, established.

consagrar *vt* **-1.** RELIG to consecrate. **-2.** [dedicar]: **~ algo a algo/alguien** [tiempo, espacio] to devote sthg to sthg/sb; [monumento, lápida] to dedicate sthg to sthg/sb. **-3.** [acreditar, confirmar] to confirm, to establish.

◆ **consagrarse** *vpr* **-1.** [dedicarse]: **~se (a)** to devote ○ dedicate o.s. (to). **-2.** [alcanzar reconocimiento] to establish o.s.

consanguíneo, -nea *adj* related by blood; **hermano ~** half-brother (*of same father*).

consanguinidad *f* **-1.** [de hermanos] sharing of the same father. **-2.** [de parientes] blood relation.

consciencia = **conciencia**.

consciente *adj* conscious; **ser ~ de** to be aware of; **estar ~** [físicamente] to be conscious.

consecución *f* [de un deseo] realization; [de un objetivo] attainment; [de un premio] winning.

consecuencia *f* **-1.** [resultado] consequence; **a ○ como ~ de** as a consequence ○ result of; **en ~** consequently; **tener ~s** to have consequences. **-2.** [coherencia] consistency.

consecuente *adj* [coherente] consistent.

consecutivo, -va *adj* consecutive.

conseguir [43] *vt* [gen] to obtain, to get; [un objetivo] to achieve; **~ hacer algo** to manage to do sthg.

consejería *f* department.

consejero, -ra *m y f* **-1.** [en asuntos personales] counsellor; [en asuntos técnicos] adviser, consultant. **-2.** [de un consejo de administración] member; POLIT councillor.

consejo *m* **-1.** [advertencia] advice (U); **dar un ~** to give some advice; **te voy a dar un ~** I've got a piece of advice for you. **-2.** [organismo] council; **~ de administración** board of directors. **-3.** [reunión] meeting.

◆ **consejo de guerra** *m* court martial.

◆ **consejo de ministros** *m* cabinet.

consenso *m* [acuerdo] consensus; [consentimiento] consent.

consensuado, -da *adj* approved by consensus.

consensual *adj* consensual.

consensuar [6] *vt* to approve by consensus.

consentido, -da ◇ *adj* spoilt, spoiled. ◇ *m y f* spoiled brat.

consentimiento *m* consent.

consentir [27] ◇ *vt* -**1.** [tolerar] to allow, to permit. -**2.** [mimar] to spoil. ◇ *vi*: ~ **en algo/en hacer algo** to agree to sthg/to do sthg; **consintió en que se quedaran** he agreed to let them stay.

conserje *m y f* [portero] porter; [encargado] caretaker.

conserjería *f* -**1.** [de un hotel] reception desk. -**2.** [de un edificio público o privado] porter's lodge.

conserva *f* tinned ○ canned food; ~ **de carne** tinned meat; **en** ~ tinned, canned.

conservación *f* -**1.** [gen] conservation; [de alimentos] preservation. -**2.** [mantenimiento] maintenance.

conservador, -ra ◇ *adj* [gen] conservative; [del partido conservador] Conservative. ◇ *m y f* -**1.** [por ideología] conservative; [miembro del partido conservador] Conservative. -**2.** [de museo] curator.

conservadurismo *m* conservatism.

conservante *m y f* preservative.

conservar *vt* -**1.** [gen & CULIN] to preserve; [amistad] to sustain, to keep up; [salud] to look after; [calor] to retain. -**2.** [guardar - libros, cartas, secreto] to keep.
◆ **conservarse** *vpr* to keep; **se conserva bien** he's keeping well.

conservatorio *m* conservatoire.

conservero, -ra *adj* canning (*antes de sust*).

considerable *adj* [gen] considerable; [importante, eminente] notable.

consideración *f* -**1.** [valoración] consideration; **tomar en** ~ to take into consideration. -**2.** [respeto] respect; **tratar a alguien con** ~ to be nice to sb; **en** ~ **a algo** in recognition of sthg. -**3.** [importancia]: **de** ~ serious; **hubo varios heridos de** ~ several people were seriously injured.

considerado, -da *adj* [atento] considerate, thoughtful; [respetado] respected, highly-regarded.

considerar *vt* -**1.** [valorar] to consider. -**2.** [juzgar, estimar] to think. -**3.** [respetar] to esteem, to treat with respect.

consienta *etc* → **consentir**.

consiga → **conseguir**.

consigna *f* -**1.** [órdenes] instructions (*pl*). -**2.** [para el equipaje] left-luggage office.

consignar *vt* -**1.** [poner por escrito] to record, to write down. -**2.** [asignar] to allocate. -**3.** [enviar - mercancía] to consign, to dispatch. -**4.** [equipaje] to deposit in the left-luggage office.

consignatario, -ria *m y f* -**1.** [de una mercancía] consignee. -**2.** [representante]: ~ **de buques** shipping agent.

consigo ◇ *v* → **conseguir**. ◇ *pron pers* with him/her, (*pl*) with them; [con usted] with you; [con uno mismo] with o.s.; **lleva siempre la pistola** ~ she always carries the gun with her; ~ **mismo/misma** with himself/herself; **hablar** ~ **mismo** to talk to o.s.

consiguiente *adj* consequent; **por** ~ consequently, therefore.

consiguiera *etc* → **conseguir**.

consintiera *etc* → **consentir**.

consistencia *f lit & fig* consistency.

consistente *adj* -**1.** [sólido - material] solid. -**2.** [coherente - argumento] sound, convincing. -**3.** [compuesto]: ~ **en** consisting of.

consistir
◆ **consistir en** *vi* -**1.** [gen] to consist of. -**2.** [deberse a] to lie in, to be based on.

consistorial *adj* of a town hall; **casa** ~ town hall.

consistorio *m* town council.

consola *f* -**1.** [mesa] console table. -**2.** IN-FORM & TECN console; ~ **de videojuegos** video console.

consolación *f* consolation.

consolador, -ra *adj* consoling, comforting.

consolar [23] *vt* to console.
◆ **consolarse** *vpr* to console o.s., to take comfort.

consolidación *f* consolidation.

consolidar *vt* to consolidate.

consomé *m* consommé.

consonancia *f* harmony; **en** ~ **con** in keeping with.

consonante *f* consonant.

consonántico, -ca *adj* consonantal.

consorcio *m* consortium; ~ **bancario** bankers' consortium.

consorte *m y f* spouse; **príncipe** ~ prince consort.

conspicuo, -cua *adj* [evidente] conspicuous; [ilustre] eminent.

conspiración *f* plot, conspiracy.

conspirador, -ra *m y f* conspirator, plotter.

conspirar *vi* to conspire, to plot.

constancia *f* -**1.** [perseverancia - en una empresa] perseverance; [- en las ideas, opiniones] steadfastness; **hacer algo con** ~ to persevere with sthg. -**2.** [testimonio] record; **dejar**

~ **de algo** [registrar] to put sthg on record; [probar] to demonstrate sthg.

constante ◇ *adj* **-1.** [persona - en una empresa] persistent; [- en ideas, opiniones] steadfast. **-2.** [acción] constant. ◇ *f* constant; **mantener las ~s vitales de alguien** MED to keep sb alive.

Constanza *m*: **el lago ~** Lake Constance.

constar *vi* **-1.** [una información]: ~ **(en)** to appear (in), to figure (in); ~**le a alguien** to be clear to sb; **me consta que** I am quite sure that; **que conste que** ... let it be clearly understood that ..., let there be no doubt that ...; **hacer ~** to put on record. **-2.** [estar constituido por]: ~ **de** to consist of.

constatar *vt* [observar] to confirm; [comprobar] to check.

constelación *f* constellation.

consternación *f* consternation, dismay.

consternar *vt* to dismay.

constipado, -da *adj*: **estar ~** to have a cold.
◆ **constipado** *m* cold.

constiparse *vpr* to catch a cold.

constitución *f* constitution.
◆ **Constitución** *f* [de un Estado] Constitution.

constitucional *adj* constitutional.

constitucionalidad *f* constitutionality.

constituir [51] *vt* **-1.** [componer] to make up. **-2.** [ser] to be. **-3.** [crear] to set up, to constitute.

constitutivo, -va *adj* constituent; **ser ~ de algo** to constitute sthg.

constituyente *adj* & *m* constituent.

constreñir *vt* **-1.** [obligar]: ~ **a alguien a hacer algo** to compel O force sb to do sthg. **-2.** [oprimir, limitar] to restrict.

construcción *f* **-1.** [gen] construction; **en ~** under construction. **-2.** [edificio] building.

constructivo, -va *adj* constructive.

constructor, -ra *adj* building (*antes de sust*), construction (*antes de sust*).
◆ **constructor** *m* [de edificios] builder.

construir [51] *vt* [edificio, barco] to build; [aviones, coches] to manufacture; [frase, teoría] to construct.

consubstancial = **consustancial**.

consuegro, -gra *m y f* father-in-law or mother-in-law of one's son or daughter.

consuela *etc* → **consolar**.

consuelo *m* consolation, solace.

consuetudinario, -ria *adj* customary; **derecho ~** common law.

cónsul, consulesa *m y f* consul.

consulado *m* [oficina] consulate; [cargo] consulship.

consular *adj* consular.

consulta *f* **-1.** [sobre un problema] consultation; **hacer una ~ a alguien** to seek sb's advice. **-2.** [despacho de médico] consulting room; **horas de ~** surgery hours; **pasar ~** to hold a surgery.

consultar ◇ *vt* [dato, fecha] to look up; [libro, persona] to consult. ◇ *vi*: ~ **con** to consult, to seek advice from.

consultivo, -va *adj* consultative, advisory.

consultor, -ra *m y f* consultant.

consultoría *f* consultancy firm.

consultorio *m* **-1.** [de un médico] consulting room. **-2.** [en periódico] problem page; [en radio] *programme answering listeners' questions*. **-3.** [asesoría] advice bureau.

consumación *f* [gen] consummation; [de un crimen] perpetration.

consumado, -da *adj* consummate, perfect; **es un granuja ~** he's a complete scoundrel.

consumar *vt* [gen] to complete; [un crimen] to perpetrate; [el matrimonio] to consummate.

consumición *f* **-1.** [acción] consumption. **-2.** [bebida] drink; [comida] food.

consumido, -da *adj* [flaco] emaciated.

consumidor, -ra *m y f* [gen] consumer; [en un bar, restaurante] patron.

consumir ◇ *vt* **-1.** [gen] to consume. **-2.** [destruir - suj: fuego] to destroy; [- suj: enfermedad] to eat away at. ◇ *vi* to consume.
◆ **consumirse** *vpr* **-1.** [persona] to waste away. **-2.** [fuego] to burn out.

consumismo *m* consumerism.

consumo *m* consumption; **bienes/sociedad de ~** consumer goods/society; ~ **de drogas** taking of drugs.

consustancial, consubstancial *adj*: **ser ~** to be an integral part.

contabilidad *f* **-1.** [oficio] accountancy. **-2.** [de persona, empresa] bookkeeping, accounting; **llevar la ~** to do the accounts; **doble ~** double-entry bookkeeping.

contabilización *f* COM entering.

contabilizar [13] *vt* COM to enter.

contable *m y f* accountant.

contactar
◆ **contactar con** *vi* to contact.

contacto *m* **-1.** [gen] contact; **ponerse en ~ con** to get in touch with; **perder el ~** to lose touch. **-2.** AUTOM ignition.

contado, -da *adj* **-1.** [raro] rare, infrequent; **contadas veces** very rarely. **-2.** [enumerado] counted.
◆ **al contado** *loc adv*: **pagar al ~** to pay (in) cash.

contador, -ra *m y f Amer* [persona] accountant.

◆ **contador** *m* [aparato] meter.

contagiar [8] *vt* [persona] to infect; [enfermedad] to transmit.

◆ **contagiarse** *vpr* [enfermedad, risa] to be contagious; [persona] to become infected.

contagio *m* infection, contagion.

contagioso, -sa *adj* [enfermedad] contagious, infectious; [risa etc] infectious.

container = contenedor.

contaminación *f* [gen] contamination; [del medio ambiente] pollution; ~ **acústica** noise pollution.

contaminante *adj* contaminating, polluting.

◆ **contaminantes** *mpl* pollutants.

contaminar *vt* -1. [gen] to contaminate; [el medio ambiente] to pollute. -2. *fig* [pervertir] to corrupt.

contante → dinero.

contar [23] ◇ *vt* -1. [enumerar, incluir] to count. -2. [narrar] to tell. ◇ *vi* to count.

◆ **contar con** *vi* -1. [confiar en] to count on. -2. [tener, poseer] to have; **cuenta con dos horas para hacerlo** he has two hours to do it. -3. [tener en cuenta] to take into account; **con esto no contaba** I hadn't reckoned with that.

contemplación *f* contemplation.

◆ **contemplaciones** *fpl* consideration (*U*); **no andarse con contemplaciones** not to beat about the bush.

contemplar *vt* [mirar, considerar] to contemplate.

contemplativo, -va *adj* contemplative.

contemporáneo, -a *adj, m y f* contemporary.

contemporizar [13] *vi* to be accommodating.

contención *f* -1. CONSTR: **muro de** ~ retaining wall. -2. [moderación] restraint, self-restraint.

contencioso, -sa *adj* -1. [tema, cuestión] contentious. -2. DER litigious.

◆ **contencioso** *m* dispute, conflict.

contender [20] *vi* [competir] to contend; [pelear] to fight.

contendiente ◇ *adj* [en una competición] contending (*antes de sust*); [en una guerra] warring (*antes de sust*). ◇ *m y f* [en una competición] contender; [en una guerra] warring faction.

contenedor, -ra *adj* containing.

◆ **contenedor, container** *m* [gen] container; [para escombros] skip; ~ **de basura** large

rubbish bin for collecting rubbish from blocks of flats etc.

contener [72] *vt* -1. [encerrar] to contain. -2. [detener, reprimir] to restrain, to hold back.

◆ **contenerse** *vpr* to restrain o.s., to hold o.s. back.

contenido *m* [gen] contents (*pl*); [de discurso, redacción] content.

contentar *vt* to please, to keep happy.

◆ **contentarse** *vpr*: ~**se con** to make do with.

contento, -ta *adj* [alegre] happy; [satisfecho] pleased.

◆ **contento** *m* happiness, joy; **no caber uno en sí de** ~ to be beside o.s. with joy.

conteo *m* counting-up.

contertulio, -lia *m y f* companion (*at a social gathering*).

contestación *f* answer.

contestador

◆ **contestador (automático)** *m* answering machine.

contestar *vt* to answer.

contestatario, -ria *adj* anti-establishment.

contexto *m* context.

contextualizar [13] *vt* to contextualize.

contextura *f* [textura] texture; [complexión] build.

contienda ◇ *v* → contender. ◇ *f* [competición, combate] contest; [guerra] conflict, war.

contiene → contener.

contigo *pron pers* with you; ~ **mismo/misma** with yourself.

contiguo, -gua *adj* adjacent.

continencia *f* continence, self-restraint.

continental *adj* continental.

continente *m* -1. GEOGR continent. -2. [recipiente] container.

contingencia *f* [eventualidad] eventuality; [imprevisibilidad] unpredictability.

contingente ◇ *adj* unforeseeable. ◇ *m* -1. [grupo] contingent. -2. COM quota.

continuación *f* continuation; **a** ~ next, then.

continuar [6] ◇ *vt* to continue, to carry on with. ◇ *vi* to continue, to go on; ~ **haciendo algo** to continue doing ○ to do sthg; **continúa lloviendo** it's still raining.

continuidad *f* [en una sucesión] continuity; [permanencia] continuation.

continuo, -nua *adj* -1. [ininterrumpido] continuous. -2. [constante, perseverante] continual.

contonearse *vpr* [hombre] to swagger; [mujer] to sway one's hips.

contoneo *m* [de hombre] swagger; [de mujer] sway of the hips.

contornear *vt* [seguir el contorno de] to go round; [perfilar] to outline.

contorno *m* **-1.** GEOGR contour; [línea] outline. **-2.** (*gen pl*) [vecindad] neighbourhood; [de una ciudad] outskirts (*pl*).

contorsión *f* contortion.

contorsionarse *vpr* [gen] to do contortions; [de dolor] to writhe.

contorsionista *m y f* contortionist.

contra ◇ *prep* against; **un jarabe ~ la tos** a cough syrup; **en ~** against; **estar en ~ de algo** to be opposed to sthg; **en ~ de** [a diferencia de] contrary to. ◇ *m*: **los pros y los ~s** the pros and cons.

contraatacar [10] *vt* to counterattack.

contraataque *m* counterattack.

contrabajo ◇ *m* **-1.** [instrumento] double-bass. **-2.** [voz, cantante] low bass. ◇ *m y f* [instrumentista] double bass player.

contrabandista *m y f* smuggler.

contrabando *m* [acto] smuggling; [mercancías] contraband; **pasar algo de ~** to smuggle sthg in; **~ de armas** gunrunning; **tabaco de ~** contraband cigarettes.

contracción *f* contraction.

contracepción *f* contraception.

contraceptivo, **-va** *adj* contraceptive (*antes de sust*).

contrachapado, **-da** *adj* made of plywood.
◆ **contrachapado** *m* plywood.

contracorriente *f* crosscurrent; **ir a ~** to go against the current ○ tide.

contráctil *adj* contractile.

contractual *adj* contractual.

contracultura *f* counter-culture.

contracultural *adj* counter-culture (*antes de sust*).

contradecir [66] *vt* to contradict.
◆ **contradecirse** *vpr* to contradict o.s.

contradicción *f* contradiction; **estar en ~ con** to be in (direct) contradiction to.

contradicho, **-cha** *pp* → **contradecir**.

contradictorio, **-ria** *adj* contradictory.

contraer [73] *vt* **-1.** [gen] to contract. **-2.** [costumbre, acento etc] to acquire. **-3.** [enfermedad] to catch.
◆ **contraerse** *vpr* to contract.

contraespionaje *m* counterespionage.

contrafuerte *m* **-1.** ARQUIT buttress. **-2.** [del calzado] heel reinforcement. **-3.** GEOGR foothill.

contragolpe *m* counter-attack.

contrahecho, **-cha** *adj* deformed.

contraindicación *f*: "**contraindicaciones:** ..." "not to be taken with ...".

contraindicado, **-da** *adj*: **está ~ beber durante el embarazo** alcohol should be avoided during pregnancy.

contralmirante *m* rear admiral.

contralor *m Amer* inspector of public spending.

contraloría *f Amer* office controlling public spending.

contralto ◇ *m* [voz] contralto. ◇ *m y f* [cantante] counter tenor (*f* contralto).

contraluz *m* back lighting; **a ~** against the light.

contramaestre *m* **-1.** NÁUT boatswain; MIL warrant officer. **-2.** [capataz] foreman.

contraofensiva *f* counteroffensive.

contraorden *f* countermand.

contrapartida *f* compensation; **como ~** to make up for it.

contrapelo
◆ **a contrapelo** *loc adv* **-1.** [acariciar] the wrong way. **-2.** [vivir, actuar] against the grain.

contrapesar *vt* **-1.** [físicamente] to counterbalance. **-2.** *fig* [contrarrestar] to compensate for.

contrapeso *m* **-1.** [en ascensores, poleas] counterweight. **-2.** *fig* [fuerza que iguala] counterbalance.

contraponer [65] *vt* **-1.** [oponer]: **~ (a)** to set up (against). **-2.** [cotejar] to compare.
◆ **contraponerse** *vpr* to oppose.

contraportada *f* [de periódico, revista] back page; [de libro, disco] back cover.

contraposición *f* **-1.** [oposición] conflict. **-2.** [comparación] comparison.

contraproducente *adj* counterproductive.

contrapuesto, **-ta** ◇ *pp* → **contraponer**. ◇ *adj* conflicting.

contrapunto *m* **-1.** MÚS counterpoint. **-2.** *fig* [contraste] contrast.

contrariado, **-da** *adj* upset.

contrariar [9] *vt* **-1.** [contradecir] to go against. **-2.** [disgustar] to upset.

contrariedad *f* **-1.** [dificultad] setback. **-2.** [disgusto] annoyance. **-3.** [oposición] contrary ○ opposing nature.

contrario, **-ria** *adj* **-1.** [opuesto - dirección, sentido] opposite; [- parte] opposing; [- opinión] contrary; **ser ~ a algo** to be opposed to sthg. **-2.** [perjudicial]: **~ a** contrary to. **-3.** *loc*: **llevar la contraria** to be awkward ○ contrary.
◆ **contrario** *m* **-1.** [rival] opponent. **-2.** [opuesto] opposite; **al ~**, **por el ~** on the

contrary; **de lo** ~ otherwise; **todo lo** ~ quite the contrary.

contrarreembolso = contrarrembolso.

contrarreforma f Counter-Reformation.

contrarreloj adj inv: **etapa** ~ time trial; **ir** ~ to be working against the clock.

contrarrembolso, **contrarreembolso** m cash on delivery.

contrarrestar vt [neutralizar] to counteract.

contrarrevolución f counterrevolution.

contrarrevolucionario, **-ria** adj, m y f counterrevolutionary.

contrasentido m nonsense (U); **es un** ~ **hacer eso** it doesn't make sense to do that.

contraseña f password.

contrastar ⋄ vi to contrast. ⋄ vt **-1.** [probar - hechos] to check, to verify. **-2.** [resistir] to resist.

contraste m contrast.

contrata f (fixed price) contract.

contratación f [de personal] hiring.

contratante m y f contracting party.

contratar vt **-1.** [obreros, personal, detective] to hire; [deportista] to sign. **-2.** [servicio, obra, mercancía]: ~ **algo a alguien** to contract for sthg with sb.

contraterrorismo m counterterrorism.

contraterrorista adj, m y f counterterrorist.

contratiempo m [accidente] mishap; [dificultad] setback.

contratista m y f contractor; ~ **de obras** building contractor.

contrato m contract; ~ **indefinido/laboral/mercantil** indefinite/work/commercial contract; ~ **administrativo** administrative contract; ~ **de arrendamiento** lease; ~ **de compraventa** contract of sale; ~ **temporal** temporary ○ short-term contract; ~ **verbal** oral contract.

contravenir [75] vi: ~ **a** to contravene.

contraventana f shutter.

contrayente m y f person getting married.

contribución f **-1.** [gen] contribution. **-2.** [impuesto] tax; ~ **directa/indirecta** direct/indirect tax; ~ **urbana** ≃ council tax Br.

contribuir [51] vi **-1.** [gen]: ~ **(a)** to contribute (to); ~ **con algo para** to contribute sthg towards. **-2.** [pagar impuestos] to pay taxes.

contribuyente m y f taxpayer.

contrición f contrition.

contrincante m y f rival, opponent.

contrito, **-ta** adj **-1.** [arrepentido] contrite. **-2.** fig [triste, compungido] downcast.

control m **-1.** [gen] control; **bajo** ~ under control; **perder el** ~ to lose one's temper; ~ **de cambios** ECON foreign exchange regulation; ~ **de natalidad** birth control. **-2.** [verificación] examination, inspection; **(bajo)** ~ **médico** (under) medical supervision; ~ **antidoping** drug test; ~ **de calidad** quality control. **-3.** [puesto policial] checkpoint.

controlador, **-ra** m y f [gen & INFORM] controller; ~ **aéreo** air traffic controller.

◆ **controlador** m: ~ **de disco** disk controller.

controlar vt **-1.** [gen] to control; [cuentas] to audit. **-2.** [comprobar] to check. **-3.** [vigilar] to watch, to keep an eye on.

◆ **controlarse** vpr to control o.s., to restrain o.s.

controversia f controversy.

contubernio m fig conspiracy.

contumacia f obstinacy, stubbornness.

contumaz adj stubborn, obstinate.

contundencia f **-1.** [de golpes, patadas] force. **-2.** fig [de palabras, argumentos] forcefulness.

contundente adj **-1.** [arma, objeto] blunt; [golpe] thudding. **-2.** fig [razonamiento, argumento] forceful.

conturbar vt to trouble, to perturb.

contusión f bruise.

contusionar vt to bruise.

contuviera etc → **contener**.

conurbación f conurbation.

convalecencia f convalescence.

convalecer [30] vi: ~ **(de)** to convalesce (after).

convaleciente adj convalescent.

convalidación f [de estudios] recognition; [de asignaturas] validation.

convalidar vt [estudios] to recognize; [asignaturas] to validate.

convección f convection.

convector m convector.

convencer [11] vt to convince; ~ **a alguien de algo** to convince sb of sthg.

◆ **convencerse** vpr: ~**se de** to become convinced of.

convencimiento m [certeza] conviction; [acción] convincing.

convención f convention.

convencional adj conventional.

convencionalismo m conventionality.

conveniencia f **-1.** [utilidad] usefulness; [oportunidad] suitability. **-2.** [interés] convenience; **sólo mira su** ~ he only looks after his own interests.

◆ **conveniencias** fpl conventions.

conveniente *adj* [útil] useful; [oportuno] suitable, appropriate; [lugar, hora] conveniente; [aconsejable] advisable; **sería ~ asistir** it would be a good idea to go.

convenio *m* agreement; **~ colectivo** collective bargaining.

convenir [75] ◇ *vi* **-1.** [venir bien] to be suitable; **conviene analizar la situación** it would be a good idea to analyse the situation; **no te conviene hacerlo** you shouldn't do it. **-2.** [acordar]: **~ en** to agree on. ◇ *vt* to agree on.

convento *m* [de monjas] convent; [de monjes] monastery.

convergencia *f* convergence.

convergente *adj* converging, convergent.

converger [14] *vi* to converge.

conversación *f* conversation; **dar ~ a alguien** to keep sb talking.

◆ **conversaciones** *fpl* [negociaciones] talks.

conversada *f Amer* chat.

conversador, -ra ◇ *adj* talkative. ◇ *m y f* conversationalist.

conversar *vi* to talk, to converse.

conversión *f* conversion.

converso, -sa ◇ *adj* converted. ◇ *m y f* convert.

convertibilidad *f* ECON convertibility.

convertible *adj* convertible.

convertir [21] *vt* **-1.** RELIG to convert. **-2.** [transformar]: **~ algo/a alguien en** to convert sthg/sb into, to turn sthg/sb into.

◆ **convertirse** *vpr* **-1.** RELIG: **~se (a)** to convert (to). **-2.** [transformarse]: **~se en** to become, to turn into.

convexo, -xa *adj* convex.

convicción *f* conviction; **tener la ~ de que** to be convinced that.

convicto, -ta *adj* convicted.

convidado, -da *m y f* guest.

convidar *vt* [invitar] to invite.

◆ **convidar a** *vi* [mover, incitar] to be conducive to.

conviene → convenir.

convierta *etc* → convertir.

convincente *adj* convincing.

conviniera *etc* → convenir.

convite *m* **-1.** [invitación] invitation. **-2.** [fiesta] banquet.

convivencia *f* living together.

convivir *vi* to live together; **~ con** to live with.

convocar [10] *vt* [reunión] to convene; [huelga, elecciones] to call.

convocatoria *f* **-1.** [anuncio, escrito] notice. **-2.** [de examen] diet.

convoy (*pl* **convoyes**) *m* **-1.** [gen] convoy. **-2.** [tren] train.

convulsión *f* **-1.** [de músculos] convulsion. **-2.** [política, social] upheaval (*U*). **-3.** [de tierra] tremor.

convulsionar *vt* to convulse.

convulso, -sa *adj* convulsed.

conyugal *adj* conjugal; **vida ~** married life.

cónyuge *m y f* spouse; **los ~s** husband and wife.

coña *f fam* **-1.** [guasa] joke; **está de ~** she's joking. **-2.** [molestia] drag, pain.

coñá, coñac (*pl* **coñacs**), **cognac** (*pl* **cognacs**) *m* brandy, cognac.

coñazo *m fam* pain, drag; **dar el ~** to be a pain.

coño *vulg* ◇ *m* **-1.** [genital] cunt. **-2.** [para enfatizar]: **¿dónde/qué ~ ...?** where/what the fuck ...? ◇ *interj* **-1.** [enfado]: **¡~!** for fuck's sake! **-2.** [asombro]: **¡~!** fucking hell!

cooperación *f* cooperation.

cooperador, -ra *adj* cooperative.

cooperante *adj* cooperating.

cooperar *vi*: **~ (con alguien en algo)** to cooperate (with sb in sthg).

cooperativa → cooperativo.

cooperativismo *m* cooperative movement.

cooperativo, -va *adj* cooperative.

◆ **cooperativa** *f* cooperative; **cooperativa agrícola** farming cooperative.

coordenada *f* (*gen pl*) coordinate.

coordinación *f* coordination.

coordinado, -da *adj* coordinated.

coordinador, -ra ◇ *adj* coordinating. ◇ *m y f* coordinator.

coordinar *vt* **-1.** [movimientos, gestos] to coordinate. **-2.** [esfuerzos, medios] to combine, to pool.

copa *f* **-1.** [vaso] glass; **ir de ~s** to go out drinking; **¿quieres (tomar) una ~?** would you like (to have) a drink? **-2.** [de árbol] top. **-3.** [de sombrero] crown. **-4.** [en deporte] cup.

◆ **copas** *fpl* [naipes] *suit with pictures of goblets in Spanish playing cards,* ≈ hearts.

COPA (*abrev de* **Compañía Panameña de Aviación**) *f Panamanian state airline.*

copar *vt fig* **-1.** [puestos · en competición] to win. **-2.** [cargos] to monopolize.

COPE (*abrev de* **Cadena de Ondas Populares Españolas**) *f private Spanish radio station.*

copear *vi* to have a few drinks.

COPEL (*abrev de* **Coordinadora de Presos Españoles en Lucha**) *f Spanish coordinating committee for the defence of prisoners' rights.*

Copenhague Copenhagen.

copeo *m* drinking.

copero, -ra *adj* [competición, partido] cup (*antes de sust*); [equipo] cupwinning (*antes de sust*).

copete *m* **-1.** [de ave] crest. **-2.** [de pelo] tuft. **-3.** *loc*: **de alto** ~ upper-class.

copetín *m Amer* cocktail.

copia *f* **-1.** [reproducción] copy; ~ **de seguridad** INFORM backup. **-2.** [acción] copying. **-3.** [persona] (spitting) image.

copiador, -ra *adj* copying.

copiar [8] ◇ *vt* [gen] to copy; [al dictado] to take down. ◇ *vi* [en examen] to cheat, to copy.

copiloto *m y f* copilot.

copión, -ona *m y f* [imitador] copycat; [en examen] cheat.

copioso, -sa *adj* copious.

copista *m y f* copyist.

copla *f* **-1.** [canción] folksong, popular song. **-2.** [estrofa] verse, stanza.

copo *m* **-1.** [de nieve, cereales]. flake; ~**s de avena** rolled oats. **-2.** [de algodón] ball.

copón *m* ciborium; **un lío del** ~ *fam* a hell of a mess.

coprocesador *m* INFORM coprocessor; ~ **matemático** maths chip ○ coprocessor.

coproducción *f* coproduction.

copropiedad *f* joint ownership.

copropietario, -ria *m y f* co-owner, joint owner.

copto, -ta *adj* Coptic.
◆ **copto** *m* [lengua] Coptic.

cópula *f* **-1.** [sexual] copulation. **-2.** GRAM copula.

copulación *f* copulation.

copular *vi* to copulate.

copulativo, -va *adj* copulative.

coque *m* coke.

coqueta → coqueto.

coquetear *vi* to flirt.

coquetería *f* coquetry.

coqueto, -ta *adj* **-1.** [persona - que flirtea] flirtatious, coquettish; [- que se arregla mucho] concerned with one's appearance. **-2.** [cosa] charming, delightful.
◆ **coqueta** *f* [tocador] dressing table.

coraje *m* **-1.** [valor] courage. **-2.** [rabia] anger; **me da mucho** ~ it makes me furious.

coral ◇ *adj* choral. ◇ *m* coral. ◇ *f* **-1.** [coro] choir. **-2.** [composición] chorale.

coralino, -na *adj* coral.

Corán *m*: **el** ~ the Koran.

coraza *f* **-1.** [de soldado] cuirasse, armour. **-2.** [de tortuga] shell. **-3.** *fig* [protección] shield.

corazón *m* **-1.** [gen] heart; **de buen** ~ kindhearted; **no tener** ~ to have no heart, to be heartless. **-2.** [de frutas] core. **-3.** → **dedo. -4.** *loc*: **con el** ~ **en la mano** frankly, openly; **de (todo)** ~ from the bottom of one's heart, quite sincerely; **se me encoge el** ~ **al ver ...** it breaks my heart to see ...; **llevar el** ~ **en la mano** to wear one's heart on one's sleeve; **romper** ○ **partir el** ~ **a alguien** to break sb's heart.
◆ **Sagrado Corazón** *m* Sacred Heart.

corazonada *f* **-1.** [presentimiento] feeling, hunch. **-2.** [impulso] sudden impulse.

corbata *f* tie; ~ **de pajarita** bow tie.

corbeta *f* corvette.

Córcega Corsica.

corcel *m* steed.

corchea *f* quaver.

corchera *f* rope with cork floats to divide lanes in swimming pool.

corchete *m* **-1.** [broche] hook and eye. **-2.** [signo ortográfico] square bracket. **-3.** *Amer* [grapa] staple.

corchetera *f Amer* stapler.

corcho *m* cork.

corcholata *f Amer* metal bottle top.

córcholis *interj* **-1.** [para expresar sorpresa]: ¡~! good heavens! **-2.** [para expresar enfado]: ¡~! for Heaven's sake!

corcova *f* hump.

corcovado, -da *m y f* hunchback.

cordada *f* roped party of mountaineers.

cordaje *m* **-1.** [de guitarra, raqueta] strings (*pl*). **-2.** NÁUT rigging.

cordel *m* cord.

cordero, -ra *m y f* *lit & fig* lamb.

cordial *adj* cordial.

cordialidad *f* cordiality.

cordillera *f* mountain range; **la** ~ **Cantábrica** the Cantabrian Mountains.

cordón *m* **-1.** [gen & ANAT] cord; [de zapato] lace; ~ **umbilical** umbilical cord. **-2.** [cable eléctrico] flex. **-3.** *fig* [para protección, vigilancia] cordon; ~ **sanitario** cordon sanitaire. **-4.** *Amer* [de la acera] kerb; **aparcar en** ~ to park end-to-end.

cordura *f* [juicio] sanity; [sensatez] sense.

corear *vt* to chorus.

coreografía *f* choreography.

coreógrafo, -fa *m y f* choreographer.

corintio, -tia *adj, m y f* Corinthian.

corista ◇ *m y f* [en coro] chorus singer. ◇ *f* [en cabaret] chorus girl.

cormorán m cormorant.

cornada f goring.

cornamenta f -1. [de toro] horns (pl); [de ciervo] antlers (pl). -2. fam [del marido engañado] cuckold's horns (pl).

cornamusa f -1. [trompeta] hunting horn. -2. [gaita] bagpipe.

córnea f cornea.

cornear, acornear vt to gore.

córner m corner (kick).

corneta ◇ f [instrumento] bugle. ◇ m y f [persona] bugler.

cornete m -1. ANAT turbinate bone. -2. [helado] cornet, cone.

cornetín ◇ m [instrumento] cornet. ◇ m y f [persona] cornet player.

cornflakes® ['konfleiks] mpl Cornflakes®.

cornisa f -1. ARQUIT cornice. -2. GEOGR: la ~ cantábrica the Cantabrian Coast.

cornucopia f -1. [espejo] small decorative mirror. -2. [cuerno] cornucopia, horn of plenty.

cornudo, -da adj -1. [animal] horned. -2. fam fig [marido] cuckolded.
◆ **cornudo** m fam fig cuckold.

coro m -1. [gen] choir; **contestar a** ~ to answer all at once. -2. [de obra musical] chorus.

coroides f inv choroid.

corola f corolla.

corolario m corollary.

corona f -1. [gen] crown. -2. [de flores] garland; ~ **fúnebre/de laurel** funeral/laurel wreath. -3. [de santos] halo. -4. [de comida] ring.

coronación f -1. [de monarca] coronation. -2. fig [remate, colmo] culmination.

coronamiento m -1. fig [remate, fin] culmination. -2. ARQUIT crown.

coronar vt -1. [persona] to crown. -2. fig [terminar] to complete; [culminar] to crown, to cap. -3. fig [cima] to reach.

coronario, -ria adj coronary.

coronel m colonel.

coronilla f crown (of the head); **estar hasta la** ~ **(de)** to be sick and tired (of).

corotos mpl Amer things, whatnots.

corpiño m bodice.

corporación f corporation.

corporal adj corporal.

corporativismo m self-interested behaviour, usu. of professional groups.

corporativo, -va adj corporate.

corpóreo, -a adj corporeal.

corpulencia f corpulence.

corpulento, -ta adj corpulent.

Corpus Christi ['korpus 'kristi] m Corpus Christi.

corpúsculo m corpuscle.

corral m -1. [gen] yard; [para cerdos, ovejas] pen. -2. [para teatro] open-air theatre in courtyard.

correa f -1. [de bolso, reloj] strap; [de pantalón] belt; [de perro] lead, leash. -2. TECN belt; ~ **del ventilador** fan belt.

correaje m [de un caballo] harness.

correcalles m y f inv fam loafer.

corrección f -1. [de errores] correction; ~ **de pruebas** proofreading. -2. [de exámenes] marking. -3. [de texto] revision. -4. [de comportamiento] correctness, courtesy. -5. [reprimenda] reprimand.

correccional m reform school.

correctivo, -va adj corrective.
◆ **correctivo** m punishment.

correcto, -ta adj -1. [resultado, texto, respuesta] correct. -2. [persona] polite; [conducta] proper.

corrector, -ra ◇ adj corrective. ◇ m y f: ~ **(de pruebas)** proofreader.
◆ **corrector** m INFORM: ~ **de estilo** stylechecker; ~ **ortográfico** spellchecker.

corredero, -ra adj sliding.
◆ **corredera** f [ranura] runner; **puerta de corredera** sliding door.

corredizo, -za adj sliding.

corredor, -ra ◇ adj running. ◇ m y f -1. [deportista] runner. -2. [intermediario]: ~ **de bolsa** stockbroker; ~ **de comercio** COM registered broker; ~ **de fincas** land agent; ~ **de seguros** COM insurance broker.
◆ **corredor** m [pasillo] corridor, passage.

corregidor, -ra m y f magistrate appointed by king, especially in former Spanish colonies.

corregir [42] vt -1. [gen] to correct; [exámenes] to mark. -2. [reprender] to reprimand.
◆ **corregirse** vpr to change for the better.

correlación f correlation.

correlacionar vt to correlate.

correlativo, -va adj correlative.

correligionario, -ria adj [en religión] fellow (antes de sust); [en política, ideología] like-minded.

correo ◇ m post, mail; **echar al** ~ to post; **a vuelta de** ~ by return (of post); ~ **aéreo** air mail; ~ **certificado** registered post o mail; ~ **comercial** direct mail; ~ **electrónico** electronic mail; ~ **urgente** special delivery; ~ **de voz** voice mail. ◇ adj: **tren** ~ mail train.
◆ **Correos** m [organismo] the post office.

correoso, -sa adj leathery.

correr ◇ *vi* **-1.** [andar de prisa] to run; **a todo ~** at full speed ○ pelt; **(ella) corre que se las pela** she runs like the wind. **-2.** [conducir de prisa] to drive fast. **-3.** [pasar por - río] to flow; [- camino, agua del grifo] to run. **-4.** [el tiempo, las horas] to pass, to go by. **-5.** [propagarse - noticia etc] to spread. **-6.** [ser válido - moneda] to be legal tender. **-7.** [encargarse de]: **~ con** [los gastos] to bear; [la cuenta] to pay; **~ a cargo de** to be taken care of by. **-8.** [sueldo etc] to be payable. ◇ *vt* **-1.** [recorrer - una distancia] to cover; **corrió los 100 metros** he ran the 100 metres. **-2.** [deslizar - mesa, silla] to move ○ pull up. **-3.** [cortinas] to draw; **~ el pestillo** to bolt the door. **-4.** [experimentar - aventuras, vicisitudes] to have; [- riesgo] to run.
◆ **correrse** *vpr* **-1.** [desplazarse - persona] to move over; [- cosa] to slide. **-2.** [pintura, colores] to run. **-3.** *vulg* [tener un orgasmo] to come.

correría *f* foray.

correspondencia *f* **-1.** [gen] correspondence. **-2.** [de metro, tren] connection.

corresponder *vi* **-1.** [compensar]: **~ (con algo) a alguien/algo** to repay sb/sthg (with sthg). **-2.** [pertenecer] to belong. **-3.** [coincidir]: **~ (a/con)** to correspond (to/with). **-4.** [tocar]: **~le a alguien hacer algo** to be sb's responsibility to do sthg. **-5.** [a un sentimiento] to reciprocate.
◆ **corresponderse** *vpr* **-1.** [escribirse] to correspond. **-2.** [amarse] to love each other.

correspondiente *adj* **-1.** [gen]: **~ (a)** corresponding (to). **-2.** [respectivo] respective.

corresponsal *m y f* **-1.** PRENS correspondent. **-2.** COM agent.

corresponsalía *f* post of correspondent.

corretaje *m* brokerage.

corretear *vi* **-1.** [correr] to run about. **-2.** *fam* [vagar] to hang about.

correveidile *m y f* gossip.

corrido, -da *adj* **-1.** [cortinas] drawn. **-2.** [avergonzado] embarrassed. **-3.** [continuo] continuous.
◆ **corrida** *f* **-1.** TAUROM bull fight; *ver también* **tauromaquia.** **-2.** [acción de correr] run.
◆ **de corrido** *loc prep* by heart; **recitar algo de ~** to recite sthg parrot-fashion.

corriente ◇ *adj* **-1.** [normal] ordinary, normal; **~ y moliente** run-of-the-mill. **-2.** [agua] running. **-3.** [mes, año, cuenta] current. ◇ *f* **-1.** [de río, electricidad] current; **~ alterna/continua** alternating/direct current. **-2.** [de aire] draught. **-3.** *fig* [tendencia] trend, current; [de opinión] tide. **-4.** *loc:* **dejarse llevar de** ○ **por la ~** to follow the crowd; **ir**

contra ~ to go against the tide ◇ *m:* **estar al ~ de** to be up to date with.

corrige, corrigió *etc* → **corregir.**

corrillo *m* knot ○ small group of people.

corrimiento *m* shift, slipping; **~ de tierras** landslide.

corro *m* **-1.** [círculo] circle, ring; **en ~** in a circle; **hacer ~** to form a circle. **-2.** FIN [cotizaciones] stocks (*pl*).

corroborar *vt* to corroborate.

corroer [69] *vt* **-1.** [gen] to corrode; GEOL to erode. **-2.** *fig* [consumir] to consume, to eat away at.

corromper *vt* **-1.** [pudrir - madera] to rot; [- alimentos] to turn bad, to spoil. **-2.** [pervertir] to corrupt. **-3.** [sobornar] to bribe.
◆ **corromperse** *vpr* **-1.** [pudrirse] to rot. **-2.** [pervertirse] to become corrupted.

corrosión *f* [gen] corrosion; [de un metal] rust; GEOL erosion.

corrosivo, -va *adj lit & fig* corrosive.

corrupción *f* **-1.** [gen] corruption; **~ de menores** corruption of minors. **-2.** [soborno] bribery. **-3.** [de una substancia] decay.

corruptela *f* corruption.

corrupto, -ta *adj* corrupt.

corruptor, -ra ◇ *adj* corrosive. ◇ *m y f* corrupter.

corrusco *m* hard crust.

corsario, -ria *adj* pirate (*antes de sust*).
◆ **corsario** *m* corsair, pirate.

corsé *m* corset.

corsetería *f* ladies' underwear shop.

corso, -sa *adj, m y f* Corsican.
◆ **corso** *m* [dialecto] Corsican.

cortacésped (*pl* **cortacéspedes**) *m* lawnmower.

cortacircuitos *m inv* circuit breaker.

cortacorriente *m* AUTOM immobilizer.

cortado, -da *adj* **-1.** [labios, manos] chapped. **-2.** [leche] sour, off; [salsa] curdled. **-3.** *fam fig* [tímido] inhibited; **quedarse ~** to be left speechless.
◆ **cortado** *m* [café] *small coffee with just a little milk.*

cortador, -ra *adj* cutting.
◆ **cortadora** *f* cutter.

cortadura *f* cut.

cortafuego *m* firebreak.

cortante *adj* **-1.** [afilado] sharp. **-2.** *fig* [frase] cutting; [viento] biting; [frío] bitter.

cortapisa *f* limitation, restriction.

cortaplumas *m inv* penknife.

cortapuros *m inv* cigar cutter.

cortar ◇ *vt* **-1.** [seccionar - pelo, uñas] to cut; [- papel] to cut up; [- ramas] to cut off;

[- árbol] to cut down. **-2.** [amputar] to amputate, to cut off. **-3.** [tela, figura de papel] to cut out. **-4.** [interrumpir - retirada, luz, teléfono] to cut off; [- carretera] to block (off); [- hemorragia] to stop, to staunch; [- discurso, conversación] to interrupt. **-5.** [atravesar - calle, territorio] to cut across. **-6.** [labios, piel] to crack, to chap. **-7.** [hender - aire, olas] to slice through. **-8.** [alimento] to curdle. **-9.** [recortar - gastos etc] to cut back. **-10.** [poner fin a - beca etc] to cut; [- abusos etc] to put a stop to. **-11.** [avergonzar]: **este hombre me corta un poco** I find it hard to be myself when that man's around. **-12.** [censurar] to censor; [película] to cut. **-13.** INFORM to cut off.
◇ vi **-1.** [producir un corte] to cut. **-2.** [atajar] to take a short cut. **-3.** [cesar una relación] to break ○ split up.
◆ **cortarse** vpr **-1.** [herirse] to cut o.s.; **~se el pelo** to have a haircut. **-2.** [labios, piel] to become chapped ○ cracked. **-3.** [alimento] to curdle. **-4.** [comunicación] to get cut off. **-5.** [turbarse] to become tongue-tied.

cortaúñas m inv nail clippers (pl).

corte ◇ m **-1.** [raja] cut; [en pantalones, camisa etc] tear; **~ y confección** [para mujeres] dressmaking; [para hombres] tailoring. **-2.** [retal de tela] length. **-3.** [contorno] shape. **-4.** [interrupción]: **~ de luz** power cut. **-5.** [sección] section. **-6.** [concepción, estilo] style. **-7.** [pausa] break. **-8.** [filo] (cutting) edge. **-9.** fam [respuesta ingeniosa] put-down; **dar un ~ a alguien** to cut sb dead; **hacer un ~ de mangas** mfam ≃ to stick two fingers up, ≃ to make a V-sign. **-10.** fam [vergüenza] embarrassment; **dar ~ a alguien** to embarrass sb. ◇ f [palacio] court; **hacer la ~ a alguien** fig to court sb.
◆ **Cortes** fpl POLIT the Spanish parliament.

cortedad f **-1.** [de extensión] shortness. **-2.** fig [timidez] shyness.

cortejar vt to court.

cortejo m retinue; **~ fúnebre** funeral cortège ○ procession.

cortés adj polite, courteous.

cortesano, -na ◇ adj [fiestas, vida] court (antes de sust); [modales] courtly. ◇ m y f [personaje de la corte] courtier.
◆ **cortesana** f [meretriz] courtesan.

cortesía f courtesy; **de ~** courtesy; **por ~ de** courtesy of.

corteza f **-1.** [del árbol] bark. **-2.** [de pan] crust; [de queso, tocino, limón] rind; [de naranja etc] peel. **-3.** [terrestre] crust. **-4.** ANAT cortex.

cortical adj cortical.

corticoide m corticoid.

cortijo m [finca] farm; [casa] farmhouse.

cortina f [de tela] curtain; fig: **~ de agua** sheet of water; **~ de humo** smoke screen.

cortinaje m curtains (pl).

cortisona f cortisone.

corto, -ta adj **-1.** [gen] short. **-2.** [escaso - raciones] small, meagre; [- disparo] short of the target; **~ de** [dinero etc] short of; **~ de vista** short-sighted. **-3.** fig [bobo] dim, simple. **-4.** loc: **a la corta o a la larga** sooner or later; **quedarse ~** [al calcular] to underestimate; **decir que es bueno es quedarse ~** it's an understatement to call it good.
◆ **corto** m CIN short (film).

cortocircuito m short circuit.

cortometraje m short (film).

corvo, -va adj [gen] curved; [nariz] hooked.
◆ **corva** f back of the knee.

corzo, -za m y f roe buck (f roe deer).

cosa f **-1.** [gen] thing; **¿queréis alguna ~?** is there anything you want?; **no es gran ~** it's not important, it's no big deal; **poca ~** nothing much. **-2.** [asunto] matter. **-3.** [ocurrencia] funny remark; **¡qué ~s tienes!** you do say some funny things! **-4.** loc: **hacer algo como quien no quiere la ~** [disimuladamente] to do sthg as if one wasn't intending to; [sin querer] to do sthg almost without realizing it; **como si tal ~** as if nothing had happened; **no sea ~ que** just in case; **eso es ~ mía** that's my affair ○ business; **son cosas de mamá** that's just the way Mum is, that's just one of Mum's little idiosyncrasies.
◆ **cosa de** loc adv about.

cosaco, -ca adj, m y f Cossack; **beber como un ~** to drink like a fish.

coscorrón m bump on the head.

cosecante f cosecant.

cosecha f **-1.** [gen] harvest; **ser de la (propia) ~ de alguien** to be made up ○ invented by sb. **-2.** [del vino] vintage.

cosechadora f combine harvester.

cosechar ◇ vt **-1.** [cultivar] to grow. **-2.** [recolectar] to harvest. **-3.** fig [obtener] to win, to reap. ◇ vi to (bring in the) harvest.

cosechero, -ra m y f [de cereales] harvester, reaper; [de frutos] picker.

coseno m cosine.

coser ◇ vt **-1.** [con hilo] to sew; **~ un botón** to sew on a button. **-2.** [con grapas] to staple (together). **-3.** loc: **~ a balazos** to riddle with bullets; **~ a cuchilladas** to stab repeatedly; **ser cosa de ~ y cantar** to be child's play ○ a piece of cake. ◇ vi to sew.

cosido m stitching.

cosmético, -ca adj cosmetic (antes de sust).

◆ **cosmético** m cosmetic.

◆ **cosmética** f cosmetics (U).

cósmico, -ca adj cosmic.

cosmogonía f cosmogony.

cosmografía f cosmography.

cosmología f cosmology.

cosmonauta m y f cosmonaut.

cosmopolita adj, m y f cosmopolitan.

cosmos m cosmos.

coso m **-1.** [plaza] bullring. **-2.** Amer [chisme] whatnot, thing.

cosquillas fpl: **hacer ~** to tickle; **tener ~** to be ticklish; **buscarle las ~ a alguien** to wind sb up, to irritate sb.

cosquilleo m tickling sensation.

costa f GEOGR coast.

◆ **costas** fpl DER costs.

◆ **Costa Azul** f: **la ~ Azul** the Côte d'Azur.

◆ **Costa Brava** f: **la ~ Brava** the Costa Brava.

◆ **a costa de** loc prep at the expense of; **lo hizo a ~ de grandes esfuerzos** he did it by dint of much effort.

◆ **a toda costa** loc prep at all costs.

Costa de Marfil Ivory Coast.

costado m side.

costal ◇ adj rib (antes de sust), costal. ◇ m sack.

costalada f, **costalazo** m heavy fall.

costanera f Amer seaside promenade.

costar [23] ◇ vt **-1.** [dinero] to cost; **¿cuánto cuesta?** how much is it? **-2.** [tiempo] to take. **-3.** loc: **le costó la vida** it cost him his life; **~ un ojo de la cara** ○ **un riñón** to cost an arm and a leg. ◇ vi [ser difícil]: **~le a alguien hacer algo** to be difficult for sb to do sthg; **~ caro a alguien** to cost sb dear; **cueste lo que cueste** whatever the cost.

Costa Rica Costa Rica.

costarricense, costarriqueño, -ña adj, m y f Costa Rican.

coste m [de producción] cost; [de un objeto] price; **~ de la vida** cost of living; **~ unitario** ECON unit cost.

costear vt **-1.** [pagar] to pay for. **-2.** NÁUT [la costa] to hug, to keep close to.

◆ **costearse** vpr: **~se algo** [pagárselo] to pay for sthg o.s.; [permitírselo] to be able to afford sthg.

costeño, -ña, costero, -ra adj [gen] coastal; [pueblo] seaside (antes de sust).

costilla f **-1.** [de persona, barco] rib. **-2.** [de animal] cutlet. **-3.** fam fig [cónyuge] better half.

◆ **costillas** fpl fam [espalda] back (sg).

costillar m [de persona] ribs (pl), rib cage; [de carne] side.

costo m [de una mercancía] price; [de un producto, de la vida] cost.

costoso, -sa adj **-1.** [operación, maquinaria] expensive. **-2.** fig [trabajo] exhausting; [triunfo] costly.

costra f **-1.** [de pan] crust; [de queso] rind. **-2.** [de herida] scab.

costumbre f habit, custom; **coger/perder la ~ de hacer algo** to get into/out of the habit of doing sthg; **como de ~** as usual.

◆ **costumbres** fpl [de país, cultura] customs; [de persona] habits.

costumbrista adj describing the customs of a country or region.

costura f **-1.** [labor] sewing, needlework. **-2.** [puntadas] seam. **-3.** [oficio] dressmaking; **alta ~** haute couture.

costurera f dressmaker, seamstress.

costurero m [caja] sewing box.

cota f **-1.** [altura] altitude, height above sea level. **-2.** [armadura]: **~ de mallas** coat of mail. **-3.** fig [nivel] level, height.

cotangente f cotangent.

cotarro m riotous gathering; **dirigir el ~** to rule the roost, to be the boss.

cotejar vt to compare.

cotejo m comparison.

cotice etc → cotizar.

cotidianidad f [vida cotidiana] everyday life; [monotonía] monotony.

cotidiano, -na adj daily.

cotiledón m cotyledon.

cotilla m y f fam gossip, busybody.

cotillear vi fam to gossip.

cotilleo m fam gossip, tittle-tattle.

cotillón m New Year's Eve party.

cotizable adj quotable.

cotización f **-1.** [valor] price. **-2.** [en Bolsa] quotation, price.

cotizado, -da adj **-1.** [en la Bolsa] quoted. **-2.** [persona] sought-after.

cotizar [13] vt **-1.** [valorar] to quote, to price. **-2.** [pagar] to pay.

◆ **cotizarse** vpr **-1.** [estimarse - persona] to be valued ○ prized. **-2.** **~se a** [producto] to sell for, to fetch; [bonos, valores] to be quoted at.

coto m preserve; **~ de caza** game preserve; **poner ~ a** to put a stop to.

cotorra f **-1.** [ave] parrot. **-2.** fam fig [persona] chatterbox; **hablar como una ~** to talk nineteen to the dozen.

cotorrear vi to chatter.

coturno m buskin.

COU (*abrev de* **curso de orientación univer-sitaria**) *m the last year of secondary education in Spain.*

COU:
In Spain, 'COU' refers to the academic year which follows the school-leaving examina-tion; its purpose is to prepare the pupil for university entrance examinations. Pupils have to study a set of compulsory subjects and several optional ones according to whether they are opting to study arts or sci-ences

covacha *f* hovel.

coxal *m* hipbone.

coxis = **cóccix**.

coyote *m* coyote.

coyuntura *f* **-1.** [situación] moment; **la ~ económica** the economic situation. **-2.** ANAT joint.

coyuntural *adj* transitional.

coz *f* kick; **tratar a alguien a coces** *fam fig* to treat sb like dirt.

cozamos → **cocer**.

CPME (*abrev de* **Confederación de Peque-ñas y Medianas Empresas**) *f Spanish confed-eration of SMEs.*

CPN (*abrev de* **Cuerpo de la Policía Nacio-nal**) *m Spanish police force.*

CPU (*abrev de* **central processing unit**) *f* CPU.

crac (*pl* **cracs**), **crack** (*pl* **cracks**) *m* FIN crash.

crack (*pl* **cracks**) *m* **-1.** *fig* [estrella] star, superstar. **-2.** FIN → **crac**. **-3.** [droga] crack.

crampón *m* crampon.

craneal *adj* cranial.

cráneo *m* cranium, skull; **ir de ~** *fam* to be doing badly.

crápula *m y f* libertine.

craso, -sa *adj* **-1.** [grueso] fat. **-2.** *fig* [grave] gross, crass.

cráter *m* crater.

creación *f* creation.

creador, -ra ◇ *adj* creative. ◇ *m y f* crea-tor; **~ gráfico** creator (*of cartoon etc*).
◆ **Creador** *m*: **el Creador** the Creator.

crear *vt* **-1.** [gen] to create. **-2.** [inventar] to invent. **-3.** [fundar - una academia] to found.

creatividad *f* creativity.

creativo, -va ◇ *adj* creative. ◇ *m y f* [en publicidad] ideas man (*f* ideas woman).

crecer [30] *vi* **-1.** [persona, planta] to grow. **-2.** [días, noches] to grow longer. **-3.** [río, marea] to rise. **-4.** [aumentar - animosidad etc]

to grow, to increase; [- rumores] to spread. **-5.** [la luna] to wax.
◆ **crecerse** *vpr* to become more self-confident.

creces
◆ **con creces** *adv* with interest.

crecido, -da *adj* [cantidad] large; [hijo] grown-up.
◆ **crecida** *f* spate, flood.

creciente ◇ *adj* [gen] growing; [luna] cres-cent. ◇ *m* crescent.

crecimiento *m* [gen] growth; [de precios] rise; **~ económico** ECON economic growth.

credencial ◇ *adj* accrediting. ◇ *f* [de acce-so a un lugar] pass.
◆ **credenciales** *fpl* [diplomáticas] creden-tials.

credibilidad *f* credibility.

crediticio, -cia *adj* credit (*antes de sust*).

crédito *m* **-1.** [préstamo] loan; **a ~** on cred-it; **~ al consumo** ECON consumer credit; **~ blando** ECON soft loan; **~ a la exportación** ECON export credit; **~ hipotecario** ECON mortgage credit; **~ oficial** ECON official credit; **~ personal** ECON personal loan. **-2.** [plazo de préstamo] credit. **-3.** [confianza] trust, belief; **digno de ~** trustworthy; **dar ~ a algo** to believe sthg. **-4.** [fama] stand-ing, reputation. **-5.** [en universidad] credit.

credo *m* **-1.** [religioso] creed. **-2.** [ideológico, político] credo.

credulidad *f* credulity.

crédulo, -la *adj* credulous.

creencia *f* belief.

creer [50] *vt* **-1.** [gen] to believe. **-2.** [supo-ner] to think.
◆ **creer en** *vi* to believe in.
◆ **creerse** *vpr* **-1.** [considerarse] to believe o.s. to be. **-2.** [dar por cierto] to believe completely.

creíble *adj* credible, believable.

creído, -da *m y f* [presumido] conceited.

crema ◇ *f* **-1.** [gen] cream; **la ~ del mundo literario** the cream of the literary world. **-2.** [betún] shoe polish. **-3.** [licor] crème. **-4.** [dulce, postre] custard. ◇ *adj* cream (*antes de sust*).

cremación *f* cremation.

cremallera *f* **-1.** [para cerrar] zip (fastener). **-2.** TECN rack.

crematístico, -ca *adj* financial.

crematorio, -ria *adj*: **horno ~** cremator.
◆ **crematorio** *m* crematorium.

cremoso, -sa *adj* creamy.

crepe [krep] *f* crepe.

crepé *m* **-1.** [tejido] crepe. **-2.** [pelo] hair-piece.

crepitar *vi* to crackle.

crepuscular *adj* crepuscular, twilight (*antes de sust*).

crepúsculo *m* **-1.** [al amanecer] first light; [al anochecer] twilight, dusk. **-2.** *fig* [fin] twilight.

crescendo *m* crescendo.
◆ **in crescendo** [inkres'tfendo] *loc adv* growing.

crespo, -pa *adj* tightly curled, frizzy.

crespón *m* crepe.

cresta *f* **-1.** [gen] crest; **estar en la ~ (de la ola)** to be riding high. **-2.** [del gallo] comb.

creta *f* chalk.

Creta Crete.

cretense *adj, m y f* Cretan.

cretino, -na *m y f* cretin.

cretona *f* cretonne.

creyente *m y f* believer.

creyera *etc* → **creer**.

crezca *etc* → **crecer**.

cría → **crío**.

criadero *m* **-1.** [de animales] farm (*breeding place*); [de árboles, plantas] nursery. **-2.** [de mineral] seam.

criadillas *fpl* bull's testicles.

criado, -da ◇ *adj* brought up; **niño mal ~** spoilt child. ◇ *m y f* servant (*f* maid).

criador, -ra ◇ *adj* producing. ◇ *m y f* [de animales] breeder; [de vinos] grower.

crianza *f* **-1.** [de bebé] nursing, breastfeeding. **-2.** [de animales] breeding, rearing. **-3.** [del vino] vintage. **-4.** [educación] breeding.

criar [9] *vt* **-1.** [amamantar - suj: mujer] to breastfeed; [- suj: animal] to suckle. **-2.** [animales] to breed, to rear; [flores, árboles] to grow. **-3.** [vino] to mature, to make. **-4.** [educar] to bring up.
◆ **criarse** *vpr* **-1.** [crecer] to grow up. **-2.** [reproducirse] to breed.

criatura *f* **-1.** [niño] child; [bebé] baby. **-2.** [ser vivo] creature.

criba *f* **-1.** [tamiz] sieve. **-2.** [selección] screening.

cribar *vt* **-1.** [con el tamiz] to sieve. **-2.** [seleccionar] to screen out, to select.

cricket = **criquet**.

crimen *m* crime; **cometer un ~** to commit a crime; **~ de guerra** war crime; **~ pasional** crime of passion.

criminal *adj, m y f* criminal.

criminalidad *f* **-1.** [cualidad] criminality. **-2. (índice de) ~** crime rate.

criminalista ◇ *adj* criminal. ◇ *m y f* criminal lawyer.

criminología *f* criminology.

crin *f* mane.

crío, cría *m y f* [niño] kid.
◆ **cría** *f* **-1.** [hijo del animal] young. **-2.** [crianza - de animales] breeding; [- de plantas] growing.

criollo, -lla ◇ *adj* **-1.** [persona] native to Latin America. **-2.** [comida, lengua] creole. ◇ *m y f* [persona] *person (black or white) born in Latin America*.
◆ **criollo** *m* [idioma] creole.

cripta *f* crypt.

críptico, -ca *adj* cryptic.

criptograma *m* cryptogram.

criptón *m* krypton.

criquet, cricket ['kriket] *m* cricket.

crisálida *f* chrysalis.

crisantemo *m* chrysanthemum.

crisis *f inv* **-1.** [gen] crisis; **~ económica** recession; **~ nerviosa** nervous breakdown. **-2.** [escasez] shortage.

crisma *f fam* bonce, nut.

crismas, christmas *m inv* Christmas card.

crisol *m* **-1.** [de metales] crucible. **-2.** *fig* [lugar donde se mezclan cosas] melting pot.

crispación *f* [de nervios] tension; [de músculos] tenseness.

crispar *vt* [los nervios] to set on edge; [los músculos] to tense; [las manos] to clench.
◆ **crisparse** *vpr* to become tense.

cristal *m* **-1.** [material] glass (*U*); [vidrio fino] crystal; **~ tintado** tinted glass. **-2.** [en la ventana] (window) pane. **-3.** MIN crystal. **-4.** *fig* [espejo] mirror.

cristalera *f* [puerta] French window; [techo] glass roof; [armario] glass-fronted cabinet.

cristalería *f* **-1.** [objetos] glassware. **-2.** [tienda] glassware shop; [fábrica] glassworks (*sg*).

cristalero *m* glazier.

cristalino, -na *adj* crystalline.
◆ **cristalino** *m* crystalline lens.

cristalización *f lit & fig* crystallization.

cristalizar [13] *vt* **-1.** [una sustancia] to crystallize. **-2.** *fig* [un asunto] to bring to a head.
◆ **cristalizarse** *vpr* to crystallize.
◆ **cristalizarse en** *vpr fig* to develop into.

cristiandad *f* Christianity.

cristianismo *m* Christianity.

cristianización *f* Christianization, conversion to Christianity.

cristianizar [13] *vt* to Christianize, to convert to Christianity.

cristiano, -na *adj, m y f* Christian.
◆ **cristiano** *m*: **hablar en ~** to speak (proper) Spanish.

cristo *m* crucifix.

◆ **Cristo** *m* Christ; **armar un Cristo** to kick up a fuss; **donde Cristo dio las tres voces/perdió el gorro** in the back of beyond.

criterio *m* **-1.** [norma] criterion. **-2.** [juicio] taste, discernment. **-3.** [opinión] opinion.

crítica → **crítico**.

criticable *adj* censurable, open to criticism.

criticar [10] *vt* **-1.** [enjuiciar - literatura, arte] to review. **-2.** [censurar] to criticize.

crítico, -ca ◇ *adj* critical. ◇ *m y f* [persona] critic.

◆ **crítica** *f* **-1.** [juicio - sobre arte, literatura] review. **-2.** [conjunto de críticos]: **la ~** the critics (*pl*). **-3.** [ataque] criticism.

criticón, -ona ◇ *adj* nit-picking, over-critical. ◇ *m y f* nitpicker.

Croacia Croatia.

croar *vi* to croak.

croata ◇ *adj* Croatian. ◇ *m y f* Croat, Croatian.

croché [kro'tʃe], **crochet** *m* **-1.** [labor] crochet. **-2.** [en boxeo] hook.

croissant [krwa'san] (*pl* **croissants**) *m* croissant.

croissantería [krwasante'ria] *f shop selling filled croissants.*

crol *m* DEP crawl.

cromado *m* chromium-plating.

cromar *vt* to chrome, to chromium-plate.

cromático, -ca *adj* chromatic.

cromatismo *m* colouring.

cromo *m* **-1.** [metal] chrome. **-2.** [estampa] transfer.

cromosoma *m* chromosome.

cromosómico, -ca *adj* chromosomal.

crónico, -ca *adj* chronic.

◆ **crónica** *f* **-1.** [de la historia] chronicle. **-2.** [de un periódico] column; [de la televisión] feature, programme.

cronicón *m brief, usually anonymous, chronicle.*

cronista *m y f* [historiador] chronicler; [periodista] columnist.

crono *m* DEP time.

cronología *f* chronology.

cronológico, -ca *adj* chronological.

cronometrador, -ra *m y f* timekeeper.

cronometraje *m* timing.

cronometrar *vt* to time.

cronométrico, -ca *adj* [puntual] extremely punctual.

cronómetro *m* DEP stopwatch; TECN chronometer.

croquet *m* croquet.

croqueta *f* croquette.

croquis *m inv* sketch.

cross *m inv* [DEP - carrera] cross-country race; [- deporte] cross-country (running).

crótalo *m* rattlesnake.

croupier = **crupier**.

cruce ◇ *v* → **cruzar**. ◇ *m* **-1.** [de líneas] crossing, intersection; [de carreteras] crossroads. **-2.** [de animales] cross, crossbreeding (*U*). **-3.** [de teléfono] crossed line. **-4.** [de electricidad] short circuit.

crucero *m* **-1.** [viaje] cruise. **-2.** [barco] cruiser. **-3.** [de iglesias] transept.

cruceta *f* **-1.** [de una cruz] crosspiece. **-2.** [en fútbol] angle (of crossbar and goalpost).

crucial *adj* crucial.

crucificar [10] *vt* **-1.** [en una cruz] to crucify. **-2.** *fig* [atormentar] to torment.

crucifijo *m* crucifix.

crucifixión *f* crucifixion.

crucigrama *m* crossword (puzzle).

crudeza *f* **-1.** [gen] harshness. **-2.** [de descripción, imágenes] brutality, harsh realism.

crudo, -da *adj* **-1.** [natural] raw; [petróleo] crude. **-2.** [sin cocer completamente] undercooked. **-3.** [realidad, clima, tiempo] harsh; [novela] harshly realistic, hard-hitting. **-4.** [cruel] cruel. **-5.** [color] beige.

◆ **crudo** *m* crude (oil).

cruel *adj* **-1.** [gen] cruel. **-2.** [dolor] excruciating, terrible; [clima] harsh.

crueldad *f* **-1.** [gen] cruelty; [del clima] harshness. **-2.** [acción cruel] act of cruelty.

cruento, -ta *adj* bloody.

crujido *m* [de madera] creak, creaking (*U*); [de hojas secas] crackle, crackling (*U*).

crujiente *adj* [madera] creaky; [hojas secas] rustling; [patatas fritas] crunchy.

crujir *vi* [madera] to creak; [patatas fritas, nieve] to crunch; [hojas secas] to crackle; [dientes] to grind.

crupier, croupier [kru'pier] *m* croupier.

crustáceo *m* crustacean.

cruz *f* **-1.** [gen] cross; **~ gamada** swastika. **-2.** [de una moneda] tails (*U*). **-3.** *fig* [aflicción] burden, torment. **-4.** *loc*: **hacer ~ y raya** to break off relations.

◆ **Cruz Roja** *f* Red Cross.

cruza *f Amer* cross, cross-breed.

cruzado, -da *adj* **-1.** [cheque, piernas, brazos] crossed. **-2.** [atravesado]: **~ en la carretera** blocking the road. **-3.** [un animal] crossbred. **-4.** [abrigo, chaqueta] double-breasted.

◆ **cruzado** *m* crusader.

◆ **cruzada** *f lit & fig* crusade.

cruzar [13] *vt* **-1.** [gen] to cross. **-2.** [unas palabras] to exchange.

◆ **cruzarse** *vpr* **-1.** [gen] to cross; ~**se de brazos** to fold one's arms. **-2.** [personas]: ~**se con alguien** to pass sb.

CSCE (*abrev de* **Conferencia de Seguridad y Cooperación Europeas**) *f* CSCE.

CSD (*abrev de* **Consejo Superior de Deportes**) *m* *Spanish national sports council*.

CSIC (*abrev de* **Consejo Superior de Investigaciones Científicas**) *m* *Spanish council for scientific research*.

CSN (*abrev de* **Consejo de Seguridad Nuclear**) *m* *Spanish nuclear safety council*.

CSP (*abrev de* **Cuerpo Superior de Policía**) *m* *Spanish police force*.

CSPM (*abrev de* **Consejo Superior de Protección de Menores**) *m* *Spanish council for the protection of minors*.

cta. (*abrev de* **cuenta**) a/c.

cte. (*abrev de* **corriente**) inst.

CTNE (*abrev de* **Compañía Telefónica Nacional de España**) *f* *Spanish state telephone company*.

c/u *abrev de* **cada uno**.

cuaderna *f* NÁUT rib.

cuaderno *m* [gen] notebook; [en el colegio] exercise book.

◆ **cuaderno de bitácora** *m* logbook.

cuadra *f* **-1.** [de caballos] stable. **-2.** *fam* [lugar sucio] pigsty. **-3.** *Amer* [manzana] block.

cuadrado, -da *adj* **-1.** [gen & MAT] square. **-2.** [una persona] square-built, stocky.

◆ **cuadrado** *m* square.

cuadrafonía *f* quadraphonics (U).

cuadrafónico, -ca *adj* quadraphonic.

cuadragésimo, -ma *núm* fortieth.

cuadrangular *adj* quadrangular.

cuadrángulo *m* quadrangle.

cuadrante *m* **-1.** [gen] quadrant. **-2.** [reloj de sol] sundial.

cuadrar ◇ *vi* **-1.** [información, hechos]: ~ **(con)** to square ○ agree (with). **-2.** [números, cuentas] to tally, to add up. ◇ *vt* **-1.** [gen] to square. **-2.** *Amer* [aparcar] to park.

◆ **cuadrarse** *vpr* **-1.** MIL to stand to attention. **-2.** [mostrar firmeza] to make a stand.

cuadratura *f* GEOM quadrature; **la ~ del círculo** *fam* squaring the circle.

cuádriceps *m inv* quadriceps.

cuadrícula *f* grid.

cuadriculado, -da *adj* squared.

cuadricular *vt* to divide into squares.

cuadriga, cuádriga *f* four-in-hand.

cuadrilátero *m* **-1.** GEOM quadrilateral. **-2.** DEP ring.

cuadrilla *f* **-1.** [de amigos, trabajadores] group; [de maleantes] gang. **-2.** [de un torero] *team of helpers*; *ver también* **tauromaquia**.

cuadro *m* **-1.** [pintura] painting, picture. **-2.** [escena] scene, spectacle. **-3.** [descripción] portrait. **-4.** [cuadrado] square; [de flores] bed; **a ~s** check (*antes de sust*). **-5.** [equipo] team. **-6.** [gráfico] chart, diagram; ~ **sinóptico** (synoptic) chart. **-7.** [de la bicicleta] frame. **-8.** [de un aparato]: ~ **de distribución** switchboard; ~ **de mandos** control panel. **-9.** TEATR scene; ~ **flamenco** flamenco group.

cuadrúpedo *m* quadruped.

cuádruple *m* quadruple.

cuadruplicar [10] *vt* to quadruple.

cuádruplo *m* quadruple.

cuajado, -da *adj* **-1.** [leche] curdled; [huevo] set. **-2.** [lleno]: ~ **de** full of.

◆ **cuajada** *f* curd (cheese).

cuajar ◇ *vt* **-1.** [solidificar - leche] to curdle; [- huevo] to set; [- sangre] to clot, to coagulate. **-2.** ~ **de** [llenar] to fill with; [cubrir] to cover with. ◇ *vi* **-1.** [lograrse - acuerdo] to be settled; [- negocio] to take off, to get going. **-2.** [ser aceptado - persona] to fit in; [- moda] to catch on. **-3.** [nieve] to settle.

◆ **cuajarse** *vpr* **-1.** [leche] to curdle; [sangre] to clot, to coagulate. **-2.** [llenarse]: ~**se de** to fill (up) with.

cuajo *m* rennet.

◆ **de cuajo** *loc adv*: **arrancar de ~** [árbol] to uproot; [brazo etc] to tear right off.

cual *pron relat*: **el/la ~** *etc* [de persona] (*sujeto*) who; (*complemento*) whom; [de cosa] which; **lo ~** which; **conoció a una española, la ~ vivía en Buenos Aires** he met a Spanish girl who lived in Buenos Aires; **está muy enfadada, lo ~ es comprensible** she's very angry, which is understandable; **todo lo ~** all of which; **sea ~ sea ○ fuere su decisión** whatever his decision (may be): **los tres son a ~ más inteligente** all three are equally intelligent.

cuál *pron* **-1.** (*interrogativo*) what; [en concreto, especificando] which one; ¿~ **es tu nombre?** what is your name?; ¿~ **es la diferencia?** what's the difference?; **no sé ~s son mejores** I don't know which are best; ¿~ **prefieres?** which one do you prefer? **-2.** (*en oraciones distributivas*): **todos contribuyeron, ~ más, ~ menos** everyone contributed, although some more than others.

cualesquiera *pl* → **cualquiera**.

cualidad *f* quality.

cualificación *f* degree of skill (*of a worker*).

cualificado, -da *adj* skilled.

cualificar [10] *vt* to qualify.

cualitativo, **-va** *adj* qualitative.

cualquiera (*pl* **cualesquiera**) ◇ *adj* (*antes de sust*: **cualquier**) any; **cualquier día vendré a visitarte** I'll drop by one of these days; **en cualquier momento** at any time; **en cualquier lugar** anywhere. ◇ *pron* anyone; ~ **te lo dirá** anyone will tell you; ~ **que** [persona] anyone who; [cosa] whatever; ~ **que te vea se reiría** anyone who saw you would laugh; ~ **que sea la razón** whatever the reason (may be). ◇ *m y f* [don nadie] nobody. ◇ *f fam* [prostituta] tart.

cuan *adv* [todo lo que]: **se desplomó** ~ **largo era** he fell flat on the ground.

cuán *adv* how.

cuando ◇ *adv* when; **de** ~ **en** ~, **de vez en** ~ from time to time, now and again. ◇ *conj* **-1.** [de tiempo] when; ~ **llegue el verano iremos de viaje** when summer comes we'll go travelling. **-2.** [si] if; ~ **tú lo dices será verdad** it must be true if you say so. **-3.** (*después de "aun"*) [aunque]: **no mentiría aun** ~ **le fuera en ello la vida** she wouldn't lie even if her life depended on it.

◆ **cuando más** *loc adv* at the most.

◆ **cuando menos** *loc adv* at least.

◆ **cuando quiera que** *loc conj* whenever.

cuándo ◇ *adv* when; **¿**~ **vas a venir?** when are you coming?; **quisiera saber a qué hora sale el tren** I'd like to know when ○ at what time the train leaves. ◇ *m*: **ignorará el cómo y el** ~ **de la operación** he won't know how or when the operation will take place.

cuantía *f* [suma] amount, quantity; [alcance] extent.

cuántico, **-ca**, **quántico**, **-ca** *adj* quantum.

cuantificable *adj* quantifiable.

cuantificar [10] *vt* to quantify.

cuantioso, **-sa** *adj* large, substantial.

cuantitativo, **-va** *adj* quantitative.

cuanto, **-ta** ◇ *adj* **-1.** [todo]: **despilfarra** ~ **dinero gana** he squanders all the money he earns; **soporté todas cuantas críticas me hizo** I put up with every single criticism he made of me. **-2.** (*antes de adv*) [compara cantidades]: **cuantas más mentiras digas, menos te creerán** the more you lie, the less people will believe you.

◇ *pron relat* (*gen pl*) [de personas] everyone who; [de cosas] everything (that); ~**s fueron alabaron el espectáculo** everyone who went said the show was excellent; **dio las gracias a todos** ~**s le ayudaron** he thanked everyone who helped him.

◆ **cuanto** ◇ *pron relat* (*neutro*) **-1.** [todo lo que] everything, as much as; **come** ~ **quie-** ras eat as much as you like; **comprendo** ~ **dice** I understand everything he says; **todo** ~ everything. **-2.** [compara cantidades]: ~ **más se tiene, más se quiere** the more you have, the more you want. ◇ *adv* [compara cantidades]: ~ **más come, más gordo está** the more he eats, the fatter he gets.

◆ **cuanto antes** *loc adv* as soon as possible.

◆ **en cuanto** ◇ *loc conj* [tan pronto como] as soon as; **en** ~ **acabe** as soon as I've finished. ◇ *loc prep* [en calidad de] as; **en** ~ **cabeza de familia** as head of the family.

◆ **en cuanto a** *loc prep* as regards; **en** ~ **a tu petición** as regards your request, as far as your request is concerned.

cuánto, **-ta** ◇ *adj* **-1.** (*interrogativo*) how much, (*pl*) how many; **¿cuántas manzanas tienes?** how many apples do you have?; **¿**~ **pan quieres?** how much bread do you want?; **no sé** ~**s hombres había** I don't know how many men were there. **-2.** (*exclamativo*) what a lot of; **¡cuánta gente (había)!** what a lot of people (were there)!

◇ *pron* (*gen pl*) **-1.** (*interrogativo*) how much, (*pl*) how many; **¿**~**s han venido?** how many came?; **dime cuántas quieres** tell me how many you want. **-2.** (*exclamativo*): **¡**~**s quisieran conocerte!** there are so many people who would like to meet you!

◆ **cuánto** *pron* (*neutro*) **-1.** (*interrogativo*) how much; **¿**~ **quieres?** how much do you want?; **me gustaría saber** ~ **te costarán** I'd like to know how much they'll cost you. **-2.** (*exclamativo*): **¡**~ **han cambiado las cosas!** how things have changed!; **¡**~ **me gusta!** I really like it!

cuáquero, **-ra** *m y f* Quaker.

cuarenta *núm* forty; **los (años)** ~ the forties; **cantar a alguien las** ~ to give sb a piece of one's mind; *ver también* **seis**.

cuarentena *f* **-1.** [por epidemia] quarantine; **poner en** ~ [enfermos] to (put in) quarantine; [noticia] to put on hold. **-2.** [cuarenta unidades] forty; **una** ~ **de personas** about forty people.

cuarentón, **-ona** *m y f* person in his/her forties.

cuaresma *f* Lent.

cuartear *vt* to cut ○ chop up.

◆ **cuartearse** *vpr* to crack.

cuartel *m* **-1.** MIL barracks (*pl*); ~ **general** headquarters (*pl*). **-2.** *fig* [piedad]: **sin** ~ [guerra] all-out; **lucha sin** ~ fight to the death.

cuartelada *f* minor military uprising.

cuartelazo *m* *Amer* military uprising, revolt.

cuartelero, **-ra** *adj* [gen] barracks (*antes de sust*); [lenguaje] vulgar, coarse.

cuartelillo *m* [de policia] police station.

cuarteto *m* quartet.

cuartilla *f* sheet of quarto.

cuarto, **-ta** *núm* fourth; **la cuarta parte** a quarter.
◆ **cuarto** *m* **-1.** [parte] quarter; **un ~ de hora** a quarter of an hour; **son las dos y/menos ~** it's a quarter past/to two; **~ creciente/menguante** first/last quarter; **ser tres ~s de lo mismo** to be exactly the same ○ no different. **-2.** [habitación] room; **~ de aseo** washroom, small bathroom; **~ de baño** bathroom; **~ de estar** living room. **-3.** *loc*: **estar sin un ~** to be skint.
◆ **cuartos** *mpl* **-1.** *fam* [dinero] dough (*U*), readies. **-2.** DEP: **~s de final** quarter finals.
◆ **cuarta** *f* [palmo] span.

cuarzo *m* quartz.

cuate, *m y f inv Amer* [amigo] friend.

cuaternario, **-ria** *adj* Quaternary.
◆ **cuaternario** *m*: **el ~** the Quaternary (era).

cuatrero, **-ra** *m y f* [de caballos] horse thief; [de ganado] cattle rustler.

cuatrillizo, **-za** *m y f* quadruplet, quad.

cuatrimestral *adj* **-1.** [en frecuencia] four-monthly. **-2.** [en duración] four-month (*antes de sust*), lasting four months.

cuatrimestre *m* period of four months.

cuatrimotor *m* four-engined plane.

cuatripartito, **-ta** *adj* four-part.

cuatro ◇ *núm* four; *ver también* **seis**. ◇ *adj fig* [poco] a few; **hace ~ días** a few days ago.

cuatrocientos, **-tas** *núm* four hundred; *ver también* **seis**.

cuba *f* barrel, cask; **estar como una ~** to be legless ○ blind drunk.

Cuba Cuba.

cubalibre *m* rum and coke.

cubano, **-na** *adj, m y f* Cuban.

cubata *m fam* rum and coke.

cubero *m*: **a ojo de buen ~** roughly.

cubertería *f* set of cutlery, cutlery (*U*).

cubeta *f* [cuba pequeña] bucket, pail; [de barómetro] bulb; FOT tray.

cubicaje *m* cylinder capacity.

cúbico, **-ca** *adj* cubic.

cubierto, **-ta** ◇ *pp* → **cubrir**. ◇ *adj* **-1.** [gen]: **~ (de)** covered (with); **estar a ~** [protegido] to be under cover; [con saldo acreedor] to be in the black; **ponerse a ~** to take cover. **-2.** [cielo] overcast. **-3.** [vacante] filled.

◆ **cubierto** *m* **-1.** [pieza de cubertería] piece of cutlery. **-2.** [juego de cubertería] set of cutlery. **-3.** [para cada persona] place setting. **-4.** [comida] set menu.
◆ **cubierta** *f* **-1.** [gen] cover. **-2.** [de neumático] tyre. **-3.** [de barco] deck.

cubil *m* **-1.** [de animales] den, lair. **-2.** *fig* [de personas] poky room.

cubilete *m* [en juegos] cup; [molde] mould.

cubismo *m* cubism.

cubista *adj, m y f* cubist.

cubito *m* [de hielo] ice cube.

cúbito *m* ulna.

cubo *m* **-1.** [recipiente] bucket; **~ de la basura** rubbish bin. **-2.** GEOM & MAT cube; **elevar al ~** to cube. **-3.** [de rueda] hub.

cubrecama *m* bedspread.

cubrir *vt* **-1.** [gen] to cover. **-2.** [proteger] to protect. **-3.** [disimular] to cover up, to hide. **-4.** [puesto, vacante] to fill.
◆ **cubrir de** *vt*: **~ de algo a alguien** to heap sthg on sb.
◆ **cubrirse** *vpr* **-1.** [taparse]: **~se (de)** to become covered (with). **-2.** [protegerse]: **~se (de)** to shelter (from). **-3.** [con sombrero] to put one's hat on. **-4.** [con ropa]: **~se (con)** to cover o.s. (with). **-5.** [cielo] to cloud over. **-6.** *loc*: **~se de gloria** [triunfar] to cover o.s. in ○ with glory; *irón* to land o.s. in it.

cuca → **cuco**.

cucaña *f* greasy pole.

cucaracha *f* cockroach.

cuchara *f* **-1.** [para comer] spoon. **-2.** [cucharada] spoonful.

cucharada *f* spoonful.

cucharilla *f* teaspoon.

cucharón *m* ladle.

cuchichear *vi* to whisper.

cuchicheo *m* whispering.

cuchilla *f* blade; **~ de afeitar** razor blade.

cuchillada *f* [golpe] stab; [herida] stab wound.

cuchillo *m* knife; **~ eléctrico** electric carving knife.

cuchipanda *f fam*: **salir de ~** to go out on the town.

cuchitril *m* hovel.

cuchufleta *f fam* joke.

cuclillas
◆ **en cuclillas** *loc adv* squatting; **ponerse en ~** to squat (down).

cuclillo *m* cuckoo.

cuco, **-ca** *adj fam* **-1.** [bonito] pretty. **-2.** [astuto] shrewd, canny.
◆ **cuco** *m* cuckoo.

◆ **cuca** *f fam* peseta.

cucú *m* **-1.** [canto] cuckoo. **-2.** [reloj] cuckoo clock.

cucurucho *m* **-1.** [de papel] paper cone. **-2.** [para helado] cornet, cone. **-3.** [gorro] pointed hat.

cuece → cocer.

cuela *etc* → colar.

cuelga *etc* → colgar.

cuello *m* **-1.** [gen] neck; ~ de botella bottleneck. **-2.** [de prendas] collar; ~ de pajarita wing collar.

cuenca *f* **-1.** [de río] basin. **-2.** [del ojo] (eye) socket. **-3.** [región minera] coalfield.

cuenco *m* earthenware bowl.

cuenta ◇ *v* → contar.

◇ *f* **-1.** [acción de contar] count; **echar ~s** to reckon up; **llevar/perder la ~** de to keep/lose count of; ~ **atrás** countdown. **-2.** [cálculo] sum; ~ de la vieja *fam* counting on one's fingers. **-3.** BANCA & COM account; **abonar algo en ~ a alguien** to credit sthg to sb's account; **abrir una ~** to open an account; ~ de gastos expenditure account; **llevar las ~s** to keep the books; **pagar mil pesetas a ~** to pay a thousand pesetas down; ~ de ahorros savings account; ~ de ahorro vivienda home loan; ~ corriente current account; ~ de crédito current account with an overdraft facility; ~ deudora overdrawn account; ~ de explotación operating statement; ~ a plazo fijo deposit account. **-4.** [factura] bill; **domiciliar una ~** to pay an account by standing order/direct debit; **pasar la ~** to send the bill; ~ por cobrar/pagar account receivable/payable. **-5.** [obligación, cuidado] responsibility; **déjalo de mi ~** leave it to me. **-6.** [bolita - de collar, rosario] bead. **-7.** *loc:* **a fin de ~s** in the end; **ajustarle a alguien las ~s** to settle an account ◯ a score with sb; **caer en la ~ de algo** to realize sthg; **dar ~ de algo** [comunicar] to report sthg; [terminar] to account for sthg, to finish sthg off; **darse ~ de algo** to realize sthg; **en resumidas ~s** in short; **más de la ~** too much; **pedir ~s a alguien** to call sb to account; **por mi/tu** *etc* ~ on my/your *etc* own; **salir de ~s** to be due to give birth; **tener en ~ algo** to bear sthg in mind.

cuentagotas *m inv* dropper; **a ◯ con ~** in dribs and drabs.

cuentakilómetros *m inv* [de distancia recorrida] ≈ milometer; [de velocidad] speedometer.

cuentarrevoluciones *m inv* tachometer, rev counter.

cuentista *m y f* **-1.** [escritor] short story writer. **-2.** [mentiroso] fibber, story-teller.

cuento *m* **-1.** [fábula] tale; ~ de hadas fairy tale; el ~ de la lechera *fig* wishful thinking. **-2.** [narración] short story. **-3.** [mentira, exageración] story, lie; ~ chino tall story. **-4.** *loc:* **quitarse ◯ dejarse de ~s** to stop beating about the bush; **ser el ~ de nunca acabar** to be the same old story; **tener ~** to put it on; **venir a ~** to be relevant; **venir con ~s** to tell fibs ◯ stories; **vivir del ~** to live by one's wits.

cuerda *f* **-1.** [para atar - fina] string; [- más gruesa] rope; ~ floja tightrope. **-2.** [de instrumento] string. **-3.** [de reloj] spring; **dar ~ a** [reloj] to wind up. **-4.** GEOM chord. **-5.** *loc:* **bajo ~** secretly, in an underhand manner; **estar en la ~ floja** to be hanging by a thread; **tener mucha ~, tener ~ para rato** to go on and on; **tirar de la ~** to go too far, to push it.

◆ **cuerdas vocales** *fpl* vocal cords.

cuerdo, -da ◇ *adj* **-1.** [sano de juicio] sane. **-2.** [sensato] sensible. ◇ *m y f* sane person.

cueriza *f Amer* beating.

cuerno *m* [gen] horn; [de ciervo] antler; **mandar al ~ a alguien** *fam* to send sb packing.

◆ **cuernos** *mpl fam:* **poner ~s a alguien** to be unfaithful to sb; [a un hombre] to cuckold sb.

cuero *m* **-1.** [piel de animal] skin; [piel curtida] hide; ~ cabelludo scalp; **en ~s, en ~s vivos** stark naked. **-2.** [material] leather. **-3.** *Amer vulg* [prostituta] whore.

cuerpo *m* **-1.** [gen] body; ~ extraño foreign body; **de ~ entero** [persona] complete, consummate; [retrato] full-length; **a ~** without a coat on; **luchar ~ a ~** to fight hand-to-hand; **tomar ~** to take shape; **vivir a ~ de rey** to live like a king; **en ~ y alma** body and soul. **-2.** [tronco] trunk. **-3.** [parte principal] main body. **-4.** [grosor] thickness. **-5.** [cadáver] corpse; **de ~ presente** (lying) in state. **-6.** [corporación consular, militar etc] corps; ~ de bomberos fire brigade; ~ diplomático diplomatic corps; ~ de policía police force. **-7.** [parte de armario, edificio] section.

cuervo *m* crow.

cuesco *m fam* fart.

cuesta ◇ *v* → costar. ◇ *f* slope; ~ arriba uphill; ~ abajo downhill; **a ~s** on one's back, over one's shoulders; **hacérsele ~ arriba a alguien** to be hard going ◯ an uphill struggle for sb.

cuestación *f* collection (for charity).

cueste → costar.

cuestión f -1. [pregunta] question. -2. [problema] problem. -3. [asunto] matter, issue; **en ~ de** [en materia de] as regards; **en ~ de una hora** in no more than an hour.

cuestionable adj questionable, debatable.

cuestionar vt to question.

◆ **cuestionarse** vpr to (call into) question.

cuestionario m questionnaire.

cueva f cave.

cueza etc → cocer.

cuicos mpl Amer fam cops.

cuidado ◇ m care; **de ~** dangerous; **estar al ~ de** to be in charge of; **tener ~ con** to be careful with; **~s intensivos** intensive care (U); **eso me tiene ○ trae sin ~** I couldn't care less about that. ◇ interj: ¡~! careful!, look out!

cuidador, -ra m y f DEP trainer.

cuidadoso, -sa adj careful.

cuidar vt [gen] to look after; [estilo etc] to take care over; [detalles] to pay attention to.

◆ **cuidar de** vi to look after; **cuida de que no lo haga** make sure she doesn't do it.

◆ **cuidarse** vpr to take care of ○ to look after oneself; **~se de** to worry about.

cuita f trouble, worry.

culata f -1. [de arma] butt. -2. [de animal] hindquarters. -3. [de motor] cylinder head.

culatazo m [golpe] blow with the butt of a rifle; [retroceso] recoil, kick.

culé (pl **culés**) adj fam DEP of/relating to the Barcelona Football Club.

culebra f snake.

culebrón m TV soap opera.

culinario, -ria adj culinary.

culminación f culmination.

culminante adj culminating; **punto ~** high point.

culminar ◇ vt: ~ **(con)** to crown (with). ◇ vi to finish, to culminate.

culo m fam -1. [de personas] backside, bum Br. -2. [de objetos] bottom. -3. [líquido]: **queda un ~** there are a few drops left in the bottom.

culpa f -1. [responsabilidad] fault; **tener la ~ de algo** to be to blame for sthg; **echar la ~ a alguien (de)** to blame sb (for); **por ~ de** because of. -2. [falta]: **~s** sins.

culpabilidad f guilt.

culpabilizar [13] vt to blame.

◆ **culpabilizarse** vpr: **~se (de)** to accept the blame (for).

culpable ◇ adj: ~ **(de)** guilty (of); **declarar ~ a alguien** to find sb guilty; **declararse ~**

to plead guilty. ◇ m y f DER guilty party; **tú eres el ~** you're to blame.

culpar vt: ~ **a alguien (de)** [atribuir la culpa] to blame sb (for); [acusar] to accuse sb (of).

culteranismo m Gongorism.

culterano, -na ◇ adj Gongoristic. ◇ m y f Gongorist.

cultismo m literary ○ learned word.

cultivable adj cultivable, arable.

cultivado, -da adj cultivated.

cultivador, -ra m y f grower.

cultivar vt -1. [tierra] to farm, to cultivate; [plantas] to grow. -2. [amistad, inteligencia] to cultivate. -3. [arte] to practise. -4. [germen] to culture.

◆ **cultivarse** vpr [persona] to improve o.s.

cultivo m -1. [de tierra] farming; [de plantas] growing. -2. [plantación] crop. -3. [de gérmenes] culture.

culto, -ta adj [persona] cultured, educated; [estilo] refined; [palabra] literary, learned.

◆ **culto** m -1. [devoción] worship; **rendir ~ a** [dios etc] to worship; [persona, valentía etc] to pay homage ○ tribute to. -2. [religión] cult.

cultura f -1. [de sociedad] culture. -2. [sabiduría] learning, knowledge.

cultural adj cultural.

culturismo m body-building.

culturista m y f body-builder.

culturizar [13] vt to educate.

cumbia f Colombian dance.

cumbre ◇ adj greatest. ◇ f -1. [de montaña] summit. -2. fig [punto culminante] peak, pinnacle. -3. POLIT summit (conference).

cumpleaños m inv birthday.

cumplido, -da adj -1. [acabado - orden] carried out; [- promesa, deber, profecía] fulfilled; [- plazo] expired. -2. [completo, lleno] full, complete. -3. [cortés] courteous.

◆ **cumplido** m compliment.

cumplidor, -ra ◇ adj reliable, dependable. ◇ m y f reliable ○ dependable person.

cumplimentar vt -1. [saludar] to greet. -2. [felicitar] to congratulate. -3. [cumplir - orden] to carry out; [- contrato] to fulfil.

cumplimiento m [de un deber] performance; [de contrato, promesa] fulfilment; [de la ley] observance; [de órdenes] carrying out; [de condena] completion; [de plazo] expiry.

cumplir ◇ vt -1. [orden] to carry out; [promesa] to keep; [ley] to observe; [contrato] to fulfil. -2. [años] to reach; **mañana cumplo los 20** I'm 20 ○ it's my 20th birthday tomorrow. -3. [condena] to serve; [servicio militar] to do. ◇ vi -1. [plazo, garantía] to expire. **-2.** [realizar el deber] to do one's duty; ~ **con alguien** to do one's duty by sb; **para** O **por** ~ out of politeness; ~ **con el deber** to do one's duty; ~ **con la palabra** to keep one's word.

cúmulo *m* **-1.** [de objetos] pile, heap. **-2.** [nube] cumulus. **-3.** *fig* [de asuntos, acontecimientos] accumulation, series.

cuna *f* **-1.** [para dormir] cot, cradle. **-2.** *fig* [de movimiento, civilización] cradle; [de persona] birthplace.

cundir *vi* **-1.** [propagarse] to spread. **-2.** [dar de sí - comida, reservas, tiempo] to go a long way; [- trabajo, estudio] to go well.

cuneiforme *adj* cuneiform.

cuneta *f* [de una carretera] ditch; [de una calle] gutter.

cunilinguo *m* cunnilingus.

cuña *f* **-1.** [pieza] wedge. **-2.** [de publicidad] commercial break. **-3.** [orinal] bedpan. **-4.** *Amer* [enchufe]: **tener** ~ to have friends in high places.

cuñado, -da *m y f* brother-in-law (*f* sister-in-law).

cuño *m* **-1.** [troquel] die. **-2.** [sello, impresión] stamp. **-3.** *loc*: **ser de nuevo** ~ to be a new coinage.

cuota *f* **-1.** [contribución - a entidad, club] membership fee, subscription; [- a Hacienda] tax (payment). **-2.** [precio, gasto] fee, cost. **-3.** [cupo] quota.
◆ **cuota de mercado** *f* ECON market share.

cupaje *m* blending of wines.

cupé *m* coupé.

cupido *m fig* lady's man.

cupiera *etc* → **caber**.

cuplé *m* popular song.

cupletista *m y f* singer of popular songs.

cupo ◇ *v* → **caber**. ◇ *m* **-1.** [cantidad máxima] quota. **-2.** [cantidad proporcional] share; [de una cosa racionada] ration.

cupón *m* [gen] coupon; [de lotería, rifa] ticket.

cúprico, -ca *adj* copper (*antes de sust*).

cúpula *f* **-1.** ARQUIT dome, cupola. **-2.** *fig* [mandos] leaders (*pl*).

cura ◇ *m* priest. ◇ *f* **-1.** [curación] recovery. **-2.** [tratamiento] treatment, cure; **necesitar una** ~ **de sueño** to need a good sleep. **-3.** *loc*: **no tener** ~ [ser incurable] to be incurable; *fam* [ser incorregible] to be incorrigible.

curación *f* **-1.** [de un enfermo - recuperación] recovery; [- tratamiento] treatment; [de una herida] healing. **-2.** [de jamón] curing.

curado, -da *adj* [alimento] cured; [pieles] tanned; ~ **de espanto** unshockable.
◆ **curado** *m* [de alimentos] curing; [de pieles] tanning.

curandería *f* quackery.

curandero, -ra *m y f* quack.

curar ◇ *vt* **-1.** [gen] to cure. **-2.** [herida] to dress. **-3.** [pieles] to tan. ◇ *vi* [enfermo] to get well, to recover; [herida] to heal up.
◆ **curarse** *vpr* **-1.** [sanar]: ~**se (de)** to recover (from); ~**se en salud** to play safe. **-2.** [alimento] to cure.

curare *m* curare.

curasao, curazao [kura'sao] *m* curaçao.

curativo, -va *adj* curative.

curazao = **curasao**.

curco *m Amer* **-1.** [joroba] hump. **-2.** [jorobado] hunchback.

curcucho *m Amer* hunchback.

curcuncho *Amer m* **-1.** [joroba] hump. **-2.** [jorobado] hunchback.

curda *fam* ◇ *f*: **coger** O **agarrar una** ~ to get plastered. ◇ *adj Amer* drunk. ◇ *m y f Amer* boozer, wino.

curdo, -da ◇ *adj* Kurdish. ◇ *m y f* [persona] Kurd.
◆ **curdo** *m* [lengua] Kurdish.

curia *f* **-1.** HIST & RELIG curia. **-2.** DER court.

curiosear ◇ *vi* [fisgonear] to nose around; [por una tienda] to browse round. ◇ *vt* [libros, revistas] to browse through.

curiosidad *f* **-1.** [gen] curiosity; **sentir** O **tener** ~ **por** to be curious about. **-2.** [limpieza] neatness, tidiness.

curioso, -sa ◇ *adj* **-1.** [por saber, averiguar] curious, inquisitive. **-2.** [raro] odd, strange. **-3.** [limpio] neat, tidy; [cuidadoso] careful. ◇ *m y f* onlooker.

curita *f Amer* sticking plaster.

currante *fam* ◇ *adj* hard-working. ◇ *m y f* worker.

currar, currelar *vi fam* to work.

curre = **curro**.

currelar = **currar**.

currículum (vitae) [ku'rrikulum ('bite)] (*pl* **currícula (vitae)** O **currículums**), **currículo** (*pl* **currículos**) *m* curriculum vitae.

curro, curre *m fam* work.

curruscar [10] *vi* to crunch.

curry *m* curry.

cursar *vt* **-1.** [estudiar] to study. **-2.** [enviar] to send. **-3.** [dar - órdenes etc] to give, to issue. **-4.** [tramitar] to submit.

cursi ◇ *adj fam* [vestido, canción etc] naff, tacky; [modales, persona] affected. ◇ *m y f fam* affected O pretentious person.

cursilada *f* [acto, comportamiento] pretentious ◇ affected act; [comentario] naff remark; [decoración, objeto] tacky thing.

cursilería *f* **-1.** [objeto] tacky thing; [comentario] naff remark; [acto, comportamiento] pretentious ◇ affected act. **-2.** [cualidad] tackiness, naffness.

cursillo *m* **-1.** [curso] short course. **-2.** [conferencias] series of lectures.

cursiva → **letra.**

curso *m* **-1.** [año académico] year. **-2.** [asignatura] course; ~ **intensivo** crash course. **-3.** [texto, manual] textbook. **-4.** [dirección - de río, acontecimientos] course; [- de la economía] trend; **seguir su** ~ to go on, to continue; **en el** ~ **de** during (the course of); **en** ~ [mes, año] current; [trabajo] in progress; **dar** ~ **a algo** [dar rienda suelta] to give free rein to sthg; [tramitar] to process ◇ deal with sthg. **-5.** [circulación]: **moneda de** ~ **legal** legal tender.

cursor *m* INFORM cursor.

CURT *(abrev de* **centro urbano de rehabilitación de toxicómanos)** *m urban drug-users' rehabilitation centre.*

curtido, -da *adj* **-1.** [piel, cuero] tanned. **-2.** *fig* [experimentado] seasoned.
◆ **curtido** *m* tanning.

curtir *vt* **-1.** [piel] to tan. **-2.** *fig* [persona] to harden.
◆ **curtirse** *vpr* **-1.** [piel] to tan. **-2.** *fig* [persona] to become hardened.

curva → **curvo.**

curvado, -da *adj* [gen] curved; [doblado] bent.

curvar *vt* to bend; [espalda, cejas] to arch.
◆ **curvarse** *vpr* to become bent.

curvatura *f* curvature.

curvilíneo, -a *adj* [gen] curved; [forma del cuerpo] curvaceous.

curvo, -va *adj* [gen] curved; [doblado] bent.
◆ **curva** *f* [gen] curve; [en carretera] bend; ~ **de la felicidad** *fig* [barriga] paunch; ~ **de nivel** contour line.

cuscurro *m* [trozo de pan frito] crouton; [punta de pan] end *(of baguette).*

cuscús *m inv* couscous.

cúspide *f* **-1.** [de montaña] summit, top. **-2.** *fig* [apogeo] peak, height. **-3.** GEOM apex.

custodia *f* **-1.** [de cosas] safe keeping. **-2.** [de personas] custody; **estar bajo la** ~ **de** to be in the custody of.

custodiar [8] *vt* **-1.** [vigilar] to guard. **-2.** [proteger] to look after.

custodio *m* guard.

cutáneo, -a *adj* skin *(antes de sust).*

cutícula *f* cuticle.

cutis *m inv* skin, complexion.

cutre *adj fam* **-1.** [de bajo precio, calidad] cheap and nasty. **-2.** [sórdido] shabby. **-3.** [tacaño] tight, stingy.

cutter *(pl* **cutters)** *m* (artist's) scalpel *(with retractable blade).*

cuyo, -ya *adj* [posesión - por parte de personas] whose; [- por parte de cosas] of which, whose; **ésos son los amigos en cuya casa nos hospedamos** those are the friends in whose house we spent the night; **ese señor,** ~ **hijo conociste ayer** that man, whose son you met yesterday; **un equipo cuya principal estrella ...** a team, the star player of which ◇ whose star player ...; **en** ~ **caso** in which case.

CV *(abrev de* **curriculum vitae)** *m* CV.

D

d, D *f* [letra] d, D.

D. *abrev de* **don.**

Dacca Dacca.

dactilar → **huella.**

dactilografía *f* typing.

dadá, dadaísmo *m* Dada, Dadaism.

dádiva *f* [regalo] gift; [donativo] donation.

dadivoso, -sa *adj* generous.

dado, -da *adj* given; **en un momento** ~ at a certain point; **ser** ~ **a** to be fond of.
◆ **dado** *m* dice, die.
◆ **dado que** *loc conj* since, seeing as.

dador, -ra *m y f* **-1.** [de letra de cambio] drawer. **-2.** [de carta] bearer.

daga *f* dagger.

daguerrotipo *m* daguerreotype.

Dakar Dakar.

dal *(abrev de* **decalitro)** dal.

dale *interj*: ¡~! - ¡otra vez con lo mismo! there you go again!

dalia *f* dahlia.

Dallas ['dalas] Dallas.

dálmata *adj, m y f* **-1.** [persona] Dalmatian. **-2.** [perro] Dalmatian.

daltónico, -ca ◇ *adj* colour-blind. ◇ *m y f* person with colour blindness.

daltonismo *m* colour blindness.

dam *(abrev de* **decámetro)** dam.

dama *f* **-1.** [mujer] lady; ~ **de honor** [de novia] bridesmaid; [de reina] lady-in-waiting; **primera** ~ TEATR leading lady; POLÍT first lady *Am.* **-2.** [en damas] king; [en ajedrez, naipes] queen.

◆ **damas** *fpl* [juego] draughts (*U*).

damajuana *f* demijohn.

damasco *m* **-1.** [tela] damask. **-2.** *Amer.* [albaricoque] apricot.

Damasco Damascus.

damasquinado *m* damascene.

damero *m* draughts board.

damisela *f desus* damsel.

damnificado, -da ◇ *adj* affected, damaged. ◇ *m y f* victim.

damnificar [10] *vt* [cosa] to damage; [persona] to harm, to injure.

dance *etc* → **danzar**.

dandi, dandy *m* dandy.

danés, -esa ◇ *adj* Danish. ◇ *m y f* [persona] Dane.

◆ **danés** *m* [lengua] Danish.

dantesco, -ca *adj lit* & *fig* Dantesque.

Danubio *m*: **el** ~ **the** (River) Danube.

danza *f* [gen] dancing; [baile] dance; **estar siempre en** ~ to be always on the go ◇ doing sthg; **estar metido en** ~ to be up to no good.

danzar [13] *vi* **-1.** [bailar] to dance. **-2.** *fig* [ir de un sitio a otro] to run about.

danzarín, -ina *m y f* dancer.

dañar *vt* [vista, cosecha] to harm, to damage; [persona] to hurt; [pieza, objeto] to damage.

◆ **dañarse** *vpr* [persona] to hurt o.s.; [cosa] to become damaged.

dañino, -na *adj* harmful.

daño *m* **-1.** [dolor] pain, hurt; **hacer** ~ **a alguien** to hurt sb; **hacerse** ~ to hurt o.s.. **-2.** [perjuicio - a algo] damage; [- a persona] harm; ~**s y perjuicios** damages.

dar [56] ◇ *vt* **-1.** [gen] to give; [baile, fiesta] to hold, to give; [naipes] to deal; ~ **algo a alguien** to give sthg to sb, to give sb sthg. **-2.** [producir - gen] to give, to produce; [- frutos, flores] to bear; [- beneficios, intereses] to yield. **-3.** [suj: reloj] to strike; **el reloj ha dado las doce** the clock struck twelve. **-4.** [suministrar luz etc - por primera vez] to connect; [- tras un corte] to turn back on; [encender] to turn ◇ switch on. **-5.** CIN, TEATR & TV to show; [concierto, interpretación] to give. **-6.** [mostrar - señales etc] to show; ~ **pruebas de sensatez** to show good sense. **-7.** [untar con] to apply; ~ **barniz a una silla** to varnish a chair. **-8.** [provocar - gusto, escalofríos etc] to give; **me da vergüenza/pena** it

makes me ashamed/sad; **me da risa** it makes me laugh; **me da miedo** it frightens me; **si no se calla me va a** ~ **algo** *fam* if he doesn't shut up soon, I'll go mad; **si sigues trabajando así te va a** ~ **algo** *fam* you can't go on working like that. **-9.** *fam* [fastidiar] to ruin; **es tan pesado que me dio la tarde** he's so boring that he ruined the afternoon for me. **-10.** [expresa acción] ~ **un grito** to give a cry; ~ **un vistazo a** to have a look at; ~**le un golpe/una puñalada a alguien** to hit/stab sb; **voy a** ~ **un paseo** I'm going (to go) for a walk. **-11.** [considerar]: ~ **algo por** to consider sthg as; **eso lo doy por hecho** I take that for granted; ~ **a alguien por muerto** to give sb up for dead. **-12.** *loc*: **donde las dan las toman** you get what you deserve; **no** ~ **una** to get everything wrong.

◇ *vi* **-1.** [repartir - en naipes] to deal. **-2.** [horas] to strike; **han dado las tres en el reloj** three o'clock struck. **-3.** [golpear]: **le dieron en la cabeza** they hit him on the head; **la piedra dio contra el cristal** the stone hit the window. **-4.** [accionar]: ~ **a** [llave de paso] to turn; [botón, timbre] to press. **-5.** [estar orientado]: ~ **a** [suj: ventana, balcón] to look out onto, to overlook; [suj: pasillo, puerta] to lead to; [suj: casa, fachada] to face. **-6.** [encontrar]: ~ **con algo/alguien** to find sthg/sb; **he dado con la solución** I've hit upon the solution. **-7.** [proporcionar]: ~ **de beber a alguien** to give sb sthg to drink; **le da de mamar a su hijo** she breast-feeds her son. **-8.** [ser suficiente]: ~ **para** to be enough for. **-9.** [motivar]: ~ **que hablar** to set people talking; **aquello me dio que pensar** that made me think. **-10.** [expresa repetición]: ~ **de** (+ *sust*): **le dieron de palos** they beat him repeatedly with a stick. **-11.** [coger costumbre]: ~**le a uno por hacer algo** to get it into one's head to do sthg; **le dio por la gimnasia** she's taken it into her head to start gymnastics. **-12.** *loc*: ~ **de sí** [ropa, calzado] to give, to stretch; **no** ~ **más de sí** ◇ **para más** [persona, animal] not to be up to much any more; **te digo que pares y tú ¡dale (que dale)!** I've told you to stop, but you just carry on and on!

◆ **darse** *vpr* **-1.** [suceder] to occur, to happen; **se da pocas veces** it rarely happens. **-2.** [entregarse]: ~**se a** [droga etc] to take to. **-3.** [golpearse]: ~**se contra** to bump into. **-4.** [tener aptitud]: **se me da bien/mal el latín** I'm good/bad at Latin. **-5.** [considerarse]: ~**se por** to consider o.s. (to be); ~**se por vencido** to give in. **-6.** *loc*: **dársela a alguien** [engañar] to take sb in; **se las da de listo** he makes out (that) he is clever.

dardo m dart.

dársena f dock.

darvinismo m Darwinism.

datar vt to date.

◆ **datar de** vi to date back to, to date from.

dátil m BOT & CULIN date.

◆ **dátiles** mpl fam [dedos] fingers.

◆ **dátil (de mar)** m date mussel.

dato m **-1.** [gen] piece of information, fact; **~s** [gen] information; INFORM data; **~s personales** personal details. **-2.** MAT datum.

dcha. (abrev de **derecha**) rt.

d. de JC., d.JC. (abrev de **después de Jesucristo**) AD.

de prep (de + el = **del**) **-1.** [posesión, pertenencia] of; **el coche ~ mi padre/mis padres** my father's/parents' car; **es ~ ella** it's hers; **la pata ~ la mesa** the table leg. **-2.** [materia (made)] of; **un vaso ~ plástico** a plastic cup; **un reloj ~ oro** a gold watch. **-3.** [en descripciones]: **un vaso ~ agua** a glass of water; **~ fácil manejo** user-friendly; **la señora ~ verde** the lady in green; **el chico ~ la coleta** the boy with the ponytail; **he comprado las peras ~ 100 ptas el kilo** I bought the pears that were ○ at 100 pesetas a kilo; **un sello ~ 50 ptas** a 50 peseta stamp. **-4.** [asunto] about; **hablábamos ~ ti** we were talking about you; **libros ~ historia** history books. **-5.** [uso]: **una bici ~ carreras** a racer; **ropa ~ deporte** sportswear. **-6.** [en calidad de] as; **trabaja ~ bombero** he works as a fireman. **-7.** [tiempo · desde] from; [· durante] in; **trabaja ~ nueve a cinco** she works from nine to five; **~ madrugada** early in the morning; **a las cuatro ~ la tarde** at four in the afternoon; **trabaja ~ noche y duerme ~ día** he works at night and sleeps during the day. **-8.** [procedencia, distancia] from; **salir ~ casa** to leave home; **soy ~ Bilbao** I'm from Bilbao; **~ la playa al apartamento hay 100 metros** it's 100 metres from the beach to the apartment. **-9.** [causa, modo] with; **morirse ~ hambre** to die of hunger; **llorar ~ alegría** to cry with joy; **una patada con un kick; ~ una sola vez** in one go. **-10.** [con superlativos]: **el mejor ~ todos** the best of all; **el más importante del mundo** the most important in the world. **-11.** [en comparaciones]: **más/menos ~ ...** more/less than .... **-12.** (antes de infin) [condición] if; **~ querer ayudarme, lo haría** if she wanted to help me, she'd do it; **~ no ser por ti, me hubiese hundido** if it hadn't been for you, I wouldn't have made it. **-13.** (después de adj y antes de sust) [enfatiza cualidad]: **el idiota ~ tu hermano** your stu-

pid brother. **-14.** (después de adj y antes de infin): **es difícil ~ creer** it's hard to believe.

dé → **dar.**

deambular vi to wander (about).

deán m dean.

debacle f debacle.

debajo adv underneath; **~ de** underneath, under; **por ~ de lo normal** below normal.

debate m debate.

debatir vt to debate.

◆ **debatirse** vpr [luchar] to struggle.

debe m debit (side); **~ y haber** debit and credit.

deber ◇ vt [adeudar] to owe; **~ algo a alguien** to owe sb sthg, to owe sthg to sb. ◇ vi **-1.** (antes de infin) [expresa obligación]: **debo hacerlo** I have to do it, I must do it; **deberían abolir esa ley** they ought to ○ should abolish that law; **debes dominar tus impulsos** you must ○ should control your impulses. **-2.** [expresa posibilidad]: **~ de: el tren debe de llegar alrededor de las diez** the train should arrive at about ten; **deben de ser las diez** it must be ten o'clock; **no debe de ser muy mayor** she can't be very old. ◇ m duty.

◆ **deberse a** vpr **-1.** [ser consecuencia de] to be due to. **-2.** [dedicarse a] to have a responsibility towards.

◆ **deberes** mpl [trabajo escolar] homework (U); **hacer los ~es** to do one's homework.

debidamente adv properly.

debido, -da adj **-1.** [adeudado] owing. **-2.** [justo, conveniente] due, proper; **como es ~** properly.

◆ **debido a** loc conj (a principio de frase) owing to; (en mitad de frase) due to.

débil ◇ adj **-1.** [persona · sin fuerzas] weak; [· condescendiente] lax, lenient. **-2.** [voz, sonido] faint; [luz] dim. **-3.** GRAM weak. ◇ m y f weak person.

debilidad f **-1.** [gen] weakness; **tener ~ por** to have a soft spot for. **-2.** [condescendencia] laxness.

debilitación f weakening.

debilitar vt to weaken.

◆ **debilitarse** vpr to become ○ grow weak.

débito m [debe] debit; [deuda] debt.

debut m [de persona] debut; [de obra] premiere.

debutante m y f person making his/her debut.

debutar vi to make one's debut.

década f decade.

decadencia f [gen] decadence; **en ~** [moda]

on the way out; [cultura, sociedad] in decline.

decadente *adj* decadent.

decaer [55] *vi* [gen] to decline; [enfermo] to get weaker; [salud] to fail; [entusiasmo] to flag; [restaurante etc] to go downhill; ¡que no decaiga! don't lose heart!

decágono *m* decagon.

decaído, -da *adj* [desalentado] gloomy, downhearted; [débil] frail.

decaiga *etc* → **decaer.**

decaimiento *m* [desaliento] gloominess; [decadencia] decline; [falta de fuerzas] weakness.

decalitro *m* decalitre.

decálogo *m* **-1.** RELIG Decalogue. **-2.** *fig* [normas] golden ○ basic rules (*pl*).

decámetro *m* decametre.

decanato *m* **-1.** [cargo] deanship. **-2.** [despacho] dean's office.

decano, -na *m y f* **-1.** [de corporación, facultad] dean. **-2.** [veterano] doyen (*f* doyenne), senior member.

decantar *vt* to decant.
◆ **decantarse** *vpr* **-1.** [inclinarse]: ~se (a) to lean (towards). **-2.** [optar]: ~se por to opt for.

decapitar *vt* to decapitate, to behead.

decatlón, decathlón *m* decathlon.

decayera *etc* → **decaer.**

deceleración *f* deceleration.

decena *f* ten; una ~ de veces about ten times.

decencia *f* **-1.** [gen] decency; [en el vestir] modesty. **-2.** [dignidad] dignity.

decenio *m* decade.

decente *adj* **-1.** [gen] decent. **-2.** [en el comportamiento] proper; [en el vestir] modest. **-3.** [limpio] clean.

decepción *f* disappointment.

decepcionante *adj* disappointing.

decepcionar *vt* to disappoint.

deceso *m* decease, death.

dechado *m*: ser un ~ de virtudes to be a paragon of virtue.

decibelio *m* decibel.

decidido, -da *adj* determined.

decidir ◇ *vt* **-1.** [gen] to decide; ~ hacer algo to decide to do sthg. **-2.** [determinar] to determine. ◇ *vi* to decide, to choose.
◆ **decidirse** *vpr* to decide, to make up one's mind; ~se a hacer algo to decide to do sthg; ~se por to decide on, to choose.

decigramo *m* decigram.

decilitro *m* decilitre.

décima → **décimo.**

decimal ◇ *adj* **-1.** [sistema] decimal. **-2.** [parte] tenth. ◇ *m* decimal.

decímetro *m* decimetre.

décimo, -ma *núm* tenth; **la décima parte** a tenth.
◆ **décimo** *m* **-1.** [fracción] tenth. **-2.** [en lotería] tenth part of a lottery ticket.
◆ **décima** *f* [en medidas] tenth; **tiene 3 décimas de fiebre** she has a slight fever; **una décima de segundo** a tenth of a second.

decimoctavo, -va *núm* eighteenth.

decimocuarto, -ta *núm* fourteenth.

decimonónico, -ca *adj* **-1.** [del siglo XIX] nineteenth-century. **-2.** [anticuado] old-fashioned.

decimonoveno, -na *núm* nineteenth.

decimoquinto, -ta *núm* fifteenth.

decimoséptimo, -ma *núm* seventeenth.

decimosexto, -ta *núm* sixteenth.

decimotercero, -ra *núm* thirteenth.

decir [57] ◇ *vt* **-1.** [gen] to say; ~ que sí/no to say yes/no; **dice que no viene** she says (that) she is not coming; ¿cómo se dice "estación" en inglés? how do you say "estación" in English?; ¿diga?, ¿dígame? [al teléfono] hello? **-2.** [contar, ordenar] to tell; ~ a alguien que haga algo to tell sb to do sthg; se dice que they ○ people say (that); ~ la verdad to tell the truth. **-3.** [recitar] to recite, to read. **-4.** *fig* [revelar] to tell, to show; **eso lo dice todo** that says it all. **-5.** [llamar] to call. **-6.** *loc:* como quien no dice nada as if it were nothing; **como quien dice, como si dijéramos** so to speak; ~ para sí to say to o.s.; ~le a alguien cuatro verdades to tell sb a few home truths; preocuparse por el qué dirán to worry about what people will say; es ~ that is, that's to say; ni que ~ tiene needless to say; ¡no me digas! no!, never!; ¡no me digas que no te gusta! don't tell me you don't like it!; no me dice nada el tenis tennis doesn't do anything for me; no hay más que ~ that's all there is to it, that's that; (o) mejor dicho or rather; por ~lo así, por así ~lo in other words, so to speak; no llueve mucho que digamos it's not exactly raining; querer ~ to mean; ¿qué quieres ~ con eso? what do you mean by that?; ¡y que lo digas! you can say that again!
◇ *m*: es un ~ it's not strictly true.

decisión *f* **-1.** [dictamen, resolución] decisión; **tomar una** ~ to make ○ take a decision. **-2.** [empeño, tesón] determination, resolve; [seguridad, resolución] decisiveness.

decisivo, -va *adj* decisive.

declamar *vt & vi* to declaim, to recite.

declaración f **-1.** [gen] statement; [de amor, impuestos, guerra] declaration; **prestar** ~ to give evidence; **tomar** ~ to take (down) a statement; ~ **del impuesto sobre la renta** income tax return. **-2.** [comienzo - de incendio] outbreak.

declarar ◇ vt [gen] to declare; [afirmar] to state, to say; ~ **la verdad** to tell the truth; ~ **culpable/inocente a alguien** to find sb guilty/not guilty. ◇ vi DER to testify, to give evidence.

◆ **declararse** vpr **-1.** [incendio, epidemia] to break out. **-2.** [confesar el amor] to declare one's feelings ○ love. **-3.** [dar una opinión]: ~**se a favor de algo** to say that one supports sthg; ~**se en contra de algo** to say one is opposed to sthg; ~**se culpable/inocente** to plead guilty/not guilty.

declinación f **-1.** [caída] decline. **-2.** GRAM declension.

declinar ◇ vt [gen & GRAM] to decline; [responsabilidad] to disclaim. ◇ vi [día, tarde] to draw to a close; [fiebre] to subside, to abate; [economía] to decline.

declive m **-1.** [decadencia] decline, fall; **cn** ~ in decline. **-2.** [pendiente] slope.

decodificador = **descodificador**.

decodificar = **descodificar**.

decolaje m Amer take-off.

decolar vi Amer to take off.

decolorante ◇ adj bleaching. ◇ m bleaching agent.

decolorar vt to bleach.

◆ **decolorarse** vpr to fade.

decomisar vt to confiscate, to seize.

decoración f **-1.** [acción] decoration; [efecto] décor. **-2.** [adorno] decorations (pl). **-3.** TEATR set, scenery.

decorado m CIN & TEATR set.

decorador, -ra m y f interior designer; TEATR set designer.

decorar vt to decorate.

decorativo, -va adj decorative.

decoro m **-1.** [pudor] decency, decorum. **-2.** [dignidad] dignity; **vivir con** ~ to live decently.

decoroso, -sa adj [decente] decent; [correcto] seemly, proper.

decrecer [30] vi [gen] to decrease, to decline; [caudal del río] to go down.

decreciente adj declining, decreasing.

decrépito, -ta adj despec [viejo] decrepit; [civilización] decadent, declining.

decrepitud f despec [de un viejo] decrepitude; [de una civilización] decline.

decretar vt to decree.

decreto m decree; **por real** ~ by royal decree; ~ **ley** decree, ≃ order in council Br.

decúbito m horizontal position.

dedal m thimble.

dédalo m labyrinth, maze.

dedicación f dedication; **con** ~ **(en) exclusiva** full-time.

dedicar [10] vt **-1.** [tiempo, dinero, energía] to devote. **-2.** [libro, monumento] to dedicate.

◆ **dedicarse a** vpr **-1.** [a una profesión]: ¿**a qué se dedica usted?** what do you do for a living?; **se dedica a la enseñanza** she works as a teacher. **-2.** [a una actividad, persona] to spend time on; **los domingos me dedico al estudio** I spend Sundays studying.

dedicatoria f dedication.

dedillo m: **saber algo al** ~ fam to know sthg (off) by heart.

dedique etc → **dedicar**.

dedo m **-1.** [de la mano] finger; **dos** ~**s de whisky** two fingers of whisky; ~ **anular/corazón** ring/middle finger; ~ **gordo** ○ **pulgar** thumb; ~ **índice/meñique** index/little finger. **-2.** [del pie] toe; ~ **gordo/pequeño** big/little toe. **-3.** loc: **escaparse de entre los** ~**s** to slip through one's fingers; **estar para chuparse los** ~**s** to be mouthwatering; **hacer** ~ fam to hitchhike; **mamarse** ○ **chuparse el** ~ to be a fool; **no creas que me chupo el** ~ I wasn't born yesterday, you know; **nombrar a alguien a** ~ to handpick sb; **no tener dos** ~**s de frente** to be as thick as two short planks; **pillarse** ○ **cogerse los** ~**s** fig to get one's fingers burnt; **poner el** ~ **en la llaga** to put one's finger on it; **señalar a alguien con el** ~ to criticize sb.

deducción f deduction; ~ **fiscal** ECON tax-deductible expenditure.

deducible adj **-1.** [idea] deducible. **-2.** [dinero] deductible.

deducir [33] vt **-1.** [inferir] to guess, to deduce. **-2.** [descontar] to deduct.

deductivo, -va adj deductive.

dedujera, deduzca etc → **deducir**.

defecar [10] vi to defecate.

defección f defection, desertion.

defectivo, -va adj defective.

defecto m [físico] defect; [moral] fault, shortcoming; ~ **de forma** administrative error; ~ **de pronunciación** speech defect.

◆ **por defecto** loc adv by default.

defectuoso, -sa adj [mercancía] defective, faulty; [trabajo] inaccurate.

defender [20] vt **-1.** [gen] to defend; [amigo etc] to stand up for. **-2.** [proteger - del frío etc]: ~ **a alguien (de)** to protect sb (against).

◆ **defenderse** *vpr* **-1.** [protegerse]: ~**se (de)** to defend o.s. (against). **-2.** *fig* [apañarse] to get by; **se defiende con su trabajo** he's getting along okay at work.

defendible *adj* defensible.

defenestrar *vt fig* to throw out, to get rid of.

defensa ◇ *f* defence; **en ~ propia, en legítima ~** in self-defence; **en ~ de** in defence of. ◇ *m y f* DEP defender; ~ **central** centreback.

defensivo, -va *adj* defensive.

◆ **defensiva** *f*: **ponerse/estar a la ~** to go/be on the defensive.

defensor, -ra ◇ *adj* → **abogado.** ◇ *m y f* [gen] defender; [abogado] counsel for the defence; [adalid] champion; ~ **del pueblo** ≃ ombudsman; ~ **del soldado** *public body created to defend soldiers' rights, especially those of young soldiers doing military service.*

defeque *etc* → **defecar.**

deferencia *f* deference; **por ~ a** in deference to.

deferente *adj* [cortés] deferential.

deferir [27] ◇ *vi:* ~ **(a)** to defer (to). ◇ *vt* DER to refer.

deficiencia *f* [defecto] deficiency, shortcoming; [insuficiencia] lack.

deficiente *adj* **-1.** [defectuoso · gen] deficient; ~ **en** lacking ○ deficient in; [audición, vista] defective. **-2.** [mediocre] poor, unsatisfactory.

◆ **deficiente (mental)** *m y f* mentally handicapped person.

◆ **muy deficiente** *m* EDUC very poor, ≃ E.

déficit (*pl* **déficits**) *m* **-1.** ECON deficit. **-2.** [falta] lack, shortage.

deficitario, -ria *adj* [empresa, operación] loss-making; [balance] negative, showing a deficit.

defienda *etc* → **defender.**

defiera *etc* → **deferir.**

definición *f* **-1.** [gen] definition. **-2.** [descripción] description. **-3.** [en televisión] resolution; **alta ~** high resolution.

definido, -da ◇ *adj* **-1.** [gen] defined. **-2.** GRAM → **artículo.**

definir *vt* **-1.** [gen] to define. **-2.** [describir] to describe.

◆ **definirse** *vpr* to take a clear stance.

definitivamente *adv* **-1.** [sin duda] definitely. **-2.** [para siempre] for good.

definitivo, -va *adj* [texto etc] definitive; [respuesta] definite; **en definitiva** in short, anyway.

defiriera *etc* → **deferir.**

deflación *f* deflation.

deflacionario, -ria *adj* deflationary.

deflector *m* baffle board ○ plate.

defoliación *f* defoliation.

deforestación *f* deforestation.

deformación *f* [de huesos, objetos etc] deformation; [de la verdad etc] distortion; ~ **física** (physical) deformity; **tener ~ profesional** to be always acting as if one were still at work.

deformar *vt* **-1.** [huesos, objetos etc] to deform. **-2.** *fig* [la verdad etc] to distort.

◆ **deformarse** *vpr* to go out of shape.

deforme *adj* [cuerpo] deformed, disfigured; [imagen] distorted; [objeto] misshapen.

deformidad *f* deformity.

defraudación *f* [fraude] tax evasion.

defraudar *vt* **-1.** [decepcionar] to disappoint. **-2.** [estafar] to defraud; ~ **a Hacienda** to practise tax evasion.

defunción *f* decease, death.

DEG (*abrev de* **derecho especial de giro**) *m* SDR.

degeneración *f* degeneration.

degenerado, -da *adj, m y f* degenerate.

degenerar *vi:* ~ **(en)** to degenerate (into).

deglutir *vt & vi* to swallow.

degolladero *m* slaughterhouse.

degollar [23] *vt* [cortar la garganta] to cut ○ slit the throat of; [decapitar] to behead.

degradación *f* **-1.** [moral] (moral) degradation. **-2.** [de un cargo] demotion.

degradante *adj* degrading.

degradar *vt* **-1.** [moralmente] to degrade, to debase. **-2.** [de un cargo] to demote.

◆ **degradarse** *vpr* to degrade ○ lower o.s.

degüella *etc* → **degollar.**

degüello *m* [decapitación] beheading; [degolladura] slaughter.

degustación *f* tasting (*of wines etc*).

degustar *vt* to taste (*wines etc*).

dehesa *f* meadow.

deidad *f* deity.

deificar [10] *vt* to deify.

dejada → **dejado.**

dejadez *f* neglect; [en aspecto] slovenliness.

dejado, -da ◇ *adj* careless; [aspecto] slovenly. ◇ *m y f* [persona] slovenly person.

◆ **dejada** *f* [en tenis] drop shot.

dejar ◇ *vt* **-1.** [gen] to leave; **deja esa pera en el plato** put that pear on the plate; **deja el abrigo en la percha** leave your coat on the hanger; ~ **a alguien en algún sitio** [con el coche] to drop sb off somewhere; **deja algo de café para mí** leave some coffee for me; ~ **algo/a alguien a alguien** [encomendar]

to leave sthg/sb with sb. **-2.** [prestar]: ~ **algo a alguien** to lend sb sthg, to lend sthg to sb. **-3.** [abandonar - casa, trabajo, país] to leave; [- tabaco, estudios] to give up; [- familia] to abandon; ~ **algo por imposible** to give sthg up as a lost cause; ~ **a alguien atrás** to leave sb behind. **-4.** [permitir]: ~ **a alguien hacer algo** to let sb do sthg, to allow sb to do sthg; **sus gritos no me dejaron dormir** his cries prevented me from sleeping; **deja que tu hijo venga con nosotros** let your son come with us; ~ **correr algo** *fig* to let sthg be. **-5.** [omitir] to leave out; ~ **algo por ○ sin hacer** to fail to do sthg; **dejó lo más importante por resolver** he left the most important question unsolved. **-6.** (*en imperativo*) [prescindir de] to forget (about); **déjalo, no importa** forget it, it doesn't matter. **-7.** (*en imperativo*) [no molestar] to leave alone ○ in peace; **¡déjame!, que tengo trabajo** leave me alone, I'm busy!; **déjame tranquilo** leave me alone ○ in peace. **-8.** [esperar]: ~ **que** to wait until; **dejó que acabara de llover para salir** he waited until it had stopped raining before going out.
◇ *vi* **-1.** [parar]: ~ **de hacer algo** to stop doing sthg; **no deja de venir ni un solo día** he never fails to come. **-2.** [expresando promesa]: **no** ~ **de** to be sure to; **¡no dejes de escribirme!** be sure to write to me! **-3.** *loc:* ~ **(mucho ○ bastante) que desear** to leave a lot to be desired.
◆ **dejarse** *vpr* **-1.** [olvidar]: ~**se algo en algún sitio** to leave sthg somewhere. **-2.** [permitir]: ~**se engañar** to allow o.s. to be taken in. **-3.** [cesar]: ~**se de hacer algo** to stop doing sthg; **¡déjate de tonterías!** stop messing about! **-4.** [descuidarse] to let o.s. go. **-5.** *loc:* ~**se llevar (por algo)** to get carried away (with sthg).

deje *m* **-1.** [acento] accent. **-2.** *fig* [resabio] touch, hint.

dejo *m* **-1.** [acento] accent. **-2.** [sabor] aftertaste.

del → **de**.

delación *f* denunciation.

delantal *m* apron.

delante *adv* **-1.** [en primer lugar, en la parte delantera] in front; **el de** ~ the one in front; **el asiento de** ~ the seat in front. **-2.** [enfrente] opposite. **-3.** [presente] present.
◆ **delante de** *loc prep* in front of.

delantero, -ra ◇ *adj* front. ◇ *m y f* DEP forward. ◇ *m y f* centro centre forward.
◆ **delantera** *f* **-1.** DEP forwards (*pl*), attack. **-2.** *fam* [de una mujer] bust. **-3.** *loc:* **coger ○ tomar la delantera** to take the lead; **coger ○ tomar la delantera a alguien**

beat sb to it; **llevar la delantera** to be in the lead.

delatar *vt* to denounce; *fig* [suj: sonrisa, ojos etc] to betray, to give away; **le delaté a la policía** I reported him to the police.
◆ **delatarse** *vpr* to give o.s. away.

delator, -ra *m y f* informer.

delco *m* distributor.

delegación *f* **-1.** [autorización, embajada] delegation; ~ **de poderes** devolution (of power). **-2.** [sucursal] branch. **-3.** [oficina pública] local office.

delegado, -da *m y f* **-1.** [gen] delegate; ~ **de curso** form monitor. **-2.** COM representative.

delegar [16] *vt:* ~ **algo (en ○ a)** to delegate sthg (to).

deleitar *vt* to delight.
◆ **deleitarse** *vpr:* ~**se con ○ en algo** to take pleasure in sthg; ~**se haciendo algo** to take pleasure in ○ enjoy doing sthg.

deleite *m* delight.

deletrear *vt* to spell (out).

deleznable *adj fig* [malo - clima, libro, actuación] appalling; [- excusa, razón] contemptible.

delfín *m* **-1.** [animal] dolphin. **-2.** [título] dauphin.

delgadez *f* [gen] thinness; [esbeltez] slimness.

delgado, -da *adj* [gen] thin; [esbelto] slim.

deliberación *f* deliberation.

deliberado, -da *adj* deliberate.

deliberar *vi* to deliberate.

delicadeza *f* **-1.** [miramiento - con cosas] care; [- con personas] kindness, attentiveness. **-2.** [finura - de perfume, rostro] delicacy; [- de persona] sensitivity. **-3.** [de un asunto, situación] delicacy.

delicado, -da *adj* **-1.** [gen] delicate; [perfume, gusto] subtle; [paladar] refined. **-2.** [persona - sensible] sensitive; [- muy exigente] fussy; [- educado] polite; **estar** ~ **de salud** to be very weak.

delicia *f* delight; **hacer las** ~**s de alguien** to delight sb.

delicioso, -sa *adj* [comida] delicious; [persona] lovely, delightful.

delictivo, -va *adj* criminal.

delimitar *vt* [finca etc] to set out the boundaries of; [funciones etc] to define.

delincuencia *f* crime; ~ **juvenil** juvenile delinquency.

delincuente *m y f* criminal.

delineante *m y f* draughtsman (*f* draughtswoman).

delinear *vt* to draw; *fig* to outline.

delinquir [18] *vi* to commit a crime.

delirante *adj* **-1.** [gen] delirious. **-2.** [idea] wild, crazy.

delirar *vi* [un enfermo] to be delirious; [desbarrar] to talk nonsense.

delirio *m* [por la fiebre] delirium; [de un enfermo mental] ravings (*pl*); **~s de grandeza** delusions of grandeur.

delito *m* crime, offence; **cometer un ~** to commit a crime ○ an offence.

delta ◇ *m* delta. ◇ *f* delta.

demacrado, -da *adj* gaunt.

demagogia *f* demagoguery.

demagogo, -ga *m y f* demagogue.

demanda *f* **-1.** [petición] request; [reivindicación] demand; **~ salarial** wage claim; **en ~ de** asking for. **-2.** ECON demand. **-3.** DER lawsuit; [por daños y perjuicios] claim; **presentar una ~ contra** to take legal action against.

demandado, -da *m y f* defendant.

demandante *m y f* plaintiff.

demandar *vt* **-1.** DER: **~ a alguien (por)** to sue sb (for). **-2.** [pedir] to ask for, to seek.

demarcación *f* **-1.** [señalización] demarcation. **-2.** [territorio demarcado] area; [jurisdicción] district.

demás ◇ *adj* other; **los ~ invitados** the other ○ remaining guests. ◇ *pron*: **lo ~** the rest; **todo lo ~** everything else; **los/las ~** the others, the rest; **por lo ~** apart from that, otherwise; **y ~** and so on.

demasía
◆ **en demasía** *loc adv* in excess, too much.

demasiado, -da ◇ *adj* too much, (*pl*) too many; **demasiada comida** too much food; **~s niños** too many children. ◇ *adv* [gen] too much; (*antes de adj o adv*) too; **habla ~** she talks too much; **iba ~ rápido** he was going too fast.

demencia *f* madness, insanity.

demencial *adj* [disparatado] chaotic.

demente ◇ *adj* mad. ◇ *m y f* MED mental patient; [loco] lunatic.

demérito *m* black mark.

demiurgo *m* demiurge.

democracia *f* democracy.

demócrata ◇ *adj* democratic. ◇ *m y f* democrat.

democratacristiano, -na *adj, m y f* Christian Democrat.

democrático, -ca *adj* democratic.

democratización *f* democratization.

democratizar [13] *vt* to democratize.

democristiano, -na = **democratacristiano**.

demografía *f* demography.

demográfico, -ca *adj* [estudio, instituto] demographic; [concentración, explosión] population (*antes de sust*).

demoledor, -ra *adj* [huracán, críticas] devastating; [razones] overwhelming.

demoler [24] *vt* [edificio] to demolish, to pull down; *fig* to destroy.

demolición *f* demolition.

demoniaco, -ca, demoníaco, -ca *adj* devilish, diabolic.

demonio *m* **-1.** *lit & fig* devil; **saber a ~s** to taste disgusting. **-2.** [para enfatizar]: **¿qué/dónde ~s ...?** what/where the hell ...?
◆ **demonios** *interj*: **¡~s!** damn (it)!

demora *f* delay.

demorar *vt* to delay.
◆ **demorarse** *vpr* **-1.** [retrasarse] to be delayed. **-2.** [detenerse] to stop (somewhere).

demostración *f* **-1.** [gen] demonstration; **hacer una ~** [de cómo funciona algo] to demonstrate; [de gimnasia etc] to put on a display. **-2.** [de un teorema] proof. **-3.** [exhibición] display; [señal] sign; [prueba] proof.

demostrar [23] *vt* **-1.** [hipótesis, teoría, verdad] to prove. **-2.** [alegría, impaciencia, dolor] to show. **-3.** [funcionamiento, procedimiento] to demonstrate, to show.

demostrativo, -va *adj* **-1.** [representativo] representative. **-2.** GRAM demonstrative.

demudar *vt* to change, to alter.
◆ **demudarse** *vpr* to change colour.

demuela *etc* → **demoler**.

demuestra *etc* → **demostrar**.

denegar [35] *vt* to turn down, to reject.

denigrante *adj* [humillante] degrading; [insultante] insulting.

denigrar *vt* [humillar] to denigrate, to vilify; [insultar] to insult.

denodado, -da *adj* [decidido] determined; [valiente] brave, intrepid.

denominación *f* naming; **"~ de origen"** "appellation d'origine".

denominador *m* denominator; **~ común** MAT & *fig* common denominator.

denominar *vt* to call.

denostar [23] *vt* to insult.

denotar *vt* to indicate, to show.

densidad *f* [gen & INFORM] density; **~ de población** population density; **alta/doble ~** INFORM high/double density.

denso, -sa *adj* [gen] dense; [líquido] thick.

dentado, -da adj [rueda] cogged, toothed; [filo, cuchillo] serrated; [sello] perforated; [hojas] dentate.

dentadura f teeth (pl); ~ **postiza** false teeth (pl), dentures (pl).

dental adj dental.

dentellada f **-1.** [mordisco] bite. **-2.** [herida] toothmark.

dentera f: dar ~ **a alguien** to set sb's teeth on edge.

dentición f **-1.** [proceso] teething. **-2.** [conjunto] teeth (pl).

dentífrico, -ca adj tooth (antes de sust).
◆ **dentífrico** m toothpaste.

dentista m y f dentist.

dentistería f Amer dental surgery.

dentística f Amer dentistry.

dentro adv inside; **está ahí** ~ it's in there; **de** ~ inside; **el bolsillo de** ~ the inside pocket; **hacia/para** ~ inwards; **por** ~ (on the) inside; fig inside, deep down.
◆ **dentro de** loc prep in; ~ **del coche** in ○ inside the car; ~ **de poco/un año** in a while/a year; ~ **de lo posible** as far as possible.

denuedo m [valor] courage; [esfuerzo] resolve.

denuesta etc → **denostar**.

denuncia f [acusación] accusation; [condena] denunciation; [a la policía] complaint; **presentar una** ~ **contra** to file a complaint against.

denunciante m y f person who reports a crime.

denunciar [8] vt to denounce; [delito] to report.

deontología f deontology.

deparar vt [gen] to bring; [oportunidad, placer] to afford.

departamento m **-1.** [gen] department. **-2.** [división territorial] administrative district; [en Francia] department. **-3.** [de maleta, cajón, tren] compartment.

departir vi to chat, to talk.

depauperar vt **-1.** [moralmente] to impoverish. **-2.** [físicamente - persona] to debilitate, to weaken; [- salud] to undermine.

dependencia f **-1.** [de una persona] dependence; [de país, drogas, alcohol] dependency. **-2.** [departamento] section; [sucursal] branch.
◆ **dependencias** fpl [habitaciones] rooms; [edificios] outbuildings.

depender vi to depend; **depende ...** it depends ... .
◆ **depender de** vi: ~ **de algo** to depend on sthg; ~ **de alguien** to be dependent on sb; **depende de ti** it's up to you.

dependienta f shop assistant, saleswoman.

dependiente ◇ adj dependent. ◇ m shop assistant, salesman.

depilación f hair removal; ~ **a la cera** waxing.

depilar vt [gen] to remove the hair from; [cejas] to pluck; [con cera] to wax.
◆ **depilarse** vpr [gen] to remove one's body hair; [las piernas] to wax one's legs.

depilatorio, -ria adj hair-removing.
◆ **depilatorio** m hair-remover.

deplorable adj [suceso, comportamiento] deplorable; [aspecto] sorry, pitiful.

deplorar vt to regret deeply.

deponer [65] vt **-1.** [abandonar - actitud] to drop, to set aside; [las armas] to lay down. **-2.** [destituir - ministro, secretario] to remove from office; [- líder, rey] to depose; ~ **a alguien de su cargo** to strip sb of his/her office.

deportación f deportation.

deportar vt to deport.

deporte m sport; **hacer** ~ to do ○ practise sports; **practicar un** ~ to do a sport; **hacer algo por** ~ to do sthg as a hobby.

deportista ◇ adj sporty, sports-loving. ◇ m y f sportsman (f sportswoman).

deportividad f sportsmanship.

deportivo, -va adj **-1.** [revista, evento] sports (antes de sust). **-2.** [conducta, espíritu] sportsmanlike.
◆ **deportivo** m sports car.

deposición f **-1.** [destitución - de ministro, secretario] removal from office; [- de líder, rey] overthrow. **-2.** [defecación] defecation.

depositar vt **-1.** [gen] to place; ~ **algo en alguien** [confianza, ilusiones] to place sthg in sb. **-2.** [en el banco etc] to deposit.
◆ **depositarse** vpr [asentarse] to settle.

depositario, -ria m y f **-1.** [de dinero] trustee. **-2.** [de confianza etc] repository. **-3.** [de mercancías etc] depositary.

depósito m **-1.** [almacén - de mercancías] store, warehouse; [- de armas] dump, arsenal; ~ **de cadáveres** morgue, mortuary. **-2.** [recipiente] tank. **-3.** [de dinero] deposit.
◆ **depósito legal** m copy of a publication legally required to be sent to the authorities.

depravación f depravity.

depravado, -da ◇ adj depraved. ◇ m y f depraved person.

depravar vt to corrupt, to deprave.
◆ **depravarse** vpr to become depraved.

depreciación f depreciation.

depreciar [8] vt to (cause to) depreciate.
◆ **depreciarse** vpr to depreciate.

depredación *f* depredation, pillaging.

depredador, -ra ◇ *adj* predatory. ◇ *m y f* predator.

depredar *vt* to pillage.

depresión *f* -1. [gen] depression; ~ **nerviosa** nervous breakdown. -2. [en superficie, terreno] hollow, depression.

depresivo, -va ◇ *adj* PSICOL depressive; [deprimente] depressing. ◇ *m y f* depressive.

deprimente *adj* depressing.

deprimido, -da *adj* depressed.

deprimir *vt* to depress.

◆ **deprimirse** *vpr* to get depressed.

deprisa, de prisa *adv* fast, quickly; ¡~! quick!

depuesto, -ta ◇ *pp* → **deponer.** ◇ *adj* [destituido ministro, secretario] removed from office; [- líder, rey] deposed.

depuración *f* -1. [de agua, metal, gas] purification. -2. *fig* [de organismo, sociedad] purge.

depurador, -ra *adj* purifying.

◆ **depurador** *m* purifier.

◆ **depuradora** *f* purifier.

depurar *vt* -1. [agua, metal, gas] to purify. -2. *fig* [organismo, sociedad] to purge. -3. [estilo, gusto] to refine.

depusiera *etc* → **deponer.**

derby *m* -1. [en hípica] derby. -2. [en fútbol] (local) derby.

derecha → **derecho.**

derechazo *m* [en boxeo] right.

derechista ◇ *adj* right-wing. ◇ *m y f* right-winger.

derecho, -cha ◇ *adj* -1. [diestro] right. -2. [vertical] upright. -3. [recto] straight. ◇ *adv* -1. [en posición vertical] upright. -2. [directamente] straight.

◆ **derecho** *m* -1. [leyes, estudio] law; ~ **administrativo/mercantil** administrative/mercantile law; ~ **canónico/fiscal** canon/tax law; ~ **civil/penal** civil/criminal law; ~ **natural** natural law. -2. [prerrogativa] right; **el** ~ **al voto** the right to vote; ¡**no hay** ~! it's not fair!; **reservado el** ~ **de admisión** the management reserves the right of admission; **tener** ~ **a algo** to have a right to sthg; **tener** ~ **a hacer algo** to have the right to do sthg; ~ **de retención** ECON right of retention; ~**s civiles/humanos** civil/human rights; **me queda el** ~ **al pataleo** all I can do now is complain. -3. [de una tela, prenda] right side; **del** ~ right side out.

◆ **derecha** *f* -1. [contrario de izquierda] right, right-hand side; **a la** ~ to the right; **girar a la** ~ to turn right. -2. POLÍT right (wing); **ser de** ~**s** to be right-wing. -3. *loc*: **no hacer nada a** ~**s** to do nothing right.

◆ **derechos** *mpl* [tasas] duties, taxes; [profesionales] fees; ~**s de aduana** customs duty (*U*); ~**s de inscripción** membership fee (*sg*); ~**s de autor** [potestad] copyright (*U*); [dinero] royalties; ~**s reales** death duty (*U*).

deriva *f* drift; **a la** ~ adrift; **ir a la** ~ to drift.

derivación *f* -1. [cable, canal, carretera] branch. -2. ELECTR shunt. -3. GRAM derivation.

derivado, -da *adj* GRAM derived.

◆ **derivado** *m* -1. [producto] by-product. -2. QUÍM derivative.

◆ **derivada** *f* MAT derivative.

derivar ◇ *vt* -1. [desviar] to divert. -2. MAT to derive. ◇ *vi* [desviarse] to change direction, to drift.

◆ **derivar de** *vi* -1. [proceder] to derive from. -2. GRAM to be derived from.

dermatología *f* dermatology.

dermatológico, -ca *adj* dermatological.

dermatólogo, -ga *m y f* dermatologist.

dérmico, -ca *adj* skin (*antes de sust*).

dermis *f inv* dermis.

derogación *f* repeal.

derogar [16] *vt* [ley] to repeal; [contrato] to rescind.

derramamiento *m* spilling; ~ **de sangre** bloodshed.

derramar *vt* [por accidente] to spill; [verter] to pour; ~ **lágrimas/sangre** to shed tears/blood.

◆ **derramarse** *vpr* [por accidente] to spill.

derrame *m* -1. MED discharge; ~ **cerebral** brain haemorrhage; ~ **sinovial** water on the knee. -2. [de líquido] spilling; [de sangre] shedding.

derrapar *vi* to skid.

derrengar *vt* [cansar] to exhaust, to tire out.

derretir [26] *vt* [gen] to melt; [nieve] to thaw.

◆ **derretirse** *vpr* -1. [metal, mantequilla] to melt; [hielo, nieve] to thaw. -2. *fam fig* [enamorarse]: ~**se (por alguien)** to be madly in love (with sb).

derribar *vt* -1. [construcción] to knock down, to demolish. -2. [hacer caer - árbol] to cut down, to fell; [- avión] to bring down. -3. [gobierno, gobernante] to overthrow.

derribo *m* -1. [de edificio] demolition; [de árbol] felling; [de avión] bringing down; [de gobierno, gobernante] overthrow. -2. [material] rubble.

derrita, derritiera *etc* → **derretir.**

derrocar [10] *vt* [gobierno] to bring down, to overthrow; [ministro] to oust.

derrochador, **-ra** ◇ *adj* wasteful. ◇ *m y f* spendthrift.

derrochar *vt* **-1.** [malgastar] to squander. **-2.** [rebosar de] to ooze, to be full of.

derroche *m* **-1.** [malgaste] waste, squandering. **-2.** [abundancia] profusion.

derrota *f* **-1.** [fracaso] defeat. **-2.** NÁUT [rumbo] course.

derrotar *vt* to defeat.

derrotero *m* **-1.** [camino] direction; **tomar diferentes ~s** to follow a different course. **-2.** NÁUT course.

derrotista *adj, m y f* defeatist.

derruir [51] *vt* to demolish, to knock down.

derrumbamiento *m* **-1.** [de puente, edificio - por accidente] collapse; [- intencionado] demolition. **-2.** *fig* [de imperio] fall; [de empresa etc] collapse. **-3.** *fig* [de persona] devastation.

derrumbar *vt* **-1.** [puente, edificio] to demolish. **-2.** [persona - moralmente] to destroy, to devastate.

◆ **derrumbarse** *vpr* **-1.** [puente, edificio] to collapse; [techo] to fall o cave in. **-2.** [persona] to be devastated; [esperanzas] to be shattered.

derrumbe *m* collapse.

desabastecer [30] *vt*: **~ a alguien de** to leave sb short of.

desabastecido, **-da** *adj* without supplies; **~ de** short o out of.

desaborido, **-da** *fam* ◇ *adj* boring, dull. ◇ *m y f* bore.

desabotonar *vt* to unbutton.

◆ **desabotonarse** *vpr* [suj: persona] to undo one's unbuttons; [suj: ropa] to come undone.

desabrido, **-da** *adj* **-1.** [tiempo] unpleasant, bad. **-2.** [persona] surly; [tono] harsh.

desabrigar [16] *vt* to wrap up insufficiently.

◆ **desabrigarse** *vpr* **-1.** [al salir a la calle]: **¡no te desabrigues!** make sure you wrap up warmly! **-2.** [en la cama] to throw off the covers.

desabrochar *vt* to undo.

◆ **desabrocharse** *vpr* [suj: persona] to undo one's buttons; [suj: ropa] to come undone.

desacatar *vt* [ley, regla] to disobey; [costumbre, persona] not to respect.

desacato *m* **-1.** [gen]: **~ (a)** lack of respect (for), disrespect (for). **-2.** DER contempt of court.

desacertado, **-da** *adj* [inoportuno] unwise, ill-considered; [erróneo] mistaken, wrong.

desacierto *m* [error] error.

desaconsejar *vt*: **~ algo (a alguien)** to advise (sb) against sthg; **~ a alguien que haga algo** to advise sb not to do sthg.

desacoplar *vt* ELECTR to disconnect; TECN to uncouple.

desacorde *adj* [opiniones] differing, conflicting.

desacostumbrado, **-da** *adj* unusual, uncommon.

desacreditar *vt* to discredit.

◆ **desacreditarse** *vpr* to become discredited.

desactivar *vt* to defuse.

desacuerdo *m* disagreement; **estar en ~ (con)** to disagree (with).

desafiante *adj* defiant.

desafiar [9] *vt* **-1.** [persona] to challenge; **~ a alguien a algo/a que haga algo** to challenge sb to sthg/to do sthg. **-2.** [peligro] to defy.

desafinar *vi* MUS to be out of tune.

desafío *m* challenge.

desaforadamente *adv* **-1.** [con exceso - comer, beber] to excess. **-2.** [con furia - gritar, protestar] furiously.

desaforado, **-da** *adj* **-1.** [excesivo - apetito] uncontrolled. **-2.** [furioso - grito] furious, wild.

desafortunado, **-da** ◇ *adj* **-1.** [gen] unfortunate. **-2.** [sin suerte] unlucky. ◇ *m y f* unlucky person.

desafuero *m* outrage, atrocity.

desagradable *adj* unpleasant.

desagradar *vi* to displease; **me desagrada su actitud** I don't like her attitude.

desagradecido, **-da** *m y f* ungrateful person.

desagrado *m* displeasure; **con ~** reluctantly.

desagraviar [8] *vt*: **~ a alguien por algo** [por una ofensa] to make amends to sb for sthg; [por un perjuicio] to compensate sb for sthg.

desagravio *m*: **en señal de ~** (in order) to make amends.

desaguadero *m* drain.

desaguar [45] *vi* [suj: bañera, agua] to drain; [suj: river]: **~ en** to flow into.

desagüe *m* [vaciado] drain; [cañería] drainpipe.

desaguisado *m* [destrozo] damage (*U*).

desahogado, **-da** *adj* **-1.** [de espacio] spacious, roomy. **-2.** [de dinero] well-off, comfortable.

desahogar [16] *vt* [ira] to vent; [pena] to relieve, to ease.

◆ **desahogarse** *vpr* **-1.** [contar penas]: ~**se con alguien** to pour out one's woes ○ to tell one's troubles to sb. **-2.** [desfogarse] to let off steam.

desahogo *m* **-1.** [moral] relief, release. **-2.** [de espacio] space, room. **-3.** [económico] ease; **vivir con** ~ to be comfortably off.

desahuciar [8] *vt* **-1.** [inquilino] to evict. **-2.** [enfermo]: ~ **a alguien** to give up all hope of saving sb.

desahucio *m* eviction.

desairado, -da *adj* **-1.** [poco airoso - actuación] unimpressive, unsuccessful. **-2.** [humillado] spurned.

desairar *vt* [person] to snub, to slight; [cosa] not to think much of, to be unimpressed by.

desaire *m* snub, slight; **hacer un** ~ **a alguien** to snub sb.

desajustar *vt* **-1.** [piezas] to disturb, to knock out of place. **-2.** [planes] to upset.

desajuste *m* **-1.** [de piezas] misalignment; [de máquina] breakdown. **-2.** [de declaraciones] inconsistency; [económico etc] imbalance.

desalentar [19] *vt* to dishearten, to discourage.

◆ **desalentarse** *vpr* to be discouraged, to lose heart.

desaliento *m* dismay, dejection.

desalinearse *vpr* to go out of line.

desaliñado, -da *adj* [aspecto] scruffy; [pelo] dishevelled.

desaliño *m* [del aspecto] scruffiness; [del pelo] dishevelment.

desalmado, -da ◇ *adj* heartless. ◇ *m y f* heartless person.

desalojar *vt* **-1.** [por una emergencia - edificio, personas] to evacuate. **-2.** [por la fuerza - suj: policía, ejército] to clear; [inquilinos etc] to evict. **-3.** [por propia voluntad] to abandon, to move out of.

desamarrar *vt* to cast off.

desambientado, -da *adj* [persona] out of place.

desamor *m* [falta de afecto] indifference, coldness; [odio] dislike.

desamortización *f* disentailment, alienation.

desamortizar [13] *vt* to disentail, to alienate.

desamparado, -da ◇ *adj* [niño] helpless; [lugar] desolate, forsaken. ◇ *m y f* helpless person.

desamparar *vt* to abandon.

desamparo *m* [abandono] abandonment; [aflicción] helplessness.

desamueblar *vt* to remove the furniture from.

desandar [52] *vt* to go back over; ~ **lo andado** to retrace one's steps.

desangelado, -da *adj* [casa, habitación] dull, uninspiring.

desangrar *vt* **-1.** [animal, persona] to bleed. **-2.** *fig* [económicamente] to bleed dry.

◆ **desangrarse** *vpr* to lose a lot of blood.

desanimado, -da *adj* **-1.** [persona] downhearted. **-2.** [fiesta, lugar] quiet, lifeless.

desanimar *vt* to discourage.

◆ **desanimarse** *vpr* to get downhearted ○ discouraged.

desánimo *m* [gen] dejection; [depresión] depression.

desanudar *vt* to untie.

desapacible *adj* unpleasant.

desaparecer [30] *vi* **-1.** [gen] to disappear. **-2.** [en guerra, accidente] to go missing.

desaparecido, -da *m y f* missing person.

desaparición *f* disappearance.

desapasionado, -da *adj* dispassionate.

desapego *m* indifference.

desapercibido, -da *adj*: **pasar** ~ to go unnoticed.

desaprensión *f* unscrupulousness.

desaprensivo, -va *m y f* unscrupulous person.

desaprobación *f* disapproval.

desaprobar [23] *vt* [gen] to disapprove of; [un plan etc] to reject.

desaprovechado, -da *adj* **-1.** [estudiante] lacking in application, idle. **-2.** [tiempo, ocasión] wasted; [casa, jardín] not properly used.

desaprovechamiento *m* **-1.** [de estudiante] lack of application, idleness. **-2.** [de tiempo, ocasión] waste; [de casa, jardín] failure to exploit fully.

desaprovechar *vt* to waste.

desarmador *m Amer* screwdriver.

desarmar *vt* **-1.** [gen] to disarm. **-2.** [desmontar] to take apart, to dismantle.

desarme *m* **-1.** MIL & POLÍT disarmament; ~ **nuclear** nuclear disarmament. **-2.** [desarticulación - de reloj, máquina] taking apart, dismantling.

desarraigar [16] *vt* **-1.** [vicio, costumbre] to root out. **-2.** [persona, pueblo] to banish, to drive (out).

desarraigo *m* [de árbol] uprooting; [de vicio, costumbre] rooting out; [de persona, pueblo] banishment.

desarreglado, **-da** adj [cuarto, armario, persona] untidy; [vida] disorganized.

desarreglar vt [armario, pelo] to mess up; [planes, horario] to upset.

desarreglo m [de cuarto, persona] untidiness; [de vida] disorder.

desarrollado, **-da** adj developed.

desarrollar vt **-1.** [mejorar - crecimiento, país] to develop. **-2.** [exponer - teoría, tema, fórmula] to expound, to explain. **-3.** [realizar - actividad, trabajo] to carry out. **-4.** MAT to expand.

♦ **desarrollarse** vpr **-1.** [crecer, mejorar] to develop. **-2.** [suceder - reunión] to take place; [- película] to be set.

desarrollismo m policy of development at all costs.

desarrollo m **-1.** [mejora] development. **-2.** [crecimiento] growth.

desarrugar [16] vt [alisar] to smooth out; [planchar] to iron out the creases in.

desarticulación f **-1.** [de huesos] dislocation. **-2.** fig [de organización, banda] breaking up.

desarticular vt **-1.** [huesos] to dislocate. **-2.** fig [organización, banda] to break up; [plan] to foil.

desaseado, **-da** adj [sucio] dirty; [desarreglado] untidy.

desasosegar [35] vt to disturb, to make uneasy.

♦ **desasosegarse** vpr to become uneasy.

desasosiego m **-1.** [mal presentimiento] unease. **-2.** [nerviosismo] restlessness.

desastrado, **-da** adj [desaseado] scruffy; [sucio] dirty.

desastre m disaster; **su madre es un** ~ her mother is hopeless; **¡vaya** ~**!** what a shambles!

desastroso, **-sa** adj disastrous.

desatar vt **-1.** [nudo, lazo] to untie; [paquete] to undo; [animal] to unleash. **-2.** fig [tormenta, iras, pasión] to unleash; [entusiasmo] to arouse; [lengua] to loosen.

♦ **desatarse** vpr **-1.** [nudo, lazo] to come undone. **-2.** fig [desencadenarse - tormenta] to break; [- ira, cólera] to erupt.

desatascar [10] vt to unblock.

desatención f [falta de atención] lack of attention; [descortesía] discourtesy, impoliteness.

desatender [20] vt **-1.** [obligación, persona] to neglect. **-2.** [ruegos, consejos] to ignore.

desatento, **-ta** adj **-1.** [distraído] inattentive. **-2.** [descortés] impolite.

desatino m **-1.** [locura] foolishness. **-2.** [desacierto] foolish act.

desatrancar [10] vt [puerta, ventana] to unbolt; [tubería] to unblock.

desautorizar [13] vt **-1.** [desmentir - noticia] to deny. **-2.** [prohibir - manifestación, huelga] to ban. **-3.** [desacreditar] to discredit.

desavenencia f [desacuerdo] friction, tension; [riña] quarrel.

desavenirse [75] vpr to fall out.

desayunar ◇ vi to have breakfast. ◇ vt to have for breakfast.

desayuno m breakfast.

desazón f unease, anxiety.

desazonar vt to worry, to cause anxiety to.

desbancar [10] vt fig [ocupar el puesto de] to oust, to replace.

desbandada f breaking up, scattering; **a la** ~ in great disorder.

desbandarse vpr to scatter.

desbarajuste m disorder, confusion; **¡vaya** ~**!** what a mess!

desbaratar vt to ruin, to wreck.

desbarrar vi to talk nonsense.

desbloquear vt [cuenta] to unfreeze; [país] to lift the blockade on; [negociación] to end the deadlock in.

desbocado, **-da** adj **-1.** [caballo] runaway. **-2.** [prenda de vestir] stretched around the neck.

desbocarse [10] vpr [caballo] to bolt.

desbordamiento m **-1.** [de río] overflowing. **-2.** fig [de sentimiento] loss of control.

desbordar vt **-1.** [cauce, ribera] to overflow, to burst. **-2.** [límites, previsiones] to exceed; [paciencia] to push beyond the limit. **-3.** [contrario, defensa] to get past, to pass.

♦ **desbordar de** vi to overflow with.

♦ **desbordarse** vpr **-1.** [líquido]: ~**se (de)** to overflow (from). **-2.** [río] to overflow. **-3.** fig [sentimiento] to erupt.

descabalgar [16] vi to dismount.

descabellado, **-da** adj crazy.

descabellar vt TAUROM to give the coup de grâce to.

descabezar [13] vt **-1.** [quitar la cabeza - persona] to behead; [- cosa] to break the head off. **-2.** [quitar la punta - planta, árbol] to top.

descacharrar vt fam to smash up.

descafeinado, **-da** adj **-1.** [sin cafeína] decaffeinated. **-2.** fig [sin fuerza] watered down.

♦ **descafeinado** m decaffeinated coffee.

descafeinar vt **-1.** [quitar cafeína] to decaffeinate. **-2.** fig [quitar fuerza] to water down.

descalabrar *vt* **-1.** [herir] to wound in the head. **-2.** *fam fig* [perjudicar] to harm, to damage.
◆ **descalabrarse** *vpr* to hurt one's head.
descalabro *m* setback, damage (*U*).
descalcificar [10] *vt* to decalcify.
◆ **descalcificarse** *vpr* to decalcify.
descalificar [10] *vt* **-1.** [en una competición] to disqualify. **-2.** [desprestigiar] to discredit.
descalzar [13] *vt*: ~ **a alguien** to take sb's shoes off.
◆ **descalzarse** *vpr* to take off one's shoes.
descalzo, -za *adj* barefoot.
descaminado, -da *adj* **-1.** *fig* [equivocado]: **andar** ○ **ir** ~ to be on the wrong track. **-2.** [caminante, excursionista] heading in the wrong direction.
descaminar *vt* [suj: malas compañías] to lead astray; [suj: guía] to take the wrong way.
◆ **descaminarse** *vpr* [por malas compañías] to go astray; [en una excursión] to go the wrong way.
descamisado, -da ◇ *adj* **-1.** [sin camisa] barechested. **-2.** *fig* [pobre] wretched. ◇ *m y f* poor wretch.
descampado *m* open country.
descangallado, -da *adj Amer fam* shabby.
descansar *vi* **-1.** [reposar] to rest. **-2.** [dormir] to sleep; **¡que descanses!** sleep well! **-3.** *fig* [viga, teoría etc]: ~ **en** to rest on.
descansillo *m* landing.
descanso *m* **-1.** [reposo] rest; **tomarse un** ~ to take a rest; **día de** ~ day off. **-2.** [pausa] break; CIN & TEATR interval; DEP half-time, interval. **-3.** *fig* [alivio] relief. **-4.** [calzado] *boot worn after skiing*. **-5.** MIL: **adoptar la posición de** ~ to stand at ease.
descapitalizar [13] *vt* COM to undercapitalize.
◆ **descapitalizarse** *vpr* to be undercapitalized.
descapotable *adj & m* convertible.
descarado, -da ◇ *adj* **-1.** [desvergonzado - persona] cheeky, impertinent. **-2.** [flagrante - intento etc] barefaced, blatant; **¡es un robo** ~**!** it's daylight robbery! ◇ *m y f* cheeky devil.
descarga *f* **-1.** [de mercancías] unloading. **-2.** [de electricidad] shock. **-3.** [disparo] firing, shots (*pl*).
descargar [16] ◇ *vt* **-1.** [vaciar - mercancías, pistola] to unload. **-2.** [disparar - munición, arma, ráfaga] ~ **(sobre)** to fire (at). **-3.** [puntapié, puñetazo] to deal, to land. **-4.** ELECTR to run down. **-5.** [exonerar]: ~ **a alguien de algo** to free ○ release sb from sthg. **-6.** DER

[absolver]: ~ **a alguien de algo** to clear sb of sthg. ◇ *vi* to burst; [tormenta] to break.
◆ **descargarse** *vpr* **-1.** [desahogarse]: ~**se con alguien** to take it out on sb. **-2.** DER: ~**se (de)** to clear oneself (of). **-3.** ELECTR to go flat.
descargo *m* **-1.** [excusa]: ~ **a** argument against. **-2.** DER defence; **en su** ~ in his/her defence. **-3.** [COM - de deuda] discharge; [- recibo] receipt.
descarnado, -da *adj* **-1.** [descripción] brutal. **-2.** [persona, animal] scrawny.
descaro *m* cheek, impertinence.
descarriarse [9] *vpr* **-1.** [ovejas, ganado] to stray. **-2.** *fig* [pervertirse] to lose one's way, to go astray.
descarrilamiento *m* derailment.
descarrilar *vi* to be derailed.
descartar *vt* [ayuda] to refuse, to reject; [posibilidad] to rule out.
◆ **descartarse** *vpr*: ~**se (de)** to discard.
descarte *m* [de naipes] discard.
descastado, -da *m y f* ungrateful person.
descendencia *f* **-1.** [hijos] offspring; **morir sin** ~ to die without issue. **-2.** [linaje] lineage, descent.
descendente *adj* [gen] descending; [movimiento, posición] downward.
descender [20] *vi* **-1.** [en estimación] to go down; ~ **a segunda** to be relegated to the second division. **-2.** [cantidad, valor, temperatura, nivel] to fall, to drop.
◆ **descender de** *vi* **-1.** [avión] to get off. **-2.** [linaje] to be descended from.
descenso *m* **-1.** [en el espacio] descent. **-2.** [de cantidad, valor, temperatura, nivel] drop. **-3.** [en esquí] downhill. **-4.** [en fútbol etc] relegation.
descentrado, -da *adj* **-1.** [geométricamente] off-centre. **-2.** [mentalmente] unsettled, disorientated.
descentralización *f* decentralization.
descentralizar [13] *vt* to decentralize.
descentrar *vt* **-1.** [sacar del centro] to knock off-centre. **-2.** *fig* [desconcentrar] to distract.
descienda *etc* → **descender**.
descifrable *adj* [mensaje, jeroglífico] decipherable; [letra] legible.
descifrar *vt* **-1.** [clave, mensaje] to decipher. **-2.** [motivos, intenciones] to work out; [misterio] to solve; [problemas] to puzzle out.
descocado, -da *adj* outrageous.
descodificador, -ra, decodificador, -ra *adj* decoding (*antes de sust*).
◆ **descodificador, decodificador** *m* decoder.
descodificar, decodificar [10] *vt* decode.

descojonarse *vpr vulg*: ~se (de) to piss oneself laughing (at).

descolgar [39] *vt* -1. [una cosa colgada] to take down. -2. [teléfono] to pick up, to take off the hook.

◆ **descolgarse** *vpr* -1. [bajar]: ~se (por algo) to let oneself down ○ to slide down (sthg). -2. DEP: ~se de to break away from. -3. *fam* [mencionar]: ~se con que to come out with the idea that.

descollar *vi fig* [sobresalir] to stand out.

descolocado, -da *adj* [objeto] out of place.

descolocar *vt* [objeto] to put out of place, to disturb.

descolonización *f* decolonization.

descolonizar [13] *vt* to decolonize.

descolorar *vt* to fade.

descolorido, -da *adj* faded.

descomedido, -da *adj* excessive, uncontrollable.

descompasado, -da *adj* excessive, uncontrollable.

descompensación *f* imbalance.

descompensar *vt* to unbalance.

descomponer [65] *vt* -1. [pudrir - fruta] to rot; [- cadáver] to decompose. -2. [dividir] to break down; ~ algo en to break sthg down into. -3. [desordenar] to mess up. -4. [estropear] to damage, to break. -5. *fig* [enojar] to annoy.

◆ **descomponerse** *vpr* -1. [pudrirse - fruta] to rot; [- cadáver] to decompose. -2. [irritarse] to get annoyed. -3. *Amer* [averiarse] to break down.

descomposición *f* -1. [de elementos] decomposition. -2. [putrefacción - de fruta] rotting; [- de cadáver] decomposition. -3. [alteración] distortion. -4. [diarrea] diarrhoea.

descompostura *f* -1. [falta de mesura] lack of respect, rudeness. -2. *Amer* [avería] breakdown.

descompresión *f* decompression.

descompuesto, -ta ◇ *pp* → **descomponer**. ◇ *adj* -1. [putrefacto - fruta] rotten; [- cadáver] decomposed. -2. [alterado - rostro] distorted, twisted.

descomunal *adj* tremendous, enormous.

desconcentrar *vt* to distract.

◆ **desconcentrarse** *vpr* to get distracted.

desconcertante *adj* disconcerting.

desconcertar [19] *vt* to disconcert, to throw.

◆ **desconcertarse** *vpr* to be thrown ○ bewildered.

desconchado *m* [de pintura] peeling paint; [de enyesado] peeling plaster.

desconchar *vt* to chip.

◆ **desconcharse** *vpr* [pintura] to flake off; [pared, loza] to chip.

desconcierto *m* [desorden] disorder; [desorientación, confusión] confusion.

desconectar *vt* [aparato] to switch off; [línea] to disconnect; [desenchufar] to unplug.

◆ **desconectarse** *vpr fig* [aislarse, olvidarse] to forget about one's worries; ~se de algo to shut sthg out, to forget (about) sthg.

desconfiado, -da ◇ *adj* distrustful. ◇ *m y f* distrustful person.

desconfianza *f* distrust.

desconfiar [9]

◆ **desconfiar de** *vi* -1. [sospechar de] to distrust; **desconfía de él** don't trust him. -2. [no confiar en] to have no faith in.

descongelar *vt* -1. [producto] to thaw; [nevera] to defrost. -2. *fig* [precios] to free; [créditos, salarios] to unfreeze.

descongestionar *vt* -1. MED to clear. -2. *fig* [calle, centro de ciudad] to make less congested; ~ el tráfico to reduce congestion.

desconocer [31] *vt* [ignorar] not to know.

desconocido, -da ◇ *adj* -1. [no conocido] unknown. -2. [muy cambiado]: **estar ~** to have changed beyond all recognition. ◇ *m y f* stranger.

desconocimiento *m* ignorance, lack of knowledge.

desconsideración *f* thoughtlessness.

desconsiderado, -da ◇ *adj* thoughtless, inconsiderate. ◇ *m y f* thoughtless ○ inconsiderate person.

desconsolado, -da *adj* disconsolate.

desconsolar [23] *vt* to distress.

desconsuelo *m* distress, grief.

descontado, -da *adj* discounted.

◆ **por descontado** *loc adv* obviously, needless to say; **dar algo por ~** to take sthg for granted.

descontaminar *vt* to decontaminate.

descontar [23] *vt* -1. [una cantidad] to deduct. -2. COM to discount.

descontentar *vt* to upset, to make unhappy.

descontento, -ta *adj* unhappy, dissatisfied.

◆ **descontento** *m* dissatisfaction.

descontrol *m* lack of control.

descontrolarse *vpr* [coche, inflación] to go out of control; [persona] to lose control.

desconvocar [10] *vt* to cancel, to call off.

descorazonador, -ra *adj* discouraging.

descorazonamiento *m* discouragement.

descorazonar *vt* to discourage.

◆ **descorazonarse** *vpr* to be discouraged, to lose heart.

descorchar *vt* to uncork.

descorrer *vt* **-1.** [cortinas] to draw back, to open. **-2.** [cerrojo, pestillo] to draw back.

descortés *adj* rude.

descortesía *f* discourtesy.

descoser *vt* to unstitch.

◆ **descoserse** *vpr* to come unstitched.

descosido, -da *adj* unstitched.

◆ **descosido** *m* [roto - a propósito] open seam; [- por accidente] tear; **como un ~** [hablar] endlessly, non-stop; [beber, comer] to excess; [gritar] wildly.

descoyuntar *vt* to dislocate.

◆ **descoyuntarse** *vpr* to dislocate.

descrédito *m* discredit; **ir en ~ de algo/ alguien** to count against sthg/sb; **estar en ~** to be discredited.

descreído, -da *m y f* non-believer, disbeliever.

descremado, -da *adj* skimmed.

descremar *vt* to skim.

describir *vt* to describe.

descripción *f* description.

descriptivo, -va *adj* descriptive.

descrito, -ta *pp* → describir.

descuajar *vt* **-1.** [derretir] to melt. **-2.** [arrancar] to uproot.

descuajaringar [16] *vt* to break into pieces.

◆ **descuajaringarse** *vpr* **-1.** [descomponerse] to fall apart ○ to pieces. **-2.** [troncharse de risa] to fall about laughing.

descuartizar [13] *vt* [persona] to quarter; [res] to carve up.

descubierto, -ta ◇ *pp* → descubrir. ◇ *adj* **-1.** [gen] uncovered; [coche] open. **-2.** [cielo] clear. **-3.** [sin sombrero] bareheaded.

◆ **descubierto** *m* [FIN - de empresa] deficit; [- de cuenta bancaria] overdraft.

◆ **al descubierto** *loc adv* **-1.** [al raso] in the open. **-2.** BANCA overdrawn; **quedar al ~** *fig* to be exposed ○ uncovered.

◆ **en descubierto** *loc adv* BANCA overdrawn.

descubridor, -ra *m y f* discoverer.

descubrimiento *m* **-1.** [de continentes, invenciones] discovery. **-2.** [de placa, busto] unveiling. **-3.** [de complots] uncovering; [de asesinos] detection.

descubrir *vt* **-1.** [gen] to discover; [petróleo] to strike; [complot] to uncover. **-2.** [destapar - estatua, placa] to unveil. **-3.** [vislumbrar] to spot, to spy. **-4.** [delatar] to give away.

◆ **descubrirse** *vpr* **-1.** [quitarse el sombrero] to take one's hat off; **~se ante algo** *fig* to

take one's hat off to sthg. **-2.** [cielo, horizonte] to clear.

descuelga *etc* → descolgar.

descuenta *etc* → descontar.

descuento *m* discount; **hacer ~** to give a discount; **con ~** at a discount; **un ~ del 10%** 10% off.

descuerar *vt* *Amer* to slam, to criticize.

descuidado, -da *adj* **-1.** [desaseado - persona, aspecto] untidy; [- jardín] neglected. **-2.** [negligente] careless. **-3.** [distraído] off one's guard.

descuidar ◇ *vt* [desatender] to neglect. ◇ *vi* [no preocuparse] not to worry; **descuida, que yo me encargo** don't worry, I'll take care of it.

◆ **descuidarse** *vpr* **-1.** [abandonarse] to neglect one's appearance; **~se de algo/de hacer algo** to neglect sthg/to do sthg. **-2.** [despistarse] not to be careful.

descuido *m* **-1.** [falta de aseo] carelessness. **-2.** [olvido] oversight; [error] slip; **al menor ~** if you let your attention wander for even a moment.

desde *prep* **-1.** [tiempo] since; **no lo veo ~ el mes pasado/~ ayer** I haven't seen him since last month/yesterday; **~ ahora** from now on; **~ hace mucho/un mes** for ages/a month; **~ ... hasta ...** from ... until ...; **~ el lunes hasta el viernes** from Monday till Friday; **~ entonces** since then; **~ que** since; **~ que murió mi madre** since my mother died; **~ ya** [inmediatamente] right now. **-2.** [espacio] from; **desde ... hasta ...** from ... to ...; **desde aquí hasta el centro** from here to the centre.

◆ **desde luego** *loc adv* **-1.** [por supuesto] of course. **-2.** [en tono de reproche] for goodness' sake!; **¡~ luego tienes cada idea!** you really come out with some funny ideas!

desdecir [66]

◆ **desdecir de** *vi* [desmerecer] to be unworthy of; [no cuadrar con] not to go with, to clash with.

◆ **desdecirse** *vpr* to go back on one's word; **~se de** to go back on.

desdén *m* disdain, scorn.

desdentado, -da *adj* toothless.

desdentar [19] *vt* to remove the teeth of.

desdeñable *adj* contemptible; **una cantidad nada ~** a considerable amount.

desdeñar *vt* to scorn.

desdeñoso, -sa *adj* scornful, disdainful.

desdibujado, -da *adj* blurred.

desdibujarse *vpr* to blur, to become blurred.

desdice → desdecir.

desdicha *f* [desgracia - situación] misery; [- suceso] misfortune.

desdichado, -da ◇ *adj* [decisión, situación] unfortunate; [persona - sin suerte] unlucky; [- sin felicidad] unhappy. ◇ *m y f* poor wretch.

desdicho, -cha *pp* → desdecir.

desdienta *etc* → desdentar.

desdiga, desdijera *etc* → desdecir.

desdoblamiento *m* -1. [de objeto] unfolding. -2. [de imagen, personalidad] splitting.

desdoblar *vt* -1. [servilleta, carta] to unfold; [alambre] to straighten out. -2. *fig* [dividir] to split.

desdramatizar [13] *vt* to play down.

deseable *adj* desirable.

desear *vt* -1. [querer] to want; [anhelar] to wish; **¿qué desea?** [en tienda] what can I do for you?; **desearía estar allí** I wish I was there; **estoy deseando que llegue** I can't wait for her to arrive; **dejar mucho/no dejar nada que** ~ to leave much/nothing to be desired. -2. [sexualmente] to desire.

desecar [10] *vt* to dry out.

◆ **desecarse** *vpr* to dry out.

desechable *adj* disposable.

desechar *vt* -1. [tirar - ropa, piezas] to throw out, to discard. -2. [rechazar - ayuda, oferta] to refuse, to turn down. -3. [desestimar - idea] to reject; [- plan, proyecto] to drop. -4. [despreciar] to ignore, to take no notice of.

desecho *m* -1. [objeto usado] unwanted object; [ropa] castoff; **material de** ~ [gen] waste products (*pl*); [metal] scrap. -2. [escoria] dregs (*pl*).

◆ **desechos** *mpl* [basura] rubbish (*U*); [residuos] waste products.

desembalar *vt* to unpack.

desembarazar [13] *vt* to clear.

◆ **desembarazarse** *vpr*: ~**se de** to get rid of.

desembarazo *m* ease.

desembarcadero *m* pier, landing stage.

desembarcar [10] ◇ *vt* [pasajeros] to disembark; [mercancías] to unload. ◇ *vi* -1. [de barco, avión] to disembark. -2. *Amer* [de autobús, tren] to get off.

◆ **desembarcarse** *vpr Amer* to get off.

desembarco *m* -1. [de pasajeros] disembarkation. -2. MIL landing.

desembarque *m* [de mercancías] unloading.

desembarrancar [10] *vt* to refloat.

desembocadura *f* [de río] mouth; [de calle] opening.

desembocar [10]

◆ **desembocar en** *vi* -1. [río] to flow into. -2. [calle] to lead onto. -3. [asunto] to lead to, to result in.

desembolsar *vt* to pay out.

desembolso *m* payment; ~ **inicial** down payment.

desembozar [13] *vt* -1. [rostro] to unmask, to uncover. -2. [cañería] to unblock.

desembragar [16] *vi* AUTOM to disengage the clutch, to declutch.

desembrollar *vt fam* [lío, malentendido] to straighten out; [ovillo] to disentangle.

desembuchar ◇ *vt* [suj: ave] to disgorge. ◇ *vi fam fig* to spit it out.

desempacar [10] *vt* to unpack.

desempalmar *vt* to disconnect.

desempañar *vt* [con trapo etc] to wipe the steam off; [electrónicamente] to demist.

desempaquetar *vt* [paquete] to unwrap; [caja] to unpack.

desempatar *vi* to decide the contest; **jugar para** ~ to have a play-off.

desempate *m* final result; **partido de** ~ decider.

desempeñar *vt* -1. [función, misión] to carry out; [cargo, puesto] to hold. -2. [papel] to play. -3. [joyas] to redeem.

◆ **desempeñarse** *vpr* to get oneself out of debt.

desempeño *m* -1. [de función] carrying out. -2. [de papel] performance. -3. [de objeto] redemption.

desempleado, -da ◇ *adj* unemployed. ◇ *m y f* unemployed person.

desempleo *m* unemployment.

desempolvar *vt* -1. [mueble, jarrón] to dust. -2. *fig* [recuerdos] to revive.

desenamorarse *vpr*: ~ **(de)** to fall out of love (with).

desencadenar ◇ *vt* -1. [preso, perro] to unchain. -2. *fig* [suceso, polémica] to give rise to, to spark off; [pasión, furia] to unleash.

◆ **desencadenarse** *vpr* -1. [pasiones, odios, conflicto] to erupt; [guerra] to break out. -2. [viento] to blow up; [tormenta] to burst; [terremoto] to strike.

desencajar *vt* -1. [mecanismo, piezas - sin querer] to knock out of place; [- intencionadamente] to take apart. -2. [hueso] to dislocate.

◆ **desencajarse** *vpr* -1. [piezas] to come apart. -2. [rostro] to distort, to become distorted.

desencajonar *vt* to take out of a box.

desencantar *vt* -1. [decepcionar] to disappoint. -2. [romper el hechizo] to disenchant.

◆ **desencantarse** *vpr* to be disappointed.

desencanto *m* disappointment.

desencapotarse *vpr* to clear.

desenchufar *vt* [quitar el enchufe] to unplug ; [apagar] to switch off.

desenfadado, -da *adj* [persona, conducta] relaxed, easy-going; [comedia, programa de TV] light-hearted; [estilo] light; [en el vestir] casual.

desenfadar *vt* to pacify, to appease.

desenfado *m* [seguridad en sí mismo] self-assurance; [desenvoltura] ease; [desparpajo] forwardness, uninhibited nature.

desenfocado, -da *adj* [imagen] out of focus; [visión] blurred.

desenfocar [10] *vt* [objeto] to focus incorrectly; [foto] to take out of focus.

desenfrenado, -da *adj* [ritmo, baile] frantic, frenzied; [comportamiento] uncontrolled; [apetito] insatiable.

desenfrenar *vt* [coche] to take the brake off; [caballo] to unbridle.

◆ **desenfrenarse** *vpr* [persona] to lose one's self-control.

desenfreno *m* **-1.** [gen] lack of restraint. **-2.** [vicio] debauchery.

desenfundar *vt* **-1.** [pistola] to draw. **-2.** [mueble] to uncover.

desenganchar *vt* **-1.** [vagón] to uncouple. **-2.** [caballo] to unhitch. **-3.** [pelo, jersey] to free.

◆ **desengancharse** *vpr fam* [de un vicio] to kick the habit.

desengañado, -da *adj*: ~ **(de)** disillusioned (with).

desengañar *vt* **-1.** [a una persona equivocada]: ~ **a alguien** to reveal the truth to sb. **-2.** [a una persona esperanzada] to disillusion.

◆ **desengañarse** *vpr*: ~**se (de)** to become disillusioned (with); **desengáñate** stop kidding yourself.

desengaño *m* disappointment; **llevarse un** ~ **con alguien** to be disappointed in sb; ~ **amoroso** unhappy affair.

desengarzar [13] *vt* [perlas] to unstring; [diamante] to remove from its setting.

desengrasar *vt* to remove the grease from.

desenlace *m* denouement, ending.

desenlazar [13] *vt* to undo.

desenmarañar *vt* **-1.** [ovillo, pelo] to untangle. **-2.** *fig* [asunto] to sort out; [problema] to resolve.

desenmascarar *vt* [descubrir] to unmask.

desenredar *vt* **-1.** [hilos, pelo] to untangle. **-2.** *fig* [asunto] to sort out; [problema] to resolve.

◆ **desenredarse** *vpr*: ~**se (de algo)** to extricate oneself (from sthg); ~**se el pelo** to unknot one's hair.

desenrollar *vt* [hilo, cinta] to unwind; [persiana] to roll down; [pergamino, papel] to unroll.

desenroscar [10] *vt* to unscrew.

desensillar *vt* to unsaddle.

desentenderse [20] *vpr* to pretend not to hear/know *etc*; ~**se de** to refuse to have anything to do with.

desenterrar [19] *vt* **-1.** [cadáver] to disinter; [tesoro, escultura] to dig up. **-2.** *fig* [recordar]: ~ **algo (de)** to recall ○ revive sthg (from).

desentonar *vi* **-1.** [MÚS - cantante] to sing out of tune; [- instrumento] to be out of tune. **-2.** [color, cortinas, edificio]: ~ **(con)** to clash (with). **-3.** [persona, modales] to be out of place.

desentrañar *vt* to unravel, to figure out.

desentrenado, -da *adj* [bajo de forma] out of training; [falto de práctica] out of practice.

desentrenarse *vpr* [bajar de forma] to get of training.

desentubar *vt fam*: ~ **a alguien** to switch off sb's life-support machine.

desentumecer [30] *vt* to stretch.

◆ **desentumecerse** *vpr* to loosen up.

desenvainar *vt* to draw.

desenvoltura *f* [al moverse, comportarse] ease; [al hablar] fluency.

desenvolver [24] *vt* to unwrap.

◆ **desenvolverse** *vpr* **-1.** [asunto, proceso] to progress; [trama] to unfold; [entrevista] to pass off. **-2.** [persona] to cope, to manage.

desenvuelto, -ta ◇ *pp* → **desenvolver**. ◇ *adj* [al moverse, comportarse] natural; [al hablar] fluent.

desenzarzar [13] *vt* [prenda] to untangle.

deseo *m* **-1.** [pasión] desire; **arder en** ~**s de hacer algo** to be burning with desire to do sthg. **-2.** [anhelo] wish; **buenos** ~**s** good intentions.

deseoso, -sa *adj*: **estar** ~ **de algo/hacer algo** to long for sthg/to do sthg.

deseque *etc* → **desecar**.

desequilibrado, -da ◇ *adj* **-1.** [persona] unbalanced. **-2.** [balanza, eje] off-centre. ◇ *m y f* unbalanced person.

desequilibrar *vt* **-1.** [persona, mente] to unbalance. **-2.** [objeto] to knock off balance.

desequilibrio *m* [mecánico] lack of balance; [mental] mental instability.

deserción *f* desertion.

desertar *vi* to desert.

desértico, -ca *adj* [del desierto] desert (*antes de sust*); [despoblado] deserted.

desertificación *f* desertification.

desertización *f* [del terreno] desertification; [de la población] depopulation.

desertor, -ra *m y f* deserter.

desescolarización *f* lack of schooling.

desesperación *f* -1. [falta de esperanza] despair, desperation; **con ~** in despair. -2. *fig* [enojo]: **es una ~ lo lento que van los trenes** it's maddening how slowly the trains go.

desesperado, -da *adj* [persona, intento] desperate; [estado, situación] hopeless; [esfuerzo] furious; **(hacer algo) a la desesperada** (to do sthg) in desperation.

desesperante *adj* infuriating.

desesperanzar [13] ◇ *vt* to cause to lose hope. ◇ *vi*: **~ de hacer algo** to have lost all hope of doing sthg.

◆ **desesperanzarse** *vpr* to lose hope.

desesperar *vt* ◇ -1. [quitar la esperanza] to drive to despair. ◇ -2. [irritar, enojar] to exasperate, to drive mad.

◆ **desesperarse** *vpr* -1. [perder la esperanza] to be driven to despair. -2. [irritarse, enojarse] to get mad ◇ exasperated.

desestabilizar [13] *vt* to destabilize.

desestimar *vt* -1. [rechazar] to turn down. -2. [despreciar] to turn one's nose up at.

desfachatez *f fam* cheek.

desfalcar [10] *vt* to embezzle.

desfalco *m* embezzlement.

desfallecer [30] *vi* -1. [debilitarse] to be exhausted; **~ de** to feel faint from. -2. [desmayarse] to faint.

desfallecimiento *m* -1. [desmayo] fainting fit. -2. [debilidad] faintness.

desfasado, -da *adj* [persona] out of touch; [libro, moda] out of date.

desfasar *vt* ELECTR to phase out; **estar desfasado** *fig* to be out of touch.

desfase *m* [diferencia] gap.

desfavorable *adj* unfavourable.

desfavorecer [30] *vt* -1. [perjudicar] to go against the interest of. -2. [sentar mal] not to suit.

desfiguración *f* [de rostro, cuerpo] disfigurement; [de la verdad] distortion.

desfigurar *vt* -1. [rostro, cuerpo] to disfigure. -2. *fig* [la verdad] to distort.

desfiladero *m* narrow mountain pass.

desfilar *vi* -1. MIL to parade. -2. *fig* [marcharse] to head off, to leave.

desfile *m* MIL parade; [de carrozas] procession; **~ de modelos** fashion show.

desflorar *vt* to deflower.

desfogar [16] *vt* to vent.

◆ **desfogarse** *vpr* to let off steam.

desfogue *m* letting off of steam.

desfondar *vt* -1. [caja, bolsa] to knock the bottom out of. -2. [agotar] to wear out.

◆ **desfondarse** *vpr* [persona] to become completely exhausted.

desforestación *f* deforestation.

desforestar *vt* to deforest.

desgajar *vt* [página] to tear out; [rama] to break off; [libro, periódico] to rip up; [naranja] to split into segments.

◆ **desgajarse** *vpr* [rama] to break off; [hoja] to fall.

desgana *f* -1. [falta de hambre] lack of appetite. -2. [falta de ánimo] lack of enthusiasm; **con ~** unwillingly, reluctantly.

desganado, -da *adj* -1. [sin apetito]: **estar ~** to be off one's food. -2. [sin ganas] listless, apathetic.

desgañitarse *vpr* to scream oneself hoarse.

desgarbado, -da *adj* clumsy, ungainly.

desgarrador, -ra *adj* harrowing.

desgarrar *vt* to rip; **~ el corazón** to break one's heart.

◆ **desgarrarse** *vpr* to rip.

desgarro *m* tear.

desgarrón *m* big tear.

desgastar *vt* to wear out.

◆ **desgastarse** *vpr* to wear oneself out.

desgaste *m* -1. [de tela, muebles etc] wear and tear; [de roca] erosion; [de pilas] running down; [de cuerdas] fraying; [de metal] corrosion. -2. [de persona] wear and tear; [de dirigentes] losing of one's touch.

desglosar *vt* to break down.

desglose *m* breakdown.

desgobernar [19] *vt* [país] to govern badly.

desgobierno *m* [de país] misgovernment, misrule.

desgracia *f* -1. [mala suerte] misfortune; **por ~** unfortunately. -2. [catástrofe] disaster; **~s personales** casualties; **es una ~ que ...** it's a terrible shame that .... -3. *loc*: **caer en ~** to fall into disgrace.

desgraciadamente *adv* unfortunately.

desgraciado, -da ◇ *adj* -1. [gen] unfortunate. -2. [sin suerte] unlucky. -3. [infeliz] unhappy. ◇ *m y f* -1. [persona sin suerte] born loser. -2. *fig* [pobre infeliz] miserable wretch.

desgraciar [8] *vt* -1. [cosa] to spoil. -2. [persona - deshonrar] to demean; [- herir] to injure seriously.

◆ **desgraciarse** *vpr* [plan, proyecto] to be a complete disaster, to fall through.

desgranar *vt* **-1.** [insultos, frases, oraciones] to spout, to come out with. **-2.** [maíz, trigo] to thresh.

desgravable *adj* tax-deductible.

desgravación *f* deduction; ~ fiscal tax deduction, tax relief (U).

desgravar *vt* to deduct from one's tax bill.

desgreñado, -da *adj* dishevelled.

desguace *m* [de coches] scrapping; [de buques] breaking.

desguarnecer [30] *vt* **-1.** [quitar los adornos] to strip. **-2.** MIL to leave unprotected o without troops.

desguazar [13] *vt* [coche] to scrap; [buque] to break up.

deshabillé *m* negligée.

deshabitado, -da *adj* uninhabited.

deshabitar *vt* **-1.** [casa] to leave. **-2.** [territorio] to depopulate, to empty of people.

deshabituar [6] *vt*: ~ a alguien (de) to get sb out of the habit (of).

◆ **deshabituarse** *vpr*: ~se (de) to break the habit (of).

deshacer [60] *vt* **-1.** [costura, nudo, paquete] to undo; [maleta] to unpack; [tarta, castillo de arena] to destroy. **-2.** [disolver - helado, mantequilla] to melt; [- pastilla, terrón de azúcar] to dissolve. **-3.** [despedazar - libro] to tear up; [- res, carne] to cut up. **-4.** [poner fin a - contrato, negocio] to cancel; [- pacto, tratado] to break; [- plan, intriga] to foil; [- organización] to dissolve. **-5.** [destruir - enemigo] to rout; [- matrimonio] to ruin. **-6.** *fig* [afligir] to devastate.

◆ **deshacerse** *vpr* **-1.** [desvanecerse] to disappear. **-2.** [afligirse] to be devastated. **-3.** *fig* [librarse]: ~se de to get rid of. **-4.** *fig*: ~se en algo (con o hacia alguien) [cumplidos] to lavish sthg (on sb); [insultos] to heap sthg (on sb). **-5.** *fig*: ~se por alguien [desvivirse] to bend over backwards for sb; [estar enamorado] to be madly in love with sb.

desharrapado, -da ◇ *adj* ragged. ◇ *m y f* person dressed in rags.

deshecho, -cha ◇ *pp* → deshacer. ◇ *adj* **-1.** [costura, nudo, paquete] undone; [cama] unmade; [maleta] unpacked. **-2.** [enemigo] destroyed; [tarta, matrimonio] ruined. **-3.** [derretido - pastilla, terrón de azúcar] dissolved; [- helado, mantequilla] melted. **-4.** [anulado - contrato, negocio] cancelled; [- pacto, tratado] broken; [- plan, intriga] foiled; [- organización] dissolved. **-5.** [afligido] devastated. **-6.** [cansado] tired out.

deshelar [19] *vt* [nieve, lago, hielo] to thaw, to melt; [parabrisas] to de-ice.

◆ **deshelarse** *vpr* to thaw, to melt.

desheredado, -da ◇ *adj* [excluido de herencia] disinherited; *fig* [indigente] underprivileged. ◇ *m y f* [indigente] deprived person; los ~s the underprivileged.

desheredar *vt* to disinherit.

deshice *etc* → deshacer.

deshidratación *f* dehydration.

deshidratante ◇ *adj* dehydrating. ◇ *m* dehydrating agent.

deshidratar *vt* to dehydrate.

◆ **deshidratarse** *vpr* to become dehydrated.

deshiela *etc* → deshelar.

deshielo *m* thaw.

deshilachar *vt* to unravel.

◆ **deshilacharse** *vpr* to fray.

deshilar *vt* to unravel.

deshilvanado, -da *adj* **-1.** [tela] untacked. **-2.** *fig* [discurso, guión] disjointed.

deshilvanar *vt* to untack.

deshinchar *vt* **-1.** [globo, rueda] to let down, to deflate. **-2.** [hinchazón] to reduce the swelling in.

◆ **deshincharse** *vpr* **-1.** [globo, hinchazón] to go down; [neumático] to go flat. **-2.** *fig* [desanimarse] to get off one's high horse.

deshizo → deshacer.

deshojar *vt* [árbol] to strip the leaves off; [flor] to pull the petals off; [libro] to pull the pages out of.

◆ **deshojarse** *vpr* [árbol] to shed its leaves; [flor] to drop its petals.

deshollinar *vt* to sweep.

deshonestidad *f* dishonesty.

deshonesto, -ta *adj* [sin honradez] dishonest; [sin pudor] indecent.

deshonor *m*, **deshonra** *f* dishonour.

deshonrar *vt* to dishonour.

◆ **deshonrarse** *vpr* to be shamed.

deshonroso, -sa *adj* dishonourable, shameful.

deshora

◆ **a deshora, a deshoras** *loc adv* [en momento inoportuno] at a bad time; [en horas poco habituales] at an unearthly hour.

deshuesar *vt* [carne] to bone; [fruto] to stone.

deshumanizar [13] *vt* to dehumanize.

◆ **deshumanizarse** *vpr* to become dehumanized, to lose one's humanity.

desiderátum *m inv* greatest wish.

desidia *f* [en el trabajo] neglect; [en el aspecto] slovenliness.

desidioso, -sa *adj* [en el trabajo] neglectful; [en el aspecto] slovenly.

desierto, -ta *adj* **-1.** [gen] deserted. **-2.** [vacante - concurso] void; [- premio] deferred.
◆ **desierto** *m* desert; **el ~ de Gobi** the Gobi Desert; **es como predicar en el ~** it's like talking to a brick wall.

designación *f* **-1.** [nombre] designation. **-2.** [nombramiento] appointment.

designar *vt* **-1.** [nombrar] to appoint. **-2.** [fijar, determinar] to name, to fix.

designio *m* intention, plan.

desigual *adj* **-1.** [diferente] different; [terreno] uneven. **-2.** [tiempo, persona, humor] changeable; [alumno, actuación] inconsistent; [lucha] unevenly matched, unequal; [tratamiento] unfair, unequal.

desigualdad *f* [gen] inequality; [diferencia] difference; [del terreno] roughness; [de carácter] changeability; [de actuación, rendimiento] inconsistency.

desilusión *f* disappointment, disillusionment (*U*); **llevarse una ~** to be disappointed.

desilusionar *vt* [desengañar] to reveal the truth to; [decepcionar] to disappoint, to disillusion.
◆ **desilusionarse** *vpr* [decepcionarse] to be disappointed ○ disillusioned; [desengañarse] to realize the truth.

desincrustar *vt* to descale.

desinencia *f* ending.

desinfección *f* disinfection.

desinfectante ◇ *adj* disinfectant (*antes de sust*). ◇ *m* disinfectant.

desinfectar *vt* to disinfect.

desinflamar *vt* to reduce the inflammation in.
◆ **desinflamarse** *vpr* to become less inflamed.

desinflar *vt* **-1.** [quitar aire] to let down, to deflate. **-2.** *fig* [quitar importancia] to play down. **-3.** [desanimar] to depress.
◆ **desinflarse** *vpr* **-1.** [perder aire - gen] to go down; [- neumático] to go flat. **-2.** [desanimarse] to get depressed.

desinformación *f* misinformation.

desinformar *vi* to misinform.

desintegración *f* **-1.** [de objetos] disintegration; **~ nuclear** nuclear fission. **-2.** [de grupos, organizaciones] breaking up.

desintegrar *vt* **-1.** [objetos] to disintegrate; [átomo] to split. **-2.** [grupos, organizaciones] to break up.
◆ **desintegrarse** *vpr* **-1.** [objetos] to disintegrate. **-2.** [grupos, organizaciones] to break up.

desinterés *m* **-1.** [indiferencia] disinterest, lack of interest. **-2.** [generosidad] unselfishness.

desinteresado, -da *adj* unselfish.

desinteresarse *vpr*: **~ de ○ por algo** to lose interest in sthg.

desintoxicación *f* detoxification.

desintoxicar [10] *vt* to detoxify.
◆ **desintoxicarse** *vpr* to detoxify oneself.

desistir *vi*: **~ (de hacer algo)** to give up ○ to stop (doing sthg).

desleal *adj*: **~ (con)** disloyal (to); [competencia] unfair.

deslealtad *f* disloyalty.

desleír [28] *vt* [sólido] to dissolve; [líquido] to dilute.

deslenguado, -da *adj fig* foul-mouthed.

deslía → **desleír**.

desliar [9] *vt* to unwrap.

deslíe *etc* → **desleír**.

desligar [16] *vt* **-1.** [desatar] to untie. **-2.** *fig* [separar]: **~ algo (de)** to separate sthg (from).
◆ **desligarse** *vpr* **-1.** [desatarse] to untie oneself. **-2.** *fig* [separarse]: **~se de** to become separated from; **~se de un grupo** to distance o.s. from a group.

deslindar *vt* **-1.** [limitar] to mark out (the boundaries of). **-2.** *fig* [separar] to define.

deslió → **desleír**.

desliz *m* slip, error; **tener ○ cometer un ~** to slip up.

deslizante *adj* slippery.

deslizar [13] *vt* **-1.** [mano, objeto]: **~ algo en** to slip sthg into; **~ algo por algo** to slide sthg along sthg. **-2.** [indirecta, comentario] to let slip in.
◆ **deslizarse** *vpr* **-1.** [resbalar]: **~se por** to slide along. **-2.** [introducirse]: **~se en** [persona] to slip into; [error] to creep into. **-3.** [tiempo] to slip away ○ by.

deslomar *vt* [a golpes] to thrash.
◆ **deslomarse** *vpr fam* to break one's back, to wear oneself out.

deslucido, -da *adj* **-1.** [sin brillo] faded; [plata] tarnished. **-2.** [sin gracia - acto, ceremonia] dull; [- actuación] lacklustre, uninspired.

deslucir [32] *vt* [espectáculo] to spoil, to ruin.

deslumbrante *adj* dazzling.

deslumbrar *vt lit & fig* to dazzle.

deslustrar *vt* [zapatos etc] to take the shine off.

desmadejar *vt* to wear ○ tire out.

desmadrarse *vpr fam* to go wild.

desmadre *m fam* chaos, utter confusion.

desmán *m* **-1.** [con la bebida, comida etc] exceso. **-2.** [abuso de poder] abuse (of power).

desmandado, -da *adj* [desobediente] unruly.

desmandarse *vpr* **-1.** [desobedecer] to be disobedient. **-2.** [insubordinarse] to get out of hand.

desmano
◆ **a desmano** *loc adv* [fuera de alcance] out of reach; [fuera del camino seguido] out of the way.

desmantelado, -da *adj* dismantled.

desmantelamiento *m* [de casa, fábrica] stripping; [de organización] disbanding; [de arsenal, andamiaje] dismantling; [de barco] unrigging.

desmantelar *vt* [casa, fábrica] to clear out, to strip; [organización] to disband; [arsenal, andamio] to dismantle; [barco] to unrig.

desmaquillador, -ra *adj* cleansing.
◆ **desmaquillador** *m* make-up remover.

desmaquillar *vt* to remove the make-up from.
◆ **desmaquillarse** *vpr* to take one's make-up off.

desmarcar [10] *vt* DEP to draw the marker away from.
◆ **desmarcarse** *vpr* DEP to lose one's marker.

desmayado, -da *adj* **-1.** [persona] unconscious; **caer ~** to faint. **-2.** [color] pale.

desmayar *vi* to lose heart.
◆ **desmayarse** *vpr* to faint.

desmayo *m* **-1.** [físico] fainting fit; **sufrir ~** to have fainting fits. **-2.** [moral] loss of heart; **sin ~** unfalteringly.

desmedido, -da *adj* excessive, disproportionate.

desmedirse [26] *vpr* to go too far, to go over the top.

desmejorar ◇ *vt* to spoil. ◇ *vi* to go downhill, to deteriorate.
◆ **desmejorarse** *vpr* to go downhill, to deteriorate.

desmelenado, -da *adj* **-1.** [persona] reckless, wild. **-2.** [cabello] tousled, dishevelled.

desmelenar *vt* [cabello] to dishevel.
◆ **desmelenarse** *vpr* to go wild.

desmembramiento *m* [de cuerpo] dismemberment; [de miembro, extremidad] loss; [de estados, partidos] breaking up.

desmembrar [19] *vt* **-1.** [trocear - cuerpo] to dismember; [- miembro, extremidad] to cut off. **-2.** [disgregar] to break up.

desmemoriado, -da ◇ *adj* forgetful. ◇ *m y f* forgetful person.

desmentido *m* denial.

desmentir [27] *vt* **-1.** [negar] to deny. **-2.** [no corresponder] to belie.

desmenuzar [13] *vt* **-1.** [trocear - pan, pastel, roca] to crumble; [- carne] to chop up; [- papel] to tear up into little pieces. **-2.** *fig* [examinar, analizar] to scrutinize.

desmerecer [30] ◇ *vt* not to deserve, to be unworthy of. ◇ *vi* to lose value; **~ (en algo) de alguien** to be inferior to sb (in sthg).

desmesurado, -da *adj* [excesivo] excessive, disproportionate; [enorme] enormous.

desmida, desmidiera *etc* → **desmedirse**.

desmiembra *etc* → **desmembrar**.

desmienta *etc* → **desmentir**.

desmigajar *vt* to crumble.
◆ **desmigajarse** *vpr* to crumble.

desmilitarizar [13] *vt* to demilitarize.

desmintiera *etc* → **desmentir**.

desmitificar [10] *vt* to demythologize.

desmontable *adj* that can be dismantled; **una librería ~** a self-assembly bookcase.

desmontar ◇ *vt* **-1.** [desarmar - máquina] to take apart o to pieces; [- motor] to strip down; [- piezas] to dismantle; [- rueda] to remove, to take off; [- tienda de campaña] to take down; [- arma] to uncock. **-2.** [jinete - suj: caballo] to unseat; [- suj: persona] to help down. ◇ *vi*: **~ de** [caballo] to dismount from; [moto, bicicleta] to get off; [coche] to get out of.
◆ **desmontarse** *vpr*: **~se de** [caballo] to dismount from; [moto, bicicleta] to get off; [coche] to get out of.

desmonte *m* **-1.** (*gen pl*) [terreno] levelled ground (U). **-2.** [allanamiento] levelling. **-3.** [de bosque] clearing.

desmoralización *f* demoralization.

desmoralizador, -ra *adj* demoralizing.

desmoralizar [13] *vt* to demoralize.
◆ **desmoralizarse** *vpr* to become demoralized.

desmoronamiento *m* [de edificios, rocas, ideales] crumbling; [de imperios] fall.

desmoronar *vt* [edificios, rocas] to cause to crumble.
◆ **desmoronarse** *vpr* **-1.** [edificio, roca, ideales] to crumble. **-2.** *fig* [persona] to be devastated; [imperio] to fall.

desmovilizar [13] *vt* to demobilize.

desnacionalizar [13] *vt* to denationalize, to privatize.

desnatado, -da *adj* skimmed.

desnatar *vt* to skim.

desnaturalizado, -da *adj* **-1.** [sustancia] adulterated; [alcohol] denatured. **-2.** [persona] inhuman.

desnaturalizar [13] *vt* **-1.** [sustancia] to adulterate. **-2.** [persona] to deny the natural rights of.

desnivel *m* **-1.** [cultural, social etc] difference, inequality. **-2.** [del terreno] irregularity, unevenness (*U*).

desnivelar *vt* to make uneven; [balanza] to tip.

◆ **desnivelarse** *vpr* to become uneven.

desnucar [10] *vt* to break the neck of.

◆ **desnucarse** *vpr* to break one's neck.

desnuclearizar [13] *vt* to make nuclear-free.

desnudar *vt* **-1.** [persona] to undress. **-2.** *fig* [cosa] to strip.

◆ **desnudarse** *vpr* to undress, to get undressed.

desnudez *f* [de persona] nakedness, nudity; [de cosa] bareness.

desnudismo *m* nudism.

desnudo, **-da** *adj* **-1.** [persona, cuerpo] naked. **-2.** *fig* [salón, hombro, árbol] bare; [verdad] plain; [paisaje] bare, barren.

◆ **desnudo** *m* nude.

desnutrición *f* malnutrition.

desnutrido, **-da** *adj* undernourished.

desnutrirse *vpr* to suffer from malnutrition.

desobedecer [30] *vt* to disobey.

desobediencia *f* disobedience.

desobediente *adj* disobedient.

desocupado, **-da** *adj* **-1.** [persona - ocioso] free, unoccupied; [- sin empleo] unemployed. **-2.** [lugar] vacant, unoccupied.

desocupar *vt* [edificio] to vacate; [habitación, mesa] to leave.

desodorante *m* deodorant.

desodorizar [13] *vt* to deodorize.

desoír *vt* not to listen to, to take no notice of.

desolación *f* **-1.** [destrucción] desolation. **-2.** [desconsuelo] distress, grief.

desolador, **-ra** *adj* [imagen, espectáculo] desolate; [noticia etc] devastating.

desolar [80] *vt* **-1.** [destruir] to devastate, to lay waste. **-2.** [afligir] to cause anguish to.

◆ **desolarse** *vpr* to be devastated.

desollar [23] *vt* to skin.

desorbitado, **-da** *adj* **-1.** [gen] disproportionate; [precio] exorbitant. **-2.** *loc*: con los ojos ~s pop-eyed.

desorbitar *vt* *fig* [exagerar] to exaggerate, to blow out of proportion.

desorden *m* **-1.** [confusión] disorder, chaos; [falta de orden] mess. **-2.** [disturbio] disturbance. **-3.** [vida desenfrenada] excess.

desordenado, **-da** *adj* **-1.** [habitación, persona] untidy, messy; [documentos, fichas] jumbled (up). **-2.** *fig* [sin regla] chaotic.

desordenar *vt* [habitación, cajón] to mess up; [documentos, fichas] to jumble up; [pelo] to ruffle.

desorganización *f* disorganization.

desorganizar [13] *vt* to disrupt, to disorganize.

desorientación *f* **-1.** [en el espacio] disorientation. **-2.** *fig* [en la mente] confusion.

desorientar *vt* **-1.** [en el espacio] to disorientate, to mislead. **-2.** *fig* [en la mente] to confuse.

◆ **desorientarse** *vpr* to lose one's way ○ bearings.

desovar *vi* [peces, anfibios] to spawn; [insectos] to lay eggs.

desoxirribonucléico → ácido.

despabilado, **-da** *adj* **-1.** [despierto] wide-awake. **-2.** [listo] smart, quick.

despabilar *vt* **-1.** [despertar] to wake up. **-2.** [hacer más avispado] to make streetwise.

◆ **despabilarse** *vpr* **-1.** [despertarse] to wake up. **-2.** [darse prisa] to hurry up.

despachar ◇ *vt* **-1.** [mercancía] to dispatch. **-2.** [en tienda - cliente] to serve; [- entradas, bebidas etc] to sell. **-3.** *fam fig* [terminar - trabajo, discurso] to finish off; [- comida] to polish off. **-4.** [del trabajo]: ~ a alguien (de) to dismiss ○ sack sb (from). **-5.** [asunto, negocio] to settle. **-6.** *Amer* [facturar] to check in. ◇ *vi* **-1.** [sobre un asunto] to do business. **-2.** [en una tienda] to serve.

◆ **despacharse** *vpr* **-1.** [hablar francamente]: ~se con alguien to give sb a piece of one's mind. **-2.** [desembarazarse]: ~se de to get rid of.

despacho *m* **-1.** [oficina] office; [en casa] study. **-2.** [muebles] set of office furniture. **-3.** [comunicación oficial] dispatch. **-4.** [venta] sale; [lugar de venta]: ~ de billetes/localidades ticket/box office.

despachurrar *vt* *fam* to squash.

despacio ◇ *adv* slowly. ◇ *interj*: ¡~! take it easy!

despampanante *adj* stunning.

despanzurrar *vt* *fam* to cause to burst open.

desparejar *vt* to mix up.

desparpajo *m* *fam* forwardness, self-assurance.

desparramar *vt* **-1.** [líquido] to spill; [objetos] to spread, to scatter. **-2.** *fig* [dinero] to squander.

◆ **desparramarse** *vpr* [líquido] to spill; [objetos, personas] to scatter, to spread out.

despatarrarse *vpr* to open one's legs wide.

despavorido, -da *adj* terrified.

despavorir [80] *vt* to terrify.

despecharse *vpr* to get angry.

despecho *m* [rencor, venganza] spite; [desengaño] bitterness; **(hacer algo) por ~** (to do sthg) out of spite.
◆ **a despecho de** *loc prep* in spite of, despite.

despechugarse [16] *vpr fam fig* to bare one's breast.

despectivo, -va *adj* **-1.** [despreciativo] scornful, contemptuous. **-2.** GRAM pejorative.
◆ **despectivo** *m* GRAM pejorative.

despedazar [13] *vt* **-1.** [físicamente] to tear apart. **-2.** *fig* [moralmente] to shatter.

despedida *f* **-1.** [adiós] goodbye, farewell. **-2.** [fiesta] farewell party; **~ de soltero/de soltera** stag/hen party.

despedir [26] *vt* **-1.** [decir adiós] to say goodbye to; **fuimos a ~le a la estación** we went to see him off at the station. **-2.** [echar - de un empleo] to dismiss, to sack; [- de un club] to throw out. **-3.** [lanzar, arrojar] to fling; **salir despedido de/por/hacia algo** to fly out of/through/towards sthg. **-4.** *fig* [difundir, desprender] to give off.
◆ **despedirse** *vpr*: **~se (de)** to say goodbye (to).

despegado, -da *adj fig* cold, detached.

despegar [16] ◇ *vt* to unstick. ◇ *vi* [avión] to take off.
◆ **despegarse** *vpr* **-1.** [etiqueta, pegatina, sello] to come unstuck. **-2.** [alejarse - persona]: **~se de alguien** to break away ○ withdraw from sb.

despego *m* detachment, indifference.

despegue *m* takeoff; **~ económico** economic takeoff.

despeinar *vt* [pelo] to ruffle; **~ a alguien** to mess up sb's hair.
◆ **despeinarse** *vpr* to mess up one's hair.

despejado, -da *adj* **-1.** [tiempo, día] clear. **-2.** *fig* [persona, mente] alert. **-3.** [espacio - ancho] spacious; [- sin estorbos] clear, uncluttered.

despejar *vt* **-1.** [gen] to clear. **-2.** MAT [incógnita] to find.
◆ **despejarse** *vpr* **-1.** [persona - espabilarse] to clear one's head; [- despertarse] to wake o.s. up. **-2.** [tiempo] to clear up; [cielo] to clear.

despeje *m* DEP clearance.

despellejar *vt* **-1.** [animal] to skin. **-2.** *fig* [criticar] to pull to pieces.

despelotarse *vpr fam* **-1.** [desnudarse] to strip. **-2.** [mondarse]: **~ (de risa)** to laugh one's head off.

despelote *m fam* **-1.** [desmadre] chaos (*U*). **-2.** [desnudo] strip.

despenalización *f* decriminalization.

despenalizar [13] *vt* to decriminalize.

despensa *f* larder, pantry.

despeñadero *m* precipice.

despeñar *vt* to throw over a cliff.
◆ **despeñarse** *vpr* to fall over a cliff.

desperdiciar [8] *vt* [tiempo, comida] to waste; [dinero] to squander; [ocasión] to throw away.

desperdicio *m* **-1.** [acción] waste. **-2.** [residuo]: **~s** scraps. **-3.** *loc*: **no tener ~** to be excellent from start to finish.

desperdigar [16] *vt* to scatter, to disperse.
◆ **desperdigarse** *vpr* to scatter.

desperezarse [13] *vpr* to stretch.

desperfecto *m* [deterioro] damage (*U*); [defecto] flaw, imperfection; **sufrir ~s** to get damaged.

despersonalizar [13] *vt* to depersonalize.

despertador *m* alarm clock.

despertar [19] ◇ *vt* **-1.** [persona, animal] to wake (up). **-2.** *fig* [reacción] to arouse. **-3.** *fig* [recuerdo] to revive, to awaken. ◇ *vi* to wake up. ◇ *m* awakening.
◆ **despertarse** *vpr* to wake up.

despiadado, -da *adj* pitiless, merciless.

despida, despidiera *etc* → **despedir**.

despido *m* dismissal, sacking; **~ improcedente** wrongful dismissal.

despiece *m* cutting-up.

despierta *etc* → **despertar**.

despierto, -ta *adj* **-1.** [sin dormir] awake. **-2.** *fig* [espabilado, listo] bright, sharp.

despilfarrar *vt* [dinero] to squander; [electricidad, agua etc] to waste.

despilfarro *m* [de dinero] squandering; [de energía, agua etc] waste.

despintar *vt* to take the paint off.

despiojar *vt* to delouse.

despiole *m Amer fam* rumpus, shindy.

despistado, -da ◇ *adj* absent-minded. ◇ *m y f* scatterbrain.

despistar *vt* **-1.** [dar esquinazo] to throw off the scent. **-2.** *fig* [confundir] to mislead.
◆ **despistarse** *vpr* **-1.** [perderse] to lose one's way, to get lost. **-2.** *fig* [distraerse] to get confused.

despiste *m* **-1.** [distracción] absent-mindedness; [error] mistake, slip. **-2.** [persona]: **Marta es un ~** Marta is very absent-minded.

desplante *m* rude remark.

desplazado, -da *adj fig* [persona] out of place.

desplazamiento *m* **-1.** [viaje] journey; [traslado] move. **-2.** NÁUT displacement.

desplazar [13] *vt* **-1.** [trasladar] to move. **-2.** *fig* [desbancar] to take the place of; ~ **a alguien/algo de** to remove sb/sthg from. **-3.** NÁUT to displace.

◆ **desplazarse** *vpr* [viajar] to travel.

desplegar [35] *vt* **-1.** [tela, periódico, mapa] to unfold; [alas] to spread, to open; [bandera] to unfurl. **-2.** [cualidad] to display. **-3.** MIL to deploy.

despliegue *m* **-1.** [de cualidad] display. **-2.** MIL deployment; ~ **de misiles** missile deployment.

desplomarse *vpr* [gen] to collapse; [techo] to fall in.

desplumar *vt* **-1.** [ave] to pluck. **-2.** *fig* [estafar] to fleece.

despoblación *f* depopulation.

despoblado, -da *adj* unpopulated, deserted.

◆ **despoblado** *m* deserted spot.

despojar *vt*: ~ **a alguien de algo** to strip sb of sthg.

◆ **despojarse** *vpr*: ~**se de algo** [bienes, alimentos] to give sthg up; [abrigo, chandal] to take sthg off.

despojo *m* [acción] stripping, plundering.

◆ **despojos** *mpl* **-1.** [sobras, residuos] leftovers. **-2.** [de animales] offal (*U*). **-3.** [restos mortales] remains.

despolitizar [13] *vt* to depoliticize.

desposar *vt* to marry.

◆ **desposarse** *vpr* to get married, to marry.

desposeer [50] *vt*: ~ **a alguien de** to dispossess sb of.

desposorios *mpl* **-1.** [compromiso] betrothal (*sg*). **-2.** [matrimonio] marriage (*sg*), wedding (*sg*).

déspota *m y f* despot.

despotismo *m* despotism; ~ **ilustrado** enlightened despotism.

despotricar [10] *vi*: ~ **(contra)** to rant on (at).

despreciar [8] *vt* **-1.** [desdeñar] to scorn. **-2.** [rechazar] to spurn.

desprecio *m* scorn, contempt; **hacer un** ~ **a alguien** to snub sb.

desprender *vt* **-1.** [lo que estaba fijo] to remove, to detach. **-2.** [olor, luz] to give off.

◆ **desprenderse** *vpr* **-1.** [caerse, soltarse] to come ○ fall off. **-2.** *fig* [deducirse]: **de sus palabras se desprende que ...** from his

words it is clear ○ it can be seen that .... **-3.** [librarse]: ~**se de** to get rid of. **-4.** [renunciar]: ~**se de algo** to part with sthg, to give sthg up.

desprendido, -da *adj* [generoso] generous.

desprendimiento *m* **-1.** [separación] detachment; ~ **de tierras** landslide; ~ **de retina** detachment of the retina. **-2.** *fig* [generosidad] generosity.

despreocupado, -da ◇ *adj* [libre de preocupaciones] unworried, unconcerned; [en el vestir] casual. ◇ *m y f* [en el vestir] *person who doesn't care too much about his/her appearance*.

despreocuparse

◆ **despreocuparse de** *vpr* **-1.** [asunto] to stop worrying about. **-2.** [persona] to be neglectful of.

desprestigiar [8] *vt* to discredit.

desprestigio *m* discredit.

desprevenido, -da *adj* unprepared; **coger** ○ **pillar** ~ **a alguien** to catch sb unawares, to take sb by surprise.

desproporción *f* disproportion.

desproporcionado, -da *adj* disproportionate.

despropósito *m* stupid remark, nonsense (*U*).

desprovisto, -ta *adj*: ~ **de** lacking in, devoid of.

después *adv* **-1.** [en el tiempo - más tarde] afterwards, later; [- entonces] then; [- justo lo siguiente] next; **poco** ~ soon after; **años** ~ years later; **ellos llegaron** ~ they arrived later; **llamé primero y** ~ **entré** I knocked first and then I went in; **yo voy** ~ it's my turn next. **-2.** [en el espacio] next, after; **¿qué viene** ~? what comes next ○ after?; **hay una farmacia y** ~ **está mi casa** there's a chemist's and then there's my house; **varias manzanas** ~ several blocks further on. **-3.** [en una lista] further down.

◆ **después de** *loc prep* after; **llegó** ~ **de ti** she arrived after you; ~ **de él, nadie lo ha conseguido** since he did it, no one else has; ~ **de hacer algo** after doing sthg.

◆ **después de que** *loc conj* after; ~ **de que amanezca** after dawn; ~ **de que te fueras a la cama** after you went to bed; ~ **de que lo hice** after I did it, after doing it.

◆ **después de todo** *loc adv* after all.

despuntar ◇ *vt* [romper] to break the point off; [desgastar] to blunt. ◇ *vi* **-1.** [brotar - flor, capullo] to bud; [- planta] to sprout. **-2.** *fig* [persona] to excel, to stand out. **-3.** [alba] to break; [día] to dawn.

desquiciar [8] *vt* **-1.** [puerta, ventana] to unhinge. **-2.** *fig* [desequilibrar] to derange, to disturb mentally; [sacar de quicio] to drive mad.

desquitarse *vpr*: ~ (de algo/alguien) to get one's own back (for sthg/on sb).

desquite *m* revenge.

desratizar [13] *vt* to clear of rats.

desriñonarse *vpr* to break one's back.

destacado, -da *adj* -1. [notable - persona] distinguished, prominent; [- acto] outstanding. -2. MIL detached; ~ **en** stationed in.

destacamento *m* detachment.

destacar [10] ◇ *vt* -1. [poner de relieve] to emphasize, to highlight; **cabe** ~ **que** ... it is important to point out that .... -2. MIL to detach, to detail. -3. ARTE to cause to stand out, to highlight. ◇ *vi* [sobresalir] to stand out.
◆ **destacarse** *vpr*: ~se (de/por) to stand out (from/because of).

destajo *m* piecework; **trabajar a** ~ [por trabajo hecho] to do piecework; *fig* [afanosamente] to work flat out.

destapar *vt* -1. [abrir - caja, botella] to open; [olla] to take the lid off; [descorchar] to uncork. -2. [descubrir] to uncover.
◆ **destaparse** *vpr* -1. [desabrigarse] to lose the covers. -2. *fig* [revelarse] to open up.

destape *m* [en revistas] nude photos (*pl*); [en películas, teatro etc] striptease.

destartalado, -da *adj* [viejo, deteriorado] dilapidated; [desordenado] untidy.

destellar *vi* [diamante, ojos] to sparkle; [estrellas] to twinkle.

destello *m* -1. [de luz, brillo] sparkle; [de estrella] twinkle. -2. *fig* [manifestación momentánea] glimmer.

destemplado, -da *adj* -1. [persona] out of sorts, off colour. -2. [instrumento] out of tune. -3. [tiempo, clima] unpleasant. -4. [carácter, actitud] irritable. -5. [voz] sharp.

destemplar *vt* [instrumento] to put out of tune.
◆ **destemplarse** *vpr* -1. [coger frío] to catch a chill. -2. [irritarse] to get upset.

desteñir ◇ *vt* to fade, to bleach. ◇ *vi* to run, not to be colour fast.
◆ **desteñirse** *vpr* to fade.

desternillarse *vpr*: ~ **de risa** to split one's sides laughing ○ with laughter.

desterrar [19] *vt* -1. [persona] to banish, to exile. -2. *fig* [idea] to dismiss. -3. *fig* [costumbre, hábito] to do away with.

destetar *vt* to wean.

destete *m* weaning.

destiempo
◆ **a destiempo** *loc adv* at the wrong time.

destierra *etc* → **desterrar**.

destierro *m* exile; **en el** ~ in exile.

destilación *f* distillation.

destilar ◇ *vt* -1. [agua, petróleo] to distil. -2. [sangre, pus] to ooze. -3. *fig* [cualidad, sentimiento] to exude, to ooze. ◇ *vi* [gotear] to trickle, to drip.

destilería *f* distillery.

destinar *vt* -1. ~ **algo a** ○ **para** [cantidad, edificio] to set sthg aside for; [empleo, cargo] to assign sthg to; [carta] to address sthg to; [medidas, programa, publicación] to aim sthg at. -2. ~ **a alguien a** [cargo, empleo] to appoint sb to; [plaza, lugar] to post sb to.

destinatario, -ria *m y f* addressee.

destino *m* -1. [sino] destiny, fate. -2. [rumbo] destination; **(ir) con** ~ **a** (to be) bound for ○ going to; **un vuelo con** ~ **a** ... a flight to .... -3. [empleo, plaza] position, post. -4. [finalidad] use, function.

destitución *f* dismissal.

destituir [51] *vt* to dismiss.

destornillador *m* screwdriver.

destornillar *vt* to unscrew.

destreza *f* skill, dexterity.

destripar *vt* -1. [sacar las tripas - animal, persona] to disembowel; [- pescado] to gut. -2. *fig* [despanzurrar] to rip open.

destronar *vt* [rey] to dethrone, to depose; *fig* [rival] to unseat, to replace at the top.

destrozar [13] *vt* -1. [físicamente - romper] to smash; [- estropear] to ruin. -2. [moralmente - persona] to shatter, to devastate; [- vida] to ruin.

destrozo *m* damage (*U*); **ocasionar grandes** ~**s** to cause a lot of damage.

destrucción *f* destruction.

destructivo, -va *adj* destructive.

destructor, -ra *adj* destructive.
◆ **destructor** *m* destroyer.

destruir [51] *vt* -1. [gen] to destroy; [casa, argumento] to demolish. -2. [proyecto] to ruin, to wreck; [ilusión] to dash.

desuella *etc* → **desollar**.

desunión *f* -1. [separación] separation. -2. [división, discordia] disunity.

desunir *vt* -1. [separar] to separate. -2. [enemistar - grupos] to divide, to cause a rift between.

desusado, -da *adj* -1. [pasado de moda] old-fashioned, obsolete. -2. [desacostumbrado] unusual.

desuso *m* disuse; **caer en** ~ to become obsolete, to fall into disuse.

desvaído, -da *adj* [color] pale, washed-out; [forma, contorno] blurred; [mirada] vague.

desvalido, -da ◇ *adj* needy, destitute. ◇ *m y f* needy ○ destitute person.

desvalijar *vt* [casa] to burgle; [persona] to rob.

desvalimiento *m* destitution.

desvalorizar [13] *vt* to devalue.

desván *m* attic, loft.

desvanecer [30] *vt* **-1.** [humo, nubes] to dissipate. **-2.** [sospechas, temores] to dispel.

◆ **desvanecerse** *vpr* **-1.** [desmayarse] to faint. **-2.** [disiparse - humo, nubes] to clear, to disappear; [- sonido, sospechas, temores] to fade away.

desvanecimiento *m* [desmayo] fainting fit.

desvariar [9] *vi* [delirar] to be delirious; [decir locuras] to talk nonsense, to rave.

desvarío *m* **-1.** [dicho] raving; [hecho] act of madness. **-2.** [delirio] delirium.

desvelar *vt* **-1.** [quitar el sueño] to keep awake. **-2.** [noticia, secreto etc] to reveal, to tell.

◆ **desvelarse por** *vpr*: ~se por hacer algo to make every effort to do sthg.

desvelo *m* **-1.** [insomnio] sleeplessness, insomnia. **-2.** [esfuerzo] effort.

desvencijado, -da *adj* [silla, mesa] rickety; [camión, coche] battered.

desvencijar *vt* [romper] to break; [desencajar] to cause to come apart.

desventaja *f* disadvantage; **en** ~ at a disadvantage.

desventura *f* misfortune.

desventurado, -da ◇ *adj* unfortunate. ◇ *m y f* poor wretch.

desvergonzado, -da ◇ *adj* shameless, insolent. ◇ *m y f* shameless person.

desvergüenza *f* **-1.** [atrevimiento, frescura] shamelessness. **-2.** [dicho] shameless remark; [hecho] shameless act.

desvestir [26] *vt* to undress.

◆ **desvestirse** *vpr* to undress (o.s.).

desviación *f* **-1.** [de dirección, cauce, norma] deviation. **-2.** [en la carretera] diversion, detour. **-3.** MED: ~ **de columna** slipped disc.

desviacionismo *m* deviationism.

desviar [9] *vt* [río, carretera, tráfico] to divert; [dirección] to change; [golpe] to parry; [pelota, disparo] to deflect; [pregunta] to evade; [conversación] to change the direction of; [mirada, ojos] to avert.

◆ **desviarse** *vpr* **-1.** [cambiar de dirección - conductor] to take a detour; [- avión, barco] to go off course; ~se de to turn off. **-2.** [cambiar]: ~se de [tema] to wander ○ digress from; [propósito, idea] to lose sight of.

desvincular *vt*: ~ **a alguien de** to release ○ discharge sb from.

◆ **desvincularse de** *vpr* to cut oneself off from.

desvío *m* diversion, detour.

desvirgar [16] *vt* to deflower.

desvirtuar [6] *vt* [gen] to detract from; [estropear] to spoil; [verdadero sentido] to distort.

desvista, desvistiera *etc* → **desvestir**.

desvivirse *vpr* [desvelarse]: ~ **(por alguien/algo)** to do everything one can (for sb/sthg); ~ **por hacer algo** to bend over backwards to do sthg.

detalladamente *adv* in (great) detail.

detallado, -da *adj* detailed, thorough.

detallar *vt* [historia, hechos] to detail, to give a rundown of; [cuenta, gastos] to itemize.

detalle *m* **-1.** [gen] detail; **con** ~ in detail; **entrar en** ~s to go into detail. **-2.** [atención] kind gesture ○ thought; **tener un** ~ **con alguien** to be thoughtful ○ considerate to sb.

◆ **al detalle** *loc adv* COM retail.

detallista ◇ *adj* **-1.** [meticuloso] painstaking. **-2.** [atento] thoughtful. ◇ *m y f* COM retailer.

detección *f* detection.

detectar *vt* to detect.

detective *m y f* detective; ~ **privado** private detective.

detector, -ra *adj* detecting (*antes de sust*).

◆ **detector** *m* detector; ~ **de mentiras** / **de incendios** lie/fire detector.

detención *f* **-1.** [arresto] arrest. **-2.** [parada] stopping, holding-up.

detener [72] *vt* **-1.** [arrestar] to arrest. **-2.** [parar] to stop; [retrasar] to hold up. **-3.** [entretener] to keep, to delay.

◆ **detenerse** *vpr* **-1.** [pararse] to stop; ~se a hacer algo to stop to do sthg. **-2.** [demorarse] to hang about, to linger.

detenidamente *adv* carefully, thoroughly.

detenido, -da ◇ *adj* **-1.** [detallado] careful, thorough. **-2.** [arrestado]: **(estar)** ~ (to be) under arrest. ◇ *m y f* prisoner, person under arrest.

detenimiento

◆ **con detenimiento** *loc adv* carefully, thoroughly.

detentar *vt* to hold unlawfully.

detergente *m* detergent.

deteriorar *vt* to damage, to spoil.

◆ **deteriorarse** *vpr fig* [empeorar] to deteriorate, to get worse.

deterioro *m* [daño] damage; [empeoramiento] deterioration.

determinación *f* **-1.** [fijación - de precio etc] settling, fixing. **-2.** [resolución] determination, resolution. **-3.** [decisión]: **tomar una ~** to take a decision.

determinado, -da *adj* **-1.** [concreto] specific; [en particular] particular. **-2.** [resuelto] determined. **-3.** GRAM definite.

determinante ◇ *adj* decisive, determining. ◇ *m* **-1.** GRAM determiner. **-2.** MAT determinant.

determinar *vt* **-1.** [fijar - fecha, precio] to settle, to fix. **-2.** [averiguar] to determine; **~ las causas de la muerte** to establish the cause of death. **-3.** [motivar] to cause, to bring about. **-4.** [decidir] to decide; **~ hacer algo** to decide to do sthg.
◆ **determinarse** *vpr*: **~se a hacer algo** to make up one's mind to do sthg.

determinismo *m* determinism.

detestable *adj* detestable.

detestar *vt* to detest.

detiene → **detener**.

detonación *f* [acción] detonation; [sonido] explosion.

detonador *m* detonator.

detonante ◇ *adj* explosive. ◇ *m* **-1.** [explosivo] explosive. **-2.** *fig* [desencadenante]: **ser el ~ de algo** to spark sthg off.

detonar *vi* to detonate, to explode.

detractor, -ra ◇ *adj*: **~ (de)** disparaging (about). ◇ *m y f* detractor.

detrás *adv* **-1.** [en el espacio] behind; **tus amigos vienen ~** your friends are coming on behind; **el interruptor está ~** the switch is at the back. **-2.** [en el orden] then, afterwards; **Portugal y ~ Puerto Rico** Portugal and then Puerto Rico.
◆ **detrás de** *loc prep* **-1.** [gen] behind. **-2.** [a espaldas de]: **~ de alguien** behind sb's back.
◆ **por detrás** *loc adv* at the back; **hablar de alguien por ~** to talk about sb behind his/her back.

detrimento *m* damage; **en ~ de** to the detriment of.

detrito *m* BIOL detritus.
◆ **detritos** *mpl* [residuos] waste (*U*).

detuviera *etc* → **detener**.

deuda *f* debt; **contraer una ~** to get into debt; **estar en ~ con alguien** *fig* [moral] to be indebted to sb; **~ exterior** ECON foreign debt; **~ pública** ECON national debt *Br*, public debt *Am*.

deudo, -da *m y f* relative, relation.

deudor, -ra ◇ *adj* [saldo] debit (*antes de sust*); [entidad] indebted. ◇ *m y f* debtor.

devaluación *f* devaluation.

devaluar [6] *vt* to devalue.
◆ **devaluarse** *vpr* to go down in value.

devanar *vt* to wind.

devaneos *mpl* **-1.** [distracción] idle pursuits. **-2.** [amoríos] affairs; [coqueteos] flirting (*U*).

devastador, -ra *adj* devastating.

devastar *vt* to devastate.

devengar [16] *vt* [intereses] to yield, to earn; [sueldo] to earn.

devenir [75] ◇ *m* transformation. ◇ *vi* **-1.** [convertirse]: **~ en** to become, to turn into. **-2.** [ocurrir] to come to pass, to happen.

devoción *f*: **~ (por)** devotion (to).

devocionario *m* prayer book.

devolución *f* [gen] return; [de dinero] refund; **~ fiscal** tax rebate ○ refund.

devolver [24] ◇ *vt* **-1.** [restituir]: **~ algo (a)** [coche, dinero etc] to give sthg back (to); [producto defectuoso, carta] to return sthg (to). **-2.** [restablecer, colocar en su sitio]: **~ algo a** to return sthg to. **-3.** [favor, agravio] to pay back for; [visita] to return. **-4.** [vomitar] to bring ○ throw up. ◇ *vi* to throw up.
◆ **devolverse** *vpr Amer* to come back.

devorar *vt lit & fig* to devour; **la culpabilidad le devora** he is consumed with guilt.

devoto, -ta ◇ *adj* **-1.** [piadoso] devout; **ser ~ de** to have a devotion for. **-2.** [admirador]: **~ (de alguien)** devoted (to sb). **-3.** [imagen, templo, lugar] devotional. ◇ *m y f* **-1.** [beato]: **los ~s** the faithful. **-2.** [admirador] devotee.

devuelto, -ta *pp* → **devolver**.

devuelva *etc* → **devolver**.

deyección *f* [GEOL - de una montaña] debris (*U*); [- de un volcán] ejecta (*pl*).
◆ **deyecciones** *fpl* MED stools, faeces.

deyector *m* antiscale device.

dg (*abrev de* **decigramo**) dg.

DGS (*abrev de* **Dirección General de Seguridad**) *f Spanish police headquarters*.

di *etc* **-1.** → **dar. -2.** → **decir**.

día *m* **-1.** [gen] day; **me voy el ~ ocho** I'm going on the eighth; **¿a qué ~ estamos?** what day is it today?; **¿qué tal ~ hace?** what's the weather like today?; **todos los ~s** every day; **el ~ que se entere nos mata** when he finds out, he'll kill us; **~ de deuda** COM pay-by date; **~ de los inocentes** ≃ April Fools' Day; **~ de pago** payday; **~ festivo** (public) holiday; **~ hábil** ○ **laborable** ○ **de trabajo** working day; **~ lectivo** school ○ teaching day; **~ libre** day off; **de ~ en ~** from day to day, day by day; **del ~** fresh; **en su ~** in due course; **hoy (en) ~** nowadays; **todo el (santo) ~** all day long; **el ~ de mañana** in the future; **al ~ siguiente** on the following day; **un ~ sí y otro no** every other day; **menú del ~** today's menu. **-2.**

[luz] daytime, day; **es de ~** it's daytime; **hacer algo de ~** to do sthg in the daytime ○ during the day; **~ y noche** day and night; **en pleno ~, a plena luz del ~** in broad daylight. **-3.** *loc:* **dar el ~ a alguien** to ruin sb's day (for them); **mañana será otro ~** tomorrow is another day; **no pasar los ~s para alguien** not to look one's age; **tener ~s** to have one's good days and one's bad days; **un ~ es un ~** this is a special occasion; **el ~ menos pensado** when you least expect it; **estar/ponerse al ~ (de)** to be/get up to date (with); **poner algo/a alguien al ~** to update sthg/sb; **vivir al ~** to live from hand to mouth.

◆ **días** *mpl* **-1.** [vida] days, life (*sg*). **-2.** [época]: **en mis ~s** in my day; **en aquellos ~s de felicidad** in those happy times.

◆ **buen día** *interj Amer:* **¡buen ~!** good morning!

◆ **buenos días** *interj:* **¡buenos ~s!** [gen] hello!; [por la mañana] good morning!

DÍA DE LOS INOCENTES:
The 'Día de los Inocentes' falls on 28th December; it commemorates the slaughter of innocent children ordered by Herod. Children and adults traditionally play jokes and tricks known as 'inocentadas' on one another

diabetes *f inv* diabetes (*U*).

diabético, -ca *adj, m y f* diabetic.

diablo *m lit* & *fig* devil; **pobre ~** poor devil; **tener el ~ en el cuerpo, ser la piel del ~** to be a little devil; **mandar al ~ a alguien** to send sb packing; **más sabe el ~ por viejo que por ~** experience is what really counts.

◆ **diablos** *fam* ◇ *mpl* [para enfatizar]: **¿dónde/cómo ~s ...?** where/how the hell ...? ◇ *interj:* **¡~s!** damn it!

diablura *f* prank.

diabólico, -ca *adj* **-1.** [del diablo] diabolic. **-2.** *fig* [muy malo, difícil] diabolical.

diácono *m* deacon.

diacronía *f* diachrony.

diacrónico, -ca *adj* diachronic.

diadema *f* [para el pelo] hairband.

diáfano, -na *adj* **-1.** [transparente] transparent, diaphanous. **-2.** *fig* [claro] clear.

diafragma *m* diaphragm.

diagnosis *f inv* diagnosis.

diagnosticar [10] *vt* to diagnose.

diagnóstico *m* diagnosis.

diagonal *adj* & *f* diagonal.

diagrama *m* diagram.

dial *m* dial.

dialectal *adj* dialect (*antes de sust*).

dialecto *m* dialect.

diálisis *f inv* dialysis.

dialogante *adj:* **persona ~** interlocutor.

dialogar [16] *vi:* **~ (con)** [hablar] to have a conversation (with), to talk (to); [negociar] to hold a dialogue ○ talks (with).

diálogo *m* [conversación] conversation; LITER & POLIT dialogue; **~ de besugos** mindless chatter (*U*); **fue un ~ de sordos** nobody listened to anyone else.

diamante *m* [piedra preciosa] diamond.

◆ **diamantes** *mpl* [naipes] diamonds.

diametralmente *adv* diametrically; **~ opuesto a** diametrically opposed to.

diámetro *m* diameter.

diana *f* **-1.** [en blanco de tiro] bull's-eye, bull; **hacer ~** to hit the bull's-eye. **-2.** [en cuartel] reveille; **tocar ~** to sound the reveille.

diantre *interj:* **¡~!** dash it!

diapasón *m* tuning fork.

diapositiva *f* slide, transparency.

diario, -ria *adj* daily; **a ~** every day; **ropa de ~** everyday clothes.

◆ **diario** *m* **-1.** [periódico] newspaper, daily; **~ hablado/televisado** radio/television news (bulletin). **-2.** [relación día a día] diary; **~ de a bordo** logbook; **~ de sesiones** parliamentary report.

diarrea *f* diarrhoea; **tener una ~ mental** *fam* not to be thinking straight.

diástole *f* diastole, dilation of the heart.

diatriba *f* diatribe.

dibujante *m y f* [gen] drawer, sketcher; [de dibujos animados] cartoonist; [de dibujo técnico] draughtsman (*f* draughtswoman).

dibujar *vt* & *vi* to draw, to sketch.

dibujo *m* **-1.** [gen] drawing; **~s animados** cartoons; **~ artístico** art; **~ lineal** technical drawing. **-2.** [de tela, prenda etc] pattern.

dic., dicbre. (*abrev de* **diciembre**) Dec.

dicción *f* diction.

diccionario *m* dictionary.

dice → **decir**.

dicha *f* **-1.** [alegría] joy. **-2.** [suerte] good fortune.

dicharachero, -ra *adj fam* talkative.

dicho, -cha ◇ *pp* → **decir**. ◇ *adj* said, aforementioned; **~s hombres** the said men, these men; **lo ~** what I/we *etc* said; **o mejor ~** or rather; **~ y hecho** no sooner said than done.

◆ **dicho** *m* saying; **del ~ al hecho hay un gran** ○ **mucho trecho** it's easier said than done.

dichoso, **-sa** *adj* **-1.** [feliz] happy; [afortunado] fortunate. **-2.** [para enfatizar - maldito] blessed, confounded.

diciembre *m* December; *ver también* **septiembre**.

dicotomía *f* dichotomy.

dictado *m* dictation; **escribir al** ~ to take dictation.

◆ **dictados** *mpl* [órdenes] dictates.

dictador, **-ra** *m y f* dictator.

dictadura *f* dictatorship; ~ **del proletariado** dictatorship of the proletariat.

dictáfono *m* Dictaphone®.

dictamen *m* [opinión] opinion, judgment; [informe] report.

dictar *vt* **-1.** [texto] to dictate. **-2.** [emitir - sentencia, fallo] to pronounce, to pass; [- ley] to enact; [- decreto] to issue.

dictatorial *adj* dictatorial.

didáctico, **-ca** *adj* didactic.

◆ **didáctica** *f* didactics (*U*).

diecinueve *núm* nineteen; *ver también* **seis**.

diecinueveavo, **-va** *núm* nineteenth; **la diecinueveava parte** a nineteenth.

dieciocho *núm* eighteen; *ver también* **seis**.

dieciochoavo, **-va** *núm* eighteenth; **la dieciochoava parte** an eighteenth.

dieciséis *núm* sixteen; *ver también* **seis**.

dieciseisavo, **-va** *núm* sixteenth; **la dieciseisava parte** a sixteenth.

diecisiete *núm* seventeen; *ver también* **seis**.

diecisieteavo, **-va** *núm* seventeenth; **la diecisieteava parte** a seventeenth.

diente *m* tooth; ~ **de leche** milk tooth; ~ **incisivo** incisor; ~ **molar** molar; **armado hasta los** ~**s** armed to the teeth; **enseñar los** ~**s** to bare one's teeth; **hablar entre** ~**s** to mumble, to mutter; **hincar el** ~ **a algo** to sink one's teeth into sthg; *fig* to get one's teeth into sthg; **ponerle a alguien los** ~**s largos** to turn sb green with envy; **me rechinan los** ~**s** it sets my teeth on edge.

◆ **diente de ajo** *m* clove of garlic.

◆ **diente de león** *m* dandelion.

diera → **dar**.

diéresis *f inv* diaeresis.

dieron *etc* → **dar**.

diesel, **diésel** *adj* diesel.

diestro, **-tra** *adj* [hábil]: ~ **(en)** skilful (at); **a** ~ **y siniestro** *fig* left, right and centre, all over the place.

◆ **diestro** *m* TAUROM matador.

◆ **diestra** *f* right hand; **a la diestra** on the right ○ right-hand side.

dieta *f* MED diet; **estar a** ~ to be on a diet.

◆ **dietas** COM *fpl* expenses.

dietario *m* housekeeping book.

dietético, **-ca** *adj* dietetic, dietary.

◆ **dietética** *f* dietetics (*U*).

dietista *m y f Amer* dietician.

diez ◇ *núm* ten; *ver también* **seis**. ◇ *m* [en la escuela] A, top marks (*pl*).

diezmar *vt* to decimate.

diezmo *m* tithe.

difamación *f* [verbal] slander; [escrita] libel.

difamar *vt* [verbalmente] to slander; [por escrito] to libel.

difamatorio, **-ria** *adj* [declaraciones, críticas] defamatory; [texto, carta, escrito] libellous.

diferencia *f* difference; **a** ~ **de** unlike; **establecer** ○ **hacer una** ~ **entre** to make a distinction between; **limar** ~**s** to settle one's differences.

diferencial ◇ *adj* distinguishing. ◇ *m* MEC differential. ◇ *f* MAT differential.

diferenciar [7] ◇ *vt*: ~ **(de)** to distinguish (from). ◇ *vi*: ~ **(entre)** to distinguish ○ differentiate (between).

◆ **diferenciarse** *vpr* **-1.** [diferir]: ~**se (de/en)** to differ (from/in), to be different (from/in). **-2.** [descollar]: ~**se de** to stand out from.

diferente ◇ *adj*: ~ **(de** ○ **a)** different (from ○ to). ◇ *adv* differently.

diferido

◆ **en diferido** *loc adv* TV recorded.

diferir [27] ◇ *vt* [posponer] to postpone, to put off. ◇ *vi* [diferenciarse] to differ, to be different; ~ **de alguien en algo** to differ from sb in sthg.

difícil *adj* difficult; ~ **de hacer** difficult to do; **es** ~ **que ganen** they are unlikely to win.

dificultad *f* **-1.** [calidad de difícil] difficulty. **-2.** [obstáculo] problem; **poner** ~**es** to raise objections.

◆ **dificultades** *fpl* [problemas] trouble (*U*); **pasar** ~**es** to suffer hardship.

dificultar *vt* [estorbar] to hinder; [obstruir] to obstruct.

dificultoso, **-sa** *adj* hard, fraught with difficulties.

difiera, **difiriera** *etc* → **diferir**.

difteria *f* diphtheria.

difuminar *vt* to blur.

difundir *vt* **-1.** [noticia, doctrina, epidemia] to spread. **-2.** [luz, calor] to diffuse; [emisión radiofónica] to broadcast.

◆ **difundirse** *vpr* **-1.** [noticia, doctrina, epidemia] to spread. **-2.** [luz, calor] to be diffused.

difunto, **-ta** ◇ *adj* [gen] deceased, dead; **el**

~ **Sr. Pérez** the late Mr Pérez. ◇ *m y f*: **el**
~ the deceased.

difusión *f* **-1.** [de cultura, noticia, doctrina]
dissemination. **-2.** [de luz, calor, ondas] diffusion. **-3.** [de programa] broadcasting.

difuso, -sa *adj* [luz] diffuse; [estilo, explica-
ción] wordy.

difusor, -ra ◇ *adj* [medio, agencia] broadcasting. ◇ *m y f* propagator.

diga → **decir.**

digerir [27] *vt* to digest; *fig* [hechos] to assimilate, to take in.

digestión *f* digestion.

digestivo, -va *adj* digestive.
◆ **digestivo** *m* digestive (drink).

digiera, digiriera *etc* → **digerir.**

digital *adj* **-1.** [del dedo] finger (*antes de
sust*). **-2.** INFORM & TECN digital.

digitalización *f* INFORM digitizing.

digitalizar *vt* INFORM to digitize.

dígito *m* digit.

dignarse *vpr*: ~ **a** to deign to.

dignatario, -ria *m y f* dignitary.

dignidad *f* **-1.** [cualidad] dignity. **-2.** [cargo]
office. **-3.** [personalidad] dignitary.

dignificar [10] *vt* to dignify.

digno, -na *adj* **-1.** [noble · actitud, respuesta]
dignified; [- persona] honourable, noble. **-2.**
[merecedor]: ~ **de** worthy of; ~ **de elogio**
praiseworthy; ~ **de mención/de ver** worth
mentioning/seeing. **-3.** [adecuado]: ~ **de** appropriate for, fitting for. **-4.** [decente · sueldo, actuación etc] decent, good.

digo → **decir.**

digresión *f* digression.

dije *adj Amer* nice, pleasant.

dijera *etc* → **decir.**

dilación *f* delay; **sin** ~ without delay, at
once.

dilapidar *vt* to squander, to waste.

dilatación *f* [gen] expansion; [de partes del
cuerpo] dilation.

dilatar *vt* **-1.** [extender] to expand; [partes
del cuerpo] to dilate. **-2.** [prolongar] to prolong. **-3.** [demorar] to delay.
◆ **dilatarse** *vpr* **-1.** [extenderse] to expand;
[partes del cuerpo] to dilate. **-2.** [prolongarse]
to be prolonged, to go on. **-3.** [demorarse]
to be delayed.

dilema *m* dilemma.

diletante *adj, m y f* dilettante.

diligencia *f* **-1.** [esmero, cuidado] diligence.
-2. [prontitud] speed. **-3.** [trámite, gestión]
business (*U*). **-4.** [vehículo] stagecoach.
◆ **diligencias** *fpl* DER proceedings; **instruir**
~**s** to start proceedings.

diligente *adj* diligent.

dilucidar *vt* to elucidate.

diluir [51] *vt* to dilute.
◆ **diluirse** *vpr* to dissolve.

diluviar [8] *v impers* to pour with rain.

diluvio *m lit* & *fig* flood.

diluya, diluyera *etc* → **diluir.**

dimanar
◆ **dimanar de** *vi* [alegría] to emanate
from; [medidas, consecuencias] to arise from.

dimensión *f* dimension; **las dimensiones
de la tragedia** the extent of the tragedy.

diminutivo *m* diminutive.

diminuto, -ta *adj* tiny, minute.

dimisión *f* resignation; **presentar la** ~ to
hand in one's resignation.

dimitir *vi*: ~ **(de)** to resign (from).

dimos → **dar.**

Dinamarca Denmark.

dinámico, -ca *adj* dynamic.
◆ **dinámica** *f* **-1.** [gen] dynamics (*pl*). **-2.**
FÍS dynamics (*U*).

dinamismo *m* dynamism.

dinamita *f* dynamite.

dinamitar *vt* to dynamite.

dinamizar [13] *vt* to speed up.

dinamo, dínamo *f* dynamo.

dinar *m* dinar.

dinastía *f* dynasty.

dinástico, -ca *adj* dynastic.

dineral *m fam* fortune.

dinero *m* money; **andar bien/mal de** ~ to
be well off for/short of money; **una familia
de** ~ a family of means; ~ **circulante** ECON
money in circulation; ~ **de curso legal** legal tender; ~ **en metálico** cash; ~ **negro** ○
sucio illegally obtained money; ~ **contante
(y sonante)** hard cash.

dinosaurio *m* dinosaur.

dintel *m* ARQUIT lintel.

diñar *vt fam*: ~**la** to snuff it.

dio → **dar.**

diócesis *f* diocese.

dioptría *f* dioptre.

dios, -sa *m y f* god (*f* goddess).
◆ **Dios** *m* God; **¡a Dios gracias!** thank
heavens!; **a la buena de Dios** any old how;
¡anda ○ **ve con Dios!** God be with you!;
armar la de Dios es Cristo to raise hell, to
make an almighty racket; **como Dios le da
a entender** as best one can; **como Dios
manda** properly; **Dios dirá** it's in the lap of
the gods; **Dios los cría y ellos se juntan**
proverb birds of a feather flock together
proverb; **Dios mediante, si Dios quiere** God
willing; **¡Dios mío!** good God!, (oh) my

God!; **Dios sabe, sabe Dios** God (alone) knows; **necesitar Dios y ayuda** to have one's work cut out; **¡por Dios!** for God's sake!; **sin encomendarse a Dios ni al diablo** throwing caution to the winds; **¡vaya por Dios!** for Heaven's sake!, honestly!

diplodoco m diplodocus.

diploma m diploma.

diplomacia f -1. [gen] diplomacy. -2. [carrera] diplomatic service.

diplomado, -da ◇ adj qualified. ◇ m y f holder of a diploma.

diplomático, -ca ◇ adj lit & fig diplomatic. ◇ m y f diplomat.

dipsomanía f dipsomania.

diptongo m diphthong.

diputación f -1. [corporación] committee; ~ **permanente** standing committee; ~ **provincial** ≈ county council Br. -2. [cargo] post of member of parliament.

DIPUTACIÓN:

In Spain, the governing and administrative body of each province of an autonomous region is called a 'diputación'. The representatives and president of the 'diputación' are elected by the members of the autonomous parliaments

---

diputado, -da m y f ≈ Member of Parliament, MP Br, representative Am.

dique m -1. [en río] dike; ~ **de contención** dam. -2. [en puerto] dock; ~ **seco** dry dock.

dirá → decir.

dirección f -1. [sentido, rumbo] direction; **calle de** ~ **única** one-way street; **en** ~ **a** towards, in the direction of. -2. [domicilio] address. -3. [mando - de empresa, hospital] management; [- de partido] leadership; [- de colegio] headship; [- de periódico] editorship; [- de una película] direction; [- de una obra de teatro] production; [- de una orquesta] conducting. -4. [junta directiva] management; ~ **comercial** commercial department; ~ **general** head office. -5. [de un vehículo] steering; ~ **asistida** power steering.

◆ **Dirección** f: **Dirección General de Tráfico** traffic department (part of the Ministry of the Interior).

direccional ◇ adj directional. ◇ m Amer AUTOM indicator.

direccionar vt INFORM to address.

directivo, -va ◇ adj managerial. ◇ m y f [jefe] manager.

◆ **directiva** f [junta] board (of directors).

directo, -ta adj -1. [gen] direct. -2. [derecho] straight.

◆ **directo** ◇ m [tren] through train. ◇ adv straight; ~ **a** straight to.

◆ **directa** f AUTOM top gear; **poner** ○ **meter la directa** to go into top gear; fig to really get a move on.

◆ **en directo** loc adv live.

director, -ra m y f -1. [de empresa] director; [de hotel, hospital] manager (f manageress); [de periódico] editor; [de cárcel] governor; ~ **general** general manager. -2. [de obra artística]: ~ **de cine** film director; ~ **de escena** producer, stage manager; ~ **de orquesta** conductor. -3. [de colegio] headmaster (f headmistress). -4. [de tesis, trabajo de investigación] supervisor; ~ **espiritual** father confessor; ~ **técnico** DEP trainer.

directorio m [gen & INFORM] directory; ~ **raíz** root directory.

directriz f GEOM directrix.

◆ **directrices** fpl [normas] guidelines.

diría → decir.

dirigente ◇ adj [en partido] leading; [en empresa] management (antes de sust). ◇ m y f [de partido político] leader; [de empresa] manager.

dirigible m airship.

dirigir [15] vt -1. [conducir - coche, barco] to steer; [- avión] to pilot; fig [- mirada] to direct. -2. [llevar - empresa, hotel, hospital] to manage; [- colegio, cárcel, periódico] to run; [- partido, revuelta] to lead; [- expedición] to head. -3. [película, obra de teatro] to direct; [orquesta] to conduct. -4. [carta, paquete] to address. -5. [guiar - persona] to guide. -6. [dedicar]: ~ **algo a** to aim sthg at.

◆ **dirigirse** vpr -1. [encaminarse]: ~**se a** ○ **hacia** to head for. -2. [hablar]: ~**se a** to address, to speak to. -3. [escribir]: ~**se a** to write to.

dirigismo m state control.

dirija etc → dirigir.

dirimir vt -1. [resolver] to resolve. -2. [disolver] to annul, to dissolve.

discar [10] vt Amer to dial.

discernimiento m discernment.

discernir [21] vt to discern, to distinguish; ~ **algo de algo** to distinguish sthg from sthg.

disciplina f discipline.

disciplinar vt to discipline.

disciplinario, -ria adj disciplinary.

discípulo, -la m y f disciple.

disc-jockey [dis'jokei] m y f disc jockey.

disco m -1. ANAT, ASTRON & GEOM disc. -2. [de música] record; ~ **compacto** compact disc; ~ **de larga duración** LP, long-playing record. -3. [semáforo] (traffic) light. -4. DEP discus. **-5.** INFORM disk; ~ **de arranque/del sistema** startup/system disk; ~ **duro/ flexible** hard/floppy disk; ~ **magnético** magnetic disk; ~ **óptico** optical disk, CD-ROM; ~ **removible/rígido** removable/hard disk; ~ **virtual** virtual disk. **-6.** [del teléfono] dial.

discóbolo *m* discus thrower.

discografía *f* records previously released (*by an artist or group*).

discográfico, -ca *adj* record (*antes de sust*).

díscolo, -la *adj* disobedient, rebellious.

disconforme *adj* in disagreement; **estar ~ con** to disagree with.

disconformidad *f* disagreement.

discontinuidad *f* lack of continuity.

discontinuo, -nua *adj* [esfuerzo] intermittent; [línea] broken, dotted.

discordante *adj* [sonidos] discordant; [opiniones] clashing.

discordar [23] *vi* **-1.** [desentonar - colores. opiniones] to clash; [- instrumentos] to be out of tune. **-2.** [discrepar]: ~ **de alguien (en)** to disagree with sb (on ○ about).

discorde *adj* [colores. opiniones] clashing; MUS discordant.

discordia *f* discord.

discoteca *f* **-1.** [local] disco, discotheque. **-2.** [colección] record collection.

discotequero, -ra ◇ *adj* disco (*antes de sust*). ◇ *m y f* nightclubber.

discreción *f* discretion.

◆ **a discreción** *loc adv* as much as one wants, freely.

discrecional *adj* [gen] optional; [parada] request (*antes de sust*).

discrepancia *f* [diferencia] difference, discrepancy; [desacuerdo] disagreement.

discrepar *vi*: ~ **(de)** [diferenciarse] to differ (from); [disentir] to disagree (with).

discreto, -ta *adj* **-1.** [prudente] discreet. **-2.** [cantidad] moderate, modest. **-3.** [no extravagante] modest. **-4.** [normal - actuación] fair, reasonable.

discriminación *f* discrimination; ~ **racial** racial discrimation.

discriminar *vt* **-1.** [cosa]: ~ **algo de** to discriminate ○ distinguish sthg from. **-2.** [persona, colectividad] to discriminate against.

discriminatorio, -ria *adj* discriminatory.

discuerda *etc* → **discordar**.

disculpa *f* [pretexto] excuse; [excusa, perdón] apology; **dar ~s** to make excuses; **pedir ~s a alguien (por)** to apologize to sb (for).

disculpar *vt* to excuse; ~ **a alguien (de** ○ **por algo)** to forgive sb (for sthg).

◆ **disculparse** *vpr*: ~**se (de** ○ **por algo)** to apologize (for sthg).

discurrir ◇ *vi* **-1.** [pasar - personas] to wander, to walk; [- tiempo, vida, sesión] to go by, to pass; [- río, tráfico] to flow. **-2.** [pensar] to think, to reflect. ◇ *vt* to come up with.

discurso *m* speech.

discusión *f* [conversación] discussion; [pelea] argument.

discutible *adj* debatable.

discutir ◇ *vi* **-1.** [hablar] to discuss. **-2.** [pelear]: ~ **(de)** to argue (about). ◇ *vt* [hablar] to discuss; [contradecir] to dispute.

disecar [10] *vt* [cadáver] to dissect; [animal] to stuff; [planta] to dry.

disección *f* [de cadáver] dissection.

diseminar *vt* [semillas] to scatter; [ideas] to disseminate.

disensión *f* disagreement, dissension.

disentería *f* dysentery.

disentir [27] *vi*: ~ **(de/en)** to disagree (with/on).

diseñador, -ra *m y f* designer; ~ **gráfico** graphic designer.

diseñar *vt* to design.

diseño *m* design; **ropa de ~** designer clothes; ~ **asistido por ordenador** INFORM computer aided design; ~ **gráfico** graphic design.

diseque *etc* → **disecar**.

disertación *f* [oral] lecture, discourse; [escrita] dissertation.

disertar *vi*: ~ **(sobre)** to speak ○ to lecture (on).

disfraz *m* [gen] disguise; [para baile. fiesta etc] fancy dress (*U*).

disfrazar [13] *vt* to disguise; ~ **a alguien de** to dress sb up as.

◆ **disfrazarse** *vpr* to disguise o.s.; ~**se de** to dress up as.

disfrutar ◇ *vi* **-1.** [sentir placer] to enjoy o.s. **-2.** [disponer de]: ~ **de algo** to enjoy sthg. ◇ *vt* to enjoy.

disfrute *m* **-1.** [placer] enjoyment. **-2.** [provecho] benefit, use.

disfunción *f* malfunction.

disgregar [16] *vt* **-1.** [multitud, manifestación] to disperse, to break up. **-2.** [roca, imperio, estado] to break up; [átomo] to split.

◆ **disgregarse** *vpr* **-1.** [multitud, manifestación] to disperse, to break up. **-2.** [roca, imperio, estado] to break up.

disgustar *vt* **-1.** [suj: comentario, críticas, noticia] to upset. **-2.** [suj: mal olor] to disgust.

◆ **disgustarse** *vpr*: ~**se (con alguien/por algo)** [sentir enfado] to get upset (with sb/

about sthg); [enemistarse] to fall out (with sb/over sthg).

disgusto *m* **-1.** [enfado] annoyance; [pesadumbre] sorrow, grief; **dar un ~ a alguien** to upset sb; **llevarse un ~** to be upset; **matar a alguien a ~s** to worry sb to death. **-2.** [desinterés, incomodidad]: **hacer algo a ~** to do sthg unwillingly ○ reluctantly; **estar a ~** to feel uncomfortable ○ uneasy. **-3.** [pelea]: **tener un ~ con alguien** to have a quarrel with sb.

disidencia *f* [política, religiosa] dissidence; [desacuerdo] disagreement.

disidente ◇ *adj* [en política] dissident; [en religión] dissenting. ◇ *m y f* [político] dissident; [religioso] dissenter.

disienta *etc* → **disentir**.

disimulado, -da *adj* hidden, concealed; **hacerse el ~** to pretend not to notice.

disimular ◇ *vt* to hide, to conceal. ◇ *vi* to pretend.

disimulo *m* pretence, concealment; **con ~** furtively.

disintiera *etc* → **disentir**.

disipar *vt* **-1.** [dudas, sospechas] to dispel; [ilusiones] to shatter. **-2.** [fortuna, herencia] to squander, to throw away. **-3.** [niebla, humo, vapor] to drive ○ blow away.
◆ **disiparse** *vpr* **-1.** [dudas, sospechas] to be dispelled; [ilusiones] to be shattered. **-2.** [niebla, humo, vapor] to vanish.

diskette = **disquete**.

dislate *m* nonsense (*U*), absurdity.

dislexia *m* dyslexia.

disléxico, -ca *adj, m y f* dyslexic.

dislocación *f* dislocation.

dislocar [10] *vt* to dislocate.
◆ **dislocarse** *vpr* to dislocate.

disminución *f* decrease, drop.

disminuido, -da ◇ *adj* handicapped. ◇ *m y f* handicapped person.

disminuir [51] ◇ *vt* to reduce, to decrease. ◇ *vi* [gen] to decrease; [precios, temperatura] to drop, to fall; [vista, memoria] to fail; [días] to get shorter; [beneficios] to fall off.

disnea *f* dyspnoea, difficulty in breathing.

disociar [8] *vt*: **~ (de)** to dissociate (from).

disolución *f* **-1.** [en un líquido] dissolving. **-2.** [de matrimonio, sociedad, partido] dissolution. **-3.** [mezcla] solution.

disoluto, -ta ◇ *adj* dissolute. ◇ *m y f* dissolute person.

disolvente *adj & m* solvent.

disolver [24] *vt* **-1.** [gen] to dissolve. **-2.** [reunión, manifestación, familia] to break up.
◆ **disolverse** *vpr* **-1.** [gen] to dissolve. **-2.** [reunión, manifestación, familia] to break up.

dispar *adj* disparate, dissimilar.

disparadero *m*: **poner a alguien en el ~** to push sb too far.

disparado, -da *adj*: **salir/entrar ~** to shoot out/in.

disparador *m* **-1.** [de armas] trigger. **-2.** FOT shutter release.

disparar ◇ *vt* to shoot; [pedrada] to throw. ◇ *vi* to shoot, to fire.
◆ **dispararse** *vpr* **-1.** [arma] to go off. **-2.** [precipitarse - persona] to rush off; [- caballo] to bolt. **-3.** [perder los estribos] to get carried away. **-4.** [precios, inflación] to shoot up.

disparatado, -da *adj* absurd, crazy.

disparatar *vi* [decir tonterías] to talk nonsense; [hacer tonterías] to behave foolishly.

disparate *m* **-1.** [comentario, acción] silly thing; [idea] crazy idea. **-2.** [precio]: **gastar un ~** to spend a ridiculous amount.

disparidad *f* difference, disparity.

disparo *m* shot.

dispendio *m* extravagance, spending on luxuries.

dispensa *f* [de examen] exemption; [para casarse] dispensation.

dispensar *vt* **-1.** [disculpar] to excuse, to forgive. **-2.** [rendir]: **~ algo (a alguien)** [honores] to confer sthg (upon sb); [bienvenida, ayuda] to give sthg (to sb). **-3.** [eximir]: **~ a alguien de** to excuse ○ exempt sb from.

dispensario *m* dispensary.

dispepsia *f* dyspepsia.

dispersar *vt* **-1.** [esparcir - objetos] to scatter. **-2.** [disolver - gentío] to disperse; [- manifestación] to break up; [- esfuerzos] to dissipate.
◆ **dispersarse** *vpr* to scatter.

dispersión *f* **-1.** [de objetos] scattering. **-2.** [de gentío, luz] scattering; [de manifestación] breaking up.

disperso, -sa *adj* scattered.

display [dis'plei] *m* INFORM display.

displicencia *f* **-1.** [desagrado] contempt. **-2.** [negligencia] carelessness; [desgana] lack of enthusiasm.

displicente *adj* **-1.** [desagradable] contemptuous. **-2.** [negligente] careless; [desganado] unenthusiastic.

disponer [65] ◇ *vt* **-1.** [gen] to arrange. **-2.** [cena, comida] to lay on. **-3.** [decidir - suj: persona] to decide; [suj: ley] to stipulate. ◇ *vi* **-1.** [poseer]: **~ de** to have. **-2.** [usar]: **~ de** to make use of.
◆ **disponerse a** *vpr*: **~se a hacer algo** to prepare ○ get ready to do sthg.

disponibilidad *f* **-1.** [gen] availability. **-2.** [a ayudar] readiness to help.

◆ **disponibilidades** *fpl* [medios] financial resources.

disponible *adj* [gen] available; [tiempo] free, spare.

disposición *f* **-1.** [colocación] arrangement, layout. **-2.** [estado]: **estar** ○ **hallarse en** ~ **de hacer algo** to be prepared ○ ready to do sthg. **-3.** [orden] order; [de ley] provision. **-4.** [uso]: **a** ~ **de** at the disposal of. **-5.** *fig* [aptitud] talent.

dispositivo *m* device; ~ **intrauterino** intrauterine device, IUD.

dispuesto, -ta ◇ *pp* → **disponer**. ◇ *adj* **-1.** [preparado] ready; **estar** ~ **a hacer algo** to be prepared to do sthg. **-2.** [capaz] capable; [a ayudar] ready to help.

dispusiera *etc* → **disponer**.

disputa *f* dispute.

disputar *vt* **-1.** [cuestión, tema] to argue about. **-2.** [trofeo, puesto] to compete for, to dispute; [carrera, partido] to compete in.

disquete, diskette [dis'kete] *m* INFORM diskette, floppy disk.

disquetera *f* INFORM disk drive.

disquisición *f* [exposición] disquisition.

◆ **disquisiciones** *fpl* [digresión] digressions.

distancia *f* **-1.** [gen] distance; **a** ~ from a distance; **mantener a** ~ to keep at a distance. ~ **de seguridad** safe distance. **-2.** [en el tiempo] gap, space. **-3.** [diferencia] difference. **-4.** *loc*: **acortar las** ~s to come closer (to an agreement); **guardar las** ~s to keep one's distance; **salvando las** ~s only up to a point.

distanciamiento *m* [afectivo] distance, coldness.

distanciar [8] *vt* [gen] to drive apart; [rival] to forge ahead of.

◆ **distanciarse** *vpr* [alejarse - afectivamente] to grow apart; [- físicamente] to distance o.s.

distante *adj* **-1.** [en el espacio]: ~ **(de)** far away (from). **-2.** [en el trato] distant.

distar *vi* **-1.** [hallarse a]: **ese sitio dista varios kilómetros de aquí** that place is several kilometres away from here. **-2.** *fig* [diferenciarse]: ~ **de** to be far from.

diste *etc* → **dar**.

distender [20] *vt* [situación, relaciones] to ease; [cuerda] to slacken.

distendido, -da *adj* [informal] relaxed, informal.

distensión *f* **-1.** [entre países] détente; [entre personas] easing of tension. **-2.** [de arco, cuerda] slackening. **-3.** MED strain.

distienda *etc* → **distender**.

distinción *f* **-1.** [diferencia] distinction; **a** ~ **de** in contrast to, unlike; **sin** ~ alike; **hacer distinciones** not to treat everyone the same. **-2.** [privilegio] privilege. **-3.** [modales] refinement.

distinguido, -da *adj* **-1.** [notable] distinguished. **-2.** [elegante] refined.

distinguir [17] *vt* **-1.** [diferenciar] to distinguish; ~ **algo de algo** to tell sthg from sthg. **-2.** [separar] to pick out. **-3.** [caracterizar] to characterize. **-4.** [premiar] to honour. **-5.** [vislumbrar] to make out.

◆ **distinguirse** *vpr* **-1.** [destacarse] to stand out. **-2.** [vislumbrarse] to be visible.

distintivo, -va *adj* distinctive; [señal] distinguishing.

◆ **distintivo** *m* badge.

distinto, -ta *adj* [diferente] different.

◆ **distintos, -tas** *adj pl* [varios] various.

distorsión *f* [de tobillo, rodilla] sprain; [de imágenes, sonidos, palabras] distortion.

distorsionar *vt* to distort.

distracción *f* **-1.** [entretenimiento] entertainment; [pasatiempo] hobby, pastime. **-2.** [despiste] slip; [falta de atención] absentmindedness.

distraer [73] *vt* **-1.** [divertir] to amuse, to entertain. **-2.** [despistar] to distract.

◆ **distraerse** *vpr* **-1.** [divertirse] to enjoy o.s.; [pasar el tiempo] to pass the time. **-2.** [despistarse] to let one's mind wander.

distraído, -da ◇ *adj* **-1.** [entretenido] amusing, entertaining. **-2.** [despistado] absentminded. ◇ *m y f* daydreamer, absentminded person.

distribución *f* **-1.** [gen] distribution; ~ **de premios** prizegiving. **-2.** [de correo, mercancías] delivery; ~ **comercial** commercial distribution. **-3.** [de casa, habitaciones] layout.

distribuidor, -ra ◇ *adj* [entidad] wholesale; [red] supply (*antes de sust*). ◇ *m y f* [persona] deliveryman (*f* deliverywoman).

◆ **distribuidor** *m* [aparato] vending machine.

◆ **distribuidora** *f* [firma] wholesaler, supplier.

distribuir [51] *vt* **-1.** [gen] to distribute; [carga, trabajo] to spread; [pastel, ganancias] to divide up. **-2.** [correo, mercancías] to deliver. **-3.** [casa, habitaciones] to arrange.

distributivo, -va *adj* distributive.

distrito *m* district; ~ **electoral** constituency; ~ **postal** postal district.

disturbio *m* disturbance; [violento] riot.

disuadir *vt*: ~ **(de)** to dissuade (from).

disuasión *f* deterrence.

disuasivo, -va *adj* deterrent.

disuelto, **-ta** *pp* → disolver.

disuelva *etc* → disolver.

disyuntivo, **-va** *adj* GRAM disjunctive.

◆ **disyuntiva** *f* straight choice.

DIU (*abrev de* **dispositivo intrauterino**) *m* IUD.

diurético, **-ca** *adj & m* diuretic.

diurno, **-na** *adj* [gen] daytime (*antes de sust*); [planta, animal] diurnal.

diva → divo.

divagación *f* digression.

divagar [16] *vi* to digress.

diván *m* divan; [de psiquiatra] couch.

divergencia *f* **-1.** [de líneas] divergence. **-2.** [de opinión] difference of opinion.

divergir [15] *vi* **-1.** [calles, líneas] to diverge. **-2.** *fig* [opiniones]: ~ **(en)** to differ (on).

diversidad *f* diversity.

diversificación *f* diversification.

diversificar [10] *vt* to diversify.

◆ **diversificarse** *vpr* to grow apart.

diversión *f* entertainment, amusement.

diverso, **-sa** *adj* [diferente] different.

◆ **diversos**, **-sas** *adj pl* [varios] several, various.

divertido, **-da** *adj* [entretenido - película, libro] entertaining; [- fiesta] enjoyable; [que hace reír] funny.

divertimiento *m* entertainment, amusement.

divertir [27] *vt* to entertain, to amuse.

◆ **divertirse** *vpr* to enjoy o.s.

dividendo *m* FIN & MAT dividend; ~ **a cuenta** interim dividend.

dividir *vt*: ~ **(en)** to divide (into); ~ **entre** [gen] to divide between; MAT to divide by.

divierta *etc* → divertir.

divinidad *f* divinity, god.

divino, **-na** *adj* lit & *fig* divine.

divirtiera *etc* → divertir.

divisa *f* **-1.** (*gen pl*) [moneda] foreign currency; ~ **convertible** convertible currency. **-2.** [distintivo] emblem.

divisar *vt* to spy, to make out.

división *f* [gen] division; [partición] splitting up; ~ **del trabajo** ECON division of labour.

divisor *m* MAT divisor; **máximo común** ~ highest common factor.

divisorio, **-ria** *adj* dividing.

divo, **-va** *m y f* **-1.** [MÚS - mujer] diva, prima donna; [- hombre] opera singer. **-2.** [celebridad] star.

divorciado, **-da** ◇ *adj* divorced. ◇ *m y f* divorcé (*f* divorcée).

divorciar [8] *vt* lit & *fig* to divorce.

◆ **divorciarse** *vpr* to get divorced.

divorcio *m* **-1.** DER divorce. **-2.** *fig* [diferencia] difference, inconsistency.

divulgación *f* [de noticia, secreto] revelation; [de rumor] spreading; [de cultura, ciencia, doctrina] popularization.

divulgar [16] *vt* [noticia, secreto] to reveal; [rumor] to spread; [cultura, ciencia, doctrina] to popularize.

dizque *adv Amer* apparently.

dl (*abrev de* **decilitro**) dl.

dm (*abrev de* **decímetro**) dm.

Dm. (*abrev de* **Dios mediante**) DV.

DNI (*abrev de* **documento nacional de identidad**) *m* ID card.

Dña *abrev de* **doña**.

do *m* MÚS C; [en solfeo] doh; **dar el** ~ **de pecho** *fam fig* to give one's all.

doberman *m* Doberman (pinscher).

dobladillo *m* [de traje, vestido] hem; [de pantalón] turn-up *Br*, cuff *Am*.

doblado, **-da** *adj* **-1.** [papel, camisa] folded. **-2.** [voz, película] dubbed.

doblaje *m* dubbing.

doblar ◇ *vt* **-1.** [duplicar] to double. **-2.** [plegar] to fold. **-3.** [torcer] to bend. **-4.** [esquina] to turn, to go round. **-5.** [voz, actor] to dub. ◇ *vi* **-1.** [girar] to turn. **-2.** [campanas] to toll.

◆ **doblarse** *vpr* [someterse]: ~**se a** to give in to.

doble ◇ *adj* double; **tiene** ~ **número de habitantes** it has double O twice the number of inhabitants; **es** ~ **de ancho** it's twice as wide; **una frase de** ~ **sentido** a phrase with a double meaning. ◇ *m y f* [gen & CIN] double. ◇ *m* [duplo]: **el** ~ twice as much; **gana el** ~ **que yo** she earns twice as much as I do, she earns double what I do. ◇ *adv* double; **trabajar** ~ to work twice as hard.

◆ **dobles** *mpl* DEP doubles.

doblegar [16] *vt* [someter] to bend, to cause to give in.

◆ **doblegarse** *vpr*: ~**se (ante)** to give in O yield (to).

doblete *m* [joya] fake, imitation; LING doublet.

doblez ◇ *m* [pliegue] fold, crease. ◇ *m o f* *fig* [falsedad] deceit.

doblón *m* doubloon.

doc. (*abrev de* **documento**) doc.

doce *núm* twelve; *ver también* **seis**.

◆ **Doce** *mpl*: **los Doce** POLÍT the Twelve, *the member states of the EC*.

doceavo, **-va** *núm* twelfth; **la doceava parte** a twelfth.

docena *f* dozen; **a** ~**s** by the dozen.

docencia f teaching.

docente ◇ adj teaching. ◇ m y f teacher.

dócil adj obedient.

docilidad f obedience.

docto, -ta ◇ adj learned. ◇ m y f learned person, scholar.

doctor, -ra m y f: ~ **(en)** doctor (of).

doctorado m doctorate.

doctoral adj doctoral.

doctorar vt to confer a doctorate on.

◆ **doctorarse** vpr: ~**se (en)** to get one's doctorate (in).

doctrina f doctrine.

doctrinal adj doctrinal.

documentación f **-1.** [en archivos] documentation. **-2.** [identificación personal] papers (pl).

documentado, -da adj **-1.** [informado - película, informe] researched; [- persona] informed. **-2.** [con papeles encima] having identification.

documental adj & m documentary.

documentalista m y f archivist.

documentar vt **-1.** [evidenciar] to document. **-2.** [informar] to brief.

◆ **documentarse** vpr to do research.

documento m **-1.** [escrito] document; ~ **nacional de identidad** identity card. **-2.** [testimonio] record.

dodecaedro m dodecahedron.

dodecafonismo m dodecaphonism.

dogma m dogma.

dogmático, -ca adj dogmatic.

dogmatismo m dogmatism.

dogmatizar [13] vi to see everything in a dogmatic way.

dogo m y f bull mastiff.

dólar m dollar.

dolby® m Dolby®.

dolencia f pain.

doler [24] vi to hurt; **me duele la pierna** my leg hurts; **¿te duele?** does it hurt?; **me duele la garganta/la cabeza** I have a sore throat/a headache; **me duele ver tanta injusticia** it pains me to see so much injustice; **¡ahí le duele!** that has really got him/her etc!

◆ **dolerse** vpr: ~**se de** ○ **por algo** [quejarse] to complain about sthg; [arrepentirse] to be sorry about sthg.

dolido, -da adj hurt.

doliente adj [enfermo] ill; [afligido] grieving.

dolmen m dolmen.

dolo m fraud.

dolor m **-1.** [físico] pain; **siento un ~ en el brazo** I have a pain in my arm; **(tener) ~** **de cabeza** (to have a) headache; ~ **de estómago** stomachache; ~ **de muelas** toothache. **-2.** [moral] grief, sorrow.

dolorido, -da adj [físicamente] sore; [moralmente] grieving, sorrowing.

doloroso, -sa adj [físicamente] painful; [moralmente] distressing.

doma f taming; [de caballos] breaking-in.

domador, -ra m y f [de caballos] breaker; [de leones] tamer.

domar vt [gen] to tame; [caballo] to break in; fig [personas] to control.

domesticar [10] vt lit & fig to tame.

doméstico, -ca adj domestic.

domiciliación f: ~ **(bancaria)** standing order, direct debit (U).

domiciliar [8] vt **-1.** [pago] to pay by direct debit ○ standing order. **-2.** [persona] to put up.

domiciliario, -ria adj house (antes de sust).

domicilio m **-1.** [vivienda] residence, home; **servicio a** ~ home delivery; **venta a** ~ door-to-door selling. **-2.** [dirección] address; **sin** ~ **fijo** of no fixed abode; ~ **fiscal** registered office; ~ **social** head office. **-3.** [localidad] residence.

dominación f rule, dominion.

dominador, -ra adj dominating.

dominante ◇ adj **-1.** [nación, religión, tendencia] dominant; [vientos] prevailing. **-2.** [persona] domineering. ◇ f predominant feature.

dominar ◇ vt **-1.** [controlar - país, territorio] to dominate, to rule (over); [- pasión, nervios, caballo] to control; [- situación] to be in control of; [- incendio] to bring under control; [- rebelión] to put down. **-2.** [divisar] to overlook. **-3.** [conocer - técnica, tema] to master; [- lengua] to be fluent in. ◇ vi [predominar] to predominate.

◆ **dominarse** vpr to control o.s.

domingo m Sunday; ~ **de Ramos** Palm Sunday; ~ **de Resurrección** ○ **de Pascua** Easter Sunday; ver también **sábado**.

dominguero, -ra fam despec ◇ adj Sunday (antes de sust). ◇ m y f Sunday tripper/driver etc.

Dominica Dominica.

dominical adj Sunday (antes de sust).

dominicano, -na adj, m y f Dominican.

dominico, -ca adj, m y f Dominican.

dominio m **-1.** [dominación, posesión]: ~ **(sobre)** control (over). **-2.** [autoridad] authority, power. **-3.** fig [territorio] domain; [ámbito] realm. **-4.** [conocimiento - de arte, técnica] mastery; [- de idiomas] command.

-5. *loc*: **ser del ~ público** to be public knowledge.
◆ **dominios** *mpl* [territorio] dominions.

dominó *m* **-1.** [juego] dominoes (*U*). **-2.** [fichas] set of dominoes.

don *m* **-1.** [tratamiento]: **~ Luis García** [gen] Mr Luis García; [en cartas] Luis García Esquire; **~ Luis** *not translated in modern English or translated as "Mr" + surname, if known*. **-2.** [habilidad] gift; **~ de mando** leadership qualities; **el ~ de la palabra** the gift of the gab; **tener ~ de gentes** to have a way with people.

donación *f* donation.

donaire *m* [al expresarse] wit; [al andar etc] grace.

donante *m y f* donor; **~ de sangre** blood donor.

donar *vt* to donate.

donativo *m* donation.

doncel *m* page.

doncella *f* maid.

donde ◇ *adv* where; **el bolso está ~ lo dejaste** the bag is where you left it; **puedes marcharte ~ quieras** you can go wherever you want; **hasta ~** as far as, up to where; **llegaré hasta ~ pueda** I'll get as far as I can; **por ~** wherever; **iré por ~ me manden** I'll go wherever they send me. ◇ *pron* where; **la casa ~ nací** the house where I was born; **la ciudad de ~ viene** the town (where) she comes from, the town from which she comes; **hacia ~** towards where, towards which; **hasta ~** as far as where, as far as which.
◆ **de donde** *loc adv* [de lo cual] from which.

dónde *adv* (*interrogativo*) where; **¿~ está el niño?** where's the child?; **no sé ~ se habrá metido** I don't know where she can be; **¿a ~ vas?** where are you going?; **¿de ~ eres?** where are you from?; **¿hacia ~ vas?** where are you heading?; **¿por ~?** whereabouts?; **¿por ~ se va al teatro?** how do you get to the theatre from here?

dondequiera
◆ **dondequiera que** *adv* wherever.

doña *f*: **~ Luisa García** Mrs Luisa García; **~ Luisa** *not translated in modern English or translated as "Mrs" + surname, if known*.

dopado, -da *adj* having taken performance-enhancing drugs.

dopar *vt* to dope.
◆ **doparse** *vpr* to take artificial stimulants.

doping ['dopiŋ] *m* doping.

doquier
◆ **por doquier** *loc adv* everywhere.

dorado, -da *adj lit* & *fig* golden.
◆ **dorado** *m* [material] gilt.
◆ **dorada** *f* [pez] gilthead.

dorar *vt* **-1.** [cubrir con oro] to gild. **-2.** [alimento] to brown. **-3.** [piel] to turn golden brown.
◆ **dorarse** *vpr* **-1.** [comida] to glaze. **-2.** [piel] to tan.

dórico, -ca *adj* Doric.

dorio, -ria *adj, m y f* Dorian.

dormilón, -ona *fam* ◇ *adj* fond of sleeping. ◇ *m y f* [persona] sleepyhead.
◆ **dormilona** *f Amer* [prenda] nightshirt, nightdress.

dormir [25] ◇ *vt* [niño, animal] to put to bed; **~ la siesta** to have an afternoon nap; **~la** *fam* to sleep it off. ◇ *vi* to sleep.
◆ **dormirse** *vpr* **-1.** [persona] to fall asleep. **-2.** [brazo, mano] to go to sleep. **-3.** *fig* [despistarse] to be slow to react.

dormitar *vi* to doze.

dormitorio *m* **-1.** [de casa] bedroom; [de colegio] dormitory. **-2.** [muebles] bedroom suite.

dorsal ◇ *adj* dorsal. ◇ *m* number (*on player's back*).

dorso *m* back; **al ~, en el ~** on the back; **"véase al ~"** "see overleaf".

dos *núm* two; **de ~ en ~** in twos, two by two; **en un ~ por tres** in no time at all; **cada ~ por tres** every five minutes, continually; *ver también* **seis**.

DOS (*abrev de* **disk operating system**) *m* DOS.

doscientos, -tas *núm* two hundred; *ver también* **seis**.

dosel *m* canopy.

dosificador *m* dispenser.

dosificar [10] *vt* **-1.** FARM & QUÍM to measure out. **-2.** *fig* [fuerzas, palabras] to use sparingly.

dosis *f inv lit* & *fig* dose.

dossier [do'sjer] *m inv* dossier, file.

dotación *f* **-1.** [de dinero, armas, medios] amount granted. **-2.** [personal] staff, personnel; [tripulantes] crew; [patrulla] squad.

dotado, -da *adj* gifted; **~ de** [persona] blessed with; [edificio, instalación, aparato] equipped with.

dotar *vt* **-1.** [proveer]: **~ algo de** to provide sthg with. **-2.** [tripular]: **~ algo de** to man sthg with. **-3.** *fig* [suj: la naturaleza]: **~ a algo/alguien de** to endow sthg/sb with. **-4.** [dar una dote] to give a dowry to.

dote *f* [en boda] dowry.
◆ **dotes** *fpl* [dones] qualities.

doy → **dar**.

Dr. (*abrev de* **doctor**) Dr.

Dra. (*abrev de* **doctora**) Dr.

draconiano, -na *adj fig* draconian.

DRAE (*abrev de* **Diccionario de la Real Academia Española**) *m dictionary of the Spanish Royal Academy.*

draga *f* [máquina] dredge; [barco] dredger.

dragado *m* dredging.

dragaminas *m inv* minesweeper.

dragar [16] *vt* to dredge.

dragón *m* dragon.

drague *etc* → **dragar**.

drama *m* [gen] drama; [obra] play.

dramático, -ca *adj* dramatic.

dramatismo *m* dramatic nature, drama.

dramatizar [13] *vt* to dramatize.

dramaturgo, -ga *m y f* playwright, dramatist.

dramón *m fam* melodrama.

drástico, -ca *adj* drastic.

drenaje *m* drainage.

drenar *vt* to drain.

dribbling ['drißlin] *m* DEP dribbling.

driblar *vt* DEP to dribble.

dril *m* drill.

drive [draif] *m* DEP drive.

droga *f* drug; **la ~** drugs (*pl*); **~ blanda/dura** soft/hard drug.

drogadicción *f* drug addiction.

drogadicto, -ta ◇ *adj* addicted to drugs. ◇ *m y f* drug addict.

drogar [16] *vt* to drug.

◆ **drogarse** *vpr* to take drugs.

drogodependencia *f* drug dependence, drug addiction.

drogue *etc* → **drogar**.

droguería *f shop selling paint, cleaning materials etc.*

droguero, -ra *m y f owner of a shop selling paint, cleaning materials etc.*

dromedario *m* dromedary.

drugstore ['drugstor] *m establishment comprising late-night shop and bar.*

druida, druidesa *m y f* druid (*f* druidess).

dto. *abrev de* **descuento**.

dual *adj* dual.

dualidad *f* duality.

dualismo *m* dualism.

dubitativo, -va *adj* hesitant.

Dublín Dublin.

dublinés, -esa ◇ *adj* of/relating to Dublin. ◇ *m y f* Dubliner.

ducado *m* **-1.** [tierras] duchy. **-2.** [moneda] ducat.

ducal *adj* ducal.

ducha *f* shower; **tomar** ○ **darse una ~** to have ○ take a shower; **una ~ de agua fría** *fam fig* a bucket of cold water.

duchar *vt* to shower.

◆ **ducharse** *vpr* to have a shower.

ducho, -cha *adj*: **ser ~ en** [entendido] to know a lot about; [diestro] to be skilled at.

dúctil *adj* **-1.** [metal] ductile. **-2.** [persona] malleable.

ductilidad *f* **-1.** [de metal] ductility. **-2.** [de persona] malleability.

duda *f* doubt; **poner algo en ~** to call sthg into question; **sacar a alguien de la ~** to remove sb's doubts; **salir de ~s** to set one's mind at rest; **sin ~** doubtless; **tener uno sus ~s** to have one's doubts; **no cabe ~** there is no doubt about it; **no te quepa ~** don't doubt it, make no mistake about it.

dudar ◇ *vi* **-1.** [desconfiar]: **~ de algo/alguien** to have one's doubts about sthg/sb. **-2.** [no estar seguro]: **~ sobre algo** to be unsure about sthg. **-3.** [vacilar] to hesitate; **~ entre hacer una cosa u otra** to be unsure whether to do one thing or another. ◇ *vt* to doubt; **dudo que venga** I doubt whether he'll come.

dudoso, -sa *adj* **-1.** [improbable]: **ser ~ (que)** to be doubtful (whether), to be unlikely (that). **-2.** [vacilante] hesitant, indecisive. **-3.** [sospechoso] questionable, suspect.

duela *etc* → **doler**.

duelo *m* **-1.** [combate] duel. **-2.** [sentimiento] grief, sorrow; **en señal de ~** to show one's grief.

duende *m* **-1.** [personaje] imp, goblin. **-2.** *fig* [encanto] charm.

dueño, -ña *m y f* [gen] owner; [de piso etc] landlord (*f* landlady); **hacerse ~ de algo** to take control of sthg; **ser ~ de sí mismo** to be self-possessed; **ser muy ~ de hacer una cosa** to be free to do sthg.

duerma *etc* → **dormir**.

Duero *m*: **el ~** the Douro.

dueto *m* duet.

dulce ◇ *adj* **-1.** [gen] sweet. **-2.** [agua] fresh. **-3.** [mirada] tender. ◇ *m* [caramelo, postre] sweet; [pastel] cake, pastry; **a nadie le amarga un ~** *fig* anything's better than nothing.

dulcificar [10] *vt* **-1.** [endulzar] to sweeten. **-2.** *fig* [suavizar] to soften.

dulzura *f* **-1.** [gen] sweetness. **-2.** [palabra cariñosa] sweet nothing.

dumping ['dumpin] *m* dumping.

duna *f* dune.

dúo *m* **-1.** MÚS duet. **-2.** [pareja] duo; **a ~** together.

duodécimo, -ma *núm* twelfth.

duodeno *m* duodenum.

dupdo. *abrev de* **duplicado.**

dúplex, duplex *m inv* **-1.** [piso] duplex. **-2.** ELECTRÓN linkup.

duplicado, -da *adj* in duplicate.
◆ **duplicado** *m*: **(por) ~ (in)** duplicate.

duplicar [10] *vt* **-1.** [cantidad] to double. **-2.** [documento] to duplicate.
◆ **duplicarse** *vpr* to double.

duplicidad *f* **-1.** [repetición] duplication. **-2.** [falsedad] duplicity.

duplo, -pla *adj & m* double.

duque, -sa *m y f* duke (*f* duchess).

duración *f* length.

duradero, -ra *adj* [gen] lasting; [ropa, zapatos] hard-wearing.

duralex® *m* resistant glass-like plastic used for making glasses, dishes etc.

durante *prep* during; **le escribí ~ las vacaciones** I wrote to him during the holidays; **estuve escribiendo ~ una hora** I was writing for an hour; **~ toda la semana** all week.

durar *vi* [gen] to last; [permanecer, subsistir] to remain, to stay; [ropa] to wear well; **aún dura la fiesta** the party's still going on.

dureza *f* **-1.** [de objeto, metal etc] hardness. **-2.** [de clima, persona] harshness. **-3.** [callosidad] callus, hard skin (*U*).

durmiente *adj* sleeping; **la Bella Durmiente** Sleeping Beauty.

durmiera *etc* → **dormir.**

duro, -ra *adj* **-1.** [gen] hard; [carne] tough. **-2.** [resistente] tough. **-3.** [palabras, clima] harsh. **-4.** *loc*: **estar a las duras y a las maduras** to be there through thick and thin; [sin quejarse] to take the rough with the smooth; **ser ~ de pelar** to be a hard nut to crack.
◆ **duro** ◇ *m* **-1.** [moneda] five-peseta piece; **estar sin un ~** to be flat broke. **-2.** [persona] tough guy. **-3.** *loc*: **lo que faltaba para el ~** that's all I/we *etc* need. ◇ *adv* hard.

Düsseldorf Dusseldorf.

d/v (*abrev de* **días vista**): **15 ~** within 15 days.

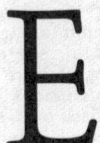

e¹, E *f* [letra] e, E.

e² *conj* (*en lugar de "y" ante palabras que empiecen por "i" o "hi"*) and.

EA (*abrev de* **Eusko Alkartasuna**) *f* Basque nationalist political party.

EAU (*abrev de* **Emiratos Árabes Unidos**) *mpl* UAE.

ebanista *m y f* cabinet-maker.

ebanistería *f* **-1.** [oficio] cabinet-making. **-2.** [taller] cabinet-maker's.

ébano *m* ebony.

ebonita *f* ebonite, vulcanite.

ebrio, ebria *adj* **-1.** [borracho] drunk. **-2.** *fig* [ofuscado]: **~ de** blind with.

Ebro *m*: **el ~** the Ebro.

ebullición *f* boiling.

ebúrneo, -a *adj* ivory.

eccema *m* eczema.

ECG (*abrev de* **electrocardiograma**) *m* ECG.

echar ◇ *vt* **-1.** [tirar] to throw; [red] to cast. **-2.** [meter] to put. **-3.** [añadir]: **~ algo (a ○ en algo)** [vino etc] to pour sthg (into sthg); [sal, azúcar etc] to add sthg (to sthg). **-4.** [decir - discurso] to give; [- reprimenda] to dish out. **-5.** [carta, postal] to post. **-6.** [humo, vapor, chispas] to give off, to emit. **-7.** [hojas, flores] to sprout, to shoot. **-8.** [expulsar]: **~ a alguien (de)** to throw sb out (of). **-9.** [despedir]: **~ a alguien (de)** to sack sb (from). **-10.** [accionar]: **~ la llave/el cerrojo** to lock/bolt the door; **~ el freno** to brake, to put the brakes on. **-11.** [acostar] to lie (down). **-12.** [una condena] to give, to slap on. **-13.** [calcular]: **¿cuántos años le echas?** how old do you reckon he is? **-14.** *fam* [en televisión, cine] to show; **¿qué echan esta noche en la tele?** what's on telly tonight? **-15.** [buenaventura] to tell. **-16.** *loc*: **~ abajo** [edificio] to pull down, to demolish; [gobierno] to bring down; [proyecto] to ruin; **~ a perder** [vestido, alimentos, plan] to ruin; [ocasión] to waste; **~ de menos** to miss.
◇ *vi* **-1.** [dirigirse]: **~ por** to go ○ head along. **-2.** [empezar]: **~ a hacer algo** to begin to do sthg, to start doing sthg; **~ a co-**

rrer to break into a run; ~ **a llorar** to burst into tears; ~ **a reír** to burst out laughing.

◆ **echarse** *vpr* **-1.** [lanzarse]: ~**se a** to throw o.s. ○ jump into. **-2.** [acostarse] to lie down. **-3.** [empezar]: ~**se a hacer algo** to begin to do sthg, to start doing sthg. **-4.** [apartarse]: ~**se a (un lado)** to move (aside); ~**se atrás** *fig* to back out. **-5.** [obtener]: ~**se (un) novio** to get o.s. a boyfriend. **-6.** *loc*: ~**se a perder** [comida] to go off, to spoil; [plan] to fall through.

echarpe *m* shawl.

eclecticismo *m* eclecticism.

ecléctico, -ca *adj, m y f* eclectic.

eclesiástico, -ca *adj* ecclesiastical.

◆ **eclesiástico** *m* clergyman.

eclipsar *vt lit* & *fig* to eclipse.

eclipse *m* eclipse.

eclíptica *f* ecliptic.

eclosión *f culto* emergence.

eco *m* **-1.** [gen] echo; **hacerse ~ de** to report; **tener ~** to arouse interest. **-2.** [rumor] rumour; ~**s de sociedad** society column (*sg*).

ecografía *f* ultrasound scanning.

ecología *f* ecology.

ecológico, -ca *adj* [gen] ecological; [alimentos] organic.

ecologismo *m* Green movement.

ecologista ◇ *adj* environmental, ecological. ◇ *m y f* environmentalist, ecologist.

economato *m* company cooperative shop.

econometría *f* ECON econometrics (*U*).

economía *f* **-1.** [gen] economy; ~ **doméstica** housekeeping; ~ **de libre mercado** free-market economy; ~ **de mercado** market economy; ~ **mixta** mixed economy; ~ **planificada** planned economy; ~ **sumergida** black economy ○ market. **-2.** [estudio] economics (*U*); ~ **aplicada** applied economics; ~ **familiar** home economics; ~ **política** political economy. **-3.** [ahorro] saving.

económico, -ca *adj* **-1.** [problema, doctrina etc] economic. **-2.** [barato] cheap, low-cost. **-3.** [que gasta poco - motor etc] economical; [- persona] thrifty.

economista *m y f* economist.

economizar [13] *vt lit* & *fig* to save.

ecosistema *m* ecosystem.

ecoturismo *m* ecotourism.

ecu (*abrev de* **unidad de cuenta europea**) *m* ecu.

ecuación *f* equation; ~ **de segundo grado** quadratic equation.

ecuador *m* equator.

Ecuador Ecuador.

ecualizador *m* equalizer.

ecuánime *adj* **-1.** [en el ánimo] level-headed, even. **-2.** [en el juicio] impartial.

ecuanimidad *f* **-1.** [del ánimo] equanimity, composure. **-2.** [del juicio] impartiality, fairness.

ecuatorial *adj* equatorial.

ecuatoriano, -na *adj, m y f* Ecuadorian, Ecuadoran.

ecuestre *adj* equestrian.

ecuménico, -ca *adj* ecumenical.

ed. -1. (*abrev de* **editor**) ed. **-2.** (*abrev de* **edición**) edit. **-3.** *abrev de* **editorial**.

edad *f* age; **¿qué ~ tienes?** how old are you?; **tiene 25 años de ~** she's 25 (years old); **una persona de ~** an elderly person; ~ **del juicio** ○ **de la razón** age of reason; ~ **escolar** school age; **Edad Media** Middle Ages (*pl*); ~ **del pavo** awkward age; **Edad de piedra** Stone Age; **la tercera ~** [ancianos] senior citizens (*pl*); **estar en ~ de merecer** to be of marriageable age.

edelweiss ['eðelweis] *m inv* edelweiss.

edema *m* oedema.

edén *m* RELIG Eden; *fig* paradise.

edición *f* **-1.** [acción - IMPRENTA] publication; [- INFORM, RADIO & TV] editing. **-2.** [ejemplares] edition; ~ **extraordinaria/de bolsillo** special/pocket edition; ~ **crítica** critical edition; ~ **pirata** pirate edition. **-3.** [celebración periódica] staging.

edicto *m* edict.

edificación *f* building.

edificante *adj* [conducta] exemplary; [libro, discurso] edifying.

edificar [10] *vt* **-1.** [construir] to build. **-2.** [aleccionar] to edify.

edificio *m* building; ~ **inteligente** intelligent building.

edil *m* (town) councillor.

Edimburgo Edinburgh.

editar *vt* **-1.** [libro, periódico] to publish; [disco] to release. **-2.** INFORM, RADIO & TV to edit.

editor, -ra ◇ *adj* publishing (*antes de sust*). ◇ *m y f* **-1.** [de libro, periódico] publisher. **-2.** RADIO & TV editor.

◆ **editor** *m* INFORM editor; ~ **de textos** text editor.

editorial ◇ *adj* publishing (*antes de sust*). ◇ *m* editorial, leader. ◇ *f* publisher, publishing house.

editorialista *m y f* leader writer.

edredón *m* duvet, eiderdown.

educación *f* **-1.** [enseñanza] education; **escuela de ~ especial** special school; ~ **física/sexual** physical/sex education; ~ **primaria/secundaria** primary/secondary education. **-2.** [modales] good manners (*pl*); ¡qué poca ~! how rude!; **mala** ~ bad manners (*pl*).

EDUCACIÓN PRIMARIA:
In Spain, primary education is compulsory for children between the ages of 6 and 12. Science and arts subjects are both covered

educado, -da *adj* polite, well-mannered; **mal** ~ rude, ill-mannered.

educador, -ra *m y f* teacher.

educar [10] *vt* **-1.** [enseñar] to educate. **-2.** [criar] to bring up. **-3.** [cuerpo, voz, oído] to train.

educativo, -va *adj* [juego, libro, método] educational; [sistema] education (*antes de sust*).

edulcorante ◇ *adj* sweetening (*antes de sust*). ◇ *m* sweetener.

edulcorar *vt* to sweeten.

eduque *etc* → **educar.**

EE (*abrev de* **Euskadiko Ezquerra**) *m* Basque political party to the left of the political spectrum.

EEE (*abrev de* **espacio económico europeo**) *m* EEA.

EE UU (*abrev de* **Estados Unidos**) *mpl* USA.

EFA (*abrev de* **Eurofighter Aircraft**) *m* EFA.

efebo *m culto* ephebe.

efectista *adj* designed for effect, dramatic.

efectivamente *adv* [en respuestas] precisely, exactly.

efectividad *f* effectiveness.

efectivo, -va *adj* **-1.** [útil] effective. **-2.** [real] actual, true; **hacer** ~ [gen] to carry out; [promesa] to keep; [dinero, crédito] to pay; [cheque] to cash.
◆ **efectivo** *m* [dinero] cash; **en** ~ in cash.
◆ **efectivos** *mpl* [personal] forces.

efecto *m* **-1.** [gen] effect; **hacer** ○ **surtir** ~ to have the desired effect; **tener** ~ [vigencia] to come into ○ take effect; ~ **invernadero** greenhouse effect; ~ **óptico** optical illusion; ~**s sonoros/visuales** sound/visual effects; ~**s especiales** special effects; ~**s secundarios** side effects. **-2.** [finalidad] aim, purpose; **a tal** ~ to that end; **a** ~**s** ○ **para los** ~**s de algo** as far as sthg is concerned. **-3.** [impresión] impression; **producir buen/mal** ~ to make a good/bad impression. **-4.** [de balón, bola] spin; **dar** ~ **a** to put spin on. **-5.** COM [documento] bill; ~ **de comercio** commercial paper; ~ **de favor** accommodation bill.
◆ **efectos personales** *mpl* personal possessions ○ effects.
◆ **en efecto** *loc adv* indeed.

efectuar [6] *vt* [gen] to carry out; [compra, pago, viaje] to make.
◆ **efectuarse** *vpr* to take place.

efeméride *f* [suceso] major event; [conmemoración] anniversary.
◆ **efemérides** *fpl* PRENS list of the day's anniversaries published in a newspaper.

efervescencia *f* **-1.** [de líquido] effervescence; [de bebida] fizziness. **-2.** *fig* [agitación, inquietud] unrest.

efervescente *adj* [bebida] fizzy.

eficacia *f* [eficiencia] efficiency; [efectividad] effectiveness.

eficaz *adj* **-1.** [eficiente] efficient. **-2.** [efectivo] effective.

eficiencia *f* efficiency.

eficiente *adj* efficient.

efigie *f* [gen] effigy; [en monedas etc] image, picture.

efímero, -ra *adj* ephemeral.

efluvio *m* **-1.** [emanación] vapour; [aroma] scent. **-2.** *fig* [de alegría, simpatía etc] aura.

EFTA (*abrev de* **European Free Trade Association**) *f* EFTA.

efusión *f* [cordialidad] effusiveness, warmth.

efusividad *f* effusiveness.

efusivo, -va *adj* effusive.

e.g. (*abrev de* **exempli gratia**) e.g.

EGB (*abrev de* **educación general básica**) *f* former Spanish primary education system.

Egeo *m* → **mar.**

egipcio, -cia *adj, m y f* Egyptian.

Egipto Egypt.

égloga *f* eclogue.

ego *m* ego.

egocéntrico, -ca ◇ *adj* egocentric, self-centred. ◇ *m y f* egocentric ○ self-centred person.

egocentrismo *m* egocentricity.

egoísmo *m* selfishness, egoism.

egoísta ◇ *adj* egoistic, selfish. ◇ *m y f* egoist, selfish person.

ególatra ◇ *adj* egotistical. ◇ *m y f* egotist.

egolatría *f* egotism.

egregio, -gia *adj culto* egregious, illustrious.

egresado, -da *m y f Amer* **-1.** [de escuela] student who has completed a course. **-2.** [de universidad] graduate.

egresar *vi Amer* **-1.** [de escuela] to leave school after graduation. **-2.** [de universidad] to graduate.

egreso *m Amer* **-1.** [de escuela] completion of course. **-2.** [de universidad] graduation.

eh *interj*: ¡~! hey!

ej. *abrev de* **ejemplar.**

eje *m* **-1.** [de rueda] axle; [de máquina] shaft. **-2.** GEOM axis. **-3.** *fig* [idea central] central idea, basis.

ejecución *f* **-1.** [realización] carrying out. **-2.** [de condenado] execution. **-3.** [de concierto] performance, rendition. **-4.** INFORM [de un programa] execution.

ejecutar *vt* **-1.** [realizar] to carry out. **-2.** [condenado] to execute. **-3.** [concierto] to perform. **-4.** INFORM [programa] to execute, to run.

ejecutivo, -va ◇ *adj* executive. ◇ *m y f* [persona] executive; ~ **agresivo** thrusting executive; ~ **de cuentas** account administrator.
◆ **ejecutivo** *m* POLÍT: **el** ~ the government.
◆ **ejecutiva** *f* [junta] executive.

ejecutor, -ra *m y f* **-1.** DER executor. **-2.** [verdugo] executioner.

ejecutorio, -ria *adj* DER final.

ejem *interj:* ¡~! [expresa duda] um!; [expresa ironía] ahem!

ejemplar ◇ *adj* exemplary. ◇ *m* [de libro] copy; [de revista] issue; [de moneda] example; [de especie, raza] specimen.

ejemplaridad *f* exemplary nature.

ejemplificar [10] *vt* to exemplify.

ejemplo *m* example; **por** ~ for example; **dar** ~ to set an example; **predicar con el** ~ to practise what one preaches.

ejercer [11] ◇ *vt* **-1.** [profesión] to practise; [cargo] to hold. **-2.** [poder, derecho] to exercise; [influencia, dominio] to exert; ~ **presión sobre** to put pressure on. ◇ *vi* to practise (one's profession); ~ **de** to practise ○ work as.

ejercicio *m* **-1.** [gen] exercise; **hacer** ~ to (do) exercise. **-2.** [de profesión] practising; [de cargo, funciones] carrying out. **-3.** [de poder, derecho] exercising. **-4.** MIL drill. **-5.** ECON: ~ **económico/fiscal** financial/tax year.
◆ **ejercicios espirituales** *mpl* retreat (*U*).

ejercitar *vt* [derecho] to exercise.
◆ **ejercitarse** *vpr:* ~**se (en)** to train (in).

ejército *m* MIL & *fig* army.

ejerza *etc* → **ejercer.**

ejote *m Amer* green bean.

el, la (*pl* **los, las**) *art* (**el** *antes de sustantivo femenino que empiece por "a" o "ha" tónica; a* + *el* = **al**; *de* + *el* = **del**) **-1.** [gen] the; [en sentido genérico] *no se traduce;* ~ **coche** the car; **la casa** the house; **los niños** the children; ~ **agua/hacha/águila** the water/axe/eagle; **fui a recoger a los niños** I went to pick up the children; **los niños imitan a los adultos** children copy adults. **-2.** [con sustantivo abstracto] *no se traduce;* ~ **amor** love; **la vida** life. **-3.** [indica posesión, pertenencia]: **se partió la pierna** he broke his leg; **se quitó los zapatos** she took her shoes off; **tiene** ~ **pelo oscuro** he has dark hair. **-4.** [con días de la semana]: **vuelven** ~ **sábado** they're coming back on Saturday. **-5.** [con nombres propios geográficos] the; ~ **Sena** the (River) Seine; ~ **Everest** (Mount) Everest; **la España de la postguerra** post-war Spain. **-6.** *fam* [con nombre propio de persona]: **llama a la María** call Maria. **-7.** [con complemento de nombre, especificativo]: ~ **de** the one; **he perdido** ~ **tren, cogeré** ~ **de las nueve** I've missed the train, I'll get the nine o'clock one; ~ **de azul** the one in blue. **-8.** [con complemento de nombre, posesivo]: **mi hermano y** ~ **de Juan** my brother and Juan's. **-9.** [antes de frase]: ~ **que** [cosa] the one, whichever; [persona] whoever; **coge** ~ **que quieras** take whichever you like; ~ **que más corra** whoever runs fastest. **-10.** [antes de adjetivo]: **prefiero** ~ **rojo al azul** I prefer the red one to the blue one.

él, ella *pron pers* **-1.** [sujeto, predicado-persona] he (*f* she); [- animal, cosa] it; **mi hermana es ella** she is the one who is my sister. **-2.** (*después de prep*) [complemento] him (*f* her); **voy a ir de vacaciones con ella** I'm going on holiday with her; **díselo a ella** tell her it. **-3.** [posesivo]: **de** ~ his; **de ella** hers.

elaboración *f* [de producto] manufacture; [de idea] working out; [de plan, informe] drawing up; **de** ~ **casera** home-made.

elaborar *vt* [producto] to make, to manufacture; [idea] to work out; [plan, informe] to draw up.

elasticidad *f* **-1.** [gen] elasticity. **-2.** *fig* [falta de rigor] flexibility.

elástico, -ca *adj* **-1.** [gen] elastic. **-2.** *fig* [sin rigor] flexible.
◆ **elástico** *m* [cinta] elastic.
◆ **elásticos** *mpl* [tirantes] braces.

Elba *m:* **el** ~ the Elbe.

El Cairo Cairo.

elección *f* **-1.** [nombramiento] election. **-2.** [opción] choice.
◆ **elecciones** *fpl* POLÍT election (*sg*); **elecciones autonómicas** *elections to the regional parliament;* **elecciones generales** general election; **elecciones municipales** local elections.

electo, -ta *adj* elect; **el presidente** ~ the president elect.

elector, -ra *m y f* voter, elector.

electorado *m* electorate.

electoral *adj* electoral.

electoralismo *m* electioneering.

electoralista *adj* electioneering (*antes de sust*).

electricidad *f* electricity.

electricista ◇ *adj* electrical. ◇ *m y f* electrician.

eléctrico, -ca *adj* electric.

electrificación *f* electrification.

electrificar [10] *vt* to electrify.

electrizar [13] *vt* *fig* [exaltar] to electrify.

electrocardiograma *m* electrocardiogram.

electrochoque, electroshock [elektro'ʃok] (*pl* **electroshocks**) *m* electric shock therapy.

electrocución *f* electrocution.

electrocutar *vt* to electrocute.

◆ **electrocutarse** *vpr* to electrocute o.s.

electrodo *m* electrode.

electrodoméstico *m* (*gen pl*) electrical household appliance.

electroencefalógrafo *m* electroencephalograph.

electroencefalograma *m* electroencephalogram.

electrógeno, -na *adj* generating.

◆ **electrógeno** *m* generator.

electrólisis *f inv* electrolysis.

electrólito *m* electrolyte.

electromagnético, -ca *adj* electromagnetic.

electromagnetismo *m* electromagnetism.

electrón *m* electron.

electrónico, -ca *adj* **-1.** [de la electrónica] electronic. **-2.** [del electrón] electron (*antes de sust*).

◆ **electrónica** *f* electronics (U).

electroscopio *m* electroscope.

electroshock = electrochoque.

electrostático, -ca *adj* electrostatic.

◆ **electrostática** *f* electrostatics (U).

elefante, -ta *m y f* elephant.

◆ **elefante marino** *m* sea cow, walrus.

elefantiasis *f inv* elephantiasis.

elegancia *f* elegance.

elegante *adj* **-1.** [persona, traje, estilo] elegant. **-2.** [conducta, actitud, respuesta] dignified.

elegantoso, -sa *adj* *Amer* elegant.

elegía *f* elegy.

elegiaco, -ca, elegíaco, -ca *adj* elegiac.

elegible *adj* eligible.

elegido, -da *adj* [escogido] selected, chosen; POL elected.

elegir [42] *vt* **-1.** [escoger] to choose, to select. **-2.** [por votación] to elect.

elemental *adj* **-1.** [básico] basic. **-2.** [obvio] obvious.

elemento *m* **-1.** [gen] element; **estar (uno) en su ~** to be in one's element. **-2.** [factor] factor. **-3.** [persona - en equipo, colectivo] individual. **-4.** *fam* [persona] chap *Br*, guy *Am*; **un ~ de cuidado** a bad lot.

◆ **elementos** *mpl* [fundamentos] rudiments.

elenco *m* **-1.** [reparto] cast. **-2.** [catálogo] list, index.

elepé *m* LP (record).

elevación *f* **-1.** [de pesos, objetos etc] lifting; [de nivel, altura, precios] rise. **-2.** [de terreno] elevation, rise.

elevado, -da *adj* [alto] high; *fig* [sublime] lofty.

elevador, -ra *adj* [gen] lifting; [músculo] elevator (*antes de sust*).

◆ **elevador** *m* **-1.** [montacargas] hoist. **-2.** *Amer* [ascensor] lift *Br*, elevator *Am*.

elevadorista *m y f* *Amer* lift operator *Br*, elevator operator *Am*.

elevalunas *m inv* window winder; **~ eléctrico** electric window.

elevar *vt* **-1.** [gen & MAT] to raise; [peso, objeto] to lift. **-2.** [ascender]: **~ a alguien (a)** to elevate sb (to). **-3.** *fig* [propuesta, quejas] to present.

◆ **elevarse** *vpr* [gen] to rise; [edificio, montaña] to rise up; **~se a** [altura] to reach; [gastos, daños] to amount O come to.

elidir *vt* to elide.

elige, eligió *etc* → elegir.

eliminación *f* elimination.

eliminar *vt* [gen] to eliminate; [contaminación, enfermedad] to get rid of.

eliminatorio, -ria *adj* qualifying (*antes de sust*).

◆ **eliminatoria** *f* [gen] qualifying round; [en atletismo] heat.

elipse *f* ellipse.

elipsis *f inv* ellipsis.

elipsoide *m* ellipsoid.

elíptico, -ca *adj* elliptical.

élite, elite *f* elite.

elitismo *m* elitism.

elitista *adj, m y f* elitist.

elixir, elíxir *m* **-1.** FARM: **~ bucal** mouthwash. **-2.** *fig* [remedio milagroso] elixir.

ella → él.

ellas → ellos.

ello *pron pers* (*neutro*) it; **no nos llevamos bien, pero ~ no nos impide formar un buen equipo** we don't get on very well, but it ○ that doesn't stop us making a good team; **no quiero hablar de** ~ I don't want to talk about it; **por** ~ for that reason.

ellos, **ellas** *pron pers* **-1.** [sujeto, predicado] they; **los invitados son** ~ they are the guests, it is they who are the guests. **-2.** (*después de prep*) [complemento] them; **me voy al bar con ellas** I'm going with them to the bar; **díselo a** ~ tell them it. **-3.** [posesivo]: **de** ~/**ellas** theirs.

elocuencia *f* eloquence.

elocuente *adj* eloquent; **se hizo un silencio** ~ the silence said it all.

elogiar [8] *vt* to praise.

elogio *m* praise.

elogioso, **-sa** *adj* [palabras] appreciative, eulogistic.

elongación *f* elongation.

El Salvador El Salvador.

elucidar *vt* to elucidate, to throw light upon.

elucubración *f* **-1.** [reflexión] reflection, meditation. **-2.** *despec* [divagación] mental meandering.

elucubrar *vt* **-1.** [reflexionar] to reflect ○ meditate upon. **-2.** *despec* [divagar] to theorize about.

eludir *vt* [gen] to avoid; [perseguidores] to escape.

e.m. (*abrev de* **en mano**) by hand.

Em. *f abrev de* **Eminencia**.

EM (*abrev de* **Estado Mayor**) *m* GS.

emanación *f* emanation, emission.

emanar
◆ **emanar de** *vi* to emanate from.

emancipación *f* [de mujeres, esclavos] emancipation; [de menores de edad] coming of age; [de países] obtaining of independence.

emancipar *vt* [gen] to emancipate, to free; [países] to grant independence (to).
◆ **emanciparse** *vpr* to free o.s., to become independent.

embadurnar *vt*: ~ **algo (de)** to smear sthg (with).
◆ **embadurnarse** *vpr*: ~**se (de)** to smear o.s. (with).

embajada *f* **-1.** [edificio] embassy. **-2.** [cargo] ambassadorship. **-3.** [empleados] embassy staff.

embajador, **-ra** *m y f* ambassador.

embalaje *m* **-1.** [acción] packing. **-2.** [caja] packaging.

embalar *vt* to wrap up, to pack.
◆ **embalarse** *vpr* **-1.** [acelerar - corredor] to

race away; [- vehículo] to pick up speed. **-2.** *fig* [entusiasmarse] to get carried away.

embaldosar *vt* [piso] to tile; [calle] to pave.

embalsamamiento *m* embalming.

embalsamar *vt* to embalm.

embalsar *vt* to dam (up).
◆ **embalsarse** *vpr* to collect, to form puddles.

embalse *m* reservoir.

embarazada ◇ *adj f* pregnant; **dejar** ~ **a alguien** to get sb pregnant; **estar** ~ **de ocho meses** to be eight months pregnant; **quedarse** ~ to get pregnant. ◇ *f* pregnant woman.

embarazar [13] *vt* **-1.** [preñar] to get pregnant. **-2.** [impedir] to restrict. **-3.** [cohibir] to inhibit.

embarazo *m* **-1.** [preñez] pregnancy. **-2.** [timidez] embarrassment. **-3.** [impedimento] obstacle.

embarazoso, **-sa** *adj* awkward, embarrassing.

embarcación *f* **-1.** [barco] craft, boat. **-2.** [embarque] embarkation.

embarcadero *m* jetty.

embarcar [10] ◇ *vt* **-1.** [personas] to board; [mercancías] to ship. **-2.** *fig* [involucrar]: ~ **a alguien en algo** to involve sb in sthg. ◇ *vi* to board.
◆ **embarcarse** *vpr* **-1.** [para viajar] to board. **-2.** *fig* [aventurarse]: ~**se en algo** to become involved in sthg.

embargar [16] *vt* **-1.** DER to seize. **-2.** [suj: emoción etc] to overcome.

embargo *m* **-1.** DER seizure. **-2.** ECON embargo.
◆ **sin embargo** *loc adv* however, nevertheless.

embarque *m* [de personas] boarding; [de mercancías] embarkation.

embarrancar [10] *vi* to run aground.
◆ **embarrancarse** *vpr* [barco] to run aground; [coche etc] to get stuck.

embarrar *vt* to cover with mud.
◆ **embarrarse** *vpr fam* to get covered in mud.

embarullar *vt fam* to mess up.
◆ **embarullarse** *vpr fam* to get into a muddle.

embate *m* [del mar] pounding (U).

embaucador, **-ra** ◇ *adj* deceitful. ◇ *m y f* swindler.

embaucar [10] *vt* to swindle, to deceive.

embeber *vt* to soak up.
◆ **embeberse** *vpr*: ~**se (en algo)** [ensimismarse] to become absorbed (in sthg); *fig* [empaparse] to immerse o.s. (in sthg).

embelesar *vt* to captivate.
◆ **embelesarse** *vpr* to be captivated.
embellecedor *m* [moldura] go-faster stripes (*pl*); [tapacubos] hubcap.
embellecer [30] *vt* to adorn, to embellish.
embellecimiento *m* embellishment.
embestida *f* [gen] attack; [de toro] charge.
embestir [26] *vt* [gen] to attack; [toro] to charge.
emblanquecer [30] *vt* to whiten.
emblema *m* -1. [divisa, distintivo] emblem, badge. -2. [símbolo] symbol.
embobar *vt* to captivate.
◆ **embobarse** *vpr* to be captivated.
embocadura *f* -1. [de río, puerto] mouth. -2. [de instrumento] mouthpiece.
embocar [10] *vt* to enter (*a narrow space*), to squeeze into.
emboce *etc* → **embozar**.
embolado *m fam* -1. [mentira] fib. -2. [follón] jam, mess.
embolador *m Amer* boot black, shoeshine boy.
embolia *f* clot, embolism.
émbolo *m* AUTOM piston.
embolsarse *vpr* [ganar] to make, to earn.
embonar *vt Amer fam* to suit.
emboque *etc* → **embocar**.
emborrachar *vt* to make drunk.
◆ **emborracharse** *vpr* to get drunk.
emborrascarse [10] *vpr* to cloud over, to turn black.
emborronar *vt* -1. [garabatear] to scribble on; [manchar] to smudge. -2. [escribir de prisa] to scribble.
emboscada *f lit* & *fig* ambush; **tender una ~** to lay an ambush.
emboscar [10] *vt* to ambush.
embotamiento *m* dullness.
embotar *vt* [sentidos] to dull.
embotellado, -da *adj* bottled.
◆ **embotellado** *m* bottling.
embotellamiento *m* -1. [de tráfico] traffic jam. -2. [de líquidos] bottling.
embotellar *vt* -1. [tráfico] to block. -2. [líquido] to bottle.
embozar [13] *vt* -1. [conducto] to block. -2. [rostro] to cover (up).
◆ **embozarse** *vpr* -1. [conducto] to get blocked (up). -2. [persona] to cover one's face.
embozo *m* [de sábana] turnover.
embragar [16] *vi* to engage the clutch.
embrague *m* clutch.
embravecer [30] *vt* to enrage.

◆ **embravecerse** *vpr* -1. [animal] to become enraged. -2. [mar] to become rough.
embriagador, -ra *adj* intoxicating.
embriagar [16] *vt* -1. [extasiar] to intoxicate. -2. [emborrachar] to make drunk.
◆ **embriagarse** *vpr* -1. [extasiarse]: **~se (de)** to become drunk (with). -2. [emborracharse]: **~se (con)** to get drunk (on).
embriaguez *f* -1. [borrachera] drunkenness. -2. [éxtasis] intoxication.
embriología *f* embryology.
embrión *m* embryo.
embrionario, -ria *adj fig* [inicial] embryonic.
embrollar *vt* [asunto] to confuse, to complicate; [hilos] to tangle up.
◆ **embrollarse** *vpr* to get muddled up ○ confused.
embrollo *m* -1. [de hilos] tangle. -2. *fig* [lío] mess; [mentira] lie.
embromado, -da *adj Amer fam* tricky.
embromar *vt* -1. [burlarse de] to tease. -2. *Amer fam* [fastidiar] to annoy.
embrujamiento *m* bewitchment.
embrujar *vt lit* & *fig* to bewitch.
embrujo *m* [maleficio] curse, spell; *fig* [de ciudad, ojos] charm, magic.
embrutecer [30] *vt* to brutalize.
◆ **embrutecerse** *vpr* to become brutalized.
embrutecimiento *m* [acción] brutalization; [cualidad] brutishness.
embuchado, -da *adj*: **carne embuchada** cured cold meat.
embuchar *vt* -1. *fam* [comer] to wolf down, to gobble up. -2. [embutir] to process into sausages.
embudo *m* funnel.
embuste *m* lie.
embustero, -ra ◇ *adj* lying. ◇ *m y f* liar.
embute *m Amer fam* bribe.
embutido *m* -1. [comida] cold cured meat. -2. [acción] sausage-making, stuffing.
embutir *vt lit* & *fig* to stuff.
eme *f fam* [mierda] sugar, fudge; **¡vete a la ~!** eff off!
emergencia *f* -1. [urgencia] emergency; **en caso de ~** in case of emergency. -2. [brote] emergence.
emergente *adj* emerging.
emerger [14] *vi* [salir del agua] to emerge; [aparecer] to come into view, to appear.
emeritense *adj* of/relating to Mérida.
emérito, -ta *adj* emeritus.
emerja *etc* → **emerger**.

emigración f -1. [de personas] emigration; [de aves] migration. -2. [grupo de personas] emigrant community.

emigrado, -da m y f emigrant.

emigrante adj, m y f emigrant.

emigrar vi [persona] to emigrate; [ave] to migrate.

eminencia f [persona] eminent figure, leading light; ~ **gris** éminence grise.
◆ **Eminencia** f: **Su Eminencia** His Eminence.

eminente adj -1. [distinguido] eminent. -2. [elevado] high.

emir m emir.

emirato m emirate.

Emiratos Árabes Unidos mpl: los ~ United Arab Emirates.

emisario, -ria m y f emissary.

emisión f -1. [de energía, rayos etc] emission. -2. [de bonos, sellos, monedas] issue; ~ **de obligaciones** COM debentures issue. -3. [RADIO & TV - transmisión] broadcasting; [- programa] programme, broadcast.

emisor, -ra adj transmitting (antes de sust).
◆ **emisor** m transmitter.
◆ **emisora** f radio station.

emitir ◇ vt -1. [rayos, calor, sonidos] to emit. -2. [moneda, sellos, bonos] to issue. -3. [expresar - juicio, opinión] to express; [- fallo] to pronounce. -4. RADIO & TV to broadcast. ◇ vi to broadcast.

emoción f -1. [conmoción, sentimiento] emotion. -2. [expectación] excitement; ¡qué ~! how exciting!

emocional adj emotional.

emocionante adj -1. [conmovedor] moving, touching. -2. [apasionante] exciting, thrilling.

emocionar vt -1. [conmover] to move. -2. [excitar, apasionar] to thrill, to excite.
◆ **emocionarse** vpr -1. [conmoverse] to be moved. -2. [excitarse, apasionarse] to get excited.

emolumento m (gen pl) emolument.

emotividad f emotional impact, emotiveness.

emotivo, -va adj [persona] emotional; [escena, palabras] moving.

empacar [10] vt to pack.

empachar vt to give indigestion to.
◆ **empacharse** vpr [hartarse] to stuff o.s.; [sufrir indigestión] to get indigestion.

empacho m -1. [indigestión] upset stomach, indigestion. -2. fig [hartura]: **tener un ~ de** to have had one's fill o enough of.

empadronamiento m ≃ registration on the electoral roll.

empadronar vt ≃ to register on the electoral roll.
◆ **empadronarse** vpr ≃ to register on the electoral roll.

empalagar [16] vt: **los bombones me empalagan** I find chocolates sickly.
◆ **empalagarse** vpr: ~**se de** o **con** to get sick of.

empalago m cloying taste.

empalagoso, -sa adj sickly, cloying.

empalizada f [cerca] fence; MIL stockade.

empalmar ◇ vt -1. [tubos, cables] to connect, to join. -2. [planes, ideas] to link. -3. [en fútbol] to volley. ◇ vi -1. [autocares, trenes] to connect. -2. [carreteras] to link o join (up). -3. [sucederse]: ~ **(con)** to follow on (from).

empalme m -1. [entre cables, tubos] joint, connection. -2. [de líneas férreas, carreteras] junction.

empanada f pasty; **tener una ~ mental** to be in a real muddle, not to be able to think straight.

empanadilla f small pasty.

empanar vt CULIN to coat in breadcrumbs.

empantanar vt to flood.
◆ **empantanarse** vpr -1. [inundarse] to be flooded o waterlogged. -2. fig [atascarse] to get bogged down.

empañado, -da adj -1. [cristal] misted o steamed up. -2. [reputación] tarnished.

empañar vt -1. [cristal] to mist o steam up. -2. fig [reputación] to tarnish.
◆ **empañarse** vpr to mist o steam up.

empapar vt -1. [humedecer] to soak. -2. [absorber] to soak up.
◆ **empaparse** vpr [persona, traje] to get soaked.

empapelado m -1. [acción] papering. -2. [papel] wallpaper.

empapelar vt -1. [pared] to paper. -2. fam fig [procesar] to have up (before the courts).

empaque etc → empacar.

empaquetar vt to pack, to package.

emparedado, -da adj confined.
◆ **emparedado** m sandwich.

emparedar vt to shut up, to lock away.

emparejamiento m pairing.

emparejar vt -1. [aparejar - personas] to pair off; [- zapatos etc] to match (up). -2. [nivelar] to make level.
◆ **emparejarse** vpr [personas] to find a partner.

emparentar [19] vi: ~ **con** to marry into.

emparrado m [pérgola] bower.

emparrar *vt* to train.

empastar *vt* to fill.

empaste *m* filling.

empatar ◇ *vi* DEP to draw; [en elecciones etc] to tie; ~ **a cero** to draw nil-nil. ◇ *vt* Amer to join, to link.

empate *m* **-1.** [resultado] draw; **un** ~ **a cero/dos** a goalless/two-two draw. **-2.** Amer [empalme] joint, link.

empecé *etc* → empezar.

empecinado, -da *adj* stubborn.

empecinamiento *m* stubbornness.

empecinarse *vpr*: ~ **(en hacer algo)** to insist (on doing sthg).

empedernido, -da *adj* [bebedor, fumador] heavy; [criminal, jugador] hardened.

empedrado *m* paving.

empedrar [19] *vt* to pave.

empeine *m* [de pie, zapato] instep.

empeñado, -da *adj* **-1.** [en préstamo] in pawn. **-2.** [obstinado] determined; **estar** ~ **en hacer algo** to be determined to do sthg.

empeñar *vt* **-1.** [joyas etc] to pawn. **-2.** [palabra, honor] to give.

◆ **empeñarse** *vpr* **-1.** [obstinarse] to insist; ~**se en hacer algo** [obstinarse] to insist on doing sthg; [persistir] to persist in doing sthg. **-2.** [endeudarse] to get into debt.

empeño *m* **-1.** [de joyas etc] pawning; **casa de** ~**s** pawnshop. **-2.** [obstinación] determination; **tener** ~ **en hacer algo** to be determined to do sthg; **en el** ~ in the attempt.

empeoramiento *m* worsening, deterioration.

empeorar *vi* to get worse, to deteriorate.

empequeñecer [30] *vt* [quitar importancia] to diminish; [en una comparación] to overshadow, to dwarf.

emperador, emperatriz *m y f* emperor (*f* empress).

◆ **emperador** *m* [pez] swordfish.

emperifollar *vt fam* to doll ○ tart up.

◆ **emperifollarse** *vpr fam* to doll ○ tart o.s. up.

empero *conj culto* but; [sin embargo] nevertheless.

emperrarse *vpr*: ~ **(en hacer algo)** to insist (on doing sthg).

empezar [34] ◇ *vt* to begin, to start. ◇ *vi*: ~ **(a hacer algo)** to begin ○ start (to do sthg); ~ **(por hacer algo)** to begin ○ start (by doing sthg); **para** ~ to begin ○ start with.

empiedra *etc* → empedrar.

empiezo → empezar.

empinado, -da *adj* steep.

empinar *vt* **-1.** [inclinar] to tip up. **-2.** [levantar] to raise.

◆ **empinarse** *vpr* **-1.** [animal] to stand up on its hind legs. **-2.** [persona] to stand on tiptoe. **-3.** *mfam* [miembro viril]: **se le empinó** he got a hard-on.

empingorotado, -da *adj* stuck-up, posh.

empírico, -ca ◇ *adj* empirical. ◇ *m y f* empiricist.

empirismo *m* empiricism.

emplasto *m* FARM poultice.

emplazamiento *m* **-1.** [ubicación] location. **-2.** DER summons.

emplazar [13] *vt* **-1.** [situar] to locate; MIL to position. **-2.** [citar] to summon; DER to summons.

empleado, -da *m y f* [gen] employee; [de banco, administración, oficina] clerk; **empleada de hogar** maid.

empleador, -ra *m y f* employer.

emplear *vt* **-1.** [usar - objetos, materiales etc] to use; [- tiempo] to spend; ~ **algo en hacer algo** to use sthg to do sthg. **-2.** [contratar] to employ. **-3.** *loc*: **lo tiene** ○ **le está bien empleado** he deserves it, it serves him right.

◆ **emplearse** *vpr* **-1.** [colocarse] to find a job. **-2.** [usarse] to be used.

empleo *m* **-1.** [uso] use. **-2.** [trabajo] employment; [puesto] job; **estar sin** ~ to be out of work; ~ **comunitario** community service; ~ **juvenil** youth employment; **pleno** ~ full employment.

emplomadura *f Amer* [diente] filling.

emplomar *vt* **-1.** [cubrir con plomo] to lead. **-2.** *Amer* [diente] to fill.

emplumar *vt* to adorn with feathers.

empobrecer [30] *vt* to impoverish.

◆ **empobrecerse** *vpr* to get poorer.

empobrecimiento *m* impoverishment.

empollar ◇ *vt* **-1.** [huevo] to incubate. **-2.** *fam* [estudiar] to swot up on. ◇ *vi fam* to swot.

◆ **empollarse** *vpr fam* to swot up on.

empollón, -ona *fam* ◇ *adj* swotty. ◇ *m y f* swot.

empolvarse *vpr* to powder one's face.

emponzoñar *vt* to poison.

emporio *m centre of commerce, finance etc.*

emporrado, -da *adj fam* stoned.

emporrarse *vpr fam* to get stoned (on cannabis).

empotrado, -da *adj* fitted, built-in.

empotrar *vt* to fit, to build in.

emprendedor, -ra *adj* enterprising.

emprender *vt* [trabajo] to start; [viaje, marcha] to set off on; ~ **vuelo** to fly off.

empresa *f* **-1.** [sociedad] company; ~ **de seguridad** security firm; ~ **júnior** junior enterprise, *firm set up and run by business studies students*; ~ **mixta/privada** mixed/private company; ~ **filial** subsidiary; ~ **libre, libre** ~ free enterprise; ~ **matriz** parent company; **pequeña y mediana** ~ small and medium-sized business; ~ **pública** public sector firm. **-2.** [acción] enterprise, undertaking.

empresariado *m* employers (*pl*).

empresarial *adj* management (*antes de sust*).

◆ **empresariales** *fpl* business studies.

empresario, -ria *m y f* [patrono] employer; [hombre, mujer de negocios] businessman (*f* businesswoman); [de teatro] impresario; **pequeño** ~ small businessman.

empréstito *m* debenture loan.

empujar *vt* to push; ~ **a alguien a que haga algo** to push sb into doing sthg.

empuje *m* **-1.** [presión] pressure. **-2.** [energía] energy, drive.

empujón *m* **-1.** [empellón] shove, push; **dar un** ~ **a alguien** to give sb a push ○ a shove; **abrirse paso a empujones** to shove ○ push one's way through. **-2.** *fig* [impulso] effort; **dar un último** ~ **a** to make one last effort with.

empuñadura *f* handle; [de espada] hilt.

empuñar *vt* to take hold of, to grasp.

emulación *f* [gen & INFORM] emulation.

emulador *m* INFORM emulator.

emular *vt* [gen & INFORM] to emulate.

émulo, -la *m y f* rival.

emulsión *f* emulsion.

en *prep* **-1.** [lugar - en el interior de] in; [- sobre la superficie de] on; [- en un punto concreto de] at; **viven** ~ **la capital** they live in the capital; **tiene el dinero** ~ **el banco** he keeps his money in the bank; ~ **la mesa/el plato** on the table/plate; ~ **casa/el trabajo** at home/work. **-2.** [dirección] into; **el avión cayó** ~ **el mar** the plane fell into the sea; **entraron** ~ **la habitación** they came into the room. **-3.** [tiempo - mes, año etc] in; [- día] on; **nació** ~ **1940/mayo** he was born in 1940/May; ~ **aquel día** on that day; ~ **Nochebuena** on Christmas Eve; ~ **Navidades** at Christmas; ~ **aquella época** at that time, in those days; ~ **un par de días** in a couple of days. **-4.** [medio de transporte] by; **ir** ~ **tren/coche/avión/barco** to go by train/car/plane/boat. **-5.** [modo] in; ~ **voz baja** in a low voice; **lo dijo** ~ **inglés** she said it in English; **pagar** ~ **libras** to pay in pounds;

la inflación aumentó ~ **un 10%** inflation increased by 10%; **todo se lo gasta** ~ **ropa** he spends everything on clothes. **-6.** [precio] in; **las ganancias se calculan** ~ **millones** profits are calculated in millions; **te lo dejo en 5.000** I'll let you have it for 5,000. **-7.** [tema]: **es un experto** ~ **la materia** he's an expert on the subject; **es doctor** ~ **medicina** he's a doctor of medicine. **-8.** [causa] from; **lo detecté** ~ **su forma de hablar** I could tell from the way he was speaking. **-9.** [materia] in, made of; ~ **seda** in silk. **-10.** [cualidad] in terms of; **le supera** ~ **inteligencia** she is more intelligent than he is.

enagua *f* (*gen pl*) petticoat.

enajenación *f*, **enajenamiento** *m* **-1.** [locura] mental derangement, insanity; [éxtasis] rapture. **-2.** [de una propiedad] transfer of ownership, alienation.

enajenar *vt* **-1.** [volver loco] to drive mad; [extasiar] to enrapture. **-2.** [propiedad] to transfer ownership of, to alienate.

enaltecer [30] *vt* to praise.

enamoradizo, -za ◇ *adj* who falls in love easily. ◇ *m y f* person who falls in love easily.

enamorado, -da ◇ *adj*: ~ **(de)** in love (with). ◇ *m y f* lover.

enamoramiento *m* falling in love.

enamorar *vt* to win the heart of.

◆ **enamorarse** *vpr*: ~**se (de)** to fall in love (with).

enanismo *m* dwarfism.

enano, -na *adj, m y f* dwarf.

enarbolar *vt* [bandera] to raise, to hoist; [pancarta] to hold up; [arma] to brandish.

enarcar [10] *vt* to arch.

enardecer [30] *vt* [gen] to inflame; [persona, multitud] to fill with enthusiasm.

enarque *etc* → **enarcar**.

encabezamiento *m* [de carta, escrito] heading; [de artículo periodístico] headline; [preámbulo] foreword.

encabezar [13] *vt* **-1.** [artículo de periódico] to headline; [libro] to write the foreword for. **-2.** [lista, carta] to head. **-3.** [marcha, expedición] to lead.

encabritarse *vpr* **-1.** [caballo, moto] to rear up. **-2.** *fam* [persona] to get shirty.

encabronarse *vpr vulg* to get pissed off.

encadenado *m* **-1.** CIN fade, dissolve. **-2.** CONSTR buttress.

encadenamiento *m* linking.

encadenar *vt* **-1.** [atar] to chain (up). **-2.** [enlazar] to link (together). **-3.** *fig* [esclavizar] to chain.

encajar ◇ *vt* **-1.** [meter ajustando]: ~ **(en)** to fit (into). **-2.** [meter con fuerza]: ~ **(en)** to push (in). **-3.** [hueso dislocado] to set. **-4.** [recibir - goipe, noticia, críticas] to take. **-5.** [soltar]: ~ **algo a alguien** [discurso] to force sb to listen to ○ sit through sthg; [insultos] to hurl sthg at sb; ~**le un golpe a alguien** to land sb a blow. ◇ *vi* **-1.** [piezas, objetos] to fit. **-2.** [hechos, declaraciones, datos]: ~ **(con)** to square (with), to match. **-3.** [ser oportuno, adecuado]: ~ **(con)** to fit nicely (with).

encaje *m* **-1.** [ajuste] insertion, fitting-in. **-2.** [tejido] lace.

encajonar *vt* **-1.** [en cajas, cajones] to pack, to put in boxes. **-2.** [en sitio estrecho]: ~ **algo/a alguien (en)** to squeeze sthg/sb (into).

encalado *m* whitewash.

encalar *vt* to whitewash.

encallar *vi* **-1.** [barco] to run aground. **-2.** *fig* [solicitud, proyecto] to founder.

encallecer [30] *vi* to become calloused ○ hard.

encamarse *vpr* **-1.** [enfermo] to take to one's bed. **-2.** *fam* [pareja]: ~ **con alguien** to sleep with sb.

encaminar *vt* **-1.** [persona, pasos] to direct. **-2.** [medidas, leyes, actividades] to aim; **encaminado a** aimed at.

◆ **encaminarse** *vpr*: ~**se a/hacia** to set off for/towards.

encamotarse *vpr Amer fam* to fall in love with.

encandilar *vt* to dazzle, to impress greatly.

◆ **encandilarse** *vpr* to be dazzled.

encanecer [30] *vi* to go grey.

◆ **encanecerse** *vpr* to go grey.

encantado, -da *adj* **-1.** [contento] delighted; ~ **de conocerle** pleased to meet you. **-2.** [hechizado - casa, lugar] haunted; [- persona] bewitched.

encantador, -ra *adj* delightful, charming.

encantamiento *m* enchantment.

encantar *vt* **-1.** [gustar]: ~**le a alguien algo/hacer algo** to love sthg/doing sthg. **-2.** [embrujar] to bewitch, to cast a spell on.

encanto *m* **-1.** [atractivo] charm; **ser un** ~ to be a treasure ○ a delight. **-2.** [apelativo cariñoso] darling. **-3.** [hechizo] spell; **como por** ~ as if by magic.

encañonar *vt* [persona] to point a gun at.

encapotado, -da *adj* overcast.

encapotarse *vpr* to cloud over.

encapricharse *vpr* **-1.** [obstinarse]: ~ **con algo/hacer algo** to set one's mind on sthg/

doing sthg. **-2.** [enamorarse]: ~ **(con alguien)** to become infatuated (with sb).

encapuchado, -da ◇ *adj* hooded. ◇ *m y f* hooded person.

encapuchar *vt* to put a hood on.

◆ **encapucharse** *vpr* to put one's hood on.

encarado, -da *adj*: **bien** ~ good-looking; **mal** ~ plain, ugly.

encaramar *vt* to lift up.

◆ **encaramarse** *vpr*: ~**se (a ○ en)** to climb up (onto).

encarar *vt* **-1.** [hacer frente a] to confront, to face up to. **-2.** [poner frente a frente] to bring face to face.

◆ **encararse** *vpr* [enfrentarse]: ~**se a ○ con** to stand up to.

encarcelamiento *m* imprisonment.

encarcelar *vt* to imprison.

encarecer [30] *vt* **-1.** [productos, precios] to make more expensive. **-2.** [rogar]: ~ **a alguien que haga algo** to beg ○ implore sb to do sthg.

◆ **encarecerse** *vpr* to become more expensive.

encarecidamente *adv* earnestly.

encarecimiento *m* **-1.** [de producto, coste] increase in price. **-2.** [empeño]: **con** ~ insistently.

encargado, -da ◇ *adj*: ~ **(de)** responsible (for), in charge (of). ◇ *m y f* [gen] person in charge; COM manager (*f* manageress).

encargar [16] *vt* **-1.** [poner al cargo]: ~ **a alguien de algo** to put sb in charge of sthg; ~ **a alguien que haga algo** to tell sb to do sthg. **-2.** [pedir] to order.

◆ **encargarse** *vpr* **-1.** [ocuparse]: ~**se de** to be in charge of; **yo me encargaré de eso** I'll take care of ○ see to that. **-2.** [pedir] to order.

encargo *m* **-1.** [pedido] order; **por** ~ to order; **es como hecho de** ~ it's tailor-made. **-2.** [recado] errand. **-3.** [tarea] task, assignment.

encariñarse *vpr*: ~ **con** to become fond of.

encarnación *f* [personificación - cosa] embodiment; [- persona] personification.

◆ **Encarnación** *f* RELIG Incarnation.

encarnado, -da *adj* **-1.** [personificado] incarnate. **-2.** [color] red.

◆ **encarnado** *m* red.

encarnar ◇ *vt* [ideal, doctrina] to embody; [personaje, papel] to play. ◇ *vi* RELIG to become flesh.

encarnizado, -da *adj* bloody, bitter.

encarnizarse [13] *vpr*: ~ **con** [presa] to fall upon; [prisionero, enemigo] to treat savagely.

encarpetar *vt* to file away.

encarrilar *vt* **-1.** [tren] to put back on the rails; [coche] to put back on the road. **-2.** *fig* [negocio, situación] to put on the right track, to point in the right direction.

◆ **encarrilarse** *vpr* [persona] to find out what one wants to do in life.

encarte *m* [en naipes] lead.

encartonar *vt* to pack with cardboard.

encasillado *m* grid.

encasillamiento *m* pigeonholing.

encasillar *vt* **-1.** [clasificar] to pigeonhole; TEATR to typecast. **-2.** [poner en casillas] to put in a box, to enter into a grid.

encasquetar *vt* **-1.** [imponer]: ~ **algo a alguien** [idea, teoría] to drum sthg into sb; [discurso, lección] to force sb to sit through sthg. **-2.** [sombrero] to pull on. **-3.** [endilgar - bultos, objetos]: ~ **algo a alguien** to lumber sb with sthg.

◆ **encasquetarse** *vpr* [sombrero] to pull on.

encasquillarse *vpr* to get jammed.

encausar *vt* to prosecute.

encauzar [13] *vt* **-1.** [corriente] to channel. **-2.** [orientar] to direct.

encebollado *m stew of meat and onions.*

encebollar *vt* to add onions to.

encefálico, -ca *adj* brain (*antes de sust*).

encéfalo *m* encephalon.

encefalograma *m* encephalogram.

encendedor *m* lighter.

encender [20] *vt* **-1.** [vela, cigarro, chimenea] to light. **-2.** [aparato] to switch on. **-3.** *fig* [avivar - entusiasmo, ira] to arouse; [- pasión, discusión] to inflame.

◆ **encenderse** *vpr* **-1.** [fuego, gas] to ignite; [luz, estufa] to come on. **-2.** *fig* [ojos] to light up; [persona, rostro] to go red, to blush; [de ira] to flare up.

encendido, -da *adj* **-1.** [luz, colilla] burning; **la luz está encendida** the light is on. **-2.** *fig* [deseos, mirada, palabras] passionate, ardent. **-3.** [mejillas] red, flushed.

◆ **encendido** *m* AUTOM ignition.

encerado, -da *adj* waxed, polished.

◆ **encerado** *m* **-1.** [acción] waxing, polishing. **-2.** [pizarra] blackboard.

encerar *vt* to wax, to polish.

encerrar [19] *vt* **-1.** [recluir - gen] to shut (up ○ in); [- con llave] to lock (up ○ in); [- en la cárcel] to lock away ○ up. **-2.** [contener] to contain.

◆ **encerrarse** *vpr* [gen] to shut o.s. away; [con llave] to lock o.s. away.

encerrona *f* **-1.** [trampa] trap. **-2.** TAUROM private bullfight.

encestar *vt & vi* to score (*in basketball*).

enceste *m* basket.

enchapado *m* veneer.

encharcamiento *m* flooding, swamping.

encharcar [10] *vt* to waterlog.

◆ **encharcarse** *vpr* **-1.** [terreno] to become waterlogged. **-2.** [pulmones] to become flooded.

enchastrar *vt Amer* to make dirty.

enchilarse *vpr Amer fam* to get angry.

enchinar *vt Amer* to curl.

enchironar *vt fam* to put in (the) nick.

enchufado, -da ◇ *adj fam*: **estar** ~ to get where one is through connections. ◇ *m y f fam* person who got where they are through connections.

enchufar *vt* **-1.** [aparato] to plug in. **-2.** *fam* [a una persona] to pull strings for.

enchufe *m* **-1.** [ELECTR - macho] plug; [- hembra] socket. **-2.** *fam* [recomendación] connections (*pl*); **obtener algo por** ~ to get sthg by pulling strings ○ ' ᵾugh one's connections.

enchufismo *m fam* ᵾ ᵾ ᵾg-pulling.

encía *f* gum.

encíclica *f* encyclical.

enciclopedia *f* encyclopedia.

enciclopédico, -ca *adj* encyclopedic.

encienda *etc* → **encender**.

encierra *etc* → **encerrar**.

encierro *m* **-1.** [protesta] sit-in. **-2.** TAUROM running of the bulls.

encima *adv* **-1.** [arriba] on top; **yo vivo** ~ I live upstairs; **por** ~ [superficialmente] superficially. **-2.** [además] on top of that. **-3.** [sobre sí]: **lleva un abrigo** ~ she has a coat on; **¿llevas dinero** ~? have you got any money on you?

◆ **encima de** *loc prep* **-1.** [en lugar superior que] above; **vivo** ~ **de tu casa** I live upstairs from you. **-2.** [sobre, en] on (top of); **el pan está** ~ **de la mesa** the bread is on (top of) the table; **estar** ~ **de alguien** *fig* to be on at sb. **-3.** [además] on top of; ~ **de ser tonto, es feo** on top of being stupid, he's also ugly.

◆ **por encima de** *loc prep* **-1.** [gen] over; **vive por** ~ **de sus posibilidades** he lives beyond his means. **-2.** *fig* [más que] more than; **por** ~ **de todo** more than anything else.

encimero, -ra *adj* top.

◆ **encimera** *f* worktop.

encina *f* holm oak.

encinta *adj f* pregnant.

enclaustrar *vt* to shut up in a convent.

◆ **enclaustrarse** *vpr* to shut o.s. up in a convent; *fig* [encerrarse] to lock o.s. up in a room.

enclavado, -da *adj* set, situated.

enclavar *vt* [clavar] to nail.

enclave *m* enclave.

enclenque *adj* sickly, frail.

encoger [14] ◇ *vt* **-1.** [ropa] to shrink. **-2.** [miembro, músculo] to contract. ◇ *vi* to shrink.

◆ **encogerse** *vpr* **-1.** [ropa] to shrink; [músculos etc] to contract; ~**se de hombros** to shrug one's shoulders. **-2.** *fig* [apocarse] to cringe.

encogido, -da *adj* [tímido] shy; [pusilánime] fearful, faint-hearted.

encoja *etc* → **encoger**.

encolado *m* [de silla etc] glueing; [de pared] sizing.

encolar *vt* [silla etc] to glue; [pared] to size, to paste.

encolerizar [13] *vt* to infuriate, to enrage.

◆ **encolerizarse** *vpr* to get angry.

encomendar [19] *vt* to entrust.

◆ **encomendarse** *vpr*: ~**se a** [persona] to entrust o.s. to; [Dios, santos] to put one's trust in.

encomiar [8] *vt* to praise, to extol.

encomienda *f* **-1.** [encargo] assignment, mission. **-2.** *Amer* [paquete] package, parcel.

encomio *m* praise.

enconado, -da *adj* [lucha] bitter; [partidario] passionate, ardent.

enconar *vt* to inflame.

◆ **enconarse** *vpr* **-1.** [persona] to get angry. **-2.** [herida] to become inflamed.

encono *m* rancour, animosity.

encontradizo, -za *adj*: **hacerse el** ~ to contrive a meeting.

encontrado, -da *adj* conflicting.

encontrar [23] *vt* **-1.** [gen] to find. **-2.** [dificultades] to encounter. **-3.** [persona] to meet, to come across.

◆ **encontrarse** *vpr* **-1.** [hallarse] to be; **se encuentra en París** she's in Paris. **-2.** [coincidir]: ~**se (con alguien)** to meet (sb); **me encontré con Juan** I ran into ◇ met Juan. **-3.** *fig* [de ánimo] to feel. **-4.** [chocar] to collide.

encontronazo *m* collision, crash.

encopetado, -da *adj fig* posh, upper-class.

encorchar *vt* to cork.

encorsetar *vt* to corset; *fig* [poner límites] to straitjacket.

encorvar *vt* to bend.

◆ **encorvarse** *vpr* to bend down ◇ over.

encrespar *vt* **-1.** [pelo] to curl; [mar] to make choppy ◇ rough. **-2.** [irritar] to irritate.

◆ **encresparse** *vpr* **-1.** [mar] to get rough. **-2.** [persona] to get irritated.

encrucijada *f lit* & *fig* crossroads (*sg*).

encuadernación *f* binding.

encuadernador, -ra *m y f* bookbinder.

encuadernar *vt* to bind.

encuadrar *vt* **-1.** [enmarcar · cuadro, tema] to frame. **-2.** [encerrar] to contain. **-3.** [encajar] to fit.

encuadre *m* FOT composition.

encubierto, -ta ◇ *pp* → **encubrir**. ◇ *adj* [intento] covert; [insulto, significado] hidden.

encubridor, -ra *m y f*: ~ **(de)** accessory (to).

encubrimiento *m* [de delito] concealment; [de persona] harbouring.

encubrir *vt* [delito] to conceal; [persona] to harbour.

encuentra *etc* → **encontrar**.

encuentro *m* **-1.** [acción] meeting, encounter; **salir al** ~ **de alguien** [para recibir] to go to meet sb; [para atacar] to confront sb. **-2.** DEP game, match. **-3.** [hallazgo] find.

encuesta *f* **-1.** [de opinión] survey, opinion poll. **-2.** [investigación] investigation, inquiry.

encuestado, -da *m y f* person polled.

encuestador, -ra *m y f* pollster.

encuestar *vt* to poll.

encumbrado, -da *adj* exalted, distinguished.

encumbramiento *m* [acción] rise; [posición] distinguished ◇ exalted position.

encumbrar *vt* to elevate ◇ raise to a higher position.

◆ **encumbrarse** *vpr* to rise to a higher position.

encurtidos *mpl* pickles.

encurtir *vt* to pickle.

endeble *adj* [persona, argumento] weak, feeble; [objeto] fragile.

endemia *f* endemic disease.

endémico, -ca *adj* MED & *fig* endemic.

endemoniado, -da ◇ *adj* **-1.** *fam fig* [molesto · niño] wicked; [- trabajo] very tricky. **-2.** [desagradable] terrible, foul. **-3.** [poseído] possessed (of the devil). ◇ *m y f* person possessed of the devil.

endenantes *adv Amer fam* before.

enderezamiento *m* [acción de poner derecho] straightening; [acción de poner vertical] putting upright.

enderezar [13] *vt* **-1.** [poner derecho] to straighten. **-2.** [poner vertical] to put upright. **-3.** *fig* [corregir] to set right, to straighten out.

◆ **enderezarse** *vpr* [sentado] to sit up straight; [de pie] to stand up straight.

ENDESA (*abrev de* **Empresa Nacional de Electricidad, SA**) *f Spanish electricity company.*

endeudamiento *m* debt.

endeudarse *vpr* to get into debt.

endiablado, -da *adj* [persona] wicked; [tiempo, genio] foul; [problema, crucigrama] fiendishly difficult.

endibia = **endivia**.

endilgar [16] *vt fam*: ~ **algo a alguien** [sermón, bronca] to dish sth out to sb; [bulto, tarea] to lumber sb with sth.

endiñar *vt fam*: ~ **algo a alguien** [golpe] to land ○ deal sb sth; [trabajo, tarea] to lumber sb with sth.

endiosamiento *m* self-importance, conceit.

endiosarse *vpr* to become conceited ○ full of o.s.

endivia, endibia *f* endive.

endocrino, -na ◇ *adj* endocrine (*antes de sust*). ◇ *m y f* endocrinologist.

endocrinología *f* endocrinology.

endocrinólogo, -ga *m y f* endocrinologist.

endogamia *f* endogamy.

endógeno, -na *adj* endogamous.

endomingado, -da *adj fam* dressed-up, dolled-up.

endomingar [16] *vt fam* to dress ○ doll up.

◆ **endomingarse** *fam vpr* to get dressed ○ dolled up in one's best clothes.

endosar *vt* **-1.** *fig* [tarea, trabajo]: ~ **algo a alguien** to lumber sb with sth. **-2.** COM to endorse.

endosatario, -ria *m y f* COM endorsee *Br*, indorsee *Am*.

endoscopia *f* endoscopy.

endoso *m* COM endorsement.

endulzar [13] *vt* [con azúcar] to sweeten; *fig* [con dulzura] to ease, to make more bearable.

endurecer [30] *vt* **-1.** [gen] to harden. **-2.** [fortalecer] to strengthen.

endurecimiento *m lit & fig* hardening.

ene. (*abrev de* **enero**) Jan.

enebro *m* juniper.

enema *f* enema.

enemigo, -ga ◇ *adj* enemy (*antes de sust*); **ser** ~ **de algo** to hate sth. ◇ *m y f* enemy.

enemistad *f* enmity.

enemistar *vt* to make enemies of.

◆ **enemistarse** *vpr*: ~**se (con)** to fall out (with).

energético, -ca *adj* energy (*antes de sust*).

◆ **energética** *f* energetics (*U*).

energía *f* **-1.** [gen] energy; ~ **atómica** ○ **nuclear** nuclear power; ~ **eólica/hidráulica** wind/water power; ~ **solar** solar energy ○ power. **-2.** [fuerza] strength.

enérgico, -ca *adj* [gen] energetic; [carácter] forceful; [gesto, medida] vigorous; [decisión, postura] emphatic.

energúmeno, -na *m y f fig* madman (*f* madwoman).

enero *m* January; *ver también* **septiembre**.

enervante *adj* [debilitador] draining; [exasperante] exasperating.

enervar *vt* **-1.** [debilitar] to sap, to weaken. **-2.** [poner nervioso] to exasperate.

enésimo, -ma *adj* **-1.** MAT nth. **-2.** *fig* umpteenth; **por enésima vez** for the umpteenth time.

enfadar *vt* to anger.

◆ **enfadarse** *vpr*: ~**se (con)** to get angry (with).

enfado *m* anger.

enfangar [16] *vt* to cover in mud.

◆ **enfangarse** *vpr* **-1.** [con fango] to get covered in mud. **-2.** *fam fig* [en un asunto sucio] to get mixed up in shady business.

énfasis *m inv* emphasis; **poner** ~ **en algo** to emphasize sth.

enfático, -ca *adj* emphatic.

enfatizar [13] *vt* to emphasize, to stress.

enfermar ◇ *vt* **-1.** [causar enfermedad] to make ill. **-2.** *fig* [irritar] to make sick. ◇ *vi* to fall ill; ~ **del pecho** to develop a chest complaint.

enfermedad *f* **-1.** [física] illness; ~ **infecciosa/venérea** infectious/venereal disease. **-2.** *fig* [sentimiento] sickness; [problema - de sociedad etc] ill.

enfermera → **enfermero**.

enfermería *f* sick bay.

enfermero, -ra *m y f* male nurse (*f* nurse).

enfermizo, -za *adj lit & fig* unhealthy.

enfermo, -ma ◇ *adj* ill, sick. ◇ *m y f* [gen] invalid, sick person; [en el hospital] patient.

enfervorizar [13] *vt* to inflame, to rouse.

enfilar ◇ *vt* **-1.** [ir por - camino] to go ○ head straight along. **-2.** [apuntar - arma] to aim. ◇ *vi*: ~ **hacia** to go ○ head straight towards.

enfisema *m* emphysema.

enflaquecer [30] ◇ *vt* to make thin. ◇ *vi* to grow thin, to lose weight.

enfocar [10] *vt* **-1.** [imagen, objetivo] to focus. **-2.** [suj: luz, foco] to shine on. **-3.** *fig* [tema, asunto] to approach, to look at.

enfoque *m* **-1.** [de una imagen] focus. **-2.** *fig* [de un asunto] approach, angle.

enfrascado, -da *adj*: **estar ~ (en)** to be totally absorbed (in).

enfrascar [10] *vt* to bottle.
◆ **enfrascarse en** *vpr* [riña] to get embroiled in; [lectura, conversación] to become engrossed in.

enfrentamiento *m* confrontation.

enfrentar *vt* **-1.** [hacer frente] to confront, to face. **-2.** [poner frente a frente] to bring face to face.
◆ **enfrentarse** *vpr* **-1.** [luchar, encontrarse] to meet, to clash. **-2.** [oponerse]: **~se con alguien** to confront sb.

enfrente *adv* **-1.** [delante] opposite; **la tienda de ~** the shop across the road; **~ de** opposite. **-2.** [en contra]: **tiene a todos ~** everyone's against her.

enfriamiento *m* **-1.** [catarro] cold. **-2.** [acción] cooling.

enfriar [9] *vt lit & fig* to cool.
◆ **enfriarse** *vpr* **-1.** [líquido, pasión, amistad] to cool down. **-2.** [quedarse demasiado frío] to go cold. **-3.** MED to catch a cold.

enfundar *vt* [espada] to sheathe; [pistola] to put away.
◆ **enfundarse** *vpr*: **~se algo** to wrap o.s. up in sthg.

enfurecer [30] *vt* to infuriate, to madden.
◆ **enfurecerse** *vpr* **-1.** [gen] to get furious. **-2.** *fig* [mar] to become rough.

enfurecimiento *m* anger.

enfurruñarse *vpr fam* to sulk.

engalanar *vt* to decorate.
◆ **engalanarse** *vpr* to dress up.

enganchar *vt* **-1.** [agarrar - vagones] to couple; [- remolque, caballos] to hitch up; [- pez] to hook. **-2.** [colgar de un gancho] to hang up. **-3.** *fam fig* [atraer]: **~ a alguien para que haga algo** to rope sb into doing sthg. **-4.** [pillar - empleo, marido] to land (o.s.).
◆ **engancharse** *vpr* **-1.** [prenderse]: **~se algo con algo** to catch sthg on sthg. **-2.** [alistarse] to enlist, to join up. **-3.** [hacerse adicto]: **~se (a)** to get hooked (on).

enganche *m* **-1.** [de trenes] coupling. **-2.** [gancho] hook. **-3.** [reclutamiento] enlistment. **-4.** *Amer* [depósito] deposit.

enganchón *m* [de ropa etc] snag.

engañabobos *m inv* **-1.** [cosa] con (trick). **-2.** [persona] con man, con artist.

engañar *vt* **-1.** [gen] to deceive; **engaña a su marido** she cheats on her husband. **-2.**

[estafar] to cheat, to swindle. **-3.** [hacer más llevadero] to appease; **~ el hambre** to cheat one's stomach.
◆ **engañarse** *vpr* **-1.** [hacerse ilusiones] to delude o.s. **-2.** [equivocarse] to be wrong.

engañifa *f fam* [gen] trick; [estafa] swindle.

engaño *m* [gen] deceit; [estafa] swindle; **llamarse a ~** to claim one has been cheated.

engañoso, -sa *adj* [persona, palabras] deceitful; [aspecto, apariencia] deceptive.

engarce *m* setting.

engarzar [13] *vt* **-1.** [encadenar - abalorios] to thread; [- perlas] to string. **-2.** [engastar] to set. **-3.** [enlazar - palabras] to string together.

engatusador, -ra *fam* ◇ *adj* coaxing, cajoling. ◇ *m y f* coaxer.

engatusamiento *m fam* coaxing, cajoling.

engatusar *vt fam* to get round; **~ a alguien para que haga algo** to coax O cajole sb into doing sthg.

engendrar *vt* **-1.** [procrear] to give birth to, to beget. **-2.** *fig* [originar] to give rise to.

engendro *m* **-1.** [obra de mala calidad] monstrosity. **-2.** [ser deforme] freak, deformed creature; [niño] malformed child.

englobar *vt* to bring together.

engolosinarse *vpr*: **~ con** to develop a taste for.

engomar *vt* **-1.** [pegar] to stick, to glue. **-2.** [dar apresto] to size.

engordar ◇ *vt* **-1.** to fatten up. **-2.** *fig* [aumentar] to swell. ◇ *vi* to put on weight.

engorde *m* fattening (up).

engorro *m* nuisance.

engorroso, -sa *adj* bothersome.

engranaje *m* **-1.** [acción] gearing. **-2.** [piezas - de reloj, piñón] cogs (*pl*); AUTOM gears (*pl*). **-3.** *fig* [enlace - de ideas] chain, sequence; [aparato - político, burocrático] machinery.

engranar *vt* **-1.** [piezas] to engage. **-2.** *fig* [ideas] to link, to connect.

engrandecer [30] *vt* **-1.** *fig* [enaltecer] to exalt. **-2.** [aumentar] to increase, to enlarge.

engrandecimiento *m* **-1.** [enaltecimiento] enhancement. **-2.** [aumento] increase.

engrasar *vt* [gen] to lubricate; [bisagra, mecanismo] to oil; [eje, bandeja] to grease.

engrase *m* **-1.** [acción - gen] lubrication; [- de goznes] oiling; [- de bandeja] greasing. **-2.** [sustancia] lubricant.

engreído, -da ◇ *adj* conceited, full of one's own importance. ◇ *m y f* conceited person.

engrescar [10] *vt* to egg on, to incite.

engrosar [23] *vt* **-1.** *fig* [aumentar] to swell.

-2. [engordar - animal] to fatten; [- texto] to bump up the size of.

engrudo *m* paste.

engruesa *etc* → engrosar.

engrumecerse [30] *vpr* to go lumpy.

enguantarse *vpr* to put one's gloves on.

engullir *vt* to gobble up, to wolf down.

enharinar *vt* to flour.

enhebrar *vt* **-1.** [gen] to thread; [perlas] to string. **-2.** *fig* [palabras] to string together.

enhiesto, -ta *adj* [derecho] erect, upright; [bandera] raised.

enhorabuena ◇ *f* congratulations (*pl*). ◇ *adv*: ¡~ (por ...)! congratulations (on ...)!

enigma *m* enigma.

enigmático, -ca *adj* enigmatic.

enjabonado, -da *adj* soapy.
◆ **enjabonado** *m* washing.

enjabonar *vt* **-1.** [con jabón] to soap. **-2.** *fig* [dar coba] to soft-soap.

enjambre *m lit* & *fig* swarm.

enjaular *vt* [en jaula] to cage; *fam fig* [en prisión] to jail, to lock up.

enjoyar *vt* to adorn with jewels.
◆ **enjoyarse** *vpr* to put on (one's) jewels.

enjuagar [16] *vt* to rinse.
◆ **enjuagarse** *vpr* to rinse o.s./one's mouth/one's hands *etc*.

enjuague *m* rinse.

enjugar [16] *vt* **-1.** [secar] to dry, to wipe away. **-2.** *fig* [pagar - deuda] to pay off; [- déficit] to cancel out.

enjuiciamiento *m* **-1.** DER trial. **-2.** [opinión] judgment.

enjuiciar [8] *vt* **-1.** DER to try. **-2.** [opinar] to judge.

enjuto, -ta *adj* [delgado] lean.

enlace ◇ *v* → enlazar. ◇ *m* **-1.** [acción] link. **-2.** [persona] go-between; ~ **sindical** shop steward. **-3.** QUÍM bond. **-4.** [casamiento]: ~ **(matrimonial)** marriage. **-5.** [de trenes] connection; **estación de** ~ junction; **vía de** ~ crossover. **-6.** INFORM: ~ **hipertextual** ○ **de hipertexto** hypertext link.

enladrillado *m* brick paving.

enladrillar *vt* to pave with bricks.

enlatar *vt* to can, to tin.

enlazar [13] ◇ *vt*: ~ **algo a** [atar] to tie sthg up to; [trabar, relacionar] to link ○ connect sthg with. ◇ *vi*: ~ **en** [trenes] to connect at.
◆ **enlazarse** *vpr* to become linked.

enlodar *vt* to cover in mud.

enloquecedor, -ra *adj* maddening.

enloquecer [30] ◇ *vt* **-1.** [volver loco] to drive mad. **-2.** *fig* [gustar mucho] to drive wild ○ crazy. ◇ *vi* to go mad.

enloquecimiento *m* madness.

enlosar *vt* to tile.

enlutado, -da *adj* in mourning.

enlutar *vt* **-1.** [vestir de luto] to dress in mourning. **-2.** *fig* [entristecer] to cast a shadow over.

enmaderar *vt* [pared] to panel; [suelo] to lay the floorboards of.

enmadrarse *vpr* to become too tied to one's mother.

enmarañar *vt* **-1.** [enredar] to tangle (up). **-2.** [complicar] to complicate, to confuse.
◆ **enmarañarse** *vpr* **-1.** [enredarse] to become tangled. **-2.** [complicarse] to become confused ○ complicated.

enmarcar [10] *vt* to frame.

enmascarado, -da ◇ *adj* masked. ◇ *m y f* masked man (*f* masked woman).

enmascarar *vt* [rostro] to mask; *fig* [encubrir] to disguise.

enmendar [19] *vt* [error] to correct; [ley, dictamen] to amend; [comportamiento] to mend; [daño, perjuicio] to redress.
◆ **enmendarse** *vpr* to mend one's ways.

enmienda *f* **-1.** [acción]: **hacer propósito de** ~ to promise to mend one's ways. **-2.** [en un texto] corrections (*pl*). **-3.** POLÍT amendment.

enmiende → enmendar.

enmohecer [30] *vt* [gen] to turn mouldy; [metal] to rust.
◆ **enmohecerse** *vpr* [gen] to grow mouldy; [metal, conocimientos] to go rusty.

enmohecimiento *m* [gen] mould; [de metal] rust.

enmoquetado *m* carpeting.

enmoquetar *vt* to carpet.

enmudecer [30] ◇ *vt* to silence. ◇ *vi* [callarse] to fall silent, to go quiet; [perder el habla] to be struck dumb.

enmudecimiento *m* silence.

ennegrecer [30] *vt* [gen] to blacken; [suj: nubes] to darken.
◆ **ennegrecerse** *vpr* [gen] to become blackened; [nublarse] to grow dark.

ennoblecer [30] *vt* **-1.** *fig* [dignificar] to lend distinction to. **-2.** [dar un título] to ennoble.

enojadizo, -za *adj* irritable, touchy.

enojar *vt* [enfadar] to anger; [molestar] to annoy.
◆ **enojarse** *vpr*: ~**se (con)** [enfadarse] to get angry (with); [molestarse] to get annoyed (with).

enojo *m* [enfado] anger; [molestia] annoyance.

enojoso, -sa *adj* [molesto] annoying; [delicado, espinoso] awkward.

enología *f* oenology, study of wine.

enólogo, -ga *m y f* oenologist, wine expert.

enorgullecer [30] *vt* to fill with pride.
◆ **enorgullecerse de** *vpr* to be proud of.

enorme *adj* [en tamaño] enormous, huge; [en gravedad] monstrous.

enormidad *f* **-1.** [de tamaño] enormity, hugeness. **-2.** *fig* [despropósito] crass remark/mistake *etc*.

ENPETROL (*abrev de* **Empresa Nacional de Petróleos**) *f Spanish petroleum company*.

enquistado, -da *adj*: **tiene la mano enquistada** he has a cyst on his hand.

enquistamiento *m* encystment.

enquistarse *vpr* to develop into a cyst.

enraizar [13] *vi* [árbol] to take root; [persona] to put down roots.

enramada *f* **-1.** [espesura] branches (*pl*), canopy. **-2.** [cobertizo] bower.

enrarecer [30] *vt* **-1.** [contaminar] to pollute. **-2.** [rarificar] to rarefy.
◆ **enrarecerse** *vpr* **-1.** [contaminarse] to become polluted. **-2.** [rarificarse] to become rarefied. **-3.** *fig* [situación, ambiente] to become tense.

enredadera *f* creeper.

enredador, -ra ◇ *adj* [travieso] naughty, mischievous; [chismoso] gossiping. ◇ *m y f* [travieso] mischief-maker; [chismoso] gossip.

enredar ◇ *vt* **-1.** [madeja, pelo] to tangle up; [situación, asunto] to complicate, to confuse. **-2.** *fig* [implicar]: ~ **a alguien (en)** to embroil sb (in), to involve sb (in). **-3.** *fig* [entretener] to bother, to annoy. ◇ *vi* to get up to mischief.
◆ **enredarse** *vpr* **-1.** [plantas] to climb; [madeja, pelo] to get tangled up; [situación, asunto] to become confused. **-2.** [empezar]: ~**se en algo** to get involved in sthg; ~**se a hacer algo** to start doing sthg. **-3.** *fam* [amancebarse]: ~**se con** to get involved ○ have an affair with.

enredo *m* **-1.** [maraña] tangle, knot. **-2.** [lío] mess, complicated affair; [asunto ilícito] shady affair. **-3.** [amoroso] (love) affair. **-4.** LITER plot.

enrejado *m* **-1.** [barrotes - de balcón, verja] railings (*pl*); [- de jaula, celda, ventana] bars (*pl*). **-2.** [de cañas] trellis.

enrejar *vt* [ventanas] to bar.

enrevesado, -da *adj* complex, complicated.

enriquecedor, -ra *adj* enriching.

enriquecer [30] *vt* **-1.** [hacer rico] to bring wealth to, to make rich. **-2.** *fig* [engrandecer] to enrich.
◆ **enriquecerse** *vpr* to get rich.

enriquecimiento *m* enrichment.

enrojecer [30] ◇ *vt* [gen] to redden, to turn red; [rostro, mejillas] to cause to blush. ◇ *vi* [por calor] to flush; [por turbación] to blush.
◆ **enrojecerse** *vpr* [por calor] to flush; [por turbación] to blush.

enrojecimiento *m* **-1.** [rubor] blushing. **-2.** [irritación] redness, red mark.

enrolar *vt* to enlist.
◆ **enrolarse en** *vpr* [la marina] to enlist in; [un buque] to sign up for.

enrollar *vt* **-1.** [arrollar] to roll up. **-2.** *fam* [gustar]: **me enrolla mucho** I love it, I think it's great.
◆ **enrollarse** *vpr fam* **-1.** [tener relaciones]: ~**se (con)** to get involved ○ have an affair (with). **-2.** [hablar] to go on (and on).

enroscar [10] *vt* **-1.** [atornillar] to screw in. **-2.** [enrollar] to roll up; [cuerpo, cola] to curl up.

ensaimada *f cake made of sweet coiled pastry*.

ensalada *f* **-1.** [de lechuga etc] salad. **-2.** *fam fig* [lío] mishmash.

ensaladera *f* salad bowl.

ensaladilla *f*: ~ **(rusa)** Russian salad.

ensalmo *m* incantation, spell; **como por** ~ as if by magic.

ensalzar [13] *vt* to praise.

ensamblado *m* assembly.

ensamblador, -ra *m y f* [persona] joiner.
◆ **ensamblador** *m* INFORM assembler.

ensambladura *f*, **ensamblaje** *m* [acción] assembly; [pieza] joint.

ensamblar *vt* [gen & INFORM] to assemble; [madera] to join.

ensanchamiento *m* [de orificio, calle] widening; [de ropa] letting out.

ensanchar *vt* [orificio, calle] to widen; [ropa] to let out; [ciudad] to expand.

ensanche *m* **-1.** [de calle etc] widening. **-2.** [en la ciudad] new suburb.

ensangrentado, -da *adj* bloodstained.

ensangrentar [19] *vt* to cover with blood.

ensañamiento *m* ferocity.

ensañarse *vpr*: ~ **con** to torment, to treat cruelly.

ensartar *vt* **-1.** [perlas] to string; [aguja] to thread. **-2.** [atravesar - torero] to gore; [puñal] to plunge, to bury.

ensayar *vt* **-1.** [gen] to test. **-2.** TEATR to rehearse.

ensayista *m y f* essayist.

ensayo *m* **-1.** TEATR rehearsal; ~ **general** dress rehearsal. **-2.** [prueba] test. **-3.** LITER essay. **-4.** [en rugby] try.

enseguida *adv* [inmediatamente] immediately, at once; [pronto] very soon; **llegará** ~ he'll be here any minute now.

ensenada *f* cove, inlet.

enseña *f* ensign.

enseñante *m y f* teacher.

enseñanza *f* [gen] education; [instrucción] teaching; ~ **estatal** O **pública** state education; ~ **privada** private (sector) education; ~ **superior/universitaria** higher/university education; ~ **primaria/media** primary/secondary education; ~ **personificada** personal O individual tutoring.

◆ **enseñanzas** *fpl* [de maestro] teachings.

enseñar *vt* **-1.** [instruir, aleccionar] to teach; ~ **a alguien a hacer algo** to teach sb (how) to do sthg. **-2.** [mostrar] to show.

enseñorearse *vpr*: ~ **(de)** to take possession (of).

enseres *mpl* **-1.** [efectos personales] belongings. **-2.** [utensilios] equipment (*U*).

ensillado, -da *adj* saddled.

ensillar *vt* to saddle up.

ensimismado, -da *adj* [enfrascado] absorbed; [pensativo] lost in thought.

ensimismamiento *m* absorption.

ensimismarse *vpr* [enfrascarse] to become absorbed; [abstraerse] to be lost in thought.

ensoberbecer [30] *vt* to fill with pride.

ensombrecer [30] *vt lit & fig* to cast a shadow over.

◆ **ensombrecerse** *vpr* to darken.

ensoñación *f* daydream.

ensopar *vt Amer* to soak.

ensordecedor, -ra *adj* deafening.

ensordecer [30] ◇ *vt* **-1.** [causar sordera] to cause to go deaf. **-2.** [suj: sonido] to deafen. ◇ *vi* to go deaf.

ensordecimiento *m* deafness.

ensortijar *vt* to curl.

ensuciar [8] *vt* to (make) dirty; *fig* [desprestigiar] to sully, to tarnish.

◆ **ensuciarse** *vpr* to get dirty.

ensueño *m lit & fig* dream; **de** ~ dream (*antes de sust*), ideal.

entablado *m* [armazón] wooden platform; [suelo] floorboards (*pl*).

entablar *vt* **-1.** [suelo] to put down floorboards on. **-2.** [iniciar - conversación, amistad] to strike up; [- negocio] to start up. **-3.** [entablillar] to put in a splint.

entablillar *vt* to put in a splint.

entallar ◇ *vt* **-1.** [prenda] to cut, to tailor. **-2.** [madera] to carve, to sculpt. ◇ *vi* to fit.

entarimado *m* [plataforma] wooden platform; [suelo] floorboards (*pl*).

entarimar *vt* [suelo] to put down floorboards on.

ente *m* **-1.** [ser] being. **-2.** [corporación] body, organization; ~ **público** state-owned body O institution; [televisión] Spanish state broadcasting company. **-3.** *fam* [personaje] odd bod.

Entel (*abrev de* **Empresa Nacional de Telecomunicaciones**) *f Spanish telecommunications company*.

entelequia *f* **-1.** FILOSOFÍA entelechy. **-2.** [fantasía] pipe dream.

entendederas *fpl fam* brains.

entendedor, -ra *m y f*: **al buen** ~ **sobran las palabras** O **pocas palabras bastan** a word to the wise is sufficient.

entender [20] ◇ *vt* **-1.** [gen] to understand; **¿tú qué entiendes por "amistad"?** what do you understand by "friendship"?; **dar a** ~ **que ...** to imply (that) .... **-2.** [darse cuenta] to realize. **-3.** [oír] to hear. **-4.** [juzgar] to think; **yo no lo entiendo así** I don't see it that way. ◇ *vi* **-1.** [comprender] to understand. **-2.** [saber]: ~ **de** O **en algo** to be an expert on sthg; ~ **poco/algo de** to know very little/a little about. ◇ *m*: **a mi** ~ **...** the way I see it ....

◆ **entenderse** *vpr* **-1.** [comprenderse - uno mismo] to know what one means; [- dos personas] to understand each other. **-2.** [llevarse bien] to get on. **-3.** [ponerse de acuerdo] to reach an agreement. **-4.** [comunicarse] to communicate (with each other). **-5.** [amorosamente]: ~**se (con)** to have an affair (with).

entendido, -da ◇ *adj* **-1.** [comprendido] understood. **-2.** [versado] expert. ◇ *m y f*: ~ **(en)** expert (on).

◆ **entendido** *interj*: ¡~! all right!, okay!

entendimiento *m* [comprensión] understanding; [juicio] judgment; [inteligencia] mind, intellect.

entente *f* POLIT entente cordiale; COM agreement.

enterado, -da ◇ *adj*: ~ **(en)** well-informed (about); **estar** ~ **de algo** to be aware of sthg; **no darse por** ~ to turn a deaf ear. ◇ *m y f* expert.

enterar *vt*: ~ **a alguien de algo** to inform sb about sthg.

◆ **enterarse** *vpr* **-1.** [descubrir]: ~**se (de)** to find out (about). **-2.** *fam* [comprender] to get it, to understand. **-3.** [darse cuenta]: ~**se (de algo)** to realize (sthg). **-4.** *loc*: **¡para que te**

enteres! I'll have you know!, as a matter of fact!; **¡te vas a ~!** you'll know all about it!, you'll catch it!

entereza f [serenidad] composure; [honradez] integrity; [firmeza] firmness.

enternecedor, -ra adj touching.

enternecer [30] vt to move, to touch.
◆ **enternecerse** vpr to be moved.

enternecimiento m compassion.

entero, -ra adj -1. [completo] whole; **por ~** entirely, completely. -2. [sereno] composed. -3. [honrado] upright, honest.
◆ **entero** m BOLSA point.

enterrador, -ra m y f gravedigger.

enterramiento m burial.

enterrar [19] vt -1. [gen] to bury. -2. fig [olvidar] to forget about.
◆ **enterrarse** vpr fig to hide o.s. away.

entibiar [8] vt -1. [enfriar] to cool. -2. [templar] to warm.
◆ **entibiarse** vpr [sentimiento] to cool.

entidad f -1. [corporación] body; [empresa] firm, company; **~ bancaria** bank. -2. FILOSOFIA entity. -3. [importancia] importance.

entienda etc → entender.

entierra etc → enterrar.

entierro m [acción] burial; [ceremonia] funeral.

entlo. abrev de entresuelo.

entoldado m [toldo] awning; [para fiestas, bailes] marquee.

entoldar vt to cover with an awning.

entomología f entomology.

entomólogo, -ga m y f entomologist.

entonación f intonation.

entonar ◇ vt -1. [cantar] to sing. -2. [tonificar] to pick up. ◇ vi -1. [al cantar] to sing in tune. -2. [armonizar]: **~ (con algo)** to match (sthg).

entonces ◇ adv then; **desde ~** since then; **en O por aquel ~** at that time. ◇ interj: **¡~!** well, then!

entontecer [30] vt: **~ a alguien** to dull sb's brain.

entornar vt to half-close.

entorno m environment, surroundings (pl).

entorpecer [30] vt -1. [debilitar - movimientos] to hinder; [- miembros] to numb; [- mente] to cloud. -2. [dificultar] to obstruct, to hinder.

entorpecimiento m -1. [debilitamiento - físico] numbness; [- mental] haziness. -2. [dificultad] hindrance.

entrada f -1. [acción] entry; [llegada] arrival; "**prohibida la ~**" "no entry". -2. [lugar] entrance; [puerta] doorway. -3. TECN inlet, intake. -4. [en espectáculos - billete] ticket; [- recaudación] receipts (pl), takings (pl); **~ libre** admission free; **sacar una ~** to buy a ticket. -5. [público] audience; DEP attendance. -6. [pago inicial] down payment. -7. [en contabilidad] income. -8. [plato] starter. -9. [en la frente]: **tener ~s** to have a receding hairline. -10. [en un diccionario] entry. -11. [principio] beginning, start; **de ~** right from the beginning O the word go. -12. INFORM input.

entrado, -da adj -1. [gen]: **~ el otoño** once autumn has started; **~ en años** elderly; **~ en carnes** portly, rather large. -2. INFORM input.

entramado m framework.

entramar vt to make the framework of.

entrante ◇ adj [año, mes] coming; [presidente, gobierno] incoming. ◇ m -1. [plato] starter. -2. [hueco] recess.

entraña f (gen pl) -1. [víscera] entrails (pl), insides (pl). -2. fig [centro, esencia] heart. -3. loc: **arrancársele a uno las ~s** to break sb's heart; **no tener ~s** to be heartless.

entrañable adj intimate.

entrañar vt to involve.

entrar ◇ vi -1. [introducirse - viniendo] to enter, to come in; [- yendo] to enter, to go in; **~ en algo** to enter sthg, to come/go into sthg; **entré por la ventana** I got in through the window. -2. [penetrar - clavo etc] to go in; **~ en algo** to go into sthg. -3. [caber]: **~ (en)** to fit (in); **este anillo no te entra** this ring won't fit you. -4. [incorporarse]: **~ (en algo)** [colegio, empresa] to start (at sthg); [club, partido político] to join (sthg); **~ de** [botones etc] to start off as. -5. [empezar]: **~ a hacer algo** to start doing sthg. -6. [participar] to join in; **~ en** [discusión, polémica] to join in; [negocio] to get in on. -7. [estar incluido]: **~ en** to be included in. -8. [figurar]: **~ en** to belong to; **entro en el grupo de los disconformes** I number among the dissidents. -9. [estado físico o de ánimo]: **le entraron ganas de hablar** he suddenly felt like talking; **me está entrando frío** I'm getting cold; **me entró mucha pena** I was filled with pity. -10. [periodo de tiempo] to start; **el verano entra el 21 de junio** summer starts on 21st June; **~ en** [edad, vejez] to reach; [año nuevo] to enter. -11. [cantidad]: **¿cuántos entran en un kilo?** how many do you get to the kilo? -12. [concepto, asignatura etc]: **no le entra la geometría** he can't get the hang of geometry. -13. AUTOM to engage; **no entra la tercera** it won't go into third gear.

◇ *vt* **-1.** [introducir] to bring in. **-2.** [prenda de vestir] to take in. **-3.** [acometer] to approach, to deal with; **a ése no hay por donde** ~**le** there's no way of getting through to him.

entre *prep* **-1.** [gen] between; ~ **nosotros** [en confianza] between you and me, between ourselves; **era un color** ~ **verde y azul** the colour was somewhere between green and blue; **su estado de ánimo estaba** ~ **la alegría y la emoción** his state of mind was somewhere between ○ was a mixture of joy and excitement; ~ **una cosa y otra** what with one thing and another. **-2.** [en medio de muchos] among, amongst; **estaba** ~ **los asistentes** she was among those who were there; **estuvo** ~ **los mejores** he was one of ○ amongst the best; ~ **hombres y mujeres somos más de cien** there are over a hundred of us, men and women together; ~ **sí** amongst themselves; **discutían** ~ **sí** they were arguing with each other.

entreabierto, -ta *pp* → entreabrir.

entreabrir *vt* to half-open.

entreacto *m* interval.

entrecejo *m* space between the brows; **fruncir el** ~ to frown.

entrecerrar [19] *vt* to half-close.

entrechocar [10] ◇ *vt* [espadas] to clash. ◇ *vi* [dientes] to chatter.

entrecomillado, -da *adj* in quotation marks.

◆ **entrecomillado** *m* text in quotation marks.

entrecomillar *vt* to put in quotation marks.

entrecortado, -da *adj* [voz, habla] faltering; [respiración] laboured; [señal, sonido] intermittent.

entrecot, entrecote *m* entrecôte.

entrecruzar [13] *vt* to interweave; [miradas] to meet; [dedos] to link together.

◆ **entrecruzarse** *vpr* to interweave; [miradas, caminos] to meet.

entredicho *m*: **estar en** ~ to be in doubt; **poner en** ~ to question, to call into question.

entrega *f* **-1.** handing over; [de pedido, paquete] delivery; [de premios] presentation; **hacer** ~ **de algo a alguien** to hand sthg over to sb; ~ **a domicilio** home delivery. **-2.** [dedicación]: ~ **(a)** devotion (to). **-3.** [fascículo] instalment.

entregar [16] *vt* [gen] to hand over; [pedido, paquete] to deliver; [examen, informe] to hand in; [persona] to turn over.

◆ **entregarse** *vpr* [rendirse · soldado, ejército] to surrender; [- criminal] to turn o.s. in.

◆ **entregarse a** *vpr* **-1.** [persona, trabajo] to devote o.s. to. **-2.** [vicio, pasión] to give o.s. over to.

entreguerras

◆ **de entreguerras** *loc adj* between the wars.

entrelazar [13] *vt* to interlace, to interlink.

entrelínea *f* space between two lines.

entremedio, entremedias *adv* in between.

entremés *m* CULIN (*gen pl*) hors d'œuvres.

entremeter *vt* to insert, to put in.

◆ **entremeterse** *vpr* [inmiscuirse]: ~**se (en)** to meddle (in).

entremetido, -da ◇ *adj* meddling. ◇ *m y f* meddler.

entremezclar *vt* to mix up.

◆ **entremezclarse** *vpr* to mix.

entrenador, -ra *m y f* coach; [seleccionador] manager.

entrenamiento *m* training.

entrenar *vt & vi* to train.

◆ **entrenarse** *vpr* to train.

entreoír [62] *vt* to half-hear.

entrepierna *f* crotch.

entresacar [10] *vt* to pick out.

entresijos *mpl* ins and outs.

entresuelo *m* mezzanine.

entretanto ◇ *adv* meanwhile. ◇ *m*: **en el** ~ in the meantime.

entretecho *m Amer* loft, attic.

entretejer *vt* to interweave.

entretela *f* [de ropa] inner lining.

◆ **entretelas** *fpl fig* innermost heart (*sg*).

entretención *f Amer* entertainment.

entretener [72] *vt* **-1.** [despistar] to distract. **-2.** [retrasar] to hold up, to keep. **-3.** [divertir] to entertain. **-4.** [mantener] to keep alive, to sustain.

◆ **entretenerse** *vpr* **-1.** [despistarse] to get distracted. **-2.** [divertirse] to amuse o.s. **-3.** [retrasarse] to be held up.

entretenido, -da *adj* entertaining, enjoyable.

entretenimiento *m* **-1.** [acción] entertainment. **-2.** [pasatiempo] pastime.

entretiempo *m*: **de** ~ mild-weather (*antes de sust*).

entrever [76] *vt* **-1.** [vislumbrar] to barely make out; [por un instante] to glimpse. **-2.** *fig* [adivinar] to see signs of.

◆ **entreverse** *vpr* to be barely visible; **no se entreve una solución** *fig* there's no sign of a solution.

entreverar *vt Amer* to mix.

◆ **entreverarse** *vpr Amer* to get tangled.

entrevero *m Amer* tangle, mess.

entrevista *f* interview; **~ de selección** job interview.

entrevistador, -ra *m y f* interviewer.

entrevistar *vt* to interview.

◆ **entrevistarse** *vpr*: **~se (con)** to have a meeting (with).

entrevisto, -ta *pp* → **entrever**.

entristecer [30] *vt* to make sad.

◆ **entristecerse** *vpr* to become sad.

entristecimiento *m* sadness.

entrometerse *vpr*: **~ (en)** to interfere (in).

entrometido, -da ◇ *adj* interfering. ◇ *m y f* meddler.

entrometimiento *m* meddling.

entromparse *vpr fam* to get legless.

entroncamiento *m* [parentesco] relationship, connection.

entroncar [10] *vi* **-1.** [emparentarse]: **~ (con)** to become related (to). **-2.** [trenes etc] to connect. **-3.** *fig* [relacionarse]: **~ (con)** to be related (to).

entronización *f*, **entronizamiento** *m* coronation.

entronizar [13] *vt* to crown.

entubar *vt* to fit tubes to, to tube.

entuerto *m* wrong, injustice; **deshacer ~s** to right wrongs.

entumecer [30] *vt* to numb.

◆ **entumecerse** *vpr* to become numb.

entumecido, -da *adj* numb.

entumecimiento *m* numbness.

enturbiar [8] *vt lit & fig* to cloud.

◆ **enturbiarse** *vpr lit & fig* to become cloudy.

entusiasmar *vt* **-1.** [animar] to fill with enthusiasm. **-2.** [gustar]: **le entusiasma la música** he loves music.

◆ **entusiasmarse** *vpr*: **~se (con)** to get excited (about).

entusiasmo *m* enthusiasm.

entusiasta ◇ *adj* enthusiastic. ◇ *m y f* enthusiast.

entusiástico, -ca *adj* enthusiastic.

enumeración *f* enumeration, listing.

enumerar *vt* to enumerate, to list.

enunciación *f*, **enunciado** *m* formulation, enunciation.

enunciar [8] *vt* to formulate, to enunciate.

envainar *vt* to sheathe.

envalentonamiento *m* boldness.

envalentonar *vt* to urge on, to fill with courage.

◆ **envalentonarse** *vpr* to become daring.

envanecer [30] *vt* to make vain.

◆ **envanecerse** *vpr* to become vain.

envanecimiento *m* vanity.

envarado, -da ◇ *adj* stiff, formal. ◇ *m y f* stiff ○ formal person.

envasado *m* [en botellas] bottling; [en latas] canning; [en paquetes] packing.

envasar *vt* [gen] to pack; [en latas] to can; [en botellas] to bottle.

envase *m* **-1.** [envasado - en botellas] bottling; [- en latas] canning; [- en paquetes] packing. **-2.** [recipiente] container; [botella] bottle; **~ desechable** disposable container; **~ sin retorno** non-returnable bottle.

envejecer [30] ◇ *vi* [hacerse viejo] to grow old; [parecer viejo] to age. ◇ *vt* to age.

envejecido, -da *adj* [de edad] old; [de aspecto] aged.

envejecimiento *m* ageing.

envenenamiento *m* poisoning.

envenenar *vt* to poison.

envergadura *f* **-1.** [importancia] size, extent; [complejidad] complexity; **una reforma de gran ~** a wide-ranging reform. **-2.** [anchura] span.

envés *m* reverse (side), back; [de tela] wrong side.

enviado, -da *m y f* POLÍT envoy; PRENS correspondent; **~ especial** PRENS special correspondent.

enviar [9] *vt* to send.

enviciar [8] *vt* to addict, to get hooked.

◆ **enviciarse** *vpr* to become addicted.

envidia *f* envy; **tener ~ de** to envy.

envidiable *adj* enviable.

envidiar [8] *vt* to envy.

envidioso, -sa ◇ *adj* envious. ◇ *m y f* envious person.

envilecer [30] *vt* to debase.

◆ **envilecerse** *vpr* to become debased.

envilecimiento *m* debasement.

envío *m* **-1.** COM dispatch; [de correo] delivery; [de víveres, mercancías] consignment. **-2.** [paquete] package.

envite *m* **-1.** [en el juego] raise. **-2.** [ofrecimiento] offer.

enviudar *vi* to be widowed.

envoltorio *m*, **envoltura** *f* wrapper, wrapping.

envolvente *adj* enveloping.

envolver [24] *vt* **-1.** [embalar] to wrap (up). **-2.** [enrollar] to wind. **-3.** [implicar]: **~ a alguien en** to involve sb in. **-4.** *fig* [dominar] to envelop, to take over.

◆ **envolverse** *vpr*: **~se en** ○ **con algo** to wrap o.s. in sthg.

envuelto, -ta *pp* → **envolver**.

envuelva *etc* → **envolver**.

enyesar vt -1. MED to put in plaster. -2. CONSTR to plaster.

enzarzar [13] vt to entangle, to embroil.

◆ **enzarzarse** vpr: ~**se en** to get entangled O embroiled in.

enzima f enzyme.

eólico, -ca adj wind (antes de sust).

epatar vt to shock.

e.p.d. (abrev de en paz descanse) RIP.

épica → épico.

epicentro m epicentre.

épico, -ca adj epic.

◆ **épica** f epic.

epicureísmo m Epicureanism.

epicúreo, -a adj, m y f Epicurean.

epidemia f epidemic.

epidémico, -ca adj epidemic.

epidemiología f epidemiology.

epidérmico, -ca adj epidermic.

epidermis f inv epidermis.

Epifanía f Epiphany.

epífisis f inv epiphysis.

epiglotis f inv epiglottis.

epígrafe m heading.

epigrafía f epigraphy.

epigrama m epigram.

epilepsia f epilepsy.

epiléptico, -ca adj, m y f epileptic.

epílogo m epilogue.

episcopado m -1. [gen] episcopate, episcopacy. -2. [territorio] diocese.

episcopal adj episcopal.

episodio m -1. [gen] episode. -2. [suceso] event.

epistemología f epistemology.

epístola f culto [carta] epistle; RELIG Epistle.

epistolar adj culto epistolary.

epistolario m collected letters (pl).

epitafio m epitaph.

epitelio m epithelium.

epíteto m epithet.

epítome m summary, synopsis.

e.p.m. abrev de en propia mano.

época f period; [estación] season; **de** ~ period (antes de sust); **en aquella** ~ at that time; **hacer** ~ to become a symbol of its time.

epónimo, -ma adj eponymous.

◆ **epónimo** m eponym.

epopeya f -1. [gen] epic. -2. fig [hazaña] feat.

épsilon f epsilon.

equidad f fairness.

equidistante adj equidistant.

equidistar vi: ~ (**de**) to be equidistant (from).

équidos mpl members of the horse family.

equilátero, -ra adj equilateral.

equilibrado, -da adj -1. [gen] balanced. -2. [sensato] sensible.

equilibrar vt to balance.

◆ **equilibrarse** vpr to balance.

equilibrio m balance; **mantener algo en** ~ to balance sthg; **mantenerse/perder el** ~ to keep/lose one's balance; ~ **ecológico** ecological balance; **hacer** ~**s** fig to perform a balancing act.

equilibrismo m [en trapecio] trapeze; [funambulismo] tightrope walking.

equilibrista m y f [trapecista] trapeze artist; [funambulista] tightrope walker.

equino, -na adj equine.

equinoccial adj equinoctial.

equinoccio m equinox.

equipaje m luggage Br, baggage Am; **hacer el** ~ to pack; ~ **de mano** hand luggage.

equipamiento m [acción] equipping; [equipo] equipment.

equipar vt: ~ (**de**) [gen] to equip (with); [ropa] to fit out (with).

◆ **equiparse** vpr to equip o.s.

equiparable adj: ~ (**a**) comparable (to).

equiparar vt to compare.

◆ **equipararse** vpr to be compared.

equipo m -1. [equipamiento] equipment; ~ **de oficina** office equipment. -2. [uniforme - de novia] trousseau; [- de soldado] kit; [- colegial] uniform. -3. [personas, jugadores] team; ~ **de rescate** rescue team. -4. [de música] system; ~ **de sonido** sound system.

equis adj X; **un número** ~ **de personas** x number of people.

equitación f [arte] equestrianism; [actividad] horse riding.

equitativo, -va adj fair, even-handed.

equivalencia f equivalence.

equivalente adj & m equivalent.

equivaler [74]

◆ **equivaler a** vi to be equivalent to; fig [significar] to amount to.

equivocación f mistake; **por** ~ by mistake.

equivocado, -da adj mistaken.

equivocar [10] vt to choose wrongly; ~ **algo con algo** to mistake sthg for sthg.

◆ **equivocarse** vpr to be wrong; ~**se en** to make a mistake in; **se equivocó de nombre** he got the wrong name.

equívoco, -ca adj -1. [ambiguo] ambiguous, equivocal. -2. [sospechoso] suspicious.

◆ **equívoco** *m* misunderstanding.

era ◇ *v* → ser. ◇ *f* **-1.** [periodo] era; ~ cristiana/geológica Christian/geological era. **-2.** [campo] threshing floor.

erario *m* funds (*pl*); ~ público exchequer.

ERASMUS (*abrev de European Action Scheme for the Mobility of University Students*) *m* ERASMUS.

erección *f* erection.

eréctil *adj* erectile.

erecto, -ta *adj* erect.

eremita *m y f* hermit.

eres → ser.

ergonomía *f* ergonomics (*U*).

ergonómico, -ca *adj* ergonomic.

erguir [58] *vt* to raise.
◆ **erguirse** *vpr* to rise up.

erial ◇ *adj* uncultivated. ◇ *m* uncultivated land.

erice *etc* → erizar.

erigir [15] *vt* **-1.** [construir] to erect, to build. **-2.** [nombrar] to name.
◆ **erigirse en** *vpr* to set o.s. up as.

eritema *m* skin rash.

erizado, -da *adj* **-1.** [de punta] on end; [con púas o espinas] spiky. **-2.** *fig* [lleno]: ~ de plagued with.

erizar [13] *vt* to cause to stand on end.
◆ **erizarse** *vpr* [pelo] to stand on end; [persona] to stiffen.

erizo *m* **-1.** [mamífero] hedgehog. **-2.** [pez] globefish; ~ de mar sea urchin.

ermita *f* hermitage.

ermitaño, -ña *m y f* hermit.

erógeno, -na *adj* erogenous.

eros *m inv* eros.

erosión *f* erosion.

erosionar *vt* to erode.
◆ **erosionarse** *vpr* to erode.

erosivo, -va *adj* erosive.

erótico, -ca *adj* erotic.
◆ **erótica** *f*: la erótica del poder the thrill of power.

erotismo *m* eroticism.

erradicación *f* eradication.

erradicar [10] *vt* to eradicate.

errado, -da *adj* [disparo] wide of the mark, missed; [razonamiento] mistaken.

errante *adj* wandering.

errar [47] ◇ *vt* [vocación, camino] to choose wrongly; [disparo, golpe] to miss. ◇ *vi* **-1.** [vagar] to wander. **-2.** [equivocarse] to make a mistake. **-3.** [al disparar] to miss.

errata *f* misprint.

errático, -ca *adj* [errante] wandering; MED erratic.

erre *f*: ~ que ~ stubbornly.

erróneo, -a *adj* mistaken.

error *m* mistake, error; **estar en un** ~ to be mistaken; **por** ~ by mistake; **salvo** ~ **u** omisión errors and omissions excepted; ~ de imprenta misprint.

ertzaina [er'tʃaina] *f member of Basque regional police force*.

ertzaintza [er'tʃaintʃa] *f Basque regional police force*.

eructar *vi* to belch.

eructo *m* belch.

erudición *f* erudition.

erudito, -ta ◇ *adj* erudite. ◇ *m y f* scholar.

erupción *f* **-1.** GEOL eruption; **en** ~ erupting. **-2.** MED rash.

eruptivo, -va *adj* [roca] volcanic; [volcán] active.

es → ser.

E/S *abrev de* entrada/salida.

esa → ese².

ésa → ése.

esbeltez *f* slenderness, slimness.

esbelto, -ta *adj* slender, slim.

esbirro *m* henchman.

esbozar [13] *vt* to sketch, to outline; [sonrisa] to give a hint of.

esbozo *m* sketch, outline.

escabechado, -da *adj* CULIN marinated.
◆ **escabechado** *m* CULIN marinade.

escabechar *vt* CULIN to marinate.

escabeche *m* CULIN marinade.

escabechina *f* destruction; [en examen] huge number of failures.

escabroso, -sa *adj* **-1.** [abrupto] rough. **-2.** [obsceno] risqué. **-3.** [espinoso] awkward, thorny.

escabullirse *vpr* **-1.** [desaparecer]: ~ (de) to slip away (from). **-2.** [escurrirse]: ~le a alguien to slip out of sb's hands.

escacharrar *vt fam* to knacker.
◆ **escacharrarse** *vpr fam* to get knackered.

escafandra *f* diving suit; ~ espacial spacesuit.

escafandrista *m y f* diver.

escala *f* **-1.** [gen] scale; [de colores] range; **a** ~ [gráfica] to scale; **a** ~ **mundial** *fig* on a worldwide scale; **a gran** ~ on a large scale; ~ **de popularidad** popularity stakes (*pl*). **-2.** [en un viaje] stopover; **hacer** ~ to stop over. **-3.** [escalera] ladder.

escalada f **-1.** [de montaña] climb. **-2.** [de violencia, precios] escalation, rise.

escalador, -ra ◇ adj climbing (antes de sust). ◇ m y f **-1.** [alpinista] climber. **-2.** fam [de puestos] careerist.

escalafón m scale, ladder.

escalar vt to climb.

escaldado, -da adj **-1.** CULIN scalded. **-2.** fig wary.

escaldar vt to scald.

◆ **escaldarse** vpr to get burned.

escaleno adj scalene.

escalera f **-1.** [gen] stairs (pl), staircase; [escala] ladder; ~ **mecánica** ○ **automática** escalator; ~ **de caracol** spiral staircase; ~ **de incendios** fire escape; ~ **de mano** ladder; ~ **de servicio** service stairs (pl); ~ **de tijera** step ladder. **-2.** [en naipes] run; ~ **de color** straight flush.

escalerilla f [de avión] stairs (pl).

escalfar vt to poach.

escalinata f staircase.

escalofriante adj spine-chilling.

escalofrío m (gen pl) shiver; **dar ~s a alguien** to give sb the shivers.

escalón m step; fig grade.

escalonado, -da adj **-1.** [en el tiempo] spread out. **-2.** [terreno] terraced; [pelo] layered.

escalonar vt **-1.** [gen] to spread out. **-2.** [terreno] to terrace.

escalope m escalope.

escalpelo m scalpel.

escama f **-1.** [de peces, reptiles] scale. **-2.** [de jabón, en la piel] flake.

escamado, -da adj fam suspicious, wary.

escamar vt **-1.** [pescado] to scale. **-2.** fam fig [mosquear] to make suspicious.

◆ **escamarse** vpr fam to smell a rat, to get suspicious.

escamotear vt: ~ **algo a alguien** [estafar] to do ○ swindle sb out of sth; [hurtar] to rob sb of sth.

escampar v impers to clear up, to stop raining.

escanciar [8] vt to serve, to pour out.

escandalizar [13] vt to scandalize, to shock.

◆ **escandalizarse** vpr to be shocked.

escándalo m **-1.** [inmoralidad] scandal; [indignación] outrage. **-2.** [alboroto] uproar, racket; **armar un ~** to kick up a fuss.

escandaloso, -sa ◇ adj **-1.** [inmoral] outrageous, shocking. **-2.** [ruidoso] very noisy. ◇ m y f very noisy ○ loud person.

escandinavo, -va adj, m y f Scandinavian.

escandio m scandium.

escáner (pl **escáners**) m INFORM & MED scanner.

escaño m **-1.** [cargo] seat (in parliament). **-2.** [asiento] bench (in parliament).

escapada f **-1.** [huida] escape, flight; DEP breakaway. **-2.** [viaje] quick trip.

escapar vi **-1.** [huir]: ~ **(de)** to get away ○ escape (from). **-2.** [quedar fuera del alcance]: ~ **a alguien** to be beyond sb.

◆ **escaparse** vpr **-1.** [huir]: ~**se (de)** to get away ○ escape (from); ~**se de casa** to run away from home. **-2.** [salir - gas, agua etc] to leak. **-3.** [perder]: **se me escapó la risa/un taco** I let out a laugh/an expletive; **se me escapó el tren** I missed the train; **se me escapó la ocasión** the opportunity slipped by.

escaparate m (shop) window.

escaparatista m y f window dresser.

escapatoria f **-1.** [fuga] escape; **no tener ~** to have no way out. **-2.** fam [evasiva] way (of getting out).

escape m [de gas etc] leak; [de coche] exhaust; **a ~** in a rush, at high speed.

escapismo m escapism.

escapista adj escapist.

escapulario m scapular.

escaquearse vpr fam to duck out; ~ **de algo/de hacer algo** to worm one's way out of sth/doing sth.

escarabajo m beetle.

escaramuza f MIL & fig skirmish.

escarapela f rosette, cockade.

escarbar vt to scratch, to scrape.

escarceos mpl forays; ~ **amorosos** flirtations.

escarcha f frost.

escarchado, -da adj [fruta] candied, crystallized.

escarchar v impers to freeze (over).

escardar vt to weed.

escarlata adj & m scarlet.

escarlatina f scarlet fever.

escarmentar [19] vi to learn (one's lesson).

escarmiento m lesson; **servir de ~** to serve as a lesson.

escarnecer [30] vt to mock, to ridicule.

escarnecimiento m mockery, ridicule.

escarnio m mockery, ridicule.

escarola f endive.

escarpado, -da adj [inclinado] steep; [abrupto] craggy.

escasear vi to be scarce, to be in short supply.

escasez f [insuficiencia] **shortage**; [pobreza] **poverty**.

escaso, -sa adj **-1.** [insuficiente, conocimientos, recursos] **limited, scant**; [- tiempo] **short**; [- cantidad, número] **low**; [- víveres, trabajo] **scarce, in short supply**; [- visibilidad, luz] **poor**; **andar ~ de** to be short of. **-2.** [casi completo]: **un metro ~** barely a metre.

escatimar vt [gastos, comida] **to be sparing with, to skimp on**; [esfuerzo, energías] **to use as little as possible**; **no ~ gastos** to spare no expense.

escatología f [sobre excrementos] **scatology**.

escatológico, -ca adj [de excrementos] **scatological**.

escay, skai m **Leatherette®**.

escayola f CONSTR **plaster of Paris**; MED **plaster**.

escayolar vt **to put in plaster**.

escayolista m y f **decorative plasterer**.

escena f **-1.** [gen] **scene**; **hacer una ~** to make a scene. **-2.** [escenario] **stage**; **llevar a la ~** to dramatize; **poner en ~** to stage.

escenario m **-1.** [tablas, escena] **stage**; CIN & TEATR [lugar de la acción] **setting**. **-2.** fig [de suceso] **scene**.

escénico, -ca adj **scenic**.

escenificación f [de novela] **dramatization**; [de obra de teatro] **staging**.

escenificar [10] vt [novela] **to dramatize**; [obra de teatro] **to stage**.

escenografía f **set design**.

escenógrafo, -fa m y f **set designer**.

escepticismo m **scepticism**.

escéptico, -ca ◇ adj **-1.** FILOSOFÍA **sceptic**. **-2.** [incrédulo] **sceptical**. ◇ m y f **sceptic**.

escindir vt **to split**.
◆ **escindirse** vpr: **~se (en)** to split (into).

escisión f [del átomo] **splitting**; [de partido político] **split**.

esclarecedor, -ra adj **illuminating**.

esclarecer [30] vt **to clear up, to shed light on**.

esclarecimiento m **clearing up, elucidation**.

esclava → **esclavo**.

esclavina f **short cape**.

esclavismo m **(system of) slavery**.

esclavista ◇ adj **pro-slavery**. ◇ m y f **supporter of slavery**.

esclavitud f lit & fig **slavery**.

esclavizar [13] vt lit & fig **to enslave**.

esclavo, -va ◇ adj **enslaved**. ◇ m y f lit & fig [persona] **slave**.
◆ **esclava** f [pulsera] **bangle, bracelet**.

esclerosis f inv MED **sclerosis**.

esclerótica f **sclera, sclerotic**.

esclusa f [de canal] **lock**; [compuerta] **floodgate**.

escoba f **broom**.

escobazo m **blow with a broom**; **echar a alguien a ~s** to kick sb out.

escobilla f **brush**.

escocedura f **-1.** [herida] **sore**. **-2.** [sensación] **smarting, stinging**.

escocer [41] vi lit & fig **to sting**.
◆ **escocerse** vpr [piel] **to get sore**.

escocés, -esa ◇ adj [gen] **Scottish**; [whisky] **Scotch**; [tejido] **tartan, plaid**. ◇ m y f [persona] **Scot, Scotsman** (f **Scotswoman**); **los escoceses** **the Scottish, the Scots**.
◆ **escocés** m [lengua] **Scots** (U).

Escocia **Scotland**.

escoger [14] vt **to choose**.

escogido, -da adj [elegido] **selected, chosen**; [selecto] **choice, select**.

escoja etc → **escoger**.

escolanía f **choirboys** (pl).

escolapio, -pia adj, m y f **member of the religious order of the Escuelas Pías**.

escolar ◇ adj **school** (antes de sust). ◇ m y f **pupil, schoolboy** (f **schoolgirl**).

escolaridad f **schooling**.

escolarización f **schooling**.

escolarizar [13] vt **to provide with schools**.

escolástico, -ca adj **scholastic**.
◆ **escolástica** f **scholasticism**.

escoliosis f inv **scoliosis**.

escollera f **breakwater**.

escollo m **-1.** [en el mar] **reef**. **-2.** fig **stumbling block**.

escolta f **escort**.

escoltar vt **to escort**.

escombros mpl **rubble** (U), **debris** (U).

esconder vt **to hide, to conceal**.
◆ **esconderse** vpr: **~se (de)** to hide (from).

escondido, -da adj [lugar] **secluded**.
◆ **a escondidas** loc adv **in secret**.

escondite m **-1.** [lugar] **hiding place**. **-2.** [juego] **hide-and-seek**.

escondrijo m **hiding place**.

escoñar vt fam **to knacker, to break**.
◆ **escoñarse** vpr fam **to get knackered**.

escopeta f **shotgun**; **~ de aire comprimido** **air gun**; **~ de cañones recortados** **sawn-off shotgun**.

escopetazo m [disparo] **gunshot**; [herida] **gunshot wound**.

escorar *vi* NÁUT to list.

escorbuto *m* scurvy.

escoria *f fig* dregs (*pl*), scum.

Escorpio, Escorpión ◇ *m* [zodiaco] Scorpio; **ser ~** to be (a) Scorpio. ◇ *m y f* [persona] Scorpio.

escorpión *m* scorpion.

◆ **Escorpión** = **Escorpio**.

escotado, -da *adj* low-cut, low-necked.

escotadura *f* low neckline.

escotar *vt* to lower the neckline of.

escote *m* [de prendas] neckline; [de persona] neck; **pagar a ~** to go Dutch.

escotilla *f* hatch, hatchway.

escozamos → **escocer**.

escozor *m* stinging.

escriba *m* RELIG scribe.

escribanía *f* [profesión] clerkship.

escribano, -na *m y f* DER clerk of the court.

escribiente *m y f* clerk.

escribir *vt & vi* to write.

◆ **escribirse** *vpr* **-1.** [personas] to write to one another. **-2.** [palabras]: **se escribe con "h"** it is spelt with an "h".

escrito, -ta ◇ *pp* → **escribir**. ◇ *adj* written; **por ~** in writing.

◆ **escrito** *m* [gen] text; [documento] document; [obra literaria] writing, work.

escritor, -ra *m y f* writer.

escritorio *m* **-1.** [mueble] desk, bureau. **-2.** [habitación] office.

escritura *f* **-1.** [arte] writing. **-2.** [sistema de signos] script. **-3.** DER deed.

◆ **Sagrada Escritura** *f* (*gen pl*): **La Sagrada Escritura** Holy Scripture.

escriturar *vt* to execute by deed.

escroto *m* scrotum.

escrúpulo *m* **-1.** [duda, recelo] scruple; **sin escrúpulos** unscrupulous. **-2.** [minuciosidad] scrupulousness, great care. **-3.** [aprensión] qualm; **le da ~** he has qualms about it.

escrupuloso, -sa *adj* **-1.** [gen] scrupulous. **-2.** [aprensivo] particular, fussy.

escrutar *vt* [con la mirada] to scrutinize, to examine; [votos] to count.

escrutinio *m* count (*of votes*).

escuadra *f* **-1.** GEOM square. **-2.** [de buques] squadron. **-3.** [de soldados] squad.

escuadrilla *f* squadron.

escuadrón *m* squadron; **~ de la muerte** death squad.

escuálido, -da *adj culto* emaciated.

escucha *f* listening-in, monitoring; **estar** O **permanecer a la ~** to listen in; **~s telefónicas** telephone tapping (*U*).

escuchar ◇ *vt* to listen to. ◇ *vi* to listen.

escuchimizado, -da ◇ *adj* skinny, thin as a rake. ◇ *m y f* skinny person.

escudar *vt fig* to shield.

◆ **escudarse** *vpr*: **~se en algo** *fig* to hide behind sthg, to use sthg as an excuse.

escudería *f* team (*in motor racing*).

escudero *m* squire.

escudo *m* **-1.** [arma] shield. **-2.** [moneda] escudo. **-3.** [emblema] coat of arms.

escudriñar *vt* [examinar] to scrutinize, to examine; [otear] to search.

escuece → **escocer**.

escuela *f* school; **~ normal** teacher training college; **~ privada** private school, public school *Br*; **~ pública** state school; **~ universitaria** *university which awards degrees after three years of study*; **formar** O **hacer ~** to have a following; **ser de la vieja ~** to be of the old school.

escueto, -ta *adj* [sucinto] concise; [sobrio] plain, unadorned.

escueza *etc* → **escocer**.

escuincle, -cla *m y f Amer* nipper, kid.

esculpir *vt* to sculpt, to carve.

escultor, -ra *m y f* sculptor (*f* sculptress).

escultórico, -ca *adj* sculptural.

escultura *f* sculpture.

escultural *adj* **-1.** ARTE sculptural. **-2.** [atractivo] statuesque.

escupidera *f* spittoon.

escupir ◇ *vi* to spit. ◇ *vt* [suj: persona, animal] to spit out; [suj: volcán, chimenea etc] to belch out.

escupitajo *m* gob, spit.

escurreplatos *m inv* dish rack.

escurridero *m* draining board.

escurridizo, -za *adj lit & fig* slippery.

escurrido, -da *adj* **-1.** [ropa - en lavadora] spun-dry; [- estrujando] wrung-out. **-2.** [verdura] drained.

escurridor *m* colander.

escurrir ◇ *vt* [gen] to drain; [ropa] to wring out; [en lavadora] to spin-dry. ◇ *vi* [gotear] to drip.

◆ **escurrirse** *vpr* [resbalarse] to slip.

escúter (*pl* escúters), **scooter** (*pl* scooters) *m* (motor) scooter.

esdrújulo, -la *adj* proparoxytone.

ese[1] *f* [figura] zigzag; **hacer ~s** [en carretera] to zigzag; [al andar] to stagger about.

ese[2] (*pl* esos), **esa** *adj demos* **-1.** [gen] that, (*pl*) those. **-2.** (*después de sust*) *fam* [despectivo] that, (*pl*) those; **el hombre ~ no me inspira confianza** I don't trust that guy.

ése (*pl* **ésos**), **ésa** *pron demos* **-1.** [gen] that one, (*pl*) those ones. **-2.** [mencionado antes] the former. **-3.** *fam* [despectivo]: ~ **fue el que me pegó** that's the guy who hit me. **-4.** *loc*: ¡a ~! stop that man!; **ni por ésas** not even then; **no me lo vendió ni por ésas** even then he wouldn't sell me it.

esencia *f* essence; **quinta** ~ quintessence.

esencial *adj* essential; **lo** ~ the fundamental thing.

esfera *f* **-1.** [gen] sphere; ~ **celeste** celestial sphere; ~ **terrestre** (terrestrial) globe. **-2.** [de reloj] face. **-3.** [círculo social] circle. **-4.** INFORM: ~ **de arrastre** ○ **de desplazamiento** trackball.

esférico, -ca *adj* spherical.
◆ **esférico** *m* DEP ball.

esfinge *f* sphinx.

esfínter (*pl* **esfínteres**) *m* sphincter.

esforzar [37] *vt* [voz] to strain.
◆ **esforzarse** *vpr* to make an effort; ~**se en** ○ **por hacer algo** to try very hard to do sthg, to do one's best to do sthg.

esfuerzo *m* effort; **sin** ~ effortlessly.

esfumarse *vpr* [esperanzas, posibilidades] to fade away; [persona] to vanish, to disappear.

esgrima *f* fencing.

esgrimir *vt* **-1.** [arma] to brandish, to wield. **-2.** [argumento, hecho, idea] to use.

esguince *m* sprain.

eslabón *m* link; **el** ~ **perdido** the missing link.

eslabonar *vt lit* & *fig* to link together.

eslálom (*pl* **esláloms**) *m* slalom.

eslavo, -va ◇ *adj* slav, Slavonic. ◇ *m y f* [persona] Slav.
◆ **eslavo** *m* [lenguas] Slavonic.

eslip (*pl* **eslips**) *m* briefs (*pl*).

eslogan (*pl* **eslóganes**) *m* slogan.

eslora *f* NÁUT length.

eslovaco, -ca *adj, m y f* Slovak, Slovakian.
◆ **eslovaco** *m* [lengua] Slovak.

Eslovaquia Slovakia.

esmaltado, -da *adj* enamelled.
◆ **esmaltado** *m* enamelling.

esmaltar *vt* to enamel.

esmalte *m* **-1.** [sustancia - en dientes, cerámica etc] enamel; [- de uñas] (nail) varnish ○ polish. **-2.** [objeto, joya etc] enamelwork.

esmerado, -da *adj* [persona] painstaking, careful; [trabajo] carefully done, polished.

esmeralda ◇ *f* emerald. ◇ *adj & m inv* emerald.

esmerarse *vpr*: ~**se (en algo/hacer algo)** [esforzarse] to take great pains (over sthg/ doing sthg).

esmeril *m* emery.

esmerilado, -da *adj* [pulido] polished with emery; [translúcido] ground.

esmerilar *vt* [pulir] to polish with emery.

esmero *m* great care.

esmirriado, -da *adj* puny, weak.

esmoquin (*pl* **esmóquines**) *m* dinner jacket *Br*, tuxedo *Am*.

esnac (*pl* **esnacs**) *m* snack bar.

esnifada *f fam* sniff (*of a drug*).

esnifar *vt fam* to sniff (*drugs*).

esnob (*pl* **esnobs**) ◇ *adj* trying to be trendy. ◇ *m y f* person who wants to be trendy.

esnobismo *m* desire to be trendy.

eso *pron demos* (*neutro*) that; ~ **es la Torre Eiffel** that's the Eiffel Tower; ~ **es lo que yo pienso** that's just what I think; ~ **que propones es irrealizable** what you're proposing is impossible; ~ **de vivir solo no me gusta** I don't like the idea of living on my own; ¡~, ~! that's right!, yes!; ¡~ **es!** that's it; ¿**cómo es** ~?, ¿**y** ~? [¿por qué?] how come?; **para** ~ **es mejor no ir** if that's all it is, you might as well not go; **por** ~ **vine** that's why I came.
◆ **a eso de** *loc prep* (at) about ○ around.
◆ **en eso** *loc adv* just then, at that very moment.
◆ **y eso que** *loc conj* even though.

esófago *m* oesophagus.

esos, -sas → ese².

ésos, -sas → ése.

esotérico, -ca *adj* esoteric.

esoterismo *m* **-1.** [impenetrabilidad] esoteric nature. **-2.** [ciencias ocultas] esotericism.

espabilar *vt* **-1.** [despertar] to wake up. **-2.** [avispar]: ~ **a alguien** to sharpen sb's wits.
◆ **espabilarse** *vpr* **-1.** [despertarse] to wake up, to brighten up. **-2.** [darse prisa] to get a move on. **-3.** [avisparse] to sharpen one's wits.

espachurrar *fam vt* to squash.
◆ **espachurrarse** *vpr* to get squashed.

espaciado, -da *adj* at regular intervals.

espaciador *m* space bar.

espacial *adj* space (*antes de sust*).

espaciar [8] *vt* to space out.

espacio *m* **-1.** [gen] space; **no tengo mucho** ~ I don't have much room; **a doble** ~ double-spaced; **por** ~ **de** over a period of; ~ **aéreo** air space; ~ **verde** park; ~ **vital** living space. **-2.** RADIO & TV programme; ~ **publicitario** advertising spot.

espacioso, -sa *adj* spacious.

espada ◇ *f* [arma] sword; ~ **de dos filos** *fig* double-edged sword; **estar entre la ~ y la pared** to be between the devil and the deep blue sea. ◇ *m* TAUROM matador; *ver también* **tauromaquia**.
◆ **espadas** *fpl* [naipes] ≃ spades.

espadachín *m* swordsman.

espagueti *m* spaghetti (*U*).

espalda *f* **-1.** [gen] back; **cargado de ~s** round-shouldered; **de ~s a alguien** with one's back turned on sb; **por la ~** from behind; *fig* behind one's back; **tumbarse de ~s** to lie on one's back; **cubrirse las ~s** to cover o.s.; **echarse algo sobre las ~s** to take sthg on; **hablar de alguien a sus ~s** to talk about sb behind their back; **tener buenas ~s** to be mentally tough; **tirar O tumbar de ~s** to be amazing O stunning; **volver la ~ a alguien** to turn one's back on sb. **-2.** [en natación] backstroke.

espaldarazo *m* blow to the back; **eso le dio el ~ (definitivo)** that finally earned her widespread recognition.

espalderas *fpl* wall bars.

espaldilla *f* shoulder (of lamb *etc*).

espantada *f* stampede; [de caballo] bolt.

espantadizo, -za *adj* nervous, easily frightened.

espantajo *m* **-1.** [espantapájaros] scarecrow. **-2.** [persona fea] fright, sight.

espantapájaros *m inv* scarecrow.

espantar *vt* **-1.** [ahuyentar] to frighten O scare away. **-2.** [asustar] to frighten, to scare.
◆ **espantarse** *vpr* to get frightened O scared.

espanto *m* fright; **¡qué ~!** how terrible!; **estar curado de ~s** to be unshockable.

espantoso, -sa *adj* **-1.** [terrorífico] horrific. **-2.** [enorme] terrible. **-3.** [feísimo] frightful, horrible.

España Spain.

español, -la ◇ *adj* Spanish. ◇ *m y f* [persona] Spaniard.
◆ **español** *m* [lengua] Spanish.

españolada *f despec* exaggerated portrayal of Spain.

españolismo *m* **-1.** [apego, afecto] affinity for things Spanish. **-2.** [carácter, naturaleza] Spanishness, Spanish character.

españolizar [13] *vt* to make Spanish, to hispanicize.
◆ **españolizarse** *vpr* to adopt Spanish ways.

esparadrapo *m* (sticking) plaster, Band-Aid® *Am*.

esparcido, -da *adj* scattered.

esparcimiento *m* **-1.** [diseminación] scattering. **-2.** [ocio] relaxation, time off.

esparcir [12] *vt* [gen] to spread; [semillas, papeles, objetos] to scatter.
◆ **esparcirse** *vpr* to spread (out).

espárrago *m* asparagus (*U*); ~ **triguero** wild asparagus; **mandar a alguien a freír ~s** *fam* to tell sb to get lost.

esparraguera *f* asparagus (plant).

espartano, -na ◇ *adj* **-1.** [de Esparta] Spartan. **-2.** *fig* [severo] spartan. ◇ *m y f* Spartan.

esparto *m* esparto (grass).

espasmo *m* spasm.

espasmódico, -ca *adj* spasmodic.

espatarrarse *vpr fam* to sprawl (with one's legs wide open).

espátula *f* **-1.** CULIN & MED spatula; ARTE palette knife; CONSTR bricklayer's trowel; [de empapelador] stripping knife. **-2.** [animal] spoonbill.

especia *f* spice.

especial *adj* **-1.** [gen] special; ~ **para** specially for; **en ~** especially, particularly; **¿alguno en ~?** any one in particular? **-2.** [peculiar - carácter, gusto, persona] peculiar, strange.

especialidad *f* speciality, specialty *Am*; ~ **de la casa** house speciality.

especialista ◇ *adj*: ~ **(en)** specializing (in). ◇ *m y f* **-1.** [experto]: ~ **(en)** specialist (in). **-2.** CIN stuntman (*f* stuntwoman).

especialización *f* specialization.

especializado, -da *adj*: ~ **en** specialized (in).

especializar [13] *vt* to specialize.
◆ **especializarse** *vpr*: ~**se (en)** to specialize (in).

especie *f* **-1.** BIOL species (*sg*). **-2.** [clase] kind, sort; **pagar en ~ O ~s** to pay in kind.

especificación *f* specification.

especificar [10] *vt* to specify.

especificidad *f* specificity.

específico, -ca *adj* specific.
◆ **específicos** *mpl* FARM patent medicines.

espécimen (*pl* **especímenes**) *m* specimen.

espectacular *adj* spectacular.

espectacularidad *f* spectacular nature.

espectáculo *m* **-1.** [diversión] entertainment. **-2.** [función] show, performance; ~ **de variedades** variety show. **-3.** [suceso, escena] sight. **-4.** *loc*: **dar el ~** to cause a scene.

espectador *m y f* TV viewer; CIN & TEATR member of the audience; DEP spectator; [de suceso, discusión] onlooker.

◆ **espectadores** *mpl* TV viewers; CIN & TEATR audience (*sg*); DEP spectators; [de suceso, discusión] onlookers.

espectral *adj* **-1.** FÍS spectral. **-2.** *fig* ghostly.

espectro *m* **-1.** [fantasma] spectre, ghost. **-2.** FÍS & MED spectrum.

especulación *f* speculation.

especulador, -ra ◇ *adj* speculating. ◇ *m y f* speculator.

especular *vi*: ~ **(sobre)** to speculate (about); ~ **en** COM to speculate on.

especulativo, -va *adj* speculative.

espejismo *m* mirage; *fig* illusion.

espejo *m lit* & *fig* mirror.

espeleología *f* potholing.

espeleólogo, -ga *m y f* potholer.

espeluznante *adj* hair-raising, lurid.

espera *f* **-1.** [acción] wait; **en ~ de, a la ~ de** waiting for, awaiting; **seguimos a la ~ de su respuesta** [en cartas] we await your reply. **-2.** [paciencia] patience.

esperanto *m* Esperanto.

esperanza *f* [deseo, ganas] hope; [confianza, expectativas] expectation; **perder la ~** to lose hope; **tener ~ de hacer algo** to hope to be able to do sthg; ~ **de vida** life expectancy.

esperanzador, -ra *adj* encouraging, hopeful.

esperanzar [13] *vt* to give hope to, to encourage.

◆ **esperanzarse** *vpr* to be encouraged.

esperar ◇ *vt* **-1.** [aguardar] to wait for; ~ **a que alguien haga algo** to wait for sb to do sthg. **-2.** [tener esperanza de]: ~ **que** to hope that; **espero que sí** I hope so; ~ **hacer algo** to hope to do sthg. **-3.** [tener confianza en] to expect; ~ **que** to expect (that); ~ **algo de alguien** to expect sthg from sb, to hope for sthg from sb. ◇ *vi* **-1.** [aguardar] to wait; **quien espera desespera** *proverb* a watched pot never boils *proverb*. **-2.** [ser inevitable] to await, to be in store for; **le esperan dificultades** many difficulties await him; **como era de ~** as was to be expected.

◆ **esperarse** *vpr* **-1.** [imaginarse, figurarse] to expect. **-2.** [aguardar] to wait; ~**se a que alguien haga algo** to wait for sb to do sthg.

esperma ◇ *m o f* BIOL sperm. ◇ *f Amer* [vela] candle.

espermaticida ◇ *adj* spermicidal. ◇ *m* spermicide.

espermatozoide, espermatozoo *m* sperm, spermatozoon.

esperpéntico, -ca *adj* grotesque.

esperpento *m* [persona] grotesque sight; [cosa] absurdity, piece of nonsense.

espesar *vt* to thicken.

espeso, -sa *adj* [gen] thick; [bosque, niebla] dense; [nieve] deep.

espesor *m* **-1.** [grosor] thickness; **tiene 2 metros de ~** it's 2 metres thick. **-2.** [densidad - de niebla, bosque] density; [- de nieve] depth.

espesura *f* **-1.** [vegetación] thicket. **-2.** [grosor] thickness; [densidad] density.

espetar *vt* **-1.** [palabras] to blurt out, to tell straight out. **-2.** [carne] to skewer.

espía *m y f* spy.

espiar [9] *vt* to spy on.

espiga *f* **-1.** [de trigo etc] ear. **-2.** [en telas] herringbone. **-3.** [pieza - de madera] peg; [- de hierro] pin.

espigado, -da *adj* **-1.** [persona] tall and slim. **-2.** [planta] ripe.

espigarse [16] *vpr* **-1.** [persona] to shoot up. **-2.** [planta] to go to seed.

espigón *m* breakwater.

espigue *etc* → **espigarse**.

espiguilla *f* herringbone.

espín *m* FÍS spin.

espina *f* [de pez] bone; [de planta] thorn; **me da mala ~** it makes me uneasy, there's something fishy about it; **tener una ~ clavada** to bear a great burden.

◆ **espina dorsal** *f* spine.

espinaca *f* (*gen pl*) spinach (*U*).

espinal *adj* spinal.

espinazo *m* spine, backbone; **doblar el ~** *fig* [humillarse] to kow-tow.

espinilla *f* **-1.** [hueso] shin, shinbone. **-2.** [grano] blackhead.

espinillera *f* shin pad.

espino *m* **-1.** [planta] hawthorn. **-2.** [alambre] barbed wire.

espinoso, -sa *adj lit* & *fig* thorny.

espionaje *m* espionage; ~ **industrial** industrial espionage.

espiración *f* exhalation, breathing out.

espiral *f lit* & *fig* spiral; **en ~** [escalera, forma] spiral; ~ **inflacionaria** ECON inflationary spiral.

espirar *vi & vt* to exhale, to breathe out.

espiritismo *m* spiritualism.

espiritista *adj* spiritualist.

espíritu *m* **-1.** [gen] spirit; RELIG soul. **-2.** [fantasma] ghost. **-3.** [modo de pensar] attitudes (*pl*); ~ **de cuerpo** esprit de corps.

◆ **Espíritu Santo** *m* Holy Ghost.

espiritual *adj & m* spiritual.

espiritualidad *f* spirituality.

espita f spigot, tap, faucet *Am.*

esplendidez f **-1.** [generosidad] generosity. **-2.** [magnificencia] splendour.

espléndido, -da *adj* **-1.** [magnífico] splendid, magnificent. **-2.** [generoso] generous, lavish.

esplendor m **-1.** [magnificencia] splendour. **-2.** [apogeo] greatness.

esplendoroso, -sa *adj* magnificent.

espliego m lavender.

espolear *vt* lit & *fig* to spur on.

espoleta f [de proyectil] fuse.

espolón m **-1.** [de ave] spur. **-2.** ARQUIT buttress; [de un puente] cutwater.

espolvorear *vt* to dust, to sprinkle.

esponja f sponge.

esponjar *vt* to fluff up.

esponjosidad f sponginess.

esponjoso, -sa *adj* spongy.

esponsales *mpl* betrothal (*sg*).

espontaneidad f spontaneity.

espontáneo, -a ◇ *adj* spontaneous. ◇ m y f *spectator who tries to join in a bullfight*.

esporádico, -ca *adj* sporadic.

esport *adj inv*: **(de)** ~ sports (*antes de sust*).

esposa → esposo.

esposado, -da *adj* handcuffed.

esposar *vt* to handcuff.

esposo, -sa m y f [persona] husband (f wife).
◆ **esposas** *fpl* [objeto] handcuffs.

espot (*pl* espots) m advertising spot, commercial.

espray (*pl* esprays) m spray.

esprint (*pl* esprints) m sprint.

esprínter (*pl* esprínters) m y f sprinter.

ESPRIT (*abrev de* **European Strategic Programme for Research and Development for Information Technology**) m ESPRIT.

espuela f **-1.** [gen] spur. **-2.** *fam fig* [última copa]: **tomar la** ~ to have one for the road.

espuerta f [recipiente] basket.
◆ **a espuertas** *loc adv* by the sackful ○ bucket.

espuma f **-1.** [gen] foam; [de cerveza] head; [de jabón] lather; [de olas] surf; [de un caldo] scum. **-2.** [para pelo] (styling) mousse.

espumadera f skimmer.

espumar *vt* [cerveza] to skim.

espumarajo m froth, foam; **echar** ~s to foam at the mouth.

espumoso, -sa *adj* [gen] foamy, frothy; [vino] sparkling; [jabón] lathery.
◆ **espumoso** m sparkling wine.

espúreo, -a, **espurio, -ria** *adj* **-1.** [bastar-

do] illegitimate. **-2.** *fig* [falso] spurious, false.

esputar *vi* to cough up ○ spit phlegm.

esputo m [gen] spittle; MED sputum.

esquech (*pl* esqueches), **esquetch** (*pl* esquetches) m (comic) sketch.

esqueje m cutting.

esquela f obituary.

esquelético, -ca *adj* ANAT skeletal; *fam* [muy delgado] skinny.

esqueleto m **-1.** [de persona] skeleton; **menear** ○ **mover el** ~ *fam* to boogie (on down). **-2.** [armazón] framework.

esquema m [gráfico] diagram; [resumen] outline.

esquemático, -ca *adj* schematic.

esquí (*pl* esquíes ○ esquís) m **-1.** [instrumento] ski. **-2.** [deporte] skiing; ~ **de fondo** ○ **nórdico** cross-country skiing; ~ **náutico** ○ **acuático** water-skiing; ~ **alpino** downhill skiing.

esquiador, -ra m y f skier.

esquiar [9] *vi* to ski.

esquilador, -ra m y f sheepshearer.

esquilar *vt* to shear.

esquimal ◇ *adj, m y f* Eskimo. ◇ m [lengua] Eskimo.

esquina f corner; **a la vuelta de la** ~ just round the corner; **doblar la** ~ to turn the corner; **hacer** ~ **(con)** to be on the corner (of).

esquinado, -da *adj* on the corner.

esquinazo m corner; **dar (el)** ~ **a alguien** to give sb the slip.

esquirla f splinter.

esquirol m *fam* blackleg, scab.

esquivar *vt* [gen] to avoid; [golpe] to dodge.

esquivez f shyness.

esquivo, -va *adj* shy.

esquizofrenia f schizophrenia.

esquizofrénico, -ca *adj, m y f* schizophrenic.

esquizoide *adj* schizoid.

esta → este².

ésta → éste.

estabilidad f stability; ~ **de precios** price stability.

estabilización f stabilization.

estabilizador, -ra *adj* stabilizing.
◆ **estabilizador** m stabilizer.

estabilizar [13] *vt* to stabilize.
◆ **estabilizarse** *vpr* to stabilize, to become stable.

estable *adj* **-1.** [firme] stable. **-2.** [permanente - huésped] permanent; [- cliente] regular.

establecer [30] *vt* **-1.** [gen] to establish; [récord] to set. **-2.** [negocio, campamento] to set up. **-3.** [inmigrantes etc] to settle.
◆ **establecerse** *vpr* **-1.** [instalarse] to settle. **-2.** [poner un negocio] to set up a business.

establecimiento *m* **-1.** [gen] establishment; [de récord] setting. **-2.** [de negocio, colonia] setting up. **-3.** [de emigrantes, colonos] settlement.

establo *m* cowshed.

estaca *f* **-1.** [para clavar, delimitar] stake; [de tienda de campaña] peg. **-2.** [garrote] cudgel.

estación *f* **-1.** [gen & INFORM] station; ~ **de autocares/de tren** coach/railway station; ~ **de esquí** ski resort; ~ **de gasolina** petrol station; ~ **de servicio** service station; ~ **de trabajo** workstation; ~ **meteorológica** weather station. **-2.** [del año, temporada] season.

estacionamiento *m* AUTOM parking; ~ **indebido** parking offence.

estacionar *vt* AUTOM to park.

estacionario, -ria *adj* [gen] stationary; ECON stagnant.

estadio *m* **-1.** DEP stadium. **-2.** [fase] stage.

estadista *m y f* statesman (*f* stateswoman).

estadístico, -ca *adj* statistical.
◆ **estadística** *f* **-1.** [ciencia] statistics (*U*). **-2.** [datos] statistics (*pl*).

estado *m* state; **su** ~ **es grave** his condition is serious; **estar en buen/mal** ~ [coche, terreno etc] to be in good/bad condition; [alimento, bebida] to be fresh/off; ~ **de ánimo** state of mind; ~ **civil** marital status; ~ **de bienestar** welfare state; ~ **de cuentas** statement of accounts; ~ **de excepción** o **emergencia** state of emergency; ~ **de salud** (state of) health; ~ **de sitio** state of siege; **en** ~ **de guerra** at war; **estar en** ~ **(de esperanza** o **buena esperanza)** to be expecting.
◆ **Estado** *m* [gobierno] State; **Estado Mayor** MIL general staff.
◆ **Estados Unidos (de América)** United States (of America).

estadounidense ◇ *adj* United States (*antes de sust*). ◇ *m y f* United States citizen.

estaf (*pl* estafs) *m* staff.

estafa *f* [gen] swindle; COM fraud.

estafador, -ra *m y f* swindler.

estafar *vt* [gen] to swindle; COM to defraud.

estafeta *f* sub-post office.

estafilococo *m* staphylococcus.

estalactita *f* stalactite.

estalagmita *f* stalagmite.

estalinismo *m* Stalinism.

estalinista *adj, m y f* Stalinist.

estallar *vi* **-1.** [reventar - bomba] to explode; [- neumático] to burst; [- volcán] to erupt; [- cristal] to shatter. **-2.** [sonar - ovación] to break out; [- látigo] to crack. **-3.** *fig* [guerra, epidemia etc] to break out. **-4.** *fig* [persona]: ~ **en sollozos** to burst into tears; ~ **en una carcajada** to burst out laughing.

estallido *m* **-1.** [de bomba] explosion; [de trueno] crash; [de látigo] crack. **-2.** *fig* [de guerra etc] outbreak.

Estambul Istanbul.

estamento *m* stratum, class.

estampa *f* **-1.** [imagen, tarjeta] print. **-2.** [aspecto] appearance. **-3.** [retrato, ejemplo] image.

estampado, -da *adj* printed.
◆ **estampado** *m* **-1.** [acción] printing. **-2.** [dibujo] (cotton) print.

estampar *vt* **-1.** [imprimir - gen] to print; [- metal] to stamp. **-2.** [escribir]: ~ **la firma** to sign one's name. **-3.** *fig* [arrojar]: ~ **algo/a alguien contra** to fling sthg/sb against, to hurl sthg/sb against. **-4.** *fig* [dar - beso] to plant; [- bofetada] to land.

estampida *f* stampede; **de** ~ suddenly, in a rush.

estampido *m* report, bang.

estampilla *f* **-1.** [para marcar] rubber stamp. **-2.** *Amer* [de correos] stamp.

estampillar *vt* [gen] to stamp; [documentos] to rubber-stamp.

estampita → **timo**.

estancado, -da *adj* [agua] stagnant; [situación, proyecto] at a standstill.

estancamiento *m* stagnation.

estancarse [10] *vpr* [líquido] to stagnate, to become stagnant; [situación] to come to a standstill.

estancia *f* **-1.** [tiempo] stay. **-2.** [habitación] room. **-3.** *Amer* [hacienda] cattle ranch.

estanciera *f* *Amer* van.

estanciero *m* *Amer* ranch owner.

estanco, -ca *adj* watertight.
◆ **estanco** *m* tobacconist's.

estand (*pl* estands) *m* stand, stall.

estándar (*pl* estándares) *adj* & *m* standard.

estandarización *f* standardization.

estandarizar [13] *vt* to standardize.

estandarte *m* standard, banner.

estanding (*pl* estandings) *m* standing, social status.

estanflación *f* ECON stagflation.

estanque *m* **-1.** [alberca] pond; [para riego]

reservoir. **-2.** *Amer* [depósito] tank (*of petrol*).

estanquero *m y f* tobacconist.

estante *m* shelf.

estantería *f* [gen] shelves (*pl*), shelving (*U*); [para libros] bookcase.

estañar *vt* to tin-plate.

estaño *m* tin.

estar [59] ◇ *vi* **-1.** [hallarse] to be; **¿dónde está la llave?** where is the key?; **¿está María?** is Maria in?; **no está** she's not in. **-2.** [con fechas]: **¿a qué estamos hoy?** what's the date today?; **hoy estamos a martes/a 15 de julio** today is Tuesday/the 15th of July; **estábamos en octubre** it was October. **-3.** [quedarse] to stay, to be; **estaré un par de horas y me iré** I'll stay a couple of hours and then I'll go. **-4.** (*antes de "a"*) [expresa valores, grados]: **estamos a veinte grados** it's twenty degrees here; **el dólar está a 95 pesetas** the dollar is at 95 pesetas; **están a 100 ptas el kilo** they're 100 pesetas a kilo. **-5.** [hallarse listo] to be ready; **¿aún no está ese trabajo?** is that piece of work still not ready? **-6.** [servir]: ~ **para** to be (there) for; **para eso están los amigos** that's what friends are for; **para eso estoy** that's what I'm there for. **-7.** (*antes de gerundio*) [expresa duración] to be; **están golpeando la puerta** they're banging on the door. **-8.** (*antes de "sin" + infin*) [expresa negación]: **estoy sin dormir desde ayer** I haven't slept since yesterday; **está sin acabar** it's not finished. **-9.** [faltar]: **eso está aún por escribir** that has yet to be written. **-10.** [hallarse a punto de]: ~ **por hacer algo** to be on the verge of doing sthg; **estuve por pegarle** I was on the verge of hitting him. **-11.** [expresa disposición]: ~ **para algo** to be in the mood for sthg; **no estoy para bromas** I'm not in the mood for jokes.

◇ *v copulativo* **-1.** (*antes de adj*) [expresa cualidad, estado] to be; **los pasteles están ricos** the cakes are delicious; **esta calle está sucia** this street is dirty. **-2.** (*antes de "con" o "sin" + sust*) [expresa estado] to be; **estamos sin agua** we have no water, we're without water. **-3.** [expresa situación, acción]: ~ **de: ~ de camarero** to work as a waiter, to be a waiter; ~ **de vacaciones** to be on holiday; ~ **de viaje** to be on a trip; ~ **de mudanza** to be (in the process of) moving; **estamos de suerte** we're in luck. **-4.** [expresa permanencia]: ~ **en uso** to be in use; ~ **en guardia** to be on guard. **-5.** [expresa apoyo, predilección]: ~ **por** to be in favour of. **-6.** [expresa ocupación]: ~ **como** to be; **está como cajera** she's a checkout girl. **-7.** [consistir]: ~

en to be, to lie in; **el problema está en la fecha** the problem is the date. **-8.** [sentar, ropa]: **este traje te está bien** this suit looks good on you. **-9.** (*antes de "que" + verbo*) [expresa actitud]: **está que muerde porque ha suspendido** he's furious because he failed.

◆ **estarse** *vpr* [permanecer] to stay; **te puedes ~ con nosotros unos días** you can stay O spend a few days with us.

estarcir *vt* to stencil.

estárter (*pl* **estárters**) *m* starter.

estatal *adj* state (*antes de sust*).

estatalizar [13] *vt* to nationalize.

estático, -ca *adj* **-1.** FÍS static. **-2.** [inmóvil] stock-still.

estatismo *m* **-1.** POLÍT statism, state interventionism. **-2.** [inmovilidad] stillness.

estatua *f* statue.

estatura *f* height.

estatus *m inv* status.

estatutario, -ria *adj* statutory.

estatuto *m* [gen] statute; [de empresa] article (of association); [de ciudad] by-law.

este¹ ◇ *adj* [posición, parte] east, eastern; [dirección, viento] easterly. ◇ *m* east; **los países del ~** the Eastern bloc countries.

este² (*pl* **estos**), **esta** *adj demos* **-1.** [gen] this, (*pl*) these; **esta camisa** this shirt; ~ **año** this year. **-2.** *fam* [despectivo] that, (*pl*) those; **no soporto a la niña esta** I can't stand that girl.

éste (*pl* **éstos**), **ésta** *pron demos* **-1.** [gen] this one, (*pl*) these (ones); **dame otro boli; ~ no funciona** give me another pen; this one doesn't work; **aquellos cuadros no están mal, aunque éstos me gustan más** those paintings aren't bad, but I like these (ones) better; **ésta ha sido la semana más feliz de mi vida** this has been the happiest week of my life. **-2.** [recién mencionado] the latter; **entraron Juan y Pedro, ~ con un abrigo verde** Juan and Pedro came in, the latter wearing a green coat. **-3.** *fam* [despectivo]: ~ **es el que me pegó** this is the guy who hit me; **éstos son los culpables de todo lo ocurrido** it's this lot who are to blame for everything.

◆ **en éstas** *loc adv fam* just then, at that very moment.

estela *f* **-1.** [de barco] wake; [de avión, estrella fugaz] trail. **-2.** *fig* [rastro] trail.

estelar *adj* **-1.** ASTRON stellar. **-2.** CIN & TEATR star (*antes de sust*).

estelaridad *f Amer* popularity.

estenografía *f* shorthand.

estenotipia *f* **-1.** [arte] stenotypy. **-2.** [máquina] Stenotype®.

estenotipista *m y f* stenotypist.

estenotipo *m* Stenotype®.

estentóreo, -a *adj* [culto] stentorian.

estepa *f* steppe.

estepario, -ria *adj* steppe (*antes de sust*).

éster *m* ester.

estera *f* [tejido] matting; [alfombrilla] mat.

estercolero *m* dunghill; *fig* [lugar sucio] pigsty.

estéreo *adj inv & m* stereo.

estereofonía *f* stereo.

estereofónico, -ca *adj* stereophonic, stereo.

estereoscopio *m* stereoscope.

estereotipado, -da *adj* stereotyped, stereotypical.

estereotipar *vt* to stereotype.

estereotipo *m* stereotype.

estéril *adj* -1. [persona, terreno, imaginación] sterile. -2. [gasa] sterilized. -3. *fig* [inútil] futile, fruitless.

esterilete *m* coil, I.U.D.

esterilidad *f* sterility.

esterilización *f* sterilization.

esterilizar [13] *vt* to sterilize.

esterilla *f* small mat.

esterlina → libra.

esternón *m* breastbone, sternum.

esteroides *mpl* steroids.

estertor *m* death rattle.

esteta *m y f* aesthete.

estética → estético.

esteticista, esthéticienne [esteti'θjen] *f* beautician.

estético, -ca *adj* aesthetic.

◆ **estética** *f* -1. FILOSOFÍA aesthetics (*U*). -2. [belleza] beauty.

estetoscopio *m* stethoscope.

esthéticienne = esteticista.

estiba *f* stowage.

estibador, -ra *m y f* stevedore.

estibar *vt* to stow.

estiércol *m* [excrementos] dung; [abono] manure.

estigma *m* -1. [marca] mark, scar. -2. *fig* [deshonor] stigma.

◆ **estigmas** *mpl* RELIG stigmata.

estigmatización *f* [marca] branding; *fig* [deshonra] stigmatization.

estigmatizar [13] *vt* -1. [marcar] to scar; [- con hierro candente] to brand. -2. *fig* [deshonrar] to stigmatize.

estilarse *vpr fam* to be in (fashion).

estilete *m* -1. [daga] stiletto. -2. MED stylet.

estilismo *m* stylism.

estilista *m y f* -1. [escritor] stylist. -2. [de moda, accesorios] fashion designer.

estilístico, -ca *adj* stylistic.

◆ **estilística** *f* stylistics (*U*).

estilizar [13] *vt* to stylize.

estilo *m* -1. [gen] style; ~ de vida lifestyle. -2. [en natación] stroke. -3. GRAM speech; ~ directo/indirecto direct/indirect speech. -4. *loc*: algo por el ~ something of the sort; ser por el ~ a to be similar to.

estilográfica *f* fountain pen.

estima *f* esteem, respect.

estimable *adj* [cantidad] considerable; [digno de estimación] worthy of appreciation.

estimación *f* -1. [aprecio] esteem, respect. -2. [valoración] valuation. -3. [en impuestos] assessment.

estimado, -da *adj* [querido] esteemed, respected; **Estimado señor** Dear Sir.

estimar *vt* -1. [valorar - gen] to value; [- valor] to estimate. -2. [apreciar] to think highly of. -3. [creer] to consider, to think.

◆ **estimarse** *vpr* [tener dignidad] to have self-respect.

estimativo, -va *adj* approximate, rough.

estimulador, -ra *adj* encouraging.

estimulante ◇ *adj* -1. [que anima] encouraging. -2. [que excita] stimulating. ◇ *m* stimulant.

estimular *vt* -1. [animar] to encourage. -2. [excitar] to stimulate.

estímulo *m* -1. [aliciente] incentive; [ánimo] encouragement. -2. [de un órgano] stimulus.

estío *m culto* summer.

estipendio *m* stipend, remuneration.

estipulación *f* -1. [acuerdo] agreement. -2. DER stipulation.

estipular *vt* to stipulate.

estirado, -da *adj* -1. [persona - altanero] haughty; [- adusto] uptight. -2. [brazos, piernas] outstretched.

estiramiento *m* stretching.

estirar ◇ *vt* -1. [alargar - gen] to stretch; [- el cuello] to crane; ~ **las piernas** to stretch one's legs. -2. [desarrugar] to straighten. -3. *fig* [el dinero etc] to make last; [discurso, tema] to spin out. ◇ *vi*: ~ (de) to pull.

◆ **estirarse** *vpr* -1. [desperezarse] to stretch. -2. [tumbarse] to stretch out. -3. [crecer] to shoot up.

estirón *m* -1. [acción] tug, pull. -2. [al crecer]: **dar** ○ **pegar un** ~ to shoot up suddenly.

estirpe *f* stock, lineage.

estival *adj* summer (*antes de sust*).

esto *pron demos (neutro)* this thing; ~ **es tu regalo de cumpleaños** this is your birthday present; ~ **que acabas de decir no tiene sentido** what you just said doesn't make sense; ~ **de trabajar de noche no me gusta** I don't like this business of working at night; ~ **es** that is (to say).
◆ **en esto** *loc adv* just then, at that very moment.

estoc (*pl* **estocs**) *m* stock.

estocada *f* [en esgrima] stab; TAUROM (sword) thrust.

Estocolmo Stockholm.

estofa *f*: **de baja** ~ [gente] low-class; [cosas] poor-quality.

estofado *m* stew.

estofar *vt* CULIN to stew.

estoicismo *m* stoicism.

estoico, -ca *adj* stoic, stoical.

estola *f* stole.

estomacal ◇ *adj* [dolencia] stomach (*antes de sust*); [bebida] digestive. ◇ *m* digestive (*drink*).

estómago *m* stomach.

Estonia Estonia.

estonio, -nia *adj, m y f* Estonian.

estop = **stop**.

estopa *f* [fibra] tow; [tela] burlap.

estoque *m* rapier.

estoquear *vt* to stab.

estor *m* Venetian blind.

estorbar ◇ *vt* [obstaculizar] to hinder; [molestar] to bother. ◇ *vi* [estar en medio] to be in the way.

estorbo *m* [obstáculo] hindrance; [molestia] nuisance.

estornino *m* starling.

estornudar *vi* to sneeze.

estornudo *m* sneeze.

estos, -tas → **este²**.

éstos, -tas → **éste**.

estoy → **estar**.

estrábico, -ca ◇ *adj* squint-eyed. ◇ *m y f* person with a squint.

estrabismo *m* squint.

estrado *m* platform.

estrafalario, -ria *adj* outlandish, eccentric.

estragón *m* tarragon.

estragos *mpl*: **causar** ○ **hacer** ~ **en** [físicos] to wreak havoc with; [morales] to destroy, to ruin.

estrambótico, -ca *adj* outlandish.

estramonio *m* thorn apple.

estrangulador, -ra *m y f* strangler.

estrangulamiento *m* strangulation.

estrangular *vt* **-1.** [ahogar] to strangle; MED to strangulate. **-2.** [proyecto] to stifle, to nip in the bud.
◆ **estrangularse** *vpr* to strangle o.s.

estraperlista *m y f* black marketeer.

estraperlo *m* black market; **de** ~ black market (*antes de sust*).

estratagema *f* MIL stratagem; *fig* [astucia] artifice, trick.

estratega *m y f* strategist.

estrategia *f* strategy.

estratégico, -ca *adj* strategic.

estratificación *f* stratification.

estratificar [10] *vt* to stratify.
◆ **estratificarse** *vpr* to form strata.

estrato *m* GEOL & *fig* stratum.

estratosfera *f* stratosphere.

estrechamiento *m* **-1.** [de calle, tubo] narrowing. **-2.** *fig* [de relaciones] rapprochement, tightening.

estrechar *vt* **-1.** [hacer estrecho - gen] to narrow; [- ropa] to take in. **-2.** *fig* [relaciones] to make closer. **-3.** [apretar] to squeeze, to hug; ~ **la mano a alguien** to shake sb's hand.
◆ **estrecharse** *vpr* **-1.** [hacerse estrecho] to narrow. **-2.** [abrazarse] to embrace. **-3.** [apretarse] to squeeze up.

estrechez *f* **-1.** [falta de anchura] narrowness; [falta de espacio] lack of space; [de ropa] tightness; ~ **de miras** narrow-mindedness. **-2.** *fig* [falta de dinero] hardship; **pasar estrecheces** to be hard up. **-3.** [intimidad] closeness.

estrecho, -cha ◇ *adj* **-1.** [no ancho - gen] narrow; [- ropa] tight; [- habitación] cramped; ~ **de miras** narrow-minded. **-2.** *fig* [íntimo] close. ◇ *m y f fam* [persona] prude.
◆ **estrecho** *m* GEOGR strait.

estregar [35] *vt* to rub.

estrella ◇ *adj inv* (*después de sust*) star (*antes de sust*). ◇ *f* **-1.** [gen] star; *fig* [destino] fate; ~ **fugaz** shooting star; ~ **polar** Pole Star; **ver las** ~**s** to see stars. **-2.** *loc*: **tener buena/mala** ~ to be lucky/unlucky.
◆ **estrella de mar** *f* starfish.

estrellado, -da *adj* **-1.** [con estrellas] starry. **-2.** [por la forma] star-shaped. **-3.** [que ha chocado] smashed.

estrellar *vt* [arrojar] to smash.
◆ **estrellarse** *vpr* **-1.** [chocar]: ~**se (contra)** [gen] to smash (against); [avión, coche] to crash (into). **-2.** *fig* [fracasar] to come to nothing.

estrellato *m* stardom.

estrellón *m Amer* crash.

estremecer [30] *vt* to shake.
◆ **estremecerse** *vpr*: ~**se (de)** [horror, miedo] to tremble ○ shudder (with); [frío] to shiver (with).

estremecimiento *m* [de miedo] shudder; [de frío] shiver.

estrenar *vt* **-1.** [gen] to use for the first time; [ropa] to wear for the first time; [piso] to move into. **-2.** CIN to release, to show for the first time; TEATR to premiere.
◆ **estrenarse** *vpr* [persona] to make one's debut, to start.

estreno *m* [de espectáculo] premiere, first night; [de cosa] first use; [en un empleo] debut.

estreñido, -da *adj* constipated.

estreñimiento *m* constipation.

estreñir *vt* to constipate.

estrépito *m* [ruido] racket, din; *fig* [ostentación] fanfare.

estrepitoso, -sa *adj* **-1.** [gen] noisy; [aplausos] deafening. **-2.** [derrota] resounding; [fracaso] spectacular.

estreptomicina *f* streptomycin.

estrés *m inv* stress.

estresado, -da *adj* suffering from stress.

estresante *adj* stressful.

estresar *vt* to cause stress to.

estría *f* [gen] groove; [en la piel] stretch mark.

estribación *f* (*gen pl*) foothills (*pl*).

estribar
◆ **estribar en** *vi* to be based on, to lie in.

estribillo *m* **-1.** MUS chorus; LITER refrain. **-2.** *fam* [coletilla] pet word ○ phrase.

estribo *m* **-1.** [de montura] stirrup. **-2.** [de coche, tren] step. **-3.** *loc*: **perder los** ~**s** to fly off the handle.

estribor *m* starboard; **a** ~ (to) starboard.

estricnina *f* strychnine.

estricto, -ta *adj* strict.

estridencia *f* **-1.** [ruido] stridency, shrillness. **-2.** *fig* [de colores] loudness.

estridente *adj* **-1.** [ruido] strident, shrill. **-2.** [color] garish, loud.

estriega *etc* → **estregar**.

estrofa *f* stanza, verse.

estrógeno, -na *adj* oestrogenic.
◆ **estrógeno** *m* oestrogen.

estroncio *m* strontium.

estropajo *m* scourer.

estropajoso, -sa *adj* **-1.** [habla] indistinct, mumbled. **-2.** [persona - andrajoso] ragged. **-3.** [filete] tough, chewy.

estropear *vt* **-1.** [averiar] to break. **-2.** [da-

ñar] to damage. **-3.** [echar a perder] to ruin, to spoil.
◆ **estropearse** *vpr* **-1.** [máquina] to break down. **-2.** [comida] to go off, to spoil; [piel] to get damaged. **-3.** [plan] to fall through.

estropicio *m*: **hacer** ○ **causar un** ~ to wreak havoc.

estructura *f* structure; ~ **profunda/superficial** deep/surface structure.

estructuración *f* structuring, organization.

estructural *adj* structural.

estructurar *vt* to structure, to organize.

estruendo *m* **-1.** [estrépito] din, roar; [de trueno] crash. **-2.** [alboroto] uproar, tumult.

estrujar *vt* **-1.** [limón] to squeeze; [trapo, ropa] to wring (out); [papel] to screw up; [caja] to crush. **-2.** [abrazar - persona, mano] to squeeze. **-3.** *fig* [sacar partido] to bleed dry.
◆ **estrujarse** *vpr* [apretujarse] to huddle together.

estuario *m* estuary.

estucado *m* stucco, stuccowork.

estucar [10] *vt* to stucco.

estuche *m* **-1.** [caja] case; [de joyas] jewellery box. **-2.** [utensilios] set.

estuco *m* stucco.

estudiado, -da *adj* studied.

estudiante *m y f* student.

estudiantil *adj* student (*antes de sust*).

estudiar [8] ◇ *vt* **-1.** [gen] to study. **-2.** [observar] to observe. ◇ *vi* to study; ~ **para médico** to be studying to be a doctor.

estudio *m* **-1.** [gen] study; **estar en** ~ to be under consideration; ~ **de mercado** [técnica] market research; [investigación] market survey. **-2.** [oficina] study; [de fotógrafo, pintor] studio. **-3.** [apartamento] studio apartment. **-4.** (*gen pl*) CIN, RADIO & TV studio.
◆ **estudios** *mpl* [serie de cursos] studies; [educación] education (*U*); ~**s primarios/secundarios** primary/secondary education.

estudioso, -sa ◇ *adj* studious. ◇ *m y f* [especialista] specialist, expert.

estufa *f* heater, fire.

estupa *m fam* drug squad detective.

estupefacción *f* astonishment.

estupefaciente *m* narcotic, drug.

estupefacto, -ta *adj* astonished.

estupendamente *adv* wonderfully; **estoy** ~ I feel wonderful.

estupendo, -da *adj* great, fantastic.
◆ **estupendo** *interj*: ¡~! great!

estupidez *f* stupidity; **decir/hacer una** ~ to say/do sthg stupid.

estúpido, -da ◇ *adj* stupid. ◇ *m y f* idiot.

estupor *m* astonishment.

estupro *m* rape of a minor.

estuque *etc* → **estucar.**

esturión *m* sturgeon.

estuviera *etc* → **estar.**

esvástica *f* swastika.

ETA (*abrev de* **Euskadi ta Askatasuna**) *f* ETA, *terrorist Basque separatist organization.*

etano *m* ethane.

etapa *f* stage; **por ~s** in stages; **quemar ~s** to come on in leaps and bounds, to progress rapidly.

etarra ◇ *adj* ETA (*antes de sust*). ◇ *m y f* member of ETA.

ETB (*abrev de* **Euskal Telebista**) *f* Basque television network.

etc. (*abrev de* **etcétera**) etc.

etcétera ◇ *adv* etcetera. ◇ *m*: **y un largo ~ de ...** and a long list of ....

éter *m* **-1.** [gas] ether. **-2.** *culto* [cielo]: **el ~** the ether, the heavens (*pl*).

etéreo, -a *adj* **-1.** QUÍM etheric. **-2.** *fig* ethereal.

eternidad *f* eternity; **hace una ~ que no la veo** *fam* it's ages since I last saw her.

eternizar [13] *vt*: **~ algo** to make sthg last forever.

♦ **eternizarse** *vpr*: **~se (haciendo algo)** to spend ages (doing sthg).

eterno, -na *adj* eternal; *fam* [larguísimo] never-ending, interminable.

ético, -ca *adj* ethical.

♦ **ética** *f* **-1.** FILOSOFÍA ethics (*U*). **-2.** [moralidad] ethics (*U*); **ética profesional** (professional) ethics.

etileno *m* ethylene.

etílico, -ca *adj* QUÍM ethyl (*antes de sust*); **intoxicación etílica** alcohol poisoning.

etilismo *m* intoxication.

etilo *m* ethyl.

étimo *m* etymon.

etimología *f* etymology.

etimológico, -ca *adj* etymological.

etimólogo, -ga *m y f* etymologist.

etiología *f* MED etiology.

etíope *adj, m y f* Ethiopian.

Etiopía Ethiopia.

etiqueta *f* **-1.** [gen & INFORM] label. **-2.** [ceremonial] etiquette; **de ~** formal.

etiquetado *m* labelling.

etiquetadora *f* pricing gun.

etiquetar *vt lit* & *fig* to label; **~ a alguien de algo** to label sb sthg.

etiquetero, -ra *adj* ceremonious, formal.

etnia *f* ethnic group.

étnico, -ca *adj* ethnic.

etnografía *f* ethnography.

etnología *f* ethnology.

etnólogo, -ga *m y f* ethnologist.

etrusco, -ca *adj, m y f* Etruscan.

EUA (*abrev de* **Estados Unidos de América**) *mpl* USA.

eucalipto *m* eucalyptus.

eucaristía *f*: **la ~** the Eucharist.

eucarístico, -ca *adj* Eucharistic.

eufemismo *m* euphemism.

euforia *f* euphoria, elation.

eufórico, -ca *adj* euphoric, elated.

Éufrates *m*: **el ~** the Euphrates.

eunuco *m* eunuch.

EURATOM (*abrev de* **Comunidad Europea de la Energía Atómica**) *f* EURATOM.

eureka *interj*: **¡~!** eureka!

euro *m* [unidad monetaria] euro.

eurocheque *m* eurocheque *Br*, eurocheck *Am*.

eurocomunismo *m* Eurocommunism.

eurocomunista *adj, m y f* Eurocommunist.

eurócrata *adj, m y f* Eurocrat.

eurodiputado, -da *m y f* Euro-M.P., M.E.P.

eurodivisa *f* ECON eurocurrency.

Europa Europe.

europarlamentario, -ria ◇ *adj* of the European Parliament. ◇ *m y f* Euro-M.P., M.E.P.

europeidad *f* Europeanness.

europeísmo *m* Europeanism.

europeísta *adj, m y f* pro-European.

europeización *f* Europeanization.

europeizar [13] *vt* to Europeanize.

europeo, -a *adj, m y f* European.

eurovisión *f* Eurovision.

Euskadi the Basque Country.

euskara, euskera *m* Basque.

eutanasia *f* euthanasia.

EUTI (*abrev de* **Escuela Universitaria de Traductores e Intérpretes**) *f* Spanish university college of translators and interpreters.

evacuación *f* evacuation.

evacuado, -da ◇ *adj* evacuated. ◇ *m y f* evacuee.

evacuador, -ra *adj* evacuative.

evacuar [7] *vt* [gen] to evacuate; [vientre] to empty, to void.

evadido, -da ◇ *adj* [persona] escaped; [divisas, impuestos] evaded. ◇ *m y f* escapee, fugitive.

evadir *vt* to evade; [respuesta, peligro] to avoid.
◆ **evadirse** *vpr*: ~se (de) to escape (from).
evaluable *adj* calculable.
evaluación *f* -1. [gen] evaluation. -2. [EDUC - examen] **assessment**; [- periodo] *period of continuous assessment.*
evaluador, -ra *adj* evaluating, evaluative.
evaluar [6] *vt* to evaluate, to assess.
evanescencia *f culto* evanescence.
evanescente *adj culto* evanescent.
evangélico, -ca *adj, m y f* evangelical.
evangelio *m* -1. RELIG gospel. -2. *fig* beliefs (*pl*).
evangelista *m* Evangelist.
evangelización *f* evangelization, evangelizing.
evangelizar [13] *vt* to envangelize.
evaporación *f* evaporation.
evaporar *vt* to evaporate.
◆ **evaporarse** *vpr* -1. [líquido etc] to evaporate. -2. *fam fig* [persona] to disappear into thin air.
evaporizar [13] *vt* to vaporize.
evasión *f* -1. [huida] escape. -2. [de dinero] ~ de capitales ○ divisas capital flight; ~ fiscal tax evasion. -3. *fig* [entretenimiento] amusement, recreation; [escapismo] escapism; de ~ escapist.
evasivo, -va *adj* evasive.
◆ **evasiva** *f* evasive answer; **responder con evasivas** not to give a straight answer.
evasor, -ra ◇ *adj* guilty of evasion. ◇ *m y f* [de la cárcel] jailbreaker.
evento *m* event.
eventual *adj* -1. [no fijo - trabajador] temporary, casual; [- gastos] incidental. -2. [posible] possible.
eventualidad *f* -1. [temporalidad] temporariness. -2. [hecho incierto] eventuality; [posibilidad] possibility.
Everest *m*: el ~ (Mount) Everest.
evidencia *f* -1. [prueba] evidence, proof. -2. [claridad] obviousness; **poner algo en** ~ to demonstrate sthg; **poner a alguien en** ~ to show sb up.
evidenciar [8] *vt* to show, to demonstrate.
◆ **evidenciarse** *vpr* to be obvious ○ evident.
evidente *adj* evident, obvious.
evitar *vt* [gen] to avoid; [desastre, accidente] to avert; ~ **que alguien haga algo** to prevent sb from doing sthg.
evocación *f* recollection, evocation.
evocador, -ra *adj* evocative.

evocar [10] *vt* -1. [recordar] to evoke. -2. [espíritu] to invoke, to call up.
evolución *f* -1. [gen] evolution; [de enfermedad] development, progress. -2. MIL manoeuvre.
evolucionar *vi* -1. [gen] to evolve; [enfermedad] to develop, to progress; [cambiar] to change. -2. MIL to carry out manoeuvres.
evolucionismo *m* evolutionism.
evolucionista *adj, m y f* evolutionist.
evolutivo, -va *adj* evolutionary.
evoque *etc* → **evocar**.
ex ◇ *m y f* [cónyuge etc] ex. ◇ *prep* ex; **el ~ presidente** the ex-president, the former president.
exabrupto *m* sharp word ○ remark.
exacción *f* [de impuestos. multas] exaction, collection.
exacerbar *vt* -1. [agudizar] to exacerbate, to aggravate. -2. [irritar] to irritate, to infuriate.
exactamente *adv* exactly, precisely.
exactas → **exacto**.
exactitud *f* accuracy, precision; [puntualidad] punctuality.
exacto, -ta *adj* -1. [justo - cálculo, medida] exact; **tres metros** ~s exactly three metres. -2. [preciso] accurate, precise; [correcto] correct, right; **para ser** ~s to be precise. -3. [idéntico]: ~ (a) identical (to), exactly the same (as).
◆ **exacto** *interj*: ¡~! exactly!, precisely!
◆ **exactas** *fpl* exact ○ pure sciences.
exageración *f* exaggeration; **este precio es una** ~ this price is over the top.
exagerado, -da *adj* [gen] exaggerated; [persona] overly dramatic; [precio] exorbitant; [gesto] flamboyant.
exagerar *vt & vi* to exaggerate.
exaltación *f* -1. [júbilo] elation, intense excitement; [acaloramiento] overexcitement. -2. [ensalzamiento] exaltation.
exaltado, -da ◇ *adj* [jubiloso] elated; [acalorado - persona] worked up; [- discusión] heated; [excitable] hotheaded. ◇ *m y f* [fanático] fanatic; POLIT extremist.
exaltar *vt* -1. [elevar] to promote, to raise. -2. [glorificar] to exalt.
◆ **exaltarse** *vpr* to get excited ○ worked up.
examen *m* -1. [ejercicio] exam, examination; **presentarse a un** ~ to sit an exam; ~ **de conducir** driving test; ~ **de ingreso** entrance examination; ~ **final/oral** final/oral (exam); ~ **parcial** ≃ end-of-term exam. -2. [indagación] consideration, examination; **hacer** ~ **de conciencia** to take a good look at

o.s.; ~ **médico** medical examination o check-up; **libre** ~ personal interpretation.

examinador, -ra *m y f* examiner.

examinando, -da *m y f* examinee, candidate.

examinar *vt* to examine.

◆ **examinarse** *vpr* to sit o take an exam.

exangüe *adj culto* exhausted.

exánime *adj* **-1.** [muerto] dead. **-2.** [desmayado] lifeless. **-3.** *fig* [agotado] exhausted, worn-out.

exasperación *f* exasperation.

exasperante *adj* exasperating, infuriating.

exasperar *vt* to exasperate, to infuriate.

◆ **exasperarse** *vpr* to get exasperated.

Exc *abrev de* **Excelencia.**

excarcelar *vt* to release (from prison).

excavación *f* **-1.** [acción] excavation. **-2.** [lugar] dig, excavation.

excavador, -ra ◇ *adj* excavating, digging. ◇ *m y f* [persona] excavator, digger.

◆ **excavadora** *f* [máquina] digger.

excavar *vt* [gen] to dig; [en arqueología] to excavate.

excedencia *f* leave (of absence); EDUC sabbatical.

excedente ◇ *adj* **-1.** [producción etc] surplus. **-2.** [funcionario etc] on leave; EDUC on sabbatical. ◇ *m* COM surplus. ◇ *m y f* [persona] person on leave; ~ **de cupo** *person excused from military service because there are already enough new recruits.*

exceder ◇ *vt* to exceed, to surpass. ◇ *vi* to be greater; ~ **a** o **de** to exceed.

◆ **excederse** *vpr* **-1.** [pasarse de la raya]: ~**se (en)** to go too far o overstep the mark (in). **-2.** [rebasar el límite]: **se excede en el peso** it's too heavy.

excelencia *f* [cualidad] excellence; **por** ~ par excellence.

◆ **Su Excelencia** *m y f* His Excellency (*f* Her Excellency).

excelente *adj* excellent.

excelentísimo, -ma *adj* most excellent.

excelso, -sa *adj culto* sublime, elevated.

excentricidad *f* eccentricity.

excéntrico, -ca *adj, m y f* eccentric.

excepción *f* exception; **a** o **con** ~ **de** with the exception of, except for; **hacer una** ~ to make an exception; **la** ~ **confirma la regla** *proverb* the exception proves the rule.

◆ **de excepción** *loc adj* exceptional.

excepcional *adj* exceptional.

excepto *adv* except (for).

exceptuar [6] *vt*: ~ **(de)** [excluir] to exclude

(from); [eximir] to exempt (from); **exceptuando a ...** excluding ....

◆ **exceptuarse** *v impers*: **se exceptúa a los menores de 16 años** children under the age of 16 are exempt.

excesivo, -va *adj* excessive.

exceso *m* [demasía] excess; **en** ~ excessively, to excess; ~ **de equipaje** excess baggage; ~ **de peso** [obesidad] excess weight; ~ **de velocidad** speeding.

excipiente *m* excipient.

excisión *f* MED excision.

excitación *f* **-1.** [nerviosismo] agitation; [por enfado, sexo] arousal. **-2.** BIO & ELECTR excitation.

excitado, -da *adj* [nervioso] agitated; [por enfado, sexo] aroused.

excitante ◇ *adj* [emocionante] exciting; [sexualmente] arousing; [café, tabaco] stimulating. ◇ *m* stimulant.

excitar *vt* **-1.** [inquietar] to upset, to agitate. **-2.** [incitar]: ~ **a** to incite to. **-3.** [estimular - sentidos] to stimulate; [- apetito] to whet; [- pasión, curiosidad, persona] to arouse.

◆ **excitarse** *vpr* [alterarse] to get worked up o excited.

exclamación *f* [interjección] exclamation; [grito] cry.

exclamar *vt & vi* to exclaim, to shout out.

exclamativo, -va *adj* exclamatory.

excluir [51] *vt* to exclude; [hipótesis, opción] to rule out; [hacer imposible] to preclude; ~ **a alguien de algo** to exclude sb from sthg.

exclusión *f* exclusion.

exclusiva → **exclusivo.**

exclusive *adv* exclusive.

exclusividad *f* **-1.** [gen] exclusiveness. **-2.** [privilegio] exclusive o sole right.

exclusivo, -va *adj* exclusive.

◆ **exclusiva** *f* **-1.** PRENS exclusive. **-2.** COM exclusive o sole right.

excluyente *adj* excluding.

Excma. *abrev de* **Excelentísima.**

Excmo. *abrev de* **Excelentísimo.**

excombatiente *m y f* ex-serviceman (*f* ex-servicewoman) *Br*, war veteran *Am*.

excomulgar [16] *vt* to excommunicate.

excomunión *f* excommunication.

excrecencia *f* growth.

excremento *m* (*gen pl*) excrement (*U*).

excretar ◇ *vt* [soltar] to secrete. ◇ *vi* [evacuar] to excrete.

excretorio, -ria *adj* excretory.

exculpación *f* exoneration; DER acquittal.

exculpar *vt* to exonerate; DER to acquit.

◆ **exculparse de** *vpr* to declare o.s. innocent of.

exculpatorio, -ria *adj* exonerative.

excursión *f* **-1.** [viaje] excursion, trip; **ir de** ~ to go on an outing o a trip. **-2.** *fam* [paseo] walk, stroll.

excursionismo *m* rambling; [de montaña] hiking.

excursionista *m y f* [en la ciudad] sightseer, tripper; [en el campo] rambler; [en la montaña] hiker.

excusa *f* **-1.** [gen] excuse. **-2.** [petición de perdón] apology; **presentar uno sus** ~**s** to apologize, to make one's excuses.

excusado, -da *adj* **-1.** [disculpado] excused. **-2.** [secreto] secret.

◆ **excusado** *m* bathroom, lavatory.

excusar *vt* **-1.** [disculpar a] to excuse; [disculpar por] to apologize for. **-2.** [evitar] to avoid.

◆ **excusarse** *vpr* to apologize, to excuse o.s.

execrable *adj culto* abominable, execrable.

execrar *vt culto* to abhor.

exégesis *f inv* exegesis, explanation.

exención *f* exemption; ~ **fiscal** tax exemption.

exento, -ta *adj* exempt; ~ **de** [sin] free from, without; [eximido de] exempt from.

exequias *fpl* funeral (*sg*), funeral rites.

exfoliación *f* exfoliation.

exfoliante ◇ *adj* exfoliating. ◇ *m* exfoliating cream/lotion *etc.*

exhalación *f* **-1.** [emanación] exhalation, vapour; [suspiro] breath. **-2.** [centella]: **como una** ~ as quick as a flash.

exhalar *vt* **-1.** [aire] to exhale, to breathe out; [suspiros] to heave; ~ **el último suspiro** to breathe one's last (breath). **-2.** [olor] to give off. **-3.** [quejas] to utter.

exhaustivo, -va *adj* exhaustive.

exhausto, -ta *adj* exhausted.

exhibición *f* **-1.** [demostración] show, display. **-2.** [deportiva, artística etc] exhibition. **-3.** [de películas] showing.

exhibicionismo *m* exhibitionism.

exhibicionista *adj, m y f* exhibitionist.

exhibir *vt* **-1.** [exponer - cuadros, fotografías] to exhibit; [- modelos] to show; [- productos] to display. **-2.** [lucir - joyas, cualidades etc] to show off. **-3.** [película] to show, to screen.

◆ **exhibirse** *vpr* [alardear] to show off.

exhortación *f* exhortation.

exhortar *vt*: ~ **a** to exhort to.

exhumación *f* exhumation, disinterment.

exhumar *vt* to exhume, to disinter.

exigencia *f* **-1.** [obligación] demand, requirement. **-2.** [capricho] fussiness (*U*).

exigente ◇ *adj* demanding. ◇ *m y f* demanding person.

exigir [15] ◇ *vt* **-1.** [gen] to demand; ~ **algo de** o **a alguien** to demand sthg from sb. **-2.** [requerir, necesitar] to call for, to require. ◇ *vi* to be demanding.

exiguo, -gua *adj* [escaso] meagre, paltry; [pequeño] minute.

exija *etc* → **exigir**.

exiliado, -da ◇ *adj* exiled, in exile. ◇ *m y f* exile.

exiliar [8] *vt* to exile.

◆ **exiliarse** *vpr* to go into exile.

exilio *m* exile.

eximente ◇ *adj* absolutory, absolving. ◇ *f* case for acquittal.

eximio, -mia *adj culto* eminent, illustrious.

eximir *vt*: ~ **(de)** to exempt (from).

existencia *f* existence.

◆ **existencias** *fpl* COM stock (*U*); **en** ~ in stock.

existencial *adj* existential.

existencialismo *m* existentialism.

existencialista *adj, m y f* existentialist.

existente *adj* existing, existent.

existir *vi* to exist; **existe mucha pobreza** there is a lot of poverty.

éxito *m* **-1.** [gen] success; **con** ~ successfully; **tener** ~ to be successful. **-2.** [libro] bestseller; [canción] hit.

exitoso, -sa *adj* successful.

éxodo *m* exodus.

exonerar *vt culto*: ~ **a alguien (de)** [culpa, responsabilidad] to exonerate sb (from); [carga, obligación] to free sb (from); [empleo, cargo] to dismiss o remove sb (from).

exorbitante *adj* exorbitant.

exorbitar *vt* to exaggerate.

exorcismo *m* exorcism.

exorcista *m y f* exorcist.

exorcizar [13] *vt* to exorcize.

exordio *m culto* exordium.

exótico, -ca *adj* exotic.

exotismo *m* exoticism.

expandir *vt* to spread; FÍS to expand.

◆ **expandirse** *vpr* to spread; FÍS to expand.

expansión *f* **-1.** FÍS expansion. **-2.** ECON growth; **en** ~ expanding. **-3.** *fig* [difusión] spread, spreading. **-4.** [recreo] relaxation, amusement.

expansionarse *vpr* **-1.** [desahogarse]: ~ **(con)** to open one's heart (to). **-2.** [divertirse] to relax, to let off steam. **-3.** [desarrollarse] to expand.

expansionismo *m* expansionism.

expansionista *adj* expansionist.

expansivo, -va *adj* **-1.** [gen] expansive. **-2.** *fig* [persona] open, frank.

expatriación *f* expatriation; [exilio] exile.

expatriado, -da ◇ *adj* expatriate (*antes de sust*); [exiliado] exiled. ◇ *m y f* expatriate; [exiliado] exile.

expatriar [9] *vt* to expatriate; [exiliar] to exile.

◆ **expatriarse** *vpr* to leave one's country, to emigrate; [exiliarse] to go into exile.

expectación *f* expectancy, anticipation.

expectante *adj* expectant.

expectativa *f* [espera] expectation; [esperanza] hope; [perspectiva] prospect; **estar a la ~** to wait and see; **estar a la ~ de** [atento] to be on the lookout for; [a la espera] to be hoping for; **~ de vida** life expectancy.

expectoración *f* **-1.** [acción] expectoration. **-2.** [esputo] sputum (*U*).

expectorante *adj & m* expectorant.

expectorar *vi* to expectorate.

expedición *f* **-1.** [viaje, grupo] expedition. **-2.** [envío] shipment, sending.

expedicionario, -ria *adj* expeditionary.

expedidor, -ra *m y f* sender, dispatcher.

expedientar *vt* [castigar] to take disciplinary action against; [investigar] to start proceedings against.

expediente *m* **-1.** [documentación] documents (*pl*); [ficha] file. **-2.** [historial] record; **~ académico** academic record. **-3.** [investigación] inquiry; **abrir ~ a alguien** [castigar] to take disciplinary action against sb; [investigar] to start proceedings against sb. **-4.** ECON: **~ de regulación de empleo** streamlining (of the workforce). **-5.** *loc*: **cubrir el ~** *fam fig* to do the bare minimum.

expedir [26] *vt* [carta, pedido] to send, to dispatch; [pasaporte, decreto] to issue; [contrato, documento] to draw up.

expeditivo, -va *adj* expeditious.

expedito, -ta *adj* clear, free.

expeler *vt* [humo - suj: persona] to blow out; [- suj: chimenea, tubo de escape] to emit; [- suj: extractor, volcán] to expel.

expendedor, -ra ◇ *adj* [máquina] vending (*antes de sust*); [taquilla, establecimiento] sales (*antes de sust*). ◇ *m y f* dealer, retailer; [de lotería] seller, vendor.

expendeduría *f* [de tabaco] tobacconist's *Br*, cigar store *Am*.

expender *vt* to sell, to retail.

expensas *fpl* [gastos] expenses, costs.

◆ **a expensas de** *loc prep* at the expense of.

experiencia *f* **-1.** [gen] experience; **por (propia) ~** from (one's own) experience. **-2.** [experimento] experiment.

experimentación *f* experimentation.

experimentado, -da *adj* [persona] experienced; [método] tried and tested.

experimentador, -ra ◇ *adj* experimenting. ◇ *m y f* experimenter.

experimental *adj* experimental.

experimentar *vt* **-1.** [gen] to experience; [derrota, pérdidas] to suffer. **-2.** [probar] to test; [hacer experimentos con] to experiment with ○ on.

experimento *m* experiment.

experto, -ta *adj, m y f* expert.

expiación *f* atonement, expiation.

expiar [9] *vt* to atone for, to expiate.

expiatorio, -ria *adj* expiatory.

expida, expidiera *etc* → **expedir**.

expiración *f* expiry.

expirar *vi* to expire.

explanación *f* levelling.

explanada *f* **-1.** [llanura] flat ○ level ground (*U*). **-2.** [paseo marítimo] esplanade.

explanar *vt* [terreno] to level.

explayar *vt* to extend.

◆ **explayarse** *vpr* **-1.** [divertirse] to amuse o.s., to enjoy o.s. **-2.** [hablar mucho] to talk at length. **-3.** [desahogarse] **~se (con)** to pour out one's heart (to).

explicación *f* explanation; **dar/pedir explicaciones** to give/demand an explanation.

explicar [10] *vt* **-1.** [gen] to explain; [teoría] to expound. **-2.** [enseñar] to teach, to lecture in.

◆ **explicarse** *vpr* **-1.** [comprender] to understand; **no me lo explico** I can't understand it. **-2.** [dar explicaciones] to explain o.s. **-3.** [expresarse] to make o.s. understood.

explicativo, -va *adj* explanatory.

explícito, -ta *adj* explicit.

exploración *f* **-1.** [gen & MED] exploration. **-2.** MIN prospecting.

explorador, -ra *m y f* explorer; [scout] boy scout (*f* girl guide).

explorar *vt* **-1.** [gen] to explore; MIL to scout. **-2.** MIN to prospect. **-3.** MED to examine; [internamente] to explore, to probe.

exploratorio, -ria *adj* exploratory; [conversaciones] preliminary.

explosión *f lit & fig* explosion; **hacer ~** to explode; **~ atómica/termonuclear** atomic/

thermonuclear explosion; ~ **demográfica** population explosion.

explosionar *vt & vi* to explode, to blow up.

explosivo, -va *adj* **-1.** [gen] explosive. **-2.** GRAM plosive.
◆ **explosivo** *m* explosive.

explotación *f* **-1.** [acción] exploitation; [de fábrica etc] running; [de yacimiento minero] mining; [agrícola] farming; [de petróleo] drilling. **-2.** [instalaciones]: ~ **agrícola** farm; ~ **minera** mine; ~ **petrolífera** oil field.

explotador, -ra ◇ *adj* exploiting. ◇ *m y f* exploiter.

explotar ◇ *vt* **-1.** [gen] to exploit. **-2.** [fábrica] to run, to operate; [terreno] to farm; [mina] to work. ◇ *vi* to explode.

expoliación *f* pillaging, plundering.

expoliar [8] *vt* to pillage, to plunder.

expolio *m* pillaging, plundering.

exponencial *adj & f* exponential.

exponente *m* MAT & *fig* exponent.

exponer [65] *vt* **-1.** [gen] to expose. **-2.** [teoría] to expound; [ideas, propuesta] to set out, to explain. **-3.** [cuadro, obra] to exhibit; [objetos en vitrinas] to display. **-4.** [vida, prestigio] to risk.
◆ **exponerse** *vpr* [arriesgarse]: ~**se (a)** [gen] to run the risk (of); [a la muerte] to expose o.s. (to).

exportación *f* **-1.** [acción] export. **-2.** [mercancías] exports (*pl*); **exportaciones invisibles** invisible exports.

exportador, -ra ◇ *adj* exporting (*antes de sust*). ◇ *m y f* exporter.

exportar *vt* COM & INFORM to export.

exposición *f* **-1.** [gen & FOT] exposure. **-2.** [de arte etc] exhibition; [de objetos en vitrina] display; ~ **universal** world fair. **-3.** [de teoría] exposition; [de ideas, propuesta] setting out, explanation.

exposímetro *m* exposure meter.

expositivo, -va *adj* explanatory.

expósito, -ta ◇ *adj* foundling (*antes de sust*). ◇ *m y f* foundling.

expositor, -ra ◇ *adj* exponent. ◇ *m y f* [de arte] exhibitor; [de teoría] exponent.

exprés ◇ *adj* **-1.** [tren] express. **-2.** [café] espresso. ◇ *m* = **expreso**.

expresado, -da *adj* [mencionado] above-mentioned.

expresamente *adv* [a propósito] expressly; [explícitamente] explicitly, specifically.

expresar *vt* to express; [suj: rostro] to show.
◆ **expresarse** *vpr* to express o.s.

expresión *f* expression; **reducir a la mínima** ~ to cut down to the bare minimum.

expresionismo *m* expressionism.

expresionista *adj, m y f* expressionist.

expresividad *f* expressiveness.

expresivo, -va *adj* expressive; [cariñoso] affectionate.

expreso, -sa *adj* [explícito] specific; [deliberado] express; [claro] clear.
◆ **expreso** ◇ *m* **-1.** [tren] express train. **-2.** [café] expresso. ◇ *adv* on purpose, expressly.

exprimelimones *m inv* lemon squeezer.

exprimidor *m* squeezer.

exprimir *vt* **-1.** [fruta] to squeeze; [zumo] to squeeze out. **-2.** *fig* to exploit.

expropiación *f* expropriation.

expropiar [8] *vt* to expropriate.

expuesto, -ta ◇ *pp* → **exponer**. ◇ *adj* **-1.** [dicho] stated, expressed. **-2.** [desprotegido]: ~ **(a)** exposed (to). **-3.** [arriesgado] dangerous, risky. **-4.** [exhibido] on display.

expugnar *vt culto* to (take by) storm.

expulsar *vt* **-1.** [persona - de clase, local, asociación] to throw out; [- de colegio] to expel. **-2.** DEP to send off. **-3.** [humo] to emit, to give off.

expulsión *f* [gen] expulsion; [de clase, local, asociación] throwing-out; DEP sending-off.

expulsor, -ra *adj* ejector (*antes de sust*).
◆ **expulsor** *m* ejector.

expurgación *f* expurgation.

expurgar [16] *vt* expurgate.

expusiera *etc* → **exponer**.

exquisitez *f* **-1.** [cualidad] exquisiteness. **-2.** [cosa] exquisite thing; [comida] delicacy.

exquisito, -ta *adj* exquisite; [comida] delicious, sublime.

extasiarse [9] *vpr*: ~ **(ante** ◇ **con)** to go into ecstasies (over).

éxtasis *m inv* ecstasy.

extemporáneo, -a *adj* **-1.** [clima] unseasonable. **-2.** [comentario etc] inopportune, untimely.

extender [20] *vt* **-1.** [desplegar - tela, plano, alas] to spread (out); [- brazos, piernas] to stretch out. **-2.** [esparcir - mantequilla] to spread; [pintura] to smear; [objetos etc] to spread out. **-3.** [ampliar - castigo, influencia etc] to extend, to widen. **-4.** [documento] to draw up; [cheque] to make out; [pasaporte, certificado] to issue.
◆ **extenderse** *vpr* **-1.** [ocupar]: ~**se (por)** to stretch ◇ extend across. **-2.** [hablar mucho]: ~**se (en)** to enlarge ◇ expand (on). **-3.** [durar] to extend, to last. **-4.** [difundirse]:

~**se (por)** to spread (across). **-5.** [tenderse] to stretch out.

extensión f **-1.** [superficie - de terreno etc] area, expanse. **-2.** [amplitud - de país etc] size; [- de conocimientos] extent. **-3.** [duración] duration, length. **-4.** [sentido - de concepto, palabra] range of meaning; **en toda la** ~ **de la palabra** in every sense of the word; **por** ~ by extension. **-5.** INFORM & TELECOM extension.

extensivo, -va adj extensive; **hacer algo** ~ **a** to extend sthg to.

extenso, -sa adj extensive; [país] vast; [libro, película] long.

extensor m **-1.** [aparato] chest expander. **-2.** [músculo] extensor.

extenuación f severe exhaustion (U).

extenuado, -da adj completely exhausted, drained.

extenuante . adj completely exhausting, draining.

extenuar [6] vt to exhaust completely, to drain.

◆ **extenuarse** vpr to exhaust o.s., to tire o.s. out.

exterior ◇ adj **-1.** [de fuera] outside; [capa] outer, exterior. **-2.** [visible] outward. **-3.** [extranjero] foreign. ◇ m **-1.** [superficie] outside; **en el** ~ outside. **-2.** [extranjero] foreign countries (pl); **en el** ~ abroad. **-3.** [aspecto] appearance.

◆ **exteriores** mpl CIN outside shots; **rodar en** ~**es** to film on location.

exterioridad f outward appearance.

exteriorización f outward demonstration, manifestation.

exteriorizar [13] vt to show, to reveal.

exterminación f extermination.

exterminador, -ra adj exterminating.

exterminar vt **-1.** [aniquilar] to exterminate. **-2.** [devastar] to destroy, to devastate.

exterminio m extermination.

externado m day school.

externo, -na adj **-1.** [gen] external; [parte, capa] outer; [influencia] outside; [signo, aspecto] outward. **-2.** [alumno] day (antes de sust).

extienda etc → **extender**.

extinción f **-1.** [gen] extinction; [de esperanzas] loss. **-2.** [de plazos, obligaciones] termination, end.

extinguir [17] vt [incendio] to put out, to extinguish; [raza] to wipe out; [afecto, entusiasmo] to put an end to.

◆ **extinguirse** vpr [fuego, luz] to go out; [animal, raza] to become extinct, to die out; [ruido] to die out; [afecto] to die.

extinto, -ta adj extinguished; [animal, volcán] extinct.

extintor m fire extinguisher.

extirpación f MED removal; fig eradication, stamping out.

extirpar vt [tumor] to remove; [muela] to extract; fig to eradicate, to stamp out.

extornar vt COM to rebate.

extorno m COM rebate.

extorsión f **-1.** [molestia] trouble, bother. **-2.** DER extortion.

extorsionador, -ra adj extortive.

extorsionar vt **-1.** [perjudicar - persona] to inconvenience; [- plan] to mess up. **-2.** DER to extort.

extorsionista m y f extortionist.

extra ◇ adj **-1.** [adicional] extra. **-2.** [de gran calidad] top quality, superior. ◇ m y f CIN extra. ◇ m [gasto etc] extra. ◇ f → **paga**.

extra- prefijo extra-.

extracción f **-1.** [gen] extraction. **-2.** [en sorteos] draw. **-3.** [de carbón] mining.

extractar vt to summarize, to shorten.

extracto m **-1.** [resumen] summary, résumé; ~ **de cuentas** statement (of account). **-2.** [concentrado] extract.

extractor, -ra adj extractor (antes de sust).

◆ **extractor** m extractor fan.

extracurricular adj extracurricular.

extradición f extradition.

extraditar vt to extradite.

extraer [73] vt: ~ **(de)** [gen] to extract (from); [sangre] to draw (from); [carbón] to mine (from); [conclusiones] to come to O draw (from).

extrafino, -na adj top quality, de luxe.

extrajudicial adj extrajudicial.

extralegal adj extralegal.

extralimitación f abuse (of power, authority).

extralimitarse vpr fig to go too far.

extramuros adv outside the city O town.

extranjería f foreign status.

extranjerismo m foreign word.

extranjerizar [13] vt to introduce foreign customs to.

extranjero, -ra ◇ adj foreign. ◇ m y f [persona] foreigner.

◆ **extranjero** m [territorio] foreign countries (pl); **estar en el** ~ to be abroad.

extranjis

◆ **de extranjis** loc adv fam on the quiet.

extrañamiento m banishment.

extrañar vt **-1.** [sorprender] to surprise; **me extraña (que digas esto)** I'm surprised (that you should say that). **-2.** [echar de menos] to miss. **-3.** [desterrar] to banish.

◆ **extrañarse de** *vpr* [sorprenderse de] to be surprised at.

extrañeza *f* **-1.** [sorpresa] surprise. **-2.** [rareza] strangeness (*U*).

extraño, -ña ◇ *adj* **-1.** [gen] strange. **-2.** [ajeno] detached, uninvolved. **-3.** MED foreign. ◇ *m y f* stranger.

extraoficial *adj* unofficial.

extraordinario, -ria *adj* **-1.** [gen] extraordinary. **-2.** [gastos] additional; [edición, suplemento] special.

◆ **extraordinario** *m* **-1.** CULIN special dish. **-2.** PRENS special edition. **-3.** [correo] special delivery.

◆ **extraordinaria** *f* → **paga**.

extraparlamentario, -ria *adj* non-parliamentary.

extraplano, -na *adj* super-slim, extra-thin.

extrapolación *f* generalization.

extrapolar *vt* to generalize about, to jump to conclusions about.

extrarradio *m* outskirts (*pl*), suburbs (*pl*).

extraterrestre *adj, m y f* extraterrestrial.

extraterritorial *adj* extraterritorial.

extraterritorialidad *f* extraterritorial rights (*pl*).

extravagancia *f* eccentricity.

extravagante *adj* eccentric, outlandish.

extravasarse *vpr* to flow out.

extraversión = **extroversión**.

extravertido, -da = **extrovertido**.

extraviado, -da *adj* **-1.** [perdido] lost; [animal] stray. **-2.** *fig* [de vida airada] debauched.

extraviar [9] *vt* **-1.** [objeto] to lose, to mislay. **-2.** [excursionista] to mislead, to cause to lose one's way. **-3.** [mirada, vista] to allow to wander.

◆ **extraviarse** *vpr* **-1.** [persona] to get lost. **-2.** [objeto] to be mislaid, to go missing.

extravío *m* **-1.** [pérdida] loss, mislaying. **-2.** [desenfreno] excess.

extremado, -da *adj* extreme.

Extremadura Estremadura.

extremar *vt* to go to extremes with.

◆ **extremarse** *vpr* to take great pains ○ care.

extremaunción *f* extreme unction.

extremeño, -ña *adj, m y f* Estremaduran.

extremidad *f* [extremo] end.

◆ **extremidades** *fpl* ANAT extremities.

extremis

◆ **in extremis** *loc adv* right at the very last moment.

extremismo *m* extremism.

extremista *adj, m y f* extremist.

extremo, -ma *adj* [gen] extreme; [en el espacio] far, furthest.

◆ **extremo** *m* **-1.** [punta] end. **-2.** [límite] extreme; **en último ~** as a last resort; **ir** ○ **pasar de un ~ al otro** to go from one extreme to the other. **-3.** DEP: **~ derecho/izquierdo** outside right/left.

◆ **extremos** *mpl* [efusiones] exaggerations.

extremosidad *f* [efusividad] effusiveness.

extremoso, -sa *adj* [efusivo] effusive, gushing.

extrínseco, -ca *adj* extrinsic.

extroversión, extraversión *f* extroversion.

extrovertido, -da, extravertido, -da *adj, m y f* extrovert.

exuberancia *f* exuberance.

exuberante *adj* exuberant.

exudación *f* exudation.

exudado, -da *adj* exuding, oozing.

exudar *vt* to exude, to ooze.

exultación *f* exultation.

exultante *adj* exultant.

exultar

◆ **exultar de** *vi* to exult with, to rejoice with.

exvoto *m* votive offering, ex voto.

eyaculación *f* ejaculation; **~ precoz** premature ejaculation.

eyacular *vi* to ejaculate.

eyección *f* ejection, expulsion.

eyectar *vt* to eject, to expel.

eyector *m* [de armas] ejector; [de aire, gases] extractor.

f, F *f* [letra] f, F.
♦ **23 F** *m day of the failed coup d'état in Spain in 1981.*

23 F:
On 23rd February 1981, a failed coup d'état was perpetrated in the Spanish parliament by a group of civil guards with the support of certain sectors of the Spanish army; the group took all the members of parliament hostage until the following morning. Late at night, the King appeared before the television cameras to pledge his support for democracy. On the morning of the 24th, the rebel group surrendered. By extension, 23 F has come to mean 'coup d'état'

f. -1. (*abrev de* **factura**) inv. **-2.** (*abrev de* **folio**) f.
fa *m* MÚS F; [en solfeo] fa.
fabada *f* Asturian stew made of beans, pork sausage and bacon.
fábrica *f* **-1.** [establecimiento] factory; ~ **de papel** paper mill; ~ **siderúrgica** iron and steelworks (*sg*). **-2.** [fabricación] manufacture. **-3.** *fig* [de mentiras etc] fabrication.
fabricación *f* manufacture; **de** ~ **casera** home-made; ~ **en serie** mass production.
fabricante ◇ *adj* manufacturing (*antes de sust*). ◇ *m y f* manufacturer.
fabricar [10] *vt* **-1.** [producir] to manufacture, to make. **-2.** [construir] to build, to construct. **-3.** *fig* [inventar] to fabricate, to make up.
fabril *adj* manufacturing (*antes de sust*).
fábula *f* **-1.** LITER fable; [leyenda] legend, myth. **-2.** [rumor] piece of gossip.
fabular *vi* to make things up.
fabulista *m y f* author of fables.
fabuloso, -sa *adj* **-1.** [ficticio] mythical, fantastic. **-2.** [muy bueno] fabulous, fantastic.
facción *f* POLÍT faction.
♦ **facciones** *fpl* [rasgos] features.
faccioso, -sa ◇ *adj* factious, rebellious. ◇ *m y f* rebel.

faceta *f* facet.
facha ◇ *f* **-1.** [aspecto] appearance, look. **-2.** [mamarracho] mess; **vas hecho una** ~ you look a mess. ◇ *m y f fam despec* [ultraderechista] fascist pig.
fachada *f* **-1.** ARQUIT façade. **-2.** *fig* outward appearance; **es pura** ~ it's just a show.
facial *adj* facial.
fácil *adj* **-1.** [gen] easy; ~ **de hacer** easy to do. **-2.** [tratable] easy-going. **-3.** [probable] probable, likely.
facilidad *f* **-1.** [simplicidad] ease, easiness. **-2.** [aptitud] aptitude; **tener** ~ **para algo** to have a gift for sthg.
♦ **facilidades** *fpl* [comodidades] facilities; ~**es de pago** easy (payment) terms.
facilitar *vt* **-1.** [simplificar] to facilitate, to make easy; [posibilitar] to make possible. **-2.** [proporcionar] to provide.
facilón, -ona *adj fam* dead easy.
facineroso, -sa *m y f* miscreant, criminal.
facsímil, facsímile *m* facsimile.
factible *adj* feasible.
fáctico, -ca → **poder**.
facto
♦ **de facto** *loc adv* de facto.
factor *m* **-1.** [gen] factor. **-2.** FERROC luggage clerk.
factoría *f* **-1.** [fábrica] factory. **-2.** COM outlet, agency.
factótum (*pl* **factotums**) *m y f* factotum.
factura *f* **-1.** [por mercancías, trabajo realizado] invoice; ~ **pro forma** O **proforma** COM proforma invoice. **-2.** [de gas, teléfono] bill; [en tienda, hotel] bill.
facturación *f* **-1.** [cobro] invoicing. **-2.** [ventas] turnover. **-3.** [de equipaje - en aeropuerto] checking-in; [- en estación] registration; **mostrador de** ~ check-in desk.
facturar *vt* **-1.** [cobrar]: ~**le a alguien algo** to invoice O bill sb for sthg. **-2.** [vender] to turn over. **-3.** [equipaje - en aeropuerto] to check in; [- en estación] to register.
facultad *f* **-1.** [gen] faculty. **-2.** [poder] power, right.
facultar *vt* to authorize.
facultativo, -va ◇ *adj* **-1.** [voluntario] optional. **-2.** [médico] medical. ◇ *m y f* doctor.
FAD (*abrev de* **Fondo de Ayuda al Desarrollo**) *m* Spanish development aid fund.
fado *m* melancholy Portuguese folk song.
faena *f* **-1.** [tarea] task, work (*U*); ~**s domésticas** housework (*U*), household chores; **hacerle una (mala)** ~ **a alguien** to play a dirty trick on sb. **-2.** TAUROM

bullfighter's performance; *ver también* **tauromaquia**.

faenar *vi* to fish.

fagocito *m* phagocyte.

fagot ◇ *m* [instrumento] bassoon. ◇ *m y f* [músico] bassoonist.

FAH (*abrev de* **factor antihemofílico**) *m* antihaemophilic factor, factor VIII.

fair play ['ferplei] *m* fair play.

faisán *m* pheasant.

faja *f* **-1.** [prenda de mujer, terapéutica] corset; [banda] sash, cummerbund. **-2.** [de terreno - pequeña] strip; [- grande] belt. **-3.** [de libro] band (*around new book*).

fajar *vt* [periódico] to put a wrapper on; [libro] to put a band on.

fajín *m* sash.

fajo *m* [de billetes, papel] wad; [de leña, cañas] bundle.

fakir = **faquir**.

falacia *f* deceit, trick.

falange *f* **-1.** ANAT & MIL phalanx. **-2.** POLÍT: **la Falange (Española)** the Falange.

LA FALANGE ESPAÑOLA:
The 'Falange Española' was a totalitarian political group, founded in Spain in 1933. It played a major role in the Spanish Civil War and later occupied an important position in Franco's Spain

falangismo *m* Falangist movement.

falangista *adj, m y f* Falangist.

falaz *adj* false.

falda *f* **-1.** [prenda] skirt; ~ **escocesa** kilt; ~ **pantalón** culottes (*pl*). **-2.** [de montaña] slope, mountainside. **-3.** [regazo] lap. **-4.** [de mesa camilla] cover.

◆ **faldas** *fpl fam* [chicas] girls.

faldero, -ra *adj* **-1.** [dócil]: **perro** ~ lapdog. **-2.** [mujeriego] keen on women.

faldón *m* **-1.** [de ropa] tail; [de cortina, mesa camilla] folds (*pl*). **-2.** [de tejado] gable.

falibilidad *f* fallibility.

falible *adj* fallible.

fálico, -ca *adj* phallic.

falla *f* [gen & GEOL] fault.

◆ **fallas** *fpl* [fiesta] *celebrations in Valencia during which cardboard figures are burnt.*

fallar ◇ *vt* **-1.** [sentenciar] to pass sentence on; [premio] to award. **-2.** [equivocar - respuesta] to get wrong; [- tiro] to miss. ◇ *vi* **-1.** [equivocarse] to get it wrong; [no acertar] to miss. **-2.** [fracasar, flaquear] to fail; [- plan] to go wrong. **-3.** [decepcionar]: ~**le a alguien** to let sb down. **-4.** [quebrarse, ceder]

to give way. **-5.** [sentenciar]: ~ **a favor/en contra de** to find in favour of/against.

fallecer [30] *vi* to pass away, to die.

fallecimiento *m* decease, death.

fallero, -ra *adj relating to the celebrations in Valencia during which cardboard figures are burnt.*

fallido, -da *adj* [esfuerzo, intento] unsuccessful, failed; [esperanza] vain; [disparo] missed.

fallo *m* **-1.** [error] mistake; DEP miss. **-2.** [sentencia - de juez, jurado] verdict. **-3.** [opinión] judgment.

fallutería *f Amer fam* hypocrisy.

falluto, -ta *adj Amer fam* phoney, hypocritical.

falo *m* phallus.

falocracia *f* male chauvinism.

falócrata *m* male chauvinist.

falsario, -ria ◇ *adj* false. ◇ *m y f* liar.

falsear *vt* [hechos, historia] to falsify, to distort; [moneda, firma] to forge.

falsedad *f* **-1.** [falta de verdad, autenticidad] falseness. **-2.** [mentira] falsehood, lie.

falsete *m* falsetto.

falsificación *f* forgery.

falsificador, -ra *m y f* forger.

falsificar [10] *vt* to forge.

falsilla *f* guide sheet (*for writing paper*).

falso, -sa *adj* **-1.** [rumor, excusa etc] false, untrue. **-2.** [dinero, firma, cuadro] forged; [joyas] fake; **jurar en** ~ to commit perjury. **-3.** [hipócrita] deceitful. **-4.** [inadecuado] wrong, incorrect.

falta *f* **-1.** [carencia] lack; **hacer** ~ to be necessary; **me hace** ~ **suerte** I need some luck; **por** ~ **de** for want ○ lack of. **-2.** [escasez] shortage. **-3.** [ausencia] absence; **echar en** ~ **algo/a alguien** [notar la ausencia de] to notice that sthg/sb is missing; [echar de menos] to miss sthg/sb. **-4.** [imperfección] fault; [error] mistake; ~ **de educación** bad manners (*pl*); ~ **de ortografía** spelling mistake. **-5.** DEP foul; [en tenis] fault; ~ **libre directa** direct free kick offence; ~ **personal** personal foul. **-6.** DER offence. **-7.** [en la menstruación] missed period.

◆ **a falta de** *loc prep* in the absence of.

◆ **sin falta** *loc adv* without fail.

faltar *vi* **-1.** [no haber] to be lacking, to be needed; **falta aire** there's not enough air; **falta sal** it needs a bit of salt. **-2.** [estar ausente] to be absent ○ missing; **falta Elena** Elena is missing. **-3.** [carecer]: **le faltan las fuerzas** he lacks ○ doesn't have the strength. **-4.** [hacer falta] to be necessary; **me falta tiempo** I need time. **-5.** [quedar]:

falta un mes para las vacaciones there's a month to go till the holidays; **sólo te falta firmar** all you have to do is sign; **¿cuánto falta para Leeds?** how much further is it to Leeds?; **falta mucho por hacer** there is still a lot to be done; **falta poco para que llegue** it won't be long till he arrives; **faltó poco para que le matase** I very nearly killed him. **-6.** *loc:* **¡no faltaba** ◇ **faltaría más!** [asentimiento] of course!; [rechazo] that tops it all!, that's a bit much!

◆ **faltar a** *vi* **-1.** [palabra, promesa] to break, not to keep; [deber, obligación] to neglect. **-2.** [cita, trabajo] not to turn up at; **¡no faltes (a la cita)!** don't miss it!, be there! **-3.** [no respetar] to be disrespectful towards; ~ **a alguien en algo** to offend sb in sthg. **-4.** [defraudar] to betray, to disappoint.

falto, -ta *adj:* ~ **de** lacking in, short of.

fama *f* **-1.** [renombre] fame. **-2.** [reputación] reputation; **cría** ~ **y échate a dormir** [proverb] *build yourself a good reputation, then you can rest on your laurels.*

famélico, -ca *adj* starving, famished.

familia *f* family; **en** ~ privately, in private; ~ **numerosa** large family.

familiar ◇ *adj* **-1.** [de familia] family (*antes de sust*). **-2.** [en el trato - agradable] friendly; [- en demasía] overly familiar. **-3.** [lenguaje, estilo] informal, colloquial. **-4.** [conocido] familiar. ◇ *m y f* relative, relation.

familiaridad *f* familiarity.

familiarizar [13] *vt:* ~ **(con)** to familiarize (with).

◆ **familiarizarse** *vpr:* ~**se con** [estudiar] to familiarize o.s. with; [acostumbrarse a] to get used to.

famoso, -sa ◇ *adj* famous. ◇ *m y f* famous person, celebrity.

fan *m y f* fan.

fanático, -ca ◇ *adj* fanatical. ◇ *m y f* [gen] fanatic; DEP fan.

fanatismo *m* fanaticism.

fanatizar [13] *vt* to arouse fanaticism in.

fandango *m* [baile] fandango.

fandanguillo *m type of fandango.*

fané *adj Amer* worn out.

fanega *f grain measure which varies from region to region.*

fanfarria *f* **-1.** *fam* [jactancia] boasting, bragging. **-2.** [de música] fanfare; [banda] brass band.

fanfarrón, -ona ◇ *adj* boastful. ◇ *m y f* braggart, show-off.

fanfarronada *f* brag.

fanfarronear *vi:* ~ **(de)** to boast ◇ brag (about).

fanfarronería *f* showing-off, bragging.

fango *m* mud.

fangoso, -sa *adj* muddy.

fantasear ◇ *vi* to fantasize. ◇ *vt* to imagine, to fantasize about.

fantasía *f* **-1.** [imaginación] imagination; [cosa imaginada] fantasy; **de** ~ [ropa] fancy; [bisutería] imitation, costume (*antes de sust*). **-2.** MÚS fantasia.

fantasioso, -sa *adj* imaginative.

fantasma ◇ *m* [espectro] ghost, phantom. ◇ *m y f fam* [fanfarrón] show-off.

fantasmada *f fam* brag.

fantasmal *adj* ghostly.

fantasmón, -ona *m y f fam* show-off.

fantástico, -ca *adj* fantastic.

fantochada *f* crazy ◇ mad thing.

fantoche *m* **-1.** [títere] puppet. **-2.** [mamarracho] (ridiculous) sight.

FAO (*abrev de* **Food and Agriculture Organization**) *f* FAO.

faquir, fakir *m* fakir.

faradio *m* farad.

farándula *f:* **la** ~ the theatre, the stage.

faraón *m* pharaoh.

faraónico, -ca *adj* pharaonic; *fig* [fastuoso] lavish, magnificent.

fardada *f fam* showing-off (*U*).

fardar *vi fam:* ~ **(de algo)** to show (sthg) off.

fardo *m* bundle.

fardón, -ona *fam* ◇ *adj* flashy. ◇ *m y f* flash Harry.

farero, -ra *m y f* lighthouse keeper.

farfullar *vt & vi* to gabble, to splutter.

faringe *f* pharynx.

faringitis *f inv* sore throat.

fariseo, -a *m y f* **-1.** HIST Pharisee. **-2.** *fig* [hipócrita] hypocrite.

farmacéutico, -ca ◇ *adj* pharmaceutical. ◇ *m y f* chemist, pharmacist.

farmacia *f* **-1.** [ciencia] pharmacy. **-2.** [establecimiento] chemist's (shop) *Br*, pharmacy, drugstore *Am*; ~ **de turno** ◇ **de guardia** duty chemist's.

fármaco *m* medicine, drug.

farmacología *f* pharmacology.

farmacopea *f* pharmacopoeia.

farmacoterapia *f treatment using course of drugs.*

faro *m* **-1.** [para barcos] lighthouse. **-2.** [de coche] headlight, headlamp; ~ **antiniebla** foglamp.

farol *m* **-1.** [farola] street lamp ◇ light; [linterna] lantern, lamp. **-2.** [en el juego] bluff. **-3.** *fam* [mentira] fib, lie.

farola *f* [farol] street lamp ○ light; [poste] lamppost.

farolear *vi fam* to fib.

farolero, -ra ○ *adj fam* boastful. ○ *m y f* **-1.** [oficio] lamplighter. **-2.** *fam* [fanfarrón] show-off.

farolillo *m* **-1.** [de papel] paper ○ Chinese lantern. **-2.** [planta] Canterbury bell.

farra *f fam* binge, spree; **ir de ~** to paint the town red.

farragoso, -sa *adj* confused, rambling.

farruco, -ca *adj* [valiente] cocky.

farsa *f lit &* *fig* farce.

farsante ○ *adj* deceitful. ○ *m y f* deceitful person.

FAS (*abrev de* **Fondo de Asistencia Social**) *m Spanish social welfare fund.*

fascículo *m* part, instalment (*of serialization*).

fascinación *f* fascination.

fascinante *adj* fascinating.

fascinar *vt* to fascinate.

fascismo *m* fascism.

fascista *adj, m y f* fascist.

fase *f* phase.

fastidiado, -da *adj* [de salud] ill; **ando ~ del estómago** I've got a bad stomach.

fastidiar [8] ○ *vt* **-1.** [estropear - fiesta etc] to spoil, to ruin; [- máquina, objeto etc] to break. **-2.** [molestar] to annoy, to bother. ○ *vi:* **¡no fastidies!** you're having me on!

◆ **fastidiarse** *vpr* **-1.** [estropearse - fiesta etc] to be ruined; [- máquina] to break down. **-2.** [aguantarse] to put up with it.

fastidio *m* **-1.** [molestia] nuisance, bother. **-2.** [enfado] annoyance. **-3.** [aburrimiento] bore.

fastidioso, -sa *adj* **-1.** [molesto] annoying. **-2.** [aburrido] boring, tedious.

fasto *m* pomp, extravagance.

fastuosidad *f* lavishness, sumptuousness.

fastuoso, -sa *adj* lavish, sumptuous.

fatal ○ *adj* **-1.** [mortal] fatal. **-2.** [muy malo] terrible, awful. **-3.** [inevitable] inevitable. **-4.** [seductor]: **mujer ~ femme fatale.** ○ *adv* terribly; **sentirse ~** to feel terrible.

fatalidad *f* **-1.** [destino] fate, destiny. **-2.** [desgracia] misfortune.

fatalismo *m* fatalism.

fatalista ○ *adj* fatalistic. ○ *m y f* fatalist.

fatídico, -ca *adj* fateful, ominous.

fatiga *f* [cansancio] tiredness, fatigue.

◆ **fatigas** *fpl* [penas] troubles, hardships.

fatigado, -da *adj* tired, weary.

fatigante *adj* tiring.

fatigar [16] *vt* to tire, to weary.

◆ **fatigarse** *vpr* to get tired.

fatigoso, -sa *adj* tiring, fatiguing.

fatigue *etc →* **fatigar.**

fatuidad *f* **-1.** [necedad] fatuousness, foolishness. **-2.** [vanidad] conceit.

fatuo, -tua *adj* **-1.** [necio] fatuous, foolish. **-2.** [engreído] conceited.

fauces *fpl* fig jaws.

fauna *f* fauna.

fauno *m* faun.

fausto, -ta *adj* happy, fortunate.

fauvismo [fo'ßismo] *m* fauvism.

favor *m* favour; **a ~ de** in favour of; **hacerle un ~ a alguien** [ayudar a] to do sb a favour; *fam fig* [acostarse con] to go to bed with sb; **hágame el ~ de cerrar la puerta** would you mind shutting the door, please?; **pedir un ~ a alguien** to ask sb a favour; **tener a** ○ **en su ~ a alguien** to enjoy sb's support.

◆ **favores** *mpl* [de una mujer] favours.

◆ **por favor** *loc adv* please.

favorable *adj* favourable; **ser ~ a algo** to be in favour of sthg.

favorecedor, -ra *adj* flattering, becoming.

favorecer [30] *vt* **-1.** [gen] to favour; [ayudar] to help, to assist. **-2.** [sentar bien] to suit.

favoritismo *m* favouritism.

favorito, -ta *adj, m y f* favourite.

fax *m inv* **-1.** [aparato] fax (machine); **mandar algo por ~** to fax sthg. **-2.** [documento] fax.

fayuquero *m Amer* dealer in contraband.

faz *f culto* **-1.** [cara] countenance, face. **-2.** [del mundo, de la tierra] face.

FBI (*abrev de* **Federal Bureau of Investigation**) *m* FBI.

f.c. *abrev de* **ferrocarril.**

FCI (*abrev de* **Fondo de Compensación Interterritorial**) *m fund created to promote the economies of the poorer autonomous regions in Spain.*

fe *f* **-1.** [gen] faith; **hacer algo de buena ~** to do sthg in good faith. **-2.** [documento] certificate; **~ de erratas** errata (*pl*). **-3.** *loc:* **dar ~ de que** to testify that; **la ~ mueve montañas** faith can move mountains.

FE *abrev de* **Falange Española.**

fealdad *f* **-1.** [de rostro etc] ugliness. **-2.** [de conducta etc] unworthiness.

feb., febr. (*abrev de* **febrero**) Feb.

febrero *m* February; *ver también* **septiembre.**

febril *adj* feverish; *fig* [actividad] hectic.

fecal *adj* faecal.

fecha *f* [gen] date; [momento actual] current date; **en ~ próxima** in the next few days; **hasta la ~** to date, so far; **ocurrió por estas ~s** it happened around this time of year; **~ de caducidad** [de alimentos] sell-by date; [de carné, pasaporte] expiry date; [de medicamento] "use before" date; **~ tope ○ límite** deadline.

fechador *m* postmark.

fechar *vt* to date.

fechoría *f* bad deed, misdemeanour.

fécula *f* starch (*in food*).

fecundación *f* fertilization; **~ artificial** artificial insemination; **~ in vitro** in vitro fertilization.

fecundar *vt* **-1.** [fertilizar] to fertilize. **-2.** [hacer productivo] to make fertile.

fecundidad *f* **-1.** [fertilidad] fertility. **-2.** [productividad] productiveness.

fecundo, -da *adj* [gen] fertile; [artista] prolific.

FED (*abrev de* **Fondo Europeo de Desarrollo**) *m* EDF.

FEDER (*abrev de* **Fondo Europeo de Desarrollo Regional**) *m* ERDF.

federación *f* federation.

federal *adj, m y f* federal.

federalismo *m* federalism.

federalista *adj, m y f* federalist.

federar *vt* to federate.

◆ **federarse** *vpr* **-1.** [formar federación] to become ○ form a federation. **-2.** [ingresar en federación] to join a federation.

federativo, -va ◇ *adj* federative. ◇ *m y f* member of a federation.

feedback ['fidbak] (*pl* **feedbacks**) *m* feedback.

fehaciente *adj* irrefutable.

felación *f* fellatio.

feldespato *m* feldspar.

felicidad *f* happiness.

◆ **felicidades** *interj* **¡~es!** [gen] congratulations!; [en cumpleaños] happy birthday!

felicitación *f* **-1.** [acción]: **felicitaciones** congratulations. **-2.** [postal] greetings card.

felicitar *vt* to congratulate.

◆ **felicitarse** *vpr*: **~se (por)** to be pleased ○ glad (about).

félidos *mpl* felines, cats.

feligrés, -esa *m y f* parishioner.

felino, -na *adj* feline.

◆ **felino** *m* feline, cat.

feliz *adj* **-1.** [gen] happy. **-2.** [afortunado] lucky. **-3.** [oportuno] timely.

felonía *f* [traición] treachery, betrayal; [infamia] vile deed.

felpa *f* [de seda] plush; [de algodón] towelling.

felpudo *m* doormat.

femenino, -na *adj* [gen] feminine; BOT & ZOOL female.

◆ **femenino** *m* GRAM feminine.

fémina *f* woman, female.

feminidad, femineidad *f* femininity.

feminismo *m* feminism.

feminista *adj, m y f* feminist.

feminizar [13] *vt* to make feminine.

femoral ◇ *adj* femoral. ◇ *f* femoral artery.

fémur (*pl* **fémures**) *m* femur, thighbone.

fenecer [30] *vi culto* to pass away, to die.

fenicio, -cia *adj, m y f* Phoenician.

◆ **fenicio** *m* [lengua] Phoenician.

fénix *m inv* [ave] phoenix.

fenomenal *adj* [magnífico] wonderful, fantastic.

fenómeno ◇ *m* **-1.** [gen] phenomenon. **-2.** [monstruo] freak. ◇ *adv fam* brilliantly, fantastically; **pasarlo ~** to have a great time. ◇ *interj*: **¡~!** great!, terrific!

fenomenología *f* phenomenology.

Fenosa (*abrev de* **Fuerzas Eléctricas del Noroeste, SA**) *f electricity company of north-east Spain.*

fenotipo *m* phenotype.

feo, -a ◇ *adj* **-1.** [persona] ugly. **-2.** [aspecto, herida, conducta] nasty; **es ~ escupir** it's rude to spit. **-3.** [tiempo] foul, horrible. ◇ *m y f* [persona] ugly person.

◆ **feo** *m* [desaire] slight, insult; **hacer un ~ a alguien** to offend ○ slight sb.

féretro *m* coffin.

feria *f* **-1.** [gen] fair; **~ (de muestras)** trade fair. **-2.** [fiesta popular] festival.

ferial *adj* fair (*antes de sust*); **recinto ~** fairground.

feriante *m y f* [vendedor] trader; [comprador] fairgoer.

fermentación *f* fermentation.

fermentar *vt & vi* to ferment.

fermento *m* ferment.

ferocidad *f* ferocity, fierceness.

feroz *adj* **-1.** [animal, bestia] fierce, ferocious. **-2.** *fig* [criminal, asesino] cruel, savage. **-3.** *fig* [dolor, angustia] terrible. **-4.** *fig* [enorme] massive.

férreo, -a *adj lit & fig* iron (*antes de sust*).

ferretería *f* ironmonger's (shop) *Br*, hardware store.

ferretero, -ra *m y f* ironmonger, hardware dealer.

férrico, -ca *adj* ferric.

ferrocarril *m* [sistema, medio] railway, railroad *Am*; [tren] train; **por** ~ by train.

ferroso, -sa *adj* ferrous.

ferroviario, -ria ◇ *adj* railway (*antes de sust*) *Br*, rail (*antes de sust*), railroad (*antes de sust*) *Am*. ◇ *m y f* railway worker.

ferry *m* ferry.

fértil *adj lit* & *fig* fertile.

fertilidad *f lit* & *fig* fertility.

fertilización *f* fertilization.

fertilizante ◇ *adj* fertilizing. ◇ *m* fertilizer.

fertilizar [13] *vt* to fertilize.

ferviente *adj* fervent.

fervor *m* fervour.

fervoroso, -sa *adj* fervent.

festejar *vt* **-1.** [celebrar] to celebrate. **-2.** [agasajar] to entertain.

◆ **festejarse** *vpr* [celebrarse] to be celebrated.

festejo *m* **-1.** [fiesta] party. **-2.** [agasajo] entertaining.

◆ **festejos** *mpl* [fiestas] public festivities.

festín *m* banquet, feast.

festival *m* festival.

festividad *f* festivity.

festivo, -va *adj* **-1.** [de fiesta] festive; **día** ~ (public) holiday. **-2.** [alegre] cheerful, jolly; [chistoso] funny, witty.

festón *m* [en costura] scallop.

festonear *vt* [en costura] to scallop.

fetal *adj* foetal.

fetén *adj inv fam* brilliant, great.

fetiche *m* fetish.

fetichismo *m* fetishism.

fetichista ◇ *adj* fetishistic. ◇ *m y f* fetishist.

fétido, -da *adj* fetid, foul-smelling.

feto *m* foetus.

feudal *adj* feudal.

feudalismo *m* feudalism.

feudo *m* HIST fief; *fig* [dominio] domain, area of influence.

FEVE (*abrev de* **Ferrocarriles Españoles de Vía Estrecha**) *m Spanish narrow-gauge railways.*

fez *m* fez.

FF AA (*abrev de* **Fuerzas Armadas**) *fpl Spanish armed forces.*

fiabilidad *f* reliability.

fiable *adj* [máquina] reliable; [persona] trustworthy.

fiador, -ra *m y f* guarantor, surety; **salir** ~ **por** to vouch for.

fiambre *m* **-1.** [comida] cold meat *Br*, cold cut *Am*. **-2.** *fam* [cadáver] stiff, corpse.

fiambrera *f* lunch ○ sandwich box.

fianza *f* **-1.** [depósito] deposit. **-2.** DER bail; **bajo** ~ on bail. **-3.** [garantía] security, bond.

fiar [9] ◇ *vt* COM to sell on credit. ◇ *vi* COM to sell on credit; **ser de** ~ *fig* to be trustworthy.

◆ **fiarse** *vpr*: ¡no te fíes! don't be too sure (about it)!; ~**se de algo/alguien** to trust sthg/sb.

fiasco *m* fiasco.

FIBA (*abrev de* **Federación Internacional de Baloncesto Amateur**) *f* IABF.

fibra *f* **-1.** [gen] fibre; [de madera] grain; ~ **de vidrio** fibreglass; ~ **óptica** INFORM optic fibre. **-2.** [energía] character, vigour.

fibroma *m* fibroma.

fibrosis *f inv* fibrosis.

fibroso, -sa *adj* fibrous.

ficción *f* **-1.** [gen] fiction. **-2.** [simulación] pretence, make-believe.

ficha *f* **-1.** [tarjeta] (index) card; [con detalles personales] file, record card. **-2.** [de guardarropa, aparcamiento] ticket. **-3.** [de teléfono] token. **-4.** [de juego - gen] counter; [en ajedrez] piece; [en un casino] chip. **-5.** DEP [contrato] contract. **-6.** INFORM card; ~ **perforada** perforated card.

fichaje *m* DEP [contratación] signing (up); [importe] transfer fee.

fichar ◇ *vt* **-1.** [archivar] to note down on an index card, to file. **-2.** [suj: policía] to put on police files ○ records. **-3.** DEP to sign up. **-4.** *fam* [calar] to suss out, to see through. ◇ *vi* **-1.** [suj: trabajador - al entrar] to clock in; [- al salir] to clock out. **-2.** DEP: ~ **(por)** to sign up (for).

fichero *m* INFORM file.

ficticio, -cia *adj* **-1.** [imaginario] fictitious. **-2.** [convencional] imaginary.

ficus *m inv* rubber plant.

fidedigno, -na *adj* reliable.

fideicomisario, -ria ◇ *adj* trust (*antes de sust*). ◇ *m y f* trustee.

fideicomiso *m* trust.

fidelidad *f* **-1.** [lealtad] loyalty; [de cónyuge, perro] faithfulness. **-2.** [precisión] accuracy; **alta** ~ high fidelity.

fideo *m* noodle; **estar** ○ **quedarse como un** ~ to be as thin as a rake.

Fidji ['fidʒi] Fiji.

fiduciario, -ria ◇ *adj* DER & ECON fiduciary. ◇ *m y f* DER & ECON fiduciary.

fiebre f fever; **tener** ~ to have a temperature; ~ **amarilla/de Malta** yellow/Malta fever; ~ **del heno** hay fever; **la** ~ **del oro** the gold rush.

fiel ◇ adj **-1.** [leal - amigo, seguidor] loyal; [- cónyuge, perro] faithful. **-2.** [preciso] accurate. ◇ m [de balanza] needle, pointer.
◆ **fieles** mpl RELIG: **los** ~es the faithful.

fieltro m felt.

fiero, -ra adj savage, ferocious.
◆ **fiera** f **-1.** [animal] wild animal. **-2.** fig [persona - genial] demon; [- cruel] brute; **estar/ponerse hecho una fiera** to be/go wild with anger.

fierro m Amer **-1.** [hierro] iron. **-2.** [navaja] penknife.

fiesta f **-1.** [reunión] party; [de pueblo etc] (local) festivities (pl); ~ **mayor** local celebrations (pl); **la** ~ **nacional** bull fighting; **aguar la** ~ **a alguien** to spoil sb's fun. **-2.** [día] public holiday; **ser** ~ to be a public holiday; **hacer** ~ to be on holiday. **-3.** fig [alegría] joy, delight.
◆ **fiestas** fpl [vacaciones] holidays.

FIESTA MAYOR:
The 'fiesta mayor' consists of a round of cultural and recreational events organized in a town to celebrate the festival of its patron saint

FIFA (abrev de **Federación Internacional de Fútbol Asociación**) f FIFA.

fifí m Amer fam playboy.

figura f **-1.** [gen] figure; [forma] shape. **-2.** [en naipes] picture card.

figuraciones fpl imaginings; **son** ~ **tuyas** it's all in your imagination.

figurado, -da adj figurative.

figurante, -ta m y f extra.

figurar ◇ vi **-1.** [aparecer] ~ **(en)** to appear (in), to figure (in). **-2.** [ser importante] to be prominent ○ important. ◇ vt **-1.** [representar] to represent. **-2.** [simular] to feign, to simulate.
◆ **figurarse** vpr [imaginarse] to imagine; **ya me lo figuraba yo** I thought as much.

figurativo, -va adj ARTE figurative.

figurín m fashion sketch; **ir/estar hecho un** ~ fig to be dressed up to the nines.

figurón m **-1.** [fanfarrón] poseur. **-2.** [mangoneador] person who wants to be the centre of attention.

fijación f **-1.** [gen & FOT] fixing. **-2.** [obsesión] fixation.
◆ **fijaciones** fpl [en esquí] bindings.

fijador, -ra adj fixing.

fijador m **-1.** [líquido] fixative; ~ **de pelo** [crema] hair gel; [espray] hair spray. **-2.** [en esquí] ski-clip.

fijar vt **-1.** [gen] to fix; [asegurar] to fasten; [cartel] to stick up; [sello] to stick on. **-2.** [significado] to establish; ~ **el domicilio** to take up residence; ~ **la mirada/la atención en** to fix one's gaze/attention on.
◆ **fijarse** vpr to pay attention; ~**se en algo** [darse cuenta] to notice sthg; [prestar atención] to pay attention to sthg.

fijeza f firmness.
◆ **con fijeza** loc adv **-1.** [con seguridad] definitely, for sure. **-2.** [con persistencia] fixedly.

fijo, -ja ◇ adj **-1.** [gen] fixed; [sujeto] secure. **-2.** [cliente] regular. **-3.** [fecha] firm, definite. **-4.** [empleado, trabajo] permanent. ◇ adv fam definitely.

fila f **-1.** [hilera - gen] line; [- de asientos] row; **en** ~, **en** ~ **india** in line, in single file; **ponerse en** ~ to line up. **-2.** MIL rank. **-3.** [manía] dislike.
◆ **filas** fpl MIL ranks; **cerrar** ~s fig to close ranks; **en** ~s doing military service; **llamar a** ~s **a alguien** to call sb up; **romper** ~s to fall out.

filamento m filament.

filantropía f philanthropy.

filantrópico, -ca adj philanthropic.

filantropismo m philanthropy.

filántropo, -pa m y f philanthropist.

filarmónico, -ca adj philharmonic.
◆ **filarmónica** f philharmonic (orchestra).

filatelia f philately.

filatélico, -ca ◇ adj philatelic. ◇ m y f philatelist.

filete m **-1.** [CULIN - grueso] (fillet) steak; [- delgado] fillet; [solomillo] sirloin. **-2.** [de tornillo] thread.

filiación f **-1.** [ficha militar, policial] record, file. **-2.** POLIT affiliation. **-3.** [parentesco] relationship.

filial ◇ adj **-1.** [de hijo] filial. **-2.** [de empresa] subsidiary. ◇ f subsidiary.

filibustero m pirate.

filiforme adj thread-like.

filigrana f **-1.** [en orfebrería] filigree. **-2.** fig [habilidad] skilful work. **-3.** [en billetes] watermark.

Filipinas fpl: **(las)** ~ the Philippines (sg).

filipino, -na adj, m y f Filipino.
◆ **filipino** m [lengua] Filipino.

filisteo, -a adj, m y f Philistine.

film = **filme**.

filmación f filming, shooting.

filmador, -ra adj film (antes de sust).
◆ **filmadora** f [cámara] cine camera.

filmar *vt* to film, to shoot.

filme (*pl* **filmes**), **film** (*pl* **films**) *m* film *Br*, movie *Am*.

filmografía *f* filmography.

filmoteca *f* [archivo] film library; [sala de cine] film institute.

filo *m* (cutting) edge; **de doble ~, de dos ~s** *lit* & *fig* double-edged.

● **al filo de** *loc prep* just before.

filología *f* **-1.** [ciencia] philology. **-2.** [carrera] language and literature.

filológico, -ca *adj* philological.

filólogo, -ga *m y f* philologist.

filón *m* **-1.** [de carbón etc] seam. **-2.** *fig* [mina] gold mine.

filoso, -sa, filudo, -da *adj Amer* sharp.

filosofar *vi* to philosophize.

filosofía *f* **-1.** [ciencia] philosophy. **-2.** [resignación]: **tomarse algo con ~** to be philosophical about sthg.

filosófico, -ca *adj* philosophical.

filósofo, -fa *m y f* philosopher.

filoxera *f* phylloxera.

filtración *f* **-1.** [de agua] filtration. **-2.** *fig* [de noticia etc] leak.

filtrante *adj* filtering.

filtrar *vt* **-1.** [tamizar] to filter. **-2.** *fig* [datos, noticia] to leak.

● **filtrarse** *vpr* **-1.** [penetrar]: **~se (por)** to filter ○ seep (through). **-2.** *fig* [datos, noticia] to be leaked.

filtro *m* **-1.** [gen] filter; [de cigarrillo] filter, filter tip. **-2.** [pócima] philtre.

filudo, -da = **filoso**.

fimosis *f inv* phimosis.

fin *m* **-1.** [final] end; **dar** ○ **poner ~ a algo** to put an end to sthg; **tocar a su ~** to come to a close; **~ de fiesta** grand finale; **~ de semana** weekend; **a ~es de** at the end of; **al** ○ **por ~** at last, finally; **a ~ de cuentas** after all; **al ~ y al cabo** after all; **sin ~** endless; **al ~ del mundo** to the end of the earth (and back). **-2.** [objetivo] aim, goal.

● **a fin de** *loc conj* in order to.

● **en fin** *loc adv* anyway.

finado, -da *m y f*: **el ~** the deceased.

final ◇ *adj* final, end (*antes de sust*). ◇ *m* end; **~ feliz** happy ending; **a ~es de** at the end of; **al ~** [en conclusión] in the end; **al ~ de** at the end of. ◇ *f* final.

finalidad *f* aim, purpose.

finalista ◇ *adj* amongst the finalists. ◇ *m y f* finalist.

finalización *f* [gen] end; [de contrato] termination.

finalizar [13] ◇ *vt* to finish, to complete. ◇ *vi*: **~ (con)** to end ○ finish (in).

financiación *f* financing.

financiar [8] *vt* to finance.

financiero, -ra ◇ *adj* financial. ◇ *m y f* [persona] financier.

● **financiera** *f* [firma] finance company.

financista *m y f Amer* financier.

finanzas *fpl* finance (*U*).

finar *vi culto* to pass away.

finca *f* [gen] property; [casa de campo] country residence.

fineza *f* **-1.** [cualidad] (fine) quality. **-2.** [cortesía] courtesy.

finger (*pl* **fingers**) *m* finger (*at airport*), jetway.

fingido, -da *adj* feigned, apparent.

fingimiento *m* pretence.

fingir [15] ◇ *vt* to feign. ◇ *vi* to pretend.

finiquitar *vt* to settle.

finiquito *m* settlement.

finito, -ta *adj* finite.

finja *etc* → **fingir**.

finlandés, -esa ◇ *adj* Finnish. ◇ *m y f* [persona] Finn.

● **finlandés** *m* [lengua] Finnish.

Finlandia Finland.

fino, -na *adj* **-1.** [gen] fine; [delgado] thin; [cintura] slim. **-2.** [cortés] refined. **-3.** [agudo - oído, olfato] sharp, keen; [- gusto, humor, ironía] refined.

● **fino** *m* dry sherry.

finolis *fam* ◇ *adj inv* affected. ◇ *m y f inv* affected person.

finura *f* [gen] fineness; [delgadez] thinness; [cortesía] refinement; [de oído, olfato] sharpness, keenness; [de gusto, humor, ironía] refinement.

fiordo *m* fiord.

firma *f* **-1.** [rúbrica] signature; [acción] signing; **estampar la ~** to sign, to write one's signature. **-2.** [empresa] firm.

firmamento *m* firmament.

firmante ◇ *adj* signatory. ◇ *m y f* signatory; **el abajo ~** the undersigned.

firmar *vt* to sign; **~ algo en blanco** *fig* to rubber-stamp sthg.

firme ◇ *adj* **-1.** [gen] firm; [mueble, andamio, edificio] stable. **-2.** [argumento, base] solid. **-3.** [carácter, actitud, paso] resolute. ◇ *adv* hard; **mantenerse ~ en** to hold fast to; ◇ *m* road surface.

● **firmes** *interj*: **¡~s!** MIL attention!

firmeza *f* **-1.** [gen] firmness; [de mueble, edificio] stability. **-2.** [de argumento] solidity. **-3.** [de carácter, actitud] resolution.

fiscal ◇ *adj* tax (*antes de sust*), fiscal. ◇ *m y f* public prosecutor *Br*, district attorney *Am*.

fiscalía *f* **-1.** [cargo] post of public prosecutor *Br* ○ district attorney *Am*. **-2.** [oficina] office of public prosecutor *Br* ○ district attorney *Am*.

fiscalización *f* investigation, inquiry.

fiscalizador, -ra ◇ *adj* investigating (*antes de sust*). ◇ *m y f* investigator.

fiscalizar [13] *vt* to inquire into ○ investigate the affairs of.

fisco *m* treasury, exchequer.

fisgar [16], **fisgonear** *vi* [gen] to pry; [escuchando] to eavesdrop.

fisgón, -ona ◇ *adj* nosey, prying. ◇ *m y f* busybody, nosy parker *Br*.

fisgonear = fisgar.

fisgoneo *m* prying.

fisgue *etc* → fisgar.

fisible *adj* fissile.

físico, -ca ◇ *adj* physical. ◇ *m y f* [persona] physicist.
◆ **físico** *m* [complexión] physique.
◆ **física** *f* [ciencia] physics (*U*).

fisiología *f* physiology.

fisiológico, -ca *adj* physiological.

fisión *f* fission.

fisionomía, fisonomía *f* features (*pl*), appearance.

fisionomista, fisonomista *m y f* person who is good at remembering faces.

fisioterapeuta *m y f* physiotherapist.

fisioterapia *f* physiotherapy.

FISL (*abrev de* **Federación Internacional de Sindicatos Libres**) *f* international federation of free trade unions.

fisonomía = fisionomía.

fisonomista = fisionomista.

fístula *f* fistula.

fisura *f* **-1.** [grieta] fissure. **-2.** *fig* weakness, weak point.

fitología *f* botany.

FITUR (*abrev de* **Feria Internacional del Turismo**) *f* international tourism fair.

flacidez, flaccidez *f* flabbiness.

flácido, -da, fláccido, -da *adj* flaccid, flabby.

flaco, -ca *adj* thin, skinny.

flagelación *f* flagellation.

flagelar *vt* to flagellate.
◆ **flagelarse** *vpr* to flagellate o.s.

flagelo *m* **-1.** [látigo] whip. **-2.** BIOL flagellum.

flagrante *adj* flagrant.

flamante *adj* [vistoso] resplendent; [nuevo] brand-new.

flambear *vt* to flambé.

flamear ◇ *vi* **-1.** [fuego] to blaze ○ flare (up). **-2.** [bandera, vela] to flap. ◇ *vt* to sterilize by passing through a flame.

flamenco, -ca ◇ *adj* **-1.** MÚS flamenco (*antes de sust*). **-2.** [de Flandes] Flemish. ◇ *m y f* [de Flandes] Fleming.
◆ **flamenco** *m* **-1.** [ave] flamingo. **-2.** [lengua] Flemish. **-3.** MÚS flamenco.

flamencología *f* study of flamenco.

flamencólogo, -ga *m y f* expert in flamenco.

flan *m* crème caramel; **estar hecho** ○ **como un ~** to shake like a jelly, to be a bundle of nerves.

flanco *m* flank.

flanera *f* crème caramel mould.

flanquear *vt* to flank.

flaquear *vi* to weaken; *fig* to flag.

flaqueza *f* weakness.

flash [flaʃ] (*pl* **flashes**) *m* **-1.** FOT flash. **-2.** [informativo] newsflash. **-3.** *fam* [imagen mental] flash of inspiration.

flato *m*: **tener ~** to have a stitch.

flatulencia *f* flatulence, wind.

flatulento, -ta *adj* flatulent.

flauta ◇ *f* flute; **~ dulce** recorder; **de la gran ~** *Amer fig* tremendous. ◇ *interj*: **¡(la gran) ~!** *Amer* good grief!, good heavens!

flautín *m* piccolo.

flautista *m y f* flautist.

flebitis *f inv* phlebitis.

flecha ◇ *f* [gen] arrow; ARQUIT spire. ◇ *m y f fam*: **ser un ~** to be red hot, to be extremely good.

flechazo *m* **-1.** [disparo] arrow shot; [herida] arrow wound. **-2.** *fam fig* [amoroso]: **fue un ~** it was love at first sight.

fleco *m* **-1.** [adorno] fringe. **-2.** [de tela gastada] frayed edge.

flema *f* phlegm.

flemático, -ca *adj* **-1.** [con mucosidad] phlegmy. **-2.** [tranquilo] phlegmatic.

flemón *m* gumboil.

flequillo *m* fringe.

fletamiento *m* [alquiler] charter, chartering (*U*).

fletar *vt* **-1.** [alquilar] to charter. **-2.** [cargar] to load.

flete *m* **-1.** [precio] freightage. **-2.** [carga] cargo, freight.

flexibilidad *f* flexibility.

flexibilizar [13] *vt* to make flexible.

flexible *adj* flexible.

flexión f **-1.** [doblegamiento] bending. **-2.**
GRAM inflection.

flexionar vt to bend.

flexo m adjustable table lamp ○ light.

flexor, -ra adj flexional.

◆ **flexor** m flexor.

flipado, -da adj fam [drogado] stoned, high;
[asombrado] gobsmacked.

flipar fam ◇ vi **-1.** [disfrutar] to have a wild
time. **-2.** [asombrarse] to be gobsmacked.
-3. [con una droga] to be stoned ○ high. ◇
vt [gustar]: **me flipan los videojuegos** I'm
wild about video games.

◆ **fliparse** fam vpr **-1.** [disfrutar]: ~**se (con)**
to go wild (about). **-2.** [drogarse] to get
stoned ○ high.

flipper m pinball machine.

flirtear vi to flirt.

flirteo m flirtation, flirting (U).

FLN (abrev de **Frente de Liberación Nacional**) m FLN.

flojear vi **-1.** [decaer - piernas, fuerzas etc] to
weaken; [- memoria] to be failing; [- película,
libro] to flag; [- calor, trabajo] to ease off;
[- ventas] to fall off. **-2.** [no ser muy apto]: ~
en algo to get worse at sthg.

flojedad f weakness.

flojera f lethargy, feeling of weakness.

flojo, -ja adj **-1.** [suelto] loose. **-2.** [débil -
persona, bebida] weak; [- sonido] faint; [- tela]
thin; [- salud] poor; [- viento] light. **-3.** [sin
calidad, aptitudes] poor; **estar** ~ **en algo** to
be poor ○ weak at sthg. **-4.** [inactivo - mercado, negocio] slack.

flor f **-1.** BOT flower; **en** ~ in flower; ~ **de
lis** fleur-de-lis; ~ **de un día** fig flash in the
pan; **echar** ~**es a alguien** to pay sb compliments. **-2.** [lo mejor]: **la** ~ **(y nata)** the
crème de la crème, the cream; **en la** ~ **de
la edad** ○ **de la vida** in the prime of life.

◆ **a flor de** loc adv: **a** ~ **de agua/tierra** at
water/ground level; **a** ~ **de piel** fig just below the surface.

flora f flora; ~ **intestinal** ○ **microbiana** mi-
crobes (pl).

floración f flowering, blossoming.

floral adj floral.

floreado, -da adj flowery.

florecer [30] vi to flower; fig to flourish.

floreciente adj fig flourishing.

florecimiento m flowering; fig flourishing.

Florencia Florence.

florentino, -na adj, m y f Florentine.

florero m vase.

floricultor, -ra m y f flower grower ○ producer.

floricultura f flower growing.

florido, -da adj [con flores] flowery; [estilo,
lenguaje] florid.

florín m florin.

florista m y f florist.

floristería f florist's (shop).

floritura f flourish.

flota f fleet.

flotabilidad f **-1.** [en el agua] buoyancy. **-2.**
ECON floatability.

flotación f [gen & ECON] flotation.

flotador m **-1.** [para nadar] rubber ring. **-2.**
[de caña de pescar] float. **-3.** [de cisternas]
ballcock.

flotante adj [gen & ECON] floating.

flotar vi [gen & ECON] to float; [banderas] to
flutter.

flote

◆ **a flote** loc adv afloat; **mantenerse a** ~ to
stay afloat; **sacar algo a** ~ fig to get sthg
back on its feet; **salir a** ~ fig to get back
on one's feet.

flotilla f flotilla.

fluctuación f **-1.** [variación] fluctuation. **-2.**
[vacilación] wavering.

fluctuante adj fluctuating.

fluctuar [6] vi **-1.** [variar] to fluctuate. **-2.**
[vacilar] to waver.

fluidez f **-1.** [gen] fluidity; [del tráfico] free
flow; [de relaciones] smoothness. **-2.** fig [en
el lenguaje] fluency.

fluido, -da adj **-1.** [gen] fluid; [tráfico] free-
flowing. **-2.** [relaciones] smooth. **-3.** fig [len-
guaje] fluent.

◆ **fluido** m fluid; ~ **eléctrico** electric current ○ power.

fluir [51] vi to flow.

flujo m flow; ~ **de caja** cash flow.

flúor m fluorine.

fluorescencia f fluorescence.

fluorescente ◇ adj fluorescent. ◇ m strip
light.

fluoruro m fluoride.

fluvial adj river (antes de sust).

fluya, fluyera etc → **fluir**.

FM (abrev de **frecuencia modulada**) f FM.

FMI (abrev de **Fondo Monetario Internacional**) m IMF.

FMLN (abrev de **Movimiento Farabundo
Martí de Liberación Nacional**) m FMLN.

FN (abrev de **Fuerza Nueva**) f Spanish political party to the extreme right of the political
spectrum.

FNMT (abrev de **Fábrica Nacional de Moneda y Timbre**) f Spanish national mint.

fobia f phobia.

foca *f* seal.

focal *adj* focal.

focalizar [13] *vt* to focus.

foco *m* **-1.** *fig* [centro] centre, focal point. **-2.** [lámpara - para un punto] spotlight; [- para una zona] floodlight. **-3.** FÍS & GEOM focus. **-4.** *Amer* [bombilla] light bulb. **-5.** *Amer* [farola] street light. **-6.** *Amer* AUTOM (car) headlight.

fofo, -fa *adj* flabby.

fogata *f* bonfire, fire.

fogón *m* **-1.** [para cocinar] stove. **-2.** [de máquina de vapor] firebox.

fogonazo *m* flash.

fogonero, -ra *m y f* stoker.

fogosidad *f* passion.

fogoso, -sa *adj* passionate.

foguео *m*: de ~ blank.

foie-gras [fwa'ɣras] *m* (pâté de) foie-gras.

fol. (*abrev de* **folio**) f.

folclore, folclor, folklor *m* folklore.

folclórico, -ca ◇ *adj* traditional, popular. ◇ *m y f* flamenco singer.

folclorismo *m* folklore.

foliación *f* foliation.

foliado, -da *adj* leafy.

folículo *m* follicle.

folio *m* [hoja] leaf, sheet; [tamaño] folio.

folklor = **folclore**.

follaje *m* foliage.

follar *vi vulg* to fuck.

folletín *m* [dramón] melodrama.

folletinesco, -ca *adj* melodramatic.

folleto *m* [turístico, publicitario] brochure; [explicativo, de instrucciones] leaflet.

follón *m fam* **-1.** [discusión] row; se armó ~ there was an almighty row. **-2.** [lío] mess; ¡vaya ~! what a mess!

fomentar *vt* to encourage, to foster.

fomento *m* encouragement, fostering.

fonación *f* phonation.

fonda *f* boarding house.

fondeadero *m* anchorage.

fondear ◇ *vi* to anchor. ◇ *vt* [sondear] to sound; [registrar - barco] to search.

fondista *m y f* **-1.** [propietario de fonda] landlord (*f* landlady). **-2.** [DEP - corredor] long-distance runner; [- nadador] long-distance swimmer; [- esquiador] cross-country skier.

fondo *m* **-1.** [de recipiente, mar, piscina] bottom; **tocar** ~ [embarcación] to scrape along the sea/river bed; *fig* to hit rock bottom; **doble** ~ false bottom. **-2.** [de habitación etc] back; **al** ~ **de** [calle, pasillo] at the end of; [sala] at the back of. **-3.** [dimensión] depth. **-4.** [de tela, cuadro, foto] background; **al** ~ **in** the background. **-5.** [de asunto, tema] heart, bottom; **llegar al** ~ **de** to get to the heart o bottom of. **-6.** [de una persona]: **tener buen** ~ to have a good heart. **-7.** [de obra literaria] substance. **-8.** ECON fund; **a** ~ **perdido** non-returnable; ~ **común** kitty; ~ **de amortización/de inversión/de pensiones** ECON sinking/investment/pension fund; ~ **de garantía de depósito** BANCA deposit guarantee fund. **-9.** [fundamento] reason, basis. **-10.** [de biblioteca, archivo] catalogue, collection; ~ **editorial** collection of published works. **-11.** DEP stamina; **de** ~ long-distance; **de medio** ~ middle-distance. **-12.** *Amer* [combinación] petticoat.

◆ **fondos** *mpl* **-1.** ECON [capital] funds; **estar mal de** ~s [persona] to be badly off; [empresa] to be short of funds; **recaudar** ~s to raise funds. **-2.** [de embarcación] bottom (*sg*).

◆ **bajos fondos** *mpl* underworld (*U*).

◆ **a fondo** ◇ *loc adv* thoroughly; **emplearse a** ~ *fig* to do one's utmost. ◇ *loc adj* thorough.

◆ **en el fondo** *loc adv* **-1.** [en lo más íntimo] deep down. **-2.** [en lo esencial] basically.

fonendoscopio *m* stethoscope.

fonético, -ca *adj* phonetic.

◆ **fonética** *f* **-1.** [ciencia] phonetics (*U*). **-2.** [sonidos] sound.

fonetista *m y f* phonetician.

fónico, -ca *adj* phonic.

fono *m Amer* phone.

fonógrafo *m* gramophone, phonograph *Am*.

fonología *f* phonology.

fonometría *f* phonometry.

fonoteca *f* record library.

fontanería *f* plumbing.

fontanero, -ra *m y f* plumber.

football = **fútbol**.

footing ['futin] *m* jogging; **hacer** ~ to go jogging.

FOP (*abrev de* **Fuerzas de Orden Público**) *fpl* police (*force*).

foque *m* NÁUT jib.

forajido, -da *m y f* outlaw.

foral *adj relating to ancient regional laws still existing in some parts of Spain.*

foráneo, -a *adj* foreign.

forastero, -ra *m y f* stranger.

FORATOM (*abrev de* **Foro Atómico Europeo**) *m* European Atomic Forum.

forcé → **forzar**.

forcejear *vi* to struggle.

forcejeo *m* struggle.

forcemos → forzar.

fórceps *m inv* forceps.

forense ◇ *adj* forensic. ◇ *m y f* pathologist.

forestal *adj* forest (*antes de sust*).

forfait [for'fe] *m* **-1.** DEP default. **-2.** [abono] pass. **-3.** [precio invariable] fixed rate; **a ~** fixed price.

forja *f* [fragua] forge; [forjadura] forging.

forjado, -da *adj* wrought.

forjador, -ra *m y f* (metal) forger.

forjar *vt* **-1.** [metal] to forge. **-2.** *fig* [inventarse] to invent; [crear] to build up.

◆ **forjarse** *vpr fig* [labrarse] to carve out for o.s.

forma *f* **-1.** [gen] shape, form; **en ~ de** in the shape of; **guardar las ~s** to keep up appearances. **-2.** [manera] way, manner; **de cualquier ~, de todas ~s** anyway, in any case; **de esta ~** in this way; **de ~ que** in such a way that, so that; **~ de pago** method of payment. **-3.** ARTE & LITER form. **-4.** [condición física] fitness; **estar en ~** to be fit. **-5.** RELIG host.

◆ **formas** *fpl* **-1.** [silueta] figure (*sg*), curves. **-2.** [modales] manners, social conventions.

formación *f* **-1.** [gen & MIL] formation. **-2.** [educación] training; **~ profesional** vocational training. **-3.** [conjunto] grouping.

formador, -ra *adj* forming, constituting.

formal *adj* **-1.** [gen] formal. **-2.** [que se porta bien] well-behaved, good. **-3.** [de confianza] reliable. **-4.** [serio] serious.

formalidad *f* **-1.** [gen] formality. **-2.** [educación] (good) manners (*pl*). **-3.** [fiabilidad] reliability. **-4.** [seriedad] seriousness.

formalismo *m* formalism.

formalista ◇ *adj* formal. ◇ *m y f* formalist.

formalización *f* formalization.

formalizar [13] *vt* to formalize.

formar ◇ *vt* **-1.** [gen] to form. **-2.** [educar] to train, to educate. **-3.** MIL to form up. ◇ *vi* MIL to fall in.

◆ **formarse** *vpr* **-1.** [gen] to form. **-2.** [educarse] to be trained o educated.

formatear *vt* INFORM to format.

formateo *m* INFORM formatting.

formativo, -va *adj* formative.

formato *m* [gen & INFORM] format.

formica® *f* Formica®.

formidable *adj* [enorme] tremendous; [extraordinario] amazing, fantastic.

formol *m* formalin.

fórmula *f* formula; **~ uno** formula one.

formulación *f* formulation.

formular *vt* to formulate; **~ una pregunta** to ask a question.

formulario *m* form.

formulismo *m* [apego - a las formas] formalism; [- a las normas] sticking to the rules.

fornicación *f culto* fornication.

fornicar [10] *vi culto* to fornicate.

fornido, -da *adj* well-built.

foro *m* **-1.** [tribunal] court (of law). **-2.** TEATR back of the stage. **-3.** [debate] forum; **~ de discusión** INFORM forum.

forofo, -fa *m y f fam* fan, supporter.

FORPA (*abrev de* **Fondo de Ordenación y Regulación de Precios y Productos Agrarios**) *m Spanish fund for the regulation of agricultural prices and products.*

forrado, -da *adj* [libro] covered; [ropa] lined; [asiento] upholstered; **estar ~** *fam* to be rolling in it.

forraje *m* fodder.

forrar *vt*: **~ (de)** [libro] to cover (with); [ropa] to line (with); [asiento] to upholster (with).

◆ **forrarse** *vpr fam* to make a packet.

forro *m* [de libro] cover; [de ropa] lining; [de asiento] upholstery; **ni por el ~** *fam* at all.

fortachón, -ona *adj* strapping, well-built.

fortalecer [30] *vt* to strengthen.

fortalecimiento *m* strengthening.

fortaleza *f* **-1.** [gen] strength. **-2.** [recinto] fortress.

fortificación *f* fortification.

fortificar [10] *vt* to fortify.

fortín *m* small fort.

FORTRAN *m* INFORM FORTRAN.

fortuito, -ta *adj* chance (*antes de sust*).

fortuna *f* **-1.** [suerte] (good) luck; **por ~** fortunately, luckily; **probar ~** to try one's luck. **-2.** [destino] fortune, fate. **-3.** [riqueza] fortune.

forúnculo, furúnculo *m* boil.

forzado, -da *adj* forced.

forzar [37] *vt* **-1.** [gen] to force; **~ a alguien a hacer algo** to force sb to do sthg; **~ la vista** to strain one's eyes. **-2.** [violar] to rape.

forzoso, -sa *adj* [obligatorio] obligatory, compulsory; [inevitable] inevitable; [necesario] necessary.

forzudo, -da ◇ *adj* strong. ◇ *m y f* strong man (*f* strong woman).

fosa *f* **-1.** [sepultura] grave; **~ común** common grave. **-2.** ANAT cavity; **~s nasales** nostrils. **-3.** [hoyo] pit; **~ marina** ocean trough; **~ séptica** septic tank.

fosfatar *vt* [fertilizar] to fertilize with phosphates.

fosfato *m* phosphate.

fosforescencia *f* phosphorescence.

fosforescente *adj* phosphorescent.

fósforo *m* **-1.** QUÍM phosphorus. **-2.** [cerilla] match.

fósil ◇ *adj* fossil (*antes de sust*). ◇ *m* **-1.** CIENCIA fossil. **-2.** *fam* [viejo] old fossil.

fosilización *f* fossilization.

fosilizarse [13] *vpr* **-1.** CIENCIA to fossilize. **-2.** *fig* [persona] to turn into an old fossil.

foso *m* [hoyo] ditch; [de fortaleza] moat; [de garaje] pit; DEP & TEATR pit.

foto *f* photo.

fotocélula *f* photocell, photoelectric cell.

fotocomponedora *f* IMPRENTA typesetter, typesetting machine.

fotocomponer *vt* IMPRENTA to typeset.

fotocomposición *f* IMPRENTA typesetting.

fotocopia *f* **-1.** [objeto] photocopy. **-2.** [procedimiento] photocopying.

fotocopiadora *f* photocopier.

fotocopiar [8] *vt* to photocopy.

fotoeléctrico, -ca *adj* photoelectric.

fotofobia *f* photophobia.

fotogenia *f* photogenic qualities (*pl*).

fotogénico, -ca *adj* photogenic.

fotograbado *m* photogravure.

fotografía *f* **-1.** [arte] photography. **-2.** [objeto] photograph.

fotografiar [9] *vt* to photograph, to take a photograph of.

fotográfico, -ca *adj* photographic.

fotógrafo, -fa *m y f* photographer.

fotograma *m* still.

fotolito *m* photolithograph.

fotomatón *m* passport photo machine.

fotometría *f* photometry.

fotómetro *m* light meter.

fotomodelo *m y f* photographic model.

fotomontaje *m* photomontage.

fotonovela *f* photo story.

fotorrobot (*pl* **fotorrobots**) *f* Identikit® picture.

fotosensible *adj* photosensitive.

fotosíntesis *f inv* photosynthesis.

fotuto *m* *Amer* AUTOM horn.

foulard = **fular**.

foxterrier [fokste'rjer] *m* fox terrier.

foxtrot *m* foxtrot.

FP (*abrev de* **formación profesional**) *f* vocational training.

FP:
In Spain, vocational training can be entered either at 16, at the end of compulsory education, or at 18, after the *bachillerato*. It aims to provide flexible training programmes for students, as well as retraining schemes for adults

FPLP (*abrev de* **Frente Popular para la Liberación de Palestina**) *m* Popular Front for the Liberation of Palestine.

fra. (*abrev de* **factura**) *inv*.

frac (*pl* **fracs**) *m* tails (*pl*), dress coat.

fracasado, -da ◇ *adj* failed. ◇ *m y f* failure.

fracasar *vi*: ~ **(en/como)** to fail (at/as).

fracaso *m* failure; **todo fue un** ~ the whole thing was a disaster.

fracción *f* **-1.** [gen] fraction; ~ **decimal** decimal fraction. **-2.** POLÍT faction.

fraccionadora *f* *Amer* estate agent.

fraccionamiento *m* **-1.** [división] division, breaking up. **-2.** *Amer* [urbanización] housing estate.

fraccionar *vt* to divide, to break up.

fraccionario, -ria *adj* fractional; **moneda fraccionaria** small change.

fractura *f* fracture.

fracturarse *vpr* to fracture.

fragancia *f* fragrance.

fragante *adj* fragrant.

fraganti
◆ **in fraganti** *loc adv*: **coger a alguien in** ~ to catch sb red-handed ○ in the act.

fragata *f* frigate.

frágil *adj* [objeto] fragile; [persona] frail.

fragilidad *f* [de objeto] fragility; [de persona] frailty.

fragmentación *f* [rotura] fragmentation; [división] division.

fragmentar *vt* [romper] to fragment; [dividir] to divide.

fragmentario, -ria *adj* [incompleto] fragmentary.

fragmento *m* fragment, piece; [de obra] excerpt.

fragor *m* [de batalla] clamour; [de trueno] crash.

fragua *f* forge.

fraguar [45] ◇ *vt* **-1.** [forjar] to forge. **-2.** *fig* [idear] to think up. ◇ *vi* to set, to harden.
◆ **fraguarse** *vpr* to be in the offing.

fraile *m* friar.

frambuesa *f* raspberry.

francés, **-esa** ◇ *adj* French. ◇ *m y f*
Frenchman (*f* Frenchwoman); **los franceses**
the French; **marcharse ○ despedirse a la
francesa** to leave without even saying
goodbye.
◆ **francés** *m* [lengua] French.

francesada *f fam exaggerated portrayal of
French life.*

franchute, **-ta** *m y f despec* Frog, *pejorative
term referring to a French person.*

Francia France.

franciscano, **-na** *adj, m y f* Franciscan.

francmasón *m* Freemason.

francmasonería *f* Freemasonry.

francmasónico, **-ca** *adj* masonic.

franco, **-ca** ◇ *adj* **-1.** [sincero] frank, open;
[directo] frank. **-2.** [sin obstáculos, gastos]
free. **-3.** HIST Frankish. ◇ *m y f* HIST Frank.
◆ **franco** *m* **-1.** [moneda] franc. **-2.** [lengua]
Frankish.

francófono, **-na** ◇ *adj* francophone. ◇ *m
y f* Francophone.

francotirador, **-ra** *m y f* **-1.** MIL sniper. **-2.**
fig [rebelde] maverick.

franela *f* flannel.

franja *f* strip; [en bandera, uniforme] stripe.

franquear *vt* **-1.** [paso, camino] to clear. **-2.**
[río, montaña etc] to negotiate, to cross. **-3.**
[correo] to frank.

franqueo *m* postage.

franqueza *f* **-1.** [sinceridad] frankness,
openness. **-2.** [confianza] familiarity.

franquicia *f* exemption.

franquismo *m*: **el ~** [régimen] the Franco
regime; [doctrina] Franco's doctrine.

FRANQUISMO:
'Franquismo' refers to the dictatorship established in Spain by General Franco in
1939 at the end of the civil war and lasting
until his death in 1975

---

franquista ◇ *adj* pro-Franco. ◇ *m y f* supporter of Franco.

frasco *m* small bottle.

frase *f* **-1.** [oración] sentence. **-2.** [locución]
expression; **~ hecha** [modismo] set phrase;
[tópico] cliché.

fraseología *f* **-1.** [estilo] phraseology. **-2.**
[palabrería] verbiage.

fraternal *adj* brotherly, fraternal.

fraternidad, **fraternización** *f* brotherhood, fraternity.

fraternizar [13] *vi* to get on like brothers.

fraterno, **-na** *adj* brotherly, fraternal.

fratricida ◇ *adj* fratricidal. ◇ *m y f* fratricide.

fratricidio *m* fratricide.

fraude *m* fraud; **~ fiscal** tax evasion.

fraudulento, **-ta** *adj* fraudulent.

fray *m* brother.

frazada *f Amer* blanket; **~ eléctrica** electric
blanket.

frecuencia *f* frequency; **con ~** often; **alta/
baja ~** high/low frequency; **~ modulada,
modulación de ~** frequency modulation.

frecuentación *f* frequenting.

frecuentado, **-da** *adj* popular.

frecuentar *vt* [lugar] to frequent; [persona]
to see, to visit.

frecuente *adj* [reiterado] frequent; [habitual]
common.

freelance ['frilens] *adj* freelance.

Freetown ['fritaun] Freetown.

fregadero *m* (kitchen) sink.

fregado, **-da** *adj Amer fam* troublesome,
annoying.
◆ **fregado** *m* **-1.** [lavado - gen] wash; [- fro-
tando] scrub. **-2.** *fam* [lío] mess. **-3.** *fam* [dis-
cusión] row, rumpus.

fregar [35] *vt* **-1.** [limpiar] to wash; **~ los
platos** to do the washing-up. **-2.** [frotar]
scrub. **-3.** *Amer fam* [molestar] to bother, to
pester.

fregona *f* **-1.** *despec* [criada] skivvy. **-2.** *despec* [verdulera]: **es una ~** she's as common
as muck. **-3.** [utensilio] mop.

fregotear *vt* to give a quick wash ○ wipe.

fregué *etc* → fregar.

freidora *f* [gen] deep fat fryer; [para patatas
fritas] chip pan.

freiduría *f shop where fried food, especially
fish, is cooked and served.*

freír [28] *vt* **-1.** CULIN to fry. **-2.** *fam* [moles-
tar]: **~ a alguien (a)** to pester sb (with). **-3.**
fam [matar]: **~ a alguien (a tiros)** to gun sb
down.
◆ **freírse** *vpr* to be frying.

frenado *m* braking.

frenar ◇ *vt* **-1.** AUTOM to brake. **-2.** [conte-
ner] to check. ◇ *vi* to stop; AUTOM to brake.

frenazo *m* **-1.** AUTOM: **dar un ~** to brake
hard. **-2.** *fig* [parón] sudden stop.

frenesí (*pl* frenesíes) *m* frenzy.

frenético, **-ca** *adj* **-1.** [colérico] furious,
mad. **-2.** [enloquecido] frenzied, frantic.

frenillo *m* fraenum.

freno *m* **-1.** AUTOM brake; **~ automático**
automatic brake; **~s ABS** ABS brakes; **~s
de disco** disc brakes. **-2.** [de caballerías] bit.

-3. *fig* [contención] check; **poner** ~ **a** to put a stop to.

frenopatía *f* psychiatry.

frenopático, -ca *adj* psychiatric.

frente ◇ *f* forehead; ~ **a** ~ face to face. ◇ *m* front; **estar al** ~ **(de)** to be at the head (of); **hacer** ~ **a** to face up to; ~ **frío** cold front.

◆ **de frente** *loc adv* **-1.** [hacia delante] forwards. **-2.** [uno contra otro] head on.

◆ **frente a** *loc prep* **-1.** [enfrente de] opposite. **-2.** [con relación a] towards.

fresa *f* **-1.** [planta, fruto] strawberry. **-2.** [herramienta - de dentista] drill; [- de orfebre etc] milling cutter.

fresco, -ca ◇ *adj* **-1.** [gen] fresh; [temperatura] cool; [pintura, tinta] wet. **-2.** [caradura] cheeky. **-3.** *loc*: **quedarse tan** ~ not to bat an eyelid. ◇ *m y f* [caradura] cheeky person.

◆ **fresco** *m* **-1.** ARTE fresco; **al** ~ in fresco. **-2.** [frescor] coolness; **hace** ~ it's chilly; **tomar el** ~ to get a breath of fresh air.

◆ **fresca** *f* [insolencia]: **soltarle una fresca** O **cuatro frescas a alguien** to tell sb a few home truths.

frescor *m* coolness, freshness.

frescura *f* **-1.** [gen] freshness. **-2.** [descaro] cheek, nerve; **¡qué** ~**!** what a cheek!

fresno *m* ash (tree).

fresón *m* large strawberry.

freudiano, -na [froi'ðjano, -na] *adj* Freudian.

fría → **freír**.

frialdad *f lit* & *fig* coldness.

fricandó *m* fricandeau.

fricasé *m* fricassee.

fricativo, -va *adj* fricative.

◆ **fricativa** *f* fricative.

fricción *f* [gen] friction; [friega] rub, massage.

friccionar *vt* to rub, to massage.

frie → **freír**.

friega ◇ *v* → **fregar**. ◇ *f* massage.

friera *etc* → **freír**.

frígida *adj f* frigid.

frigider, friyider *m Amer* refrigerator, fridge *Br*, icebox *Am*.

frigidez *f* frigidity.

frigorífico, -ca *adj* [camión] refrigerator (*antes de sust*); [cámara] cold.

◆ **frigorífico** *m* refrigerator, fridge *Br*, icebox *Am*.

frijol, fríjol *m Amer* bean.

frío, -a *adj* [gen] cold; [inmutable] cool; **dejar a alguien** ~ to leave sb cold.

◆ **frío** *m* cold; **hacer un** ~ **que pela** to be freezing cold; **pelarse de** ~ to be freezing

to death; **tener** ~ to be cold; **coger a alguien en** ~ *fig* to catch sb on the hop; **no darle a alguien ni** ~ **ni calor** *fig* to leave sb cold.

frió → **freír**.

friolento, -ta *adj Amer* sensitive to the cold.

friolero, -ra ◇ *adj* sensitive to the cold. ◇ *m y f* person who feels the cold.

◆ **friolera** *f fam*: **costó la friolera de 20.000 pesetas** it cost a cool 20,000 pesetas.

frisar *vt* to be around, to be getting on for (*a certain age*).

friso *m* **-1.** ARQUIT frieze. **-2.** [zócalo] skirting board.

frisón, -ona *adj, m y f* Frisian.

fritada *f* fry-up, dish of fried food.

frito, -ta ◇ *pp* → **freír**. ◇ *adj* **-1.** [alimento] fried. **-2.** *fam fig* [persona - harta] fed up (to the back teeth); [- dormida] flaked out, asleep.

◆ **frito** *m* (*gen pl*) fried food (*U*).

fritura *f* fry-up, dish of fried food.

frivolidad *f* frivolity.

frívolo, -la *adj* frivolous.

friyider = **frigider**.

frondosidad *f* leafiness.

frondoso, -sa *adj* leafy.

frontal *adj* frontal.

frontera *f* border; *fig* [límite] bounds (*pl*).

fronterizo, -za *adj* border (*antes de sust*).

frontis *m inv* façade.

frontispicio *m* **-1.** [de edificio - fachada] façade; [- remate] pediment. **-2.** [de libro] frontispiece.

frontón *m* **-1.** [deporte] pelota; [cancha] pelota court. **-2.** ARQUIT pediment.

frotamiento *m* rubbing.

frotar *vt* to rub.

◆ **frotarse** *vpr*: ~**se las manos** to rub one's hands.

fructífero, -ra *adj* fruitful.

fructificar [10] *vi lit* & *fig* to bear fruit.

fructosa *f* fructose.

fructuoso, -sa *adj* fruitful.

frugal *adj* frugal.

frugalidad *f* frugality.

fruición *f* gusto, delight.

fruncido, fruncimiento *m* gathering, shirring.

fruncir [12] *vt* **-1.** [labios] to purse; ~ **el ceño** to frown. **-2.** [tela] to gather.

fruslería *f* triviality, trifle.

frustración *f* frustration.

frustrado, -da *adj* frustrated; [fracasado] failed.

frustrante *adj* frustrating.

frustrar *vt* **-1.** [persona] to frustrate. **-2.** [posibilidades, ilusiones] to thwart, to put paid to.
◆ **frustrarse** *vpr* **-1.** [persona] to get frustrated. **-2.** [ilusiones] to be thwarted; [proyecto] to fail.

fruta *f* fruit.

frutal ◇ *adj* fruit (*antes de sust*). ◇ *m* fruit tree.

frutería *f* fruit shop.

frutero, -ra ◇ *adj* fruit (*antes de sust*). ◇ *m y f* [persona] fruiterer.
◆ **frutero** *m* [recipiente] fruit bowl.

fruticultura *f* fruit farming.

frutilla *f* *Amer* strawberry.

fruto *m* **-1.** [naranja, plátano etc] fruit; [nuez, avellana etc] nut; ~s **secos** dried fruit and nuts. **-2.** [resultado] fruit; **dar** ~ to bear fruit; **sacar** ~ **a** ○ **de algo** to profit from sthg.

FSLN (*abrev de* **Frente Sandinista de Liberación Nacional**) *m* FSLN.

FSM *f* (*abrev de* **Federación Sindical Mundial**) WFTU.

fu
◆ **ni fu ni fa** *loc adv* so-so.

fucsia ◇ *f* [planta] fuchsia. ◇ *adj inv & m inv* [color] fuchsia.

fue -1. → **ir. -2.** → **ser.**

fuego *m* **-1.** [gen & MIL] fire; [de cocina, fogón] ring, burner; **a** ~ **lento/vivo** CULIN over a low/high heat; **atizar el** ~ to poke the fire; **pegar** ~ **a algo** to set sthg on fire, to set fire to sthg; **pedir/dar** ~ to ask for/give a light; ¿**tiene** ~? have you got a light?; ~ **fatuo** will-o'-the-wisp; ~s **artificiales** fireworks; **estar entre dos** ~s to be between the devil and the deep blue sea; **jugar con** ~ to play with fire. **-2.** [apasionamiento] passion, ardour. **-3.** [sensación de ardor] heat, burning.

fuel = **fuel-oil.**

fuelle *m* **-1.** [gen] bellows (*pl*). **-2.** [de maleta, bolso] accordion pleats (*pl*). **-3.** [entre vagones] connecting corridor, concertina vestibule.

fuel-oil, fuel *m* fuel oil.

fuente *f* **-1.** [manantial] spring. **-2.** [construcción] fountain. **-3.** [bandeja] (serving) dish. **-4.** *fig* [origen] source; ~s **oficiales** official sources. **-5.** ELECTRÓN: ~ **de alimentación** feed source.

fuera ◇ *v* **-1.** → **ir. -2.** → **ser.** ◇ *adv* **-1.** [en el exterior] outside; **le echó** ~ she threw him out; **hacia** ~ outwards; **por** ~ (on the) outside. **-2.** [en otro lugar] away; [en el extranjero] abroad; **de** ~ [extranjero] from abroad. **-3.** *fig* [alejado]: ~ **de** [alcance, peligro] out of; [cálculos, competencia] outside; **estar** ~ **de sí** to be beside o.s. (with rage). **-4.** DEP: ~ **de banda** out of play; ~ **de combate** knocked out; *fig* out of action; ~ **de juego** offside.
◇ *interj* ¡~! [gen] (get) out!; [en el teatro] (get) off!; ¡~ **de aquí!** get out of my sight!
◆ **fuera de** *loc prep* [excepto] except for, apart from.
◆ **fuera de serie** ◇ *adj* exceptional, out of the ordinary. ◇ *m y f*: **ser un** ~ **de serie** to be one of a kind.

fueraborda *m inv* outboard motor ○ engine.

fuerce → **forzar.**

fuero *m* **-1.** [ley local] (*gen pl*) ancient regional law still existing in some parts of Spain. **-2.** [jurisdicción] code of laws. **-3.** *loc*: **en el** ~ **interno de alguien** in sb's heart of hearts, deep down.

fuerte ◇ *adj* **-1.** [gen] strong. **-2.** [carácter] unpleasant. **-3.** [frío, dolor, color] intense; [lluvia] heavy; [ruido] loud; [golpe, pelea] hard. **-4.** [comida, salsa] rich. **-5.** [nudo] tight. **-6.** [grave]: **esto es** ~ that's a bit much. ◇ *adv* **-1.** [intensamente - gen] hard; [- abrazar, agarrar] tight. **-2.** [abundantemente] a lot. **-3.** [en voz alta] loudly. ◇ *m* **-1.** [fortificación] fort. **-2.** [punto fuerte] strong point, forte.

fuerza ◇ *v* → **forzar.**
◇ *f* **-1.** [gen] strength; [violencia] force; [de sonido] loudness; [de dolor] intensity; **por** ~ of necessity; **tener** ~s **para** to have the strength to; ~ **mayor** DER force majeure; [en seguros] act of God; **no llegué por un caso de** ~ **mayor** I didn't make it due to circumstances beyond my control; ~ **de voluntad** willpower; **a** ~ **de** by dint of, **a la** ~ [contra la voluntad] by force; [por necesidad] of necessity; **por la** ~ by force; **sacar** ~s **de flaqueza** to screw up one's courage. **-2.** FÍS & MIL force; ~s **armadas** armed forces; ~s **del orden público** police (*pl*). **-3.** ELECTR power.
◆ **fuerzas** *fpl* [grupo] forces.

fuese -1. → **ir. -2.** → **ser.**

fuga *f* **-1.** [huida] escape; **darse a la** ~ to take flight; ~ **de cerebros** brain drain. **-2.** [escape] leak. **-3.** MÚS fugue.

fugacidad *f* fleeting nature.

fugarse [16] *vpr* to escape; ~ **de casa** to run away from home; ~ **con alguien** to run off with sb.

fugaz *adj* fleeting.
fugitivo, **-va** ◇ *adj* -1. [en fuga] fleeing. -2. [fugaz] fleeting. ◇ *m y f* fugitive.
fugue *etc* → **fugarse**.
führer ['firer] (*pl* **führers**) *m* führer.
fui → **ir**.
fulano, **-na** *m y f* what's his/her name, so-and-so.
◆ **fulana** *f* [prostituta] tart, whore.
fular, **foulard** [fu'lar] *m* headscarf.
fulero, **-ra** ◇ *adj* -1. [chapucero] shoddy. -2. [tramposo] dishonest. ◇ *m y f* trickster.
fulgor *m* shining; [de disparo] flash.
fulgurante *adj* -1. [rápido] rapid. -2. [resplandeciente] flashing.
fulgurar *vi* to gleam; [intermitentemente] to flash.
fullero, **-ra** ◇ *adj* cheating, dishonest. ◇ *m y f* cheat.
fulminante *adj* -1. *fig* [despido, muerte] sudden; [enfermedad] devastating; [mirada] withering. -2. [explosivo] fulminating.
fulminar *vt* [suj: enfermedad] to strike down; **un rayo la fulminó** she was struck by lightning; ~ **a alguien con la mirada** to look daggers at sb.
fumadero *m* [de opio] den.
fumador, **-ra** *m y f* smoker; ~ **pasivo** passive smoker; **no** ~ nonsmoker.
fumar *vt & vi* to smoke.
fumeta *m y f fam* pot-head, pot smoker.
fumigación *f* fumigation.
fumigador *m* fumigator.
fumigar [16] *vt* to fumigate.
funámbulo, **-la** *m y f* tightrope walker.
Funchal Funchal.
función *f* -1. [gen] function; [trabajo] duty; **director en funciones** acting director; **entrar en funciones** to take up one's duties. -2. CIN & TEATR show.
◆ **en función de** *loc prep* depending on.
funcional *adj* functional.
funcionalidad *f* functional qualities (*pl*).
funcionalismo *m* functionalism.
funcionamiento *m* operation, functioning; **entrar/estar en** ~ to come into/be in operation; **poner algo en** ~ to start sthg (working).
funcionar *vi* to work; ~ **con gasolina** to run on petrol; **"no funciona"** "out of order".
funcionariado *m* civil service.
funcionario, **-ria** *m y f* civil servant.
funda *f* [de sofá, máquina de escribir] cover; [de almohada] case; [de disco] sleeve; [de pistola] sheath.

fundación *f* foundation.
fundado, **-da** *adj* well-founded.
fundador, **-ra** ◇ *adj* founding. ◇ *m y f* founder.
fundamentación *f* foundation, basis.
fundamental *adj* fundamental.
fundamentalismo *m* fundamentalism.
fundamentalista *adj, m y f* fundamentalist.
fundamentar *vt* -1. *fig* [basar] to base. -2. CONSTR to lay the foundations of.
◆ **fundamentarse en** *vpr fig* [basarse] to be based ○ founded on.
fundamento *m* -1. [base] foundation, basis. -2. [razón] reason, grounds (*pl*); **sin** ~ unfounded, groundless.
◆ **fundamentos** *mpl* -1. [principios] basic principles. -2. [cimientos] foundations.
fundar *vt* -1. [crear] to found. -2. [basar]: ~ **(en)** to base (on).
◆ **fundarse** *vpr* [basarse]: ~**se (en)** to be based (on).
fundición *f* -1. [fusión - de vidrio] melting; [- de metal] smelting. -2. [taller] foundry.
fundido *m* [apareciendo] fade-in; [desapareciendo] fade-out.
fundir *vt* -1. [METAL - plomo] to melt; [- hierro] to smelt. -2. ELECTR to fuse; [bombilla, fusible] to blow. -3. COM & *fig* to merge.
◆ **fundirse** *vpr* -1. ELECTR to blow. -2. [derretirse] to melt. -3. COM & *fig* to merge.
fúnebre *adj* funeral (*antes de sust*).
funeral *m* (*gen pl*) funeral.
funerario, **-ria** *adj* funeral (*antes de sust*).
◆ **funeraria** *f* undertaker's *Br*, mortician's *Am*.
funesto, **-ta** *adj* fateful, disastrous.
fungible *adj* perishable.
fungicida ◇ *adj* fungicidal. ◇ *m* fungicide.
fungir [15] *vi Amer* to act, to serve.
funicular ◇ *adj* funicular. ◇ *m* -1. [por tierra] funicular. -2. [por aire] cable car.
furcia *f vulg* slag, whore.
furgón *m* AUTOM van; FERROC wagon, van.
furgoneta *f* van.
furia *f* fury; **ponerse hecho una** ~ to fly into a rage.
furibundo, **-da** *adj* furious.
furioso, **-sa** *adj* furious.
furor *m* -1. [enfado] fury, rage. -2. [ímpetu] fever, urge. -3. *loc*: **hacer** ~ to be all the rage.
furtivo, **-va** *adj* [mirada, sonrisa] furtive.
furúnculo = **forúnculo**.
fusa *f* demisemiquaver.
fuseaux *m inv* ski pants (*pl*).

fuselaje *m* fuselage.
fusible ◇ *adj* fusible. ◇ *m* fuse.
fusil *m* rifle.
fusilamiento *m* **-1.** [ejecución] execution by firing squad. **-2.** *fam* [plagio] plagiarism.
fusilar *vt* **-1.** [ejecutar] to execute by firing squad, to shoot. **-2.** *fam* [plagiar] to plagiarize.
fusilero *m* fusilier, rifleman.
fusión *f* **-1.** [agrupación] merging. **-2.** [de empresas, bancos] merger. **-3.** [derretimiento] melting. **-4.** FÍS fusion; ~ **nuclear** nuclear fusion.
fusionar ◇ *vt* **-1.** [gen & ECON] to merge. **-2.** FÍS to fuse. ◇ *vi* to fuse.
◆ **fusionarse** *vpr* ECON to merge.
fusta *f* riding crop.
fustán *m Amer* petticoat.
fuste *m* shaft.
fustigar [16] *vt* **-1.** [azotar] to whip. **-2.** [censurar] to criticize harshly.
fútbol, football ['fudbol] *m* football; ~ **sala** indoor five-a-side.
futbolero, -ra *adj* football-crazy.
futbolín *m* table football.
futbolista *m y f* footballer.
futbolístico, -ca *adj* football (*antes de sust*).
fútil *adj* trivial.
futilidad *f* triviality.
futón *m* futon.
futurible *adj* potential.
futuro, -ra *adj* future.
◆ **futuro** *m* [gen & GRAM] future; ~ **perfecto** future perfect.
◆ **futuros** *mpl* ECON futures.
futurología *f* futurology.
futurólogo, -ga *m y f* futurologist.

g¹, G *f* [letra] g, G.
g² (*abrev de* **gramo**) g.
g/ *abrev de* **giro**.
gabacho, -cha *fam despec* ◇ *adj* Froggy, *pejorative term meaning 'French'.* ◇ *m y f* Frog, *pejorative term referring to a French person.*
gabán *m* overcoat.
gabardina *f* **-1.** [tela] gabardine. **-2.** [prenda] raincoat, mac.
gabinete *m* **-1.** [gobierno] cabinet. **-2.** [despacho] office. **-3.** [sala] study.
Gabón Gabon.
Gaborone Gaborone.
gacela *f* gazelle.
gaceta *f* gazette.
gachas *fpl* CULIN (corn) porridge (*U*).
gachí *f fam* bird, chick.
gacho, -cha *adj* drooping.
gachó *m fam* bloke *Br*, guy.
gaélico, -ca *adj* Gaelic.
◆ **gaélico** *m* [lengua] Gaelic.
gafar *vt fam* to jinx, to bring bad luck to.
gafas *fpl* glasses; ~ **graduales** prescription glasses; ~ **de sol** sunglasses; ~ **submarinas** [para submarinismo] diving mask; [para nadar] goggles.
gafe ◇ *adj* jinxed; **ser** ~ to be jinxed. ◇ *m y f* jinxed person.
gag *m inv* gag.
gaita *f* **-1.** [instrumento] bagpipes (*pl*). **-2.** *fam* [pesadez] drag, pain.
gaitero, -ra *m y f* piper.
gajes *mpl*: ~ **del oficio** occupational hazards.
gajo *m* **-1.** [trozo de fruta] segment. **-2.** [racimo] bunch. **-3.** [rama] broken-off branch.
GAL (*abrev de* **Grupos Antiterroristas de Liberación**) *mpl former right-wing Spanish terrorist group that directed its attacks against ETA.*
gala → **galo**.
galáctico, -ca *adj* galactic.
galaico, -ca *adj culto* Galician.
galán *m* **-1.** [hombre atractivo] attractive young man. **-2.** TEATR leading man, lead.

galante adj gallant.

galantear vt to court, to woo.

galanteo m courting, wooing.

galantería f -1. [cualidad] politeness. -2. [acción] gallantry, compliment.

galápago m turtle.

Galápagos fpl: **las (islas)** ~ the Galapagos Islands.

galardón m award, prize.

galardonado, -da adj award-winning, prize-winning.

galardonar vt to award a prize to.

galaxia f galaxy.

galena f galena, lead sulphide.

galeno m doctor.

galeón m galleon.

galera f galley.

galerada f (gen pl) galley proof.

galería f -1. [gen] gallery; [corredor descubierto] verandah. -2. [para cortinas] curtain rail. -3. fig [vulgo] masses (pl); **hacer algo para la** ~ to play to the gallery.
◆ **galerías (comerciales)** fpl shopping arcade (sg).

galerna f strong north-west wind.

Gales: (el país de) ~ Wales.

galés, -esa ◇ adj Welsh. ◇ m y f Welshman m (f Welshwoman); **los galeses** the Welsh.
◆ **galés** m [lengua] Welsh.

galgo m greyhound.

Galicia Galicia.

galicismo m gallicism.

galimatías m inv [lenguaje] gibberish (U); [lío] jumble.

gallardete m pennant.

gallardía f -1. [valentía] bravery. -2. [elegancia] elegance.

gallardo, -da adj -1. [valiente] brave. -2. [bien parecido] elegant.

gallear vi to strut about, to show off.

gallego, -ga adj, m y f Galician.
◆ **gallego** m [lengua] Galician.

galleguismo m [palabra] Galician expression.

galleta f -1. CULIN biscuit. -2. fam [cachete] slap, smack.

gallina ◇ f [ave] hen; **la** ~ **ciega** blind man's buff; **matar la** ~ **de los huevos de oro** to kill the goose that lays the golden eggs. ◇ m y f fam [persona] chicken, coward.

gallináceo, -a adj gallinaceous.

gallinero m -1. [corral] henhouse. -2. fam TEATR gods (sg). -3. fam [alboroto] madhouse.

gallito m fig cock of the walk.

gallo m -1. [ave] cock, cockerel; ~ **de pelea** fighting cock; **en menos que canta un** ~ fam in no time at all. -2. [al cantar] false note; [al hablar] squeak. -3. [pez] John Dory. -4. fig [mandón] cock of the walk.

galo, -la ◇ adj HIST Gallic; [francés] French. ◇ m y f [persona] Gaul.

◆ **gala** f -1. [fiesta] gala; **ropa/uniforme de gala** [ropa] full dress/uniform; **cena de gala** black tie dinner, formal dinner. -2. [ropa]: **galas** finery (U), best clothes. -3. [actuación] show. -4. loc: **hacer gala de algo** [preciarse] to be proud of sthg; [exhibir] to demonstrate sthg; **tener a gala algo** to be proud of sthg.

galón m -1. [adorno] braid; MIL stripe. -2. [medida] gallon.

galopada f gallop.

galopante adj galloping.

galopar vi to gallop.

galope m gallop; **al** ~ at a gallop; **a** ~ **tendido** at full gallop.

galpón m Amer shed.

galvanización f galvanization.

galvanizar [13] vt to galvanize.

gama f [gen] range; MÚS scale.

gamba f prawn.

gamberrada f act of vandalism.

gamberrismo m vandalism; [en fútbol etc] hooliganism.

gamberro, -rra ◇ adj loutish. ◇ m y f vandal; [en fútbol etc] hooligan.

Gambia (The) Gambia.

gameto m gamete.

gamín m Amer child.

gamma f gamma.

gamo m fallow deer.

gamonal m Amer village chief.

gamuza f -1. [tejido] chamois (leather); [trapo] duster. -2. [animal] chamois.

gana f -1. [afán]: ~ **(de)** desire ○ wish (to); **de buena** ~ willingly; **de mala** ~ unwillingly; **me da/no me da la** ~ **hacerlo** I damn well feel like/don't damn well feel like doing it. -2. [apetito] appetite.

◆ **ganas** fpl [deseo]: **tener** ~**s de algo/hacer algo**, **sentir** ~**s de algo/hacer algo** to feel like sthg/doing sthg; **quedarse con** ~**s de hacer algo** not to manage to do sthg; **no tengo** ~**s de que me pongan una multa** I don't fancy getting a fine; **tenerle** ~**s a alguien** to have it in for sb.

ganadería f -1. [actividad] livestock farming. -2. [ganado] livestock. -3. [lugar] livestock farm.

ganadero, -ra ◇ adj livestock-farming (antes de sust); [industria] livestock (antes de sust). ◇ m y f livestock farmer.

ganado m livestock, stock; ~ **porcino** pigs (pl); ~ **vacuno** cattle (pl).

ganador, -ra ◇ adj winning. ◇ m y f winner.

ganancia f [rendimiento] profit; [ingreso] earnings (pl); ~**s y pérdidas** profit and loss; ~ **líquida** net profit.

ganancial → bien.

ganapán m odd-job man.

ganar ◇ vt -1. [gen] to win; [sueldo, dinero] to earn; [peso, tiempo, terreno] to gain. -2. [derrotar] to beat. -3. [aventajar]: ~ **a alguien en algo** to be better than sb as regards sthg. -4. [alcanzar - cima etc] to reach, to make it to. -5. [conquistar - ciudad etc] to take, to capture. ◇ vi -1. [vencer] to win. -2. [lograr dinero] to earn money. -3. [mejorar]: ~ **(con)** to benefit (from); ~ **en algo** to gain in sthg.
♦ **ganarse** vpr -1. [conquistar - simpatía, respeto] to earn; [- persona] to win over. -2. [merecer] to deserve.

ganchillo m [aguja] crochet hook; [labor] crochet; **hacer** ~ to crochet.

gancho m -1. [gen] hook; [de percha] peg. -2. [cómplice - de timador] decoy; [- de vendedor] person who attracts buyers. -3. fam [atractivo] charm, sex appeal; **tener** ~ **to** have charm ◇ sex appeal.

ganchudo, -da adj hooked.

gandul, -la fam ◇ adj lazy. ◇ m y f lazybones, layabout.

gandulear vi to loaf around.

gandulería f idleness.

ganga f fam snip, bargain.

Ganges m: **el** ~ the Ganges.

ganglio m ganglion.

gangoso, -sa adj nasal.

gangrena f gangrene.

gangrenado, -da adj gangrenous.

gangrenarse vpr to become gangrenous.

gangrenoso, -sa adj gangrenous.

gángster (pl gángsters) m gangster.

gangsterismo m gangsterism.

gansada f fam silly thing.

ganso, -sa m y f -1. [ave - hembra] goose; [- macho] gander. -2. fam [persona] idiot, fool.

ganzúa f picklock.

gañido m yelp.

garabatear vi & vt to scribble.

garabato m scribble; **hacer** ~**s** to scribble.

garaje m garage.

garante m y f guarantor; **salir** ~ to act as guarantor.

garantía f -1. [gen] guarantee; **de** ~ reliable, dependable; **ser** ~ **de algo** to guarantee sthg; ~**s constitucionales** constitutional rights. -2. [fianza] surety.

garantizado, -da adj guaranteed.

garantizar [13] vt -1. [gen] to guarantee; ~ **algo a alguien** to assure sb of sthg. -2. [avalar] to vouch for.

garbanzo m chickpea.

garbeo m fam stroll; **dar un** ~ to go for ◇ take a stroll.

garbo m [de persona] grace; [de escritura] stylishness, style.

garboso, -sa adj [persona] graceful; [escritura] stylish.

gardenia f gardenia.

garduña f marten.

garete m: **ir** ◇ **irse al** ~ fam to come adrift.

garfio m hook.

gargajo m phlegm.

garganta f -1. ANAT throat; **lo tengo atravesado en la** ~ he/it sticks in my gullet. -2. [desfiladero] gorge.

gargantilla f choker, necklace.

gargantúa m big eater, glutton.

gárgara f (gen pl) gargle, gargling (U); **hacer** ~**s** to gargle; **mandar a alguien a hacer** ~**s** fam to send sb packing; **¡vete a hacer** ~**s!** fam get lost!

gárgola f gargoyle.

garita f [gen] cabin; [de conserje] porter's lodge; MIL sentry box.

garito m despec [casa de juego] gambling den; [establecimiento] dive.

garnacha f [uva] purplish grape from Pyrenees.

Garona m: **el** ~ the Garonne.

garra f [de animal] claw; [de ave de rapiña] talon; despec [de persona] paw, hand; **caer en las** ~**s de alguien** to fall into sb's clutches; **tener** ~ [persona] to have charisma; [novela, canción etc] to be gripping.

garrafa f carafe.

garrafal adj monumental, enormous.

garrafón m demijohn.

garrapata f tick.

garrapiña f sugar coating.

garrapiñar vt [fruta] to candy; [almendras etc] to coat with sugar.

garrocha f pike, lance.

garrotazo m blow with a club ◇ stick.

garrote m -1. [palo] club, stick. -2. [torniquete] tourniquet. -3. [instrumento] garotte.

garúa f Amer drizzle.

garza f heron; ~ **real** grey heron.

gas m gas; ~ **ciudad/natural** town/natural gas; ~ **butano** butane (gas); ~ **lacrimógeno** tear gas.

♦ **gases** mpl [en el estómago] wind (U).

♦ **a todo gas** loc adv flat out, at top speed.

gasa f gauze.

gaseado, -da adj gassed.

gasear vt to gas.

gaseoducto m gas pipeline.

gaseoso, -sa adj gaseous; [bebida] fizzy.

♦ **gaseosa** f lemonade.

gásfiter, gasfitero m Amer plumber.

gasfitería f Amer plumber's (shop).

gasificación f gasification.

gasificar [10] vt to gasify; [bebida] to carbonate.

gasóleo m diesel oil.

gasolina f petrol Br, gas Am; **poner** ~ to fill up (with petrol).

gasolinera f petrol station Br, gas station Am.

gastado, -da adj [ropa, pieza etc] worn out; [frase, tema] hackneyed; [persona] broken, burnt out.

gastar ◇ vt **-1.** [consumir - dinero, tiempo] to spend; [- gasolina, electricidad] to use (up); [- ropa, zapatos] to wear out. **-2.** fig [usar - gen] to use; [- ropa] to wear; [- número de zapatos] to take; ~ **una broma (a alguien)** to play a joke (on sb). **-3.** [malgastar] to waste. **-4.** loc: ~**las** to carry on, to behave. ◇ vi **-1.** [despilfarrar] to spend (money). **-2.** [desgastar] to be wearing.

♦ **gastarse** vpr **-1.** [deteriorarse] to wear out. **-2.** [terminarse] to run out.

gasto m [acción de gastar] outlay, expenditure; [cosa que pagar] expense; [de energía, gasolina] consumption; [despilfarro] waste; **cubrir** ~**s** to cover costs, to break even; **no reparar en** ~**s** to spare no expense; ~ **amortizable** ECON capitalized expense; ~ **deducible** ECON tax-deductible expense; ~ **público** public expenditure; ~**s fijos** COM fixed charges ○ costs; [en una casa] overheads; ~**s generales** overheads; ~**s de mantenimiento** maintenance costs; ~**s de representación** entertainment allowance (sg).

gástrico, -ca adj gastric.

gastritis f inv gastritis.

gastroenteritis f inv gastroenteritis.

gastrointestinal adj gastrointestinal.

gastronomía f gastronomy.

gastronómico, -ca adj gastronomic.

gastrónomo, -ma m y f gourmet, gastronome.

gatas

♦ **a gatas** loc adv on all fours.

gatear vi to crawl.

gatera f cat flap ○ door.

gatillero m Amer hired gunman.

gatillo m trigger.

gato, -ta m y f cat; ~ **montés** wildcat; **dar** ~ **por liebre a alguien** to swindle ○ cheat sb; **buscar tres pies al** ~ to overcomplicate matters; **sólo había cuatro** ~**s** there was hardly a soul there; **aquí hay** ~ **encerrado** there's something fishy going on here.

♦ **gato** m AUTOM jack.

GATT (abrev de **General Agreement on Tariffs and Trade**) m GATT.

gatuno, -na adj catlike, feline.

gauchada f Amer favour.

gaucho, -cha adj, m y f gaucho.

gavilán m sparrowhawk.

gavilla f sheaf.

gaviota f seagull.

gay adj inv, m y f gay (homosexual).

gazapo m **-1.** [animal] young rabbit. **-2.** [error] misprint.

gazmoñería f sanctimoniousness.

gazmoño, -ña adj sanctimonious.

gaznate m gullet.

gazpacho m gazpacho, Andalusian soup made from tomatoes, peppers, cucumbers and bread, served chilled.

GB (abrev de **Gran Bretaña**) f GB.

géiser, géyser (pl **géyseres**) m geyser.

geisha ['geiʃa] f inv geisha.

gel m gel.

gelatina f [de carne] gelatine; [de fruta] jelly.

gema f gem.

gemelo, -la ◇ adj twin (antes de sust). ◇ m y f [persona] twin.

♦ **gemelo** m [músculo] calf.

♦ **gemelos** mpl **-1.** [de camisa] cufflinks. **-2.** [prismáticos] binoculars; [para teatro] opera glasses.

gemido m [de persona] moan, groan; [de animal] whine.

Géminis ◇ m [zodiaco] Gemini; **ser** ~ to be (a) Gemini. ◇ m y f [persona] Gemini.

gemir [26] vi **-1.** [persona] to moan, to groan; [animal] to whine. **-2.** [viento] to howl.

gemología f gemology.

gen = **gene**.

gendarme m y f gendarme.

gendarmería f gendarmerie.

gene, gen m gene.

genealogía f genealogy.

genealógico, -ca *adj* genealogical.

generación *f* generation; **~ espontánea** spontaneous generation, autogenesis.

generacional *adj* generation (*antes de sust*).

generador, -ra *adj* generating.

◆ **generador** *m* generator.

general ◇ *adj* **-1.** [gen] general; **por lo ~, en ~** in general, generally. **-2.** [usual] usual. ◇ *m* MIL general; **~ de brigada** brigadier *Br*, brigadier general *Am*; **~ de división** major general.

generala *f* MIL call to arms.

generalidad *f* **-1.** [mayoría] majority. **-2.** [vaguedad] generalization.

◆ **generalidades** *fpl* [principios básicos] basic principles.

generalísimo *m* supreme commander, generalissimo.

generalista *adj* [médico] general.

Generalitat [ʒenerali'tat] *f* Generalitat, *autonomous government of Catalonia or Valencia*.

generalización *f* **-1.** [comentario amplio] generalization. **-2.** [extensión - de conflicto] escalation, widening; [- de prácticas, enseñanza] spread.

generalizar [13] ◇ *vt* to spread, to make widespread. ◇ *vi* to generalize.

◆ **generalizarse** *vpr* to become widespread.

generalmente *adv* generally.

generar *vt* [gen] to generate; [engendrar] to create.

generatriz *f* generatrix.

genérico, -ca *adj* **-1.** [común] generic. **-2.** GRAM gender (*antes de sust*).

género *m* **-1.** [clase] kind, type. **-2.** GRAM gender. **-3.** BIOL genus; **el ~ humano** the human race. **-5.** MUS: **~ chico** zarzuela, *Spanish light opera*; **~ lírico** opera. **-6.** [productos] merchandise, goods (*pl*). **-7.** [tejido] cloth, material.

generosidad *f* generosity.

generoso, -sa *adj* generous.

génesis *f inv* genesis.

◆ **Génesis** *m* Genesis.

genético, -ca *adj* genetic.

◆ **genética** *f* genetics (U).

genial *adj* **-1.** [autor, compositor etc] of genius. **-2.** *fig* [estupendo] brilliant, great.

genialidad *f* **-1.** [capacidad] genius. **-2.** [acción] stroke of genius.

genio *m* **-1.** [talento] genius. **-2.** [carácter] nature, disposition. **-3.** [personalidad fuerte] spirit. **-4.** [mal carácter] bad temper; **estar de/tener mal ~** to be in a mood/bad-tempered. **-5.** [ser sobrenatural] genie.

genital *adj* genital.

◆ **genitales** *mpl* genitals.

genitivo *m* genitive.

genocidio *m* genocide.

genotipo *m* genotype.

genovés, -esa *adj, m y f* Genoese.

gente *f* **-1.** [gen] people (*pl*); **~ bien** well-to-do people; **~ menuda** kids (*pl*). **-2.** *fam* [familia] folks (*pl*).

gentil ◇ *adj* [amable] kind, nice. ◇ *m y f* gentile.

gentileza *f* courtesy, kindness; **¿tendría la ~ de decirme ...?** would you be so kind as to tell me ...?; **por ~ de** by courtesy of.

gentilhombre *m* HIST gentleman (*in the royal court*).

gentilicio *m* term referring to the natives or inhabitants of a particular place.

gentío *m* crowd.

gentuza *f* riffraff.

genuflexión *f* genuflection; **hacer una ~** to genuflect.

genuino, -na *adj* genuine.

GEO (*abrev de* **Grupo Especial de Operaciones**) *m* specially trained police force, ≃ SAS *Br*, ≃ SWAT *Am*.

geodesia *f* geodesy.

geodinámica *f* geodynamics (U).

geofísico, -ca ◇ *adj* geophysical. ◇ *m y f* [persona] geophysicist.

◆ **geofísica** *f* [ciencia] geophysics (U).

geografía *f* geography; *fig*: **varios puntos de la ~ nacional** several parts of the country.

geográfico, -ca *adj* geographical.

geógrafo, -fa *m y f* geographer.

geología *f* geology.

geológico, -ca *adj* geological.

geólogo, -ga *m y f* geologist.

geometría *f* geometry.

geométrico, -ca *adj* geometric.

geopolítico, -ca *adj* geopolitical.

◆ **geopolítica** *f* geopolitics (U).

Georgetown ['ɔrdʒtaun] Georgetown.

georgiano, -na *adj, m y f* Georgian.

◆ **georgiano** *m* [lengua] Georgian.

geranio *m* geranium.

gerencia *f* **-1.** [gen] management. **-2.** [cargo] post of manager. **-3.** [oficina] manager's office.

gerente *m y f* manager, director.

geriatra *m y f* geriatrician.

geriatría *f* geriatrics (U).

gerifalte, jerifalte *m* **-1.** ZOOL gerfalcon. **-2.** *fig* [persona] bigwig.

germanía f culto thieves' slang.

germánico, -ca ◇ adj [gen] Germanic; [pueblos, carácter] Teutonic. ◇ m y f [alemán] German; HIST Teuton.

◆ **germánico** m [lengua] Germanic.

germanismo m Germanism.

germanista m y f German scholar.

germano, -na ◇ adj [gen] Germanic; [pueblos, carácter] Teutonic. ◇ m y f [alemán] German; HIST Teuton.

germen m lit & fig germ.

germicida m germicide.

germinación f germination.

germinar vi lit & fig to germinate.

gerontocracia f gerontocracy.

gerontología f gerontology.

gerundense ◇ adj of/relating to Gerona. ◇ m y f native/inhabitant of Gerona.

gerundio m gerund.

gesta f exploit, feat.

gestación f lit & fig gestation.

gestar vi to gestate.

◆ **gestarse** vpr: se estaba gestando un cambio sin precedentes the seeds of an unprecedented change had been sown.

gesticulación f gesticulation; [de cara] face-pulling.

gesticular vi to gesticulate; [con la cara] to pull faces.

gestión f -1. [diligencia] step, thing that has to be done; tengo que hacer unas gestiones I have a few things to do. -2. [administración] management; ¡~ de cartera ECON portfolio management.

gestionar vt -1. [tramitar] to negotiate. -2. [administrar] to manage.

gesto m -1. [gen] gesture. -2. [mueca] face, grimace; hacer un ~ to pull a face.

gestor, -ra ◇ adj managing (antes de sust). ◇ m y f person who carries out dealings with public bodies on behalf of private customers or companies, combining the role of solicitor and accountant.

gestoría f office of a "gestor".

gestual adj using gestures.

géyser = **géiser**.

Ghana Ghana.

ghetto = **gueto**.

giba f -1. [de camello] hump. -2. [de persona] hunchback, hump.

giboso, -sa ◇ adj hunchbacked. ◇ m y f hunchback.

Gibraltar Gibraltar.

gibraltareño, -ña adj, m y f Gibraltarian.

gigabyte [xiva'ßait] m INFORM gigabyte.

gigante, -ta m y f giant.

◆ **gigante** adj gigantic.

gigantesco, -ca adj gigantic.

gigantismo m gigantism.

gigoló [jixo'lo] m gigolo.

gil, -la m y f Amer fam twit, idiot.

gilí fam ◇ adj stupid. ◇ m y f pillock, prat.

gilipollada, jilipollada f fam: hacer/decir una ~ to do/say sthg bloody stupid.

gilipollas, jilipollas fam ◇ adj inv daft, dumb Am. ◇ m y f inv pillock, prat.

gilipollez, jilipollez f inv fam: hacer/decir una ~ to do/say sthg bloody stupid.

gima, gimiera etc → **gemir**.

gimnasia f [deporte] gymnastics (U); [ejercicio] gymnastics (pl); ~ correctiva ○ médica ○ terapéutica physiotherapeutic exercises (pl); ~ deportiva gymnastics (U); ~ rítmica rhythmic gymnastics (U); ~ sueca free exercise, callisthenics (U); confundir la ~ con la magnesia to get the wrong end of the stick.

gimnasio m gymnasium.

gimnasta m y f gymnast.

gimnástico, -ca adj gymnastic.

gimotear vi to whine, to whimper.

gimoteo m whining, whimpering.

gin [jin]

◆ **gin tonic** m gin and tonic.

gincana, gymkhana [jin'kana] f [de caballos] gymkhana; [de automóviles] rally.

ginebra f gin.

Ginebra Geneva.

ginecología f gynaecology.

ginecológico, -ca adj gynaecological.

ginecólogo, -ga m y f gynaecologist.

ginger ale [jinje'reil] (pl inv) m ginger ale.

gingivitis f inv gingivitis.

gira f tour.

giralda f weather vane.

girar ◇ vi -1. [dar vueltas, torcer] to turn; [rápidamente] to spin. -2. fig [centrarse]: ~ en torno a ○ alrededor de to be centred around, to centre on. -3. COM to remit payment. ◇ vt -1. [hacer dar vueltas] to turn; [rápidamente] to spin. -2. COM to draw. -3. [dinero - por correo, telégrafo] to transfer.

girasol m sunflower.

giratorio, -ria adj revolving; [silla] swivel (antes de sust).

giro m -1. [gen] turn. -2. [postal, telegráfico] money order; ~ postal postal order. -3. [de letras, órdenes de pago] draft. -4. [expresión] turn of phrase.

gis m Amer chalk.

gitanería f -1. [engaño] wiliness, craftiness. -2. [gitanos] gypsies (pl).

gitano, **-na** ◇ adj gypsy (antes de sust); fig wily, crafty. ◇ m y f gypsy.

glaciación f glaciation.

glacial adj glacial; [viento, acogida] icy.

glaciar ◇ adj glacial. ◇ m glacier.

gladiador m gladiator.

gladiolo, **gladíolo** m gladiolus.

glande m glans penis.

glándula f gland.

glasé ◇ adj glacé. ◇ m glacé silk.

glaseado, **-da** adj glacé.
◆ **glaseado** m glazing.

glasear vt to glaze.

gleba f feudal land.

glicerina f glycerine.

global adj global, overall.

globalizar [13] vt to give an overall view of.

globo m **-1.** [Tierra] globe, earth; ~ **terráqueo** O **terrestre** globe. **-2.** [aeróstato, juguete] balloon; ~ **sonda** weather balloon. **-3.** [lámpara] round glass lampshade. **-4.** [esfera] sphere; ~ **ocular** eyeball.

globulina f globulin.

glóbulo m MED corpuscle; ~ **blanco/rojo** white/red corpuscle.

gloria f **-1.** [gen] glory. **-2.** [celebridad] celebrity, star. **-3.** [placer] delight; **estar en la** ~ **to** be in seventh heaven; **saber a** ~ to taste divine O heavenly.

glorieta f **-1.** [de casa, jardín] arbour. **-2.** [plaza - gen] square; [- redonda] circus, roundabout Br, traffic circle Am.

glorificación f glorification.

glorificar [10] vt to glorify.

glorioso, **-sa** adj **-1.** [importante] glorious. **-2.** RELIG Blessed.

glosa f marginal note.

glosador, **-ra** m y f commentator (on text).

glosar vt **-1.** [anotar] to annotate. **-2.** [comentar] to comment on.

glosario m glossary.

glotis f inv glottis.

glotón, **-ona** ◇ adj gluttonous, greedy. ◇ m y f glutton.

glotonería f gluttony, greed.

glucemia f glycaemia.

glúcido m carbohydrate.

glucosa f glucose.

gluglú m glug-glug.

gluten m gluten.

glúteo, **-a** adj gluteal.
◆ **glúteo** m gluteus.

gnomo, **nomo** m gnome.

gobernabilidad f governability.

gobernable adj governable.

gobernación f governing.

gobernador, **-ra** ◇ adj governing (antes de sust). ◇ m y f governor.

gobernanta f cleaning and laundry manageress.

gobernante ◇ adj ruling (antes de sust). ◇ m y f ruler, leader.

gobernar [19] ◇ vt **-1.** [gen] to govern, to rule; [casa, negocio] to run, to manage. **-2.** [barco] to steer; [avión] to fly. ◇ vi NAUT to steer.

Gobi → desierto.

gobierno m **-1.** [gen] government; ~ **autónomo/central** autonomous/central government; ~ **militar** military command; ~ **de transición** caretaker O interim government. **-2.** [edificio] government buildings (pl). **-3.** [administración, gestión] running, management. **-4.** [control] control.

goce ◇ v → gozar. ◇ m pleasure.

godo, **-da** ◇ adj Gothic. ◇ m y f **-1.** HIST Goth. **-2.** despec [español peninsular] pejorative term for a mainland Spaniard.

GOE (abrev de **Grupo de Operaciones Especiales**) m army special operations unit.

gol (pl **goles**) m goal.

goleada f high score, cricket score.

goleador, **-ra** m y f goalscorer.

golear vt to score a lot of goals against, to thrash.

goleta f schooner.

golf m golf.

golfa → golfo.

golfante m y f scoundrel, rascal.

golfear vi fam [vaguear] to loaf around.

golfería f **-1.** [golfos] layabouts (pl), good-for-nothings (pl). **-2.** [granujada] loutish behaviour (U).

golfista m y f golfer.

golfo, **-fa** ◇ adj [gamberro] loutish; [vago] idle. ◇ m y f [gamberro] lout; [vago] layabout.
◆ **golfo** m GEOGR gulf, bay.
◆ **golfa** f mfam [prostituta] tart, whore, hooker Am.
◆ **Golfo Pérsico** m: **el Golfo Pérsico** the Persian Gulf.

gollete m neck.

golondrina f **-1.** [ave] swallow. **-2.** [barco] motor launch.

golondrino m **-1.** MED boil in the armpit. **-2.** ZOOL young swallow.

golosina f [dulce] sweet; [exquisitez] titbit, delicacy.

goloso, -sa ◇ *adj* sweet-toothed. ◇ *m y f* sweet-toothed person.

golpe *m* **-1.** [gen] blow; [bofetada] smack; [con puño] punch; [en puerta etc] knock; [en tenis, golf] shot; [entre coches] bump, collision; **a ~s** by force; *fig* in fits and starts; **moler a alguien a ~s** to beat sb up; **un ~ bajo** DEP & *fig* a blow below the belt; **~ de castigo** [en rugby] penalty (kick); **~ franco** free kick. **-2.** [disgusto] blow. **-3.** [atraco] raid, job, heist *Amer*. **-4.** POLIT: **~ (de Estado)** coup (d'état). **-5.** [ocurrencia] witticism. **-6.** *loc:* **errar** ○ **fallar el ~** to miss the mark; **no dar** ○ **pegar ~** not to lift a finger, not to do a stroke of work.

◆ **de golpe** *loc adv* suddenly.

◆ **de golpe y porrazo** *loc adv* without warning, just like that.

◆ **de un golpe** *loc adv* at one fell swoop, all at once.

◆ **golpe de gracia** *m* coup de grâce.

◆ **golpe de suerte** *m* stroke of luck.

◆ **golpe de vista** *m* glance; **al primer ~ de vista** at a glance.

golpear *vt & vi* [gen] to hit; [puerta] to bang; [con puño] to punch.

golpeteo *m* [de dedos, lluvia] drumming; [de puerta, persiana] banging.

golpismo *m* tendency to military coups.

golpista ◇ *adj* in favour of military coups. ◇ *m y f* person involved in military coup.

golpiza *f Amer* beating.

goma *f* **-1.** [sustancia viscosa, pegajosa] gum; **~ arábiga** gum arabic; **~ de mascar** chewing gum; **~ de pegar** glue, gum. **-2.** [tira elástica] rubber band, elastic band *Br*; **~ elástica** elastic. **-3.** [caucho] rubber; **~ espuma** foam rubber; **~ de borrar** rubber *Br*, eraser *Am*. **-4.** *fam* [preservativo] rubber.

◆ **Goma 2** *f* plastic explosive.

gomero *m Amer* **-1.** [persona] rubber plantation worker. **-2.** [árbol] rubber tree.

gomina *f* hair gel.

gomoso, -sa *adj* gummy.

gónada *f* gonad.

góndola *f* **-1.** [embarcación] gondola. **-2.** *Amer* [autobús] bus.

gondolero *m* gondolier.

gong *m inv* gong.

gonorrea *f* gonorrhoea.

gordinflón, -ona ◇ *adj* chubby, tubby. ◇ *m y f* fatty.

gordo, -da ◇ *adj* **-1.** [persona] fat; **me cae ~** I can't stand him. **-2.** [grueso] thick. **-3.** [grande] big. **-4.** [grave] big, serious. ◇ *m y f* **-1.** [persona obesa] fat man (*f* fat woman); **armar la gorda** *fig* to kick up a row ○

stink. **-2.** *Amer* [querido] sweetheart, darling.

◆ **gordo** *m* [en lotería] first prize, jackpot.

EL GORDO:
This is the top prize awarded in the Spanish National Lottery, particularly in the Christmas draw

gordura *f* fatness.

gorgonzola [gorɣon'tsola] *m* gorgonzola.

gorgorito *m* warble.

gorgoteo *m* gurgle, gurgling (*U*).

gorila *m* **-1.** ZOOL gorilla. **-2.** *fig* [guardaespaldas] bodyguard. **-3.** *fig* [en discoteca etc] bouncer.

gorjear *vi* to chirp, to twitter.

gorjeo *m* chirping, twittering.

gorra ◇ *f* (peaked) cap. ◇ *m fam* scrounger, sponger; **de ~** for free; **vivir de ~** to scrounge.

gorrear = **gorronear**.

gorrinada *f* **-1.** [guarrada - acción] disgusting behaviour (*U*); [- lugar] pigsty. **-2.** *fig* [mala pasada] dirty trick.

gorrino, -na *m y f lit & fig* pig.

gorrión *m* sparrow.

gorro *m* [gen] cap; [de niño] bonnet; **estar hasta el ~ (de)** *fig* to be fed up (with).

gorrón, -ona *fam* ◇ *adj* sponging, scrounging. ◇ *m y f* sponger, scrounger.

gorronear, gorrear *vt & vi fam* to sponge, to scrounge.

gorronería *f* sponging, scrounging.

gota *f* **-1.** [gen] drop; [de sudor] bead; **caer cuatro ~s** to spit (with rain); **ni ~** anything; **no se veía ni ~** you couldn't see a thing; **parecerse como dos ~s de agua** to be as like as two peas in a pod; **sudar la gorda** to sweat blood, to work very hard. **-2.** *fig* [de aire] breath; [de sensatez etc] ounce. **-3.** MED gout.

◆ **gota a gota** *m* MED intravenous drip.

◆ **gota fría** *f* METEOR *cold front that remains in one place for some time, causing continuous heavy rain.*

gotear ◇ *vi* [líquido] to drip; [techo, depósito etc] to leak; *fig* to trickle through. ◇ *v impers* [chispear] to spit, to drizzle.

goteo *m* dripping.

gotera *f* **-1.** [filtración] leak. **-2.** [mancha] stain (*left by leaking water*).

gótico, -ca *adj* Gothic.

◆ **gótico** *m* [arte] Gothic.

gourmet → **gurmet**.

goyesco, -ca *adj* relating to ○ like Goya.

gozada *f fam* absolute delight.

gozar [13] *vi* to enjoy o.s.; ~ **de algo** to enjoy sthg; ~ **con** to take delight in.

gozne *m* hinge.

gozo *m* joy, pleasure; **mi** ~ **en un pozo** *fig* that's just my (bad) luck.

g/p, g.p. (*abrev de* **giro postal**) p.o.

GP (*abrev de* **gran premio**) *m* GP.

gr *abrev de* **grado**.

grabación *f* recording.

grabado *m* -1. [gen] engraving; [en madera] carving. -2. [en papel - acción] printing; [- lámina] print.

grabador, -ra ◇ *adj* [gen] engraving; [en papel] printing. ◇ *m y f* [gen] engraver; [en madera] carver; [en papel] printer.

◆ **grabadora** *f* [casete] tape recorder.

grabar *vt* -1. [gen] to engrave; [en madera] to carve; [en papel] to print; **grabado en su memoria** engraved on his mind. -2. [sonido, cinta] to record, to tape. -3. INFORM to save.

◆ **grabarse en** *vpr fig*: **grabársele a alguien en la memoria** to become engraved on sb's mind.

gracia *f* -1. [humor, comicidad] humour; **hacer** ~ **a alguien** to amuse sb; **no me hizo** ~ I didn't find it funny; **tener** ~ [ser divertido] to be funny; **tiene** ~ [es curioso] it's funny; **caer en** ~ to be liked. -2. [arte, habilidad] skill, natural ability. -3. [encanto] grace, elegance. -4. [chiste] joke. -5. [favor] favour; [indulto] pardon.

◆ **gracias** *fpl* thank you, thanks; ~**s a** thanks to; **dar las** ~**s a alguien (por)** to thank sb (for); **muchas** ~ thank you, thanks very much.

grácil *adj* [gen] graceful; [delicado] delicate.

gracioso, -sa ◇ *adj* -1. [divertido] funny, amusing. -2. [curioso] funny; **es** ~ **que ...** it's funny how .... ◇ *m y f* -1. [persona divertida] funny ○ amusing person. -2. TEATR fool, clown.

grada *f* -1. [peldaño] step. -2. TEATR row.

◆ **gradas** *fpl* DEP terraces.

gradación *f* -1. [en retórica] climax. -2. [escalonamiento] scale.

gradería *f*, **graderío** *m* TEATR rows (*pl*); DEP terraces (*pl*).

grado *m* -1. [gen] degree; ~ **centígrado** degree centigrade. -2. [fase] stage, level; [índice, nivel] extent, level; **en** ~ **sumo** greatly. -3. [rango - gen] degree; MIL rank. -4. EDUC year, class, grade *Am*. -5. [voluntad]: **hacer algo de buen/mal** ~ to do sthg willingly/unwillingly.

graduable *adj* adjustable.

graduación *f* -1. [acción] grading; [de la vista] eye-test. -2. EDUC graduation. -3. [de bebidas] strength, ≃ proof. -4. MIL rank.

graduado, -da ◇ *adj* -1. [termómetro etc] graded. -2. [universitario] graduate. ◇ *m y f* [persona] graduate.

◆ **graduado** *m* [título - gen] certificate; [- universitario] degree; ~ **escolar** *basic school-leaving certificate*.

gradual *adj* gradual.

graduar [6] *vt* -1. [medir] to gauge, to measure; [regular] to regulate; [vista] to test. -2. [escalonar] to stagger; [publicación] to serialize. -3. EDUC to confer a degree on. -4. MIL to confer a rank on, to commission.

◆ **graduarse** *vpr*: ~**se (en)** to graduate (in).

grafía *f* written symbol.

gráfico, -ca *adj* graphic.

◆ **gráfico** *m* [gráfica] graph, chart; [dibujo] diagram.

◆ **gráfica** *f* graph, chart.

grafismo *m* -1. [diseño gráfico] graphics (*U*). -2. ARTE graphic art.

grafista *m y f* graphic artist ○ designer.

grafito *m* graphite.

grafología *f* graphology.

grafólogo, -ga *m y f* graphologist.

gragea *f* -1. MED pill, tablet. -2. [confite] sugar-coated sweet.

grajo *m* rook.

gral. (*abrev de* **general**) gen.

gramática → **gramático**.

gramatical *adj* grammatical.

gramático, -ca ◇ *adj* grammatical. ◇ *m y f* [persona] grammarian.

◆ **gramática** *f* [disciplina, libro] grammar.

◆ **gramática parda** *f* native wit.

gramo *m* gram.

gramófono *m* gramophone.

gramola *f* gramophone.

grampa *f Amer* staple.

gran = **grande**.

granada *f* -1. [fruta] pomegranate. -2. [proyectil] grenade; ~ **de mano** hand grenade.

Granada -1. [en España] Granada. -2. [en las Antillas] Grenada.

granadino, -na *adj* -1. [en España] of/relating to Granada. -2. [en las Antillas] Grenadian.

◆ **granadina** *f* -1. [bebida] grenadine. -2. [cante] *type of flamenco from Granada*.

granar *vi* to seed.

granate ◇ *m* garnet. ◇ *adj inv* garnet-coloured.

Gran Barrera del Coral f: la ~ the Great Barrier Reef.

Gran Bretaña f Great Britain.

Gran Cañón m Grand Canyon.

grande ◇ adj (antes de sust: **gran**) **-1.** [de tamaño] big, large; [de altura] tall; [de intensidad, importancia] great; **este traje me está** ~ this suit is too big for me. **-2.** fig & irón [enojoso] just great, a bit rich. **-3.** Amer [fantástico] great. **-4.** Amer [divertido] amusing. **-5.** loc: **pasarlo en** ~ fam to have a great time. ◇ m [noble] grandee.
◆ **grandes** mpl [adultos] grown-ups, adults.
◆ **a lo grande** loc adv in a big way, in style.
◆ **en grande** loc adv on a large scale.

Grandes Lagos mpl: los ~ the Great Lakes.

grandeza f **-1.** [de tamaño] (great) size. **-2.** [de sentimientos] generosity, graciousness. **-3.** [aristocracia] aristocracy, nobility.

grandilocuencia f grandiloquence.

grandilocuente adj grandiloquent.

grandiosidad f grandeur.

grandioso, -sa adj grand, splendid.

grandullón, -ona ◇ adj overgrown. ◇ m y f big boy (f big girl).

granel
◆ **a granel** loc adv **-1.** [sin envase - gen] loose; [- en gran cantidad] in bulk. **-2.** [sin orden] any old how, in a rough and ready manner. **-3.** [en abundancia] in abundance.

granero m granary.

granito m granite.

granizada f **-1.** METEOR hailstorm. **-2.** fig [abundancia] hail, shower.

granizado m iced drink.

granizar [13] v impers to hail.

granizo m hail.

granja f farm.

granjearse vpr to gain, to earn.

granjero, -ra m y f farmer.

grano m **-1.** [semilla - de cereales] grain; ~ **de café** coffee bean; ~ **de pimienta** peppercorn. **-2.** [partícula] grain. **-3.** [en la piel] spot, pimple. **-4.** loc: **aportar** O **poner uno su** ~ **de arena** to do one's bit; **ir al** ~ to get to the point.

granuja m y f [pillo] rogue, scoundrel; [canalla] trickster, swindler.

granujada f dirty trick.

granulado, -da adj granulated.
◆ **granulado** m granules (pl).

granuloso, -sa adj bumpy.

grapa f [para papeles etc] staple; [para heridas] stitch, (wire) suture.

grapadora f stapler.

grapar vt to staple.

GRAPO (abrev de **Grupos de Resistencia Antifascista Primero de Octubre**) mpl former left-wing Spanish terrorist group.

grasa → **graso**.

grasiento, -ta adj greasy.

graso, -sa adj [gen] greasy; [con alto contenido en grasas] fatty.
◆ **grasa** f **-1.** [en comestibles] fat; [de cerdo] lard; **grasa vegetal** vegetable fat. **-2.** [lubricante] grease, oil. **-3.** [suciedad] grease.

gratén m gratin; **al** ~ au gratin.

gratificación f **-1.** [moral] reward. **-2.** [monetaria] bonus.

gratificante adj rewarding.

gratificar [10] vt [complacer] to reward; [retribuir] to give a bonus to; [dar propina] to tip.

gratinado, -da adj au gratin.
◆ **gratinado** m gratin.

gratinar vt to cook a dish au gratin.

gratis adv [sin dinero] free, for nothing; [sin esfuerzo] for nothing.

gratitud f gratitude.

grato, -ta adj pleasant; **nos es** ~ **comunicarle que ...** we are pleased to inform you that ....

gratuito, -ta adj **-1.** [sin dinero] free. **-2.** [arbitrario] gratuitous; [infundado] unfair, uncalled for.

grava f gravel.

gravamen m **-1.** [impuesto] tax. **-2.** [obligación moral] burden.

gravar vt **-1.** [con impuestos] to tax. **-2.** [agravar] to worsen.

grave adj **-1.** [gen] serious; [estilo] formal; **estar** ~ to be seriously ill. **-2.** [sonido, voz] low, deep. **-3.** [GRAM - acento prosódico] with the stress on the penultimate syllable; [- tilde] grave.

gravedad f **-1.** [cualidad de grave] seriousness. **-2.** FÍS gravity.

gravidez f pregnancy.

grávido, -da adj full.

gravilla f gravel.

gravitación f gravitation.

gravitar vi to gravitate; fig [pender]: ~ **sobre** to hang O loom over.

gravoso, -sa adj burdensome; [costoso] expensive, costly.

graznar vi [cuervo] to caw; [ganso] to honk; [pato] to quack; fig [persona] to squawk.

graznido m [de cuervo] caw, cawing (U); [de ganso] honk, honking (U); [de pato]

quack, quacking (*U*); *fig* [de personas] squawk, squawking (*U*).

Grecia Greece.

grecorromano, -na *adj* Greco-Roman.

gregario, -ria *adj* gregarious; *fig* incapable of independent thought.

gregoriano, -na *adj* Gregorian.

gremial *adj* [gen] (trade) union (*antes de sust*); HIST guild (*antes de sust*).

gremialismo *m* trade unionism.

gremio *m* **-1.** [sindicato] (trade) union; [profesión] profession, trade; HIST guild. **-2.** *fam* [grupo] league, club.

greña *f* (*gen pl*) tangle of hair.

gres *m* stoneware.

gresca *f* row.

griego, -ga *adj, m y f* Greek.
◆ **griego** *m* [lengua] Greek.

grieta *f* crack; [entre montañas] crevice; [que deja pasar luz] chink.

grifa *f fam* marijuana.

grifería *f* taps (*pl*), plumbing.

grifero, -ra *m y f Amer* petrol pump attendant *Br*, gas pump attendant *Am*.

grifo *m* **-1.** [llave] tap *Br*, faucet *Am*. **-2.** [gasolinera] *Amer* petrol station *Br*, gas station *Am*.

grill [gril] (*pl* grills) *m* grill.

grillado, -da *adj fam* crazy, loopy.

grillete *m* shackle.

grillo *m* cricket.

grima *f* **-1.** [disgusto] annoyance; **dar ~ to** get on one's nerves. **-2.** [dentera] **dar ~ to** set one's teeth on edge.

gringo, -ga *adj, m y f* gringo.

gripa *f Amer* flu.

gripe *f* flu.

griposo, -sa *adj* fluey.

gris ◇ *adj* grey; *fig* [triste] gloomy, miserable. ◇ *m* grey; **~ marengo** dark grey; **~ perla** pearl grey.

grisáceo, -a *adj* greyish.

grisalla *f Amer* scrap metal.

grisear *vi* to become grey.

grisú (*pl* grisúes) *m* firedamp.

gritar ◇ *vi* [hablar alto] to shout; [chillar] to scream, to yell. ◇ *vt*: **~ (algo) a alguien** to shout (sthg) at sb.

griterío *m* screaming, shouting.

grito *m* [gen] shout; [de dolor, miedo] cry, scream; [de sorpresa, de animal] cry; **dar** ◇ **pegar un ~** to shout ○ scream (out); **a ~ limpio** ○ **pelado** at the top of one's voice; **pedir algo a ~s** *fig* to be crying out for sthg; **poner el ~ en el cielo** to hit the roof;

ser el último ~ to be the latest fashion ○ craze, to be the in thing.

Groenlandia Greenland.

grog *m* grog.

grogui *adj lit* & *fig* groggy.

grosella *f* redcurrant; **~ negra** blackcurrant; **~ silvestre** gooseberry.

grosería *f* [cualidad] rudeness; [acción] rude thing; [palabrota] swear word.

grosero, -ra ◇ *adj* **-1.** [maleducado] rude, crude. **-2.** [tosco] coarse, rough. ◇ *m y f* rude person.

grosor *m* thickness.

grosso
◆ **a grosso modo** *loc adv* roughly.

grotesco, -ca *adj* grotesque.

grúa *f* **-1.** CONSTR crane. **-2.** AUTOM breakdown truck.

grueso, -sa *adj* **-1.** [espeso] thick. **-2.** [corpulento] thickset; [obeso] fat. **-3.** [grande] large, big. **-4.** [mar] stormy.
◆ **grueso** *m* **-1.** [grosor] thickness. **-2.** [la mayor parte]: **el ~ de** the bulk of.

grulla *f* crane.

grumete *m* cabin boy.

grumo *m* [gen] lump; [de sangre] clot.

grumoso, -sa *adj* lumpy.

gruñido *m* **-1.** [gen] growl; [del cerdo] grunt. **-2.** *fig* [de personas] grumble.

gruñir *vi* **-1.** [gen] to growl; [cerdo] to grunt. **-2.** *fig* [personas] to grumble.

gruñón, -ona *fam* ◇ *adj* grumpy. ◇ *m y f* old grump.

grupa *f* hindquarters.

grupo *m* [gen] group; [de árboles] cluster; TECN unit, set; **en ~** in a group; **~ de discusión** INFORM forum; **~ electrógeno** generator; **~ de empresas** ECON (corporate) group; **~ de noticias** INFORM newsgroup; **~ de presión** pressure group.
◆ **grupo sanguíneo** *m* blood group.

grupúsculo *m* small group; POLÍT splinter group.

gruta *f* grotto.

gruyère [gru'jer] *m* gruyère.

gta. *abrev de* glorieta.

guacal *m Amer* **-1.** [calabaza] pumpkin. **-2.** [jaula] cage.

guacamol, guacamole *m* guacamole, avocado dip.

guachada *f Amer fam* mean trick.

guachafita *f Amer fam* racket, uproar.

guachimán *m Amer* night watchman.

guachinango *m Amer* [pez] red snapper.

guacho, -cha *m y f Amer fam* illegitimate child.

Guadalquivir *m*: el ~ the Guadalquivir.
guadaña *f* scythe.
Guadiana *m*: el ~ the Guadiana.
guagua *f Amer* **-1.** [autobús] bus. **-2.** [niño] baby.
guajiro, -ra *m y f Amer fam* peasant.
guajolote *m Amer* turkey.
gualdo, -da *adj* yellow.
guampa *f Amer* horn.
guampudo, -da *adj Amer* horned.
guanajo *m Amer* turkey.
guanche *adj, m y f* Guanche.
guantazo *m fam* slap.
guante *m* glove; ~ **de boxeo** boxing glove; **arrojar** ○ **tirar el** ~ to throw down the gauntlet; **de** ~ **blanco** gentlemanly; **echarle el** ~ **a algo** to get hold of sthg, to get one's hands on sthg; **estar más suave que un** ~ to be as meek as a lamb.
guantera *f* glove compartment.
guaperas *fam* ○ *adj inv* pretty-pretty. ○ *m inv* **-1.** [presumido] pretty boy. **-2.** [artista, cantante] heart-throb.
guapo, -pa ○ *adj* [gen] good-looking; [hombre] handsome; [mujer] pretty. ○ *m y f* **-1.** [valiente]: **a ver quién es el** ~ **que ...** let's see who's brave enough to .... **-2.** [fanfarrón] braggart.
guapura *f* [de hombre] handsomeness; [de mujer] prettiness.
guarangada *f Amer* rude remark.
guarango, -ga *adj Amer* coarse, vulgar.
guaraní ○ *adj inv, m y f* Guarani. ○ *m* **-1.** [lengua] Guarani. **-2.** [moneda] guarani.
guarda ○ *m y f* [vigilante] guard, keeper; ~ **forestal** gamekeeper, forest ranger; ~ **jurado** security guard. ○ *f* **-1.** [tutela] guardianship. **-2.** [de libros] flyleaf.
guardabarrera *m y f* level crossing keeper.
guardabarros *m inv* mudguard *Br*, fender *Am*.
guardabosque *m y f* forest ranger.
guardacoches *m y f inv* parking attendant.
guardacostas *m inv* [barco] coastguard boat.
guardador, -ra *m y f* keeper.
guardaespaldas *m y f inv* bodyguard.
guardafrenos *m y f inv* brakeman (*f* brakewoman).
guardagujas *m y f inv* switchman (*f* switchwoman).
guardameta *m y f* goalkeeper.
guardamuebles *m inv* furniture warehouse (*for storage*).
guardapolvo *m* overalls (*pl*).

guardar *vt* **-1.** [gen] to keep; [en su sitio] to put away. **-2.** [vigilar] to keep watch over; [proteger] to guard. **-3.** [reservar, ahorrar]: ~ **algo (a** ○ **para alguien)** to save sthg (for sb). **-4.** [cumplir - ley] to observe; [- secreto, promesa] to keep.
◆ **guardarse** *vpr*: **guardársela a alguien** to have it in for sb.
◆ **guardarse de** *vpr*: ~**se de hacer algo** [evitar] to avoid doing sthg; [abstenerse de] to be careful not to do sthg.
guardarropa *m* [gen] wardrobe; [de cine, discoteca etc] cloakroom.
guardarropía *f* TEATR wardrobe.
guardería *f* nursery; [en el lugar de trabajo] crèche.
guardia ○ *f* **-1.** [gen] guard; [vigilancia] watch, guard; **en** ~ on guard; **montar (la)** ~ to mount guard; ~ **municipal** urban police; **aflojar** ○ **bajar la** ~ to lower ○ drop one's guard; **la vieja** ~ the old guard. **-2.** [turno] duty; **estar de** ~ to be on duty. ○ *m y f* [policía] policeman (*f* policewoman); ~ **de tráfico** traffic warden.
◆ **guardia marina** *m* sea cadet in final two years of training.
◆ **Guardia Civil** *f*: **la Guardia Civil** the Civil Guard.

GUARDIA CIVIL:
The 'Guardia Civil' is a military-style security force operating under the control of the Spanish Ministry of the Interior and responsible for policing rural areas and highways. They also form the Spanish customs police and are easily recognizable by their traditional black three-cornered hat

guardián, -ana *m y f* [de persona] guardian; [de cosa] watchman, keeper.
guarecer [30] *vt*: ~ **(de)** to protect ○ shelter (from).
◆ **guarecerse** *vpr*: ~**se (de)** to shelter (from).
guarida *f* lair; *fig* hideout.
guarismo *m* figure, number.
guarnecer [30] *vt* **-1.** [adornar] to decorate; [ropa] to trim; CULIN to garnish. **-2.** [vigilar] to be garrisoned in.
guarnición *f* **-1.** CULIN garnish. **-2.** MIL garrison. **-3.** [adorno] decoration; [de ropa] trimming; [de joya] setting.
guarrada *f fam* filthy thing; [mala pasada] filthy ○ dirty trick.
guarrería *f* **-1.** [suciedad] filth, muck. **-2.** [acción] filthy thing. **-3.** *fig* [mala pasada] filthy ○ dirty trick.

guarro, **-rra** ◇ *adj* filthy. ◇ *m y f* **-1.** [animal] pig. **-2.** *fam* [persona] filthy ○ dirty pig.

guarura *m Amer fam* bodyguard.

guasa *f* **-1.** *fam* [gracia] humour; [ironía] irony; **estar de** ~ to be joking. **-2.** *fam* [pesadez]: **tener mucha** ~ to be a pain in the neck.

guasca *f Amer* whip.

guasearse *vpr fam*: ~ **(de)** to take the mickey (out of).

guasón, **-ona** ◇ *adj* fond of teasing. ◇ *m y f* joker, tease.

guata *f* **-1.** [de algodón] cotton padding. **-2.** *Amer fam* [barriga] belly.

guateado, **-da** *adj* padded.

Guatemala **-1.** [país] Guatemala. **-2.** [ciudad] Guatemala City.

guatemalteco, **-ca**, **guatemaltés**, **-esa** *adj*, *m y f* Guatemalan.

guateque *m* private party.

guatón, **-ona** *adj Amer fam* potbellied.

guau *m* woof.

guay *adj fam* cool, neat.

guayabo, **-ba** *m y f Amer fam* [persona] gorgeous person.

◆ **guayabo** *m* [árbol] guava tree

◆ **guayaba** *f* [fruta] guava.

guayín *m Amer fam* van.

gubernamental *adj* government (*antes de sust*).

gubernativo, **-va** *adj* government (*antes de sust*).

guepardo *m* cheetah.

güero, **-ra** *adj Amer fam* blond (*f* blonde).

guerra *f* war; [referido al tipo de conflicto] warfare; [pugna] struggle, conflict; [de intereses, ideas] conflict; **declarar la** ~ to declare war; **en** ~ at war; ~ **sin cuartel** all-out war; ~ **bacteriológica/química** germ/chemical warfare; ~ **civil/mundial** civil/world war; ~ **atómica** ○ **nuclear** nuclear war; ~ **espacial** ○ **de las galaxias** star wars; ~ **fría** cold war; ~ **de guerrillas** guerrilla warfare; ~ **de precios** price war; ~ **santa** Holy War, crusade; **dar** ~ to be a pain, to be annoying.

guerrear *vi* to (wage) war.

guerrero, **-ra** ◇ *adj* warlike. ◇ *m y f* [luchador] warrior.

◆ **guerrera** *f* [prenda] (military) jacket.

guerrilla *f* [grupo] guerrilla group.

guerrillero, **-ra** *m y f* guerrilla.

gueto, **ghetto** ['geto] *m* ghetto.

güevón *m Amer vulg* bloody idiot.

guía ◇ *m y f* [persona] guide; ~ **turístico** tourist guide. ◇ *f* **-1.** [indicación] guidance.

-2. [libro] guide (book); ~ **de ferrocarriles** train timetable; ~ **telefónica** telephone book ○ directory. **-3.** [de bicicleta] handlebars (*pl*). **-4.** [para cortinas] rail.

guiahilos *m inv* thread guide.

guiar [9] *vt* **-1.** [indicar dirección] to guide, to lead; [aconsejar] to guide, to direct. **-2.** AUTOM to drive; NÁUT to steer. **-3.** [plantas, ramas] to train.

◆ **guiarse** *vpr*: ~**se por algo** to be guided by ○ to follow sthg.

guija *f* pebble.

guijarro *m* pebble.

guijarroso, **-sa** *adj* pebbly.

guillado, **-da** *adj* crazy.

guilladura *f* craziness (*U*).

guillotina *f* guillotine.

guillotinar *vt* to guillotine.

guinda *f* morello cherry.

guindar *vt fam*: ~ **algo a alguien** to pinch ○ nick sthg off sb.

guindilla *f* chilli (pepper).

guindo *m* morello cherry tree.

guinea *f* guinea.

Guinea-Bissau Guinea-Bissau.

Guinea Ecuatorial Equatorial Guinea.

guineano, **-na** *adj*, *m y f* Guinean.

guiñapo *m* **-1.** [andrajo] rag. **-2.** [persona] (physical) wreck.

guiñar *vt* to wink.

◆ **guiñarse** *vpr* to wink at each other.

guiño *m* wink.

guiñol *m* puppet theatre.

guiñolesco, **-ca** *adj* puppet theatre (*antes de sust*).

guión *m* **-1.** [resumen] framework, outline. **-2.** CIN & TV script. **-3.** GRAM [signo] hyphen.

guionista *m y f* scriptwriter.

guiri *fam despec* ◇ *adj* foreign. ◇ *m y f* foreigner.

guirigay *m* **-1.** *fam* [jaleo] racket. **-2.** [lenguaje ininteligible] gibberish.

guirlache *m brittle sweet made of roasted almonds or hazelnuts and toffee*.

guirnalda *f* garland.

guisa *f* way, manner; **a** ~ **de** by way of, as; **de esta** ~ in this way.

guisado *m* stew.

guisante *m* pea.

guisar *vt & vi* to cook.

◆ **guisarse** *vpr fig* to be cooking, to be going on.

guiso *m* dish.

güisqui, **whisky** *m* whisky.

guita *f fam* dosh.

guitarra ◇ *f* guitar; ~ **eléctrica** electric guitar; **chafar la ~ a alguien** to mess things up for sb. ◇ *m y f* guitarist.

guitarrero, -ra *m y f* guitar maker.

guitarrista *m y f* guitarist.

gula *f* gluttony.

gulasch [gu'laʃ] *m* goulash.

gulden *m* guilder, florin.

gurí, -isa *m y f Amer fam* kid, child.

guripa *m fam* cop.

gurmet, gourmet [gur'met] *m y f* gourmet.

guru, gurú *m* guru.

gusanillo *m fam*: **el ~ de la conciencia** conscience; **entrarle a uno el ~ de los videojuegos** to be bitten by the videogame bug; **matar el ~** [bebiendo] to have a drink on an empty stomach; [comiendo] to have a snack between meals; **sentir un ~ en el estómago** to have butterflies (in one's stomach).

gusano *m lit* & *fig* worm; ~ **de luz** glow worm; ~ **de (la) seda** silkworm.

gusarapo, -pa *m y f* creepy-crawly.

gustar ◇ *vi* [agradar] to be pleasing; **me gusta esa chica/ir al cine** I like that girl/going to the cinema; **me gustan las novelas** I like novels; ~ **de hacer algo** to like ○ enjoy doing sthg; **como guste** as you wish. ◇ *vt* to taste, to try.

gustativo, -va *adj* taste (*antes de sust*).

gustazo *m fam* great pleasure; **darse el ~ de algo/hacer algo** to allow o.s. the pleasure of sthg/doing sthg.

gustillo *m* **-1.** [sabor] aftertaste. **-2.** [satisfacción] malicious sense of satisfaction.

gusto *m* **-1.** [gen] taste; [sabor] taste, flavour; **de buen/mal ~** in good/bad taste; **tener buen/mal ~** to have good/bad taste; **sobre ~s no hay nada escrito** there's no accounting for taste, each to his own. **-2.** [placer] pleasure; **con mucho ~** gladly, with pleasure; **da ~ estar aquí** it's a real pleasure to be here; **mucho ~** pleased to meet you; **tomar ~ a algo** to take a liking to sthg.

◆ **a gusto** *loc adv*: **hacer algo a ~** [de buena gana] to do sthg willingly ○ gladly; [cómodamente] to do sthg comfortably; **estar a ~** to be comfortable ○ at ease.

gustoso, -sa *adj* **-1.** [sabroso] tasty. **-2.** [con placer]: **hacer algo ~** to do sthg gladly ○ willingly.

gutural *adj* guttural.

Guyana Guyana.

Guyana francesa *f*: **la ~** French Guyana.

guyanés, -esa *adj, m y f* Guyanese.

gymkhana = **gincana**.

h¹, H *f* [letra] h, H; **por h o por b** *fig* for one reason or another.
◆ **H** (*abrev de* **Hermano**) Br.

h², h. (*abrev de* **hora**) hr, h.

ha ◇ *v* → **haber**. ◇ (*abrev de* **hectárea**) ha.

haba *f* broad bean.

habanero, -ra *adj* of/relating to Havana.
◆ **habanera** *f* MÚS habanera.

habano, -na *adj* Havanan.
◆ **habano** *m* Havana cigar.

hábeas corpus *m* habeas corpus.

haber [4] ◇ *v aux* **-1.** [en tiempos compuestos] to have; **lo he/había hecho** I have/had done it; **los niños ya han comido** the children have already eaten; **en el estreno ha habido mucha gente** there were a lot of people at the premiere. **-2.** [expresa reproche]: ~ **venido antes** you could have come a bit earlier; **¡~lo dicho!** why didn't you say so? **-3.** [expresa obligación]: ~ **de hacer algo** to have to do sthg; **has de estudiar más** you have to study more.

◇ *v impers* **-1.** [existir, estar]: **hay** there is/are; **hay mucha gente en la calle** there are a lot of people in the street; **había/hubo muchos problemas** there were many problems; **habrá dos mil** [expresa futuro] there will be two thousand; [expresa hipótesis] there must be two thousand. **-2.** [expresa obligación]: ~ **que hacer algo** to have to do sthg; **hay que hacer más ejercicio** one ○ you should do more exercise; **habrá que soportar su mal humor** we'll have to put up with his bad mood. **-3.** *loc*: **algo habrá** there must be something in it; **allá se las haya** that's his/her/your *etc* problem; **habérselas con alguien** to face ○ confront sb; **¡hay que ver!** well I never!; **lo habido y por ~** everything under the sun; **no hay de qué** don't mention it; **¿qué hay?** *fam* [saludo] how are you doing?

◇ *m* **-1.** [bienes] assets (*pl*). **-2.** [en cuentas, contabilidad] credit (side).
◆ **haberes** *mpl* [sueldo] remuneration (*U*).

habichuela *f* bean.

habido, -da *adj* occurred; **los accidentes**

~s este verano the number of accidents this summer.

hábil *adj* **-1.** [diestro] skilful; [inteligente] clever. **-2.** [utilizable - lugar] suitable, fit. **-3.** DER: **días ~es** working days.

habilidad *f* [destreza] skill; [inteligencia] cleverness; **tener ~ para algo** to be good at sthg.

habilidoso, -sa *adj* skilful, clever.

habilitación *f* **-1.** [acondicionamiento] fitting out. **-2.** DER [autorización] authorization, right.

habilitado, -da ◇ *adj* DER authorized. ◇ *m y f* paymaster.

habilitar *vt* **-1.** [acondicionar] to fit out, to equip. **-2.** [autorizar] to authorize. **-3.** [financiar] to finance.

habiloso, -sa *adj Amer* shrewd, astute.

habitabilidad *f* habitability.

habitable *adj* habitable, inhabitable.

habitación *f* [gen] room; [dormitorio] bedroom; **~ doble** [con cama de matrimonio] double room; [con dos camas] twin room; **~ individual** ○ **simple** single room.

habitáculo *m* dwelling.

habitante *m* [de ciudad, país] inhabitant; [de barrio] resident.

habitar ◇ *vi* to live. ◇ *vt* to live in, to inhabit.

hábitat (*pl* **hábitats**) *m* **-1.** [gen] habitat. **-2.** [vivienda] housing conditions (*pl*).

hábito *m* habit; **tener el ~ de hacer algo** to be in the habit of doing sthg; **colgar los ~s** RELIG to leave the priesthood, to give up the cloth; *fig* [renunciar] to give it up; **el ~ no hace al monje** clothes don't make the man.

habituación *f* [a drogas etc] addiction; **la ~ al nuevo trabajo fue difícil** getting used to the new job was difficult.

habitual *adj* habitual; [cliente, lector] regular.

habituar [6] *vt*: **~ a alguien a** to accustom sb to.

◆ **habituarse** *vpr*: **~se a** [gen] to get used ○ accustomed to; [drogas etc] to become addicted to.

habla *f* (*el*) **-1.** [idioma] language; [dialecto] dialect; **de ~ española** Spanish-speaking. **-2.** [facultad] speech; **quedarse sin ~** to be left speechless. **-3.** LING discourse. **-4.** [al teléfono]: **estar al ~ con alguien** to be on the line to sb.

hablador, -ra ◇ *adj* talkative. ◇ *m y f* chatterbox.

habladurías *fpl* [rumores] rumours; [chismes] gossip (*U*).

hablante ◇ *adj* speaking. ◇ *m y f* speaker.

hablar ◇ *vi*: **~ (con)** to talk (to), to speak (to); **~ por ~** to talk for the sake of talking; **~ de** to talk about; **~ bien/mal de** to speak well/badly of; **~ en voz alta/baja** to speak loudly/softly; **dar que ~** to make people talk; **¡ni ~!** no way! ◇ *vt* **-1.** [idioma] to speak. **-2.** [asunto]: **~ algo (con)** to discuss sthg (with).

◆ **hablarse** *vpr* to speak (to each other); **no ~se** not to be speaking, not to be on speaking terms; **"se habla inglés"** "English spoken".

habrá *etc* → **haber**.

hacedor, -ra *m y f* maker.

◆ **Hacedor** *m*: **el Hacedor** the Maker.

hacendado, -da *m y f* landowner.

hacendoso, -sa *adj* houseproud.

hacer [60] ◇ *vt* **-1.** [elaborar, crear, cocinar] to make; **~ un vestido/planes** to make a dress/plans; **~ un poema/una sinfonía** to write a poem/symphony; **para ~ la carne ...** to cook the meat .... **-2.** [construir] to build; **han hecho un edificio nuevo** they've put up a new building. **-3.** [generar] to produce; **el árbol hace sombra** the tree gives shade; **la carretera hace una curva** there's a bend in the road. **-4.** [movimientos, sonidos, gestos] to make; **le hice señas** I signalled to her; **el reloj hace tic-tac** the clock goes tick-tock; **~ ruido** to make a noise. **-5.** [obtener - fotocopia] to make; [- retrato] to paint; [- fotografía] to take. **-6.** [realizar - trabajo, estudios] to do; [- viaje] to make; [- comunión] to take; **hoy hace guardia** she's on duty today; **estoy haciendo segundo** I'm in my second year. **-7.** [practicar - gen] to do; [- tenis, fútbol] to play; **debes ~ deporte** you should start doing some sport. **-8.** [arreglar - casa, colada] to do; [- cama] to make. **-9.** [dar aspecto] to cause to look ○ seem; **este espejo te hace gordo** that mirror makes you look ○ seem fat. **-10.** [transformar en]: **~ a alguien feliz** to make sb happy; **la guerra no le hizo un hombre** the war didn't make him (into) a man; **hizo pedazos el papel** he tore the paper to pieces; **~ de algo/alguien algo** to make sthg/sb into sthg; **hizo de ella una buena cantante** he made a good singer of her. **-11.** [comportarse como]: **~ el tonto** to act the fool; **~ el vándalo** to act like a hooligan. **-12.** [causar]: **~ daño a alguien** to hurt sb; **me hizo gracia** I thought it was funny. **-13.** CIN & TEATR to play; **hace el papel de la hija del rey** she plays (the part of) the king's daughter. **-14.** [suponer] to think, to reckon; **a estas horas yo te hacía en París** I thought ○ reckoned you'd be in Paris by now. **-15.**

[ser causa de]: ~ **que alguien haga algo** to make sb do sthg; **me hizo reír** it made me laugh; **has hecho que se enfadara** you've made him angry. **-16.** [mandar]: ~ **que se haga algo** to have sthg done; **voy a ~ teñir este traje** I'm going to have the dress dyed.

◇ *vi* **-1.** [intervenir]: **déjame ~ a mí** let me do it. **-2.** [actuar]: ~ **de** CIN & TEATR to play; [trabajar] to act as. **-3.** [aparentar]: ~ **como si** to act as if; **haz como que no te importa** act as if you don't care. **-4.** [procurar, intentar]: ~ **por hacer algo** to try to do sthg; **haré por verle esta noche** I'll try to see him tonight. **-5.** *loc*: **¿hace?** all right?

◇ *v impers* **-1.** [tiempo meteorológico]: **hace frío/sol/viento** it's cold/sunny/windy; **hace un día precioso** it's a beautiful day. **-2.** [tiempo transcurrido]: **hace diez años** ten years ago; **hace mucho/poco** a long time/not long ago; **hace un mes que llegué** it's a month since I arrived; **no la veo desde hace un año** I haven't seen her for a year.

◆ **hacerse** *vpr* **-1.** [formarse] to form. **-2.** [desarrollarse, crecer] to grow. **-3.** [guisarse, cocerse] to cook. **-4.** [convertirse] to become; ~**se musulmán** to become a Moslem. **-5.** [resultar] to get; **se hace muy pesado** it gets very tedious. **-6.** [crearse en la mente]: ~**se ilusiones** to get one's hopes up; ~**se una idea de algo** to imagine what sthg is like. **-7.** [mostrarse]: **se hace el gracioso/el simpático** he tries to act the comedian/the nice guy; ~**se el distraído** to pretend to be miles away.

hacha *f* (*el*) axe; **desenterrar el ~ de guerra** *fig* to sharpen one's sword; **ser un ~** *fam* to be a whizz ○ an ace.

hachazo *m* blow of an axe, hack.

hache *f*: **llamémosle ~** call it what you like.

hachís, hash [xaʃ] *m* hashish.

hacia *prep* **-1.** [dirección, tendencia, sentimiento] towards; ~ **aquí/allí** this/that way; ~ **abajo** downwards; ~ **arriba** upwards; ~ **atrás** backwards; ~ **adelante** forwards. **-2.** [tiempo] around, about; ~ **las diez** around ○ about ten o'clock.

hacienda *f* **-1.** [finca] country estate ○ property. **-2.** [bienes] property; ~ **pública** public purse.

◆ **Hacienda** *f*, **Ministerio de Hacienda** *m* the Treasury.

hacinamiento *m* [de personas] overcrowding; [de objetos] heaping, piling.

hacinar *vt* to pile ○ heap (up).

◆ **hacinarse** *vpr* [gente] to be crowded together; [cosas] to be piled ○ heaped (up).

hada *f* (*el*) fairy.

hado *m* fate, destiny.

haga *etc* → **hacer**.

Haití Haiti.

haitiano, -na *adj, m y f* Haitian.

hala *interj*: ¡~! [para dar ánimo, prisa] come on!; [para expresar incredulidad] no!, you're joking!; [para expresar admiración, sorpresa] wow!

halagador, -ra ◇ *adj* flattering. ◇ *m y f* flatterer.

halagar [16] *vt* to flatter.

halago *m* flattery.

halague *etc* → **halagar**.

halagüeño, -ña *adj* [prometedor] promising, encouraging.

halcón *m* **-1.** ZOOL falcon, hawk. **-2.** *Amer fam* [matón] government-paid killer.

halconería *f* falconry.

hale *interj*: ¡~! come on!

hálito *m* **-1.** [aliento] breath. **-2.** *fig* [aire] zephyr, gentle breeze.

halitosis *f inv* bad breath.

hall [xol] (*pl* **halls**) *m* entrance hall, foyer.

hallar *vt* [gen] to find; [averiguar] to find out.

◆ **hallarse** *vpr* **-1.** [en un casa etc - persona] to be, to find o.s.; [- lugar] to be (situated). **-2.** [en una situación] to be; ~**se enfermo** to be ill.

hallazgo *m* **-1.** [descubrimiento] discovery. **-2.** [objeto] find.

halo *m* [de astros, santos] halo; [de objetos, personas] aura.

halógeno, -na *adj* QUÍM halogenous; [faro] halogen (*antes de sust*).

halterofilia *f* weightlifting.

hamaca *f* **-1.** [para colgar] hammock. **-2.** [tumbona - silla] deckchair; [- canapé] sun-lounger.

hambre *f* **-1.** [apetito] hunger; [inanición] starvation; **tener ~** to be hungry; ~ **canina** ravenous hunger; **matar el ~** to satisfy one's hunger. **-2.** [epidemia] famine. **-3.** *fig* [deseo]: ~ **de** hunger ○ thirst for. **-4.** *loc*: **se juntan el ~ con las ganas de comer** it's one thing on top of another; **ser más listo que el ~** to be nobody's fool.

hambreador *m Amer* exploiter.

hambriento, -ta ◇ *adj* starving. ◇ *m y f* starving person; **los ~s** the hungry.

hamburguesa *f* hamburger.

hamburguesería *f* hamburger joint.

hampa *f* (*el*) underworld.

hampón *m* thug.

hámster ['xamster] (*pl* **hámsters**) *m* hamster.

hándicap ['xandikap] (*pl* **hándicaps**) *m* handicap.

hangar *m* hangar.

Hanoi Hanoi.

hará *etc* → hacer.

haragán, -ana ◇ *adj* lazy, idle. ◇ *m y f* layabout, idler.

haraganear *vi* to laze about, to lounge around.

haraganería *f* laziness, idleness.

harakiri = haraquiri.

harapiento, -ta *adj* ragged, tattered.

harapo *m* rag, tatter.

haraquiri, harakiri *m* harakiri.

Harare Harare.

hardware ['xarwar] *m* INFORM hardware.

harén *m* harem.

harina *f* flour; **ser ~ de otro costal** *fig* to be a different kettle of fish.

harinoso, -sa *adj* floury; [manzana] mealy.

hartar *vt* **-1.** [atiborrar] to stuff (full). **-2.** [fastidiar]: **~ a alguien** to annoy sb, to get on sb's nerves.

◆ **hartarse** *vpr* **-1.** [atiborrarse] to stuff ◇ gorge o.s. **-2.** [cansarse]: **~se (de)** to get fed up (with). **-3.** [no parar]: **~se de algo** to do sthg non-stop.

hartazgo, hartón *m* fill; **darse un ~ (de)** to have one's fill (of).

harto, -ta *adj* **-1.** [de comida] full. **-2.** [cansado]: **~ (de)** tired (of), fed up (with).

◆ **harto** *adv* somewhat, rather.

hartón = hartazgo.

hash = hachís.

hasta ◇ *prep* **-1.** [en el espacio] as far as, up to; **desde aquí ~ allí** from here to there; **¿~ dónde va este tren?** where does this train go? **-2.** [en el tiempo] until, till; **~ ahora** (up) until now, so far; **~ el final** right up until the end; **~ luego** ◇ **pronto** ◇ **la vista** see you (later). **-3.** [con cantidades] up to. ◇ *adv* [incluso] even.

◆ **hasta que** *loc conj* until, till.

hastiar [9] *vt* [aburrir] to bore; [asquear] to sicken, to disgust.

◆ **hastiarse de** *vpr* to tire of, to get fed up with.

hastío *m* [tedio] boredom (*U*); [repugnancia] disgust.

hatajo *m* load, bunch; **un ~ de** [gamberros] a bunch of; [mentiras] a pack of.

hatillo *m* bundle of clothes.

hato *m* **-1.** [de ganado] herd; [de ovejas] flock. **-2.** [de ropa] bundle.

Hawai [xa'wai] Hawaii.

hawaiano, -na [xawai'ano] *adj, m y f* Hawaiian.

haya ◇ *v* → **haber.** ◇ *f* [árbol] beech (tree); [madera] beech (wood).

hayal *m* beech grove ◇ wood.

haz ◇ *v* → **hacer.** ◇ *m* **-1.** [de leña] bundle; [de cereales] sheaf. **-2.** [de luz] beam.

hazaña *f* feat, exploit.

hazmerreír *m* laughing stock.

HB (*abrev de* **Herri Batasuna**) *f political wing of ETA.*

he → **haber.**

hebdomadario, -ria *adj* weekly.

hebilla *f* buckle.

hebra *f* [de hilo] thread; [de judías, puerros] string; [de tabaco] strand (of tobacco).

hebreo, -a *adj, m y f* Hebrew.

◆ **hebreo** *m* [lengua] Hebrew.

hecatombe *f* carnage (*U*), disaster.

hechicería *f* **-1.** [arte] witchcraft, sorcery. **-2.** [maleficio] spell.

hechicero, -ra ◇ *adj* enchanting, bewitching. ◇ *m y f* wizard (*f* witch), sorcerer (*f* sorceress).

hechizar [13] *vt* to cast a spell on; *fig* to bewitch, to captivate.

hechizo *m* **-1.** [maleficio] spell. **-2.** *fig* [encanto] magic, charm.

hecho, -cha ◇ *pp* → **hacer.** ◇ *adj* **-1.** [acabado - persona] mature; [- cuerpo feminino] shapely; **estás ~ un artista** you've become quite an artist; **una mujer hecha y derecha** a fully-grown woman. **-2.** [carne] done; **quiero el filete muy/poco ~** I'd like the steak well done/rare.

◆ **hecho** *m* ◇ **-1.** [obra] action, deed; **a lo ~, pecho** it's no use crying over spilt milk. **-2.** [suceso] event; **~ consumado** fait accompli. **-3.** [realidad, dato] fact. ◇ *interj*: **¡~!** it's a deal!, you're on!

◆ **de hecho** *loc adv* in fact, actually.

hechura *f* **-1.** [de traje] cut. **-2.** [forma] shape.

hectárea *f* hectare.

hectolitro *m* hectolitre.

hectómetro *m* hectometre.

heder [20] *vi* **-1.** [apestar] to stink, to reek. **-2.** *fig* [fastidiar] to be annoying ◇ irritating.

hediondez *f* stench, stink.

hediondo, -da *adj* **-1.** [pestilente] stinking, foul-smelling. **-2.** *fig* [insoportable] unbearable.

hedonismo *m* hedonism.

hedonista ◇ *adj* hedonistic. ◇ *m y f* hedonist.

hedor *m* stink, stench.

hegemonía *f* [gen] dominance; POLÍT hegemony.

hegemónico, -ca *adj* [gen] dominant; [clase, partido] ruling.

hégira, héjira *f* hegira.

helada → helado.

heladería *f* [tienda] ice-cream parlour; [puesto] ice-cream stall.

heladero, -ra *m y f* ice-cream seller.

helado, -da *adj* **-1.** [hecho hielo - agua] frozen; [- lago] frozen over. **-2.** [muy frío - manos, agua] freezing. **-3.** *fig* [atónito] dumbfounded, speechless.
◆ **helado** *m* ice-cream.
◆ **helada** *f* frost.

helar [19] ◇ *vt* **-1.** [líquido] to freeze. **-2.** *fig* [dejar atónito] to dumbfound. ◇ *v impers:* **ayer heló** there was a frost last night.
◆ **helarse** *vpr* to freeze; [plantas] to be frostbitten.

helecho *m* fern, bracken.

helénico, -ca *adj* Hellenic, Greek.

helenismo *m* Hellenism.

helenista *m y f* Hellenist.

heleno, -na *adj* Hellenic, Greek.

hélice *f* **-1.** TECN propeller. **-2.** [espiral] spiral.

helicóptero *m* helicopter.

helio *m* helium.

helipuerto *m* heliport.

Helsinki Helsinki.

helvético, -ca *adj, m y f* Swiss.

hematíe *m* red blood cell.

hematología *f* haematology.

hematológico, -ca *adj* haematological.

hematólogo, -ga *m y f* haematologist.

hematoma *m* bruise, haematoma (MED).

hembra *f* **-1.** BIOL female; [mujer] woman; [niña] girl. **-2.** [del enchufe] socket.

hembrilla *f* [de corchete] eye.

hemeroteca *f* newspaper library ○ archive.

hemiciclo *m* **-1.** [semicírculo] semicircle. **-2.** [en el parlamento] floor.

hemiplejia, hemiplejía *f* hemiplegia.

hemipléjico, -ca *adj, m y f* hemiplegic.

hemisférico, -ca *adj* hemispheric.

hemisferio *m* hemisphere.

hemofilia *f* haemophilia.

hemofílico, -ca *adj, m y f* haemophiliac.

hemoglobina *f* haemoglobin.

hemograma *m* blood test.

hemopatía *f* blood disease ○ disorder.

hemorragia *f* haemorrhage; ~ **nasal** nosebleed.

hemorrágico, -ca *adj* haemorrhagic.

hemorroides *fpl* haemorrhoids, piles.

henchido, -da *adj* bloated.

henchir [26] *vt* to fill (up).
◆ **henchirse** *vpr* **-1.** [hartarse] to stuff o.s. **-2.** *fig* [llenarse]: ~**se (de)** to be full (of).

hender [20], **hendir** [27] *vt* [carne, piel] to carve open, to cleave; [piedra, madera] to crack open; [aire, agua] to cut ○ slice through.

hendido, -da *adj* split (open).

hendidura *f* [en carne, piel] cut, split; [en piedra, madera] crack.

hendir = hender.

heno *m* hay.

hepático, -ca *adj* liver (*antes de sust*), hepatic.

hepatitis *f inv* hepatitis.

heptagonal *adj* heptagonal.

heptágono *m* heptagon.

heráldico, -ca *adj* heraldic.
◆ **heráldica** *f* heraldry.

heraldista *m y f* heraldist.

heraldo *m* herald.

herbario, -ria *adj* herbal.
◆ **herbario** *m* [colección] herbarium.

herbicida *m* weedkiller.

herbívoro, -ra ◇ *adj* herbivorous. ◇ *m y f* herbivore.

herbolario, -ria *m y f* [persona] herbalist.
◆ **herbolario** *m* [tienda] herbalist's (shop).

herboristería *f* herbalist's (shop).

hercio, hertz ['erθjo] *m* hertz.

hercúleo, -a *adj* very powerful, incredibly strong.

hércules *m* ox, very strong man.

Hércules Hercules.

heredar *vt:* ~ **(de)** to inherit (from).

heredero, -ra ◇ *m y f* heir (*f* heiress).

hereditario, -ria *adj* hereditary.

hereje *m y f* heretic.

herejía *f* [gen] heresy; [disparate] stupid ○ ridiculous thing.

herencia *f* [de bienes] inheritance; [de características] legacy; BIOL heredity.

herético, -ca *adj* heretical.

herido, -da ◇ *adj* [gen] injured; [en lucha, atentado] wounded; [sentimentalmente] hurt, wounded. ◇ *m y f* [gen] injured person; [en lucha, atentado] wounded person; **no hubo** ~**s** there were no casualties; **los** ~**s** the wounded.

◆ **herida** f -1. [lesión] injury; [en lucha, atentado] wound. -2. [ofensa] injury, offence (U); [pena] hurt (U), pain (U).

herir [27] vt -1. [físicamente] to injure; [en lucha, atentado] to wound; [vista] to hurt; [oído] to pierce. -2. [sentimentalmente] to hurt.

hermafrodita adj, m y f hermaphrodite.

hermanado, -da adj [gen] united, joined; [ciudades] twinned.

hermanamiento m [gen] union; [de ciudades] twinning.

hermanar vt -1. [esfuerzos, personas] to unite. -2. [ciudades] to twin.

◆ **hermanarse** vpr [ciudades] to be twinned.

hermanastro, -tra m y f stepbrother (f stepsister).

hermandad f -1. [asociación] association; [RELIG - de hombres] brotherhood; [- de mujeres] sisterhood. -2. [amistad] intimacy, close friendship.

hermano, -na ◇ adj related, connected. ◇ m y f brother (f sister); ~s siameses Siamese twins.

hermenéutico, -ca adj hermeneutic.

◆ **hermenéutica** f hermeneutics (U).

hermético, -ca adj -1. [al aire] airtight, hermetic; [al agua] watertight, hermetic. -2. fig [persona] inscrutable.

hermetismo m inscrutability.

hermoso, -sa adj [gen] beautiful, lovely; [hombre] handsome; [excelente] wonderful.

hermosura f [gen] beauty; [de hombre] handsomeness.

hernia f hernia, rupture.

herniado, -da ◇ adj ruptured. ◇ m y f person suffering from a hernia.

herniarse [8] vpr -1. MED to rupture o.s. -2. fam [esforzarse]: ~se (a hacer algo) to bust a gut (doing sthg).

héroe m hero.

heroicidad f -1. [cualidad] heroism. -2. [hecho] heroic deed.

heroico, -ca adj heroic.

heroína f -1. [mujer] heroine. -2. [droga] heroin.

heroinomanía f heroin addiction.

heroinómano, -na m y f heroin addict.

heroísmo m heroism.

herpes m inv herpes (U).

herradura f horseshoe.

herraje m iron fittings (pl), ironwork.

herramienta f tool.

herrería f -1. [taller] smithy, forge. -2. [oficio] smithery, blacksmith's trade.

herrero m blacksmith, smith.

herrín m rust.

herrumbrarse vpr to rust, to go rusty.

herrumbre f -1. [óxido] rust. -2. [sabor] iron taste.

herrumbroso, -sa adj rusty.

hertz = **hercio**.

hervidero m -1. [de pasiones, intrigas] hotbed. -2. [de gente - muchedumbre] swarm, throng; [- sitio] place throbbing o swarming with people.

hervido m stew.

hervir [27] ◇ vt to boil. ◇ vi -1. [líquido] to boil. -2. fig [lugar]: ~ de to swarm with. -3. fig [persona]: ~ en to be burning with.

hervor m boiling; dar un ~ a algo to blanch sthg.

heterodoxia f heterodoxy, unorthodox nature.

heterodoxo, -xa ◇ adj heterodox, unorthodox. ◇ m y f heterodox o unorthodox person.

heterogeneidad f heterogeneity.

heterogéneo, -a adj heterogeneous.

heteromorfo, -fa adj heteromorphous.

heterosexual adj, m y f heterosexual.

heterosexualidad f heterosexuality.

hevea m hevea.

hexadecimal adj INFORM hexadecimal.

hexagonal adj hexagonal.

hexágono m hexagon.

hez f lit & fig dregs (pl).

◆ **heces** fpl [excrementos] faeces, excrement (sg).

hg (abrev de **hectogramo**) hg.

hiato m hiatus.

hibernación f [de animales] hibernation.

hibernal adj winter (antes de sust).

hibernar vi to hibernate.

hibridación f hybridization.

híbrido, -da adj lit & fig hybrid.

◆ **híbrido** m -1. [animal, planta] hybrid. -2. fig [mezcla] cross.

hice etc → **hacer**.

hidalgo, -ga ◇ adj -1. [nobiliar] noble. -2. fig [caballeroso] courteous, gentlemanly. ◇ m y f nobleman (f noblewoman).

hidalguía f -1. [aristocracia] nobility. -2. fig [caballerosidad] courtesy, chivalry.

hidra f fig [peligro] threat.

hidratación f [de la piel] moisturizing; [de persona] rehydration; [de sustancia] hydration.

hidratado, -da adj [piel] moist; QUÍM hydrated.

hidratante ◇ *adj* moisturizing. ◇ *m* moisturizing cream.

hidratar *vt* [piel] to moisturize; QUÍM to hydrate.

hidrato *m* hydrate; ~ **de carbono** carbohydrate.

hidráulico, -ca *adj* hydraulic.
◆ **hidráulica** *f* hydraulics (U).

hídrico, -ca *adj* hydric.

hidroavión *m* seaplane.

hidrocarburo *m* hydrocarbon.

hidrocefalia *f* water on the brain, hydrocephalus (MED).

hidrodinámico, -ca *adj* hydrodynamic.
◆ **hidrodinámica** *f* hydrodynamics (U).

hidroelectricidad *f* hydroelectricity.

hidroeléctrico, -ca *adj* hydroelectric.

hidrófilo, -la *adj* absorbent; **algodón** ~ cotton wool *Br*, cotton *Am*.

hidrofobia *f* hydrophobia.

hidrófobo, -ba *adj* hydrophobic, rabid.

hidrófugo, -ga *adj* [contra filtraciones] waterproof; [contra humedad] dampproof.

hidrogenar *vt* to hydrogenate.

hidrógeno *m* hydrogen.

hidrografía *f* hydrography.

hidrográfico, -ca *adj* hydrographic.

hidrólisis *f inv* hydrolysis.

hidromecánico, -ca *adj* hydrodynamic, water-powered.

hidrometría *f* hydrometry.

hidroplano *m* **-1.** [barco] hydrofoil. **-2.** [avión] seaplane.

hidrosfera *f* hydrosphere.

hidrosoluble *adj* water-soluble.

hidrostático, -ca *adj* hydrostatic.
◆ **hidrostática** *f* hydrostatics (U).

hidroterapia *f* hydrotherapy.

hidróxido *m* hydroxide.

hidruro *m* hydride.

hieda *etc* → **heder**.

hiedra *f* ivy.

hiel *f* **-1.** [bilis] bile. **-2.** *fig* [mala intención] spleen, bitterness.

hiela *etc* → **helar**.

hielo *m* ice; **romper el** ~ *fig* to break the ice.

hiena *f* hyena.

hienda *etc* → **hender, hendir**.

hiera *etc* → **herir**.

hierático, -ca *adj* solemn.

hierba, yerba *f* **-1.** [planta] herb; **mala** ~ weed; ~ **mate** maté; ~**s medicinales** medicinal herbs. **-2.** [césped] grass. **-3.** *fam* [droga] grass. **-4.** *loc*: **ser mala** ~ to be a nasty piece of work; **mala** ~ **nunca muere** *proverb* ill weeds grow apace *proverb*; **y otras** ~**s** and so on.

hierbabuena *f* mint.

hierro *m* **-1.** [metal] iron; **de** ~ [severo] iron (*antes de sust*); ~ **forjado** wrought iron; ~ **fundido** cast iron. **-2.** [de puñal] blade; [de flecha] point; **quien a** ~ **mata a** ~ **muere** *proverb* he who lives by the sword dies by the sword *proverb*.

hierva *etc* → **hervir**.

HI-FI (*abrev de* **high fidelity**) *f* hi-fi.

higadillo *m*: ~**s de pollo** chicken livers.

hígado *m* liver; **echar los** ~**s** to nearly kill o.s. (with the effort); **tener** ~**s** to have guts.

higiene *f* hygiene; ~ **mental** mental health.

higiénico, -ca *adj* hygienic.

higienista *m y f* hygienist.

higienización *f* sterilization.

higienizar [13] *vt* to sterilize.

higo *m* fig; ~ **chumbo** prickly pear; **de** ~**s a brevas** once in a blue moon.

higrometría *f* hygrometry.

higrómetro *m* hygrometer.

higuera *f* fig tree; ~ **chumba** prickly pear; **estar en la** ~ *fig* to live in a world of one's own.

hijastro, -tra *m y f* stepson (*f* stepdaughter).

hijo, -ja *m y f* **-1.** [descendiente] son (*f* daughter); ~ **de la chingada** *Amer* o **de puta** *vulg* bastard *Br*, mother-fucker *Am*; ~ **de papá** *fam* daddy's boy; ~ **ilegítimo** illegitimate child; ~ **pródigo** prodigal son; ~ **único** only child; **cualquier** o **todo** ~ **de vecino** *fam fig* any Tom, Dick or Harry. **-2.** [natural] native. **-3.** [como forma de dirigirse a alguien]: **¡pues** ~, **podrías haber avisado!** you could at least have told me, couldn't you?; **¡hija mía, qué bruta eres!** God, you're stupid!
◆ **hijo** *m* [hijo o hija] child.
◆ **hijos** *mpl* children.

hilacha *f* loose thread.

hilada *f* row.

hilandería *f* **-1.** [arte] spinning. **-2.** [taller] (spinning) mill.

hilandero, -ra *m y f* spinner.

hilar *vt* [hilo, tela] to spin; [ideas, planes] to think up; ~ **delgado** o **muy fino** *fig* to split hairs.

hilarante *adj* hilarious.

hilaridad *f* hilarity.

hilatura *f* spinning.

hilera *f* row; **en** ~ in a row.

hilo *m* **-1.** [fibra, hebra] thread; **colgar** o **pender de un** ~ to be hanging by a thread; **mover los** ~**s** to pull some strings. **-2.** [tejido] linen. **-3.** [de metal, teléfono] wire. **-4.** [de agua, sangre] trickle; **apenas le salía un** ~ **de voz** *fig* he was barely able to speak. **-5.** *fig* [de pensamiento] train; [de discurso, conversación] thread; **perder el** ~ to lose the thread; **seguir el** ~ to follow (the thread).
◆ **hilo musical**® *m* piped music.

hilván *m* **-1.** [costura] tacking *Br*, basting *Am*. **-2.** [hilo] tacking stitch *Br*, basting stitch *Am*.

hilvanado *m* tacking *Br*, basting *Am*.

hilvanar *vt* **-1.** [ropa] to tack *Br*, to baste *Am*. **-2.** *fig* [coordinar - ideas] to piece together. **-3.** *fig* [improvisar] to throw together.

Himalaya *m*: **el** ~ the Himalayas (*pl*).

himen *m* hymen.

himeneo *m* LITER wedding.

himno *m* hymn; ~ **nacional** national anthem.

hincapié *m*: **hacer** ~ **en** [insistir] to insist on; [subrayar] to emphasize, to stress.

hincar [10] *vt*: ~ **algo en** to stick sthg into.
◆ **hincarse** *vpr*: ~**se de rodillas** to fall to one's knees.

hincha ◇ *v* → **henchir.** ◇ *m y f* [seguidor] fan. ◇ *f* [rabia]: **tener** ~ **a alguien** to have it in for sb.

hinchado, -da *adj* **-1.** [rueda, globo] inflated; [cara, tobillo] swollen. **-2.** *fig* [persona] bigheaded, conceited; [lenguaje, estilo] bombastic.
◆ **hinchada** *f* fans (*pl*).

hinchar *vt lit* & *fig* to blow up.
◆ **hincharse** *vpr* **-1.** [pierna, mano] to swell (up). **-2.** *fig* [persona] to become bigheaded. **-3.** *fig* [de comida]: ~**se (a)** to stuff o.s. (with).
◆ **hincharse a** *vpr* [no parar de]: ~**se a hacer algo** to do sthg a lot.

hinchazón *f* swelling.

hinche, hinchiera *etc* → **henchir.**

hindi *m* Hindi.

hindiera *etc* → **hendir.**

hindú (*pl* **hindúes**) *adj, m y f* **-1.** [de la India] Indian. **-2.** RELIG Hindu.

hinduismo *m* Hinduism.

hinojo *m* fennel.

hinque *etc* → **hincar.**

hip *interj*: ¡~! ¡~! ¡hurra! hip, hip, hooray!

hipar *vi* to hiccup, to have hiccups.

hiper *m fam* hypermarket.

hiperactividad *f* hyperactivity.

hiperactivo, -va *adj* hyperactive.

hipérbaton (*pl* **hipérbatos** o **hiperbatones**) *m* hyperbaton.

hipérbola *f* hyperbola.

hipérbole *f* hyperbole.

hiperbólico, -ca *adj* hyperbolic.

hiperfunción *f* MED increase in normal rate of functioning.

hiperglucemia *f* hyperglycæmia.

hiperinflación *f* hyperinflation.

hipermercado *m* hypermarket.

hipermetropía *f* long-sightedness.

hiperrealismo *m artistic movement concerned with almost photographic representation of reality.*

hipersensibilidad *f* hypersensitivity.

hipersensible *adj* hypersensitive.

hipersónico, -ca *adj* hypersonic.

hipertensión *f* high blood pressure.

hipertenso, -sa ◇ *adj* with high blood pressure. ◇ *m y f* person with high blood pressure.

hipertermia *f* hyperthermia.

hipertexto *m* INFORM hypertext.

hipertrofia *f* hypertrophy; *fig* overexpansion.

hip-hop *m* hip-hop.

hípico, -ca *adj* [de las carreras] horseracing (*antes de sust*); [de la equitación] showjumping (*antes de sust*).
◆ **hípica** *f* [carreras de caballos] horseracing; [equitación] showjumping.

hipnosis *f inv* hypnosis.

hipnótico, -ca *adj* hypnotic.
◆ **hipnótico** *m* hypnotic, narcotic.

hipnotismo *m* hypnotism.

hipnotización *f* hypnotization.

hipnotizador, -ra ◇ *adj* hypnotic; *fig* spellbinding, mesmerizing. ◇ *m y f* hypnotist.

hipnotizar [13] *vt* to hypnotize; *fig* to mesmerize.

hipo *m* hiccups (*pl*); **tener** ~ to have (the) hiccups; **quitar el** ~ **a uno** *fig* to take one's breath away.

hipocentro *m* hypocentre, focus.

hipocondría *f* hypochondria.

hipocondriaco, -ca *adj, m y f* hypochondriac.

hipocondrio *m* hypochondrium.

hipocrático, -ca *adj*: **juramento** ~ Hippocratic oath.

hipocresía *f* hypocrisy.

hipócrita ◇ *adj* hypocritical. ◇ *m y f* hypocrite.

hipodérmico, -ca *adj* hypodermic.

hipodermis *f inv* hypodermis.

hipódromo *m* racecourse, racetrack.

hipófisis *f inv* pituitary gland.

hipofunción *f* MED decrease in normal rate of functioning.

hipoglucemia *f* hypoglycaemia.

hipopótamo *m* hippopotamus.

hipotálamo *m* hypothalamus.

hipoteca *f* mortgage; **levantar una ~** to pay off a mortgage.

hipotecable *adj* mortgageable.

hipotecar [10] *vt* **-1.** [bienes] to mortgage. **-2.** *fig* [poner en peligro] to compromise, to jeopardize.

hipotecario, -ria *adj* mortgage (*antes de sust*).

hipotensión *f* low blood pressure.

hipotenso, -sa ◇ *adj* with low blood pressure. ◇ *m y f* person with low blood pressure.

hipotensor *m* hypotensive drug.

hipotenusa *f* hypotenuse.

hipotermia *f* hypothermia.

hipótesis *f inv* hypothesis.

hipotético, -ca *adj* hypothetic, hypothetical.

hippy, hippie ['xipi] (*pl* **hippies**) *adj, m y f* hippy.

hiriente *adj* [palabras] hurtful, cutting.

hiriera *etc* → **herir**.

hirsuto, -ta *adj* **-1.** [cabello] wiry; [brazo, pecho] hairy. **-2.** *fig* [persona] gruff, surly.

hirviera *etc* → **hervir**.

hisopo *m* **-1.** RELIG aspergillum, sprinkler. **-2.** BOT hyssop.

hispalense *adj, m y f* Sevillian.

hispánico, -ca *adj, m y f* Hispanic, Spanish-speaking.

hispanidad *f* [cultura] Spanishness; [pueblos] Spanish-speaking world.

hispanista *m y f* Hispanist, student of Hispanic culture.

hispano, -na ◇ *adj* [español] Spanish; [hispanoamericano] Spanish-American; [en Estados Unidos] Hispanic. ◇ *m y f* [español] Spaniard; [estadounidense] Hispanic.

hispanoamericano, -na ◇ *adj* Spanish-American. ◇ *m y f* Spanish American.

hispanoárabe ◇ *adj* Hispano-Arabic. ◇ *m y f* Spanish Arab.

hispanohablante ◇ *adj* Spanish-speaking. ◇ *m y f* Spanish speaker.

hispanojudío, -a ◇ *adj* Spanish-Jewish. ◇ *m y f* Spanish Jew.

histamina *f* histamine.

histerectomía *f* hysterectomy.

histeria *f* MED & *fig* hysteria.

histérico, -ca ◇ *adj* MED & *fig* hysterical; **ponerse ~** to get hysterical. ◇ *m y f* MED hysteric; *fig* hysterical person.

histerismo *m* MED & *fig* hysteria.

histerotomía *f* hysterotomy.

histograma *m* histogram.

histología *f* histology.

historia *f* **-1.** [gen] history; **~ antigua/universal** ancient/world history; **~ del arte** art history; **pasar a la ~** to go down in history. **-2.** [narración, chisme] story; **dejarse de ~s** to stop beating about the bush.
 ◆ **historia natural** *f* natural history.

historiador, -ra *m y f* historian.

historial *m* [gen] record; [profesional] curriculum vitae, résumé *Am*; **~ médico** ○ **clínico** medical ○ case history.

historicidad *f* historicity, historical authenticity.

historicismo *m* historicism.

histórico, -ca *adj* **-1.** [de la historia] historical. **-2.** [verídico] factual. **-3.** [importante] historic.

historieta *f* **-1.** [chiste] funny story, anecdote. **-2.** [tira cómica] comic strip.

historiografía *f* historiography.

historiógrafo, -fa *m y f* historiographer.

histrión *m* **-1.** [actor] actor. **-2.** [persona afectada] play-actor.

histriónico, -ca *adj* histrionic.

histrionismo *m* histrionics (*pl*).

hit [xit] (*pl* **hits**) *m* hit.

hitita *adj, m y f* Hittite.

hitleriano [xitle'rjano], **-na** *adj, m y f* Hitlerite.

hito *m* lit & *fig* milestone; **mirar a alguien de ~ en ~** to stare at sb.

hizo → **hacer**.

hl (*abrev de* **hectolitro**) hl.

hm (*abrev de* **hectómetro**) hm.

hmnos. (*abrev de* **hermanos**) bros.

hobby ['xoβi] (*pl* **hobbies**) *m* hobby.

hocico *m* **-1.** [de perro] muzzle; [de gato] nose; [de cerdo] snout. **-2.** *despec* [de personas - boca] rubber lips (*pl*); [- cara] mug.

hockey ['xokei] *m* hockey; **~ sobre hielo/patines** ice/roller hockey; **~ sobre hierba** (field) hockey.

hogar *m* **-1.** [de chimenea] fireplace; [de horno, cocina] grate. **-2.** [domicilio] home. **-3.** [familia] family.

hogareño, -ña *adj* [gen] family (*antes de sust*); [amante del hogar] home-loving, homely.

hogaza *f* large loaf.

hoguera *f* bonfire; **morir en la ~** to be burned at the stake.

hoja *f* **-1.** [de plantas] leaf; [de flor] petal; [de hierba] blade. **-2.** [de papel] sheet (of paper); [de libro] page; **~ de paga** pay slip; **~ de servicios** record (of service), track record. **-3.** [de cuchillo] blade; **~ de afeitar** razor blade. **-4.** [de puertas, ventanas] leaf.
◆ **hoja de cálculo** *f* INFORM spreadsheet.

hojalata *f* tinplate.

hojalatería *f* tinsmith's.

hojalatero *m* tinsmith.

hojaldre *m* puff pastry.

hojarasca *f* **-1.** [hojas secas] (dead) leaves (*pl*); [frondosidad] tangle of leaves. **-2.** *fig* [paja] rubbish.

hojear *vt* to leaf through.

hola *interj*: ¡~! hello!

Holanda Holland.

holandés, -esa ◇ *adj* Dutch. ◇ *m y f* [persona] Dutchman (*f* Dutchwoman).
◆ **holandés** *m* [lengua] Dutch.
◆ **holandesa** *f* [papel] *piece of paper measuring 22 x 28cm.*

holding ['xoldin] (*pl* **holdings**) *m* holding company.

holgado, -da *adj* **-1.** [ropa] baggy, loose-fitting; [habitación, espacio] roomy. **-2.** [victoria, situación económica] comfortable.

holganza *f* leisure.

holgar [39] *vi* [sobrar] to be unnecessary; **huelga decir que ...** needless to say ....

holgazán, -ana ◇ *adj* idle, good-for-nothing. ◇ *m y f* good-for-nothing.

holgazanear *vi* to laze about.

holgazanería *f* idleness.

holgué *etc* → **holgar**.

holgura *f* **-1.** [anchura - de espacio] room; [- de ropa] bagginess, looseness; [- entre piezas] play, give. **-2.** [bienestar] comfort, affluence; **vivir con ~** to be comfortably off.

hollar [23] *vt* to tread (on).

hollejo *m* skin (*of grape, olive etc*).

hollín *m* soot.

holocausto *m* holocaust.

holografía *f* holography.

holograma *m* hologram.

hombre ◇ *m* man; **el ~** [la humanidad] man, mankind; **~ de acción** man of action; **el ~ de la calle** ○ **de a pie** the man in the street; **~ de las cavernas** caveman; **~ de estado** statesman; **~ de mundo** man of the world; **~ de negocios** businessman; **~ de paja** front (man); **~ de palabra** man of his word; **~ del saco** *fam* bogeyman; **el abominable ~ de las nieves** the abominable snowman; **un pobre ~** a nobody; ¡**pobre ~**! poor chap *Br* ○ guy!; **de ~ a ~** a man to man; **ser muy ~** to be a (real) man; **ser todo un ~** to be every bit a man.
◇ *interj*: ¡~! ¡**qué alegría verte!** (hey,) how nice to see you!
◆ **hombre lobo** (*pl* **hombres lobo**) *m* werewolf.
◆ **hombre orquesta** (*pl* **hombres orquesta**) *m* one-man band.
◆ **hombre rana** (*pl* **hombres rana**) *m* frogman.

hombrear *vi* to act the man.

hombrera *f* [de traje, vestido] shoulder pad; [de uniforme] epaulette.

hombría *f* manliness.

hombro *m* shoulder; **a ~s** over one's shoulders; **al ~** across one's shoulder; **encogerse de ~s** to shrug one's shoulders; **arrimar el ~** *fig* to lend a hand; **mirar por encima del ~ a alguien** *fig* to look down one's nose at sb.

hombruno, -na *adj* masculine, mannish.

homenaje *m* [gen] tribute; [al soberano] homage; **partido (de) ~** testimonial (match); **en ○ de ○ a** in honour of, as a tribute to; **rendir ~ a** to pay tribute to.

homenajeado, -da ◇ *adj* honoured. ◇ *m y f* guest of honour.

homenajear *vt* to pay tribute to, to honour.

homeópata *m y f* homeopath.

homeopatía *f* homeopathy.

homeopático, -ca *adj* homeopathic.

homérico, -ca *adj* **-1.** LITER Homeric. **-2.** [épico] epic.

homicida ◇ *adj* [mirada etc] murderous; **arma ~** murder weapon. ◇ *m y f* murderer.

homicidio *m* homicide, murder.

homilía *f* homily, sermon.

homínido *m* hominid.

homofonía *f* homophony.

homófono, -na *adj* homophonic.

homogeneidad *f* homogeneity.

homogeneización *f* homogenization.

homogeneizador, -ra *adj* homogenizing.

homogeneizar [13] *vt* to homogenize.

homogéneo, -a *adj* homogenous.

homografía *f* homography.

homógrafo, -fa *adj* homographic.
◆ **homógrafo** *m* homograph.

homologable *adj*: ~ **(a)** comparable (to).

homologación *f* **-1.** [equiparación] bringing into line. **-2.** [ratificación - de un producto] official authorization; [- de un récord] official confirmation.

homologar [16] *vt* **-1.** [equiparar]: ~ **(con)** to bring into line (with), to make comparable (with). **-2.** [dar por válido - producto] to authorize officially; [- récord] to confirm officially.

homólogo, -ga ◇ *adj* **-1.** [semejante] equivalent. **-2.** GEOM & QUIM homologous. ◇ *m y f* counterpart.

homonimia *f* homonymy.

homónimo, -ma ◇ *adj* homonymous. ◇ *m y f* [tocayo] namesake.

◆ **homónimo** *m* GRAM homonym.

homoplastia *f* homoplasty.

homosexual *adj, m y f* homosexual.

homosexualidad *f* homosexuality.

hondo, -da *adj* **-1.** *lit & fig* [gen] deep; **lo** ~ the depths *(pl)*; **calar** ~ **en** to strike a chord with; **en lo más** ~ **de** in the depths of. **-2.** → **cante**.

◆ **honda** *f* sling.

hondonada *f* hollow.

hondura *f* depth.

Honduras Honduras.

hondureño, -ña *adj, m y f* Honduran.

honestamente *adv* [con honradez] honestly; [con decencia] modestly, decently; [con justicia] fairly.

honestidad *f* [honradez] honesty; [decencia] modesty, decency; [justicia] fairness.

honesto, -ta *adj* [honrado] honest; [decente] modest, decent; [justo] fair.

hongo *m* **-1.** [planta - comestible] mushroom; [- no comestible] toadstool. **-2.** [enfermedad] fungus. **-3.** [sombrero] bowler (hat) *Br*, derby *Am*.

Honolulu Honolulu.

honor *m* honour; **en** ~ **de** in honour of; **hacer** ~ **a** to live up to; **en** ~ **a la verdad** to be (quite) honest.

◆ **honores** *mpl* [ceremonial] honours; **hacer los** ~**es de la casa** *fig* to do the honours, to look after the guests.

honorabilidad *f* honour.

honorable *adj* honourable.

honorar *vt* to honour.

honorario, -ria *adj* honorary.

◆ **honorarios** *mpl* fees.

honorífico, -ca *adj* honorific.

honra *f* honour; **es la** ~ **de su país** she's the pride ○ toast of her country; **tener algo**

a mucha ~ to be honoured by sthg; **¡y a mucha** ~! and proud of it!

◆ **honras fúnebres** *fpl* funeral *(sg)*.

honradez *f* honesty.

honrado, -da *adj* honest.

honrar *vt* to honour.

◆ **honrarse** *vpr*: ~**se (con algo/de hacer algo)** to be honoured (by sthg/to do sthg).

honrilla *f* pride, concern about what people say.

honroso, -sa *adj* **-1.** [que da honra] honorary. **-2.** [respetable] honourable, respectable.

hora *f* **-1.** [del día] hour; **a primera** ~ first thing in the morning; **a última** ~ [al final del día] at the end of the day; [en el último momento] at the last moment; **dar la** ~ to strike the hour; **de última** ~ [noticia] latest, up-to-the-minute; [preparativos] last-minute; **"última** ~**"** "stop press"; **(pagar) por** ~**s** (to pay) by the hour; **poner el reloj en** ~ to set one's watch ○ clock; ~**s de oficina/trabajo** office/working hours; ~ **oficial** official time; ~ **punta** rush hour; ~**s extraordinarias** overtime *(U)*; ~**s de visita** visiting times; **media** ~ half an hour. **-2.** [momento determinado] time; **¿a qué** ~ **sale?** what time ○ when does it leave?; **es** ~ **de irse** it's time to go; **a la** ~ on time; **en su** ~ when the time comes, at the appropriate time; **¿qué** ~ **es?** what time is it?; ~ **H** zero hour. **-3.** [cita] appointment; **pedir/dar** ~ to ask for/give an appointment; **tener** ~ **en/con** to have an appointment at/with. **-4.** [muerte]: **llegó mi** ~ my time has come. **-5.** *loc*: **a altas** ~**s de la noche** in the small hours; **a buenas** ~**s (mangas verdes)** it's a bit late now; **en mala** ~ unluckily; **la** ~ **de la verdad** the moment of truth; **no ver la** ~ **de hacer algo** [no tener tiempo] not to know when one is going to find time to do sthg; [estar ansioso] not to be able to wait to do sthg; **tener las** ~**s contadas** to have one's days numbered; **¡ya era** ~! and about time too!

horadar *vt* to pierce; [con máquina] to bore through.

horario, -ria *adj* time *(antes de sust)*.

◆ **horario** *m* timetable; ~ **comercial/laboral** opening/working hours *(pl)*; ~ **flexible** flexitime *(U)*; ~ **intensivo** *working day without a long break for lunch*; ~ **de visitas** visiting hours *(pl)*.

horca *f* **-1.** [patíbulo] gallows *(pl)*. **-2.** AGR pitchfork.

horcajadas

◆ **a horcajadas** *loc adv* astride.

horchata *f* *cold drink made from ground tiger nuts or almonds, milk and sugar.*

horchatería f bar where "horchata" is served.

horda f horde.

horizontal adj horizontal.

horizontalidad f flatness.

horizonte m horizon.

horma f [gen] mould, pattern; [para arreglar zapatos] last; [para conservar zapatos] shoe tree; [de sombrero] hat block; **encontrar alguien la ~ de su zapato** fig to meet one's match.

hormiga f ant; **ser una ~** fig to be hardworking and thrifty.

hormigón m concrete; **~ armado** reinforced concrete.

hormigonar vt to construct with concrete.

hormigonera f concrete mixer.

hormiguear vi **-1.** [dar hormigueo]: **me hormiguean las piernas** I've got pins and needles in my legs. **-2.** [bullir] to swarm.

hormigueo m pins and needles (pl).

hormiguero ◇ adj → **oso**. ◇ m ants' nest.

hormiguita f fam hard-working and thrifty person.

hormona f hormone.

hormonal adj hormonal.

hornada f lit & fig batch.

hornear vt to bake.

hornillo m [para cocinar] camping ○ portable stove; [de laboratorio] small furnace.

horno m CULIN oven; TECN furnace; [de cerámica, ladrillos] kiln; **alto ~** blast furnace; **altos ~s** [factoría] iron and steelworks; **~ crematorio** crematorium; **~ eléctrico** electric oven; **~ microondas** microwave (oven); **no está el ~ para bollos** fig the time is not right.

horóscopo m **-1.** [signo zodiacal] star sign. **-2.** [predicción] horoscope.

horquilla f **-1.** [para el pelo] hairgrip, hairpin. **-2.** [de bicicleta etc] fork.

horrendo, -da adj [gen] horrendous; [muy malo] terrible, awful.

hórreo m raised granary typical of Asturias and Galicia.

horrible adj [gen] horrible; [muy malo] terrible, awful.

horripilante adj **-1.** [terrorífico] horrifying, spine-chilling. **-2.** fam [muy malo, feo] dreadful, awful.

horripilar vt to terrify, to scare to death.

horror m **-1.** [miedo] terror, horror; **¡qué ~!** how awful! **-2.** (gen pl) [atrocidad] atrocity.

◆ **horrores** adv fam terribly, an awful lot.

horrorizado, -da adj terrified, horrified.

horrorizar [13] vt to terrify, to horrify.

◆ **horrorizarse** vpr to be terrified ○ horrified.

horroroso, -sa adj **-1.** [gen] awful, dreadful. **-2.** [muy feo] horrible, hideous. **-3.** fam [enorme] terrible.

hortaliza f (garden) vegetable.

hortelano, -na ◇ adj market garden (antes de sust). ◇ m y f market gardener.

hortensia f hydrangea.

hortera fam ◇ adj tasteless, tacky. ◇ m y f person with no taste.

horterada f fam tacky thing.

hortícola adj horticultural.

horticultor, -ra m y f horticulturalist.

horticultura f horticulture.

hosanna m [himno] hymn sung on Palm Sunday.

hosco, -ca adj [persona] sullen, gruff; [lugar] grim, gloomy.

hospedaje m **-1.** [alojamiento] accommodation, lodgings (pl). **-2.** [dinero] (cost of) board and lodging.

hospedar vt to put up.

◆ **hospedarse** vpr to stay.

hospedería f guest house; [de convento] hospice.

hospiciano, -na m y f resident of an orphanage ○ a children's home.

hospicio m [para niños] orphanage, children's home; [para pobres] poorhouse.

hospital m hospital.

hospitalario, -ria adj **-1.** [acogedor] hospitable. **-2.** [de hospital] hospital (antes de sust).

hospitalidad f hospitality.

hospitalización f hospitalization.

hospitalizar [13] vt to hospitalize, to take ○ send to hospital.

hosquedad f sullenness, gruffness.

hostal m guesthouse.

hostelería f catering.

hostelero, -ra ◇ adj catering (antes de sust). ◇ m y f landlord (f landlady).

hostería f guesthouse.

hostia f **-1.** RELIG host. **-2.** vulg [bofetada] bash, punch. **-3.** vulg [accidente] smash-up.

◆ **hostias** interj vulg: **¡~s!** bloody hell!, damn it!

hostiar [9] vt vulg to bash.

hostigamiento m harassment.

hostigar [16] vt **-1.** [acosar] to pester, to bother. **-2.** MIL to harass.

hostil adj hostile.

hostilidad f [sentimiento] hostility.

◆ **hostilidades** fpl MIL hostilities.

hostilizar [13] *vt* to harass.

hot dog ['xotdoɣ] *m* hot dog.

hotel *m* hotel.

hotelería *f* hotel industry ○ trade.

hotelero, -ra ◇ *adj* hotel (*antes de sust*). ◇ *m y f* hotel manager (*f* hotel manageress), hotelier.

hoy *adv* **-1.** [en este día] today; **de ~ en adelante** from now on. **-2.** [en la actualidad] nowadays, today; **~ día, ~ en día, ~ por ~** these days, nowadays.

hoyo *m* **-1.** [gen] hole, pit; [de golf] hole. **-2.** *fam* [sepultura] grave.

hoyuelo *m* dimple.

hoz *f* sickle; **la ~ y el martillo** the hammer and sickle.

HTML (*abrev de* **hypertext markup language**) *m* INFORM HTML.

huacal *m Amer* **-1.** [jaula] cage. **-2.** [cajón] drawer.

huachafería *f Amer fam* **-1.** [hecho] tacky thing. **-2.** [dicho] naff comment.

huachafo, -fa *adj Amer fam* tacky.

huacho, -cha *m y f Amer fam* illegitimate child.

huasca *f Amer* whip.

huaso, -sa *m y f Amer fam* peasant.

hubiera *etc* → **haber**.

hucha *f* moneybox.

hueco, -ca *adj* **-1.** [vacío] hollow. **-2.** [sonido] resonant, hollow. **-3.** [sin ideas] empty.
◆ **hueco** *m* **-1.** [cavidad - gen] hole; [- en pared] recess. **-2.** [tiempo libre] spare moment. **-3.** [espacio libre] space, gap; [de escalera] well; [de ascensor] shaft.

huela *etc* → **oler**.

huelga ◇ *v* → **holgar**. ◇ *f* strike; **estar/declararse en ~** to be/to go on strike; **~ de brazos caídos** ○ **cruzados** sit-down (strike); **~ de celo** work-to-rule; **~ de hambre** hunger strike; **~ general** general strike; **~ salvaje** wildcat strike.

huelguista ◇ *adj* strike (*antes de sust*). ◇ *m y f* striker.

huella ◇ *v* → **hollar**. ◇ *f* **-1.** [de persona] footprint; [de animal, rueda] track; **~ digital** ○ **dactilar** fingerprint; **seguir las ~s de alguien** to follow in sb's footsteps. **-2.** *fig* [vestigio] trace. **-3.** *fig* [impresión profunda] mark; **dejar ~** to leave one's mark.

huérfano, -na *adj, m y f* orphan.

huero, -ra *adj* hollow; *fig* empty.

huerta *f* **-1.** [huerto] market garden *Br*, truck farm *Am*. **-2.** [tierra de regadío] *irrigated crop-growing region*.

huertano, -na *m y f* **-1.** [murciano] Murcian. **-2.** [valenciano] Valencian.

huertero, -ra *m y f* market gardener.

huerto *m* [de hortalizas] vegetable garden; [de frutales] orchard.

hueso *m* **-1.** [del cuerpo] bone; **acabar** ○ **dar con sus ~s en** to end up in; **estar en los ~s** to be all skin and bones; **no poder alguien con sus ~s** to be ready to drop, to be exhausted; **ser un ~ duro de roer** to be a hard nut to crack. **-2.** [de fruto] stone *Br*, pit *Am*. **-3.** *fam* [persona] very strict person; [asignatura] difficult subject. **-4.** *Amer fam* [enchufe] contacts (*pl*), influence.
◆ **hueso de santo** *m* CULIN *small marzipan roll filled with egg yolk*.

huésped, -da *m y f* guest.

huestes *fpl* [gen] army (*sg*); [seguidores] followers.

huesudo, -da *adj* bony.

hueva *f* roe.

huevada *f Amer vulg* bollocks (*U*), crap.

huevear *vi Amer fam* to muck about.

huevero, -ra *m y f* egg seller.
◆ **huevera** *f* **-1.** [para servir] egg cup. **-2.** [para guardar] egg box.

huevo *m* **-1.** [de animales] egg; **~ a la copa** ○ **tibio** *Amer* boiled egg; **~ escalfado/frito** poached/fried egg; **~ pasado por agua/duro** soft-boiled/hard-boiled egg; **~s al plato** *eggs cooked in the oven in an earthenware dish*; **~s revueltos** scrambled eggs. **-2.** (*gen pl*) *vulg* [testículos] balls (*pl*); **costar un ~** [ser caro] to cost a packet ○ bomb; [ser difícil] to be bloody hard; **saber un ~** to know a hell of a lot; **tener ~s** to have (a lot of) balls; **¡y un ~!** bollocks!, like hell!

huevón *m Amer vulg* stupid bastard.

hugonote, -ta *adj, m y f* Huguenot.

huida *f* escape, flight.

huidizo, -za *adj* shy, elusive.

huir [51] ◇ *vi* **-1.** [escapar]: **~ (de)** [gen] to flee (from); [de cárcel etc] to escape (from); **huir del país** to flee the country. **-2.** [evitar]: **~ de algo** to avoid sthg, to keep away from sthg. ◇ *vt* to avoid.

huiro *m Amer* seaweed.

hule *m* oilskin.

hulla *f* soft coal.

hullero, -ra *adj* soft coal (*antes de sust*).

humanidad *f* humanity.
◆ **humanidades** *fpl* [letras] humanities.

humanismo *m* humanism.

humanista ◇ *adj* humanist, humanistic. ◇ *m y f* humanist.

humanitario, -ria *adj* humanitarian.

humanitarismo *m* humanitarianism.
humanización *f* humanization, making more human.
humanizar [13] *vt* to humanize, to make more human.
◆ **humanizarse** *vpr* to become more human.
humano, **-na** *adj* **-1.** [del hombre] human. **-2.** [compasivo] humane.
◆ **humano** *m* human being; **los** ~**s** mankind (*U*).
humareda *f* cloud of smoke.
humazo *m* clouds (*pl*) of smoke.
humeante *adj* [lleno de humo] smoky; [que echa humo] smoking; [que echa vapor] steaming.
humear *vi* [salir humo] to (give off) smoke; [salir vapor] to steam.
humedad *f* **-1.** [gen] dampness; [en pared, techo] damp; [de algo chorreando] wetness; [de piel, ojos etc] moistness. **-2.** [de atmósfera etc] humidity.
humedecer [30] *vt* to moisten.
◆ **humedecerse** *vpr* to become moist; ~**se los labios** to moisten one's lips.
humedecimiento *m* moistening.
húmedo, **-da** *adj* **-1.** [gen] damp; [chorreando] wet; [piel, ojos etc] moist. **-2.** [aire, clima, atmósfera] humid.
húmero *m* humerus.
humidificador *m* humidifier.
humidificar [10] *vt* to humidify.
humildad *f* humility.
humilde *adj* humble.
humillación *f* humiliation.
humillado, **-da** *adj* humiliated.
humillante *adj* humiliating.
humillar *vt* to humiliate.
◆ **humillarse** *vpr* to humble o.s.; ~**se a hacer algo** [rebajarse] to lower o.s. to do sthg, to stoop to doing sthg.
humo *m* [gen] smoke; [vapor] steam; [de coches etc] fumes (*pl*).
◆ **humos** *mpl* *fig* [aires] airs; **bajarle a alguien los** ~**s** *fig* to take sb down a peg or two.
humor *m* **-1.** [estado de ánimo] mood; [carácter] temperament; **estar de buen/mal** ~ to be in a good/bad mood; **tener un** ~ **de perros** to be in a filthy mood. **-2.** [gracia] humour; **un programa de** ~ a comedy programme; ~ **negro** black humour. **-3.** [ganas] mood; **no estoy de** ~ I'm not in the mood. **-4.** ANAT humour.
humorismo *m* humour; TEATR & TV comedy.

humorista *m y f* humorist; TEATR & TV comedian (*f* comedienne).
humorístico, **-ca** *adj* humorous.
humoso, **-sa** *adj* smoky; [de vapor] steamy.
humus *m inv* humus.
hundimiento *m* **-1.** [naufragio] sinking. **-2.** [ruina] collapse.
hundir *vt* **-1.** [gen] to sink; ~ **algo en el agua** to put sthg underwater. **-2.** *fig* [afligir] to devastate, to destroy. **-3.** *fig* [hacer fracasar] to ruin.
◆ **hundirse** *vpr* **-1.** [sumergirse] to sink; [intencionadamente] to dive. **-2.** [derrumbarse] to collapse; [techo] to cave in. **-3.** *fig* [fracasar] to be ruined.
húngaro, **-ra** *adj, m y f* Hungarian.
◆ **húngaro** *m* [lengua] Hungarian.
Hungría Hungary.
huno, **-na** ◇ *adj* Hunnish. ◇ *m y f* Hun.
huracán *m* hurricane.
huracanado, **-da** *adj* violent; METEOR hurricane-force.
huraño, **-ña** *adj* unsociable.
hurgar [16] *vi*: ~ (**en**) [gen] to rummage around (in); [con el dedo, un palo] to poke around (in).
◆ **hurgarse** *vpr*: ~**se la nariz** to pick one's nose; ~**se los bolsillos** to rummage around in one's pockets.
hurgón *m* poker.
hurgonear *vt* to poke.
hurgue *etc* → **hurgar**.
hurón *m* **-1.** ZOOL ferret. **-2.** *fig* [persona] unsociable person.
Huron *m*: **lago** ~ Lake Huron.
hurra *interj*: ¡~! hurray!
hurtadillas
◆ **a hurtadillas** *loc adv* on the sly, stealthily.
hurtar *vt* to steal.
hurto *m* theft.
húsar *m* hussar.
husmeador, **-ra** *adj* [perro] sniffer (*antes de sust*); [persona] nosey, prying.
husmear ◇ *vt* [olfatear] to sniff out, to scent. ◇ *vi* [curiosear] to nose around.
huso *m* spindle; [en máquina] bobbin.
◆ **huso horario** *m* time zone.
huy *interj*: ¡~! [dolor] ouch!; [sorpresa] gosh!
huya, **huyera** *etc* → **huir**.

I

i, I f [letra] i, I.
IAE (*abrev de* **Impuesto sobre Actividades Económicas**) *m Spanish tax paid by professionals and shop owners.*
ib., ibíd. (*abrev de* ibidem) ibid.
iba → ir.
ibérico, -ca *adj* Iberian.
íbero, -ra *adj, m y f* Iberian.
◆ **íbero, ibero** *m* [lengua] Iberian.
iberoamericano, -na *adj, m y f* Latin American.
ibídem, ibidem *adv* ibidem, ibid.
ice *etc* → izar.
ICE (*abrev de* **Instituto de Ciencias de la Educación**) *m Spanish institute for educational sciences.*
iceberg (*pl* **icebergs**) *m* iceberg.
ICI (*abrev de* **Instituto de Cooperación Iberoamericana**) *m institute for Latin American cooperation.*
Icona (*abrev de* **Instituto Nacional para la Conservación de la Naturaleza**) *m Spanish national institute for conservation,* ≃ NCC *Br.*
icono *m* icon.
iconoclasta ◇ *adj* iconoclastic. ◇ *m y f* iconoclast.
iconografía *f* iconography.
iconográfico, -ca *adj* iconographical.
ictericia *f* jaundice.
ictiología *f* ichthyology.
id → ir.
ida *f* outward journey; **(billete de)** ~ y vuelta return (ticket); ~**s y venidas** *fig* comings and goings.
IDE (*abrev de* **Iniciativa de Defensa Estratégica**) *f* SDI.
idea *f* **-1.** [gen] idea; [propósito] intention; **a mala** ~ maliciously; **con la** ~ **de** with the idea ○ intention of; **tener** ~ **de hacer algo** to intend to do sthg; ~ **fija** obsession; ~ **luminosa** brilliant idea, brainwave; **no tener ni** ~ **(de)** not to have a clue (about); **tener** ~**s de bombero** to have wild ○ crazy ideas. **-2.** [opinión] impression; **cambiar de** ~ to change one's mind.

◆ **ideas** *fpl* [ideología] ideas.
ideal *adj & m* ideal.
idealismo *m* idealism.
idealista ◇ *adj* idealistic. ◇ *m y f* idealist.
idealización *f* idealization.
idealizar [13] *vt* to idealize.
idear *vt* **-1.** [planear] to think up, to devise. **-2.** [inventar] to invent.
ideario *m* ideology.
ídem *pron* ditto; ~ **de** ~ exactly the same.
IDEM (*abrev de* **Instituto de los Derechos de la Mujer**) *m Spanish institute for women's rights.*
idéntico, -ca *adj*: ~ **(a)** identical (to).
identidad *f* **-1.** [gen] identity. **-2.** [igualdad] identical nature.
identificación *f* identification.
identificar [10] *vt* to identify.
◆ **identificarse** *vpr*: ~**se (con)** to identify (with).
ideograma *m* ideogram, ideograph.
ideología *f* ideology.
ideológico, -ca *adj* ideological.
ideólogo, -ga *m y f* ideologist.
idílico, -ca *adj* idyllic.
idilio *m* love affair.
idioma *m* language.
idiomático, -ca *adj* idiomatic.
idiosincrasia *f* individual character.
idiosincrásico, -ca *adj* characteristic.
idiota ◇ *adj* **-1.** *despec* [tonto] stupid. **-2.** [enfermo] mentally deficient. ◇ *m y f* idiot.
idiotez *f* **-1.** [tontería] stupid thing, stupidity (*U*). **-2.** [enfermedad] mental deficiency.
idiotizar [13] *vt* to turn into an idiot, to zombify.
ido, ida *adj* mad, touched.
idólatra ◇ *adj lit & fig* idolatrous. ◇ *m y f* idolater (*f* idolatress); *fig* idolizer.
idolatrar *vt* to worship; *fig* to idolize.
idolatría *f lit & fig* idolatry.
ídolo *m* idol.
idoneidad *f* suitability.
idóneo, -a *adj*: ~ **(para)** suitable (for).
i.e. (*abrev de* **id est**) i.e.
IEM (*abrev de* **instituto de enseñanza media**) *m Spanish state secondary school.*
iglesia *f* church; **con la** ~ **hemos topado** now we're really up against it.
iglú (*pl* **iglúes**) *m* igloo.
ígneo, -a *adj* igneous.
ignición *f* ignition.
ignominia *f* ignominy.
ignominioso, -sa *adj* ignominious.

ignorancia *f* ignorance; ~ **supina** blind ignorance.

ignorante ◇ *adj* ignorant. ◇ *m y f* ignoramus.

ignorar *vt* **-1.** [desconocer] not to know, to be ignorant of. **-2.** [no tener en cuenta] to ignore.

ignoto, -ta *adj* unknown, undiscovered.

igual ◇ *adj* **-1.** [idéntico]: ~ **(que)** the same (as); **llevan jerseys ~es** they're wearing the same jumper; **son ~es** they're the same. **-2.** [parecido]: ~ **(que)** similar (to). **-3.** [equivalente]: ~ **(a)** equal (to). **-4.** [liso] even. **-5.** [constante - velocidad] constant; [- clima, temperatura] even. **-6.** MAT: **A más B es ~ a C** A plus B equals C. ◇ *m y f* equal; **sin** ~ without equal, unrivalled. ◇ *adv* **-1.** [de la misma manera] the same; **yo pienso** ~ I think the same, I think so too; **al ~ que** just like; **por** ~ equally. **-2.** [posiblemente] perhaps; ~ **llueve** it could well rain. **-3.** DEP: **van ~es** the scores are level. **-4.** *loc*: **dar** ○ **ser** ~ **a alguien** to be all the same to sb; **es** ○ **da** ~ it doesn't matter, it doesn't make any difference.

igualación *f* **-1.** [de terreno] levelling; [de superficie] smoothing. **-2.** [de cantidades] equalizing.

igualado, -da *adj* level.

igualar *vt* **-1.** [gen] to make equal, to equalize; DEP to equalize; ~ **algo a** ○ **con** to equate sthg with. **-2.** [persona] to be equal to; **nadie le iguala en generosidad** nobody is as generous as he is. **-3.** [terreno] to level; [superficie] to smooth.

◆ **igualarse** *vpr* **-1.** [gen] to be equal, to equal one another; ~**se a** ○ **con** to be equated with. **-2.** [a otra persona]: ~**se a** ○ **con alguien** to treat sb as an equal.

igualdad *f* **-1.** [equivalencia] equality; **en** ~ **de condiciones** on equal terms; ~ **de oportunidades** equal opportunities. **-2.** [identidad] sameness.

igualitario, -ria *adj* egalitarian.

igualitarismo *m* egalitarianism.

igualmente *adv* **-1.** [también] also, likewise. **-2.** [fórmula de cortesía] the same to you, likewise.

iguana *f* iguana.

Iguazú: **(las cataratas del)** ~ the Iguaçu Falls.

ijada *f*, **ijar** *m* flank, side.

ikastola *f* primary school in the Basque country where classes are given entirely in Basque.

ikurriña *f* Basque national flag.

ilación *f* cohesion.

ilegal *adj* illegal.

ilegalidad *f* **-1.** [acción] unlawful act. **-2.** [cualidad] illegality.

ilegible *adj* illegible.

ilegitimidad *f* illegitimacy.

ilegítimo, -ma *adj* **-1.** illegitimate. **-2.** → **hijo**.

ileso, -sa *adj* unhurt, unharmed; **salir** ○ **resultar** ~ to escape unharmed.

iletrado, -da *adj*, *m y f* illiterate.

ilícito, -ta *adj* illicit.

ilimitado, -da *adj* unlimited, limitless.

ilógico, -ca *adj* illogical.

iluminación *f* **-1.** [gen] lighting; [acción] illumination. **-2.** RELIG enlightenment.

iluminado, -da ◇ *adj* **-1.** [gen] lit (up). **-2.** RELIG enlightened. ◇ *m y f* RELIG enlightened person.

iluminador, -ra ◇ *adj* illuminating. ◇ *m y f* lighting technician.

iluminar *vt* **-1.** [gen] to illuminate, to light up. **-2.** RELIG to enlighten.

◆ **iluminarse** *vpr* **-1.** to light up. **-2.** RELIG to become enlightened.

ilusión *f* **-1.** [esperanza - gen] hope; [- infundada] delusion, illusion; **hacerse** ○ **forjarse ilusiones** to build up one's hopes. **-2.** [emoción] thrill, excitement (*U*); **¡qué ~!** how exciting!; **me hace mucha** ~ I'm really looking forward to it. **-3.** [espejismo] illusion.

ilusionar *vt* **-1.** [esperanzar]: ~ **a alguien (con algo)** to build up sb's hopes (about sthg). **-2.** [emocionar] to excite, to thrill.

◆ **ilusionarse** *vpr* **-1.** [esperanzarse]: ~**se (con)** to get one's hopes up (about). **-2.** [emocionarse]: ~**se (con)** to get excited (about).

ilusionismo *m* conjuring.

ilusionista ◇ *adj* conjuring (*antes de sust*). ◇ *m y f* illusionist, conjurer.

iluso, -sa ◇ *adj* gullible. ◇ *m y f* gullible person.

ilusorio, -ria *adj* illusory; [promesa] empty.

ilustración *f* **-1.** [estampa] illustration. **-2.** [cultura] learning.

◆ **Ilustración** *f* HIST: **la Ilustración** the Enlightenment.

ilustrado, -da *adj* **-1.** [publicación] illustrated. **-2.** [persona] learned. **-3.** HIST enlightened.

ilustrador, -ra ◇ *adj* illustrative. ◇ *m y f* illustrator.

ilustrar *vt* **-1.** [explicar] to illustrate, to explain. **-2.** [publicación] to illustrate. **-3.** [educar] to enlighten.

ilustrativo, -va *adj* illustrative.

ilustre *adj* **-1.** [gen] illustrious, distinguished. **-2.** [título]: **el ~ señor alcalde** his Worship, the mayor.

ilustrísimo, -ma *adj* most illustrious.
◆ **Ilustrísima** *f*: **Su Ilustrísima** Your/His Grace, Your/His Worship.

imagen *f* [gen] image; TV picture; **a ~ y semejanza de** identical to, exactly the same as; **ser la viva ~ de alguien** to be the spitting image of sb.

imaginable *adj* imaginable, conceivable.

imaginación *f* **-1.** [facultad] imagination; **pasar por la ~ de alguien** to occur to sb, to cross sb's mind; **no me pasó por la ~** it never occurred to me. **-2.** (*gen pl*) [idea falsa] delusion, imagining; **son imaginaciones tuyas** you're just imagining things, it's all in your mind.

imaginar *vt* **-1.** [gen] to imagine. **-2.** [idear] to think up, to invent.
◆ **imaginarse** *vpr* to imagine; **¡imagínate!** just think ○ imagine!; **me imagino que sí** I suppose so.

imaginario, -ria *adj* imaginary.

imaginativo, -va *adj* imaginative.

imaginería *f religious image-making.*

imán *m* **-1.** [para atraer] magnet. **-2.** [entre musulmanes] imam.

imanación *f* magnetization.

imanar, imantar *vt* to magnetize.

imbatible *adj* unbeatable.

imbatido, -da *adj* unbeaten.

imbebible *adj* undrinkable.

imbécil ○ *adj* stupid. ○ *m y f* idiot.

imbecilidad *f* stupidity; **decir/hacer una ~** to say/do sthg stupid.

imberbe *adj* beardless.

imbornal *m* scupper.

imborrable *adj fig* indelible; [recuerdo] unforgettable.

imbricación *f* overlapping.

imbricado, -da *adj* overlapping.

imbricar [10] *vt* to overlap.

imbuir [51] *vt*: **~ (de)** to imbue (with).

imitación *f* imitation; [de humorista] impersonation; **a ~ de** in imitation of; **piel de ~** imitation leather.

imitador, -ra *m y f* imitator; [humorista] impersonator.

imitar *vt* [gen] to imitate, to copy; [a personajes famosos] to impersonate; [producto, material] to simulate.

imitativo, -va *adj* imitative.

imp *abrev de* **imprenta.**

impaciencia *f* impatience.

impacientar *vt* to make impatient, to exasperate.
◆ **impacientarse** *vpr* to grow impatient.

impaciente *adj* impatient; **~ por hacer algo** impatient ○ anxious to do sthg.

impactar ○ *vt* [noticia] to have an impact on. ○ *vi* [bala] to hit.

impacto *m* **-1.** [gen] impact; [de bala] hit. **-2.** [señal] (impact) mark; **~s de bala** bullethole; **~ ambiental** environmental impact.

impagable *adj* invaluable.

impagado, -da *adj* unpaid.
◆ **impagado** *m* unpaid bill.

impago *m* non-payment.

impalpable *adj* impalpable.

impar *adj* **-1.** MAT odd. **-2.** [sin igual] unequalled.

imparable *adj* unstoppable.

imparcial *adj* impartial.

imparcialidad *f* impartiality.

impartir *vt* to give.

impase, impasse [im'pas] *m* impasse.

impasibilidad *f* impassivity.

impasible *adj* impassive.

impavidez *f* [valor] fearlessness, courage; [impasibilidad] impassivity.

impávido, -da *adj* [valeroso] fearless, courageous; [impasible] impassive.

impecable *adj* impeccable.

impedancia *f* impedance.

impedido, -da ○ *adj* disabled; **estar ~ de un brazo** to only have the use of one arm. ○ *m y f* disabled person.

impedimento *m* [gen] obstacle; [contra un matrimonio] impediment; **no hay ningún ~ para hacerlo** there's no reason why we shouldn't do it.

impedir [26] *vt* **-1.** [imposibilitar] to prevent; **~ a alguien hacer algo** to prevent sb from doing sthg. **-2.** [dificultar] to hinder, to obstruct.

impeler *vt* **-1.** [hacer avanzar] to propel. **-2.** [estimular]: **~ a alguien a algo/hacer algo** to drive sb to sthg/to do sthg.

impenetrabilidad *f lit & fig* impenetrability.

impenetrable *adj lit & fig* impenetrable.

impenitencia *f* impenitence.

impenitente *adj* unrepentant, impenitent; *fig* [incorregible] inveterate.

impensable *adj* unthinkable.

impensado, -da *adj* unexpected.

impepinable *adj fam* clear as clear can be, undeniable.

imperante *adj* prevailing.

imperar *vi* to prevail.

imperativo, **-va** *adj* **-1.** [gen & GRAM] imperative. **-2.** [autoritario] imperious.
◆ **imperativo** *m* [gen & GRAM] imperative.
imperceptible *adj* imperceptible.
imperdible *m* safety pin.
imperdonable *adj* unforgivable.
imperecedero, **-ra** *adj* non-perishable; *fig* [eterno] immortal, eternal.
imperfección *f* **-1.** [cualidad] imperfection. **-2.** [defecto] flaw, defect.
imperfecto, **-ta** *adj* [gen] imperfect; [defectuoso] faulty, defective.
◆ **imperfecto** *m* GRAM imperfect.
imperial *adj* imperial.
imperialismo *m* imperialism.
imperialista *adj*, *m y f* imperialist.
impericia *f* lack of skill; [inexperiencia] inexperience.
imperio *m* **-1.** [territorio] empire. **-2.** [dominio] rule; **valer un** ~ to be worth a fortune. **-3.** [mandato] emperorship.
imperioso, **-sa** *adj* **-1.** [autoritario] imperious. **-2.** [apremiante] urgent, pressing.
impermeabilidad *f* impermeability.
impermeabilización *f* waterproofing.
impermeabilizar [13] *vt* to (make) waterproof.
impermeable ◇ *adj* waterproof. ◇ *m* raincoat, mac *Br*.
impersonal *adj* impersonal.
impertérrito, **-ta** *adj* unperturbed, unmoved; [ante peligros] fearless.
impertinencia *f* **-1.** [gen] impertinence. **-2.** [comentario] impertinent remark.
impertinente ◇ *adj* impertinent. ◇ *m y f* [persona] impertinent person.
◆ **impertinentes** *mpl* [anteojos] lorgnette (*sg*).
imperturbabilidad *f* imperturbability.
imperturbable *adj* imperturbable.
ímpetu *m* **-1.** [brusquedad] force. **-2.** [energía] energy. **-3.** FÍS impetus.
impetuosidad *f* [precipitación] impetuosity.
impetuoso, **-sa** ◇ *adj* **-1.** [olas, viento, ataque] violent. **-2.** *fig* [persona] impulsive, impetuous. ◇ *m y f* impulsive person.
impida, **impidiera** *etc* → **impedir**.
impío, **-a** *adj* godless, impious.
implacable *adj* implacable, relentless.
implantación *f* **-1.** [establecimiento] introduction. **-2.** BIOL implantation. **-3.** MED insertion.
implantar *vt* **-1.** [establecer] to introduce. **-2.** MED to insert.
◆ **implantarse** *vpr* **-1.** [establecerse] to be introduced. **-2.** BIOL to become implanted.

implante *m* implant; [dental] dental plate.
implementar *vt* to implement.
implemento *m* implement.
implicación *f* **-1.** [participación] involvement. **-2.** (*gen pl*) [consecuencia] implication.
implicar [10] *vt* **-1.** [involucrar]: ~ **(en)** to involve (in); DER to implicate (in). **-2.** [significar] to mean.
◆ **implicarse** *vpr* DER to incriminate o.s.; ~**se en** to become involved in.
implícito, **-ta** *adj* implicit.
imploración *f* entreaty, plea.
implorar *vt* to implore.
impoluto, **-ta** *adj* unpolluted, pure; *fig* unblemished, untarnished.
imponderabilidad *f* imponderability.
imponderable ◇ *adj* [incalculable] invaluable; [imprevisible] imponderable. ◇ *m* imponderable.
imponente *adj* **-1.** [impresionante] imposing, impressive. **-2.** [estupendo] sensational, terrific.
imponer [65] ◇ *vt* **-1.** ~ **algo (a alguien)** [gen] to impose sthg (on sb); [respeto] to command sthg (from sb); **el profesor impuso silencio en la clase** the teacher silenced the class. **-2.** [moda] to set; [costumbre] to introduce. ◇ *vi* to be imposing.
◆ **imponerse** *vpr* **-1.** [hacerse respetar] to command respect, to show authority. **-2.** [prevalecer] to prevail. **-3.** [asumir - obligación, tarea] to take on. **-4.** [ser necesario] to be necessary. **-5.** DEP to win, to prevail.
imponible → **base**.
impopular *adj* unpopular.
impopularidad *f* unpopularity.
importación *f* [acción] importing; [artículo] import; **de** ~ imported.
importador, **-ra** ◇ *adj* importing (*antes de sust*). ◇ *m y f* importer.
importancia *f* importance; **dar** ~ **a algo** to attach importance to sthg; **de** ~ important, of importance; **quitar** ~ **a algo** to play sthg down; **sin** ~ unimportant; **darse** ~ to give o.s. airs, to show off.
importante *adj* **-1.** [gen] important; [lesión] serious. **-2.** [cantidad] considerable.
importar ◇ *vt* **-1.** [gen & INFORM] to import. **-2.** [suj: factura, coste] to amount to, to come to.
◇ *vi* **-1.** [preocupar] to matter; **no me importa** I don't care, it doesn't matter to me; **¿y a ti qué te importa?** what's it got to do with you?; **me importa un bledo** ○ **comino** ○ **pito** *fam* I don't give a damn, I couldn't care less. **-2.** [en preguntas] to mind; **¿le im-**

porta que me siente? do you mind if I sit down?; **¿te importaría acompañarme?** would you mind coming with me?
◇ *v impers* to matter; **no importa** it doesn't matter; **¡qué importa que llueva!** who cares if it's raining.

importe *m* [gen] price, cost; [de factura] total; ~ **total** total cost.

importunar ◇ *vt* to bother, to pester. ◇ *vi* to be tiresome ○ a nuisance.

importuno, -na = **inoportuno**.

imposibilidad *f* impossibility; **su ~ para contestar la pregunta** his inability to answer the question; ~ **física** physical disability.

imposibilitado, -da *adj* disabled; **estar ~ para hacer algo** to be unable to do sthg.

imposibilitar *vt*: ~ **a alguien para hacer algo** to make it impossible for sb to do sthg, to prevent sb from doing sthg.

imposible ◇ *adj* **-1.** [irrealizable] impossible. **-2.** [insoportable] unbearable, impossible. ◇ *m*: **pedir ~s** to ask for the impossible; **hacer lo ~** to do everything possible and more.

imposición *f* **-1.** [obligación] imposition. **-2.** [impuesto] tax. **-3.** BANCA deposit; **hacer** ○ **efectuar una ~** to make a deposit.

impositivo, -va *adj* tax (*antes de sust*).

impostor, -ra ◇ *adj* [suplantador] fraudulent. ◇ *m y f* [suplantador] impostor.

impostura *f* **-1.** [suplantación] fraud. **-2.** [calumnia] slander.

impotencia *f* impotence.

impotente ◇ *adj* impotent. ◇ *m* impotent man.

impracticable *adj* **-1.** [irrealizable] impracticable. **-2.** [intransitable] impassable.

imprecación *f* imprecation.

imprecar [10] *vt* to imprecate.

imprecatorio, -ria *adj* imprecatory.

imprecisión *f* imprecision, vagueness (*U*).

impreciso, -sa *adj* imprecise, vague.

impredecible *adj* unforeseeable; [variable] unpredictable.

impregnar *vt*: ~ **(de)** to impregnate (with).
◆ **impregnarse** *vpr*: ~**se (de)** to become impregnated (with).

imprememeditación *f* lack of premeditation.

imprememeditado, -da *adj* unpremeditated.

imprenta *f* **-1.** [arte] printing. **-2.** [máquina] (printing) press. **-3.** [establecimiento] printing house.

imprescindible *adj* indispensable, essential.

impresentable *adj* unpresentable.

impresión *f* **-1.** [gen] impression; [sensación física] feeling; **cambiar impresiones** to compare notes, to exchange views; **causar (una) buena/mala ~** to make a good/bad impression; **dar la ~ de** to give the impression of; **tener la ~ de que** to have the impression that. **-2.** [huella] imprint; ~ **digital** ○ **dactilar** fingerprint. **-3.** [IMPRENTA - acción] printing; [- edición] edition.

impresionable *adj* impressionable.

impresionante *adj* impressive; [error] enormous.

impresionar ◇ *vt* **-1.** [maravillar] to impress. **-2.** [conmocionar] to move. **-3.** [horrorizar] to shock. **-4.** FOT to expose. ◇ *vi* **-1.** [maravillar] to make an impression. **-2.** [conmocionar] to be moving. **-3.** [horrorizar] to be shocking.
◆ **impresionarse** *vpr* **-1.** [maravillarse] to be impressed. **-2.** [conmocionarse] to be moved. **-3.** [horrorizarse] to be shocked.

impresionismo *m* impressionism.

impresionista *adj, m y f* impressionist.

impreso, -sa ◇ *pp* → **imprimir**. ◇ *adj* printed.
◆ **impreso** *m* **-1.** [texto] printed sheet, printed matter (*U*). **-2.** [formulario] form.

impresor, -ra ◇ *adj* printing (*antes de sust*). ◇ *m y f* [persona] printer.
◆ **impresora** *f* INFORM printer; **impresora láser/térmica** laser/thermal printer; **impresora de matriz** ○ **de agujas** dot-matrix printer; **impresora de chorro de tinta** ink-jet printer; **impresora de margarita** daisywheel printer.

imprevisible *adj* unforeseeable; [variable] unpredictable.

imprevisión *f* lack of foresight.

imprevisto, -ta *adj* unexpected.
◆ **imprevisto** *m* [hecho] unforeseen circumstance; **salvo ~s** barring accidents.
◆ **imprevistos** *mpl* [gastos] unforeseen expenses.

imprimir ◇ *vt* **-1.** [gen] to print; [huella, paso] to leave, to make. **-2.** *fig* [transmitir]: ~ **algo a** to impart ○ bring sthg to. ◇ *vi* to print.

improbabilidad *f* improbability, unlikelihood.

improbable *adj* improbable, unlikely.

ímprobo, -ba *adj culto* Herculean, strenuous.

improcedencia *f* **-1.** [gen] inappropriateness. **-2.** DER inadmissibility.

improcedente *adj* **-1.** [inoportuno] inappropriate. **-2.** DER inadmissible.

improductivo, **-va** *adj* unproductive.
impronta *f* mark, impression.
impronunciable *adj* unpronounceable.
improperio *m* insult.
impropiedad *f* impropriety.
impropio, **-pia** *adj*: ~ **(de)** improper (for), unbecoming (to).
improrrogable *adj* unable to be extended; [plazo] final.
improvisación *f* improvisation.
improvisado, **-da** *adj* [gen] improvised; [discurso, truco] impromptu; [comentario] adlib; [cama etc] makeshift.
improvisar ◇ *vt* [gen] to improvise; [comida] to rustle up; ~ **una cama** to make (up) a makeshift bed. ◇ *vi* [gen] to improvise; MUS to extemporize.
improviso
◆ **de improviso** *loc adv* unexpectedly, suddenly; **coger a alguien de** ~ to catch sb unawares.
imprudencia *f* [en los actos] carelessness (U); [en los comentarios] indiscretion; ~ **temeraria** DER criminal negligence.
imprudente ◇ *adj* [en los actos] careless, rash; [en los comentarios] indiscreet. ◇ *m y f* [en los actos] rash person; [en los comentarios] indiscreet person.
impúber ◇ *adj* pre-pubescent. ◇ *m y f* pre-pubescent child.
impudicia *f* immodesty.
impúdico, **-ca** *adj* immodest, indecent.
impudor *m* immodesty.
impuesto, **-ta** *pp* → **imponer**.
◆ **impuesto** *m* tax; ~ **al consumo** tax on the consumer; ~ **directo/indirecto** direct/indirect tax; ~ **de lujo** luxury tax; ~ **municipal** local tax; ~ **revolucionario** *fig protection money paid by businessmen to terrorists*; ~ **sobre el capital** capital tax; ~ **sobre el valor añadido** value-added tax; ~ **sobre la renta** ≃ income tax.
impugnable *adj* contestable.
impugnación *f* contestation, challenge.
impugnar *vt* to contest, to challenge.
impulsar *vt* **-1.** [empujar] to propel, to drive. **-2.** [incitar]: ~ **a alguien (a algo/a hacer algo)** to drive sb (to sthg/to do sthg). **-3.** [promocionar] to stimulate.
impulsión *f* impulsion.
impulsivo, **-va** ◇ *adj* impulsive. ◇ *m y f* impulsive person, hothead.
impulso *m* **-1.** [progreso] stimulus, boost. **-2.** [fuerza] momentum; **tomar** ~ to take a run-up. **-3.** [motivación] impulse, urge.

impulsor, **-ra** ◇ *adj* driving (*antes de sust*). ◇ *m y f* dynamic force.
impune *adj* unpunished; **quedar** ~ to go unpunished.
impunemente *adv* with impunity.
impunidad *f* impunity.
impuntualidad *f* unpunctuality.
impureza *f* (*gen pl*) impurity.
impuro, **-ra** *adj lit* & *fig* impure.
impusiera *etc* → **imponer**.
imputabilidad *f* imputability.
imputable *adj*: ~ **a** attributable to.
imputación *f* accusation.
imputar *vt* **-1.** [atribuir]: ~ **algo a alguien** [delito] to accuse sb of sthg; [fracaso, error] to attribute sthg to sb. **-2.** COM to allocate, to assign.
in → **fraganti, vitro**.
inabarcable *adj* unmanageable.
inabordable *adj* inaccessible.
inacabable *adj* interminable, endless.
inacabado, **-da** *adj* unfinished.
inaccesible *adj* inaccessible.
inacción *f* inaction, inactivity.
inaceptable *adj* unacceptable.
inactividad *f* inactivity.
inactivo, **-va** *adj* inactive.
inadaptación *f* maladjustment.
inadaptado, **-da** ◇ *adj* maladjusted. ◇ *m y f* misfit.
inadecuado, **-da** *adj* [inapropiado] unsuitable, inappropriate.
inadmisible *adj* inadmissible.
inadvertido, **-da** *adj* unnoticed; **pasar** ~ to go unnoticed.
inagotable *adj* inexhaustible.
inaguantable *adj* unbearable.
inalámbrico, **-ca** *adj* cordless.
inalcanzable *adj* unattainable.
inalienable *adj* inalienable.
inalterable *adj* **-1.** [gen] unalterable; [salud] stable; [amistad] undying. **-2.** [color] fast. **-3.** [rostro, carácter] impassive. **-4.** [resultado, marcador] unchanged.
inamovible *adj* immovable, fixed.
inane *adj* useless, pointless.
inanición *f* starvation.
inanimado, **-da** *adj* inanimate.
inánime *adj* lifeless.
inapagable *adj* unextinguishable.
inapelable *adj* **-1.** [inevitable] inevitable. **-2.** DER not open to appeal.
inapetencia *f* lack of appetite.
inapetente *adj* lacking in appetite.

inaplazable *adj* [reunión, sesión] that cannot be postponed; [necesidad] urgent, pressing.

inaplicable *adj* inapplicable, not applicable.

inapreciable *adj* **-1.** [incalculable] invaluable, inestimable. **-2.** [insignificante] imperceptible.

inapropiado, -da *adj* inappropriate.

inaptitud *f* unsuitability.

inarrugable *adj* crease-resistant.

inasequible *adj* **-1.** [por el precio] prohibitive. **-2.** [inalcanzable - meta, ambición] unattainable; [- persona] unapproachable.

inatacable *adj* unassailable; *fig* irrefutable.

inaudible *adj* inaudible.

inaudito, -ta *adj* unheard-of.

inauguración *f* inauguration, opening.

inaugurar *vt* to inaugurate, to open.

inca *adj, m y f* Inca.

incaico, -ca *adj* Inca.

incalculable *adj* incalculable.

incalificable *adj* unspeakable, indescribable.

incandescente *adj* incandescent.

incansable *adj* untiring, tireless.

incapacidad *f* **-1.** [imposibilidad] inability. **-2.** [inaptitud] incompetence. **-3.** DER incapacity; ~ **laboral** industrial disablement o disability.

incapacitado, -da ◇ *adj* [DER · gen] disqualified; [- para testar] incapacitated; [- para trabajar] unfit. ◇ *m y f* DER disqualified person, person declared unfit.

incapacitar *vt*: ~ **(para)** [gen] to disqualify (from); [para trabajar etc] to render unfit (for).

incapaz *adj* **-1.** [gen]: ~ **de** incapable of. **-2.** [sin talento]: ~ **para** incompetent at, no good at. **-3.** DER incompetent; **declarar** ~ **a alguien** to declare sb incompetent.

incautación *f* seizure, confiscation.

incautarse
◆ **incautarse de** *vpr* **-1.** DER to seize, to confiscate. **-2.** [apoderarse de] to grab.

incauto, -ta ◇ *adj* gullible. ◇ *m y f* gullible person.

incendiar [8] *vt* to set fire to.
◆ **incendiarse** *vpr* to catch fire.

incendiario, -ria ◇ *adj* **-1.** [bomba etc] incendiary. **-2.** *fig* [artículo, libro etc] inflammatory. ◇ *m y f* arsonist, fire-raiser.

incendio *m* fire; ~ **provocado** arson.

incensario *m* censer.

incentivar *vt* to motivate.

incentivo *m* incentive.

incertidumbre *f* uncertainty.

incesante *adj* incessant, ceaseless.

incesto *m* incest.

incestuoso, -sa *adj* incestuous.

incidencia *f* **-1.** [repercusión] impact, effect. **-2.** [suceso] event.

incidental *adj* incidental, chance (*antes de sust*).

incidente *m* incident.

incidir
◆ **incidir en** *vi* **-1.** [incurrir en] to fall into, to lapse into. **-2.** [insistir en] to focus on. **-3.** [influir en] to have an impact on, to affect. **-4.** [suj: rayo] to fall on. **-5.** [suj: cirujano] to make an incision into.

incienso *m* incense.

incierto, -ta *adj* **-1.** [dudoso] uncertain. **-2.** [falso] untrue.

incineración *f* [de cadáver] cremation; [de basura] incineration.

incinerador *m* [para basura] incinerator.

incinerar *vt* [cadáver] to cremate; [basura] to incinerate.

incipiente *adj* incipient; [estado, etapa] early.

incisión *f* incision.

incisivo, -va *adj* **-1.** [instrumento] sharp, cutting. **-2.** *fig* [mordaz] incisive. **-3.** [diente] incisive.
◆ **incisivo** *m* incisor.

inciso, -sa *adj* cut.
◆ **inciso** *m* passing remark.

incitación *f* incitement.

incitante *adj* [instigador] inciting; [provocativo] provocative.

incitar *vt*: ~ **a alguien a algo** [violencia, rebelión etc] to incite sb to sthg; ~ **a alguien a la fuga/venganza** to urge sb to flee/avenge himself; ~ **a alguien a hacer algo** [rebelarse etc] to incite sb to do sthg; [fugarse, vengarse] to urge sb to do sthg.

incívico, -ca *adj* antisocial.

inclasificable *adj* unclassifiable.

inclemencia *f* harshness, inclemency.

inclemente *adj* harsh, inclement.

inclinación *f* **-1.** [desviación] slant, inclination; [de terreno] slope. **-2.** *fig* [afición]: ~ **(a** o **por)** penchant o propensity (for). **-3.** [cariño]: ~ **hacia alguien** fondness towards sb. **-4.** [saludo] bow.

inclinar *vt* **-1.** [doblar] to bend; [ladear] to tilt. **-2.** [cabeza] to bow. **-3.** [influir]: ~ **a alguien a hacer algo** to persuade sb to do sthg.
◆ **inclinarse** *vpr* **-1.** [doblarse] to lean. **-2.** [para saludar]: ~**se (ante)** to bow (before).

◆ **inclinarse a** *vi* [tender a] to be ○ feel inclined to.

◆ **inclinarse por** *vi* [preferir] to favour, to lean towards.

incluir [51] *vt* [gen] to include; [adjuntar - en cartas] to enclose.

inclusa → **incluso**.

inclusión *f* inclusion.

inclusive *adv* inclusive.

incluso, -sa *adj* enclosed.

◆ **incluso** *adv & prep* even.

◆ **inclusa** *f* foundling hospital.

incógnito, -ta *adj* unknown.

◆ **incógnita** *f* **-1.** MAT unknown quantity. **-2.** [misterio] mystery.

◆ **de incógnito** *loc adv* incognito.

incoherencia *f* **-1.** [cualidad] incoherence. **-2.** [comentario] nonsensical remark.

incoherente *adj* **-1.** [inconexo] incoherent. **-2.** [inconsecuente] inconsistent.

incoloro, -ra *adj lit & fig* colourless.

incólume *adj culto* unscathed.

incombustible *adj* fire-resistant.

incomestible, incomible *adj* inedible.

incomodar *vt* **-1.** [causar molestia] to bother, to inconvenience. **-2.** [enfadar] to annoy.

◆ **incomodarse** *vpr* [enfadarse]: ~**se (por)** to get annoyed (about).

incomodidad *f* **-1.** [de silla etc] uncomfortableness. **-2.** [de situación, persona] awkwardness, discomfort. **-3.** [molestia - de visita etc] inconvenience.

incómodo, -da *adj* **-1.** [silla etc] uncomfortable. **-2.** [situación, persona] awkward, uncomfortable; **sentirse** ~ to feel awkward ○ uncomfortable. **-3.** [visita] inconvenient.

incomparable *adj* incomparable.

incomparecencia *f* failure to appear (in court).

incompatibilidad *f* incompatibility.

incompatible *adj*: ~ **(con)** incompatible (with).

incompetencia *f* incompetence.

incompetente *adj* incompetent.

incompleto, -ta *adj* **-1.** [gen] incomplete. **-2.** [inacabado] unfinished.

incomprendido, -da ◇ *adj* misunderstood. ◇ *m y f* misunderstood person.

incomprensible *adj* incomprehensible.

incomprensión *f* lack of understanding.

incomprensivo, -va *adj* unsympathetic.

incompresible *adj* incompressible.

incomunicación *f* **-1.** [gen] lack of communication. **-2.** [de detenido] solitary confinement. **-3.** [de una localidad] isolation.

incomunicado, -da *adj* **-1.** [gen] isolated. **-2.** [por la nieve etc] cut off. **-3.** [preso] in solitary confinement.

incomunicar [10] *vt* [gen] to cut off; [detenido] to place in solitary confinement.

inconcebible *adj* inconceivable.

inconciliable *adj* irreconcilable.

inconcluso, -sa *adj* unfinished.

incondicional ◇ *adj* unconditional; [ayuda] wholehearted; [seguidor] staunch. ◇ *m y f* staunch supporter.

inconexo, -xa *adj* [gen] unconnected; [pensamiento, texto] disjointed.

inconfesable *adj* shameful.

inconformismo *m* nonconformism.

inconformista *adj, m y f* nonconformist.

inconfundible *adj* unmistakable; [prueba] irrefutable.

incongruencia *f* incongruity; **hacer/decir una** ~ to do/say sthg incongruous.

incongruente *adj* incongruous.

inconmensurable *adj* immeasurable; [espacio] vast.

inconquistable *adj* unassailable, impregnable.

inconsciencia *f* **-1.** [gen] unconsciousness. **-2.** *fig* [falta de juicio] thoughtlessness.

inconsciente ◇ *adj* **-1.** [gen] unconscious. **-2.** *fig* [irreflexivo] thoughtless. ◇ *m y f* thoughtless person. ◇ *m* PSICOL: **el** ~ the unconscious.

inconsecuencia *f* inconsistency.

inconsecuente ◇ *adj* inconsistent. ◇ *m y f* inconsistent person.

inconsistencia *f* [de tela, pared etc] flimsiness; [de una salsa] runniness; [de argumento, discurso etc] lack of substance.

inconsistente *adj* [tela, pared etc] flimsy; [salsa] runny; [argumento, discurso etc] lacking in substance.

inconsolable *adj* disconsolate.

inconstancia *f* **-1.** [en el trabajo, la conducta] unreliability. **-2.** [de opinión, ideas] changeability.

inconstante *adj* **-1.** [en el trabajo, la conducta] unreliable. **-2.** [de opinión, ideas] changeable.

inconstitucional *adj* unconstitutional.

inconstitucionalidad *f* unconstitutionality.

incontable *adj* [innumerable] countless.

incontenible *adj* [alegría] unbounded; [llanto] uncontrollable; [dolor] unbearable.

incontestable *adj* indisputable, undeniable.

incontinencia f -1. [vicio] lack of restraint. -2. MED incontinence.

incontinente adj -1. [insaciable] lacking all restraint. -2. MED incontinent.

incontrolable adj uncontrollable.

incontrolado, -da adj [velocidad] furious; [situación] out of hand; [comando] maverick, not controlled by the leadership; [aumento de precios etc] spiralling.

incontrovertible adj incontrovertible, indisputable.

inconveniencia f -1. [inoportunidad] inappropriateness. -2. [comentario] tactless remark, faux pas; [acto] mistake.

inconveniente ◇ adj -1. [inoportuno] inappropriate. -2. [descortés] rude. ◇ m -1. [dificultad] obstacle, problem; **no tener ~ en hacer algo** to have no objection to doing sthg. -2. [desventaja] disadvantage, drawback.

incordiar [8] vt fam to bother, to pester.

incordio m fam pain, nuisance.

incorporación f: ~ **(a)** [gen] incorporation (into); [a un puesto] induction (into).

incorporado, -da adj TECN built-in.

incorporar vt -1. [añadir]: ~ **(a)** [gen] to incorporate (into); CULIN to mix (into). -2. [anexionar]: ~ **a** to annex as part of. -3. [levantar] to sit up.
◆ **incorporarse** vpr -1. [empezar]: ~**se (a)** [equipo] to join; [trabajo] to start. -2. [levantarse] to sit up.

incorpóreo, -a adj incorporeal, intangible.

incorrección f -1. [inexactitud] incorrectness; [error gramatical] mistake. -2. [descortesía] lack of courtesy, rudeness (U).

incorrecto, -ta adj -1. [equivocado] incorrect, wrong. -2. [descortés] rude, impolite.

incorregible adj incorrigible.

incorruptible adj -1. [substancia] imperishable. -2. fig [persona] incorruptible.

incorrupto, -ta adj [cadáver] uncorrupted, not decomposed.

incredulidad f incredulity.

incrédulo, -la ◇ adj sceptical, incredulous; RELIG unbelieving. ◇ m y f unbeliever.

increíble adj -1. [difícil de creer] unconvincing, lacking credibility. -2. fig [extraordinario] incredible. -3. fig [inconcebible] unbelievable; **es ~ que pasen cosas así** it's hard to believe that such things can happen.

incrementar vt to increase.
◆ **incrementarse** vpr to increase.

incremento m increase; [de temperatura] rise.

increpar vt -1. [reprender] to reprimand. -2. [insultar] to abuse, insult.

incriminación f accusation.

incriminar vt to accuse.

incruento, -ta adj bloodless.

incrustación f inlay.

incrustar vt -1. TECN to inlay; [en joyería] to set. -2. fam fig [empotrar]: ~ **algo en algo** to sink sthg into sthg.
◆ **incrustarse** vpr [cal etc] to become encrusted.

incubación f incubation; ~ **artificial** artificial incubation.

incubadora f incubator.

incubar vt -1. [huevo] to incubate. -2. [enfermedad] to be sickening for.

incuestionable adj [teoría, razón] irrefutable; [deber] bounden.

inculcar [10] vt: ~ **algo a alguien** to instil sthg into sb.

inculpación f accusation; JUR charge.

inculpado, -da ◇ adj accused; JUR charged. ◇ m y f accused.

inculpar vt: ~ **a alguien (de)** [gen] to accuse sb (of); DER to charge sb (with).

inculto, -ta ◇ adj -1. [persona] uneducated. -2. [tierra] uncultivated. ◇ m y f ignoramus.

incultura f lack of education.

incumbencia f: **es/no es de nuestra ~** it is/isn't a matter for us, it falls/doesn't fall within our area of responsibility; **no es asunto de tu ~** it's none of your business.

incumbir
◆ **incumbir a** vi: ~ **a alguien** to be a matter for sb, to be within sb's area of responsibility; **esto no te incumbe** this is none of your business.

incumplimiento m [de deber] failure to fulfil; [de orden, ley] non-compliance; [de promesa] failure to keep; ~ **de contrato** breach of contract.

incumplir vt [deber] to fail to fulfil, to neglect; [orden, ley] to fail to comply with; [promesa] to break; [contrato] to breach.

incunable ◇ adj incunabular. ◇ m incunabulum.

incurable adj incurable.

incurrir
◆ **incurrir en** vi -1. [delito, falta] to commit; [error] to make. -2. [desprecio etc] to incur.

incursión f incursion.

indagación f investigation, inquiry.

indagar [16] ◇ vt to investigate, to inquire into. ◇ vi to investigate, to inquire.

indebido, -da adj -1. [incorrecto] improper. -2. [ilegal] unlawful, illegal.

indecencia f **-1.** [cualidad] indecency. **-2.** [acción] outrage, crime.

indecente adj **-1.** [impúdico] indecent. **-2.** [indigno] miserable, wretched.

indecible adj [alegría] indescribable; [dolor] unspeakable.

indecisión f indecisiveness.

indeciso, -sa adj **-1.** [persona - inseguro] indecisive; [- que está dudoso] undecided, unsure. **-2.** [pregunta, respuesta] hesitant; [resultado] undecided.

indecoroso, -sa adj unseemly.

indefectible adj culto unfailing.

indefensión f defencelessness.

indefenso, -sa adj defenceless.

indefinible adj indefinable; [edad] uncertain.

indefinido, -da adj **-1.** [ilimitado] indefinite; [contrato] open-ended. **-2.** [impreciso] vague. **-3.** GRAM indefinite.

indeleble adj culto indelible.

indemne adj unhurt, unharmed.

indemnidad f culto indemnity.

indemnización f [gen] compensation; [por despido] severance pay; ~ **por daños y perjuicios** DER damages (pl).

indemnizar [13] vt: ~ **a alguien (por)** to compensate sb (for).

indemostrable adj unprovable.

independencia f independence; **con ~ de** independently of.

independentismo m independence movement.

independentista ◇ adj advocating independence. ◇ m y f supporter of independence.

independiente adj **-1.** [gen] independent. **-2.** [aparte] separate.

independizar [13] vt to grant independence to.
◆ **independizarse** vpr: ~**se (de)** to become independent (of).

indescifrable adj [gen] indecipherable; [misterio] inexplicable, impenetrable.

indescriptible adj indescribable.

indeseable adj undesirable.

indestructible adj indestructible.

indeterminación f indecisiveness.

indeterminado, -da adj **-1.** [sin determinar] indeterminate; **por tiempo ~** indefinitely. **-2.** [impreciso] vague. **-3.** GRAM → **artículo**.

indexación f INFORM indexing.

indexar vt INFORM to index.

India: (la) ~ India.

indiano, -na ◇ adj (Latin American) Indian. ◇ m y f **-1.** [indígena] (Latin Ameri-

can) Indian. **-2.** [emigrante] Spanish emigrant to Latin America who returned to Spain having made his fortune.

indicación f **-1.** [señal, gesto] sign, signal. **-2.** (gen pl) [instrucción] instruction; [para llegar a un sitio] directions (pl). **-3.** [nota, corrección] note.

indicado, -da adj suitable, appropriate.

indicador, -ra adj indicating (antes de sust).
◆ **indicador** m [gen] indicator; TECN gauge, meter; ~ **económico** economic indicator.

indicar [10] vt **-1.** [señalar] to indicate; [suj: aguja etc] to read. **-2.** [explicar] to tell, to explain to. **-3.** [prescribir] to prescribe.

indicativo, -va adj indicative.
◆ **indicativo** m GRAM indicative.

índice m **-1.** [gen] index; [proporción] level, rate; ~ **bursátil** stock market index; ~ **del coste de la vida** cost of living index; ~ **de natalidad** birth rate; ~ **de precios al consumo** retail price index. **-2.** [señal] sign, indicator; ~ **económico** economic indicator. **-3.** [catálogo] catalogue. **-4.** [dedo] index finger.

indicio m sign; [pista] clue; [cantidad pequeña] trace.

Índico m: **el (océano)** ~ the Indian Ocean.

indiferencia f indifference.

indiferente adj indifferent; **me es** ~ [me da igual] I don't mind, it's all the same to me; [no me interesa] I'm not interested in it.

indígena ◇ adj indigenous, native. ◇ m y f native.

indigencia f culto destitution, poverty.

indigente ◇ adj destitute, poor. ◇ m y f poor person.

indigestarse vpr to get indigestion; **se me ha indigestado esa chica** fam fig I can't stomach that girl.

indigestión f indigestion.

indigesto, -ta adj indigestible; fam fig [pesado] stodgy, heavy.

indignación f indignation.

indignante adj shocking, outrageous.

indignar vt to anger.
◆ **indignarse** vpr: ~**se (por)** to get angry o indignant (about).

indigno, -na adj **-1.** [gen]: ~ **(de)** unworthy (of). **-2.** [impropio] not fitting, wrong. **-3.** [vergonzoso] contemptible, shameful.

indio, -dia ◇ adj Indian. ◇ m y f Indian; **hacer el** ~ to play the fool.

indique etc → **indicar**.

indirecto, -ta adj indirect.
◆ **indirecta** f hint; **lanzar una indirecta a alguien** to drop a hint to sb.

indisciplina f indiscipline.
indisciplinado, -da ◇ adj undisciplined. ◇ m y f undisciplined person.
indiscreción f -1. [cualidad] indiscretion. -2. [comentario] indiscreet remark; **si no es ~** if you don't mind my asking.
indiscreto, -ta ◇ adj indiscreet. ◇ m y f indiscreet person.
indiscriminado, -da adj indiscriminate.
indiscutible adj [gen] indisputable; [poder] undisputed.
indisolubilidad f indissolubility.
indisoluble adj -1. [substancia] insoluble. -2. [unión, ley] indissoluble.
indispensable adj indispensable, essential.
indisponer [65] vt -1. [enfermar] to make ill, to upset. -2. [enemistar] to set at odds.
indisposición f -1. [malestar] indisposition. -2. [reticencia] unwillingness.
indispuesto, -ta ◇ pp → indisponer. ◇ adj indisposed, unwell.
indistinto, -ta adj -1. [indiferente]: **es ~** it doesn't matter, it makes no difference. -2. [cuenta, cartilla] joint. -3. [perfil, figura] indistinct, blurred.
individual adj -1. [gen] individual; [habitación, cama] single; [despacho] personal. -2. [prueba, competición] singles (antes de sust).
◆ **individuales** mpl DEP singles.
individualidad f individuality.
individualismo m individualism.
individualista ◇ adj individualistic. ◇ m y f individualist.
individualizar [13] vi to single people out.
individuo, -dua m y f person; despec individual.
indivisibilidad f indivisibility.
indivisible adj indivisible.
indiviso, -sa adj undivided.
indochino, -na adj, m y f Indochinese.
indocumentado, -da ◇ adj -1. [sin documentación] without identity papers. -2. [ignorante] ignorant. ◇ m y f [ignorante] ignoramus.
indoeuropeo, -a adj Indo-European.
◆ **indoeuropeo** m [lengua] Indo-European.
índole f [naturaleza] nature; [tipo] type, kind.
indolencia f indolence, laziness.
indolente adj culto indolent, lazy.
indoloro, -ra adj painless.
indomable adj -1. [animal] untameable. -2. [carácter] rebellious; [pueblo] unruly.
indómito, -ta adj -1. [animal] untameable. -2. [carácter] rebellious; [pueblo] unruly.
Indonesia Indonesia.

indonesio, -sia adj, m y f Indonesian.
◆ **indonesio** m [lengua] Indonesian.
inducción f -1. [gen & FÍS] induction. -2. [incitación] instigation.
inducir [33] vt -1. [incitar]: **~ a alguien a algo/a hacer algo** to lead sb into sthg/into doing sthg; **~ a error** to mislead. -2. [deducir] to infer. -3. FÍS to induce.
inductor, -ra adj instigating.
◆ **inductor** m inductor.
indudable adj undoubted; **es ~ que ...** there is no doubt that ....
indujera etc → inducir.
indulgencia f indulgence; **~ plenaria** plenary indulgence.
indulgente adj indulgent.
indultar vt to pardon.
indulto m pardon.
indumentaria f attire.
industria f -1. [gen] industry; **~ automotriz/pesada/punta** motor/heavy/sunrise industry. -2. [fábrica] factory.
industrial ◇ adj industrial. ◇ m y f industrialist.
industrialismo m industrialism.
industrialización f industrialization.
industrializar [13] vt to industrialize.
◆ **industrializarse** vpr to become industrialized.
industrioso, -sa adj industrious.
induzca etc → inducir.
INE (abrev de **Instituto Nacional de Estadística**) m organization that publishes official statistics about Spain, ≃ HMSO Br.
inédito, -ta adj -1. [no publicado] unpublished. -2. [sorprendente] unheard-of, unprecedented.
INEF (abrev de **Instituto Nacional de Educación Física**) m Spanish university for training physical education teachers.
inefable adj ineffable, inexpressible.
ineficacia f -1. [bajo rendimiento] inefficiency. -2. [baja efectividad] ineffectiveness.
ineficaz adj -1. [de bajo rendimiento] inefficient. -2. [de baja efectividad] ineffective.
ineficiencia f -1. [bajo rendimiento] inefficiency. -2. [baja efectividad] ineffectiveness.
ineficiente adj -1. [de bajo rendimiento] inefficient. -2. [de baja efectividad] ineffective.
ineluctable adj inevitable, inescapable.
ineludible adj unavoidable.
INEM (abrev de **Instituto Nacional de Empleo**) m Spanish department of employment.
inenarrable adj spectacular.
ineptitud f ineptitude.

inepto, -ta ◇ *adj* inept. ◇ *m y f* inept person.

inequívoco, -ca *adj* [apoyo, resultado] unequivocal; [señal, voz] unmistakeable.

inercia *f lit* & *fig* inertia.

inerme *adj* [sin armas] unarmed; [sin defensa] defenceless.

inerte *adj* **-1.** [materia] inert. **-2.** [cuerpo, cadáver] lifeless.

inescrutable *adj* **-1.** [persona, rostro] inscrutable. **-2.** [misterio, verdad] impenetrable.

inesperado, -da *adj* unexpected.

inestabilidad *f* instability.

inestable *adj lit* & *fig* unstable.

inestimable *adj* inestimable, invaluable.

inevitable *adj* inevitable.

inexactitud *f* inaccuracy.

inexacto, -ta *adj* **-1.** [impreciso] inaccurate. **-2.** [erróneo] incorrect, wrong.

inexcusable *adj* **-1.** [imperdonable] inexcusable. **-2.** [ineludible] unavoidable.

inexistencia *f* nonexistence.

inexistente *adj* nonexistent.

inexorabilidad *f* inexorability.

inexorable *adj* **-1.** [inevitable] inexorable. **-2.** [inflexible] unyielding.

inexperiencia *f* inexperience.

inexperto, -ta ◇ *adj* **-1.** [falto de experiencia] inexperienced. **-2.** [falto de habilidad] unskilful, inexpert. ◇ *m y f* person without experience.

inexplicable *adj* inexplicable.

inexpresivo, -va *adj* expressionless.

inexpugnable *adj* unassailable, impregnable.

inextinguible *adj* [fuego] unquenchable; [sentimiento] undying.

inextricable *adj* intricate.

infalibilidad *f* infallibility.

infalible *adj* infallible.

infamar *vt culto* to defame.

infame *adj* vile, base.

infamia *f* **-1.** [deshonra] infamy, disgrace. **-2.** [mala acción] vile ○ base deed.

infancia *f* **-1.** [periodo] childhood. **-2.** [todos los niños] children (*pl*).

infante, -ta *m y f* **-1.** [niño] infant. **-2.** [hijo del rey] infante (*f* infanta), prince (*f* princess).
◆ **infante** *m* [soldado] infantryman.

infantería *f* infantry; ~ **de marina** marines (*pl*); ~ **ligera** light infantry.

infanticida ◇ *adj* infanticidal. ◇ *m y f* infanticide, child-murderer.

infanticidio *m* infanticide.

infantil *adj* **-1.** [para niños] children's; [de niños] child (*antes de sust*). **-2.** *fig* [inmaduro] infantile, childish.

infantilismo *m* infantilism.

infarto *m*: ~ **(de miocardio)** heart attack.

infatigable *adj* indefatigable, tireless.

infatuación *f* vanity.

infatuar [6] *vt* to make conceited.

infausto, -ta *adj* ill-starred.

infección *f* infection.

infeccioso, -sa *adj* infectious.

infectar *vt* to infect.
◆ **infectarse** *vpr* to become infected.

infecto, -ta *adj* **-1.** [agua, carroña] putrid. **-2.** [población, zona] infected. **-3.** *fig* [desagradable] foul, terrible.

infecundo, -da *adj* **-1.** [tierra] infertile. **-2.** [mujer] sterile.

infelicidad *f* unhappiness.

infeliz ◇ *adj* **-1.** [desgraciado] unhappy. **-2.** *fig* [ingenuo] gullible. ◇ *m y f* [ingenuo] gullible person; **un pobre** ~ a poor wretch.

inferior ◇ *adj*: ~ **(a)** [en espacio, cantidad] lower (than); [en calidad] inferior (to); **una cifra** ~ **a 100** a figure under ○ below 100. ◇ *m y f* inferior.

inferioridad *f* inferiority; **estar en** ~ **de condiciones** to be at a disadvantage.

inferir [27] *vt* **-1.** [deducir]: ~ **(de)** to deduce (from), to infer (from). **-2.** [ocasionar - herida] to inflict; [- mal] to cause.

infernal *adj lit* & *fig* infernal.

infestar *vt* to infest; [suj: carteles, propaganda etc] to be plastered across.

infidelidad *f* [conyugal] infidelity, unfaithfulness; [a la patria, un amigo] disloyalty.

infiel ◇ *adj* **-1.** [desleal - cónyuge] unfaithful; [- amigo] disloyal. **-2.** [inexacto] inaccurate, unfaithful. ◇ *m y f* RELIG infidel.

infiera *etc* → **inferir**.

infiernillo *m* portable stove.

infierno *m lit* & *fig* hell; **en el quinto** ~ in the middle of nowhere; **¡vete al** ~! go to hell!

infiltración *f* **-1.** [de líquido] seeping. **-2.** [de persona, ideas] infiltration.

infiltrado, -da ◇ *adj* infiltrated. ◇ *m y f* infiltrator.

infiltrar *vt* **-1.** [inyectar] to inject. **-2.** *fig* [ideas] to infiltrate.
◆ **infiltrarse en** *vpr* to infiltrate.

ínfimo, -ma *adj* [calidad, categoría] extremely low; [precio] giveaway, knockdown; [importancia] minimal.

infinidad *f*: **una ~ de** an infinite number of; *fig* masses of; **en ~ de ocasiones** on countless occasions.

infinitesimal *adj* infinitesimal.

infinitivo, -va *adj* infinitive.

◆ **infinitivo** *m* infinitive.

infinito, -ta *adj lit* & *fig* infinite; **infinitas veces** hundreds of times.

◆ **infinito** ◇ *m* infinity. ◇ *adv* [mucho] extremely, infinitely.

infiriera *etc* → **inferir**.

inflación *f* ECON inflation.

inflacionario, -ria, inflacionista *adj* inflationary.

inflamable *adj* inflammable, flammable.

inflamación *f* MED inflammation.

inflamar *vt* **-1.** MED & *fig* to inflame. **-2.** [encender] to set alight.

◆ **inflamarse** *vpr* [hincharse] to become inflamed.

inflamatorio, -ria *adj* inflammatory.

inflar *vt* **-1.** [soplando] to blow up, to inflate; [con bomba] to pump up. **-2.** *fig* [exagerar] to blow up, to exaggerate.

◆ **inflarse** *vpr*: **~se (de)** [hartarse] to stuff o.s. (with).

inflexibilidad *f lit* & *fig* inflexibility.

inflexible *adj lit* & *fig* inflexible.

inflexión *f* inflection.

infligir [15] *vt* to inflict; [castigo] to impose.

influencia *f* influence.

influenciar [8] *vt* to influence, to have an influence on.

influenza *f* influenza.

influir [51] ◇ *vt* to influence. ◇ *vi* to have influence; **~ en** to influence, to have an influence on.

influjo *m* influence.

influyente *adj* influential.

información *f* **-1.** [conocimiento] information; **para tu ~** for your information. **-2.** [PRENS - noticias] news (U); [- noticia] report, piece of news; [- sección] section, news (U); **~ meteorológica** weather report o forecast. **-3.** [oficina] information office; [mostrador] information desk. **-4.** TELECOM directory enquiries (pl) *Br*, directory assistance *Am*.

informador, -ra ◇ *adj* informing, reporting. ◇ *m y f* reporter.

informal *adj* **-1.** [desenfadado] informal. **-2.** [irresponsable] unreliable.

informalidad *f* **-1.** [desenfado] informality. **-2.** [irresponsabilidad] unreliability.

informante ◇ *adj* informing. ◇ *m y f* informant, informer.

informar ◇ *vt*: **~ a alguien (de)** to inform o tell sb (about). ◇ *vi* to inform; PRENS to report.

◆ **informarse** *vpr* to find out (details); **~se de** to find out about.

informático, -ca ◇ *adj* computer (antes de sust). ◇ *m y f* [persona] computer expert.

◆ **informática** *f* [ciencia] information technology, computing.

informativo, -va *adj* **-1.** [instructivo, esclarecedor] informative. **-2.** [que da noticias] news (antes de sust); [que da información] information (antes de sust).

◆ **informativo** *m* news (bulletin).

informatización *f* computerization.

informatizar [13] *vt* to computerize.

informe ◇ *adj* shapeless. ◇ *m* **-1.** [gen] report. **-2.** DER plea.

◆ **informes** *mpl* [gen] information (U); [sobre comportamiento] report (sg); [para un empleo] references.

infortunado, -da ◇ *adj* unfortunate, unlucky; [encuentro, conversación] ill-fated. ◇ *m y f* unfortunate o unlucky person.

infortunio *m* misfortune, bad luck (U).

infracción *f* infringement; [de circulación] offence.

infractor, -ra ◇ *adj* offending. ◇ *m y f* offender.

infraestructura *f* **-1.** [de organización] infrastructure. **-2.** [de construcción] foundations (pl).

infrahumano, -na *adj* subhuman.

infranqueable *adj* impassable; *fig* insurmountable.

infrarrojo, -ja *adj* infrared.

infrautilizar [13] *vt* to underuse.

infravalorar *vt* to undervalue, to underestimate.

infrecuente *adj* infrequent.

infringir [15] *vt* [quebrantar] to infringe, to break.

infructuoso, -sa *adj* fruitless, unsuccessful.

ínfulas *fpl* pretensions, presumption (U).

infumable *adj* unsmokable; *fam fig* unbearable, intolerable.

infundado, -da *adj* unfounded.

infundio *m culto* untruth, lie.

infundir *vt*: **~ algo a alguien** to fill sb with sthg, to inspire sthg in sb; **~ miedo** to inspire fear.

infusión *f* infusion; **~ de manzanilla** camomile tea.

infuso, -sa *adj* inspired.

ingeniar [8] *vt* to invent, to devise.

◆ **ingeniarse** *vpr*: **ingeniárselas** to manage, to engineer it; **ingeniárselas para hacer algo** to manage ○ contrive to do sthg.

ingeniería *f* engineering; ~ **genética** genetic engineering.

ingeniero, -ra *m y f* engineer; ~ **agrónomo** agronomist; ~ **de caminos, canales y puertos** civil engineer; ~ **industrial/de telecomunicaciones** industrial/telecommunications engineer; ~ **de sistemas/sonido** systems/sound engineer.

ingenio *m* -1. [inteligencia] ingenuity; **aguzar el** ~ to sharpen one's wits. -2. [agudeza] wit, wittiness. -3. [máquina] device.

ingenioso, -sa *adj* [inteligente] ingenious, clever; [agudo] witty.

ingente *adj* enormous, huge.

ingenuidad *f* ingenuousness, naivety.

ingenuo, -nua ○ *adj* ingenuous, naive. ○ *m y f* ingenuous ○ naive person.

ingerencia = injerencia.

ingerir [27] *vt* to consume, to ingest.

ingestión *f* consumption.

ingiera *etc*, **ingiriera** *etc* → ingerir.

Inglaterra England.

ingle *f* groin.

inglés, -esa ○ *adj* English. ○ *m y f* [persona] Englishman (*f* Englishwoman); **los ingleses** the English.

◆ **inglés** *m* [lengua] English.

ingobernable *adj* [país] ungovernable; [niño] uncontrollable, unmanageable.

ingratitud *f* ingratitude, ungratefulness.

ingrato, -ta *adj* ungrateful; [trabajo] thankless.

ingravidez *f* weightlessness.

ingrávido, -da *adj* weightless.

ingrediente *m* ingredient.

ingresar ○ *vt* BANCA to deposit, to pay in. ○ *vi*: ~ **(en)** [asociación, ejército] to join; [hospital] to be admitted (to); [convento, universidad] to enter; ~ **cadáver** to be dead on arrival.

ingreso *m* -1. [gen] entry; [en asociación, ejército] joining; [en hospital, universidad] admission. -2. BANCA deposit.

◆ **ingresos** *mpl* -1. [sueldo etc] income (*U*); ~**s brutos/netos** gross/net income. -2. [recaudación] revenue (*U*).

inhábil *adj* -1. [torpe] clumsy, unskilful. -2. [incapacitado - por defecto físico] unfit; [- por la edad] disqualified. -3. [festivo]: **día** ~ *weekend day or public holiday*.

inhabilitación *f* disqualification; [minusvalía] disablement.

inhabilitar *vt* to disqualify.

inhabitable *adj* uninhabitable.

inhabitado, -da *adj* uninhabited.

inhalación *f* inhalation.

inhalador *m* inhaler.

inhalar *vt* to inhale.

inherente *adj*: ~ **(a)** inherent (in).

inhibición *f* inhibition.

inhibir *vt* to inhibit.

◆ **inhibirse de** *vpr* [gen] to keep out of, to stay away from; [responsabilidades] to avoid, to shirk.

inhóspito, -ta *adj* inhospitable.

inhumano, -na *adj* [despiadado] inhuman; [desconsiderado] inhumane.

inhumar *vt* to inter, to bury.

INI (*abrev de* **Instituto Nacional de Industria**) *m Spanish governmental organization that promotes industry.*

iniciación *f* -1. [gen] initiation. -2. [de suceso, curso] start, beginning.

iniciado, -da ○ *adj* started; [neófito] initiated. ○ *m y f* initiate.

inicial *adj & f* initial.

inicialización *f* INFORM initialization.

inicializar [13] *vt* INFORM to initialize.

iniciar [8] *vt* [gen] to start, to initiate; [debate, discusión] to start off; ~ **a alguien en** to initiate sb into.

iniciativa *f* initiative; **tomar la** ~ to take the initiative; ~ **privada** private enterprise.

inicio *m* start, beginning.

inicuo, -cua *adj* iniquitous.

inigualable *adj* unrivalled.

inigualado, -da *adj* unequalled.

inimaginable *adj* unimaginable.

inimitable *adj* inimitable.

ininteligible *adj* unintelligible.

ininterrumpido, -da *adj* uninterrupted, continuous.

iniquidad *f* iniquity.

INIT (*abrev de* **Instituto Nacional de Ingenieros Técnicos**) *m Spanish professional body of engineers.*

injerencia, ingerencia *f* interference, meddling.

injerir [27] *vt* to introduce, to insert.

◆ **injerirse** *vpr* [entrometerse]: ~**se (en)** to interfere (in), to meddle (in).

injertar *vt* to graft.

injerto *m* graft.

injiera, injiriera *etc* → injerir.

injuria *f* [insulto] insult, abuse (*U*); [agravio] offence; DER slander.

injuriar [8] *vt* [insultar] to insult, to abuse; [agraviar] to offend; DER to slander.

injurioso, -sa *adj* insulting, abusive; DER slanderous.

injusticia *f* injustice.

injustificado, -da *adj* unjustified.

injusto, -ta *adj* unfair, unjust.

INM (*abrev de* **Instituto Nacional de Meteorología**) *m Spanish meteorology institute,* ≈ Weather Centre *Br.*

inmaculado, -da *adj* immaculate.

◆ **Inmaculada** *f*: **la Inmaculada** the Virgin Mary.

inmadurez *f* immaturity.

inmaduro, -ra *adj* **-1.** [fruta] unripe. **-2.** [persona] immature.

inmaterial *adj* immaterial.

inmediaciones *fpl* [de localidad] surrounding area (*sg*); [de lugar, casa] vicinity (*sg*).

inmediatamente *adv* immediately, at once.

inmediatez *f* immediateness, immediacy.

inmediato, -ta *adj* **-1.** [gen] immediate; **de** ~ immediately, at once. **-2.** [contiguo] next, adjoining.

inmejorable *adj* unbeatable, that cannot be bettered.

inmemorial *adj* immemorial.

inmensidad *f* **-1.** [grandeza] immensity. **-2.** [multitud] huge amount, sea.

inmenso, -sa *adj* **-1.** [gen] immense. **-2.** *fig* [profundo] deep.

inmerecido, -da *adj* undeserved.

inmersión *f* immersion; [de submarinista] dive.

inmerso, -sa *adj*: ~ **(en)** immersed (in).

inmigración *f* immigration.

inmigrante *m y f* immigrant.

inmigrar *vi* to immigrate.

inminencia *f* imminence.

inminente *adj* imminent, impending.

inmiscuirse [51] *vpr*: ~ **(en)** to interfere o meddle (in).

inmobiliario, -ria *adj* property (*antes de sust*), real estate *Am* (*antes de sust*).

◆ **inmobiliaria** *f* **-1.** [agencia] estate agency *Br*, real estate agent *Am*. **-2.** [constructora] construction company.

inmolación *f* immolation, sacrifice.

inmolar *vt* to immolate, to sacrifice.

inmoral *adj* immoral.

inmortal *adj* immortal.

inmortalidad *f* immortality.

inmortalizar [13] *vt* to immortalize.

inmóvil *adj* motionless, still; [coche, tren] stationary.

inmovilidad *f* immobility.

inmovilismo *m* defence of the status quo.

inmovilizado, -da ◇ *adj* immobilized; [pierna, brazo] immobile. ◇ *m* ECON fixed assets (*pl*).

inmovilizar [13] *vt* to immobilize.

inmueble ◇ *adj*: **bienes ~s** real estate (*U*). ◇ *m* [edificio] building.

inmundicia *f* [suciedad] filth, filthiness; [basura] rubbish.

inmundo, -da *adj* filthy, dirty.

inmune *adj* **-1.** MED immune. **-2.** [exento] exempt.

inmunidad *f* immunity; ~ **diplomática/parlamentaria** diplomatic/parliamentary immunity.

inmunitario, -ria *adj* immune.

inmunizar [13] *vt* to immunize.

inmunodeficiencia *f* MED immunodeficiency.

inmunodepresor, -ra *adj* immunodepressant.

inmunología *f* immunology.

inmunoterapia *f* immunotherapy.

inmutabilidad *f* immutability.

inmutable *adj* immutable, unchangeable.

inmutar *vt* to upset, to perturb.

◆ **inmutarse** *vpr* to get upset, to be perturbed; **ni se inmutó** he didn't bat an eyelid.

innato, -ta *adj* innate.

innecesario, -ria *adj* unnecessary.

innegable *adj* undeniable.

innegociable *adj* unnegotiable, not negotiable.

innoble *adj* ignoble.

innombrable *adj* unmentionable.

innovación *f* innovation.

innovador, -ra ◇ *adj* innovative, innovatory. ◇ *m y f* innovator.

innovar *vt* [método, técnica] to improve on.

innumerable *adj* countless, innumerable.

inobservancia *f* breaking, violation.

inocencia *f* innocence.

inocentada *f* practical joke, trick.

inocente ◇ *adj* **-1.** [gen] innocent. **-2.** [ingenuo - persona] naive, innocent. **-3.** [sin maldad - persona] harmless. ◇ *m y f* innocent person; [sin maldad] harmless person.

inocuidad *f* innocuousness, harmlessness.

inocular *vt* to inoculate.

inocuo, -cua *adj* innocuous, harmless.

inodoro, -ra *adj* odourless.

◆ **inodoro** *m* toilet *Br*, washroom *Am*.

inofensivo, -va *adj* inoffensive, harmless.

inolvidable *adj* unforgettable.

inoperancia *f* ineffectiveness.

inoperante *adj* ineffective.

inopia *f*: **estar en la** ~ to be miles away, to be day-dreaming.

inopinado, -da *adj* unexpected.

inoportuno, -na, importuno, -na *adj* **-1.** [en mal momento] inopportune, untimely. **-2.** [molesto] inconvenient. **-3.** [inadecuado] inappropriate.

inorgánico, -ca *adj* inorganic.

inoxidable *adj* rustproof; [acero] stainless.

input ['imput] (*pl* **inputs**) *m* input (*U*).

inquebrantable *adj* unshakeable; [lealtad] unswerving.

inquiera *etc* → inquirir.

inquietante *adj* worrying.

inquietar *vt* to worry, to trouble.

◆ **inquietarse** *vpr* to worry, to get anxious.

inquieto, -ta *adj* **-1.** [preocupado]: ~ **(por)** worried ○ anxious (about). **-2.** [agitado, emprendedor] restless.

inquietud *f* [preocupación] worry, anxiety.

◆ **inquietudes** *fpl* [afán de saber]: **tener** ~**es** to have an inquiring mind.

inquilino, -na *m y f* tenant.

inquina *f* antipathy, aversion; **tener** ~ **a** to feel aversion towards.

inquirir [22] *vt culto* to inquire into, to investigate.

inquisición *f* [indagación] inquiry, investigation.

◆ **Inquisición** *f* [tribunal] Inquisition.

inquisidor, -ra *adj* inquisitive, inquiring.

◆ **inquisidor** *m* inquisitor.

inquisitivo, -va *adj* inquisitive.

inri *m*: **para más** ~ *fam fig* to add insult to injury, to crown it all.

insaciable *adj* insatiable.

insalubre *adj culto* insalubrious, unhealthy.

insalubridad *f culto* insalubrity, unhealthiness.

Insalud (*abrev de* **Instituto Nacional de la Salud**) *m* ≃ NHS *Br*, ≃ Medicaid *Am*.

insano, -na *adj* [gen] unhealthy; [loco] insane.

insatisfacción *f* dissatisfaction.

insatisfecho, -cha *adj* **-1.** [descontento] dissatisfied. **-2.** [no saciado] not full, unsatisfied.

inscribir *vt* **-1.** [grabar]: ~ **algo (en)** to engrave ○ inscribe sthg (on). **-2.** [apuntar]: ~ **algo/a alguien (en)** to register sthg/sb (on).

◆ **inscribirse** *vpr*: ~**se (en)** [gen] to enrol (on); [asociación] to enrol (with); [concurso] to enter.

inscripción *f* **-1.** EDUC registration, enrolment; [en censo, registro] registration; [en partido etc] enrolment; [en concursos etc] entry. **-2.** [escrito] inscription.

inscrito, -ta *pp* → inscribir.

insecticida ◇ *adj* insecticidal. ◇ *m* insecticide.

insectívoro, -ra *adj* insectivorous.

insecto *m* insect.

inseguridad *f* **-1.** [falta de confianza] insecurity. **-2.** [duda] uncertainty. **-3.** [peligro] lack of safety; ~ **ciudadana** lack of law and order.

inseguro, -ra *adj* **-1.** [sin confianza] insecure. **-2.** [dudoso] uncertain. **-3.** [peligroso] unsafe.

inseminación *f* insemination; ~ **artificial** artificial insemination.

inseminar *vt* to inseminate.

insensatez *f* foolishness, senselessness; **hacer/decir una** ~ to do/say sthg foolish.

insensato, -ta ◇ *adj* foolish, senseless. ◇ *m y f* foolish ○ senseless person, fool.

insensibilidad *f* [emocional] insensitivity; [física] numbness.

insensibilizar *vt* MED to numb.

◆ **insensibilizarse** *vpr* [emocionalmente] to become desensitized.

insensible *adj* **-1.** [indiferente]: ~ **(a)** insensitive (to). **-2.** [entumecido] numb. **-3.** [imperceptible] imperceptible.

inseparable *adj* inseparable.

insepulto, -ta *adj culto* unburied.

inserción *f* insertion.

insertar *vt* [gen & COMPUT]: ~ **(en)** to insert (into).

inservible *adj* useless, unserviceable.

insidia *f* **-1.** [trampa] trap, snare. **-2.** [mala acción] malicious act.

insidioso, -sa *adj* malicious.

insigne *adj* distinguished, illustrious.

insignia *f* **-1.** [distintivo] badge; MIL insignia. **-2.** [bandera] flag, banner.

insignificancia *f* **-1.** [cualidad] insignificance. **-2.** [cosa, hecho] trifle, insignificant thing.

insignificante *adj* insignificant.

insinuación *f* hint, insinuation.

◆ **insinuaciones** *fpl* [amorosas] innuendo (*U*).

insinuante *adj* suggestive, full of innuendo.

insinuar [6] *vt*: ~ **algo (a)** to hint at ○ insinuate sthg (to).

◆ **insinuarse** *vpr* **-1.** [amorosamente]: ~**se (a)** to make advances (to). **-2.** [asomar]: ~**se** detrás de algo to peep out from behind sthg.

insípido, -da *adj lit* & *fig* insipid.

insistencia *f* insistence.

insistente *adj* insistent.

insistir *vi*: ~ **(en)** to insist (on).

insobornable *adj* incorruptible.

insociable *adj* unsociable.

insolación *f* **-1.** MED sunstroke (*U*). **-2.** METEOR sunshine.

insolencia *f* insolence; **hacer/decir una** ~ to do/say sthg insolent.

insolente ◇ *adj* [descarado] insolent; [orgulloso] haughty. ◇ *m y f* insolent person.

insolidaridad *f* lack of solidarity.

insolidario, -ria ◇ *adj* lacking in solidarity. ◇ *m y f* person lacking in solidarity.

insólito, -ta *adj* very unusual.

insoluble *adj* insoluble.

insolvencia *f* insolvency.

insolvente *adj* insolvent.

insomne *adj* sleepless.

insomnio *m* insomnia, sleeplessness.

insondable *adj lit* & *fig* unfathomable.

insonorización *f* soundproofing.

insonorizar [13] *vt* to soundproof.

insoportable *adj* unbearable, intolerable.

insoslayable *adj* inevitable, unavoidable.

insospechable *adj* impossible to tell, unforeseeable.

insospechado, -da *adj* unexpected, unforeseen.

insostenible *adj* untenable.

inspección *f* inspection; [policial] search; ~ **de calidad** quality control inspection.

inspeccionar *vt* to inspect; [suj: policía] to search.

inspector, -ra *m y f* inspector; ~ **de aduanas** customs official; ~ **de Hacienda** tax inspector.

inspiración *f* **-1.** [gen] inspiration. **-2.** [respiración] inhalation, breath.

inspirado, -da *adj* inspired.

inspirar *vt* **-1.** [gen] to inspire. **-2.** [respirar] to inhale, to breathe in.
◆ **inspirarse** *vpr*: ~**se (en)** to be inspired (by).

instalación *f* **-1.** [gen] installation; ~ **eléctrica** wiring. **-2.** [de gente] settling.
◆ **instalaciones** *fpl* [deportivas etc] facilities.

instalador, -ra ◇ *adj* installing, fitting. ◇ *m y f* fitter.

instalar *vt* **-1.** [montar - antena etc] to instal,

to fit; [- local, puesto etc] to set up. **-2.** [situar - objeto] to place; [- gente] to settle.
◆ **instalarse** *vpr* [establecerse]: ~ **en** to settle (down) in; [nueva casa] to move into.

instancia *f* **-1.** [solicitud] application (form). **-2.** [ruego] request; **a** ~**s de** at the request O bidding of; **en última** ~ as a last resort. **-3.** DER: **juzgado de primera** ~ court of first instance.

instantáneo, -a *adj* **-1.** [momentáneo] momentary. **-2.** [rápido] instantaneous.
◆ **instantánea** *f* snapshot, snap.

instante *m* moment; **a cada** ~ all the time, constantly; **al** ~ instantly, immediately; **en un** ~ in a second.

instar *vt*: ~ **a alguien a que haga algo** to urge O press sb to do sthg.

instauración *f* establishment, foundation.

instaurar *vt* to establish, to set up.

instigador, -ra ◇ *adj* instigating. ◇ *m y f* instigator.

instigar [16] *vt*: ~ **a alguien (a que haga algo)** to instigate sb (to do sthg); ~ **a algo** to incite to sthg.

instintivo, -va *adj* instinctive.

instinto *m* instinct; **por** ~ instinctively.

institución *f* **-1.** [gen] institution; ~ **benéfica** charitable organization; ~ **pública** public institution; **ser una** ~ *fig* to be an institution. **-2.** [de ley, sistema] introduction; [de organismo] establishment; [de premio] foundation.

institucional *adj* institutional.

institucionalizar [13] *vt* to institutionalize.

instituir [51] *vt* **-1.** [fundar - gobierno] to establish; [- premio, sociedad] to found; [- sistema, reglas] to introduce. **-2.** [nombrar] to appoint, to name.

instituto *m* **-1.** [corporación] institute. **-2.** EDUC: ~ **(de Bachillerato** O **Enseñanza Media)** state secondary school; ~ **de Formación Profesional** ≃ technical college; ~ **politécnico** polytechnic.
◆ **instituto de belleza** *m* beauty salon.

institutriz *f* governess.

instrucción *f* **-1.** [conocimientos] education; [docencia] instruction; ~ **militar** military training. **-2.** [DER - investigación] preliminary investigation; [- curso del proceso] proceedings (*pl*).
◆ **instrucciones** *fpl* [de uso] instructions.

instructivo, -va *adj* [gen] instructive; [juguete, película] educational.

instructor, -ra ◇ *adj* training, instructing. ◇ *m y f* [gen] instructor, teacher; DEP coach.

instruido, -da *adj* educated.

instruir [51] *vt* **-1.** [enseñar] to instruct. **-2.** DER to prepare.

instrumental ◇ *adj* instrumental. ◇ *m* instruments (*pl*).

instrumentar *vt* to orchestrate, to score.

instrumentista *m* y *f* **-1.** MUS instrumentalist. **-2.** MED surgeon's assistant.

instrumento *m* **-1.** MUS & *fig* instrument. **-2.** [herramienta] tool, instrument; ~ **de precisión** precision tool.

insubordinación *f* insubordination.

insubordinado, -da ◇ *adj* insubordinate. ◇ *m* y *f* insubordinate (person), rebel.

insubordinar *vt* to stir up, to incite to rebellion.

◆ **insubordinarse** *vpr* to rebel.

insubstancial = **insustancial**.

insubstituible = **insustituible**.

insuficiencia *f* **-1.** [escasez] lack, shortage. **-2.** MED failure, insufficiency; ~ **cardiaca/renal** heart/kidney failure.

insuficiente ◇ *adj* insufficient. ◇ *m* [nota] fail.

insufrible *adj* intolerable, insufferable.

ínsula *f* island.

insular ◇ *adj* insular, island (*antes de sust*). ◇ *m* y *f* islander.

insulina *f* insulin.

insulso, -sa *adj lit* & *fig* bland, insipid.

insultante *adj* insulting, offensive.

insultar *vt* to insult.

insulto *m* insult; **proferir** ~**s** to hurl insults.

insumisión *f* rebelliousness.

insumiso, -sa ◇ *adj* rebellious. ◇ *m* y *f* [gen] rebel; MIL *person who refuses to do military or community service.*

insuperable *adj* **-1.** [inmejorable] unsurpassable. **-2.** [sin solución] insurmountable, insuperable.

insurgente *adj* insurgent.

insurrección *f* insurrection, revolt.

insurrecto, -ta *adj, m* y *f* insurgent, rebel.

insustancial, insubstancial *adj* insubstantial.

insustituible, insubstituible *adj* irreplaceable.

INTA (*abrev de* **Instituto Nacional de Técnicas Aeroespaciales**) *m Spanish national aerospace institute.*

intachable *adj* irreproachable.

intacto, -ta *adj* untouched; *fig* intact.

intangible *adj* intangible.

integración *f* integration; ~ **racial** racial integration.

integral ◇ *adj* **-1.** [total] total, complete. **-2.** [sin refinar - pan, harina, pasta] wholemeal; [- arroz] brown. **-3.** MAT → **cálculo**. ◇ *f* MAT integral.

integrante ◇ *adj* integral, constituent; **estado** ~ **de la CE** member state of the EC. ◇ *m* y *f* member.

integrar *vt* **-1.** [gen & MAT] to integrate. **-2.** [componer] to make up.

◆ **integrarse** *vpr* to integrate; ~**se en** to become integrated into.

integridad *f* [gen] integrity; [totalidad] wholeness.

integrismo *m* reaction, traditionalism.

integrista *adj, m* y *f* **-1.** POLIT reactionary, traditionalist. **-2.** RELIG fundamentalist.

íntegro, -gra *adj* **-1.** [completo] whole, entire; [versión etc] unabridged. **-2.** [honrado] upright, honourable.

intelecto *m* intellect.

intelectual *adj, m* y *f* intellectual.

intelectualidad *f* intelligentsia, intellectuals (*pl*).

intelectualizar [13] *vt* to intellectualize.

inteligencia *f* intelligence; ~ **artificial** INFORM artificial intelligence.

inteligente *adj* [gen & COMPUT] intelligent.

inteligibilidad *f* intelligibility.

inteligible *adj* intelligible.

intelligentsia *f* intelligentsia.

Intelsat (*abrev de* **International Telecommunications Satellite Organization**) *m* Intelsat.

intemperancia *f* intemperance, immoderation.

intemperie *f*: **a la** ~ in the open air.

intempestivo, -va *adj* [clima, comentario] harsh; [hora] ungodly, unearthly; [proposición, visita] inopportune.

intemporal *adj* timeless, independent of time.

intención *f* intention; **tener la** ~ **de** to intend to; **buena/mala** ~ good/bad intentions (*pl*); **la** ~ **es lo que cuenta** it's the thought that counts.

intencionado, -da *adj* intentional, deliberate; **bien** ~ [acción] well-meant; [persona] well-meaning; **mal** ~ [acción] ill-meant, ill-intentioned; [persona] malevolent.

intencional *adj* intentional, deliberate.

intencionalidad *f* intent.

intendencia *f* management, administration; ~ **militar** service corps.

intendente *m* [militar] quartermaster.

intensidad *f* [gen] intensity; [de lluvia]

heaviness; [de luz, color] brightness; [de amor] passion, strength.

intensificación *f* intensification.

intensificar [10] *vt* to intensify.

◆ **intensificarse** *vpr* to intensify.

intensivo, -va *adj* intensive.

intenso, -sa *adj* [gen] intense; [lluvia] heavy; [luz, color] bright; [amor] passionate, strong.

intentar *vt*: ~ (**hacer algo**) to try (to do sthg).

intento *m* [tentativa] attempt; [intención] intention; ~ **de golpe/robo** attempted coup/robbery.

intentona *f*: ~ (**golpista**) POLÍT attempted coup.

interacción *f* interaction.

interaccionar *vi* to interact.

interactivo, -va *adj* INFORM interactive.

intercalar *vt* to insert, to put in.

intercambiable *adj* interchangeable.

intercambiar [8] *vt* to exchange; [lugares, posiciones] to change, to swap.

intercambio *m* exchange; ~ **comercial** trade.

interceder *vi*: ~ (**por alguien**) to intercede (on sb's behalf).

interceptar *vt* **-1.** [detener] to intercept. **-2.** [obstruir] to block.

interceptor, -ra ◇ *adj* intercepting. ◇ *m* interceptor.

intercesión *f* intercession.

intercesor, -ra ◇ *adj* interceding. ◇ *m y f* interceder, intercessor.

interconexión *f* interconnection.

intercostal *adj* intercostal, between the ribs.

interdicción *f* interdiction.

interés *m* **-1.** [gen & FIN] interest; **de** ~ interesting; **tener** ~ **en** O **por** to be interested in; **tengo** ~ **en que venga pronto** it's in my interest that he should come soon; ~ **interbancario** interbank deposit rate; ~ **preferencial** preferential interest rate; **intereses creados** vested interests. **-2.** [egoísmo] self-interest, selfishness; **por** ~ out of selfishness.

interesado, -da ◇ *adj* **-1.** [gen]: ~ (**en** O **por**) interested (in). **-2.** [egoísta] selfish, self-interested. **-3.** [implicado]: **las partes interesadas** the interested parties. ◇ *m y f* **-1.** [deseoso] interested person; **los** ~**s** those interested. **-2.** [egoísta] selfish O self-interested person.

interesante *adj* interesting.

interesar *vi* to interest; **le interesa el arte** she's interested in art.

◆ **interesarse** *vpr*: ~**se** (**por**) to take an interest (in), to be interested (in); **se interesó por tu salud** she asked after your health.

interestatal *adj* interstate.

interfaz *f* INFORM interface.

interfecto, -ta *m y f* murder victim.

interferencia *f* interference.

interferir [27] ◇ *vt* **-1.** RADIO, TELECOM & TV to jam. **-2.** [interponerse] to interfere with. ◇ *vi*: ~ (**en**) to interfere (in).

interfono *m* intercom.

ínterin (*pl* **ínterines**) *m culto* interim; **en el** ~ in the meantime.

interina → **interino**.

interinidad *f* **-1.** [cualidad] temporariness. **-2.** [tiempo] (period of) temporary employment.

interino, -na ◇ *adj* [gen] temporary; [presidente, director etc] acting; [gobierno] interim. ◇ *m y f* [gen] stand-in; [médico, juez] locum; [profesor] supply teacher.

◆ **interina** *f* [asistenta] cleaning lady.

interior ◇ *adj* **-1.** [gen] inside, inner; [patio, jardín etc] interior, inside; [habitación, vida] inner. **-2.** POLÍT domestic. **-3.** GEOGR inland. ◇ *m* **-1.** [parte de dentro] inside, interior. **-2.** GEOGR interior, inland area. **-3.** [de una persona] inner self, heart; **en mi** ~ deep down. **-4.** *Amer* [calzoncillos] underpants (*pl*).

interioridad *f* [carácter] inner self.

◆ **interioridades** *fpl* [asuntos] private affairs.

interiorismo *m* interior design.

interiorista *m y f* interior designer.

interiorización *f* internalization; [de sentimientos] bottling-up.

interiorizar [13] *vt* to internalize; [sentimientos] to bottle up.

interjección *f* interjection.

interlineado *m* space between the lines.

interlocutor, -ra *m y f* interlocutor, speaker; **su** ~ the person she was speaking to.

interludio *m* [gen & MÚS] interlude.

intermediar [8] *vi* to mediate.

intermediario, -ria ◇ *adj* intermediary. ◇ *m y f* [gen] intermediary; COM middleman; [en disputas] mediator.

intermedio, -dia *adj* **-1.** [etapa] intermediate, halfway; [calidad] average; [tamaño] medium. **-2.** [tiempo] intervening; [espacio] in between.

◆ **intermedio** *m* [gen & TEATR] interval; CIN intermission.

interminable *adj* endless, interminable.

intermitencia *f* intermittence.
intermitente ◇ *adj* intermittent. ◇ *m* indicator.
internacional *adj* international.
◆ **Internacional** *f* POLÍT International; **La Internacional** [himno] the Internationale.
internacionalismo *m* internationalism.
internado, -da ◇ *adj* [en manicomio] confined; [en colegio] boarding; POLÍT interned. ◇ *m y f* [en manicomio] inmate; [en colegio] boarder; POLÍT internee.
◆ **internado** *m* **-1.** [internamiento - en manicomio] confinement; [- en colegio] boarding. **-2.** [colegio] boarding school.
◆ **internada** *f* DEP break, breakaway.
internamiento *m* [en manicomio] confinement; [en escuela] boarding; POLÍT internment.
internar *vt:* ~ **(en)** [internado] to send to boarding school (at); [manicomio] to commit (to); [campo de concentración] to intern (in).
◆ **internarse** *vpr:* ~**se (en)** [un lugar] to go O penetrate deep (into); [un tema] to become deeply involved (in).
internauta *m y f* Internet user.
Internet *f:* **(la red)** ~ the Internet.
internista *adj, m y f* internist.
interno, -na ◇ *adj* **-1.** [gen] internal; POLÍT domestic. **-2.** [alumno] boarding. **-3.** → **medicina.** ◇ *m y f* **-1.** [alumno] boarder. **-2.** → **médico. -3.** [preso] prisoner, inmate.
interparlamentario, -ria *adj* interparliamentary.
interpelación *f* formal question.
interpelar *vt* to question formally.
interplanetario, -ria *adj* interplanetary.
Interpol (*abrev de* **International Criminal Police Organization**) *f* Interpol.
interpolar *vt* to interpolate, to put in.
interponer [65] *vt* **-1.** [gen] to interpose, to put in. **-2.** DER to lodge, to make.
◆ **interponerse** *vpr* to intervene.
interposición *f* **-1.** [gen] interposition. **-2.** DER lodging (*of an appeal*).
interpretación *f* **-1.** [explicación] interpretation. **-2.** [artística] performance. **-3.** [traducción] interpreting.
interpretar *vt* **-1.** [gen] to interpret. **-2.** [artísticamente] to perform.
intérprete *m y f* **-1.** [traductor & INFORM] interpreter. **-2.** [artista] performer. **-3.** [comentarista] commentator.
interpuesto, -ta *pp* → **interponer.**
interregno *m* interregnum.
interrelación *f* interrelation.

interrelacionar *vt* to interrelate.
interrogación *f* **-1.** [acción] questioning. **-2.** [signo] question mark. **-3.** [pregunta] question.
interrogador, -ra ◇ *adj* questioning. ◇ *m y f* [gen] questioner; [que usa amenazas etc] interrogator.
interrogante *m o f* [incógnita] question mark.
interrogar [16] *vt* [gen] to question; [con amenazas etc] to interrogate.
interrogativo, -va *adj* interrogative.
interrogatorio *m* [gen] questioning; [con amenazas] interrogation.
interrumpir *vt* **-1.** [gen] to interrupt. **-2.** [discurso, trabajo] to break off; [viaje, vacaciones] to cut short. **-3.** [circulación] to block.
◆ **interrumpirse** *vpr* to be interrupted; [tráfico] to be blocked.
interrupción *f* **-1.** [gen] interruption. **-2.** [de discurso, trabajo] breaking-off; [de viaje, vacaciones] cutting-short. **-3.** [de circulación etc] blocking.
interruptor *m* switch; ~ **general** mains switch.
intersección *f* intersection.
interurbano, -na *adj* inter-city; TELECOM long-distance.
intervalo *m* **-1.** [gen & MÚS] interval; [de espacio] space, gap; **a** ~**s** at intervals. **-2.** [duración]: **en el** ~ **de un mes** in the space of a month.
intervención *f* **-1.** [gen] intervention. **-2.** [discurso] speech; [interpelación] contribution. **-3.** COM auditing. **-4.** MED operation. **-5.** TELECOM tapping.
intervencionismo *m* interventionism.
intervencionista *adj, m y f* interventionist.
intervenir [75] ◇ *vi* **-1.** [participar]: ~ **(en)** [gen] to take part (in); [pelea] to get involved (in); [discusión etc] to make a contribution (to). **-2.** [dar un discurso] to make a speech. **-3.** [interferir]: ~ **(en)** to intervene (in). **-4.** MED to operate. ◇ *vt* **-1.** MED to operate on. **-2.** TELECOM to tap. **-3.** [incautar] to seize. **-4.** COM to audit.
interventor, -ra *m y f* **-1.** COM auditor. **-2.** [en elecciones] scrutineer.
interviú (*pl* **interviús**) *f* interview.
intestado, -da *adj, m y f* intestate.
intestinal *adj* intestinal.
intestino, -na *adj* internecine.
◆ **intestino** *m* intestine; ~ **delgado/grueso** small/large intestine.
intimar *vi:* ~ **(con)** to become intimate O very friendly (with).
intimidación *f* intimidation.

intimidad *f* **-1.** [vida privada] private life; [privacidad] privacy; **en la** ~ in private. **-2.** [amistad] intimacy.

intimidar *vt* to intimidate.

intimista *adj* Intimist.

íntimo, -ma ◇ *adj* **-1.** [vida, fiesta] private; [ambiente, restaurante] intimate. **-2.** [relación, amistad] close. **-3.** [sentimiento etc] innermost; **en lo (más)** ~ **de su corazón/alma** deep down in her heart/soul. ◇ *m y f* close friend.

intitular *vt* to entitle, to call.

intocable *adj* untouchable.

◆ **intocables** *mpl y fpl* [en la India] untouchables.

intolerable *adj* intolerable, unacceptable; [dolor, ruido] unbearable.

intolerancia *f* **-1.** [actitud] intolerance. **-2.** MED allergy.

intolerante ◇ *adj* intolerant. ◇ *m y f* intolerant person.

intoxicación *f* poisoning (U); ~ **alimenticia** food poisoning.

intoxicar [10] *vt* to poison.

◆ **intoxicarse** *vpr* to poison o.s.

intraducible *adj* untranslatable.

intramuros *adv* within the city walls.

intranquilidad *f* unease, anxiety.

intranquilizar [13] *vt* to worry, to make uneasy.

◆ **intranquilizarse** *vpr* to get worried.

intranquilo, -la *adj* [preocupado] worried, uneasy; [nervioso] restless.

intranscendencia = intrascendencia.

intranscendente = intrascendente.

intransferible *adj* non-transferable, untransferable.

intransigencia *f* intransigence.

intransigente *adj* intransigent.

intransitable *adj* impassable.

intransitivo, -va *adj* intransitive.

intrascendencia, intranscendencia *f* insignificance, unimportance.

intrascendente, intranscendente *adj* insignificant, unimportant.

intratable *adj* unsociable, difficult to get on with.

intrauterino, -na *adj* intrauterine.

intravenoso, -sa *adj* intravenous.

intrépido, -da *adj* intrepid.

intriga *f* **-1.** [curiosidad] curiosity; **de** ~ suspense (*antes de sust*). **-2.** [maquinación] intrigue. **-3.** [trama] plot.

intrigado, -da *adj* intrigued.

intrigante *adj* intriguing.

intrigar [16] *vt & vi* to intrigue.

intrincado, -da *adj* **-1.** [bosque etc] thick, dense. **-2.** [problema etc] intricate.

intrincar [10] *vt* to complicate, to confuse.

intríngulis *m inv fam* [dificultad] snag, catch; [quid] nub, crux.

intrínseco, -ca *adj* intrinsic.

introducción *f*: ~ **(a)** introduction (to).

introducir [33] *vt* **-1.** [meter - llave, carta etc] to put in, to insert; [mercancías etc] to bring in, to introduce. **-2.** [dar a conocer]: ~ **a alguien en** to introduce sb to; ~ **algo en** to introduce ○ bring sthg to.

◆ **introducirse** *vpr*: ~**se en** to get into.

introductor, -ra ◇ *adj* introductory; **el país** ~ **de esta moda** the country that brought in this fashion. ◇ *m y f* introducer.

introductorio, -ria *adj* introductory.

intromisión *f* meddling, interfering.

introspección *f* introspection.

introspectivo, -va *adj* introspective.

introvertido, -da *adj, m y f* introvert.

intrusión *f* intrusion.

intrusismo *m* illegal practice of a profession.

intruso, -sa ◇ *adj* intrusive. ◇ *m y f* intruder.

intubar *vt* to intubate.

intuición *f* intuition.

intuir [51] *vt* to know by intuition, to sense.

intuitivo, -va *adj* intuitive.

intuya, intuyera *etc* → intuir.

inundación *f* flood, flooding (U).

inundar *vt* to flood; *fig* to inundate, to swamp.

◆ **inundarse** *vpr* to flood; ~**se de** *fig* to be inundated ○ swamped with.

inusitado, -da *adj* uncommon, rare.

inusual *adj* unusual.

inútil ◇ *adj* **-1.** [gen] useless; [intento, esfuerzo] unsuccessful, vain. **-2.** [inválido] disabled. **-3.** [no apto] unfit. ◇ *m y f* hopeless case, useless person.

inutilidad *f* **-1.** [gen] uselessness; [falta de sentido] pointlessness. **-2.** [invalidez] disablement.

inutilizar [13] *vt* [gen] to make unusable; [máquinas, dispositivos] to disable, to put out of action.

invadir *vt* to invade; **le invade la tristeza** she's overcome by sadness.

invalidación *f* invalidation.

invalidar *vt* to invalidate.

invalidez *f* **-1.** MED disablement, disability; ~ **permanente/temporal** permanent/temporary disability. **-2.** DER invalidity.

inválido, -da ◇ *adj* **-1.** MED disabled. **-2.** DER invalid. ◇ *m y f* invalid, disabled person; **los ~s** the disabled.

invariable *adj* invariable.

invasión *f* invasion.

invasor, -ra ◇ *adj* invading. ◇ *m y f* invader.

invectiva *f* invective (*U*).

invencible *adj* invincible; [timidez etc] insurmountable, insuperable.

invención *f* invention.

invendible *adj* unsaleable.

inventar *vt* [gen] to invent; [narración, falsedades] to make up.

◆ **inventarse** *vpr* to make up.

inventario *m* inventory; **hacer el ~** COM to do the stocktaking.

inventiva *f* inventiveness.

invento *m* invention.

inventor, -ra *m y f* inventor.

invernadero, invernáculo *m* greenhouse.

invernal *adj* winter (*antes de sust*); [tiempo, paisaje] wintry.

invernar [19] *vi* [pasar el invierno] to (spend the) winter; [hibernar] to hibernate.

inverosímil *adj* unlikely, improbable.

inverosimilitud *f* unlikeliness, improbability.

inversión *f* **-1.** [del orden] inversion. **-2.** [de dinero, tiempo] investment; **inversiones extranjeras** ECON foreign investments.

inverso, -sa *adj* opposite, inverse; **~ a** opposite to; **a la inversa** the other way round; **en orden ~** in reverse order.

inversor, -ra ◇ *adj* investing. ◇ *m y f* COM & FIN investor.

◆ **inversor** *m* ELECTR inverter.

invertebrado, -da *adj* **-1.** ZOOL invertebrate. **-2.** *fig* [incoherente] disjointed.

◆ **invertebrado** *m* invertebrate.

invertido, -da ◇ *adj* **-1.** [al revés] reversed, inverted; [sentido, dirección] opposite. **-2.** [dinero] invested. **-3.** [homosexual] homosexual. ◇ *m y f* homosexual.

invertir [27] *vt* **-1.** [gen] to reverse, to invert; [poner boca abajo] to turn upside down, to invert. **-2.** [dinero, tiempo, esfuerzo] to invest. **-3.** [tardar - tiempo] to spend.

investidura *f* investiture.

investigación *f* **-1.** [estudio] research; **~ y desarrollo** research and development. **-2.** [indagación] investigation, inquiry.

investigador, -ra ◇ *adj* **-1.** [que estudia] research (*antes de sust*). **-2.** [que indaga] investigating. ◇ *m y f* **-1.** [estudioso] re-

searcher. **-2.** [detective] investigator; **~ privado** private investigator ◯ detective.

investigar [16] ◇ *vt* **-1.** [estudiar] to research. **-2.** [indagar] to investigate. ◇ *vi* **-1.** [estudiar] to do research. **-2.** [indagar] to investigate.

investir [26] *vt*: **~ a alguien con algo** to invest sb with sthg.

inveterado, -da *adj* deep-rooted.

inviabilidad *f* impracticability.

inviable *adj* impractical, unviable.

invicto, -ta *adj culto* unconquered, unbeaten.

invidente ◇ *adj* blind, sightless. ◇ *m y f* blind ◯ sightless person; **los ~s** the blind.

invierna *etc* → **invernar**.

invierno *m* winter.

invierta *etc* → **invertir**.

inviolabilidad *f* inviolability.

inviolable *adj* inviolable.

invirtiera *etc* → **invertir**.

invisible *adj* invisible.

invista, invistiera *etc* → **investir**.

invitación *f* invitation.

invitado, -da ◇ *adj* invited. ◇ *m y f* guest.

invitar ◇ *vt* **-1.** [convidar]: **~ a alguien (a algo/a hacer algo)** to invite sb (to sthg/to do sthg). **-2.** [pagar]: **os invito** it's my treat, this one's on me; **~ a alguien a algo** to buy sb sthg (*food, drink*); **te invito a cenar fuera** I'll take you out for dinner. ◇ *vi* to pay; **invita la casa** it's on the house.

◆ **invitar a** *vi fig* [incitar]: **~ a algo** to encourage sthg; **la lluvia invita a quedarse en casa** the rain makes you want to stay at home.

in vitro *loc adv* **-1.** [de probeta] in vitro. **-2.** → **fecundación**.

invocación *f* invocation.

invocar [10] *vt* to invoke.

involución *f* regression.

involucionista ◇ *adj* regressive, reactionary. ◇ *m y f* reactionary.

involucrar *vt*: **~ a alguien (en)** to involve sb (in).

◆ **involucrarse** *vpr*: **~se (en)** to get involved (in).

involuntario, -ria *adj* [espontáneo] involuntary; [sin querer] unintentional.

invoque *etc* → **invocar**.

invulnerabilidad *f* invulnerability.

invulnerable *adj*: **~ (a)** immune (to), invulnerable (to).

inyección *f* injection; **poner una ~** to give an injection.

inyectable ◇ *adj* injectable. ◇ *m* injection.

inyectar *vt* to inject.
◆ **inyectarse** *vpr* [drogas] to take drugs intravenously; ~**se algo** to inject o.s. with sthg.

iodo = **yodo**.

ion *m* ion.

ionice *etc* → **ionizar**.

iónico, -ca *adj* ionic.

ionizar [13] *vt* to ionize.

ionosfera *f* ionosphere.

IORTV (*abrev de* **Instituto Oficial de Radiodifusión y Televisión**) *m Spanish broadcasting institute.*

IPA (*abrev de* **International Phonetic Association**) *f* IPA.

IPC (*abrev de* **índice de precios al consumo**) *m Spanish cost of living index,* ≃ RPI *Br.*

ipso facto *loc adv* immediately.

ir [61] *vi* **-1.** [gen] to go; ~ **hacia el sur/al cine** to go south/to the cinema; ~ **en autobús/coche** to go by bus/car; ~ **andando** to go on foot, to walk; ¡**vamos!** let's go! **-2.** [expresa duración gradual]: ~ **haciendo algo** to be (gradually) doing sthg; **va anocheciendo** it's getting dark; **voy mejorando mi estilo** I'm working on improving my style. **-3.** [expresa intención, opinión]: ~ **a hacer algo** to be going to do sthg; **voy a decírselo a tu padre** I'm going to tell your father; **te voy a echar de menos** I'm going to miss you. **-4.** [cambiar]: ~ **a mejor/peor** *etc* to get better/worse *etc.* **-5.** [funcionar] to work; **la manivela va floja** the crank is loose; **la televisión no va** the television isn't working. **-6.** [desenvolverse] to go; **le va bien en su nuevo trabajo** things are going well for him in his new job; **su negocio va mal** his business is going badly; ¿**cómo te va?** how are you doing? **-7.** [vestir]: ~ **en/con** to wear; **iba en camisa y con corbata** he was wearing a shirt and tie; ~ **de azul/de uniforme** to be dressed in blue/in uniform. **-8.** [tener aspecto físico] to look like; **iba hecho un pordiosero** he looked like a beggar. **-9.** [vacaciones, tratamiento]: ~**le bien a alguien** to do sb good. **-10.** [ropa]: ~**le (bien) a alguien** to suit sb; ~ **con algo** to go with sthg. **-11.** [comentario, indirecta]: ~ **con** ○ **por alguien** to be meant for sb, to be aimed at sb. **-12.** *loc:* **fue y dijo que ...** he went and said that ...; **ni me va ni me viene** *fam* I don't care; ¡**qué va!** you must be joking!; **ser el no va más** to be the ultimate.
◆ **ir de** *vi* **-1.** película, novela] to be about. **-2.** *fig* [persona] to think o.s.; **va de listo** he thinks he's clever.

◆ **ir por** *vi* **-1.** [buscar]: ~ **por algo/alguien** to go and get sthg/sb, to go and fetch sthg/sb. **-2.** [alcanzar]: **va por el cuarto vaso de vino** he's already on his fourth glass of wine; **vamos por la mitad de la asignatura** we covered about half the subject.

◆ **irse** *vpr* **-1.** [marcharse] to go, to leave; ~**se a** to go to; ¡**vete!** go away! **-2.** [gastarse, desaparecer] to go. **-3.** *loc:* ~**se abajo** [edificio] to fall down; [negocio] to collapse; [planes] to fall through.

ira *f* anger, rage.

IRA (*abrev de* **Irish Republican Army**) *m* IRA.

iracundo, -da *adj* angry, irate; [irascible] irascible.

Irán: (**el**) ~ Iran.

iraní (*pl* **iraníes**) *adj, m y f* Iranian.
◆ **iraní** *m* [lengua] Iranian.

Iraq: (**el**) ~ Iraq.

iraquí (*pl* **iraquíes**) *adj, m y f* Iraqi.

irascible *adj* irascible.

irga, irguiera *etc* → **erguir**.

iridiscencia *f* iridescence.

iridólogo, -ga *m y f* MED iridologist.

iris *m inv* iris.

Irlanda Ireland.

irlandés, -esa ◇ *adj* Irish. ◇ *m y f* [persona] Irishman (*f* Irishwoman); **los irlandeses** the Irish.
◆ **irlandés** *m* [lengua] Irish.

ironía *f* irony.

irónico, -ca *adj* ironic, ironical.

ironizar [13] ◇ *vt* to ridicule. ◇ *vi:* ~ (**sobre**) to be ironical (about).

IRPF (*abrev de* **Impuesto sobre la Renta de las Personas Físicas**) *m Spanish personal income tax.*

irracional *adj* irrational.

irracionalidad *f* irrationality.

irradiación *f* **-1.** [gen] irradiation. **-2.** [de cultura, ideas] dissemination, spreading.

irradiar [8] *vt lit & fig* to radiate.

irrazonable *adj* unreasonable.

irreal *adj* unreal.

irrealidad *f* unreality.

irrealizable *adj* [sueño, objetivo] unattainable; [plan] impractical.

irrebatible *adj* irrefutable, indisputable.

irreconciliable *adj* irreconcilable.

irreconocible *adj* unrecognizable.

irrecuperable *adj* irretrievable.

irreemplazable = **irremplazable**.

irreflexión *f* rashness.

irreflexivo, -va *adj* rash.

irrefrenable *adj* irrepressible, uncontainable.

irrefutable *adj* irrefutable.

irregular *adj* [gen] irregular; [terreno, superficie] uneven.

irregularidad *f* [gen] irregularity; [de terreno, superficie] unevenness.

irrelevancia *f* irrelevance.

irrelevante *adj* irrelevant.

irremediable *adj* irremediable.

irremisible *adj* [imperdonable] unpardonable; [irremediable] irremediable.

irremplazable, irreemplazable *adj* irreplaceable.

irreparable *adj* irreparable.

irrepetible *adj* unique, unrepeatable.

irreprimible *adj* irrepressible.

irreprochable *adj* irreproachable.

irresistible *adj* irresistible.

irresoluble *adj* unsolvable.

irresoluto, -ta ◇ *adj culto* irresolute. ◇ *m y f* irresolute person.

irrespetuoso, -sa *adj* disrespectful.

irrespirable *adj* unbreathable.

irresponsabilidad *f* irresponsibility.

irresponsable ◇ *adj* irresponsible. ◇ *m y f* irresponsible person.

irreverente *adj* irreverent.

irreversible *adj* irreversible.

irrevocable *adj* irrevocable.

irrigación *f* irrigation.

irrigador *m* MED irrigator.

irrigar [16] *vt* to irrigate.

irrisorio, -ria *adj* -1. [excusa etc] laughable, derisory. -2. [precio etc] ridiculously low.

irritabilidad *f* irritability.

irritable *adj* irritable.

irritación *f* irritation.

irritante *adj* irritating.

irritar *vt* to irritate.
◆ **irritarse** *vpr* -1. [enfadarse] to get angry o annoyed. -2. [suj: piel etc] to become irritated.

irrompible *adj* unbreakable.

irrumpir *vi*: ~ **en** to burst into.

irrupción *f* bursting in.

IRYDA (*abrev de* **Instituto Nacional de Reforma y Desarrollo**) *m Spanish government body providing financial aid to the agricultural sector.*

isabelino, -na *adj* [en España] Isabelline; [en Inglaterra] Elizabethan.

ISBN (*abrev de* **international standard book number**) *m* ISBN.

isla *f* island; **la ~ de Pascua** Easter Island.

islam *m* Islam.

Islamabad Islamabad.

islámico, -ca *adj* Islamic.

islamismo *m* Islam.

islamizar [13] *vt* to Islamize, to convert to Islam.
◆ **islamizarse** *vpr* to convert to Islam.

islandés, -esa ◇ *adj* Icelandic. ◇ *m y f* [persona] Icelander.
◆ **islandés** *m* [lengua] Icelandic.

Islandia Iceland.

isleño, -ña ◇ *adj* island (*antes de sust*). ◇ *m y f* islander.

islote *m* small, rocky island.

ISO (*abrev de* **International Standards Organization**) *f* ISO.

isobara, isóbara *f* isobar.

isomorfo, -fa *adj* MIN isomorphic.

isósceles ◇ *adj inv* isosceles. ◇ *m inv* isosceles triangle.

isótopo ◇ *adj* isotopic. ◇ *m* isotope.

Israel Israel.

israelí (*pl* **israelíes**) *adj, m y f* Israeli.

israelita *adj, m y f* Israelite.

istmo *m* isthmus.

Italia Italy.

italianismo *m* Italianism.

italianizar [13] *vt* to Italianize.

italiano, -na *adj, m y f* Italian.
◆ **italiano** *m* [lengua] Italian.

itálico, -ca ◇ *adj* -1. HIST Italic. -2. → letra. ◇ *m y f* HIST Italic.

item, ítem *m* item.

itinerante *adj* itinerant; [embajador] roving.

itinerario *m* route, itinerary.

ITT (*abrev de* **International Telegraph and Telephone (Corporation)**) *f* ITT.

ITV (*abrev de* **inspección técnica de vehículos**) *f annual technical inspection for motor vehicles of ten years or more,* ≃ MOT *Br.*

IVA (*abrev de* **impuesto sobre el valor añadido**) *m* VAT.

izar [13] *vt* to raise, to hoist.

izda (*abrev de* **izquierda**) L, l.

izquierda → izquierdo.

izquierdismo *m* left-wing views (*pl*).

izquierdista ◇ *adj* left-wing. ◇ *m y f* left-winger.

izquierdo, -da *adj* left.
◆ **izquierda** *f* -1. [lado] left; **a la izquierda (de)** on o to the left (of); **girar a la izquierda** to turn left. -2. [mano] left hand. -3. POLÍT left (wing); **de izquierdas** left-wing.

izquierdoso, -sa *adj fam* leftish.

J

j, J f [letra] j, J.
ja *interj*: ¡~! ha!
jabalí (*pl* jabalíes) *m y* f wild boar.
jabalina f DEP javelin.
jabato, -ta *adj* brave.
◆ **jabato** *m* ZOOL baby wild boar.
jabón *m* soap; ~ **de afeitar/tocador** shaving/toilet soap; ~ **líquido** liquid soap; **dar** ~ **a alguien** to soft-soap sb.
jabonar *vt* to soap.
jaboncillo *m* tailor's chalk.
jabonero, -ra *adj* soap (*antes de sust*).
◆ **jabonera** f soap dish.
jabonoso, -sa *adj* soapy.
jaca f [caballo pequeño] pony; [yegua] mare.
jacal *m Amer* hut.
jacinto *m* hyacinth.
jaco *m mfam* junk, heroin.
jacobeo, -a *adj* of/relating to St James.
jacobinismo *m* Jacobinism.
jacobino, -na *adj, m y* f Jacobin.
jactancia f boasting.
jactancioso, -sa *adj* boastful.
jactarse *vpr*: ~ **(de)** to boast (about ○ of).
jaculatoria f short prayer.
jacuzzi® [ʤa'kusi] (*pl* jacuzzis) *m* Jacuzzi®.
jade *m* jade.
jadeante *adj* panting.
jadear *vi* to pant.
jadeo *m* panting.
jaguar (*pl* jaguars) *m* jaguar.
jaiba f *Amer* [cangrejo de río] crayfish.
jaibol *m Amer* highball.
Jakarta [ʤa'karta] Jakarta.
jalar *mfam vi* to pig (out), to scoff.
◆ **jalarse** *vpr mfam* to scoff (down).
jalea f jelly; ~ **real** royal jelly.
jalear *vt* to cheer on.
jaleo *m* **-1.** *fam* [alboroto] row, rumpus; **armar** ~ to kick up a row ○ fuss. **-2.** *fam* [lío] mess, confusion. **-3.** [aplausos, gritos] cheering.
jalón *m* [palo] marker pole.

jalonar *vt* to stake ○ mark out; *fig* to mark.
Jamaica Jamaica.
jamaicano, -na *adj, m y* f Jamaican.
jamás *adv* never; **no le he visto** ~ I've never seen him; **la mejor película que** ~ **se haya hecho** the best film ever made; ~ **de los jamases** never ever.
jamba f jamb, door post.
jamelgo *m fam* nag.
jamón *m* ham; ~ **del país** local homemade ham; ~ **(de) York** ○ **(en) dulce** boiled ham; ~ **serrano** cured ham, ≈ Parma ham; **¡y un** ~! *fam fig* you've got to be joking!, not on your life!
jamona *fam* ◇ *adj* generously built. ◇ f generously-built woman.
jam-session [ʤam'sesjon] f MÚS jam.
jansenismo *m* Jansenism.
Japón: **(el)** ~ Japan.
japonés, -esa *adj, m y* f Japanese.
◆ **japonés** *m* [lengua] Japanese.
jaque *m*: ~ **(al rey)** check; ~ **mate** checkmate; **tener en** ~ **a alguien** *fig* to keep sb in a state of anxiety.
jaqueca f migraine; **dar** ~ **(a alguien)** *fam* to bother (sb), to pester (sb).
jarabe *m* syrup; ~ **para la tos** cough mixture ○ syrup; ~ **de palo** beating; **tener mucho** ~ **de pico** to have the gift of the gab, to be a smooth talker.
jarana f **-1.** [juerga]: **estar/irse de** ~ to be/go out on the town. **-2.** [alboroto] row, rumpus.
jaranero, -ra ◇ *adj* fond of partying. ◇ *m y* f party-goer.
jarcia f NÁUT rigging.
jardín *m* garden; ~ **botánico** botanical garden.
◆ **jardín de infancia** *m* kindergarten, nursery school.
jardinera → **jardinero**.
jardinería f gardening.
jardinero, -ra *m y* f gardener.
◆ **jardinera** f flowerpot stand; **a la jardinera** CULIN garnished with vegetables.
jarra f **-1.** [para servir] jug. **-2.** [para beber] tankard.
◆ **en jarras** *loc adv* [postura] hands on hips.
jarrete *m* hock.
jarro *m* jug; **fue como un** ~ **de agua fría** *fig* it was a bolt from the blue.
jarrón *m* vase.
Jartum Khartoum.
jaspe *m* jasper.

jogging

jaspeado, -da *adj* mottled, speckled.
◆ **jaspeado** *m* mottling.
jaspear *vt* to mottle, to speckle.
jauja *f fam* paradise, heaven on earth; **ser**
~ to be heaven on earth ○ paradise.
jaula *f* cage.
jauría *f* pack of dogs.
Java Java.
javanés, -esa *adj, m y f* Javanese.
jazmín *m* jasmine.
jazz [jas] *m* jazz.
JC (*abrev de* **Jesucristo**) JC.
je *interj*: ¡~! ha!
jeans [jins] *mpl* jeans.
jeep [jip] (*pl* **jeeps**) *m* jeep.
jefa → **jefe**.
jefatura *f* **-1.** [cargo] leadership. **-2.** [organismo] headquarters, head office.
jefazo, -za *m y f fam* big boss.
jefe, -fa *m y f* [gen] boss; COM manager (*f* manageress); [líder] leader; [de tribu, ejército] chief; [de departamento etc] head; **en** ~ MIL in-chief; ~ **de cocina** chef; ~ **de estación** stationmaster; ~ **de Estado** head of state; ~ **de estudios** deputy head; ~ **de producción/ventas** production/sales manager; ~ **de redacción** editor-in-chief.
JEME (*abrev de* **Jefe del Estado Mayor del Ejército**) *m Spanish military chief of staff*.
JEN (*abrev de* **Junta de Energía Nuclear**) *f Spanish nuclear energy board*.
jengibre *m* ginger.
jeque *m* sheikh.
jerarca *m* high-ranking person, leader.
jerarquía *f* **-1.** [organización] hierarchy. **-2.** [persona] high-ranking person, leader.
jerárquico, -ca *adj* hierarchical.
jerarquizar [13] *vt* to structure in a hierarchical manner.
jerez *m* sherry; ~ **fino** dry sherry.
jerga *f* jargon; [argot] slang.
jergón *m* straw mattress.
jerifalte = **gerifalte**.
jerigonza *f* [galimatías] gibberish; [jerga] jargon; [argot] slang.
jeringa *f* syringe.
jeringuilla *f* syringe; ~ **hipodérmica** hypodermic syringe.
jeroglífico, -ca *adj* hieroglyphic.
◆ **jeroglífico** *m* **-1.** [inscripción] hieroglyphic. **-2.** [pasatiempo] rebus.
jerséi (*pl* **jerséis**), **jersey** *m* (*pl* **jerseys**) jumper, pullover.
Jerusalén Jerusalem.
jesuita *adj & m* Jesuit.

jesuítico, -ca *adj* Jesuitic.
jesús *interj* ¡~! [sorpresa] gosh!, good heavens!; [tras estornudo] bless you!
jet [jet] (*pl* **jets**) ◇ *m* jet. ◇ *f* → **jet-set**.
jeta *mfam* ◇ *f* [cara] mug, face; **romperle la** ~ **a alguien** to smash sb's face in; **tener (mucha)** ~ to be a cheeky bugger. ◇ *m y f* cheeky bugger.
jet lag ['jetlak] *m* jet lag.
jet-set ['jetset] *f* jet set.
jíbaro, -ra ◇ *adj* Jívaro (*antes de sust*). ◇ *m y f* Jívaro.
Jibuti Djibouti.
jiddisch ['jiðiʃ] = **yiddish**.
jijona *m type of nougat made in Jijona*.
jilguero *m* goldfinch.
jilipollada = **gilipollada**.
jilipollas = **gilipollas**.
jilipollez = **gilipollez**.
jinete *m y f* rider; [yóquey] jockey.
jiote *m Amer* rash.
jirafa *f* **-1.** ZOOL giraffe. **-2.** CIN & TV boom.
jirón *m* **-1.** [andrajo] shred, rag; **hecho jirones** in tatters. **-2.** *Amer* [calle] street.
jitomate *m Amer variety of tomato*.
jiu-jitsu [jiu'jitsu] = **yiu-yitsu**.
jívaro, -ra = **jíbaro**.
JJ OO (*abrev de* **juegos olímpicos**) *mpl Olympic Games*.
JME (*abrev de* **Juventudes Musicales Españolas**) *fpl Spanish national organization of young musicians*.
jo *interj fam*: ¡~! [asombro, admiración] wow!; [enfado, molestia] hell!, Christ!
jockey ['jokei] = **yóquey**.
jocosidad *f* **-1.** [humor] funniness, humour. **-2.** [chiste] quip.
jocoso, -sa *adj* jocular.
jocundo, -da *adj culto* jovial, cheerful.
joder *vulg* ◇ *vi* **-1.** [copular] to fuck. **-2.** [fastidiar] to be a pain in the arse; **¡no jodas!** [incredulidad] bollocks!, pull the other one! ◇ *vt* **-1.** [fastidiar] to fuck about ○ around. **-2.** [disgustar] to fuck ○ piss off. **-3.** [estropear] to fuck (up). ◇ *interj*: ¡~! fuck it!, fucking hell!
◆ **joderse** *vpr vulg* **-1.** [aguantarse] to fucking well put up with it; **¡que se joda!** he can fuck off! **-2.** [estropearse] to get fucked (up).
jodido, -da *adj vulg* **-1.** [gen] fucked; [anímicamente] fucked up. **-2.** [difícil] fucking difficult. **-3.** [maldito] fucking.
jodienda *f vulg* fucking pain (in the arse).
jofaina *f* wash basin.
jogging ['joɣin] *m* jogging.

jóker ['joker] (*pl* **jokers**) *m* joker (*in cards*).

jolgorio *m* merrymaking.

jolín, jolines *interj fam*: ¡~!, ¡jolines! hell!, Christ!

jondo → **cante**.

jónico, -ca *adj* Ionic.

JONS (*abrev de* **Juntas de Ofensiva Nacional Sindicalista**) *fpl* Spanish right-wing youth movement founded in 1931.

jornada *f* -1. [de trabajo] working day; ~ **intensiva** working day from 8 to 3 with only a short lunch break; **media** ~ half day. ~ **partida** typical Spanish working day from 9 to 1 and 4 to 7; ~ **de reflexión** day of reflection before elections when campaigning is forbidden. -2. [de viaje] day's journey. -3. DEP round of matches, programme.
◆ **jornadas** *fpl* [conferencia] conference (*sg*).

jornal *m* day's wage.

jornalero, -ra *m y f* day labourer.

joroba *f* hump.

jorobado, -da ◇ *adj* -1. *fam* [estropeado] knackered; **tengo el estómago** ~ I've got gut-rot. -2. [con joroba] hunchbacked. ◇ *m y f* hunchback.

jorobar *vt fam* -1. [molestar] to cheese off, to annoy. -2. [estropear] to knacker; **me ha jorobado el estómago** it's given me gut-rot.
◆ **jorobarse** *vpr fam*: **pues te jorobas** you can like it or lump it.

jorongo *m Amer* -1. [manta] blanket. -2. [poncho] poncho.

jota *f* [baile] Aragonese folk song and dance; **no entender** ○ **saber ni** ~ *fam fig* not to understand ○ know a thing; **no ver ni** ~ *fam fig* [por defecto visual] to be as blind as a bat; [por oscuridad etc] not to be able to see a thing.

jotero, -ra *m y f* jota dancer.

joto *m y f Amer fam despec* queer *Br*, faggot *Am*.

joven ◇ *adj* young; **de** ~ as a young man/woman. ◇ *m y f* young man (*f* young woman); **los jóvenes** young people.

jovenzuelo, -la *m y f* youngster.

jovial *adj* jovial, cheerful.

jovialidad *f* joviality, cheerfulness.

joya *f* jewel; *fig* gem.

joyería *f* -1. [tienda] jeweller's (shop). -2. [arte, comercio] jewellery.

joyero, -ra *m y f* [persona] jeweller.
◆ **joyero** *m* [estuche] jewellery box.

JPI (*abrev de* **juzgado de primera instancia**) *m* court of first instance.

JPT (*abrev de* **Jefatura Provincial de Tráfico**) *f* Spanish provincial headquarters for traffic police.

Jr. (*abrev de* **junior**) Jr.

JSP (*abrev de* **Junta Superior de Precios**) *f* Spanish government watchdog on prices.

juanete *m* bunion.

jubilación *f* -1. [retiro] retirement; ~ **anticipada** early retirement. -2. [dinero] pension.

jubilado, -da ◇ *adj* retired. ◇ *m y f* pensioner *Br*, senior citizen.

jubilar *vt*: ~ **a alguien (de)** to pension sb off ○ retire sb (from).
◆ **jubilarse** *vpr* to retire.

jubileo *m* RELIG jubilee.

júbilo *m* jubilation, joy.

jubiloso, -sa *adj* jubilant, joyous.

judaico, -ca *adj* Judaic, Jewish.

judaísmo *m* Judaism.

judas *m inv* Judas, traitor.

judeocristiano, -na *adj* Judaeo-Christian.

judeoespañol, -la ◇ *adj* Sephardic. ◇ *m y f* [persona] Sephardic Jew.
◆ **judeoespañol** *m* [lengua] Sephardi.

judería *f* Jewish ghetto ○ quarter.

judía *f* bean; ~ **blanca/verde** haricot/green bean.

judiada *f fam* dirty trick.

judicatura *f* -1. [cargo] office of judge. -2. [institución] judiciary.

judicial *adj* judicial.

judío, -a ◇ *adj* Jewish. ◇ *m y f* Jew (*f* Jewess).

judo = **yudo**.

judoka = **yudoka**.

juega → **jugar**.

juego *m* -1. [gen & DEP] game; [acción] play, playing; [con dinero] gambling; **abrir/cerrar el** ~ to begin/finish the game; **estar/poner en** ~ to be/put at stake; ¡hagan ~! place your bets!; **ser un** ~ **de niños** to be child's play; ~ **de azar** game of chance; ~ **de manos** conjuring trick; ~ **de palabras** play on words, pun; ~ **de prendas** game of forfeit; ~**s malabares** juggling (*U*); *fig* [piruetas] balancing act (*sg*); **Juegos Olímpicos** Olympic Games; ~ **sucio/limpio** foul/clean play; **descubrirle el** ~ **a alguien** to see through sb; **doble** ~, **doble** double game, double dealing (*U*); **estar (en) fuera de** ~ DEP to be offside; *fig* not to know what's going on. -2. [mano - de cartas] hand; **me salió un buen** ~ I was dealt a good hand. -3. [conjunto de objetos] set; ~ **de herramientas** tool kit; ~ **de llaves/sábanas** set of keys/sheets; ~ **de té/café** tea/coffee service; **zapatos a** ~

con el bolso shoes with matching handbag; hacer ~ (con) to match.
◆ juegos florales *mpl* poetry competition (*sg*).

juegue → jugar.

juerga *f fam* rave-up, binge; irse/estar de ~ to go/be out on the town; tomar algo a ~ to take sthg as a joke.

juerguista *fam* ◇ *adj* fond of partying. ◇ *m y f* party-goer, reveller.

jueves *m inv* Thursday; ~ lardero Thursday before Shrovetide; Jueves Santo Maundy Thursday; no ser nada del otro ~ to be nothing out of this world; *ver también* sábado.

juez *m y f* -1. DER judge; ~ de instrucción, ~ de primera instancia examining magistrate; ~ de paz Justice of the Peace. -2. [DEP - gen] judge; [- en atletismo] official; ~ de línea [fútbol] linesman; [rugby] touch judge; ~ de salida starter; ~ de silla umpire.

jugada *f* -1. DEP period of play; [en tenis, ping-pong] rally; [en fútbol, rugby etc] move; [en ajedrez etc] move; [en billar] shot. -2. [treta] dirty trick; hacer una mala ~ a alguien to play a dirty trick on sb.

jugador, -ra ◇ *adj* [gen] playing; [de juego de azar] gambling. ◇ *m y f* [gen] player; [de juego de azar] gambler.

jugar [40] ◇ *vi* -1. [gen] to play; ~ al ajedrez to play chess; ~ en un equipo to play for a team; te toca ~ it's your turn ○ go; ~ limpio/sucio to play clean/dirty. -2. [con dinero]: ~ (a) to gamble (on); ~ (a la Bolsa) to speculate (on the Stock Exchange). -3. [ser desconsiderado]: ~ con to play (around) with. ◇ *vt* -1. [gen] to play; [ficha, pieza] to move. -2. [dinero]: ~ algo (a algo) to gamble sthg (on sthg).
◆ jugarse *vpr* -1. [apostarse] to bet. -2. [arriesgar] to risk. -3. *loc*: jugársela a alguien to play a dirty trick on sb.

jugarreta *f fam* dirty trick.

juglar *m* minstrel.

juglaresco, -ca *adj* minstrel (*antes de sust*).

juglaría *f* minstrelsy.

jugo *m* -1. [gen & ANAT] juice; BOT sap. -2. [interés] meat, substance; sacar ~ a algo/alguien to get the most out of sthg/sb.

jugosidad *f* juiciness.

jugoso, -sa *adj* -1. [con jugo] juicy. -2. *fig* [picante] juicy; [sustancioso] meaty, substantial.

jugué *etc* → jugar.

juguete *m lit & fig* toy; de ~ toy (*antes de sust*); ~s bélicos war toys.

juguetear *vi* to play (around); ~ con algo to toy with sthg.

juguetería *f* toy shop.

juguetón, -ona *adj* playful.

juicio *m* -1. DER trial; llevar a alguien a ~ to take sb to court. -2. [sensatez] (sound) judgement; [cordura] sanity, reason; estar/no estar en su (sano) ~ to be/not to be in one's right mind; perder el ~ to lose one's reason, to go mad. -3. [opinión] opinion; a mi ~ in my opinion.
◆ Juicio Final *m*: el Juicio Final the Last Judgement.

juicioso, -sa *adj* sensible, wise.

Jujem (*abrev de* Junta de Jefes de Estado Mayor) *f* Spanish military joint chiefs of staff.

jul. (*abrev de* julio) Jul.

juliana *f* CULIN *soup made with chopped vegetables and herbs*; en ~ julienne.

julio *m* -1. [mes] July. -2. FÍS joule; *ver también* septiembre.

jumbo *m* jumbo (jet).

jun. (*abrev de* junio) Jun.

juncal *f* bed of rushes.

junco *m* -1. [planta] rush, reed. -2. [embarcación] junk.

jungla *f* jungle.

junio *m* June; *ver también* septiembre.

júnior (*pl* juniors) ◇ *adj* -1. DEP under-21. -2. [hijo] junior. ◇ *m y f* DEP under-21.

junta *f* -1. [gen] committee; [de empresa, examinadores] board; ~ directiva board of directors; ~ de gobierno *government and administrative body in certain autonomous regions*; ~ militar military junta. -2. [reunión] meeting; ~ (general) de accionistas shareholders' meeting. -3. [juntura] joint; ~ de culata gasket.

juntamente *adv*: ~ con together with.

juntar *vt* [gen] to put together; [fondos] to raise; [personas] to bring together.
◆ juntarse *vpr* -1. [reunirse - personas] to get together; [- ríos, caminos] to meet. -2. [arrimarse] to draw ○ move closer. -3. [convivir] to live together.

junto, -ta ◇ *adj* -1. [gen] together. -2. [próximo] close together. ◇ *adv*: todo ~ [ocurrir etc] all at the same time; [escribirse] as one word.
◆ junto a *loc prep* -1. [al lado de] next to. -2. [cerca de] right by, near.
◆ junto con *loc prep* together with.

juntura *f* joint.

Júpiter *m* Jupiter.

jura *f* [gen] oath; [de un cargo] swearing in; ~ de bandera oath of allegiance to the flag.

Jura *m*: el ~ the Jura mountains (*pl*).

jurado, -da *adj* **-1.** [declaración etc] sworn. **-2.** → **guarda. -3.** → **traductor.**

◆ **jurado** *m* **-1.** [tribunal] jury. **-2.** [miembro] member of the jury.

juramentar *vt* to swear in.

juramento *m* **-1.** [promesa] oath; **bajo ~** on ○ under oath; **prestar ~** to take the oath; **tomar ~ a alguien** to swear sb in; **~ hipocrático** Hippocratic oath. **-2.** [blasfemia] oath, curse.

jurar ◇ *vt* to swear; [constitución etc] to pledge allegiance to; **te lo juro** I promise, I swear it; **~ por ... que** to swear by ... that; **~ que** to swear that. ◇ *vi* [blasfemar] to swear.

jurel *m* scad, horse mackerel.

jurídico, -ca *adj* legal.

jurisconsulto, -ta *m y f* jurist.

jurisdicción *f* jurisdiction.

jurisdiccional *adj* jurisdictional; [aguas] territorial.

jurisprudencia *f* [ciencia] jurisprudence; [casos previos] case law; **sentar ~** to set a legal precedent.

jurista *m y f* jurist.

justa *f* HIST joust.

justamente *adv* **-1.** [con justicia] justly. **-2.** [exactamente] exactly; **~, eso es lo que estaba pensando** exactly, that's just what I was thinking.

justicia *f* **-1.** [gen] justice; [equidad] fairness, justice; **administrar ~** to administer justice; **en ~** in (all) fairness; **hacer ~** to do justice; **~ social** social justice; **ser de ~** to be only fair; **tomarse la ~ por su mano** to take the law into one's own hands. **-2.** [organización]: **la ~** the law.

justiciero, -ra ◇ *adj* righteous. ◇ *m y f* angel of justice.

justificable *adj* justifiable.

justificación *f* [gen & IMPRENTA] justification; **~ automática** automatic justification.

justificado, -da *adj* justified.

justificante *m* written proof (*U*), documentary evidence (*U*).

justificar [10] *vt* **-1.** [gen & IMPRENTA] to justify. **-2.** [excusar]: **~ a alguien** to make excuses for sb.

◆ **justificarse** *vpr* **-1.** [suj: actitud etc] to be justified. **-2.** [suj: persona] to justify ○ excuse o.s.; **~se de algo** to excuse o.s. for sthg; **~se con alguien** to make one's excuses to sb.

justificativo, -va *adj* providing evidence, supporting (*antes de sust*).

justiprecio *m* valuation.

justo, -ta *adj* **-1.** [equitativo] fair. **-2.** [merecido - recompensa, victoria] deserved; [- castigo] just. **-3.** [exacto - medida, hora] exact. **-4.** [idóneo] right. **-5.** [apretado] tight; **estar** ○ **venir ~** to be a tight fit. **-6.** RELIG righteous.

◆ **justo** ◇ *m* RELIG: **los ~s** the righteous. ◇ *adv* just; **~ ahora iba a llamarte** I was just about to ring you; **~ en medio** right in the middle.

juvenil ◇ *adj* youthful; DEP youth (*antes de sust*). ◇ *m y f* (*gen pl*) DEP player in the youth team.

juventud *f* **-1.** [edad] youth. **-2.** [conjunto] young people (*pl*).

juzgado *m* **-1.** [tribunal] court; **~ municipal** magistrates' court; **~ de guardia** *court open during the night or at other times when ordinary courts are shut*; **ser de ~ de guardia** *fam* to be criminal ○ a crime. **-2.** [jurisdicción] jurisdiction.

juzgar [16] *vt* **-1.** [enjuiciar] to judge; DER to try; **~ mal a alguien** to misjudge sb; **a ~ por (como)** judging by (how). **-2.** [estimar] to consider, to judge.

k, K *f* [letra] k, K.

Kabul Kabul.

kafkiano, -na *adj* *fig* kafkaesque.

káiser (*pl* **káisers**) *m* kaiser.

kaki = **caqui.**

Kalahari *m*: el (desierto) ~ the Kalahari Desert.

kamikaze *m* **-1.** MIL kamikaze. **-2.** *fig* [arriesgado] daredevil.

Kampala Kampala.

kantiano, -na *adj, m y f* Kantian.

kárate, cárate *m* karate.

karateka *m y f* karateist.

kart (*pl* **karts**) *m* go-kart.

KAS (*abrev de* **Koordinadora Abertzale Sozialista**) *f Basque left-wing nationalist political group which includes the terrorist organization ETA.*

katiusca, katiuska *f ankle-length rubber boot.*

Katmandú Katmandu.

kayac (*pl* **kayacs**) *m* kayak.
kelvin (*pl* **kelvins**) *m* kelvin.
Kenia Kenya.
keniata *adj, m y f* Kenyan.
kepis = **quepis**.
kermesse [ker'mes] *f* kermis.
keroseno = **queroseno**.
ketchup ['ketʃup] *m* ketchup.
keynesianismo *m* Keynesianism.
keynesiano, -na *adj* Keynesian.
kg (*abrev de* **kilogramo**) kg.
KGB *m* KGB.
kibutz [ki'ßuθ] (*pl* **kibutzim**) *m* kibbutz.
kif = **quif**.
Kilimanjaro *m*: **el ~** (Mount) Kilimanjaro.
kilo, quilo *m* **-1.** [peso] kilo. **-2.** *fam* [millón] tonne, million.
kilocaloría, quilocaloría *f* kilocalorie.
kilogramo, quilogramo *m* kilogram.
kilolitro, quilolitro *m* kilolitre.
kilometraje, quilometraje *m* ≃ mileage, distance in kilometres.
kilometrar, quilometrar *vt* to measure in kilometres.
kilométrico, -ca, quilométrico, -ca *adj* **-1.** [distancia] kilometric. **-2.** *fig* [largo] very long.
kilómetro, quilómetro *m* kilometre; **~ cuadrado** square kilometre.
kilovatio, quilovatio *m* kilowatt.
kilovoltio, quilovoltio *m* kilovolt.
kimono = **quimono**.
Kingston Kingston.
Kinshasa Kinshasa.
KIO (*abrev de* **Kuwait Investment Office**) *f* KIO.
kiosco = **quiosco**.
kirial *m* RELIG plainsong book.
kirsch [kirʃ] *m* kirsch.
kiwi (*pl* **kiwis**) *m* [fruto] kiwi (fruit).
KKK (*abrev de* **Ku-Klux-Klan**) *m* KKK.
km (*abrev de* **kilómetro**) km.
km/h (*abrev de* **kilómetro por hora**) km/h.
knockout [no'kaut] *m* knockout.
KO (*abrev de* **knockout**) *m* KO.
kopeck (*pl* **kopecks**) *m* kopeck.
Kuala Lumpur Kuala Lumpur.
kuchen *m* Amer cake.
Kurdistán *m* Kurdistan.
kurdo, -da ◇ *adj* Kurdish. ◇ *m y f* Kurd.
Kuwait [ku'ßait] Kuwait.
kuwaití (*pl* **kuwaitíes**) *adj, m y f* Kuwaiti.

l¹, L *f* [letra] l, L.
l² (*abrev de* **litro**) l.
L/ *abrev de* **letra**.
la¹ *m* MÚS A; [en solfeo] lah.
la² ◇ *art* → **el**. ◇ *pron* → **lo**.
laberíntico, -ca *adj* *lit* & *fig* labyrinthine.
laberinto *m* *lit* & *fig* labyrinth.
labia *f* *fam* smooth talk; **tener mucha ~** to have the gift of the gab.
labial *adj* & *f* labial.
labio *m* **-1.** ANAT lip; **~ leporino** harelip; **estar pendiente de los ~s de alguien** to hang on sb's every word; **no despegar los ~s** not to utter a word. **-2.** [borde] edge.
labiodental *adj* & *f* labiodental.
labor *f* **-1.** [trabajo] work; [tarea] task; **~ de equipo** teamwork (*U*); **~es domésticas** household chores; **ser de profesión sus ~es** to be a housewife; **no estar por la ~** [distraerse] not to have one's mind on the job; [ser reacio] not to be keen on the idea. **-2.** [de costura] needlework.
laborable → **día**.
laboral *adj* labour; [semana, condiciones] working (*antes de sust*).
laboralista ◇ *adj* labour (*antes de sust*). ◇ *m y f* labour lawyer.
laboratorio *m* laboratory; **~ de idiomas** O **lenguas** language laboratory.
laborioso, -sa *adj* **-1.** [difícil] laborious, arduous. **-2.** [trabajador] hard-working.
laborismo *m*: **el ~** the Labour party.
laborista ◇ *adj* Labour. ◇ *m y f* Labour Party supporter O member; **los ~s** Labour.
labrador, -ra *m y f* [agricultor] farmer; [trabajador] farm worker.
labranza *f* farming.
labrar *vt* **-1.** [campo - cultivar] to cultivate; [- arar] to plough. **-2.** [piedra, metal etc] to work. **-3.** *fig* [desgracia etc] to bring about; [porvenir, fortuna] to carve out.
◆ **labrarse** *vpr* [porvenir etc] to carve out for o.s.
labriego, -ga *m y f* farmworker.

laca f -1. [gen] lacquer; [para cuadros] lake. -2. [para el pelo] hairspray. -3. [de uñas] nail varnish.

lacado m lacquering.

lacar [10] vt to lacquer.

lacayo m footman; fig lackey.

lacerante adj [dolor] excruciating, stabbing; [palabras etc] hurtful, cutting; [grito etc] piercing.

lacerar vt to lacerate; fig to wound.

lacio, -cia adj -1. [cabello - liso] straight; [- sin fuerza] lank. -2. [planta] wilted. -3. fig [sin fuerza] limp.

lacón m shoulder of pork.

lacónico, -ca adj laconic.

laconismo m terseness.

lacra f scourge.

lacrar vt to seal with sealing wax.

lacre m sealing wax.

lacrimal adj lacrimal, tear (antes de sust).

lacrimógeno, -na adj -1. [novela etc] weepy, tear-jerking. -2. → gas.

lacrimoso, -sa adj -1. [ojos etc] tearful. -2. [historia etc] weepy, tear-jerking.

LACSA (abrev de Líneas Aéreas Costarricenses, SA) f Costa Rican state airline.

lactancia f lactation; ~ materna breastfeeding.

lactante m y f breast-fed baby.

lactar vt & vi to suckle, to breastfeed.

lácteo, -a adj -1. [gen] milk (antes de sust); [industria, productos] dairy. -2. fig [blanco] milky.

láctico, -ca adj lactic.

lactosa f lactose.

ladeado, -da adj tilted, at an angle.

ladear vt to tilt.

ladera f slope, mountainside.

ladilla f crab (louse).

ladino, -na adj crafty.
◆ **ladino** m [dialecto] Ladino.

lado m -1. [gen] side; **en el ~ de arriba/abajo** on the top/bottom; **a ambos ~s** on both sides; **estoy de su ~** I'm on her side; **de ~** [torcido] crooked; **dormir de ~** to sleep on one's side; **echarse ○ hacerse a un ~** to move aside; **por un ~** on the one hand; **por otro ~** on the other hand. -2. [lugar] place; **debe estar en otro ~** it must be somewhere else; **de un ~ para ○ a otro** to and fro. -3. loc: **dar de ~ a alguien** to cold-shoulder sb; **dejar algo de ~ ○ a un ~** [prescindir] to leave sthg to one side; **mirar de ~ a alguien** [despreciar] to look askance at sb.
◆ **al lado** loc adv [cerca] nearby.

◆ **al lado de** loc prep [junto a] beside.
◆ **de al lado** loc adj next door; **la casa de al ~** the house next door.

ladrador, -ra adj barking.

ladrar vi lit & fig to bark; **estar alguien que ladra** to be in a foul mood.

ladrido m lit & fig bark, barking (U).

ladrillo m -1. CONSTR brick. -2. fam fig [pesadez] drag, bore.

ladrón, -ona ◇ adj thieving. ◇ m y f [persona] thief, robber.
◆ **ladrón** m [para varios enchufes] adapter.

lady ['leiði] (pl ladies) f Lady.

lagar m [de vino] winepress; [de aceite] oil press.

lagarta → lagarto.

lagartija f (small) lizard.

lagarto, -ta m y f ZOOL lizard.
◆ **lagarta** f fam fig [mujer] scheming woman.

lago m lake.

Lagos Lagos.

Lago Superior m Lake Superior.

lágrima f tear; **hacer saltar las ~s** to bring tears to the eyes; **llorar a ~ viva** to cry buckets; **~s de cocodrilo** crocodile tears.

lagrimal ◇ adj lacrimal, tear (antes de sust). ◇ m corner of the eye.

lagrimear vi [suj: persona] to weep; [suj: ojos] to water.

laguna f -1. [lago] lagoon. -2. fig [en colección, memoria] gap; [en leyes, reglamento] loophole.

La Habana Havana.

La Haya The Hague.

laicismo m laicism.

laico, -ca ◇ adj lay, secular. ◇ m y f layman (f laywoman).

laísmo m the use of "la" and "las" instead of "le" as indirect objects.

lama m lama.

lambada f lambada.

lamber vt Amer fam to lick.

lamé m lamé.

La Meca Mecca.

lameculos m & f inv vulg arse-licker.

lamentable adj -1. [triste] terribly sad. -2. [malo] lamentable, deplorable.

lamentación f moaning (U).

lamentar vt to regret, to be sorry about; **lo lamento** I'm very sorry; **lamentamos comunicarle ... we regret to inform you ....**
◆ **lamentarse** vpr: ~se (de ○ por) to complain (about).

lamento m moan, cry of pain.

lamer *vt* to lick.
◆ **lamerse** *vpr* to lick o.s.
lametón *m* (big) lick.
lamido, -da *adj* skinny.
◆ **lamido** *m* lick.
lámina *f* **-1.** [plancha] sheet; [placa] plate.
-2. [rodaja] slice. **-3.** [plancha grabada] engraving. **-4.** [dibujo] plate.
laminado, -da *adj* **-1.** [cubierto por láminas] laminated. **-2.** [reducido a láminas] rolled.
◆ **laminado** *m* **-1.** [cubrir con láminas] lamination. **-2.** [reducir a láminas] rolling.
laminador *m*, **laminadora** *f* rolling mill.
laminar ◇ *adj* laminar. ◇ *vt* **-1.** [hacer láminas] to roll. **-2.** [cubrir con láminas] to laminate.
lámpara *f* **-1.** [aparato] lamp; ~ **de mesa** table lamp; ~ **de pie** standard lamp. **-2.** [bombilla] bulb. **-3.** TECN valve.
lamparilla *f* small lamp.
lamparón *m* grease stain.
lampazo *m* Amer cloth.
lampiño, -ña *adj* [sin barba] beardless, smooth-cheeked; [sin vello] hairless.
lamprea *f* lamprey.
lana ◇ *f* wool; **de** ~ woollen; **ir a por** ~ **y volver trasquilado** *proverb* to go for wool and come home shorn. ◇ *m* Amer fam dosh, dough.
lanar *adj* wool-bearing.
lance ◇ *v* → **lanzar**. ◇ *m* **-1.** [en juegos, deportes] incident; [acontecimiento] event. **-2.** [riña] dispute.
lancero *m* lancer.
lanceta *f* Amer sting.
lancha *f* **-1.** [embarcación - grande] launch; [- pequeña] boat; ~ **neumática** rubber dinghy; ~ **patrullera** patrol boat; ~ **salvavidas** lifeboat. **-2.** [piedra] slab.
lancinante *adj* piercing, stabbing.
landa *f* moor.
landó (*pl* **landós**) *m* landau.
lanero, -ra *adj* wool (*antes de sust*).
langosta *f* **-1.** [crustáceo] lobster. **-2.** [insecto] locust.
langostino *m* king prawn.
languidecer [30] *vi* to languish; [conversación, entusiasmo] to flag.
languidez *f* [debilidad] listlessness; [falta de ánimo] disinterest.
lánguido, -da *adj* [débil] listless; [falto de ánimo] disinterested.
lanilla *f* **-1.** [pelillo] nap. **-2.** [tejido] flannel.
lanolina *f* lanolin.
lanudo, -da *adj* woolly.

lanza *f* **-1.** [arma - arrojadiza] spear; [- en justas, torneos] lance. **-2.** [de carruaje] shaft.
lanzacohetes *m inv* rocket launcher.
lanzadera *f* [de telar] shuttle.
◆ **lanzadera espacial** *f* space shuttle.
lanzado, -da *adj* **-1.** [atrevido] forward; [valeroso] fearless. **-2.** [rápido]: **ir** ~ to hurtle along.
lanzagranadas *m inv* grenade launcher.
lanzallamas *m inv* flamethrower.
lanzamiento *m* **-1.** [de objeto] throwing; [de cohete] launching. **-2.** [DEP - con la mano] throw; [- con el pie] kick; [- en béisbol] pitch; ~ **de disco** discus; ~ **de jabalina** javelin; ~ **de martillo** hammer; ~ **de peso** shot put. **-3.** [de producto, artista] launch; [de disco] release.
lanzamisiles *m inv* rocket launcher.
lanzaplatos *m inv* DEP (clay pigeon) trap.
lanzar [13] *vt* **-1.** [gen] to throw; [con fuerza] to hurl, to fling; [de una patada] to kick; [bomba] to drop; [flecha, misil] to fire; [cohete] to launch. **-2.** [proferir] to let out; [acusación, insulto] to hurl; [suspiro] to heave. **-3.** [COM - producto, artista, periódico] to launch; [- disco] to release.
◆ **lanzarse** *vpr* **-1.** [tirarse] to throw o.s. **-2.** [abalanzarse]: ~**se (sobre)** to throw o.s. (upon). **-3.** [empezar]: ~**se (a hacer algo)** to get started (doing sthg).
lanzatorpedos *m inv* torpedo tube.
LAP (*abrev de* **Líneas Aéreas Paraguayas**) *f* Paraguayan state airline.
lapa *f* **-1.** ZOOL limpet. **-2.** fam fig [persona] hanger-on, pest; **pegarse como una** ~ to cling like a leech.
La Paz La Paz.
lapicera *f* Amer [bolígrafo] biro, pen.
lapicero *m* pencil.
lápida *f* memorial stone; ~ **mortuoria** tombstone.
lapidación *f* stoning.
lapidar *vt* to stone.
lapidario, -ria *adj* solemn.
lapislázuli *m* lapis lazuli.
lápiz (*pl* **lápices**) *m* pencil; ~ **de labios** lipstick; ~ **de ojos** eyeliner; ~ **óptico** INFORM light pen.
lapo *m* fam gob, spit.
lapón, -ona *adj, m y f* Lapp.
◆ **lapón** *m* [lengua] Lapp.
lapso *m* space, interval.
lapsus *m inv* lapse, slip.
laque *etc* → **lacar**.
laquear *vt* to lacquer.

lar *m* **-1.** [lumbre] hearth. **-2.** MITOL household god.

◆ **lares** *mpl* [hogar] hearth and home.

lardero → **jueves.**

larga → **largo.**

largar [16] *vt* **-1.** [aflojar] to pay out. **-2.** *fam* [dar, decir] to give; **le largué un bofetón** I gave him a smack.

◆ **largarse** *vpr fam* to clear off.

largavistas *m inv Amer* binoculars (*pl*).

largo, -ga *adj* **-1.** [en espacio, tiempo] long; **estarle ~ a alguien** to be too long for sb. **-2.** [alto] tall. **-3.** [sobrado]: **media hora larga** a good half hour. **-4.** *fam* [astuto] sly, crafty. **-5.** *fam* [generoso]: **~ en hacer algo** generous in doing sthg.

◆ **largo** ◇ *m* length; **a lo ~** lengthways; **tiene dos metros de ~** it's two metres long; **pasar de ~** to pass by; **vestirse de ~** to dress up, to dress formally; **a lo ~ de** [en el espacio] along; [en el tiempo] throughout; **a lo ~ y a lo ancho de** right across, throughout; **¡~ de aquí!** go away!, get out of here! ◇ *adv* at length; **~ y tendido** at great length.

◆ **larga** *f*: **a la larga** in the long run; **dar largas a algo** to put sthg off.

largometraje *m* feature film.

largue *etc* → **largar.**

larguero *m* **-1.** CONSTR main beam. **-2.** DEP crossbar.

larguirucho, -cha *adj fam* lanky.

largura *f* length.

laringe *f* larynx.

laringitis *f inv* laryngitis.

laringología *f* laryngology.

laringólogo, -ga *m y f* laryngologist.

La Rioja La Rioja.

larva *f* larva.

larvado, -da *adj* latent.

las ◇ *art* → **el.** ◇ *pron* → **lo.**

lasaña *f* lasagne, lasagna.

lascivia *f* lasciviousness, lechery.

lascivo, -va ◇ *adj* lascivious, lewd. ◇ *m y f* lascivious o lewd person.

láser ◇ *adj inv* → **rayo.** ◇ *m inv* laser.

laserterapia *f* laser therapy.

lasitud *f* lassitude.

laso, -sa *adj* **-1.** [cansado] weary. **-2.** [liso] straight.

Las Palmas (de Gran Canaria) Las Palmas.

lástex *m inv* Lastex®.

lástima *f* **-1.** [compasión] pity. **-2.** [pena] shame, pity; **dar ~** to be a crying shame; **da ~ ver gente así** it's sad to see people in that state; **¡qué ~!** what a shame o pity!; **quedarse hecho una ~** to be a sorry o pitiful sight.

lastimar *vt* to hurt.

◆ **lastimarse** *vpr* to hurt o.s.

lastimoso, -sa *adj* pitiful, woeful.

lastrar *vt* to ballast.

lastre *m* **-1.** [peso] ballast; **soltar ~** to discharge ballast. **-2.** *fig* [estorbo] burden.

lata *f* **-1.** [envase] can, tin; [de bebidas] can; **en ~** tinned, canned. **-2.** *fam* [fastidio] pain; **¡qué ~!** what a pain!; **dar la ~ a alguien** to pester sb.

latente *adj* latent.

lateral ◇ *adj* **-1.** [del lado - gen] lateral; [- puerta, pared] side. **-2.** [indirecto] indirect. ◇ *m* **-1.** [lado] side. **-2.** DEP: **~ derecho/izquierdo** right/left back.

látex *m inv* latex.

latido *m* [del corazón] beat; [en dedo etc] throb, throbbing (*U*).

latiente *adj* [corazón] beating.

latifundio *m* large rural estate.

latifundismo *m* *the system of land tenure characterized by the "latifundio".*

latigazo *m* **-1.** [golpe] lash. **-2.** [chasquido] crack (of the whip). **-3.** *fam* [trago] swig.

látigo *m* whip.

latín *m* Latin; **~ clásico/vulgar** Classical/Vulgar Latin; **~ de cocina** o **macarrónico** dog Latin; **saber (mucho) ~** *fig* to be sharp, to be on the ball.

latinajo *m fam despec* Latin word used in an attempt to sound academic.

latinismo *m* Latinism.

latinista *m y f* Latinist.

latinizar [13] *vt* to Latinize.

latino, -na *adj, m y f* Latin.

latinoamericano, -na *adj, m y f* Latin American.

latir *vi* **-1.** [suj: corazón] to beat. **-2.** [estar latente] to be concealed, to lie.

latitud *f* GEOGR latitude.

◆ **latitudes** *fpl* [parajes] region (*sg*), area (*sg*).

lato, -ta *adj* **-1.** [discurso etc] extensive, lengthy. **-2.** [sentido etc] broad.

latón *m* brass.

latoso, -sa *fam* ◇ *adj* tiresome. ◇ *m y f* pain (in the neck).

latrocinio *m* larceny.

laúd *m* lute.

laudable *adj* praiseworthy.

láudano *m* laudanum.

laudatorio, -ria *adj* laudatory.

laureado, -da *adj* prize-winning.

laurear *vt:* ~ **a alguien (con)** to honour sb (with).

laurel *m* BOT laurel; CULIN bay leaf.

◆ **laureles** *mpl* [honores] laurels; **dormirse en los ~es** *fig* to rest on one's laurels.

LAV (*abrev de* **Línea Aeropostal Venezolana**) *f Venezuelan state airline.*

lava *f* lava.

lavable *adj* washable.

lavabo *m* **-1.** [objeto] washbasin. **-2.** [habitación] lavatory *Br*, washroom *Am*.

lavacoches *m & f inv* car washer.

lavadero *m* [en casa] laundry room; [público] washing place.

lavado *m* wash, washing (*U*); ~ **de cerebro** brainwashing; ~ **de estómago** stomach pumping.

lavadora *f* washing machine.

lavafrutas *m inv* finger bowl.

La Valeta Valetta.

lavamanos *m inv* washbasin.

lavanda *f* lavender.

lavandería *f* laundry; [automática] launderette.

lavandero, -ra *m* laundryman (*f* laundress).

lavaplatos ◇ *m y f inv* [persona] dishwasher, washer-up. ◇ *m inv* [aparato] dishwasher.

lavar *vt* **-1.** [limpiar] to wash; ~ **y marcar** shampoo and set. **-2.** *fig* [honor] to clear; [ofensa] to make up for.

◆ **lavarse** *vpr* [gen] to wash o.s.; [cara, manos, pelo] to wash; [dientes] to clean.

lavaseco *m Amer* dry cleaner's.

lavativa *f* enema.

lavavajillas *m inv* dishwasher.

laxante ◇ *adj* **-1.** MED laxative. **-2.** [relajante] relaxing. ◇ *m* MED laxative.

laxar *vt* [vientre] to loosen.

laxativo, -va *adj* laxative.

◆ **laxativo** *m* laxative.

laxitud *f* [de músculo, cable] slackness; *fig* laxity.

laxo, -xa *adj* [músculo, cable] slack; *fig* lax.

lazada *f* bow.

lazarillo *m* **-1.** [persona] blind person's guide. **-2.** → **perro**.

lazo *m* **-1.** [atadura] bow. **-2.** [trampa] snare; [de vaquero] lasso. **-3.** (*gen pl*) *fig* [vínculo] tie, bond.

l.c. = loc. cit.

LCD (*abrev de* **liquid crystal display**) *f* LCD.

Lda. *abrev de* **licenciada**.

Ldo. *abrev de* **licenciado**.

le *pron pers* **-1.** (*complemento indirecto*) [- hombre] (to) him; [- mujer] (to) her; [- cosa] to it; [- usted] to you; ~ **expliqué el motivo** I explained the reason to him/her; ~ **tengo miedo** I'm afraid of him/her; **ya** ~ **dije lo que pasaría** I told you what would happen. **-2.** (*complemento directo*) him; [usted] you. **-3.** → **se**.

leal ◇ *adj:* ~ **(a)** loyal (to). ◇ *m y f:* ~ **(a)** loyal supporter (of).

lealtad *f:* ~ **(a)** loyalty (to).

leasing ['lisin] (*pl* **leasings**) *m system of leasing whereby the lessee has the option of purchasing the property after a certain time.*

lebrel *m* whippet.

lección *f* lesson; **dar a alguien una** ~ [como advertencia] to teach sb a lesson; [como ejemplo] to give sb a lesson; **servir de** ~ to serve as a lesson.

lechal ◇ *adj* sucking. ◇ *m* sucking lamb.

leche *f* **-1.** [gen] milk; ~ **condensada/en polvo** condensed/powdered milk; ~ **de almendras** almond milk; ~ **descremada** O **desnatada** skimmed milk; ~ **esterilizada/homogeneizada** sterilized/homogenized milk; ~ **merengada** *drink made from milk, egg whites, sugar and cinnamon*; ~ **pasterizada** O **pasteurizada** pasteurized milk; ~ **semidesnatada** semiskimmed milk. **-2.** [de plantas] (milky) sap. **-3.** *mfam* [bofetada]: **pegar una** ~ **a alguien** to belt O clobber sb. **-4.** *mfam* [accidente] smash-up. **-5.** *mfam* [malhumor]: bloody awful mood; **estar de mala** ~ to be in a bloody awful mood; **tener mala** ~ to be a miserable git. **-6.** *mfam* [suerte]: **tener mala** ~ to have bloody awful luck. **-7.** *vulg* [semen] spunk. **-8.** *loc mfam:* **ser la** ~ [ser raro] to be a nutcase; [ser molesto] to be a pain (in the neck); **¡una** ~! no way!

lechera → **lechero**.

lechería *f* dairy.

lechero, -ra ◇ *adj* milk (*antes de sust*), dairy. ◇ *m y f* [persona] milkman (*f* milkwoman).

◆ **lechera** *f* [para transportar] milk churn; [para beber] milk jug.

lecho *m* **-1.** [gen] bed; **ser un** ~ **de rosas** to be a bed of roses. **-2.** [capa] layer.

lechón *m* sucking pig.

lechoso, -sa *adj* milky.

lechuga *f* **-1.** [planta] lettuce. **-2.** *fam* [billete] *thousand peseta note*.

lechuza *f* (barn) owl.

lecitina *f* lecithin.

lectivo, -va *adj* school (*antes de sust*).

lector, -ra *m y f* **-1.** [gen] reader. **-2.** EDUC language assistant.

◆ **lector** *m* [de microfilms etc] reader, scanner; ~ **óptico** optical scanner.

lectorado *m* post of language assistant.

lectura *f* **-1.** [gen] reading. **-2.** [de tesis] viva voce. **-3.** [escrito] reading (matter) (*U*). **-4.** [de datos] scanning; ~ **óptica** optical scanning.

leer [50] ◇ *vt* [gen & INFORM] to read. ◇ *vi* to read; ~ **de corrido** to read fluently.

legación *f* legation.

legado *m* **-1.** [herencia] legacy. **-2.** [representante - cargo] legation; [- persona] legate.

legajo *m* file.

legal *adj* **-1.** [gen] legal; [hora] standard. **-2.** [forense] forensic. **-3.** *fam* [persona] honest, decent.

legalidad *f* legality.

legalismo *m* fine legal point, legalism.

legalista ◇ *adj* legalistic. ◇ *m y f* legalist.

legalización *f* **-1.** [gen] legalization. **-2.** [certificado] (certificate of) authentication.

legalizar [13] *vt* **-1.** [gen] to legalize. **-2.** [certificar] to authenticate.

legañas *fpl* sleep (*U*) (*in the eyes*).

legañoso, -sa *adj* full of sleep.

legar [16] *vt* **-1.** [gen] to bequeath. **-2.** [delegar] to delegate.

legatario, -ria *m y f* legatee.

legendario, -ria *adj* legendary.

legible *adj* legible.

legión *f lit & fig* legion.
◆ **Legión de Honor** *f* Legion of Honour.

legionario, -ria *adj* legionary.
◆ **legionario** *m* HIST legionary; MIL legionnaire.

legislación *f* **-1.** [leyes] legislation. **-2.** [ciencia] law.

legislador, -ra ◇ *adj* legislative. ◇ *m y f* legislator.

legislar *vi* to legislate.

legislativo, -va *adj* legislative.

legislatura *f* **-1.** [periodo] period of office. **-2.** [órganos] parliament, legislature.

legitimación *f* **-1.** [legalización] legitimation. **-2.** [certificación] authentication.

legitimar *vt* **-1.** [legalizar] to legitimize. **-2.** [certificar] to authenticate.

legitimidad *f* legitimacy.

legítimo, -ma *adj* [gen] legitimate; [auténtico] real, genuine; [oro] pure.

lego, -ga ◇ *adj* **-1.** [gen] lay. **-2.** [ignorante] ignorant; **ser** ~ **en** to know nothing about. ◇ *m y f* **-1.** [gen] layman (*f* laywoman). **-2.** [ignorante] ignorant person.

legua *f* league; ~ **marina** marine league; **verse a la** ~ to stand out a mile.

legue *etc* → **legar**.

leguleyo, -ya *m y f despec* bad lawyer.

legumbre *f* (*gen pl*) pulse, pod vegetable; ~**s secas** dried pulses; ~**s verdes** green vegetables.

leguminosas *fpl* pulses, leguminous vegetables.

lehendakari [lenda'kari] *m president of the Basque government*.

leído, -da *adj* **-1.** [obra]: **muy/poco** ~ much/little read. **-2.** [persona] well-read.
◆ **leída** *f* reading.

leísmo *m* GRAM *use of "le" as direct object instead of "lo"*.

leitmotiv [leitmo'tif] (*pl* **leitmotivs**) *m* leitmotiv.

lejanía *f* distance.

lejano, -na *adj* distant; **no está** ~ it's not far (away).

lejía *f* bleach.

lejos *adv* **-1.** [en el espacio] far (away); **¿está** ~**?** is it far?; **a lo** ~ in the distance; **de** ◇ **desde** ~ from a distance. **-2.** [en el pasado] long ago; [en el futuro] far in the future; **eso queda ya** ~ that happened a long time ago.
◆ **lejos de** ◇ *loc conj* far from; ~ **de mejorar ...** far from getting better .... ◇ *loc prep* far (away) from.

lelo, -la ◇ *adj* stupid, slow. ◇ *m y f* idiot.

lema *m* **-1.** [norma] motto; [político, publicitario] slogan. **-2.** LING & MAT lemma.

Léman *m*: **el lago** ~ Lake Geneva.

lempira *m* lempira.

lencería *f* **-1.** [ropa] linen; ~ **fina** lingerie. **-2.** [tienda] draper's.

lendakari *m president of the autonomous Basque government*.

lengua *f* **-1.** [gen] tongue; ~ **de gato** CULIN ≈ chocolate finger (biscuit); ~ **de víbora** ◇ **viperina** malicious tongue; **irse de la** ~ to let the cat out of the bag; **morderse la** ~ to bite one's tongue; **se le trabó la** ~ she stumbled over her words; **ser largo de** ~ to be a gossip; **tirar a alguien de la** ~ to draw sb out. **-2.** [idioma, lenguaje] language; ~ **materna** mother tongue; ~ **muerta** dead language.

lenguado *m* sole.

lenguaje *m* [gen & INFORM] language; ~ **coloquial/comercial** colloquial/business language; ~ **cifrado** code; ~ **corporal** body language; ~ **gestual** gestures (*pl*); ~ **máquina** machine language; ~ **de alto nivel/ de bajo nivel** high-level/low-level language; ~ **de programación** programming language; ~ **de los sordomudos** sign language.

lenguaraz *adj* **-1.** [malhablado] foul-mouthed. **-2.** [charlatán] talkative.

lengüeta *f* [gen & MÚS] tongue.

lengüetazo *m*, **lengüetada** *f* lick.

lenidad *f* leniency.

leninismo *m* Leninism.

leninista *adj, m y f* Leninist.

lenitivo, -va *adj* soothing, lenitive.
◆ **lenitivo** *m* **-1.** [físico] lenitive. **-2.** [moral] balm.

lenocinio *m* procuring, pimping.

lente *f* lens; ~s **de contacto** contact lenses.
◆ **lentes** *mpl* [gafas] glasses.

lenteja *f* lentil.

lentejuela *f* sequin.

lenticular *adj* lenticular.

lentilla *f* (*gen pl*) contact lens.

lentitud *f* slowness; **con** ~ slowly.

lento, -ta *adj* slow; [veneno] slow-working; [agonía, enfermedad] lingering, long drawn out.

leña *f* **-1.** [madera] firewood; **echar** ~ **al fuego** to add fuel to the flames ○ fire. **-2.** *fam* [golpes] beating; **dar** ~ **a alguien** to beat sb up.

leñador, -ra *m y f* woodcutter.

leñazo *m fam* **-1.** [garrotazo] blow with a stick; [golpe] bang, bash. **-2.** [choque] smash-up, crash.

leñe *interj fam*: ¡~! for heaven's sake!

leñera *f* woodshed.

leño *m* **-1.** [de madera] log; **dormir como un** ~ to sleep like a log. **-2.** *fam fig* [persona] blockhead.

leñoso, -sa *adj* woody.

Leo ◇ *m* [zodiaco] Leo; **ser** ~ to be (a) Leo. ◇ *m y f* [persona] Leo.

león, -ona *m y f* lion (*f* lioness); *fig* fierce person; **no es tan fiero el** ~ **como lo pintan** *proverb* he/it *etc* is not as bad as he/it *etc* is made out to be.
◆ **león marino** *m* sea lion.

leonera *f* **-1.** [jaula] lion's cage. **-2.** *fam fig* [cuarto sucio] pigsty.

leonino, -na *adj* **-1.** [rostro, aspecto] leonine. **-2.** [contrato, condiciones] one-sided, unfair.

leopardo *m* leopard.

leotardo *m* **-1.** (*gen pl*) [medias] stockings (*pl*), thick tights (*pl*). **-2.** [de gimnasta etc] leotard.

lépero, -ra *adj Amer fam* coarse, vulgar.

leporino → **labio**.

lepra *f* leprosy.

leprosería *f* leper colony.

leproso, -sa ◇ *adj* leprous. ◇ *m y f* leper.

lerdo, -da ◇ *adj* [idiota] dim, slow-witted; [torpe] useless, hopeless. ◇ *m y f* [idiota] fool, idiot; [torpe] useless idiot.

les *pron pers pl* **-1.** (*complemento indirecto*) (to) them; [ustedes] (to) you; ~ **expliqué el motivo** I explained the reason to them; ~ **tengo miedo** I'm afraid of them; **ya** ~ **dije lo que pasaría** [a ustedes] I told you what would happen. **-2.** (*complemento directo*) them; [ustedes] you. **-3.** → **se**.

lesbianismo *m* lesbianism.

lesbiano, -na *adj* lesbian.
◆ **lesbiana** *f* lesbian.

leseras *fpl Amer* rubbish (U), nonsense (U).

lesión *f* **-1.** [herida] injury. **-2.** *fig* [perjuicio] damage, harm. **-3.** DER: ~ **grave** grievous bodily harm.

lesionado, -da ◇ *adj* injured. ◇ *m y f* injured person.

lesionar *vt* to injure; *fig* to damage, to harm.
◆ **lesionarse** *vpr* to injure o.s.

lesivo, -va *adj* damaging, harmful.

leso, -sa *adj*: **crimen de lesa humanidad** crime against humanity; **crimen de lesa patria** high treason (U).

letal *adj* lethal.

letanía *f* (*gen pl*) *lit* & *fig* litany.

letárgico, -ca *adj* **-1.** MED lethargic. **-2.** ZOOL hibernating.

letargo *m* **-1.** MED lethargy. **-2.** ZOOL hibernation.

Letonia Latvia.

letonio, -nia, letón, -ona *adj, m y f* Latvian.
◆ **letonio, letón** *m* [lengua] Latvian.

letra *f* **-1.** [signo] letter. **-2.** [caligrafía] handwriting. **-3.** [estilo] script; IMPRENTA type, typeface; ~ **bastardilla** ○ **cursiva** ○ **itálica** italic type, italics (*pl*); ~ **de imprenta** ○ **molde** IMPRENTA print; [en formularios etc] block capitals (*pl*); ~ **mayúscula/minúscula** capital/small letter; ~ **negrita** ○ **negrilla** bold (face); **leer la** ~ **pequeña** *fig* to read the small print; **mandar cuatro** ~**s a alguien** to drop sb a line. **-4.** [de una canción] lyrics (*pl*). **-5.** COM: ~ **(de cambio)** bill of exchange; **girar una** ~ to draw a bill of exchange; **protestar una** ~ to protest a bill; ~ **avalada** guaranteed bill of exchange; ~ **de cambio a la vista** sight bill. **-6.** [sentido] literal meaning; **al pie de la** ~ to the letter.
◆ **letras** *fpl* EDUC arts; **ser de** ~**s** to study an arts subject.

letrado, -da ◇ *adj* learned. ◇ *m y f* lawyer.

letrero *m* sign.
letrina *f* latrine.
letrista *m y f* lyricist.
leucemia *f* leukaemia.
leucémico, -ca ◇ *adj* leukaemia (*antes de sust*). ◇ *m y f* person suffering from leukaemia.
leucocito *m* (*gen pl*) leucocyte.
leva *f* **-1.** MIL levy. **-2.** NÁUT weighing anchor. **-3.** MEC cam.
levadizo → **puente**.
levadura *f* yeast, leaven; ~ **de cerveza** brewer's yeast.
levantador, -ra ◇ *adj* lifting. ◇ *m y f*: ~ **de pesas** DEP weightlifter.
levantamiento *m* **-1.** [sublevación] uprising. **-2.** [elevación] raising; ~ **de pesas** DEP weightlifting. **-3.** [supresión] lifting, removal.
levantar *vt* **-1.** [gen] to raise; [peso, capó, trampilla] to lift; ~ **el ánimo** to cheer up; ~ **la vista** o **mirada** to look up. **-2.** [separar - pintura, venda, tapa] to remove. **-3.** [recoger - campamento] to strike; [- tienda de campaña, puesto] to take down; [- mesa] to clear. **-4.** [encender - protestas, polémica] to stir up; ~ **a alguien contra** to stir sb up against. **-5.** [suspender - embargo, prohibición] to lift; [- pena, castigo] to suspend; [- sesión] to adjourn. **-6.** [redactar - acta, atestado] to draw up.
◆ **levantarse** *vpr* **-1.** [ponerse de pie] to stand up. **-2.** [de la cama] to get up. **-3.** [elevarse - avión etc] to lift off, to take off; [- niebla] to lift. **-4.** [sublevarse] to rise up. **-5.** [empezar - viento, oleaje] to get up, to rise; [- tormenta] to gather.
levante *m* **-1.** [este] east; [región] east coast. **-2.** [viento] east wind.
◆ **Levante** *m* GEOGR *the east coast of Spain between Castellón and Cartagena*.
levar *vt* to weigh.
leve *adj* **-1.** light; [olor, sabor, temblor] slight. **-2.** [pecado, falta, herida] minor. **-3.** [enfermedad] mild, slight.
levedad *f* lightness; [de temblor etc] slightness; [de pecado, falto, herida] minor nature; [de enfermedad] mildness.
levita *f* frock coat.
levitación *f* levitation.
levitar *vi* to levitate.
lexema *m* lexeme.
léxico, -ca *adj* lexical.
◆ **léxico** *m* **-1.** [vocabulario] vocabulary. **-2.** [diccionario] lexicon, dictionary.
lexicografía *f* lexicography.
lexicográfico, -ca *adj* lexicographical.

lexicógrafo, -fa *m y f* lexicographer.
lexicología *f* lexicology.
lexicólogo, -ga *m y f* lexicologist.
lexicón *m* lexicon.
ley *f* **-1.** [gen] law; [parlamentaria] act; ~ **de extranjería** Aliens Act; ~ **de incompatibilidades** *act regulating which other positions may be held by people holding public office*; ~ **sálica** Salic law; ~ **seca** prohibition law; **hecha la ~, hecha la trampa** laws are made to be broken; **con todas las de la** ~ in due form, properly. **-2.** [regla] rule; ~ **del embudo** one law for o.s. and another for everyone else; ~ **de la ventaja** DEP advantage (law); ~ **de la oferta y de la demanda** law of supply and demand; **de buena** ~ reliable, sterling. **-3.** [de un metal]: **de** ~ [oro] pure; [plata] sterling.
◆ **leyes** *fpl* [derecho] law (*sg*).
leyenda *f* **-1.** [narración] legend. **-2.** [inscripción] inscription, legend.
leyera *etc* → **leer**.
liar [9] *vt* **-1.** [atar] to tie up. **-2.** [envolver - cigarrillo] to roll; ~ **algo en** [papel] to wrap sthg up in; [toalla etc] to roll sthg up in. **-3.** [involucrar]: ~ **a alguien (en)** to get sb mixed up (in). **-4.** [complicar - asunto etc] to confuse; **¡ya me has liado!** now you've really got me confused!
◆ **liarse** *vpr* **-1.** [enredarse] to get muddled up. **-2.** [empezar] to begin, to start; ~**se a hacer algo** to start o begin doing sthg. **-3.** *fam* [sexualmente]: ~**se (con)** to get involved (with), to have an affair (with).
libación *f* libation.
libanés, -esa *adj, m y f* Lebanese.
Líbano *m*: **el** ~ the Lebanon.
libar *vt* to sip, to suck.
libelo *m* lampoon.
libélula *f* dragonfly.
liberación *f* **-1.** [gen] liberation; [de preso] release; ~ **de la mujer** women's liberation; ~ **sexual** sexual liberation. **-2.** [de una hipoteca] redemption.
liberado, -da *adj* [gen] liberated; [preso] freed.
liberal *adj, m y f* liberal.
liberalidad *f* liberality.
liberalismo *m* liberalism.
liberalización *f* liberalization; COM deregulation.
liberalizar [13] *vt* to liberalize; COM to deregulate.
liberar *vt* [gen] to liberate; [preso] to free; ~ **de algo a alguien** to free sb from sthg.
◆ **liberarse** *vpr* to liberate o.s.; ~**se de algo** to free o liberate o.s. from sthg.

Liberia Liberia.

libertad f freedom, liberty; **dejar** ○ **poner a alguien en** ~ to set sb free, to release sb; **estar en** ~ to be free; **tener** ~ **para hacer algo** to be free to do sthg; **tomarse la** ~ **de hacer algo** to take the liberty of doing sthg; **tomarse** ~**es** to take liberties; ~ **de circulación de capitales/trabajadores** ECON free movement of capital/workers; ~ **condicional** probation; ~ **de expresión** freedom of speech; ~ **de imprenta** ○ **prensa** freedom of the press; ~ **provisional (bajo fianza)** bail; ~ **provisional (bajo palabra)** parole.

libertador, -ra ◇ adj liberating. ◇ m y f liberator.

libertar vt [gen] to liberate, to deliver; [preso] to set free.

libertario, -ria adj, m y f libertarian.

libertinaje m licentiousness.

libertino, -na ◇ adj licentious. ◇ m y f libertine.

liberto, -ta m y f freedman (f freedwoman).

Libia Libya.

libidinoso, -sa adj libidinous, lewd.

libido f libido.

libio, -bia adj, m y f Libyan.

libra f [peso, moneda] pound; ~ **esterlina** pound sterling.

◆ **Libra** ◇ m [zodiaco] Libra; **ser Libra** to be (a) Libra. ◇ m y f [persona] Libran.

librado, -da ◇ m y f COM drawee. ◇ adj: **salir bien** ~ to get off lightly; **salir mal** ~ to come off badly.

librador, -ra m y f drawer.

libramiento m, **libranza** f order of payment.

librar ◇ vt -1. [eximir]: ~ **a alguien (de algo/de hacer algo)** [gen] to free sb (from sthg/from doing sthg); [pagos, impuestos] to exempt sb (from sthg/from doing sthg). -2. [entablar - pelea, lucha] to engage in; [- batalla, combate] to join, to wage. -3. COM to draw. ◇ vi [no trabajar] to be off work.

◆ **librarse** vpr -1. [salvarse]: ~**se (de hacer algo)** to escape (from doing sthg); **de buena te libraste** you had a narrow escape. -2. [deshacerse]: ~**se de algo/alguien** to get rid of sthg/sb.

libre adj -1. [gen] free; [rato, tiempo] spare; [camino, vía] clear; [espacio, piso, lavabo] empty, vacant; **200 metros** ~ 200 metres freestyle; ~ **de** [gen] free from; [exento] exempt from; ~ **de franqueo** post-free; ~ **de impuestos** tax-free; **ser** ~ **de** ○ **para hacer algo** to be free to do sthg; **ir por** ~ to go it

alone. -2. [alumno] external; **estudiar por** ~ to be an external student.

librea f livery.

librecambio m free trade.

librecambismo m (doctrine of) free trade.

librepensador, -ra ◇ adj freethinking. ◇ m y f freethinker.

librepensamiento m freethinking.

librería f -1. [tienda] bookshop. -2. [oficio] bookselling. -3. [mueble] bookcase.

librero, -ra ◇ adj book (antes de sust). ◇ m y f [persona] bookseller. ◇ m Amer [mueble] bookshelf.

libreta f -1. [para escribir] notebook. -2. [del banco]: ~ **(de ahorros)** savings book.

libreto m -1. MÚS libretto. -2. Amer CIN script.

Libreville [libre'ßil] Libreville.

libro m [gen & COM] book; **llevar los** ~**s** to keep the books; ~ **blanco** POLÍT white paper; ~ **de bolsillo** paperback; ~ **de cabecera/cocina** bedside/cookery book; ~ **de caja** cashbook; ~ **de comercio** ledger; ~ **de consulta/cuentos** reference/story book; ~ **de cuentas** ○ **contabilidad** accounts book; ~ **de escolaridad** school report; ~ **de familia** document containing personal details of the members of a family; ~ **de reclamaciones** complaints book; ~ **de registro (de entradas)** register; ~ **sagrado** Book (in Bible); ~ **de texto** textbook; **hablar como un** ~ to express oneself very clearly.

Lic. abrev de **licenciado**.

licantropía f lycanthropy.

licántropo, -pa ◇ adj werewolf (antes de sust). ◇ m y f werewolf.

licencia f -1. [documento] licence, permit; [autorización] permission; ~ **de armas/caza** gun/hunting licence; ~ **de exportación/importación** export/import licence; ~ **de obras** planning permission; ~ **fiscal** official authorization to practise a profession; ~ **poética** poetic licence. -2. MIL discharge. -3. [confianza] licence, freedom; **tomarse** ~**s con alguien** to take liberties with sb.

licenciado, -da ◇ adj -1. EDUC graduate (antes de sust); **estar** ~ **en derecho** to be a law graduate. -2. MIL discharged. ◇ m y f -1. EDUC graduate; ~ **en económicas** economics graduate. -2. MIL discharged soldier.

licenciamiento m MIL discharge.

licenciar [8] vt MIL to discharge.

◆ **licenciarse** vpr -1. EDUC: ~**se (en)** to graduate (in). -2. MIL to be discharged.

licenciatura f degree.

licencioso, -sa adj licentious.

liceo *m* **-1.** EDUC lycée. **-2.** [de recreo] ≃ social club.

licitación *f* bid, bidding (*U*).

licitador, -ra *m y f* bidder.

licitar *vt* to bid for.

lícito, -ta *adj* **-1.** [legal] lawful. **-2.** [correcto] right. **-3.** [justo] fair.

licor *m* liquor.

licorera *f* **-1.** [botella] decanter. **-2.** [mueble] cocktail cabinet.

licorería *f* **-1.** [fábrica] distillery. **-2.** [tienda] ≃ off-licence.

licuadora *f* liquidizer, blender.

licuar [6] *vt* **-1.** CULIN to liquidize. **-2.** TECN to liquefy.

licuefacción *f* liquefaction.

lid *f* fight; **experto en estas ~es** *fig* an old hand in these matters.

líder ◇ *adj* leading. ◇ *m y f* leader.

liderar *vt* to lead.

liderato, liderazgo *m* **-1.** [primer puesto] lead; [en liga] first place. **-2.** [dirección] leadership.

lidia *f* **-1.** [arte] bullfighting. **-2.** [corrida] bullfight; *ver también* **tauromaquia.**

lidiador, -ra *m y f* bullfighter.

lidiar [8] ◇ *vi* [luchar]: **~ (con)** to struggle (with). ◇ *vt* TAUROM to fight.

liebre *f* **-1.** ZOOL hare; **correr como una ~** *fig* to run like a hare; **levantar la ~** *fig* to let the cat out of the bag. **-2.** *Amer* [microbús] minibus.

Liechtenstein ['litʃenstain] Liechtenstein.

liendre *f* nit.

lienzo *m* **-1.** [tela] (coarse) cloth; [paño] piece of cloth. **-2.** [para pintar] canvas. **-3.** [cuadro] painting.

lifting ['liftin] (*pl* **liftings**) *m* facelift.

liga *f* **-1.** [gen] league. **-2.** [de medias] suspender.

ligadura *f* **-1.** MED & MÚS ligature; **~ de trompas** MED tubal ligation. **-2.** [atadura] bond, tie.

ligamento *m* ANAT ligament.

ligar [16] ◇ *vt* **-1.** [gen & CULIN] to bind; [atar] to tie (up). **-2.** MED to put a ligature on. **-3.** MÚS to slur. ◇ *vi* **-1.** [coincidir]: **~ (con)** to tally (with). **-2.** *fam* [conquistar]: **~ (con)** to get off (with).

ligazón *f* link, connection.

ligereza *f* **-1.** [levedad - gen] lightness; [- de dolor] slightness. **-2.** [agilidad] agility. **-3.** [rapidez] speed. **-4.** [irreflexión - cualidad] rashness; [- acto] rash act.

ligero, -ra *adj* **-1.** [gen] light; [dolor, rumor, descenso] slight; [traje, tela] thin. **-2.** [ágil]

agile, nimble. **-3.** [rápido] quick, swift. **-4.** [irreflexivo] flippant; **a la ligera** lightly; **juzgar a alguien a la ligera** to be quick to judge sb.

light [lait] *adj inv* [comida] low-calorie; [refresco] diet (*antes de sust*); [cigarrillos] light.

ligón, -ona *fam* ◇ *adj*: **es muy ~** he's always getting off with sb or other. ◇ *m y f* goer, raver.

ligue ◇ *v* → **ligar.** ◇ *mfam* **-1.** [acción]: **ir de ~** to go cruising. **-2.** [persona] pick-up.

liguero, -ra *adj* DEP league (*antes de sust*).

◆ **liguero** *m* suspender belt *Br*, garter belt *Am*.

liguilla *f* DEP mini-league, round-robin tournament.

lija *f* **-1.** [papel] sandpaper. **-2.** [pez] dogfish.

lijadora *f* sander.

lijar *vt* to sand down.

lila ◇ *f* [flor] lilac. ◇ *adj inv & m* [color] lilac.

liliputiense *fam* ◇ *adj* dwarfish. ◇ *m y f* midget.

lima *f* **-1.** [utensilio] file; **~ de uñas** nail file; **comer como una ~** to eat like a horse. **-2.** BOT lime.

Lima Lima.

limadora *f* polisher.

limar *vt* **-1.** [pulir] to file down. **-2.** [perfeccionar] to polish, to add the finishing touches to.

limbo *m* **-1.** RELIG limbo; **estar en el ~** *fig* to be miles away. **-2.** ASTRON & BOT limb.

limeño, -ña ◇ *adj* of/relating to Lima. ◇ *m y f* native/inhabitant of Lima.

limitación *f* **-1.** [restricción] limitation, limit; **~ de velocidad** speed limit. **-2.** [distrito] boundaries (*pl*).

limitado, -da *adj* **-1.** [gen] limited. **-2.** *fig* [poco inteligente] dim-witted.

limitar ◇ *vt* **-1.** [gen] to limit. **-2.** [terreno] to mark out. **-3.** [atribuciones, derechos etc] to set out, to define. ◇ *vi*: **~ (con)** to border (on).

◆ **limitarse a** *vpr* to limit o.s. to.

límite ◇ *adj inv* **-1.** [precio, velocidad, edad] maximum. **-2.** [situación] extreme; [caso] borderline. ◇ *m* **-1.** [tope] limit; **dentro de un ~** within limits; **su pasión no tiene ~** her passion knows no bounds; **~ de velocidad** speed limit. **-2.** [confín] boundary.

limítrofe *adj* [país, territorio] bordering; [terreno, finca] neighbouring.

limón *m* lemon.

limonada *f* lemonade.

limonar *m* lemon grove.

limonero, -ra *adj* lemon (*antes de sust*).
◆ **limonero** *m* lemon tree.
limosna *f* alms (*pl*); **pedir** ~ to beg.
limosnear *vi* to beg.
limousine = **limusina**.
limpia *f Amer* cleaning.
limpiabotas *m y f inv* shoeshine, boot-black *Br.*
limpiacristales *m inv* window-cleaning fluid.
limpiador, -ra ◇ *adj* cleaning. ◇ *m y f* cleaner.
limpiamente *adv* **-1.** [con destreza] cleanly. **-2.** [honradamente] honestly.
limpiaparabrisas *m inv* windscreen wiper *Br*, windshield wiper *Am.*
limpiar [8] *vt* **-1.** [gen] to clean; [con trapo] to wipe; [mancha] to wipe away; [zapatos] to polish. **-2.** *fig* [desembarazar]: ~ **algo de algo** to clear sthg of sthg. **-3.** *fam* [en el juego] to clean out. **-4.** *fam* [robar] to snipe, to pinch.
límpido, -da *adj culto* limpid.
limpieza *f* **-1.** [cualidad] cleanliness. **-2.** [acción] cleaning; **hacer la** ~ to do the cleaning; ~ **en seco** dry cleaning. **-3.** *fig* [destreza] skill, cleanness. **-4.** *fig* [honradez] honesty.
limpio, -pia *adj* **-1.** [gen] clean; [pulcro] neat; [cielo, imagen] clear. **-2.** [neto - sueldo etc] net. **-3.** [honrado] **honest**; [intenciones] honourable; [juego] **clean**. **-4.** [sin culpa]: **estar** ~ to be in the clear; ~ **de** [sospecha etc] free of. **-5.** *fam* [sin dinero] broke, skint. **-6.** *fig* [puro]: **a puñetazo** ~ with bare fists; **a pedrada limpia** with nothing more than stones.
◆ **limpio** *adv* cleanly, fair; **pasar a** ◇ **poner en** ~ to make a fair copy of, to write out neatly; **sacar algo en** ~ **de** to make sthg out from.
limusina, limousine [limu'sin] *f* limousine.
linaje *m* lineage.
linaza *f* linseed.
lince *m* lynx; **ser un** ~ **para algo** to be very sharp at sthg.
linchamiento *m* lynching.
linchar *vt* to lynch.
lindante *adj*: ~ **(con)** [espacios] bordering; [conceptos] bordering (on).
lindar
◆ **lindar con** *vi* **-1.** [terreno] to adjoin, to be next to. **-2.** [conceptos, ideas] to border on.
linde *m o f* boundary.
lindero, -ra *adj* **-1.** [terreno] adjoining, bordering. **-2.** [concepto] bordering.

◆ **lindero** *m* boundary.
lindeza *f* [belleza] prettiness.
◆ **lindezas** *fpl irón* [insultos] insults.
lindo, -da *adj* pretty, lovely; **de lo** ~ a great deal.
línea *f* **-1.** [gen, DEP & TELECOM] line; **cortar la** ~ **(telefónica)** to cut off the phone; ~ **aérea** airline; ~ **de banda** sideline, touch-line; ~ **de conducta** course of action; ~ **continua** AUTOM solid white line; ~ **de crédito/de descubierto** BANCA credit/overdraft limit; ~ **divisoria** dividing line; ~ **de flotación** waterline; ~ **de meta** [en fútbol] goal line; [en carrera] finishing line; ~ **de mira** ◇ **tiro** line of fire; ~ **de puntos** dotted line; ~ **recta** straight line; ~ **de saque** base line, service line. **-2.** [de un coche etc] lines (*pl*), shape. **-3.** [silueta] figure; **guardar la** ~ to watch one's figure. **-4.** [estilo] style; **de** ~ **clásica** classical. **-5.** [categoría] class, category; **de primera** ~ first-rate. **-6.** INFORM: **en** ~ on-line; **fuera de** ~ off-line. **-7.** *loc*: **en** ~**s generales** in broad terms; **en toda la** ~ [completamente] all along the line; **leer entre** ~**s** to read between the lines.
lineal *adj* **-1.** [gen] linear; [dibujo] line. **-2.** [aumento] across-the-board.
linfa *f* lymph.
linfático, -ca *adj* lymphatic.
lingotazo *m fam* swig.
lingote *m* ingot.
lingüista *m y f* linguist.
lingüístico, -ca *adj* linguistic.
◆ **lingüística** *f* linguistics.
linier [li'njer] (*pl* **liniers**) *m* linesman.
linimento *m* liniment.
lino *m* **-1.** [planta] flax. **-2.** [tejido] linen.
linóleo, linóleum (*pl* **linóleums**) *m* linoleum (*U*).
linotipia *f* Linotype®.
linotipista *m y f* linotypist.
linotipo *m* Linotype®.
linterna *f* **-1.** [farol] lantern, lamp. **-2.** [de pilas] torch *Br*, flashlight *Am.*
◆ **linterna mágica** *f* magic lantern.
lío *m* **-1.** [paquete] bundle. **-2.** *fam* [enredo] mess; **hacerse un** ~ to get muddled up; **meterse en** ~**s** to get into trouble. **-3.** *fam* [jaleo] racket, row; **armar un** ~ to kick up a fuss. **-4.** *fam* [amorío] affair.
liofilización *f* freeze-drying.
liofilizar [13] *vt* to freeze-dry.
lioso, -sa *adj fam* **-1.** [enredado - asunto] messy; [- explicación] muddled. **-2.** [persona] troublemaking.
lípido *m* lipid.
liposoma *m* liposome.

liposucción f liposuction.
lipotimia f fainting fit.
liquen m lichen.
liquidación f **-1.** [pago] settlement, payment; ~ **de bienes** COM liquidation of assets. **-2.** [rebaja] clearance sale. **-3.** [fin] liquidation.
liquidar vt **-1.** [pagar - deuda] to pay; [- cuenta] to settle. **-2.** [rebajar] to sell off. **-3.** [malgastar] to throw away. **-4.** [acabar - asunto] to settle; [- negocio, sociedad] to wind up. **-5.** fam [matar] to liquidate.
liquidez f ECON & FÍS liquidity.
líquido, -da adj **-1.** [gen] liquid. **-2.** ECON [neto] net.
◆ **líquido** m **-1.** [gen] liquid. **-2.** ECON liquid assets (pl). **-3.** MED fluid.
lira f **-1.** MÚS lyre. **-2.** [moneda] lira.
lírico, -ca adj **-1.** LITER lyric, lyrical. **-2.** [musical] musical.
◆ **lírica** f lyric poetry.
lirio m iris.
lirismo m lyricism.
lirón m ZOOL dormouse; **dormir como un ~** fig to sleep like a log.
lis f iris.
Lisboa Lisbon.
lisboeta adj of/relating to Lisbon.
lisiado, -da ◇ adj crippled. ◇ m y f cripple.
lisiar [8] vt to maim, to cripple.
◆ **lisiarse** vpr to be maimed ○ crippled.
liso, -sa ◇ adj **-1.** [llano] flat; [sin asperezas] smooth; [pelo] straight; **los 400 metros ~s** the 400 metres; **lisa y llanamente** quite simply; **hablando lisa y llanamente** to put it plainly. **-2.** [no estampado] plain. ◇ m y f Amer coarse ○ rude person.
lisonja f flattering remark.
lisonjear vt to flatter.
lisonjero, -ra adj flattering; [perspectiva] promising.
lista f **-1.** [enumeración] list; **pasar ~** to call the register; ~ **de boda/de espera/de precios** wedding/waiting/price list; ~ **electoral** electoral roll; ~ **negra** black list. **-2.** [de tela, madera] strip; [de papel] slip; [de color] stripe.
◆ **lista de correos** f poste restante.
listado, -da adj striped.
◆ **listado** m INFORM listing.
listar vt INFORM to list.
listín
◆ **listín (de teléfonos)** m (telephone) directory.
listo, -ta adj **-1.** [inteligente, hábil] clever, smart; **dárselas de ~** to make o.s. out to

be clever; **pasarse de ~** to be too clever by half; **ser más ~ que el hambre** to be nobody's fool. **-2.** [preparado] ready; **¿estáis ~s?** are you ready?; **estás** ○ **vas ~ (si crees que ...)** you've got another think coming (if you think that ...).
listón m lath; DEP bar; **poner el ~ muy alto** fig to set very high standards.
lisura f Amer rude remark, bad language (U).
litera f **-1.** [cama] bunk (bed); [- de barco] berth; [- de tren] couchette. **-2.** [vehículo] litter.
literal adj literal.
literario, -ria adj literary.
literato, -ta m y f writer.
literatura f literature.
litigante adj, m y f litigant.
litigar [16] vi to go to law.
litigio m DER litigation (U); fig dispute; **en ~** in dispute.
litigue etc → litigar.
litio m lithium.
litografía f **-1.** [arte] lithography. **-2.** [grabado] lithograph. **-3.** [taller] lithographer's (workshop).
litografiar [9] vt to lithograph.
litoral ◇ adj coastal. ◇ m coast.
litosfera f lithosphere.
litro m litre.
litrona f mfam litre bottle of beer.
Lituania Lithuania.
lituano, -na adj, m y f Lithuanian.
◆ **lituano** m [language] Lithuanian.
liturgia f liturgy.
litúrgico, -ca adj liturgical.
liviano, -na adj **-1.** [ligero - blusa] thin; [- carga] light. **-2.** [sin importancia] slight. **-3.** [superficial] frivolous.
lividez f [palidez] pallor.
lívido, -da adj **-1.** [pálido] very pale, white as a sheet. **-2.** [amoratado] livid.
living ['lißin] (pl **livings**) m living room.
liza f [lucha] battle; **en ~** in opposition.
ll, Ll f [letra] ll, Ll.
llaga f lit & fig wound.
llagar [16] vt to wound.
◆ **llagarse** vpr to become covered in sores.
llama f **-1.** [de fuego, pasión] flame; **en ~s** ablaze. **-2.** ZOOL llama.
llamada f **-1.** [gen] call; [a la puerta] knock; [con timbre] ring. **-2.** TELECOM telephone call; **hacer una ~** to make a phone call; **~ urbana/interrurbana/a cobro revertido**

local/long-distance/reverse-charge call. **-3.** [en un libro] reference mark.

llamado, -da *adj* so-called.
◆ **llamado** *m Amer* [de teléfono] call.

llamador *m* [aldaba] door knocker; [timbre] doorbell.

llamamiento *m* **-1.** [apelación] appeal, call; **hacer un** ∼ **a alguien para que haga algo** to call upon sb to do sthg. **-2.** MIL call-up.

llamar ◇ *vt* **-1.** [gen] to call; [con gestos] to beckon. **-2.** [por teléfono] to phone, to call. **-3.** [convocar] to summon, to call; ∼ **(a filas)** MIL to call up. **-4.** [atraer] to attract, to call. ◇ *vi* **-1.** [a la puerta etc - con golpes] to knock; [- con timbre] to ring; **están llamando** there's somebody at the door. **-2.** [por teléfono] to phone.
◆ **llamarse** *vpr* [tener por nombre] to be called; **¿cómo te llamas?** what's your name?; **me llamo Pepe** my name's Pepe.

llamarada *f* **-1.** [de fuego, ira etc] blaze. **-2.** [de rubor] flush.

llamativo, -va *adj* [color] bright, gaudy; [ropa] showy.

llamear *vi* to burn, to blaze.

llana → **llano**.

llanear *vi* to roam the plains.

llanero, -ra ◇ *adj* of the plainspeople. ◇ *m y f* plainsman (*f* plainswoman).

llaneza *f* naturalness, straightforwardness.

llano, -na *adj* **-1.** [campo, superficie] flat. **-2.** [trato, persona] natural, straightforward. **-3.** [pueblo, clase] ordinary. **-4.** [lenguaje, expresión] simple, plain. **-5.** GRAM paroxytonic.
◆ **llana** *f* CONSTR trowel.
◆ **llano** *m* [llanura] plain.

llanta *f* rim.

llantera, llantina *f fam* blubbing (*U*).

llanto *m* tears (*pl*), crying.

llanura *f* plain.

llave *f* **-1.** [gen] key; **bajo** ∼ under lock and key; **echar la** ∼ to lock up; ∼ **en mano** [vivienda] ready for immediate occupation; ∼ **de contacto** ignition key; ∼ **maestra** master key. **-2.** [del agua, gas] tap *Br*, faucet *Am*; [de la electricidad] switch; **cerrar la** ∼ **de paso** to turn the water/gas off at the mains. **-3.** [herramienta] spanner; ∼ **inglesa** monkey wrench. **-4.** [de judo etc] hold, lock. **-5.** [signo ortográfico] curly bracket.

llavero *m* keyring.

llavín *m* latchkey.

llegada *f* **-1.** [gen] arrival. **-2.** DEP finish.

llegar [16] *vi* **-1.** [a un sitio] ∼ **(de)** to arrive (from); ∼ **a un hotel/una ciudad** to arrive at a hotel/in a city; **llegaré pronto** I'll be there early. **-2.** [un tiempo, la noche etc] to

come. **-3.** [durar] ∼ **a** ○ **hasta** to last until. **-4.** [alcanzar] ∼ **a** to reach; **no llego al techo** I can't reach the ceiling; ∼ **hasta** to reach up to. **-5.** [ser suficiente] ∼ **(para)** to be enough (for). **-6.** [lograr] ∼ **a (ser) algo** to get to be sthg, to become sthg; **si llego a saberlo** if I get to know of it. **-7.** [atreverse]: **llegó a decirme ...** he went as far as to say to me ....
◆ **llegarse a** *vpr* to go round to.

llenar *vt* **-1.** [ocupar]: ∼ **algo (de)** [vaso, hoyo, habitación] to fill sthg (with); [pared, suelo] to cover sthg (with). **-2.** [satisfacer] to satisfy. **-3.** [rellenar - impreso] to fill in ○ out. **-4.** [colmar]: ∼ **a alguien de** to fill sb with.
◆ **llenarse** *vpr* **-1.** [ocuparse] to fill up. **-2.** [saciarse] to be full. **-3.** [cubrirse]: ∼ **de** to become covered in.

llenazo *m* full house.

lleno, -na *adj* **-1.** [gen] full; [cubierto] covered; ∼ **de** [gen] full of; [manchas, pósters] covered in. **-2.** *fam* [regordete] chubby.
◆ **lleno** *m* full house.
◆ **de lleno** *loc adv* full in the face; **acertó de** ∼ he was bang on target.

llevadero, -ra *adj* bearable.

llevar ◇ *vt* **-1.** [gen] to carry. **-2.** [acompañar, coger y depositar] to take; ∼ **algo/a alguien a** to take sthg/sb to; **me llevó en coche** he drove me there. **-3.** [prenda, objeto personal] to wear; **llevo gafas** I wear glasses; **no llevo dinero** I haven't got any money on me. **-4.** [caballo, coche etc] to handle. **-5.** [conducir]: ∼ **a alguien a algo** to lead sb to sthg; ∼ **a alguien a hacer algo** to lead ○ cause sb to do sthg. **-6.** [ocuparse de, dirigir] to be in charge of, to look after; [casa, negocio] to run; **lleva la contabilidad** she keeps the books. **-7.** [hacer - de alguna manera]: **lleva muy bien sus estudios** he's doing very well in his studies. **-8.** [tener - de alguna manera] to have; ∼ **el pelo largo** to have long hair; **llevas las manos sucias** your hands are dirty. **-9.** [soportar] to deal ○ cope with. **-10.** [mantener] to keep; ∼ **el paso** to keep in step. **-11.** [pasarse - tiempo]: **lleva tres semanas sin venir** she hasn't come for three weeks now, it's three weeks since she came last. **-12.** [ocupar - tiempo] to take; **me llevó un día hacer este guiso** it took me a day to make this dish. **-13.** [sobrepasar en]: **te llevo seis puntos** I'm six points ahead of you; **me lleva dos centímetros** he's two centimetres taller than me. **-14.** *loc*: ∼ **consigo** [implicar] to lead to, to bring about; ∼ **las de perder** to be heading for defeat.

◇ *vi* **-1.** [conducir]: ~ **a** to lead to; **esta carretera lleva al norte** this road leads north.
-2. (*antes de participio*) [haber]: **llevo leída
media novela** I'm halfway through the
novel; **llevo dicho esto mismo docenas de
veces** I've said the same thing time and
again **-3.** (*antes de gerundio*) [estar]: ~ **mucho tiempo haciendo algo** to have been
doing sthg for a long time.

◆ **llevarse** *vpr* **-1.** [coger] to take, to steal;
alguien se ha llevado mi sombrero someone has taken my hat. **-2.** [conseguir] to
get; **se ha llevado el premio** she has carried
off the prize; **yo me llevo siempre las cul-
pas** I always get the blame. **-3.** [recibir -
susto, sorpresa etc] to get, to receive; **me llevé un disgusto** I was upset. **-4.** [entenderse]:
~**se bien/mal (con alguien)** to get on well/
badly (with sb). **-5.** [estar de moda] to be in
(fashion); **este año se lleva el verde** green
is in this year. **-6.** MAT: **me llevo una** carry
(the) one.

llorar ◇ *vi* **-1.** [con lágrimas] to cry. **-2.** *fam*
[quejarse] to whinge. ◇ *vt*: ~ **la muerte de
alguien** to mourn sb's death.

llorera *f fam* crying fit.

llorica *despec* ◇ *adj*: **ser** ~ to be a crybaby. ◇ *m y f* crybaby.

lloriquear *vi* to whine, to snivel.

lloriqueo *m* whining (*U*), snivelling (*U*).

lloro *m* crying (*U*), tears (*pl*).

llorón, -ona ◇ *adj* who cries a lot. ◇ *m y
f* crybaby.

lloroso, -sa *adj* tearful.

llover [24] ◇ *v impers* to rain; **está lloviendo** it's raining. ◇ *vi fig*: **le llueven las ofertas** offers are raining down on him.

llovizna *f* drizzle.

lloviznar *v impers* to drizzle.

llueva *etc* → llover.

lluvia *f* **-1.** METEOR rain; **bajo la** ~ in the
rain; ~ **ácida** acid rain; ~ **radiactiva** (nuclear) fallout. **-2.** *fig* [de panfletos, regalos etc]
shower; [de preguntas] barrage.

lluvioso, -sa *adj* rainy.

lo, la (*pl* **los, las**) *pron pers* (*complemento directo*) [cosa] it, (*pl*) them; [persona] him (*f*
her), (*pl*) them; [usted] you.

◆ **lo** ◇ *pron pers* (*neutro*) (*predicado*) it; **su
hermana es muy guapa pero él no** ~ **es** his
sister is very good-looking, but he isn't; **es
muy bueno aunque no** ~ **parezca** it's very
good, even if it doesn't look it. ◇ *art det*
(*neutro*): ~ **antiguo me gusta más que** ~
moderno I like old things better than modern things; ~ **mejor/peor** the best/worst
part; **no te imaginas** ~ **grande que era** you
can't imagine how big it was.

◆ **lo de** *loc prep*: ¿**y** ~ **de la fiesta?** what
about the party, then?; **siento** ~ **de ayer**
I'm sorry about yesterday.

◆ **lo que** *loc conj* what; **acepté** ~ **que me
ofrecieron** I accepted what they offered
me.

loa *f* **-1.** [gen] praise. **-2.** LITER eulogy.

loable *adj* praiseworthy.

LOAPA (*abrev de* **Ley Orgánica para la Ar-
monización del Proceso Autonómico**) *f
Spanish act governing the development of the
autonomous communities.*

loar *vt* to praise.

lobato = lobezno.

lobby ['loßi] (*pl* **lobbies**) *m* lobby, pressure
group.

lobezno, lobato *m* wolf cub.

lobo, -ba *m y f* wolf.

◆ **lobo de mar** [marinero] *m* sea dog.

lobotomía *f* lobotomy.

lóbrego, -ga *adj* gloomy, murky.

lobulado, -da *adj* lobulate.

lóbulo *m* lobe.

lobuno, -na *adj* wolf-like.

local ◇ *adj* local. ◇ *m* **-1.** [edificio] premises (*pl*). **-2.** [sede] headquarters (*pl*).

localidad *f* **-1.** [población] place, town. **-2.**
[asiento] seat. **-3.** [entrada] ticket; "**no hay**
~**es**" "sold out".

localismo *m* **-1.** [sentimiento] parochialism.
-2. LING localism.

localista *adj* parochial.

localización *f* localization, tracking down.

localizar [13] *vt* **-1.** [encontrar] to locate, to
track down. **-2.** [circunscribir] to localize.

◆ **localizarse en** *vpr* to become localized
in.

locatis *fam* ◇ *adj inv* nutty. ◇ *m y f .inv*
nutcase.

locativo *m* locative.

loc. cit., l.c. (*abrev de* **loco citato**) loc. cit.

loción *f* lotion.

loco, -ca ◇ *adj* **-1.** [gen] mad; **estar** ~ **de/
por** to be mad with/about; **volver** ~ **a alguien** to drive sb mad; **volverse** ~ **por** to
be mad about; ~ **de atar** ○ **remate** stark
raving mad; **a lo** ~ [sin pensar] hastily; [te-
merariamente] wildly. **-2.** [extraordinario - interés, ilusión] tremendous; [- suerte, precio]
extraordinary; [- amor, alegría] wild.
◇ *m y f lit* & *fig* madman (*f* madwoman),
lunatic; **hacerse el** ~ to play dumb, to pretend not to understand.

locomoción *f* transport; [de tren] loco-
motion.

locomotor, -ra ○ **-triz** *adj* locomotive.

lotero

◆ **locomotora** *f* engine, locomotive.

locuacidad *f* loquacity, talkativeness.

locuaz *adj* loquacious, talkative.

locución *f* phrase.

locura *f* -1. [demencia] madness. -2. [imprudencia] folly. -3. [exageración]: **con** ~ madly.

locutor, **-ra** *m y f* [de radio] announcer; [de televisión] presenter.

locutorio *m* -1. [para visitas] visiting room. -2. TELECOM phone box o booth. -3. RADIO studio.

lodazal *m* quagmire.

LODE (*abrev de* **Ley Orgánica del Derecho a la Educación**) *f Spanish Education Act.*

loden *m* loden coat.

lodo *m lit & fig* mud.

logarítmico, **-ca** *adj* logarithmic.

logaritmo *m* logarithm.

logia *f* -1. [masónica] lodge. -2. ARQUIT loggia.

lógico, **-ca** ◇ *adj* logical; **es** ~ **que se enfade** it stands to reason that he should get angry. ◇ *m y f* [persona] logician.

◆ **lógica** *f* [ciencia] logic.

logístico, **-ca** *adj* logistic.

◆ **logística** *f* logistics (*pl*).

logopeda *m y f* speech therapist.

logopedia *f* speech therapy.

logos *m inv* -1. FILOSOFÍA logos. -2. RELIG Logos, Word of God.

logotipo *m* logo.

logrado, **-da** *adj* [bien hecho] accomplished.

lograr *vt* [gen] to achieve; [puesto, beca, divorcio] to get, to obtain; [resultado] to obtain, to achieve; [perfección] to attain; [victoria, premio] to win; [deseo, aspiración] to fulfil; ~ **hacer algo** to manage to do sthg; ~ **que alguien haga algo** to manage to get sb to do sthg.

logro *m* achievement.

logroñés, **-esa** *adj* of or relating to Logroño.

Logroño Logroño.

LOGSE (*abrev de* **Ley Orgánica de Ordenación General del Sistema Educativo**) *f Spanish Education Act.*

Loira *m*: **el** ~ the (river) Loire.

loísmo *m* incorrect use of "lo" as indirect object instead of "le".

loma *f* hillock.

lombardo, **-da** *adj, m y f* [de Lombardía] Lombard.

◆ **lombarda** *f* [verdura] red cabbage.

lombriz *f* earthworm, worm; **tener lombrices** to have worms; ~ **de tierra** earthworm; ~ **intestinal** tapeworm.

Lomé Lomé.

lomo *m* -1. [espalda] back. -2. [carne] loin. -3. [de libro] spine. -4. [de cuchillo] blunt edge.

lona *f* canvas.

loncha *f* slice; [de beicon] rasher.

londinense ◇ *adj* London (*antes de sust*). ◇ *m y f* Londoner.

Londres London.

longaniza *f type of spicy, cold pork sausage.*

longevidad *f* longevity.

longevo, **-va** *adj* long-lived.

longitud *f* -1. [dimensión] length; **tiene medio metro de** ~ it's half a metre long; ~ **de onda** wavelength. -2. ASTRON & GEOGR longitude.

longitudinal *adj* longitudinal.

long play ['lomplai] (*pl* **long plays**) *m* LP, album.

longui, **longuis** *m fam*: **hacerse el** ~ to act dumb, to pretend not to understand.

lonja *f* -1. [loncha] slice. -2. [edificio] exchange; ~ **de pescado** fish market.

lontananza *f* background; **en** ~ in the distance.

loquería *f Amer fam* mental home.

loquero, **-ra** *m y f fam* [persona] psychiatric nurse.

◆ **loquero** *m Amer* [escándalo] row, uproar.

lord (*pl* **lores**) *m* lord.

loro *m* -1. [animal] parrot. -2. *fam fig* [charlatán] chatterbox; [mujer fea] fright, ugly old bag.

los ◇ *art* → **el.** ◇ *pron* → **lo.**

losa *f* paving stone, flagstone; [de tumba] tombstone.

loseta *f* floor tile.

lote *m* -1. [parte] share. -2. [conjunto] batch, lot. -3. *fam* [magreo]: **darse** o **pegarse el** ~ to kiss and canoodle.

lotería *f* -1. [gen] lottery; **jugar a la** ~ to play the lottery; **le tocó la** ~ she won the lottery; ~ **primitiva** *weekly state-run lottery.* -2. [tienda] lottery booth. -3. [juego de mesa] lotto.

LOTERÍA PRIMITIVA:
This lottery, run by the Spanish State, is drawn twice a week. Participants try to guess a combination of six numbers between one and forty-nine. A seventh number, the 'número de reintegro', is also drawn. Participants who have chosen that number are reimbursed for the price of their ticket

lotero, **-ra** *m y f* seller of lottery tickets.

loto f fam weekly state-run lottery.

loza f -1. [material] earthenware; [porcelana] china. -2. [objetos] crockery.

lozanía f -1. [de plantas] luxuriance. -2. [de persona] youthful vigour.

lozano, -na adj -1. [planta] lush, luxuriant. -2. [persona] youthfully vigorous.

LRU (abrev de **Ley de Reforma Universitaria**) f act governing changes to the Spanish university system.

LSD (abrev de **lysergic diethylamide**) m LSD.

Ltd., ltda. (abrev de **limitada**) Ltd.

Luanda Luanda.

lubina f sea bass.

lubricación f lubrication.

lubricante, lubrificante ◇ adj lubricating. ◇ m lubricant.

lubricar [10], **lubrificar** [10] vt to lubricate.

lucero m bright star; ~ **del alba/de la tarde** morning/evening star; **como un** ~ as bright as a new pin.

lucha f fight; fig struggle; ~ **libre** all-in wrestling; ~ **de clases** class struggle O war.

luchador, -ra ◇ adj fighting. ◇ m y f DEP wrestler; fig fighter.

luchar vi to fight; fig to struggle; ~ **contra/por** to fight against/for.

lucidez f lucidity, clarity.

lucido, -da adj splendid.

lúcido, -da adj lucid.

luciérnaga f glow-worm.

Lucifer m Lucifer.

lucimiento m [de ceremonia etc] sparkle; [de actriz etc] brilliant performance.

lucio m pike.

lucir [32] ◇ vi -1. [gen] to shine. -2. [compensar]: **no me lucían tantas horas de trabajo** working so many hours didn't do me much good. -3. [llevar puesto] to wear. -4. Amer [parecer] to seem. -5. Amer [tener] to have. ◇ vt [gen] to show off; [ropa] to sport.
◆ **lucirse** vpr -1. [destacar]: ~**se (en)** to shine (at). -2. fam fig & irón [quedar mal] to really go and do it, to mess things up.

lucrarse vpr: ~ **(de)** to profit (from).

lucrativo, -va adj lucrative; **no** ~ non profit-making.

lucro m profit, gain.

lucubrar vt to rack one's brains over.

lúdico, -ca adj [del juego] game (antes de sust); [ocioso] of enjoyment, of pleasure.

ludópata m y f pathological gambling addict.

ludopatía f pathological addiction to gambling.

ludoteca f toy library.

luego ◇ adv -1. [justo después] then, next; **primero aquí y** ~ **allí** first here and then there; ~ **de** immediately after. -2. [más tarde] later; **hazlo** ~ do it later. -3. Amer [pronto] soon. ◇ conj [así que] so, therefore.
◆ **luego luego** loc adv Amer right away.

lugar m -1. [gen] place; [localidad] place, town; [del crimen, accidente etc] scene; [para acampar, merendar etc] spot; **en primer** ~ in the first place, firstly; **fuera de** ~ out of place; **no hay** ~ **a duda** there's no room for doubt; **tener** ~ to take place; **yo en tu** ~ if I were you. -2. [motivo] cause, reason; **dar** ~ **a** to bring about, to cause. -3. [puesto] position.
◆ **en lugar de** loc prep instead of.
◆ **lugar común** m platitude, commonplace.

lugareño, -ña ◇ adj village (antes de sust). ◇ m y f villager.

lugarteniente m deputy.

lúgubre adj gloomy, mournful.

lujo m luxury; fig profusion; **con todo** ~ **de detalles** in great detail; **de** ~ luxury (antes de sust); **permitirse el** ~ **de algo/de hacer algo** to be able to afford sthg/to do sthg.

lujoso, -sa adj luxurious.

lujuria f lust.

lujurioso, -sa ◇ adj lecherous. ◇ m y f lecher.

lulú → perro.

lumbago m lumbago.

lumbar adj lumbar.

lumbre f -1. [fuego] fire; **dar** ~ **a alguien** to give sb a light. -2. fig [resplandor] brightness.

lumbrera f fam leading light.

luminaria f light, lighting (U).

luminiscencia f luminescence.

luminosidad f brightness; [fig] brilliance.

luminoso, -sa adj -1. [gen] bright; [fuente, energía] light (antes de sust). -2. fig [idea etc] brilliant.

luminotecnia f lighting.

luna f -1. [astro] moon; ~ **creciente** crescent moon (when waxing); ~ **llena/nueva** full/new moon; ~ **menguante** crescent moon (when waning); **media** ~ half moon. -2. [cristal] window (pane). -3. [espejo] mirror. -4. loc: **estar en la** ~ to be miles away; **pedir la** ~ to ask the impossible.
◆ **luna de miel** f honeymoon.

lunar ◇ adj lunar. ◇ m -1. [en la piel]

mole, beauty spot. **-2.** [en telas] spot; **a ~es** spotted.

lunático, -ca ◇ *adj* crazy. ◇ *m y f* lunatic.

lunch [lantʃ] (*pl* **lunches**) *m* buffet lunch.

lunes *m inv* Monday; *ver también* **sábado**.

luneta *f* [de coche] windscreen; ~ **trasera** rear windscreen; ~ **térmica** demister.

lupa *f* magnifying glass.

lupanar *m culto* brothel.

lúpulo *m* hops (*pl*).

Lusaka Lusaka.

lusitano, -na, luso, -sa *adj, m y f* **-1.** [de Lusitania] Lusitanian. **-2.** [de Portugal] Portuguese.

lustrabotas *m inv*, **lustrador** *m Amer* bootblack.

lustrar *vt* to polish.

lustre *m* **-1.** [brillo] shine. **-2.** *fig* [gloria] glory.

lustrín *m Amer* shoeshine box.

lustro *m* five-year period.

lustroso, -sa *adj* shiny.

luteranismo *m* Lutheranism.

luterano, -na *adj, m y f* Lutheran.

luto *m* mourning; **de ~** in mourning.

luxación *f* dislocation.

Luxemburgo Luxembourg.

luxemburgués, -esa ◇ *adj* Luxembourg (*antes de sust*). ◇ *m y f* Luxembourger.

Luxor Luxor.

luz *f* [gen] light; [electricidad] electricity; [destello] flash (of light); **apagar la ~** to switch off the light; **cortar la ~** to cut off the electricity supply; **dar** ○ **encender la ~** to switch on the light; **pagar (el recibo de) la ~** to pay the electricity (bill); **se ha ido la ~** the lights have gone out; **~ solar** sunlight; **a la ~ de** in the light of; **arrojar ~ sobre** to shed light on; **a todas luces** whichever way you look at it; **dar a ~ (un niño)** to give birth (to a child); **dar ~ verde** to give the green light ○ the go-ahead; **sacar a la ~** to bring to light.

◆ **luces** *fpl* **-1.** [cultura] enlightenment (*U*). **-2.** [inteligencia] intelligence (*U*); **de pocas luces** dim-witted. **-3.** AUTOM lights; **darle las luces a alguien** to flash (one's lights) at sb; **poner las luces de carretera** ○ **largas** to put (one's) headlights) on full beam; **luces de cruce** ○ **cortas** dipped headlights; **luces de freno** brake lights; **luces de posición** ○ **situación** sidelights; **luces de tráfico** ○ **de señalización** traffic lights.

luzca *etc* → **lucir**.

lycra® *f* Lycra®.

Lyon Lyons, Lyon.

m¹, M *f* [letra] m, M.

m² (*abrev de* **metro**) m.

maca *f* **-1.** [de fruta] bruise. **-2.** [de objetos] flaw.

macabro, -bra *adj* macabre.

macana *f Amer fam* [disparate] stupid thing.

macarra *m fam* [de prostitutas] pimp; [rufián] thug.

macarrón *m* [tubo] sheath (*of cable*).

◆ **macarrones** *mpl* [pasta] macaroni (*U*).

macarrónico, -ca *adj fam* macaronic.

macedonia *f* salad; ~ **de frutas** fruit salad.

maceración *f* CULIN soaking, maceration.

macerar *vt* CULIN to soak, to macerate.

maceta *f* **-1.** [tiesto] flowerpot. **-2.** [herramienta] mallet.

macetero *m* flowerpot holder.

machaca *m y f fam* **-1.** [pesado] pain. **-2.** [currante] dogsbody.

machacador, -ora *adj* crushing.

◆ **machacadora** *f* crusher.

machacante *m fam* [moneda] *five peseta coin*.

machacar [10] ◇ *vt* **-1.** [triturar] to crush. **-2.** *fig* [insistir] to keep going on about. **-3.** *fig* [empollar] to swot up on. ◇ *vi fig*: ~ **(sobre)** to go on (about).

machacón, -ona ◇ *adj* tiresome. ◇ *m y f* pain.

machaconería *f* annoying insistence.

machada *f* act of bravado.

machamartillo

◆ **a machamartillo** *loc adv* very firmly; **creer algo a ~** to be firm in one's belief of sthg.

machete *m* machete.

machismo *m* machismo.

machista *adj, m y f* male chauvinist.

macho ◇ *adj* **-1.** BIOL male. **-2.** *fig* [hombre] macho. ◇ *m.* **-1.** BIOL male. **-2.** *fig* [hombre] macho man, he-man. **-3.** TECN male part; [de enchufe] pin. **-4.** ~ **cabrío** billy goat. ◇ *interj fam*: ¡oye, ~! oy, mate!

machote, -ta *fam* ◇ *adj* brave. ◇ *m y f* [niño] big boy (*f* big girl).

◆ **machote** *m Amer* [modelo] rough draft.

macilento, -ta *adj culto* wan.

macizo, -za *adj* solid; **estar ~** [hombre] to be hunky; [mujer] to be gorgeous.

◆ **macizo** *m* **-1.** GEOGR massif. **-2.** BOT: **~ de flores** flowerbed.

Macom (*abrev de* **Mando Aéreo de Combate**) *m Spanish air combat command.*

macramé *m* macramé.

macro *f* INFORM macro.

macrobiótico, -ca *adj* macrobiotic.

◆ **macrobiótica** *f* macrobiotics (*U*).

macrocefalia *f* macrocephaly.

macroeconomía *f* macroeconomics (*U*).

mácula *f* spot; *fig* blemish.

macuto *m* backpack, knapsack.

Madagascar Madagascar.

Madeira Madeira.

madeja *f* hank, skein; **estar hecho una ~ de nervios** to be a bundle of nerves.

madera *f* **-1.** [gen] wood; CONSTR timber; [tabla] piece of wood; **de ~** wooden; **~ contrachapada** plywood. **-2.** *fig* [disposición]: **tener ~ de algo** to have the makings of sthg.

maderaje, maderamen *m* timbers (*pl*).

maderero, -ra *adj* timber (*antes de sust*).

madero *m* **-1.** [tabla] log. **-2.** *fig* [necio] halfwit. **-3.** *mfam* [policía] cop, pig.

madrás *m* madras.

madrastra *f* stepmother.

madrazo *m Amer* hard blow.

madre *f* **-1.** [gen] mother; **~ adoptiva/de alquiler** foster/surrogate mother; **~ política** mother-in-law; **~ soltera** single mother; **~ superiora** mother superior; **la ~ patria** the motherland; **éramos ciento y la ~** *fam* there were hundreds of us there; **me vale ~** *Amer fig* I couldn't care less; **ser la ~ del cordero** *fig* to be at the very root of the problem. **-2.** [poso] dregs (*pl*). **-3.** [cauce] bed; **salirse de ~** [río] to burst its banks; *fig* [persona] to go too far.

◆ **madre mía** *interj* **¡~ mía!** Jesus!, Christ!

madreperla *f* [ostra] pearl oyster; [nácar] mother-of-pearl.

madreselva *f* honeysuckle.

Madrid Madrid.

madrigal *m* madrigal.

madriguera *f* [gen & *fig*] den; [de conejo] burrow.

madrileño, -ña ◇ *adj* of/relating to Madrid. ◇ *m y f* native/inhabitant of Madrid.

madrina *f* [gen] patroness; [de boda] bridesmaid; [de bautizo] godmother.

madroño *m* **-1.** [árbol] strawberry tree. **-2.** [fruto] strawberry-tree berry.

madrugada *f* **-1.** [amanecer] dawn. **-2.** [noche] early morning; **las tres de la ~** three in the morning. **-3.** [madrugón] early rise.

madrugador, -ra ◇ *adj* early-rising. ◇ *m y f* early riser.

madrugar [16] *vi* to get up early; *fig* to be quick off the mark; **no por mucho ~ amanece más temprano** *proverb* time must take its course.

madrugón *m* early rise.

madurar ◇ *vt* **-1.** [gen] to mature; [fruta, mies] to ripen. **-2.** [idea, proyecto etc] to think through. ◇ *vi* [gen] to mature; [fruta] to ripen.

madurez *f* **-1.** [cualidad - gen] maturity; [- de fruta, mies] ripeness. **-2.** [edad adulta] adulthood.

maduro, -ra *adj* [gen] mature; [fruta, mies] ripe; **de edad madura** middle-aged.

maestra → **maestro.**

maestranza *f* MIL arsenal.

maestrazgo *m office and territory of the master of a military order.*

maestre *m* MIL master.

maestría *f* [habilidad] mastery, skill.

maestro, -tra ◇ *adj* **-1.** [perfecto] masterly. **-2.** [principal] main; [llave] master (*antes de sust*). ◇ *m y f* **-1.** [profesor] teacher. **-2.** [sabio] master. **-3.** MÚS maestro. **-4.** [director]: **~ de ceremonias** master of ceremonies; **~ de cocina** chef; **~ de obras** foreman; **~ de orquesta** conductor.

◆ **maestro** *m* TAUROM matador.

mafia *f* mafia.

mafioso, -sa ◇ *adj* mafia (*antes de sust*). ◇ *m y f* mafioso.

magazine [maɣa'sin] *m* magazine.

magdalena *f* fairy cake.

magenta *adj inv & m* magenta.

magia *f* magic; **~ blanca/negra** white/ black magic.

magiar ◇ *adj, m y f* Magyar. ◇ *m* [lengua] Magyar.

mágico, -ca *adj* **-1.** [con magia] magic. **-2.** [atractivo] magical.

magisterio *m* **-1.** [título] teaching certificate. **-2.** [enseñanza] teaching. **-3.** [profesión] teaching profession.

magistrado, -da *m y f* [juez] judge.

◆ **magistrado** *m Amer* [primer ministro] Prime Minister.

magistral *adj* **-1.** [de maestro] magisterial. **-2.** [genial] masterly.

magistratura *f* **-1.** [oficio] judgeship. **-2.** [jueces] magistrature. **-3.** [tribunal] tribunal; **~ de trabajo** industrial tribunal.

magma *m* magma.

magnanimidad *f* magnanimity.

magnánimo, -ma *adj* magnanimous.

magnate *m* magnate; ~ **del petróleo/de la prensa** oil/press baron.

magnesia *f* magnesia.

magnesio *m* magnesium.

magnético, -ca *adj lit* & *fig* magnetic.

magnetismo *m lit* & *fig* magnetism.

magnetizar [13] *vt* to magnetize; *fig* to mesmerize.

magnetofónico, -ca *adj* [cinta] magnetic.

magnetófono *m* tape recorder.

magnetoscopio *m* video recorder.

magnicida *m y f* assassin (*of somebody important*).

magnicidio *m* assassination (*of somebody important*).

magnificación *f* great praise.

magnificar [10] *vt* to praise highly.

magnificencia *f* magnificence.

magnífico, -ca *adj* wonderful, magnificent.

magnitud *f* magnitude.

magno, -na *adj* great.

magnolia *f* magnolia.

magnolio *m* magnolia (tree).

mago, -ga *m y f* **-1.** [prestidigitador] magician. **-2.** [en cuentos etc] wizard.

magra → **magro.**

magrear *vt vulg* to touch up.

magreo *m vulg* touching up.

magro, -gra *adj* **-1.** [sin grasa] lean. **-2.** [pobre] poor.

◆ **magro** *m* lean meat.

◆ **magra** *f* slice of ham.

magulladura *f* bruise.

magullar *vt* to bruise.

maharajá [mara'xa] *m* maharajah.

maharaní [mara'ni] *f* maharani.

mahatma [ma'xaðma] *m* mahatma.

mahometano, -na *adj, m y f* Muslim.

mahonesa = mayonesa.

maicena *f* cornflour *Br*, cornstarch *Am*.

maillot [ma'jot] (*pl* **maillots**) *m* **-1.** [prenda femenina] maillot. **-2.** [para ciclistas] jersey; ~ **amarillo** DEP yellow jersey.

maitines *mpl* matins.

maître ['metre] *m* maître.

maíz *m* maize *Br*, corn *Am*; ~ **dulce** sweetcorn.

maizal *m* maize field.

maja → **majo.**

majadería *f* idiocy.

majadero, -ra *m y f* idiot.

majar *vt* [machacar] to crush; [moler] to grind.

majareta *fam* ◇ *adj* nutty. ◇ *m y f* nutcase.

majestad *f* majesty.

◆ **Su Majestad** *f* His/Her Majesty.

majestuosidad *f* majesty.

majestuoso, -sa *adj* majestic.

majo, -ja ◇ *adj* **-1.** [simpático] nice. **-2.** [bonito] pretty. ◇ *m y f* ARTE & HIST Majo (*f* Maja).

majorette [majo'ret] *f* majorette.

mal ◇ *adj* → **malo.**

◇ *m* **-1.** [perversión]: **el** ~ evil. **-2.** [daño] harm, damage. **-3.** [enfermedad] illness; ~ **de montaña** altitude ○ mountain sickness; ~ **de ojo** evil eye. **-4.** [inconveniente] bad thing; **un** ~ **necesario** a necessary evil. **-5.** *loc:* **a grandes ~es, grandes remedios** drastic situations demand drastic action; **del** ~, **el menos** it's the lesser of two evils; ~ **de muchos, consuelo de todos** *proverb* at least I'm not the only one; **no hay** ~ **que por bien no venga** *proverb* every cloud has a silver lining *proverb.*

◇ *adv* **-1.** [incorrectamente] wrong; **esto está** ~ **hecho** this has been done wrong; **has escrito** ~ **esta palabra** you've spelt that word wrong. **-2.** [inadecuadamente] badly; **la fiesta salió** ~ the party went off badly; **oigo/veo** ~ I can't hear/see very well; **encontrarse** ~ [enfermo] to feel ill; [incómodo] to feel uncomfortable; **oler** ~ [tener mal olor] to smell bad; *fam* [tener mal cariz] to smell fishy; **saber** ~ [tener mal sabor] to taste bad; **me supo** ~ **que no vinieses a mi fiesta** I was none too pleased that you didn't come to my party; **sentar** ~ **a alguien** [ropa] not to suit sb; [comida] to disagree with sb; [comentario, actitud] to upset sb; **tomar algo a** ~ to take sthg the wrong way. **-3.** [difícilmente] hardly; ~ **puede saberlo si no se lo cuentas** he's hardly going to know it if you don't tell him. **-4.** *loc:* **estar a** ~ **con alguien** to have fallen out with sb; **ir de** ~ **en peor** to go from bad to worse; **no estaría** ~ **que ...** it would be nice if ....

◆ **mal que** *loc conj* although, even though; ~ **que te pese, las cosas están así** whether you like it or not, that's the way things are.

◆ **mal que bien** *loc adv* somehow or other.

malabar *adj*: **juego** ~ juggling (*U*).

malabarismo *m lit* & *fig* juggling (*U*); **hacer** ~**s** to juggle.

malabarista *m y f* juggler.

malacostumbrado, -da *adj* spoiled.

malacostumbrar *vt* to spoil.

malaleche *m y f vulg* miserable sod.

malapata *fam* ◇ *m y f* clumsy oaf. ◇ *f* tough luck.

malaria *f* malaria.

malasangre ◇ *m y f* [persona] evil-minded person. ◇ *f* mala intención] evil spirit; **hacerse ~** *fam* to get cheesed off.

Malasia Malaysia.

malasio, -sia *adj* Malaysian.

malasombra *fam* ◇ *m y f* [persona] pest. ◇ *f* [falta de gracia] lack of charm.

malayo, -ya *adj, m y f* Malay, Malayan.

◆ **malayo** *m* [lengua] Malay, Malayan.

malcomer *vi* to eat poorly.

malcriado, -da ◇ *adj* spoiled. ◇ *m y f* spoilt brat.

malcriar [9] *vt* to spoil.

maldad *f* **-1.** [cualidad] evil. **-2.** [acción] evil thing.

maldecir [66] ◇ *vt* to curse. ◇ *vi* to curse; **~ de** to speak ill of.

maldición *f* curse.

maldiga, maldijera *etc* → **maldecir**.

maldito, -ta *adj* **-1.** [embrujado] cursed, damned. **-2.** *fam* [para enfatizar] damned; **¡maldita sea!** damn it! **-3.** [marginado - escritor etc] ostracized.

maleable *adj lit & fig* malleable.

maleado, -da *adj* corrupt.

maleante ◇ *adj* wicked. ◇ *m y f* crook.

malear *vt* to corrupt.

malecón *m* [atracadero] jetty.

maledicencia *f* cursing; [difamación] slander.

maleducado, -da ◇ *adj* rude. ◇ *m y f* rude person.

maleficio *m* curse.

maléfico, -ca *adj* evil.

malentendido *m* misunderstanding.

malestar *m* **-1.** [dolor] upset, discomfort; **siento un ~ en el estómago** I've got an upset stomach; **sentir ~ general** to feel unwell. **-2.** *fig* [inquietud] uneasiness, unrest.

maleta *f* suitcase; **hacer** ○ **preparar la ~** to pack (one's bags).

maletera *f Amer* boot *Br*, trunk *Am*.

maletero *m* boot *Br*, trunk *Am*.

maletilla *m y f* apprentice bullfighter.

maletín *m* briefcase.

malevolencia *f* malevolence, wickedness.

malévolo, -la *adj* malevolent, wicked.

maleza *f* [arbustos] undergrowth; [malas hierbas] weeds (*pl*).

malformación *f* malformation.

malgastar *vt* [dinero, tiempo] to waste; [salud] to ruin.

malhablado, -da ◇ *adj* foul-mouthed. ◇ *m y f* foul-mouthed person.

malhechor, -ra *adj, m y f* criminal.

malherir [27] *vt* to injure seriously.

malhumor *m* bad mood; **de ~** in a bad mood.

malhumorado, -da *adj* bad-tempered; [enfadado] in a bad mood.

malicia *f* **-1.** [maldad] wickedness, evil; [mala intención] malice. **-2.** [agudeza] sharpness, alertness.

malicioso, -sa *adj* **-1.** [malo] wicked, evil; [malintencionado] malicious. **-2.** [avispado] sharp, alert.

malignidad *f* malignance.

maligno, -na *adj* malignant.

malintencionado, -da ◇ *adj* ill-intentioned. ◇ *m y f* ill-intentioned person.

malla *f* **-1.** [tejido] mesh; **~ de alambre** wire mesh. **-2.** [red] net. **-3.** *Amer* [traje de baño] swimsuit.

◆ **mallas** *fpl* **-1.** [de gimnasia] leotard (*sg*); [de ballet] tights. **-2.** [de portería] net (*sg*).

Mallorca Majorca.

malnacido, -da ◇ *adj* undesirable, nasty. ◇ *m y f* nasty type.

malnutrido, -da *adj* undernourished.

malo, -la, mal (*compar* peor, *superl* el peor) *adj* (*antes de sust masc sg: "mal"*) **-1.** [gen] bad; [calidad] poor, bad; **lo ~ fue que ...** the problem was (that) .... **-2.** [malicioso] wicked. **-3.** [enfermo] ill, sick; **estar/ponerse ~** to be/fall ill. **-4.** [molesto] unpleasant. **-5.** [travieso] naughty.

◆ **malo, -la** *m y f* [de película etc] villain, baddie.

◆ **malas** *fpl*: **ponerse a (las) malas con** to fall out with; **estar de malas** to be in a bad mood; **por las malas** by force.

malogrado, -da *adj* **-1.** [desaprovechado] wasted. **-2.** [difunto]: **un ~ poeta** a poet who died before his time.

malograr *vt* to waste.

◆ **malograrse** *vpr* **-1.** [fracasar] to fail. **-2.** [morir] to die before one's time.

maloliente *adj* smelly.

malparado, -da *adj*: **salir ~ de algo** to come out of sthg badly.

malpensado, -da ◇ *adj* malicious, evil-minded. ◇ *m y f* evil-minded person.

malquerencia *f* dislike.

malsano, -na *adj* unhealthy.

malsonante *adj* rude.

malta *m* malt.

Malta Malta.

malteado, -da *adj* malted.

maltés, -esa *adj, m y f* Maltese.

maltraer [73] *vt* [maltratar] to ill-treat; **llevar** ○ **traer a** ~ to cause headaches.

maltratar *vt* **-1.** [pegar, insultar] to ill-treat. **-2.** [estropear] to damage.

maltrato *m* ill-treatment.

maltrecho, -cha *adj* battered.

maltusianismo *m* malthusianism.

malva ◇ *f* BOT mallow; **criar** ~**s** *fam fig* to push up daisies. ◇ *adj inv* mauve. ◇ *m* [color] mauve.

malvado, -da ◇ *adj* evil, wicked. ◇ *m y f* villain, evil person.

malvavisco *m* marshmallow.

malvender *vt* to sell at a loss.

malversación *f*: ~ **(de fondos)** embezzlement (of funds).

malversador, -ra *m y f* embezzler.

malversar *vt* to embezzle.

Malvinas *fpl*: **las (islas)** ~ the Falkland Islands, the Falklands.

malvivir *vi* to live badly, to scrape together an existence.

mama *f* **-1.** [de mujer] breast; [ZOOL] udder. **-2.** *fam* [madre] mum, mummy.

mamá (*pl* **mamás**) *f fam* mum, mummy; ~ **grande** *Amer fam* grandma.

mamadera *f Amer* (baby's) bottle.

mamado, -da *adj fam* [ebrio] pissed.

◆ **mamada** *f* [de bebé] (breast) feed, (breast) feeding (*U*).

mamar ◇ *vt* **-1.** [suj: bebé] to suckle. **-2.** *fig* [aprender]: **lo mamó desde pequeño** he was immersed in it as a child. **-3.** *mfam fig* [beber] to knock back. ◇ *vi* to suckle; **dar de** ~ to breast-feed.

◆ **mamarse** *vpr mfam* [emborracharse] to get plastered.

mamario, -ria *adj* mammary.

mamarrachada *f fam* **-1.** [acción] stupid ○ idiotic thing. **-2.** [cuadro etc] rubbish (*U*).

mamarracho *m* **-1.** [fantoche] sight, mess. **-2.** [imbécil] idiot. **-3.** [bodrio] rubbish (*U*).

mambo *m* mambo.

mameluco *m* **-1.** HIST mameluke. **-2.** *fam* [torpe, necio] idiot.

mamífero, -ra *adj* mammal.

◆ **mamífero** *m* mammal.

mamografía *f MED* **-1.** [técnica] breast scanning, mammography. **-2.** [resultado] breast scan.

mamón, -ona ◇ *adj* **-1.** [que mama] unweaned. **-2.** *vulg* [necio] prattish. ◇ *m y f* **-1.** [que mama] unweaned baby. **-2.** *vulg* [necio] prat.

mamotreto *m* **-1.** *despec* [libro] hefty tome. **-2.** [objeto grande] monstrosity.

mampara *f* screen.

mamporro *m fam* punch, clout; [al caer] bump.

mampostería *f* masonry.

mamut (*pl* **mamuts**) *m* mammoth.

maná *m inv* manna; *fig* cheap and plentiful food.

manada *f* **-1.** [ZOOL - gen] herd; [- de lobos] pack; [- de ovejas] flock; [- de leones] pride. **-2.** *fam* [de gente] crowd, mob.

manager (*pl* **managers**) *m* manager.

Managua Managua.

manantial *m* spring; *fig* source.

manar *vi lit* & *fig*: ~ **(de)** to flow (from).

manazas ◇ *adj inv* clumsy. ◇ *m y f inv* clumsy person.

mancebo, -ba *m y f* young person.

◆ **manceba** *f* [concubina] concubine.

mancha *f* **-1.** [gen] stain, spot; [de tinta] blot; [de color] spot, mark. **-2.** ASTRON spot. **-3.** *fig* [deshonra] blemish.

manchado, -da *adj* [sucio] dirty; [con manchas] stained; [emborronado] smudged.

manchar *vt* **-1.** [ensuciar]: ~ **algo (de** ○ **con)** [gen] to make sthg dirty (with); [con manchas] to stain sthg (with); [emborronar] to smudge sthg (with). **-2.** *fig* [deshonrar] to tarnish.

◆ **mancharse** *vpr* [ensuciarse] to get dirty.

manchego, -ga ◇ *adj* of/relating to La Mancha. ◇ *m y f* native/inhabitant of La Mancha.

◆ **manchego** *m* → **queso**.

mancillar *vt* to tarnish, to sully.

manco, -ca *adj* **-1.** [sin una mano] one-handed; [sin manos] handless; [sin un brazo] one-armed; [sin brazos] armless; *fig*: **no ser** ~ **para** ○ **en** to be a dab hand at. **-2.** *fig* [incompleto] imperfect, defective.

mancomunar *vt* to pool (together).

◆ **mancomunarse** *vpr* to join together, to unite.

mancomunidad *f* association.

mancorna, mancuerna *f Amer* cufflink.

mandado, -da *m y f* [subordinado] underling.

◆ **mandado** *m* [recado] errand.

mandamás (*pl* **mandamases**) *m y f* bigwig, boss.

mandamiento *m* **-1.** [orden - militar] order, command; [- judicial] writ. **-2.** RELIG commandment.

mandanga *f fam* **-1.** (*gen pl*) [cuento, tontería] story. **-2.** [calma] sluggishness, lethargy.

mandar ◇ *vt* **-1.** [dar órdenes] to order; ~ **a alguien hacer algo** to order sb to do sthg; ~ **hacer algo** to have sthg done. **-2.** [enviar] to send. **-3.** [dirigir, gobernar] to lead, to be in charge of; [país] to rule. ◇ *vi* **-1.** [gen] to be in charge; [jefe de estado] to rule. **-2.** *despec* [dar órdenes] to order people around. **-3.** *loc:* **¿mande?** *fam* eh?, you what?

mandarín (*pl* **mandarines**) *m* **-1.** [título] mandarin. **-2.** [dialecto] Mandarin.

mandarina *f* mandarin.

mandarinero *m* mandarin tree.

mandatario, -ria *m y f* representative, agent; **primer** ~ [jefe de estado] head of state.

mandato *m* **-1.** [gen] order, command. **-2.** [poderes de representación, disposición] mandate; ~ **judicial** warrant. **-3.** POLÍT term of office; [reinado] period of rule.

mandíbula *f* jaw; **reír a** ~ **batiente** *fig* to laugh one's head off.

mandil *m* [delantal] apron.

mandioca *f* **-1.** [planta] cassava. **-2.** [fécula] tapioca.

mando *m* **-1.** [poder] command, authority; **al** ~ **de** in charge of. **-2.** [periodo en poder] term of office. **-3.** (*gen pl*) [autoridades] leadership (*U*); MIL command (*U*); **alto** ~ MIL high command; ~**s intermedios** middle management (*sg*). **-4.** [dispositivo] control; ~ **automático/a distancia** automatic/remote control.

mandolina *f* mandolin.

mandón, -ona ◇ *adj* bossy. ◇ *m y f* bossy-boots.

mandrágora *f* mandrake.

mandril *m* **-1.** [animal] mandrill. **-2.** [pieza] mandrel.

manduca *f fam* grub, scoff.

manecilla *f* **-1.** [del reloj] hand. **-2.** [cierre] clasp.

manejable *adj* [gen] manageable; [herramienta] easy to use.

manejador *m*: ~ **de dispositivos** device (driver).

manejar *vt* **-1.** [conocimientos, datos] to use, to marshal. **-2.** [máquina, mandos] to operate; [caballo, bicicleta] to handle; [arma] to wield. **-3.** [negocio etc] to manage, to run; [gente] to handle. **-4.** *fig* [dominar] to boss about. **-5.** *Amer* [conducir] to drive.

◆ **manejarse** *vpr* **-1.** [moverse] to move ○ get about. **-2.** [desenvolverse] to manage, to get by.

manejo *m* **-1.** [de máquina, mandos] operation; [de armas, herramientas] use; **de fácil** ~ user-friendly. **-2.** [de conocimientos, datos] marshalling; [de idiomas] command. **-3.** [de caballo, bicicleta] handling. **-4.** [de negocio etc] management, running. **-5.** (*gen pl*) *fig* [intriga] intrigue.

manera *f* way, manner; **a mi** ~ **de ver** the way I see it; **de cualquier** ~ [sin cuidado] any old how; [de todos modos] anyway, in any case; **de mala** ~ badly; **de ninguna** ~, **en** ~ **alguna** [refuerza negación] by no means, under no circumstances; [respuesta exclamativa] no way!, certainly not!; **de todas** ~**s** anyway; **de una** ~ **o de otra** one way or another; **en cierta** ~ in a way; ~ **de ser** way of being, nature; **a la** ~ **de** in the style of, after the fashion of; **a** ~ **de** [como] as, by way of; **de** ~ **que** [para] so (that); **no hay** ~ there is no way, it's impossible.

◆ **maneras** *fpl* [modales] manners.

manga *f* **-1.** [de prenda] sleeve; **en** ~**s de camisa** in shirt sleeves; ~ **corta/larga** short/long sleeve; ~ **raglán** ○ **ranglán** raglan sleeve; **sacarse algo de la** ~ [improvisar] to make sthg up on the spur of the moment; [idear] to come up with sthg; **ser de** ~ **ancha, tener** ~ **ancha** to be overindulgent. **-2.** [manguera] hosepipe. **-3.** [filtro] muslin strainer. **-4.** [medidor de viento] wind sock. **-5.** [de pastelería] forcing ○ piping bag. **-6.** DEP stage, round.

manganeso *m* manganese.

mangante *fam* ◇ *adj* thieving. ◇ *m y f* thief.

mangar [16] *vt fam* to pinch, to nick.

mango *m* **-1.** [asa] handle. **-2.** [árbol] mango tree; [fruta] mango.

mangonear *vi fam* **-1.** [entrometerse] to meddle. **-2.** [mandar] to push people around, to be bossy. **-3.** [manipular] to fiddle about.

mangoneo *m fam* **-1.** [intromisión] bossing ○ pushing around. **-2.** [manipulación] fiddling.

mangosta *f* mongoose.

mangue *etc* → **mangar**.

manguera *f* hosepipe; [de bombero] fire hose.

mangui *mfam* ◇ *adj* [persona no fiable] sneaky. ◇ *m y f* **-1.** [ladrón] crook, thief. **-2.** [persona no fiable] crook.

manguito *m* **-1.** [para el frío] muff. **-2.** [media manga] protective sleeve, oversleeve.

maní (*pl* **manises**) *m Amer* peanut.

manía *f* **-1.** [idea fija] obsession; ~ **persecutoria** persecution complex. **-2.** [peculiaridad] idiosyncracy. **-3.** [mala costumbre] bad habit. **-4.** [afición exagerada] mania, craze. **-5.** *fam* [ojeriza] dislike; **coger** ~ **a alguien** to take a dislike to sb; **tener** ~ **a alguien** not to be able to stand sb. **-6.** PSICOL mania.

maniaco, -ca, **maníaco, -ca** ◇ *adj* manic. ◇ *m y f* maniac; ~ **sexual** sex maniac.

maniacodepresivo, -va *adj*, *m y f* manic-depressive.

maniatar *vt* to tie the hands of.

maniático, -ca ◇ *adj* fussy. ◇ *m y f* fussy person; **es un** ~ **del fútbol** he's football-crazy.

manicomio *m* mental o psychiatric hospital *Br*, insane asylum *Am*.

manicuro, -ra *m y f* [persona] manicurist.
◆ **manicura** *f* [técnica] manicure.

manido, -da *adj* [tema etc] hackneyed.

manierismo *m* ARTE mannerism.

manifestación *f* **-1.** [de alegría, dolor etc] show, display; [de opinión] declaration, expression; [indicio] sign. **-2.** [por la calle] demonstration.

manifestante *m y f* demonstrator.

manifestar [19] *vt* **-1.** [alegría, dolor etc] to show. **-2.** [opinión etc] to express.
◆ **manifestarse** *vpr* **-1.** [por la calle] to demonstrate. **-2.** [hacerse evidente] to become clear o apparent.

manifiesto, -ta *adj* clear, evident; **poner de** ~ **algo** [revelar] to reveal sthg; [hacer patente] to make sthg clear.
◆ **manifiesto** *m* manifesto.

manija *f* handle.

Manila Manila.

manilargo, -ga *adj* **-1.** [generoso] generous. **-2.** [ladrón] light-fingered.

manileño, -ña *adj* of/relating to Manila.

manilla *f* (*gen pl*) **-1.** [del reloj] hand. **-2.** [grilletes] manacle.

manillar *m* handlebars (*pl*).

maniobra *f* **-1.** [gen] manoeuvre; **hacer ~s** to manoeuvre. **-2.** *fig* [treta] trick.

maniobrar *vi* to manoeuvre.

manipulación *f* **-1.** [gen] handling. **-2.** [engaño] manipulation.

manipulador, -ra ◇ *adj* handling. ◇ *m y f* handler.

manipular *vt* **-1.** [manejar] to handle. **-2.** [mangonear - información, resultados] to manipulate; [- negocios, asuntos] to interfere in.

maniqueísmo *m* **-1.** [doctrina] Manicheism. **-2.** [actitud] seeing things in black and white.

maniqueo, -a ◇ *adj* Manichean. ◇ *m y f* Manichee.

maniquí (*pl* **maniquíes**) ◇ *m* dummy. ◇ *m y f* **-1.** [modelo] model. **-2.** [persona manipulada] puppet.

manirroto, -ta ◇ *adj* extravagant. ◇ *m y f* spendthrift.

manitas ◇ *adj inv* handy, good with one's hands. ◇ *m y f inv* handy person; **ser un** ~ **(de plata)** to be (very) good with one's hands; **hacer** ~ to fondle, to touch each other up.

manito, **mano** *m Amer fam* mate, chum.

manivela *f* crank.

manjar *m* delicious food (*U*).

mano *f* **-1.** [gen] hand; **a** ~ [cerca] to hand, handy; [sin máquina] by hand; **votación a** ~ **alzada** show of hands; **a** ~ **armada** armed; **dar** o **estrechar la** ~ **a alguien** to shake hands with sb; **darse** o **estrecharse la** ~ to shake hands; **echar/tender una** ~ to give/ offer a hand; **¡~s arriba!**, **¡arriba las ~s!** hands up!; ~ **de obra** [capacidad de trabajo] labour; [trabajadores] workforce; ~ **de obra especializada** skilled labour. **-2.** [ZOOL - gen] forefoot; [- de perro, gato] (front) paw; [- de cerdo] (front) trotter. **-3.** [lado]: **a** ~ **derecha/izquierda** on the right/left. **-4.** [de pintura etc] coat. **-5.** [influencia] influence. **-6.** [de mortero] pestle. **-7.** [partida de naipes] game; **ser** ~ to (be the) lead. **-8.** *fig* [serie, tanda] series. **-9.** *loc*: **alzar la** ~ **contra alguien** to raise one's hand to sb; **bajo** ~ secretly; **caer en ~s de alguien** to fall into sb's hands; **cargar la** ~ to go over the top; **con las ~s cruzadas**, ~ **sobre** ~ sitting around doing nothing; **coger a alguien con las ~s en la masa** to catch sb red-handed o in the act; **de primera** ~ [coche etc] brand new; [noticias etc] first-hand; **de segunda** ~ second-hand; **dejar de la** ~ to abandon; **dejar algo en ~s de alguien** to leave sthg in sb's hands; **echar** ~ **de algo** to make use of sthg, to resort to sthg; **ensuciarse las ~s** to get one's hands dirty; **escaparse de las ~s a alguien** [oportunidad etc] to slip through sb's hands; [control, proyecto] to get out of hand for sb; **estar dejado de la** ~ **de Dios** [gen] to be godforsaken; [persona] to be a total failure; **ganar por la** ~ **a alguien** to beat sb to it; **írsele a uno la** ~ [perder el control] to lose control; [exagerar] to go too far; **lavarse las ~s (de algo)** to wash one's hands (of sthg); **llevarse las ~s a la cabeza** [gesticular] to throw one's hands in the air (in horror); *fig* to be horrified; ~ **a** ~ tête-à-tête; **¡~s a la obra!** let's get down to it!;

meter ~ a alguien [investigar] to get onto sb, to start to investigate sb; [magrear sin consentimiento] **to grope sb;** [magrear con consentimiento] to touch sb up; **meter ~ a algo** [gen] to fiddle about ○ meddle with sthg; [problema, asunto] to tackle sthg; **pedir la ~ de una mujer** to ask for a woman's hand (in marriage); **ponerse en ~s de alguien** to put o.s. in sb's hands; **ser la ~ derecha de alguien** to be sb's right hand man; **tener buena ~ para algo** to have a knack for sthg; **tener las ~s largas** to be fond of a fight; **tener ~ izquierda con la gente** to know how to deal with people; **traerse entre ~s algo** to be up to sthg; **venir ○ llegar a las ~s** to come to blows.

manojo *m* bunch; **estar hecho un ~ de nervios** *fig* to be a bundle of nerves; **ser un ~ de nervios** *fig* to be hyperactive.

manoletina *f* **-1.** TAUROM *pass with the cape in bullfighting invented by the Spanish bullfighter, Manolete; ver también* **tauromaquia.** **-2.** [zapato] *type of open, low-heeled shoe, often with a bow.*

manómetro *m* pressure gauge.

manopla *f* mitten.

manoseado, -da *adj* shabby, worn.

manosear *vt* **-1.** [gen] to handle roughly; [papel, tela] to rumple. **-2.** [persona] to fondle.

manoseo *m* fingering, touching.

manotazo *m* slap.

mansalva

◆ **a mansalva** *loc adv* [en abundancia] in abundance.

mansarda *f* attic.

mansedumbre *f* [gen] calmness, gentleness; [de animal] tameness.

mansión *f* mansion.

manso, -sa *adj* **-1.** [apacible] calm, gentle. **-2.** [domesticado] tame. **-3.** *Amer* [extraordinario] great.

manta ◇ *f* [abrigo] blanket; **liarse la ~ a la cabeza** *fig* to take the plunge; **tirar de la ~** *fig* to let the cat out of the bag. ◇ *m y f fam* [persona] hopeless ○ useless person.

manteca *f* fat; [mantequilla] butter; **~ de cacao** cocoa butter; **~ de cerdo** lard.

mantecado *m* **-1.** [pastel] shortcake. **-2.** [helado] *ice-cream made of milk, eggs and sugar.*

mantecoso, -sa *adj* fatty, greasy.

mantel *m* tablecloth.

mantelería *f* table linen.

manteleta *f* shawl.

mantener [72] *vt* **-1.** [sustentar, aguantar] to support. **-2.** [conservar] to keep; [en buen estado] to maintain, to service. **-3.** [tener - relaciones, conversación] to have. **-4.** [defender - opinión] to stick to, to maintain; [- candidatura] to refuse to withdraw.

◆ **mantenerse** *vpr* **-1.** [sustentarse] to subsist, to support o.s. **-2.** [permanecer, continuar] to remain; [edificio] to remain standing; **~se aparte** [en discusión] to stay out of it.

mantenido, -da ◇ *adj* sustained. ◇ *m y f* [hombre] gigolo; [mujer] kept woman.

mantenimiento *m* **-1.** [sustento] sustenance. **-2.** [conservación] upkeep, maintenance.

mantequera *f* butter dish.

mantequería *f* **-1.** [fábrica] dairy, butter factory. **-2.** [tienda] grocer's (shop).

mantequilla *f* butter.

mantiene *etc* → **mantener.**

mantilla *f* **-1.** [de mujer] mantilla. **-2.** [de bebé] shawl. **-3.** *loc* **estar en ~s** [persona] to be wet behind the ears; [plan] to be in its infancy.

manto *m* **-1.** [gen] cloak. **-2.** GEOL mantle.

mantón *m* shawl; **~ de Manila** embroidered silk shawl.

mantuviera *etc* → **mantener.**

manual ◇ *adj* **-1.** [con las manos] manual. **-2.** [manejable] easy-to-use. ◇ *m* manual.

manubrio *m* crank.

manufacturado, -da *adj* manufactured.

manufacturar *vt* to manufacture.

manumisión *f* liberation.

manuscrito, -ta *adj* handwritten.

◆ **manuscrito** *m* manuscript.

manutención *f* **-1.** [sustento] support, maintenance. **-2.** [alimento] food.

manzana *f* **-1.** [fruta] apple; **~ de la discordia** *fig* bone of contention. **-2.** [grupo de casas] block (of houses).

manzanilla *f* **-1.** [planta] camomile. **-2.** [infusión] camomile tea. **-3.** [vino] manzanilla (sherry). **-4.** [aceituna] manzanilla, *type of small olive.*

manzano *m* apple tree.

maña *f* **-1.** [destreza] skill; **más vale ~ que fuerza** *proverb* brain is better than brawn. **-2.** [astucia] wits (*pl*), guile (*U*); **darse ~ para hacer algo** to contrive to do sthg. **-3.** [engaño] ruse, trick.

mañana ◇ *f* morning; **(muy) de ~** (very) early in the morning; **a las dos de la ~** at two in the morning. ◇ *m*: **el ~** tomorrow, the future. ◇ *adv* tomorrow; **¡hasta ~!** see you tomorrow!; **~ por la ~** tomorrow morning; **pasado ~** the day after tomorrow.

marcar

mañanero, -ra *adj* **-1.** [madrugador] early rising. **-2.** [matutino] morning (*antes de sust*).

mañanitas *f Amer* birthday song *sg.*

maño, -ña *m y f fam* Aragonese.

mañoso, -sa *adj* skilful.

maoísmo *m* Maoism.

maoísta *adj, m y f* Maoist.

mapa *m* map; ~ **físico/mudo/político** geographic/blank/political map; ~ **de bits** INFORM bit map; **desaparecer del** ~ *fam fig* to vanish into thin air.

mapamundi *m* world map.

Maputo Maputo.

maqueta *f* **-1.** [reproducción a escala] (scale) model. **-2.** [de libro] dummy.

maqui = **maquis.**

maquiavélico, -ca *adj* Machiavellian.

maquiavelismo *m* Machiavellianism.

maquillador, -ra ◇ *adj* make-up (*antes de sust*). ◇ *m y f* make-up artist.

maquillaje *m* **-1.** [producto] make-up. **-2.** [acción] making-up.

maquillar *vt* **-1.** [pintar] to make up. **-2.** *fig* [disimular] to cover up, to disguise.
◆ **maquillarse** *vpr* to make o.s. up.

máquina *f* **-1.** [gen] machine; **a toda** ~ at full pelt; **escrito a** ~ typewritten; **escribir a** ~ to type; **hecho a** ~ machine-made; ~ **de coser** sewing machine; ~ **de escribir** typewriter; ~ **fotográfica** camera; ~ **registradora** cash register; ~ **tragaperras**, ~ **traganíqueles** *Amer* slot machine, fruit machine. **-2.** [locomotora] engine; ~ **de vapor** steam engine. **-3.** [mecanismo] mechanism. **-4.** *Amer* [coche] car. **-5.** *fig* [de estado, partido etc] machinery (*U*).

maquinación *f* machination.

maquinal *adj* mechanical.

maquinar *vt* to machinate, to plot; ~ **algo contra alguien** to plot sth against sb.

maquinaria *f* **-1.** [gen] machinery. **-2.** [de reloj etc] mechanism.

maquinilla *f*: ~ **de afeitar** razor; ~ **eléctrica** electric razor.

maquinismo *m* mechanization.

maquinista *m y f* [de tren] engine driver *Br*, engineer *Am*; [de barco] engineer.

maquinizar [13] *vt* to mechanize.

maquis, **maqui** *m y f inv* guerrilla.

mar *m o f lit* & *fig* sea; **hacerse a la** ~ to set sail, to put (out) to sea; ~ **adentro** out to sea; **alta** ~ high seas (*pl*); ~ **de fondo** *lit* & *fig* groundswell; ~ **Egeo** the Aegean Sea; **el** ~ **del Norte** the North Sea; ~ **Tirreno** the Tyrrhenian Sea; **a** ~**es** a lot; **llover a** ~**es** to rain buckets; **la** ~ **de** really, very; **es la** ~ **de inteligente** she's really intelligent.

mar. (*abrev de* **marzo**) Mar.

marabunta *f* **-1.** [de hormigas] plague of ants. **-2.** *fig* [muchedumbre] crowd.

maraca *f* maraca.

maraña *f* **-1.** [maleza] thicket. **-2.** *fig* [enredo] tangle.

marasmo *m* **-1.** MED marasmus, wasting. **-2.** *fig* [de ánimo] apathy; [de negocio] stagnation.

maratón *m lit* & *fig* marathon.

maratoniano, -na *adj* marathon.

maravilla *f* **-1.** [gen] marvel, wonder; **es una** ~ it's wonderful; **hacer** ~**s** to do o work wonders; **a las mil** ~**s**, **de** ~ wonderfully; **venir de** ~ to be just the thing o ticket. **-2.** BOT marigold.

maravillar *vt* to amaze.
◆ **maravillarse** *vpr*: ~**se (con)** to be amazed (by).

maravilloso, -sa *adj* marvellous, wonderful.

marca *f* **-1.** [señal] mark; [de rueda, animal] track; [en ganado] brand; [en papel] watermark. **-2.** [COM - de tabaco, café etc] brand; [- de coche, ordenador etc] make; **de** ~ designer (*antes de sust*); ~ **de fábrica** trademark; ~ **registrada** registered trademark. **-3.** [etiqueta] label. **-4.** [DEP - gen] performance; [- en carreras] time; [- plusmarca] record. **-5.** *loc*: **de** ~ **mayor** [muy grande] enormous; [excelente] outstanding.

marcado, -da *adj* **-1.** [gen] marked. **-2.** [pelo] set.
◆ **marcado** *m* **-1.** [señalado] marking. **-2.** [peinado] set.

marcador, -ra *adj* marking.
◆ **marcador** *m* **-1.** [tablero] scoreboard; ~ **electrónico** electronic scoreboard. **-2.** [DEP - defensor] marker; [- goleador] scorer. **-3.** [para libros] bookmark.

marcaje *m* DEP marking.

marcapasos *m inv* pacemaker.

marcar [10] ◇ *vt* **-1.** [gen] to mark. **-2.** [poner precio a] to price. **-3.** [indicar] to indicate. **-4.** [anotar] to note down. **-5.** [resaltar] to emphasise. **-6.** [número de teléfono] to dial. **-7.** [suj: termómetro, contador etc] to read; [suj: reloj] to say. **-8.** [DEP - tanto] to score; [- a un jugador] to mark. **-9.** [cabello] to set. ◇ *vi* **-1.** [dejar secuelas] to leave a mark. **-2.** DEP [anotar un tanto] to score.
◆ **marcarse** *vpr fam*: ~**se un detalle** to do sth nice o kind; ~**se un tanto** to earn a Brownie point.

marcha f **-1.** [partida] departure. **-2.** [ritmo] speed; **a ~s forzadas** [contra reloj] against the clock; **a toda ~** at top speed; **en ~** [motor] running; [plan] underway; **poner en ~** [gen] to start; [dispositivo, alarma] to activate; **hacer algo sobre la ~** to do sthg as one goes along. **-3.** AUTOM gear; **cambiar de ~** to change gear; **~ atrás** reverse; **dar ~ atrás** AUTOM to reverse; fig to back out. **-4.** MIL & POLÍT march; **abrir la ~** to head the procession; **cerrar la ~** to bring up the rear. **-5.** MÚS march; **~ fúnebre/nupcial** funeral/wedding march; **Marcha Real** Spanish national anthem. **-6.** [transcurso] course; [progreso] progress. **-7.** DEP walk. **-8.** fam [animación] liveliness, life; **hay mucha ~** there's a great atmosphere; **ir de ~** to go out on the town; **tener (mucha) ~** to be a (real) raver.

marchante, -ta m y f dealer.

marchar vi **-1.** [andar] to walk. **-2.** [partir] to leave, to go. **-3.** [funcionar] to work. **-4.** [desarrollarse] to progress; **el negocio marcha** business is going well.

◆ **marcharse** vpr to leave, to go.

marchitar vt lit & fig to wither.

◆ **marchitarse** vpr **-1.** [planta] to fade, to wither. **-2.** fig [persona] to languish, to fade away.

marchito, -ta adj **-1.** [planta] faded. **-2.** fig [persona] worn.

marchoso, -sa fam ◇ adj lively. ◇ m y f livewire.

marcial adj martial.

marcialidad f martial nature.

marcianitos mpl [juego] space invaders.

marciano, -na adj, m y f Martian.

marco m **-1.** [cerco] frame. **-2.** fig [ambiente, paisaje] setting. **-3.** [ámbito] framework. **-4.** [moneda] mark. **-5.** [portería] goalmouth.

marea f **-1.** [del mar] tide; **~ alta/baja** high/low tide; **~ negra** oil slick. **-2.** fig [multitud] flood.

mareado, -da adj **-1.** [con náuseas] sick, queasy; [en coche, avión etc] travelsick. **-2.** [aturdido] dizzy. **-3.** fig [fastidiado] fed up to the back teeth.

marear vt **-1.** [provocar náuseas] to make sick; [en coche, avión etc] to make travelsick. **-2.** [aturdir] to make dizzy. **-3.** fam fig [fastidiar] to annoy.

◆ **marearse** vpr **-1.** [tener náuseas] to feel sick; [en coche, avión etc] to feel travelsick. **-2.** [estar aturdido] to get dizzy. **-3.** [emborracharse] to get drunk.

marejada f **-1.** [mar rizada] heavy sea. **-2.** fig [agitación] wave of discontent.

marejadilla f slight swell.

mare mágnum m jumble.

maremoto m tidal wave.

marengo → gris.

mareo m **-1.** [náuseas] sickness; [en coches, aviones etc] travelsickness. **-2.** [aturdimiento] dizziness, giddiness. **-3.** fam fig [fastidio] drag, pain.

marfil m ivory.

marfileño, -ña adj ivory (antes de sust).

marga f marl.

margarina f margarine.

margarita f **-1.** BOT daisy; **deshojar la ~** fig to hum and haw, to shillyshally. **-2.** IMPRENTA daisy wheel.

margen m o f **-1.** (gen f) [de río] bank; [de camino] side. **-2.** (gen m) [de página] margin. **-3.** (gen m) COM margin; **~ de beneficio** profit margin. **-4.** (gen m) [límites] leeway; **al ~ de eso, hay otros factores** over and above this, there are other factors; **al ~ de la ley** outside the law; **dejar al ~** to exclude; **estar al ~ de** to have nothing to do with; **mantenerse al ~ de** to keep out of; **~ de error** margin of error; **~ de seguridad** degree of certainty. **-5.** (gen m) [ocasión]: **dar ~ a alguien para hacer algo** to give sb the chance to do sthg.

marginación f exclusion; **~ social** exclusion from society.

marginado, -da ◇ adj excluded. ◇ m y f outcast.

marginal adj **-1.** [nota] marginal; [tema] minor. **-2.** ARTE & POLÍT fringe.

marginalidad f exclusion.

marginar vt **-1.** [excluir] to exclude, to make an outcast; [dar de lado] to give the cold shoulder. **-2.** [omitir] to omit.

maría f Amer fam migrant from country to urban areas.

mariachi m **-1.** [música] mariachi (music). **-2.** [orquesta] mariachi band.

marianismo m Marianism.

mariano, -na adj Marian.

marica m mfam despec queer, poof.

Maricastaña → tiempo.

maricón m mfam despec queer, poof.

mariconada f mfam despec [mala jugada] dirty trick.

mariconear vi mfam despec to camp it up.

mariconera f fam (man's) clutch bag.

marido m husband.

marihuana f marijuana.

marimacho m fam mannish woman; despec butch woman.

marimorena f row; **armar la ~** fig to kick up a row.

marina → marino.

marinar *vt* to marinate.

marine *m* MIL marine.

marinería *f* **-1.** [profesión] sailoring. **-2.** [marineros] crew, seamen (*pl*).

marinero, **-ra** *adj* [gen] sea (*antes de sust*); [buque] seaworthy; [pueblo] seafaring.
◆ **marinero** *m* sailor.

marino, **-na** *adj* sea (*antes de sust*), marine.
◆ **marino** *m* sailor.
◆ **marina** *f* **-1.** [náutica] seamanship. **-2.** MIL: ~ **(de guerra)** navy; ~ **mercante** merchant navy. **-3.** ARTE seascape.

marioneta *f* [muñeco] marionette, puppet.
◆ **marionetas** *fpl* [teatro] puppet show (*sg*).

mariposa *f* **-1.** [insecto] butterfly. **-2.** [tuerca] wing nut. **-3.** [candela, luz] oil lamp. **-4.** [en natación] butterfly. **-5.** *loc*: **a otra cosa** ~ let's move on.

mariposear *vi* **-1.** [ser inconstante] to flit about. **-2.** [galantear] to flirt.

mariposón *m fam* flirt, wolf.

mariquita ◇ *f* [insecto] ladybird *Br*, ladybug *Am*. ◇ *m mfam despec* [homosexual] poof, queer.

marisabidilla *f* know-all.

mariscada *f* seafood dish.

mariscal *m* marshal; ~ **de campo** field marshal.

marisco *m* seafood (*U*), shellfish (*U*).

marisma *f* salt marsh.

marismeño, **-ña** *adj* marshy.

marisquería *f* seafood restaurant.

marista *adj & m* Marist.

marital *adj* marital.

marítimo, **-ma** *adj* [del mar] maritime; [cercano al mar] seaside (*antes de sust*).

marketing ['marketin] *m* marketing.

marmita *f* pot.

mármol *m* marble; **de** ~ *fig* cold, insensitive.

marmota *f* marmot; **dormir como una** ~ to sleep like a log.

mar Muerto *npr m*: **el** ~ the Dead Sea.

mar Negro *m*: **el** ~ the Black Sea.

maroma *f* rope.

maromo *m fam* bloke, guy.

maronita *adj, m y f* Maronite.

marque *etc* → marcar.

marqués, **-esa** *m* marquis (*f* marchioness).

marquesina *f* glass canopy; [parada de autobús] bus-shelter.

marquetería *f* marquetry.

marranada *fam f* **-1.** [porquería - estado] filthy mess; [- dicho] filthy thing, filth (*U*). **-2.** [mala jugada] dirty trick.

marrano, **-na** *m y f* **-1.** [animal] pig. **-2.** *fam fig* [sucio] (filthy) pig. **-3.** *fam fig* [sin escrúpulos] swine.

marras
◆ **de marras** *loc adj* aforementioned, said.

mar Rojo *m*: **el** ~ the Red Sea.

marrón *adj & m* brown.

marron glacé [ma'rroŋ gla'se] (*pl* **marrons glacés**) *m* marron glacé.

marroquí (*pl* **marroquíes**) *adj, m y f* Moroccan.

marroquinería *f* **-1.** [arte] leatherwork. **-2.** [artículos] leather goods (*pl*).

Marruecos Morocco.

Marsellesa *f* Marseillaise.

Marte *m* Mars.

martes *m inv* Tuesday; ~ **de Carnaval** Shrove Tuesday; ~ **y trece** ≃ Friday 13th; *ver también* sábado.

martillear, **martillar** *vt* to hammer.

martillo *m* hammer; ~ **neumático** pneumatic drill *Br*, jackhammer *Am*.

martinete *m* heron.

martín pescador (*pl* **martín pescadores**) *m* kingfisher.

mártir *m y f lit & fig* martyr.

martirio *m* **-1.** RELIG martyrdom. **-2.** *fig* [sufrimiento] trial, torment.

martirizar [13] *vt* **-1.** [torturar] to martyr. **-2.** *fig* [hacer sufrir] to torment, to torture.

marxismo *m* Marxism.

marxista *adj, m y f* Marxist.

marzo *m* March; *ver también* septiembre.

mas *conj* but.

más ◇ *adv* **-1.** (*comparativo*) more; **Pepe es** ~ **alto/ambicioso** Pepe is taller/more ambitious; **tener** ~ **hambre** to be hungrier ○ more hungry; ~ **de/que** more than; ~ ... **que** ... more ... than ...; **Juan es** ~ **alto que tú** Juan is taller than you; **de** ~ [de sobra] left over; **hay 100 ptas de** ~ there are 100 pesetas left over; **eso está de** ~ that's not necessary. **-2.** (*superlativo*): **el/la/lo** ~ the most; **el** ~ **listo/ambicioso** the cleverest/ most ambitious. **-3.** (*en frases negativas*) any more; **no necesito** ~ **(trabajo)** I don't need any more (work). **-4.** (*con pron interrogativos e indefinidos*) else; ¿**qué/quién** ~? what/who else?; **nadie** ~ **vino** nobody else came. **-5.** [indica suma] plus; **dos** ~ **dos igual a cuatro** two plus two is four. **-6.** [indica intensidad]: **no le aguanto, ¡es** ~ **tonto!** I can't stand him, he's so stupid!; ¡**qué día** ~ **bonito!** what a lovely day! **-7.** [indica pre-

ferencia]: ~ **vale que nos vayamos a casa** it would be better for us to go home. **-8.** *loc*: **el que ~ y el que menos** everyone; **es ~** indeed, what is more; **~ bien** rather; **~ o menos** more or less; **¿qué ~ da?** what difference does it make?; **sin ~ (ni ~)** just like that.
◇ *m inv* MAT plus (sign); **tiene sus ~ y sus menos** it has its good points and its bad points.
◆ **a más de** *loc adv* in addition to, as well as.
◆ **por más que** *loc conj* however much; **por ~ que lo intente no lo conseguirá** however much ○ hard she tries, she'll never manage it.

masa ◇ *f* **-1.** [gen] mass; **~ atómica** atomic mass; **~ salarial** total wages bill. **-2.** [multitud] throng; **en ~** en masse. **-3.** CULIN dough. **-4.** ELECTR earth. **-5.** *Amer* [pastelillo] *small cake*.
◆ **masas** *fpl*: **las ~s** the masses.

masacrar *vt* to massacre.

masacre *f* massacre.

masaje *m* massage.

masajista *m* masseur (*f* masseuse).

mascar [10] *vt & vi* to chew.

máscara *f* **-1.** [gen] mask; **~ antigás** gas mask. **-2.** *fig* [pretexto] front, pretence; **quitar la ~ a alguien** to unmask sb; **quitarse la ~ to reveal o.s.

mascarada *f* **-1.** [fiesta] masquerade. **-2.** *fig* [farsa] farce.

mascarilla *f* **-1.** MED mask. **-2.** [cosmética] face pack.

mascarón *m* **-1.** [máscara] large mask. **-2.** ARQUIT grotesque head; **~ de proa** figurehead.

Mascate Muscat.

mascota *f* mascot.

masculinidad *f* masculinity.

masculinizar [13] *vt* to make mannish.

masculino, -na *adj* **-1.** BIOL male. **-2.** [varonil] manly. **-3.** GRAM masculine.

mascullar *vt* to mutter.

masía *f* *traditional Catalan or Aragonese farmhouse*.

masificación *f* overcrowding.

masificar [10] *vt* to cause overcrowding in.
◆ **masificarse** *vpr* to become overcrowded.

masilla *f* putty.

masivo, -va *adj* mass (*antes de sust*).

masoca *m y f* *fam* masochist.

masón, -ona ◇ *adj* masonic. ◇ *m y f* mason, freemason.

masonería *f* masonry, freemasonry.

masoquismo *m* masochism.

masoquista ◇ *adj* masochistic. ◇ *m y f* masochist.

masque *etc* → **mascar**.

mass media, **mass-media** *mpl* mass media.

mastectomía *f* mastectomy.

máster (*pl* masters) *m* Master's (degree).

masticar [10] *vt* **-1.** [mascar] to chew. **-2.** *fig* [pensar] to chew over, to ponder.

mástil *m* **-1.** NÁUT mast. **-2.** [palo] pole. **-3.** MUS neck.

mastín *m* mastiff.

mastitis *f inv* mastitis.

mastodonte ◇ *m* mastodon. ◇ *m y f fam* giant.

masturbación *f* masturbation.

masturbar *vt* to masturbate.
◆ **masturbarse** *vpr* to masturbate.

MAT (*abrev de* **Ministerio de Administración Territorial**) *m Spanish ministry for relations with the autonomous regions*.

mata *f* [arbusto] bush, shrub; [matojo] tuft; **~s** scrub.
◆ **mata de pelo** *f* mop of hair.

Matac (*abrev de* **Mando Aéreo Táctico**) *m Spanish tactical air command*.

matadero *m* abattoir, slaughterhouse.

matador, -ra *fam adj* **-1.** [cansado] killing, exhausting. **-2.** [feo] awful, horrendous.
◆ **matador** *m* matador; *ver también* **tauromaquia**.

matambre *m Amer* cold cooked meat.

matamoscas *m inv* [pala] flyswat; [esprai] flyspray.

matanza *f* **-1.** [masacre] slaughter. **-2.** [del cerdo] pig-killing.

matar *vt* **-1.** [gen] to kill; **estar a ~ con alguien** to be at daggers drawn with sb; **~las callando** to be up to sthg on the quiet. **-2.** [molestar] to drive mad. **-3.** [apagar - color] to tone down; [- sed] to slake, to quench; [- hambre] to stay. **-4.** [redondear, limar] to round (off).
◆ **matarse** *vpr* **-1.** [morir] to die. **-2.** [suicidarse, esforzarse] to kill o.s.; **~se a trabajar** to work o.s. to death; **~se por hacer algo** to kill o.s. in order to do sthg.

matarratas *m inv* **-1.** [veneno] rat poison. **-2.** *fig* [bebida] rotgut.

matasanos *m y f inv despec* quack.

matasellos *m y f inv* postmark.

matasuegras *m inv* (party) cracker.

match [matʃ] (*pl* matches) *m* match.

◆ **match ball** ['matʃßol] (pl **match balls**) m match ball.

mate ◇ adj matt. ◇ m **-1.** [en ajedrez] mate, checkmate. **-2.** [en baloncesto] dunk; [en tenis] smash. **-3.** BOT [bebida] maté.

matemático, -ca ◇ adj mathematical. ◇ m y f [científico] mathematician.

◆ **matemáticas** fpl [ciencia] mathematics (U).

materia f **-1.** [sustancia, asunto] matter; ~ **gris** grey matter. **-2.** [material] material; ~ **prima, primera** ~ raw material. **-3.** [asignatura] subject; **en** ~ **de** on the subject of, concerning; **entrar en** ~ to get down to business.

material ◇ adj **-1.** [gen] physical; [daños, consecuencias] material. **-2.** [real] real, actual. ◇ m **-1.** [gen] material; ~ **de desecho** waste material; ~ **refractario** heat-resistant material. **-2.** [instrumentos] equipment; ~ **bélico** ○ **de guerra** war material.

materialismo m materialism; ~ **dialéctico/histórico** dialectical/historical materialism.

materialista ◇ adj materialistic. ◇ m y f materialist.

materializar [13] vt **-1.** [idea, proyecto] to realize. **-2.** [hacer tangible] to produce.

◆ **materializarse** vpr to materialize.

maternal adj motherly, maternal.

maternidad f **-1.** [cualidad] motherhood. **-2.** [hospital] maternity hospital.

materno, -na adj maternal; [lengua] mother (antes de sust).

matice etc → matizar.

matinal adj morning (antes de sust).

matinée [mati'ne] f matinée.

matiz m **-1.** [variedad - de color, opinión] shade; [- de sentido] nuance, shade of meaning. **-2.** [atisbo] trace, hint.

matizar [13] vt **-1.** [teñir]: ~ **(de)** to tinge (with). **-2.** fig [distinguir - rasgos, aspectos] to distinguish; [- tema] to explain in detail. **-3.** fig [dar tono especial] to tinge, to colour. **-4.** ARTE to blend.

matojo m [mata] tuft; [arbusto] bush, shrub.

matón, -ona m y f fam bully.

matorral m thicket.

Matra (abrev de **Mando Aéreo de Transporte**) m Spanish air transport command.

matraca f [instrumento] rattle; **dar la** ~ fam fig to go on, to be a nuisance; **ser una** ~ fam to be a pain.

matraz m flask.

matriarcado m matriarchy.

matrícula f **-1.** [inscripción] registration. **-2.**

[documento] registration document. **-3.** AUTOM number plate.

◆ **matrícula de honor** f top marks (pl).

matriculación f [inscripción] registration.

matricular vt to register.

◆ **matricularse** vpr to register.

matrimonial adj marital; [vida] married.

matrimonio m **-1.** [gen] marriage; **consumar el** ~ to consummate one's marriage; **contraer** ~ to get married; ~ **civil** civil marriage. **-2.** [pareja] married couple.

matriz ◇ f **-1.** ANAT womb. **-2.** [de talonario (cheque] stub. **-3.** [molde] mould. **-4.** MAT matrix. ◇ adj [empresa] parent (antes de sust); [casa] head (antes de sust); [iglesia] mother (antes de sust).

matrona f **-1.** [madre] matron. **-2.** [comadrona] midwife. **-3.** [en aduanas] female customs officer responsible for frisking women travellers. **-4.** [en cárceles] female prison warden.

matusalén m very old person; **ser más viejo que** ~ fig to be as old as Methuselah.

matutino, -na adj morning (antes de sust).

maullar vi to miaow.

maullido m miaow, miaowing (U).

Mauricio Mauritius.

máuser® (pl **máuseres** ○ **máusers**) m Mauser®.

mausoleo m mausoleum.

maxilar ◇ adj maxillary, jaw (antes de sust). ◇ m jaw.

máxima → máximo.

maximalismo m maximalism.

maximalista ◇ adj, m y f maximalist.

máxime adv especially.

máximo, -ma ◇ superl → **grande**. ◇ adj maximum; [galardón, puntuación] highest.

◆ **máximo** m maximum; **al** ~ to the utmost; **llegar al** ~ to reach the limit; **como** ~ [a más tardar] at the latest; [como mucho] at the most.

◆ **máxima** f **-1.** [sentencia, principio] maxim. **-2.** [temperatura] high, highest temperature.

maxisingle [maxi'singel] (pl **maxisingles**) m twelve inch (single).

maya ◇ adj Mayan. ◇ m y f Maya, Mayan. ◇ m [lengua] Maya.

mayestático, -ca adj majestic.

mayo m May; ver también **septiembre**.

mayonesa, mahonesa f mayonnaise.

mayor ◇ adj **-1.** (comparativo): ~ **(que)** [tamaño] bigger (than); [de importancia etc] greater (than); [de edad] older (than); [de número] higher (than). **-2.** (superlativo): **el/la** ~

... [de tamaño] the biggest ...; [de importancia etc] the greatest ...; [de edad] the oldest ...; [de número] the highest .... **-3.** [adulto] grown-up; **ser ~ de edad** to be an adult. **-4.** [anciano] elderly. **-5.** MÚS: **en do ~ in C** major. **-6.** *loc*: **al por ~** COM wholesale. ◇ *m y f*: **el/la ~** [hijo, hermano] the eldest. ◇ *m* MIL major.

◆ **mayores** *mpl* **-1.** [adultos] grown-ups. **-2.** [antepasados] ancestors, forefathers.

mayoral *m* **-1.** [pastor] chief herdsman. **-2.** [capataz] foreman, overseer.

mayorazgo *m* **-1.** [institución] primogeniture. **-2.** [bienes] entailed estate. **-3.** [persona] *heir to an entailed estate*; [primogénito] eldest son.

mayordomo *m* butler.

mayoreo *m Amer* wholesale.

mayoría *f*: **la ~ de** most of; **la ~ de los españoles** most Spaniards; **en su ~** in the main; **~ absoluta/relativa** absolute/relative majority; **~ silenciosa** silent majority.

◆ **mayoría de edad** *f*: **llegar a la ~ de edad** to come of age.

mayorista ◇ *adj* wholesale. ◇ *m y f* wholesaler.

mayoritario, -ria *adj* majority (*antes de sust*).

mayúscula → **letra**.

mayúsculo, -la *adj* tremendous, enormous.

maza *f* mace; [del bombo] drumstick.

mazacote *m* dry, sticky food.

mazapán *m* marzipan.

mazazo *m* lit & fig heavy blow.

mazmorra *f* dungeon.

mazo *m* **-1.** [martillo] mallet. **-2.** [de mortero] pestle. **-3.** [conjunto - de cartas, papeles] bundle; [- de billetes] wad; [- de naipes] balance (of the deck).

mazorca *f* cob.

mazurca *f* mazurka.

MC (*abrev de* **Movimiento Comunista**) *m Spanish communist party*.

MCE *m* **-1.** (*abrev de* **Mercado Común Europeo**) ECM. **-2.** (*abrev de* **Movimiento Comunista de España**) *Spanish communist party*.

me *pron pers* **-1.** (*complemento directo*) me; **le gustaría verme** she'd like to see me. **-2.** (*complemento indirecto*) (to) me; **~ lo dio** he gave it to me; **~ tiene miedo** he's afraid of me. **-3.** (*reflexivo*) myself.

meada *f vulg* piss; [mancha] urine stain.

meandro *m* meander.

mear *vi vulg* to piss.

◆ **mearse** *vpr vulg* to piss o.s.; **~se en la cama** to wet one's bed; **~se (de risa)** to piss o.s. laughing.

MEC (*abrev de* **Ministerio de Educación y Ciencia**) *m Spanish ministry of education and science*.

meca *f* mecca.

mecachis *interj fam eufemismo*: **¡~!** sugar! *Br*, shoot! *Am*.

mecánica → **mecánico**.

mecanicismo *m* mechanism.

mecánico, -ca ◇ *adj* mechanical. ◇ *m y f* [persona] mechanic; **~ dentista** dental technician.

◆ **mecánica** *f* **-1.** [ciencia] mechanics (*U*). **-2.** [funcionamiento] mechanics (*pl*).

mecanismo *m* **-1.** [estructura] mechanism. **-2.** [funcionamiento] way of working, modus operandi.

mecanización *f* mechanization.

mecanizado, -da *adj* mechanized.

mecanizar [13] *vt* to mechanize.

mecano® *m* Meccano®.

mecanografía *f* typing; **~ al tacto** touch typing.

mecanografiar [9] *vt* to type.

mecanógrafo, -fa *m y f* typist.

mecapal *m Amer* porter's leather harness.

mecedora *f* rocking chair.

mecenas *m y f inv* patron.

mecenazgo *m* patronage.

mecer [11] *vt* to rock.

◆ **mecerse** *vpr* to rock back and forth; [en columpio] to swing.

mecha *f* **-1.** [de vela] wick. **-2.** [de explosivos] fuse; **a toda ~** *fam* flat out; **aguantar ~** *fam* to grin and bear it. **-3.** [de pelo] streak.

mechero *m* (cigarette) lighter.

mechón *m* [de pelo] lock; [de lana] tuft.

medalla *f* medal; **ponerse ~s** *fig* to show off.

medallero *m* medals table.

medallista *m y f* **-1.** [oficio] maker of medals. **-2.** DEP medallist.

medallón *m* **-1.** [joya] medallion. **-2.** [rodaja] médaillon; **~ de pescado** [empanado] fishcake.

médano *m* (sand) dune.

media → **medio**.

mediación *f* mediation; **por ~ de** through.

mediado, -da *adj* [medio lleno] half-full; **mediada la película** halfway through the film.

◆ **a mediados de** *loc prep* in the middle of, halfway through.

mediador, -ra ◇ *adj* mediating. ◇ *m y f* mediator.

mediagua *f Amer* shack, hut.

mediana → mediano.

medianía *f* average ○ mediocre person.

mediano, -na *adj* **-1.** [intermedio - de tamaño] medium; [- de calidad] average. **-2.** [mediocre] average, ordinary.

◆ **mediana** *f* **-1.** GEOM median. **-2.** [de carretera] central reservation.

medianoche (*pl* **mediasnoches**) *f* **-1.** [hora] midnight; **a ~** at midnight. **-2.** [bollo] *sandwich made with a small bun.*

mediante *prep* by means of.

mediar [8] *vi* **-1.** [llegar a la mitad] to be halfway through; **mediaba julio** it was mid-July. **-2.** [estar en medio - tiempo, distancia, espacio] **~ entre** to be between; **media un jardín/un kilómetro entre las dos casas** there is a garden/one kilometre between the two houses; **medió una semana a** week passed by. **-3.** [intervenir]: **~ (en/entre)** to mediate (in/between). **-4.** [interceder]: **~ (en favor de** ○ **por)** to intercede (on behalf of ○ for). **-5.** [ocurrir] to intervene, to happen; **media la circunstancia de que ...** it so happens that ....

mediatizar [13] *vt* to determine.

medicación *f* medication.

medicamento *m* medicine.

medicar [10] *vt* to give medicine to.

◆ **medicarse** *vpr* to take medicine.

medicina *f* medicine; **~ alternativa** alternative medicine; **~ interna** general medicine ○ practice; **~ preventiva/social** preventive/community medicine.

medicinal *adj* medicinal.

medición *f* measurement.

médico, -ca ◇ *adj* medical. ◇ *m y f* doctor; **ir al ~** to go to the doctor; **~ de cabecera** ○ **familia** family doctor, general practitioner; **~ forense** specialist in forensic medicine; **~ interno** houseman *Br*, intern *Am*.

medida *f* **-1.** [gen] measure; [medición] measurement; **a (la) ~** [gen] custom-built; [ropa] made-to-measure; **~ de capacidad** measure (*liquid or dry*). **-2.** [disposición] measure, step; **tomar ~s** to take measures ○ steps; **~s represivas** clampdown (*sg*). **-3.** [moderación] moderation; **sin ~** without moderation. **-4.** [grado] extent, degree; **en cierta/gran ~** to some/a large extent; **en la ~ de lo posible** as far as possible; **a ~ que** entraban as they were coming in.

◆ **medidas** *fpl* [del cuerpo] measurements; **tomar las ~s a alguien** to take sb's measurements.

medieval *adj* medieval.

medievalismo *m* medievalism.

medievalista *m y f* medievalist.

medievo, medioevo *m* Middle Ages (*pl*).

medina *f* medina.

medio, -dia *adj* **-1.** [gen] half; **a ~ camino** [en viaje] halfway there; [en trabajo etc] halfway through; **media docena/hora** half a dozen/an hour; **~ pueblo estaba allí** half the town was there; **a media luz** in the half-light; **hacer algo a medias** to half-do sthg; **pagar a medias** to go halves, to share the cost; **un kilo y ~** one and a half kilos; **son (las dos) y media** it's half past (two). **-2.** [intermedio - estatura, tamaño] medium; [- posición, punto] middle. **-3.** [de promedio - temperatura, velocidad] average. **-4.** [corriente] ordinary, average.

◆ **medio** ◇ *adv* half; **~ borracho** half drunk; **a ~ hacer** half done. ◇ *m* **-1.** [mitad] half. **-2.** [centro] middle, centre; **en ~ (de)** in the middle (of); **estar por (en) ~** to be in the way; **equivocarse de ~ a ~** to be completely wrong; **meterse** ○ **ponerse de por ~** to get in the way; *fig* to interfere; **quitar de en ~ a alguien** to get rid of sb, to get sb out of the way. **-3.** [sistema, manera] means, method; **por ~ de** by means of, through. **-4.** [elemento físico] environment; **~ ambiente** environment. **-5.** [ambiente social] circle; **en ~s bien informados** in well-informed circles. **-6.** DEP midfielder.

◆ **medios** *mpl* [recursos] means, resources; **los ~s de comunicación** ○ **información** the media; **~s de producción/transporte** means of production/transport.

◆ **media** *f* **-1.** [promedio] average; **media aritmética/proporcional** arithmetic/proportional mean; **media horaria** hourly average. **-2.** [hora]: **al dar la ~** on the half-hour. **-3.** (*gen pl*) [prenda] tights (*pl*), stockings (*pl*). **-4.** DEP midfielders (*pl*).

medioambiental *adj* environmental.

mediocampista *m y f* midfielder.

mediocre *adj* mediocre, average.

mediocridad *f* mediocrity.

mediodía (*pl* **mediodías**) *m* **-1.** [hora] midday, noon; **al ~** at noon ○ midday. **-2.** [sur] south.

medioevo = medievo.

mediofondista *m y f* middle-distance runner.

mediofondo *m* middle-distance running.

mediopensionista *m y f child who has lunch at school.*

medique *etc* → medicar.

medir [26] *vt* **-1.** [gen] to measure; **¿cuánto mides?** how tall are you?; **mido 1,80** ≃ I'm

6 foot (tall); **mide diez metros** it's ten metres long. **-2.** [pros, contras etc] to weigh up. **-3.** [palabras] weigh carefully. **-4.** [fuerzas] to test out against each other.

◆ **medirse** *vpr* **-1.** [tomarse medidas] to measure o.s. **-2.** [moderarse] to show restraint. **-3.** [enfrentarse]: ~**se con** to meet, to compete against.

meditabundo, -da *adj* thoughtful, pensive.

meditación *f* meditation.

meditar ◇ *vi*: ~ **(sobre)** to meditate (on). ◇ *vt* **-1.** [gen] to meditate, to ponder. **-2.** [planear] to plan, to think through.

meditativo, -va *adj* pensive.

mediterráneo, -a *adj* Mediterranean.

◆ **Mediterráneo** *m*: **el (mar) Mediterráneo** the Mediterranean (Sea).

médium *m y f inv* medium.

medrar *vi* **-1.** [prosperar] to prosper. **-2.** [enriquecerse] to get rich. **-3.** [crecer] to grow.

medroso, -sa ◇ *adj* [miedoso] fearful. ◇ *m y f* fearful person.

médula *f* **-1.** ANAT (bone) marrow; ~ **espinal** spinal cord. **-2.** [esencia] core.

medusa *f* jellyfish.

mefistotélico, -ca *adj* diabolical.

megabyte [meɣa'ßait] (*pl* **megabytes**) *m* INFORM megabyte.

megafonía *f* public-address system.

megáfono *m* megaphone.

megalito *m* megalith.

megalomanía *f* megalomania.

megalómano, -na *adj, m y f* megalomaniac.

megatón *m* megaton.

mejicanismo = **mexicanismo**.

mejicano, -na = **mexicano**.

Méjico = **México**.

mejilla *f* cheek.

mejillón *m* mussel; **mejillones a la marinera** *mussels cooked in a tomato, onion and garlic sauce.*

mejor ◇ *adj* **-1.** (*comparativo*): ~ **(que)** better (than). **-2.** (*superlativo*): **el/la** ~ ... the best ....

◇ *m y f*: **el/la** ~ **(de)** the best (in); **el** ~ **de todos** the best of all; **lo** ~ **fue que** ... the best thing was that ....

◇ *adv* **-1.** (*comparativo*): ~ **(que)** better (than); **ahora veo** ~ I can see better now; **es** ~ **que no vengas** it would be better if you didn't come; **estar** ~ [no tan malo] to feel better; [recuperado] to be better; ~ **que** ~ so much the better. **-2.** (*superlativo*) best; **el que la conoce** ~ the one who knows her best.

◆ **a lo mejor** *loc adv* maybe, perhaps.

◆ **mejor dicho** *loc adv* (or) rather.

mejora *f* **-1.** [progreso] improvement. **-2.** [aumento] increase.

mejorable *adj* improvable.

mejorana *f* sweet marjoram.

mejorar ◇ *vt* **-1.** [gen] to improve; [enfermo] to make better. **-2.** [aumentar] to increase. ◇ *vi* to improve, to get better.

◆ **mejorarse** *vpr* to improve, to get better; **¡qué te mejores!** get well soon!

mejoría *f* improvement.

mejunje *m lit & fig* concoction.

melancolía *f* melancholy.

melancólico, -ca ◇ *adj* melancholic. ◇ *m y f* melancholic person.

melanina *f* melanin.

melaza *f* molasses (*pl*).

Melbourne [mel'burne] Melbourne.

melena *f* **-1.** [de persona] long hair (*U*). **-2.** [de león] mane.

◆ **melenas** *fpl despec* mop (*sg*) of hair.

melenudo, -da *despec* ◇ *adj* with a mop of hair. ◇ *m y f* person with a mop of hair.

melifluo, -flua *adj* honeyed, mellifluous.

Melilla Melilla.

melillense *adj* of/relating to Melilla.

melindre *m* CULIN *fried cake made from honey and sugar.*

◆ **melindres** *mpl* [escrúpulos] affected scrupulousness (*U*).

melindroso, -sa ◇ *adj* affectedly scrupulous. ◇ *m y f* affectedly scrupulous person.

melisa *f* lemon balm.

mella *f* [gen] nick; [en dentadura] gap; **hacer** ~ **en algo** [dañar] to dent sthg; **hacer** ~ **en alguien** to make an impression on sb.

mellado, -da *adj* **-1.** [con hendiduras] nicked. **-2.** [sin dientes] gap-toothed.

mellar *vt* **-1.** [hacer mellas] to nick, to chip. **-2.** [menoscabar] to damage.

mellizo, -za *adj, m y f* twin.

melocotón *m* peach.

melocotonero *m* peach tree.

melodía *f* melody, tune.

melódico, -ca *adj* melodic.

melodioso, -sa *adj* melodious.

melodrama *m* melodrama.

melodramático, -ca *adj* melodramatic.

melomanía *f* love of music.

melómano, -na *m y f* music lover.

melón *m* **-1.** [fruta] melon. **-2.** *fam fig* [persona] lemon, idiot.

melopea *f fam*: **agarrar una** ~ to get legless.

melosidad *f* sweetness; [empalago] sickliness.

meloso, -sa *adj* **-1.** [como la miel] honey; *fig* sweet. **-2.** [empalagoso] sickly.

membrana *f* membrane.

membranoso, -sa *adj* membranous.

membrete *m* letterhead.

membrillo *m* **-1.** [fruto] quince. **-2.** [dulce] quince jelly.

memez *f* stupidity; [acción, dicho] silly ○ stupid thing.

memo, -ma ◇ *adj* stupid. ◇ *m y f* idiot, fool.

memorable *adj* memorable.

memorándum (*pl* **memorándums** ○ **memorandos**) *m* **-1.** [cuaderno] notebook. **-2.** [nota diplomática] memorandum.

memoria *f* **-1.** [gen & INFORM] memory; **de ~** by heart; **hacer ~** to try to remember; **traer a la ~** to call to mind; **~ de acceso aleatorio/de sólo lectura** INFORM random-access/read only memory; **~ expandida/extendida/programable** INFORM expanded/extended/programmable memory; **~ RAM/ROM** INFORM RAM/ROM; **ser flaco de ~** to be forgetful. **-2.** [recuerdo] remembrance, remembering; **ser de feliz/ingrata ~** to be a happy/an unhappy memory. **-3.** [disertación] (academic) paper. **-4.** [informe]: **~ (anual)** (annual) report. **-5.** [lista] list, record.
◆ **memorias** *fpl* [biografía] memoirs.

memorial *m* petition, request.

memorístico, -ca *adj* memory (*antes de sust*).

memorización *f* memorizing.

memorizar [13] *vt* to memorize.

menaje *m* household goods and furnishings (*pl*); **~ de cocina** kitchenware.

mención *f* mention; **hacer ~ de** to mention.

mencionar *vt* to mention.

menda ◇ *pron fam* [el que habla] yours truly. ◇ *m y f* [uno cualquiera]: **vino un ~ y ...** this bloke came along and ....

mendicidad *f* begging.

mendigar [16] ◇ *vt* to beg for. ◇ *vi* to beg.

mendigo, -ga *m y f* beggar.

mendrugo *m* crust (of bread).

menear *vt* **-1.** [mover - gen] to move; [- la cabeza] to shake; [- la cola] to wag; [- las caderas] to wiggle. **-2.** *fig* [activar] to get moving.
◆ **menearse** *vpr* **-1.** [moverse] to move (about); [agitarse] to shake; [oscilar] to sway. **-2.** [darse prisa, espabilarse] to get a move on. **-3.** *loc*: **un susto de no te menees** *fam* a hell of a scare.

meneo *m* [gen] movement; [de cabeza] shake; [de cola] wag, wagging (*U*); [de caderas] wiggling (*U*); **dar un ~ a algo** *fam* to knock sthg; **dar un ~ a alguien** *fam* to give sb a hiding.

menester *m* necessity; **haber ~ de algo** to be in need of sthg; **ser ~ que alguien haga algo** to be necessary for sb to do sthg.
◆ **menesteres** *mpl* [asuntos] business (*U*), matters (*pl*).

menesteroso, -sa ◇ *adj* needy, poor. ◇ *m y f* needy ○ poor person.

menestra *f* vegetable stew.

mengano, -na *m y f* so-and-so.

mengua *f* [reducción] reduction; [falta] lack; [descrédito] discredit; **sin ~ de** without detriment to.

menguado, -da *adj* reduced, diminished.

menguante *adj* [luna] waning.

menguar [45] ◇ *vi* **-1.** [disminuir] to decrease, to diminish; [luna] to wane. **-2.** [en labor de punto] to decrease. ◇ *vt* **-1.** [disminuir] to lessen, to diminish. **-2.** [en labor de punto] to decrease.

menhir *m* menhir.

meninge *f* meninx.

meningitis *f inv* meningitis.

menisco *m* meniscus.

menopausia *f* menopause.

menor ◇ *adj* **-1.** (*comparativo*): **~ (que)** [de tamaño] smaller (than); [de edad] younger (than); [de importancia etc] less ○ lesser (than); [de número] lower (than). **-2.** (*superlativo*): **el/la ~ ...** [de tamaño] the smallest ...; [de edad] the youngest ...; [de importancia] the slightest ...; [de número] the lowest .... **-3.** [de poca importancia] minor; **un problema ~** a minor problem. **-4.** [joven]: **ser ~ de edad** [para votar, conducir] to be under age; DER to be a minor. **-5.** MÚS: **en do ~** in C minor. **-6.** *loc*: **al por ~** COM retail.
◇ *m y f* **-1.** (*superlativo*): **el/la ~** [hijo, hermano] the youngest. **-2.** DER [niño] minor.

Menorca Minorca.

menos ◇ *adj inv* **-1.** (*comparativo*) [cantidad] less; [número] fewer; **~ aire** less air; **~ manzanas** fewer apples; **~ ... que ...** less/fewer ... than ...; **tiene ~ experiencia que tú** she has less experience than you; **hace ~ calor que ayer** it's not as hot as it was yesterday. **-2.** (*superlativo*) [cantidad] the least; [número] the fewest; **el que compró ~ acciones** the one who bought the fewest shares; **lo que ~ tiempo llevó** the thing that took the least time. **-3.** *fam* [peor]: **éste**

es ~ **coche que el mío** that car isn't as good as mine.
◇ *adv* **-1.** (*comparativo*) less; ~ **de/que** less than; **estás ~ gordo** you're no as fat. **-2.** (*superlativo*): **el/la/lo ~** the least; **él es el ~ indicado para criticar** he's the last person who should be criticizing; **ella es la ~ adecuada para el cargo** she's the least suitable person for the job; **es lo ~ que puedo hacer** it's the least I can do. **-3.** [expresa resta] minus; **tres ~ dos igual a uno** three minus two is one. **-4.** [con las horas] to; **son (las dos) ~ diez** it's ten to (two). **-5.** *loc*: **es lo de ~** that's the least of it, that's of no importance; **hacer de ~ a alguien** to snub sb; **¡~ mal!** just as well!, thank God!; **no es para ~** not without (good) reason; **venir a ~** to go down in the world.
◇ *m inv* MAT minus (sign).
◇ *prep* [excepto] except (for); **todo ~ eso** anything but that.
◆ **al menos, por lo menos** *loc adv* at least.
◆ **a menos que** *loc conj* unless; **no iré a ~ que me acompañes** I won't go unless you come with me.
◆ **de menos** *loc adj* [que falta] missing; **hay 100 ptas de ~** there's 100 pesetas missing.

menoscabar *vt* [fama, honra etc] to damage; [derechos, intereses, salud] to harm; [belleza, perfección] to diminish.

menoscabo *m* [de fama, honra etc] damage; [de derechos, intereses, salud] harm; [de belleza, perfección] diminishing; **(ir) en ~ de** (to be) to the detriment of.

menospreciar [8] *vt* [despreciar] to scorn, to despise; [infravalorar] to undervalue.

menosprecio *m* scorn, contempt.

mensáfono *m* pager.

mensaje *m* [gen & INFORM] message.

mensajería *f* courier service.

mensajero, -ra ◇ *adj* message-carrying; *fig* announcing, presaging. ◇ *m y f* [gen] messenger; [de mensajería] courier.

menstruación *f* menstruation.

menstrual *adj* menstrual.

menstruar [6] *vi* to menstruate, to have a period.

menstruo *m* menstruation.

mensual *adj* monthly; **5.000 ptas ~es** 5,000 pesetas a month.

mensualidad *f* **-1.** [sueldo] monthly salary. **-2.** [pago] monthly payment ○ instalment.

mensualizar [13] *vt* to make on a monthly basis.

menta *f* mint.

mentado, -da *adj* **-1.** [mencionado] above-mentioned, aforementioned. **-2.** [famoso] famous.

mental *adj* mental.

mentalidad *f* mentality.

mentalización *f* mental preparation.

mentalizar [13] *vt* to put into a frame of mind.
◆ **mentalizarse** *vpr* to get into a frame of mind.

mentar [19] *vt* to mention.

mente *f* **-1.** [gen] mind; **tener en ~ algo** to have sthg in mind; **tener en ~ hacer algo** to intend to do sthg; **traer a la ~** to bring to mind. **-2.** [mentalidad] mentality.

mentecato, -ta *m y f* idiot.

mentir [27] *vi* to lie.

mentira *f* lie; [acción] lying; **aunque parezca ~** strange as it may seem; **de ~** pretend, false; **parece ~ (que ...)** it hardly seems possible (that ...), it's scarcely credible (that ...); **una ~ como una casa** a whopping great lie.

mentirijillas
◆ **de mentirijillas** *fam* ◇ *loc adv* [en broma] as a joke, in fun. ◇ *loc adj* [falso] pretend, make-believe.

mentiroso, -sa ◇ *adj* lying; [engañoso] deceptive. ◇ *m y f* liar.

mentís *m inv* denial; **dar un ~ (a)** to issue a denial (of).

mentol *m* menthol.

mentolado, -da *adj* mentholated.

mentón *m* chin.

mentor *m* mentor.

menú (*pl* **menús**) *m* **-1.** [lista] menu; [comida] food; **~ del día** set meal. **-2.** INFORM menu; **~ desplegable** pull-down menu.

menudear ◇ *vi* to happen frequently. ◇ *vt* to repeat, to do repeatedly.

menudencia *f* trifle, insignificant thing.

menudeo *m* Amer retailing.

menudillos *mpl* giblets.

menudo, -da *adj* **-1.** [pequeño] small. **-2.** [insignificante] trifling, insignificant. **-3.** (*antes de sust*) [para enfatizar] what!; **¡~ lío/gol!** what a mess/goal!
◆ **a menudo** *loc adv* often.

meñique → **dedo**.

meollo *m* core, heart.

meón, -ona *m y f fam* person who wets themselves.

mequetrefe *m y f fam* good-for-nothing.

mercachifle *m y f despec* **-1.** [comerciante] pedlar. **-2.** [usurero] money-grabber, shark.

mercader *m y f* trader.

mercadería f merchandise, goods (pl).

mercadillo m flea market.

mercado m market; ~ **alcista/bajista** bull/bear market; ~ **bursátil** stock market; ~ **común** Common Market; ~ **de abastos** COM wholesale food market; ~ **de capitales/divisas/valores** capital/currency/securities market; ~ **de futuros** futures market; ~ **de trabajo** labour ○ job market; ~ **interbancario** interbank market; ~ **libre/negro** free/black market.

mercadología f marketing.

mercadotecnia f marketing.

mercancía f merchandise (U), goods (pl).
◆ **mercancías** m inv FERROC goods train, freight train Am.

mercante adj merchant.

mercantil adj mercantile, commercial.

mercantilismo m ECON mercantilism; fig commercialism.

mercantilizar [13] vt to commercialize.

merced f favour; ~ **a** thanks to; **a la** ~ **de algo/alguien** at the mercy of sthg/sb.

mercenario, -ria ◇ adj, m y f mercenary.

mercería f -1. [género] haberdashery Br, notions Am. -2. [tienda] haberdasher's (shop) Br, notions store Am.

mercurio m mercury.

Mercurio m Mercury.

mercurocromo m mercurochrome.

merecedor, -ra adj: ~ **de** worthy of.

merecer [30] ◇ vt to deserve, to be worthy of; **la isla merece una visita** the island is worth a visit; **no merece la pena** it's not worth it. ◇ vi to be worthy.

merecido m: **recibir su** ~ to get one's just deserts.

merendar [19] ◇ vi to have tea (as a light afternoon meal). ◇ vt to have for tea.
◆ **merendarse** vpr fam fig: ~**se a alguien** to thrash sb.

merendero m open-air café or bar (in the country or on the beach).

merendola f fam slap-up tea.

merengue ◇ m -1. CULIN meringue. -2. [baile] merengue. ◇ adj fam DEP of/relating to Real Madrid Football Club.

meretriz f prostitute.

merezca etc → merecer.

Mérida Merida.

meridiano, -na adj -1. [hora etc] midday. -2. fig [claro] crystal-clear.
◆ **meridiano** m meridian.

meridional ◇ adj southern. ◇ m y f southerner.

merienda ◇ v → **merendar**. ◇ f tea (as a light afternoon meal); [en el campo] picnic; ~ **de negros** free-for-all.

mérito m -1. [cualidad] merit; **hacer** ~**s para** do to everything possible to. -2. [valor] value, worth; **tiene mucho** ~ it's no mean achievement; **de** ~ worthy, deserving.

meritorio, -ria ◇ adj worthy, deserving. ◇ m y f unpaid trainee ○ apprentice.

merluza f -1. [pez, pescado] hake. -2. fam [borrachera]: **agarrar una** ~ to get sozzled.

merma f decrease, reduction.

mermar ◇ vi to diminish, to lessen. ◇ vt to reduce, to diminish.

mermelada f jam; ~ **de naranja** marmalade.

mero, -ra adj (antes de sust) mere.
◆ **mero** m grouper.

merodeador, -ra m y f prowler, snooper.

merodear vi: ~ **(por)** to snoop ○ prowl (about).

mes m -1. [del· año] month. -2. [salario] monthly salary. -3. [menstruación] period.

mesa f -1. [gen] table; [de oficina, despacho] desk; **bendecir la** ~ to say grace; **poner/quitar la** ~ to set/clear the table; ~ **camilla** small round table under which a heater is placed; ~ **de mezclas** mixing desk; **(de) nido** nest of tables; ~ **de operaciones** operating table; ~ **plegable** folding table. -2. [comité] board, committee; [en un debate etc] panel; ~ **directiva** executive board ○ committee.
◆ **mesa electoral** f polling station.
◆ **mesa redonda** f [coloquio] round table.

mesana f -1. [mástil] mizenmast. -2. [vela] mizensail.

mescalina f mescalin.

mescolanza = mezcolanza.

mesero, -ra m y f Amer waiter m (f waitress).

meseta f plateau, tableland.

mesianismo m RELIG messianism; fig blind faith in one person.

mesías m fig Messiah.
◆ **Mesías** m: **el Mesías** the Messiah.

mesilla f small table; ~ **de noche** bedside table.

mesnada f armed retinue.

mesocracia f government by the middle classes.

mesón m -1. HIST inn. -2. [bar-restaurante] old, country-style restaurant and bar.

mesonero, -ra m y f innkeeper.

Mesopotamia Mesopotamia.

mester *m desus* trade, craft.

mestizaje *m* cross-breeding; *fig* mixing.

mestizo, -za ◇ *adj* [persona] half-caste; [animal, planta] cross-bred. ◇ *m y f* half-caste.

mesura *f* **-1.** [moderación] moderation, restraint; **con ~** [moderadamente] in moderation. **-2.** [cortesía] courtesy, politeness. **-3.** [gravedad] dignity, seriousness.

mesurado, -da *adj* moderate, restrained.

mesurarse *vpr* to restrain o.s.

meta *f* **-1.** [DEP - llegada] finishing line; [- portería] goal; **~ volante** [en ciclismo] hot spot sprint. **-2.** *fig* [objetivo] aim, goal; **fijarse una ~** to set o.s. a target ◇ goal.

metabólico, -ca *adj* metabolic.

metabolismo *m* metabolism.

metadona *f* methadone.

metafísico, -ca ◇ *adj* metaphysical. ◇ *m y f* [filósofo] metaphysicist.

◆ **metafísica** *f* [disciplina] metaphysics (*U*).

metáfora *f* metaphor.

metafórico, -ca *adj* metaphorical.

metal *m* **-1.** [material] metal; **~ blanco** white metal; **~es preciosos** precious metals. **-2.** MUS brass.

metalenguaje *m* INFORM & LING meta-language.

metálico, -ca ◇ *adj* [sonido, color] metallic; [objeto] metal. ◇ *m*: **pagar en ~** to pay (in) cash.

metalizado, -da *adj* [pintura] metallic.

metalurgia *f* metallurgy.

metalúrgico, -ca ◇ *adj* metallurgical. ◇ *m y f* metallurgist.

metamórfico, -ca *adj* metamorphic.

metamorfismo *m* metamorphism.

metamorfosis *f inv lit* & *fig* metamorphosis.

metano *m* methane.

metanol *m* methanol.

metástasis *f inv* MED metastasis.

metedura

◆ **metedura de pata** *f* clanger.

meteórico, -ca *adj lit* & *fig* meteoric.

meteorito *m* meteorite.

meteoro *m* meteor.

meteorología *f* meteorology.

meteorológico, -ca *adj* meteorological.

meteorólogo, -ga *m y f* meteorologist; RADIO & TV weatherman (*f* weatherwoman).

meter *vt* **-1.** [gen] to put in; **~ algo/a alguien en algo** to put sthg/sb in sthg; **~ la llave en la cerradura** to get the key into the lock; **le metieron en la cárcel** they put him in prison; **~ dinero en el banco** to put money in the bank; **he metido mis ahorros en esa empresa** I've put all my savings into this venture. **-2.** [hacer participar]: **~ a alguien en algo** to get sb into sthg. **-3.** [obligar a]: **~ a alguien a hacer algo** to make sb start doing sthg. **-4.** [causar]: **~ prisa/miedo a alguien** to rush/scare sb; **~ ruido** to make a noise. **-5.** *fam* [asestar] to give; **le metió un puñetazo** he gave him a punch. **-6.** *fam* [echar] to give; **~ una bronca a alguien** to tell sb off. **-7.** [estrechar - prenda] to take in; **~ el bajo de una falda** to take up a skirt. **-8.** *loc*: **a todo ~** as quickly as possible.

◆ **meterse** *vpr* **-1.** [entrar] to get in; **~se en** to get into. **-2.** (*en frase interrogativa*) [estar] to get to; **¿dónde se ha metido ese chico?** where has that boy got to? **-3.** [dedicarse]: **~se a** to become; **~se a torero** to become a bullfighter. **-4.** [involucrarse]: **~se (en)** to get involved (in). **-5.** [entrometerse] to meddle, to interfere; **se mete en todo** he never minds his own business; **~se por medio** to interfere. **-6.** [empezar]: **~se a hacer algo** to get started on doing sthg.

◆ **meterse con** *vpr* **-1.** [incordiar] to hassle. **-2.** [atacar] to go for.

meterete, metete *adj Amer fam* meddling, meddlesome.

meticulosidad *f* meticulousness.

meticuloso, -sa *adj* meticulous.

metido, -da *adj* **-1.** [envuelto]: **andar** ◇ **estar ~ en** to be involved in. **-2.** [abundante]: **~ en años** elderly; **~ en carnes** plump.

metódico, -ca *adj* methodical.

metodismo *m* Methodism.

metodista *adj, m y f* Methodist.

método *m* **-1.** [sistema] method. **-2.** EDUC course.

metodología *f* methodology.

metodológico, -ca *adj* methodological.

metomentodo *fam* ◇ *adj inv* meddlesome. ◇ *m y f* busybody.

metonimia *f* metonymy.

metraje *m* length, running time.

metralla *f* shrapnel.

metralleta *f* submachine gun.

métrico, -ca *adj* **-1.** [del metro] metric. **-2.** LITER metrical.

◆ **métrica** *f* LITER metrics (*U*).

metro *m* **-1.** [gen] metre; **~ cuadrado/cúbico** square/cubic metre; **~s por segundo** metres *per* second. **-2.** [transporte] underground *Br*, tube *Br*, subway *Am*. **-3.** [cinta métrica] tape measure.

metrópoli *f*, **metrópolis** *f inv* **-1.** [ciudad] metropolis. **-2.** [nación] home country.

metropolitano, **-na** *adj* metropolitan.
◆ **metropolitano** *m desus* tube, underground *Br*, subway *Am*.

mexicanismo, **mejicanismo** *m* Mexicanism.

mexicano, **-na**, **mejicano**, **-na** *adj, m y f* Mexican.

México, **Méjico** Mexico.

meza *etc* → **mecer**.

mezcla *f* **-1.** [gen] mixture; [tejido] blend; [de una grabación] mix. **-2.** [acción] mixing.

mezclador, **-ra** *m y f* [persona] sound mixer.
◆ **mezclador** *m* [aparato] mixer; ~ de imagen/sonido vision/sound mixer.

mezclar *vt* **-1.** [gen] to mix; [combinar, armonizar] to blend. **-2.** [confundir, desordenar] to mix up. **-3.** *fig* [implicar]: ~ a alguien en to get sb mixed up in.
◆ **mezclarse** *vpr* **-1.** [gen]: ~se (con) to mix (with). **-2.** [esfumarse]: ~se entre to disappear ○ blend into. **-3.** *fig* [implicarse]: ~se en to get mixed up in.

mezcolanza, **mescolanza** *f fam* hotchpotch, mishmash.

mezquindad *f* **-1.** [cualidad] meanness. **-2.** [acción] mean action.

mezquino, **-na** *adj* mean.

mezquita *f* mosque.

mg (*abrev de* **miligramo**) mg.

mi[1] *m* MÚS E; [en solfeo] mi.

mi[2] (*pl* **mis**) *adj poses* my; ~ casa my house; ~s libros my books.

mí *pron pers* (*después de prep*) **-1.** [gen] me; este trabajo no es para ~ this job isn't for me; no se fía de ~ he doesn't trust me. **-2.** (*reflexivo*) myself. **-3.** *loc*: ¡a ~ qué! so what?, why should I care?; para ~ [yo creo] as far as I'm concerned, in my opinion; por ~ as far as I'm concerned; por ~, no hay inconveniente it's fine by me.

mía → **mío**.

miaja *f* crumb; *fig* tiny bit.

mialgia *f* MED myalgia.

miasma *m* (*gen pl*) miasma.

miau *m* miaow.

mica *f* mica.

micción *f* [MED - acción] urination; [- orina] urine.

micénico, **-ca** *adj* Mycenaean.

michelines *mpl fam* spare tyre (*sg*).

Michigan *m*: el lago ~ Lake Michigan.

mico *m* **-1.** [animal] (long-tailed) monkey. **-2.** *fam* [persona] ugly devil; ser el último ~ *fig* to be the lowest of the low.

micología *f* mycology.

micosis *f inv* mycosis.

micra *f* micron.

micrero, **-ra** *m y f Amer* minibus driver.

micro ◇ *m fam* (*abrev de* **micrófono**) mike. ◇ *m o f Amer* [microbús] minibus.

microbio *m* germ, microbe.

microbiología *f* microbiology.

microbús *m* minibus.

microcirugía *f* microsurgery.

microclima *m* microclimate.

microeconomía *f* microeconomics (*U*).

microelectrónica *f* microelectronics (*U*).

microficha *f* microfiche.

microfilm (*pl* **microfilms**), **microfilme** *m* microfilm.

micrófono *m* microphone.

microfotografía *f* microphotography.

microinformática *f* INFORM microcomputing.

microonda *f* microwave.

microondas *m inv* microwave (oven).

microordenador *m* INFORM microcomputer.

microorganismo *m* microorganism.

microprocesador *m* INFORM microprocessor.

microscópico, **-ca** *adj* microscopic.

microscopio *m* microscope; ~ electrónico electron microscope.

microsurco *m* microgroove.

mida *etc* → **medir**.

midiera *etc* → **medir**.

MIE (*abrev de* **Ministerio de Industria y Energía**) *m Spanish ministry of industry and energy*.

miedo *m* fear; dar ~ to be frightening; me da ~ conducir I'm afraid ○ frightened of driving; meter ~ a to frighten; temblar de ~ to tremble with fear; tener ~ a ○ de (hacer algo) to be afraid of (doing sthg); ~ cerval terrible fear, terror; de ~ *fam fig* [estupendo] smashing; estar cagado de ~ *vulg* to be shit-scared; morirse de ~ to die of fright, to be terrified.

miedoso, **-sa** ◇ *adj* fearful. ◇ *m y f* fearful person.

miel *f* honey; ~ sobre hojuelas all the better.

miembro *m* **-1.** [gen] member. **-2.** [extremidad] limb, member; ~s superiores/inferiores upper/lower limbs; ~ (viril) penis.

mienta *etc* **-1.** → **mentar**. **-2.** → **mentir**.

mientes *fpl* mind (*sg*); parar ~ (en algo) to consider (sthg); traer a las ~ to bring to mind.

mientras ◇ *conj* **-1.** [al tiempo que] while; leía ~ comía she was reading while eating; ~ más ando más sudo the more I walk, the more I sweat. **-2.** [hasta que]: ~ **no se pruebe lo contrario** until proved otherwise. **-3.** [por el contrario]: ~ **(que)** whereas, whilst. ◇ *adv:* ~ **(tanto)** meanwhile, in the meantime.

miércoles *m* Wednesday; ~ **de ceniza** Ash Wednesday; *ver también* **sábado**.

mierda *vulg* ◇ *f* **-1.** [excremento] shit. **-2.** [suciedad] filth, shit. **-3.** [cosa sin valor]: **es una** ~ it's (a load of) crap; **de** ~ shitty, crappy. **-4.** *loc:* **irse a la** ~ [proyecto etc] to go down the tubes; **mandar a alguien a la** ~ to tell sb to piss off; **¡vete a la** ~**!** go to hell!, piss off! ◇ *m y f vulg* shithead.

mies *f* [cereal] ripe corn.
◆ **mieses** *fpl* [campo] cornfields.

miga *f* [de pan] crumb; **tener** ~ *fam* [ser sustancioso] to have a lot to it; [ser complicado] to have more to it than meets the eye.
◆ **migas** *fpl* CULIN fried breadcrumbs; **hacer buenas/malas** ~**s** *fam* to get on well/badly; **hacerse** ~**s** *fam* [cosa] to be smashed to bits; **hacer** ~**s a alguien** *fam* [desmoralizar] to shatter sb.

migaja *f* **-1.** [trozo] bit; [de pan] crumb. **-2.** *fig* [pizca] scrap.
◆ **migajas** *fpl* [restos] leftovers.

migración *f* migration.

migraña *f* migraine.

migrar *vi* to migrate.

migratorio, -ria *adj* migratory.

mijo *m* millet.

mil *núm* thousand; **dos** ~ two thousand; ~ **pesetas** a thousand pesetas; ~ **y una/uno** *fig* a thousand and one; *ver también* **seis**.
◆ **miles** *mpl* [gran cantidad]: ~**es (de)** thousands (of).

milagrero, -ra *despec* ◇ *adj* who believes in miracles. ◇ *m y f* person who believes in miracles.

milagro *m* miracle; **de** ~ miraculously, by a miracle; **hacer** ~**s** *fig* to work wonders.

milagroso, -sa *adj* miraculous; *fig* amazing.

milamores *f inv* valerian.

milano *m* kite.

milenario, -ria *adj* ancient.
◆ **milenario** *m* millennium.

milenio *m* millennium.

milésimo, -ma *núm* thousandth; **la milésima parte** a thousandth.

milhojas *m inv* CULIN mille feuille.

mili *f fam* military service; **hacer la** ~ to do one's military service.

milicia *f* **-1.** [profesión] military (profession). **-2.** [grupo armado] militia; ~**s universitarias** *formerly in Spain, military service for students.*

miliciano, -na ◇ *adj* militia (*antes de sust*). ◇ *m y f* militiaman (*f* female soldier).

miligramo *m* milligram.

mililitro *m* millilitre.

milimetrado *adj* → **papel**.

milimétrico, -ca *adj* millimetric.

milímetro *m* millimetre.

militancia *f* militancy.

militante *adj, m y f* militant.

militar ◇ *adj* military. ◇ *m y f* soldier; **los** ~**es** the military. ◇ *vi:* ~ **(en)** to be active (in).

militarismo *m* militarism.

militarista *adj, m y f* militarist.

militarización *f* militarization.

militarizar [13] *vt* to militarize.

milla *f* mile; ~ **(marina)** nautical mile.

millar *m* thousand; **un** ~ **de personas** a thousand people.

millón *núm* million; **dos millones** two million; **un** ~ **de personas** a million people; **un** ~ **de cosas que hacer** a million things to do; **un** ~ **de gracias** thanks a million.
◆ **millones** *mpl* [dineral] millions, a fortune (*sg*).

millonada *f fam* fortune, millions (*pl*).

millonario, -ria ◇ *adj:* **es** ~ he's a millionaire. ◇ *m y f* millionaire (*f* millionairess).

millonésimo, -ma *núm* millionth; **la millonésima parte** a millionth.

mimado, -da *adj* spoilt.

mimar *vt* to spoil, to pamper.

mimbre *m* wicker; **de** ~ wickerwork.

mimético, -ca *adj* **-1.** [animal, planta] mimetic. **-2.** [persona]: **ser** ~ to be a copycat.

mimetismo *m* **-1.** [de animal, planta] mimetism. **-2.** [de persona] mimicry.

mimetizar [13] *vt* to copy, to imitate.

mímico, -ca *adj* mime (*antes de sust*).
◆ **mímica** *f* **-1.** [mimo] mime. **-2.** [lenguaje] sign language.

mimo *m* **-1.** [zalamería] mollycoddling. **-2.** [cariño] show of affection. **-3.** TEATR mime; **hacer** ~ to perform mime.

mimosa *f* BOT mimosa.

mimoso, -sa *adj* affectionate.

min (*abrev de* **minuto**) min.

mina *f* **-1.** GEOL & MIL mine; ~ **de carbón** coalmine. **-2.** *fig* [chollo] goldmine. **-3.** [de lápiz] lead.

minar *vt* **-1.** MIL to mine. **-2.** *fig* [aminorar] to undermine.

mineral ◇ *adj* mineral. ◇ *m* **-1.** GEOL mineral. **-2.** MIN ore.

mineralizar [13] *vt* to mineralize.

◆ **mineralizarse** *vpr* to become mineralized.

mineralogía *f* minerology.

minería *f* **-1.** [técnica] mining. **-2.** [sector] mining industry.

minero, -ra ◇ *adj* mining (*antes de sust*); [producción, riqueza] mineral. ◇ *m y f* miner.

minestrone *f* minestrone.

miniatura *f* miniature; **el piso es una** ~ the flat is tiny; **en** ~ in miniature.

miniaturista *m y f* miniaturist.

miniaturizar [13] *vt* to miniaturize.

minicadena *f* midi system.

mini disk, mini disc *m inv* mini disc.

minifalda *f* mini skirt.

minifundio *m* small holding.

minigolf (*pl* **minigolfs**) *m* **-1.** [lugar] crazy golf course. **-2.** [juego] crazy golf.

mínima → **mínimo**.

minimalismo *m* MÚS minimalism.

minimalista *adj* MÚS minimalist.

minimizar [13] *vt* to play down.

mínimo, -ma ◇ *superl* → **pequeño**. ◇ *adj* **-1.** [lo más bajo posible o necesario] minimum. **-2.** [lo más bajo temporalmente] lowest. **-3.** [muy pequeño - efecto, importancia etc] minimal, very small; [- protesta, ruido etc] slightest; **no tengo la más mínima idea** I haven't the slightest idea; **como** ~ at the very least; **en lo más** ~ in the slightest.

◆ **mínimo** *m* [límite] minimum; ~ **común múltiplo** lowest common multiple.

◆ **mínima** *f* METEOR low, lowest temperature.

minino, -na *m y f fam* pussy (cat).

ministerial *adj* ministerial.

ministerio *m* **-1.** POLÍT ministry *Br*, department *Am*. **-2.** RELIG ministry.

◆ **ministerio público, ministerio fiscal** *m* ≃ Department of Public Prosecution.

◆ **Ministerio de Asuntos Exteriores** *m* ≃ Foreign Office *Br*, ≃ State Department *Am*.

◆ **Ministerio de Economía y Hacienda** *m* ≃ Treasury *Br*, ≃ Treasury Department *Am*.

◆ **Ministerio del Interior** *m* ≃ Home Office *Br*, ≃ Department of the Interior *Am*.

ministro, -tra *m y f* **-1.** POLÍT minister *Br*, secretary *Am*; ~ **sin cartera** minister without portfolio; **primer** ~ prime minister. **-2.** RELIG minister; ~ **de Dios** minister of God.

minoría *f* minority; ~**s étnicas** ethnic minorities.

minorista ◇ *adj* retail. ◇ *m y f* retailer.

minoritario, -ria *adj* minority (*antes de sust*).

mintiera *etc* → **mentir**.

minucia *f* trifle, insignificant thing.

minuciosidad *f* meticulousness, attention to detail.

minucioso, -sa *adj* **-1.** [meticuloso] meticulous. **-2.** [detallado] highly detailed.

minué *m* minuet.

minuendo *m* minuend.

minúsculo, -la *adj* **-1.** [tamaño] tiny, minute. **-2.** [letra] small; IMPRENTA lower-case.

◆ **minúscula** *f* small letter; IMPRENTA lower-case letter.

minusvalía *f* **-1.** ECON depreciation. **-2.** [física] handicap, disability.

minusválido, -da ◇ *adj* disabled, handicapped. ◇ *m y f* disabled ○ handicapped person.

minusvalorar *vt* to underestimate.

minuta *f* **-1.** [factura] fee. **-2.** [menú] menu.

minutero *m* minute hand.

minuto *m* minute; **al** ~ a moment later.

Miño *m*: **el (río)** ~ the River Miño.

mío, mía ◇ *adj poses* mine; **este libro es** ~ this book is mine; **un amigo** ~ a friend of mine; **no es asunto** ~ it's none of my business. ◇ *pron poses*: **el** ~ mine; **el** ~ **es rojo** mine is red; **esta es la mía** *fam* this is the chance I've been waiting for; **lo** ~ **es el teatro** [lo que me va] theatre is what I should be doing; **los** ~**s** *fam* [mi familia] my folks; [mi bando] my lot, my side.

miocardio *m* myocardium.

miope ◇ *adj* shortsighted, myopic. ◇ *m y f* shortsighted ○ myopic person.

miopía *f* shortsightedness, myopia.

MIR (*abrev de* **médico interno y residente**) *m* ≃ houseman *Br*, ≃ intern *Am*.

mira ◇ *f* sight; *fig* intention; **con** ~**s a** with a view to, with the intention of. ◇ *interj*: ¡~! look!

mirado, -da *adj* [prudente] careful; **bien** ~ [bien pensado] if you look at it closely.

◆ **mirada** *f* [gen] look; [rápida] glance; [de cariño, placer, admiración] gaze; **mirada fija** stare; **apartar la mirada** to look away; **dirigir** ○ **lanzar la mirada** to look at; **echar una mirada (a algo)** to glance ○ to have a quick look (at sthg); **fulminar con la mirada a alguien** to look daggers at sb; **levantar la mirada** to look up.

mirador *m* **-1.** [balcón] enclosed balcony. **-2.** [para ver un paisaje] viewpoint.

miramiento *m* consideration, circumspection; **andarse con ~s** to stand on ceremony; **sin ~s** just like that, without the least consideration.

mirar ◇ *vt* **-1.** [gen] to look at; [observar] to watch; [fijamente] to stare at; **~ algo de cerca/lejos** to look at sthg closely/from a distance; **~ algo por encima** to glance over sthg, to have a quick look at sthg; **~ a alguien bien/mal** to think highly/poorly of sb; **~ a alguien de arriba abajo** to look sb up and down; **de mírame y no me toques** very fragile. **-2.** [fijarse en] to keep an eye on, to watch. **-3.** [examinar, averiguar] to check, to look through; **le miraron todas las maletas** they searched all her luggage; **mira si ha llegado la carta** go and see if the letter has arrived. **-4.** [considerar] to consider, to take a look at.
◇ *vi* **-1.** [gen] to look; [observar] to watch; [fijamente] to stare; **mira, yo creo que ...** look, I think that .... **-2.** [buscar] to check, to look; **he mirado en todas partes** I've looked everywhere. **-3.** [orientarse]: **~ a** to face. **-4.** [cuidar]: **~ por alguien/algo** to look after sb/sthg.
◆ **mirarse** *vpr* [uno mismo] to look at o.s.; **si bien se mira** *fig* if you really think about it.

miríada *f* myriad.

mirilla *f* spyhole.

mirlo *m* blackbird; **ser un ~ blanco** *fig* to be one in a million.

mirón, -ona *fam* ◇ *adj* nosey; [con lascivia] peeping. ◇ *m y f* **-1.** [espectador] onlooker. **-2.** [curioso] noseyparker. **-3.** [voyeur] peeping Tom.

mirra *f* myrrh.

mirto *m* myrtle.

misa *f* mass; **cantar/decir/oír ~** to sing/say/hear mass; **ir a ~** to go to mass ○ church; *fam fig* **to be gospel**; **~ cantada/de campaña** sung/open-air mass; **~ de difuntos** requiem, mass for the dead; **~ del gallo** midnight mass (*on Christmas Eve*); **no saber de la ~ la mitad** *fam fig* not to know half the story.

misal *m* missal.

misantropía *f* misanthropy.

misántropo, -pa *m y f* misanthrope, misanthropist.

miscelánea *f* miscellany.

miserable ◇ *adj* **-1.** [pobre] poor; [vivienda] wretched, squalid. **-2.** [penoso, insuficiente] miserable. **-3.** [vil] contemptible, base. **-4.** [tacaño] mean. ◇ *m y f* **-1.** [ruin] wretch, vile person. **-2.** [tacaño] mean person, miser.

miseria *f* **-1.** [pobreza] poverty. **-2.** [desgracia] misfortune. **-3.** [tacañería] meanness. **-4.** [vileza] baseness, wretchedness. **-5.** [poco dinero] pittance.

misericordia *f* compassion; **pedir ~** to beg for mercy.

misericordioso, -sa ◇ *adj* compassionate, merciful. ◇ *m y f*: **los ~s** the merciful.

mísero, -ra *adj* [pobre] wretched; **ni un ~ ...** not even a measly ○ miserable ....

misil (*pl* **misiles**) *m* missile; **~ de crucero** cruise missile.

misión *f* **-1.** [gen] mission; [cometido] task. **-2.** [expedición científica] expedition.
◆ **misiones** *fpl* RELIG (overseas) missions.

misionero, -ra *m y f* missionary.

misiva *f culto* missive.

mismo, -ma ◇ *adj* **-1.** [igual] same; **el ~ piso** the same flat; **del ~ color que** the same colour as. **-2.** [para enfatizar]: **yo ~** I myself; **en este ~ cuarto** in this very room; **en su misma calle** right in the street where he lives; **por mí/ti ~** by myself/yourself; **¡tú ~!** it's up to you.
◇ *pron*: **el ~** the same; **el ~ que vi ayer** the same one I saw yesterday; **lo ~** the same (thing); **lo ~ que** the same as; **da ○ es lo ~** it doesn't matter, it doesn't make any difference; **me da lo ~** I don't care; **estar en las mismas** *fig* to be no further forward.
◆ **mismo** *adv* (*después de sust*) **-1.** [para enfatizar]: **lo vi desde mi casa ~** I saw it from my own house; **ahora/aquí ~** right now/here; **ayer ~** only yesterday; **por eso ~** precisely for that reason. **-2.** [por ejemplo]: **escoge uno cualquiera — este ~** choose any — this one, for instance.

misoginia *f* misogyny.

misógino, -na ◇ *adj* misogynistic. ◇ *m y f* misogynist.

miss (*pl* **misses**) *f* beauty queen.

Mississippi [misi'sipi] *m*: **el ~** the Mississippi.

Missouri [mi'suri] *m*: **el (río) ~** the (river) Missouri.

míster (*pl* **místers**) *m* DEP ≃ manager.

misterio *m* mystery.

misterioso, -sa *adj* mysterious.

mística → **místico**.

misticismo *m* mysticism.

místico, -ca ◇ *adj* mystical. ◇ *m y f* [persona] mystic.
◆ **mística** *f* [práctica] mysticism.

mistificación *f* mystification.

mistificar [10], **mixtificar** *vt* to mystify.

MIT (*abrev de* **Massachusetts Institute of Technology**) *m* MIT.

mitad *f* **-1.** [gen] half; **a ~ de precio** at half price; **a ~ de camino** halfway there; **a ~ de película** halfway through the film; **a ~ de** half (of); **la ~ del tiempo no está** half the time she's not in; **~ y ~** half and half. **-2.** [centro] middle; **en ~ de** in the middle of; **(cortar algo) por la ~** (to cut sthg) in half.

mítico, -ca *adj* mythical.

mitificar [10] *vt* to mythologize.

mitigador, -ra *adj* calming.

mitigar [16] *vt* **-1.** [gen] to alleviate, to reduce; [ánimos] to calm; [sed] to slake; [hambre] to take the edge off; [choque, golpe] to soften; [dudas, sospechas] to allay. **-2.** [justificar] to mitigate.

mitin (*pl* **mítines**) *m* rally, meeting.

mito *m* **-1.** [gen] myth. **-2.** [personaje] mythical figure.

mitología *f* mythology.

mitológico, -ca *adj* mythological.

mitomanía *f* mythomania.

mitómano, -na *adj, m y f* mythomaniac.

mitón *m* (fingerless) mitten.

mitote *m Amer fam* [alboroto] racket.

mitra *f* **-1.** [tocado] mitre. **-2.** [cargo] office of archbishop/bishop.

mixtificar [10] = **mistificar**.

mixto, -ta *adj* mixed; [comisión] joint.

mixtura *f* mixture.

mízcalo *m* milk fungus.

ml (*abrev de* **mililitro**) ml.

mm (*abrev de* **milímetro**) mm.

m/n (*abrev de* **moneda nacional**) national currency.

mnemónico, -ca, nemónico, -ca *adj* mnemonic.

mnemotecnia, nemotecnia *f* mnemonics (*U*).

moaré = **muaré**.

mobiliario *m* furniture.

moca *f* mocha.

mocasín *m* moccasin.

mocedad *f* youth.

mocetón, -ona *m y f fam* strapping lad (*f* strapping lass).

moche → **troche**.

mochila *f* backpack.

mocho, -cha *adj* [gen] blunt; [árbol] lopped.
◆ **mocho** *m* [fregona] mop.

mochuelo *m* little owl; **cargar con el ~** *fam* to be landed with it.

moción *f* motion; **~ de censura** censure motion.

moco *m fam* snot (*U*); MED mucus (*U*); **limpiarse los ~s** to wipe one's nose; **tener ~s** to have a runny nose; **llorar a ~ tendido** *fam fig* to cry one's eyes out; **no ser ~ de pavo** *fam fig* to be sthg not to be sneezed at, to be no mean feat.

mocoso, -sa ◇ *adj* runny-nosed. ◇ *m y f fam despec* brat.

moda *f* [gen] fashion; [furor pasajero] craze; **estar de ~** to be fashionable ○ in fashion; **estar pasado de ~** to be unfashionable ○ out of fashion; **ir a la última ~** to wear the latest fashion.

modal *adj* modal.
◆ **modales** *mpl* manners; **tener buenos/malos ~es** to have good/bad manners.

modalidad *f* form, type; DEP discipline; **~ de pago** method of payment.

modelado *m* modelling.

modelar *vt* to model; *fig* to form, to shape.

modelismo *m* modelling.

modelo ◇ *adj* model. ◇ *m y f* model. ◇ *m* **-1.** [gen] model; **~ económico** ECON economic model. **-2.** [prenda de vestir] number.

modem ['moðem] (*pl* **modems**) *m* INFORM modem; **~ fax** fax modem.

moderación *f* moderation.

moderado, -da *adj, m y f* moderate.

moderador, -ra ◇ *adj* moderating. ◇ *m y f* chair, chairperson.

moderar *vt* **-1.** [gen] to moderate; [velocidad] to reduce. **-2.** [debate] to chair.
◆ **moderarse** *vpr* to restrain o.s.; **~se en algo** to moderate sthg.

modernidad *f* modernity.

modernismo *m* **-1.** [gen & LITER] modernism. **-2.** [ARQUIT etc - en España] Modernismo, ≈ Art Nouveau.

modernista *adj, m y f* **-1.** [gen & LITER] modernist. **-2.** [ARQUIT etc - en España] Modernista.

modernización *f* modernization.

modernizar [13] *vt* to modernize.
◆ **modernizarse** *vpr* to modernize.

moderno, -na ◇ *adj* modern. ◇ *m y f fam* trendy (person).

modestia *f* modesty; **falsa ~** false modesty.

modesto, -ta ◇ *adj* modest. ◇ *m y f* modest person.

módico, -ca *adj* modest.

modificación *f* alteration.

modificar [10] *vt* **-1.** [variar] to alter. **-2.** GRAM to modify.

modismo *m* idiom.

modista *m y f* **-1.** [diseñador] fashion designer. **-2.** [que cose] tailor (*f* dressmaker).

modisto *m* **-1.** [diseñador] fashion designer. **-2.** [sastre] tailor.

modo *m* **-1.** [manera, forma] way; **a ~ de** as, by way of; **al ~ de** in the style of; **de ese ~** in that way; **de ningún ~** in no way; **de todos ~s** in any case, anyway; **de un ~ u otro** one way or another; **en cierto ~** in some ways; **~ de empleo** instructions (*pl*) for use; **de ~ que** [de manera que] in such a way that; [así que] so. **-2.** GRAM mood; **~ adverbial** adverbial phrase.
◆ **modos** *mpl* [modales] manners; **buenos/malos ~s** good/bad manners.

modorra *f fam* drowsiness.

modoso, -sa *adj* [recatado] modest; [formal] well-behaved.

modulación *f* modulation; **~ de frecuencia** frequency modulation.

modulador, -ra *adj* modulating.
◆ **modulador** *m* modulator.

modular ◇ *adj* modular. ◇ *vt* to modulate.

módulo *m* **-1.** [gen] module. **-2.** [de muebles] unit.

modus operandi *m* modus operandi.

modus vivendi *m* way of life.

mofa *f* mockery; **hacer ~ de** to mock.

mofarse *vpr* to scoff; **~ de** to mock.

moflete *m* chubby cheek.

Mogadiscio [moɣaˈðisθio] Mogadishu.

mogol, -la, mongol, -la ◇ *adj* Mongolian. ◇ *m y f* [persona] Mongol, Mongolian.
◆ **mogol** *m* [lengua] Mongol, Mongolian.

mogollón *m mfam* **-1.** [muchos]: **~ de tons** (*pl*) of, loads (*pl*) of. **-2.** [lío] row, commotion; **entraron/salieron a ~** everyone rushed in/out at once.

mohair [moˈer] *m* mohair.

mohín *m* grimace, face.

moho *m* **-1.** [hongo] mould. **-2.** [herrumbre] rust.

mohoso, -sa *adj* **-1.** [con hongo] mouldy. **-2.** [oxidado] rusty.

moisés *m inv* Moses basket.

mojado, -da *adj* wet; [húmedo] damp; **llover sobre ~** *fig* to be just too much.

mojama *f* dried salted tuna.

mojar *vt* to wet; [humedecer] to dampen; [comida] to dunk.
◆ **mojarse** *vpr* **-1.** [con agua] to get wet. **-2.** *fam* [comprometerse] to commit o.s.

mojigatería *f* **-1.** [beatería] prudery. **-2.** [falsa humildad] sanctimoniousness.

mojigato, -ta ◇ *adj* **-1.** [beato] prudish. **-2.** [con falsa humildad] sanctimonious. ◇ *m y f* **-1.** [beato] prude. **-2.** [con falsa humildad] sanctimonious person.

mojón *m* [piedra] milestone; [poste] milepost.

molar¹ → **diente**.

molar² *mfam* ◇ *vt*: **¡cómo me mola esa moto/ese chico!** I think that motorbike/that guy is bloody gorgeous. ◇ *vi* to be bloody gorgeous.

molcajete *m Amer* mortar.

Moldavia Moldavia.

moldavo, -va *adj, m y f* Moldavian.

molde *m* mould.

moldeado *m* **-1.** [del pelo] soft perm, bodywave. **-2.** [de figura, cerámica] moulding.

moldear *vt* **-1.** [gen] to mould. **-2.** [modelar] to cast. **-3.** [cabello] to give a soft perm to.

moldura *f* moulding.

mole *f* hulk.

molécula *f* molecule.

molecular *adj* molecular.

moler [24] *vt* **-1.** [gen] to grind; [aceitunas] to press; [trigo] to mill. **-2.** *fam fig* [cansar] to wear out.

molestar *vt* **-1.** [perturbar] to annoy; **¿le molesta que fume?** do you mind if I smoke?; **perdone que le moleste ...** I'm sorry to bother you .... **-2.** [doler] to hurt. **-3.** [ofender] to offend.
◆ **molestarse** *vpr* **-1.** [incomodarse] to bother; **no te molestes, yo lo haré** don't bother, I'll do it; **~se en hacer algo** to bother to do sthg; **~se por alguien/algo** to put o.s. out for sb/sthg. **-2.** [ofenderse]: **~se (por algo)** to take offence (at sthg).

molestia *f* **-1.** [incomodidad] nuisance; **si no es demasiada ~** if it's not too much trouble; **tomarse la ~ de hacer algo** to take the trouble to do sthg. **-2.** [malestar] discomfort.

molesto, -ta *adj* **-1.** [incordiante] annoying; [- visita] inconvenient. **-2.** [irritado]: **~ (con)** annoyed (with). **-3.** [con malestar] in discomfort.

molido, -da *adj* **-1.** [gen] ground; [trigo] milled. **-2.** *fam fig* [cansado] worn out; **estar ~ de** to be worn out from.

molienda *f* grinding; [de trigo] milling.

molinero, -ra ◇ *adj* milling. ◇ *m y f* miller.

molinete *m* **-1.** [ventilador] extractor fan. **-2.** [juguete] toy windmill.

molinillo *m* grinder.

molino *m* mill; **~ de viento** windmill.

molla f -1. [parte blanda] flesh. -2. [gordura] flab.

molleja f gizzard.

mollera f fam [juicio] brains (pl); **ser duro de** ~ [estúpido] to be thick in the head; [testarudo] to be pig-headed.

molusco m mollusc.

momentáneo, -a adj [de un momento] momentary; [pasajero] temporary.

momento m [gen] moment; [periodo] time; **llegó un** ~ **en que ...** there came a time when ...; **a cada** ~ all the time; **al** ~ straightaway; **de** ~, **por el** ~ for the time being ○ moment; **del** ~ [actual] of the day; **de un** ~ **a otro** any minute now; **desde el** ~ **(en) que ...** [tiempo] from the moment that ...; [causa] seeing as ...; **por** ~s by the minute.

momia f mummy.

momificar [10] vt to mummify.

◆ **momificarse** vpr to mummify.

momio, -mia adj Amer fam [carcamal] square, untrendy.

mona → **mono**.

monacal adj monastic.

Mónaco Monaco.

monada f -1. [persona] little beauty. -2. [cosa] lovely thing. -3. [gracia] antic.

monaguillo m altar boy.

monarca m monarch.

monarquía f monarchy; ~ **absoluta/ constitucional/parlamentaria** absolute/constitutional/parliamentary monarchy.

monárquico, -ca ◇ adj monarchic. ◇ m y f monarchist.

monasterio m [de monjes] monastery; [de monjas] convent.

monástico, -ca adj monastic.

Moncloa f: **la** ~ residence of the Spanish premier.

LA MONCLOA:

This palace in Madrid is the residence of the Spanish premier, and the place where the 'pactos de la Moncloa', economic and social agreements drawn up between 1977 and 1978, were signed. By extension, the phrase refers to the Spanish government

monda f [acción] peeling; [piel] peel; **ser la** ~ mfam [extraordinario] to be amazing; [gracioso] to be a scream.

mondadientes m inv toothpick.

mondadura f -1. [acción] peeling. -2. [piel] peel.

mondar vt to peel.

◆ **mondarse** vpr: ~**se (de risa)** fam to laugh one's head off.

mondongo m innards (pl).

moneda f -1. [pieza] coin; ~ **suelta** small change (U); **pagar a alguien con** ○ **en la misma** ~ to pay sb back in kind; **ser** ~ **corriente** to be commonplace. -2. [divisa] currency; ~ **débil/fuerte** weak/strong currency; ~ **corriente** legal tender; ~ **divisionaria** ○ **fraccionaria** minor unit of currency.

monedero m purse; ~ **electrónico** electronic purse.

monegasco, -ca adj, m y f Monacan, Monegasque.

monería f -1. [de una persona - gracia] antic; [- bobada] foolish act. -2. [de un mono] monkey's trick.

monetario, -ria adj monetary.

monetarismo m monetarism.

monetarista adj monetarist.

mongol = **mogol**.

Mongolia Mongolia.

mongólico, -ca MED ◇ adj Down's syndrome (antes de sust). ◇ m y f Down's syndrome person.

mongolismo m Down's syndrome.

monigote m -1. [muñeco] rag ○ paper doll. -2. [dibujo] doodle. -3. fig [persona] puppet.

monitor, -ra m y f [persona] instructor.

◆ **monitor** m INFORM & TECN monitor; ~ **en color** colour monitor.

monitorio, -ria adj culto admonitory.

monja f nun.

monje m monk.

monjil adj [de monje] monk's; [de monja] nun's.

mono, -na ◇ adj lovely. ◇ m y f [animal] monkey; **aunque la mona se vista de seda, mona se queda** you can't make a silk purse out of a sow's ear; **ser el último** ~ to be bottom of the heap.

◆ **mono** m -1. [prenda - con peto] dungarees (pl); [- con mangas] overalls (pl). -2. fam [abstinencia] cold turkey.

◆ **mona** f fam [borrachera]: **coger una mona** to get legless; **dormir la mona** to sleep it off.

monocarril adj & m monorail.

monocolor adj monochrome.

monocorde adj -1. fig [monótono] monotonous. -2. MÚS single-stringed.

monóculo m monocle.

monoesquí (pl monoesquís) m monoski.

monofásico, -ca adj single-phase.

monogamia f monogamy.

monógamo, **-ma** ◇ adj monogamous. ◇ m y f monogomous person.

monografía f monograph.

monográfico, **-ca** adj monographic.

monokini m monokini.

monolingüe adj monolingual.

monolítico, **-ca** adj monolithic.

monolito m monolith.

monologar [16] vi to give a monologue.

monólogo m monologue; TEATR soliloquy.

monomanía f obsession.

monomaniaco, **-ca**, **monomaníaco**, **-ca** adj, m y f obsessive.

monopatín m skateboard.

monoplano adj & m monoplane.

monoplaza ◇ adj single-seat (antes de sust). ◇ m single-seater.

monopolio m monopoly.

monopolización f monopolization.

monopolizador, **-ra** ◇ adj monopolistic. ◇ m y f monopolist.

monopolizar [13] vt lit & fig to monopolize.

monorraíl adj & m monorail.

monosilábico, **-ca** adj monosyllabic.

monosílabo, **-ba** adj monosyllabic.
◆ **monosílabo** m monosyllable.

monoteísmo m monotheism.

monoteísta ◇ adj monotheistic. ◇ m y f monotheist.

monotipo m IMPRENTA Monotype®.

monotonía f **-1.** [uniformidad] monotony. **-2.** [entonación] monotone.

monótono, **-na** adj monotonous.

monóxido m monoxide; ~ de carbono carbon monoxide.

Monrovia Monrovia.

Mons. abrev de **Monseñor**.

monseñor m Monsignor.

monserga f fam drivel (U).

monstruo ◇ adj inv **-1.** [grande] enormous, monster (antes de sust). **-2.** [prodigioso] fantastic. ◇ m **-1.** [gen] monster. **-2.** [prodigio] giant, marvel.

monstruosidad f **-1.** [crueldad] monstrosity, atrocity. **-2.** [fealdad] hideousness. **-3.** [anomalía] freak. **-4.** [enormidad] hugeness.

monstruoso, **-sa** adj **-1.** [cruel] monstrous. **-2.** [feo] hideous. **-3.** [enorme] huge, enormous. **-4.** [deforme] terribly deformed.

monta f **-1.** [suma] total. **-2.** [importancia] importance; de poca/mucha ~ of little/great importance. **-3.** [en un caballo] ride, riding (U).

montacargas m inv goods lift Br, freight elevator Am.

montador, **-ra** m y f **-1.** [obrero] fitter. **-2.** CIN editor.

montaje m **-1.** [de una máquina] assembly. **-2.** TEATR staging. **-3.** FOT montage. **-4.** CIN editing. **-5.** [farsa] put-up job.

montante m **-1.** [ARQUIT - de armazón] upright; [- de ventana] mullion; [- de puerta] jamb. **-2.** [ventanuco] fanlight. **-3.** [importe] total; ~s compensatorios COM compensating duties.

montaña f lit & fig mountain; ir de excursión a la ~ to go camping in the mountains; ~ rusa roller coaster, big dipper; hacer una ~ de algo to make a big thing of sthg; hacer una ~ de un grano de arena to make a mountain out of a molehill.

Montañas Rocosas fpl: las ~ the Rocky Mountains.

montañero, **-ra** ◇ adj mountaineering. ◇ m y f mountaineer.

montañés, **-esa** ◇ adj **-1.** [santanderino] of or relating to Santander. **-2.** [de la montaña] highland (antes de sust), mountain (antes de sust). ◇ m y f **-1.** [santanderino] person from Santander. **-2.** [de la montaña] highlander.

montañismo m mountaineering.

montañoso, **-sa** adj mountainous.

montar ◇ vt **-1.** [ensamblar - máquina, estantería] to assemble; [- tienda de campaña, tenderete] to put up. **-2.** [encajar]: ~ algo en algo to fit sthg into sthg. **-3.** [organizar - negocio, piso] to set up. **-4.** [cabalgar] to ride. **-5.** [poner encima]: ~ a alguien en to lift sb onto. **-6.** [CULIN - nata] to whip; [- claras, yemas] to beat. **-7.** TEATR to stage. **-8.** CIN to cut, to edit.

◇ vi **-1.** [subir] to get on; [en un coche] to get in; ~ en [gen] to get onto; [coche] to get into; [animal] to mount. **-2.** [ir montado] to ride; ~ en bicicleta/a caballo to ride a bicycle/a horse. **-3.** [sumar]: ~ a to come to, to total; tanto monta it's all the same.

◆ **montarse** vpr **-1.** [gen] to get on; [en un coche] to get in; [en un animal] to mount; ~se en [gen] to get onto; [coche] to get into; [animal] to mount. **-2.** loc montárselo fam to work it, to organize things.

montaraz adj mountain (antes de sust).

Mont Blanc m: el ~ Mont Blanc.

monte m [elevación] mountain; [terreno] woodland; ~ bajo scrub; echarse o tirarse al ~ to take to the hills; fig to go to extremes; no todo el ~ es orégano life's not a bowl of cherries.

◆ **monte de piedad** m state pawnbroker's.

◆ **monte de Venus** *m* mons veneris.

montepío *m* mutual aid society.

montera *f* bullfighter's hat; *ver también* **tauromaquia.**

montés *adj* wild.

Montevideo Montevideo.

montículo *m* hillock.

montilla *m* Montilla, *dry sherry from Montilla near Córdoba.*

monto *m* total.

montón *m* -1. [pila] heap, pile; **a** ○ **en** ~ everything together ○ at once; **del** ~ *fig* ordinary, run-of-the-mill. -2. *fig* [muchos] loads; **un** ~ **de** loads of; **a montones** by the bucketload.

Montreal Montreal.

montura *f* -1. [cabalgadura] mount. -2. [arreos] harness; [silla] saddle. -3. [soporte - de gafas] frame; [- de joyas] mounting.

monumental *adj* -1. [ciudad, lugar] famous for its monuments. -2. [fracaso etc] *fig* monumental.

monumento *m* monument.

monzón *m* monsoon.

moña ◇ *f* -1. *fam* [borrachera]: **coger una** ~ to get smashed. -2. [adorno] ribbon. ◇ *m mfam* poof.

moño *m* bun (*of hair*); **agarrarse del** ~ [pegarse] to pull each other's hair out; **estar hasta el** ~ **(de)** to be sick to death (of).

MOPU (*abrev de* **Ministerio de Obras Públicas y Urbanismo**) *m Spanish ministry of public works and town planning.*

moquear *vi* to have a runny nose.

moqueta *f* fitted carpet.

moquillo *m* VETER distemper.

mora *f* -1. [de la zarzamora] blackberry. -2. [del moral] mulberry.

morada *f culto* dwelling.

morado, -da *adj* purple; **pasarlas moradas** *fam fig* to have a bad time of it; **ponerse** ~ *fam* to stuff o.s.

◆ **morado** *m* -1. [color] purple. -2. [golpe] bruise.

morador, -ra *m y f culto* inhabitant.

moral ◇ *adj* moral. ◇ *f* -1. [ética] morality. -2. [ánimo] morale; **estar bajo de** ~ to be in poor spirits. ◇ *m* [árbol] mulberry tree.

moraleja *f* moral.

moralidad *f* morality.

moralismo *m* moralism.

moralista *m y f* moralist.

moralizar [13] *vi* to moralize.

morapio *m fam* cheap red wine, plonk.

morar *vi culto:* ~ **(en)** to dwell (in).

moratoria *f* moratorium.

mórbido, -da *adj* -1. [gen & MED] morbid. -2. [delicado] delicate.

morbo *m* -1. *fam* [placer malsano] morbid pleasure. -2. MED disease.

morbosidad *f* morbidity.

morboso, -sa *adj* morbid.

morcilla *f* CULIN ≃ black pudding *Br*, ≃ blood sausage *Am*; **¡que te/os den** ~**!** *mfam* you can stuff it, then!

morcillo *m* foreknuckle.

mordacidad *f* sharpness, mordacity.

mordaz *adj* caustic, biting.

mordaza *f* gag.

mordedura *f* bite.

morder [24] ◇ *vt* -1. [con los dientes] to bite. -2. [gastar] to eat into. ◇ *vi* to bite; **estar que muerde** to be hopping mad.

◆ **morderse** *vpr:* ~**se la lengua/las uñas** to bite one's tongue/nails.

mordida *f Amer fam* [soborno] bribe.

mordisco *m* bite; **a** ~**s** by biting.

mordisquear *vt* to nibble (at).

moreno, -na ◇ *adj* -1. [pelo, piel] dark; [por el sol] tanned; **ponerse** ~ to get a tan. -2. [pan, azúcar] brown. ◇ *m y f* [por el pelo] dark-haired person; [por la piel] dark-skinned person.

◆ **morena** *f* [pez] moray eel.

morera *f* white mulberry.

morería *f* Moorish quarter.

moretón *m* bruise.

morfema *m* morpheme.

morfina *f* morphine.

morfinómano, -na ◇ *adj* addicted to morphine. ◇ *m y f* morphine addict.

morfología *f* morphology.

morganático, -ca *adj* morganatic.

morgue *f* morgue.

moribundo, -da ◇ *adj* dying. ◇ *m y f* dying person.

morir [25] *vi* -1. [gen] to die. -2. [río, calle] to come out. -3. [fuego] to die down; [luz] to go out; [día] to come to a close.

◆ **morirse** *vpr* -1. [fallecer]: ~**se (de)** to die (of). -2. *fig* [sentir con fuerza]: ~**se de envidia/ira** to be burning with envy/rage; **me muero de ganas de ir a bailar** I'm dying to go dancing; **me muero de hambre/frío** I'm starving/freezing; ~**se por algo** to be dying for sthg; ~**se por alguien** to be crazy about sb.

morisco, -ca ◇ *adj referring to Moors in Spain baptized after the Reconquest.* ◇ *m y f* baptized Moor.

mormón, -ona ◇ *adj, m y f* Mormon.

moro, **-ra** ◇ *adj* **-1.** HIST Moorish. **-2.** *fam* [machista] sexist. ◇ *m y f* **-1.** HIST Moor; ~s **y cristianos** *Spanish festival*. **-2.** [árabe] Arab (*N.B.: the term 'moro' is considered to be racist*); **no hay** ~s **en la costa** the coast is clear.
◆ **moro** *m fam fig* [machista] sexist (man).

MOROS Y CRISTIANOS:
This traditional festival is especially popular in the east of Spain. A mock battle is held to simulate the battles which took place between Moors and Christians during the Spanish Reconquest

morocho, **-cha** *adj Amer* [moreno] dark-haired.

morochos *mpl Amer* [gemelos] twins.

morosidad *f* **-1.** COM defaulting, failure to pay on time. **-2.** [lentitud] slowness.

moroso, **-sa** COM ◇ *adj* defaulting. ◇ *m y f* defaulter, bad debtor.

morral *m* MIL haversack; [de cazador] game-bag.

morralla *f* **-1.** *despec* [personas] scum; [cosas] junk. **-2.** [pescado] small fry. **-3.** *Amer* [suelto] loose change.

morrear *mfam vt & vi* to snog.
◆ **morrearse** *vpr* to snog.

morriña *f* [por el país de uno] homesickness; [por el pasado] nostalgia.

morro *m* **-1.** [hocico] snout. **-2.** (*gen pl*) *fam* [labios] (thick) lips (*pl*); **estar de** ~s to be angry; **romperle los** ~s **a alguien** to smash sb's face in; **¡qué** ~ **tiene!** *fam* he's got a cheek! **-3.** *fam* [de coche, avión] nose.

morrocotudo, **-da** *adj fam* tremendous.

morsa *f* walrus.

morse *m* (*en aposición inv*) Morse (code).

mortadela *f* Mortadella.

mortaja *f* shroud.

mortal ◇ *adj* mortal; [caída, enfermedad] fatal; [aburrimiento, susto, enemigo] deadly. ◇ *m y f* mortal.

mortalidad *f* mortality.

mortandad *f* mortality.

mortecino, **-na** *adj* [luz, brillo] faint; [color, mirada] dull.

mortero *m* mortar.

mortífero, **-ra** *adj* deadly.

mortificación *f* mortification.

mortificante *adj* mortifying.

mortificar [10] *vt* to mortify.

mortuorio, **-ria** *adj* death (*antes de sust*).

moruno, **-na** *adj* Moorish.

mosaico, **-ca** *adj* Mosaic.
◆ **mosaico** *m* mosaic.

mosca *f* fly; ~ **tse-tsé** tsetse fly; **aflojar** o **soltar la** ~ to cough up, to fork out; **cazar** ~s to twiddle one's thumbs; **estar con** o **tener la** ~ **detrás de la oreja** *fam* to be suspicious o distrustful; **estar** ~ *fam* [enfadado] to be in a mood; [con sospechas] to smell a rat; **no se oía ni una** ~ you could have heard a pin drop; **por si las** ~s just in case; **¿qué** ~ **te ha picado?** what's up with you?
◆ **mosca muerta** *m y f* slyboots, hypocrite.

moscardón *m* **-1.** ZOOL blowfly. **-2.** *fam fig* [persona] pest, creep.

moscatel *m* Muscatel, *dessert wine made from muscat grapes.*

moscón *m* **-1.** ZOOL meatfly, bluebottle. **-2.** *fam fig* [persona] pest, creep.

moscovita *adj, m y f* Muscovite.

Moscú Moscow.

mosén (*pl* **mosenes**) *m* RELIG father, reverend.

mosqueado, **-da** *adj fam* [enfadado] cross, in a mood.

mosquearse *vpr fam* [enfadarse] to get cross; [sospechar] to smell a rat.

mosqueo *m fam* annoyance, anger.

mosquete *m* musket.

mosquetero *m* musketeer.

mosquetón *m* short carbine.

mosquitero *m* mosquito net.

mosquito *m* mosquito.

mosso d'Esquadra *m member of the Catalan police force.*

mostacho *m* moustache.

mostaza *f* mustard.

mosto *m* [residuo] must; [zumo de uva] grape juice.

mostrador *m* [en tienda] counter; [en bar] bar.

mostrar [23] *vt* to show.
◆ **mostrarse** *vpr* to appear, to show o.s.; **se mostró muy interesado** he expressed great interest.

mostrenco, **-ca** ◇ *adj* [sin dueño] without an owner, unclaimed. ◇ *m y f fam* [torpe] thick o stupid person.

mota *f* [de polvo] speck; [en una tela] dot.

mote *m* nickname.

moteado, **-da** *adj* speckled; [vestido] dotted.

motear *vt* [poner mote] to nickname.

motejar *vt*: ~ **a alguien de algo** to brand sb sthg.

motel *m* motel.

motín *m* [del pueblo] uprising, riot; [de las tropas] mutiny.

motivación *f* motive, motivation (*U*).

motivar *vt* **-1.** [causar] to cause; [impulsar] to motivate. **-2.** [razonar] to explain, to justify.

motivo *m* **-1.** [causa] reason, cause; [de crimen] motive; **con** ~ **de** [por causa de] because of; [para celebrar] on the occasion of; [con el fin de] in order to; **dar** ~ **a** to give reason to; **tener** ~**s para** to have reason to; **sin** ~ for no reason. **-2.** ARTE, LITER & MÚS motif.

moto *f* motorbike *Br*, motorcycle.

motocicleta *f* motorbike, motorcycle.

motociclismo *m* motorcycling.

motociclista *m y f* motorcyclist.

motociclo *m* motorcycle.

motocross *m* motocross.

motocultivo *m* mechanized farming.

motonáutico, -ca *adj* speedboat (*antes de sust*).
◆ **motonáutica** *f* speedboat racing.

motoneta *f Amer* scooter, moped.

motor (*f* **motora** ○ **motriz**) *adj* motor.
◆ **motor** *m* **-1.** [aparato] motor, engine; ~ **diesel/de gasolina** diesel/fuel engine; ~ **de inyección/reacción** fuel-injection/jet engine; ~ **de arranque** starter, starting motor; ~ **de combustión interna** internal combustion engine; ~ **eléctrico** electric motor; ~ **de explosión** spark-ignition engine; ~ **fuera borda** outboard motor. **-2.** [fuerza] dynamic force. **-3.** *fig* [causa] instigator, cause.
◆ **motora** *f* motorboat.

motorismo *m* motorcycling.

motorista *m y f* motorcyclist.

motorizado, -da *adj* motorized.

motorizar [13] *vt* to motorize.
◆ **motorizarse** *vpr fam* to get o.s. some wheels.

motosierra *f* power saw.

motricidad *f* motivity.

motriz → motor.

motu propio *adv*: **(de)** ~ of one's own accord.

mountain bike ['maunten 'bike] *m* DEP mountain biking.

mousse [mus] *m inv* CULIN mousse.

movedizo, -za *adj* **-1.** [movible] movable, easily moved. **-2.** [inestable] unsteady, unstable.

mover [24] *vt* **-1.** [gen & INFORM] to move; [mecánicamente] to drive. **-2.** [cabeza - afirmativamente] to nod; [- negativamente] to shake. **-3.** [suscitar] to arouse, to provoke. **-4.** *fig* [empujar]: ~ **a alguien a algo/a hacer algo** to drive sb to sthg/to do sthg.

◆ **mover a** *vi* **-1.** [incitar] to incite to. **-2.** [causar] to provoke, to cause.
◆ **moverse** *vpr* **-1.** [gen] to move; [en la cama] to toss and turn. **-2.** [darse prisa] to get a move on. **-3.** [hacer gestiones] to make an effort. **-4.** [relacionarse]: ~**se en/entre** to move in/among.

movible *adj* movable.

movido, -da *adj* **-1.** [debate, torneo] lively; [persona] active, restless; [jornada, viaje] hectic. **-2.** FOT blurred, fuzzy.
◆ **movida** *f fam* [ambiente] scene; **la** ~ **madrileña** *the Madrid scene of the 1970s*.

LA MOVIDA MADRILEÑA:
This movement, which emerged in Madrid at the end of the 1970s, brought new cultural life to the city in the fields of music and cinema. Its most celebrated exponents were cinema directors such as Pedro Almodóvar, pop groups such as Radio Futura and so on

móvil ◇ *adj* mobile, movable. ◇ *m* **-1.** [motivo] motive. **-2.** [juguete] mobile.

movilidad *f* mobility.

movilización *f* mobilization.

movilizar [13] *vt* to mobilize.

movimiento *m* **-1.** [gen & POLÍT] movement; ~ **obrero** working-class movement. **-2.** FÍS & TECN motion; ~ **continuo/de rotación** perpetual/rotational motion; ~ **sísmico** earth tremor. **-3.** [circulación - gen] activity; [- de personal, mercancías] turnover; [- de vehículos] traffic; ~ **de capital** cash flow. **-4.** [MÚS - parte de la obra] movement; [- velocidad del compás] tempo.

moviola *f* editing projector.

moza → mozo.

mozalbete *m* young lad.

Mozambique Mozambique.

mozárabe ◇ *adj* Mozarabic, *Christian in the time of Moorish Spain*. ◇ *m y f* [habitante] Mozarab, *Christian of Moorish Spain*. ◇ *m* [lengua] Mozarabic.

mozo, -za ◇ *adj* [joven] young; [soltero] single, unmarried. ◇ *m y f* young boy (*f* young girl), young lad (*f* young lass).
◆ **mozo** *m* **-1.** [trabajador] assistant (worker); ~ **de cordel** ○ **de cuerda** porter; ~ **de estación** (station) porter. **-2.** [recluta] conscript. **-3.** *Amer* [camarero] waiter.
◆ **moza** *f* **-1.** [sirvienta] girl, maid. **-2.** *Amer* [camarera] waitress.

MPAIAC (*abrev de* **Movimiento para la Autodeterminación y la Independencia del Archipiélago Canario**) *m Canarian independence movement*.

m.s. (*abrev de* **manuscrito**) ms., MS.

Mtro. *abrev de* **maestro**.

mu *m* [mugido] moo; **no decir ni** ~ not to say a word.

muaré, **moaré** *m* moiré.

mucamo, -ma *m y f Amer* servant.

muchachada *f Amer* group of youngsters.

muchacho, -cha *m y f* boy (*f* girl).
◆ **muchacha** *f* [sirvienta] maid.

muchedumbre *f* [de gente] crowd, throng; [de cosas] great number, masses (*pl*).

mucho, -cha ◇ *adj* **-1.** [gran cantidad] (*en sg*) a lot of; (*en pl*) many, a lot of; (*en interrogativas y negativas*) much, a lot of; **tengo** ~ **sueño** I'm very sleepy; **~s días** several days; **no tengo** ~ **tiempo** I haven't got much time. **-2.** (*en sg*) [demasiado]: **hay** ~ **niño aquí** there are too many kids here.
◇ *pron* (*en sg*) a lot; (*en pl*) many, a lot; **tengo** ~ **que contarte** I have a lot to tell you; **¿queda dinero? - no** ~ is there any money left? - not much ○ not a lot; **~s piensan igual** a lot of ○ many people think the same.
◆ **mucho** *adv* **-1.** [gen] a lot; **habla** ~ he talks a lot; **me canso** ~ I get really ○ very tired; **me gusta** ~ I like it a lot ○ very much; **no me gusta** ~ I don't like it much; **(no)** ~ **más tarde** (not) much later. **-2.** [largo tiempo]: **hace** ~ **que no vienes** I haven't seen you for a long time; **¿vienes** ~ **por aquí?** do you come here often?; **¿dura** ~ **la obra?** is the play long?; ~ **antes/después** long before/after. **-3.** *loc:* **como** ~ at the most; **con** ~ by far, easily; **ni** ~ **menos** far from it, by no means; **no está ni** ~ **menos decidido** it is by no means decided.
◆ **por mucho que** *loc conj* no matter how much, however much; **por** ~ **que insistas** no matter how much ○ however much you insist.

mucosidad *f* mucus.

mucoso, -sa *adj* mucous.
◆ **mucosas** *fpl* mucous membranes.

mucus *m inv* mucus.

muda *f* **-1.** [de la voz] breaking; [de piel, plumas] moulting. **-2.** [ropa interior] change of underwear.

mudable *adj* [persona] changeable; [carácter] fickle.

mudanza *f* **-1.** [cambio] change; [de carácter] changeability, fickleness; [de plumas, piel] moulting. **-2.** [de casa] move; **estar de** ~ to be moving.

mudar ◇ *vt* **-1.** [gen] to change; [casa] to move; **cuando mude la voz** when his voice breaks. **-2.** [piel, plumas] to moult. ◇ *vi*

[cambiar]: ~ **de** [opinión, color] to change; [domicilio] to move.
◆ **mudarse** *vpr:* ~**se (de casa)** to move (house); ~**se (de ropa)** to change.

mudéjar *adj, m y f* Mudejar.

mudo, -da ◇ *adj* **-1.** [sin habla] dumb. **-2.** [callado] silent, mute; **se quedó** ~ he was left speechless. **-3.** [sin sonido] silent. ◇ *m y f* dumb person, mute.

mueble ◇ *m* piece of furniture; **los** ~**s** the furniture (*U*); ~ **bar** cocktail cabinet. ◇ *adj* → **bien**.

mueca *f* [gen] face, expression; [de dolor] grimace.

muela ◇ *v* → **moler**. ◇ *f* **-1.** [diente - gen] tooth; [- molar] molar; ~ **del juicio** wisdom tooth. **-2.** [de molino] millstone; [para afilar] grindstone.

muelle *m* **-1.** [de colchón, reloj] spring. **-2.** [en el puerto] dock, quay; [en el río] wharf.

muera → **morir**.

muerda *etc* → **morder**.

muérdago *m* mistletoe.

muere → **morir**.

muermo *m fam* bore, drag; **tener** ~ to be bored.

muerte *f* **-1.** [gen] death; **a** ~ to the death, to the bitter end; **un susto de** ~ a terrible shock; ~ **natural/violenta** natural/violent death; **de mala** ~ third-rate, lousy. **-2.** [homicidio] murder.

muerto, -ta ◇ *pp* → **morir**. ◇ *adj* **-1.** [gen] dead; **estar** ~ **de miedo/frío** to be scared/freezing to death; **estar** ~ **de hambre** to be starving. **-2.** [color] dull. ◇ *m y f* dead person; [cadáver] corpse; **hubo dos** ~**s** two people died; **hacerse el** ~ to pretend to be dead, to play dead; **cargar con el** ~ [trabajo, tarea] to be left holding the baby; [culpa] to get the blame; **hacer el** ~ to float on one's back; **más** ~ **que vivo** frightened half to death; **medio** ~ [cansado] dead beat; **no tener donde caerse** ~ not to have a penny to one's name.

muesca *f* **-1.** [concavidad] notch, groove. **-2.** [corte] nick.

muestra ◇ *v* → **mostrar**. ◇ *f* **-1.** [pequeña cantidad] sample; ~ **gratuita** free sample; **para** ~ **(basta) un botón** one example is enough. **-2.** [señal] sign, show; [prueba] proof; [de cariño, aprecio] token; **dar** ~**s de** to show signs of. **-3.** [modelo] model, pattern. **-4.** [exposición] show, exhibition.

muestrario *m* collection of samples.

muestreo *m* sample; [acción] sampling.

mueva *etc* → **mover**.

Muface (*abrev de* **Mutualidad General de Funcionarios Civiles del Estado**) *f mutual benefit society for Spanish civil servants.*

mugido *m* [de vaca] moo, mooing (*U*); [de toro] bellow, bellowing (*U*).

mugir [15] *vi* [vaca] to moo; [toro] to bellow.

mugre *f* filth, muck.

mugriento, -ta *adj* filthy.

muguete *m* lily of the valley.

muja → **mugir**.

mujer *f* woman; [cónyuge] wife; ~ **de su casa** good housewife; ~ **fatal** femme fatale; ~ **de la limpieza** cleaning lady; ~ **de negocios** businesswoman; ~ **pública** prostitute.

mujeriego, -ga *adj* fond of the ladies.
◆ **mujeriego** *m* womanizer, lady's man.

mujerzuela *f despec* loose woman.

muladí (*pl* **muladíes**) *adj, m y f* renegade.

mulato, -ta *adj, m y f* mulatto.

muleta *f* -1. [para andar] crutch; *fig* prop, support. -2. TAUROM muleta, *red cape hanging from a stick used to tease the bull; ver también* **tauromaquia**.

muletilla *f* [frase] pet phrase; [palabra] pet word.

Mulhacén *m*: **el** ~ Mulhacén.

mullido, -da *adj* soft, springy.

mullir *vt* to soften; [lana, almohada] to fluff up.

mulo, -la *m y f* -1. ZOOL mule. -2. *fam fig* [persona] brute, beast.

multa *f* fine; **poner una** ~ **a alguien** to fine sb.

multar *vt* to fine.

multicolor *adj* multicoloured.

multicopista *f* duplicator, duplicating machine.

multidisciplinar,   multidisciplinario, -ria *adj* multidisciplinary.

multiestación *f*: ~ **(de musculación)** multigym.

multiforme *adj* multiform, differently shaped.

multigrado *adj* multigrade.

multilateral *adj* multilateral.

multimedia *adj inv* INFORM multimedia.

multimillonario, -ria ◇ *adj*: **un negocio** ~ **a** multimillion pound ◇ dollar business. ◇ *m y f* multimillionaire.

multinacional *adj & f* multinational.

múltiple *adj* [variado] multiple.
◆ **múltiples** *adj pl* [numerosos] many, numerous.

multiplicación *f* multiplication.

multiplicador, -ra *adj* multiplying.
◆ **multiplicador** *m* MAT multiplier.

multiplicando *m* multiplicand.

multiplicar [10] *vt & vi* to multiply.
◆ **multiplicarse** *vpr* -1. [esforzarse] to do lots of things at the same time. -2. BIOL to multiply.

multiplicidad *f* multiplicity.

múltiplo, -pla *adj* multiple.
◆ **múltiplo** *m* multiple.

multipuesto *adj inv* INFORM multi-terminal (*antes de sust*).

multisalas *m inv* [cine] multiplex cinema.

multitarea *adj inv* INFORM multitasking.

multitud *f* [de personas] crowd; **una** ~ **de cosas** loads of ◇ countless things.

multitudinario,   -ria *adj* extremely crowded; [manifestación] mass (*antes de sust*).

multiuso *adj inv* multipurpose.

mundanal *adj* worldly.

mundano, -na *adj* -1. [del mundo] worldly, of the world. -2. [de la vida social] (high) society.

mundial ◇ *adj* [política, economía, guerra] world (*antes de sust*); [tratado, organización, fama] worldwide. ◇ *m* World Championships (*pl*); [en fútbol] World Cup.

mundillo *m* world, circles (*pl*); **el** ~ **literario** the literary world, literary circles.

mundo *m* -1. [gen] world; **el nuevo** ~ the New World; **el otro** ~ the next world, the hereafter; **el tercer** ~ the Third World; **desde que el** ~ **es** ~ since the dawn of time; **el** ~ **anda al revés** the world has been turned on its head; **el** ~ **es un pañuelo** it's a small world; **medio** ~ half the world, a lot of people; **no es cosa** ◇ **nada del otro** ~ it's nothing special; **ponerse el** ~ **por montera** not to give a damn what people think; **por nada del** ~ not for (all) the world; **se le cayó el** ~ **encima** his world fell apart; **todo el** ~ everyone, everybody; **venir al** ~ to come into the world, to be born. -2. *fig* [diferencia]: **hay un** ~ **entre ellos** they are worlds apart. -3. [experiencia]: **hombre/mujer de** ~ man/woman of the world; **tener** ~ to be worldly-wise, to know the ways of the world; **ver** ◇ **correr** ~ to see life.

mundología *f* worldly wisdom, experience of life.

Munich ['munik] Munich.

munición *f* ammunition.

municipal ◇ *adj* town (*antes de sust*), municipal; [elecciones] local; [instalaciones] public. ◇ *m y f* → **guardia**.

municipalizar [13] *vt* to municipalize, to bring under municipal authority.

municipio *m* **-1.** [corporación] town council. **-2.** [edificio] town hall. **-3.** [territorio] town, municipality. **-4.** [habitantes] inhabitants of a town ○ municipality.

munificencia *f* munificence.

muñeco, -ca *m y f* [juguete] doll; [marioneta] puppet.
◆ **muñeco** *m fig* puppet.
◆ **muñeca** *f* **-1.** ANAT wrist. **-2.** *fig* [mujer] doll. **-3.** *Amer fam* [enchufe]: **tener** ~ to have friends in high places.
◆ **muñeco de nieve** *m* snowman.

muñeira *f popular Galician dance and music.*

muñequera *f* wristband.

muñón *m* stump.

mural ◇ *adj* [pintura] mural; [mapa] wall. ◇ *m* mural.

muralla *f* wall.

Murcia Murcia.

murciano, -na *adj, m y f* Murcian.

murciélago *m* bat.

murga *f* **-1.** [charanga] band of street musicians. **-2.** *fam* [pesadez] drag, pain; **dar la** ~ to be a pain.

muriera *etc* → morir.

murmullo *m* [gen] murmur, murmuring (*U*); [de hojas] rustle, rustling (*U*); [de insectos] buzz, buzzing (*U*).

murmuración *f* backbiting (*U*), gossip (*U*).

murmurador, -ra ◇ *adj* backbiting, gossiping. ◇ *m y f* backbiter, gossip.

murmurar ◇ *vt* to murmur. ◇ *vi* **-1.** [susurrar - persona] to murmur, to whisper; [- agua, viento] to murmur, to gurgle; [- hojas] to rustle. **-2.** [criticar]: ~ **(de)** to gossip ○ backbite (about). **-3.** [rezongar, quejarse] to grumble.

muro *m lit & fig* wall; ~ **de contención** retaining wall; ~ **de las lamentaciones** Wailing Wall.
◆ **muro del sonido** *m* sound barrier.

mus *m inv card game played in pairs with bidding and in which players communicate by signs.*

musa *f* **-1.** [inspiración] muse. **-2.** MITOL Muse.
◆ **musas** *fpl* [artes] arts.

musaraña *f* ZOOL shrew; **mirar a las** ~**s** to stare into space ○ thin air; **pensar en las** ~**s** to have one's head in the clouds.

musculación *f* body-building.

muscular *adj* muscular.

musculatura *f* muscles (*pl*).

músculo *m* muscle.

musculoso, -sa *adj* muscular.

muselina *f* muslin.

museo *m* museum; ~ **de arte** art gallery.

museología *f* museology.

musgo *m* moss.

música → músico.

musical *adj & m* musical.

musicalidad *f* musicality.

music-hall ['musik'xol] (*pl* **music-halls**) *m* music hall.

músico, -ca ◇ *adj* musical. ◇ *m y f* [persona] musician.
◆ **música** *f* music; **música clásica/de cámara** classical/chamber music; **música instrumental/vocal** instrumental/choral music; **música ligera/pop** light/pop music; **música ambiental** background music; **música celestial** *fig* hot air, empty words (*pl*); **irse con la música a otra parte** to clear off; **mandar a alguien con la música a otra parte** to send sb packing.

musitar *vt* to mutter, to mumble.

muslo *m* thigh; [de pollo] drumstick.

mustela *f* **-1.** [comadreja] weasel. **-2.** [pez] dogfish.

mustiar [8] *vt* to wither, to wilt.
◆ **mustiarse** *vpr* to wither, to wilt.

mustio, -tia *adj* **-1.** [flor, planta] withered, wilted. **-2.** [persona] down, gloomy.

musulmán, -ana *adj, m y f* Muslim, Moslem.

mutable *adj* changeable, mutable.

mutación *f* [cambio] sudden change; BIOL mutation.

mutante *adj, m y f* mutant.

mutar *vt* to mutate.

mutilación *f* mutilation (*U*).

mutilado, -da ◇ *adj* mutilated. ◇ *m y f* cripple.

mutilar *vt* [gen] to mutilate; [estatua] to deface, to spoil.

mutis *m inv* TEATR exit; **hacer** ~ [marcharse] to leave, to go away; [callar] to keep quiet, to say nothing; TEATR to exit.

mutismo *m* **-1.** [mudez] muteness, dumbness. **-2.** [silencio] silence.

mutua → mutuo.

mutualidad *f* **-1.** [asociación] mutual benefit society. **-2.** [reciprocidad] mutuality.

mutualista ◇ *adj* mutual benefit society (*antes de sust*). ◇ *m y f* member of a mutual benefit society.

mutuo, -tua *adj* mutual.
◆ **mutua** *f* mutual benefit society.

muy *adv* very; ~ **bueno/cerca** very good/ near; ~ **de mañana** very early in the morning; ¡~ **bien!** [vale] OK!, all right!; [qué bien] very good!, well done!; **eso es** ~ **de ella**

that's just like her; **eso es ~ de los ameri-canos** that's typically American; **¡el ~ idio-ta!** what an idiot!

n¹, N *f* [letra] n, N.
◆ **N** *m*: **el 20 N** *date of Franco's death.*

---

20 N:
The day of General Franco's death, 20th November 1975, is commemorated every year by far-right groups. This date is considered to be the starting point of Spain's transition to a democratic state

---

n² *f* MAT: **n pesetas** n (number of) pesetas.

n/ *abrev de* **nuestro.**

nabo *m* turnip.

nácar *m* mother-of-pearl.

nacarado, -da *adj* mother-of-pearl (*antes de sust*).

nacer [29] *vi* **-1.** [venir al mundo - niño, animal] to be born; [- planta] to sprout, to begin to grow; [- pájaro] to hatch (out); ~ **de/en** to be born of/in; ~ **de familia humilde** to be born into a poor family; ~ **para algo** to be born to be sthg; **ha nacido cantante** she's a born singer; **volver a** ~ to have a lucky escape. **-2.** [surgir - pelo] to grow; [- río] to rise, to have its source; [- costumbre, actitud, duda] to have its roots.

nacido, -da ◇ *adj* born. ◇ *m y f*: **los ~s hoy** those born today; **recién** ~ new-born baby; **ser un mal** ~ to be a wicked o vile person.

naciente *adj* **-1.** [día] dawning; [sol] rising. **-2.** [gobierno, estado] new, fledgling; [interés] growing.

nacimiento *m* **-1.** [gen] birth; [de planta] sprouting; **de** ~ from birth. **-2.** [de río] source. **-3.** [origen] origin, beginning. **-4.** [belén] Nativity scene.

nación *f* [gen] nation; [territorio] country.
◆ **Naciones Unidas** *fpl* United Nations.

nacional ◇ *adj* national; [mercado, vuelo] domestic; [asuntos] home (*antes de sust*). ◇ *m y f* HIST Francoist.

nacionalidad *f* nationality; **doble** ~ dual nationality.

nacionalismo *m* nationalism.

nacionalista *adj, m y f* nationalist.

nacionalización *f* [de educación, bienes] nationalization; [de persona] naturalization.

nacionalizar [13] *vt* **-1.** [banca, bienes] to nationalize. **-2.** [persona] to naturalize.
◆ **nacionalizarse** *vpr* to become naturalized.

nacionalsocialismo *m* National Socialism.

nada ◇ *pron* nothing; (*en negativas*) anything; **no he leído** ~ **de este autor** I haven't read anything by this author; ~ **más** nothing else, nothing more; **no quiero** ~ **más** I don't want anything else; **no dijo** ~ **de** ~ he didn't say anything at all; **te he traído un regalito de** ~ I've brought you a little something; **de** ~ [respuesta a "gracias"] not at all, you're welcome; **como si** ~ as if nothing had happened; **esto no es** ~ that's nothing.
◇ *adv* **-1.** [en absoluto] at all; **la película no me ha gustado** ~ I didn't like the film at all. **-2.** [poco] a little, a bit; **no hace** ~ **que salió** he left just a minute ago; ~ **menos que** [cosa] no less than; [persona] none other than.
◇ *f*: **la** ~ nothingness, the void.
◆ **nada más** *loc conj* no sooner, as soon as; ~ **más salir de casa se puso a llover** no sooner had I left the house than it started to rain, as soon as I left the house, it started to rain.

nadador, -ra ◇ *adj* swimming. ◇ *m y f* swimmer.

nadar *vi* **-1.** [gen] to swim; [flotar] to float. **-2.** [abundar]: ~ **en** [dinero] to be rolling in; [deudas] to be up to one's neck in.

nadería *f* trifle, little thing.

nadie ◇ *pron* nobody, no one; ~ **lo sabe** nobody knows; **no se lo dije a** ~ I didn't tell anybody; **no ha llamado** ~ nobody phoned. ◇ *m*: **un don** ~ a nobody.

nado
◆ **a nado** *loc adv* swimming.

nafta *f* **-1.** QUÍM naphtha. **-2.** *Amer* [gasolina] petrol.

naftalina *f* naphthalene, naphthaline.

naïf [na'if] *adj* naïve, primitivistic.

nailon, nilón, nylon® *m* nylon.

naipe *m* (playing) card.
◆ **naipes** *mpl* cards.

Nairobi Nairobi.

nalga *f* buttock.

nana *f* **-1.** [canción] lullaby. **-2.** *fam* [abuela] grandma, nana.

nanay *interj fam*: ¡~! no way!, not likely!

nao *f* vessel.

napa *f* nappa (leather).

napalm [na'palm] *m* napalm.

napia *f* (*gen pl*) *fam* snout, conk.

napoleón *m Amer* pliers *pl*.

napoleónico, -ca *adj* Napoleonic.

naranja ◇ *adj inv* orange. ◇ *m* [color] orange. ◇ *f* [fruto] orange; ¡~s de la china! no way!
◆ **media naranja** *f fam fig* other ○ better half.

naranjal *m* orange grove.

naranjo *m* **-1.** [árbol] orange tree. **-2.** [madera] orange (wood).

narcisismo *m* narcissism.

narcisista *m y f* narcissist.

narciso *m* **-1.** BOT narcissus. **-2.** *fig* [hombre] narcissist.

narcomanía *f* narcotism.

narcótico, -ca *adj* narcotic.
◆ **narcótico** *m* narcotic; [droga] drug.

narcotismo *m* narcotism.

narcotizar [13] *vt* to drug.

narcotraficante *m y f* drug trafficker.

narcotráfico *m* drug trafficking.

nardo *m* nard, spikenard.

narices *interj*: ¡~! no way!, not on your life!

narigudo, -da ◇ *adj* big-nosed. ◇ *m y f* big-nosed person.

nariz *f* **-1.** [órgano] nose; ~ aguileña/chata/respingona Roman/snub/turned-up nose. **-2.** [orificio] nostril. **-3.** *fig* [olfato] sense of smell. **-4.** *loc*: me da en la ~ que ... I've got a feeling that ...; dar a alguien en las narices con algo *fig* to rub sb's nose in sthg; darse de narices contra algo to bump into sthg, to go flat into sthg; de narices [estupendo] great, brilliant; estar hasta las narices (de algo) to be fed up to the back teeth (with sthg); me estás hinchando las narices you're beginning to get up my nose; meter las narices en algo to poke ○ stick one's nose into sthg; romper las narices a alguien to smash sb's face in; romperse las narices to fall flat on one's face.

narizotas *m y f inv fam* big-nose.

narración *f* **-1.** [cuento, relato] narrative, story. **-2.** [acción] narration.

narrador, -ra *m y f* narrator.

narrar *vt* [contar] to recount, to tell.

narrativo, -va *adj* narrative.
◆ **narrativa** *f* narrative.

Na S (*abrev de* **Nuestra Señora**) Our Lady.

NASA (*abrev de* **National Aeronautics and Space Administration**) *f* NASA.

nasal *adj* nasal.

nasalizar [13] *vt* to nasalize.

Nassau Nassau.

nata *f* **-1.** [gen & *fig*] cream; ~ batida ○ montada whipped cream. **-2.** [de leche hervida] skin.

natación *f* swimming.

natal *adj* [país] native; [ciudad, pueblo] home (*antes de sust*).

natalicio *m* [cumpleaños] birthday.

natalidad *f* birth rate.

natillas *fpl* custard (*U*).

natividad *f* nativity.
◆ **Natividad** *f*: la Natividad Christmas.

nativo, -va ◇ *adj, m y f* native.

nato, -ta *adj* [gen] born; [cargo, título] ex officio.

natura *f* nature; contra ~ against nature, unnatural.

natural ◇ *adj* **-1.** [gen] natural; [flores, fruta, leche] fresh; al ~ [persona] in one's natural state; [fruta] in its own juice; ser ~ en alguien to be natural ○ normal for sb. **-2.** [nativo] native; ser ~ de to come from. **-3.** [ilegítimo] illegitimate. ◇ *m y f* [nativo] native. ◇ *m* [talante] nature, disposition.

naturaleza *f* **-1.** [gen] nature; por ~ by nature; la madre ~ Mother Nature; ~ muerta still life. **-2.** [complexión] constitution.

naturalidad *f* naturalness; con ~ naturally.

naturalismo *m* naturalism.

naturalización *f* naturalization.

naturalizado, -da *adj* naturalized.

naturalizar [13] *vt* to naturalize.
◆ **naturalizarse** *vpr* to become naturalized.

naturismo *m way of life promoting return to nature.*

naturista *m y f person favouring return to nature.*

naturópata *m y f* naturopath.

naufragar [16] *vi* **-1.** [barco] to sink, to be wrecked; [persona] to be shipwrecked. **-2.** *fig* [fracasar] to fail, to collapse.

naufragio *m* **-1.** [de barco] shipwreck. **-2.** *fig* [fracaso] failure, collapse.

náufrago, -ga ◇ *adj* shipwrecked. ◇ *m y f* shipwrecked person, castaway.

náusea *f* (*gen pl*) nausea (*U*), sickness (*U*); me da ~s it makes me sick.

nauseabundo, -da *adj* nauseating, sickening.

náutico, -ca adj [gen] nautical; DEP water (antes de sust).
◆ **náutica** f navigation, seamanship.

navaja f -1. [cuchillo - pequeño] penknife; [- más grande] jackknife; ~ **de afeitar** razor. -2. [molusco] razor-shell, razor clam.

navajazo m stab, slash.

navajero, -ra m y f thug who carries a knife.

naval adj naval.

Navarra Navarre.

navarro, -rra adj, m y f Navarrese.

nave f -1. [barco] ship; **quemar las** ~**s** to burn one's boats O bridges. -2. [vehículo] craft; ~ **espacial** spaceship, spacecraft; ~ **extraterrestre** (extraterrestrial) spaceship. -3. [de fábrica] shop, plant; [almacén] warehouse. -4. [de iglesia] nave.

navegable adj navigable.

navegación f navigation; ~ **aérea/fluvial/ marítima** air/river/sea navigation; ~ **de altura** ocean navigation.

navegante ◇ adj sailing; [pueblo] seafaring. ◇ m y f navigator.

navegar [16] ◇ vi & vt [barco] to sail; [avión] to fly.

naveta f prehistoric burial monument on Menorca.

Navidad f -1. [día] Christmas (Day). -2. (gen pl) [periodo] Christmas (time); **felices Navidades** Merry Christmas.

navideño, -ña adj Christmas (antes de sust).

naviero, -ra adj shipping.
◆ **naviero** m [armador] shipowner.
◆ **naviera** f [compañía] shipping company.

navío m large ship.

nazareno, -na adj, m y f Nazarene.
◆ **nazareno** m penitent in Holy Week processions.
◆ **Nazareno** m: **el Nazareno** Jesus of Nazareth.

nazca etc → **nacer**.

nazi adj, m y f Nazi.

nazismo m Nazism.

NB (abrev de **nota bene**) NB.

NBA (abrev de **National Basketball Association**) f NBA.

NBC (abrev de **National Broadcasting Company**) f NBC.

neblina f mist.

nebulosidad f [de nubes] cloudiness; [de niebla] fogginess.

nebuloso, -sa adj -1. [con nubes] cloudy; [de niebla] foggy. -2. fig [idea, mirada] vague.
◆ **nebulosa** f ASTRON nebula.

necedad f -1. [estupidez] stupidity, foolishness. -2. [dicho, hecho] stupid O foolish thing; **decir necedades** to talk nonsense.

necesario, -ria adj necessary; **es** ~ **hacerlo** it needs to be done; **no es** ~ **que lo hagas** you don't need to do it; **si fuera** ~ if need be.

neceser m toilet bag O case.

necesidad f -1. [gen] need; **de (primera)** ~ essential; **obedecer a la** ~ **(de)** to arise from the need (to). -2. [obligación] necessity; **por** ~ out of necessity. -3. [hambre] hunger.
◆ **necesidades** fpl: **hacer (uno) sus** ~ eufemismo to answer the call of nature.

necesitado, -da ◇ adj needy; ~ **de** in need of. ◇ m y f needy O poor person; **los** ~**s** the poor.

necesitar vt to need; **necesito que me lo digas** I need you to tell me; **"se necesita piso"** "flat wanted".
◆ **necesitar de** vi to have need of.

necio, -cia ◇ adj stupid, foolish. ◇ m y f idiot, fool.

nécora f fiddler crab.

necrófago, -ga adj necrophagous.

necrofilia f necrophilia.

necrología f obituary; [lista de esquelas] obituaries (pl), obituary column.

necrológico, -ca adj obituary (antes de sust).

necrópolis f inv necropolis.

necrosis f inv necrosis.

néctar m nectar.

nectarina f nectarine.

nefando, -da adj abominable, odious.

nefasto, -ta adj [funesto] ill-fated; [dañino] bad, harmful; [pésimo] terrible, awful.

nefrítico, -ca adj nephritic.

nefrología f nephrology.

negación f -1. [desmentido] denial. -2. [negativa] refusal. -3. [lo contrario] antithesis, negation. -4. GRAM negative.

negado, -da ◇ adj useless, inept. ◇ m y f useless person, dead loss.

negar [35] vt -1. [rechazar] to deny. -2. [denegar] to refuse, to deny; ~**le algo a alguien** to refuse O deny sb sthg.
◆ **negarse** vpr: ~**se (a)** to refuse (to).

negativo, -va ◇ adj -1. [gen] negative. -2. MAT minus (antes de sust), negative.
◆ **negativo** m FOT negative.
◆ **negativa** f -1. [rechazo] refusal. -2. [mentís] denial.

negligé [neʒli'ʒe] m negligée.

negligencia f negligence.

negligente *adj* negligent.

negociable *adj* negotiable.

negociación *f* negotiation; ~ **colectiva** collective bargaining.

negociado *m* department, section.

negociador, -ra ◇ *adj* negotiating. ◇ *m y f* negotiator.

negociante *m y f* [comerciante] businessman (*f* businesswoman); ~ **en coches** car dealer; ~ **en vinos** wine merchant.

negociar [8] ◇ *vi* **-1.** [comerciar] to do business; ~ **en** to deal ⊙ trade in; ~ **con** to deal ⊙ trade with. **-2.** [discutir] to negotiate. ◇ *vt* to negotiate.

negocio *m* **-1.** [gen] business; **el mundo de los** ~**s** the business world. **-2.** [transacción] deal, (business) transaction; ~ **sucio** shady deal, dirty business (*U*). **-3.** [operación ventajosa] good deal, bargain; **hacer** ~ to do well; ~ **redondo** great bargain, excellent deal. **-4.** [comercio] trade.

negra → negro.

negrero, -ra ◇ *adj fig* [explotador] tyrannical. ◇ *m y f* **-1.** HIST slave trader. **-2.** *fig* [explotador] slave driver.

negrita, negrilla → letra.

negro, -gra ◇ *adj* **-1.** [gen] black. **-2.** [moreno] tanned. **-3.** [suerte] awful, rotten; [porvenir] black, gloomy; **pasarlas negras** to have a hard time. **-4.** [furioso] furious, fuming; **ponerse** ~ to get mad ⊙ angry. **-5.** CIN: **cine** ~ film noir. ◇ *m y f* black man (*f* black woman); **trabajar como un** ~ *fig* to work like a slave.

◆ **negro** *m* [color] black.

◆ **negra** *f* **-1.** MÚS crotchet. **-2.** *loc*: **tener la negra** to have bad luck.

negroide *adj* negroid.

negrura *f* blackness.

negruzco, -ca *adj* blackish.

negué *etc* → negar.

nemónico, -ca = mnemónico.

nemotecnia = mnemotecnia.

nene, -na *m y f* **-1.** *fam* [niño] baby. **-2.** [apelativo cariñoso] dear, darling.

nenúfar *m* water lily.

neocapitalismo *m* neocapitalism.

neocelandés, -esa, neozelandés, -esa ◇ *adj* New Zealand (*antes de sust*), of/relating to New Zealand. ◇ *m y f* New Zealander.

neoclasicismo *m* neoclassicism.

neoclásico, -ca ◇ *adj* neoclassical. ◇ *m y f* neoclassicist.

neofascismo *m* neofascism.

neofascista ◇ *adj, m y f* neofascist.

neófito, -ta *m y f* **-1.** RELIG neophyte. **-2.** [aprendiz] novice.

neogótico, -ca *adj* Neo-Gothic.

◆ **neogótico** *m* Neo-Gothic movement.

neolatino, -na *adj* [gen] Neo-Latin; [lengua] Romance.

neoliberalismo *m* neoliberalism.

neolítico, -ca *adj* Neolithic.

◆ **neolítico** *m* Neolithic (period).

neologismo *m* neologism.

neón *m* **-1.** QUÍM neon. **-2.** [luz] neon light.

neonato, -ta *adj culto* newborn.

neonazi *adj, m y f* neo-Nazi.

neoplasma *m* neoplasm, tumour.

neorrealismo *m* neorealism.

neoyorquino, -na ◇ *adj* New York (*antes de sust*), of/relating to New York. ◇ *m y f* New Yorker.

neozelandés, -esa = neocelandés.

Nepal: **el** ~ Nepal.

nepalés, -esa, nepalí (*pl* **nepalíes**) *adj, m y f* Nepalese.

◆ **nepalés, nepalí** *m* [lengua] Nepalese.

nepotismo *m* nepotism.

Neptuno Neptune.

nervio *m* **-1.** ANAT nerve; ~ **ciático** sciatic nerve. **-2.** [de carne] sinew. **-3.** BOT vein, rib. **-4.** [vigor] energy, vigour. **-5.** ARQUIT rib.

◆ **nervios** *mpl* [estado mental] nerves; **tener** ~**s** to be nervous; **poner los** ~**s de punta a alguien** to get on sb's nerves; **tener los** ~**s de punta** to be on edge; **tener** ~**s de acero** to have nerves of steel.

nerviosismo *m* nervousness, nerves (*pl*).

nervioso, -sa *adj* **-1.** [ANAT - sistema, enfermedad] nervous; [- tejido, célula, centro] nerve (*antes de sust*). **-2.** [inquieto] nervous; **ponerse** ~ to get nervous. **-3.** [muy activo] highly-strung. **-4.** [irritado] worked-up, uptight; **poner** ~ **a alguien** to get on sb's nerves; **ponerse** ~ to get uptight ⊙ worked up.

nervudo, -da *adj* sinewy.

neto, -ta *adj* **-1.** [claro] clear, clean; [verdad] simple, plain. **-2.** [peso, sueldo] net.

neumático, -ca *adj* pneumatic.

◆ **neumático** *m* tyre; ~ **de repuesto** spare tyre.

neumonía *f* pneumonia.

neuralgia *f* neuralgia.

neurálgico, -ca *adj* **-1.** MED neuralgic. **-2.** *fig* [importante] critical.

neurastenia *f* nervous exhaustion.

neurasténico, -ca MED ◇ *adj* neurasthenic. ◇ *m y f* neurasthenic person.

neurobiología *f* neurobiology.

neurocirugía f neurosurgery.

neurocirujano, -na m y f neurosurgeon.

neurofisiología f neurophysiology.

neurología f neurology.

neurológico, -ca adj neurological.

neurólogo, -ga m y f neurologist.

neurona f neuron, nerve cell.

neuropatía f neuropathy.

neuropsicología f neuropsychology.

neuropsiquiatría f neuropsychiatry.

neurosis f inv neurosis.

neurótico, -ca adj, m y f neurotic.

neurotransmisor m neurotransmitter.

neutral adj, m y f neutral.

neutralidad f neutrality.

neutralizable adj [efecto, consecuencia] remediable.

neutralización f neutralization.

neutralizador, -ra adj neutralizing.

neutralizar [13] vt to neutralize.

◆ **neutralizarse** vpr to neutralize each other.

neutro, -tra adj -1. [gen] neutral. -2. BIOL & GRAM neuter.

neutrón m neutron.

nevado, -da adj snowy.

◆ **nevada** f snowfall.

nevar [19] v impers to snow.

nevera f fridge Br, icebox Am.

nevisca f snow flurry.

neviscar [10] v impers to snow lightly.

newton ['niuton] m newton.

nexo m link, connection; [relación] relation, connection.

ni ◇ conj: ~ ... ~ ... neither ... nor ...; ~ mañana ~ pasado neither tomorrow nor the day after; **no** ... ~ ... neither ... nor ..., not ... or ... (either); **no es alto** ~ **bajo** he's neither tall nor short, he's not tall or short (either); **no es rojo** ~ **verde** ~ **azul** it's neither red nor green nor blue; ~ **un/una** ... not a single ...; **no me quedaré** ~ **un minuto más** I'm not staying a minute longer; ~ **uno/una** not a single one; **no he aprobado** ~ **una** I haven't passed a single one; ~ **que as if**; **¡~ que yo fuera tonto!** as if I were that stupid!
◇ adv not even; **anda tan atareado que** **tiene tiempo para comer** he's so busy he doesn't even have time to eat.

Niágara m: **las cataratas del** ~ the Niagara Falls.

Niamey Niamey.

Nicaragua Nicaragua.

nicaragüense adj, m y f Nicaraguan.

nicho m niche.

Nicosia Nicosia.

nicotina f nicotine.

nidada f [de críos] brood; [de huevos] clutch.

nidal m nest.

nidificar [10] vi to (build a) nest.

nido m -1. [gen] nest; ~ **de víboras** fig nest of vipers. -2. fig [escondrijo] hiding-place.

niebla f -1. [densa] fog; [neblina] mist; **hay** ~ it's foggy. -2. fig [confusión] fogginess, cloudiness.

niega etc → **negar**.

nieto, -ta m y f grandson (f granddaughter).

nieva etc → **nevar**.

nieve f -1. METEOR snow. -2. fam [cocaína] snow.
◆ **nieves** fpl [nevada] snows, snowfall (sg).
◆ **nieve carbónica** f carbon dioxide snow.

NIF (abrev de **número de identificación fiscal**) m ≃ National Insurance number Br, identification number for tax purposes.

Níger m Niger.

Nigeria Nigeria.

night-club ['naitklub] (pl **night-clubs**) m nightclub.

nigromancia f necromancy.

nigromante m y f necromancer.

nihilismo m nihilism.

Nilo m: **el** ~ the (river) Nile.

nilón = **nailon**.

nimbo m -1. METEOR nimbus. -2. [de astro, santo] halo, nimbus.

nimiedad f -1. [cualidad] insignificance, triviality. -2. [dicho, hecho] trifle.

nimio, -mia adj insignificant, trivial.

ninfa f nymph.

ninfómana ◇ adj f nymphomaniac. ◇ f nymphomaniac.

ninfomanía f nymphomania.

ninguno, -na ◇ adj (antes de sust masculino: **ningún**) no; **ninguna respuesta se dio** no answer was given; **no tengo ningún interés en hacerlo** I've no interest in doing it, I'm not at all interested in doing it; **no tengo ningún hijo/ninguna buena idea** I don't have any children/good ideas; **no tiene ninguna gracia** it's not funny. ◇ pron [cosa] none, not any; [persona] nobody, no one; ~ **funciona** none of them works; **no hay** ~ there aren't any, there are none; ~ **lo sabrá** no one ○ nobody will know; ~ **de** none of; ~ **de ellos** none of them; ~ **de los dos** neither of them.

niña → **niño**.

niñato, -ta *m y f* kid, baby.

niñería *f* **-1.** [cualidad] childishness (*U*). **-2.** *fig* [tontería] silly ○ childish thing.

niñero, -ra *adj* fond of children.
◆ **niñera** *f* nanny.

niñez *f* **-1.** [infancia] childhood. **-2.** *fig* [tontería] silly ○ childish thing.

niño, -ña ◇ *adj* young.
◇ *m y f* **-1.** [crío] child, boy (*f* girl); [bebé] baby; **los ~s** the children; **~ bien** *despec* spoilt brat; **~ probeta** test-tube baby; **~ prodigio** child prodigy; **~ de teta** ○ **pecho** tiny baby; **estar como un ~ con zapatos nuevos** to be as pleased as punch; **es culpa de la crisis - ¡qué crisis ni qué ~ muerto!** it's the fault of the recession - don't talk to me about recessions!; **ser el ~ bonito de alguien** to be sb's pet ○ blue-eyed boy. **-2.** [joven] young boy (*f* young girl).
◆ **niña** *f* [del ojo] pupil; **la niña de los ojos** *fig* the apple of one's eye.

nipón, -ona *adj, m y f* Japanese.

níquel *m* nickel.

niquelar *vt* to nickel-plate.

niqui *m* T-shirt.

nirvana *m* nirvana.

níspero *m* medlar.

nitidez *f* clarity; [de imágenes, colores] sharpness.

nítido, -da *adj* clear; [imágenes, colores] sharp.

nitratación *f* nitration.

nitrato *m* nitrate; **~ de Chile** Chile saltpetre, nitre.

nítrico, -ca *adj* nitric.

nitrificar [10] *vt* to nitrify.

nitrogenado, -da *adj* nitrogenous.

nitrógeno *m* nitrogen.

nitroglicerina *f* nitroglycerine.

nitroso, -sa *adj* nitrous.

nivel *m* **-1.** [gen] level; [altura] height; **al ~ de** level with; **al ~ del mar** at sea level. **-2.** [grado] level, standard; **al mismo ~ (que)** on a level ○ par (with); **a ~ europeo** at a European level; **~ mental** level of intelligence; **~ de vida** standard of living. **-3.** [herramienta] spirit level.

nivelación *f* **-1.** [allanamiento] levelling. **-2.** [equilibrio] levelling out, evening out.

nivelador, -ra *adj* levelling.
◆ **niveladora** *f* bulldozer.

nivelar *vt* **-1.** [allanar] to level. **-2.** [equilibrar] to even out; FIN to balance.

níveo, -a *adj culto* snow-white.

no ◇ *adv* **-1.** [expresa negación - gen] not; [- en respuestas] no; [- con sustantivos] non-;

~ sé I don't know; **~ veo nada** I can't see anything; **~ es fácil** it's not easy, it isn't easy; **~ tiene dinero** he has no money, he hasn't got any money; **todavía ~** not yet; **¿~ vienes? - ~, ~ creo** aren't you coming? - no, I don't think so; **~ fumadores** nonsmokers; **~ bien** as soon as; **~ ya ... sino que ...** not only ... but (also) ...; **¡a que ~ lo haces!** I bet you don't do it!; **¿cómo ~?** of course; **pues ~, eso sí que ~** certainly not; **¡que ~!** I said no! **-2.** [expresa duda, extrañeza]: **¿~ irás a venir?** you're not coming, are you?; **estamos de acuerdo, ¿~?** we're agreed then, are we?; **es español, ¿~?** he's Spanish, isn't he?
◇ *m* no.

n.º (*abrev de* **número**) no.

nobiliario, -ria *adj* noble, nobiliary.
◆ **nobiliario** *m* [libro] ≃ Debretts' Peerage.

noble *adj, m y f* noble; **los ~s** the nobility.

nobleza *f* nobility.

noche *f* night; [atardecer] evening; **ayer por la ~** last night; **esta ~** tonight; **hacerse ~ en** to stay the night in; **hacerse de ~** to get dark; **pasar la ~ en claro** ○ **vela** to have a sleepless night; **por la ~, de ~** at night; **buenas ~s** [despedida] good night; [saludo] good evening; **de la ~ a la mañana** overnight; **ser la ~ y el día** to be as different as night and day.

Nochebuena *f* Christmas Eve.

nochero *m Amer* **-1.** [vigilante] night watchman. **-2.** [mesita] bedside table.

Nochevieja *f* New Year's Eve.

noción *f* [concepto] notion; **tener ~ (de)** to have an idea (of).
◆ **nociones** *fpl* [conocimiento básico] **tener nociones de** to have a smattering of.

nocividad *f* [gen] harmfulness; [de gas] noxiousness.

nocivo, -va *adj* [gen] harmful; [gas] noxious.

noctambulismo *m* being out and about at night.

noctámbulo, -la ◇ *adj* active at night; [vida] night (*antes de sust*). ◇ *m y f* night owl.

nocturnidad *f* DER: **con ~** under cover of darkness.

nocturno, -na *adj* **-1.** [club, tren, vuelo] night (*antes de sust*); [clase] evening (*antes de sust*). **-2.** [animales, plantas] nocturnal.
◆ **nocturno** *m* MÚS nocturne.

nodo *m* node.

nodriza *f* wet nurse.

nódulo *m* nodule.

Noel → **papá.**

nogal *m* walnut.

nómada ◇ *adj* nomadic. ◇ *m y f* nomad.

nomadismo *m* nomadism.

nombrado, -da *adj* **-1.** [citado] mentioned. **-2.** [famoso] famous, well-known.

nombramiento *m* appointment.

nombrar *vt* **-1.** [citar] to mention. **-2.** [designar] to appoint.

nombre *m* **-1.** [gen] name; **a ~ de** [carta] addressed to; [cheque] made out to; **de ~ Juan** called Juan, Juan by name; **~ artístico/comercial** stage/trade name; **~ y apellidos** full name; **~ compuesto** compound name; **~ de pila** first O Christian name; **~ de soltera** maiden name; **en ~ de** on behalf of; **llamar a las cosas por su ~** to call a spade a spade; **no tener ~** *fig* to be unspeakable. **-2.** [fama] reputation; **tener mucho ~** to be renowned O famous. **-3.** GRAM noun; **~ abstracto/colectivo** abstract/collective noun; **~ común/propio** common/proper noun.

nomenclátor *m* catalogue of names.

nomenclatura *f* nomenclature.

nomeolvides *m inv* **-1.** BOT forget-me-not. **-2.** [pulsera] identity bracelet.

nómina *f* **-1.** [lista de empleados] payroll; **estar en ~** to be on the staff. **-2.** [pago] wage packet, wages (*pl*). **-3.** [hoja de salario] payslip.

nominación *f* nomination.

nominado, -da *adj* nominated.

nominal *adj* nominal.

nominar *vt* to nominate.

nominativo, -va *adj* COM bearing a person's name, nominal.

◆ **nominativo** *m* GRAM nominative.

nomo, gnomo *m* gnome.

non ◇ *adj* odd, uneven. ◇ *m* odd number.

◆ **nones** *adv* [no] no way, absolutely not.

nonagenario, -ria ◇ *adj* ninety-year old. ◇ *m y f* person in his/her nineties.

nonagésimo, -ma *núm* ninetieth.

nono, -na *núm culto* ninth.

noquear *vt* DEP to knock out.

nordeste = noreste.

nórdico, -ca ◇ *adj* **-1.** [del norte] northern, northerly. **-2.** [escandinavo] Nordic. ◇ *m y f* Nordic person.

noreste, nordeste ◇ *adj* [posición, parte] northeast, northeastern; [dirección, viento] northeasterly. ◇ *m* north-east.

noria *f* **-1.** [para agua] water wheel. **-2.** [de feria] big wheel *Br*, Ferris wheel.

norma *f* standard; [regla] rule; **es la ~ hacerlo así** it's usual to do it this way; **por ~** as a rule; **~ de conducta** [principios] standards (of behaviour) (*pl*); [pauta] pattern of behaviour.

normal *adj* normal.

normalidad *f* normality.

normalización *f* **-1.** [vuelta a la normalidad] normalization. **-2.** [regularización] standardization.

normalizar [13] *vt* **-1.** [volver normal] to return to normal. **-2.** [estandarizar] to standardize.

◆ **normalizarse** *vpr* to return to normal.

normando, -da ◇ *adj* **-1.** [de Normandía] Norman. **-2.** HIST [nórdico] Norse. ◇ *m y f* **-1.** [habitante de Normandía] Norman. **-2.** HIST [nórdico] Norseman (*f* Norsewoman).

normativo, -va *adj* normative.

◆ **normativa** *f* regulations (*pl*).

noroeste ◇ *adj* [posición, parte] northwest, northwestern; [dirección, viento] northwesterly. ◇ *m* northwest.

norte ◇ *adj* [posición, parte] north, northern; [dirección, viento] northerly. ◇ *m* **-1.** GEOGR north. **-2.** [objetivo] goal, objective; **perder el ~** to lose one's bearings O way.

norteamericano, -na *adj, m y f* North American, American.

norteño, -ña ◇ *adj* northern. ◇ *m y f* northerner.

Noruega Norway.

noruego, -ga *adj, m y f* Norwegian.

◆ **noruego** *m* [lengua] Norwegian.

nos *pron pers* **-1.** (*complemento directo*) us; **le gustaría vernos** she'd like to see us. **-2.** (*complemento indirecto*) (to) us; **~ lo dio** he gave it to us; **~ tiene miedo** he's afraid of us. **-3.** (*reflexivo*) ourselves. **-4.** (*recíproco*) each other; **~ enamoramos** we fell in love (with each other).

nosocomio *m Amer* hospital.

nosotros, -tras *pron pers* **-1.** (*sujeto*) we. **-2.** (*predicado*): **somos ~** it's us. **-3.** (*después de prep*) (*complemento*) us; **vente a comer con ~** come and eat with us. **-4.** *loc*: **entre ~** between you and me, just between the two of us.

nostalgia *f* [del pasado] nostalgia; [de país, amigos] homesickness.

nostálgico, -ca ◇ *adj* [del pasado] nostalgic; [de país, amigos] homesick. ◇ *m y f* nostalgic person.

nota *f* **-1.** [gen & MÚS] note; **tomar ~ de algo** [apuntar] to note sthg down; [fijarse] to take note of sthg; **~ a pie de página** footnote; **~ dominante** prevailing mood; **~s de sociedad** society column (*sg*). **-2.** EDUC mark; **ir para ~** to go for top marks; **sacar**

○ **tener buenas** ~s to get good marks; ~ **de corte** *minimum marks for entry into university*. **-3.** [cuenta] bill; ~ **de gastos** expenses claim. **-4.** *loc:* **dar la** ~ to make o.s. conspicuous; **de mala** ~ of ill repute; **forzar la** ~ to go too far.

◆ **nota bene** *f* [correspondencia] nota bene, N.B.

notable ◇ *adj* remarkable, outstanding. ◇ *m* **-1.** EDUC merit, second class. **-2.** (*gen pl*) [persona] notable, distinguished person.

notar *vt* **-1.** [advertir] to notice; **te noto cansado** you look tired to me; **hacer** ~ **algo** to point sthg out. **-2.** [sentir] to feel.

◆ **notarse** *vpr* to be apparent; **se nota que le gusta** you can tell she likes it; **¡pues no se nota!** you could have fooled me!

notaría *f* **-1.** [profesión] profession of notary. **-2.** [oficina] notary's office.

notariado *m* [profesión] profession of notary.

notarial *adj* notarial.

notario, -ria *m y f* notary (public).

noticia *f* news (*U*); **una** ~ a piece of news; **tener** ~s to have news; **¿tienes** ~s **suyas?** have you heard from him?

◆ **noticias** *fpl:* **las** ~s RADIO & TV the news.

noticiario, noticiero *m* CIN newsreel; RADIO & TV news bulletin.

notición *m fam* bombshell.

notificación *f* notification.

notificar [10] *vt* to notify, to inform.

notoriedad *f* **-1.** [fama] fame. **-2.** [evidencia] obviousness.

notorio, -ria *adj* **-1.** [evidente] obvious. **-2.** [conocido] widely-known.

nov., novbre. (*abrev de* **noviembre**) Nov.

novatada *f* **-1.** [broma] ragging (*U*). **-2.** [error] beginner's mistake; **pagar la** ~ to learn the hard way.

novato, -ta ◇ *adj* inexperienced. ◇ *m y f* novice, beginner.

novecientos, -tas *núm* nine hundred; *ver también* **seis**.

novedad *f* **-1.** [cualidad - de nuevo] newness; [- de novedoso] novelty. **-2.** [cambio] change. **-3.** [noticia] news (*U*); **sin** ~ without incident; MIL all quiet. **-4.** [cosa nueva] new thing; [innovación] innovation.

◆ **novedades** *fpl* [libros, discos] new releases; [moda] latest fashion (*sg*).

novedoso, -sa *adj* novel, new.

novel *adj* new, first-time.

novela *f* novel; ~ **de caballerías** tales of chivalry (*pl*); ~ **por entregas** serial; ~ **policíaca** detective story; ~ **rosa** romance, romantic novel.

novelar *vt* to fictionalize, to make into a novel.

novelero, -ra ◇ *adj* **-1.** [fantasioso] very imaginative. **-2.** [aficionado a las novelas] fond of novels. ◇ *m y f* **-1.** [fantasioso] very imaginative person. **-2.** [aficionado a las novelas] person fond of novels.

novelesco, -ca *adj* **-1.** [de la novela] fictional. **-2.** [fantástico] fantastic, extraordinary.

novelista *m y f* novelist.

novelón *m fam* hefty and badly written novel.

noveno, -na *núm* ninth; **la novena parte** a ninth.

◆ **novena** *f* RELIG novena.

noventa *núm* ninety; **los (años)** ~ the nineties; *ver también* **seis**.

noviar [8] *vi Amer* to go out.

noviazgo *m* engagement.

noviciado *m* RELIG novitiate; *fig* [aprendizaje] apprenticeship.

novicio, -cia RELIG & *fig* ◇ *adj* novice (*antes de sust*). ◇ *m y f* novice.

noviembre *m* November; *ver también* **septiembre**.

novillada *f* TAUROM bullfight with young bulls.

novillero, -ra *m y f* TAUROM apprentice bullfighter.

novillo, -lla *m y f* young bull or cow; **hacer** ~s *fam* to play truant *Br*, to play hooky *Am*.

novio, -via *m y f* **-1.** [antes de la boda - amigo] boyfriend (*f* girlfriend); [- prometido] fiancé (*f* fiancée). **-2.** [recién casado] bridegroom (*f* bride); **los** ~s the newly-weds.

novocaína *f* FARM Novocaine®.

NS (*abrev de* **Nuestro Señor**) Our Lord.

NSJC (*abrev de* **Nuestro Señor Jesucristo**) Our Lord Jesus Christ.

ntro. *abrev de* **nuestro**.

nubarrón *m* storm cloud.

nube *f* **-1.** [gen & *fig*] cloud; ~ **de verano** *fig* short fit of anger; **caído de las** ~s out of the blue; **estar en las** ~s *fig* to have one's head in the clouds; **poner algo/a alguien por las** ~s *fig* to praise sthg/sb to the skies; **por las** ~s [caro] sky-high, terribly expensive. **-2.** [de personas, moscas] swarm.

núbil *adj culto* nubile.

nublado, -da *adj* **-1.** [encapotado] cloudy, overcast. **-2.** *fig* [turbado] clouded, darkened.

nublar *vt lit* & *fig* to cloud.

◆ **nublarse** *vpr* **-1.** [suj: cielo] to cloud over. **-2.** *fig* [turbarse, oscurecerse] to become clouded.

nubloso, -sa *adj* cloudy.
nubosidad *f* cloudiness, clouds (*pl*).
nuboso, -sa *adj* cloudy.
nuca *f* nape, back of the neck.
nuclear *adj* nuclear.
nuclearización *f* IND introduction of nuclear power; MIL acquisition of nuclear weapons.
nuclearizar [13] *vt* IND to introduce nuclear power into; MIL to acquire nuclear weapons for.
núcleo *m* **-1.** [centro] nucleus; *fig* centre. **-2.** [grupo] core.
nucléolo *m* nucleolus.
nudillo *m* knuckle.
nudismo *m* nudism.
nudista *adj, m y f* nudist.
nudo *m* **-1.** [gen] knot; ~ **corredizo** slipknot; **se le hizo un ~ en la garganta** she got a lump in her throat. **-2.** [cruce] junction; ~ **de comunicaciones** communications centre. **-3.** *fig* [vínculo] tie, bond. **-4.** *fig* [punto principal] crux, nub. **-5.** [de una planta] node.
nudopropiedad *f* DER bare legal title.
nudopropietario, -ria *m y f* DER remainder man (*f* remainder woman).
nudosidad *f* MED nodosity.
nudoso, -sa *adj* knotty, gnarled.
nuera *f* daughter-in-law.
nuestro, -tra ◇ *adj poses* our; ~ **coche** our car; **este libro es** ~ this book is ours, this is our book; **un amigo** ~ a friend of ours; **no es asunto** ~ it's none of our business. ◇ *pron poses*: **el** ~ ours; **el** ~ **es rojo** ours is red; **esta es la nuestra** *fam* this is the chance we have been waiting for; **lo** ~ **es el teatro** [lo que nos va] theatre is what we should be doing; **los** ~**s** *fam* [nuestra familia] our folks; [nuestro bando] our lot, our side.
nueva → **nuevo**.
Nueva Delhi New Delhi.
Nueva York New York.
Nueva Zelanda New Zealand.
nueve *núm* nine; *ver también* **seis**.
nuevo, -va ◇ *adj* [gen] new; [patatas, legumbres] new, fresh; [vino] young; **ser** ~ **en** to be new to; **estar/quedar como** ~ to be as good as new. ◇ *m y f* newcomer.
◆ **buena nueva** *f* good news (U).
◆ **de nuevo** *loc adv* again.
nuez *f* **-1.** BOT [gen] nut; [de nogal] walnut. **-2.** ANAT Adam's apple.
◆ **nuez moscada** *f* nutmeg.
nulidad *f* **-1.** [no validez] nullity. **-2.** [inepti-tud] incompetence. **-3.** *fam* [persona] nonentity; **ser una** ~ to be useless.
nulo, -la *adj* **-1.** [sin validez] null and void, invalid. **-2.** *fam* [incapacitado]: ~ **(para)** useless (at).
núm. (*abrev de* **número**) No.
numen *m culto* inspiration, muse.
numeración *f* **-1.** [acción] numbering. **-2.** [sistema] numerals (*pl*), numbers (*pl*); ~ **arábiga** ○ **decimal** Arabic numerals; ~ **binaria** binary numbers (*pl*); ~ **romana** Roman numerals.
numerador *m* MAT numerator.
numeral *adj* numeral.
numerar *vt* to number.
◆ **numerarse** *vpr* [suj: personas] to number off.
numerario, -ria *adj* [profesor, catedrático] tenured, permanent; [miembro] full.
numérico, -ca *adj* numerical.
número *m* **-1.** [gen] number; **sin** ~ [muchos] countless, innumerable; ~ **abstracto** abstract number; ~ **cardinal/ordinal** cardinal/ordinal number; ~ **complejo/irracional** complex/irrational number; ~ **complementario** complementary number; ~ **de matrícula** AUTOM registration number; ~ **dígito** digit; ~ **entero** whole number, integer; ~ **fraccionario** ○ **quebrado** fraction; ~ **par/impar** even/odd number; ~ **primo** prime number; ~ **redondo** round number; ~ **romano** Roman numeral; **en** ~**s rojos** in the red; **hacer** ~**s** to reckon up; **ser el** ~ **uno** to be number one. **-2.** [tamaño, talla] size. **-3.** [de publicación] issue, number; ~ **atrasado** back number. **-4.** [de lotería] ticket. **-5.** MIL member. **-6.** [de un espectáculo] turn, number; **montar el** ~ *fam* to make ○ cause a scene.
◆ **número atómico** *m* QUÍM atomic number.
numeroso, -sa *adj* numerous; **un grupo** ~ a large group.
numerus clausus ['numerus 'klausus] *m restricted number of places on university course.*
numismático, -ca ◇ *adj* numismatic. ◇ *m y f* [persona] numismatist.
◆ **numismática** *f* [estudio] numismatics (U).
nunca *adv* (*en frases afirmativas*) never; (*en frases negativas*) ever; **casi** ~ **viene** he almost never comes, he hardly ever comes; ¿~ **le has visto?** have you never seen her?, haven't you ever seen her?; **más que** ~ more than ever; ~ **jamás** ○ **más** never more ○ again.
nunciatura *f* **-1.** [cargo] nunciature. **-2.**

[edificio] **nuncio's residence. -3.** [tribunal de Rota] *ecclesiastical court in Spain*.

nuncio *m* nuncio.

nupcial *adj* wedding (*antes de sust*).

nupcias *fpl* wedding (*sg*), nuptials.

nurse ['nurse] *f* nurse, nanny.

nutria *f* otter.

nutrición *f* nutrition.

nutrido, -da *adj* **-1.** [alimentado] nourished. fed; **mal** ~ undernourished. **-2.** [numeroso] large.

nutrir *vt* **-1.** [alimentar]: ~ **(con** ○ **de)** to nourish ○ feed (with). **-2.** *fig* [fomentar] to feed, to nurture. **-3.** *fig* [suministrar]: ~ **(de)** to supply (with).

◆ **nutrirse** *vpr* **-1.** [gen]: ~se de ○ con to feed on. **-2.** *fig* [proveerse]: ~se de ○ con to supply ○ provide o.s. with.

nutritivo, -va *adj* nutritious.

NY (*abrev de* **Nueva York**) *f* NY.

nylon® ['nailon] = **nailon**.

ñ, Ñ *f* [letra] ñ, Ñ, *15th letter of the Spanish alphabet*.

ñato, -ta *adj Amer* snub.

ñoñería, ñoñez *f* inanity, insipidness (*U*).

ñoño, -ña *adj* **-1.** [remilgado] squeamish; [quejica] whining. **-2.** [soso] dull, insipid.

ñoqui *m* (*gen pl*) CULIN gnocchi (*pl*).

ñu *m* gnu.

ñudo *Amer*

◆ **al ñudo** *loc adv* in vain.

o¹, O *f* [letra] o, O.

o² *conj* ("u" *en vez de* "o" *antes de palabras que empiezan por* "o" *u* "ho") or; ~ ... ~ either ... or; ~ **sea (que)** in other words.

o/ *abrev de* **orden**.

OACI (*abrev de* **Organización de la Aviación Civil Internacional**) *f* ICAO.

oasis *m inv lit* & *fig* oasis.

obcecación *f* blindness, stubbornness.

obcecado, -da *adj* **-1.** [tozudo] stubborn. **-2.** [obsesionado]: ~ **por** ○ **con** blinded by.

obcecar [10] *vt* to blind.

◆ **obcecarse** *vpr* to become stubborn; ~se en hacer algo to insist on doing sthg.

obedecer [30] ◇ *vt*: ~ **(a alguien)** to obey (sb). ◇ *vi* **-1.** [acatar] to obey, to do as one is told. **-2.** [someterse]: ~ **a** to respond to. **-3.** [estar motivado]: ~ **a** to be due to.

obediencia *f* obedience.

obediente *adj* obedient.

obelisco *m* obelisk.

obenque *m* NÁUT shroud.

obertura *f* overture.

obesidad *f* obesity.

obeso, -sa ◇ *adj* obese. ◇ *m y f* obese person.

óbice *m*: no ser ~ para not to be an obstacle to.

obispado *m* bishopric.

obispo *m* bishop.

óbito *m culto* decease, demise.

obituario *m* obituary.

objeción *f* objection; **poner objeciones a** to raise objections to; **tener objeciones** to have objections; ~ **de conciencia** conscientious objection.

objetar ◇ *vt* to object to; **no tengo nada que** ~ I have no objection. ◇ *vi* MIL to be a conscientious objector.

objetivar *vt* to treat objectively.

objetividad *f* objectivity.

objetivo, -va *adj* objective.

◆ **objetivo** *m* **-1.** [finalidad] objective, aim. **-2.** MIL target. **-3.** FOT lens.

objeto *m* **-1.** [gen] object; **ser** ~ **de** to be the object of; **~s de valor** valuables; **~s perdidos** lost property (*U*). **-2.** [propósito] purpose, object; **sin** ~ [inútilmente] to no purpose, pointlessly; **al** ○ **con** ~ **de** [para] in order to, with the aim of.

objetor, -ra *m y f* objector; ~ **de conciencia** conscientious objector.

oblación *f* oblation.

oblicuidad *f* oblique angle, obliqueness.

oblicuo, -cua *adj* **-1.** [inclinado] oblique, slanting; [mirada] sidelong. **-2.** GEOM oblique.

obligación *f* **-1.** [gen] obligation, duty; **por** ~ out of a sense of duty. **-2.** FIN (*gen pl*) bond, security; ~ **convertible** convertible bond; ~ **del Estado** Treasury bond.

obligacionista *m y f* COM bondholder.

obligado, -da *adj* obligatory, compulsory.

obligar [16] *vt*: ~ **a alguien (a hacer algo)** to oblige ○ force sb (to do sthg).

◆ **obligarse** *vpr*: **~se a hacer algo** to undertake to do sthg.

obligatoriedad *f* obligatory ○ compulsory nature.

obligatorio, -ria *adj* obligatory, compulsory.

obligue *etc* → **obligar**.

obliterar *vt* MED to obliterate.

oblongo, -ga *adj* oblong.

obnubilación *f* bewilderment.

obnubilar *vt* to bewilder, to daze.

oboe ◇ *m* [instrumento] oboe. ◇ *m y f* [persona] oboist.

óbolo *m* small contribution.

obra *f* **-1.** [gen] work (*U*); **es** ~ **suya** it's his doing; **poner en** ~ to put into effect; ~ **de caridad** [institución] charity; **~s sociales** community work (*U*); **por** ~ **(y gracia) de** thanks to. **-2.** ARTE work (of art); TEATR play; LITER book; MÚS opus; ~ **maestra** masterpiece; **~s completas** complete works. **-3.** CONSTR [lugar] building site; [reforma] alteration; **"cerrado por ~s"** "closed for alterations"; **"~s"** [en carretera] "roadworks"; **~s públicas** public works.

obrador *m* workshop.

obrar ◇ *vi* **-1.** [actuar] to act. **-2.** [causar efecto] to work, to take effect. **-3.** [estar en poder]: ~ **en manos de** to be in the possession of. ◇ *vt* to work.

obrero, -ra ◇ *adj* [clase] working; [movimiento] labour (*antes de sust*). ◇ *m y f* [en fábrica] worker; [en obra] workman, labourer; ~ **cualificado** skilled worker.

obscenidad *f* obscenity.

obsceno, -na *adj* obscene.

obscurantismo = oscurantismo.

obscurecer [30] = oscurecer.

obscuridad = oscuridad.

obscuro, -ra = oscuro.

obsequiar [8] *vt*: ~ **a alguien con algo** to present sb with sthg.

obsequio *m* gift, present; ~ **de empresa** complimentary gift.

obsequiosidad *f* attentiveness, helpfulness.

obsequioso, -sa *adj* obliging, attentive.

observación *f* **-1.** [gen] observation. **-2.** [nota] note. **-3.** [cumplimiento] observance.

observador, -ra ◇ *adj* observant. ◇ *m y f* observer.

observancia *f* observance.

observar *vt* **-1.** [contemplar] to observe, to watch. **-2.** [advertir] to notice, to observe. **-3.** [acatar - ley, normas] to observe, to respect; [- conducta, costumbre] to follow.

◆ **observarse** *vpr* to be noticed.

observatorio *m* observatory.

obsesión *f* obsession.

obsesionar *vt* to obsess.

◆ **obsesionarse** *vpr* to be obsessed.

obsesivo, -va *adj* obsessive.

obseso, -sa ◇ *adj* obsessed. ◇ *m y f* obsessed ○ obsessive person.

obsoleto, -ta *adj culto* obsolete.

obstaculizar [13] *vt* to hinder, to hamper.

obstáculo *m* obstacle; **un** ~ **para** an obstacle to; **poner ~s a algo/alguien** to hinder sthg/sb.

obstante

◆ **no obstante** *loc adv* nevertheless, however.

obstar *vi*: **eso no obsta para que vengas si quieres** that isn't to say that you can't come if you want to.

obstetricia *f* obstetrics (*U*).

obstinación *f* [persistencia] perseverence; [terquedad] obstinacy, stubbornness.

obstinado, -da *adj* [persistente] persistent; [terco] obstinate, stubborn.

obstinarse *vpr* to refuse to give way; ~ **en** to persist in.

obstrucción *f lit* & *fig* obstruction.

obstruccionismo *m* obstructionism, stonewalling.

obstruccionista *adj, m y f* obstructionist.

obstruir [51] *vt* **-1.** [bloquear] to block, to obstruct. **-2.** [obstaculizar] to obstruct, to impede.

◆ **obstruirse** *vpr* to get blocked (up).

obtención *f* obtaining.

obtener [72] *vt* [beca, cargo, puntos] to get; [premio, victoria] to win; [ganancias] to make; [satisfacción] to gain.

obturación *f* blockage, obstruction.

obturador *m* FOT shutter.

obturar *vt* to block.

obtuso, -sa ◇ *adj* **-1.** [sin punta] blunt. **-2.** *fig* [tonto] obtuse, stupid. ◇ *m y f fig* dimwit.

obtuviera *etc* → obtener.

obús (*pl* **obuses**) *m* **-1.** [cañón] howitzer. **-2.** [proyectil] shell.

obviar [8] *vt* to avoid, to get round.

obvio, -via *adj* obvious.

oca *f* **-1.** [animal] goose. **-2.** [juego] ≃ snakes and ladders.

ocasión *f* **-1.** [oportunidad] opportunity, chance; **tener ~ de hacer algo** to have the chance to do sthg; **la ~ la pintan calva** *fam* this is my/your *etc* big chance. **-2.** [momento] moment, time; [vez] occasion; **en dos ocasiones** on two occasions; **en alguna ~** sometimes; **en cierta ~** once; **en otra ~** some other time. **-3.** [motivo]: **con ~ de** on the occasion of; **dar ~ para algo/hacer algo** to give cause for sthg/to do sthg. **-4.** [ganga] bargain; **de ~** [precio, artículos etc] bargain (*antes de sust*).

ocasional *adj* **-1.** [accidental] accidental. **-2.** [irregular] occasional.

ocasionar *vt* to cause.

ocaso *m* **-1.** [puesta del sol] sunset. **-2.** *fig* [decadencia] decline.

occidental ◇ *adj* western. ◇ *m y f* westerner.

occidentalismo *m* western nature.

occidentalizar [13] *vt* to westernize.

◆ **occidentalizarse** *vpr* to become westernized.

occidente *m* west.

◆ **Occidente** *m* [bloque de países] the West.

occipital *adj* occipital.

OCDE (*abrev de* **Organización para la Cooperación y el Desarrollo Económico**) *f* OECD.

Oceanía Oceania.

oceánico, -ca *adj* **-1.** [de un océano] oceanic. **-2.** [de Oceanía] Oceanian.

océano *m* ocean; *fig* [inmensidad] sea, host.

oceanografía *f* oceanography.

oceanográfico, -ca *adj* oceanographical.

ochenta *núm* eighty; **los (años) ~** the eighties; *ver también* **seis**.

ocho *núm* eight; **de aquí en ~ días** [en una semana] a week today; *ver también* **seis**.

ochocientos, -tas *núm* eight hundred; *ver también* **seis**.

ocio *m* [tiempo libre] leisure; [inactividad] idleness.

ociosidad *f* idleness.

ocioso, -sa *adj* **-1.** [inactivo] idle. **-2.** [innecesario] unnecessary; [inútil] pointless.

oclusión *f* blockage.

oclusivo, -va *adj* occlusive.

◆ **oclusiva** *f* occlusive.

ocre ◇ *m* ochre. ◇ *adj inv* ochre.

octaedro *m* octahedron.

octagonal *adj* octagonal.

octágono, -na *adj* octagonal.

◆ **octágono** *m* octagon.

octanaje *m* octane number.

octano *m* octane.

octava *f* → octavo.

octavilla *f* **-1.** [de propaganda política] pamphlet, leaflet. **-2.** [tamaño] octavo.

octavo, -va *núm* eighth; **la octava parte** an eighth.

◆ **octavo** *m* **-1.** [parte] eighth. **-2.** DEP: **~s de final** *round before the quarter final*.

◆ **octava** *f* MÚS octave.

octeto *m* **-1.** MÚS octet. **-2.** INFORM byte.

octogenario, -ria *adj, m y f* octogenarian.

octogésimo, -ma *núm* eightieth.

octogonal *adj* octagonal.

octubre *m* October; *ver también* **septiembre**.

OCU (*abrev de* **Organización de Consumidores y Usuarios**) *f Spanish consumer organization*, ≃ CAB *Br*.

ocular *adj* eye (*antes de sust*).

oculista *m y f* ophthalmologist.

ocultar *vt* **-1.** [gen] to hide; **~ algo a alguien** to hide sthg from sb. **-2.** *fig* [delito] to cover up.

◆ **ocultarse** *vpr* to hide.

ocultismo *m* occultism.

ocultista *m y f* occultist.

oculto, -ta *adj* hidden.

ocupación *f* **-1.** [gen] occupation; **~ ilegal de viviendas** squatting. **-2.** [empleo] job.

ocupacional *adj* occupational.

ocupado, -da *adj* **-1.** [persona] busy. **-2.** [teléfono, lavabo etc] engaged. **-3.** [lugar - gen, por ejército] occupied; [plaza] taken; **tengo las manos ocupadas** I've got my hands full.

ocupante ◇ *adj* occupying. ◇ *m y f* ocupant; **~ ilegal de viviendas** squatter.

ocupar *vt* **-1.** [gen] to occupy. **-2.** [superficie, espacio] to take up; [habitación, piso] to live in; [mesa] to sit at; [sillón] to sit in. **-3.** [suj: actividad] to take up. **-4.** [cargo] to hold.

-5. [dar trabajo a] to find o provide work for.

◆ **ocuparse** *vpr* [encargarse]: **ocúpate tú, yo no puedo** you do it, I can't; ~**se de** [gen] to deal with; [niños, enfermos, finanzas] to look after; **¡tú ocúpate de lo tuyo!** mind your own business!

ocurrencia *f* **-1.** [idea] bright idea. **-2.** [dicho gracioso] witty remark.

ocurrente *adj* witty.

ocurrir *vi* **-1.** [acontecer] to happen. **-2.** [pasar, preocupar]: **¿qué le ocurre a Juan?** what's up with Juan?; **¿te ocurre algo?** is anything the matter?

◆ **ocurrirse** *vpr* [venir a la cabeza]: **no se me ocurre ninguna solución** I can't think of a solution; **¡ni se te ocurra!** don't even think about it!; **se me ocurre que ...** it occurs to me that ....

oda *f* ode.

odalisca *f* odalisque.

ODECA (*abrev de* **Organización de Estados Centroamericanos**) *f* OCAS.

odeón *m* odeon.

odiar [8] *vt & vi* to hate.

odio *m* hatred; **tener** ~ **a algo/alguien** to hate sthg/sb.

odioso, -sa *adj* hateful, horrible.

odisea *f* odyssey.

odontología *f* dentistry.

odontólogo, -ga *m y f* dentist, dental surgeon.

odre *m* [de vino] wineskin.

OEA (*abrev de* **Organización de Estados Americanos**) *f* OAS.

oeste ◇ *adj* [posición, parte] west, western; [dirección, viento] westerly. ◇ *m* west; **el lejano** ~ the wild west.

ofender ◇ *vt* **-1.** [injuriar] to insult; [suj: palabras] to offend, to hurt. **-2.** [a la vista, al oído etc] to offend. ◇ *vi* to cause offence.

◆ **ofenderse** *vpr*: ~**se (por)** to take offence (at).

ofendido, -da ◇ *adj* offended. ◇ *m y f* offended party.

ofensa *f* **-1.** [acción]: ~ **(a)** offence (against). **-2.** [injuria] slight, insult.

ofensivo, -va *adj* offensive.

◆ **ofensiva** *f* offensive; **pasar a la** ~ to go on the offensive.

ofensor, -ra *m y f* offender.

oferta *f* **-1.** [gen] offer; **"~s de trabajo"** "situations vacant". **-2.** ECON [suministro] supply; **la** ~ **y la demanda** supply and demand; ~ **monetaria** money supply. **-3.** [rebaja] bargain, special offer; **de** ~ bargain (*antes de sust*), on offer. **-4.** FIN [proposición]

bid, tender; ~ **pública de adquisición** COM takeover bid.

ofertar *vt* to offer.

ofertorio *m* RELIG offertory.

office ['ofis] *m inv* scullery.

oficial, -la *m y f* [obrero] journeyman; [aprendiz] trainee.

◆ **oficial** ◇ *adj* official. ◇ *m* **-1.** MIL officer. **-2.** [funcionario] clerk.

oficialidad *f* official nature.

oficialismo *m Amer* [gobierno]: **el** ~ the Government.

oficializar [13] *vt* to make official.

oficiante *m y f* RELIG officiant.

oficiar [8] ◇ *vt* to officiate at. ◇ *vi* **-1.** [sacerdote] to officiate. **-2.** [actuar de]: ~ **de** to act as.

oficina *f* office; ~ **de correos** post office; ~ **de empleo** job centre; ~ **de turismo** tourist office; ~ **inteligente** INFORM intelligent office.

oficinista *m y f* office worker.

oficio *m* **-1.** [profesión manual] trade; **de** ~ by trade. **-2.** [trabajo] job; **no tener** ~ **ni beneficio** to have no trade. **-3.** [experiencia]: **tener mucho** ~ to be very experienced. **-4.** RELIG service. **-5.** [función] function, role.

◆ **Santo Oficio** *m*: **el Santo Oficio** the Holy Office, the Inquisition.

oficioso, -sa *adj* unofficial.

ofimática *f* office automation.

ofrecer [30] *vt* **-1.** [gen] to offer; [una fiesta] to give, to throw; ~**le algo a alguien** to offer sb sthg. **-2.** [un aspecto] to present.

◆ **ofrecerse** *vpr* **-1.** [presentarse] to offer, to volunteer; ~**se a** o **para hacer algo** to offer to do sthg. **-2.** *loc*: **¿qué se le ofrece?** what can I do for you?

ofrecimiento *m* offer.

ofrenda *f* RELIG offering; *fig* [por gratitud, amor] gift.

ofrendar *vt* to offer up.

ofrezca *etc* → **ofrecer**.

oftalmología *f* ophthalmology.

oftalmólogo, -ga *m y f* ophthalmologist.

ofuscación *f* blindness, confusion.

ofuscar [10] *vt* **-1.** [deslumbrar] to dazzle. **-2.** [turbar] to blind.

◆ **ofuscarse** *vpr*: ~**se (con)** to be blinded (by).

ogro *m* ogre.

oh *interj*: ¡~! oh!

ohmio *m* ohm.

oídas

◆ **de oídas** *loc adv* by hearsay.

oído *m* **-1.** [órgano] ear; **abrir los** ~**s** to pay close attention; **de** ~ by ear; **entrar por un**

~ **y salir por el otro** to go in one ear and out the other; **hacer** ~**s sordos** to turn a deaf ear; **lastimar los** ~**s** to offend one's ears; **si llega a** ~**s de ella** ... if she gets to hear about this ...; **me zumban los** ~**s** my ears are burning; **ser todo** ~**s** to be all ears. **-2.** [sentido] (sense of) hearing; **ser duro de** ~ to be hard of hearing; **tener** ~, **tener buen** ~ to have a good ear.

OIEA (*abrev de* **Organismo Internacional para la Energía Atómica**) *m* IAEA.

oír [62] ◇ *vt* **-1.** [gen] to hear; **como quien oye llover** without paying the least attention. **-2.** [atender] to listen to. ◇ *vi* to hear; **¡oiga, por favor!** excuse me!; **¡oye!** *fam* hey!; ~, **ver y callar** *fig* hear no evil, see no evil, speak no evil.

OIT (*abrev de* **Organización Internacional del Trabajo**) *f* ILO.

ojal *m* buttonhole.

ojalá *interj*: **¡**~**!** if only (that were so)!; **¡**~ **lo haga!** I hope she does it!; **¡**~ **fuera ya domingo!** I wish it were Sunday!

OJE (*abrev de* **Organización Juvenil Española**) *f Spanish youth organization created by Franco.*

ojeada *f* glance, look; **echar una** ~ **a algo/alguien** to take a quick glance at sthg/sb, to take a quick look at sthg/sb.

ojear *vt* to have a look at.

ojera *f* (*gen pl*) bags (*pl*) under the eyes.

ojeriza *f fam* dislike; **tener** ~ **a alguien** to have it in for sb.

ojeroso, -sa *adj* with bags under the eyes, haggard.

ojete *m* **-1.** [bordado] eyelet. **-2.** *vulg* arsehole.

ojiva *f* **-1.** ARQUIT ogive. **-2.** MIL warhead.

ojo ◇ *m* **-1.** ANAT eye; **poner los** ~**s en blanco** *lit* & *fig* to roll one's eyes; ~ **a la funerala** ○ **a la virulé** black eye; ~**s rasgados** almond eyes; ~**s saltones** popping eyes. **-2.** [agujero - de aguja] eye; [- de puente] span; ~ **de la cerradura** keyhole; ~ **de la escalera** stairwell. **-3.** *loc*: **a** ~ **(de buen cubero)** roughly, approximately; **a** ~**s vistas** visibly; **abrir los** ~**s a alguien** to open sb's eyes; **andar con (mucho)** ~ to be (very) careful; **cerrar los** ~**s** [morir] to pass away; **cerrar los** ~**s ante algo** [ignorar] to close one's eyes to sthg; **comerse con los** ~**s a alguien** *fam* to drool over sb; **¡dichosos los** ~**s que te ven!** *fam* how lovely to see you again!; **echar el** ~ **a algo** to have one's eye on sthg; **en un abrir y cerrar de** ~**s** in the twinkling of an eye; **estar** ~ **alerta** ○ **avizor** to be on the lookout; **mirar algo con buenos/malos** ~**s** to look favourably/unfavourably on sthg; **no pegar** ~ not to get a wink of sleep; **no quitar los** ~**s de encima a alguien** not to take one's eyes off sb; **tener** ~ **de iince** to have eyes like a hawk; **poner los** ~**s en alguien** to set one's sights on sb; **ser todo** ~**s** to be all eyes; **tener (buen)** ~ to have a good eye; **tener** ~ **clínico para algo** to be a good judge of sthg; ~ **por** ~, **diente por diente** *proverb* an eye for an eye, a tooth for a tooth; ~**s que no ven, corazón que no siente** *proverb* what the eye doesn't see, the heart doesn't grieve over. ◇ *interj*: **¡**~**!** be careful!, watch out!

◆ **ojo de buey** *m* [ventana] porthole.

◆ **ojo de gallo** *m* MED corn.

◆ **ojo de pez** *m* FOT fish-eye lens.

OK, okey [o'kei] (*abrev de* **all correct**) *interj* OK.

okupa *m y f mfam* squatter.

ola *f* wave; ~ **de calor** heatwave; ~ **de frío** cold spell.

◆ **nueva ola** *f*: **la nueva** ~ the New Wave.

ole, olé *interj*: **¡**~**!** bravo!

oleada *f* **-1.** [del mar] swell. **-2.** *fig* [abundancia] wave.

oleaginoso, -sa *adj* oleaginous.

oleaje *m* swell.

óleo *m* oil (painting); **al** ~ in oils.

oleoducto *m* oil pipeline.

oleoso, -sa *adj* oily.

oler [49] ◇ *vt* to smell. ◇ *vi* **-1.** [despedir olor]: ~ **(a)** to smell (of). **-2.** *fig* [parecer]: ~ **a** to smack of.

◆ **olerse** *vpr*: ~**se algo** *fig* to sense sthg.

olfatear *vt* **-1.** [olisquear] to sniff. **-2.** *fig* [barruntar] to smell, to sense.

◆ **olfatear en** *vi* [indagar] to pry into.

olfativo, -va *adj* olfactory.

olfato *m* **-1.** [sentido] sense of smell. **-2.** *fig* [sagacidad] nose, instinct; **tener** ~ **para algo** to be a good judge of sthg.

oligarca *m y f* oligarch.

oligarquía *f* oligarchy.

oligárquico, -ca *adj* oligarchic.

oligofrenia *f* mental handicap.

oligofrénico, -ca ◇ *adj* mentally handicapped. ◇ *m y f* mentally handicapped person.

olimpiada, olimpíada *f* Olympiad, Olympic Games (*pl*); **las** ~**s** the Olympics.

olímpicamente *adv fam* blithely.

olímpico, -ca *adj* **-1.** DEP olympic. **-2.** *fig* [altanero] Olympian, haughty.

olimpismo *m* Olympic movement.

olisquear *vt* to sniff (at).

oliva f olive.

oliváceo, -a adj olive.

olivar m olive grove.

olivarero, -ra ◇ adj olive (antes de sust). ◇ m y f olive-grower.

olivera f olive tree.

olivo m olive tree.

olla f pot; ~ **exprés** O **a presión** pressure cooker; ~ **podrida** CULIN stew; ~ **de grillos** fig bedlam, madhouse.

olmeda f elm grove.

olmo m elm (tree).

olor m smell; ~ **a** smell of; ~ **corporal** body odour; **en** ~ **de multitud** (considerado incorrecto) enjoying popular acclaim.

oloroso, -sa adj fragrant.

◆ **oloroso** m oloroso (sherry).

OLP (abrev de **Organización para la Liberación de Palestina**) f PLO.

olvidadizo, -za adj forgetful.

olvidar vt **-1.** [gen] to forget. **-2.** [dejarse] to leave; **olvidé las llaves en la oficina** I left my keys at the office.

◆ **olvidarse** vpr **-1.** [gen] to forget; **~se de algo/hacer algo** to forget sthg/to do sthg. **-2.** [dejarse] to leave.

olvido m **-1.** [de un nombre, hecho etc] forgetting; **caer en el** ~ to fall into oblivion. **-2.** [descuido] oversight.

Omán Oman.

ombligo m **-1.** ANAT navel. **-2.** fig [centro] centre.

ombudsman ['ombuðsman] m ombudsman.

ominoso, -sa adj abominable.

omisión f omission.

omiso, -sa → **caso**.

omitir vt to omit.

OMM (abrev de **Organización Meteorológica Mundial**) f WMO.

ómnibus m inv omnibus; FERROC local train.

omnipotencia f omnipotence.

omnipotente adj omnipotent.

omnipresente adj omnipresent.

omnívoro, -ra ◇ adj omnivorous. ◇ m y f omnivore.

omoplato, omóplato m shoulder-blade.

OMPI (abrev de **Organización Mundial de la Propiedad Intelectual**) f WIPO.

OMS (abrev de **Organización Mundial de la Salud**) f WHO.

onanismo m onanism.

once núm eleven; ver también **seis**.

ONCE (abrev de **Organización Nacional de Ciegos Españoles**) f Spanish association for the blind.

ONCE:
The ONCE is an independent organization which was originally set up to help the blind, although it now covers other handicapped people as well. One of its functions is to provide work for its members, and to this end it runs a national lottery, tickets for which are sold by the blind. The lottery is also one of the ONCE's main sources of income

onceavo, -va núm eleventh; **la onceava parte** an eleventh.

oncología f oncology.

oncólogo, -ga m y f oncologist.

onda f wave; ~ **corta/larga/media** short/long/medium wave; ~ **eléctrica** O **hertziana** Hertzian wave; ~ **expansiva** shock wave; ~ **luminosa/sonora** light/sound wave; **estar en la** ~ fam to be on the ball.

ondeante adj rippling.

ondear vi to ripple.

ondulación f **-1.** [acción] rippling. **-2.** [onda] ripple; [del pelo] wave.

ondulado, -da adj wavy.

ondulante adj undulating.

ondular ◇ vi [agua] to ripple; [terreno] to undulate. ◇ vt to wave.

ondulatorio, -ria adj wavelike.

oneroso, -sa adj burdensome.

ónice, ónix m o f onyx.

onírico, -ca adj dream (antes de sust).

ónix = **ónice**.

onomástico, -ca adj culto onomastic.

◆ **onomástica** f culto name day.

onomatopeya f onomatopoeia.

onomatopéyico, -ca adj onomatopoeic.

Ontario m: **el lago** ~ Lake Ontario.

ontología f ontology.

ONU (abrev de **Organización de las Naciones Unidas**) f UN.

ONUDI (abrev de **Organización de las Naciones Unidas para el Desarrollo Industrial**) f UNIDO.

onza f **-1.** [unidad de peso] ounce. **-2.** [de chocolate] square.

op. abrev de **opus**.

OPA f (abrev de **oferta pública de adquisición**) takeover bid.

opacidad f opacity.

opaco, -ca adj opaque.

OPAEP (*abrev de* **Organización de los Países Árabes Exportadores de Petróleo**) *f* OAPEC.

opalino, -na *adj* opaline.

◆ **opalina** *f* opaline.

ópalo *m* opal.

opción *f* **-1.** [elección] option; **no hay ~** there is no alternative. **-2.** [derecho] right; **dar ~ a** to give the right to; **tener ~ a** [empleo, cargo] to be eligible for.

opcional *adj* optional.

OPEP (*abrev de* **Organización de Países Exportadores de Petróleo**) *f* OPEC.

ópera *f* opera; **~ bufa** comic opera, opera buffa; **~ rock** rock opera.

operación *f* **-1.** [gen] operation; **~ quirúrgica** (surgical) operation; **~ retorno** *police operation to assist return of holidaymakers to their city homes, minimizing traffic congestion and maximizing road safety.* **-2.** COM transaction.

operacional *adj* operational.

operador, -ra *m y f* **-1.** INFORM & TELECOM operator. **-2.** [de la cámara] cameraman; [del proyector] projectionist.

◆ **operador** *m* MAT operator.

◆ **operador turístico** *m* tour operator.

operar ◇ *vt* **-1.** [enfermo]: **~ a alguien (de algo)** [enfermedad] to operate on sb (for sthg); **le operaron del hígado** they've operated on his liver. **-2.** [cambio etc] to bring about, to produce. ◇ *vi* **-1.** [gen] to operate. **-2.** [actuar] to act. **-3.** COM & FIN to deal.

◆ **operarse** *vpr* **-1.** [enfermo] to be operated on, to have an operation; **~ se de algo** to be operated on for sthg; **me voy a ~ del hígado** I'm going to have an operation on my liver. **-2.** [cambio etc] to occur, to come about.

operario, -ria *m y f* worker.

operatividad *f* feasibility.

operativo, -va *adj* operative.

opereta *f* operetta.

operístico, -ca *adj* operatic.

opiáceo, -a *adj* opiate.

◆ **opiáceo** *m* opiate.

opinar ◇ *vt* to believe, to think. ◇ *vi* to give one's opinion; **~ de algo/alguien**, **~ sobre algo/alguien** to think about sthg/sb; **~ bien de alguien** to think highly of sb.

opinión *f* [parecer] opinion; **expresar** O **dar una ~** to give an opinion; **reservarse la ~** to reserve judgment; **la ~ pública** public opinion.

opio *m* opium.

opíparo, -ra *adj* sumptuous.

opondrá *etc* → **oponer**.

oponente *m y f* opponent.

oponer [65] *vt* **-1.** [resistencia] to put up. **-2.** [argumento, razón] to put forward, to give.

◆ **oponerse** *vpr* **-1.** [no estar de acuerdo] to be opposed; **~ se a algo** [desaprobar] to be opposed to sthg, to oppose sthg; [contradecir] to contradict sthg; **me opongo a creerlo** I refuse to believe it. **-2.** [obstaculizar]: **~ se a** to stand in the way of, to impede.

oporto *m* port (wine).

oportunidad *f* **-1.** [ocasión] opportunity, chance; **aprovechar la ~** to seize the opportunity. **-2.** [conveniencia] timeliness.

oportunismo *m* opportunism.

oportunista ◇ *adj* opportunistic. ◇ *m y f* opportunist.

oportuno, -na *adj* **-1.** [pertinente] appropriate. **-2.** [propicio] timely; **el momento ~** the right time.

oposición *f* **-1.** [gen] opposition. **-2.** [resistencia] resistance. **-3.** (*gen pl*) [examen] public entrance examination; **~ a profesor** public examination to be a teacher; **preparar oposiciones** to be studying for a public entrance examination.

opositar *vi*: **~ (a)** to sit a public entrance examination (for).

opositor, -ra *m y f* **-1.** [a un cargo] *candidate in a public entrance examination.* **-2.** [oponente] opponent.

opresión *f* **-1.** [de un botón] press. **-2.** *fig* [represión] oppression. **-3.** *fig* [ahogo] difficulty in breathing.

opresivo, -va *adj* oppressive.

opresor, -ra ◇ *adj* oppressive. ◇ *m y f* oppressor.

oprimir *vt* **-1.** [apretar - botón etc] to press; [- garganta, brazo etc] to squeeze. **-2.** [suj: zapatos, cinturón] to pinch, to be too tight for. **-3.** *fig* [reprimir] to oppress. **-4.** *fig* [angustiar] to weigh down on, to burden.

oprobio *m* shame, disgrace.

optar *vi* **-1.** [escoger]: **~ (por algo)** to choose (sthg); **~ por hacer algo** to choose to do sthg; **~ entre** to choose between. **-2.** [aspirar]: **~ a** to aim for, to go for.

optativo, -va *adj* optional.

◆ **optativa** *f* EDUC option, optional subject.

óptico, -ca ◇ *adj* optic. ◇ *m y f* [persona] optician.

◆ **óptica** *f* **-1.** FÍS optics (U). **-2.** [tienda] optician's (shop). **-3.** *fig* [punto de vista] point of view.

optimismo *m* optimism.

optimista ◇ *adj* optimistic. ◇ *m y f* optimist.

optimización *f* optimization.

optimizar *vt* to optimize.

óptimo, -ma ◇ *superl* → **bueno.** ◇ *adj* optimum.

opuesto, -ta ◇ *pp* → **oponer.** ◇ *adj* **-1.**
[contrario] conflicting; ~ **a** opposed ○ contrary to. **-2.** [de enfrente] opposite.

opulencia *f* [riqueza] opulence; [abundancia] abundance; **vivir en la** ~ to live in luxury; **nadar en la** ~ to be filthy rich.

opulento, -ta *adj* **-1.** [rico] opulent. **-2.** [abundante] abundant.

opus *m* MÚS opus.

◆ **Opus Dei** *m*: **el Opus Dei** the Opus Dei, *traditionalist religious organization, the members of which are usually professional people or public figures.*

opusiera *etc* → **oponer.**

ora *conj desus*: ~ ... ~ ... now ... now ....

oración *f* **-1.** [rezo] prayer; ~ **fúnebre** memorial speech. **-2.** GRAM sentence; ~ **principal/subordinada** main/subordinate clause.

oráculo *m* **-1.** [gen] oracle. **-2.** *fig* [persona] fount of wisdom.

orador, -ra *m y f* speaker.

oral ◇ *adj* oral. ◇ *m* → **examen.**

órale *interj Amer fam*: ¡~! come on!

orangután *m* orangutang.

orar *vi* to pray.

oratorio, -ria *adj* oratorical.

◆ **oratorio** *m* **-1.** [lugar] oratory. **-2.** MÚS oratorio.

◆ **oratoria** *f* oratory.

orbe *m* world, globe.

órbita *f* **-1.** ASTRON orbit; **entrar/poner en** ~ to go/put into orbit. **-2.** [de ojo] eye socket. **-3.** *fig* [ámbito] sphere, realm.

orca *f* killer whale.

órdago *m* all-or-nothing stake in the game of ''*mus*''; **de** ~ *fig* magnificent.

orden ◇ *m* **-1.** [gen] order; **en** ~ [bien colocado] tidy, in its place; [como debe ser] in order; **llamar al** ~ **a alguien** to call sb to order; **poner en** ~ **algo** to tidy sthg up; **por** ~ in order; **sin** ~ **ni concierto** in a haphazard way; **las fuerzas del** ~ the forces of law and order; ~ **de compra** COM purchase order; ~ **público** law and order. **-2.** [tipo] type, order; **problemas de** ~ **económico** economic problems; **en otro** ~ **de cosas** on the other hand.

◇ *f* order; **dar órdenes** to give orders; **por** ~ **de** by order of; ~ **de busca y captura** warrant for search and arrest; ~ **de caballería** order of knighthood; ~ **militar** military order; ~ **de pago** payment order; **¡a la** ~! MIL (yes) sir!; **estar a la** ~ **del día** to be the order of the day.

◆ **del orden de** *loc prep* around, approximately.

◆ **orden del día** *m* agenda.

ordenación *f* **-1.** [organización] ordering, arranging; [disposición] order, arrangement; [de recursos, edificios] planning. **-2.** RELIG ordination.

ordenado, -da ◇ *adj* [lugar, persona] tidy. ◇ *m y f* RELIG ordained person.

◆ **ordenada** *f* MAT ordinate.

ordenador *m* INFORM computer; ~ **central** mainframe computer; ~ **personal** personal computer; ~ **portátil** laptop computer.

ordenamiento *m* legislation, regulations (*pl*).

ordenanza ◇ *m* **-1.** [de oficina] messenger. **-2.** MIL orderly. ◇ *f* (*gen pl*) ordinance, law; ~**s municipales** by-laws.

ordenar *vt* **-1.** [poner en orden - gen] to arrange, to put in order; [- habitación, armario etc] to tidy (up). **-2.** [mandar] to order. **-3.** RELIG to ordain.

◆ **ordenarse** *vpr* RELIG to be ordained.

ordeñadora *f* milking machine.

ordeñar *vt* to milk.

ordeño *m* milking.

ordinal ◇ *adj* ordinal. ◇ *m* → **número.**

ordinariez *f* commonness, coarseness; **decir/hacer una** ~ to say/do sthg rude.

ordinario, -ria ◇ *adj* **-1.** [común] ordinary, usual; **de** ~ usually. **-2.** [vulgar] common, coarse. **-3.** [no selecto] unexceptional. **-4.** [no especial - presupuesto, correo] daily; [- tribunal] of first instance. ◇ *m y f* common ○ coarse person.

orear *vt* to air.

◆ **orearse** *vpr* [ventilarse] to air.

orégano *m* oregano.

oreja *f* **-1.** ANAT ear; **calentarle a alguien las** ~**s** to box sb's ears; **con las** ~**s gachas** with one's tail between one's legs; **tirar a alguien de las** ~**s** to give sb a good telling-off; **verle las** ~**s al lobo** to see what's coming. **-2.** [de sillón] wing.

orejera *f* earflap.

orejudo, -da *adj* big-eared.

orfanato, orfelinato *m* orphanage.

orfandad *f* orphanhood; *fig* abandonment, neglect.

orfebre *m y f* [de plata] silversmith; [de oro] goldsmith.

orfebrería *f* [obra - de plata] silver work; [- de oro] gold work.

orfelinato = **orfanato.**

orfeón *m* choral group ○ society.

organdí (*pl* **organdíes**) *m* organdie.

orgánico, **-ca** *adj* organic.

organigrama *m* [gen & INFORM] flowchart.

organillero, **-ra** *m y f* organ-grinder.

organillo *m* barrel organ.

organismo *m* **-1.** BIOL organism. **-2.** ANAT body. **-3.** *fig* [entidad] organization, body.

organista *m y f* organist.

organización *f* organization.

organizador, **-ra** ◇ *adj* organizing. ◇ *m y f* organizer.

organizar [13] *vt* to organize.

✦ **organizarse** *vpr* **-1.** [persona] to organize o.s. **-2.** [pelea etc] to break out, to happen suddenly.

organizativo, **-va** *adj* organizing.

órgano *m* organ.

orgasmo *m* orgasm.

orgía *f* orgy.

orgiástico, **-ca** *adj* orgiastic.

orgullo *m* pride.

orgulloso, **-sa** ◇ *adj* proud. ◇ *m y f* proud person.

orientación *f* **-1.** [dirección - acción] guiding; [- rumbo] direction. **-2.** [posicionamiento - acción] positioning; [- lugar] position. **-3.** *fig* [información] guidance; ~ **profesional** careers advice ○ guidance. **-4.** *fig* [tendencia] tendency, leaning.

oriental ◇ *adj* [gen] eastern; [del Lejano Oriente] oriental. ◇ *m y f* oriental.

orientalismo *m* orientalism.

orientalista *m y f* orientalist.

orientar *vt* **-1.** [dirigir] to direct; [casa] to build facing. **-2.** *fig* [medidas etc]: ~ **hacia** to direct towards ○ at. **-3.** *fig* [aconsejar] to give advice ○ guidance to.

✦ **orientarse** *vpr* **-1.** [dirigirse - foco etc]: ~**se a** to point towards ○ at. **-2.** [encontrar el camino] to get one's bearings, to find one's way around. **-3.** *fig* [encaminarse]: ~**se hacia** to be aiming at.

oriente *m* east.

✦ **Oriente** *m*: **el Oriente** the East, the Orient; **Oriente Medio/Próximo** Middle/Near East; **Lejano** ○ **Extremo Oriente** Far East.

orificio *m* hole; TECN opening.

origen *m* **-1.** [gen] origin; [ascendencia] origins (*pl*), birth; **de** ~ **español** of Spanish origin. **-2.** [causa] cause; **dar** ~ **a** to give rise to.

original ◇ *adj* **-1.** [gen] original. **-2.** [raro] eccentric, different. ◇ *m* original.

originalidad *f* **-1.** [gen] originality. **-2.** [extravagancia] eccentricity.

originar *vt* to cause.

✦ **originarse** *vpr* to be caused.

originario, **-ria** *adj* **-1.** [inicial, primitivo] original. **-2.** [procedente]: **ser** ~ **de** [costumbres etc] to come from (originally); [persona] to be a native of.

orilla *f* **-1.** [ribera - de río] bank; [- de mar] shore; **a** ~**s de** [río] on the banks of; **a** ~**s del mar** by the sea. **-2.** [borde] edge. **-3.** [acera] pavement.

orillar *vt* **-1.** [dificultad, obstáculo] to skirt around. **-2.** [tela] to edge.

orín *m* [herrumbre] rust.

✦ **orines** *mpl* [orina] urine (*U*).

orina *f* urine.

orinal *m* chamberpot.

orinar *vi & vt* to urinate.

✦ **orinarse** *vpr* to wet o.s.

Orinoco *m*: **el** ~ the Orinoco.

oriundo, **-da** ◇ *adj*: ~ **de** native of. ◇ *m y f* DEP *non-Spanish footballer whose mother or father is Spanish*.

orla *f* **-1.** [adorno] (decorative) trimming. **-2.** [fotografía] graduation photograph.

orlar *vt* to decorate with trimmings.

ornamentación *f* ornamentation.

ornamental *adj* ornamental.

ornamentar *vt* to decorate, to adorn.

ornamento *m* [objeto] ornament.

✦ **ornamentos** *mpl* RELIG vestments (*pl*).

ornar *vt* to decorate, to adorn.

ornato *m* decoration.

ornitología *f* ornithology.

ornitólogo, **-ga** *m y f* ornithologist.

oro *m* gold; *fig* money, riches (*pl*); **de** ~ gold; ~ **en barras** bullion; ~ **en polvo** gold dust; **guardar algo como** ~ **en paño** to treasure sthg; **hacerse de** ~ to make one's fortune; **no es** ~ **todo lo que reluce** all that glitters is not gold; **pedir el** ~ **y el moro** to ask the earth.

✦ **oros** *mpl* [naipes] *suit of Spanish cards bearing gold coins*.

✦ **oro negro** *m* oil.

orogénesis *f inv* orogenesis.

orografía *f* **-1.** GEOGR orography. **-2.** [relieve] terrain.

orondo, **-da** *adj fam* **-1.** [gordo] plump. **-2.** [satisfecho] self-satisfied, smug.

oropel *m* tinsel.

oropéndola *f* golden oriole.

orquesta *f* **-1.** [músicos] orchestra; ~ **de cámara/sinfónica** chamber/symphony orchestra. **-2.** [lugar] orchestra pit.

orquestación *f* orchestration.

orquestar *vt* to orchestrate.

orquestina *f* dance band.

orquídea *f* orchid.

ortiga *f* (stinging) nettle.

ortodoncia *f* orthodontics (*U*).

ortodoxia *f* orthodoxy.

ortodoxo, -xa ◇ *adj* orthodox. ◇ *m y f* RE-LIG member of the Orthodox Church.

ortografía *f* spelling.

ortográfico, -ca *adj* spelling (*antes de sust*).

ortopedia *f* orthopaedics (*U*).

ortopédico, -ca ◇ *adj* orthopaedic. ◇ *m y f* orthopaedist.

ortopedista *m y f* orthopaedist.

oruga *f* caterpillar.

orujo *m strong spirit made from grape pressings.*

orzuelo *m* stye.

os *pron. pers* **-1.** (*complemento directo*) you; me gustaría veros I'd like to see you. **-2.** (*complemento indirecto*) (to) you; ~ **lo dio** he gave it to you; ~ **tengo miedo** I'm afraid of you. **-3.** (*reflexivo*) yourselves. **-4.** (*recíproco*) each other; ~ **enamorasteis** you fell in love (with each other).

osa → oso.

osadía *f* **-1.** .[valor] boldness, daring. **-2.** [descaro] audacity, cheek.

osado, -da *adj* **-1.** [valeroso] daring, bold. **-2.** [descarado] impudent, cheeky.

osamenta *f* skeleton.

osar *vi* to dare.

osario *m* ossuary.

Óscar *m* CIN Oscar.

oscilación *f* **-1.** [movimiento] swinging; FÍS oscillation. **-2.** [espacio recorrido] swing. **-3.** *fig* [variación] fluctuation.

oscilador *m* oscillator.

oscilar *vi* **-1.** [moverse] to swing; FÍS to oscillate. **-2.** *fig* [variar] to fluctuate.

oscilatorio, -ria *adj* swinging; FÍS oscillating.

ósculo *m culto* kiss.

oscurantismo *m* obscurantism.

oscurecer [30] ◇ *vt* **-1.** [privar de luz] to darken. **-2.** *fig* [mente] to confuse, to cloud. **-3.** *fig* [deslucir] to overshadow. ◇ *v impers* [anochecer] to get dark.
◆ **oscurecerse** *vpr* to grow dark.

oscuridad *f* **-1.** [falta de luz] darkness. **-2.** [zona oscura]: **en la** ~ in the dark. **-3.** *fig* [falta de claridad] obscurity.

oscuro, -ra *adj* **-1.** [gen] dark; **a oscuras** in the dark. **-2.** [nublado] overcast. **-3.** *fig* [inusual] obscure. **-4.** *fig* [incierto] uncertain, unclear. **-5.** *fig* [intenciones, asunto] shady.

óseo, -a *adj* bone (*antes de sust*).

osezno *m* bear cub.

osificarse [10] *vpr* to ossify.

Oslo Oslo.

ósmosis *f inv* FÍS & *fig* osmosis.

oso, osa *m y f* bear (*f* she-bear); ~ **de felpa** O **peluche** teddy bear; ~ **hormiguero** anteater; ~ **panda** panda; ~ **polar** polar bear; **hacer el** ~ to act the fool.
◆ **Osa Mayor** *f* Great Bear.
◆ **Osa Menor** *f* Little Bear.

ossobuco [oso'βuko] *m* CULIN osso bucco.

ostensible *adj* evident, clear.

ostentación *f* ostentation, show; **hacer** ~ **de algo** to show sthg off, to parade sthg.

ostentador, -ra *m y f* show-off, ostentatious person.

ostentar *vt* **-1.** [poseer] to hold, to have. **-2.** [exhibir] to show off, to parade.

ostentoso, -sa *adj* ostentatious.

osteópata *m y f* osteopath.

osteopatía *f* [terapia] osteopathy.

osteoplastia *f* osteoplasty.

ostra *f* oyster; **aburrirse como una** ~ *fam* to be bored to death.
◆ **ostras** *interj fam:* ¡~**s**! blimey!

ostracismo *m* ostracism; ~ **político** political wilderness.

OTAN (*abrev de* **Organización del Tratado del Atlántico Norte**) *f* NATO.

otear *vt* to survey, to scan; *fig* to study.

otero *m* hillock.

OTI (*abrev de* **Organización de Televisiones Iberoamericanas**) *f association of all Spanish-speaking television networks.*

otitis *f inv* inflammation of the ear.

otomano, -na *adj, m y f* Ottoman.
◆ **otomana** *f* [sofá] ottoman.

otoñal *adj* autumn *Br* (*antes de sust*), autumnal *Br*, fall *Am* (*antes de sust*).

otoño *m lit* & *fig* autumn *Br*, fall *Am*.

otorgamiento *m* granting, conferring; [de un premio] award, presentation; DER execution.

otorgar [16] *vt* to grant; [premio] to award, to present; DER to execute.

otorrino, -na *m y f fam* ear, nose and throat specialist.

otorrinolaringología *f* ear, nose and throat medicine.

otorrinolaringólogo, -ga *m y f* ear, nose and throat specialist.

otro, -tra ◇ *adj* **-1.** [distinto] (*sg*) another, (*pl*) other; ~ **chico** another boy; **el** ~ **chico** the other boy; **(los)** ~**s chicos** (the) other boys; **no hacer otra cosa que llorar** to do nothing but cry; **el** ~ **día** [pasado] the other day. **-2.** [nuevo] another; **estamos ante ~ Dalí** this is another Dalí; **~s tres goles** another three goals.

◇ *pron* (*sg*) another (one), (*pl*) others; **dame ~** give me another (one); **el ~** the other one; **(los) ~s** (the) others; **yo no lo hice, fue ~** it wasn't me, it was somebody else; **~ habría abandonado, pero no él** anyone else would have given up, but not him; **¡otra!** [en conciertos] encore!, more!

otrora *adv culto* formerly.

otrosí *adv culto* besides, moreover.

Ottawa [o'taßa] Ottawa.

OUA (*abrev de* **Organización para la Unidad Africana**) *f* OAU.

output ['autput] (*pl* **outputs**) *m* INFORM output (*U*).

ovación *f* ovation.

ovacionar *vt* to give an ovation to, to applaud.

oval *adj* oval.

ovalado, -da *adj* oval.

óvalo *m* oval.

ovario *m* ovary.

oveja *f* sheep, ewe.
◆ **oveja descarriada** *f* lost sheep.
◆ **oveja negra** *f* black sheep.

overbooking [oßer'ßukin] *m* overbooking.

ovetense *adj* of/relating to Oviedo.

OVI (*abrev de* **objeto volador identificado**) *m identified flying object.*

Oviedo Oviedo.

ovillar *vt* to roll ○ wind into a ball.
◆ **ovillarse** *vpr* to curl up into a ball.

ovillo *m* ball (*of wool etc*); **hacerse un ~** to curl up into a ball.

ovino, -na ◇ *adj* ovine, sheep (*antes de sust*). ◇ *m y f* sheep.

ovíparo, -ra *adj* oviparous.

ovni ['ofni] *m* (*abrev de* **objeto volador no identificado**) UFO.

ovoide *adj* ovoid.

ovulación *f* ovulation.

ovular ◇ *adj* ovular. ◇ *vi* to ovulate.

óvulo *m* ovum.

oxidación *f* rusting.

oxidante ◇ *adj* oxidizing. ◇ *m* oxidizing agent.

oxidar *vt* to rust; QUÍM to oxidize.
◆ **oxidarse** *vpr* to get rusty.

óxido *m* **-1.** QUÍM oxide. **-2.** [herrumbre] rust.

oxigenación *f* oxygenation.

oxigenado, -da *adj* **-1.** QUÍM oxygenated.

-2. [cabello] peroxide (*antes de sust*), bleached.

oxigenar *vt* QUÍM to oxygenate.
◆ **oxigenarse** *vpr* **-1.** [airearse] to get a breath of fresh air. **-2.** [cabello] to bleach.

oxígeno *m* oxygen.

oye → **oír.**

oyente *m y f* **-1.** RADIO listener. **-2.** [alumno] unregistered student.

oyera *etc* → **oír.**

ozono *m* ozone.

ozonosfera *f* ozonosphere.

P

p, P *f* [letra] p, P.

p. -1. = **pág. -2.** *abrev de* **paseo.**

p.a. -1. *abrev de* **por ausencia. -2.** (*abrev de* **por autorización**) pp.

PAAU (*abrev de* **pruebas de aptitud para el acceso a la universidad**) *fpl university entrance examinations.*

pabellón *m* **-1.** [edificio] pavilion. **-2.** [parte de un edificio] block, section. **-3.** [en parques, jardines] summerhouse. **-4.** [tienda de campaña] bell tent. **-5.** [dosel] canopy. **-6.** [bandera] flag. **-7.** *fam* [oreja] ear.

pábilo *m* wick.

pábulo *m* food, fuel; **dar ~ a** to feed, to encourage.

PAC (*abrev de* **política agrícola común**) *f* CAP.

pacato, -ta ◇ *adj* **-1.** [mojigato] prudish. **-2.** [tímido] shy. ◇ *m y f* [mojigato] prude.

paceño, -ña ◇ *adj* of/relating to La Paz. ◇ *m y f* native/inhabitant of La Paz.

pacer [29] *vi* to graze.

pachá (*pl* **pachaes**) *m* pasha; **vivir como un ~** *fam* to live like a lord.

pachanga *f fam* rowdy celebration.

pachanguero, -ra *adj fam* [música] catchy but mindless.

pacharán *m liqueur made from brandy and sloes.*

pachorra *f fam* calmness.

pachucho, -cha *adj fam* off-colour.

pachulí (*pl* **pachulíes**) *m* patchouli.

paciencia *f* patience; **armarse de** ~ to summon up one's patience; **perder la** ~ to lose one's patience; **tener más** ~ **que un santo** to have the patience of a saint.

paciente *adj, m y f* patient.

pacificación *f* pacification.

pacificar [10] *vt* **-1.** [país] to pacify. **-2.** [ánimos] to calm.

◆ **pacificarse** *vpr* [persona] to calm down.

pacífico, -ca *adj* [gen] peaceful; [persona] peaceable.

Pacífico *m*: **el (océano)** ~ the Pacific (Ocean).

pacifismo *m* pacifism.

pacifista *adj, m y f* pacifist.

paco, -ca *m y f Amer fam* cop.

pacotilla *f*: **de** ~ trashy, third-rate.

pactar ◇ *vt* to agree to. ◇ *vi*: ~ **(con)** to strike a deal (with).

pacto *m* [gen] agreement, pact; [entre países] treaty; ~ **social** social contract.

paddle = **pádel.**

padecer [30] ◇ *vt* to suffer, to endure; [enfermedad] to suffer from. ◇ *vi* to suffer; [enfermedad]: ~ **de** to suffer from.

padecimiento *m* suffering.

pádel, paddle ['paðel] *m ball game for two or four players, played with a small rubber bat on a two-walled court.'*

padezca *etc* → **padecer.**

padrastro *m* **-1.** [pariente] stepfather. **-2.** [pellejo] hangnail.

padrazo *m fam* adoring father.

padre ◇ *m* [gen & RELIG] father; ~ **de familia** head of the family; ~ **espiritual** confessor; **de** ~ **y muy señor mío** tremendous. ◇ *adj inv fam* tremendous.

◆ **padres** *mpl* **-1.** [padre y madre] parents. **-2.** [antepasados] ancestors, forefathers.

◆ **Padres de la Iglesia** *mpl* RELIG Fathers of the Christian Church.

◆ **Santo Padre** *m* RELIG Holy Father, Pope.

padrenuestro (*pl* **padrenuestros**) *m* Lord's Prayer.

padrino *m* **-1.** [de bautismo] godfather; [de boda] best man. **-2.** [en duelos, torneos etc] second. **-3.** *fig* [protector] patron.

◆ **padrinos** *mpl* [padrino y madrina] godparents.

padrísimo *adj Amer fam* fantastic, great.

padrón *m* [censo] census; [para votar] electoral roll ○ register.

padrote *m Amer fam* pimp.

paella *f* paella.

paellera *f large frying-pan or earthenware dish for cooking paella.*

paf *interj* bang!, crash!

pág., p. (*abrev de* **página**) p.

paga *f* payment; [salario] salary, wages (*pl*); [de niño] pocket money; ~ **extra** ○ **extraordinaria** ≃ bonus.

PAGA EXTRA:

This is a bonus, equivalent to one month's wages, which is added to employees' salaries twice a year, in the summer and at Christmas, to help people over these periods of heavy expenditure. It is considered as part of an employee's annual salary

pagadero, -ra *adj* payable; ~ **a 90 días/a la entrega** payable within 90 days/on delivery.

pagado, -da *adj* paid.

pagador, -ra ◇ *adj* paying. ◇ *m y f* [de obreros etc] paymaster.

paganismo *m* paganism.

pagano, -na *adj, m y f* pagan, heathen.

pagar [16] ◇ *vt* [gen] to pay; [deuda] to pay off, to settle; [ronda, gastos, delito] to pay for; [ayuda, favor] to repay; **me las pagarás** *fam* you'll pay for this; **el que la hace la paga** he/she *etc* will pay for it in the end. ◇ *vi* to pay.

pagaré (*pl* **pagarés**) *m* COM promissory note, IOU; ~ **del Tesoro** Treasury note.

pagel *m* sea bream.

página *f* page; ~ **inicial** ○ **de inicio** INFORM home page; **las** ~**s amarillas** the Yellow Pages.

paginación *f* pagination.

paginar *vt* INFORM to paginate.

pago *m* payment; *fig* reward, payment; **en** ~ **de** [en recompensa por] as a reward for; [a cambio de] in return for; ~ **anticipado/inicial** advance/down payment.

◆ **pagos** *mpl* [lugar]: **por estos** ~**s** around here.

pague *etc* → **pagar.**

paila *f Amer* **-1.** [sartén] frying pan. **-2.** [huevos fritos] fried eggs (*pl*).

paipai (*pl* **paipais**), **paipay** *m* (*pl* **paipays**) *fan made from a palm leaf.*

pair → **au pair.**

país *m* country; ~ **natal** native country, homeland; ~ **satélite** satellite state; ~**es desarrollados/en vías de desarrollo/subdesarrollados** developed/developing/underdeveloped countries.

paisaje *m* [gen] landscape; [vista panorámica] scenery (*U*), view.

paisajista ◇ *adj* landscape (*antes de sust*). ◇ *m y f* landscape painter.

paisajístico, -ca *adj* landscape (*antes de sust*).

paisanaje *m* civilians (*pl*).

paisano, -na ◇ *adj* [del mismo país] from the same country. ◇ *m y f* [del mismo país] compatriot, fellow countryman (*f* fellow countrywoman).
◆ **paisano** *m* [civil] civilian; **de** ~ MIL in civilian clothes; **de** ~ [policía] in plain clothes.

Países Bajos *mpl*: **los** ~ the Netherlands.

País Valenciano *m*: **el** ~ the autonomous region of Valencia.

País Vasco *m*: **el** ~ the Basque Country.

paja *f* -**1.** [gen] straw. -**2.** *fig* [relleno] waffle. -**3.** *vulg* [masturbación] wank; **hacerse una** ~ to have a wank.

pajar *m* straw loft.

pájara *f fig* crafty ◇ sly woman.

pajarera *f* aviary.

pajarería *f* pet shop.

pajarita *f* -**1.** [corbata] bow tie. -**2.** [de papel] paper bird.

pájaro *m* -**1.** ZOOL bird; ~ **bobo** penguin; ~ **carpintero** woodpecker; ~ **de mal agüero** bird of ill omen; **más vale** ~ **en mano que ciento volando** *proverb* a bird in the hand is worth two in the bush; **matar dos** ~**s de un tiro** to kill two birds with one stone; **tener** ~**s en la cabeza** to be scatterbrained ◇ empty-headed. -**2.** *fig* [persona] crafty devil, sly old fox.

pajarraco *m despec* -**1.** [pájaro] big, ugly bird. -**2.** [persona] nasty piece of work.

paje *m* page.

pajilla, pajita *f* (drinking) straw.

pajizo, -za *adj* [de paja] straw (*antes de sust*); [color] straw-coloured; [techo] thatched.

pajolero, -ra *adj fam* damn, blessed; **no tengo ni pajolera idea** I haven't got the foggiest.

Pakistán, Paquistán Pakistan.

pakistaní (*pl* pakistaníes), **paquistaní** (*pl* paquistaníes) *adj, m y f* Pakistani.

pala *f* -**1.** [herramienta] spade; [para recoger] shovel; CULIN slice; ~ **mecánica** ◇ **excavadora** excavator, digger. -**2.** [de frontón, pingpong] bat. -**3.** [de remo, hélice] blade. -**4.** [de calzado] instep.

palabra *f* -**1.** [gen] word; **bajo** ~ on one's word; **de** ~ by word of mouth, verbally; **mantener uno su** ~ to keep one's word; **no tener** ~ to go back on one's word; ~ **por** ~ word for word; **sin mediar** ~ without a single word; **tomar** ◇ **coger la** ~ **a alguien** to hold sb to their word; ~ **clave** IN-FORM key word; ~ **divina** ◇ **de Dios** word of God; ~ **de honor** word of honour. -**2.** [habla] speech. -**3.** [derecho de hablar] right to speak; **dar la** ~ **a alguien** to give the floor to sb. -**4.** *loc*: **dejar a alguien con la** ~ **en la boca** to cut sb off in mid-sentence; **en cuatro** ◇ **dos** ~**s** in a few words; **en una** ~ in a word; **medir las** ~**s** weigh one's words (carefully); **ser** ~**s mayores** to be an important matter.
◆ **palabras** *fpl* [discurso] words.

palabrería *f fam* hot air.

palabrota *f* swearword, rude word; **decir** ~**s** to swear.

palacete *m* mansion, small palace.

palaciego, -ga *adj* palace (*antes de sust*), court (*antes de sust*).

palacio *m* palace; ~ **de congresos** conference centre; ~ **de Justicia** Law Courts (*pl*).

palada *f* -**1.** [al cavar] spadeful, shovelful. -**2.** [de remo] stroke. -**3.** [de hélice] rotation.

paladar *m* palate.

paladear *vt* to savour.

paladín *m* -**1.** HIST paladin, heroic knight. -**2.** *fig* [adalid] champion, defender.

palanca *f* -**1.** [barra, mando] lever; ~ **de cambio** gear lever ◇ stick, gearshift *Am*; ~ **de mando** joystick. -**2.** [trampolín] diving board.

palangana *f* [para fregar] washing-up bowl; [para lavarse] wash bowl.

palangre *m* fishing line with hooks.

palanqueta *f* jemmy, crowbar.

palatal *adj* palatal.

palatino, -na *adj* -**1.** [de paladar] palatine. -**2.** [de palacio] palace (*antes de sust*), court (*antes de sust*).

palco *m* box (*at theatre*).

paleocristiano, -na *adj* early Christian.

paleografía *f* paleography.

paleográfico, -ca *adj* paleographic.

paleógrafo, -fa *m y f* paleographer.

paleolítico, -ca *adj* paleolithic.
◆ **paleolítico** *m* Paleolithic period.

paleontología *f* paleontology.

paleontólogo, -ga *m y f* paleontologist.

Palermo Palermo.

Palestina Palestine.

palestino, -na *adj, m y f* Palestinian.

palestra *f* arena; **salir** ◇ **saltar a la** ~ to enter the fray.

paleta *f* [gen] small shovel, small spade; [llana] trowel; CULIN slice; ARTE palette.

paletada *f* [gen] shovelful, spadeful; [de yeso] trowelful; [de pintura] palette.

paletilla *f* shoulder blade.

pampa

paleto, -ta ◇ *adj* coarse, uncouth. ◇ *m y f* country bumpkin, yokel.

paletón *m* bit.

paliar [8] *vt* **-1.** [atenuar] to ease, to relieve. **-2.** [disculpar] to excuse, to justify.

paliativo, -va *adj* palliative.
◆ **paliativo** *m* **-1.** [excusa] excuse, mitigation (*U*). **-2.** MED palliative.

palidecer [30] *vi* **-1.** [ponerse pálido] to go ○ turn pale. **-2.** [perder importancia] to pale, to fade.

palidez *f* paleness.

pálido, -da *adj* pale; *fig* dull.

palier [pa'ljer] *m* AUTOM bearing.

palillero *m* toothpick holder.

palillo *m* **-1.** [mondadientes] toothpick. **-2.** [baqueta] drumstick. **-3.** [para comida china] chopstick. **-4.** *fig* [persona delgada] matchstick.

palio *m* canopy.

palique *m* *fam* chat, natter; **estar de** ~ to have a chat ○ a natter.

palisandro *m* rosewood.

palito *m*: ~ **(de pescado)** CULIN fish finger.

paliza *f* **-1.** [golpes, derrota] beating. **-2.** [esfuerzo] hard grind. **-3.** *fam* [rollo] drag.

palma *f* **-1.** [de mano] palm; **conocer algo como la** ~ **de la mano** to know sthg like the back of one's hand. **-2.** [palmera] palm (tree); [hoja de palmera] palm leaf; **llevarse la** ~ to be the best; *irón* to take the biscuit.
◆ **palmas** *fpl* [aplausos] clapping (*U*), applause (*U*); **batir** ~**s** to clap (one's hands).

palmada *f* **-1.** [golpe] pat; [más fuerte] slap. **-2.** [aplauso] clap; ~**s** clapping (*U*).

palmar¹ ◇ *adj* of the palm (*of the hand*). ◇ *m* palm grove.

palmar² *fam* ◇ *vi* to kick the bucket, to snuff it. ◇ *vt*: ~**la** to kick the bucket, to snuff it.

palmarés *m* **-1.** [historial] record. **-2.** [lista] list, roll.

palmear ◇ *vt* **-1.** [aplaudir] to applaud. **-2.** [espalda] to slap, to pat. ◇ *vi* to clap, to applaud.

palmeño, -ña *adj* of/relating to Las Palmas.

palmera *f* **-1.** [árbol] palm (tree); [datilera] date palm. **-2.** [pastel] *flat, butterfly-shaped pastry.*

palmeral *m* palm grove.

palmesano, -na *adj* of/relating to Palma (Mallorca).

palmito *m* **-1.** [árbol] palmetto, fan palm. **-2.** CULIN palm heart. **-3.** *fam fig* [buena plan-

ta] good looks (*pl*); **lucir el** ~ to show off one's good looks.

palmo *m* handspan; *fig* small amount; ~ **a** ~ bit by bit; **dejar a alguien con un** ~ **de narices** to let sb down.

palmotear *vi* to clap.

palmoteo *m* clapping.

palo *m* **-1.** [gen] stick; [de golf] club; [de portería] post; [de la escoba] handle. **-2.** [mástil] mast. **-3.** [golpe] blow (*with a stick*); **moler a alguien a** ~**s** to thrash sb. **-4.** *fig* [mala crítica] bad review. **-5.** [de baraja] suit. **-6.** [madera]: **de** ~ wooden. **-7.** BOT tree; ~ **santo** lignum vitae. **-8.** *fig* [pesadez] bind, drag; **dar** ~ *fam* to be a bind ○ a drag. **-9.** *loc*: **a** ~ **seco** [gen] without anything else; [bebida] neat; **dar** ~**s de ciego** [criticar] to lash out (wildly); [no saber qué hacer] to grope around in the dark; **de tal** ~ **tal astilla** like father, like son.

paloma → **palomo**.

palomar *m* dovecote; [grande] pigeon shed.

palomilla *f* **-1.** [insecto] grain moth. **-2.** [tornillo] butterfly nut, wing nut. **-3.** [soporte] bracket.

palomino *m* young dove ○ pigeon.

palomita *f*: ~**s** popcorn (*U*).

palomo, -ma *m y f* dove, pigeon; **paloma mensajera** carrier ○ homing pigeon; **paloma torcaz** ringdove, wood pigeon.

palote *m* [trazo] downstroke.

palpable *adj* touchable, palpable; *fig* obvious, clear.

palpación *f* palpation.

palpar ◇ *vt* **-1.** [tocar] to feel, to touch; MED to palpate. **-2.** *fig* [percibir] to feel. ◇ *vi* to feel around.

palpitación *f* beat, beating (*U*); [con fuerza] throb, throbbing (*U*).
◆ **palpitaciones** *fpl* MED palpitations.

palpitante *adj* **-1.** [que palpita] beating; [con fuerza] throbbing. **-2.** *fig* [interesante - discusión, competición] lively; [- interés, deseo, cuestión] burning.

palpitar *vi* **-1.** [latir] to beat; [con fuerza] to throb. **-2.** *fig* [suj: sentimiento] to be evident.

pálpito *m* feeling, hunch.

palta *f* *Amer* avocado.

palúdico, -ca *adj* **-1.** MED malarial. **-2.** [pantanoso] marshy, swampy.

paludismo *m* malaria.

palurdo, -da ◇ *adj* *fam* coarse, uncouth. ◇ *m y f* country bumpkin, yokel, hick *Am*.

pamela *f* sun hat.

pampa *f*: **la** ~ the pampas (*pl*).

pampero, **-ra** ◇ *adj* of/relating to the pampas. ◇ *m y f* inhabitant of the pampas.

pamplina *f* (*gen pl*) *fam* trifle, unimportant thing.

Pamplona Pamplona.

pamplonés, **-esa** *adj* of/relating to Pamplona.

pan *m* **-1.** [alimento] bread; ~ **de molde** ○ **inglés** sliced bread; ~ **francés** French bread; ~ **integral** wholemeal bread; ~ **moreno** ○ **negro** [integral] brown bread; [con centeno] black ○ rye bread; ~ **rallado** breadcrumbs (*pl*). **-2.** [hogaza] loaf. **-3.** *loc*: **a falta de** ~ **buenas son tortas** you have to make the most of what you've got; **a** ~ **y agua** on bread and water; *fig* on the breadline; **contigo** ~ **y cebolla** I'll go through thick and thin with you; **llamar al** ~ ~ **y al vino vino** to call a spade a spade; **ser** ~ **comido** to be a piece of cake, to be as easy as pie; **ser el** ~ **nuestro de cada día** to be a regular occurrence, to be commonplace; **ser más bueno que el** ~ to be kindness itself.

pana *f* corduroy.

panacea *f lit* & *fig* panacea.

panadería *f* bakery, baker's.

panadero, **-ra** *m y f* baker.

panal *m* honeycomb.

panamá (*pl* **panamaes**) *m* panama (hat).

Panamá Panama.

panameño, **-ña** *adj, m y f* Panamanian.

panamericanismo *m* Pan-Americanism.

pancarta *f* placard, banner.

panceta *f* bacon.

pancho, **-cha** *adj fam* calm, unruffled; **estar/quedarse tan** ~ to be/remain perfectly calm.

páncreas *m inv* pancreas.

pancreático, **-ca** *adj* pancreatic.

panda ◇ *m* → **oso**. ◇ *f* gang.

pandemónium (*pl* **pandemóniums**) *m* pandemonium.

pandereta *f* tambourine.

pandero *m* **-1.** MÚS tambourine. **-2.** *fam* [culo] bum.

pandilla *f* gang.

pandillero, **-ra** *m y f* member of a gang.

panecillo *m* bread roll.

panegírico, **-ca** *adj* panegyrical, eulogistic.
◆ **panegírico** *m* panegyric, eulogy.

panel *m* **-1.** [gen] panel. **-2.** [pared, biombo] screen. **-3.** [tablero] board.

panera *f* bread basket.

panero *m* bread tray.

paneuropeísmo *m* Europeanism.

pánfilo, **-la** ◇ *adj* simple, foolish. ◇ *m y f* fool, simpleton.

panfletario, **-ria** *adj* propagandist.

panfleto *m* pamphlet.

pánico *m* panic; **ser presa del** ~ to be panic-stricken.

panificadora *f* (large) bakery.

panocha *f* ear, cob.

panoplia *f* **-1.** [armadura] panoply. **-2.** [armas] collection of arms ○ weapons.

panorama *m* **-1.** [vista] panorama. **-2.** *fig* [situación] overall state; [perspectiva] outlook.

panorámico, **-ca** *adj* panoramic.
◆ **panorámica** *f* panorama.

pantagruélico, **-ca** *adj* gargantuan, enormous.

pantaletas *fpl Amer* knickers.

pantalla *f* **-1.** [gen & INFORM] screen; **mostrar en** ~ to show on the screen; ~ **acústica** baffle; ~ **de cristal líquido** liquid crystal display; ~ **de radar** radar screen; ~ **táctil** touch screen; **la pequeña** ~ the small screen, television. **-2.** [de lámpara] lampshade. **-3.** [de chimenea] fireguard. **-4.** *fig* [encubridor] front.

pantalón *m* (*gen pl*) trousers (*pl*), pants (*pl*) *Am*; ~ **tejano** ○ **vaquero** jeans (*pl*); ~ **pitillo** drainpipe trousers (*pl*); **bajarse los pantalones** to give in; **llevar los pantalones** to wear the trousers.

pantano *m* **-1.** [ciénaga] marsh; [laguna] swamp. **-2.** [embalse] reservoir.

pantanoso, **-sa** *adj* **-1.** [cenagoso] marshy, boggy. **-2.** *fig* [difícil] tricky.

panteísta ◇ *adj* pantheistic. ◇ *m y f* pantheist.

panteón *m* pantheon; [familiar] mausoleum, vault.

pantera *f* panther; ~ **negra** black panther.

pantimedias *fpl Amer* tights.

pantocrátor *m* Christ Pantocrator.

pantomima *f* mime; *fig* pantomime (*U*), acting (*U*).

pantorrilla *f* calf.

pantufla *f* (*gen pl*) slipper.

panty (*pl* **pantys**) *m* tights (*pl*).

panza *f* belly.

panzada *f* **-1.** [en el agua] belly flop. **-2.** *fam* [hartura] bellyful.

pañal *m* nappy *Br*, diaper *Am*; **estar en** ~**es** [en sus inicios] to be in its infancy; [sin conocimientos] not to have a clue; **dejar a alguien en** ~**es** to leave sb standing ○ behind.

pañería *f* [producto] drapery; [tienda] draper's (shop), dry-goods store *Am*.

paño *m* **-1.** [tela] cloth, material. **-2.** [trapo] cloth; [para polvo] duster; [de cocina] tea towel. **-3.** [lienzo] panel, length. **-4.** *loc*: conocer el ~ to know the score; ser el ~ de lágrimas de alguien to be a shoulder to cry on for sb.

◆ **paños** *mpl* **-1.** [vestiduras] drapes; ~s menores underwear (*U*). **-2.** MED swabs. **-3.** *loc*: ~s calientes half-measures.

pañol *m* NÁUT storeroom.

pañoleta *f* shawl, wrap.

pañuelo *m* [de nariz] handkerchief; [para el cuello] scarf; [para la cabeza] headscarf; ~ de papel paper handkerchief, tissue.

papa *f* potato; **no saber ni** ~ *fam* not to have a clue.

◆ **Papa** *m* Pope.

papá *m fam* dad, daddy, pop *Am*; ~ **grande** *Amer* grandpa.

◆ **Papá Noel** [pa'pa no'el] *m* Father Christmas.

papachador, -ra *adj Amer* comforting.

papachar *vt Amer* to spoil.

papada *f* [de persona] double chin; [de animal] dewlap.

papado *m* papacy.

papagayo *m* parrot; **como un** ~ parrot-fashion.

papal *adj* papal.

papalote *m Amer* [cometa] kite.

papamoscas *m inv* flycatcher.

papanatas *m y f inv fam* sucker.

papaya *f* [fruta] papaya, pawpaw.

papear *vi fam* to scoff, to pig out.

papel *m* **-1.** [gen] paper; [hoja] sheet of paper; ~ **carbón/cuché/secante** carbon/coated/blotting paper; ~ **cebolla** onionskin; ~ **celofán** Cellophane; ~ **continuo** INFORM continuous paper; ~ **de barba** bloom; ~ **de embalar** o **de embalaje** wrapping paper; ~ **de estaño** o **de aluminio** o **de plata** tin o aluminium foil; ~ **de estraza** brown paper; ~ **de fumar** cigarette paper; ~ **de lija** sandpaper; ~ **higiénico** toilet paper; ~ **madera** *Amer* cardboard; ~ **milimetrado** graph paper; ~ **pintado** wallpaper; ~ **sellado** o **timbrado** stamp, stamped paper; ~ **vegetal** tracing paper; **ser** ~ **mojado** to be worthless. **-2.** CIN, TEATR & *fig* role, part; **desempeñar** o **hacer el** ~ **de** to play the role o part of; ~ **principal/secundario** main/minor part; **hacer buen/mal** ~ to do well/badly. **-3.** FIN stocks and shares (*pl*); ~ **de pagos** *special stamps for making certain payments to the State*; ~ **del Estado** government bonds (*pl*); ~ **moneda** paper money, banknotes (*pl*).

◆ **papeles** *mpl* [documentos] papers.

papela *f fam* [documentación] I.D. card.

papeleo *m* paperwork, red tape.

papelera → papelero.

papelería *f* stationer's (shop).

papelero, -ra *adj* paper (*antes de sust*).

◆ **papelera** *f* **-1.** [cesto - en oficina etc] wastepaper basket o bin; [- en la calle] litter bin. **-2.** [fábrica] paper mill.

papeleta *f* **-1.** [boleto] ticket, slip (of paper); [de votación] ballot paper. **-2.** EDUC *slip of paper with university exam results*. **-3.** *fig* [problema]: **¡menuda** ~! that's a nasty one!

papelina *f fam sachet of paper containing drugs*.

papelón *m fam* spectacle; **hacer un** ~ to make a fool of o.s., to be left looking ridiculous.

paperas *fpl* mumps.

papi *m fam* daddy, dad.

papilla *f* **-1.** [para niños] baby food; **echar** o **arrojar la primera** ~ to be as sick as a dog; **hecho** ~ [cansado] shattered, exhausted; [roto] smashed to bits, ruined. **-2.** MED barium meal.

papiloma *m* papilloma.

papiro *m* papyrus.

papiroflexia *f* origami.

papista *m y f* papist; **ser más** ~ **que el Papa** to be more Catholic than the Pope.

paprika *f* paprika.

papú (*pl* papúes) *adj, m y f* Papuan.

Papúa-Nueva Guinea Papua New Guinea.

paquebote *m* packet boat.

paquete *m* **-1.** [de libros, regalos etc] parcel; ~ **bomba** parcel bomb; ~ **postal** parcel. **-2.** [de cigarrillos, klínex, folios etc] pack, packet; [de azúcar, arroz] bag. **-3.** [maleta, bulto etc] bag. **-4.** [de medidas] package; ~ **de acciones** share holding; ~ **turístico** package tour. **-5.** *fam* [cosa fastidiosa]: **me ha tocado el** ~ **de hacer** ... I've been lumbered with doing .... **-6.** INFORM package. **-7.** *fam* [pañales] nappies. **-8.** [en una moto]: **ir de** ~ to ride pillion. **-9.** *loc*: **meter un** ~ **a alguien** *fam* [castigar] to come down on sb like a ton of bricks.

paquidermo *m* pachyderm.

Paquistán = Pakistán.

paquistaní = pakistaní.

par ◇ *adj* **-1.** MAT even; **jugar a** ~**es o nones** *to play a game involving guessing the number of fingers that another person is holding out behind his/her back*. **-2.** [igual] equal. ◇ *m* **-1.**

[pareja - de zapatos etc] pair. **-2.** [dos - veces etc] couple. **-3.** [número indeterminado] few, couple; **un ~ de copas** a couple of ◇ a few drinks. **-4.** [en golf] par. **-5.** [noble] peer.
◆ **a la par** *loc adv* **-1.** [simultáneamente] at the same time. **-2.** [a igual nivel] at the same level. **-3.** FIN at par.
◆ **de par en par** *loc adj*: **abierto de ~ en ~** wide open.
◆ **sin par** *loc adj* without equal, matchless.
PAR (*abrev de* **Partido Aragonés Regionalista**) *m Aragonese regionalist party.*

para *prep* **-1.** [finalidad] for; **es ~ ti** it's for you; **una mesa ~ el salón** a table for the living room; **esta agua no es buena ~ beber** this water isn't fit for drinking ◇ to drink; **te lo repetiré ~ que te enteres** I'll repeat it so you understand; **¿~ qué?** what for? **-2.** [motivación] (in order) to; **~ conseguir sus propósitos** in order to achieve his aims; **lo he hecho ~ agradarte** I did it to please you. **-3.** [dirección] towards; **ir ~ casa** to head (for) home; **salir ~ el aeropuerto** to leave for the airport. **-4.** [tiempo] for; **tiene que estar acabado ~ mañana** it has to be finished by ◇ for tomorrow. **-5.** [comparación]: **está muy delgado ~ lo que come** he's very thin considering how much he eats; **~ ser verano hace mucho frío** considering it's summer, it's very cold. **-6.** (*después de adj y antes de infin*) [inminencia, propósito] to; **la comida está lista ~ servir** the meal is ready to be served; **el atleta está preparado ~ ganar** the athlete is ready to win.
◆ **para con** *loc prep* towards; **es buena ~ con los demás** she is kind towards other people.
parabién (*pl* **parabienes**) *m* congratulations (*pl*).
parábola *f* **-1.** [alegoría] parable. **-2.** GEOM parabola.
parabólico, -ca *adj* parabolic.
parabrisas *m inv* windscreen, windshield *Am.*
paracaídas *m inv* parachute.
paracaidismo *m* parachuting, parachute jumping.
paracaidista *m y f* parachutist; MIL paratrooper.
parachispas *m inv* fireguard.
parachoques *m inv* AUTOM bumper, fender *Am*; FERROC buffer.
parada → **parado.**
paradero *m* **-1.** [de persona] whereabouts (*pl*). **-2.** *Amer* [parada de autobús] bus stop.
paradigma *m* paradigm, example.

paradisiaco, -ca, paradisíaco, -ca *adj* heavenly.
parado, -da ◇ *adj* **-1.** [inmóvil - coche] stationary, standing; [- persona] still, motionless; [- fábrica, proyecto] at a standstill. **-2.** [pasivo] lacking in initiative. **-3.** *fam* [sin empleo] unemployed, out of work. **-4.** *loc*: **salir bien/mal ~ de algo** to come off well/badly out of sthg. ◇ *m y f fam* [desempleado] unemployed person; **los ~s** the unemployed.
◆ **parada** *f* **-1.** [detención] stop, stopping (*U*). **-2.** DEP save. **-3.** [de autobús] (bus) stop; [de taxis] taxi rank; [de metro] (underground) station; **parada discrecional** request stop. **-4.** MIL parade.
paradoja *f* paradox.
paradójico, -ca *adj* paradoxical, ironical.
parador *m* **-1.** [mesón] roadside inn. **-2.** [hotel]: **~ (nacional)** *state-owned hotel.*

PARADOR NACIONAL:
A 'parador nacional' is a building of artistic or historic interest which has been converted into a luxury hotel and is administered by the Spanish government. 'Paradores' are found throughout Spain, both in cities and the countryside. They are considered to be flagships of the government's policy on tourism

parafernalia *f* paraphernalia.
parafina *f* paraffin.
parafrasear *vt* to paraphrase.
paráfrasis *f inv* paraphrase.
paraguas *m inv* umbrella.
Paraguay: **(el) ~** Paraguay.
paraguayo, -ya *adj, m y f* Paraguayan.
paragüero *m* umbrella stand.
paraíso *m* RELIG Paradise; *fig* paradise; **~ fiscal** tax haven; **~ terrenal** earthly Paradise.
paraje *m* spot, place.
paralelismo *m* **-1.** GEOM parallelism. **-2.** [semejanza] similarity, parallels (*pl*).
paralelo, -la *adj*: **~ (a)** parallel (to).
◆ **paralelo** *m* **-1.** GEOGR parallel. **-2.** [comparación] comparison. **-3.** ELECTR: **estar en ~** to be in parallel.
◆ **paralela** *f* GEOM parallel (line).
◆ **paralelas** *fpl* DEP parallel bars.
paralelogramo *m* parallelogram.
parálisis *f inv* paralysis; **~ cerebral** cerebral palsy; **~ infantil** polio.
paralítico, -ca *adj, m y f* paralytic.
paralización *f* paralysis; *fig* halting.
paralizar [13] *vt* to paralyse.

◆ **paralizarse** *vpr* to become paralysed; [producción etc] to come to a standstill.

Paramaribo Paramaribo.

paramento *m* -1. [adorno] adornment. -2. CONSTR facing (*of a wall*).

parámetro *m* parameter.

paramilitar *adj* paramilitary.

páramo *m* moor, moorland (*U*); *fig* wilderness.

parangón *m* paragon; **sin** ~ unparalleled; **tener** ~ **con** to be comparable with.

paraninfo *m* assembly hall, auditorium.

paranoia *f* paranoia.

paranoico, -ca *adj, m y f* paranoic.

paranoide *adj* paranoid.

paranormal *adj* paranormal.

parapente *m* parapente, paraskiing.

parapetarse *vpr lit & fig*: ~ **(tras)** to take refuge (behind).

parapeto *m* [antepecho] parapet; [barandilla] bannister; [barricada] barricade.

paraplejía *f* paraplegia.

parapléjico, -ca *adj, m y f* paraplegic.

parapsicología *f* parapsychology.

parapsicológico, -ca *adj* parapsychological.

parapsicólogo, -ga *m y f* parapsychologist.

parar ◇ *vi* -1. [gen] to stop; ~ **de hacer algo** to stop doing sthg; **no para de molestarme** she keeps annoying me; **no** ~ *fam* to be always on the go; **sin** ~ non-stop. -2. [alojarse] to stay. -3. [recaer]: ~ **en manos de alguien** to come into the possession of sb. -4. [acabar] to end up; **¿en qué parará este lío?** where will it all end?; **ir a** ~ **a** to end up in.
◇ *vt* -1. [gen] to stop; [golpe] to parry. -2. [preparar] to prepare, to lay. -3. *Amer* [levantar] to raise.

◆ **pararse** *vpr* -1. [detenerse] to stop; ~**se a hacer algo** to stop to do sthg. -2. *Amer* [ponerse de pie] to stand up.

pararrayos *m inv* lightning conductor.

parasitario, -ria *adj* parasitic.

parasitismo *m* parasitism.

parásito, -ta *adj* BIOL parasitic.

◆ **parásito** *m* BIOL & *fig* parasite.

◆ **parásitos** *mpl* [interferencias] statics (*pl*).

parasitología *f* parasitology.

parasol *m* parasol.

parcela *f* plot (of land).

parcelación *f* parcelling out, division into plots.

parcelar *vt* to parcel out, to divide into plots.

parcelario, -ria *adj of or relating to plots of land*.

parche *m* -1. [gen] patch. -2. [emplasto] poultice. -3. [chapuza - mal hecha] botch job; [- para salir del paso] makeshift solution.

parchear *vt fig* to patch up.

parchís *m inv* ludo.

parcial ◇ *adj* -1. [no total] partial. -2. [no ecuánime] biased. ◇ *m* [examen] *end-of-term exam at university*.

parcialidad *f* -1. [tendenciosidad] bias, partiality. -2. [bando] faction.

parco, -ca *adj* -1. [moderado]: ~ **(en)** sparing (in). -2. [escaso] meagre; [cena] frugal; [explicación] brief, concise.

pardiez *interj desus*: ¡~! good gracious!

pardillo, -lla ◇ *adj* -1. [ingenuo] naive. -2. [palurdo] countrified. ◇ *m y f* -1. [ingenuo] naive person. -2. [palurdo] bumpkin.

◆ **pardillo** *m* ZOOL linnet.

pardo, -da *adj* greyish-brown, dull brown.

◆ **pardo** *m* greyish-brown, dull brown.

parear *vt* to pair.

parecer [30] ◇ *m* -1. [opinión] opinion. -2. [apariencia]: **de buen** ~ good-looking.
◇ *vi* (*antes de sust*) to look like; **parece un palacio** it looks like a palace.
◇ *v copulativo* to look, to seem; **pareces cansado** you look ○ seem tired.
◇ *v impers* -1. [opinar]: **me parece que ...** I think ○ it seems to me that ...; **me parece que sí/no** I think/don't think so; **¿qué te parece?** what do you think (of it)? -2. [tener aspecto de]: **parece que va a llover** it looks as if it's going to rain; **parece que le gusta** it looks as if ○ it seems that she likes it; **eso parece so it seems**; **al** ~ apparently.

◆ **parecerse** *vpr*: ~**se (en)** to be alike (in); ~**se a alguien** [físicamente] to look like sb; [en carácter] to be like sb.

parecido, -da *adj* similar; ~ **a** similar to, like; **bien** ~ [atractivo] good-looking.

◆ **parecido** *m*: ~ **(con/entre)** resemblance (to/between).

pared *f* -1. [gen] wall; ~ **maestra** main wall; **entre cuatro** ~**es** cooped-up at home; **las** ~**es oyen** walls have ears; **si las** ~**es hablasen ...** if the walls could talk ...; **subirse por las** ~**es** to hit the roof, to go up the wall. -2. [de montaña] side. -3. DEP one-two.

paredón *m* (thick) wall; [de fusilamiento] (execution) wall.

parejo, -ja *adj*: ~ **(a)** similar (to).

◆ **pareja** *f* -1. [gen] pair; [de novios] couple; **por parejas** in pairs; ~ **de hecho** *common-law heterosexual or homosexual relationship*. -2. [miembro del par - persona] partner; [- guante etc] other one; **la pareja de este calcetín** the other sock of this pair.

parentela f relations (pl), family.

parentesco m relationship.

paréntesis m inv **-1.** [signo] bracket; **entre** ~ in brackets, in parentheses. **-2.** [intercalación] digression. **-3.** [interrupción] break; **hacer un** ~ to have a break.

pareo m wraparound skirt.

parezca etc → **parecer.**

pargo m porgy.

paria m y f pariah.

parida f fam tripe (U), nonsense (U).

paridad f **-1.** [semejanza] similarity; [igualdad] evenness. **-2.** ECON parity; ~ **de cambio** parity of exchange. **-3.** INFORM parity check.

pariente, -ta m y f **-1.** [familiar] relation, relative. **-2.** fam [cónyuge] old man (f missus).

parietal m parietal.

parihuela f stretcher.

paripé m fam: **hacer el** ~ to put on an act, to pretend.

parir ◇ vi to give birth. ◇ vt to give birth to.

paritorio m delivery room.

parking ['parkin] (pl **parkings**) m car park, parking lot Am.

parlamentar vi to negotiate.

parlamentario, -ria ◇ adj parliamentary. ◇ m y f member of parliament.

parlamentarismo m parliamentary system.

parlamento m **-1.** POLÍT parliament. **-2.** TEATR speech.

parlanchín, -ina ◇ adj talkative. ◇ m y f chatterbox.

parlante adj talking.

parlotear vi fam to chatter.

parloteo m fam chatter.

parmesano, -na adj, m y f Parmesan.
◆ **parmesano** m → **queso.**

parnaso m culto parnassus.

paro m **-1.** [desempleo] unemployment; **estar en** ~ to be unemployed; ~ **cíclico/encubierto/estructural** cyclical/hidden/structural unemployment; ~ **forzoso** compulsory redundancy. **-2.** [cesación - acción] shutdown; [- estado] stoppage; ~ **cardiaco** cardiac arrest; ~ **de imagen** [de vídeo] freeze-frame function; ~ **laboral** industrial action (U).

parodia f parody.

parodiar [8] vt to parody.

parón m sudden stoppage.

paroxismo m paroxysm.

paroxítono, -na adj paroxytone, word where the penultimate syllable is stressed.

parpadeante adj [luz] flickering.

parpadear vi **-1.** [pestañear] to blink. **-2.** [centellear] to flicker.

parpadeo m **-1.** [pestañeo] blinking. **-2.** fig [centelleo] flickering.

párpado m eyelid.

parque m **-1.** [gen] park; ~ **acuático** waterpark; ~ **de atracciones** amusement park; ~ **nacional** national park; ~ **tecnológico** science park; (~) **zoológico** zoo. **-2.** [vehículos] fleet; ~ **de bomberos** fire station; ~ **móvil** car pool. **-3.** [para niños] playpen.

parqué (pl **parqués**), **parquet** [par'ke] (pl **parquets**) m parquet (floor).

parqueadero m Amer car park.

parquear vt Amer to park.

parquedad f moderation; **con** ~ sparingly.

parquet = **parqué.**

parquímetro m parking meter.

parra f grapevine; **subirse a la** ~ fig fam to hit the roof.

parrafada f earful, dull monologue; **soltar una** ~ to go on (and on).

párrafo m paragraph.

parral m **-1.** [emparrado] vine arbour. **-2.** [terreno] vineyard.

parrampán m Amer fam [tonto] daft.

parranda f **-1.** fam [juerga]: **irse de** ~ to go out on the town. **-2.** [banda] group of musicians who go out on the town.

parrandear vi to go out on the town.

parricida m y f parricide.

parricidio m parricide.

parrilla f **-1.** [utensilio] grill; **a la** ~ grilled. **-2.** [sala de restaurante] grillroom. **-3.** DEP: ~ **(de salida)** (starting) grid. **-4.** Amer [baca] roof rack.

parrillada f mixed grill.

párroco m parish priest.

parroquia f **-1.** [iglesia] parish church. **-2.** [jurisdicción] parish. **-3.** [fieles] parishioners (pl), parish. **-4.** [clientela] clientele.

parroquial adj parish (antes de sust).

parroquiano, -na m y f **-1.** [feligrés] parishioner. **-2.** [cliente] customer.

parsimonia f deliberation, calmness; **con** ~ unhurriedly.

parsimonioso, -sa adj unhurried, deliberate.

parte ◇ m report; **dar** ~ **(a alguien de algo)** to report (sthg to sb); ~ **facultativo** o **médico** medical report; ~ **meteorológico** weather forecast. ◇ f [gen] part; [bando]

side; DER party; **la mayor** ~ **de la gente** most people; **la tercera** ~ **de a** third of; **en alguna** ~ somewhere; **no lo veo por ninguna** ~ I can't find it anywhere; **en** ~ to a certain extent, partly; **estar/ponerse de** ~ **de alguien** to be on/to take sb's side; **formar** ~ **de** to be part of; **por mi** ~ for my part; **por** ~ **de padre/madre** on one's father's/mother's side; **por** ~s bit by bit; **por una** ~ ... **por la otra** ... on the one hand ... on the other (hand) ...; **tener a alguien de** ~ **de uno** to have sb on one's side; **tomar** ~ **en algo** to take part in sthg; **en todas** ~s **cuecen habas** it's the same the whole world over.

◆ **partes** *fpl* [genitales] private parts.

◆ **de parte de** *loc prep* on behalf of, for; **¿de** ~ **de (quién)?** TELECOM who is calling, please?

◆ **por otra parte** *loc adv* [además] what is more, besides.

partenaire [parte'ner] *m y f* partner.

partera *f* midwife.

parterre *m* flowerbed.

partición *f* **-1.** [reparto] sharing out; [- de territorio] partitioning. **-2.** MAT division.

participación *f* **-1.** [colaboración] participation. **-2.** [de lotería] share of a lottery ticket. **-3.** [comunicación] notice. **-4.** ECON: ~ **en los beneficios** profit-sharing.

participante ◇ *adj* participating. ◇ *m y f* participant.

participar ◇ *vi* **-1.** [colaborar]: ~ **(en)** to take part O participate (in); FIN to have a share (in). **-2.** [recibir]: ~ **(de** O **en)** to receive a share (of). **-3.** [compartir]: ~ **de** to share. ◇ *vt*: ~ **algo a alguien** to notify sb of sthg.

partícipe ◇ *adj*: ~ **(de)** involved (in); **hacer** ~ **de algo a alguien** [notificar] to notify sb of sthg; [compartir] to share sthg with sb. ◇ *m y f* participant.

participio *m* participle; ~ **pasado/presente** past/present participle.

partícula *f* particle.

particular ◇ *adj* **-1.** [gen] particular; **tiene su sabor** ~ it has its own particular taste; **en** ~ in particular. **-2.** [no público - domicilio, clases etc] private. **-3.** [no corriente - habilidad etc] uncommon. ◇ *m y f* [persona] member of the public. ◇ *m* [asunto] matter; **sin otro** ~ without further ado.

particularidad *f* [cualidad] peculiarity; [rasgo] special O distinctive feature.

particularizar [13] ◇ *vt* [caracterizar] to characterize. ◇ *vi* **-1.** [detallar] to go into details. **-2.** [personalizar]: ~ **en alguien** to single sb out.

◆ **particularizarse** *vpr* [caracterizarse]: ~se **por** to be characterized by.

partida *f* **-1.** [marcha] departure. **-2.** [en juego] game; **echar una** ~ to have a game. **-3.** [documento] certificate; ~ **de defunción/matrimonio/nacimiento** death/marriage/birth certificate. **-4.** [COM - mercancía] consignment; [- entrada] item, entry.

partidario, -ria ◇ *adj*: ~ **de** in favour of, for. ◇ *m y f* supporter.

partidismo *m* partisanship, bias.

partidista *adj* partisan, biased.

partido *m* **-1.** POLÍT party. **-2.** DEP match; ~ **amistoso** friendly (match). **-3.** [futuro cónyuge] match; **buen/mal** ~ good/bad match. **-4.** *loc*: **sacar** ~ **de** to make the most of; **tomar** ~ **por** to side with.

partir ◇ *vt* **-1.** [dividir] to divide, to split. **-2.** [repartir] to share out. **-3.** [romper] to break open; [cascar] to crack; [tronco, loncha etc] to cut. ◇ *vi* **-1.** [marchar] to leave, to set off. **-2.** [basarse]: ~ **de** to start from.

◆ **partirse** *vpr* **-1.** [romperse] to split. **-2.** [rajarse] to crack.

◆ **a partir de** *loc prep* starting from; **a** ~ **de aquí** from here on.

partisano, -na *adj, m y f* partisan.

partitivo, -va *adj* partitive.

◆ **partitivo** *m* partitive.

partitura *f* score.

parto *m* birth; **estar de** ~ to be in labour; ~ **natural/prematuro** natural/premature birth.

parturienta *f* woman in labour.

parvulario *m* nursery school, kindergarten.

párvulo, -la *m y f* infant.

pasa *f* [fruta] raisin; ~ **de Corinto** currant; ~ **de Esmirna** sultana.

pasable *adj* passable.

pasabocas *m inv* *Amer* snack.

pasada → pasado.

pasadizo *m* passage.

pasado, -da *adj* **-1.** [gen] past; ~ **un año a** year later; **lo** ~, ~ **está** let bygones be bygones. **-2.** [último] last; **el año** ~ last year. **-3.** [podrido] off, bad. **-4.** [hecho - filete, carne] well done.

◆ **pasado** *m* [gen] past; GRAM past (tense).

◆ **pasada** *f* **-1.** [con el trapo] wipe; [con la brocha] coat. **-2.** *fam* [barbaridad]: **es una pasada** it's way over the top.

◆ **de pasada** *loc adv* in passing.

◆ **mala pasada** *f* dirty trick.

pasador *m* **-1.** [cerrojo] bolt. **-2.** [para el pelo] slide. **-3.** *Amer* [cordón] shoelace.

pasaje *m* **-1.** [billete] ticket, fare. **-2.** [pasajeros] passengers (*pl*). **-3.** [calle] passage. **-4.** [fragmento] passage.

pasajero, -ra ◇ *adj* passing. ◇ *m y f* passenger.

pasamano *m* [adorno] braid.

pasamanos *m inv* [de escalera interior] bannister; [de escalera exterior] handrail.

pasamontañas *m inv* balaclava (helmet).

pasante *m y f* articled clerk.

pasapalos *m inv Amer* snack.

pasaporte *m* passport.

pasapuré *m*, **pasapurés** *m inv* food mill.

pasar ◇ *vt* **-1.** [gen] to pass; [noticia, aviso] to pass on; **¿me pasas la sal?** would you pass me the salt?; ~ **algo por** [filtrar] to pass sthg through. **-2.** [cruzar] to cross; ~ **la calle** to cross the road; **pasé el río a nado** I swam across the river. **-3.** [traspasar] to pass through. **-4.** [trasladar]: ~ **algo a** to move sthg to. **-5.** [llevar adentro] to show in; **el criado nos pasó al salón** the butler showed us into the living room. **-6.** [contagiar]: ~ **algo a alguien** to give sthg to sb, to infect sb with sthg; **me has pasado la tos** you've given me your cough. **-7.** [admitir - instancia etc] to accept. **-8.** [consentir]: ~ **algo a alguien** to let sb get away with sthg. **-9.** [rebasar - en el espacio] to go through; [- en el tiempo] to have been through; ~ **un semáforo en rojo** to go through a red light. **-10.** [emplear - tiempo] to spend; **pasó dos años en Roma** he spent two years in Rome. **-11.** [padecer] to go through, to suffer; **pasarlo mal** to have a hard time of it. **-12.** [sobrepasar]: **ya ha pasado los veinticinco** he's over twenty-five now; **mi hijo me pasa ya dos centímetros** my son is already two centimetres taller than me. **-13.** [adelantar - coche, contrincante etc] to overtake. **-14.** CIN to show.

◇ *vi* **-1.** [gen] to pass, to go; **pasó por mi lado** he passed by my side; **el autobús pasa por mi casa** the bus goes past ○ passes in front of my house; **el Manzanares pasa por Madrid** the Manzanares goes ○ passes through Madrid; **he pasado por tu calle** I went down your street; ~ **de ... a ...** to go ○ pass from ... to ...; ~ **de largo** to go by. **-2.** [entrar] to go/come in; **¡pase!** come in! **-3.** [poder entrar]: ~ **(por)** to go (through); **por ahí no pasa** it won't go through there. **-4.** [ir un momento] to pop in; **pasaré por mi oficina/por tu casa** I'll pop into my office/round to your place. **-5.** [suceder] to happen; **¿qué pasa aquí?** what's going on here?; **¿qué pasa?** what's the matter?; **pase lo que pase** whatever happens, come what

may. **-6.** [terminarse] to be over; **pasó la Navidad** Christmas is over. **-7.** [transcurrir] to go by. **-8.** [cambiar - acción]: ~ **a** to move on to; **pasemos a otra cosa** let's move on to something else. **-9.** [conformarse]: ~ **(con/sin algo)** to make do (with/without sthg); **tendrá que** ~ **sin coche** she'll have to make do without a car. **-10.** [servir] to be all right, to be usable; **puede** ~ it'll do. **-11.** *fam* [prescindir]: ~ **de algo/alguien** to want nothing to do with sthg/sb; **paso de política** I'm not into politics. **-12.** [tolerar]: ~ **por algo** to put up with sthg.

◆ **pasarse** *vpr* **-1.** [acabarse] to pass; **siéntate hasta que se te pase** sit down until you feel better. **-2.** [emplear - tiempo] to spend, to pass; **se pasaron el día hablando** they spent all day talking. **-3.** [desaprovecharse] to slip by; **se me pasó la oportunidad** I missed my chance. **-4.** [estropearse - comida] to go off; [- flores] to fade. **-5.** [cambiar de bando]: ~**se a** to go over to. **-6.** [omitir] to miss out; **te has pasado una página** you've missed a page out. **-7.** [olvidarse]: **pasársele a alguien** to slip sb's mind; **se me pasó decírtelo** I forgot to mention it to you. **-8.** [no fijarse]: **pasársele a alguien** to escape sb's attention; **no se le pasa nada** he never misses a thing. **-9.** [excederse]: ~**se de generoso/bueno** to be far too generous/kind. **-10.** *fam* [propasarse] to go too far, to go over the top; **te has pasado diciéndole eso** what you said went too far ○ was over the top. **-11.** [divertirse]: **¿qué tal te lo estás pasando?** how are you enjoying yourself?; **pasárselo bien/mal** to have a good/bad time.

pasarela *f* **-1.** [puente] footbridge; [para desembarcar] gangway. **-2.** [en un desfile] catwalk.

pasatiempo *m* [hobby] pastime, hobby.

◆ **pasatiempos** *mpl* PRENS crossword and puzzles section (*sg*).

Pascua *f* **-1.** [de los judíos] Passover. **-2.** [de los cristianos] Easter; **hacer la** ~ **a alguien** *fam* [ser pesado] to pester sb; [poner en apuros] to land sb in it.

◆ **Pascuas** *fpl* [Navidad] Christmas (*sg*); **¡felices Pascuas!** Merry Christmas!; **de Pascuas a Ramos** once in a blue moon.

pascual *adj* Easter (*antes de sust*).

pase *m* **-1.** [gen, DEP & TAUROM] pass; *ver también* **tauromaquia. -2.** [proyección] showing, screening. **-3.** [desfile] parade; ~ **de modelos** fashion parade.

paseante *m y f* person out for a stroll.

pasear ◇ *vi* to go for a walk. ◇ *vt* to take for a walk; [perro] to walk; *fig* to show off, to parade.

◆ **pasearse** *vpr* [gandulear] to loaf about.

paseíllo *m* *parade of bullfighters when they come out into the ring before the bullfight starts*; *ver también* **tauromaquia**.

paseo *m* **-1.** [acción - a pie] walk; [- en coche] drive; [- a caballo] ride; [- en barca] row; **dar un** ~ [a pie] to go for a walk. **-2.** [lugar] avenue; ~ **marítimo** promenade. **-3.** *loc:* **mandar** ○ **enviar a alguien a** ~ to send sb packing.

pasillo *m* corridor; ~ **deslizante** travelator; **hacer el** ~ to form a corridor (*for people to walk down*); **hacer** ~**s** to creep up to the boss.

pasión *f* passion.

◆ **Pasión** *f* RELIG Passion.

pasional *adj* passionate.

pasionaria *f* passion flower.

pasividad *f* passivity.

pasivo, -va *adj* **-1.** [gen & GRAM] passive. **-2.** [haber] (received) from a pension. **-3.** [población etc] inactive.

◆ **pasivo** *m* COM liabilities (*pl*).

pasma *f* *fam* fuzz (*pl*), cops (*pl*).

pasmado, -da ◇ *adj* **-1.** [asombrado] astonished, astounded. **-2.** [atontado] stunned. ◇ *m y f* halfwit.

pasmar *vt* to astound.

◆ **pasmarse** *vpr* to be astounded.

pasmarote *m y f fam* twit.

pasmo *m* astonishment.

pasmoso, -sa *adj* astonishing.

paso *m* **-1.** [gen] step; [huella] footprint. **-2.** [acción] passing; [cruce] crossing; [camino de acceso] way through, thoroughfare; **abrir** ~ **a alguien** *lit & fig* to make way for sb; **ceder el** ~ **(a alguien)** to let sb past; AUTOM to give way (to sb); "**ceda el** ~" "give way"; "**prohibido el** ~" "no entry"; ~ **elevado** flyover; ~ **a nivel** level crossing; ~ **peatonal** ○ **de peatones** pedestrian crossing; ~ **subterráneo** subway, underpass *Am*; ~ **de cebra** zebra crossing. **-3.** [forma de andar] walk; [ritmo] pace; **marcar el** ~ to keep time. **-4.** [GEOGR - en montaña] pass; [- en el mar] strait. **-5.** (*gen pl*) [gestión] step; [progreso] step forward, advance; **dar los** ~**s necesarios** to take the necessary steps. **-6.** [mal momento]: **(mal)** ~ difficult situation. **-7.** *loc:* **a cada** ~ every other minute; **está a dos** ○ **cuatro** ~**s** it's just down the road; **¡a este** ~ ...!** *fig* at that rate ...!; **a** ~ **de tortuga** at a snail's pace; **abrirse** ~ **en la vida** to get on in life; **dar un** ~ **en falso** to make a false move ○ a mistake; **estar de** ~ to be passing through; **a** ~ step by step; **salir del** ~ to get out of trouble.

◆ **de paso** *loc adv* in passing.

◆ **paso del ecuador** *m* *halfway stage in a university course.*

PASO DEL ECUADOR:
In Spain, the mid-point in a university course is called the 'paso del ecuador'. Students celebrate by organizing parties, and the money spent by party-goers at these affairs finances a trip students take together at the end of the academic year

pasodoble *m* paso doble.

pasota *fam* ◇ *adj* apathetic. ◇ *m y f* dropout.

pasotismo *m fam* couldn't-care-less attitude.

pasquín *m* lampoon.

pasta *f* **-1.** [masa] paste; [de papel] pulp; ~ **dentífrica** toothpaste. **-2.** [CULIN - espaguetti etc] pasta; [- de pasteles] pastry; [- de pan] dough; ~**s alimenticias** pasta (*U*). **-3.** [pastelillo] pastry. **-4.** *fam* [dinero] dough. **-5.** [encuadernación]: **en** ~ hardback. **-6.** *loc:* **ser de buena** ~ *fam* to be good-natured.

pastar *vi* to graze.

pastel *m* **-1.** [CULIN - dulce] cake; [- salado] pie. **-2.** ARTE pastel. **-3.** *fam* [chapucería] botch-up. **-4.** *loc:* **descubrir el** ~ to let the cat out of the bag; **repartirse el** ~ to share things out.

pastelería *f* **-1.** [establecimiento] cake shop, patisserie. **-2.** [repostería] pastries (*pl*).

pastelero, -ra ◇ *adj* pastry (*antes de sust*). ◇ *m y f* [cocinero] pastry cook; [vendedor] owner of a patisserie.

pasteurizado [pasteuri'θaðo], **-da** *adj* pasteurized.

pasteurizar [pasteuri'θar] [13] *vt* to pasteurize.

pastiche *m* pastiche.

pastilla *f* **-1.** MED pill, tablet. **-2.** [de jabón, chocolate] bar. **-3.** AUTOM shoe (*of brakes*). **-4.** ELECTRÓN microchip. **-5.** *loc:* **a toda** ~ at full pelt.

pastizal *m* pasture.

pasto *m* **-1.** [acción] grazing; [sitio] pasture. **-2.** [hierba] fodder. **-3.** [motivo] food. **-4.** *loc:* **a todo** ~ in abundance; **ser** ~ **de las llamas** to go up in flames.

pastón *m fam:* **vale un** ~ it costs a bomb.

pastor, -ra *m y f* [de ganado] shepherd (*f* shepherdess).

◆ **pastor** *m* **-1.** [sacerdote] minister; ~ **protestante** Protestant minister. **-2.** → **perro**.

pastoral *adj* pastoral.

pastorear *vt* to put out to pasture.

pastoreo *m* shepherding.

pastoso, **-sa** *adj* **-1.** [blando] pasty; [arroz] sticky. **-2.** [seco] dry.

pata *f* **-1.** [pierna] leg. **-2.** [pie - gen] foot; [- de perro, gato] paw; [- de vaca, caballo] hoof. **-3.** *fam* [de persona] leg; **a cuatro ~s** on all fours; **a ~ on foot; ir a la ~ coja** to hop. **-4.** [de mueble] leg; [de gafas] arm. **-5.** *Amer* [etapa] stage. **-6.** [ave] duck. **-7.** *loc:* **estirar la ~** to kick the bucket; **meter la ~** to put one's foot in it; **poner/estar ~s arriba** to turn/be upside down; **tener mala ~** to be unlucky.
◆ **patas** *fpl Amer fam* [poca vergüenza] cheek (*U*).
◆ **pata de gallo** *f* **-1.** [en la cara] crow's feet (*pl*). **-2.** [tejido] hound's-tooth check material.
◆ **pata negra** *m* CULIN *type of top-quality cured ham.*

patada *f* kick; [en el suelo] stamp; **dar una ~ a** to kick; **dar cien ~s a alguien** to drive sb mad; **dar la ~ a alguien** to kick sb out; **sentar como una ~ en el estómago** to be like a kick in the teeth; **tratar a alguien a ~s** to treat sb like dirt.

patagón, **-ona** *adj, m y f* Patagonian.

Patagonia *f:* **la ~** Patagonia.

patalear *vi* to kick about; [en el suelo] to stamp one's feet.

pataleo *m* kicking (*U*); [en el suelo] stamping (*U*).

pataleta *f* tantrum.

patán ◇ *adj m* uncivilized, uncouth. ◇ *m* bumpkin.

patata *f* potato; **~s fritas** [de sartén] chips; [de bolsa] crisps; **~ caliente** *fig* hot potato.

patatero, **-ra** ◇ *adj* potato (*antes de sust*). ◇ *m y f* potato farmer.

patatús *m fam* funny turn.

paté *m* paté.

patear ◇ *vt* [dar un puntapié] to kick; [pisotear] to stamp on. ◇ *vi* **-1.** [patalear] to stamp one's feet. **-2.** *fam fig* [andar] to tramp.
◆ **patearse** *vpr* [recorrer] to tramp.

patena *f* paten; **limpio** ○ **blanco como una ~** as clean as a new pin.

patentado, **-da** *adj* patent, patented.

patentar *vt* to patent.

patente ◇ *adj* obvious; [demostración, prueba] clear. ◇ *f* **-1.** [de invento] patent. **-2.** [autorización] licence. **-3.** *Amer* [matrícula] number plate.

pateo *m* stamping.

paternal *adj* fatherly, paternal; *fig* paternal.

paternalismo *m* **-1.** [actitud protectora] paternalism. **-2.** [de padre] fatherliness.

paternalista *adj* paternalistic.

paternidad *f·*fatherhood; DER paternity.

paterno, **-na** *adj* paternal.

patético, **-ca** *adj* pathetic, moving.

patetismo *m* pathos (*U*).

patíbulo *m* scaffold, gallows (*pl*).

patilla *f* **-1.** [de pelo] sideboard, sideburn. **-2.** [de gafas] arm.

patín *m* **-1.** [calzado - de cuchilla] ice skate; [- de ruedas] roller skate. **-2.** [patinete] scooter. **-3.** [embarcación] pedal boat.

pátina *f* patina.

patinador, **-ra** *m y f* skater.

patinaje *m* skating; **~ artístico** figure skating; **~ sobre hielo** ice skating; **~ sobre ruedas** roller skating.

patinar *vi* **-1.** [sobre hielo] to skate; [sobre ruedas] to roller-skate. **-2.** [resbalar - coche] to skid; [- persona] to slip. **-3.** *fam fig* [meter la pata] to put one's foot in it.

patinazo *m* **-1.** [de coche] skid; [de persona] slip. **-2.** *fam fig* [planchazo] blunder.

patinete *m* scooter.

patio *m* [gen] patio, courtyard; [de escuela] playground; [de cuartel] parade ground; **~ (de butacas)** stalls (*pl*); **¡cómo está el ~!** *fam* what a fine state of affairs!

patita *f:* **poner a alguien de ~s en la calle** *fam fig* to kick sb out.

patitieso, **-sa** *adj* **-1.** [de frío] frozen stiff. **-2.** [de sorpresa] aghast, amazed.

patizambo, **-ba** *adj* knock-kneed.

pato, **-ta** *m y f* duck; **pagar el ~** to carry the can.

patógeno, **-na** *adj* infectious.

patología *f* pathology.

patológico, **-ca** *adj* pathological.

patoso, **-sa** *adj fam* clumsy.

patraña *f fam* fib, lie.

patria → patrio.

patriarca *m* patriarch.

patriarcado *m* patriarchy.

patriarcal *adj* patriarchal.

patricio, **-cia** *adj, m y f* patrician.

patrimonial *adj* hereditary.

patrimonio *m* **-1.** [bienes - heredados] inheritance; [- propios] wealth; **~ nacional** [artístico] national heritage; [económico] national wealth. **-2.** *fig* [de una colectividad] exclusive birthright.

patrio, **-tria** *adj* native.

◆ **patria** f native country, fatherland; **patria chica** home town.

◆ **patria potestad** f DER parental authority.

patriota ◇ adj patriotic. ◇ m y f patriot.

patriotero, -ra adj despec jingoistic.

patriótico, -ca adj patriotic.

patriotismo m patriotism.

patrocinador, -ra ◇ adj sponsoring. ◇ m y f sponsor.

patrocinar vt to sponsor.

patrocinio m sponsorship.

patrón, -ona m y f **-1.** [de obreros] boss; [de criados] master (f mistress). **-2.** [de pensión etc] landlord (f landlady). **-3.** [santo] patron saint.

◆ **patrón** m **-1.** [de barco] skipper. **-2.** [medida] standard; ~ **oro** ECON gold standard. **-3.** [en costura] pattern; **estar cortados por el mismo** ~ fig to be cast in the same mould.

patronal ◇ adj **-1.** [empresarial] management (antes de sust). **-2.** RELIG patron saint (antes de sust). ◇ f **-1.** [de empresa] management. **-2.** [de país] employers' organisation.

patronato m [gen] board; [con fines benéficos] trust.

patronímico, -ca adj patronymic.

patronista m y f pattern cutter.

patrono, -na m y f **-1.** [de empresa - encargado] boss; [- empresario] employer. **-2.** [santo] patron saint.

patrulla ◇ adj → **coche**. ◇ f patrol; **estar de** ~ to be on patrol; ~ **urbana** vigilante group.

patrullar vt & vi to patrol.

patrullero, -ra adj patrol (antes de sust).

◆ **patrullero** m [barco] patrol boat; [avión] patrol plane.

patuco m (gen pl) bootee.

paulatino, -na adj gradual.

pauperización f impoverishment.

paupérrimo, -ma adj very poor, impoverished.

pausa f pause, break; MÚS rest; **con** ~ unhurriedly.

pausado, -da adj deliberate, slow.

pauta f **-1.** [gen] standard, model; **seguir una** ~ to follow an example. **-2.** [en un papel] guideline.

pautado, -da adj lined, ruled.

pava → **pavo**.

pavero, -ra ◇ adj boastful. ◇ m y f braggart.

pavimentación f [de una carretera] road surfacing; [de la acera] paving; [de un suelo] flooring.

pavimentar vt [carretera] to surface; [acera] to pave; [suelo] to floor.

pavimento m [de carretera] road surface; [de acera] paving; [de suelo] flooring.

pavo, -va ◇ adj fam despec wet, drippy. ◇ m y f **-1.** [ave] turkey; ~ **real** peacock (f peahen). **-2.** fam despec [persona] drip.

pavonearse vpr despec: ~ **(de)** to boast ○ brag (about).

pavoneo m despec showing off, boasting.

pavor m terror.

pavoroso, -sa adj terrifying.

paya f Amer improvised poem accompanied by guitar.

payasada f clowning (U); **hacer** ~**s** to clown around.

payaso, -sa ◇ adj clownish. ◇ m y f clown.

payés, -esa m y f peasant farmer from Catalonia or the Balearic Islands.

payo, -ya m y f non-gipsy.

paz f peace; [tranquilidad] peacefulness; **dejar a alguien en** ~ to leave sb alone ○ in peace; **estar** ○ **quedar en** ~ to be quits; **firmar la** ~ to sign a peace treaty; **hacer las paces** to make (it) up; **que en** ~ **descanse, que descanse en** ~ may he/she rest in peace.

pazca etc → **pacer**.

pazguato, -ta fam despec ◇ adj simple. ◇ m y f simpleton.

pazo m Galician country mansion.

PC m **-1.** (abrev de **personal computer**) PC. **-2.** (abrev de **Partido Carlista**) Carlist Party.

PCC m (abrev de **Partido Comunista Cubano**) Cuban communist party.

PCE m (abrev de **Partido Comunista de España**) m Spanish communist party.

PCUS (abrev de **Partido Comunista de la Unión Soviética**) m Soviet communist party.

PD, PS (abrev de **posdata**) PS.

pdo. abrev de **pasado**.

pe f: **de** ~ **a pa** fam fig from beginning to end.

peaje m toll.

peana f pedestal.

peatón m pedestrian.

peatonal adj pedestrian (antes de sust).

peca f freckle.

pecado m sin; ~ **original** original sin; ~**s capitales** mortal sins; **ser un** ~ to be a sin ○ crime.

pecador, -ra ◇ adj sinful. ◇ m y f sinner.

pecaminoso, -sa adj sinful.

pecar [10] *vi* **-1.** RELIG to sin. **-2.** [pasarse]: ~ de confiado/generoso to be overconfident/ too generous.

pecera *f* fish tank; [redonda] fish bowl.

pechera *f* [de camisa] shirt front; [de blusa, vestido] bust.

pecho *m* **-1.** [gen] chest; [de mujer] bosom. **-2.** [mama] breast; **dar el** ~ **a** to breastfeed. **-3.** *fig* [interior] heart. **-4.** *loc*: **a lo hecho,** ~ it's no use crying over spilt milk; **a** ~ **descubierto** without protection ○ any form of defence; **tomarse algo a** ~ to take sthg to heart.

pechuga *f* **-1.** [de ave] breast (*meat*). **-2.** *mfam* [de mujer] tits (*pl*).

pechugón, -ona *adj mfam* big-chested (*f* buxom).

pécora *f*: **ser una mala** ~ to be a bitch ○ cow.

pecoso, -sa *adj* freckly.

pectoral ◇ *adj* **-1.** ANAT pectoral, chest (*antes de sust*). **-2.** FARM cough (*antes de sust*). ◇ *m* FARM cough mixture ○ medicine.

pecuario, -ria *adj* livestock (*antes de sust*).

peculiar *adj* **-1.** [característico] typical, characteristic. **-2.** [curioso] peculiar.

peculiaridad *f* **-1.** [cualidad] uniqueness. **-2.** [detalle] particular feature ○ characteristic.

pecuniario, -ria *adj* pecuniary.

pedagogía *f* education, pedagogy.

pedagógico, -ca *adj* educational.

pedagogo, -ga *m y f* educator; [profesor] teacher.

pedal *m* pedal.

pedalada *f* pedal, pedalling (*U*).

pedalear *vi* to pedal.

pedante ◇ *adj* pompous. ◇ *m y f* pompous person.

pedantería *f* pomposity (*U*).

pedazo *m* piece, bit; **hacer** ~**s** to break to bits; *fig* to destroy; **saltar en (mil)** ~**s** to be smashed to pieces; ~ **de alcornoque** ○ **de animal** ○ **de bruto** stupid oaf ○ brute; **ser un** ~ **de pan** *fig* to be an angel.

pederasta *m* pederast.

pedernal *m* flint.

pedestal *m* pedestal, stand; **poner/tener a alguien en un** ~ to put sb on a pedestal.

pedestre *adj* on foot.

pediatra *m y f* pediatrician.

pediatría *f* pediatrics (*U*).

pedicuro, -ra *m y f* chiropodist *Br*, podiatrist *Am*.

pedido *m* COM order; **hacer un** ~ to place an order.

pedigrí, pedigree [peðiˈɣɾi] *m* pedigree.

pedigüeño, -ña ◇ *adj* demanding, clamouring. ◇ *m y f* demanding person.

pedir [26] ◇ *vt* **-1.** [gen] to ask for; [en comercios, restaurantes] to order; ~ **a alguien que haga algo** to ask sb to do sthg; ~ **a alguien (en matrimonio)** to ask for sb's hand (in marriage); ~ **prestado algo a alguien** to borrow sthg from sb. **-2.** [exigir] to demand. **-3.** [requerir] to call for, to need. **-4.** [poner precio]: ~ **(por)** to ask (for); **pide un millón por la moto** he's asking a million for the motorbike. ◇ *vi* [mendigar] to beg.

pedo ◇ *m* **-1.** *vulg* [ventosidad] fart; **tirarse un** ~ to fart. **-2.** *mfam* [borrachera]: **cogerse un** ~ to get pissed. ◇ *adj mfam*: **estar** ~ to be pissed.

pedofilia *f* paedophilia.

pedorrear *vi vulg* to fart a lot.

pedorreta *f fam* raspberry (*sound*).

pedrada *f* **-1.** [acción] throw of a stone. **-2.** [golpe] blow ○ hit with a stone; **a** ~**s** by stoning.

pedrea *f* **-1.** [en lotería] *group of smaller prizes in the Spanish national lottery.* **-2.** [apedreamiento] stone fight.

pedregal *m* stony ground.

pedregullo *m Amer* gravel.

pedrera *f* stone quarry.

pedrería *f* precious stones (*pl*).

pedrisco *m* hail.

pedrusco *m* rough stone.

PEE (*abrev de* **Partido Ecologista Español**) *m Spanish ecologist party.*

peeling [ˈpilin] (*pl* **peelings**) *m* face mask ○ pack.

pega *f* **-1.** [pegamento] glue. **-2.** [obstáculo] difficulty, hitch; **poner** ~**s (a)** to find problems (with).
♦ **de pega** *loc adj* false, fake.

pegadizo, -za *adj* **-1.** [música] catchy. **-2.** *fig* [contagioso] catching.

pegado *m* **-1.** [parche] plaster. **-2.** [comida] burnt bits (*pl*).

pegajoso, -sa *adj* sticky; *despec* clinging.

pegamento *m* glue.

pegar [16] ◇ *vt* **-1.** [adherir] to stick; [con pegamento] to glue; [póster, cartel] to fix, to put up; [botón] to sew on. **-2.** [arrimar]: ~ **algo a** to put ○ place sthg against. **-3.** [golpear] to hit. **-4.** [propinar - bofetada, paliza etc] to give; [- golpe] to deal. **-5.** [contagiar]: ~ **algo a alguien** to give sb sthg, to pass sthg on to sb. **-6.** INFORM to paste.
◇ *vi* **-1.** [adherir] to stick. **-2.** [golpear] to hit. **-3.** [armonizar] to go together, to match; ~ **con** to go with. **-4.** [sol] to beat down.

◆ **pegarse** *vpr* **-1.** [adherirse] to stick. **-2.** [agredirse] to fight, to hit one another. **-3.** [golpearse]: ~se (un golpe) con algo to hit o.s. against sthg. **-4.** *fig* [contagiarse - enfermedad] to be transmitted, to be passed on; [- canción] to be catchy; **se me pegó su acento** I picked up his accent. **-5.** *despec* [engancharse]: ~se a alguien to stick to sb. **-6.** *loc*: **pegársela a alguien** *fam* to have sb on, to deceive sb; [cónyuge] to cheat on sb.

pegatina *f* sticker.

pego *m*: **dar el ~** *fam fig* to look like the real thing.

pegote *m fam* **-1.** [masa pegajosa] sticky mess. **-2.** [chapucería] botch.

pegue *etc* → **pegar**.

peinado *m* hairdo; [estilo, tipo] hairstyle.

peinador *m* hairdressing gown.

peinar *vt lit & fig* to comb.

◆ **peinarse** *vpr* to comb one's hair.

peine *m* comb; **enterarse de** ○ **saber lo que vale un ~** *fam fig* to find out what's what ○ a thing or two.

peineta *f comb worn in the back of the hair.*

p.ej. (*abrev de* **por ejemplo**) e.g.

pejiguera *f fam* drag, pain.

Pekín Peking, Beijing.

pela *f fam* peseta; **no tengo ~s** I'm skint.

peladilla *f* sugared almond.

pelado, -da *adj* **-1.** [cabeza] shorn. **-2.** [piel, cara etc] peeling; [fruta] peeled. **-3.** [habitación, monte, árbol] bare. **-4.** [número] exact, round; **saqué un aprobado ~** I passed, but only just. **-5.** *fam* [sin dinero] broke, skint.

peladura *f* peeling.

pelagatos *m y f inv fam despec* nobody.

pelaje *m* [de gato, oso, conejo] fur; [de perro, caballo] coat.

pelambre *m* mane ○ mop of hair.

pelambrera *f* long thick hair (*U*).

pelandusca *f fam despec* tart, slut.

pelar *vt* **-1.** [persona] to cut the hair of. **-2.** [fruta, patatas] to peel; [guisantes, marisco] to shell. **-3.** [aves] to pluck; [conejos etc] to skin. **-4.** *fam fig* [dejar sin dinero] to fleece.

◆ **pelarse** *vpr* **-1.** [cortarse el pelo] to have one's hair cut. **-2.** [piel, espalda etc] to peel.

peldaño *m* step; [de escalera de mano] rung.

pelea *f* **-1.** [a golpes] fight. **-2.** [riña] row, quarrel.

pelear *vi* **-1.** [a golpes] to fight. **-2.** [a gritos] to have a row ○ quarrel. **-3.** [esforzarse] to struggle.

◆ **pelearse** *vpr* **-1.** [a golpes] to fight. **-2.** [a gritos] to have a row ○ quarrel.

pelele *m* **-1.** *fam despec* [persona] puppet. **-2.** [muñeco] guy, straw doll. **-3.** [prenda de bebé] rompers (*pl*).

peleón, -ona *adj* **-1.** [persona] aggressive. **-2.** [vino] rough.

peletería *f* **-1.** [tienda] fur shop, furrier's. **-2.** [oficio] furriery. **-3.** [pieles] furs (*pl*).

peletero, -ra *m y f* furrier.

peliagudo, -da *adj* tricky.

pelicano, pelícano *m* pelican.

película *f* **-1.** [gen] film; **echar** ○ **poner una ~** to show a film; **~ muda/de terror** silent/horror film; **~ del Oeste** western; **de ~** amazing; **~ virgen** FOT blank film. **-2.** *fam* [historia increíble] (tall) story.

peliculero, -ra *m y f fam* teller of tall stories.

peligrar *vi* to be in danger.

peligro *m* danger; **correr ~ (de)** to be in danger (of); **estar/poner en ~** to be/put at risk; **fuera de ~** out of danger; **¡~ de muerte!** danger!

peligrosidad *f* danger.

peligroso, -sa *adj* dangerous.

pelín *m fam* mite, tiny bit.

pelirrojo, -ja ◇ *adj* ginger, red-headed. ◇ *m y f* redhead.

pellejo *m* **-1.** [piel, vida] skin. **-2.** [padrastro] hangnail; **estar/ponerse en el ~ de otro** to be/put o.s. in someone else's shoes; **salvar el ~** to save one's skin.

pelliza *f* fur jacket.

pellizcar [10] *vt* **-1.** [gen] to pinch. **-2.** [pan] to pick at.

pellizco *m* pinch.

pelma, pelmazo, -za *fam despec* ◇ *adj* annoying, tiresome. ◇ *m y f* bore, pain.

pelo *m* **-1.** [gen] hair. **-2.** [de oso, conejo, gato] fur; [de perro, caballo] coat. **-3.** [de melocotón] down. **-4.** [de una tela] nap. **-5.** *loc*: **con ~s y señales** with all the details; **de medio ~** second-rate; **le luce el ~** he's as fit as a fiddle; **montar a caballo a ~** to ride bareback; **presentarse a un examen a ~** to enter an exam unprepared; **no tener un ~ de tonto** *fam* to be nobody's fool; **no tener ~s en la lengua** *fam* not to mince one's words; **no verle el ~ a alguien** *fam* not to see hide nor hair of sb; **poner a alguien los ~s de punta** *fam* to make sb's hair stand on end; **por los ~s, por un ~** by the skin of one's teeth, only just; **ser un hombre de ~ en pecho** to be a real man; **soltarse el ~** to let one's hair down; **tomar el ~ a alguien** *fam* to pull sb's leg; **venir al ~ a alguien** *fam* to be just right for sb.

◆ **a contra pelo** *loc adv lit* & *fig* against the grain.

pelota ◇ *f* **-1.** [gen & DEP] ball; **jugar a la ~** to play ball; **~ base** baseball; **~ vasca** pelota; **devolver la ~ a alguien** to put the ball back into sb's court; **hacer la ~ (a alguien)** *fam* to suck up (to sb). **-2.** *fam* [cabeza] nut. ◇ *m y f* [persona] crawler, creep.

◆ **pelotas** *fpl vulg* balls; **en ~s** *mfam* starkers, in the nude.

pelotari *m y f* pelota player.

pelotazo *m* kick ○ throw of a ball.

pelotear *vi* to have a kickabout; [en tenis] to knock up.

pelotera *f fam* scrap, fight.

pelotón *m* [de soldados] squad; [de gente] crowd; DEP pack; **~ de ejecución** firing squad.

pelotudo, -da *adj Amer fam* stupid.

peluca *f* wig.

peluche *m* plush.

peludo, -da *adj* hairy.

peluquería *f* **-1.** [establecimiento] hairdresser's (shop). **-2.** [oficio] hairdressing.

peluquero, -ra *m y f* hairdresser.

peluquín *m* toupee.

pelusa *f* **-1.** [de tela] fluff. **-2.** [vello] down.

pélvico, -ca *adj* pelvic.

pelvis *f inv* pelvis.

Pemex (*abrev de* **Petróleos Mexicanos**) *f* Mexican state oil company.

PEN (*abrev de* **Plan Energético Nacional**) *m* Spanish national energy plan.

pena *f* **-1.** [lástima] shame, pity!; **¡qué ~!** what a shame ○ pity!; **dar ~** to inspire pity; **el pobre me da ~** I feel sorry for the poor chap. **-2.** [tristeza] sadness, sorrow. **-3.** (*gen pl*) [desgracia] problem, trouble. **-4.** (*gen pl*) [dificultad] struggle (*U*); **a duras ~s** with great difficulty. **-5.** [castigo] punishment; **so ○ bajo ~ de** under penalty of; **~ capital ○ de muerte** death penalty. **-6.** *Amer* [vergüenza] shame, embarrassment; **me da ~** I'm ashamed of it. **-7.** *loc:* **(no) valer ○ merecer la ~** (not) to be worthwhile ○ worth it; **una película que merece la ~** a film that is worth seeing; **sin ~ ni gloria** without distinction.

penacho *m* **-1.** [de pájaro] crest. **-2.** [adorno] plume.

penado, -da *m y f* convict.

penal ◇ *adj* criminal. ◇ *m* prison.

penalidad *f* (*gen pl*) suffering (*U*), hardship.

penalista *m y f* [abogado] criminal lawyer.

penalización *f* **-1.** [acción] penalization. **-2.** [sanción] penalty.

penalizar [13] *vt* [gen & DEP] to penalize.

penalti, penalty *m* DEP penalty; **casarse de ~** *fam* to have a shotgun wedding.

penar ◇ *vt* [castigar] to punish. ◇ *vi* [sufrir] to suffer.

pendejo *m fam* **-1.** [cobarde] coward. **-2.** [tonto] prat, idiot.

pendenciero, -ra ◇ *adj* who always gets into a fight. ◇ *m y f* person who is always getting into fights.

pender *vi* **-1.** [colgar]: **~ (de)** to hang (from). **-2.** *fig* [amenaza etc]: **~ sobre** to hang over. **-3.** *fig* [sentencia etc] to be pending.

pendiente ◇ *adj* **-1.** [por resolver] pending; [deuda] outstanding; **estar ~ de** [atento a] to keep an eye on; [a la espera de] to be waiting for. **-2.** [asignatura] failed. ◇ *m* earring. ◇ *f* slope.

péndola *f* pendulum.

pendón, -ona *m y f fam* libertine.

pendonear *vi fam* to hang out.

pendular *adj* **-1.** [gen] swinging, swaying. **-2.** [tren] high-speed.

péndulo *m* pendulum.

pene *m* penis.

penene *m y f* untenured teacher or lecturer.

penetración *f* **-1.** [gen] penetration; **~ de mercado** ECON market penetration. **-2.** [sagacidad] astuteness, sharpness.

penetrante *adj* **-1.** [intenso - dolor] acute; [- olor] sharp; [- frío] biting; [- mirada] penetrating; [- voz, sonido etc] piercing. **-2.** [sagaz] sharp, penetrating.

penetrar ◇ *vi:* **~ en** [internarse en] to enter; [filtrarse por] to get into, to penetrate; [perforar] to pierce; [llegar a conocer] to get to the bottom of. ◇ *vt* **-1.** [introducirse en - suj: arma, sonido etc] to pierce, to penetrate; [- suj: humedad, líquido] to permeate; [- suj: emoción, sentimiento] to pierce. **-2.** [llegar a conocer - secreto etc] to get to the bottom of. **-3.** [sexualmente] to penetrate.

peneuvista ◇ *adj* of/relating to the Basque nationalist party PNV. ◇ *m y f* member/supporter of the Basque nationalist party PNV.

penicilina *f* penicillin.

península *f* peninsula.

peninsular ◇ *adj* peninsular. ◇ *m y f* peninsular Spaniard.

penique *m* penny; **~s** pence.

penitencia *f* penance; **hacer ~** to do penance.

penitenciaría *f* penitentiary.

penitenciario, **-ria** *adj* prison (*antes de sust*).

penitente *m y f* penitent.

penoso, **-sa** *adj* **-1.** [trabajoso] laborious. **-2.** [lamentable] distressing; [aspecto, espectáculo] sorry.

pensado, **-da** *adj*: **mal** ~ twisted, evil-minded; **en el día/momento menos** ~ when you least expect it; **un mal** ~ a twisted person.

◆ **bien pensado** *loc adv* on reflection.

pensador, **-ra** *m y f* thinker.

pensamiento *m* **-1.** [gen] thought; [mente] mind; [idea] idea; **leer el** ~ **a alguien** to read sb's mind ○ thoughts. **-2.** BOT pansy.

pensar [19] ◇ *vi* to think; ~ **en algo/en alguien/en hacer algo** to think about sthg/about sb/about doing sthg; ~ **sobre algo** to think about sthg; **piensa en un número/buen regalo** think of a number/good present; **dar que** ~ **a alguien** to give sb food for thought.

◇ *vt* **-1.** [reflexionar] to think about ○ over. **-2.** [opinar, creer] to think; ~ **algo de alguien/algo** to think sthg of sb/sthg; **pienso que no vendrá** I don't think she'll come. **-3.** [idear] to think up. **-4.** [tener la intención de]: ~ **hacer algo** to intend to do sthg.

◆ **pensarse** *vpr*: ~**se algo** to think about sthg, to think sthg over.

pensativo, **-va** *adj* pensive, thoughtful.

pensión *f* **-1.** [dinero] pension; ~ **alimenticia** ○ **alimentaria** maintenance; ~ **de jubilación/de viudedad** retirement/widow's pension. **-2.** [de huéspedes] ≃ guest house; **media** ~ [en hotel] half board; **estar a media** ~ [en colegio] to have school dinners; ~ **completa** full board.

pensionado *m* boarding school.

pensionista *m y f* **-1.** [jubilado] pensioner. **-2.** [en una pensión] guest, lodger. **-3.** [en un colegio] boarder.

pentaedro *m* pentahedron.

pentagonal *adj* pentagonal.

pentágono *m* pentagon.

pentagrama *m* MÚS stave.

pentatlón *m* pentathlon.

Pentecostés *m* (*no se usa pl*) **-1.** [católico] Whitsun, Whitsuntide. **-2.** [judío] Pentecost.

pentotal® *m* Pentothal®.

penúltimo, **-ma** *adj*, *m y f* penultimate, last but one.

penumbra *f* semi-darkness, half-light; **en** ~ in semi-darkness.

penuria *f* **-1.** [pobreza] penury, poverty. **-2.** [escasez] paucity, dearth.

peña *f* **-1.** [roca] crag, rock; [monte] cliff. **-2.** [grupo de amigos] circle, group; [club] club; [quinielística] pool.

peñasco *m* large crag ○ rock.

peñón *m* rock.

◆ **Peñón** *m*: **el Peñón** (**de Gibraltar**) the Rock (of Gibraltar).

peón *m* **-1.** [obrero] unskilled labourer; ~ **caminero** navvy. **-2.** [en ajedrez] pawn. **-3.** [peonza] (spinning) top.

peonada *f* **-1.** [día de trabajo] day's work. **-2.** [sueldo] day's wages (*pl*). **-3.** *Amer* [obreros] group of workers.

peonza *f* (spinning) top.

peor ◇ *adj* **-1.** (*comparativo*): ~ (**que**) worse (than). **-2.** (*superlativo*): **el/la** ~ ... the worst ....

◇ *pron*: **el/la** ~ (**de**) the worst (in); **el** ~ **de todos** the worst of all; **lo** ~ **fue que** ... the worst thing was that ....

◇ *adv* **-1.** (*comparativo*): ~ (**que**) worse (than); **ahora veo** ~ I see worse now; **estar** ~ [enfermo] to get worse; **estoy** ~ [de salud] I feel worse; ~ **que** ~ so much the worse. **-2.** (*superlativo*) worst; **el que lo hizo** ~ the one who did it (the) worst.

pepinillo *m* gherkin.

pepino *m* **-1.** BOT cucumber; **me importa un** ~ I couldn't care less. **-2.** *fam* [obús] shell.

pepita *f* **-1.** [de fruta] pip. **-2.** [de oro] nugget.

pepito *m* grilled meat sandwich.

pepona *f* large cardboard doll.

peppermint = **pipermín**.

peque *etc* → **pecar**.

pequeñez *f* **-1.** [gen] smallness. **-2.** *fig* [insignificancia] trifle.

pequeño, **-ña** ◇ *adj* small, little; [hermano] little; [posibilidad] slight; [ingresos, cifras etc] low. ◇ *m y f* [niño] little one; **de** ~ as a child; **el** ~, **la pequeña** [benjamín] the youngest, the baby.

pequeñoburgués, **-esa** ◇ *adj* petit bourgeois. ◇ *m y f* petit bourgeois (*f* petite bourgeoise).

pequinés, **-esa** ◇ *adj*, *m y f* Pekinese. ◇ *m* [perro] Pekinese.

pera ◇ *f* **-1.** [fruta] pear. **-2.** [para ducha etc] (rubber) bulb. **-3.** [interruptor] pear-shaped switch. **-4.** *loc*: **partir** ~**s** to fall out; **pedir** ~**s al olmo** to ask (for) the impossible; **ser la** ~ *fam* to be the limit. ◇ *adj inv fam* posh; **niño** ~ spoilt ○ posh brat.

peral *m* pear-tree.

perborato *m* perborate.

perca *f* perch.

percal *m* percale; **conocer el ~** to know what one is doing.

percance *m* mishap.

percatarse *vpr*: **~ (de algo)** to notice (sthg).

percebe *m* **-1.** [pez] barnacle. **-2.** *fam* [persona] twit.

percepción *f* **-1.** [de los sentidos] perception. **-2.** [cobro] receipt, collection.

perceptible *adj* **-1.** [por los sentidos] noticeable, perceptible. **-2.** [que se puede cobrar] receivable, payable.

perceptivo, -va *adj* sensory.

percha *f* **-1.** [de armario] (coat) hanger. **-2.** [de pared] coat rack. **-3.** [de pie] coat stand. **-4.** [para pájaros] perch.

perchero *m* [de pared] coat rack; [de pie] coat stand.

percibir *vt* **-1.** [con los sentidos] to perceive, to notice; [por los oídos] to hear; [ver] to see. **-2.** [cobrar] to receive, to get.

percusión *f* percussion.

percusionista *m y f* percussionist.

percutor, percusor *m* hammer, firing pin.

perdedor, -ra ◇ *adj* losing. ◇ *m y f* loser.

perder [20] ◇ *vt* **-1.** [gen] to lose. **-2.** [desperdiciar] to waste. **-3.** [tren, oportunidad] to miss. **-4.** [perjudicar] to be the ruin of. ◇ *vi* **-1.** [salir derrotado] to lose. **-2.** [empeorar] to go downhill. **-3.** [dejar escapar aire] to deflate, to go down. **-4.** *loc*: **echar algo a ~** to spoil sthg; **echarse a ~** [alimento] to go off, to spoil.

◆ **perderse** *vpr* **-1.** [gen] to get lost. **-2.** [desaparecer] to disappear. **-3.** [desperdiciarse] to be wasted. **-4.** [desaprovechar]: **~se algo** to miss out on sthg; **¡no te lo pierdas!** don't miss it! **-5.** *fig* [por los vicios] to be beyond salvation. **-6.** *fig* [anhelar]: **~se por** to be mad about.

perdición *f* ruin, undoing.

pérdida *f* **-1.** [gen] loss; **no tiene ~** you can't miss it. **-2.** [de tiempo, dinero] waste. **-3.** [escape] leak.

◆ **pérdidas** *fpl* **-1.** FIN & MIL losses. **-2.** [daños] damage (*U*). **-3.** [de sangre] haemorrhage (*sg*).

perdidamente *adv* hopelessly.

perdido, -da ◇ *adj* **-1.** [extraviado] lost; [animal, bala] stray. **-2.** [sucio] filthy. **-3.** [tiempo] wasted; [ocasión] missed. **-4.** *fam* [de remate] complete, utter. **-5.** *loc*: **estar ~** to be done for ◇ lost. ◇ *m y f* reprobate.

perdigón *m* pellet.

perdigonada *f* **-1.** [tiro] shot. **-2.** [herida] gunshot wound.

perdiguero *m* English setter.

perdiz *f* partridge; **fueron felices y comieron perdices** they all lived happily ever after.

perdón *m* pardon, forgiveness; **con ~** if you'll forgive the expression; **no tener ~** to be unforgivable; **pedir ~** to apologize; **¡~!** sorry!

perdonar *vt* **-1.** [gen] to forgive; **~le algo a alguien** to forgive sb for sthg; **perdone que le moleste** sorry to bother you. **-2.** [eximir de - deuda, condena]: **~ algo a alguien** to let sb off sthg; **~le la vida a alguien** to spare sb their life. **-3.** [desperdiciar]: **no ~ algo** not to miss sthg.

perdonavidas *m y f inv fam* bully.

perdurable *adj* **-1.** [que dura siempre] eternal. **-2.** [que dura mucho] long-lasting.

perdurar *vi* **-1.** [durar mucho] to endure, to last. **-2.** [persistir] to persist.

perecedero, -ra *adj* **-1.** [productos] perishable. **-2.** [naturaleza] transitory.

perecer [30] *vi* to perish, to die.

perejil *m* parsley.

perenne *adj* **-1.** BOT perennial. **-2.** [recuerdo] enduring. **-3.** [continuo] constant.

perentorio, -ria *adj* urgent, pressing; [gesto, tono] peremptory; **plazo ~** fixed time limit.

pereza *f* idleness; **me da ~ ir a pie** I can't be bothered walking; **sacudirse la ~** to wake o.s. up.

perezca *etc* → **perecer**.

perezoso, -sa ◇ *adj* **-1.** [vago] lazy. **-2.** [lento] slow, sluggish. ◇ *m y f* [vago] lazy person, idler.

perfección *f* perfection; **es de una gran ~** it's exceptionally good; **a la ~** perfectly, to perfection.

perfeccionamiento *m* **-1.** [acabado] perfecting. **-2.** [mejoramiento] improvement.

perfeccionar *vt* **-1.** [redondear] to perfect. **-2.** [mejorar] to improve.

perfeccionismo *m* perfectionism.

perfeccionista *adj, m y f* perfectionist.

perfectamente *adv* **-1.** [sobradamente] perfectly. **-2.** [muy bien] fine; **¿cómo estas?** -

estoy ~ how are you? - I'm fine. **-3.** [de acuerdo]: ¡~! fine!, great!

perfectivo, -va adj perfective.

perfecto, -ta adj perfect.

perfidia f perfidy, treachery.

pérfido, -da ◇ adj perfidious, treacherous. ◇ m y f treacherous person.

perfil m **-1.** [contorno] outline, shape. **-2.** [de cara, cuerpo] profile; **de** ~ in profile. **-3.** fig [característica] characteristic. **-4.** fig [retrato moral] profile. **-5.** GEOM cross section.

perfilar vt to outline.
◆ **perfilarse** vpr **-1.** [destacarse] to be outlined. **-2.** [concretarse] to shape up.

perforación f **-1.** [gen & MED] perforation. **-2.** [taladro] bore-hole.

perforador, -ra adj drilling.
◆ **perforadora** f **-1.** [herramienta] drill. **-2.** INFORM card punch.

perforar vt [horadar] to perforate; [agujero] to drill; INFORM to punch.

perfumar vt to perfume.
◆ **perfumarse** vpr to put perfume on.

perfume m perfume.

perfumería f **-1.** [tienda, arte] perfumery. **-2.** [productos] perfumes (pl).

pergamino m parchment.

pérgola f pergola.

pericia f skill.

pericial adj expert.

perico m **-1.** fam [pájaro] parakeet. **-2.** mfam [cocaína] snow. **-3.** Amer [café con leche] white coffee.

periferia f periphery; [alrededores] outskirts (pl).

periférico, -ca adj peripheral; [barrio] outlying.
◆ **periférico** m INFORM peripheral.

perifollos mpl fam frills (and fripperies).

perífrasis f inv: ~ **(verbal)** wordy explanation.

perifrástico, -ca adj long-winded.

perilla f goatee; **venir de** ~**(s)** to be just the right thing.

perímetro m perimeter.

periodicidad f frequency; TECN periodicity.

periódico, -ca adj **-1.** [gen] periodic. **-2.** MAT recurrent.
◆ **periódico** m newspaper.

periodismo m journalism.

periodista m y f journalist.

periodístico, -ca adj journalistic.

periodo, período m period; DEP half; ~ **de prácticas** trial period.

peripatético, -ca ◇ adj **-1.** FILOSOFÍA Peri-

patetic. **-2.** fam [ridículo] ludicrous. ◇ m y f Peripatetic.

peripecia f incident, sudden change.

periplo m journey, voyage.

peripuesto, -ta adj fam dolled-up, tarted-up.

periquete m: **en un** ~ fam in a jiffy.

periquito ◇ m parakeet. ◇ adj fam of/relating to the Español Football Club.

periscopio m periscope.

perista m y f fam fence, receiver of stolen goods.

peritaje m **-1.** [trabajo] expert work; [informe] expert's report. **-2.** [estudios] professional training.

peritar vt [casa] to value, to assess the value of; [coche] to assess the damage to.

perito m **-1.** [experto] expert; ~ **agrónomo** agronomist. **-2.** [ingeniero técnico] technician.

perjudicar [10] vt to damage, to harm.

perjudicial adj: ~ **(para)** harmful (to).

perjuicio m harm (U), damage (U); **ir en** ~ **de** to be detrimental to; **sin** ~ **de** despite.

perjurar vi **-1.** [jurar mucho] to swear blind. **-2.** [jurar en falso] to commit perjury.

perjurio m perjury.

perjuro, -ra ◇ adj perjured. ◇ m y f perjuror.

perla f pearl; fig [maravilla] gem, treasure; **de** ~s great, fine; **me viene de** ~s it's just the right thing.

perlado, -da adj **-1.** [con perlas] pearly; [collar] pearl (antes de sust). **-2.** [con gotas] beaded.

perlé m beading.

permanecer [30] vi **-1.** [en un lugar] to stay. **-2.** [en un estado] to remain, to stay.

permanencia f **-1.** [en un lugar] staying, continued stay. **-2.** [en un estado] continuation.

permanente ◇ adj permanent; [comisión] standing. ◇ f perm; **hacerse la** ~ to have a perm.

permeabilidad f permeability.

permeable adj permeable.

permisible adj permissible, acceptable.

permisividad f permissiveness.

permisivo, -va adj permissive.

permiso m **-1.** [autorización] permission; **con** ~ if I may, if you'll excuse me; **pedir** ~ **para hacer algo** to ask permission to do sthg. **-2.** [documento] licence, permit; ~ **de armas** gun licence; ~ **de conducir** driving licence Br, driver's license Am; ~ **de traba-**

jo work permit. **-3.** [vacaciones] leave; **estar de** ~ to be on leave.

permitido, -da *adj* permitted, allowed.

permitir *vt* to allow; ~ **a alguien hacer algo** to allow sb to do sthg; **¿me permite?** may I?

◆ **permitirse** *vpr* to allow o.s. (the luxury of); **no puedo permitírmelo** I can't afford it.

permuta, permutación *f* exchange.

permutable *adj* exchangeable.

permutación = **permuta**.

permutar *vt* to exchange, to swap.

pernera *f* trouser leg.

pernicioso, -sa *adj* damaging, harmful.

pernil *m* leg of ham.

perno *m* bolt.

pernoctar *vi* to stay overnight.

pero ◇ *conj* but; **la casa es vieja** ~ **céntrica** the house may be old, but it's central; ~ **¿qué es tanto ruido?** what on earth is all this noise about? ◇ *m* snag, fault; **poner** ~**s a todo** to find fault with everything.

perogrullada *f fam* truism.

perol *m* casserole (dish).

peroné *m* fibula.

peronismo *m* Peronism.

peronista *adj, m y f* Peronist.

perorata *f* long-winded speech.

peróxido *m* peroxide.

perpendicular *adj* perpendicular; **ser** ~ **a algo** to be at right angles to sthg.

perpetrar *vt* to perpetrate, to commit.

perpetuar [6] *vt* to perpetuate.

◆ **perpetuarse** *vpr* to last, to endure.

perpetuidad *f* perpetuity; **a** ~ in perpetuity; **presidente a** ~ president for life; **condenado a** ~ condemned to life imprisonment.

perpetuo, -tua *adj* **-1.** [gen] perpetual. **-2.** [para toda la vida] lifelong; DER life (*antes de sust*).

perplejidad *f* perplexity, bewilderment.

perplejo, -ja *adj* perplexed, bewildered.

perra *f* **-1.** [rabieta] tantrum; **coger una** ~ to throw a tantrum. **-2.** [dinero] penny; **estoy sin una** ~ I'm flat broke. **-3.** → **perro**.

perrera → **perrero**.

perrería *f fam*: **hacer** ~**s a alguien** to play dirty tricks on sb.

perrero, -ra *m y f* [persona] dogcatcher.

◆ **perrera** *f* **-1.** [lugar] kennels (*pl*). **-2.** [vehículo] dogcatcher's van.

perro, -rra ◇ *m y f* **-1.** [animal] dog (*f* bitch); ~ **callejero** stray dog; ~ **de caza** hunting dog; ~ **lazarillo** guide dog; ~ **lobo** alsatian; ~ **lulú** Pomeranian; ~ **pastor**

sheepdog; ~ **policía** police dog; **allí no atan los** ~**s con longaniza** money doesn't grow on trees there; **andar como el** ~ **y el gato** to fight like cat and dog; **de** ~**s** [tiempo etc] wretched, lousy; ~ **ladrador poco mordedor** his bark is worse than his bite; **ser** ~ **viejo** to be an old hand. **-2.** *despec* [persona] swine, dog. ◇ *adj* wretched, lousy.

◆ **perro caliente** *m* hot dog.

perruno, -na *adj* canine.

persecución *f* **-1.** [seguimiento] pursuit. **-2.** [acoso] persecution.

persecutorio, -ria *adj* [manía] persecution (*antes de sust*).

perseguir [43] *vt* **-1.** [seguir, tratar de obtener] to pursue. **-2.** [acosar] to persecute. **-3.** [suj: mala suerte, problema etc] to dog.

perseverancia *f* perseverance.

perseverante *adj* persistent.

perseverar *vi*: ~ **(en)** to persevere (with), to persist (in).

Persia Persia.

persiana *f* blind.

persiga → **perseguir**.

persignarse *vpr* to cross o.s.

persigo, persiguiera *etc* → **perseguir**.

persistencia *f* persistence.

persistente *adj* persistent.

persistir *vi*: ~ **(en)** to persist (in).

persona *f* **-1.** [individuo] person; **cien** ~**s** a hundred people; **en** ~ in person; **por** ~ per head; **ser buena** ~ to be nice; ~ **mayor** adult, grown-up. **-2.** DER party; ~ **física** private individual; ~ **jurídica** legal entity ○ person. **-3.** GRAM person.

personaje *m* **-1.** [persona importante] important person, celebrity. **-2.** [de obra] character.

personal ◇ *adj* [gen] personal; [teléfono, dirección] private, home (*antes de sust*). ◇ *m* **-1.** [trabajadores] staff, personnel. **-2.** *fam* [gente] people (*pl*). ◇ *f* [en baloncesto] personal foul.

personalidad *f* **-1.** [características] personality. **-2.** [identidad] identity. **-3.** [persona importante] important person, celebrity. **-4.** DER legal personality ○ status.

personalismo *m* **-1.** [parcialidad] favouritism. **-2.** [egocentrismo] self-centredness.

personalizar [13] *vi* **-1.** [nombrar] to name names. **-2.** [aludir] to get personal.

personarse *vpr* to turn up.

personero, -ra *m y f Amer* government representative.

personificación *f* personification.

personificar *vt* to personify.

perspectiva *f* -**1.** [gen] perspective. -**2.** [paisaje] view. -**3.** [futuro] prospect; **en ~** in prospect.

perspicacia *f* insight, perceptiveness.

perspicaz *adj* sharp, perceptive.

persuadir *vt* to persuade; **~ a alguien para que haga algo** to persuade sb to do sthg.
◆ **persuadirse** *vpr* to convince o.s.; **~se de algo** to become convinced of sthg.

persuasión *f* persuasion.

persuasivo, -va *adj* persuasive.
◆ **persuasiva** *f* persuasive power.

pertenecer [30] *vi* -**1.** [gen]: **~ a** to belong to. -**2.** [corresponder] to be up to, to be a matter for.

perteneciente *adj*: **ser ~ a** to belong to.

pertenencia *f* -**1.** [propiedad] ownership. -**2.** [afiliación] membership.
◆ **pertenencias** *fpl* [enseres] belongings.

pértiga *f* -**1.** [vara] pole. -**2.** DEP pole-vault.

pertinaz *adj* -**1.** [terco] stubborn. -**2.** [persistente] persistent.

pertinencia *f* -**1.** [adecuación] appropriateness. -**2.** [relevancia] relevance.

pertinente *adj* -**1.** [adecuado] appropriate. -**2.** [relativo] relevant, pertinent.

pertrechar *vt* MIL to supply with food and ammunition.
◆ **pertrecharse** *vpr*: **~se de** to equip o.s. with.

pertrechos *mpl* -**1.** MIL supplies and ammunition. -**2.** *fig* [utensilios] gear (*U*).

perturbación *f* -**1.** [desconcierto] disquiet, unease. -**2.** [disturbio] disturbance; **~ del orden público** breach of the peace. -**3.** MED mental imbalance. -**4.** METEOR unsettled weather (*U*).

perturbado, -da ◇ *adj* -**1.** MED disturbed, mentally unbalanced. -**2.** [desconcertado] perturbed. ◇ *m y f* MED mentally unbalanced person.

perturbador, -ra ◇ *adj* unsettling. ◇ *m y f* troublemaker.

perturbar *vt* -**1.** [trastornar] to disrupt. -**2.** [inquietar] to disturb, to unsettle. -**3.** [enloquecer] to perturb.

Perú: (el) ~ Peru.

peruano, -na *adj, m y f* Peruvian.

perversidad *f* wickedness.

perversión *f* perversion.

perverso, -sa *adj* depraved.

pervertido, -da *m y f* pervert.

pervertidor, -ra ◇ *adj* pernicious, corrupting. ◇ *m y f* reprobate, corrupter.

pervertir [27] *vt* to corrupt.

◆ **pervertirse** *vpr* to become corrupt, to be corrupted.

pervivir *vi* to survive.

pesa *f* -**1.** [gen] weight. -**2.** (*gen pl*) DEP weights (*pl*).

pesabebés *m inv* baby-weighing scales (*pl*).

pesacartas *m inv* letter-weighing scales (*pl*).

pesada → pesado.

pesadez *f* -**1.** [peso] weight. -**2.** [sensación] heaviness. -**3.** [molestia, fastidio] drag, pain. -**4.** [aburrimiento] ponderousness.

pesadilla *f* nightmare.

pesado, -da ◇ *adj* -**1.** [gen] heavy. -**2.** [caluroso] sultry. -**3.** [lento] ponderous, sluggish. -**4.** [duro] difficult, tough. -**5.** [aburrido] boring. -**6.** [molesto] annoying, tiresome; **¡qué ~ eres!** you're so annoying!; **ponerse ~** to be a pain. ◇ *m y f* bore, pain.

pesadumbre *f* grief, sorrow.

pésame *m* sympathy, condolences (*pl*); **dar el ~** to offer one's condolences.

pesar ◇ *m* -**1.** [tristeza] grief. -**2.** [arrepentimiento] remorse. -**3.** *loc*: **a ~ mío** against my will. ◇ *vt* -**1.** [determinar el peso de] to weigh. -**2.** [examinar] to weigh up. ◇ *vi* -**1.** [tener peso] to weigh. -**2.** [ser pesado] to be heavy. -**3.** [importar] to play an important part. -**4.** [molestar]: **me pesa tener que hacerlo** it grieves me to have to do it; **pese a quien pese** in spite of everything. -**5.** [entristecer]: **me pesa tener que decirte esto** I'm sorry to have to tell you this.
◆ **pesarse** *vpr* to weigh o.s.
◆ **a pesar de** *loc prep* despite.
◆ **a pesar de que** *loc conj* in spite of the fact that.

pesaroso, -sa *adj* -**1.** [arrepentido] remorseful. -**2.** [afligido] sad.

pesca *f* -**1.** [acción] fishing; **ir de ~** to go fishing; **~ de bajura/altura** coastal/deep-sea fishing; **~ submarina** underwater fishing. -**2.** [lo pescado] catch.

pescadería *f* fishmonger's (shop).

pescadero, -ra *m y f* fishmonger.

pescadilla *f* whiting.

pescado *m* fish; **~ azul/blanco** blue/white fish.

pescador, -ra *m y f* fisherman (*f* fisherwoman).

pescante *m* -**1.** [de carruaje] driver's seat. -**2.** NÁUT davit.

pescar [10] ◇ *vt* -**1.** [peces] to catch. -**2.** *fig* [enfermedad] to catch. -**3.** *fam fig* [conseguir] to get o.s., to land. -**4.** *fam fig* [atrapar] to catch. **-5.** *fam* *fig* [entender] to pick up, to understand. ◇ *vi* to fish, to go fishing.

pescuezo *m* neck; **retorcer el ~ a alguien** *fam* to wring sb's neck.

pese

◆ **pese a** *loc prep* despite.

pesebre *m* **-1.** [para los animales] manger. **-2.** [belén] crib, Nativity scene.

pesero *m Amer fixed-rate taxi service.*

peseta *f* [unidad] peseta.

◆ **pesetas** *fpl fig* [dinero] money (*U*).

pesetero, -ra ◇ *adj* money-grubbing. ◇ *m y f* moneygrubber.

pesimismo *m* pessimism.

pesimista ◇ *adj* pessimistic. ◇ *m y f* pessimist.

pésimo, -ma ◇ *superl* → **malo**. ◇ *adj* terrible, awful.

peso *m* **-1.** [gen] weight; **siento ~ en las piernas** my legs feel heavy; **tiene un kilo de ~** it weighs a kilo; **de ~** [razones] weighty, sound; [persona] influential; **~ atómico/molecular** atomic/molecular weight; **~ bruto/neto** gross/net weight; **~ muerto** dead weight; **~ ligero** lightweight; **~ medio** middleweight; **~ mosca** flyweight; **~ pesado** heavyweight; **caer por su propio ~** to be self-evident; **pagar algo a ~ de oro** to pay a fortune for sthg; **quitarse un ~ de encima** to take a weight off one's mind. **-2.** [moneda] peso. **-3.** [de atletismo] shot. **-4.** [balanza] scales (*pl*).

pespunte *m* backstitch.

pespuntear *vt* to backstitch.

pesque *etc* → **pescar**.

pesquero, -ra *adj* fishing.

◆ **pesquero** *m* fishing boat.

pesquisa *f* investigation, inquiry.

pestaña *f* **-1.** [de párpado] eyelash; **quemarse las ~s** *fig* to burn the midnight oil. **-2.** [saliente - de vestido] hem; [- de libro] flap. **-3.** TECN flange.

pestañear *vi* to blink; **sin ~** [con serenidad] without batting an eyelid; [con atención] without losing concentration once.

peste *f* **-1.** [enfermedad, plaga] plague; **~ bubónica** bubonic plague. **-2.** *fam* [mal olor] stink, stench. **-3.** [molestia] pest. **-4.** *loc:* **decir ~s de alguien** to heap abuse on sb.

pesticida ◇ *adj* pesticidal. ◇ *m* pesticide.

pestilencia *f* stench.

pestilente *adj* foul-smelling.

pestillo *m* [cerrojo] bolt; [mecanismo, en verjas] latch; **correr** O **echar el ~** to shoot the bolt.

petaca *f* **-1.** [para cigarrillos] cigarette case; [para tabaco] tobacco pouch. **-2.** [para bebi-] das] flask. **-3.** *Amer* [maleta] suitcase. **-4.** *loc:* **hacer la ~** to make an apple-pie bed.

pétalo *m* petal.

petanca *f game similar to bowls played in parks, on beach etc.*

petardo ◇ *m* **-1.** [cohete] banger, firecracker. **-2.** *fam* [aburrimiento] bore. **-3.** *mfam* [porro] joint. ◇ *m y f fam* [persona fea] horror, ugly person.

petate *m* kit bag; **liar el ~** *fam* [marcharse] to pack one's bags and go; [morir] to kick the bucket.

petenera *f Andalusian popular song;* **salir por ~s** to go off at a tangent.

petición *f* **-1.** [acción] request; **a ~ de** at the request of. **-2.** DER [escrito] petition; **~ de mano** proposal (of marriage).

petimetre, -tra *m y f* fop, dandy.

petirrojo *m* robin.

petiso, -sa *adj Amer fam* short.

peto *m* **-1.** [de prenda] bib. **-2.** [de armadura] breastplate. **-3.** DEP breastguard.

pétreo, -a *adj* [de piedra] stone; [como piedra] stony.

petrificar [10] *vt lit & fig* to petrify.

petrodólar *m* petrodollar.

petróleo *m* oil, petroleum.

petrolero, -ra *adj* oil (*antes de sust*).

◆ **petrolero** *m* oil tanker.

petrolífero, -ra *adj* oil (*antes de sust*).

petroquímico, -ca *adj* petrochemical.

◆ **petroquímica** *f* petrochemistry.

petulancia *f* arrogance.

petulante ◇ *adj* opinionated, arrogant. ◇ *m y f* opinionated person.

petunia *f* petunia.

peúco *m* (*gen pl*) bootee.

peyorativo, -va *adj* pejorative.

pez ◇ *m* fish; **~ de río** freshwater fish; **~ espada** swordfish; **estar uno como ~ en el agua** to be in one's element; **estar ~ (en algo)** to have no idea (about sthg). ◇ *f* pitch, tar.

◆ **pez gordo** *m fam fig* big shot.

pezón *m* **-1.** [de pecho] nipple. **-2.** BOT stalk. **-3.** [de eje] tip.

pezuña *f* hoof.

Phnom Penh [nom'pen] Phnom Penh.

pi *f* MAT pi.

piadoso, -sa *adj* **-1.** [compasivo] kindhearted. **-2.** [religioso] pious.

pianista *m y f* pianist.

piano ◇ *m* piano; **~ bar** piano bar; **~ de cola** grand piano; **~ de media cola** baby grand. ◇ *adv* piano.

pianola *f* pianola.

piar [9] *vi* to cheep, to tweet.

piara *f* herd.

piastra *f* piastre, piaster.

PIB (*abrev de* **producto interior bruto**) *m* GDP.

pibe, -ba *m y f Amer fam* kid, boy (*f* girl).

PIC (*abrev de* **punto de información cultural**) *m tourist information point*.

pica *f* **-1.** [naipe] spade. **-2.** [lanza] pike; poner una ~ **en Flandes** to do the impossible. **-3.** TAUROM goad, picador's spear.

◆ **picas** *fpl* [palo de baraja] spades.

picada → **picado**.

picadero *m* **-1.** [de caballos] riding school. **-2.** *fam* [de soltero] bachelor pad.

picadillo *m* [de carne] mince; [de verdura] chopped vegetables (*pl*).

picado, -da *adj* **-1.** [marcado - piel] pockmarked; [- fruta] bruised. **-2.** [agujereado] perforated; ~ **de polilla** moth-eaten. **-3.** [triturado - alimento] chopped; [- carne] minced; [- tabaco] cut. **-4.** [vino] sour. **-5.** [diente] decayed. **-6.** [mar] choppy. **-7.** *fig* [enfadado] annoyed. **-8.** AERON: **descender en ~** to dive; **caer en ~** *fig* to plummet.

◆ **picada** *f* [de mosquito, serpiente] bite; [de avispa, escorpión, ortiga] sting.

picador, -ra *m y f* **-1.** TAUROM picador; *ver también* **tauromaquia**. **-2.** [domador] (horse) trainer. **-3.** [minero] face worker.

picadora *f* mincer.

picadura *f* **-1.** [de mosquito, serpiente] bite; [de avispa, ortiga, escorpión] sting. **-2.** [de viruela] pockmark. **-3.** [de diente] decay (*U*). **-4.** [tabaco] (cut) tobacco (*U*).

picante ◇ *adj* **-1.** [comida etc] spicy, hot. **-2.** *fig* [obsceno] saucy. ◇ *m* [comida] spicy food; [sabor] spiciness.

picantería *f Amer* cheap restaurant.

picapica → **polvo**.

picapleitos *m y f inv despec* bad lawyer.

picaporte *m* [aldaba] doorknocker; [barrita] latch.

picar [10] ◇ *vt* **-1.** [suj: mosquito, serpiente] to bite; [suj: avispa, escorpión, ortiga] to sting. **-2.** [escocer] to itch; **me pican los ojos** my eyes are stinging. **-3.** [triturar - verdura] to chop; [- carne] to mince. **-4.** [suj: ave] to peck. **-5.** [aperitivo] to pick at. **-6.** [tierra, piedra, hielo] to hack at. **-7.** *fig* [enojar] to irritate. **-8.** *fig* [estimular - persona, caballo] to spur on; [- curiosidad] to prick. **-9.** [perforar - billete, ficha] to punch. **-10.** [teclear] to type. **-11.** TAUROM to goad.

◇ *vi* **-1.** [alimento] to be spicy ○ hot. **-2.** [pez] to bite. **-3.** [escocer] to itch. **-4.** [ave] to peck. **-5.** [tomar un aperitivo] to nibble. **-6.**

[sol] to burn. **-7.** [dejarse engañar] to take the bait. **-8.** *loc:* ~ **(muy) alto** to have great ambitions.

◆ **picarse** *vpr* **-1.** [vino] to turn sour. **-2.** [ropa] to become moth-eaten. **-3.** [mar] to get choppy. **-4.** [diente] to get a cavity. **-5.** [oxidarse] to go rusty. **-6.** *fig* [enfadarse] to get annoyed ○ cross. **-7.** *fam* [inyectarse droga] to shoot up.

picardía *f* **-1.** [astucia] sharpness, craftiness. **-2.** [travesura] naughty trick, mischief (*U*). **-3.** [atrevimiento] brazenness. **-4.** [prenda femenina] negligee.

picaresco, -ca *adj* mischievous, roguish.

◆ **picaresca** *f* **-1.** LITER picaresque literature. **-2.** [modo de vida] roguery.

PICARESCA:

The picaresque was a popular and influential Spanish literary genre during the 16th and 17th centuries. Its principal characteristics are its episodic form and the ingenuity and roguish qualities of the low-life hero. In the course of the hero's adventures, a vivid and often critical picture of all strata of Spanish society is presented. In modern Spanish the term 'pícaro' is still used to describe people with the same qualities as the picaresque hero

---

pícaro, -ra *m y f* **-1.** [astuto] sly person, rogue. **-2.** [travieso] rascal. **-3.** [atrevido] brazen person. **-4.** *ver también* **picaresca**.

picatoste *m* crouton.

picazón *f* **-1.** [en el cuerpo] itch. **-2.** *fam fig* [inquietud] uneasiness.

picha *f mfam* dick, knob.

pichi *m* pinafore (dress).

pichichi *m* DEP top scorer.

pichincha *f Amer fam* snip, bargain.

pichón *m* **-1.** ZOOL young pigeon. **-2.** *fam fig* [apelativo cariñoso] darling, sweetheart.

pichula *f Amer vulg* prick, cock.

picnic (*pl* **picnics**) *m* picnic.

pico *m* **-1.** [de ave] beak. **-2.** [punta, saliente] corner. **-3.** [herramienta] pick, pickaxe. **-4.** [cumbre] peak. **-5.** [cantidad indeterminada]: **cincuenta y** ~ fifty-odd, fifty-something; **llegó a las cinco y** ~ he got there just after five. **-6.** *fam* [boca] gob, mouth; **cerrar el** ~ [callar] to shut up; **ser** ○ **tener un** ~ **de oro** to be a smooth talker, to have the gift of the gab. **-7.** *loc:* **andar/irse de** ~**s pardos** to be/go out on the town; **le costó un** ~ it cost her a fortune.

picor *m* [del calor] burning; [que irrita] itch.

picoso, -sa *adj Amer* spicy, hot.

picota f **-1.** [de ajusticiados] pillory; **poner a alguien en la** ~ fig to pillory sb. **-2.** [cereza] cherry.

picotazo m peck.

picotear vt **-1.** [suj: ave] to peck. **-2.** fig [comer] to pick at.

pictórico, -ca adj pictorial.

pida, pidiera etc → pedir.

pie m **-1.** [gen & ANAT] foot; **a** ~ on foot; **estar de** ○ **en** ~ to be on one's feet ○ standing; **ponerse de** ○ **en** ~ to stand up; **de** ~s **a cabeza** fig from head to toe; **seguir en** ~ [vigente] to be still valid; **en** ~ **de igualdad** on an equal footing; **en** ~ **de guerra** at war; **perder/no hacer** ~ to go/to be out of one's depth; ~ **de atleta** athlete's foot; ~ **de foto** caption; ~s **de cerdo** (pig's) trotters; ~s **planos** flat feet. **-2.** [de micrófono, lámpara etc] stand; [de copa] stem. **-3.** TEATR cue. **-4.** loc: **al** ~ **de la letra** to the letter, word for word; **al** ~ **del cañón** ready for action; **andar con** ~s **de plomo** to tread carefully; **a** ~s **juntillas** unquestioningly; **a sus** ~s at your service; **buscarle (los) tres** ~s **al gato** to split hairs; **cojear del mismo** ~ to fall at the same fence; **con buen** ~ on the right footing; **dar** ~ **a alguien para que haga algo** to give sb cause to do sthg; **el ciudadano de a** ~ the man in the street; **levantarse con el** ~ **izquierdo** to get out of bed on the wrong side; **no dar** ~ **con bola** to get everything wrong; **no tener ni** ~s **ni cabeza** to make no sense at all; **no tenerse de** ○ **en** ~ [por cansancio] not to be able to stand up a minute longer; fig [por ser absurdo] not to stand up; **pararle los** ~s **a alguien** to put sb in their place; **poner** ~s **en polvorosa** to make a run for it; **saber de qué** ~ **cojea alguien** to know sb's weaknesses; **tener un** ~ **en la tumba** to have one foot in the grave.

piedad f **-1.** [compasión] pity; **tener** ~ **de** to take pity on. **-2.** [religiosidad] piety.
◆ **Piedad** f ARTE Pietà.

piedra f **-1.** [gen] stone; ~ **angular** lit & fig cornerstone; ~ **pómez** pumice stone; ~ **preciosa** precious stone; **poner la primera** ~ [inaugurar] to lay the foundation stone; fig to lay the foundations; **no dejar** ~ **sobre** ~ to leave no stone standing; **quedarse de** ~ to be thunderstruck; **tirar la** ~ **y esconder la mano** to play the innocent. **-2.** [de mechero] flint.

piel f **-1.** ANAT skin; ~ **roja** redskin (N.B: the term "piel roja" is considered to be racist); **dejar** ○ **jugarse la** ~ to risk one's neck; **ser de la** ~ **del diablo** to be a little devil. **-2.** [cuero] leather. **-3.** [pelo] fur. **-4.** [cáscara] skin, peel.

piensa etc → pensar.

pienso m fodder.

pierda etc → perder.

pierna f leg; **dormir a** ~ **suelta** to sleep like a log; **estirar las** ~s to stretch one's legs.

pieza f **-1.** [gen] piece; [de mecanismo] part; ~ **de recambio** ○ **repuesto** spare part, extra Am; **un dos** ~s a two-piece suit; **dejar/quedarse de una** ~ to leave/be thunderstruck. **-2.** [presa] specimen. **-3.** irón [persona]: **ser una buena** ~ to be a fine one ○ a right one. **-4.** [parche] patch. **-5.** [obra dramática] play. **-6.** [habitación] room.

pifia f blunder.

pifiar [8] vt: ~**la** fam to put one's foot in it.

pigmentación f pigmentation.

pigmento m pigment.

pigmeo, -a m y f pygmy.

pijada f fam [dicho] trivial remark; [hecho] trifle.

pijama m pyjamas (pl).

pijería f fam [dicho] trivial remark; [hecho] trifle.

pijo, -ja fam ◇ adj posh. ◇ m y f spoilt rich brat.
◆ **pijo** m vulg prick, cock.

pila f **-1.** [generador] battery; ~ **atómica** atomic pile; ~ **solar** solar cell. **-2.** [montón] pile; **tiene una** ~ **de deudas** he's up to his neck in debt. **-3.** [fregadero] sink; ~ **bautismal** (baptismal) font. **-4.** ARQUIT pile.

pilar m lit & fig pillar.

pilastra f pilaster.

píldora f pill; [anticonceptivo]: **la** ~ the pill; **dorar la** ~ to sugar the pill.

pileta f Amer swimming pool.

pillaje m pillage.

pillar ◇ vt **-1.** [gen] to catch. **-2.** [chiste, explicación] to get. **-3.** [atropellar] to knock down. ◇ vi [hallarse]: **me pilla lejos** it's out of the way for me; **me pilla de camino** it's on my way.
◆ **pillarse** vpr [dedos etc] to catch.

pillastre m y f fam rogue, crafty person.

pillo, -lla fam ◇ adj **-1.** [travieso] mischievous. **-2.** [astuto] crafty. ◇ m y f **-1.** [pícaro] rascal. **-2.** [astuto] crafty person.

pilón m **-1.** [pila - para lavar] basin; [- para animales] trough. **-2.** [torre eléctrica] pylon. **-3.** [pilar grande] post.

pilotar vt [avión] to fly, to pilot; [coche] to drive; [barco] to steer.

piloto ◇ m y f [gen] pilot; [de coche] driver; ~ **automático** automatic pilot; ~ **de pruebas** test pilot. ◇ m [luz - de coche] tail light;

[- de aparato] **pilot lamp**. ◇ *adj inv* pilot (*antes de sust*).

piltra *f mfam* pit, bed.

piltrafa *f* (*gen pl*) scrap; *fam* [persona débil] wreck.

pimentón *m* paprika.

pimienta *f* pepper; ~ **blanca/negra** white/ black pepper.

pimiento *m* [fruto] pepper, capsicum; [planta] pimiento, pepper plant; ~ **morrón** sweet pepper.

pimpante *adj* **-1.** [satisfecho] well-pleased. **-2.** [garboso] swish, smart.

pimpinela *f* pimpernel.

pimpollo *m* **-1.** [de rama, planta] shoot; [de flor] bud. **-2.** *fam fig* [persona atractiva] gorgeous person.

PIN (*abrev de* **producto interior neto**) *m* NDP.

pinacoteca *f* art gallery.

pináculo *m* **-1.** [gen] pinnacle. **-2.** [juego de naipes] pinochle.

pinar *m* pine wood ○ grove.

pinaza *f* pine needles (*pl*).

pincel *m* **-1.** [para pintar] paintbrush; [para maquillar etc] brush. **-2.** *fig* [estilo] style.

pincelada *f* brushstroke; **a grandes ~s** *fig* in broad terms.

pinchadiscos *m y f inv* disc jockey.

pinchar ◇ *vt* **-1.** [punzar - gen] to prick; [- rueda] to puncture; [- globo, balón] to burst. **-2.** [penetrar] to pierce. **-3.** [fijar]: ~ **algo en la pared** to pin sthg to the wall. **-4.** *fam* [teléfono] to tap. **-5.** *fig* [irritar] to torment. **-6.** *fig* [incitar]: ~ **a alguien para que haga algo** to urge sb to do sthg. ◇ *vi* **-1.** [rueda] to get a puncture. **-2.** [barba] to be prickly. **-3.** *loc*: **ella ni pincha ni corta** she cuts no ice.

◆ **pincharse** *vpr* **-1.** [punzarse - persona] to prick o.s.; [- rueda] to get a puncture. **-2.** *fig* [irritarse] to get annoyed. **-3.** [inyectarse]: ~**se (algo)** [medicamento] to inject o.s. (with sthg); *fam* [droga] to shoot up (with sthg).

pinchazo *m* **-1.** [punzada] prick. **-2.** [marca] needle mark. **-3.** [de neumático, balón etc] puncture, flat *Am*.

pinche ◇ *m y f* kitchen boy (*f* kitchen maid). ◇ *adj Amer fam* damned.

pinchito *m* CULIN **-1.** [tapa] aperitif on a stick. **-2.** [pincho moruno] shish kebab.

pincho *m* **-1.** [punta] (sharp) point. **-2.** [espina - de planta] prickle, thorn. **-3.** [varilla] pointed stick. **-4.** CULIN aperitif on a stick; ~ **moruno** shish kebab.

pindonguear *vi fam* to loaf about.

pineda *f* pine wood ○ grove.

pinedo *m* pine wood ○ grove.

pinga *f Amer vulg* prick, cock.

pingajo *m fam despec* rag.

pingo *m* **-1.** *fam despec* [pingajo] rag. **-2.** [mamarracho]: **ir hecho un** ~ to look a state, to be dressed in rags. **-3.** *fam* [persona despreciable] rotter, dog.

pingonear *vi fam* to loaf about.

pingüe *adj* plentiful; ~**s ganancias** fat profit (*sg*).

ping-pong [pin'pon] *m* ping-pong, table-tennis.

pingüino *m* penguin.

pinitos *mpl*: **hacer** ~ *lit & fig* to take one's first steps.

pino *m* pine; **en el quinto** ~ in the middle of nowhere; **hacer el** ~ to do a handstand.

pinta → pinto.

pintado, -da *adj* **-1.** [coloreado] coloured; "**recién** ~" "wet paint". **-2.** [maquillado] made-up. **-3.** [moteado] speckled. **-4.** *loc*: **el más** ~ the best person around; **venir que ni** ~ to be just the thing.

◆ **pintada** *f* **-1.** [escrito] graffiti (*U*). **-2.** [ave] guinea fowl.

pintalabios *m inv* lipstick.

pintar ◇ *vt* to paint. ◇ *vi* **-1.** [con pintura] to paint. **-2.** [significar, importar] to count; **aquí no pinto nada** there's no place for me here; **¿qué pinto yo en este asunto?** where do I come in?

◆ **pintarse** *vpr* **-1.** [maquillarse] to make o.s. up. **-2.** [manifestarse] to show, to be evident. **-3.** *loc*: **pintárselas uno solo para algo** to be a past master at sthg.

pintarrajear *vt fam despec* to daub.

pinto, -ta *adj* speckled, spotted.

◆ **pinta** ◇ *f* **-1.** [lunar] spot. **-2.** *fig* [aspecto] appearance; **tener pinta de algo** to look ○ seem sthg; **tiene buena pinta** it looks good. **-3.** [unidad de medida] pint. **-4.** *Amer* [pintada] graffiti (*U*). ◇ *m y f fam* [caradura] cheeky so-and-so, shameless person.

pintor, -ra *m y f* painter; ~ **de brocha gorda** painter and decorator; *despec* dauber.

pintoresco, -ca *adj* picturesque; *fig* [extravagante] colourful.

pintura *f* **-1.** ARTE painting; ~ **a la acuarela** watercolour; ~ **al óleo** oil painting; ~ **rupestre** cave painting; **no poder ver a alguien ni en** ~ *fig* not to be able to stand the sight of sb. **-2.** [materia] paint. **-3.** *fig* [descripción] description, portrayal.

pinza *f* (*gen pl*) **-1.** [gen] tweezers (*pl*); [de tender ropa] peg, clothespin *Am*; **coger algo con** ~**s** to handle sthg with great care. **-2.** [de animal] pincer, claw. **-3.** [pliegue] fold.

piña f **-1.** [del pino] pine cone. **-2.** [ananás] pineapple; ~ **colada** piña colada. **-3.** fig [conjunto de gente] close-knit group. **-4.** fam [golpe] knock, bash.

piñata f pot full of sweets.

piñón m **-1.** [fruto] pine nut; **estar a partir un** ~ **con alguien** to be hand in glove with sb. **-2.** [rueda dentada] pinion; **ser de** ~ **fijo** to be fixed ○ rigid.

pío, -a adj pious.

◆ **pío** m cheep, cheeping (U); [de gallina] cluck, clucking (U); **no decir ni** ~ fig not to make a peep.

piojo m louse.

piojoso, -sa ◇ adj lousy, covered in lice; fig [sucio] flea-bitten, filthy. ◇ m y f [con piojos] louse-ridden person; fig [sucio] filthy person.

piola adj Amer fam **-1.** [astuto] shrewd. **-2.** [estupendo] fabulous.

piolín m Amer cord.

pionero, -ra m y f pioneer.

piorrea f pyorrhoea.

pipa f **-1.** [para fumar] pipe; **fumar en** ~ to smoke a pipe. **-2.** [pepita] seed, pip; ~**s (de girasol)** sunflower seeds coated in salt. **-3.** [tonel] barrel. **-4.** loc: **pasarlo** ○ **pasárselo** ~ to have a whale of a time.

pipermín, peppermint [piper'min] m peppermint liqueur.

pipeta f pipette.

pipí m fam wee-wee; **hacer** ~ to have a wee-wee.

pipón, -ona m y f Amer fam nipper, kid.

pipote m Amer rubbish bin Br, garbage can Am.

pique ◇ v → **picar**. ◇ m **-1.** [enfado] grudge; **tener un** ~ **con alguien** to have a grudge against sb. **-2.** [rivalidad] rivalry. **-3.** loc: **irse a** ~ [barco] to sink; [negocio] to go under; [plan] to fail.

piqué (pl **piqués**) m piqué.

piquera f Amer [antro] dive, seedy bar.

piqueta f pickaxe.

piquete m **-1.** [herramienta] peg, stake. **-2.** [grupo]: ~ **de ejecución** firing squad; ~ **(de huelga)** picket.

pira f pyre.

pirado, -da adj fam crazy.

piragua f canoe.

piragüismo m canoeing.

piramidal adj pyramid-shaped, pyramidal.

pirámide f pyramid.

piraña f piranha.

pirarse vpr fam to clear off.

pirata ◇ adj pirate (antes de sust); [disco] bootleg. ◇ m y f lit & fig pirate; ~ **del aire** hijacker; ~ **informático** hacker.

piratear ◇ vi **-1.** [gen] to be involved in piracy. **-2.** INFORM to hack. ◇ vt INFORM to hack into.

piratería f lit & fig piracy; ~ **aérea** hijacking; ~ **informática** hacking.

pirenaico, -ca adj Pyrenean.

pírex, pyrex® m Pyrex®.

pirindolo m fam fig thingamabob.

Pirineos mpl: **los** ~ the Pyrenees.

piripi adj fam tipsy.

pirita f pyrite.

piro m fam: **darse el** ~ to scarper, to clear off.

piromanía f pyromania.

pirómano, -na ◇ adj pyromaniacal. ◇ m y f pyromaniac.

piropear vt fam to make flirtatious comments to, ≈ to wolf-whistle at.

piropo m fam flirtatious remark, ≈ wolf whistle.

pirotecnia f pyrotechnics (U).

pirotécnico, -ca ◇ adj firework (antes de sust). ◇ m y f firework specialist.

pirrarse vpr fam: ~ **por algo/alguien** to be dead keen on sthg/sb.

pírrico, -ca adj Pyrrhic.

pirueta f pirouette; **hacer** ~**s** fig [esfuerzo] to perform miracles.

piruleta f lollipop.

pirulí (pl **pirulís**) m lollipop.

pis (pl **pises**) m fam pee; **hacer** ~ fam to have a pee.

pisada f **-1.** [acción] footstep; **seguir las** ~**s de alguien** to follow in sb's footsteps. **-2.** [huella] footprint.

pisadura f footprint.

pisapapeles m inv paperweight.

pisar vt **-1.** [con el pie] to tread on; ~ **fuerte** fig to be firing on all cylinders. **-2.** [uvas] to tread. **-3.** fig [llegar a] to set foot in. **-4.** fig [despreciar] to trample on. **-5.** fig [anticiparse]: ~ **un contrato a alguien** to beat sb to a contract; ~ **una idea a alguien** to think of something before sb.

piscicultura f fish farming.

piscifactoría f fish farm.

piscina f swimming pool.

Piscis ◇ m [zodiaco] Pisces; **ser** ~ to be (a) Pisces. ◇ m y f [persona] Pisces.

piscolabis m inv fam snack.

piso m **-1.** [vivienda] flat; ~ **franco** safe house. **-2.** [planta] floor. **-3.** [suelo - de carre-

plancha

tera] **surface**; [- de edificio] **floor**. **-4.** [capa] layer.

pisotear vt **-1.** [con el pie] to **trample on**. **-2.** [humillar] to **scorn**. **-3.** [desobedecer] to **trample over**.

pisotón m fam **stamp** (of the foot).

pista f **-1.** [gen] **track**; ~ **de aterrizaje** runway; ~ **de baile** dance floor; ~ **de esquí** ski slope; ~ **de hielo** ice rink; ~ **de tenis** tennis court. **-2.** fig [indicio] **clue**; **seguir la** ~ **a alguien** to be on sb's trail.

pistacho m pistachio.

pistilo m pistil.

pisto m ≃ ratatouille.

pistola f **-1.** [arma - con cilindro] **gun**; [- sin cilindro] **pistol**; ~ **de agua** water pistol. **-2.** [pulverizador] **spraygun**; **pintar a** ~ to spray-paint. **-3.** [herramienta] **gun**.

pistolero, -ra m y f [persona] **gunman**.
◆ **pistolera** f [funda] **holster**.

pistón m **-1.** MEC **piston**. **-2.** [MÚS - corneta] **cornet**; [- llave] **key**. **-3.** [de arma] **percussion cap**.

pita f agave.

pitada f Amer fam **drag, puff**.

pitanza f **-1.** [ración de comida] **daily rations** (pl). **-2.** fam [alimento] **grub**.

pitar ◇ vt **-1.** [arbitrar - partido] to **referee**; [- falta] to **blow for**. **-2.** [abuchear]: ~ **a alguien** to whistle at sb in disapproval. **-3.** Amer fam [dar una calada a] to **puff (on)**. ◇ vi **-1.** [tocar el pito] to **blow a whistle**; [del coche] to **toot one's horn**. **-2.** [funcionar - cosa] to **work**; [- persona] to **get on**. **-3.** loc: **salir/irse pitando** to **rush out/off**; **venir pitando** to come rushing.

pitido m whistle.

pitillera f cigarette case.

pitillo m **-1.** [cigarrillo] **cigarette**. **-2.** Amer [paja] drinking **straw**.

pito m **-1.** [silbato] **whistle**. **-2.** [claxon] **horn**. **-3.** fam [cigarrillo] **fag**. **-4.** fam [pene] **willie**. **-5.** loc: **(no) me importa un** ~ I couldn't give a damn; **por** ~**s o por flautas** for one reason or another; **tomar a alguien por el** ~ **del sereno** not to take sb seriously.

pitón ◇ m **-1.** [cuerno] **horn**. **-2.** [pitorro] **spout**. ◇ f → **serpiente**.

pitonisa f fortune-teller.

pitorrearse vpr fam: ~ **(de)** to take the mickey (out of).

pitorreo m making fun (U), joking (U).

pitorro m spout.

pituitario, -ria adj pituitary.

pívot = **pivote**.

pivotar vi DEP to **pivot**.

pivote (pl **pivotes**), **pívot** (pl **pivots**) m y f DEP **pivot**.

pizarra f **-1.** [roca, material] **slate**. **-2.** [encerado] **blackboard**.

pizca f fam **-1.** [gen] **tiny bit**; [de sal] **pinch**; **ni** ~ **not one bit**. **-2.** Amer [cosecha] **harvest, crop**.

pizpireta adj f fam **brassy, spirited**.

pizza ['pitsa] f pizza.

pizzería [pitse'ria] f pizzeria.

placa f **-1.** [lámina] **plate**; [de madera] **sheet**; ~ **solar** solar panel. **-2.** [inscripción] **plaque**; [de policía] **badge**. **-3.** [matrícula] **number plate**. **-4.** [de cocina] **ring**; ~ **de vitrocerámica** glass enamel **hob**. **-5.** GEOL **plate**. **-6.** ELECTRÓN **board**; ~ **madre** INFORM **motherboard**. **-7.** ~ **dental** dental **plaque**.

placaje m tackle.

placar [10] vt to **tackle**.

placebo m placebo.

placenta f placenta.

placentero, -ra adj pleasant.

placer m **pleasure**; **ha sido un** ~ **(conocerle)** it has been a pleasure meeting you.

placidez f [de persona] **placidness**; [de día, vida, conversación] **peacefulness**.

plácido, -da adj [persona] **placid**; [día, vida, conversación] **peaceful**.

plafón m ARQUIT soffit.

plaga f **-1.** [gen] **plague**; AGR **blight**; [animal] **pest**. **-2.** fig [de gente] **swarm**. **-3.** [epidemia] **epidemic**.

plagado, -da adj: ~ **(de)** infested (with).

plagar [16] vt: ~ **de** [propaganda etc] to **swamp with**; [moscas etc] to **infest with**.

plagiar [8] vt **-1.** [copiar] to **plagiarize**. **-2.** Amer [secuestrar] to **kidnap**.

plagiario, -ria m y f Amer kidnapper.

plagio m **-1.** [copia] **plagiarism**. **-2.** Amer [secuestro] **kidnapping**.

plague etc → **plagar**.

plaguicida ◇ adj **pesticidal**. ◇ m **pesticide**.

plan m **-1.** [proyecto, programa] **plan**; ~ **de estudios** syllabus; ~ **de pensiones** pension plan. **-2.** fam [ligue] **date**. **-3.** fam [modo, forma]: **lo dijo en** ~ **serio** he was serious about it; **¡vaya** ~ **de vida!** what a life!; **si te pones en ese** ~ ... if you're going to be like that about it ...; **no es** ~ it's just not on.

plana → **plano**.

plancha f **-1.** [para planchar] **iron**. **-2.** [para cocinar] **grill**; **a la** ~ **grilled**. **-3.** [placa] **plate**; [de madera] **sheet**. **-4.** fam [metedura de pata] boob, blunder. **-5.** [en fútbol] **diving header. -6.** IMPRENTA **plate.**

planchado *m* ironing.

planchar *vt* to iron.

planchazo *m fam* boob, blunder.

plancton *m* plankton.

planeador *m* glider.

planeadora *f* [de madera] plane.

planear ◇ *vt* to plan. ◇ *vi* **-1.** [hacer planes] to plan. **-2.** [en el aire] to glide.

planeta *m* planet.

planetario, **-ria** *adj* **-1.** [de un planeta] planetary. **-2.** [mundial] world (*antes de sust*).

◆ **planetario** *m* planetarium.

planicie *f* plain.

planificación *f* planning; ~ **familiar** family planning.

planificar [10] *vt* to plan.

planilla *f Amer* [formulario] form.

planisferio *m* planisphere.

planning ['planin] (*pl* **plannings**) *m* scheduling.

plano, **-na** *adj* flat.

◆ **plano** *m* **-1.** [diseño, mapa] plan. **-2.** [nivel, aspecto] level. **-3.** CIN shot; **primer** ~ close-up; **en segundo** ~ *fig* in the background. **-4.** GEOM plane. **-5.** *loc:* **de** ~ [golpear] right, directly; [negar] flatly; **cantar de** ~ to make a full confession.

◆ **plana** *f* **-1.** [página] page; **en primera plana** on the front page. **-2.** [llanura] plain. **-3.** MIL: **plana mayor** staff.

planta *f* **-1.** BOT & IND plant; ~ **depuradora** purification plant; ~ **de envase** ◇ **envasadora** packaging plant. **-2.** [piso] floor; ~ **baja** ground floor. **-3.** [del pie] sole. **-4.** *loc:* **de nueva** ~ brand new; **tener buena** ~ to be good-looking.

plantación *f* **-1.** [terreno] plantation. **-2.** [acción] planting.

plantado, **-da** *adj* standing, planted; **dejar** ~ **a alguien** *fam* [cortar la relación] to walk out on sb; [no acudir] to stand sb up; **ser bien** ~ to be good-looking.

plantar *vt* **-1.** [sembrar]: ~ **algo (de)** to plant sthg (with). **-2.** [fijar - tienda de campaña] to pitch; [- poste] to put in. **-3.** *fam* [asestar] to deal, to land. **-4.** *fam* [decir con brusquedad]: **le plantó cuatro frescas** she gave him a piece of her mind. **-5.** *fam* [abandonar] to dump, to leave.

◆ **plantarse** *vpr* **-1.** [gen] to plant o.s. **-2.** [en un sitio con rapidez]: ~**se en** to get to, to reach. **-3.** [en una actitud]: ~**se en algo** to stick to sthg, to insist on sthg. **-4.** [en naipes] to stick.

plante *m* **-1.** [para protestar] protest. **-2.** [plantón]: **dar** ◇ **hacer un** ~ **a alguien** to stand sb up.

planteamiento *m* **-1.** [exposición] raising, posing. **-2.** [enfoque] approach.

plantear *vt* **-1.** [exponer - problema] to pose; [- posibilidad, dificultad, duda] to raise. **-2.** [enfocar] to approach.

◆ **plantearse** *vpr:* ~**se algo** to consider sthg, to think about sthg.

plantel *m* **-1.** [criadero] nursery bed. **-2.** *fig* [conjunto] group.

plantilla *f* **-1.** [de empresa] staff; **estar en** ~ to be on the staff. **-2.** [suela interior] insole. **-3.** [patrón] pattern, template.

plantío *m* plot (of land).

plantón *m:* **dar un** ~ **a alguien** *fam* to stand sb up.

plañidero, **-ra** *adj* plaintive, whining.

plañido *m* moan.

plañir ◇ *vt* to bewail. ◇ *vi* to moan, to wail.

plaque *etc* → **placar**.

plaqueta *f* BIOL platelet.

plasma *m* plasma.

plasmar *vt* **-1.** *fig* [reflejar] to give shape to. **-2.** [modelar] to shape, to mould.

◆ **plasmarse** *vpr* to emerge, to take shape.

plasta ◇ *adj mfam:* **ser** ~ to be a pain. ◇ *m y f mfam* [pesado] pain, drag. ◇ *f* **-1.** [cosa blanda] mess. **-2.** *fam fig* [cosa mal hecha] botch-up.

plástica → **plástico**.

plasticidad *f* **-1.** [gen] plasticity. **-2.** [expresividad] expressiveness.

plástico, **-ca** *adj* **-1.** [gen] plastic. **-2.** [expresivo] expressive.

◆ **plástico** *m* **-1.** [gen] plastic. **-2.** *fam* [tarjetas de crédito] plastic (money).

◆ **plástica** *f* plastic art.

plastificar [10] *vt* to plasticize.

plastilina® *f* ≃ Plasticine®.

plata *f* **-1.** [metal] silver; ~ **de ley** sterling silver; **hablar en** ~ *fam* to speak bluntly. **-2.** [objetos de plata] silverware. **-3.** *Amer* [dinero] money.

plataforma *f* **-1.** [gen] platform. **-2.** ~ **petrolífera** oil rig. **-3.** *fig* [punto de partida] launching pad. **-4.** GEOL shelf; ~ **continental** continental shelf.

platal *m Amer fam:* **un** ~ a fortune, loads of money.

platanal, **platanar** *m* banana plantation.

platanero *m* banana tree.

plátano *m* **-1.** [fruta] banana. **-2.** [árbol] banana tree.

platea *f* stalls (*pl*).

plateado, -da *adj* **-1.** [con plata] silver-plated. **-2.** *fig* [color] silvery.

plateresco *m* plateresque.

platería *f* **-1.** [arte u oficio] silversmithing. **-2.** [tienda] jeweller's (shop).

platero, -ra *m y f* silversmith.

plática *f* **-1.** [charla] talk, chat. **-2.** RELIG sermon.

platicar [10] *vi* to talk, to chat.

platillo *m* **-1.** [plato pequeño] small plate; [de taza] saucer. **-2.** [de una balanza] pan. **-3.** (*gen pl*) MÚS cymbal.
◆ **platillo volante** *m* flying saucer.

platina *f* **-1.** [de tocadiscos] turntable. **-2.** [de microscopio] slide.

platino *m* [metal] platinum.
◆ **platinos** *mpl* AUTOM & MEC contact points.

plato *m* **-1.** [recipiente] plate, dish; **lavar los ~s** to do the washing-up; **~ de postre** dessert plate; **~ hondo** ○ **sopero** soup dish ○ plate; **~ llano** plate; **comer en el mismo ~** to be great friends; **pagar los ~s rotos** to carry the can; **parecer que alguien no ha roto un ~ en su vida** to look as if butter wouldn't melt in one's mouth. **-2.** [parte de una comida] course; **primer ~** first course, starter; **de primer ~** for starters; **segundo ~** second course, main course; **~ fuerte** [en una comida] main course; *fig* main part. **-3.** [comida] dish; **~ combinado** *single-course meal which usually consists of meat or fish accompanied by chips and vegetables*; **~ preparado** ready-prepared meal. **-4.** [de tocadiscos, microondas] turntable. **-5.** [de bicicleta] chain wheel.

plató *m* set.

platónico, -ca *adj* Platonic.

platudo, -da *adj Amer fam* loaded, rolling in it.

plausibilidad *f* **-1.** [admisibilidad] acceptability. **-2.** [posibilidad] plausibility.

plausible *adj* **-1.** [admisible] acceptable. **-2.** [posible] plausible.

playa *f* **-1.** [en el mar] beach; **ir a la ~ de vacaciones** to go on holiday to the seaside. **-2.** *Amer* [aparcamiento]: **~ de estacionamiento** car park.

play-back ['pleiβak] (*pl* **play-backs**) *m*: **hacer ~** to mime (the lyrics).

play-boy [plei'βoi] (*pl* **play-boys**) *m* playboy.

playero, -ra *adj* beach (*antes de sust*).
◆ **playeras** *fpl* **-1.** [de deporte] tennis

shoes. **-2.** [para la playa] canvas shoes.

plaza *f* **-1.** [en una población] square. **-2.** [sitio] place; **tenemos ~s limitadas** there are a limited number of places available. **-3.** [asiento] seat; **de dos ~s** two-seater (*antes de sust*). **-4.** [puesto de trabajo] position, job; **~ vacante** vacancy. **-5.** [mercado] market, marketplace. **-6.** TAUROM: **~ (de toros)** bull-ring. **-7.** COM [zona] area. **-8.** [fortificación]: **~ fuerte** stronghold.

plazo *m* **-1.** [de tiempo] period (of time); **en un ~ de un mes** within a month; **mañana termina el ~ de inscripción** the deadline for registration is tomorrow; **a corto/largo ~** [gen] in the short/long term; ECON short/long term; **~ de entrega** COM delivery time. **-2.** [de dinero] instalment; **a ~s** in instalments, on hire purchase.

plazoleta *f* small square.

pleamar *f* high tide.

plebe *f*: **la ~** *lit & fig* the plebs.

plebeyo, -ya *adj* **-1.** HIST plebeian. **-2.** [vulgar] common.

plebiscito *m* plebiscite.

plegable *adj* collapsible, foldaway; [chair] folding.

plegar [35] *vt* to fold; [mesita, hamaca] to fold away.
◆ **plegarse** *vpr*: **~se a algo** to give in ○ yield to sthg.

plegaria *f* prayer.

plegue *etc* → **plegar**.

pleitear *vi* DER to litigate, to conduct a lawsuit.

pleitesía *f* homage; **rendir ~ a alguien** to pay homage to sb.

pleito *m* DER [litigio] legal action (*U*), lawsuit; [disputa] dispute; **poner un ~ (a alguien)** to take legal action (against sb).

plenario, -ria *adj* plenary.

plenilunio *m* full moon.

plenipotenciario, -ria ◇ *adj* plenipotentiary. ◇ *m y f* envoy.

plenitud *f* **-1.** [totalidad] completeness, fullness; **en la ~ de** at the height of. **-2.** [abundancia] abundance.

pleno, -na *adj* full, complete; [derecho] perfect; **en ~ día** in broad daylight; **en plena guerra** in the middle of the war; **le dio en plena cara** she hit him right in the face; **en ~ uso de sus facultades** in full command of his faculties; **la reunión en ~** the meeting as a whole, everyone at the meeting; **en plena forma** on top form.
◆ **pleno** *m* **-1.** [reunión] plenary meeting. **-2.** [en las quinielas] full claim, ≈ 24 points.

pletórico, -ca *adj*: **~ de** full of.

pleura *f* pleural membrane.

pleuresía *f* pleurisy.

plexiglás® *m inv* ≃ Perspex®.

pléyade *f* [conjunto] cluster.

pliega *etc* → **plegar**.

pliego *m* **-1.** [hoja] sheet (of paper). **-2.** [carta, documento] *sealed document* ○ *letter*; ~ **de condiciones** specifications (*pl*); ~ **de descargos** list of rebuttals. **-3.** IMPRENTA signature.

pliegue *m* **-1.** [gen & GEOL] fold. **-2.** [en un plisado] pleat.

plisado *m* pleating.

plisar *vt* to pleat.

plomada *f* plumb line.

plomería *f Amer* plumber's.

plomero *m Amer* plumber.

plomizo, -za *adj* [color] leaden.

plomo *m* **-1.** [metal] lead; **caer a** ~ to fall ○ drop like a stone. **-2.** [pieza de metal] lead weight. **-3.** [fusible] fuse. **-4.** *fam* [pelmazo] bore, drag.

plotter (*pl* **plotters**) *m* INFORM plotter.

pluma ◇ *f* **-1.** [de ave] feather. **-2.** [para escribir] (fountain) pen; HIST quill; ~ **estilográfica** fountain pen. **-3.** *fig* [estilo de escribir] style. **-4.** *loc*: **tener mucha** ~ to be camp. ◇ *adj inv* DEP featherweight.

plumaje *m* **-1.** [de ave] plumage. **-2.** [adorno] plume.

plumazo *m* stroke of the pen; **de un** ~ [al tachar] with a stroke of one's pen; *fig* [al hacer algo] in one fell swoop, at a stroke.

plúmbeo, -a *adj fig* tedious, heavy.

plum-cake [pluŋ'keik] (*pl* **plum-cakes**) *m* fruit cake.

plumero *m* feather duster; **vérsele a alguien el** ~ *fam* to see through sb.

plumier (*pl* **plumiers**) *m* pencil box.

plumilla *f* nib.

plumín *m* nib.

plumón *m* **-1.** [de ave] down. **-2.** [anorak] feather-lined anorak.

PLUNA (*abrev de* **Primeras Líneas Uruguayas de Navegación Aérea**) *f Uruguayan state airline.*

plural *adj & m* plural.

pluralidad *f* diversity.

pluralismo *m* pluralism.

pluralizar [13] *vi* to generalize.

pluriempleado, -da *adj*: **estar** ~ to have more than one job.

pluriempleo *m*: **hacer** ~ to have more than one job.

pluripartidismo *m* multi-party system.

plurivalente *adj* polyvalent.

plus (*pl* **pluses**) *m* bonus; ~ **de peligrosidad** danger money (*U*); ~ **familiar** family allowance.

pluscuamperfecto *adj & m* pluperfect.

plusmarca *f* record.

plusmarquista *m y f* record-holder.

plusvalía *f* ECON appreciation, added value.

plutocracia *f* plutocracy.

Plutón Pluto.

plutonio *m* plutonium.

pluvial *adj* rain (*antes de sust*).

pluviómetro *m* rain gauge.

pluviosidad *f* rainfall.

pluvioso, -sa *adj culto* rainy.

p.m. (*abrev de* **post meridiem**) p.m.

PM (*abrev de* **policía militar**) *f* MP.

p.n. (*abrev de* **peso neto**) nt. wt.

PN (*abrev de* **policía naval**) *f* naval police.

PNB (*abrev de* **producto nacional bruto**) *m* GNP.

PND (*abrev de* **personal no docente**) *m non-academic staff.*

PNN (*abrev de* **profesor no numerario**) *m y f teacher who does not have tenure.*

PNV (*abrev de* **Partido Nacionalista Vasco**) *m Basque nationalist party.*

Po *m*: **el** ~ **the** (River) Po.

p.o., p/o *abrev de* **por orden**.

población *f* **-1.** [ciudad] town, city; [pueblo] village. **-2.** [habitantes] population; ~ **activa** working population; ~ **flotante** floating population. **-3.** [acción de poblar] settlement, populating.

poblado, -da *adj* **-1.** [habitado] inhabited; **una zona muy poblada** a densely populated area. **-2.** *fig* [lleno] full; [barba, cejas] bushy.

◆ **poblado** *m* settlement.

poblador, -ra *m y f* settler.

poblar [23] *vt* **-1.** [establecerse en] to settle, to colonize. **-2.** *fig* [llenar]: ~ **(de)** [plantas, árboles] to plant (with); [peces etc] to stock (with). **-3.** [habitar] to inhabit.

◆ **poblarse** *vpr*: ~**se (de)** to fill up (with).

pobre ◇ *adj* poor; **¡~ hombre!** poor man!; ~ **en** lacking in; **¡~ de mí!** poor me! ◇ *m y f* **-1.** [gen] poor person; **los** ~**s** the poor, poor people; **¡el** ~**!** poor thing! **-2.** [mendigo] beggar.

pobreza *f* [escasez] poverty; ~ **de** lack ○ scarcity of; ~ **de espíritu** weakness of character.

pochismo *m Amer fam language mistake caused by English influence.*

pocho, **-cha** *adj* **-1.** [persona] off-colour. **-2.** [fruta] over-ripe. **-3.** *Amer fam* [americanizado] Americanized.

pocilga *f lit* & *fig* pigsty.

pocillo *m Amer* small cup.

pócima *f* **-1.** [poción] potion. **-2.** *despec* [bebida de mal sabor] concoction.

poción *f* potion.

poco, **-ca** ◇ *adj* little, not much; (*pl*) few, not many; **poca agua** not much water; **de poca importancia** of little importance; **hay ~s árboles** there aren't many trees; **pocas personas lo saben** few ○ not many people know it; **tenemos ~ tiempo** we don't have much time; **hace ~ tiempo** not long ago; **dame unos ~s días** give me a few days.
◇ *pron* little, not much; (*pl*) few, not many; **queda ~** there's not much left; **tengo muy ~s** I don't have very many, I have very few; **~s hay que sepan tanto** not many people know so much; **un ~** a bit; **¿me dejas un ~?** can I have a bit?; **un ~ de** a bit of; **un ~ de sentido común** a bit of common sense; **unos ~s** a few.
◆ **poco** *adv* **-1.** [escasamente] not much; **este niño come ~** this boy doesn't eat much; **es ~ común** it's not very common; **es un ~ triste** it's rather sad; **~ más o menos** more or less; **por ~** almost, nearly; **tener en ~ a alguien** not to think much of sb. **-2.** [brevemente] **tardaré muy ~** I won't be long; **al ~ de ...** shortly after ...; **dentro de ~** soon, in a short time; **hace ~** a little while ago, not long ago; **~ a ~** [progresivamente] little by little, bit by bit; **¡~ a ~!** [despacio] steady on!, slow down!

poda *f* **-1.** [acción] pruning. **-2.** [tiempo] pruning time.

podadera *f* pruning knife.

podar *vt* to prune.

podenco *m* hound.

poder [64] ◇ *m* **-1.** [gen] power; **estar en/hacerse con el ~** to be in/to seize power; **~ adquisitivo** purchasing power; **~ calorífico** calorific value; **tener ~ de convocatoria** to be a crowd-puller; **~es fácticos** *the church, military and press*. **-2.** [posesión]: **estar en ~ de alguien** to be in sb's hands. **-3.** (*gen pl*) [autorización] power, authorization; **dar ~es a alguien para que haga algo** to authorize sb to do sthg; **por ~es** by proxy.
◇ *vi* **-1.** [tener facultad] can, to be able to; **no puedo decírtelo** I can't tell you, I'm unable to tell you. **-2.** [tener permiso] can, may; **no puedo salir por la noche** I'm not allowed to ○ I can't go out at night; **¿se puede fumar aquí?** may I smoke here? **-3.** [ser capaz moralmente] can; **no podemos por-**

tarnos así con él we can't treat him like that. **-4.** [tener posibilidad, ser posible] may, can; **podías haber cogido el tren** you could have caught the train; **puede estallar la guerra** war could ○ may break out; **¡hubiera podido invitarnos!** [expresa enfado] she could ○ might have invited us! **-5.** *loc*: **a ○ hasta más no ~** as much as can be; **es avaro a más no ~** he's as miserly as can be; **no ~ más** [estar cansado] to be too tired to carry on; [estar harto de comer] to be full (up); [estar enfadado] to have had enough; **¿se puede?** may I come in?
◇ *v impers* [ser posible] may; **puede que llueva** it may ○ might rain; **¿vendrás mañana? - puede** will you come tomorrow? - I may do; **puede ser** perhaps, maybe.
◇ *vt* [ser más fuerte que] to be stronger than; **tú eres más alto, pero yo te puedo** you may be taller than me, but I could still beat you up.
◆ **poder con** *vi* + *prep* **-1.** [enfermedad, rival] to be able to overcome. **-2.** [tarea, problema] to be able to cope with. **-3.** [soportar]: **no ~ con algo/alguien** not to be able to stand sthg/sb; **no puedo con la hipocresía** I can't stand hypocrisy.

poderío *m* **-1.** [poder] power. **-2.** [riqueza] riches (*pl*).

poderoso, **-sa** *adj* powerful.

podio, **podium** *m* podium.

podología *f* chiropody.

podólogo, **-ga** *m y f* chiropodist.

podrá → **poder**.

podredumbre *f* **-1.** [putrefacción] putrefaction. **-2.** *fig* [inmoralidad] corruption.

podría → **poder**.

podrido, **-da** ◇ *pp* → **pudrir**. ◇ *adj* rotten.

poema *m* poem; **ser todo un ~** to be pathetic.

poesía *f* **-1.** [género literario] poetry. **-2.** [poema] poem.

poeta *m y f* poet.

poético, **-ca** *adj* poetic.
◆ **poética** *f* poetics (*U*).

poetisa *f* female poet.

póker = **póquer**.

polaco, **-ca** *adj, m y f* Polish.
◆ **polaco** *m* [lengua] Polish.

polaina *f* leggings (*pl*).

polar *adj* polar.

polaridad *f* polarity.

polarizar [13] *vt* **-1.** *fig* [miradas, atención, esfuerzo] to concentrate. **-2.** FÍS to polarize.
◆ **polarizarse** *vpr* [vida política, opinión pública] to become polarized.

polaroid® *f inv* Polaroid®.
polca *f* polka.
polea *f* pulley.
polémico, -ca *adj* controversial.
◆ **polémica** *f* controversy.
polemizar [13] *vi* to argue, to debate.
polen *m* pollen.
polenta *f* cornflour.
poleo *m* pennyroyal.
polera *f Amer* T-shirt.
poli *fam* ◇ *m y f* cop. ◇ *f* cops (*pl*).
poliamida *f* polyamide.
polichinela *m* **-1.** [personaje] Punchinello. **-2.** [títere] puppet, marionette.
policía ◇ *m y f* policeman (*f* police-woman). ◇ *f*: **la** ~ the police; ~ **militar/secreta/urbana** military/secret/local police; ~ **antidisturbios** riot police; ~ **de tráfico** traffic police.
policiaco, -ca, policíaco, -ca *adj* police (*antes de sust*); [novela, película] detective (*antes de sust*).
policial *adj* police (*antes de sust*).
policlínica *f* general hospital.
policromo, -ma, polícromo, -ma *adj* polychromatic.
polideportivo, -va *adj* multi-sport; [gimnasio] multi-use.
◆ **polideportivo** *m* sports centre.
poliedro *m* polyhedron.
poliéster *m inv* polyester.
polietileno *m* polythene *Br*, polyethylene *Am*.
polifacético, -ca *adj* multifaceted, versatile.
polifónico, -ca *adj* polyphonic.
poligamia *f* polygamy.
polígamo, -ma ◇ *adj* polygamous. ◇ *m y f* polygamist.
poligloto, -ta, polígloto, -ta *adj, m y f* polyglot.
poligonal *adj* polygonal.
polígono *m* **-1.** GEOM polygon. **-2.** [terreno]: ~ **industrial/residencial** industrial/housing estate; ~ **de tiro** firing range.
polilla *f* moth.
polinización *f* pollination.
polinomio *m* polynomial.
poliomelitis, polio *f inv* polio.
polipiel *f* artificial skin.
pólipo *m* polyp.
Polisario (*abrev de* **Frente Popular para la Liberación de Sakiet el Hamra y Río de Oro**) *m*: **el (Frente)** ~ the Polisario Front.
polisemia *f* polysemy.

polisílabo, -ba *adj* polysyllabic.
◆ **polisílabo** *m* polysyllable.
politburó *m* politburo.
politécnico, -ca *adj* polytechnic.
◆ **politécnica** *f* polytechnic.
politeísta *adj* polytheistic.
política → **político**.
politicastro *m despec* bad politician.
político, -ca *adj* **-1.** [de gobierno] political. **-2.** *fig* [prudente] tactful. **-3.** [pariente]: **hermano** ~ brother-in-law; **familia política** in-laws (*pl*).
◆ **político** *m* politician.
◆ **política** *f* **-1.** [arte de gobernar] politics (*U*). **-2.** [modo de gobernar, táctica] policy; **política monetaria** monetary policy; **la política de avestruz** burying one's head in the sand.
politiqueo *m despec* politicking.
politización *f* politicization.
politizar [13] *vt* to politicize.
◆ **politizarse** *vpr* to become politicized.
poliuretano *m* polyurethane.
polivalencia *f* polyvalency.
polivalente *adj* [vacuna, suero] polyvalent.
póliza *f* **-1.** [de seguro] (insurance) policy. **-2.** [sello] *stamp on a document showing that a certain tax has been paid.*
polizón *m* stowaway.
polizonte *m fam despec* cop.
polla → **pollo**.
pollera *f Amer* skirt.
pollería *f* poultry shop.
pollito *m* chick.
pollo, -lla *m y f* **-1.** ZOOL chick. **-2.** (*gen m*) *fig* [joven] young kid.
◆ **pollo** *m* CULIN chicken.
◆ **polla** *f vulg* cock, prick.
◆ **polla de agua** *f* [ave] moorhen.
polo *m* **-1.** [gen] pole; ~ **magnético** magnetic pole; ~ **norte/sur** North/South Pole; ~ **de atracción** ○ **de atracción** *fig* centre of attraction; **ser** ~**s opuestos** *fig* to be poles apart. **-2.** ELECTR terminal; ~ **negativo/positivo** negative/positive terminal. **-3.** [helado] ice lolly. **-4.** [jersey] polo shirt. **-5.** DEP polo.
pololear *vi Amer fam* to go out (together).
pololeo *m Amer fam* small job.
pololo, -la *m y f Amer fam* boyfriend (*f* girlfriend).
Polonia Poland.
poltrón, -ona *adj* lazy.
◆ **poltrona** *f* easy chair.
polución *f* **-1.** [contaminación] pollution. **-2.** [eyaculación]: ~ **nocturna** wet dream.

polucionar *vt* to pollute.

polvareda *f* dust cloud; **levantar una gran** ~ *fig* to cause a commotion.

polvera *f* powder compact.

polvo *m* **-1.** [en el aire] dust; **limpiar** O **quitar el** ~ to do the dusting. **-2.** [de un producto] powder; **en** ~ powdered; ~**s de talco** talcum powder; ~**s picapica** itching powder; **estar hecho** ~ *fam* to be knackered; **hacer** ~ **algo** to smash sthg; **morder el** ~ to be humiliated. **-3.** *vulg* [coito] fuck, screw; **echar un** ~ to have a screw.
 ◆ **polvos** *mpl* [maquillaje] powder (*U*); **ponerse** ~**s** to powder one's face.

pólvora *f* [sustancia explosiva] gunpowder; **correr como la** ~ to spread like wildfire; **no ha inventado la** ~ *fam* he's not the most intelligent person in the world.

polvoriento, -ta *adj* [superficie] dusty; [sustancia] powdery.

polvorín *m* munitions dump.

polvorón *m* crumbly sweet made from flour, butter and sugar.

pomada *f* ointment.

pomelo *m* **-1.** [fruto] grapefruit. **-2.** [árbol] grapefruit tree.

pómez → **piedra**.

pomo *m* knob.

pompa *f* **-1.** [suntuosidad] pomp. **-2.** [ostentación] show, ostentation.
 ◆ **pompa de jabón** *f* (*gen pl*) soap bubble.
 ◆ **pompas fúnebres** *fpl* **-1.** [servicio] undertaker's (*sg*). **-2.** [ceremonia] funeral (*sg*).

Pompeya Pompeii.

pompis *m inv fam* bottom, backside.

pompón *m* pompom.

pomposidad *f* **-1.** [suntuosidad] splendour; [ostentación] showiness. **-2.** [en el lenguaje] pomposity.

pomposo, -sa *adj* **-1.** [suntuoso] sumptuous, magnificent; [ostentoso] showy. **-2.** [lenguaje] pompous.

pómulo *m* **-1.** [hueso] cheekbone. **-2.** [mejilla] cheek.

pon → **poner**.

ponchar *vt Amer* to puncture.
 ◆ **poncharse** *vpr Amer* to get a puncture.

ponche *m* punch.

ponchera *f* punch bowl.

poncho *m* poncho.

ponderación *f* **-1.** [alabanza] praise. **-2.** [moderación] deliberation, considered nature. **-3.** [en estadística] weighting.

ponderado, -da *adj* **-1.** [moderado] considered. **-2.** [en estadística] weighted.

ponderar *vt* **-1.** [alabar] to praise. **-2.** [considerar, to consider, to weigh up. **-3.** [en estadística] to weight.

pondrá *etc* → **poner**.

ponedero *m* nesting box.

ponedor, -ra *adj* egg-laying.
 ◆ **ponedor** *m* [ponedero] nesting box.

ponencia *f* **-1.** [conferencia] lecture, paper; [informe] report. **-2.** [cargo] position of reporter. **-3.** [comisión] reporting committee.

ponente *m y f* reporter, rapporteur; [en congreso] speaker.

poner [65] ◇ *vt* **-1.** [gen] to put; [colocar] to place, to put. **-2.** [vestir]: ~ **algo a alguien** to put sthg on sb. **-3.** [contribuir, invertir] to put in; ~ **dinero en el negocio** to put money into the business; ~ **algo de mi/tu** *etc* **parte** to do my/your *etc* bit. **-4.** [hacer estar de cierta manera]: ~ **a alguien en un aprieto/de mal humor** to put sb in a difficult position/in a bad mood; **le has puesto colorado** you've made him blush. **-5.** [calificar]: ~ **a alguien de algo** to call sb sthg. **-6.** [oponer]: ~ **obstáculos a algo** to hinder sthg; ~ **pegas a algo** to raise objections to sthg. **-7.** [asignar - precio, medida] to fix, to settle; [- multa, tarea] to give; **le pusieron Mario** they called him Mario. **-8.** [TELECOM - telegrama, fax] to send; [- conferencia] to make; **¿me pones con él?** can you put me through to him? **-9.** [conectar - televisión etc] to switch O put on; [- despertador] to set; [- instalación, gas] to put in. **-10.** CIN, TEATR & TV to show; **¿qué ponen en la tele?** what's on the telly? **-11.** [montar - negocio] to set up; **ha puesto una tienda** she has opened a shop. **-12.** [decorar] to do up; **han puesto su casa con mucho lujo** they've done up their house in real style. **-13.** [suponer] to suppose; **pongamos que sucedió así** (let's) suppose that's what happened; **pon que necesitemos cinco días** suppose we need five days; **poniendo que todo salga bien** assuming everything goes according to plan. **-14.** [decir] to say; **¿qué pone ahí?** what does it say? **-15.** [huevo] to lay.
◇ *vi* [ave] to lay (eggs).
 ◆ **ponerse** ◇ *vpr* **-1.** [colocarse] to put o.s.; ~**se de pie** to stand up; **ponte en la ventana** stand by the window. **-2.** [ropa, gafas, maquillaje] to put on. **-3.** [estar de cierta manera] to go, to become; **se puso rojo de ira** he went red with anger; **se puso colorado** he blushed; **se puso muy guapa** she made herself attractive. **-4.** [iniciar]: ~**se a hacer algo** to start doing sthg. **-5.** [de salud]: ~**se malo** O **enfermo** to fall ill; ~**se bien** to get

better. **-6.** [llenarse]: ~**se de algo** to get covered in sthg; **se puso de barro hasta las rodillas** he got covered in mud up to the knees. **-7.** [suj: astro] to set. **-8.** [llegar]: ~**se en** to get to.
◇ *v impers Amer fam* [parecer]: **se me pone que ...** it seems to me that ....

poney = **poni**.

pongo → **poner**.

poni, poney ['poni] *m* pony.

poniente *m* [occidente] West; [viento] west wind.

pontificado *m* papacy.

pontifical *adj* papal.

pontífice *m* Pope, Pontiff.

pontificio, -cia *adj* papal.

pontón *m* pontoon.

ponzoña *f* [veneno] venom, poison.

ponzoñoso, -sa *adj* [venenoso] venomous, poisonous.

pop ◇ *adj* pop. ◇ *m* → **música**.

popa *f* stern.

pope *m* **-1.** RELIG *priest of the Orthodox church.* **-2.** *fam fig* [pez gordo] big shot.

popelina *f*, **popelín** *m* poplin.

popote *m Amer* drinking straw.

populachero, -ra *adj despec* **-1.** [fiesta] common, popular. **-2.** [discurso] populist.

populacho *m despec* mob, masses (*pl*).

popular *adj* **-1.** [del pueblo] of the people; [arte, música] folk. **-2.** [famoso] popular.

popularidad *f* popularity.

popularizar [13] *vt* to popularize.
◆ **popularizarse** *vpr* to become popular.

populista *adj, m y f* populist.

populoso, -sa *adj* populous, crowded.

popurrí *m* potpourri.

póquer, póker *m* **-1.** [juego] poker. **-2.** [jugada] four of a kind.

por *prep* **-1.** [causa] because of; **se enfadó ~ tu comportamiento** she got angry because of your behaviour. **-2.** [finalidad] (*antes de infin*) (in order) to; (*antes de sust, pron*) for; **lo hizo ~ complacerte** he did it to please you; **lo hice ~ ella** I did it for her. **-3.** [medio, modo, agente] by; **~ mensajero/fax** by courier/fax; **~ escrito** in writing; **lo cogieron ~ el brazo** they took him by the arm; **el récord fue batido ~ el atleta** the record was broken by the athlete. **-4.** [tiempo aproximado]: **creo que la boda será ~ abril** I think the wedding will be some time in April. **-5.** [tiempo concreto]: **~ la mañana/tarde** in the morning/afternoon; **~ la noche** at night; **ayer salimos ~ la noche** we went out last night; **~ unos días** for a few days. **-6.** [lugar - aproximadamente en]: **¿~ dónde vive?** whereabouts does he live?; **vive ~ las afueras** he lives somewhere on the outskirts; **había papeles ~ el suelo** there were papers all over the floor. **-7.** [lugar - a través de] through; **iba paseando ~ el bosque/la calle** she was walking through the forest/along the street; **pasar ~ la aduana** to go through customs. **-8.** [a cambio de, en lugar de] for; **lo ha comprado ~ poco dinero** she bought it for very little; **cambió el coche ~ la moto** he exchanged his car for a motorbike; **él lo hará ~ mí** he'll do it for me. **-9.** [distribución] per; **cien pesetas ~ unidad** a hundred pesetas each; **20 kms ~ hora** 20 km an ○ per hour. **-10.** MAT: **dos ~ dos igual a cuatro** two times two is four. **-11.** [en busca de] for; **baja ~ tabaco** go down to the shops for some cigarettes, go down to get some cigarettes; **a ~ for; vino a ~ las entradas** she came for the tickets. **-12.** [concesión]: **~ más ○ mucho que lo intentes no lo conseguirás** however hard you try ○ try as you might, you'll never manage it; **no me cae bien, ~ (muy) simpático que te parezca** you may think he's nice, but I don't like him.
◆ **por qué** *pron* why; **¿~ qué lo dijo?** why did she say it?; **¿~ qué no vienes?** why don't you come?

porcelana *f* **-1.** [material] porcelain, china. **-2.** [objeto] piece of porcelain ○ china.

porcentaje *m* percentage.

porcentual *adj* percentage (*antes de sust*).

porche *m* [soportal] arcade; [entrada] porch.

porcino, -na *adj* pig (*antes de sust*).

porción *f* portion, piece.

pordiosero, -ra ◇ *adj* begging. ◇ *m y f* beggar.

porfía *f* **-1.** [disputa] dispute. **-2.** [insistencia] persistence; [tozudez] stubbornness.

porfiado, -da *adj* persistent; [tozudo] stubborn.

porfiar [9] *vi* **-1.** [disputar] to argue obstinately. **-2.** [empeñarse]: **~ en** to be insistent on.

pormenor *m* (*gen pl*) detail.

pormenorizar [13] ◇ *vt* to describe in detail. ◇ *vi* to go into detail.

porno *adj fam* porno.

pornografía *f* pornography.

pornográfico, -ca *adj* pornographic.

poro *m* pore.

poroso, -sa *adj* porous.

porque *conj* **-1.** [debido a que] because. **-2.** [para que] so that, in order that.

porqué *m* reason; **el ~ de** the reason for.

porquería f **-1.** [suciedad] filth. **-2.** [cosa de mala calidad] rubbish (U). **-3.** despec [golosina] junk food, rubbish (U).

porquero, -ra m y f swineherd.

porra ◇ f **-1.** [palo] club; [de policía] truncheon. **-2.** CULIN deep-fried pastry sticks. **-3.** loc: **mandar a alguien a la ~** fam to tell sb to go to hell. ◇ interj (gen pl) fam: **¡~s!** hell!, damn it!

porrada f fam: **una ~ (de)** heaps (pl) ○ tons (pl) (of).

porrazo m [golpe] bang, blow; [caída] bump.

porreta ◇ m y f mfam [fumador de porros] pothead. ◇ f fam [nariz] hooter.

porrillo
◆ **a porrillo** loc adv fam by the bucket.

porro m fam [de droga] joint.

porrón m glass wine jar used for drinking wine from its long spout.

portaaviones = **portaviones**.

portabustos m inv Amer bra (sg).

portada f **-1.** [de libro] title page; [de revista] (front) cover; [de periódico] front page. **-2.** [de disco] sleeve. **-3.** ARQUIT facade.

portador, -ra ◇ adj carrying, bearing. ◇ m y f carrier, bearer; **al ~** COM to the bearer.

portaequipajes m inv boot Br, trunk Am.

portaestandarte m standard-bearer.

portafolios m inv, **portafolio** m [carpeta] file; [maletín] attaché case.

portal m **-1.** [entrada] entrance hall; [puerta] main door. **-2.** [belén] crib, Nativity scene.

portalámparas m inv socket.

portaligas m inv suspender belt.

portalón m monumental gate.

portamaletas m inv Amer boot Br, trunk Am.

portamonedas m inv purse.

portar vt to carry.
◆ **portarse** vpr to behave; **se ha portado bien conmigo** she has treated me well; **~se mal** to misbehave.

portátil adj portable.

portaviones, portaaviones m inv aircraft carrier.

portavoz ◇ m y f [persona] spokesman (f spokeswoman). ◇ m [periódico] voice.

portazo m: **dar un ~** to slam the door.

porte m **-1.** (gen pl) [gasto de transporte] carriage, transport costs (pl); **~ debido/pagado** COM carriage due/paid. **-2.** [transporte] carriage, transport. **-3.** [aspecto] bearing, demeanour.

porteador, -ra ◇ adj bearing, carrying. ◇ m y f porter.

portento m wonder, marvel.

portentoso, -sa adj wonderful, amazing.

portería f **-1.** [de casa, colegio] caretaker's office ○ lodge; [de hotel, ministerio] porter's office ○ lodge. **-2.** DEP goal, goalmouth.

portero, -ra m y f **-1.** [de casa, colegio] caretaker; [de hotel, ministerio] porter; **~ automático** ○ **electrónico** ○ **eléctrico** entryphone. **-2.** DEP goalkeeper.

pórtico m **-1.** [fachada] portico. **-2.** [arcada] arcade.

portilla f NÁUT porthole.

portillo m **-1.** [abertura] opening, gap. **-2.** [puerta pequeña] wicket gate.

Port Louis [por'luis] Port Louis.

Port Moresby Port Moresby.

portón m large door ○ entrance.

portuario, -ria adj port (antes de sust); [de los muelles] dock (antes de sust); **trabajador ~** docker.

Portugal Portugal.

portugués, -esa adj, m y f Portuguese.
◆ **portugués** m [lengua] Portuguese.

porvenir m future.

pos
◆ **en pos de** loc prep **-1.** [detrás de] behind. **-2.** [en busca de] after.

posada f **-1.** [fonda] inn, guest house. **-2.** [hospedaje] lodging, accommodation.

posaderas fpl fam backside (sg), bottom (sg).

posadero, -ra m y f innkeeper.

posar ◇ vt to put ○ lay down; [mano, mirada] to rest. ◇ vi to pose.
◆ **posarse** vpr **-1.** [gen] to settle. **-2.** [pájaro] to perch; [nave, helicóptero] to come down.

posavasos m inv coaster; [en pub] beer mat.

posdata, postdata f postscript.

pose f pose.

poseedor, -ra ◇ adj owning, possessing; [de cargo, acciones, récord] holding. ◇ m y f owner; [de cargo, acciones, récord] holder.

poseer [50] vt **-1.** [ser dueño de] to own; [estar en poder de] to have, to possess. **-2.** [sexualmente] to have.

poseído, -da ◇ adj: **~ por** possessed by. ◇ m y f possessed person.

posesión f possession; **tomar ~ de un cargo** to take up a position ○ post.

posesivo, -va adj possessive.
◆ **posesivo** m GRAM possessive.

poseso, -sa ◇ *adj* possessed. ◇ *m y f* possessed person.

poseyera *etc* → poseer.

posgraduado, -da, postgraduado, -da *adj, m y f* postgraduate.

posguerra, postguerra *f* post-war period.

posibilidad *f* possibility, chance; **cabe la ~ de que ...** there is a chance that ....

♦ **posibilidades económicas** *fpl* financial means ○ resources.

posibilitar *vt* to make possible.

posible *adj* possible; **es ~ que llueva** it could rain; **dentro de lo ~, en lo ~** as far as possible; **de ser ~** if possible; **hacer (todo) lo ~** to do everything possible; **lo antes ~** as soon as possible.

♦ **posibles** *mpl* (financial) means.

posición *f* -1. [gen] position. -2. [categoría - social] status (*U*); [- económica] situation.

posicionarse *vpr* to take a position ○ stance.

positivar *vt* FOT to develop.

positivismo *m* -1. [realismo] pragmatism. -2. FILOSOFÍA positivism.

positivo, -va *adj* [gen & ELECTR] positive.

♦ **positivo** *m* FOT print.

posmeridiano, -na, postmeridiano, -na *adj* afternoon (*antes de sust*).

posmodernidad *f* post-modernism.

posmoderno, -na *adj, m y f* postmodernist.

poso *m* sediment; *fig* trace.

posología *f* dosage.

posponer [65] *vt* -1. [relegar] to put behind, to relegate. -2. [aplazar] to postpone.

pospuesto, -ta *pp* → posponer.

pospusiera *etc* → posponer.

posta

♦ **a posta** *loc adv* on purpose.

postal ◇ *adj* postal. ◇ *f* postcard.

postdata = posdata.

poste *m* post, pole; DEP post.

póster (*pl* posters) *m* poster.

postergar [16] *vt* -1. [retrasar] to postpone. -2. [relegar] to put behind, to relegate.

posteridad *f* -1. [generación futura] posterity. -2. [futuro] future.

posterior *adj* -1. [en el espacio] rear, back; **~ a** behind. -2. [en el tiempo] subsequent, later; **~ a** subsequent to, after.

posteriori

♦ **a posteriori** *loc adv* later, afterwards.

posterioridad *f*: **con ~** later, subsequently.

postgraduado, -da = posgraduado.

postguerra = posguerra.

postigo *m* -1. [contraventana] shutter. -2. [puerta pequeña] wicket gate.

postín *m* showiness, boastfulness; **darse ~** to show off; **de ~** posh.

post-it® *m inv* Post-it®.

postizo, -za *adj* -1. [falso] false. -2. [añadido] detachable.

♦ **postizo** *m* hairpiece.

postmeridiano, -na = posmeridiano.

post meridiem *adj* post meridiem.

postoperatorio, -ria *adj* post-operative.

postor, -ra *m y f* bidder; **mejor ~** highest bidder.

postración *f* prostration.

postrado, -da *adj* prostrate.

postrar *vt* to weaken, to (make) prostrate.

♦ **postrarse** *vpr* to prostrate o.s.

postre *m* dessert, pudding; **de ~** for dessert; **a la ~** *fig* in the end; **para ~** *fig* to cap it all.

postrero, -ra *adj* (*antes de sust masculino sg:* **postrer**) *culto* last.

postrimerías *fpl* final stages.

postulado *m* postulate.

postulante, -ta *m y f* [para colectas] collector; RELIG postulant.

postular ◇ *vt* [exigir] to call for. ◇ *vi* [colectas] to collect.

póstumo, -ma *adj* posthumous.

postura *f* -1. [posición] position, posture. -2. [actitud] attitude, stance. -3. [en subasta] bid.

posventa, postventa *adj inv* after-sales (*antes de sust*).

potable *adj* -1. [bebible] drinkable; **agua ~** drinking water. -2. *fam* [aceptable] acceptable, passable.

potaje *m* [CULIN - guiso] vegetable stew; [- caldo] vegetable stock.

potasa *f* potash.

potasio *m* potassium.

pote *m* pot.

potencia *f* -1. [gen, MAT & POLÍT] power; **tiene mucha ~** it's very powerful; **las grandes ~s** the major (world) powers. -2. [posibilidad]: **en ~** potentially; **una campeona en ~** a potential champion.

potencial ◇ *adj* [gen & FÍS] potential. ◇ *m* -1. [fuerza] power. -2. [posibilidades] potential. -3. GRAM conditional. -4. ELECTR (electric) potential.

potenciar [8] *vt* -1. [fomentar] to encourage, to promote. -2. [reforzar] to boost, to strengthen.

potentado, -da *m y f* potentate.

potente *adj* powerful.

potestad *f* authority, power.

potingue *m fam* concoction.

potra → potro.

potranco, -ca *m y f* horse under three years of age.

potrero *m Amer* field, pasture.

potrillo *m Amer* large glass.

potro, -tra *m y f* ZOOL colt (*f* filly).
♦ **potro** *m* DEP vaulting horse.
♦ **potra** *f mfam* [suerte] luck; **tener ~** to be jammy.

pozo *m* well; [de mina] shaft; **~ negro** cesspool; **~ de petróleo** oil well; **ser un ~ de algo** *fig* to be a fountain of sthg.

p.p. -1. (*abrev de* **por poder**) pp. **-2.** (*abrev de* **porte pagado**) c/p.

PP (*abrev de* **Partido Popular**) *m Spanish political party to the right of the political spectrum.*

PPA (*abrev de* **Partido Peronista Auténtico**) *m Argentinian political party which follows the Perón ideology.*

práctica → práctico.

practicable *adj* **-1.** [realizable] practicable. **-2.** [transitable] passable.

practicante ◇ *adj* practising. ◇ *m y f* **-1.** [de deporte] practitioner; [de religión] practising member of a Church. **-2.** MED medical assistant.

practicar [10] ◇ *vt* **-1.** [gen] to practise; [deporte] to play. **-2.** [realizar] to carry out, to perform. ◇ *vi* to practise.

práctico, -ca *adj* practical.
♦ **práctico** *m* NÁUT pilot.
♦ **práctica** *f* **-1.** [gen] practice; [de un deporte] playing; **llevar algo a la práctica, poner algo en práctica** to put sthg into practice; **en la práctica** in practice. **-2.** [clase no teórica] practical.

pradera *f* large meadow, prairie.

prado *m* meadow.
♦ **Prado** *m*: **el (Museo del) Prado** the Prado (Museum).

Praga Prague.

pragmático, -ca ◇ *adj* pragmatic. ◇ *m y f* [persona] pragmatist.
♦ **pragmática** *f* **-1.** [edicto] royal edict. **-2.** LING pragmatics (*U*).

pragmatismo *m* pragmatism.

pral. *abrev de* **principal**.

praliné *m* praline.

praxis *f inv* practice; FILOSOFÍA praxis.

preacuerdo *m* draft agreement.

preámbulo *m* **-1.** [introducción - de libro] foreword, preface; [- de congreso, conferencia] introduction, preamble. **-2.** [rodeo] digression.

preaviso *m* prior notice.

prebenda *f* **-1.** RELIG prebend. **-2.** [favor] special favour.

preboste *m* provost.

precalentamiento *m* DEP warm-up.

precalentar [19] *vt* **-1.** CULIN to pre-heat. **-2.** DEP to warm up.

precampaña *f* preliminary campaign.

precariedad *f* precariousness.

precario, -ria *adj* precarious.

precaución *f* **-1.** [prudencia] caution, care. **-2.** [medida] precaution; **tomar precauciones** to take precautions.

precaver *vt* to guard against.
♦ **precaverse** *vpr* to take precautions; **~se de ○ contra** to guard (o.s.) against.

precavido, -da *adj* **-1.** [prevenido] prudent; **es muy ~** he always comes prepared. **-2.** [cauteloso] wary.

precedente ◇ *adj* previous, preceding. ◇ *m* precedent; **sentar ~** to set a precedent; **sin ~s** unprecedented.

preceder *vt* to go before, to precede.

preceptivo, -va *adj* obligatory, compulsory.
♦ **preceptiva** *f* rules (*pl*).

precepto *m* precept; **fiestas de ~** RELIG days of obligation.

preceptor, -ra *m y f* (private) tutor.

preces *fpl* prayers.

preciado, -da *adj* valuable, prized.

preciar [8] *vt* to appreciate.
♦ **preciarse** *vpr* to have self-respect; **~se de** to be proud of.

precintado *m* sealing.

precintadora *f* sealing machine.

precintar *vt* to seal.

precinto *m* seal.

precio *m lit & fig* price; **a cualquier ~** at any price; **al ~ de** *fig* at the cost of; **~ de fábrica/de coste** factory/cost price; **~ de compra** purchase price; **~ indicativo** ECON guide price; **~ de mercado** market price; **~ prohibitivo** prohibitively high price; **~ de salida** starting price; **~ de venta (al público)** retail price; **no tener ~** to be priceless.

preciosidad *f* **-1.** [valor] value. **-2.** [cosa bonita]: **¡es una ~!** it's lovely ○ beautiful!

precioso, -sa *adj* **-1.** [valioso] precious. **-2.** [bonito] lovely, beautiful.

precipicio *m* precipice.

precipitación *f* **-1.** [apresuramiento] haste. **-2.** [lluvia] rainfall (*U*). **-3.** QUÍM precipitation.

precipitado, -da *adj* hasty.
♦ **precipitado** *m* QUÍM precipitate.

precipitar *vt* **-1.** [arrojar] to throw ○ hurl down. **-2.** [acelerar] to hasten, to speed up. **-3.** QUÍM to precipitate.
◆ **precipitarse** *vpr* **-1.** [caer] to plunge (down). **-2.** [acelerarse - acontecimientos etc] to speed up. **-3.** [apresurarse]: ~se **(hacia)** to rush (towards). **-4.** [obrar irreflexivamente] to act rashly.

precisamente *adv* **-1.** [con precisión] precisely. **-2.** [justamente] ¡~! exactly!, precisely!; ~ **por eso** for that very reason; ~ **tú lo sugeriste** in fact it was you who suggested it.

precisar *vt* **-1.** [determinar] to fix, to set; [aclarar] to specify exactly. **-2.** [necesitar] to need, to require.

precisión *f* accuracy, precision.

preciso, -sa *adj* **-1.** [determinado, conciso] precise. **-2.** [necesario]: **ser ~ para (algo/hacer algo)** to be necessary (for sthg/to do sthg); **es ~ que vengas** you must come.

precocidad *f* precociousness.

precocinado, -da *adj* pre-cooked.

precolombino, -na *adj* pre-Columbian.

preconcebido, -da *adj* [idea] preconceived; [plan] drawn up in advance.

preconcebir [26] *vt* draw up in advance.

preconizar [13] *vt* to recommend, to advise.

preroz *adj* **-1.** [persona] precocious. **-2.** [lluvias, frutos etc] early.

precursor, -ra *m y f* precursor.

predador, -ra *adj* predatory.
◆ **predador** *m* predator.

predatorio, -ria *adj* [animal, instinto] predatory.

predecesor, -ra *m y f* predecessor.

predecible *adj* predictable.

predecir [66] *vt* to predict.

predestinado, -da *adj*: ~ **(a)** predestined (to).

predestinar *vt* to predestine.

predeterminación *f* predetermination.

predeterminar *vt* to predetermine.

prédica *f* sermon.

predicado *m* GRAM predicate.

predicador, -ra *m y f* preacher.

predicar [10] *vt & vi* to preach.

predicción *f* prediction; [del tiempo] forecast.

predice → predecir.

predicho, -cha *pp* → predecir.

prediga, predijera → predecir.

predilección *f*: ~ **(por)** preference (for).

predilecto, -ta *adj* favourite.

predio *m* **-1.** [finca] estate, property. **-2.** *Amer* [edificio] building.

predisponer [65] *vt*: ~ **(a)** to predispose (to).

predisposición *f* **-1.** [aptitud]: ~ **para** aptitude for. **-2.** [tendencia]: ~ **a** a predisposition to.

predispuesto, -ta ◇ *pp* → predisponer. ◇ *adj*: ~ **(a)** predisposed (to).

predominancia *f* predominance.

predominante *adj* predominant; [viento, actitudes] prevailing.

predominar *vi*: ~ **(sobre)** to predominate ○ prevail (over).

predominio *m* preponderance, predominance (*U*).

preelectoral *adj* pre-election (*antes de sust*).

preeminencia *f* preeminence.

preeminente *adj* preeminent.

preescolar ◇ *adj* nursery (*antes de sust*), preschool. ◇ *m* nursery school, kindergarten.

preestreno *m* preview.

preexistente *adj* pre-existing.

prefabricado, -da *adj* prefabricated.

prefabricar [10] *vt* to prefabricate.

prefacio *m* preface.

prefecto *m* prefect.

prefectura *f* prefecture; ~ **de tráfico** traffic division.

preferencia *f* preference; **con** ○ **de** ~ preferably; **tener** ~ AUTOM to have right of way; **tener** ~ **por** to have a preference for.

preferente *adj* preferential.

preferentemente *adv* preferably.

preferible *adj*: ~ **(a)** preferable (to).

preferido, -da *adj* favourite.

preferir [27] *vt*: ~ **algo (a algo)** to prefer sthg (to sthg).

prefigurar *vt* to prefigure.

prefijar *vt* to fix in advance.

prefijo *m* **-1.** GRAM prefix. **-2.** TELECOM (telephone) dialling code.

prefiriera *etc* → preferir.

pregón *m* [discurso] speech; [bando] proclamation, announcement.

pregonar *vt* **-1.** [bando etc] to proclaim, to announce. **-2.** *fig* [secreto] to spread about.

pregonero, -ra *m y f* **-1.** [de pueblo] town crier. **-2.** *despec* [bocazas] blabbermouth.

pregunta *f* question; **hacer una ~** to ask a question; ~ **capciosa** catch question; **andar a la cuarta** ○ **última ~** to be broke.

preguntar ◇ *vt* to ask; ~ **algo a alguien** to ask sb sthg. ◇ *vi*: ~ **por** to ask about ○ after.

◆ **preguntarse** *vpr*: ~**se (si)** to wonder (whether).

prehistoria *f* prehistory.

prehistórico, -ca *adj* prehistoric.

prejuicio *m* prejudice.

prejuzgar [16] *vt & vi* to prejudge.

prelado *m* prelate.

preliminar ◇ *adj* preliminary. ◇ *m* (*gen pl*) preliminary.

◆ **preliminares** *mpl* [de tratado de paz] results of preliminary negotiations.

preludio *m* [gen & MÚS] prelude.

prematrimonial *adj* premarital.

prematuro, -ra *adj* premature.

premeditación *f* premeditation; ~ **y alevosía** malice aforethought.

premeditado, -da *adj* premeditated.

premeditar *vt* to think out in advance.

premiar [8] *vt* **-1.** [recompensar] to reward. **-2.** [dar un premio a] to give a prize to.

premier (*pl* **premiers**) *m* British prime minister.

premio *m* **-1.** [en competición] prize; [recompensa] reward; ~ **de consolación** consolation prize; ~ **gordo** first prize. **-2.** [ganador] prize-winner.

premisa *f* premise.

premolar *adj & m* premolar.

premonición *f* premonition.

premonitorio, -ria *adj* warning.

premura *f* **-1.** [urgencia] urgency. **-2.** [escasez] lack, shortage.

prenatal *adj* prenatal, antenatal.

prenda *f* **-1.** [vestido] garment, article of clothing. **-2.** [garantía] pledge; **dejar algo en** ~ to leave sthg as a pledge. **-3.** [de un juego] forfeit. **-4.** [virtud] talent, gift. **-5.** [apelativo cariñoso] darling, treasure. **-6.** *loc*: **no soltar** ~ not to say a word.

prendar *vt* to enchant.

◆ **prendarse de** *vpr* to fall in love with.

prendedor *m* brooch.

prender ◇ *vt* **-1.** [arrestar] to arrest, to apprehend. **-2.** [sujetar] to fasten. **-3.** [encender] to light. **-4.** [agarrar] to grip. ◇ *vi* **-1.** [arder] to catch (fire). **-2.** [planta] to take root. **-3.** *fig* [propagarse] to spread, to take root.

◆ **prenderse** *vpr* [arder] to catch fire.

prendido, -da *adj* caught; **quedar** ~ **de** *fig* to be captivated by.

prensa *f* **-1.** [gen] press; ~ **amarilla** the gutter press, ≃ the tabloids; ~ **del corazón** romantic magazines (*pl*); **tener buena/mala** ~ *fig* to have a good/bad press. **-2.** [imprenta] printing press.

prensar *vt* to press.

prenupcial *adj* premarital.

preñado, -da *adj* **-1.** [mujer] pregnant. **-2.** *fig* [lleno]: ~ **de** full of.

◆ **preñada** *f* pregnant woman.

preñar *vt* **-1.** [mujer] to make pregnant. **-2.** *fig* [llenar]: ~ **de** to fill with.

preñez *f* pregnancy.

preocupación *f* concern, worry.

preocupado, -da *adj*: ~ **(por)** worried ○ concerned (about).

preocupante *adj* worrying.

preocupar *vt* **-1.** [inquietar] to worry. **-2.** [importar] to bother.

◆ **preocuparse** *vpr* **-1.** [inquietarse]: ~**se (por)** to worry (about), to be worried (about). **-2.** [encargarse]: ~**se de algo** to take care of sthg; ~**se de hacer algo** to see to it that sthg is done; ~**se de que ...** to make sure that ....

preolímpico, -ca *adj* in the run-up to the Olympics; **torneo** ~ Olympic qualifying competition.

preparación *f* **-1.** [gen] preparation. **-2.** [conocimientos] training. **-3.** [para el microscopio] specimen.

preparado, -da *adj* **-1.** [dispuesto] ready; [de antemano] prepared; **¡~s, listos, ya!** ready, steady, go! **-2.** [capacitado]: ~ **(para)** competent ○ talented (in). **-3.** CULIN ready-cooked.

◆ **preparado** *m* FARM preparation.

preparar *vt* **-1.** [gen] to prepare; [trampa] to set, to lay; [maletas] to pack. **-2.** [examen] to prepare for. **-3.** DEP to train.

◆ **prepararse** *vpr*: ~**se (para algo)** to prepare o.s. ○ get ready (for sthg); ~**se para hacer algo** to prepare ○ get ready to do sthg.

preparativo, -va *adj* preparatory, preliminary.

◆ **preparativos** *mpl* preparations.

preparatorio, -ria *adj* preparatory.

preponderancia *f* preponderance; **tener** ~ **(sobre)** to predominate (over).

preponderante *adj* prevailing.

preponderar *vi* to prevail.

preposición *f* preposition.

preposicional *adj* prepositional.

prepotencia *f* **-1.** [arrogancia] arrogance. **-2.** [poder] dominance, power.

prepotente *adj* **-1.** [arrogante] domineering, overbearing. **-2.** [poderoso] very powerful.

prepucio *m* foreskin.

prerrogativa *f* prerogative.

presa *f* **-1.** [captura - de cazador] catch; [- de animal] prey; **hacer ~ en alguien** to seize O grip sb; **ser ~ de** to be prey to; **ser ~ del pánico** to be panic-stricken. **-2.** [dique] dam.

presagiar [8] *vt* [felicidad, futuro] to foretell; [tormenta, problemas] to warn of.

presagio *m* **-1.** [premonición] premonition. **-2.** [señal] omen.

Presb. *abrev de* **Presbítero**.

presbiterianismo *m* Presbyterianism.

presbiteriano, -na *adj, m y f* Presbyterian.

presbiterio *m* presbytery.

presbítero *m* priest.

prescindir
◆ **prescindir de** *vi* **-1.** [renunciar a] to do without. **-2.** [omitir] to dispense with.

prescribir ◇ *vt* to prescribe. ◇ *vi* **-1.** [ordenar] to prescribe. **-2.** DER to expire, to lapse.

prescripción *f* prescription; ~ **facultativa** medical prescription.

prescrito, -ta *pp* → **prescribir**.

preselección *f* short list, shortlisting (U).

preseleccionar *vt* to shortlist; DEP to name in the squad.

presencia *f* [asistencia, aspecto] presence; **en ~ de** in the presence of; **buena/mala ~** good/bad looks (*pl*); **mucha/poca ~** great/little presence.
◆ **presencia de ánimo** *f* presence of mind.

presencial → **testigo**.

presenciar [8] *vt* [asistir] to be present at; [ser testigo de] to witness.

presentable *adj* presentable.

presentación *f* **-1.** [gen] presentation. **-2.** [entre personas] introduction.

presentador, -ra *m y f* presenter.

presentar *vt* **-1.** [gen] to present; [dimisión] to tender, to hand in; [tesis, pruebas, propuesta] to submit; [solicitud, recurso, denuncia] to lodge; [moción] to propose. **-2.** [ofrecer - disculpas, excusas] to make; [- respetos] to pay. **-3.** [persona, amigos etc] to introduce; **me presentó a sus amigos** she introduced me to her friends. **-4.** [tener - aspecto etc] to have, to show; **presenta difícil solución** it's going to be difficult to solve. **-5.** [proponer]: ~ **a alguien para** to propose sb for, to put sb forward for.
◆ **presentarse** *vpr* **-1.** [aparecer] to turn up, to appear. **-2.** [en juzgado, comisaría]: ~**se (en)** to report (to); ~**se a un examen** to sit an exam. **-3.** [darse a conocer] to introduce o.s. **-4.** [para un cargo]: ~**se (a)** to stand O run (for). **-5.** [futuro] to appear, to

look. **-6.** [problema etc] to arise, to come up.

presente ◇ *adj* **-1.** [gen] present; **aquí ~** here present; **hacer ~ algo a alguien** to notify sb of sthg; **tener ~** [recordar] to remember; [tener en cuenta] to bear in mind. **-2.** [en curso] current; **del ~ mes** of this month.
◇ *m y f* **-1.** [en un lugar]: **los (aquí) ~s** all those present. **-2.** [escrito]: **por la ~ le informo ...** I hereby inform you ....
◇ *m* **-1.** [gen & GRAM] present; ~ **histórico** historical present. **-2.** [regalo] gift, present. **-3.** [corriente]: **el ~** [mes] the current month; [año] the current year. **-4.** *loc*: **mejorando lo ~** without wishing to detract from anyone present; **¡~!** present!

presentimiento *m* presentiment, feeling.

presentir [27] *vt* to foresee; ~ **que algo va a pasar** to have a feeling that sthg is going to happen; ~ **lo peor** to fear the worst.

preservación *f* preservation.

preservar *vt* to protect.
◆ **preservarse de** *vpr* to protect o.s. O shelter from.

preservativo, -va *adj* protective.
◆ **preservativo** *m* condom; ~ **femenino** female condom.

presidencia *f* [de nación] presidency; [de asamblea, empresa] chairmanship.

presidencialismo *m* presidential system.

presidencialista ◇ *adj* presidential. ◇ *m y f* supporter of the presidential system.

presidente, -ta *m y f* [de nación] president; [de asamblea, empresa] chairman (*f* chairwoman); ~ **(del gobierno)** ≃ prime minister.

presidiario, -ria *m y f* convict.

presidio *m* prison.

presidir *vt* **-1.** [ser presidente de] to preside over; [reunión] to chair. **-2.** [predominar] to dominate.

presienta, presintiera *etc* → **presentir**.

presintonía *f* [de radio] pre-set station selector.

presión *f* pressure; **a ~** under pressure; ~ **atmosférica** atmospheric pressure; ~ **arterial** O **sanguínea** blood pressure; ~ **fiscal** ECON tax burden.

presionar *vt* **-1.** [apretar] to press. **-2.** *fig* [coaccionar] to pressurize, to put pressure on.

preso, -sa ◇ *adj* imprisoned. ◇ *m y f* prisoner.

prestación *f* **-1.** [de servicio - acción] provision; [- resultado] service; ~ **social** social security benefit. **-2.** [de dinero] lending.

◆ **prestaciones** *fpl* [de coche etc] performance features.

prestado, -da *adj* on loan; **dar** ~ **algo** to lend sthg; **pedir/tomar** ~ **algo** to borrow sthg; **de** ~ [con cosas prestadas] with borrowed things; [de modo precario] on borrowed time.

prestamista *m y f* moneylender.

préstamo *m* -1. [acción - de prestar] lending; [- de pedir prestado] borrowing. -2. [cantidad] loan.

prestancia *f* excellence, distinction.

prestar *vt* -1. [dejar - dinero etc] to lend, to loan. -2. [dar - ayuda etc] to give, to offer; [- servicio] to offer, to provide; [- atención] to pay; [- declaración, juramento] to make. -3. [transmitir - encanto etc] to lend.
◆ **prestarse a** *vpr* -1. [ofrecerse a] to offer to. -2. [acceder a] to consent to. -3. [dar motivo a] to be open to.

presteza *f* promptness, speed.

prestidigitación *f* conjuring.

prestidigitador, -ra *m y f* conjuror.

prestigiar [8] *vt* to honour, to give prestige to.

prestigio *m* prestige.

prestigioso, -sa *adj* prestigious.

presto, -ta *adj* -1. [dispuesto]: ~ **(a)** ready (to). -2. [rápido] prompt.

presumible *adj* probable, likely.

presumido, -da ◇ *adj* conceited, vain. ◇ *m y f* conceited ○ vain person.

presumir ◇ *vt* [suponer] to presume, to assume. ◇ *vi* -1. [jactarse] to show off; **presume de guapa** she thinks she's pretty. -2. [ser vanidoso] to be conceited ○ vain.

presunción *f* -1. [suposición] presumption. -2. [vanidad] conceit, vanity.

presunto, -ta *adj* presumed, supposed; [criminal, robo etc] alleged, suspected.

presuntuoso, -sa ◇ *adj* [vanidoso] conceited; [pretencioso] pretentious. ◇ *m y f* conceited person.

presuponer [65] *vt* to presuppose.

presuposición *f* assumption.

presupuestar *vt* [gen] to estimate; FIN to budget for.

presupuestario, -ria *adj* budgetary, budget (*antes de sust*).

presupuesto, -ta *pp* → presuponer.
◆ **presupuesto** *m* -1. [cálculo] budget; [de costo] estimate; ~**s generales del Estado** ECON *Spanish national budget*. -2. [suposición] assumption.

presuroso, -sa *adj* in a hurry.

prêt-à-porter [pretapor'te] (*pl* **prêts-à-porter**) *m* off-the-peg clothing.

pretencioso, -sa ◇ *adj* [persona] pretentious; [cosa] showy. ◇ *m y f* pretentious person.

pretender *vt* -1. [intentar]: ~ **hacer algo** to try to do sthg. -2. [aspirar a]: ~ **hacer algo** to aspire ○ want to do sthg; ~ **que alguien haga algo** to want sb to do sthg; **¿qué pretendes decir?** what do you mean? -3. [afirmar] to claim. -4. [solicitar] to apply for. -5. [cortejar] to court.

pretendido, -da *adj* supposed.

pretendiente ◇ *m y f* -1. [aspirante]: ~ **(a)** candidate (for). -2. [a un trono]: ~ **(a)** pretender (to). ◇ *m* [a una mujer] suitor.

pretensión *f* -1. [intención] aim, intention. -2. [aspiración] aspiration. -3. [supuesto derecho]: ~ **(a** ○ **sobre)** claim (to). -4. [afirmación] claim. -5. (*gen pl*) [exigencia] demand.

pretérito, -ta *adj* past.
◆ **pretérito** *m* GRAM preterite, past; ~ **imperfecto** imperfect; ~ **indefinido** simple past; ~ **perfecto** (present) perfect; ~ **pluscuamperfecto** pluperfect.

pretextar *vt* to use as a pretext, to claim.

pretexto *m* pretext, excuse.

pretil *m* parapet.

preuniversitario, -ria *adj* pre-university.
◆ **preuniversitario** *m in Spain, former one-year course of study, successful completion of which allowed pupils to go to university.*

prevalecer [30] *vi*: ~ **(sobre)** to prevail (over).

prevaler [74] *vi*: ~ **(sobre)** to prevail (over).
◆ **prevalerse de** *vpr* to take advantage of.

prevaricación *f* breach of trust.

prevaricar [10] *vi* to betray one's trust.

prevención *f* -1. [acción] prevention; [medida] precaution; **en** ~ **de** as a precaution against. -2. [prejuicio] prejudice.

prevenido, -da *adj* -1. [previsor]: **ser** ~ to be cautious. -2. [avisado, dispuesto]: **estar** ~ to be prepared.

prevenir [75] *vt* -1. [evitar] to prevent; **más vale** ~ **que curar** *proverb* prevention is better than cure *proverb*. -2. [avisar] to warn. -3. [prever] to foresee, to anticipate. -4. [predisponer]: ~ **a alguien contra algo/alguien** to prejudice sb against sthg/sb.

preventivo, -va *adj* [medicina, prisión] preventive; [medida] precautionary.

prever [76] *vt* -1. [conjeturar] to foresee, to anticipate. -2. [planear] to plan. -3. [predecir] to forecast.

previene → prevenir.

previera *etc* → prever.

previniera *etc* → prevenir.

previo, -via *adj* prior; **~ pago de multa** on payment of a fine.

◆ **previo** *m* CIN prescoring, playback.

previó → prever.

previsible *adj* foreseeable.

previsión *f* **-1.** [predicción] forecast. **-2.** [visión de futuro] foresight. **-3.** [precaución]: **en ~ de** as a precaution against.

previsor, -ra *adj* prudent, farsighted.

previsto, -ta ◇ *pp* → prever. ◇ *adj* [conjeturado] predicted, forecast; [planeado] expected, planned.

prieto, -ta *adj* **-1.** [ceñido] tight. **-2.** *Amer fam* [moreno] dark-haired.

prima → primo.

primacía *f* primacy.

primado *m* primate.

primar ◇ *vi*: **~ (sobre)** to have priority (over). ◇ *vt* to give a bonus to.

primario, -ria *adj* primary; *fig* primitive.

primates *mpl* Primates.

primavera *f* **-1.** [estación] spring. **-2.** *fig* [juventud] springtime. **-3.** *fig* [año]: **tiene diez ~s** she is ten years old, she has seen ten summers.

primaveral *adj* spring (*antes de sust*).

primer, primera → primero.

primerizo, -za ◇ *adj* **-1.** [principiante] novice. **-2.** [embarazada] first-time. ◇ *m y f* [principiante] beginner.

◆ **primeriza** *f* [madre] first-time mother.

primero, -ra ◇ *núm adj* (*antes de sust masculino sg*: **primer**) **-1.** [para ordenar] first. **-2.** [en importancia] main, basic; **lo ~** the most important ◇ main thing; **lo ~ es lo ~** first things first. ◇ *núm m y f* **-1.** [en orden]: **el ~** the first one; **llegó el ~** he came first; **es el ~ de la clase** he's top of the class; **a ~s de mes** at the beginning of the month. **-2.** [mencionado antes]: **vinieron Pedro y Juan, el ~ con ...** Pedro and Juan arrived, the former with ....

◆ **primero** ◇ *adv* **-1.** [en primer lugar] first. **-2.** [antes, todo menos]: **~ ... que ...** rather ... than ...; **~ morir que traicionarle** I'd rather die than betray him. ◇ *m* **-1.** [piso] first floor. **-2.** [curso] first year.

◆ **primera** *f* **-1.** AUTOM first (gear). **-2.** AERON & FERROC first class. **-3.** DEP first division. **-4.** *loc*: **de primera** first-class, excellent.

primicia *f* scoop, exclusive.

primitivo, -va *adj* **-1.** [gen] primitive. **-2.** [original] original.

primo, -ma *m y f* **-1.** [pariente] cousin. **-2.** *fam* [tonto] sucker; **hacer el ~** to be taken for a ride.

◆ **prima** *f* **-1.** [paga extra] bonus. **-2.** [de un seguro] premium; **~ de riesgo** risk premium. **-3.** [subvención] subsidy. **-4.** MÚS first string.

◆ **prima dona** *f* prima donna.

primogénito, -ta *adj, m y f* first-born.

primor *m* fine thing; **con ~** with skill.

primordial *adj* fundamental.

primoroso, -sa *adj* **-1.** [delicado] exquisite, fine. **-2.** [hábil] skilful.

princesa *f* princess.

principado *m* principality.

principal ◇ *adj* main, principal; [puerta] front. ◇ *m* **-1.** [piso] first floor. **-2.** [jefe] chief, boss.

príncipe *m* prince; **~ consorte** prince consort; **~ heredero** crown prince.

◆ **príncipe azul** *m* Prince Charming.

principesco, -ca *adj* princely.

principiante ◇ *adj* novice, inexperienced. ◇ *m y f* novice, beginner.

principio *m* **-1.** [comienzo] beginning, start; **a ~s de** at the beginning of; **en un ~** at first. **-2.** [fundamento, ley] principle; **en ~** in principle; **por ~** on principle. **-3.** [origen] origin, source. **-4.** [elemento] element.

◆ **principios** *mpl* **-1.** [reglas de conducta] principles. **-2.** [nociones] rudiments, first principles.

pringar [16] ◇ *vt* **-1.** [ensuciar] to make greasy. **-2.** [mojar] to dip. **-3.** *fam fig* [comprometer] to involve. ◇ *vi fam fig* to get stuck in.

◆ **pringarse** *vpr* **-1.** [ensuciarse] to get covered in grease. **-2.** *fam fig* [en asunto sucio] to get one's hands dirty.

pringoso, -sa *adj* [grasiento] greasy; [pegajoso] sticky.

pringue ◇ *v* → pringar. ◇ *m* [suciedad] muck, dirt; [grasa] grease.

prior, -ra *m y f* prior (*f* prioress).

priorato *m* **-1.** RELIG priorate. **-2.** [vino] *wine from El Priorato in Tarragona*.

priori

◆ **a priori** *loc adv* in advance, a priori.

prioridad *f* priority; AUTOM right of way.

prioritario, -ria *adj* priority (*antes de sust*).

prisa *f* haste, hurry; **a ◇ de ~** quickly; **a toda ~** very quickly; **correr ~** to be urgent; **darse ~** to hurry (up); **meter ~ a alguien** to hurry ◇ rush sb; **tener ~** to be in a hurry; **de ~ y corriendo** in a slapdash way.

prisión *f* **-1.** [cárcel] prison. **-2.** [encarcelamiento] imprisonment.

prisionero, **-ra** *m y f* prisoner.

prisma *m* **-1.** FÍS & GEOM prism. **-2.** *fig* [perspectiva] viewpoint, perspective.

prismático, **-ca** *adj* prismatic.

◆ **prismáticos** *mpl* binoculars.

privación *f* [gen] deprivation; [de libertad] loss; **pasar privaciones** to suffer hardship.

privado, **-da** *adj* private; **en** ~ in private.

privar ◇ *vt* **-1.** [quitar]: ~ **a alguien/algo de** to deprive sb/sthg of. **-2.** [prohibir]: ~ **a alguien de hacer algo** to forbid sb to do sthg. ◇ *vi* **-1.** [gustar]: **le privan los pasteles** he adores cakes. **-2.** [estar de moda] to be in (fashion). **-3.** *fam* [beber] to booze.

◆ **privarse de** *vpr* to go without.

privativo, **-va** *adj* exclusive.

privatizar [13] *vt* to privatize.

privilegiado, **-da** ◇ *adj* **-1.** [favorecido] privileged. **-2.** [excepcional] exceptional. ◇ *m y f* **-1.** [afortunado] privileged person. **-2.** [muy dotado] very gifted person.

privilegiar [8] *vt* [persona] to favour; [intereses] to put first.

privilegio *m* privilege.

pro ◇ *prep* for, supporting; **una asociación** ~ **derechos humanos** a human rights organization. ◇ *m* advantage; **los** ~**s y los contras** the pros and cons.

◆ **en pro de** *loc prep* for, in support of.

proa *f* NÁUT prow, bows (*pl*); AERON nose.

probabilidad *f* probability, likelihood; [oportunidad] chance.

probable *adj* probable, likely; **es** ~ **que llueva** it'll probably rain; **es** ~ **que no diga nada** he probably won't say anything.

probador *m* fitting room.

probar [23] ◇ *vt* **-1.** [demostrar, indicar] to prove. **-2.** [comprobar] to test, to check. **-3.** [experimentar] to try. **-4.** [degustar] to taste, to try. ◇ *vi*: ~ **a hacer algo** to try to do sthg.

◆ **probarse** *vpr* [ropa] to try on.

probeta *f* test tube.

probidad *f culto* integrity.

problema *m* problem.

problemático, **-ca** *adj* problematic.

◆ **problemática** *f* problems (*pl*).

probo, **-ba** *adj culto* honest.

procacidad *f* obscenity; [acto] indecent act.

procaz *adj* indecent, obscene.

procedencia *f* **-1.** [origen] origin. **-2.** [punto de partida] point of departure; **con** ~ **de** (arriving) from. **-3.** [pertinencia] properness, appropriateness.

procedente *adj* **-1.** [originario]: ~ **de** [gen] originating in; AERON & FERROC (arriving) from. **-2.** [oportuno] appropriate, fitting; DER right and proper.

proceder ◇ *m* conduct, behaviour. ◇ *vi* **-1.** [originarse]: ~ **de** to come from. **-2.** [actuar]: ~ **(con)** to act (with). **-3.** [empezar]: ~ **(a algo/a hacer algo)** to proceed (with sthg/to do sthg). **-4.** [ser oportuno] to be appropriate.

procedimiento *m* **-1.** [método] procedure, method. **-2.** DER proceedings (*pl*).

prócer *m* great person.

procesado, **-da** *m y f* accused, defendant.

procesador *m* INFORM processor; ~ **Pentium®** Pentium® processor; ~ **de textos** word processor.

procesamiento *m* **-1.** DER prosecution. **-2.** INFORM processing; ~ **de textos** word processing.

procesar *vt* **-1.** DER to prosecute. **-2.** INFORM to process.

procesión *f* **-1.** RELIG & *fig* procession; **la** ~ **va por dentro** he/she is putting on a brave face. **-2.** [transcurso] succession.

proceso *m* **-1.** [gen] process. **-2.** [desarrollo, intervalo] course. **-3.** [DER - juicio] trial; [- causa] lawsuit; **abrir un** ~ **contra** to bring an action against.

◆ **proceso de datos** *m* data processing.

◆ **proceso de textos** *m* word processing.

proclama *f* proclamation.

proclamación *f* **-1.** [anuncio] notification. **-2.** [ceremonia] proclamation.

proclamar *vt* **-1.** [nombrar] to proclaim. **-2.** *fig* [aclamar] to acclaim. **-3.** [anunciar] to declare.

◆ **proclamarse** *vpr* **-1.** [nombrarse] to proclaim o.s. **-2.** [conseguir un título]: ~**se campeón** to become champion.

proclive *adj*: ~ **a** prone to.

procreación *f* procreation.

procrear ◇ *vi* to procreate. ◇ *vt* to generate, to bear.

procurador, **-ra** *m y f* DER attorney; ~ **en Cortes** Member of Spanish Parliament.

procurar *vt* **-1.** [intentar]: ~ **hacer algo** to try to do sthg; ~ **que ...** to make sure that .... **-2.** [proporcionar] to get, to secure.

◆ **procurarse** *vpr* to get, to obtain (for o.s.).

prodigalidad *f* **-1.** [derroche] prodigality. **-2.** [abundancia] profusion.

prodigar [16] *vt*: ~ **algo a alguien** to lavish sthg on sb.

◆ **prodigarse** *vpr* **-1.** [exhibirse] to appear

a lot in public. **-2.** [excederse]: ~**se en** to be lavish with.

prodigio *m* [suceso] miracle, wonder; [persona] prodigy.

prodigioso, -sa *adj* **-1.** [sobrenatural] miraculous. **-2.** [extraordinario] wonderful, marvellous.

pródigo, -ga ◇ *adj* **-1.** [derrochador] extravagant. **-2.** [generoso] generous, lavish. ◇ *m y f* spendthrift.

producción *f* **-1.** [gen & CIN] production. **-2.** [productos] products (*pl*); ~ **en serie** ECON mass production.

producir [33] *vt* **-1.** [gen & CIN] to produce. **-2.** [causar] to cause, to give rise to. **-3.** [interés, fruto] to yield, to bear.

◆ **producirse** *vpr* [ocurrir] to take place, to come about.

productividad *f* productivity.

productivo, -va *adj* productive; [que da beneficio] profitable.

producto *m* **-1.** [gen & MAT] product; AGR produce (*U*); ~ **acabado/manufacturado** finished/manufactured product; ~ **interior/nacional bruto** gross domestic/national product; ~ **químico** chemical. **-2.** [ganancia] profit. **-3.** *fig* [resultado] result.

productor, -ra ◇ *adj* producing; **país** ~ **de petróleo** oil-producing country. ◇ *m y f* CIN [persona] producer.

◆ **productora** *f* CIN [firma] production company.

proeza *f* exploit, deed.

prof. (*abrev de* **profesor**) Prof.

profanación *f* desecration.

profanar *vt* to desecrate.

profano, -na ◇ *adj* **-1.** [no sagrado] profane, secular. **-2.** [ignorante] ignorant, uninitiated. ◇ *m y f* layman (*f* laywoman), lay person.

profecía *f* [predicción] prophecy.

◆ **profecías** *fpl* [libros] Prophets.

proferir [22] *vt* [gen] to utter; [insultos] to hurl.

profesar ◇ *vt* **-1.** [una religión] to follow; [una profesión] to practise. **-2.** [admiración etc] to profess. ◇ *vi* RELIG to take one's vows.

profesión *f* profession; **de** ~ by profession; ~ **liberal** liberal profession.

profesional *adj, m y f* professional.

profesionalidad *f*, **profesionalismo** *m* professionalism.

profesionalización *f* professionalization.

profesionalizar [13] *vt* to professionalize.

profesionista *m y f Amer* professional.

profeso, -sa ◇ *adj* professed. ◇ *m y f* professed monk (*f* professed nun).

◆ **ex profeso** *loc adv* intentionally, expressly.

profesor, -ra *m y f* [gen] teacher; [de universidad] lecturer; [de autoescuela, esquí etc] instructor; ~ **agregado** lecturer; ~ **asociado** associate lecturer; ~ **ayudante** assistant lecturer; ~ **particular** (private) tutor; ~ **titular** (full) lecturer.

profesorado *m* **-1.** [plantilla] teaching staff, faculty *Am*; [profesión] teachers (*pl*), teaching profession. **-2.** [cargo] post of teacher; [- en la universidad] lectureship.

profeta *m* prophet.

profético, -ca *adj* prophetic.

profetisa *f* prophetess.

profetizar [13] *vt* to prophesy.

profiera *etc* → **proferir**.

profiláctico, -ca *adj* prophylactic.

◆ **profiláctico** *m* prophylactic, condom.

profilaxis *f inv* prophylaxis.

prófugo, -ga *adj, m y f* fugitive.

◆ **prófugo** *m* MIL deserter.

profundidad *f lit* & *fig* depth; **tiene dos metros de** ~ it's two metres deep.

profundizar [13] ◇ *vt fig* to study in depth. ◇ *vi* to go into detail; ~ **en** to study in depth.

profundo, -da *adj* **-1.** [gen] deep. **-2.** *fig* [respeto, libro, pensamiento] profound, deep; [dolor] intense.

profusión *f* profusion.

profuso, -sa *adj* profuse.

progenie *f* **-1.** [familia] lineage. **-2.** [descendencia] offspring.

progenitor, -ra *m y f* father (*f* mother).

◆ **progenitores** *mpl* parents.

progesterona *f* progesterone.

programa *m* **-1.** [gen] programme; ~ **espacial** space programme; ~ **de intercambio** exchange (programme). **-2.** [de actividades] schedule, programme; [de estudios] syllabus. **-3.** INFORM program.

programación *f* **-1.** INFORM programming. **-2.** TV scheduling; **la** ~ **del lunes** Monday's programmes.

programador, -ra *m y f* [persona] programmer.

◆ **programador** *m* [aparato] programmer.

programar *vt* **-1.** [vacaciones, reforma etc] to plan. **-2.** CIN & TV to put on, to show. **-3.** TECN to programme; INFORM to program.

progre *fam* ◇ *adj* liberal, permissive. ◇ *m y f* progressive.

progresar *vi* to progress, to make progress; ~ **en** to make progress in.

progresión *f* [gen & MAT] progression; [mejora] progress, advance; ~ **aritmética/geométrica** arithmetic/geometric progression.

progresismo *m* progressivism.

progresista *adj, m y f* progressive.

progresivo, -va *adj* progressive.

progreso *m* progress; **hacer** ~**s** to make progress.

prohibición *f* ban, banning (*U*).

prohibido, -da *adj* prohibited, banned; "~ aparcar/fumar" "no parking/smoking", "parking/smoking prohibited"; "**prohibida la entrada**" "no entry"; "**dirección prohibida**" AUTOM "no entry".

prohibir *vt* **-1.** [gen] to forbid; ~ **a alguien hacer algo** to forbid sb to do sthg; "**se prohíbe el paso**" "no entry". **-2.** [por ley - de antemano] to prohibit; [- a posteriori] to ban.

prohibitivo, -va *adj* prohibitive.

prohijar *vt* to adopt.

prohombre *m* great man.

prójimo *m* fellow human being, neighbour.

pról. *abrev de* **prólogo**.

prole *f* offspring.

prolegómenos *mpl* [de una obra] preface (*sg*).

proletariado *m* proletariat.

proletario, -ria *adj, m y f* proletarian.

proliferación *f* proliferation; ~ **nuclear** proliferation (of nuclear arms).

proliferar *vi* to proliferate.

prolífico, -ca *adj* prolific.

prolijo, -ja *adj* **-1.** [extenso] long-winded. **-2.** [esmerado] meticulous; [detallado] exhaustive.

prologar *vt* to preface.

prólogo *m* [de libro] preface, foreword; [de obra de teatro] prologue; *fig* prelude.

prolongación *f* extension.

prolongado, -da *adj* long; *fig* [dilatado] lengthy.

prolongar [16] *vt* [gen] to extend; [espera, visita, conversación] to prolong; [cuerda, tubo] to lengthen.

promedio *m* average.

promesa *f* **-1.** [compromiso] promise. **-2.** *fig* [persona] promising talent.

prometedor, -ra *adj* promising.

prometer ◇ *vt* to promise. ◇ *vi* [tener futuro] to show promise.
◆ **prometerse** *vpr* to get engaged.

prometido, -da ◇ *m y f* fiancé (*f* fiancée). ◇ *adj* **-1.** [para casarse] engaged. **-2.** [asegura-

do]: **lo** ~ what has been promised, promise; **cumplir lo** ~ to keep one's promise.

prominencia *f* **-1.** [abultamiento] protuberance. **-2.** [elevación] rise. **-3.** [importancia] prominence.

prominente *adj* **-1.** [abultado] protruding. **-2.** [elevado, ilustre] prominent.

promiscuidad *f* promiscuity.

promiscuo, -cua *adj* promiscuous.

promoción *f* **-1.** [gen & DEP] promotion; ~ **de ventas** sales promotion. **-2.** [curso] class, year.

promocional *adj* promotional.

promocionar *vt* to promote.
◆ **promocionarse** *vpr* to put o.s. forward, to promote o.s.

promontorio *m* promontory.

promotor, -ra ◇ *adj* promoting. ◇ *m y f* promoter; [de una rebelión] instigator; ~ **inmobiliario** COM real estate developer.

promover [24] *vt* **-1.** [iniciar - fundación etc] to set up; [- rebelión] to stir up. **-2.** [ocasionar] to cause. **-3.** [ascender]: ~ **a alguien a** to promote sb to.

promulgación *f* [de ley] passing.

promulgar [16] *vt* [ley] to pass.

pronombre *m* pronoun; (~) **demostrativo** demonstrative pronoun; (~) **indefinido** indefinite pronoun; ~ **interrogativo/personal** interrogative/personal pronoun; (~) **posesivo** possessive pronoun; ~ **relativo** relative pronoun.

pronominal ◇ *adj* pronominal. ◇ *m* pronominal verb.

pronosticar [10] *vt* to predict, to forecast.

pronóstico *m* **-1.** [predicción] forecast. **-2.** MED prognosis; **de** ~ **leve** suffering from a mild condition; **de** ~ **grave** serious, in a serious condition; **de** ~ **reservado** under observation.

prontitud *f* promptness.

pronto, -ta *adj* quick, fast; [respuesta] prompt, early; [curación, tramitación] speedy.
◆ **pronto** ◇ *adv* **-1.** [rápidamente] quickly; **tan** ~ **como** as soon as. **-2.** [temprano] early; **salimos** ~ we left early. **-3.** [dentro de poco] soon; **¡hasta** ~**!** see you soon! ◇ *m fam* sudden impulse.
◆ **al pronto** *loc adv* at first.
◆ **de pronto** *loc adv* suddenly.
◆ **por lo pronto** *loc adv* **-1.** [de momento] for the time being. **-2.** [para empezar] to start with.

pronunciación *f* pronunciation.

pronunciado, -da *adj* [facciones] pronounced; [curva] sharp; [pendiente, cuesta] steep; [nariz] prominent.

pronunciamiento *m* **-1.** [sublevación] uprising. **-2.** DER pronouncement.

pronunciar [8] *vt* **-1.** [decir - palabra] to pronounce; [- discurso] to deliver, to make. **-2.** [realzar] to accentuate. **-3.** DER to pronounce, to pass.
◆ **pronunciarse** *vpr* **-1.** [definirse]: ~se **(sobre)** to state an opinion (on). **-2.** [sublevarse] to rise up, to revolt.

propagación *f* **-1.** [gen] spreading (U). **-2.** BIOL & FIS propagation.

propaganda *f* **-1.** [publicidad] advertising (U). **-2.** [prospectos - gen] publicity leaflets (U); [- por correo] junk mail. **-3.** [política, religiosa] propaganda.

propagandístico, **-ca** *adj* advertising (*antes de sust*); POLÍT propaganda (*antes de sust*).

propagar [16] *vt* [gen] to spread; [razas, especies] to propagate.
◆ **propagarse** *vpr* **-1.** [gen] to spread. **-2.** BIOL & FIS to propagate

propalar *vt* to divulge.

propano *m* propane.

propasarse *vpr*: ~ **(con algo)** to go too far (with sthg); ~ **con alguien** [sexualmente] to take liberties with sb.

propensión *f* propensity, tendency.

propenso, **-sa** *adj*: ~ a algo/a hacer algo prone to sthg/doing sthg.

propiamente *adv* [adecuadamente] properly; [verdaderamente] really, strictly; ~ **dicho** strictly speaking; **el pueblo** ~ **dicho es sólo esto** strictly speaking, the town is just this area.

propiciar [8] *vt* to be conducive to.

propiciatorio, **-ria** *adj* propitiatory.

propicio, **-cia** *adj* **-1.** [favorable] propitious, favourable. **-2.** [adecuado] suitable, appropriate.

propiedad *f* **-1.** [derecho] ownership; [bienes] property; **tener algo en** ~ to own sthg; ~ **horizontal** joint-ownership (*in a block of flats*); ~ **industrial** patent rights (*pl*); ~ **intelectual** copyright; ~ **privada** private property; ~ **pública** public ownership. **-2.** [facultad] property. **-3.** [exactitud] accuracy; **usar una palabra con** ~ to use a word properly.

propietario, **-ria** *m y f* [de bienes] owner; [de cargo] holder.

propina *f* tip.

propinar *vt* [paliza] to give; [golpe] to deal.

propio, **-pia** *adj* **-1.** [gen] own; **tiene coche** ~ she has a car of her own, she has her own car; **por tu** ~ **bien** for your own good. **-2.** [peculiar]: ~ **de** typical ○ characteristic of; **no es** ~ **de él** it's not like him.

-3. [apropiado]: ~ **(para)** suitable ○ right (for). **-4.** [correcto] proper, true. **-5.** [en persona] himself (*f* herself); **el** ~ **compositor** the composer himself. **-6.** [semejante] true to life.

proponer [65] *vt* to propose; [candidato] to put forward.
◆ **proponerse** *vpr*: ~se hacer algo to plan ○ intend to do sthg.

proporción *f* **-1.** [gen & MAT] proportion; **guardar** ~ **(con)** to be in proportion (to). **-2.** (*gen pl*) [importancia] extent, size.
◆ **proporciones** *fpl* [tamaño] size (*sg*).

proporcionado, **-da** *adj*: ~ **(a)** [estatura, sueldo] commensurate (with); [medidas] proportionate (to); **bien** ~ well-proportioned.

proporcional *adj* proportional.

proporcionar *vt* **-1.** [ajustar]: ~ **algo a algo** to adapt sthg to sthg. **-2.** [facilitar]: ~ **algo a alguien** to provide sb with sthg. **-3.** *fig* [conferir] to lend, to add.

proposición *f* **-1.** [propuesta] proposal. **-2.** GRAM clause.
◆ **proposiciones** *fpl* [sugerencias] propositions; **hacer proposiciones a alguien** to proposition sb; **proposiciones deshonestas** improper suggestions.

propósito *m* **-1.** [intención] intention. **-2.** [objetivo] purpose.
◆ **a propósito** ◇ *loc adj* [adecuado] suitable. ◇ *loc adv* **-1.** [adrede] on purpose. **-2.** [por cierto] by the way.
◆ **a propósito de** *loc prep* with regard to, concerning.

propuesta *f* proposal; [de empleo] offer.

propuesto, **-ta** *pp* → **proponer**.

propugnar *vt* to advocate, to support.

propulsar *vt* **-1.** [impeler] to propel. **-2.** *fig* [promover] to promote.

propulsión *f* propulsion; ~ **a chorro** jet propulsion.

propulsor, **-ra** ◇ *adj* propulsive. ◇ *m y f* [persona] promoter.
◆ **propulsor** *m* **-1.** [dispositivo] engine. **-2.** [combustible] propellent.

propusiera *etc* → **proponer**.

prorrata *f* quota, share; **a** ~ pro rata.

prórroga *f* **-1.** [gen] extension; [de estudios, servicio militar] deferment. **-2.** DEP extra time.

prorrogable *adj* which can be extended.

prorrogar [16] *vt* [alargar] to extend; [aplazar] to defer, to postpone.

prorrumpir *vi*: ~ **en** to burst into.

prosa *f* **-1.** LITER prose; **en** ~ in prose. **-2.** *fig* [monotonía] monotony.

prosaico, **-ca** *adj* prosaic.

prosapia *f* lineage, ancestry.

proscribir *vt* **-1.** [prohibir] to ban. **-2.** [desterrar] to banish.

proscrito, -ta ◇ *pp* → **proscribir**. ◇ *adj* **-1.** [prohibido] banned. **-2.** [desterrado] banished. ◇ *m y f* **-1.** [desterrado] exile. **-2.** [fuera de la ley] outlaw.

prosecución *f* continuation.

proseguir [43] ◇ *vt* to continue. ◇ *vi* to go on, to continue.

proselitismo *m* proselytism.

prosélito, -ta *m y f* proselyte.

prosiga *etc* → **proseguir**.

prosiguiera *etc* → **proseguir**.

prosista *m y f* prose writer.

prosodia *f* prosody.

prospección *f* **-1.** [gen] exploration; [petrolífera, minera] prospecting. **-2.** [de clientes]: ~ (de) canvassing (for).

prospectivo, -va *adj* exploratory.

prospecto *m* leaflet; COM & EDUC prospectus.

prosperar *vi* **-1.** [mejorar] to prosper, to thrive. **-2.** [triunfar] to be successful.

prosperidad *f* **-1.** [mejora] prosperity. **-2.** [éxito] success.

próspero, -ra *adj* prosperous, flourishing.

próstata *f* prostate.

prosternarse *vpr* to prostrate o.s.

prostíbulo *m* brothel.

prostitución *f* **-1.** [gen] prostitution. **-2.** *fig* [corrupción] corruption.

prostituir [51] *vt lit* & *fig* to prostitute.
◆ **prostituirse** *vpr* to become a prostitute.

prostituta *f* prostitute.

protagonismo *m* leading role.

protagonista *m y f* **-1.** [gen] main character, hero (*f* heroine); TEATR lead, leading role. **-2.** *fig* [de crimen, hazaña] person responsible.

protagonizar [13] *vt* **-1.** [obra, película] to play the lead in, to star in. **-2.** *fig* [crimen, hazaña] to be responsible for.

protección *f* protection; ~ **civil** civil defence.

proteccionismo *m* protectionism.

protector, -ra ◇ *adj* protective. ◇ *m y f* [persona] protector.
◆ **protector** *m* **-1.** [en boxeo] gumshield. **-2.** ~ **labial** lip salve.

protectorado *m* protectorate.

proteger [14] *vt* **-1.** [gen] to protect; ~ **algo de algo** to protect sthg from sthg. **-2.** [apoyar] to support.
◆ **protegerse** *vpr* to take cover ○ refuge.

protege-slips *m inv* panty pad ○ liner.

protegido, -da ◇ *adj* protected. ◇ *m y f* protégé (*f* protégée).

proteico, -ca *adj* protean.

proteína *f* protein.

protésico, -ca ◇ *adj* prosthetic. ◇ *m y f* prosthetist.

prótesis *f inv* **-1.** MED prosthesis; [miembro] artificial limb. **-2.** GRAM prothesis.

protesta *f* protest; DER objection.

protestante *adj, m y f* Protestant.

protestantismo *m* Protestantism.

protestar *vi* **-1.** [quejarse]: ~ **(por/contra)** to protest (about/against); ¡protesto! DER objection! **-2.** [refunfuñar] to grumble.

protesto *m* COM: ~ **de letra** noting bill of exchange.

protocolario, -ria *adj* formal.

protocolo *m* **-1.** [gen & INFORM] protocol; ~ **de comunicación** communications protocol. **-2.** [ceremonial] etiquette. **-3.** DER *documents handled by a solicitor.*

protohistoria *f* protohistory.

protón *m* proton.

prototipo *m* **-1.** [modelo] archetype. **-2.** [primer ejemplar] prototype.

protozoo *m* protozoan, protozoon.

protuberancia *f* protuberance, bulge.

provecho *m* **-1.** [gen] benefit; **buen ~** enjoy your meal!; **de ~** [persona] worthy; **hacer ~** to do good; **sacar ~ de** to make the most of, to take advantage of. **-2.** [rendimiento] good effect.

provechoso, -sa *adj* **-1.** [ventajoso] beneficial, advantageous. **-2.** [lucrativo] profitable.

proveedor, -ra *m y f* supplier.

proveer [50] *vt* **-1.** [abastecer] to supply, to provide; ~ **a alguien de algo** to provide sb with sthg. **-2.** [puesto, cargo] to fill.
◆ **proveerse de** *vpr* **-1.** [ropa, víveres] to stock up on. **-2.** [medios, recursos] to arm o.s. with.

proveniente *adj*: ~ **de** (coming) from.

provenir [75] *vi* ~ **de** to come from.

provenzal ◇ *adj, m y f* Provençal. ◇ *m* [lengua] Provençal.

proverbial *adj* proverbial.

proverbio *m* proverb.

providencia *f* **-1.** [medida] measure, step. **-2.** DER ruling.
◆ **Providencia** *f* Providence.

providencial *adj lit* & *fig* providential.

proviene *etc* → **provenir**.

provincia *f* [división administrativa] province.

◆ **provincias** *fpl* [no la capital] the provinces.

provincial *adj & m* provincial.

provincianismo *m* provincialism.

provinciano, -na *adj, m y f despec* provincial.

proviniera *etc* → **provenir**.

provisión *f* **-1.** (*gen pl*) [suministro] supply, provision; [de una plaza] filling (*U*). **-2.** [disposición] measure; ~ **de fondos** financial reserves (*pl*).

provisional *adj* provisional.

provisto, -ta *pp* → **proveer**.

provocación *f* **-1.** [hostigamiento] provocation. **-2.** [ocasionamiento - de incendio] starting; [- de incidente] causing; [- de revuelta] instigation.

provocador, -ra ◇ *adj* provocative. ◇ *m y f* agitator.

provocar [10] *vt* **-1.** [incitar] to incite; ~ **a alguien a hacer algo** [gen] to cause sb to do sthg, to make sb do sthg; [matar, luchar etc] to provoke sb to do sthg. **-2.** [irritar] to provoke. **-3.** [ocasionar - gen] to cause; [- incendio, rebelión] to start. **-4.** [excitar sexualmente] to arouse. **-5.** *Amer fig* [apetecer]: **¿te provoca hacerlo?** do you feel like doing it?

provocativo, -va *adj* provocative.

proxeneta *m y f* pimp (*f* procuress).

proxenetismo *m* pimping (*U*), procuring (*U*).

próximamente *adv* soon, shortly; CIN coming soon.

proximidad *f* [cercanía] closeness, proximity.

◆ **proximidades** *fpl* **-1.** [de ciudad] surrounding area (*sg*). **-2.** [de lugar] vicinity (*sg*).

próximo, -ma *adj* **-1.** [cercano] near, close; [casa, ciudad] nearby, neighbouring; **en fecha próxima** shortly. **-2.** [parecido] similar, close. **-3.** [siguiente] next; **el** ~ **año** next year.

proyección *f* **-1.** [gen & GEOM] projection. **-2.** CIN screening, showing. **-3.** [lanzamiento] throwing forwards. **-4.** *fig* [trascendencia] importance.

proyectar *vt* **-1.** [dirigir - focos etc] to shine, to direct. **-2.** [mostrar - película] to project, to screen; [- sombra] to cast; [- diapositivas] to show. **-3.** [planear - viaje, operación, edificio] to plan; [- puente, obra] to design. **-4.** [arrojar] to throw forwards. **-5.** GEOM to project.

proyectil *m* projectile, missile.

proyectista *m y f* designer.

proyecto *m* **-1.** [intención] project. **-2.** [plan] plan; **tener en** ~ **hacer algo** to be planning to do sthg. **-3.** [diseño - ARQUIT] design; [- IND & TECN] plan. **-4.** [borrador] draft; ~ **de ley** bill. **-5.** EDUC: ~ **fin de carrera** *design project forming part of doctoral thesis for architecture students etc*; ~ **de investigación** [de un grupo] research project; [de una persona] dissertation.

proyector, -ra *adj* projecting.

◆ **proyector** *m* **-1.** [de cine, diapositivas] projector. **-2.** [reflector] searchlight; [en el teatro] spotlight.

prudencia *f* [cuidado] caution, care; [previsión, sensatez] prudence; [moderación] moderation; **con** ~ in moderation.

prudencial *adj* [sensato] sensible; [moderado] moderate.

prudente *adj* **-1.** [cuidadoso] careful, cautious; [previsor, sensato] sensible. **-2.** [razonable] reasonable.

prueba ◇ *v* → **probar**.
◇ *f* **-1.** [demostración] proof; DER evidence, proof; **no tengo** ~**s** I have no proof. **-2.** [manifestación] sign, token; **en** ○ **como** ~ **de** in ○ as proof of. **-3.** [trance] ordeal, trial. **-4.** EDUC & MED test; ~ **de acceso** entrance examination. **-5.** [comprobación] test; **a** ○ **de** ~ [trabajador] on trial; [producto comprado] on approval; **es a** ~ **de agua/balas** it's waterproof/bulletproof; **paciencia a toda** ~ unwavering patience; **poner a** ~ to (put to the) test; **la** ~ **de fuego** the acid test. **-6.** DEP event. **-7.** IMPRENTA proof.

prurito *m* MED itch, itching (*U*); *fig* urge.

prusiano, -na *adj, m y f* Prussian.

PS = **PD**.

pseudo *adj* pseudo.

pseudónimo *m* pseudonym.

psicoanálisis *m inv* psychoanalysis.

psicoanalista *m y f* psychoanalyst.

psicoanalizar [13] *vt* to psychoanalyze.

psicodélico, -ca *adj* psychedelic.

psicodrama *m* psychodrama.

psicología *f lit* & *fig* psychology.

psicológico, -ca *adj* psychological.

psicólogo, -ga *m y f* psychologist.

psicometría *f* psychometrics (*U*).

psicomotor, -ra *adj* psychomotor.

psicomotricidad *f* psychomotricity.

psicópata *m y f* psychopath.

psicopatía *f* psychopathy, psychopathic personality.

psicosis *f inv* psychosis; ~ **maniacodepresiva** manic-depressive psychosis.

psicosomático, -ca *adj* psychosomatic.

psicotécnico, -ca ◇ *adj* psychotechnical. ◇ *m y f* psychotechnician.

◆ **psicotécnico** *m* [prueba] psychotechnical test.

psicoterapia *f* psychotherapy.

psique *f* psyche.

psiquiatra *m y f* psychiatrist.

psiquiatría *f* psychiatry.

psiquiátrico, -ca *adj* psychiatric.

◆ **psiquiátrico** *m* psychiatric ○ mental hospital.

psíquico, -ca *adj* psychic.

psiquis *f inv* psyche.

PSOE [pe'soe, soe] (*abrev de* **Partido Socialista Obrero Español**) *m major Spanish political party to the centre-left of the political spectrum.*

PSUC [pe'suk] (*abrev de* **Partit Socialista Unificat de Catalunya**) *m Catalan political party now conflated into Iniciativa per Catalunya and to the left of the political spectrum.*

pta. (*abrev de* **peseta**) pta.

púa *f* **-1.** [de planta] thorn, barb; [de erizo] quill, spine; [de peine] tooth; [de tenedor] prong. **-2.** MÚS plectrum.

pub [pap] (*pl* **pubs**) *m upmarket pub,* ≈ wine bar.

púber, -ra *adj, m y f culto* adolescent.

pubertad *f* puberty.

pubis *m inv* pubes (*pl*).

publicación *f* publication.

publicar [10] *vt* **-1.** [editar] to publish. **-2.** [difundir] to publicize, to make public; [ley] to pass; [aviso] to issue.

publicidad *f* **-1.** [difusión] publicity; **dar ~ a algo** to publicize sthg. **-2.** COM advertising; TV adverts (*pl*), commercials (*pl*); **~ directa** direct mailing.

publicista *m y f* advertising agent.

publicitar *vt* to advertise.

publicitario, -ria ◇ *adj* advertising (*antes de sust*). ◇ *m y f* advertising agent.

público, -ca *adj* public; **ser ~** [conocido] to be common knowledge; **en ~** in public; **hacer algo ~** to make sthg public.

◆ **público** *m* **-1.** CIN, TEATR & TV audience; DEP crowd. **-2.** [comunidad] public; **el gran ~** the (general) public.

publirreportaje *m* [anuncio de televisión] promotional film; [en revista] advertising spread.

pucha *interj Amer* good heavens!

pucherazo *m fig* electoral fraud (*U*).

puchero *m* **-1.** [perola] cooking pot. **-2.** [comida] stew.

◆ **pucheros** *mpl* [gesto] pout (*sg*); **hacer ~s** to pout.

pucho *m Amer* [colilla] cigarette butt.

pudding = pudin.

pudendo, -da *adj*: **partes pudendas** private parts.

pudibundez *f* prudishness.

pudibundo, -da *adj* prudish.

púdico, -ca *adj* modest.

pudiente ◇ *adj* wealthy, well-off. ◇ *m y f* wealthy person.

pudiera *etc* → poder.

pudin (*pl* púdines), **pudding** ['puðin] (*pl* puddings) *m* (plum) pudding.

pudor *m* **-1.** [recato] (sense of) shame. **-2.** [timidez] bashfulness.

pudoroso, -sa *adj* **-1.** [recatado] modest. **-2.** [tímido] bashful.

pudridero *m* rubbish dump.

pudrir *vt* to rot.

◆ **pudrirse** *vpr* to rot.

puebla *etc* → poblar.

pueblerino, -na ◇ *adj* village (*antes de sust*); *despec* rustic, provincial. ◇ *m y f* villager; *despec* yokel.

pueblo *m* **-1.** [población - pequeña] village; [- grande] town. **-2.** [nación] people. **-3.** [proletariado] (common) people.

pueda *etc* → poder.

puente *m* **-1.** [gen] bridge; **~ colgante** suspension bridge; **~ levadizo** drawbridge. **-2.** [días festivos]: **hacer ~** *to take an extra day off between two public holidays.*

◆ **puente aéreo** *m* [civil] air shuttle; [militar] airlift.

puenting *m* bungee-jumping.

puerco, -ca ◇ *adj* dirty, filthy. ◇ *m y f* **-1.** [animal] pig (*f* sow). **-2.** *fam fig* [persona] pig, swine.

puercoespín *m* porcupine.

puericultor, -ra *m y f* pediatrician.

puericultura *f* pediatrics (*U*).

pueril *adj fig* childish.

puerilidad *f fig* childishness.

puerperio *m* puerperium.

puerro *m* leek.

puerta *f* **-1.** [de casa] door; [de jardín, ciudad etc] gate; **de ~ en ~** from door to door; **~ principal/trasera** front/back door; **~ corrediza/giratoria** sliding/revolving door; **~ blindada/vidriera** reinforced/glass door. **-2.** *fig* [posibilidad] gateway, opening. **-3.** DEP goal, goalmouth. **-4.** *loc*: **a las ~s de** on the verge of; **a ~ cerrada** [gen] behind closed doors; [juicio] in camera; **coger la ~ y marcharse** to up and go; **dar a alguien**

con las ~s en las narices to slam the door in sb's face; **estar en** ~s to be knocking on the door, to be imminent.

puerto *m* -1. [de mar] port; **llegar a** ~ to come into port; *fig* to make it in the end; ~ **deportivo** marina; ~ **franco** ○ **libre** free port. -2. [de montaña] pass. -3. INFORM port; ~ **paralelo/serie** parallel/serial port. -4. *fig* [refugio] haven.

Puerto España Port of Spain.

Puerto Príncipe Port-au-Prince.

Puerto Rico Puerto Rico.

pues *conj* -1. [dado que] since, as. -2. [por lo tanto] therefore, so; **creo**, ~, **que ... so**, so I think that .... -3. [así que] so; **querías verlo**, ~ **ahí está** you wanted to see it, so here it is. -4. [enfático]: **¡~ ya está!** well, that's it!; **¡~ claro!** but of course!; **¡~ vaya amigo que tienes!** some friend he is!

puesto, -ta ◇ *pp* → **poner**. ◇ *adj*: **ir muy** ~ to be all dressed up; **iba sólo con lo** ~ all she had with her were the clothes on her back.

◆ **puesto** *m* -1. [empleo] post, position; **escalar** ~s to work one's way up. -2. [en fila, clasificación etc] place. -3. [tenderete] stall, stand. -4. MIL post; ~ **de mando/vigilancia** command/sentry post; ~ **de policía** police station; ~ **de socorro** first-aid post.

◆ **puesta** *f* -1. [acción]: **puesta a punto** [de una técnica] perfecting; [de un motor] tuning; **puesta al día** updating; **puesta de largo** debut (in society); **puesta en escena** staging, production; **puesta en marcha** [de máquina] starting, start-up; [de acuerdo, proyecto] implementation; **puesta en órbita** putting into orbit. -2. [de ave] laying.

◆ **puesta de sol** *f* sunset.

◆ **puesto que** *loc conj* since, as.

puf (*pl* **pufs**) *m* pouf, pouffe.

púgil *m* boxer.

pugilato *m* boxing.

pugilístico, -ca *adj* boxing (*antes de sust*).

pugna *f* fight, battle.

pugnar *vi* -1. [luchar] to fight. -2. *fig* [esforzarse]: ~ **por** to struggle ○ fight (for).

puja *f* [en subasta - acción] bidding; [- cantidad] bid.

pujante *adj* vigorous.

pujanza *f* vigour, strength.

pujar ◇ *vi* -1. [en subasta] to bid higher. -2. *fig* [luchar] to struggle. ◇ *vt* to bid.

pulcritud *f* neatness, tidiness.

pulcro, -cra *adj* neat, tidy.

pulga *f* flea; **tener malas** ~s *fig* to be bad-tempered.

pulgada *f* inch.

pulgar → **dedo**.

pulgón *m* plant louse, aphid.

pulido, -da *adj* polished, clean.

◆ **pulido** *m* polish.

pulidor, -ra *adj* polishing.

◆ **pulidora** *f* polisher.

pulimentar *vt* to polish.

pulimento *m* polish, polishing (*U*).

pulir *vt* to polish.

◆ **pulirse** *vpr* [gastarse] to blow, to throw away.

pulla *f* gibe.

pulmón *m* lung; ~ **de acero** ○ **artificial** iron lung; **a pleno** ~ [gritar] at the top of one's voice; [respirar] deeply.

◆ **pulmones** *mpl* *fig* [vozarrón] powerful voice.

pulmonar *adj* pulmonary, lung (*antes de sust*).

pulmonía *f* pneumonia.

pulpa *f* pulp; [de fruta] flesh.

púlpito *m* pulpit.

pulpo *m* -1. [animal] octopus. -2. *fam* [hombre]: **es un** ~ he can't keep his hands off women. -3. [correa elástica] spider strap.

pulque *m* *Amer* fermented maguey juice.

pulsación *f* -1. [del corazón] beat, beating (*U*). -2. [en máquina de escribir] keystroke, tap; [en piano] touch; **pulsaciones por minuto** keystrokes per minute.

pulsador *m* button, push button.

pulsar *vt* -1. [botón, timbre etc] to press; [teclas de ordenador] to hit, to strike; [teclas de piano] to play; [cuerdas de guitarra] to pluck. -2. *fig* [opinión pública etc] to sound out.

pulsera *f* bracelet.

pulso *m* -1. [latido] pulse; **tomar el** ~ **a alguien** to take sb's pulse; **tomar el** ~ **a algo/alguien** *fig* to sound sthg/sb out. -2. [firmeza]: **tener buen** ~ to have a steady hand; **a** ~ unaided; **echar un** ~ (**con alguien**) to arm-wrestle (with sb). -3. *fig* [cuidado] tact.

pulular *vi* to swarm.

pulverización *f* [de sólido] pulverization; [de líquido] spraying.

pulverizador, -ra *adj* spray (*antes de sust*).

◆ **pulverizador** *m* spray.

pulverizar [13] *vt* -1. [líquido] to spray. -2. [sólido] to reduce to dust; TECN to pulverize. -3. *fig* [aniquilar] to pulverize.

pum *interj*: **¡~!** bang!

puma *m* puma.

pumba *interj*: **¡~!** wham!, bang!

punce *etc* → **punzar**.

punción *f* puncture.

pundonor *m* pride.

punible *adj* punishable.

punición *f* punishment.

púnico, -ca *adj* Punic.

punitivo, -va *adj* punitive.

punk [paŋk] (*pl* punks), **punki** *adj, m y f* punk.

punta *f* **-1.** [extremo - gen] point; [- de pan, pelo] end; [- de dedo, cuerno] tip; **a ~ de pistola** at gunpoint; **sacar ~ a (un lápiz)** to sharpen (a pencil); **a ~ (de) pala** by the dozen ○ bucket; **estar de ~ con alguien** to be on edge with sb; **ir de ~ en blanco** to be dressed up to the nines; **la ~ del iceberg** *fig* the tip of the iceberg; **tener algo en la ~ de la lengua** *fig* to have sthg on the tip of one's tongue. **-2.** [pizca] touch, bit; [de sal] pinch. **-3.** [clavo] small nail. **-4.** GEOGR point, headland.
◆ **puntas** *fpl* [en costura] point lace (*U*).

puntada *f* **-1.** [agujero] hole ○ mark left by needle. **-2.** [pespunte] stitch.

puntal *m* [madero] prop; *fig* [apoyo] mainstay.

puntapié *m* kick; **echar a alguien a ~s** to kick sb out; **tratar a alguien a ~s** *fig* to be nasty to sb.

punteado *m* MÚS plucking.

puntear *vt* to pluck.

punteo *m* guitar solo.

puntera → puntero.

puntería *f* **-1.** [destreza] marksmanship; **tener ~** to be a good shot. **-2.** [orientación] aim.

puntero, -ra ◇ *adj* leading. ◇ *m y f* [líder] leader.
◆ **puntero** *m* [para señalar] pointer.
◆ **puntera** *f* [de zapato] toecap.

puntiagudo, -da *adj* pointed.

puntilla *f* point lace; **dar la ~** *fig* to give the coup de grâce.
◆ **de puntillas** *loc adv* on tiptoe.

puntillismo *m* pointillism.

puntillo *m* pride.

puntilloso, -sa *adj* **-1.** [susceptible] touchy. **-2.** [meticuloso] punctilious.

punto *m* **-1.** [gen] point; **~ débil/fuerte** weak/strong point; **~ de ebullición/fusión** boiling/melting point; **~ cardinal** cardinal point; **~ de apoyo** fulcrum; *fig* backup, support; **~s a tratar** matters to be discussed; **poner ~ final a algo** to bring sthg to a close; **y ~** *fam* and that's that. **-2.** [signo ortográfico] dot; **~ y aparte** full stop, new paragraph; **~ y coma** semi-colon; **~ y seguido** full stop; **~s suspensivos** dots, suspension

points; **dos ~s** colon; **poner los ~s sobre las íes** to dot the i's and cross the t's. **-3.** [marca] spot, dot. **-4.** [lugar] spot, place; **~ de venta** COM point of sale. **-5.** [momento] point, moment; **estar a ~** to be ready; **estar a ~ de hacer algo** to be on the point of doing sthg; **llegar a ~ (para hacer algo)** to arrive just in time (to do sthg); **al ~** at once, there and then. **-6.** [estado] state, condition; **estando las cosas en este ~** things being as they are; **llegar a un ~ en que ...** to reach the stage where ...; **estar a ~ de caramelo para** to be ripe for; **estar en su ~** [gen] to be just right; [comida] to be done to a turn; **poner a ~** [gen] to fine-tune; [motor] to tune. **-7.** [grado] degree; **hasta tal ~ que** to such an extent that. **-8.** [cláusula] clause. **-9.** [puntada - en costura, cirugía] stitch; **~ de cruz** cross-stitch; **hacer ~** to knit; **un jersey de ~** a knitted jumper. **-10.** [estilo de tejer] knitting; **~ de ganchillo** crochet. **-11.** [pizca, toque] touch. **-12.** [objetivo] end, target.
◆ **en punto** *loc adv* exactly, on the dot.
◆ **hasta cierto punto** *loc adv* to some extent, up to a point.
◆ **punto de partida** *m* starting point.
◆ **punto de referencia** *m* point of reference.
◆ **punto de vista** *m* point of view, viewpoint.
◆ **punto muerto** *m* **-1.** AUTOM neutral. **-2.** [en un proceso] deadlock; **estar en un ~ muerto** to be deadlocked.

puntuable *adj*: **~ para** that counts towards.

puntuación *f* **-1.** [calificación] mark; [- en concursos, competiciones] score. **-2.** [ortográfica] punctuation.

puntual *adj* **-1.** [en el tiempo] punctual. **-2.** [exacto, detallado] detailed. **-3.** [aislado] isolated, one-off.

puntualidad *f* **-1.** [en el tiempo] punctuality. **-2.** [exactitud] exactness.

puntualizar [13] *vt* to specify, to clarify.

puntuar [6] ◇ *vt* **-1.** [calificar] to mark; DEP to award marks to. **-2.** [escrito] to punctuate. ◇ *vi* **-1.** [calificar] to mark. **-2.** [entrar en el cómputo] **~ (para)** to count (towards).

punzada *f* **-1.** [pinchazo] prick. **-2.** [dolor intenso] stabbing pain (*U*); *fig* pang, twinge.

punzante *adj* **-1.** [que pincha] sharp. **-2.** [intenso] sharp, stabbing. **-3.** [mordaz] caustic.

punzar [13] *vt* **-1.** [pinchar] to prick. **-2.** [suj: dolor] to stab; *fig* [suj: actitud] to wound.

punzón *m* punch.

puñado *m* handful; **a ~s** *fig* hand over fist.

puñal *m* dagger.

puñalada *f* stab; [herida] stab wound; **coser a ~s** *fig* to stab repeatedly; **~ trapera** *fig* stab in the back.

puñeta ◇ *f* **-1.** *fam* [tontería]: **hacer la ~** to be a pain; **mandar a alguien a hacer ~s** to tell sb to get lost. **-2.** [bocamanga] border. ◇ *interj fam*: **¡~!, ¡~s!** damn it!

puñetazo *m* punch.

puñetería *f fam* **-1.** [molestia] bloody-mindedness. **-2.** [menudencia] trifle, unimportant thing.

puñetero, -ra *fam* ◇ *adj* **-1.** [persona] damn. **-2.** [cosa] tricky, awkward. ◇ *m y f* pain.

puño *m* **-1.** [mano cerrada] fist; **son verdades como ~s** it's as clear as daylight; **de su ~ y letra** in his/her own handwriting; **meter** ○ **tener a alguien en un ~** to have sb under one's thumb. **-2.** [de manga] cuff. **-3.** [empuñadura - de espada] hilt; [- de paraguas] handle.

pupa *f* **-1.** [erupción] blister. **-2.** [daño] pain; **hacerse ~** to hurt o.s.

pupila *f* pupil.

pupilaje *m* reserved ○ long-term parking.

pupilo, -la *m y f* **-1.** [discípulo] pupil. **-2.** [huérfano] ward.

pupitre *m* desk.

purasangre *m inv* thoroughbred.

puré *m* CULIN purée; [sopa] thick soup; **~ de patatas** mashed potatoes (*pl*); **estar hecho ~** *fam* to be knackered.

pureta *fam* ◇ *adj* fogeyish. ◇ *m y f* old fogey.

pureza *f* purity.

purga *f* **-1.** MED purgative. **-2.** *fig* [depuración] purge.

purgación *f* (*gen pl*) MED gonorrhoea (*U*).

purgante *adj & m* purgative.

purgar [16] *vt lit & fig* to purge.

◆ **purgarse** *vpr* to take a purge.

purgatorio *m* purgatory.

purgue *etc* → **purgar**.

purificación *f* purification.

purificar [10] *vt* to purify; [mineral, metal] to refine.

purina *f* QUÍM purine.

purista ◇ *adj* purist (*antes de sust*). ◇ *m y f* purist.

puritanismo *m* puritanism.

puritano, -na *adj, m y f* puritan.

puro, -ra *adj* **-1.** [gen] pure; [oro] solid. **-2.** [cielo, atmósfera] clear. **-3.** [conducta, persona] decent, honourable. **-4.** [mero] sheer; [verdad] plain; **por pura casualidad** by pure chance.

◆ **puro** *m* cigar.

púrpura ◇ *adj inv* purple. ◇ *m* purple.

purpúreo, -a *adj culto* purple.

purpurina *f* purpurin.

purulencia *f culto* purulence.

purulento, -ta *adj culto* purulent.

pus *m* pus.

pusiera *etc* → **poner**.

pusilánime *adj* cowardly.

puso → **poner**.

pústula *f* pimple, spot.

puta ◇ *adj* → **puto**. ◇ *f vulg* whore.

putada *f vulg*: **hacerle una ~ a alguien** to be a mean bastard to sb; **¡qué ~!** what a bummer!

putativo, -va *adj* putative.

puteado, -da *adj vulg* pissed off.

putear *vulg* ◇ *vt* [fastidiar] to piss off. ◇ *vi* [salir con prostitutas] to go whoring.

puteo *m vulg* **-1.** [enfado] stroppy mood. **-2.** [con prostitutas]: **ir de ~** to go whoring.

putero, -ra *adj vulg* whoremonger.

puto, -ta *adj vulg* **-1.** [maldito] bloody. **-2.** [difícil] bloody difficult.

◆ **puto** *m vulg* male prostitute.

putrefacción *f* rotting, putrefaction.

putrefacto, -ta *adj* rotting.

pútrido, -da *adj* putrid.

puya *f* goad.

puzzle ['puθle], **puzle** *m* jigsaw puzzle.

PVC (*abrev de* **polyvinyl-chloride**) *m* PVC.

PVP (*abrev de* **precio de venta al público**) *m* ≃ RRP.

PYME (*abrev de* **Pequeña y Mediana Empresa**) *f* SME.

pyrex® = **pírex**.

pza. (*abrev de* **plaza**) Sq.

Q

q, **Q** *f* [letra] q, Q.

Qatar Qatar.

q.e.g.e. (*abrev de* que en gloria esté) RIP.

q.e.p.d. (*abrev de* que en paz descanse) RIP.

q.e.s.m. (*abrev de* que estrecha su mano) *polite formula in letters*.

quántico, -ca = cuántico.

que ◇ *pron relat* **-1.** (*sujeto*) [persona] who, that; [cosa] that, which; **la mujer ~ me saluda** the woman (who ○ that is) waving to me; **el ~ me lo compró** the one who bought it from me; **la moto ~ me gusta** the motorbike (that) I like. **-2.** (*complemento directo*) [persona] whom, that; [cosa] that, which; **el hombre ~ conociste ayer** the man (whom ○ that) you met yesterday; **ese coche es el ~ me quiero comprar** that car is the one (that ○ which) I want to buy. **-3.** (*complemento indirecto*): **al/a la ~** (to) whom; **ese es el chico al ~ presté dinero** that's the boy to whom I lent some money. **-4.** (*complemento circunstancial*): **la playa a la ~ fui** the beach where ○ to which I went; **la mujer con la ~ hablas** the woman to whom you are talking; **la mesa sobre la ~ escribes** the table on which you are writing. **-5.** (*complemento de tiempo*): **(en) ~** when; **el día (en) ~ me fui** the day (when) I left.
◇ *conj* **-1.** (*con oraciones de sujeto*) that; **es importante ~ me escuches** it's important that you listen to me. **-2.** (*con oraciones de complemento directo*) that; **me ha confesado ~ me quiere** he has told me that he loves me. **-3.** (*comparativo*) than; **es más rápido ~ tú** he's quicker than you; **antes morir ~ vivir la guerra** I'd rather die than live through a war. **-4.** [expresa causa]: **hemos de esperar, ~ todavía no es la hora** we'll have to wait, as it isn't time yet. **-5.** [expresa consecuencia] that; **tanto me lo pidió ~ se lo di** he asked me for it so insistently that I gave it to him. **-6.** [expresa finalidad] so (that); **ven aquí ~ te vea** come over here so (that) I can see you. **-7.** (+ *subjuntivo*) [expresa deseo] that; **quiero ~ lo hagas** I

want you to do it; **espero ~ te diviertas** I hope (that) you have fun. **-8.** (*en oraciones exclamativas*): **¡~ te diviertas!** have fun!; **¡~ te doy un bofetón!** do that again and I'll slap you! **-9.** (*en oraciones interrogativas*): **¿~ quiere venir? pues que venga** so she wants to come? then let her. **-10.** [expresa disyunción] or; **quieras ~ no, harás lo que yo mando** you'll do what I tell you, whether you like it or not. **-11.** [expresa hipótesis] if; **~ no quieres hacerlo, pues no pasa nada** it doesn't matter if you don't want to do it. **-12.** [expresa reiteración] and; **estaban charla ~ charla** they were talking and talking.

qué ◇ *adj* [gen] what; [al elegir, al concretar] which; **¿~ hora es?** what's the time?; **¿~ coche prefieres?** which car do you prefer? ◇ *pron* (*interrogativo*) what; **¿~ te dijo?** what did he tell you?; **no sé ~ hacer** I don't know what to do; **¿~?** [¿cómo?] sorry?, pardon? ◇ *adv* **-1.** [exclamativo] how; **¡~ horror!** how awful!; **¡~ tonto eres!** how stupid you are!, you're so stupid!; **¡~ casa más bonita!** what a lovely house!; **¡y ~!** so what? **-2.** [expresa gran cantidad]: **¡~ de ...!** what a lot of ...!; **¡~ de gente hay aquí!** what a lot of people there are here!, there are so many people here!

Québec *m*: (el) ~ Quebec.

quebrada → quebrado.

quebradero
◆ **quebradero de cabeza** *m* headache, problem.

quebradizo, -za *adj* **-1.** [frágil] fragile, brittle. **-2.** [débil] frail. **-3.** [voz] weak.

quebrado, -da *adj* **-1.** [terreno] rough, uneven; [perfil] rugged. **-2.** MAT fractional. **-3.** LITER broken.
◆ **quebrado** *m* MAT fraction.
◆ **quebrada** *f* **-1.** [desfiladero] gorge. **-2.** *Amer* [arroyo] stream.

quebradura *f* **-1.** [grieta] crack, fissure. **-2.** MED rupture.

quebrantado, -da *adj* frail.

quebrantahuesos *m inv* bearded vulture, lammergeier.

quebrantar *vt* **-1.** [incumplir - promesa, ley] to break; [- obligación] to fail in. **-2.** [romper] to crack. **-3.** [debilitar] to weaken; [- moral, resistencia] to break.
◆ **quebrantarse** *vpr* **-1.** [romperse] to crack. **-2.** [debilitarse] to decline, to deteriorate.

quebranto *m* **-1.** [pérdida] loss. **-2.** [debilitamiento] weakening, debilitation. **-3.** [pena] grief.

quebrar [19] ◇ *vt* **-1.** [romper] to break. **-2.** [color] to make paler. ◇ *vi* FIN to go bankrupt.

◆ **quebrarse** *vpr* **-1.** [romperse] to break. **-2.** [color] to pale. **-3.** [voz] to break, to falter. **-4.** [deslomarse] to rupture o.s.

quechua ◇ *adj* Quechuan. ◇ *m y f* [persona] Quechua. ◇ *m* [idioma] Quechua.

quedar ◇ *vi* **-1.** [permanecer] to remain, to stay; **el viaje quedó en proyecto** the trip never got beyond the planning stage. **-2.** [haber aún, faltar] to be left, to remain; **¿queda azúcar?** is there any sugar left?; **nos quedan 100 pesetas** we have 100 pesetas left; **¿cuánto queda para León?** how much further is it to León?; **~ por hacer** to remain to be done; **queda por fregar el suelo** the floor has still to be cleaned. **-3.** [mostrarse]: **~ como** to come across as; **~ bien/mal (con alguien)** to make a good/bad impression (on sb). **-4.** [llegar a ser, resultar]: **el trabajo ha quedado perfecto** the job turned out perfectly; **el cuadro queda muy bien ahí** the picture looks great there. **-5.** [acabar]: **~ en** to end in; **~ en nada** to come to nothing. **-6.** [sentar] to look; **te queda un poco corto el traje** your suit is a bit too short; **~ bien/mal a alguien** to look good/bad on sb; **~ bien/mal con algo** to go well/badly with sthg. **-7.** [citarse]: **~ (con alguien)** to arrange to meet (sb); **hemos quedado el lunes** we've arranged to meet on Monday. **-8.** [acordar]: **~ en algo/en hacer algo** to agree on sthg/to do sthg; **~ en que ...** to agree that ...; **¿en qué quedamos?** what's it to be, then? **-9.** *fam* [estar situado] to be; **queda por las afueras** it's somewhere on the outskirts; **¿por dónde queda?** whereabouts is it?

◇ *v impers*: **por mí que no quede** don't let me be the one to stop you; **que no quede por falta de dinero** we don't want it to fall through for lack of money.

◆ **quedarse** *vpr* **-1.** [permanecer - en un lugar] to stay, to remain. **-2.** [terminar - en un estado]: **~se ciego/sordo** to go blind/deaf; **~se triste** to be ○ feel sad; **~se sin dinero** to be left penniless; **la pared se ha quedado limpia** the wall is clean now. **-3.** [comprar] to take; **me quedo éste** I'll take this one.

◆ **quedarse con** *vpr* **-1.** [retener, guardarse] to keep. **-2.** [preferir] to go for, to prefer. **-3.** *mfam* [burlarse de]: **~se con alguien** to wind sb up.

quedo, -da *adj* quiet, soft.
◆ **quedo** *adv* quietly, softly.

quehacer *m* (*gen pl*) task; **~es domésticos** housework (*U*).

queimada *f* punch made from lemon juice, sugar and brandy.

queja *f* **-1.** [lamento] moan, groan. **-2.** [protesta] complaint.

quejarse *vpr* **-1.** [lamentar] to groan, to cry out; **~ de algo/alguien** to bemoan sthg/sb. **-2.** [protestar] to complain; **~ de** to complain about.

quejica *despec* ◇ *adj* whining, whingeing. ◇ *m y f* whinger.

quejido *m* cry, moan.

quejoso, -sa *adj*: **~ (de)** annoyed ○ upset (with).

quejumbroso, -sa *adj* whining.

quema *f* burning.

quemado, -da *adj* **-1.** [gen] burnt; [por agua hirviendo] scalded; [por electricidad] burntout; [fusible] blown. **-2.** [por sol] sunburnt. **-3.** *loc*: **estar ~** [agotado] to be burnt-out; [harto] to be fed up.

quemador *m* burner.

quemadura *f* [por fuego] burn; [por agua hirviendo] scald.

quemar ◇ *vt* **-1.** [gen] to burn; [suj: agua hirviendo] to scald; [suj: electricidad] to blow. **-2.** [suj: frío] to wither. **-3.** *fig* [malgastar] to go through, to fritter away. **-4.** *fig* [desgastar] to burn out. **-5.** *fig* [hartar] to make fed up. ◇ *vi* **-1.** [estar caliente] to be (scalding) hot. **-2.** *fig* [desgastar]: **la política quema** politics burns you out.

◆ **quemarse** *vpr* **-1.** [por fuego] to burn down; [por agua hirviendo] to get scalded; [por calor] to burn; [por electricidad] to blow. **-2.** [por el sol] to get burned. **-3.** *fig* [desgastarse] to burn out. **-4.** *fig* [hartarse] to get fed up.

quemarropa
◆ **a quemarropa** *loc adv* point-blank.

quemazón *f* burning; [picor] itch.

quepa → caber.

quepis, kepis *m* kepi.

quepo → caber.

queratina *f* keratin.

querella *f* **-1.** DER [acusación] charge. **-2.** [discordia] dispute.

querellante *adj, m y f* DER plaintiff.

querellarse *vpr* to bring an action.

querencia *f* homing instinct.

querer [67] ◇ *vt* **-1.** [gen] to want; **quiero una bicicleta** I want a bicycle; **¿quieren ustedes algo más?** would you like anything else?; **~ que alguien haga algo** to want sb to do sthg; **quiero que lo hagas tú** I want you to do it; **~ que pase algo** to want sthg to happen; **queremos que las cosas te vayan bien** we want things to go well for

you; **quisiera hacerlo, pero ...** I'd like to do it, but .... **-2.** [amar] to love. **-3.** [en preguntas - con amabilidad]: **¿quiere decirle a su amigo que pase?** could you tell your friend to come in, please? **-4.** [pedir - precio]: **algo (por)** to want sthg (for); **¿cuánto quieres por el coche?** how much do you want for the car? **-5.** *fig* & *iron* [dar motivos para]: **tú lo que quieres es que te pegue** you're asking for a smack. **-6.** *loc*: **como quien no quiere la cosa** as if it were nothing; **quien bien te quiere te hará llorar** *proverb* you have to be cruel to be kind *proverb*.
◇ *vi* to want; **ven cuando quieras** come whenever you like ○ want; **no me voy porque no quiero** I'm not going because I don't want to; **queriendo** on purpose; **sin ~ accidentally**; **~ decir** to mean; **¿qué quieres decir con eso?** what do you mean by that?; **~ es poder** where there's a will there's a way. ◇ *v impers* [haber atisbos]: **parece que quiere llover** it looks like rain. ◇ *m* love.
◆ **quererse** *vpr* to love each other.

querido, -da ◇ *adj* dear. ◇ *m y f* lover; [apelativo afectuoso] darling.

quermes *m* kermes.

quermés, quermese *f* kermiss.

queroseno, keroseno *m* kerosene.

querrá *etc* → querer.

querubín *m* cherub.

quesera → quesero.

quesería *f* cheese shop.

quesero, -ra ◇ *adj* cheese (*antes de sust*). ◇ *m y f* [persona] cheese maker.
◆ **quesera** *f* [recipiente] cheese dish.

queso *m* cheese; **~ gruyère/parmesano/roquefort** Gruyère/Parmesan/Roquefort (cheese); **~ de bola** Dutch cheese; **~ manchego** *hard mild yellow cheese made in La Mancha*; **~ rallado** grated cheese.

quetzal [ket'sal] *m* quetzal.

quevedos *mpl* pince-nez.

quia *interj fam*: ¡~! huh!, ha!

quibutz [ki'ßuθ] (*pl* **quibutzs**), **kibutz** (*pl* **kibutzim**) *m* kibbutz.

quicio *m* jamb; **estar fuera de ~** *fig* to be out of kilter; **sacar de ~ a alguien** *fig* to drive sb mad.

quid (*pl* **quids**) *m* crux; **el ~ de la cuestión** the crux of the matter.

quiebra ◇ *v* → quebrar. ◇ *f* **-1.** [ruina] bankruptcy; [en bolsa] crash; **~ fraudulenta** DER fraudulent bankruptcy. **-2.** *fig* [pérdida] collapse.

quiebro *m* **-1.** [ademán] swerve. **-2.** MÚS trill.

quien *pron* **-1.** (*relativo*) [sujeto] who; [complemento] whom; **fue mi hermano ~ me lo explicó** it was my brother who explained it to me; **era Pepe a ~ vi/de ~ no me fiaba** it was Pepe (whom) I saw/didn't trust. **-2.** (*indefinido*): **~es quieran verlo que se acerquen** whoever wants to see it will have to come closer; **hay ~ lo niega** there are those who deny it. **-3.** *loc*: **~ más ~ menos** everyone.

quién *pron* **-1.** (*interrogativo*) [sujeto] who; [complemento] who, whom; **¿~ es ese hombre?** who's that man?; **no sé ~ viene** I don't know who is coming; **¿a ~es has invitado?** who ○ whom have you invited?; **¿~ es?** [en la puerta] who is it?; [al teléfono] who's calling? **-2.** (*exclamativo*): ¡**~ pudiera verlo!** if only I could have seen it!

quienquiera (*pl* **quienesquiera**) *pron* whoever; **~ que venga** whoever comes.

quiera *etc* → querer.

quieto, -ta *adj* **-1.** [parado] still; ¡**estáte ~!** keep still!; ¡**~ ahí!** don't move! **-2.** *fig* [tranquilo] quiet.

quietud *f* **-1.** [inmovilidad] stillness. **-2.** [tranquilidad] quietness.

quif, kif *m* hashish.

quijada *f* jaw.

quijotada *f* quixotic deed.

quijote *m despec* do-gooder.

quijotesco, -ca *adj* quixotic.

quijotismo *m* quixotism.

quilate *m* carat.

quilla *f* **-1.** NÁUT keel. **-2.** [de ave] breastbone.

quilo *etc* = kilo.

quimbambas *fpl*: **irse a las ~** to go to the ends of the earth.

quimera *f* fantasy.

quimérico, -ca *adj* fanciful, unrealistic.

químico, -ca ◇ *adj* chemical. ◇ *m y f* [científico] chemist.
◆ **química** *f* [ciencia] chemistry.

quimioterapia *f* chemotherapy.

quimono, kimono *m* kimono.

quina *f* **-1.** [planta] cinchona. **-2.** [bebida] quinine; **ser más malo que la ~** to be truly horrible; **tragar ~** to grin and bear it.

quincalla *f* trinket.

quincallería *f* [quincallas] trinkets (*pl*).

quince *núm* fifteen; *ver también* seis.

quinceañero, -ra ◇ *adj* teenage. ◇ *m y f* teenager.

quinceavo, -va *núm* fifteenth; **la quinceava parte** a fifteenth.

quincena *f* fortnight.

quincenal adj fortnightly.

quincuagésimo, -ma núm fiftieth.

quiniela f [boleto] pools coupon.

◆ **quinielas** fpl [apuestas] (football) pools.

◆ **quiniela hípica** f sweepstake.

quinielista m y f punter who does the pools.

quinientos, -tas núm five hundred; ver también seis.

quinina f quinine.

quinqué m oil lamp.

quinquenal adj five-year (antes de sust).

quinquenio m -1. [período] five-year period. -2. [paga] five-yearly increment of salary.

quinqui m y f fam delinquent.

quinta → quinto.

quintacolumnista m y f fifth columnist.

quintaesencia f inv quintessence.

quintal m weight measure equivalent to 46 kilos; ~ métrico 100 kilos.

quinteto m quintet.

quintillizo, -za adj, m y f quintuplet.

quinto, -ta núm fifth; la quinta parte a fifth.

◆ **quinto** m -1. [parte] fifth. -2. MIL recruit, conscript.

◆ **quinta** f -1. [finca] country house. -2. MIL call-up year; entrar en quintas to be called up.

quíntuple = quíntuplo.

quintuplicar [10] vt to increase fivefold.

◆ **quintuplicarse** vpr to increase fivefold.

quíntuplo, -pla, quíntuple adj quintuple.

◆ **quíntuplo** m quintuple.

quiosco, kiosco m kiosk; [de periódicos] newspaper stand; ~ de música bandstand.

quiosquero, -ra m y f owner of a newspaper stand.

quiquiriquí (pl quiquiriquíes) m cock-a-doodle-do.

quirófano m operating theatre.

quiromancia f palmistry, chiromancy.

quiromántico, -ca ◇ adj chiromantic. ◇ m y f palmist.

quiromasaje m (manual) massage.

quirúrgico, -ca adj surgical.

quisiera etc → querer.

quisque m: cada ○ todo ~ every man Jack, everyone.

quisquilloso, -sa ◇ adj -1. [detallista] pernickety. -2. [susceptible] touchy, oversensitive. ◇ m y f -1. [detallista] nit picker. -2. [susceptible] touchy person.

quiste m cyst.

quitaesmalte m nail-polish remover.

quitaipón

◆ **de quitaipón** loc adj removable; [capucha] detachable.

quitamanchas m inv stain remover.

quitanieves m inv snow plough.

quitar vt -1. [gen] to remove; [ropa, zapatos etc] to take off; ~le algo a alguien to take sthg away from sb; de quita y pon removable; [capucha] detachable. -2. [dolor, ansiedad] to take away, to relieve; [sed] to quench. -3. [tiempo] to take up. -4. [robar] to take, to steal. -5. [impedir]: esto no quita que sea un vago that doesn't change the fact that he's a layabout. -6. [exceptuar]: quitando el queso, me gusta todo apart from cheese, I'll eat anything. -7. [desconectar] to switch off.

◆ **quitarse** vpr -1. [apartarse] to get out of the way. -2. [ropa] to take off. -3. [suj: mancha] to come out. -4. loc: ~se a alguien de encima ○ de en medio to get rid of sb.

quitasol m sunshade Br, parasol.

quite m DEP parry; estar al ~ to be on hand to help.

quiteño, -ña adj of/relating to Quito.

Quito Quito.

quizá, quizás adv perhaps; ~ llueva mañana it might rain tomorrow; ~ no lo creas you may not believe it; ~ sí maybe; ~ no maybe not.

quórum m quorum.

r, R f [letra] r, R.

rabadilla f coccyx.

rábano m radish; me importa un ~ I couldn't care less, I don't give a damn.

Rabat Rabat.

rabel m rebec.

rabí m rabbi.

rabia f -1. [ira] rage; me da ~ it makes me mad; tenerle ~ a alguien fig not to be able to stand sb. -2. [enfermedad] rabies.

rabiar [8] vi -1. [sufrir] to writhe in pain; ~ de ○ por to writhe in. -2. [enfadarse] to be furious; estar a ~ (con alguien) to be furious (with sb); hacer ~ a alguien to make sb furious. -3. [desear]: ~ por algo/hacer

algo to be dying for sthg/to do sthg; **me gusta a** ~ I'm crazy about it.

rabicorto, -ta *adj* short-tailed.

rabieta *f fam* tantrum.

rabilargo, -ga *adj* long-tailed.

rabillo *m* corner; **mirar algo con el** ~ **del ojo** to look at sthg out of the corner of one's eye.

rabino *m* rabbi.

rabiosamente *adv* **-1.** [mucho] terribly. **-2.** [con enfado] furiously, in a rage.

rabioso, -sa *adj* **-1.** [furioso] furious. **-2.** [excesivo] terrible. **-3.** [enfermo de rabia] rabid. **-4.** [chillón] loud, gaudy.

rabo *m* **-1.** [de animal] tail; ~ **de buey** oxtail; **irse** ○ **salir con el** ~ **entre las piernas** to go off with one's tail between one's legs. **-2.** [de hoja, fruto] stem. **-3.** *vulg* [pene] prick, cock.

racanear *vi fam* **-1.** [holgazanear] to idle, to laze about. **-2.** [ser tacaño] to be stingy.

rácano, -na *fam* ○ *adj* **-1.** [tacaño] mean, stingy. **-2.** [gandul] idle, lazy. ○ *m y f* **-1.** [tacaño] mean devil. **-2.** [gandul] lazybones.

RACE (*abrev de* **Real Automóvil Club de España**) *m Spanish automobile association,* ≃ AA *Br,* ≃ AAA *Am.*

racha *f* **-1.** [ráfaga] gust (of wind). **-2.** [época] spell; [serie] string; **buena/mala** ~ good/bad patch; **a** ~**s** in fits and starts.

racheado, -da *adj* gusty, squally.

racial *adj* racial.

racimo *m* **-1.** [de frutos] bunch. **-2.** [de flores] raceme.

raciocinio *m* **-1.** [razón] (power of) reason. **-2.** [razonamiento] reasoning (*U*).

ración *f* **-1.** [porción] portion. **-2.** [en bar, restaurante] *large portion of a dish served as a snack.*

racionado, -da *adj* rationed.

racional *adj* rational.

racionalidad *f* rationality.

racionalismo *m* rationalism.

racionalización *f* rationalization.

racionalizar [13] *vt* to rationalize.

racionamiento *m* rationing.

racionar *vt* to ration.

racismo *m* racism.

racista *adj, m y f* racist.

rada *f* roadstead.

radar (*pl* **radares**) *m* radar.

radiación *f* radiation; ~ **solar** solar radiation.

radiactividad, radioactividad *f* radioactivity.

radiactivo, -va, radioactivo, -va *adj* radioactive.

radiado, -da *adj* **-1.** [por radio - mensaje] radioed; [- programa etc] radio (*antes de sust*). **-2.** [radial] radiate.

radiador *m* radiator.

radial *adj* **-1.** [gen] radial. **-2.** *Amer* RADIO radio (*antes de sust*).

radiante *adj* radiant.

radiar [9] *vt* **-1.** [irradiar] to radiate. **-2.** FÍS to irradiate; MED to give X-ray treatment to. **-3.** [por radio] to broadcast.

radicación *f* [establecimiento] settling.

radical ○ *adj, m y f* radical. ○ *m* **-1.** GRAM & MAT root. **-2.** QUÍM free radical.

radicalismo *m* **-1.** [intransigencia] severity. **-2.** POLÍT radicalism.

radicalización *f* radicalization.

radicalizar [13] *vt* to harden, to make more radical.

◆ **radicalizarse** *vpr* to become more radical ○ extreme.

radicar [10] *vi:* ~ **en** [suj: problema etc] to lie in; [suj: población] to be (situated) in.

◆ **radicarse** *vpr* [establecerse]: ~**se (en)** to settle (in).

radio ○ *m* **-1.** ANAT & GEOM radius; **en un** ~ **de** within a radius of; ~ **de acción** TECN range; *fig* sphere of influence. **-2.** [de rueda] spoke. **-3.** QUÍM radium. ○ *f* radio; **oír algo por la** ~ to hear sthg on the radio.

radioactividad = **radiactividad**.

radioactivo, -va = **radiactivo**.

radioaficionado, -da *m y f* radio ham.

radiocasete *m* radio cassette (player).

radiocontrol *m* remote control.

radiodespertador *m* clock radio.

radiodifusión *f* broadcasting.

radioemisor, -ra *adj* radio broadcasting.

◆ **radioemisora** *f* radio station, radio transmitter.

radioenlace *m* radio link.

radioescucha *m y f inv* listener.

radiofonía *f* radio (*technology*).

radiofónico, -ca *adj* radio (*antes de sust*).

radiofrecuencia *f* radio frequency.

radiografía *f* [fotografía] X-ray; [ciencia] radiography.

radiografiar [9] *vt* to X-ray.

radiología *f* radiology.

radiólogo, -ga *m y f* radiologist.

radionovela *f* radio soap opera.

radiooperador, -ra *m y f* radio operator.

radiorreceptor *m* radio (receiver).

radiorreloj *m* clock radio.

radiotaxi *m* taxi (with radio link).
radioteléfono *m* radiotelephone.
radiotelegrafía *f* radiotelegraphy.
radiotelegrafista *m y f* wireless operator.
radioterapia *f* radiotherapy.
radiotransmisión *f* broadcasting.
radiotransmisor *m* radio transmitter.
radioyente *m y f* listener.
radique *etc* → radicar.
RAE *abrev de* **Real Academia Española**.
raer [68] *vt* to scrape (off).
ráfaga *f* [de aire, viento] gust; [de disparos] burst; [de luces] flash.
rafting *m* DEP rafting.
raglán → manga.
ragout (*pl* ragouts) = ragú.
ragtime [rak'taim] *m* ragtime.
ragú, ragout [ra'ɣu] *m* (*pl* ragouts) ragout.
raído, -da *adj* threadbare; [por los bordes] frayed.
raiga → raer.
raigambre *f* -1. [tradición] tradition. -2. BOT root system.
raigo → raer.
raíl, rail *m* rail.
raíz (*pl* raíces) *f* [gen & MAT] root; ~ **cuadrada/cúbica** square/cube root; **a ~ de** as a result of, following; **arrancar algo de** ~ to root sthg out completely; **cortar algo de** ~ to nip sthg in the bud; **echar raíces** to put down roots.
raja *f* -1. [porción] slice. -2. [grieta] crack.
rajá (*pl* rajaes) *m* rajah.
rajado, -da *adj, m y f fam* chicken.
rajar *vt* -1. [partir] to crack; [melón] to slice. -2. *mfam* [apuñalar] to slash, to cut up.
◆ **rajarse** *vpr* -1. [partirse] to crack. -2. *fam* [echarse atrás] to chicken out.
rajatabla
◆ **a rajatabla** *loc adv* to the letter, strictly.
ralea *f despec* breed, ilk.
ralentí *m* neutral; **al** ~ AUTOM ticking over; CIN in slow motion.
rallado, -da *adj* grated.
◆ **rallado** *m* grating.
rallador *m* grater.
ralladura *f* (*gen pl*) grating; ~**s de limón** grated lemon rind.
rallar *vt* to grate.
rally ['rali] (*pl* rallys) *m* rally.
ralo, -la *adj* [pelo, barba] sparse, thin; [dientes] with gaps between them.
RAM (*abrev de* **random access memory**) *f* RAM.

rama *f* branch; **en** ~ raw; **andarse por las** ~**s** *fam* to beat about the bush.
ramada *f Amer* stall.
ramadán *m* Ramadan.
ramaje *m* branches (*pl*).
ramal *m* [de carretera, ferrocarril] branch.
ramalazo *m* -1. *fam* [hecho que delata] give-away sign. -2. [ataque] fit.
rambla *f* -1. [avenida] avenue, boulevard. -2. [río] watercourse.
ramera *f* whore, hooker *Am*.
ramificación *f* -1. [gen] ramification. -2. [de carretera, ferrocarril, ciencia] branch.
ramificarse [10] *vpr* -1. [bifurcarse] to branch out. -2. [subdividirse]: ~ **(en)** to subdivide (into).
ramillete *m* bunch, bouquet.
ramo *m* -1. [de flores] bunch, bouquet. -2. [rama] branch; **el** ~ **de la construcción** the building industry.
rampa *f* -1. [para subir y bajar] ramp; ~ **de lanzamiento** launch pad. -2. [cuesta] steep incline. -3. [calambre] cramp (*U*).
rampante *adj* ARQUIT rampant.
rampla *f Amer* trailer.
ramplón, -ona *adj* vulgar, coarse.
rana *f* frog; **salir** ~ *fam* to turn out sadly, to be a disappointment.
ranchero, -ra *m y f* rancher.
◆ **ranchera** *f* -1. MÚS *popular Mexican song*. -2. AUTOM estate car. -3. *Amer* [furgoneta] van.
rancho *m* -1. [comida] mess. -2. [granja] ranch.
rancio, -cia *adj* -1. [pasado] rancid. -2. [antiguo] ancient. -3. [añejo - vino] mellow.
ranglán → manga.
rango *m* -1. [social] standing. -2. [jerárquico] rank.
Rangún Rangoon.
raní *f* rani.
ranking ['rankin] (*pl* rankings) *m* ranking.
ranúnculo *m* buttercup.
ranura *f* groove; [de máquina tragaperras, cabina telefónica] slot.
rapaces *fpl* → rapaz.
rapacidad *f* rapacity, greed.
rapado, -da *adj* shaven.
rapapolvo *m fam* ticking-off; **dar** ○ **echar un** ~ **a alguien** to tick sb off.
rapar *vt* [barba, bigote] to shave off; [cabeza] to shave; [persona] to shave the hair of.
◆ **raparse** *vpr* to shave one's head.
rapaz, -za *m y f fam* lad (*f* lass).
◆ **rapaz** *adj* -1. [que roba] rapacious, greedy. -2. ZOOL → ave.

◆ **rapaces** *fpl* ZOOL birds of prey.

rape *m* angler fish; **cortar el pelo al ~ a alguien** to crop sb's hair.

rapé *m* (*en aposición inv*) snuff.

rapidez *f* speed; **con ~** quickly.

rápido, -da *adj* quick, fast; [coche] fast; [beneficio, decisión] quick.

◆ **rápido** ◇ *adv* quickly; **más ~** quicker; **¡ven, ~!** come, quick! ◇ *m* [tren] express train.

◆ **rápidos** *mpl* [de río] rapids.

rapiña *f* **-1.** [robo] robbery with violence. **-2.** → **ave**.

rapiñar *vt* to steal.

raposa *f* vixen.

rappel ['rapel] (*pl* **rappels**) *m* DEP abseiling; **hacer ~** to abseil.

rapsodia *f* rhapsody.

raptar *vt* to abduct, to kidnap.

rapto *m* **-1.** [secuestro] abduction, kidnapping. **-2.** [ataque] fit.

raptor, -ra *m y f* abductor, kidnapper.

raqueta *f* **-1.** [para jugar - al tenis] racquet; [- al ping pong] bat. **-2.** [para la nieve] snowshoe. **-3.** [de croupier] rake.

raquídeo, -a *adj* ANAT rachideal.

raquis *m* vertebral column.

raquítico, -ca ◇ *adj* **-1.** MED rachitic. **-2.** [insuficiente] miserable. ◇ *m y f* MED rickets sufferer.

raquitismo *m* MED rickets (*U*).

rareza *f* **-1.** [poco común, extraño] rarity. **-2.** [poco frecuente] infrequency. **-3.** [extravagancia] idiosyncracy, eccentricity.

raro, -ra *adj* **-1.** [extraño] strange; **¡qué ~!** how odd ○ strange! **-2.** [excepcional] unusual, rare; [visita] infrequent. **-3.** [extravagante] odd, eccentric. **-4.** [escaso] rare; **rara vez** rarely.

◆ **rara avis** *m y f* oddity.

ras *m*: **a ~ de** level with; **a ~ de tierra** at ground level; **volar a ~ de tierra** to fly low.

rasante ◇ *adj* [vuelo] low-level; [tiro] grazing. ◇ *f* [de carretera] gradient.

rasar *vt* to skim, to graze.

rascacielos *m inv* skyscraper.

rascador *m* **-1.** [herramienta] scraper. **-2.** [para las cerillas] striking surface.

rascar [10] ◇ *vt* **-1.** [con uñas, clavo] to scratch. **-2.** [con espátula] to scrape (off); [con cepillo] to scrub. **-3.** *despec* [instrumento] to scrape away at. ◇ *vi* to be rough.

◆ **rascarse** *vpr* to scratch o.s.

RASD (*abrev de* **República Árabe Saharaui Democrática**) *f Democratic Arab Republic of the Western Sahara.*

rasera *f* fish slice.

rasero *m* strickle; **medir por el mismo ~** to treat alike.

rasgado, -da → **ojo**.

rasgar [16] *vt* to tear; [sobre] to tear open.

◆ **rasgarse** *vpr* to tear.

rasgo *m* **-1.** [característica] trait, characteristic. **-2.** [acto elogiable] act. **-3.** [trazo] flourish, stroke.

◆ **rasgos** *mpl* **-1.** [del rostro] features. **-2.** [letra] handwriting (*U*).

◆ **a grandes rasgos** *loc adv* in general terms; **explicar algo a grandes ~s** to outline sthg.

rasgón *m* tear.

rasgue *etc* → **rasgar**.

rasguear *vt* to strum.

rasguñar *vt* to scratch.

◆ **rasguñarse** *vpr* to scratch.

rasguño *m* scratch; **sin un ~** without a scratch.

rasilla *f* **-1.** [tela] serge. **-2.** [ladrillo] tile.

raso, -sa *adj* **-1.** [terreno] flat. **-2.** [cucharada etc] level. **-3.** [cielo] clear. **-4.** [a poca altura] low. **-5.** MIL: **soldado ~** private.

◆ **raso** *m* **-1.** [tela] satin. **-2.** *loc*: **al ~** in the open air.

raspa *f* backbone (of fish).

raspado *m* **-1.** MED scrape. **-2.** [de pieles etc] scraping.

raspador *m* scraper.

raspadura *f* (*gen pl*) scraping; [señal] scratch.

raspar ◇ *vt* **-1.** [rascar] to scrape (off). **-2.** [rasar] to graze, to shave. ◇ *vi* to be rough.

rasposo, -sa *adj* rough.

rasque *etc* → **rascar**.

rastras

◆ **a rastras** *loc adv*: **llevar algo/a alguien a ~** *lit* & *fig* to drag sthg/sb along.

rastreador, -ra ◇ *adj* tracker (*antes de sust*). ◇ *m y f* tracker.

rastrear ◇ *vt* **-1.** [seguir las huellas de] to track. **-2.** *fig* [buscar pistas en - suj: persona] to search, to comb; [- suj: reflector, foco] to sweep. ◇ *vi fig* [indagar] to make enquiries.

rastreo *m* [de una zona] searching, combing.

rastrero, -ra *adj* despicable.

rastrillar *vt* to rake (over).

rastrillo *m* **-1.** [en jardinería] rake. **-2.** [mercado] flea market; [benéfico] jumble sale.

rastro *m* **-1.** [pista] trail; **perder el ~ de alguien** to lose track of sb; **sin dejar ~** without trace; **no hay** ○ **queda ni ~ de él**

there's no sign of him. **-2.** [vestigio] trace. **-3.** [mercado] flea market.

rastrojo *m* stubble.

rasurar *vt* to shave.

♦ **rasurarse** *vpr* to shave.

rata ◇ *adj fam* stingy, mean. ◇ *m y f fam* stingy person. ◇ *f* rat; ~ **de sacristía** *fam* fanatical churchgoer; **más pobre que una ~** *fam* as poor as a church mouse.

ratafía *f* ratafia.

rataplán *m* ratatat.

ratear *vi* to pilfer, to steal.

ratería *f* pilfering, stealing.

ratero, -ra *m y f* petty thief.

raticida *m* rat poison.

ratificar [10] *vt* to ratify.

♦ **ratificarse en** *vpr* to stand by, to stick to.

rato *m* while; **estuvimos hablando mucho ~** we were talking for quite a while; **al poco ~ (de)** shortly after; **con esto hay para ~** that should keep us going for a while; **pasar el ~** to kill time, to pass the time; **pasar un mal ~** to have a hard time of it; **~s libres** spare time (*U*); **a ~s** at times; **a ~s perdidos** at odd moments; **un ~ (largo)** *fig* really, terribly.

ratón *m* [gen & INFORM] mouse.

♦ **ratón de biblioteca** *m* bookworm.

ratonera *f* **-1.** [para ratas] mousetrap. **-2.** *fig* [trampa] trap.

RAU (*abrev de* **República Árabe Unida**) *f* UAR.

raudal *m* **-1.** [de agua] torrent. **-2.** *fig* [montón] abundance; [de lágrimas] flood; [de desgracias] string; **a ~es** in abundance, by the bucket.

raudo, -da *adj* fleet, swift.

ravioli *m* (*gen pl*) ravioli (*U*).

raya ◇ *v* → **raer**. ◇ *f* **-1.** [línea] line; [en tejido] stripe; **a ~s** striped. **-2.** [del pelo] parting; **hacerse la ~** to part one's hair. **-3.** [de pantalón] crease. **-4.** *fig* [límite] limit; **pasarse de la ~** to overstep the mark; **mantener** ○ **tener a ~ a alguien** to keep sb in line. **-5.** [señal - en disco, pintura etc] scratch. **-6.** [pez] ray. **-7.** [guión] dash.

rayado, -da *adj* **-1.** [a rayas - tela] striped; [- papel] ruled. **-2.** [estropeado] scratched.

♦ **rayado** *m* **-1.** [rayas] stripes (*pl*). **-2.** [acción] ruling.

rayano, -na *adj fig*: ~ **en** bordering on.

rayar ◇ *vt* **-1.** [marcar] to scratch. **-2.** [trazar rayas] to rule lines on. ◇ *vi* **-1.** [aproximarse]: ~ **en algo** to border on sthg; **raya en los cuarenta** he's pushing forty. **-2.** [alba] to break.

♦ **rayarse** *vpr* to get scratched.

rayera *etc* → **raer**.

rayo ◇ *v* → **raer**. ◇ *m* **-1.** [de luz] ray; ~ **solar** sunbeam. **-2.** FÍS beam, ray; ~ **láser** laser beam; ~**s infrarrojos/ultravioleta/uva** infrared/ultraviolet/UVA rays; ~**s X** X-rays; **caer como un ~** *fig* to be a bombshell. **-3.** METEOR bolt of lightning; ~**s** lightning (*U*); **¡que te parta un ~!** *fam* go to hell! **-4.** [persona]: **ser un ~** to be like greased lightning; **pasar como un ~** to flash by. **-5.** [de rueda] spoke.

rayón *m* rayon.

rayuela *f* **-1.** [juego en que se tiran monedas] pitch and toss. **-2.** *Amer* [juego en que se salta a la pata coja] hopscotch.

raza *f* **-1.** [humana] race; ~ **humana** human race. **-2.** [animal] breed; **de ~** [caballo] thoroughbred; [perro] pedigree. **-3.** *Amer fam* [cara] cheek, nerve.

razón *f* **-1.** [gen] reason; **atender a razones** to listen to reason; **dar la ~ a alguien** to say that sb is right; **en ~ de** ○ **a** in view of; ~ **de ser** raison d'être; **hacer entrar en ~ a alguien** to make sb see reason; **perder la ~** to lose one's reason ○ mind; **tener ~ (en hacer algo)** to be right (to do sthg); **no tener ~** to be wrong; **y con ~** and quite rightly so. **-2.** [información]: **se vende piso; ~ aquí** flat for sale: enquire within; **dar ~ de** to give an account of. **-3.** MAT ratio.

♦ **razón de Estado** *f* reasons (*pl*) of state.

♦ **razón social** *f* COM trade name.

♦ **a razón de** *loc adv* at a rate of.

razonable *adj* reasonable.

razonamiento *m* reasoning (*U*).

razonar ◇ *vt* [argumentar] to reason out. ◇ *vi* [pensar] to reason.

RDA (*abrev de* **República Democrática Alemana**) *f* GDR.

re *m* MÚS D; [en solfeo] re.

reacción *f* reaction; ~ **en cadena** chain reaction.

reaccionar *vi* to react.

reaccionario, -ria *adj, m y f* reactionary.

reacio, -cia *adj* stubborn; ~ **a algo** resistant to sthg; **ser ~ a** ○ **en hacer algo** to be reluctant to do sthg.

reactivación *f* revival.

reactivar *vt* to revive.

reactivo, -va *adj* reactive.

♦ **reactivo** *m* QUÍM reagent.

reactor *m* **-1.** [propulsor] reactor. **-2.** [avión] jet (plane).

readaptación *f* rehabilitation.

readaptar *vt* to rehabilitate.

◆ **readaptarse** *vpr* to readjust.

readmitir *vt* to accept O take back.

reafirmar *vt* to confirm; ~ **a alguien en algo** to confirm sb in sthg.

◆ **reafirmarse** *vpr* to assert o.s.; ~**se en algo** to become confirmed in sthg.

reagrupar *vt* to regroup, to reorganize.

reajustar *vt* **-1.** [corregir] to rearrange. **-2.** [ECON - precios, impuestos] to make changes to, to raise; [- plantilla] to cut back; [- sector] to streamline; [- salarios] to cut.

reajuste *m* **-1.** [cambio] readjustment; ~ **ministerial** cabinet reshuffle. **-2.** [ECON - precios, impuestos] increase; [- de sector] streamlining; [- de salarios] reduction; ~ **de plantilla** redundancies (*pl*).

real ◇ *adj* **-1.** [verdadero] real. **-2.** [de monarquía] royal. ◇ *m desus old Spanish coin worth one quarter of a peseta;* **no valer un** ~ to be worthless.

realce ◇ *v* → **realzar.** ◇ *m* **-1.** [esplendor] glamour; **dar** ~ **a algo/alguien** to enhance sthg/sb. **-2.** [en pintura] highlight. **-3.** [en arquitectura, escultura] relief.

realeza *f* **-1.** [monarcas] royalty. **-2.** [magnificencia] magnificence.

realidad *f* **-1.** [mundo real] reality; ~ **virtual** INFORM virtual reality. **-2.** [verdad] truth; **en** ~ actually, in fact.

realismo *m* realism.

realista ◇ *adj* realistic. ◇ *m y f* ARTE realist.

realización *f* **-1.** [ejecución] carrying-out; [de proyecto, medidas] implementation; [de sueños, deseos] fulfilment; ~ **de beneficios** profit-taking. **-2.** [obra] achievement. **-3.** CIN production.

realizado, -da *adj* **-1.** [hecho] carried out, performed. **-2.** [satisfecho] fulfilled.

realizador, -ra *m y f* CIN & TV director.

realizar [13] *vt* **-1.** [ejecutar - esfuerzo, viaje, inversión] to make; [- operación, experimento, trabajo] to perform; [- encargo] to carry out; [- plan, reformas] to implement; [- desfile] to go on. **-2.** [hacer real] to fulfil, to realize. **-3.** CIN to produce.

◆ **realizarse** *vpr* **-1.** [en un trabajo] to find fulfilment. **-2.** [hacerse real - sueño, predicción, deseo] to come true; [- esperanza, ambición] to be fulfilled. **-3.** [ejecutarse] to be carried out.

realmente *adv* **-1.** [en verdad] in fact, actually. **-2.** [muy] really, very.

realquilado, -da ◇ *adj* sub-let. ◇ *m y f* sub-tenant.

realquilar *vt* to sublet.

realzar [13] *vt* **-1.** [resaltar] to enhance. **-2.** [en pintura] to highlight.

reanimación *f* **-1.** [física, moral] recovery. **-2.** MED resuscitation.

reanimar *vt* **-1.** [físicamente] to revive. **-2.** [moralmente] to cheer up. **-3.** MED to resuscitate.

◆ **reanimarse** *vpr* to revive.

reanudación *f* resumption; [de amistad] renewal.

reanudar *vt* [conversación, trabajo] to resume; [amistad] to renew.

◆ **reanudarse** *vpr* [conversación, trabajo] to resume; [amistad] to be renewed.

reaparecer [30] *vi* to reappear.

reaparición *f* reappearance.

reapertura *f* reopening.

rearmar *vt* to rearm.

rearme *m* rearmament.

reaseguro *m* reinsurance.

reavivar *vt* to revive.

rebaja *f* **-1.** [acción] reduction. **-2.** [descuento] discount.

◆ **rebajas** *fpl* COM sales; **"grandes ~s"** "massive reductions"; **estar de** ~**s** to have a sale on.

rebajado, -da *adj* **-1.** [precio] reduced. **-2.** [humillado] humiliated. **-3.** ARQUIT depressed.

rebajar *vt* **-1.** [precio] to reduce; **te rebajo 100 pesetas** I'll knock 100 pesetas off for you. **-2.** [persona] to humiliate. **-3.** [intensidad] to tone down. **-4.** [altura] to lower.

◆ **rebajarse** *vpr* [persona] to humble o.s.; ~**se a hacer algo** to lower o.s. O stoop to do sthg.

rebanada *f* slice.

rebanar *vt* [pan] to slice; [dedo etc] to slice off.

rebañar *vt* to scrape clean.

rebaño *m* flock; [de vacas] herd.

rebasar *vt* to exceed, to surpass; [agua] to overflow; AUTOM to overtake.

rebatible *adj* refutable.

rebatir *vt* to refute.

rebato *m* alarm; **tocar a** ~ to sound the alarm.

rebeca *f* cardigan.

rebelarse *vpr* to rebel.

rebelde ◇ *adj* **-1.** [sublevado] rebel (*antes de sust*). **-2.** [desobediente] rebellious. **-3.** [difícil de dominar - pelo] unmanageable; [- tos] persistent; [- pasiones] unruly. **-4.** DER defaulting. ◇ *m y f* **-1.** [sublevado, desobediente] rebel. **-2.** DER defaulter.

rebeldía *f* **-1.** [cualidad] rebelliousness. **-2.** [acción] (act of) rebellion. **-3.** DER default; **declarar a alguien en** ~ to declare sb in default.

rebelión *f* rebellion.

rebenque *m Amer* [látigo] whip.

reblandecer [30] *vt* to soften.

◆ **reblandecerse** *vpr* to get soft.

rebobinado *m* rewinding.

rebobinar *vt* to rewind.

reboce *etc* → rebozar.

reborde *m* edge.

rebosante *adj*: ~ **(de)** brimming ○ overflowing (with).

rebosar ◇ *vt* to overflow with, to brim with. ◇ *vi* to overflow; ~ **de** to be overflowing with; *fig* [persona] to brim with.

rebotado, -da *adj* [cura] who has given up the cloth ○ left the priesthood.

rebotar ◇ *vi*: ~ **(en)** to bounce (off), to rebound (off) ◇ *vt fam* [irritar] to cheese off.

◆ **rebotarse** *vpr fam* [irritarse] to get cheesed off.

rebote *m* **-1.** [bote] bounce, bouncing (*U*). **-2.** DEP rebound; **de** ~ on the rebound.

rebozado, -da *adj* CULIN coated in batter ○ breadcrumbs.

rebozar [13] *vt* CULIN to coat in batter ○ breadcrumbs.

rebozo *m* wrap, muffler.

rebrotar *vi* BOT to sprout; [fenómeno] to reappear.

rebuscado, -da *adj* recherché, pretentious.

rebuscamiento *m* pretentiousness.

rebuscar [10] *vt* to search (around in).

rebuznar *vi* to bray.

rebuzno *m* bray, braying (*U*).

recabar *vt* [pedir] to ask for; [conseguir] to manage to get.

recadero, -ra *m y f* messenger.

recado *m* **-1.** [mensaje] message. **-2.** [encargo] errand; **hacer** ~s to run errands.

recaer [55] *vi* **-1.** [enfermo] to have a relapse. **-2.** [ir a parar]: ~ **sobre** to fall on. **-3.** [reincidir]: ~ **en** to relapse into.

recaída *f* relapse.

recaiga *etc* → recaer.

recalar ◇ *vt* to soak through. ◇ *vi* NÁUT to sight land.

recalcar [10] *vt* to stress, to emphasize.

recalcitrante *adj* recalcitrant.

recalentar [19] *vt* **-1.** [volver a calentar] to warm up. **-2.** [calentar demasiado] to overheat.

◆ **recalentarse** *vpr* to overheat.

recámara *f* **-1.** [habitación] dressing room. **-2.** [de arma de fuego] chamber. **-3.** *Amer* [dormitorio] bedroom.

recamarera *f Amer* maid.

recambiar [8] *vt* to replace.

recambio *m* spare (part); [para pluma] refill; **de** ~ spare.

recapacitar *vi* to reflect, to think.

recapitalización *f* recapitalization.

recapitulación *f* recap, recapitulation.

recapitular *vt* to recapitulate, to summarize.

recargable *adj* [batería] rechargeable; [encendedor] refillable.

recargado, -da *adj* [estilo etc] overelaborate, affected.

recargar [16] *vt* **-1.** [volver a cargar - encendedor, recipiente] to refill; [- batería, pila] to recharge; [- fusil, camión] to reload. **-2.** [cargar demasiado] to overload. **-3.** [adornar en exceso] to overelaborate. **-4.** [cantidad]: ~ **1.000 pesetas a alguien** to charge sb 1,000 pesetas extra. **-5.** [poner en exceso]: ~ **algo de algo** to put too much of sthg in sthg.

recargo *m* extra charge, surcharge.

recatado, -da *adj* [pudoroso] modest, demure.

recatarse *vpr*: ~ **de hacer algo** to shy away from doing sthg; **sin** ~ openly.

recato *m* **-1.** [pudor] modesty, demureness. **-2.** [reserva]: **sin** ~ openly, without reserve. **-3.** [cautela] prudence, caution.

recauchutar *vt* to retread.

recaudación *f* **-1.** [acción] collection, collecting; ~ **de impuestos** tax collection. **-2.** [cantidad] takings (*pl*); DEP gate.

recaudador, -ra *m y f*: ~ **(de impuestos)** tax collector.

recaudar *vt* to collect.

recaudo

◆ **a buen recaudo** *loc adv* in safe-keeping; **poner a buen** ~ to put in a safe place.

recayera *etc* → recaer.

rece *etc* → rezar.

recelar ◇ *vt* **-1.** [sospechar] to suspect. **-2.** [temer] to fear. ◇ *vi* to be mistrustful; ~ **de** to mistrust.

recelo *m* mistrust, suspicion.

receloso, -sa *adj* mistrustful, suspicious.

recensión *f* review, write-up.

recepción *f* **-1.** [gen] reception. **-2.** [de carta, paquete] receipt.

recepcionista *m y f* receptionist.

receptáculo *m* receptacle.

receptividad *f* receptiveness.

receptivo, -va *adj* receptive.

receptor, -ra ◇ *adj* receiving. ◇ *m* y *f* [persona] recipient; ~ **de órgano** organ recipient.
◆ **receptor** *m* [aparato] receiver.
recesión *f* recession.
recesivo, -va *adj* **-1.** ECON recessionary. **-2.** BIOL recessive.
receta *f* **-1.** CULIN & *fig* recipe. **-2.** MED prescription.
recetar *vt* to prescribe.
recetario *m* **-1.** MED prescription record. **-2.** CULIN recipe book.
rechazar [13] *vt* **-1.** [gen & MED] to reject; [oferta] to turn down. **-2.** [repeler - a una persona] to push away; MIL to drive back, to repel.
rechazo *m* **-1.** [gen & MED] rejection; [hacia una ley, un político] disapproval; ~ **a hacer algo** refusal to do sthg. **-2.** [negación] denial.
rechinar *vi* **-1.** [puerta] to creak; [dientes] to grind; [frenos, ruedas] to screech; [metal] to clank. **-2.** [dando dentera] to grate.
rechistar *vi* to answer back; **sin** ~ without a word of protest.
rechoncho, -cha *adj fam* tubby, chubby.
rechupete
◆ **de rechupete** *loc adv fam* [gen] brilliant, great; [comida] delicious, scrumptious.
recibí *m*: "~" [en documentos] "received".
recibidor *m* entrance hall.
recibimiento *m* reception, welcome.
recibir ◇ *vt* **-1.** [gen] to receive; [clase, instrucción] to have. **-2.** [dar la bienvenida a] to welcome. **-3.** [ir a buscar] to meet. ◇ *vi* [atender visitas] to receive visitors.
recibo *m* receipt; **acusar** ~ **de** to acknowledge receipt of.
reciclado, -da *adj* recycled.
reciclaje *m* **-1.** [de residuos] recycling. **-2.** [de personas] retraining.
reciclar *vt* **-1.** [residuos] to recycle. **-2.** [personas] to retrain.
reciedumbre *f* strength.
recién *adv* recently, newly; **el** ~ **casado** the newly-wed; **los** ~ **llegados** the newcomers; **el** ~ **nacido** the newborn baby.
reciente *adj* **-1.** [acontecimiento etc] recent. **-2.** [pintura, pan etc] fresh.
recinto *m* [zona cercada] enclosure; [área] place, area; [alrededor de edificios] grounds (*pl*); ~ **ferial** fairground (*of trade fair*).
recio, -cia *adj* **-1.** [persona] robust. **-2.** [voz] gravelly. **-3.** [objeto] solid. **-4.** [material, tela] tough, strong. **-5.** [lluvia, viento, etc] harsh.
recipiente *m* container, receptacle.

reciprocidad *f* reciprocity; **en** ~ **a** in return for.
recíproco, -ca *adj* mutual, reciprocal.
recital *m* **-1.** [de música clásica] recital; [de rock] concert. **-2.** [de lectura] reading. **-3.** *fig* [exhibición] display, exhibition.
recitar *vt* to recite.
reclamación *f* **-1.** [petición] claim, demand. **-2.** [queja] complaint.
reclamar ◇ *vt* **-1.** [pedir, exigir] to demand, to ask for. **-2.** [necesitar] to demand, to need. ◇ *vi* [protestar]: ~ **(contra)** to protest (against), to complain (about).
reclamo *m* **-1.** [para atraer] inducement. **-2.** [para cazar] decoy, lure. **-3.** [de ave] call.
reclinable *adj* reclining.
reclinar *vt*: ~ **algo (sobre)** to lean sthg (on).
◆ **reclinarse** *vpr* to lean back.
reclinatorio *m* prie-dieu, prayer stool.
recluir [51] *vt* to shut ◇ lock away, to imprison.
◆ **recluirse** *vpr* to shut o.s. away.
reclusión *f* **-1.** [encarcelamiento] imprisonment. **-2.** *fig* [encierro] seclusion.
recluso, -sa *m* y *f* **-1.** [preso] prisoner. **-2.** [anacoreta] recluse, hermit.
recluta *m* [obligatorio] conscript; [voluntario] recruit.
reclutamiento *m* **-1.** [de soldados - obligatorio] conscription; [- voluntario] recruitment. **-2.** [de trabajadores] recruitment.
reclutar *vt* **-1.** [soldados - obligatoriamente] to conscript; [- voluntariamente] to recruit. **-2.** [trabajadores] to recruit.
recobrar *vt* [gen] to recover; [conocimiento] to regain; [tiempo perdido] to make up for.
◆ **recobrarse** *vpr*: ~**se (de)** to recover (from).
recochinearse *vpr fam*: ~ **de alguien** to take the mickey out of sb.
recochineo *m fam* mickey-taking (*U*).
recodo *m* bend.
recogedor *m* dustpan.
recogemigas *m inv* crumb scoop.
recogepelotas *m* y *f inv* ball boy (*f* ball girl).
recoger [14] *vt* **-1.** [coger] to pick up. **-2.** [reunir] to collect, to gather. **-3.** [ordenar, limpiar - mesa] to clear; [- habitación, cosas] to tidy ◇ clear up. **-4.** [ir a buscar] to pick up, to fetch. **-5.** [albergar] to take in. **-6.** [cosechar] to gather, to harvest; [fruta] to pick. **-7.** [acortar - prenda] to take up, to shorten.
◆ **recogerse** *vpr* **-1.** [a dormir, meditar] to retire. **-2.** [cabello] to put up.

recogido, **-da** *adj* **-1.** [lugar] withdrawn, secluded. **-2.** [cabello] tied back.

◆ **recogida** *f* **-1.** [gen] collection. **-2.** [cosecha] harvest, gathering; [de fruta] picking.

recogimiento *m* **-1.** [concentración] concentration, absorption. **-2.** [retiro] withdrawal, seclusion.

recoja *etc* → **recoger**.

recolección *f* **-1.** [cosecha] harvest, gathering. **-2.** [recogida] collection.

recolectar *vt* **-1.** [cosechar] to harvest, to gather; [fruta] to pick. **-2.** [reunir] to collect.

recolector, **-ra** ◇ *adj* harvesting. ◇ *m y f* **-1.** [gen] collector. **-2.** [de cosecha] harvester; [de fruta] picker.

recoleto, **-ta** *adj* quiet, secluded.

recomendable *adj* recommendable; **no ser ~** not to be a good idea.

recomendación *f* (*gen pl*) **-1.** [gen] recommendation. **-2.** [referencia] reference.

recomendado, **-da** *m y f* protégé (*f* protégée).

recomendar [19] *vt* to recommend; **~ a alguien que haga algo** to recommend that sb do sthg.

recomenzar [34] *vt* to begin ◇ start again, to recommence.

recompensa *f* reward; **en ~ por** in return for.

recompensar *vt* **-1.** [premiar] to reward. **-2.** [compensar]: **~ a alguien algo** to compensate ◇ reward sb for sthg.

recomponer [65] *vt* to repair, to mend.

recompuesto, **-ta** *pp* → **recomponer**.

reconcentrar *vt* **-1.** [reunir] to bring together. **-2.** [concentrar]: **~ algo en** to centre ◇ concentrate sthg on. **-3.** [hacer denso] to thicken.

◆ **reconcentrarse** *vpr*: **~se (en)** to concentrate (on), to be absorbed (in).

reconciliación *f* reconciliation.

reconciliar [8] *vt* to reconcile.

◆ **reconciliarse** *vpr* to be reconciled.

reconcomerse *vpr*: **~ (de)** to be consumed (with ◇ by).

reconcomio *m* grudge, resentment (*U*).

recóndito, **-ta** *adj* hidden, secret; **en lo más ~ de mi corazón** in the depths of my heart.

reconducir [33] *vt* to redirect.

reconfortante *adj* **-1.** [anímicamente] comforting. **-2.** [físicamente] revitalizing.

reconfortar *vt* **-1.** [anímicamente] to comfort. **-2.** [físicamente] to revitalize.

reconocer [31] *vt* **-1.** [gen] to recognize. **-2.** MED to examine. **-3.** [terreno] to survey.

◆ **reconocerse** *vpr* **-1.** [identificarse] to recognize each other. **-2.** [confesarse]: **se reconoció culpable** he admitted to being guilty.

reconocido, **-da** *adj* **-1.** [admitido] recognized, acknowledged. **-2.** [agradecido] grateful.

reconocimiento *m* **-1.** [gen] recognition; **~ del habla** INFORM & LING speech recognition. **-2.** [agradecimiento] gratitude. **-3.** MED examination. **-4.** MIL reconnaissance.

reconquista *f* reconquest, recapture.

◆ **Reconquista** *f*: **la Reconquista** HIST *the Reconquest of Spain, when the Christian Kings retook the country from the Muslims.*

reconquistar *vt* to recapture, to reconquer; *fig* to regain, to win back.

reconsiderar *vt* to reconsider.

reconstituir [51] *vt* **-1.** [rehacer] to reconstitute. **-2.** [reproducir] to reconstruct.

◆ **reconstituirse** *vpr* [rehacerse - país] to rebuild.

reconstituyente FARM ◇ *adj* tonic (*antes de sust*). ◇ *m* tonic.

reconstrucción *f* **-1.** [de edificios, país etc] rebuilding. **-2.** [de sucesos] reconstruction.

reconstruir [51] *vt* **-1.** [edificio, país etc] to rebuild. **-2.** [suceso] to reconstruct.

reconvención *f* reprimand, reproach.

reconvenir [75] *vt* to reprimand, to reproach.

reconversión *f* restructuring; **~ industrial** rationalization of industry.

reconvertir [27] *vt* [gen] to restructure; [industria] to rationalize.

recopilación *f* **-1.** [acción] collecting, gathering. **-2.** [texto - de poemas, artículos] compilation, collection; [- de leyes] code.

recopilar *vt* **-1.** [recoger] to collect, to gather. **-2.** [escritos, leyes] to compile.

récord (*pl* **récords**) ◇ *m* record; **batir un ~** to break a record; **establecer un ~** to set a new record; **tener el ~** to hold the record. ◇ *adj inv* record.

recordar [23] ◇ *vt* **-1.** [acordarse de] to remember. **-2.** [traer a la memoria] to remind; **me recuerda a un amigo mío** he reminds me of a friend of mine. ◇ *vi* to remember; **si mal no recuerdo** as far as I can remember.

recordatorio *m* **-1.** [aviso] reminder. **-2.** [estampa] *card given to commemorate sb's first communion, a death etc.*

recordman (*pl* **recordmen** ◇ **recordmans**) *m* record holder.

recorrer *vt* **-1.** [atravesar - lugar, país] to travel through ◇ across, to cross; [- ciudad] to go round. **-2.** [distancia] to cover. **-3.** *fig* [con la mirada] to look over.

recorrida *f Amer* trip.

recorrido *m* **-1.** [trayecto] route, path. **-2.** [viaje] journey. **-3.** *fig* [examen]: ~ **(por)** summary ○ résumé (of).

recortable *m* cutout.

recortado, -da *adj* **-1.** [cortado] cut. **-2.** [borde] jagged.

recortar *vt* **-1.** [cortar - lo que sobra] to cut off ○ away; [- figuras de un papel] to cut out. **-2.** [pelo, flequillo] to trim. **-3.** *fig* [reducir] to cut.
◆ **recortarse** *vpr* [figura etc] to stand out, to be outlined.

recorte *m* **-1.** [pieza cortada] cut, trimming; [de periódico, revista] cutting, clipping. **-2.** [reducción] cut, cutback. **-3.** [cartulina] cutout. **-4.** DEP swerve, sidestep.

recostar [23] *vt* to lean (back).
◆ **recostarse** *vpr* to lie down.

recoveco *m* **-1.** [rincón] nook, hidden corner. **-2.** [curva] bend. **-3.** *fig* [complicación]: **sin** ~**s** uncomplicated. **-4.** *fig* [lo más oculto]: **los** ~**s del alma** the innermost recesses of the mind.

recreación *f* re-creation.

recrear *vt* **-1.** [volver a crear] to recreate. **-2.** [entretener] to amuse, to entertain.
◆ **recrearse** *vpr* **-1.** [entretenerse] to amuse o.s., to entertain o.s. **-2.** [regodearse] to take delight ○ pleasure.

recreativo, -va *adj* recreational.

recreo *m* **-1.** [entretenimiento] recreation, amusement. **-2.** [EDUC - en primaria] playtime; [- en secundaria] break.

recriminar *vt* to reproach.
◆ **recriminarse** *vpr* to reproach each other.

recrudecer [30] *vi* to get worse.
◆ **recrudecerse** *vpr* to get worse.

recrudecimiento *m* worsening, accentuation; [de criminalidad etc] upsurge.

recta → recto.

rectal *adj* rectal.

rectangular *adj* **-1.** [de forma] rectangular. **-2.** GEOM right-angled.

rectángulo *m* rectangle.

rectificable *adj* rectifiable.

rectificación *f* rectification; [en periódico] correction.

rectificar [10] *vt* **-1.** [error] to rectify, to correct. **-2.** [conducta, actitud etc] to improve. **-3.** [ajustar] to put right.

rectilíneo, -a *adj* rectilinear.

rectitud *f* straightness; *fig* rectitude, uprightness.

recto, -ta *adj* **-1.** [sin curvas, vertical] straight. **-2.** *fig* [íntegro] upright, honourable. **-3.** *fig* [justo, verdadero] true, correct. **-4.** *fig* [literal] literal, true.
◆ **recto** ◇ *m* ANAT rectum. ◇ *adv* straight on ○ ahead.
◆ **recta** *f* straight line; **la recta final** *lit* & *fig* the home straight.

rector, -ra ◇ *adj* governing, guiding. ◇ *m y f* **-1.** [de universidad] vice-chancellor *Br*, president *Am*. **-2.** [dirigente] leader, head.
◆ **rector** *m* RELIG rector.

rectorado *m* **-1.** [cargo] vice-chancellorship *Br*, presidency *Am*. **-2.** [lugar] vice-chancellor's office, rector's office.

rectoría *f* **-1.** [cargo] rectorate, rectorship. **-2.** [casa] rectory.

recuadro *m* box.

recubierto, -ta *pp* → recubrir.

recubrimiento *m* covering, coating.

recubrir *vt* [gen] to cover; [con pintura, barniz] to coat.

recuento *m* recount.

recuerda *etc* → recordar.

recuerdo *m* **-1.** [rememoración] memory; **traer** ~**s a alguien de algo** to bring back memories of sthg to sb. **-2.** [objeto - de viaje] souvenir; [- de persona] keepsake.
◆ **recuerdos** *mpl* [saludos] regards; **dale** ~**s de mi parte** give her my regards.

recuesta *etc* → recostar.

recular *vi* **-1.** [retroceder] to go ○ move back. **-2.** *fig* [ceder] to back down.

recuperable *adj* [gen] recoverable; [fiestas, horas de trabajo] that can be made up later.

recuperación *f* **-1.** [de lo perdido, la salud, la economía] recovery. **-2.** [fisioterapia] physiotherapy. **-3.** EDUC → clase.

recuperar *vt* [lo perdido] to recover; [horas de trabajo] to catch up; [conocimiento] to regain.
◆ **recuperarse** *vpr* **-1.** [enfermo] to recuperate, to recover. **-2.** [de una crisis] to recover; [negocio] to pick up; ~**se de algo** to get over sthg.

recurrente ◇ *adj* **-1.** DER appellant. **-2.** [repetido] recurrent. ◇ *m y f* DER appellant.

recurrir *vi* **-1.** [buscar ayuda]: ~ **a alguien** to turn to sb; ~ **a algo** to resort to sthg. **-2.** DER to appeal.

recurso *m* **-1.** [medio] resort; **como último** ~ as a last resort. **-2.** DER appeal; ~ **de alzada** appeal (against an official decision); ~ **de apelación** appeal; ~ **de casación** High Court appeal.

◆ **recursos** *mpl* [fondos] resources; [financieros] means; ~**s propios** ECON equities.

recusar *vt* **-1.** DER to challenge. **-2.** [rechazar] to reject, to refuse.

red *f* **-1.** [malla] net; [para cabello] hairnet. **-2.** [sistema] network, system; [de electricidad, agua] mains (*sg*); ~ **viaria** road network ◇ system. **-3.** [organización de espionaje] ring; [- de tiendas] chain. **-4.** INFORM network; ~ **local/neuronal** local (area)/ neural network. **-5.** *loc:* **caer en las** ~**es de alguien** to fall into sb's trap.

◆ **Red** *f* INFORM: **la Red** the Net; **navegar por la Red** to surf the Net.

redacción *f* **-1.** [acción - gen] writing; [- de periódico etc] editing. **-2.** [estilo] wording. **-3.** [equipo de redactores] editorial team ◇ staff. **-4.** [oficina] editorial office. **-5.** EDUC essay, composition.

redactar *vt* to write (up); [carta] to draft.

redactor, -ra *m y f* [PRENS - escritor] writer; [- editor] editor; ~ **jefe** editor-in-chief.

redada *f* **-1.** [de pesca] catch, haul. **-2.** *fig* [de policía - en un solo lugar] raid; [- en varios lugares] round-up.

redecilla *f* [de pelo] hairnet.

redención *f* redemption.

redentor, -ra *m y f* [persona] redeemer.

◆ **Redentor** *m*: **el Redentor** RELIG the Redeemer.

redicho, -cha *adj fam* affected.

rediez *interj* ¡~! for Heaven's sake!

redil *m* fold, pen.

redimir *vt* **-1.** [gen] to redeem. **-2.** [librar] to free. **-3.** [pagar el rescate de] to ransom.

◆ **redimirse** *vpr* to redeem o.s.

redireccionar *vt* INFORM to redirect.

redistribuir [51] *vt* to redistribute.

rédito *m* interest (*U*), yield (*U*).

redoblar ◇ *vt* to redouble. ◇ *vi* to roll.

redoble *m* roll, drumroll.

redomado, -da *adj* out-and-out.

redonda → **redondo**.

redondeado, -da *adj* rounded.

redondear *vt* **-1.** [hacer redondo] to round, to make round. **-2.** [negocio, acuerdo] to round off. **-3.** [cifra, precio] to round up/down.

redondel *m* **-1.** [gen] circle, ring. **-2.** TAUROM bullring.

redondo, -da *adj* **-1.** [circular, esférico] round; **a la redonda** around; **caerse** ~ *fig* to collapse in a heap. **-2.** [perfecto] excellent. **-3.** [rotundo] categorical. **-4.** [cantidad] round; **mil pesetas redondas** a round thousand pesetas.

◆ **redondo** *m* CULIN topside.

◆ **redonda** *f* [letra] roman type ◇ print.

reducción *f* **-1.** [gen] reduction. **-2.** [sometimiento] suppression.

reducido, -da *adj* **-1.** [pequeño] small. **-2.** [limitado] limited. **-3.** [estrecho] narrow.

reducir [33] ◇ *vt* **-1.** [gen] to reduce; ~ **algo a algo** to reduce sthg to sthg. **-2.** [someter - país, ciudad] to suppress, to subdue; [- sublevados, atracadores] to bring under control. **-3.** MAT [convertir] to convert. **-4.** MED to set. ◇ *vi* AUTOM to change down.

◆ **reducirse a** *vpr* **-1.** [limitarse a] to be reduced to. **-2.** [equivaler a] to boil ◇ come down to.

reducto *m* **-1.** [fortificación] redoubt. **-2.** *fig* [refugio] stronghold, bastion.

redujera *etc* → **reducir**.

redundancia *f* redundancy, superfluousness.

redundante *adj* redundant, superfluous.

redundar *vi*: ~ **en algo** to have an effect on sthg; **redunda en beneficio nuestro** it is to our advantage.

reduplicar [10] *vt* to redouble.

reduzca *etc* → **reducir**.

reedición *f* new edition; [reimpresión] reprint.

reeditar *vt* to bring out a new edition of; [reimprimir] to reprint.

reelección *f* re-election.

reelegir [42] *vt* to re-elect.

reembolsable *adj* [gastos] reimbursable; [fianza, dinero] refundable; [deuda] repayable.

reembolsar, rembolsar *vt* [gastos] to reimburse; [fianza, dinero] to refund; [deuda] to repay.

◆ **reembolsarse** *vpr* to be reimbursed.

reembolso, rembolso *m* [de gastos] reimbursement; [de fianza, dinero] refund; [de deuda] repayment; **contra** ~ cash on delivery.

reemplazar [13], **remplazar** *vt* [gen & INFORM] to replace.

reemplazo, remplazo *m* **-1.** [gen & INFORM] replacement. **-2.** MIL call-up, draft.

reemprender *vt* to start again.

reencarnación *f* reincarnation.

reencarnar *vt* to reincarnate.

◆ **reencarnarse en** *vpr* to be reincarnated as.

reencontrar [23] *vt* to find again.

◆ **reencontrarse** *vpr* [varias personas] to meet again.

reencuentro *m* reunion.

reengancharse *vpr* MIL to re-enlist.

reestrenar *vt* CIN to re-run; TEATR to revive.

reestreno *m* CIN re-run; TEATR revival.

reestructuración *f* restructuring.

reestructurar *vt* to restructure.

reexpedir [26] *vt* to forward, to send on.

reexportación *f* re-exportation.

reexportar *vt* to re-export.

refacción *f Amer* **-1.** [reparaciones] repairs (*pl*). **-2.** [recambios] spare parts (*pl*).

refaccionar *vt Amer* to repair, to fix.

refaccionaria *f Amer* repair workshop.

refectorio *m* refectory.

referencia *f* reference; **con** ~ **a** with reference to; **hacer** ~ **a** to make reference to, to refer to.

◆ **referencias** *fpl* [información] information (*U*).

referéndum (*pl* **referéndums**) *m* referendum.

referente *adj*; ~ **a** concerning, relating to.

referir [27] *vt* **-1.** [narrar] to tell, to recount. **-2.** [remitir]: ~ **a alguien a** to refer sb to. **-3.** [relacionar]: ~ **algo a** to relate sthg to. **-4.** COM [convertir]: ~ **algo a** to convert sthg into.

◆ **referirse a** *vpr* to refer to; **¿a qué te refieres?** what do you mean?; **por lo que se refiere a ...** as far as ... is concerned.

refilón

◆ **de refilón** *loc adv* **-1.** [de lado] sideways; **mirar algo de** ~ to look at sthg out of the corner of one's eye. **-2.** *fig* [de pasada] briefly.

refinado, -da *adj* refined.

◆ **refinado** *m* refining.

refinamiento *m* refinement.

refinanciación *f* refinancing.

refinanciar [8] *vt* to refinance.

refinar *vt* to refine.

refinería *f* refinery.

refiriera *etc* → **referir**.

reflectar *vt* to reflect.

reflector *m* **-1.** ELECTR spotlight; MIL searchlight. **-2.** [telescopio] reflector.

reflejar *vt lit* & *fig* to reflect.

◆ **reflejarse** *vpr lit* & *fig*: ~**se (en)** to be reflected (in).

reflejo, -ja *adj* **-1.** [onda, rayo] reflected. **-2.** [movimiento, dolor] reflex (*antes de sust*).

◆ **reflejo** *m* **-1.** [gen] reflection. **-2.** [destello] glint, gleam. **-3.** ANAT reflex; ~ **condicional** ◇ **condicionado** conditioned reflex ◇ response.

◆ **reflejos** *mpl* [de peluquería] highlights (*pl*); **hacerse** ~**s** to have highlights put in one's hair.

réflex ◇ *adj inv* reflex. ◇ *f inv* FOT [cámara] reflex camera.

reflexión *f* reflection; **con** ~ on reflection; **sin previa** ~ without thinking.

reflexionar *vi* to reflect, to think.

reflexivo, -va *adj* **-1.** [que piensa] reflective, thoughtful. **-2.** GRAM reflexive.

refluir [51] *vi* to flow back ◇ out.

reflujo *m* ebb (tide).

reforma *f* **-1.** [modificación] reform; ~ **agraria** agrarian reform. **-2.** [en local, casa etc] alterations (*pl*).

◆ **Reforma** *f*: **la Reforma** RELIG the Reformation.

reformar *vt* **-1.** [gen & RELIG] to reform. **-2.** [local, casa etc] to renovate, to do up.

◆ **reformarse** *vpr* to mend one's ways.

reformatorio *m* ≃ youth custody centre, ≃ borstal; [de menores de 15 años] ≃ remand home.

reformismo *m* reformism.

reformista *adj, m y f* reformist.

reformular *vt* to reformulate, to put another way.

reforzado, -da *adj* reinforced.

reforzar [37] *vt* to reinforce.

refracción *f* refraction.

refractar *vt* to refract.

refractario, -ria *adj* **-1.** [material] refractory, heat-resistant. **-2.** [opuesto]: ~ **a** averse to. **-3.** [inmune]: ~ **a** immune to.

refrán *m* proverb, saying.

refranero *m* collection of proverbs ◇ sayings.

refregar [35] *vt* **-1.** [frotar] to scrub. **-2.** *fig* [reprochar]: ~ **algo a alguien** to reproach sb for sthg.

refreír [28] *vt* **-1.** [volver a freír] to re-fry. **-2.** [freír en exceso] to over-fry.

refrenar *vt* to curb, to restrain.

◆ **refrenarse** *vpr* to hold back, to restrain o.s.

refrendar *vt* **-1.** [aprobar] to approve. **-2.** [legalizar] to endorse, to countersign.

refrescante *adj* refreshing.

refrescar [10] ◇ *vt* **-1.** [gen] to refresh; [bebidas] to chill. **-2.** *fig* [conocimientos] to brush up. ◇ *vi* **-1.** [tiempo] to cool down. **-2.** [bebida] to be refreshing.

◆ **refrescarse** *vpr* **-1.** [tomar aire fresco] to get a breath of fresh air. **-2.** [beber algo] to have a drink. **-3.** [mojarse con agua fría] to splash o.s. down.

refresco *m* **-1.** [bebida] soft drink; ~**s** refreshments. **-2.** MIL: **de** ~ new, fresh.

refría *etc* → **refreír**.

refriega ◇ *v* → **refregar**. ◇ *f* scuffle, fracas; MIL skirmish.

refriera *etc* → **refreír**.

refrigeración *f* **-1.** [aire acondicionado] air-conditioning. **-2.** [de alimentos] refrigeration. **-3.** [de máquinas] cooling.

refrigerado, -da *adj* [gen] cooled; [local] air-conditioned; [alimentos] refrigerated.

refrigerador, -ra *adj* cooling.
◆ **refrigerador** *m* **-1.** [de alimentos] refrigerator, fridge *Br*, icebox *Am*. **-2.** [de máquinas] cooling system.

refrigerante *adj* [gen] cooling; [para alimentos] refrigerating.

refrigerar *vt* **-1.** [alimentos] to refrigerate. **-2.** [local] to air-condition. **-3.** [máquina] to cool.

refrigerio *m* snack.

refrito, -ta ◇ *pp* → **refreír**. ◇ *adj* [demasiado frito] over-fried; [frito de nuevo] re-fried.
◆ **refrito** *m* **-1.** CULIN *sauce made from fried tomato and onion*. **-2.** *fig* [cosa rehecha] rehash.

refucilo, refusilo *m Amer* flash of lightning.

refuerce *etc* → **reforzar**.

refuerzo *m* reinforcement, strengthening (U).
◆ **refuerzos** *mpl* MIL reinforcements.

refugiado, -da ◇ *adj* refugee (*antes de sust*). ◇ *m y f* refugee.

refugiar [8] *vt* to give refuge to.
◆ **refugiarse** *vpr* to take refuge; ~**se de** **algo** to shelter from sthg.

refugio *m* **-1.** [lugar] shelter, refuge; ~ **antiaéreo** air-raid shelter; ~ **atómico** nuclear bunker; ~ **subterráneo** bunker, underground shelter. **-2.** *fig* [amparo, consuelo] refuge, comfort. **-3.** AUTOM traffic island.

refulgencia *f* brilliance.

refulgente *adj* brilliant.

refulgir [15] *vi* to shine brightly.

refundir *vt* **-1.** [material] to re-cast. **-2.** LITER to adapt. **-3.** *fig* [unir] to bring together.

refunfuñar *vi* to grumble.

refunfuñón, -ona ◇ *adj* grumpy. ◇ *m y f* grumbler.

refusilo *m* = **refucilo**.

refutable *adj* refutable.

refutación *f* refutation.

refutar *vt* to refute.

regadera *f* **-1.** [para regar] watering can; **estar como una** ~ *fig* to be as mad as a hatter. **-2.** *Amer* [chubasco] shower.

regadío *m* irrigated land; **de** ~ irrigated, irrigable.

regalado, -da *adj* **-1.** [muy barato] dirt cheap; **te lo doy** ~ I'm giving it away to you. **-2.** [agradable] comfortable, easy.

regalar *vt* **-1.** [dar - de regalo] to give (as a present); [- gratis] to give away. **-2.** [agasajar]: ~ **a alguien con algo** to shower sb with sthg.
◆ **regalarse con** *vpr* to treat o.s. to.

regalía *f* royal prerogative.

regaliz *m* liquorice.

regalo *m* **-1.** [obsequio] present, gift. **-2.** [placer] joy, delight.

regalón, -ona *adj Amer fam* spoilt.

regalonear *vt Amer fam* to spoil.

regañadientes
◆ **a regañadientes** *loc adv fam* unwillingly, reluctantly.

regañar ◇ *vt* [reprender] to tell off. ◇ *vi* [pelearse] to fall out, to argue.

regañina *f* **-1.** [reprimenda] ticking off. **-2.** [enfado] argument, row.

regaño *m* telling off.

regañón, -ona ◇ *adj* grumpy. ◇ *m y f* grumbler.

regar [35] *vt* **-1.** [con agua - planta] to water; [- calle] to hose down. **-2.** [suj: río] to flow through. **-3.** *fig* [desparramar] to sprinkle, to scatter.

regata *f* **-1.** NÁUT regatta, boat race. **-2.** [reguera] irrigation channel.

regate *m* **-1.** DEP swerve, sidestep. **-2.** *fig* [evasiva] dodge.

regatear ◇ *vt* **-1.** [escatimar] to be sparing with; **no ha regateado esfuerzos** he has spared no effort. **-2.** DEP to beat, to dribble past. **-3.** [precio] to haggle over. ◇ *vi* **-1.** [negociar el precio] to barter, to haggle. **-2.** NÁUT to race.

regateo *m* bartering, haggling.

regazo *m* lap.

regencia *f* **-1.** [reinado] regency. **-2.** [administración] running, management.

regeneración *f* regeneration; [moral] reform.

regeneracionismo *m* political reform movement.

regenerar *vt* to regenerate; [moralmente] to reform.

regenta *f* wife of the regent.

regentar *vt* [país] to run, to govern; [negocio] to run, to manage; [puesto] to hold.

regente ◇ *adj* regent. ◇ *m y f* **-1.** [de un país] regent. **-2.** [administrador - de tienda] manager; [- de colegio] governor. **-3.** *Amer* [alcalde] mayor (*f* mayoress).

reggae ['riɣi] *m* reggae.

regicida *m y f* regicide.

regicidio *m* regicide.

regidor, -ra *m y f* **-1.** [concejal] councillor. **-2.** TEATR stage manager; CIN & TV assistant director.

régimen (*pl* **regímenes**) *m* **-1.** [sistema político] regime; **Antiguo ~** ancien régime; **-2.** **parlamentario** parliamentary system. **-2.** [normativa] rules (*pl*). **-3.** [dieta] diet; **estar/ ponerse a ~** to be/go on a diet. **-4.** [de vida, lluvias etc] pattern, usual routine. **-5.** LING government.

regimiento *m* MIL & *fig* regiment.

regio, -gia *adj* lit & *fig* royal.

región *f* region; MIL district.

regional *adj* regional.

regionalismo *m* regionalism.

regionalizar [13] *vt* to regionalize.

regir [42] ◇ *vt* **-1.** [reinar en] to rule, to govern. **-2.** [administrar] to run, to manage. **-3.** LING to govern. **-4.** *fig* [determinar] to govern, to determine. ◇ *vi* **-1.** [ley] to be in force, to apply. **-2.** *fig* [persona] to be of sound mind.
◆ **regirse por** *vpr* to trust in, to be guided by.

registrado, -da *adj* **-1.** [grabado] recorded. **-2.** [patentado] registered.

registrador, -ra ◇ *adj* registering. ◇ *m y f* registrar.

registrar ◇ *vt* **-1.** [inspeccionar - zona, piso] to search; [- persona] to frisk. **-2.** [nacimiento, temperatura etc] to register, to record. **-3.** [grabar] to record. ◇ *vi* to search.
◆ **registrarse** *vpr* **-1.** [suceder] to occur, to happen. **-2.** [observarse] to be recorded.

registro *m* **-1.** [oficina] registry (office); **~ civil** registry (office); **~ de la propiedad** land registry office; **~ mercantil** ○ **de comercio** business registry office. **-2.** [libro] register. **-3.** [inspección] search, searching (*U*). **-4.** [de libro] bookmark. **-5.** INFORM record. **-6.** LING & MÚS register.

regla *f* **-1.** [para medir] ruler, rule; **~ de cálculo** slide rule. **-2.** [norma] rule; **en ~** in order; **por ~ general** as a rule, generally; **salirse de la ~** to overstep the mark ○ line. **-3.** MAT operation; **~ de tres** rule of three. **-4.** *fam* [menstruación] period; **tener la ~** to have one's period. **-5.** [modelo] example, model.

reglamentación *f* [acción] regulation; [reglas] rules (*pl*), regulations (*pl*).

reglamentar *vt* to regulate.

reglamentario, -ria *adj* lawful, within the rules; [arma, balón] regulation (*antes de sust*); DER statutory.

reglamento *m* regulations (*pl*), rules (*pl*).

reglar *vt* to regulate.

regocijar
◆ **regocijarse** *vpr*: **~se (de ○ con)** to rejoice (in).

regocijo *m* joy, delight.

regodearse *vpr*: **~ (con)** to take pleasure ○ delight (in).

regodeo *m* delight, pleasure; [malicioso] (cruel) delight ○ pleasure.

regordete *adj* chubby, tubby.

regresar ◇ *vi* [yendo] to go back, to return; [viniendo] to come back, to return. ◇ *vt* *Amer* [devolver] to give back.
◆ **regresarse** *vpr* *Amer* [volver] to come back.

regresión *f* **-1.** [de epidemia] regression. **-2.** [de exportaciones] drop, decline.

regresivo, -va *adj* regressive.

regreso *m* return; **estar de ~** to be back.

regué *etc* → **regar**.

reguero *m* [de sangre, agua] trickle, dribble; [de harina etc] trail; **correr como un ~ de pólvora** to spread like wildfire.

regulación *f* [gen] regulation; [de nacimientos, tráfico] control; [de mecanismo] adjustment; **~ de empleo** streamlining, redundancies (*pl*).

regulador, -ra *adj* regulating, regulatory.

regular ◇ *adj* **-1.** [gen] regular; [de tamaño] medium; **de un modo ~** regularly. **-2.** [mediocre] average, fair. **-3.** [normal] normal, usual. ◇ *m* MIL regular. ◇ *adv* all right; [de salud] so-so. ◇ *vt* [gen] to control, to regulate; [mecanismo] to adjust.
◆ **por lo regular** *loc adv* as a rule, generally.

regularidad *f* regularity; **con ~** regularly.

regularización *f* regularization.

regularizar [13] *vt* **-1.** [volver a la normalidad] to get back to normal. **-2.** [legalizar] to regularize.
◆ **regularizarse** *vpr* **-1.** [volver a la normalidad] to return to normal. **-2.** [legalizarse] to become legitimate.

regurgitar *vt & vi* to regurgitate.

regusto *m* aftertaste; [semejanza, aire] flavour, hint.

rehabilitación *f* **-1.** [de personas] rehabilitation; [en un puesto] reinstatement. **-2.** [de local] restoration.

rehabilitar *vt* **-1.** [personas] to rehabilitate; [en un puesto] to reinstate. **-2.** [local] to restore.

rehacer [60] *vt* **-1.** [volver a hacer] to redo, to do again. **-2.** [reconstruir] to rebuild.
◆ **rehacerse** *vpr* [recuperarse] to recuperate, to recover.

rehecho, -cha *pp* → rehacer.

rehén (*pl* rehenes) *m* hostage.

rehíce → rehacer.

rehiciera *etc* → rehacer.

rehogar [16] *vt* to fry over a low heat.

rehuir [51] *vt* to avoid.

rehusar *vt & vi* to refuse.

rehuya *etc* → rehuir.

rehuyera *etc* → rehuir.

Reikiavik Reykjavik.

reimplantar *vt* **-1.** [reintroducir] to reintroduce. **-2.** MED to implant again.

reimportación *f* reimporting.

reimpresión *f* [tirada] reprint; [acción] reprinting.

reimprimir *vt* to reprint.

reina *f* **-1.** [monarca] queen. **-2.** → abeja.

reinado *m* lit & fig reign.

reinante *adj* **-1.** [monarquía, persona] reigning, ruling. **-2.** [viento] prevailing; [frío, calor] current.

reinar *vi* lit & fig to reign.

reincidencia *f* relapse; [en un delito] recidivism.

reincidente *adj, m y f* recidivist.

reincidir *vi*: ~ **en** [falta, error] to relapse into, to fall back into; [delito] to repeat.

reincorporar *vt* to reincorporate.
◆ **reincorporarse** *vpr*: ~**se (a)** to rejoin, to go back to.

reingresar *vi*: ~ **en** to return to.

reinicializar [13] *vt* INFORM to reset.

reino *m* CIENCIA & POLÍT kingdom; fig realm; **el ~ de los cielos** the kingdom of Heaven.

Reino Unido United Kingdom.

reinserción *f*: ~ **(social)** (social) rehabilitation ○ reintegration.

reinsertar *vt* to reintegrate, to rehabilitate.

reinstaurar *vt* to reestablish.

reintegración *f* **-1.** [a puesto] reinstatement. **-2.** [de dinero] repayment, reimbursement.

reintegrar *vt* **-1.** [a un puesto] to reinstate. **-2.** [dinero] to repay, to reimburse. **-3.** [timbrar] to stick a fiscal stamp on.
◆ **reintegrarse** *vpr*: ~**se (a)** to return (to).

reintegro *m* **-1.** [de dinero] repayment, reimbursement; BANCA withdrawal. **-2.** [en lotería] return of one's stake (*in lottery*). **-3.** [póliza] fiscal stamp.

reinvertir [27] *vt* to reinvest.

reír [28] ◇ *vi* to laugh; **dar que ~** to ask to be laughed at. ◇ *vt* to laugh at.
◆ **reírse** *vpr*: ~**se (de)** to laugh (at).

reiterar *vt* to reiterate, to repeat.
◆ **reiterarse** *vpr*: ~**se en** to reaffirm.

reiterativo, -va *adj* repetitive, repetitious.

reivindicación *f* claim, demand.

reivindicar [10] *vt* **-1.** [derechos, salario etc] to claim, to demand. **-2.** [atentado] to claim responsibility for. **-3.** [herencia] to claim (the right to).

reivindicativo, -va *adj*: **plataforma reivindicativa** (set of) demands; **jornada reivindicativa** day of protest.

reja *f* [gen] bars (*pl*); [en el suelo] grating; [celosía] grille; **estar entre ~s** to be behind bars.

rejego, -ga *adj Amer fam* [terco] stubborn.

rejilla *f* **-1.** [enrejado] grid, grating; [de ventana] grille; [de cocina] grill (*on stove*); [de horno] gridiron. **-2.** [para sillas, muebles] wickerwork. **-3.** [para equipaje] luggage rack.

rejón *m* TAUROM *type of "banderilla" used by mounted bullfighter.*

rejoneador, -ra *m y f* TAUROM *bullfighter on horseback who uses the "rejón".*

rejuntarse *vpr fam* to live together.

rejuvenecer [30] *vt & vi* to rejuvenate.
◆ **rejuvenecerse** *vpr* to be rejuvenated.

relación *f* **-1.** [nexo] relation, connection; **con ~ a, en ~ con** in relation to, with regard to; ~ **precio-calidad** value for money. **-2.** [comunicación, trato] relations (*pl*), relationship; **relaciones amorosas** (love) affair (*sg*); **relaciones comerciales** [entre individuos] business relationship (*sg*); [entre países, empresas] trade (*U*); **relaciones diplomáticas/públicas** diplomatic/public relations; **relaciones laborales** industrial relations. **-3.** [lista] list. **-4.** [descripción] account. **-5.** [informe] report. **-6.** (*gen pl*) [noviazgo] relationship; **llevan cinco años de relaciones** they've been going out together for five years. **-7.** MAT ratio.
◆ **relaciones** *fpl* [contactos] contacts, connections.

relacionar *vt* **-1.** [vincular] to relate, to connect. **-2.** [relatar] to tell, to relate.
◆ **relacionarse** *vpr*: ~**se (con)** [alternar] to mix (with).

relajación *f* relaxation.

relajante *adj* relaxing.

relajar *vt* to relax.
◆ **relajarse** *vpr* to relax.

relajo *m Amer fam* [alboroto] racket, din.

relamer *vt* to lick repeatedly.

◆ **relamerse** *vpr* **-1.** [persona] to lick one's lips. **-2.** [animal] to lick its chops.

relamido, -da *adj* prim and proper.

relámpago *m* **-1.** [descarga] flash of lightning, lightning (*U*). [destello] flash. **-2.** *fig* [exhalación]: **pasar como un** ~ to pass by as quick as lightning, to flash past.

relampaguear ◇ *v impers*: **relampagueó** lightning flashed. ◇ *vi fig* to flash.

relampagueo *m* METEOR lightning; [destello] flashing.

relanzamiento *m* relaunch.

relanzar [13] *vt* to relaunch.

relatar *vt* [suceso] to relate, to recount; [historia] to tell.

relatividad *f* relativity.

relativismo *m* relativism.

relativizar [13] *vt* to put into perspective.

relativo, -va *adj* **-1.** [gen] relative; **en lo** ~ **a** regarding. **-2.** [escaso] limited.

relato *m* [exposición] account, report; [cuento] tale, story.

relax *m inv* **-1.** [relajación] relaxation. **-2.** [sección de periódico] personal column.

releer [50] *vt* to re-read.

relegar [16] *vt*: ~ **(a)** to relegate (to); ~ **algo al olvido** to banish sthg from one's mind.

relente *m* (night) dew.

relevancia *f* relevance, importance.

relevante *adj* outstanding, important.

relevar *vt* **-1.** [sustituir] to relieve, to take over from. **-2.** [destituir]: ~ **(de)** to dismiss (from), to relieve (of). **-3.** [eximir]: ~ **(de)** to free (from). **-4.** [DEP - en partidos] to substitute; [- en relevos] to take over from.

relevo *m* **-1.** MIL relief, changing. **-2.** DEP [acción] relay. **-3.** *loc*: **tomar el** ~ to take over.

◆ **relevos** *mpl* DEP [carrera] relay (race) (*sg*).

releyera *etc* → **releer**.

relicario *m* RELIG reliquary; [estuche] locket.

relieve *m* **-1.** [gen, ARTE & GEOGR] relief; **alto** ~ high relief; **bajo** ~ bas-relief. **-2.** [importancia] importance; **de** ~ important; **poner de** ~ to underline (the importance of), to highlight.

religión *f* religion.

religiosamente *adv lit & fig* religiously.

religiosidad *f lit & fig* religiousness.

religioso, -sa ◇ *adj* religious. ◇ *m y f* [monje] monk (*f* nun).

relinchar *vi* to neigh, to whinny.

relincho *m* neigh, neighing (*U*).

reliquia *f* relic; [familiar] heirloom.

rellano *m* **-1.** [de escalera] landing. **-2.** [de terreno] shelf.

rellenar *vt* **-1.** [volver a llenar] to refill. **-2.** [documento, formulario] to fill in ○ out. **-3.** [pollo, cojín etc] to stuff; [- tarta, pastel] to fill.

relleno, -na *adj* [gen] stuffed; [tarta, pastel] filled.

◆ **relleno** *m* [de pollo] stuffing; [de pastel] filling; **de** ~ *fig* as padding, as a filler.

reloj *m* [de pared] clock; [de pulsera] watch; ~ **analógico/digital** analogue/digital watch; ~ **de arena** hourglass; ~ **de bolsillo** pocket watch; ~ **de cuarzo** quartz watch; ~ **de cuco** cuckoo clock; ~ **interno** INFORM internal clock; ~ **de pulsera** watch, wristwatch; ~ **de sol** sun dial; **hacer algo contra** ~ to do sthg against the clock; **ser como un** ~ *fig* to be like clockwork.

relojería *f* **-1.** [tienda] watchmaker's (shop). **-2.** [arte] watchmaking.

relojero, -ra *m y f* watchmaker.

reluciente *adj* shining, gleaming.

relucir [32] *vi lit & fig* to shine; **sacar algo a** ~ to bring sthg up, to mention sthg.

relumbrar *vi* to shine brightly.

reluzca *etc* → **relucir**.

REM (*abrev de* **Roentgen Equivalent Man**) *m* REM.

remachar *vt* **-1.** [machacar] to rivet. **-2.** *fig* [recalcar] to drive home, to stress.

remache *m* **-1.** [acción] riveting. **-2.** [clavo] rivet.

remake [ri'meik] (*pl* **remakes**) *m* remake.

remanente *m* **-1.** [de géneros] surplus stock; [de productos agrícolas] surplus. **-2.** [en cuenta bancaria] balance. **-3.** [de beneficios] net profit.

remangar [16] = **arremangar**.

remanso *m* still pool; ~ **de paz** oasis of peace.

remar *vi* to row.

remarcar [10] *vt* [recalcar] to underline, to stress.

rematadamente *adv* absolutely, utterly.

rematado, -da *adj* utter, complete.

rematar ◇ *vt* **-1.** [acabar] to finish. **-2.** [matar - persona] to finish off; [- animal] to put out of its misery. **-3.** DEP to shoot. **-4.** [liquidar, vender] to sell off cheaply. **-5.** [adjudicar en subasta] to knock down. ◇ *vi* [en fútbol] to shoot; [de cabeza] to head at goal.

remate *m* **-1.** [fin, colofón] end; **para** ~ [colmo] to cap it all. **-2.** ARQUIT top. **-3.** [en fútbol] shot; [de cabeza] header at goal.

◆ **de remate** *loc adv* totally, completely.

rembolsar = **reembolsar**.

rembolsarse = **reembolsarse**.

rembolso = reembolso.

remecer [11] *vi Amer* to shake.

remedar *vt* to imitate; [por burla] to ape, to mimic.

remediar [8] *vt* [daño] to remedy, to put right; [problema] to solve; [peligro] to avoid, to prevent.

remedio *m* **-1.** [solución] solution, remedy; **como último ~** as a last resort; **no hay** ◊ **queda más ~ que ...** there's nothing for it but ...; **no tener más ~** to have no alternative ◊ choice; **poner ~ a algo** to do sthg about sthg; **sin ~** [sin cura, solución] hopeless; [ineludiblemente] inevitably. **-2.** [consuelo] comfort, consolation. **-3.** [medicamento] remedy, cure; **~ casero** home remedy.

remedo *m* imitation; [por burla] parody.

rememorar *vt* to remember, to recall.

remendado, -da *adj* patched.

remendar [19] *vt* to mend, to darn.

remendón, -ona *adj* → zapatero.

remero, -ra *m y f* [persona] rower.

◆ **remera** *f Amer* [prenda] T-shirt.

remesa *f* [de productos] consignment, shipment; [de dinero] remittance.

remeter *vt* to tuck in.

remezón *m Amer* earth tremor.

remienda *etc* → remendar.

remiendo *m* **-1.** [parche] mend, darn. **-2.** *fam* [apaño] patching up, makeshift mending.

remigio *m card game where players aim to collect ten particular cards.*

remilgado, -da *adj* **-1.** [afectado] affected. **-2.** [escrupuloso] squeamish; [- con comida] fussy, finicky.

remilgo *m* **-1.** [afectación] affectation. **-2.** [escrupulosidad] squeamishness; [- con comida] fussiness.

reminiscencia *f* reminiscence; **tener ~s de** to be reminiscent of.

remisión *f* **-1.** [envío] sending. **-2.** [en texto] cross-reference, reference. **-3.** [perdón] remission, forgiveness.

◆ **sin remisión** *loc adv* without hope of a reprieve.

remiso, -sa *adj*: **ser ~ a hacer algo** to be reluctant to do sthg.

remite *m* sender's name and address.

remitente *m y f* sender.

remitir ◊ *vt* **-1.** [enviar] to send. **-2.** [perdonar] to forgive, to remit. **-3.** [traspasar]: **~ algo a** to refer sthg to. ◊ *vi* **-1.** [en texto]: **~ a** to refer to. **-2.** [disminuir] to subside.

◆ **remitirse a** *vpr* **-1.** [atenerse a] to comply with, to abide by. **-2.** [referirse a] to refer to.

remo *m* **-1.** [pala] oar. **-2.** [deporte] rowing. **-3.** (*gen pl*) [extremidad] limb.

remoción *f Amer* dismissal, sacking.

remodelación *f* [gen] to redesign; [de gobierno] reshuffle.

remodelar *vt* [gen] to redesign; [gobierno] to reshuffle.

remojar *vt* **-1.** [humedecer] to soak. **-2.** *fam* [festejar] to drink to, to celebrate with a drink.

remojo *m*: **poner en ~** to leave to soak; **estar en ~** to be soaking.

remojón *m fam* [en la piscina, el mar] dip; [bajo la lluvia] soaking, drenching.

remolacha *f* beetroot *Br*, beet *Am*; [azucarera] (sugar) beet.

remolcador, -ra *adj* [coche] tow (*antes de sust*); [barco] tug (*antes de sust*).

◆ **remolcador** *m* [camión] breakdown lorry; [barco] tug, tugboat.

remolcar [10] *vt* [coche] to tow; [barco] to tug.

remolino *m* **-1.** [de agua] eddy, whirlpool; [de viento] whirlwind; [de humo] cloud, swirl. **-2.** [de gente] throng, mass. **-3.** [de ideas] confusion. **-4.** [de pelo] cowlick.

remolón, -ona ◊ *adj* lazy. ◊ *m y f*: **hacerse el ~** to shirk.

remolonear *vi fam* to laze.

remolque *m* **-1.** [acción] towing; **ir a ~** *fig* [voluntariamente] to go in tow, to tag along; [obligado] to be dragged along. **-2.** [vehículo] trailer.

remontar *vt* [pendiente, río] to go up; [obstáculo] to get over, to overcome; [puestos] to pull back, to catch up.

◆ **remontarse** *vpr* **-1.** [ave, avión] to soar, to climb high. **-2.** [gastos]: **~se a** to amount ◊ come to. **-3.** *fig* [datar]: **~se a** to go ◊ date back to.

rémora *f* **-1.** [pez] remora. **-2.** *fam fig* [obstáculo] drawback, hindrance.

remorder [24] *vt fig*: **~le a alguien** to fill sb with remorse.

remordimiento *m* remorse.

remoto, -ta *adj* remote; **no tengo ni la más remota idea** I haven't got the faintest idea.

remover [24] *vt* **-1.** [agitar - sopa, café] to stir; [- ensalada] to toss; [- bote, frasco] to shake; [- tierra] to turn over, to dig up. **-2.** [desplazar] to move, to shift. **-3.** [reavivar - caso policial] to re-open; [- recuerdos, pasado] to stir up, to rake up. **-4.** *Amer* [despedir] to dismiss, to sack.

◆ **removerse** *vpr* to move about; [mar] to get rough.

remozar *vt* [edificio, fachada] to renovate.
remplazar [13] = reemplazar.
remplazo = reemplazo.
remuerda *etc* → remorder.
remueva *etc* → remover.
remuneración *f* remuneration.
remunerado, -da *adj*: **bien** ~ well-paid;
mal ~ badly-paid.
remunerar *vt* **-1.** [pagar] to remunerate. **-2.**
[recompensar] to reward.
renacentista *adj* Renaissance (*antes de sust*).
renacer [29] *vi* **-1.** [gen] to be reborn; [flores, hojas] to grow again. **-2.** [alegría, esperanza] to return, to revive.
renacimiento *m* **-1.** [gen] rebirth; [de flores, hojas] budding. **-2.** [de alegría, esperanza] revival, return.
◆ **Renacimiento** *m*: **el Renacimiento** the Renaissance.
renacuajo *m* tadpole; *fam fig* tiddler.
renal *adj* renal, kidney (*antes de sust*).
renazca *etc* → renacer.
rencilla *f* quarrel.
rencor *m* resentment, bitterness; **guardar** ~ **a** to bear a grudge.
rencoroso, -sa ◇ *adj* resentful, bitter. ◇ *m y f* resentful ○ bitter person.
rendición *f* surrender.
rendido, -da *adj* **-1.** [agotado] exhausted, worn-out. **-2.** [sumiso] submissive, servile; [admirador] devoted.
rendija *f* crack, gap.
rendimiento *m* **-1.** [de inversión, negocio] yield, return; [de trabajador, fábrica] productivity, performance; [de tierra, cosecha] yield. **-2.** [de motor] performance.
rendir [26] ◇ *vt* **-1.** [cansar] to wear out, to tire out. **-2.** [rentar] to yield. **-3.** [vencer] to defeat, to subdue. **-4.** [ofrecer] to give, to present; [pleitesía] to pay. ◇ *vi* [máquina] to perform well; [negocio] to be profitable; [fábrica, trabajador] to be productive.
◆ **rendirse** *vpr* **-1.** [entregarse] to give o.s. up, to surrender. **-2.** [ceder]: ~**se a** to submit to, to give in to; ~**se a la evidencia** to bow to the evidence. **-3.** [desanimarse] to give in ○ up.
renegado, -da *adj, m y f* renegade.
renegar [35] ◇ *vt* to deny strongly. ◇ *vi* **-1.** [repudiar]: ~ **de** RELIG to renounce; [familia] to disown. **-2.** *fam* [gruñir] to grumble.
renegociar [8] *vt* to renegotiate.
renegué *etc* → renegar.
Renfe (*abrev de* **Red Nacional de los Ferro-**

carriles Españoles) *f Spanish state railway network*.
renglón *m* line; COM item; **a** ~ **seguido** *fig* in the same breath, straight after.
◆ **renglones** *mpl fam fig* [escrito] lines, words.
reniega *etc* → renegar.
reno *m* reindeer.
renombrado, -da *adj* renowned, famous.
renombrar *vt* INFORM to rename.
renombre *m* renown, fame.
renovable *adj* renewable.
renovación *f* [de carné, contrato] renewal; [de mobiliario, local] renovation.
renovador, -ra ◇ *adj* radical; POLÍT reformist. ◇ *m y f* radical; POLÍT reformer.
renovar [24] *vt* **-1.** [cambiar - mobiliario, local] to renovate; [- vestuario] to clear out; [- personal, plantilla] to make changes to, to shake out. **-2.** [rehacer - carné, contrato, ataques] to renew. **-3.** [restaurar] to restore. **-4.** [innovar] to rethink, to revolutionize; POLÍT to reform.
renqueante *adj* limping, hobbling.
renquear *vi* to limp, to hobble; *fig* to struggle along.
renta *f* **-1.** [ingresos] income; **vivir de las** ~**s** to live off one's (private) income; ~ **fija** fixed income; ~ **per cápita** ○ **por habitante** per capita income; ~ **variable/vitalicia** variable/life annuity. **-2.** [alquiler] rent. **-3.** [beneficios] return. **-4.** [intereses] interest. **-5.** [deuda pública] national ○ public debt.
rentabilidad *f* profitability.
rentabilizar [13] *vt* to make profitable.
rentable *adj* profitable.
rentar ◇ *vt* **-1.** [rendir] to produce, to yield. **-2.** *Amer* [alquilar] to rent. ◇ *vi* to be profitable.
rentista *m y f* person of independent means.
renuencia *f* reluctance, unwillingness.
renuente *adj*: ~ **a** reluctant to, unwilling to.
renueva *etc* → renovar.
renuncia *f* [abandono] giving up; [dimisión] resignation.
renunciar [8] *vi* **-1.** [abandonar] to give up. **-2.** [dimitir] to resign.
◆ **renunciar a** *vi* **-1.** [prescindir de] to give up; [plan, proyecto] to drop; ~ **al tabaco** to give up ○ stop smoking. **-2.** [rechazar]: ~ **(a hacer algo)** to refuse (to do sthg).
reñido, -da *adj* **-1.** [enfadado]: ~ **(con)** on bad terms ○ at odds (with); **están** ~**s** they've fallen out. **-2.** [disputado] fierce, hard-fought. **-3.** [incompatible]: **estar** ~ **con**

to be at odds with, to be incompatible with.

reñir [26] ◇ *vt* **-1.** [regañar] to tell off. **-2.** [disputar] to fight. ◇ *vi* [enfadarse] to argue, to fall out; ~ **con** to fall out with.

reo, -a *m y f* [culpado] offender, culprit; [acusado] accused, defendant.

reoca *f fam:* **ser la** ~ [gracioso] to be a scream; [el colmo] to be the limit.

reojo *m:* **mirar algo de** ~ to look at sthg out of the corner of one's eye.

reordenación *f* restructuring, reorganization.

reorganización *f* [gen] reorganization; [del gobierno] reshuffle.

reorganizar [13] *vt* [gen] to reorganize; [gobierno] to reshuffle.

reorientar *vt* to give a new direction to, to re-focus.

repanchigarse [16] *vpr fam* to sprawl out.

repanocha *f fam:* **ser la** ~ [gracioso] to be a scream; [el colmo] to be the limit.

repantigarse [16] *vpr* to sprawl out.

reparación *f* **-1.** [arreglo] repair, repairing (*U*); **en** ~ under repair. **-2.** [compensación] reparation, redress.

reparador, -ra *adj* [descanso, sueño] refreshing.

reparar ◇ *vt* [coche etc] to repair, to fix; [error, daño etc] to make amends for, to make up for; [fuerzas] to restore. ◇ *vi* [advertir]: ~ **en algo** to notice sthg; **no** ~ **en gastos** to spare no expense.

reparo *m* **-1.** [objeción] objection; **poner** ~**s a algo** to raise objections to sthg. **-2.** [apuro]: **con** ~**s** with hesitation ○ reservations; **me da** ~ I feel awkward about it; **no tener** ~**s en** not to be afraid to; **sin** ~**s** without reservation, with no holds barred.

repartición *f* [reparto] sharing out.

repartidor, -ra ◇ *adj* distributing. ◇ *m y f* [gen] distributor; [de butano, carbón] deliveryman (*f* deliverywoman); [de leche] milkman (*f* milklady); [de periódicos] paperboy (*f* papergirl).

repartir *vt* **-1.** [dividir - gen] to share out, to divide; [- territorio, nación] to partition. **-2.** [distribuir - leche, periódicos, correo] to deliver; [- naipes] to deal (out). **-3.** [esparcir - pintura, mantequilla] to spread. **-4.** [asignar - trabajo, órdenes] to give out, to allocate; [- papeles] to assign. **-5.** *fig* [administrar] to administer, to dish out.

reparto *m* **-1.** [división] division, distribution; ~ **de beneficios** ECON profit sharing; ~ **de premios** prizegiving. **-2.** [distribución - de leche, periódicos, correo] **delivery**; [- de naipes]

dealing. **-3.** [asignación] giving out, allocation. **-4.** CIN & TEATR cast.

repasador *m Amer* tea towel.

repasar *vt* **-1.** [revisar] to go over; [lección] to revise. **-2.** [zurcir] to darn, to mend. **-3.** [volver a pasar - trapo etc] to run over again.

repaso *m* **-1.** [revisión] revision; [de ropa] darning, mending; **curso de** ~ refresher course. **-2.** *fam* [reprimenda] telling off, ticking off.

repatear *vt fam* to bug.

repatriación *f* repatriation.

repatriar [9] *vt* to repatriate.

◆ **repatriarse** *vpr* to be repatriated.

repecho *m* steep slope.

repelencia *f* repulsion.

repelente *adj* **-1.** [desagradable, repugnante] repulsive. **-2.** [ahuyentador] repellent.

repeler *vt* **-1.** [rechazar] to repel. **-2.** [repugnar] to repulse, to disgust.

repelús *m:* **me da** ~ it gives me the shivers.

repeluzno *m* shiver.

repente *m* [arrebato] fit.

◆ **de repente** *loc adv* suddenly.

repentinamente *adv* suddenly.

repentino, -na *adj* sudden.

repera *f fam:* **ser la** ~ to be the limit.

repercusión *f* **-1.** *fig* [consecuencia] repercussion. **-2.** [resonancia] echoes (*pl*).

repercutir *vi* **-1.** *fig* [afectar]: ~ **en** to have repercussions on. **-2.** [resonar] to resound, to echo.

repertorio *m* **-1.** [obras] repertoire. **-2.** *fig* [serie] selection.

repesca *f* **-1.** EDUC resit. **-2.** DEP repêchage.

repescar [10] *vt* **-1.** EDUC to allow a resit. **-2.** DEP to allow into the repêchage.

repetición *f* repetition; [de una jugada] action replay.

repetido, -da *adj* **-1.** [gen] repeated; **repetidas veces** time and time again. **-2.** [cromo etc] duplicated.

repetidor, -ra ◇ *adj* repeating the year. ◇ *m y f* EDUC student repeating a year.

◆ **repetidor** *m* ELECTR repeater.

repetir [26] ◇ *vt* to repeat; [ataque] to renew; [en comida] to have seconds of. ◇ *vi* **-1.** [alumno] to repeat a year. **-2.** [sabor, alimento]: ~ **(a alguien)** to repeat (on sb). **-3.** [comensal] to have seconds.

◆ **repetirse** *vpr* **-1.** [fenómeno] to recur. **-2.** [persona] to repeat o.s.

repetitivo, -va *adj* repetitive.

repicar [10] ◇ *vt* [campanas] to ring; [tambor] to beat. ◇ *vi* [campanas] to ring; [tambor] to sound.

repipi *fam* ◇ *adj* precocious. ◇ *m y f* precocious brat.

repique ◇ *v* → repicar. ◇ *m* peal, ringing (*U*).

repiquetear *vi* [campanas] to ring out; [tambor] to beat; [timbre] to ring; [lluvia, dedos] to drum.

repiqueteo *m* [de campanas] pealing; [de tambor] beating; [de timbre] ringing; [de lluvia, dedos] drumming.

repisa *f* **-1.** [estante] shelf; [sobre chimenea] mantelpiece. **-2.** ARQUIT bracket.

repita *etc* → repetir.

repitiera *etc* → repetir.

replantar *vt* to replant.

replanteamiento *m* restatatement, reconsideration.

replantear *vt* **-1.** [reenfocar] to reconsider, to restate. **-2.** [volver a mencionar] to bring up again.

replay [ri'plei] (*pl* replays) *m* replay.

replegar [35] *vt* [ocultar] to retract.
◆ **replegarse** *vpr* [retirarse] to withdraw, to retreat.

repleto, -ta *adj*: ~ (de) packed (with).

réplica *f* **-1.** [respuesta] reply. **-2.** [copia] replica.

replicar [10] ◇ *vt* [responder] to answer; [objetar] to answer back, to retort. ◇ *vi* [objetar] to answer back.

repliega *etc* → replegar.

repliegue *m* **-1.** [retirada] withdrawal, retreat. **-2.** [pliegue] fold.

repoblación *f* [con gente] repopulation; [con peces] restocking; ~ **forestal** reafforestation.

repoblar [23] *vt* [con gente] to repopulate; [con peces] to restock; [con árboles] to replant, to reafforest.
◆ **repoblarse** *vpr*: ~se de [gente] to be repopulated with; [peces] to be restocked with; [árboles] to be replanted ○ reafforested with.

repollo *m* cabbage.

reponer [65] *vt* **-1.** [gen] to replace. **-2.** CIN & TEATR to re-run; TV to repeat. **-3.** [replicar]: ~ **que** to reply that.
◆ **reponerse** *vpr*: ~se (de) to recover (from).

reportaje *m* RADIO & TV report; PRENS article; ~ **gráfico** illustrated feature.

reportar *vt* **-1.** [traer] to bring; **no le ha reportado más que problemas** it has caused

him nothing but problems. **-2.** *Amer* [informar] to report.

reporte *m Amer* report.

reportero, -ra, repórter *m y f* reporter; ~ **gráfico** press photographer.

reposacabezas *m inv* headrest.

reposado, -da *adj* relaxed, calm.

reposapiés *m inv* footrest.

reposar *vi* **-1.** [descansar] to (have a) rest. **-2.** [sedimentarse] to stand. **-3.** *fig* [yacer] to lie.

reposera *f Amer* easy chair.

reposición *f* **-1.** CIN rerun; TEATR revival; TV repeat. **-2.** [de existencias, pieza etc] replacement.

reposo *m* [descanso] rest; **en** ~ [cuerpo, persona] at rest; [máquina] not in use; CULIN standing.

repostar ◇ *vi* [coche] to fill up; [avión] to refuel. ◇ *vt* **-1.** [coche] to fill up; [avión] to refuel. **-2.** [gasolina] to fill up with. **-3.** [provisiones] to stock up on.

repostería *f* **-1.** [establecimiento] confectioner's (shop). **-2.** [oficio, productos] confectionery.

repostero, -ra *m y f* [persona] confectioner.
◆ **repostero** *m Amer* [armario] larder, pantry.

reprender *vt* [a niños] to tell off; [a empleados] to reprimand.

reprensible *adj* reprehensible.

reprensión *f* [a niños] telling-off; [a empleados] reprimand.

represa *f* dam.

represalia *f* (*gen pl*) reprisal; **tomar** ~**s** to retaliate, to take reprisals.

representación *f* **-1.** [gen & COM] representation; **en** ~ **de** on behalf of; **tener la** ~ **de** COM to act as a representative for. **-2.** TEATR performance.

representante ◇ *adj* representative. ◇ *m y f* **-1.** [gen & COM] representative. **-2.** [de artista] agent.

representar *vt* **-1.** [gen & COM] to represent. **-2.** [aparentar] to look; **representa unos 40 años** she looks about 40. **-3.** [significar] to mean; **representa el 50% del consumo interno** it accounts for 50% of domestic consumption. **-4.** [TEATR - función] to perform; [- papel] to play.

representatividad *f* representativeness.

representativo, -va *adj* **-1.** [simbolizador]: **ser** ~ **de** to represent. **-2.** [característico, relevante]: ~ **(de)** representative (of).

represión *f* repression.

represivo, -va *adj* repressive.

reprimenda f reprimand.
reprimido, -da ◇ adj repressed. ◇ m y f repressed person.
reprimir vt [gen] to suppress; [minorías, disidentes] to repress.
◆ **reprimirse** vpr: ~**se (de hacer algo)** to restrain o.s. (from doing sthg).
reprís, reprise (pl **reprises**) m acceleration.
reprobable adj reprehensible.
reprobación f reproof, censure.
reprobar [23] vt to censure, to condemn.
réprobo, -ba ◇ adj damned. ◇ m y f lost soul.
reprochar vt: ~ **algo a alguien** to reproach sb for sthg.
◆ **reprocharse** vpr: ~**se algo (uno mismo)** to reproach o.s. for sthg.
reproche m reproach; **hacer un** ~ **a alguien** to reproach sb.
reproducción f reproduction.
reproducir [33] vt [gen & ARTE] to reproduce; [gestos] to copy, to imitate.
◆ **reproducirse** vpr **-1.** [volver a suceder] to recur. **-2.** [procrear] to reproduce.
reproductor, -ra adj reproductive.
reprueba etc → reprobar.
reptar vi to crawl.
reptil m reptile.
república f republic.
◆ **República Centroafricana** f Central African Republic.
◆ **República Dominicana** f Dominican Republic.
republicanismo m republicanism.
republicano, -na adj, m y f republican.
repudiar [8] vt **-1.** [condenar] to repudiate. **-2.** [rechazar] to disown.
repudio m disowning.
repuebla etc → repoblar.
repuesto, -ta ◇ pp → reponer. ◇ adj: ~ **(de)** recovered (from).
◆ **repuesto** m [gen] reserve; AUTOM spare part; **de** ~ spare, in reserve; **la rueda de** ~ the spare wheel.
repugnancia f disgust.
repugnante adj disgusting.
repugnar ◇ vi to be disgusting. ◇ vt **me repugna ese olor/su actitud** I find that smell/her attitude disgusting; **me repugna hacerlo** I'm loathe to do it.
repujado, -da adj embossed.
◆ **repujado** m embossed work.
repujar vt to emboss.
repulsa f [censura] condemnation.
repulsión f repulsion.

repulsivo, -va adj repulsive.
repusiera etc → reponer.
reputación f reputation; **tener mucha** ~ to be very famous.
reputado, -da adj highly reputed.
reputar vt to consider.
requemado, -da adj burnt.
requemar vt to burn; [planta, tierra] to scorch.
◆ **requemarse** vpr to get burnt, to burn.
requerimiento m **-1.** [demanda] entreaty. **-2.** [DER - intimación] writ, injunction; [- aviso] summons (sg).
requerir [27] vt **-1.** [necesitar] to require. **-2.** [ordenar] to demand. **-3.** [pedir] ~ **a alguien (para) que haga algo** to ask sb to do sthg. **-4.** DER to order.
◆ **requerirse** vpr [ser necesario] to be required ◇ necessary.
requesón m cottage cheese.
requiebro m flirtatious remark.
réquiem (pl **réquiems**) m requiem.
requiera etc → requerir.
requiriera etc → requerir.
requisa f **-1.** [requisición - MIL] requisition; [- en aduana] seizure. **-2.** [inspección] inspection.
requisar vt MIL to requisition; [en aduana] to seize.
requisito m requirement; **cumplir los** ~**s** to fulfil all the requirements; ~ **previo** prerequisite.
res f beast, animal.
resabiado, -da adj fam know-all (antes de sust).
resabio m **-1.** [sabor] nasty aftertaste. **-2.** [vicio] persistent bad habit.
resaca f **-1.** fam [de borrachera] hangover. **-2.** [de las olas] undertow.
resalado, -da adj fam charming.
resaltar ◇ vi **-1.** [destacar] to stand out. **-2.** [en edificios - balcón] to stick out; [- decoración] to stand out. ◇ vt [destacar] to highlight.
resarcir [12] vt: ~ **a alguien (de)** to compensate sb (for).
◆ **resarcirse** vpr to be compensated; ~**se de** [daño, pérdida] to be compensated for; [desengaño, derrota] to make up for.
resbalada f Amer fam slip.
resbaladizo, -za adj lit & fig slippery.
resbalar vi **-1.** [caer]: ~ **(con** ◇ **sobre)** to slip (on). **-2.** [deslizarse] to slide; ~**le a alguien** fam fig to leave sb cold. **-3.** [estar resbaladizo] to be slippery.
◆ **resbalarse** vpr to slip (over).

resbalón *m* slip; **dar** ○ **pegar un** ~ to slip.
resbaloso, **-sa** *adj* slippery.
rescatar *vt* **-1.** [liberar, salvar] to rescue; [pagando rescate] to ransom. **-2.** [recuperar - herencia etc] to recover.
rescate *m* **-1.** [liberación, salvación] rescue. **-2.** [dinero] ransom. **-3.** [recuperación] recovery.
rescindir *vt* to rescind.
rescisión *f* cancellation.
rescoldo *m* ember; *fig* lingering feeling, flicker.
resecar [10] *vt* **-1.** [piel] to dry out. **-2.** [tierra] to parch.
◆ **resecarse** *vpr* **-1.** [piel] to dry out. **-2.** [tierra] to become parched.
reseco, **-ca** *adj* **-1.** [piel, garganta, pan] very dry. **-2.** [tierra] parched. **-3.** [flaco] emaciated.
resentido, **-da** ◇ *adj* bitter, resentful; **estar** ~ **con alguien** to be really upset with sb. ◇ *m y f* bitter ○ resentful person.
resentimiento *m* resentment, bitterness.
resentirse [27] *vpr* **-1.** [debilitarse] to be weakened; [salud] to deteriorate. **-2.** [sentir molestias]: ~ **de** to be suffering from. **-3.** [ofenderse] to be offended.
reseña *f* [de libro, concierto] review; [de partido, conferencia] report.
reseñar *vt* **-1.** [criticar - libro, concierto] to review; [- partido, conferencia] to report on. **-2.** [describir] to describe.
reseque *etc* → **resecar**.
reserva ◇ *f* **-1.** [de hotel, avión etc] reservation. **-2.** [provisión] reserves (*pl*); **tener algo de** ~ to keep sthg in reserve; ~**s de divisas/monetarias** ECON foreign currency/monetary reserves. **-3.** [objeción] reservation; **sin** ~**s** without reservation. **-4.** [discreción] discretion. **-5.** [de indígenas] reservation. **-6.** [de animales] reserve; ~ **natural** nature reserve. **-7.** MIL reserve; **pasar a la** ~ to become a reservist.
◇ *m y f* DEP reserve, substitute.
◇ *m* [vino] vintage.
◆ **reservas** *fpl* **-1.** [energía acumulada] energy reserves. **-2.** [recursos] resources.
reservado, **-da** *adj* **-1.** [gen] reserved. **-2.** [tema, asunto] confidential.
◆ **reservado** *m* [en restaurante] private room; FERROC reserved compartment.
reservar *vt* **-1.** [habitación, asiento etc] to reserve, to book. **-2.** [guardar - dinero, pasteles etc] to set aside; [- sorpresa] to keep. **-3.** [callar - opinión, comentarios] to reserve.
◆ **reservarse** *vpr* **-1.** [esperar]: ~**se para** to save o.s. for. **-2.** [guardar para sí - secreto] to

keep to o.s.; [- dinero, derecho] to retain (for o.s.).
reservista MIL ◇ *adj* reserve. ◇ *m y f* reservist.
resfriado, **-da** *adj*: **estar** ~ to have a cold.
◆ **resfriado** *m* cold.
resfriar [9] *vt* to make cold.
◆ **resfriarse** *vpr* [constiparse] to catch a cold.
resfrío *m* *Amer* cold.
resguardar *vt & vi*: ~ **de** to protect against.
◆ **resguardarse** *vpr*: ~**se de** [en un portal] to shelter from; [con abrigo, paraguas] to protect o.s. against.
resguardo *m* **-1.** [documento] receipt. **-2.** [protección] protection; **al** ~ **de** safe from.
residencia *f* **-1.** [estancia] stay. **-2.** [localidad, domicilio] residence. **-3.** [establecimiento - de estudiantes] hall of residence; [- de ancianos] old people's home; [- de oficiales] residence. **-4.** [hotel] boarding house. **-5.** [hospital] hospital. **-6.** [permiso para extranjeros] residence permit. **-7.** [periodo de formación] residency.
residencial *adj* residential.
residente *adj, m y f* resident.
residir *vi* **-1.** [vivir] to reside. **-2.** [radicar]: ~ **en** to lie in, to reside in.
residual *adj* (*gen pl*) residual; **aguas** ~**es** sewage (*U*).
residuo *m* **-1.** (*gen pl*) [material inservible] waste; QUÍM residue; ~**s nucleares** nuclear waste (*U*). **-2.** [restos] leftovers (*pl*).
resienta *etc* → **resentirse**.
resignación *f* resignation.
resignarse *vpr*: ~ (**a hacer algo**) to resign o.s. (to doing sthg).
resina *f* resin.
resinoso, **-sa** *adj* resinous.
resintiera *etc* → **resentirse**.
resistencia *f* **-1.** [gen, ELECTR & POLÍT] resistance; **ofrecer** ~ to put up resistance; ~ **pasiva** passive resistance. **-2.** [de puente, cimientos] strength. **-3.** [física - para correr etc] stamina.
resistente *adj* [gen] tough, strong; ~ **al calor** heat-resistant.
resistir ◇ *vt* **-1.** [dolor, peso, críticas] to withstand. **-2.** [tentación, impulso, deseo] to resist. **-3.** [tolerar] to tolerate, to stand; **no lo resisto más, me voy** I can't stand it any longer, I'm off.
◇ *vi* **-1.** [ejército, ciudad etc]: ~ (**a algo/a alguien**) to resist (sthg/sb). **-2.** [corredor etc] to keep going; ~ **a algo** to stand up to sthg, to withstand sthg. **-3.** [mesa, dique etc]

to take the strain; ~ **a algo** to withstand sthg. **-4.** [mostrarse firme - ante tentaciones etc] to resist (it); ~ **a algo** to resist sthg.
◆ **resistirse** *vpr*: ~**se (a algo)** to resist (sthg); ~**se a hacer algo** to refuse to do sthg; **me resisto a creerlo** I refuse to believe it; **no hay hombre que se le resista** no man can resist her; **se le resisten las matemáticas** she just can't get the hang of maths.

resma *f* ream.

resol *m* (sun's) glare.

resollar [23] *vi* to gasp (for breath); [jadear] to pant.

resolución *f* **-1.** [solución - de una crisis] resolution; [- de un crimen] solution. **-2.** [firmeza] determination. **-3.** [decisión] decision; DER ruling; **tomar una** ~ to take a decision. **-4.** [de Naciones Unidas etc] resolution.

resoluto, -ta *adj* resolute.

resolver [24] *vt* **-1.** [solucionar - duda, crisis] to resolve; [- problema, caso] to solve. **-2.** [decidir]: ~ **hacer algo** to decide to do sthg. **-3.** [partido, disputa, conflicto] to settle.
◆ **resolverse** *vpr* **-1.** [solucionarse - duda, crisis] to be resolved; [- problema, caso] to be solved. **-2.** [decidirse]: ~**se a hacer algo** to decide to do sthg. **-3.** [en disputa, conflicto]: ~**se en** to come to nothing more than.

resonancia *f* **-1.** [gen & FÍS] resonance (*U*); ~ **magnética** MED magnetic resonance. **-2.** *fig* [importancia] repercussions (*pl*).

resonante *adj* resounding; FÍS resonant; *fig* important.

resonar [23] *vi* to resound, to echo.

resoplar *vi* [de cansancio] to pant; [de enfado] to snort.

resoplido *m* [por cansancio] pant; [por enfado] snort.

resorte *m* spring; *fig* means (*pl*); **tocar todos los** ~**s** to pull out all the stops.

respaldar *vt* to back, to support.
◆ **respaldarse** *vpr* **-1.** [en asiento] to lean back. **-2.** *fig* [apoyarse]: ~**se en** to fall back on.

respaldo *m* **-1.** [de asiento] back. **-2.** *fig* [apoyo] backing, support.

respectar *v impers*: **por lo que respecta a alguien/a algo, en lo que respecta a alguien/a algo** as far as sb/sthg is concerned.

respectivo, -va *adj* respective; **en lo** ~ **a** with regard to.

respecto *m*: **al** ~**, a este** ~ in this respect; **no sé nada al** ~ I don't know anything about it; **(con)** ~ **a,** ~ **de** regarding.

respetable *adj* [venerable] respectable.

respetar *vt* **-1.** [gen] to respect; [la palabra] to honour; **hacerse** ~ to make o.s. respected. **-2.** [no destruir] to spare; **"respetad las plantas"** "keep off the flowerbeds".

respeto *m*: ~ **(a ○ por)** respect (for); **es una falta de** ~ it shows a lack of respect; **faltar al** ~ **a alguien** to be disrespectful to sb; **por** ~ **a** out of consideration for; **presentar uno sus** ~**s a alguien** to pay one's respects to sb.

respetuoso, -sa *adj*: ~ **(con)** respectful (of).

respingar [16] *vi* [protestar] to make a fuss, to complain.

respingo *m* **-1.** [movimiento] start, jump; **dar un** ~ to start. **-2.** [contestación] shrug (of annoyance).

respingón, -ona *adj* snub.

respiración *f* breathing; MED respiration; ~ **artificial** ○ **asistida** artificial respiration; **quedarse sin** ~ [asombrado] to be stunned.

respiradero *m* [hueco] vent; [conducto] ventilation shaft.

respirar ◇ *vt* **-1.** [aire] to breathe. **-2.** *fig* [bondad etc] to exude. ◇ *vi* to breathe; *fig* [sentir alivio] to breathe again; **no dejar** ~ **a alguien** *fig* not to allow sb a moment's peace; **sin** ~ [sin descanso] without a break; [atentamente] with great attention.

respiratorio, -ria *adj* respiratory.

respiro *m* **-1.** [descanso] rest. **-2.** [alivio] relief, respite.

resplandecer [30] *vi* **-1.** [brillar] to shine. **-2.** *fig* [destacar] to shine, to stand out; ~ **de algo** to shine with sthg.

resplandeciente *adj* shining; [sonrisa] beaming; [época] glittering; [vestimenta, color] resplendent.

resplandor *m* **-1.** [luz] brightness; [de fuego] glow. **-2.** [brillo] gleam.

responder ◇ *vt* to answer. ◇ *vi* **-1.** [contestar]: ~ **(a algo)** to answer (sthg). **-2.** [reaccionar]: ~ **(a)** to respond (to). **-3.** [responsabilizarse]: ~ **de algo/por alguien** to answer for sthg/for sb. **-4.** [replicar] to answer back. **-5.** [corresponder]: ~ **a** to correspond to; **las medidas responden a la crisis** the measures are in keeping with the nature of the crisis.

respondón, -ona ◇ *adj* insolent. ◇ *m y f* insolent person.

responsabilidad *f* responsibility; DER liability; **de** ~ responsible; **tener la** ~ **de algo** to be responsible for sthg; ~ **civil/penal** DER civil/criminal liability; ~ **limitada** limited liability.

responsabilizar [13] vt: ~ **a alguien (de algo)** to hold sb responsible (for sthg).
◆ **responsabilizarse** vpr: ~**se (de)** to accept responsibility (for).

responsable ◇ adj responsible; ~ **de** responsible for; **hacerse ~ de** [gen] to take responsibility for; [atentado, secuestro] to claim responsibility for. ◇ m y f -**1.** [culpable] person responsible. -**2.** [encargado] person in charge.

responso m prayer for the dead.

respuesta f -**1.** [gen] answer, reply; [en exámenes] answer; **en ~ a** in reply to. -**2.** fig [reacción] response.

resquebrajamiento m, **resquebrajadura** f crack.

resquebrajar vt to crack.
◆ **resquebrajarse** vpr to crack.

resquemor m resentment, bitterness.

resquicio m -**1.** [abertura] chink; [grieta] crack. -**2.** fig [pizca] glimmer.

resta f MAT subtraction.

restablecer [30] vt to reestablish, to restore.
◆ **restablecerse** vpr -**1.** [curarse] ~**se (de)** to recover (from). -**2.** [reimplantarse] to be reestablished.

restablecimiento m -**1.** [reimplantación] restoration, reestablishment. -**2.** [cura] recovery.

restallar vt & vi [látigo] to crack; [lengua] to click.

restante adj remaining; **lo ~** the rest.

restar ◇ vt -**1.** MAT to subtract; ~ **una cantidad de otra** to subtract one figure from another. -**2.** [disminuir]: ~ **importancia a algo/méritos a alguien** to play down the importance of sthg/sb's qualities. ◇ vi [faltar] to be left.

restauración f restoration.

restaurador, -ra m y f restorer.

restaurante m restaurant.

restaurar vt to restore.

restitución f return.

restituir [51] vt -**1.** [devolver - objeto] to return; [- salud] to restore. -**2.** [restaurar] to restore.
◆ **restituirse a** vpr [regresar] to return to.

resto m: **el ~** [gen] the rest; MAT the remainder; **echar el ~** fig to do one's utmost.
◆ **restos** mpl -**1.** [sobras] leftovers. -**2.** [cadáver] remains; ~**s mortales** mortal remains. -**3.** [ruinas] ruins.

restregar [35] vt to rub hard; [para limpiar] to scrub.
◆ **restregarse** vpr [frotarse] to rub.

restricción f restriction.

restrictivo, -va adj restrictive.

restringir [15] vt to limit, to restrict.

resucitar ◇ vt [person] to bring back to life, to resurrect; [costumbre] to revive, to resurrect. ◇ vi [persona] to rise from the dead.

resuella etc → **resollar**.

resuello m gasp, gasping (U); [jadeo] pant, panting (U).

resuelto, -ta ◇ pp → **resolver**. ◇ adj -**1.** [solucionado] solved. -**2.** [decidido] determined; **estar ~ a hacer algo** to be determined to do sthg.

resuelva etc → **resolver**.

resuena etc → **resonar**.

resulta f: **de ~s de** as a result of.

resultado m result; **dar ~** to work (out), to have the desired effect; **dar buen/mal ~** to be a success/failure.

resultante adj & f resultant.

resultar ◇ vi -**1.** [acabar siendo]: ~ **(ser)** to turn out (to be); **resultó ileso** he was uninjured; **nuestro equipo resultó vencedor** our team came out on top. -**2.** [salir bien] to work (out), to be a success. -**3.** [originarse]: ~ **de** to come of, to result from. -**4.** [ser] to be; **resulta sorprendente** it's surprising; **me resultó imposible terminar antes** I was unable to finish earlier. -**5.** [venir a costar]: ~ **a** to come to, to cost.
◇ v impers [suceder]: ~ **que** to turn out that; **ahora resulta que no quiere alquilarlo** now it seems that she doesn't want to rent it.

resultón, -ona adj fam who knows how to make the most of his/her assets.

resumen m summary; **en ~** in short.

resumir vt to summarize; [discurso] to sum up.
◆ **resumirse en** vpr -**1.** [sintetizarse en] to be able to be summed up in. -**2.** [reducirse a] to boil down to.

resurgimiento m resurgence.

resurgir [15] vi to undergo a resurgence, to be revived.

resurrección f resurrection.

retablo m altarpiece.

retaco m despec o hum shorty, midget.

retaguardia f [tropa] rearguard; [territorio] rear.

retahíla f string, series.

retal m remnant.

retama f broom.

retar vt: ~ **(a)** to challenge (to).

retardado, -da adj delayed.

retardar vt [retrasar] to delay; [frenar] to hold up, to slow down.

retazo *m* remnant; *fig* fragment.

RETD (*abrev de* **Red Especial de Transmisión de Datos**) *f special data transmission network*.

rete *adv Amer fam* very.

retén *m* reserve.

retención *f* **-1.** [en comisaría] detention. **-2.** [en el sueldo] deduction. **-3.** (*gen pl*) [de tráfico] hold-up. **-4.** MED retention.

retener [72] *vt* **-1.** [detener] to hold back; [en comisaría] to detain. **-2.** [contener - impulso, ira] to hold back, to restrain; [- aliento] to hold. **-3.** [conservar] to retain. **-4.** [quedarse con] to hold on to, to keep. **-5.** [memorizar] to remember. **-6.** [deducir del sueldo] to deduct.

reticencia *f* **-1.** [resistencia] unwillingness. **-2.** [insinuación] insinuation, innuendo (*U*).

reticente *adj* **-1.** [reacio] unwilling, reluctant. **-2.** [con insinuaciones] full of insinuation.

reticular *adj* ANAT reticular.

retículo *m* reticle.

retiene → retener.

retina *f* retina.

retintín *m* **-1.** [ironía] sarcastic tone; **con ~** sarcastically. **-2.** [tintineo] ringing.

retirado, -da ◇ *adj* **-1.** [jubilado] retired. **-2.** [solitario, alejado] isolated, secluded. ◇ *m y f* [jubilado] retired person.

◆ **retirada** *f* **-1.** MIL retreat; **batirse en retirada** to beat a retreat; **cubrir la retirada** MIL to cover the retreat; *fig* [tomar precauciones] not to burn one's bridges, to cover o.s. **-2.** [de fondos, moneda, carné] withdrawal. **-3.** [de competición, actividad] withdrawal.

retirar *vt* **-1.** [quitar - gen] to remove; [- dinero, moneda, carné] to withdraw; [- nieve] to clear; [- mano] to withdraw. **-2.** [jubilar - a deportista] to force to retire; [- a empleado] to retire. **-3.** [retractarse de] to take back.

◆ **retirarse** *vpr* **-1.** [gen] to retire. **-2.** [de competición, elecciones] to withdraw; [de reunión] to leave. **-3.** [de campo de batalla] to retreat. **-4.** [apartarse] to move away.

retiro *m* **-1.** [jubilación] retirement; [pensión] pension. **-2.** [refugio, ejercicio] retreat.

reto *m* challenge.

retocar [10] *vt* to touch up; [prenda de vestir] to alter.

retoce *etc* → retozar.

retomar *vt* to take up again.

retoño *m* BOT sprout, shoot; *fig* offspring (*U*).

retoque ◇ *v* → retocar. ◇ *m* touching-up (*U*); [de prenda de vestir] alteration; **dar los** últimos **~s a** to put the finishing touches to.

retorcer [41] *vt* **-1.** [torcer - brazo, alambre] to twist; [- ropa, cuello] to wring. **-2.** *fig* [tergiversar] to twist.

◆ **retorcerse** *vpr* [contraerse]: **~se (de)** [risa] to double up (with); [dolor] to writhe about (in).

retorcido, -da *adj* **-1.** [torcido - brazo, alambre] twisted; [- ropa] wrung out. **-2.** *fig* [rebuscado] complicated, involved. **-3.** *fig* [malintencionado] twisted, warped.

retórico, -ca ◇ *adj* rhetorical. ◇ *m y f* [persona] rhetorician.

◆ **retórica** *f lit* & *fig* [discurso] rhetoric.

retornable *adj* returnable; **no ~** nonreturnable.

retornar *vt* & *vi* to return.

retorno *m* [gen & INFORM] return; **~ de carro** carriage return.

retortijón *m* (*gen pl*) stomach cramp.

retozar [13] *vi* to gambol, to frolic; [amantes] to romp about.

retozón, -ona *adj* playful.

retractación *f* retraction.

retractarse *vpr* [de una promesa] to go back on one's word; [de una opinión] to take back what one has said; **~ de** [lo dicho] to retract, to take back.

retráctil *adj* retractable; [uña] retractile.

retraer [73] *vt* **-1.** [encoger] to retract. **-2.** [disuadir]: **~ a alguien de hacer algo** to persuade sb not to do sthg.

◆ **retraerse** *vpr* **-1.** [encogerse] to retract. **-2.** [retirarse]: **~se de** to withdraw from. **-3.** [retroceder] to withdraw, to retreat.

retraído, -da *adj* withdrawn, retiring.

retraimiento *m* shyness, reserve.

retransmisión *f* broadcast; **~ en directo/diferido** live/recorded broadcast.

retransmitir *vt* to broadcast.

retrasado, -da ◇ *adj* **-1.** [país, industria] backward; [reloj] slow; [tren] late, delayed. **-2.** [en el pago, los estudios] behind. **-3.** MED retarded, backward. ◇ *m y f*: **~ (mental)** mentally retarded person.

retrasar ◇ *vt* **-1.** [aplazar] to postpone. **-2.** [demorar] to delay, to hold up. **-3.** [hacer más lento] to slow down, to hold up. **-4.** [en el pago, los estudios] to set back. **-5.** [reloj] to put back. ◇ *vi* [reloj] to be slow.

◆ **retrasarse** *vpr* **-1.** [llegar tarde] to be late. **-2.** [quedarse atrás] to fall behind. **-3.** [aplazarse] to be put off. **-4.** [reloj] to lose time.

retraso *m* **-1.** [por llegar tarde] delay; **llegar con (15 minutos de) ~** to be (15 minutes)

late. **-2.** [por sobrepasar una fecha] time behind schedule; **llevo en mi trabajo un** ~ **de
20 páginas** I'm 20 pages behind with my
work. **-3.** [subdesarrollo] backwardness; **llevar (siglos de)** ~ to be (centuries) behind.
-4. MED mental deficiency.

retratar *vt* **-1.** [fotografiar] to photograph.
-2. [dibujar] to do a portrait of. **-3.** *fig* [des-
cribir] to portray.
◆ **retratarse** *vpr fig* [describirse] to describe
o.s.

retratista *m y f* ARTE portraitist; FOT (portrait) photographer.

retrato *m* **-1.** [dibujo] portrait; [fotografía]
photograph; ~ **robot** photofit picture; **ser
el vivo** ~ **de alguien** to be the spitting
image of sb. **-2.** *fig* [reflejo] portrayal.

retreta *f* retreat.

retrete *m* toilet.

retribución *f* [pago] payment; [recompensa]
reward.

retribuir [51] *vt* [pagar] to pay; [recompensar]
to reward.

retro *adj* reactionary.

retroactividad *f* [de ley] retroactivity; [del
pago] backdating.

retroactivo, -va *adj* [ley] retrospective,
retroactive; [pago] backdated.

retroceder *vi* to go back; *fig* to back
down; **no retrocederé ante nada** there's no
stopping me now.

retroceso *m* **-1.** [regresión - gen] backward
movement; [- en negociaciones] setback;
[- en la economía] recession. **-2.** [en enferme-
dad] deterioration.

retrógrado, -da *adj, m y f* reactionary.

retropropulsión *f* jet propulsion.

retroproyector *m* overhead projector.

retrospección *f* retrospection.

retrospectivo, -va *adj* retrospective; **echar
una mirada retrospectiva a** to look back
over.
◆ **retrospectiva** *f* retrospective.

retrotraer [73] *vt* [relato] to set in the past.

retrovisor *m* rear-view mirror.

retuerce *etc* → retorcer.

retumbante *adj* resounding.

retumbar *vi* **-1.** [resonar] to resound. **-2.**
[hacer ruido] to thunder, to boom.

retuviera *etc* → retener.

reuma, reúma *m o f* rheumatism.

reumático, -ca *adj, m y f* rheumatic.

reumatismo *m* rheumatism.

reumatología *f* rheumatology.

reumatólogo, -ga *m y f* rheumatologist.

reunificación *f* reunification.

reunificar [10] *vt* to reunify.
◆ **reunificarse** *vpr* to reunify.

reunión *f* meeting.

reunir *vt* **-1.** [público, accionistas etc] to
bring together. **-2.** [objetos, textos etc] to
collect, to bring together; [fondos] to raise.
-3. [requisitos] to meet; [cualidades] to possess, to combine. **-4.** [volver a unir] to put
back together.
◆ **reunirse** *vpr* [congregarse] to meet.

reutilizar [13] *vt* to reuse.

reválida *f* final exam.

revalidar *vt* to confirm.

revalorar = revalorizar.

revalorización *f* **-1.** [aumento del valor] appreciation; [de moneda] revaluation. **-2.** [res-
titución del valor] favourable reassessment.

revalorizar [13], **revalorar** *vt* **-1.** [aumentar
el valor] to increase the value of; [moneda]
to revalue. **-2.** [restituir el valor] to reassess
in a favourable light.
◆ **revalorizarse** *vpr* **-1.** [aumentar de valor]
to appreciate; [moneda] to be revalued. **-2.**
[recuperar valor] to be reassessed favourably.

revancha *f* **-1.** [venganza] revenge; **tomarse
la** ~ to take revenge. **-2.** DEP return match.

revanchismo *m* vengefulness.

revelación *f* revelation.

revelado *m* FOT developing.

revelador, -ra *adj* [aclarador] revealing.
◆ **revelador** *m* FOT developer.

revelar *vt* **-1.** [declarar] to reveal. **-2.** [evi-
denciar] to show. **-3.** FOT to develop.
◆ **revelarse** *vpr*: ~**se como** to show o.s.
to be.

revendedor, -ra *m y f* ticket tout.

revender *vt* to resell; [entradas] to tout.

reventa *f* resale; [de entradas] touting.

reventado, -da *adj fam* shattered,
whacked.

reventar [19] ◇ *vt* **-1.** [explotar] to burst.
-2. [echar abajo] to break down; [con explosi-
vos] to blow up. **-3.** [hacer fracasar] to ruin,
to spoil. **-4.** *fam* [fastidiar] to annoy. ◇ *vi*
-1. [explotar] to burst. **-2.** [estar lleno]: ~ **de**
to be bursting with. **-3.** [desear mucho]: ~
por hacer algo to be bursting to do sthg.
-4. *fam fig* [perder los nervios]: ~ **(de)** to explode (with).
◆ **reventarse** *vpr* **-1.** [explotar] to explode;
[rueda] to burst. **-2.** *fam* [cansarse] to get
whacked, to tire o.s. to death.

reventón *m* **-1.** [pinchazo] blowout, flat
Am, puncture *Br*. **-2.** [estallido] burst.

reverberación *f* [de sonido] reverberation;
[de luz, calor] reflection.

reverberar vi [sonido] to reverberate; [luz, calor] to reflect.

reverdecer [30] vi -1. [campos etc] to become green again. -2. fig [amor] to revive.

reverencia f -1. [respeto] reverence. -2. [saludo - inclinación] bow; [- flexión de piernas] curtsy.

reverenciar [8] vt to revere.

reverendo, -da adj reverend.
◆ **reverendo** m reverend.

reverente adj reverent.

reversibilidad f reversibility.

reversible adj reversible.

reverso m back, other side; **ser el ~ de la medalla** to be the other side of the coin.

revertir [27] vi -1. [volver, devolver] to revert. -2. [resultar]: **~ en** to result in; **~ en beneficio/perjuicio de** to be to the advantage/detriment of.

revés m -1. [parte opuesta - de papel, mano] back; [- de tela] other ○ wrong side; **al ~** [en sentido contrario] the wrong way round; [en forma opuesta] the other way round; **del ~** [lo de detrás, delante] the wrong way round, back to front; [lo de dentro, fuera] inside out; [lo de arriba, abajo] upside down. -2. [bofetada] slap. -3. DEP backhand. -4. [contratiempo] setback, blow.

revestimiento m covering.

revestir [26] vt -1. [recubrir]: **~ (de)** [gen] to cover (with); [pintura] to coat (with); [forro] to line (with). -2. [poseer - solemnidad, gravedad etc] to take on, to have. -3. fig [aparentar] to disguise, to cover up.
◆ **revestirse** vpr: **~se de** [valor, paciencia] to arm o.s. with.

revienta etc → reventar.

revierta, revirtiera etc → revertir.

revisar vt -1. [repasar] to go over again. -2. [inspeccionar] to inspect; [cuentas] to audit. -3. [modificar] to revise.

revisión f -1. [repaso] revision. -2. [inspección] inspection; **~ de cuentas** audit; **~ médica** check-up. -3. [modificación] amendment. -4. [AUTOM - puesta a punto] service; [- anual] ≃ MOT (test).

revisionismo m revisionism.

revisor, -ra m y f [en tren] ticket inspector; [en autobús] (bus) conductor.

revista ○ v → revestir. ○ f -1. [publicación] magazine; **~ del corazón** gossip magazine. -2. [sección de periódico] section, review. -3. [espectáculo teatral] revue. -4. [inspección] inspection; **pasar ~ a** MIL to inspect, to review; [examinar] to examine.

revistero m [mueble] magazine rack.

revistiera etc → revestir.

revitalizar [13] vt to revitalize.

revival m inv revival.

revivificar [10] vt to revive.

revivir ○ vi to revive. ○ vt [recordar] to revive memories of.

revocable adj revocable.

revocación f revocation.

revocar [10] vt -1. [gen] to revoke. -2. CONSTR to plaster.

revolcar [36] vt to throw to the ground, to upend.
◆ **revolcarse** vpr to roll about.

revolcón m tumble, fall.

revolotear vi to flutter (about).

revoloteo m fluttering (about).

revoltijo, revoltillo m jumble.

revoltoso, -sa ○ adj rebellious. ○ m y f troublemaker.

revolución f revolution.

revolucionar vt -1. [crear conflicto] to cause a stir in. -2. [transformar] to revolutionize.

revolucionario, -ria adj, m y f revolutionary.

revolver [24] vt -1. [dar vueltas] to turn around; [líquido] to stir. -2. [mezclar] to mix; [ensalada] to toss. -3. [desorganizar] to turn upside down, to mess up; [cajones] to turn out. -4. [irritar] to upset; **me revuelve el estómago** ○ **las tripas** it makes my stomach turn.
◆ **revolver en** vi [cajones etc] to rummage around in.
◆ **revolverse** vpr -1. [moverse] to move around; [en la cama] to toss and turn. -2. [volverse] to turn around; **~se contra** to turn against. -3. [el mar] to become rough; [el tiempo] to turn stormy.

revólver m revolver.

revoque etc → revocar.

revuelca → revolcar.

revuelco m fall, tumble.

revuelo m [agitación] commotion; **armar un gran ~** to cause a great stir.

revuelque → revolcar.

revuelto, -ta ○ pp → revolver. ○ adj -1. [desordenado] upside down, in a mess. -2. [alborotado - época etc] troubled, turbulent. -3. [clima] unsettled. -4. [aguas] choppy, rough.
◆ **revuelto** m CULIN scrambled eggs (pl).
◆ **revuelta** f -1. [disturbio] riot, revolt. -2. [curva] bend.

revuelva etc → revolver.

revulsión f revulsion.

revulsivo, -va adj fig stimulating, revitalizing.

revulsivo, -va *adj fig* stimulating, revitalizing.
◆ **revulsivo** *m fig* kick-start, stimulus.
rey *m* king.
◆ **Reyes** *mpl*: los Reyes the King and Queen.
◆ **Reyes Católicos** *mpl*: los Reyes Católicos *the Spanish Catholic monarchs Ferdinand V and Isabella.*
◆ **Reyes Magos** *mpl*: los Reyes Magos the Three Kings, the Three Wise Men.

REYES MAGOS:
On 6th January Spanish children traditionally receive presents, supposedly brought by the Three Wise Men. Tradition has it that children should leave a few crumbs of bread in their slippers to feed the camels on which the Wise Men ride. This custom is still very much alive, although some people now welcome the Three Wise Men on Christmas Day

---

reyerta *f* fight, brawl.
rezagado, -da ◇ *adj*: ir ~ to lag behind. ◇ *m y f* straggler.
rezagarse [16] *vpr* to lag ○ fall behind.
rezar [13] ◇ *vt* [oración] to say. ◇ *vi* **-1.** [orar]: ~ **(a)** to pray (to). **-2.** [decir] to read, to say. **-3.** [corresponderse]: ~ **con** to have to do with.
rezo *m* **-1.** [acción] praying. **-2.** [oración] prayer.
rezongar [16] *vi* to grumble, to moan.
rezumar ◇ *vt* **-1.** [transpirar] to ooze. **-2.** *fig* [manifestar] to be overflowing with. ◇ *vi* to ooze ○ seep out.
RF (*abrev de* **radiofrecuencia**) *f* rf.
RFA (*abrev de* **República Federal de Alemania**) *f* FRG.
RFEF (*abrev de* **Real Federación Española de Fútbol**) *f* Spanish football federation.
RH (*abrev de* **recursos humanos**) *mpl* personnel.
Rhin *m*: el (río) ~ the Rhine.
ría ◇ *v* → reír. ◇ *f* estuary.
riachuelo *m* brook, stream.
riada *f lit* & *fig* flood.
ribeiro *m wine from the province of Orense, Spain.*
ribera *f* [del río] bank; [del mar] shore.
ribereño, -ña *adj* [de río] riverside; [de mar] coastal.
ribete *m* edging (*U*), trimming (*U*); *fig* touch, nuance.
ribeteado, -da *adj* edged, trimmed.
ribetear *vt* to edge, to trim.

ribonucleico → ácido.
ricamente *adv*: tan ~ quite happily.
rice *etc* → rizar.
ricino *m* [planta] castor oil plant.
rico, -ca ◇ *adj* **-1.** [gen] rich. **-2.** [abundante]: ~ **(en)** rich (in). **-3.** [sabroso] delicious. **-4.** [simpático] cute. **-5.** *fam* [apelativo]: ¡oye ~! hey, sunshine! ◇ *m y f* rich person; los ~s the rich; los nuevos ~s the nouveaux riches.
rictus *m inv* **-1.** [de ironía] smirk. **-2.** [de desprecio] sneer. **-3.** [de dolor] wince.
ricura *f* [persona] delight, lovely person.
ridiculez *f* **-1.** [payasada] silly thing, nonsense (*U*). **-2.** [nimiedad] trifle; cuesta una ~ it costs next to nothing.
ridiculizar [13] *vt* to ridicule.
ridículo, -la *adj* ridiculous; [precio, suma] laughable, derisory.
◆ **ridículo** *m* ridicule; hacer el ~ to make a fool of o.s.; poner ○ dejar en ~ a alguien to make sb look stupid; quedar en ~ to look like a fool.
ríe → reír.
riega → regar.
riego *m* [de campo] irrigation; [de jardín] watering; ~ **sanguíneo** (blood) circulation.
riegue → regar.
riel *m* **-1.** [de vía] rail. **-2.** [de cortina] (curtain) rail.
rienda *f* **-1.** [de caballería] rein; dar ~ suelta a *fig* to give free rein to. **-2.** [moderación] restraint.
◆ **riendas** *fpl fig* [dirección] reins; aflojar las ~s to ease up; llevar ○ tener las ~s to hold the reins, to be in control.
riera *etc* → reír.
riesgo *m* risk; a todo ~ [seguro, póliza] comprehensive; correr (el) ~ de to run the risk of.
rifa *f* raffle.
rifar *vt* to raffle.
◆ **rifarse** *vpr fig* to fight over, to contest.
rifle *m* rifle.
Riga Riga.
rige → regir.
rigidez *f* **-1.** [de un cuerpo, objeto etc] rigidity. **-2.** [del rostro] stoniness. **-3.** *fig* [severidad] strictness, harshness.
rígido, -da *adj* **-1.** [cuerpo, objeto etc] rigid. **-2.** [rostro] stony. **-3.** [severo - normas etc] harsh; [- carácter] inflexible.
rigiera *etc* → regir.
rigor *m* **-1.** [severidad] strictness. **-2.** [exactitud] accuracy, rigour; en ~ strictly (speaking). **-3.** [inclemencia] harshness.

◆ **de rigor** *loc adj* essential.

rigurosidad *f* **-1.** [severidad] strictness. **-2.** [exactitud] accuracy, rigour. **-3.** [inclemencia] harshness.

riguroso, -sa *adj* **-1.** [severo] strict. **-2.** [exacto] rigorous, disciplined. **-3.** [inclemente] harsh.

rija *etc* → regir.

rijoso, -sa *adj* **-1.** [pendenciero] always getting into fights. **-2.** [lujurioso] lustful.

rima *f* rhyme.

rimar *vt & vi* to rhyme.

rimbombante *adj* **-1.** [estilo, frases] pompous. **-2.** [desfile, fiesta etc] ostentatious.

rímel, rimmel *m* mascara.

Rimini Rimini.

rin *m Amer* **-1.** [ficha telefónica] telephone token. **-2.** [llanta] wheel rim.

rincón *m* corner (*inside*).

rinconera *f* corner piece.

rinda, rindiera *etc* → rendir.

ring (*pl* **rings**) *m* (boxing) ring.

rinitis *f inv* rhinitis.

rinoceronte *m* rhinoceros.

riña ◇ *v* → reñir. ◇ *f* [disputa] quarrel; [pelea] fight.

riñera *etc* → reñir.

riñón *m* kidney; ~ **artificial** kidney machine; **costar un** ~ *fig* to cost a packet; **tener el** ~ **bien cubierto** *fig* to be well-heeled.

◆ **riñones** *mpl* [región lumbar] lower back (*sg*).

riñonada *f* [región lumbar] lower back.

riñonera *f* [pequeño bolso] bum bag *Br*, fanny pack *Am*.

río ◇ *v* → reír. ◇ *m lit & fig* river; **ir** ~ **arriba/abajo** to go upstream/downstream; **a** ~ **revuelto, ganancia de pescadores** *proverb* it's an ill wind that blows nobody any good *proverb*; **cuando el** ~ **suena, agua lleva** *proverb* there's no smoke without fire *proverb*.

Río de Janeiro *m* Rio de Janeiro.

Río de la Plata *m* River Plate.

rioja *m* Rioja (wine).

riojano, -na *adj, m y f* Riojan.

rioplatense *adj* of/relating to the River Plate region.

RIP (*abrev de* **requiescat in pace**) RIP.

ripio *m* **-1.** LITER *word or phrase included to complete a rhyme.* **-2.** [relleno] padding (*U*). **-3.** [cascote] rubble (*U*).

riqueza *f* **-1.** [fortuna] wealth. **-2.** [abundancia] richness.

risa *f* laugh, laughter (*U*); **me da** ~ I find it funny; **¡qué** ~! how funny!; **de** ~ funny; **mondarse** ◇ **morirse** ◇ **partirse de** ~ to die of laughter; **se me escapó la** ~ I burst out laughing; **tomar algo a** ~ to take sthg as a joke.

risco *m* cliff, crag.

risible *adj* laughable.

risotada *f* guffaw.

ristra *f lit & fig* string.

ristre

◆ **en ristre** *loc adv* at the ready.

risueño, -ña *adj* **-1.** [alegre] smiling. **-2.** [próspero] sunny, promising.

rítmico, -ca *adj* rhythmic.

ritmo *m* **-1.** [gen] rhythm; [cardíaco] beat. **-2.** [velocidad] pace.

rito *m* **-1.** RELIG rite. **-2.** [costumbre] ritual.

ritual *adj & m* ritual.

rival *adj, m y f* rival.

rivalidad *f* rivalry.

rivalizar [13] *vi*: ~ **(con)** to compete (with).

rivera *f* brook, stream.

Riyadh Riyadh.

rizado, -da *adj* **-1.** [pelo] curly. **-2.** [mar] choppy.

◆ **rizado** *m* [en peluquería]: **hacerse un** ~ to have one's hair curled.

rizar [13] *vt* **-1.** [pelo] to curl. **-2.** [mar] to ripple.

◆ **rizarse** *vpr* [pelo] to curl.

rizo, -za *adj* **-1.** [pelo] curly. **-2.** [mar] choppy.

◆ **rizo** *m* **-1.** [de pelo] curl. **-2.** [del agua] ripple. **-3.** [de avión] loop. **-4.** [tela] towelling, terry. **-5.** *loc*: **rizar el** ~ to split hairs.

Rmo. (*abrev de* **Reverendísimo**) Rt Revd.

RNE (*abrev de* **Radio Nacional de España**) *f Spanish national radio station.*

RO (*abrev de* **Real Orden**) *f* royal decree.

roast-beef [ros'ßif] (*pl* **roast-beefs**), **rosbif** (*pl* **rosbifs**) *m* roast beef.

róbalo, robalo *m* sea bass.

robar *vt* **-1.** [gen] to steal; [casa] to burgle; ~ **a alguien** to rob sb. **-2.** [en naipes] to draw. **-3.** [cobrar caro] to rob.

roble *m* **-1.** BOT oak. **-2.** *fig* [persona] strong person.

robledal, robledo *m* oak wood ◇ grove.

robo *m* **-1.** [delito] robbery, theft; [en casa] burglary; ~ **a mano armada** armed robbery; **ser un** ~ [precios etc] to be daylight robbery. **-2.** [cosa robada] stolen goods (*pl*).

robot (*pl* **robots**) *m* [gen & INFORM] robot.

◆ **robot de cocina** *m* food processor.

robótica f robotics (U).

robotización f automation.

robotizar [13] vt to automate.

robustecer [30] vt to strengthen.

◆ **robustecerse** vpr to get stronger.

robustez f robustness.

robusto, -ta adj robust.

roca f rock.

rocalla f rubble.

rocambolesco, -ca adj ludicrous.

roce ◇ v → rozar. ◇ m **-1.** [rozamiento - gen] rub, rubbing (U); [- suave] brush, brushing (U); FÍS friction. **-2.** [desgaste] wear. **-3.** [rasguño - en piel] graze; [- en zapato, puerta] scuffmark; [- en metal] scratch. **-4.** [trato] close contact. **-5.** [desavenencia] brush.

rociada f **-1.** [rocío] dew. **-2.** [aspersión] sprinkling. **-3.** [de insultos, perdigones etc] shower.

rociar [9] ◇ vt **-1.** [arrojar gotas] to sprinkle; [con espray] to spray. **-2.** [arrojar cosas]: ~ algo (de) to shower sthg (with). ◇ v impers [caer rocío]: **roció anoche** a dew fell last night.

rocín m nag.

rocío m dew.

rock, rock and roll m inv **-1.** [baile] rock and roll. **-2.** [estilo] rock; [de los 50] rock and roll.

rockero, -ra, roquero, -ra ◇ adj rock (antes de sust). ◇ m y f **-1.** [músico] rock musician. **-2.** [fan] rock fan.

rococó adj inv & m rococo.

rocoso, -sa adj rocky.

roda f NÁUT stem.

rodaballo m turbot.

rodado, -da adj **-1.** [piedra] rounded. **-2.** [tráfico] road (antes de sust). **-3.** loc: **estar muy** ~ [persona] to be very experienced; **venir** ~ **para** to be the perfect opportunity to.

◆ **rodada** f tyre track.

rodaja f slice; **en** ~**s** sliced.

rodaje m **-1.** [filmación] shooting. **-2.** [de motor] running-in. **-3.** [experiencia] experience.

Ródano m: **el** ~ the (River) Rhône.

rodapié m skirting board.

rodar [23] ◇ vi **-1.** [deslizar] to roll. **-2.** [circular] to travel, to go. **-3.** [girar] to turn. **-4.** [caer]: ~ **(por)** to tumble (down). **-5.** [ir de un lado a otro] to go around. **-6.** CIN to shoot. ◇ vt **-1.** CIN to shoot. **-2.** [automóvil] to run in.

Rodas Rhodes.

rodear vt **-1.** [gen] to surround; **le rodeó el cuello con los brazos** she put her arms around his neck. **-2.** [dar la vuelta a] to go around. **-3.** [eludir] to skirt around.

◆ **rodearse** vpr: ~**se de** to surround o.s. with.

rodeo m **-1.** [camino largo] detour; **dar un** ~ to make a detour. **-2.** (gen pl) [evasiva] evasiveness (U); **andar** ○ **ir con** ~**s** to beat about the bush; **hablar sin** ~**s** to come straight to the point. **-3.** [reunión de ganado] rounding up. **-4.** [espectáculo] rodeo.

rodete m round pad.

rodilla f knee; **de** ~**s** on one's knees; **doblar** ○ **hincar la** ~ [arrodillarse] to go down on one knee; fig to bow (down), to humble o.s.; **hincarse de** ~**s** to kneel (down).

rodillera f **-1.** [protección] knee pad. **-2.** [remiendo] knee patch.

rodillo m [gen] roller; [para repostería] rolling pin.

rododendro m rhododendron.

rodrigón m stake, prop.

rodríguez m inv grass widower; **estar** ○ **quedarse de** ~ to be a grass widower.

RODRÍGUEZ:
'Rodríguez' is the name given to a man who stays working in town whilst his wife and children spend the summer holidays elsewhere

---

roedor, -ra adj ZOOL rodent (antes de sust).

◆ **roedor** m rodent.

roedura f **-1.** [acción] gnawing. **-2.** [señal] gnaw mark.

roer [69] vt **-1.** [con dientes] to gnaw (at). **-2.** fig [gastar] to eat away (at). **-3.** fig [atormentar] to nag ○ gnaw (at). **-4.** loc: **ser duro de** ~ to be a tough nut to crack.

rogar [39] vt [implorar] to beg; [pedir] to ask; ~ **a alguien que haga algo** to ask ○ beg sb to do sthg; **le ruego me perdone** I beg your pardon; **hacerse (de)** ~ to play hard to get; "**se ruega silencio**" "silence, please".

rogativa f (gen pl) rogation.

rogué etc → rogar.

roiga etc → roer.

rojez f **-1.** [cualidad] redness. **-2.** [roncha] (red) blotch.

rojizo, -za adj reddish.

rojo, -ja ◇ adj red; **ponerse** ~ [gen] to turn red; [ruborizarse] to blush. ◇ m y f POLÍT red.

◆ **rojo** m [color] red; **al** ~ **vivo** [en incandescencia] red hot; fig heated.

rol (pl **roles**) m **-1.** [papel] role. **-2.** NÁUT muster.

rollizo, **-za** *adj* chubby, plump.

rollo *m* **-1.** [cilindro] roll; ~ **de primavera** CULIN spring roll. **-2.** CIN roll. **-3.** *fam* [discurso]: **el** ~ **de costumbre** the same old story; **soltar el** ~ to go on and on; **tener mucho** ~ to witter on. **-4.** *fam* [embuste] tall story. **-5.** *fam* [pelmazo, pesadez] bore, drag. **-6.** *fam* [tema] stuff; **¿de qué va el** ~? what's it all about? **-7.** *fam* [relación] relationship; **tener buen/mal** ~ **(con alguien)** to get on/not to get on with sb. **-8.** *fam* [ambiente, tipo de vida] scene; **traerse un mal** ~ to be into a bad scene.

ROM (*abrev de* **read-only memory**) *f* ROM.

Roma Rome.

romance ◇ *adj* Romance. ◇ *m* **-1.** LING Romance language. **-2.** LITER romance. **-3.** [idilio] romance.

romancero *m* LITER collection of romances.

románico, **-ca** *adj* **-1.** ARQUIT & ARTE Romanesque. **-2.** LING Romance.

◆ **románico** *m*: **el (estilo)** ~ the Romanesque (style).

romanización *f* Romanization.

romanizar [13] *vt* to Romanize.

romano, **-na** ◇ *adj* Roman; RELIG Roman Catholic. ◇ *m y f* Roman.

romanticismo *m* **-1.** ARTE & LITER Romanticism. **-2.** [sentimentalismo] romanticism.

romántico, **-ca** *adj, m y f* **-1.** ARTE & LITER Romantic. **-2.** [sentimental] romantic.

romanza *f* MÚS ballad.

rombo *m* **-1.** GEOM rhombus. **-2.** IMPRENTA lozenge.

romeo *m fig person* very much in love.

romería *f* **-1.** [peregrinación] pilgrimage. **-2.** [fiesta] *open-air festivities to celebrate a religious event.* **-3.** *fig* [mucha gente] long line.

romero, **-ra** *m y f* [peregrino] pilgrim.

◆ **romero** *m* BOT rosemary.

romo, **-ma** *adj* **-1.** [sin filo] blunt. **-2.** [de nariz] snub-nosed.

rompecabezas *m inv* **-1.** [juego] jigsaw. **-2.** *fam* [problema] puzzle.

rompehielos *m inv* ice-breaker.

rompeolas *m inv* breakwater.

romper ◇ *vt* **-1.** [gen] to break; [hacer añicos] to smash; [rasgar] to tear. **-2.** [desgastar] to wear out. **-3.** [interrumpir - monotonía, silencio, hábito] to break; [- hilo del discurso] to break off; [- tradición] to put an end to, to stop. **-4.** [terminar - relaciones etc] to break off.

◇ *vi* **-1.** [terminar una relación]: ~ **(con alguien)** to break ○ split up (with sb). **-2.** [olas, el día] to break; [hostilidades] to break out; **al** ~ **el alba** ○ **día** at day break. **-3.**

[empezar]: ~ **a hacer algo** to suddenly start doing sthg; ~ **a llorar** to burst into tears; ~ **a reír** to burst out laughing. **-4.** *loc*: **de rompe y rasga** [persona] determined.

◆ **romperse** *vpr* **-1.** [partirse] to break; [rasgarse] to tear; **se ha roto una pierna** he has broken a leg. **-2.** [desgastarse] to wear out.

rompiente *m* reef, shoal.

rompimiento *m* breaking; [de relaciones] breaking-off.

ron *m* rum.

roncar [10] *vi* to snore.

roncha *f* red blotch.

ronco, **-ca** *adj* **-1.** [afónico] hoarse. **-2.** [bronco] harsh.

ronda *f* **-1.** [de vigilancia, visitas] rounds (*pl*); **hacer la** ~ to do one's rounds. **-2.** [carretera] ring road. **-3.** [avenida] avenue. **-4.** *fam* [de bebidas, en el juego etc] round.

rondalla *f* group of minstrels.

rondar ◇ *vt* **-1.** [vigilar] to patrol. **-2.** [estar próximo]: **me ronda un resfriado** I've got a cold coming on. **-3.** [rayar - edad] to be around. **-4.** [cortejar] to court. ◇ *vi* [merodear]: ~ **(por)** to wander ○ hang around.

rondín *m Amer* **-1.** [vigilante] watchman, guard. **-2.** [armónica] mouth organ.

ronque *etc* → **roncar**.

ronquear *vi* to be hoarse.

ronquera *f* hoarseness.

ronquido *m* snore, snoring (*U*).

ronroneante *adj* purring.

ronronear *vi* to purr.

ronroneo *m* purr, purring (*U*).

roña ◇ *adj fam* [tacaño] stingy, tight. ◇ *m y f fam* [tacaño] stingy person. ◇ *f* **-1.** [suciedad] filth, dirt. **-2.** *fam* [tacañería] stinginess. **-3.** VETER mange.

roñería *f fam* stinginess.

roñica *fam* ◇ *adj* stingy, tight. ◇ *m y f* stingy person.

roñoso, **-sa** ◇ *adj* **-1.** [sucio] dirty. **-2.** [tacaño] mean. ◇ *m y f* miser, mean person.

ropa *f* clothes (*pl*); **aligerarse de** ~ [semidesnudo] to strip half-naked; **ligero de** ~ scantily clad; ~ **blanca** linen; ~ **de abrigo** warm clothes (*pl*); ~ **de cama** bed linen; ~ **hecha** ready-to-wear clothes; ~ **interior** underwear; **lavar la** ~ **sucia en público** *fig* to wash one's dirty linen in public; **nadar y guardar la** ~ *fig* to cover one's back.

ropaje *m* robes (*pl*).

ropero *m* **-1.** [armario] wardrobe. **-2.** [habitación] walk-in wardrobe; TEATR cloakroom.

roque *m* [en ajedrez] castle; **estar/quedarse** ~ *fig* to be/fall fast asleep.

rublo

roquefort [roke'for] *m* Roquefort (cheese).

roquero = rockero.

rorro *m* baby.

rosa ◇ *f* [flor] rose; **estar (fresco) como una** ~ to be as fresh as a daisy. ◇ *m* [color] pink. ◇ *adj inv* [color] pink; **verlo todo de color (de)** ~ *fig* to see everything through rose-tinted spectacles.

◆ **rosa de los vientos** *f* NÁUT compass.

rosáceo, -a *adj* pinkish.

rosado, -da *adj* pink.

◆ **rosado** *m* → vino.

rosal *m* [arbusto] rose bush.

rosaleda *f* rose garden.

rosario *m* **-1.** RELIG rosary; **rezar el** ~ to say one's rosary. **-2.** [sarta] string. **-3.** *loc*: **acabar como el** ~ **de la aurora** to finish up badly.

rosbif = roast-beef.

rosca *f* **-1.** [de tornillo] thread. **-2.** [forma de anillo] ring; [- espiral] coil. **-3.** CULIN ring doughnut. **-4.** *loc*: **hacerle la** ~ **a alguien** to suck up to sb; **pasarse de** ~ [persona] to go over the top.

rosco *m* ring-shaped bread roll; **no comerse un** ~ *mfam* never to get off with anyone.

roscón *m* ring-shaped bread roll; ~ **de reyes** *roll eaten on 6th January*.

Roseau [ro'só] Roseau.

roseta *f* **-1.** [rubor] flush. **-2.** ARQUIT rosette. **-3.** [de regadera] nozzle.

◆ **rosetas** *fpl* [palomitas] popcorn (*U*).

rosetón *m* **-1.** [ventana] rose window. **-2.** [adorno] ceiling rose.

rosquete *adj Amer fam despec* queer.

rosquilla *f* ring doughnut; **venderse como** ~**s** *fam* to sell like hot cakes.

rostro *m* face; **tener (mucho)** ~ *fam fig* to have a lot of nerve.

rotación *f* **-1.** [giro] rotation; ~ **de cultivos** crop rotation. **-2.** [alternancia] rota; **por** ~ in turn.

rotativo, -va *adj* rotary, revolving.

◆ **rotativo** *m* newspaper.

◆ **rotativa** *f* rotary press.

rotatorio, -ria *adj* rotary, revolving.

roto, -ta ◇ *pp* → romper. ◇ *adj* **-1.** [gen] broken; [tela, papel] torn. **-2.** *fig* [deshecho - vida etc] destroyed; [- corazón] broken. **-3.** *fig* [exhausto] shattered. ◇ *m y f Amer* [trabajador] worker.

◆ **roto** *m* [en tela] tear, rip.

rotonda *f* **-1.** [plaza] circus. **-2.** [edificio] rotunda.

rotoso, -sa *adj Amer* ragged, in tatters.

Rotterdam Rotterdam.

rótula *f* kneecap.

rotulador *m* felt-tip pen; [fluorescente] marker pen.

rotular¹ *adj* kneecap (*antes de sust*).

rotular² *vt* **-1.** [con rotulador] to highlight. **-2.** [calle] to put up a sign on. **-3.** [carta, artículo] to head with fancy lettering. **-4.** [letrero] to letter.

rótulo *m* **-1.** [letrero] sign. **-2.** [encabezamiento] headline, title.

rotundidad *f* firmness, categorical nature.

rotundo, -da *adj* **-1.** [categórico - negativa, persona] categorical; [- lenguaje, estilo] emphatic, forceful. **-2.** [completo] total.

rotura *f* [gen] break, breaking (*U*); [de hueso] fracture; [en tela] rip, hole.

roturar *vt* to plough.

roulotte [ru'lot], **rulot** *f* caravan *Br*, trailer *Am*.

round [raund] (*pl* **rounds**) *m* DEP round.

roya → roer.

royalty [ro'jalti] (*pl* **royalties**) *m* royalty.

royera, royo *etc* → roer.

rozadura *f* **-1.** [señal] scratch, scrape. **-2.** [herida] graze.

rozamiento *m* **-1.** [fricción] rub, rubbing (*U*); FÍS friction (*U*). **-2.** *fig* [enfado] disagreement, friction (*U*).

rozar [13] *vt* **-1.** [gen] to rub; [suavemente] to brush; [suj: zapato] to graze. **-2.** [pasar cerca de] to skim, to shave. **-3.** *fig* [estar cerca de] to border on; **roza los cuarenta** he's almost forty.

◆ **rozar con** *vi* **-1.** [tocar] to brush against. **-2.** *fig* [relacionarse con] to touch on.

◆ **rozarse** *vpr* **-1.** [tocarse] to touch. **-2.** [pasar cerca] to brush past each other. **-3.** [herirse - rodilla etc] to graze. **-4.** *fig* [tener trato]: ~**se con** to rub shoulders with.

Rte. *abrev de* remitente.

RTVE (*abrev de* **Radiotelevisión Española**) *f Spanish state broadcasting company*.

rúa *f* street.

ruana *f Amer* poncho.

rubeola, rubéola *f* German measles (*U*).

rubí (*pl* **rubís** o **rubíes**) *m* ruby.

rubia → rubio.

rubicundo, -da *adj* ruddy.

rubio, -bia ◇ *adj* **-1.** [pelo, persona] blond (*f* blonde), fair. **-2.** [tabaco] Virginia (*antes de sust*). **-3.** [cerveza] lager (*antes de sust*). ◇ *m y f* [persona] blond (*f* blonde), fair-haired person.

◆ **rubia** *f* [moneda] *fam* peseta.

rublo *m* rouble.

rubor *m* **-1.** [vergüenza] embarrassment. **-2.** [sonrojo] blush.

ruborizar [13] *vt* [avergonzar] to embarrass.
◆ **ruborizarse** *vpr* to blush.

ruboroso, -sa *adj* blushing.

rúbrica *f* **-1.** [de firma] flourish. **-2.** [título] title. **-3.** [conclusión] final flourish; **poner** ~ **a algo** to complete sthg.

rubricar [10] *vt* **-1.** [firmar] to sign with a flourish. **-2.** *fig* [confirmar] to confirm. **-3.** *fig* [concluir] to complete.

rucio, -cia *adj* **-1.** [gris] grey. **-2.** *Amer fam* blond (*f* blonde).
◆ **rucio** *m* ass, donkey.

rudeza *f* **-1.** [tosquedad] roughness. **-2.** [grosería] coarseness.

rudimentario, -ria *adj* rudimentary.

rudimentos *mpl* rudiments.

rudo, -da *adj* **-1.** [tosco] rough. **-2.** [brusco] sharp, brusque. **-3.** [grosero] rude, coarse.

rueca *f* distaff.

rueda ◇ *v* → **rodar.** ◇ *f* **-1.** [pieza] wheel; ~ **delantera/trasera** front/rear wheel; ~ **de repuesto** spare wheel; **la** ~ **de la fortuna** ○ **del destino** *fig* the wheel of fortune; **comulgar con** ~**s de molino** *fig* to be very gullible; **ir sobre** ~**s** *fig* to go smoothly. **-2.** [corro] circle. **-3.** [rodaja] slice.
◆ **rueda de prensa** *f* press conference.
◆ **rueda de reconocimiento** *f* identification parade.

ruedo *m* **-1.** TAUROM bullring; *ver también* **tauromaquia. -2.** *fig* [mundo] sphere, world; **echarse al** ~ to enter the fray.

ruega *etc* → **rogar.**

ruego *m* request; ~**s y preguntas** any other business.

rufián *m* villain.

rufianesco, -ca *adj* villainous.
◆ **rufianesca** *f*: **la rufianesca** the underworld.

rugby *m* rugby.

rugido *m* [gen] roar; [de persona] bellow.

rugir [15] *vi* [gen] to roar; [persona] to bellow.

rugosidad *f* **-1.** [cualidad] roughness. **-2.** [arruga - de persona] wrinkle; [- de tejido] crinkle.

rugoso, -sa *adj* **-1.** [áspero - material, terreno] rough. **-2.** [con arrugas - rostro etc] wrinkled; [- tejido] crinkled.

Ruhr *m*: **el** ~ the (River) Ruhr.

ruibarbo *m* rhubarb.

ruido *m* **-1.** [gen] noise; [sonido] sound; ~ **de fondo** background noise; **mucho** ~ **y pocas nueces** much ado about nothing. **-2.**

fig [escándalo] row; **hacer** ○ **meter** ~ **to cause a stir.**

ruidoso, -sa *adj* **-1.** [que hace ruido] noisy. **-2.** *fig* [escandaloso] controversial, sensational.

ruin *adj* **-1.** [vil] low, contemptible. **-2.** [avaro] mean.

ruina *f* **-1.** [gen] ruin; **amenazar** ~ [edificio] to be about to collapse; **dejar en** ○ **llevar a la** ~ **a alguien** to ruin sb; **estar en la** ~ to be ruined. **-2.** [destrucción] destruction. **-3.** [fracaso - persona] wreck; **estar hecho una** ~ to be a wreck.
◆ **ruinas** *fpl* [históricas] ruins.

ruindad *f* **-1.** [cualidad] meanness, baseness. **-2.** [acto] vile deed.

ruinoso, -sa *adj* **-1.** [poco rentable] ruinous. **-2.** [edificio] ramshackle.

ruiseñor *m* nightingale.

ruja *etc* → **rugir.**

ruleta *f* roulette.
◆ **ruleta rusa** *f* Russian roulette.

ruletear *vi Amer* to drive a taxi.

ruletero *m Amer* taxi driver.

rulo *m* **-1.** [para el pelo] roller. **-2.** [rizo] curl.

rulot = **roulotte.**

ruma *f Amer* heap, pile.

Rumanía Rumania.

rumano, -na *adj, m y f* Rumanian.
◆ **rumano** *m* [lengua] Rumanian.

rumba *f* rumba.

rumbo *m* **-1.** [dirección] direction, course; **ir con** ~ **a** to be heading for; **poner** ~ **a** to set course for; **perder el** ~ [barco] to go off course; *fig* [persona] to lose one's way. **-2.** *fig* [camino] path, direction.

rumboso, -sa *adj fam* generous.

rumiante *adj & m* ruminant.

rumiar [8] ◇ *vt* [suj: rumiante] to chew; *fig* to ruminate, to chew over. ◇ *vi* [masticar] to ruminate, to chew the cud.

rumor *m* **-1.** [ruido sordo] murmur. **-2.** [chisme] rumour.

rumorearse *v impers*: ~ **que** ... to be rumoured that ....

runrún *m* **-1.** [ruido confuso] hum, humming (*U*). **-2.** [chisme] rumour.

runrunearse *v impers* to be rumoured.

runruneo *m* [ruido] hum, humming (*U*).

rupestre *adj* cave (*antes de sust*).

rupia *f* rupee.

ruptura *f* [gen] break; [de relaciones, conversaciones] breaking-off; [de contrato] breach.

rural *adj* rural.

Rusia Russia.

ruso, -sa *adj, m y f* Russian.

◆ **ruso** m [lengua] Russian.

rústico, -ca adj **-1.** [del campo] country (antes de sust). **-2.** [tosco] rough, coarse.
◆ **en rústica** loc adj paperback.

ruta f route; fig way, course.

rutilante adj shining.

rutilar vi to shine brightly.

rutina f [gen & INFORM] routine; **de ~** routine; **por ~** as a matter of course.

rutinario, -ria adj routine.

Rvda. (abrev de **Reverenda**) Rev. (Mother etc).

Rvdo. (abrev de **Reverendo**) Rev. (Father etc).

S

s¹, S f [letra] s, S.
◆ **S** (abrev de **san**) St.

s² (abrev de **segundo**) s.

s., sig. (abrev de **siguiente**) foll.

s.a. (abrev de **sinne anno**) s.a.

SA (abrev de **sociedad anónima**) f ≃ Ltd, ≃ PLC.

sábado m Saturday; **¿qué día es hoy? - (es) ~** what day is it (today)? - (it's) Saturday; **cada ~, todos los ~s** every Saturday; **cada dos ~s, un ~ sí y otro no** every other Saturday; **caer en ~** to be on a Saturday; **te llamo el ~** I'll call you on Saturday; **el próximo ~, el ~ que viene** next Saturday; **el ~ pasado** last Saturday; **el ~ por la mañana/ tarde/noche** Saturday morning/afternoon/ night; **en ~** on Saturdays; **nací en ~** I was born on a Saturday; **este ~** [pasado] last Saturday; [próximo] this (coming) Saturday; **¿trabajas los ~s?** do you work (on) Saturdays?; **trabajar un ~** to work on a Saturday; **un ~ cualquiera** on any Saturday; **hacer ~** to have a good clean.

sabana f savannah.

sábana f sheet; **~ bajera/encimera** bottom/top sheet; **se le pegan las ~s** she's not good at getting up.

sabandija f **-1.** [animal] creepy-crawly, bug. **-2.** fig [persona] worm.

sabañón m chilblain.

sabático, -ca adj **-1.** [del sábado] Saturday (antes de sust). **-2.** → **año**.

Sabbat ['saßat] m Sabbath.

sabedor, -ra adj: **ser ~ de** to be aware of.

sabelotodo m y f inv fam know-all.

saber [70] ◇ m knowledge.
◇ vt **-1.** [conocer] to know; **ya lo sé** I know; **hacer ~ algo a alguien** to inform sb of sthg, to tell sb sthg. **-2.** [ser capaz de]: **~ hacer algo** to know how to do sthg, to be able to do sthg; **sabe hablar inglés/montar en bici** she can speak English/ride a bike. **-3.** [enterarse] to learn, to find out; **lo supe ayer** I only found out yesterday. **-4.** [entender] to know about; **sabe mucha física** he knows a lot about physics. **-5.** loc: **no ~ dónde meterse** not to know where to put o.s.
◇ vi **-1.** [tener sabor]: **~ (a)** to taste (of); **~ mal a alguien** fig to upset ○ annoy sb. **-2.** [entender]: **~ de algo** to know about sthg; **ése sí que sabe** he's a canny one. **-3.** [tener noticia]: **~ de alguien** to hear from sb; **~ de algo** to learn of sthg. **-4.** [parecer]: **eso me sabe a disculpa** that sounds like an excuse to me. **-5.** Amer fam [soler]: **~ hacer algo** to be wont to do sthg. **-6.** loc: **no ~ uno por dónde se anda** not to have a clue; **que yo sepa** as far as I know; **¡quién sabe!, ¡vete a ~!** who knows!
◆ **saberse** vpr: **~se algo** to know sthg; **sabérselas todas** fig to know all the tricks.
◆ **a saber** loc adv [es decir] namely.

sabido, -da adj: **como es (bien) ~** as everyone knows.

sabiduría f **-1.** [conocimientos] knowledge, learning. **-2.** [prudencia] wisdom.

sabiendas
◆ **a sabiendas** loc adv knowingly; **a ~ de que ...** knowing that ..., quite aware of the fact that ....

sabihondo, -da, sabiondo, -da adj; m y f know-all, know-it-all.

sabina f [planta] savin.

sabio, -bia ◇ adj **-1.** [sensato, inteligente] wise. **-2.** [docto] learned. **-3.** [amaestrado] trained. ◇ m y f [listo] wise person; [docto] learned person.

sabiondo, -da = sabihondo.

sablazo m **-1.** [golpe] blow with a sabre. **-2.** [herida] sabre wound. **-3.** fam fig [de dinero] scrounging (U); **dar un ~ a alguien** to scrounge money off sb.

sable m sabre.

sablear vi fam to scrounge money.

sablista m y f fam scrounger.

sabor m **-1.** [gusto] taste, flavour; **tener ~ a algo** to taste of sthg; **dejar mal/buen ~ (de boca)** fig to leave a nasty taste in one's mouth/a warm feeling. **-2.** *fig* [estilo] flavour.

saborear *vt lit* & *fig* to savour.

sabotaje *m* sabotage.

saboteador, -ra *m y f* saboteur.

sabotear *vt* to sabotage.

sabrá *etc* → **saber**.

sabroso, -sa *adj* **-1.** [gustoso] tasty. **-2.** *fig* [substancioso] tidy, considerable. **-3.** *fig* [malicioso] malicious.

sabueso *m* **-1.** [perro] bloodhound. **-2.** *fig* [policía] sleuth, detective.

saca *f* sack.

sacacorchos *m inv* corkscrew.

sacamuelas *m inv fam* dentist.

sacapuntas *m inv* pencil sharpener.

sacar [10] ◇ *vt* **-1.** [poner fuera, hacer salir] to take out; [lengua] to stick out; ~ **algo de** to take sthg out of; **nos sacaron algo de comer** they gave us something to eat. **-2.** [quitar]: ~ **algo (de)** to remove sthg (from). **-3.** [librar, salvar]: ~ **a alguien de** to get sb out of. **-4.** [obtener - carné, buenas notas] to get, to obtain; [- premio] to win; [- foto] to take; [- fotocopia] to make; [- dinero del banco] to withdraw. **-5.** [sonsacar]: ~ **algo a alguien** to get sthg out of sb. **-6.** [extraer - producto]: ~ **algo de** to extract sthg from. **-7.** [fabricar] to produce. **-8.** [crear - modelo, disco etc] to bring out. **-9.** [exteriorizar] to show. **-10.** [resolver - crucigrama etc] to do, to finish. **-11.** [deducir] to gather, to understand; [- conclusión] to come to. **-12.** [mostrar] to show; **le sacaron en televisión** he was on television. **-13.** [comprar - entradas etc] to get, to buy. **-14.** [prenda - de ancho] to let out; [- de largo] to let down. **-15.** [aventajar]: **sacó tres minutos a su rival** he was three minutes ahead of his rival. **-16.** [DEP - con la mano] to throw in; [- con la raqueta] to serve.
◇ *vi* DEP to put the ball into play; [con la raqueta] to serve.

◆ **sacarse** *vpr* **-1.** [poner fuera]: ~**se algo (de)** to take sthg out (of). **-2.** [carné etc] to get.

◆ **sacar adelante** *vt* **-1.** [hijos] to bring up. **-2.** [negocio] to make a go of.

sacárido *m* saccharide.

sacarino, -na *adj* sugary.

◆ **sacarina** *f* saccharine.

sacarosa *f* sucrose.

sacerdocio *m* priesthood; *fig* vocation.

sacerdotal *adj* priestly.

sacerdote, -tisa *m y f* [pagano] priest (*f* priestess).

◆ **sacerdote** *m* [cristiano] priest.

saciar [8] *vt* **-1.** [satisfacer - sed] to quench; [- hambre] to satisfy, to sate. **-2.** *fig* [colmar] to fulfil.

◆ **saciarse** *vpr* to have had one's fill; *fig* to be satisfied.

saciedad *f* satiety; **hasta la** ~ *fig* over and over again.

saco *m* **-1.** [bolsa] sack, bag; ~ **de dormir** sleeping bag. **-2.** *fig* [persona]: **ser un** ~ **de mentiras** to be full of lies. **-3.** *Amer* jacket. **-4.** *loc:* **entrar a** ~ **en** to sack, to pillage; **no echar algo en** ~ **roto** to take good note of sthg.

sacralizar [13] *vt* to consecrate.

sacramental *adj* sacramental.

sacramentar *vt* to administer the last rites to.

sacramento *m* sacrament.

sacrificar [10] *vt* **-1.** [gen] to sacrifice; ~ **algo a** *lit* & *fig* to sacrifice sthg to. **-2.** [animal - para consumo] to slaughter.

◆ **sacrificarse** *vpr*: ~**se (para hacer algo)** to make sacrifices (in order to do sthg); ~**se por** to make sacrifices for.

sacrificio *m lit* & *fig* sacrifice.

sacrilegio *m lit* & *fig* sacrilege.

sacrílego, -ga ◇ *adj* sacrilegious. ◇ *m y f* sacrilegious person.

sacristán, -ana *m y f* sacristan, sexton.

sacristía *f* sacristy.

sacro, -cra *adj* **-1.** [sagrado] holy, sacred. **-2.** ANAT sacral.

◆ **sacro** *m* ANAT sacrum.

sacrosanto, -ta *adj* sacrosanct.

sacudida *f* **-1.** [gen] shake; [de la cabeza] toss; [de tren, coche] jolt; ~ **eléctrica** electric shock. **-2.** [terremoto] tremor. **-3.** *fig* [conmoción] shock.

sacudidor *m* carpet beater.

sacudir *vt* **-1.** [agitar] to shake. **-2.** [golpear - alfombra etc] to beat. **-3.** *fig* [conmover] to shake, to shock. **-4.** *fam fig* [pegar] to smack, to give a hiding.

◆ **sacudirse** *vpr* [persona] to get rid of; [responsabilidad, tarea] to get out of.

sádico, -ca ◇ *adj* sadistic. ◇ *m y f* sadist.

sadismo *m* sadism.

sadomasoquismo *m* sadomasochism.

sadomasoquista ◇ *adj* sadomasochistic. ◇ *m y f* sadomasochist.

saeta *f* **-1.** [flecha] arrow. **-2.** [de reloj] hand. **-3.** MÚS *flamenco-style song sung on religious occasions.*

safari *m* **-1.** [expedición] safari. **-2.** [zoológico] safari park.

saga *f* saga.

sagacidad *f* astuteness.

sagaz *adj* astute, shrewd.

Sagitario ◇ *m* [zodiaco] Sagittarius; **ser** ~ to be (a) Sagittarius. ◇ *m y f* [persona] Sagittarian.

sagrado, -da *adj* holy, sacred; *fig* sacred.

sagrario *m* -1. [parte del templo] shrine. -2. [de las hostias] tabernacle.

Sahara *m*: **el (desierto del)** ~ the Sahara (Desert).

sahariana [saxa'rjana] *f* [prenda] safari jacket.

sahariano, -na *adj, m y f* Saharan.

SAI *m* -1. INFORM (*abrev de* **sistema de alimentación ininterrumpida**) continuous feed. -2. (*abrev de* **Su Alteza Imperial**) HIH.

sainete *m* TEATR *short, popular comic play.*

Saint George's [sen'jorjes] Saint George's.

Saint John's [sen'jons] Saint John's.

sajar *vt* to cut open.

sajón, -ona *adj, m y f* Saxon.

Sajonia *f* Saxony.

sal *f* -1. CULIN & QUÍM salt; ~ **común** O **de cocina** cooking salt; ~ **marina** sea salt. -2. *fig* [gracia] wit. -3. *fig* [garbo] charm.
◆ **sales** *fpl* -1. [para reanimar] smelling salts. -2. [para baño] bath salts.

sala *f* -1. [habitación - gen] room; [- de una casa] lounge, living room; [- de hospital] ward; ~ **de espera** waiting room; ~ **de estar** lounge, living room; ~ **de juntas** boardroom; ~ **de máquinas** machine room; ~ **de operaciones** operating theatre; ~ **de partos** delivery room. -2. [mobiliario] lounge suite. -3. [local - de conferencias, conciertos] hall; [- de cine, teatro] auditorium; ~ **de fiestas** discothèque. -4. [DER - lugar] court (room); [- magistrados] bench.

saladero *m* salting room.

saladillo, -lla *adj* salted.

salado, -da *adj* -1. [con sal] salted; [agua] salt (*antes de sust*); [con demasiada sal] salty; **estar** ~ to be (too) salty. -2. *fig* [gracioso] witty. -3. *Amer* unfortunate.

salamandra *f* [animal] salamander.

salami, salame *m* salami.

salar *vt* -1. [para conservar] to salt. -2. [para cocinar] to add salt to.

salarial *adj* wage (*antes de sust*).

salario *m* salary, wages (*pl*); [semanal] wage; ~ **base** O **básico** basic wage; ~ **bruto/neto** gross/net wage; ~ **mínimo (interprofesional)** minimum wage.

salaz *adj* salacious.

salazón *f* [acción] salting.

◆ **salazones** *fpl* [carne] salted meat (*U*); [pescado] salted fish (*U*).

salchicha *f* sausage.

salchichón *m* ≃ salami.

saldar *vt* -1. [pagar - cuenta] to close; [- deuda] to settle. -2. *fig* [poner fin a] to settle. -3. COM to sell off.
◆ **saldarse** *vpr* [acabar]: ~**se con** to produce; **la pelea se saldó con 11 heridos** 11 people were injured in the brawl.

saldo *m* -1. [de cuenta] balance; ~ **acreedor/deudor** credit/debit balance; ~ **negativo** overdraft. -2. [de deudas] settlement. -3. (*gen pl*) [restos de mercancías] remnant; [rebajas] sale; **de** ~ bargain. -4. *fig* [resultado] balance.

saldrá *etc* → salir.

saledizo, -za *adj* projecting.
◆ **saledizo** *m* overhang.

salero *m* -1. [recipiente] salt cellar. -2. *fig* [gracia] wit; [donaire] charm.

saleroso, -sa *adj* [gracioso] witty; [garboso] charming.

salga *etc* → salir.

sálico → ley.

salida *f* -1. [acción de partir - gen] leaving; [- de tren, avión] departure. -2. DEP start; ~ **nula** false start. -3. [lugar] exit, way out; ~ **de emergencia/incendios** emergency/fire exit. -4. [momento]: **quedamos a la** ~ **del trabajo** we agreed to meet after work. -5. [viaje] trip. -6. [aparición - de sol, luna] rise; [- de revista, nuevo modelo] appearance. -7. [COM - posibilidades] market; [- producción] output. -8. INFORM output. -9. *fig* [solución] way out; **si no hay otra** ~ if there's no alternative. -10. [pretexto] excuse. -11. [ocurrencia]: **tener** ~**s** to be witty; ~ **de tono** out-of-place remark. -12. *fig* [futuro - de carreras etc] opening, opportunity.

salido, -da ◇ *adj* -1. [saliente] projecting, sticking out; [- ojos] bulging. -2. [animal] on heat. -3. *mfam* [persona] horny. ◇ *m y f* *mfam* [persona] horny bugger.

saliente ◇ *adj* -1. [destacable] salient, important. -2. POLÍT outgoing. ◇ *m* projection.

salina → salino.

salinidad *f* salinity.

salino, -na *adj* saline.
◆ **salina** *f* -1. MIN salt mine. -2. (*gen pl*) [en el mar] saltworks (*sg*).

salir [71] *vi* -1. [ir fuera] to go out; [venir fuera] to come out; ~ **de** to go/come out of; **¿salimos al jardín?** shall we go out into the garden?; **¡sal aquí fuera!** come out here! -2. [ser novios]: ~ **(con alguien)** to go out (with sb). -3. [marcharse]: ~ **(de/para)** to leave

(from/for). **-4.** [desembocar - calle]: ~ **a** to open out onto. **-5.** [separarse - tapón, anillo etc]: ~ **(de)** to come off. **-6.** [resultar] to turn out; **ha salido muy estudioso** he has turned out to be very studious; **¿qué salió en la votación?** what was the result of the vote?; ~ **elegida actriz del año** to be voted actress of the year; ~ **bien/mal** to turn out well/badly; ~ **ganando/perdiendo** to come off well/badly. **-7.** [proceder]: ~ **de** to come from; **el vino sale de la uva** wine comes from grapes. **-8.** [surgir - luna, estrellas, planta] to come out; [- sol] to rise; [- dientes] to come through; **le ha salido un sarpullido en la espalda** her back has come out in a rash. **-9.** [aparecer - publicación, producto, traumas] to come out; [- moda, ley] to come in; [- en imagen, prensa, televisión] to appear; **¡qué bien sales en la foto!** you look great in the photo!; **ha salido en los periódicos** it's in the papers; ~ **de** CIN & TEATR to appear as. **-10.** [en sorteo] to come up. **-11.** [presentarse - ocasión, oportunidad] to turn up, to come along; [- problema, contratiempo] to arise; **a lo que salga, salga lo que salga** *fig* whatever happens. **-12.** [costar]: ~ **(a** ○ **por)** to work out (at); ~ **caro** [de dinero] to be expensive; [por las consecuencias] to be costly. **-13.** [decir u obrar inesperadamente]: **nunca se sabe por dónde va a** ~ you never know what she's going to do/come out with next. **-14.** [parecerse]: ~ **a alguien** to turn out like sb, to take after sb. **-15.** [en juegos] to lead; **te toca** ~ **a ti** it's your lead. **-16.** [quitarse - manchas] to come out. **-17.** [librarse]: ~ **de** [gen] to get out of; [problema] to get round. **-18.** INFORM: ~ **(de)** to quit, to exit.
◆ **salirse** *vpr* **-1.** [marcharse - de lugar, asociación etc]: ~**se (de)** to leave. **-2.** [filtrarse]: ~**se (por)** [líquido, gas] to leak ○ escape (through); [humo, aroma] to come out (through). **-3.** [rebosar] to overflow; [leche] to boil over; **el río se salió del cauce** the river broke its banks. **-4.** [desviarse]: ~**se (de)** to come off; **el coche se salió de la carretera** the car came off ○ left the road. **-5.** *fig* [escaparse]: ~**se de** [gen] to deviate from; [límites] to go beyond; ~**se del tema** to digress. **-6.** *loc:* ~**se con la suya** to get one's own way.
◆ **salir adelante** *vi* **-1.** [persona, empresa] to get by. **-2.** [proyecto, propuesta, ley] to be successful.

salitre *m* saltpetre.

salitroso, -sa *adj* containing saltpetre.

saliva *f* saliva; **gastar** ~ **en balde** *fig* to waste one's breath; **tragar** ~ *fig* to bite one's tongue.

salivación *f* salivation.

salivadera *f Amer* spitoon.

salival, **salivar** *adj* salivary.

salivar *vi* to salivate.

salmo *m* psalm.

salmodia *f* singing of psalms; *fig* drone.

salmodiar [8] *vt* to sing in a monotone.

salmón ◇ *m* [pez] salmon. ◇ *adj & m inv* [color] salmon (pink).

salmonelosis *f inv* MED salmonella.

salmonete *m* red mullet.

salmuera *f* brine.

salobre *adj* salty.

salobridad *f* saltiness.

salomón *m fig* sage, wise person.

salomónico, -ca *adj* equitable, even-handed.

salón *m* **-1.** [habitación - en casa] lounge, sitting room; [- en residencia, edificio público] reception hall. **-2.** [mobiliario] lounge suite. **-3.** [local - de sesiones etc] hall; ~ **de actos** assembly hall. **-4.** [feria] show, exhibition. **-5.** [establecimiento] shop; ~ **de belleza/masaje** beauty/massage parlour; ~ **de té** tea-room.
◆ **de salón** *loc adj fig* pretentious.

salpicadera *f Amer* mudguard *Br*, fender *Am*.

salpicadero *m* dashboard.

salpicadura *f* [acción] splashing, spattering; [mancha] spot, spatter.

salpicar [10] *vt* **-1.** [rociar] to splash, to spatter. **-2.** *fig* [diseminar]: ~ **(de)** to pepper (with).

salpicón *m* CULIN *cold dish of chopped fish, seasoned with pepper, salt, vinegar and onion.*

salpimentar [19] *vt* to season.

salpullido = sarpullido.

salsa *f* **-1.** [CULIN - gen] sauce; [- de carne] gravy; ~ **bearnesa/tártara** bearnaise/tartar sauce; ~ **bechamel** ○ **besamel** bechamel ○ white sauce; ~ **muselina** *sauce made from egg yolk, butter and whipped cream;* ~ **rosa** thousand island dressing; **en su propia** ~ *fig* in one's element. **-2.** *fig* [interés] spice. **-3.** MÚS salsa.

salsera *f* gravy boat.

SALT (*abrev de* **Strategic Arms Limitation Talks**) *fpl* SALT.

saltador, -ra ◇ *adj* jumping. ◇ *m y f* DEP jumper.

saltamontes *m inv* grasshopper.

saltar ◇ *vt* **-1.** [obstáculo] to jump (over). **-2.** [omitir] to skip, to miss out. **-3.** [hacer estallar] to blow up.

san

◇ *vi* **-1.** [gen] to jump; [a la comba] to skip; [al agua] to dive; ~ **sobre alguien** [abalanzarse] to set upon sb; ~ **de un tema a otro** to jump (around) from one subject to another. **-2.** [levantarse] to jump up; ~ **de la silla** to jump out of one's seat. **-3.** [salir para arriba - objeto] to jump (up); [- champán, aceite] to spurt (out); [- corcho, válvula] to pop out. **-4.** [explotar] to explode, to blow up. **-5.** [romperse] to break. **-6.** [sorprender]: ~ **con** to suddenly come out with. **-7.** [reaccionar violentamente] to explode. **-8.** [suj: agua, cascada]: ~ **por** to gush down, to pour down. **-9.** *loc*: **estar a la que salta** to be always on the lookout.
◆ **saltarse** *vpr* **-1.** [omitir] to skip, to miss out. **-2.** [salir despedido] to pop off. **-3.** [no respetar - cola, semáforo] to jump; [- ley, normas] to break.

salteado, -da *adj* **-1.** CULIN sautéed. **-2.** [espaciado] unevenly spaced.

salteador, -ra *m y f*: ~ **de caminos** highwayman.

saltear *vt* **-1.** [asaltar] to assault. **-2.** CULIN to sauté.

saltimbanqui *m y f* acrobat.

salto *m* **-1.** [gen & DEP] jump; [grande] leap; [al agua] dive; **dar** ○ **pegar un** ~ to jump; [grande] to leap; ~ **de altura/longitud** high/long jump; ~ **mortal** somersault; ~ **con pértiga** pole vault. **-2.** *fig* [diferencia, omisión] gap. **-3.** *fig* [progreso] leap forward. **-4.** [despeñadero] precipice. **-5.** *loc*: **vivir a** ~ **de mata** to live from one day to the next; **dar** ~**s de alegría** ○ **contento** to jump with joy.
◆ **salto de agua** *m* waterfall.
◆ **salto de cama** *m* negligée.

saltón, -ona *adj* [ojos] bulging; [dientes] sticking out.

salubre *adj* healthy.

salubridad *f* **-1.** [cualidad] healthiness. **-2.** *culto* [salud pública] public health.

salud ◇ *f lit & fig* health; **estar bien/mal de** ~ to be well/unwell; **rebosar de** ~ to glow with health; **beber** ○ **brindar a la** ~ **de alguien** to drink to sb's health; **curarse en** ~ to cover one's back. ◇ *interj*: **¡~!** [para brindar] cheers!; [después de estornudar] bless you!

saludable *adj* **-1.** [sano] healthy. **-2.** *fig* [provechoso] beneficial.

saludar *vt* to greet; MIL to salute; **saluda a Ana de mi parte** give my regards to Ana; **le saluda atentamente** yours faithfully.
◆ **saludarse** *vpr* to greet one another.

saludo *m* greeting; MIL salute; **Ana te manda** ~**s** [en cartas] Ana sends you her regards; [al teléfono] **Ana says hello; un** ~ **afectuoso** [en cartas] yours sincerely.

salva *f* MIL salvo; **una** ~ **de aplausos** *fig* a round of applause.

salvación *f* **-1.** [remedio]: **no tener** ~ to be beyond hope. **-2.** [rescate] rescue. **-3.** RELIG salvation.

salvado *m* bran.

salvador, -ra ◇ *adj* saving. ◇ *m y f* [persona] saviour.
◆ **Salvador** *m* **-1.** RELIG: **el Salvador** the Saviour. **-2.** GEOGR: **El Salvador** El Salvador.

salvadoreño, -ña *adj, m y f* Salvadoran.

salvaguarda *f* INFORM backup.

salvaguardar *vt* to safeguard.

salvaguardia *f* **-1.** [defensa] safeguard. **-2.** [salvoconducto] safe-conduct, pass.

salvajada *f* atrocity.

salvaje ◇ *adj* **-1.** [gen] wild. **-2.** [pueblo, tribu] savage. ◇ *m y f* **-1.** [primitivo] savage. **-2.** [bruto] maniac.

salvamanteles *m inv* [llano] table mat; [con pies] trivet.

salvamento *m* rescue, saving; **equipo de** ~ rescue team.

salvar *vt* **-1.** [gen & INFORM] to save. **-2.** [rescatar] to rescue. **-3.** [superar - moralmente] to overcome; [- físicamente] to go over ○ around. **-4.** [recorrer] to cover. **-5.** [exceptuar]: **salvando algunos detalles** except for a few details.
◆ **salvarse** *vpr* **-1.** [librarse] to escape; **sálvese quien pueda** every man for himself. **-2.** RELIG to be saved.

salvavidas ◇ *adj inv* life (*antes de sust*). ◇ *m* [chaleco] lifejacket; [flotador] lifebelt.

salve[1] *interj* hail!

salve[2] *f prayer dedicated to the Virgin Mary.*

salvedad *f* exception; **con la** ~ **de** with the exception of.

salvia *f* sage.

salvo, -va *adj* safe; **estar a** ~ to be safe; **poner algo a** ~ to put sthg in a safe place.
◆ **salvo** *adv* except; ~ **que** unless.

salvoconducto *m* safe-conduct, pass.

Salzburgo [sals'ßurɣo] Salzburg.

SAM (*abrev de* **surface-to-air missile**) *m* SAM.

samaritano, -na *adj, m y f* Samaritan.

samba *f* samba.

sambenito *m fig* [descrédito] disgrace; **poner** ○ **colgar a alguien el** ~ **de borracho** to brand sb a drunk.

samovar *m* samovar.

samurái (*pl* **samuráis**) *m* samurai.

san *adj* Saint; ~ **José** Saint Joseph.

Sana Sana.

sanar ◇ vt [persona] to cure; [herida] to heal. ◇ vi [persona] to get better; [herida] to heal.

sanatorio m sanatorium, nursing home.

sanción f -1. [castigo] punishment; ECON sanction. -2. [aprobación] approval.

sancionar vt -1. [castigar] to punish. -2. [aprobar] to approve, to sanction.

sanctasanctórum m inv lit & fig sanctum.

sandalia f sandal.

sándalo m sandalwood.

sandez f silly thing, nonsense (U).

sandía f watermelon.

sandinismo m Sandinista movement.

sandinista adj, m y f Sandinista.

sandunguero, -ra adj witty, charming.

sándwich ['sanwitʃ] (pl sándwiches) m toasted sandwich.

saneado, -da adj [FIN - bienes] written off, written down; [- economía] back on a sound footing; [- cuenta] regularized.

saneamiento m -1. [higienización - de tierras] drainage; [- de edificio] disinfection. -2. fig [FIN - de bienes] write-off, write-down; [- de moneda etc] stabilization; [- de economía] putting back on a sound footing.

sanear vt -1. [higienizar - tierras] to drain; [- un edificio] to disinfect. -2. fig [FIN - bienes] to write off ○ down; [- moneda] to stabilize; [- economía] to put back on a sound footing.

sanfermines mpl festival held in Pamplona when bulls are run through the streets of the town.

sangrante adj bleeding.

sangrar ◇ vi to bleed. ◇ vt -1. [sacar sangre] to bleed. -2. [vaciar - conducto] to drain off; [- árbol] to tap. -3. [robar] to bleed dry. -4. IMPRENTA to indent.

sangre f blood; **de ~ caliente** ZOOL warm-blooded; **de ~ fría** ZOOL cold-blooded; **~ azul** blue blood; **chuparle a alguien la ~** to bleed sb dry; **encender ○ quemar la ~ a alguien** to make sb's blood boil; **llevar algo en la ~** to have sthg in one's blood; **no llegó la ~ al río** it didn't get too nasty; **no tiene ~ en las venas** he's got no life in him; **se le subió la ~ a la cabeza** he saw red; **sudar ~** to sweat blood; **tener mala ~** to be malicious; **tener ~ de horchata** to be as cool as a cucumber.

◆ **sangre fría** f sangfroid; **a ~ fría** in cold blood.

sangría f -1. [bebida] sangria. -2. MED bloodletting. -3. fig [ruina] drain.

sangriento, -ta adj -1. [ensangrentado, cruento] bloody. -2. [despiadado, cruel, hiriente] cruel.

sanguijuela f lit & fig leech.

sanguinario, -ria adj bloodthirsty.

sanguíneo, -a adj blood (antes de sust).

sanguinolento, -ta adj [que echa sangre] bleeding; [bañado en sangre] bloody; [manchado de sangre] bloodstained; [ojos] bloodshot.

sanidad f -1. [salubridad] health, healthiness. -2. [servicio] public health; [ministerio] health department.

sanitario, -ria ◇ adj health (antes de sust). ◇ m y f [persona] health officer.
◆ **sanitarios** mpl [instalación] bathroom fittings (pl).

San José San José.

San Marino San Marino.

sano, -na adj -1. [saludable] healthy; **~ y salvo** safe and sound. -2. [positivo - principios, persona etc] sound; [- ambiente, educación] wholesome. -3. [entero] intact, undamaged. -4. loc: **cortar por lo ~** to make a clean break.

San Salvador San Salvador.

sánscrito, -ta adj Sanskrit.
◆ **sánscrito** m Sanskrit.

sanseacabó interj fam: **¡~!** that's an end to it!

sansón m very strong man.

Santander Santander.

santanderino, -na adj of/relating to Santander.

santero, -ra adj pious.

Santiago Santiago.

Santiago de Compostela Santiago de Compostela.

Santiago de Cuba Santiago de Cuba.

santiaguino, -na ◇ adj of/relating to Santiago. ◇ m y f native/inhabitant of Santiago.

santiamén
◆ **en un santiamén** loc adv fam in a flash.

santidad f saintliness, holiness.
◆ **Santidad** f: **Su** ○ **Vuestra Santidad** His Holiness.

santificación f sanctification.

santificar [10] vt -1. [consagrar] to sanctify. -2. [guardar] to keep, to respect.

santiguar [45] vt to make the sign of the cross over.
◆ **santiguarse** vpr -1. [persignarse] to cross o.s. -2. fam fig [de asombro] to be shocked ○ horrified.

santo, -ta ◇ *adj* **-1.** [sagrado] holy. **-2.** [virtuoso] saintly. **-3.** *fam fig* [beneficioso] miraculous. **-4.** *fam fig* [dichoso] damn; **todo el ~ día** all day long. ◇ *m y f* RELIG saint.
◆ **santo** *m* **-1.** [onomástica] saint's day. **-2.** [ilustración] illustration. **-3.** [estatua] (statue of a) saint. **-4.** *loc*: **¿a ~ de qué?** why on earth?; **se le fue el ~ al cielo** *fam* he/she completely forgot; **llegar y besar el ~** to get sthg at the first attempt; **no ser ~ de su devoción** not to be his/her *etc* cup of tea; **quedarse para vestir ~s** to be left on the shelf.
◆ **santo y seña** *m* MIL password.

Santo Domingo Santo Domingo.

santón *m* **-1.** RELIG Muslim holy man. **-2.** *fig* [persona influyente] guru.

santoral *m* **-1.** [libro de vidas de santos] *book containing lives of saints*. **-2.** [onomásticas] *list of saints' days*.

Santo Tomé São Tomé.

Santo Tomé y Príncipe São Tomé and Príncipe.

santuario *m* shrine; *fig* sanctuary.

santurrón, -ona ◇ *adj* excessively pious. ◇ *m y f* excessively pious person.

santurronería *f* sanctimoniousness.

saña *f* viciousness, malice.

sañudo, -da *adj* vicious, malicious.

Sao Paulo Sao Paulo.

sapiencia *f culto* knowledge.

sapo *m* toad; **echar ~s y culebras** *fig* to rant and rave.

saque ◇ *v* → **sacar**. ◇ *m* **-1.** [en fútbol]: **~ de banda** throw-in; **~ inicial** O **de centro** kick-off; **~ de esquina/meta** corner/goal kick. **-2.** [en tenis *etc*] serve; **tener buen ~** to have a good serve; *fig* to have a hearty appetite.

saqueador, -ra ◇ *adj* looting, plundering. ◇ *m y f* looter.

saquear *vt* **-1.** [rapiñar - ciudad] to sack; [- tienda *etc*] to loot. **-2.** *fam* [vaciar] to ransack.

saqueo *m* [de ciudad] sacking; [de tienda *etc*] looting.

SAR (*abrev de* **Su Alteza Real**) HRH.

sarampión *m* measles (*U*).

sarao *m* **-1.** [fiesta] party. **-2.** *fam* [jaleo] row, rumpus.

sarasa *m fam despec* poof, queer.

sarcasmo *m* sarcasm.

sarcástico, -ca ◇ *adj* sarcastic. ◇ *m y f* sarcastic person.

sarcófago *m* sarcophagus.

sarcoma *m* sarcoma.

sardana *f traditional Catalan dance and music*.

sardina *f* sardine; **como ~s en canasta** O **en lata** like sardines.

sardinero, -ra *adj* sardine (*antes de sust*).

sardo, -da *adj, m y f* Sardinian.
◆ **sardo** *m* [lengua] Sardinian.

sardónico, -ca *adj* sardonic.

sargento ◇ *m y f* **-1.** MIL ≃ sergeant. **-2.** *despec* [mandón] dictator, little Hitler. ◇ *m* [herramienta] handscrew.

sari *m* sari.

sarmiento *m* vine shoot.

sarna *f* MED scabies (*U*); VETER mange; **~ con gusto no pica** *proverb* some things are a necessary evil.

sarnoso, -sa ◇ *adj* [perro] mangy. ◇ *m y f* [persona] scabies sufferer.

sarpullido, salpullido *m* rash.

sarraceno, -na *adj, m y f* Saracen.

sarro *m* **-1.** [de dientes] tartar. **-2.** [poso] sediment.

sarta *f lit & fig* string.

sartén *f* frying pan; **tener la ~ por el mango** to be in control.

SAS (*abrev de* **Su Alteza Serenísima**) HSH.

sastre, -tra *m y f* tailor.

sastrería *f* [oficio] tailoring; [taller] tailor's (shop).

Satanás *m* Satan.

satánico, -ca *adj* satanic.

satanismo *m* Satanism.

satélite ◇ *m* satellite; **~ artificial** satellite. ◇ *adj fig* satellite (*antes de sust*).

satelización *f* putting into orbit.

satén *m* satin; [de algodón] sateen.

satinado, -da *adj* glossy.
◆ **satinado** *m* gloss.

satinar *vt* to make glossy.

sátira *f* satire.

satírico, -ca ◇ *adj* satirical. ◇ *m y f* satirist.

satirizar [13] *vt* to satirize.

sátiro *m* **-1.** MITOL satyr. **-2.** *fig* [lujurioso] lecher.

satisfacción *f* satisfaction.

satisfacer [60] *vt* **-1.** [gen] to satisfy; [sed] to quench. **-2.** [deuda, pago] to pay, to settle. **-3.** [ofensa, daño] to redress. **-4.** [duda, pregunta] to answer. **-5.** [cumplir - requisitos, exigencias] to meet.
◆ **satisfacerse** *vpr* to be satisified.

satisfactorio, -ria *adj* satisfactory.

satisfecho, -cha ◇ *pp* → **satisfacer**. ◇ *adj*

satisfied; ~ **de sí mismo** self-satisfied; **darse por** ~ to be satisfied.

saturación *f* saturation.

saturado, -da *adj*: ~ **(de)** saturated (with).

saturar *vt* to saturate.

◆ **saturarse** *vpr*: ~**se (de)** to become saturated (with).

saturnismo *m* lead poisoning.

Saturno Saturn.

sauce *m* willow; ~ **llorón** weeping willow.

saúco *m* elder.

saudí (*pl* **saudíes**), **saudita** *adj, m y f* Saudi.

sauna *f* sauna.

savia *f* sap; *fig* vitality; ~ **nueva** *fig* new blood.

savoir-faire [sa'ßwar fer] *m* savoir-faire.

saxo ◇ *m* [instrumento] sax. ◇ *m y f* [persona] sax player.

saxofón, saxófono ◇ *m* [instrumento] saxophone. ◇ *m y f* [persona] saxophonist.

saxofonista *m y f* saxophonist.

saxófono = saxofón.

saya *f desus* petticoat.

sayal *m desus* sackcloth.

sayo *m desus* smock.

sazón *f* **-1.** [madurez] ripeness; **en** ~ ripe. **-2.** [sabor] seasoning, flavouring.

◆ **a la sazón** *loc adv* then, at that time.

sazonado, -da *adj* seasoned.

sazonar *vt* to season.

scanner [es'kaner] = **escáner**.

schilling = **chelín**.

scooter [es'kuter] = **escúter**.

scotch [es'kotʃ] (*pl* **scotchs**) *m* scotch (whisky).

scout [es'kaut] (*pl* **scouts**) *m* scout.

script [es'kript] (*pl* **scripts**) *m* script.

SDN (*abrev de* **Sociedad de Naciones**) *f* Society of Nations.

se *pron pers* **-1.** (*reflexivo*) [de personas] himself (*f* herself), (*pl*) themselves; [usted mismo] yourself, (*pl*) yourselves; [de cosas, animales] itself, (*pl*) themselves; ~ **está lavando, está lavándo**~ she is washing (herself); ~ **lavó los dientes** she cleaned her teeth; **espero que** ~ **diviertan** I hope you enjoy yourselves; **el perro** ~ **lame** the dog is licking itself; ~ **lame la herida** it's licking its wound; ~ **levantaron y** ~ **fueron** they got up and left. **-2.** (*reflexivo impersonal*) oneself; **hay que afeitar**~ **todos los días** one has to shave every day, you have to shave every day. **-3.** (*recíproco*) each other, one another; ~ **aman** they love each other; ~ **escriben cartas** they write to each other.

-4. [en construcción pasiva]: ~ **ha suspendido la reunión** the meeting has been cancelled; "~ **prohíbe fumar**" "no smoking"; "~ **habla inglés**" "English spoken". **-5.** (*impersonal*): **en esta sociedad ya no** ~ **respeta a los ancianos** in our society old people are no longer respected; ~ **dice que ...** it is said that ..., people say that .... **-6.** (*en vez de "le" o "les" antes de "lo", "la", "los" o "las"*) (*complemento indirecto*) [gen] to him (*f* to her), (*pl*) to them; [de cosa, animal] to it, (*pl*) to them; [usted, ustedes] to you; ~ **lo dio** he gave it to him/her *etc*; ~ **lo dije, pero no me hizo caso** I told her, but she didn't listen; **si usted quiere, yo** ~ **lo arreglo en un minuto** if you like, I'll sort it out for you in a minute.

sé -1. → **saber. -2.** → **ser.**

SE (*abrev de* **Su Excelencia**) HE.

sebáceo, -a *adj* sebaceous.

sebo *m* fat; [para jabón, velas] tallow.

seborrea *f* seborrhoea.

seboso, -sa *adj* fatty.

secadero *m* drying room.

secado *m* drying.

secador *m* dryer; ~ **de pelo** hair-dryer.

secadora *f* clothes ○ tumble dryer.

secano *m* unirrigated ○ dry land.

secante ◇ *adj* **-1.** [secador] drying. **-2.** → **papel. -3.** GEOM secant (*antes de sust*). ◇ *f* GEOM secant.

secar [10] *vt* **-1.** [desecar] to dry. **-2.** [enjugar] to wipe away; [con fregona] to mop up.

◆ **secarse** *vpr* [gen] to dry up; [ropa, vajilla, suelo] to dry.

sección *f* **-1.** [gen & GEOM] section. **-2.** [departamento] department.

seccionar *vt* **-1.** [cortar] to cut; TECN to section. **-2.** [dividir] to divide (up).

sececionismo *m* secessionism.

secesión *f* secession.

seco, -ca *adj* **-1.** [gen] dry; [plantas, flores] withered; [higos, pasas] dried; **lavar en** ~ to dry-clean; **lavado en** ~ dry-cleaning. **-2.** [tajante] brusque. **-3.** [flaco] thin, lean. **-4.** [ruido] dull; [tos] dry; [voz] sharp. **-5.** *loc*: **dejar a alguien** ~ [matar] to kill sb stone dead; [pasmar] to stun sb; **parar en** ~ to stop dead.

◆ **a secas** *loc adv* simply, just; **llámame Juan a secas** just call me Juan.

secreción *f* secretion.

secretar *vt* to secrete.

secretaría *f* **-1.** [cargo] post of secretary. **-2.** [oficina, lugar] secretary's office. **-3.** [organismo] secretariat.

secretariado *m* **-1.** EDUC secretarial skills (*pl*). **-2.** [cargo] post of secretary. **-3.** [oficina, lugar] secretary's office. **-4.** [organismo] secretariat.

secretario, -ria *m y f* secretary; ~ **de Estado** Secretary of State; ~ **general** General Secretary.

secretear *vi* to talk in secret.

secreter *m* bureau, writing desk.

secreto, -ta *adj* [gen] secret; [tono] confidential; **en** ~ in secret.
◆ **secreto** *m* **-1.** [gen] secret; ~ **a voces** open secret; ~ **de confesión** confessional secret; ~ **de estado** State secret; ~ **profesional** professional secret. **-2.** [sigilo] secrecy.

secta *f* sect.

sectario, -ria ◇ *adj* sectarian. ◇ *m y f* **-1.** [miembro de secta] sect member. **-2.** [fanático] fanatic.

sectarismo *m* sectarianism.

sector *m* **-1.** [gen] sector; [grupo] group; ~ **primario/secundario** primary/secondary sector; ~ **privado/público** private/public sector; ~ **terciario** service industries (*pl*). **-2.** [zona] area.

sectorial *adj* sectorial.

secuaz *m y f despec* minion.

secuela *f* consequence.

secuencia *f* sequence.

secuestrador, -ra *m y f* kidnapper.

secuestrar *vt* **-1.** [raptar] to kidnap. **-2.** [avión, barco] to hijack. **-3.** [embargar] to seize.

secuestro *m* **-1.** [rapto] kidnapping. **-2.** [de avión, barco] hijack. **-3.** [de bienes etc] seizure, confiscation.

secula
◆ **secula seculorum** *loc adv* for ever and ever.

secular ◇ *adj* **-1.** [seglar] secular, lay. **-2.** [centenario] age-old. ◇ *m* lay person.

secularización *f* secularization.

secularizar [13] *vt* to secularize.

secundar *vt* to support, to back (up); [propuesta] to second.

secundario, -ria *adj* secondary.

sed ◇ *v* → **ser.** ◇ *f* thirst; **tener** ~ to be thirsty; ~ **de** *fig* thirst for.

seda *f* silk; ~ **artificial** rayon, artificial silk; ~ **cruda/natural** raw/pure silk; **ir como una** ~ to go smoothly.

sedal *m* fishing line.

sedán *m* saloon.

sedante ◇ *adj* MED sedative; [música] soothing. ◇ *m* sedative.

sedar *vt* MED to sedate; [suj: música] to soothe, to calm.

sedativo, -va *adj* MED sedative; [música] soothing.

sede *f* **-1.** [emplazamiento] headquarters (*pl*); [de gobierno] seat; ~ **social** head office. **-2.** RELIG see.
◆ **Santa Sede** *f*: **la Santa Sede** the Holy See.

sedentario, -ria *adj* sedentary.

sedente *adj* seated.

sedición *f* sedition.

sedicioso, -sa ◇ *adj* seditious. ◇ *m y f* rebel.

sediento, -ta *adj* **-1.** [de agua] thirsty. **-2.** *fig* [deseoso]: ~ **de** hungry for.

sedimentación *f* sedimentation.

sedimentar *vt* to deposit.
◆ **sedimentarse** *vpr* [líquido] to settle.

sedimentario, -ria *adj* sedimentary.

sedimento *m* **-1.** [poso] sediment. **-2.** GEOL deposit. **-3.** *fig* [huella] residue.

sedoso, -sa *adj* silky.

seducción *f* **-1.** [cualidad] seductiveness. **-2.** [acción - gen] attraction, charm; [- sexual] seduction.

seducir [33] *vt* **-1.** [atraer] to attract, to charm; [- sexualmente] to seduce. **-2.** [persuadir]: ~ **a alguien para que haga algo** to tempt sb to do sthg.

seductor, -ra ◇ *adj* [gen] attractive, charming; [sexualmente] seductive; [persuasivo] tempting. ◇ *m y f* seducer.

sedujera, seduzca *etc* → **seducir.**

sefardí (*pl* **sefardíes**), **sefardita** ◇ *adj* Sephardic. ◇ *m y f* [persona] Sephardi. ◇ *m* [lengua] Sephardi.

segador, -ra *m y f* [agricultor] reaper.
◆ **segadora** *f* [máquina] reaping machine.

segar [35] *vt* **-1.** AGR to reap. **-2.** [cortar] to cut off. **-3.** *fig* [truncar] to put an end to.

seglar ◇ *adj* secular, lay. ◇ *m* lay person.

segmentación *f* division.

segmentar *vt* to cut o divide into pieces.

segmento *m* **-1.** GEOM & ZOOL segment. **-2.** [trozo] piece.

segregación *f* **-1.** [separación, discriminación] segregation; ~ **racial** racial segregation. **-2.** [secreción] secretion.

segregacionismo *m* racial segregation.

segregar [16] *vt* **-1.** [separar, discriminar] to segregate. **-2.** [secretar] to secrete.

segué *etc* → **segar.**

seguidilla *f* **-1.** LITER *poem containing four or seven verses used in popular songs.* **-2.** (*gen pl*) [baile] *traditional Spanish dance.* **-3.** [cante] *mournful flamenco song.*

seguido, -da *adj* **-1.** [consecutivo] consecutive; **diez años ~s** ten years in a row. **-2.** [sin interrupción - gen] one after the other; [- línea, pitido etc] continuous.
◆ **seguido** *adv* **-1.** [inmediatamente después] straight after. **-2.** [en línea recta] straight on.
◆ **en seguida** *loc adv* straight away, at once; **en seguida nos vamos** we're going in a minute.

seguidor, -ra *m y f* follower.

seguimiento *m* [de noticia] following; [de clientes] follow-up.

seguir [43] ◇ *vt* **-1.** [gen] to follow. **-2.** [perseguir] to chase. **-3.** [reanudar] to continue, to resume. **-4.** [cursar]: **sigue un curso de italiano** he's doing an Italian course.
◇ *vi* **-1.** [sucederse]: **~ a algo** to follow sthg; **a la tormenta siguió la lluvia** the storm was followed by rain. **-2.** [continuar] to continue, to go on; **¡sigue!** go O carry on, don't stop!; **sigo trabajando en la fábrica** I'm still working at the factory; **debes ~ haciéndolo** you should keep on O carry on doing it; **sigo pensando que está mal** I still think it's wrong; **sigue enferma/en el hospital** she's still ill/at the hospital.
◆ **seguirse** *vpr* to follow; **~se de algo** to follow O be deduced from sthg; **de esto se sigue que estás equivocado** it therefore follows that you are wrong.

según ◇ *prep* **-1.** [de acuerdo con] according to; **~ su opinión, ha sido un éxito** in his opinion O according to him, it was a success; **~ yo/tú** *etc* in my/your *etc* opinion. **-2.** [dependiendo de] depending on; **~ la hora que sea** depending on the time.
◇ *adv* **-1.** [como] (just) as; **todo permanecía ~ lo recordaba** everything was just as she remembered it; **actuó ~ se le recomendó** he did as he had been advised. **-2.** [a medida que] as; **entrarás en forma ~ vayas entrenando** you'll get fit as you train. **-3.** [dependiendo]: **¿te gusta la música? - ~** do you like music? - it depends; **lo intentaré ~ esté de tiempo** I'll try to do it, depending on how much time I have.
◆ **según que** *loc adv* depending on whether.
◆ **según qué** *loc adj* certain; **~ qué días la clase es muy aburrida** some days the class is really boring.

segunda → segundo.

segundero *m* second hand.

segundo, -da ◇ *núm adj* second. ◇ *núm m y f* **-1.** [en orden]: **el ~** the second one; **llegó el ~** he came second. **-2.** [mencionado

antes]: **vinieron Pedro y Juan, el ~ con ...** Pedro and Juan arrived, the latter with .... **-3.** [ayudante] number two; **~ de abordo** NÁUT first mate.
◆ **segundo** *m* **-1.** [gen] second. **-2.** [piso] second floor.
◆ **segunda** *f* **-1.** AUTOM second (gear). **-2.** AERON & FERROC second class. **-3.** DEP second division.
◆ **con segundas** *loc adv* with an ulterior motive.

segundón *m* second son; *fig & despec* failure, second best.

seguramente *adv* probably; **~ iré, pero aún no lo sé** the chances are I'll go, but I'm not sure yet.

seguridad *f* **-1.** [fiabilidad, ausencia de peligro] safety; [protección, estabilidad] security; **de ~** [cinturón, cierre] safety (*antes de sust*); [puerta, guardia] security (*antes de sust*); **~ vial** road safety. **-2.** [certidumbre] certainty; **con ~** for sure, definitely. **-3.** [confianza] confidence; **~ en sí mismo** self-confidence.
◆ **Seguridad Social** *f* Social Security.

seguro, -ra *adj* **-1.** [fiable, sin peligro] safe; [protegido, estable] secure; **sobre ~** safely, without risk. **-2.** [infalible - prueba, negocio etc] reliable. **-3.** [confiado] sure; **estar ~ de algo** to be sure about sthg. **-4.** [indudable - nombramiento, fecha etc] definite, certain; **tener por ~ que** to be sure that.
◆ **seguro** ◇ *m* **-1.** [contrato] insurance (*U*); **~ a todo riesgo/a terceros** comprehensive/ third party insurance; **~ de incendios/de vida** fire/life insurance; **~ de paro** O **de desempleo** unemployment benefit; **~ de cambio** exchange rate hedge; **~ del coche** car insurance; **~ de invalidez** O **incapacidad** disability insurance; **~ mutuo** joint insurance. **-2.** [seguridad social] *health service office.* **-3.** [dispositivo] safety device; [de armas] safety catch. **-4.** *Amer* [imperdible] safety pin.
◇ *adv* for sure, definitely; **~ vendrá** she's bound to come.

seis ◇ *núm adj inv* **-1.** [para contar] six; **tiene ~ años** she's six (years old). **-2.** [para ordenar] (number) six; **la página ~** page six.
◇ *núm m* **-1.** [número] six; **el ~** number six; **doscientos ~** two hundred and six; **treinta y ~** thirty-six. **-2.** [en fechas] sixth; **el ~ de agosto** the sixth of August. **-3.** [en direcciones]: **calle Mayor (número) ~** number six calle Mayor. **-4.** [en naipes] six; **el ~ de diamantes** the six of diamonds; **echar** O **tirar un ~** to play a six.
◇ *núm mpl* **-1.** [referido a grupos]: **invité a diez y sólo vinieron ~** I invited ten and only six came along; **somos ~** there are six

of us; **de** ~ **en** ~ in sixes; **los** ~ the six of them. **-2.** [en temperaturas]: **estamos a** ~ **bajo cero** the temperature is six below zero. **-3.** [en puntuaciones]: **empatar a** ~ to draw six all; ~ **a cero** six-nil.
◇ *núm fpl* [hora]: **las** ~ six o'clock; **son las** ~ it's six o'clock.

seiscientos, -tas *núm* six hundred; *ver también* **seis**.

seísmo *m* earthquake.

selección *f* **-1.** [gen] selection; [de personal] recruitment; ~ **natural** natural selection. **-2.** [equipo] team; ~ **nacional** national team.

seleccionador, -ra ◇ *adj* **-1.** DEP selecting. **-2.** [de personal] recruiting. ◇ *m y f* **-1.** DEP selector, ≈ manager. **-2.** [de personal] recruiter.

seleccionar *vt* to pick, to select.

selectividad *f* **-1.** [selección] selectivity. **-2.** [examen] university entrance examination.

SELECTIVIDAD:
The 'selectividad' is a series of exams which take place after the end of secondary education. The mark obtained in these exams is one of the factors which determines whether a student is admitted to his or her preferred field of study at university

selectivo, -va *adj* selective.

selecto, -ta *adj* **-1.** [excelente] fine, excellent. **-2.** [escogido] exclusive, select.

selector, -ra *adj* selecting.
◆ **selector** *m* selector (button).

selenio *m* selenium.

selenita ◇ *f* selenite. ◇ *m y f* [habitante] moon dweller.

self-service *m inv* self-service restaurant.

sellado, -da *adj* [documento] sealed; [pasaporte, carta] stamped.
◆ **sellado** *m* [de documento] sealing; [de pasaporte, carta] stamping.

sellar *vt* **-1.** [timbrar] to stamp. **-2.** [lacrar] to seal. **-3.** *fig* [pacto, labios] to seal.

sello *m* **-1.** [gen] stamp. **-2.** [tampón] rubber stamp. **-3.** [lacre] seal. **-4.** [sortija] signet ring. **-5.** *fig* [carácter] hallmark.
◆ **sello discográfico** *m* record label.

selva *f* [gen] jungle; [bosque] forest; ~ **virgen** virgin forest.

Selva Negra *f*: **la** ~ the Black Forest.

selvático, -ca *adj* woodland (*antes de sust*).

semáforo *m* traffic lights (*pl*).

semana *f* week; **entre** ~ during the week; ~ **laboral** working week.

◆ **Semana Santa** *f* Easter; RELIG Holy Week.

semanal *adj* weekly.

semanario, -ria *adj* weekly.
◆ **semanario** *m* [publicación semanal] weekly.

semántico, -ca *adj* semantic.
◆ **semántica** *f* semantics (*U*).

semblante *m* countenance, face.

semblanza *f* portrait, profile.

sembrado, -da *adj* **-1.** [plantado] sown. **-2.** *fig* [lleno]: ~ **de** scattered ○ plagued with.
◆ **sembrado** *m* sown field.

sembrador, -ra ◇ *adj* sowing (*antes de sust*). ◇ *m y f* [persona] sower.
◆ **sembradora** *f* [máquina] seed drill.

sembrar [19] *vt* **-1.** [plantar] to sow. **-2.** *fig* [llenar] to scatter, to strew. **-3.** *fig* [confusión, pánico etc] to sow.

semejante ◇ *adj* **-1.** [parecido]: ~ **(a)** similar (to). **-2.** [tal] such; **jamás aceptaría** ~ **invitación** I would never accept such an invitation. ◇ *m* (*gen pl*) fellow (human) being.

semejanza *f* similarity.

semejar *vt* to resemble.
◆ **semejarse** *vpr* to be alike, to resemble each other; ~**se a alguien** to resemble sb.

semen *m* semen.

semental ◇ *adj* stud (*antes de sust*). ◇ *m* stud; [caballo] stallion.

sementera *f* [tierra] sown land.

semestral *adj* half-yearly, six-monthly.

semestre *m* period of six months, semester *Am*; **cada** ~ every six months.

semiautomático, -ca *adj* semiautomatic.

semicírculo *m* semicircle.

semiconductor *m* semiconductor.

semiconsonante *f* semiconsonant.

semicorchea *f* semiquaver.

semidirecto ◇ *adj* express. ◇ *m* → **tren**.

semifinal *f* semifinal.

semifinalista ◇ *adj* semifinalist (*antes de sust*). ◇ *m y f* semifinalist.

semilla *f* seed.

semillero *m* **-1.** [para plantar] seedbed. **-2.** [para guardar] seed box.

seminario *m* **-1.** [escuela para sacerdotes] seminary. **-2.** [EDUC - curso, conferencia] seminar; [- departamento] department, school.

seminarista *m* seminarist.

semioculto, -ta *adj* partially hidden.

semiología *f* LING & MED semiology.

semiólogo, -ga *m y f* LING & MED semiologist.

semiótica *f* LING & MED semiotics (*U*).

semipesado DEP ◇ *adj* light heavyweight (*antes de sust*). ◇ *m* light heavyweight.

semiseco, -ca *adj* medium-dry.

semita ◇ *adj* Semitic. ◇ *m y f* Semite.

semítico, -ca *adj* Semitic.

semitismo *m* Semitism.

semitono *m* semitone.

semitransparente *adj* translucent.

semivocal *f* LING semivowel.

sémola *f* semolina.

sempiterno, -na *adj culto* eternal.

Sena *m*: el ~ the (river) Seine.

senado *m* senate.

senador, -ra *m y f* senator.

senatorial *adj* -1. [del senado] senate (*antes de sust*). -2. [de senador] senatorial.

sencillez *f* -1. [facilidad] simplicity. -2. [modestia] unaffectedness, naturalness. -3. [discreción] plainness.

sencillo, -lla *adj* -1. [fácil, sin lujo, llano] simple. -2. [campechano] natural, unaffected. -3. [billete, unidad etc] single.
◆ **sencillo** *m* -1. [disco] single. -2. *Amer fam* [cambio] loose change.

senda *f*, **sendero** *m* path.

sendos, -das *adj pl* each, respective; **llegaron los dos con ~ paquetes** they arrived each carrying a parcel, they both arrived with their respective parcels.

senectud *f culto* old age.

Senegal: **(el)** ~ Senegal.

senil *adj* senile.

senilidad *f* senility.

senior (*pl* **seniors**) *adj & m* senior.

seno *m* -1. [pecho] breast. -2. [pechera] bosom; **en el ~ de** *fig* within. -3. [útero]: ~ **(materno)** womb. -4. *fig* [amparo, cobijo] refuge, shelter. -5. [concavidad] hollow. -6. MAT sine. -7. ANAT [de la nariz] sinus.

SENPA (*abrev de* **Servicio Nacional de Productos Agrarios**) *m Spanish agricultural products service*.

sensación *f* -1. [percepción] feeling, sensation. -2. [efecto] sensation; **causar ~ to** cause a sensation; **causar una gran ~ a alguien** to make a great impression on sb. -3. [premonición] feeling; **tener la ~ de que** to have a feeling that.

sensacional *adj* sensational.

sensacionalismo *m* sensationalism.

sensacionalista *adj* sensationalist.

sensatez *f* wisdom, common sense.

sensato, -ta *adj* sensible.

sensibilidad *f* -1. [perceptibilidad] feeling. -2. [sentimentalismo] sensitivity. -3. [don especial] feel. -4. [de emulsión fotográfica, balanza etc] sensitivity.

sensibilización *f* -1. [concienciación] increased awareness. -2. FOT to sensitization.

sensibilizar [13] *vt* -1. [concienciar] to raise the awareness of. -2. FOT sensitize.

sensible *adj* -1. [gen] sensitive. -2. [evidente] perceptible; [pérdida] significant.

sensiblería *f despec* mushiness.

sensiblero, -ra *adj despec* mushy, sloppy.

sensitivo, -va *adj* -1. [de los sentidos] sensory. -2. [receptible] sensitive.

sensor *m* sensor.

sensorial *adj* sensory.

sensual *adj* sensual.

sensualidad *f* sensuality.

sentado, -da *adj* -1. [en asiento] seated; **estar ~** to be sitting down. -2. [establecido]: **dar algo por ~** to take sthg for granted; **dejar ~ que ...** to make it clear that .... -3. [sensato] sensible.
◆ **sentada** *f* sit-in.

sentar [19] ◇ *vt* -1. [en asiento] to seat, to sit. -2. [establecer] to establish. ◇ *vi* -1. [ropa, color] to suit. -2. [comida]: ~ **bien/mal a alguien** to agree/disagree with sb. -3. [vacaciones, medicamento]: ~ **bien a alguien** to do sb good. -4. [comentario, consejo]: **le sentó mal** it upset her; **le sentó bien** she appreciated it.
◆ **sentarse** *vpr* to sit down; **~se a hacer algo** to sit down and do sthg.

sentencia *f* -1. DER sentence; **visto para ~** ready for judgment. -2. [máxima] maxim.

sentenciar [8] *vt* -1. DER: ~ **(a alguien a algo)** to sentence (sb to sthg). -2. *fig* [condenar, juzgar] to condemn.

sentencioso, -sa *adj* sententious.

sentido, -da *adj* -1. [profundo] heartfelt. -2. [sensible]: **ser muy ~** to be very sensitive.
◆ **sentido** *m* -1. [gen] sense; **tener ~ to** make sense; ~ **común** common sense; ~ **del humor** sense of humour; **sexto ~** sixth sense. -2. [conocimiento] consciousness; **perder/recobrar el ~** to lose/regain consciousness; **sin ~** unconscious. -3. [significado] meaning, sense; **sin ~** [ilógico] meaningless; [inútil, irrelevante] pointless; **doble ~** double meaning. -4. [dirección] direction; **de ~ único** one-way.
◆ **sin sentido** *m* nonsense (*U*).

sentimental *adj* sentimental.

sentimentalismo *m* sentimentality.

sentimentaloide *adj* mushy, sloppy.

sentimiento *m* -1. [gen] feeling; **dejarse llevar por los ~s** to get carried away. -2.

[pena, aflicción]: **le acompaño en el** ~ my deepest sympathy.

sentir [27] ◇ *vt* **-1.** [gen] to feel. **-2.** [lamentar] to regret, to be sorry about; **siento que no puedas venir** I'm sorry you can't come; **lo siento (mucho)** I'm (really) sorry. **-3.** [oír] to hear. ◇ *vi* to feel; **sin** ~ *fig* without noticing. ◇ *m* feelings (*pl*), sentiments (*pl*).
◆ **sentirse** *vpr* to feel; **me siento mareada** I feel sick; **se siente superior** she considers herself superior.

seña *f* [gesto, indicio, contraseña] sign, signal.
◆ **señas** *fpl* **-1.** [dirección] address (*sg*); ~**s personales** (personal) description (*sg*). **-2.** [gesto, indicio] signs; **dar** ~**s de algo** to show signs of sthg; **(hablar) por** ~**s** (to talk) in sign language; **hacer** ~**s (a alguien)** to signal (to sb). **-3.** [detalle] details; **para** ο **por más** ~**s** to be precise.

señal *f* **-1.** [gen & TELECOM] signal; [de teléfono] tone; ~ **de alarma/salida** alarm/starting signal. **-2.** [indicio, símbolo] sign; **dar** ~**es de vida** to show signs of life; ~ **de la Cruz** sign of the Cross; ~ **de tráfico** road sign; **en** ~ **de** as a mark ο sign of. **-3.** [marca, huella] mark; **no quedó ni** ~ **de él** there was no sign of him left; **no dejó ni** ~ she didn't leave a trace. **-4.** [cicatriz] scar, mark. **-5.** [fianza] deposit.

señalado, -da *adj* **-1.** [importante - fecha] special; [- personaje] distinguished. **-2.** [con cicatrices] scarred, marked.

señalar *vt* **-1.** [marcar, denotar] to mark; [hora, temperatura etc] to indicate, to say. **-2.** [indicar - con el dedo, con un comentario] to point out. **-3.** [fijar] to set, to fix; **señaló su valor en 1.000 dólares** he set ο fixed its value at $1,000.
◆ **señalarse** *vpr* [perfilarse] to stand out.

señalización *f* **-1.** [conjunto de señales] signs (*pl*). **-2.** [colocación de señales] signposting.

señalizar [13] *vt* to signpost.

señera *f Catalan flag.*

señor, -ra *adj* **-1.** [refinado] noble, refined. **-2.** (*antes de sust*) *fam* [gran] real.
◆ **señor** *m* **-1.** [tratamiento - antes de nombre, cargo] Mr; [- al dirigir la palabra] Sir; **el** ~ **López** Mr López; **¡**~ **presidente!** Mr President!; **¿qué desea el** ~**?** what would you like, Sir?; **Muy señor mío** [en cartas] Dear Sir. **-2.** [hombre] man. **-3.** [caballero] gentleman. **-4.** [dueño] owner. **-5.** [amo - de criado] master.
◆ **señora** *f* **-1.** [tratamiento - antes de nombre, cargo] Mrs; [- al dirigir la palabra] Madam; **la** ~**a López** Mrs López; **¡**~**a presidenta!** Madam President!; **¿qué desea la** ~**a?**

what would you like, Madam?; **¡**~**as y** ~**es! ...** Ladies and Gentlemen! ...; **Estimada** ~**a** [en cartas] Dear Madam; **¿es usted** ~**a** ο ~**ita?** are you a Mrs or a Miss? **-2.** [mujer] lady; ~**a de compañía** female companion. **-3.** [dama] lady. **-4.** [dueña] owner. **-5.** [ama - de criado] mistress. **-6.** [esposa] wife.
◆ **señores** *mpl* [matrimonio]: **los** ~**es Ruiz** Mr & Mrs Ruiz.
◆ **Señor** *m*: **el Señor** RELIG the Lord.
◆ **Nuestra Señora** *f* RELIG Our Lady.

señorear *vt* [dominar] to control, to rule.

señoría *f* lordship (*f* ladyship); **su** ~ [gen] his lordship; [al dirigirse - a un noble] your lordship; [- a un parlamentario] the right honourable gentleman/lady; [- a un juez] your Honour.

señorial *adj* **-1.** [majestuoso] stately. **-2.** [del señorío] lordly.

señorío *m* **-1.** [dominio] dominion, rule. **-2.** [distinción] nobility.

señorito, -ta *adj fam despec* [refinado] lordly.
◆ **señorito** *m* **-1.** *desus* [hijo del amo] master. **-2.** *fam despec* [niñato] rich kid.
◆ **señorita** *f* **-1.** [soltera, tratamiento] Miss. **-2.** [joven] young lady. **-3.** [maestra]: **la** ~ miss, the teacher. **-4.** *desus* [hija del amo] mistress.

señuelo *m* **-1.** [reclamo] decoy. **-2.** *fig* [trampa] bait, lure.

sep., sept. (*abrev de* **septiembre**) Sept.

sepa → **saber**.

sépalo *m* sepal.

separación *f* **-1.** [gen] separation. **-2.** [espacio] space, distance.
◆ **separación de bienes** *f* DER separate estates (*pl*) (in matrimony).

separado, -da ◇ *adj* **-1.** [gen] separate; **está muy** ο **de la pared** it's too far away from the wall; **por** ~ separately. **-2.** [del cónyuge] separated. ◇ *m y f* separated person.

separar *vt* **-1.** [gen] to separate; ~ **algo de** to separate sthg from. **-2.** [desunir] to take off, to remove. **-3.** [apartar - silla etc] to move away. **-4.** [reservar] to put aside. **-5.** [destituir]: ~ **de** to remove ο dismiss from.
◆ **separarse** *vpr* **-1.** [apartarse] to move apart; ~**se de** to move away from. **-2.** [ir por distinto lugar] to separate, to part company. **-3.** [matrimonio]: ~**se (de alguien)** to separate (from sb). **-4.** [desprenderse] to come away ο off.

separatismo *m* separatism.

separo *m Amer* cell.

sepelio *m* burial.

sepia *f* [molusco] cuttlefish.

sept = sep.

septentrional ◇ *adj* northern. ◇ *m y f* northerner.

septicemia *f* septicaemia.

séptico, -ca *adj* septic.

septiembre, setiembre *m* September; **el 1 de ~** the 1st of September; **uno de los ~s más lluviosos de la última década** one of the rainiest Septembers in the last decade; **a principios/mediados/finales de ~** at the beginning/in the middle/at the end of September; **el pasado/próximo (mes de) ~** last/next September; **en ~** in September; **en pleno ~** in mid-September; **este (mes de) ~** [pasado] (this) last September; [próximo] next September, this coming September; **para ~** by September.

séptimo, -ma, sétimo, -ma *núm* seventh; **la séptima parte** a seventh.

septuagésimo, -ma *núm* seventieth.

septuplicar [10] *vt* to multiply by seven.
◆ **septuplicarse** *vpr* to increase sevenfold.

sepulcral *adj* **-1.** [del sepulcro] tomb (*antes de sust*). **-2.** *fig* [profundo - voz, silencio] lugubrious, gloomy; [- frío] deathly.

sepulcro *m* tomb.

sepultar *vt* to bury.

sepultura *f* **-1.** [enterramiento] burial. **-2.** [fosa] grave.

sepulturero, -ra *m y f* gravedigger.

seque *etc* → secar.

sequedad *f* **-1.** [falta de humedad] dryness. **-2.** *fig* [antipatía] abruptness, brusqueness.

sequía *f* drought.

séquito *m* [comitiva] retinue, entourage.

ser [5] ◇ *vaux* (*antes de participio forma la voz pasiva*) to be; **fue visto por un testigo** he was seen by a witness.

◇ *v copulativo* **-1.** [gen] to be; **es alto/gracioso** he is tall/funny; **es azul/difícil** it's blue/difficult; **es un amigo/el dueño** he is a friend/the owner. **-2.** [empleo, dedicación] to be; **soy abogado/actriz** I'm a lawyer/an actress; **son estudiantes** they're students.

◇ *vi* **-1.** [gen] to be; **fue aquí** it was here; **lo importante es decidirse** the important thing is to reach a decision; **~ de** [estar hecho de] to be made of; [provenir de] to be from; [ser propiedad de] to belong to; [formar parte de] to be a member of; **¿de dónde eres?** where are you from?; **los juguetes son de mi hijo** the toys are my son's. **-2.** [con precios, horas, números] to be; **¿cuánto es?** how much is it?; **son 300 pesetas** that'll be 300 pesetas; **¿qué (día) es hoy?** what day is it today?, what's today?; **mañana será 15 de julio** tomorrow (it) will be the 15th of July; **¿qué hora es?** what time is it?, what's the time?; **son las tres (de la tarde)** it's three o'clock (in the afternoon), it's three (pm). **-3.** [servir, ser adecuado]: **~ para** to be for; **este trapo es para (limpiar) las ventanas** this cloth is for (cleaning) the windows; **este libro es para niños** this book is (meant) for children. **-4.** (*uso partitivo*): **~ de los que ...** to be one of those (people) who ...; **ése es de los que están en huelga** he is one of those on strike.

◇ *v impers* **-1.** [expresa tiempo] to be; **es muy tarde** it's rather late; **era de noche/de día** it was night/day. **-2.** [expresa necesidad, posibilidad]: **es de desear que ...** it is to be hoped that ...; **es de suponer que aparecerá** presumably, he'll turn up. **-3.** [expresa motivo]: **es que no vine porque estaba enfermo** the reason I didn't come is that I was ill. **-4.** *loc*: **a no ~ que** unless; **como sea** one way or another, somehow or other; **de no ~ por** had it not been for; **érase una vez, érase que se era** once upon a time; **no es para menos** not without reason; **o sea** that is (to say), I mean; **por si fuera poco** as if that wasn't enough.

◇ *m* [ente] being; **~ humano/vivo** human/living being.

SER (*abrev de* **Sociedad Española de Radiodifusión**) *f Spanish independent radio company.*

serafín *m* seraph.

SEREM (*abrev de* **Servicio Especial de Rehabilitación de Enfermos y Minusválidos**) *m Spanish special rehabilitation service for the sick and disabled.*

serenar *vt* [calmar] to calm.
◆ **serenarse** *vpr* **-1.** [calmarse] to calm down. **-2.** [estabilizarse - tiempo] to clear up; [- viento] to die down; [- aguas] to grow calm.

serenata *f* MUS serenade.

serenidad *f* **-1.** [tranquilidad] calm. **-2.** [quietud] tranquility.

sereno, -na *adj* calm.
◆ **sereno** *m* **-1.** [vigilante] night watchman. **-2.** [humedad] night dew.

serial *m* serial.

serie *f* **-1.** [gen & TV] series (*sg*); [de hechos, sucesos] chain; [de mentiras] string. **-2.** [de sellos, monedas] set. **-3.** *loc*: **ser un fuera de ~** to be unique.
◆ **de serie** *loc adj* [equipamiento] (fitted) as standard.
◆ **en serie** *loc adv* **-1.** [fabricación]: **fabricar en ~** to mass-produce. **-2.** ELECTR in series.

seriedad *f* **-1.** [gravedad] seriousness. **-2.** [responsabilidad] sense of responsibility. **-3.** [formalidad - de persona] reliability.

serigrafía *f* silkscreen printing.

serio, -ria *adj* **-1.** [gen] serious; **estar** ~ to look serious. **-2.** [responsable, formal] responsible. **-3.** [sobrio] sober.

◆ **en serio** *loc adv* seriously; **lo digo en** ~ I'm serious; **tomar(se) algo/a alguien en** ~ to take sthg/sb seriously.

sermón *m lit* & *fig* sermon.

sermoneador, -ra *adj* sermonizing.

sermonear *vt* to give a lecture O ticking-off to.

seropositivo, -va MED ◇ *adj* HIV-positive. ◇ *m y f* HIV-positive person.

serpentear *vi* **-1.** [río, camino] to wind, to snake. **-2.** [culebra] to wriggle.

serpentina *f* streamer.

serpiente *f* [culebra] snake; LITER serpent; ~ **de cascabel** rattlesnake; ~ **pitón** python.

serrallo *m* seraglio.

serranía *f* mountainous region.

serrano, -na ◇ *adj* **-1.** [de la sierra] mountain (*antes de sust*), highland (*antes de sust*). **-2.** [jamón] cured. ◇ *m y f* highlander.

serrar [19] *vt* to saw (up).

serrería *f* sawmill.

serrín *m* sawdust.

serrucho *m* handsaw.

servicial *adj* attentive, helpful.

servicio *m* **-1.** [gen] service; ~ **de inteligencia** O **secreto** intelligence O secret service; ~ **de prensa/de urgencias** press/casualty department; ~ **discrecional/público** private/public service; ~ **a domicilio** home delivery service; ~ **de mesa** dinner service; ~ **militar** military service; ~ **de paquetería** parcel service; ~ **posventa** after-sales service; ~ **de té** tea set. **-2.** [servidumbre] servants (*pl*); ~ **doméstico** domestic help. **-3.** [turno] duty; **estar de** ~ to be on duty. **-4.** (*gen pl*) [WC] toilet, lavatory. **-5.** DEP serve, service. **-6.** [cubierto] place setting.

servidor, -ra *m y f* **-1.** [criado] servant. **-2.** [en cartas]: **su seguro** ~ yours faithfully. **-3.** [yo] yours truly, me; **¿quién es el último?** - ~ who's last? - I am.

◆ **servidor** *m* INFORM server.

servidumbre *f* **-1.** [criados] servants (*pl*). **-2.** [dependencia] servitude.

servil *adj* servile.

servilismo *m* subservience.

servilleta *f* serviette, napkin.

servilletero *m* serviette O napkin ring.

servir [26] ◇ *vt* to serve; **sírvanos dos cer-** vezas bring us two beers; **¿te sirvo más patatas?** would you like some more potatoes?; **¿en qué puedo** ~**le?** what can I do for you?

◇ *vi* **-1.** [gen] to serve; ~ **en el gobierno** to be a government minister. **-2.** [valer, ser útil] to serve, to be useful; **no sirve para estudiar** he's no good at studying; **de nada sirve que se lo digas** it's no use telling him; ~ **de algo** to serve as sthg. **-3.** [como criado] to be in service.

◆ **servirse** *vpr* **-1.** [aprovecharse]: ~**se de** to make use of; **sírvase llamar cuando quiera** please call whenever you want. **-2.** [comida, bebida] to help o.s.

servoasistido, -da *adj* AUTOM servo (*antes de sust*).

servodirección *f* power steering.

servofreno *m* servo brake.

sésamo *m* sesame.

sesear *vi* GRAM *to pronounce "c" and "z" as "s", as in Andalusia and Latin America.*

sesenta *núm* sixty; **los (años)** ~ the sixties; *ver también* **seis.**

seseo *m pronunciation of "c" and "z" as an "s".*

sesera *f fam* **-1.** [cabeza] skull, nut. **-2.** *fig* [inteligencia] brains (*pl*).

sesgar [16] *vt* to cut on the bias.

sesgo *m* **-1.** [oblicuidad] slant; **al** ~ [gen] on a slant; [costura] on the bias. **-2.** *fig* [rumbo] course, path.

sesgue *etc* → **sesgar.**

sesión *f* **-1.** [reunión] meeting, session; DER sitting, session; **abrir/levantar la** ~ to open/to adjourn the meeting. **-2.** [proyección, representación] show, performance; ~ **continua** continuous showing; ~ **matinal** matinée; ~ **de tarde** afternoon matinée; ~ **de noche** evening showing. **-3.** [periodo] session.

seso *m* (*gen pl*) **-1.** [cerebro] brain. **-2.** [sensatez] brains (*pl*), sense; **calentarse** O **devanarse los** ~**s** to rack one's brains; **sorber el** ~ O **los** ~**s a alguien** to brainwash sb.

sestear *vi* to have a nap.

sesudo, -da *adj* **-1.** [inteligente] brainy. **-2.** [sensato] wise, sensible.

set (*pl* **sets**) *m* DEP set.

seta *f* mushroom; ~ **venenosa** toadstool.

setecientos, -tas *núm* seven hundred; *ver también* **seis.**

setenta *núm* seventy; **los (años)** ~ the seventies; *ver también* **seis.**

setiembre = **septiembre.**

sétimo, -ma = **séptimo.**

seto *m* fence; ~ **vivo** hedge.

setter ['seter] *m* setter.
SEU (*abrev de* **Sindicato Español Universitario**) *m Francoist students' union in Spain.*
seudo = pseudo.
seudónimo = pseudónimo.
s.e.u.o. (*abrev de* **salvo error u omisión**) E. & O.E.
severidad *f* -1. [rigor] severity. -2. [intransigencia] strictness.
severo, -ra *adj* -1. [castigo] severe, harsh. -2. [persona] strict.
Sevilla Seville.
sevillano, -na *adj, m y f* Sevillian.
◆ **sevillanas** *fpl Andalusian dance and song.*
sexagenario, -ria *adj, m y f* sexagenarian.
sexagésimo, -ma *núm* sixtieth.
sex-appeal [seksa'pil] *m inv* sex appeal.
sexi, sexy (*pl* **sexys**) *adj* sexy.
sexismo *m* sexism.
sexista *adj, m y f* sexist.
sexo *m* -1. [gen] sex; **bello ~, ~ débil** fair sex. -2. [genitales] genitals (*pl*).
sexología *f* sexology.
sexólogo, -ga *m y f* sexologist.
sex-shop [se'ʃop] (*pl* **sex-shops**) *m* sex shop.
sextante *m* sextant.
sexteto *m* -1. MÚS sextet. -2. LITER sestina.
sexto, -ta *núm* sixth; **la sexta parte** a sixth.
sextuplicar [10] *vt* to multiply by six.
◆ **sextuplicarse** *vpr* to increase sixfold.
séxtuplo, -pla *adj* sixfold.
◆ **séxtuplo** *m* sextuple.
sexuado, -da *adj* sexed.
sexual *adj* [gen] sexual; [educación, vida] sex (*antes de sust*).
sexualidad *f* sexuality.
sexy = sexi.
Seychelles [sei'ʃels] *fpl*: **las (islas) ~** the Seychelles.
SGAE *f* -1. (*abrev de* **Sociedad General Azucarera de España**) *Spanish Sugar Company.* -2. (*abrev de* **Sociedad General de Autores de España**) *society that safeguards the interests of Spanish authors, musicians etc.*
SGBD *m abrev de* **sistema de gestión de bases de datos.**
sha [sa, ʃa] *m* shah.
shakesperiano, -na [ʃespi'rjano] *adj* Shakespearian.
Shanghai [ʃaŋ'gai] Shanghai.
SHAPE (*abrev de* **Supreme Headquarters Allied Powers in Europe**) *m* SHAPE.
sheriff ['ʃerif] *m* sheriff.
sherry ['ʃeri] (*pl* **sherries**) *m* sherry.

shock = choc.
shorts [ʃorts] *mpl* shorts.
show [ʃou] (*pl* **shows**) *m* show; **montar un ~** *fig* to cause a scene.
si¹ (*pl* **sis**) *m* MÚS B; [en solfeo] ti.
si² *conj* -1. (*condicional*) if; **~ viene él yo me voy** if he comes, then I'm going; **~ hubieses venido te habrías divertido** if you had come, you would have enjoyed yourself. -2. (*en oraciones interrogativas indirectas*) if, whether; **ignoro ~ lo sabe** I don't know if O whether she knows. -3. [expresa protesta] but; **¡~ te dije que no lo hicieras!** but I told you not to do it!
sí (*pl* **síes**) ◇ *adv* -1. [afirmación] yes; **¿vendrás? - ~, iré** will you come? - yes, I will; **claro que ~** of course; **creo que ~** I think so; **¿están de acuerdo? - algunos ~** do they agree? - some do. -2. [uso enfático]: **~ que** really, certainly; **~ que me gusta** I really O certainly like it. -3. *loc*: **no creo que puedas hacerlo - ¡a que ~!** I don't think you can do it - I bet I can!; **porque ~** [sin razón] because (I/you *etc* felt like it); **van a subir la gasolina - ¡pues ~ que ...!** petrol prices are going up - what a pain!; **¿~?** [incredulidad] really?
◇ *pron pers* -1. (*reflexivo*) [de personas] himself (*f* herself), (*pl*) themselves; [usted] yourself, (*pl*) yourselves; [de cosas, animales] itself, (*pl*) themselves; **lo quiere todo para ~ (misma)** she wants everything for herself; **se acercó la silla hacia ~** he drew the chair nearer (himself); **de (por) ~** [cosa] in itself. -2. (*reflexivo impersonal*) oneself; **cuando uno piensa en ~ mismo** when one thinks about oneself, when you think about yourself.
◇ *m* consent; **dar el ~** to give one's consent.
Siam Siam.
siamés, -esa ◇ *adj* Siamese. ◇ *m y f* -1. [de Siam] Siamese person, Thai. -2. [gemelo] Siamese twin.
◆ **siamés** *m* [gato] Siamese.
sibarita ◇ *adj* sybaritic. ◇ *m y f* sybarite, epicure.
sibaritismo *m* sybaritism, epicureanism.
Siberia Siberia.
siberiano, -na *adj, m y f* Siberian.
sibila *f* MITOL sibyl.
sibilante *adj* sibilant.
sibilino, -na *adj* [incomprensible] mysterious, cryptic.
SICAB (*abrev de* **sistema de información para catálogos informatizados de bibliotecas**) *m information system for computerized library catalogues.*

sicario *m* hired assassin.
Sicilia Sicily.
siciliano, -na *adj, m y f* Sicilian.
sicoanálisis *etc* = psicoanálisis.
sicodélico, -ca = psicodélico.
sicodrama = psicodrama.
sicología *etc* = psicología.
sicometría = psicometría.
sicomoro *m* [planta] sycamore.
sicomotricidad = psicomotricidad.
sicópata = psicópata.
sicopatía = psicopatía.
sicosis = psicosis.
sicosomático, -ca = psicosomático.
sicotécnico, -ca = psicotécnico.
sicoterapia = psicoterapia.
sida (*abrev de* **síndrome de inmunodeficiencia adquirida**) *m* AIDS.
sidecar (*pl* **sidecares**) *m* sidecar.
sideral *adj* sidereal.
siderurgia *f* iron and steel industry.
siderúrgico, -ca *adj* IND iron and steel (*antes de sust*).
sidra *f* cider.
siega ◇ *v* → segar. ◇ *f* **-1.** [acción] reaping, harvesting. **-2.** [época] harvest (time).
siembra ◇ *v* → sembrar. ◇ *f* **-1.** [acción] sowing. **-2.** [época] sowing time.
siempre *adv* **-1.** [gen] always; **como ~** as usual; **de ~** usual; **lo de ~** the usual; **somos amigos de ~** we've always been friends; **es así desde ~** it has always been that way; **para ~, para ~ jamás** for ever and ever. **-2.** *Amer* [sin duda] really.
◆ **siempre que** *loc conj* **-1.** [cada vez que] whenever. **-2.** [con tal de que] provided that, as long as.
◆ **siempre y cuando** *loc conj* provided that, as long as.
siempreviva *f* everlasting flower.
sien *f* temple.
sienta *etc* **-1.** → sentar. **-2.** → sentir.
sierpe *f desus* serpent.
sierra ◇ *v* → serrar. ◇ *f* **-1.** [herramienta] saw; **~ eléctrica** power saw. **-2.** [cordillera] mountain range. **-3.** [región montañosa] mountains (*pl*).
Sierra Leona Sierra Leone.
siervo, -va *m y f* **-1.** [esclavo] serf. **-2.** RELIG servant.
siesta *f* siesta, nap; **dormir** O **echarse la ~** to have an afternoon nap.
siete *núm* seven; *ver también* **seis** ◇ *f Amer fig*: **de la gran ~** amazing, incredible; **¡la gran ~!** good heavens!

◆ **siete y media** *fpl card game in which players aim to get 7½ points, court cards counting for ½ point.*
sietemesino, -na ◇ *adj* premature. ◇ *m y f* premature baby.
sífilis *f inv* syphilis.
sifilítico, -ca MED *adj, m y f* syphilitic.
sifón *m* **-1.** [agua carbónica] soda (water). **-2.** [de WC] trap, U-bend. **-3.** [tubo] siphon.
sig. = s.
siga → seguir.
sigilo *m* [gen] secrecy; [al robar, escapar] stealth.
sigiloso, -sa *adj* [discreto] secretive; [al robar, escapar] stealthy.
siglas *fpl* acronym.
siglo *m* **-1.** [cien años] century; **el ~ XX** the 20th century; **el ~ de las Luces** the Age of Enlightenment; **el ~ de Oro** the Golden Age. **-2.** *fig* [mucho tiempo]: **hace ~s que no la veo** I haven't seen her for ages; **por los ~s de los ~s** for ever and ever.
signatario, -ria *adj, m y f* signatory.
signatura *f* **-1.** [en biblioteca] catalogue number. **-2.** [firma] signature.
significación *f* **-1.** [importancia] significance. **-2.** [significado] meaning.
significado, -da *adj* important.
◆ **significado** *m* **-1.** [sentido] meaning. **-2.** LING signifier.
significante *m* LING signifiant.
significar [10] ◇ *vt* **-1.** [gen] to mean. **-2.** [expresar] to express. ◇ *vi* [tener importancia]: **no significa nada para mí** it means nothing to me.
◆ **significarse por** *vpr* to become known for.
significativo, -va *adj* significant.
signo *m* **-1.** [gen] sign; **~ de multiplicar/dividir** multiplication/division sign; **~ del zodíaco** sign of the zodiac. **-2.** [en la escritura] mark; **~ de admiración/interrogación** exclamation/question mark. **-3.** [símbolo] symbol.
sigo *etc* → seguir.
siguiente ◇ *adj* **-1.** [en el tiempo, espacio] next. **-2.** [a continuación] following. ◇ *m y f* **-1.** [el que sigue]: **el ~** the next one; **¡el ~!** next, please! **-2.** [lo que sigue]: **lo ~** the following.
siguiera *etc* → seguir.
sij (*pl* **sijs**) *adj, m y f* Sikh.
sílaba *f* syllable.
silabear ◇ *vt* to spell out syllable by syllable. ◇ *vi* to read syllable by syllable.
silábico, -ca *adj* syllabic.

silbar ◇ *vt* **-1.** [gen] to whistle. **-2.** [abuchear] to hiss, to catcall. ◇ *vi* **-1.** [gen] to whistle. **-2.** [abuchear] to hiss, to catcall. **-3.** *fig* [oídos] to ring.

silbato *m* whistle.

silbido, silbo *m* **-1.** [gen] whistle. **-2.** [para abuchear, del serpiente] hiss, hissing (*U*).

silenciador *m* silencer.

silenciar [8] *vt* to hush up, to keep quiet.

silencio *m* **-1.** [gen] silence; **en ~** in silence; **guardar ~ (sobre algo)** to keep silent (about sthg); **guardaron un minuto de ~** they held a minute's silence; **imponer ~ a alguien** to make sb be silent; **romper el ~** to break the silence. **-2.** MÚS rest.

silencioso, -sa *adj* silent, quiet.

sílex *m inv* flint.

sílfide *f* sylph.

silicato *m* silicate.

sílice *f* silica.

silicio *m* silicon.

silicona *f* silicone.

silicosis *f inv* silicosis.

silla *f* **-1.** [gen] chair; **~ de la reina** seat made by two people joining hands; **~ de ruedas** wheelchair; **~ eléctrica** electric chair. **-2.** [de caballo]: **~ (de montar)** saddle.

sillería *f* set of chairs; [de coro] choir stalls (*pl*).

sillín *m* saddle, seat.

sillón *m* armchair.

silo *m* silo.

silogismo *m* syllogism.

silueta *f* **-1.** [cuerpo] figure. **-2.** [contorno] outline. **-3.** [dibujo] silhouette.

silvestre *adj* wild.

sima *f* chasm.

simbiosis *f inv* symbiosis.

simbólico, -ca *adj* symbolic.

simbolismo *m* symbolism.

simbolizar [13] *vt* to symbolize.

símbolo *m* symbol.

simbología *f* system of symbols.

simetría *f* symmetry.

simétrico, -ca *adj* symmetrical.

simiente *f culto* seed.

simiesco, -ca *adj* simian, apelike.

símil *m* **-1.** [paralelismo] similarity, resemblance. **-2.** LITER simile.

similar *adj*: **~ (a)** similar (to).

similitud *f* similarity.

simio, -mia *m y f* simian, ape.

simpatía *f* **-1.** [cordialidad] friendliness. **-2.** [cariño] affection; **coger ~ a alguien** to take a liking to sb; **tener ~ a, sentir ~ por** to like. **-3.** MED sympathy.

simpático, -ca *adj* **-1.** [gen] nice, likeable; [abierto, cordial] friendly. **-2.** [anécdota, comedia etc] amusing, entertaining. **-3.** [reunión, velada etc] pleasant, agreeable. **-4.** ANAT sympathetic.

simpatizante ◇ *adj* sympathizing. ◇ *m y f* sympathizer.

simpatizar [13] *vi*: **~ (con)** [persona] to hit it off (with), to get on (with); [cosa] to sympathize (with).

simple ◇ *adj* **-1.** [gen] simple. **-2.** [fácil] easy, simple. **-3.** [único, sin componentes] single; **dame una ~ razón** give me one single reason. **-4.** [mero] mere; **por ~ estupidez** through sheer stupidity. **-5.** MAT prime. ◇ *m y f* [persona] simpleton.

simplemente *adv* simply.

simpleza *f* **-1.** [de persona] simplemindedness. **-2.** [tontería] trifle.

simplicidad *f* simplicity.

simplificación *f* simplification.

simplificar [10] *vt* to simplify.

◆ **simplificarse** *vpr* to be simplified.

simplista ◇ *adj* simplistic. ◇ *m y f* naïve person.

simplón, -ona ◇ *adj* simple, simpleminded. ◇ *m y f* simpleminded person.

simposio, simposium *m* symposium.

simulación *f* pretence, simulation.

simulacro *m* simulation; **~ de combate** mock battle.

simulado, -da *adj* **-1.** [sentimiento, desmayo etc] feigned. **-2.** [combate, salvamento] simulated.

simular *vt* **-1.** [sentimiento, desmayo etc] to feign; **simuló que no me había visto** he pretended not to have seen me. **-2.** [combate, salvamento] to simulate.

simultanear *vt* to do at the same time.

simultaneidad *f* simultaneousness.

simultáneo, -nea *adj* simultaneous.

sin *prep* without; **~ alcohol** alcohol-free; **estoy ~ una peseta** I'm penniless; **ha escrito cinco libros ~ (contar) las novelas** he has written five books, not counting his novels; **está ~ hacer** it hasn't been done yet; **estamos ~ vino** we're out of wine; **~ que** (+ *subjuntivo*) without (+ *gerund*); **~ que nadie se enterara** without anyone noticing.

◆ **sin embargo** *conj* however.

sinagoga *f* synagogue.

Sinaí *m*: **el ~** Sinai.

sincerarse *vpr*: **~ (con alguien)** to open one's heart (to sb).

sinceridad *f* sincerity; [llaneza, franqueza] frankness; **con toda** ~ in all honesty.

sincero, -ra *adj* sincere; [abierto, directo] frank; **para ser** ~ to be honest.

síncopa *f* -1. [en palabra] syncope. -2. MÚS syncopation.

sincopado, -da *adj* syncopated.

sincopar *vt* to syncopate.

síncope *m* blackout.

sincretismo *m* synchretism.

sincronía *f* -1. [simultaneidad] synchronousness. -2. LING synchrony.

sincrónico, -ca *adj* -1. [simultáneo] simultaneous. -2. [coordinado] synchronous. -3. LING synchronic.

sincronismo *m* -1. [simultaneidad] simultaneity. -2. FÍS tuning.

sincronización *f* synchronization.

sincronizar [13] *vt* -1. [regular] to synchronize. -2. FÍS to tune.

sindicación *f* trade union membership.

sindicado, -da *adj* belonging to a trade union.

sindical *adj* (trade) union (*antes de sust*).

sindicalismo *m* trade unionism.

sindicalista ◇ *adj* (trade) union (*antes de sust*). ◇ *m y f* trade unionist.

sindicar [10] *vt* to unionize.
◆ **sindicarse** *vpr* to join a union.

sindicato *m* trade union, labor union *Am*; ~ **amarillo** yellow union, *conservative trade union that leans towards the employers' interests*; ~ **vertical** *workers' and employers' union during the Franco period*.

síndico *m* -1. [representante] community representative. -2. [administrador] (official) receiver. -3. ECON trustee.

síndrome *m* syndrome; ~ **de abstinencia** withdrawal symptoms (*pl*); ~ **de Down** Down's syndrome; ~ **de Estocolmo** Stockholm syndrome; ~ **tóxico** *toxic syndrome caused by ingestion of adulterated rapeseed oil*.

sine
◆ **sine die** *loc adv* indefinitely.

sinecura *f* sinecure.

sinergia *f* synergy.

sinestesia *f* synaesthesia.

sinfín *m* vast number; **un** ~ **de problemas** no end of problems.

sinfonía *f* symphony.

sinfónico, -ca *adj* symphonic.

Singapur Singapore.

singladura *f* NÁUT [distancia] day's run; *fig* [dirección] course.

single ['siŋgel] *m* single.

singular ◇ *adj* -1. [raro] peculiar, odd. -2. [único] unique. -3. GRAM singular. ◇ *m* GRAM singular; **en** ~ in the singular.

singularidad *f* -1. [rareza, peculiaridad] peculiarity. -2. [exclusividad] uniqueness.

singularizar [13] *vt* to distinguish, to single out.
◆ **singularizarse** *vpr* to stand out, to be conspicuous.

siniestrado, -da ◇ *adj* [coche, avión etc] crashed, smashed up; [edificio] ruined, destroyed. ◇ *m y f* victim.

siniestralidad *f* accident rate.

siniestro, -tra *adj* -1. [perverso] sinister. -2. [desgraciado] disastrous.
◆ **siniestro** *m* disaster; [accidente de coche] accident, crash; [incendio] fire.
◆ **siniestra** *f desus* left hand.

sinnúmero *m*: **un** ~ **de** countless.

sino[1] *m* fate, destiny.

sino[2] *conj* -1. [para contraponer] but; **no lo hizo él,** ~ **ella** he didn't do it, she did; **no sólo es listo,** ~ **también trabajador** he's not only clever but also hardworking. -2. [para exceptuar] except, but; **¿quién** ~ **tú lo haría?** who else but you would do it?; **no quiero** ~ **que se haga justicia** I only want justice to be done.

sínodo *m* synod.

sinonimia *f* synonymy.

sinónimo, -ma *adj* synonymous.
◆ **sinónimo** *m* synonym.

sinopsis *f inv* synopsis.

sinóptico, -ca *adj* synoptic.

sinovial *adj* synovial.

sinrazón *f* (*gen pl*) injustice.

sinsabor *m* (*gen pl*) trouble.

sintáctico, -ca *adj* syntactic.

sintagma *m* syntagma.

sintaxis *f inv* syntax.

síntesis *f inv* synthesis; **en** ~ in short; ~ **del habla** INFORM & LING speech synthesis.

sintético, -ca *adj* -1. [artificial] synthetic. -2. [resumido] summarized.

sintetizador, -ra *adj* synthesizing.
◆ **sintetizador** *m* synthesizer.

sintetizar [13] *vt* -1. [resumir] to summarize. -2. [fabricar artificialmente] to synthesize.

sintiera *etc* → sentir.

sintoísmo *m* Shintoism.

síntoma *m* symptom.

sintomático, -ca *adj* symptomatic.

sintomatología *f* symptoms (*pl*).

sintonía *f* -1. [música] signature tune. -2.

[conexión] tuning. **-3.** *fig* [compenetración] harmony.

sintonización *f* **-1.** [conexión] tuning. **-2.** *fig* [compenetración] harmonization.

sintonizador *m* tuner, tuning dial.

sintonizar [13] ◇ *vt* [conectar] to tune in to. ◇ *vi* **-1.** [conectar]: ~ **(con)** to tune in (to). **-2.** *fig* [compenetrarse]: ~ **en algo (con alguien)** to be on the same wavelength (as sb) about sthg.

sinuosidad *f* bend, wind.

sinuoso, -sa *adj* **-1.** [camino] winding. **-2.** [movimiento] sinuous. **-3.** *fig* [disimulado] devious.

sinusitis *f inv* sinusitis.

sinvergüenza ◇ *adj* **-1.** [canalla] shameless. **-2.** [fresco, descarado] cheeky. ◇ *m y f* **-1.** [canalla] rogue. **-2.** [fresco, descarado] cheeky person.

sionismo *m* Zionism.

sionista *adj, m y f* Zionist.

sioux ['siuks] *adj inv & m y f inv* Sioux.

sique = **psique**.

siquiatra = **psiquiatra**.

siquiatría = **psiquiatría**.

siquiátrico, -ca = **psiquiátrico**.

síquico, -ca = **psíquico**.

siquiera ◇ *conj* [aunque] even if; **ven ~ por pocos días** do come, even if it's only for a few days. ◇ *adv* [por lo menos] at least; **dime ~ tu nombre** (you could) at least tell me your name.
◆ **ni (tan) siquiera** *loc conj* not even; **ni (tan) ~ me hablaron** they didn't even speak to me.

siquis = **psiquis**.

sirena *f* **-1.** MITOL mermaid, siren. **-2.** [señal] siren.

Siria Syria.

sirimiri *m* drizzle.

sirio, -ria *adj, m y f* Syrian.

siroco *m* sirocco.

sirva *etc* → **servir**.

sirviente, -ta *m y f* servant.

sirviera *etc* → **servir**.

sisa *f* **-1.** [de dinero] pilfering. **-2.** [en costura] dart; [de manga] armhole.

sisar ◇ *vt* **-1.** [dinero] to pilfer. **-2.** [costura] to take in. ◇ *vi* to pilfer.

sisear *vt & vi* to hiss.

siseo *m* hiss, hissing (*U*).

sísmico, -ca *adj* seismic.

sismo *m* earthquake.

sismógrafo *m* seismograph.

sisón, -ona ◇ *adj* pilfering. ◇ *m y f* [ladrón] pilferer, petty thief.
◆ **sisón** *m* [ave] little bustard.

sistema *m* **-1.** [gen & INFORM] system; ~ **nervioso/solar** nervous/solar system; ~ **experto/operativo** INFORM expert/operating system; ~ **fiscal** ○ **impositivo** tax system; ~ **ABS** AUTOM ABS (brake) system; ~ **dual** TV *system enabling dubbed TV programmes to be heard in the original language;* ~ **de gestión de bases de datos** INFORM database management system; ~ **internacional de unidades** SI units (*pl*); ~ **métrico (decimal)** metric (decimal) system; ~ **monetario europeo** European Monetary System; ~ **montañoso** mountain chain ○ range; ~ **periódico de los elementos** periodic table of elements. **-2.** [método, orden] method.
◆ **por sistema** *loc adv* systematically.

Sistema Ibérico *m*: **el ~** the Iberian mountain chain.

sistemático, -ca *adj* systematic.

sistematización *f* systematization.

sistematizar [13] *vt* to systematize.

sístole *f* systole.

sitiado, -da *adj* besieged.

sitial *m culto* seat of honour.

sitiar [8] *vt* **-1.** [cercar] to besiege. **-2.** *fig* [acorralar] to surround.

sitio *m* **-1.** [lugar] place; **cambiar de ~ (con alguien)** to change places (with sb). **-2.** [espacio] room, space; **hacer ~ a alguien** to make room for sb. **-3.** [cerco] siege. **-4.** INFORM: ~ **Web** Web site.

sito, -ta *adj* located.

situ
◆ **in situ** *loc adv* on the spot.

situación *f* **-1.** [circunstancias] situation; [legal, social] status; **estar en ~ de hacer algo** [gen] to be in a position to do sthg; [suj: enfermo, borracho] to be in a fit state to do sthg; ~ **límite** extreme situation. **-2.** [condición, estado] state, condition. **-3.** [ubicación] location.

situado, -da *adj* **-1.** [acomodado] comfortably off. **-2.** [ubicado] located.

situar [6] *vt* **-1.** [colocar] to place, to put; [edificio, ciudad] to site, to locate. **-2.** [en clasificación] to place, to rank. **-3.** [localizar] to locate, to find.
◆ **situarse** *vpr* **-1.** [colocarse] to take up position. **-2.** [ubicarse] to be located. **-3.** [acomodarse, establecerse] to get o.s. established. **-4.** [en clasificación] to be placed; **se sitúa entre los mejores** he's (ranked) amongst the best.

siútico, -ca *adj Amer fam* naff, tacky.

SJ (*abrev de* **Societatis Jesus**) *f* SJ.

skai [es'kai] = **escay**.

skateboard [es'keiðʃor] (*pl* **skateboards**) *m* **-1.** [tabla] skateboard. **-2.** [deporte] skateboarding.

sketch [es'ketʃ] (*pl* **sketches**) *m* CIN & TEATR sketch.

ski [es'ki] = **esquí**.

skin head [es'kinxeð] (*pl* **skin heads**) *m y f* skinhead.

s.l. *abrev de* **sus labores**.

SL (*abrev de* **sociedad limitada**) *f* ≃ Ltd.

slalom [es'lalom] = **eslálom**.

slip [es'lip] = **eslip**.

SLMM (*abrev de* **Sindicato Libre de la Marina Mercante**) *m Spanish merchant navy union*.

slogan [es'loʏan] = **eslogan**.

SM (*abrev de* **Su Majestad**) HM.

smash [es'maʃ] (*pl* **smashes**) *m* DEP smash.

SME (*abrev de* **sistema monetario europeo**) *m* EMS.

SMI (*abrev de* **sistema monetario internacional**) *m* IMS.

smoking [es'mokin] = **esmoquin**.

s/n *abrev de* **sin número**.

snob = **esnob**.

snobismo = **esnobismo**.

so ◇ *prep* under; ~ **pretexto de** under the pretext of. ◇ *adv*: ¡~ **tonto!** you idiot! ◇ *interj*: ¡~! whoa!

sobaco *m* armpit.

sobado, -da *adj* **-1.** [cuello, puños etc] worn, shabby; [libro] dog-eared. **-2.** *fig* [argumento, excusa] well-worn, hackneyed. **-3.** CULIN short (*antes de sust*).
◆ **sobado** *m* CULIN shortcrust pastry.

sobaquera *f* armhole.

sobaquina *f fam* body odour.

sobar ◇ *vt* **-1.** [tocar] to finger, to paw. **-2.** *despec* [acariciar, besar] to touch up, to fondle. **-3.** [ablandar] to soften. ◇ *vi mfam* to kip.

soberanía *f* sovereignty.

soberano, -na ◇ *adj* **-1.** [independiente] sovereign. **-2.** *fig* [grande] massive; [paliza] thorough; [belleza, calidad] supreme, unrivalled. ◇ *m y f* sovereign.

soberbio, -bia ◇ *adj* **-1.** [arrogante] proud, arrogant. **-2.** [magnífico] superb. **-3.** [grande] huge. ◇ *m y f* [persona] arrogant ○ proud person.
◆ **soberbia** *f* **-1.** [arrogancia] pride, arrogance. **-2.** [magnificencia] grandeur, splendour.

sobón, -ona *adj, m y f fam* groper.

sobornar *vt* to bribe.

soborno *m* **-1.** [acción] bribery. **-2.** [dinero, regalo] bribe.

sobra *f* excess, surplus; **de** ~ [en exceso] more than enough; [de más] superfluous; **aquí estoy de** ~, **me voy** I'm off, it's obvious I'm not wanted here; **lo sabemos de** ~ we know it only too well.
◆ **sobras** *fpl* **-1.** [de comida] leftovers. **-2.** [de tela] remnants.

sobrado, -da *adj* **-1.** [de sobra] more than enough, plenty of. **-2.** [de dinero] well off.

sobrante ◇ *adj* remaining. ◇ *m* surplus.

sobrar *vi* **-1.** [quedar, restar] to be left over, to be spare; **nos sobró comida** we had some food left over. **-2.** [haber de más] to be more than enough; **parece que van a** ~ **bocadillos** it looks like there are going to be too many sandwiches. **-3.** [estar de más] to be superfluous; **lo que dices sobra** that goes without saying.

sobrasada *f Mallorcan spiced sausage*.

sobre[1] *m* **-1.** [para cartas] envelope. **-2.** [para alimentos] sachet, packet. **-3.** *mfam* [cama] sack; **irse al** ~ to hit the sack.

sobre[2] *prep* **-1.** [encima de] on (top of); **el libro está** ~ **la mesa** the book is on (top of) the table. **-2.** [por encima de] over, above; **el pato vuela** ~ **el lago** the duck is flying over the lake. **-3.** [superioridad] above; **su opinión está** ~ **las de los demás** his opinion is more important than that of the others. **-4.** [acerca de] about, on; **un libro** ~ **el amor** a book about ○ on love; **una conferencia** ~ **el desarme** a conference on disarmament. **-5.** [alrededor de] about; **llegarán** ~ **las diez** they'll arrive at about ten o'clock. **-6.** [acumulación] upon; **nos contó mentira** ~ **mentira** he told us lie upon lie ○ one lie after another. **-7.** [cerca de] upon; **la desgracia estaba ya** ~ **nosotros** the disaster was already upon us.

sobreabundancia = **superabundancia**.

sobreabundante = **superabundante**.

sobreabundar = **superabundar**.

sobrealimentación *f* overfeeding.

sobrealimentar *vt* to overfeed.

sobreañadir *vt* to add on top of.

sobrecalentar [19] *vt* to overheat.

sobrecarga *f* **-1.** [exceso de carga] excess weight. **-2.** [saturación] overload.

sobrecargar [16] *vt* [gen] to overload; [decoración etc] to overdo.

sobrecargo *m* **-1.** NÁUT supercargo. **-2.** COM surcharge.

sobrecogedor, -ra *adj* frightening, startling.

sobrecoger [14] *vt* to frighten, to startle.
◆ **sobrecogerse** *vpr* to be frightened, to be startled.
sobrecongelar *vt* to deep-freeze.
sobrecosto *m* extra costs (*pl*).
sobrecubierta *f* -1. [de libro] (dust) jacket. -2. [de barco] upper deck.
sobredosis *f inv* overdose.
sobreentender = sobrentender.
sobreentendido = sobrentendido.
sobreexcitar = sobrexcitar.
sobreexponer = sobrexponer.
sobreexposición = sobrexposición.
sobrefusión *f* supercooling.
sobregiro *m* COM overdraft.
sobrehilar *vt* to whipstitch.
sobrehumano, -na *adj* superhuman.
sobreimpresión *f* superimposing (*U*).
sobreimprimir *vt* to superimpose.
sobrellevar *vt* to bear, to endure.
sobremanera *adv* exceedingly.
sobremesa *f* after-dinner period; **de ~** [programación etc] mid-afternoon (*antes de sust*).

SOBREMESA:
The time after a meal, when the dishes are cleared away and coffee and liqueurs are served, is called the 'sobremesa'. People remain at the table chatting over their drinks; sometimes they play a game of cards or watch television

sobrenadar *vi* to float.
sobrenatural *adj* [extraordinario] supernatural.
sobrenombre *m* nickname.
sobrentender, sobreentender [20] *vt* to understand, to deduce.
◆ **sobrentenderse** *vpr* to be inferred O implied.
sobrentendido, -da, sobreentendido, -da *adj* implied, implicit.
sobrepasar *vt* -1. [exceder] to exceed. -2. [aventajar]: **~ a alguien** to overtake sb.
sobrepeso *m* excess weight.
sobreponer, superponer [65] *vt* -1. [poner encima] to put on top. -2. *fig* [anteponer]: **~ algo a algo** to put sthg before sthg.
◆ **sobreponerse** *vpr*: **~se a algo** to overcome sthg.
sobreposición, superposición *f* superimposing.
sobreproducción, superproducción *f* ECON overproduction (*U*).
sobreproteger [14] *vt* to overprotect.

sobrepuesto, -ta, superpuesto, -ta *adj* superimposed.
◆ **sobrepuesto, -ta** *pp* → sobreponer.
sobrepujar *vt* to outdo, to surpass.
sobresaliente ◇ *adj* [destacado] outstanding. ◇ *m* [en escuela] excellent, ≃ A; [en universidad] ≃ first class.
sobresalir [71] *vi* -1. [en tamaño] to jut out. -2. [en importancia] to stand out.
sobresaltar *vt* to startle.
◆ **sobresaltarse** *vpr* to be startled, to start.
sobresalto *m* start, fright; **dar un ~ a alguien** to make sb start, to give sb a fright.
sobresaturar *vt* to supersaturate.
sobrescribir *vt* to overwrite.
sobrescrito, -ta *pp* → sobrescribir.
sobreseer [50] *vt* DER to discontinue, to stay.
sobreseimiento *m* DER stay.
sobrestimar *vt* to overestimate.
sobresueldo *m* extra money on the side (*U*).
sobretasa *f* surcharge.
sobretodo *m* overcoat.
sobrevenir [75] *vi* to happen, to ensue; **sobrevino la guerra** the war intervened.
sobreviviente = superviviente.
sobrevivir *vi* to survive; **~ a alguien** to outlive sb.
sobrevolar [23] *vt* to fly over.
sobrexcitar, sobreexcitar *vt* to overexcite.
◆ **sobrexcitarse** *vpr* to get overexcited.
sobrexponer, sobreexponer [65] *vt* to overexpose.
sobrexposición, sobreexposición *f* overexposure.
sobriedad *f* -1. [moderación] restraint, moderation. -2. [no embriaguez] soberness.
sobrino, -na *m y f* nephew (*f* niece).
sobrio, -bria *adj* -1. [moderado] restrained; **~ en** moderate in. -2. [no excesivo] simple. -3. [austero, no borracho] sober.
SOC (*abrev de* **Sindicato de Obreros del Campo**) *m* Spanish farm-workers' union.
socaire *m* NÁUT lee; **al ~ de** *fig* under the protection of.
socarrón, -ona *adj* sarcastic.
socarronería *f* sarcasm.
socavar *vt* [excavar por debajo] to dig under; *fig* [debilitar] to undermine.
socavón *m* -1. [hoyo] hollow; [en la carretera] pothole. -2. MIN gallery.
sociabilidad *f* sociability.
sociable *adj* sociable.

social *adj* **-1.** [gen] social. **-2.** COM company (*antes de sust*).

socialdemocracia *f* social democracy.

socialdemócrata ◇ *adj* social democratic. ◇ *m y f* social democrat.

socialismo *m* socialism.

socialista *adj, m y f* socialist.

socialización *f* ECON nationalization.

socializar [13] *vt* ECON to nationalize.

sociedad *f* **-1.** [gen] society; **entrar** ○ **presentarse en** ~ to come out, to make one's debut; **alta** ~ high society; ~ **de consumo** consumer society; ~ **deportiva** sports club; ~ **literaria** literary society. **-2.** COM [empresa] company; ~ **anónima** public (limited) company *Br*, incorporated company *Am*; ~ **civil** non-profit making company; ~ **colectiva** general partnership; ~ **comanditaria** ○ **en comandita** general and limited partnership; (~) **cooperativa** cooperative; ~ **de cartera** portfolio company; ~ **(de responsabilidad) limitada** private limited company; ~ **industrial** industrial society.

socio, -cia *m y f* **-1.** COM partner; ~ **capitalista** ○ **comanditario** sleeping partner *Br*, silent partner *Am*; ~ **fundador** founding partner. **-2.** [miembro] member. **-3.** *fam* [amigo] mate.

sociocultural *adj* sociocultural.

socioeconomía *f* socioeconomics (*U*).

socioeconómico, -ca *adj* socioeconomic.

sociolingüístico, -ca *adj* sociolinguistic.

◆ **sociolingüística** *f* sociolinguistics (*U*).

sociología *f* sociology.

sociólogo, -ga *m y f* sociologist.

sociopolítico, -ca *adj* sociopolitical.

socorrer *vt* to help.

socorrido, -da *adj* [útil] useful, handy.

socorrismo *m* first aid; [en la playa] life-saving.

socorrista *m y f* first aid worker; [en la playa] lifeguard.

socorro ◇ *m* help, aid. ◇ *interj*: ¡~! help!

soda *f* [bebida] soda water.

sódico, -ca *adj* sodium (*antes de sust*).

sodio *m* sodium.

sodomía *f* sodomy.

sodomita *adj, m y f* sodomite.

sodomizar [13] *vt* to sodomize.

SOE (*abrev de* **seguro obligatorio de enfermedad**) *m* *compulsory sickness insurance in Spain*.

soez *adj* vulgar, dirty.

sofá (*pl* **sofás**) *m* sofa; ~ **cama** ○ **nido** sofa bed.

Sofía Sofia.

sofisma *m* sophism.

sofisticación *f* sophistication.

sofisticado, -da *adj* sophisticated.

sofocado, -da *adj* **-1.** [por cansancio] gasping for breath; [por calor] suffocating. **-2.** [por vergüenza] mortified. **-3.** [por irritación] hot under the collar.

sofocante *adj* suffocating, stifling.

sofocar [10] *vt* **-1.** [ahogar] to suffocate, to stifle. **-2.** [incendio] to put out, to smother. **-3.** *fig* [rebelión] to suppress, to quell. **-4.** *fig* [avergonzar] to mortify.

◆ **sofocarse** *vpr* **-1.** [ahogarse] to suffocate. **-2.** *fig* [avergonzarse] to go red as a beetroot. **-3.** *fig* [irritarse]: ~**se (por)** to get hot under the collar (about).

sofoco *m* **-1.** [ahogo] breathlessness (*U*); [sonrojo, bochorno] hot flush. **-2.** *fig* [vergüenza] mortification. **-3.** *fig* [disgusto]: **llevarse un** ~ to have a fit.

sofocón *m* *fam*: **llevarse un** ~ to get hot under the collar.

sofoque *etc* → **sofocar**.

sofreír [28] *vt* to fry lightly over a low heat.

sofría *etc* → **sofreír**.

sofriera *etc* → **sofreír**.

sofrito, -ta *pp* → **sofreír**.

◆ **sofrito** *m* *fried tomato and onion sauce*.

sofrología *f* relaxation therapy.

software ['sofwer] *m* INFORM software; ~ **integrado** integrated software.

soga *f* rope; [para ahorcar] noose; **estar con la** ~ **al cuello** *fig* to be in dire straits; **no hay que mentar la** ~ **en casa del ahorcado** use a little tact.

sois → **ser**.

soja *f* soya.

sojuzgar [16] *vt* to subjugate.

sol *m* **-1.** [astro] sun; **hace** ~ it's sunny; ~ **naciente/poniente** rising/setting sun; **de** ~ **a** ~ from dawn to dusk; **no dejar a alguien ni a** ~ **ni a sombra** not to give sb a moment's peace. **-2.** [rayos, luz] sunshine, sun; **tomar el** ~ to sunbathe. **-3.** TAUROM *seats in the sun, the cheapest in the bullring*. **-4.** *fig* [ángel, ricura] darling, angel. **-5.** MÚS G; [en solfeo] so. **-6.** [moneda] sol.

◆ **sol y sombra** *m* [bebida] *mixture of brandy and anisette*.

solace *etc* → **solazar**.

solamente *adv* only, just; **vino** ~ **él** only he came.

solana *f* **-1.** [lugar] sunny spot. **-2.** [galería] sun lounge.

solano *m* east wind.

solapa *f* **-1.** [de prenda] lapel. **-2.** [de libro, sobre] flap.

solapado, -da *adj* underhand, devious.

solapar *vt* to cover up.

solar ◇ *adj* solar. ◇ *m* undeveloped plot (of land).

solariego, -ga *adj* ancestral.

solario, solárium (*pl* **solariums**) *m* solarium.

solaz *m* **-1.** [entretenimiento] amusement, entertainment. **-2.** [descanso] rest.

solazar [13] *vt* to amuse, to entertain.
◆ **solazarse** *vpr* to enjoy o.s.

soldada *f* pay.

soldado *m* soldier; ~ **de primera** ≃ lance corporal; ~ **raso** private.

soldador, -ra *m y f* [persona] welder.
◆ **soldador** *m* [aparato] soldering iron.

soldadura *f* **-1.** [acción] soldering, welding. **-2.** [juntura] weld, soldered joint.

soldar [23] *vt* to solder, to weld.

soleado, -da *adj* sunny.

solear *vt* to put in the sun.

solecismo *m* solecism.

soledad *f* loneliness; *culto* solitude.

solemne *adj* **-1.** [con pompa] formal. **-2.** [grave] solemn. **-3.** *fig* [enorme] utter, complete.

solemnidad *f* **-1.** [suntuosidad] pomp, solemnity. **-2.** [acto] ceremony.

solemnizar [13] *vt* to celebrate, to commemorate.

soler [81] *vi*: ~ **hacer algo** to do sthg usually; **aquí suele llover mucho** it usually rains a lot here; **solíamos ir a la playa cada día** we used to go to the beach every day.

solera *f* **-1.** [tradición] tradition. **-2.** [del vino] sediment; **de** ~ vintage.

solfa *f* **-1.** MÚS tonic sol-fa. **-2.** *fam* [paliza] thrashing.

solfeo *m* MÚS solfeggio, singing of scales.

solicitante ◇ *adj* applying. ◇ *m y f* applicant.

solicitar *vt* **-1.** [pedir] to request; [un empleo] to apply for; ~ **algo a** ○ **de alguien** to request sthg of sb. **-2.** [persona] to pursue; **estar muy solicitado** to be very popular, to be much sought after.

solícito, -ta *adj* solicitous, obliging.

solicitud *f* **-1.** [petición] request. **-2.** [documento] application. **-3.** [atención] care.

solidaridad *f* solidarity.

solidario, -ria *adj* **-1.** [adherido]: ~ **(con)** sympathetic (to), supporting (of). **-2.** [obligación, compromiso] mutually binding.

solidarizarse [13] *vpr* to make common cause, to show one's solidarity.

solidez *f* **-1.** [física] solidity. **-2.** [moral] firmness.

solidificación *f* solidification.

solidificar [10] *vt* to solidify.
◆ **solidificarse** *vpr* to solidify.

sólido, -da *adj* **-1.** [gen] solid; [cimientos, fundamento] firm. **-2.** [argumento, conocimiento, idea] sound. **-3.** [color] fast.
◆ **sólido** *m* solid.

soliloquio *m* soliloquy.

solista ◇ *adj* solo. ◇ *m y f* soloist.

solitario, -ria ◇ *adj* **-1.** [sin compañía] solitary. **-2.** [lugar] lonely, deserted. ◇ *m y f* [persona] loner.
◆ **solitario** *m* **-1.** [diamante] solitaire. **-2.** [juego] patience.
◆ **solitaria** *f* [tenia] tapeworm.

soliviantar *vt* **-1.** [excitar] to stir up. **-2.** [indignar] to exasperate.
◆ **soliviantarse** *vpr* to be infuriated.

solla *f* plaice.

sollozar [13] *vi* to sob.

sollozo *m* sob.

solo, -la *adj* **-1.** [sin nadie] alone; **se quedó** ~ **a temprana edad** he was on his own from an early age; **a solas** alone, by oneself. **-2.** [sin nada] on its own; [café] black; [whisky] neat. **-3.** [único] single, sole; **ni una sola gota** not a (single) drop; **dame una sola cosa** give me just one thing. **-4.** [solitario] lonely.
◆ **solo** *m* MÚS solo.

sólo *adv* only, just; **no** ~ **... sino (también)** ... not only ... but (also) ...; **con** ~, ~ **con** just by; ~ **que** ... only ....

solomillo *m* sirloin.

solsticio *m* solstice.

soltar [23] *vt* **-1.** [desasir] to let go of. **-2.** [desatar - gen] to unfasten; [- nudo] to untie; [- hebilla, cordones] to undo. **-3.** [dejar libre] to release. **-4.** [desenrollar - cable etc] to let ○ pay out. **-5.** [patada, grito, suspiro etc] to give; **no suelta ni un duro** you can't get a penny out of her. **-6.** [decir bruscamente] to come out with.
◆ **soltarse** *vpr* **-1.** [desasirse] to break free. **-2.** [desatarse] to come undone. **-3.** [desprenderse] to come off. **-4.** *fam* [adquirir habilidad] to get the hang of it; ~**se en algo** to get the hang of sthg. **-5.** [perder timidez] to let go.

soltería *f* [de hombre] bachelorhood; [de mujer] spinsterhood.

soltero, -ra ◇ *adj* single, unmarried. ◇ *m y f* bachelor (*f* single woman).

solterón, -ona ◇ *adj* unmarried. ◇ *m y f* old bachelor (*f* spinster, old maid).

soltura *f* **-1.** [gen] fluency. **-2.** [seguridad de sí mismo] assurance.

soluble *adj* **-1.** [que se disuelve] soluble. **-2.** [que se soluciona] solvable.

solución *f* solution.
♦ **solución de continuidad** *f* interruption; **sin ~ de continuidad** uninterrupted.

solucionar *vt* to solve; [disputa] to resolve.

solvencia *f* **-1.** [económica] solvency. **-2.** [capacidad] reliability.

solventar *vt* **-1.** [pagar] to settle. **-2.** [resolver] to resolve.

solvente *adj* **-1.** [económicamente] solvent. **-2.** *fig* [fuentes etc] reliable.

Somalia Somalia.

somático, -ca *adj* somatic.

somatizar [13] *vt* MED to convert into physical symptoms.

sombra *f* **-1.** [proyección - fenómeno] shadow; [- zona] shade; **a la ~** in the shade; *fam* [en la cárcel] in the slammer; **dar ~ a** to cast a shadow over; **hacer ~ a alguien** to overshadow sb; **ser la ~ de alguien** to be sb's shadow. **-2.** [en pintura] shade. **-3.** *fig* [animato] background; **permanecer en la ~** to stay out of the limelight. **-4.** *fig* [imperfección] stain, blemish. **-5.** *fig* [atisbo] trace, touch; **no tener ni ~ de** not to have the slightest bit of. **-6.** [mancha] spot. **-7.** [suerte]: **buena/mala ~** good/bad luck. **-8.** TAUROM *most expensive seats in bullring, located in the shade.*
♦ **sombras** *fpl* **-1.** [oscuridad, inquietud] darkness (*U*). **-2.** [ignorancia] gaps in one's knowledge.

sombreado *m* shading.

sombrerería *f* **-1.** [fábrica] hat factory. **-2.** [tienda] hat shop.

sombrero *m* **-1.** [prenda] hat; **~ de copa** top hat; **~ hongo** bowler hat, derby *Am*; **quitarse el ~** *fig* to take one's hat off. **-2.** [de setas] cap.

sombrilla *f* sunshade, parasol; **me vale ~** *Amer fig* I couldn't care less.

sombrío, -a *adj* **-1.** [oscuro] gloomy, dark. **-2.** *fig* [triste] sombre, gloomy.

somero, -ra *adj* superficial.

someter *vt* **-1.** [a rebeldes] to subdue. **-2.** [presentar]: **~ algo a la aprobación de alguien** to submit sthg for sb's approval; **~ algo a votación** to put sthg to the vote. **-3.** [subordinar] to subordinate. **-4.** [a operación, interrogatorio etc]: **~ a alguien a algo** to subject sb to sthg.

♦ **someterse** *vpr* **-1.** [rendirse] to surrender. **-2.** [conformarse]: **~se a algo** to yield ○ bow to sthg. **-3.** [a operación, interrogatorio etc]: **~se a algo** to undergo sthg.

sometimiento *m* **-1.** [gen] submission. **-2.** [dominio] subjugation.

somier (*pl* **somieres**) *m* [de muelles] bed springs (*pl*); [de tablas] slats (*of bed*).

sommelier = **sumiller**.

somnífero, -ra *adj* somniferous.
♦ **somnífero** *m* sleeping pill.

somnolencia *f* sleepiness, drowsiness.

somnoliento, -ta *adj* drowsy, sleepy.

somos → ser.

son ◇ *v* → ser. ◇ *m* **-1.** [sonido] sound; **bailar al ~ que le tocan** *fig* to toe the line. **-2.** [estilo] way; **en ~ de** in the manner of; **en ~ de paz** in peace.

sonado, -da *adj* **-1.** [renombrado] famous. **-2.** [loco] crazy. **-3.** [boxeador] punch drunk.

sonajero *m* rattle.

sonambulismo *m* sleepwalking.

sonámbulo, -la ◇ *adj* sleepwalking (*antes de sust*). ◇ *m y f* sleepwalker.

sonante *adj* → dinero.

sonar[1] *m* sonar.

sonar[2] [23] *vi* **-1.** [gen] to sound; **suena a falso/chiste** it sounds false/like a joke; **(así ○ tal) como suena** literally, in so many words. **-2.** [timbre] to ring. **-3.** [hora]: **sonaron las doce** the clock struck twelve. **-4.** [ser conocido, familiar] to be familiar; **me suena** it rings a bell; **no me suena su nombre** I don't remember hearing her name before. **-5.** [pronunciarse - letra] to be pronounced. **-6.** [rumorearse] to be rumoured.
♦ **sonarse** *vpr* to blow one's nose.

sonata *f* sonata.

sonda *f* **-1.** MED & TECN probe; **~ espacial** space probe. **-2.** NÁUT sounding line. **-3.** MIN drill, bore.

sondar *vt* **-1.** MED to sound, to probe. **-2.** NÁUT to sound. **-3.** [MIN - terreno] to test; [- roca] to drill.

sondear *vt* **-1.** [indagar] to sound out. **-2.** [MIN - terreno] to test; [- roca] to drill.

sondeo *m* **-1.** [encuesta] (opinion) poll. **-2.** MIN drilling (*U*), boring (*U*). **-3.** NÁUT sounding.

soneto *m* sonnet.

sónico, -ca *adj* sonic, sound (*antes de sust*).

sonido *m* sound.

SONIMAG (*abrev de* **Sonido e Imagen**) *m* SONIMAG, *sound and vision technology trade fair held in Spain.*

soniquete *m* monotonous noise.

sonora → sonoro.

sonoridad f -1. [gen] sonority. -2. [acústica] acoustics (pl). -3. [resonancia] resonance.

sonorización f soundtrack recording.

sonorizar [13] vt -1. [con amplificadores] to fit with a public address system. -2. CIN [poner sonido] to record the soundtrack for. -3. GRAM to voice.

sonoro, -ra adj -1. [gen] sound (antes de sust); [película] talking. -2. [ruidoso, resonante, vibrante] resonant. -3. GRAM voiced.
◆ **sonora** f GRAM voiced consonant.

sonreír [28] vi -1. [reír levemente] to smile. -2. fig [ser favorable] to smile on.
◆ **sonreírse** vpr to smile.

sonriente adj smiling.

sonriera etc → sonreír.

sonrisa f smile.

sonrojar vt to cause to blush.
◆ **sonrojarse** vpr to blush.

sonrojo m blush, blushing (U).

sonrosado, -da adj rosy.

sonrosar vt to colour pink.

sonsacar [10] vt: ~ algo a alguien [conseguir] to wheedle sthg out of sb; [hacer decir] to extract sthg from sb; ~ a alguien to pump sb for information.

sonso, -sa adj Amer fam silly.

sonsonete m -1. [ruido] tapping (U). -2. fig [entonación] monotonous intonation. -3. fig [cantinela] old tune. -4. fig [sarcasmo] hint of sarcasm.

soñador, -ra ◇ adj dreamy. ◇ m y f dreamer.

soñar [23] ◇ vt lit & fig to dream; ¡ni ~lo! not on your life! ◇ vi lit & fig: ~ (con) to dream (of ○ about); ~ con los angelitos to have sweet dreams; ~ despierto to daydream.

soñoliento, -ta adj sleepy, drowsy.

sopa f -1. [guiso] soup; ~ de ajo garlic soup; ~ juliana ○ de verduras vegetable soup. -2. [de pan] sop, piece of soaked bread. -3. loc: andar a la ~ boba to scrounge; dar ~ con hondas a alguien to knock the spots off sb; encontrarse a alguien hasta en la ~ not to be able to get away from sb; estar como una ~ to be sopping wet.

sopapo m slap.

sopero, -ra adj soup (antes de sust).
◆ **sopero** m [plato] soup plate.
◆ **sopera** f [recipiente] soup tureen.

sopesar vt to try the weight of; fig to weigh up.

sopetón
◆ **de sopetón** loc adv suddenly, abruptly.

soplado m [del vidrio] glassblowing.

soplagaitas fam ◇ adj inv [quisquilloso] fussy. ◇ m y f inv [quisquilloso] fuss-pot.

soplamocos m inv punch on the nose.

soplar ◇ vt -1. [vela, fuego] to blow out. -2. [ceniza, polvo] to blow off. -3. [globo etc] to blow up. -4. [vidrio] to blow. -5. fig [pregunta, examen] to prompt. -6. fig [denunciar] to squeal. -7. fig [hurtar] to pinch, to nick. ◇ vi -1. [gen] to blow. -2. fam [beber] to booze.
◆ **soplarse** vpr fam [comer] to gobble up; [beber] to knock back.

soplete m blowlamp.

soplido m blow, puff.

soplo m -1. [soplido] blow, puff. -2. fig [instante] breath, moment. -3. MED murmur. -4. fam [chivatazo] tip-off; dar el ~ to squeal, to grass.

soplón, -ona m y f fam grass.

soponcio m fam fainting fit; le dio un ~ she passed out.

sopor m drowsiness.

soporífero, -ra adj lit & fig soporific.

soportal m [pórtico] porch.
◆ **soportales** mpl [arcadas] arcade (sg).

soportar vt -1. [sostener] to support. -2. [resistir, tolerar] to stand; ¡no le soporto! I can't stand him! -3. [sobrellevar] to endure, to bear.
◆ **soportarse** vpr to stand one another.

soporte m -1. [apoyo] support; ~ publicitario publicity medium. -2. INFORM medium; ~ físico hardware; ~ lógico software.

soprano m y f soprano.

sor f sister (RELIG).

sorber vt -1. [beber] to sip; [haciendo ruido] to slurp. -2. [absorber] to soak up, to absorb. -3. [atraer] to draw ○ suck in. -4. fig [escuchar atentamente] to drink in.

sorbete m sorbet.

sorbo m -1. [acción] gulp, swallow; [pequeño] sip; beber a ~s to sip. -2. [trago] mouthful; [pequeño] sip. -3. [cantidad pequeña] drop.

sorda → sordo.

sordera f deafness.

sordidez f -1. [miseria] squalor. -2. [obscenidad, perversión] sordidness.

sórdido, -da adj -1. [miserable] squalid. -2. [obsceno, perverso] sordid.

sordina f -1. MÚS [en instrumentos de viento, cuerda] mute; [en pianos] damper. -2. [de reloj] muffle.

sordo, -da ◇ adj -1. [que no oye] deaf; permanecer ~ a ○ ante algo fig to be deaf to sthg; estar más ~ que una tapia to be stone deaf. -2. [pasos] quiet, muffled. -3.

[ruido, dolor] dull. **-4.** GRAM voiceless, un-voiced. ◇ *m y f* [persona] deaf person; **los ~s** the deaf; **hacerse el ~** to turn a deaf ear.

◆ **sorda** *f* GRAM voiceless consonant.

sordomudo, -da ◇ *adj* deaf and dumb. ◇ *m y f* deaf-mute.

soriasis *f inv* psoriasis.

sorna *f* sarcasm.

sorprendente *adj* surprising.

sorprender *vt* **-1.** [asombrar] to surprise. **-2.** [atrapar]: ~ **a alguien (haciendo algo)** to catch sb (doing sthg). **-3.** [coger desprevenido] to catch unawares. **-4.** [descubrir] to discover.

◆ **sorprenderse** *vpr* to be surprised.

sorprendido, -da *adj* surprised.

sorpresa *f* surprise; **dar una ~ a alguien** to surprise sb; **llevarse una ~** to get a surprise; **de** ○ **por ~** by surprise.

sorpresivo, -va *adj Amer* unexpected.

sortear *vt* **-1.** [rifar] to raffle. **-2.** [echar a suertes] to draw lots for. **-3.** *fig* [superar] to get round. **-4.** *fig* [esquivar] to dodge.

sorteo *m* **-1.** [lotería] draw. **-2.** [rifa] raffle.

sortija *f* ring.

sortilegio *m* **-1.** [hechizo] spell. **-2.** *fig* [atractivo] charm, magic.

SOS (*abrev de* **save our souls**) *m* SOS.

sosa *f* soda; ~ **cáustica** caustic soda.

sosegado, -da *adj* calm.

sosegar [35] *vt* to calm.

◆ **sosegarse** *vpr* to calm down.

soseras *m y f inv fam* dull person, bore.

sosería *f* lack of sparkle.

sosias *m inv* double, lookalike.

sosiega *etc* → **sosegar**.

sosiego *m* calm.

soslayar *vt* to avoid.

soslayo

◆ **de soslayo** *loc adv* [oblicuamente] sideways, obliquely; **mirar a alguien de ~** to look at sb out of the corner of one's eye.

soso, -sa ◇ *adj* **-1.** [sin sal] bland, tasteless. **-2.** [sin gracia] dull, insipid. ◇ *m y f* dull person, bore.

sospecha *f* suspicion; **despertar ~s** to arouse suspicion.

sospechar ◇ *vt* [creer, suponer] to suspect; **sospecho que no lo terminará** I doubt whether she'll finish it. ◇ *vi*: ~ **de** to suspect.

sospechoso, -sa ◇ *adj* suspicious. ◇ *m y f* suspect.

sostén *m* **-1.** [apoyo] support. **-2.** [sustento] main support; [alimento] sustenance. **-3.** [sujetador] bra, brassiere.

sostener [72] *vt* **-1.** [sujetar] to support, to hold up. **-2.** [defender - idea, opinión, tesis] to defend; [- promesa, palabra] to stand by, to keep; ~ **que ...** to maintain that .... **-3.** [mantener, costear] to support. **-4.** [tener - conversación] to hold, to have; [- correspondencia] to keep up.

◆ **sostenerse** *vpr* to hold o.s. up; [en pie] to stand up; [en el aire] to hang.

sostenido, -da *adj* **-1.** [persistente] sustained. **-2.** MÚS sharp.

◆ **sostenido** *m* MÚS sharp.

sostiene, sostuviera *etc* → **sostener**.

sota *f* ≈ jack.

sotabanco *m* attic.

sotabarba *f* double chin.

sotana *f* cassock.

sótano *m* basement.

sotavento *m* leeward.

soterrar [19] *vt* [enterrar] to bury; *fig* to hide.

sotto voce [soto'ßotʃe] *loc adv* sotto voce.

soufflé [su'fle] (*pl* **soufflés**) *m* soufflé.

soul *m* MÚS soul (music).

SOV (*abrev de* **seguro obligatorio de viajeros**) *m compulsory travel insurance*.

soviet (*pl* **soviets**) *m* soviet.

soviético, -ca ◇ *adj* **-1.** [del soviet] soviet. **-2.** [de la URSS] Soviet. ◇ *m y f* Soviet.

soy → **ser**.

SP *abrev de* **servicio público**.

spaghetti [espa'ɣeti] = **espagueti**.

spaniel [es'paniel] *m* spaniel.

sparring [es'parrin] (*pl* **sparrings**) *m* DEP sparring partner.

sport [es'port] = **esport**.

spot [es'pot] = **espot**.

spray [es'prai] = **espray**.

sprint [es'prin] = **esprint**.

sprinter [es'printer] = **esprínter**.

squash [es'kwaʃ] *m inv* squash.

squatter [es'kwater] (*pl* **squatters**) *m* squatter.

Sr. (*abrev de* **señor**) Mr.

Sra. (*abrev de* **señora**) Mrs.

Sres. (*abrev de* **señores**) Messrs.

Sri Lanka Sri Lanka.

SRM (*abrev de* **Su Real Majestad**) HRM.

Srta. (*abrev de* **señorita**) Miss.

SS (*abrev de* **Su Santidad**) HH.

s.s.s. (*abrev de* **su seguro servidor**) *formula used in letters*.

Sta. (*abrev de* **santa**) St.

staff [es'taf] = estaf.

stalinismo [estali'nismo] = estalinismo.

stalinista [estali'nista] = estalinista.

stand [es'tand] = estand.

standard [es'tandar] = estándar.

standarización [estandariθa'θjon] = estandarización.

standarizar [estandari'θar] [13] = estandarizar.

standing [es'tandin] = estanding.

starter [es'tarter] = estárter.

statu quo [es'tatu 'kwo] *m inv* status quo.

status [es'tatus] = estatus.

stereo [es'tereo] = estéreo.

sterling [es'terlin] = esterlina.

stick [es'tik] (*pl* **sticks**) *m* DEP hockey stick.

Sto. (*abrev de* **santo**) St.

stock [es'tok] = estoc.

stop, estop [es'top] *m* **-1.** AUTOM stop sign. **-2.** [en telegrama] stop.

stress [es'tres] = estrés.

strip-tease [es'triptis] *m inv* striptease.

su (*pl* **sus**) *adj poses* [de él] his; [de ella] her; [de cosa, animal] its; [de uno] one's; [de ellos, ellas] their; [de usted, ustedes] your.

suahili [sua'xili] *m* [lengua] Swahili.

suave *adj* **-1.** [gen] soft. **-2.** [liso] smooth. **-3.** [sabor, olor, color] delicate. **-4.** [apacible - persona, carácter] gentle; [- clima] mild. **-5.** [fácil - cuesta, tarea, ritmo] gentle; [- dirección de un coche] smooth.

suavidad *f* **-1.** [gen] softness. **-2.** [lisura] smoothness. **-3.** [de sabor, olor, color] delicacy. **-4.** [de carácter] gentleness. **-5.** [de clima] mildness. **-6.** [de cuesta, tarea, ritmo] gentleness; [de la dirección de un coche] smoothness.

suavizante ◇ *adj* [para ropa, cabello] conditioning; [para piel] moisturizing. ◇ *m* conditioner; ~ **para la ropa** fabric conditioner.

suavizar [13] *vt* **-1.** [gen] to soften; [ropa, cabello] to condition. **-2.** [hacer dócil] to temper. **-3.** [ascensión, conducción, tarea] to ease; [clima] to make milder. **-4.** [sabor, olor, color] to tone down. **-5.** [alisar] to smooth.

subacuático, -ca *adj* subaquatic.

subafluente *m* tributary.

subalimentación *f* undernourishment.

subalimentar *vt* to undernourish.

subalquilar *vt* to sublet.

subalterno, -na ◇ *adj* [subordinado] auxiliary. ◇ *m y f* [empleado] subordinate.
♦ **subalterno** *m* TAUROM *assistant to bullfighter; ver también* **tauromaquia.**

subarrendar [19] *vt* to sublet.

subarrendatario, -ria *m y f* subtenant.

subarriendo *m* **-1.** [acción] subtenancy. **-2.** [contrato] sublease (agreement).

subasta *f* **-1.** [venta pública] auction; **sacar algo a** ~ to put sthg up for auction. **-2.** [contrata pública] tender; **sacar algo a** ~ to put sthg out to tender.

subastador, -ra ◇ *adj* auction (*antes de sust*). ◇ *m y f* auctioneer.

subastar *vt* to auction.

subcampeón, -ona *m y f* runner-up.

subcampeonato *m* second place, runner-up's position.

subclase *f* subclass.

subcomisión *f* subcommittee.

subconjunto *m* MAT subset.

subconsciencia *f* subconscious.

subconsciente *adj & m* subconscious.

subcontratar *vt* to subcontract.

subcontrato *m* subcontract.

subcutáneo, -a *adj* subcutaneous.

subdelegación *f* subdelegation.

subdelegado, -da *m y f* subdelegate.

subdesarrollado, -da *adj* underdeveloped.

subdesarrollo *m* underdevelopment.

subdirección *f* [puesto] post of assistant manager.

subdirector, -ra *m y f* assistant manager.

subdirectorio *m* INFORM subdirectory.

súbdito, -ta ◇ *adj*: **ser** ~ **de** to be subject to. ◇ *m y f* **-1.** [subordinado] subject. **-2.** [ciudadano] citizen, national.

subdividir *vt* to subdivide.
♦ **subdividirse** *vpr* to be subdivided.

subdivisión *f* subdivision.

subemplear *vt* to underemploy.

subempleo *m* underemployment.

subespecie *f* subspecies.

subestimar *vt* to underestimate; [infravalorar] to underrate.
♦ **subestimarse** *vpr* to underrate o.s.

subgénero *m* subgenus.

subgrupo *m* subgroup.

subido, -da *adj* **-1.** [intenso] strong, intense. **-2.** *fam* [en cantidad]: **tiene el guapo** ~ he really fancies himself; **está de un imbécil** ~ he has been acting like an idiot recently. **-3.** *fam* [atrevido] risqué; ~ **de tono** [impertinente] impertinent.
♦ **subida** *f* **-1.** [cuesta] hill. **-2.** [ascensión] ascent, climb. **-3.** [aumento] increase, rise.

subíndice *m* subscript.

subinspector, -ra *m y f* deputy inspector.

subir ◇ *vi* **-1.** [a piso, azotea] to go/come up; [a montaña, cima] to climb. **-2.** [aumentar

- precio, temperatura] to go up, to rise; [- cauce, marea] to rise. **-3.** [montar - en avión, barco] to get on; [- en coche] to get in; **sube al coche** get into the car. **-4.** [cuenta, importe]: ~ **a** to come ○ amount to. **-5.** [de categoría] to be promoted. **-6.** CULIN [crecer] to rise.
◇ *vt* **-1.** [ascender - calle, escaleras] to go/come up; [- pendiente, montaña] to climb. **-2.** [poner arriba] to lift up; [llevar arriba] to take/bring up. **-3.** [aumentar - precio, peso] to put up, to increase; [- volumen de radio etc] to turn up. **-4.** [montar]: ~ **algo/a alguien a** to lift sthg/sb onto. **-5.** [alzar - mano, bandera, voz] to raise; [- persiana] to roll up; [- ventanilla] to wind up. **-6.** MÚS to raise the pitch of.
◆ **subirse** *vpr* **-1.** [ascender]: ~**se a** [árbol] to climb up; [mesa] to climb onto; [piso] to go/come up to. **-2.** [montarse]: ~**se a** [tren, avión] to get on, to board; [caballo, bicicleta] to mount; [coche] to get into; **el taxi paró y me subí** the taxi stopped and I got in. **-3.** [alzarse - pernera, mangas] to roll up; [- cremallera] to do up; [- pantalones, calcetines] to pull up. **-4.** *fam* [emborrachar] to go to one's head.

súbito, -ta *adj* sudden.

subjefe, -fa *m y f* second-in-command.

subjetividad *f* subjectivity.

subjetivismo *m* subjectivism.

subjetivo, -va *adj* subjective.

sub júdice [suß'djuðiθe] *adj* DER sub judice.

subjuntivo, -va *adj* subjunctive.
◆ **subjuntivo** *m* subjunctive.

sublevación *f*, **sublevamiento** *m* uprising.

sublevar *vt* **-1.** [amotinar] to stir up. **-2.** [indignar] to infuriate.
◆ **sublevarse** *vpr* [amotinarse] to rise up, to rebel.

sublimación *f* **-1.** [exaltación] exaltation. **-2.** PSICOL & QUÍM sublimation.

sublimar *vt* **-1.** [exaltar] to exalt. **-2.** PSICOL & QUÍM to sublimate.

sublime *adj* sublime.

sublimidad *f* sublimity.

subliminal *adj* subliminal.

submarinismo *m* skin-diving.

submarinista ◇ *adj* skin-diving (*antes de sust*). ◇ *m y f* skin-diver.

submarino, -na *adj* underwater.
◆ **submarino** *m* submarine.

submúltiplo, -pla *adj* submultiple.
◆ **submúltiplo** *m* submultiple.

subnormal ◇ *adj* **-1.** *ofensivo* [minusválido] subnormal. **-2.** *fig* & *despec* [imbécil] moronic. ◇ *m y f* **-1.** *ofensivo* [minusválido]

subnormal person. **-2.** *fig* & *despec* [imbécil] moron, cretin.

subnormalidad *f* subnormality.

suboficial *m* MIL non-commissioned officer.

suborden *m* BIOL suborder.

subordinación *f* [gen & GRAM] subordination.

subordinado, -da *adj*, *m y f* subordinate.

subordinante *adj* GRAM subordinating.

subordinar *vt* [gen & GRAM] to subordinate.
◆ **subordinarse** *vpr* to subordinate o.s.

subproducto *m* by-product.

subrayado, -da *adj* underlined.
◆ **subrayado** *m* underlining.

subrayar *vt* *lit* & *fig* to underline.

subrepticio, -cia *adj* surreptitious.

subrogación *f* subrogation.

subrogar [16] *vt* to subrogate.

subsanable *adj* **-1.** [solucionable] solvable. **-2.** [corregible] rectifiable.

subsanar *vt* **-1.** [solucionar] to resolve. **-2.** [corregir] to correct. **-3.** [disculpar] to excuse.

subscribir = suscribir.

subscripción = suscripción.

subscriptor = suscriptor.

subscrito = suscrito.

subsecretaría *f* **-1.** [oficina] undersecretary's office. **-2.** [cargo] undersecretaryship.

subsecretario, -ria *m y f* **-1.** [de secretario] assistant secretary. **-2.** [de ministro] undersecretary.

subsector *m* subsection.

subsidiar [8] *vt* to subsidize.

subsidiario, -ria *adj* **-1.** [de subvención] paid for by the State. **-2.** DER ancillary.

subsidio *m* benefit, allowance; ~ **de invalidez** disability allowance; ~ **de paro** unemployment benefit.

subsiguiente *adj* subsequent.

subsistencia *f* **-1.** [vida] subsistence. **-2.** [conservación] continued existence.
◆ **subsistencias** *fpl* [provisiones] provisions.

subsistente *adj* surviving.

subsistir *vi* **-1.** [vivir] to live, to exist. **-2.** [sobrevivir] to survive.

substancia = sustancia.

substancial = sustancial.

substanciar [8] = sustanciar.

substancioso = sustancioso.

substantivación = sustantivación.

substantivar = sustantivar.

substantivo = sustantivo.

substitución = sustitución.
substituible = sustituible.
substituir [51] = sustituir.
substitutivo = sustitutivo.
substituto = sustituto.
substracción = sustracción.
substraer [73] = sustraer.
substrato = sustrato.
subsuelo *m* subsoil.
subteniente *m* sub-lieutenant.
subterfugio *m* subterfuge.
subterráneo, -a *adj* subterranean, underground.
◆ **subterráneo** *m* underground tunnel.
subtipo *m* BIOL subtype.
subtitular *vt* [gen & CIN] to subtitle.
subtítulo *m* [gen & CIN] subtitle.
subtropical *adj* subtropical.
suburbano, -na *adj* suburban.
suburbial *adj*: **barrio** ~ poor suburb.
suburbio *m* poor suburb.
subvalorar *vt* to undervalue, to underrate.
subvención *f* subsidy.
subvencionar *vt* to subsidize.
subversión *f* subversion.
subversivo, -va *adj* subversive.
subvertir [27] *vt* to subvert.
subyacente *adj* underlying.
subyacer *vi* [ocultarse]: ~ **bajo algo** to underlie sthg.
subyugador, -ra *adj* -1. [dominador] conquering. -2. [atrayente] captivating.
subyugar [16] *vt* -1. [someter] to subjugate. -2. *fig* [dominar] to quell, to master. -3. *fig* [atraer] to captivate.
succión *f* suction.
succionar *vt* [suj: raíces] to suck up, to absorb; [suj: bebé] to suck.
sucedáneo, -a *adj* ersatz, substitute.
◆ **sucedáneo** *m* substitute.
suceder ◇ *v impers* [ocurrir] to happen; **suceda lo que suceda** whatever happens. ◇ *vt* [sustituir]: ~ **a alguien (en)** to succeed sb (in). ◇ *vi* [venir después]: ~ **a** to come after, to follow; **a la guerra sucedieron años muy tristes** the war was followed by years of misery.
sucedido *m* event.
sucesión *f* -1. [gen] succession. -2. [descendencia] issue.
sucesivamente *adv* successively; **y así** ~ and so on.
sucesivo, -va *adj* -1. [consecutivo] successive, consecutive. -2. [siguiente]: **en días** ~s

les informaremos we'll let you know over the next few days; **en lo** ~ in future.
suceso *m* -1. [acontecimiento] event. -2. (*gen pl*) [hecho delictivo] crime; [incidente] incident.
sucesor, -ra ◇ *adj* succeeding. ◇ *m y f* successor.
sucesorio, -ria *adj* succession (*antes de sust*).
suciedad *f* -1. [cualidad] dirtiness (*U*). -2. [porquería] dirt, filth (*U*).
sucinto, -ta *adj* -1. [conciso] succinct. -2. [pequeño - biquini etc] skimpy.
sucio, -cia *adj* -1. [gen] dirty; [al comer, trabajar] messy; **el blanco es un color muy** ~ white is a colour that gets dirty easily; **en** ~ in rough. -2. [juego] dirty. -3. [conciencia] bad, guilty.
sucre *m* [moneda] sucre.
suculento, -ta *adj* tasty.
sucumbir *vi* -1. [rendirse, ceder]: ~ **(a)** to succumb (to). -2. [fallecer] to die.
sucursal *f* branch.
sudaca *adj, m y f fam* racist term referring to a Latin American.
sudadera *f* -1. [sudor] sweat. -2. [prenda] sweatshirt.
sudado *m Amer* stew.
Sudáfrica South Africa.
sudafricano, -na *adj, m y f* South African.
Sudán Sudan.
sudanés, -esa *adj, m y f* Sudanese.
sudar ◇ *vi* -1. [gen] to sweat. -2. *fam* [trabajar duro] to sweat blood. ◇ *vt* -1. [empapar] to make sweaty. -2. *fam* [trabajar duro por] to work hard for.
sudario *m* shroud.
sudeste, sureste ◇ *adj* [posición, parte] south-east, southeastern; [dirección, viento] southeasterly. ◇ *m* southeast.
sudista ◇ *adj* Southern (*in US Civil War*). ◇ *m y f* Southerner (*in US Civil War*).
sudoeste, suroeste ◇ *adj* [posición, parte] southwest, southwestern; [dirección, viento] southwesterly. ◇ *m* southwest.
sudor *m* -1. [gen] sweat (*U*); **con el** ~ **de su frente** by the sweat of his/her *etc* brow. -2. [de botijo etc] condensation.
sudoriento, -ta *adj* sweaty.
sudoríparo, -ra *adj* sweat (*antes de sust*).
sudoroso, -sa *adj* sweaty.
Suecia Sweden.
sueco, -ca ◇ *adj* Swedish. ◇ *m y f* [persona] Swede; **hacerse el** ~ *fig* to play dumb, to pretend not to understand.
◆ **sueco** *m* [lengua] Swedish.

suegro, -gra *m y f* father-in-law (*f* mother-in-law).

suela *f* sole; **no llegarle a alguien a la ~ del zapato** *fig* not to hold a candle to sb.

suelda *etc* → **soldar**.

sueldo *m* salary, wages (*pl*); [semanal] wage; **a ~** [asesino] hired; [empleado] salaried; **~ base** basic salary; [semanal] basic wage.

suelo ◇ *v* → **soler**. ◇ *m* **-1.** [pavimento - en interiores] floor; [- en el exterior] ground. **-2.** [terreno, territorio] soil; [para edificar] land. **-3.** [base] bottom. **-4.** *loc*: **arrastrarse por el ~** to grovel, to humble o.s.; **echar por el ~ un plan** to ruin a project; **estar por los ~s** [persona, precio] to be at rock bottom; [productos] to be dirt cheap; **poner ○ tirar por los ~s** to run down, to criticize.

suelto, -ta *adj* **-1.** [gen] loose; [cordones] undone; **¿tienes cinco duros ~s?** have you got 25 pesetas in loose change?; **andar ~** [en libertad] to be free; [en fuga] to be at large; [con diarrea] to have diarrhoea. **-2.** [separado] separate; [desparejado] odd; **no los vendemos ~s** we don't sell them separately. **-3.** [arroz] fluffy. **-4.** [lenguaje, estilo] fluent, fluid. **-5.** [desenvuelto] comfortable, at ease.
◆ **suelto** *m* [calderilla] loose change.
◆ **suelta** *etc v* → **soltar**.

suena *etc* → **sonar²**.

sueña *etc* → **soñar**.

sueño *m* **-1.** [ganas de dormir] sleepiness; [por medicamento etc] drowsiness; **¡qué ~!** I'm really sleepy!; **tener ~** to be sleepy. **-2.** [estado] sleep; **coger el ~** to get to sleep; **descabezar un ~** to have a nap; **~ eterno** *fig* eternal rest; **~ pesado/ligero** heavy/light sleep. **-3.** [imagen mental, objetivo, quimera] dream; **esta casa es un ~** *fam* this house is a dream; **en ~s** in a dream; **ni en ~s** *fig* no way, under no circumstances.

suero *m* **-1.** MED serum; **~ artificial** saline solution. **-2.** [de la leche] whey.

suerte *f* **-1.** [azar] chance; **echar ○ tirar algo a ~s** to draw lots for sthg; **la ~ está echada** the die is cast. **-2.** [fortuna] luck; **por ~** luckily; **probar ~** to try one's luck; **¡qué ~!** that was lucky!; **tener ~** to be lucky. **-3.** [destino] fate; **tentar a la ~** to tempt fate; **tocar ○ caer en ~ a alguien** to fall to sb's lot. **-4.** [situación] situation, lot. **-5.** *culto* [clase]: **toda ~ de** all manner of. **-6.** *culto* [manera] manner, fashion; **de ~ que** in such a way that.

suéter (*pl* **suéteres**) *m* sweater.

Suez Suez.

suficiencia *f* **-1.** [capacidad] proficiency. **-2.** [idoneidad] suitability; [de medidas, esfuerzos] adequacy. **-3.** [presunción] smugness, self-importance.

suficiente ◇ *adj* **-1.** [bastante] enough; [medidas, esfuerzos] adequate; **no llevo (dinero) ~** I don't have enough (money) on me; **no tienes la estatura ~** you're not tall enough. **-2.** [presuntuoso] smug, full of o.s. ◇ *m* [nota] pass.

sufijo *m* suffix.

sufragar [16] *vt* to defray.

sufragio *m* suffrage; **~ directo/indirecto** direct/indirect suffrage; **~ universal** universal suffrage.

sufragismo *m* suffragette movement.

sufragista ◇ *adj* suffragette (*antes de sust*). ◇ *m y f* suffragette.

sufrido, -da *adj* **-1.** [resignado] patient, uncomplaining; [durante mucho tiempo] long-suffering. **-2.** [resistente - tela] hardwearing; [- color] that does not show the dirt.

sufridor, -ra *adj* easily worried.

sufrimiento *m* suffering.

sufrir ◇ *vt* **-1.** [gen] to suffer; [accidente] to have. **-2.** [soportar] to bear, to stand; **tengo que ~ sus manías** I have to put up with his idiosyncrasies. **-3.** [experimentar - cambios etc] to undergo. ◇ *vi* [padecer] to suffer; **~ de** [enfermedad] to suffer from; **~ del estómago** *etc* to have a stomach *etc* complaint.

sugerencia *f* suggestion.

sugerente *adj* evocative.

sugerir [27] *vt* **-1.** [proponer] to suggest. **-2.** [evocar] to evoke.

sugestión *f* suggestion.

sugestionable *adj* impressionable.

sugestionar *vt* to influence.
◆ **sugestionarse** *vpr* **-1.** [obsesionarse] to become obsessed. **-2.** PSICOL to use auto-suggestion.

sugestivo, -va *adj* attractive.

sugiera, sugiriera *etc* → **sugerir**.

suich *m Amer* switch.

suicida ◇ *adj* suicidal. ◇ *m y f* [por naturaleza] suicidal person; [suicidado] person who has committed suicide.

suicidarse *vpr* to commit suicide.

suicidio *m* suicide.

sui generis [sui 'xeneris] *adj* individual.

suite [suit] *f* [gen & MÚS] suite.

Suiza Switzerland.

suizo, -za *adj, m y f* Swiss.

sujeción *f* **-1.** [atadura] fastening. **-2.** [sometimiento] subjection.

sujetador *m* bra, brassiere.

sujetapapeles *m inv* paper clip.

sujetar *vt* **-1.** [agarrar] to hold down. **-2.** [aguantar] to fasten; [papeles] to fasten together. **-3.** [someter] to subdue; [a niños] to control.
◆ **sujetarse** *vpr* **-1.** [agarrarse]: ~**se a** to hold on to, to cling to. **-2.** [aguantarse] to keep in place. **-3.** [someterse]: ~**se a** to keep O stick to.

sujeto, -ta *adj* **-1.** [agarrado - objeto] fastened. **-2.** [expuesto]: ~ **a** subject to.
◆ **sujeto** *m* **-1.** [gen & GRAM] subject. **-2.** [individuo] individual; ~ **pasivo** ECON taxpayer.

sulfamida *f* MED sulphonamide.

sulfatarse *vpr* [pilas] to leak.

sulfato *m* sulphate.

sulfurar *vt* **-1.** [encolerizar] to infuriate. **-2.** QUÍM to sulphurate.
◆ **sulfurarse** *vpr* [encolerizarse] to get mad.

sulfúrico, -ca *adj* sulphuric.

sulfuro *m* sulphide.

sulfuroso, -sa *adj* QUÍM sulphurous.

sultán *m* sultan.

sultana *f* sultana.

suma *f* **-1.** [MAT - acción] addition; [- resultado] total. **-2.** [conjunto - de conocimientos, datos] total, sum; [- de dinero] sum. **-3.** [resumen]: **en** ~ in short.

sumamente *adv* extremely.

sumando *m* addend.

sumar *vt* **-1.** MAT to add together; **tres y cinco suman ocho** three and five are O make eight. **-2.** [costar] to come to.
◆ **sumarse** *vpr*: ~**se (a)** to join (in).

sumarial *adj* pertaining to an indictment.

sumario, -ria *adj* **-1.** [conciso] brief. **-2.** DER summary.
◆ **sumario** *m* **-1.** DER indictment. **-2.** [resumen] summary.

sumarísimo, -ma *adj* DER swift, expeditious.

Sumatra Sumatra.

sumergible ◇ *adj* waterproof. ◇ *m* submarine.

sumergir [15] *vt* [hundir] to submerge; [- con fuerza] to plunge; [bañar] to dip.
◆ **sumergirse** *vpr* **-1.** [hundirse] to submerge. [- con fuerza] to plunge. **-2.** [abstraerse]: ~**se (en)** to immerse o.s. (in).

sumidero *m* drain.

sumiller (*pl* **sumillers**), **sommelier** [sumi'jer] (*pl* **sommeliers**) *m* sommelier, wine waiter.

suministrador, -ra ◇ *adj* supply (*antes de sust*). ◇ *m y f* supplier.

suministrar *vt* to supply; ~ **algo a alguien** to supply sb with sthg.

suministro *m* [gen] supply; [acto] supplying.

sumir *vt*: ~ **a alguien en** to plunge sb into.
◆ **sumirse en** *vpr* **-1.** [depresión, sueño etc] to sink into. **-2.** [estudio, tema] to immerse o.s. in.

sumisión *f* **-1.** [obediencia - acción] submission; [- cualidad] submissiveness. **-2.** [rendición] surrender.

sumiso, -sa *adj* submissive.

súmmum *m* height.

sumo, -ma *adj* **-1.** [supremo] highest, supreme. **-2.** [gran] extreme, great.
◆ **a lo sumo** *loc adv* at most.

sunnita ◇ *adj* Sunni. ◇ *m y f* Sunnite, Sunni Moslem.

suntuosidad *f* sumptuousness, magnificence.

suntuoso, -sa *adj* sumptuous, magnificent.

supeditación *f* subordination.

supeditar *vt*: ~ **(a)** to subordinate (to); **estar supeditado a** to be dependent on.
◆ **supeditarse** *vpr*: ~**se a** to submit to.

súper ◇ *adj fam* great, super. ◇ *adv fam* really. ◇ *m fam* supermarket. ◇ *f*: (gasolina) ~ ≃ four-star (petrol).

superable *adj* surmountable.

superabundancia, **sobreabundancia** *f* excess.

superabundante, **sobreabundante** *adj* excessive.

superabundar, **sobreabundar** *vi* to abound.

superación *f* overcoming; **afán de** ~ drive to improve.

superar *vt* **-1.** [gen] to beat; [récord] to break; ~ **algo/a alguien en algo** to beat sthg/sb in sthg. **-2.** [adelantar - corredor] to overtake, to pass. **-3.** [época, técnica]: **estar superado** to have been superseded. **-4.** [resolver - dificultad etc] to overcome.
◆ **superarse** *vpr* **-1.** [mejorar] to better o.s. **-2.** [lucirse] to excel o.s.

superávit *m inv* surplus.

supercarburante *m* high-grade fuel.

superchería *f* fraud, hoax.

superdotado, -da ◇ *adj* extremely gifted. ◇ *m y f* extremely gifted person.

superestructura *f* superstructure.

superficial *adj lit* & *fig* superficial.

superficialidad *f* superficiality.

superficie f **-1.** [gen] surface. **-2.** [área] area.

superfino, -na adj superfine.

superfluo, -flua adj superfluous; [gasto] unnecessary.

superhombre m superman.

superintendente m y f superintendent.

superior, -ra RELIG ◇ adj superior. ◇ m y f superior (f mother superior).
◆ **superior** ◇ adj **-1.** [de arriba] top. **-2.** [mayor]: ~ **(a)** higher (than). **-3.** [mejor]: ~ **(a)** superior (to). **-4.** [excelente] excellent. **-5.** ANAT & GEOGR upper. **-6.** EDUC higher. ◇ m (gen pl) [jefe] superior.

superioridad f lit & fig superiority.

superlativo, -va adj **-1.** [belleza etc] exceptional. **-2.** GRAM superlative.

superman [super'man] m superman.

supermercado m supermarket.

supernova f supernova.

superpoblación f overpopulation.

superpoblado, -da adj overpopulated.

superponer [65] = **sobreponer**.

superposición = **sobreposición**.

superpotencia f superpower.

superproducción f **-1.** ECON overproduction (U). **-2.** CIN blockbuster.

superpuesto, -ta ◇ adj = **sobrepuesto**. ◇ pp → **superponer**.

supersónico, -ca adj supersonic.

superstición f superstition.

supersticioso, -sa adj superstitious.

supervalorar vt to overvalue, to overrate.
◆ **supervalorarse** vpr to have too high opinion of o.s.

supervisar vt to supervise.

supervisión f supervision.

supervisor, -ra ◇ adj supervisory. ◇ m y f supervisor.

supervivencia f survival.

superviviente, sobreviviente ◇ adj surviving. ◇ m y f survivor.

supiera etc → **saber**.

supino, -na adj **-1.** [tendido] supine. **-2.** fig [excesivo] utter.
◆ **supino** m GRAM supine.

suplantación f: ~ **(de personalidad)** impersonation.

suplantador, -ra m y f impostor.

suplantar vt to take the place of.

suplementario, -ria adj supplementary, extra.

suplemento m **-1.** [gen & PRENS] supplement; ~ **dominical** Sunday supplement. **-2.** [complemento] attachment.

suplencia f EDUC: **hacer** ~**s** ≈ to do supply teaching (U).

suplente ◇ adj stand-in (antes de sust). ◇ m y f **-1.** [gen] stand-in. **-2.** TEATR understudy. **-3.** DEP substitute.

supletorio, -ria adj additional, extra.
◆ **supletorio** m TELECOM extension.

súplica f **-1.** [ruego] plea, entreaty. **-2.** DER petition.

suplicar [10] vt **-1.** [rogar]: ~ **algo (a alguien)** to plead for sthg (with sb); ~ **a alguien que haga algo** to beg sb to do sthg. **-2.** DER to appeal to.

suplicatorio m letters (pl) rogatory.

suplicio m lit & fig torture.

suplique etc → **suplicar**.

suplir vt **-1.** [sustituir]: ~ **algo/a alguien (con)** to replace sthg/sb (with). **-2.** [compensar]: ~ **algo (con)** to compensate for sthg (with).

supo → **saber**.

suponer [65] ◇ vt **-1.** [creer, presuponer] to suppose. **-2.** [implicar] to involve, to entail. **-3.** [significar] to mean. **-4.** [conjeturar] to imagine; **lo suponía** I guessed as much; **te suponía mayor** I thought you were older. ◇ vi to be important. ◇ m: **ser un** ~ to be conjecture.
◆ **suponerse** vpr to suppose.

suposición f assumption.

supositorio m suppository.

suprarrenal adj suprarenal.

supremacía f supremacy.

supremo, -ma adj lit & fig supreme.
◆ **Supremo** m DER: **el Supremo** the High Court Br, the Supreme Court Am.

supresión f **-1.** [de ley, impuesto, derecho] abolition; [de sanciones, restricciones] lifting. **-2.** [de palabras, texto] deletion. **-3.** [de puestos de trabajo, proyectos] axing.

suprimir vt **-1.** [ley, impuesto, derecho] to abolish; [sanciones, restricciones] to lift. **-2.** [palabras, texto] to delete. **-3.** [puestos de trabajo, proyectos] to axe.

supuesto, -ta ◇ pp → **suponer**. ◇ adj supposed; [culpable, asesino] alleged; [nombre] falso; **dar algo por** ~ to take sthg for granted; **por** ~ of course.
◆ **supuesto** m assumption; **en el** ~ **de que ... assuming ....**

supuración f suppuration.

supurar vi to suppurate, to fester.

supusiera etc → **suponer**.

sur ◇ adj [posición, parte] south, southern; [dirección, viento] southerly. ◇ m south.

surcar [10] vt [tierra] to plough; [aire, agua] to cut ○ slice through.

surco *m* **-1.** [zanja] furrow. **-2.** [señal - de disco] groove; [- de rueda] rut. **-3.** [arruga] line, wrinkle.

sureño, -ña ◇ *adj* southern; [viento] southerly. ◇ *m y f* southerner.

sureste = sudeste.

surf, surfing *m* surfing.

surgir [15] *vi* **-1.** [brotar] to spring forth. **-2.** [aparecer] to appear. **-3.** *fig* [producirse] to arise.

Surinam Surinam.

suroeste = sudoeste.

surque *etc* → surcar.

surrealismo *m* surrealism.

surrealista *adj, m y f* surrealist.

surtido, -da *adj* **-1.** [bien aprovisionado] well-stocked. **-2.** [variado] assorted.

◆ **surtido** *m* **-1.** [gama] range. **-2.** [caja surtida] assortment.

surtidor *m* [de gasolina] pump; [de un chorro] spout.

surtir ◇ *vt* [proveer]: ~ **a alguien (de)** to supply sb (with). ◇ *vi* [brotar]: ~ **(de)** to spout ○ spurt (from).

◆ **surtirse de** *vpr* [proveerse de] to stock up on.

susceptibilidad *f* oversensitivity.

susceptible *adj* **-1.** [sensible] oversensitive. **-2.** [posible]: ~ **de** liable to.

suscitar *vt* to provoke; [interés, dudas, sospechas] to arouse.

suscribir *vt* **-1.** [firmar] to sign. **-2.** [ratificar] to endorse. **-3.** COM [acciones] to subscribe for.

◆ **suscribirse** *vpr* **-1.** PRENS: ~se (a) to subscribe (to). **-2.** COM: ~se a to take out an option on.

suscripción *f* subscription.

suscriptor, -ra *m y f* subscriber.

suscrito, -ta ◇ *pp* → suscribir. ◇ *adj*: estar ~ a to subscribe to.

susodicho, -cha *adj* above-mentioned.

suspender *vt* **-1.** [colgar] to hang (up). **-2.** EDUC to fail. **-3.** [interrumpir] to suspend; [sesión] to adjourn. **-4.** [aplazar] to postpone. **-5.** [de un cargo] to suspend; ~ **de empleo y sueldo** to suspend without pay.

suspense *m* suspense.

suspensión *f* **-1.** [gen & AUTOM] suspension; **en** ~ in suspension; ~ **de empleo** suspension on full pay; ~ **de pagos** suspension of payments. **-2.** [aplazamiento] postponement; [de reunión, sesión] adjournment.

suspenso, -sa *adj* **-1.** [colgado]: ~ **de** hanging from. **-2.** [no aprobado]: **estar** ~ to have failed. **-3.** *fig* [interrumpido]: **en** ~ pending.

◆ **suspenso** *m* failure.

suspensores *mpl Amer* braces.

suspensorio *m* jockstrap.

suspicacia *f* suspicion.

suspicaz *adj* suspicious.

suspirar *vi* **-1.** [dar suspiros] to sigh; ~ **de** to sigh with. **-2.** *fig* [desear]: ~ **por algo/por hacer algo** to long for sthg/to do sthg.

suspiro *m* **-1.** [aspiración] sigh; **dar un** ~ to heave a sigh. **-2.** [instante]: **en un** ~ in no time at all. **-3.** [pizca] pinch.

sustancia *f* **-1.** [gen] substance; **sin** ~ lacking in substance. **-2.** [esencia] essence. **-3.** [de alimento] nutritional value.

◆ **sustancia gris** *f* grey matter.

sustancial *adj* substantial, significant.

sustanciar [8] *vt* **-1.** [resumir] to summarize. **-2.** DER to substantiate.

sustancioso, -sa *adj* substantial.

sustantivación *f* substantivization, use as a noun.

sustantivar *vt* to substantivize, to use as a noun.

sustantivo, -va *adj* GRAM noun (*antes de sust*).

◆ **sustantivo** *m* GRAM noun.

sustentar *vt* **-1.** [gen] to support. **-2.** *fig* [mantener - la moral] to keep up; [- argumento, teoría] to defend.

sustento *m* **-1.** [alimento] sustenance; [mantenimiento] livelihood; **ganarse el** ~ to earn one's living. **-2.** [apoyo] support.

sustitución *f* **-1.** [cambio] replacement. **-2.** DER subrogation.

sustituible *adj* replaceable.

sustituir [51] *vt*: ~ **(por)** to replace (with).

sustitutivo, -va *adj* substitute.

◆ **sustitutivo** *m*: ~ **(de)** substitute (for).

sustituto, -ta *m y f* substitute, replacement.

susto *m* fright; **dar** ○ **pegar un** ~ **a alguien** to give sb a fright; **darse** ○ **pegarse un** ~ to get a fright.

sustracción *f* **-1.** [robo] theft. **-2.** MAT subtraction.

sustraer [73] *vt* **-1.** [robar] to steal. **-2.** MAT to subtract.

◆ **sustraerse** *vpr*: ~se a ○ de [obligación, problema] to avoid.

sustrato *m* substratum.

susurrador, -ra, susurrante *adj* whispering.

susurrar *vt & vi* to whisper.

susurro *m* whisper; *fig* murmur.

sutil *adj* [gen] subtle; [velo, tejido] delicate, thin; [brisa] gentle; [hilo, línea] fine.

sutileza *f* subtlety; [de velo, tejido] delicacy, thinness; [de brisa] gentleness; [de hilo, línea] fineness.

sutura *f* suture.

suturar *vt* to stitch.

Suva Suva.

suyo, -ya ◇ *adj poses* [de él] his; [de ella] hers; [de uno] one's (own); [de ellos, ellas] theirs; [de usted, ustedes] yours; **este libro es** ~ this book is his/hers *etc*; **un amigo** ~ a friend of his/hers *etc*; **no es asunto** ~ it's none of his/her *etc* business; **es muy** ~ *fam fig* he/she is really selfish.
◇ *pron poses* **-1. el** ~ [de él] his; [de ella] hers; [de cosa, animal] its (own); [de uno] one's own; [de ellos, ellas] theirs; [de usted, ustedes] yours. **-2.** [*loc*]: **de** ~ in itself; **hacer de las suyas** to be up to his/her *etc* usual tricks; **hacer** ~ to make one's own; **lo** ~ **es el teatro** he/she *etc* should be on the stage; **lo** ~ **sería volver** the proper thing to do would be to go back; **los** ~**s** *fam* [su familia] his/her *etc* folks; [su bando] his/her *etc* lot.

svástica = **esvástica**.

SW (*abrev de* **short wave**) *f* SW.

SWAPO (*abrev de* **South West African People's Organization**) *m* SWAPO.

swing [swin] *m* MÚS swing.

Sydney Sydney.

T

t¹, T *f* [letra] t, T.

t² **-1.** (*abrev de* **tonelada**) t. **-2.** *abrev de* **tomo**.

tabacalero, -ra *adj* tobacco (*antes de sust*).
◆ **Tabacalera** *f* state tobacco monopoly in Spain.

tabaco ◇ *m* **-1.** [planta] tobacco plant. **-2.** [picadura] tobacco; ~ **de pipa** pipe tobacco; ~ **negro/rubio** dark/Virginia tobacco. **-3.** [cigarrillos] cigarettes (*pl*). ◇ *adj inv* [color] light brown.

tábano *m* horsefly.

tabaquería *f* tobacconist's (shop) *Br*, cigar store *Am*.

tabaquismo *m* nicotine poisoning.

tabardo *m* (coarse) cloak.

tabarra *f fam*: **dar la** ~ to be a pest.

tabasco® *m* Tabasco®.

taberna *f country-style bar, usually cheap*.

tabernáculo *m* tabernacle.

tabernario, -ria *adj* coarse.

tabernero, -ra *m y f* [propietario] landlord (*f* landlady); [encargado] bartender, barman (*f* barmaid).

tabicar [10] *vt* to wall up.

tabique *m* **-1.** [pared] partition (wall). **-2.** ANAT: ~ **nasal** nasal septum.

tabla *f* **-1.** [plancha] plank; ~ **de planchar** ironing board. **-2.** [pliegue] pleat. **-3.** [lista, gráfico] table; ~ **de multiplicación** ○ **pitagórica** multiplication ○ Pythagorean table. **-4.** CULIN: ~ **de cocina** chopping board; ~ **de queso** cheeseboard. **-5.** NÁUT [de surf, vela etc] board. **-6.** ARTE panel. **-7.** *loc*: **ser una** ~ **de salvación** to be a last resort ○ hope; **hacer** ~ **rasa** to wipe the slate clean.
◆ **tablas** *fpl* **-1.** [en ajedrez]: **quedar en** ○ **hacer** ~**s** to end in stalemate. **-2.** TEATR stage (*sg*), boards; **tener** ~**s** TEATR to be an experienced actor; *fig* to be an old hand. **-3.** TAUROM *fence surrounding bullring*.

tablado *m* [de teatro] stage; [de baile] dancefloor; [plataforma] platform.

tablao *m* flamenco show.

tablero *m* **-1.** [gen] board; ~ **de ajedrez** chessboard. **-2.** [en baloncesto] backboard. **-3.** ~ **(de mandos)** [de avión] instrument panel; [de coche] dashboard.

tableta *f* **-1.** MED tablet. **-2.** [de chocolate] bar.

tablilla *f* MED splint.

tablón *m* plank; [en el techo] beam; ~ **de anuncios** notice board.

tabú (*pl* **tabúes** ○ **tabús**) *adj & m* taboo.

tabulación *f* tabulation.

tabulador *m*, **tabuladora** *f* tabulator.

tabular *vt & vi* to tabulate.

taburete *m* stool.

tacañería *f* meanness, miserliness.

tacaño, -ña ◇ *adj* mean, miserly. ◇ *m y f* mean ○ miserly person.

tacataca, tacatá *m* babywalker.

tacha *f* **-1.** [defecto] flaw, fault; **sin** ~ faultless. **-2.** [clavo] tack.

tachadura *f* correction, crossing out.

tachar *vt* **-1.** [lo escrito] to cross out. **-2.** *fig* [acusar]: ~ **a alguien de mentiroso** *etc* to accuse sb of being a liar *etc*.

tacho *m Amer* bucket.

tachón *m* **-1.** [tachadura] correction, crossing out. **-2.** [clavo] stud.

tachonar *vt* **-1.** [poner clavos] to decorate

with studs. **-2.** *fig* [salpicar] to stud; **tacho-nado de** studded with.

tachuela *f* tack.

tácito, -ta *adj* tacit; [norma, regla] unwritten.

taciturno, -na *adj* taciturn.

taco *m* **-1.** [tarugo] plug. **-2.** [cuña] wedge. **-3.** *fam fig* [palabrota] swearword. **-4.** *fam fig* [confusión] mess, muddle; **armarse un ~ (con algo)** to get into a muddle (over sthg). **-5.** [de billar] cue. **-6.** [de hojas, billetes de banco] wad; [de billetes de autobús, metro] book. **-7.** [de jamón, queso] hunk. **-8.** *Amer* CULIN taco. **-9.** *Amer* [tacón] heel.
◆ **tacos** *mpl mfam* [años] years (of age).

tacógrafo *m* tachograph.

tacón *m* heel; **de ~ alto** high-heeled; **~ de aguja** stiletto heel.

taconear *vi* **-1.** [bailarín] to stamp one's feet. **-2.** MIL to click one's heels.

taconeo *m* [de bailarín] foot-stamping.

táctico, -ca *adj* tactical.
◆ **táctica** *f lit* & *fig* tactics (*pl*).

táctil *adj* tactile.

tacto *m* **-1.** [sentido] sense of touch. **-2.** [textura] feel. **-3.** *fig* [delicadeza] tact. **-4.** MED manual examination.

TAE (*abrev de* **tasa anual equivalente**) *f* Annual Equivalent Rate.

taekwondo [tae'kwondo] *m* tae kwon do.

tafetán *m* taffeta.

tafilete *m* morocco leather.

tagalo, -la *adj, m y f* Tagalog.
◆ **tagalo** *m* [lengua] Tagalog.

tahona *f* bakery.

tahúr, -ra *m y f* cardsharp.

taifa *f* HIST *independent Muslim kingdom in Iberian peninsula.*

taiga *f* taiga.

tailandés, -esa *adj, m y f* Thai.
◆ **tailandés** *m* [lengua] Thai.

Tailandia Thailand.

taimado, -da ◇ *adj* crafty. ◇ *m y f* crafty person.

Taipei Taipei.

Taiwán [tai'wan] Taiwan.

taiwanés, -esa *adj, m y f* Taiwanese.

tajada *f* **-1.** [rodaja] slice. **-2.** *fig* [parte] share; **sacar ~ de algo** to get sthg out of sthg. **-3.** *fam fig* [borrachera]: **agarrarse una ~** to get plastered ○ legless.

tajante *adj* [categórico] categorical.

tajar *vt* to cut ○ slice up; [en dos] to slice in two.

tajo *m* **-1.** [corte] deep cut. **-2.** [trabajo] workplace, work. **-3.** [acantilado] precipice.

Tajo *m*: **el (río) ~** the (River) Tagus.

tal ◇ *adj* **-1.** [semejante, tan grande] such; **¡jamás se vio cosa ~!** you've never seen such a thing!; **lo dijo con ~ seguridad que ...** he said it with such conviction that ...; **dijo cosas ~es como ...** he said such things as .... **-2.** [sin especificar] such and such; **a ~ hora** at such and such a time. **-3.** [desconocido]: **un ~ Pérez** a (certain) Mr Pérez.
◇ *pron* **-1.** [alguna cosa] such a thing. **-2.** *loc*: **que si ~ que si cual** this, that and the other; **ser ~ para cual** to be two of a kind; **~ y cual, ~ y ~** this and that; **y ~** [etcétera] and so on.
◇ *adv*: **¿qué ~?** how's it going?, how are you doing?; **déjalo ~ cual** leave it just as it is.
◆ **con tal de** *loc prep* as long as, provided; **con ~ de volver pronto ...** as long as we're back early ....
◆ **con tal (de) que** *loc conj* as long as, provided.
◆ **tal (y) como** *loc conj* just as ○ like.
◆ **tal que** *loc prep fam* [como por ejemplo] like.

tala *f* felling.

taladrador, -ra *adj* drilling.
◆ **taladradora** *f* drill.

taladrar *vt* to drill; *fig* [suj: sonido] to pierce.

taladro *m* **-1.** [taladradora] drill. **-2.** [agujero] drill hole.

tálamo *m* **-1.** *culto* [cama] bed. **-2.** ANAT & BOT thalamus.

talante *m* **-1.** [humor] mood; **estar de buen ~** to be in good humour. **-2.** [carácter] character, disposition.

talar¹ *adj* full-length.

talar² *vt* to fell.

talayote *m* *megalithic monument found in the Balearic Islands.*

talco *m* talc, talcum powder.

talega *f* sack.

talego *m* **-1.** [talega] sack. **-2.** *fam* [gordo] fatty. **-3.** *mfam* [cárcel] nick, slammer. **-4.** *mfam* [mil pesetas] 1000 peseta note.

talento *m* **-1.** [don natural] talent. **-2.** [inteligencia] intelligence.

talentoso, -sa *adj* talented.

talgo (*abrev de* **tren articulado ligero de Goicoechea Oriol**) *m Spanish intercity high-speed train.*

talidomida *f* thalidomide.

talión *m*: **la ley del ~** *an eye for an eye and a tooth for a tooth.*

talismán *m* talisman.

talla *f* **-1.** [medida] size; **¿qué ~ usas?** what size are you? **-2.** [estatura] height. **-3.** *fig* [capacidad] stature; **dar la ~** to be up to it. **-4.** [ARTE - en madera] carving; [- en piedra] sculpture. **-5.** [de piedras preciosas] cutting.

tallado, -da *adj* [madera] carved; [piedras preciosas] cut.
◆ **tallado** *m* [de madera, piedra] carving; [de piedras preciosas] cutting.

tallar *vt* **-1.** [esculpir - madera, piedra] to carve; [- piedra preciosa] to cut. **-2.** [medir] to measure (the height of).

tallarín *m* (*gen pl*) noodle.

talle *m* **-1.** [cintura] waist. **-2.** [figura, cuerpo] figure. **-3.** [medida] measurement.

taller *m* **-1.** [gen] workshop. **-2.** AUTOM garage. **-3.** ARTE studio.

tallista *m y f* [de madera] wood carver; [de metales] engraver.

tallo *m* stem; [brote] sprout, shoot.

talludo, -da *adj* thick-stemmed; *fig* tall.

Talmud *m*: **el ~** the Talmud.

talón *m* **-1.** [gen & ANAT] heel; **~ de Aquiles** *fig* Achilles' heel; **pisarle a alguien los talones** to be hot on sb's heels. **-2.** [cheque] cheque; [matriz] stub; **~ cruzado/devuelto/en blanco** crossed/bounced/blank cheque; **~ bancario** cashier's cheque *Br*, cashier's check *Am*; **~ sin fondos** bad cheque.

talonario *m* [de cheques] cheque book; [de recibos] receipt book.

talonera *f* heelpiece.

talud *m* bank, slope.

tamaño, -ña *adj* such; **¡cómo pudo decir tamaña estupidez!** how could he say such a stupid thing!
◆ **tamaño** *m* size; **de gran ~** large; **de ~ natural** life-size.

tamarindo *m* tamarind.

tambaleante *adj* **-1.** [inestable - silla etc] wobbly, unsteady; [- persona] staggering. **-2.** *fig* [gobierno, sistema] unstable.

tambalearse *vpr* **-1.** [bambolearse - persona] to stagger, to totter; [- mueble] to wobble, to be unsteady; [- tren] to sway. **-2.** *fig* [gobierno, sistema] to totter.

tambaleo *m* [de tren etc] swaying; [de mueble] wobble; [de persona] staggering.

también *adv* also, too; **yo ~ me too; ~ a mí me gusta** I like it too, I also like it.

tambor ◇ *m* **-1.** MÚS & TECN drum; [de pistola] cylinder. **-2.** ANAT eardrum. **-3.** AUTOM brake drum. ◇ *m y f* [tamborilero] drummer.

tamboril *m* small drum.

tamborilear *vi* MÚS & *fig* to drum.

tamborileo *m* drumming.

tamborilero, -ra *m y f* drummer.

Támesis *m*: **el ~ (río)** the (River) Thames.

tamice *etc* → **tamizar**.

tamiz *m* **-1.** [cedazo] sieve. **-2.** *fig* [selección] screening procedure.

tamizar [13] *vt* **-1.** [cribar] to sieve. **-2.** *fig* [seleccionar] to screen.

tampoco *adv* neither, not ... either; **ella no va y tú ~** she's not going and neither are you, she's not going and you aren't either; **¿no lo sabías? - yo ~** didn't you know? - me neither ○ neither did I.

tampón *m* **-1.** [sello] stamp; [almohadilla] inkpad. **-2.** [para la menstruación] tampon; **~ contraceptivo** contraceptive sponge.

tam-tam *m* tom tom.

tan *adv* **-1.** [mucho] so; **~ grande/deprisa** so big/quickly; **¡qué película ~ larga!** what a long film!; **~ ... que ...** so ... that ...; **~ es así que ...** so much so that .... **-2.** [en comparaciones]: **~ ... como ...** as ... as ....
◆ **tan sólo** *loc adv* only.

Tananarive Antananarivo.

tanda *f* **-1.** [grupo, lote] group, batch. **-2.** [serie] series; [de inyecciones] course. **-3.** [turno de trabajo] shift.

tándem (*pl* **tándemes**) *m* **-1.** [bicicleta] tandem. **-2.** [pareja] duo, pair.

tanga *m* tanga.

Tanganica *m*: **el lago ~** Lake Tanganyika.

tangencial *adj* tangential.

tangente ◇ *adj* tangential. ◇ *f* tangent; **irse** ○ **salirse por la ~** to go off at a tangent.

tangible *adj* tangible.

tango *m* tango.

tanino *m* tannin.

tanque *m* **-1.** MIL tank. **-2.** [vehículo cisterna] tanker. **-3.** [depósito] tank.

tanqueta *f* armoured car.

tantear ◇ *vt* **-1.** [sopesar - peso, precio, cantidad] to try to guess; [- problema, posibilidades, ventajas] to weigh up. **-2.** [probar, sondear] to test (out). **-3.** [toro, contrincante etc] to size up. ◇ *vi* **-1.** [andar a tientas] to feel one's way. **-2.** [apuntar los tantos] to (keep) score.

tanteo *m* **-1.** [prueba, sondeo] testing out. **-2.** [de posibilidades, ventajas] weighing up. **-3.** [de contrincante, puntos débiles] sizing up. **-4.** [puntuación] score. **-5.** DER first option (*on a purchase*).
◆ **a tanteo** *loc adv* roughly.

tanto, -ta ◇ *adj* **-1.** [gran cantidad] so much, (*pl*) so many; **~ dinero** so much money, such a lot of money; **tanta gente** so many people; **tiene ~ entusiasmo/~s amigos que ...** she has so much

enthusiasm/so many friends that .... **-2.** [cantidad indeterminada] so much, (*pl*) so many; **nos daban tantas pesetas al día** they used to give us so many pesetas per day; **cuarenta y ~s** forty-something, forty-odd; **nos conocimos en el sesenta y ~s** we met sometime in the Sixties. **-3.** [en comparaciones]: **~ ... como** as much ... as, (*pl*) as many ... as.
◇ *pron* **-1.** [gran cantidad] so much, (*pl*) so many; **¿cómo puedes tener ~s?** how can you have so many? **-2.** [cantidad indeterminada] so much, (*pl*) so many; **a ~s de agosto** on such and such a date in August. **-3.** [igual cantidad] as much, (*pl*) as many; **había mucha gente aquí, allí no había tanta** there were a lot of people here, but not as many there; **otro ~** as much again; **otro ~ le ocurrió a los demás** the same thing happened to the rest of them. **-4.** *loc:* **ser uno de ~s** to be nothing special.
◆ **tanto** ◇ *m* **-1.** [punto] point; [gol] goal; **marcar un ~** to score. **-2.** *fig* [ventaja] point; **apuntarse un ~ a favor** to earn o.s. a point in one's favour. **-3.** [cantidad indeterminada] **un ~** so much, a certain amount; **~ por ciento** percentage. **-4.** *loc:* **estar al ~ (de)** to be on the ball (about).
◇ *adv* **-1.** [mucho]: **~ (que ...)** [cantidad] so much (that ...); [tiempo] so long (that ...); **no bebas ~** don't drink so much; **de eso hace ~ que ya no me acordaba** it's been so long since that happened that I don't even remember; **~ mejor/peor** so much the better/worse; **~ más cuanto que ...** all the more so because .... **-2.** [en comparaciones]: **~ como** as much as; **~ hombres como mujeres** both men and women; **~ si estoy como si no** whether I'm there or not. **-3.** *loc:* **¡y ~!** most certainly!, you bet!
◆ **tantas** *fpl fam:* **eran las tantas** it was very late.
◆ **en tanto (que)** *loc conj* while.
◆ **entre tanto** *loc adv* meanwhile.
◆ **por (lo) tanto** *loc conj* therefore, so.
◆ **tanto (es así) que** *loc conj* so much so that.
◆ **un tanto** *loc adv* [un poco] a bit, rather.
Tanzania Tanzania.
tañer ◇ *vt* [tocar] to play; [campana] to ring. ◇ *vi* [repicar] to ring.
tañido *m* **-1.** MÚS sound. **-2.** [de campana] ringing.
taoísmo *m* Taoism.
tapa *f* **-1.** [para cerrar] lid; **levantarse la ~ de los sesos** *fam* to blow one's brains out. **-2.** CULIN snack, tapa. **-3.** [portada - de libro] cover; [- de disco] sleeve. **-4.** [de zapato] heel

plate. **-5.** [trozo de carne] topside. **-6.** *Amer* [de botella] top; [de frasco] stopper.
tapabarro *m Amer* mudguard.
tapacubos *m inv* hubcap.
tapadera *f* **-1.** [para encubrir] front. **-2.** [tapa] lid.
tapadillo
◆ **de tapadillo** *loc adv* on the sly.
tapado *m Amer* [abrigo] overcoat.
tapar *vt* **-1.** [cerrar - ataúd, cofre] to close (the lid of); [- olla, caja] to put the lid on; [- botella] to put the top on. **-2.** [ocultar, cubrir] to cover; [no dejar ver] to block out. **-3.** [abrigar - en la cama] to tuck in; [- con ropa] to wrap up. **-4.** [encubrir] to cover up.
◆ **taparse** *vpr* **-1.** [cubrirse] to cover (up). **-2.** [abrigarse - con ropa] to wrap up; [- en la cama] to tuck o.s. in.
taparrabos *m inv* **-1.** [de hombre primitivo] loincloth. **-2.** [tanga] tanga briefs (*pl*).
tapete *m* [paño] runner; [en mesa de billar, para cartas] baize; **estar sobre el ~** *fig* to be up for discussion; **poner algo sobre el ~** to put sthg up for discussion.
◆ **tapete verde** *m* [mesa] card table.
tapia *f* (stone) wall; **estar sordo como una ~** *fam* to be (as) deaf as a post.
tapiar [8] *vt* **-1.** [obstruir] to brick up. **-2.** [cercar] to wall in.
tapice *etc* → **tapizar**.
tapicería *f* **-1.** [tela] upholstery. **-2.** [tienda - para muebles] upholsterer's; [- para cortinas] draper's. **-3.** [tapices] tapestries (*pl*). **-4.** [oficio] tapestry making.
tapicero, -ra *m y f* **-1.** [de muebles] upholsterer. **-2.** [de tapices] tapestry maker.
tapioca *f* tapioca.
tapiz *m* [para la pared] tapestry; [para el suelo] carpet.
tapizado *m* **-1.** [de mueble] upholstery. **-2.** [de pared] tapestries (*pl*).
tapizar [13] *vt* [mueble] to upholster.
tapón *m* **-1.** [para tapar - botellas, frascos] stopper; [- de corcho] cork; [- de metal, plástico] cap, top; [- de bañera, lavabo] plug; **~ de rosca** screw-top. **-2.** [atasco] traffic jam. **-3.** [en el oído - de cerumen] wax (*U*) in the ear; [- de algodón] earplug. **-4.** *fam* [persona rechoncha] tubby person. **-5.** [en baloncesto] block.
taponamiento *m* **-1.** MED tamponage. **-2.** TECN plugging.
taponar *vt* **-1.** [cerrar - botella] to put the top on; [- lavadero] to put the plug in; [- salida] to block; [- tubería] to stop up. **-2.** MED to tampon.
◆ **taponarse** *vpr* to get blocked.

tapujo *m* subterfuge; **hacer algo con/sin ~s** to do sthg deceitfully/openly.

taquicardia *f* tachycardia.

taquigrafía *f* shorthand, stenography.

taquigrafiar [9] *vt* to write (down) in shorthand.

taquígrafo, -fa *m y f* shorthand writer, stenographer.

taquilla *f* **-1.** [ventanilla - gen] ticket office, booking office; [- CIN & TEATR] box office. **-2.** [armario] locker. **-3.** [recaudación] takings (*pl*). **-4.** [casillero] set of pigeonholes.

taquillero, -ra ◇ *adj*: **es un espectáculo ~** the show is a box-office hit. ◇ *m y f* ticket clerk.

taquimecanografía *f* shorthand and typing.

taquimecanógrafo, -fa *m y f* shorthand typist.

taquímetro *m* **-1.** [en topografía] tacheometer. **-2.** [velocímetro] speedometer.

tara *f* **-1.** [defecto] defect. **-2.** [peso] tare.

tarado, -da ◇ *adj* **-1.** [defectuoso] defective. **-2.** [tonto] thick. ◇ *m y f* idiot.

tarántula *f* tarantula.

tarar *vt* to tare.

tararear *vt* to hum.

tarareo *m* humming.

tardanza *f* lateness.

tardar *vi* **-1.** [llevar tiempo] to take; **tardó un año en hacerlo** she took a year to do it; **¿cuánto tardarás (en hacerlo)?** how long will you be (doing it)?, how long will it take you (to do it)? **-2.** [retrasarse] to be late; [ser lento] to be slow; **~ en hacer algo** to take a long time to do sthg; **no tardaron en hacerlo** they were quick to do it; **a más ~** at the latest.

tarde ◇ *f* [hasta las cinco] afternoon; [después de las cinco] evening; **por la ~** [hasta las cinco] in the afternoon; [después de las cinco] in the evening; **buenas ~s** [hasta las cinco] good afternoon; [después de las cinco] good evening; **de ~ en ~** from time to time. ◇ *adv* [gen] late; [en demasía] too late; **ya es ~ para eso** it's too late for that now; **llegar ~** to be late; **se está haciendo ~** it's getting late; **~ o temprano** sooner or later; **más vale ~ que nunca** better late than never.

tardío, -día *adj* [gen] late; [consejo, decisión] belated.

tardo, -da *adj* **-1.** [lento] slow. **-2.** [torpe] dull; **~ de oído** hard of hearing.

tardón, -ona *m y f* **-1.** [impuntual] person who is always late. **-2.** [lento] slowcoach.

tarea *f* [gen] task; EDUC homework.

tarifa *f* **-1.** [precio] charge; COM tariff; [en transportes] fare. **-2.** (*gen pl*) [lista] price list.

tarifar *vt* to price.

tarima *f* platform.

tarjeta *f* [gen & INFORM] card; **~ amarilla/roja** DEP yellow/red card; **~ con chip** smart O intelligent card; **~ de crédito** credit card; **~ de embarque** boarding pass; **~ multiviaje** travel pass; **~ perforada** INFORM punch card; **~ postal** postcard; **~ de visita** visiting O calling card.

tarot *m* tarot.

tarrina *f* terrine.

tarro *m* **-1.** [recipiente] jar. **-2.** *mfam* [cabeza] nut, bonce.

tarso *m* tarsus.

tarta *f* [gen] cake; [plana, con base de pasta dura] tart; [plana, con base de bizcocho] flan; **~ de cumpleaños** birthday cake.

tartajear *vi* to stammer, to stutter.

tartajeo *m* stammer, stammering (*U*).

tartaleta *f* tartlet.

tartamudear *vi* to stammer, to stutter.

tartamudeo *m* stammer, stammering (*U*).

tartamudez *f* stammerer, stutterer.

tartamudo, -da ◇ *adj* stammering, stuttering. ◇ *m y f* stammerer, stutterer.

tartán *m inv* tartan.

tartana *f* **-1.** [carruaje] trap. **-2.** *fam* [coche viejo] banger.

tártaro, -ra ◇ *adj* **-1.** [pueblo] Tartar. **-2.** → **salsa.** ◇ *m y f* Tartar.

tartera *f* **-1.** [fiambrera] lunch box. **-2.** [cazuela] flan dish.

tarugo *m* **-1.** *fam* [necio] blockhead. **-2.** [de madera] block of wood. **-3.** [de pan] chunk (of stale bread).

tarumba *adj fam* crazy.

tasa *f* **-1.** [índice] rate; **~ de mortalidad/natalidad** death/birth rate; **~ de paro** O **desempleo** (level of) unemployment; **~ de crecimiento** growth rate. **-2.** [impuesto] tax. **-3.** EDUC fee. **-4.** [tasación] valuation.

tasación *f* valuation.

tasador, -ra ◇ *adj* evaluating. ◇ *m y f* valuer.

tasar *vt* **-1.** [valorar] to value. **-2.** [fijar precio] to fix a price for.

tasca *f* ≃ pub; **ir de ~s** to go on a pub crawl.

Tasmania *f* Tasmania.

tasquear *vi* to go on a pub crawl.

tasqueo *m* pubcrawling.

TASS (*abrev de* **Telegrafnoe Agentstvo Sovetskogo Sojuza**) *f* TASS.

tata → **tato.**

tatarabuelo, **-la** *m* y *f* great-great-grandfather (*f* great-great-grandmother).

tataranieto, **-ta** *m* y *f* great-great-grandson (*f* great-great-granddaughter).

tate *interj*: ¡~! [¡cuidado!] watch out!; [¡ya comprendo!] I see!

tato, **-ta** *fam* m y *f* [hermano] big brother (*f* big sister).

◆ **tata** *f* [niñera] nanny.

tatuaje *m* **-1.** [dibujo] tattoo. **-2.** [acción] tattooing.

tatuar [6] ◇ *vt* to tattoo. ◇ *vi* to make a tattoo.

◆ **tatuarse** *vpr* to have a tattoo done.

taumaturgia *f* miracle-working.

taumaturgo, **-ga** *m* y *f* miracle-worker.

taurino, **-na** *adj* bullfighting (*antes de sust*).

tauro ◇ *m* [zodiaco] Taurus; **ser** ~ to be (a) Taurus. ◇ *m* y *f* [persona] Taurean.

tauromaquia *f* bullfighting.

TAUROMAQUIA:

'Tauromaquia' is the name given to the art and the world of bullfighting. The bullfight, or 'corrida', is opened by a procession, the 'paseíllo', which is headed by mounted officials called 'alguacilillos'. The bullfighters, dressed in splendid traditional costumes called 'trajes de luces', parade diagonally across the bullring. Each of the three principal bullfighters, the 'matadores' or 'espadas', is attended by his assistants or 'subalternos' (known collectively as the 'cuadrilla'), and by the mounted 'picadores'.

The bullfight itself, the 'lidia', follows a strict order and is divided into three main parts or 'tercios'. Six bulls are involved; each in turn is released into the bullring (the 'ruedo') and is greeted by the 'matador', who performs a series of passes with his long cape (the 'capa') so that he can study the way the bull moves and can slow down its momentum.

The first stage of the bullfight, the 'tercio de varas', belongs to the 'picador'; sitting on his horse, the 'picador' pricks the bull with a lance, or 'vara', up to three times to goad and weaken it. Next, in the 'tercio de banderillas', the bull is stuck in the neck or shoulder with long decorated barbed darts ('banderillas') by specialized bullfighters called 'banderilleros'. The 'matador' himself may also take part. If he judges that the 'tercio de varas' or the 'tercio de banderillas' has gone on long enough, he may ask the permission of the president of the bullring to move on to the next stage, and he does this by removing his 'montera' or hat.

In the third and final part of the 'lidia', the 'tercio de muerte', the 'matador' takes his 'muleta', a small cape attached to a stick, and performs the 'faena', his final series of passes. This consists of set pieces like the 'manoletina', a particular type of pass invented by one of Spain's famous 'matadors', Manolete. It is on this stage of the proceedings that the performance of the bullfighter - and of the bull - will be judged.

Bullfighting is extremely popular in both Spain and Latin America, where it is seen by many as a true art form. It does have its detractors, however, who consider it a cruel and inhuman spectacle

tautología *f* tautology.

tautológico, **-ca** *adj* tautological.

TAV (*abrev de* **tren de alta velocidad**) *m* Spanish high-speed train.

taxativo, **-va** *adj* precise, exact.

taxi *m* taxi.

taxidermia *f* taxidermy.

taxidermista *m* y *f* taxidermist.

taxímetro *m* taximeter.

taxista *m* y *f* taxi driver.

taxonomía *f* taxonomy.

taxonomista *m* y *f* taxonomist.

taza *f* **-1.** [para beber] cup. **-2.** [de retrete] bowl.

tazón *m* bowl.

TC *m abrev de* **Tribunal Constitucional**.

te *pron pers* **-1.** (*complemento directo*) you; **le gustaría verte** she'd like to see you. **-2.** (*complemento indirecto*) (to) you; ~ **lo dio** he gave it to you; ~ **tiene miedo** he's afraid of you. **-3.** (*reflexivo*) yourself. **-4.** *fam* [valor impersonal]: **si** ~ **dejas pisar, estás perdido** if you let people walk all over you, you've had it.

té (*pl* **tés**) *m* tea.

tea *f* [antorcha] torch.

teatral *adj* **-1.** [de teatro - gen] theatre (*antes de sust*); [- grupo] drama (*antes de sust*). **-2.** [exagerado] theatrical.

teatralidad *f* theatrical nature.

teatralizar [13] *vt* to exaggerate.

teatro *m* **-1.** [gen] theatre; ~ **de variedades** music hall *Br*, variety, vaudeville *Am*; ~ **lírico** opera and light opera. **-2.** *fig* [fingimiento] playacting; **hacer** ~ to playact. **-3.** *fig* [escenario] scene.

tebeo® *m* (children's) comic; **estar más visto que el** ~ to be old hat.

teca *f* teak.

techado *m* roof; **bajo** ~ under cover.

techar *vt* to roof.

techo *m* **-1.** [gen] roof; [dentro de casa] ceiling; ~ **deslizante** O **corredizo** AUTOM sun roof; **bajo** ~ under cover. **-2.** *fig* [límite] ceiling.

techumbre *f* roof.

tecla *f* [gen, INFORM & MÚS] key; ~ **de borrado/control/función/retorno** erase/control/function/return key; **pulsar** O **tocar una** ~ to press O strike a key; **tocar muchas** ~**s** [contactar] to pull lots of strings; [abarcar mucho] to have too many things on the go at once.

teclado *m* [gen & MÚS] keyboard; ~ **expandido/numérico** expanded/numeric keyboard.

teclear *vt & vi* [en ordenador etc] to type; [en piano] to play.

tecleo *m* [en piano] playing; [en máquina de escribir] clattering.

teclista *m y f* keyboard player.

tecnicismo *m* **-1.** [cualidad] technical nature. **-2.** [término] technical term.

técnico, -ca ◇ *adj* technical. ◇ *m y f* **-1.** [mecánico] technician. **-2.** [experto] expert.
◆ **técnica** *f* **-1.** [gen] technique. **-2.** [tecnología] technology.

tecnicolor *m* Technicolor®.

tecnificación *f* application of technology.

tecnificar [10] *vt* to apply technology to.

tecno *m inv* MÚS techno (music).

tecnocracia *f* technocracy.

tecnócrata ◇ *adj* technocratic. ◇ *m y f* technocrat.

tecnocratización *f* technocratization.

tecnología *f* technology; ~ **punta** state-of-the-art technology.

tecnológico, -ca *adj* technological.

tecnólogo, -ga *m y f* technologist.

tecolote *m Amer* owl.

tectónico, -ca *adj* tectonic.
◆ **tectónica** *f* tectonics (*U*).

tedéum *m inv* Te Deum.

tedio *m* boredom, tedium.

tedioso, -sa *adj* tedious.

teflón® *m* Teflon®.

Tegucigalpa Tegucigalpa.

tegumento *m* integument.

Teherán Teheran.

Teide *m*: **el** ~ (Mount) Teide.

teísmo *m* theism.

teja *f* **-1.** [de tejado] tile. **-2.** CULIN potato waffle.

tejado *m* roof.

tejano, -na ◇ *adj* **-1.** [de Texas] Texan. **-2.** [tela] denim. ◇ *m y f* [persona] Texan.
◆ **tejanos** *mpl* [pantalones] jeans.

tejar ◇ *m* brickworks (*sg*). ◇ *vt & vi* to tile.

tejedor, -ra ◇ *adj* weaving. ◇ *m y f* weaver.

tejeduría *f* **-1.** [arte] weaving. **-2.** [taller] weaver's shop.

tejemaneje *m fam* **-1.** [maquinación] intrigue. **-2.** [ajetreo] to-do, fuss.

tejer ◇ *vt* **-1.** [gen] to weave. **-2.** [labor de punto] to knit. **-3.** [telaraña] to spin. **-4.** *fig* [labrar - porvenir] to carve out; [- ruina] to bring about. ◇ *vi* [hacer ganchillo] to crochet; [hacer punto] to knit; ~ **y destejer** *fig* to chop and change.

tejido *m* **-1.** [tela] fabric, material; IND textile. **-2.** ANAT tissue.

tejo *m* **-1.** [juego] hopscotch. **-2.** BOT yew. **-3.** *loc*: **tirar los** ~**s a alguien** *fam* to try it on with sb.

tejón *m* badger.

tel., **teléf.** (*abrev de* **teléfono**) tel.

tela *f* **-1.** [tejido] fabric, material; [retal] piece of material; ~ **de araña** cobweb; ~ **asfáltica** asphalt roofing/flooring; ~ **metálica** wire netting. **-2.** ARTE [lienzo] canvas. **-3.** *fam* [dinero] dough. **-4.** *fam* [cosa complicada]: **el examen era** ~ the exam was really tricky; **tener (mucha)** ~ [ser difícil] to be (very) tricky; **hay** ~ **(para rato)** [trabajo] there's no shortage of things to do; **¡~ marinera!** that's too much! **-5.** *loc*: **poner en** ~ **de juicio** to call into question.

Telam (*abrev de* **Telenoticias Americanas**) *f Argentinian news agency.*

telar *m* **-1.** [máquina] loom. **-2.** TEATR gridiron. **-3.** (*gen pl*) [fábrica] textiles mill.

telaraña *f* spider's web, cobweb.

tele *f fam* telly.

teleadicto, -ta *m y f* telly-addict.

telearrastre *m* ski-tow.

telecabina *f* cable-car.

telecomedia *f* television comedy programme.

telecomunicación *f* [medio] telecommunication.
◆ **telecomunicaciones** *fpl* [red] telecommunications.

telecontrol *m* remote control.

telediario *m* television news (*U*).

teledifusión *f* telecast, telecasting (*U*).

teledirigido, -da *adj* remote-controlled.

teledirigir [15] *vt* to operate by remote control.

teléf. = tel.

telefax *m inv* telefax, fax.

teleférico *m* cable-car.

telefilme, **telefilm** (*pl* **telefilms**) *m* TV film.

telefonazo *m fam* ring, buzz; **dar un ~ a alguien** to give sb a ring ○ buzz.

telefonear *vi* to phone.

telefonía *f* telephony; **~ móvil** mobile phones (*pl*).

telefónico, **-ca** *adj* telephone (*antes de sust*).

◆ **Telefónica** *f Spanish national telephone monopoly*.

telefonista *m y f* telephonist.

teléfono *m* telephone, phone; **hablar por ~** to be on the phone; **~ inalámbrico/móvil** cordless/mobile phone; **~ modular** ○ **inteligente** cellphone; **~ público** public phone; **~ rojo** hot line; **~ sin manos** phone with hands-free dialling.

telefotografía *f* telephotography.

telegrafía *f* telegraphy.

telegrafiar [9] *vt & vi* to telegraph.

telegráfico, **-ca** *adj lit & fig* telegraphic.

telegrafista *m y f* telegraphist.

telégrafo *m* [medio, aparato] telegraph.

◆ **telégrafos** *mpl* [oficina] telegraph office (*sg*).

telegrama *m* telegram.

teleinformática *f* telematics (*U*).

telejuego *m* television game show.

telele *m*: **le dio un ~** [desmayo] he had a fainting fit; [enfado] he had a fit.

telemando *m* remote control.

telémetro *m* telemeter.

telenovela *f* television soap opera.

teleobjetivo *m* telephoto lens.

telepatía *f* telepathy.

telepático, **-ca** *adj* telepathic.

telequinesia *f* telekinesis (*U*).

telescópico, **-ca** *adj* telescopic.

telescopio *m* telescope.

telesilla *m* chair lift.

telespectador, **-ra** *m y f* viewer.

telesquí *m* ski lift.

teletexto *m* Teletext®.

teletipo *m* **-1.** [aparato] teleprinter. **-2.** [texto] Teletype®.

teletrabajo *m* teleworking.

televendedor, **-ra** *m y f* telesales assistant.

televenta *f* **-1.** [por teléfono] telesales (*pl*). **-2.** [por televisión] *TV advertising in which a phone number is given for clients to contact*.

televidente *m y f* viewer.

televisado, **-da** *adj* televised.

televisar *vt* to televise.

televisión *f* television; **~ en blanco y negro/en color** black and white/colour television; **~ por cable/vía satélite** cable/satellite television; **~ privada/pública** commercial/public television; **~ a la carta** pay TV.

televisivo, **-va** *adj* television (*antes de sust*).

televisor *m* television (set).

télex *m inv* telex; **mandar por ~** to telex.

telón *m* [de escenario - delante] curtain; [- detrás] backcloth; **~ de acero** *fig* Iron Curtain; **~ de fondo** *fig* backdrop.

telonero, **-ra** ◇ *adj* support (*antes de sust*). ◇ *m y f* [cantante] support artist; [grupo] support band.

tema *m* **-1.** [gen] subject; **~s de actualidad** current affairs. **-2.** MÚS theme.

temario *m* [de una asignatura] curriculum; [de oposiciones] list of topics; [de reunión, congreso] agenda.

temático, **-ca** *adj* thematic.

◆ **temática** *f* subject matter.

tembladera *f* trembling fit.

temblar [19] *vi* **-1.** [tiritar]: **~ (de)** [gen] to tremble (with); [de frío] to shiver (with). **-2.** [vibrar - suelo etc] to shudder, to shake. **-3.** *fig* [sentir temor] to tremble; **tiemblo por lo que pueda pasarle** I shudder to think what could happen to him.

tembleque *m* trembling fit; **le dio** ○ **entró un ~** he got the shakes.

temblón, **-ona** *adj* shaky, trembling.

temblor *m* shaking (*U*), trembling (*U*); **~ de tierra** earthquake.

tembloroso, **-sa** *adj* trembling, shaky.

temer ◇ *vt* **-1.** [tener miedo de] to fear, to be afraid of. **-2.** [sospechar] to fear. ◇ *vi* to be afraid; **no temas** don't worry; **~ por** to fear for.

◆ **temerse** *vpr*: **~se que** to be afraid that, to fear that; **me temo que no vendrá** I'm afraid she won't come; **~se lo peor** to fear the worst.

temerario, **-ria** *adj* rash; [conducción] reckless.

temeridad *f* **-1.** [cualidad] recklessness. **-2.** [acción] folly (*U*), reckless act.

temeroso, **-sa** *adj* **-1.** [receloso] fearful. **-2.** [temible] terrifying, fearsome.

temible *adj* fearsome.

temor *m*: **~ (a** ○ **de)** fear (of); **por ~ a** ○ **de** for fear of.

témpano *m*: **~ (de hielo)** ice floe.

temperado, -da *adj* temperate.

temperamental *adj* **-1.** [cambiante] temperamental. **-2.** [impulsivo] impulsive.

temperamento *m* temperament.

temperancia *f* temperance.

temperar *vt* **-1.** [enfriar] to cool down. **-2.** [moderar] to temper.

temperatura *f* temperature; **tomar la ~ a alguien** to take sb's temperature; **~ máxima/mínima** highest/lowest temperature; **~ ambiental** room temperature.

tempestad *f* storm.

tempestuoso, -sa *adj* *lit* & *fig* stormy.

templado, -da *adj* **-1.** [tibio - agua, bebida, comida] lukewarm. **-2.** GEOGR [clima, zona] temperate. **-3.** [nervios] steady. **-4.** [persona, carácter] calm, composed. **-5.** MÚS in tune.

templanza *f* **-1.** [serenidad] composure. **-2.** [moderación] moderation. **-3.** [benignidad - del clima] mildness.

templar ◇ *vt* **-1.** [entibiar - lo frío] to warm (up); [- lo caliente] to cool down. **-2.** [calmar - nervios, ánimos] to calm; [- ira, pasiones] to restrain; [- voz] to soften. **-3.** TECN [metal etc] to temper. **-4.** [diluir - café etc] to water down, to dilute. **-5.** MÚS to tune. **-6.** [tensar] to tighten (up). ◇ *vi* [entibiar] to get milder.
◆ **templarse** *vpr* to warm up.

templario *m* Templar.

temple *m* **-1.** [serenidad] composure; **estar de buen/mal ~** to be in a good/bad mood. **-2.** TECN tempering. **-3.** ARTE tempera; **al ~** in tempera.

templete *m* pavilion.

templo *m* **-1.** [edificio - gen] temple; [- católico, protestante] church; [- judío] synagogue. **-2.** *fig* [lugar mitificado] temple.

tempo *m* tempo.

temporada *f* **-1.** [periodo concreto] season; [de exámenes] period; **de ~** [fruta, trabajo] seasonal; [en turismo] peak (*antes de sust*); **~ alta/baja** high/low season; **~ media** mid-season. **-2.** [periodo indefinido] (period of) time; **pasé una ~ en el extranjero** I spent some time abroad.

temporal ◇ *adj* **-1.** [provisional] temporary. **-2.** ANAT & RELIG temporal. ◇ *m* **-1.** [tormenta] storm; **capear el ~** *lit* & *fig* to ride out the storm. **-2.** ANAT temporal bone.

temporalidad *f* temporary nature.

témporas *fpl* RELIG Ember days.

temporero, -ra ◇ *adj* temporary. ◇ *m y f* casual labourer.

temporizador *m* timing device.

tempranero, -ra *adj* [persona] early-rising.

temprano, -na *adj* early.
◆ **temprano** *adv* early.

ten *v* → tener.
◆ **ten con ten** *m* *fam* tact.

tenacidad *f* tenacity.

tenacillas *fpl* tongs; [para vello] tweezers; [para rizar el pelo] curling tongs.

tenaz *adj* **-1.** [perseverante] tenacious. **-2.** [persistente] stubborn.

tenaza *f* (*gen* *pl*) **-1.** [herramienta] pliers (*pl*). **-2.** [pinzas] tongs (*pl*). **-3.** ZOOL pincer.

tendal *m* awning.

tendedero *m* **-1.** [armazón] clothes horse; [cuerda] clothes line. **-2.** [lugar] drying place.

tendencia *f* tendency, trend; **~ a hacer algo** tendency to do sthg **~ a la depresión** tendency to get depressed.

tendenciosidad *f* tendentiousness.

tendencioso, -sa *adj* tendentious.

tender [20] *vt* **-1.** [colgar - ropa] to hang out. **-2.** [tumbar] to, lay (out). **-3.** [extender] to stretch (out); [mantel] to spread. **-4.** [dar - cosa] to hand; [- mano] to hold out, to offer. **-5.** [entre dos puntos - cable, vía] to lay; [- puente] to build; [- cuerda] to stretch. **-6.** *fig* [preparar - trampa etc] to lay.
◆ **tender a** *vi*: **~ a hacer algo** to tend to do something; **~ a la depresión** to have a tendency to get depressed.
◆ **tenderse** *vpr* to stretch out, to lie down.

tenderete *m* [presto] stall.

tendero, -ra *m y f* shopkeeper.

tendido, -da *adj* **-1.** [extendido, tumbado] stretched out. **-2.** [colgado - ropa] hung out, on the line.
◆ **tendido** *m* **-1.** [de puente] construction; [- de cable] laying; **~ eléctrico** electrical installation. **-2.** TAUROM front rows (*pl*).

tendón *m* tendon.

tendrá *etc* → tener.

tenebrismo *m* tenebrism.

tenebroso, -sa *adj* dark, gloomy; *fig* shady, sinister.

tenedor[1] *m* [utensilio] fork.

tenedor[2]**, -ra** *m y f* [poseedor] holder; **~ de acciones** shareholder; **~ de libros** COM bookkeeper.

teneduría *f* COM bookkeeping.

tenencia *f* possession; **~ ilícita de armas** illegal possession of arms.

tener [72] ◇ *vaux* **-1.** (*antes de participio*) [haber]: **teníamos pensado ir al teatro** we had thought of going to the theatre. **-2.** (*antes de adj*) [hacer estar]: **me tuvo despierto it kept me awake; eso la tiene despistada** that has confused her. **-3.** [expresa obligación]: **~ que hacer algo** to have to do sthg; **tiene que ser así** it has to be this way. **-4.** [expresa propósito]: **tenemos que ir a cenar un día** we ought to ○ should go for dinner some time.

◇ *vt* **-1.** [gen] to have; **tengo un hermano** I have ○ I've got a brother; ~ **fiebre** to have a temperature; **tuvieron una pelea** they had a fight; ~ **un niño** to have a baby; **¡que tengan buen viaje!** have a good journey!; **hoy tengo clase** I have to go to school today. **-2.** [medida, años, sensación, cualidad] to be; **tiene 3 metros de ancho** it's 3 metres wide; **¿cuántos años tienes?** how old are you?; **tiene diez años** she's ten (years old); ~ **hambre/miedo** to be hungry/afraid; ~ **mal humor** to be bad-tempered; **le tiene lástima** he feels sorry for her. **-3.** [sujetar] to hold; **tenlo por el asa** hold it by the handle. **-4.** [tomar]: **ten el libro que me pediste** here's the book you asked me for; **¡aquí tienes!** here you are! **-5.** [recibir] to get; **tuve un verdadero desengaño** I was really disappointed; **tendrá una sorpresa** he'll get a surprise. **-6.** [valorar]: **me tienen por tonto** they think I'm stupid; ~ **a alguien en mucho** to think the world of sb. **-7.** [guardar, contener] to keep. **-8.** *loc*: **no las tiene todas consigo** he is not too sure about it; ~ **a bien hacer algo** to be kind enough to do sthg; ~ **que ver con algo/alguien** [existir relación] to have something to do with sthg/sb; [existir semejanza] to be in the same league as sthg/sb.

◆ **tenerse** *vpr* **-1.** [sostenerse]: ~**se de pie** to stand upright. **-2.** [considerarse]: **se tiene por listo** he thinks he's clever.

tengo → tener.

tenia *f* tapeworm.

tenida *f Amer* suit.

teniente *m* lieutenant; ~ **coronel/general** lieutenant colonel/general.

◆ **teniente (de) alcalde** *m y f* deputy mayor.

tenis *m inv* tennis; ~ **de mesa** table tennis.

tenista *m y f* tennis player.

tenístico, -ca *adj* tennis (*antes de sust*).

Tenochtitlán Tenochtitlan.

tenor *m* **-1.** MÚS tenor. **-2.** [estilo] tone; **a este** ~ along those lines.

◆ **a tenor de** *loc prep* in view of.

tenorio *m* ladies' man, Casanova.

tensado *m* tightening.

tensar *vt* to tauten; [arco] to draw.

tensión *f* **-1.** [gen] tension; ~ **nerviosa** nervous tension. **-2.** TECN [estiramiento] stress; **en** ~ tensed. **-3.** MED: ~ **(arterial)** blood pressure; **tener la** ~ **alta/baja** to have high/low blood pressure. **-4.** ELECTR voltage; **alta** ~ high voltage.

tenso, -sa *adj* taut; *fig* tense.

tensor, -ra *adj* tightening.

◆ **tensor** *m* **-1.** [dispositivo] turnbuckle. **-2.** ANAT tensor.

tentación *f* **-1.** [deseo] temptation; **caer en la** ~ to give in to temptation; **tener la** ~ **de** to be tempted to. **-2.** [punto débil] weakness.

tentáculo *m* tentacle.

tentador, -ra *adj* tempting.

tentar [19] *vt* **-1.** [palpar] to feel. **-2.** [atraer, incitar] to tempt.

tentativa *f* attempt; ~ **de asesinato** attempted murder.

tentempié (*pl* **tentempiés**) *m* snack.

tenue *adj* **-1.** [tela, hilo, lluvia] fine. **-2.** [luz, sonido, dolor] faint. **-3.** [relación] tenuous.

teñido *m* dyeing.

teñir [26] *vt* **-1.** [ropa, pelo]: ~ **algo (de rojo** *etc*) to dye sthg (red *etc*). **-2.** *fig* [matizar]: ~ **algo (de)** to tinge sthg (with).

◆ **teñirse** *vpr*: ~**se (el pelo)** to dye one's hair.

teocracia *f* theocracy.

teología *f* theology; ~ **de la liberación** liberation theology.

teológico, -ca *adj* theological.

teólogo, -ga *m y f* theologian.

teorema *m* theorem.

teorético, -ca *adj* theoretical.

teoría *f* theory; **en** ~ in theory; ~ **del conocimiento** epistemology; ~ **de la información** information theory; ~ **monetaria** monetary theory.

teóricamente *adv* theoretically.

teórico, -ca ◇ *adj* theoretical. ◇ *m y f* [persona] theorist.

◆ **teórica** *f* [teoría] theory (*U*).

teorizador, -ra *adj* theorizing.

teorizar [13] *vi* to theorize.

tequila *m o f* tequila.

TER (*abrev de* **tren español rápido**) *m Spanish high-speed train.*

terapeuta *m y f* therapist.

terapéutico, -ca *adj* therapeutic.

◆ **terapéutica** *f* therapeutics (*U*).

terapia *f* therapy; ~ **ocupacional/de grupo** occupational/group therapy.

tercer → tercero.

tercera → tercero.

tercermundista *adj* third-world (*antes de sust*).

tercero, -ra *núm* (*antes de sust masculino sg*: **tercer**) third; **a la tercera va la vencida** third time lucky.

terreno

◆ **tercero** *m* **-1.** [piso] third floor. **-2.** [curso] third year. **-3.** [mediador, parte interesada] third party; **el ~ en discordia** the third party.

◆ **tercera** *f* AUTOM third (gear).

terceto *m* **-1.** [estrofa] tercet. **-2.** MÚS trio.

terciar [8] ◇ *vt* **-1.** [poner en diagonal - gen] to place diagonally; [- sombrero] to tilt. **-2.** [dividir] to divide into three. ◇ *vi* **-1.** [mediar]: **~ (en)** to mediate (in). **-2.** [participar] to intervene, to take part.

◆ **terciarse** *vpr* to arise; **si se tercia** if the opportunity arises.

terciario, -ria *adj* tertiary.

◆ **terciario** *m* GEOL Tertiary (period).

tercio *m* **-1.** [tercera parte] third. **-2.** MIL ≈ regiment; **~ de la guardia civil** Civil Guard division. **-3.** TAUROM stage (*of bullfight*); *ver también* **tauromaquia.**

terciopelo *m* velvet.

terco, -ca ◇ *adj* stubborn. ◇ *m y f* stubborn person.

tergal® *m* Tergal®.

tergiversación *f* distortion.

tergiversador, -ra ◇ *adj* distorting. ◇ *m y f* person who distorts the facts.

tergiversar *vt* to distort, to twist.

termal *adj* thermal.

termas *fpl* **-1.** [baños] hot baths, spa (*sg*). **-2.** HIST thermae.

termes = **termita.**

térmico, -ca *adj* thermal.

terminación *f* **-1.** [finalización] completion. **-2.** [parte final] end. **-3.** GRAM ending.

terminal ◇ *adj* [gen] final; [enfermo] terminal. ◇ *m* ELECTR & INFORM terminal; **~ video-texto** videotext terminal. ◇ *f* [de aeropuerto] terminal; [de autobuses] terminus.

terminante *adj* categorical; [prueba] conclusive.

terminar ◇ *vt* to finish. ◇ *vi* **-1.** [acabar] to end; [tren] to stop, to terminate; **~ en** [objeto] to end in. **-2.** [reñir] to finish, to split up. **-3.** [ir a parar]: **~ (de/en)** to end up (as/in); **~ por hacer algo** to end up doing sthg.

◆ **terminarse** *vpr* **-1.** [finalizarse] to finish. **-2.** [agotarse] to run out.

término *m* **-1.** [fin, extremo] end; **dar ~ a algo** to bring sthg to a close; **poner ~ a algo** to put a stop to sthg. **-2.** [territorio]: **~ (municipal)** district. **-3.** [plazo] period; **en el ~ de un mes** within (the space of) a month. **-4.** [lugar, posición] place; **en primer ~** ARTE & FOT in the foreground; **en último ~** ARTE & FOT in the background; *fig* [si es necesario] as a last resort; [en resumidas cuentas] in the final analysis. **-5.** [elemento] point; **~ medio** [media] average; [compromiso] compromise, happy medium; **por ~ medio** on average. **-6.** LING & MAT term; **en ~s generales** generally speaking. **-7.** [de transportes] terminus.

◆ **términos** *mpl* [palabras] terms; **los ~s del contrato** the terms of the contract; **estar en buenos/malos ~s** to be on good/bad terms.

terminología *f* terminology.

terminológico, -ca *adj* terminological.

termita *f*, **termes** *m inv* termite.

termo *m* Thermos® (flask).

termoaislante *adj* heat insulating.

termodinámico, -ca *adj* thermodynamic.

◆ **termodinámica** *f* thermodynamics (*U*).

termometría *f* thermometry.

termométrico, -ca *adj* thermometric.

termómetro *m* thermometer; **~ centígrado/clínico** centigrade/clinical thermometer.

termonuclear *adj* thermonuclear.

termorregulador *m* thermostat.

termostato *m* thermostat.

terna *f* POLÍT shortlist of three candidates.

ternario, -ria *adj* ternary.

ternasco *f* suckling lamb.

ternero, -ra *m y f* [animal] calf.

◆ **ternera** *f* [carne] veal.

ternilla *f* **-1.** CULIN gristle. **-2.** ANAT cartilage.

terno *m* **-1.** [trío] trio. **-2.** [traje] three-piece suit.

ternura *f* tenderness.

terquedad *f* stubbornness.

terracota *f* terracotta.

terrado *m* terrace roof.

terral, tierral *m* Amer dust cloud.

Terranova Newfoundland.

terraplén *m* embankment.

terráqueo, -a *adj* Earth (*antes de sust*), terrestrial.

terrario, terrarium *m* terrarium.

terrateniente *m y f* landowner.

terraza *f* **-1.** [balcón] balcony. **-2.** [de café] terrace, patio. **-3.** [azotea] terrace roof. **-4.** [bancal] terrace.

terrazo *m* terrazzo.

terremoto *m* earthquake.

terrenal *adj* earthly.

terreno, -na *adj* earthly.

◆ **terreno** *m* **-1.** [suelo - gen] land; [- GEOL] terrain; [- AGR] soil. **-2.** [solar] plot (of land). **-3.** DEP: **~ (de juego)** field, pitch. **-4.** *fig* [ámbito] field. **-5.** *loc:* **estar** O **encontrarse en**

su propio ~ to be on home ground; **ganar** ~ [imponerse] to gain ground; [progresar] to make up ground; **perder** ~ to lose ground; **preparar** ○ **trabajar el** ~ **(para)** to pave the way (for); **reconocer** ○ **tantear el** ~ to see how the land lies; **saber uno el** ~ **que pisa** to know what one is about; **ser** ~ **abonado (para algo)** to be fertile ground (for sthg); **sobre el** ~ on the spot.

térreo, -a adj earthy.

terrestre ◇ adj **-1.** [del planeta] terrestrial. **-2.** [de la tierra] land (antes de sust). ◇ m y f terrestrial, Earth-dweller.

terrible adj **-1.** [gen] terrible. **-2.** [aterrador] terrifying.

terrícola ◇ adj land (antes de sust). ◇ m y f earthling.

terrier m terrier.

territorial adj territorial.

territorialidad f DER territoriality.

territorio m territory; **por todo el** ~ **nacional** across the country, nationwide.

terrón m **-1.** [de tierra] clod of earth. **-2.** [de harina etc] lump; ~ **de azúcar** sugar lump.

terror m terror; CIN horror; **dar** ~ to terrify.

terrorífico, -ca adj terrifying.

terrorismo m terrorism.

terrorista adj, m y f terrorist.

terroso, -sa adj **-1.** [parecido a la tierra] earthy. **-2.** [con tierra] muddy.

terruño m **-1.** [terreno] plot of land. **-2.** [patria] homeland.

terso, -sa adj **-1.** [piel, superficie] smooth. **-2.** [aguas, mar] clear. **-3.** [estilo, lenguaje] polished.

tersura f **-1.** [de piel, superficie] smoothness. **-2.** [de aguas, mar] clarity. **-3.** [de estilo, lenguaje] polish.

tertulia f regular meeting of people for informal discussion of a particular issue of common interest; ~ **literaria** literary circle.

Tesalónica f Thessalonica.

tesina f (undergraduate) dissertation.

tesis f inv thesis.

tesitura f **-1.** [circunstancia] circumstances (pl). **-2.** MÚS tessitura, pitch.

tesón m **-1.** [tenacidad] tenacity, perseverance. **-2.** [firmeza] firmness.

tesorería f **-1.** [cargo] treasurership. **-2.** [oficina] treasurer's office. **-3.** COM liquid capital.

tesorero, -ra m y f treasurer.

tesoro m **-1.** [botín] treasure. **-2.** [hacienda pública] treasury, exchequer. **-3.** fig [persona valiosa] gem, treasure. **-4.** fig [apelativo] my treasure.

◆ **Tesoro** m ECON: **el Tesoro** the Treasury.

test (pl **tests**) m test; ~ **de embarazo** pregnancy test.

testa f head.

testado, -da adj [persona] testate; [herencia] testamentary.

testaferro m front man.

testamentaría f **-1.** [documentos] documentation (of a will). **-2.** [bienes] estate, inheritance.

testamentario, -ria ◇ adj testamentary. ◇ m y f executor.

testamento m will; **hacer** ~ to write one's will.

◆ **Antiguo Testamento** m Old Testament.

◆ **Nuevo Testamento** m New Testament.

testar vi to make a will.

testarudez f stubbornness.

testarudo, -da ◇ adj stubborn. ◇ m y f stubborn person.

testículo m testicle.

testificar [10] ◇ vt to testify; fig to testify to. ◇ vi to testify, to give evidence.

testigo ◇ m y f [persona] witness; **poner por** ~ **a alguien** to cite sb as a witness; ~ **de cargo/descargo** witness for the prosecution/defence; ~ **ocular** ○ **presencial** eyewitness. ◇ m **-1.** fig [prueba]: ~ **de** proof of. **-2.** DEP baton.

◆ **testigo de Jehová** m y f Jehovah's Witness.

testimonial adj **-1.** [documento, prueba etc] testimonial. **-2.** fig [simbólico] token, symbolic.

testimoniar [8] ◇ vt to testify; fig to testify to. ◇ vi to testify, to give evidence.

testimonio m **-1.** DER testimony; **falso** ~ perjury, false evidence. **-2.** [prueba] proof; **como** ~ **de** as proof of; **dar** ~ **de** to prove.

testosterona f testosterone.

testuz m o f **-1.** [frente] brow. **-2.** [nuca] nape.

teta f **-1.** fam [de mujer] tit; **dar la** ~ to breast-feed; **de** ~ nursing. **-2.** [de animal] teat.

tétanos m inv tetanus.

tetera f teapot.

tetilla f **-1.** [de hombre, animal] nipple. **-2.** [de biberón] teat.

tetina f teat.

tetrabrick (pl **tetrabricks**) m tetrabrick.

tetraedro m tetrahedron.

tetralogía f tetralogy.

tetraplejía f quadriplegia.

tetrapléjico, -ca adj, m y f quadriplegic.

tétrico, -ca adj gloomy.

teutón, -ona ◇ adj Teutonic. ◇ m y f Teuton.

teutónico, -ca adj HIST Teutonic.

textil adj & m textile.

texto m **-1.** [gen] text. **-2.** [pasaje] passage.

textual adj **-1.** [del texto] textual. **-2.** [exacto] exact.

textura f **-1.** [de tela etc] texture. **-2.** fig [estructura] structure.

tez f complexion.

thriller ['θriler] (pl thrillers) m thriller.

ti pron pers (después de prep) **-1.** [gen] you; siempre pienso en ~ I'm always thinking about you; **me acordaré de** ~ I'll remember you. **-2.** [reflexivo] yourself; **sólo piensas en** ~ **(mismo)** you only think about yourself.

tía → **tío.**

tianguis m inv Amer open-air market.

TIAR (abrev de **Tratado Interamericano de Asistencia Recíproca**) m inter-American co-operation treaty.

tiara f tiara.

Tibet m: **el** ~ Tibet.

tibetano, -na adj, m y f Tibetan.

tibia f shinbone, tibia.

tibieza f **-1.** [calidez] warmth; [falta de calor] lukewarmness. **-2.** fig [frialdad] lack of enthusiasm.

tibio, -bia adj **-1.** [cálido] warm; [falto de calor] tepid, lukewarm. **-2.** fig [frío] lukewarm. **-3.** loc: **poner** ~ **a alguien** to speak ill of sb.

tiburón m **-1.** [gen] shark. **-2.** FIN raider.

tic m tic.

ticket = **tíquet.**

tictac m tick tock.

tiembla etc → **temblar.**

tiempo m **-1.** [gen] time; **al poco** ~ soon afterwards; **a** ~ **(de hacer algo)** in time (to do sthg); **a un** ~ at the same time; **cada cierto** ~ every so often; **con el** ~ in time; **del** ~ [fruta] of the season; [bebida] at room temperature; **en mis** ~**s** in my day o time; **estar a o tener** ~ **de** to have time to; **fuera de** ~ at the wrong moment; **ganar** ~ to save time; **hacer** ~ to pass the time; **perder el** ~ to waste time; ~ **libre** o **de ocio** spare time; ~ **parcial** o **partido** part-time; ~ **de acceso** INFORM access time; ~ **real** INFORM real time; **dar** ~ **al** ~ to give things time; **en** ~**s de Maricastaña** donkey's years ago; **engañar** o **matar el** ~ to kill time. **-2.** [periodo largo] long time; **con** ~ in good time; **hace** ~ **que** it is a long time since; **hace** ~ **que no vive aquí** he hasn't lived here for some time; **tomarse uno su** ~ to take one's time. **-3.** [edad] age; **¿qué** ~ **tiene?** how old is he? **-4.** [movimiento] movement; **motor de cuatro** ~**s** four-stroke engine. **-5.** METEOR weather; **hizo buen/mal** ~ the weather was good/bad; **si el** ~ **lo permite** o **no lo impide** weather permitting; **hace un** ~ **de perros** it's a foul day; **poner a** o **al mal** ~ **buena cara** to put a brave face on things. **-6.** DEP half. **-7.** GRAM tense. **-8.** [MÚS - compás] time; [- ritmo] tempo.

tienda ◇ v → **tender.** ◇ f **-1.** [establecimiento] shop; ~ **libre de impuestos** duty-free shop. **-2.** [para acampar]: ~ **(de campaña)** tent.

tiene → **tener.**

tienta ◇ v → **tentar.** ◇ f TAUROM trial (of the bulls).

◆ **a tientas** loc adv blindly; **andar a tientas** to grope along.

tiento m **-1.** [cuidado] care; [tacto] tact. **-2.** [de ciego] white stick. **-3.** [de equilibrista] balancing pole.

tierno, -na adj **-1.** [blando, cariñoso] tender. **-2.** [del día] fresh.

tierra f **-1.** [gen] land; ~ **adentro** inland; ~ **de nadie** no-man's-land; ~ **de promisión** Promised Land; ~ **firme** terra firma, dry land; ~ **virgen** virgin land. **-2.** [materia inorgánica] earth, soil; **un camino de** ~ a dirt track. **-3.** [suelo] ground; **besar la** ~ fig to fall flat on one's face; **caer a** ~ to fall to the ground; **tomar** ~ to touch down. **-4.** [patria] homeland, native land. **-5.** ELECTR earth Br, ground Am. **-6.** loc: **echar por** ~ **algo** to ruin sthg; **echar** ~ **a un asunto** to hush up an affair; **poner** ~ **por medio** to make o.s. scarce; **¡trágame** ~! fam I wish the earth would swallow me up!; **venir** o **venirse a** ~ to come to nothing.

◆ **Tierra** f: **la Tierra** the Earth.

◆ **Tierra del Fuego** f Tierra del Fuego.

◆ **Tierra Santa** f the Holy Land.

tierral = **terral.**

tieso, -sa adj **-1.** [rígido] stiff; **dejar** ~ **a alguien** fig to kill sb; **quedarse** ~ [de frío] to freeze. **-2.** [erguido] erect. **-3.** fig [engreído] haughty. **-4.** fig [distante] distant.

tiesto m flowerpot.

tifoideo, -a adj typhoid (antes de sust).

tifón m typhoon.

tifus m inv typhus.

tigre m tiger; **oler a** ~ fam to stink.

tigresa *f* tigress.

Tigris *m*: **el** ~ the (River) Tigris.

TIJ (*abrev de* **Tribunal Internacional de Justicia**) *m* ICJ.

tijera *f* (*gen pl*) scissors (*pl*); [de jardinero, esquilador] shears (*pl*); **unas ~s** a pair of scissors/shears; **de** ~ [escalera, silla] folding.

tijereta *f* **-1.** [insecto] earwig. **-2.** DEP scissors (*sg*).

tijeretazo *m* snip.

tijeretear *vt* to snip.

tila *f* **-1.** [flor] lime blossom. **-2.** [infusión] lime blossom tea.

tildar *vt*: ~ **a alguien de algo** to brand ○ call sb sthg.

tilde *f* **-1.** [signo ortográfico] tilde. **-2.** [acento gráfico] accent.

tiliches *mpl Amer* bits and pieces.

tilín *m* tinkle, tinkling (*U*); **me hace** ~ *fam* I fancy him.

tilo *m* **-1.** [árbol] linden ○ lime tree. **-2.** [madera] lime.

timador, -ra *m y f* confidence trickster, swindler.

timar *vt* **-1.** [estafar]: ~ **a alguien** to swindle sb; ~ **algo a alguien** to swindle sb out of sthg. **-2.** *fig* [engañar] to cheat, to con.

timba *f* game of cards.

timbal *m* [MÚS - de orquesta] kettledrum, timbal; [- tamboril] small drum.

timbrado, -da *adj* **-1.** [sellado] stamped. **-2.** [sonido] clear, true.

timbrar *vt* to stamp.

timbrazo *m* loud ring.

timbre *m* **-1.** [aparato] bell; **tocar el** ~ to ring the bell; ~ **de alarma** alarm (bell). **-2.** [de voz, sonido] tone; TECN timbre. **-3.** [sello - de documentos] stamp; [- de impuestos] seal.

timidez *f* shyness.

tímido, -da ◇ *adj* shy. ◇ *m y f* shy person.

timing ['taimen] (*pl* **timings**) *m* work schedule.

timo *m* **-1.** [estafa] swindle; ~ **de la estampita** *confidence trick where fake notes are used to buy a watch*. **-2.** *fam* [engaño] trick. **-3.** ANAT thymus.

timón *m* **-1.** AERON & NÁUT rudder. **-2.** *fig* [gobierno] helm; **llevar el** ~ **de** to be at the helm of. **-3.** *Amer* [volante] steering wheel.

timonear *vi* to steer.

timonel, timonero *m* NÁUT helmsman.

timorato, -ta *adj* **-1.** [mojigato] prudish. **-2.** [tímido] fearful.

tímpano *m* **-1.** ANAT eardrum. **-2.** [MÚS -

tamboril] small drum; [- de cuerda] hammer dulcimer. **-3.** ARQUIT tympanum.

tina *f* **-1.** [tinaja] pitcher. **-2.** [gran cuba] vat. **-3.** [bañera] bathtub.

tinaja *f* (large) pitcher.

tinglado *m* **-1.** [cobertizo] shed. **-2.** [armazón] platform. **-3.** *fig* [lío] fuss. **-4.** *fig* [maquinación] plot.

tinieblas *fpl* darkness (*U*); *fig* confusion (*U*), uncertainty (*U*); **estar en** ~ **sobre algo** to be in the dark about sthg.

tino *m* **-1.** [puntería] good aim. **-2.** *fig* [habilidad] skill. **-3.** *fig* [juicio] sense, good judgment. **-4.** *fig* [moderación] moderation.

tinta *f* ink; ~ **china** Indian ink; ~ **simpática** invisible ink; **cargar** ○ **recargar las** ~ **s** to exaggerate; **saberlo de buena** ~ to have it on good authority; **sudar** ~ to sweat blood.

◆ **medias tintas** *fpl*: **andarse con medias** ~**s** to be wishy-washy.

tintar *vt* to dye.

tinte *m* **-1.** [sustancia] dye. **-2.** [operación] dyeing. **-3.** [tintorería] dry cleaner's. **-4.** *fig* [tono] shade, tinge. **-5.** *fig* [apariencia] suggestion, semblance.

tintero *m* [frasco] ink pot; [en la mesa] inkwell; **dejarse algo en el** ~ to leave sthg unsaid.

tintinear *vi* to jingle, to tinkle.

tintineo *m* tinkle, tinkling (*U*).

tinto, -ta *adj* **-1.** [teñido] dyed. **-2.** [manchado] stained. **-3.** [vino] red.

◆ **tinto** *m* [vino] red wine.

tintorera *f* blue shark.

tintorería *f* dry cleaner's.

tintorero, -ra *m y f* dry cleaner.

tintorro *m fam* red plonk.

tintura *f* **-1.** FARM tincture. **-2.** [tinte] dye; [proceso] dyeing.

tiña ◇ *v* → **teñir**. ◇ *f* MED ringworm.

tiñera *etc* → **teñir**.

tiñoso, -sa *adj* MED suffering from ringworm.

tío, -a *m y f* **-1.** [familiar] uncle (*f* aunt); ~ **abuelo** great uncle (*f* great aunt); ~ **carnal** blood uncle (*f* blood aunt); **el** ~ **Sam** *fig* Uncle Sam. **-2.** *fam* [individuo] guy (*f* bird). **-3.** *mfam* [apelativo] mate (*f* darling). **-4.** *loc*: **no hay tu tía** *mfam* there's no way.

tiovivo *m* merry-go-round.

tipazo *m fam* [de mujer] great figure; [de hombre] good build.

tipejo, -ja *m y f despec* individual, character.

típico, -ca *adj* typical; [traje, restaurante etc] traditional; ~ **de** typical of.

tipificación *f* **-1.** [gen & DER] classification. **-2.** [normalización] standardization.

tipificar [10] *vt* **-1.** [gen & DER] to classify. **-2.** [normalizar] to standardize. **-3.** [simbolizar] to typify.

tipismo *m* local colour.

tiple ◇ *m y f* [cantante] soprano. ◇ *m* **-1.** [voz] soprano. **-2.** [guitarra] treble guitar.

tipo, -pa *m y f mfam* guy (*f* bird).
◆ **tipo** *m* **-1.** [clase] type, sort; **no es mi** ~ he is not my type; **todo** ~ **de** all sorts of. **-2.** [cuerpo - de mujer] figure; [- de hombre] build; **aguantar** ○ **mantener el** ~ to keep one's calm; **jugarse el** ~ to risk one's neck. **-3.** ECON rate; ~ **de descuento** base rate; ~ **de interés/cambio** interest/exchange rate; ~ **impositivo** tax band. **-4.** IMPRENTA & ZOOL type.

tipografía *f* **-1.** [procedimiento] printing. **-2.** [taller] printing works (*sg*).

tipográfico, -ca *adj* typographical, printing (*antes de sust*).

tipógrafo, -fa *m y f* printer.

tipología *f* typology.

tíquet (*pl* **tíquets**), **ticket** ['tiket] (*pl* **tickets**) *m* ticket; ~ **de compra** receipt.

tiquismiquis ◇ *adj inv fam* [maniático] pernickety. ◇ *m y f inv fam* [maniático] fusspot. ◇ *mpl* **-1.** [riñas] squabbles. **-2.** [bagatelas] trifles.

TIR (*abrev de* **transport international routier**) *m* International Road Transport, ≈ HGV *Br*.

tira *f* **-1.** [banda cortada] strip. **-2.** [tirante] strap. **-3.** [de viñetas] comic strip. **-4.** *loc:* **la** ~ **de** *fam* loads (*pl*) of.

tirabuzón *m* **-1.** [rizo] curl. **-2.** [sacacorchos] corkscrew.

tirachinas *m inv* catapult.

tiradero *m Amer* rubbish dump.

tirado, -da ◇ *adj* **-1.** *fam* [barato] dirt cheap. **-2.** *fam* [fácil] simple, dead easy; **estar** ~ to be a cinch. **-3.** *fam* [débil, cansado] worn-out. **-4.** *fam* [miserable] seedy. **-5.** *loc:* **dejar** ~ **a alguien** to leave sb in the lurch. ◇ *m y f fam* [persona] wretch.
◆ **tirada** *f* **-1.** [lanzamiento] throw. **-2.** [IMPRENTA - número de ejemplares] print run; [- reimpresión] reprint; [- número de lectores] circulation. **-3.** [sucesión] series. **-4.** [distancia]: **hay una** ~ **hasta allí** it's a fair way ○ quite a stretch; **de** ○ **en una tirada** in one go.

tirador, -ra *m y f* [persona] marksman.

◆ **tirador** *m* **-1.** [mango] handle. **-2.** [de campanilla] bell rope.
◆ **tiradores** *mpl Amer* [tirantes] braces.

Tirana Tirana.

tiranía *f* tyranny.

tiránico, -ca *adj* tyrannical.

tiranizar [13] *vt* to tyrannize.

tirano, -na ◇ *adj* tyrannical. ◇ *m y f* tyrant.

tirante ◇ *adj* **-1.** [estirado] taut. **-2.** *fig* [violento, tenso] tense; **estoy** ~ **con él** there's tension between us. ◇ *m* **-1.** [de tela] strap. **-2.** ARQUIT brace.
◆ **tirantes** *mpl* [para pantalones] braces *Br*, suspenders *Am*.

tirantez *f fig* tension.

tirar ◇ *vt* **-1.** [lanzar] to throw; ~ **algo a alguien/algo** [para hacer daño] to throw sthg at sb/sthg; **tírame una manzana** throw me an apple. **-2.** [dejar caer] to drop; [derramar] to spill; [volcar] to knock over. **-3.** [desechar, malgastar] to throw away. **-4.** [disparar] to fire; [- bomba] to drop; [- petardo, cohete] to let off. **-5.** [derribar] to knock down. **-6.** [jugar - carta] to play; [- dado] to throw. **-7.** [DEP - falta, penalti etc] to take; [- balón] to pass. **-8.** [imprimir] to print.
◇ *vi* **-1.** [estirar, arrastrar]: ~ **(de algo)** to pull (sthg); **tira y afloja** give and take. **-2.** [disparar] to shoot; ~ **a matar** to shoot to kill. **-3.** *fam* [atraer] to have a pull; **me tira la vida del campo** I feel drawn towards life in the country; ~ **de algo** to attract sthg. **-4.** [cigarrillo, chimenea etc] to draw. **-5.** *fam* [funcionar] to go, to work. **-6.** [dirigirse] to go, to head. **-7.** *fam* [apañárselas] to get by; **ir tirando** to get by; **voy tirando** I'm O.K., I've been worse. **-8.** [durar] to last. **-9.** [parecerse]: **tira a gris** it's greyish; **tira a su abuela** she takes after her grandmother; **tirando a** approaching, not far from. **-10.** [tender]: ~ **para algo** [persona] to have the makings of sthg; **este programa tira a (ser) hortera** this programme is a bit on the tacky side; **el tiempo tira a mejorar** the weather looks as if it's getting better. **-11.** [jugar] to (have one's) go. **-12.** [DEP - con el pie] to kick; [- con la mano] to throw; [- a meta, canasta etc] to shoot.
◆ **tirarse** *vpr* **-1.** [lanzarse]: ~**se (a)** [agua] to dive (into); [aire] to jump (into); ~**se sobre alguien** to jump on top of sb; ~**se de** [gen] to jump from; [para bajar] to jump down from; [para matarse] to throw o.s. from. **-2.** [tumbarse] to stretch out. **-3.** [tiempo] to spend. **-4.** *vulg* [fornicar]: ~**se a alguien** to screw sb.

tirita® *f* (sticking) plaster *Br*, ≃ Bandaid®
Am.

tiritar *vi*: ~ **(de)** to shiver (with).

tiritera, **tiritona** *f* shivering.

tiro *m* **-1.** [gen] shot; **pegar un ~ a alguien**
to shoot sb; **pegarse un ~** to shoot o.s.; ~
de gracia coup de grâce; ~ **libre** DEP free
kick; **ni a ~s** never in a million years; **me
salió el ~ por la culata** it backfired on me;
no por ahí los ~s you're a bit wide of the
mark there; **sentar como un ~ (a alguien)**
fam to go down badly (with sb). **-2.** [acción] shooting; ~ **al blanco** [deporte] target
shooting; [lugar] shooting range; ~ **al plato**
clay-pigeon shooting; ~ **con arco** archery.
-3. [huella, marca] bullet mark; [herida] gunshot wound. **-4.** [alcance] range; **a ~ de**
within the range of; **a ~ de piedra** a
stone's throw away; **ponerse/estar a ~** [de
arma] to come/be within range; *fig* [de persona] to come/be within one's reach. **-5.**
[de chimenea, horno] draw. **-6.** [de pantalón]
distance between crotch and waist; **vestirse** ○
ponerse de ~s largos to dress o.s. up to
the nines. **-7.** [de caballos] team.

tiroideo, -a *adj* thyroid (*antes de sust*).

tiroides *m inv* thyroid (gland).

tirón *m* **-1.** [estirón] pull. **-2.** [robo] bagsnatching.

◆ **de un tirón** *loc adv* in one go.

tirotear ○ *vt* to fire at. ○ *vi* to shoot.

◆ **tirotearse** *vpr* to fire at each other.

tiroteo *m* [tiros] shooting; [intercambio de
disparos] shootout.

Tirreno *m*: **el (mar) ~** the Tyrrhenian Sea.

tirria *f fam* dislike; **tenerle ~ a alguien** to
have a grudge against sb.

tisana *f* herbal tea.

tísico, -ca *adj, m y f* MED consumptive.

tisis *f inv* MED (pulmonary) tuberculosis.

tisú (*pl* **tisús**) *m* [tela] lamé.

titán *m fig* giant.

titánico, -ca *adj* titanic.

titanio *m* titanium.

títere *m lit* & *fig* puppet; **no dejar ~ con
cabeza** [destrozar] to destroy everything in
sight; [criticar] to spare nobody.

◆ **títeres** *mpl* [guiñol] puppet show (*sg*).

Titicaca *m*: **el lago ~** Lake Titicaca.

titilar, **titilear** *vi* **-1.** [temblar] to tremble.
-2. [estrella, luz] to flicker.

titipuchal *m Amer fam* hubbub.

titiritar *vi*: ~ **(de)** to shiver (with).

titiritero, -ra *m y f* **-1.** [de títeres] puppeteer. **-2.** [acróbata] acrobat.

titubeante *adj* **-1.** [actitud] hesitant. **-2.**
[voz] stuttering. **-3.** [al andar] tottering.

titubear *vi* **-1.** [dudar] to hesitate. **-2.** [al hablar] to stutter. **-3.** [tambalearse] to totter.

titubeo *m* (*gen pl*) **-1.** [duda] hesitation. **-2.**
[al hablar] stutter, stuttering (*U*). **-3.** [al andar] tottering.

titulación *f* [académica] qualifications (*pl*).

titulado, -da ○ *adj* [diplomado] qualified;
[licenciado] graduate (*antes de sust*); ~ **en**
with a qualification/degree in. ○ *m y f*
[diplomado] holder of a qualification; [licenciado] graduate.

titular ○ *adj* [profesor, médico] official. ○ *m
y f* [poseedor] holder. ○ *m* (*gen pl*) PRENS
headline; **con grandes ~es** splashed across
the front page. ○ *vt* [llamar] to title, to call.

◆ **titularse** *vpr* **-1.** [llamarse] to be titled ○
called. **-2.** [licenciarse]: ~**se (en)** to graduate
(in). **-3.** [diplomarse]: ~**se (en)** to obtain a
qualification (in).

titulillo *m despec* useless little qualification.

título *m* **-1.** [gen] title; ~ **de propiedad** title
deed. **-2.** [licenciatura] degree; [diploma] diploma; **tiene muchos ~s** she has a lot of
qualifications. **-3.** *fig* [derecho] right; **a ~ de**
as. **-4.** ECON bond, security.

tiza *f* chalk; **una ~** a piece of chalk.

tiznadura *f* **-1.** [acción] blackening, dirtying. **-2.** [mancha] black mark.

tiznar *vt* to blacken.

◆ **tiznarse** *vpr* to be blackened.

tizne *m o f* soot.

tizón *m* burning stick ○ log.

tizona *f* sword.

tlapalería *f Amer* ironmonger's (shop).

TNT (*abrev de* **trinitrotolueno**) *m o f* TNT.

toalla *f* **-1.** [para secarse] towel; ~ **de
ducha/manos** bath/hand towel; **arrojar** ○
tirar la ~ to throw in the towel. **-2.** [tejido]
towelling.

toallero *m* towel rail.

tobera *f* nozzle.

tobillera *f* ankle support.

tobillo *m* ankle.

tobogán *m* **-1.** [rampa] slide; [en parque de
atracciones] helter-skelter; [en piscina] chute,
flume. **-2.** [trineo] toboggan. **-3.** [pista] toboggan run.

toca *f* wimple.

tocadiscos *m inv* record player.

tocado, -da *adj* **-1.** [chiflado] soft in the
head. **-2.** [fruta] bad, rotten.

◆ **tocado** *m* **-1.** [prenda] headgear (*U*). **-2.**
[peinado] hairdo.

tocador *m* **-1.** [mueble] dressing table. **-2.**
[habitación - en lugar público] powder room;
[- en casa] boudoir.

tocante *adj*: (en lo) ~ a regarding.

tocar [10] ◇ *vt* **-1.** [gen] to touch; [palpar] to feel; [suj: país, jardín] to border on. **-2.** [instrumento, canción] to play; [bombo] to bang; [sirena, alarma] to sound; [campana, timbre] to ring; **el reloj tocó las doce** the clock struck twelve. **-3.** [abordar - tema etc] to touch on. **-4.** *fig* [conmover] to touch; [herir] to wound. **-5.** *fig* [concernir]: **por lo que a mí me toca/a eso le toca** as far as I'm/that's concerned; ~ **a alguien de cerca** to concern sb closely.
◇ *vi* **-1.** [entrar en contacto] to touch. **-2.** [estar próximo]: ~ **(con)** [gen] to be touching; [país, jardín] to border (on). **-3.** [llamar - a la puerta, ventana] to knock. **-4.** [corresponder - en un reparto]: ~ **a alguien** to be due to sb; **tocamos a mil cada uno** we're due a thousand each; **le tocó la mitad** he got half of it; **te toca a ti hacerlo** [turno] it's your turn to do it; [responsabilidad] it's up to you to do it. **-5.** [caer en suerte]: **me ha tocado la lotería** I've won the lottery; **le ha tocado sufrir mucho** he has had to suffer a lot. **-6.** [llegar el momento]: **nos toca pagar ahora** it's time (for us) to pay now.
◆ **tocarse** *vpr* to touch.

tocata *m* **-1.** *fam* [tocadiscos] record player. **-2.** MÚS toccata.

tocateja
◆ **a tocateja** *loc adv* in cash.

tocayo, -ya *m y f* namesake.

tocho *m* **-1.** *fam* [libro] boring tome. **-2.** [hierro] iron ingot.

tocinería *f* pork butcher's.

tocinero, -ra *m y f* pork butcher.

tocineta *f Amer* bacon.

tocino *m* [para cocinar] lard; [para comer] fat (*of bacon*); ~ **entreverado** streaky bacon.
◆ **tocino de cielo** *m* CULIN *dessert made of syrup and eggs.*

tocología *f* obstetrics (*U*).

tocólogo, -ga *m y f* obstetrician.

tocomocho *m confidence trick involving the sale of a lottery ticket, claimed to be a certain winner, for a large amount of money.*

tocón *m* stump.

todavía *adv* **-1.** [aún] still; [con negativo] yet, still; ~ **no lo he recibido** I still haven't got it, I haven't got it yet; ~ **ayer** as late as yesterday; ~ **no** not yet. **-2.** [sin embargo] still. **-3.** [incluso] even.

todo, -da ◇ *adj* **-1.** [gen] all; ~ **el mundo** everybody; ~ **el libro** the whole book, (of) the book; ~ **el día** all day. **-2.** [cada, cualquier]: ~**s los días/lunes** every day/Monday; ~ **español** every Spaniard, all Spaniards. **-3.** [para enfatizar]: **es** ~ **un hom-**

bre he's every bit a man; **ya es toda una mujer** she's a big girl now; **fue** ~ **un éxito** it was a great success.
◇ *pron* **-1.** [todas las cosas] everything, (*pl*) all of them; **lo vendió** ~ he sold everything, he sold it all; ~**s están rotos** they're all broken, all of them are broken; **de** ~ everything (you can think of); **en** ~ **y por** ~ entirely; **ante** ~ [sobre todo] above all; [en primer lugar] first of all; **con** ~ despite everything; **después de** ~ after all; **de todas todas** without a shadow of a doubt; **sobre** ~ above all; **está en** ~ he/she always makes sure everything is just so; **me invitó a cenar y** ~ she even asked me to dinner. **-2.** [todas las personas]: ~**s** everybody; **todas vinieron** everybody ○ they all came.
◆ **todo** ◇ *m* whole; **jugarse el** ~ **por el** ~ to stake everything. ◇ *adv* completely, all.
◆ **del todo** *loc adv*: **no estoy del** ~ **contento** I'm not entirely happy; **no lo hace mal del** ~ she doesn't do it at all badly.
◆ **todo terreno** *m* Jeep®.

todopoderoso, -sa *adj* almighty.
◆ **Todopoderoso** *m*: **el Todopoderoso** the Almighty.

toffee ['tofi] (*pl* **toffees**) *m* coffee-flavoured toffee.

toga *f* **-1.** [manto] toga. **-2.** [traje] gown. **-3.** [en el pelo] method of combing one's hair so it becomes straight.

togado, -da *adj* robed.

Togo Togo.

toilette [tua'let] (*pl* **toilettes**) *f* toilet.

toisón
◆ **toisón de oro** *m* **-1.** [insignia] golden fleece. **-2.** [orden] Order of the Golden Fleece.

tojo *m* gorse.

Tokio Tokyo.

toldo *m* [de tienda] awning; [de playa] sunshade.

toledano, -na *adj* of/relating to Toledo.

Toledo Toledo.

tolerable *adj* **-1.** [aguantable] tolerable. **-2.** [perdonable] acceptable.

tolerancia *f* tolerance.

tolerante ◇ *adj* tolerant. ◇ *m y f* tolerant person.

tolerar *vt* **-1.** [consentir, aceptar] to tolerate; ~ **que alguien haga algo** to tolerate sb doing sthg. **-2.** [aguantar] to stand.

tolva *f* hopper.

toma *f* **-1.** [de biberón, papilla] feed. **-2.** [de medicamento] dose; [de sangre] sample. **-3.** [de ciudad etc] capture. **-4.** [de agua, aire] inlet; ~ **de corriente** ELECTR socket; ~ **de tie-**

rra ELECTR earth. **-5.** CIN [de escena] take. **-6.** *loc:* **ser un ~ y daca** to be give and take.
◆ **toma de conciencia** *f* realization.
◆ **toma de posesión** *f* **-1.** [de gobierno, presidente] investiture. **-2.** [de cargo] undertaking.

tomadura *f:* **~ de pelo** hoax.

tomahawk [toma'xauk] (*pl* **tomahawks**) *m* tomahawk.

tomar ◇ *vt* **-1.** [gen] to take; [actitud, costumbre] to adopt. **-2.** [datos, información] to take down. **-3.** [comida, bebida] to have; **¿qué quieres ~?** what would you like (to drink/eat)? **-4.** [autobús, tren etc] to catch; [taxi] to take. **-5.** [contratar] to take on. **-6.** [considerar, confundir]: **~ a alguien por algo/alguien** to take sb for sthg/sb. **-7.** *loc:* **~la ○ ~las con alguien** *fam* to have it in for sb; **¡toma!** [al dar algo] here you are!; [expresando sorpresa] well I never!; **¡toma (ésa)!** *fam* [expresa venganza] take that!
◇ *vi* [encaminarse] to go, to head.
◆ **tomarse** *vpr* **-1.** [comida, bebida] to have; [medicina, drogas] to take. **-2.** [interpretar] to take; **~se algo a mal/bien** to take sthg badly/well.

tomate *m* **-1.** [fruto] tomato; **~ frito** *unconcentrated puree made by frying peeled tomatoes;* **ponerse como un ~** to go as red as a beetroot. **-2.** [de calcetín] hole. **-3.** *fam* [jaleo] uproar, commotion.

tomatera *f* tomato plant.

tomavistas *m inv* cine camera.

tómbola *f* tombola.

tomillo *m* thyme.

tomo *m* **-1.** [volumen] volume. **-2.** [libro] tome.

tomografía *f* tomography.

ton
◆ **sin ton ni son** *loc adv* for no apparent reason.

tonada *f* tune.

tonadilla *f* ditty.

tonadillero, -ra *m y f* ditty singer/writer.

tonal *adj* tonal.

tonalidad *f* **-1.** MÚS key. **-2.** [de color] tone.

tonel *m* [recipiente] barrel; **estar/ponerse como un ~** to be/become (as fat as) a barrel.

tonelada *f* tonne; **~ métrica** metric ton, tonne; **pesar una ~** to weigh a ton.

tonelaje *m* tonnage.

tongada *f* layer.

tongo *m* **-1.** [engaño]: **en la pelea hubo ~** the fight was fixed. **-2.** *Amer fam* [sombrero hongo] bowler hat.

tónico, -ca *adj* **-1.** [reconstituyente] revitalizing. **-2.** GRAM & MÚS tonic.
◆ **tónico** *m* **-1.** [reconstituyente] tonic. **-2.** [cosmético] skin toner.
◆ **tónica** *f* **-1.** [tendencia] trend. **-2.** MÚS tonic. **-3.** [bebida] tonic water.

tonificación *f* invigoration.

tonificador, -ra, tonificante *adj* invigorating.

tonificar [10] *vt* to invigorate.

tonillo *m despec* [retintín] sarcastic tone of voice.

tono *m* **-1.** [gen] tone; **estar a ~ (con)** to be appropriate (for); **fuera de ~** out of place. **-2.** [MÚS - tonalidad] key; [- altura] pitch. **-3.** [de color] shade; **~ de piel** complexion. **-4.** *loc:* **darse ~** *fam* to give o.s. airs; **ponerse a ~ con algo** [emborracharse] to get drunk on sthg; [ponerse al día] to get to grips with sthg; **subir el ~, subirse de ~** to get angrier and angrier.

tonsura *f* tonsure.

tontaina ◇ *adj fam* daft. ◇ *m y f fam* daft idiot.

tontear *vi* **-1.** [hacer el tonto] to fool about. **-2.** [coquetear]: **~ (con alguien)** to flirt (with sb).

tontería *f* **-1.** [estupidez] stupid thing; **decir una ~** to talk nonsense; **hacer una ~** to do sthg foolish. **-2.** [cosa sin importancia o valor] trifle.

tonto, -ta ◇ *adj* stupid; **ponerse ~** to be difficult; **~ de capirote ○ remate** daft as a brush. ◇ *m y f* idiot; **hacer el ~** to play the fool; **hacerse el ~** to act innocent.
◆ **a lo tonto** *loc adv* [sin notarlo] without realizing it.
◆ **a tontas y a locas** *loc adv* haphazardly.

tontorrón, -ona ◇ *adj* daft. ◇ *m y f* daft idiot.

top (*pl* **tops**) *m* [prenda] short top.

topacio *m* topaz.

topadora *f Amer* bulldozer.

topar *vi* **-1.** [chocar] to bump into each other. **-2.** [encontrarse]: **~ con alguien** to bump into sb; **~ con algo** to come across sthg.
◆ **toparse con** *vpr* [persona] to bump into; [cosa] to come across.

tope ◇ *adj inv* **-1.** [máximo] top, maximum; [fecha] last. **-2.** *mfam* [molón] brill, ace. ◇ *adv mfam* [muy] mega, really. ◇ *m* **-1.** [pieza] block; [para puerta] doorstop. **-2.** FERROC buffer. **-3.** [límite máximo] limit; [de plazo] deadline. **-4.** [freno]: **poner ~ a** to rein in, to curtail. **-5.** *loc:* **estar hasta los ~s** to be bursting at the seams.

◆ **a tope** *loc adv* **-1.** [de velocidad, intensidad] flat out. **-2.** *fam* [lleno - lugar] packed.

topera *f* molehill.

topetazo *m* bump; **darse un** ~ [en la cabeza] to bump o.s. on the head.

topetear *vi* to butt.

tópico, -ca *adj* **-1.** MED topical. **-2.** [manido] clichéd.
◆ **tópico** *m* cliché.

topless ['toβles] *m inv* topless bathing; **en** ~ topless.

topo *m* ZOOL & *fig* mole.

topografía *f* topography.

topográfico, -ca *adj* topographical.

topógrafo, -fa *m y f* topographer.

toponimia *f* **-1.** [nombres] place names (*pl*). **-2.** [ciencia] toponymy.

toponímico, -ca *adj* toponymical.

topónimo *m* place name.

toque ◇ *v* → tocar. ◇ *m* **-1.** [gen] touch; **dar los (últimos) ~s a algo** to put the finishing touches to sthg. **-2.** [aviso] warning; **dar un** ~ **a alguien** [llamar] to call sb; [amonestar] to prod sb, to warn sb; ~ **de atención** warning. **-3.** [sonido - de campana] chime, chiming (*U*); [- de tambor] beat, beating (*U*); [- de sirena etc] blast; ~ **de diana** reveille; ~ **de difuntos** death knell; ~ **de queda** curfew.

toquetear ◇ *vt* [manosear - cosa] to fiddle with; [- persona] to fondle. ◇ *vi fam* [sobar] to fiddle about.

toqueteo *m* [de cosa] fiddling; [a persona] fondling.

toquilla *f* shawl.

torácico, -ca *adj* thoracic.

tórax *m inv* thorax.

torbellino *m* **-1.** [remolino - de aire] whirlwind; [- de agua] whirlpool; [- de polvo] dustcloud. **-2.** *fig* [mezcla confusa] spate. **-3.** *fig* [persona inquieta] whirlwind.

torcaz *adj* → paloma.

torcedura *f* **-1.** [torsión] twist, twisting (*U*). **-2.** [esguince] sprain.

torcer [41] ◇ *vt* **-1.** [gen] to twist; [doblar] to bend. **-2.** [girar] to turn. **-3.** [desviar] to deflect; *fig* [persona] to corrupt. ◇ *vi* [girar] to turn.
◆ **torcerse** *vpr* **-1.** [retorcerse] to twist; [doblarse] to bend; **me tuerzo al andar/escribir** I can't walk/write in a straight line. **-2.** [dislocarse] to sprain. **-3.** [ir mal - esperanzas, negocios, día] to go wrong; [- persona] to go astray.

torcido, -da *adj* [enroscado] twisted; [doblado] bent; [cuadro, corbata] crooked.

tordo, -da ◇ *adj* dappled. ◇ *m y f* [caballo] dapple (horse).
◆ **tordo** *m* [pájaro] thrush.

toreador, -ra *m y f* bullfighter.

torear ◇ *vt* **-1.** [lidiar] to fight (*bulls*). **-2.** *fig* [eludir] to dodge. **-3.** *fig* [burlarse de]: ~ **a alguien** to mess sb about. ◇ *vi* [lidiar] to fight bulls.

toreo *m* bullfighting.

torero, -ra ◇ *adj* bullfighting (*antes de sust*). ◇ *m y f* [persona] bullfighter; **saltarse algo a la torera** *fig* to flout sthg.
◆ **torera** *f* [prenda] bolero (jacket).

toril *m* bullpen.

tormenta *f lit* & *fig* storm.

tormento *m* torment; **ser un** ~ [persona] to be a torment; [cosa] to be torture.

tormentoso, -sa *adj* stormy; [sueño] troubled.

tornadizo, -za *adj* fickle.

tornado *m* tornado.

tornar *culto* ◇ *vt* **-1.** [convertir]: ~ **algo en** (algo) to turn sthg into (sthg). **-2.** [devolver] to return. ◇ *vi* **-1.** [regresar] to return. **-2.** [volver a hacer]: ~ **a hacer algo** to do sthg again.
◆ **tornarse** *vpr* [convertirse]: ~**se (en)** to turn (into), to become.

tornas *fpl*: **volver las** ~ to turn the tables.

tornasol *m* **-1.** [girasol] sunflower. **-2.** [reflejo] sheen.

tornasolado, -da *adj* iridescent.

torneado, -da *adj* **-1.** [cerámica] turned. **-2.** [brazos, piernas] shapely.
◆ **torneado** *m* turning.

tornear *vt* to turn.

torneo *m* tournament.

tornero, -ra *m y f* [con madera] lathe operator.

tornillo *m* screw; [con tuerca] bolt; **le falta un** ~ *fam* he has a screw loose.

torniquete *m* **-1.** MED tourniquet. **-2.** [en entrada] turnstile.

torno *m* **-1.** [de alfarero] (potter's) wheel. **-2.** [de carpintero] lathe. **-3.** [para pesos] winch.
◆ **en torno a** *loc prep* **-1.** [alrededor de] around. **-2.** [acerca de] about; **girar en** ~ **a** to be about.

toro *m* bull; ~ **de lidia** fighting bull; **agarrar** ○ **coger el** ~ **por los cuernos** to take the bull by the horns; **ver los** ~**s desde la barrera** to watch from the wings.
◆ **toros** *mpl* [lidia] bullfight (*sg*), bullfighting (*U*).

toronja *f* grapefruit.

torpe *adj* **-1.** [gen] clumsy. **-2.** [necio] slow, dim-witted.

torpedear *vt* to torpedo.

torpedero, -ra *adj* torpedo-firing.
◆ **torpedero** *m* torpedo boat.

torpedo *m* **-1.** [proyectil] torpedo. **-2.** [pez] electric ray.

torpeza *f* **-1.** [gen] clumsiness; **fue una ~ hacerlo/decirlo** it was a clumsy thing to do/say. **-2.** [falta de inteligencia] slowness.

torrar *vt* to roast.

torre *f* **-1.** [construcción] tower; ELECTR pylon; **~ (de apartamentos)** tower block; **~ de control** control tower; **~ de homenaje** keep; **~ de marfil** *fig* ivory tower; **~ de perforación** oil derrick. **-2.** [en ajedrez] rook, castle. **-3.** MIL turret. **-4.** [chalé] cottage.

torrefacto, -ta *adj* high roast (*antes de sust*).

torrencial *adj* torrential.

torrente *m* torrent; **un ~ de** *fig* [gente, palabras etc] a stream ○ flood of; [dinero, energía] masses of.

torreón *m* large fortified tower.

torreta *f* **-1.** MIL turret. **-2.** ELECTR pylon.

torrezno *m* chunk of fried bacon.

tórrido, -da *adj* torrid.

torrija *f* French toast (*U*).

torsión *f* **-1.** [del cuerpo, brazo] twist, twisting (*U*). **-2.** MEC torsion.

torso *m* *culto* torso.

torta *f* **-1.** CULIN cake; **nos costó la ~ un pan** it cost us an arm and a leg. **-2.** *fam* [bofetada] thump; **dar** ○ **pegar una ~ a alguien** to thump sb.
◆ **ni torta** *loc adv fam* not a thing.

tortazo *m* **-1.** [bofetada] thump; **dar** ○ **pegar un ~ a alguien** to thump sb; **liarse a ~s** to come to blows. **-2.** [accidente] crash; **darse** ○ **pegarse un ~** to crash.

tortícolis *f inv* crick in the neck.

tortilla *f* omelette; **~ (a la) española** Spanish ○ potato omelette; **~ (a la) francesa** French ○ plain omelette; **cambió** ○ **se volvió la ~** the tables turned.

tortillera *f mfam despec* dyke, lesbian.

tortillería *f* [restaurante] omelette restaurant.

tórtola *f* turtledove.

tortolito, -ta *m y f* **-1.** [inexperto] novice. **-2.** (*gen pl*) *fam* [enamorado] lovebird.

tortuga *f* [terrestre] tortoise; [marina] turtle; [fluvial] terrapin.

tortuosidad *f* **-1.** [sinuosidad] tortuousness. **-2.** *fig* [perversidad] deviousness.

tortuoso, -sa *adj* **-1.** [sinuoso] tortuous, winding. **-2.** *fig* [perverso] devious.

tortura *f* torture.

torturador, -ra ◇ *adj* torturing. ◇ *m y f* torturer.

torturar *vt* to torture.
◆ **torturarse** *vpr* to torture o.s.

torvo, -va *adj* fierce.

torzamos → torcer.

tos *f* cough; **~ ferina** = tosferina.

tosco, -ca *adj* **-1.** [basto] crude. **-2.** *fig* [ignorante] coarse.

toser *vi* to cough.

tosferina, tos ferina *f* whooping cough.

tosquedad *f* **-1.** [vulgaridad] crudeness. **-2.** *fig* [ignorancia] coarseness.

tostadero *m* roaster.

tostado, -da *adj* **-1.** [pan, almendras] toasted. **-2.** [color] brownish. **-3.** [piel] tanned.
◆ **tostada** *f* piece of toast.

tostador *m*, **tostadora** *f* toaster.

tostar [23] *vt* **-1.** [dorar, calentar - pan, almendras] to toast; [- carne] to brown. **-2.** [broncear] to tan.
◆ **tostarse** *vpr* to get brown.

tostón *m* **-1.** CULIN crouton. **-2.** *fam fig* [rollo, aburrimiento] bore, drag. **-3.** *fam fig* [persona molesta] pain.

total ◇ *adj* total. ◇ *m* **-1.** [suma] total. **-2.** [totalidad, conjunto] whole; **el ~ del grupo** the whole group; **en ~** in all. ◇ *adv* anyway; **~ que me marché** so anyway, I left.

totalidad *f* whole; **en su ~** as a whole.

totalitario, -ria *adj* totalitarian.

totalitarismo *m* totalitarianism.

totalizar [13] *vt* to add up to, to amount to.

tótem (*pl* **tótems** ○ **tótemes**) *m* totem.

totémico, -ca *adj* totemic.

tour [tur] (*pl* **tours**) *m* tour.
◆ **tour de force** ['turðefors] *m* tour de force.
◆ **tour operador** *m* tour operator.

tournedos [turne'ðo] *m inv* tournedos.

tournée [tur'ne] (*pl* **tournées**) *f* tour.

toxicidad *f* toxicity.

tóxico, -ca *adj* toxic, poisonous.
◆ **tóxico** *m* poison.

toxicología *f* toxicology.

toxicológico, -ca *adj* toxicological.

toxicomanía *f* drug addiction.

toxicómano, -na ◇ *adj* addicted to drugs. ◇ *m y f* drug addict.

toxina *f* toxin.

tozudez f stubbornness, obstinacy.

tozudo, -da ◇ adj stubborn. ◇ m y f stubborn person.

traba f **-1.** [para coche] chock. **-2.** [de mesa] crosspiece. **-3.** fig [obstáculo] obstacle; **poner ~s (a alguien)** to put obstacles in the way (of sb).

trabado, -da adj **-1.** [unido - salsa] smooth; [- discurso] coherent. **-2.** [atascado] jammed. **-3.** GRAM ending in a consonant.

trabajado, -da adj **-1.** [obra] carefully worked. **-2.** [músculo] developed.

trabajador, -ra ◇ adj hard-working. ◇ m y f worker; **~ por cuenta propia** self-employed person.

trabajar ◇ vi **-1.** [gen] to work; **~ de/en** to work as/in; **~ en una empresa** to work for a firm. **-2.** CIN & TEATR to act. ◇ vt **-1.** [hierro, barro, tierra] to work; [masa] to knead. **-2.** [mejorar] to work on ○ at. **-3.** fig [engatusar, convencer]: **~ a alguien (para que haga algo)** to work on sb (so that they do sthg).

trabajo m **-1.** [gen] work; **hacer un buen ~** to do a good job; **~ intelectual/físico** mental/physical effort; **~ manual** manual labour; **~s forzados** ○ **forzosos** hard labour (U); **~s manuales** [en el colegio] arts and crafts; **ser un ~ de chinos** to be a finicky job. **-2.** [empleo] job; **no tener ~** to be out of work. **-3.** [estudio escrito] piece of work, essay. **-4.** POLÍT labour. **-5.** fig [esfuerzo] effort; **costar mucho ~** to take a lot of effort.

trabajoso, -sa adj **-1.** [difícil] hard, difficult. **-2.** [molesto] tiresome.

trabalenguas m inv tongue-twister.

trabar vt **-1.** [sujetar] to fasten; [a preso] to shackle. **-2.** [unir] to join. **-3.** [iniciar - conversación, amistad] to strike up. **-4.** [obstaculizar] to obstruct, to hinder. **-5.** CULIN to thicken.

◆ **trabarse** vpr **-1.** [enredarse] to get tangled. **-2.** [espesarse] to thicken. **-3.** loc: **se le trabó la lengua** he got tongue-tied.

trabazón f **-1.** [unión, enlace] assembly. **-2.** fig [conexión, enlace] link, connection.

trabilla f [de pantalón] foot strap; [de chaqueta] half belt.

trabucar vt to mix up.

trabuco m [arma de fuego] blunderbuss.

traca f string of firecrackers.

tracción f traction; **~ delantera/trasera** front-wheel/rear-wheel drive.

trace etc → **trazar**.

tracoma m trachoma.

tractor, -ra adj tractive.

◆ **tractor** m tractor.

tractorista m y f tractor driver.

tradición f tradition.

tradicional adj traditional.

tradicionalismo m traditionalism; POLÍT conservatism.

tradicionalista adj, m y f traditionalist.

traducción f translation; **~ automática/simultánea** machine/simultaneous translation.

traducir [33] ◇ vt **-1.** [a otro idioma] to translate. **-2.** fig [expresar] to express. ◇ vi: **~ (de/a)** to translate (from/into).

◆ **traducirse** vpr [a otro idioma]: **~se (por)** to be translated (by ○ as).

◆ **traducirse en** vpr [ocasionar] to lead to.

traductor, -ra ◇ adj translating. ◇ m y f translator; **~ jurado** translator qualified to work at court.

traer [73] vt **-1.** [trasladar, provocar] to bring; [consecuencias] to carry, to have; **~ consigo** [implicar] to mean, to lead to. **-2.** [llevar] to carry; **¿qué traes ahí?** what have you got there? **-3.** [llevar adjunto, dentro] to have; **trae un artículo interesante** it has an interesting article in it. **-4.** [llevar puesto] to wear.

◆ **traerse** vpr: **traérselas** fam fig to be a real handful.

tráfago m drudgery.

traficante m y f [de drogas, armas etc] trafficker.

traficar [10] vi: **~ (en/con algo)** to traffic (in sthg).

tráfico m [gen] traffic; **~ rodado** road traffic; **~ de influencias** political corruption.

tragaderas fpl fam: **tener (buenas) ~** [ser crédulo] to fall for anything; [ser tolerante] to be able to stomach anything.

tragaluz m skylight.

traganíqueles f inv Amer fam → **máquina**.

tragaperras f inv slot machine.

tragar [16] ◇ vt **-1.** [ingerir, creer] to swallow. **-2.** [absorber] to swallow up. **-3.** fig [soportar] to put up with; **no (poder) ~ a alguien** not to be able to stand sb. **-4.** fig [disimular] to contain, to keep to o.s.; [lágrimas] to choke back. **-5.** fam [consumir mucho - suj: persona, coche] to devour, to guzzle. ◇ vi to swallow.

◆ **tragarse** vpr fig [soportarse]: **no se tragan** they can't stand each other.

tragedia f tragedy.

trágico, -ca ◇ adj tragic. ◇ m y f tragedian.

tragicomedia f tragicomedy.

tragicómico, -ca adj tragicomic.

trago *m* **-1.** [de líquido] mouthful; **de un ~** in one gulp. **-2.** *fam* [copa] drink; **echar un ~** to have a quick drink. **-3.** *fam fig* [disgusto]: **ser un ~ para alguien** to be tough on sb; **pasar un mal ~** to have a tough time of it.

tragón, -ona ◇ *adj fam* greedy. ◇ *m y f fam* pig, glutton.

trague *etc* → tragar.

traición *f* **-1.** [infidelidad] betrayal; **a ~** treacherously. **-2.** DER treason; **alta ~** high treason.

traicionar *vt lit* & *fig* [ser infiel] to betray.

traicionero, -ra ◇ *adj* [desleal] treacherous; DER treasonous. ◇ *m y f* traitor.

traído, -da *adj* worn-out; **~ y llevado** well-worn, hackneyed.

traidor, -ra ◇ *adj* treacherous; DER treasonous. ◇ *m y f* traitor.

traiga *etc* → traer.

trailer ['trailer] (*pl* **trailers**) *m* **-1.** CIN trailer. **-2.** AUTOM articulated lorry.

trainera *f small Basque fishing boat.*

training ['trainin] (*pl* **trainings**) *m* training.

traje *m* **-1.** [con chaqueta] suit; [de una pieza] dress; **~ de baño** swimsuit; **~ de ceremonia** ○ **de gala** dress suit, formal dress (*U*); **~ de chaqueta** woman's two-piece suit; **~ de etiqueta** evening dress (*U*); **~ de noche** evening dress; **~ pantalón** trouser suit. **-2.** [regional, de época etc] costume; **~ de luces** matador's outfit; *ver también* tauromaquia. **-3.** [ropa] clothes (*pl*); **~ de diario** everyday clothes; **~ de paisano** [de militar] civilian clothes; [de policía] plain clothes.

trajeado, -da *adj* **-1.** [con chaqueta] wearing a jacket. **-2.** *fam* [arreglado] spruced up.

trajear *vt* to clothe.

trajera *etc* → traer.

trajín *m* **-1.** *fam fig* [ajetreo] bustle. **-2.** [transporte] haulage, transport.

trajinar ◇ *vi fam fig* to bustle about. ◇ *vt* to transport.

◆ **trajinarse a** *vpr fam* [ligarse a] to get off with.

trajo → traer.

trama *f* **-1.** [de hilos] weft. **-2.** *fig* [confabulación] intrigue. **-3.** LITER plot.

tramar *vt* **-1.** [hilo] to weave. **-2.** *fam fig* [planear] to plot; [complot] to hatch; **estar tramando algo** to be up to something.

tramitación *f* [acción] processing.

tramitar *vt* **-1.** [suj: autoridades - pasaporte, permiso] to take the necessary steps to obtain; [- solicitud, dimisión] to process. **-2.**

[suj: solicitante]: **~ un permiso** to be in the process of applying for a licence.

trámite *m* [gestión] formal step; **de ~** routine, formal.

◆ **trámites** *mpl* **-1.** [proceso] procedure (*sg*). **-2.** [papeleo] paperwork (*U*).

tramo *m* **-1.** [espacio] section, stretch. **-2.** [de escalera] flight (of stairs).

tramontana *f* north wind.

tramoya *f* **-1.** TEATR stage machinery (*U*). **-2.** *fig* [enredo] intrigue.

tramoyista *m y f* **-1.** TEATR stagehand. **-2.** *fig* [tramposo] schemer.

trampa *f* **-1.** [para cazar] trap. **-2.** [trampilla] trapdoor. **-3.** *fig* [engaño] trick; **caer en la ~** to fall into the trap; **tender una ~ (a alguien)** to set ○ lay a trap (for sb); **hacer ~s** to cheat. **-4.** *fig* [deuda] debt.

trampear *vi fam* **-1.** [estafar] to swindle money. **-2.** [ir tirando] to struggle along.

trampilla *f* [en el suelo] trapdoor.

trampolín *m* **-1.** [de piscina] diving board; [de esquí] ski jump; [en gimnasia] springboard. **-2.** *fig* [medio, impulso] springboard.

tramposo, -sa ◇ *adj* [fullero] cheating. ◇ *m y f* **-1.** [fullero] cheat. **-2.** [moroso] bad debtor.

tranca *f* **-1.** [de puerta o ventana] bar. **-2.** [arma] cudgel, stick. **-3.** *fam* [borrachera]: **coger una ~** to get plastered. **-4.** *loc*: **a ~s y barrancas** with great difficulty.

trancazo *m* **-1.** [golpe] blow (with a stick). **-2.** *fam fig* [gripe] bout of the flu.

trance *m* **-1.** [apuro] difficult situation; **estar en ~ de hacer algo** to be about to do sthg; **pasar por un mal ~** to go through a bad patch. **-2.** [estado hipnótico] trance; **estar en ~** to be in a trance.

◆ **a todo trance** *loc adv* at all costs.

tranco *m* stride.

tranquilidad *f* peacefulness, calmness; **para mayor ~** to be on the safe side.

tranquilizador, -ra *adj* calming.

tranquilizante ◇ *adj* **-1.** [música, color etc] soothing. **-2.** FARM tranquilizing. ◇ *m* FARM tranquilizer.

tranquilizar [13] *vt* **-1.** [calmar] to calm (down). **-2.** [dar confianza] to reassure.

◆ **tranquilizarse** *vpr* **-1.** [calmarse] to calm down. **-2.** [ganar confianza] to feel reassured.

tranquillo *m fam*: **coger el ~ a algo** to get the knack of sthg.

tranquilo, -la *adj* **-1.** [sosegado - lugar, música] peaceful; [- persona, tono de voz, mar] calm; [- viento] gentle; **¡(tú) ~!** *fam* don't you worry! **-2.** [velada, charla, negocio] quiet.

-3. [mente] untroubled; [conciencia] clear. **-4.** [despreocupado] casual, laid back; **quedarse tan ~** not to bat an eyelid.

transacción *f* COM transaction.

transalpino, -na *adj* transalpine.

transar *vi Amer* to compromise, to give in.

transatlántico, -ca *adj* transatlantic.

◆ **transatlántico** *m* NÁUT (ocean) liner.

transbordador *m* **-1.** NÁUT ferry. **-2.** AE-RON: **~ (espacial)** space shuttle.

transbordar ◇ *vt* to transfer. ◇ *vi* to change (*trains etc*).

transbordo *m*: **hacer ~** to change (*trains etc*).

transcendencia *f* importance; **tener una gran ~** to be deeply significant.

transcendental *adj* **-1.** [importante] momentous. **-2.** [meditación] transcendental.

transcendente *adj* momentous.

transcender [20] *vi* **-1.** [extenderse]: **~ (a algo)** to spread (across sthg). **-2.** [filtrarse] to be leaked. **-3.** [sobrepasar]: **~ de** to transcend, to go beyond. **-4.** [oler]: **~ a** to smell of.

transcontinental *adj* transcontinental.

transcribir *vt* **-1.** [escribir] to transcribe. **-2.** *fig* [expresar] to express in writing.

transcripción *f* transcription.

transcriptor, -ra *m y f* [persona] transcriber.

◆ **transcriptor** *m* [aparato] transcriber.

transcrito, -ta *adj* transcribed.

transcurrir *vi* **-1.** [tiempo] to pass, to go by. **-2.** [ocurrir] to take place, to go off.

transcurso *m* **-1.** [paso de tiempo] passing. **-2.** [periodo de tiempo]: **en el ~ de** in the course of.

transeúnte ◇ *adj* passing. ◇ *m y f* **-1.** [paseante] passer-by. **-2.** [transitorio] temporary resident.

transexual *adj, m y f* transsexual.

transferencia *f* transfer; **~ electrónica de fondos** electronic banking.

transferir [27] *vt* to transfer.

transfiguración *f* transfiguration.

transfigurar *vt* to transfigure.

◆ **transfigurarse** *vpr* to become transfigured.

transformable *adj* convertible (*furniture*).

transformación *f* transformation.

transformador, -ra *adj* transforming.

◆ **transformador** *m* ELECTRÓN transformer.

transformar *vt* **-1.** [cambiar radicalmente]: **~ algo/a alguien (en)** to transform sthg/sb (into). **-2.** [convertir]: **~ algo (en)** to convert sthg (into). **-3.** [en rugby] to convert.

◆ **transformarse** *vpr* **-1.** [cambiar radicalmente] to be transformed. **-2.** [convertirse]: **~se en algo** to be converted into sthg.

transformismo *m* evolution.

transformista ◇ *adj* evolutionary. ◇ *m y f* **-1.** [seguidor] evolutionist. **-2.** [artista] quick-change artist.

tránsfuga *m y f* **-1.** POLÍT defector. **-2.** MIL deserter.

transfusión *f* transfusion.

transfusor, -ra *adj* transfusion (*antes de sust*).

◆ **transfusor** *m* [aparato] transfuser.

transgredir [78] *vt* to transgress.

transgresión *f* transgression.

transgresor, -ra *m y f* transgressor.

transiberiano *m* Trans-Siberian railway.

transición *f* transition; **periodo de ~** transition period; **~ democrática** transition to democracy.

TRANSICIÓN:

The 'transición' is the name given to the stage in Spain's history which began after "franquismo". It was characterized by the setting up of representative political institutions and the modernization of prevailing legislation. One of the important landmarks of this period was the establishment of a constitution in 1978, which the Spanish people approved by referendum

---

transido, -da *adj*: **~ (de)** stricken (with); **~ de pena** grief-stricken.

transigencia *f* willingness to compromise.

transigente *adj* **-1.** [que cede] compromising. **-2.** [tolerante] tolerant.

transigir [15] *vi* **-1.** [ceder] to compromise. **-2.** [ser tolerante] to be tolerant.

transistor *m* transistor.

transitable *adj* [franqueable] passable; [no cerrado al tráfico] open to traffic.

transitar *vi* to go (along).

transitivo, -va *adj* transitive.

tránsito *m* **-1.** [circulación - gen] movement; [- de coches] traffic; **~ rodado** road traffic. **-2.** [transporte] transit.

transitorio, -ria *adj* [gen] transitory; [residencia] temporary; [régimen, medida] transitional, interim.

translúcido, -da *adj* translucent.

translucirse [32] **-1.** [cristal etc] to be translucent. **-2.** *fig* [motivos etc] to show through, to be obvious.

transmediterráneo, -a *adj* transmediterranean.

transmisible *adj* **-1.** [enfermedad] transmittible. **-2.** [título, posesiones] transferrable.

transmisión *f* **-1.** [gen & AUTOM] transmission; [de saludos, noticias] passing on; ~ **del pensamiento** telepathy. **-2.** RADIO & TV broadcast, broadcasting (*U*). **-3.** [de herencia, poderes etc] transference.

transmisor, -ra *adj* transmission (*antes de sust*).
◆ **transmisor** *m* transmitter.

transmitir *vt* **-1.** [gen] to transmit; [saludos, noticias] to pass on. **-2.** RADIO & TV to broadcast. **-3.** [ceder] to transfer.
◆ **transmitirse** *vpr* to be transmitted.

transmutación *f* transmutation.

transmutar *vt* to transmute.

transnacional *adj* transnational.

transoceánico, -ca *adj* transoceanic.

transparencia *f* transparency.

transparentarse *vpr* **-1.** [tela] to be seethrough; [vidrio, líquido] to be transparent. **-2.** *fig* [manifestarse] to show through.

transparente *adj* [gen] transparent; [tela] see-through.

transpiración *f* perspiration; BOT transpiration.

transpirar *vi* to perspire; BOT to transpire.

transpirenaico, -ca *adj* trans-Pyrenean.

transplantar *vt* to transplant.

transplante *m* transplant, transplanting (*U*).

transponer [65] *vt* **-1.** [cambiar] to switch. **-2.** [desaparecer detrás de] to disappear behind.
◆ **transponerse** *vpr* **-1.** [adormecerse] to doze off. **-2.** [ocultarse] to disappear; [sol] to set.

transportable *adj* portable.

transportador *m* **-1.** [para transportar]: ~ **aéreo** cableway; ~ **de cinta** conveyor belt. **-2.** [para medir ángulos] protractor.

transportar *vt* **-1.** [trasladar] to transport. **-2.** [embelesar] to captivate.
◆ **transportarse** *vpr* [embelesarse] to go into raptures.

transporte *m* transport; ~ **público** O **colectivo** public transport.

transportista *m y f* carrier.

transposición *f* transposition.

transpuesto, -ta *adj* dozing.

transvasar *vt* **-1.** [líquido] to decant. **-2.** [río] to transfer.

transvase *m* **-1.** [de líquido] decanting. **-2.** [de río] transfer.

transversal ◇ *adj* transverse. ◇ *f* GEOM transversal.

tranvía *m* tram, streetcar *Am*.

trapecio *m* **-1.** GEOM trapezium. **-2.** [de gimnasia] trapeze. **-3.** [músculo] trapezius.

trapecista *m y f* trapeze artist.

trapense *adj, m y f* RELIG Trappist.

trapero, -ra *m y f* rag-and-bone man (*f* woman).

trapezoide *m* ANAT & GEOM trapezoid.

trapichear *vi fam* to be on the fiddle.

trapicheo *m fam* **-1.** [negocio sucio] fiddle. **-2.** [tejemaneje] scheme, scheming (*U*).

trapío *m culto* **-1.** [garbo] elegance. **-2.** TAUROM good bearing.

trapisonda *f fam* **-1.** [riña] row, commotion. **-2.** [enredo] scheme.

trapisondear *vi fam* **-1.** [reñir] to kick up a row. **-2.** [liar, enredar] to scheme.

trapisondista *m y f fam* **-1.** [camorrista] troublemaker. **-2.** [liante] schemer.

trapo *m* **-1.** [trozo de tela] rag. **-2.** [gamuza, bayeta] cloth; **los ~s sucios se lavan en casa** you should not wash your dirty linen in public; **poner a alguien como un** ~ to tear sb to pieces. **-3.** TAUROM cape. **-4.** *loc*: **a todo** ~ at full pelt.
◆ **trapos** *mpl fam* [ropa] clothes.

tráquea *f* windpipe, trachea (MED).

traqueotomía *f* tracheotomy.

traquetear ◇ *vt* to shake. ◇ *vi* [hacer ruido] to rattle.

traqueteo *m* [ruido] rattling.

tras *prep* **-1.** [detrás de] behind. **-2.** [después de, en pos de] after; **uno** ~ **otro** one after the other; **andar** ~ **algo** to be after sthg.

trasalpino, -na = transalpino.

trasatlántico, -ca = transatlántico.

trasbordador = transbordador.

trasbordar = transbordar.

trasbordo = transbordo.

trascendencia = transcendencia.

trascendental = transcendental.

trascendente = transcendente.

trascender [20] = transcender.

trascontinental = transcontinental.

trascribir = transcribir.

trascripción = transcripción.

trascriptor = transcriptor.

trascrito, -ta = transcrito.

trascurrir = transcurrir.

trascurso = transcurso.

trasegar [35] *vt* **-1.** [desordenar] to rummage about amongst. **-2.** [transvasar] to decant.

trasero, -ra *adj* back (*antes de sust*), rear (*antes de sust*).
◆ **trasero** *m fam* backside.
◆ **trasera** *f* rear.
trasferencia = transferencia.
trasferir [27] = transferir.
trasfiguración = transfiguración.
trasfigurar = transfigurar.
trasfondo *m* background; [de palabras, intenciones] undertone.
trasformable = transformable.
trasformación = transformación.
trasformador, -ra = transformador.
trasformar = transformar.
trasformismo = transformismo.
trasformista = transformista.
trásfuga = tránsfuga.
trasfusión = transfusión.
trasfusor, -ra = transfusor.
trasgredir [78] = transgredir.
trasgresión = transgresión.
trasgresor, -ra = transgresor.
trashumancia *f* seasonal migration (*of livestock*).
trashumante *adj* seasonally migratory.
trashumar *vi* to migrate seasonally.
trasiega → trasegar.
trasiego *m* -1. [movimiento] comings and goings (*pl*). -2. [trasvase] decanting.
trasiegue → trasegar.
traslación *f* ASTRON passage.
trasladar *vt* -1. [desplazar] to move. -2. [a empleado, funcionario] to transfer. -3. [reunión, fecha] to postpone, to move back. -4. [traducir] to translate. -5. *fig* [expresar]: ~ algo al papel to transfer sthg onto paper.
◆ **trasladarse** *vpr* -1. [desplazarse] to go. -2. [mudarse] to move; me traslado de piso I'm moving flat.
traslado *m* -1. [de casa, empresa, muebles] move, moving (*U*). -2. [de trabajo] transfer. -3. [de personas] movement.
traslúcido, -da = translúcido.
traslucirse [32] = translucirse.
trasluz *m* reflected light; al ~ against the light.
trasmano
◆ **a trasmano** *loc adv* -1. [fuera de alcance] out of reach. -2. [lejos] out of the way.
trasmediterráneo, -a = transmediterráneo.
trasmisible = transmisible.
trasmisión = transmisión.
trasmisor, -ra = transmisor.
trasmitir = transmitir.

trasmutación = transmutación.
trasmutar = transmutar.
trasnacional = transnacional.
trasnochador, -ra ◇ *adj* given to staying up late. ◇ *m y f* night owl.
trasnochar *vi* to stay up late, to go to bed late.
trasoceánico, -ca = transoceánico.
traspapelar *vt* [papeles, documentos] to mislay, to misplace.
◆ **traspapelarse** *vpr* to get mislaid ○ misplaced.
trasparencia = transparencia.
trasparentarse = transparentarse.
trasparente = transparente.
traspasable *adj* [camino] passable; [río] crossable.
traspasar *vt* -1. [atravesar] to go through, to pierce. -2. [cruzar] to cross (over); [puerta] to pass through. -3. [suj: líquido] to soak through. -4. [jugador] to transfer. -5. [negocio] to sell (as a going concern). -6. *fig* [exceder] to go beyond.
traspaso *m* -1. [venta - de jugador] transfer; [- de negocio] sale (as a going concern). -2. [precio - de jugador] transfer fee; [- de negocio] takeover fee.
traspié (*pl* **traspiés**) *m* -1. [resbalón] trip, stumble; dar un ~ to trip up. -2. *fig* [error] blunder, slip.
traspiración = transpiración.
traspirar = transpirar.
traspirenaico, -ca = transpirenaico.
trasplantar = transplantar.
trasplante = transplante.
trasponer [65] = transponer.
trasportar *etc* = transportar.
trasposición = transposición.
traspuesto, -ta = transpuesto.
trasquilado, -da *adj*: salir ~ *fig* to come off badly.
trasquilar *vt* [esquilar] to shear.
trasquilón *m*: hacerle un ~ a alguien to cut sb's hair crooked.
trastabillar *vi Amer* to stagger.
trastada *f* dirty trick; hacer una ~ a alguien to play a dirty trick on sb.
trastazo *m* bump, bang; darse ○ pegarse un ~ to bang ○ bump o.s.
traste *m* -1. MÚS fret. -2. *Amer fam* [trasero] bottom. -3. *loc*: dar al ~ con algo to ruin sthg; irse al ~ to fall through.
trastero *m* junk room.
trastienda *f* backroom.
trasto *m* -1. [utensilio inútil] piece of junk, junk (*U*). -2. *fam fig* [persona traviesa]

menace, nuisance. **-3.** *fam fig* [persona inútil]: ~ **(viejo)** dead loss.

◆ **trastos** *mpl fam* [pertenencias, equipo] things, stuff (*U*); **tirarse los ~s a la cabeza** to have a flaming row.

trastocar [36] *vt* [cambiar] to turn upside down.

◆ **trastocarse** *vpr* [enloquecer] to go mad.

trastornado, **-da** *adj* disturbed, unbalanced.

trastornar *vt* **-1.** [volver loco] to drive mad. **-2.** [inquietar] to worry, to trouble. **-3.** [alterar] to turn upside down; [planes] to disrupt, to upset. **-4.** [estómago] to upset.

◆ **trastornarse** *vpr* [volverse loco] to go mad.

trastorno *m* **-1.** [mental] disorder; [digestivo] upset. **-2.** [alteración - por huelga, nevada] trouble (*U*), disruption (*U*); [- por guerra etc] upheaval.

trastrocar [36] *vt* **-1.** [cambiar de orden] to switch ○ change round. **-2.** [cambiar de sentido] to change.

trasvasar = transvasar.

trasvase = transvase.

trata *f* slave trade; ~ **de blancas** white slave trade.

tratable *adj* easy-going, friendly.

tratadista *m y f* treatise writer, essayist.

tratado *m* **-1.** [convenio] treaty. **-2.** [escrito] treatise.

tratamiento *m* **-1.** [gen & MED] treatment; ~ **del dolor** pain relief. **-2.** [título] title, form of address; **apear el ~ a alguien** to drop sb's title. **-3.** INFORM processing; ~ **de datos/textos** data/word processing; ~ **por lotes** batch processing.

tratante *m y f* dealer; [de vinos] merchant.

tratar ◇ *vt* **-1.** [gen & MED] to treat. **-2.** [discutir] to discuss. **-3.** INFORM to process. **-4.** [dirigirse a]: ~ **a alguien de** [usted, tú etc] to address sb as. **-5.** [llamar]: ~ **a alguien de algo** [cretino etc] to call sb sthg.
◇ *vi* **-1.** [versar]: ~ **de/sobre** to be about. **-2.** [tener relación]: ~ **con alguien** to mix with sb, to have dealings with sb. **-3.** [intentar]: ~ **de hacer algo** to try to do sthg. **-4.** [utilizar]: ~ **con** to deal with, to use. **-5.** [comerciar]: ~ **en** to deal in.

◆ **tratarse** *vpr* **-1.** [relacionarse]: ~**se con** to mix with, to have dealings with sthg. **-2.** [versar]: ~**se de** to be about; **¿de qué se trata?** what's it about?

tratativas *fpl Amer* procedure (*sg*).

trato *m* **-1.** [comportamiento, conducto] treatment; **de ~ agradable** pleasant; **malos ~s** battering (*U*) (*of child, wife*). **-2.** [relación] dealings (*pl*); **tener ~ con alguien** to associate with, to be friendly with. **-3.** [acuerdo] deal; **cerrar** ○ **hacer un ~** to do ○ make a deal; **¡~ hecho!** it's a deal! **-4.** [tratamiento] title, term of address.

trauma *m* trauma.

traumático, **-ca** *adj* traumatic.

traumatismo *m* traumatism.

traumatizante *adj* traumatic.

traumatizar [13] *vt* to traumatize.

◆ **traumatizarse** *vpr* to be devastated.

traumatología *f* traumatology.

traumatólogo, **-ga** *m y f* traumatologist.

través

◆ **a través de** *loc prep* **-1.** [de un lado a otro de] across, over. **-2.** [por, por medio de] through.

◆ **al través** *loc adv* crossways, crosswise.

◆ **de través** *loc adv* [transversalmente] crossways, crosswise; [de lado] sideways; **mirar de ~** *fig* to give a sidelong glance.

travesaño *m* **-1.** ARQUIT crosspiece. **-2.** DEP crossbar.

travesero, **-ra** *adj*: **flauta travesera** flute.

travesía *f* **-1.** [viaje - por mar] voyage, crossing; [- por aire] flight. **-2.** [calle] cross-street.

travestido, **-da**, **travestí** (*pl* **travestís**) *m y f* transvestite.

travestirse [26] *vpr* to cross-dress.

travestismo *m* transvestism.

travesura *f* prank, mischief (*U*).

traviesa *f* **-1.** FERROC sleeper (*on track*). **-2.** CONSTR crossbeam, tie beam.

travieso, **-sa** *adj* mischievous.

travista, **travistiera** *etc* → travestirse.

trayecto *m* **-1.** [distancia] distance; **final de ~** end of the line. **-2.** [viaje] journey, trip. **-3.** [ruta] route.

trayectoria *f* **-1.** [recorrido] trajectory. **-2.** *fig* [evolución] path.

traza *f* **-1.** [boceto, plano] plan, design. **-2.** [aspecto] appearance (*U*), looks (*pl*). **-3.** [habilidad]: **tener buena/mala ~ (para algo)** to be good/no good (at sthg).

trazado ◇ *adj* designed, laid out. ◇ *m* **-1.** [trazo] outline, sketching. **-2.** [diseño] plan, design. **-3.** [recorrido] route.

trazar [13] *vt* **-1.** [dibujar] to draw, to trace; [ruta] to plot. **-2.** [indicar, describir] to outline. **-3.** [idear] to draw up.

trazo *m* **-1.** [de dibujo, rostro] line. **-2.** [de letra] stroke.

trébol *m* **-1.** [planta] clover. **-2.** [naipe] club.
◆ **tréboles** *mpl* [naipes] clubs.

trece *núm* thirteen; **mantenerse** O **seguir en sus** ~ to stick to one's guns; *ver también* **seis**.

treceavo, -va *núm* thirteenth; **la treceava parte** a thirteenth.

trecho *m* [espacio] distance; [tiempo] time, while; **de** ~ **en** ~ every so often.

tregua *f* truce; *fig* respite.

treinta *núm* thirty; **los (años)** ~ the thirties; *ver también* **seis**.

treintena *f* thirty.

tremebundo, -da *adj* terrifying.

tremendismo *m* **-1.** [exageración] quality of always imagining the worst. **-2.** LITER tremendismo, *gloomy Spanish post-war realism*.

tremendo, -da *adj* **-1.** [enorme] tremendous, enormous. **-2.** [travieso] mischievous.
◆ **tremenda** *f*: **tomar** O **tomarse algo a la tremenda** to take sthg hard.

trementina *f* turpentine.

tremolar *vi culto* to wave, to flutter.

tremolina *f* row, uproar.

trémolo *m* tremolo.

trémulo, -la *adj* [voz] trembling; [luz] flickering.

tren *m* **-1.** [ferrocarril] train; ~ **de alta velocidad/largo recorrido** high-speed/long-distance train; ~ **de cercanías** local train, suburban train; ~ **correo** mail train; ~ **de mercancías** freight O goods train; ~ **mixto** passenger and goods train; ~ **semidirecto** *through train, a section of which becomes a stopping train*; **estar como (para parar) un** ~ to be really gorgeous; **perder el** ~ *fig* to miss the boat. **-2.** TECN line; ~ **de aterrizaje** undercarriage, landing gear; ~ **de lavado** car wash. **-3.** *fig* [estilo]: ~ **de vida** lifestyle; **vivir a todo** ~ to live in style.

trena *f mfam* nick, slammer.

trenca *f* duffle coat.

trence *etc* → **trenzar**.

trenza *f* **-1.** [de pelo] plait. **-2.** [de fibras] braid.

trenzar [13] *vtr* **-1.** [pelo] to plait. **-2.** [fibras] to braid.

trepa *m y f fam* social climber.

trepador, -ra ◇ *adj*: **planta trepadora** climber, creeper. ◇ *m y f fam* social climber.

trepanación *f* trepanation.

trepanar *vt* to trepan.

trepar ◇ *vt* to climb. ◇ *vi* **-1.** [subir] to climb. **-2.** *fam fig* [medrar] to be a social climber.

trepidación *f* shaking, vibration.

trepidante *adj* **-1.** [rápido, vivo] frenetic. **-2.** [que tiembla] shaking, vibrating.

trepidar *vi* to shake, to vibrate.

tres *núm* three; **de** ~ **al cuarto** cheap, third-rate; **ni a la de** ~ for anything in the world, no way; **no ver** ~ **en un burro** to be as blind as a bat; ~ **cuartos de lo mismo** the same thing; *ver también* **seis**.
◆ **tres cuartos** *m inv* [abrigo] three-quarter length coat.
◆ **tres en raya** *m* noughts and crosses (U) *Br*, tick-tack-toe *Am*.

trescientos, -tas *núm* three hundred; *ver también* **seis**.

tresillo *m* **-1.** [sofá] three-piece suite. **-2.** [juego de naipes] ombre. **-3.** MÚS triplet.

treta *f* [engaño] trick.

tríada *f* triad.

trial *m* DEP trial; ~ **indoor** indoor trial.

trialsin *m* DEP BMX, bicycle motocross.

triangular *adj* triangular.

triángulo *m* **-1.** GEOM & MÚS triangle; ~ **equilátero/escaleno/isósceles/rectángulo** equilateral/scalene/isosceles/right-angled triangle. **-2.** *fam* [amoroso] ménage à trois.

triates *mpl Amer* triplets.

tribal *adj* tribal.

tribu *f* tribe; ~ **urbana** *identifiable social group, such as punks or yuppies, made up of young people living in urban areas*.

tribulación *f* tribulation.

tribuna *f* **-1.** [estrado] rostrum, platform; [del jurado] jury box. **-2.** [DEP - localidad] stand; [- graderío] grandstand. **-3.** PRENS: ~ **de prensa** press box; ~ **libre** open forum.

tribunal *m* **-1.** [gen] court; **llevar a alguien/acudir a los** ~**es** to take sb/go to court; **Tribunal Constitucional** Constitutional Court; **Tribunal Supremo** High Court *Br*, Supreme Court *Am*; **Tribunal tutelar de menores** Juvenile Court. **-2.** [de examen] board of examiners; [de concurso] panel.

tributable *adj* taxable.

tributación *f* **-1.** [impuesto] tax. **-2.** [sistema] taxation.

tributar ◇ *vt* [homenaje] to pay; [respeto, admiración] to have. ◇ *vi* [pagar impuestos] to pay taxes.

tributario, -ria ◇ *adj* tax (*antes de sust*). ◇ *m y f* taxpayer.

tributo *m* **-1.** [impuesto] tax. **-2.** *fig* [precio] price. **-3.** [homenaje] tribute.

tricéfalo, -la *adj* three-headed.

tríceps *m inv* triceps.

triciclo *m* tricycle.

tricolor *adj* tricolour, three-coloured.

tricornio *m* three-cornered hat.

tricot *m inv* knitting (*U*).

tricotar *vt & vi* to knit.

tricotosa *f* knitting machine.

tridente *m* trident.

tridimensional *adj* three-dimensional.

trienal *adj* triennial, three-yearly.

trienio *m* **-1.** [tres años] three years (*pl*). **-2.** [paga] *three-yearly salary increase.*

trifásico, -ca *adj* **-1.** ELECTR three-phase. **-2.** [de tres fases] three-part.

trifulca *f fam* row, squabble.

trigal *m* wheat field.

trigésimo, -ma *núm* thirtieth.

trigo *m* wheat.

trigonometría *f* trigonometry.

trigueño, -ña *adj* [tez] olive; [cabello] corn-coloured.

triguero, -ra *adj* [del trigo] wheat (*antes de sust*).

trilateral *adj* trilateral.

trilingüe *adj* trilingual.

trilla *f* **-1.** [acción] threshing. **-2.** [tiempo] threshing time ○ season.

trillado, -da *adj fig* well-worn, trite.

trillador, -ra ◇ *adj* threshing. ◇ *m y f* [persona] thresher.
◆ **trilladora** *f* [máquina] threshing machine.

trillar *vt* to thresh.

trillizo, -za *m y f* triplet.

trilogía *f* trilogy.

trimestral *adj* three-monthly, quarterly; [exámenes, notas] end-of-term (*antes de sust*).

trimestre *m* three months (*pl*), quarter; [en escuela, universidad] term.

trimotor ◇ *adj* three-engined. ◇ *m* three-engined aeroplane.

trinar *vi* to chirp, to warble; **está que trina** *fig* she's fuming.

trinca *f* trio.

trincar [10] *fam* ◇ *vt* [detener] to nick, to arrest. ◇ *vi* [beber] to guzzle.
◆ **trincarse** *vpr fam* [beberse] to guzzle, to down.

trincha *f* strap.

trinchante *m* **-1.** [cuchillo] carving knife. **-2.** [tenedor] meat fork.

trinchar *vt* to carve.

trinchera *f* MIL trench.

trineo *m* [pequeño] sledge; [grande] sleigh.

Trinidad *f*: **la (Santísima) ~** the (Holy) Trinity.

Trinidad y Tobago Trinidad and Tobago.

trinitario, -ria *adj, m y f* Trinitarian.

trino *m* [de pájaros] chirp, chirping (*U*); MÚS trill.

trinque *etc* → **trincar**.

trinquete *m* NÁUT foremast.

trío *m* **-1.** [gen] trio. **-2.** [de naipes] three of a kind.

tripa *f* **-1.** [intestino] gut, intestine. **-2.** *fam* [barriga] gut, belly; **revolverle las ~s a alguien** *fig* to turn sb's stomach.
◆ **tripas** *fpl fig* [interior] insides; **hacer de ~s corazón** to pluck up one's courage.

tripartito, -ta *adj* tripartite.

triple ◇ *adj* triple. ◇ *m*: **el ~** three times as much; **el ~ de gente** three times as many people.

triplicado *m* second copy, triplicate; **por ~** in triplicate.

triplicar [10] *vt* to triple, to treble.
◆ **triplicarse** *vpr* to triple, to treble.

trípode *m* tripod.

Trípoli Tripoli.

tríptico *m* **-1.** ARTE triptych. **-2.** [folleto] three-part document.

triptongo *m* GRAM triphthong.

tripulación *f* crew.

tripulante *m y f* crew member.

tripular *vt* to man.

triquina *f* trichina.

triquinosis *f inv* trichinosis.

triquiñuela *f* (*gen pl*) *fam* [truco] trick.

tris *m*: **estar en un ~ de** *fig* to be within a whisker of.

trisílabo, -ba *adj* GRAM trisyllabic.

triste *adj* **-1.** [gen] sad; [día, tiempo, paisaje] gloomy, dreary; **es ~ que** it's a shame ○ pity that. **-2.** *fig* [color, vestido, luz] pale, faded. **-3.** (*antes de sust*) [humilde] poor; [sueldo] sorry, miserable. **-4.** *loc*: **ni un ~** not a single.

tristeza *f* **-1.** [gen] sadness; [de paisaje, día] gloominess, dreariness. **-2.** [de color, vestido, luz] paleness.

tristón, -ona *adj* rather sad ○ miserable.

tritón *m* newt.

trituración *f* grinding, crushing.

triturador *m* [de basura] waste-disposal unit; [de papeles] shredder.

trituradora *f* crushing machine, grinder.

triturar *vt* **-1.** [moler, desmenuzar] to crush, to grind; [papel] to shred. **-2.** [mascar] to chew.

triunfador, -ra ◇ *adj* winning, victorious. ◇ *m y f* winner.

triunfal *adj* triumphant.

triunfalismo *m* extreme bullishness.

triunfante *adj* victorious.

triunfar *vi* **-1.** [vencer] to win, to triumph. **-2.** [tener éxito] to succeed, to be successful.

triunfo *m* **-1.** [gen] triumph; [en encuentro, elecciones] victory, win. **-2.** [trofeo] trophy. **-3.** [en juegos de naipes] trump; **sin** ~ no trump.

triunvirato *m* triumvirate.

trivial *adj* trivial.

trivialidad *f* triviality.

trivializar [13] *vt* to trivialize.

trizas *fpl* piece (*sg*), bit (*sg*); **hacer** ~ **algo** [hacer añicos] to smash sthg to pieces; [desgarrar] to tear sthg to shreds; **hacer** ~ **a alguien** to tear ○ pull sb to pieces; **estar hecho** ~ [persona] to be shattered.

trocar [36] *vt* **-1.** [transformar]: ~ **algo (en algo)** to change sthg (into sthg). **-2.** [intercambiar] to swap, to exchange. **-3.** [malinterpretar] to mix up.

◆ **trocarse** *vpr* [transformarse]: ~**se (en)** to change (into).

trocear *vt* to cut up (into pieces).

trocha *f Amer* path.

troche

◆ **a troche y moche** *loc adv* haphazardly.

trofeo *m* trophy.

troglodita ◇ *adj* **-1.** [cavernícola] cave dwelling, troglodytic. **-2.** *fam* [bárbaro, tosco] rough, brutish. ◇ *m y f* **-1.** [cavernícola] cave dweller, troglodyte. **-2.** *fam* [bárbaro, tosco] roughneck, brute.

troika *f* troika.

trola *f fam* fib, lie.

trolebús *m* trolleybus.

trolero, -ra *fam* ◇ *adj* fibbing, lying. ◇ *m y f* fibber, liar.

tromba *f* waterspout; ~ **de agua** heavy downpour.

trombo *m* thrombus.

trombón *m* [MÚS - instrumento] trombone; [- músico] trombonist; ~ **de pistones** ○ **de llaves** valve trombone; ~ **de varas** slide trombone.

trombosis *f inv* thrombosis.

trompa ◇ *f* **-1.** MÚS horn. **-2.** [de elefante] trunk; [de oso hormiguero] snout. **-3.** [de insecto] proboscis. **-4.** ANAT tube; ~ **de Eustaquio/de Falopio** Eustachian/Fallopian tube. **-5.** *fam* [borrachera]: **coger** ○ **pillar una** ~ to get plastered. ◇ *adj fam* [borracho] plastered.

trompazo *m* bang; **darse** ○ **pegarse un** ~ **con** to bang into.

trompear *vt Amer fam* to punch.

◆ **trompearse** *vpr Amer fam* to have a fight.

trompeta ◇ *f* trumpet. ◇ *m y f* trumpeter.

trompetilla *f* ear trumpet.

trompetista *m y f* trumpeter.

trompicón *m* [tropezón] stumble; **a trompicones** in fits and starts.

trompo *m* spinning top.

tronado, -da *adj fam* [radio etc] old, broken-down.

◆ **tronada** *f* thunderstorm.

tronar [23] *v impers & vi* to thunder.

◆ **tronarse** *vpr Amer fam* to shoot o.s.

tronchante *adj fam* hilarious.

tronchar *vt* [partir] to snap.

◆ **troncharse** *vpr fam*: ~**se (de risa)** to split one's sides laughing.

tronco *m* ANAT & BOT trunk; [talado y sin ramas] log; **dormir como un** ~, **estar hecho un** ~ to sleep like a log.

tronera *f* **-1.** ARQUIT & HIST embrasure. **-2.** [en billar] pocket.

trono *m* throne.

tropa *f* **-1.** (*gen pl*) MIL troops (*pl*). **-2.** *fam* [multitud] troop, flock.

tropear *vt Amer* to herd.

tropel *m* **-1.** [de personas] mob, crowd; **en** ~ in a mad rush, en masse. **-2.** [de cosas] mass, heap.

tropelía *f* outrage.

tropero *m Amer* cowboy.

tropezar [34] *vi* [con pie]: ~ **(con)** to trip ○ stumble (on).

◆ **tropezarse** *vpr fam* [encontrarse] to bump into each other, to come across one another; ~**se con alguien** to bump into sb.

◆ **tropezar con** *vi* [problema, persona] to run into, to come across.

tropezón *m* **-1.** [tropiezo] trip, stumble; **dar un** ~ to trip up, to stumble. **-2.** *fig* [desacierto] slip-up, blunder.

◆ **tropezones** *mpl* CULIN small chunks of meat.

tropical *adj* tropical.

trópico *m* tropic.

tropiece *etc* → **tropezar**.

tropiezo *m* **-1.** [tropezón] trip, stumble; **dar un** ~ to trip up, to stumble. **-2.** *fig* [impedimento] obstacle, stumbling block. **-3.** *fig* [equivocación] blunder, slip-up. **-4.** [revés] setback. **-5.** *fig* [desliz sexual] indiscretion; **tener un** ~ to commit an indiscretion.

tropismo *m* tropism.

tropo *m* figure of speech, trope.

troqué → **trocar**.

troquel *m* **-1.** [molde] mould, die. **-2.** [cuchilla] cutter.

troquelado *m* **-1.** [acuñado] [de moneda] minting, mintage; [de medallas] die-casting. **-2.** [recorte] cutting.

troquelar *vt* **-1.** [acuñar] [monedas] to mint; [medallas] to cast. **-2.** [recortar] to cut.

troquemos → trocar.

trotamundos *m y f inv* globe-trotter.

trotar *vi* to trot; *fam fig* [andar mucho] to dash ○ run around.

trote *m* **-1.** [de caballo] trot; **al** ~ at a trot. **-2.** *fam* [actividad]: **no estar para** ~s not to be up to it.

trotskismo [tros'kismo] *m* Trotskyism.

trotskista [tros'kista] *adj, m y f* Trotskyite.

troupe [trup, 'trupe] (*pl* **troupes**) *f* troupe.

trova *f* LITER lyric.

trovador *m* troubadour.

troyano, -na *adj, m y f* Trojan.

trozo *m* [gen] piece; [de obra, película] extract; **cortar algo a** ~s to cut sthg into pieces.

trucaje *m* [gen] trick effect; [fotografía] trick photography.

trucar [10] *vt* to doctor; [motor] to soup up.

trucha *f* [pez] trout; ~ **a la navarra** *fried trout stuffed with ham.*

truco *m* **-1.** [trampa, engaño] trick. **-2.** [habilidad, técnica] knack; **coger el** ~ to get the knack; ~ **publicitario** advertising gimmick.

truculencia *f* horror, terror.

truculento, -ta *adj* horrifying, terrifying.

trueca → trocar.

truena *etc* → tronar.

trueno *m* **-1.** METEOR clap of thunder, thunder (*U*). **-2.** *fig* [ruido] thunder, boom.

trueque ◇ *v* → trocar. ◇ *m* **-1.** COM & HIST barter. **-2.** [intercambio] exchange, swap.

trufa *f* [hongo, bombón] truffle.

trufar *vt* CULIN to stuff with truffles.

truhán, -ana ◇ *adj* crooked. ◇ *m y f* rogue, crook.

trullo *m mfam* slammer, nick.

truncado, -da *adj* **-1.** [frustrado - vida, carrera] cut short; [- planes, ilusiones] ruined. **-2.** GEOM truncated.

truncar [10] *vt* **-1.** [frustrar - vida, carrera] to cut short; [- planes, ilusiones] to spoil, to ruin. **-2.** [dejar incompleto - texto, frase] to leave unfinished.

truque *etc* → trucar.

trusa *f Amer* **-1.** [calzoncillos] underpants (*pl*). **-2.** [bragas] knickers (*pl*).

trust [trust] (*pl* **trusts**) *m* trust, cartel.

TS (*abrev de* **Tribunal Supremo**) *m* SC.

tse-tsé → mosca.

tu (*pl* **tus**) *adj poses* (*antes de sust*) your.

tú *pron pers* you; **es más alta que** ~ she's taller than you; **de** ~ **a** ~ [lucha] evenly matched; **hablar** ○ **tratar de** ~ **a alguien** to address sb as "tú".

tuareg *adj inv & m y f inv* Tuareg.

tuba *f* tuba.

tuberculina *f* tuberculin.

tubérculo *m* tuber, root vegetable.

tuberculosis *f inv* tuberculosis.

tuberculoso, -sa ◇ *adj* **-1.** MED tuberculous. **-2.** BOT tuberous. ◇ *m y f* tuberculosis sufferer.

tubería *f* **-1.** [cañerías] pipes (*pl*), pipework. **-2.** [tubo] pipe.

tubo *m* **-1.** [tubería] pipe; ~ **de escape** AUTOM exhaust (pipe); ~ **del desagüe** drainpipe. **-2.** [recipiente] tube; ~ **de ensayo** test tube. **-3.** ANAT tract; ~ **digestivo** digestive tract, alimentary canal. **-4.** *loc*: **pasar por el** ~ to put up with it.
◆ **por un tubo** *loc adv fam* a hell of a lot.

tubular ◇ *adj* tubular. ◇ *m* bicycle tyre.

tucán *m* toucan.

tuerca *f* nut; **apretar las** ~s **a alguien** to tighten the screws on sb.

tuerce → torcer.

tuerto, -ta ◇ *adj* [sin un ojo] one-eyed; [ciego de un ojo] blind in one eye. ◇ *m y f* [sin un ojo] one-eyed person; [ciego de un ojo] person who is blind in one eye.

tuerza *etc* → torcer.

tuesta *etc* → tostar.

tuétano *m* **-1.** ANAT (bone) marrow. **-2.** *fig* [meollo] crux, heart; **hasta el** ~ ○ **los** ~s to the core.

tufarada *f* waft.

tufillo *m* whiff.

tufo *m* **-1.** [mal olor] stench, foul smell. **-2.** [emanación] vapour.

tugurio *m* hovel.

tul *m* tulle.

tulipa *f* **-1.** [tulipán] tulip. **-2.** [de lámpara] tulip-shaped lampshade.

tulipán *m* tulip.

tullido, -da ◇ *adj* paralyzed, crippled. ◇ *m y f* cripple, disabled person.

tullir *vt* to paralyze, to cripple.

tumba *f* grave, tomb; **a** ~ **abierta** at breakneck speed; **ser (como) una** ~ to be as silent as the grave.

tumbar *vt* **-1.** [derribar] to knock over ○ down. **-2.** *fam fig* [suspender] to fail. **-3.** *fam*

fig [suj: noticia] to knock back; [suj: olor] to overpower.
◆ **tumbarse** *vpr* **-1.** [acostarse] to lie down. **-2.** [repantigarse] to lounge, to stretch out.

tumbo *m* jolt, jerk; **dar ~s** o **un ~** [coche etc] to jolt, to jerk; **ir dando ~s** *fig* [persona] to have a lot of ups and downs.

tumbona *f* [en la playa] deck chair; [en el jardín] (sun) lounger.

tumefacción *f* swelling.

tumefacto, -ta *adj* swollen.

tumor *m* tumour.

túmulo *m* **-1.** [sepulcro] tomb. **-2.** [montecillo] burial mound. **-3.** [catafalco] catafalque.

tumulto *m* **-1.** [disturbio] riot, disturbance. **-2.** [alboroto] uproar, tumult.

tumultuoso, -sa *adj* **-1.** [conflictivo] tumultuous, riotous. **-2.** [turbulento] rough, stormy.

tuna *f* → tuno.

tunante, -ta *m y f* crook, scoundrel.

tunda *f fam* **-1.** [paliza] beating, thrashing. **-2.** [esfuerzo] drag, exhausting job.

tundra *f* tundra.

tunecino, -na *adj, m y f* Tunisian.

túnel *m* tunnel; **salir del ~** *fig* to turn the corner.
◆ **túnel de lavado** *m* AUTOM car wash.

Túnez -1. [capital] Tunis. **-2.** [país] Tunisia.

tungsteno *m* tungsten.

túnica *f* tunic.

Tunicia Tunisia.

tuno, -na *m y f* rogue, scoundrel.
◆ **tuno** *m* student minstrel.
◆ **tuna** *f* group of student minstrels.

TUNA:

A 'tuna' is a musical group made up of university students who wear black capes and coloured ribbons; they wander the streets singing and playing various instruments for pleasure or to collect money

---

tuntún
◆ **al tuntún** *loc adv* without thinking.

tupamaro *m* POLÍT Tupamaro, *Marxist urban guerrillas in Uruguay.*

tupé *m* **-1.** [cabello] quiff. **-2.** *fig* [atrevimiento] cheek, nerve.

tupido, -da *adj* thick, dense.

tupir *vt* to pack tightly.

Tupungato *m* Tupungato.

turba *f* **-1.** [combustible] peat, turf. **-2.** [muchedumbre] mob.

turbación *f* **-1.** [desconcierto] upset, disturbance. **-2.** [azoramiento] embarrassment.

turbador, -ra *adj* **-1.** [desconcertante] disconcerting, troubling. **-2.** [emocionante] upsetting, disturbing.

turbante *m* turban.

turbar *vt* **-1.** [alterar] to disturb. **-2.** [emocionar] to upset. **-3.** [desconcertar] to trouble, to disconcert.
◆ **turbarse** *vpr* [emocionarse] to get upset.

turbiedad *f* **-1.** [de agua etc] cloudiness. **-2.** *fig* [de negocios etc] shadiness.

turbina *f* turbine.

turbio, -bia *adj* **-1.** [agua etc] cloudy. **-2.** [vista] blurred. **-3.** *fig* [negocio etc] shady. **-4.** *fig* [época etc] turbulent, troubled.

turbión *m* downpour.

turbopropulsor *m* turboprop.

turborreactor *m* turbojet (engine).

turbulencia *f* **-1.** [de fluido] turbulence. **-2.** [alboroto] uproar, clamour.

turbulento, -ta *adj* **-1.** [gen] turbulent. **-2.** [revoltoso] unruly, rebellious.

turco, -ca ◇ *adj* Turkish. ◇ *m y f* [persona] Turk.
◆ **turco** *m* [lengua] Turkish.

turgente *adj* [formas, muslos] well-rounded.

turismo *m* **-1.** [gen] tourism; **hacer ~ (por)** to go touring (round). **-2.** AUTOM private car.

turista *m y f* tourist.

turístico, -ca *adj* tourist (*antes de sust*).

turmalina *f* tourmaline.

túrmix® *f inv* blender, liquidizer.

turnarse *vpr*: **~ (con alguien)** to take turns (with sb).

turnedó (*pl* turnedós) *m* tournedos.

turno *m* **-1.** [tanda] turn, go. **-2.** [de trabajo] shift; **~ de día/noche** day/night shift.

turón *m* polecat.

turquesa ◇ *f* [mineral] turquoise. ◇ *adj inv* [color] turquoise. ◇ *m* [color] turquoise.

Turquía Turkey.

turrón *m Christmas sweet similar to marzipan or nougat, made with almonds and honey.*

turulato, -ta *adj fam* flabbergasted, dumbfounded.

tururú *interj fam*: ¡~! get away!, you must be joking!

tute *m* **-1.** [juego] *card game similar to whist.* **-2.** *fam fig* [trabajo intenso] hard slog; **darse un ~** to slog away.

tutear *vt* to address as "tú".
◆ **tutearse** *vpr* to address each other as "tú".

tutela *f* **-1.** DER guardianship. **-2.** [cargo]: **~ (de)** responsibility (for); **bajo la ~ de** under the protection of.

tutelaje *m* DER guardianship.

tutelar ◇ *adj* **-1.** DER tutelary. **-2.** [protector] protecting. ◇ *vt* to act as guardian to.

tuteo *m* use of "tú", familiar form of address.

tutiplén
◆ **a tutiplén** *loc adv fam* to excess, in abundance.

tutor, -ra *m y f* **-1.** DER guardian. **-2.** [profesor - privado] tutor; [- de un curso] form teacher.

tutoría *f* **-1.** DER guardianship. **-2.** [de un curso] role of form teacher.

tutti frutti, tuttifrutti *m* tutti frutti.

tutú (*pl* tutús) *m* tutu.

tutuma *f Amer fam* variety of nut.

tuviera *etc* → tener.

tuyo, -ya ◇ *adj poses* yours; **este libro es** ~ this book is yours; **un amigo** ~ a friend of yours; **no es asunto** ~ it's none of your business. ◇ *pron poses*: **el** ~ yours; **el** ~ **es rojo** yours is red; **ésta es la tuya** *fam* this is the chance you've been waiting for; **lo** ~ **es el teatro** [lo que haces bien] you should be on the stage; **los** ~**s** *fam* [tu familia] your folks; [tu bando] your lot, your side.

TV (*abrev de* televisión) *f* TV.

TV3 (*abrev de* Televisión de Cataluña, SA) *f Catalan television channel.*

TVA (*abrev de* tasa sobre el valor añadido) *f* VAT.

TVE (*abrev de* Televisión Española) *f Spanish state television network.*

TVG (*abrev de* Televisión de Galicia) *f Galician television channel.*

TVV (*abrev de* Televisión Valenciana, SA) *f* Valencian television channel.

twist [tuist] *m inv* twist (*dance*).

u¹, U *f* [letra] u, U.

u² *conj* or; *ver también* o².

UAB (*abrev de* Universidad Autónoma de Barcelona) *f Autonomous University of Barcelona.*

UB (*abrev de* Universidad de Barcelona) *f University of Barcelona.*

ubérrimo, -ma *adj culto* [tierra] extremely fertile; [vegetación] luxuriant, abundant.

ubicación *f* position, location.

ubicar [10] *vt* to place, to position; [edificio etc] to locate.
◆ **ubicarse** *vpr* [edificio etc] to be situated, to be located.

ubicuo, -cua *adj* ubiquitous.

ubique *etc* → ubicar.

ubre *f* udder.

UCD (*abrev de* Unión de Centro Democrático) *f former Spanish political party at the centre of the political spectrum.*

UCP (*abrev de* unidad central de proceso) *f* CPU.

Ud., Vd. *abrev de* usted.

UDC (*abrev de* universal decimal classification) *f* UDC.

Uds., Vds. *abrev de* ustedes.

UE (*abrev de* Unión Europea) *f* EU.

UEFA (*abrev de* Unión de Asociaciones Europeas de Fútbol) *f* UEFA.

UEM (*abrev de* unión económica y monetaria) *f* EMU.

UEO (*abrev de* Unión Europea Occidental) *f* WEU.

UER (*abrev de* Unión Europea de Radiodifusión) *f* EBU.

uf *interj*: ¡~! [expresa cansancio, calor] phew!; [expresa fastidio] tut!; [expresa repugnancia] ugh!

ufanarse *vpr*: ~ de to boast about.

ufano, -na *adj* **-1.** [satisfecho] proud, pleased. **-2.** [engreído] boastful, conceited. **-3.** [lozano] luxuriant, lush.

UFO (*abrev de* unidentified flying object) *m* UFO.

ufología *f* ufology.

Uganda Uganda.

ugetista ◇ *adj* of or belonging to the "UGT". ◇ *m y f* member of the "UGT".

UGT (*abrev de* **Unión General de los Trabajadores**) *f* major socialist Spanish trade union.

UHF (*abrev de* **ultra high frequency**) *f* UHF.

UIMP (*abrev de* **Universidad Internacional Menéndez Pelayo**) *f* Menéndez Pelayo International University in Santander.

UIT (*abrev de* **Unión Internacional de Telecomunicaciones**) *f* ITU.

ujier (*pl* **ujieres**) *m* usher.

újule *interj Amer:* ¡~! wow!

ukelele *m* ukelele.

Ulan-Bator Ulan-Bator.

úlcera *f* MED ulcer; ~ **de estómago** stomach ulcer.

ulceración *f* ulceration.

ulcerar *vt* to ulcerate.
◆ **ulcerarse** *vpr* MED to ulcerate.

ulterior *adj* [culto] **-1.** [en el tiempo] subsequent, ulterior. **-2.** [en el espacio] further.

ulteriormente *adv* [culto] subsequently.

ultimación *f* conclusion, completion.

ultimador, -ra *m y f Amer* killer.

últimamente *adv* recently, of late.

ultimar *vt* **-1.** [gen] to conclude, to complete. **-2.** *Amer* [matar] to kill.

ultimátum (*pl* **ultimátums** ○ **ultimatos**) *m* ultimatum.

último, -ma ◇ *adj* **-1.** [gen] last; **por** ~ lastly, finally; **ser lo** ~ [lo final] to come last; [el último recurso] to be a last resort; [el colmo] to be the last straw. **-2.** [más reciente] latest, most recent. **-3.** [más remoto] furthest, most remote. **-4.** [más bajo] bottom. **-5.** [más alto] top. **-6.** [de más atrás] back.
◇ *m y f* **-1.** [en fila, carrera etc]: **el** ~ the last (one); **llegar el** ~ to come last. **-2.** (*en comparaciones, enumeraciones*): **éste** ~ ... the latter ....
◆ **última** *f*: **estar en las últimas** [muriéndose] to be on one's deathbed; [sin dinero] to be down to one's last penny; [sin provisiones] to be down to one's last provisions; **ir a la última** *fam* to wear the latest fashion.

ultra ◇ *adj* POLÍT extreme right-wing. ◇ *m y f* POLÍT right-wing extremist.
◆ **non plus ultra** *m* epitome, height.

ultraderecha *f* extreme right (wing).

ultraizquierda *f* extreme left (wing).

ultrajante *adj* insulting, offensive.

ultrajar *vt* to insult, to offend.

ultraje *m* insult.

ultraligero *m* microlight.

ultramar *m* overseas (*pl*); **de** ~ overseas (*antes de sust*).

ultramarino, -na *adj* overseas (*antes de sust*).
◆ **ultramarinos** ◇ *mpl* **-1.** [comestibles] groceries. ◇ *m inv* [tienda] grocer's (shop).

ultramicroscopio *m* ultramicroscope.

ultramontano, -na ◇ *adj* **-1.** [gen & RELIG] ultramontane. **-2.** *fig* [reaccionario] reactionary. ◇ *m y f* **-1.** RELIG ultramontane. **-2.** *fig* [reaccionario] **reactionary.**

ultranza
◆ **a ultranza** *loc adv* **-1.** [con decisión] to the death. **-2.** [acérrimamente] out-and-out.

ultrasonido *m* ultrasound.

ultratumba *f*: **de** ~ from beyond the grave.

ultravioleta *adj inv* ultraviolet.

ulular *vi* **-1.** [viento, lobo] to howl. **-2.** [búho] to hoot.

umbilical *adj* → **cordón.**

umbral *m* **-1.** [gen] threshold. **-2.** *fig* [límite] bounds (*pl*), realms (*pl*).

umbrío, -a *adj* shady.

un, una ◇ *art* (*antes de sust femenino que empiece por "a" o "ha" tónica: "un"*) a, an (*ante sonido vocálico*): ~ **hombre/coche** a man/car; **una mujer/mesa** a woman/table; ~ **águila/hacha** an eagle/axe; **una hora** an hour. ◇ *adj* → **uno.**

unánime *adj* unanimous.

unanimidad *f* unanimity; **por** ~ unanimously.

unción *f* unction.

uncir [12] *vt* to yoke.

undécimo, -ma *núm* eleventh.

underground [ander'graun] *adj inv* underground.

UNED (*abrev de* **Universidad Nacional de Educación a Distancia**) *f* Spanish open university.

Unesco (*abrev de* **United Nations Educational, Scientific and Cultural Organization**) *f* UNESCO.

ungimiento *m* unction.

ungir [15] *vt* to put ointment on; RELIG to anoint.

ungüento *m* ointment.

únicamente *adv* only, solely.

Unicef (*abrev de* **United Nations Children's Fund**) *m* UNICEF.

unicelular *adj* single-cell, unicellular.

unicidad *f* uniqueness.

único, -ca *adj* **-1.** [sólo] only; **es lo** ~ **que**

quiero it's all I want. **-2.** [excepcional] unique. **-3.** [precio, función, razón] single.

unicornio *m* unicorn.

unidad *f* **-1.** [gen, MAT & MIL] unit; **25 pesetas la** ~ 25 pesetas each; ~ **de cuidados intensivos** O **vigilancia intensiva** intensive care (unit); ~ **central de proceso** INFORM central processing unit; ~ **de combate** combat unit; ~ **de disco** INFORM disk drive; ~ **móvil** TV mobile unit. **-2.** [cohesión, acuerdo] unity.

unidireccional *adj* unidirectional, one-way.

unido, -da *adj* united; [familia, amigo] close.

UNIDO (*abrev de* United Nations Industrial Development Organization) *f* UNIDO.

unifamiliar *adj* detached.

unificación *f* **-1.** [unión] unification. **-2.** [uniformización] standardization.

unificador, -ra *adj* unifying.

unificar [10] *vt* **-1.** [unir] to unite; [países] to unify. **-2.** [uniformar] to standardize.

uniformado, -da *adj* uniformed.

uniformar *vt* **-1.** [igualar] to standardize. **-2.** [poner uniforme] to put into uniform.

uniforme ◇ *adj* uniform; [superficie] even. ◇ *m* uniform.

uniformidad *f* uniformity; [de superficie] evenness.

uniformización *f* standardization.

uniformizar [13] *vt* to standardize.

unilateral *adj* unilateral.

unión *f* **-1.** [gen] union; **en** ~ **de** together with. **-2.** [suma, adherimiento] joining together. **-3.** TECN join, joint.

◆ **Unión Europea** *f*: **la Unión Europea** the European Union.

unir *vt* **-1.** [pedazos, habitaciones etc] to join. **-2.** [empresas, estados, facciones] to unite. **-3.** [comunicar - ciudades etc] to link. **-4.** [suj: amistad, circunstancias etc] to bind. **-5.** [casar] to join, to marry. **-6.** [combinar] to combine. **-7.** [mezclar] to mix O blend in.

◆ **unirse** *vpr* **-1.** [gen] to join together; ~**se a algo** to join sthg. **-2.** [casarse]: ~**se en matrimonio** to be joined in wedlock.

unisexo, unisex *adj inv* unisex.

unisexual *adj* unisexual.

unísono

◆ **al unísono** *loc adv* in unison.

UNITA (*abrev de* Unión Nacional para la Independencia Total de Angola) *f* UNITA.

unitario, -ria ◇ *adj* **-1.** [de una unidad - estado, nación] single; [- precio] unit (*antes de sust*). **-2.** POLÍT unitarian. ◇ *m y f* POLÍT unitarian.

UNIVAC (*abrev de* universal automatic computer) *m* UNIVAC.

universal *adj* **-1.** [gen] universal. **-2.** [mundial] world (*antes de sust*).

◆ **universales** *mpl* FILOSOFÍA universals.

universalidad *f* universality.

universalismo *m* universalism.

universalizar [13] *vt* to make widespread.

universidad *f* university; ~ **a distancia** ≃ Open University *Br*.

universitario, -ria ◇ *adj* university (*antes de sust*). ◇ *m y f* **-1.** [estudiante] university student. **-2.** [professor] university lecturer. **-3.** [licenciado] university graduate.

universo *m* **-1.** ASTRON universe. **-2.** *fig* [mundo] world.

unívoco, -ca *adj* univocal, unambiguous.

unja *etc* → **ungir**.

uno, una ◇ *adj* (*antes de sust masculino sg*: **un**) **-1.** [indefinido] one; **un día volveré** one O some day I'll return; **había** ~**s coches mal aparcados** there were some badly parked cars; **había** ~**s 12 muchachos** there were about O some 12 boys there. **-2.** [numeral] one; **un hombre, un voto** one man, one vote; **la fila** ~ row one. ◇ *pron* **-1.** [indefinido] one; **coge** ~ take one; ~ **de vosotros** one of you; ~**s ... otros ...** some ... others ...; ~ **a otro**, ~**s a otros** each other, one another; ~ **y otro** both; ~**s y otros** all of them. **-2.** *fam* [cierta persona] someone, somebody; **hablé con** ~ **que te conoce** I spoke to someone who knows you; **me lo han contado** ~**s** certain people told me so. **-3.** [yo] one; ~ **ya no está para estos trotes** one isn't really up to this sort of thing any more. **-4.** *loc*: **a una** [en armonía, a la vez] together; **de** ~ **en** ~, ~ **a** ~, ~ **por** ~ one by one; **juntar varias cosas en una** to combine several things into one; **lo** ~ **por lo otro** it all evens out in the end; **más de** ~ many people; **una de dos** it's either one thing or the other; ~**s cuantos** a few; **una y no más** once was enough, once bitten, twice shy.

◆ **uno** *m* [número] (number) one; **el** ~ number one; *ver también* **seis**.

◆ **una** *f* [hora]: **la una** one o'clock.

untar *vt* **-1.** [pan, tostada]: ~ **(con)** to spread (with); [piel, cara etc] to smear (with). **-2.** [máquina, bisagra etc] to grease, to oil. **-3.** *fam fig* [sobornar] to grease the palm of, to bribe.

◆ **untarse** *vpr fam* [enriquecerse] to line one's pockets.

unto *m* **-1.** [ungüento] ointment. **-2.** [grasa] grease.

untuosidad *f* greasiness, oiliness.

untuoso, -sa *adj* greasy, oily.

untura *f* **-1.** [ungüento] ointment. **-2.** [grasa] grease.

unza *etc* → **uncir**.

uña *f* **-1.** [de mano] fingernail, nail; **hacerse las ~s** to do one's nails; **comerse las ~s** [por preocupación, nerviosismo] to bite one's nails; **ser ~ y carne** to be as thick as thieves. **-2.** [de pie] toenail. **-3.** [garra] claw; **enseñar ○ sacar las ~s** to get one's claws out. **-4.** [casco] hoof.

uñero *m* **-1.** [inflamación] whitlow. **-2.** [uña encarnada] ingrowing nail. **-3.** [de libro] thumb-index.

UPC (*abrev de* **Universidad Politécnica de Cataluña**) *f polytechnic university of Catalonia.*

UPE (*abrev de* **Unión Parlamentaria Europea**) *f* EPU.

uperización *f* U.H.T. treatment.

uperizar [13] *vt* to give U.H.T. treatment.

UPG (*abrev de* **Unión del Pueblo Gallego**) *f Galician nationalist party.*

UPM (*abrev de* **Universidad Politécnica de Madrid**) *f polytechnic university of Madrid.*

UPN (*abrev de* **Unión del Pueblo Navarro**) *f Navarrese nationalist party.*

UPU (*abrev de* **Unión Postal Universal**) *f* UPU.

Ural *m*: **el ~** the River Ural.

Urales *mpl*: **los ~** the Urals.

uralita® *f* CONSTR *material made of asbestos and cement, usually corrugated and used mainly for roofing.*

uranio *m* uranium.

Urano Uranus.

urbanidad *f* politeness, courtesy.

urbanismo *m* town planning.

urbanista *m y f* town planner.

urbanístico, -ca *adj* town-planning (*antes de sust*).

urbanización *f* **-1.** [acción] urbanization. **-2.** [zona residencial] (housing) estate.

urbanizador, -ra ◇ *adj* developing. ◇ *m y f* developer.

urbanizar [13] *vt* to develop, to urbanize.

urbano, -na ◇ *adj* urban, city (*antes de sust*). ◇ *m y f* traffic policeman (*f* traffic policewoman).

urbe *f* large city.

urdido *m* warp.

urdimbre *f* warp.

urdir *vt* **-1.** [planear] to plot, to forge. **-2.** [hilos] to warp.

urea *f* urea.

uremia *f* uraemia.

uréter *m* ureter.

uretra *f* urethra.

urgencia *f* **-1.** [cualidad] urgency. **-2.** [necesidad] urgent need; **en caso de ~** in case of emergency.

◆ **urgencias** *fpl* MED casualty (department) (*sg*).

urgente *adj* **-1.** [apremiante] urgent. **-2.** [correo] express.

urgir [15] *vi* to be urgently necessary; **me urge hacerlo** I urgently need to do it.

úrico, -ca *adj* uric.

urinario, -ria *adj* urinary.

◆ **urinario** *m* urinal, comfort station *Am*.

urja *etc* → **urgir**.

urna *f* **-1.** [vasija] urn; **~ cineraria** urn (*for sb's ashes*). **-2.** [caja de cristal] glass case. **-3.** [para votar] ballot box; **acudir a la ~s** to go to the polls.

uro *m* aurochs, urus.

urogallo *m* capercaillie.

urología *f* urology.

urólogo, -ga *m y f* urologist.

urraca *f* magpie.

URSS (*abrev de* **Unión de Repúblicas Socialistas Soviéticas**) *f* USSR.

ursulina *f* **-1.** RELIG Ursuline (nun). **-2.** *fig* [mujer recatada] prudish woman.

urticaria *f* nettle rash.

Uruguay: **(el) ~** Uruguay.

uruguayo, -ya *adj, m y f* Uruguayan.

usado, -da *adj* **-1.** [utilizado] used; **muy ~** widely-used. **-2.** [gastado] worn-out, worn.

usanza *f* custom, usage; **a la vieja ~** in the old way ○ style.

usar ◇ *vt* **-1.** [gen] to use. **-2.** [prenda] to wear. ◇ *vi*: **~ de** to use, to make use of.

◆ **usarse** *vpr* **-1.** [emplearse] to be used. **-2.** [estar de moda] to be worn.

usía *m y f desus* Your Lordship (*f* Your Ladyship).

uso *m* **-1.** [gen] use; **al ~** fashionable; **al ~ andaluz** in the Andalusian style; **"de ~ externo"** FARM "for external use only"; **fuera de ~** out of use, obsolete; **hacer ~ de** [utilizar] to make use of, to use; [de prerrogativa, derecho] to exercise; **tener el ~ de la palabra** to have the floor. **-2.** (*gen pl*) [costumbre] custom. **-3.** LING usage. **-4.** [desgaste] wear and tear.

◆ **uso de razón** *m* age of reason.

USO (*abrev de* **Unión Sindical Obrera**) *f Spanish trade union.*

USP (*abrev de* **Unión Sindical de Policía**) *f Spanish police union.*

usted *pron pers* **-1.** [tratamiento de respeto · *sg*] you; [- *pl*]: **~es** you (*pl*); **contesten ~es a**

las preguntas please answer the questions; **me gustaría hablar con** ~ I'd like to talk to you. **-2.** [tratamiento de respeto - posesivo]: **de** ~/~**es** yours.

usual *adj* usual.

usuario, -ria *m y f* user.

usufructo *m* DER usufruct, use.

usufructuar [6] *vt* DER to have the usufruct O use of.

usufructuario, -ria *adj, m y f* DER usufructuary.

usura *f* usury.

usurero, -ra *m y f* usurer.

usurpación *f* usurpation.

usurpador, -ra ◇ *adj* usurping. ◇ *m y f* usurper.

usurpar *vt* to usurp.

utensilio *m* [gen] tool, implement; CULIN utensil; ~**s de pesca** fishing tackle.

uterino, -na *adj* uterine.

útero *m* womb, uterus MED.

útil ◇ *adj* **-1.** [beneficioso, aprovechable] useful. **-2.** [eficiente] helpful. **-3.** [hábil] working. ◇ *m* (*gen pl*) [herramienta] tool; AGR implement.

utilería *f* equipment; CIN & TEATR props (*pl*).

utilidad *f* **-1.** [cualidad] usefulness. **-2.** [beneficio] profit.

utilitario, -ria *adj* **-1.** [persona] utilitarian. **-2.** AUTOM run-around, utility.
◆ **utilitario** *m* AUTOM run-around car, utility car.

utilitarismo *m* utilitarianism.

utilización *f* use.

utilizar [13] *vt* [gen] to use.

utillaje *m* tools (*pl*).

utopía *f* utopia.

utópico, -ca *adj* utopian.

uva *f* grape; **de** ~**s a peras** once in a blue moon; **estar de mala** ~ to be in a bad mood; **tener mala** ~ to be a bad sort, to be a nasty piece of work; ~**s de la suerte** *grapes eaten on New Year's Eve.*

UVAS DE LA SUERTE:
Tradition dictates that on New Year's Eve twelve grapes must be eaten as midnight is struck, one for each of the twelve chimes, in the belief that whoever manages to do so will have good luck in the coming year

UVI (*abrev de* **unidad de vigilancia intensiva**) *f* ICU.

úvula *f* uvula.

uvular *adj* uvular.

uy *interj*: ¡~! ahh!, oh!

v ['uße], **V** *f* [letra] v, V.
◆ **v doble** *f* W.

v. = **vid.**

va → **ir.**

vaca *f* **-1.** [animal] cow; ~ **lechera/sagrada** dairy/sacred cow. **-2.** [carne] beef.
◆ **vacas flacas** *fpl fig* lean years.
◆ **vacas gordas** *fpl fig* years of plenty.

vacaciones *fpl* holiday (*sg*), holidays *Br*, vacation (*sg*) *Am*; **coger (las)** ~ to take one's holidays; **estar/irse de** ~ to be/go on holiday.

vacante ◇ *adj* vacant. ◇ *f* vacancy.

vaciado *m* **-1.** [de recipiente] emptying. **-2.** [de estatua] casting, moulding.

vaciar [9] *vt* **-1.** [gen]: ~ **algo (de)** to empty sthg (of). **-2.** [dejar hueco] to hollow (out). **-3.** ARTE to cast, to mould. **-4.** [texto] to copy out.

vaciedad *f* [tontería] trifle.

vacilación *f* **-1.** [duda] hesitation; [al elegir] indecision. **-2.** [oscilación] swaying; [de la luz] flickering.

vacilante *adj* **-1.** [gen] hesitant; [al elegir] indecisive. **-2.** [luz] flickering; [pulso] irregular; [paso] swaying, unsteady.

vacilar ◇ *vi* **-1.** [dudar] to hesitate; [al elegir] to be indecisive. **-2.** [voz, principios, régimen] to falter. **-3.** [fluctuar - luz] to flicker; [- pulso] to be irregular. **-4.** [tambalearse] to wobble, to sway. **-5.** *fam* [chulear] to swank, to show off. **-6.** *fam* [bromear] to take the mickey. ◇ *vt fam* [tomar el pelo]: ~ **a alguien** to take the mickey out of sb.

vacilón, -ona *fam* ◇ *adj* **-1.** [chulo] swanky. **-2.** [bromista] jokey, teasing. ◇ *m y f* **-1.** [chulo] show-off. **-2.** [bromista] tease.
◆ **vacilón** *m Amer fam* [fiesta] party.

vacío, -a *adj* empty; ~ **de** [contenido etc] devoid of.
◆ **vacío** *m* **-1.** FÍS vacuum; **envasar al** ~ to vacuum-pack. **-2.** [abismo, carencia] void. **-3.** [hueco] space, gap. **-4.** *loc*: **caer en el** ~ to fall on deaf ears; **hacer el** ~ **a alguien** to

send sb to Coventry; **tener un ~ en el estómago** to feel hungry.

vacuidad *f* [trivialidad] shallowness, vacuity.

vacuna *f* vaccine.

vacunación *f* vaccination.

vacunar *vt* to vaccinate.

◆ **vacunarse** *vpr* to get vaccinated.

vacuno, -na *adj* bovine.

vacuo, -cua *adj* [trivial] shallow, vacuous.

vadeable *adj* fordable.

vadear *vt* to ford; *fig* to overcome.

vademécum (*pl* **vademecums**) *m* vade mecum, handbook.

vado *m* **-1.** [en acera] lowered kerb; "~ **permanente**" "keep clear". **-2.** [de río] ford.

Vaduz Vaduz.

vagabundear *vi* **-1.** [ser un vagabundo] to lead a vagrant's life. **-2.** [vagar]: ~ **(por)** to wander, to roam.

vagabundeo *m* vagrant's life.

vagabundo, -da ◇ *adj* [persona] vagrant; [perro] stray. ◇ *m y f* tramp, vagrant, bum *Am*.

vagamente *adv* vaguely.

vagancia *f* **-1.** [holgazanería] laziness, idleness. **-2.** [vagabundeo] vagrancy.

vagar [16] *vi*: ~ **(por)** to wander, to roam.

vagido *m* cry of a newborn baby.

vagina *f* vagina.

vaginal *adj* vaginal.

vago, -ga ◇ *adj* **-1.** [perezoso] lazy, idle. **-2.** [impreciso] vague. ◇ *m y f* lazy person, idler.

vagón *m* [de pasajeros] carriage; [de mercancías] wagon; ~ **cisterna** tanker, tank wagon; ~ **de mercancías** goods wagon O van; ~ **de primera/segunda** first-class/second-class carriage; ~ **restaurante** dining car, restaurant car.

vagoneta *f* wagon.

vaguada *f* valley floor.

vague *etc* → **vagar**.

vaguear *vi* to laze around.

vaguedad *f* **-1.** [cualidad] vagueness. **-2.** [dicho] vague remark.

vahído *m* blackout, fainting fit; **me dio un ~** I fainted.

vaho *m* **-1.** [vapor] steam. **-2.** [aliento] breath.

◆ **vahos** *mpl* MED inhalation (*sg*).

vaina *f* **-1.** [gen] sheath. **-2.** [BOT - envoltura] pod. **-3.** *Amer fam* [engreído] pain in the neck.

vainica *f* hemstitch.

vainilla *f* vanilla.

vaivén *m* **-1.** [balanceo - de barco] swaying, rocking; [- de péndulo, columpio] swinging. **-2.** [altibajo] ups-and-downs (*pl*).

vajilla *f* crockery; **una ~** a dinner service.

valdepeñas *m inv* Valdepeñas, *Spanish wine from the La Mancha region, usually red*.

valdrá *etc* → **valer**.

vale ◇ *m* **-1.** [bono] coupon, voucher. **-2.** [entrada gratuita] free ticket. **-3.** [comprobante] receipt. **-4.** [pagaré] I.O.U. **-5.** *Amer fam* [compañero] mate. ◇ *interj* → **valer**.

valedero, -ra *adj* valid.

valedor, -ra *m y f* protector.

valemadrista *adj Amer* **-1.** [apático] apathetic. **-2.** [cínico] cynical.

valencia *f* QUÍM valency.

Valencia Valencia.

valenciano, -na *adj, m y f* [de Valencia] Valencian.

◆ **valenciana** *f Amer* [de pantalón] (trouser) turn-up.

valentía *f* **-1.** [valor] bravery. **-2.** [hazaña] act of bravery.

valentón, -ona *m y f*: **hacerse el ~** to boast of one's bravery.

valer [74] ◇ *vt* **-1.** [costar - precio] to cost; [tener un valor de] to be worth; **¿cuánto vale?** [de precio] how much does it cost?, how much is it? **-2.** [suponer] to earn. **-3.** [merecer] to deserve, to be worth. **-4.** [equivaler] to be equivalent O equal to.

◇ *vi* **-1.** [merecer aprecio] to be worthy; **hacerse ~** to show one's worth. **-2.** [servir]: ~ **para algo** to be for sthg; **eso aún vale** you can still use that; **¿para qué vale?** what's it for? **-3.** [ser válido] to be valid; [en juegos] to be allowed. **-4.** [ayudar] to help, to be of use. **-5.** [tener calidad] to be worth; **no ~ nada** to be worthless O useless. **-6.** [equivaler]: ~ **por** to be worth. **-7.** *loc*: **más vale tarde que nunca** better late than never; **más vale que te calles/vayas** it would be better if you shut up/left; **¿vale?** okay?, all right?; **¡vale!** okay!, all right!; **¡vale (ya)!** that's enough!

◇ *m* worth, value.

◆ **valerse** *vpr* **-1.** [servirse]: ~**se de algo/alguien** to use sthg/sb. **-2.** [desenvolverse]: ~**se (por sí mismo)** to manage on one's own.

valeriana *f* valerian, allheal.

valeroso, -sa *adj* brave, courageous.

valga *etc* → **valer**.

valía *f* value, worth.

validar *vt* to validate.

validez *f* validity; **dar ~ a** to validate.

valido *m* favourite.

válido, **-da** *adj* valid.

valiente ◇ *adj* **-1.** [valeroso] brave. **-2.** *irón* [menudo]: ¡**en** ~ **lío te has metido!** you've got yourself into some mess ○ into a fine mess!
◇ *m y f* [valeroso] brave person.

valija *f* **-1.** [maleta] case, suitcase; ~ **diplomática** diplomatic bag. **-2.** [de correos] mailbag.

valioso, **-sa** *adj* **-1.** [gen] valuable. **-2.** [intento, esfuerzo] worthy.

valla *f* **-1.** [cerca] fence. **-2.** DEP hurdle.
◆ **valla publicitaria** *f* billboard, hoarding.

vallado *m* fence.

Valladolid Valladolid.

vallar *vt* to put a fence round.

valle *m* valley.

vallisoletano, **-na** *adj* of/relating to Valladolid.

valor *m* **-1.** [gen, MAT & MÚS] value; **de** ~ valuable; **joyas por** ~ **de ...** jewels worth ...; **sin** ~ worthless; ~ **adquisitivo** purchasing power; ~ **añadido** ECON added value; ~ **nominal** face ○ nominal value; ~ **nutritivo** nutritional value. **-2.** [importancia] importance; **dar** ~ **a** to give ○ attach importance to; **quitar** ~ **a algo** to take away from sthg, to diminish the importance of sthg. **-3.** [valentía] bravery; **armarse de** ~ to pluck up one's courage. **-4.** [desvergüenza] cheek, nerve. **-5.** *fam* [personaje - DEP etc]: **un joven** ~ a young prospect.
◆ **valores** *mpl* **-1.** [principios] values. **-2.** FIN securities, bonds; ~**es en cartera** investments.

valoración *f* **-1.** [de precio, pérdidas] valuation. **-2.** [de mérito, cualidad, ventajas] evaluation, assessment.

valorar *vt* **-1.** [tasar, apreciar] to value. **-2.** [evaluar] to evaluate, to assess.

valorización *f* appreciation.

valorizar [13] *vt* to increase the value of.
◆ **valorizarse** *vpr* to increase in value.

valquiria *f* Valkyrie.

vals (*pl* **valses**) *m* waltz.

valuar [6] *vt* to value.

valva *f* BOT & ZOOL valve.

válvula *f* valve; ~ **de seguridad** safety valve.
◆ **válvula de escape** *f* *fig* means of letting off steam.

vampiresa *f* *fam* vamp, femme fatale.

vampirismo *m* vampirism.

vampiro *m* **-1.** [personaje] vampire. **-2.** [murciélago] vampire bat.

vanagloriarse [8] *vpr*: ~ (**de**) to boast (about), to show off (about).

vandálico, **-ca** *adj* [salvaje] vandalistic; **un acto** ~ an act of vandalism.

vandalismo *m* vandalism.

vándalo, **-la** ◇ *adj* vandal (*antes de sust*).
◇ *m y f* HIST Vandal.
◆ **vándalo** *m* *fig* [salvaje] vandal.

vanguardia *f* **-1.** MIL vanguard; **ir a la** ~ **de** *fig* to be at the forefront of. **-2.** [cultural] avant-garde, vanguard.

vanguardismo *m* avant-garde.

vanidad *f* **-1.** [orgullo] vanity. **-2.** [inutilidad] futility.

vanidoso, **-sa** ◇ *adj* vain, conceited. ◇ *m y f* vain person.

vano, **-na** *adj* **-1.** [gen] vain; **en** ~ in vain. **-2.** [vacío, superficial] shallow, superficial.
◆ **vano** *m* ARQUIT bay.

vapor *m* **-1.** [emanación] vapour; [de agua] steam; **al** ~ CULIN steamed; **de** ~ [máquina etc] steam (*antes de sust*); ~ **de agua** FÍS & QUÍM water vapour. **-2.** [barco] steamer, steamship.

vaporización *f* **-1.** FÍS vaporization. **-2.** [pulverización] spraying.

vaporizador *m* **-1.** [pulverizador] spray. **-2.** [para evaporar] vaporizer.

vaporizar [13] *vt* **-1.** FÍS to vaporize. **-2.** [pulverizar] to spray.
◆ **vaporizarse** *vpr* FÍS to evaporate, to vaporize.

vaporoso, **-sa** *adj* **-1.** [con vapor - ducha, baño] steamy; [- cielo] hazy, misty. **-2.** [fino - tela etc] diaphanous, sheer.

vapulear *vt* to beat, to thrash; *fig* to slate, to tear apart.

vapuleo *m* beating, thrashing; *fig* slating, tearing apart.

vaquería *f* dairy.

vaquero, **-ra** ◇ *adj* cowboy (*antes de sust*).
◇ *m y f* [persona] cowboy (*f* cowgirl), cowherd.
◆ **vaqueros** *mpl* [pantalón] jeans.

vaquilla *f* [vaca] heifer; [toro] young bull.

vara *f* **-1.** [rama, palo] stick. **-2.** [pértiga] pole. **-3.** [de metal etc] rod. **-4.** [tallo] stem, stalk. **-5.** [de trombón] slide. **-6.** [insignia] staff.

varadero *m* dry dock.

varado, **-da** *adj* [NÁUT - encallado] aground, stranded; [- en el dique seco] in dry dock.

varar *vi* NÁUT to run aground.

varear *vt* [árboles] to beat (with a pole); [fruta] to knock ○ beat down.

variabilidad *f* changeability, variability.

variable ◇ *adj* changeable, variable. ◇ *f* MAT variable.

variación f variation; [del tiempo] change.

◆ **variación magnética** f magnetic declination.

variado, -da adj varied; [galletas, bombones] assorted.

variante ◇ adj variant. ◇ f -1. [variación] variation; [versión] version. -2. AUTOM bypass. -3. [en quiniela] draw or away win.

variar [9] ◇ vt -1. [modificar] to alter, to change. -2. [dar variedad] to vary. ◇ vi -1. [cambiar]: ~ (de) to change; **para** ~ irón (just) for a change. -2. [ser diferente]: ~ (de) to vary ○ differ (from).

varicela f chickenpox.

varicoso, -sa adj varicose.

variedad f variety.

◆ **variedades, varietés** fpl TEATR variety (U), music hall (U).

varilla f -1. [barra larga] rod, stick. -2. [tira larga - de abanico, paraguas] spoke, rib; [- de gafas] arm; [- de corsé] bone, stay.

varillaje m [de abanico, paraguas] spokes (pl), ribbing; [de gafas] arms (pl); [de corsé] bones (pl), stays (pl).

vario, -ria adj [variado] varied, different; (pl) various, several.

◆ **varios, -rias** pron pl several.

variopinto, -ta adj diverse.

varita f wand; ~ **mágica** magic wand.

variz f (gen pl) varicose vein.

varón m [hombre] male, man; [chico] boy.

varonil adj masculine, male.

Varsovia Warsaw.

varsoviano, -na ◇ adj of/relating to Warsaw. ◇ m y f native/inhabitant of Warsaw.

vasallo, -lla m y f -1. [siervo] vassal. -2. [súbdito] subject.

vasco, -ca adj, m y f Basque.

◆ **vasco** m [lengua] Basque.

vascuence m [lengua] Basque.

vascular adj vascular.

vasectomía f vasectomy.

vaselina® f Vaseline®.

vasija f [de barro] earthenware vessel.

vaso m -1. [recipiente, contenido] glass; **un ~ de plástico** a plastic cup; **ahogarse en un ~ de agua** to make a mountain out of a molehill. -2. ANAT vessel; **~s capilares** capillaries; **~s sanguíneos** blood vessels. -3. BOT vein.

vástago m -1. [descendiente] offspring (U). -2. [brote] shoot. -3. [varilla] rod.

vasto, -ta adj vast.

vate m cult bard.

váter = wáter.

vaticano, -na adj Vatican (antes de sust).

◆ **Vaticano** m: **el Vaticano** the Vatican.

vaticinar vt to prophesy, to predict.

vaticinio m culto prophecy, prediction.

vatio, watio ['batio] m watt.

vaudeville = vodevil.

vaya ◇ v → ir. ◇ interj -1. [sorpresa]: ¡~! well! -2. [énfasis]: ¡~ moto! what a motorbike!

VB abrev de **visto bueno**.

Vd. = Ud.

Vda. abrev de **viuda**.

Vds. = Uds.

ve → ir.

véase → ver.

vecinal adj -1. [relaciones, trato] neighbourly. -2. [camino, impuestos] local.

vecindad f -1. [vecindario] neighbourhood. -2. [cualidad] neighbourliness. -3. [alrededores] vicinity.

vecindario m [de barrio] neighbourhood; [de población] community, inhabitants (pl).

vecino, -na ◇ adj [cercano] neighbouring; ~ **a** next to. ◇ m y f -1. [de la misma casa, calle] neighbour; [de un barrio] resident. -2. [de una localidad] inhabitant.

vector m vector.

vectorial adj vectorial.

veda f -1. [prohibición] ban (on hunting and fishing); **levantar la** ~ to open the season. -2. [periodo] close season.

vedado, -da adj prohibited.

◆ **vedado** m reserve.

vedar vt to prohibit.

vedette [be'ðet] (pl vedettes) f star.

vedismo m Vedaism.

vega f fertile plain.

vegetación f vegetation.

◆ **vegetaciones** fpl MED adenoids.

vegetal ◇ adj -1. BIOL vegetable, plant (antes de sust). -2. [sandwich] salad (antes de sust). ◇ m vegetable.

vegetar vi to vegetate.

vegetarianismo m vegetarianism.

vegetariano, -na adj, m y f vegetarian.

vegetativo, -va adj vegetative.

vehemencia f -1. [pasión, entusiasmo] vehemence. -2. [irreflexión] impulsiveness, impetuosity.

vehemente adj -1. [apasionado, entusiasta] vehement. -2. [irreflexivo] impulsive, impetuous.

vehículo m [gen] vehicle; [de infección] carrier.

veinte núm twenty; **los (años)** ~ the twenties; ver también **seis**.

veinteañero, -ra ◇ *adj* about twenty years old. ◇ *m y f* person about twenty years old.

veinteavo, -va *núm* twentieth; **la veinteava parte** a twentieth.

veintena *f* **-1.** [veinte] twenty. **-2.** [aproximadamente]: **una ~ (de)** about twenty.

vejación *f*, **vejamen** *m* humiliation.

vejar *vt* to humiliate.

vejatorio, -ria *adj* humiliating.

vejestorio *m despec* old fogey.

vejez *f* old age; **¡a la ~ viruelas!** fancy that at his/her age!

vejiga *f* bladder; **~ de la bilis** gall bladder.

vela *f* **-1.** [para dar luz] candle; **estar a dos ~s** not to have two halfpennies to rub together. **-2.** [de barco] sail; **a toda ~** under full sail. **-3.** DEP sailing. **-4.** [vigilia] vigil; **pasar la noche en ~** [adrede] to stay awake all night; [desvelado] to have a sleepless night.
◆ **velas** *fpl fam* [mocos] bogies, snot (U).

velada *f* evening.

velado, -da *adj* **-1.** [oculto] veiled, hidden. **-2.** FOT blurred.

velador, -ra *adj* watching.
◆ **velador** *m* [mesa] pedestal table.
◆ **veladora** *f Amer* [vela] candle.

velamen *m* sails (*pl*).

velar¹ *adj* ANAT & LING velar.

velar² ◇ *vi* **-1.** [cuidar]: **~ por** to look after, to watch over. **-2.** [no dormir] to stay awake. ◇ *vt* **-1.** [de noche - muerto] to keep a vigil over; [- enfermo] to sit up with. **-2.** [ocultar] to mask, to veil. **-3.** FOT to blur.
◆ **velarse** *vpr* FOT to blur.

velatorio *m* wake, vigil.

veleidad *f* **-1.** [inconstancia] fickleness, capriciousness. **-2.** [antojo, capricho] whim, caprice.

veleidoso, -sa *adj* **-1.** [inconstante] fickle. **-2.** [caprichoso] capricious.

velero *m* sailing boat/ship.

veleta ◇ *f* weather vane. ◇ *m y f fam* capricious person.

vello *m* **-1.** [pelusilla] down. **-2.** [pelo] hair.

vellocino *m* fleece.

vellón *m* **-1.** [lana] fleece. **-2.** [aleación] silver and copper alloy.

velloso, -sa *adj* hairy.

velludo, -da *adj* hairy.

velo *m lit & fig* veil; **correr** ○ **echar un (tupido) ~ sobre algo** to draw a veil over sthg.
◆ **velo del paladar** *m* soft palate.

velocidad *f* **-1.** [gen] speed; TECN velocity; **a toda ~** at full speed; **de alta ~** high-

speed; **~ de crucero** cruising speed; **~ punta** top speed; **con la ~ de un rayo** as quick as lightning. **-2.** AUTOM [marcha] gear; **cambiar de ~** to change gear.

velocímetro *m* speedometer.

velocípedo *m* velocipede.

velocista *m y f* sprinter.

velódromo *m* cycle track, velodrome.

velomotor *m* moped.

velorio *m* wake.

veloz *adj* fast, quick.

ven → **venir.**

vena *f* **-1.** [gen, ANAT & MIN] vein. **-2.** [inspiración] inspiration; **tener la ~** to be inspired. **-3.** [don] vein, streak; **tener ~ de algo** to have a gift for doing sthg. **-4.** *loc*: **si se le da la ~** if the mood takes him/her.

venado *m* ZOOL deer; CULIN venison.

venal *adj* **-1.** [sobornable] venal, corrupt. **-2.** [vendible] for sale, saleable.

vencedor, -ra ◇ *adj* winning, victorious. ◇ *m y f* winner.

vencer [11] ◇ *vt* **-1.** [ganar] to beat, to defeat. **-2.** [derrotar - suj: sueño, cansancio, emoción] to overcome. **-3.** [aventajar]: **~ a alguien a** ○ **en algo** to outdo sb at sthg. **-4.** [superar - miedo, obstáculos] to overcome; [- tentación] to resist. ◇ *vi* **-1.** [ganar] to win, to be victorious. **-2.** [caducar - garantía, contrato, plazo] to expire; [- deuda, pago] to fall due, to be payable; [- bono] to mature. **-3.** [prevalecer] to prevail.
◆ **vencerse** *vpr* [estante etc] to give way, to collapse.

vencido, -da ◇ *adj* **-1.** [derrotado] defeated; **darse por ~** to give up. **-2.** [caducado - garantía, contrato, plazo] expired; [- pago, deuda] due, payable; [- bono] mature. ◇ *m y f* [en guerra] conquered ○ defeated person; [en deportes, concursos] loser.

vencimiento *m* **-1.** [término - de garantía, contrato, plazo] expiry; [- de pago, deuda] falling due; [- de bono] maturing. **-2.** [expiración] due date. **-3.** [inclinación] giving way, collapse.

venda *f* bandage; **tener una ~ en** ○ **delante de los ojos** *fig* to be blind.

vendaje *m* bandaging.

vendar *vt* to bandage; **~ los ojos a alguien** to blindfold sb.

vendaval *m* gale.

vendedor, -ra ◇ *adj* selling. ◇ *m y f* [gen] seller; [en tienda] shop ○ sales assistant; [de coches, seguros] salesman (*f* saleswoman); **~ ambulante** pedlar, hawker.

vender *vt lit & fig* to sell; **~ algo a** ○ **por** to sell sthg for.

◆ **venderse** *vpr* **-1.** [ser vendido] to be sold ○ on sale; "se vende" "for sale". **-2.** [dejarse sobornar] to sell o.s., to be bribed.

vendido, -da *adj* sold; **estar** ○ **ir** ~ *fig* not to stand a chance.

vendimia *f* grape harvest.

vendimiador, -ra *m y f* grape picker.

vendimiar [8] ◇ *vt* to harvest (*grapes*). ◇ *vi* to pick grapes.

vendrá *etc* → venir.

Venecia Venice.

veneciano, -na *adj, m y f* Venetian.

veneno *m* **-1.** [gen] poison; [de serpiente, insecto] venom. **-2.** *fig* [mala intención] venom.

venenoso, -sa *adj* **-1.** [gen] poisonous. **-2.** *fig* [malintencionado] venomous.

venerable *adj* venerable.

veneración *f* veneration, worship.

venerador, -ra ◇ *adj* venerational. ◇ *m y f* venerator.

venerar *vt* to venerate, to worship.

venéreo, -a *adj* venereal.

venezolano, -na *adj, m y f* Venezuelan.

Venezuela Venezuela.

venga ◇ *v* → venir. ◇ *interj* ¡~! come on!

vengador, -ra ◇ *adj* avenging. ◇ *m y f* avenger.

venganza *f* vengeance, revenge.

vengar [16] *vt* to avenge.

◆ **vengarse** *vpr*: ~se (de) to take revenge (on), to avenge o.s. (on).

vengativo, -va *adj* vengeful, vindictive.

vengo → venir.

vengue *etc* → vengar.

venia *f* **-1.** [permiso] permission. **-2.** DER [perdón] pardon; **con la** ~ [tomando la palabra] by your leave.

venial *adj* petty, venial.

venialidad *f* veniality, pettiness.

venida *f* **-1.** [llegada] arrival. **-2.** [regreso] return.

venidero, -ra *adj* coming, future.

venir [75] ◇ *vi* **-1.** [gen] to come; ~ **a/de hacer algo** to come to do sthg/from doing sthg; ~ **de algo** [proceder, derivarse] to come from sthg; ~ **a alguien con algo** to come to sb with sthg; **no me vengas con exigencias** don't come to me making demands; **el año que viene** next year. **-2.** [llegar] to arrive; **vino a las doce** he arrived at twelve o'clock. **-3.** [hallarse] to be; **su foto viene en primera página** his photo is ○ appears on the front page; **el texto viene en inglés** the text is in English. **-4.** [acometer, sobrevenir]: **me viene sueño** I'm getting sleepy; **le vinieron ganas de reír** he was seized by a

desire to laugh; **le vino una tremenda desgracia** he suffered a great misfortune. **-5.** [ropa, calzado]: ~ **a alguien** to fit sb; **¿qué tal te viene?** does it fit all right?; **el abrigo le viene pequeño** the coat is too small for her. **-6.** [convenir]: ~ **bien/mal a alguien** to suit/not to suit sb. **-7.** [aproximarse]: **viene a costar un millón** it costs almost a million. **-8.** *loc*: **¿a qué viene esto?** what do you mean by that?, what's that in aid of?; ~ **a menos** [negocio] to go downhill; [persona] to go down in the world; ~ **a parar en** to end in; ~ **a ser** to amount to.

◇ *vaux* **-1.** (*antes de gerundio*) [haber estado]: ~ **haciendo algo** to have been doing sthg; **las peleas vienen sucediéndose desde hace tiempo** fighting has been going on for some time. **-2.** (*antes de participio*) [estar]: **los cambios vienen motivados por la presión de la oposición** the changes have resulted from pressure on the part of the opposition.

◆ **venirse** *vpr* **-1.** [volver]: ~se (de) to come back ○ return (from). **-2.** *loc*: ~se **abajo** [techo, estante etc] to collapse; [ilusiones] to be dashed.

venoso, -sa *adj* venous.

venta *f* **-1.** [acción] sale, selling; **de** ~ **en ...** on sale at ...; **estar en** ~ to be for sale; **poner a la** ~ [casa] to put up for sale; [producto] to put on sale; ~ **por correo** ○ **por correspondencia** mail-order sale; ~ **automatizada** vending-machine sale; ~ **al contado** cash sale; ~ **a crédito** credit sale; ~ **a domicilio** door-to-door selling; ~ **a plazos** sale by instalments; ~ **pública** public auction; ~ **sobre plano** sale of customized goods. **-2.** (*gen pl*) [cantidad] sales (*pl*). **-3.** [posada] country inn.

ventaja *f* **-1.** [hecho favorable] advantage. **-2.** [en competición] lead; **dar** ~ to give a start; **llevar** ~ **a alguien** to have a lead over sb.

ventajista *adj, m y f* opportunist.

ventajoso, -sa *adj* advantageous.

ventana *f* **-1.** [gen & INFORM] window; ~ **de guillotina** sash window. **-2.** [de nariz] nostril.

ventanal *m* large window.

ventanilla *f* **-1.** [de vehículo, sobre] window. **-2.** [taquilla] counter.

ventear ◇ *v impers* to be very windy. ◇ *vi* to sniff the air.

ventilación *f* ventilation.

ventilador *m* ventilator, fan.

ventilar *vt* **-1.** [airear] to air. **-2.** [resolver] to clear up. **-3.** [discutir] to air. **-4.** [difundir] to spread, to make public.

◆ **ventilarse** *vpr* **-1.** [airearse] to air. **-2.** *fam* [terminarse] to knock ○ finish off.

ventisca *f* blizzard.

ventiscar [10], **ventisquear** *v impers* to blow a blizzard.

ventisquero *m* [nieve amontonada] snow-drift.

ventolera *f* **-1.** [viento] gust of wind. **-2.** [idea extravagante] wild idea; **se le ha dado la ~ de hacerlo** she has taken it into her head to do it.

ventosa *f* [gen & ZOOL] sucker.

ventosear *vi* to break wind.

ventosidad *f* wind, flatulence.

ventoso, -sa *adj* windy.

ventrículo *m* ventricle.

ventrílocuo, -cua *m y f* ventriloquist.

ventriloquía *f* ventriloquism.

ventura *f* **-1.** [suerte] luck; **a la (buena) ~** [al azar] at random, haphazardly; [sin nada previsto] without planning ○ a fixed plan; **echar la buena ~ a alguien** to tell sb's fortune. **-2.** [casualidad] fate, fortune.

venturoso, -sa *adj* happy, fortunate.

Venus Venus.

venza *etc* → **vencer.**

ver [76] ◇ *vi* **-1.** [gen] to see. **-2.** *loc*: **a ~** [veamos] let's see; **¿a ~?** [mirando con interés] let me see, let's have a look; **¡a ~!** [¡pues claro!] what do you expect?; [al empezar algo] right!; **dejarse ~ (por un sitio)** to show one's face (somewhere); **eso está por ~** that remains to be seen; **ni visto ni oído** in the twinkling of an eye; **ya veremos** we'll see.
◇ *vt* **-1.** [gen] to see; [mirar] to look at; [televisión, partido de fútbol] to watch; **¿ves algo?** can you see anything?; **he estado viendo tu trabajo** I've been looking at your work; **ya veo que estás de mal humor** I can see you're in a bad mood; **¿ves lo que quiero decir?** do you see what I mean?; **ir a ~ lo que pasa** to go and see what's going on; **es una manera de ~ las cosas** that's one way of looking at it; **yo no lo veo tan mal** I don't think it's that bad. **-2.** *loc*: **eso habrá que ~** to that remains to be seen; **¡hay que ~ qué lista es!** you wouldn't believe how clever she is!; **no puedo verle (ni en pintura)** *fam* I can't stand him; **si no lo veo, no lo creo** you'll never believe it; **si te vi, no me acuerdo** he/she *etc* doesn't want anything to do with me; **~ venir a alguien** to see what sb is up to.
◇ *m*: **estar de buen ~** to be good-looking.

◆ **verse** *vpr* **-1.** [mirarse, imaginarse] to see o.s.; **~se en el espejo** to see o.s. in the mirror; **ya me veo cargando el camión yo solo** I can see myself having to load the lorry on my own. **-2.** [percibirse]: **desde aquí se ve el mar** you can see the sea from here. **-3.** [encontrarse] to meet, to see each other; **hace mucho que no nos vemos** we haven't seen each other for a long time. **-4.** [darse, suceder] to be seen. **-5.** *loc*: **vérselas y deseárselas para hacer algo** to have a real struggle doing sthg.

◆ **véase** *vpr* [en textos] see.

◆ **por lo visto, por lo que se ve** *loc adv* apparently.

vera *f* **-1.** [orilla - de río, lago] bank; [- de camino] edge, side. **-2.** *fig* [lado] side; **a la ~ de** next to.

veracidad *f* truthfulness.

veranda *f* verandah.

veraneante ◇ *adj* holiday-making. ◇ *m y f* holidaymaker, (summer) vacationer *Am*.

veranear *vi*: **~ en** to spend one's summer holidays in.

veraneo *m* summer holidays (*pl*); **de ~** holiday (*antes de sust*).

veraniego, -ga *adj* summer (*antes de sust*).

verano *m* summer.

veras *fpl* truth (*U*); **de ~** [verdaderamente] really; [en serio] seriously.

veraz *adj* truthful.

verbal *adj* verbal.

verbalizar [13] *vt* to verbalize.

verbena *f* **-1.** [fiesta] street-party (*on the eve of certain saints' days*). **-2.** [planta] verbena.

verbenero, -ra *adj* street-party (*antes de sust*).

verbigracia *adv culto* for example, for instance.

verbo *m* **-1.** GRAM verb. **-2.** [lenguaje] language.

verborrea *f* verbal diarrhoea, verbosity.

verbosidad *f* verbosity.

verboso, -sa *adj* verbose.

verdad *f* **-1.** [gen] truth; **a decir ~** to tell the truth; **en ~** truly, honestly. **-2.** [principio aceptado] fact. **-3.** *loc*: **no te gusta, ¿~?** you don't like it, do you?; **está bueno, ¿~?** it's good, isn't it?; **una ~ como un puño** an undeniable fact.

◆ **verdades** *fpl* [opinión sincera] true thoughts; **cantar las ~es** *fig* to speak one's mind; **cantarle** ○ **decirle a alguien cuatro ~es** *fig* to tell sb a few home truths.

◆ **de verdad** ◇ *loc adv* **-1.** [en serio] seriously. **-2.** [realmente] really. ◇ *loc adj* [auténtico] real.

verdadero, -ra *adj* **-1.** [cierto, real] true,

real; fue un ~ **lío** it was a real mess. **-2.** [sin falsificar] real. **-3.** [enfático] real.

verde ◇ *adj* **-1.** [gen] green; ~ **oliva** olive (green); **poner** ~ **a alguien** to criticize sb. **-2.** [fruta] unripe, green. **-3.** [ecologista] Green, green. **-4.** *fig* [obsceno] blue, dirty. **-5.** *fig* [inmaduro - proyecto etc] in its early stages. ◇ *m* [color] green.
◆ **Verdes** *mpl* [partido]: **los Verdes** the Greens.
VERDE (*abrev de* **Vértice Español de Reivindicación y Desarrollo Ecológico**) *m* Spanish ecology party.
verdear *vi* **-1.** [parecer verde] to look green. **-2.** [brotar plantas] to turn ○ go green.
verdecer [30] *vi* to turn ○ go green.
verdinegro, -gra *adj* very dark green.
verdor *m* **-1.** [color] greenness. **-2.** [madurez] lushness.
verdoso, -sa *adj* greenish.
verdugo *m* **-1.** [de preso] executioner; [que ahorca] hangman. **-2.** *fig* [tirano] tyrant. **-3.** [pasamontañas] balaclava helmet.
verdulería *f* greengrocer's (shop).
verdulero, -ra *m y f* [tendero] greengrocer.
◆ **verdulera** *f fam* *fig* [ordinaria] fishwife.
verdura *f* vegetables (*pl*), greens (*pl*).
verdusco, -ca *adj despec* dirty green.
vereda *f* **-1.** [senda] path; **hacer entrar** ○ **meter a alguien en** ~ to bring sb into line. **-2.** *Amer* [acera] pavement *Br*, sidewalk *Am*.
veredicto *m* verdict.
verga *f* **-1.** ANAT penis. **-2.** NÁUT yard. **-3.** [vara] stick.
vergel *m* lush, fertile place.
vergonzante *adj* shameful.
vergonzoso, -sa ◇ *adj* **-1.** [deshonroso] shameful. **-2.** [tímido] bashful. ◇ *m y f* bashful person.
vergüenza *f* **-1.** [turbación] embarrassment; **dar** ~ to embarrass; **¡qué** ~**!** how embarrassing!; **sentir** ~ to feel embarrassed; **sentir** ~ **ajena** to feel embarrassed for sb. **-2.** [timidez] bashfulness; **perder la** ~ to lose one's inhibitions. **-3.** [remordimiento] shame; **sentir** ~ to feel ashamed. **-4.** [dignidad] pride, dignity. **-5.** [deshonra, escándalo] disgrace; **¡es una** ~**!** it's disgraceful!
◆ **vergüenzas** *fpl* [genitales] private parts.
vericueto *m* (*gen pl*) rough track.
verídico, -ca *adj* **-1.** [cierto] true, truthful. **-2.** *fig* [verosímil] true-to-life, real.
verificación *f* check, checking (*U*).
verificador, -ra ◇ *adj* [confirmador] checking; [examinador] testing, inspecting. ◇ *m y f* tester, inspector.

verificar [10] *vt* **-1.** [comprobar - verdad, autenticidad] to check, to verify. **-2.** [examinar - funcionamiento, buen estado] to check, to test. **-3.** [confirmar - fecha, cita] to confirm. **-4.** [llevar a cabo] to carry out.
◆ **verificarse** *vpr* **-1.** [tener lugar] to take place. **-2.** [resultar cierto - predicción] to come true; [comprobarse] to be verified.
verja *f* **-1.** [puerta] iron gate. **-2.** [valla] railings (*pl*). **-3.** [enrejado] grille.
vermú (*pl* **vermús**), **vermut** (*pl* **vermuts**) *m* **-1.** [bebida] vermouth. **-2.** *Amer* CIN & TEATR matinee.
vernáculo, -la *adj* vernacular.
verónica *f* **-1.** TAUROM *pass in which matador swings cape away from bull.* **-2.** [planta] veronica.
verosímil *adj* **-1.** [creíble] believable, credible. **-2.** [probable] likely, probable.
verosimilitud *f* **-1.** [credibilidad] credibility. **-2.** [probabilidad] likeliness.
verruga *f* wart.
verrugosidad *f* [lesión] area of warts.
verrugoso, -sa *adj* warty.
versado, -da *adj*: ~ (**en**) versed (in).
Versalles Versailles.
versallesco, -ca *adj fam* [cortés] gallant, chivalrous.
versar *vi*: ~ **sobre** to be about, to deal with.
versátil *adj* **-1.** [voluble] changeable, fickle. **-2.** (*considerado incorrecto*) [polifacético] versatile.
versatilidad *f* **-1.** [volubilidad] changeability, fickleness. **-2.** (*considerado incorrecto*) [adaptabilidad] versatility.
versículo *m* verse.
versificación *f* versification.
versificar [10] ◇ *vi* to write (in) verse. ◇ *vt* to put into verse.
versión *f* **-1.** [gen] version; [en música pop] cover version; ~ **original** CIN original (version). **-2.** [traducción] translation, version.
verso *m* **-1.** [género] verse; **en** ~ in verse; ~ **blanco/libre** blank/free verse. **-2.** [unidad rítmica] line (*of poetry*). **-3.** [poema] poem.
versus *prep culto* versus.
vértebra *f* vertebra.
vertebrado, -da *adj* vertebrate.
◆ **vertebrados** *mpl* ZOOL vertebrates.
vertebral *adj* vertebral.
vertedero *m* **-1.** [de basuras] rubbish tip ○ dump; [de agua] overflow. **-2.** [de pantano] drain, spillway.

verter [20] ◇ *vt* **-1.** [derramar] to spill. **-2.**
[vaciar - líquido] to pour (out); [- recipiente]
to empty. **-3.** [tirar - basura, residuos] to
dump. **-4.** [traducir]: ~ **(a)** translate (into).
-5. *fig* [decir] to tell. ◇ *vi*: ~ **a** to flow into.
◆ **verterse** *vpr* [derramarse] to spill.

vertical ◇ *adj* GEOM vertical; [derecho] upright. ◇ *m* ASTRON vertical circle. ◇ *f* GEOM
vertical.

verticalidad *f* verticality, vertical position.

vértice *m* [gen] vertex; [de cono] apex.

vertido *m* **-1.** (*gen pl*) [residuo] waste (*U*).
-2. [acción] dumping.

vertiente *f* **-1.** [pendiente] slope. **-2.** *fig* [as-
pecto] side, aspect. **-3.** *Amer* [manantial]
spring.

vertiginosidad *f* dizziness.

vertiginoso, -sa *adj* **-1.** [mareante] dizzy.
-2. *fig* [raudo] giddy.

vértigo *m* **-1.** [enfermedad] vertigo; [mareo]
dizziness; **trepar me da** ~ climbing makes
me dizzy. **-2.** *fig* [apresuramiento] mad rush,
hectic pace. **-3.** *fig* [asombro]: **dar** ~ **a alguien** to make sb's head spin; **de** ~ [veloci-
dad, altura] giddy; [cifras] mindboggling.

vesícula *f*: ~ **biliar** gall bladder.

vesicular *adj* vesicular.

vespertino, -na *adj* evening (*antes de sust*).

vestal *f* vestal (virgin).

vestíbulo *m* [de casa] (entrance) hall; [de
hotel, oficina] lobby, foyer.

vestido, -da *adj* dressed.
◆ **vestido** *m* **-1.** [indumentaria] clothes (*pl*).
-2. [prenda femenina] dress.

vestidor *m* dressing room.

vestidura *f* (*gen pl*) clothes (*pl*); RELIG vestments (*pl*); **rasgarse las** ~**s** to make a fuss.

vestigio *m* vestige; *fig* sign, trace.

vestimenta *f* clothes (*pl*), wardrobe.

vestir [26] ◇ *vt* **-1.** [gen] to dress. **-2.** [llevar
puesto] to wear. **-3.** [cubrir] to cover. **-4.** *fig*
[encubrir]: ~ **algo de** to invest sth with. ◇
vi **-1.** [ser elegante] to be dressy; **de (mucho)**
~ (very) dressy. **-2.** [llevar ropa] to dress. **-3.**
fig [estar bien visto] to be the done thing. **-4.**
loc: **el mismo que viste y calza** the very
same, none other; **vísteme despacio que
tengo prisa** *proverb* more haste, less speed
proverb.
◆ **vestirse** *vpr* **-1.** [ponerse ropa] to get
dressed, to dress. **-2.** [adquirir ropa]: ~**se en**
to buy one's clothes at. **-3.** *fig* [cubrirse]:
~**se de** to be covered in.

vestuario *m* **-1.** [vestimenta] clothes (*pl*),
wardrobe; TEATR costumes (*pl*). **-2.** [guarda-
rropa] cloakroom. **-3.** [para cambiarse]
changing room; [de actores] dressing room.

veta *f* **-1.** [filón] vein, seam. **-2.** [faja, lista]
grain.

vetar *vt* to veto.

veteado, -da *adj* grained.

vetear *vt* to grain.

veteranía *f* seniority, age.

veterano, -na ◇ *adj*, *m y f* veteran.

veterinario, -ria ◇ *adj* veterinary. ◇ *m y f*
[persona] vet, veterinary surgeon.
◆ **veterinaria** *f* [ciencia] veterinary science
○ medicine.

veto *m* veto; **poner** ~ **a algo** to veto sth.

vetusto, -ta *adj* culto ancient, very old.

vez *f* **-1.** [gen] time; **una** ~ once; **dos veces**
twice; **tres veces** three times; **¿has estado
allí alguna** ~? have you ever been there?; **a
mi/tu** *etc* ~ in my/your *etc* turn; **a la** ~
(que) at the same time (as); **cada** ~ **(que)**
every time; **cada** ~ **más** more and more;
cada ~ **menos** less and less; **cada** ~ **la veo
más feliz** she seems happier and happier;
de una ~ in one go; **de una** ~ **para siempre** ○ **por todas** once and for all; **muchas
veces** often, a lot; **otra** ~ again; **pocas veces, rara** ~ rarely, seldom; **por última** ~ for
the last time; **una** ○ **alguna que otra** ~ occasionally; **una** ~ **más** once again; **una y
otra** ~ time and again; **érase una** ~ once
upon a time. **-2.** [turno] turn. **-3.** *loc*: **hacer
las veces de** to act as.
◆ **a veces, algunas veces** *loc adv* sometimes, at times.
◆ **de vez en cuando** *loc adv* from time to
time, now and again.
◆ **en vez de** *loc prep* instead of.
◆ **tal vez** *loc adv* perhaps, maybe.
◆ **una vez que** *loc conj* once, after.

v.g., v.gr. (*abrev de* **verbigracia**) v.gr.

VHF (*abrev de* **very high frequency**) *f* VHF.

VHS (*abrev de* **video home system**) *m* VHS.

vía ◇ *f* **-1.** [medio de transporte] route; **por**
~ **aérea** [gen] by air; [correo] (by) airmail;
por ~ **marítima** by sea; **por** ~ **terrestre**
overland, by land; ~ **de comunicación**
communication route; ~ **fluvial** waterway.
-2. [calzada, calle] road; ~ **pública** public
thoroughfare. **-3.** [FERROC - raíl] rails (*pl*),
track; [- andén] platform; ~ **estrecha** narrow gauge; ~ **férrea** [ruta] railway line; ~
muerta siding. **-4.** [proceso]: **estar en** ~**s de**
to be in the process of; **país en** ~**s de desarrollo** developing country; **una especie en**
~**s de extinción** an endangered species. **-5.**
ANAT tract; **por** ~ **oral** orally. **-6.** [opción]
channel, path; **por** ~ **oficial/judicial**
through official channels/the courts. **-7.**
[camino] way; **dar** ~ **libre** [dejar paso] to give

way; [dar libertad de acción] to give a free rein. **-8.** DER procedure.
◇ *prep* via.
◆ **Vía Láctea** *f* Milky Way.

viabilidad *f* viability.

viable *adj fig* [posible] viable.

viacrucis *m inv* RELIG Stations (*pl*) of the Cross, Way of the Cross.

viaducto *m* viaduct.

viajante *m y f* travelling salesperson.

viajar *vi* **-1.** [trasladarse, irse]: ~ **(en)** to travel (by). **-2.** [circular] to run.

viaje *m* **-1.** [gen] journey, trip; [en barco] voyage; ¡buen ~! have a good journey ○ trip !; **estar de** ~ to be away (on a trip); **hay 11 días de** ~ it's an 11-day journey; ~ **de ida/de vuelta** outward/return journey; ~ **de ida y vuelta** return journey ○ trip; ~ **de novios** honeymoon; ~ **relámpago** lightning trip ○ visit. **-2.** *fig* [recorrido] trip; **di varios** ~**s para trasladar los muebles** it took me a good few trips to move all the furniture. **-3.** *fam fig* [alucinación] trip. **-4.** *fam fig* [golpe] bang, bump.
◆ **viajes** *mpl* [singladuras] travels.

viajero, -ra ◇ *adj* [persona] travelling; [ave] migratory. ◇ *m y f* [gen] traveller; [en transporte público] passenger.

vial ◇ *adj* road (*antes de sust*). ◇ *m* FARM phial.

vianda *f* food (*U*).

viandante *m y f* **-1.** [peatón] pedestrian. **-2.** [transeúnte] passer-by.

viaraza *f Amer* **-1.** [enfado] fit of anger. **-2.** [ocurrencia] absurd idea.

viario, -ria *adj* road (*antes de sust*).

VIASA (*abrev de* **Venezolana Internacional de Aviación, SA**) *f Venezuelan state airline.*

viático *m* **-1.** [dieta] expenses allowance. **-2.** RELIG last rites (*pl*), viaticum.

víbora *f* viper.

vibración *f* vibration.

vibrador, -ra *adj* vibrating.
◆ **vibrador** *m* vibrator.

vibráfono *m* vibraphone.

vibrante ◇ *adj* **-1.** [oscilante] vibrating. **-2.** *fig* [emocionante] vibrant. ◇ *f* LING rolled, trilled.

vibrar *vi* **-1.** [oscilar] to vibrate. **-2.** *fig* [voz, rodillas etc] to shake. **-3.** *fig* [público] to get excited.

vibrátil *adj* vibratile.

vibratorio, -ria *adj* vibratory.

vicaría *f* **-1.** [cargo] vicarship, vicariate. **-2.** [residencia] vicarage.

vicario *m* vicar.

vicealmirante *m* vice-admiral.

vicecónsul *m* vice-consul.

vicepresidencia *f* [de país, asociación] vice-presidency; [de comité, empresa] vice-chairmanship.

vicepresidente, -ta *m y f* [de país, asociación] vice-president; [de comité, empresa] vice-chairman.

vicerrector, -ra *m y f* ≈ vice-rector.

vicesecretario, -ria *m y f* assistant secretary.

viceversa *adv* vice versa.

vichy [bi'tʃi] (*pl* vichys) *m* gingham.

vichysoisse [bitʃi'swas] (*pl* vichysoisses) *f* CULIN vichysoisse.

viciado, -da *adj* [maloliente] foul; [contaminado] polluted.

viciar [8] *vt* **-1.** [pervertir] to corrupt. **-2.** [contaminar] to pollute. **-3.** [adulterar] to adulterate. **-4.** *fig* [falsear] to falsify; [tergiversar] to distort, to twist.
◆ **viciarse** *vpr* **-1.** [pervertirse] to become ○ get corrupted; [enviciarse] to take to vice. **-2.** [contaminarse] to become polluted. **-3.** [deformarse] to warp.

vicio *m* **-1.** [mala costumbre] bad habit, vice; **llorar** ○ **quejarse de** ~ to complain for no (good) reason. **-2.** [libertinaje] vice. **-3.** [defecto físico, de dicción etc] defect. **-4.** *fam fig* [mimo] over-indulgence. **-5.** *loc*: **de** ~ *fam* [fenomenal] brilliant.

vicioso, -sa ◇ *adj* **-1.** [depravado] depraved. **-2.** [defectuoso] defective. ◇ *m y f* [depravado] depraved person.

vicisitud *f* [inestabilidad] instability, changeability.
◆ **vicisitudes** *fpl* [avatares] vicissitudes, ups and downs.

víctima *f* victim; [en accidente, guerra] casualty; **ser** ~ **de** to be the victim of; ~ **propiciatoria** scapegoat.

victoria *f* victory; **adjudicarse la** ~ to win a victory; **cantar** ~ to claim victory.
◆ **Victoria** *m*: **el lago** ~ Lake Victoria.

victoriano, -na *adj* Victorian.

victorioso, -sa *adj* victorious.

vicuña *f* vicuña.

vid *f* vine.

vid., v. (*abrev de* **véase**) v., vid.

vida *f* life; **amargarse la** ~ to make one's life a misery; **buscarse la** ~ to try to earn one's own living; **dar la** ~ **por** *fig* to give one's life for; **de toda la** ~ [amigo etc] lifelong; **le conozco de toda la** ~ I've known him all my life; **de por** ~ for life; **en** ~ **de** during the life ○ lifetime of; **en mi/tu** *etc* ~ never (in my/your *etc* life); **estar con** ~ to be alive; **estar entre la ~ y la muerte** to be at death's door; **ganarse la ~** to earn a living; **pasar a mejor ~** to pass away; **perder la ~** to lose one's life; **quitar la ~ a alguien** to kill sb; **~ privada/sentimental** private/love life; **~ eterna** eternal life; **la otra ~** the next life; **¡así es la ~!** that's life!, such is life!; **darse** ○ **pegarse la gran ~, darse** ○ **pegarse la ~ padre** to live the life of Riley; **enterrarse en ~** to forsake the world; **la ~ y milagros de alguien** sb's life story; **llevar una ~ de perros** to lead a dog's life; **¡mi ~!, ¡~ mía!** my darling!; **¿qué es de tu ~?** how's life?; **tener la ~ pendiente de un hilo** to have one's life hanging by a thread; **tener siete ~s como los gatos** to have nine lives.

vidente m y f clairvoyant.

vídeo, video ◇ m -1. [gen] video; **grabar en ~** to videotape, to record on video; **~ comunitario** system enabling one video to be shown simultaneously on different television sets in one block of flats; **~ doméstico** home video. -2. [aparato filmador] camcorder. ◇ adj inv video (antes de sust).

videocámara f camcorder.

videocasete m video, videocassette.

videocinta f video, videotape.

videoclip m (pop) video.

videoclub (pl **videoclubes**) m video club.

videodisco m videodisc.

videoedición f video editing.

videojuego m video game.

videoteca f video library.

videoteléfono m videophone.

videoterminal m video terminal.

videotexto m, **videotex** m inv [por señal de televisión] teletext; [por línea telefónica] videotext, viewdata.

vidorra f fam: **pegarse una gran ~** to live the life of Riley.

vidriado, -da adj glazed.
◆ **vidriado** m -1. [técnica] glazing. -2. [material] glaze.

vidriero, -ra m y f -1. [que fabrica cristales] glass merchant ○ manufacturer. -2. [que coloca cristales] glazier.
◆ **vidriera** f [puerta] glass door; [ventana] glass window; [en catedrales] stained glass window.

vidrio m -1. [material] glass. -2. [cristal] window (pane); **pagar los ~s rotos** to carry the can.

vidrioso, -sa adj -1. [quebradizo] brittle. -2. fig [tema, asunto] thorny, delicate. -3. fig [ojos] glazed.

vieira f scallop.

viejo, -ja ◇ adj old; **hacerse ~** to get ○ grow old. ◇ m y f -1. [anciano] old man (old lady); **los ~s** the elderly; **~ verde** dirty old man (f dirty old woman). -2. fam [padres] old man (f old girl); **mis ~s** my folks. -3. Amer fam [amigo] pal, mate.
◆ **Viejo de Pascua** m Amer Father Christmas.

Viena Vienna.

viene → venir.

vienés, -esa adj, m y f Viennese.

viento m -1. [aire] wind; (~) **alisio** trade wind; **~ de costado** ○ **de lado** crosswind. -2. [cuerda] guy (rope). -3. NÁUT [rumbo] course, bearing. -4. loc: **a los cuatro ~s** from the rooftops; **contra ~ y marea** in spite of everything; **despedir** ○ **echar a alguien con ~ fresco** to send sb packing; **mis esperanzas se las llevó el ~** my hopes flew out of the window; **~ en popa** splendidly, very nicely.

vientre m -1. ANAT stomach; **hacer de ~** to have a bowel movement; **bajo ~** lower stomach. -2. [de vasija etc] belly, rounded part.

viera → ver.

viernes m inv Friday; ver también **sábado**.
◆ **Viernes Santo** m RELIG Good Friday.

vierta etc → verter.

viese → ver.

Vietnam Vietnam.

vietnamita adj, m y f Vietnamese.

viga f [de madera] beam, rafter; [de metal] girder; **~ maestra** main beam.

vigencia f [de ley etc] validity; [de costumbre] use; **estar/entrar en ~** to be in/come into force.

vigente adj [ley etc] in force; [costumbre] in use.

vigésimo, -ma núm twentieth.

vigía ◇ f -1. [atalaya] watch tower. -2. [vigilancia] watch. ◇ m y f lookout.

vigilancia f -1. [cuidado] vigilance, care. -2. [vigilantes] guards (pl).

vigilante ◇ adj vigilant. ◇ m y f guard; **~ nocturno** night watchman.

vigilar ◇ vt [enfermo] to watch over; [presos, banco] to guard; [niños, bolso] to keep an eye on; [proceso] to oversee. ◇ vi to keep watch.

vigilia f -1. [vela] wakefulness; **estar de ~** to be awake. -2. [insomnio] sleeplessness. -3. [víspera] vigil.

vigor m -1. [gen] vigour. -2. [vigencia]: **en ~** in force; **entrar en ~** to come into force, to take effect.

vigorizador, -ra, vigorizante adj [medicamento] fortifying; [actividad] invigorating.

vigorizar [13] vt **-1.** [fortalecer] to fortify. **-2.** fig [animar] to animate, to encourage.

vigoroso, -sa adj [gen] vigorous; [colorido] strong.

vikingo, -ga adj, m y f Viking.

vil adj vile, despicable; [metal] base.

vileza f **-1.** [acción] vile O despicable act. **-2.** [cualidad] vileness.

vilipendiar [8] vt desus **-1.** [despreciar] to despise; [humillar] to humiliate. **-2.** [ofender] to vilify, to revile.

vilipendio m desus **-1.** [desprecio] scorn, contempt; [humillación] humiliation. **-2.** [ofensa] vilification.

vilipendioso, -sa adj desus **-1.** [despreciativo] scornful, contemptuous; [humillante] humiliating. **-2.** [ofensivo] vilifying.

villa f **-1.** [población] small town. **-2.** [casa] villa, country house.

villadiego m: **coger** O **tomar las de** ~ fig to take to one's heels.

villancico m [navideño] Christmas carol.

villanía f vile O despicable act, villainy (U).

villano, -na ◇ adj villainous. ◇ m y f villain.

villorrio m despec dump, hole.

Vilna Vilnius.

vilo
◆ **en vilo** loc adv **-1.** [suspendido] in the air, suspended. **-2.** [inquieto] on tenterhooks; **tener a alguien en** ~ to keep sb in suspense.

vinagre m vinegar.

vinagrera f [vasija] vinegar bottle.
◆ **vinagreras** fpl CULIN [convoy] cruet (sg).

vinagreta f vinaigrette, French dressing.

vinatero, -ra ◇ adj wine (antes de sust). ◇ m y f vintner, wine merchant.

vinculación f link, linking (U).

vinculante adj DER binding.

vincular vt **-1.** [enlazar] to link; [por obligación] to tie, to bind. **-2.** DER to entail.
◆ **vincularse** vpr [enlazarse] to be linked.

vínculo m **-1.** [lazo - entre hechos, países] link; [- personal, familiar] tie, bond. **-2.** DER entail.

vindicación f **-1.** [venganza] vengeance, revenge. **-2.** [defensa] vindication.

vindicar [10] vt **-1.** [vengar] to avenge, to revenge. **-2.** [defender] to vindicate. **-3.** [reivindicar] to claim.

vindicativo, -va adj [reivindicativo]: ~ **(de)** in defence (of).

vinícola adj [país, región] wine-producing (antes de sust); [industria] wine (antes de sust).

vinicultor, -ra m y f wine producer.

vinicultura f wine producing.

viniera etc → venir.

vinilo m vinyl.

vino ◇ v → venir. ◇ m wine; ~ **blanco/tinto** white/red wine; ~ **dulce/seco** sweet/dry wine; ~ **espumoso/generoso** sparkling/full-bodied wine; ~ **clarete** light red wine; ~ **de mesa** table wine; ~ **peleón** plonk, cheap wine; ~ **rosado** rosé.

viña f vineyard.

viñedo m (large) vineyard.

viñeta f **-1.** [de tebeo] (individual) cartoon. **-2.** [de libro] vignette.

vio → ver.

viola ◇ f viola. ◇ m y f viola player.

violáceo, -a adj violet.
◆ **violáceo** m violet.

violación f **-1.** [de ley, derechos] violation, infringement. **-2.** [de persona] rape. **-3.** ~ **de domicilio** unlawful entry.

violador, -ra adj, m y f rapist.

violar vt **-1.** [ley, derechos, domicilio] to violate, to infringe. **-2.** [persona] to rape.

violencia f **-1.** [agresividad] violence. **-2.** [fuerza - de viento, pasiones] force. **-3.** [incomodidad] embarrassment, awkwardness.

violentar vt **-1.** [incomodar] to embarrass, to cause to feel awkward. **-2.** [forzar - cerradura] to force; [- domicilio] to break into.
◆ **violentarse** vpr [incomodarse] to get embarrassed, to feel awkward.

violentismo m Amer subversiveness.

violentista adj Amer subversive.

violento, -ta adj **-1.** [gen] violent; [goce] intense. **-2.** [incómodo] awkward.

violeta ◇ f [flor] violet. ◇ adj inv & m [color] violet.

violetera f violet seller.

violín ◇ m violin. ◇ m y f violinist.

violinista m y f violinist.

violón ◇ m double bass. ◇ m y f double bass player.

violonchelista, violoncelista m y f cellist.

violonchelo, violoncelo ◇ m cello. ◇ m y f cellist.

VIP (abrev de **very important person**) m y f VIP.

viperino, -na adj fig venomous.

viraje m **-1.** [giro - AUTOM] turn; NÁUT tack. **-2.** [curva] bend, curve. **-3.** FOT toning. **-4.** fig [cambio] change of direction.

virar ◇ *vt* **-1.** [girar] to turn (round); NÁUT to tack, to put about. **-2.** FOT to tone. ◇ *vi* [girar] to turn (round).

virgen ◇ *adj* [gen] virgin; [cinta] blank; [película] unused. ◇ *m y f* persona] virgin. ◇ *f* ARTE Madonna.

◆ **Virgen** *f*: **la Virgen** RELIG the (Blessed) Virgin.

virginal *adj* **-1.** [puro] virginal. **-2.** RELIG Virgin (*antes de sust*).

virginidad *f* virginity.

virgo *m* [virginidad] virginity.

◆ **Virgo** ◇ *m* [zodiaco] Virgo; **ser Virgo** to be (a) Virgo. ◇ *m y f* [persona] Virgo.

virguería *f fam* gem; **hacer ~s** to do wonders.

vírico, -ca *adj* viral.

viril *adj* virile, manly.

virilidad *f* virility.

virola *f* ferrule.

virolento, -ta *adj* pockmarked.

virreina *f* vicereine.

virreinato, virreino *m* viceroyalty.

virrey *m* viceroy.

virtual *adj* **-1.** [posible] possible, potential. **-2.** [casi real] virtual.

virtualidad *f* potential.

virtud *f* **-1.** [cualidad] virtue; **~ cardinal/ teologal** cardinal/theological virtue. **-2.** [poder] power; **tener la ~ de** to have the power ○ ability to.

◆ **en virtud de** *loc prep* by virtue of.

virtuosismo *m* virtuosity.

virtuoso, -sa ◇ *adj* [honrado] virtuous. ◇ *m y f* [genio] virtuoso.

viruela *f* **-1.** [enfermedad] smallpox. **-2.** [pústula] pockmark; **picado de ~s** pockmarked.

virulé

◆ **a la virulé** *loc adj* **-1.** [torcido] crooked. **-2.** [hinchado]: **un ojo a la ~** a black eye.

virulencia *f* MED & *fig* virulence.

virulento, -ta *adj* MED & *fig* virulent.

virus *m inv* [gen & INFORM] virus.

viruta *f* shaving.

vis

◆ **vis a vis** *loc adv* face-to-face.

◆ **vis cómica** *f* sense of humour.

visado *m* visa.

visar *vt* to endorse.

víscera *f* internal organ; **~s** entrails.

visceral *adj* ANAT & *fig* visceral; **un sentimiento/una reacción ~** a gut feeling/ reaction.

viscosidad *f* **-1.** [cualidad] viscosity. **-2.** [substancia] slime.

viscoso, -sa *adj gen* viscous; [baboso] slimy.

◆ **viscosa** *f* [tejido] viscose.

visera *f* **-1.** [de gorra] peak. **-2.** [de casco, suelta] visor. **-3.** [de automóvil] sun visor.

visibilidad *f* visibility.

visible *adj* visible; **estar ~** [presentable] to be decent ○ presentable.

visigodo, -da ◇ *adj* Visigothic. ◇ *m y f* Visigoth.

visillo *m* (*gen pl*) net/lace curtain.

visión *f* **-1.** [sentido, lo que se ve] sight. **-2.** [alucinación, lucidez] vision; **ver visiones** to be seeing things. **-3.** [punto de vista] (point of) view.

visionar *vt* to view privately.

visionario, -ria *adj, m y f* visionary.

visir (*pl* **visires**) *m* vizier.

visita *f* **-1.** [gen] visit; [breve] call; **hacer una ~ a alguien** to visit sb, to pay sb a visit; **ir de ~** to go visiting; **pasar ~** MED to see one's patients; **~s médicas** doctor's rounds (*pl*); **~ de cumplido** courtesy visit ○ call; **~ relámpago** flying visit. **-2.** [visitante] visitor; **tener ~** ○ **~s** to have visitors.

visitador, -ra ◇ *adj* fond of visiting. ◇ *m y f* **-1.** [visitante] visitor. **-2.** [de laboratorio] medical sales representative.

visitante ◇ *adj* DEP visiting, away. ◇ *m y f* visitor.

visitar *vt* [gen] to visit; [suj: médico] to call on.

vislumbrar *vt* **-1.** [entrever] to make out, to discern. **-2.** [adivinar] to have an inkling of.

◆ **vislumbrarse** *vpr* **-1.** [entreverse] to be barely visible. **-2.** [adivinarse] to become a little clearer.

vislumbre *m o f lit* & *fig* glimmer.

viso *m* **-1.** [aspecto]: **tener ~s de** to seem; **tiene ~s de verdad** it seems pretty true; **tiene ~s de hacerse realidad** it could become a reality. **-2.** [reflejo - de tejido] sheen; [- de metal] glint. **-3.** [de prenda] lining.

visón *m* mink.

visor *m* **-1.** FOT viewfinder. **-2.** [de arma] sight. **-3.** [en fichero] file tab.

víspera *f* **-1.** [día antes] day before, eve; **en ~s de** on the eve of. **-2.** (*gen pl*) RELIG evensong (*U*), vespers (*U*).

vista → **visto**.

vistazo *m* glance, quick look; **echar** ○ **dar un ~ a** to have a quick look at.

viste → **ver**.

vistiera *etc* → **vestir**.

visto, -ta ◇ *pp* → **ver**. ◇ *adj*: **estar muy ~** to be old-fashioned; **estar bien/mal ~** to be considered good/frowned upon; **es lo**

no ○ nunca ~ you've never seen anything like it; fue ~ y no ~ it happened just like that, it was over in a flash.

◆ **vista** ◇ *v* → **vestir.**

◇ *f* **-1.** [sentido] sight, eyesight; [ojos] eyes (*pl*); **perder la vista** to lose one's sight, to go blind; **corto de vista** short-sighted; **vista cansada** eyestrain. **-2.** [observación] watching. **-3.** [mirada] gaze; **fijar la vista en** to fix one's eyes on, to stare at; **a la vista de** in full view of; **a primera** ○ **simple vista** [aparentemente] at first sight, on the face of it; **estar a la vista** [visible] to be visible; [muy cerca] to be staring one in the face. **-4.** [panorama] view. **-5.** DER hearing. **-6.** *loc*: **a vista de pájaro** from a bird's eye view; **conocer a alguien de vista** to know sb by sight; **hacer la vista gorda** to turn a blind eye; **¡hasta la vista!** see you!; **no perder de vista a alguien/algo** [vigilar] not to let sb/sthg out of one's sight; [tener en cuenta] not to lose sight of sb/sthg, not to forget about sb/sthg; **perder de vista** [dejar de ver] to lose sight of; [perder contacto] to lose touch with; **saltar a la vista** to be blindingly obvious; **tener vista** to have vision ○ foresight; **volver la vista atrás** to look back.

◆ **vistas** *fpl* [panorama] view (*sg*); **con vistas al mar** with a sea view.

◆ **visto bueno** *m*: **el ~ bueno** the go-ahead; **dar el ~ bueno (a algo)** to give the go-ahead (to sthg); "~ **bueno**" "approved".

◆ **a la vista** *loc adv* BANCA at sight.

◆ **con vistas a** *loc prep* with a view to.

◆ **en vista de** *loc prep* in view of, considering.

◆ **en vista de que** *loc conj* since, seeing as.

◆ **por lo visto** *loc adv* apparently.

◆ **visto que** *loc conj* seeing ○ given that.

vistoso, -sa *adj* eye-catching.

Vístula *m*: **el ~** the Vistula.

visual ◇ *adj* visual. ◇ *f* line of sight.

visualización *f* **-1.** [gen] visualization. **-2.** INFORM display.

visualizar [13] *vt* **-1.** [gen] to visualize. **-2.** INFORM to display.

vital *adj* [gen] vital; [ciclo] life (*antes de sust*); [persona] full of life, vivacious.

vitalicio, -cia *adj* for life, life (*antes de sust*).

◆ **vitalicio** *m* **-1.** [pensión] life annuity. **-2.** [seguro] life insurance policy.

vitalidad *f* vitality.

vitalizar [13] *vt* to vitalize.

vitamina *f* vitamin.

vitaminado, -da *adj* with added vitamins, vitamin-enriched.

vitamínico, -ca *adj* vitamin (*antes de sust*).

viticultor, -ra *m y f* wine grower, viticulturist.

viticultura *f* wine growing, viticulture.

vítor *m* (*gen pl*) *desus* cheer.

vitorear *vt* to cheer.

Vitoria GEOGR Vitoria.

vitoriano, -no *adj* of/relating to Vitoria.

vitral *m* stained-glass window.

vítreo, -a *adj* vitreous.

vitrificar [10] *vt* to vitrify.

vitrina *f* [en casa] display cabinet; [en tienda] showcase, glass case.

vitriolo *m* vitriol.

vitro

◆ **in vitro** *loc adv* in vitro.

vituallas *fpl* provisions.

vituperar *vt* to criticize harshly, to condemn.

vituperio *m* harsh criticism, condemnation.

viudedad *f* **-1.** [viudez - de mujer] widowhood; [- de hombre] widowerhood. **-2.** **(pensión de) ~** widow's/widower's pension.

viudo, -da ◇ *adj* widowed. ◇ *m y f* widower (*f* widow).

viva ◇ *m* cheer. ◇ *interj*: **¡~!** hurrah!; **¡~ el rey!** long live the King!

vivac = **vivaque.**

vivacidad *f* liveliness.

vivalavirgen *m y f inv* happy-go-lucky person.

vivales *m y f inv* crafty person.

vivamente *adv* **-1.** [relatar, describir] vividly. **-2.** [afectar, emocionar] deeply.

vivaque, vivac *m* bivouac.

vivaracho, -cha *adj* lively, vivacious.

vivaz *adj* **-1.** [despierto] alert, sharp. **-2.** BOT perennial.

vivencia *f* (*gen pl*) experience.

víveres *mpl* provisions, supplies.

vivero *m* **-1.** [de plantas] nursery. **-2.** [de peces] fish farm; [de moluscos] bed.

viveza *f* **-1.** [de colorido, descripción] vividness. **-2.** [de persona, discusión, ojos] liveliness; [de ingenio, inteligencia] sharpness.

vívido, -da *adj* real-life, true.

vívido, -da *adj* vivid.

vividor, -ra *m y f despec* parasite, scrounger.

vivienda *f* **-1.** [alojamiento] housing. **-2.** [morada] dwelling; **~ de protección oficial**

≈ council house; ~ **de renta limitada** ≈ council house with fixed maximum rent ○ price.

viviente *adj* living.

vivificante *adj* [que da vida] life-giving; [que reanima] revitalizing.

vivificar [10] *vt* [dar vida] to give life to; [reanimar] to revitalize.

vivíparo, -ra *adj* viviparous.

vivir ◇ *vt* [experimentar] to experience, to live through. ◇ *vi* [gen] to live; [estar vivo] to be alive; ~ **de** to live on ○ off; ~ **para algo/alguien** to live for sthg/sb; ~ **bien** [económicamente] to be well-off; [en armonía] to be happy; **no dejar ~ a alguien** not to give sb any peace; **¿quién vive?** who goes there?; ~ **para ver** who'd have thought it?

vivisección *f* vivisection.

vivito *adj*: ~ **y coleando** *fam* alive and kicking.

vivo, -va *adj* **-1.** [existente - ser, lengua etc] living; **estar ~** [persona, costumbre, recuerdo] to be alive. **-2.** [dolor, deseo, olor] intense; [luz, color, tono] bright. **-3.** [gestos, ojos, descripción] lively, vivid. **-4.** [activo - ingenio, niño] quick, sharp; [- ciudad] lively. **-5.** [pronunciado - ángulo etc] sharp. **-6.** [genio] quick, hot.
◆ **vivos** *mpl*: **los ~s** the living.
◆ **en vivo** *loc adv* **-1.** [en directo] live. **-2.** [sin anestesia] without anaesthetic.

vizcaíno, -na *adj*, *m y f* Biscayan; **a la vizcaína** CULIN → **bacalao**.

Vizcaya Vizcaya, **Golfo de ~** Bay of Biscay.

vizconde, -desa *m y f* viscount (*f* viscountess).

VM (*abrev de* **Vuestra Majestad**) Your Majesty.

VO *f abrev de* **versión original**.

vocablo *m* word, term.

vocabulario *m* **-1.** [riqueza léxica] vocabulary. **-2.** [diccionario] dictionary.

vocación *f* vocation, calling.

vocacional *adj* vocational.

vocal ◇ *adj* vocal. ◇ *m y f* member. ◇ *f* vowel.

vocalista *m y f* vocalist.

vocalización *f* vocalization.

vocalizar [13] *vi* to vocalize.

vocativo *m* vocative.

vocear ◇ *vt* **-1.** [gritar] to shout ○ call out. **-2.** [llamar] to shout ○ call to. **-3.** [vitorear] to cheer. **-4.** [pregonar - mercancía] to hawk; [- secreto] to publicize. ◇ *vi* [gritar] to shout.

vocerío *m* shouting.

vociferante *adj* shouting.

vociferar *vi* to shout.

vodevil, vaudeville [boðe'ßil] *m* vaudeville.

vodka ['boθka] *m o f* vodka.

vol. (*abrev de* **volumen**) vol.

volado, -da *adj fam* [ido]: **estar ~** to be away with the fairies.

volador, -ra *adj* flying.
◆ **volador** *m* **-1.** [pez] flying fish. **-2.** [cohete] rocket.

voladura *f* [en guerras, atentados] blowing-up; [de edificio en ruinas] demolition (*with explosives*); MIN blasting.

volandas
◆ **en volandas** *loc. adv* in the air, off the ground.

volante ◇ *adj* flying. ◇ *m* **-1.** [para conducir] (steering) wheel; **estar** ○ **ir al ~** to be at the wheel. **-2.** [automovilismo] motor racing. **-3.** [de tela] frill, flounce. **-4.** [del médico] (referral) note. **-5.** [en bádminton] shuttlecock.

volantín *m Amer* kite.

volapié *m* TAUROM *method of killing the bull*.

volar [23] ◇ *vt* [en guerras, atentados] to blow up; [caja fuerte, puerta] to blow open; [edificio en ruinas] to demolish (*with explosives*); MIN to blast.
◇ *vi* **-1.** [gen] to fly; [papeles etc] to blow away; ~ **a** [una altura] to fly at; [un lugar] to fly to; **echar(se) a ~** to fly away ○ off. **-2.** *fam* [desaparecer] to disappear, to vanish. **-3.** *fig* [correr] to fly (off), to rush (off); **hacer algo volando** to do sthg at top speed; **me voy volando** I must fly ○ dash. **-4.** *fig* [días, años] to fly by.
◆ **volarse** *vpr* [papeles etc] to be blown away.

volatería *f* birds (*pl*), fowl.

volátil *adj* QUÍM & *fig* volatile.

volatilización *f* volatilization.

volatilizar [13] *vt* to volatilize.
◆ **volatilizarse** *vpr* **-1.** FÍS to volatilize, to evaporate. **-2.** *fam fig* [persona] to vanish into thin air.

volatinero, -ra *m y f* acrobat.

vol-au-vent = **volován**.

volcado *m* INFORM: ~ **de pantalla** screen dump; ~ **de pantalla en impresora** hard copy.

volcán *m* volcano.

volcánico, -ca *adj* volcanic.

volcar [36] ◇ *vt* **-1.** [tirar] to knock over; [- carretilla] to tip up. **-2.** [vaciar] to empty out. ◇ *vi* [coche, camión] to overturn; [barco] to capsize.

◆ **volcarse** *vpr* **-1.** [esforzarse]: ~**se (con/ en)** to bend over backwards (for/in). **-2.** [caerse] to fall over.

volea *f* volley.

voleibol *m* volleyball.

voleo *m* volley; **a** ○ **al** ~ [arbitrariamente] randomly, any old how.

Volga *m*: **el** ~ the (River) Volga.

volitivo, -va *adj* voluntary.

volován (*pl* **volovanes**), **vol-au-vent** [bolo'ßan] (*pl* **vol-au-vents**) *m* vol-au-vent.

volqué *etc* → **volcar**.

volquete *m* dumper truck, dump truck *Am*.

Volta *m*: **el (río)** ~ the (River) Volta.

voltaico, -ca *adj* voltaic.

voltaje *m* voltage.

volteador, -ra *m y f* acrobat.

voltear *vt* **-1.** [heno, crepe, torero] to toss; [tortilla - con plato] to turn over; [mesa, silla] to turn upside-down. **-2.** *Amer* [derribar] to knock over.

◆ **voltearse** *vpr Amer* **-1.** [volverse] to turn around. **-2.** [volcarse] to overturn.

voltereta *f* [en el suelo] handspring; [en el aire] somersault; **dar una** ~ to do a somersault; ~ **lateral** cartwheel.

voltímetro *m* voltmeter.

voltio *m* volt.

volubilidad *f* changeability, fickleness.

voluble *adj* changeable, fickle.

volumen *m* **-1.** [gen & COM] volume; **subir/bajar el** ~ [de aparato] to turn up/ down the volume; **sube el** ~ **que no te oímos** speak up, please, we can't hear you; ~ **de contratación** ECON trading volume; ~ **de negocio** ○ **ventas** turnover. **-2.** [espacio ocupado] size, bulk.

voluminoso, -sa *adj* bulky.

voluntad *f* **-1.** [determinación] will, willpower; ~ **de hierro** iron will. **-2.** [intención] intention; **buena** ~ goodwill; **mala** ~ ill will. **-3.** [deseo] wishes (*pl*); **contra la** ~ **de alguien** against sb's will. **-4.** [albedrío] free will; **a** ~ [cuanto se quiere] as much as one likes; **por** ~ **propia** of one's own free will. **-5.** [cantidad]: **¿qué le debo? - la** ~ what do I owe you? - whatever you think fit.

voluntariado *m* voluntary enlistment.

voluntariedad *f* **-1.** [intencionalidad] volition. **-2.** [no obligatoriedad] voluntary nature.

voluntario, -ria ◇ *adj* voluntary. ◇ *m y f* volunteer.

voluntarioso, -sa *adj* [esforzado] willing.

voluptuosidad *f* voluptuousness.

voluptuoso, -sa *adj* voluptuous.

voluta *f* spiral.

volver [24] ◇ *vt* **-1.** [dar la vuelta a] to turn round; [lo de arriba abajo] to turn over. **-2.** [poner del revés - boca abajo] to turn upside down; [- lo de dentro fuera] to turn inside out; [- lo de detrás delante] to turn back to front. **-3.** [cabeza, ojos etc] to turn. **-4.** [convertir en]: **eso le volvió un delincuente** that made him a criminal, that turned him into a criminal.

◇ *vi* [ir de vuelta] to go back, to return; [venir de vuelta] to come back, to return; **yo allí no vuelvo** I'm not going back there; **vuelve, no te vayas** come back, don't go; ~ **en sí** to come to, to regain consciousness.

◆ **volver a** *vi* [reanudar] to return to; ~ **a hacer algo** [hacer otra vez] to do sthg again.

◆ **volverse** *vpr* **-1.** [darse la vuelta, girar la cabeza] to turn round. **-2.** [ir de vuelta] to go back, to return; [venir de vuelta] to come back, to return. **-3.** [convertirse en] to become; ~**se loco/pálido** to go mad/pale. **-4.** *loc*: ~**se atrás** [de una afirmación, promesa] to go back on one's word; [de una decisión] to change one's mind, to back out; ~**se (en) contra (de) alguien** to turn against sb.

vomitar ◇ *vt* **-1.** to vomit, to bring up. **-2.** *fig* [expresar] to come out with. ◇ *vi* to vomit, to be sick.

vomitera *f* acute vomiting (*U*).

vomitivo, -va *adj* **-1.** MED emetic. **-2.** *fig* [asqueroso] sickening, repulsive.

◆ **vomitivo** *m* emetic.

vómito *m* **-1.** [acción] vomiting. **-2.** [substancia] vomit (*U*).

voracidad *f* voraciousness.

vorágine *f fig* confusion, whirl.

voraz *adj* **-1.** [persona, apetito] voracious. **-2.** *fig* [fuego, enfermedad] raging.

vórtice *m* **-1.** [de agua] whirlpool, vortex. **-2.** [de aire] whirlwind.

vos *pron pers* [tú] you.

VOSE (*abrev de* **versión original subtitulada en español**) *f* CIN *original language version subtitled in Spanish*.

vosotros, -tras *pron pers* you (*pl*).

votación *f* vote, voting (*U*); **decidir algo por** ~ to put sthg to the vote; ~ **a mano alzada** show of hands.

votante *m y f* voter.

votar ◇ *vt* **-1.** [partido, candidato] to vote for; [ley] to vote on. **-2.** [aprobar] to pass, to approve (*by vote*). ◇ *vi* to vote; ~ **por** [emitir un voto por] to vote for; *fig* [estar a favor de] to be in favour of; ~ **por que ...** to vote (that) ...; ~ **en blanco** to return a blank ballot paper.

voto *m* **-1.** [gen] vote; ~ **de confianza/ censura** vote of confidence/no confidence; ~ **por correspondencia** O **correo** postal vote; ~ **de calidad** casting vote; ~ **de castigo** vote against one's own party; ~ **secreto** secret ballot. **-2.** RELIG vow; **hacer** ~ **de** to vow to; ~ **de castidad/pobreza/silencio** vow of chastity/poverty/silence. **-3.** [ruego] prayer, plea; **hacer** ~**s por** to pray for; ~**s de felicidad** best wishes.

voy → **ir.**

voyeur [bwa'jer] (*pl* **voyeurs**) ◇ *adj* voyeuristic. ◇ *m y f* voyeur.

voyeurismo [bwaje'rismo] *m* voyeurism.

vóytelas *interj Amer fam* good grief!

voz *f* **-1.** [gen & GRAM] voice; **a media** ~ in a low voice, under one's breath; **a** ~ **en cuello** O **grito** at the top of one's voice; **aclarar** O **aclararse la** ~ to clear one's throat; **alzar** O **levantar la** ~ **a alguien** to raise one's voice to sb; **en** ~ **alta** aloud; **en** ~ **baja** softly, in a low voice; **mudó la** ~ his voice broke; **tener la** ~ **tomada** to be hoarse; ~ **activa/pasiva** GRAM active/passive voice; **la** ~ **de la conciencia** the voice of conscience; ~ **en off** CIN voice-over; TEATR voice offstage. **-2.** [grito] shout; **a voces** shouting; **dar voces** to shout. **-3.** [vocablo] word; **dar la** ~ **de alerta** to raise the alarm; ~ **de mando** order, command. **-4.** [derecho a expresarse] say, voice; **no tener ni** ~ **ni voto** to have no say in the matter. **-5.** [rumor] rumour. **-6.** *loc:* **correr la** ~ to spread the word; **estar pidiendo algo a voces** to be crying out for sthg; **llevar la** ~ **cantante** to be the boss.

vozarrón *m fam* loud voice.

VPO (*abrev de* **vivienda de protección oficial**) *f* ≈ council house/flat *Br*, ≈ public housing unit *Am*.

VTR (*abrev de* **videotape recording**) *f* VTR.

vudú *m* (*en aposición inv*) voodoo.

vuela → **volar.**

vuelca → **volcar.**

vuelco *m* upset; **dar un** ~ [coche] to overturn; [relaciones] to change completely; [empresa] to go to ruin; **me dio un** ~ **el corazón** my heart missed O skipped a beat.

vuele → **volar.**

vuelo *m* **-1.** [gen & AERON] flight; **alzar** O **emprender** O **levantar el** ~ [despegar] to take flight, to fly off; *fig* [irse de casa] to fly the nest; **coger algo al** ~ [en el aire] to catch sthg in flight; *fig* [rápido] to catch on to sthg very quickly; **remontar el** ~ to soar; ~ **chárter/regular** charter/scheduled flight; ~

espacial space flight; ~ **libre** hang gliding; ~ **sin motor** gliding; ~**s nacionales** domestic flights; **de altos** ~**s, de mucho** ~ of great importance; **no se oía el** ~ **de una mosca** you could have heard a pin drop. **-2.** [de vestido] fullness; **una falda de** ~ **a** full skirt. **-3.** ARQUIT projection. **-4.** [envergadura - de alas] wingspan.

vuelque → **volcar.**

vuelta *f* **-1.** [gen] turn; [acción] turning; **dar una** ~ (**a algo**) [recorriéndolo] to go round (sthg); **darse la** ~ to turn round; **dar** ~**s (a algo)** [girándolo] to turn (sthg) round; **media** ~ MIL about-turn; AUTOM U-turn; ~ **al ruedo** TAUROM bullfighter's lap of honour. **-2.** DEP lap; ~ **(ciclista)** tour. **-3.** [regreso, devolución] return; **a la** ~ [volviendo] on the way back; [al llegar] on one's return; **estar de** ~ to be back. **-4.** [paseo] **dar una** ~ to go for a walk. **-5.** [dinero sobrante] change. **-6.** [ronda, turno] round. **-7.** [parte opuesta] back, other side; **a la** ~ **de la esquina** *lit & fig* round the corner; **a la** ~ **de la página** over the page. **-8.** [cambio, avatar] change; **dar la** O **una** ~ *fig* to turn around completely. **-9.** [de pantalón] turn-up *Br*, cuff *Am*; [de manga] cuff. **-10.** [en labor de punto] row. **-11.** *loc:* **a la** ~ **de** [tras] at the end of; **a** ~ **de correo** by return of post; **dar la** ~ **a la tortilla** *fam* to turn the tables; **darle cien** ~**s a alguien** to knock spots off sb; **dar una** ~**/dos** *etc* ~**s de campana** [coche] to turn over once/twice *etc*; **darle** ~**s a algo** to turn sthg over in one's mind; **estar de** ~ **de algo** to be blasé about sthg; **estar de** ~ **de todo** to be in the know; **la cabeza me da** ~**s** my head's spinning; **no tiene** ~ **de hoja** there are no two ways about it; **poner a alguien de** ~ **y media** [criticar] to call sb all the names under the sun; [regañar] to give sb a good telling-off; **sin** ~ **de hoja** irrevocable.

vuelto, -ta ◇ *pp* → **volver.** ◇ *adj* turned.
◆ **vuelto** *m Amer* change.

vuelva *etc* → **volver.**

vuestro, -tra ◇ *adj poses* your; ~ **libro/ amigo** your book/friend; **este libro es** ~ this book is yours; **un amigo** ~ a friend of yours; **no es asunto** ~ it's none of your business. ◇ *pron poses:* **el** ~ yours; **los** ~**s están en la mesa** yours are on the table; **lo** ~ **es el teatro** [lo que hacéis bien] you should be on the stage; **los** ~**s** *fam* [vuestra familia] your folks; [vuestro bando] your lot, your side.

vulcanología *f* vulcanology.

vulgar *adj* **-1.** [no refinado] vulgar. **-2.** [corriente, ordinario] ordinary, common. **-3.** [no técnico] non-technical, lay.

vulgaridad *f* **-1.** [grosería] vulgarity; **hacer/ decir una** ~ to do/say sthg vulgar. **-2.** [banalidad] banality.

vulgarismo *m* GRAM vulgarism.

vulgarización *f* popularization.

vulgarizar [13] *vt* to popularize.

◆ **vulgarizarse** *vpr* to become popular o common.

vulgo *m despec*: **el** ~ [plebe] the masses (*pl*), the common people (*pl*); [no expertos] the lay public (*U*).

vulnerabilidad *f* vulnerability.

vulnerable *adj* vulnerable.

vulneración *f* **-1.** [de prestigio etc] harming, damaging. **-2.** [de ley, pacto etc] violation, infringement.

vulnerar *vt* **-1.** [prestigio etc] to harm, to damage. **-2.** [ley, pacto etc] to violate, to break.

vulva *f* vulva.

VV *abrev de* **ustedes**.

x, X *f* [letra] x, X.

◆ **X** *m y f*: **la señora X** Mrs X.

xenofobia *f* xenophobia.

xenófobo, -ba ◇ *adj* xenophobic. ◇ *m y f* xenophobe.

xerografía *f* photocopying, xerography.

xilofón, xilófono *m* xylophone.

xilografía *f* **-1.** [técnica] xylography, wood engraving. **-2.** [impresión] xylograph, wood engraving.

w, W *f* [letra] w, W.

wagon-lit [baˈγonˈlit] (*pl* **wagons-lits**) *m* sleeping car.

walkie-talkie [ˈwalkiˈtalki] (*pl* **walkie-talkies**) *m* walkie-talkie.

walkman® [ˈwalman] (*pl* **walkmans**) *m* Walkman®.

Washington [ˈwaʃiŋton] Washington.

wáter [ˈbater] (*pl* **wáteres**), **váter** (*pl* **váteres**) *m* toilet.

waterpolo [waterˈpolo] *m* water polo.

watio = **vatio**.

WC (*abrev de* **water closet**) *m* WC.

Web [web] *f*: **la (World Wide)** ~ the (World Wide) Web.

Wellington [ˈweliŋton] Wellington.

western [ˈwester] (*pl* **westerns**) *m* CIN western.

whisky [ˈwiski] = **güisqui**.

windsurf [ˈwinsurf], **windsurfing** [ˈwinsurfin] *m* windsurfing.

WWW (*abrev de* **World Wide Web**) *f* WWW.

y¹, Y *f* [letra] y, Y.

y² *conj* **-1.** [gen] and; **un ordenador** ~ **una impresora** a computer and a printer; **horas** ~ **horas de espera** hours and hours of waiting. **-2.** [pero] and yet; **sabía que no lo conseguiría** ~ **seguía intentándolo** she knew she wouldn't manage it and yet she kept on trying. **-3.** [en preguntas] what about; **¿**~ **tu mujer?** what about your wife?

ya ◇ *adv* **-1.** [en el pasado] already; ~ **me lo habías contado** you had already told me; ~ **en 1926** as long ago as 1926. **-2.** [ahora] now; [inmediatamente] at once; **hay que hacer algo** ~ something has to be done now/at once; **bueno, yo** ~ **me voy** right, I'm off now; ~ **no es así** it's no longer like that. **-3.** [en el futuro]: ~ **te llamaré** I'll give you a ring some time; ~ **hablaremos** we'll talk later; ~ **nos habremos ido** we'll already have gone; ~ **verás** you'll (soon) see. **-4.** [refuerza al verbo]: ~ **entiendo/lo sé** I understand/know.

◇ *conj* [distributiva]: ~ **(sea) por ...** ~ **(sea) por ...** whether for ... or ....

◇ *interj*: ¡~! [expresa asentimiento] right!; [expresa comprensión] yes!; ¡~, ~! *irón* sure!, yes, of course!

◆ **ya no** *loc adv*: ~ **no ... sino** not only ..., but.

◆ **ya que** *loc conj* since; ~ **que has venido, ayúdame con esto** since you're here, give me a hand with this.

yacente, **yaciente** *adj* [gen] lying; ARTE recumbent, reclining.

yacer [77] *vi* to lie.

yaciente = yacente.

yacimiento *m* -1. [minero] bed, deposit; ~ **de petróleo** oilfield. -2. [arqueológico] site.

yaga *etc* → yacer.

Yakarta Jakarta.

yanqui ◇ *adj* -1. HIST Yankee (*antes de sust*). -2. *fam* [estadounidense] *pejorative term relating to the US*, yank (*antes de sust*). ◇ *m y f* -1. HIST Yankee. -2. *fam* [estadounidense] *pejorative term referring to a person from the US*, yank.

yantar *desus* ◇ *m* fare, food. ◇ *vt* to eat.

Yaoundé [jaun'de] Yaoundé.

yarda *f* yard.

yate *m* yacht.

yayo, -ya *m y f fam* grandad (*f* grandma).

yazca, **yazga** *etc* → yacer.

yegua *f* mare.

yeísmo *m* *pronunciation of Spanish "ll" as "y"*.

yelmo *m* helmet.

yema *f* -1. [de huevo] yolk. -2. [de planta] bud, shoot. -3. [de dedo] fingertip. -4. CULIN *sweet made from sugar and egg yolk*.

Yemen: (el) ~ Yemen.

yemenita *adj, m y f* Yemeni.

yen (*pl* yenes) *m* yen.

yerba = hierba.

yerbatero *m Amer* healer.

yerga *etc* → erguir.

yermo, -ma *adj* -1. [estéril] barren. -2. [despoblado] uninhabited.

◆ **yermo** *m* wasteland.

yerno *m* son-in-law.

yerra *etc* → errar.

yerro *m desus* mistake, error.

yerto, -ta *adj* rigid, stiff.

yesca *f* tinder.

yesería *f* [fábrica] gypsum kiln.

yesero, -ra ◇ *adj* plaster (*antes de sust*). ◇ *m y f* -1. [fabricante] plaster manufacturer. -2. [obrero] plasterer.

yeso *m* -1. GEOL gypsum. -2. CONSTR plaster. -3. ARTE gesso.

yeti *m* yeti.

yeyé (*pl* yeyés) *adj* sixties.

Yibuti Djibouti.

yiddish, **jiddisch** *m* Yiddish.

yiu-yitsu, **jiu-jitsu** *m* jujitsu.

yo ◇ *pron pers* -1. (*sujeto*) I; ~ **me llamo Luis** I'm called Luis. -2. (*predicado*): **soy ~** it's me. -3. *loc*: ~ **que tú/él** *etc* if I were you/him *etc*. ◇ *m* PSICOL: **el** ~ the ego.

yodado, -da *adj* iodized.

yodo, **iodo** *m* iodine.

yoga *m* yoga.

yogui *m y f* yogi.

yogur (*pl* yogures), **yogurt** (*pl* yogurts) *m* yoghurt.

yogurtera *f* yoghurt maker.

yonqui *m y f fam* junkie.

yóquey (*pl* yóqueys), **jockey** (*pl* jockeys) *m* jockey.

yoyó *m* yoyo.

yuca *f* -1. BOT yucca. -2. CULIN cassava, manioc.

yudo, **judo** ['juðo] *m* judo.

yudoka, **judoka** [ju'ðoka] *m y f* judoist, judoka.

yugo *m lit & fig* yoke.

Yugoslavia Yugoslavia.

yugoslavo, -va ◇ *adj* Yugoslavian. ◇ *m y f* Yugoslav.

yugular *adj & f* jugular.

yunque *m* anvil.

yunta *f* -1. [de bueyes etc] yoke, team. -2. *Amer* [esposas] cufflink.

yuppie (*pl* yuppies), **yuppi** *m y f* yuppie.

yute *m* jute.

yuxtaponer [65] *vt* to juxtapose.

◆ **yuxtaponerse** *vpr*: ~**se (a)** to be juxtaposed (with).

yuxtaposición *f* juxtaposition.

yuxtapuesto, -ta *pp* → yuxtaponer.

Z

z, **Z** f [letra] z, Z.

zafacón m *Amer* rubbish bin.

zafarrancho m **-1.** NÁUT clearing of the decks; ~ **de combate** MIL call to action stations. **-2.** *fig* [destrozo] mess. **-3.** *fig* [riña] row, fracas.

zafarse *vpr* to get out of it, to escape; ~ **de** [persona] to get rid of; [obligación] to get out of.

zafiedad f roughness, uncouthness.

zafio, **-fia** *adj* rough, uncouth.

zafiro m sapphire.

zaga f DEP defence; **a la** ~ behind, at the back; **no irle a la** ~ **a alguien** to be every bit ○ just as good as sb.

zagal, **-la** m y f **-1.** [muchacho] adolescent, teenager. **-2.** [pastor] shepherd (f shepherdess).

zaguán m (entrance) hall.

zaherir *vt* **-1.** [herir] to hurt. **-2.** [burlarse de] to mock. **-3.** [criticar] to pillory.

zahorí (*pl* zahoríes) m y f **-1.** [de agua] water diviner. **-2.** *fig* [clarividente] mind reader.

zaino, **-na** *adj* **-1.** [caballo] chestnut. **-2.** [res] black.

Zaire Zaire.

zalamería f (*gen pl*) flattery (*U*).

zalamero, **-ra** ◇ *adj* flattering; *despec* smooth-talking. ◇ m y f flatterer; *despec* smooth talker.

zamarra f sheepskin jacket.

Zambia Zambia.

zambo, **-ba** ◇ *adj* knock-kneed. ◇ m y f knock-kneed person.

zambomba ◇ f MUS *type of rustic drum*. ◇ *interj*: ¡~! *fam* wow!

zambombazo m bang.

zambullida f dive; **darse una** ~ [baño] to go for a dip.

zambullir *vt* to dip, to submerge.

◆ **zambullirse** *vpr*: ~se (en) [agua] to dive (into); [actividad] to immerse o.s. (in).

zampar *fam vi* to gobble.

◆ **zamparse** *vpr* to scoff, to wolf down.

zanahoria f carrot.

zanca f [de ave] leg, shank.

zancada f stride.

zancadilla f trip; **poner una** ○ **la** ~ **a alguien** [hacer tropezar] to trip sb up; [engañar] to trick sb.

zancadillear *vt* **-1.** [hacer tropezar] to trip up. **-2.** *fig* [engañar] to trick.

zanco m stilt.

zancudo, **-da** *adj* long-legged.

◆ **zancuda** f wader.

◆ **zancudo** m *Amer* mosquito.

zanganear *vi fam* to laze about.

zángano, **-na** m y f *fam* [persona] lazy oaf, idler.

◆ **zángano** m [abeja] drone.

zanja f ditch.

zanjar *vt* [poner fin a] to put an end to; [resolver] to settle, to resolve.

zapallo m *Amer* courgette.

zapapico m pickaxe.

zapata f **-1.** [cuña] wedge. **-2.** [de freno] shoe.

zapateado m *type of flamenco music and dance*.

zapatear *vi* to stamp one's feet.

zapatería f **-1.** [oficio] shoemaking. **-2.** [taller] shoemaker's. **-3.** [tienda] shoe shop.

zapatero, **-ra** m y f **-1.** [fabricante] shoemaker. **-2.** [reparador]: ~ **(de viejo** ○ **remendón)** cobbler; ¡~ **a tus zapatos!** mind your own business! **-3.** [vendedor] shoe seller.

zapatilla f **-1.** [de baile] shoe, pump; [de estar en casa] slipper; [de deporte] sports shoe, trainer. **-2.** [de grifo] washer.

zapato m shoe; **saber alguien dónde le aprieta el** ~ to know which side one's bread is buttered.

zapping ['θapin] m *inv* channel-hopping; **hacer** ~ to channel-hop.

zar, **zarina** m y f tsar (f tsarina), czar (f czarina).

zarabanda f **-1.** [danza] saraband. **-2.** *fig* [jaleo] commotion, uproar.

Zaragoza Saragossa.

zaragozano, **-na** *adj* of/relating to Saragossa.

zarandajas *fpl fam* nonsense (*U*), trifles.

zarandear *vt* **-1.** [cosa] to shake. **-2.** [persona] to jostle, to knock about.

zarandeo m **-1.** [sacudida] shake, shaking (*U*). **-2.** [empujón] pushing (*U*) ○ knocking (*U*) about.

zarcillo m (*gen pl*) earring.

zarista *adj, m y f* Tsarist, Czarist.

zarpa *f* **-1.** [de animal - uña] claw; [- mano] paw. **-2.** *fam* [de persona] paw, hand.

zarpar *vi* to weigh anchor, to set sail.

zarpazo *m* clawing (*U*).

zarrapastroso, -sa ◇ *adj* scruffy, shabby. ◇ *m y f* scruff.

zarza *f* bramble, blackberry bush.

zarzal *m* bramble patch.

zarzamora *f* blackberry.

zarzaparrilla *f* sarsaparilla.

zarzuela *f* **-1.** MÚS zarzuela, *Spanish light opera.* **-2.** CULIN *fish stew in a spicy sauce.*

ZARZUELA:

'Zarzuela' in the musical sense is a form of light opera which combines song, dance and spoken dialogue. It usually portrays everyday life in Spain, and the music is often based on traditional Spanish folk songs

zas *interj*: ¡~! wham!, bang!

zen ◇ *adj inv* Zen (*antes de sust*). ◇ *m* Zen.

zenit, cenit *m lit* & *fig* zenith.

zepelín (*pl* zepelines) *m* zeppelin.

zigzag (*pl* zigzags O zigzagues) *m* zigzag.

zigzaguear *vi* to zigzag.

Zimbabue Zimbabwe.

zinc = cinc.

zíngaro, -ra = cíngaro.

zíper *m Amer* zip.

zipizape *m fam* squabble, set-to.

zócalo *m* **-1.** [de pared] skirting board. **-2.** [de edificio, pedestal] plinth. **-3.** [pedestal] pedestal.

zoco *m* souk, Arabian market.

zodiacal *adj* zodiacal.

zodiaco, zodíaco *m* zodiac.

ZOE (*abrev de* zona de ordenación de explotaciones) *f development zone.*

zombi, zombie *m y f lit* & *fig* zombie.

zona *f* zone, area; ~ **azul** AUTOM restricted parking zone; ~ **catastrófica** disaster area; ~ **franca** COM free-trade zone; ~ **de urgente reindustrialización** ECON *region given priority status for industrial investment,* ≃ enterprise zone *Br*; ~ **verde** [grande] park; [pequeño] lawn.

zoo *m* zoo.

zoología *f* zoology.

zoológico, -ca *adj* zoological.
◆ **zoológico** *m* zoo.

zoólogo, -ga *m y f* zoologist.

zoom [θum] (*pl* zooms) *m* FOT zoom.

zopenco, -ca *fam* ◇ *adj* idiotic, daft. ◇ *m y f* idiot, nitwit.

zoquete ◇ *adj* stupid. ◇ *m* [calcetín] *Amer* ankle sock. ◇ *m y f* [tonto] blockhead, idiot.

zorro, -rra ◇ *adj* foxy, crafty. ◇ *m y f lit* & *fig* fox; ~ **azul** blue fox.
◆ **zorro** *m* [piel] fox (fur).
◆ **zorra** *f mfam despec* [ramera] whore, tart, hooker *Am*.
◆ **zorros** *mpl* [utensilio] feather duster (*sg*); **estar hecho unos** ~**s** *fam* [cansado, maltrecho] to be whacked, to be done in; [enfurecido] to be fuming.

zozobra *f* anxiety, worry.

zozobrar *vi* **-1.** [naufragar] to be shipwrecked. **-2.** *fig* [fracasar] to fall through.

zueco *m* clog.

zulo *m* hideout.

zulú (*pl* zulúes) *adj, m y f* Zulu.

zumbador *m* buzzer.

zumbar ◇ *vi* [gen] to buzz; [máquinas] to whirr, to hum; **me zumban los oídos** my ears are buzzing. ◇ *vt fam* to bash, to thump.

zumbido *m* [gen] buzz, buzzing (*U*); [de máquinas] whirr, whirring (*U*).

zumbón, -ona *fam* ◇ *adj* funny, joking. ◇ *m y f* joker, tease.

zumo *m* juice.

ZUR *abrev de* zona de urgente reindustrialización.

zurcido *m* **-1.** [acción] darning. **-2.** [remiendo] darn.

zurcidor, -ra *m y f* darner, mender.

zurcir [12] *vt* to darn; ¡**anda y que te zurzan!** *fam* on your bike!, get lost!

zurdo, -da ◇ *adj* [mano etc] left; [persona] left-handed. ◇ *m y f* [persona] left-handed person.
◆ **zurda** *f* **-1.** [mano] left hand. **-2.** [pie] left foot.

Zurich ['θurik] Zurich.

zurra *f* beating, hiding.

zurrar *vt* **-1.** [pegar] to beat, to thrash. **-2.** [curtir] to tan.

zurza *etc* → zurcir.

zutano, -na *m y f* so-and-so, what's-his-name (*f* what's-her-name).

Living in Spain and Spanish-speaking America

CONTENTS

SPAIN

■ State capital
● Regional capital

0   125 miles

ASTURIAS   CANTABRIA   PAÍS VASCO   NAVARRA
Oviedo ●   Santander ●   Vitoria ●   Pamplona ●
Santiago de Compostela ●
GALICIA   LA RIOJA   Logroño ●   ANDORRA
CASTILLA Y LEÓN   Zaragoza ●   CATALUÑA
Valladolid ●   ARAGÓN   Barcelona ●
COMUNIDAD DE MADRID
■ Madrid
PORTUGAL   Toledo ●   Palma de Mallorca ●
EXTREMADURA   CASTILLA-LA MANCHA   COMUNIDAD ● Valencia
Mérida ●   VALENCIANA   BALEARES
Sevilla ●   Murcia ●
ANDALUCÍA   MURCIA
Ceuta
Melilla
MARRUECOS

CANARIAS
Santa Cruz de Tenerife
Las Palmas de Gran Canaria
0   125 miles

City	Population
Madrid	2 866 850
Barcelona	1 508 810
Valencia	746 690
Seville	697 490
Zaragoza	601 670
Málaga	549 140

Spain is situated on the Iberian Peninsula, in the southwest corner of Europe; it has a surface area of 195 300 square miles, making it one of the largest European countries. It occupies most of the peninsula, and also includes the Balearic Islands in the Mediterranean, the Canary Islands in the Atlantic and the North African enclaves of Ceuta and Melilla. To the north it is bordered by France and the Bay of Biscay; to the east by the Mediterranean; to the south by the Straits of Gibraltar, which separate it from Africa; and to the west by Portugal. Sandwiched between the Atlantic Ocean and the Mediterranean Sea – the former giving rise to a damp, cold climate, the latter to warm, drier weather – Spain's climate combines with its physical geography to create some striking contrasts: from the *rías* (the Spanish equivalent of *fjords*) in Galicia to the Almería desert, from the Castilian tableland to the peaks of the Pyrenees, from the volcanic landscape of Tenerife to the rugged Majorcan coastline.

> **Official Languages**
>
> ■ Throughout Spain: *Spanish (Castilian)*
> ■ Catalonia, Balearic Islands: *Catalan*
> ■ Galicia: *Galician*
> ■ Basque Country: *Basque*
> ■ Valencia: *Valencian*

Language   Spanish (Castilian) is the official language spoken throughout Spain, but it is not the only language. In certain regions, there are two official languages (*see right*). Most linguists consider Valencian to be a variety of Catalan. *Euskera*, or Basque, is the joint official language in Basque-speaking areas of Navarre. Other minority languages are spoken in very specific areas, such as *bable* in parts of Asturias. Until the 1960s, French was the most widely taught foreign language, but it has now been overtaken by English.

Political Administration   The 1978 Constitution was the product of a broad and hard-won consensus amongst the major political parties which won parliamentary representation in the first democratic elections since the civil war. According to that Constitution, Spain is a parliamentary monarchy. The King is the head of state; he plays a mediating role in the workings of the institutions and is the highest representative of the Spanish state at international level, although actual political leadership remains the role of the Government.

▶ **Parliament (*las Cortes Generales*)**, usually called *las Cortes*, consists of the lower house, the Congress of Deputies (*Congreso de los Diputados*), and the upper house, the Senate (*Senado*). Members of both chambers are elected by universal suffrage every four years in a general election, but their responsibilities are very different.

The Congress of Deputies is made up of 350 deputies elected by proportional representation. Its political dominance is evident not only in the legislative process, but also in the fact that it votes to accept a new Prime Minister (*presidente del Gobierno*) and can force him or her to resign, either by a censure motion or a vote of no confidence.

The Prime Minister determines both the actions of the Government and its actual composition. The prime ministerial candidate first submits his manifesto to the Congress and then, once he has obtained the approval of the deputies and been appointed by the King, puts forward to the King the names of his chosen ministers.

The Senate serves as a 'cooling-off' chamber in the legislative process. Here, bills coming from the Congress of Deputies can technically be amended or vetoed, but in practice the Congress always has the last word. Composed of 208 elected members and 49 members chosen by the parliaments in the autonomous regions (*see page 4*), the Senate is becoming more and more involved with representing the interests of the different regions at national level.

▶ **The Constitution** was passed in 1978, bringing to an end the 'Transition' period (1975–8), which bridged the gap between the Franco regime and democracy. At present, the regional map of Spain is made up of 17 *comunidades* (autonomous regions), each with its own government and parliament, plus two autonomous municipalities (Ceuta and Melilla in North Africa).

▶ **The autonomous regions** were set up in an attempt to preserve and foster the cultural and historical diversity which remains such a strong feature of 20th-century Spain. For legal and administrative purposes, the regions are divided up into provinces and municipalities. The Constitution does not set out a list of responsibilities (*competencias*) for the regional governments; within preset limits, it allows each to take on whatever it considers necessary. The State draws up the national budget and is responsible for foreign affairs and trade, defence and the armed forces, the legal system, the monetary system, economic planning, public works of national scope and so on. The autonomous regions have the right to implement national guidelines in, for example, the areas of education and health, in a way which is suited to regional circumstances.

The Legal System

At local level, legal cases are heard at the *juzgados de primera instancia e instrucción*, which cover single or several municipalities, towns and cities. A step further up the ladder, each province has an *audiencia provincial*, and each autonomous region has a *tribunal superior de justicia*. Finally, the *Tribunal Supremo* operates at national level as the highest court in the land. The *Audiencia Nacional* is based in Madrid and has jurisdiction over the whole of Spain in matters of special significance for the nation: terrorism, arms dealing, smuggling, drug trafficking, large-scale fraud, immigration etc. Slightly apart from the rest of the legal system, the *Tribunal Constitucional* safeguards constitutional rights and interprets the constitution.

The Main Political Parties

After Franco, the forces of the centre right formed the *UCD* (*Unión de Centro Democrático*), a coalition which won the first democratic elections since the civil war and was in power from 1977 to 1982. After the *UCD*'s dissolution, the *CDS* (*Centro Democrático y Social*) attempted to fill the void between left and right wings; its downfall left the *PP* (*Partido Popular*, formerly *AP*, *Alianza Popular*) as Spain's largest centre-right party. To the left of the spectrum, the *PSOE* (*Partido Socialista Obrero Español* – the Spanish Socialist Party), founded in 1879, is the oldest party in Spain and formed the Government from 1982 to 1995; its policies are more or less in line with those of the other Western European socialist parties. The *PCE* (*Partido Comunista de España* – the Spanish Communist Party) was set up in 1920 and is currently the largest member of the coalition party, *IU* (*Izquierda Unida* – United Left).

▶ **In the autonomous regions** the big nationwide parties are complemented by regional ones, some of whom play a major role in the government of the regions and even carry some weight at national level; these include *Convergència i Unió* (*CiU*), a nationalist Catalan coalition, and the *PNV* (*Partido Nacionalista Vasco* – Basque Nationalist Party). Other regional parties represented in Parliament are *Coalición Canaria*, *BNG* (*Bloque Nacional Galego*), *Unió Valenciana*, the Basque *Eusko Alkartasuna* (*EA*) and *Herri Batasuna* (the latter the political wing of the terrorist organization *ETA*), and the Catalan *Esquerra Republicana*. There are also regional parties in Andalusia, Navarre and Aragon.

Main Political Parties and Coalitions	
PP	Partido Popular
PSOE	Partido Socialista Obrero Español
IU	Izquierda Unida
CiU	Convergència i Unió
PNV	Partido Nacionalista Vasco
CC	Coalición Canaria

With the economic expansion of the 1980s, it became clear that if Spain was to meet the challenges presented by the single European market, it would have to bring its communications infrastructure into line with that of the other member states.

Telephones Telecommunications in Spain are no longer run by state monopoly. With its huge turnover, however, *Telefónica* remains one of Spain's most important companies. Other companies include *Airtel* and *Retevisión*.

▶ **If you are making a telephone call** you will hear the ringing tone – a long tone repeated at regular intervals – once you are through. The engaged tone (busy signal) is a short tone repeated at regular intervals. A more rapid intermittent tone means all lines are busy.

▶ **For local calls** within a province dial the subscriber's number without an area code.

▶ **For calls to another province** first dial the area code. All area codes in Spain start with 9, which is dropped when calling from abroad.

Telephone Charges *(not mobile phones)*
Standard or 'A':
5 p.m. to 10 p.m. Monday to Friday
Cheap or 'B':
10 p.m. to 8 a.m. Monday to Friday
12 p.m. to 8 a.m., 2 p.m. to 12 p.m. Saturdays
All day Sundays and public holidays
Peak or 'C':
8 a.m. to 5 p.m. Monday to Friday
8 a.m. to 2 p.m. Saturdays

▶ **For international calls** dial the international code 07 and wait for a second, sharper tone; now dial the country code, local code and finally subscriber number.

▶ **Reverse charge (collect) calls** within Spain are made by dialling 009; you should then tell the operator the name of the subscriber, his or her telephone number and your own name and telephone number. For international calls, dial 008 (Europe, Algeria, Libya, Morocco, Tunisia and Turkey) or 005 (the rest of the world).

Useful Numbers	
Operator	*003*
International operator	*025*
Accident and emergency	*061*
Fire service	*080*
Police	*091*
Speaking clock	*093*
Alarm call	*096*

▶ **Freefone numbers** all begin with 900.

▶ **Public telephones** are signposted with a large 'T' (for *Telefónica*). Some are coin-operated; some require a phonecard. You can also use charge cards and some credit cards. Phonecards can be bought in tobacconists' (*estancos*) and post offices. Some hotels, restaurants and bars meter calls; you may be charged up to 35% more.

Post Offices The post office is usually called *correos*. Monday to Friday post offices open between 8.30 a.m. and 7 p.m. (sub-post offices close at 2.30 p.m.); both open from 9.30 a.m. to 1 p.m. on Saturdays. The central post office in major cities opens from 8 a.m. to 9 p.m. Monday to Friday and 8 a.m. to 7 p.m. on Saturdays.

▶ **Stamps** can be bought at a post office, but most people buy them at *estancos* which have more flexible opening hours. They are easy to spot because of the orange and red 'T' (for *Tabacalera*, the state tobacco monopoly) displayed on shop fronts.

▶ **Postal services** include *Postal Exprés*, which guarantees delivery within Spain in less than 24 hours; delivery to other European countries takes only slightly longer. You can also send telegrams, telexes and faxes from post offices.

Travelling in Spain has become considerably easier in the last 15 years. New motorways (freeways) and other major roads have been opened, and a national road network now connects all major Spanish cities. Rail travel has also been much improved by the introduction of high-speed trains.

Madrid → Barcelona	
Train	7 hours
Coach	8 hours
Car	6 hours
Air	50 minutes

Air Spain's airports are based around the needs of tourists, which largely explains the heavy international traffic. Busy domestic routes include the Madrid–Barcelona shuttle *(see below)*, Madrid to the Balearic and Canary Islands, and Barcelona to Palma de Mallorca. Other major cities are served by smaller airports with good connections. The capital's Barajas airport is the most important stopover point between Latin America and Europe.

▶ **Shuttle services** carry around 2 million passengers a year between Madrid and Barcelona. At peak times there are flights every 30 minutes; you can book in advance or turn up without a reservation. The majority of shuttle flights are with *Iberia*, the national airline, but *Air Europa* and *Spanair* operate a similar service.

Sea *Transmediterránea*, 95% state-owned, is the largest passenger ferry company in Spain. Ferries travel daily from Barcelona and Valencia to the Balearic Islands. The journey takes between six and eight hours, and for most of the year is made overnight. Other private companies run services too. In the high season you can travel by day, and can also leave from other ports, such as Denia and Alicante; *Transmediterránea* runs fast ferry services which take only four hours. If you opt for a reclining seat on the ferry, fares are much cheaper than by plane, but with a cabin there is very little difference. All companies provide transport between the islands in the Balearic group.

The Canary Islands lie 750 miles from the Spanish mainland and so the sea route is not the most popular option for most visitors. There are weekly ferry departures between Cádiz and Arrecife (Lanzarote), Las Palmas de Gran Canaria and Santa Cruz de Tenerife; the journey takes three days. As with the Balearics, there are plenty of ferry and jetfoil services linking the different islands to each other.

The fast ferries linking Africa and Europe make Algeciras and Ceuta very busy passenger ports, especially during the summer, since this is the favoured route home for North Africans now resident in Europe. Ferries leave every half-hour.

Rail The Spanish rail network covers over 8700 miles of track, of which around 7640 miles belong to *RENFE (Red Nacional de Ferrocarriles Españoles)*, the state-owned rail company. The rest are owned by *FEVE (Ferrocarriles de Vía Estrecha)*, which operates along the Atlantic coast, and by regional networks in Valencia, Catalonia, the Basque Country and the Balearic Islands.

The centre of the rail network is Madrid. Lines run north with branches to Galicia, Cantabria and the Basque Country; east to Valencia; west to Extremadura – including a service to Lisbon; south to Andalusia *(see below)*; and towards the French border (through Catalonia or the Basque Country). Other main lines link Galicia with Catalonia, and Barcelona with Valencia and Alicante.

As in Portugal, the track in Spain is a wider gauge than in the rest of Europe. The *Talgo*, however, can run on tracks of different gauges. One of its many routes extends beyond the French border to Paris and Geneva. New high-speed lines running on the international gauge will eventually link Madrid with the French border via Zaragoza and Barcelona; the first high-speed train, the *AVE (Alta Velocidad Española)*, was intro-

duced in 1992 and travels from the capital to Seville in less than two-and-a-half hours.

Trains are classified according to journey length, as follows.

▶ **Cercanías** (local or suburban trains) cover short journeys between provincial capitals and other towns within the same province. They run from Asturias, Barcelona, Bilbao, Cádiz, Madrid, Málaga, Murcia, San Sebastián, Santander, Seville and Valencia.

▶ **Regionales** (regional trains) cover medium distances and go beyond the provincial boundaries of large cities, e.g. Seville to the other provinces in Andalusia.

▶ **Trenes de largo recorrido** (fast long-distance trains) are divided into *estrellas* (known as *expresos*), *Intercity* and the *Talgo*. *Estrellas* are equipped with sleeping cars and couchettes for overnight travel, and have a buffet service. *Talgo* trains have sleeping cars, a buffet, restaurant and videos. *Intercity* trains do not usually run at night.

Return (round-trip) tickets work out cheaper than buying two single (one-way) tickets. A *tarjeta joven* (young person's railcard) or *tarjeta dorada* (for senior citizens) can give you big reductions. For local trains (*cercanías*), weekly or monthly season tickets or even books of ten tickets can be considerably cheaper.

Coaches The coach (bus) network is more comprehensive than the rail system and links almost all towns and cities. For some journeys coaches can prove faster and cheaper than trains. There are many private companies that operate all over Spain, several of them running international services too.

Car Roads are divided into different categories:

❏ *autopistas* (motorways, or freeways) or *autovías* (like British dual carriageways, with two lanes going in each direction): road signs for both are blue

❏ *carreteras nacionales* (like British trunk roads/US state highways): red signs

❏ *autonómicas de 1ª* or *de 2ª* (smaller roads between towns): orange signs for the former, green for the latter

❏ *autonómicas locales* (local roads): yellow signs

Some *autopistas* and *autovías* are toll roads (turnpikes).

In Spain you drive on the right. Seat belts are compulsory for drivers and both front-seat and back-seat passengers at all times.

Urban Transport You can buy a single (one-way) bus ticket from the driver, but it is cheaper to buy a ten-trip ticket (called *bonobús* in some cities) or a travelcard/season ticket, from *estancos* (tobacconists), *quioscos de periódicos* (newsagents) or even bus company offices, though this varies from one city to another. Public transport services usually start at 6 a.m. and run through until 1 a.m.; in big cities there is usually a skeleton bus service throughout the night. Madrid, Barcelona, Valencia and Bilbao all have Underground rail (subway) networks.

Taxis can be hailed in the street if their green light is indicating that they are free (*libre*). They also wait in taxi ranks or can be booked by phone. When you get into the taxi, the meter will indicate the minimum fare for the trip; the driver will then start the meter. There may be supplements for transporting luggage or pets, trips to and from stations and airports, or journeys late at night, on Sundays or public holidays.

Speed Limits
■ *Motorways (freeways) and dual carriageways: 75 miles (120 km) per hour*
■ *Other roads: 55 or 60 miles (90 or 100 km) per hour*
■ *Built-up areas: 30 miles (50 km) per hour*

The normal working week in Spain is 40 hours. People working the *jornada partida* (split working day) normally start at 9 a.m. and finish at 7 p.m., taking a two-hour break for lunch from around 2 to 4 p.m. Amongst civil servants, however, the *jornada intensiva* (intensive working day) from 8 a.m. to 3 p.m. has become the norm, and many companies adopt this system during the summer months because of the afternoon heat.

Salaries Employees in Spain have their annual salary divided into 14 parts: 1 for each month, plus two additional payments (*pagas extraordinarias*) in June and December. In this way, workers have more money to spend on their summer holidays (vacation) and at Christmas. The Government sets a minimum wage (*Salario Mínimo Interprofesional*); management and trade unions use this sum as a baseline when negotiating collective wage agreements. Some workers, like waiters, rely heavily on tips to supplement their income. Unlike in the UK and the USA, however, you are not expected to leave a fixed percentage of the bill in cafes and restaurants; it is up to you how much you leave.

Income Tax Tax reforms in 1978 brought Spanish tax laws into line with those in the rest of the European Union and resulted in the introduction in Spain of personal income tax (*Impuesto sobre la Renta de las Personas Físicas – IRPF*) and VAT (sales tax) (*IVA*). The tax year runs from 1 January to 31 December. Anyone earning above a given minimum in any one year is obliged to declare their income and expenditure on a tax return (*Declaración de la Renta*). You can either calculate your own tax or ask the tax office to do it for you, but if you need to pay extra or want to claim a refund, then you must do so by June of the following year.

Instituto Nacional de Empleo (INEM) (Department of Employment and Social Security) In Spain, you become eligible for four months' unemployment benefit after contributing to social security for a minimum of a year; you can claim the maximum of two years' benefit after contributing for at least six years. If you have not paid enough contributions or if the two-year period has elapsed without your finding work, you can apply for other family benefits or, if applicable, for a special benefit payable to people over 52 years old. As well as administering these various benefits, *INEM* plays an important role in training the unemployed and getting them back on to the job market. Nowadays, though, private employment agencies are taking on more and more of the responsibilities that were previously *INEM*'s sole preserve.

Sickness and Maternity Benefit Whether you are an employee or self-employed, only your family doctor can issue a medical certificate that gives you the right to benefit during the period you are unable to work. Maternity leave (*baja de maternidad*) allows for 16 weeks off work before or after the birth, although at least 40 days of the total must be taken after it. Breast-feeding mothers who work are allowed up to one hour off during each working day.

Trade Unions Since 1978 democratic trade unions have been legal again in Spain. Spaniards initially flocked to join the union of their choice, but the 1980s saw a considerable drop in membership.

Historically, trade unionism has always been very strong in Spain. The two largest unions are the *Unión General de Trabajadores (UGT)*, founded in 1888, and *Comisiones Obreras (CC OO)*, founded in 1962. The *UGT* is basically socialist and the *CC OO* communist, but social changes have forced them both to become increasingly inde-

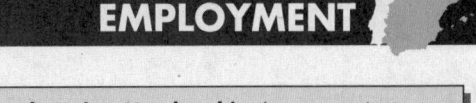
pendent of political parties. Other trade unions include the anarchist *Confederación Nacional del Trabajo (CNT)*, founded in 1910; the *Confederación General del Trabajo (CGT)*, formed

Trade Union Membership *(fee-paying members)*	
CC OO *(Comisiones Obreras)*	790 000
UGT *(Unión General de Trabajadores)*	730 000
USO *(Unión Sindical Obrera)*	75 000
CGT *(Confederación General del Trabajo)*	50 000

by a breakaway group that left the *CNT* in 1989; the *Unión Sindical Obrera (USO)*; and others which are more regionally based. Agricultural workers have various unions, like the Andalusian *Sindicato de Obreros del Campo (SOC)* and the Catalan *Unió de Pagesos*. White-collar unions have also played an important part in certain spheres (amongst civil servants, pilots, doctors etc.). The Spanish employers' organization is called the *Confederación Española de Organizaciones Empresariales (CEOE)*.

Public Holidays In addition to the paid holiday (vacation) every worker is entitled to, there are also public holidays on certain dates throughout the year. As well

National Public Holidays	
Año Nuevo (New Year)	1 January
Viernes Santo (Good Friday)	varies each year
Fiesta del Trabajo (International Labour Day)	1 May
Asunción de la Virgen (Assumption)	15 August
Fiesta de la Hispanidad/Día del Pilar (Columbus/St Pilar's Day)	12 October
Todos los Santos (All Saints' Day)	1 November
Fiesta de la Constitución (Constitution Day)	6 December
Inmaculada Concepción (Immaculate Conception)	8 December
Navidad (Christmas Day)	25 December

as those listed above, which are common to the whole country, each autonomous region has the right to another four days, and each town or city to a further two days chosen by the local council. At present, Epiphany (*los Reyes Magos*) on 6 January can be considered a national public holiday, since it is still observed in all the autonomous regions. If a public holiday falls on a Thursday or a Tuesday, employers usually agree to make a long weekend of it and give staff the intervening Friday or Monday off as well. These *puentes* are usually marked by a mass exodus from the cities.

Holiday Periods Although it is still true that most people take their holidays as shown below, it is becoming more common for Spaniards to follow the European trend towards a shorter summer break and longer holidays at Christmas and Easter.

– *Summer*: three to four weeks for all workers, usually taken during July and August, and about three months for schoolchildren and students, from the end of June to the middle of September. Many small shops close for August.

– *Christmas*: a minimum of three or four days for workers, and from 23 December to 7 January for students.

– *Easter* (*Semana Santa* – Holy Week): in March or April, usually a four-day weekend for workers and two weeks for students.

Under the Spanish Constitution, access to health care is the right of all citizens. Around 99 per cent of the population was covered by the national health system in 1995. Health care is publicly funded and free: around 90% of its budget comes from general taxation, and only 6% from social security contributions. Health care is currently being decentralized and responsibility gradually devolved to the autonomous regions: services for two-thirds of the population are now administered by those regions for whom health is part of their remit (*see below*). The remaining third is covered by *Insalud* – the National Institute for Health, which is slowly being phased out. *Insalud* is answerable to the *Ministerio de Sanidad* (Ministry for Health).

For health purposes Spain is split up geographically into units called *áreas de salud* (health districts); in each of these the service is divided into *atención primaria* (primary health care) and *asistencia especializada* (specialized services).

> **Autonomous Regions with Responsibility for Health Services**
>
> - Catalonia
> - Andalusia
> - Basque Country
> - Valencia
> - Navarre
> - Galicia
> - Canary Islands

Atención Primaria Primary health care is provided at *centros de salud* (health centres) or *consultorios rurales* (small country surgeries) by a team consisting of *médicos de cabecera* or *de familia* (family doctors or GPs), paediatricians and nursing staff. The latter are still popularly known as *ATS – ayudante técnico sanitario*, although the proper term has once again reverted to *enfermero/enfermera*. As well as providing the usual health services, the *centros de salud* play an important role in preventive medicine and health education, running family planning clinics, vaccination and immunization programmes, and antenatal and postnatal classes, and providing basic physiotherapy.

Spaniards can change to another doctor if they do not want to stay with the one allocated to them, but they must stay within the same centre or area. This system also works for certain types of specialist; however, patients are not able to choose which hospital they attend.

Asistencia Especializada More specialized health care is provided at hospitals and *centros de especialidades* (outpatient centres still popularly known by their old name, a*mbulatorios*). Services at the latter vary, ranging from blood tests and appointments with the specialist to whom your doctor has referred you, to surgery, transplantation and in vitro fertilization. Hospitals deal with both outpatients and inpatients. They are generally well equipped and offer very specialized medical care, as well as the more sophisticated diagnostic tests and investigations.

Tarjeta Sanitaria (Medical Card) Every Spaniard using the health service is issued with a medical card; looking rather like a credit card, this bears your full name along with your identity card and national insurance numbers. On the back are printed the name of your doctor and the address and phone number of your health centre, as well as the telephone number of your local accident and emergency department. Your doctor will ask for this card when making out a prescription.

Prescriptions With any prescriptions made out by your GP or specialist, you only have to pay 40% of the price; the state pays the remainder. If you suffer from a serious chronic disease or have AIDS, you only pay 10% of the price. Pensioners, the handicapped and people who have had an industrial accident get all their prescribed medicines completely free of charge. In the past doctors have been accused of prescribing far too liberally. The Government is trying to bring this under control and so certain types of medication for minor ailments are no longer free; these include hygiene and dermatological products, nutritional supplements and so on.

Emergency Services   In a medical emergency dial 061. There are accident and emergency departments (emergency rooms) at some health centres, and in theory emergencies are the responsibility of the primary health care team. In practice, however, the accident and emergency department of the local hospital is often the first port of call, and all hospitals run a 24-hour emergency service.

Chemists (Pharmacies)   These sell all kinds of branded and unbranded medicines and can dispense prescriptions. They also sell baby food, certain special food items and cosmetics. If you need to buy drugs or medicines outside normal hours, you will find a list on the door of any chemist's, giving the name and address of the nearest *farmacia de guarda* (duty chemist's).

Private Medicine   This provides an alternative or complementary service to the national health service.

Opening Hours for Chemists (Pharmacies)	
Monday–Friday	9.30 a.m.–1.45 p.m. and 5–8 p.m.
Saturday	10 a.m.–1.45 p.m.

Private medical services are sometimes run by friendly societies, and these are known as *mutuas*. Private medicine has grown rapidly in recent years, its main attraction being that patients can bypass the often overcrowded state system.

When you have chosen a private service, you are given a list of all available doctors, GPs and specialists alike, listed by town or city and according to their medical specialty. You also receive a book of vouchers or a receipt proving your membership of the private health care scheme, and you use these when paying for a consultation. You are also supplied with a prescription pad; when completed by the doctor, a prescription entitles you to discounts on certain medicines. Depending on the kind of arrangement you have with the private health care company, you may receive total cover which will include both primary health care and hospital treatment. If you choose to take out private medical insurance, then you qualify for a certain amount of tax relief. Alternative medicine – homeopathy, acupuncture, Chinese medicine, naturopathy – is usually only available in the private sector.

Medical Care for Citizens of the European Union   If EU citizens have with them the relevant document provided in their country of origin (form E111, available at post offices in the UK), they are eligible for free medical treatment in Spain. If they come from a country where free medical treatment is not available, patients will be given a bill which they will have to pay on the spot, but which they should keep to use later on to apply for reimbursement from their own health service when they return home.

Dentists and Opticians   For anything other than very basic dental treatment, which is provided by the primary health care team, you need to go to a private surgery. Most Spaniards consider treatment here to be very expensive.

You can have your eyes tested either at the ophthalmologist's or the optician's (*la óptica*) but you will have to pay for your glasses or contact lenses, as they are not provided by the national health service.

The *Banco de España* (Bank of Spain), which dates back to 1782, is Spain's national bank. It is the only bank that is permitted to issue money. One of its functions is to formulate and implement monetary policy in order to control inflation, as well as supervising the way that private banks operate. Since 1994 it has been wholly independent of the Government.

Currency

The Spanish unit of currency is the peseta. Coins are issued in denominations of 1, 5, 10, 25, 50, 100, 200, 500 and (rarely seen) 2000 pesetas. Notes are issued in denominations of 1000, 2000, 5000 and 10 000 pesetas. The 5-peseta coin is popularly known as a *duro*.

Banks and Savings Banks

In 1974 the banking system was deregulated, giving banks the freedom to open new branches and to set their own interest rates. At present, there are 165 banks in Spain, a substantial proportion of which are foreign-owned. The legal framework established by the European Union will put foreign banks operating in Spain on a par with Spanish banks.

The Five Largest Banks

- *Banco Bilbao-Vizcaya (BBV)*
- *Banco Central Hispano (BCH)*
- *Banco de Santander*
- *Banco Español de Crédito (Banesto)*
- *Banco Exterior de España (Bex)*

There are also about 51 savings banks (*cajas de ahorros*), which make up the second most important group within the Spanish financial system. They were set up originally as charitable organizations but although they are still involved in charitable work (centres for retired people, museums etc.), the way they operate and the services they offer are now very similar to banks.

Banking hours are Monday to Friday from 8.30 a.m. to 2 p.m. and Saturdays from 8.30 a.m. to 1 p.m.; opening hours for savings banks are Monday to Friday from 8.15 a.m. to 2.30 p.m. Savings banks also open on Thursday evenings from 5 to 7.30 p.m., except during the period June to September.

The Five Largest Savings Banks

- *Caja de Ahorros y Pensiones de Barcelona ('la Caixa')*
- *Caja de Ahorros y M.P. de Madrid*
- *Caja de Ahorros de Cataluña*
- *Bilbao Bizkaia Kutxa*
- *Caja de Ahorros de Valencia, Castellón y Alicante ('Bancaja')*

There has been a huge increase in the number of cash machines (ATMs) in Spain. All machines indicate which cards they accept and normally, since they are part of a national and international computerized network, you can make withdrawals anywhere, at any time. More and more businesses now accept payment by credit card and debit card too (with the latter, the business debits money directly from your account without you having to write a cheque). In fact, very few outlets accept payment by cheque, and cheques are almost exclusively used in major business deals or when paying out large sums of money.

Home Banking

Called *banca telefónica* or sometimes *telebanco*, home banking is becoming more and more popular. In Spain it normally works via the telephone rather than via a home computer.

The Stock Exchange

There are four buildings which house the Spanish stock exchange, in Madrid, Bilbao, Barcelona and Valencia.

Over recent years, the Spanish education system has seen many changes: the 1970 *Ley General de Educación* (*LGE* – General Education Act) has been replaced by the *Ley Orgánica de Ordenación General del Sistema Educativo* (*LOGSE* – General Organization of the Educational System Act), which came into force in 1990. The new system has been gradually phased in and is expected to have superseded the old one by the turn of the century. The reforms are intended to expand free, compulsory education up to the age of 16; bring infant schooling (0–6 years) into the state system; bring vocational training more into line with the needs of business and industry; place special emphasis on the development of training in the arts; and generally bring the education system up to date and into line with other European Union countries.

According to the Constitution, central government has general responsibility for education in the following areas: basic legislation, degrees and diplomas, organization of grades, courses and minimum course content, requirements for passing from one grade to the next, minimum standards for schools, and general planning. Other responsibilities can and have been taken over by the autonomous regions. In those regions with their own language (Catalonia, Galicia, the Basque Country, Valencia, Navarre [in bilingual areas] and the Balearic Islands), the teaching of that language is one of the main organizational tasks of their regional authorities. In this respect a special effort has been made to revive the Basque language at the *ikastolas* (schools where all teaching is in Basque).

State Schools and Private Schools

Private education has traditionally been very important at primary (elementary) and secondary (high school) levels and used to have close links with the Catholic Church, although nowadays non-denominational private schools predominate. At pre-school level and primary, 32% of pupils attend private schools; in secondary, 28% of students are privately educated; but at university level, only 4%.

As stated above, under the new Education Act, *LOGSE*, education has become compulsory until 16 years of age. The aim is to put an end to the situation in which the wealthy middle classes typically send their children to *escuelas de pago* (fee-paying schools), whilst working-class children attend state schools. Yet the coexistence of the two different systems, along with the transfer of power to the autonomous regions, has created various anomalies. The *Ley Orgánica del Derecho a la Educación* (*LODE* – Right to Education Act), which came into force in 1985, states that all private schools funded with public money should provide their services free. In practice, this process of *concertación* (harmonization) varies considerably, according to the agreement between individual schools and the education authorities. 'Harmonized' schools remain private and offer free education. It is, however, still up to the family to buy books and to pay a proportion of the cost of transport, food and some extra-curricular activities.

Ley General de Educación (Old System)

▶ **Preescolar** (pre-school) was divided into *Jardín de Infancia* (nursery school – for 2- and 3-year-olds) and *Escuela de Párvulos* (infant school – for 4- and 5-year-olds). Although not compulsory, it was free at state-provided centres.

▶ **Educación general básica (EGB)** (primary, or elementary) was compulsory and therefore free at state and 'harmonized' schools. Education began at 6 years old and lasted for eight years. If pupils failed their end-of-year exams, they had to repeat the year, but those who completed the course before 16 qualified for the diploma of *graduado escolar* and could then enrol in either *BUP* or *FP*.

▶ **Bachillerato unificado polivalente (BUP)** (secondary, or high school) was a three-year course aiming to provide general education in arts and sciences; students also began to specialize, with a view to higher education. *BUP* was not compulsory.

▶ **Formación profesional (FP)** (vocational training) was also optional; it followed on from *EGB* and provided vocational training. *FP I* consisted of a two-year course and *FP II* of a three-year course, after which you could apply to university.

▶ **Curso de orientación universitaria (COU)** is a pre-university course following on from *BUP* or *FP II*.

▶ **Pruebas de acceso a la Universidad** are not a course but a two-part exam known as *la Selectividad*, taken in June or September. The first part is taken by all students, and the second focuses on the speciality chosen by the student in *COU* or *FP*.

Ley Orgánica de Ordenación General del Sistema Educativo (New System)

▶ **Educación infantil** (pre-school education – 0–6 years) is not compulsory, but the new system aims to attract as many children as possible.

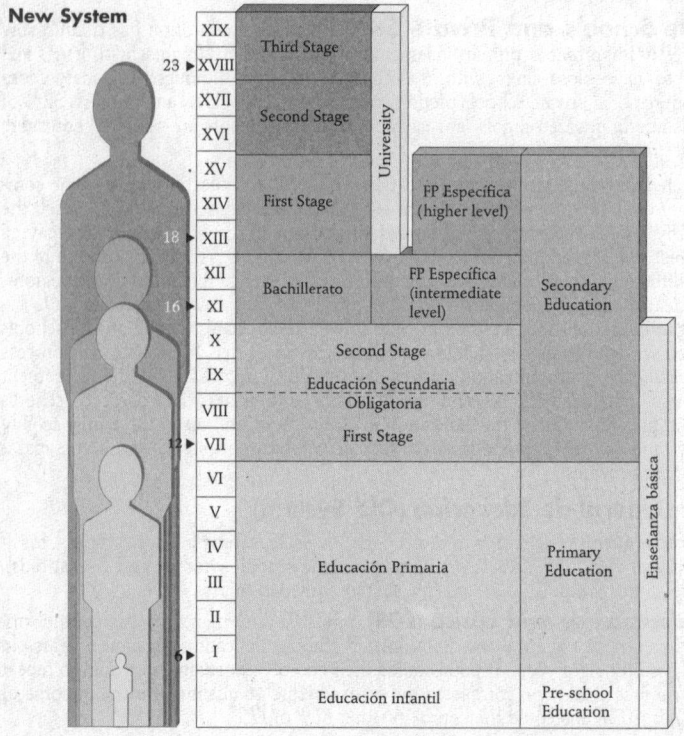

▶ **Educación primaria** (primary education – 6–12 years) constitutes the first part of compulsory education. It consists of three stages of two years each. As well as the usual subjects, physical education (PE), music and a foreign language are taught.

▶ **Educación secundaria obligatoria (ESO)** (secondary education – 12–16 years) consists of two stages of two years each. At the end of *ESO*, students are awarded the qualification of *graduado en educación secundaria* (graduate in secondary education), which signals successful completion of compulsory education.

▶ **Bachillerato** (16–18 years) lasts for two years and offers four options: natural sciences and health, humanities and social sciences, technology, and art. All students follow certain core courses (language and literature; a foreign language; and PE, philosophy and history for one year each), as well as studying a number of optional subjects. Students who complete the *bachillerato* obtain a single qualification that allows them either to go on to university or to enter the higher level of *FP*.

▶ **FP** is made up of two levels: *grado medio* (intermediate level), which students can enter at the end of compulsory education and from which they can go straight on to the job market; and *grado superior* (higher level), which students can enter after completing their *bachillerato* and from which they can either go into work or go on to university. The new *FP* aims to provide more flexible training for students, enabling them to respond to the changing needs of business and industry. It also seeks to undertake retraining programmes for professionals.

University   The University of Salamanca, founded in the early 13th century, was one of the first universities in Europe.The School of Translators in Toledo, where many scientific works from the East were translated during the 12th and 13th centuries, is evidence of the vigorous cultural life of medieval Spain and of the country's role as a multicultural meeting place. Other Spanish universities with a long history are Santiago de Compostela (1504) and Alcalá de Henares (1507); the latter became the Universidad Complutense de Madrid in 1707.

Most universities (47 out of 60) are public: the private ones tend to concentrate on specific subjects such as economics and business administration. Students usually stay in their home town if there is a university which offers the course they are interested in.

Higher education courses last from three to six years. On completing a university course of four, five or six years, the student becomes a *licenciado* (graduate). *Escuelas universitarias* offer shorter three-year courses, at the end of which the student becomes a *diplomado*. Students over 25 wishing to enter university have to take exams similar to the *Selectividad*.

Another institution, the Universidad Internacional Menéndez Pelayo, was

The Top Ten Universities
(by number of students)
■ Universidad Complutense de Madrid
■ Universidad Nacional de Educación a Distancia (Spanish Open University)
■ Universitat de Barcelona
■ Universitat de València (Estudi General)
■ Universidad de Sevilla
■ Universidad de Santiago de Compostela
■ Universidad de Granada
■ Universidad del País Vasco
■ Universitat Autònoma de Barcelona
■ Universidad de Zaragoza

founded in Santander in 1932; it runs summer courses for students of all nationalities.

I n Spain, as in most countries in Western Europe, there is a pitched battle amongst political and economic interests for control of the media.

Television Television now broadcasts almost 24 hours a day. There are two national channels owned and run by the State: *TVE-1* is aimed at a broad audience and provides mainstream viewing, whilst *TVE-2* concentrates on cultural and educational programmes. *Televisión Española (TVE)* provides a separate Catalan channel. There are also several locally run channels in the autonomous regions (*see below*).

Programmes on the independent channels are broadly similar to those on the State-owned channels, with whom they have been in competition since 1990. In that same year, *Canal+* began broadcasting in Spain. This is an independent subscription channel offering mainly films, special reports, documentaries, news, sports and music; films are shown with no commercial breaks. To receive most of its programmes you need to buy a decoder, for which you pay a subscription and a monthly fee.

Satellite television is becoming more and more popular in Spain, and there are around 60 satellite channels available, including *Canal Clásico, Antena 3 satélite, Canal 31, Documanía, Cinemanía, Cineclassics, Minimax, Teledeporte* and *Galavisión* (the latter a Latin American channel), all broadcasting in Spanish. You can also receive foreign channels, such as the *BBC, CNN, RTL* or *Eurosport*.

Main Television Channels
■ State-owned: *TVE-1, TVE-2 (La 2)*
■ Independent: *Antena 3, Tele 5, Canal+*
■ Regional: *Telemadrid, Canal Sur* (Andalusia), *TVE-3* and *Canal 33* (Catalonia), *TVG* (Galicia), *Canal 9* and *Noticias 9* (Valencia), *ETB1* and *ETB2* (Basque Country)

The main players on the digital TV scene are *Canal Satélite Digital* (belonging to the owners of *Canal+* and the newspaper *El País*) and *Vía Digital* (owned by *Telefónica* and other shareholders like the newspaper *El Mundo*). They broadcast by satellite, but are expected to go over to cable. Both companies offer a wide range of channels (around 35) and require a decoder, for which you pay a subscription.

Teletexto (Teletext) provides text-only information on the weather, news, sports, entertainment listings etc.

Radio There are two frequencies available: *Onda Media* (Medium Wave), which is used less and less, and *Frecuencia Modulada* (FM), which has a growing number of stations providing programmes 24 hours a day. The State-owned *Radio Nacional de España (RNE)* has five stations: *Radio 1* produces chat shows, news bulletins, game shows and sports programmes; *Radio 2* specializes in classical music; *Radio 3* broadcasts mainly rock and pop but also has 'alternative' versions of chat shows etc.; *Radio 4* is in Catalan and only goes out in Catalonia; and *Radio 5* is dedicated to news.

Main Radio Stations
■ *RNE Radio 1*: chat shows, news, game shows, sport
■ *RNE Radio 2*: classical music
■ *RNE Radio 3*: rock and pop music
■ *COPE, SER* and *Onda Cero*: chat shows, news, music

Independent stations enjoy very large audiences and they too offer

chat shows, discussion programmes, music, game shows and news. The most popular stations are *SER*, *COPE* and *Onda Cero*. *SER*'s *Cuarenta Principales*, specializing in rock and pop music, also has a large following, especially amongst young people.

State-owned radio in the autonomous regions has undergone a massive expansion in recent years: *Euskadi Irratia*, *Radio Galega*, *Catalunya Ràdio*, *Canal Sur* (in Andalusia), *Onda Regional de Murcia* and *Canal Nou* (in Valencia) are just a few of the stations available in the regions.

The Press Newspaper circulation in Spain is one of the lowest in Europe: only 100 newspapers are sold for every 1000 people. Nevertheless, the press is very influential and there is a wide variety of newspapers available: more than 150 dailies. Although some of these are distributed nationally and some – e.g. *El País*, *El Mundo* or *ABC* – produce special editions in some of the autonomous regions, most are purely local or regional.

At regional level, the main newspapers published wholly or partially in languages other than Spanish are: *Avui* and *El Punt* in Catalan; *Egin* and *Deia* in Basque; and *O Correo Galego*

Major Daily Newspapers and their Circulation	
El País	414 000
ABC	303 000
El Mundo	261 000
El Periódico de Cataluña	211 000
La Vanguardia	197 000

in Galician. Some newspapers are even published in English: *Majorca Daily Bulletin* and *Sur in English*, for example. Sports newspapers (*As*, *Marca*, *Sport*, *Mundo Deportivo*) have a wide circulation, as do the new financial and economic papers like *Expansión*, *Gaceta de los Negocios* and *Cinco Días*. The weekend editions of most newspapers carry a supplement which sometimes includes part works (guides, maps, dictionaries etc.), although this makes for a higher cover price. The dailies also frequently come in separate sections, often printed in different colours and on different paper, focusing on local issues or on a topic such as science, medicine, culture etc.

The magazine market is a thriving one, with more than 300 registered titles. Those with the highest circulation figures are the so-called *revistas del corazón* (real-life or true-romance magazines), such as *¡Hola!*, *Lecturas* and *Semana*, which report on the love lives of actors and other celebrities. *Pronto* and *Diez Minutos* have the same subject matter but take a more sensationalist line. Next come the television guides (*Teleprograma*, *Supertele*), which are cheap and provide complete coverage of TV programmes as well as short news items. The TV listings magazines are losing in popularity, as the TV ratings wars mean that the schedules are constantly changing, often from one day to the next. Magazines providing general news coverage come only third, since the weekend newspaper supplements now have the lion's share of this market. The most popular of these magazines is *Interviú*, followed by *Tiempo*, *Cambio 16* and *Época*. The best-selling monthly magazine is *Muy Interesante*, which specializes in articles on scientific or popular science topics. For readers interested in the arts, *El Europeo* and *El Paseante* are amongst the most appealing titles. There is also a vast choice of publications catering for the specialist reader, on subjects ranging from computing to knitting.

Nearly all newspaper and magazine sales are made through the ubiquitous *quioscos* (newsstands), since subscriptions are almost unknown (although certain professional journals are sold in this way).

Away from the ubiquitous shopping centres (malls), department stores, hypermarkets and supermarkets, you will discover an array of smaller shops catering for the typical Spanish lifestyle. *Bodeguillas* sell table wine from the barrel, as well as bottles of more upmarket vintages, beers, soft drinks etc. Some even serve drinks at the counter, typically a *chato* (a small glass of wine) or *botellín* (a small beer). Here you will find *cava*, the Spanish version of champagne, and wines from Rioja, Ribera del Duero, Penedés and Valdepeñas alongside Spain's most famous export, sherry. Try your wine with some cheese: *manchego* (from La Mancha), *queso de Mahón*

Shopping Hours	
Shops may choose their own opening hours, but must not exceed 72 hours per week. The ones below are the most usual. Sunday and bank holiday opening is very restricted (except for bakers, newsagents, florists and petrol (gas) stations).	
Department stores	10 a.m.–9/10 p.m.
Hypermarkets	10 a.m.–9/10 p.m.
Shopping centres	10 a.m.–10 p.m.
Smaller shops	9/10 a.m.–1.30/2 p.m.,
	4.30/5 p.m.–8/8.30 p.m.
Markets	9 a.m.–2 p.m.,
	5–8 p.m.

(from Menorca), *cabrales* (from Asturias) or *queso de tetilla* (from Galicia), or visit the *charcutería* or *salchichería* for some cold meats. Choose from *jamón serrano* (cured ham – the best is from Jabugo in the south), *chorizo* (spicy red sausage), *lomo ibérico* (pork loin), or *fuet* from Catalonia. Shops selling *frutos secos y variantes* lure Spanish children with their displays of *pipas* (salted sunflower seeds, whose husks you will see littering streets and cafes), sweets, popcorn and crisps, while adults buy pickles (onions, gherkins or *banderillas* – cocktail sticks on which are speared gherkins, pieces of chilli pepper, onions, olives and perhaps anchovies). The stars of the show in these shops are undoubtedly olives. *Herbolarios* or *herboristerías* are herbalists which also stock health foods, organic and vegetarian products, diet foods, herbal teas and so on.

On a more practical note, *droguerías* stock cosmetics and toiletries as well as cleaning products, whilst you can find the two-prong plugs and adapters you will need to use the 220-volt electric current in a *ferretería* (an ironmonger's shop, more like a small DIY store) or a *tienda de electrodomésticos*.

Markets Every town has its covered markets: either big municipal ones or smaller food markets serving a particular neighbourhood. The latter are called *galerías de alimentación*. In villages, there may well be travelling markets that set up one day a week in the main square or in the streets to sell food and clothes from open-air stalls.

For bargain antiques or unusual artifacts, it is best to go to street markets like the famous *Rastro* in Madrid, *Los Encantes* in Barcelona, or their equivalents in other cities.

Sales These take place mainly in the months of January and August.

Payment VAT (sales tax) is normally included in the price of all goods bought in shops, supermarkets etc. You can pay in cash or with a credit or debit card (*see page 12*). Some large stores have their own charge cards, but they also accept the better-known credit cards (Visa®, MasterCard®, American Express® and so on). Cheques are not normally accepted in shops. Although it is not the usual custom, the shop assistant is obliged to give the customer a bill or receipt if requested. If you buy faulty goods, you can usually exchange them if you still have your receipt.

The *siesta*, a rest period after lunch when most people take a nap, is a very Spanish phenomenon. Modern working hours, however, mean that most people can no longer keep up the tradition. Lunch is usually eaten between 2 and 3 p.m.

Given the fine weather during most of the year, a large part of people's leisure time is spent out of doors, either playing sports or chatting with friends and having a drink at an open-air bar. The *paseo*, a late afternoon or early evening stroll, is a tradition that many Spaniards keep up when work permits. Dinner is eaten late, from 9 p.m. onwards. If you can't last out till then, you can sample some of Spain's delicious bar snacks: *tapas* are small portions of food which sometimes – but not always – come free with your drink. *Raciones* are the same but bigger, whilst *pinchos* come on a cocktail stick. *Montados* and *bocadillos* (small or large filled baguettes, or subs) are also sold in bars. You pay for your food and drinks when you are ready to leave.

Entertainment and Culture

Bullfights remain a distinctive feature of the country and still have a large following, especially in central and southern Spain. The season is mainly spring and summer. Football is still the most popular sport overall, however, closely followed by basketball, cycling and tennis.

Cinemas are very popular, especially at weekends and on Wednesdays, the so-called *día del espectador* (when seats are cheaper). The theatre is more of a minority interest, although independent and alternative theatre groups have flourished in recent years.

Spain is home to several museums of international standing, including the Prado in Madrid, the Picasso museum in Barcelona, and the new Guggenheim in Bilbao.

Gambling

The *Quiniela*, a sports lottery based on the Spanish football (soccer) league (rather like the football pools in Britain), is very popular. There are other lotteries too: the one organized by *ONCE* (the Spanish Association for the Blind), with daily draws from Monday to Friday; the *Primitiva*; *Bonoloto*; and the National Lottery, famous for its Christmas draw for which almost everyone in Spain buys a ticket. Since the transition to democracy, the casinos have opened their doors again, as have bingo halls, which are very popular.

Local Fiestas

Each village or town has its annual celebration, the *fiesta mayor*, usually in summer. Local people, businesses and institutions pool their resources to stage cultural and recreational events which vary according to the traditions

---

Local Fiestas

- *Carnaval* (Cádiz and Santa Cruz de Tenerife)
- *Fallas* (Valencia)
- *Semana Santa* (Holy Week) (Andalusia and Aragon)
- *Rocío* (Andalusia and Estremadura)
- *Feria de abril* (Andalusia)
- *Sanfermines* (Pamplona)
- *Noche de San Juan* (St John's Eve) (Mediterranean coast)

---

and customs of each particular place. They include the colourful *Carnavales* in Cádiz and Santa Cruz de Tenerife; the *Fallas* in Valencia (19 March), when gigantic papier-mâché figures called *ninots* are burned; the religious processions of *Semana Santa* (Holy Week) in Andalusia or Aragon and the *Rocío* in Huelva; the *Feria* in Seville in April, with flamenco, horses and sherry; and the *Sanfermines*, a bullrunning festival in the streets of Pamplona, that takes place in July. Lastly, on the eve of *San Juan* (24 June), there are spectacular bonfires and fireworks all along Spain's Mediterranean coast.

SPANISH-SPEAKING AMERICA

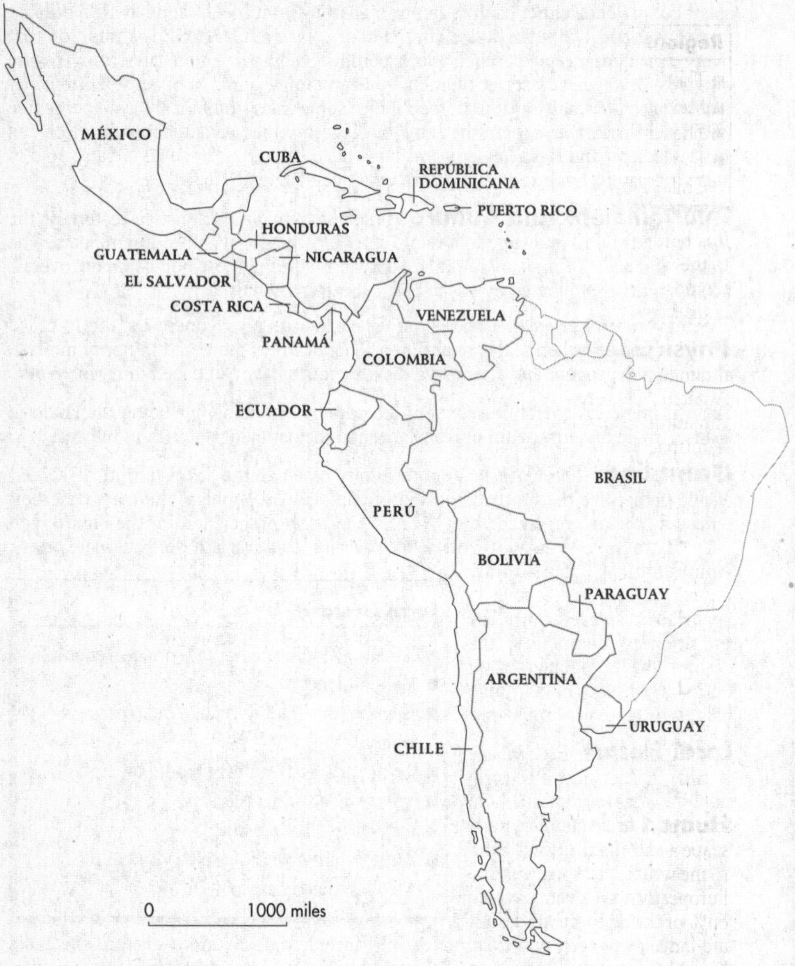

MÉXICO

CUBA

REPÚBLICA
DOMINICANA

PUERTO RICO

HONDURAS

GUATEMALA

NICARAGUA

EL SALVADOR

COSTA RICA

VENEZUELA

PANAMÁ

COLOMBIA

ECUADOR

BRASIL

PERÚ

BOLIVIA

PARAGUAY

ARGENTINA

URUGUAY

CHILE

0   1000 miles

The Americas are divided into three geographical regions: North America, Central America and South America. Spanish-speakers can be found in all three of these areas. People sometimes tend to forget, perhaps because of its powerful neighbour to the north, that Mexico is actually part of North America.

Regions of Spanish America

- The Caribbean
- Mexico and Central America
- The Andean countries
- The Southern Cone (Argentina, Chile, Uruguay) and Paraguay

The term 'Spanish America' is used to describe the group of Spanish-speaking nations in Latin America that were colonized by the Spanish from the 16th century onwards. It covers a very large area: the southernmost part of North America and almost the whole of Central and South America, with the exception of Haiti, Belize, Surinam, Guyana, French Guiana and Brazil. It is bordered to the east by the Atlantic Ocean and to the west by the Pacific Ocean; to the north, Mexico shares a border with the United States of America, and the southernmost point of Spanish America – Tierra del Fuego – is only a relatively short distance from Antarctica.

Physical Geography South America is a land of contrasts, from the high, cold mountains of the Andes (that run for 6000 miles from the Caribbean Sea to the Antarctic) to the warm beaches of the Caribbean and the Pacific. There is tremendous climatic variety: in Mexico and Central America the seasons are those of the northern hemisphere, whilst in South America the summer runs from December to March and the winter from June to September. There are four main types of landscape in this part of the Americas:

❏ The Pacific region is dominated by extremely high mountain ranges (the highest peak is Aconcagua at 23 000 feet) and partially volcanic ranges that mark the edge of the *altiplanos* (the high plateaux), such as the Andes.

❏ The Atlantic coast is characterized by coastal plains like the Pampas. The mountainous areas consist mainly of high plateaux, none of which exceeds 10 000 feet.

❏ The central region consists of very low-lying areas, like the Amazon Jungle, which are criss-crossed by vast river systems.

❏ The Caribbean Islands are volcanic in origin, with no natural defences against a climate characterized by strong winds, high temperatures, heavy rainfall and extreme humidity.

Human Geography The population of this vast region is as varied as the landscape and climate; in most countries you can find ethnic groups from almost anywhere in the world. The majority of the population are *mestizos*, a mixture of Spanish or other European and the native Indian population. In Mexico, for example, *mestizos* make up 60% of the total population. In Bolivia and Guatemala, more than half the population are Indian, whilst in Argentina and Uruguay most of the population are white and of European descent.

Religion The principal religion is Roman Catholicism. In some countries, like Nicaragua, El Salvador and Peru, Liberation Theology – the belief that poverty is a sin and that the Church should side with the poor against the rich – is very influential. More recently, evangelical Christianity has found growing popularity, especially amongst the poorer sections of society.

	Population	Area (square miles)	Currency	Major Cities (and Populations)
The Caribbean				
Cuba	10 841 000	42 800	peso	Havana (2 015 000) Santiago de Cuba (403 000)
Puerto Rico	3 573 000	3 500	US dollar	San Juan (424 600)
Dominican Republic	7 321 000	19 000	peso	Santo Domingo (1 410 000)
Mexico and Central America				
Mexico	84 967 000	755 800	nuevo peso	Mexico City (15 700 000) Guadalajara (2 245 000)
Guatemala	9 746 000	42 000	quetzal	Guatemala City (1 130 000)
Honduras	5 418 000	43 200	lempita	Tegucigalpa (571 400)
El Salvador	5 387 000	8 100	colón	San Salvador (2 000 000)
Nicaragua	3 916 000	50 200	córdoba oro	Managua (650 000)
Costa Rica	3 135 000	19 700	colón	San José (1 068 206)
Panama	2 514 000	29 700	balboa	Panama City (546 000)
The Andean Countries				
Venezuela	20 310 000	352 000	bolivar	Caracas (1 817 000)
Colombia	33 405 000	439 700	peso	Bogotá (2 015 000) Medellín (2 096 000) Cali (1 955 000)
Ecuador	11 028 000	109 600	sucre	Quito (1 387 887)
Peru	22 370 000	496 000	nuevo sol	Lima (4 165 000)
Bolivia	7 527 000	424 200	boliviano	La Paz (993 000)
The Southern Cone and Paraguay				
Paraguay	4 519 000	157 100	guarani	Asunción (729 307)
Argentina	33 099 000	1 068 000	peso	Buenos Aires (2 209 000; with suburbs 10 881 000) Rosario (955 000) Córdoba (990 000)
Uruguay	3 131 000	68 200	nuevo peso	Montevideo (1 248 000)
Chile	13 599 000	292 200	peso	Santiago (4 913 000)

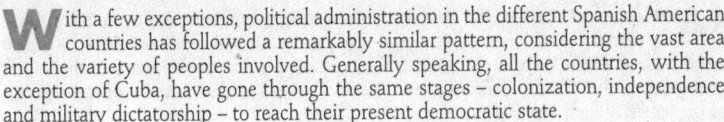

With a few exceptions, political administration in the different Spanish American countries has followed a remarkably similar pattern, considering the vast area and the variety of peoples involved. Generally speaking, all the countries, with the exception of Cuba, have gone through the same stages – colonization, independence and military dictatorship – to reach their present democratic state.

Politics All the Spanish-speaking countries in the Americas (except Puerto Rico) are independent republics which, apart from Cuba, are governed by democratically elected parliaments. Under the multiparty system, people vote every four or – in the case of Mexico – six years to elect their representatives. In most countries, the President is only elected for one term of office. Puerto Rico is a self-governing part of the USA, with the same control over internal affairs as the other states. Until the 1980s, Spanish America suffered under a series of oppressive military dictatorships.

Economics Most of the countries in Spanish-speaking America have vast natural resources, although in general their economies are not very developed. Despite the fact that much of the population lives in towns and cities, Spanish-speaking America is not highly industrialized, agriculture and mining still playing an important part in the economy. Common factors are high inflation, a massive foreign debt, an extensive black economy, and tremendous inequalities in the distribution of wealth, with the indigenous populations usually coming off worst. A large part of Spanish America is poor and many people live on very meagre incomes. The Central American republics are amongst the poorest, especially Nicaragua and Honduras, with a per capita gross national product (GNP) of 360 US dollars and 580 US dollars respectively. Argentina and Puerto Rico are the wealthiest, with a GNP of 7290 and 6700 dollars respectively, followed by Uruguay on 3910 dollars and Mexico on 3750 dollars.

Language Spanish is the official language spoken by the majority of people in all of Spanish-speaking America. In countries where there is a large indigenous population, such as Peru, Bolivia, Guatemala and Mexico, various Amerindian languages are also spoken.

Some Amerindian Languages
■ *Quechua* (Peru, Bolivia, Ecuador)
■ *Aimara* (Peru and Bolivia)
■ *Náhuatl* (El Salvador and Mexico)

The Spanish spoken in Spanish America has many distinguishing features, but only two are common to the whole continent, namely the *seseo* (the pronunciation of 'c' before 'i' and 'e' as 's', not 'th' as in Spain) and the use of *ustedes* instead of *vosotros* in informal as well as formal speech. Other characteristics are shared by some regions and countries, but not by all. *Vos* replaces *tú* in many regions, and the corresponding verb forms differ from area to area. In the River Plate and most of Central America, the present indicative and imperative forms are affected, e.g. *vos hablás* (for *tú hablas*), *vos tenés* (for *tú tienes*), *vení* (for *ven*) and *levantate* (for *levántate*).

Spanish in the USA In the southern states of the USA there are still a few pockets of Spanish-speakers, descended from the first Spanish settlers to arrive there in the 14th century. The growing importance of Spanish in America, however, is due to the modern-day Spanish-speaking immigrants who come from Mexico, Cuba and Puerto Rico. They now make up about 9% of the whole population, the second largest ethnic minority after Black Americans, and for most of them Spanish is their mother tongue. The most notable thing about the Spanish spoken in the USA is the influence English has had on vocabulary and syntax.

Most experts agree that the first settlers to arrive in the Americas came from Asia. Out of these diverse tribes arose the pre-Columbian civilizations, the most important of which were the Aztecs in the north of Mexico, the Mayans in the south of Mexico and in Central America, and the Incas, who settled in the Andean regions of present-day Peru and Bolivia.

Discovery and Colonization The discovery of the Americas by Cristóbal Colón (Christopher Columbus) in 1492 was followed by the conquest of its people and its lands. Many European explorers and conquistadors made the journey across the Atlantic, but it was Spanish colonization and the imposition of Christianity which destroyed the indigenous civilizations. By the 1530s Hernán Cortés had conquered the Aztecs and Francisco Pizarro the Incas. Pedro de Mendoza founded Buenos Aires in 1536 and, around the same time, a colony was set up in Paraguay. The colonization of other parts of the continent was much slower due to the difficulty of the terrain.

Independence Spanish and Portuguese colonization created a new social class, the *criollo*, someone of European descent born in a Spanish American colony. It was the *criollos* who formed the revolutionary juntas in revolt against Spanish rule after 1808. The most famous of the independence leaders, who began their campaigns of liberation at around the same time, were General Simón Bolívar (Venezuela, 1783–1830), whose unrealized dream was to form a confederation of Latin American states, and General José Sanmartín (Argentina, 1778–1850), who liberated Chile and contributed to the independence of Peru. Other countries soon joined them in declaring their independence.

Dates of Independence
■ *Argentina:* 9 July 1816
■ *Bolivia:* 6 August 1825
■ *Chile:* 18 September 1810
■ *Colombia:* 20 July 1810
■ *Costa Rica:* 15 September 1821
■ *Cuba:* 20 May 1902
■ *Dominican Republic:* 27 February 1844
■ *Ecuador:* 24 May 1822
■ *El Salvador:* 15 September 1821
■ *Guatemala:* 15 September 1821
■ *Honduras:* 15 September 1821
■ *Mexico:* 16 September 1810
■ *Nicaragua:* 15 September 1821
■ *Panama:* 3 November 1903
■ *Paraguay:* 14 May 1811
■ *Peru:* 28 July 1821
■ *Uruguay:* 25 August 1825
■ *Venezuela:* 5 July 1811

The Present Day Once fragmented, Spanish America underwent a long period of internal political upheavals and border wars. In 1898 Spain lost its last colonies, Cuba and Puerto Rico, signalling the end of four centuries of domination. Since 1898 the United States army has intervened in Spanish American countries on numerous occasions, sometimes on its own initiative, at others at the request of Spanish Americans themselves. The condition of permanent economic crisis and poverty was a breeding ground for military dictatorships and for the revolutionary movements that sprang up to combat them. Finally, in the 1980s, democracy was restored to almost every country in Spanish America. As for relations between the different states, the creation of the *Organización de Estados Americanos* (Organization of American States) in 1948 in Bogotá was proof of a desire for cooperation. Some countries, like Argentina, Brazil, Uruguay and Paraguay, went further, and moved towards economic integration through the creation of *Mercosur*, which represents about 200 million people and has a GDP of 800 000 million dollars. Another far-reaching international treaty was the *Tratado de Libre Comercio* (TLC – North American Free Trade Agreement, NAFTA), to which the USA, Canada and Mexico are signatories.

Railways (railroads) are generally in decline due to competition from the road network and high maintenance costs, especially in areas where the terrain is difficult. Most road systems are extensive (although largely unpaved), but there are few international road and rail links; travelling between countries is far easier by air.

Air Most countries have good and reasonably priced external and internal connections by air. In countries such as Colombia, Ecuador and Uruguay internal flights are the cheapest and most efficient method of getting around.

Rail Cuba is the only Caribbean country with a functioning railway – there are trains to all of the regional capitals and they are much more reliable than buses. In Mexico, Honduras and Guatemala trains are cheap but often slow and unreliable; they can also be unsafe. The train service in Panama (mainly consisting of a line between Panama City and Colón) was destroyed in the 1989 US invasion and is being rebuilt. In Costa Rica the railway network was severely damaged during the 1991 earthquake and remains closed. The railway system in Ecuador is unreliable but features a dramatic ascent from Alausí to Guayaquil which is one of the most spectacular in the world. The eastern and western rail networks in Bolivia are disorganized and all trains apart from the *ferrobús* are extremely slow. Peru has a limited passenger network, including a short line from Huancayo to Huancavelica and the Southern Railroad between Arequipa to Lake Titicaca and Cuzco. Both Argentina and Chile have extensive, if rather neglected, railway systems. Paraguay's ancient, wood-burning trains are extremely cheap but slow, except for the line from Asunción to Areguá, on Lake Ypacaraí.

Road Road conditions vary from excellent in many national capitals to appalling in many of the more rural areas.

▶ **Buses** are the main form of public transport in most countries, with long-distance services the most comfortable and local buses frequent, inexpensive but often crowded. In Cuba services are limited and tickets difficult to obtain without queueing.

▶ **Minibuses**, called variously *colectivos, combis* or *peseros*, are often used for local transport on popular routes. They are usually more expensive than buses although they do not leave until they are full.

▶ **Trucks** (*camiones*) are also a popular mode of transport in many countries and are usually half the price of buses, but less comfortable.

▶ **Taxis** are not always metered and fares may have to be negotiated before starting the journey. It is common to share taxis for local trips; for longer journeys taxis are good value and can usually be chartered by the day or half-day.

▶ **Car** ownership is still a luxury in the poorer countries and road networks are primitive. Even in wealthier nations roads outside the cities are often unpaved and driving is dangerous due to potholes, poor lighting, lack of road signs and stray animals. Roads can become very dusty or muddy or may even disappear altogether depending on the season. In Mexico City car use is restricted to lessen air pollution – the last number of your licence plate determines which days of the week you can drive. Parking is a major problem in most national capitals and major cities.

▶ **Hitchhiking** is popular in many countries. In Cuba government vehicles are legally required to pick up hitchhikers if they have room. In Andean countries drivers may insist on payment, even if giving the initial impression that the lift is free.

Sea The most important ports are Montevideo (Uruguay) and Buenos Aires (Argentina) on the Atlantic coast, and Valparaíso and Callao (Peru) on the Pacific.

Telephone and postal services vary in quality throughout Spanish American countries, the most advanced being in the richer nations such as Argentina and Mexico, and the least developed in the poorest countries such as Cuba. Services are operated by private or state-owned companies or a mixture of the two. In general, increasing competition in the provision of telecommunication and postal services has led to major improvements in the quality of facilities in many countries in recent years.

Standard Time Zones (hours before GMT)	
■ Puerto Rico	4
■ Cuba	5
■ Dominican Republic	4
■ Mexico	6–8
■ Panama	5
■ Costa Rica	6
■ El Salvador	6
■ Guatemala	6
■ Honduras	6
■ Nicaragua	6
■ Venezuela	4
■ Peru	5
■ Colombia	5
■ Ecuador	5
■ Bolivia	4
■ Argentina	3
■ Uruguay	3
■ Chile	4
■ Paraguay	4

Telephones The telephone service is often erratic and delays are quite commonly experienced when making both local and long-distance calls.

▶ **Public telephones** are available in streets, public buildings, transport terminals and some shops, bars and restaurants in towns and cities, but are less common in the countryside. They operate on coins, tokens (*fichas*) or phonecards which are usually available at tobacco kiosks, bars and post offices; in some countries they can be bought from street vendors.

▶ **Long-distance calls** are expensive, especially if made from a hotel. It is cheaper to use the long-distance call direct services of AT&T, MCI, Sprint and BT which bypass local exchanges and surcharges. Overseas calls can also be made from public phone booths in telephone company offices in main towns. The minimum duration is usually three minutes and you pay the attendant when the call is completed.

▶ **Reverse charges/Collect calls** are not always possible; it depends on where you are and who you are calling.

Telegrams, Telex and Fax These services are available in main post offices, in telecom offices and in larger hotels. Telegrams are still commonly used throughout Spanish America.

Postal Services In general, postal systems are not very efficient: long delays are common, it is not unusual for stamps to be removed and mail often goes missing. It is better to avoid using post boxes and small post offices. Any letter or package of importance should be sent registered or certified (*con certificado*) from a main post office, and air mail is generally much more reliable than surface mail. Many businesses use courier services run by private companies or rely on faxes to ensure the safe delivery of important items.

▶ **Stamps** can be bought at post offices and in hotels.

▶ **Post office box numbers** (usually called *apartados* or *casillas*) are commonly used in Spanish American countries instead of street addresses.

▶ **Poste restante/General delivery** services (*lista de correos*) are available in main post offices in national capitals, but can be unreliable.

Most of the working population is employed in various forms of agriculture, either on small peasant farms, large banana, coffee and cotton plantations, or *haciendas*, or in commercial ranching operations or vegetable and flower production. Despite growing industrialization, manufacturing output is small by world standards. Japan alone, for example, produces more manufactured goods than all of Spanish America combined. Manufacturing continues to be poorly paid, labour-intensive and low-technology. Mining, important during the colonial period, continues to employ large numbers of people. Tourism is expanding throughout the region, and is an increasingly important source of income and employment.

GNP per capita ($US)	
■ Puerto Rico	6700
■ Cuba	1580
■ Dominican Republic	1080
■ Mexico	3750
■ Panama	2610
■ Costa Rica	2160
■ El Salvador	1320
■ Guatemala	1100
■ Honduras	580
■ Nicaragua	360
■ Venezuela	2840
■ Peru	1490
■ Colombia	1350
■ Ecuador	1170
■ Bolivia	770
■ Argentina	7290
■ Uruguay	3910
■ Chile	3070
■ Paraguay	1500

Social Security State benefits for families and the unemployed are minimal or non-existent. The social security system provides only limited benefits: old age pensions, sick pay and maternity leave.

Employment

▶ **Agriculture** is the dominant economic sector, with most countries heavily dependent on primary exports including sugar, coffee, bananas, beef, cotton, tobacco, corn, soya, fresh fruit, timber and cut flowers.

▶ **Mining** has traditionally been important and remains an area of high investment and growth. Many countries in Spanish America possess vast metallic and non-metallic mineral resources. Mexico is the world's leading producer of silver, fluorite and arsenic; Peru has the largest gold mine in South America; Chile has been the world's largest producer of copper since 1982; and Colombia has the largest coal reserves in South America.

▶ **Manufacturing** in most countries is closely allied to agricultural activity. Leading manufacturing industries include food processing and beverages, cotton processing, sugar refining, meat packing, textiles and clothing.

▶ **Oil and gas** production is a major source of income in the region. Mexico is the world's sixth largest producer; Venezuela has the largest oil reserves in the Western hemisphere and was a founding member of OPEC (Organization of Petroleum Exporting Countries); and Argentina, Bolivia, Colombia and Ecuador are all net exporters of oil.

▶ **Tourism** is an important source of foreign exchange, with growing numbers of visitors and the development of new tourist attractions. In Mexico tourism is the largest employer, with about a third of the workforce. The Spanish-speaking Caribbean islands and Central American countries attract increasing numbers of tourists, stimulating economic growth in those regions, as well as creating jobs in areas of high unemployment.

▶ **Narcotics** are big business. Colombia is a major producer of cocaine, heroin and marijuana for the international drug market; most of the coca leaves, coca paste and cocaine base used for processing into Colombian cocaine comes from Bolivia and Peru.

The banks and other financial institutions in Spanish America are mostly State-owned, and are usually regulated by a central bank or an official body such as a superintendency of banks. Recurrent political and economic instability in many Spanish American countries means that the banking and financial sectors are not very robust.

Business Hours These vary according to climate and local custom. In most countries the afternoon *siesta* is sacred and offices, shops and businesses close for two or three hours in the afternoon, although in the big cities the custom is no longer so well observed. In general many businesses open early in the morning and after the *siesta* stay open until early evening. At weekends most businesses and offices are closed.

▶ **Banks** are usually open from 8 or 9 a.m. to early or mid-afternoon Mondays to Fridays. Head offices in some countries may open on Saturday mornings as well.

Inflation	
■ Puerto Rico (av. 1989–94)	3.6
■ Cuba	n.a.
■ Dominican Republic (av. 1989–94)	23.9
■ Mexico (av. 1989–94)	16.1
■ Panama (av. 1989–94)	1.1
■ Costa Rica (av. 1989–94)	18.4
■ El Salvador (av. 1989–94)	15.6
■ Guatemala (av. 1988–93)	20.8
■ Honduras (av. 1989–94)	19.4
■ Nicaragua (av. 1989–94)	418.0
■ Venezuela (av. 1989–94)	40.7
■ Peru (av. 1991–94)	746.7
■ Colombia (av. 1989–94)	26.6
■ Ecuador (av. 1989–94)	44.5
■ Bolivia (av. 1989–94)	13.3
■ Argentina (av. 1991–94)	13.3
■ Uruguay (av. 1988–93)	74.4
■ Chile (av. 1989–94)	17.5
■ Paraguay (av. 1988–93)	24.2

▶ **Shops** are usually open from 8 or 9 a.m. to 2 p.m. and then from 4 or 5 p.m. to 7 p.m. Mondays to Saturdays. On Saturdays shops in some Spanish American countries may only open in the morning.

Credit Cards American Express®, Diners Club®, Mastercard® and Visa® are generally accepted in most countries, although acceptance can be patchy and credit card transactions may be subject to high surcharges. Outside urban areas credit cards are of limited use and transactions require cash. In general, American Express® is less useful than Visa®. In Cuba credit cards issued in the USA and American Express® cards, wherever issued, are not accepted.

Cash Machines (ATMs) The Cirrus®, Plus®, Visa®, MasterCard® and other networks (*cajero automático*) are available in most large towns and cities but are not as common as in the UK and USA.

Shopping Hypermarkets have not yet made any real impact, and wholesale and retail outlets tend to be family-run.

Tipping In general taxi drivers should be tipped if the taxi has a meter but there is no need to do so if the fare has been agreed in advance. Porters at airports should be tipped per item of luggage. In restaurants a tip of between 5 and 10% of the bill is usual, but tends to be discretionary where a service charge is already included. In many Spanish American countries tips are also usually given to cinema usherettes, cloakroom attendants and hairdressers.

Most Spanish American countries have a national health system. However, private hospitals exist alongside state ones and tend to offer much better-quality care, though only a rich minority can afford to use them. Hospital facilities in rural areas are, for the most part, limited.

Public Health In rural areas public sanitation is rudimentary and the risk of contracting infections and diseases is greater than in Europe or the USA. By country the leading causes of death are dysentery (especially in Colombia), tuberculosis (Peru), whooping cough (Bolivia, Ecuador and Peru) and measles (Ecuador, Bolivia and Colombia). Among notifiable diseases, the main causes of death in South America are syphilis and typhoid fever.

▶ **Nutrition** is inadequate in terms of calorie and protein intake in poorer countries in Central America and the Andes. Even in some of the wealthier nations food shortages are not uncommon.

▶ **Infant mortality** rates are exceptionally high in some countries despite continuing medical progress. For example, in Bolivia and Peru more than 70 of every 1000 infants under the age of one died in 1995. In the more developed nations, though, life expectancy exceeds 70 years.

Common Health Risks The following inoculations are recommended before visiting any of the countries in Spanish-speaking America: yellow fever, typhoid, poliomyelitis, tetanus and hepatitis.

▶ **Insects** such as chiggers, mites, ticks and mosquitoes are a nuisance, particularly in tropical regions, and may be carriers of serious diseases. Mosquito nets and chemical repellents are essential in many regions.

▶ **Intestinal upsets** are common. Tap water is rarely safe outside large cities and is best avoided, as are ice cubes in drinks. Filtered and bottled water is widely available and safe. Amoebic dysentery is a real risk in some countries and it is also best to avoid uncooked vegetables, fruit with a thin peel, salads, unpasteurized milk and unpasteurized milk products.

▶ **Altitude sickness** is a threat at altitudes above 10 000 feet. Acute symptoms (*soroche*) include headaches, dizziness, lassitude, nausea and vomiting. Visitors to Mexico City, Bolivia and Peru should allow half a day or more of rest for acclimatization. A local Peruvian remedy for *soroche* is *mate de coca*, tea made from coca leaf.

▶ **Malaria** is uncommon and restricted to coastal and jungle zones, but has been on the increase in recent years. Medical advice should be taken if visiting malarial regions.

▶ **Dengue fever** is a viral disease which can require hospitalization. There is no vaccine against the *Aedes* mosquito that carries the virus; you must just avoid bites.

▶ **Rabies** is endemic, so if bitten by a dog seek medical assistance at once.

▶ **Sunburn** is a serious problem at high altitudes.

▶ **Air pollution** levels in Mexico City are extremely high between December and May. The smog is considered a serious health threat so caution is necessary.

Chemists (Pharmacies) There are large numbers of chemists offering a wide range of treatments for stomach bugs and tropical diseases. Many medicines can be bought over the counter without a prescription, and pharmacists often diagnose and treat minor ailments.

Spanish America has a state education system at primary (elementary), secondary (high school) and university levels, which coexists with a large private sector. While some state universities enjoy great prestige, primary and secondary schools are generally inferior to private schools, which are beyond the means of most of the population.

Pre-school Education Only a small proportion of children under the age of five are enrolled in pre-school programmes (*see table below*).

Primary and Secondary Education In general, increased government expenditure on state schools since the 1960s has improved the quantity and quality of primary and secondary education and reduced the importance of private schools. Vocational training and technical and professional education have also been expanded at secondary level to help provide students with practical skills to prepare them for the job market.

Higher Education This has seen rapid growth since the 1960s and there are now over 400 major universities (including technical universities) among several thousand institutions of higher learning. This increase has been achieved by greater public expenditure and through the expansion and proliferation of private universities

Enrolment in Education (%)				
	1960	1970	1980	1990
■ Pre-school (0–5 age group)	2.4	3.3	7.8	16.7
■ Primary (6–11 age group)	57.7	71	82.9	87.1
■ Secondary (12–17 age group)	36.3	49.8	62.9	66.2
■ Tertiary (18–23 age group)	5.7	11.6	24.1	26.9

funded by tuition fees and lucrative contract research. Degrees are offered in virtually every field, and traditionally law, medicine and engineering have attracted large numbers of students. As a result, many graduates in these and other specialized professions have difficulty finding employment due to the underdeveloped nature of most national economies. In Cuba technical and scientific subjects are emphasized over more traditional studies and in this respect the Cuban university system can be said to come closest to serving national economic development and the interests of the poorest people in society.

Literacy Although schooling at all levels has increased since the 1960s, the quality of education that most children receive is inadequate. This is particularly the case in public schools, which enrol most primary and secondary students, and for virtually all of the poor. Illiteracy is still a big problem, especially in rural areas and amongst women; incomplete primary education is more the rule than the exception and secondary or higher education rates are very low compared to the developed world. Poverty, the dispersed nature of rural populations, discrimination against indigenous peoples and lack of political will to educate the rural population all conspire to prevent access to basic education. Cuba, Argentina, Costa Rica, Peru and Uruguay do the most effective job of educating their citizens; each has a literacy rate of 90% or greater. Much further down the scale are the Central American republics. In Guatemala, for example, 50% of the population over 25 have had no formal education and a further 22% fail to complete elementary schooling. The exception in this region is Nicaragua, where in the 1980s the Sandinista Government organized a nationwide drive for literacy, based on the Cuban example after the 1959 revolution.

Most of the media in Spanish America (except Cuba) tend to be privately owned.

Newspapers Most countries offer a wide range of newspapers and magazines, although they are only read by the middle and upper classes. The oldest newspapers date back to the early nineteenth century: Chile's *El Mercurio* (still the country's leading newspaper) was founded in 1827 and Peru's *El Comercio* in 1839. In several countries political upheavals produced complete breaks with the past; in Mexico, for example, the oldest existing newspapers – *El Universal* (1916), *El Excelsior* (1917) and *La Prensa* (1928) – all postdate the 1910 revolution, and in Cuba the oldest existing paper is *Granma*, founded in 1965. Despite the common linguistic and cultural heritage there are only a few region-wide publications, the most successful being the news magazine *Visión*.

> **Major Spanish Language Newspapers**
>
> *La Nación* (Buenos Aires)
> *El Excelsior* (Mexico City)
> *La Jornada* (Mexico City)
> *El Comercio* (Lima)

▶ **English language newspapers** are among the oldest and most prestigious of publications. Panama's oldest paper is the *Star and Herald* (1849); in Argentina the *Buenos Aires Herald* (1876) maintains an enviable reputation for political independence; and in Venezuela the *Daily Journal* is also highly regarded.

▶ **Censorship** has varied according to time and place, and at its most extreme has led to abductions, imprisonment, forced exile and assassinations of journalists, as in Argentina in the mid-1970s. Less extreme censorship persists in some countries in the form of economic coercion and bribery. In Cuba all media are controlled by the State.

Television As everywhere else in the world, television is the staple of popular information and entertainment, and is largely funded by advertising. Most countries have two or three commercial networks and often a government or educational channel. Programmes used to consist entirely of reruns of US output dubbed into Spanish, but the share of national programmes has increased dramatically in the last 20 years. Programmes characteristic of Spanish American TV include marathon variety shows presented live before a studio audience, live regional music, comedy and *telenovelas*.

▶ **Telenovelas** are popular TV soap operas which dominate prime-time viewing in most countries. They are not clones of US soaps or movies but adaptations of older forms of Spanish American popular culture such as radio melodramas (*radionovelas*) and the serial novel. As well as family dramas and romance, *telenovelas* often feature more realistic themes such as economic corruption, health and family planning.

▶ **Cable and satellite** television is expanding most rapidly in Argentina and Mexico. In Argentina, for example, 60% of households have cable TV.

Radio There are many thousands of radio stations in Spanish America. The majority are small commercial operations with simple output, although in cities there are larger FM and AM stations offering a variety of programmes including news, popular music, sport, talk shows and *radionovelas*.

▶ **National radio**, the official state network, is often poorly funded and equipped. It carries more political discussions and educational material than commercial stations.

▶ **University stations** are aimed at an educated minority. They broadcast a mixture of educational programmes, classical music and cultural programmes taken from leading international radio networks such as the *BBC* and *Voice of America*.

▶ **Religious stations** run by the Roman Catholic and Protestant churches are numerous. They provide a wide range of news, and cultural and evangelical material.

Popular culture throughout Spanish America is based on a complex fusion of European Spanish, indigenous, African and *criollo* folklore. Music and dance are particularly important in the region, and are an essential part of any celebration of a traditional or popular nature.

Festivals Independence Day (*see page 24*) is the main festival in all Spanish American countries; also known as the *Fiesta Patria*, it commemorates independence from the Spanish Crown.

Other important festivals tend to be linked to religious occasions, for example, *el Día de los Muertos* (2 November, All Souls' Day) and the *Virgen de Guadalupe* (12 December) in Mexico, or *Nuestro Señor de los Milagros* (Our Lord of Miracles, in October) in Peru.

El Día de los Muertos (Day of the Dead) reflects Aztec traditions and attitudes with regard to death. In most homes and public places, people leave offerings for their dead relatives and friends: flowers and candles, as well as the dead person's favourite food and drink and objects that were of sentimental value to him or her. It is a celebration full of colour and joy, a vision of death that has none of the tragic overtones of the Judaeo-Christian tradition.

The festival of the *Virgen de Guadalupe* attracts devotees from miles around to the Basilica of La Villa in Mexico City, where the image of the Virgin Mary is kept.

Nuestro Señor de los Milagros in Peru is another deeply religious festival. Throughout the month of October, many devotees in Lima dress in purple, the colour of *El Señor*. The festival culminates in a massive procession that packs the city centre.

Music Spanish American music is very varied and usually has close links with dance. Popular music is characterized by its lively, impassioned rhythms, for example, the *tango* in Argentina, the *cumbia* in Colombia, the *salsa*, popular everywhere, *rancheras*, sung by mariachi bands in Mexico, and the rhythms of the Caribbean: the calypso, the Cuban *son* and the *bachata* from the Dominican Republic. There are more ancient musical traditions too: for example, the *guaíno* in Peru and Bolivia, that originated with the pre-Columbian Indians. The symbiosis between *criollo* and indigenous music has produced new rhythms like the *chicha* in Peru. *Nueva canción* (called *nueva trova* in Cuba) developed in Chile and Argentina in the 1960s and is political in nature, although its message is expressed in a variety of forms.

Food Most Spanish American countries have an excellent, rich and varied cuisine that combines indigenous, Asian, African, *criollo* and European flavours. Argentina and Uruguay produce excellent beef, which they normally serve grilled (fish is hardly eaten at all in these places), and you can eat wonderful seafood in the countries on the Caribbean and the Pacific coasts. Mexican cooking is known around the world for its quality and originality. It uses a wide variety of fruit and vegetables as well as spices, especially the many types of chilli pepper; some savoury dishes are even based on chocolate (discovered by the Aztecs and brought to Europe via Spain around 1500).

Sports Various sports are played in Spanish America, but football is the most popular, both to watch and to play. Professional football here is of an extremely high standard and several nations are internationally renowned; fans flock to the stadiums in their thousands to watch their local and national teams. Some countries have achieved great success in other sports too, e.g. athletics in Cuba, basketball in Puerto Rico and cycling in Colombia.

ENGLISH–SPANISH
INGLÉS–ESPAÑOL

a¹ (*pl* **as** OR **a's**), **A** (*pl* **As** OR **A's**) [eɪ] *n* [letter] a *f*, A *f*; **from A to B** de un sitio a otro; **from A to Z** de cabo a rabo.
◆ **A** *n* **-1.** MUS la *m*. **-2.** SCH [mark] ≃ sobresaliente *m*.

a² [*stressed* eɪ, *unstressed* ə] (*before vowel or silent "h":* **an** [*stressed* æn, *unstressed* ən]) *indef art* **-1.** [gen] un (una); **a boy** un chico; **a table** una mesa; **an orange** una naranja; **an eagle** un águila; **a hundred/thousand pounds** cien/mil libras. **-2.** [referring to occupation]: **to be a dentist/teacher** ser dentista/maestra. **-3.** [to express prices, ratios etc] por; **£10 a person** 10 libras por persona; **50 km an hour** 50 kms. por hora; **20p a kilo** 20 peniques el kilo; **twice a week/month** dos veces a la semana/al mes. **-4.** [preceding person's name] un (una) tal; **a Mr Jones** un tal señor Jones.

a. (*abbr of* **acre**) a.

A-1 *adj inf* [excellent] de primera, fetén (*inv*).

A4 *n Br* DIN *m* A4.

AA ◇ *adj abbr of* **anti-aircraft.** ◇ *n* **-1.** (*abbr of* **Automobile Association**) *asociación británica del automóvil*, ≃ RACE *m*. **-2.** (*abbr of* **Associate in Arts**) *titular de una licenciatura de letras en Estados Unidos.* **-3.** (*abbr of* **Alcoholics Anonymous**) AA *mpl*.

AAA *n* **-1.** (*abbr of* **Amateur Athletics Association**) *federación británica de atletismo aficionado.* **-2.** (*abbr of* **American Automobile Association**) *asociación estadounidense del automóvil*, ≃ RACE *m*.

AAUP (*abbr of* **American Association of University Professors**) *n sindicato estadounidense de profesores universitarios.*

AB (*abbr of* **Bachelor of Arts**) *n Am* (*titular de una*) *licenciatura de letras.*

aback [ə'bæk] *adv*: **to be taken ~** quedarse atónito(ta) OR estupefacto(ta).

abacus ['æbəkəs] (*pl* **-cuses** OR **-ci** [-saɪ]) *n* ábaco *m*.

abandon [ə'bændən] ◇ *vt* abandonar. ◇ *n*: **with ~** con desenfreno.

abandoned [ə'bændənd] *adj* abandonado(da).

abashed [ə'bæʃt] *adj* avergonzado(da).

abate [ə'beɪt] *vi* [storm] amainar; [noise] debilitarse; [fear] apaciguarse.

abattoir ['æbətwɑːr] *n* matadero *m*.

abbess ['æbes] *n* abadesa *f*.

abbey ['æbɪ] *n* abadía *f*.

abbot ['æbət] *n* abad *m*.

abbreviate [ə'briːvɪeɪt] *vt* abreviar.

abbreviation [ə,briːvɪ'eɪʃn] *n* abreviatura *f*.

ABC *n* **-1.** *lit* & *fig* abecé *m*. **-2.** (*abbr of* **American Broadcasting Company**) ABC *f*, *cadena de televisión estadounidense.*

abdicate ['æbdɪkeɪt] ◇ *vi* abdicar. ◇ *vt* [responsibility] abdicar de.

abdication [,æbdɪ'keɪʃn] *n* abdicación *f*.

abdomen ['æbdəmen] *n* abdomen *m*.

abdominal [æb'dɒmɪnl] *adj* abdominal.

abduct [əb'dʌkt] *vt* raptar.

abduction [æb'dʌkʃn] *n* rapto *m*.

aberration [,æbə'reɪʃn] *n* aberración *f*, anomalía *f*; **a mental ~** un despiste.

abet [ə'bet] (*pt* & *pp* **-ted**, *cont* **-ting**) *vt* → **aid.**

abeyance [ə'beɪəns] *n*: **in ~** [custom] en desuso; [law] en suspenso.

abhor [əb'hɔːr] (*pt* & *pp* **-red**, *cont* **-ring**) *vt* aborrecer.

abhorrent [əb'hɒrənt] *adj* aborrecible.

abide [ə'baɪd] *vt* soportar, aguantar.

◆ **abide by** *vt fus* [law, ruling] acatar; [principles, own decision] atenerse a.

abiding [ə'baɪdɪŋ] *adj* [feeling, interest] inagotable; [memory] perdurable.

ability [ə'bɪlətɪ] (*pl* **-ies**) *n* **-1.** [capability] capacidad *f*, facultad *f*; **to do sthg to the best of one's** ~ hacer algo lo mejor posible OR lo mejor que uno puede. **-2.** [skill] aptitud *f*, dotes *fpl*.

abject ['æbdʒekt] *adj* **-1.** [poverty] vil, indigente. **-2.** [person] sumiso(sa); [apology] humillante.

ablaze [ə'bleɪz] *adj* **-1.** [on fire] en llamas. **-2.** [bright]: **to be** ~ **with** resplandecer de.

able ['eɪbl] *adj* **-1.** [capable]: **to be** ~ **to do sthg** poder hacer algo. **-2.** [skilful] capaz, competente.

able-bodied [-,bɒdɪd] *adj* (físicamente) sano(na).

ablutions [ə'bluːʃnz] *npl fml* abluciones *fpl*.

ably ['eɪblɪ] *adv* eficientemente.

ABM (*abbr of* **anti-ballistic missile**) *n* ABM *m*, misil antibalístico.

abnormal [æb'nɔːml] *adj* anormal.

abnormality [,æbnɔː'mælətɪ] (*pl* **-ies**) *n* anormalidad *f*, anomalía *f*.

abnormally [æb'nɔːməlɪ] *adv* [unusually] extraordinariamente.

aboard [ə'bɔːd] ◇ *adv* a bordo. ◇ *prep* [ship, plane] a bordo de; [bus, train] en.

abode [ə'bəʊd] *n fml*: **of no fixed** ~ sin domicilio fijo.

abolish [ə'bɒlɪʃ] *vt* abolir.

abolition [,æbə'lɪʃn] *n* abolición *f*.

A-bomb (*abbr of* **atom bomb**) *n* bomba *f* A.

abominable [ə'bɒmɪnəbl] *adj* abominable, deplorable.

abominable snowman *n*: **the** ~ el Abominable Hombre de las Nieves.

abominably [ə'bɒmɪnəblɪ] *adv* de forma abominable OR deplorable.

aborigine [,æbə'rɪdʒənɪ] *n* aborigen *m y f* de Australia.

abort [ə'bɔːt] ◇ *vt* **-1.** [pregnancy, plan, project] abortar; [pregnant woman] provocar el aborto a. **-2.** COMPUT abortar. ◇ *vi* COMPUT abortar.

abortion [ə'bɔːʃn] *n* aborto *m*; **to have an** ~ abortar.

abortive [ə'bɔːtɪv] *adj* frustrado(da), fracasado(da).

abound [ə'baʊnd] *vi* **-1.** [be plentiful] abundar. **-2.** [be full]: **to** ~ **with** OR **in** abundar en.

about [ə'baʊt] ◇ *adv* **-1.** [approximately] más o menos, como; **there were** ~ **fifty/a** hundred había (como) unos cincuenta/cien o así; **at** ~ **five o'clock** a eso de las cinco. **-2.** [referring to place] por ahí; **to leave things lying** ~ dejar las cosas por ahí; **to walk** ~ ir andando por ahí; **to jump** ~ dar saltos. **-3.** [on the point of]: **to be** ~ **to do sthg** estar a punto de hacer algo.
◇ *prep* **-1.** [relating to, concerning] sobre, acerca de; **a film** ~ **Paris** una película sobre París; **what is it** ~? ¿de qué trata?; **tell me** ~ **your problems** háblame de tus problemas; **there's something odd** ~ **that man** hay algo raro en ese hombre; **how** ~ ...? → **how**; **what** ~ ...? → **what**. **-2.** [referring to place] por; **to wander** ~ **the streets** vagar por las calles.

about-turn, **about-face** *n* MIL media vuelta *f*; *fig* cambio *m* radical, giro *m* de 180 grados.

above [ə'bʌv] ◇ *adv* **-1.** [on top, higher up] arriba; **the flat** ~ el piso de arriba; **see** ~ [in text] véase más arriba. **-2.** [more, over]: **children aged five and** ~ niños de cinco años en adelante.
◇ *prep* **-1.** [on top of] encima de. **-2.** [higher up than, over] por encima de; **the plane flew** ~ **them** el avión pasó por encima de ellos. **-3.** [more than, superior to] por encima de; **children** ~ **the age of 15** niños mayores de 15 años; **she's not** ~ **lying** es muy capaz de mentir.

◆ **above all** *adv* sobre todo, por encima de todo.

aboveboard [ə,bʌv'bɔːd] *adj* honrado(da), sin tapujos.

abracadabra [,æbrəkə'dæbrə] *excl* ¡abracadabra!

abrasion [ə'breɪʒn] *n fml* [graze] abrasión *f*.

abrasive [ə'breɪsɪv] ◇ *adj* **-1.** [substance] abrasivo(va). **-2.** [person] cáustico(ca), mordaz. ◇ *n* abrasivo *m*.

abreast [ə'brest] ◇ *adv* en línea, hombro con hombro. ◇ *prep*: **to keep** ~ **of** mantenerse OR estar al día de.

abridged [ə'brɪdʒd] *adj* abreviado(da), reducido(da).

abroad [ə'brɔːd] *adv* en el extranjero; **to go** ~ ir al extranjero.

abrupt [ə'brʌpt] *adj* **-1.** [sudden] repentino(na), súbito(ta). **-2.** [brusque] brusco(ca), seco(ca).

abruptly [ə'brʌptlɪ] *adv* **-1.** [suddenly] bruscamente, de repente. **-2.** [brusquely] secamente, con brusquedad.

ABS (*abbr of* **Antiblockiersystem**) *n* ABS *m*.

abscess ['æbsɪs] *n* absceso *m*.

abscond [əb'skɒnd] *vi*: **to** ~ **(with/from)** escaparse OR fugarse (con/de).

abseil ['æbseɪl] *vi*: **to ~ (down sthg)** descolgarse OR descender haciendo rappel (por algo).

absence ['æbsəns] *n* **-1.** [of person] ausencia *f*; **in sb's ~** en ausencia de alguien. **-2.** [of thing] falta *f*; **in the ~ of** ante la falta de.

absent ['æbsənt] *adj* **-1.** [not present] ausente; **to be ~ from** faltar a, ausentarse de; **to be ~ without leave** MIL ausentarse sin permiso. **-2.** [absent-minded] distraído(da).

absentee [,æbsən'tiː] *n* ausente *m y f*.

absenteeism [,æbsən'tiːɪzm] *n* absentismo *m*.

absent-minded [-'maɪndɪd] *adj* [person] despistado(da); [behaviour] distraído(da).

absent-mindedly [-'maɪndɪdlɪ] *adv* distraídamente.

absinth(e) ['æbsɪnθ] *n* absenta *f*, ajenjo *m*.

absolute ['æbsəluːt] *adj* absoluto(ta).

absolutely ['æbsəluːtlɪ] ◇ *adv* [completely] completamente, absolutamente. ◇ *excl* ¡desde luego!, ¡por supuesto!

absolute majority *n* mayoría *f* absoluta.

absolution [,æbsə'luːʃn] *n* absolución *f*.

absolve [əb'zɒlv] *vt*: **to ~ sb (from)** absolver a alguien (de).

absorb [əb'sɔːb] *vt* **-1.** [gen] absorber; **to be ~ed in sthg** *fig* estar absorto OR embebido en algo. **-2.** *fig* [learn] asimilar.

absorbent [əb'sɔːbənt] *adj* absorbente.

absorbing [əb'sɔːbɪŋ] *adj* absorbente.

absorption [əb'sɔːpʃn] *n* [of liquid] absorción *f*.

abstain [əb'steɪn] *vi*: **to ~ (from)** abstenerse (de).

abstemious [æb'stiːmjəs] *adj fml* sobrio(bria), moderado(da).

abstention [əb'stenʃn] *n* abstención *f*.

abstinence ['æbstɪnəns] *n*: **~ (from)** abstinencia *f* (de).

abstract [*adj & n* 'æbstrækt, *vb* æb'strækt] ◇ *adj* abstracto(ta). ◇ *n* [summary] resumen *m*, sinopsis *f*. ◇ *vt* [summarize] resumir, sintetizar.

abstraction [æb'strækʃn] *n* abstracción *f*.

abstruse [æb'struːs] *adj* abstruso(sa).

absurd [əb'sɜːd] *adj* absurdo(da).

absurdity [əb'sɜːdətɪ] (*pl* **-ies**) *n* irracionalidad *f*.

absurdly [əb'sɜːdlɪ] *adv* [ridiculously] inconcebiblemente.

ABTA ['æbtə] (*abbr of* **Association of British Travel Agents**) *n* asociación británica de agencias de viajes.

Abu Dhabi [,æbu'dɑːbɪ] *n* Abu Dhabi.

abundance [ə'bʌndəns] *n*: **(in) ~ (en)** abundancia *f*.

abundant [ə'bʌndənt] *adj* abundante.

abundantly [ə'bʌndəntlɪ] *adv* **-1.** [extremely]: **it's ~ clear** está clarísimo. **-2.** [in large amounts] abundantemente, en abundancia.

abuse [*n* ə'bjuːs, *vb* ə'bjuːz] ◇ *n* (U) **-1.** [offensive remarks] insultos *mpl*. **-2.** [misuse, maltreatment] abuso *m*. ◇ *vt* **-1.** [insult] insultar. **-2.** [maltreat, misuse] abusar de.

abusive [ə'bjuːsɪv] *adj* [person] grosero(ra); [behaviour, language] insultante, ofensivo(va).

abut [ə'bʌt] (*pt & pp* **-ted**, *cont* **-ting**) *vi*: **to ~ on to** lindar con.

abysmal [ə'bɪzml] *adj* pésimo(ma), nefasto(ta).

abysmally [ə'bɪzməlɪ] *adv* pésimamente.

abyss [ə'bɪs] *n* abismo *m*, sima *f*.

Abyssinia [,æbɪ'sɪnɪə] *n* Abisinia.

Abyssinian [,æbɪ'sɪnɪən] ◇ *adj* abisinio(nia). ◇ *n* abisinio *m*, -nia *f*.

a/c (*abbr of* **account (current)**) c/c.

AC *n* **-1.** *Br* (*abbr of* **athletics club**) CA *m*. **-2.** (*abbr of* **alternating current**) CA *f*.

acacia [ə'keɪʃə] *n* acacia *f*.

academic [,ækə'demɪk] ◇ *adj* **-1.** [of college, university] académico(ca). **-2.** [studious] estudioso(sa). **-3.** [hypothetical] teórico(ca). ◇ *n* [university lecturer] profesor *m* universitario, profesora *f* universitaria.

academically [,ækə'demɪklɪ] *adv* [gifted, qualified] en el terreno académico.

academic year *n* año *m* académico.

academy [ə'kædəmɪ] (*pl* **-ies**) *n* academia *f*.

ACAS ['eɪkæs] (*abbr of* **Advisory, Conciliation and Arbitration Service**) *n* organización británica para el arbitraje en conflictos laborales, ≃ IMAC *m*.

accede [æk'siːd] *vi* **-1.** [agree]: **to ~ to** acceder a. **-2.** [monarch]: **to ~ to the throne** subir al trono.

accelerate [ək'seləreɪt] *vi* **-1.** [car, driver] acelerar. **-2.** [inflation, growth] dispararse.

acceleration [ək,selə'reɪʃn] *n* aceleración *f*.

accelerator [ək'seləreɪtə'] *n* acelerador *m*.

accelerator board *n* COMPUT placa *f* aceleradora.

accelerator card *n* COMPUT tarjeta *f* aceleradora.

accent ['æksent] *n lit & fig* acento *m*.

accentuate [æk'sentjueɪt] *vt* acentuar, poner de relieve.

accept [ək'sept] *vt* **-1.** [gen] aceptar. **-2.** [difficult situation, problem] asimilar. **-3.** [defeat, blame, responsibility] asumir, admitir.

-4. [agree]: **to ~ that** admitir que. **-5.** [subj: machine - coins] funcionar con, admitir.

acceptable [ək'septəbl] *adj* aceptable.

acceptably [ək'septəblɪ] *adv* [allowably, adequately] aceptablemente.

acceptance [ək'septəns] *n* **-1.** [gen] aceptación *f*. **-2.** [of piece of work, article] aprobación *f*. **-3.** [of defeat, blame, responsibility] asunción *f*, reconocimiento *m*. **-4.** [of person - as part of group etc] admisión *f*.

accepted [ək'septɪd] *adj* [ideas, truth] reconocido(da) por todos.

access ['ækses] ◇ *n* **-1.** [entry] acceso *m*; **to gain ~ to** [place] acceder a, conseguir acceso a. **-2.** [opportunity to use or see] libre acceso *m*; **to have ~ to** tener acceso a. ◇ *vt* COMPUT acceder a.

accessibility [ək,sesə'bɪlətɪ] *n* **-1.** [of place] accesibilidad *f*. **-2.** [of service, amenity] facilidad *f* de acceso.

accessible [ək'sesəbl] *adj* **-1.** [place] accesible. **-2.** [service, book, film] asequible.

accession [æk'seʃn] *n* [of monarch] advenimiento *m* OR subida *f* (al trono).

accessory [ək'sesərɪ] (*pl* **-ies**) *n* **-1.** [of car, vacuum cleaner] accesorio *m*. **-2.** JUR cómplice *m y f*.
◆ **accessories** *npl* complementos *mpl*.

access road *n* Br vía *f* OR carretera *f* de acceso.

access time *n* COMPUT tiempo *m* de acceso.

accident ['æksɪdənt] *n* accidente *m*; **to have an ~** [gen] tener un accidente; [in car] tener un accidente de coche; **it was an ~** fue sin querer; **~ and emergency department** urgencias *fpl*; **by ~** [by chance] por casualidad.

accidental [,æksɪ'dentl] *adj* accidental.

accidentally [,æksɪ'dentəlɪ] *adv* **-1.** [by chance] por casualidad. **-2.** [unintentionally] sin querer.

accident-prone *adj* propenso(sa) a los accidentes.

acclaim [ə'kleɪm] ◇ *n* (*U*) elogio *m*, alabanza *f*. ◇ *vt* elogiar, alabar.

acclamation [,æklə'meɪʃn] *n* (*U*) aclamación *f*, vítores *mpl*.

acclimatize, -ise [ə'klaɪmətaɪz], **acclimate** *Am* ['æklɪmeɪt] ◇ *vt*: **to become ~d to sthg** aclimatarse a algo. ◇ *vi*: **to ~ (to)** aclimatarse (a).

accolade ['ækəleɪd] *n* [praise] elogio *m*, halago *m*; [award] galardón *m*.

accommodate [ə'kɒmədeɪt] *vt* **-1.** [provide room for people - subj: person] alojar; [- subj: building, place] albergar. **-2.** [provide room for things] acomodar. **-3.** [oblige] complacer.

accommodating [ə'kɒmədeɪtɪŋ] *adj* complaciente, servicial.

accommodation [ə,kɒmə'deɪʃn] *n* Br, **accommodations** [ə,kɒmə'deɪʃnz] *npl* Am **-1.** [lodging] alojamiento *m*. **-2.** [work space] espacio *m*.

accompaniment [ə'kʌmpənɪmənt] *n* MUS acompañamiento *m*.

accompanist [ə'kʌmpənɪst] *n* MUS acompañante *m y f*.

accompany [ə'kʌmpənɪ] (*pt & pp* **-ied**) *vt* acompañar.

accomplice [ə'kʌmplɪs] *n* cómplice *m y f*.

accomplish [ə'kʌmplɪʃ] *vt* [achieve] conseguir, alcanzar.

accomplished [ə'kʌmplɪʃt] *adj* competente, experto(ta).

accomplishment [ə'kʌmplɪʃmənt] *n* **-1.** [action] realización *f*. **-2.** [achievement] logro *m*.
◆ **accomplishments** *npl* dotes *fpl*.

accord [ə'kɔːd] ◇ *n*: **in ~** de acuerdo; **with one ~** al unísono; **to do sthg of one's own ~** hacer algo por propia voluntad. ◇ *vt*: **to ~ sb sthg, to ~ sthg to sb** conceder algo a alguien. ◇ *vi*: **to ~ with sthg** concordar con algo.

accordance [ə'kɔːdəns] *n*: **in ~ with** acorde con, conforme a.

according [ə'kɔːdɪŋ]
◆ **according to** *prep* **-1.** [as stated or shown by] según; **to go ~ to plan** ir según lo planeado. **-2.** [with regard to] de acuerdo con, conforme a.

accordingly [ə'kɔːdɪŋlɪ] *adv* **-1.** [appropriately] como corresponde. **-2.** [consequently] por lo tanto, en consecuencia.

accordion [ə'kɔːdjən] *n* acordeón *m*.

accordionist [ə'kɔːdjənɪst] *n* acordeonista *m y f*.

accost [ə'kɒst] *vt* abordar.

account [ə'kaʊnt] *n* **-1.** [with bank, shop etc] cuenta *f*. **-2.** [report - spoken] relato *m*; [- written] informe *m*. **-3.** *phr*: **to call sb to ~** pedir cuentas a alguien; **to give a good ~ of o.s.** hacer un buen papel; **to take ~ of sthg, to take sthg into ~** tener en cuenta algo; **of no ~** indiferente, de poca importancia; **on no ~** bajo ningún pretexto OR concepto.
◆ **accounts** *npl* [of business] cuentas *fpl*.
◆ **by all accounts** *adv* a decir de todos, según todo el mundo.
◆ **on account of** *prep* debido a, a causa de.
◆ **account for** *vt fus* **-1.** [explain] justificar, dar razón de. **-2.** [represent] configurar, representar.

accountability [ə,kaʊntə'bɪlətɪ] *n* (*U*) responsabilidad *f*.

accountable [ə'kaʊntəbl] *adj* **-1.** [responsible]: ~ **(for)** responsable (de). **-2.** [answerable]: ~ **to** obligado(da) a rendir cuentas ante.

accountancy [ə'kaʊntənsɪ] *n* contabilidad *f*.

accountant [ə'kaʊntənt] *n* contable *m y f*, contador *m*, -ra *f Amer*.

accounting [ə'kaʊntɪŋ] *n* contabilidad *f*.

accoutrements *Br* [ə'ku:trəmənts], **accouterments** *Am* [ə'ku:tərmənts] *npl fml* impedimenta *f*, pertrechos *mpl*.

accredited [ə'kredɪtɪd] *adj* [ambassador] acreditado(da); [dealer, spokesperson] oficial.

accrue [ə'kru:] *vi* acumularse.

accumulate [ə'kju:mjʊleɪt] ◇ *vt* acumular, juntar. ◇ *vi* [money, things] acumularse; [problems] amontonarse.

accumulation [ə,kju:mjʊ'leɪʃn] *n* **-1.** (*U*) [act of accumulating] acumulación *f*. **-2.** [collection of things] cúmulo *m*, montón *m*.

accuracy ['ækjʊrəsɪ] *n* **-1.** [of description, report] veracidad *f*, rigor *m*. **-2.** [of weapon, marksman] precisión *f*; [of typing, figures] exactitud *f*, corrección *f*.

accurate ['ækjʊrət] *adj* **-1.** [description, report] veraz, riguroso(sa). **-2.** [weapon, marksman, typist] preciso(sa); [figures, estimate] exacto(ta), correcto(ta).

accurately ['ækjʊrətlɪ] *adv* **-1.** [truthfully] verazmente, rigurosamente. **-2.** [precisely] con precisión.

accusation [,ækju:'zeɪʃn] *n* **-1.** [charge] acusación *f*. **-2.** JUR denuncia *f*.

accuse [ə'kju:z] *vt*: **to** ~ **sb of sthg/of doing sthg** acusar a alguien de algo/de hacer algo.

accused [ə'kju:zd] (*pl inv*) *n* JUR: **the** ~ el acusado, la acusada.

accusing [ə'kju:zɪŋ] *adj* acusador(ra).

accusingly [ə'kju:zɪŋlɪ] *adv* [look at] acusatoriamente; [speak to] en tono acusador.

accustomed [ə'kʌstəmd] *adj*: ~ **to** acostumbrado(da) a.

ace [eɪs] ◇ *adj*: **an** ~ **athlete** un as del atletismo. ◇ *n* [playing card] as *m*; **to be within an** ~ **of** *fig* estar al borde de.

ACE (*abbr of* **American Council on Education**) *n* organización estadounidense privada que en las escuelas ofrece asesoramiento a los padres de alumnos.

acerbic [ə'sɜ:bɪk] *adj* mordaz.

acetate ['æsɪteɪt] *n* acetato *m*.

acetic acid [ə'si:tɪk-] *n* ácido *m* acético.

acetone ['æsɪtəʊn] *n* acetona *f*.

acetylene [ə'setɪli:n] *n* acetileno *m*.

ACGB (*abbr of* **Arts Council of Great Britain**) *n* organismo británico para la promoción de las artes.

ache [eɪk] ◇ *n* [pain] dolor *m*. ◇ *vi* **-1.** [hurt] doler; **my back** ~**s** me duele la espalda. **-2.** *fig* [want]: **to be aching for sthg/to do sthg** morirse de ganas de algo/de hacer algo.

achieve [ə'tʃi:v] *vt* [success, goal, fame] alcanzar, lograr; [ambition] realizar.

achievement [ə'tʃi:vmənt] *n* **-1.** [accomplishment] logro *m*, éxito *m*. **-2.** [act of achieving] consecución *f*, realización *f*.

achiever [ə'tʃi:və*] *n* triunfador *m*, -ra *f*; **low** ~ [at school] estudiante *m y f* de bajo rendimiento escolar.

Achilles' heel [ə'kɪli:z-] *n* talón *m* de Aquiles.

Achilles' tendon [ə'kɪli:z-] *n* tendón *m* de Aquiles.

acid ['æsɪd] ◇ *adj* **-1.** CHEM ácido(da). **-2.** [sharp-tasting] agrio (agria). **-3.** *fig* [person, remark] mordaz, corrosivo(va). ◇ *n* ácido *m*.

acidic [ə'sɪdɪk] *adj* ácido(da).

acidity [ə'sɪdətɪ] *n* **-1.** [of substance, liquid, soil] acidez *f*. **-2.** *fig* [of person, remark] mordacidad *f*.

acid rain *n* lluvia *f* ácida.

acid test *n fig* prueba *f* de fuego.

acknowledge [ək'nɒlɪdʒ] *vt* **-1.** [accept] reconocer. **-2.** [greet] saludar. **-3.** [letter etc]: **to** ~ **receipt of** acusar recibo de. **-4.** [recognize]: **to** ~ **sb as** reconocer OR considerar a alguien como.

acknowledg(e)ment [ək'nɒlɪdʒmənt] *n* **-1.** [acceptance] reconocimiento *m*. **-2.** [confirmation of receipt] acuse *m* de recibo. **-3.** [thanks]: **in** ~ **of** en señal de agradecimiento por.
   ◆ **acknowledg(e)ments** *npl* agradecimientos *mpl*.

ACLU (*abbr of* **American Civil Liberties Union**) *n* asociación estadounidense para la defensa de las libertades civiles.

acme ['ækmɪ] *n* cenit *m*, súmmum *m*.

acne ['æknɪ] *n* acné *m*.

acorn ['eɪkɔ:n] *n* bellota *f*.

acoustic [ə'ku:stɪk] *adj* acústico(ca).
   ◆ **acoustics** *npl* acústica *f*.

acoustic guitar *n* guitarra *f* acústica.

ACPO ['ækpəʊ] (*abbr of* **Association of Chief Police Officers**) *n* asociación británica de jefes de policía.

acquaint [ə'kweɪnt] *vt* **-1.** [make familiar]: **to** ~ **sb with sthg** [information] poner a alguien al corriente de algo; [method, technique] familiarizar a alguien con algo. **-2.** [make known]: **to be ~ed with sb** conocer a alguien.

acquaintance [ə'kweɪntəns] *n* conocido *m*, -da *f*; **to make sb's ~** *fml* conocer a alguien.

acquiesce [ˌækwɪ'es] *vi*: **to ~ (to** OR **in sthg)** acceder (a algo).

acquiescence [ˌækwɪ'esns] *n* consentimiento *m*.

acquire [ə'kwaɪə^r] *vt* **-1.** [buy, adopt] adquirir. **-2.** [obtain - information, document] hacerse con, procurarse.

acquired taste [ə'kwaɪəd-] *n gusto que se adquiere con el tiempo*.

acquisition [ˌækwɪ'zɪʃn] *n* adquisición *f*.

acquisitive [ə'kwɪzɪtɪv] *adj* consumista.

acquit [ə'kwɪt] (*pt* & *pp* **-ted**, *cont* **-ting**) *vt* **-1.** JUR: **to ~ sb of sthg** absolver a alguien de algo. **-2.** [perform]: **to ~ o.s. well/badly** hacer un buen/mal papel.

acquittal [ə'kwɪtl] *n* JUR absolución *f*.

acre ['eɪkə^r] *n* acre *m*.

acreage ['eɪkərɪdʒ] *n* medida *f* en acres.

acrid ['ækrɪd] *adj lit* & *fig* acre.

acrimonious [ˌækrɪ'məʊnjəs] *adj* [words] áspero(ra); [dispute] agrio (agria), enconado(da).

acrobat ['ækrəbæt] *n* acróbata *m y f*.

acrobatic [ˌækrə'bætɪk] *adj* **-1.** [somersault, display] acrobático(ca). **-2.** [person] ágil.

◆ **acrobatics** *npl* acrobacias *fpl*.

acronym ['ækrənɪm] *n* siglas *fpl*.

across [ə'krɒs] ◇ *adv* **-1.** [from one side to the other] de un lado a otro; **to walk/run ~** cruzar andando/corriendo; **to look ~** mirar al otro lado. **-2.** [in measurements]: **the river is 2 km ~** el río tiene 2 kms de ancho. **-3.** [in crossword]: **"21 ~"** "21 horizontal". **-4.** *phr*: **to get sthg ~ (to sb)** hacer entender algo (a alguien).
◇ *prep* **-1.** [from one side to the other of] a través de, de un lado a otro de; **to walk/run ~ the road** cruzar la carretera andando/corriendo; **the bridge ~ the river** el puente que cruza el río; **he drew a line ~ the page** trazó una línea a través de la página; **to look ~ sthg** mirar hacia el otro lado de algo. **-2.** [on the other side of] al otro lado de.

◆ **across from** *prep* enfrente de.

across-the-board *adj* global; [salary rise] lineal.

acrylic [ə'krɪlɪk] ◇ *adj* acrílico(ca). ◇ *n* acrílico *m*.

act [ækt] ◇ *n* **-1.** [action, deed] acto *m*, acción *f*; **to be in the ~ of doing sthg** estar haciendo algo; **to catch sb in the ~** coger a alguien con las manos en la masa. **-2.** [pre-

tence] farsa *f*, fachada *f*. **-3.** [in parliament] ley *f*. **-4.** [THEATRE - part of play] acto *m*; [- routine, turn] número *m*. **-5.** *phr*: **to get in on the ~** apuntarse al carro; **to get one's ~ together** organizarse.
◇ *vi* **-1.** [gen] actuar; **to ~ as** [person] hacer de, fungir de *Amer*; [thing] actuar como. **-2.** [behave]: **to ~ (as if/like)** comportarse (como si/como). **-3.** *fig* [pretend] fingir. **-4.** JUR [lawyer, estate agent]: **to ~ for sb**, **to ~ on behalf of sb** actuar en representación OR nombre de alguien.
◇ *vt* [part - in play, film] interpretar; **to ~ the fool** hacer el tonto; **to ~ the innocent** hacerse el inocente; **~ your age!** ¡deja de portarte como un crío!

◆ **act out** *vt sep* **-1.** [feelings, thoughts] exteriorizar. **-2.** [scene, event] representar.

◆ **act up** *vi* **-1.** [machine] no ir bien. **-2.** [child] dar guerra.

acting ['æktɪŋ] ◇ *adj* [interim] temporal, en funciones. ◇ *n* actuación *f*; **I like ~** me gusta actuar.

action ['ækʃn] *n* **-1.** [gen & MIL] acción *f*; **to take ~** tomar medidas; **in ~** [person] en acción; [machine] en funcionamiento; **to be killed in ~** caer muerto en combate OR en acto de servicio; **to put sthg into ~** poner algo en práctica OR marcha; **out of ~** [person] fuera de combate; [machine] averiado(da). **-2.** [deed] acto *m*, acción *f*. **-3.** JUR demanda *f*.

action group *n* grupo *m* de presión.

action replay *n* repetición *f* (de la jugada).

activate ['æktɪveɪt] *vt* [device] activar; [machine] poner en funcionamiento.

active ['æktɪv] *adj* **-1.** [person, campaigner] activo(va). **-2.** [encouragement etc] enérgico(ca), decidido(da). **-3.** [volcano] en actividad; [bomb] activado(da).

actively ['æktɪvlɪ] *adv* [encourage, discourage] enérgicamente.

active service *n* MIL servicio *m* activo.

activist ['æktɪvɪst] *n* activista *m y f*.

activity [æk'tɪvətɪ] (*pl* **-ies**) *n* **-1.** [movement, action] actividad *f*. **-2.** [pastime, hobby] afición *f*.

◆ **activities** *npl* [actions] actividades *fpl*.

act of God *n* caso *m* de fuerza mayor.

actor ['æktə^r] *n* actor *m*.

actress ['æktrɪs] *n* actriz *f*.

actual ['æktʃʊəl] *adj* [emphatic]: **the ~ cost is £10** el coste real es de 10 libras; **the ~ game starts at three pm** el partido en sí empieza a las tres; **the ~ spot where it happened** el sitio mismo en que ocurrió.

actuality [ˌæktʃʊ'ælətɪ] *n*: **in ~** de hecho.

actually ['æktʃʊəlɪ] *adv* **-1.** [really, in truth]: **do you ~ like him?** ¿de verdad que te gusta?; **no-one ~ saw her** en realidad, nadie la vio; **~ it's not that good** la verdad es que no está tan bien. **-2.** [by the way]: **~, I was there yesterday** pues yo estuve ayer por allí.

actuary ['æktjʊərɪ] (*pl* **-ies**) *n* actuario *m*, -ria *f* de seguros.

actuate ['æktjʊeɪt] *vt* [mechanism] activar, accionar.

acuity [ə'kjuːətɪ] *n fml* agudeza *f*.

acumen ['ækjʊmen] *n*: **business ~ vista** *f* para los negocios.

acupuncture ['ækjʊpʌŋktʃəʳ] *n* acupuntura *f*.

acute [ə'kjuːt] *adj* **-1.** [illness] agudo(da); [pain, danger] extremo(ma). **-2.** [perceptive - person] perspicaz. **-3.** [hearing, smell] muy fino(na). **-4.** LING: **e ~ e** *f* acentuada.

acute accent *n* acento *m* agudo.

acutely [ə'kjuːtlɪ] *adv* [extremely] extremadamente, profundamente.

ad [æd] (*abbr of* **advertisement**) *n* anuncio *m*.

AD (*abbr of* **Anno Domini**) d. C.

adage ['ædɪdʒ] *n* refrán *m*, adagio *m*.

adamant ['ædəmənt] *adj*: **to be ~ (that)** mostrarse inflexible (en que).

Adam's apple ['ædəmz-] *n* bocado *m* OR nuez *f* de Adán.

adapt [ə'dæpt] ◇ *vt* adaptar. ◇ *vi*: **to ~ (to)** adaptarse OR amoldarse (a).

adaptability [ə,dæptə'bɪlətɪ] *n* capacidad *f* de adaptación, adaptabilidad *f*.

adaptable [ə'dæptəbl] *adj* [person] capaz de adaptarse.

adaptation [,ædæp'teɪʃn] *n* adaptación *f*.

adapter, adaptor [ə'dæptəʳ] *n* [ELEC - for several devices] ladrón *m*; [- for different socket] adaptador *m*.

ADC *n* **-1.** *abbr of* **aide-de-camp. -2.** (*abbr of* **Aid to Dependent Children**) *organización estadounidense de ayuda a niños necesitados.* **-3.** (*abbr of* **analogue-digital converter**) *convertidor analógico-digital.*

add [æd] *vt* **-1.** [gen]: **to ~ sthg (to sthg)** añadir algo (a algo). **-2.** [numbers] sumar.

◆ **add in** *vt sep* añadir, sumar.

◆ **add on** *vt sep* **-1.** [to building]: **to ~ sthg on (to sthg)** adosar OR incorporar algo (a algo). **-2.** [to bill, total]: **to ~ sthg on (to sthg)** añadir OR incluir algo (en algo).

◆ **add to** *vt fus* aumentar, acrecentar.

◆ **add up** ◇ *vt sep* [numbers] sumar. ◇ *vi inf* [make sense]: **it doesn't ~ up** no tiene sentido.

◆ **add up to** *vt fus* venir a ser.

addendum [ə'dendəm] (*pl* **-da** [-də]) *n* addenda *m* o *f*.

adder ['ædəʳ] *n* víbora *f*.

addict ['ædɪkt] *n* **-1.** [taking drugs] adicto *m*, -ta *f*; **drug ~** drogadicto *m*, -ta *f*, toxicómano *m*, -na *f*; **heroin ~** heroinómano *m*, -na *f*. **-2.** *fig* [fan] fanático *m*, -ca *f*.

addicted [ə'dɪktɪd] *adj* **-1.** [to drug]: **~ (to)** adicto(ta) (a). **-2.** *fig* [to food, TV]: **to be ~ (to)** ser un fanático (de).

addiction [ə'dɪkʃn] *n* **-1.** [to drug]: **~ (to)** adicción *f* (a). **-2.** *fig* [to food, TV]: **~ (to)** vicio *m* (por).

addictive [ə'dɪktɪv] *adj* *lit* & *fig* adictivo(va).

Addis Ababa ['ædɪs 'æbəbə] *n* Addis Abeba.

addition [ə'dɪʃn] *n* **-1.** MATH suma *f*. **-2.** [extra thing] adición *f*. **-3.** [act of adding] incorporación *f*; **in ~** además; **in ~ to** además de.

additional [ə'dɪʃənl] *adj* adicional.

additive ['ædɪtɪv] *n* aditivo *m*.

addled ['ædld] *adj* **-1.** [egg] podrido(da). **-2.** [brain] hecho(cha) un lío.

add-on COMPUT ◇ *adj* externo(na), complementario(ria). ◇ *n* expansión *f*, circuito *m* complementario.

address [ə'dres] ◇ *n* **-1.** [of person, organization] dirección *f*, domicilio *m*. **-2.** [speech] discurso *m*, conferencia *f*. ◇ *vt* **-1.** [letter, parcel, remark]: **to ~ sthg to** dirigir algo a; **to be ~ed to** ir dirigido a. **-2.** [meeting, conference] dirigirse a, hablar ante. **-3.** [issue]: **to ~ o.s. to sthg** enfrentarse a OR abordar algo.

address book *n* agenda *f* de direcciones.

addressee [,ædre'siː] *n* destinatario *m*, -ria *f*.

Aden ['eɪdn] *n* Adén.

adenoids ['ædɪnɔɪdz] *npl* vegetaciones *fpl* (adenoideas).

adept ['ædept] *adj*: **to be ~ (at sthg/at doing sthg)** ser experto(ta) (en algo/en hacer algo).

adequacy ['ædɪkwəsɪ] *n* **-1.** [sufficiency] suficiencia *f*. **-2.** [suitability] capacitación *f*, idoneidad *f*.

adequate ['ædɪkwət] *adj* **-1.** [sufficient] suficiente. **-2.** [good enough] aceptable, satisfactorio(ria).

adequately ['ædɪkwətlɪ] *adv* **-1.** [sufficiently] suficientemente. **-2.** [well enough] aceptablemente, satisfactoriamente.

adhere [əd'hɪəʳ] *vi* **-1.** [to surface, principle]:

to ~ (to) adherirse (a). **-2.** [to rule, decision]: **to ~ to** respetar, observar.

adherence [əd'hɪərəns] *n* **-1.** [to rule, decision]: **~ to** observancia *f* OR cumplimiento *m* de. **-2.** [to principle, belief]: **~ to** adhesión *f* a.

adhesive [əd'hiːsɪv] ◇ *adj* adhesivo(va), adherente. ◇ *n* adhesivo *m*.

adhesive tape *n* cinta *f* adhesiva, celo® *m*.

ad hoc [,æd'hɒk] *adj* ad hoc, a propósito.

ad infinitum [,ædɪnfɪ'naɪtəm] *adv* ad infinitum, hasta el infinito.

adjacent [ə'dʒeɪsənt] *adj*: **~ (to)** adyacente OR contiguo(gua) (a).

adjective ['ædʒɪktɪv] *n* adjetivo *m*.

adjoin [ə'dʒɔɪn] *vt* [land] lindar con; [room] estar contiguo(gua) a.

adjoining [ə'dʒɔɪnɪŋ] ◇ *adj* [table] adyacente; [room] contiguo(gua). ◇ *prep* junto a.

adjourn [ə'dʒɜːn] ◇ *vt* [decision] aplazar; [session] levantar; [meeting] interrumpir. ◇ *vi* aplazarse, suspenderse.

adjournment [ə'dʒɜːnmənt] *n* aplazamiento *m*.

Adjt *abbr of* **adjutant**.

adjudge [ə'dʒʌdʒ] *vt* declarar, juzgar.

adjudicate [ə'dʒuːdɪkeɪt] ◇ *vt* actuar como juez en. ◇ *vi* actuar como juez; **to ~ on** OR **upon sthg** emitir un fallo OR un veredicto sobre algo.

adjudication [ə,dʒuːdɪ'keɪʃn] *n* fallo *m*, decisión *f*.

adjunct ['ædʒʌŋkt] *n* complemento *m*, apéndice *m*.

adjust [ə'dʒʌst] ◇ *vt* [machine, setting] ajustar; [clothing] arreglarse. ◇ *vi*: **to ~ (to)** adaptarse OR amoldarse (a).

adjustable [ə'dʒʌstəbl] *adj* [machine, chair] regulable, graduable.

adjustable spanner *n* llave *f* inglesa.

adjusted [ə'dʒʌstɪd] *adj*: **to be well ~** ser una persona equilibrada.

adjustment [ə'dʒʌstmənt] *n* **-1.** [modification] modificación *f*, reajuste *m*; **to make an ~ to sthg** hacerle un reajuste a algo. **-2.** (U) [change in attitude]: **~ (to)** adaptación *f* OR amoldamiento *m* (a).

adjutant ['ædʒʊtənt] *n* ayudante *m*.

ad lib [,æd'lɪb] (*pt* & *pp* **-bed**, *cont* **-bing**) ◇ *adj* [improvised] improvisado(da). ◇ *n* improvisación *f*. ◇ *adv* [without preparation] improvisando; [without limit] a voluntad, sin trabas.

◆ **ad-lib** *vi* improvisar.

adman ['ædmæn] (*pl* **admen** ['ædmen]) *n* publicista *m*.

admin ['ædmɪn] (*abbr of* **administration**) *n* Br *inf* papeleo *m*.

administer [əd'mɪnɪstəʳ] *vt* [gen] administrar; [punishment] aplicar.

administration [əd,mɪnɪ'streɪʃn] *n* [gen] administración *f*; [of punishment] aplicación *f*.

◆ **Administration** *n* Am: **the Administration** la Administración.

administrative [əd'mɪnɪstrətɪv] *adj* administrativo(va).

administrator [əd'mɪnɪstreɪtəʳ] *n* administrador *m*, -ra *f*.

admirable ['ædmərəbl] *adj* admirable.

admirably ['ædmərəblɪ] *adv* admirablemente.

admiral ['ædmərəl] *n* almirante *m*.

Admiralty ['ædmərəltɪ] *n* Br: **the ~** el Almirantazgo.

admiration [,ædmə'reɪʃn] *n* admiración *f*.

admire [əd'maɪəʳ] *vt*: **to ~ sb (for)** admirar a alguien (por).

admirer [əd'maɪərəʳ] *n* admirador *m*, -ra *f*.

admiring [əd'maɪərɪŋ] *adj* lleno(na) de admiración.

admiringly [əd'maɪərɪŋlɪ] *adv* con admiración.

admissible [əd'mɪsəbl] *adj* JUR admisible, aceptable.

admission [əd'mɪʃn] *n* **-1.** [permission to enter] admisión *f*, ingreso *m*. **-2.** [cost of entrance] entrada *f*. **-3.** [of guilt, mistake] reconocimiento *m*; **by his/her** *etc* **own ~** como él mismo/ella misma *etc* reconoce.

admit [əd'mɪt] (*pt* & *pp* **-ted**, *cont* **-ting**) ◇ *vt* **-1.** [acknowledge, confess]: **to ~ (that)** admitir OR reconocer (que); **to ~ doing sthg** reconocer haber hecho algo; **to ~ defeat** *fig* darse por vencido. **-2.** [allow to enter or join] admitir; **to be admitted to hospital** Br OR **to the hospital** Am ser ingresado en el hospital; **"~s two"** [on ticket] "válido para dos (personas)". ◇ *vi*: **to ~ to sthg** confesar algo.

admittance [əd'mɪtəns] *n*: **to gain ~ to** conseguir entrar en; **"no ~"** "prohibido el paso".

admittedly [əd'mɪtɪdlɪ] *adv* sin duda, indudablemente.

admixture [æd'mɪkstʃəʳ] *n* componente *m* (*de mezcla*).

admonish [əd'mɒnɪʃ] *vt* amonestar, apercibir.

ad nauseam [,æd'nɔːzɪæm] *adv* hasta la saciedad.

ado [ə'duː] *n*: **without further** OR **more ~** sin más preámbulos, sin mayor dilación.

adolescence [,ædə'lesns] *n* adolescencia *f*.

adolescent [ˌædəˈlesnt] ◇ *adj* **-1.** [teenage] adolescente. **-2.** *pej* [immature] pueril, infantil. ◇ *n* [teenager] adolescente *m y f*.

adopt [əˈdɒpt] *vt & vi* adoptar.

adoption [əˈdɒpʃn] *n* adopción *f*.

adoptive [əˈdɒptɪv] *adj* adoptivo(va).

adorable [əˈdɔːrəbl] *adj* encantador(ra), adorable.

adoration [ˌædəˈreɪʃn] *n* adoración *f*.

adore [əˈdɔːr] *vt* **-1.** [love deeply] adorar, querer con locura. **-2.** [like very much]: **I ~** chocolate me encanta el chocolate.

adoring [əˈdɔːrɪŋ] *adj* lleno(na) de adoración.

adorn [əˈdɔːn] *vt* adornar.

adornment [əˈdɔːnmənt] *n* adorno *m*.

ADP (*abbr of* **automatic data processing**) *n* proceso automático de datos.

adrenalin [əˈdrenəlɪn] *n* adrenalina *f*.

Adriatic [ˌeɪdrɪˈætɪk] *n*: **the ~ (Sea)** el (mar) Adriático.

adrift [əˈdrɪft] ◇ *adj* [boat] a la deriva. ◇ *adv*: **to go ~** *fig* irse a la deriva.

adroit [əˈdrɔɪt] *adj* diestro(tra).

ADT (*abbr of* **Atlantic Daylight Time**) *n* hora de verano de la costa este estadounidense.

adulation [ˌædjʊˈleɪʃn] *n* adulación *f*.

adult [ˈædʌlt] ◇ *adj* **-1.** [fully grown] adulto(ta). **-2.** [mature] maduro(ra). **-3.** [suitable for adults only] para adultos OR mayores. ◇ *n* adulto *m*, -ta *f*.

adult education *n* educación *f* de adultos.

adulterate [əˈdʌltəreɪt] *vt* adulterar.

adulteration [əˌdʌltəˈreɪʃn] *n* adulteración *f*.

adulterer [əˈdʌltərər] *n* adúltero *m*, -ra *f*.

adultery [əˈdʌltəri] *n* adulterio *m*.

adulthood [ˈædʌlthʊd] *n* madurez *f*, edad *f* adulta.

advance [ədˈvɑːns] ◇ *n* **-1.** [gen] avance *m*. **-2.** [money] adelanto *m*, anticipo *m*. ◇ *comp*: **~ notice** OR **warning** previo aviso *m*; **~ booking** reserva *f* anticipada; **~ payment** pago *m* anticipado. ◇ *vt* **-1.** [improve] promover, favorecer. **-2.** [bring forward in time] adelantar. **-3.** [give in advance]: **to ~ sb sthg** adelantarle a alguien algo. ◇ *vi* avanzar.
◆ **advances** *npl*: **to make ~s to sb** [sexual] hacerle proposiciones a alguien, insinuarse a alguien; [business] hacerle una propuesta a alguien.
◆ **in advance** *adv* [pay] por adelantado; [book] con antelación; [know] de antemano; **to arrive half an hour in ~** llegar con media hora de adelanto.
◆ **in advance of** *prep* **-1.** [ahead of] por delante de. **-2.** [prior to] con anterioridad a.

advanced [ədˈvɑːnst] *adj* **-1.** [developed] avanzado(da); **~ in years** *euphemism* entrado(da) en años. **-2.** [student, pupil] adelantado(da), aventajado(da); [studies] superior.

advancement [ədˈvɑːnsmənt] *n* **-1.** [in job] ascenso *m*. **-2.** [of cause etc] fomento *m*, desarrollo *m*.

advantage [ədˈvɑːntɪdʒ] *n*: **~ (over)** ventaja *f* (sobre); **to be to one's ~** ir en beneficio de uno; **to take ~ of sthg** aprovechar algo; **to take ~ of sb** aprovecharse de alguien; **to have** OR **hold the ~ (over sb)** tener OR llevar ventaja (sobre alguien).

advantageous [ˌædvənˈteɪdʒəs] *adj* ventajoso(sa).

advent [ˈædvənt] *n* [arrival] advenimiento *m*.
◆ **Advent** *n* RELIG Adviento *m*.

Advent calendar *n* calendario *m* de Adviento.

adventure [ədˈventʃər] *n* aventura *f*.

adventure holiday *n* vacaciones *fpl* de aventura.

adventure playground *n* Br parque *m* infantil.

adventurer [ədˈventʃərər] *n* **-1.** [adventurous person] aventurero *m*, -ra *f*. **-2.** [unscrupulous person] sinvergüenza *m y f*.

adventurous [ədˈventʃərəs] *adj* **-1.** [daring] aventurero(ra). **-2.** [dangerous] arriesgado(da).

adverb [ˈædvɜːb] *n* adverbio *m*.

adversary [ˈædvəsəri] (*pl* **-ies**) *n* adversario *m*, -ria *f*.

adverse [ˈædvɜːs] *adj* adverso(sa).

adversely [ˈædvɜːslɪ] *adv* de manera adversa.

adversity [ædˈvɜːsətɪ] *n* adversidad *f*.

advert [ˈædvɜːt] Br = advertisement.

advertise [ˈædvətaɪz] ◇ *vt* anunciar. ◇ *vi* anunciarse, poner un anuncio; **to ~ for** buscar (*mediante anuncio*).

advertisement [ədˈvɜːtɪsmənt] *n* anuncio *m*; **to be a great ~ for** *fig* hacerle una propaganda excelente a.

advertiser [ˈædvətaɪzər] *n* anunciante *m y f*.

advertising [ˈædvətaɪzɪŋ] *n* publicidad *f*.

advertising agency *n* agencia *f* de publicidad.

advertising campaign *n* campaña *f* publicitaria.

advice [ədˈvaɪs] *n* (*U*) consejos *mpl*; **to take sb's ~** seguir el consejo de alguien; **a piece of ~** un consejo; **to give sb ~** aconsejar a alguien.

advice note *n* aviso *m* de envío.

advisability [əd,vaɪzə'bɪlətɪ] *n* conveniencia *f*.

advisable [əd'vaɪzəbl] *adj* aconsejable, conveniente.

advise [əd'vaɪz] ◇ *vt* **-1.** [give advice to]: **to ~ sb to do sthg** aconsejar a alguien que haga algo; **to ~ sb against sthg/against doing sthg** desaconsejar a alguien algo/que haga algo. **-2.** [professionally]: **to ~ sb on sthg** asesorar a alguien en algo. **-3.** *fml* [inform]: **to ~ sb (of sthg)** informar a alguien (de algo). ◇ *vi* **-1.** [give advice]: **to ~ against sthg** desaconsejar algo; **to ~ against doing sthg** aconsejar no hacer algo. **-2.** [professionally]: **to ~ on** asesorar en (materia de).

advisedly [əd'vaɪzɪdlɪ] *adv* [deliberately] deliberadamente; [after careful consideration] con conocimiento de causa.

adviser *Br*, **advisor** *Am* [əd'vaɪzər] *n* consejero *m*, -ra *f*, asesor *m*, -ra *f*.

advisory [əd'vaɪzərɪ] *adj* [body] consultivo(va), asesor(ra); **in an ~ capacity** OR **role** en calidad de asesor.

advocacy ['ædvəkəsɪ] *n* apoyo *m*, defensa *f*.

advocate [*n* 'ædvəkət, *vb* 'ædvəkeɪt] ◇ *n* **-1.** JUR abogado *m*, -da *f*, defensor *m*, -ra *f*. **-2.** [supporter] defensor *m*, -ra *f*, partidario *m*, -ria *f*. ◇ *vt* abogar por.

advt. *abbr of* **advertisement**.

AEA (*abbr of* **Atomic Energy Authority**) *n* organismo británico de energía nuclear, ≈ CSN *m*.

AEC (*abbr of* **Atomic Energy Commission**) *n* organismo estadounidense de energía nuclear, ≈ CSN *m*.

AEEU (*abbr of* **Amalgamated Engineering and Electrical Union**) *n* sindicato británico de ingeniería.

Aegean [iː'dʒiːən] *n*: **the ~ (Sea)** el mar Egeo.

aegis ['iːdʒɪs] *n*: **under the ~ of** bajo el patrocinio OR la égida de.

Aeolian Islands [iː'əʊljən-] *npl*: **the ~** las islas Eoli, las islas Lipari.

aeon *Br*, **eon** *Am* ['iːən] *n fig*: **it's been ~s since I saw you** hace siglos que no te veo.

aerial ['eərɪəl] ◇ *adj* aéreo(a). ◇ *n Br* [antenna] antena *f*.

aerobatics [,eərəʊ'bætɪks] *n* (*U*) acrobacia *f* aérea.

aerobics [eə'rəʊbɪks] *n* (*U*) aerobic *m*.

aerodrome ['eərədrəʊm] *n* aeródromo *m*.

aerodynamic [,eərəʊdaɪ'næmɪk] *adj* aerodinámico(ca).
◆ **aerodynamics** ◇ *n* (*U*) [science] aerodi-

námica *f*. ◇ *npl* [aerodynamic qualities] aerodinámica *f*.

aerogramme ['eərəgræm] *n* aerograma *m*.

aeronautics [,eərə'nɔːtɪks] *n* (*U*) aeronáutica *f*.

aeroplane ['eərəpleɪn] *n Br* avión *m*.

aerosol ['eərəsɒl] *n* aerosol *m*.

aerospace ['eərəʊspeɪs] *n*: **the ~ industry** la industria aeroespacial.

aesthete, **esthete** *Am* ['iːsθiːt] *n* esteta *m* y *f*.

aesthetic, **esthetic** *Am* [iːs'θetɪk] *adj* estético(ca).

aesthetically, **esthetically** *Am* [iːs'θetɪklɪ] *adv* estéticamente.

aesthetics, **esthetics** *Am* [iːs'θetɪks] *n* (*U*) estética *f*.

afar [ə'fɑːr] *adv*: **from ~** desde lejos.

AFB (*abbr of* **Air Force Base**) *n Am* base de las fuerzas aéreas.

AFDC (*abbr of* **Aid to Families with Dependent Children**) *n* organización estadounidense que ofrece ayuda a familias de niños necesitados.

affable ['æfəbl] *adj* afable.

affair [ə'feər] *n* **-1.** [event, do] acontecimiento *m*. **-2.** [concern, matter] asunto *m*. **-3.** [extra-marital relationship] aventura *f* (amorosa).
◆ **affairs** *npl* asuntos *mpl*.

affect [ə'fekt] *vt* **-1.** [influence, move emotionally] afectar. **-2.** [put on] fingir, simular.

affectation [,æfek'teɪʃn] *n* afectación *f*.

affected [ə'fektɪd] *adj* [insincere] afectado(da).

affection [ə'fekʃn] *n* cariño *m*, afecto *m*.

affectionate [ə'fekʃnət] *adj* cariñoso(sa), afectuoso(sa).

affectionately [ə'fekʃnətlɪ] *adv* cariñosamente, afectuosamente.

affidavit [,æfɪ'deɪvɪt] *n* declaración *f* jurada.

affiliate [*n* ə'fɪlɪət, *vb* ə'fɪlɪeɪt] ◇ *n* filial *f*. ◇ *vt*: **to be ~d to** OR **with** estar afiliado(da) a.

affiliation [ə,fɪlɪ'eɪʃn] *n* afiliación *f*.

affinity [ə'fɪnətɪ] (*pl* **-ies**) *n* **-1.** [close feeling] afinidad *f*; **to have an ~ with** sentirse afín a. **-2.** [similarity] similitud *f*; **to have an ~ with** tener un parecido con.

affirm [ə'fɜːm] *vt* afirmar.

affirmation [,æfə'meɪʃn] *n* **-1.** [declaration] afirmación *f*. **-2.** [confirmation] confirmación *f*.

affirmative [ə'fɜːmətɪv] ◇ *adj* afirmativo(va). ◇ *n* respuesta *f* afirmativa; **in the ~** afirmativamente.

affix [ə'fɪks] *vt* fijar, pegar.

afflict [ə'flɪkt] *vt* aquejar, afligir; **to be ~ed with sthg** estar aquejido de algo.

affliction [ə'flɪkʃn] *n* aflicción *f*, padecimiento *m*.

affluence ['æfluəns] *n* opulencia *f*.

affluent ['æfluənt] *adj* pudiente, adinerado(da).

affluent society *n* sociedad *f* próspera.

afford [ə'fɔːd] *vt* **-1.** [gen]: **to be able to ~** poder permitirse (el lujo de); **I can't ~ the time** no tengo tiempo; **we can't ~ to let this happen** no podemos permitirnos el lujo de dejar que esto ocurra. **-2.** *fml* [provide, give] brindar.

affordable [ə'fɔːdəbl] *adj* asequible.

afforestation [æ,fɒrɪ'steɪʃn] *n* repoblación *f* forestal.

affray [ə'freɪ] *n Br* reyerta *f*.

affront [ə'frʌnt] ◇ *n* afrenta *f*. ◇ *vt* afrentar.

Afghan ['æfgæn], **Afghani** [æf'gænɪ] ◇ *adj* afgano(na). ◇ *n* afgano *m*, -na *f*.

Afghan hound *n* galgo *m* afgano.

Afghanistan [æf'gænɪstæn] *n* Afganistán.

afield [ə'fiːld] *adv*: **far ~** lejos.

AFL-CIO (*abbr of* **American Federation of Labor and Congress of Industrial Organizations**) *n* confederación estadounidense de sindicatos de la industria.

afloat [ə'fləʊt] *adj lit & fig* a flote.

afoot [ə'fʊt] *adj* [plan] en marcha; **there is a rumour ~ that** corre el rumor de que.

aforementioned [ə,fɔː'menʃənd], **aforesaid** [ə'fɔːsed] *adj* susodicho(cha), arriba mencionado(da).

afraid [ə'freɪd] *adj* **-1.** [gen] asustado(da); **to be ~ of sb** tenerle miedo a alguien; **to be ~ of sthg** tener miedo de algo; **to be ~ of doing** OR **to do sthg** tener miedo de hacer algo. **-2.** [in apologies]: **to be ~ that** temerse que; **I'm ~ so/not** me temo que sí/no.

afresh [ə'freʃ] *adv* de nuevo.

Africa ['æfrɪkə] *n* África.

African ['æfrɪkən] ◇ *adj* africano(na). ◇ *n* africano *m*, -na *f*.

African American *n* negro *m* americano, negra *f* americana.

Afrikaans [,æfrɪ'kɑːns] *n* africaans *m*.

Afrikaner [,æfrɪ'kɑːnər] *n* africánder *m y f*.

aft [ɑːft] *adv* en popa.

AFT (*abbr of* **American Federation of Teachers**) *n* sindicato estadounidense de profesores.

after ['ɑːftər] ◇ *prep* **-1.** [gen] después de; **~ having ... después de haber ...; ~ all my efforts** después de todos mis esfuerzos; **~**

you! ¡usted primero!; **day ~ day** día tras día; **the day ~ tomorrow** pasado mañana; **the week ~ next** no la semana que viene sino la otra. **-2.** *inf* [in search of]: **to be ~ sthg** buscar algo; **to be ~ sb** andar detrás de alguien. **-3.** [with the name of]: **to be named ~ sb/sthg** llamarse así por alguien/ algo. **-4.** [towards retreating person]: **to call ~ sb** llamar a alguien (*desde detrás*); **to run ~ sb** correr tras alguien. **-5.** ART: **~ Titian** copia de Tiziano. **-6.** *Am* [telling the time]: **it's twenty ~ three** son las tres y veinte.
◇ *adv* más tarde, después.
◇ *conj* después (de) que; **~ you had done it** después de que lo hubieras hecho.
◆ **afters** *npl Br inf* postre *m*.
◆ **after all** *adv* **-1.** [in spite of everything] después de todo. **-2.** [it should be remembered] al fin y al cabo.

afterbirth ['ɑːftəbɜːθ] *n* placenta *f* (*tras el parto*).

aftercare ['ɑːftəkeər] *n* ayuda oficial prestada a una persona que sale de la prisión o del hospital.

aftereffects ['ɑːftərɪˌfekts] *npl* secuelas *fpl*, efectos *mpl* secundarios.

afterlife ['ɑːftəlaɪf] (*pl* **-lives** [-laɪvz]) *n* más allá *m*, vida *f* de ultratumba.

aftermath ['ɑːftəmæθ] *n* [time] período *m* posterior; [situation] situación *f* posterior.

afternoon [,ɑːftə'nuːn] *n* tarde *f*; **in the ~** por la tarde; **good ~** buenas tardes.
◆ **afternoons** *adv Am* por la tarde.

aftershave ['ɑːftəʃeɪv] *n* loción *f* para después del afeitado.

aftershock ['ɑːftəʃɒk] *n* pequeño temblor de tierra después de un terremoto.

aftertaste ['ɑːftəteɪst] *n* **-1.** [of food, drink] regusto *m*, resabio *m*. **-2.** *fig* [of unpleasant experience] mal sabor *m* de boca.

afterthought ['ɑːftəθɔːt] *n* idea *f* a posteriori.

afterward(s) ['ɑːftəwəd(z)] *adv* después, más tarde.

again [ə'gen] *adv* **-1.** [gen] otra vez, de nuevo; **never ~** nunca jamás; **he's well ~ now** ya está bien; **to do sthg ~** volver a hacer algo; **to say sthg ~** repetir algo; **~ and ~** una y otra vez; **all over ~** otra vez desde el principio; **time and ~** una y otra vez. **-2.** [asking for repetition]: **what's his name ~?** ¿cómo has dicho que se llama? **-3.** *phr*: **half as much ~** la mitad otra vez; **twice as much ~** dos veces lo mismo otra vez; **come ~?** *inf* ¿cómo?; **then** OR **there ~** por otro lado, por otra parte.

against [ə'genst] ◇ *prep* contra; **I'm** ~ **it** estoy (en) contra (de) ello; **to lean** ~ **sthg** apoyarse en algo; **(as)** ~ a diferencia de, en contraste con. ◇ *adv* en contra.

age [eɪdʒ] (*cont* ageing OR aging) ◇ *n* **-1.** [gen] edad *f*; **to be of** ~ *Am* ser mayor de edad; **to come of** ~ hacerse mayor de edad; **to be under** ~ ser menor (de edad); **what** ~ **are you?** ¿qué edad tienes? **-2.** [state of being old] vejez *f*. ◇ *vt & vi* envejecer.

◆ **ages** *npl* [long time] un montón de tiempo, siglos *mpl*; ~**s ago** hace siglos; **I haven't seen her for** ~**s** hace siglos que no la veo.

aged [*adj sense 1* eɪdʒd, *adj sense 2 & npl* 'eɪdʒɪd] ◇ *adj* **-1.** [of the stated age]: **children** ~ **between 8 and 15** niños de entre 8 y 15 años de edad. **-2.** [very old] anciano(na). ◇ *npl*: **the** ~ los ancianos.

age group *n* (grupo *m* de) edad *f*.

ageing ['eɪdʒɪŋ] ◇ *adj* viejo(ja). ◇ *n* envejecimiento *m*.

ageless ['eɪdʒlɪs] *adj* [person] eternamente joven; [thing] imperecedero(ra).

agency ['eɪdʒənsɪ] (*pl* -ies) *n* **-1.** [business] agencia *f*; **employment/travel** ~ agencia de trabajo/viajes. **-2.** [organization, body] organismo *m*, instituto *m*.

agenda [ə'dʒendə] *n* orden *m* del día; **what's on the** ~? ¿cuál es el orden del día?

agent ['eɪdʒənt] *n* **-1.** COMM [of company] representante *m y f*, delegado *m*, -da *f*; [of actor] agente *m y f*. **-2.** [substance] agente *m*. **-3.** [secret agent] agente *m* (secreto).

age-old *adj* secular.

aggravate ['ægrəveɪt] *vt* **-1.** [make worse] agravar, empeorar. **-2.** [annoy] irritar.

aggravating ['ægrəveɪtɪŋ] *adj* [annoying] irritante, exasperante.

aggravation [,ægrə'veɪʃn] *n* **-1.** (*U*) [trouble] irritación *f*. **-2.** [annoying thing] molestia *f*, incomodidad *f*.

aggregate ['ægrɪgət] ◇ *adj* global, total. ◇ *n* **-1.** [total] conjunto *m*, total *m*. **-2.** [material] conglomerado *m*.

aggression [ə'greʃn] *n* agresividad *f*; **act of** ~ agresión *f*.

aggressive [ə'gresɪv] *adj* **-1.** [belligerent person] agresivo(va). **-2.** [forceful · person, campaign] audaz, emprendedor(ra).

aggressively [ə'gresɪvlɪ] *adv* con agresividad.

aggressor [ə'gresər] *n* agresor *m*, -ra *f*.

aggrieved [ə'gri:vd] *adj* ofendido(da), herido(da).

aggro ['ægrəʊ] *n Br inf* camorra *f*, follón *m*.

aghast [ə'gɑːst] *adj*: ~ **(at)** horrorizado(da) (ante).

agile [*Br* 'ædʒaɪl, *Am* 'ædʒəl] *adj* ágil.

agility [ə'dʒɪlətɪ] *n* agilidad *f*.

aging = ageing.

agitate ['ædʒɪteɪt] ◇ *vt* **-1.** [disturb, worry] inquietar, perturbar. **-2.** [shake about] agitar. ◇ *vi* [campaign]: **to** ~ **for/against** hacer campaña a favor de/en contra de.

agitated ['ædʒɪteɪtɪd] *adj* inquieto(ta), nervioso(sa).

agitation [,ædʒɪ'teɪʃn] *n* **-1.** [anxiety] inquietud *f*, nerviosismo *m*. **-2.** POL [campaigning] campaña *f*.

agitator ['ædʒɪteɪtər] *n* [political activist] agitador *m*, -ra *f*.

AGM *n abbr of* **annual general meeting**.

agnostic [æg'nɒstɪk] ◇ *adj* agnóstico(ca). ◇ *n* agnóstico *m*, -ca *f*.

ago [ə'gəʊ] *adv*: **a long time/three days/three years** ~ hace mucho tiempo/tres días/tres años.

agog [ə'gɒg] *adj* ansioso(sa), expectante; ~ **with excitement** vibrante de emoción.

agonize, -ise ['ægənaɪz] *vi* titubear largamente; **to** ~ **over** OR **about sthg** atormentarse con algo.

agonized ['ægənaɪzd] *adj* agónico(ca), angustioso(sa).

agonizing ['ægənaɪzɪŋ] *adj* angustioso(sa).

agonizingly ['ægənaɪzɪŋlɪ] *adv* angustiosamente.

agony ['ægənɪ] (*pl* -ies) *n* **-1.** [physical pain] dolor *m* muy intenso; **to be in** ~ tener tremendos dolores. **-2.** [mental pain] angustia *f*; **to be in** ~ estar angustiado.

agony aunt *n Br inf* consejera *f* sentimental.

agony column *n Br inf* consultorio *m* sentimental.

agoraphobia [,ægərə'fəʊbjə] *n* agorafobia *f*.

agree [ə'griː] ◇ *vi* **-1.** [be of same opinion]: **to** ~ **(with sb about sthg)** estar de acuerdo (con alguien acerca de algo); **to** ~ **on sthg** ponerse de acuerdo en algo. **-2.** [consent]: **to** ~ **(to sthg)** acceder (a algo). **-3.** [approve]: **to** ~ **with sthg** estar de acuerdo con algo. **-4.** [be consistent] concordar. **-5.** [food]: **to** ~ **with sb** sentarle bien a alguien. **-6.** GRAMM: **to** ~ **(with)** concordar (con). ◇ *vt* **-1.** [fix] acordar, convenir. **-2.** [be of same opinion]: **to** ~ **that** estar de acuerdo en que. **-3.** [agree, consent]: **to** ~ **to do sthg** acordar hacer algo. **-4.** [concede]: **to** ~ **(that)** reconocer que.

agreeable [ə'griːəbl] *adj* **-1.** [pleasant] agradable. **-2.** [willing]: **to be ~ to** sthg/doing sthg estar conforme con algo/hacer algo.

agreeably [əˈgrɪəblɪ] *adv* agradablemente.

agreed [əˈgriːd] ◇ *adj*: **to be ~ on** sthg estar de acuerdo sobre algo. ◇ *adv* **-1.** [decided] de acuerdo. **-2.** [admittedly] de acuerdo que.

agreement [əˈgriːmənt] *n* **-1.** [accord, settlement, contract] acuerdo *m*; **to be in ~ with** estar de acuerdo con; **to reach an ~** llegar a un acuerdo. **-2.** [consent] aceptación *f*. **-3.** [consistency] correspondencia *f*. **-4.** GRAMM concordancia *f*.

agricultural [ˌægrɪˈkʌltʃərəl] *adj* agrícola.

agriculture [ˈægrɪkʌltʃəˈ] *n* agricultura *f*.

aground [əˈgraʊnd] *adv*: **to run ~** encallar.

ah [ɑː] *excl* ¡ah!

aha [ɑːˈhɑː] *excl* ¡ajá!

ahead [əˈhed] *adv* **-1.** [in front] delante; **to go on ~** ir por delante; **to be sent on ~** ser enviado por delante. **-2.** [forwards] adelante, hacia delante; **go ~!** ¡por supuesto!; **right** OR **straight ~** todo recto OR de frente. **-3.** [winning]: **to be ~** [in race] ir en cabeza; [in football, rugby etc] ir ganando; **they went ~ in the fifth minute** a los cinco minutos ganaban por un gol. **-4.** [in better position] por delante; **to get ~** [be successful] abrirse camino. **-5.** [in time]: **to look** OR **think ~** mirar hacia el futuro.
◆ **ahead of** *prep* **-1.** [in front of] frente a. **-2.** [beating]: **to be two points ~ of** llevar dos puntos de ventaja a. **-3.** [in better position than] por delante de. **-4.** [in time] antes de, con anterioridad a; **~ of schedule** por delante de lo previsto.

ahoy [əˈhɔɪ] *excl* NAUT: **land/ship ~!** ¡tierra/barco a la vista!

AI *n* **-1.** (*abbr of* **Amnesty International**) AI *f*. **-2.** (*abbr of* **artificial intelligence**) IA *f*. **-3.** *abbr of* **artificial insemination**.

AIB (*abbr of* **Accident Investigation Bureau**) *n* comisión investigadora de accidentes en Gran Bretaña.

aid [eɪd] ◇ *n* ayuda *f*; **medical ~** asistencia *f* médica; **with the ~ of** con (la) ayuda de; **to go to the ~ of** sb OR **to sb's ~** ir en auxilio de alguien; **in ~ of** a beneficio de. ◇ *vt* **-1.** [help] ayudar. **-2.** JUR: **to ~ and abet** ser cómplice de.

AID *n* **-1.** (*abbr of* **artificial insemination by donor**) inseminación artificial con semen de donante anónimo. **-2.** (*abbr of* **Agency for International Development**) organismo estadounidense para el desarrollo internacional.

aide [eɪd] *n* POL ayudante *m y f*.

aide-de-camp [eɪddəˈkɑ̃ː] (*pl* **aides-de-camp**) *n* ayudante *m* de campo.

AIDS, Aids [eɪdz] (*abbr of* **acquired immune deficiency syndrome**) ◇ *n* SIDA *m*, sida *m*. ◇ *comp*: **~ specialist** especialista de sida; **~ patient** sidoso *m*, -sa *f*.

AIH (*abbr of* **artificial insemination by husband**) *n* inseminación artificial con semen del marido.

ail [eɪl] ◇ *vt literary* afligir. ◇ *vi* enfermar.

ailing [ˈeɪlɪŋ] *adj* **-1.** [ill] enfermo(ma), achacoso(sa). **-2.** *fig* [economy] debilitado(da), renqueante.

ailment [ˈeɪlmənt] *n* achaque *m*, molestia *f*.

aim [eɪm] ◇ *n* **-1.** [objective] objetivo *m*, intención *f*. **-2.** [in firing gun] puntería *f*; **to take ~** at apuntar a.
◇ *vt* **-1.** [weapon]: **to ~** sthg **at** apuntar algo a. **-2.** [plan, action]: **to be ~ed at doing** sthg ir dirigido OR encaminado a hacer algo. **-3.** [campaign, publicity, criticism]: **to ~** sthg **at** sb dirigir algo a alguien.
◇ *vi* **-1.** [point weapon]: **to ~ (at** sthg**)** apuntar (a algo). **-2.** [intend]: **to ~ at** OR **for** sthg apuntar a OR pretender algo; **to ~ to do** sthg aspirar a OR pretender hacer algo.

aimless [ˈeɪmlɪs] *adj* sin un objetivo claro.

aimlessly [ˈeɪmlɪslɪ] *adv* sin rumbo fijo.

ain't [eɪnt] *inf* = **am not, are not, is not, have not, has not**.

air [eəˈ] ◇ *n* **-1.** [gen] aire *m*; **into the ~** al aire; **by ~** en avión; **(up) in the ~** *fig* en el aire; **to clear the ~** *fig* aclarar las cosas. **-2.** [tune] melodía *f*. **-3.** RADIO & TV: **on the ~** en el aire. ◇ *comp* aéreo(a). ◇ *vt* **-1.** [clothes, sheets] airear; [cupboard, room] ventilar. **-2.** [views, opinions] expresar. **-3.** *Am* [broadcast] emitir. ◇ *vi* [clothes, sheets] airearse; [cupboard, room] ventilarse.
◆ **airs** *npl*: **~s and graces** aires *mpl*; **to give o.s. ~s, to put on ~s** darse aires, presumir.

airbag [ˈeəbæg] *n* AUT colchón que se infla automáticamente en caso de accidente para proteger a los pasajeros.

airbase [ˈeəbeɪs] *n* base *f* aérea.

airbed [ˈeəbed] *n Br* colchón *m* inflable.

airborne [ˈeəbɔːn] *adj* **-1.** [troops] aerotransportado(da); [attack] aéreo(a). **-2.** [plane] en el aire, en vuelo.

airbrake [ˈeəbreɪk] *n* freno *m* neumático.

airbus [ˈeəbʌs] *n* aerobús *m*.

air-conditioned [-kənˈdɪʃnd] *adj* climatizado(da), con aire acondicionado.

air-conditioning [-kənˈdɪʃnɪŋ] *n* aire *m* acondicionado.

aircraft [ˈeəkrɑːft] (*pl inv*) *n* [plane] avión *m*; [any flying machine] aeronave *m*.

aircraft carrier *n* portaaviones *m inv*.

air cushion *n* cojín *m* neumático.

airfield ['eəfiːld] *n* campo *m* de aviación.

airforce ['eəfɔːs] ◇ *n:* **the ~** las fuerzas aéreas. ◇ *comp* de las fuerzas aéreas.

air freight *n* transporte *m* por vía aérea.

airgun ['eəgʌn] *n* pistola *f* de aire comprimido.

airhostess ['eə,həustɪs] *n* azafata *f*, aeromoza *f Amer*.

airily ['eərəlɪ] *adv* alegremente.

airing ['eərɪŋ] *n:* **to give sthg an ~** [clothes, linen] **orear** OR **airear algo;** [room] **ventilar algo;** [opinions] **expresar algo.**

airing cupboard *n Br* armario seco y caliente para guardar la ropa.

airkiss ['eəkɪs] *vi* besarse sin llegar a tocar con los labios.

airlane ['eəleɪn] *n* ruta *f* aérea.

airless ['eəlɪs] *adj* mal ventilado(da).

airletter ['eəletər] *n* aerograma *m*.

airlift ['eəlɪft] ◇ *n* puente *m* aéreo. ◇ *vt* aerotransportar, transportar por avión.

airline ['eəlaɪn] *n* línea *f* aérea.

airliner ['eəlaɪnər] *n* avión *m* (grande) de pasajeros.

airlock ['eəlɒk] *n* **-1.** [in tube, pipe] bolsa *f* de aire. **-2.** [airtight chamber] cámara *f* OR esclusa *f* de aire.

airmail ['eəmeɪl] *n* correo *m* aéreo; **by ~** por correo aéreo.

airman ['eəmən] (*pl* **-men** [-mən]) *n* [aviator] soldado *m* de aviación.

air mattress *n* colchón *m* inflable.

airplane ['eəpleɪn] *n Am* avión *m*.

airplay ['eəpleɪ] *n* tiempo *m* de emisión, cobertura *f* radiofónica.

airpocket ['eəpɒkɪt] *n* bolsa *f* de aire.

airport ['eəpɔːt] ◇ *n* aeropuerto *m*. ◇ *comp* de aeropuerto.

air raid *n* ataque *m* aéreo.

air-raid shelter *n* refugio *m* antiaéreo.

air rifle *n* fusil *m* de aire comprimido.

airship ['eəʃɪp] *n* dirigible *m*.

airsick ['eəsɪk] *adj:* **to be ~** marearse (en el avión).

airspace ['eəspeɪs] *n* espacio *m* aéreo.

airspeed ['eəspiːd] *n* velocidad *f* de vuelo.

air steward *n* auxiliar *m* de vuelo.

air stewardess *n* azafata *f*.

airstrip ['eəstrɪp] *n* pista *f* de aterrizaje.

air terminal *n* terminal *f* aérea.

airtight ['eətaɪt] *adj* hermético(ca).

airtime ['eətaɪm] *n* [on radio] espacio *m* radiofónico, cobertura *f* radiofónica.

air-to-air *adj* [missile] aire-aire (*inv*).

air-traffic control *n* control *m* del tráfico aéreo.

air-traffic controller *n* controlador aéreo *m*, controladora aérea *f*.

air travel *n* (*U*) viaje *m* en avión.

airwaves ['eəweɪvz] *npl* ondas *fpl*; **on the ~** en antena.

airy ['eərɪ] (*compar* **-ier**, *superl* **-iest**) *adj* **-1.** [room] espacioso(sa) y bien ventilado(da). **-2.** [fanciful] vano(na), ilusorio(ria). **-3.** [nonchalant] despreocupado(da).

aisle [aɪl] *n* **-1.** [in church] nave *f* lateral. **-2.** [in plane, theatre, supermarket] pasillo *m*.

ajar [əˈdʒɑːr] *adj* entreabierto(ta).

AK *abbr of* **Alaska.**

aka (*abbr of* **also known as**) alias.

akin [əˈkɪn] *adj:* **~ to sthg/to doing sthg** semejante a algo/a hacer algo.

AL *abbr of* **Alabama.**

Alabama [,æləˈbæmə] *n* Alabama.

alabaster [,æləˈbɑːstər] *n* alabastro *m*.

à la carte *adj & adv* a la carta.

alacrity [əˈlækrətɪ] *n* presteza *f*, prontitud *f*.

alarm [əˈlɑːm] ◇ *n* alarma *f*; **to raise** OR **sound the ~** dar la (voz de) alarma. ◇ *vt* alarmar, asustar.

alarm clock *n* despertador *m*.

alarming [əˈlɑːmɪŋ] *adj* alarmante.

alarmingly [əˈlɑːmɪŋlɪ] *adv* de manera alarmante.

alarmist [əˈlɑːmɪst] *adj* alarmista.

alas [əˈlæs] *excl literary* ¡ay!

Alaska [əˈlæskə] *n* Alaska.

Albania [ælˈbeɪnjə] *n* Albania.

Albanian [ælˈbeɪnjən] ◇ *adj* albanés(esa). ◇ *n* **-1.** [person] albanés *m*, -esa *f*. **-2.** [language] albanés *m*.

albatross ['ælbətrɒs] (*pl inv* OR **-es**) *n* albatros *m*.

albeit [ɔːlˈbiːɪt] *conj fml* aunque, si bien.

Alberta [ælˈbɜːtə] *n* Alberta.

Albert Hall ['ælbət-] *n:* **the ~** el Albert Hall.

ALBERT HALL:
El 'Albert Hall' es un gran edificio londinense que acoge conciertos y manifestaciones diversas, incluidas pruebas deportivas; fue bautizado en honor al príncipe Alberto, esposo de la reina Victoria

---

albino [ælˈbiːnəu] (*pl* **-s**) ◇ *n* albino *m*, -na *f*. ◇ *comp* albino(na).

album ['ælbəm] *n* **-1.** [of stamps, photos] álbum *m*. **-2.** [record] elepé *m*.

albumen ['ælbjumɪn] *n* albúmina *f*.

alchemy ['ælkəmɪ] *n* alquimia *f*.

alcohol ['ælkəhɒl] *n* alcohol *m*.

alcoholic [,ælkə'hɒlɪk] ◇ *adj* alcohólico(ca). ◇ *n* alcohólico *m*, -ca *f*.

alcoholism ['ælkəhɒlɪzm] *n* alcoholismo *m*.

alcopop ['ælkəʊpɒp] *n* refresco gaseoso que contiene un cierto porcentaje de alcohol.

alcove ['ælkəʊv] *n* hueco *m*.

alderman ['ɔːldəmən] (*pl* **-men** [-mən]) *n* ≈ concejal *m*, -la *f*.

ale [eɪl] *n* tipo de cerveza.

alert [ə'lɜːt] ◇ *adj* **-1.** [vigilant] atento(ta). **-2.** [perceptive] despierto(ta). **-3.** [aware]: **to be ~ to** ser consciente de. ◇ *n* [gen & MIL] alerta *f*; **on the ~** alerta. ◇ *vt* alertar; **to ~ sb to sthg** alertar a alguien de algo.

Aleutian Islands [ə'luːʃjən-] *npl*: **the ~** las islas Aleutianas.

A-level (*abbr of* **Advanced level**) *n* Br SCH nivel escolar necesario para acceder a la universidad.

A-LEVEL:
Cada 'A-level' es un examen bastante especializado sobre una materia concreta escogida previamente por el alumno. Se suele hacer a los 18 años tras un curso de dos años. Las universidades suelen requerir tres 'A-levels' para acceder a ellas, no obstante mucha gente estudia 'A-levels' simplemente para mejorar su currículum

Alexandria [,ælɪg'zɑːndrɪə] *n* Alejandría.

alfalfa [æl'fælfə] *n* alfalfa *f*.

alfresco [æl'freskəʊ] *adj & adv* al aire libre.

algae ['ældʒiː] *npl* algas *fpl*.

Algarve [æl'gɑːv] *n*: **the ~** el Algarve.

algebra ['ældʒɪbrə] *n* álgebra *f*.

Algeria [æl'dʒɪərɪə] *n* Argelia.

Algerian [æl'dʒɪərɪən] ◇ *adj* argelino(na). ◇ *n* argelino *m*, -na *f*.

Algiers [æl'dʒɪəz] *n* Argel.

algorithm ['ælgərɪðm] *n* algoritmo *m*.

alias ['eɪlɪəs] (*pl* **-es**) ◇ *adv* alias. ◇ *n* alias *m*.

alibi ['ælɪbaɪ] *n* coartada *f*.

alien ['eɪljən] ◇ *adj* **-1.** [foreign] foráneo(a), extranjero(ra). **-2.** [from outer space] extraterrestre. **-3.** [unfamiliar] extraño(ña), ajeno(na). ◇ *n* **-1.** [from outer space] extraterrestre *m y f*. **-2.** JUR [foreigner] extranjero *m*, -ra *f*.

alienate ['eɪljəneɪt] *vt* **-1.** [make unsympathetic] ganarse la antipatía de. **-2.** [distance emotionally]: **to be ~d from** estar distanciado(da) de.

alienation [,eɪljə'neɪʃn] *n* **-1.** [separation] separación *f*, alejamiento *m*. **-2.** [not belonging] alienación *f*, desarraigo *m*.

alight [ə'laɪt] (*pt & pp* **-ed** OR **alit**) ◇ *adj* [on fire] prendido(da), ardiendo. ◇ *vi fml* **-1.** [land] posarse. **-2.** [get off]: **to ~ from** apearse de.

align [ə'laɪn] *vt* **-1.** [line up] alinear, poner en línea. **-2.** [ally]: **to ~ o.s. with** alinearse con.

alignment [ə'laɪnmənt] *n* **-1.** [arrangement] alineación *f*. **-2.** [alliance] alineamiento *m*.

alike [ə'laɪk] ◇ *adj* parecido(da). ◇ *adv* de la misma forma, por igual; **to look ~** parecerse; **to think ~** pensar igual.

alimentary canal [,ælɪ'mentərɪ-] *n* tubo *m* digestivo.

alimony ['ælɪmənɪ] *n* pensión *f* alimenticia.

A-line *adj* de vuelo.

alive [ə'laɪv] *adj* **-1.** [living] vivo(va). **-2.** [tradition] con vida. **-3.** [active, lively] lleno(na) de vida; **to come ~** [story, description] cobrar vida; [person, place] animarse. **-4.** [aware]: **to be ~ to** ser consciente de. **-5.** [rats, insects]: **to be ~ with** estar infestado(da) de; [rumour, speculation] bullir de.

alkali ['ælkəlaɪ] (*pl* **-s** OR **-ies**) *n* álcali *m*.

alkaline ['ælkəlaɪn] *adj* alcalino(na).

all [ɔːl] ◇ *adj* **-1.** (*with sg noun*) todo(da); **~ the drink** toda la bebida; **~ violence is to be condemned** toda forma de violencia es condenable; **~ day** todo el día; **~ night** toda la noche; **~ the time** todo el tiempo OR el rato. **-2.** (*with pl noun*) todos(das); **~ the boxes** todas las cajas; **~ men** todos los hombres; **~ three died** los tres murieron. ◇ *pron* **-1.** (*sg*) [the whole amount] todo *m*, -da *f*; **she drank it ~, she drank ~ of it** se lo bebió todo. **-2.** (*pl*) [everybody, everything] todos *mpl*, -das *fpl*; **~ of them came, they ~ came** vinieron todos. **-3.** (*with superl*): **he's the cleverest of ~** es el más listo de todos; **best/worst of ~ ...** lo mejor/peor de todo es que ...; **above ~ →** above; **after ~ →** after; **at ~ →** at. ◇ *adv* **-1.** [entirely] completamente; **I'd forgotten ~ about that** me había olvidado completamente de eso; **it spilled ~ over the carpet** se derramó por toda la alfombra; **she was dressed ~ in red** iba vestida toda de rojo; **~ alone** completamente solo(la); **that's ~ very well, but ...** sí, eso está muy bien, pero .... **-2.** [in sport, competitions]: **the score is two ~** el resultado es de empate a dos. **-3.** (*with compar*): **the situation was made ~ the worse by his arrival** la situación se hizo peor si cabe con su llegada; **to run ~ the faster** correr aun más rápido.

◆ **all but** *adv* casi.

◆ **all in all** *adv* en conjunto.

◆ **all that** *adv* tan; **she's not ~ that pretty** no es tan guapa.

◆ **for all** ◇ *prep* a pesar de. ◇ *conj*: **for ~ I know** por lo que yo sé; **do it, for ~ I care!** pues hazlo, ¡a mí qué me importa!

◆ **in all** *adv* en total.

Allah ['ælə] *n* Alá *m*.

all-around *Am* = **all-round**.

allay [ə'leɪ] *vt fml* apaciguar, mitigar.

all clear *n* **-1.** [signal] señal *f* de cese de peligro. **-2.** *fig* [go-ahead] luz *f* verde.

allegation [,ælɪ'geɪʃn] *n* acusación *f*; **to make ~s (about)** hacer acusaciones (acerca de).

allege [ə'ledʒ] *vt* alegar; **to ~ that** alegar que; **to be ~d to have done/said** ser acusado de haber hecho/dicho.

alleged [ə'ledʒd] *adj* presunto(ta).

allegedly [ə'ledʒɪdlɪ] *adv* presuntamente.

allegiance [ə'liːdʒəns] *n* fidelidad *f*.

allegorical [,ælɪ'gɒrɪkl] *adj* alegórico(ca).

allegory ['ælɪgərɪ] (*pl* **-ies**) *n* alegoría *f*.

alleluia [,ælɪ'luːjə] *excl* ¡aleluya!

allergic [ə'lɜːdʒɪk] *adj lit & fig*: **~ (to sthg)** alérgico(ca) (a algo).

allergy ['ælədʒɪ] (*pl* **-ies**) *n* alergia *f*; **to have an ~ to** tener alergia a.

alleviate [ə'liːvɪeɪt] *vt* aliviar.

alley(way) ['ælɪ(weɪ)] *n* callejuela *f*.

alliance [ə'laɪəns] *n* alianza *f*.

allied ['ælaɪd] *adj* **-1.** [powers, troops] aliado(da). **-2.** [subjects] análogo(ga), afín.

alligator ['ælɪgeɪtə^r] (*pl inv* OR **-s**) *n* caimán *m*.

all-important *adj* de suma importancia, crucial.

all-in *adj Br* [inclusive] todo incluido.

◆ **all in** ◇ *adj inf* [tired] hecho(cha) polvo, derrengado(da). ◇ *adv* [inclusive] todo incluido.

all-in wrestling *n* lucha *f* libre.

alliteration [ə,lɪtə'reɪʃn] *n* aliteración *f*.

all-night *adj* que dura toda la noche.

allocate ['æləkeɪt] *vt*: **to ~ sthg to sb** [money, resources] destinar algo a alguien; [task, tickets, seats] asignar algo a alguien.

allocation [,ælə'keɪʃn] *n* **-1.** [sharing out - of money, resources] distribución *f*, reparto *m*; [- of task, tickets, seats] asignación *f*. **-2.** [share - of money, resources] presupuesto *m*; [- of tickets, seats] asignación *f*.

allot [ə'lɒt] (*pt & pp* **-ted**, *cont* **-ting**) *vt* [job, time] asignar; [money, resources] destinar.

allotment [ə'lɒtmənt] *n* **-1.** *Br* [garden] parcela municipal arrendada para su cultivo. **-2.** [sharing out - of job, time] asignación *f*; [- of money, resources] distribución *f*. **-3.** [share - of money, resources] porción *f*, asignación *f*; [- of time] espacio *m* (de tiempo) concedido.

all-out *adj* [effort] supremo(ma); [war] sin cuartel.

allow [ə'laʊ] *vt* **-1.** [permit] permitir, dejar; **to ~ sb to do sthg** permitir OR dejar a alguien hacer algo; **~ me** permítame. **-2.** [set aside - money] apartar, destinar; [- time] dejar. **-3.** [officially accept - subj: person] conceder; [- subj: law] admitir, permitir. **-4.** [concede]: **to ~ that** admitir OR reconocer que.

◆ **allow for** *vt fus* tener en cuenta, contar con.

allowable [ə'laʊəbl] *adj* permisible.

allowance [ə'laʊəns] *n* **-1.** [money received - from government] subsidio *m*; [- from employer] dietas *fpl*; **clothing ~** asignación *f* para ropa. **-2.** *Am* [pocket money] paga *f*, asignación *f* semanal. **-3.** FIN desgravación *f*. **-4.** **to make ~s for sthg/sb** [forgive] disculpar algo/a alguien; [take into account] tener en cuenta algo/a alguien.

alloy ['ælɔɪ] *n* aleación *f*.

all-powerful *adj* todopoderoso(sa), omnipotente.

all right ◇ *adv* **-1.** [gen] bien. **-2.** *inf* [only just acceptably] (más o menos) bien. **-3.** *inf* [in answer - yes] vale, bueno. **-4.** *inf* [certainly] seguro, sin duda; **it's her ~** seguro que es ella. **-5.** [do you understand?]: **~?** ¿vale? **-6.** [now then] bueno, vale; **~, children, stop talking now!** ¡venga, niños, callaos de una vez!

◇ *adj* **-1.** [gen] bien. **-2.** *inf* [not bad]: **it's ~, but ...** no está mal, pero .... **-3.** [allowable]: **is it ~ if ...?** ¿te importa si ...? **-4.** *inf* [OK]: **sorry — that's ~** lo siento — no importa.

all-round *Br*, **all-around** *Am adj* **-1.** [multi-skilled] completo(ta), polifacético(ca). **-2.** [comprehensive] amplio(plia), extenso(sa).

all-rounder ['raʊndə^r] *n* **-1.** [versatile person] persona *f* que hace de todo. **-2.** [sportsman, sportswoman] deportista completo *m*, deportista completa *f*.

all-time *adj* de todos los tiempos.

allude [ə'luːd] *vi*: **to ~ to** aludir a.

allure [ə'ljʊə^r] *n* encanto *m*, atractivo *m*.

alluring [ə'ljʊərɪŋ] *adj* [person] atrayente; [thing] tentador(ra).

allusion [ə'luːʒn] *n* alusión *f*.

ally [*n* 'ælaɪ, *vb* ə'laɪ] (*pl* **-ies**, *pt & pp* **-ied**) ◇ *n* aliado *m*, **-da** *f*. ◇ *vt*: **to ~ o.s. with** aliarse con.

almanac ['ɔːlmənæk] *n* [yearbook] anuario *m*; [calendar] almanaque *m*.

almighty [ɔːl'maɪtɪ] *adj inf* [very big] descomunal.

◆ **Almighty** ◇ *adj* todopoderoso(sa). ◇ *n*: the Almighty el Todopoderoso.

almond ['ɑːmənd] *n* **-1.** [nut] almendra *f*. **-2.** [tree] almendro *m*.

almond paste *n* mazapán *m*, pasta *f* de almendras.

almost ['ɔːlməʊst] *adv* casi.

alms [ɑːmz] *npl dated* limosna *f*.

aloft [ə'lɒft] *adv* **-1.** [in the air] en lo alto. **-2.** NAUT entre el velamen.

alone [ə'ləʊn] ◇ *adj* solo(la); **to be ~ with** estar a solas con; **all ~** completamente solo. ◇ *adv* **-1.** [without others] solo(la). **-2.** [only] sólo. **-3.** *phr*: **to go it ~** ir por cuenta propia OR por libre; **to leave sthg/sb ~** dejar algo/a alguien en paz.

◆ **let alone** *conj* no digamos, y mucho menos.

along [ə'lɒŋ] ◇ *adv* **-1.** [forward] hacia delante; **to go** OR **walk ~** avanzar; **she was walking ~** iba andando. **-2.** [with others or oneself]: **bring it ~** tráetelo. **-3.** [to this or that place]: **to come ~** venir; **to go ~** ir. ◇ *prep* **-1.** [towards one end of, beside] por, a lo largo de. **-2.** [in] en; **he lives ~ Dalry Rd** vive en Dalry Rd.

◆ **all along** *adv* todo el rato, siempre.

◆ **along with** *prep* junto con.

alongside [ə,lɒŋ'saɪd] ◇ *prep* **-1.** [next to] junto a. **-2.** [together with] junto con. ◇ *adv*: **to come ~** ponerse a la misma altura; **to work ~** trabajar juntos(tas).

aloof [ə'luːf] ◇ *adj* frío(a), distante. ◇ *adv* distante, a distancia; **to remain ~ (from)** mantenerse a distancia (de).

aloud [ə'laʊd] *adv* en alto, en voz alta.

alpaca [æl'pækə] *n* [animal] alpaca *f*.

alphabet ['ælfəbet] *n* alfabeto *m*.

alphabetical [,ælfə'betɪkl] *adj* alfabético(ca); **in ~ order** en OR por orden alfabético.

alphabetically [,ælfə'betɪklɪ] *adv* alfabéticamente.

alphabetize, -ise ['ælfəbətaɪz] *vt* ordenar alfabéticamente.

alphanumeric [,ælfənjuː'merɪk] *adj* COMPUT alfanumérico(ca).

alpine ['ælpaɪn] *adj* alpino(na).

Alps [ælps] *npl*: **the ~** los Alpes.

already [ɔːl'redɪ] *adv* ya.

alright [,ɔːl'raɪt] = **all right**.

Alsace [æl'sæs] *n* Alsacia.

Alsatian [æl'seɪʃn] ◇ *adj* [of Alsace] alsacia-

no(na). ◇ *n* **-1.** [person] alsaciano *m*, -na *f*. **-2.** [dog] pastor *m* alemán.

also ['ɔːlsəʊ] *adv* también.

also-ran *n* comparsa *m* y *f*.

Alta. *abbr of* **Alberta**.

altar ['ɔːltər] *n* altar *m*.

alter ['ɔːltər] ◇ *vt* [modify] alterar, modificar; **to have a dress ~ed** mandar arreglar un vestido. ◇ *vi* cambiar.

alteration [,ɔːltə'reɪʃn] *n* alteración *f*; **to make an ~/~s** hacer una modificación/ modificaciones en.

altercation [,ɔːltə'keɪʃn] *n* altercado *m*.

alter ego (*pl* **-s**) *n* álter ego *m*.

alternate [*adj Br* ɔːl'tɜːnət, *Am* 'ɔːltərnət, *vb* 'ɔːltərneɪt] ◇ *adj* **-1.** [by turns] alternativo(va), alterno(na). **-2.** [every other]: **on ~ days/weeks** cada dos días/semanas. ◇ *vt* alternar. ◇ *vi*: **to ~ (with/between)** alternar (con/entre).

alternately [ɔːl'tɜːnətlɪ] *adv* alternativamente.

alternating current ['ɔːltəneɪtɪŋ-] *n* ELEC corriente *f* alterna.

alternation [,ɔːltə'neɪʃn] *n* alternancia *f*.

alternative [ɔːl'tɜːnətɪv] ◇ *adj* alternativo(va). ◇ *n* alternativa *f*, opción *f*; **to have no ~ (but to do sthg)** no tener más remedio (que hacer algo).

alternatively [ɔːl'tɜːnətɪvlɪ] *adv* o bien, por otra parte.

alternative medicine *n* medicina *f* alternativa.

alternator ['ɔːltəneɪtər] *n* ELEC alternador *m*.

although [ɔːl'ðəʊ] *conj* aunque.

altitude ['æltɪtjuːd] *n* altitud *f*.

alto ['æltəʊ] (*pl* **-s**) ◇ *n* [male voice] contralto *m*; [female voice] contralto *f*. ◇ *comp* alto.

altogether [,ɔːltə'geðər] *adv* **-1.** [completely] completamente, totalmente; **not ~** no del todo. **-2.** [considering all things] en conjunto, en general. **-3.** [in total] en total.

altruism ['æltruːɪzm] *n* altruismo *m*.

altruistic [,æltrʊ'ɪstɪk] *adj* altruista.

aluminium *Br* [,æljʊ'mɪnɪəm], **aluminum** *Am* [ə'luːmɪnəm] ◇ *n* aluminio *m*. ◇ *comp* de aluminio.

alumnus [ə'lʌmnəs] (*pl* **-ni** [-naɪ]) *n* exalumno *m*, -na *f* (de una universidad).

always ['ɔːlweɪz] *adv* siempre.

am [æm] → **be**.

a.m. (*abbr of* **ante meridiem**) antes de mediodía; **at 3 ~** a las tres de la mañana.

AM (*abbr of* **amplitude modulation**) *n* AM *f*.

AMA (*abbr of* **American Medical Association**) *n colegio estadounidense de médicos.*

amalgam [ə'mælgəm] *n fml & TECH* amalgama *f*.

amalgamate [ə'mælgəmeɪt] ◇ *vt* [unite] amalgamar. ◇ *vi* [unite] amalgamarse.

amalgamation [ə,mælgə'meɪʃn] *n* fusión *f*, unión *f*.

amass [ə'mæs] *vt* amasar.

amateur ['æmətə'] ◇ *adj* aficionado(da); *pej* chapucero(ra), poco profesional. ◇ *n* aficionado *m*, -da *f*; *pej* chapucero *m*, -ra *f*.

amateurish [,æmə'tɜːrɪʃ] *adj* chapucero(ra), poco profesional.

amaze [ə'meɪz] *vt* asombrar.

amazed [ə'meɪzd] *adj* asombrado(da), pasmado(da).

amazement [ə'meɪzmənt] *n* asombro *m*; **to my ~** para gran sorpresa mía.

amazing [ə'meɪzɪŋ] *adj* asombroso(sa).

amazingly [ə'meɪzɪŋlɪ] *adv* asombrosamente.

Amazon ['æməzn] *n* **-1.** [river]: **the ~** el Amazonas. **-2.** [region]: **the ~ (Basin)** la Amazonia, la cuenca amazónica; **the ~ rain forest** la selva amazónica. **-3.** [woman] amazona *f*.

Amazonian [,æmə'zəʊnjən] *adj* amazónico(ca).

ambassador [æm'bæsədə'] *n* embajador *m*, -ra *f*.

amber ['æmbə'] ◇ *adj* **-1.** [amber-coloured] de color ámbar, ambarino(na). **-2.** *Br* [traffic light] ámbar. ◇ *n* ámbar *m*. ◇ *comp* [made of amber] de ámbar.

ambiance ['æmbɪəns] = **ambience**.

ambidextrous [,æmbɪ'dekstrəs] *adj* ambidiestro(tra).

ambience ['æmbɪəns] *n* ambiente *m*.

ambiguity [,æmbɪ'gjuːətɪ] (*pl* **-ies**) *n* ambigüedad *f*.

ambiguous [æm'bɪgjʊəs] *adj* ambiguo(gua).

ambiguously [æm'bɪgjʊəslɪ] *adv* ambiguamente.

ambition [æm'bɪʃn] *n* ambición *f*.

ambitious [æm'bɪʃəs] *adj* ambicioso(sa).

ambivalence [æm'bɪvələns] *n* ambivalencia *f*.

ambivalent [æm'bɪvələnt] *adj* ambivalente.

amble ['æmbl] *vi* [walk] deambular, pasear.

ambulance ['æmbjʊləns] ◇ *n* ambulancia *f*. ◇ *comp*: **~ man** ambulanciero *m*; **~ woman** ambulanciera *f*.

ambush ['æmbʊʃ] ◇ *n* emboscada *f*. ◇ *vt* emboscar.

ameba *Am* = **amoeba**.

ameliorate [ə'miːljəreɪt] *vt & vi fml* mejorar.

amen [,ɑː'men] *excl* amén.

amenable [ə'miːnəbl] *adj* razonable; **~ to** favorable a.

amend [ə'mend] *vt* [law] enmendar; [text] corregir.

◆ **amends** *npl*: **to make ~s for sthg** reparar algo.

amendment [ə'mendmənt] *n* **-1.** [change - to law] enmienda *f*; [- to text] corrección *f*. **-2.** [act of changing] enmienda *f*, rectificación *f*.

amenities [ə'miːnətɪz] *npl* [of town] facilidades *fpl*; [of building] comodidades *fpl*.

America [ə'merɪkə] *n* América.

◆ **Americas** *npl*: **the ~s** las Américas.

American [ə'merɪkn] ◇ *adj* americano(na). ◇ *n* [person] americano *m*, -na *f*.

American Indian *n* amerindio *m*, -dia *f*.

Americanism [ə'merɪkənɪzm] *n* americanismo *m*.

americanize, **-ise** [ə'merɪkənaɪz] *vt* americanizar.

amethyst ['æmɪθɪst] *n* amatista *f*.

Amex ['æmeks] *n* **-1.** (*abbr of* **American Stock Exchange**) *segundo mercado bursátil estadounidense*. **-2.** *abbr of* **American Express**.

amiable ['eɪmjəbl] *adj* amable, agradable.

amiably ['eɪmjəblɪ] *adv* amablemente.

amicable ['æmɪkəbl] *adj* amigable, amistoso(sa).

amicably ['æmɪkəblɪ] *adv* amigablemente, amistosamente.

amid(st) [ə'mɪd(st)] *prep fml* entre, en medio de.

amino acid [ə'miːnəʊ-] *n* aminoácido *m*.

amiss [ə'mɪs] ◇ *adj* mal. ◇ *adv*: **to take sthg ~** tomarse algo a mal.

ammo ['æməʊ] *n* (*U*) *inf* MIL munición *f*.

ammonia [ə'məʊnjə] *n* amoníaco *m*.

ammunition [,æmjʊ'nɪʃn] *n* (*U*) **-1.** MIL municiones *fpl*. **-2.** *fig* [information, argument] argumentos *mpl*.

ammunition dump *n* arsenal *m* OR depósito *m* de municiones.

amnesia [æm'niːzjə] *n* amnesia *f*.

amnesty ['æmnəstɪ] (*pl* **-ies**) *n* amnistía *f*.

Amnesty International *n* Amnistía *f* Internacional.

amoeba *Br* (*pl* **-bas** OR **-bae** [-biː]), **ameba** *Am* (*pl* **-bas** OR **-bae** [-biː]) [ə'miːbə] *n* ameba *f*.

amok [ə'mɒk] *adv*: **to run ~** *enloquecer atacando a gente de forma indiscriminada*.

among(st) [ə'mʌŋ(st)] *prep* entre.

amoral [,eɪ'mɒrəl] *adj* amoral.

amorous ['æmərəs] *adj* amoroso(sa).

amorphous [ə'mɔːfəs] *adj* amorfo(fa).

amortize [ə'mɔːtaɪz] *vt* FIN amortizar.

amount [ə'maʊnt] *n* cantidad *f*.
▶ **amount to** *vt fus* **-1.** [total] ascender a. **2.** [be equivalent to] venir a ser.
amp [æmp] *n* **-1.** *abbr of* **ampere**. **-2.** *inf abbr of* **amplifier**) amplificador *m*.
amperage ['æmpərɪdʒ] *n* ELEC amperaje *m*.
ampere ['æmpeər] *n* amperio *m*.
ampersand ['æmpəsænd] *n* ampersand *m*.
amphetamine [æm'fetəmiːn] *n* anfetamina *f*.
amphibian [æm'fɪbɪən] *n* anfibio *m*.
amphibious [æm'fɪbɪəs] *adj* anfibio(bia).
amphitheatre *Br*, **amphitheater** *Am* 'æmfɪ,θɪətər] *n* anfiteatro *m*.
ample ['æmpl] *adj* **-1.** [enough] suficiente; more than enough] sobrado(da). **-2.** [garment, oom] amplio(plia); [stomach, bosom] abundante.
amplification [,æmplɪfɪ'keɪʃn] *n* **-1.** [of ound] amplificación *f*. **-2.** [of idea, statement] desarrollo *m*, explicación *f*.
amplifier ['æmplɪfaɪər] *n* amplificador *m*.
amplify ['æmplɪfaɪ] (*pt & pp* **-ied**) ◇ *vt* **-1.** sound] amplificar. **-2.** [idea, statement] desarrollar, ampliar. ◇ *vi*: **to ~ (on sthg)** ampliar (algo).
amply ['æmplɪ] *adv* **-1.** [sufficiently] suficientemente; [more than sufficiently] sobradamente. **-2.** [considerably] abundantemente, ampliamente.
ampoule *Br*, **ampule** *Am* ['æmpuːl] *n* ampolla *f*.
amputate ['æmpjʊteɪt] *vt & vi* amputar.
amputation [,æmpjʊ'teɪʃn] *n* amputación *f*.
Amsterdam [,æmstə'dæm] *n* Amsterdam.
amt *abbr of* **amount**.
Amtrak ['æmtræk] *n organismo que regula y coordina las líneas férreas en Estados Unidos*.
amuck [ə'mʌk] = **amok**.
amulet ['æmjʊlɪt] *n* amuleto *m*.
amuse [ə'mjuːz] *vt* **-1.** [make laugh, smile] divertir. **-2.** [entertain] distraer; **to ~ o.s. (by doing sthg)** distraerse (haciendo algo).
amused [ə'mjuːzd] *adj* **-1.** [person, look] divertido(da); **I was not ~ at** OR **by that** no me hizo gracia eso. **-2.** [entertained]: **to keep o.s. ~** entretenerse, distraerse.
amusement [ə'mjuːzmənt] *n* **-1.** [enjoyment] regocijo *m*, diversión *f*. **-2.** [diversion, game] atracción *f*.
amusement arcade *n* salón *m* de juegos.
amusement park *n* parque *m* de atracciones.
amusing [ə'mjuːzɪŋ] *adj* divertido(da), gracioso(sa).
an [*stressed* æn, *unstressed* ən] → **a²**.

ANA *n* **-1.** (*abbr of* **American Newspaper Association**) *sindicato estadounidense de la prensa escrita*. **-2.** (*abbr of* **American Nurses Association**) *sindicato estadounidense de enfermeros*.
anabolic steroid [,ænə'bɒlɪk-] *n* esteroide *m* anabolizante.
anachronism [ə'nækrənɪzm] *n* anacronismo *m*.
anachronistic [ə,nækrə'nɪstɪk] *adj* anacrónico(ca).
anaemia *Br*, **anemia** *Am* [ə'niːmjə] *n* anemia *f*.
anaemic *Br*, **anemic** *Am* [ə'niːmɪk] *adj* **-1.** [ill] anémico(ca). **-2.** *fig & pej* [weak, poor] pobre.
anaesthesia *Br*, **anesthesia** *Am* [,ænɪs'θiːzjə] *n* anestesia *f*.
anaesthetic *Br*, **anesthetic** *Am* [,ænɪs'θetɪk] *n* anestesia *f*; **under ~** anestesiado; **local/general ~** anestesia local/general.
anaesthetist *Br*, **anesthetist** *Am* [æ'niːsθətɪst] *n* anestesista *m y f*.
anaesthetize *Br*, **-ise** *Br*, **anesthetize** *Am* [æ'niːsθətaɪz] *vt* anestesiar.
anagram ['ænəgræm] *n* anagrama *m*.
anal ['eɪnl] *adj* anal.
analgesic [,ænæl'dʒiːsɪk] ◇ *adj* analgésico(ca). ◇ *n* analgésico *m*.
analog *Am* = **analogue**.
analogous [ə'næləgəs] *adj fml*: **~ (to)** análogo(ga) (a).
analogue, **analog** *Am* ['ænəlɒg] ◇ *adj* [watch, clock] analógico(ca). ◇ *n fml* equivalente *m*.
analogy [ə'nælədʒɪ] (*pl* **-ies**) *n* analogía *f*; **to draw an ~ with/between** establecer una analogía con/entre; **by ~** por analogía.
analyse *Br*, **analyze** *Am* ['ænəlaɪz] *vt* analizar.
analysis [ə'næləsɪs] (*pl* **analyses** [ə'næləsiːz]) *n* análisis *m inv*; **in the final** OR **last ~** en resumidas cuentas.
analyst ['ænəlɪst] *n* **-1.** [gen] analista *m y f*. **-2.** [psychoanalyst] psicoanalista *m y f*.
analytic(al) [,ænə'lɪtɪk(l)] *adj* analítico(ca).
analyze *Am* = **analyse**.
anarchic [æ'nɑːkɪk] *adj* anárquico(ca).
anarchist ['ænəkɪst] *n* anarquista *m y f*.
anarchy ['ænəkɪ] *n* anarquía *f*.
anathema [ə'næθəmə] *n*: **the idea is ~ to me** la idea me parece aberrante.
anatomical [,ænə'tɒmɪkl] *adj* anatómico(ca).
anatomy [ə'nætəmɪ] (*pl* **-ies**) *n* anatomía *f*.

ANC (*abbr of* **African National Congress**) *n* ANC *m*.

ancestor ['ænsestər] *n lit* & *fig* antepasado *m*.

ancestral home [æn'sestrəl-] *n* casa *f* solariega.

ancestry ['ænsestrɪ] (*pl* **-ies**) *n* ascendencia *f*.

anchor ['æŋkər] ◇ *n* NAUT ancla *f*; **to drop** ~ echar el ancla; **to weigh** ~ levar anclas. ◇ *vt* **-1.** [secure] sujetar, aferrar. **-2.** TV presentar. ◇ *vi* NAUT anclar.

anchorage ['æŋkərɪdʒ] *n* **-1.** NAUT fondeadero *m*. **-2.** [means of securing] sujeción *f*.

anchorman ['æŋkəmæn] (*pl* **-men** [-men]) *n* TV presentador *m*, locutor *m*.

anchorwoman ['æŋkə,wʊmən] (*pl* **women** [-,wɪmɪn]) *n* presentadora *f*, locutora *f*.

anchovy ['æntʃəvɪ] (*pl inv* OR **-ies**) *n* [salted] anchoa *f*; [fresh] boquerón *m*.

ancient ['eɪnʃənt] *adj* **-1.** [gen] antiguo(gua). **-2.** *hum* [very old] vetusto(ta).

ancillary [æn'sɪlərɪ] *adj* auxiliar.

and [*strong form* ænd, *weak form* ənd, ən] *conj* **-1.** [gen] y, (*before* "*i*" *or* "*hi*") e; **faster** ~ **faster** cada vez más rápido; **it's nice** ~ **easy** es sencillito. **-2.** [in numbers]: **one hundred** ~ **eighty** ciento ochenta; **one** ~ **a half** uno y medio; **2** ~ **2 is 4** 2 y 2 son 4. **-3.** [to]: **try** ~ **come** intenta venir; **come** ~ **see the kids** ven a ver a los niños; **wait** ~ **see** espera a ver.

♦ **and so on, and so forth** *adv* etcétera, y cosas así.

Andalusia [,ændə'luːzɪə] *n* Andalucía.

Andalusian [,ændə'luːzɪən] ◇ *adj* andaluz(za). ◇ *n* andaluz *m*, -za *f*.

Andes ['ændiːz] *npl*: **the** ~ los Andes.

Andorra [æn'dɔːrə] *n* Andorra.

androgynous [æn'drɒdʒɪnəs] *adj* andrógino(na).

android ['ændrɔɪd] *n* androide *m*.

anecdote ['ænɪkdəʊt] *n* anécdota *f*.

anemia *Am* = **anaemia**.

anemic *Am* = **anaemic**.

anemone [ə'nemənɪ] *n* anémona *f*.

anesthesia *etc Am* = **anaesthesia** *etc*.

anew [ə'njuː] *adv* de nuevo, nuevamente.

angel ['eɪndʒəl] *n* **-1.** RELIG ángel *m*. **-2.** *inf* [delightful person] cielo *m*, sol *m*.

Angeleno [,ændʒə'liːnəʊ] *n* habitante *de Los Angeles*.

angelic [æn'dʒelɪk] *adj* angelical.

anger ['æŋgər] ◇ *n* ira *f*, furia *f*. ◇ *vt* enfurecer.

angina [æn'dʒaɪnə] *n* angina *f* de pecho.

angle ['æŋgl] ◇ *n* **-1.** [gen] ángulo *m*; **at an** ~ [aslant] torcido. **-2.** [point of view] enfoque *m*. ◇ *vi* **-1.** [fish] pescar (*con caña*). **-2.** [manoeuvre]: **to** ~ **for** andar detrás de OR a la caza de.

angler ['æŋglər] *n* pescador *m*, -ra *f* (*con caña*).

Anglican ['æŋglɪkən] ◇ *adj* anglicano(na) ◇ *n* anglicano *m*, -na *f*.

anglicism ['æŋglɪsɪzm] *n* anglicismo *m*.

angling ['æŋglɪŋ] *n* pesca *f* con caña.

Anglo- ['æŋgləʊ] *prefix* anglo-.

Anglo-Saxon ◇ *adj* anglosajón(ona). ◇ *n* **-1.** [person] anglosajón *m*, -ona *f*. **-2.** [language] anglosajón *m*.

Angola [æŋ'gəʊlə] *n* Angola.

Angolan [æŋ'gəʊlən] ◇ *adj* angoleño(ña). ◇ *n* angoleño *m*, -ña *f*.

angora [æŋ'gɔːrə] *n* **-1.** [goat] cabra *f* de angora; [rabbit] conejo *m* de angora. **-2.** [material] angora *f*.

angrily ['æŋgrəlɪ] *adv* airadamente, con furia.

angry ['æŋgrɪ] (*compar* **-ier**, *superl* **-iest**) *adj* [person] enfadado(da); [letter, look, face] furioso(sa), airado(da); **to be** ~ **at** OR **with sb** estar enfadado con alguien; **to get** ~ **with** sb enfadarse con alguien.

angst [æŋst] *n* angustia *f* vital.

anguish ['æŋgwɪʃ] *n* angustia *f*.

anguished ['æŋgwɪʃt] *adj* angustiado(da).

angular ['æŋgjʊlər] *adj* [face, body] anguloso(sa).

animal ['ænɪml] ◇ *adj* animal. ◇ *n* animal *m*; *pej* animal *m* y *f*.

animate ['ænɪmət] *adj* animado(da).

animated ['ænɪmeɪtɪd] *adj* animado(da).

animated cartoon *n* dibujos *mpl* animados.

animation [,ænɪ'meɪʃn] *n* **-1.** [excitement] emoción *f*, entusiasmo *m*. **-2.** [of cartoons] animación *f*.

animosity [,ænɪ'mɒsətɪ] (*pl* **-ies**) *n* animosidad *f*, animadversión *f*.

aniseed ['ænɪsiːd] *n* anís *m*.

ankle ['æŋkl] ◇ *n* tobillo *m*. ◇ *comp*: ~ **boots** botines *mpl*; ~ **socks** calcetines *mpl* por el tobillo.

annals ['ænlz] *npl* anales *mpl*.

annex ['æneks] ◇ *n* edificio *m* anejo. ◇ *vt* anexionar.

annexation [,ænek'seɪʃn] *n* anexión *f*.

annexe ['æneks] = **annex**.

annihilate [ə'naɪəleɪt] *vt* [destroy] aniquilar.

annihilation [ə,naɪə'leɪʃn] *n* [destruction] aniquilación *f*.

anniversary [,ænɪ'vɜːsərɪ] (*pl* -ies) *n* aniversario *m*.

annotate ['ænəteɪt] *vt fml* anotar.

announce [ə'naʊns] *vt* anunciar.

announcement [ə'naʊnsmənt] *n* anuncio *m*.

announcer [ə'naʊnsər] *n*: radio/television ~ presentador *m*, -ra *f* OR locutor *m*, -ra *f* de radio/televisión.

annoy [ə'nɔɪ] *vt* fastidiar, molestar, cargosear *Amer*.

annoyance [ə'nɔɪəns] *n* molestia *f*.

annoyed [ə'nɔɪd] *adj*: ~ at sthg/with sb molesto(ta) por algo/con alguien.

annoying [ə'nɔɪɪŋ] *adj* fastidioso(sa), irritante, cargoso(sa) *Amer*.

annual ['ænjʊəl] ◇ *adj* anual. ◇ *n* -1. [plant] planta *f* anual. -2. [book] anuario *m*.

annual general meeting *n* junta *f* general anual.

annually ['ænjʊəlɪ] *adv* anualmente.

annuity [ə'njuːɪtɪ] (*pl* -ies) *n* FIN anualidad *f*.

annul [ə'nʌl] (*pt* & *pp* -led, *cont* -ling) *vt* anular.

annulment [ə'nʌlmənt] *n* anulación *f*.

annum ['ænəm] *n*: per ~ al año.

Annunciation [ə,nʌnsɪ'eɪʃn] *n*: the ~ la Anunciación *f*.

anode ['ænəʊd] *n* ánodo *m*.

anoint [ə'nɔɪnt] *vt* ungir.

anomalous [ə'nɒmələs] *adj* anómalo(la).

anomaly [ə'nɒməlɪ] (*pl* -ies) *n* anomalía *f*.

anon. [ə'nɒn] (*abbr of* **anonymous**) anón.

anonymity [,ænə'nɪmətɪ] *n* anonimato *m*.

anonymous [ə'nɒnɪməs] *adj* anónimo(ma).

anonymously [ə'nɒnɪməslɪ] *adv* anónimamente.

anorak ['ænəræk] *n* chubasquero *m*, anorak *m*.

anorexia (nervosa) [,ænə'reksɪə(nɜː'vəʊsə)] *n* anorexia *f*.

anorexic [,ænə'reksɪk] ◇ *adj* anoréxico(ca). ◇ *n* anoréxico *m*, -ca *f*.

another [ə'nʌðər] ◇ *adj* otro(tra); in ~ few minutes en unos minutos más. ◇ *pron* otro *m*, -tra *f*; one after ~ uno tras otro, una tras otra; one ~ el uno al otro, la una a la otra; we love one ~ nos queremos; with one ~ el uno con el otro, la una con la otra.

ANSI (*abbr of* **American National Standards Institute**) *n instituto estadounidense de normalización*.

answer ['ɑːnsər] ◇ *n* respuesta *f*; in ~ to en respuesta a. ◇ *vt* -1. [reply to] responder a, contestar a. -2. [respond to]: to ~ the

door abrir la puerta; to ~ the phone coger OR contestar el teléfono. ◇ *vi* responder, contestar.

◆ **answer back** *vt sep* & *vi* replicar.

◆ **answer for** *vt fus* -1. [accept responsibility for] responder por. -2. [suffer consequences of] responder de.

answerable ['ɑːnsərəbl] *adj*: ~ (to sb/for sthg) responsable (ante alguien/de algo).

answering machine ['ɑːnsərɪŋ-] *n* contestador *m* automático.

ant [ænt] *n* hormiga *f*.

ANTA (*abbr of* **American National Theatre and Academy**) *n centro dramático nacional estadounidense*.

antacid [,ænt'æsɪd] *n* antiácido *m*.

antagonism [æn'tægənɪzm] *n* antagonismo *m*.

antagonist [æn'tægənɪst] *n* antagonista *m* y *f*.

antagonistic [æn,tægə'nɪstɪk] *adj* antagónico(ca), hostil.

antagonize, -ise [æn'tægənaɪz] *vt* provocar la hostilidad de.

Antarctic [æn'tɑːktɪk] ◇ *adj* antártico(ca). ◇ *n*: the ~ el Antártico.

Antarctica [æn'tɑːktɪkə] *n* (la) Antártida.

Antarctic Circle *n*: the ~ el Círculo Polar Antártico.

Antarctic Ocean *n*: the ~ el océano Antártico.

ante ['æntɪ] *n inf fig*: to up OR raise the ~ subir la apuesta.

anteater ['ænt,iːtər] *n* oso *m* hormiguero.

antecedent [,æntɪ'siːdənt] *n fml* antecedente *m*.

antediluvian [,æntɪdɪ'luːvjən] *adj hum* antediluviano(na).

antelope ['æntɪləʊp] (*pl inv* OR -s) *n* antílope *m*.

antenatal [,æntɪ'neɪtl] *adj* prenatal.

antenatal clinic *n* maternidad *f*.

antenna [æn'tenə] (*pl sense 1* -nae [-niː], *pl sense 2* -s) *n* -1. antena *f*. -2. *Am* [aerial] antena *f*.

anteroom ['æntɪrʊm] *n* [antechamber] antesala *f*; [waiting room] sala *f* de espera.

anthem ['ænθəm] *n* himno *m*.

anthill ['ænthɪl] *n* hormiguero *m*.

anthology [æn'θɒlədʒɪ] (*pl* -ies) *n* antología *f*.

anthrax ['ænθræks] *n* ántrax *m inv*.

anthropologist [,ænθrə'pɒlədʒɪst] *n* antropólogo *m*, -ga *f*.

anthropology [,ænθrə'pɒlədʒɪ] *n* antropología *f*.

anti- ['æntɪ] *prefix* anti-.

antiaircraft [,æntɪ'eəkrɑːft] *adj* antiaéreo(a).

antiapartheid [,æntɪə'pɑːtheɪt] *adj* contra el apartheid.

antiballistic missile [,æntɪbə'lɪstɪk-]´ *n* misil *m* antibalístico.

antibiotic [,æntɪbaɪ'ɒtɪk] *n* antibiótico *m*.

antibody ['æntɪ,bɒdɪ] (*pl* **-ies**) *n* anticuerpo *m*.

anticipate [æn'tɪsɪpeɪt] *vt* **-1.** [expect] prever. **-2.** [look forward to] esperar ansiosamente. **-3.** [competitor] adelantarse a.

anticipation [æn,tɪsɪ'peɪʃn] *n* expectación *f*; **in** ~ con impaciencia; **in** ~ **of** en previsión de.

anticlimax [,æntɪ'klaɪmæks] *n* anticlímax *m*.

anticlockwise [,æntɪ'klɒkwaɪz] *Br* ◇ *adj* contrario(ria) al sentido de las agujas del reloj. ◇ *adv* en sentido contrario al de las agujas del reloj.

antics ['æntɪks] *npl* payasadas *fpl*.

anticyclone [,æntɪ'saɪkləun] *n* anticiclón *m*.

antidepressant [,æntɪdə'presnt] *n* antidepresivo *m*.

antidote ['æntɪdəut] *n lit* & *fig*: ~ **(to)** antídoto *m* (contra).

antifreeze ['æntɪfriːz] *n* anticongelante *m*.

Antigua [æn'tiːgə] *n* Antigua; ~ **and Barbuda** Antigua y Barbuda.

antihero ['æntɪ,hɪərəu] (*pl* **-es**) *n* antihéroe *m*.

antihistamine [,æntɪ'hɪstəmɪn] *n* antihistamínico *m*.

antinuclear [,æntɪ'njuːklɪəʳ] *adj* antinuclear.

antipathy [æn'tɪpəθɪ] *n*: ~ **(to** OR **towards)** antipatía *f* (hacia OR por).

antipersonnel ['æntɪ,pɜːsə'nel] *adj* MIL antipersonal.

antiperspirant [,æntɪ'pɜːspərənt] *n* antitranspirante *m*.

Antipodes [æn'tɪpədiːz] *npl*: **the** ~ las antípodas.

antiquarian [,æntɪ'kweərɪən] ◇ *adj* de viejo. ◇ *n* anticuario *m*, -ria *f*.

antiquated ['æntɪkweɪtɪd] *adj* anticuado(da).

antique [æn'tiːk] ◇ *adj* [furniture, object] antiguo(gua). ◇ *n* antigüedad *f*.

antique dealer *n* anticuario *m*, -ria *f*.

antique shop *n* tienda *f* de antigüedades.

antiquity [æn'tɪkwətɪ] (*pl* **-ies**) *n* antigüedad *f*.

anti-Semitic [-sɪ'mɪtɪk] *adj* antisemita.

anti-Semitism [-'semɪtɪzm] *n* antisemitismo *m*.

antiseptic [,æntɪ'septɪk] ◇ *adj* antiséptico(ca). ◇ *n* antiséptico *m*.

antisocial [,æntɪ'səuʃl] *adj* **-1.** [against society] antisocial. **-2.** [unsociable] poco sociable.

antistatic [,æntɪ'stætɪk] *adj* antiestático(ca).

antitank [,æntɪ'tæŋk] *adj* antitanque (*inv*).

antithesis [æn'tɪθɪsɪs] (*pl* **-theses** [-θɪsiːz]) *n* antítesis *f inv*.

antlers ['æntləz] *npl* cornamenta *f*.

antonym ['æntənɪm] *n* antónimo *m*.

Antwerp ['æntwɜːp] *n* Amberes.

anus ['eɪnəs] *n* ano *m*.

anvil ['ænvɪl] *n* yunque *m*.

anxiety [æŋ'zaɪətɪ] (*pl* **-ies**) *n* **-1.** [worry] ansiedad *f*, inquietud *f*. **-2.** [cause of worry] preocupación *f*. **-3.** [keenness] afán *m*, ansia *f*.

anxious ['æŋkʃəs] *adj* **-1.** [worried] preocupado(da); **to be** ~ **about** estar preocupado por. **-2.** [keen]: **to be** ~ **that/to do sthg** estar ansioso(sa) por que/por hacer algo.

anxiously ['æŋkʃəslɪ] *adv* con inquietud.

any ['enɪ] ◇ *adj* **-1.** (*with negative*) ninguno(na); **I haven't read** ~ **books** no he leído ningún libro; **I haven't got** ~ **money** no tengo nada de dinero. **-2.** [some] algún(una); **are there** ~ **cakes left?** ¿queda algún pastel?; **is there** ~ **milk left?** ¿queda algo de leche?; **can I be of** ~ **help?** ¿le puedo ayudar en algo?; **have you got** ~ **money?** ¿tienes dinero? **-3.** [no matter which] cualquier; ~ **box will do** cualquier caja vale; *see also* **case, day, moment, rate**. ◇ *pron* **-1.** (*with negative*) ninguno *m*, -na *f*; **I didn't get** ~ **a mí no me tocó ninguno. -2.** [some] alguno *m*, -na *f*; **can** ~ **of you do it?** ¿sabe alguno de vosotros hacerlo?; **I need some matches, do you have** ~? necesito cerillas, ¿tienes?; **few foreign films, if** ~, **are successful here** muy pocas películas extranjeras, por no decir ninguna, tienen éxito aquí. **-3.** [no matter which] cualquiera; **take** ~ **you like** coge cualquiera que te guste. ◇ *adv* **-1.** (*with negative*): **I can't see it** ~ **more** ya no lo veo; **he's not feeling** ~ **better** no se siente nada mejor; **I can't stand it** ~ **longer** no lo aguanto más. **-2.** [some, a little]: **do you want** ~ **more potatoes?** ¿quieres más patatas?; **is that** ~ **better/different?** ¿es así mejor/diferente?

anybody ['enɪ,bɒdɪ] = **anyone**.

anyhow ['enɪhau] *adv* **-1.** [in spite of that] de todos modos. **-2.** [carelessly] de cualquier manera. **-3.** [in any case] en cualquier caso.

anyone ['enɪwʌn] *pron* **-1.** (*in negative sentences*) nadie; **I don't know** ~ no conozco a nadie. **-2.** (*in questions*) alguien. **-3.** [any person] cualquiera.

anyplace *Am* = **anywhere**.

anything ['enιθιŋ] *pron* **-1.** (*in negative sentences*) nada; **I don't want** ~ no quiero nada. **-2.** (*in questions*) algo; **would you like** ~ **else?** ¿quiere algo más? **-3.** [any object, event] cualquier cosa; **it could be** ~ **between two and five** no sé, de dos a cinco.
♦ **anything but** *adv* cualquier cosa menos.

anyway ['enιweι] *adv* **-1.** [in any case] de todas formas OR maneras. **-2.** [in conversatic.n] en cualquier caso.

anywhere ['enιweəᵊ], **anyplace** *Am* ['enιpleιs] *adv* **-1.** (*in negative sentences*) en ningún sitio; **I didn't go** ~ no fui a ninguna parte. **-2.** (*in questions*) en algún sitio; **did you go** ~? ¿fuiste a algún sitio? **-3.** [any place] cualquier sitio; ~ **you like** donde quieras. **-4.** [any amount, number]: ~ **between 10 and 100 people** de 10 a 100 personas.

Anzac ['ænzæk] (*abbr of* **Australia-New Zealand Army Corps**) *n soldado australiano o neocelandés.*

AOB, a.o.b. (*abbr of* **any other business**) *ruegos y preguntas.*

Apache [ə'pætʃι] *n* apache *m y f.*

apart [ə'pɑːt] *adv* **-1.** [separated] aparte, separado(da); **they're not very far** ~ están bastante juntos; **we're living** ~ vivimos separados. **-2.** [in several parts]: **to take sthg** ~ desmontar algo; **to fall** ~ hacerse pedazos. **-3.** [aside] aparte; **joking** ~ bromas aparte.
♦ **apart from** *prep* **-1.** [except for] salvo. **-2.** [as well as] aparte de.

apartheid [ə'pɑːtheιt] *n* apartheid *m.*

apartment [ə'pɑːtmənt] *n* piso *m*, apartamento *m.*

apartment building *n Am* bloque *m* de pisos.

apathetic [,æpə'θetιk] *adj* apático(ca).

apathy ['æpəθι] *n* apatía *f.*

APB (*abbr of* **all points bulletin**) *n mensaje policial radiado referente a la busca y captura de alguien.*

ape [eιp] ◇ *n* simio *m.* ◇ *vt pej* copiar, imitar.

Apennines ['æpιnaιnz] *npl*: **the** ~ los Apeninos.

aperitif [əperə'tiːf] *n* aperitivo *m.*

aperture ['æpə,tjυəᵊ] *n* abertura *f.*

apex ['eιpeks] (*pl* **-es** OR **apices**) *n* [top] vértice *m.*

APEX ['eιpeks] (*abbr of* **advance purchase excursion**) *n Br* (tarifa *f*) APEX *f.*

aphid ['eιfιd] *n* pulgón *m.*

aphorism ['æfərιzm] *n* aforismo *m.*

aphrodisiac [,æfrə'dιzιæk] *n* afrodisíaco *m.*

API (*abbr of* **American Press Institute**) *n asociación de prensa estadounidense.*

apices ['eιpιsiːz] *pl* → **apex**.

apiece [ə'piːs] *adv* cada uno(na).

aplomb [ə'plɒm] *n* aplomo *m.*

APO (*abbr of* **Army Post Office**) *n servicio de correos de las fuerzas armadas estadounidenses.*

apocalypse [ə'pɒkəlιps] *n* apocalipsis *m inv.*

apocalyptic [ə,pɒkə'lιptιk] *adj* apocalíptico(ca).

apogee ['æpədʒiː] *n* ASTRON & *fig* apogeo *m.*

apolitical [,eιpə'lιtιkəl] *adj* apolítico(ca).

apologetic [ə,pɒlə'dʒetιk] *adj* [tone, look] lleno(na) de disculpas; **to be** ~ **(about)** no hacer más que disculparse (por).

apologetically [ə,pɒlə'dʒetιklι] *adv* pidiendo disculpas OR perdón.

apologize, -ise [ə'pɒlədʒaιz] *vi*: **to** ~ **(to sb for sthg)** disculparse (con alguien por algo).

apology [ə'pɒlədʒι] (*pl* **-ies**) *n* disculpa *f.*

apoplectic [,æpə'plektιk] *adj* **-1.** MED apoplético(ca). **-2.** *inf* [very angry] encendido(da), enfurecido(da).

apoplexy ['æpəpleksι] *n* apoplejía *f.*

apostle [ə'pɒsl] *n* RELIG apóstol *m.*

apostrophe [ə'pɒstrəfι] *n* apóstrofo *m.*

appal *Br* (*pt* & *pp* **-led**, *cont* **-ling**), **appall** *Am* [ə'pɔːl] *vt* horrorizar.

Appalachian [,æpə'leιtʃən] ◇ *adj* apalache. ◇ *n*: **the** ~**s, the** ~ **Mountains** los (montes) Apalaches.

appall *Am* = **appal**.

appalled [ə'pɔːld] *adj* horrorizado(da).

appalling [ə'pɔːlιŋ] *adj* **-1.** [shocking] horroroso(sa). **-2.** *inf* [very bad] pésimo(ma), fatal.

appallingly [ə'pɔːlιŋlι] *adv* **-1.** [shockingly] horrorosamente. **-2.** *inf* [very badly] pésimamente.

apparatus [,æpə'reιtəs] (*pl inv* OR **-es**) *n* [gen & POL] aparato *m.*

apparel [ə'pærəl] *n Am* ropa *f.*

apparent [ə'pærənt] *adj* **-1.** [evident] evidente, patente; **for no** ~ **reason** sin motivo aparente. **-2.** [seeming] aparente.

apparently [ə'pærəntlι] *adv* **-1.** [it seems] al parecer, por lo visto, diz que *Amer.* **-2.** [seemingly] aparentemente.

apparition [,æpə'rιʃn] *n fml* aparición *f*, espectro *m.*

appeal [ə'piːl] ◇ *vi* **-1.** [request]: **to** ~ **(to sb for sthg)** solicitar (de alguien algo). **-2.** [to sb's honour, common sense]: **to** ~ **to** apelar a. **-3.** JUR: **to** ~ **(against)** apelar (contra). **-4.**

[attract, interest]: **to ~ (to)** atraer (a). ◇ *n* **-1.** [request] llamamiento *m*, súplica *f*; [fundraising campaign] campaña *f* para recaudar fondos. **-2.** JUR apelación *f*. **-3.** [charm, interest] atractivo *m*.

appealing [ə'piːlɪŋ] *adj* **-1.** [attractive] atractivo(va). **-2.** [touching] enternecedor(ra).

appear [ə'pɪəʳ] *vi* **-1.** [gen] aparecer. **-2.** [seem]: **to ~ (to be/to do sthg)** parecer (ser/hacer algo); **it would ~ that ...** parece que .... **-3.** [in play, film, on TV]: **to ~ on TV/in a film** salir en televisión/en una película. **-4.** JUR: **to ~ (before)** comparecer (ante).

appearance [ə'pɪərəns] *n* **-1.** [gen] aparición *f*; **to make an ~** aparecer; **to put in an ~** hacer acto de presencia. **-2.** [look - of person, place, object] aspecto *m*; **by** OR **to all ~s** por lo que parece; **to keep up ~s** guardar las apariencias.

appease [ə'piːz] *vt* aplacar, apaciguar.

appeasement [ə'piːzmənt] *n* **-1.** [placating] apaciguamiento *m*. **-2.** POL pacificación *f*.

append [ə'pend] *vt fml*: **to ~ sthg (to sthg)** agregar algo (a algo).

appendage [ə'pendɪdʒ] *n* apéndice *m*, añadido *m*.

appendices [ə'pendɪsiːz] *pl* → **appendix**.

appendicitis [ə,pendɪ'saɪtɪs] *n* (*U*) apendicitis *f inv*.

appendix [ə'pendɪks] (*pl* **-dixes** OR **-dices**) *n* [gen & MED] apéndice *m*; **to have one's ~ out** OR **removed** operarse de apendicitis.

appertain [,æpə'teɪn] *vi fml*: **to ~ to** concernir OR atañer a.

appetite ['æpɪtaɪt] *n* **-1.** [for food] apetito *m*; **~ for** ganas *fpl* de. **-2.** *fig* [enthusiasm]: **~ for** entusiasmo *m* OR ilusión *f* por.

appetizer, -iser ['æpɪtaɪzəʳ] *n* aperitivo *m*, pasapalos *m inv Amer*.

appetizing, -ising ['æpɪtaɪzɪŋ] *adj* [food] apetitoso(sa).

applaud [ə'plɔːd] *vt & vi lit & fig* aplaudir.

applause [ə'plɔːz] *n* (*U*) aplausos *mpl*.

apple ['æpl] *n* manzana *f*; **she's the ~ of my eye** *inf* es la niña de mis ojos.

apple pie *n* pastel *m* OR tarta *f* de manzana.

appliance [ə'plaɪəns] *n* aparato *m*; **domestic ~** electrodoméstico *m*.

applicable [ə'plɪkəbl] *adj*: **to be ~ (to)** aplicarse (a).

applicant ['æplɪkənt] *n*: **~ (for)** solicitante *m y f* (de).

application [,æplɪ'keɪʃn] *n* **-1.** [gen] aplicación *f*. **-2.** [for job, college, club]: **~ (for)** solicitud *f* (para). **-3.** COMPUT: **~ (program)** aplicación *f*.

application form *n* impreso *m* de solicitud.

applicator ['æplɪkeɪtəʳ] *n* aplicador *m*.

applied [ə'plaɪd] *adj* [science] aplicado(da).

appliqué [ə'pliːkeɪ] *n* SEWING aplicación *f*, sobrepuesto *m*.

apply [ə'plaɪ] (*pt & pp* **-ied**) ◇ *vt* [gen] aplicar; [brakes] echar; **to ~ o.s. (to sthg)** aplicarse (en algo). ◇ *vi* **-1.** [for work, grant] presentar una solicitud; **to ~ to sb for sthg** solicitar a alguien algo. **-2.** [be relevant] aplicarse; **to ~ to** concernir a.

appoint [ə'pɔɪnt] *vt* **-1.** [to job, position]: **to ~ sb (to sthg)** nombrar a alguien (para algo); **to ~ sb as sthg** nombrar a alguien algo. **-2.** *fml* [time, place] señalar, fijar.

appointment [ə'pɔɪntmənt] *n* **-1.** [to job, position] nombramiento *m*; **"by ~ to Her Majesty the Queen"** ≃ "proveedor de la familia real". **-2.** [job, position] puesto *m*, cargo *m*. **-3.** [with businessman, lawyer] cita *f*; [with doctor, hairdresser] hora *f*; **to have an ~** [with businessman] tener una cita; [with doctor] tener hora; **to make an ~** concertar una cita; **by ~** mediante cita.

apportion [ə'pɔːʃn] *vt* [money] repartir; [blame] adjudicar.

apposite ['æpəzɪt] *adj fml* oportuno(na).

appraisal [ə'preɪzl] *n* evaluación *f*, valoración *f*.

appraise [ə'preɪz] *vt fml* evaluar, valorar.

appreciable [ə'priːʃəbl] *adj* apreciable.

appreciably [ə'priːʃəblɪ] *adv* de manera apreciable.

appreciate [ə'priːʃɪeɪt] ◇ *vt* **-1.** [value, like] apreciar. **-2.** [recognize, understand] entender, darse cuenta de. **-3.** [be grateful for] agradecer. ◇ *vi* FIN encarecerse.

appreciation [ə,priːʃɪ'eɪʃn] *n* **-1.** [liking] aprecio *m*. **-2.** [recognition, understanding] entendimiento *m*. **-3.** [gratitude] gratitud *f*, agradecimiento *m*. **-4.** FIN encarecimiento *m*, plusvalía *f*. **-5.** [of novel, play] valoración *f*.

appreciative [ə'priːʃjətɪv] *adj* [person, remark] agradecido(da); [audience] entendido(da).

apprehend [,æprɪ'hend] *vt fml* [arrest] capturar, aprehender.

apprehension [,æprɪ'henʃn] *n* [anxiety] aprensión *f*.

apprehensive [,æprɪ'hensɪv] *adj* aprensivo(va).

apprehensively [,æprɪ'hensɪvlɪ] *adv* con aprensión.

apprentice [ə'prentɪs] ◇ *n* aprendiz *m*, -za

f. ◇ *vt*: **to be ~d to sb** ser puesto de aprendiz con alguien.

apprenticeship [ə'prentɪʃɪp] *n* aprendizaje *m*.

appro ['æprəʊ] (*abbr of* **approval**) *n Br inf*: **on ~** a prueba.

approach [ə'prəʊtʃ] ◇ *n* **-1.** [arrival] llegada *f*. **-2.** [way in] acceso *m*. **-3.** [method] enfoque *m*, planteamiento *m*. **-4.** [to person]: **to makes ~es to sb** hacerle propuestas a alguien. ◇ *vt* **-1.** [come near to] acercarse a. **-2.** [ask]: **to ~ sb about sthg** hacer una propuesta OR dirigirse a alguien acerca de algo. **-3.** [problem, situation] abordar. **-4.** [level, speed] aproximarse a. ◇ *vi* aproximarse, acercarse.

approachable [ə'prəʊtʃəbl] *adj* accesible.

approaching [ə'prəʊtʃɪŋ] *adj* próximo(ma), cercano(na).

approbation [,æprə'beɪʃn] *n fml* aprobación *f*.

appropriate [*adj* ə'prəʊprɪət, *vb* ə'prəʊprɪeɪt] ◇ *adj* apropiado(da). ◇ *vt* **-1.** JUR [take] apropiarse de. **-2.** [allocate] destinar.

appropriately [ə'prəʊprɪətlɪ] *adv* de manera apropiada.

appropriation [ə,prəʊprɪ'eɪʃn] *n* **-1.** [taking] apropiación *f*. **-2.** [allocation] asignación *f*.

approval [ə'pruːvl] *n* **-1.** [admiration] aprobación *f*. **-2.** [official sanctioning] visto *m* bueno. **-3.** COMM: **on ~** a prueba.

approve [ə'pruːv] ◇ *vi* estar de acuerdo; **to ~ of sthg/sb** ver con buenos ojos algo/a alguien. ◇ *vt* aprobar, autorizar.

approved [ə'pruːvd] *adj* aprobado(da), reconocido(da).

approving [ə'pruːvɪŋ] *adj* aprobatorio(ria).

approx. [ə'prɒks] (*abbr of* **approximately**) aprox.

approximate [*adj* ə'prɒksɪmət, *vb* ə'prɒksɪmeɪt] ◇ *adj* aproximado(da). ◇ *vi*: **to ~ to** aproximarse a.

approximately [ə'prɒksɪmətlɪ] *adv* aproximadamente.

approximation [ə,prɒksɪ'meɪʃn] *n* **-1.** [of number, position] cálculo *m* aproximado. **-2.** [similarity]: **~ (to)** aproximación *f* (a).

Apr. (*abbr of* **April**) abr.

APR *n* **-1.** (*abbr of* **annualized percentage rate**) tasa de interés anual. **-2.** (*abbr of* **annual purchase rate**) tasa de adquisición anual.

après-ski [,æpreɪ'skiː] *n* alterne nocturno en una estación de esquí.

apricot ['eɪprɪkɒt] ◇ *n* **-1.** [fruit] albaricoque *m*, chabacano *m Amer*. **-2.** [colour] color *m* albaricoque. ◇ *comp* de albaricoque.

April ['eɪprəl] *n* abril *m*; *see also* **September**.

April Fools' Day *n* primero *m* de abril, ≃ Día *m* de los Santos Inocentes.

APRIL FOOLS' DAY:
En Gran Bretaña, el 1 de abril es el día en que se hacen todo tipo de bromas, aunque no existe la tradición del monigote de papel pegado a la espalda y las bromas deben hacerse antes de las 12h del mediodía

apron ['eɪprən] *n* **-1.** [clothing] delantal *m*, mandil *m*; **to be tied to sb's ~ strings** *inf* estar pegado a las faldas de alguien. **-2.** AERON pista *f* de servicio.

apropos ['æprəpəʊ] ◇ *adj* oportuno(na). ◇ *prep*: **~ (of)** hablando de.

apt [æpt] *adj* **-1.** [pertinent] acertado(da). **-2.** [likely]: **~ to do sthg** propenso(sa) a hacer algo.

Apt. (*abbr of* **apartment**) Apto.

APT (*abbr of* **advanced passenger train**) *n* tren de alta velocidad, ≃ AVE *m*.

aptitude ['æptɪtjuːd] *n* aptitud *f*; **to have an ~ for** tener aptitudes para.

aptitude test *n* prueba *f* de aptitud.

aptly ['æptlɪ] *adv* apropiadamente.

aqualung ['ækwəlʌŋ] *n* escafandra *f* autónoma.

aquamarine [,ækwəmə'riːn] *n* [colour] color *m* aguamarina.

aquaplane ['ækwəpleɪn] *vi Br* AUT patinar.

aquarium [ə'kweərɪəm] (*pl* **-riums** OR **-ria** [-rɪə]) *n* acuario *m*.

Aquarius [ə'kweərɪəs] *n* Acuario *m*; **to be (an) ~** ser Acuario.

aquatic [ə'kwætɪk] *adj* acuático(ca).

aqueduct ['ækwɪdʌkt] *n* acueducto *m*.

AR *abbr of* **Arkansas**.

ARA (*abbr of* **Associate of the Royal Academy**) *n* miembro de la Royal Academy; *see also* **RA**.

Arab ['ærəb] ◇ *adj* árabe. ◇ *n* **-1.** [person] árabe *m y f*. **-2.** [horse] caballo *m* árabe.

Arabia [ə'reɪbjə] *n* Arabia.

Arabian [ə'reɪbjən] *adj* árabe, arábigo(ga).

Arabian desert *n*: **the ~** el Desierto de Arabia.

Arabian Peninsula *n*: **the ~** la península Arábiga.

Arabian Sea *n*: **the ~** el Mar de Omán.

Arabic ['ærəbɪk] ◇ *adj* árabe. ◇ *n* [language] árabe *m*.

Arabic numeral *n* número *m* arábigo.

arable ['ærəbl] *adj* cultivable.

Aragon ['ærəgən] *n* Aragón.

ARAM (*abbr of* **Associate of the Royal Academy of Music**) *n miembro de la Royal Academy of Music, academia británica de música.*

arbiter ['ɑːbɪtəʳ] *n fml* árbitro *m*.

arbitrary ['ɑːbɪtrərɪ] *adj* [random] arbitrario(ria).

arbitrate ['ɑːbɪtreɪt] *vi* arbitrar.

arbitration [,ɑːbɪ'treɪʃn] *n* arbitraje *m*; **to go to** ~ acudir a arbitraje.

arc [ɑːk] *n* arco *m*.

ARC (*abbr of* **AIDS-related complex**) *n enfermedad relacionada con el sida.*

arcade [ɑː'keɪd] *n* **-1.** [shopping arcade] galería *f* OR centro *m* comercial. **-2.** [covered passage] arcada *f*, galería *f*.

arch [ɑːtʃ] ◇ *adj* travieso(sa), pícaro(ra). ◇ *n* **-1.** ARCHIT arco *m*. **-2.** [of foot] puente *m*. ◇ *vt* arquear. ◇ *vi* arquearse, combarse.

arch- [ɑːtʃ] *prefix*: ~**rival** máximo rival.

archaeological [,ɑːkɪə'lɒdʒɪkl] *adj* arqueológico(ca).

archaeologist [,ɑːkɪ'ɒlədʒɪst] *n* arqueólogo *m*, -ga *f*.

archaeology [,ɑːkɪ'ɒlədʒɪ] *n* arqueología *f*.

archaic [ɑː'keɪɪk] *adj* arcaico(ca).

archangel ['ɑːk,eɪndʒəl] *n* arcángel *m*.

archbishop [,ɑːtʃ'bɪʃəp] *n* arzobispo *m*.

archduchess [,ɑːtʃ'dʌtʃɪs] *n* archiduquesa *f*.

archduke [,ɑːtʃ'djuːk] *n* archiduque *m*.

arched [ɑːtʃt] *adj* [gen] arqueado(da); [roof] abovedado(da).

archenemy [,ɑːtʃ'enɪmɪ] (*pl* **-ies**) *n* peor enemigo *m*, enemigo acérrimo.

archeology *etc* [,ɑːkɪ'ɒlədʒɪ] = **archaeology** *etc*.

archer ['ɑːtʃəʳ] *n* arquero *m*.

archery ['ɑːtʃərɪ] *n* tiro *m* con arco.

archetypal [,ɑːkɪ'taɪpl] *adj* arquetípico(ca).

archetype ['ɑːkɪtaɪp] *n* arquetipo *m*.

archipelago [,ɑːkɪ'pelɪgəʊ] (*pl* **-es** OR **-s**) *n* archipiélago *m*.

architect ['ɑːkɪtekt] *n* **-1.** [of buildings] arquitecto *m*, -ta *f*. **-2.** *fig* [of plan, event] artífice *m y f*.

architectural [,ɑːkɪ'tektʃərəl] *adj* arquitectónico(ca).

architecture ['ɑːkɪtektʃəʳ] *n* [gen & COMPUT] arquitectura *f*.

archive file ['ɑːkaɪv-] *n* COMPUT fichero *m* archivado.

archives ['ɑːkaɪvz] *npl* [of documents] archivos *mpl*.

archivist ['ɑːkɪvɪst] *n* archivero *m*, -ra *f*.

archway ['ɑːtʃweɪ] *n* [passage] arcada *f*; [entrance] entrada *f* en forma de arco.

ARCM (*abbr of* **Associate of the Royal College of Music**) *n miembro del Royal College of Music, conservatorio nacional británico.*

Arctic ['ɑːktɪk] ◇ *adj* **-1.** GEOGR ártico(ca). **-2.** *inf* [very cold] gélido(da). ◇ *n*: **the** ~ **el** Ártico.

Arctic Circle *n*: **the** ~ el Círculo Polar Ártico.

Arctic Ocean *n*: **the** ~ el océano Ártico.

ardent ['ɑːdənt] *adj* ardoroso(sa), ferviente.

ardour *Br*, **ardor** *Am* ['ɑːdəʳ] *n* ardor *m*.

arduous ['ɑːdjʊəs] *adj* arduo(dua).

are [weak form əʳ, strong form ɑːʳ] → **be**.

area ['eərɪə] *n* **-1.** [region, designated space] zona *f*, área *f*; **in the** ~ en la zona. **-2.** *fig* [approximate size, number]: **in the** ~ **of** del orden de, alrededor de. **-3.** [surface size] superficie *f*, área *f*. **-4.** [of knowledge, interest] campo *m*.

area code *n* prefijo *m* (telefónico).

arena [ə'riːnə] *n* **-1.** SPORT palacio *m*, pabellón *m*. **-2.** *fig* [area of activity]: **she entered the political** ~ saltó al ruedo político.

aren't [ɑːnt] = **are not**.

Argentina [,ɑːdʒən'tiːnə] *n* (la) Argentina.

Argentine ['ɑːdʒəntaɪn] ◇ *adj* argentino(na). ◇ *n* argentino *m*, -na *f*.

Argentinian [,ɑːdʒən'tɪnɪən] ◇ *adj* argentino(na). ◇ *n* argentino *m*, -na *f*.

arguable ['ɑːgjʊəbl] *adj* [questionable] discutible.

arguably ['ɑːgjʊəblɪ] *adv* probablemente.

argue ['ɑːgjuː] ◇ *vi* **-1.** [quarrel]: **to** ~ (**with sb about sthg**) discutir (con alguien por algo). **-2.** [reason]: **to** ~ (**for/against**) argumentar (a favor de/contra). ◇ *vt*: **to** ~ **that** argumentar que.

argument ['ɑːgjʊmənt] *n* **-1.** [gen] discusión *f*; **to have an** ~ (**with**) tener una discusión (con). **-2.** [reason] argumento *m*.

argumentative [,ɑːgjʊ'mentətɪv] *adj* muy propenso(sa) a discutir.

aria ['ɑːrɪə] *n* aria *f*.

arid ['ærɪd] *adj lit* & *fig* árido(da).

Aries ['eəriːz] *n* Aries *m*; **to be (an)** ~ ser Aries.

arise [ə'raɪz] (*pt* **arose**, *pp* **arisen** [ə'rɪzn]) *vi* [appear]: **to** ~ (**from**) surgir (de).

aristocracy [,ærɪ'stɒkrəsɪ] (*pl* **-ies**) *n* aristocracia *f*.

aristocrat [*Br* 'ærɪstəkræt, *Am* ə'rɪstəkræt] *n* aristócrata *m y f*.

aristocratic [*Br* ,ærɪstə'krætɪk, *Am* ə,rɪstə'krætɪk] *adj* aristocrático(ca).

arithmetic [ə'rɪθmətɪk] *n* aritmética *f*.

Arizona [ˌærɪ'zəʊnə] *n* Arizona.

ark [ɑːk] *n* arca *f*.

Arkansas ['ɑːkənsɔː] *n* Arkansas.

arm [ɑːm] ◇ *n* **-1.** [of person, chair] brazo *m*; ~ **in** ~ del brazo; **to chance one's** ~ *fig* jugársela; **to keep sb at** ~**'s length** *fig* guardar las distancias con alguien; **to twist sb's** ~ *fig* persuadir a alguien. **-2.** [of garment] manga *f*. **-3.** [of organization] rama *f*. ◇ *vt* armar.

◆ **arms** *npl* [weapons] armas *fpl*; **to take up** ~**s** tomar las armas; **he's up in** ~**s (about it)** está que se sube por las paredes (por ello).

armada [ɑː'mɑːdə] *n* armada *f*.

armadillo [ˌɑːmə'dɪləʊ] (*pl* **-s**) *n* armadillo *m*.

Armageddon [ˌɑːmə'gedn] *n* guerra *f* del fin del mundo.

armaments ['ɑːməmənts] *npl* armamento *m*.

armchair ['ɑːmtʃeəʳ] *n* sillón *m*.

armed [ɑːmd] *adj* **-1.** [police, thieves] armado(da). **-2.** *fig* [with information]: ~ **with** provisto(ta) de.

armed forces *npl* fuerzas *fpl* armadas.

Armenia [ɑː'miːnjə] *n* Armenia.

Armenian [ɑː'miːnjən] ◇ *adj* armenio(nia). ◇ *n* **-1.** [person] armenio *m*, -nia *f*. **-2.** [language] armenio *m*.

armhole ['ɑːmhəʊl] *n* sobaquera *f*, sisa *f*.

armistice ['ɑːmɪstɪs] *n* armisticio *m*.

armour *Br*, **armor** *Am* ['ɑːməʳ] *n* **-1.** [for person] armadura *f*. **-2.** [for military vehicle] blindaje *m*.

armoured *Br*, **armored** *Am* ['ɑːməd] *adj* MIL blindado(da).

armoured car *n* MIL carro *m* blindado.

armour-plated [-'pleɪtɪd] *adj* MIL blindado(da), acorazado(da).

armoury *Br* (*pl* **-ies**), **armory** *Am* (*pl* **-ies**) ['ɑːmərɪ] *n* arsenal *m*.

armpit ['ɑːmpɪt] *n* sobaco *m*, axila *f*.

armrest ['ɑːmrest] *n* brazo *m*.

arms control ['ɑːmz-] *n* control *m* armamentístico.

army ['ɑːmɪ] (*pl* **-ies**) *n lit* & *fig* ejército *m*.

A road *n Br* ≃ carretera *f* nacional.

aroma [ə'rəʊmə] *n* aroma *m*.

aromatherapy [ərəʊmə'θerəpɪ] *n* aromaterapia *f*.

aromatic [ˌærə'mætɪk] *adj* aromático(ca).

arose [ə'rəʊz] *pt* → **arise**.

around [ə'raʊnd] ◇ *adv* **-1.** [about, round] por ahí; **to walk/look** ~ andar/mirar por ahí. **-2.** [on all sides] alrededor. **-3.** [present, available]: **is John** ~? [there] ¿está John por ahí?; [here] ¿está John por aquí? **-4.** [turn, look]: **to turn** ~ volverse; **to look** ~ volver la cabeza. **-5.** *phr*: **to have been** ~ *inf* haber visto mundo.

◇ *prep* **-1.** [on all sides of] alrededor de. **-2.** [about, round - place] por. **-3.** [in the area of] cerca de. **-4.** [approximately] alrededor de.

arousal [ə'raʊzl] *n* excitación *f*.

arouse [ə'raʊz] *vt* **-1.** [excite - feeling] levantar, despertar; [- person] excitar. **-2.** [wake] despertar.

arrange [ə'reɪndʒ] *vt* **-1.** [flowers, books, furniture] colocar. **-2.** [event, meeting, party] organizar; **to** ~ **to do sthg** acordar hacer algo; **to** ~ **sthg for sb** organizarle algo a alguien; **to** ~ **for sb to do sthg** hacer lo necesario para que alguien haga algo. **-3.** MUS arreglar.

arranged marriage [ə'reɪndʒd-] *n* matrimonio *m* concertado.

arrangement [ə'reɪndʒmənt] *n* **-1.** [agreement] acuerdo *m*; **to come to an** ~ llegar a un acuerdo. **-2.** [of flowers, furniture] disposición *f*, colocación *f*. **-3.** MUS arreglo *m*.

◆ **arrangements** *npl* preparativos *mpl*; **to make** ~**s** hacer los preparativos.

array [ə'reɪ] ◇ *n* **-1.** [of objects] surtido *m*. **-2.** COMPUT matriz *f*. ◇ *vt* [ornaments etc] disponer.

arrears [ə'rɪəz] *npl* [money owed] atrasos *mpl*; **in** ~ [retrospectively] con retraso; [late] atrasado en el pago.

arrest [ə'rest] ◇ *n* arresto *m*, detención *f*; **under** ~ bajo arresto. ◇ *vt* **-1.** [subj: police] arrestar, detener. **-2.** [sb's attention] captar, atraer. **-3.** *fml* [stop] detener, poner freno a.

arresting [ə'restɪŋ] *adj* llamativo(va).

arrival [ə'raɪvl] *n* llegada *f*; **late** ~ [of train, bus, mail] retraso *m*; **new** ~ [person] recién llegado *m*, recién llegada *f*; [baby] recién nacido *m*, recién nacida *f*.

arrive [ə'raɪv] *vi* **-1.** [gen] llegar; **to** ~ **at** [conclusion, decision] llegar a. **-2.** [baby] nacer.

arrogance ['ærəgəns] *n* arrogancia *f*.

arrogant ['ærəgənt] *adj* arrogante.

arrogantly ['ærəgəntlɪ] *adv* con arrogancia.

arrow ['ærəʊ] *n* flecha *f*.

arrowroot ['ærəʊruːt] *n* arrurruz *m*.

arse *Br* [ɑːs], **ass** *Am* [æs] *n v inf* [bottom] culo *m*.

arsenal ['ɑːsənl] *n* arsenal *m*.

arsenic ['ɑːsnɪk] *n* arsénico *m*.

arson ['ɑːsn] *n* incendio *m* premeditado.

arsonist ['ɑːsənɪst] *n* incendiario *m*, -ria *f*.

art [ɑːt] ◇ n arte m. ◇ comp [student, college, exhibition] de arte.
◆ **arts** ◇ npl **-1.** SCH & UNIV [humanities] letras fpl. **-2.** [fine arts]: **the ~s** las bellas artes. ◇ comp SCH & UNIV de letras.

art deco [-'dekəʊ] n art deco m.

artefact ['ɑːtɪfækt] = artifact.

arterial [ɑː'tɪərɪəl] adj **-1.** [blood] arterial. **-2.** [road] principal.

arteriosclerosis [ɑː,tɪərɪəʊsklɪ'rəʊsɪs] n arteriosclerosis f inv.

artery ['ɑːtərɪ] (pl **-ies**) n arteria f.

artful ['ɑːtfʊl] adj astuto(ta).

art gallery n [public] museo m (de arte); [commercial] galería f (de arte).

arthritic [ɑː'θrɪtɪk] adj artrítico(ca).

arthritis [ɑː'θraɪtɪs] n artritis f inv.

artic [ɑː'tɪk] (abbr of articulated lorry) n Br inf camión m articulado.

artichoke ['ɑːtɪtʃəʊk] n alcachofa f.

article ['ɑːtɪkl] n artículo m; ~ **of clothing** prenda f de vestir; ~ **of furniture** mueble m.

articled clerk ['ɑːtɪkld-] n Br abogado contratado m, abogada contratada f en prácticas.

articles of association ['ɑːtɪklz-] npl estatutos mpl sociales.

articulate [adj ɑː'tɪkjʊlət, vb ɑː'tɪkjʊleɪt] ◇ adj [person] elocuente; [speech] claro(ra), bien articulado(da). ◇ vt [express clearly] expresar.

articulated lorry [ɑː'tɪkjʊleɪtɪd-] n Br camión m articulado.

articulation [ɑː,tɪkjʊ'leɪʃn] n **-1.** [speech] articulación f. **-2.** [of idea, feeling] expresión f.

artifact ['ɑːtɪfækt] n artefacto m.

artifice ['ɑːtɪfɪs] n **-1.** [trick] artificio m. **-2.** [trickery] artificiosidad f.

artificial [,ɑːtɪ'fɪʃl] adj artificial.

artificial insemination n inseminación f artificial.

artificial intelligence n inteligencia f artificial.

artificially [,ɑːtɪ'fɪʃəlɪ] adv de modo artificial.

artificial respiration n respiración f artificial.

artillery [ɑː'tɪlərɪ] n [guns] artillería f.

artisan [,ɑːtɪ'zæn] n artesano m, -na f.

artist ['ɑːtɪst] n artista m y f.

artiste [ɑː'tiːst] n artista m y f.

artistic [ɑː'tɪstɪk] adj **-1.** [gen] artístico(ca). **-2.** [good at art] con sensibilidad artística.

artistically [ɑː'tɪstɪklɪ] adv artísticamente.

artistry ['ɑːtɪstrɪ] n maestría f.

artless ['ɑːtlɪs] adj ingenuo(nua), cándido(da).

art nouveau [,ɑːnuː'vəʊ] n art nouveau m.

ARV (abbr of American Revised Version) n traducción estadounidense de la Biblia.

as [unstressed əz, stressed æz] ◇ conj **-1.** [referring to time - while] mientras; [- when] cuando; **she told it to me ~ we walked along** me lo contó mientras paseábamos; ~ **time goes by** a medida que pasa el tiempo; **she rang (just) ~ I was leaving** llamó justo cuando iba a salir. **-2.** [referring to manner, way] como; **leave it ~ it is** déjalo como está; **do ~ I say** haz lo que te digo. **-3.** [introducing a statement] como; ~ **you see, ...** como puedes ver, ...; ~ **you know, ...** como (ya) sabes, ... **-4.** [because] como, ya que. **-5.** phr: ~ **it is** (ya) de por sí; **things are bad enough ~ it is** las cosas ya están mal de por sí; ~ **it turns out** resulta que; ~ **things stand** tal como están las cosas.
◇ prep como; **I'm speaking ~ a friend** te hablo como amigo; **she works ~ a nurse** trabaja de OR como enfermera; ~ **a boy, I lived in Spain** de niño vivía en España; **she treats it ~ a game** se lo toma como un juego; **it came ~ a shock** fue una gran sorpresa.
◇ adv (in comparisons): ~ **... ~** tan ... como; ~ **tall ~ I am** tan alto como yo; **I've lived ~ long ~ she has** he vivido durante tanto tiempo como ella; **twice ~ big** el doble de grande; **it's just ~ fast** es igual de rápido; ~ **much ~** tanto como; ~ **many ~** tantos(tas) como; ~ **much wine ~ you like** tanto vino como quieras.
◆ **as it were** adv por así decirlo.
◆ **as for, as to** prep en cuanto a, por lo que se refiere a.
◆ **as from, as of** prep a partir de.
◆ **as if, as though** conj como si.
◆ **as to** prep Br con respecto a.

AS ◇ n (abbr of Associate in Science) titular de una licenciatura de ciencias en Estados Unidos. ◇ abbr of American Samoa.

ASA (abbr of American Standards Association) n instituto estadounidense de normalización.

a.s.a.p. (abbr of as soon as possible) a la mayor brevedad posible.

asbestos [æs'bestəs] n asbesto m, amianto m.

asbestosis [,æsbes'təʊsɪs] n asbestosis f inv.

ascend [ə'send] ◇ vt subir; **to ~ the throne** subir al trono. ◇ vi ascender.

ascendancy [ə'sendənsɪ] n ascendiente m.

ascendant [ə'sendənt] *n*: **in the** ~ en auge.

ascendency [ə'sendənsɪ] = **ascendancy**.

ascending [ə'sendɪŋ] *adj* ascendiente; **in** ~ **order** en orden ascendiente.

ascension [ə'senʃn] *n* [to throne] subida *f*.
◆ **Ascension** *n* RELIG Ascensión *f*.

Ascension Island *n* Isla de la Ascensión.

ascent [ə'sent] *n* **-1.** [climb] ascensión *f*. **-2.** [upward slope] subida *f*, cuesta *f*. **-3.** *fig* [progress] ascenso *m*.

ascertain [,æsə'teɪn] *vt* determinar.

ascetic [ə'setɪk] ◇ *adj* ascético(ca). ◇ *n* asceta *m y f*.

ASCII ['æskɪ] (*abbr of* **American Standard Code for Information**) *n* ASCII *m*.

ascorbic acid [ə'skɔːbɪk-] *n* ácido *m* ascórbico.

ascribe [ə'skraɪb] *vt*: **to** ~ **sthg to** atribuir algo a.

ASCU (*abbr of* **Association of State Colleges and Universities**) *n* asociación estadounidense de centros estatales de enseñanza superior.

ASE (*abbr of* **American Stock Exchange**) *n* mercado bursátil estadounidense.

aseptic [,eɪ'septɪk] *adj* aséptico(ca).

asexual [,eɪ'sekʃʊəl] *adj* asexual, asexuado(da).

ash [æʃ] *n* **-1.** [from cigarette, fire] ceniza *f*. **-2.** [tree] fresno *m*.
◆ **ashes** *npl* [from cremation] cenizas *fpl*.

ASH [æʃ] (*abbr of* **Action on Smoking and Health**) *n* asociación británica contra el tabaco.

ashamed [ə'ʃeɪmd] *adj* avergonzado(da), apenado(da) *Amer*; **I'm** ~ **to do it** me avergüenza hacerlo; **to be** ~ **of** avergonzarse de, achuncharse de *Amer*.

ashcan ['æʃkæn] *n Am* cubo *m* de la basura.

ashen-faced ['æʃn,feɪst] *adj*: **to be** ~ tener la cara pálida.

ashore [ə'ʃɔːr] *adv* [swim] hasta la orilla; **to go** ~ desembarcar.

ashtray ['æʃtreɪ] *n* cenicero *m*.

Ash Wednesday *n* miércoles *m inv* de ceniza.

Asia [*Br* 'eɪʃə, *Am* 'eɪʒə] *n* Asia.

Asia Minor *n* Asia Menor.

Asian [*Br* 'eɪʃn, *Am* 'eɪʒn] ◇ *adj* asiático(ca). ◇ *n* asiático *m*, -ca *f*.

Asiatic [*Br* ,eɪʃɪ'ætɪk, *Am* ,eɪʒɪ'ætɪk] *adj* asiático(ca).

aside [ə'saɪd] ◇ *adv* **-1.** [to one side] a un lado; **to move** ~ apartarse; **to take sb** ~ llevar a alguien aparte; **to brush** OR **sweep sthg** ~ dejar algo aparte OR de lado. **-2.** [apart] aparte; ~ **from** aparte de. ◇ *n* **-1.** [in

play] aparte *m*. **-2.** [remark] inciso *m*, comentario *m* al margen.

ask [ɑːsk] ◇ *vt* **-1.** [question - person]: **to** ~ (**sb sthg**) preguntar (a alguien algo); **if you** ~ **me ...** si quieres que te diga la verdad .... **-2.** [put - question]: **to** ~ **a question** hacer una pregunta. **-3.** [request, demand] pedir; **to** ~ **sb (to do sthg)** pedir a alguien (que haga algo); **to** ~ **sb for sthg** pedirle algo a alguien. **-4.** [invite] invitar. ◇ *vi* **-1.** [question] preguntar. **-2.** [request] pedir.
◆ **ask after** *vt fus* preguntar por.
◆ **ask for** *vt fus* **-1.** [person] preguntar por. **-2.** [thing] pedir.

askance [ə'skæns] *adv*: **to look** ~ **at sb** mirar a alguien con recelo.

askew [ə'skjuː] *adj* torcido(da).

asking price ['ɑːskɪŋ-] *n* precio *m* inicial.

asleep [ə'sliːp] *adj* dormido(da); **to fall** ~ quedarse dormido; **to be fast** OR **sound** ~ estar profundamente dormido.

ASLEF ['æzlef] (*abbr of* **Associated Society of Locomotive Engineers and Firemen**) *n* sindicato británico de ferroviarios.

ASM (*abbr of* **air-to-surface missile**) *n* misil aire-tierra.

asparagus [ə'spærəgəs] *n* (U) [plant] espárrago *m*; [shoots] espárragos *mpl*.

aspartame [*Br* ə'spɑːteɪm, *Am* 'æspərteɪm] *n* edulcorante de ácido aspártico.

ASPCA (*abbr of* **American Society for the Prevention of Cruelty to Animals**) *n* sociedad estadounidense protectora de animales, ≈ SPA *f*.

aspect ['æspekt] *n* **-1.** [of subject, plan] aspecto *m*. **-2.** [appearance] cariz *m*, aspecto *m*. **-3.** [of building] orientación *f*.

aspen ['æspən] *n* álamo *m* alpino OR temblón.

aspersions [ə'spɔːʃnz] *npl*: **to cast** ~ **on sthg** poner en duda algo.

asphalt ['æsfælt] *n* asfalto *m*.

asphyxiate [əs'fɪksɪeɪt] *vt* asfixiar.

aspic ['æspɪk] *n* gelatina *f* de carne.

aspirate ['æspərət] *adj* aspirado(da).

aspiration [,æspə'reɪʃn] *n* aspiración *f*.

aspire [ə'spaɪər] *vi*: **to** ~ **to** aspirar a.

aspirin ['æsprɪn] *n* aspirina *f*.

aspiring [ə'spaɪərɪŋ] *adj* aspirante; **an** ~ **actor** un aspirante a actor.

ass [æs] *n* **-1.** [donkey] asno *m*, -na *f*. **-2.** *Br inf* [idiot] burro *m*, -rra *f*. **-3.** *Am v inf* = **arse**.

assail [ə'seɪl] *vt* **-1.** [attack] atacar, arremeter contra. **-2.** *fig* [trouble] asaltar.

assailant [ə'seɪlənt] *n* agresor *m*, -ra *f*.

assassin [əˈsæsɪn] n asesino m, -na f.

assassinate [əˈsæsɪneɪt] vt asesinar.

assassination [ə,sæsɪˈneɪʃn] n asesinato m.

assault [əˈsɔːlt] ◇ n **-1.** MIL: ~ **(on)** ataque m (contra). **-2.** [physical attack]: ~ **(on sb)** agresión f (contra alguien); ~ **and battery** JUR lesiones fpl. ◇ vt [physically] asaltar, agredir; [sexually] abusar de.

assault course n pista f americana.

assemble [əˈsembl] ◇ vt **-1.** [gather] juntar, reunir. **-2.** [fit together] montar. ◇ vi reunirse.

assembler language = assembly language.

assembly [əˈsemblɪ] (pl **-ies**) n **-1.** [meeting, law-making body] asamblea f. **-2.** [gathering together] reunión f. **-3.** [fitting together] montaje m.

assembly language, assembler language n COMPUT lenguaje m ensamblador.

assembly line n cadena f de montaje.

assent [əˈsent] ◇ n consentimiento m. ◇ vi: to ~ **(to)** asentir (a).

assert [əˈsɜːt] vt **-1.** [fact, belief] afirmar. **-2.** [authority] imponer; to ~ **o.s.** imponerse.

assertion [əˈsɜːʃn] n aserto m, afirmación f.

assertive [əˈsɜːtɪv] adj enérgico(ca).

assess [əˈses] vt evaluar.

assessment [əˈsesmənt] n **-1.** [evaluation] evaluación f. **-2.** [calculation] cálculo m.

assessor [əˈsesəʳ] n tasador m, -ra f.

asset [ˈæset] n **-1.** [valuable quality - of person] cualidad f; [- of thing] ventaja f. **-2.** [valuable person] elemento m importante.
◆ **assets** npl COMM activo m, bienes mpl.

asset-stripping [-,strɪpɪŋ] n adquisición de una empresa para la venta de sus activos y posterior cierre.

assiduous [əˈsɪdjuəs] adj [gen] dedicado(da); [student] aplicado(da).

assiduously [əˈsɪdjuəslɪ] adv con dedicación.

assign [əˈsaɪn] vt **-1.** [gen]: to ~ **sthg (to sb)** asignar OR encomendar algo (a alguien); to ~ **sb to sthg** asignar OR encomendar a alguien algo; to ~ **sb to do sthg** asignar OR encomendar a alguien que haga algo. **-2.** [designate for specific use, purpose]: to ~ **sthg (to)** destinar algo (a).

assignation [,æsɪgˈneɪʃn] n fml cita f a escondidas.

assignment [əˈsaɪnmənt] n **-1.** [task] misión f; SCH trabajo m. **-2.** [act of assigning] asignación f.

assimilate [əˈsɪmɪleɪt] vt **-1.** [learn] asimilar. **-2.** [absorb]: to ~ **sb (into)** integrar a alguien (en).

assimilation [ə,sɪmɪˈleɪʃn] n **-1.** [of ideas, facts] asimilación f. **-2.** [of people] incorporación f.

assist [əˈsɪst] vt: to ~ **sb (with sthg/in doing sthg)** ayudar a alguien (con algo/a hacer algo).

assistance [əˈsɪstəns] n ayuda f, asistencia f; to be of ~ **(to)** ayudar (a).

assistant [əˈsɪstənt] ◇ n ayudante m y f; **(shop)** ~ dependiente m, -ta f. ◇ comp adjunto(ta); ~ **manager** director adjunto m, directora adjunta f.

associate [adj & n əˈsəuʃɪət, vb əˈsəuʃɪeɪt] ◇ adj asociado(da). ◇ n socio m, -cia f. ◇ vt asociar; to ~ **sthg/sb with** asociar algo/a alguien con; to be ~**d with** [organization, plan, opinion] estar relacionado con; [people] estar asociado con. ◇ vi: to ~ **with sb** relacionarse con alguien.

association [ə,səusɪˈeɪʃn] n **-1.** [organization, act of associating] asociación f; in ~ **with** en colaboración con. **-2.** [in mind] connotación f.

assonance [ˈæsənəns] n asonancia f.

assorted [əˈsɔːtɪd] adj [of various types] variado(da).

assortment [əˈsɔːtmənt] n surtido m.

Asst. abbr of **assistant**.

assuage [əˈsweɪdʒ] vt fml [grief] aliviar; [thirst, hunger] saciar.

assume [əˈsjuːm] vt **-1.** [suppose] suponer. **-2.** [power, responsibility] asumir. **-3.** [appearance, attitude] adoptar.

assumed name [əˈsjuːmd-] n nombre m falso.

assuming [əˈsjuːmɪŋ] conj suponiendo que.

assumption [əˈsʌmpʃn] n **-1.** [supposition] suposición f; on the ~ **that** suponiendo que. **-2.** [of power] asunción f.
◆ **Assumption** n RELIG: the Assumption la Asunción.

assurance [əˈʃuərəns] n **-1.** [promise] garantía f. **-2.** [confidence] seguridad f de sí mismo. **-3.** [insurance] seguro m.

assure [əˈʃuəʳ] vt asegurar, garantizar; to ~ **sb of sthg** garantizar a alguien algo; to be ~**d of sthg** tener algo garantizado.

assured [əˈʃuəd] adj [confident] seguro(ra).

AST (abbr of **Atlantic Standard Time**) n hora oficial de la costa este estadounidense.

asterisk [ˈæstərɪsk] n asterisco m.

astern [əˈstɜːn] adv NAUT a popa.

asteroid [ˈæstərɔɪd] n asteroide m.

asthma [ˈæsmə] n asma f.

asthmatic [æsˈmætɪk] ◇ adj asmático(ca). ◇ n asmático m, -ca f.

astigmatism [ə'stɪgmətɪzm] *n* astigmatismo *m*.

astonish [ə'stɒnɪʃ] *vt* asombrar.

astonishing [ə'stɒnɪʃɪŋ] *adj* asombroso(sa).

astonishment [ə'stɒnɪʃmənt] *n* asombro *m*.

astound [ə'staʊnd] *vt* asombrar, pasmar.

astounding [ə'staʊndɪŋ] *adj* asombroso(sa), pasmoso(sa).

astrakhan [ˌæstrə'kæn] *n* astracán *m*.

astray [ə'streɪ] *adv*: **to go** ~ [become lost] extraviarse; **to lead sb** ~ [into bad ways] llevar a alguien por el mal camino.

astride [ə'straɪd] ◇ *adv* a horcajadas. ◇ *prep* a horcajadas en.

astringent [ə'strɪndʒənt] ◇ *adj* astringente. ◇ *n* astringente *m*.

astrologer [ə'strɒlədʒə'] *n* astrólogo *m*, -ga *f*.

astrological [ˌæstrə'lɒdʒɪkl] *adj* astrológico(ca).

astrologist [ə'strɒlədʒɪst] *n* astrólogo *m*, -ga *f*.

astrology [ə'strɒlədʒɪ] *n* astrología *f*.

astronaut ['æstrənɔːt] *n* astronauta *m y f*.

astronomer [ə'strɒnəmə'] *n* astrónomo *m*, -ma *f*.

astronomical [ˌæstrə'nɒmɪkl] *adj* astronómico(ca).

astronomy [ə'strɒnəmɪ] *n* astronomía *f*.

astrophysics [ˌæstrəʊ'fɪzɪks] *n* astrofísica *f*.

Asturias [æ'stʊərɪæs] *n* Asturias; **the prince of** ~ el príncipe de Asturias.

astute [ə'stjuːt] *adj* astuto(ta), abusado(da) *Amer*.

asunder [ə'sʌndə'] *adv literary* [apart]: **to tear** ~ hacer trizas.

ASV (*abbr of* **American Standard Version**) *n* traducción estadounidense de la Biblia.

asylum [ə'saɪləm] *n* **-1.** [mental hospital] manicomio *m*. **-2.** [protection] asilo *m*.

asymmetrical [ˌeɪsɪ'metrɪkl] *adj* asimétrico(ca).

at [*unstressed* ət, *stressed* æt] *prep* **-1.** [indicating place] en; ~ **my father's** en casa de mi padre; **standing** ~ **the window** de pie junto a la ventana; ~ **the bottom of the hill** al pie de la colina; **to arrive** ~ llegar a; ~ **school/work/home** en la escuela/el trabajo/casa. **-2.** [indicating direction] a; **to look** ~ **sthg/sb** mirar algo/a alguien; **she smiled** ~ **me** me sonrió. **-3.** [indicating a particular time] en; ~ **a more suitable time** en un momento más oportuno; ~ **midnight/noon/eleven o'clock** a medianoche/mediodía/las once; ~ **night** por la noche; ~ **Christmas/Easter** en Navidades/Semana

Santa. **-4.** [indicating speed, rate, price] a; ~ **100mph/high speed** a 100 millas por hora/gran velocidad; ~ **£50 (a pair)** a 50 libras (el par). **-5.** [indicating particular state, condition]: ~ **peace/war** en paz/guerra; **she's** ~ **lunch** está comiendo; **to work hard** ~ **sthg** trabajar duro en algo. **-6.** [indicating a particular age] a; ~ **52/your age** a los 52/tu edad. **-7.** [indicating tentativeness, noncompletion]: **to snatch** ~ **sthg** intentar agarrar algo; **to nibble** ~ **sthg** mordisquear algo. **-8.** (*after adjectives*): **delighted** ~ encantado con; **clever/experienced** ~ listo/experimentado en; **puzzled/horrified** ~ perplejo/horrorizado ante; **he's good/bad** ~ **sport** se le dan bien/mal los deportes.
◆ **at all** *adv* **-1.** (*with negative*): **not** ~ **all** [when thanked] de nada; [when answering a question] en absoluto; **she's not** ~ **all happy** no está nada contenta. **-2.** [in the slightest]: **anything** ~ **all will do** cualquier cosa valdrá; **do you know her** ~ **all?** ¿la conoces (de algo)?

ATC (*abbr of* **Air Training Corps**) *n* unidad de formación de las fuerzas aéreas británicas.

ate [*Br* et, *Am* eɪt] *pt* → **eat**.

atheism ['eɪθɪɪzm] *n* ateísmo *m*.

atheist ['eɪθɪɪst] *n* ateo *m*, -a *f*.

Athenian [ə'θiːnjən] ◇ *adj* ateniense. ◇ *n* ateniense *m y f*.

Athens ['æθɪnz] *n* Atenas.

athlete ['æθliːt] *n* atleta *m y f*.

athlete's foot *n* pie *m* de atleta.

athletic [æθ'letɪk] *adj* atlético(ca).
◆ **athletics** *npl* atletismo *m*.

Atlantic [ət'læntɪk] ◇ *adj* atlántico(ca). ◇ *n*: **the** ~ **(Ocean)** el (océano) Atlántico.

Atlantis [ət'læntɪs] *n* (la) Atlántida.

atlas ['ætləs] *n* atlas *m inv*.

Atlas ['ætləs] *n*: **the** ~ **Mountains** el Atlas.

atm. (*abbr of* **atmosphere**) atm.

ATM (*abbr of* **automatic teller machine**) *n* cajero automático.

atmosphere ['ætmə,sfɪə'] *n* **-1.** [of planet] atmósfera *f*. **-2.** [air in room, mood of place] ambiente *m*, atmósfera *f*.

atmospheric [ˌætməs'ferɪk] *adj* **-1.** [pressure, pollution] atmosférico(ca). **-2.** [attractive, mysterious] cautivador(ra).

atoll ['ætɒl] *n* atolón *m*.

atom ['ætəm] *n* **-1.** TECH átomo *m*. **-2.** *fig* [tiny amount] pizca *f*.

atom bomb *n* bomba *f* atómica.

atomic [ə'tɒmɪk] *adj* atómico(ca).

atomic bomb = **atom bomb**.

atomic energy *n* energía *f* atómica.

atomic number *n* número *m* atómico.

atomizer, **-iser** ['ætəmaɪzəʳ] *n* atomizador *m*.

atone [ə'təun] *vi*: **to ~ for** reparar.

atonement [ə'təunmənt] *n*: **~ (for)** reparación *f* (por).

A to Z *n* guía *f* alfabética; [map] callejero *m*.

ATP (*abbr of* **Association of Tennis Professionals**) *n* ATP *f*.

atrocious [ə'trəuʃəs] *adj* [very bad] atroz.

atrocity [ə'trɒsəti] (*pl* **-ies**) *n* [terrible act] atrocidad *f*.

attach [ə'tætʃ] *vt* **-1.** [with pin, clip]: **to ~ sthg (to)** sujetar algo (a); [with string] atar algo (a). **-2.** [importance, blame]: **to ~ sthg (to sthg)** atribuir algo (a algo).

attaché [ə'tæʃeɪ] *n* agregado *m*, -da *f*.

attaché case *n* portafolios *m inv*, maletín *m*.

attached [ə'tætʃt] *adj* **-1.** [fastened on]: **~ (to)** adjunto(ta) (a). **-2.** [for work, job]: **~ to** destinado(da) a. **-3.** [fond]: **~ to** encariñado(da) con.

attachment [ə'tætʃmənt] *n* **-1.** [device] accesorio *m*. **-2.** [fondness]: **~ (to)** cariño *m* (por).

attack [ə'tæk] ◇ *n*: **~ (on)** ataque *m* (contra). ◇ *vt* **-1.** [gen] atacar. **-2.** [job, problem] acometer. ◇ *vi* atacar.

attacker [ə'tækəʳ] *n* atacante *m y f*.

attain [ə'teɪn] *vt* lograr, alcanzar.

attainment [ə'teɪnmənt] *n* logro *m*.

attempt [ə'tempt] ◇ *n*: **~ (at sthg)** intento *m* (de algo); **~ on sb's life** atentado *m*. ◇ *vt*: **to ~ sthg/to do sthg** intentar algo/hacer algo.

attend [ə'tend] ◇ *vt* asistir a. ◇ *vi* **-1.** [be present] asistir. **-2.** [pay attention]: **to ~ (to)** atender (a).

◆ **attend to** *vt fus* **-1.** [matter] ocuparse de. **-2.** [customer] atender a; [patient] asistir a.

attendance [ə'tendəns] *n* asistencia *f*.

attendant [ə'tendənt] ◇ *adj* relacionado(da), concomitante. ◇ *n* [at museum] vigilante *m y f*; [at petrol station] encargado *m*, -da *f*.

attention [ə'tenʃn] ◇ *n* (*U*) **-1.** [gen] atención *f*; **to bring sthg to sb's ~**, **to draw sb's ~ to sthg** llamar la atención de alguien sobre algo; **to attract** OR **catch sb's ~** atraer OR captar la atención de alguien; **to pay/pay no ~ (to)** prestar/no prestar atención (a); **for the ~ of** COMM a la atención de. **-2.** [care] asistencia *f*. **-3.** MIL: **to stand to ~** ponerse en la posición de firmes, cuadrarse. ◇ *excl* MIL ¡firmes!

attentive [ə'tentɪv] *adj* atento(ta).

attentively [ə'tentɪvlɪ] *adv* atentamente.

attenuate [ə'tenjueɪt] *fml* ◇ *vt* atenuar. ◇ *vi* atenuarse.

attest [ə'test] ◇ *vt* atestiguar. ◇ *vi*: **to ~ to sthg** atestiguar algo.

attic ['ætɪk] *n* desván *m*, entretecho *m* Amer.

attire [ə'taɪəʳ] *n* (*U*) atuendo *m*, atavío *m*.

attitude ['ætɪtjuːd] *n* **-1.** [way of thinking, acting]: **~ (to** OR **towards)** actitud *f* (hacia). **-2.** [posture] postura *f*.

attn. (*abbr of* **for the attention of**) a/a.

attorney [ə'tɜːnɪ] *n Am* abogado *m*, -da *f*.

attorney general (*pl* **attorneys general**) *n* fiscal *m* general del estado.

attract [ə'trækt] *vt* **-1.** [gen] atraer; **to be ~d to** sentirse atraído por. **-2.** [support, criticism] atraerse, ganarse.

attraction [ə'trækʃn] *n* **-1.** [gen]: **~ (to sb)** atracción *f* (hacia OR por alguien). **-2.** [attractiveness - of thing] atractivo *m*.

attractive [ə'træktɪv] *adj* atractivo(va).

attractively [ə'træktɪvlɪ] *adv* de un modo atractivo.

attributable [ə'trɪbjutəbl] *adj* [of thing]: **~ to** atribuible a.

attribute [*vb* ə'trɪbjuːt, *n* 'ætrɪbjuːt] ◇ *vt*: **to ~ sthg to** atribuir algo a. ◇ *n* atributo *m*.

attribution [ˌætrɪ'bjuːʃn] *n*: **~ (to)** atribución *f* (a).

attrition [ə'trɪʃn] *n* desgaste *m*; **war of ~** guerra de desgaste.

attuned [ə'tjuːnd] *adj* **-1.** [accustomed]: **~ (to)** acostumbrado(da) (a). **-2.** [ears]: **~ to** sensible a.

Atty. Gen. *abbr of* **Attorney General**.

ATV *n* **-1.** (*abbr of* **Associated Television**) compañía británica de televisión. **-2.** (*abbr of* **all terrain vehicle**) todo terreno.

atypical [ˌeɪ'tɪpɪkl] *adj* atípico(ca).

atypically [ˌeɪ'tɪpɪklɪ] *adv* de manera atípica.

aubergine ['əubəʒiːn] *n Br* berenjena *f*.

auburn ['ɔːbən] *adj* castaño rojizo.

auction ['ɔːkʃn] ◇ *n* subasta *f*; **at** OR **by ~** mediante subasta; **to put sthg up for ~** sacar algo a subasta. ◇ *vt* subastar.

◆ **auction off** *vt sep* subastar.

auctioneer [ˌɔːkʃə'nɪəʳ] *n* subastador *m*, -ra *f*.

audacious [ɔː'deɪʃəs] *adj* [daring] audaz; [cheeky] atrevido(da).

audacity [ɔː'dæsəti] *n* osadía *f*, atrevimiento *m*.

audible ['ɔːdəbl] *adj* audible.

audience ['ɔːdjəns] n -1. [of play, film] público m. -2. [formal meeting, TV viewers] audiencia f.

audio ['ɔːdɪəʊ] adj de audio.

audio frequency n audiofrecuencia f.

audiotyping ['ɔːdɪəʊ,taɪpɪŋ] n mecanografía f por dictáfono.

audiotypist ['ɔːdɪəʊ,taɪpɪst] n mecanógrafo m, -fa f por dictáfono.

audio-visual adj audiovisual.

audit ['ɔːdɪt] ◇ n auditoría f. ◇ vt auditar.

audition [ɔː'dɪʃn] ◇ n prueba f (a un artista). ◇ vi: to ~ for hacer una prueba para.

auditor ['ɔːdɪtəʳ] n auditor m, -ra f.

auditorium [,ɔːdɪ'tɔːrɪəm] (pl **-riums** OR **-ria** [-rɪə]) n auditorio m.

au fait [,əʊ'feɪ] adj: ~ with familiarizado(da) con.

Aug. (abbr of August) ago.

augment [ɔːg'ment] vt acrecentar, aumentar.

augur ['ɔːgəʳ] vi: to ~ well/badly traer buenos/malos augurios.

august [ɔː'gʌst] adj augusto(ta).

August ['ɔːgəst] n agosto m; see also September.

Auld Lang Syne [,ɔːldlæŋ'saɪn] n canción escocesa en alabanza de los viejos tiempos.

aunt [ɑːnt] n tía f.

auntie, aunty ['ɑːntɪ] (pl **-ies**) n inf tita f.

au pair [,əʊ'peəʳ] n au pair f.

aura ['ɔːrə] n aura f, halo m.

aural ['ɔːrəl] adj auditivo(va).

aurally ['ɔːrəlɪ] adv: ~ handicapped con deficiencia auditiva.

auspices ['ɔːspɪsɪz] npl: under the ~ of bajo los auspicios de.

auspicious [ɔː'spɪʃəs] adj prometedor(ra).

Aussie ['ɒzɪ] n inf australiano m, -na f.

austere [ɒ'stɪəʳ] adj austero(ra).

austerity [ɒ'sterətɪ] n austeridad f.

austerity measures npl medidas fpl restrictivas.

Australasia [,ɒstrə'leɪʒə] n Australasia.

Australia [ɒ'streɪljə] n Australia.

Australian [ɒ'streɪljən] ◇ adj australiano(na). ◇ n australiano m, -na f.

Austria ['ɒstrɪə] n Austria.

Austrian ['ɒstrɪən] ◇ adj austriaco(ca). ◇ n austriaco m, -ca f.

AUT (abbr of **Association of University Teachers**) n sindicato británico de profesores universitarios.

authentic [ɔː'θentɪk] adj auténtico(ca).

authenticate [ɔː'θentɪkeɪt] vt autentificar.

authentication [ɔː,θentɪ'keɪʃn] n autentificación f.

authenticity [,ɔːθen'tɪsətɪ] n autenticidad f.

author ['ɔːθəʳ] n autor m, -ra f.

authoritarian [ɔː,θɒrɪ'teərɪən] adj autoritario(ria).

authoritative [ɔː'θɒrɪtətɪv] adj -1. [person, voice] autoritario(ria). -2. [study] autorizado(da).

authority [ɔː'θɒrətɪ] (pl **-ies**) n -1. [gen] autoridad f; to be an ~ on ser una autoridad en. -2. [permission] autorización f. -3. phr: to have it on good ~ saberlo de buena tinta.

◆ **authorities** npl: the authorities las autoridades fpl.

authorize, -ise ['ɔːθəraɪz] vt: to ~ (sb to do sthg) autorizar (a alguien a hacer algo).

Authorized Version ['ɔːθəraɪzd-] n: the ~ la versión oficial de la Biblia en inglés.

authorship ['ɔːθəʃɪp] n autoría f.

autistic [ɔː'tɪstɪk] adj autista.

auto ['ɔːtəʊ] (pl **-s**) n Am coche m, auto m.

autobiographical ['ɔːtə,baɪə'græfɪkl] adj autobiográfico(ca).

autobiography [,ɔːtəbaɪ'ɒgrəfɪ] (pl **-ies**) n autobiografía f.

autocrat ['ɔːtəkræt] n autócrata m y f.

autocratic [,ɔːtə'krætɪk] adj autocrático(ca).

autocross ['ɔːtəʊkrɒs] n Br autocross m.

Autocue® ['ɔːtəʊkjuː] n Br teleapuntador m.

autograph ['ɔːtəgrɑːf] ◇ n autógrafo m. ◇ vt autografiar.

Automat® ['ɔːtəmæt] n Am restaurante con servicio automatizado.

automata [ɔː'tɒmətə] pl → automaton.

automate ['ɔːtəmeɪt] vt automatizar.

automatic [,ɔːtə'mætɪk] ◇ adj automático(ca). ◇ n -1. Br [car] coche m automático. -2. [gun] arma f automática. -3. [washing machine] lavadora f automática.

automatically [,ɔːtə'mætɪklɪ] adv automáticamente.

automatic pilot n -1. AERON & NAUT piloto m automático. -2. fig: on ~ [automatically] con el piloto automático puesto.

automation [,ɔːtə'meɪʃn] n automatización f.

automaton [ɔː'tɒmətən] (pl **-tons** OR **-ta**) n -1. [robot] autómata m. -2. pej [person] autómata m y f, máquina f.

automobile ['ɔːtəməbiːl] n Am coche m, automóvil m.

automotive [,ɔːtə'məʊtɪv] adj automovilístico(ca).

autonomous [ɔː'tɒnəməs] *adj* autóno-mo(ma).

autonomy [ɔː'tɒnəmɪ] *n* autonomía *f*.

autopilot ['ɔːtəʊpaɪlət] *n* piloto *m* automáti-co.

autopsy ['ɔːtɒpsɪ] (*pl* **-ies**) *n* autópsia *f*.

autumn ['ɔːtəm] ◇ *n* otoño *m*; **in** ~ en otoño. ◇ *comp* otoñal.

autumnal [ɔː'tʌmnəl] *adj* otoñal.

auxiliary [ɔːg'zɪljərɪ] (*pl* **-ies**) ◇ *adj* auxi-liar. ◇ *n* **-1.** [medical worker] auxiliar sanita-rio *m*, auxiliar sanitaria *f*. **-2.** [soldier] solda-do *m* auxiliar.

Av. (*abbr of* **avenue**) Av.

AV -1. *abbr of* **Authorized Version**. **-2.** *abbr of* **audiovisual**.

avail [ə'veɪl] ◇ *n*: **to no** ~ en vano. ◇ *vt*: **to** ~ **o.s. of sthg** aprovechar algo.

availability [ə,veɪlə'bɪlətɪ] *n* disponibilidad *f*.

available [ə'veɪləbl] *adj* **-1.** [product, service] disponible. **-2.** [person] libre, disponible.

avalanche ['ævəlɑːnʃ] *n* lit & fig avalancha *f*, alud *m*.

avant-garde [,ævɒŋ'gɑːd] *adj* de vanguar-dia, vanguardista.

avarice ['ævərɪs] *n* avaricia *f*.

avaricious [,ævə'rɪʃəs] *adj* avaricioso(sa).

avdp. (*abbr of* **avoirdupois**) *sistema de peso basado en la libra.*

Ave. (*abbr of* **avenue**) Avda.

avenge [ə'vendʒ] *vt* vengar.

avenue ['ævənjuː] *n* **-1.** [wide road] avenida *f*. **-2.** fig [method, means] camino *m*, vía *f*.

average ['ævərɪdʒ] ◇ *adj* **-1.** [mean, typical] medio(dia). **-2.** [mediocre] regular. ◇ *n* me-dia *f*, promedio *m*; **on** ~ de media, por tér-mino medio. ◇ *vt* alcanzar un promedio de.

◆ **average out** ◇ *vt sep* sacar la media de. ◇ *vi*: **to** ~ **out at** salir a una media de.

averse [ə'vɜːs] *adj*: **not to be** ~ **to sthg/to doing sthg** no hacerle ascos a algo/a hacer algo.

aversion [ə'vɜːʃn] *n* **-1.** [dislike]: ~ **(to)** aversión *f* (a). **-2.** [object of dislike]: **football is my pet** ~ el fútbol es lo que más odio.

avert [ə'vɜːt] *vt* **-1.** [problem, accident] evitar, prevenir. **-2.** [eyes, glance] apartar, desviar.

aviary ['eɪvjərɪ] (*pl* **-ies**) *n* pajarera *f*.

aviation [,eɪvɪ'eɪʃn] *n* aviación *f*.

aviator ['eɪvɪeɪtə] *n* dated aviador *m*, -ra *f*.

avid ['ævɪd] *adj*: ~ **(for)** ávido(da) (de).

avocado [,ævə'kɑːdəʊ] (*pl* **-s** OR **-es**) *n*: ~ **(pear)** aguacate *m*, palta *f* Amer.

avoid [ə'vɔɪd] *vt*: **to** ~ **(sthg/doing sthg)** evitar (algo/hacer algo).

avoidable [ə'vɔɪdəbl] *adj* evitable.

avoidance [ə'vɔɪdəns] → **tax avoidance**.

avowed [ə'vaʊd] *adj* declarado(da).

AVP (*abbr of* **assistant vice-president**) *n* vi-cepresidente segundo.

AWACS ['eɪwæks] (*abbr of* **airborne warn-ing and control system**) *n* AWACS *m*.

await [ə'weɪt] *vt* esperar, aguardar.

awake [ə'weɪk] (*pt* **awoke** OR **awaked**, *pp* **awoken**) ◇ *adj* **-1.** [not sleeping] despier-to(ta); **wide** ~ completamente despierto. **-2.** fig [aware]: ~ **to sthg** consciente de algo. ◇ *vt lit* & fig despertar. ◇ *vi lit* & fig despertarse.

awakening [ə'weɪknɪŋ] *n* lit & fig despertar *m*; **a rude** ~ una repentina y desagradable toma de conciencia.

award [ə'wɔːd] ◇ *n* **-1.** [prize] premio *m*, galardón *m*. **-2.** [compensation] indemniza-ción *f*. ◇ *vt*: **to** ~ **sb sthg, to** ~ **sthg to sb** [prize] conceder OR otorgar algo a alguien; [compensation] adjudicar algo a alguien.

aware [ə'weə] *adj* **-1.** [conscious]: ~ **of** consciente de. **-2.** [informed, sensitive] infor-mado(da), al día; ~ **of sthg** al día de algo; **to be** ~ **that** estar informado de que.

awareness [ə'weənɪs] *n* conciencia *f*.

awash [ə'wɒʃ] *adj* lit & fig: ~ **(with)** inun-dado(da) (de).

away [ə'weɪ] ◇ *adv* **-1.** [move, walk, drive]: **to walk** ~ **(from)** marcharse (de); **to drive** ~ **(from)** alejarse (de) (*en coche*); **to turn** OR **look** ~ apartar la vista. **-2.** [at a distance - in space, time]: ~ **from** a distancia de; **4 miles** ~ a 4 millas de distancia; **the exam is two days** ~ faltan dos días para el examen. **-3.** [not at home or office] fuera. **-4.** [in safe place]: **to put sthg** ~ poner algo en su sitio. **-5.** [indicating removal or disappearance]: **to fade** ~ desvanecerse; **to give sthg** ~ regalar algo; **to take sthg** ~ llevarse algo. **-6.** [con-tinuously]: **he was working** ~ **when ...** esta-ba muy concentrado trabajando cuando .... ◇ *adj* SPORT visitante; ~ **game** partido *m* fuera de casa.

awe [ɔː] *n* sobrecogimiento *m*; **to be in** ~ **of sb** estar sometido a alguien.

awesome ['ɔːsəm] *adj* impresionante.

awestruck ['ɔːstrʌk] *adj* sobrecogido(da), asombrado(da).

awful ['ɔːfʊl] *adj* **-1.** [terrible] terrible, es-pantoso(sa); **I feel** ~ me siento fatal. **-2.** *inf* [very great] tremendo(da).

awfully ['ɔːflɪ] *adv* inf [very] tremendamen-te.

awhile [ə'waɪl] *adv literary* un instante, un rato.

awkward ['ɔːkwəd] *adj* **-1.** [clumsy - movement] torpe; [- person] desgarbado(da). **-2.** [embarrassed, embarrassing] incómodo(da). **-3.** [unreasonable] difícil. **-4.** [inconvenient] poco manejable.

awkwardly ['ɔːkwədlɪ] *adv* **-1.** [with difficulty] torpemente. **-2.** [in an embarrassed way] incómodamente.

awkwardness ['ɔːkwədnəs] *n* **-1.** [clumsiness] torpeza *f*. **-2.** [embarrassment] incomodidad *f*. **-3.** [unreasonableness] antipatía *f*. **-4.** [inconvenience] inoportunidad *f*.

awl [ɔːl] *n* lezna *f*.

awning ['ɔːnɪŋ] *n* toldo *m*.

awoke [ə'wəʊk] *pt* → awake.

awoken [ə'wəʊkn] *pp* → awake.

AWOL ['eɪwɒl] (*abbr of* **absent without leave**) ausente sin permiso.

awry [ə'raɪ] ◇ *adj* torcido(da), ladeado(da). ◇ *adv*: **to go ~** salir mal.

axe *Br*, **ax** *Am* [æks] ◇ *n* hacha *f*; **to have an ~ to grind** tener intereses personales. ◇ *vt* [project, jobs] suprimir.

axes ['æksiːz] *pl* → axis.

axiom ['æksɪəm] *n* axioma *m*.

axis ['æksɪs] (*pl* **axes**) *n* eje *m*.

axle ['æksl] *n* eje *m*.

ayatollah [,aɪə'tɒlə] *n* ayatollah *m*.

aye [aɪ] ◇ *adv* sí. ◇ *n* sí *m*.

AYH (*abbr of* **American Youth Hostels**) *n* asociación estadounidense de albergues juveniles.

AZ *abbr of* **Arizona.**

azalea [ə'zeɪljə] *n* azalea *f*.

Azerbaijan [,æzəbaɪ'dʒɑːn] *n* Azerbaiyán.

Azerbaijani [,æzəbaɪ'dʒɑːnɪ] ◇ *adj* azerbaiyaní. ◇ *n* azerbaiyaní *m y f*.

Azeri [ə'zeri] ◇ *adj* azerí. ◇ *n* azerí *m y f*.

Azores [ə'zɔːz] *npl*: **the ~** los Azores.

AZT (*abbr of* **azidothymidine**) *n* AZT *m*.

Aztec ['æztek] ◇ *adj* azteca. ◇ *n* [person] azteca *m y f*.

azure ['æʒəʳ] *adj* azul celeste *inv*.

B

b (*pl* **b's** OR **bs**), **B** (*pl* **B's** OR **Bs**) [biː] *n* [letter] b *f*, B *f*.
◆ **B** *n* **-1.** MUS si *m*. **-2.** SCH [mark] ≃ bien *m*.

b. (*abbr of* **born**) n.

BA *n* **-1.** (*abbr of* **Bachelor of Arts**) (*titular de una*) licenciatura de letras. **-2.** (*abbr of* **British Academy**) organismo público para el fomento de la investigación en el campo de las letras. **-3.** (*abbr of* **British Airways**) líneas aéreas británicas.

BAA (*abbr of* **British Airports' Authority**) *n* organismo independiente gestor de siete grandes aeropuertos británicos.

babble ['bæbl] ◇ *n* parloteo *m*. ◇ *vi* [person] farfullar.

babe [beɪb] *n* **-1.** *literary* [baby] bebé *m*. **-2.** *Am inf* [term of affection] cariño *m*.

baboon [bə'buːn] *n* babuino *m*, papión *m*.

baby ['beɪbɪ] (*pl* **-ies**) *n* **-1.** [newborn child] bebé *m*; [infant] niño *m*. **-2.** *inf* [term of affection] cariño *m*.

baby boomer [-,buːməʳ] *n Am* niño nacido durante el boom natalicio de los sesenta.

baby buggy *n* **-1.** *Br* [foldable pushchair] sillita *f* de niño (con ruedas). **-2.** *Am* = baby carriage.

baby carriage *n Am* cochecito *m* de niños.

babyish ['beɪbɪɪʃ] *adj pej* infantil.

baby-minder *n Br* niñera *f* (durante el día).

baby-sit *vi* cuidar a niños.

baby-sitter *n* canguro *m y f*.

bachelor ['bætʃələʳ] *n* soltero *m*.

Bachelor of Arts *n* ≃ licenciado *m*, -da *f* en Letras.

Bachelor of Science *n* ≃ licenciado *m*, -da *f* en Ciencias.

bachelor's degree *n* ≃ licenciatura *f*.

back [bæk] ◇ *adv* **-1.** [in position] atrás; **stand ~!** ¡échense para atrás!; **to push ~** empujar hacia atrás. **-2.** [to former position or state] de vuelta; **to come ~** volver; **to go ~** volver; **to look ~** volver la mirada; **to walk ~** volver andando; **to give sthg ~** devolver algo; **to be ~ (in fashion)** estar de vuelta; **he has been there and ~** ha estado allí y ha vuelto; **I spent all day going ~ and forth** pasé todo el día yendo y viniendo. **-3.** [in time]: **two weeks ~** hace dos semanas; **it dates ~ to 1960** data de 1960; **~ in March** allá en marzo; **to think ~ (to sthg)** recordar (algo). **-4.** [phone, write] de vuelta; **to pay sb ~** [give back money] devolverle el dinero a alguien.

◇ **n -1.** [of person] espalda *f*; [of animal] lomo *m*; **to break the ~ of** *fig* pasar lo peor OR la peor parte de; **behind sb's ~** a espaldas de alguien; **to put sb's ~ up** poner negro a alguien; **to stab sb in the ~** *fig* darle a alguien una puñalada por la espalda OR trapera; **to turn one's ~ on sb/sthg** dar la espalda a alguien/algo, volver la espalda a alguien/algo. **-2.** [of hand, cheque] dorso *m*; [of coin, page] reverso *m*; [of car, book, head] parte *f* trasera; [of chair] respaldo *m*; [of room, cupboard] fondo *m*; **the ~ of beyond** *Br* el quinto pino; **to know somewhere like the ~ of one's hand** conocer un sitio como la palma de la mano. **-3.** SPORT [player] defensa *m*.

◇ *adj* (*in compounds*) **-1.** [at the back - door, legs, seat] trasero(ra); [- page] último(ma). **-2.** [overdue - pay, rent] atrasado(da).

◇ *vt* **-1.** [reverse] dar marcha atrás a. **-2.** [support] respaldar. **-3.** [bet on] apostar por. **-4.** [line with material] forrar.

◇ *vi* [drive backwards] ir marcha atrás; [walk backwards] ir hacia atrás.

◆ **back to back** *adv* [with backs facing] espalda con espalda.

◆ **back to front** *adv* al revés.

◆ **back away** *vi* retroceder.

◆ **back down** *vi* echarse OR volverse atrás.

◆ **back off** *vi* retirarse.

◆ **back onto** *vt Br* dar (por la parte de atrás) a.

◆ **back out** *vi* echarse OR volverse atrás.

◆ **back up** ◇ *vt sep* **-1.** [support] apoyar. **-2.** [reverse] dar marcha atrás a. **-3.** COMPUT hacer un archivo de seguridad de. ◇ *vi* [reverse] ir marcha atrás.

backache ['bækeɪk] *n* dolor *m* de espalda.

backbencher [,bæk'bentʃər] *n Br diputado sin cargo en el gabinete del gobierno o la oposición.*

backbenches [,bæk'bentʃɪz] *npl Br escaños de los diputados sin cargo en el gabinete del gobierno o la oposición.*

backbiting ['bækbaɪtɪŋ] *n* murmuración *f*, chismorreo *m*.

backbone ['bækbəʊn] *n lit & fig* columna *f* vertebral.

backbreaking ['bæk,breɪkɪŋ] *adj* derrengante.

back burner *n*: **to put sthg on the ~** aparcar algo.

backchat *Br* ['bæktʃæt], **backtalk** *Am* ['bæktɔːk] *n* (*U*) *inf* réplicas *fpl*.

backcloth ['bækklɒθ] *n Br* = **backdrop.**

backcomb ['bækkəʊm] *vt Br* cardar.

back copy *n* número *m* atrasado.

backdate [,bæk'deɪt] *vt*: **a pay rise ~d to March** un aumento de sueldo con efecto retroactivo desde marzo.

back door *n* puerta *f* trasera; **to get in through** OR **by the ~** *fig* entrar con enchufe.

backdrop ['bækdrɒp] *n lit & fig* telón *m* de fondo.

backer ['bækər] *n* promotor *m*, -ra *f*, patrocinador *m*, -ra *f*.

backfire [,bæk'faɪər] *vi* **-1.** [motor vehicle] petardear. **-2.** [go wrong]: **it ~d on him** le salió el tiro por la culata.

backgammon ['bæk,gæmən] *n* backgammon *m*.

background ['bækgraʊnd] ◇ *n* **-1.** [in picture, view] fondo *m*; **in the ~** [of painting etc] al fondo; [out of the limelight] en la sombra. **-2.** [of event, situation] trasfondo *m*. **-3.** [upbringing] origen *m*; **family ~** antecedentes *mpl* familiares. ◇ *comp* [music, noise] de fondo.

backhand ['bækhænd] *n* revés *m*.

backhanded ['bækhændɪd] *adj fig* equívoco(ca).

backhander ['bækhændər] *n Br inf*: **to give sb a ~** untarle la mano a alguien.

backing ['bækɪŋ] *n* **-1.** [support] apoyo *m*, respaldo *m*. **-2.** [lining] refuerzo *m*. **-3.** MUS acompañamiento *m*.

back issue *n* = **back number.**

backlash ['bæklæʃ] *n* reacción *f* violenta.

backless ['bæklɪs] *adj* abierto(ta) por la espalda.

backlog ['bæklɒg] *n* acumulación *f*.

back number *n* número *m* atrasado.

backpack ['bækpæk] *n* mochila *f*, macuto *m*.

backpacker ['bækpækər] *n* excursionista *m* y *f*.

backpacking ['bækpækɪŋ] *n*: **to go ~** irse de viaje con la mochila.

back passage *n euphemism* recto *m*.

back pay *n* (*U*) atrasos *mpl*.

backpedal [,bæk'pedl] (*Br pt & pp* **-led**, *cont* **-ling**, *Am pt & pp* **-ed**, *cont* **-ing**) *vi fig*: **to ~**

(on sthg) dar marcha atrás (con respecto a algo).

back seat *n* asiento *m* trasero OR de atrás; **to take a ~** *fig* situarse en segundo plano.

back-seat driver *n* persona que no para de dar consejos al conductor.

backside [,bæk'saɪd] *n* inf trasero *m*.

backslash ['bækslæʃ] *n* COMPUT barra *f* inversa.

backslide [,bæk'slaɪd] (*pt & pp* **-slid** [-'slɪd]) *vi* reincidir, recaer.

backspace ['bækspeɪs] ◇ *n* COMPUT: **~ (key)** tecla *f* de retroceso. ◇ *vi* retroceder.

backstage [,bæk'steɪdʒ] *adv* entre bastidores.

back street *n* Br callejuela *f* de barrio.

back-street abortion *n* Br aborto *m* clandestino.

backstroke ['bækstrəʊk] *n* espalda *f* (en natación).

backtalk Am = backchat.

backtrack ['bæktræk] = backpedal.

backup ['bækʌp] ◇ *adj* **-1.** [plan] de emergencia, alternativo(va); [team] de apoyo. **-2.** COMPUT de seguridad. ◇ *n* **-1.** [support] apoyo *m*. **-2.** COMPUT copia *f* de seguridad.

backward ['bækwəd] ◇ *adj* **-1.** [movement, look] hacia atrás. **-2.** [country, person] atrasado(da). ◇ *adv* Am = backwards.

backward-looking [-,lʊkɪŋ] *adj* pej retrógrado(da).

backwards ['bækwədz], **backward** Am *adv* **-1.** [move, go] hacia atrás; **~ and forwards** [movement] de un lado a otro. **-2.** [back to front] al OR del revés.

backwash ['bækwɒʃ] *n* estela *f*.

backwater ['bæk,wɔːtə'] *n* fig páramo *m*, lugar *m* atrasado.

backwoods ['bækwʊdz] *npl* zona *f* aislada.

backyard [,bæk'jɑːd] *n* **-1.** Br [yard] patio *m*. **-2.** Am [garden] jardín *m* (trasero).

bacon ['beɪkən] *n* bacon *m*, tocino *m*.

bacteria [bæk'tɪərɪə] *npl* bacterias *fpl*.

bacteriology [bæk,tɪərɪ'ɒlədʒɪ] *n* bacteriología *f*.

bad [bæd] (*compar* **worse**, *superl* **worst**) ◇ *adj* **-1.** [gen] malo(la); **he's ~ at French** se le da mal el francés; **to go ~** [food] echarse a perder; **to go from ~ to worse** ir de mal en peor; **too ~!** ¡qué pena!; **it's not ~ (at all)** no está nada mal; **how are you? — not ~** ¿qué tal? — bien. **-2.** [illness] fuerte, grave. **-3.** [guilty]: **to feel ~ about sthg** sentirse mal por algo. ◇ *adv* Am = badly.

bad blood *n* rencor *m*, resentimiento *m*.

bad cheque *n* cheque *m* sin fondos.

bad debt *n* deuda *f* incobrable.

bade [bæd] *pt & pp* → bid.

bad feeling *n* (U) rencor *m*, resentimiento *m*.

badge [bædʒ] *n* **-1.** [for decoration - metal, plastic] chapa *f*; [sewn-on] insignia *f*. **-2.** [for identification] distintivo *m*.

badger ['bædʒə'] ◇ *n* tejón *m*. ◇ *vt*: **to ~ sb (to do sthg)** ponerse pesado(da) con alguien (para que haga algo).

badly ['bædlɪ] (*compar* **worse**, *superl* **worst**) *adv* **-1.** [not well] mal; **to think ~ of sb** pensar mal de alguien. **-2.** [seriously] gravemente; **I'm ~ in need of help** necesito ayuda urgentemente.

badly-off *adj* **-1.** [poor] apurado(da) de dinero. **-2.** [lacking]: **to be ~ for sthg** estar OR andar mal de algo.

bad-mannered [-'mænəd] *adj* maleducado(da).

badminton ['bædmɪntən] *n* bádminton *m*.

bad-mouth *vt* inf poner verde.

badness ['bædnɪs] *n* [of behaviour] maldad *f*.

bad-tempered *adj* **-1.** [by nature] de mal genio. **-2.** [in a bad mood] malhumorado(da).

baffle ['bæfl] *vt* desconcertar.

baffling ['bæflɪŋ] *adj* desconcertante.

bag [bæg] (*pt & pp* **-ged**, *cont* **-ging**) ◇ *n* **-1.** [container, bagful] bolsa *f*; **he's nothing but a ~ of bones** está en los huesos; **in the ~** inf en el bote; **to pack one's ~s** fig hacer las maletas. **-2.** [handbag] bolso *m*, cartera *f* Amer. ◇ *vt* **-1.** [put into bags] meter en bolsas. **-2.** Br inf [reserve] pedirse, reservarse.

◆ **bags** *npl* **-1.** [under eyes] ojeras *fpl*. **-2.** [lots]: **~s of** inf un montón de.

bagel ['beɪgəl] *n* bollo de pan en forma de rosca.

baggage ['bægɪdʒ] *n* (U) equipaje *m*.

baggage car *n* Am furgón *m* de equipajes.

baggage reclaim *n* recogida *f* de equipajes.

baggage room *n* Am consigna *f*.

baggy ['bægɪ] (*compar* **-ier**, *superl* **-iest**) *adj* holgado(da).

Baghdad [bæg'dæd] *n* Bagdad.

bag lady *n* inf vagabunda *f*.

bagpipes ['bægpaɪps] *npl* gaita *f*.

bagsnatcher ['bægsnætʃə'] *n* ladrón que roba dando el tirón.

baguette [bə'get] *n* barra *f* de pan.

bah [bɑː] *excl* ¡bah!

Bahamas [bə'hɑːməz] *npl*: **the ~** (las) Bahamas.

Bahrain, Bahrein [bɑː'reɪn] *n* Bahrein.

Bahraini, **Bahreini** [bɑːˈreɪnɪ] ◇ adj bahreiní. ◇ n bahreiní m y f.

Bahrein = Bahrain.

Bahreini = Bahraini.

bail [beɪl] n (U) fianza f; **on** ~ bajo fianza.
◆ **bail out** ◇ vt sep **-1.** [pay bail for] obtener la libertad bajo fianza de. **-2.** [rescue] sacar de apuros. ◇ vi [from plane] tirarse en paracaídas.

bailiff [ˈbeɪlɪf] n alguacil m.

bait [beɪt] ◇ n lit & fig cebo m; **to rise to** OR **take the** ~ fig picarse, morder el anzuelo. ◇ vt **-1.** [put bait on] cebar. **-2.** [tease, torment] hacer sufrir, cebarse con.

baize [beɪz] n tapete m.

bake [beɪk] ◇ vt **-1.** [food] cocer al horno. **-2.** [bricks, clay] endurecer. ◇ vi [food] cocerse al horno.

baked beans [beɪkt-] npl alubias fpl cocidas en salsa de tomate.

baked potato [beɪkt-] n patata f asada OR al horno.

Bakelite® [ˈbeɪkəlaɪt] n baquelita f.

baker [ˈbeɪkər] n panadero m; ~'s (shop) panadería f.

bakery [ˈbeɪkərɪ] (pl **-ies**) n panadería f, tahona f.

baking [ˈbeɪkɪŋ] ◇ adj inf abrasador(ra). ◇ n cocción f.

baking powder n levadura f en polvo.

baking tin n molde m para cocinar al horno.

balaclava (helmet) [bæləˈklɑːvə-] n pasamontañas m inv, verdugo m.

balance [ˈbæləns] ◇ n **-1.** [equilibrium] equilibrio m; **to keep/lose one's** ~ mantener/perder el equilibrio; **it caught me off** ~ me pilló desprevenido(da). **-2.** fig [counterweight] contrapunto m. **-3.** [of evidence etc] peso m. **-4.** [scales] balanza f; **to be** OR **hang in the** ~ estar en el aire. **-5.** [of account] saldo m.
◇ vt **-1.** [keep in balance] poner en equilibrio. **-2.** [compare] sopesar. **-3.** [in accounting]: **to** ~ **the books/a budget** hacer que cuadren las cuentas/que cuadre un presupuesto.
◇ vi **-1.** [maintain equilibrium] sostenerse en equilibrio. **-2.** [in accounting] cuadrar.
◆ **on balance** adv tras pensarlo detenidamente.

balanced [ˈbælənst] adj [fair] equilibrado(da), ecuánime.

balanced diet n dieta f equilibrada.

balance of payments n balanza f de pagos.

balance of power n equilibrio m de fuerzas.

balance of trade n balanza f comercial.

balance sheet n balance m.

balancing act [ˈbælənsɪŋ-] n fig malabarismo m; **to perform a** ~ hacer equilibrios.

balcony [ˈbælkənɪ] (pl **-ies**) n **-1.** [on building - big] terraza f; [- small] balcón m. **-2.** [in theatre] anfiteatro m, galería f.

bald [bɔːld] adj **-1.** [without hair] calvo(va). **-2.** [without tread] desgastado(da). **-3.** fig [blunt] escueto(ta).

bald eagle n águila f calva (este pájaro es el símbolo de los Estados Unidos y aparece en todos los emblemas oficiales).

balding [ˈbɔːldɪŋ] adj con calva incipiente.

baldness [ˈbɔːldnɪs] n calvicie f.

bale [beɪl] n bala f, fardo m.
◆ **bale out** vi Br **-1.** [remove water] achicar agua. **-2.** [from plane] tirarse en paracaídas.

Balearic Islands [ˌbælɪˈærɪk-], **Balearics** [ˌbælɪˈærɪks] npl: **the** ~ las Baleares.

baleful [ˈbeɪlfʊl] adj maligno(na), siniestro(tra).

Bali [ˈbɑːlɪ] n Bali.

balk [bɔːk] vi: **to** ~ **(at doing sthg)** resistirse (a hacer algo); **I** ~ **at the idea** me repele la idea.

Balkan [ˈbɔːlkən] adj balcánico(ca).

Balkans [ˈbɔːlkənz], **Balkan States** npl: **the** ~ los países balcánicos.

ball [bɔːl] n **-1.** [for tennis, cricket] pelota f; [for golf, billiards] bola f; [for football] balón m; **to be on the** ~ fig estar al tanto de todo; **to play** ~ **with** fig colaborar con; **to start/keep the** ~ **rolling** fig poner/mantener las cosas en marcha. **-2.** [round shape] bola f. **-3.** [of foot] pulpejo m. **-4.** [dance] baile m; **to have a** ~ fig pasárselo bomba.
◆ **balls** v inf ◇ npl [testicles] pelotas fpl. ◇ n (U) [nonsense] gilipolleces fpl. ◇ excl [expressing disagreement] ¡una mierda!; [expressing annoyance] ¡mierda!

ballad [ˈbæləd] n balada f.

ball-and-socket joint n enartrosis f inv.

ballast [ˈbæləst] n lastre m.

ball bearing n cojinete m de bolas.

ball boy n recogepelotas m inv.

ballcock [ˈbɔːlkɒk] n válvula f de desagüe.

ballerina [ˌbæləˈriːnə] n bailarina f.

ballet [ˈbæleɪ] n ballet m.

ballet dancer n bailarín m, -ina f.

ball game n **-1.** Am [baseball match] partido m de béisbol. **-2.** inf [situation]: **it's a whole new** ~ es una historia totalmente distinta.

ball girl n recogepelotas f inv.

ballistic missile [bəˈlɪstɪk-] n misil m balístico.

ballistics [bə'lɪstɪks] *n* (*U*) balística *f*.

ballocks ['bɒləks] = **bollocks**.

balloon [bə'luːn] ◇ *n* -1. [toy] globo *m*. -2. [hot-air balloon] globo *m* (aerostático). -3. [in cartoon] bocadillo *m*. ◇ *vi* inflarse.

ballooning [bə'luːnɪŋ] *n* aerostación *f*.

ballot ['bælət] ◇ *n* -1. [voting paper] voto *m*. -2. [voting process] votación *f*. ◇ *vt*: **to ~ the members on an issue** someter un asunto a votación entre los miembros. ◇ *vi*: **to ~ for sthg** elegir algo por votación.

ballot box *n* -1. [container] urna *f*. -2. [voting process] urnas *fpl*.

ballot paper *n* voto *m*, papeleta *f*.

ball park *n Am* estadio *m* de béisbol.

ball-park figure *n inf* cifra *f* aproximada.

ballpoint (pen) ['bɔːlpɔɪnt-] *n* bolígrafo *m*.

ballroom ['bɔːlrum] *n* salón *m* de baile.

ballroom dancing *n* (*U*) baile *m* de salón.

balls-up *Br*, **ball-up** *Am n v inf* cagada *f*.

balm [bɑːm] *n* bálsamo *m*.

balmy ['bɑːmɪ] (*compar* **-ier**, *superl* **-iest**) *adj* apacible.

baloney [bə'ləʊnɪ] *n* (*U*) *inf* bobadas *fpl*.

balsa ['bɒlsə], **balsawood** ['bɒlsəwud] *n* balsa *f*.

balsam ['bɔːlsəm] *n* balsamero *m*.

balsamic vinegar [bɔːl'sæmɪk-] *n* vinagre *m* (balsámico) de Módena.

balsawood = **balsa**.

balti ['bɔːltɪ] *n* [pan] *cacerola utilizada en la cocina india;* [food] *plato sazonado con especias y preparado en un 'balti'.*

Baltic ['bɔːltɪk] ◇ *adj* báltico(ca). ◇ *n*: **the ~ (Sea)** el (mar) Báltico.

Baltic Republic *n*: **the ~s** las repúblicas bálticas.

Baltic State *n*: **the ~s** los países bálticos.

balustrade [ˌbæləs'treɪd] *n* balaustrada *f*.

bamboo [bæm'buː] *n* bambú *m*.

bamboozle [bæm'buːzl] *vt inf* camelar.

ban [bæn] (*pt* & *pp* **-ned**, *cont* **-ning**) ◇ *n*: **~ (on)** prohibición *f* (de). ◇ *vt*: **to ~ sb (from doing sthg)** prohibir a alguien (hacer algo).

banal [bə'nɑːl] *adj pej* banal, ordinario(ria).

banana [bə'nɑːnə] *n* plátano *m*, banana *f Amer*.

banana republic *n* república *f* bananera.

banana split *n postre de plátano con helado, nata etc.*

band [bænd] *n* -1. [musical group - pop] grupo *m*; [- jazz, military] banda *f*. -2. [of thieves etc] banda *f*. -3. [strip] cinta *f*. -4. [stripe, range] franja *f*.

◆ **band together** *vi* juntarse, agruparse.

bandage ['bændɪdʒ] ◇ *n* venda *f*. ◇ *vt* vendar.

Band-Aid® *n* ≃ tirita® *f*.

bandan(n)a [bæn'dænə] *n* pañuelo *m* (*para la cabeza*).

b and b, B and B *n abbr of* **bed and breakfast**.

bandeau ['bændəʊ] (*pl* **-x** [-z]) *n* cinta *f* elástica.

bandit ['bændɪt] *n* bandido *m*, -da *f*, bandolero *m*, -ra *f*.

bandmaster ['bænd,mɑːstər] *n* director *m* (de banda musical).

band saw *n* sierra *f* de cinta.

bandsman ['bændzmən] (*pl* **-men** [-mən]) *n* músico *m* (de banda).

bandstand ['bændstænd] *n* quiosco *m* de música.

bandwagon ['bændwægən] *n*: **to jump on the ~** subirse OR apuntarse al carro.

bandy ['bændɪ] (*compar* **-ier**, *superl* **-iest**, *pt* & *pp* **-ied**) *adj* de piernas arqueadas.

◆ **bandy about**, **bandy around** *vt sep* sacar a relucir.

bandy-legged [-,legd] *adj* de piernas arqueadas.

bane [beɪn] *n*: **to be the ~ of sb's life** ser la cruz de alguien.

bang [bæŋ] ◇ *n* -1. [blow] golpe *m*. -2. [loud noise] estampido *m*, estruendo *m*; **to go with a ~** *inf* ser la bomba. ◇ *vt* -1. [hit - drum, desk] golpear; [- knee, head] golpearse. -2. [slam] cerrar de golpe. ◇ *vi* golpear, dar golpes. ◇ *adv* -1. [exactly]: **~ in the middle of** justo en mitad de; **~ on** muy acertado(da). -2. *inf* [away]: **~ goes** OR **go ... adiós a ....** ◇ *excl* ¡pum!

◆ **bangs** *npl Am* flequillo *m*.

◆ **bang down** *vt sep* golpear con.

banger ['bæŋər] *n Br* -1. *inf* [sausage] salchicha *f*. -2. *inf* [old car] carraca *f*, cacharro *m*. -3. [firework] petardo *m*.

Bangkok [bæŋ'kok] *n* Bangkok.

Bangladesh [ˌbæŋglə'deʃ] *n* Bangladesh.

Bangladeshi [ˌbæŋglə'deʃɪ] ◇ *adj* bangladesí. ◇ *n* bangladesí *m* y *f*.

bangle ['bæŋgl] *n* pulsera *f*, brazalete *m*.

banish ['bænɪʃ] *vt lit* & *fig* desterrar.

banister ['bænɪstər] *n*, **banisters** ['bænɪstəz] *npl* barandilla *f*, pasamanos *m inv*.

banjo ['bændʒəʊ] (*pl* **-s** OR **-es**) *n* banjo *m*.

bank [bæŋk] ◇ *n* -1. [gen & FIN] banco *m*. -2. [by river, lake] ribera *f*, orilla *f*. -3. [slope] loma *f*. -4. [of clouds etc] masa *f*. ◇ *vt* FIN ingresar en el banco. ◇ *vi* -1. FIN: **to ~ with** tener una cuenta en. -2. [plane] ladearse.

◆ **bank on** *vt fus* contar con.

bank account *n* cuenta *f* bancaria.

bank balance *n* saldo *m*.

bankbook ['bæŋkbʊk] *n* libreta *f* OR cartilla *f* (del banco).

bank card = banker's card.

bank charges *npl* comisiones *fpl* bancarias.

bank draft *n* giro *m* bancario.

banker ['bæŋkə'] *n* banquero *m*, -ra *f*.

banker's card *n* Br tarjeta *f* de identificación bancaria.

banker's order *n* Br domiciliación *f* de pago.

bank holiday *n* Br día *m* festivo, fiesta *f* nacional.

banking ['bæŋkɪŋ] *n* banca *f*.

banking house *n* entidad *f* bancaria.

bank loan *n* préstamo *m* OR crédito *m* bancario.

bank manager *n* director *m*, -ra *f* de banco.

bank note *n* billete *m* de banco.

bank rate *n* tipo *m* de interés bancario.

bankrupt ['bæŋkrʌpt] ◇ *adj* [financially] quebrado(da), en quiebra; **to go ~** quebrar. ◇ *n* quebrado *m*, -da *f*, insolvente *m* y *f*. ◇ *vt* llevar a la quiebra.

bankruptcy ['bæŋkrəptsɪ] (*pl* -ies) *n* quiebra *f*, bancarrota *f*; *fig* [of ideas] agotamiento *m*, falta *f* total.

bank statement *n* extracto *m* de cuenta.

banner ['bænə'] *n* pancarta *f*.

bannister ['bænɪstə'], **bannisters** ['bænɪstəz] = banister.

banns [bænz] *npl*: **to publish the ~** correr las amonestaciones.

banquet ['bæŋkwɪt] *n* banquete *m*.

bantam ['bæntəm] *n* *tipo de gallina pequeña*.

bantamweight ['bæntəmweɪt] *n* peso *m* gallo.

banter ['bæntə'] ◇ *n* (*U*) bromas *fpl*. ◇ *vi* bromear.

BAOR (*abbr of* **British Army of the Rhine**) *n fuerzas armadas británicas en Alemania*.

bap [bæp] *n* Br bollo *m* de pan, panecillo *m*.

baptism ['bæptɪzm] *n* bautismo *m*; **~ of fire** bautismo de fuego.

Baptist ['bæptɪst] *n* bautista *m* y *f*.

baptize, -ise [*Br* bæp'taɪz, *Am* 'bæptaɪz] *vt* bautizar.

bar [baː] (*pt* & *pp* **-red**, *cont* **-ring**) ◇ *n* **-1.** [of soap] pastilla *f*; [of chocolate] tableta *f*; [of gold] lingote *m*; [of wood] tabla *f*; [of metal] barra *f*; **to be behind ~s** estar entre rejas. **-2.** *fig* [obstacle] barrera *f*; [ban] prohibición *f*. **-3.** [drinking place] bar *m*. **-4.** [counter] barra *f*. **-5.** MUS compás *m*.
◇ *vt* **-1.** [close with a bar] atrancar. **-2.** [block]: **to ~ sb's way** impedir el paso a alguien. **-3.** [ban]: **to ~ sb (from doing sthg)** prohibir a alguien (hacer algo); **to ~ sb from somewhere** prohibir a alguien la entrada en un sitio.
◇ *prep* [except] menos, salvo; **~ none** sin excepción.

◆ **Bar** *n* JUR: **the Bar** *Br conjunto de los abogados que ejercen en tribunales superiores*; *Am* la abogacía.

Barbados [baː'beɪdɒs] *n* Barbados.

barbarian [baː'beərɪən] *n lit* & *fig* bárbaro *m*, -ra *f*.

barbaric [baː'bærɪk] *adj* bárbaro(ra).

barbarous ['baːbərəs] *adj* bárbaro(ra).

barbecue ['baːbɪkjuː] ◇ *n* barbacoa *f*. ◇ *vt* asar a la parrilla.

barbed [baːbd] *adj* **-1.** [pointed, spiked] con púa OR púas. **-2.** [unkind] envenenado(da), afilado(da).

barbed wire *n* alambre *m* de espino.

barber ['baːbə'] *n* barbero *m*; **~'s** barbería *f*.

barbiturate [baː'bɪtjʊrət] *n* barbitúrico *m*.

Barcelona [ˌbaːsə'ləʊnə] *n* Barcelona.

bar chart, bar graph *Am n* gráfico *m* de barras.

bar code *n* código *m* de barras.

bare [beə'] ◇ *adj* **-1.** [without covering - legs, trees, hills] desnudo(da); [- feet] descalzo(za). **-2.** [absolute, minimum] esencial; **the ~ essentials** lo mínimo indispensable. **-3.** [empty] vacío(a). **-4.** [mere]: **a ~ 10%** tan sólo el 10%. ◇ *vt* descubrir; **to ~ one's teeth** enseñar los dientes.

bareback ['beəbæk] *adj* & *adv* a pelo.

barefaced ['beəfeɪst] *adj* descarado(da).

barefoot(ed) [ˌbeə'fʊt(ɪd)] *adj* & *adv* descalzo(za).

bareheaded [ˌbeə'hedɪd] *adj* & *adv* descubierto(ta), sin sombrero.

barelegged [ˌbeə'legd] *adj* & *adv* con las piernas desnudas.

barely ['beəlɪ] *adv* [scarcely] apenas.

Barents Sea ['bærənts-] *n*: **the ~** el mar de Barents.

bargain ['baːgɪn] ◇ *n* **-1.** [agreement] trato *m*, acuerdo *m*; **into the ~** por añadidura, además. **-2.** [good buy] ganga *f*, pichincha *f* *Amer*. ◇ *vi*: **to ~ (with sb for sthg)** negociar (con alguien para obtener algo).

◆ **bargain for, bargain on** *vt fus* contar con.

bargaining ['baːgɪnɪŋ] *n* (*U*) negociación *f*.

argaining power *n* poder *m* negociador.

arge [ba:dʒ] ◇ *n* gabarra *f*, barcaza *f*. ◇ *vi* *if* abrirse paso; **to ~ into** [person] chocarse on; [room] irrumpir en.

◆ **barge in** *vi inf*: **to ~ in (on)** [conversation xc] entrometerse (en).

arge pole *n inf*: **I wouldn't touch it with ~** no lo quiero ni regalado.

ar graph *Am* = bar chart.

aritone ['bærɪtəʊn] *n* barítono *m*.

arium meal ['beərɪəm-] *n Br* papilla *f* (*to-ada antes de radiografía*).

ark [ba:k] ◇ *n* **-1.** [of dog] ladrido *m*; **his - is worse than his bite** *inf* ≈ perro ladra-lor, poco mordedor. **-2.** [on tree] corteza *f*. ◇ *vt* gritar. ◇ *vi*: **to ~ (at)** ladrar (a).

arking ['ba:kɪŋ] *n* (*U*) ladridos *mpl*.

arley ['ba:lɪ] *n* cebada *f*.

arley sugar *n Br* azúcar *m o f* cande.

arley water *n Br* hordiate *m*.

armaid ['ba:meɪd] *n* camarera *f*.

arman ['ba:mən] (*pl* **-men** [-mən]) *n* ca-narero *m*, barman *m*.

army ['ba:mɪ] (*compar* **-ier**, *superl* **-iest**) *adj* *Br inf* chalado(da), chiflado(da).

arn [ba:n] *n* granero *m*.

arnacle ['ba:nəkl] *n* percebe *m*.

arn dance *n* baile *m* campestre.

arn owl *n* lechuza *f*.

arometer [bə'rɒmɪtə'] *n* barómetro *m*; *fig* of public opinion etc] piedra *f* de toque.

aron ['bærən] *n* barón *m*; **press/oil ~** *fig* nagnate *m* de la prensa/del petróleo.

aroness ['bærənɪs] *n* baronesa *f*.

aronet ['bærənɪt] *n* baronet *m*.

aroque [bə'rɒk] *adj* barroco(ca).

arrack ['bærək] *vt Br* abroncar, abuchear.

◆ **barracks** *npl* cuartel *m*.

barracking ['bærəkɪŋ] *n Br* bronca *f*, abu-:heo *m*.

barracuda [ˌbærə'ku:də] *n* barracuda *f*.

barrage ['bærɑ:ʒ] *n* **-1.** [of firing] bombar-leo *m*, fuego *m* intenso de artillería. **-2.** [of questions] aluvión *m*, alud *m*. **-3.** *Br* [dam] presa *f*, dique *m*.

barred [ba:d] *adj* enrejado(da).

barrel ['bærəl] *n* **-1.** [for beer, wine, oil] barril *m*. **-2.** [of gun] cañón *m*.

barrel organ *n* organillo *m*.

barren ['bærən] *adj* estéril.

barrette [bə'ret] *n Am* pasador *m*.

barricade [ˌbærɪ'keɪd] ◇ *n* barricada *f*. ◇ *vt* levantar barricadas en; **to ~ o.s. in** atrin-cherarse OR parapetarse en.

barrier ['bærɪə'] *n lit* & *fig* barrera *f*.

barrier cream *n Br* crema *f* protectora.

barring ['ba:rɪŋ] *prep* salvo.

barrister ['bærɪstə'] *n Br* abogado *m*, -da *f* (*de tribunales superiores*).

barroom ['ba:rʊm] *n Am* bar *m*.

barrow ['bærəʊ] *n* carrito *m*.

bar stool *n* taburete *m* (*de bar*).

Bart. *abbr of* baronet.

bartender ['ba:tendə'] *n* camarero *m*, -ra *f*.

barter ['ba:tə'] ◇ *n* trueque *m*. ◇ *vt*: **to ~ (sthg for sthg)** trocar (algo por algo). ◇ *vi* trocar.

base [beɪs] ◇ *n* base *f*. ◇ *vt* **-1.** [place, estab-lish] emplazar; **he's ~d in Paris** trabaja en París. **-2.** [use as starting point]: **to ~ sthg on** OR **upon** basar algo en. ◇ *adj pej* bajo(ja), vil.

baseball ['beɪsbɔ:l] *n* béisbol *m*.

baseball cap *n* gorra *f* de béisbol.

base camp *n* campamento *m* base.

Basel, Basle ['ba:zəl] *n* Basilea.

baseless ['beɪslɪs] *adj* infundado(da).

baseline ['beɪslaɪn] *n* línea *f* de fondo.

basement ['beɪsmənt] *n* sótano *m*.

base metal *n dated* metal *m* no precioso.

base rate *n* tipo *m* de interés base.

bases ['beɪsi:z] *pl* → basis.

bash [bæʃ] *inf* ◇ *n* **-1.** [painful blow] porra-zo *m*. **-2.** [attempt]: **to have a ~ at sthg** in-tentar algo. **-3.** [party] juerga *f*. ◇ *vt* **-1.** [hit - person, thing] darle un porrazo a; [- one's head, knee] darse un porrazo en. **-2.** [criti-cize] arremeter contra.

bashful ['bæʃfʊl] *adj* [person] vergonzo-so(sa); [smile] tímido(da).

basic ['beɪsɪk] *adj* básico(ca).

◆ **basics** *npl* **-1.** [rudiments] principios *mpl* básicos. **-2.** [essentials] lo imprescindible.

BASIC ['beɪsɪk] (*abbr of* **Beginner's All-purpose Symbolic Instruction Code**) *n* BA-SIC *m*.

basically ['beɪsɪklɪ] *adv* **-1.** [essentially] esen-cialmente. **-2.** [really] en resumen.

basic rate *n Br* tipo *m* base.

basic wage *n* sueldo *m* base.

basil ['bæzl] *n* albahaca *f*.

basin ['beɪsn] *n* **-1.** *Br* [bowl] balde *m*, ba-rreño *m*. **-2.** [wash basin] lavabo *m*. **-3.** GEOGR cuenca *f*.

basis ['beɪsɪs] (*pl* **bases**) *n* base *f*; **on the ~ of** de acuerdo con, a partir de; **on a weekly/monthly ~** de forma semanal/mensual.

bask [ba:sk] *vi* **-1.** [in sun]: **to ~ in the sun** tostarse al sol. **-2.** *fig*: **to ~ in** [sb's approval, praise] gozar de.

basket ['bɑːskɪt] *n* cesto *m*, cesta *f*.
basketball ['bɑːskɪtbɔːl] ◇ *n* baloncesto *m*.
◇ *comp* de baloncesto.
basketwork ['bɑːskɪtwɜːk] *n* cestería *f*.
basking shark ['bɑːskɪŋ-] *n* tiburón *m* peregrino.
Basle = Basel.
Basque [bɑːsk] ◇ *adj* vasco(ca). ◇ *n* -1. [person] vasco *m*, -ca *f*. -2. [language] vascuence *m*, euskera *m*.
Basque Country [bɑːsk-] *n*: **the ~** el País Vasco, Euskadi.
bass¹ [beɪs] ◇ *adj* bajo(ja). ◇ *n* -1. [singer, bass guitar] bajo *m*. -2. [double bass] contrabajo *m*.
bass² [bæs] (*pl inv* OR **-es**) *n* [fish] lubina *f*, róbalo *m*.
bass clef [beɪs-] *n* clave *f* de fa.
bass drum [beɪs-] *n* bombo *m*.
basset (hound) ['bæsɪt-] *n* basset *m*.
bass guitar [beɪs-] *n* bajo *m*.
bassoon [bə'suːn] *n* fagot *m*.
bastard ['bɑːstəd] *n* -1. [illegitimate child] bastardo *m*, -da *f*. -2. *v inf pej* cabrón *m*, -ona *f*, concha *f* de su madre *Amer*.
baste [beɪst] *vt* untar, pringar.
bastion ['bæstɪən] *n* bastión *m*.
BASW (*abbr of* **British Association of Social Workers**) *n* sindicato británico de trabajadores sociales.
bat [bæt] (*pt* & *pp* **-ted**, *cont* **-ting**) ◇ *n* -1. [animal] murciélago *m*. -2. [for cricket, baseball] bate *m*. -3. [for table-tennis] pala *f*, paleta *f*. -4. *phr*: **to do sthg off one's own ~** hacer algo uno por su cuenta. ◇ *vt* & *vi* batear.
batch [bætʃ] *n* -1. [of letters etc] remesa *f*. -2. [of work] montón *m*, serie *f*. -3. [of products] lote *m*, partida *f*. -4. [of people] grupo *m*, tanda *f*.
batch file *n* COMPUT fichero *m* por lotes.
batch processing *n* COMPUT proceso *m* por lotes.
bated ['beɪtɪd] *adj*: **with ~ breath** con el aliento contenido.
bath [bɑːθ] ◇ *n* -1. [bathtub] bañera *f*, bañadera *f Amer*. -2. [act of washing] baño *m*, bañada *f Amer*; **to have** OR **take a ~** darse un baño, bañarse. ◇ *vt* bañar.
◆ **baths** *npl Br* [public swimming pool] piscina *f* municipal.
bath chair *n* silla *f* de ruedas.
bath cube *n cubito con esencias aromáticas para el baño.*
bathe [beɪð] ◇ *vt* -1. [wound] lavar. -2. [suf-

fuse]: **to be ~d in** OR **with** estar bañado(da de. ◇ *vi* bañarse.
bather ['beɪðər] *n* bañista *m y f*.
bathing ['beɪðɪŋ] *n* (*U*) baños *mpl*.
bathing cap *n* gorro *m* de baño.
bathing costume, bathing suit *n* traje *m* de baño, bañador *m*, malla *f Amer*.
bathing trunks *npl* bañador *m*.
bath mat *n* alfombrilla *f* de baño.
bath oil *n* aceite *m* de baño.
bathrobe ['bɑːθrəʊb] *n* -1. [made of towelling] albornoz *m*. -2. [dressing gown] batír *m*, bata *f*.
bathroom ['bɑːθrʊm] *n* -1. *Br* [room with bath] (cuarto *m* de) baño *m*. -2. *Am* [toilet] servicio *m*.
bath salts *npl* sales *fpl* de baño.
bath towel *n* toalla *f* de baño.
bathtub ['bɑːθtʌb] *n* bañera *f*.
batik [bə'tiːk] *n método para teñir tejidos con cera.*
baton ['bætən] *n* -1. [of conductor] batuta *f*. -2. [in relay race] testigo *m*. -3. *Br* [of policeman] porra *f*.
baton charge *n Br* carga *f* policial.
batsman ['bætsmən] (*pl* **-men** [-mən]) *n* bateador *m*.
battalion [bə'tæljən] *n* batallón *m*.
batten ['bætn] *n* listón *m* (de madera).
◆ **batten down** *vt fus* sujetar con listones.
batter ['bætər] ◇ *n* pasta *f* para rebozar. ◇ *vt* -1. [child, woman] pegar. -2. [door, ship] sacudir, golpear.
◆ **batter down** *vt sep* echar abajo.
battered ['bætəd] *adj* -1. [child, woman] maltratado(da). -2. [car, hat] abollado(da).
battering ['bætərɪŋ] *n* paliza *f*.
battering ram *n* ariete *m*.
battery ['bætərɪ] (*pl* **-ies**) *n* -1. [of radio] pila *f*; [of car, guns] batería *f*. -2. [array, set] serie *f*, conjunto *m*.
battery charger *n* aparato *m* para recargar pilas.
battery hen *n* gallina *f* de granja intensiva.
battle ['bætl] ◇ *n* -1. [in war] batalla *f*. -2. [struggle]: **~ (for/against/with)** lucha *f* (por/contra/con); **~ of wits** batalla *f* dialéctica; **self-confidence is half the ~** confiar en uno mismo es llevar medio camino andado; **to be fighting a losing ~** luchar por una causa perdida. ◇ *vi*: **to ~ (for/against/with)** luchar (por/contra/con).
battledress ['bætldres] *n Br* uniforme *m*.
battlefield ['bætlfiːld], **battleground** ['bætlgraʊnd] *n lit* & *fig* campo *m* de batalla.
battlements ['bætlmənts] *npl* almenas *fpl*.

battleship ['bætlʃɪp] n acorazado m.

bauble ['bɔːbl] n baratija f.

baud [bɔːd] n baudio m.

baud rate n intensidad f de baudios.

baulk [bɔːk] = **balk**.

Bavaria [bə'veərɪə] n Baviera.

Bavarian [bə'veərɪən] ◇ adj bávaro(ra). ◇ n bávaro m, -ra f.

bawdy ['bɔːdɪ] (compar -ier, superl -iest) adj verde, picante.

bawl [bɔːl] ◇ vt vociferar. ◇ vi -1. [shout] vociferar. -2. [cry] berrear.

bay [beɪ] ◇ n -1. [of coast] bahía f. -2. [for loading] zona f de carga y descarga. -3. [for parking] plaza f, estacionamiento m. -4. [horse] caballo m bayo. -5. phr: to keep sthg/sb at ~ mantener algo/a alguien a raya. ◇ vi aullar.

bay leaf n (hoja f de) laurel m.

bayonet ['beɪənɪt] n bayoneta f.

bay tree n laurel m.

bay window n ventana f salediza.

bazaar [bə'zɑːr] n -1. [market] bazar m, zoco m. -2. Br [charity sale] mercadillo m benéfico.

bazooka [bə'zuːkə] n bazuca m, lanzagranadas m inv.

BB (abbr of **Boys' Brigade**) n asociación juvenil británica para chicos.

B & B abbr of **bed and breakfast**.

BBB (abbr of **Better Business Bureau**) n organismo para la defensa de la ética profesional en el sector terciario.

BBC (abbr of **British Broadcasting Corporation**) n BBC f, compañía estatal británica de radiotelevisión.

BC -1. (abbr of **before Christ**) a.C. -2. abbr of **British Columbia**.

BCG (abbr of **Bacillus Calmette-Guérin**) n vacuna de la tuberculosis.

BD (abbr of **Bachelor of Divinity**) n (titular de una) licenciatura de teología.

BDS (abbr of **Bachelor of Dental Science**) n (titular de una) licenciatura de odontología.

be [biː] (pt **was** OR **were**, pp **been**) ◇ aux vb -1. (in combination with present participle: to form cont tense) estar; **what is he doing?** ¿qué hace OR está haciendo?; **it's snowing** está nevando; **I'm leaving tomorrow** me voy mañana; **they've been promising it for years** han estado prometiéndolo durante años. -2. (in combination with pp: to form passive) ser; **to ~ loved** ser amado; **there was no one to ~ seen** no se veía a nadie; **ten people were killed** murieron diez personas. -3. (in question tags): **you're not going now, are you?** no irás a marcharte ya ¿no?; **the**

meal was delicious, wasn't it? la comida fue deliciosa ¿verdad? -4. (followed by "to" + infin): **I'm to be promoted** me van a ascender; **you're not to tell anyone** no debes decírselo a nadie.
◇ copulative vb -1. (with adj, n) [indicating innate quality, permanent condition] ser; [indicating state, temporary condition] estar; **snow is white** la nieve es blanca; **she's intelligent/tall** es inteligente/alta; **to ~ a doctor/plumber** ser médico/fontanero; **I'm Scottish** soy escocés; **~ quiet!** ¡cállate!; **1 and 1 are 2** 1 y 1 son 2; **your hands are cold** tus manos están frías; **I'm tired/angry** estoy cansado/enfadado; **I'm hot** tengo calor; **he's in a difficult position** está en una situación difícil. -2. [referring to health] estar; **she's ill/better** está enferma/mejor; **how are you?** ¿cómo estás?, ¿qué tal? -3. [referring to age]: **how old are you?** ¿qué edad OR cuántos años tienes?; **I'm 20 (years old)** tengo 20 años. -4. [cost] ser, costar; **how much is it?** ¿cuánto es?; **how much was it?** ¿cuánto costó?; **that will ~ £10, please** son 10 libras; **apples are only 20p a kilo today** hoy las manzanas están a tan sólo 20 peniques el kilo.
◇ vi -1. [exist] ser, existir; **the worst prime minister that ever was** el peor primer ministro que jamás existió; **~ that as it may** aunque así sea; **there is/are** hay; **is there life on Mars?** ¿hay vida en Marte? -2. [referring to place] estar; **Valencia is in Spain** Valencia está en España; **he will ~ here tomorrow** estará aquí mañana. -3. [referring to movement] estar; **where have you been?** ¿dónde has estado?
◇ impersonal vb -1. [referring to time, dates] ser; **it's two o'clock** son las dos; **it's the 17th of February** estamos a 17 de febrero. -2. [referring to distance]: **it's 3 km to the next town** hay 3 kms hasta el próximo pueblo. -3. [referring to the weather]: **it's hot/cold/windy** hace calor/frío/viento. -4. [for emphasis] ser; **it's me** soy yo; **it's the milkman** es el lechero.

B/E abbr of **bill of exchange**.

beach [biːtʃ] ◇ n playa f. ◇ vt varar.

beach ball n pelota f de playa.

beach buggy n todoterreno m para playa.

beachcomber ['biːtʃ,kəʊmər] n [person] raquero m, -ra f.

beachhead ['biːtʃhed] n MIL cabeza f de playa.

beachwear ['biːtʃweər] n ropa f de playa.

beacon ['biːkən] n -1. [warning fire] almenara f. -2. [lighthouse] faro m, fanal m. -3. [radio beacon] radiofaro m.

bead [biːd] *n* **-1.** [of wood, glass] cuenta *f*, abalorio *m*. **-2.** [of sweat] gota *f*.

beaded ['biːdɪd] *adj* adornado(da) con abalorios.

beading ['biːdɪŋ] *n* (*U*) [on furniture] moldura *f*; [on walls] astrágalo *m*.

beady ['biːdɪ] (*compar* -ier, *superl* -iest) *adj*: ~ **eyes** ojos pequeños y brillantes.

beagle ['biːgl] *n* sabueso *m*.

beak [biːk] *n* pico *m*.

beaker ['biːkə'] *n* taza *f* (*sin asa*).

be-all *n*: **the** ~ **and end-all** la razón de ser.

beam [biːm] ◇ *n* **-1.** [of wood, concrete] viga *f*. **-2.** [of light] rayo *m*. ◇ *vt* transmitir. ◇ *vi* **-1.** [smile] sonreír resplandeciente. **-2.** [shine] resplandecer, brillar.

beaming ['biːmɪŋ] *adj* radiante.

bean [biːn] *n* CULIN [haricot] judía *f*, habichuela *f*; [of coffee] grano *m*; **to be full of** ~**s** *inf* estar lleno de energía; **to spill the** ~**s** *inf* descubrir el pastel.

beanbag ['biːnbæg] *n* cojín grande relleno de polietileno.

beanshoot ['biːnʃuːt], **beansprout** ['biːnspraut] *n* brote *m* de soja.

bear [beə'] (*pt* bore, *pp* borne) ◇ *n* **-1.** [animal] oso *m*, -sa *f*. **-2.** ST EX bajista *m y f*. ◇ *vt* **-1.** [carry] llevar. **-2.** [support] soportar. **-3.** [responsibility] cargar con. **-4.** [marks, signs] llevar. **-5.** [endure] aguantar. **-6.** [fruit, crop] dar. **-7.** [child] dar a luz. **-8.** [feeling] guardar, albergar. **-9.** FIN [interest] devengar. ◇ *vi*: **to** ~ **left** torcer OR doblar a la izquierda; **to bring pressure/influence to** ~ **on** ejercer presión/influencia sobre.

◆ **bear down** *vi*: **to** ~ **down on** echarse encima de.

◆ **bear out** *vt sep* corroborar.

◆ **bear up** *vi* resistir.

◆ **bear with** *vt fus* tener paciencia con.

bearable ['beərəbl] *adj* soportable.

beard [bɪəd] *n* barba *f*.

bearded ['bɪədɪd] *adj* con barba.

bearer ['beərə'] *n* **-1.** [of stretcher, news, cheque] portador *m*, -ra *f*. **-2.** [of passport] titular *m y f*. **-3.** [of name, title] poseedor *m*, -ra *f*.

bear hug *n inf* fuerte abrazo *m*.

bearing ['beərɪŋ] *n* **-1.** [connection]: ~ **(on)** relación *f* (con). **-2.** [deportment] porte *m*. **-3.** [for shaft] cojinete *m*. **-4.** [on compass] rumbo *m*, orientación *f*; **to get one's** ~**s** orientarse; **to lose one's** ~**s** desorientarse.

bear market *n* ST EX mercado *m* a la baja.

bearskin ['beəskɪn] *n* **-1.** [fur] piel *f* de oso. **-2.** [hat] birretina *f*.

beast [biːst] *n lit* & *fig* bestia *f*.

beastly ['biːstlɪ] (*compar* -ier, *superl* -iest) *adj dated* atroz.

beat [biːt] (*pt* beat, *pp* beaten) ◇ *n* **-1.** [of drum] golpe *m*. **-2.** [of heart, pulse] latido *m*. **-3.** MUS [rhythm] ritmo *m*; [individual unit of time] golpe *m* (*de compás*). **-4.** [of wings] batido *m*. **-5.** [of policeman] ronda *f*. ◇ *adj inf* hecho(cha) polvo.

◇ *vt* **-1.** [hit - person] pegar; [- thing] golpear. **-2.** [wings, eggs, butter] batir. **-3.** [time] marcar. **-4.** [defeat] ganar; **it** ~**s me** *inf* no me lo explico. **-5.** [reach ahead of]: **to** ~ **sb (to sthg)** adelantarse a alguien (en algo). **-6.** [be better than] ser mucho mejor que. **-7.** *phr*: ~ **it!** *inf* ¡largo!.

◇ *vi* **-1.** [rain] golpear. **-2.** [heart, pulse] latir.

◆ **beat down** ◇ *vt sep* [seller] regatear con. ◇ *vi* **-1.** [sun] pegar fuerte. **-2.** [rain] descargar.

◆ **beat off** *vt sep* repeler.

◆ **beat up** *vt sep inf* apalear, dar una paliza a.

beaten ['biːtn] *adj* **-1.** [metal] batido(da). **-2.** [path] trillado(da).

beater ['biːtə'] *n* **-1.** [for eggs] batidora *f*. **-2.** [for carpet] sacudidor *m*. **-3.** [of wife, child] persona *f* que pega.

beating ['biːtɪŋ] *n* **-1.** [hitting] paliza *f*, golpiza *f* Amer. **-2.** [defeat] derrota *f*; **to take some** ~ *inf* ser difícil de superar.

beating up (*pl* beatings up) *n inf* paliza *f*.

beatnik ['biːtnɪk] *n* beatnik *m y f*.

beat-up *adj inf* destartalado(da).

beautician [bjuː'tɪʃn] *n* esteticista *m y f*, esteticienne *f*.

beautiful ['bjuːtɪful] *adj* **-1.** [person] guapo(pa). **-2.** [thing, animal] precioso(sa). **-3.** *inf* [very good - shot, weather] espléndido(da).

beautifully ['bjuːtəflɪ] *adv* **-1.** [attractively] bellamente. **-2.** *inf* [very well] espléndidamente.

beauty ['bjuːtɪ] (*pl* -ies) ◇ *n* belleza *f*. ◇ *comp* de belleza.

beauty contest *n* concurso *m* de belleza.

beauty parlour *n* salón *f* de belleza.

beauty queen *n* miss *f*.

beauty salon = beauty parlour.

beauty spot *n* **-1.** [picturesque place] bello paraje *m*. **-2.** [on skin] lunar *m*.

beaver ['biːvə'] *n* castor *m*.

◆ **beaver away** *vi*: **to** ~ **away (at)** trabajar con afán (en).

becalmed [bɪ'kɑːmd] *adj* parado(da) por falta de viento.

became [bɪ'keɪm] *pt* → become.

because [bɪ'kɒz] *conj* porque.

◆ **because of** *prep* por, a causa de.

béchamel sauce [ˌbeɪʃə'mel-] *n* besamel *f*.

beck [bek] *n*: **to be at sb's ~ and call** estar siempre a disposición de alguien.

beckon ['bekən] ◇ *vt* **-1.** [signal to] llamar (con un gesto). **-2.** *fig* [draw, attract] atraer, llamar. ◇ *vi* [signal]: **to ~ to sb** llamar (con un gesto) a alguien.

become [bɪ'kʌm] (*pt* **became**, *pp* **become**) *vi* hacerse; **to ~ happy** ponerse contento; **to ~ angry** enfadarse; **he became Prime Minister in 1991** en 1991 se convirtió en primer ministro; **what has ~ of ...?** ¿qué ha sido de ...?

becoming [bɪ'kʌmɪŋ] *adj* **-1.** [attractive] favorecedor(ra). **-2.** [appropriate] apropiado(da).

BECTU ['bektuː] (*abbr of* **Broadcasting, Entertainment, Cinematograph and Theatre Union**) *n* sindicato británico de técnicos que trabajan en el campo audiovisual.

bed [bed] (*pt* & *pp* **-ded**, *cont* **-ding**) *n* **-1.** [to sleep on] cama *f*; **to go to ~** irse a la cama; **to make the ~** hacer la cama; **to go to ~ with** *euphemism* acostarse con. **-2.** [flowerbed] macizo *m*; **a ~ of roses** *fig* un lecho de rosas. **-3.** [of sea] fondo *m*; [of river] lecho *m*, cauce *m*.

◆ **bed down** *vi* acostarse.

bed and breakfast *n* [service] cama *f* y desayuno; [hotel] pensión *f*.

bed-bath *n* lavado que se hace a alguien que está en cama.

bedbug ['bedbʌg] *n* chinche *m* o *f*.

bedclothes ['bedkləʊðz] *npl* ropa *f* de cama.

bedcover ['bed,kʌvər] *n* colcha *f*.

bedding ['bedɪŋ] *n* ropa *f* de cama.

bedding plant *n* planta *f* de jardinería.

bedeck [bɪ'dek] *vt*: **to ~ sthg with** engalanar algo con.

bedevil [bɪ'devl] (*Br pt* & *pp* **-led**, *cont* **-ling**, *Am pt* & *pp* **-ed**, *cont* **-ing**) *vt*: **to be bedevilled with** estar plagado(da) de.

bedfellow ['bed,feləʊ] *n* *fig* compañero *m*, -ra *f* de cama.

bedlam ['bedləm] *n* jaleo *m*, alboroto *m*.

bed linen *n* ropa *f* de cama.

Bedouin, Beduin ['bedʊɪn] ◇ *adj* beduino(na). ◇ *n* beduino *m*, -na *f*.

bedpan ['bedpæn] *n* orinal *m*.

bedraggled [bɪ'drægld] *adj* mojado y sucio (mojada y sucia).

bedridden ['bed,rɪdn] *adj* postrado(da) en cama.

bedrock ['bedrɒk] *n* (U) **-1.** GEOL roca *f* sólida. **-2.** *fig* [solid foundation] cimientos *mpl*.

bedroom ['bedrʊm] *n* dormitorio *m*, recámara *f* Amer.

Beds [beds] (*abbr of* **Bedfordshire**) *condado inglés*.

bedside ['bedsaɪd] *n* [side of bed] lado *m* de la cama; [of ill person] lecho *m*; **~ lamp** lámpara *f* de noche; **~ table** mesita *f* de noche, nochero *m* Amer.

bedside manner *n* actitud *f* hacia el enfermo.

bed-sit(ter) *n* Br habitación alquilada con cama.

bedsore ['bedsɔːr] *n* úlcera *f* por decúbito.

bedspread ['bedspred] *n* colcha *f*.

bedtime ['bedtaɪm] *n* hora *f* de dormir.

Beduin = **Bedouin**.

bed-wetting [-,wetɪŋ] *n* (U) enuresis *f inv* MED.

bee [biː] *n* abeja *f*; **to have a ~ in one's bonnet about** tener una fijación con.

Beeb [biːb] *n* Br inf: **the ~** la BBC.

beech [biːtʃ] *n* haya *f*.

beef [biːf] *n* carne *f* de vaca.

◆ **beef up** *vt sep inf* reforzar.

beefburger ['biːf,bɜːgər] *n* hamburguesa *f*.

Beefeater ['biːf,iːtər] *n* guardián de la Torre de Londres.

beefsteak ['biːf,steɪk] *n* bistec *m*.

beehive ['biːhaɪv] *n* **-1.** [for bees] colmena *f*. **-2.** [hairstyle] moño *m* alto.

beekeeper ['biː,kiːpər] *n* apicultor *m*, -ra *f*, colmenero *m*, -ra *f*.

beeline ['biːlaɪn] *n*: **to make a ~ for** *inf* irse derechito(ta) hacia.

been [biːn] *pp* → **be**.

beep [biːp] *inf* ◇ *n* pitido *m*. ◇ *vi* pitar.

beer [bɪər] *n* cerveza *f*.

beer garden *n* terraza *f* interior (de bar).

beeswax ['biːzwæks] *n* cera *f* de abeja.

beet [biːt] *n* remolacha *f*.

beetle ['biːtl] *n* escarabajo *m*.

beetroot ['biːtruːt] *n* remolacha *f*.

befall [bɪ'fɔːl] (*pt* **-fell** [-'fel], *pp* **-fallen** [-'fɔːlən]) *literary* ◇ *vt* acontecer a. ◇ *vi* acontecer.

befit [bɪ'fɪt] (*pt* & *pp* **-ted**, *cont* **-ting**) *vt fml* corresponder a.

before [bɪ'fɔːr] ◇ *adv* antes, endenantes Amer; **we went the year ~** fuimos el año anterior. ◇ *prep* **-1.** [in time] antes de; **they arrived ~ us** llegaron antes que nosotros. **-2.** [in space - facing] ante, frente a. ◇ *conj* antes de; **~ it's too late** antes de que sea demasiado tarde.

beforehand [bɪ'fɔːhænd] *adv* con antelación, de antemano.

befriend [bɪ'frend] vt hacer OR entablar amistad con.

befuddled [bɪ'fʌdld] adj liado(da), confundido(da).

beg [beg] (pt & pp **-ged**, cont **-ging**) ◇ vt **-1.** [money, food] mendigar, pedir. **-2.** [favour, forgiveness] suplicar; **to ~ sb to do sthg** rogar a alguien que haga algo; **to ~ sb for sthg** rogar algo a alguien. ◇ vi **-1.** [for money, food]: **to ~ (for sthg)** pedir OR mendigar (algo). **-2.** [for favour, forgiveness]: **to ~ (for sthg)** suplicar OR rogar (algo).

began [bɪ'gæn] pt → begin.

beggar ['begə'] n mendigo m, -ga f.

begin [bɪ'gɪn] (pt **began**, pp **begun**, cont **-ning**) ◇ vt: **to ~ (doing** OR **to do sthg)** empezar OR comenzar (a hacer algo). ◇ vi empezar, comenzar; **to ~ with** para empezar, de entrada.

beginner [bɪ'gɪnə'] n principiante m y f.

beginning [bɪ'gɪnɪŋ] n comienzo m, principio m; **at the ~ of the month** a principios de mes; **from ~ to end** de principio a fin.

begonia [bɪ'gəʊnjə] n begonia f.

begrudge [bɪ'grʌdʒ] vt **-1.** [envy]: **to ~ sb sthg** envidiar a alguien algo. **-2.** [give, do unwillingly]: **to ~ doing sthg** hacer algo de mala gana OR a regañadientes.

beguile [bɪ'gaɪl] vt [charm] seducir.

beguiling [bɪ'gaɪlɪŋ] adj seductor(ra).

begun [bɪ'gʌn] pp → begin.

behalf [bɪ'hɑːf] n: **on ~ of** Br, **in ~ of** Am en nombre OR en representación de.

behave [bɪ'heɪv] ◇ vt: **to ~ o.s.** portarse bien. ◇ vi **-1.** [in a particular way] comportarse, portarse. **-2.** [in an acceptable way] comportarse OR portarse bien.

behaviour Br, **behavior** Am [bɪ'heɪvjə'] n comportamiento m, conducta f.

behaviourism Br, **behaviorism** Am [bɪ'heɪvjərɪzm] n conductismo m.

behead [bɪ'hed] vt decapitar.

beheld [bɪ'held] pt & pp → behold.

behind [bɪ'haɪnd] ◇ prep **-1.** [in space] detrás de. **-2.** [causing, responsible for] detrás de. **-3.** [in support of] con; **we're ~ you** nosotros te apoyamos. **-4.** [in time]: **to be ~ schedule** ir retrasado(da). **-5.** [less successful than] por detrás de. ◇ adv **-1.** [in space] detrás. **-2.** [in time]: **to be ~ (with)** ir atrasado(da) (con). **-3.** [less successful] por detrás. ◇ n inf trasero m.

behold [bɪ'həʊld] (pt & pp **beheld**) vt literary contemplar.

beige [beɪʒ] ◇ adj beige. ◇ n (color m) beige m; **in ~** en beige.

Beijing [,beɪ'dʒɪŋ] n Pekín.

being ['biːɪŋ] n **-1.** [creature] ser m. **-2.** [state of existing]: **in ~** en vigor; **to come into ~** ver la luz, nacer.

Beirut [,beɪ'ruːt] n Beirut; **East/West ~** Beirut Este/Oeste.

belated [bɪ'leɪtɪd] adj tardío(a).

belatedly [bɪ'leɪtɪdlɪ] adv tardíamente.

belch [beltʃ] ◇ n eructo m. ◇ vt escupir, arrojar. ◇ vi **-1.** [person] eructar. **-2.** [smoke, fire] brotar.

beleaguered [bɪ'liːgəd] adj **-1.** MIL asediado(da). **-2.** fig [harassed] atosigado(da), abrumado(da).

belfry ['belfrɪ] (pl **-ies**) n campanario m.

Belgian ['beldʒən] ◇ adj belga. ◇ n belga m y f.

Belgium ['beldʒəm] n Bélgica.

Belgrade [,bel'greɪd] n Belgrado.

belie [bɪ'laɪ] (cont **belying**) vt **-1.** [disprove] contradecir, desmentir. **-2.** [give false idea of] esconder, encubrir.

belief [bɪ'liːf] n **-1.** [faith, principle]: **~ (in)** creencia f (en); **to be beyond ~** ser increíble. **-2.** [opinion] opinión f; **in the ~ that** con la idea de que.

believable [bɪ'liːvəbl] adj creíble.

believe [bɪ'liːv] ◇ vt creer; **~ it or not** lo creas o no. ◇ vi **-1.** [be religious] ser creyente. **-2.** [know to exist, be good]: **to ~ in** creer en.

believer [bɪ'liːvə'] n **-1.** [religious person] creyente m y f. **-2.** [in idea, action]: **~ in sthg** partidario m, -ria f de algo.

Belisha beacon [bɪ'liːʃə-] n Br farol intermitente junto a paso de peatones.

belittle [bɪ'lɪtl] vt subestimar, menospreciar.

Belize [be'liːz] n Belice.

bell [bel] n **-1.** [of church] campana f; [handbell, on door, bike] timbre m. **-2.** phr: **the name rings a ~** el nombre me suena.

bell-bottoms npl pantalones mpl de campana.

bellhop ['belhɒp] n Am botones m inv.

belligerence [bɪ'lɪdʒərəns] n [aggression] belicosidad f.

belligerent [bɪ'lɪdʒərənt] adj **-1.** [at war] beligerante. **-2.** [aggressive] belicoso(sa).

bellow ['beləʊ] ◇ vt gritar. ◇ vi **-1.** [person] rugir. **-2.** [bull] mugir, bramar.

bellows ['beləʊz] npl fuelle m.

bell push n Br (interruptor m del) timbre m.

bell-ringer n campanero m, -ra f.

belly ['belɪ] (pl **-ies**) n **-1.** [of person] barriga f, guata f Amer. **-2.** [of animal] vientre m.

bellyache ['belieik] *inf* ◇ *n* dolor *m* de barriga. ◇ *vi* gruñir.

belly button *n inf* ombligo *m*.

belly dancer *n bailarina que practica la danza del vientre.*

belong [bɪ'lɒŋ] *vi* **-1.** [be property]: **to ~ to** pertenecer a. **-2.** [be member]: **to ~ to** ser miembro de. **-3.** [be situated in right place]: **where does this book ~?** ¿dónde va este libro?; **he felt he didn't ~ there** sintió que no encajaba allí.

belongings [bɪ'lɒŋɪŋz] *npl* pertenencias *fpl*.

Belorussia [,beləʊ'rʌʃə] *n* Bielorrusia.

beloved [bɪ'lʌvd] ◇ *adj* querido(da). ◇ *n* amado *m*, -da *f*.

below [bɪ'ləʊ] ◇ *adv* **-1.** [gen] abajo; **the flat ~** el piso de abajo. **-2.** [in text] más abajo; **see ~** véase más abajo. ◇ *prep* **-1.** [lower than in position] (por) debajo de, bajo. **-2.** [lower than in rank, number] por debajo de.

belt [belt] ◇ *n* **-1.** [for clothing] cinturón *m*, correa *f*; *inf*: **that was below the ~** eso fue un golpe bajo; **to tighten one's ~** apretarse el cinturón; **under one's ~** a las espaldas de uno. **-2.** TECH [wide] cinta *f*; [narrow] correa *f*. **-3.** [of land, sea] cinturón *m*, franja *f*. ◇ *vt inf* arrear. ◇ *vi Br inf* ir a toda mecha.

◆ **belt out** *vt sep inf* cantar a voz en grito.

◆ **belt up** *vi Br inf* cerrar el pico.

beltway ['belt,weɪ] *n Am* carretera *f* de circunvalación.

bemused [bɪ'mju:zd] *adj* atónito(ta).

bench [bentʃ] *n* **-1.** [seat] banco *m*. **-2.** [in lab, workshop] mesa *f* de trabajo. **-3.** *Br* POL escaño *m*.

bend [bend] (*pt & pp* **bent**) ◇ *n* curva *f*; **round the ~** *inf* majareta, majara. ◇ *vt* doblar. ◇ *vi* [person] agacharse; [tree] doblarse; **to ~ over backwards for** hacer todo lo humanamente posible por.

◆ **bends** *npl*: **the ~s** *enfermedad producida por una brusca descompresión.*

bendy ['bendɪ] (*compar* **-ier**, *superl* **-iest**) *adj Br* flexible.

beneath [bɪ'ni:θ] ◇ *adv* debajo. ◇ *prep* **-1.** [under] bajo. **-2.** [unworthy of] indigno(na) de.

benediction [,benɪ'dɪkʃn] *n* bendición *f*.

benefactor ['benɪfæktər] *n* benefactor *m*.

benefactress ['benɪfæktrɪs] *n* benefactora *f*.

beneficial [,benɪ'fɪʃl] *adj*: **~ (to)** beneficioso(sa) (para).

beneficiary [,benɪ'fɪʃərɪ] (*pl* **-ies**) *n* **-1.** JUR [of will] beneficiario *m*, -ria *f*. **-2.** [of change in law, new rule] beneficiado *m*, -da *f*.

benefit ['benɪfɪt] ◇ *n* **-1.** [advantage] ventaja *f*; **for the ~ of** en atención a; **to be to sb's ~, to be of ~ to sb** ir en beneficio de alguien. **-2.** ADMIN [allowance of money] subsidio *m*. ◇ *comp* [concert, match] benéfico(ca). ◇ *vt* beneficiar. ◇ *vi*: **to ~ from** beneficiarse de.

Benelux ['benɪlʌks] *n* (el) Benelux; **the ~ countries** los países del Benelux.

benevolent [bɪ'nevələnt] *adj* benevolente.

BEng [,bi:'eŋ] (*abbr of* **Bachelor of Engineering**) *n (titular de un) título de ingeniero:*

Bengal [,beŋ'gɔːl] *n* Bengala; **the Bay of ~** el golfo de Bengala.

benign [bɪ'naɪn] *adj* **-1.** [person] bondadoso(sa). **-2.** MED benigno(na).

Benin [be'nɪn] *n* Benín.

bent [bent] ◇ *pt & pp* → **bend**. ◇ *adj* **-1.** [wire, bar] torcido(da). **-2.** [person, body] encorvado(da). **-3.** *Br inf* [dishonest] corrupto(ta). **-4.** [determined]: **to be ~ on sthg/on doing sthg** estar empeñado(da) en algo/en hacer algo. ◇ *n* [natural tendency] inclinación *f*; **~ for** don *m* OR talento *m* para.

bequeath [bɪ'kwi:ð] *vt lit & fig*: **to ~ sb sthg**, **to ~ sthg to sb** legar algo a alguien.

bequest [bɪ'kwest] *n* legado *m*.

berate [bɪ'reɪt] *vt* regañar.

Berber ['bɜːbər] ◇ *adj* bereber. ◇ *n* **-1.** [person] bereber *m y f*. **-2.** [language] bereber *m*.

bereaved [bɪ'riːvd] (*pl inv*) ◇ *adj* que llora la muerte de un ser querido; **the ~ family** la desconsolada familia. ◇ *n*: **the ~** la persona más allegada al difunto.

bereavement [bɪ'riːvmənt] *n* pérdida *f*.

bereft [bɪ'reft] *adj literary*: **~ (of)** ayuno(na) (de).

beret ['bereɪ] *n* boina *f*.

Bering Sea ['berɪŋ-] *n*: **the ~** el mar de Bering.

Bering Strait ['berɪŋ-] *n*: **the ~** el estrecho de Bering.

berk [bɜːk] *n Br inf* gilipollas *m y f inv*.

Berks (*abbr of* **Berkshire**) *condado inglés*.

Berlin [bɜː'lɪn] *n* Berlín; **East/West ~** Berlín Este/Oeste; **the ~ Wall** el muro de Berlín.

Berliner [bɜː'lɪnər] *n* berlinés *m*, -esa *f*.

berm [bɜːm] *n Am* arcén *m*.

Bermuda [bə'mjuːdə] *n* las Bermudas.

Bermuda shorts *npl* bermudas *mpl*.

Bern [bɜːn] *n* Berna.

berry ['berɪ] (*pl* **-ies**) *n* baya *f*.

berserk [bə'zɜːk] *adj*: **to go ~** ponerse hecho(cha) una fiera.

berth [bɜːθ] ◇ n **-1.** [in harbour] amarradero m, atracadero m. **-2.** [in ship, train] litera f. **-3.** phr: **to give sb a wide ~** mantenerse a distancia de alguien. ◇ vt & vi atracar.

beseech [bɪˈsiːtʃ] (pt & pp besought OR beseeched) vt literary: **to ~ (sb to do sthg)** suplicar (a alguien que haga algo).

beset [bɪˈset] (pt & pp beset, cont -ting) ◇ adj: **~ with** OR **by** [subj: person] acosado(da) por; [subj: plan] plagado(da) de. ◇ vt acosar.

beside [bɪˈsaɪd] prep **-1.** [next to] al lado de, junto a. **-2.** [compared with] comparado con. **-3.** phr: **that's ~ the point** eso no importa, eso no viene al caso; **to be ~ o.s. with rage** estar fuera de sí; **to be ~ o.s. with joy** estar loco(ca) de alegría.

besides [bɪˈsaɪdz] ◇ adv además. ◇ prep aparte de.

besiege [bɪˈsiːdʒ] vt lit & fig asediar; **to be ~d with** verse asediado por.

besotted [bɪˈsɒtɪd] adj: **~ with** borracho(cha) de.

besought [bɪˈsɔːt] pt & pp → beseech.

bespectacled [bɪˈspektəkld] adj con gafas.

bespoke [bɪˈspəʊk] adj Br **-1.** [clothes] (hecho(cha)) a medida. **-2.** [tailor] que hace ropa a medida.

best [best] ◇ adj mejor. ◇ adv mejor; **which did you like ~?** ¿cuál te gustó más? ◇ n: **to do one's ~** hacerlo lo mejor que uno puede; **to make the ~ of sthg** sacarle el mayor partido posible a algo; **for the ~** para bien; **all the ~** [ending letter] un abrazo; [saying goodbye] que te vaya bien; **to have the ~ of both worlds** tenerlo todo.
◆ **at best** adv en el mejor de los casos.

bestial [ˈbestjəl] adj [disgusting] bestial.

best man n ≃ padrino m de boda.

BEST MAN:
En los países anglosajones, el padrino de boda entrega la alianza al novio y pronuncia unas palabras en el banquete de bodas, generalmente contando algún chascarrillo sobre el novio

bestow [bɪˈstəʊ] vt fml: **to ~ sthg on sb** [gift] otorgar OR conceder algo a alguien; [praise] dirigir algo a alguien; [title] conferir algo a alguien.

best-seller n [book] best seller m, éxito m editorial.

best-selling adj de éxito.

bet [bet] (pt & pp bet OR -ted, cont -ting) ◇ n **-1.** [gen]: **~ (on)** apuesta f (a). **-2.** fig [prediction] predicción f; **it's a safe ~ that** seguro que. **-3.** phr: **to hedge one's ~s** cubrirse, guardarse las espaldas. ◇ vt apostar. ◇ vi

-1. [gamble]: **to ~ (on)** apostar (a). **-2.** [predict]: **to ~ on sthg** contar con (que pase) algo. **-3.** phr: **you ~!** inf ¡pues claro!

beta-blocker [ˈbiːtə‚blɒkər] n betabloqueante m.

Bethlehem [ˈbeθlɪhem] n Belén.

betray [bɪˈtreɪ] vt **-1.** [person, trust, principles] traicionar. **-2.** [secret] revelar. **-3.** [feeling] delatar.

betrayal [bɪˈtreɪəl] n **-1.** [of person, trust, principles] traición f. **-2.** [of secret] revelación f.

betrothed [bɪˈtrəʊðd] adj dated: **~ (to)** prometido(da) (a).

better [ˈbetər] ◇ adj (compar of good) mejor; **to get ~** mejorar. ◇ adv (compar of well) **-1.** [in quality] mejor. **-2.** [more]: **I like it ~** me gusta más; **~ known for** más conocido(da) por. **-3.** [preferably]: **we had ~ be going** más vale que nos vayamos ya. ◇ n [best one] mejor m y f; **to get the ~ of sb** poder con alguien. ◇ vt mejorar; **to ~ o.s.** mejorarse.

better half n inf media naranja f.

better off adj **-1.** [financially] mejor de dinero. **-2.** [in better situation]: **you'd be ~ going by bus** sería mejor si vas en autobús.
◆ **better-off** n: **the ~** la gente pudiente.

betting [ˈbetɪŋ] n (U) apuestas fpl.

betting shop n Br casa f de apuestas.

between [bɪˈtwiːn] ◇ prep entre; **he sat (in) ~ Paul and Anne** se sentó entre Paul y Anne; **closed ~ 1 and 2** cerrado de 1 a 2. ◇ adv: **(in) ~** en medio, entremedio.

bevelled Br, **beveled** Am [ˈbevld] adj biselado(da).

beverage [ˈbevərɪdʒ] n fml bebida f.

bevy [ˈbevɪ] (pl -ies) n [group, women] panda f.

beware [bɪˈweər] vi: **to ~ (of)** tener cuidado (con).

bewildered [bɪˈwɪldəd] adj desconcertado(da).

bewildering [bɪˈwɪldərɪŋ] adj desconcertante.

bewitched [bɪˈwɪtʃt] adj hechizado(da).

bewitching [bɪˈwɪtʃɪŋ] adj hechizante.

beyond [bɪˈjɒnd] ◇ prep más allá de; **~ midnight** pasada la medianoche; **~ my reach/responsibility** fuera de mi alcance/ competencia; **it has changed ~ recognition** está irreconocible. ◇ adv más allá.

b/f abbr of brought forward.

bhp abbr of brake horsepower.

bi- [baɪ] prefix bi-.

biannual [baɪˈænjʊəl] adj semestral.

bias ['baɪəs] *n* **-1.** [prejudice] prejuicio *m*. **-2.** [tendency] tendencia *f*, inclinación *f*.

biased ['baɪəst] *adj* parcial; **to be ~ towards/against** tener prejuicios en favor/en contra de.

bib [bɪb] *n* [for baby] babero *m*.

Bible ['baɪbl] *n*: **the ~** la Biblia.
◆ **bible** *n* biblia *f*.

biblical ['bɪblɪkl] *adj* bíblico(ca).

bibliography [,bɪblɪ'ɒɡrəfɪ] (*pl* **-ies**) *n* bibliografía *f*.

bicarbonate of soda [baɪ'kɑːbənət-] *n* bicarbonato *m*.

bicentenary *Br* [,baɪsen'tiːnərɪ] (*pl* **-ies**), **bicentennial** *Am* [,baɪsen'tenjəl] *n* bicentenario *m*.

biceps ['baɪseps] (*pl inv*) *n* bíceps *m inv*.

bicker ['bɪkə] *vi* reñir.

bickering ['bɪkərɪŋ] *n* (*U*) discusiones *fpl*.

bicycle ['baɪsɪkl] ◇ *n* bicicleta *f*. ◇ *vi* ir en bicicleta.

bicycle path *n* camino *m* para bicicletas.

bicycle pump *n* bomba *f*.

bid [bɪd] (*pt & pp vt sense 1 & vi* **bid**, *cont* **bidding**, *pt vt senses 2 & 3* **bid** OR **bade**, *pp vt senses 2 & 3* **bid** OR **bidden** ['bɪdn], *cont* **bidding**) ◇ *n* **-1.** [attempt]: **~ (for)** intento *m* (de hacerse con). **-2.** [at auction] puja *f*. **-3.** [financial offer]: **~ (for sthg)** oferta *f* (para adquirir algo). ◇ *vt* **-1.** [money] pujar. **-2.** *literary* [request]: **to ~ sb do sthg** invitar a alguien a hacer algo. **-3.** *fml*: **to ~ sb good morning** dar los buenos días a alguien. ◇ *vi* [at auction]: **to ~ (for)** pujar (por).

bidder ['bɪdə] *n* postor *m*, -ra *f*; **to sell to the highest ~** vender al mejor postor.

bidding ['bɪdɪŋ] *n* (*U*) [at auction] puja *f*.

bide [baɪd] *vt*: **to ~ one's time** esperar el momento oportuno.

bidet ['biːdeɪ] *n* bidé *m*.

biennial [baɪ'enɪəl] ◇ *adj* bienal. ◇ *n* [plant] planta *f* bienal.

bier [bɪə] *n* andas *fpl*.

bifocals [,baɪ'fəʊklz] *npl* gafas *fpl* bifocales.

big [bɪg] (*compar* **-ger**, *superl* **-gest**) *adj* **-1.** [large, important] grande; **a ~ problem** un gran problema; **~ problems** grandes problemas. **-2.** [older] mayor. **-3.** [successful] popular. **-4.** *phr*: **in a ~ way** a lo grande.

bigamist ['bɪɡəmɪst] *n* bígamo *m*, -ma *f*.

bigamy ['bɪɡəmɪ] *n* bigamia *f*.

Big Apple *n*: **the ~** Nueva York.

Big Ben *n* Big Ben *m*.

big business *n* (*U*) [large companies] grandes compañías *fpl*.

big cat *n* felino *m* grande.

big deal *inf* ◇ *n*: **it's no ~** no tiene (la menor) importancia. ◇ *excl* ¡y a mí qué!

Big Dipper [-'dɪpə] *n* **-1.** *Br* [rollercoaster] montaña *f* rusa. **-2.** *Am* ASTRON: **the ~** la Osa Mayor.

big end *n* cabeza *f* de biela.

big fish *n inf* pez *m* gordo.

big game *n* caza *f* mayor.

big hand *n* **-1.** [on clock] minutero *m*. **-2.** *inf* [applause] fuerte aplauso *m*.

bighead ['bɪghed] *n inf pej* creído *m*, -da *f*.

bigheaded [,bɪg'hedɪd] *adj inf pej* creído(da).

big-hearted [-'hɑːtɪd] *adj* de buen corazón, generoso(sa).

big money *n inf* mucha pasta *f*.

big mouth *n inf* bocazas *m y f inv*.

big name *n inf* figura *f*.

bigot ['bɪgət] *n* fanático *m*, -ca *f*.

bigoted ['bɪgətɪd] *adj* fanático(ca).

bigotry ['bɪgətrɪ] *n* fanatismo *m*.

big shot *n inf* pez *m* gordo.

big time *n inf*: **the ~** el éxito, la fama.

big toe *n* dedo *m* gordo (del pie).

big top *n* carpa *f*.

big wheel *n* **-1.** *Br* [at fairground] noria *f*. **-2.** *inf* [big shot] pez *m* gordo.

bigwig ['bɪgwɪg] *n inf pej* pope *m*, pez *m* gordo.

bike [baɪk] *n inf* [bicycle] bici *f*; [motorcycle] moto *f*.

bikeway ['baɪkweɪ] *n Am* [lane] carril-bici *m*.

bikini [bɪ'kiːnɪ] *n* biquini *m*, bikini *m*.

bilateral [,baɪ'lætərəl] *adj* bilateral.

bilberry ['bɪlbərɪ] (*pl* **-ies**) *n* arándano *m*.

bile [baɪl] *n* **-1.** [fluid] bilis *f*. **-2.** [anger] hiel *f*.

bilingual [baɪ'lɪŋgwəl] *adj* bilingüe.

bilious ['bɪljəs] *adj* **-1.** [sickening] nauseabundo(da). **-2.** [nauseous] bilioso(sa).

bill [bɪl] ◇ *n* **-1.** [statement of cost]: **~ (for)** [meal] cuenta *f* (de); [electricity, phone] factura *f* (de). **-2.** [in parliament] proyecto *m* de ley. **-3.** [of show, concert] programa *m*. **-4.** *Am* [banknote] billete *m*. **-5.** [poster]: **"post** OR **stick no ~s"** "prohibido fijar carteles". **-6.** [beak] pico *m*. **-7.** *phr*: **a clean ~ of health** MED un certificado médico favorable; *fig* el visto bueno. ◇ *vt* [send a bill]: **to ~ sb for** mandar la factura a alguien por.

billboard ['bɪlbɔːd] *n* valla *f* publicitaria, cartelera *f*.

billet ['bɪlɪt] ◇ *n* acantonamiento *m*, alojamiento *m*. ◇ *vt* acantonar, alojar.

billfold ['bɪlfəʊld] *n Am* billetera *f*.

billiards ['bɪljədz] *n* billar *m*.

billion ['bɪljən] *num* **-1.** *Am* [thousand million] millar *m* de millones. **-2.** *Br* [million million] billón *m*.

billionaire [,bɪljə'neəʳ] *n* multimillonario *m*, -ria *f*.

bill of exchange *n* letra *f* de cambio.

bill of lading [-'leɪdɪŋ] *n* conocimiento *m* de embarque.

Bill of Rights *n*: the ~ *las diez primeras enmiendas de la Constitución estadounidense.*

BILL OF RIGHTS:
Nombre colectivo con el que se conocen las diez primeras enmiendas de la Constitución estadounidense, que garantizan derechos fundamentales, tales como la libertad de expresión, de credo y de reunión

---

bill of sale *n* contrato *m* OR escritura *f* de venta.

billow ['bɪləʊ] ⬦ *n* nube *f*. ⬦ *vi* **-1.** [smoke, steam] brotar en nubes. **-2.** [sail, skirt] hincharse.

billycan ['bɪlɪkæn] *n* cazo *m*.

billy goat ['bɪlɪ-] *n* cabrón *m*, macho *m* cabrío.

bimbo ['bɪmbəʊ] (*pl* **-s** OR **-es**) *n inf pej* niña *f* mona, *mujer joven, guapa y poco inteligente.*

bimonthly [,baɪ'mʌnθlɪ] ⬦ *adj* **-1.** [every two months] bimestral. **-2.** [twice a month] bimensual. ⬦ *adv* **-1.** [every two months] bimestralmente. **-2.** [twice a month] bimensualmente.

bin [bɪn] ⬦ *n* **-1.** *Br* [for rubbish] cubo *m* de la basura; [for paper] papelera *f*. **-2.** [for grain, coal] depósito *m*. **-3.** [for bread, flour] caja *f*. ⬦ *vt inf* echar a la basura.

binary ['baɪnərɪ] *adj* binario(ria).

bind [baɪnd] (*pt* & *pp* **bound**) ⬦ *vt* **-1.** [tie up] atar. **-2.** [unite - people] unir. **-3.** [bandage] vendar. **-4.** [book] encuadernar. **-5.** [constrain] obligar, comprometer. ⬦ *n inf* **-1.** *Br* [nuisance] lata *f*, pesadez *f*. **-2.** [difficult situation] aprieto *m*.

◆ **bind over** *vt sep* conminar, obligar legalmente.

binder ['baɪndəʳ] *n* **-1.** [machine] (máquina *f*) encuadernadora *f*. **-2.** [person] encuadernador *m*, -ra *f*. **-3.** [cover] carpeta *f*.

binding ['baɪndɪŋ] ⬦ *adj* obligatorio(ria), vinculante. ⬦ *n* **-1.** [on book] encuadernación *f*. **-2.** [on dress, tablecloth] ribete *m*.

binge [bɪndʒ] *inf* ⬦ *n*: to go on a ~ irse de juerga. ⬦ *vi*: to ~ on sthg hincharse a algo.

bingo ['bɪŋgəʊ] *n* bingo *m*.

bin-liner *n Br* bolsa *f* de basura.

binoculars [bɪ'nɒkjʊləz] *npl* gemelos *mpl*, prismáticos *mpl*.

biochemistry [,baɪəʊ'kemɪstrɪ] *n* bioquímica *f*.

biodegradable [,baɪəʊdɪ'greɪdəbl] *adj* biodegradable.

biodiversity [,baɪəʊdaɪ'vɜːsətɪ] *n* biodiversidad *f*.

biographer [baɪ'ɒgrəfəʳ] *n* biógrafo *m*, -fa *f*.

biographic(al) [,baɪə'græfɪk(l)] *adj* biográfico(ca).

biography [baɪ'ɒgrəfɪ] (*pl* **-ies**) *n* biografía *f*.

biological [,baɪə'lɒdʒɪkl] *adj* biológico(ca).

biological weapon *n* arma *f* biológica.

biologist [baɪ'ɒlədʒɪst] *n* biólogo *m*, -ga *f*.

biology [baɪ'ɒlədʒɪ] *n* biología *f*.

biopic ['baɪəʊpɪk] *n inf* película *f* biográfica.

biopsy ['baɪɒpsɪ] (*pl* **-ies**) *n* biopsia *f*.

bipartite [,baɪ'pɑːtaɪt] *adj* bipartito(ta).

biplane ['baɪpleɪn] *n* biplano *m*.

birch [bɜːtʃ] *n* **-1.** [tree] abedul *m*. **-2.** [stick]: the ~ la vara.

bird [bɜːd] *n* **-1.** [animal - large] ave *f*; [- small] pájaro *m*; **to kill two ~s with one stone** matar dos pájaros de un tiro. **-2.** *inf* [woman] tía *f*, periquita *f*.

birdcage ['bɜːdkeɪdʒ] *n* jaula *f*.

birdie ['bɜːdɪ] *n* **-1.** [bird] pajarito *m*. **-2.** [in golf] birdie *m*.

bird of paradise *n* ave *f* del Paraíso.

bird of prey *n* ave *f* rapaz OR de presa.

birdseed ['bɜːdsiːd] *n* alpiste *m*.

bird's-eye view *n* vista *f* panorámica.

bird-watcher *n* observador *m*, -ra *f* de pájaros.

Biro® ['baɪərəʊ] *n* bolígrafo *m*, lapicera *f* *Amer*.

birth [bɜːθ] *n* [gen] nacimiento *m*; [delivery] parto *m*; **to give ~ (to)** dar a luz (a).

birth certificate *n* partida *f* de nacimiento.

birth control *n* control *m* de natalidad.

birthday ['bɜːθdeɪ] ⬦ *n* cumpleaños *m inv*. ⬦ *comp* de cumpleaños.

birthmark ['bɜːθmɑːk] *n* antojo *m*.

birthplace ['bɜːθpleɪs] *n* lugar *m* de nacimiento.

birthrate ['bɜːθreɪt] *n* índice *m* de natalidad.

birthright ['bɜːθraɪt] *n* derecho *m* de nacimiento.

Biscay ['bɪskɪ] *n*: **the Bay of** ~ el golfo de Vizcaya.

biscuit ['bɪskɪt] *n* [in UK] **galleta** *f*; [in US] *tipo de bollo.*

bisect [baɪ'sekt] *vt* dividir en dos.

bisexual [,baɪ'sekʃʊəl] ◇ *adj* bisexual. ◇ *n* bisexual *m y f.*

bishop ['bɪʃəp] *n* **-1.** [in church] obispo *m*. **-2.** [in chess] alfil *m*.

bison ['baɪsn] (*pl inv* OR **-s**) *n* bisonte *m.*

bistro ['bɪstrəʊ] (*pl* **-s**) *n* ≃ bar-restaurante *m.*

bit [bɪt] ◇ *pt* → **bite**.
◇ *n* **-1.** [piece - gen] trozo *m*; [- small]: **a** ~ **of** un poco de; **a** ~ **of news** una noticia; ~**s and pieces** *Br* [objects] cosillas *fpl*, tiliches *mpl Amer*; [possessions] cosas *fpl*, bártulos *mpl*; **to fall to** ~**s** [clothes, house] caerse a pedazos; **to take sthg to** ~**s** desmontar algo. **-2.** [amount]: **a** ~ **of** un poco de; **a** ~ **of shopping** algunas compras; **quite a** ~ **of** bastante. **-3.** [short time]: **(for) a** ~ un rato. **-4.** [of drill] broca *f.* **-5.** [of bridle] bocado *m*, freno *m.* **-6.** COMPUT bit *m.* **-7.** *phr*: **to do one's** ~ *Br* aportar uno su grano de arena; **every** ~ **as ... as** igual de ... que; **a** ~ **much** demasiado; **not a** ~ ni mucho menos, en absoluto.
◆ **a bit** *adv* un poco.
◆ **bit by bit** *adv* poco a poco.

bitch [bɪtʃ] ◇ *n* **-1.** [female dog] perra *f.* **-2.** *v inf pej* [unpleasant woman] bruja *f.* ◇ *vi inf* **-1.** [complain] protestar todo el rato. **-2.** [talk unpleasantly]: **to** ~ **about** poner a parir a.

bitchy ['bɪtʃɪ] (*compar* **-ier**, *superl* **-iest**) *adj inf*: **to be** ~ tener mala uva.

bite [baɪt] (*pt* **bit**, *pp* **bitten**) ◇ *n* **-1.** [by dog, person] mordisco *m*; [by insect, snake] picotazo *m.* **-2.** *inf* [food]: **a** ~ **(to eat)** un bocado. **-3.** [wound - from dog] mordedura *f*; [- from insect, snake] picadura *f.* **-4.** *Br* [sharp flavour] sabor *m* fuerte.
◇ *vt* **-1.** [subj: person, animal] morder. **-2.** [subj: insect, snake] picar.
◇ *vi* **-1.** [animal, person]: **to** ~ **(into sthg)** morder (algo); **to** ~ **off sthg** arrancar algo de un mordisco; **to** ~ **off more than one can chew** intentar abarcar demasiado. **-2.** [insect, snake] picar. **-3.** [grip] agarrar. **-4.** [take effect] pegar duro.

biting ['baɪtɪŋ] *adj* **-1.** [very cold] gélido(da), cortante. **-2.** [caustic] mordaz.

bit part *n* papel *m* secundario.

bitten ['bɪtn] *pp* → **bite**.

bitter ['bɪtər] ◇ *adj* **-1.** [coffee, chocolate] amargo(ga); [lemon] agrio(gria). **-2.** [icy] gélido(da). **-3.** [causing pain] amargo(ga); **to**

the ~ **end** hasta el final. **-4.** [acrimonious] agrio(gria), enconado(da). **-5.** [resentful] amargado(da), resentido(da). ◇ *n Br* [beer] *tipo de cerveza amarga.*

bitter lemon *n* bíter *m* de limón.

bitterly ['bɪtəlɪ] *adv*: **it's** ~ **cold** hace un frío de muerte; **to criticise** ~ criticar duramente.

bitterness ['bɪtənɪs] *n* **-1.** [of taste] amargor *m.* **-2.** [of wind, weather] gelidez *f.* **-3.** [resentment] resentimiento *m.*

bittersweet ['bɪtəswiːt] *adj* agridulce.

bitty ['bɪtɪ] (*compar* **-ier**, *superl* **-iest**) *adj Br inf* inconexo(xa).

bitumen ['bɪtjʊmɪn] *n* betún *m*, chapopote *m Amer.*

bivouac ['bɪvʊæk] (*pt & pp* **-ked**, *cont* **-king**) ◇ *n* vivaque *m.* ◇ *vi* vivaquear.

biweekly [,baɪ'wiːklɪ] ◇ *adj* **-1.** [every two weeks] quincenal. **-2.** [twice a week] bisemanal. ◇ *adv* **-1.** [every two weeks] quincenalmente. **-2.** [twice a week] dos veces por semana.

bizarre [bɪ'zɑːr] *adj* [behaviour, appearance] extravagante; [machine, remark] singular, extraordinario(ria).

bk -1. *abbr of* **bank**. **-2.** *abbr of* **book**.

bl *abbr of* **bill of lading**.

BL *n* **-1.** (*abbr of* **Bachelor of Law(s)**) *(titular de una)* licenciatura de derecho. **-2.** (*abbr of* **Bachelor of Letters**) *(titular de una)* licenciatura de letras. **-3.** (*abbr of* **Bachelor of Literature**) *(titular de una)* licenciatura de literatura.

blab [blæb] (*pt & pp* **-bed**, *cont* **-bing**) *vi inf* irse de la lengua.

black [blæk] ◇ *adj* **-1.** [gen] negro(gra); ~ **and blue** amoratado(da); ~ **and white** [films, photos] en blanco y negro; [clear-cut] extremadamente nítido(da). **-2.** [without milk] solo. **-3.** [angry] furioso(sa). ◇ *n* **-1.** [colour] negro *m.* **-2.** [person] negro *m*, -gra *f.* **-3.** *phr*: **in** ~ **and white** [in writing] por escrito; **to be in the** ~ tener saldo positivo. ◇ *vt Br* [boycott] boicotear.
◆ **black out** ◇ *vt sep* **-1.** [put out lights] dejar sin luz. **-2.** [suppress] censurar. ◇ *vi* desmayarse, perder el conocimiento.

blackball ['blækbɔːl] *vt* votar en contra de.

black belt *n* cinturón *m* negro.

blackberry ['blækbərɪ] (*pl* **-ies**) *n* mora *f*, zarzamora *f.*

blackbird ['blækbɜːd] *n* mirlo *m.*

blackboard ['blækbɔːd] *n* pizarra *f*, encerado *m.*

black box *n* [flight recorder] caja *f* negra.

black comedy *n* comedia *f* de humor negro.

blackcurrant [ˌblæk'kʌrənt] *n* grosella *f* negra, casis *m*.

black economy *n* economía *f* sumergida.

blacken ['blækn] ◇ *vt* **-1.** [make dark] ennegrecer. **-2.** [tarnish] manchar. ◇ *vi* ennegrecerse.

black eye *n* ojo *m* morado.

blackhead ['blækhed] *n* barrillo *m*.

black hole *n* agujero *m* negro.

black ice *n* hielo transparente en el suelo.

blackjack ['blækdʒæk] *n* **-1.** [card game] veintiuna *f*. **-2.** *Am* [weapon] porra *f*, cachiporra *f*.

blackleg ['blækleg] *n pej* esquirol *m*.

blacklist ['blæklɪst] ◇ *n* lista *f* negra. ◇ *vt* poner en la lista negra.

black magic *n* magia *f* negra.

blackmail ['blækmeɪl] ◇ *n lit* & *fig* chantaje *m*. ◇ *vt lit* & *fig* chantajear.

blackmailer ['blækmeɪlə'] *n* chantajista *m* y *f*.

Black Maria [-mə'raɪə] *n inf* coche *m* celular, furgón *m* policial.

black mark *n* punto *m* en contra.

black market *n* mercado *m* negro.

blackout ['blækaut] *n* **-1.** [in wartime, power cut] apagón *m*. **-2.** [of news] censura *f*. **-3.** [fainting fit] desmayo *m*.

Black Power *n* el poder negro.

black pudding *n Br* morcilla *f*.

Black Sea *n*: the ~ el mar Negro.

black sheep *n* oveja *f* negra.

blacksmith ['blæksmɪθ] *n* herrero *m*.

black spot *n* punto *m* negro.

black-tie *adj* de etiqueta.

bladder ['blædə'] *n* ANAT vejiga *f*.

blade [bleɪd] *n* **-1.** [of knife, saw] hoja *f*. **-2.** [of propeller] aleta *f*, paleta *f*. **-3.** [of grass] brizna *f*, hoja *f*.

blame [bleɪm] ◇ *n* culpa *f*; **to take the ~ for** hacerse responsable de; **to be to ~** ser el culpable de. ◇ *vt* echar la culpa a, culpar; **to ~ sthg on sthg/sb**, **to ~ sthg/sb for sthg** culpar algo/a alguien de algo.

blameless ['bleɪmlɪs] *adj* inocente.

blanch [blɑːntʃ] ◇ *vt* blanquear. ◇ *vi* palidecer.

blancmange [blə'mɒndʒ] *n* manjar *m* blanco.

bland [blænd] *adj* soso(sa).

blank [blæŋk] ◇ *adj* **-1.** [wall] liso(sa); [sheet of paper] en blanco. **-2.** *fig* [look] vacío(a); **her mind went ~** se le quedó la mente en blanco. ◇ *n* **-1.** [empty space] espacio *m* en blanco. **-2.** MIL [cartridge] cartucho *m* de fogueo. **-3.** *phr*: **to draw a ~** buscar en vano.

blank cheque *n* cheque *m* en blanco; *fi*,carta *f* blanca.

blanket ['blæŋkɪt] ◇ *adj* [TV coverage] exhaustivo(va); [ban, statement] global, general. ◇ *n* **-1.** [bed cover] manta *f*, frazada *f* Amer. **-2.** [layer] manto *m*. ◇ *vt* cubrir, tapar.

blanket bath *n Br* baño dado a un enfermo en cama.

blankly ['blæŋklɪ] *adv* [stare] con la mirada vacía.

blank verse *n* (U) versos *mpl* sueltos o blancos.

blare [bleə'] *vi* resonar, sonar.
◆ **blare out** *vi* retumbar, resonar.

blasé [Br 'blɑːzeɪ, Am ˌblɑː'zeɪ] *adj*: **to be ~ about** estar de vuelta de.

blasphemous ['blæsfəməs] *adj* blasfemo(ma).

blasphemy ['blæsfəmɪ] (*pl* **-ies**) *n* blasfemia *f*.

blast [blɑːst] ◇ *n* **-1.** [of bomb] explosión *f*. **-2.** [of wind] ráfaga *f*. ◇ *vt* [hole, tunnel] perforar (con explosivos). ◇ *excl Br inf* ¡maldita sea!
◆ **(at) full blast** *adv* a todo trapo.
◆ **blast off** *vi* despegar.

blasted ['blɑːstɪd] *adj inf* maldito(ta), puñetero(ra).

blast furnace *n* alto horno *m*.

blast-off *n* despegue *m*.

blatant ['bleɪtənt] *adj* descarado(da).

blatantly ['bleɪtəntlɪ] *adv* descaradamente.

blaze [bleɪz] ◇ *n* **-1.** [fire] incendio *m*. **-2.** *fig* [of colour] explosión *f*; [of light] resplandor *m*; **a ~ of publicity** una ola de publicidad. ◇ *vi lit* & *fig* arder.

blazer ['bleɪzə'] *n* chaqueta de sport generalmente con la insignia de un equipo, colegio etc.

blazing ['bleɪzɪŋ] *adj* **-1.** [sun, heat] abrasador(ra). **-2.** [row] encendido(da), acalorado(da).

bleach [bliːtʃ] ◇ *n* lejía *f*. ◇ *vt* [hair] blanquear; [clothes] desteñir.

bleached [bliːtʃt] *adj* [hair] teñido(da) de rubio; [jeans] desteñido(da).

bleachers ['bliːtʃəz] *npl Am* SPORT graderío *m* descubierto.

bleak [bliːk] *adj* **-1.** [future] negro(gra). **-2.** [place, person, face] sombrío(a). **-3.** [weather] desapacible.

bleary ['blɪərɪ] (*compar* **-ier**, *superl* **-iest**) *adj* nublado(da).

bleary-eyed [-'aɪd] *adj* con los ojos nublados.

bleat [bliːt] ◇ *n* [of sheep] balido *m*. ◇ *vi* **-1.** [sheep] balar. **-2.** *fig* [person] gimotear.

bleed [bli:d] (*pt* & *pp* **bled**) ◇ *vt* [radiator etc] vaciar. ◇ *vi* sangrar.

bleep [bli:p] ◇ *n* pitido *m* intermitente. ◇ *vt* llamar con el busca. ◇ *vi* pitar, dar unos pitidos.

bleeper ['bli:pər] *n* busca *m*, buscapersonas *m inv*.

blemish ['blemɪʃ] ◇ *n* [mark] señal *f*, marca *f*; *fig* mancha *f*. ◇ *vt* [reputation] manchar.

blend [blend] ◇ *n* *lit* & *fig* mezcla *f*. ◇ *vt*: to ~ (sthg with sthg) mezclar (algo con algo). ◇ *vi*: to ~ (with) combinarse (con).
◆ **blend in** *vi* confundirse.
◆ **blend into** *vt fus* confundirse con.

blender ['blendər] *n* licuadora *f*, túrmix® *f*.

bless [bles] (*pt* & *pp* **-ed** OR **blest**) *vt* **-1.** RE-LIG bendecir. **-2.** [endow]: to be ~ed with estar dotado(da) de. **-3.** *phr*: ~ you! [after sneezing] ¡jesús!; [thank you] ¡gracias!

blessed ['blesɪd] *adj* **-1.** RELIG bendito(ta). **-2.** [desirable] feliz, maravilloso(sa). **-3.** *inf* [blasted] dichoso(sa).

blessing ['blesɪŋ] *n* **-1.** RELIG bendición *f*; that's a ~ in disguise no hay mal que por bien no venga; to count one's ~s darse con un canto en los dientes; it's a mixed ~ tiene sus pros y sus contras. **-2.** *fig* [good wishes] aprobación *f*.

blest [blest] *pt* & *pp* → **bless**.

blew [blu:] *pt* → **blow**.

blight [blaɪt] ◇ *n* [plant disease] añublo *m*; *fig* plaga *f*, mal *m*. ◇ *vt* malograr, arruinar.

blimey ['blaɪmɪ] *excl* Br *inf* ¡ostias!

blind [blaɪnd] ◇ *adj* **-1.** [unsighted, irrational] ciego(ga). **-2.** *fig* [unaware]: to be ~ to sthg no ver algo. **-3.** Br *inf* [for emphasis]: it doesn't make a ~ bit of difference no cambia las cosas para nada. ◇ *adv*: ~ drunk borracho(cha) como una cuba. ◇ *n* [for window] persiana *f*. ◇ *npl*: the ~ los ciegos. ◇ *vt* [permanently] dejar ciego(ga); [temporarily] cegar; to ~ sb to sthg *fig* no dejar a alguien ver algo.

blind alley *n* *lit* & *fig* callejón *m* sin salida.

blind corner *n* curva *f* sin visibilidad.

blind date *n* cita *f* a ciegas.

blinders ['blaɪndəz] *npl* Am anteojeras *fpl*.

blindfold ['blaɪndfəʊld] ◇ *adv* con los ojos vendados. ◇ *n* venda *f*. ◇ *vt* vendar los ojos a.

blinding ['blaɪndɪŋ] *adj* deslumbrante.

blindly ['blaɪndlɪ] *adv* **-1.** [unable to see] a ciegas. **-2.** *fig* [guess] a boleo; [accept] ciegamente.

blindness ['blaɪndnɪs] *n* *lit* & *fig*: ~ (to) ceguera *f* (ante).

blind spot *n* **-1.** [when driving] ángulo *m* muerto. **-2.** *fig* [inability to understand] punto *m* débil.

blink [blɪŋk] ◇ *n* **-1.** [of eyes] parpadeo *m*. **-2.** *phr*: on the ~ *inf* estropeado(da). ◇ *vt* **-1.** [eyes]: to ~ one's eyes parpadear. **-2.** Am AUT: to ~ one's lights dar las luces (intermitentemente). ◇ *vi* parpadear.

blinkered ['blɪŋkəd] *adj* **-1.** [horse] con anteojeras. **-2.** *fig* [attitude] estrecho(cha) de miras.

blinkers ['blɪŋkəz] *npl* Br anteojeras *fpl*.

blinking ['blɪŋkɪŋ] *adj* Br *inf* condenado(da).

blip [blɪp] *n* **-1.** [sound] pitido *m*. **-2.** [image on radar] señal *f*. **-3.** *fig* [temporary problem] pequeño bache *m*.

bliss [blɪs] *n* gloria *f*, dicha *f*.

blissful ['blɪsfʊl] *adj* dichoso(sa), feliz.

blissfully ['blɪsfʊlɪ] *adv* [happy] dichosamente; [smile] extáticamente; [unaware] ingenuamente.

blister ['blɪstər] ◇ *n* ampolla *f*. ◇ *vi* ampollarse.

blistering ['blɪstərɪŋ] *adj* **-1.** [heat] abrasador(ra). **-2.** [attack] feroz.

blister pack *n* lámina con ampollas de plástico especialmente para envasar pastillas.

blithe [blaɪð] *adj* alegre.

blithely ['blaɪðlɪ] *adv* alegremente.

BLitt [,bi:'lɪt] (*abbr of* **Bachelor of Letters (Baccalaureus Litterarum)**) *n* (*titular de una*) *licenciatura de letras*.

blitz [blɪts] *n* **-1.** MIL bombardeo *m* aéreo. **-2.** Br *fig* [attack]: to have a ~ on sthg ponerse a hacer algo a tope (*para terminarlo*).

blizzard ['blɪzəd] *n* ventisca *f* (de nieve).

BLM (*abbr of* **Bureau of Land Management**) *n* *instituto estadounidense de gestión territorial*.

bloated ['bləʊtɪd] *adj* hinchado(da).

blob [blɒb] *n* **-1.** [drop] gota *f*. **-2.** [indistinct shape] bulto *m* borroso.

bloc [blɒk] *n* bloque *m*.

block [blɒk] ◇ *n* **-1.** [gen] bloque *m*. **-2.** Am [of buildings] manzana *f*, cuadra *f* Amer. **-3.** [obstruction - physical or mental] bloqueo *m*. **-4.** TECH: ~ and tackle sistema *m* de poleas. ◇ *vt* **-1.** [road] cortar; [pipe] obstruir. **-2.** [view] tapar. **-3.** [prevent] bloquear, obstaculizar.
◆ **block off** *vt sep* bloquear.
◆ **block out** *vt sep* **-1.** [from mind] apartar. **-2.** [light] tapar.
◆ **block up** ◇ *vt sep* obstruir. ◇ *vi* atascarse.

blockade [blɒ'keɪd] ◇ *n* bloqueo *m*. ◇ *vt* bloquear.

blockage ['blɒkɪdʒ] *n* obstrucción *f*.

block booking *n* reserva *f* de grupos grandes.

blockbuster ['blɒkbʌstəʳ] *n inf* [book] (gran) éxito *m* editorial; [film] (gran) éxito (de taquilla).

block capitals *npl* mayúsculas *fpl* (*de imprenta*).

blockhead ['blɒkhed] *n inf* zoquete *m* y *f*.

block letters *npl* mayúsculas *fpl* (*de imprenta*).

block release *n Br permiso para que un aprendiz en un trabajo vaya a estudiar temporalmente*.

block vote *n Br* voto *m* por delegación.

bloke [bləʊk] *n Br inf* tío *m*, tipo *m*, chavo *m Amer*.

blond [blɒnd] *adj* rubio(bia), catire(ra) *Amer*.

blonde [blɒnd] ◇ *adj* rubia. ◇ *n* [woman] rubia *f*.

blood [blʌd] *n* sangre *f*; *fig*: **in cold ~ a** sangre fría; **to make one's ~ boil** hacer que la sangre se le suba a uno a la cabeza; **to make one's ~ run cold** helarle a uno la sangre; **it's in his ~** lo lleva en la sangre; **new** OR **fresh ~** savia *f* nueva.

blood bank *n* banco *m* de sangre.

bloodbath ['blʌdbɑ:θ, *pl* -bɑ:ðz] *n* matanza *f*, carnicería *f*.

blood brother *n* hermano *m* de sangre.

blood cell *n* glóbulo *m*.

blood count *n* recuento *m* de glóbulos.

bloodcurdling ['blʌd,kɜ:dlɪŋ] *adj* espeluznante.

blood donor *n* donante *m* y *f* de sangre.

blood group *n* grupo *m* sanguíneo.

bloodhound ['blʌdhaʊnd] *n* sabueso *m*.

bloodless ['blʌdlɪs] *adj* **-1.** [face, lips] macilento(ta), mortecino(na). **-2.** [coup, victory] incruento(ta).

bloodletting ['blʌd,letɪŋ] *n* [killing] derramamiento *m* de sangre.

blood money *n* dinero pagado para que se cometa un asesinato.

blood orange *n* naranja *f* sanguina OR de sangre.

blood poisoning *n* septicemia *f*.

blood pressure *n* presión *f* sanguínea, tensión *f* arterial; **to have high/low ~** tener la tensión alta/baja.

blood relation, **blood relative** *n* familiar *m* consanguíneo.

bloodshed ['blʌdʃed] *n* derramamiento *m* de sangre.

bloodshot ['blʌdʃɒt] *adj* inyectado(da) (d sangre).

blood sports *npl* deportes en que se mata animales.

bloodstained ['blʌdsteɪnd] *adj* manchado(da) de sangre.

bloodstream ['blʌdstri:m] *n* fluj⌐ *m* sanguineo, sangre *f*.

blood test *n* análisis *m inv* de sangre.

bloodthirsty ['blʌd,θɜ:stɪ] *adj* sediento(ta de sangre.

blood transfusion *n* transfusión *f* de san gre.

blood type *n* grupo *m* sanguíneo.

blood vessel *n* vaso *m* sanguíneo.

bloody ['blʌdɪ] (*compar* **-ier**, *superl* **-iest**) < *adj* **-1.** [war, conflict] sangriento(ta). **-2.** [face hands] ensangrentado(da). **-3.** *Br v inf* mal dito(ta), puñetero(ra), pinche *Amer*. ◇ *ad Br v inf*: **he's ~ useless** es un puto inútil it's **~ brilliant** es de puta madre.

bloody-minded [-'maɪndɪd] *adj Br inf* pu ñetero(ra), que lleva la contraria.

bloom [blu:m] ◇ *n* flor *f*. ◇ *vi* florecer.

blooming ['blu:mɪŋ] ◇ *adj* **-1.** *Br inf* [t show annoyance] condenado(da). **-2** [healthy, attractive] radiante. ◇ *adv Br in* condenadamente.

blossom ['blɒsəm] ◇ *n* flor *f*; **in ~** en flor ◇ *vi lit & fig* florecer.

blot [blɒt] (*pt & pp* **-ted**, *cont* **-ting**) ◇ *n* [o ink] borrón *m*; *fig* mancha *f*. ◇ *vt* **-1.** [paper emborronar. **-2.** [ink] secar.

◆ **blot out** *vt sep* [gen] cubrir, ocultar [memories] borrar.

blotchy ['blɒtʃɪ] (*compar* **-ier**, *superl* **-iest**) *ad* lleno(na) de marcas.

blotting paper ['blɒtɪŋ-] *n* papel *m* secante

blouse [blaʊz] *n* blusa *f*.

blouson ['blu:zɒn] *n Br* blusón *m*.

blow [bləʊ] (*pt* **blew**, *pp* **blown**) ◇ *vi* **-1.** [gen] soplar. **-2.** [in wind] salir volando, vo lar. **-3.** [fuse] fundirse.

◇ *vt* **-1.** [subj: wind] hacer volar. **-2.** [whis tle, horn] tocar, hacer sonar. **-3.** [bubbles] hacer. **-4.** [kiss] mandar. **-5.** [fuse] fundir **-6.** [clear]: **to ~ one's nose** sonarse la nariz **-7.** *inf* [money] ventilarse.

◇ *n* **-1.** [hit, shock] golpe *m*; **to come to ~s** llegar a las manos; **to soften the ~** ayudar a encajar el golpe. **-2.** [for cause]: **a ~ (for)** un empujón OR adelanto (para).

◆ **blow out** ◇ *vt sep* apagar. ◇ *vi* **-1.** [can dle] apagarse. **-2.** [tyre] reventar.

◆ **blow over** *vi* **-1.** [storm] amainar. **-2.** [ar gument] disiparse.

◆ **blow up** ◇ *vt sep* -1. [inflate] inflar. -2. [destroy] volar. -3. [photograph] ampliar. ◇ *vi* saltar por los aires, estallar.

blow-by-blow *adj* paso por paso.

blow-dry ◇ *n* secado *m* (*con secador*). ◇ *vt* secar (*con secador*).

blowfly ['bləʊflaɪ] (*pl* -flies) *n* moscardón *m*, moscón *m*.

blowgun *Am* = blowpipe.

blowlamp *Br* ['bləʊlæmp], **blowtorch** ['bləʊtɔːtʃ] *n* soplete *m*.

blown [bləʊn] *pp* → blow.

blowout ['bləʊaʊt] *n* -1. [of tyre] pinchazo *m*, reventón *m*. -2. *inf* [big meal] comilona *f*.

blowpipe *Br* ['bləʊpaɪp], **blowgun** *Am* ['bləʊgʌn] *n* cerbatana *f*.

blowtorch = blowlamp.

blowzy ['blaʊzɪ] *adj*: **a ~ woman** una mujer gorda y zarrapastrosa.

BLS (*abbr of* Bureau of Labor Statistics) *n* instituto estadounidense de estadística laboral.

blubber ['blʌbə'] ◇ *n* grasa *f* de ballena. ◇ *vi pej* lloriquear.

bludgeon ['blʌdʒən] *vt* apalear.

blue [bluː] ◇ *adj* -1. [colour] azul. -2. *inf* [sad] triste. -3. [pornographic - film] equis (*inv*), porno; [- joke] verde. ◇ *n* azul *m*; **in ~** de azul; **out of the ~** en el momento menos pensado.
◆ **blues** *npl* -1. MUS blues *m inv*. -2. *inf* [sad feeling] depre *f*.

blue baby *n* bebé *m* cianótico.

bluebell ['bluːbel] *n* campanilla *f*.

blueberry ['bluːbərɪ] *n* arándano *m*.

bluebird ['bluːbɜːd] *n* azulejo *m* (*pájaro*).

blue-black *adj* azul oscuro (*inv*).

blue-blooded [-'blʌdɪd] *adj* de sangre azul.

bluebottle ['bluː,bɒtl] *n* moscardón *m*, moscón *m*.

blue channel *n* en las aduanas, vía de salida reservada a los ciudadanos de la CEE.

blue cheese *n* queso *m* azul.

blue chip *n* acción *f* de rentabilidad segura.
◆ **blue-chip** *comp* de rentabilidad segura.

blue-collar *adj*: **~ worker** obrero *m*, -ra *f*.

blue-eyed boy [-aɪd-] *n inf* niño *m* mimado.

blue jeans *npl Am* vaqueros *mpl*, tejanos *mpl*.

blue moon *n*: **once in a ~** de higos a brevas.

blueprint ['bluːprɪnt] *n* -1. CONSTR cianotipo *m*. -2. *fig* [description] proyecto *m*.

bluestocking ['bluː,stɒkɪŋ] *n pej* marisabidilla *f*, intelectualoide *f*.

blue tit *n Br* herrerillo *m*.

bluff [blʌf] ◇ *adj* brusco(ca). ◇ *n* -1. [deception] fanfarronada *f*; **to call sb's ~** desafiar a alguien a que haga lo que dice. -2. [cliff] acantilado *m*. ◇ *vt* engañar. ◇ *vi* fanfarronear.

blunder ['blʌndə'] ◇ *n* metedura *f* de pata. ◇ *vi* -1. [make mistake] meter la pata. -2. [move clumsily] ir tropezando; **to ~ into** sthg tropezar con algo.

blundering ['blʌndərɪŋ] *adj* estúpido(da).

blunt [blʌnt] ◇ *adj* -1. [knife] desafilado(da). -2. [object] romo(ma). -3. [forthright] directo(ta), franco(ca). ◇ *vt* -1. [knife] desafilar. -2. *fig* [weaken] debilitar, aflojar.

bluntly ['blʌntlɪ] *adv* sin rodeos, con franqueza.

bluntness ['blʌntnɪs] *n* [forthrightness] franqueza *f*.

blur [blɜː'] (*pt & pp* -red, *cont* -ring) ◇ *n* imagen *f* borrosa. ◇ *vt* -1. [vision] nublar. -2. [distinction] desdibujar, oscurecer.

blurb [blɜːb] *n inf* texto publicitario en la cubierta o solapa de un libro.

blurred [blɜːd] *adj* -1. [photograph] movido(da). -2. [vision, distinction] borroso(sa).

blurt [blɜːt]
◆ **blurt out** *vt sep* espetar, decir de repente.

blush [blʌʃ] ◇ *n* rubor *m*. ◇ *vi* ruborizarse.

blusher ['blʌʃə'] *n* colorete *m*.

bluster ['blʌstə'] ◇ *n* fanfarronería *f*. ◇ *vi* fanfarronear.

blustery ['blʌstərɪ] *adj* borrascoso(sa).

Blvd (*abbr of* Boulevard) *bulevar*.

BM *n* -1. (*abbr of* Bachelor of Medicine) (*titular de una*) *licenciatura de medicina*. -2. (*abbr of* British Museum) *museo nacional británico*.

BMA (*abbr of* British Medical Association) *n colegio británico de médicos*.

BMJ (*abbr of* British Medical Journal) *n publicación de la British Medical Association*.

BMus [,biː'mjuːz] (*abbr of* Bachelor of Music) *n* (*titular de una*) *licenciatura de música*.

BMX (*abbr of* bicycle motorcross) *n mountain-bike*.

BO *n* (*abbr of* body odour) OC *m*.

boa constrictor ['bəʊəkən'strɪktə'] *n* boa *f* constrictor.

boar [bɔː'] *n* -1. [male pig] verraco *m*. -2. [wild pig] jabalí *m*.

board [bɔːd] ◇ *n* -1. [plank] tabla *f*. -2. [for notices] tablón *m*. -3. [for games] tablero *m*. -4. [blackboard] pizarra *f*. -5. COMPUT placa *f*. -6. [of company]: **~ (of directors)** (junta *f*) directiva *f*. -7. [committee] comité *m*, junta *f*. -8. *Br* [at hotel, guesthouse] pensión *f*; **~**

and lodging comida y habitación; **full ~** pensión completa; **half ~** media pensión. **-9. on ~** [ship, plane] a bordo; [bus, train] dentro. **-10.** *phr:* **above ~** en regla; **across the ~** lineal, general; **to go by the ~** irse al garete; **to sweep the ~** arrasar; **to take sthg on ~** hacerse cargo de OR entender algo.
◇ *vt* [ship, plane] embarcar en; [train, bus] subirse a, embarcarse en *Amer*.

boarder ['bɔːdə] *n* **-1.** [lodger] huésped *m* y *f*. **-2.** [at school] interno *m*, -na *f*.

board game *n* juego *m* de tablero.

boarding card ['bɔːdɪŋ-] *n* tarjeta *f* de embarque.

boardinghouse ['bɔːdɪŋhaʊs, *pl* -haʊzɪz] *n* casa *f* de huéspedes.

boarding school ['bɔːdɪŋ-] *n* internado *m*.

board meeting *n* reunión *f* de la (junta) directiva.

Board of Trade *n* Br: **the ~** ≃ el Ministerio de Comercio.

boardroom ['bɔːdrʊm] *n* sala *f* de juntas.

boardwalk ['bɔːdwɔːk] *n* Am *paseo marítimo entarimado*.

boast [bəʊst] ◇ *n* alarde *m*. ◇ *vt* disfrutar de, presumir de tener. ◇ *vi:* **to ~ (about)** alardear OR jactarse (de), compadrear (de) *Amer*.

boastful ['bəʊstfʊl] *adj* presuntuoso(sa), fanfarrón(ona).

boat [bəʊt] *n* [large] barco *m*; [small] barca *f*; **by ~** en barco/barca; **to rock the ~** complicar las cosas; **to be in the same ~** estar en el mismo barco OR en la misma situación.

boater ['bəʊtə] *n* [hat] canotié *m*, sombrero *m* de paja.

boating ['bəʊtɪŋ] *n* paseo *m* en barco; **to go ~** dar un paseo en barco.

boatswain ['bəʊsn] *n* NAUT contramaestre *m*.

boat train *n* tren *que enlaza con un puerto*.

bob [bɒb] ◇ (*pt* & *pp* **-bed**, *cont* **-bing**) ◇ *n* **-1.** [hairstyle] corte *m* de chico. **-2.** Br *inf dated* [shilling] chelín *m*. **-3.** = **bobsleigh**. ◇ *vi* [boat] balancearse.

bobbin ['bɒbɪn] *n* bobina *f*.

bobble ['bɒbl] *n* pompón *m*.

bobby ['bɒbɪ] (*pl* **-ies**) *n* Br *inf* poli *m*.

bobby pin *n* Am horquilla *f*.

bobby socks, bobby sox *npl* Am calcetines *mpl* de colegiala.

bobsleigh ['bɒbsleɪ] *n* bobsleigh *m*.

bode [bəʊd] *vi literary:* **to ~ ill/well for** traer malos/buenos presagios para.

bodice ['bɒdɪs] *n* [of dress] cuerpo *m*.

bodily ['bɒdɪlɪ] ◇ *adj* corporal, físico(ca) ◇ *adv:* **to lift/move sb ~** levantar/mover a alguien por la fuerza.

body ['bɒdɪ] (*pl* **-ies**) *n* **-1.** [gen] cuerpo *m* (**to earn enough) to keep ~ and soul together** (ganar lo justo para) seguir tirando. **-2.** [corpse] cadáver *m*; **over my dead ~** por encima de mi cadáver. **-3.** [organization] entidad *f*; **a ~ of thought/opinion** una corriente de pensamiento/opinión. **-4.** [of car] carrocería *f*; [of plane] fuselaje *m*.

body building *n* culturismo *m*.

bodyguard ['bɒdɪgɑːd] *n* guardaespaldas *m inv*, guarura *m* *Amer*.

body odour *n* olor *m* corporal.

body search *n* cacheo *m*.

body shop *n* **-1.** [garage] taller *m* de reparación de carrocerías. **-2.** Am *inf* [gym] gimnasio *m*.

body stocking *n* [woman's undergarment] body *m*; [dancer's garment] malla *f*.

bodywork ['bɒdɪwɜːk] *n* carrocería *f*.

boffin ['bɒfɪn] *n* Br *inf* científico *m*, -ca *f*.

bog [bɒg] *n* **-1.** [marsh] cenagal *m*, lodazal *m*. **-2.** Br *v inf* [toilet] meódromo *m*, tigre *m*.

bogey ['bəʊgɪ] *n* [in golf] bogey *m*.

bogged down [bɒgd-] *adj* **-1.** [in details, work]: **~ (in)** empantanado(da) (en). **-2.** [in mud, snow]: **~ in** atascado(da) en.

boggle ['bɒgl] *vi:* **the mind ~s!** ¡me da vueltas la cabeza!, ¡es increíble!

boggy ['bɒgɪ] *adj* cenagoso(sa), pantanoso(sa).

bogie ['bəʊgɪ] *n* RAIL carretón *m*.

Bogotá [ˌbɒgə'tɑː] *n* Bogotá.

bogus ['bəʊgəs] *adj* falso(sa).

Bohemia [bəʊ'hiːmjə] *n* Bohemia.

bohemian [bəʊ'hiːmɪən] ◇ *adj* bohemio(mia). ◇ *n* bohemio *m*, -mia *f*.
◆ **Bohemian** ◇ *adj* bohemio(mia). ◇ *n* bohemio *m*, -mia *f*.

boil [bɔɪl] ◇ *n* **-1.** MED pústula *f*, grano *m*. **-2.** [boiling point]: **to bring sthg to the ~** poner algo a hervir; **to come to the ~** romper a hervir. ◇ *vt* **-1.** [water] hervir. **-2.** [pan, kettle] poner a hervir. **-3.** [food] cocer. ◇ *vi* hervir.
◆ **boil away** *vi* [evaporate] (hervir hasta) consumirse.
◆ **boil down to** *vt fus* reducirse a.
◆ **boil over** *vi* **-1.** [liquid] rebosar. **-2.** *fig* [feelings] desbordarse.

boiled [bɔɪld] *adj* cocido(da); **~ egg** huevo *m* pasado por agua; **~ sweets** Br caramelos *mpl* (duros).

boiler ['bɔɪlə] *n* caldera *f*.

boiler suit *n* Br mono *m*.

boiling ['bɔɪlɪŋ] *adj* -1. [liquid] hirviendo. -2. *inf* [hot]: **I'm ~** estoy asado(da) de calor; **it's ~** hace un calor de muerte. -3. [angry]: **~ with rage** ciego(ga) de ira.

boiling point *n* punto *m* de ebullición.

boisterous ['bɔɪstərəs] *adj* ruidoso(sa), alborotador(ra).

bold [bəʊld] *adj* -1. [brave, daring] audaz. -2. [lines, design] marcado(da). -3. [colour] vivo(va). -4. TYPO: **~ type** OR **print** negrita *f*.

boldly ['bəʊldlɪ] *adv* [bravely] con audacia, audazmente.

Bolivia [bə'lɪvɪə] *n* Bolivia.

Bolivian [bə'lɪvɪən] ⋄ *adj* boliviano(na). ⋄ *n* boliviano *m*, -na *f*.

bollard ['bɒlɑːd] *n* [on road] poste *m*.

bollocks ['bɒləks] *Br v inf* ⋄ *npl* cojones *mpl*. ⋄ *excl* ¡un cojón!, ¡qué cojones!

Bolshevik ['bɒlʃɪvɪk] ⋄ *adj* bolchevique. ⋄ *n* bolchevique *m* y *f*.

bolster ['bəʊlstər] ⋄ *n* cabezal *m*. ⋄ *vt* fortalecer, reforzar.

◆ **bolster up** *vt fus* reforzar.

bolt [bəʊlt] ⋄ *n* -1. [on door, window] cerrojo *m*. -2. [type of screw] tornillo *m*, perno *m*. ⋄ *adv*: **~ upright** muy derecho(cha). ⋄ *vt* -1. [fasten together] atornillar. -2. [door, window] echar el cerrojo a. -3. [food] tragarse. ⋄ *vi* salir disparado(da).

bomb [bɒm] ⋄ *n* bomba *f*. ⋄ *vt* bombardear.

bombard [bɒm'bɑːd] *vt* MIL & *fig*: **to ~ (with)** bombardear (a).

bombardment [bɒm'bɑːdmənt] *n* bombardeo *m*.

bombastic [bɒm'bæstɪk] *adj* grandilocuente, rimbombante.

bomb disposal squad *n* equipo *m* de artificieros.

bomber ['bɒmər] *n* -1. [plane] bombardero *m*. -2. [person] persona *f* que pone bombas.

bomber jacket *n* cazadora *f* (de aviador).

bombing ['bɒmɪŋ] *n* bombardeo *m*.

bombproof ['bɒmpruːf] *adj* a prueba de bombas.

bombshell ['bɒmʃel] *n fig* bombazo *m*.

bombsite ['bɒmsaɪt] *n* lugar *m* del bombardeo.

bona fide ['bəʊnə'faɪdɪ] *adj* de buena fe.

bonanza [bə'nænzə] *n* mina *f fig*.

bond [bɒnd] ⋄ *n* -1. [between people] lazo *m*, vínculo *m*. -2. [binding promise] compromiso *m*. -3. FIN bono *m*. ⋄ *vt* [glue] adherir; *fig* [people] unir; **to ~ sthg to** adherir algo a.

⋄ *vi* [stick together]: **to ~ (together)** adherirse; *fig* [people] unirse.

bondage ['bɒndɪdʒ] *n literary* [servitude] esclavitud *f*, vasallaje *m*.

bonded warehouse ['bɒndɪd-] *n almacén aduanero para mercancías que aún no han pagado impuestos*.

bone [bəʊn] ⋄ *n* [gen] hueso *m*; [of fish] raspa *f*, espina *f*; **~ of contention** manzana *f* de la discordia; **to feel** OR **know sthg in one's ~s** tener el presentimiento de algo; **to make no ~s about sthg** no andarse con rodeos acerca de algo; **to make no ~s about doing sthg** no tener problema en hacer algo. ⋄ *vt* [fish] limpiar; [meat] deshuesar.

bone china *n* porcelana *f* china.

bone-dry *adj* bien seco(ca).

bone-idle *adj* haragán(ana), gandul(la).

boneless ['bəʊnlɪs] *adj* [meat] deshuesado(da); [fish] sin raspa.

bone marrow *n* tuétano *m*.

bonfire ['bɒn,faɪər] *n* hoguera *f*.

bonfire night *n Br noche del 5 de noviembre en que se encienden hogueras y fuegos artificiales*.

bongo ['bɒŋgəʊ] (*pl* **-s** OR **-es**) *n*: **~ (drum)** bongó *m*.

Bonn [bɒn] *n* Bonn.

bonnet ['bɒnɪt] *n* -1. *Br* [of car] capó *m*. -2. [hat] toca *f*.

bonny ['bɒnɪ] (*compar* **-ier**, *superl* **-iest**) *adj Scot* majo(ja).

bonus ['bəʊnəs] (*pl* **-es**) *n* [extra money] paga *f* extra, prima *f*; *fig* beneficio *m* adicional.

bonus issue *n Br* FIN emisión *f* gratuita de acciones.

bony ['bəʊnɪ] (*compar* **-ier**, *superl* **-iest**) *adj* -1. [person, hand] huesudo(da). -2. [meat] lleno(na) de huesos; [fish] espinoso(sa).

boo [buː] (*pl* **-s**) ⋄ *excl* ¡bu! ⋄ *n* abucheo *m*. ⋄ *vt & vi* abuchear.

boob [buːb] *n inf* [mistake] metedura *f* de pata.

◆ **boobs** *npl Br v inf* [woman's breasts] tetas *fpl*.

boob tube *n* -1. *Br* [garment] ajustador *m*. -2. *Am inf* [television] tele *f*.

booby prize ['buːbɪ-] *n premio otorgado al último o al peor (en broma)*.

booby trap ['buːbɪ-] *n* -1. [bomb] bomba *f* camuflada. -2. [type of prank] trampa *f* (*broma*).

◆ **booby-trap** *vt* poner una trampa explosiva en.

boogie ['buːgɪ] *inf* ⋄ *n* baile *m*. ⋄ *vi* bailar.

book [bʊk] ◇ *n* **-1.** [for reading] libro *m*; **to do sthg by the ~** hacer algo como mandan los cánones; **to throw the ~ at sb** acusar a alguien de todo lo posible. **-2.** [of stamps] librillo *m*; [of tickets, cheques] talonario *m*; [of matches] cajetilla *f*. ◇ *vt* **-1.** [reserve] reservar; **to be fully ~ed** estar completo. **-2.** *inf* [subj: police] multar. **-3.** *Br* FTBL amonestar. ◇ *vi* hacer reserva.

◆ **books** *npl* COMM libros *mpl*; **to do the ~s** hacer las cuentas; **to be in sb's good/bad ~s** estar a bien/a mal con alguien.

◆ **book in** *Br* ◇ *vt sep* hacer una reserva a. ◇ *vi* registrarse.

◆ **book up** *vt sep*: **to be ~ed up** estar completo.

bookable ['bʊkəbl] *adj Br* **-1.** [seats, tickets] reservable con antelación. **-2.** FTBL punible, merecedor(ra) de tarjeta.

bookbinding ['bʊk,baɪndɪŋ] *n* encuadernación *f*.

bookcase ['bʊkkeɪs] *n* estantería *f*.

book club *n* ≃ círculo *m* de lectores.

bookends ['bʊkendz] *npl* sujetalibros *m inv*.

bookie ['bʊkɪ] *n inf* corredor *m*, -ra *f* de apuestas.

booking ['bʊkɪŋ] *n* **-1.** [reservation] reserva *f*. **-2.** *Br* FTBL amonestación *f*.

booking clerk *n* taquillero *m*, -ra *f*.

booking office *n* taquilla *f*.

bookish ['bʊkɪʃ] *adj* aficionado(da) a la lectura seria.

bookkeeper ['bʊk,kiːpə'] *n* contable *m y f*.

bookkeeping ['bʊk,kiːpɪŋ] *n* contabilidad *f*.

booklet ['bʊklɪt] *n* folleto *m*.

bookmaker ['bʊk,meɪkə'] *n* corredor *m*, -ra *f* de apuestas.

bookmark ['bʊkmɑːk] *n* separador *m*.

bookseller ['bʊk,selə'] *n* librero *m*, -ra *f*.

bookshelf ['bʊkʃelf] (*pl* **-shelves**) *n* [shelf] estante *m*; [bookcase] estantería *f*, librero *m* *Amer*.

bookshop *Br* ['bʊkʃɒp], **bookstore** *Am* ['bʊkstɔː'] *n* librería *f*.

bookstall ['bʊkstɔːl] *n Br* puesto *m* de libros.

bookstore = **bookshop**.

book token *n* vale *m* para comprar libros.

bookworm ['bʊkwɜːm] *n* ratón *m* de biblioteca.

boom [buːm] ◇ *n* **-1.** [loud noise] estampido *m*, estruendo *m*. **-2.** [increase] auge *m*, boom *m*. **-3.** NAUT botalón *m*. **-4.** [for TV camera, microphone] jirafa *f*. ◇ *vi* **-1.** [make noise] tronar. **-2.** ECON estar en auge.

boomerang ['buːməræŋ] *n* bumerán *m*.

boon [buːn] *n* ayuda *f*.

boor [bʊə'] *n* patán *m*.

boorish ['bʊərɪʃ] *adj* basto(ta).

boost [buːst] ◇ *n* **-1.** [in profits, production] incremento *m*. **-2.** [to popularity, spirits] empujón *m*, estímulo *m*. ◇ *vt* **-1.** [increase] incrementar. **-2.** [improve] levantar.

booster ['buːstə'] *n* MED inyección *f* de revacunación.

booster seat *n* asiento especial en coches para niños mayores de cuatro años.

boot [buːt] ◇ *n* **-1.** [item of footwear] bota *f*; [ankle boot] botín *m*. **-2.** *Br* [of car] maletero *m*, cajuela *f* *Amer*. ◇ *vt inf* dar una patada a.

◆ **to boot** *adv* además.

◆ **boot out** *vt sep inf* echar, poner (de patitas) en la calle.

booth [buːð] *n* **-1.** [at fair] puesto *m*. **-2.** [for phoning, voting] cabina *f*.

bootleg ['buːtleg] *adj inf* [recording] pirata; [whisky] de contrabando.

bootlegger ['buːt,legə'] *n inf* contrabandista *m y f*.

booty ['buːtɪ] *n literary* botín *m*.

booze [buːz] *inf* ◇ *n* (U) bebida *f*, alcohol *m*. ◇ *vi* pimplar, empinar el codo.

boozer ['buːzə'] *n inf* **-1.** [person] borracho *m*, -cha *f*, curda *m y f Amer*. **-2.** *Br* [pub] ≃ bareto *m*, ≃ tasca *f*.

bop [bɒp] (*pt & pp* **-ped**, *cont* **-ping**) *inf* ◇ *n* **-1.** [hit] castañazo *m*. **-2.** [disco, dance] baile *m*. ◇ *vt* cascar. ◇ *vi* bailar.

border ['bɔːdə'] ◇ *n* **-1.** [between countries] frontera *f*. **-2.** [edge] borde *m*, banda *f*. **-3.** [in garden] parterre *m*, arriate *m*. ◇ *vt* **-1.** [country] limitar con. **-2.** [edge] bordear.

◆ **border on** *vt fus* rayar en.

borderline ['bɔːdəlaɪn] ◇ *adj*: **a ~ case** un caso dudoso. ◇ *n fig* frontera *f*, límite *m*.

bore [bɔː'] ◇ *pt* → **bear**. ◇ *n* **-1.** *pej* [person] pelmazo *m*, -za *f*, pesado *m*, -da *f*; [situation, event] rollo *m*, lata *f*. **-2.** [of gun] calibre *m*. ◇ *vt* **-1.** [not interest] aburrir; **to ~ sb stiff** OR **to tears** OR **to death** aburrir a alguien un montón. **-2.** [drill] taladrar, horadar.

bored [bɔːd] *adj* aburrido(da); **to be ~ with sthg** estar harto de algo; **to be ~ stiff** OR **to tears** OR **to death** aburrirse como una ostra.

boredom ['bɔːdəm] *n* aburrimiento *m*.

boring ['bɔːrɪŋ] *adj* aburrido(da), cansador(ra) *Amer*.

born [bɔːn] *adj* **-1.** [given life] nacido(da); **to be ~** nacer; **~ and bred** nacido y criado. **-2.** [natural] nato(ta).

born-again *adj* converso(sa).

borne [bɔːn] *pp* → **bear**.

Borneo ['bɔːnɪəu] *n* Borneo.

borough ['bʌrə] *n* [area of town] distrito *m*; [town] municipio *m*.

borrow ['bɒrəu] *vt*: **to ~ sthg from sb** coger OR tomar algo prestado a alguien; **can I ~ your bike?** ¿me prestas tu bici?

borrower ['bɒrəuə'] *n* prestatario *m*, -ria *f*.

borrowing ['bɒrəuɪŋ] *n* (*U*) préstamos *mpl*.

borstal ['bɔːstl] *n Br* correccional *m*, reformatorio *m*.

Bosnia ['bɒznɪə] *n* Bosnia.

Bosnia-Herzegovina [-,hɜːtsəgə'viːnə] *n* Bosnia-Herzegovina.

Bosnian ['bɒznɪən] ◇ *adj* bosnio(nia). ◇ *n* bosnio *m*, -nia *f*.

bosom ['buzəm] *n* **-1.** [of woman] busto *m*, pecho *m*. **-2.** *fig* [centre of emotions] seno *m*; **~ friend** amigo *m*, -ga *f* del alma.

Bosporus ['bɒspərəs], **Bosphorus** ['bɒsfərəs] *n*: **the ~** el Bósforo.

boss [bɒs] ◇ *n* jefe *m*, -fa *f*; **to be one's own ~** trabajar por cuenta propia. ◇ *vt pej* mangonear, dar órdenes a.

◆ **boss about**, **boss around** *vt sep pej* mangonear, dar órdenes a.

bossy ['bɒsɪ] (*compar* **-ier**, *superl* **-iest**) *adj* mandón(ona).

bosun ['bəusn] = **boatswain**.

botanic(al) [bə'tænɪk(l)] *adj* botánico(ca).

botanical garden *n* jardín *m* botánico.

botanist ['bɒtənɪst] *n* botánico *m*, -ca *f*, botanista *m y f*.

botany ['bɒtənɪ] *n* botánica *f*.

botch [bɒtʃ]

◆ **botch up** *vt sep inf* estropear, hacer chapuceramente.

both [bəuθ] ◇ *adj* los dos, las dos, ambos(bas). ◇ *pron*: **~ (of them)** los dos (las dos), ambos *mpl*, -bas *fpl*; **~ of us are coming** vamos los dos. ◇ *adv*: **she is ~ pretty and intelligent** es guapa e inteligente.

bother ['bɒðə'] ◇ *vt* **-1.** [worry] preocupar; [irritate] fastidiar, fregar *Amer*; **I/she can't be ~ed to do it** no tengo/tiene ganas de hacerlo. **-2.** [pester] molestar. ◇ *vi*: **to ~ (to do** OR **doing sthg)** molestarse (en hacer algo); **to ~ about** preocuparse por. ◇ *n* (*U*) **-1.** [inconvenience] problema *m*. **-2.** [pest, nuisance] molestia *f*.

bothered ['bɒðəd] *adj* preocupado(da).

Botswana [bɒ'tswɑːnə] *n* Botsuana.

bottle ['bɒtl] ◇ *n* **-1.** [gen] botella *f*. **-2.** [of shampoo, medicine - plastic] bote *m*; [- glass] frasco *m*. **-3.** [for baby] biberón *m*. **-4.** (*U*) *Br inf* [courage] agallas *fpl*, arrestos *mpl*. ◇ *vt* **-1.** [wine] embotellar. **-2.** [fruit] envasar.

◆ **bottle out** *vi Br inf* achantarse, arrugarse.

◆ **bottle up** *vt sep* reprimir, tragarse.

bottle bank *n* contenedor *m* de vidrio (*para reciclaje*).

bottled ['bɒtld] *adj* embotellado(da).

bottle-feed *vt* criar con biberón.

bottleneck ['bɒtlnek] *n* **-1.** [in traffic] embotellamiento *m*. **-2.** [in production] freno *m*.

bottle-opener *n* abridor *m*, abrebotellas *m inv*.

bottle party *n* fiesta a la que los invitados traen bebida.

bottom ['bɒtəm] ◇ *adj* **-1.** [lowest] más bajo(ja), de abajo del todo. **-2.** [least successful] peor. ◇ *n* **-1.** [lowest part - of glass, bottle] culo *m*; [- of bag, mine, sea] fondo *m*; [- of ladder, hill] pie *m*; [- of page, list] final *m*. **-2.** [farthest point] final *m*, fondo *m*. **-3.** [of class etc] parte *f* más baja. **-4.** [buttocks] culo *m*, trasero *m*, traste *m Amer*. **-5.** [root]: **at the ~ of** detrás de; **to get to the ~ of** llegar al fondo de.

◆ **bottom out** *vi* tocar fondo.

bottomless ['bɒtəmlɪs] *adj* **-1.** [very deep] sin fondo, insondable. **-2.** [endless] inagotable.

bottom line *n fig*: **the ~ is ...** a fin de cuentas ....

botulism ['bɒtjolɪzm] *n* botulismo *m*.

bough [bau] *n* rama *f*.

bought [bɔːt] *pt & pp* → **buy**.

boulder ['bəuldə'] *n* canto *m* rodado.

boulevard ['buːləvɑːd] *n* bulevar *m*.

bounce [bauns] ◇ *vi* **-1.** [gen] rebotar. **-2.** [light] reflejarse. **-3.** [person]: **to ~ into the room** irrumpir en el cuarto; **to ~ (on sthg)** dar botes (en algo). **-4.** *inf* [cheque] ser rechazado(da) por el banco. ◇ *vt* botar. ◇ *n* bote *m*.

◆ **bounce back** *vi* recuperarse.

bouncer ['baunsə'] *n inf* matón *m*, gorila *m* (*de un local*).

bouncy ['baunsɪ] (*compar* **-ier**, *superl* **-iest**) *adj* **-1.** [lively] animado(da), dinámico(ca). **-2.** [springy] elástico(ca).

bound [baund] ◇ *pt & pp* → **bind**. ◇ *adj* **-1.** [certain]: **it's ~ to happen** seguro que va a pasar. **-2.** [obliged]: **~ (by sthg/to do sthg)** obligado(da) (por algo/a hacer algo); **I'm ~ to say** OR **admit** tengo que decir OR admitir. **-3.** [for place]: **to be ~ for** ir rumbo a. ◇ *n* salto *m*. ◇ *vt*: **to be ~ed by** estar rodeado(da) de. ◇ *vi* ir dando saltos.

◆ **bounds** *npl* [limits] límites *mpl*; **out of ~s** (en) zona prohibida.

boundary ['baʊndərɪ] (*pl* **-ies**) *n* [gen] límite *m*; [between countries] frontera *f*.

boundless ['baʊndlɪs] *adj* ilimitado(da).

bountiful ['baʊntɪful] *adj literary* [ample] generoso(sa), opulento(ta).

bounty ['baʊntɪ] *n literary* [generosity] magnificencia *f*, generosidad *f*.

bouquet [bəʊ'keɪ] *n* [of flowers] ramo *m*.

bouquet garni ['buːkeɪgɑː'niː] *n* ramo de hierbas aromáticas atadas y utilizadas en cocina.

bourbon ['bɜːbən] *n* bourbon *m*.

bourgeois ['bɔːʒwɑː] *adj pej* burgués(esa).

bourgeoisie [,bɔːʒwɑː'ziː] *n pej*: **the ~** la burguesía.

bout [baʊt] *n* **-1.** [attack] ataque *m*, acceso *m*. **-2.** [session] racha *f*. **-3.** [boxing match] pelea *f*, combate *m*.

boutique [buː'tiːk] *n* boutique *f*.

bow[1] [baʊ] ◇ *n* **-1.** [act of bowing] reverencia *f*. **-2.** [of ship] proa *f*. ◇ *vt* inclinar. ◇ *vi* **-1.** [make a bow] inclinarse. **-2.** [defer]: **to ~ to sthg** ceder OR doblegarse ante algo.
◆ **bow down** *vi* doblegarse.
◆ **bow out** *vi* retirarse.

bow[2] [bəʊ] *n* **-1.** [weapon. musical instrument] arco *m*. **-2.** [knot] lazo *m*.

bowels ['baʊəlz] *npl lit* & *fig* entrañas *fpl*.

bowl [bəʊl] ◇ *n* **-1.** [gen] cuenco *m*, bol *m*; [for soup] tazón *m*; [for washing clothes] barreño *m*, balde *m*. **-2.** [of toilet] taza *f*; [of pipe] cazoleta *f*. ◇ *vt* lanzar. ◇ *vi* lanzar la bola.
◆ **bowls** *n* (*U*) bochas *fpl*.
◆ **bowl over** *vt sep* **-1.** [knock over] atropellar. **-2.** *fig* [surprise. impress] dejar atónito(ta).

bow-legged [,bəʊ'legɪd] *adj* de piernas arqueadas, estevado(da).

bowler ['bəʊlə'] *n* **-1.** CRICKET lanzador *m*. **-2.** **~ (hat)** bombín *m*, sombrero *m* hongo, tongo *m Amer*.

bowling ['bəʊlɪŋ] *n* (*U*) bolos *mpl*.

bowling alley *n* **-1.** [building] bolera *f*. **-2.** [alley] calle *f*.

bowling green *n* campo de césped para jugar a las bochas.

bow tie [bəʊ-] *n* pajarita *f*.

bow window [bəʊ-] *n* mirador *m*.

box [bɒks] ◇ *n* **-1.** [container, boxful] caja *f*; [for jewels] estuche *m*. **-2.** THEATRE palco *m*. **-3.** *Br inf* [television]: **the ~** la caja tonta. ◇ *vt* **-1.** BOXING boxear con. **-2.** [put in boxes] encajonar. ◇ *vi* boxear.
◆ **box in** *vt sep* **-1.** [cut off] encerrar, encajonar. **-2.** [build a box around] proteger con una caja.

boxed [bɒkst] *adj* presentado(da) en una caja.

boxer ['bɒksə'] *n* **-1.** [fighter] boxeador *m*, púgil *m*. **-2.** [dog] bóxer *m*.

boxer shorts *npl* calzón *m* (de boxeo).

boxing ['bɒksɪŋ] *n* boxeo *m*, box *m Amer*.

Boxing Day *n* fiesta nacional en Inglaterra y Gales el 26 de diciembre (salvo domingos) en que tradicionalmente se da el aguinaldo.

boxing glove *n* guante *m* de boxeo.

boxing ring *n* ring *m*, cuadrilátero *m*.

box junction *n Br* parrilla *f* (en un cruce).

box number *n* apartado *m* de correos.

box office *n* taquilla *f*, boletería *f Amer*.

boxroom ['bɒksrum] *n Br* trastero *m*.

boy [bɔɪ] ◇ *n* **-1.** [male child] chico *m*, niño *m*, pibe *m Amer*. **-2.** *inf* [young man] chaval *m*. ◇ *excl*: **(oh) ~!** ¡jolín!, ¡vaya, vaya!

boycott ['bɔɪkɒt] ◇ *n* boicot *m*. ◇ *vt* boicotear.

boyfriend ['bɔɪfrend] *n* novio *m*, pololo *m Amer*.

boyish ['bɔɪɪʃ] *adj* **-1.** [man] juvenil. **-2.** [woman. figure] masculino(na).

boy scout *n* (boy) scout *m*.

bozo ['bəʊzəʊ] *n inf* tonto *m*, -ta *f*, bobo *m*, -ba *f*.

Bp (*abbr of* **Bishop**) Ob.

Br, Bro (*abbr of* **brother**) [preceding name of monk] Hno.

BR (*abbr of* **British Rail**) *n* ferrocarriles británicos, ≈ Renfe *f*.

bra [brɑː] *n* sujetador *m*, ajustadores *mpl Amer*.

brace [breɪs] ◇ *n* **-1.** [on teeth] aparato *m* corrector. **-2.** [on leg] soporte *m* para la pierna. **-3.** [pair] par *m*. ◇ *vt* [steady] tensar; **to ~ o.s. (for)** *lit* & *fig* prepararse (para).
◆ **braces** *npl Br* tirantes *mpl*, tiradores *mpl Amer*.

bracelet ['breɪslɪt] *n* brazalete *m*, pulsera *f*.

bracing ['breɪsɪŋ] *adj* tonificante.

bracken ['brækn] *n* helecho *m*.

bracket ['brækɪt] ◇ *n* **-1.** [support] soporte *m*, palomilla *f*. **-2.** [parenthesis - round] paréntesis *m inv*; [- square] corchete *m*; **in ~s** entre paréntesis. **-3.** [group] sector *m*, banda *f*. ◇ *vt* **-1.** [enclose in brackets] poner entre paréntesis. **-2.** [group]: **to ~ sthg/sb (together) with** agrupar algo/a alguien (junto) con.

brackish ['brækɪʃ] *adj* salino(na), salobre.

brag [bræg] (*pt* & *pp* **-ged**, *cont* **-ging**) *vi* fanfarronear, jactarse, compadrear *Amer*.

braid [breɪd] ◇ *n* **-1.** [on uniform] galón *m*. **-2.** [hairstyle] trenza *f*. ◇ *vt* trenzar.

bread

braille [breɪl] *n* braille *m*.

brain [breɪn] *n* lit & fig cerebro *m*; **to have sthg on the ~** tener algo metido en la cabeza.

◆ **brains** *npl* cerebro *m*, seso *m*; **to pick sb's ~s** recurrir a los conocimientos de alguien.

brainchild ['breɪntʃaɪld] *n* inf invención *f*, idea *f*.

brain death *n* muerte *f* cerebral.

brain drain *n* fuga *f* de cerebros.

brainless ['breɪnlɪs] *adj* insensato(ta), estúpido(da).

brainstorm ['breɪnstɔːm] *n* **-1.** *Br* [moment of aberration] momento *m* de atontamiento OR estupidez. **-2.** *Am* [brilliant idea] idea *f* genial, genialidad *f*.

brainstorming ['breɪn,stɔːmɪŋ] *n*: **~ session** reunión para solucionar un problema en la que todos piensan el mayor número de ideas posible en poco tiempo.

brainteaser ['breɪn,tiːzə'] *n* rompecabezas *m inv*.

brainwash ['breɪnwɒʃ] *vt* lavar el cerebro a.

brainwave ['breɪnweɪv] *n* idea *f* genial.

brainy ['breɪnɪ, (compar -ier, superl -iest) adj inf listo(ta).

braise [breɪz] *vt* cocer a fuego lento.

brake [breɪk] ◇ *n* lit & fig freno *m*. ◇ *vi* frenar.

brake horsepower *n* potencia *f* en caballos de vapor.

brake light *n* luz *f* de freno.

brake lining *n* forro *m* del freno.

brake pedal *n* pedal *m* del freno.

brake shoe *n* zapata *f* del freno.

bramble ['bræmbl] *n* [bush] zarza *f*, zarzamora *f*; [fruit] **mora** *f*.

bran [bræn] *n* salvado *m*.

branch [brɑːntʃ] ◇ *n* **-1.** [of tree, of subject] rama *f*. **-2.** [of river] afluente *m*; [of railway] ramal *m*. **-3.** [of company, bank] sucursal *f*. ◇ *vi* bifurcarse.

◆ **branch off** *vi* desviarse.

◆ **branch out** *vi* [person] ampliar horizontes; [firm] expandirse, diversificarse.

branch line *n* ramal *m*.

brand [brænd] ◇ *n* **-1.** [of product] marca *f*. **-2.** *fig* [type] tipo *m*, estilo *m*. **-3.** [mark] hierro *m*. ◇ *vt* **-1.** [cattle] marcar (con hierro). **-2.** *fig* [classify]: **to ~ sb (as sthg)** tildar a alguien (de algo).

brandish ['brændɪʃ] *vt* [weapon] blandir; [letter etc] agitar.

brand leader *n* marca *f* líder OR puntera.

brand name *n* marca *f*.

brand-new *adj* flamante.

brandy ['brændɪ] (*pl* **-ies**) *n* coñac *m*, brandy *m*.

brash [bræʃ] *adj pej* insolente.

Brasilia [brə'zɪljə] *n* Brasilia.

brass [brɑːs] *n* **-1.** [metal] latón *m*. **-2.** MUS: **the ~** el metal.

brass band *n* banda *f* de metal.

brasserie ['bræsərɪ] *n* restaurante *m*.

brassiere [*Br* 'bræsɪə', *Am* brə'zɪr] *n* sostén *m*, sujetador *m*.

brass knuckles *npl Am* guante *m* de clavos.

brass tacks *npl inf*: **to get down to ~** ir al grano.

brat [bræt] *n inf pej* mocoso *m*, -sa *f*.

bravado [brə'vɑːdəʊ] *n* bravuconería *f*.

brave [breɪv] ◇ *adj* valiente. ◇ *n* guerrero *m* indio. ◇ *vt* [weather, storm] desafiar; [sb's anger] hacer frente a.

bravely ['breɪvlɪ] *adv* valientemente.

bravery ['breɪvərɪ] *n* valentía *f*.

bravo [,brɑː'vəʊ] *excl* ¡bravo!

brawl [brɔːl] *n* gresca *f*, reyerta *f*.

brawn [brɔːn] *n* (*U*) **-1.** [muscle] musculatura *f*, fuerza *f* física. **-2.** *Br* [meat] carne de cerdo en gelatina.

brawny ['brɔːnɪ] (*comp* **-ier**, *superl* **-iest**) *adj* musculoso(sa).

bray [breɪ] *vi* [donkey] rebuznar.

brazen ['breɪzn] *adj* [person] descarado(da); [lie] burdo(da).

◆ **brazen out** *vt sep*: **to ~ it out** echarle cara.

brazier ['breɪzjə'] *n* brasero *m*.

Brazil [brə'zɪl] *n* (el) Brasil.

Brazilian [brə'zɪljən] ◇ *adj* brasileño(ña), brasilero(ra) *Amer*. ◇ *n* brasileño *m*, -ña *f*, brasilero *m*, -ra *f Amer*.

brazil nut *n* nuez *f* de Pará.

breach [briːtʃ] ◇ *n* **-1.** [act of disobedience] incumplimiento *m*; **~ of confidence** abuso *m* de confianza; **to be in ~ of sthg** incumplir algo; **breach of contract** incumplimiento de contrato. **-2.** [opening, gap] brecha *f*; **to step into the ~** echar una mano. **-3.** *fig* [in friendship, marriage] ruptura *f*. ◇ *vt* **-1.** [disobey] incumplir. **-2.** [make hole in] abrir (una) brecha en.

breach of the peace *n* alteración *f* del orden público.

bread [bred] *n* **-1.** [food] pan *m*; **~ and butter** [buttered bread] pan con mantequilla; *fig* [main income] sustento *m* diario. **-2.** *inf* [money] **pasta** *f*.

bread bin *Br*, **bread box** *Am n* panera *f*.

breadboard ['bredbɔːd] *n* tabla *f* (de cortar el pan).

bread box *Am* = **bread bin**.

breadcrumbs ['bredkrʌmz] *npl* migas *fpl* (de pan); CULIN pan *m* rallado.

breaded ['bredɪd] *adj* empanado(da).

breadline ['bredlaɪn] *n*: **to be on the ~** vivir en la miseria.

breadth [bretθ] *n* **-1.** [in measurements] anchura *f*. **-2.** *fig* [scope] amplitud *f*.

breadwinner ['bred,wɪnəʳ] *n* cabeza *m y f* de familia.

break [breɪk] (*pt* broke, *pp* broken) ◇ *n* **-1.** [gap - in clouds] claro *m*; [- in line] espacio *m* en blanco; [- in transmission] corte *m*. **-2.** [fracture] rotura *f*, fractura *f*. **-3.** [rupture]: ~ **(with)** ruptura *f* (con). **-4.** [pause]: ~ **(from)** descanso *m* (de); **to have** OR **take a ~** tomarse un descanso. **-5.** [playtime] recreo *m*. **-6.** *inf* [chance] oportunidad *f*; **a lucky ~** un golpe de suerte. **-7.** *literary*: **at ~ of day** al alba. **-8.** COMPUT: ~ **(key)** tecla *f* de interrupción.
◇ *vt* **-1.** [gen] romper; [arm, leg etc] romperse; **the river broke its banks** el río se desbordó; **to ~ sb's hold** escaparse OR liberarse de alguien. **-2.** [machine] estropear. **-3.** [journey, contact] interrumpir. **-4.** [habit, health] acabar con; [strike] reventar. **-5.** [law, rule] violar; [appointment, word] faltar a. **-6.** [record] batir. **-7.** [in tennis - service] romper. **-8.** [tell]: **to ~ the news (of sthg to sb)** dar la noticia (de algo a alguien).
◇ *vi* **-1.** [come to pieces] romperse. **-2.** [stop working] estropearse. **-3.** [pause] parar; [weather] cambiar. **-4.** [start - day] romper; [- storm] estallar, desencadenarse. **-5.** [wave] romper. **-6.** [escape]: **to ~ loose** OR **free** escaparse. **-7.** [voice] cambiar. **-8.** [news] divulgarse. **-9.** *phr*: **to ~ even** salir sin pérdidas ni beneficios.

◆ **break away** *vi* escaparse; **to ~ away (from)** [end connection] separarse (de); POL escindirse (de).

◆ **break down** ◇ *vt sep* **-1.** [destroy - gen] derribar, echar abajo; [- resistance] vencer. **-2.** [analyse] descomponer. **-3.** [cause to decompose] descomponer. ◇ *vi* **-1.** [collapse, disintegrate, fail] venirse abajo. **-2.** [stop working] estropearse. **-3.** [lose emotional control] perder el control. **-4.** [decompose] descomponerse.

◆ **break in** ◇ *vi* **-1.** [enter by force] entrar por la fuerza. **-2.** [interrupt]: **to ~ in (on sthg/sb)** interrumpir (algo/a alguien). ◇ *vt sep* **-1.** [horse, shoes] domar. **-2.** [person] amoldar, poner al tanto.

◆ **break into** *vt fus* **-1.** [house, shop] entrar (por la fuerza) en, allanar; [box, safe] forzar. **-2.** [begin suddenly]: **to ~ into song/a run** echarse a cantar/correr. **-3.** [become involved in] introducirse OR adentrarse en.

◆ **break off** ◇ *vt sep* **-1.** [detach] partir. **-2.** [end] romper; [holiday] interrumpir. ◇ *vi* **-1.** [become detached] partirse. **-2.** [stop talking] interrumpirse. **-3.** [stop working] parar (de trabajar).

◆ **break out** *vi* **-1.** [fire, fighting, panic] desencadenarse; [war] estallar. **-2.** [become covered]: **he broke out in spots** le salieron granos. **-3.** [escape]: **to ~ out (of)** escapar (de).

◆ **break through** *vt fus* abrirse paso a través de. ◇ *vi* abrirse paso.

◆ **break up** ◇ *vt sep* **-1.** [ice] hacer pedazos; [car] desguazar. **-2.** [relationship] romper; [talks] poner fin a; [fight, crowd] disolver. ◇ *vi* **-1.** [into smaller pieces] hacerse pedazos. **-2.** [relationship] deshacerse; [conference] concluir; [school, pupils] terminar el curso; **to ~ up with sb** romper con alguien. **-3.** [crowd] disolverse.

◆ **break with** *vt fus* romper con.

breakable ['breɪkəbl] *adj* frágil.

breakage ['breɪkɪdʒ] *n* rotura *f*.

breakaway ['breɪkəweɪ] *adj* disidente.

break dancing *n* break (dance) *m*.

breakdown ['breɪkdaʊn] *n* **-1.** [of car, train] avería *f*; [of talks, in communications] ruptura *f*; [of law and order] colapso *m*; **nervous ~** crisis *f* (nerviosa). **-2.** [analysis] desglose *m*.

breaker ['breɪkəʳ] *n* [wave] cachón *m*, gran ola *f*.

breakeven [,breɪk'iːvn] *n* punto *m* de equilibrio (de pérdidas y ganancias).

breakfast ['brekfəst] ◇ *n* desayuno *m*. ◇ *vi fml*: **to ~ (on sthg)** desayunar (algo).

breakfast cereal *n* cereales *mpl* (*para desayuno*).

breakfast television *n Br* programación *f* matinal de televisión.

break-in *n* robo *m* (*con allanamiento de morada*).

breaking ['breɪkɪŋ] *n*: ~ **and entering** JUR allanamiento *m* de morada.

breaking point *n*: **to be at ~** estar al límite OR a punto de estallar.

breakneck ['breɪknek] *adj*: **at ~ speed** a (una) velocidad de vértigo.

breakthrough ['breɪkθruː] *n* avance *m*, paso *m* adelante.

breakup ['breɪkʌp] *n* ruptura *f*.

breakup value *n* COMM valor *m* en liquidación.

bream [briːm] (*pl inv* OR **-s**) *n* [sea bream] besugo *m*; [freshwater] brema *f*.

breast [brest] *n* **-1.** [of woman] pecho *m*, seno *m*; [of man] pecho. **-2.** [meat of bird] pechuga *f*. **-3.** *literary* [seat of emotions] corazón *m*; **to make a clean ~ of it** confesarlo abiertamente.

breast-feed *vt & vi* amamantar, dar de mamar.

breast pocket *n* bolsillo *m* del pecho OR de arriba.

breaststroke ['breststrəʊk] *n* braza *f*.

breath [breθ] *n* respiración *f*, aliento *m*; **to take a deep ~** respirar hondo; **to be a ~ of fresh air** *fig* [person, experience] ser un soplo de aire fresco; **to get one's ~ back** recuperar el aliento; **to go for a ~ of (fresh) air** salir a tomar un poco de aire; **to hold one's ~** [stop breathing] aguantar la respiración; [wait anxiously] contener el aliento; **to say sthg under one's ~** decir algo en voz baja; **to take one's ~ away** dejar a uno sin habla OR respiración; **to waste/save one's ~** gastar/no gastar saliva; **out of ~** sin aliento.

breathable ['briːðəbl] *adj* respirable.

breathalyse *Br*, **-yze** *Am* ['breθəlaɪz] *vt* hacer la prueba del alcohol a.

Breathalyser® *Br*, **-yzer**® *Am* ['breθəlaɪzə'] *n* alcoholímetro *m*.

breathe [briːð] ◇ *vi* respirar; **to ~ more easily** *fig* respirar (más) tranquilo. ◇ *vt* **-1.** [inhale] respirar, aspirar. **-2.** [exhale] despedir.
◆ **breathe in** *vt sep & vi* aspirar.
◆ **breathe out** *vi* espirar.

breather ['briːðə'] *n inf* respiro *m*, descanso *m*.

breathing ['briːðɪŋ] *n* respiración *f*.

breathing space *n* (periodo *m* de) respiro *m*.

breathless ['breθlɪs] *adj* **-1.** [out of breath] ahogado(da), jadeante. **-2.** [with excitement] sin aliento (por la emoción).

breathtaking ['breθ,teɪkɪŋ] *adj* sobrecogedor(ra), impresionante.

breath test *n* prueba *f* del alcohol.

breed [briːd] (*pt & pp* **bred** [bred]) ◇ *n* **-1.** [of animal] raza *f*. **-2.** *fig* [sort] generación *f*, especie *f*. ◇ *vt* **-1.** [animals] criar; [plants] cultivar. **-2.** *fig* [suspicion] alimentar; [contempt, hate] concitar. ◇ *vi* procrear, reproducirse.

breeder ['briːdə'] *n* [of animals] criador *m*, -ra *f*.

breeder reactor *n* reactor *m* generador.

breeding ['briːdɪŋ] *n* **-1.** [of animals] cría *f*; [of plants] cultivo *m*. **-2.** [manners] educación *f*.

breeding-ground *n* [of ideas, activity] campo *m* de cultivo.

breeze [briːz] ◇ *n* brisa *f*. ◇ *vi*: **to ~ in/out** entrar/salir como si tal cosa.

breezeblock ['briːzblɒk] *n Br* ladrillo *grande de cemento y cenizas de coque*.

breezy ['briːzɪ] (*compar* **-ier**, *superl* **-iest**) *adj* **-1.** [windy]: **it's ~** hace aire. **-2.** [cheerful] jovial, despreocupado(da).

Breton ['bretn] ◇ *adj* bretón(ona). ◇ *n* **-1.** [person] bretón *m*, -ona *f*. **-2.** [language] bretón *m*.

brevity ['brevɪtɪ] *n* brevedad *f*.

brew [bruː] ◇ *vt* [beer] elaborar; [tea, coffee] preparar. ◇ *vi* **-1.** [tea] reposar. **-2.** [trouble] fraguarse.

brewer ['bruːə'] *n* cervecero *m*, -ra *f*.

brewery ['brʊərɪ] (*pl* **-ies**) *n* fábrica *f* de cerveza.

briar ['braɪə'] *n* brezo *m*.

bribe [braɪb] ◇ *n* soborno *m*, coima *f Amer*. ◇ *vt*: **to ~ (sb to do sthg)** sobornar (a alguien para que haga algo).

bribery ['braɪbərɪ] *n* soborno *m*.

bric-a-brac ['brɪkəbræk] *n* baratijas *fpl*.

brick [brɪk] *n* ladrillo *m*.
◆ **brick up** *vt sep* enladrillar, tapiar (con ladrillos).

bricklayer ['brɪk,leɪə'] *n* albañil *m*.

brickwork ['brɪkwɜːk] *n* enladrillado *m*, ladrillos *mpl*.

bridal ['braɪdl] *adj* nupcial; **~ dress** traje *m* de novia.

bride [braɪd] *n* novia *f*.

bridegroom ['braɪdgrʊm] *n* novio *m*.

bridesmaid ['braɪdzmeɪd] *n* dama *f* de honor.

bridge [brɪdʒ] ◇ *n* **-1.** [gen] puente *m*; **I'll cross that ~ when I come to it** ya me preocuparé de eso cuando llegue el momento. **-2.** [on ship] puente *m* de mando. **-3.** [of nose] caballete *m*. **-4.** [card game] bridge *m*. ◇ *vt* *fig* [gap] llenar.

bridging loan ['brɪdʒɪŋ-] *n Br* préstamo *m* puente.

bridle ['braɪdl] ◇ *n* brida *f*. ◇ *vt* embridar. ◇ *vi*: **to ~ (at)** indignarse (por OR ante).

bridle path *n* camino *m* de herradura.

brief [briːf] ◇ *adj* **-1.** [short, to the point] breve; **in ~** en resumen. **-2.** [clothes] corto(ta). ◇ *n* **-1.** JUR [statement] sumario *m*, resumen *m*. **-2.** *Br* [instructions] instrucciones *fpl.* ◇ *vt*: **to ~ sb (on)** informar a alguien (acerca de).

◆ **briefs** *npl* [underpants] calzoncillos *mpl*; [knickers] bragas *fpl*.

briefcase ['briːfkeɪs] *n* maletín *m*, portafolios *m inv*.

briefing ['briːfɪŋ] *n* [meeting] reunión *f* informativa; [instructions] instrucciones *fpl*.

briefly ['briːflɪ] *adv* **-1.** [for a short time] brevemente. **-2.** [concisely] en pocas palabras.

Brig. *abbr of* **brigadier**.

brigade [brɪˈgeɪd] *n* brigada *f*.

brigadier [ˌbrɪgəˈdɪəʳ] *n* brigadier *m*, general *m* de brigada.

bright [braɪt] *adj* **-1.** [light] brillante; [day, room] luminoso(sa); [weather] despejado(da). **-2.** [colour] vivo(va), fuerte. **-3.** [lively - eyes] brillante; [- smile] radiante. **-4.** [intelligent - person] listo(ta); [- idea] genial. **-5.** [hopeful] prometedor(ra).

◆ **brights** *npl* Am *inf* faros *mpl*.

◆ **bright and early** *adv* muy de mañana, muy temprano.

brighten ['braɪtn] *vi* **-1.** [become lighter] clarear, despejarse. **-2.** [become more cheerful] alegrarse.

◆ **brighten up** ◇ *vt sep* animar, alegrar. ◇ *vi* **-1.** [become more cheerful] animarse. **-2.** [weather] clarear, despejarse.

brightly ['braɪtlɪ] *adv* **-1.** [shine] de forma resplandeciente. **-2.** [coloured] vivamente. **-3.** [cheerfully] alegremente.

brightness ['braɪtnɪs] *n* **-1.** [of light] luminosidad *f*, brillo *m*. **-2.** [of colour] viveza *f*.

brilliance ['brɪljəns] *n* **-1.** [cleverness] brillantez *f*. **-2.** [of colour, light] brillo *m*.

brilliant ['brɪljənt] *adj* **-1.** [clever] genial, fantástico(ca). **-2.** [colour] vivo(va). **-3.** [light, career, future] brillante. **-4.** *inf* [wonderful] fenomenal, genial.

brilliantly ['brɪljəntlɪ] *adv* **-1.** [cleverly] de manera genial. **-2.** [coloured] vivamente. **-3.** [shine] brillantemente.

Brillo pad® ['brɪləu-] *n* estropajo *m* (jabonoso) de aluminio.

brim [brɪm] (*pt & pp* **-med**, *cont* **-ming**) ◇ *n* **-1.** [edge] borde *m*. **-2.** [of hat] ala *f*. ◇ *vi lit & fig*: **to ~ with** rebosar de.

◆ **brim over** *vi lit & fig*: **to ~ over (with)** rebosar (de).

brine [braɪn] *n* salmuera *f*.

bring [brɪŋ] (*pt & pp* **brought**) *vt* **-1.** [gen] traer; **to ~ sthg to an end** poner fin a algo. **-2.** JUR: **to ~ charges against** presentar una denuncia contra; **to ~ sb to trial** llevar a alguien a juicio. **-3.** *phr*: **I/he** *etc* **couldn't ~**

myself/himself *etc* **to do it** yo/él *etc* era incapaz de hacerlo.

◆ **bring about** *vt sep* producir.

◆ **bring along** *vt sep* traer.

◆ **bring around** *vt sep* [make conscious] reanimar, hacer recuperar el conocimiento.

◆ **bring back** *vt sep* **-1.** [books etc] devolver; [person] traer de vuelta. **-2.** [shopping] traer. **-3.** [memories] traer (a la memoria). **-4.** [practice, hanging] volver a introducir; [fashion] recuperar.

◆ **bring down** *vt sep* **-1.** [plane, bird] derribar; [government, tyrant] derrocar. **-2.** [prices] reducir.

◆ **bring forward** *vt sep* **-1.** [meeting, elections etc] adelantar. **-2.** [in bookkeeping] sumar a la siguiente columna.

◆ **bring in** *vt sep* **-1.** [introduce - law] implantar; [- bill] presentar. **-2.** [earn] ganar, ingresar. **-3.** JUR [verdict] pronunciar.

◆ **bring off** *vt sep* [plan] sacar adelante; [deal] cerrar.

◆ **bring on** *vt sep* producir, ocasionar; **you brought it on yourself** tú (solo) te lo buscaste.

◆ **bring out** *vt sep* **-1.** [new product, book] sacar. **-2.** [the worst etc in sb] revelar, despertar.

◆ **bring round**, **bring to** = **bring around**.

◆ **bring up** *vt sep* **-1.** [raise - children] criar. **-2.** [mention] sacar a relucir. **-3.** [vomit] devolver.

brink [brɪŋk] *n*: **on the ~ of** al borde de.

brisk [brɪsk] *adj* **-1.** [quick] rápido(da). **-2.** [busy] boyante, activo(va). **-3.** [efficient, confident - manner] enérgico(ca); [- person] eficaz. **-4.** [weather] fresco(ca).

brisket ['brɪskɪt] *n* carne *f* de pecho.

briskly ['brɪsklɪ] *adv* **-1.** [quickly] rápidamente. **-2.** [efficiently, confidently] con soltura y eficacia.

bristle ['brɪsl] ◇ *n* [gen] cerda *f*; [of person] pelillo *m*. ◇ *vi* **-1.** [stand up] erizarse, ponerse de punta. **-2.** [react angrily]: **to ~ (at)** enfadarse (por).

◆ **bristle with** *vt fus* estar sembrado(da) de.

bristly ['brɪslɪ] (*compar* **-ier**, *superl* **-iest**) *adj* [chin, face] con barba áspera OR de tres días; [moustache] erizado(da), pinchudo(da).

Brit [brɪt] *n inf* británico *m*, -ca *f*.

Britain ['brɪtn] *n* Gran Bretaña.

British ['brɪtɪʃ] ◇ *adj* británico(ca). ◇ *npl*: **the ~** los británicos.

British Columbia *n* (la) Columbia Británica.

British Council *n*: the ~ el British Council.

BRITISH COUNCIL:
El British Council es un organismo cultural público encargado de promover la lengua inglesa y la cultura británica, y de reforzar los lazos culturales con otros países

Britisher ['brɪtɪʃə'] *n Am* británico *m*, -ca *f*, inglés *m*, -esa *f*.
British Isles *npl*: the ~ las islas Británicas.
British Rail *n compañía ferroviaria británica*, ≃ Renfe *f*.
British Summer Time *n hora oficial británica entre finales de marzo y de octubre.*
British Telecom [-'telɪkɒm] *n principal empresa británica de telecomunicaciones*, ≃ Telefónica *f*.
Briton ['brɪtn] *n* británico *m*, -ca *f*.
Britpop ['brɪtpɒp] *n* Britpop *m, corriente de la música pop británica de los 90.*
Brittany ['brɪtənɪ] *n* (la) Bretaña.
brittle ['brɪtl] *adj* quebradizo(za), frágil.
Bro = **Br**.
broach [brəʊtʃ] *vt* abordar.
B road *n Br* ≃ carretera *f* comarcal.
broad [brɔːd] *adj* **-1.** [shoulders, river, street] ancho(cha); [grin] amplio(plia). **-2.** [range, interests] amplio(plia). **-3.** [description, outline] general, a grandes rasgos. **-4.** [hint] claro(ra). **-5.** [accent] cerrado(da), marcado(da). **-6.** *phr*: **in** ~ **daylight** a plena luz del día.
broad bean *n* haba *f*.
broadcast ['brɔːdkɑːst] (*pt* & *pp* **broadcast**) ◇ *n* emisión *f*. ◇ *vt* emitir.
broadcaster ['brɔːdkɑːstə'] *n* locutor *m*, -ra *f*.
broadcasting ['brɔːdkɑːstɪŋ] *n* (*U*) TV emisión *f* (televisiva); RADIO radiodifusión *f*.
broaden ['brɔːdn] ◇ *vt* **-1.** [road, pavement] ensanchar. **-2.** [scope, appeal] ampliar. ◇ *vi* [river, road] ensancharse; [smile] hacerse más amplia.
◆ **broaden out** ◇ *vt sep* ampliar. ◇ *vi* ampliarse.
broadly ['brɔːdlɪ] *adv* **-1.** [generally] en general; ~ **speaking** en líneas generales. **-2.** [smile] abiertamente.
broadly-based [-'beɪst] *adj* [party] de amplia base; [course] muy completo(ta), que abarca muchos temas.
broadminded [,brɔːd'maɪndɪd] *adj* abierto(ta), liberal.
broadsheet ['brɔːdʃiːt] *n periódico con hojas de gran tamaño.*

BROADSHEET:
Los principales periódicos nacionales de calidad en Gran Bretaña son los siguientes: 'The Guardian' (tendencia centroizquierda); 'The Independent' (tendencia centrista); 'The Daily Telegraph' (tendencia derechista); 'The Times' (tendencia centroderecha); 'The Financial Times' (se centra en la actualidad económica)

brocade [brə'keɪd] *n* brocado *m*.
broccoli ['brɒkəlɪ] *n* brécol *m*, bróculi *m*.
brochure ['brəʊʃə'] *n* folleto *m*.
brogues [brəʊgz] *npl zapatos gruesos de cuero con dibujo calado y estilo clásico.*
broil [brɔɪl] *vt Am* asar a la parrilla.
broiler ['brɔɪlə'] *n* **-1.** [young chicken] pollo *m*. **-2.** *Am* [grill] parrilla *f*.
broke [brəʊk] ◇ *pt* → **break**. ◇ *adj inf* sin blanca, sin un duro, bruja *Amer*; **to go** ~ ir a la ruina; **to go for** ~ jugárselo todo.
broken ['brəʊkn] ◇ *pp* → **break**. ◇ *adj* **-1.** [gen] roto(ta); ~ **home** hogar *m* OR familia *f* de padres separados. **-2.** [not working] estropeado(da). **-3.** [interrupted - sleep] entrecortado(da); [- journey] discontinuo(nua). **-4.** [hesitant, inaccurate] macarrónico(ca).
broken-down *adj* **-1.** [car, machine] averiado(da). **-2.** [building] destartalado(da).
broker ['brəʊkə'] *n* [of stock] corredor *m*; [of insurance] agente *m* y *f*.
brokerage ['brəʊkərɪdʒ] *n* corretaje *m*.
brolly ['brɒlɪ] (*pl* **-ies**) *n Br inf* paraguas *m inv*.
bronchitis [brɒŋ'kaɪtɪs] *n* (*U*) bronquitis *f*.
bronze [brɒnz] ◇ *n* **-1.** [metal, sculpture] bronce *m*. **-2.** = **bronze medal**. ◇ *comp* de bronce.
bronze medal *n* medalla *f* de bronce.
brooch [brəʊtʃ] *n* broche *m*, alfiler *m*.
brood [bruːd] ◇ *n* **-1.** [of animals] cría *f*, nidada *f*. **-2.** *inf* [of children] prole *f*. ◇ *vi*: **to** ~ **(over** OR **about)** dar vueltas (a).
broody ['bruːdɪ] (*compar* **-ier**, *superl* **-iest**) *adj* **-1.** [sad] apesadumbrado(da). **-2.** [bird] clueco(ca).
brook [brʊk] ◇ *n* arroyo *m*. ◇ *vt fml* tolerar.
broom [bruːm] *n* [brush] escoba *f*.
broomstick ['bruːmstɪk] *n* palo *m* de escoba.
Bros., bros. (*abbr of* **brothers**) Hnos.
broth [brɒθ] *n* caldo *m*.
brothel ['brɒθl] *n* burdel *m*.

brother ['brʌðəʳ] ◇ n -1. [relative, monk] hermano m. -2. fig [comrade] camarada m. ◇ excl Am inf ¡dios mío!

brotherhood ['brʌðəhʊd] n -1. [companionship] fraternidad f. -2. [religious organization] cofradía f, hermandad f; [professional association] gremio m, colegio m.

brother-in-law (pl **brothers-in-law**) n cuñado m.

brotherly ['brʌðəlɪ] adj fraternal, fraterno(na).

brought [brɔːt] pt & pp → bring.

brow [braʊ] n -1. [forehead] frente f. -2. [eyebrow] ceja f; **to knit one's ~s** fruncir el ceño OR entrecejo. -3. [of hill] cima f, cresta f.

browbeat ['braʊbiːt] (pt **-beat**, pp **-beaten**) vt intimidar, amedrentar.

browbeaten ['braʊbiːtn] adj intimidado(da), amedrentado(da).

brown [braʊn] ◇ adj -1. [gen] marrón; [hair, eyes] castaño(ña). -2. [tanned] moreno(na). ◇ n marrón m; **in ~** de marrón. ◇ vt [food] dorar.

Brownie (Guide) ['braʊnɪ-] n guía f (7–10 años).

Brownie point n: **to gain ~s** fig apuntarse tantos.

brown paper n (U) papel m de embalar.

brown rice n arroz m integral.

brown sugar n azúcar m moreno, azúcar f morena.

browse [braʊz] vi -1. [person] echar un ojo, mirar; **to ~ through** hojear. -2. [animal] pacer.

bruise [bruːz] ◇ n magulladura f, cardenal m. ◇ vt -1. [person, arm] magullar, contusionar; [fruit] estropear. -2. fig [feelings] herir. ◇ vi [person] magullarse, contusionarse; [fruit] estropearse.

bruised [bruːzd] adj -1. [arm, knee] magullado(da); [fruit] estropeado(da). -2. fig [person] dolido(da); [feelings] herido(da).

Brum [brʌm] (abbr of **Birmingham**) n inf ciudad inglesa.

Brummie, Brummy ['brʌmɪ] n Br inf natural o habitante de Birmingham.

brunch [brʌntʃ] n brunch m, combinación de desayuno y almuerzo que se toma por la mañana tarde.

Brunei ['bruːnaɪ] n Brunei.

brunette [bruːˈnet] n morena f.

brunt [brʌnt] n: **to bear** OR **take the ~ of** aguantar lo peor de.

brush [brʌʃ] ◇ n -1. [for hair, teeth] cepillo m; [for shaving, painting] brocha f; [of artist] pincel m; [broom] escoba f. -2. [encounter]

roce m. ◇ vt -1. [clean with brush] cepillar. -2. [move with hand] quitar, apartar. -3. [touch lightly] rozar.

◆ **brush aside** vt sep rechazar.

◆ **brush off** vt sep [dismiss] hacer caso omiso de.

◆ **brush up** ◇ vt sep fig [revise] repasar. ◇ vi: **to ~ up on** repasar.

brushed [brʌʃt] adj [steel, chrome] cepillado(da); [cotton, nylon] afelpado(da).

brush-off n inf: **to give sb the ~** mandar a alguien a paseo.

brush-up n inf: **to have a wash and ~** lavarse y peinarse, arreglarse.

brushwood ['brʌʃwʊd] n leña f, ramojo m.

brushwork ['brʌʃwɜːk] n (estilo m de) pincelada f.

brusque [bruːsk] adj brusco(ca).

Brussels ['brʌslz] n Bruselas.

brussels sprout n col f de Bruselas.

brutal ['bruːtl] adj brutal.

brutality [bruːˈtælətɪ] (pl **-ies**) n brutalidad f.

brutalize, -ise ['bruːtəlaɪz] vt -1. [make cruel] embrutecer. -2. [treat brutally] tratar brutalmente.

brute [bruːt] ◇ adj bruto(ta). ◇ n -1. [large animal] bestia f, bruto m. -2. [bully] bestia m y f.

bs abbr of **bill of sale**.

BS (abbr of **Bachelor of Science**) n (titular de una) licenciatura de ciencias.

BSA (abbr of **Boy Scouts of America**) n asociación estadounidense de boy scouts.

BSc (abbr of **Bachelor of Science**) n (titular de una) licenciatura de ciencias.

BSE (abbr of **bovine spongiform encephalopathy**) n encefalopatía espongiforme bovina.

BSI (abbr of **British Standards Institution**) n instituto británico de normalización.

B-side n cara f dos OR B.

BST -1. abbr of **British Summer Time**. -2. (abbr of **British Standard Time**) hora oficial británica.

Bt. abbr of **baronet**.

BT n abbr of **British Telecom**.

btu (abbr of **British thermal unit**) n btu f.

bubble ['bʌbl] ◇ n [gen] burbuja f; [of soap] pompa f. ◇ vi -1. [produce bubbles] burbujear. -2. [make a bubbling sound] borbotar. -3. [be full]: **to ~ with** rebosar de.

bubble bath n espuma f de baño.

bubble gum n chicle m (de globo).

bubblejet printer ['bʌbl,dʒet-] n COMPUT impresora f de inyección.

bubbly ['bʌblɪ] (*compar* **-ier**, *superl* **-iest**) ◇ *adj* **-1.** [full of bubbles] con burbujas. **-2.** [lively] alegre, vivo(va). ◇ *n inf* champán *m*.

Bucharest [,buːkə'rest] *n* Bucarest.

buck [bʌk] (*pl inv* OR **-s**) ◇ *n* **-1.** [male animal] macho *m*. **-2.** *inf* [dollar] dólar *m*; **to make a fast ~** hacer pasta rápidamente. **-3.** *inf* [responsibility]: **the ~ stops here** a mí me toca lidiar con eso; **to pass the ~ to sb** echarle el muerto a alguien. ◇ *vt* **-1.** [subj: horse] tirar. **-2.** *inf* [oppose] oponerse a, ir en contra de. ◇ *vi* corcovear, encabritarse.

◆ **buck up** *inf* ◇ *vt sep* **-1.** [improve] mejorar; **~ your ideas up** más vale que espabiles. **-2.** [cheer up] animar. ◇ *vi* **-1.** [hurry up] darse prisa. **-2.** [cheer up] animarse.

bucket ['bʌkɪt] *n* **-1.** [container, bucketful] cubo *m*, tacho *m Amer*. **-2.** *inf* [large quantity]: **~s of** un montón de.

Buckingham Palace ['bʌkɪŋəm-] *n* el palacio de Buckingham.

buckle ['bʌkl] ◇ *n* hebilla *f*. ◇ *vt* **-1.** [fasten] abrochar con hebilla. **-2.** [bend] combar, torcer. ◇ *vi* [wheel] combarse, torcerse; [knees] doblarse.

◆ **buckle down** *vi*: **to ~ down (to)** dedicarse seriamente (a).

Bucks [bʌks] (*abbr of* **Buckinghamshire**) *condado inglés*.

buckshot ['bʌkʃɒt] *n* perdigones *mpl*.

buckskin ['bʌkskɪn] *n* ante *m*.

buckteeth [bʌk'tiːθ] *npl* dientes *mpl* salientes.

buckwheat ['bʌkwiːt] *n* alforfón *m*.

bud [bʌd] (*pt & pp* **-ded**, *cont* **-ding**) ◇ *n* [shoot] brote *m*; [flower] capullo *m*; **to nip sthg in the ~** *fig* cortar algo de raíz. ◇ *vi* brotar, echar brotes.

Budapest [,bjuːdə'pest] *n* Budapest.

Buddha ['budə] *n* Buda *m*.

Buddhism ['budɪzm] *n* budismo *m*.

Buddhist ['budɪst] ◇ *adj* budista. ◇ *n* budista *m y f*.

budding ['bʌdɪŋ] *adj* en ciernes.

buddy ['bʌdɪ] (*pl* **-ies**) *n inf* [friend] amiguete *m*, -ta *f*, colega *m y f*, compa *m Amer*.

budge [bʌdʒ] ◇ *vt* mover. ◇ *vi* [move] moverse; [give in] ceder, hacer concesiones.

budgerigar ['bʌdʒərɪgɑːʳ] *n* periquito *m*.

budget ['bʌdʒɪt] ◇ *adj* económico(ca). ◇ *n* presupuesto *m*; **the Budget** *Br* el presupuesto nacional OR del estado. ◇ *vt* [money] presupuestar; [time] planificar. ◇ *vi* presupuestar.

◆ **budget for** *vt fus* contar con.

budget account *n Br* [with a shop] cuenta *f*; [with a bank] cuenta para domiciliaciones.

budgetary ['bʌdʒɪtrɪ] *adj* presupuestario(ria).

budgie ['bʌdʒɪ] *n inf* periquito *m*.

Buenos Aires [,bwenəs'aɪrɪz] *n* Buenos Aires.

buff [bʌf] ◇ *adj* color de ante. ◇ *n inf* [expert] aficionado *m*, -da *f*.

buffalo ['bʌfələʊ] (*pl inv* OR **-s** OR **-es**) *n* búfalo *m*.

buffer ['bʌfəʳ] *n* **-1.** *Br* [for trains] tope *m*. **-2.** [protection] defensa *f*, salvaguarda *f*. **-3.** COMPUT memoria *f* intermedia.

buffer state *n* estado *m* tapón.

buffet¹ [*Br* 'bufeɪ, *Am* bə'feɪ] *n* **-1.** [meal] bufé *m*. **-2.** [cafeteria] cafetería *f*.

buffet² ['bʌfɪt] *vt* [physically] golpear.

buffet car ['bufeɪ-] *n* coche *m* restaurante (*sólo mostrador*).

buffoon [bə'fuːn] *n* bufón *m*.

bug [bʌg] (*pt & pp* **-ged**, *cont* **-ging**) ◇ *n* **-1.** [small insect] bicho *m*. **-2.** *inf* [germ] microbio *m*, virus *m*; **stomach ~** virus del estómago. **-3.** *inf* [listening device] micrófono *m* oculto. **-4.** COMPUT error *m*. **-5.** [enthusiasm] manía *f*. ◇ *vt* **-1.** *inf* [spy on - room] poner un micrófono oculto en; [- phone] pinchar, intervenir. **-2.** *inf* [annoy] fastidiar, jorobar.

bugbear ['bʌgbeəʳ] *n* fastidio *m*, pesadilla *f*.

bugger ['bʌgəʳ] *Br v inf* ◇ *n* **-1.** [unpleasant person] cabrón *m*, -ona *f*; **lucky ~!** ¡qué suerte tiene el cabrón/la cabrona! **-2.** [difficult, annoying task] coñazo *m*. ◇ *excl* ¡mierda! ◇ *vt*: **~ it!** ¡mierda!

◆ **bugger off** *vi v inf*: **~ off!** ¡vete a tomar por culo!

buggy ['bʌgɪ] (*pl* **-ies**) *n* **-1.** [carriage] calesa *f*. **-2.** [pushchair] sillita *f* de ruedas; *Am* [pram] cochecito *m* de niño.

bugle ['bjuːgl] *n* corneta *f*, clarín *m*.

build [bɪld] (*pt & pp* **built**) ◇ *vt* **-1.** [construct] construir. **-2.** *fig* [form, create] crear. ◇ *n* complexión *f*, constitución *f*.

◆ **build into** *vt sep* **-1.** [construct as part of] empotrar. **-2.** [include in] incorporar.

◆ **build (up)on** ◇ *vt fus* [further] desarrollar. ◇ *vt sep* [base on] fundar en.

◆ **build up** ◇ *vt sep* **-1.** [business - establish] poner en pie; [- promote] fomentar. **-2.** [person] fortalecer; **to ~ up one's reputation** labrarse una reputación. ◇ *vi* acumularse.

builder ['bɪldəʳ] *n* constructor *m*, -ra *f*.

building ['bɪldɪŋ] *n* **-1.** [structure] edificio *m*. **-2.** [profession] construcción *f*.

building and loan association *n Am* ≃ caja *f* de ahorros.

building block *n* [toy] bloque *m* de construcción; *fig* [element] componente *m* esencial, pilar *m*.

building contractor *n* contratista *m* y *f* de obras.

building site *n* solar *m* (de construcción), obra *f*.

building society *n* Br ≃ caja *f* de ahorros.

BUILDING SOCIETY:
Las 'building societies' funcionan como los bancos pero no tienen un sistema de compensación. Estas organizaciones conceden préstamos inmobiliarios a particulares y desempeñan un papel muy importante en Gran Bretaña

buildup ['bɪldʌp] *n* [increase] acumulación *f*, incremento *m* gradual.

built [bɪlt] ◇ *pt & pp* → **build**. ◇ *adj*: heavily/slightly ~ de complexión fuerte/débil; to be ~ for dar el tipo para.

built-in *adj* **-1.** [physically integral] empotrado(da). **-2.** [inherent] incorporado(da).

built-up *adj* urbanizado(da).

bulb [bʌlb] *n* **-1.** [for lamp] bombilla *f*. **-2.** [of plant] bulbo *m*. **-3.** [bulb-shaped part] parte *f* redondeada.

bulbous ['bʌlbəs] *adj* bulboso(sa).

Bulgaria [bʌl'geərɪə] *n* Bulgaria.

Bulgarian [bʌl'geərɪən] ◇ *adj* búlgaro(ra). ◇ *n* **-1.** [person] búlgaro *m*, -ra *f*. **-2.** [language] búlgaro *m*.

bulge [bʌldʒ] ◇ *n* **-1.** [lump] protuberancia *f*, bulto *m*. **-2.** [sudden increase] aumento *m* súbito, alza *f*. ◇ *vi*: to ~ (with) rebosar (de), estar atestado (de).

bulging ['bʌldʒɪŋ] *adj* [muscles] fornido(da); [pocket] abultado(da).

bulimia (nervosa) [bjʊ'lɪmɪə-] *n* bulimia *f* nerviosa.

bulk [bʌlk] ◇ *n* **-1.** [mass] bulto *m*, volumen *m*. **-2.** [large body] mole *f*. **-3.** [large quantity]: **in ~** a granel. **-4.** [majority, most of]: **the ~ of** la mayor parte de. ◇ *adj* a granel.

bulk buying [-'baɪɪŋ] *n* compra *f* en gran cantidad OR al por mayor.

bulkhead ['bʌlkhed] *n* mamparo *m*.

bulky ['bʌlkɪ] (*compar* **-ier**, *superl* **-iest**) *adj* abultado(da), voluminoso(sa).

bull [bʊl] *n* **-1.** [male cow] toro *m*. **-2.** [male animal] macho *m*. **-3.** ST EX alcista *m* y *f*. **-4.** (U) *v inf* [nonsense] gilipolleces *fpl*.

bulldog ['bʊldɒg] *n* buldog *m*.

bulldog clip *n* pinza *f*.

bulldoze ['bʊldəʊz] *vt* [ground] nivelar; [building] derribar; *fig* [force] forzar; **to ~ sb into sthg/into doing sthg** *fig* forzar a alguien a algo/a hacer algo.

bulldozer ['bʊldəʊzə'] *n* bulldozer *m*.

bullet ['bʊlɪt] *n* bala *f*.

bulletin ['bʊlətɪn] *n* **-1.** [news] boletín *m*; [medical report] parte *m*. **-2.** [regular publication] boletín *m*, gaceta *f*.

bulletin board *n* tablón *m* de anuncios.

bullet-proof *adj* a prueba de balas.

bullfight ['bʊlfaɪt] *n* corrida *f* (de toros).

bullfighter ['bʊl,faɪtə'] *n* torero *m*, -ra *f*.

bullfighting ['bʊl,faɪtɪŋ] *n* toreo *m*.

bullfinch ['bʊlfɪntʃ] *n* camachuelo *m*.

bullion ['bʊljən] *n* (U) lingotes *mpl*.

bullish ['bʊlɪʃ] *adj* ST EX alcista.

bull market *n* mercado *m* en alza OR alcista.

bullock ['bʊlək] *n* buey *m*, toro *m* castrado.

bullring ['bʊlrɪŋ] *n* plaza *f* (de toros).

bullrush ['bʊlrʌʃ] = **bulrush**.

bull's-eye *n* diana *f*.

bullshit ['bʊlʃɪt] (*pt & pp* **-ted**, *cont* **-ting**) *vulg* ◇ *n* (U) gilipolleces *fpl*. ◇ *vi* decir gilipolleces.

bull terrier *n* bulterrier *m*.

bully ['bʊlɪ] (*pl* **-ies**, *pt & pp* **-ied**) ◇ *n* abusón *m*, matón *m*. ◇ *vt* abusar de, intimidar; **to ~ sb into doing sthg** obligar a alguien con amenazas a hacer algo.

bullying ['bʊlɪŋ] *n* intimidación *f*.

bulrush ['bʊlrʌʃ] *n* anea *f*.

bum [bʌm] (*pt & pp* **-med**, *cont* **-ming**) *n* **-1.** *v inf* [bottom] culo *m*. **-2.** *Am inf pej* [tramp] vagabundo *m*, -da *f*. **-3.** *Am inf pej* [idler] holgazán *m*, -ana *f*, vago *m*, -ga *f*.
◆ **bum around** *vi Am inf* **-1.** [waste time] haraganear. **-2.** [travel aimlessly] vagabundear.

bumblebee ['bʌmblbiː] *n* abejorro *m*.

bumbling ['bʌmblɪŋ] *adj inf* inútil.

bumf [bʌmf] *n* (U) *Br inf* papelotes *mpl*, papeleo *m*.

bump [bʌmp] ◇ *n* **-1.** [lump - on head] chichón *m*; [- on road] bache *m*. **-2.** [knock, blow, noise] golpe *m*. ◇ *vt* [car] chocar con OR contra; [head, knee] golpearse en; **I -ed my head on the door** me di con la cabeza en la puerta. ◇ *vi* avanzar dando sacudidas.
◆ **bump into** *vt fus* [meet by chance] toparse con, encontrarse con.
◆ **bump off** *vt sep inf* cargarse a.
◆ **bump up** *vt sep inf* aumentar, subir.

bumper ['bʌmpəʳ] ◇ *adj* abundante; ~ **edition** edición especial. ◇ *n* -**1.** AUT parachoques *m inv*. -**2.** *Am* RAIL tope *m*.

bumper-to-bumper *adj*: the cars were ~ había una caravana (de coches).

bumph [bʌmf] = **bumf**.

bumptious ['bʌmpʃəs] *adj pej* engreído(da).

bumpy ['bʌmpɪ] (*compar* -**ier**, *superl* -**iest**) *adj* -**1.** [road] lleno(na) de baches. -**2.** [ride, journey] con muchas sacudidas.

bun [bʌn] *n* -**1.** [cake, bread roll] bollo *m*. -**2.** [hairstyle] moño *m*, chongo *m Amer*.

bunch [bʌntʃ] ◇ *n* [of people] grupo *m*; [of flowers] ramo *m*; [of fruit] racimo *m*; [of keys] manojo *m*. ◇ *vt* agrupar. ◇ *vi* agruparse.

◆ **bunches** *npl* [hairstyle] coletas *fpl*.

bundle ['bʌndl] ◇ *n* [of clothes] lío *m*, bulto *m*; [of notes, papers] fajo *m*; [of wood] haz *m*. ◇ *vt* [clothes] empaquetar de cualquier manera; [person] empujar.

◆ **bundle off** *vt sep* despachar.

◆ **bundle up** *vt sep* [put into bundles] liar, envolver.

bundled software ['bʌndld-] *n* COMPUT software *m* incluido en la compra de un ordenador.

bung [bʌŋ] ◇ *n* tapón *m*. ◇ *vt Br inf* -**1.** [throw] echar, tirar. -**2.** [pass] pasar, alcanzar.

bungalow ['bʌŋɡələʊ] *n* bungalow *m*.

bunged up [bʌŋd-] *adj* [drain] atascado(da), obstruido(da); [nose] taponado(da), congestionado(da).

bungee-jumping ['bʌndʒɪ-] *n* puenting *m*.

bungle ['bʌŋɡl] *vt* chapucear.

bunion ['bʌnjən] *n* juanete *m*.

bunk [bʌŋk] *n* -**1.** [bed] litera *f*. -**2.** (*U*) *inf* [nonsense] tonterías *fpl*. -**3.** *phr*: **to do a ~** *inf* poner pies en polvorosa.

bunk bed *n* litera *f*.

bunker ['bʌŋkəʳ] *n* -**1.** [shelter, in golf] bunker *m*. -**2.** [for coal] carbonera *f*.

bunkhouse ['bʌŋkhaʊs, *pl* -haʊzɪz] *n* barracones *mpl* (de vaqueros).

bunny ['bʌnɪ] (*pl* -**ies**) *n*: ~ (**rabbit**) conejito *m*, -ta *f*.

bunny hill *n Am* SKI pista *f* (de esquí) para principiantes.

Bunsen burner ['bʌnsn-] *n* mechero *m* Bunsen.

bunting ['bʌntɪŋ] *n* (*U*) [flags] banderitas *fpl*.

buoy [*Br* bɔɪ, *Am* 'buːɪ] *n* boya *f*.

◆ **buoy up** *vt sep* [encourage] alentar, animar.

buoyancy ['bɔɪənsɪ] *n* -**1.** [ability to float] flotabilidad *f*. -**2.** [optimism] optimismo *m*.

buoyant ['bɔɪənt] *adj* -**1.** [able to float] boyante, capaz de flotar. -**2.** [optimistic - gen] optimista; [- market] con tendencia alcista.

burden ['bɜːdn] ◇ *n* -**1.** [heavy load] carga *f*. -**2.** *fig* [heavy responsibility]: ~ **on** carga *f* para. ◇ *vt*: **to ~ sb with** cargar a alguien con.

bureau ['bjʊərəʊ] (*pl* -**x**) *n* -**1.** [government department] departamento *m*, oficina *f*. -**2.** [office] oficina *f*. -**3.** *Br* [desk] secreter *m*; *Am* [chest of drawers] cómoda *f*.

bureaucracy [bjʊə'rɒkrəsɪ] (*pl* -**ies**) *n* burocracia *f*.

bureaucrat ['bjʊərəkræt] *n pej* burócrata *m* y *f*.

bureaucratic [ˌbjʊərə'krætɪk] *adj pej* burocrático(ca).

bureau de change [ˌbjʊərəʊdə'ʃɒndʒ] (*pl* **bureaux de change** [ˌbjʊərəʊdə'ʃɒndʒ]) *n* casa *f* de cambio.

bureaux ['bjʊərəʊz] *pl* → **bureau**.

burger ['bɜːɡəʳ] *n* hamburguesa *f*.

burglar ['bɜːɡləʳ] *n* ladrón *m*, -ona *f*.

burglar alarm *n* alarma *f* antirrobo.

burglarize *Am* = **burgle**.

burglary ['bɜːɡlərɪ] (*pl* -**ies**) *n* robo *m* (de una casa).

burgle ['bɜːɡl], **burglarize** ['bɜːɡləraɪz] *Am vt* robar, desvalijar (*una casa*).

burial ['berɪəl] *n* entierro *m*.

burial ground *n* cementerio *m*.

burk [bɜːk] *n Br inf* tonto *m*, -ta *f*.

Burkina Faso [bɜːˌkiːnə'fæsəʊ] *n* Burkina Faso.

burly ['bɜːlɪ] (*compar* -**ier**, *superl* -**iest**) *adj* fornido(da).

Burma ['bɜːmə] *n* Birmania.

Burmese [ˌbɜː'miːz] ◇ *adj* birmano *m*, -na *f*. ◇ *n* -**1.** [person] birmano *m*, -na *f*. -**2.** [language] birmano *m*.

burn [bɜːn] (*pt* & *pp* **burnt** OR -**ed**) ◇ *vt* -**1.** [gen] quemar. -**2.** [injure - by heat, fire] quemarse. ◇ *vi* -**1.** [gen] arder; **to ~ with passion/hatred** arder de pasión/odio. -**2.** [be alight] estar encendido(da). -**3.** [food] quemar. -**4.** [cause burning sensation] escocer. -**5.** [become sunburnt] quemarse. ◇ *n* quemadura *f*.

◆ **burn down** ◇ *vt sep* incendiar. ◇ *vi* -**1.** [be destroyed by fire] incendiarse. -**2.** [burn less brightly] apagarse.

◆ **burn out** ◇ *vt sep* [exhaust]: **to ~ o.s. out** quemarse, consumirse. ◇ *vi* apagarse, consumirse.

◆ **burn up** ◇ *vt sep* quemar. ◇ *vi* quemarse.

burner ['bɜːnəʳ] *n* quemador *m*.

burning ['bɜːnɪŋ] *adj* **-1.** [on fire] en llamas. **-2.** [heat, passion, interest] ardiente; **it was ~ hot** hacía un calor abrasador. **-3.** [cheeks, face] colorado(da). ' **-4.** [controversial]: **~ question** pregunta *f* candente.

burnish ['bɜːnɪʃ] *vt* bruñir.

Burns' Night *n* fiesta celebrada en Escocia el 25 de enero en honor del poeta escocés Robert Burns.

burnt [bɜːnt] *pt & pp* → burn.

burnt-out *adj lit & fig* quemado(da), chamuscado(da).

burp [bɜːp] *inf* ◇ *n* eructo *m*. ◇ *vi* eructar.

burrow ['bʌrəʊ] ◇ *n* madriguera *f*. ◇ *vi* **-1.** [dig] escarbar (un agujero). **-2.** *fig* [in order to search] hurgar.

bursar ['bɜːsəʳ] *n* tesorero *m*, -ra *f*, administrador *m*, -ra *f*.

bursary ['bɜːsəri] (*pl* -ies) *n Br* beca *f*.

burst [bɜːst] (*pt & pp* burst) ◇ *vi* **-1.** [gen] reventarse; [bag] romperse; [tyre] pincharse. **-2.** [explode] estallar. **-3.** [door, lid]: **to ~ open** abrirse de golpe. **-4.** [go suddenly]: **to ~ into** irrumpir en; **to ~ through** abrirse paso a través de. ◇ *vt* [gen] reventar; [tyre] pinchar. ◇ *n* [of gunfire, enthusiasm] estallido *m*; [of song] clamor *m*.
◆ **burst in on** *vt fus* interrumpir.
◆ **burst into** *vt fus* **-1.** [tears, song]: **to ~ into tears/song** romper a llorar/cantar. **-2.** [flames] estallar en. **-3.** [subj: plants]: **to ~ into flower** florecer.
◆ **burst out** ◇ *vt fus* [say suddenly] exclamar. ◇ *vi* [begin suddenly]: **to ~ out laughing/crying** echarse a reír/llorar.

bursting ['bɜːstɪŋ] *adj* **-1.** [full] lleno(na) a estallar. **-2.** [with emotion]: **~ with** rebosando de. **-3.** [eager]: **to be ~ to do sthg** estar deseando hacer algo.

Burundi [bʊ'rʊndɪ] *n* Burundi.

bury ['berɪ] (*pt & pp* -ied) *vt* **-1.** [in ground] enterrar. **-2.** [hide - face, memory] ocultar. **-3.** *fig* [immerse]: **to ~ o.s. in sthg** enfrascarse en algo.

bus [bʌs] ◇ *n* autobús *m*, góndola *f Amer*; **by ~** en autobús.

bus conductor *n* cobrador *m*, -ra *f*.

bus driver *n* conductor *m*, -ra *f*.

bush [bʊʃ] *n* **-1.** [plant] arbusto *m*. **-2.** [open country]: **the ~** el campo abierto, el monte. **-3.** *phr*: **to beat about the ~** andarse por las ramas.

bushel ['bʊʃl] *n Br* = 36,37 litros; *Am* = 35,24 litros.

bushy ['bʊʃɪ] (*compar* -ier, *superl* -iest) *adj* poblado(da), espeso(sa).

business ['bɪznɪs] ◇ *n* **-1.** (*U*) [commerce, amount of trade] negocios *mpl*; **to be away on ~** estar en viaje de negocios; **to mean ~** *inf* ir en serio; **to go out of ~** quebrar. **-2.** [company] negocio *m*, empresa *f*. **-3.** [concern, duty] oficio *m*, ocupación *f*; **to have no ~ doing** OR **to do sthg** no tener derecho a hacer algo; **mind your own ~!** *inf* ¡no te metas donde no te llaman! **-4.** (*U*) [affair, matter] asunto *m*.
◇ *comp*: **~ interests** intereses *mpl* comerciales; **~ hours** horas *fpl* de oficina.

business address *n* dirección *f* comercial.

business card *n* tarjeta *f* de visita.

business class *n* clase *f* preferente.

businesslike ['bɪznɪslaɪk] *adj* formal, práctico(ca).

businessman ['bɪznɪsmæn] (*pl* -men [-men]) *n* empresario *m*, hombre *m* de negocios.

business school *n* escuela *f* OR academia *f* comercial.

business trip *n* viaje *m* de negocios.

businesswoman ['bɪznɪs,wʊmən] (*pl* -women [-,wɪmɪn]) *n* empresaria *f*, mujer *f* de negocios.

busker ['bʌskəʳ] *n Br* músico *m* ambulante OR callejero.

bus lane *n* carril *m* de autobús.

bus-shelter *n* marquesina *f* (de parada de autobús).

bus station *n* estación *f* de autobuses.

bus stop *n* parada *f* de autobús, paradero *m Amer*.

bust [bʌst] (*pt & pp* -ed OR bust) ◇ *adj inf* **-1.** [broken] fastidiado(da), roto(ta). **-2.** [bankrupt]: **to go ~** quebrar. ◇ *n* **-1.** [bosom, statue] busto *m*. **-2.** *inf police sl* [raid] redada *f*. ◇ *vt* **-1.** *inf* [break] fastidiar, estropear. **-2.** *police sl* [arrest] pillar, empapelar; [raid] registrar, hacer una redada en.

bustle ['bʌsl] ◇ *n* bullicio *m*. ◇ *vi* apresurarse.

bustling ['bʌslɪŋ] *adj* bullicioso(sa).

bust-up *n inf* **-1.** [quarrel] trifulca *f*, camorra *f*. **-2.** [breakup] ruptura *f*.

busy ['bɪzɪ] (*compar* -ier, *superl* -iest) ◇ *adj* **-1.** [active] activo(va). **-2.** [hectic - life, week] ajetreado(da); [- town, office] concurrido(da), animado(da). **-3.** [occupied] ocupado(da); **to be ~ doing sthg** estar ocupado haciendo algo. **-4.** TELEC [engaged] comunicando. ◇ *vt*: **to ~ o.s. (doing sthg)** ocuparse (haciendo algo).

busybody ['bɪzɪ,bɒdɪ] (*pl* -ies) *n pej* entrometido *m*, -da *f*.

busy signal *n Am* TELEC señal *f* de comunicando.

but [bʌt] ⟡ *conj* pero; **we were poor ~ happy** éramos pobres pero felices; **she owns not one ~ two houses** tiene no una sino dos casas; **~ now let's talk about you** pero ahora hablemos de ti.
⟡ *prep* menos, excepto; **everyone ~ Jane was there** todos estaban allí, menos Jane; **we've had nothing ~ bad weather** no hemos tenido más que mal tiempo; **he has no one ~ himself to blame** la culpa no es de otro más que él OR sino de él.
⟡ *adv fml*: **had I ~ known** de haberlo sabido; **we can ~ try** por intentarlo que no quede; **she has ~ recently joined the firm** hace tan sólo un tiempo que entró en la empresa.
◆ **but for** *conj* de no ser por; **~ for her I'd have died** de no ser por ella, hubiera muerto.
◆ **but then** *adv*: **I really like him, ~ then I've known him for years** me gusta mucho, pero claro, nos conocemos desde hace años.

butane [ˈbjuːteɪn] *n* butano *m*.

butch [bʊtʃ] *adj Br inf* [woman] marimacho; [man] muy macho.

butcher [ˈbʊtʃər] ⟡ *n* **-1.** [occupation] carnicero *m*, -ra *f*; **~'s (shop)** carnicería *f*. **-2.** [indiscriminate killer] carnicero *m*, -ra *f*, asesino *m*, -na *f*. ⟡ *vt* [animal - for meat] matar; *fig* [kill indiscriminately] hacer una carnicería con.

butchery [ˈbʊtʃəri] *n fig* [indiscriminate killing] matanza *f*, carnicería *f*.

butler [ˈbʌtlər] *n* mayordomo *m*.

butt [bʌt] ⟡ *n* **-1.** [of cigarette, cigar] colilla *f*. **-2.** [of rifle] culata *f*. **-3.** [for water] tina *f*. **-4.** [target] blanco *m*. ⟡ *vt* topetar.
◆ **butt in** *vi* [interrupt]: **to ~ in on sb** cortar a alguien; **to ~ in on sthg** entrometerse en algo.

butter [ˈbʌtər] ⟡ *n* mantequilla *f*; **~ wouldn't melt in her mouth** *inf* parece una mosquita muerta. ⟡ *vt* untar con mantequilla.
◆ **butter up** *vt sep inf* dar coba a.

butter bean *n* judía *f* blanca.

buttercup [ˈbʌtəkʌp] *n* ranúnculo *m*.

butter dish *n* mantequera *f*.

buttered [ˈbʌtəd] *adj* con mantequilla.

butterfingers [ˈbʌtəˌfɪŋgəz] (*pl inv*) *n inf* persona *f* con manos de mantequilla.

butterfly [ˈbʌtəflaɪ] (*pl* -ies) *n* **-1.** [insect] mariposa *f*; **to have butterflies in one's stomach** *inf* estar hecho un manojo de nervios. **-2.** [swimming style] (estilo *m*) mariposa *f*.

buttermilk [ˈbʌtəmɪlk] *n* suero *m* de leche.

butterscotch [ˈbʌtəskɒtʃ] *n* dulce hecho hirviendo azúcar y mantequilla.

buttocks [ˈbʌtəks] *npl* nalgas *fpl*.

button [ˈbʌtn] ⟡ *n* **-1.** [gen & COMPUT] botón *m*. **-2.** *Am* [badge] chapa *f*. ⟡ *vt* = **button up**.
◆ **button up** *vt sep* abotonar, abrochar.

buttonhole [ˈbʌtnhəʊl] ⟡ *n* **-1.** [hole] ojal *m*. **-2.** *Br* [flower] flor *f* para el ojal. ⟡ *vt inf* enganchar, coger por banda.

button mushroom *n* champiñón *m* pequeño.

buttress [ˈbʌtrɪs] ⟡ *n* contrafuerte *m*. ⟡ *vt* [wall] poner contrafuerte a.

buxom [ˈbʌksəm] *adj* [woman] maciza, pechugona.

buy [baɪ] (*pt* & *pp* **bought**) ⟡ *vt lit* & *fig* comprar. ⟡ *n* compra *f*.
◆ **buy in** *vt sep Br* aprovisionarse de.
◆ **buy into** *vt fus* comprar acciones en.
◆ **buy off** *vt sep* sobornar, comprar.
◆ **buy out** *vt sep* **-1.** [in business] comprar la parte de. **-2.** [from army] pagar dinero para salirse del ejército.
◆ **buy up** *vt sep* acaparar.

buyer [ˈbaɪər] *n* **-1.** [purchaser] comprador *m*, -ra *f*. **-2.** [profession] jefe *m*, -fa *f* de compras.

buyer's market *n* mercado *m* de compradores.

buyout [ˈbaɪaʊt] *n* adquisición de la mayoría de las acciones de una empresa.

buzz [bʌz] ⟡ *n* [of insect, machinery] zumbido *m*; [of conversation] rumor *m*; **to give sb a ~** *inf* [on phone] dar un toque OR llamar a alguien. ⟡ *vi* **-1.** [make noise] zumbar. **-2.** *fig* [be active]: **to ~ (with)** bullir (de). ⟡ *vt* [on intercom] llamar.
◆ **buzz off** *vi Br inf*: **~ off!** ¡lárgate!

buzzard [ˈbʌzəd] *n* **-1.** *Br* [hawk] águila *f* ratonera. **-2.** *Am* [vulture] buitre *m*.

buzzer [ˈbʌzər] *n* timbre *m*.

buzzing [ˈbʌzɪŋ] *n* zumbido *m*.

buzzword [ˈbʌzwɜːd] *n inf* palabra *f* de moda.

by [baɪ] ⟡ *prep* **-1.** [indicating cause, agent] por; **caused/written ~** causado/escrito por; **a book ~ Joyce** un libro de Joyce. **-2.** [indicating means, method, manner]: **to travel ~ bus/train/plane/ship** viajar en autobús/tren/avión/barco; **to pay ~ cheque** pagar con cheque; **to take sb ~ the hand** coger a alguien de la mano; **~ candlelight** a la luz de las velas; **he got rich ~ buying land** se hizo rico comprando terrenos; **~ nature** por naturaleza; **~ profession/trade** de profesión/oficio. **-3.** [beside, close to] junto a; **~ the sea** junto al mar. **-4.** [past] por delante de; **to walk ~ sb/sthg** pasear por delante de alguien/algo; **we drove ~ the castle** pasamos por el castillo (conduciendo). **-5.** [via, through] por; **we entered ~ the back door** entramos por la puerta trasera. **-6.** [with time - at or before, during] para; **I'll be there ~ eight** estaré allí para las ocho; **~ 1916 it was all over** en 1916 ya todo estaba decidido; **~ now** ya; **~ day/night** por el día/la noche, de día/noche. **-7.** [according to] según; **~ law/my standards** según la ley/mis criterios. **-8.** [in division] entre; [in multiplication, measurements] por; **divide 20 ~ 2** dividir 20 entre 2; **multiply 20 ~ 2** multiplicar 20 por 2; **twelve feet ~ ten** doce pies por diez. **-9.** [in quantities, amounts] por; **~ the thousand** OR **thousands** por miles; **~ the metre** por metros; **~ the day/hour** por día/horas; **prices were cut ~ 50%** los precios fueron rebajados (en) un 50%. **-10.** [indicating gradual change]: **day ~ day** día a OR tras día; **one ~ one** uno a uno. **-11.** [to explain a word or expression] con, por; **what do you mean ~ "all right"?** ¿qué quieres decir con "bien"?; **what do you understand ~ the word "subsidiarity"?** ¿qué entiendes por "subsidiariedad"? **-12.** *phr:* **(all) ~ oneself** solo(la); **did you do it all ~ yourself?** ¿lo hiciste tú solo? ◇ *adv* → **go, pass** etc.

bye(-bye) [baɪ(baɪ)] *excl inf* ¡hasta luego!

bye-election = **by-election**.

byelaw ['baɪlɔː] = **bylaw**.

by-election *n* elección *f* parcial.

Byelorussia [bɪ,eləʊ'rʌʃə] = **Belorussia**.

bygone ['baɪgɒn] *adj* pasado(da).
◆ **bygones** *npl:* **let ~s be ~s** lo pasado, pasado está.

bylaw ['baɪlɔː] *n* reglamento *m* OR estatuto *m* local.

by-line *n* subtítulo *donde figura el nombre del autor.*

bypass ['baɪpɑːs] ◇ *n* **-1.** [road] carretera *f* de circunvalación. **-2.** MED: **~ (operation)** (operación *f* de) by-pass *m.* ◇ *vt* evitar.

by-product *n* **-1.** [product] subproducto *m.* **-2.** [consequence] consecuencia *f.*

bystander ['baɪ,stændər] *n* espectador *m*, -ra *f.*

byte [baɪt] *n* COMPUT byte *m*, octeto *m.*

byword ['baɪwɜːd] *n:* **~ (for)** símbolo *m* (de), equivalente *m* (a).

c¹ (*pl* **c's** OR **cs**), **C** (*pl* **C's** OR **Cs**) [siː] *n* [letter] c *f*, C *f.*
◆ **C** *n* **-1.** MUS do *m.* **-2.** (*abbr of* **celsius, centigrade**) C.

c² **-1.** (*abbr of* **century**) s. **-2.** (*abbr of* **cent(s)**) cént.

c. (*abbr of* **circa**) h.

ca. (*abbr of* **circa**) h.

c/a **-1.** *abbr of* **credit account. -2.** (*abbr of* **current account**) c/c.

CA ◇ *n* **-1.** *abbr of* **chartered accountant. -2.** (*abbr of* **Consumers' Association**) *organismo para la defensa del consumidor*, ≃ OCU *f.* ◇ **-1.** *abbr of* **Central America. -2.** *abbr of* **California.**

CAA *n* **-1.** (*abbr of* **Civil Aviation Authority**) *organismo independiente regulador de la aviación civil en Gran Bretaña.* **-2.** (*abbr of* **Civil Aeronautics Authority**) *dirección estadounidense de aviación civil.*

cab [kæb] *n* **-1.** [taxi] taxi *m.* **-2.** [of lorry] cabina *f.*

CAB (*abbr of* **Citizens' Advice Bureau**) *n oficina británica de información y asistencia al ciudadano.*

cabaret ['kæbəreɪ] *n* cabaret *m.*

cabbage ['kæbɪdʒ] *n* col *f*, repollo *m.*

cabbie, cabby ['kæbɪ] *n inf* taxista *m y f.*

caber ['keɪbər] *n Scot:* **tossing the ~** *prueba de lanzamiento de una pesada pértiga en los 'Highland Games'.*

cabin ['kæbɪn] *n* **-1.** [on ship] camarote *m.* **-2.** [in aircraft] cabina *f.* **-3.** [house] cabaña *f.*

cabin class *n* clase *f* económica OR de cámara.

cabin cruiser *n* yate *m* de motor.

cabinet ['kæbɪnɪt] *n* **-1.** [cupboard] armario *m.* **-2.** POL consejo *m* de ministros, gabinete *m.*

cabinet-maker *n* ebanista *m y f.*

cabinet minister *n* ministro *m*, -tra *f* (en el gabinete).

cable ['keɪbl] ◇ *n* **-1.** [rope, wire] cable *m.* **-2.** [telegram] cablegrama *m.* ◇ *vt* cablegrafiar.

cable car *n* teleférico *m*.

cablegram ['keɪblgræm] *n* cablegrama *m*.

cable railway *n* funicular *m* aéreo.

cable television, **cable TV** *n* televisión *f* por cable.

caboodle [kə'buːdl] *n inf*: **the whole ~** todo el rollo.

cabriolet ['kæbrɪəʊleɪ] *n* [car] cabriolé *m*.

cache [kæʃ] ◇ *n* **-1.** [store] alijo *m*. **-2.** COMPUT memoria *f* de acceso rápido. ◇ *vt* COMPUT poner en la memoria de acceso rápido.

cachet ['kæʃeɪ] *n fml* caché *m*.

cackle ['kækl] ◇ *n* **-1.** [of hen] cacareo *m*. **-2.** [of person] risotada *f*. ◇ *vi* **-1.** [hen] cacarear. **-2.** [person] reírse.

cacophony [kæ'kɒfənɪ] *n* cacofonía *f*.

cactus ['kæktəs] (*pl* **-tuses** OR **-ti** [-taɪ]) *n* cactus *m inv*.

CAD (*abbr of* **computer-aided design**) *n* CAD *m*.

caddie ['kædɪ] ◇ *n* cadi *m* y *f*. ◇ *vi*: **to ~ (for)** hacer de cadi (para).

caddy ['kædɪ] (*pl* **-ies**) *n* cajita *f* para el té.

cadence ['keɪdəns] *n* [of voice] cadencia *f*, ritmo *m*.

cadet [kə'det] *n* cadete *m*.

cadge [kædʒ] *Br inf* ◇ *vt*: **to ~ sthg (off** OR **from sb)** gorronear algo (a alguien). ◇ *vi*: **to ~ off** OR **from sb** gorronear a alguien.

Cadiz [kə'dɪz] *n* Cádiz.

Caesar ['siːzər] *n* César *m*.

caesarean (section) *Br*, **cesarean (section)** *Am* [sɪ'zeərɪən-] *n* cesárea *f*.

CAF (*abbr of* **cost and freight**) C y F.

cafe, **café** ['kæfeɪ] *n* café *m*, cafetería *f*.

cafeteria [,kæfɪ'tɪərɪə] *n* (restaurante *m*) autoservicio *m*, cantina *f*.

caffeine ['kæfiːn] *n* cafeína *f*.

cage [keɪdʒ] *n* jaula *f*.

caged [keɪdʒd] *adj* enjaulado(da).

cagey ['keɪdʒɪ] (*compar* **-ier**, *superl* **-iest**) *adj inf* reservado(da).

cagoule [kə'guːl] *n Br* chubasquero *m*, canguro *m*.

cahoots [kə'huːts] *n*: **in ~ (with)** *inf* confabulado(da) (con).

CAI (*abbr of* **computer-aided instruction**) EAO *f*.

cairn [keən] *n* hito *m* de piedras.

Cairo ['kaɪərəʊ] *n* El Cairo.

cajole [kə'dʒəʊl] *vt*: **to ~ sb (into doing sthg)** engatusar a alguien (para que haga algo).

cake [keɪk] *n* **-1.** [sweet food] pastel *m*, tarta *f*; **to be a piece of ~** *inf fig* ser pan comido; **to sell like hot ~s** *inf* venderse como rosquillas; **you can't have your ~ and eat it** *inf* no se puede estar en misa y repicando. **-2.** [of fish, potato] medallón *m* empanado. **-3.** [of soap] pastilla *f*.

caked ['keɪkt] *adj*: **~ with mud** cubierto(ta) de barro seco.

cake tin *Br*, **cake pan** *Am n* molde *m*, bandeja *f*.

cal. [kæl] (*abbr of* **calorie**) cal.

calamine lotion ['kæləmaɪn-] *n* loción *f* de calamina.

calamitous [kə'læmɪtəs] *adj fml* calamitoso(sa).

calamity [kə'læmətɪ] (*pl* **-ies**) *n fml* calamidad *f*.

calcium ['kælsɪəm] *n* calcio *m*.

calculate ['kælkjʊleɪt] *vt* **-1.** [work out] calcular. **-2.** [plan]: **to be ~d to do sthg** estar pensado(da) para hacer algo.

◆ **calculate on** *vi*: **to ~ on sthg** contar con algo; **you can't ~ on them accepting** no puedes contar con que acepten.

calculated ['kælkjʊleɪtɪd] *adj* [murder, deception] premeditado(da); [risk] calculado(da), medido(da).

calculating ['kælkjʊleɪtɪŋ] *adj pej* calculador(ra).

calculation [,kælkjʊ'leɪʃn] *n* cálculo *m*.

calculator ['kælkjʊleɪtə'] *n* calculadora *f*.

calculus ['kælkjʊləs] *n* cálculo *m*.

calendar ['kælɪndə'] *n* calendario *m*.

calendar month *n* mes *m* civil.

calendar year *n* año *m* civil.

calf [kɑːf] (*pl* **calves**) *n* **-1.** [young animal - of cow] ternero *m*, -ra *f*, becerro *m*, -rra *f*; [- of whale] ballenato *m*; [- of other animals] cría *f*. **-2.** [leather] piel *f* de becerro. **-3.** [of leg] pantorrilla *f*.

caliber *Am* = **calibre**.

calibrate ['kælɪbreɪt] *vt* calibrar.

calibre, **caliber** *Am* ['kælɪbə'] *n* **-1.** [quality] nivel *m*. **-2.** [size] calibre *m*.

calico ['kælɪkəʊ] *n* percal *m*, calicó *f*.

California [,kælɪ'fɔːnjə] *n* California.

Californian [,kælɪ'fɔːnjən] ◇ *adj* californiano(na). ◇ *n* californiano *m*, -na *f*.

calipers *Am* = **callipers**.

call [kɔːl] ◇ *n* **-1.** [cry, attraction, vocation] llamada *f*, llamado *m Amer*; [cry of bird] reclamo *m*. **-2.** [visit] visita *f*; **to pay a ~ on sb** hacerle una visita a alguien. **-3.** [demand]: **~ for** petición *f* de. **-4.** [summons]: **on ~** de guardia. **-5.** TELEC llamada *f*.

◇ *vt* **-1.** [gen & TELEC] llamar; **I'm ~ed Joan** me llamo Joan; **what is it ~ed?** ¿cómo se

llama?; **he ~ed my name** me llamó por el nombre; **we'll ~ it £10** dejémoslo en 10 libras. **-2.** [announce - flight] anunciar; [- strike, meeting, election] convocar.
◇ *vi* **-1.** [gen & TELEC] llamar; **who's ~ing?** ¿quién es? **-2.** [visit] pasar.
◆ **call back** ◇ *vt sep* **-1.** [on phone] volver a llamar. **-2.** [ask to return] hacer volver. ◇ *vi* **-1.** [on phone] volver a llamar. **-2.** [visit again] volver a pasarse.
◆ **call by** *vi inf* pasarse.
◆ **call for** *vt fus* **-1.** [collect] ir a buscar. **-2.** [demand] pedir; **this ~s for a drink** esto merece un trago.
◆ **call in** ◇ *vt sep* **-1.** [send for] llamar. **-2.** [recall - product, banknotes] retirar; [- loan] exigir pago de. ◇ *vi*: **to ~ in (at)** pasarse (por).
◆ **call off** *vt sep* **-1.** [meeting, party] suspender; [- strike] desconvocar. **-2.** [dog etc] llamar (*para que no ataque*).
◆ **call on** *vt fus* **-1.** [visit] visitar. **-2.** [ask]: **to ~ on sb to do sthg** pedir a alguien que haga algo.
◆ **call out** ◇ *vt sep* **-1.** [order to help - troops] movilizar; [- police, firemen] hacer intervenir. **-2.** [order to strike] llamar a la huelga a. **-3.** [cry out] gritar. ◇ *vi* gritar.
◆ **call round** *vi* pasarse.
◆ **call up** *vt sep* **-1.** MIL llamar a filas a. **-2.** [on telephone] llamar (por teléfono). **-3.** COMPUT pedir, hacer aparecer en pantalla.
call box *n Br* cabina *f* telefónica.
caller ['kɔːlə'] *n* **-1.** [visitor] visita *f*. **-2.** [on telephone] persona *f* que llama.
call girl *n* prostituta *f* (*que concierta sus citas por teléfono*).
calligraphy [kə'lɪɡrəfɪ] *n* caligrafía *f*.
call-in *n Am* RADIO & TV programa *m* a micrófono abierto.
calling ['kɔːlɪŋ] *n* **-1.** [profession] profesión *f*. **-2.** [vocation] vocación *f*.
calling card *n Am* tarjeta *f* de visita.
callipers *Br*, **calipers** *Am* ['kælɪpəz] *npl* **-1.** MED aparato *m* ortopédico. **-2.** MATH compás *m* de grueso.
callous ['kæləs] *adj* despiadado(da), cruel.
callously ['kæləslɪ] *adv* despiadadamente, cruelmente.
callousness ['kæləsnɪs] *n* crueldad *f*.
call-up *n Br* llamamiento *m* a filas, reclutamiento *m*.
callus ['kæləs] (*pl* **-es**) *n* callo *m*.
calm [kɑːm] ◇ *adj* **-1.** [not worried or excited] tranquilo(la). **-2.** [evening, weather] apacible. **-3.** [water] en calma. ◇ *n* calma *f*. ◇ *vt* calmar.

◆ **calm down** ◇ *vt sep* calmar. ◇ *vi* calmarse.
calmly ['kɑːmlɪ] *adv* tranquilamente, con calma.
calmness ['kɑːmnɪs] *n* calma *f*.
Calor gas® ['kælə'-] *n Br* (gas *m*) butano *m*.
calorie ['kælərɪ] *n* caloría *f*.
calorific [ˌkælə'rɪfɪk] *adj* [fattening] que engorda.
calve [kɑːv] *vi* parir (un becerro).
calves [kɑːvz] *pl* → **calf**.
cam [kæm] *n* leva *f*.
CAM (*abbr of* **computer aided manufacture**) *n* FAO *f*.
camaraderie [ˌkæmə'rɑːdərɪ] *n* camaradería *f*.
camber ['kæmbə'] *n* bombeo *m*.
Cambodia [kæm'bəʊdjə] *n* Camboya.
Cambodian [kæm'bəʊdjən] ◇ *adj* cambo-yano(na). ◇ *n* camboyano *m*, -na *f*.
Cambs (*abbr of* **Cambridgeshire**) *condado inglés*.
camcorder ['kæmˌkɔːdə'] *n* camcorder *m*, cámara *f* de vídeo con micrófono.
came [keɪm] *pt* → **come**.
camel ['kæml] ◇ *adj* pardo(da). ◇ *n* camello *m*.
camellia [kə'miːljə] *n* camelia *f*.
cameo ['kæmɪəʊ] (*pl* **-s**) *n* **-1.** [jewellery] camafeo *m*. **-2.** [in acting] actuación breve y memorable; [in writing] excelente descripción.
camera ['kæmərə] *n* cámara *f*.
◆ **in camera** *adv fml* a puerta cerrada.
cameraman ['kæmərəmæn] (*pl* **-men** [-men]) *n* cámara *m*.
Cameroon [ˌkæmə'ruːn] *n* (el) Camerún.
Cameroonian [ˌkæmə'ruːnɪən] ◇ *adj* camerunés(esa). ◇ *n* camerunés *m*, -esa *f*.
camisole ['kæmɪsəʊl] *n* combinación *f*, picardías *m inv*.
camomile ['kæməmaɪl] ◇ *n* manzanilla *f*. ◇ *comp*: **~ tea** manzanilla *f*.
camouflage ['kæməflɑːʒ] ◇ *n* camuflaje *m*. ◇ *vt* camuflar.
camp [kæmp] ◇ *n* **-1.** [gen & MIL] campamento *m*. **-2.** [temporary mass accommodation] campo *m*; **prison ~** campo de prisioneros. **-3.** [faction] bando *m*. ◇ *vi* acampar.
◆ **camp out** *vi* acampar (al aire libre).
campaign [kæm'peɪn] ◇ *n* campaña *f*. ◇ *vi*: **to ~ (for/against)** hacer campaña (a favor de/en contra de).
campaigner [kæm'peɪnə'] *n* **-1.** [supporter of cause] defensor *m*, -ra *f*. **-2.** [experienced person] veterano *m*, -na *f*.

camp bed *n* cama *f* de campaña.
camper ['kæmpə'] *n* **-1.** [person] campista *m* y *f*. **-2.** ~ **(van)** caravana *f*.
campground ['kæmpgraʊnd] *n Am* camping *m*.
camphor ['kæmfə'] *n* alcanfor *m*.
camping ['kæmpɪŋ] *n* camping *m*, acampada *f*.
camping site, **campsite** ['kæmpsaɪt] *n* camping *m*.
campus ['kæmpəs] (*pl* **-es**) *n* campus *m inv*, ciudad *f* universitaria.
camshaft ['kæmʃɑːft] *n* árbol *m* de levas.
can¹ [kæn] (*pt* & *pp* **-ned**, *cont* **-ning**) ⋄ *n* [for drink, food] lata *f*, bote *m*; [for oil, paint] lata. ⋄ *vt* enlatar.
can² [*weak form* kən, *strong form* kæn] (*pt* & *conditional* **could**, *negative* **cannot** OR **can't**) *modal vb* **-1.** [be able to] poder; ~ **you come to lunch?** ¿puedes venir a comer?; **she couldn't come** no pudo venir; **I ~'t** OR **cannot afford it** no me lo puedo permitir; ~ **you see/hear something?** ¿ves/oyes algo? **-2.** [know how to] saber; **I ~ speak French/play the piano** sé hablar francés/tocar el piano; ~ **you drive/cook?** ¿sabes conducir/cocinar? **-3.** [indicating permission, in polite requests] poder; **you ~ use my car if you like** puedes utilizar mi coche si quieres; **we ~'t wear jeans to work** no nos dejan llevar vaqueros en el trabajo; ~ **I speak to John, please?** ¿puedo hablar con John, por favor? **-4.** [indicating disbelief, puzzlement]: **you ~'t be serious** estás de broma ¿no?; **what ~ she have done with it?** ¿qué puede haber hecho con ello?; **we ~'t just leave him here** no podemos dejarlo aquí de esta forma. **-5.** [indicating possibility] poder; **you could have done it** podrías haberlo hecho; **I could see you tomorrow** podríamos vernos mañana. **-6.** [indicating usual state or behaviour] poder; **she ~ be a bit difficult sometimes** a veces puede ser un poco terca; **Edinburgh ~ be very chilly** Edimburgo puede llegar a ser muy frío.
Canada ['kænədə] *n* (el) Canadá.
Canadian [kə'neɪdjən] ⋄ *adj* canadiense. ⋄ *n* [person] canadiense *m y f*.
canal [kə'næl] *n* canal *m*.
canary [kə'neərɪ] (*pl* **-ies**) *n* canario *m*.
Canary Islands, **Canaries** [kə'neərɪz] *npl*: **the ~** las (islas) Canarias.
cancan ['kænkæn] *n* cancán *m*.
cancel ['kænsl] (*Br pt* & *pp* **-led**, *cont* **-ling**, *Am pt* & *pp* **-ed**, *cont* **-ing**) *vt* **-1.** [call off] cancelar, suspender. **-2.** [invalidate - cheque, debt] cancelar; [- stamp] matar.
◆ **cancel out** *vt sep* anular.

cancellation [,kænsə'leɪʃn] *n* suspensión *f*.
cancer ['kænsə'] ⋄ *n* [disease] cáncer *m*. ⋄ *comp* de cáncer; ~ **patient** enfermo *m*, -ma *f* de cáncer; ~ **research** investigación *f* sobre el cáncer, oncología *f*.
◆ **Cancer** *n* Cáncer *m*; **to be (a) ~** ser Cáncer.
cancerous ['kænsərəs] *adj* canceroso(sa).
candelabra [,kændɪ'lɑːbrə] *n* candelabro *m*.
C and F (*abbr of* **cost and freight**) C y F.
candid ['kændɪd] *adj* franco(ca), sincero(ra).
candidacy ['kændɪdəsɪ] *n* candidatura *f*.
candidate ['kændɪdət] *n*: ~ **(for)** candidato *m*, -ta *f* (a).
candidature ['kændɪdətʃə'] *n* candidatura *f*.
candidly ['kændɪdlɪ] *adv* con franqueza OR sinceridad.
candidness ['kændɪdnɪs] = **candour**.
candied ['kændɪd] *adj* confitado(da).
candle ['kændl] *n* vela *f*, esperma *f Amer*; **to burn the ~ at both ends** *inf* no descansar en todo el día.
candlelight ['kændllaɪt] *n* luz *f* de una vela.
candlelit ['kændllɪt] *adj* a la luz de las velas.
candlestick ['kændlstɪk] *n* candelero *m*.
candour *Br*, **candor** *Am* ['kændə'] *n* franqueza *f*, sinceridad *f*.
candy ['kændɪ] (*pl* **-ies**) *n* **-1.** (*U*) [confectionery] golosinas *fpl*; ~ **bar** chocolatina *f*. **-2.** [sweet] caramelo *m*.
candyfloss *Br* ['kændɪflɒs], **cotton candy** *Am* *n* azúcar *m* hilado, algodón *m*.
cane [keɪn] ⋄ *n* **-1.** (*U*) [for making furniture, supporting plant] caña *f*, mimbre *m*. **-2.** [walking stick] bastón *m*. **-3.** [for punishment]: **the ~** la vara. ⋄ *comp* de caña OR mimbre. ⋄ *vt* azotar (*con vara*).
cane sugar *n* azúcar *m o f* de caña.
canine ['keɪnaɪn] ⋄ *adj* canino(na). ⋄ *n*: ~ **(tooth)** (diente *m*) canino *m*, colmillo *m*.
canister ['kænɪstə'] *n* [for tea] bote *m*; [for film] lata *f*; [for gas] bombona *f*; **smoke ~** bote de humo.
cannabis ['kænəbɪs] *n* canabis *m*.
canned [kænd] *adj* **-1.** [food, drink] enlatado(da), en lata. **-2.** *inf fig* [applause, music, laughter] grabado(da).
cannelloni [,kænɪ'ləʊnɪ] *n* (*U*) canelones *mpl*.
cannery ['kænərɪ] (*pl* **-ies**) *n* fábrica *f* de conservas.
cannibal ['kænɪbl] *n* caníbal *m y f*.
cannibalize, **-ise** ['kænɪbəlaɪz] *vt desmontar para aprovechar algunas piezas*.
cannon ['kænən] (*pl inv* OR **-s**) *n* cañón *m*.

◆ **cannon into** vt fus Br chocar de lleno con.

cannonball ['kænənbɔːl] n bala f de cañón.

cannot ['kænɒt] fml → can.

canny ['kænɪ] (compar -ier, superl -iest) adj [shrewd] astuto(ta).

canoe [kə'nuː] (cont canoeing) ◇ n [gen] canoa f; SPORT piragua f. ◇ vi ir en canoa.

canoeing [kə'nuːɪŋ] n piragüismo m.

canon ['kænən] n -1. [clergyman] canónigo m. -2. [general principle] canon m. -3. [of mass]: **the Canon** el canon.

canonize, -ise ['kænənaɪz] vt canonizar.

canoodle [kə'nuːdl] vi Br inf hacerse arrumacos.

can opener n abrelatas m inv.

canopy ['kænəpɪ] (pl -ies) n -1. [over bed, seat] dosel m. -2. [of trees, branches] cubierta f frondosa.

cant [kænt] n (U) pej [insincere talk] demagogia f, hipocresías fpl.

can't [kɑːnt] = cannot.

Cantab. (abbr of cantabrigiensis) de o relativo a Cambridge, especialmente su universidad.

Cantabrian Mountains [kæn'teɪbrɪən-] npl: **the** ~ la cordillera Cantábrica.

cantaloup Br, **cantaloupe** Am ['kæntəluːp] n cantalupo m.

cantankerous [kæn'tæŋkərəs] adj [person] refunfuñón(ona); [behaviour] arisco(ca).

canteen [kæn'tiːn] n -1. [restaurant] cantina f. -2. [set of cutlery] (juego m de) cubertería f.

canter ['kæntər] ◇ n medio galope m. ◇ vi ir a medio galope.

Canterbury ['kæntəbrɪ] n Cantorbery.

cantilever ['kæntɪliːvər] n voladizo m.

Canton [kæn'tɒn] n Cantón.

Cantonese [,kæntə'niːz] ◇ adj cantonés(esa). ◇ n -1. [person] cantonés m, -esa f. -2. [language] cantonés m.

canvas ['kænvəs] n -1. [cloth] lona f; **under** ~ [in a tent] en una tienda (de campaña). -2. [for painting on, finished painting] lienzo m.

canvass ['kænvəs] ◇ vt -1. POL [person] solicitar el voto a. -2. [opinion] pulsar. ◇ vi solicitar votos yendo de puerta en puerta.

canvasser ['kænvəsər] n -1. [for political support] persona que solicita votos. -2. [for poll] encuestador m, -ra f.

canvassing ['kænvəsɪŋ] n -1. (U) [for political support]: **to go** ~ ir a solicitar votos. -2. [for poll] sondeos mpl.

canyon ['kænjən] n cañón m.

cap [kæp] (pt & pp **-ped**, cont **-ping**) ◇ -1. [hat - peaked] gorra f; [- with no peak] gorro m; **to go** ~ **in hand to sb** ir sombrero en mano a alguien, ponerle la gorra a alguien. -2. [on bottle] tapón m; [on jar] tapa f; [on pen] capuchón m. -3. Br [contraceptive device] diafragma m. ◇ vt -1. [top]: **to be capped with** estar coronado(da) de. -2 [outdo]: **to** ~ **it all** para colmo.

CAP [kæp, ,siːeɪ'piː] (abbr of **Common Agri cultural Policy**) n PAC f.

capability [,keɪpə'bɪlətɪ] (pl -ies) n capaci dad f.

capable ['keɪpəbl] adj -1. [able]: **to be** ~ o sthg/of doing sthg ser capaz de algo/de ha cer algo. -2. [competent] hábil.

capably ['keɪpəblɪ] adv competentemente.

capacious [kə'peɪʃəs] adj fml espacioso(sa).

capacitor [kə'pæsɪtər] n condensador n eléctrico.

capacity [kə'pæsɪtɪ] (pl -ies) ◇ n -1. [gen] ~ **(for)** capacidad f (de); **seating** ~ aforo m **to** ~ al completo; ~ **for doing** OR **to d** sthg capacidad de hacer algo; **within one's** ~ dentro de las posibilidades de uno. -2 [position] calidad f; **in my** ~ **as ...** en calidac de .... ◇ comp: ~ **audience** lleno m absoluto OR total.

cape [keɪp] n -1. GEOGR cabo m. -2. [cloak] capa f.

Cape Canaveral [-kə'nævərəl] n Cabo Ca ñaveral.

Cape Cod n Cabo Cod.

Cape Horn n Cabo de Hornos.

Cape of Good Hope n: **the** ~ el Cabo de Buena Esperanza.

caper ['keɪpər] ◇ n -1. [food] alcaparra f -2. inf [escapade] treta f. ◇ vi retozar.

Cape Town n Ciudad del Cabo.

Cape Verde [-vɜːd] n: **the** ~ **Islands** las is las de Cabo Verde.

capillary [kə'pɪlərɪ] (pl -ies) ◇ n capilar m.

capita → **per capita**.

capital ['kæpɪtl] ◇ adj -1. [letter] mayúscu la. -2. [punishable by death] capital. ◇ n -1. [of country, main centre] capital f. -2. ~ **(let ter)** mayúscula f; **in** ~s en mayúsculas. -3. [money] capital m; **to make** ~ **(out) of** fig sa car partido de.

capital allowance n desgravación f por inversiones.

capital assets npl bienes mpl de capital, activo m fijo.

capital expenditure n (U) inversión f de capital.

capital gains tax n impuesto m sobre plusvalías.

capital goods *npl* bienes *mpl* de capital.

capital-intensive *adj* que utiliza gran volumen de capital.

capitalism ['kæpɪtəlɪzm] *n* capitalismo *m*.

capitalist ['kæpɪtəlɪst] ◇ *adj* capitalista. ◇ *n* capitalista *m* y *f*.

capitalize, -ise ['kæpɪtəlaɪz] *vi*: **to ~ on** sthg capitalizar algo.

capital punishment *n* (U) pena *f* capital.

capital stock *n* capital *m* nominal en acciones.

capital transfer tax *n* impuesto *m* sobre las transferencias de capital.

Capitol ['kæpɪtl] *n*: **the ~** el Capitolio.

Capitol Hill *n* el Capitolio, *ubicación del Congreso estadounidense, en Washington*.

capitulate [kə'pɪtjʊleɪt] *vi*: **to ~ (to)** capitular (ante).

capitulation [kə,pɪtjʊ'leɪʃn] *n* capitulación *f*.

cappuccino [,kæpʊ'tʃiːnəʊ] (*pl* -s) *n* capuchino *m*.

capricious [kə'prɪʃəs] *adj* [person] caprichoso(sa); [behaviour] inconstante; [weather] variable.

Capricorn ['kæprɪkɔːn] *n* Capricornio *m*; **to be (a) ~** ser Capricornio.

caps [kæps] (*abbr of* **capital letters**) mayúsc.

capsicum ['kæpsɪkəm] *n* pimiento *m*.

capsize [kæp'saɪz] ◇ *vt* hacer volcar OR zozobrar. ◇ *vi* volcar, zozobrar.

capsule ['kæpsjuːl] *n* cápsula *f*.

Capt. (*abbr of* **captain**).

captain ['kæptɪn] ◇ *n* capitán *m*, -ana *f*. ◇ *vt* capitanear.

caption ['kæpʃn] *n* [under picture etc] pie *m*, leyenda *f*; [heading] encabezamiento *m*.

captivate ['kæptɪveɪt] *vt* cautivar.

captivating ['kæptɪveɪtɪŋ] *adj* cautivador(ra).

captive ['kæptɪv] ◇ *adj* **-1.** [imprisoned] en cautividad, en cautiverio. **-2.** *fig* [market] asegurado(da); **~ audience** grupo de gente forzado a ver o escuchar algo. ◇ *n* cautivo *m*, -va *f*.

captivity [kæp'tɪvətɪ] *n*: **in ~** en cautividad, en cautiverio.

captor ['kæptə'] *n* apresador *m*, -ra *f*.

capture ['kæptʃə'] ◇ *vt* **-1.** [gen & COMPUT] capturar. **-2.** [audience, share of market] hacerse con; [city] tomar. **-3.** [scene, mood, attention] captar. ◇ *n* captura *f*.

car [kɑː'] ◇ *n* **-1.** [motorcar] coche *m*, automóvil *m*, carro *m* Amer. **-2.** [on train] vagón *m*. ◇ *comp* [door, tyre etc] del coche; [industry] del automóvil; [accident] de automóvil.

Caracas [kə'rækəs] *n* Caracas.

carafe [kə'ræf] *n* garrafa *f*.

caramel ['kærəmel] *n* **-1.** [burnt sugar] caramelo *m* (líquido), azúcar *m* quemado. **-2.** [sweet] tofe *m*.

caramelize, -ise ['kærəməlaɪz] *vi* caramelizar.

carat ['kærət] *n* Br quilate *m*; **24-~ gold** oro de 24 quilates.

caravan ['kærəvæn] ◇ *n* caravana *f*, roulotte *f*. ◇ *comp* [holiday] en caravana OR roulotte; [park] para caravanas OR roulottes.

caravanning ['kærəvænɪŋ] *n* Br caravaning *m*.

caravan site *n* Br camping *m* para caravanas OR roulottes.

caraway seed ['kærəweɪ-] *n* carvi *m*.

carbohydrate [,kɑːbəʊ'haɪdreɪt] *n* CHEM hidrato *m* de carbono.

◆ **carbohydrates** *npl* [foods] féculas *fpl*.

carbon ['kɑːbən] *n* **-1.** [element] carbono *m*. **-2.** = **carbon copy**. **-3.** = **carbon paper**.

carbonated ['kɑːbəneɪtɪd] *adj* con gas, carbónico(ca).

carbon copy *n* [document] copia *f* en papel carbón; *fig* [exact copy] calco *m*.

carbon dating [-'deɪtɪŋ] *n* datación *f* por carbono 14.

carbon dioxide [-daɪ'ɒksaɪd] *n* bióxido *m* OR dióxido *m* de carbono.

carbon fibre *n* Br fibra *f* de carbono.

carbon monoxide *n* monóxido *m* de carbono.

carbon paper *n* papel *m* carbón.

car-boot sale *n* venta de objetos usados colocados en el portaequipajes del coche.

carburettor Br, **carburetor** Am [,kɑːbə'retə'] *n* carburador *m*.

carcass ['kɑːkəs] *n* [gen] cadáver *m* (de animal); [of bird] carcasa *f*; [at butcher's] canal *m*.

carcinogenic [,kɑːsɪnə'dʒenɪk] *adj* cancerígeno(na).

card [kɑːd] ◇ *n* **-1.** [playing card] carta *f*, naipe *m*; **to play one's ~s right** hacer las cosas bien; **to put** OR **lay one's ~s on the table** poner las cartas boca arriba OR sobre la mesa. **-2.** [for information, greetings, computers] tarjeta *f*. **-3.** [postcard] postal *f*. **-4.** [cardboard] cartulina *f*.

◆ **cards** *npl* las cartas, los naipes.

◆ **on the cards** Br, **in the cards** Am *adv* *inf* más que probable.

cardamom ['kɑːdəməm] *n* cardamomo *m*.

cardboard ['kɑːdbɔːd] ◇ *n* (U) cartón *m*. ◇ *comp* de cartón.

cardboard box *n* caja *f* de cartón.

card-carrying [-'kærɪŋ] *adj* con carné.
card catalog *n Am* fichero *m*.
cardiac ['kɑːdɪæk] *adj* cardíaco(ca).
cardiac arrest *n* paro *m* cardíaco.
cardigan ['kɑːdɪgən] *n* rebeca *f*, cárdigan *m*.
cardinal ['kɑːdɪnl] ◇ *adj* capital. ◇ *n* RELIG cardenal *m*.
cardinal number, **cardinal numeral** *n* número *m* cardinal.
card index *n Br* fichero *m*.
cardiograph ['kɑːdɪəgrɑːf] *n* cardiógrafo *m*.
cardiology [,kɑːdɪ'ɒlədʒɪ] *n* cardiología *f*.
cardiovascular [,kɑːdɪəʊ'væskjʊləʳ] *adj* cardiovascular.
cardsharp ['kɑːd,ʃɑːp] *n* fullero *m*, -ra *f*.
card table *n* mesita *f* plegable (*para jugar a cartas*).
card vote *n Br* voto *m* por delegación.
care [keəʳ] ◇ *n* -1. [gen] cuidado *m*; **in sb's ~** al cargo OR cuidado de alguien; **to be in/be taken into ~** estar/ser internado en un centro de protección de menores; **to take ~ of** [look after] cuidar de; [deal with] encargarse de; **take ~!** ¡nos vemos!, ¡cuídate!; **to take ~ (to do sthg)** tener cuidado (de hacer algo). -2. [cause of worry] preocupación *f*, problema *m*.
◇ *vi* -1. [be concerned]: **to ~ (about)** preocuparse (de OR por). -2. [mind]: **I don't ~** no me importa; **I couldn't ~ less** *inf* me importa un pito.
◆ **care of** *prep* al cuidado de, en casa de.
◆ **care for** *vt fus dated* [like] gustar; **I don't ~ for cheese** no me gusta el queso; **he still ~s for her** todavía la quiere.
CARE [keəʳ] (*abbr of* **Cooperative for American Relief Everywhere**) *n* organización humanitaria estadounidense.
career [kə'rɪəʳ] ◇ *n* carrera *f*. ◇ *comp* de carrera. ◇ *vi* ir a toda velocidad.
careerist [kə'rɪərɪst] *n pej* arribista *m* y *f*.
careers [kə'rɪəz] *comp* vocacional, profesional.
careers adviser *n* persona que aconseja sobre salidas profesionales.
career woman *n* mujer *f* de carrera.
carefree ['keəfriː] *adj* despreocupado(da).
careful ['keəfʊl] *adj* [gen] cuidadoso(sa); [driver] prudente; [work] esmerado(da); **to be ~ with** ser mirado OR cuidadoso con; **to be ~ to do sthg** tener cuidado de hacer algo.
carefully ['keəflɪ] *adv* -1. [cautiously] con cuidado, cuidadosamente. -2. [thoroughly] detenidamente.
careless ['keəlɪs] *adj* -1. [inattentive] descui-

dado(da). -2. [unconcerned] despreocupado(da).
carelessly ['keəlɪslɪ] -1. [inattentively - gen] descuidadamente; [- drive] con poco cuidado. -2. [unconcernedly] despreocupadamente.
carelessness ['keəlɪsnɪs] *n* -1. [inattention] descuido *m*. -2. [lack of concern] despreocupación *f*.
carer ['keərə] *n* persona que cuida de un familiar impedido o enfermo.
caress [kə'res] ◇ *n* caricia *f*, apapacho *m* Amer. ◇ *vt* acariciar.
caretaker ['keə,teɪkəʳ] *n Br* conserje *m* y *f*.
caretaker government *n* gobierno *m* provisional.
car ferry *n* transbordador *m* de coches.
cargo ['kɑːgəʊ] (*pl* **-es** OR **-s**) ◇ *n* carga *f*, cargamento *m*. ◇ *comp* de carga.
car hire *n Br* alquiler *m* de coches.
Carib ['kærɪb] *n* [language] caribe *m*.
Caribbean [*Br* kærɪ'bɪən, *Am* kə'rɪbɪən] ◇ *adj* caribe. ◇ *n*: **the ~ (Sea)** el (mar) Caribe.
caribou ['kærɪbuː] (*pl inv* OR **-s**) *n* caribú *m*.
caricature ['kærɪkə,tjʊəʳ] ◇ *n lit* & *fig* caricatura *f*. ◇ *vt* caricaturizar.
caries ['keəriːz] *n* caries *f*.
caring ['keərɪŋ] *adj* solícito(ta), dedicado(da).
caring professions *npl*: **the ~** las profesiones relacionadas con la asistencia social.
carnage ['kɑːnɪdʒ] *n* carnicería *f*, matanza *f*.
carnal ['kɑːnl] *adj literary* carnal.
carnation [kɑː'neɪʃn] *n* clavel *m*.
carnival ['kɑːnɪvl] *n* carnaval *m*.
carnivore ['kɑːnɪvɔːʳ] *n* carnívoro *m*, -ra *f*.
carnivorous [kɑː'nɪvərəs] *adj* carnívoro(ra).
carol ['kærəl] *n* villancico *m*.
carouse [kə'raʊz] *vi* andar de parranda.
carousel [,kærə'sel] *n* -1. [at fair] tiovivo *m*. -2. [at airport] cinta *f* transportadora.
carp [kɑːp] (*pl inv* OR **-s**) ◇ *n* carpa *f*. ◇ *vi*: **to ~ (about)** refunfuñar OR renegar (de).
car park *n Br* aparcamiento *m*, parqueadero *m* Amer.
Carpathians [kɑː'peɪθɪənz] *npl*: **the ~** los Cárpatos.
carpenter ['kɑːpəntəʳ] *n* carpintero *m*, -ra *f*.
carpentry ['kɑːpəntrɪ] *n* carpintería *f*.
carpet ['kɑːpɪt] ◇ *n lit* & *fig* alfombra *f*; **fitted ~** moqueta *f*; **to sweep sthg under the ~** *fig* echar tierra a algo. ◇ *vt* -1. [fit with carpet] enmoquetar. -2. *fig* [cover] cubrir.

carpet slipper *n* zapatilla *f.*

carpet sweeper *n* cepillo *m* mecánico (de alfombras).

car phone *n* teléfono *m* de coche.

car pool *n Br* [fleet of cars] *conjunto de coches de una empresa para uso de sus empleados.*

carport ['kɑː,pɔːt] *n* cobertizo *m* para coches.

car rental *n Am* alquiler *m* de coches.

carriage ['kærɪdʒ] *n* **-1.** [horsedrawn vehicle] carruaje *m.* **-2.** *Br* [railway coach] vagón *m.* **-3.** [transport of goods] transporte *m;* ~ **paid** OR **free** *Br* porte pagado; ~ **forward** *Br* porte a cuenta del destinatario. **-4.** [on typewriter] carro *m.* **-5.** *literary* [bearing] porte *m.*

carriage clock *n reloj grande con asa.*

carriage return *n* retorno *m* de carro.

carriageway ['kærɪdʒweɪ] *n Br* carril *m.*

carrier ['kærɪə'] *n* **-1.** COMM transportista *m* y *f.* **-2.** [of disease] portador *m,* -ra *f.* **-3.** MIL: (aircraft) ~ portaaviones *m inv.* **-4.** [on bicycle] portaequipajes *m inv.* **-5.** = **carrier bag.**

carrier bag *n* bolsa *f* (*de papel o plástico*).

carrier pigeon *n* paloma *f* mensajera.

carrion ['kærɪən] *n* carroña *f.*

carrot ['kærət] *n* **-1.** [vegetable] zanahoria *f.* **-2.** *inf* [incentive] señuelo *m,* aliciente *m.*

carry ['kærɪ] (*pt* & *pp* **-ied**) ◇ *vt* **-1.** [transport] llevar. **-2.** [disease] transmitir. **-3.** [involve] acarrear, conllevar. **-4.** [motion, proposal] aprobar. **-5.** [be pregnant with] estar embarazada de. **-6.** MATH llevarse. ◇ *vi* [sound] oírse.

◆ **carry away** *vt fus:* **to get carried away** exaltarse.

◆ **carry forward** *vt sep* llevar a la página siguiente; **carried forward** suma y sigue.

◆ **carry off** *vt sep* **-1.** [make a success of] llevar a cabo. **-2.** [win] llevarse.

◆ **carry on** ◇ *vt fus* **-1.** [continue] continuar, seguir; **to ~ on doing sthg** continuar OR seguir haciendo algo. **-2.** [conversation] sostener. ◇ *vi* **-1.** [continue]: **to ~ on (with)** continuar OR seguir (con). **-2.** *inf* [make a fuss] exagerar la nota. **-3.** *inf dated* [have a love affair]: **to ~ on with** tener un lío con.

◆ **carry out** *vt fus* **-1.** [perform] llevar a cabo. **-2.** [fulfil] cumplir.

◆ **carry over** *vt sep* = **carry forward.**

◆ **carry through** *vt sep* [accomplish] llevar a cabo.

carryall ['kærɪɔːl] *n Am* bolsa *f* de viaje.

carrycot ['kærɪkɒt] *n* moisés *m,* capacho *m.*

carry-on *n Br inf* lío *m,* follón *m.*

carry-out *n* comida *f* para llevar.

carsick ['kɑː,sɪk] *adj* mareado(da) (*al ir en coche*).

cart [kɑːt] ◇ *n* carro *m,* carreta *f.* ◇ *vt inf* acarrear.

carte blanche *n* carta *f* blanca.

cartel [kɑː'tel] *n pej* cártel *m.*

cartilage ['kɑːtɪlɪdʒ] *n* cartílago *m.*

carton ['kɑːtn] *n* **-1.** [strong cardboard box] caja *f* de cartón. **-2.** [for liquids] cartón *m,* envase *m.*

cartoon [kɑː'tuːn] *n* **-1.** [satirical drawing] chiste *m* (en viñeta). **-2.** [comic strip] tira *f* cómica. **-3.** [film] dibujos *mpl* animados.

cartoonist [kɑː'tuːnɪst] *n* dibujante *m* y *f.*

cartridge ['kɑːtrɪdʒ] *n* **-1.** [for gun, camera] cartucho *m.* **-2.** [for pen] recambio *m.* **-3.** [for record player] portaagujas *m inv.*

cartridge paper *n* papel *m* guarro.

cartwheel ['kɑːtwiːl] *n* voltereta *f* lateral.

carve [kɑːv] ◇ *vt* **-1.** [wood] tallar; [stone] esculpir. **-2.** [meat] trinchar. **-3.** [cut] grabar. ◇ *vi* trinchar.

◆ **carve out** *vt sep* [niche, place] conquistar; **to ~ out a career for o.s.** labrarse un porvenir.

◆ **carve up** *vt sep* repartir.

carving ['kɑːvɪŋ] *n* **-1.** [art, work - wooden] tallado *m;* [- stone] labrado *m,* cincelado *m.* **-2.** [object - wooden] talla *f;* [- stone] escultura *f.*

carving knife *n* cuchillo *m* de trinchar.

car wash *n* lavado *m* de coches.

Casablanca [,kæsə'blæŋkə] *n* Casablanca.

cascade [kæ'skeɪd] ◇ *n* cascada *f.* ◇ *vi* caer en cascada.

case [keɪs] *n* **-1.** [gen] caso *m;* **to be the ~** ser el caso; **a ~ in point** un ejemplo claro; **in that/which ~** en ese/cuyo caso; **as** OR **whatever the ~ may be** según sea el caso; **in ~ of** en caso de. **-2.** [argument] argumento *m,* razones *fpl;* **the ~ for/against (sthg)** los argumentos a favor/en contra (de algo). **-3.** JUR [trial, inquiry] pleito *m,* causa *f.* **-4.** [container of leather] funda *f;* [- of hard material] estuche *m.* **-5.** *Br* [suitcase] maleta *f.*

◆ **in any case** *adv* en cualquier caso, de todas formas.

◆ **in case** *conj & adv* por si acaso.

case-hardened [-'hɑːdnd] *adj* [person] inconmovible, inalterable.

case history *n* historial *m* (clínico).

case study *n* estudio *m* de casos prácticos.

cash [kæʃ] ◇ *n* **-1.** [notes and coins] (dinero *m*) efectivo *m,* metálico *m;* **to pay (in) ~** pagar al contado OR en efectivo. **-2.** *inf* [money] dinero *m,* lana *f Amer.* **-3.** [payment]: ~ **in advance** pago *m* al contado por adelantado; ~ **on delivery** entrega *f* contra reembolso. ◇ *vt* cobrar, hacer efectivo.

◆ **cash in** *vi*: **to ~ in on** *inf* sacar partido de.

cash and carry *n* almacén *de venta al por mayor.*

cashbook ['kæʃbʊk] *n* libro *m* de caja.

cash box *n* caja *f* con cerradura (para el dinero).

cash card *n* tarjeta *f* de cajero automático.

cash crop *n* cultivo *m* para comercialización.

cash desk *n Br* caja *f*.

cash discount *n* descuento *m* por pronto pago.

cash dispenser *n* cajero *m* automático.

cashew (nut) ['kæʃuː-] *n* (nuez *f* de) anacardo *m*.

cash flow *n* flujo *m* de fondos, cash-flow *m*.

cashier [kæ'ʃɪəʳ] *n* cajero *m*, -ra *f*.

cash machine = **cash dispenser**.

cashmere [kæʃ'mɪəʳ] ◇ *n* cachemir *m*, cachemira *f*. ◇ *comp* de cachemir OR cachemira.

cash payment *n* pago *m* en efectivo OR al contado.

cash price *n* precio *m* al contado.

cash register *n* caja *f* (registradora).

cash sale *n* venta *f* al contado.

casing ['keɪsɪŋ] *n* cubierta *f*, revestimiento *m*.

casino [kə'siːnəʊ] (*pl* **-s**) *n* casino *m*.

cask [kɑːsk] *n* tonel *m*, barril *m*.

casket ['kɑːskɪt] *n* **-1.** [for jewels] estuche *m*. **-2.** *Am* [coffin] ataúd *m*.

Caspian Sea ['kæspɪən-] *n*: **the ~** el mar Caspio.

casserole ['kæsərəʊl] *n* **-1.** [stew] guiso *m*. **-2.** [pan] cazuela *f*, cacerola *f*.

cassette [kæ'set] *n* cinta *f*, casete *f*.

cassette deck *n* platina *f*, pletina *f*.

cassette player *n* casete *m*, magnetófono *m*.

cassette recorder *n* casete *m*, magnetófono *m*.

cassock ['kæsək] *n* sotana *f*.

cast [kɑːst] (*pt* & *pp* **cast**) ◇ *n* [of play, film] reparto *m*. ◇ *vt* **-1.** [look] echar, lanzar; **to ~ doubt on sthg** poner algo en duda; **to ~ a spell on** embrujar OR hechizar a. **-2.** [light] irradiar; [shadow] proyectar. **-3.** [throw] arrojar, lanzar. **-4.** [choose for play]: **to ~ sb as** asignar a alguien el papel de. **-5.** [vote] emitir. **-6.** [metal, statue] fundir. **-7.** [shed - skin] mudar.

◆ **cast about, cast around** *vi*: **to ~ about for sthg** buscar algo.

◆ **cast aside** *vt sep* [person] abandonar; [idea] rechazar.

◆ **cast off** ◇ *vt sep* desechar, abandonar. ◇ *vi* NAUT soltar amarras.

castanets [,kæstə'nets] *npl* castañuelas *fpl*.

castaway ['kɑːstəweɪ] *n* náufrago *m*, -ga *f*.

caste [kɑːst] *n* casta *f*.

caster ['kɑːstəʳ] *n* [wheel] ruedecilla *f*, pivote *m*.

caster sugar *n Br* azúcar *m* extrafino.

castigate ['kæstɪgeɪt] *vt fml* [behaviour, report] censurar.

Castile [kæs'tiːl], **Castilla** [kæs'tiʎa] *n* Castilla.

Castilian [kæ'stiljən] ◇ *adj* castellano(na). ◇ *n* **-1.** [person] castellano *m*, -na *f*. **-2.** [language] castellano *m*.

Castilla = **Castile**.

casting ['kɑːstɪŋ] *n* [for film, play] reparto *m*.

casting vote *n* voto *m* de calidad.

cast iron *n* hierro *m* fundido.

◆ **cast-iron** *adj* **-1.** [made of cast iron] de hierro fundido. **-2.** [alibi, excuse] irrebatible, indiscutible; [will] férreo(a), de hierro.

castle ['kɑːsl] *n* **-1.** [building] castillo *m*. **-2.** [in chess] torre *f*.

castoffs ['kɑːstɒfs] *npl* ropa *f* vieja OR usada.

castor ['kɑːstəʳ] = **caster**.

castor oil *n* aceite *m* de ricino.

castor sugar = **caster sugar**.

castrate [kæ'streɪt] *vt* castrar.

castration [kæ'streɪʃn] *n* castración *f*.

casual ['kæʒʊəl] *adj* **-1.** [relaxed, indifferent] despreocupado(da). **-2.** *pej* [offhand] descuidado(da), informal. **-3.** [chance - visitor] ocasional; [- remark] casual. **-4.** [informal] de sport, informal. **-5.** [irregular - labourer etc] eventual.

casually ['kæʒʊəlɪ] *adv* **-1.** [in a relaxed manner, indifferently] con aire despreocupado. **-2.** [informally] informalmente.

casualty ['kæʒjʊəltɪ] (*pl* **-ies**) *n* **-1.** [gen] víctima *f*. **-2.** (*U*) [ward] urgencias *fpl*.

casualty department *n* unidad *f* de urgencias.

cat [kæt] *n* **-1.** [domestic] gato *m*, -ta *f*; **to let the ~ out of the bag** descubrir el pastel; **to be like a ~ on hot bricks** *Br* OR **on a hot tin roof** *Am* estar en ascuas; **to put the ~ among the pigeons** *Br* meter el lobo en el redil; **to rain ~s and dogs** llover a cántaros; **to think that one is the ~'s whiskers** *Br* creerse que uno es el oro y el moro. **-2.** [wild] felino *m*.

cataclysmic [ˌkætə'klɪzmɪk] *adj* catastrófico(ca).

catacombs ['kætəkuːmz] *npl* catacumbas *fpl*.

Catalan ['kætəˌlæn] ◇ *adj* catalán(ana). ◇ *n* **-1.** [person] catalán *m*, -ana *f*. **-2.** [language] catalán *m*.

catalogue *Br*, **catolog** *Am* ['kætəlɒg] ◇ *n* **-1.** [of items] catálogo *m*. **-2.** *fig* [list] serie *f*, cadena *f*. ◇ *vt* **-1.** [make official list of] catalogar. **-2.** *fig* [list] enumerar.

Catalonia [ˌkætə'ləʊnɪə] *n* Cataluña.

Catalonian [ˌkætə'ləʊnɪən] ◇ *adj* catalán(ana). ◇ *n* [person] catalán *m*, -ana *f*.

catalyst ['kætəlɪst] *n lit* & *fig* catalizador *m*.

catalytic convertor [ˌkætə'lɪtɪkkən'vɜːtər] *n* catalizador *m*.

catamaran [ˌkætəmə'ræn] *n* catamarán *m*.

catapult ['kætəpʌlt] *Br* ◇ *n* **-1.** HIST [handheld] tirachinas *m inv*. **-2.** HIST [machine] catapulta *f*. ◇ *vt* **-1.** [hurl] lanzar. **-2.** *fig* [propel] catapultar.

cataract ['kætərækt] *n* [in eye, waterfall] catarata *f*.

catarrh [kə'tɑːr] *n* (*U*) catarro *m*.

catastrophe [kə'tæstrəfɪ] *n* catástrofe *f*.

catastrophic [ˌkætə'strɒfɪk] *adj* catastrófico(ca).

cat burglar *n Br* ladrón *que entra trepando*.

catcall ['kætkɔːl] *n* silbido *m*, pitido *m*.

catch [kætʃ] (*pt* & *pp* **caught**) ◇ *vt* **-1.** [gen] coger, agarrar *Amer*. **-2.** [fish] pescar; [stopperson] parar. **-3.** [be in time for]: **to ~ the (last) post** *Br* llegar a la (última) recogida del correo. **-4.** [hear clearly] entender, llegar a oír. **-5.** [interest, imagination] despertar. **-6.** [see]: **to ~ sight** OR **a glimpse of** alcanzar a ver. **-7.** [hook - shirt etc] engancharse; [shut in door - finger] pillarse. **-8.** [light] reflejar. **-9.** [strike] golpear.
◇ *vi* **-1.** [become hooked, get stuck] engancharse. **-2.** [start to burn] prenderse, encenderse.
◇ *n* **-1.** [of ball etc] parada *f*. **-2.** [of fish] pesca *f*, captura *f*. **-3.** [fastener] pestillo *m*. **-4.** [snag] trampa *f*.
◆ **catch at** *vt fus* agarrarse a.
◆ **catch on** *vi* **-1.** [become popular] hacerse popular. **-2.** *inf* [understand]: **to ~ on (to)** caer en la cuenta (de).
◆ **catch out** *vt sep* [trick] pillar en un error.
◆ **catch up** ◇ *vt sep* alcanzar. ◇ *vi*: **we'll soon ~ up** pronto nos pondremos a la misma altura; **to ~ up on** [sleep] recuperar; [work, reading] ponerse al día con.
◆ **catch up with** *vt fus* **-1.** [group etc] alcanzar. **-2.** [criminal] pillar, descubrir.

catch-22 *n* callejón *m* sin salida, la pescadilla que se muerde la cola.

catch-all *adj* general.

catching ['kætʃɪŋ] *adj* contagioso(sa).

catchment area ['kætʃmənt-] *n Br* zona *f* de captación.

catchphrase ['kætʃfreɪz] *n* muletilla *f*.

catchword ['kætʃwɜːd] *n* eslogan *m*, lema *m*.

catchy ['kætʃɪ] (*compar* **-ier**, *superl* **-iest**) *adj* pegadizo(za).

catechism ['kætəkɪzm] *n* catecismo *m*.

categorical [ˌkætɪ'gɒrɪkl] *adj* [statement] categórico(ca); [denial] rotundo(da).

categorically [ˌkætɪ'gɒrɪklɪ] *adv* [state] categóricamente; [deny] rotundamente.

categorize, -ise ['kætəgəraɪz] *vt*: **to ~ sb (as)** clasificar OR catalogar a alguien (de).

category ['kætəgərɪ] (*pl* **-ies**) *n* categoría *f*.

cater ['keɪtər] *vi* proveer comida.
◆ **cater for** *vt fus Br* [tastes, needs] atender a; [social group] estar destinado(da) a; **I hadn't ~ed for that** no había contado con eso.
◆ **cater to** *vt fus* complacer.

caterer ['keɪtərər] *n* proveedor *m*, -ra *f*.

catering ['keɪtərɪŋ] *n* [at wedding etc] servicio *m* de banquetes; [trade] hostelería *f*.

caterpillar ['kætəpɪlər] *n* oruga *f*.

caterpillar tracks *npl* (rodado *m* de) oruga *f*.

cat flap *n Br* gatera *f*.

catharsis [kə'θɑːsɪs] (*pl* **catharses** [kə'θɑːsiːz]) *n fml* catarsis *f inv*.

cathedral [kə'θiːdrəl] *n* catedral *f*.

catheter ['kæθɪtər] *n* catéter *m*, sonda *f*.

cathode ray tube ['kæθəʊd-] *n* tubo *m* de rayos catódicos.

Catholic ['kæθlɪk] ◇ *adj* católico(ca). ◇ *n* católico *m*, -ca *f*.
◆ **catholic** *adj* diverso(sa), variado(da).

Catholicism [kə'θɒlɪsɪzm] *n* catolicismo *m*.

catkin ['kætkɪn] *n* candelilla *f*, amento *m*.

Catseyes® ['kætsaɪz] *npl Br* catafaros *mpl*.

catsuit ['kætsuːt] *n Br malla de manga larga hasta el tobillo*.

catsup ['kætsəp] *n Am* ketchup *m*.

cattle ['kætl] *npl* ganado *m* (vacuno).

cattle grid *n Br* reja de tubos metálicos en la calzada para impedir el paso al ganado.

catty ['kætɪ] (*compar* **-ier**, *superl* **-iest**) *adj inf pej* [spiteful] rencoroso(sa).

catwalk ['kætwɔːk] *n* pasarela *f*.

Caucasian [kɔː'keɪzjən] ◇ *adj* caucásico(ca). ◇ *n* caucásico *m*, -ca *f*.

Caucasus ['kɔːkəsəs] *n*: the ~ el Cáucaso.
caucus ['kɔːkəs] *n* [political group] comité *m*.
◆ **Caucus** *n Am* congreso *m*.

CAUCUS:
El Caucus en Estados Unidos es el congreso
multitudinario de carácter político que celebran los dos grandes partidos nacionales, en
el transcurso del cual escogen sus candidatos y definen sus objetivos

caught [kɔːt] *pt & pp* → catch.
cauliflower ['kɒlɪ,flauəʳ] *n* coliflor *f*.
causal ['kɔːzl] *adj* causal.
cause [kɔːz] ◇ *n* -1. [gen] causa *f*. -2.
[grounds]: ~ **(for)** motivo *m* (para); ~ **for**
complaint motivo de queja; ~ **to do sthg**
motivo para hacer algo. ◇ *vt* causar; **to** ~
sb to do sthg hacer que alguien haga algo.
causeway ['kɔːzweɪ] *n* carretera *f* elevada.
caustic ['kɔːstɪk] *adj* -1. CHEM cáustico(ca).
-2. [comment] mordaz, hiriente.
caustic soda *n* sosa *f* cáustica.
cauterize, -ise ['kɔːtəraɪz] *vt* cauterizar.
caution ['kɔːʃn] ◇ *n* -1. (*U*) [care] precaución *f*, cautela *f*. -2. [warning] advertencia *f*,
amonestación *f*. ◇ *vt* -1. [warn - against dan-
ger] prevenir; [- against behaving rudely etc]
advertir, avisar. -2. *Br* [subj: policeman]: **to**
~ **sb (for)** amonestar a alguien (por).
cautionary ['kɔːʃənərɪ] *adj* instructivo(va),
con moraleja.
cautious ['kɔːʃəs] *adj* prudente, precavi-
do(da).
cautiously ['kɔːʃəslɪ] *adv* prudentemente,
precavidamente.
cautiousness ['kɔːʃəsnɪs] *n* cautela *f*, precaución *f*.
cavalier [,kævə'lɪəʳ] *adj* arrogante, desdeño-
so(sa).
cavalry ['kævlrɪ] *n* caballería *f*.
cave [keɪv] *n* cueva *f*.
◆ **cave in** *vi* -1. [roof, ceiling] hundirse, derrumbarse. -2. [yield]: **to** ~ **in (to)** ceder OR
transigir (ante).
caveman ['keɪvmæn] (*pl* -men [-men]) *n*
cavernícola *m y f*, hombre *m* de las cavernas.
cavern ['kævən] *n* caverna *f*.
cavernous ['kævənəs] *adj* cavernoso(sa),
grande y profundo(da).
caviar(e) ['kævɪɑːʳ] *n* caviar *m*.
caving ['keɪvɪŋ] *n Br* espeleología *f*.
cavity ['kævɪtɪ] (*pl* -ies) *n* -1. [in object,
structure] cavidad *f*. -2. [in tooth] caries *f inv*.
-3. [in body]: **nasal** ~ fosa *f* nasal.

cavity wall insulation *n Br* aislamiento *m*
de doble pared.
cavort [kə'vɔːt] *vi* retozar, brincar.
cayenne (pepper) [keɪ'en-] *n* [powder] (pimienta *f* de) cayena *f*; [pepper] guindilla
f.
CB *n* -1. *abbr of* citizens' band. -2. (*abbr of*
Companion of (the Order of) the Bath) (*titular de*) distinción honorífica británica.
CBC (*abbr of* Canadian Broadcasting Corporation) *n* cadena canadiense de radiotelevisión.
CBE (*abbr of* Companion of (the Order of)
the British Empire) *n* (*titular de*) distinción honorífica británica.
CBI (*abbr of* Confederation of British Industry) *n* confederación británica de empresarios, ≈ CEOE *f*.
CBS (*abbr of* Columbia Broadcasting System) *n* ≈ CBS *f*, cadena estadounidense de televisión.
cc ◇ *n* (*abbr of* cubic centimetre) cc. ◇
(*abbr of* carbon copy) cc.
CC (*abbr of* county council) *n* ≈ Dip. *f*.
CCA (*abbr of* Circuit Court of Appeals) *n*
tribunal de apelación que actúa de forma itinerante en Estados Unidos.
CCTV (*abbr of* closed-circuit television) *n*
circuito cerrado de televisión.
CD ◇ *n* (*abbr of* compact disc) CD *m*. ◇
-1. *abbr of* Civil Defence. -2. (*abbr of* Corps
Diplomatique) CD.
CD drive *n* COMPUT unidad *f* de disco.
CD player *n* reproductor *m* de CD.
Cdr. (*abbr of* commander) *rango militar*, ≈
Cte.
CD-ROM [,siːdiː'rɒm] (*abbr of* compact disc
read only memory) *n* CD-ROM *m*.
CDT (*abbr of* Central Daylight Time) *hora
de verano del centro de Estados Unidos*.
CDV (*abbr of* compact disc video) *n* vídeo en
disco compacto.
CDW *n abbr of* collision damage waiver.
CE *abbr of* Church of England.
cease [siːs] *fml* ◇ *vt* cesar; **to** ~ **doing** OR **to
do sthg** dejar de hacer algo; ~ **fire!** ¡alto el
fuego! ◇ *vi* cesar.
cease-fire *n* alto *m* el fuego.
ceaseless ['siːslɪs] *adj fml* incesante.
ceaselessly ['siːslɪslɪ] *adv* incesantemente.
cedar (tree) ['siːdəʳ] *n* cedro *m*.
cede [siːd] *vt*: **to** ~ **sthg (to)** ceder algo (a).
cedilla [sɪ'dɪlə] *n* cedilla *f*.
CEEB (*abbr of* College Entry Examination
Board) *n* organismo encargado del acceso a la
enseñanza superior en Estados Unidos.

Ceefax® ['si:fæks] *n Br* servicio de teletexto de la BBC.

ceilidh ['keılı] *n* en Escocia e Irlanda, fiesta en la que se baila y se canta música regional.

ceiling ['si:lıŋ] *n* **-1.** [of room] techo *m*. **-2.** [limit] tope *m*, límite *m*.

celebrate ['selıbreıt] ◇ *vt* celebrar. ◇ *vi* divertirse.

celebrated ['selıbreıtıd] *adj* célebre, famoso(sa).

celebration [,selı'breıʃn] *n* **-1.** (*U*) [activity, feeling] celebración *f*. **-2.** [event] fiesta *f*, festejo *m*.

celebrity [sı'lebrətı] (*pl* **-ies**) *n* celebridad *f*.

celeriac [sə'leriæk] *n* apio *m* nabo.

celery ['selərı] *n* apio *m*.

celestial [sı'lestjəl] *adj* celestial.

celibacy ['selıbəsı] *n* celibato *m*.

celibate ['selıbət] *adj* célibe.

cell [sel] *n* **-1.** BIOL, COMPUT & POL célula *f*. **-2.** [prisoner's, nun's or monk's room] celda *f*, separo *m Amer*.

cellar ['selər] *n* **-1.** [basement] sótano *m*. **-2.** [stock of wine] bodega *f*.

cellist ['tʃelıst] *n* violoncelista *m y f*.

cello ['tʃeləʊ] (*pl* **-s**) *n* violoncelo *m*.

cellophane® ['seləfeın] *n* celofán® *m*.

cellphone ['selfəʊn], **cellular phone** ['səljʊlər-] *n* teléfono *m* celular.

cellulite ['seljʊlaıt] *n* adiposidad *f*, tejido *m* adiposo.

Celluloid® ['seljʊlɔıd] *n* celuloide *m*.

cellulose ['seljʊləʊs] *n* celulosa *f*.

Celsius ['selsıəs] *adj* centígrado(da); **20 degrees ~ 20** grados centígrados.

Celt [kelt] *n* celta *m y f*.

Celtic ['keltık] ◇ *adj* celta, céltico(ca). ◇ *n* celta *m*.

cement [sı'ment] ◇ *n* **-1.** [for concrete] cemento *m*. **-2.** [glue] cola *f*, pegamento *m*. ◇ *vt* **-1.** [cover with cement] cubrir con cemento. **-2.** [glue] pegar, encolar. **-3.** [agreement, relationship] cimentar, fortalecer.

cement mixer *n* hormigonera *f*.

cemetery ['semıtrı] (*pl* **-ies**) *n* cementerio *m*.

cenotaph ['senətɑːf] *n* cenotafio *m*.

censor ['sensər] ◇ *n* censor *m*, -ra *f*. ◇ *vt* censurar.

censorship ['sensəʃıp] *n* censura *f*.

censure ['senʃər] ◇ *n* censura *f*. ◇ *vt* censurar.

census ['sensəs] (*pl* **-uses**) *n* censo *m*.

cent [sent] *n* centavo *m*.

centenary *Br* [sen'ti:nərı] (*pl* **-ies**), **centennial** *Am* [sen'tenjəl] *n* centenario *m*.

center *Am* = **centre**.

centigrade ['sentıgreıd] *adj* centígrado(da); **20 degrees ~ 20** grados centígrados.

centigram(me) ['sentıgræm] *n* centigramo *m*.

centilitre *Br*, **centiliter** *Am* ['sentı,li:tər] *n* centilitro *m*.

centimetre *Br*, **centimeter** *Am* ['sentı,mi:tər] *n* centímetro *m*.

centipede ['sentıpi:d] *n* ciempiés *m inv*.

central ['sentrəl] *adj* **-1.** [gen] central; **in ~ Spain** en el centro de España; **to be ~ to** ser el eje OR la pieza clave de. **-2.** [easily reached] céntrico(ca).

Central African ◇ *adj* centroafricano(na). ◇ *n* centroafricano *m*, -na *f*.

Central African Republic *n*: **the ~** la república Centroafricana.

Central America *n* Centroamérica.

Central American ◇ *adj* centroamericano(na). ◇ *n* centroamericano *m*, -na *f*.

Central Asia *n* Asia Central.

central government *n* gobierno *m* central.

central heating *n* calefacción *f* central.

centralization [,sentrəlaı'zeıʃn] *n* centralización *f*.

centralize, -ise ['sentrəlaız] *vt* centralizar.

centralized ['sentrəlaızd] *adj* centralizado(da).

central locking [-'lɒkıŋ] *n* cierre *m* centralizado.

centrally ['sentrəlı] *adv*: **~ situated** OR **located** céntrico(ca).

centrally heated *adj* con calefacción central.

central nervous system *n* centros *mpl* nerviosos.

central processing unit *n* unidad *f* central de proceso.

central reservation *n Br* mediana *f*.

centre *Br*, **center** *Am* ['sentər] ◇ *n* centro *m*; **~ of attention/gravity** centro de atención/gravedad; **the ~** POL el centro. ◇ *adj* **-1.** [middle] central. **-2.** POL centrista. ◇ *vt* centrar.

◆ **centre around**, **centre on** *vt fus* centrarse en.

centre back *n* defensa *m y f* central.

centre-fold *n* (doble) página *f* central.

centre forward *n* delantero *m* centro.

centre half = **centre back**.

centrepiece *Br*, **centerpiece** *Am* ['sentəpiːs] *n* **-1.** [decoration] centro *m* de mesa. **-2.** [principal element] punto *m* central.

centre-spread *n* (doble) página *f* central.

centrifugal force [sentrɪ'fjuːgl-] *n* fuerza *f* centrífuga.

century ['sentʃʊrɪ] (*pl* **-ies**) *n* siglo *m*; **the 20th** ~ el siglo XX.

CEO (*abbr of* **chief executive officer**) *n Am* Dtor. Gral. *m*, Dtora. Gral. *f*.

ceramic [sɪ'ræmɪk] *adj* de cerámica, cerámico(ca).

◆ **ceramics** ◇ *n* cerámica *f*. ◇ *npl* [objects] piezas *fpl* de cerámica.

cereal ['sɪərɪəl] *n* **-1.** [crop] cereal *m*. **-2.** [breakfast food] cereales *mpl*.

cerebral ['serɪbrəl] *adj* cerebral.

cerebral palsy *n* parálisis *f inv* cerebral.

ceremonial [,serɪ'məʊnjəl] ◇ *adj* ceremonial. ◇ *n* ceremonial *m*.

ceremonious [,serɪ'məʊnjəs] *adj* ceremonioso(sa).

ceremony ['serɪmənɪ] (*pl* **-ies**) *n* ceremonia *f*; **without** ~ sin miramientos; **to stand on** ~ andarse con cumplidos OR ceremonias.

cert [sɜːt] *n Br inf* cosa *f* segura.

cert. *abbr of* **certificate**.

certain ['sɜːtn] *adj* **-1.** [gen] seguro(ra); **he's** ~ **to be late** (es) seguro que llega tarde; **to be** ~ **(of)** estar seguro (de); **to make** ~ **(of)** asegurarse (de); **for** ~ seguro, con toda seguridad. **-2.** [particular, some] cierto(ta); **to a** ~ **extent** hasta cierto punto. **-3.** [named person]: **a** ~ ... un (una) tal ....

certainly ['sɜːtnlɪ] *adv* desde luego; ~ **not!** ¡claro que no!

certainty ['sɜːtntɪ] (*pl* **-ies**) *n* seguridad *f*; **it's a** ~ **that** ... es seguro que ....

CertEd [,sɜːt'ed] (*abbr of* **Certificate in Education**) *n diploma universitario de pedagogía*.

certifiable [,sɜːtɪ'faɪəbl] *adj* [mad] demente.

certificate [sə'tɪfɪkət] *n* [gen] certificado *m*; SCH & UNIV diploma *m*, título *m*; [of birth, death] partida *f*.

certification [,sɜːtɪfɪ'keɪʃn] *n* certificación *f*.

certified ['sɜːtɪfaɪd] *adj* [document] certificado(da); [person] diplomado(da).

certified mail *n Am* correo *m* certificado.

certified public accountant *n Am* contable diplomado *m*, contable diplomada *f*.

certify ['sɜːtɪfaɪ] (*pt* & *pp* **-ied**) *vt* **-1.** [declare true] certificar. **-2.** [declare officially]: **to** ~ **sb dead** dar constancia de la muerte de alguien. **-3.** [declare insane] declarar demente.

cervical [sə'vaɪkl] *adj* cervical.

cervical smear *n* citología *f*, frotis *f* cervical.

cervix ['sɜːvɪks] (*pl* **-ices** [-ɪsiːz]) *n* [of womb] cuello *m* del útero.

cesarean (section) = **caesarean (section)**.

cessation [se'seɪʃn] *n fml* cese *m*.

cesspit ['sespɪt], **cesspool** ['sespuːl] *n* pozo *m* negro.

CET (*abbr of* **Central European Time**) *hora de Europa central*.

cf. (*abbr of* **confer**) cf., cfr.

c/f (*abbr of* **carried forward**) suma y sigue.

c & f (*abbr of* **cost and freight**) c y f.

CFC (*abbr of* **chlorofluorocarbon**) *n* CFC *m*.

cg (*abbr of* **centigram**) cg *m*.

CG *abbr of* **coastguard**.

C & G (*abbr of* **City and Guilds**) *n diploma británico de formación profesional*.

CGA (*abbr of* **colour graphics adapter**) *n* CGA *m*.

CGT (*abbr of* **capital gains tax**) *n impuesto sobre plusvalías*.

ch (*abbr of* **central heating**) cal. cent.

ch. (*abbr of* **chapter**) cap.

CH (*abbr of* **Companion of Honour**) *n (titular de) distinción honorífica británica*.

Chad [tʃæd] *n* el Chad.

chafe [tʃeɪf] ◇ *vt* [rub] rozar. ◇ *vi* **-1.** [skin] irritarse. **-2.** [person]: **to** ~ **at** irritarse por.

chaff [tʃɑːf] *n* barcia *f*.

chaffinch ['tʃæfɪntʃ] *n* pinzón *m*.

chain [tʃeɪn] ◇ *n* cadena *f*; ~ **of office** ≃ collar *m* de mando; ~ **of events** serie *f* OR cadena *f* de acontecimientos. ◇ *vt* [person, object] encadenar.

chain letter *n carta que se hace circular en cadena para obtener algún beneficio*.

chain reaction *n* reacción *f* en cadena.

chain saw *n* sierra *f* (mecánica) continua OR de cinta.

chain-smoke *vi* fumar un cigarrillo tras otro.

chain-smoker *n* fumador empedernido *m*, fumadora empedernida *f*.

chain store *n* grandes almacenes *mpl*.

chair [tʃeəʳ] ◇ *n* **-1.** [gen] silla *f*; [armchair] sillón *m*. **-2.** [university post] cátedra *f*. **-3.** [of meeting] presidencia *f*; **to take the** ~ presidir, tomar la presidencia. ◇ *vt* presidir.

chair lift *n* telesilla *m*.

chairman ['tʃeəmən] (*pl* **-men** [-mən]) *n* presidente *m*.

chairmanship ['tʃeəmənʃɪp] *n* presidencia *f*.

chairperson ['tʃeə,pɜːsn] (*pl* **-s**) *n* presidente *m*, -ta *f*.

chairwoman ['tʃeə,wʊmən] (*pl* **-women** [,wɪmɪn]) *n* presidenta *f*.

chaise longue [ʃeɪz'lɒŋ] (*pl* **chaises longues** [ʃeɪz'lɒŋ]) *n* tumbona *f*, chaise-longue *f*.

chalet ['ʃæleɪ] *n* chalé *m*, chalet *m*.

chalice ['tʃælɪs] *n* cáliz *m*.

chalk [tʃɔːk] *n* **-1.** [type of rock] creta *f*. **-2.** [for drawing] tiza *f*, gis *m Amer*.
◆ **by a long chalk** *adv* con diferencia, con mucho.
◆ **not by a long chalk** *adv* ni mucho menos, de ninguna manera.
◆ **chalk up** *vt sep* [attain] apuntarse.

chalkboard ['tʃɔːkbɔːd] *n Am* pizarra *f*, encerado *m*.

challenge ['tʃælɪndʒ] ◇ *n* desafío *m*, reto *m*. ◇ *vt* **-1.** [to fight, competition]: **to ~ sb (to sthg/to do sthg)** desafiar a alguien (a algo/a que haga algo). **-2.** [question] poner en tela de juicio.

challenger ['tʃælɪndʒə'] *n* [opponent] contrincante *m y f*; [for title, leadership] aspirante *m y f*.

challenging ['tʃælɪndʒɪŋ] *adj* **-1.** [task, job] estimulante, que supone un reto. **-2.** [look, tone of voice] desafiante.

chamber ['tʃeɪmbə'] *n* [room] cámara *f*.
◆ **chambers** *npl* despacho *m*.

chambermaid ['tʃeɪmbəmeɪd] *n* [at hotel] camarera *f*.

chamber music *n* música *f* de cámara.

chamber of commerce *n* cámara *f* de comercio.

chamber orchestra *n* orquesta *f* de cámara.

chameleon [kə'miːljən] *n* camaleón *m*.

chamois[1] ['ʃæmwaː] (*pl inv*) *n* [animal] gamuza *f*.

chamois[2] ['ʃæmɪ] *n*: ~ **(leather)** gamuza *f*.

champ [tʃæmp] ◇ *n inf* campeón *m*, -ona *f*. ◇ *vi* mordisquear.

champagne [,ʃæm'peɪn] *n* champán *m*.

champion ['tʃæmpjən] *n* **-1.** [of competition] campeón *m*, -ona *f*. **-2.** [of cause] defensor *m*, -ra *f*.

championship ['tʃæmpjənʃɪp] *n* campeonato *m*.

chance [tʃɑːns] ◇ *n* **-1.** [luck] azar *m*, suerte *f*; **by ~** por casualidad. **-2.** [likelihood] posibilidad *f*; **not to stand a ~ (of)** no tener ninguna posibilidad (de); **by any ~** por casualidad, acaso; **on the off ~** por si acaso. **-3.** [opportunity] oportunidad *f*. **-4.** [risk] riesgo *m*; **to take a ~ (on)** correr un riesgo OR arriesgarse (con).

◇ *adj* fortuito(ta), casual.
◇ *vt* arriesgar; **to ~ it** arriesgarse.
◇ *vi literary* [happen]: **to ~ to do sthg** hacer algo por casualidad.

chancellor ['tʃɑːnsələ'] *n* **-1.** [chief minister] canciller *m*. **-2.** UNIV ≃ rector *m*, -ra *f*.

Chancellor of the Exchequer *n Br* Ministro *m*, -tra *f* de Economía y Hacienda.

chancy ['tʃɑːnsɪ] (*compar* **-ier**, *superl* **-iest**) *adj inf* arriesgado(da).

chandelier [,ʃændə'lɪə'] *n* (lámpara *f* de) araña *f*, candil *m Amer*.

change [tʃeɪndʒ] ◇ *n* **-1.** [gen] cambio *m*; ~ **of clothes** muda *f*; **it makes a ~** es un cambio; **for a ~** para variar. **-2.** [from payment] vuelta *f*, cambio *m*, vuelto *m Amer*. **-3.** [coins] suelto *m*, calderilla *f*. **-4.** [money in exchange]: **have you got ~ for £5?** ¿tienes cambio de 5 libras?
◇ *vt* **-1.** [gen] cambiar; **to ~ sthg into** transformar algo en; **to ~ pounds into francs** cambiar libras en francos; **to ~ direction** cambiar de rumbo; **to ~ one's mind** cambiar de idea OR opinión. **-2.** [goods in shop] descambiar. **-3.** [switch - job, gear, train] cambiar de; **to ~ hands** COMM cambiar de mano; **to ~ one's clothes** cambiarse de ropa.
◇ *vi* **-1.** [alter] cambiar; **to ~ into sthg** transformarse en algo. **-2.** [change clothes] cambiarse. **-3.** [change trains, buses] hacer transbordo.
◆ **change over** *vi* [convert]: **to ~ over to** cambiar a.

changeable ['tʃeɪndʒəbl] *adj* variable.

changed [tʃeɪndʒd] *adj*: **he's a ~ man** es otro, es un hombre nuevo.

change machine *n* máquina *f* de cambio.

change of life *n*: **the ~** la menopausia.

changeover ['tʃeɪndʒ,əʊvə'] *n*: ~ **(to)** cambio *m* (a).

change purse *n Am* portamonedas *m inv*.

changing ['tʃeɪndʒɪŋ] *adj* cambiante.

changing room *n* vestuario *m*.

channel ['tʃænl] (*Br pt & pp* **-led**, *cont* **-ling**, *Am pt & pp* **-ed**, *cont* **-ing**) ◇ *n* canal *m*. ◇ *vt lit & fig* canalizar.
◆ **Channel** *n*: **the (English) Channel** el Canal de la Mancha.
◆ **channels** *npl* [procedure] conductos *mpl*, medios *mpl*.

Channel Islands *npl*: **the ~** las islas del canal de la Mancha.

Channel tunnel *n*: **the ~** el túnel del Canal de la Mancha.

chant [tʃɑːnt] ◇ *n* **-1.** RELIG canto *m*. **-2.** [repeated words] soniquete *m*. ◇ *vt* **-1.** RELIG

cantar. **-2.** [words] **corear.** ◇ vi **-1.** RELIG salmodiar. **-2.** [repeat words] **corear.**

chaos ['keɪɒs] n caos m.

chaotic [keɪ'ɒtɪk] adj caótico(ca).

chap [tʃæp] n Br inf chico m, tío m.

chapat(t)i [tʃə'pætɪ] n chapati m, pan indio
sin levadura.

chapel ['tʃæpl] n capilla f.

chaperon(e) ['ʃæpərəʊn] ◇ n carabina f,
acompañanta f. ◇ vt acompañar.

chaplain ['tʃæplɪn] n capellán m.

chapped [tʃæpt] adj agrietado(da).

chapter ['tʃæptər] n lit & fig capítulo m.

char [tʃɑːr] (pt & pp **-red**, cont **-ring**) ◇ n Br
[cleaner] mujer f de la limpieza. ◇ vt [burn]
carbonizar, calcinar. ◇ vi [work as cleaner]
trabajar de mujer de la limpieza.

character ['kærəktər] n **-1.** [nature, quality,
letter] carácter m; **to be out of/in ~ (for)** no
ser/ser típico de. **-2.** [in film, book, play]
personaje m. **-3.** inf [person of stated kind]
tipo m. **-4.** inf [person with strong personality]:
to be a ~ ser todo un carácter.

characteristic [,kærəktə'rɪstɪk] ◇ adj carac-
terístico(ca). ◇ n característica f.

characteristically [,kærəktə'rɪstɪklɪ] adv típicamente.

characterization [,kærəktəraɪ'zeɪʃn] n caracterización f.

characterize, -ise ['kærəktəraɪz] vt **-1.**
[typify] caracterizar. **-2.** [portray]: **to ~ sthg
as** definir algo como.

charade [ʃə'rɑːd] n farsa f.

◆ **charades** n (U) charadas fpl.

charcoal ['tʃɑːkəʊl] n [for barbecue etc] carbón m (vegetal); [for drawing] carboncillo
m.

chard [tʃɑːd] n acelga f.

charge [tʃɑːdʒ] ◇ n **-1.** [cost] precio m, coste m; **admission ~** entrada f; **free of ~** gratis. **-2.** JUR cargo m, acusación f. **-3.** [re-
sponsibility]: **to have ~ of sthg** tener algo al
cargo de uno; **to take ~ (of)** hacerse cargo
(de); **to be in ~** ser el encargado (la encargada); **in ~ of** encargado(da) de. **-4.** ELEC
carga f. **-5.** MIL [of cavalry] carga f.
◇ vt **-1.** [customer, sum] cobrar; **to ~ sthg to
sb** cargar algo en la cuenta de alguien. **-2.**
[suspect, criminal]: **to ~ sb (with)** acusar a
alguien (de). **-3.** [attack] cargar contra. **-4.**
[battery] cargar.
◇ vi **-1.** [ask in payment]: **to ~ (for)** cobrar
(por). **-2.** [rush] cargar; **to ~ in/out** entrar/
salir en tromba.

chargeable ['tʃɑːdʒəbl] adj **-1.** [costs] cobra-
ble, cobradero(ra). **-2.** [offence] punible.

charge account n cuenta f abierta.

charge card n tarjeta de crédito de un establecimiento comercial.

charged [tʃɑːdʒd] adj cargado(da).

chargé d'affaires [,ʃɑːzeɪdæ'feə] (pl **char-
gés d'affaires** [,ʃɑːzeɪdæ'feə]) n encargado
m, -da f de negocios.

charge hand n Br ayudante m y f de capataz.

charge nurse n Br enfermero m jefe.

charger ['tʃɑːdʒər] n **-1.** [for batteries] cargador m. **-2.** literary [horse] caballo m de batalla.

charge sheet n Br atestado m policial.

chariot ['tʃærɪət] n carro m, cuadriga f.

charisma [kə'rɪzmə] n carisma m.

charismatic [,kærɪz'mætɪk] adj carismáti-
co(ca).

charitable ['tʃærətəbl] adj **-1.** [person, re-
mark] caritativo(va). **-2.** [organization] benéfi-
co(ca).

charity ['tʃærətɪ] (pl **-ies**) n **-1.** [kindness,
money] caridad f. **-2.** [organization] institución f benéfica.

charlatan ['ʃɑːlətən] n charlatán m, -ana f.

charm [tʃɑːm] ◇ n **-1.** [appeal, attractiveness]
encanto m. **-2.** [spell] encantamiento m, hechizo m. **-3.** [on bracelet] dije m, amuleto m.
◇ vt dejar encantado(da).

charm bracelet n pulsera f con dijes.

charmer ['tʃɑːmər] n: **he's a real ~** es muy
cumplido.

charming ['tʃɑːmɪŋ] adj encantador(ra).

charmingly ['tʃɑːmɪŋlɪ] adv [attractive, naïve]
encantadoramente; [smile, dress] de un
modo encantador.

charred [tʃɑːd] adj carbonizado(da), calci-
nado(da).

chart [tʃɑːt] ◇ n **-1.** [diagram] gráfico m,
diagrama m; **weather ~** mapa m del tiem-
po. **-2.** [map] carta f. ◇ vt **-1.** [plot, map] representar en un mapa. **-2.** fig [record] trazar.

◆ **charts** npl: **the ~s** la lista de éxitos.

charter ['tʃɑːtər] ◇ n [document] carta f. ◇
comp chárter (inv), alquilado(da). ◇ vt
[plane, boat] fletar.

chartered accountant ['tʃɑːtəd-] n Br contable colegiado m, contable colegiada f.

charter flight n vuelo m chárter.

chart-topping adj Br número uno en la
lista de éxitos.

chary ['tʃeərɪ] (compar **-ier**, superl **-iest**) adj:
to be ~ of doing sthg ser precavido(da) a la
hora de hacer algo.

chase [tʃeɪs] ◇ n [pursuit] persecución f; **to
give ~** emprender la persecución. ◇ vt **-1.**

[pursue] **perseguir. -2.** [drive away] ahuyentar. **-3.** [money, jobs] ir detrás de, ir a la caza de. ◇ *vi:* **to ~ after** sthg/sb perseguir algo/a alguien.

◆ **chase up** *vt sep Br* [person] localizar; [information] buscar, intentar hacerse con; **to ~ sb up about** sthg ponerse en contacto con alguien para recordarle algo.

chaser ['tʃeɪsə'] *n copa de licor tomada después de una cerveza.*

chasm ['kæzm] *n* [deep crack] sima *f*; *fig* [divide] abismo *m*.

chassis ['ʃæsɪ] (*pl inv*) *n* [of vehicle] chasis *m inv*.

chaste [tʃeɪst] *adj* casto(ta).

chasten ['tʃeɪsn] *vt* escarmentar.

chastise [tʃæˈstaɪz] *vt fml* [scold] reprender.

chastity ['tʃæstətɪ] *n* castidad *f*.

chat [tʃæt] (*pt* & *pp* **-ted,** *cont* **-ting**) ◇ *n* charla *f*, conversada *f Amer*. ◇ *vi* charlar.

◆ **chat up** *vt sep Br inf* ligar con.

chat show *n Br* programa *m* de entrevistas.

chatter ['tʃætə'] ◇ *n* **-1.** [of person] cháchara *f*, parloteo *m*. **-2.** [of bird] gorjeo *m*; [of monkey] chillidos *mpl*. ◇ *vi* **-1.** [person] parlotear. **-2.** [bird] gorjear; [monkey] chillar. **-3.** [teeth] castañetear.

chatterbox ['tʃætəbɒks] *n inf* parlanchín *m*, -ina *f*.

chatty ['tʃætɪ] (*compar* **-ier,** *superl* **-iest**) *adj* **-1.** [person] dicharachero(ra). **-2.** [letter] informal.

chauffeur ['ʃəʊfə'] ◇ *n* chófer *m y f*. ◇ *vt* hacer de chófer para.

chauvinist ['ʃəʊvɪnɪst] *n* **-1.** [sexist] sexista *m y f*; **male ~** machista *m*. **-2.** [nationalist] chovinista *m y f*, chauvinista *m y f*.

chauvinistic ['ʃəʊvɪˈnɪstɪk] *adj* **-1.** [sexist] sexista. **-2.** [nationalistic] chovinista, chauvinista.

ChE *abbr of* **chemical engineer**.

cheap [tʃiːp] ◇ *adj* **-1.** [inexpensive] barato(ta). **-2.** [low-quality] de mala calidad. **-3.** [vulgar - joke etc] de mal gusto. ◇ *adv* barato. ◇ *n:* **on the ~** en plan barato.

cheapen ['tʃiːpn] *vt* [degrade] rebajar, degradar.

cheaply ['tʃiːplɪ] *adv* barato.

cheapness ['tʃiːpnɪs] *n* **-1.** [low cost] lo barato, baratura *f*. **-2.** [low quality] baja calidad *f*. **-3.** [vulgarity - of joke etc] mal gusto *m*.

cheapskate ['tʃiːpskeɪt] *n inf pej* agarrado *m*, -da *f*.

cheat [tʃiːt] ◇ *n* tramposo *m*, -sa *f*. ◇ *vt* timar, estafar; **to ~ sb out of** sthg estafar

algo a alguien; **to feel ~ed** sentirse engañado. ◇ *vi* **-1.** [in exam] copiar; [at cards] hacer trampas. **-2.** *inf* [be unfaithful]: **to ~ on** sb pegársela a alguien.

cheating ['tʃiːtɪŋ] *n* [in games] trampas *fpl*; [in business] fraude *m*.

check [tʃek] ◇ *n* **-1.** [inspection, test]: **~ (on)** inspección *f* OR comprobación *f* (de); **to keep a ~ on** llevar un control de. **-2.** [restraint]: **~ (on)** restricción *f* (en); **to put a ~ on** sthg controlar OR restringir algo; **in ~** bajo control. **-3.** *Am* [cheque] cheque *m*. **-4.** *Am* [bill] cuenta *f*, nota *f*. **-5.** [pattern] cuadros *mpl*.

◇ *vt* **-1.** [test, verify] comprobar, revisar; [inspect] inspeccionar. **-2.** [restrain, stop] refrenar, contener; **to ~ o.s.** detenerse.

◇ *vi* comprobar; **to ~ (for/on** sthg) comprobar (algo).

◆ **check in** ◇ *vt sep* [luggage, coat] facturar, despachar *Amer*. ◇ *vi* **-1.** [at hotel] inscribirse, registrarse. **-2.** [at airport] facturar.

◆ **check off** *vt sep* ir comprobando (en una lista).

◆ **check out** ◇ *vt sep* **-1.** [luggage, coat] recoger. **-2.** [investigate] comprobar. ◇ *vi* [from hotel] dejar el hotel.

◆ **check up** *vi:* **to ~ up (on)** informarse (acerca de).

checkbook *Am* = **chequebook**.

checked [tʃekt] *adj* a cuadros.

checkered *Am* = **chequered**.

checkers ['tʃekəz] *n Am* (U) damas *fpl*.

check guarantee card *n Am* tarjeta *f* de identificación bancaria.

check-in *n* facturación *f* de equipajes.

checking account ['tʃekɪŋ-] *n Am* cuenta *f* corriente.

checklist ['tʃeklɪst] *n* lista *f* (de cosas por hacer).

checkmate ['tʃekmeɪt] *n* jaque *m* mate.

checkout ['tʃekaʊt] *n* caja *f*.

checkpoint ['tʃekpɔɪnt] *n* control *m*.

checkup ['tʃekʌp] *n* chequeo *m*, revisión *f*.

Cheddar (cheese) ['tʃedə'] *n* (queso *m*) cheddar *m*.

cheek [tʃiːk] ◇ *n* **-1.** [of face] mejilla *f*. **-2.** *inf* [impudence] cara *f*, descaro *m*. ◇ *vt inf* ser descarado(da) con.

cheekbone ['tʃiːkbəʊn] *n* pómulo *m*.

cheekily ['tʃiːkɪlɪ] *adv* con descaro.

cheekiness ['tʃiːkɪnɪs] *n* descaro *m*.

cheeky ['tʃiːkɪ] (*compar* **-ier,** *superl* **-iest**) *adj* descarado(da).

cheer [tʃɪə'] ◇ *n* [shout] aclamación *f*, grito *m* de entusiasmo; **~s** vítores *mpl*. ◇ *vt* **-1.** [shout approval, encouragement at] aclamar, vitorear. **-2.** [gladden] animar. ◇ *vi* gritar con entusiasmo.

◆ **cheers** *excl* [when drinking] ¡salud!; *inf* [thank you] ¡gracias!; *inf* [goodbye] ¡hasta luego!

◆ **cheer on** *vt sep* animar con gritos de aliento.

◆ **cheer up** ◇ *vt sep* animar. ◇ *vi* animarse.

cheerful ['tʃɪəfʊl] *adj* **-1.** [gen] alegre. **-2.** [attitude, agreement] entusiasta.

cheerfully ['tʃɪəfʊlɪ] *adv* **-1.** [joyfully - smile, sing] alegremente; [- dress] con colores vivos. **-2.** [willingly] con entusiasmo.

cheerfulness ['tʃɪəfʊlnɪs] *n* [of person] buen humor *m*; [of dress, song] alegría *f*.

cheering ['tʃɪərɪŋ] ◇ *adj* [gladdening] alentador(ra). ◇ *n* (U) vítores *mpl*, aclamaciones *fpl*.

cheerio [,tʃɪərɪ'əʊ] *excl inf* ¡hasta otra!, ¡hasta luego!

cheerleader ['tʃɪə,liːdəʳ] *n* animadora *f* (de un equipo).

cheerless ['tʃɪəlɪs] *adj* triste, deprimente.

cheery ['tʃɪərɪ] (*compar* **-ier**, *superl* **-iest**) *adj* animado(da), alegre.

cheese [tʃiːz] *n* queso *m*.

cheeseboard ['tʃiːzbɔːd] *n* tabla *f* de quesos.

cheeseburger ['tʃiːz,bɜːgəʳ] *n* hamburguesa *f* de queso.

cheesecake ['tʃiːzkeɪk] *n* pastel *m* OR tarta *f* de queso.

cheesy ['tʃiːzɪ] (*compar* **-ier**, *superl* **-iest**) *adj* [tasting of cheese] con sabor a queso.

cheetah ['tʃiːtə] *n* guepardo *m*, onza *f*.

chef [ʃef] *n* chef *m*, jefe *m* de cocina.

chemical ['kemɪkl] ◇ *adj* químico(ca). ◇ *n* sustancia *f* química.

chemically ['kemɪklɪ] *adv* químicamente.

chemical weapons *npl* armas *fpl* químicas.

chemist ['kemɪst] *n* **-1.** *Br* [pharmacist] farmacéutico *m*, -ca *f*; ~'s (shop) farmacia *f*. **-2.** [scientist] químico *m*, -ca *f*.

chemistry ['kemɪstrɪ] *n* **-1.** [science] química *f*. **-2.** [composition, characteristics] composición *f* (química).

chemotherapy [,kiːməʊ'θerəpɪ] *n* quimioterapia *f*.

cheque *Br*, **check** *Am* [tʃek] *n* cheque *m*, talón *m*; **to pay by** ~ pagar con cheque.

cheque account *n* cuenta *f* corriente.

chequebook *Br*, **checkbook** *Am* ['tʃekbʊk] *n* talonario *m* de cheques, chequera *f Amer*.

cheque card *n Br* tarjeta *f* de identificación bancaria.

chequered *Br* ['tʃekəd], **checkered** *Am* ['tʃekerd] *adj* **-1.** [patterned] a cuadros. **-2.** [varied] lleno(na) de altibajos.

Chequers ['tʃekəz] *n segunda residencia oficial del primer ministro británico.*

cherish ['tʃerɪʃ] *vt* **-1.** [hope, memory] abrigar, albergar. **-2.** [privilege, right] apreciar. **-3.** [person, thing] tener mucho cariño a.

cherished ['tʃerɪʃt] *adj* [memory] querido(da); [hope] anhelado(da).

cherry ['tʃerɪ] (*pl* **-ies**) *n* [fruit] cereza *f*; ~ (tree) cerezo *m*.

cherub ['tʃerəb] (*pl* **-s** OR **-im** [-ɪm]) *n* **-1.** [angel] querubín *m*. **-2.** [child] ricura *f*, angelito *m*.

chervil ['tʃɜːvɪl] *n* perifollo *m*, cerafolio *m*.

Ches. (*abbr of* **Cheshire**) *condado inglés*.

chess [tʃes] *n* ajedrez *m*.

chessboard ['tʃesbɔːd] *n* tablero *m* de ajedrez.

chessman ['tʃesmæn] (*pl* **-men** [-men]) *n* pieza *f*.

chest [tʃest] *n* **-1.** ANAT pecho *m*; **to get sthg off one's** ~ *inf* contar algo para desahogarse. **-2.** [box, trunk - gen] arca *f*, cofre *m*; [- for tools] caja *f*.

chesterfield ['tʃestəfiːld] *n* sofá *m* de cuero.

chestnut ['tʃesnʌt] ◇ *adj* [colour] castaño(ña). ◇ *n* [nut] castaña *f*; ~ (tree) castaño *m*.

chest of drawers (*pl* chests of drawers) *n* cómoda *f*.

chesty ['tʃestɪ] (*compar* **-ier**, *superl* **-iest**) *adj* [cough] de pecho.

chevron ['ʃevrən] *n* [on uniform] galón *m*.

chew [tʃuː] ◇ *n* [sweet] gominola *f*. ◇ *vt* **-1.** [food] masticar. **-2.** [nails] morderse; [carpet] morder.

◆ **chew over** *vt sep fig* rumiar.

◆ **chew up** *vt sep* [food] masticar; [slippers] mordisquear.

chewing gum ['tʃuːɪŋ-] *n* chicle *m*, goma *f* de mascar.

chewy ['tʃuːɪ] (*compar* **-ier**, *superl* **-iest**) *adj* difícil de masticar.

chic [ʃiːk] ◇ *adj* chic (*inv*), elegante. ◇ *n* estilo *m*, elegancia *f*.

chicanery [ʃɪ'keɪnərɪ] *n* (U) supercherías *fpl*, engaños *mpl*.

chick [tʃɪk] *n* [baby bird] polluelo *m*.

chicken ['tʃɪkɪn] ◇ *adj inf* [cowardly] gallina. ◇ *n* **-1.** [bird] gallina *f*; **it's a** ~ **and egg situation** es como lo del huevo y la gallina. **-2.** [food] pollo *m*. **-3.** *inf* [coward] gallina *m* y *f*.

◆ **chicken out** *vi inf*: **to ~ out (of sthg/of doing sthg)** rajarse (a la hora de algo/de hacer algo).

chickenfeed ['tʃɪkɪnfiːd] *n* (U) *fig* minucia *f*, miseria *f*.

chickenpox ['tʃɪkɪnpɒks] *n* varicela *f*.

chicken wire *n* tela *f* metálica (con agujeros hexagonales).

chickpea ['tʃɪkpiː] *n* garbanzo *m*.

chicory ['tʃɪkəri] *n* achicoria *f*.

chide [tʃaɪd] (*pt* **chided** OR **chid** [tʃɪd], *pp* **chid** OR **chidden** ['tʃɪdn]) *vt literary*: **to ~ sb for** reprender a alguien por.

chief [tʃiːf] ◇ *adj* principal. ◇ *n* jefe *m*, -fa *f*.

chief constable *n* Br ≃ jefe *m*, -fa *f* superior de policía.

chief executive *n* [head of company] director *m*, -ra *f* general.

◆ **Chief Executive** *n* Am [US president] presidente *m*, -ta *f*.

chief justice *n* presidente *m*, -ta *f* del tribunal supremo.

chiefly ['tʃiːfli] *adv* **-1.** [mainly] principalmente. **-2.** [especially, above all] por encima de todo.

chief of staff *n* jefe *m*, -fa *f* del estado mayor.

chief superintendent *n* inspector *m*, -ra *f* jefe.

chieftain ['tʃiːftən] *n* jefe *m*, -fa *f*, cacique *m*.

chiffon ['ʃɪfɒn] *n* gasa *f*.

chihuahua [tʃɪˈwɑːwə] *n* chihuahua *m* y *f*.

chilblain ['tʃɪlbleɪn] *n* sabañón *m*.

child [tʃaɪld] (*pl* **children**) *n* **-1.** [boy, girl] niño *m*, -ña *f*. **-2.** [son, daughter] hijo *m*, -ja *f*.

childbearing ['tʃaɪld,beərɪŋ] *n*: **of ~ age** en edad de tener hijos.

child benefit *n* (U) Br subsidio *pagado a todas las familias por cada hijo*.

childbirth ['tʃaɪldbɜːθ] *n* (U) parto *m*.

childhood ['tʃaɪldhʊd] *n* infancia *f*, niñez *f*.

childish ['tʃaɪldɪʃ] *adj pej* infantil.

childishly ['tʃaɪldɪʃli] *adv pej* de manera infantil.

childless ['tʃaɪldlɪs] *adj* sin hijos.

childlike ['tʃaɪldlaɪk] *adj* [person] como un niño; [smile, trust] de niño.

childminder ['tʃaɪld,maɪndər] *n* Br niñera *f* (*durante el día*).

child prodigy *n* niño *m*, -na *f* prodigio.

childproof ['tʃaɪldpruːf] *adj* a prueba de niños.

children ['tʃɪldrən] *pl* → **child**.

children's home *n* hogar *m* infantil.

Chile ['tʃɪli] *n* Chile.

Chilean ['tʃɪliən] ◇ *adj* chileno(na). ◇ *n* chileno *m*, -na *f*.

chili ['tʃɪli] = **chilli**.

chill [tʃɪl] ◇ *adj* frío(a). ◇ *n* **-1.** [illness] resfriado *m*. **-2.** [in temperature]: **there's a ~ in the air** hace un poco de fresco. **-3.** [feeling of fear] escalofrío *m*. ◇ *vt* **-1.** [drink, food] (dejar) enfriar. **-2.** [person - with cold] enfriar; [- with fear] hacer sentir escalofríos. ◇ *vi* enfriarse.

chilli ['tʃɪli] (*pl* **-ies**) *n* guindilla *f*, chile *m*, ají *m* Amer.

chilling ['tʃɪlɪŋ] *adj* **-1.** [very cold] helado(da). **-2.** [frightening] escalofriante.

chilli powder *n* guindilla *f* en polvo.

chilly ['tʃɪli] (*compar* **-ier**, *superl* **-iest**) *adj* frío(a).

chime [tʃaɪm] ◇ *n* campanada *f*. ◇ *vt* [time] dar. ◇ *vi* [bell] repicar; [clock] sonar.

chimney ['tʃɪmni] *n* chimenea *f*.

chimneypot ['tʃɪmnipɒt] *n* cañón *m* de chimenea.

chimneysweep ['tʃɪmniswiːp] *n* deshollinador *m*, -ra *f*.

chimp [tʃɪmp], **chimpanzee** [,tʃɪmpənˈziː] *n* chimpancé *m* y *f*.

chin [tʃɪn] *n* barbilla *f*.

china ['tʃaɪnə] ◇ *n* porcelana *f*, loza *f*. ◇ *comp* de porcelana.

China ['tʃaɪnə] *n* la China; **the People's Republic of ~** la República Popular China.

china clay *n* caolín *m*.

China Sea *n*: **the ~** el mar de China.

Chinatown ['tʃaɪnətaʊn] *n* barrio *m* chino (*de la comunidad oriental*).

chinchilla [tʃɪnˈtʃɪlə] *n* chinchilla *f*.

Chinese [,tʃaɪˈniːz] ◇ *adj* chino(na). ◇ *n* **-1.** [person] chino *m*, -na *f*. **-2.** [language] chino *m*. ◇ *npl*: **the ~** los chinos.

Chinese cabbage *n* (hojas *fpl* de) col *f* china.

Chinese lantern *n* farolillo *m* chino.

Chinese leaves *npl* Br (hojas *fpl* de) col *f* china.

chink [tʃɪŋk] ◇ *n* **-1.** [narrow opening] grieta *f*; [of light] resquicio *m*. **-2.** [sound] tintineo *m*. ◇ *vi* tintinear.

chinos ['tʃiːnəʊz] *npl* pantalones *mpl* de algodón.

chintz [tʃɪnts] ◇ *n* zaraza *f*. ◇ *comp* de zaraza.

chinwag ['tʃɪnwæg] *n* inf charla *f*.

chip [tʃɪp] (*pt* & *pp* **-ped**, *cont* **-ping**) ◇ *n* **-1.** Br [fried potato chip] patata *f* frita; Am

[potato crisp] **patata** *f* **frita** (*de bolsa o de chu-rrería*). **-2.** [fragment - gen] **pedacito** *m*; [- of wood] **viruta** *f*; [- of stone] **lasca** *f*. **-3.** [flaw - in cup, glass] **mella** *f*, **desportilladura** *f*. **-4.** COMPUT **chip** *m*. **-5.** [token] **ficha** *f*. **-6.** *phr*: **when the ~s are down** cuando llega la hora de la verdad; **to have a ~ on one's shoulder** estar resentido, tener uno un poco de complejo.
◇ *vt* [damage] **mellar**, **desportillar**.
◆ **chip in** *inf* ◇ *vt fus* [pay money] **poner**.
◇ *vi* **-1.** [pay money] **poner dinero**. **-2.** [interrupt] **interrumpir**.
◆ **chip off** *vt sep* **desconchar**.

chip-based *adj* **basado(da) en el uso de chips**.

chipboard ['tʃɪpbɔːd] *n* **aglomerado** *m*.

chipmunk ['tʃɪpmʌŋk] *n* **ardilla** *f* **listada**.

chipolata [ˌtʃɪpə'lɑːtə] *n* **salchicha** *f* **pequeña**.

chipped ['tʃɪpt] *adj* [flawed] **mellado(da)**, **desconchado(da)**.

chippings ['tʃɪpɪŋz] *npl* [of stone] **gravilla** *f*; [of wood] **virutas** *fpl*; **"loose ~"** "**gravilla suelta**".

chip shop *n Br* **tienda en la que se vende pescado y patatas fritas**.

chiropodist [kɪ'rɒpədɪst] *n* **podólogo** *m*, **-ga** *f*, **pedicuro** *m*, **-ra** *f*.

chiropody [kɪ'rɒpədɪ] *n* **podología** *f*.

chirp [tʃɜːp] *vi* [bird] **piar**; [insect] **chirriar**.

chirpy ['tʃɜːpɪ] (*compar* **-ier**, *superl* **-iest**) *adj inf* **alegre**.

chisel ['tʃɪzl] (*Br pt & pp* **-led**, *cont* **-ling**, *Am pt & pp* **-ed**, *cont* **-ing**) *n* [for wood] **formón** *m*, **escoplo** *m*; [for stone] **cincel** *m*.
◇ *vt* [wood] **escoplear**; [stone] **cincelar**.

chit [tʃɪt] *n* [note] **nota** *f* **firmada**.

chitchat ['tʃɪttʃæt] *n* (*U*) *inf* **cotilleos** *mpl*.

chivalrous ['ʃɪvlrəs] *adj* **caballeroso(sa)**.

chivalry ['ʃɪvlrɪ] *n* **-1.** *literary* [of knights] **caballería** *f*. **-2.** [good manners] **caballerosidad** *f*.

chives [tʃaɪvz] *npl* **cebollana** *f*, **cebollino** *m*.

chivy (*pt & pp* **-ied**), **chivvy** (*pt & pp* **-ied**) ['tʃɪvɪ] *vt inf* **meter prisa a**.

chloride ['klɔːraɪd] *n* **cloruro** *m*.

chlorinated ['klɔːrɪneɪtɪd] *adj* **clorado(da)**.

chlorine ['klɔːriːn] *n* **cloro** *m*.

chlorofluorocarbon ['klɔːrəʊˌflʊərəʊ-'kɑːbən] *n* **clorofluorocarbono** *m*.

chloroform ['klɒrəfɔːm] *n* **cloroformo** *m*.

choc-ice ['tʃɒkaɪs] *n Br* **helado** *m* **cubierto de chocolate**.

chock [tʃɒk] *n* **cuña** *f*, **calzo** *m*.

chock-a-block, **chock-full** *adj inf*: **~ (with)** **hasta los topes (de)**.

chocolate ['tʃɒkələt] ◇ *n* **-1.** [food, drink] **chocolate** *m*. **-2.** [sweet] **bombón** *m*. ◇ *comp* **de chocolate**.

choice [tʃɔɪs] ◇ *n* **-1.** [gen] **elección** *f*; **to do sthg by** OR **from ~** **elegir hacer algo**; **to have no ~ but to do sthg** **no tener más remedio que hacer algo**. **-2.** [person chosen] **preferido** *m*, **-da** *f*; [thing chosen] **alternativa** *f* **preferida**. **-3.** [variety, selection] **surtido** *m*. ◇ *adj* **de primera calidad**.

choir ['kwaɪəʳ] *n* **coro** *m*.

choirboy ['kwaɪəbɔɪ] *n* **niño** *m* **de coro**.

choke [tʃəʊk] ◇ *n* AUT **estárter** *m*. ◇ *vt* **-1.** [subj: person, fumes] **asfixiar**, **ahogar**; [subj: fishbone etc] **hacer atragantarse**. **-2.** [block - pipes, gutter] **atascar**. ◇ *vi* [on fishbone etc] **atragantarse**; [to death] **asfixiarse**.
◆ **choke back** *vt fus* **contener**, **reprimir**.

cholera ['kɒlərə] *n* **cólera** *m*.

cholesterol [kə'lestərɒl] *n* **colesterol** *m*.

choose [tʃuːz] (*pt* **chose**, *pp* **chosen**) ◇ *vt* **-1.** [select] **elegir**, **escoger**; **there's little** OR **not much to ~ between them** **no se sabe cuál es mejor**. **-2.** [decide]: **to ~ to do sthg** **decidir hacer algo**; **do whatever you ~** **haz lo que quieras**. ◇ *vi* **elegir**, **escoger**.

choos(e)y ['tʃuːzɪ] (*compar* **-ier**, *superl* **-iest**) *adj* [gen] **quisquilloso(sa)**; [about food] **exigente**, **remilgado(da)**.

chop [tʃɒp] (*pt & pp* **-ped**, *cont* **-ping**) ◇ *n* **-1.** CULIN **chuleta** *f*. **-2.** [blow - with axe] **hachazo** *m*; [- with hand] **golpe** *m*, **tajo** *m*; **I'm for the ~** *fig* **mi puesto es uno de los que se van a cargar**. ◇ *vt* **-1.** [cut up] **cortar**. **-2.** *inf* [funding, budget] **recortar**. **-3.** *phr*: **to ~ and change** **cambiar cada dos por tres**.
◆ **chops** *npl inf* **morros** *mpl*, **jeta** *f*.
◆ **chop down** *vt sep* **talar**.
◆ **chop up** *vt sep* [vegetables, meat] **picar**; [wood] **cortar**.

chopper ['tʃɒpəʳ] *n* **-1.** [for wood] **hacha** *f*; [for meat] **cuchillo** *m* **de carnicero**. **-2.** *inf* [helicopter] **helicóptero** *m*.

chopping board ['tʃɒpɪŋ-] *n* **tajo** *m* OR **tabla** *f* **de cocina**.

choppy ['tʃɒpɪ] (*compar* **-ier**, *superl* **-iest**) *adj* **picado(da)**.

chopsticks ['tʃɒpstɪks] *npl* **palillos** *mpl*.

choral ['kɔːrəl] *adj* **coral**.

chord [kɔːd] *n* MUS **acorde** *m*; **to strike a ~ (with)** **calar hondo (en)**.

chore [tʃɔːʳ] *n* **tarea** *f*, **faena** *f*.

choreographer [ˌkɒrɪ'ɒgrəfəʳ] *n* **coreógrafo** *m*, **-fa** *f*.

choreography [ˌkɒrɪ'ɒgrəfɪ] *n* **coreografía** *f*.

chortle ['tʃɔːtl] *vi* reírse con satisfacción.

chorus ['kɔːrəs] ◇ *n* **-1.** [part of song, refrain] estribillo *m.* **-2.** [choir, group of singers or dancers] coro *m.* ◇ *vt* corear todos a una.

chose [tʃəʊz] *pt* → **choose.**

chosen ['tʃəʊzn] *pp* → **choose.**

choux pastry [ʃuː-] *n* pasta *f* brisa.

chow [tʃaʊ] *n* [dog] chow-chow *m inv.*

chowder ['tʃaʊdər] *n* sopa espesa de pescado.

Christ [kraɪst] ◇ *n* Cristo *m.* ◇ *excl* ¡vaya por Dios!

christen ['krɪsn] *vt* bautizar.

christening ['krɪsnɪŋ] ◇ *n* bautizo *m.* ◇ *comp* de bautizo.

Christian ['krɪstʃən] ◇ *adj* cristiano(na). ◇ *n* cristiano *m*, -na *f.*

Christianity [ˌkrɪstɪ'ænətɪ] *n* cristianismo *m.*

Christian name *n* nombre *m* de pila.

Christmas ['krɪsməs] ◇ *n* Navidad *f*; **happy** OR **merry ~!** ¡Felices Navidades! ◇ *comp* navideño(ña).

Christmas cake *n Br* pastel *m* de Navidad.

Christmas card *n* crismas *m inv*, christmas *m inv.*

Christmas cracker *n Br* cilindro de papel que produce un estallido al abrirlo y que tiene dentro un regalito de Navidad.

Christmas Day *n* día *m* de Navidad.

Christmas Eve *n* Nochebuena *f.*

Christmas Island *n* la isla Christmas.

Christmas pudding *n Br* pudín de frutas que se come caliente el día de Navidad.

Christmas stocking *n* calcetín largo en el que se meten regalos por Nochebuena.

Christmastime ['krɪsməstaɪm] *n* (*U*) Navidad *f*, Navidades *fpl.*

Christmas tree *n* árbol *m* de Navidad.

chrome [krəʊm], **chromium** ['krəʊmɪəm] ◇ *n* cromo *m.* ◇ *comp* cromado(da).

chromosome ['krəʊməsəʊm] *n* cromosoma *m.*

chronic ['krɒnɪk] *adj* **-1.** [illness, unemployment] crónico(ca). **-2.** [liar, alcoholic] empedernido(da).

chronically ['krɒnɪklɪ] *adv* crónicamente.

chronicle ['krɒnɪkl] ◇ *n* crónica *f.* ◇ *vt* narrar cronológicamente.

chronological [ˌkrɒnə'lɒdʒɪkl] *adj* cronológico(ca).

chronologically [ˌkrɒnə'lɒdʒɪklɪ] *adv* cronológicamente.

chronology [krə'nɒlədʒɪ] *n* [sequence] cronología *f.*

chrysalis ['krɪsəlɪs] (*pl* **-lises** [-lɪsiːz]) *n* crisálida *f.*

chrysanthemum [krɪ'sænθəməm] (*pl* **-s**) *n* crisantemo *m.*

chubbiness ['tʃʌbɪnɪs] *n* rechonchez *f.*

chubby ['tʃʌbɪ] (*compar* **-bier**, *superl* **-biest**) *adj* [person, hands] rechoncho(cha); [cheeks] mofletudo(da).

chuck [tʃʌk] *vt inf* **-1.** [throw] tirar, arrojar, aventar *Amer*; **to ~ sb out** echar a alguien. **-2.** [job, girlfriend] mandar a paseo, dejar.
◆ **chuck away, chuck out** *vt sep inf* tirar.

chuckle ['tʃʌkl] ◇ *n* risita *f.* ◇ *vi* reírse entre dientes.

chuffed [tʃʌft] *adj Br inf*: **to be ~ (with sthg/to do sthg)** estar como unas castañuelas (con algo/al hacer algo).

chug [tʃʌg] (*pt* & *pp* **-ged**, *cont* **-ging**) *vi* [train] traquetear; [car] resoplar.

chum [tʃʌm] *n inf* [gen] amiguete *m*, -ta *f*, manito *m Amer*; [at school] compañero *m*, -ra *f.*

chummy ['tʃʌmɪ] (*compar* **-mier**, *superl* **-miest**) *adj inf*: **to be ~ (with)** ser muy amiguete(ta) (de).

chump [tʃʌmp] *n inf* tontín *m*, -ina *f.*

chunk [tʃʌŋk] *n* **-1.** [piece] trozo *m.* **-2.** *inf* [large amount] tajada *f.*

chunky ['tʃʌŋkɪ] (*compar* **-ier**, *superl* **-iest**) *adj* **-1.** [person] cuadrado(da), fornido(da). **-2.** [furniture] macizo(za); [jumper] grueso(sa).

church [tʃɜːtʃ] *n* iglesia *f*; **to go to ~** ir a misa.

churchgoer ['tʃɜːtʃˌgəʊər] *n* practicante *m y f.*

churchman ['tʃɜːtʃmən] (*pl* **-men** [-mən]) *n* clérigo *m.*

Church of England *n*: **the ~** la Iglesia Anglicana.

CHURCH OF ENGLAND:

La Iglesia Anglicana es la iglesia oficial de Inglaterra; su jefe laico es el monarca y su jefe espiritual el arzobispo de Canterbury

Church of Scotland *n*: **the ~** la Iglesia de Escocia.

churchyard ['tʃɜːtʃjɑːd] *n* cementerio *m*, camposanto *m.*

churlish ['tʃɜːlɪʃ] *adj* descortés, mal educado(da).

churn [tʃɜːn] ◇ *n* **-1.** [for making butter] mantequera *f.* **-2.** [for transporting milk] lechera *f*, cántara *f* de leche. ◇ *vt* [stir up] agitar. ◇ *vi*: **my stomach ~ed** se me revolvió el estómago.
◆ **churn out** *vt sep inf* hacer como churros OR en cantidades industriales.

◆ **churn up** vt sep agitar.

chute [ʃuːt] n [for water] vertedor m, conducto m; [slide] tobogán m; [for waste] rampa f.

chutney ['tʃʌtnɪ] n salsa agridulce y picante de fruta y semillas.

CI abbr of **Channel Islands**.

CIA (abbr of **Central Intelligence Agency**) n CIA f.

CIB (abbr of **Criminal Investigation Branch**) n Am ≃ Brigada f de Policía Judicial.

cicada [sɪ'kɑːdə] n cigarra f.

CID (abbr of **Criminal Investigation Department**) n Br ≃ Brigada f de Policía Judicial.

cider ['saɪdə] n sidra f.

CIF (abbr of **cost, insurance and freight**) C. S. F.

cigar [sɪ'gɑːr] n puro m.

cigarette [ˌsɪgə'ret] n cigarrillo m.

cigarette butt n colilla f.

cigarette end Br = **cigarette butt**.

cigarette holder n boquilla f.

cigarette lighter n mechero m, encendedor m.

cigarette paper n papel m de fumar.

C-in-C n abbr of **commander-in-chief**.

cinch [sɪntʃ] n inf: **it's a ~** está tirado, es pan comido.

cinder ['sɪndə] n ceniza f.

cinderblock ['sɪndəblɒk] n Am ladrillo grande de cemento y cenizas de coque.

Cinderella [ˌsɪndə'relə] n Cenicienta f.

cine-camera ['sɪnɪ-] n cámara f cinematográfica.

cine-film ['sɪnɪ-] n película f cinematográfica.

cinema ['sɪnəmə] n cine m, biógrafo m Amer.

cinematic [ˌsɪnɪ'mætɪk] adj cinematográfico(ca).

cinnamon ['sɪnəmən] n canela f.

cipher ['saɪfə] n [secret writing system] código m, cifra f.

circa ['sɜːkə] prep hacia.

circle ['sɜːkl] ◇ n -1. [gen] círculo m; **to come full ~** volver al punto de partida; **to go round in ~s** darle (mil) vueltas al mismo tema. -2. [in theatre] anfiteatro m, segundo piso; [in cinema] entresuelo m. ◇ vt -1. [draw a circle round] rodear con un círculo. -2. [move round] describir círculos alrededor de. ◇ vi dar vueltas.

circuit ['sɜːkɪt] n -1. [gen] circuito m. -2. [of track] vuelta f.

circuit board n tarjeta f de circuito impreso.

circuit breaker n cortacircuitos m inv, (interruptor m) automático m.

circuitous [sə'kjuːɪtəs] adj tortuoso(sa).

circular ['sɜːkjʊlə] ◇ adj -1. [gen] circular. -2. [argument, discussion] que no lleva a ninguna parte. ◇ n circular f.

circulate ['sɜːkjʊleɪt] ◇ vi -1. [gen] circular. -2. [socialize] alternar. ◇ vt [rumour, document] hacer circular.

circulation [ˌsɜːkjʊ'leɪʃn] n -1. [of blood, money] circulación f; **in ~** en circulación. -2. [of magazine, newspaper] tirada f.

circumcise ['sɜːkəmsaɪz] vt circuncidar.

circumcision [ˌsɜːkəm'sɪʒn] n circuncisión f.

circumference [sə'kʌmfərəns] n circunferencia f.

circumflex ['sɜːkəmfleks] n: **~ (accent)** (acento m) circunflejo m.

circumnavigate [ˌsɜːkəm'nævɪgeɪt] vt circunnavegar.

circumscribe ['sɜːkəmskraɪb] vt fml circunscribir.

circumspect ['sɜːkəmspekt] adj circunspecto(ta).

circumstances ['sɜːkəmstənsɪz] npl circunstancias fpl; **under** OR **in no ~s** bajo ningún concepto; **in** OR **under the ~** dadas las circunstancias.

circumstantial [ˌsɜːkəm'stænʃl] adj fml: **~ evidence** prueba f indiciaria.

circumvent [ˌsɜːkəm'vent] vt fml burlar, evadir.

circus ['sɜːkəs] n -1. [for entertainment] circo m. -2. [in place names] glorieta f.

cirrhosis [sɪ'rəʊsɪs] n cirrosis f inv.

CIS (abbr of **Commonwealth of Independent States**) n CEI f.

cissy ['sɪsɪ] (pl -ies) n Br inf cobardica m y f.

cistern ['sɪstən] n -1. Br [in roof] depósito m de agua. -2. [in toilet] cisterna f.

citation [saɪ'teɪʃn] n -1. [official praise]: **~ (for)** mención f (por). -2. [quotation] cita f.

cite [saɪt] vt citar.

citizen ['sɪtɪzn] n ciudadano m, -na f.

Citizens' Band n banda de radio reservada para radioaficionados y conductores.

citizenship ['sɪtɪznʃɪp] n ciudadanía f.

citric acid ['sɪtrɪk-] n ácido m cítrico.

citrus fruit ['sɪtrəs-] n cítrico m.

city ['sɪtɪ] (pl -ies) n ciudad f.

◆ **City** n Br: **the City** la City.

THE CITY:
La City, barrio financiero de Londres, es una circunscripción administrativa autónoma de Londres y tiene su propio cuerpo de policía; por extensión, el mundo financiero británico

city centre *n* centro *m* de la ciudad.

city hall *n Am* ayuntamiento *m*.

city technology college *n Br* centro de formación profesional financiado por la industria.

civic ['sɪvɪk] *adj* **-1.** [leader, event] público(ca). **-2.** [duty, pride] cívico(ca).

civic centre *n Br* zona de la ciudad donde se encuentran los edificios públicos.

civil ['sɪvl] *adj* **-1.** [involving ordinary citizens] civil. **-2.** [polite] cortés, correcto(ta).

civil defence *n milicia civil organizada para luchar contra ataques enemigos.*

civil disobedience *n* desobediencia *f* civil.

civil engineer *n* ingeniero *m*, -ra *f* de caminos, canales y puertos.

civil engineering *n* ingeniería *f* civil.

civilian [sɪ'vɪljən] ◇ *n* civil *m* y *f*. ◇ *comp* [organization] civil; [clothes] de paisano.

civility [sɪ'vɪlətɪ] *n* urbanidad *f*, cortesía *f*.

civilization [ˌsɪvɪlaɪ'zeɪʃn] *n* civilización *f*.

civilize, -ise ['sɪvɪlaɪz] *vt* civilizar.

civilized ['sɪvɪlaɪzd] *adj* civilizado(da).

civil law *n* derecho *m* civil.

civil liberties *npl* libertades *fpl* civiles.

civil list *n Br presupuesto de la familia real votado cada año en el Parlamento.*

civil rights *npl* derechos *mpl* civiles.

civil servant *n* funcionario *m*, -ria *f*.

civil service *n* administración *f* pública.

civil war *n* guerra *f* civil.

cl (*abbr of* **centilitre**) cl.

clad [klæd] *adj literary:* ~ **in** vestido(da) de.

cladding ['klædɪŋ] *n Br* revestimiento *m*.

claim [kleɪm] ◇ *n* **-1.** [for pay, insurance, expenses] reclamación *f*. **-2.** [of right] reivindicación *f*, demanda *f*; **to have a** ~ **on sb** tener un derecho OR control sobre alguien; **to lay** ~ **to sthg** reclamar algo. **-3.** [assertion] afirmación *f*.
◇ *vt* **-1.** [allowance, expenses, lost property] reclamar. **-2.** [responsibility, credit] atribuirse. **-3.** [maintain]: **to** ~ **(that)** mantener que.
◇ *vi*: **to** ~ **on one's insurance** reclamar al seguro; **to** ~ **for sthg** reclamar algo.

claimant ['kleɪmənt] *n* [to throne] pretendiente *m* y *f*; [of unemployment benefit] solicitante *m* y *f*; JUR demandante *m* y *f*.

claim form *n* impreso *m* de solicitud.

clairvoyant [kleə'vɔɪənt] ◇ *adj* clarividente.
◇ *n* clarividente *m* y *f*.

clam [klæm] (*pt* & *pp* **-med**, *cont* **-ming**) *n* almeja *f*.
◆ **clam up** *vi inf* cerrar la boca OR el pico.

clamber ['klæmbər] *vi* trepar; **to** ~ **down a tree** bajar por un árbol.

clammy ['klæmɪ] (*compar* **-mier**, *superl* **-miest**) *adj* [hands] húmedo(da), pegajoso(sa); [weather] bochornoso(sa).

clamor *Am* = **clamour**.

clamorous ['klæmərəs] *adj* clamoroso(sa).

clamour *Br*, **clamor** *Am* ['klæmər] ◇ *n* (U) **-1.** [noise] clamor *m*. **-2.** [demand]: ~ **(for)** exigencias *fpl* OR demandas *fpl* (de). ◇ *vi*: **to** ~ **for sthg** exigir a voces algo.

clamp [klæmp] ◇ *n* [gen] abrazadera *f*; [for car wheel] cepo *m*. ◇ *vt* **-1.** [with clamp] sujetar (con abrazadera). **-2.** [with wheel clamp] poner un cepo a.
◆ **clamp down** *vi*: **to** ~ **down on** poner freno a.

clampdown ['klæmpdaʊn] *n*: ~ **(on)** restricción *f* (a).

clan [klæn] *n* clan *m*.

clandestine [klæn'destɪn] *adj* clandestino(na).

clang [klæŋ] ◇ *n* sonido *m* metálico. ◇ *vi* hacer un ruido metálico.

clanger ['klæŋər] *n Br inf* metedura *f* de pata; **to drop a** ~ meter la pata.

clank [klæŋk] ◇ *n* sonido *m* seco y metálico. ◇ *vi* retumbar con sonido metálico.

clap [klæp] (*pt* & *pp* **-ped**, *cont* **-ping**) ◇ *n* **-1.** [of hands] palmada *f*. **-2.** [of thunder] retumbo *m*, estruendo *m*. ◇ *vt* **-1.** **to** ~ **one's hands** dar palmadas. **-2.** *inf* [place]: **to** ~ **sthg onto sthg** golpear algo con algo; **to** ~ **eyes on** ver. ◇ *vi* aplaudir.

clapboard ['klæpbɔːd] *n Am* tablilla *f*.

clapped-out [klæpt-] *adj Br inf* [car] destartalado(da).

clapperboard ['klæpəbɔːd] *n* claqueta *f*.

clapping ['klæpɪŋ] *n* (U) aplausos *mpl*.

claptrap ['klæptræp] *n* (U) *inf* chorradas *fpl*.

claret ['klærət] *n* burdeos *m inv*.

clarification [ˌklærɪfɪ'keɪʃn] *n* aclaración *f*.

clarify ['klærɪfaɪ] (*pt* & *pp* **-ied**) *vt* aclarar.

clarinet [ˌklærə'net] *n* clarinete *m*.

clarity ['klærətɪ] *n* claridad *f*.

clash [klæʃ] ◇ *n* **-1.** [difference - of interests] conflicto *m*; [- of personalities] choque *m*. **-2.** [fight, disagreement]: ~ **(with)** conflicto *m* (con). **-3.** [noise] estruendo *m*, estrépito *m*. ◇ *vi* **-1.** [fight, disagree]: **to** ~ **(with)** enfrentarse (con). **-2.** [opinions, policies] estar en desacuerdo. **-3.** [date, event]: **to ~ (with)** coincidir (con). **-4.** [colour]: **to ~ (with)** desentonar (con). **-5.** [cymbals] sonar.

clasp [klɑ:sp] ◇ *n* [on necklace, bracelet] broche *m*; [on belt] cierre *m*, hebilla *f*. ◇ *vt* [person] abrazar (agarrando); [thing] agarrar.

class [klɑ:s] ◇ *n* **-1.** [gen] clase *f*. **-2.** [category] clase *f*, tipo *m*; **to be in a ~ of one's own** ser incomparable. ◇ *comp* de clases. ◇ *vt*: **to ~ sb (as)** clasificar a alguien (de).

class-conscious *adj usu pej* con conciencia de clase.

classic ['klæsɪk] ◇ *adj* [typical] clásico(ca). ◇ *n* clásico *m*.

◆ **classics** *npl* (lenguas *fpl*) clásicas *fpl*.

classical ['klæsɪkl] *adj* clásico(ca).

classical music *n* música *f* clásica.

classification [,klæsɪfɪ'keɪʃn] *n* clasificación *f*.

classified ['klæsɪfaɪd] *adj* [secret] reservado(da), secreto(ta).

classified ad *n* anuncio *m* por palabras.

classify ['klæsɪfaɪ] (*pt* & *pp* **-ied**) *vt* clasificar.

classless ['klɑ:slɪs] *adj* sin clases.

classmate ['klɑ:smeɪt] *n* compañero *m*, -ra *f* de clase.

classroom ['klɑ:srʊm] *n* aula *f*, clase *f*.

classy ['klɑ:sɪ] (*compar* **-ier**, *superl* **-iest**) *adj inf* con clase.

clatter ['klætə'] ◇ *n* [gen] estrépito; [of pots, pans, dishes] ruido *m* (de cacharros); [of hooves] chacoloteo *m*. ◇ *vi* [hooves] chacolotear; [person, car etc]: **to ~ down/into sthg** armar un gran estrépito al caer por/chocar con algo.

clause [klɔ:z] *n* **-1.** [in legal document] cláusula *f*. **-2.** GRAMM oración *f*.

claustrophobia [,klɔ:strə'fəʊbjə] *n* claustrofobia *f*.

claustrophobic [,klɔ:strə'fəʊbɪk] *adj* claustrofóbico(ca).

claw [klɔ:] ◇ *n* **-1.** [of animal, bird] garra *f*; [of cat] uña *f*. **-2.** [of crab, lobster] pinza *f*. ◇ *vt* arañar. ◇ *vi*: **to ~ at sthg** [cat] arañar algo; [person] intentar agarrarse a algo.

◆ **claw back** *vt sep Br* lograr recuperar.

clay [kleɪ] *n* arcilla *f*.

clay pigeon shooting *n* tiro *m* al plato.

clean [kli:n] ◇ *adj* **-1.** [gen] limpio(pia). **-2.** [page] en blanco. **-3.** [record, reputation] impecable, irreprochable; [driving licence] sin multas; **to come ~ about sthg** *inf* confesar algo. **-4.** [joke] inocente. **-5.** [outline] neto(ta), nítido(da); [movement] suelto(ta), ágil. ◇ *adv* totalmente. ◇ *vt* & *vi* limpiar. ◇ *n* limpieza *f*.

◆ **clean out** *vt sep* **-1.** [clear out] limpiar el interior de. **-2.** *inf* [take money from] desplumar. **-3.** *inf* [take everything from]: **they ~ed us out** (los ladrones) nos limpiaron la casa.

◆ **clean up** ◇ *vt sep* [clear up] ordenar, limpiar; **to ~ o.s. up** asearse. ◇ *vi inf* forrarse.

cleaner ['kli:nə'] *n* **-1.** [person] limpiador *m*, -ra *f*. **-2.** [substance] producto *m* de limpieza. **-3.** [shop]: **~'s** tintorería *f*.

cleaning ['kli:nɪŋ] *n* limpieza *f*.

cleaning lady *n* mujer *f* OR señora *f* de la limpieza.

cleanliness ['klenlɪnɪs] *n* limpieza *f*.

cleanly ['kli:nlɪ] *adv* limpiamente.

cleanness ['kli:nnɪs] *n* limpieza *f*.

cleanse [klenz] *vt* [gen] limpiar; [soul] purificar; **to ~ sthg/sb of sthg** limpiar algo/a alguien de algo.

cleanser ['klenzə'] *n* crema *f* OR loción *f* limpiadora.

clean-shaven *adj* [never growing a beard] barbilampiño(ña); [recently shaved] bien afeitado(da).

cleanup ['kli:nʌp] *n* limpieza *f*.

clear [klɪə'] ◇ *adj* **-1.** [gen] claro(ra); [day, road, view] despejado(da); **to make sthg ~ (to)** dejar algo claro (a); **it's ~ that ...** está claro que ...; **are you ~ about it?** ¿lo entiendes?; **to make o.s. ~** explicarse con claridad. **-2.** [transparent] transparente. **-3.** [free of blemishes - skin] terso(sa). **-4.** [free - time] libre. **-5.** [conscience] tranquilo(la), limpio(pia). **-6.** [complete - day, week] entero(ra); [- profit, wages] limpio(pia), neto(ta). ◇ *adv* [out of the way]: **stand ~!** ¡aléjate!; **to jump/step ~** saltar/dar un paso para hacerse a un lado. ◇ *n*: **in the ~** [out of danger] fuera de peligro; [free from suspicion] fuera de (toda) sospecha. ◇ *vt* **-1.** [remove objects, obstacles from] despejar; [pipe] desatascar; **to ~ sthg of sthg** quitar algo de algo; **to ~ a space** hacer sitio; **to ~ the table** quitar la mesa; **to ~ one's throat** aclararse la garganta. **-2.** [remove] quitar. **-3.** [jump] saltar. **-4.** [pay] liquidar. **-5.** [authorize] aprobar. **-6.** [prove not guilty] declarar inocente; **to be ~ed of sthg** salir absuelto de algo. **-7.** [cheque] conformar, dar por bueno. ◇ *vi* despejarse.

◆ **clear away** *vt sep* poner en su sitio.

◆ **clear off** *vi Br inf* largarse.

◆ **clear out** ◇ *vt sep* limpiar a fondo. ◇ *vi inf* largarse.

◆ **clear up** ◇ *vt sep* **-1.** [room, mess] limpiar; [toys, books] ordenar. **-2.** [mystery, disagreement] **aclarar, resolver.** ◇ *vi* **-1.** [weather] **despejarse**; [infection] **desaparecer. -2.** [tidy up] **ordenar, recoger.**

clearance ['klɪərəns] *n* **-1.** [removal - of rubbish, litter] **despeje** *m*, **limpieza** *f*; [of slums, houses] **eliminación** *f*. **-2.** [permission] **autorización** *f*, **permiso** *m*. **-3.** [free space] **distancia** *f* **de seguridad.**

clearance sale *n* (**venta** *f* de) **liquidación** *f*.

clear-cut *adj* [issue, plan] **bien definido(da)**; [division] **nítido(da).**

clear-headed [-'hedɪd] *adj* **lúcido(da).**

clearing ['klɪərɪŋ] *n* **claro** *m*.

clearing bank *n* *Br* *banco asociado a la cámara de compensación.*

clearing house *n* **-1.** [organization] **centro** *m* **de intercambio de información. -2.** [bank] **cámara** *f* **de compensación.**

clearing up *n* **limpieza** *f*.

clearly ['klɪəlɪ] *adv* **-1.** [gen] **claramente. -2.** [plainly] **obviamente.**

clearout ['klɪəraʊt] *n* *inf* **limpieza** *f*; **to have a ~ ordenar y tirar lo que no sirva.**

clear-sighted [-'saɪtɪd] *adj* **perspicaz.**

clearway ['klɪəweɪ] *n* *Br* *carretera donde no se puede parar.*

cleavage ['kliːvɪdʒ] *n* **-1.** [between breasts] **escote** *m*. **-2.** [division] **escisión** *f*.

cleaver ['kliːvər] *n* **cuchillo** *m* OR **cuchilla** *f* **de carnicero.**

clef [klef] *n* **clave** *f*.

cleft [kleft] *n* **grieta** *f*.

cleft palate *n* **fisura** *f* **de paladar.**

clematis ['klemətɪs] *n* **clemátide** *f*.

clemency ['klemənsɪ] *n* *fml* [mercy] **clemencia** *f*.

clementine ['klemantaɪn] *n* **clementina** *f*.

clench [klentʃ] *vt* **apretar.**

clergy ['klɜːdʒɪ] *npl*: **the ~ el clero.**

clergyman ['klɜːdʒɪmən] (*pl* **-men** [-mən]) *n* **clérigo** *m*.

cleric ['klerɪk] *n* **clérigo** *m*.

clerical ['klerɪkl] *adj* **-1.** [in office] **de oficina. -2.** [in church] **clerical.**

clerk [*Br* klɑːk, *Am* klɜːrk] *n* **-1.** [in office] **oficinista** *m* y *f*. **-2.** [in court] **secretario** *m*, **escribano** *m*. **-3.** *Am* [shop assistant] **dependiente** *m*, **-ta** *f*.

clever ['klevər] *adj* **-1.** [intelligent] **listo(ta), inteligente. -2.** [idea, invention] **ingenioso(sa)**; [with hands] **hábil.**

cleverly ['klevəlɪ] *adv* **-1.** [intelligently] **con inteligencia. -2.** [skilfully] **ingeniosamente.**

cleverness ['klevənɪs] *n* [intelligence] **inteligencia** *f*; [with hands] **habilidad** *f*.

cliché ['kliːʃeɪ] *n* **cliché** *m*.

click [klɪk] ◇ *n* [of tongue, fingers] **chasquido** *m*; [of camera, door] **clic** *m*. ◇ *vt* **chasquear.** ◇ *vi* **-1.** [heels] **sonar con un taconazo**; [camera] **dar un chasquido, hacer clic. -2.** *inf* [fall into place]: **suddenly, it ~ed (with me) de pronto, caí en la cuenta. -3.** COMPUT: **to ~ on an application apretar el ratón.**

client ['klaɪənt] *n* **cliente** *m*, **-ta** *f*.

clientele [,kliːən'tel] *n* **clientela** *f*.

cliff [klɪf] *n* [on coast] **acantilado** *m*; [inland] **precipicio** *m*.

cliffhanger ['klɪf,hæŋər] *n* *inf* [film, story] **historia** *f* **de suspense.**

climactic [klaɪ'mæktɪk] *adj* **culminante.**

climate ['klaɪmɪt] *n* [weather] **clima** *m*; *fig* [atmosphere] **ambiente** *m*.

climatic [klaɪ'mætɪk] *adj* **climático(ca).**

climax ['klaɪmæks] *n* [culmination] **clímax** *m*, **culminación** *f*.

climb [klaɪm] ◇ *n* **escalada** *f*. ◇ *vt* [stairs, ladder] **subir**; [tree] **trepar a**; [mountain] **escalar.** ◇ *vi* **-1.** [clamber]: **to ~ over sthg trepar por algo; to ~ into sthg subirse a algo. -2.** [plant] **trepar**; [road, plane] **subir. -3.** [increase] **subir.**

◆ **climb down** *vi* **apearse del burro, rectificar.**

climb-down *n* **rectificación** *f*.

climber ['klaɪmər] *n* **-1.** [mountaineer] **escalador** *m*, **-ra** *f*. **-2.** [plant] **enredadera** *f*.

climbing ['klaɪmɪŋ] *n* **montañismo** *m*, **alpinismo** *m*.

climbing frame *n* *Br* *barras de metal para que trepen los niños.*

climes [klaɪmz] *npl* *literary* **parajes** *mpl*.

clinch [klɪntʃ] *vt* [deal] **cerrar.**

cling [klɪŋ] (*pt* & *pp* **clung**) *vi* **-1.** [hold tightly]: **to ~ (to) agarrarse (a). -2.** [clothes, person]: **to ~ (to sb) pegarse (a alguien). -3.** [to ideas, principles]: **to ~ to aferrarse a.**

clingfilm ['klɪŋfɪlm] *n* *Br* **film** *m* **de plástico adherente.**

clinging ['klɪŋɪŋ] *adj* **-1.** [person, child] **pegajoso(sa). -2.** [clothes] **ajustado(da), ceñido(da).**

clinic ['klɪnɪk] *n* **clínica** *f*.

clinical ['klɪnɪkl] *adj* **-1.** MED **clínico(ca). -2.** [cold] **frío(a).**

clinically ['klɪnɪklɪ] *adv* MED **clínicamente.**

clink [klɪŋk] ◇ *n* **tintineo** *m*. ◇ *vi* **tintinear.**

clip [klɪp] (*pt* & *pp* **-ped**, *cont* **-ping**) ◇ *n* **-1.** [for paper] **clip** *m*; [for hair] **horquilla** *f*; [on earring] **cierre** *m*. **-2.** [of film] **fragmento** *m*, **secuencias** *fpl*. ◇ *vt* **-1.** [fasten] **sujetar. -2.** [cut - lawn, newspaper cutting] **recortar;**

[punch - tickets] picar. **-3.** *inf* [hit] dar un golpecito en.

clipboard ['klɪpbɔːd] *n* tabloncillo *m* con pinza sujetapapeles.

clip-on *adj* de enganche.

clipped [klɪpt] *adj* [staccato] entrecortado(da).

clippers ['klɪpəz] *npl* [for nails] cortaúñas *m inv*; [for hair] maquinilla *f* para cortar el pelo; [for hedges, grass] tijeras *fpl* de podar.

clipping ['klɪpɪŋ] *n* **-1.** [from newspaper] recorte *m*. **-2.** [of nails] corte *m*.

clique [kliːk] *n pej* camarilla *f*.

cloak [kləʊk] ◇ *n* **-1.** [garment] capa *f*, manto *m*. **-2.** [cover for secret] tapadera *f*. ◇ *vt*: to be ~ed in estar rodeado(da) de.

cloak-and-dagger *adj* de capa y espada.

cloakroom ['kləʊkrʊm] *n* **-1.** [for clothes] guardarropa *m*. **-2.** *Br* [toilets] servicios *mpl*.

clobber ['klɒbə] *inf* ◇ *n Br* (*U*) **-1.** [things] bártulos *mpl*, trastos *mpl*. **-2.** [clothes] indumentaria *f*, trapos *mpl*. ◇ *vt* atizar.

clock [klɒk] *n* **-1.** [timepiece] reloj *m*; round the ~ día y noche, las 24 horas; to put the ~ back *lit* atrasar el reloj OR la hora; *fig* retroceder en el tiempo; to put the ~ forward adelantar el reloj OR la hora. **-2.** [mileometer] cuentakilómetros *m inv*.

◆ **clock in, clock on** *vi Br* fichar (a la entrada).

◆ **clock off, clock out** *vi Br* fichar (a la salida).

◆ **clock up** *vt fus* [miles etc] recorrer.

clockwise ['klɒkwaɪz] *adj & adv* en el sentido de las agujas del reloj.

clockwork ['klɒkwɜːk] ◇ *n*: to go like ~ ir sobre ruedas. ◇ *comp* de cuerda.

clod [klɒd] *n* terrón *m*.

clog [klɒg] (*pt & pp* **-ged**, *cont* **-ging**) *vt* atascar, obstruir.

◆ **clogs** *npl* zuecos *mpl*.

◆ **clog up** ◇ *vt sep* [drain, pipe] atascar; [eyes, nose] congestionar. ◇ *vi* atascarse.

clogged [klɒgd] *adj* [drains, roads] atascado(da); [pores] obstruido(da).

cloister ['klɔɪstə] *n* claustro *m*.

cloistered ['klɔɪstəd] *adj literary* enclaustrado(da), recluido(da).

clone [kləʊn] ◇ *n* [gen & COMPUT] clon *m*. ◇ *vt* producir por clonación.

close¹ [kləʊs] ◇ *adj* **-1.** [near] cercano(na); ~ to cerca de; ~ to tears/laughter a punto de llorar/reír; ~ up, ~ to de cerca; ~ by, ~ at hand muy cerca; it was a ~ shave OR thing OR call nos libramos por los pelos. **-2.** [relationship, friend] íntimo(ma); to be ~ to sb estar muy unido(da) a alguien. **-3.**

[relative, family] cercano(na), próximo(ma) [resemblance] grande; [link, tie, cooperation estrecho(cha). **-4.** [questioning] minucioso(sa); [examination] detallado(da); [look] de cerca; [watch] estrecho(cha), atento(ta). **-5** [room, air] cargado(da); [weather] bochornoso(sa). **-6.** [contest, race] reñido(da); [result apretado(da).

◇ *adv* cerca.

◇ *n* [in street names] callejón *m*.

◆ **close on, close to** *prep* [almost] cerca de.

close² [kləʊz] ◇ *vt* **-1.** [gen] cerrar. **-2.** [meeting] clausurar; [discussion, speech] acabar, terminar. ◇ *vi* cerrarse. ◇ *n* final *m*; to bring sthg to a ~ dar por terminado algo; to draw to a ~ tocar a su fin.

◆ **close down** ◇ *vt sep* cerrar (definitivamente). ◇ *vi* [factory etc] cerrarse (definitivamente). **-2.** [meeting, day] acabar, terminar.

◆ **close in** *vi* acercarse; to ~ in on sthg/sb rodear OR cercar algo/a alguien.

◆ **close off** *vt fus* [road] cortar; [room] cerrar.

close-cropped [,kləʊs-] *adj* al rape.

closed [kləʊzd] *adj* cerrado(da).

closed circuit television *n* televisión *f* por circuito cerrado.

closedown ['kləʊzdaʊn] *n* cierre *m*.

closed shop *n* empresa donde sólo se contrata a miembros de un determinado sindicato.

close-fitting [,kləʊs-] *adj* ajustado(da), ceñido(da).

close-knit [,kləʊs-] *adj* muy unido(da).

closely ['kləʊslɪ] *adv* **-1.** [of connection, relation etc] estrechamente; to be ~ involved in sthg estar muy metido en algo; [of resemblance] fielmente. **-2.** [carefully] atentamente.

closeness ['kləʊsnɪs] *n* **-1.** [nearness] proximidad *f*. **-2.** [intimacy] intimidad *f*.

closeout ['kləʊzaʊt] *n Am* liquidación *f*.

close quarters [,kləʊs-] *npl*: at ~ de cerca.

close season ['kləʊs-] *n Br* (temporada *f* de) veda *f*.

closet ['klɒzɪt] ◇ *adj inf* en secreto. ◇ *n Am* armario *m*. ◇ *vt*: to be ~ed with estar encerrado(da) con.

close-up ['kləʊs-] *n* primer plano *m*.

closing ['kləʊzɪŋ] *adj* final, último(ma).

closing price *n* precio *m* OR cotización *f* de cierre.

closing time *n* hora *f* de cierre.

closure ['kləʊʒə] *n* cierre *m*.

clot [klɒt] (*pt & pp* **-ted**, *cont* **-ting**) ◇ *n* **-1.** [in blood] coágulo *m*; [in liquid] grumo *m*. **-2.**

Br inf [fool] bobo *m*, -ba *f*. ◇ *vi* [blood] coagularse.

cloth [klɒθ] *n* **-1.** (*U*) [fabric] tela *f*. **-2.** [piece of cloth] trapo *m*.

clothe [kləʊð] *vt fml* vestir; ~d in vestido(da) de.

clothes [kləʊðz] *npl* ropa *f*; **to put one's** ~ **on** vestirse; **to take one's** ~ **off** quitarse la ropa.

clothes basket *n* cesta *f* de la ropa sucia.

clothes brush *n* cepillo *m* para la ropa.

clotheshorse ['kləʊðhɔːs] *n* tendedero *m* (plegable).

clothesline ['kləʊðzlaɪn] *n* cuerda *f* para tender la ropa.

clothes peg *Br*, **clothespin** *Am* ['kləʊðzpɪn] *n* pinza *f* (para la ropa).

clothing ['kləʊðɪŋ] *n* ropa *f*.

clotted cream [ˌklɒtɪd-] *n* nata *muy espesa típica de Cornualles.*

cloud [klaʊd] ◇ *n* nube *f*; **to be under a** ~ ser mirado con malos ojos. ◇ *vt* **-1.** [mirror, window] empañar. **-2.** [memory, happiness] oscurecer. **-3.** [mind] obnubilar; [issue] complicar.

♦ **cloud over** *vi lit* & *fig* nublarse.

cloudburst ['klaʊdbɜːst] *n* chaparrón *m*.

cloudless ['klaʊdlɪs] *adj* despejado(da), sin nubes.

cloudy ['klaʊdɪ] (*compar* **-ier**, *superl* **-iest**) *adj* **-1.** [overcast] nublado(da). **-2.** [murky] turbio(bia). **-3.** [confused - idea etc] vago(ga), impreciso(sa).

clout [klaʊt] *inf* ◇ *n* **-1.** [blow] bofetón *m*, tortazo *m*. **-2.** (*U*) [influence] influencia *f*. ◇ *vt* dar un tortazo a.

clove [kləʊv] *n*: **a** ~ **of garlic** un diente de ajo.

♦ **cloves** *npl* [spice] clavos *mpl*.

clover ['kləʊvə'] *n* trébol *m*.

cloverleaf ['kləʊvəliːf] (*pl* **-leaves** [-liːvz]) *n* [plant] hoja *f* de trébol.

clown [klaʊn] ◇ *n* **-1.** [performer] payaso *m*. **-2.** [fool] payaso *m*, -sa *f*. ◇ *vi* hacer payasadas.

cloying ['klɔɪɪŋ] *adj* empalagoso(sa).

club [klʌb] (*pt* & *pp* **-bed**, *cont* **-bing**) ◇ *n* **-1.** [organization, place] club *m*. **-2.** [weapon] porra *f*, garrote *m*. **-3.** (golf) ~ palo *m* de golf. ◇ *comp* del club. ◇ *vt* apalear, aporrear.

♦ **clubs** *npl* [cards] tréboles *mpl*.

♦ **club together** *vi Br* recolectar dinero.

club car *n Am* RAIL vagón *m* restaurante.

clubhouse ['klʌbhaʊs, *pl* -haʊzɪz] *n* [for golfers] (edificio *m* del) club *m*.

cluck [klʌk] *vi* **-1.** [hen] cloquear. **-2.** [person] chasquear la lengua.

clue [kluː] *n* **-1.** [in crime] pista *f*; **not to have a** ~ **(about)** no tener ni idea (de). **-2.** [answer, solution] clave *f*. **-3.** [in crossword] pregunta *f*, clave *f*.

clued-up [kluːd-] *adj Br inf* bien informado(da), al tanto.

clueless ['kluːlɪs] *adj Br inf*: **to be** ~ **(about)** no tener ni idea (de).

clump [klʌmp] ◇ *n* **-1.** [of bushes] mata *f*; [of trees, flowers] grupo *m*. **-2.** [sound] ruido *m* de pisadas. ◇ *vi*: **to** ~ **about** andar pesadamente.

clumsily ['klʌmzɪlɪ] *adv* **-1.** [ungracefully] torpemente. **-2.** [awkwardly, unskillfully] toscamente, rudimentariamente. **-3.** [tactlessly] torpemente, sin tacto.

clumsy ['klʌmzɪ] (*compar* **-ier**, *superl* **-iest**) *adj* **-1.** [ungraceful] torpe. **-2.** [unwieldy] difícil de manejar. **-3.** [tactless] torpe, sin tacto.

clung [klʌŋ] *pt* & *pt* → **cling**.

cluster ['klʌstə'] ◇ *n* [group] grupo *m*; [of grapes] racimo. ◇ *vi* agruparse.

clutch [klʌtʃ] ◇ *n* AUT embrague *m*. ◇ *vt* [hand] estrechar; [arm, baby] agarrar. ◇ *vi*: **to** ~ **at sthg** tratar de agarrarse a algo.

♦ **clutches** *npl*: **in the** ~ **of** en las garras de.

clutch bag *n* bolso *m* de mano.

clutter ['klʌtə'] ◇ *n* desorden *m*. ◇ *vt* cubrir desordenadamente.

cm (*abbr of* **centimetre**) cm.

CNAA (*abbr of* **Council for National Academic Awards**) *n organismo británico independiente de las universidades que otorga títulos superiores.*

CND (*abbr of* **Campaign for Nuclear Disarmament**) *n organización británica contra el armamento nuclear.*

co- [kəʊ] *prefix* co-.

c/o (*abbr of* **care of**) c/d.

Co. **-1.** (*abbr of* **Company**) Cía. **-2.** *abbr of* **County**.

CO ◇ *n* **-1.** (*abbr of* **commanding officer**) *rango militar*, ≃ Cte. *m y f*. **-2.** (*abbr of* **Commonwealth Office**) *ministerio para las relaciones con la Commonwealth*. **-3.** (*abbr of* **conscientious objector**) *objetor de conciencia*. ◇ *abbr of* **Colorado**.

coach [kəʊtʃ] ◇ *n* **-1.** [bus] autocar *m*. **-2.** RAIL coche *m*, vagón *m*. **-3.** [horsedrawn] carruaje *m*. **-4.** SPORT entrenador *m*, -ra *f*. **-5.** [tutor] profesor *m*, -ra *f* particular. ◇ *vt* **-1.** SPORT entrenar. **-2.** [tutor] dar clases particulares a.

coaching ['kəʊtʃɪŋ] n (U) **-1.** SPORT entrenamiento m. **-2.** [tutoring] clases fpl particulares.

coach trip n Br excursión f en autocar.

coagulate [kəʊ'ægjʊleɪt] vi coagularse.

coal [kəʊl] n carbón m.

coalesce [ˌkəʊə'les] vi fml fundirse.

coalface ['kəʊlfeɪs] n frente m de una mina de carbón.

coalfield ['kəʊlfiːld] n cuenca f minera.

coal gas n gas m del alumbrado OR de la hulla.

coalition [ˌkəʊə'lɪʃn] n coalición f.

coalman ['kəʊlmæn] (pl **-men** [-men]) n Br carbonero m.

coalmine ['kəʊlmaɪn] n mina f de carbón.

coalminer ['kəʊlˌmaɪnəʳ] n minero m (de carbón).

coalmining ['kəʊlˌmaɪnɪŋ] n minería f del carbón.

coarse [kɔːs] adj **-1.** [skin, hair, sandpaper] áspero(ra); [fabric] basto(ta). **-2.** [person, joke] ordinario(ria), guarango(ga) Amer.

coarse fishing n Br pesca de río que exceptúa la de los salmónidos.

coarsen ['kɔːsn] ◇ vt **-1.** [person, manners] embrutecer. **-2.** [make rough] curtir. ◇ vi **-1.** [become vulgar] embrutecerse. **-2.** [become rough] curtirse.

coast [kəʊst] ◇ n costa f. ◇ vi **-1.** [in car] ir en punto muerto. **-2.** [progress easily] ir holgadamente OR sin esfuerzos.

coastal ['kəʊstl] adj costero(ra).

coaster ['kəʊstəʳ] n [small mat] posavasos m inv.

coastguard ['kəʊstɡɑːd] n **-1.** [person] guardacostas m y f inv. **-2.** [organization]: **the ~** los guardacostas (pl).

coastline ['kəʊstlaɪn] n litoral m.

coat [kəʊt] ◇ n **-1.** [garment] abrigo m. **-2.** [of animal] pelo m, pelaje m. **-3.** [layer] capa f. ◇ vt: **to ~ sthg (with)** cubrir algo (de).

coat hanger n percha f.

coating ['kəʊtɪŋ] n [of dust etc] capa f; [of chocolate, silver] baño m.

coat of arms (pl **coats of arms**) n escudo m de armas.

coauthor [kəʊ'ɔːθəʳ] n coautor m, -ra f.

coax [kəʊks] vt: **to ~ sb (to do OR into doing sthg)** engatusar a alguien (para que haga algo).

coaxial cable [kəʊ'æksɪəl-] n COMPUT cable m coaxial.

cob [kɒb] n → **corn**.

cobalt ['kəʊbɔːlt] n [colour] azul m cobalto.

cobble ['kɒbl]

◆ **cobble together** vt sep pergeñar (de cualquier manera).

cobbled ['kɒbld] adj adoquinado(da).

cobbler ['kɒbləʳ] n zapatero (remendón) m zapatera (remendona) f.

◆ **cobbles** ['kɒblz], **cobblestones** ['kɒblstəʊnz] npl adoquines mpl.

Cobol ['kəʊbɒl] (abbr of **Common Business Orientated Language**) n COMPUT cobol m.

cobra ['kəʊbrə] n cobra f.

cobweb ['kɒbweb] n telaraña f.

Coca-Cola® [ˌkəʊkə'kəʊlə] n Coca-Cola® f.

cocaine [kəʊ'keɪn] n cocaína f.

cock [kɒk] ◇ n **-1.** [male chicken] gallo m **-2.** [male bird] macho m. ◇ vt **-1.** [gun] montar, amartillar. **-2.** [head] ladear.

◆ **cock up** vt sep Br v inf jorobar, fastidiar.

cock-a-hoop adj inf [delighted]: **to be ~** estar como unas castañuelas.

cockatoo [ˌkɒkə'tuː] (pl **-s**) n cacatúa f.

cockerel ['kɒkrəl] n gallo m joven.

cocker spaniel [ˌkɒkə-] n cocker m.

cockeyed ['kɒkaɪd] adj inf **-1.** [lopsided] torcido(da). **-2.** [foolish] disparatado(da).

cockfight ['kɒkfaɪt] n pelea f de gallos.

cockle ['kɒkl] n berberecho m.

Cockney ['kɒknɪ] (pl **Cockneys**) ◇ n **-1.** [person] cockney m y f, persona procedente del este de Londres. **-2.** [dialect, accent] cockney m, dialecto del este de Londres. ◇ comp cockney, del este de Londres.

cockpit ['kɒkpɪt] n [in plane] cabina f, carlinga f.

cockroach ['kɒkrəʊtʃ] n cucaracha f.

cocksure [ˌkɒk'ʃɔːʳ] adj presuntuoso(sa).

cocktail ['kɒkteɪl] n cóctel m, copetín m Amer.

cocktail dress n vestido m de fiesta.

cocktail shaker [-ˌʃeɪkəʳ] n coctelera f.

cocktail stick n palillo m.

cock-up n v inf chapuza f, pifia f.

cocky ['kɒkɪ] (compar **-ier**, superl **-iest**) adj inf chulo(la), chuleta.

cocoa ['kəʊkəʊ] n **-1.** [powder] cacao m. **-2.** [drink] chocolate m.

coconut ['kəʊkənʌt] n coco m.

cocoon [kə'kuːn] ◇ n **-1.** ZOOL capullo m. **-2.** fig [protective environment]: **to live in a ~** vivir entre algodones. ◇ vt fig arropar.

cod [kɒd] (pl inv OR **-s**) n bacalao m.

COD (abbr of **cash on delivery**) contra reembolso, ≃ CAE.

code [kəʊd] ◇ n **-1.** [gen] código m. **-2.** [for telephone] prefijo m. ◇ vt **-1.** [encode] codificar, cifrar. **-2.** [give identifier to] clasificar.

coded ['kəʊdɪd] *adj* codificado(da).

codeine ['kəʊdiːn] *n* codeína *f*.

code name *n* nombre *m* en clave.

code of practice *n* código *m* (de ética) profesional.

cod-liver oil *n* aceite *m* de hígado de bacalao.

codswallop ['kɒdz,wɒləp] *n* (*U*) *Br inf* bobadas *fpl*.

coed [,kəʊ'ed] ⋄ *adj* (*abbr of* **coeducational**) mixto(ta). ⋄ *n* **-1.** *Am* (*abbr of* **coeducational student**) *estudiante de un colegio mixto*. **-2.** *Br* (*abbr of* **coeducational school**) *colegio mixto*.

coeducational [,kəʊedjuː'keɪʃənl] *adj* mixto(ta).

coefficient [,kəʊɪ'fɪʃnt] *n* coeficiente *m*.

coerce [kəʊ'ɜːs] *vt*: **to ~ sb (into doing sthg)** coaccionar a alguien (para que haga algo).

coercion [kəʊ'ɜːʃn] *n* coacción *f*.

coexist [,kəʊɪg'zɪst] *vi* coexistir.

coexistence [,kəʊɪg'zɪstəns] *n* coexistencia *f*.

C. of C. (*abbr of* **chamber of commerce**) *n* CC *f*.

C of E (*abbr of* **Church of England**) *n iglesia anglicana*; **she's ~** es anglicana.

coffee ['kɒfɪ] *n* café *m*.

coffee bar *n Br* cafetería *f*.

coffee beans *npl* granos *mpl* de café.

coffee break *n pausa para descansar en el trabajo por la mañana y por la tarde*.

coffee cup *n* taza *f* de café.

coffee mill *n* molinillo *m* de café.

coffee morning *n Br reunión matinal, generalmente benéfica, en la que se sirve café*.

coffeepot ['kɒfɪpɒt] *n* cafetera *f*.

coffee shop *n* **-1.** *Br* [shop] cafetería *f*. **-2.** *Am* [restaurant] café *m*.

coffee table *n* mesita *f* baja (de salón).

coffee-table book *n libro grande con fotografías o ilustraciones que se coloca a la vista, generalmente sobre la mesita del salón*.

coffers ['kɒfəz] *npl* arcas *fpl*.

coffin ['kɒfɪn] *n* ataúd *m*.

cog [kɒg] *n* [tooth on wheel] diente *m*; [wheel] rueda *f* dentada; **a ~ in the machine** una pieza insignificante del engranaje.

cogent ['kəʊdʒənt] *adj* contundente, convincente.

cogitate ['kɒdʒɪteɪt] *vi fml* meditar.

cognac ['kɒnjæk] *n* coñac *m*.

cognitive ['kɒgnɪtɪv] *adj* cognoscitivo(va).

cogwheel ['kɒgwiːl] *n* rueda *f* dentada.

cohabit [,kəʊ'hæbɪt] *vi fml*: **to ~ (with)** cohabitar (con).

coherent [kəʊ'hɪərənt] *adj* coherente.

coherently [kəʊ'hɪərəntlɪ] *adv* coherentemente.

cohesion [kəʊ'hiːʒn] *n* cohesión *f*.

cohesive [kəʊ'hiːsɪv] *adj* unido(da).

cohort ['kəʊhɔːt] *n pej* acólito *m*, -ta *f*, secuaz *m* y *f*.

COHSE ['kəʊzɪ] (*abbr of* **Confederation of Health Service Employees**) *n sindicato británico de trabajadores del sector sanitario*.

COI (*abbr of* **Central Office of Information**) *n oficina gubernamental británica de información al público*.

coil [kɔɪl] ⋄ *n* **-1.** [of rope, wire] rollo *m*; [of hair] tirabuzón *m*; [of smoke] espiral *f*. **-2.** ELEC bobina *f*. **-3.** *Br* [contraceptive device] DIU *m*, espiral *f*. ⋄ *vi* enrollarse, enroscarse. ⋄ *vt* enrollar, enroscar.

♦ **coil up** *vt sep* enrollar.

coiled [kɔɪld] *adj* [rope etc] enrollado(da); [spring] en espiral.

coin [kɔɪn] ⋄ *n* moneda *f*. ⋄ *vt* [invent] acuñar, inventar; **to ~ a phrase** como se suele decir.

coinage ['kɔɪnɪdʒ] *n* **-1.** [currency] moneda *f*. **-2.** [invention] palabra *f* de nuevo cuño.

coin-box *n Br* teléfono *m* público.

coincide [,kəʊɪn'saɪd] *vi*: **to ~ (with)** coincidir (con).

coincidence [kəʊ'ɪnsɪdəns] *n* coincidencia *f*.

coincidental [kəʊ,ɪnsɪ'dentl] *adj* fortuito(ta).

coincidentally [kəʊ,ɪnsɪ'dentəlɪ] *adv*: **~ his name was the same as mine** dio la coincidencia de que tenía el mismo nombre que yo.

coin-operated [-'ɒpə,reɪtɪd] *adj* que funciona con monedas.

coitus ['kəʊɪtəs] *n fml* coito *m*.

coke [kəʊk] *n* **-1.** [fuel] coque *m*. **-2.** *drugs sl* coca *f*.

Coke® [kəʊk] *n* Coca-Cola® *f*.

Col. (*abbr of* **colonel**) Col.

cola ['kəʊlə] *n* (bebida *f* de) cola *f*.

COLA (*abbr of* **cost-of-living adjustment**) *n actualización salarial según el coste de vida*.

colander ['kʌləndə'] *n* colador *m*, escurridor *m*.

cold [kəʊld] ⋄ *adj* frío(a); **it's ~** hace frío; **my hands are ~** tengo las manos frías; **I'm ~** tengo frío; **to get ~** enfriarse. ⋄ *n* **-1.** [illness] resfriado *m*, constipado *m*; **to catch (a) ~** resfriarse, coger un resfriado. **-2.** [low temperature] frío *m*.

cold-blooded [-'blʌdɪd] *adj* **-1.** [animal] de sangre fría. **-2.** [person] despiadado(da); [killing] a sangre fría.

cold cream *n* crema *f* facial.

cold cuts *npl* embutidos *mpl*, fiambres *mpl*.

cold feet *npl*: **he got** ~ *inf* se le arrugó el ombligo.

cold-hearted [-'hɑːtɪd] *adj* [person] duro(ra) de corazón; [action] despiadado(da).

coldly ['kəʊldlɪ] *adv* con frialdad.

coldness ['kəʊldnɪs] *n* frialdad *f*.

cold shoulder *n*: **to give sb the** ~ *inf* dar de lado a alguien.

cold sore *n* calentura *f*, pupa *f*.

cold storage *n* [of food] conservación *f* en frío.

cold sweat *n* sudor *m* frío.

cold war *n*: **the** ~ la guerra fría.

coleslaw ['kəʊlslɔː] *n* ensalada de col, zanahoria, cebolla y mayonesa.

colic ['kɒlɪk] *n* cólico *m*.

collaborate [kə'læbəreɪt] *vi*: **to** ~ **(with)** colaborar (con).

collaboration [kə,læbə'reɪʃn] *n* **-1.** [teamwork]: ~ **(with)** colaboración *f* (con). **-2.** *pej* [with enemy]: ~ **(with)** colaboracionismo *m* (con).

collaborative [kə'læbərətɪv] *adj* de colaboración.

collaborator [kə'læbəreɪtə*r*] *n* **-1.** [colleague] colaborador *m*, -ra *f*. **-2.** *pej* [traitor] colaboracionista *m* y *f*.

collage ['kɒlɑːʒ] *n* collage *m*.

collagen ['kɒlədʒən] *n* colágeno *m*.

collapse [kə'læps] ◇ *n* **-1.** [of building] derrumbamiento *m*, desplome *m*; [of roof] hundimiento *m*. **-2.** [of marriage, system] fracaso *m*; [of government, currency] caída *f*; [of empire] derrumbamiento *m*. **-3.** MED colapso *m*. ◇ *vi* **-1.** [building, person] derrumbarse, desplomarse; [roof] hundirse; **to** ~ **with laughter** partirse de risa. **-2.** [plan, business] venirse abajo. **-3.** MED sufrir un colapso. **-4.** [fold up] plegarse.

collapsible [kə'læpsəbl] *adj* plegable.

collar ['kɒlə*r*] ◇ *n* **-1.** [on clothes] cuello *m*. **-2.** [for dog] collar *m*. **-3.** TECH collar *m*. ◇ *vt* *inf* [subj: police] pescar, cazar; [subj: boss etc] pillar, parar.

collarbone ['kɒləbəʊn] *n* clavícula *f*.

collate [kə'leɪt] *vt* **-1.** [compare] cotejar. **-2.** [put in order] poner en orden.

collateral [kɒ'lætərəl] *n* garantía *f* subsidiaria, seguridad *f* colateral.

collation [kə'leɪʃn] *n* **-1.** [comparison] cotejo *m*. **-2.** [ordering] ordenación *f*.

colleague ['kɒliːg] *n* colega *m* y *f*.

collect [kə'lekt] ◇ *vt* **-1.** [gather together] reunir, juntar; **to** ~ **o.s.** recobrar el dominio de sí mismo. **-2.** [as a hobby] coleccionar. **-3.** [go to get - person, parcel] recoger. **-4.** [money, taxes] recaudar. ◇ *vi* **-1.** [gather] congregarse, reunirse. **-2.** [accumulate] acumularse. **-3.** [for charity, gift] hacer una colecta. ◇ *adv* *Am* TELEC: **to call (sb)** ~ llamar (a alguien) a cobro revertido.

◆ **collect up** *vt sep* recoger.

collectable [kə'lektəbl] ◇ *adj* interesante para un coleccionista. ◇ *n* pieza *f* interesante para un coleccionista.

collected [kə'lektɪd] *adj* **-1.** [calm] sosegado(da). **-2.** LITERATURE: ~ **works** obras *fpl* completas.

collecting [kə'lektɪŋ] *n* [hobby] coleccionismo *m*.

collection [kə'lekʃn] *n* **-1.** [of stamps, art etc] colección *f*. **-2.** [of poems, stories etc] recopilación *f*. **-3.** [of rubbish, mail] recogida *f*; [of taxes] recaudación *f*. **-4.** [of money] colecta *f*.

collective [kə'lektɪv] ◇ *adj* colectivo(va). ◇ *n* colectivo *m*.

collective bargaining *n* (*U*) convenios *mpl* colectivos.

collectively [kə'lektɪvlɪ] *adv* colectivamente.

collective ownership *n* propiedad *f* colectiva.

collector [kə'lektə*r*] *n* **-1.** [as a hobby] coleccionista *m* y *f*. **-2.** [of taxes] recaudador *m*, -ra *f*. **-3.** [of debts, rent] cobrador *m*, -ra *f*.

collector's item *n* pieza *f* de coleccionista.

college ['kɒlɪdʒ] ◇ *n* **-1.** [for further education] instituto *m*, escuela *f*. **-2.** [of university] *colegio universitario que forma parte de ciertas universidades*. **-3.** [organized body] colegio *m*. ◇ *comp* universitario(ria).

college of education *n* escuela de formación de profesores de enseñanza primaria y secundaria.

collide [kə'laɪd] *vi*: **to** ~ **(with)** [gen] chocar (con); [vehicles] colisionar OR chocar (con).

collie ['kɒlɪ] *n* collie *m*.

colliery ['kɒljərɪ] (*pl* **-ies**) *n* mina *f* de carbón.

collision [kə'lɪʒn] *n* *lit* & *fig*: ~ **(with/between)** choque *m* (con/entre), colisión *f* (con/entre); **to be on a** ~ **course (with)** *fig* estar al borde del enfrentamiento (con).

collision damage waiver *n* franquicia *f*.

colloquial [kə'ləʊkwɪəl] *adj* coloquial.

collude [kə'luːd] *vi*: **to** ~ **with** estar en connivencia con.

collusion [kə'lu:ʒn] *n*: **in ~ with** en connivencia con.

cologne [kə'ləʊn] *n* colonia *f.*

Colombia [kə'lɒmbɪə] *n* Colombia.

Colombian [kə'lɒmbɪən] ◇ *adj* colombiano(na). ◇ *n* colombiano *m*, -na *f.*

Colombo [kə'lʌmbəʊ] *n* Colombo.

colon ['kəʊlən] *n* **-1.** ANAT colon *m.* **-2.** [punctuation mark] dos puntos *mpl.*

colonel ['kɜ:nl] *n* coronel *m y f.*

colonial [kə'ləʊnjəl] *adj* colonial.

colonialism [kə'ləʊnjəlɪzm] *n* colonialismo *m.*

colonist ['kɒlənɪst] *n* colono *m.*

colonize, -ise ['kɒlənaɪz] *vt* colonizar.

colonnade [,kɒlə'neɪd] *n* columnata *f.*

colony ['kɒlənɪ] (*pl* **-ies**) *n* colonia *f.*

color *etc Am* = **colour** *etc.*

Colorado [,kɒlə'rɑ:dəʊ] *n* Colorado.

colorado beetle *n* escarabajo *m* de la patata.

colossal [kə'lɒsl] *adj* colosal.

colostomy [kə'lɒstəmɪ] (*pl* **-ies**) *n* colostomía *f.*

colour *Br*, **color** *Am* ['kʌlə'] ◇ *n* color *m*; **in ~** en color; **to change ~** cambiar de color. ◇ *adj* en color. ◇ *vt* **-1.** [give colour to] dar color a; [with pen, crayon] colorear. **-2.** [dye] teñir. **-3.** [affect] influenciar. ◇ *vi* [blush] ruborizarse.
◆ **colours** *npl* colores *mpl.*
◆ **colour in** *vt sep* colorear.

colour bar *n* discriminación *f* racial.

colour-blind *adj* daltónico(ca).

colour-coded *adj* identificado(da) por color.

coloured *Br*, **colored** *Am* ['kʌləd] *adj* **-1.** [pens, sheets etc] de colores. **-2.** [with stated colour]: **maroon-~** de color granate; **brightly-~** de vivos colores. **-3.** [person - black] de color.

colourfast *Br*, **colorfast** *Am* ['kʌləfɑ:st] *adj* que no destiñe.

colourful *Br*, **colorful** *Am* ['kʌləfʊl] *adj* **-1.** [brightly coloured] de vivos colores. **-2.** [story] animado(da). **-3.** [person] pintoresco(ca).

colouring *Br*, **coloring** *Am* ['kʌlərɪŋ] *n* **-1.** [dye] colorante *m.* **-2.** [complexion, hair] tez *f.* **-3.** [of animal's skin] color *m*, coloración *f.*

colourless *Br*, **colorless** *Am* ['kʌlələs] *adj* **-1.** [not coloured] incoloro(ra). **-2.** *fig* [uninteresting] soso(sa), anodino(na).

colour scheme *n* combinación *f* de colores.

colour supplement *n Br* suplemento *m* en color.

colt [kəʊlt] *n* potro *m.*

column ['kɒləm] *n* **-1.** [gen] columna *f.* **-2.** [of people, vehicles] hilera *f.*

columnist ['kɒləmnɪst] *n* columnista *m y f.*

coma ['kəʊmə] *n* coma *m.*

comatose ['kəʊmətəʊs] *adj* MED comatoso(sa).

comb [kəʊm] ◇ *n* peine *m.* ◇ *vt lit & fig* peinar.

combat ['kɒmbæt] ◇ *n* combate *m.* ◇ *vt* combatir.

combative ['kɒmbətɪv] *adj* combativo(va).

combination [,kɒmbɪ'neɪʃn] *n* combinación *f.*

combination lock *n* cerradura *f* de combinación.

combine [*vb* kəm'baɪn, *n* 'kɒmbaɪn] ◇ *vt*: **to ~ sthg (with)** combinar algo (con). ◇ *vi* combinarse, unirse. ◇ *n* **-1.** [group] grupo *m.* **-2.** = **combine harvester.**

combine harvester [-'hɑ:vɪstə'] *n* cosechadora *f.*

combustible [kəm'bʌstəbl] *adj* combustible.

combustion [kəm'bʌstʃn] *n* combustión *f.*

come [kʌm] (*pt* **came**, *pp* **come**) *vi* **-1.** [move] venir; [arrive] llegar; **the news came as a shock** la noticia constituyó un duro golpe; **coming!** ¡ahora voy!; **the time has ~** ha llegado la hora; **he doesn't know whether he's coming or going** *fig* no sabe si va o viene. **-2.** [reach]: **to ~ up/down to** llegar hasta; **the water came up to her thighs** el agua le llegaba hasta los muslos. **-3.** [happen] pasar; **~ what may** pase lo que pase; **how did you ~ to fail your exam?** ¿cómo es que suspendiste el examen? **-4.** [become]: **to ~ true** hacerse realidad; **to ~ unstuck** despegarse; **my shoelaces have ~ undone** se me han desatado los cordones. **-5.** [begin gradually]: **to ~ to do sthg** llegar a hacer algo. **-6.** [be placed in order]: **to ~ first/last in a race** llegar el primero/el último en una carrera; **she came second in the exam** quedó segunda en el examen; **P ~s before Q** la P viene antes de la Q. **-7.** *v inf* [sexually] correrse. **-8.** *phr*: **~ to think of it** ahora que lo pienso.
◆ **to come** *adv*: **in (the) days/years to ~** en días/años venideros.
◆ **come about** *vi* [happen] pasar, ocurrir.
◆ **come across** ◇ *vt fus* [find] cruzarse con, encontrar. ◇ *vi* [speaker, message]: **to ~ across well/badly** causar buena/mala impresión; **to ~ across as sthg** resultar ser algo.

◆ **come along** *vi* -1. [arrive by chance - opportunity] surgir; [- bus] aparecer, llegar. -2. [improve] ir; **the project is coming along nicely** el proyecto va muy bien. -3. *phr:* ~ **along!** [expressing encouragement] ¡venga!; [hurry up] ¡date prisa!

◆ **come apart** *vi* deshacerse.

◆ **come at** *vt fus* [attack] atacar.

◆ **come back** *vi* -1. [in talk, writing]: **to ~ back to sthg** volver a algo. -2. [memory]: **to ~ back to sb** volverle a la memoria a alguien. -3. [become fashionable again] volver a estar de moda.

◆ **come by** *vt fus* -1. [get, obtain] conseguir. -2. *Am* [visit, drop in on]: **they came by the house** se pasaron por nuestra casa.

◆ **come down** *vi* -1. [decrease] bajar. -2. [descend - plane, parachutist] aterrizar; [- rain] caer.

◆ **come down to** *vt fus* reducirse a.

◆ **come down with** *vt fus* coger, agarrar (*enfermedad*).

◆ **come forward** *vi* presentarse.

◆ **come from** *vt fus* [noise etc] venir de; [person] ser de.

◆ **come in** *vi* -1. [enter] entrar, pasar; ~ **in!** ¡pase! -2. [arrive - train, letters, donations] llegar. -3. [be involved] entrar; **the plan is good, but where do I ~ in?** el plan está bien pero ¿qué pinto yo en él?

◆ **come in for** *vt fus* [criticism etc] recibir, llevarse.

◆ **come into** *vt fus* -1. [inherit] heredar. -2. [begin to be]: **to ~ into being** nacer, ver la luz; **to ~ into sight** vislumbrarse.

◆ **come of** *vt fus* [result from] resultar de; **what came of your plans?** ¿qué fue de tus planes?

◆ **come off** *vi* -1. [button] descoserse; [label] despegarse; [lid] soltarse; [stain] quitarse. -2. [plan, joke] salir bien, dar resultado. -3. [person]: **to ~ off well/badly** salir bien/mal parado. -4. *phr:* ~ **off it!** *inf* ¡venga ya!

◆ **come on** *vi* -1. [start] empezar; **I have a cold coming on** creo que me estoy constipando. -2. [start working - lights, heating] encenderse. -3. [progress, improve] ir; **it's coming on nicely** va muy bien. -4. *phr:* ~ **on!** [expressing encouragement, urging haste] ¡vamos!; [expressing disbelief] ¡venga ya!

◆ **come out** *vi* -1. [become known] salir a la luz. -2. [appear - product, book, sun] salir; [- film] estrenarse. -3. [in exam, race etc] terminar, acabar; **who came out on top?** ¿quién acabó ganando? -4. [go on strike] ponerse en huelga. -5. [declare publicly]: **to ~ out for/against sthg** declararse a favor/en contra de algo. -6. [photograph] salir.

◆ **come out in** *vt fus*: **she has ~ out in spots** le han salido unos granos.

◆ **come over** *vt fus* [subj: feeling] sobrevenir; **I don't know what has ~ over her** no sé qué le pasa.

◆ **come round** *vi* -1. [change opinion]: **to ~ round (to sthg)** terminar por aceptar (algo). -2. [regain consciousness] volver en sí. -3. [happen] volver.

◆ **come through** ◇ *vt fus* [difficult situation, period] pasar por, atravesar; [operation, war] sobrevivir a. ◇ *vi* -1. [arrive] llegar. -2. [survive] sobrevivir.

◆ **come to** ◇ *vt fus* -1. [reach]: **to ~ to an end** tocar a su fin; **to ~ to power** subir al poder; **to ~ to a decision** alcanzar una decisión. -2. [amount to] ascender a. -3. [subj: memory, thought]: **the idea suddenly came to me** se me ocurrió la idea de pronto. ◇ *vi* [regain consciousness] volver en sí.

◆ **come under** *vt fus* -1. [be governed by] estar bajo. -2. [heading in book etc] venir en, estar comprendido en. -3. [suffer]: **to ~ under attack** ser víctima de críticas.

◆ **come up** *vi* -1. [name, topic, opportunity] surgir. -2. [be imminent] estar al llegar. -3. [sun, moon] salir.

◆ **come up against** *vt fus* tropezarse OR toparse con.

◆ **come upon** *vt fus* [find] cruzarse con, encontrar.

◆. **come up to** *vt fus* -1. [approach - in space] acercarse a; [- in time]: **it's coming up to Christmas/six o'clock** nos acercamos a la Navidad/a las seis de la tarde. -2. [equal] estar a la altura de.

◆ **come up with** *vt fus* [idea] salir con; [solution] encontrar.

comeback ['kʌmbæk] *n* [return] reaparición *f*; **to make a ~** [fashion] volver (a ponerse de moda); [actor] hacer una reaparición.

Comecon ['kɒmɪkɒn] (*abbr of* **Council for Mutual Economic Aid**) *n* CAME *m*.

comedian [kə'miːdjən] *n* cómico *m*, humorista *m*.

comedienne [kə,miːdɪ'en] *n* cómica *f*, humorista *f*.

comedown ['kʌmdaʊn] *n inf* desilusión *f*, decepción *f*.

comedy ['kɒmədɪ] (*pl* **-ies**) *n* comedia *f*.

comely ['kʌmlɪ] *adj literary* hermoso(sa), bello(lla).

come-on *n*: **to give sb the ~** *inf* insinuarse a alguien.

comet ['kɒmɪt] *n* cometa *m*.

come-uppance [,kʌm'ʌpəns] *n*: **to get one's ~** *inf* llevarse uno su merecido.

comfort ['kʌmfət] ◇ *n* -1. [gen] comodidad *f*; **we managed it, but it was a bit too close for ~** lo conseguimos, pero por poco. -2.

[solace] **consuelo** *m.* ◇ *vt* consolar, confortar.

comfortable ['kʌmftəbl] *adj* **-1.** [gen] cómodo(da). **-2.** [financially secure] acomodado(da). **-3.** [after operation, accident] en estado satisfactorio. **-4.** [victory, job, belief] fácil; [lead, majority] amplio(plia); **it's a ~ hour's walk away** está a una buena hora de camino.

comfortably ['kʌmftəblɪ] *adv* **-1.** [sit, sleep] cómodamente. **-2.** [without financial difficulty] sin aprietos; **~ off** acomodado(da). **-3.** [easily] fácilmente.

comforter ['kʌmfətəʳ] *n* **-1.** [person] consolador *m*, -ra *f*. **-2.** *Am* [quilt] edredón *m*.

comforting ['kʌmfətɪŋ] *adj* reconfortante.

comfort station *n Am euphemism* aseos *mpl* públicos.

comfy ['kʌmfɪ] (*compar* **-ier**, *superl* **-iest**) *adj inf* cómodo(da).

comic ['kɒmɪk] ◇ *adj* cómico(ca). ◇ *n* **-1.** [comedian] cómico *m*, -ca *f*, humorista *m y f*. **-2.** [magazine - for children] tebeo *m*; [- for adults] cómic *m*.

◆ **comics** *npl Am* [in newspaper] sección *f* de chistes OR tiras cómicas.

comical ['kɒmɪkl] *adj* cómico(ca).

comic strip *n* tira *f* cómica.

coming ['kʌmɪŋ] ◇ *adj* [future] próximo(ma). ◇ *n*: **~s and goings** idas *fpl* y venidas.

comma ['kɒmə] *n* coma *f*.

command [kə'mɑːnd] ◇ *n* **-1.** [order] orden *f*. **-2.** (*U*) [control] mando *m*; **to be in ~ of** [of people, tasks, operations] estar al mando de; [of senses] tener pleno dominio de. **-3.** [of language, skill] dominio *m*; **to have sthg at one's ~** dominar algo. **-4.** COMPUT comando *m*.

◇ *vt* **-1.** [order]: **to ~ sb (to do sthg)** ordenar OR mandar a alguien (que haga algo). **-2.** MIL [control] comandar. **-3.** [deserve - respect, attention] hacerse acreedor(ra) de; [- high price] alcanzar.

commandant [,kɒmən'dænt] *n* comandante *m y f*.

commandeer [,kɒmən'dɪəʳ] *vt* requisar.

commander [kə'mɑːndəʳ] *n* **-1.** [in army] comandante *m y f*. **-2.** [in navy] capitán *m*, -ana *f* de fragata.

commander in chief (*pl* **commanders in chief**) *n* comandante *m y f* en jefe.

commanding [kə'mɑːndɪŋ] *adj* **-1.** [lead, position, height] dominante. **-2.** [voice, manner] autoritario(ria).

commanding officer *n* jefe *m*, -fa *f* militar.

commandment [kə'mɑːndmənt] *n* RELIG mandamiento *m*.

command module *n* módulo *m* de mando.

commando [kə'mɑːndəʊ] (*pl* **-s** OR **-es**) *n* comando *m*.

command performance *n* obra teatral representada a petición del jefe de estado.

commemorate [kə'meməreɪt] *vt* conmemorar.

commemoration [kə,memə'reɪʃn] *n* conmemoración *f*.

commemorative [kə'memərətɪv] *adj* conmemorativo(va).

commence [kə'mens] *fml* ◇ *vt*: **to ~ (doing sthg)** comenzar OR empezar (a hacer algo). ◇ *vi* comenzar, empezar.

commencement [kə'mensmənt] *n fml* inicio *m*, comienzo *m*.

commend [kə'mend] *vt* **-1.** [praise] alabar. **-2.** [recommend]: **to ~ sthg (to)** recomendar algo (a).

commendable [kə'mendəbl] *adj* admirable, loable.

commendation [,kɒmen'deɪʃn] *n* [special award] distinción *f*, mención *f*.

commensurate [kə'menʃərət] *adj fml*: **~ with** acorde OR en proporción con.

comment ['kɒment] ◇ *n* comentario *m*; **no ~** sin comentarios. ◇ *vt*: **to ~ that** comentar que. ◇ *vi* comentar; **to ~ on** hacer comentarios sobre.

commentary ['kɒməntrɪ] (*pl* **-ies**) *n* comentario *m*.

commentate ['kɒmənteɪt] *vi* RADIO & TV: **to ~ (on sthg)** comentar (algo), hacer de comentarista (de algo).

commentator ['kɒmənteɪtəʳ] *n* comentarista *m y f*.

commerce ['kɒmɜːs] *n* (*U*) comercio *m*.

commercial [kə'mɜːʃl] ◇ *adj* comercial. ◇ *n* anuncio *m* (*televisivo o radiofónico*).

commercial bank *n* banco *m* comercial.

commercial break *n* pausa *f* para la publicidad.

commercial college *n* escuela *f* de comercio.

commercialism [kə'mɜːʃəlɪzm] *n* comercialismo *m*.

commercialize, -ise [kə'mɜːʃəlaɪz] *vt* comercializar.

commercialized [kə'mɜːʃəlaɪzd] *adj* comercializado(da).

commercially [kə'mɜːʃəlɪ] *adv* comercialmente.

commercial television n Br televisión f comercial.

commercial traveller n Br dated viajante m y f de comercio.

commercial vehicle n Br vehículo m comercial.

commie ['kɒmɪ] inf pej ◇ adj rojo(ja), comunista. ◇ n rojo m, -ja f, comunista m y f.

commiserate [kə'mɪzəreɪt] vi: to ~ (with) compadecerse (de).

commiseration [kə,mɪzə'reɪʃn] n conmiseración f.

commission [kə'mɪʃn] ◇ n -1. [money, investigative body] comisión f. -2. [piece of work] encargo m. ◇ vt encargar; to ~ sb (to do sthg) encargar a alguien (que haga algo).

commissionaire [kə,mɪʃə'neəʳ] n Br portero m (uniformado).

commissioned officer [kə'mɪʃnd-] n oficial o suboficial (salvo sargentos) del ejército.

commissioner [kə'mɪʃnəʳ] n comisario m, -ria f.

commit [kə'mɪt] (pt & pp -ted, cont -ting) vt -1. [crime, sin etc] cometer. -2. [pledge - money, resources] destinar; to ~ o.s. (to) comprometerse (a). -3. [consign - to mental hospital] ingresar; to ~ sb to prison encarcelar a alguien; to ~ sthg to memory aprender algo de memoria.

commitment [kə'mɪtmənt] n compromiso m.

committed [kə'mɪtɪd] adj comprometido(da); ~ to entregado(da) a.

committee [kə'mɪtɪ] n comisión f, comité m.

commode [kə'məʊd] n [with chamber pot] silla f con orinal incorporado.

commodity [kə'mɒdətɪ] (pl -ies) n mercancía f, producto m.

commodity exchange n bolsa f de mercancías.

common ['kɒmən] ◇ adj -1. [gen]: ~ (to) común (a). -2. [ordinary - man, woman] corriente, de la calle. -3. Br pej [vulgar] vulgar, ordinario(ria). ◇ n campo m común.
◆ **in common** adv en común.

commoner ['kɒmənəʳ] n plebeyo m, -ya f.

common good n: for the ~ para el bien común.

common ground n punto m en común.

common knowledge n: it's ~ es de todos sabido, es del dominio público.

common land n tierra f comunal.

common law n derecho m consuetudinario.

◆ **common-law** adj [wife, husband] de hecho.

commonly ['kɒmənlɪ] adv generalmente comúnmente.

Common Market n: the ~ el Mercado Común.

commonplace ['kɒmənpleɪs] adj corriente común.

common room n sala f de estudiantes.

Commons ['kɒmənz] npl Br: the ~ (la Cámara de) los Comunes.

common sense n sentido m común.

Commonwealth ['kɒmənwelθ] n: the ~ la Commonwealth.

Commonwealth of Independent States n: the ~ la Comunidad de Estados Independientes.

commotion [kə'məʊʃn] n alboroto m.

communal ['kɒmjʊnl] adj comunal.

commune [n 'kɒmjuːn, vb kə'mjuːn] ◇ n comuna f. ◇ vi: to ~ with estar en comunión OR comulgar con.

communicate [kə'mjuːnɪkeɪt] ◇ vt transmitir, comunicar. ◇ vi: to ~ (with) comunicarse (con).

communicating [kə'mjuːnɪkeɪtɪŋ] adj [door] que comunica.

communication [kə,mjuːnɪ'keɪʃn] n -1. [contact] comunicación f. -2. [letter, phone call] comunicado m.
◆ **communications** npl comunicaciones fpl.

communication cord n Br alarma f (de un tren o metro).

communications satellite n satélite m de comunicaciones.

communicative [kə'mjuːnɪkətɪv] adj comunicativo(va).

communicator [kə'mjuːnɪkeɪtəʳ] n: a good/ bad ~ una persona con/sin dotes para comunicar ideas.

communion [kə'mjuːnjən] n [communication] comunión f.
◆ **Communion** n (U) RELIG comunión f.

communiqué [kə'mjuːnɪkeɪ] n comunicado m oficial.

Communism ['kɒmjʊnɪzm] n comunismo m.

Communist ['kɒmjʊnɪst] ◇ adj comunista. ◇ n comunista m y f.

community [kə'mjuːnətɪ] (pl -ies) n comunidad f.

community centre n centro m social.

community charge n Br impuesto municipal pagado por todos los adultos, ≃ contribución f urbana.

community home *n* Br centro *m* docente para delincuentes menores de edad.

community policing *n* fomento de las buenas relaciones entre policía y vecindario.

community service *n* (U) servicio *m* social.

community spirit *n* civismo *m*.

commutable [kə'mju:təbl] *adj* [sentence] conmutable.

commutation ticket [ˌkɒmju:'teɪʃn-] *n* Am billete *m* de abono.

commute [kə'mju:t] ◇ *vt* JUR conmutar. ◇ *vi* [to work] *viajar diariamente al lugar de trabajo, esp en tren.*

commuter [kə'mju:təʳ] *n persona que viaja diariamente al lugar de trabajo, esp en tren.*

commy ['kɒmɪ] (*pl* **-ies**) = **commie.**

Comoro Islands ['kɒmərəʊ-] *npl:* **the** ~ las islas Comores.

compact [*adj & vb* kəm'pækt, *n* 'kɒmpækt] ◇ *adj* [small and neat] compacto(ta). ◇ *n* **-1.** [for face powder] polvera *f*. **-2.** Am [car] utilitario *m*. ◇ *vt* comprimir.

compact disc *n* disco *m* compacto, compact disc *m*.

compact disc player *n* compact *m* (disc), reproductor *m* de discos compactos.

companion [kəm'pænjən] *n* compañero *m*, -ra *f*.

companionable [kəm'pænjənəbl] *adj* [person] sociable; [evening, silence] agradable.

companionship [kəm'pænjənʃɪp] *n* compañerismo *m*.

company ['kʌmpənɪ] (*pl* **-ies**) *n* [gen] compañía *f*; [business] empresa *f*, compañía *f*; **to keep sb** ~ hacer compañía a alguien; **to part** ~ **(with)** separarse (de).

company car *n* coche *m* de la empresa.

company director *n* gerente *m* y *f* OR director *m*, -ra *f* de la empresa.

company secretary *n ejecutivo de una empresa encargado de llevar las cuentas, asuntos legales etc.*

comparable ['kɒmprəbl] *adj:* ~ **(to** OR **with)** comparable (a).

comparative [kəm'pærətɪv] *adj* **-1.** [relative] relativo(va). **-2.** [study] comparado(da). **-3.** GRAMM comparativo(va).

comparatively [kəm'pærətɪvlɪ] *adv* relativamente.

compare [kəm'peəʳ] ◇ *vt:* **to** ~ **sthg/sb (with), to** ~ **sthg/sb (to)** comparar algo/a alguien (con); ~**d with** OR **to** [as opposed to] comparado con; [in comparison with] en comparación con. ◇ *vi:* **to** ~ **(with)** compararse (con); **to** ~ **favourably/unfavourably with** ser mejor/peor que.

comparison [kəm'pærɪsn] *n* comparación *f*; **in** ~ **(with** OR **to)** en comparación (con).

compartment [kəm'pɑ:tmənt] *n* **-1.** [container] compartimento *m*, compartimiento *m*. **-2.** RAIL departamento *m*, compartimento *m*.

compartmentalize, **-ise** [ˌkɒmpɑ:t-'mentəlaɪz] *vt* dividir OR clasificar (en secciones).

compass ['kʌmpəs] *n* **-1.** [magnetic] brújula *f*. **-2.** *fml* [scope] alcance *m*.
◆ **compasses** *npl* compás *m*.

compassion [kəm'pæʃn] *n* compasión *f*.

compassionate [kəm'pæʃənət] *adj* compasivo(va).

compatibility [kəmˌpætə'bɪlətɪ] *n:* ~ **(with)** compatibilidad *f* (con).

compatible [kəm'pætəbl] *adj:* ~ **(with)** compatible (con).

compatriot [kəm'pætrɪət] *n* compatriota *m* y *f*.

compel [kəm'pel] (*pt & pp* **-led**, *cont* **-ling**) *vt* **-1.** [force] obligar; **to** ~ **sb to do sthg** forzar OR obligar a alguien a hacer algo. **-2.** [cause - feeling] despertar; [- event] ocasionar.

compelling [kəm'pelɪŋ] *adj* [forceful] convincente.

compendium [kəm'pendɪəm] (*pl* **-diums** OR **-dia** [-dɪə]) *n* [book] compendio *m*.

compensate ['kɒmpenseɪt] ◇ *vt:* **to** ~ **sb for sthg** [financially] compensar OR indemnizar a alguien por algo. ◇ *vi:* **to** ~ **for sthg** compensar algo.

compensation [ˌkɒmpen'seɪʃn] *n* **-1.** [money]: ~ **(for)** indemnización *f* (por). **-2.** [way of compensating]: ~ **(for)** compensación *f* (por).

compere ['kɒmpeəʳ] Br ◇ *n* presentador *m*, -ra *f*. ◇ *vt* presentar.

compete [kəm'pi:t] *vi* **-1.** [gen]: **to** ~ **(for/in)** competir (por/en); **to** ~ **(with** OR **against)** competir (con). **-2.** [be in conflict] rivalizar.

competence ['kɒmpɪtəns] *n* [proficiency] competencia *f*, aptitud *f*.

competent ['kɒmpɪtənt] *adj* competente, capaz.

competently ['kɒmpɪtəntlɪ] *adv* competentemente.

competing [kəm'pi:tɪŋ] *adj* [conflicting] contrapuesto(ta).

competition [ˌkɒmpɪ'tɪʃn] *n* **-1.** [rivalry] competencia *f*. **-2.** [race, sporting event] competición *f*. **-3.** [contest] concurso *m*.

competitive [kəm'petətɪv] *adj* **-1.** [person, spirit] competidor(ra). **-2.** [match, exam, prices] competitivo(va).

competitively [kəm'petətɪvlɪ] *adv* **-1.** [play] competitivamente. **-2.** COMM [price, market] de forma competitiva.

competitor [kəm'petɪtər] *n* competidor *m*, -ra *f*.

compilation [ˌkɒmpɪ'leɪʃn] *n* recopilación *f*, compilación *f*.

compile [kəm'paɪl] *vt* recopilar, compilar.

complacency [kəm'pleɪsnsɪ] *n* autosatisfacción *f*, autocomplacencia *f*.

complacent [kəm'pleɪsnt] *adj* satisfecho de sí mismo (satisfecha de sí misma), autocomplaciente.

complacently [kəm'pleɪsntlɪ] *adv* con autosatisfacción.

complain [kəm'pleɪn] *vi* **-1.** [moan]: **to ~ (about)** quejarse (de). **-2.** MED: **to ~ of sthg** sufrir algo.

complaining [kəm'pleɪnɪŋ] *adj* protestón(ona).

complaint [kəm'pleɪnt] *n* **-1.** [gen] queja *f*. **-2.** MED dolencia *f*.

complement [*n* 'kɒmplɪmənt, *vb* 'kɒmplɪˌment] ⋄ *n* **-1.** [gen & GRAMM] complemento *m*. **-2.** [number]: **a full ~ of** la totalidad de. ⋄ *vt* complementar.

complementary [ˌkɒmplɪ'mentərɪ] *adj* complementario(ria).

complete [kəm'pliːt] ⋄ *adj* **-1.** [total] total; **a ~ idiot** un auténtico idiota. **-2.** [lacking nothing] completo(ta); **bathroom ~ with shower** baño con ducha. **-3.** [finished] terminado(da). ⋄ *vt* **-1.** [make whole - collection] completar; [- disappointment, amazement] colmar, rematar. **-2.** [finish] terminar, acabar. **-3.** [form] rellenar.

completely [kəm'pliːtlɪ] *adv* completamente.

completion [kəm'pliːʃn] *n* finalización *f*, terminación *f*.

complex ['kɒmpleks] ⋄ *adj* complejo(ja). ⋄ *n* complejo *m*.

complexion [kəm'plekʃn] *n* **-1.** [of face] tez *f*, cutis *m inv*. **-2.** [nature] naturaleza *f*, carácter *m*.

complexity [kəm'pleksətɪ] (*pl* **-ies**) *n* complejidad *f*.

compliance [kəm'plaɪəns] *n* [obedience]: **~ (with)** obediencia *f* (a), acatamiento *m* (de).

compliant [kəm'plaɪənt] *adj* dócil, sumiso(sa).

complicate ['kɒmplɪkeɪt] *vt* complicar.

complicated ['kɒmplɪkeɪtɪd] *adj* complicado(da).

complication [ˌkɒmplɪ'keɪʃn] *n* complicación *f*.

complicity [kəm'plɪsətɪ] *n*: **~ (in)** complicidad *f* (en).

compliment [*n* 'kɒmplɪmənt, *vb* 'kɒmplɪment] ⋄ *n* cumplido *m*. ⋄ *vt*: **to ~ sb (on)** felicitar a alguien (por).

◆ **compliments** *npl fml* saludos *mpl*.

complimentary [ˌkɒmplɪ'mentərɪ] *adj* **-1.** [remark] elogioso(sa); [person] halagador(ra). **-2.** [drink, seats] gratis (*inv*).

complimentary ticket *n* entrada *f* gratuita.

compliments slip *n* nota *f* OR tarjeta *f* de saludos.

comply [kəm'plaɪ] (*pt* & *pp* **-ied**) *vi*: **to ~ with sthg** [standards] cumplir (con) algo; [request] acceder a algo; [law] acatar algo.

component [kəm'pəʊnənt] *n* [gen] elemento *m*, parte *f* integrante; TECH pieza *f*.

compose [kəm'pəʊz] *vt* **-1.** [constitute] componer; **to be ~d of** estar compuesto OR componerse de. **-2.** [music, poem, letter] componer. **-3.** [calm]: **to ~ o.s.** calmarse, tranquilizarse.

composed [kəm'pəʊzd] *adj* tranquilo(la).

composer [kəm'pəʊzər] *n* compositor *m*, -ra *f*.

composite ['kɒmpəzɪt] ⋄ *adj* compuesto(ta). ⋄ *n* combinación *f*, conjunto *m*.

composition [ˌkɒmpə'zɪʃn] *n* **-1.** [gen] composición *f*. **-2.** [essay] redacción *f*.

compost [*Br* 'kɒmpɒst, *Am* 'kɒmpəʊst] *n* abono *m*.

composure [kəm'pəʊʒər] *n* calma *f*.

compound [*adj* & *n* 'kɒmpaʊnd, *vb* kəm'paʊnd] ⋄ *adj* [eye] compuesto(ta); [problem] complejo(ja). ⋄ *n* **-1.** [gen & CHEM] compuesto *m*. **-2.** [enclosed area] recinto *m*. ⋄ *vt* **-1.** [mixture, substance]: **to be ~ed of** componerse de. **-2.** [exacerbate] agravar.

compound fracture *n* fractura *f* complicada.

compound interest *n* interés *m* compuesto.

comprehend [ˌkɒmprɪ'hend] *vt* comprender.

comprehension [ˌkɒmprɪ'henʃn] *n* comprensión *f*.

comprehensive [ˌkɒmprɪ'hensɪv] ⋄ *adj* **-1.** [wide-ranging] amplio(plia). **-2.** [insurance] a todo riesgo. ⋄ *n Br* = **comprehensive school**.

comprehensively [ˌkɒmprɪ'hensɪvlɪ] *adv* [cover] extensamente; [study] minuciosamente; [beat] abrumadoramente.

comprehensive school *n* instituto de enseñanza media no selectiva en Gran Bretaña.

compress [kəm'pres] *vt* **-1.** [squeeze, press] comprimir. **-2.** [shorten] reducir.

compression [kəm'preʃn] *n* **-1.** [of air] compresión *f*. **-2.** [of text] reducción *f*.

comprise [kəm'praɪz] *vt* **-1.** [consist of] comprender. **-2.** [form] constituir.

compromise ['kɒmprəmaɪz] ◇ *n* arreglo *m*, término *m* medio. ◇ *vt* comprometer; **to ~ o.s.** comprometerse. ◇ *vi* llegar a un arreglo, transigir.

compromising ['kɒmprəmaɪzɪŋ] *adj* comprometedor(ra).

compulsion [kəm'pʌlʃn] *n* **-1.** [strong desire] ganas *fpl* irrefrenables. **-2.** (U) [force] obligación *f*.

compulsive [kəm'pʌlsɪv] *adj* **-1.** [gambler] empedernido(da); [liar] compulsivo(va). **-2.** [fascinating, compelling] absorbente.

compulsory [kəm'pʌlsərɪ] *adj* [gen] obligatorio(ria); [retirement] forzoso(sa).

compulsory purchase *n Br* compra *f* forzosa.

compunction [kəm'pʌŋkʃn] *n* (U) escrúpulos *mpl*, reparos *mpl*.

computation [ˌkɒmpjuː'teɪʃn] *n* cálculo *m*.

compute [kəm'pjuːt] *vt* computar, calcular.

computer [kəm'pjuːtər] ◇ *n* ordenador *m*. ◇ *comp* de ordenadores.

computer dating [-'deɪtɪŋ] *n* cita organizada por una agencia matrimonial a través de ordenador.

computer game *n* videojuego *m*.

computerization [kəmˌpjuːtəraɪ'zeɪʃn] *n* informatización *f*.

computerize, -ise [kəm'pjuːtəraɪz] *vt* informatizar.

computerized [kəm'pjuːtəraɪzd] *adj* informatizado(da), computerizado(da).

computer language *n* lenguaje *m* de ordenador.

computer-literate *adj* con conocimientos de informática a nivel usuario.

computing [kəm'pjuːtɪŋ], **computer science** *n* informática *f*.

comrade ['kɒmreɪd] *n* camarada *m y f*.

comradeship ['kɒmreɪdʃɪp] *n* camaradería *f*.

comsat ['kɒmsæt] = **communications satellite**.

con [kɒn] (*pt & pp* **-ned**, *cont* **-ning**) *inf* ◇ *n* **-1.** [trick] timo *m*, estafa *f*. **-2.** *prison sl* presidiario *m*, -ria *f*. ◇ *vt* timar, estafar; **to ~ sb out of sthg** timarle algo a alguien; **to ~ sb into doing sthg** engañar a alguien para que haga algo.

concave [ˌkɒn'keɪv] *adj* concavo(va).

conceal [kən'siːl] *vt* [object, substance, information] ocultar; [feelings] disimular; **to ~ sthg from sb** ocultarle algo a alguien.

concede [kən'siːd] ◇ *vt* [defeat, a point] admitir, reconocer. ◇ *vi* [gen] ceder; [in sports, chess] rendirse.

conceit [kən'siːt] *n* vanidad *f*, arrogancia *f*.

conceited [kən'siːtɪd] *adj* engreído(da), vanidoso(sa).

conceivable [kən'siːvəbl] *adj* concebible, imaginable.

conceivably [kən'siːvəblɪ] *adv* posiblemente; **I can't ~ do that** no puedo hacer eso por nada del mundo.

conceive [kən'siːv] ◇ *vt* concebir. ◇ *vi* **-1.** MED concebir. **-2.** [imagine]: **to ~ of sthg** imaginarse algo.

concentrate ['kɒnsəntreɪt] ◇ *vt* concentrar. ◇ *vi*: **to ~ (on)** concentrarse (en).

concentrated ['kɒnsəntreɪtɪd] *adj* **-1.** [fruit juice, washing powder] concentrado(da). **-2.** [effort] decidido(da), intenso(sa).

concentration [ˌkɒnsən'treɪʃn] *n* concentración *f*.

concentration camp *n* campo *m* de concentración.

concentric [kən'sentrɪk] *adj* concéntrico(ca).

concept ['kɒnsept] *n* concepto *m*.

conception [kən'sepʃn] *n* **-1.** [gen] concepción *f*. **-2.** [idea] concepto *m*, idea *f*.

conceptualize, -ise [kən'septʃʊəlaɪz] *vt* formarse un concepto de, conceptualizar.

concern [kən'sɜːn] ◇ *n* **-1.** [worry, anxiety] preocupación *f*. **-2.** [matter of interest] asunto *m*; **it's no ~ of yours** no es asunto tuyo. **-3.** [company] negocio *m*, empresa *f*. ◇ *vt* **-1.** [worry] preocupar; **to be ~ed about** preocuparse por. **-2.** [involve] concernir; **to be ~ed with** [subj: person] estar involucrado en; **to ~ o.s. with sthg** preocuparse de OR por algo; **as far as ... is ~ed** por lo que a ... respecta. **-3.** [book, film etc] tratar de.

concerning [kən'sɜːnɪŋ] *prep* sobre, acerca de.

concert ['kɒnsət] *n* concierto *m*.

◆ **in concert** *adv* **-1.** MUS en directo, en concierto. **-2.** *fml* [acting as one] conjuntamente.

concerted [kən'sɜːtɪd] *adj* en común, conjunto(ta).

concertgoer ['kɒnsətˌgəʊər] *n* asiduo *m*, -dua *f* a conciertos.

concert hall *n* sala *f* de conciertos.

concertina [ˌkɒnsə'tiːnə] (*pt & pp* **-ed**, *cont* **-ing**) ◇ *n* concertina *f*. ◇ *vi* quedarse hecho(cha) un acordeón.

concerto [kən'tʃeətəʊ] (*pl* **-s**) *n* concierto *m*.

concession [kən'seʃn] *n* **-1.** [allowance, franchise] concesión *f*. **-2.** [special price] descuento *m*, rebaja *f*; [reduced ticket] entrada *f* de descuento.

concessionaire [kən,seʃə'neə'] *n* concesionario *m*, -ria *f*.

concessionary [kən'seʃnərı] *adj* de descuento, especial.

conciliation [kən,sılı'eıʃn] *n* conciliación *f*.

conciliatory [kən'sılıətrı] *adj* conciliador(ra).

concise [kən'saıs] *adj* conciso(sa).

concisely [kən'saıslı] *adv* de manera concisa.

conclave ['kɒŋkleıv] *n* cónclave *m*.

conclude [kən'kluːd] ◇ *vt* **-1.** [bring to an end] concluir, terminar. **-2.** [deduce]: **to ~ (that)** concluir que. **-3.** [agreement] llegar a; [business deal] cerrar; [treaty] firmar. ◇ *vi* terminar, concluir.

conclusion [kən'kluːʒn] *n* **-1.** [decision] conclusión *f*; **to jump to the wrong ~** sacar a la ligera una conclusión errónea. **-2.** [ending] final *m*; **a foregone ~** un final esperado OR anticipado. **-3.** [of business deal] cierre *m*; [of treaty] firma *f*; [of agreement] alcance *m*.

conclusive [kən'kluːsıv] *adj* concluyente, irrebatible.

concoct [kən'kɒkt] *vt* **-1.** [excuse, story] ingeniar. **-2.** [food] confeccionar; [drink] preparar.

concoction [kən'kɒkʃn] *n* [drink] brebaje *m*; [food] mezcla *f*.

concord ['kɒŋkɔːd] *n* concordia *f*.

concourse ['kɒŋkɔːs] *n* [of station etc] vestíbulo *m*.

concrete ['kɒŋkriːt] ◇ *adj* [definite, real] concreto(ta). ◇ *n* hormigón *m*, concreto *m* *Amer*. ◇ *comp* [made of concrete] de hormigón. ◇ *vt* cubrir con hormigón.

concrete mixer *n* hormigonera *f*.

concubine ['kɒŋkjʊbaın] *n* concubina *f*.

concur [kən'kɜː'] (*pt* & *pp* **-red**, *cont* **-ring**) *vi* [agree]: **to ~ (with)** estar de acuerdo OR coincidir (con).

concurrently [kən'kʌrəntlı] *adv* simultáneamente, al mismo tiempo.

concussed [kən'kʌst] *adj* con conmoción cerebral.

concussion [kən'kʌʃn] *n* conmoción *f* cerebral.

condemn [kən'dem] *vt* **-1.** [gen]: **to ~ sb (for/to)** condenar a alguien (por/a). **-2.** [building] declarar en ruinas.

condemnation [,kɒndem'neıʃn] *n* condena *f*.

condemned [kən'demd] *adj* **-1.** JUR [condemned to death] condenado(da) a muerte. **-2.** [building] declarado(da) en ruinas.

condensation [,kɒnden'seıʃn] *n* [on glass] vaho *m*.

condense [kən'dens] ◇ *vt* condensar. ◇ *vi* condensarse.

condensed milk [kən'denst-] *n* leche *f* condensada.

condescend [,kɒndı'send] *vi* **-1.** [talk down]: **to ~ to sb** hablar a alguien con tono de superioridad. **-2.** [deign]: **to ~ to do sthg** condescender OR rebajarse a hacer algo.

condescending [,kɒndı'sendıŋ] *adj* altanero(ra), altivo(va).

condiment ['kɒndımənt] *n* *fml* condimento *m*.

condition [kən'dıʃn] ◇ *n* **-1.** [state] estado *m*; **in good/bad ~** en buen/mal estado; **to be out of ~** no estar en forma. **-2.** MED [disease, complaint] afección *f*. **-3.** [provision] condición *f*; **on ~ that** a condición de que; **on one ~** con una condición. ◇ *vt* **-1.** [gen] condicionar. **-2.** [hair] acondicionar.
◆ **conditions** *npl* condiciones *fpl*.

conditional [kən'dıʃənl] *adj* condicional; **to be ~ on** OR **upon** depender de.

conditionally [kən'dıʃnəlı] *adv* con reservas.

conditioner [kən'dıʃnə'] *n* suavizante *m*.

conditioning [kən'dıʃnıŋ] *n* (*U*) condicionamientos *mpl*, condicionantes *mpl*.

condo ['kɒndəʊ] *n* *inf abbr of* **condominium**.

condolences [kən'dəʊlənsız] *npl* pésame *m*; **to offer one's ~** dar uno su más sentido pésame.

condom ['kɒndəm] *n* condón *m*.

condominium [,kɒndə'mınıəm] *n* *Am* **-1.** [apartment] piso *m*, apartamento *m*. **-2.** [apartment block] bloque *m* de pisos OR apartamentos.

condone [kən'dəʊn] *vt* perdonar, tolerar.

condor ['kɒndɔː'] *n* cóndor *m*.

conducive [kən'djuːsıv] *adj*: **to ~ to** favorable para.

conduct [*n* 'kɒndʌkt, *vb* kən'dʌkt] ◇ *n* **-1.** [behaviour] conducta *f*. **-2.** [carrying out] dirección *f*. ◇ *vt* **-1.** [carry out] dirigir, llevar a cabo. **-2.** [behave]: **to ~ o.s. well/badly** comportarse bien/mal. **-3.** MUS dirigir. **-4.** PHYSICS conducir. ◇ *vi* [lead orchestra, choir] dirigir.

conducted tour [kən'dʌktıd-] *n* excursión *f* con guía.

conductor [kən'dʌktəʳ] *n* **-1.** [of orchestra, choir] director *m*, -ra *f*. **-2.** [on bus] cobrador *m*. **-3.** *Am* [on train] revisor *m*, -ra *f*.

conductress [kən'dʌktrɪs] *n* cobradora *f*.

conduit ['kɒndɪt] *n* conducto *m*.

cone [kəʊn] *n* **-1.** [shape] cono *m*. **-2.** [for ice cream] cucurucho *m*. **-3.** [from tree] piña *f*.
◆ **cone off** *vt sep Br* cortar temporalmente (*un carril o carretera*) *con pivotes*.

confectioner [kən'fekʃnəʳ] *n* confitero *m*, -ra *f*; ~'s (shop) confitería *f*.

confectionery [kən'fekʃnərɪ] *n* (U) dulces *mpl*, golosinas *fpl*.

confederation [kən,fedə'reɪʃn] *n* confederación *f*.

Confederation of British Industry *n*: **the** ~ *organización patronal británica*, ≃ la CEOE.

confer [kən'fɜːʳ] (*pt* & *pp* **-red**, *cont* **-ring**) ◇ *vt fml*: **to** ~ **sthg (on)** otorgar OR conferir algo (a). ◇ *vi*: **to** ~ **(with)** consultar (con).

conference ['kɒnfərəns] *n* congreso *m*, conferencia *f*; **in** ~ reunido.

conference call *n sistema de comunicación telefónica entre tres o más personas.*

conference centre *n* centro *m* de congresos.

conference hall *n* sala *f* de conferencias OR congresos.

conferencing ['kɒnfərənsɪŋ] *n servicio que facilita comunicación telefónica entre tres o más personas.*

confess [kən'fes] ◇ *vt* confesar; **to** ~ **(that)** admitir OR confesar que. ◇ *vi* **-1.** [to crime] confesarse; **to** ~ **to sthg** confesar algo. **-2.** [admit]: **to** ~ **to sthg** admitir algo.

confession [kən'feʃn] *n* confesión *f*.

confessional [kən'feʃənl] *n* confesionario *m*.

confetti [kən'fetɪ] *n* confeti *m*.

confidant [,kɒnfɪ'dænt] *n* confidente *m*.

confidante [,kɒnfɪ'dænt] *n* confidente *f*.

confide [kən'faɪd] ◇ *vt* confiar. ◇ *vi*: **to** ~ **(in)** confiar (en).

confidence ['kɒnfɪdəns] *n* **-1.** [self-assurance] confianza *f* OR seguridad *f* (en sí mismo/misma *f*). **-2.** [trust] confianza *f*; **to have** ~ **in sb** tener confianza en alguien. **-3.** [secrecy]: **in** ~ en secreto. **-4.** [secret] intimidad *f*, secreto *m*.

confidence trick *n* timo *m*, estafa *f*.

confident ['kɒnfɪdənt] *adj* **-1.** [self-assured - person] seguro de sí mismo (segura de sí misma); [- smile, attitude] confiado(da). **-2.** [sure]: ~ **(of)** seguro(ra) (de).

confidential [,kɒnfɪ'denʃl] *adj* [gen] confidencial; [person] de confianza.

confidentiality ['kɒnfɪ,denʃɪ'ælətɪ] *n* confidencialidad *f*.

confidentially [,kɒnfɪ'denʃəlɪ] *adv* **-1.** [secretly] en confianza. **-2.** [secretively] confidencialmente.

confidently ['kɒnfɪdəntlɪ] *adv* **-1.** [with self-assurance] con seguridad. **-2.** [trustingly] con toda confianza.

configuration [kən,fɪgə'reɪʃn] *n* [gen & COM-PUT] configuración *f*.

confine [kən'faɪn] *vt* **-1.** [limit, restrict] limitar, restringir; **to be** ~**d to** limitarse a; **to** ~ **o.s. to** limitarse a. **-2.** [shut up] recluir, encerrar.
◆ **confines** *npl* confines *mpl*, límites *mpl*.

confined [kən'faɪnd] *adj* reducido(da), limitado(da).

confinement [kən'faɪnmənt] *n* **-1.** [imprisonment] reclusión *f*. **-2.** *dated* MED hospitalización *f* preparto.

confirm [kən'fɜːm] *vt* confirmar.

confirmation [,kɒnfə'meɪʃn] *n* confirmación *f*.

confirmed [kən'fɜːmd] *adj* [non-smoker] inveterado(da); [bachelor] empedernido.

confiscate ['kɒnfɪskeɪt] *vt* confiscar.

confiscation [,kɒnfɪ'skeɪʃn] *n* confiscación *f*, incautación *f*.

conflagration [,kɒnflə'greɪʃn] *n fml* conflagración *f*.

conflict [*n* 'kɒnflɪkt, *vb* kən'flɪkt] ◇ *n* conflicto *m*; ~ **of interest** conflicto de intereses. ◇ *vi*: **to** ~ **(with)** estar en desacuerdo (con).

conflicting [kən'flɪktɪŋ] *adj* contrapuesto(ta).

conform [kən'fɔːm] *vi* **-1.** [behave as expected] amoldarse a las normas sociales. **-2.** [be in accordance]: **to** ~ **(to** OR **with)** [expectations] corresponder (a); [rules] ajustarse (a).

conformist [kən'fɔːmɪst] ◇ *adj* conformista. ◇ *n* conformista *m y f*.

conformity [kən'fɔːmətɪ] *n*: ~ **(to** OR **with)** conformidad *f* (con).

confound [kən'faʊnd] *vt* [confuse, defeat] confundir, desconcertar.

confounded [kən'faʊndɪd] *adj inf* maldito(ta).

confront [kən'frʌnt] *vt* **-1.** [problem, task] afrontar, hacer frente a. **-2.** [subj: problem, task] presentarse a. **-3.** [enemy etc] enfrentarse con. **-4.** [challenge]: **to** ~ **sb (with)** poner a alguien cara a cara (con).

confrontation [,kɒnfrʌn'teɪʃn] *n* enfrentamiento *m*, confrontación *f*.

confuse [kən'fjuːz] *vt* **-1.** [bewilder] desconcertar. **-2.** [mix up]: **to** ~ **(with)** confundir (con). **-3.** [complicate, make less clear] complicar.

confused [kənˈfjuːzd] *adj* **-1.** [not clear] confuso(sa). **-2.** [bewildered] desconcertado(da).

confusing [kənˈfjuːzɪŋ] *adj* confuso(sa).

confusion [kənˈfjuːʒn] *n* **-1.** [gen] confusión *f*. **-2.** [of person] turbación *f*, desconcierto *m*.

conga [ˈkɒŋgə] *n*: **the ~** la conga.

congeal [kənˈdʒiːl] *vi* coagularse.

congenial [kənˈdʒiːnjəl] *adj* ameno(na), agradable.

congenital [kənˈdʒenɪtl] *adj* MED congénito(ta).

conger eel [ˈkɒŋgə-] *n* congrio *m*.

congested [kənˈdʒestɪd] *adj* **-1.** [area] superpoblado(da); [road] congestionado(da), colapsado(da). **-2.** MED congestionado(da).

congestion [kənˈdʒestʃn] *n* (*U*) **-1.** [of traffic] retención *f*, congestión *f*. **-2.** MED congestión *f*.

conglomerate [kənˈglɒmərət] *n* COMM conglomerado *m*.

conglomeration [kən,glɒməˈreɪʃn] *n* *fml* conglomeración *f*.

Congo [ˈkɒŋgəʊ] *n* [country, river]: **the ~** el Congo.

Congolese [,kɒŋgəˈliːz] ◇ *adj* congoleño(ña). ◇ *n* congoleño *m*, -ña *f*.

congratulate [kənˈgrætʃʊleɪt] *vt*: **to ~ sb (on)** felicitar a alguien (por); **to ~ o.s. (on)** sentirse satisfecho(cha) (con).

congratulations [kən,grætʃʊˈleɪʃənz] ◇ *npl* felicitaciones *fpl*. ◇ *excl* ¡enhorabuena!

congratulatory [kənˈgrætʃʊlətrɪ] *adj* de felicitación.

congregate [ˈkɒŋgrɪgeɪt] *vi* [people] congregarse; [animals] juntarse.

congregation [,kɒŋgrɪˈgeɪʃn] *n* RELIG feligreses *mpl*.

congress [ˈkɒŋgres] *n* congreso *m*.
◆ **Congress** *n* [in US]: **(the) Congress** el Congreso.

CONGRESS:

El Congreso, órgano legislativo estadounidense, está formado por el Senado y la Cámara de Representantes. Un proyecto de ley debe ser aprobado obligatoriamente y de manera separada por las dos cámaras

congressional [kənˈgreʃənl] *adj* Am POL del Congreso.

congressman [ˈkɒŋgresmən] (*pl* **-men** [-mən]) *n* miembro *m* del Congreso.

congresswoman [ˈkɒŋgres,wʊmən] (*pl* **-women** [-,wɪmɪn]) *n* miembro *f* del Congreso.

conical [ˈkɒnɪkl] *adj* cónico(ca).

conifer [ˈkɒnɪfə-] *n* conífera *f*.

coniferous [kəˈnɪfərəs] *adj* conífero(ra).

conjecture [kənˈdʒektʃə-] ◇ *n* conjetura *f*. ◇ *vt*: **to ~ (that)** conjeturar que. ◇ *vi* hacer conjeturas.

conjugal [ˈkɒndʒʊgl] *adj* conyugal.

conjugate [ˈkɒndʒʊgeɪt] *vt* conjugar.

conjugation [,kɒndʒʊˈgeɪʃn] *n* conjugación *f*.

conjunction [kənˈdʒʌŋkʃn] *n* **-1.** GRAMM conjunción *f*. **-2.** [combination]: **in ~ with** juntamente con.

conjunctivitis [kən,dʒʌŋktɪˈvaɪtɪs] *n* conjuntivitis *f inv*.

conjure [ˈkʌndʒə-] ◇ *vt* hacer aparecer. ◇ *vi* hacer juegos de manos.
◆ **conjure up** *vt sep* [evoke] evocar.

conjurer [ˈkʌndʒərə-] *n* prestidigitador *m*, -ra *f*.

conjuring trick [ˈkʌndʒərɪŋ-] *n* juego *m* de manos.

conjuror [ˈkʌndʒərə-] = **conjurer**.

conk [kɒŋk] *n inf* [nose] napia *f*.
◆ **conk out** *vi inf* escacharrarse.

conker [ˈkɒŋkə-] *n* Br castaña *f* (*del castaño de Indias*).

conman [ˈkɒnmæn] (*pl* **-men** [-men]) *n* estafador *m*, timador *m*.

connect [kəˈnekt] ◇ *vt* **-1.** [join]: **to ~ sthg (to)** unir algo (con). **-2.** [on telephone]: **I'll ~ you now** ahora le paso OR pongo. **-3.** [associate]: **to ~ sthg/sb (with)** asociar algo/a alguien (con). **-4.** ELEC: **to ~ sthg to** conectar algo a. ◇ *vi* [train, plane, bus]: **to ~ (with)** enlazar (con).

connected [kəˈnektɪd] *adj* [related]: **~ (with)** relacionado(da) (con).

Connecticut [kəˈnetɪkət] *n* Connecticut.

connecting [kəˈnektɪŋ] *adj* de enlace.

connection [kəˈnekʃn] *n* **-1.** [gen & ELEC]: **~ (between/with)** conexión *f* (entre/con); **in ~ with** con relación OR respecto a. **-2.** [plane, train, bus] enlace *m*. **-3.** [professional acquaintance] contacto *m*; **to have good ~s** tener mucho enchufe.

connective tissue [kəˈnektɪv-] *n* tejido *m* conjuntivo.

connexion [kəˈnekʃn] *n* Br = **connection**.

connive [kəˈnaɪv] *vi* **-1.** [plot]: **to ~ (with)** confabularse (con). **-2.** [allow to happen]: **to ~ at sthg** hacer la vista gorda con algo.

conniving [kəˈnaɪvɪŋ] *adj* intrigante.

connoisseur [,kɒnəˈsɜː-] *n* entendido *m*, -da *f*, experto *m*, -ta *f*.

connotation [,kɒnəˈteɪʃn] *n* connotación *f*.

conquer ['kɒŋkə'] vt **-1.** [take by force] conquistar. **-2.** [gain control of, overcome] doblegar, vencer.

conqueror ['kɒŋkərə'] n conquistador m, -ra f.

conquest ['kɒŋkwest] n conquista f.

cons [kɒnz] npl **-1.** Br inf: all mod ~ con todas las comodidades. **-2.** → pro.

Cons. abbr of **Conservative**.

conscience ['kɒnʃəns] n conciencia f; **in all** ~ en conciencia.

conscientious [,kɒnʃɪ'enʃəs] adj concienzudo(da).

conscientiously [,kɒnʃɪ'enʃəslɪ] adv a conciencia.

conscientiousness [,kɒnʃɪ'enʃəsnɪs] n meticulosidad f, escrupulosidad f.

conscientious objector n objetor m, -ra f de conciencia.

conscious ['kɒnʃəs] adj **-1.** [gen] consciente; **to be** ~ **of** ser consciente de. **-2.** [intentional] deliberado(da).

consciously ['kɒnʃəslɪ] adv deliberadamente.

consciousness ['kɒnʃəsnɪs] n **-1.** [gen] conciencia f. **-2.** [state of being awake] conocimiento m; **to lose/regain** ~ perder/recobrar el conocimiento.

conscript [n 'kɒnskrɪpt, vb kən'skrɪpt] ◇ n recluta m y f. ◇ vt reclutar.

conscription [kən'skrɪpʃn] n servicio m militar obligatorio.

consecrate ['kɒnsɪkreɪt] vt RELIG & fig consagrar.

consecration [,kɒnsɪ'kreɪʃn] n RELIG consagración f.

consecutive [kən'sekjʊtɪv] adj consecutivo(va); **on three** ~ **days** tres días seguidos.

consecutively [kən'sekjʊtɪvlɪ] adv consecutivamente.

consensus [kən'sensəs] n consenso m.

consent [kən'sent] ◇ n (U) **-1.** [permission] consentimiento m. **-2.** [agreement] acuerdo m; **by general** OR **common** ~ de común acuerdo. ◇ vi: **to** ~ **(to)** consentir (en).

consenting [kən'sentɪŋ] adj: ~ **adults** adultos, esp homosexuales, que aceptan tener relaciones sexuales.

consequence ['kɒnsɪkwəns] n **-1.** [result] consecuencia f; **in** ~ por consiguiente. **-2.** [importance] importancia f.

consequent ['kɒnsɪkwənt] adj consiguiente.

consequently ['kɒnsɪkwəntlɪ] adv por consiguiente.

conservation [,kɒnsə'veɪʃn] n conservación f.

conservation area n zona f protegida.

conservationist [,kɒnsə'veɪʃənɪst] n ecologista m y f (preocupado por la conservación de la naturaleza).

conservatism [kən'sɜːvətɪzm] n conservadurismo m.

◆ **Conservatism** n POL conservadurismo m.

conservative [kən'sɜːvətɪv] ◇ adj **-1.** [not modern] conservador(ra). **-2.** [estimate, guess] moderado(da). ◇ n conservador m, -ra f.

◆ **Conservative** POL ◇ adj conservador(ra). ◇ n conservador m, -ra f.

Conservative Party n: **the** ~ el partido Conservador británico.

conservatory [kən'sɜːvətrɪ] (pl **-ies**) n pequeña habitación acristalada aneja a la casa.

conserve [n 'kɒnsɜːv, vb kən'sɜːv] ◇ n compota f. ◇ vt [energy, supplies] ahorrar; [nature, wildlife] conservar, preservar.

consider [kən'sɪdə'] vt **-1.** [gen] considerar; **to** ~ **doing sthg** pensarse si hacer algo. **-2.** [take into account] tener en cuenta; **all things** ~ed teniéndolo todo en cuenta.

considerable [kən'sɪdrəbl] adj considerable.

considerably [kən'sɪdrəblɪ] adv considerablemente, sustancialmente.

considerate [kən'sɪdərət] adj considerado(da).

consideration [kən,sɪdə'reɪʃn] n consideración f; **to take sthg into** ~ tomar OR tener algo en cuenta; **several options are under** ~ se están considerando varias posibilidades.

considered [kən'sɪdəd] adj: **my** ~ **opinion is that ...** tras pensarlo detenidamente creo que ....

considering [kən'sɪdərɪŋ] ◇ prep habida cuenta de, contando con. ◇ conj después de todo.

consign [kən'saɪn] vt: **to** ~ **sthg/sb to** relegar algo/a alguien a.

consignee [,kɒnsaɪ'niː] n consignatario m, -ria f.

consignment [,kən'saɪnmənt] n remesa f.

consignment note n talón m de expedición.

consignor [kən'saɪnə'] n consignador m, -ra f.

consist [kən'sɪst]

◆ **consist in** vt fus consistir en, basarse en.

◆ **consist of** vt fus consistir en, constar de.

consistency [kən'sɪstənsɪ] (pl **-ies**) n **-1.** [coherence - of behaviour, policy] consecuen-

cia f, coherencia f; [of work] regularidad f.
-2. [texture] consistencia f.

consistent [kən'sɪstənt] adj **-1.** [regular] constante. **-2.** [coherent]: ~ **(with)** consecuente (con).

consistently [kən'sɪstəntlɪ] adv **-1.** [without exception] constantemente. **-2.** [argue, reason] consecuentemente.

consolation [ˌkɒnsə'leɪʃn] n consuelo m.

consolation prize n premio m de consolación.

console [n 'kɒnsəʊl, vt kən'səʊl] ◇ n consola f. ◇ vt consolar; **to ~ o.s. with the thought that ...** consolarse pensando que ....

consolidate [kən'sɒlɪdeɪt] ◇ vt **-1.** [strengthen] consolidar. **-2.** [merge] fusionar. ◇ vi fusionarse.

consolidation [kənˌsɒlɪ'deɪʃn] n (U) **-1.** [strengthening] consolidación f. **-2.** [merging] fusión f.

consols ['kɒnsəlz] npl Br bonos mpl consolidados.

consommé [Br kən'sɒmeɪ, Am ˌkɒnsə'meɪ] n consomé m.

consonant ['kɒnsənənt] n consonante f.

consort [vb kən'sɔːt, n 'kɒnsɔːt] ◇ vi fml: **to ~ with sb** asociarse OR frecuentar a alguien. ◇ n consorte m y f.

consortium [kən'sɔːtjəm] (pl -tiums OR -tia [-tjə]) n consorcio m.

conspicuous [kən'spɪkjʊəs] adj [building] visible; [colour] llamativo(va); **he felt ~** le pareció que llamaba mucho la atención.

conspicuously [kən'spɪkjʊəslɪ] adv ostentosamente.

conspiracy [kən'spɪrəsɪ] (pl -ies) n conspiración f.

conspirator [kən'spɪrətə'] n conspirador m, -ra f.

conspiratorial [kənˌspɪrə'tɔːrɪəl] adj cómplice.

conspire [kən'spaɪə'] ◇ vt: **to ~ to do sthg** conspirar para hacer algo. ◇ vi **-1.** [plan secretly]: **to ~ (against/with)** conspirar (contra/con). **-2.** [combine] confabularse.

constable ['kʌnstəbl] n policía m y f, agente m y f.

constabulary [kən'stæbjʊlərɪ] (pl -ies) n policía f (de una zona determinada).

constancy ['kɒnstənsɪ] n **-1.** [of purpose] constancia f; [of temperature] estabilidad f. **-2.** literary [faithfulness] fidelidad f.

constant ['kɒnstənt] adj **-1.** [gen] constante. **-2.** literary [faithful] fiel.

constantly ['kɒnstəntlɪ] adv [forever] constantemente.

constellation [ˌkɒnstə'leɪʃn] n constelación f.

consternation [ˌkɒnstə'neɪʃn] n consternación f.

constipated ['kɒnstɪpeɪtɪd] adj estreñido(da).

constipation [ˌkɒnstɪ'peɪʃn] n estreñimiento m.

constituency [kən'stɪtjʊənsɪ] (pl -ies) n [area] distrito m electoral, circunscripción f.

constituency party n Br delegación f local de un partido.

constituent [kən'stɪtjʊənt] ◇ adj integrante, constituyente. ◇ n **-1.** [voter] votante m y f, elector m, -ra f. **-2.** [element] componente m, constituyente m.

constitute ['kɒnstɪtjuːt] vt constituir.

constitution [ˌkɒnstɪ'tjuːʃn] n constitución f.
◆ **Constitution** n: the Constitution [in US] la Constitución.

CONSTITUTION:
Cabe destacar que la constitución británica, a diferencia de la estadounidense (texto escrito y definitivo), no es un documento propiamente dicho, sino el resultado virtual de la sucesión de leyes a lo largo de la historia con base en el principio de jurisprudencia

constitutional [ˌkɒnstɪ'tjuːʃənl] adj constitucional.

constrain [kən'streɪn] vt **-1.** [coerce]: **to ~ sb to do sthg** forzar a alguien a hacer algo. **-2.** [restrict] coartar, constreñir.

constrained [kən'streɪnd] adj [smile] forzado(da); [manner] inhibido(da).

constraint [kən'streɪnt] n **-1.** [restriction]: ~ **(on)** limitación f (de). **-2.** [self-control] autocontrol m. **-3.** [coercion] coacción f, constreñimiento m.

constrict [kən'strɪkt] vt **-1.** [compress] apretar. **-2.** [limit] limitar.

constricting [kən'strɪktɪŋ] adj **-1.** [clothes] que aprieta. **-2.** [circumstances, lifestyle] opresivo(va).

construct [vb kən'strʌkt, n 'kɒnstrʌkt] ◇ vt lit & fig construir. ◇ n fml concepto m.

construction [kən'strʌkʃn] ◇ n construcción f; **under ~** en construcción. ◇ comp de la construcción; **~ site** obra f.

construction industry n (industria f de la) construcción f.

constructive [kən'strʌktɪv] adj constructivo(va).

constructively [kən'strʌktɪvlɪ] *adv* de forma constructiva.

construe [kən'struː] *vt fml*: **to ~ sthg as** interpretar algo como.

consul ['kɒnsəl] *n* cónsul *m y f*.

consular ['kɒnsjʊləʳ] *adj* consular.

consulate ['kɒnsjʊlət] *n* consulado *m*.

consult [kən'sʌlt] ◇ *vt* consultar. ◇ *vi*: **to ~ with sb** consultar a OR con alguien.

consultancy [kən'sʌltənsɪ] (*pl* **-ies**) *n* [company] consultorio *m*.

consultancy fee *n* honorarios *mpl* por la consulta.

consultant [kən'sʌltənt] *n* **-1.** [expert] asesor *m*, **-ra** *f*. **-2.** *Br* [hospital doctor] (médico) especialista *m*, (médica) especialista *f*.

consultation [ˌkɒnsəl'teɪʃn] *n* **-1.** [gen] consulta *f*. **-2.** [discussion] discusión *f*.

consulting room [kən'sʌltɪŋ-] *n* consultorio *m*, consulta *f*.

consume [kən'sjuːm] *vt lit & fig* consumir.

consumer [kən'sjuːməʳ] ◇ *n* consumidor *m*, **-ra** *f*. ◇ *comp* [protection, rights] del consumidor; [advice] al consumidor.

consumer credit *n* (*U*) crédito *m* al consumidor.

consumer durables *npl* bienes *mpl* de consumo duraderos.

consumer goods *npl* bienes *mpl* de consumo.

consumerism [kən'sjuːmərɪzm] *n usu pej* [theory] consumismo *m*.

consumer society *n* sociedad *f* de consumo.

consumer spending *n* gasto *m* de bienes de consumo.

consummate [*adj* kən'sʌmət, *vb* 'kɒnsəmeɪt] ◇ *adj* **-1.** [skill, ease] absoluto(ta). **-2.** [liar, politician, snob] consumado(da). ◇ *vt* **-1.** [marriage] consumar. **-2.** [deal] cerrar; [achievement] completar, redondear.

consummation [ˌkɒnsə'meɪʃn] *n* **-1.** [of marriage] consumación *f*. **-2.** [culmination] culminación *f*.

consumption [kən'sʌmpʃn] *n* **-1.** [use] consumo *m*. **-2.** *dated* [tuberculosis] tisis *f inv*.

cont. *abbr of* **continued**.

contact ['kɒntækt] ◇ *n* contacto *m*; **in ~ (with)** en contacto (con); **to lose ~ with** perder (el) contacto con; **to make ~ with** ponerse en contacto con. ◇ *vt* ponerse en contacto con.

contact lens *n* lentilla *f*, lente *f* de contacto.

contact number *n* (número *m* de) teléfono *m* (*donde localizar a alguien en su ausencia*).

contagious [kən'teɪdʒəs] *adj* contagioso(sa).

contain [kən'teɪn] *vt* contener; **to ~ o.s.** contenerse.

contained [kən'teɪnd] *adj* [unemotional] contenido(da), mesurado(da).

container [kən'teɪnəʳ] *n* **-1.** [box, bottle etc] recipiente *m*, envase *m*. **-2.** [for transporting goods] contenedor *m*.

containerize, **-ise** [kən'teɪnəraɪz] COMM *vt* **-1.** [goods] poner en contenedores. **-2.** [port] adaptar para el uso de contenedores.

container ship *n* barco *m* OR buque *m* contenedor.

containment [kən'teɪnmənt] *n* contención *f*.

contaminate [kən'tæmɪneɪt] *vt* contaminar.

contaminated [kən'tæmɪneɪtɪd] *adj* contaminado(da).

contamination [kənˌtæmɪ'neɪʃn] *n* contaminación *f*.

cont'd *abbr of* **continued**.

contemplate ['kɒntempleɪt] ◇ *vt* **-1.** [consider] considerar, pensar en; **to ~ doing sthg** contemplar la posibilidad de hacer algo. **-2.** *fml* [look at] contemplar. ◇ *vi* reflexionar.

contemplation [ˌkɒntem'pleɪʃn] *n* **-1.** [thought] reflexión *f*. **-2.** *fml* [act of looking quietly] contemplación *f*.

contemplative [kən'templətɪv] *adj* contemplativo(va).

contemporary [kən'tempərərɪ] (*pl* **-ies**) ◇ *adj* contemporáneo(a). ◇ *n* contemporáneo *m*, **-a** *f*.

contempt [kən'tempt] *n* **-1.** [scorn]: **~ (for)** desprecio *m* OR desdén *m* (por); **to hold sb in ~** despreciar a alguien. **-2.** JUR desacato *m*.

contemptible [kən'temptəbl] *adj* despreciable.

contemptuous [kən'temptʃʊəs] *adj* despreciativo(va); **to be ~ of sthg** despreciar algo.

contend [kən'tend] ◇ *vi* **-1.** [deal]: **to ~ with** enfrentarse a; **I've got enough to ~ with** ya tengo suficientes problemas que afrontar. **-2.** [compete]: **to ~ for/against** competir por/contra. ◇ *vt fml*: **to ~ that** sostener OR afirmar que.

contender [kən'tendəʳ] *n* [gen] contendiente *m y f*; [for title] aspirante *m y f*.

content [*n* 'kɒntent, *adj & vb* kən'tent] ◇ *adj*: **~ (with)** contento(ta) OR satisfecho(cha) (con); **to be ~ to do sthg** contentarse con hacer algo; **I'd be quite ~ to go** iría de buena gana. ◇ *n* contenido *m*. ◇ *vt*:

to ~ **o.s. with sthg/with doing sthg** contentarse con algo/con hacer algo.

◆ **contents** *npl* contenido *m*.

contented [kən'tentɪd] *adj* satisfecho(cha), contento(ta).

contentedly [kən'tentɪdlɪ] *adv* con satisfacción.

contention [kən'tenʃn] *n fml* **-1.** [argument, assertion] argumento *m*; **it is my ~ that ...** en mi opinión .... **-2.** (U) [disagreement] disputas *fpl*. **-3.** [competition]: **to be in ~** entrar en liza.

contentious [kən'tenʃəs] *adj fml* controvertido(da), polémico(ca).

contentment [kən'tentmənt] *n* satisfacción *f*, contento *m*.

contest [*n* 'kɒntest, *vb* kən'test] ◇ *n* **-1.** [competition] competición *f*, concurso *m*. **-2.** [for power, control] contienda *f*, lucha *f*. ◇ *vt* **-1.** [seat, election] presentarse como candidato(ta) a. **-2.** [dispute - statement] disputar; [- decision] impugnar.

contestant [kən'testənt] *n* [in quiz show] concursante *m y f*; [in race] participante *m y f*; [in boxing match] contrincante *m y f*.

context ['kɒntekst] *n* contexto *m*; **out of ~** fuera de contexto.

continent ['kɒntɪnənt] *n* continente *m*.

◆ **the Continent** *n Br*: **the Continent** la Europa continental.

continental [,kɒntɪ'nentl] ◇ *adj* **-1.** GEOGR continental. **-2.** [European] de la Europa continental. ◇ *n inf* europeo (no británico) *m*, europea (no británica) *f*.

continental breakfast *n* desayuno *m* continental.

CONTINENTAL BREAKFAST:
Con este nombre se designa un desayuno ligero consistente en café y bollos por oposición al desayuno inglés, que es mucho más copioso y suele incluir platos calientes

continental climate *n* clima *m* continental.

continental quilt *n Br* edredón *m*.

contingency [kən'tɪndʒənsɪ] (*pl* **-ies**) *n* contingencia *f*.

contingency plan *n* plan *m* de emergencia.

contingent [kən'tɪndʒənt] ◇ *adj fml*: **~ on** OR **upon** supeditado(da) a. ◇ *n* **-1.** MIL contingente *m*. **-2.** [group] representación *f*.

continual [kən'tɪnjʊəl] *adj* continuo(nua), constante.

continually [kən'tɪnjʊəlɪ] *adv* continuamente, constantemente.

continuation [kən,tɪnjʊ'eɪʃn] *n* continuación *f*.

continue [kən'tɪnjuː] ◇ *vt*: **to ~ (doing** OR **to do sthg)** continuar (haciendo algo); **to be ~d** continuará. ◇ *vi*: **to ~ (with sthg)** continuar (con algo).

continuity [,kɒntɪ'njuːətɪ] *n* **-1.** [coherence] continuidad *f*. **-2.** CINEMA: **~ girl** script *f*, anotadora *f*.

continuous [kən'tɪnjʊəs] *adj* continuo(nua), ininterrumpido(da).

continuous assessment *n* evaluación *f* continua.

continuously [kən'tɪnjʊəslɪ] *adv* continuamente, ininterrumpidamente.

contort [kən'tɔːt] ◇ *vt* retorcer. ◇ *vi* retorcerse.

contortion [kən'tɔːʃn] *n* contorsión *f*.

contour ['kɒn,tʊər] ◇ *n* **-1.** [outline] contorno *m*. **-2.** [on map] curva *f* de nivel. ◇ *comp*: **~ map** mapa *m* topográfico; **~ line** curva *f* de nivel.

contraband ['kɒntrəbænd] ◇ *adj* de contrabando. ◇ *n* contrabando *m*.

contraception [,kɒntrə'sepʃn] *n* anticoncepción *f*.

contraceptive [,kɒntrə'septɪv] ◇ *adj* anticonceptivo(va). ◇ *n* anticonceptivo *m*.

contraceptive pill *n* píldora *f* anticonceptiva.

contract [*n* 'kɒntrækt, *vb* kən'trækt] ◇ *n* contrato *m*. ◇ *vt* **-1.** [through legal agreement]: **to ~ sb (to do sthg)** contratar a alguien (para hacer algo); **to ~ to do sthg** comprometerse a hacer algo (por contrato). **-2.** *fml* [illness, disease] contraer. **-3.** [reduce in size, length] contraer. ◇ *vi* [decrease in size, length] contraerse.

◆ **contract in** *vi* acceder formalmente a participar.

◆ **contract out** ◇ *vt sep*: **they've ~ed out refuse collection to a private firm** han contratado a una empresa privada para que se encargue de la recogida de la basura. ◇ *vi*: **to ~ out (of)** optar formalmente por no participar (en).

contraction [kən'trækʃn] *n* contracción *f*.

contractor [kən'træktər] *n* contratista *m y f*.

contractual [kən'træktʃʊəl] *adj* contractual.

contradict [,kɒntrə'dɪkt] *vt* contradecir.

contradiction [,kɒntrə'dɪkʃn] *n* contradicción *f*; **~ in terms** contradicción *f* en sí misma.

contradictory [,kɒntrə'dɪktərɪ] *adj* contradictorio(ria).

contraflow ['kɒntrəfləʊ] *n* estrechamiento *(de la autopista) a una carretera de dos direcciones*.

contralto [kən'træltəʊ] (*pl* **-s**) *n* contralto *f*.

contraption [kən'træpʃn] *n* chisme *m*, artilugio *m*.

contrary ['kɒntrəri, *adj sense 2* kən'treəri] ◇ *adj* **-1.** [opposite] contrario(ria); ~ **to** en contra de. **-2.** [awkward] obstinado(da), que lleva la contraria siempre. ◇ *n*: **the** ~ lo contrario; **on the** ~ al contrario; **to the** ~ en contra; **unless I hear to the** ~ a menos que me digan otra cosa.
◆ **contrary to** *prep* en contra de.

contrast [*n* 'kɒntrɑːst, *vb* kən'trɑːst] ◇ *n*: ~ **(between** OR **with)** contraste *m* (entre); **by** OR **in** ~ en cambio; **in** ~ **with** OR **to** a diferencia de; **to be a** ~ **(to** OR **with)** contrastar (con). ◇ *vt*: **to** ~ **sthg with** contrastar algo con. ◇ *vi*: **to** ~ **(with)** contrastar (con).

contrasting [kən'trɑːstɪŋ] *adj* [personalities, views] opuesto(ta); [colours] que contrastan.

contravene [ˌkɒntrə'viːn] *vt* contravenir.

contravention [ˌkɒntrə'venʃn] *n* contravención *f*.

contribute [kən'trɪbjuːt] ◇ *vt* **-1.** [give] contribuir, aportar. **-2.** [to magazine, newspaper]: **to** ~ **(to)** escribir (para). ◇ *vi* **-1.** [gen]: **to** ~ **(to)** contribuir (a). **-2.** [write material]: **to** ~ **to** colaborar con.

contributing [kən'trɪbjuːtɪŋ] *adj* contribuyente.

contribution [ˌkɒntrɪ'bjuːʃn] *n* **-1.** [gen]: ~ **(to)** contribución *f* (a). **-2.** [article] colaboración *f*.

contributor [kən'trɪbjʊtər] *n* **-1.** [of money] contribuyente *m y f*. **-2.** [to magazine, newspaper] colaborador *m*, -ra *f*.

contributory [kən'trɪbjʊtəri] *adj* contribuyente.

contributory pension scheme *n* plan *m* de pensiones contributivo.

contrite ['kɒntraɪt] *adj literary* contrito(ta).

contrition [kən'trɪʃn] *n literary* contrición *f*, arrepentimiento *m*.

contrivance [kən'traɪvns] *n* **-1.** [contraption] artilugio *m*. **-2.** [ploy] estratagema *m*, treta *f*.

contrive [kən'traɪv] *fml vt* **-1.** [engineer] maquinar, idear. **-2.** [manage]: **to** ~ **to do sthg** lograr hacer algo.

contrived [kən'traɪvd] *adj* inverosímil.

control [kən'trəʊl] (*pt & pp* **-led**, *cont* **-ling**) ◇ *n* **-1.** [gen & COMPUT] control *m*; [on spending] restricción *f*; **beyond** OR **outside one's** ~ fuera del control de uno; **in** ~ **of** al mando de; **to be in** ~ **of o.s.** tener el control de sí mismo; **to be in** ~ **of the situation** dominar la situación; **out of/under** ~ fuera de/bajo control; **to gain** ~

(of) hacerse con el poder (en); **to take** ~ **(of)** tomar el control OR las riendas (de). **-2.** [of emotions] dominio *m*, control *m*; **to lose** ~ perder el dominio.
◇ *vt* **-1.** [gen] controlar; **to** ~ **o.s.** dominarse, controlarse. **-2.** [operate - machine, plane] manejar; [- central heating] regular.
◇ *comp* de control.
◆ **controls** *npl* [of machine, vehicle] controles *mpl*.

control code *n* COMPUT código *m* de control.

control group *n* grupo *m* de control.

controlled [kən'trəʊld] *adj* **-1.** [person] controlado(da). **-2.** ECON dirigido(da).

controller [kən'trəʊlər] *n* FIN interventor *m*, -ra *f*; RADIO & TV director *m*, -ra *f*.

controlling [kən'trəʊlɪŋ] *adj* [factor] controlador(ra).

controlling interest *n* participación *f* mayoritaria.

control panel *n* tablero *m* de instrumentos OR de mandos.

control tower *n* torre *f* de control.

controversial [ˌkɒntrə'vɜːʃl] *adj* polémico(ca), controvertido(da).

controversy ['kɒntrəvɜːsɪ, *Br* kən'trɒvəsɪ] (*pl* **-ies**) *n* controversia *f*, polémica *f*.

conundrum [kə'nʌndrəm] (*pl* **-s**) *n fml* [problem] enigma *m*.

conurbation [ˌkɒnɜː'beɪʃn] *n* conurbación *f*.

convalesce [ˌkɒnvə'les] *vi* convalecer.

convalescence [ˌkɒnvə'lesns] *n* convalecencia *f*.

convalescent [ˌkɒnvə'lesnt] ◇ *adj* de convalecencia. ◇ *n* convaleciente *m y f*.

convection [kən'vekʃn] *n* convección *f*.

convector [kən'vektər] *n* calentador *m* de convección, convector *m*.

convene [kən'viːn] ◇ *vt* convocar. ◇ *vi* reunirse.

convener [kən'viːnər] *n Br* [trade union official] *sindicalista que supervisa a los enlaces sindicales de una empresa.*

convenience [kən'viːnjəns] *n* comodidad *f*; **do it at your** ~ hágalo cuando le venga bien.

convenience food *n* comida *f* preparada.

convenience store *n Am* tienda *f* que abre hasta tarde.

convenient [kən'viːnjənt] *adj* **-1.** [suitable] conveniente; **is Monday** ~? ¿te viene bien el lunes? **-2.** [handy - size] práctico(ca); [- position] adecuado(da); ~ **for** [well-situated] bien situado para.

conveniently [kən'viːnjəntlɪ] *adv* convenientemente.

convent ['kɒnvənt] *n* convento *m*.

convention [kən'venʃn] *n* convención *f*.

conventional [kən'venʃənl] *adj* convencional.

conventionally [kən'venʃnəlɪ] *adv* de manera convencional.

convent school *n* colegio *m* de monjas.

converge [kən'vɜːdʒ] *vi lit & fig*: **to ~ (on)** converger (en); **the protesters ~d on the palace** los manifestantes se dieron cita ante el palacio.

conversant [kən'vɜːsənt] *adj fml*: **~ with** familiarizado(da) con.

conversation [ˌkɒnvə'seɪʃn] *n* conversación *f*; **to make ~ (with)** dar conversación (a).

conversational [ˌkɒnvə'seɪʃənl] *adj* coloquial; **~ style** estilo familiar.

conversationalist [ˌkɒnvə'seɪʃnəlɪst] *n* conversador *m*, -ra *f*.

converse [*n & adj* 'kɒnvɜːs, *vb* kən'vɜːs] ◇ *adj fml* contrario(ria), opuesto(ta). ◇ *n*: **the ~** lo contrario OR opuesto. ◇ *vi fml*: **to ~ (with)** conversar (con).

conversely [kən'vɜːslɪ] *adv fml* a la inversa.

conversion [kən'vɜːʃn] *n* **-1.** [gen & RELIG] conversión *f*. **-2.** [in building] reforma *f*. **-3.** [in rugby] transformación *f*.

conversion table *n* tabla *f* de conversión.

convert [*vb* kən'vɜːt, *n* 'kɒnvɜːt] ◇ *vt* **-1.** [gen]: **to ~ sthg (to OR into)** convertir algo (en). **-2.** [change belief of]: **to ~ sb (to)** convertir a alguien (a). **-3.** [in rugby] transformar. ◇ *vi* **-1.** [change]: **to ~ from sthg to** pasarse de algo a. **-2.** [in rugby] hacer una transformación. ◇ *n* converso *m*, -sa *f*.

converted [kən'vɜːtɪd] *adj* **-1.** [building, ship] acondicionado(da). **-2.** RELIG converso(sa).

convertible [kən'vɜːtəbl] ◇ *adj* **-1.** [sofa]: **~ sofa** sofá-cama *m*. **-2.** [currency] convertible. **-3.** [car] descapotable. ◇ *n* (coche *m*) descapotable *m*.

convex [kɒn'veks] *adj* convexo(xa).

convey [kən'veɪ] *vt* **-1.** *fml* [transport] transportar, llevar. **-2.** [express]: **to ~ sthg (to)** expresar OR transmitir algo (a).

conveyancing [kən'veɪənsɪŋ] *n (U)* redacción *f* de escrituras de traspaso.

conveyer belt [kən'veɪə-] *n* cinta *f* transportadora.

convict [*n* 'kɒnvɪkt, *vb* kən'vɪkt] ◇ *n* presidiario *m*, -ria *f*. ◇ *vt*: **to ~ sb of** condenar a alguien por, declarar a alguien culpable de.

convicted [kən'vɪktɪd] *adj* convicto(ta).

conviction [kən'vɪkʃn] *n* **-1.** [belief, fervour] convicción *f*. **-2.** JUR condena *f*.

convince [kən'vɪns] *vt*: **to ~ sb (of sthg/to**

do sthg) convencer a alguien (de algo/para que haga algo).

convinced [kən'vɪnst] *adj*: **~ (of)** convencido(da) (de).

convincing [kən'vɪnsɪŋ] *adj* convincente.

convivial [kən'vɪvɪəl] *adj* [gathering, atmosphere] agradable; [group] alegre.

convoluted ['kɒnvəluːtɪd] *adj* [tortuous] retorcido(da).

convoy ['kɒnvɔɪ] *n* convoy *m*; **in ~** en convoy.

convulse [kən'vʌls] *vt*: **to be ~d with** [pain] retorcerse de; [laughter] troncharse de.

convulsion [kən'vʌlʃn] *n* MED convulsión *f*.

convulsive [kən'vʌlsɪv] *adj* convulsivo(va).

coo [kuː] *vi* arrullar.

cook [kʊk] ◇ *n* cocinero *m*, -ra *f*. ◇ *vt* **-1.** [gen] cocinar, guisar; [prepare] preparar, hacer. **-2.** [in oven] asar, hacer en el horno. **-3.** *inf* [falsify] falsificar. ◇ *vi* **-1.** [prepare food] cocinar, guisar. **-2.** [in oven] cocerse, hacerse.

◆ **cook up** *vt sep* [plan, deal] tramar, urdir; [excuse] inventarse.

cookbook ['kʊk,bʊk] = **cookery book**.

cooked [kʊkt] *adj* cocido(da).

cooker ['kʊkə'] *n* cocina *f (aparato)*.

cookery ['kʊkərɪ] *n* cocina *f (arte)*.

cookery book *n* libro *m* de cocina.

cookie ['kʊkɪ] *n Am* galleta *f*.

cooking ['kʊkɪŋ] ◇ *n* **-1.** [activity]: **do you like ~?** ¿te gusta cocinar? **-2.** [food] cocina *f*. ◇ *comp* [utensils, salt] de cocina; [oil, sherry] para cocinar OR guisar.

cooking apple *n* manzana *f* para asar.

cookout ['kʊkaʊt] *n Am* barbacoa *f* al aire libre.

cool [kuːl] ◇ *adj* **-1.** [not warm] fresco(ca). **-2.** [calm] tranquilo(la). **-3.** [unfriendly] frío(a). **-4.** *inf* [hip] guay, chachi. ◇ *vt* refrescar. ◇ *vi* **-1.** [become less warm] enfriarse. **-2.** [abate] calmarse, aplacarse. ◇ *n*: **to keep/lose one's ~** mantener/perder la calma.

◆ **cool down** ◇ *vt sep* **-1.** [make less warm] refrescar. **-2.** [make less angry] calmar. ◇ *vi* **-1.** [become less warm] enfriarse. **-2.** [become less angry] calmarse.

◆ **cool off** *vi* **-1.** [become less warm] refrescarse. **-2.** [become less angry] calmarse.

coolant ['kuːlənt] *n* líquido *m* refrigerante.

cool box *n* nevera *f* portátil.

cool-headed [-'hedɪd] *adj* [person] impasible; [reaction] calmado(da).

cooling-off period ['kuːlɪŋ-] *n* tiempo en el *que los sindicatos y la patronal pueden intentar* *llegar a un acuerdo antes de declararse una huelga.*

cooling tower ['kuːlɪŋ-] *n* torre *f* de refrigeración.

coolly ['kuːlɪ] *adv* **-1.** [calmly] con tranquilidad. **-2.** [coldly] con frialdad.

coolness ['kuːlnɪs] *n* **-1.** [in temperature] frescor *m*. **-2.** [unfriendliness] frialdad *f*.

coop [kuːp] *n* gallinero *m*.
◆ **coop up** *vt sep inf* encerrar.

Co-op ['kəʊˌɒp] *(abbr of* co-operative society) *n* Coop. *f*.

cooperate [kəʊˈɒpəreɪt] *vi:* **to ~ (with)** cooperar (con).

cooperation [kəʊˌɒpəˈreɪʃn] *n* (*U*) cooperación *f*.

cooperative [kəʊˈɒpərətɪv] ◇ *adj* **-1.** [helpful] servicial, dispuesto(ta) a ayudar. **-2.** [collective] cooperativo(va). ◇ *n* cooperativa *f*.

co-opt *vt:* **to ~ sb (into/onto)** cooptar a alguien (a).

coordinate [*n* kəʊˈɔːdɪnət, *vt* kəʊˈɔːdɪneɪt] ◇ *n* coordenada *f*. ◇ *vt* coordinar.
◆ **coordinates** *npl* [clothes] conjunto *m*.

coordination [kəʊˌɔːdɪˈneɪʃn] *n* coordinación *f*.

co-ownership *n* copropiedad *f*.

cop [kɒp] *(pt* & *pp* **-ped,** *cont* **-ping)** *n inf* poli *m*, paco *m* Amer.
◆ **cop out** *vi inf:* **to ~ out (of)** escaquearse (de).

cope [kəʊp] *vi* arreglárselas: **to ~ with** [work] poder con; [problem, situation] hacer frente a.

Copenhagen [ˌkəʊpənˈheɪgən] *n* Copenhague.

copier ['kɒpɪər] *n* copiadora *f*, fotocopiadora *f*.

copilot ['kəʊˌpaɪlət] *n* copiloto *m y f*.

copious ['kəʊpjəs] *adj* copioso(sa), abundante.

cop-out *n inf* escaqueo *m*.

copper ['kɒpər] *n* **-1.** [metal] cobre *m*. **-2.** *Br inf* [policeman] poli *m*.

coppice ['kɒpɪs], **copse** [kɒps] *n* bosquecillo *m*.

copulate ['kɒpjʊleɪt] *vi:* **to ~ (with)** copular (con).

copulation [ˌkɒpjʊˈleɪʃn] *n* cópula *f*.

copy ['kɒpɪ] *(pt* & *pp* **-ied)** ◇ *n* **-1.** [imitation, duplicate] copia *f*. **-2.** [of book, magazine] ejemplar *m*. ◇ *vt* **-1.** [imitate] copiar. **-2.** [photocopy] fotocopiar. ◇ *vi* copiar.
◆ **copy down** *vt sep* copiar (por escrito).
◆ **copy out** *vt sep* copiar, pasar a limpio.

copycat ['kɒpɪkæt] ◇ *n inf* copión *m*, -ona *f*. ◇ *comp* calcado de otro (calcada de otra).

copy protect *vt* COMPUT proteger contra copia.

copyright ['kɒpɪraɪt] *n* (*U*) derechos *mpl* de autor.

copy typist *n Br* mecanógrafo *m*, -fa *f*, escribiente *m y f*.

copywriter ['kɒpɪˌraɪtər] *n* redactor *m*, -ra *f* de textos publicitarios.

coral ['kɒrəl] ◇ *n* coral *m*. ◇ *comp* de coral.

coral reef *n* arrecife *m* de coral.

Coral Sea *n:* **the ~** el mar del Coral.

cord [kɔːd] ◇ *n* **-1.** [string] cuerda *f*; [for tying clothes] cordón *m*. **-2.** [wire] cable *m*, cordón *m*. **-3.** [fabric] pana *f*. ◇ *comp* de pana.
◆ **cords** *npl* pantalones *mpl* de pana.

cordial ['kɔːdjəl] ◇ *adj* cordial, afectuoso(sa). ◇ *n* bebida de frutas concentrada.

cordially ['kɔːdɪəlɪ] *adv* cordialmente, afectuosamente.

cordless ['kɔːdlɪs] *adj* sin cable.

Cordoba ['kɔːdəbə] *n* Córdoba.

cordon ['kɔːdn] *n* cordón *m*.
◆ **cordon off** *vt sep* acordonar.

cordon bleu [-'blɜː] *adj* de primera clase.

corduroy ['kɔːdərɔɪ] ◇ *n* pana *f*. ◇ *comp* de pana.

core [kɔːr] ◇ *n* **-1.** [of fruit] corazón *m*. **-2.** [of Earth, nuclear reactor, group] núcleo *m*. **-3.** [of issue, matter] meollo *m*; **to the ~** hasta la médula. ◇ *vt* quitar el corazón de.

CORE [kɔːr] *(abbr of* Congress on Racial Equality) *n* organización estadounidense contra el racismo.

corer ['kɔːrər] *n* deshuesadora *f*.

corespondent [ˌkəʊrɪˈspɒndənt] *n* cómplice del demandado por adulterio.

core time *n Br* periodo en el que todos deben estar trabajando en un sistema de horario flexible.

Corfu [kɔːˈfuː] *n* Corfú.

corgi ['kɔːgɪ] *(pl* **-s)** *n* perro *m* galés.

coriander [ˌkɒrɪˈændər] *n* cilantro *m*.

cork [kɔːk] *n* corcho *m*.

corkage ['kɔːkɪdʒ] *n* recargo a pagar en restaurantes si se introducen bebidas de fuera.

corked [kɔːkt] *adj* con sabor a corcho.

corkscrew ['kɔːkskruː] *n* sacacorchos *m inv*.

cormorant ['kɔːmərənt] *n* cormorán *m*.

corn [kɔːn] ◇ *n* **-1.** *Br* [wheat, barley, oats] cereal *m*. **-2.** *Am* [maize] maíz *m*, choclo *m* Amer; **~ on the cob** mazorca *f*. **-3.** [callus] callo *m*. ◇ *comp* de maíz.

Corn *abbr of* **Cornwall**.

cornea ['kɔːnɪə] (pl -s) n córnea f.

corned beef [kɔːnd-] n carne de vaca cocinada y enlatada.

corner ['kɔːnər] ◇ n -1. [angle - on outside] esquina f; [- on inside] rincón m; **to cut ~s** economizar esfuerzos, atajar. -2. [bend - in street, road] curva f; **just around the ~** a la vuelta de la esquina. -3. [faraway place] rincón m. -4. [in football] saque m de esquina, córner m. ◇ vt -1. [trap] arrinconar. -2. [monopolize] monopolizar, acaparar.

corner flag n banderín m de córner.

corner kick n FTBL saque m de esquina, córner m.

corner shop n tienda pequeña de barrio que vende comida, artículos de limpieza etc.

cornerstone ['kɔːnəstəun] n fig piedra f angular.

cornet ['kɔːnɪt] n -1. [instrument] corneta f. -2. Br [ice-cream cone] cucurucho m.

cornfield ['kɔːnfiːld] n -1. Br campo m de cereal. -2. Am maizal m.

cornflakes ['kɔːnfleɪks] npl copos mpl de maíz, cornflakes mpl.

cornflour Br ['kɔːnflauər], **cornstarch** Am ['kɔːnstɑːtʃ] n harina f de maíz, maicena f.

cornice ['kɔːnɪs] n cornisa f.

Cornish ['kɔːnɪʃ] ◇ adj de Cornualles. ◇ n [language] córnico m. ◇ npl: **the ~** los córnicos.

Cornishman ['kɔːnɪʃmən] (pl -men [-mən]) n hombre de Cornualles.

Cornishwoman ['kɔːnɪʃ,wumən] (pl -women [-,wɪmɪn]) n mujer de Cornualles.

cornstarch Am = **cornflour**.

cornucopia [,kɔːnjʊ'kəupjə] n literary cornucopia f.

Cornwall ['kɔːnwɔːl] n Cornualles.

corny ['kɔːnɪ] (compar -ier, superl -iest) adj inf trillado(da).

corollary [kə'rɒlərɪ] (pl -ies) n corolario m.

coronary ['kɒrənrɪ] (pl -ies), **coronary thrombosis** (pl coronary thromboses) n trombosis f inv coronaria.

coronation [,kɒrə'neɪʃn] n coronación f.

coroner ['kɒrənər] n ≃ juez m y f de instrucción.

Corp. (abbr of **corporation**) Corp.

corpora ['kɔːpərə] pl → **corpus**.

corporal ['kɔːpərəl] n cabo m y f.

corporal punishment n castigo m corporal.

corporate ['kɔːpərət] adj -1. [business] corporativo(va). -2. [collective] colectivo(va).

corporate hospitality n (U) atencione fpl de la compañía.

corporate identity, **corporate image** imagen f corporativa.

corporation [,kɔːpə'reɪʃn] n -1. [council] ayuntamiento m. -2. [large company] ≃ sociedad f mercantil.

corporation tax n Br impuesto m de sociedades.

corps [kɔːr] (pl inv) n cuerpo m; **press ~** gabinete m de prensa.

corpse [kɔːps] n cadáver m.

corpulent ['kɔːpjulənt] adj corpulento(ta).

corpus ['kɔːpəs] (pl -pora OR -puses) n corpus m.

corpuscle ['kɔːpʌsl] n glóbulo m.

corral [kɒ'rɑːl] n corral m.

correct [kə'rekt] ◇ adj -1. [accurate - time, amount, forecast] exacto(ta); [- answer] correcto(ta); **you're ~** tienes razón. -2. [socially acceptable] correcto(ta). -3. [appropriate, required] apropiado(da). ◇ vt corregir.

correction [kə'rekʃn] n corrección f.

correctly [kə'rektlɪ] adv -1. [gen] correctamente. -2. [appropriately, as required] apropiadamente.

correlate ['kɒrəleɪt] ◇ vt relacionar, vincular. ◇ vi: **to ~ (with)** guardar correspondencia (con).

correlation [,kɒrə'leɪʃn] n: **~ (between)** correlación f (entre).

correspond [,kɒrɪ'spɒnd] vi -1. [correlate] **to ~ (with OR to)** corresponder (con OR a). -2. [match]: **to ~ (with OR to)** coincidir (con). -3. [write letters]: **to ~ (with)** cartearse (con).

correspondence [,kɒrɪ'spɒndəns] n: **~ (with/between)** correspondencia f (con entre).

correspondence course n curso m por correspondencia.

correspondent [,kɒrɪ'spɒndənt] n [reporter] corresponsal m y f.

corresponding [,kɒrɪ'spɒndɪŋ] adj correspondiente.

corridor ['kɒrɪdɔːr] n pasillo m, corredor m.

corroborate [kə'rɒbəreɪt] vt corroborar.

corroboration [kə,rɒbə'reɪʃn] n corroboración f.

corrode [kə'rəud] ◇ vt corroer. ◇ vi corroerse.

corrosion [kə'rəuʒn] n corrosión f.

corrosive [kə'rəusɪv] adj [poison, substance] corrosivo(va).

corrugated ['kɒrəgeɪtɪd] adj ondulado(da).

corrugated iron n chapa f ondulada.

corrupt [kə'rʌpt] ◇ *adj* [gen & COMPUT] corrupto(ta). ◇ *vt* corromper; **to ~ a minor** pervertir a un menor.

corruption [kə'rʌp∫n] *n* corrupción *f*.

corsage [kɔː'sɑːʒ] *n* ramillete *m*.

corset ['kɔːsɪt] *n* corsé *m*, faja *f*.

Corsica ['kɔːsɪkə] *n* Córcega.

Corsican ['kɔːsɪkən] ◇ *adj* corso(sa). ◇ *n* **-1.** [person] corso *m*, -sa *f*. **-2.** [language] corso *m*.

cortege, cortège [kɔː'teɪʒ] *n* cortejo *m*, comitiva *f*.

cortisone ['kɔːtɪzəʊn] *n* cortisona *f*.

cos[1] [kɒz] *Br inf* = **because**.

cos[2] [kɒs] = **cos lettuce**.

cosh [kɒ∫] ◇ *n* porra *f*. ◇ *vt* aporrear.

cosignatory [,kəʊ'sɪgnətrɪ] (*pl* **-ies**) *n* cosignatario *m*, -ria *f*.

cosine ['kəʊsaɪn] *n* coseno *m*.

cos lettuce [kɒs-] *n Br* lechuga *f* romana.

cosmetic [kɒz'metɪk] ◇ *n* cosmético *m*. ◇ *adj fig* superficial.

cosmetic surgery *n* cirugía *f* estética.

cosmic ['kɒzmɪk] *adj* cósmico(ca).

cosmonaut ['kɒzmənɔːt] *n* cosmonauta *m y f*.

cosmopolitan [kɒzmə'pɒlɪtn] *adj* cosmopolita.

cosmos ['kɒzmɒs] *n*: **the ~** el cosmos.

Cossack ['kɒsæk] *n* cosaco *m*, -ca *f*.

cosset ['kɒsɪt] *vt* mimar.

cost [kɒst] (*pt & pp* **cost** OR **-ed**) ◇ *n* **-1.** [price] coste *m*, precio *m*. **-2.** *fig* [loss, damage] coste *m*, costo *m*; **at the cost of** a costa de; **at all ~s** a toda costa. ◇ *vt* **-1.** [gen] costar; **it ~ us £20/a lot of effort** nos costó 20 libras/mucho esfuerzo; **how much does it ~?** ¿cuánto cuesta OR vale? **-2.** [estimate] presupuestar, preparar un presupuesto de.

◆ **costs** *npl* JUR litisexpensas *fpl*, costas *fpl*.

cost accountant *n* contable *m y f* de costos OR costes.

co-star ◇ *n* coprotagonista *m y f*. ◇ *vt* tener de coprotagonistas a. ◇ *vi* coprotagonizar.

Costa Rica [,kɒstə'riːkə] *n* Costa Rica.

Costa Rican [,kɒstə'riːkən] ◇ *adj* costarricense. ◇ *n* costarricense *m y f*.

cost-benefit analysis *n* análisis *m inv* coste-beneficio.

cost-effective *adj* rentable.

cost-effectiveness *n* rentabilidad *f*.

costing ['kɒstɪŋ] *n* cálculo *m* del coste.

costly ['kɒstlɪ] (*compar* **-ier**, *superl* **-iest**) *adj* costoso(sa).

cost of living *n*: **the ~** el coste de la vida.

cost-of-living index *n* índice *m* del coste de la vida.

cost price *n* precio *m* de coste.

costume ['kɒstjuːm] *n* **-1.** [gen] traje *m*. **-2.** [swimming costume] traje *m* de baño.

costume jewellery *n* (*U*) joyas *fpl* de fantasía, bisutería *f*.

cosy *Br*, **cozy** *Am* ['kəʊzɪ] (*compar* **-ier**, *superl* **-iest**, *pl* **-ies**) ◇ *adj* **-1.** [warm and comfortable - room] acogedor(ra); [- clothes] cómodo(da). **-2.** [intimate] agradable, amigable. ◇ *n* funda *f* para tetera.

cot [kɒt] *n* **-1.** *Br* [for child] cuna *f*. **-2.** *Am* [folding bed] cama *f* plegable, catre *m*.

cot death *n* muerte *f* en la cuna.

cottage ['kɒtɪdʒ] *n* casa *f* de campo, chalé *m*.

cottage cheese *n* requesón *m*.

cottage hospital *n Br* hospital pequeño en el campo.

cottage industry *n* industria *f* casera.

cottage pie *n Br* pastel de carne picada con una capa de puré de patatas.

cotton ['kɒtn] ◇ *n* **-1.** [fabric] algodón *m*. **-2.** [plant] algodonero *m*. **-3.** [thread] hilo *m* (de algodón). ◇ *comp* [dress, shirt, mill] de algodón; [industry] algodonero(ra).

◆ **cotton on** *vi inf*: **to ~ on (to)** caer en la cuenta (de).

cotton bud *Br*, **cotton swab** *Am n* bastoncillo *m* de algodón.

cotton candy *n Am* azúcar *m* hilado, algodón *m*.

cotton swab *Am* = **cotton bud**.

cotton wool *n* algodón *m* (hidrófilo).

couch [kaʊt∫] ◇ *n* **-1.** [sofa] sofá *m*, diván *m*. **-2.** [in doctor's surgery] camilla *f*. ◇ *vt*: **to ~ sthg in** formular algo en.

couchette [kuː'∫et] *n Br* litera *f*.

couch potato *n inf* persona perezosa que pasa mucho tiempo en el sofá viendo la televisión.

cougar ['kuːgə] (*pl inv* OR **-s**) *n* puma *m*.

cough [kɒf] ◇ *n* tos *f*. ◇ *vi* toser. ◇ *vt* escupir.

◆ **cough up** *vt sep* **-1.** [bring up] escupir. **-2.** *v inf* [pay up] soltar.

coughing ['kɒfɪŋ] *n* (*U*) tos *f*.

cough mixture *n Br* jarabe *m* para la tos.

cough sweet *n Br* caramelo *m* para la tos.

cough syrup = **cough mixture**.

could [kʊd] *pt* → **can**.

couldn't ['kʊdnt] = **could not**.

could've ['kʊdəv] = **could have**.

council ['kaʊnsl] ◇ *n* **-1.** [of a town] ayuntamiento *m*; [of a county] ≃ diputación *f*.

-2. [group, organization] consejo *m*. **-3.** [meeting] junta *f*, consejo *m*. ◇ *comp* [meeting, leader] del ayuntamiento; [tenant] de una vivienda protegida.

council estate *n* urbanización *de viviendas de protección oficial*.

council house *n Br* ≃ casa *f* de protección oficial.

councillor ['kaʊnsələʳ] *n* concejal *m y f*.

Council of Europe *n* Consejo *m* de Europa.

council of war *n* consejo *m* de guerra.

council tax *n Br impuesto municipal basado en el valor de la propiedad*, ≃ contribución *f* urbana.

counsel ['kaʊnsəl] (*Br pt & pp* **-led**, *cont* **-ling**, *Am pt & pp* **-ed**, *cont* **-ing**) ◇ *n* **-1.** (U) *fml* [advice] consejo *m*. **-2.** [lawyer] abogado *m*, -da *f*. ◇ *vt* aconsejar; **to ~ sb to do sthg** *fig* aconsejar a alguien hacer algo.

counselling *Br*, **counseling** *Am* ['kaʊnsəlɪŋ] *n* (U) consejo *m*, orientación *f*.

counsellor *Br*, **counselor** *Am* ['kaʊnsələʳ] *n* **-1.** [gen] consejero *m*, -ra *f*. **-2.** *Am* [lawyer] abogado *m*, -da *f*.

count [kaʊnt] ◇ *n* **-1.** [total] total *m*; [of votes] recuento *m*; **to keep/lose ~ of** llevar/perder la cuenta de. **-2.** [point] punto *m*. **-3.** JUR [charge] cargo *m*. **-4.** [aristocrat] conde *m*. ◇ *vt* **-1.** [add up] contar; [total, cost] calcular. **-2.** [consider]: **to ~ sb as** considerar a alguien como. **-3.** [include] incluir, contar. ◇ *vi* contar; **to ~ (up) to** contar hasta; **to ~ for** valer; **to ~ as** contar como.

◆ **count against** *vt fus* perjudicar.
◆ **count in** *vt sep inf* incluir, contar con.
◆ **count (up)on** *vt fus* contar con.
◆ **count out** *vt sep* **-1.** [money] ir contando. **-2.** [leave out] *inf* no contar con.
◆ **count up** *vt fus* contar.

countdown ['kaʊntdaʊn] *n* cuenta *f* atrás.

countenance ['kaʊntənəns] ◇ *n literary* [face] semblante *m*, continente *m*. ◇ *vt* aprobar.

counter ['kaʊntəʳ] ◇ *n* **-1.** [in shop] mostrador *m*; [in bank] ventanilla *f*. **-2.** [in board game] ficha *f*. ◇ *vt*: **to ~ sthg with** responder a algo mediante; **to ~ sthg by doing sthg** contrarrestar algo haciendo algo. ◇ *vi*: **to ~ with sthg/by doing sthg** contestar con algo/haciendo algo.

◆ **counter to** *adv* contrario a, en contra de; **to run ~ to** ir en contra de.

counteract [,kaʊntə'rækt] *vt* contrarrestar.

counterattack [,kaʊntərə'tæk] ◇ *n* contraataque *m*. ◇ *vt & vi* contraatacar.

counterbalance [,kaʊntə'bæləns] *vt fig* contrapesar, compensar.

counterclaim ['kaʊntəkleɪm] *n* contrarréplica *f*.

counterclockwise [,kaʊntə'klɒkwaɪz] *adv Am* en sentido opuesto a las agujas del reloj.

counterespionage [,kaʊntər'espɪənɑːʒ] *n* contraespionaje *m*.

counterfeit ['kaʊntəfɪt] ◇ *adj* falsificado(da). ◇ *vt* falsificar.

counterfoil ['kaʊntəfɔɪl] *n* matriz *f*.

counterintelligence [,kaʊntərɪn'telɪdʒəns] *n* contraespionaje *m*.

countermand [,kaʊntə'mɑːnd] *vt* revocar.

countermeasure [,kaʊntə'meʒəʳ] *n* medida *f* en contra, contramedida *f*.

counteroffensive [,kaʊntərə'fensɪv] *n* contraofensiva *f*.

counterpane ['kaʊntəpeɪn] *n* cubrecama *m*, colcha *f*.

counterpart ['kaʊntəpɑːt] *n* homólogo *m*, -ga *f*.

counterpoint ['kaʊntəpɔɪnt] *n* MUS contrapunto *m*.

counterproductive [,kaʊntəprə'dʌktɪv] *adj* contraproducente.

counter-revolution *n* contrarrevolución *f*.

countersank ['kaʊntəsæŋk] *pt* → **countersink**.

countersign ['kaʊntəsaɪn] *vt* refrendar, ratificar.

countersink ['kaʊntəsɪŋk] (*pt* **-sank**, *pp* **-sunk** [-sʌŋk]) *vt* avellanar.

countess ['kaʊntɪs] *n* condesa *f*.

countless ['kaʊntlɪs] *adj* innumerable.

countrified ['kʌntrɪfaɪd] *adj pej* [person] pueblerino(na); [area] provinciano(na).

country ['kʌntrɪ] (*pl* **-ies**) ◇ *n* **-1.** [nation] país *m*. **-2.** [population]: **the ~** el pueblo. **-3.** [countryside]: **the ~** el campo. **-4.** [terrain] terreno *m*. ◇ *comp* campestre.

country and western ◇ *n* música *f* country. ◇ *comp* [music] country (*inv*); [fan] del country.

country club *n* club *m* de campo.

country dancing *n* (U) baile *m* tradicional.

country house *n* casa *f* de campo.

countryman ['kʌntrɪmən] (*pl* **-men** [-mən]) *n* [from same country] compatriota *m*.

country music *n* = **country and western**.

country park *n Br parque natural abierto al público*.

countryside ['kʌntrɪsaɪd] *n* [land] campo *m*; [landscape] paisaje *m*.

countrywoman ['kʌntrɪ,wʊmən] (*pl*

-women [-ˌwɪmɪn]) *n* [from same country] compatriota *f*.

county ['kaʊntɪ] (*pl* **-ies**) *n* condado *m*.

county council *n Br* organismo que gobierna un condado, ≃ diputación *f* provincial.

county court *n Br* tribunal de justicia de un condado, ≃ audiencia *f* provincial.

county town *Br*, **county seat** *Am n* capital de un condado.

coup [kuː] *n* **-1.** [rebellion]: ~ (**d'état**) golpe *m* (de estado). **-2.** [masterstroke] éxito *m*.

coupé ['kuːpeɪ] *n* cupé *m*.

couple ['kʌpl] ◇ *n* **-1.** [two people in relationship] pareja *f*. **-2.** [two objects, people]: **a ~ (of)** un par (de). **-3.** [a few - objects, people] **a ~ (of)** un par (de), unos(nas). ◇ *vt* **-1.** [join]: **to ~ sthg (to)** enganchar algo (con). **-2.** *fig* [associate]: **to ~ sthg with** asociar algo con; **~d with** unido(da) a, junto con.

couplet ['kʌplɪt] *n* pareado *m*.

coupling ['kʌplɪŋ] *n* RAIL enganche *m*.

coupon ['kuːpɒn] *n* [gen] cupón *m*; [for pools] boleto *m*.

courage ['kʌrɪdʒ] *n* valor *m*; **to take ~ (from)** animarse (con); **to have the ~ of one's convictions** ser consecuente con los principios de uno.

courageous [kə'reɪdʒəs] *adj* valiente.

courageously [kə'reɪdʒəslɪ] *adv* valientemente.

courgette [kɔː'ʒet] *n Br* calabacín *m*.

courier ['kʊrɪə] *n* **-1.** [on holiday] guía *m* y *f*. **-2.** [to deliver letters, packages] mensajero *m*, -ra *f*.

course [kɔːs] ◇ *n* **-1.** [gen] curso *m*; [of lectures] ciclo *m*; UNIV carrera *f*; ~ **of treatment** MED tratamiento *m*; **to be on ~ for** [ship, plane] ir rumbo a; *fig* [on target] ir camino de; **to run** OR **take its ~** seguir su curso; **off ~** fuera de su rumbo; ~ (**of action**) medida *f*, planteamiento *m* (a seguir); **in the ~ of** a lo largo de. **-2.** [of meal] plato *m*. **-3.** SPORT [for golf] campo *m* (de golf); [for horse racing] hipódromo *m*. ◇ *vi literary* [flow] correr.

◆ **of course** *adv* **-1.** [inevitably, not surprisingly] naturalmente. **-2.** [certainly] claro, por supuesto; **of ~ not** claro que no, desde luego que no.

coursebook ['kɔːsbʊk] *n* libro *m* de texto.

coursework ['kɔːswɜːk] *n* (*U*) trabajo *m* realizado durante el curso.

court [kɔːt] ◇ *n* **-1.** [place of trial, judge, jury etc] tribunal *m*; **to appear in** ~ comparecer ante el juez; **to go to** ~ ir a juicio; **to take sb to** ~ llevar a alguien a juicio. **-2.** SPORT cancha *f*, pista *f*; **on** ~ en la cancha OR pis-

ta. **-3.** [courtyard] patio *m*. **-4.** [of king, queen etc] corte *f*. ◇ *vt* [danger] exponerse a; [favour] solicitar. ◇ *vi dated* [go out together] cortejarse.

court circular *n Br* diario *m* real, noticiario *m* de la corte.

courteous ['kɜːtjəs] *adj* cortés.

courtesan [ˌkɔːtɪ'zæn] *n* cortesana *f*.

courtesy ['kɜːtɪsɪ] ◇ *n* cortesía *f*. ◇ *comp* de cortesía.

◆ **(by) courtesy of** *prep* [the author] con permiso de; [a company] por cortesía OR gentileza de.

courtesy car *n* coche *m* de cortesía.

courtesy coach *n* autobús gratuito fletado para llevar a invitados.

courthouse ['kɔːthaʊs, *pl* -haʊzɪz] *n Am* palacio *m* de justicia.

courtier ['kɔːtjə] *n* cortesano *m*.

court-martial (*pl* **court-martials** OR **courts-martial**, *Br pt & pp* **-led**, *cont* **-ling**, *Am pt & pp* **-ed**, *cont* **-ing**) ◇ *n* consejo *m* de guerra. ◇ *vt* juzgar en consejo de guerra.

court of appeal *Br*, **court of appeals** *Am n* tribunal *m* de apelación.

court of inquiry *n* comisión *f* de investigación.

court of law *n* tribunal *m* (de justicia).

courtroom ['kɔːtrʊm] *n* sala *f* del tribunal.

courtship ['kɔːtʃɪp] *n* **-1.** [of people] noviazgo *m*. **-2.** [of animals] cortejo *m*.

court shoe *n* escarpín *m*, zapato liso de tacón.

courtyard ['kɔːtjɑːd] *n* patio *m*.

cousin ['kʌzn] *n* primo *m*, -ma *f*.

couture [kuː'tʊə] *n* alta costura *f*.

cove [kəʊv] *n* cala *f*, ensenada *f*.

coven ['kʌvən] *n* aquelarre *m*.

covenant ['kʌvənənt] *n* **-1.** [of money] compromiso escrito para el pago regular de una contribución *esp con fines caritativos*. **-2.** [agreement] convenio *m*.

Covent Garden [ˌkɒvənt-] *n* el Covent Garden.

COVENT GARDEN:
El 'Covent Garden', antiguo mercado de frutas, legumbres y flores del centro de Londres, es actualmente una galería comercial, alrededor de la cual se dan cita todo tipo de artistas callejeros (magos, mimos, etc.). Este nombre también designa la 'Royal Opera House', situada cerca del antiguo mercado

Coventry ['kɒvəntrɪ] *n*: **to send sb to** ~ hacer el vacío a alguien.

cover ['kʌvəʳ] ◇ n -1. [covering] cubierta f; [lid] tapa f; [for seat, typewriter] funda f. -2. [of book] tapa f, cubierta f; [of magazine - at the front] portada f; [- at the back] contraportada f. -3. [protection, shelter] refugio m, cobijo m; **air ~** apoyo m aéreo, cobertura f aérea; **to take ~** [from weather, gunfire] ponerse a cubierto, refugiarse; **under ~** [from weather] a cubierto, bajo techo. -4. [concealment] tapadera f; **under ~ of** al amparo OR abrigo de; **to break ~** salir al descubierto. -5. [insurance] cobertura f. -6. [blanket] manta f, cobertor m.
◇ vt -1. [gen]: **to ~ sthg (with)** cubrir algo (de); [with lid] tapar algo (con). -2. [insure]: **to ~ sb (against)** cubrir OR asegurar a alguien (contra). -3. [include] abarcar. -4. [report on] informar sobre, cubrir. -5. [discuss, deal with] abarcar, cubrir.
◆ **cover up** vt sep -1. [place sthg over] tapar. -2. [conceal] encubrir.

coverage ['kʌvərɪdʒ] n [of news] reportaje m, cobertura f informativa.

coveralls ['kʌvərɔːlz] npl Am mono m.

cover charge n precio m del cubierto.

cover girl n modelo f OR chica f de portada.

covering ['kʌvərɪŋ] n -1. [for floor etc] cubierta f. -2. [of snow, dust] capa f.

covering letter Br, **cover letter** Am n [with CV] carta f de presentación; [with parcel, letter] nota f aclaratoria.

cover note n Br póliza f provisional.

cover price n [of magazine] precio m (de una revista).

covert ['kʌvət] adj [operation] encubierto(ta), secreto(ta); [glance] furtivo(va).

cover-up n encubrimiento m.

cover version n versión f.

covet ['kʌvɪt] vt codiciar.

cow [kaʊ] ◇ n -1. [female type of cattle] vaca f. -2. [female elephant, whale, seal] hembra f. -3. Br inf pej [woman] bruja f, foca f. ◇ vt acobardar, intimidar.

coward ['kaʊəd] n cobarde m y f.

cowardice ['kaʊədɪs] n cobardía f.

cowardly ['kaʊədlɪ] adj cobarde.

cowboy ['kaʊbɔɪ] ◇ n -1. [cattlehand] vaquero m, tropero m Amer. -2. Br inf [dishonest workman] chorizo m. ◇ comp de vaqueros; **~ boots** botas fpl camperas.

cower ['kaʊəʳ] vi encogerse.

cowhide ['kaʊhaɪd] n cuero m.

cowl neck [kaʊl-] n cuello m enrollado OR vuelto.

cowpat ['kaʊpæt] n boñiga f.

cowshed ['kaʊʃed] n establo m.

cox [kɒks], **coxswain** ['kɒksən] n timonel m y f.

coy [kɔɪ] adj gazmoño(ña) (con afectación).

coyly ['kɔɪlɪ] adv con gazmoñería (afectada).

coyote [kɔɪ'əʊtɪ] n coyote m.

cozy Am = **cosy**.

cp. (abbr of **compare**) cf., cfr.

c/p (abbr of **carriage paid**) pp.

CP (abbr of **Communist Party**) n PC m.

CPA n abbr of **certified public accountant**.

CPI (abbr of **Consumer Price Index**) n IPC m.

Cpl. abbr of **corporal**.

CP/M (abbr of **control program for microcomputers**) n CP/M.

c.p.s. (abbr of **characters per second**) c.p.s.

CPS (abbr of **Crown Prosecution Service**) n acusación popular.

CPSA (abbr of **Civil and Public Services Association**) n sindicato británico de funcionarios.

CPU (abbr of **central processing unit**) n COMPUT UPC f.

cr. -1. abbr of **credit**. -2. abbr of **creditor**.

crab [kræb] n cangrejo m.

crab apple n manzana f silvestre.

crack [kræk] ◇ n -1. [split - in wood, ground] grieta f; [- in glass, pottery] raja f. -2. [gap] rendija f; **at the ~ of dawn** al romper el alba. -3. [sharp noise - of whip] chasquido m; [- of twigs] crujido m. -4. [joke] chiste m. -5. inf [attempt]: **to have a ~ at sthg** intentar algo. -6. drugs sl [cocaine] crack m.
◇ adj de primera.
◇ vt -1. [cause to split] romper, partir. -2. [egg, nut] cascar. -3. [whip etc] chasquear. -4. [bang - head] golpearse. -5. inf [open - bottle] abrir; [- safe] forzar. -6. [solve] dar con la clave de, descifrar. -7. inf [make joke] contar.
◇ vi -1. [split - skin, wood, ground] agrietarse; [- pottery, glass] partirse, rajarse. -2. [break down] hundirse, venirse abajo. -3. [make sharp noise - whip] chasquear; [- twigs] crujir. -4. Br inf [act quickly]: **to get ~ing** ponerse manos a la obra.
◆ **crack down** vi: **to ~ down (on)** tomar medidas severas (contra).
◆ **crack up** vi venirse abajo.

crackdown ['krækdaʊn] n: **~ (on)** ofensiva f (contra).

cracked ['krækt] adj -1. [damaged - wall] agrietado(da); [- vase] rajado(da). -2. [harsh] cascado(da), ronco(ca). -3. inf [mad] majara.

cracker ['krækəʳ] n -1. [biscuit] galleta f (salada). -2. Br [for Christmas] tubo con sorpresa típico de Navidades.

crackers ['krækəz] *adj Br inf* majara.

cracking ['krækɪŋ] *adj inf*: **a ~ pace** un ritmo tremendo.

crackle ['krækl] ◇ *n* [of fire, cooking] crujido *m*, chasquido *m*; [on phone, radio] interferencia *f*. ◇ *vi* [fire] crujir, chasquear; [radio] sonar con interferencias.

crackling ['kræklɪŋ] *n* (*U*) **-1.** [of fire, dry leaves] crujido *m*; [on phone, radio] interferencias *fpl*. **-2.** [pork skin] corteza *f*.

crackpot ['krækpɒt] *inf* ◇ *adj* descabellado(da). ◇ *n* chiflado *m*, -da *f*.

cradle ['kreɪdl] ◇ *n* **-1.** [baby's bed, birthplace] cuna *f*. **-2.** [hoist] andamio *m* colgado, puente *m* volante. ◇ *vt* acunar, mecer.

craft [krɑːft] (*pl sense 2 inv*) *n* **-1.** [trade] oficio *m*; [skill] arte *m*. **-2.** [boat] embarcación *f*.

craftsman ['krɑːftsmən] (*pl* **-men** [-mən]) *n* artesano *m*.

craftsmanship ['krɑːftsmənʃɪp] *n* (*U*) **-1.** [skill] destreza *f*, habilidad *f*. **-2.** [skilled work] artesanía *f*.

craftsmen *pl* → craftsman.

crafty ['krɑːftɪ] (*compar* **-ier**, *superl* **-iest**) *adj* astuto(ta).

crag [kræg] *n* peñasco *m*.

craggy ['krægɪ] (*compar* **-ier**, *superl* **-iest**) *adj* **-1.** [rock] escarpado(da). **-2.** [face] anguloso(sa), de facciones pronunciadas.

Crakow ['krækaʊ] *n* Cracovia.

cram [kræm] (*pt & pp* **-med**, *cont* **-ming**) ◇ *vt* **-1.** [push - books, clothes] embutir; [people] apiñar. **-2.** [overfill]: **to ~ sthg with** atiborrar OR atestar algo de; **to be crammed (with)** estar repleto(ta) (de). ◇ *vi* empollar.

cramming ['kræmɪŋ] *n* empolladura *f*, empollada *f*.

cramp [kræmp] ◇ *n* calambre *m*; **stomach ~s** retortijones *mpl* de vientre. ◇ *vt* [restrict, hinder] coartar, limitar.

cramped [kræmpt] *adj* [flat, conditions] estrecho(cha).

crampon ['kræmpən] *n* crampón *m*.

cranberry ['krænbərɪ] (*pl* **-ies**) *n* arándano *m* (agrio).

crane [kreɪn] ◇ *n* **-1.** [machine] grúa *f*. **-2.** [bird] grulla *f*. ◇ *vt* estirar. ◇ *vi* estirarse.

crane fly *n* típula *f*.

cranium ['kreɪnjəm] (*pl* **-niums** OR **-nia** [-njə]) *n* cráneo *m*.

crank [kræŋk] ◇ *n* **-1.** TECH manivela *f*. **-2.** *inf* [eccentric] majareta *m y f*. ◇ *vt* **-1.** [wind] girar. **-2.** AUT poner en marcha con la manivela.

crankshaft ['kræŋkʃɑːft] *n* cigüeñal *m*.

cranky ['kræŋkɪ] (*compar* **-ier**, *superl* **-iest**) *adj inf* **-1.** [odd] extravagante, estrambótico(ca). **-2.** *Am* [bad-tempered] refunfuñón(ona).

cranny ['krænɪ] (*pl* **-ies**) *n* → nook.

crap [kræp] *n* (*U*) *v inf* mierda *f*.

crappy ['kræpɪ] (*compar* **-ier**, *superl* **-iest**) *adj v inf* de mierda, muy chungo(ga).

crash [kræʃ] ◇ *n* **-1.** [accident] colisión *f*, choque *m*, estrellón *m Amer*. **-2.** [loud noise] estruendo *m*. **-3.** FIN crac *m*, quiebra *f*. ◇ *vt* estrellar. ◇ *vi* **-1.** [collide - two vehicles] chocar, colisionar; [one vehicle - into wall etc] estrellarse; **to ~ into sthg** chocar OR estrellarse contra algo. **-2.** [make crashing noise] armar estruendo; **to ~ to the ground** caerse y hacerse añicos. **-3.** FIN quebrar. **-4.** COMPUT bloquearse.

crash barrier *n* valla *f* protectora.

crash course *n* cursillo *m* intensivo de introducción, curso *m* acelerado.

crash diet *n* régimen *m* drástico.

crash-dive *vi* sumergirse a gran profundidad y con gran rapidez.

crash helmet *n* casco *m* protector.

crash-land ◇ *vt* hacer un aterrizaje forzoso con. ◇ *vi* realizar un aterrizaje forzoso.

crash landing *n* aterrizaje *m* forzoso.

crass [kræs] *adj* burdo(da); **a ~ error** un craso error.

crate [kreɪt] *n* caja *f* (*para embalaje o transporte*).

crater ['kreɪtər] *n* **-1.** [hole in ground] socavón *m*. **-2.** [of volcano, on the moon] cráter *m*.

cravat [krə'væt] *n* pañuelo *m* (de hombre).

crave [kreɪv] ◇ *vt* ansiar. ◇ *vi*: **to ~ for sthg** ansiar algo.

craving ['kreɪvɪŋ] *n* [gen]: **~ (for sthg/to do sthg)** anhelo *m* (de algo/de hacer algo); [of pregnant woman]: **~ (for sthg)** antojo *m* (de algo).

crawl [krɔːl] ◇ *vi* **-1.** [baby] andar a gatas, gatear. **-2.** [insect, person] arrastrarse. **-3.** [move slowly, with difficulty] avanzar lentamente, ir a paso de tortuga. **-4.** *inf* [be covered]: **to be ~ing with sthg** estar infestado(da) de algo. **-5.** *inf* [grovel]: **to ~ (to)** arrastrarse (ante). ◇ *n* **-1.** [slow pace]: **at a ~** a paso de tortuga. **-2.** [swimming stroke]: **the ~** el crol.

crawler lane ['krɔːlər-] *n Br* carril *m* de los lentos.

crayfish ['kreɪfɪʃ] (*pl inv* OR **-es**) *n* [freshwater] cangrejo *m* de río; [spiny lobster] langosta *f*.

crayon ['kreɪɒn] *n* lápiz *m* de cera.

craze [kreɪz] *n* moda *f*.

crazed [kreɪzd] *adj* enloquecido(da); ~ **with** loco(ca) de.

crazy ['kreɪzɪ] (*compar* **-ier**, *superl* **-iest**) *adj inf* **-1.** [mad - person] loco(ca); [- idea] disparatado(da). **-2.** [enthusiastic]: **to be** ~ **about** estar loco(ca) por.

crazy paving *n Br* enlosado *m* irregular.

creak [kriːk] ◇ *n* [of floorboard, bed] crujido *m*; [of door, hinge] chirrido *m*. ◇ *vi* [floorboard, bed] crujir; [door, hinge] chirriar.

creaky ['kriːkɪ] (*compar* **-ier**, *superl* **-iest**) *adj* [floorboard, bed] que cruje; [door, hinge] chirriante.

cream [kriːm] ◇ *adj* [in colour] (color) crema (*inv*). ◇ *n* **-1.** [food] nata *f*. **-2.** [cosmetic, mixture for food] crema *f*; ~ **of tomato soup** crema de tomate. **-3.** [colour] (color *m*) crema *m*. **-4.** [elite]: **the** ~ la flor y nata, la crema. ◇ *vt* CULIN batir; ~**ed potatoes** puré *m* de patatas.

◆ **cream off** *vt sep* seleccionar, separar.

cream cake *n Br* pastel *m* de nata.

cream cheese *n* queso *m* cremoso OR blanco.

cream cracker *n Br galleta sin azúcar que generalmente se come con queso.*

cream of tartar *n* crémor *m* tártaro.

cream tea *n Br merienda de té con bollos, nata y mermelada.*

creamy ['kriːmɪ] (*compar* **-ier**, *superl* **-iest**) *adj* **-1.** [taste, texture] cremoso(sa). **-2.** [colour] (color) crema (*inv*).

crease [kriːs] ◇ *n* [deliberate - in shirt] pliegue *m*; [- in trousers] raya *f*; [accidental] arruga *f*. ◇ *vt* arrugar. ◇ *vi* [gen] arrugarse; [forehead] fruncirse.

creased [kriːst] *adj* arrugado(da).

crease-resistant *adj* inarrugable.

create [kriː'eɪt] *vt* [gen] crear; [interest] producir.

creation [kriː'eɪʃn] *n* creación *f*.

creative [kriː'eɪtɪv] *adj* [gen] creativo(va); [energy] creador(ra); ~ **writing** redacciones *fpl*.

creativity [,kriːeɪ'tɪvətɪ] *n* creatividad *f*.

creator [kriː'eɪtə*r*] *n* creador *m*, -ra *f*.

creature ['kriːtʃə*r*] *n* criatura *f*.

crèche [kreʃ] *n Br* guardería *f* (infantil).

credence ['kriːdns] *n*: **to give** OR **lend** ~ **to** dar crédito a.

credentials [krɪ'denʃlz] *npl* credenciales *fpl*.

credibility [,kredə'bɪlətɪ] *n* credibilidad *f*.

credible ['kredəbl] *adj* creíble, digno(na) de crédito.

credit ['kredɪt] ◇ *n* **-1.** [financial aid] crédito *m*; **in** ~ con saldo acreedor OR positivo; **on** ~ a crédito. **-2.** (*U*) [praise] reconocimiento *m*, mérito *m*; **to have sthg to one's** ~ [successfully completed] tener uno algo en su haber; **to be to sb's** ~ [in sb's favour] ir en favor de alguien; **to do sb credit** decir mucho en favor de alguien; **to give sb** ~ **for** reconocer a alguien el mérito de. **-3.** SCH & UNIV punto *m*, crédito *m*. **-4.** [money credited] saldo *m* acreedor OR positivo.

◇ *vt* **-1.** FIN [add] abonar; **we'll** ~ **your account** lo abonaremos en su cuenta. **-2.** *inf* [believe] creer. **-3.** [give the credit to]: **to** ~ **sb with** atribuir a alguien el mérito de.

◆ **credits** *npl* [on film] títulos *mpl*.

creditable ['kredɪtəbl] *adj fml* **-1.** [reasonable] meritorio(ria). **-2.** [respectable] digno(na) de encomio.

credit account *n Br* cuenta *f* de crédito.

credit broker *n* intermediario *m* financiero.

credit card *n* tarjeta *f* de crédito.

credit control *n* control *m* de crédito.

credit facilities *npl* facilidades *fpl* de crédito.

credit limit *Br*, **credit line** *Am n* límite *m* de crédito.

credit note *n* pagaré *m*.

creditor ['kredɪtə*r*] *n* acreedor *m*, -ra *f*.

credit rating *n* calificación *f* de solvencia.

credit squeeze *n* restricción *f* de créditos.

credit transfer *n* transferencia *f* bancaria.

creditworthy ['kredɪt,wɜːðɪ] *adj* [person] solvente; [project] fiable.

credulity [krɪ'djuːlətɪ] *n fml* credulidad *f*.

credulous ['kredjʊləs] *adj* crédulo(la).

creed [kriːd] *n* credo *m*.

creek [kriːk] *n* **-1.** [inlet] cala *f*. **-2.** *Am* [stream] riachuelo *m*.

creep [kriːp] (*pt* & *pp* **crept**) ◇ *vi* **-1.** [insect] arrastrarse; [traffic etc] avanzar lentamente. **-2.** [person] deslizarse, andar con sigilo. **-3.** *inf* [grovel]: **to** ~ **(to sb)** hacer la pelota (a alguien). ◇ *n inf* [person] pelotillero *m*, -ra *f*, pelota *m* y *f*.

◆ **creeps** *npl*: **to give sb the** ~**s** *inf* ponerle a alguien la piel de gallina.

◆ **creep in** *vi* [appear] introducirse.

◆ **creep up on** *vt* **-1.** [subj: person, animal] acercarse sigilosamente a. **-2.** [subj: old age, deadline] aproximarse a.

creeper ['kriːpə*r*] *n* enredadera *f*, bejuco *m* *Amer*.

◆ **creepers** *npl zapatos de suela de goma.*

creepy ['kriːpɪ] (*compar* **-ier**, *superl* **-iest**) *adj inf* horripilante, espeluznante.

creepy-crawly [-'krɔːlɪ] (*pl* **-ies**) *n inf* bicho *m*.

cremate [krɪ'meɪt] *vt* incinerar.

cremation [krɪ'meɪʃn] *n* incineración *f*.

crematorium *Br* [ˌkremə'tɔːrɪəm] (*pl* **-riums** OR **-ria** [-rɪə]), **crematory** *Am* ['kremətrɪ] (*pl* **-ies**) *n* (horno *m*) crematorio *m*.

creosote ['krɪəsəʊt] ◇ *n* creosota *f*. ◇ *vt* aplicar creosota a.

crepe [kreɪp] *n* **-1.** [cloth] crespón *m*. **-2.** [rubber] crepé *m*. **-3.** [thin pancake] crepe *f*.

crepe bandage *n Br* venda *f* de gasa.

crepe paper *n* papel *m* seda.

crepe-soled shoes [-səʊld-] *npl Br* zapatos *mpl* de suela de crepé.

crept [krept] *pt & pp* → **creep**.

Cres. *abbr of* **Crescent**.

crescendo [krɪ'ʃendəʊ] (*pl* **-s**) *n* crescendo *m*.

crescent ['kresnt] ◇ *adj* creciente. ◇ *n* **-1.** [shape] media luna *f*. **-2.** [street] *calle en forma de arco*.

cress [kres] *n* berro *m*.

crest [krest] *n* **-1.** [on bird's head, of wave] cresta *f*. **-2.** [of hill] cima *f*, cumbre *f*. **-3.** [on coat of arms] blasón *m*.

crestfallen ['krest,fɔːln] *adj* alicaído(da).

Crete [kriːt] *n* Creta.

cretin ['kretɪn] *n inf* [idiot] cretino *m*, -na *f*.

Creutzfeldt-Jakob disease [ˌkrɔɪtsfelt-'jækɒb-] *n* enfermedad *f* de Creutzfeldt-Jakob.

crevasse [krɪ'væs] *n* grieta *f*, fisura *f*.

crevice ['krevɪs] *n* grieta *f*, hendidura *f*.

crew [kruː] *n* **-1.** [of ship, plane] tripulación *f*. **-2.** [on film set etc] equipo *m*.

crew cut *n* rapado *m*, corte *m* al cero.

crewman ['kruːmæn] (*pl* **-men** [-men]) *n* [of ship, plane] tripulante *m*; [on film set etc] miembro *m* del equipo.

crew-neck(ed) [-nek(t)] *adj* con cuello redondo.

crib [krɪb] (*pt & pp* **-bed**, *cont* **-bing**) ◇ *n* [cot] cuna *f*. ◇ *vt inf*: **to ~ sthg off** OR **from sb** copiar algo de alguien.

cribbage ['krɪbɪdʒ] *n juego de cartas en que la puntuación se anota colocando clavijas en un tablero*.

crick [krɪk] ◇ *n* [in neck] tortícolis *f*. ◇ *vt* torcerse.

cricket ['krɪkɪt] ◇ *n* **-1.** [game] críquet *m*. **-2.** [insect] grillo *m*. ◇ *comp* de críquet.

cricketer ['krɪkɪtəʳ] *n* jugador *m*, -ra *f* de críquet.

crikey ['kraɪkɪ] *excl Br inf dated* ¡caramba!

crime [kraɪm] ◇ *n* **-1.** [criminal behaviour - serious] criminalidad *f*; [- less serious] delincuencia *f*. **-2.** [serious offence] crimen *m*; [less serious offence] delito *m*. **-3.** [immoral act] crimen *m*. ◇ *comp* de la delincuencia; ~

squad brigada *f* de investigación criminal; **~ novel** novela *f* policíaca.

Crimea [kraɪ'mɪə] *n*: **the ~** Crimea.

crime wave *n* ola *f* delictiva.

criminal ['krɪmɪnl] ◇ *adj* **-1.** JUR [act, behaviour] criminal, delictivo(va); [law] penal; [lawyer] criminalista; **~ offence** delito *m*. **-2.** *inf* [shameful] criminal. ◇ *n* [serious] criminal *m* y *f*; [less serious] delincuente *m* y *f*.

criminalize, -ise ['krɪmɪnəlaɪz] *vt* convertir en delincuente.

criminal law *n* derecho *m* penal.

criminology [ˌkrɪmɪ'nɒlədʒɪ] *n* criminología *f*.

crimp [krɪmp] *vt* ondular, rizar.

crimson ['krɪmzn] ◇ *adj* **-1.** [in colour] carmesí. **-2.** [with embarrassment] colorado(da). ◇ *n* carmesí *m*.

cringe [krɪndʒ] *vi* **-1.** [out of fear] encogerse. **-2.** *inf* [with embarrassment]: **to ~ (at)** encogerse de vergüenza (ante).

crinkle ['krɪŋkl] ◇ *n* arruga *f*. ◇ *vt* arrugar. ◇ *vi* arrugarse.

cripple ['krɪpl] ◇ *n dated & offensive* tullido *m*, -da *f*, lisiado *m*, -da *f*. ◇ *vt* **-1.** MED dejar inválido(da). **-2.** [country, industry] paralizar, inmovilizar; [ship, plane] dañar, dejar inutilizado(da).

crippling ['krɪplɪŋ] *adj* **-1.** MED postrador(ra). **-2.** [severe] abrumador(ra).

crisis ['kraɪsɪs] (*pl* **crises** ['kraɪsiːz]) *n* crisis *f inv*.

crisp [krɪsp] *adj* **-1.** [pastry, bacon, snow] crujiente; [banknote, vegetables, weather] fresco(ca). **-2.** [brisk] directo(ta), categórico(ca). ◆ **crisps** *npl* patatas *fpl* fritas (*de bolsa*).

crispbread ['krɪspbred] *n galleta salada y alargada de centeno o trigo*.

crispy ['krɪspɪ] (*compar* **-ier**, *superl* **-iest**) *adj* crujiente.

crisscross ['krɪskrɒs] ◇ *adj* entrecruzado(da). ◇ *vt* entrecruzar. ◇ *vi* entrecruzarse.

criterion [kraɪ'tɪərɪən] (*pl* **-ria** [-rɪə] OR **-rions**) *n* criterio *m*.

critic ['krɪtɪk] *n* crítico *m*, -ca *f*.

critical ['krɪtɪkl] *adj* [gen] crítico(ca); [illness] grave; **to be ~ of** criticar a; **~ acclaim** la aclamación de la crítica.

critically ['krɪtɪklɪ] *adv* [gen] críticamente; [ill] gravemente.

criticism ['krɪtɪsɪzm] *n* crítica *f*.

criticize, -ise ['krɪtɪsaɪz] *vt & vi* criticar.

critique [krɪ'tiːk] *n* crítica *f*.

croak [krəʊk] ◇ *n* **-1.** [of frog] croar *m*, canto *m*; [of raven] graznido *m*. **-2.** [hoarse voice]

ronquido *m*, estertor *m*. ◇ *vi* **-1.** [frog] croar; [raven] graznar. **-2.** [person] ronquear.

Croat ['krəʊæt], **Croatian** [krəʊ'eɪʃn] ◇ *adj* croata. ◇ *n* **-1.** [person] croata *m y f*. **-2.** [language] croata *m*.

Croatia [krəʊ'eɪʃə] *n* Croacia.

Croatian = **Croat**.

crochet ['krəʊʃeɪ] ◇ *n* ganchillo *m*. ◇ *vt* hacer a ganchillo.

crockery ['krɒkərɪ] *n* loza *f*, vajilla *f*.

crocodile ['krɒkədaɪl] (*pl inv* OR **-s**) *n* cocodrilo *m*.

crocus ['krəʊkəs] (*pl* **-es**) *n* azafrán *m*.

croft [krɒft] *n Br* granja o terreno pequeño que pertenece a una familia y les proporciona sustento.

croissant ['krwæsɑ̃] *n* croissant *m*.

crony ['krəʊnɪ] (*pl* **-ies**) *n inf* amiguete *m*, -ta *f*, amigote *m*.

crook [krʊk] ◇ *n* **-1.** [criminal] ratero *m*, -ra *f*, delincuente *m y f*. **-2.** *inf* [dishonest person] ladrón *m*, -ona *f*, sinvergüenza *m y f*. **-3.** [of arm, elbow] pliegue *m*. **-4.** [shepherd's staff] cayado *m*. ◇ *vt* doblar.

crooked ['krʊkɪd] *adj* **-1.** [back] encorvado(da); [path] sinuoso(sa). **-2.** [teeth, tie] torcido(da). **-3.** *inf* [dishonest - person, policeman] corrupto(ta); [- deal] sucio(cia).

croon [kruːn] *vt & vi* canturrear.

crop [krɒp] (*pt & pp* **-ped**, *cont* **-ping**) ◇ *n* **-1.** [kind of plant] cultivo *m*. **-2.** [harvested produce] cosecha *f*, pizca *f Amer*. **-3.** *inf* [group - of people] hornada *f*; [- of books] ristra *f*. **-4.** [whip] fusta *f*. ◇ *vt* **-1.** [cut short] cortar (muy corto). **-2.** [subj: cows, sheep] pacer.

◆ **crop up** *vi* surgir, salir.

cropper ['krɒpə'] *n inf*: **to come a ~** [fall] darse un batacazo; *fig* pegar un patinazo; [business] irse a la porra.

crop spraying [-,spreɪɪŋ] *n* fumigación *f*.

croquet ['krəʊkeɪ] *n* croquet *m*.

croquette [krɒ'ket] *n* croqueta *f*.

cross [krɒs] ◇ *adj* enfadado(da); **to get ~ (with)** enfadarse (con). ◇ *n* **-1.** [gen] cruz *f*. **-2.** [hybrid] cruce *m*, cruza *f Amer*; **a ~ between** [combination] una mezcla de. ◇ *vt* **-1.** [gen & FIN] cruzar. **-2.** [face - subj: expression] reflejarse en. **-3.** RELIG: **to ~ o.s.** santiguarse. ◇ *vi* **-1.** [intersect] cruzarse. **-2.** [boat, ship] hacer una travesía.

◆ **cross off**, **cross out** *vt sep* tachar.

crossbar ['krɒsbɑː'] *n* **-1.** [on goal] larguero *m*, travesaño *m*. **-2.** [on bicycle] barra *f*.

crossbow ['krɒsbəʊ] *n* ballesta *f*.

crossbreed ['krɒsbriːd] *n* híbrido *m*.

cross-Channel *adj* [ferry] que hace la travesía del Canal de la Mancha; [route] a través del Canal de la Mancha.

cross-check *n* verificación *f* con otro método.

◆ **crosscheck** *vt* verificar con otro método.

cross-country ◇ *adj & adv* a campo traviesa. ◇ *n* cross *m*.

cross-cultural *adj* intercultural.

cross-dressing *n* travestismo *m*.

crossed line [krɒst-] *n* cruce *m* de líneas.

cross-examination *n* interrogatorio *m* (*para comprobar veracidad*).

cross-examine *vt* interrogar (*para comprobar veracidad*).

cross-eyed ['krɒsaɪd] *adj* bizco(ca).

cross-fertilize *vt* [plants] fecundar por fertilización cruzada.

crossfire ['krɒs,faɪə'] *n* fuego *m* cruzado.

crosshead ['krɒs,hed] *adj*: **~ screw** tornillo *m* de cabeza en cruz; **~ screwdriver** destornillador *m* de cabeza en cruz.

crossing ['krɒsɪŋ] *n* **-1.** [on road] cruce *m*, paso *m* de peatones; [on railway line] paso a nivel. **-2.** [sea journey] travesía *f*.

cross-legged ['krɒslegd] *adv* con las piernas cruzadas.

crossly ['krɒslɪ] *adv* con enfado.

crossply ['krɒsplaɪ] (*pl* **-ies**) ◇ *adj* de carcasa diagonal. ◇ *n* neumático *m* de carcasa diagonal.

cross-purposes *npl*: **to be at ~ with** sufrir un malentendido con.

cross-question *vt* interrogar (*para comprobar veracidad*).

cross-refer ◇ *vt* remitir. ◇ *vi* hacer una remisión OR referencia.

cross-reference *n* remisión *f*, referencia *f*.

crossroads ['krɒsrəʊdz] (*pl inv*) *n* cruce *m*; **to be at a ~** *fig* estar en una encrucijada.

cross-section *n* **-1.** [drawing] sección *f* transversal. **-2.** [sample] muestra *f* representativa.

crosswalk ['krɒswɔːk] *n Am* paso *m* de peatones.

crossways ['krɒsweɪz] = **crosswise**.

crosswind ['krɒswɪnd] *n* viento *m* de costado.

crosswise ['krɒswaɪz] *adv* en diagonal, transversalmente.

crossword (puzzle) ['krɒswɜːd-] *n* crucigrama *m*.

crotch [krɒtʃ] *n* entrepierna *f*.

crotchet ['krɒtʃɪt] *n* negra *f*.

crotchety ['krɒtʃɪtɪ] *adj Br inf* refunfuñón(ona).

crouch [krautʃ] *vi* [gen] agacharse; [ready to spring] agazaparse.

croup [kru:p] *n* -1. [illness] crup *m*. -2. [of horse] grupa *f*.

croupier ['kru:pɪə'] *n* crupier *m y f*.

crouton ['kru:tɒn] *n* cuscurro *m*.

crow [krəu] ◇ *n* corneja *f*; **as the ~ flies** en línea recta. ◇ *vi* -1. [cock] cantar. -2. *inf* [gloat] darse pisto, vanagloriarse.

crowbar ['krəubɑ:'] *n* palanca *f*.

crowd [kraud] ◇ *n* -1. [mass of people] multitud *f*, muchedumbre *f*; [at football match etc] público *m*. -2. [particular group] gente *f*. ◇ *vi* agolparse, apiñarse; **to ~ in/out** entrar/salir en tropel. ◇ *vt* -1. [room, theatre etc] llenar. -2. [people] meter, apiñar.

crowded ['kraudɪd] *adj*: ~ **(with)** repleto(ta) OR atestado(da) (de).

crown [kraun] ◇ *n* -1. [of royalty, on tooth] corona *f*. -2. [of hat] copa *f*; [of head] coronilla *f*; [of hill] cumbre *f*, cima *f*. ◇ *vt* -1. [gen] coronar. -2. [tooth] poner una corona a.
◆ **Crown** ◇ *n*: **the Crown** [monarchy] la corona. ◇ *comp* de la corona.

crown court *n* ≃ tribunal *m* superior de lo penal.

crowning ['kraunɪŋ] *adj* supremo(ma).

crown jewels *npl* joyas *fpl* de la corona.

crown prince *n* príncipe *m* heredero.

crow's feet *npl* patas *fpl* de gallo.

crow's nest *n* cofa *f*.

crucial ['kru:ʃl] *adj* crucial.

crucially ['kru:ʃlɪ] *adv* de manera decisiva; ~ **important** de importancia crucial.

crucible ['kru:sɪbl] *n* crisol *m*.

crucifix ['kru:sɪfɪks] *n* crucifijo *m*.

Crucifixion [,kru:sɪ'fɪkʃn] *n*: **the ~** la crucifixión.

crucify ['kru:sɪfaɪ] (*pt & pp* -**ied**) *vt lit & fig* crucificar.

crude [kru:d] ◇ *adj* -1. [rubber, oil, joke] crudo(da). -2. [person, behaviour] basto(ta), vulgar. -3. [drawing, sketch] tosco(ca). ◇ *n*: ~ **(oil)** crudo *m*.

crudely ['kru:dlɪ] *adv* -1. [say, remark] vulgarmente. -2. [sketch, write] toscamente.

crude oil *n* crudo *m*.

cruel [kruəl] (*compar* -**ler**, *superl* -**lest**) *adj* [gen] cruel; [winter] crudo(da).

cruelly ['kruəlɪ] *adv* -1. [sadistically] cruelmente. -2. [painfully, harshly] dolorosamente.

cruelty ['kruəltɪ] *n* (*U*) crueldad *f*.

cruet ['kru:ɪt] *n* vinagreras *fpl*, convoy *m*.

cruise [kru:z] ◇ *n* crucero *m*. ◇ *vi* -1. [sail] hacer un crucero. -2. [drive, fly] ir a velocidad de crucero.

cruise missile *n* misil *m* de crucero.

cruiser ['kru:zə'] *n* -1. [warship] crucero *m*. -2. [cabin cruiser] yate *m* (para cruceros).

crumb [krʌm] *n* -1. [of food] miga *f*, migaja *f*. -2. [of information] migaja *f*, pizca *f*.

crumble ['krʌmbl] ◇ *n* compota de fruta con una pasta seca por encima. ◇ *vt* desmigajar. ◇ *vi* -1. [building, cliff] desmoronarse; [plaster] caerse. -2. *fig* [relationship, hopes] derrumbarse, venirse abajo.

crumbly ['krʌmblɪ] (*compar* -**ier**, *superl* -**iest**) *adj* que se desmigaja con facilidad.

crummy ['krʌmɪ] (*compar* -**mier**, *superl* -**miest**) *adj inf* [bad] chungo(ga).

crumpet ['krʌmpɪt] *n* [food] bollo que se come tostado.

crumple ['krʌmpl] ◇ *vt* [dress, suit] arrugar; [letter] estrujar. ◇ *vi* -1. [dress, suit, face] arrugarse; [car] quedarse hecho un acordeón. -2. [body] desplomarse; [army, government] sucumbir.
◆ **crumple up** *vt sep* estrujar.

crunch [krʌntʃ] ◇ *n* crujido *m*; **when it comes to the ~** *inf* a la hora de la verdad. ◇ *vt* -1. [with teeth] ronzar. -2. [underfoot] hacer crujir. ◇ *vi* crujir.

crunchy ['krʌntʃɪ] (*compar* -**ier**, *superl* -**iest**) *adj* crujiente.

crusade [kru:'seɪd] ◇ *n lit & fig* cruzada *f*. ◇ *vi*: **to ~ for/against** hacer una cruzada en pro/en contra de.

crusader [kru:'seɪdə'] *n* -1. HISTORY cruzado *m*. -2. [campaigner] paladín *m*, defensor *m*, -ra *f*.

crush [krʌʃ] ◇ *n* -1. [crowd] gentío *m*, aglomeración *f*. -2. *inf* [infatuation]: **to have a ~ on sb** estar colado(da) OR loco(ca) por alguien. -3. *Br* [drink] zumo con agua añadida. ◇ *vt* -1. [squash] aplastar. -2. [grind - garlic, grain] triturar; [- ice] picar; [- grapes] exprimir. -3. [destroy] demoler.

crush barrier *n Br* valla *f* de contención.

crushing ['krʌʃɪŋ] *adj* -1. [defeat, blow] aplastante, abrumador(ra). -2. [remark] demoledor(ra).

crust [krʌst] *n* -1. [on bread] corteza *f*. -2. [on pie] pasta *f* (dura). -3. [of snow, earth] corteza *f*.

crustacean [krʌ'steɪʃn] *n* crustáceo *m*.

crusty ['krʌstɪ] (*compar* -**ier**, *superl* -**iest**) *adj* -1. [food] crujiente. -2. [person] brusco(ca).

crutch [krʌtʃ] *n* -1. [stick] muleta *f*; *fig* [support] apoyo *m*, soporte *m*. -2. [crotch] entrepierna *f*.

crux [krʌks] *n*: **the ~ of the matter** el quid de la cuestión.

cry [kraɪ] (*pt* & *pp* **cried**, *pl* **cries**) ⋄ *n* **-1.** [weep] llanto *m*, llorera *f*. **-2.** [shout] grito *m*; **to be a far ~ from** no parecerse en nada a. **-3.** [of bird] canto *m*, trino *m*. ⋄ *vt* llorar; **to ~ o.s. to sleep** llorar hasta dormirse. ⋄ *vi* **-1.** [weep] llorar. **-2.** [shout] gritar; **to ~ for help** gritar pidiendo ayuda.
◆ **cry off** *vi* volverse atrás.
◆ **cry out** ⋄ *vt* gritar. ⋄ *vi* [call out] gritar.
◆ **cry out for** *vt fus* pedir a voces.

crybaby ['kraɪˌbeɪbɪ] (*pl* **-ies**) *n inf pej* llorón *m*, -ona *f*.

crying ['kraɪɪŋ] ⋄ *adj inf* **-1.** [shame]: **a ~ shame** una verdadera vergüenza. **-2.** [need]: **a ~ need for sthg** una necesidad imperiosa de algo. ⋄ *n* (*U*) llanto *m*.

crypt [krɪpt] *n* cripta *f*.

cryptic ['krɪptɪk] *adj* críptico(ca).

crypto- [krɪptəʊ] *prefix*: **a ~communist** un comunista de tapadillo.

crystal ['krɪstl] ⋄ *n* cristal *m*. ⋄ *comp* de cristal.

crystal ball *n* bola *f* de cristal.

crystal clear *adj* **-1.** [transparent] cristalino(na). **-2.** [clearly stated] claro(ra) como el agua.

crystallize, **-ise** ['krɪstəlaɪz] ⋄ *vi lit* & *fig* cristalizar. ⋄ *vt* **-1.** [make clear] cristalizar. **-2.** [preserve in sugar] confitar, escarchar.

CSC (*abbr of* **Civil Service Commission**) *n organismo encargado de la contratación de funcionarios.*

CSE (*abbr of* **Certificate of Secondary Education**) *n antiguo título de enseñanza secundaria en Gran Bretaña para alumnos de bajo rendimiento escolar.*

CS gas *n* gas *m* lacrimógeno.

CST (*abbr of* **Central Standard Time**) *hora oficial del centro de Estados Unidos.*

CSU (*abbr of* **Civil Service Union**) *n sindicato británico de funcionarios.*

ct (*abbr of* **carat**) quil.

CT *abbr of* **Connecticut**.

CTC *n abbr of* **city technology college**.

cu. (*abbr of* **cubic**) c.

cub [kʌb] *n* **-1.** [young animal] cachorro *m*. **-2.** [boy scout] *boy scout de entre 8 y 11 años.*

Cuba ['kjuːbə] *n* Cuba.

Cuban ['kjuːbən] ⋄ *adj* cubano(na). ⋄ *n* [person] cubano *m*, -na *f*.

cubbyhole ['kʌbɪhəʊl] *n* [room] cuchitril *m*; [cupboard] armario *m*.

cube [kjuːb] ⋄ *n* [gen] cubo *m*; [of sugar] terrón *m*. ⋄ *vt* MATH elevar al cubo.

cube root *n* raíz *f* cúbica.

cubic ['kjuːbɪk] *adj* cúbico(ca).

cubicle ['kjuːbɪkl] *n* [at swimming pool] caseta *f*; [in shop] probador *m*.

cubism ['kjuːbɪzm] *n* cubismo *m*.

cubist ['kjuːbɪst] *n* cubista *m y f*.

cub reporter *n* periodista novato *m*, periodista novata *f*.

Cub Scout *n boy scout de entre 8 y 11 años.*

cuckoo ['kʊkuː] *n* cuco *m*, cuclillo *m*.

cuckoo clock *n* reloj *m* de cuco.

cucumber ['kjuːkʌmbəʳ] *n* pepino *m*.

cud [kʌd] *n*: **to chew the ~** *lit* & *fig* rumiar.

cuddle ['kʌdl] ⋄ *n* abrazo *m*. ⋄ *vt* abrazar, apapachar *Amer*. ⋄ *vi* abrazarse.
◆ **cuddle up** *vi*: **to ~ up (to)** arrimarse (a).

cuddly ['kʌdlɪ] (*compar* **-ier**, *superl* **-iest**) *adj* [person] mimoso(sa).

cuddly toy *n* muñeco *m* de peluche.

cudgel ['kʌdʒəl] (*Br pt* & *pp* **-led**, *cont* **-ling**, *Am pt* & *pp* **-ed**, *cont* **-ing**) ⋄ *n* porra *f*; **to take up the ~s for** salir en defensa de. ⋄ *vt* aporrear; **to ~ one's brains** *Am* devanarse los sesos.

cue [kjuː] *n* **-1.** RADIO, THEATRE & TV entrada *f*; **on ~** justo en aquel instante; **to take one's ~ from** guiarse por. **-2.** *fig* [stimulus, signal] señal *f*. **-3.** [in snooker, pool] taco *m*.

cuff [kʌf] ⋄ *n* **-1.** [of sleeve] puño *m*; **off the ~** improvisado(da), sacado(da) de la manga. **-2.** *Am* [of trouser leg] vuelta *f*. **-3.** [blow] cachete *m*. ⋄ *vt* dar un cachete a.

cuff link *n* gemelo *m*, collera *f Amer*.

cu. in. (*abbr of* **cubic inch(es)**) p.c.

cuisine [kwɪ'ziːn] *n* cocina *f*.

cul-de-sac ['kʌldəsæk] *n* callejón *m* sin salida.

culinary ['kʌlɪnərɪ] *adj* culinario(ria).

cull [kʌl] ⋄ *n* eliminación *f*. ⋄ *vt* **-1.** [animals] eliminar. **-2.** *fml* [information, facts] recoger.

culminate ['kʌlmɪneɪt] *vi*: **to ~ in** culminar en.

culmination [ˌkʌlmɪ'neɪʃn] *n* culminación *f*.

culottes [kjuː'lɒts] *npl* falda *f* pantalón.

culpable ['kʌlpəbl] *adj fml*: **~ (of)** culpable (de); **~ homicide** homicidio *m* involuntario.

culprit ['kʌlprɪt] *n* culpable *m y f*.

cult [kʌlt] ⋄ *n* **-1.** RELIG culto *m*. **-2.** [person, activity, object] objeto *m* de culto. ⋄ *comp* de culto.

cultivate ['kʌltɪveɪt] *vt* **-1.** [gen] cultivar. **-2.** [get to know - person] hacer amistad con.

cultivated ['kʌltɪveɪtɪd] *adj* **-1.** [cultured] culto(ta). **-2.** [land] cultivado(da).

cultivation [ˌkʌltɪ'veɪʃn] *n* (*U*) cultivo *m*.

cultural ['kʌltʃərəl] *adj* cultural.

culture ['kʌltʃər] *n* **-1.** [gen] cultura *f*. **-2.** [of bacteria] cultivo *m*.

cultured ['kʌltʃəd] *adj* culto(ta), cultivado(da).

cultured pearl *n* perla *f* cultivada.

culture shock *n* choque *m* cultural.

culture vulture *n* inf hum devorador insaciable de cultura.

culvert ['kʌlvət] *n* alcantarilla *f*, desagüe *m*.

cumbersome ['kʌmbəsəm] *adj* **-1.** [parcel] abultado(da), voluminoso(sa); [machinery] aparatoso(sa). **-2.** [system] torpe, lento(ta).

cumin ['kʌmɪn] *n* comino *m*.

cumulative ['kju:mjʊlətɪv] *adj* acumulativo(va).

cunning ['kʌnɪŋ] ⋄ *adj* [gen] astuto(ta); [device, idea] ingenioso(sa). ⋄ *n* (U) astucia *f*.

cup [kʌp] (*pt* & *pp* -**ped**, *cont* -**ping**) ⋄ *n* **-1.** [gen] taza *f*. **-2.** [prize, of bra] copa *f*. ⋄ *vt* ahuecar.

cupboard ['kʌbəd] *n* armario *m*.

Cup Final *n*: the ~ ≃ la final de la Copa.

cup holder *n* (actual) campeón *m* de copa.

cupid ['kju:pɪd] *n* [figure] cupido *m*.

cupola ['kju:pələ] (*pl* -**s**) *n* cúpula *f*.

cup tie *n* Br partido *m* de copa.

curable ['kjʊərəbl] *adj* curable.

curate ['kjʊərət] *n* coadjutor *m*, -ra *f*, auxiliar *m* y *f*.

curator [,kjʊə'reɪtər] *n* conservador *m*, -ra *f*, director *m*, -ra *f*.

curb [kɜ:b] ⋄ *n* **-1.** [control]: ~ (on) control *m* OR restricción *f* (de); to put a ~ on sthg poner freno a algo. **-2.** Am [in road] bordillo *m*. ⋄ *vt* controlar, contener.

curd cheese [kɜ:d-] *n* Br requesón *m*.

curdle ['kɜ:dl] *vi* [milk] cuajarse; fig [blood] helarse.

cure [kjʊər] ⋄ *n* **-1.** MED: ~ (for) cura *f* (para). **-2.** [solution]: ~ (for) remedio *m* (a). ⋄ *vt* **-1.** MED curar. **-2.** [problem, inflation] remediar. **-3.** [rid]: to ~ sb of sthg hacer a alguien abandonar algo. **-4.** [food, tobacco] curar; [leather] curtir.

cure-all *n* panacea *f*.

curfew ['kɜ:fju:] *n* toque *m* de queda.

curio ['kjʊərɪəʊ] (*pl* -**s**) *n* curiosidad *f*, rareza *f*.

curiosity [,kjʊərɪ'ɒsətɪ] *n* curiosidad *f*.

curious ['kjʊərɪəs] *adj* curioso(sa); to be ~ about sentir curiosidad por; I'm ~ to know ... tengo ganas de saber ....

curiously ['kjʊərɪəslɪ] *adv* **-1.** [inquisitively] con curiosidad. **-2.** [oddly] curiosamente.

curl [kɜ:l] ⋄ *n* **-1.** [of hair] rizo *m*. **-2.** [of smoke] voluta *f*. ⋄ *vt* **-1.** [hair] rizar. **-2.** [twist] enroscar. ⋄ *vi* **-1.** [hair] rizarse. **-2.** [paper] abarquillarse, curvarse; to ~ into a ball acurrucarse, hacerse un ovillo.

◆ **curl up** *vi* [person, animal] acurrucarse, hacerse un ovillo; [leaf, paper] abarquillarse, curvarse.

curler ['kɜ:lər] *n* rulo *m*.

curling ['kɜ:lɪŋ] *n* (U) deporte que consiste en hacer deslizar piedras planas sobre el hielo.

curling tongs *npl* tenacillas *fpl* de rizar.

curly ['kɜ:lɪ] (*compar* -**ier**, *superl* -**iest**) *adj* [hair] rizado(da); [pig's tail] enroscado(da).

currant ['kʌrənt] *n* [dried grape] pasa *f* de Corinto.

currency ['kʌrənsɪ] (*pl* -**ies**) *n* **-1.** FIN moneda *f*; foreign ~ divisa *f*. **-2.** fml [acceptability]: to gain ~ ganar aceptación.

current ['kʌrənt] ⋄ *adj* [price, girlfriend] actual; [year] presente, en curso; [issue] último(ma); [ideas, customs] común, corriente; in ~ use de uso común. ⋄ *n* corriente *f*.

current account *n* Br cuenta *f* corriente.

current affairs *npl* temas *mpl* de actualidad.

current assets *npl* activo *m* disponible.

current liabilities *npl* pasivo *m* circulante.

currently ['kʌrəntlɪ] *adv* actualmente.

curricular [kə'rɪkjələr] *adj* del temario.

curriculum [kə'rɪkjələm] (*pl* -**lums** OR -**la** [-lə]) *n* [course of study] temario *m*, plan *m* de estudios.

curriculum vitae [-'vi:taɪ] (*pl* **curricula vitae**) *n* currículum *m* (vitae), currículo *m*.

curried ['kʌrɪd] *adj* al curry.

curry ['kʌrɪ] (*pl* -**ies**) *n* curry *m*.

curry powder *n* curry *m* en polvo.

curse [kɜ:s] ⋄ *n* **-1.** [evil charm] maldición *f*; to put a ~ on echar una maldición a. **-2.** [swearword] taco *m*, palabrota *f*. **-3.** [source of problems] azote *m*. ⋄ *vt* maldecir. ⋄ *vi* [swear] blasfemar, soltar tacos.

cursor ['kɜ:sər] *n* COMPUT cursor *m*.

cursory ['kɜ:sərɪ] *adj* superficial, por encima.

curt [kɜ:t] *adj* brusco(ca), seco(ca).

curtail [kɜ:'teɪl] *vt* **-1.** [visit] acortar. **-2.** [expenditure] reducir; [rights] restringir.

curtailment [kɜ:'teɪlmənt] *n* fml [of expenditure] reducción *f*; [of rights] restricción *f*.

curtain ['kɜ:tn] *n* **-1.** [gen] cortina *f*. **-2.** [in theatre] telón *m*.

◆ **curtain off** *vt sep* separar con una cortina.

curtain call *n* salida *f* a escena para saludar.

curtain raiser *n* *fig* preludio *m*, preámbulo *m*.

curts(e)y ['kɜːtsɪ] (*pt* & *pp* **curtsied**) ◇ *n* reverencia *f* (*de mujer*). ◇ *vi* hacer una reverencia (*una mujer*).

curvaceous [kɜː'veɪʃəs] *adj inf* de buenas curvas.

curvature ['kɜːvətʃəʳ] *n* (U) **-1.** [of Earth] curvatura *f*. **-2.** MED [of spine] desviación *f*.

curve [kɜːv] ◇ *n* curva *f*. ◇ *vi* [river] torcer, hacer una curva; [surface] curvarse, arquearse.

curved [kɜːvd] *adj* curvo(va).

curvy ['kɜːvɪ] (*compar* **-ier**, *superl* **-iest**) *adj* curvo(va).

cushion ['kʊʃn] ◇ *n* **-1.** [for sitting on] cojín *m*, almohadón *m*. **-2.** [protective layer] colchón *m*. ◇ *vt lit* & *fig* amortiguar; **to be ~ed against** estar protegido contra.

cushy ['kʊʃɪ] (*compar* **-ier**, *superl* **-iest**) *adj inf* cómodo(da); **a ~ job** OR **number** un chollo (de trabajo).

custard ['kʌstəd] *n* (U) [sauce] natillas *fpl*.

custard pie *n* tarta *f* de crema.

custard powder *n* (U) polvos *mpl* para natillas.

custodian [kʌ'stəʊdjən] *n* [of building, museum] conservador *m*, -ra *f*.

custody ['kʌstədɪ] *n* custodia *f*; **to take sb into ~** detener a alguien; **in ~** bajo custodia.

custom ['kʌstəm] *n* **-1.** [tradition, habit] costumbre *f*. **-2.** (U) *fml* [trade] clientela *f*.
◆ **customs** *n* [place] aduana *f*; **to go through ~s** pasar por la aduana.

customary ['kʌstəmrɪ] *adj* acostumbrado(da), habitual.

custom-built *adj* hecho(cha) de encargo.

customer ['kʌstəməʳ] *n* **-1.** [client] cliente *m* y *f*. **-2.** *inf* [person] tipo *m*, individuo *m*.

customer services *npl* servicio *m* de atención al cliente.

customize, -ise ['kʌstəmaɪz] *vt* personalizar.

custom-made *adj* [shoes, suit] hecho(cha) a la medida; [car] hecho de encargo.

Customs and Excise *n* (U) *Br* oficina del gobierno británico encargada de la recaudación de derechos arancelarios.

customs duty *n* (U) derechos *mpl* de aduana, aranceles *mpl*.

customs officer *n* empleado *m*, -da *f* de aduana.

cut [kʌt] (*pt* & *pp* **cut**, *cont* **-ting**) ◇ *n* **-1.** [gen] corte *m*. **-2.** [reduction]: **~ (in)** reducción *f* (de). **-3.** *inf* [share] parte *f*. **-4.** *phr*: **to be a ~ above the rest** *inf* ser superior al resto. ◇ *vt* **-1.** [gen] cortar; [one's finger etc] cortarse. **-2.** [spending, staff etc] reducir, recortar. **-3.** [tooth] echar. **-4.** *inf* [lecture] fumarse.
◆ **cut across** *vt fus* **-1.** [take short cut] atajar OR cortar por. **-2.** [disregard] rebasar, trascender.
◆ **cut back** ◇ *vt sep* **-1.** [plant] podar. **-2.** [expenditure, budget] reducir, recortar. ◇ *vi*: **to ~ back (on sthg)** reducir OR recortar (algo).
◆ **cut down** ◇ *vt sep* **-1.** [chop down] cortar, talar. **-2.** [reduce] reducir. ◇ *vi*: **to ~ down on smoking** OR **cigarettes** fumar menos.
◆ **cut in** *vi* **-1.** [interrupt]: **to ~ in (on sb)** cortar OR interrumpir (a alguien). **-2.** [in car] colarse.
◆ **cut off** *vt sep* **-1.** [gen] cortar. **-2.** [separate]: **to be ~ off (from)** [person] estar aislado(da) (de); [town, village] quedarse incomunicado(da) (de).
◆ **cut out** ◇ *vt sep* **-1.** [remove] recortar. **-2.** [dress, pattern etc] cortar; **to be ~ out for sthg** *fig* estar hecho para algo. **-3.** [stop]: **to ~ out smoking** OR **cigarettes** dejar de fumar; **~ it out!** *inf* ¡basta ya! **-4.** [exclude - light etc] eliminar; **to ~ sb out of one's will** desheredar a alguien. ◇ *vi* [stall] calarse, pararse.
◆ **cut through** *vt fus* **-1.** [object, liquid] cortar. **-2.** [take short cut through] atajar OR cortar por.
◆ **cut up** *vt sep* [chop up] cortar, desmenuzar.

cut-and-dried *adj* [issue, result] decidido(da); [formula, answer] pre-establecido(da).

cut and paste COMPUT ◇ *vt* definir e insertar. ◇ *vi* definir e insertar un bloque.

cutback ['kʌtbæk] *n*: **~ (in)** recorte *m* OR reducción *f* (en).

cute [kjuːt] *adj* [appealing] mono(na), lindo(da).

cut glass ◇ *n* cristal *m* labrado. ◇ *comp* de cristal labrado.

cuticle ['kjuːtɪkl] *n* cutícula *f*.

cutlery ['kʌtlərɪ] *n* (U) cubertería *f*, cubiertos *mpl*.

cutlet ['kʌtlɪt] *n* chuleta *f*.

cutoff (point) ['kʌtɒf-] *n* [limit] límite *m*.

cutout ['kʌtaʊt] *n* **-1.** [on machine] cortacircuitos *m inv*. **-2.** [shape] recorte *m*.

cut-price, cut-rate *Am adj* de oferta, rebajado(da); **~ offers** ofertas *fpl*.

cutter ['kʌtə] *n* [tool]: **wire ~s** cortaalambres *m inv*; **glass ~** diamante *m*.

cutthroat ['kʌtθrəʊt] *adj* [ruthless] encarnizado(da).

cutting ['kʌtɪŋ] ◇ *adj* [sarcastic] cortante, mordaz. ◇ *n* **-1.** [of plant] esqueje *m*. **-2.** [from newspaper] recorte *m*. **-3.** *Br* [for road, railway] desmonte *m*, paso *m* estrecho.

cuttlefish ['kʌtlfɪʃ] (*pl inv*) *n* jibia *f*, sepia *f*.

cut-up *adj Br inf* [upset] disgustado(da).

CV (*abbr of* curriculum vitae) *n* CV *m*.

C & W (*abbr of* country and western (music)) *n* música country.

cwo (*abbr of* cash with order) *pago al contado.*

cwt. *abbr of* hundredweight.

cyanide ['saɪənaɪd] *n* cianuro *m*.

cybercafe ['saɪbə,kæfeɪ] *n* cybercafé *m*.

cybernetics [,saɪbə'netɪks] *n*(*U*) cibernética *f*.

cyberspace ['saɪbəspeɪs] *n* cyberespacio *m*.

cyclamen ['sɪkləmən] (*pl inv*) *n* ciclamen *m*.

cycle ['saɪkl] ◇ *n* **-1.** [series of events, poems, songs] ciclo *m*. **-2.** [bicycle] bicicleta *f*. ◇ *comp*: **~ path** camino *m* para bicicletas; **~ race** carrera *f* ciclista. ◇ *vi* ir en bicicleta.

cyclic(al) ['saɪklɪk(l)] *adj* cíclico(ca).

cycling ['saɪklɪŋ] *n* ciclismo *m*; **to go ~** ir en bicicleta.

cyclist ['saɪklɪst] *n* ciclista *m y f*.

cyclone ['saɪkləʊn] *n* ciclón *m*.

cygnet ['sɪgnɪt] *n* pollo *m* de cisne.

cylinder ['sɪlɪndə] *n* **-1.** [shape, engine component] cilindro *m*. **-2.** [for gas] bombona *f*.

cylinder block *n* bloque *m* de cilindros.

cylinder head *n* culata *f* del cilindro.

cylinder-head gasket *n* junta *f* de la culata.

cylindrical [sɪ'lɪndrɪkl] *adj* cilíndrico(ca).

cymbals ['sɪmblz] *npl* platillos *mpl*.

cynic ['sɪnɪk] *n* cínico *m*, -ca *f*.

cynical ['sɪnɪkl] *adj* cínico(ca).

cynically ['sɪnɪklɪ] *adv* cínicamente.

cynicism ['sɪnɪsɪzm] *n* cinismo *m*.

CYO (*abbr of* Catholic Youth Association) *n* asociación estadounidense de jóvenes católicos.

cypher ['saɪfə] = cipher.

cypress ['saɪprəs] *n* ciprés *m*.

Cypriot ['sɪprɪət] ◇ *adj* chipriota. ◇ *n* chipriota *m y f*; **Greek ~** chipriota griego *m*, chipriota griega *f*; **Turkish ~** chipriota turco *m*, chipriota turca *f*.

Cyprus ['saɪprəs] *n* Chipre.

cyst [sɪst] *n* quiste *m*.

cystic fibrosis [,sɪstɪkfaɪ'brəʊsɪs] *n* (*U*) fibrosis *f inv* quística (del páncreas).

cystitis [sɪs'taɪtɪs] *n* cistitis *f inv*.

cytology [saɪ'tɒlədʒɪ] *n* citología *f*.

CZ (*abbr of* canal zone) *área del canal de Panamá.*

czar [zɑː] *n* zar *m*.

Czech [tʃek] ◇ *adj* checo(ca). ◇ *n* **-1.** [person] checo *m*, -ca *f*. **-2.** [language] checo *m*.

Czechoslovak [,tʃekə'sləʊvæk] = Czechoslovakian.

Czechoslovakia [,tʃekəslə'vækɪə] *n* Checoslovaquia.

Czechoslovakian [,tʃekəslə'vækɪən] ◇ *adj* checoslovaco(ca). ◇ *n* [person] checoslovaco *m*, -ca *f*.

d¹ (*pl* **d's** OR **ds**), **D** (*pl* **D's** OR **Ds**) [diː] *n* [letter] d *f*, D *f*.
◆ **D** ◇ *n* MUS re *m*. ◇ *Am abbr of* Democrat, Democratic.

d² [diː] (*abbr of* penny) *antiguamente, penique.*

d. (*abbr of* died) m.; **~ 1913** m. 1913.

DA *n abbr of* district attorney.

dab [dæb] (*pt & pp* -bed, *cont* -bing) ◇ *n* [small amount] toque *m*, pizca *f*; [of powder] pizca *f*. ◇ *vt* **-1.** [skin, wound] dar ligeros toques en. **-2.** [cream, ointment]: **to ~ sthg on** OR **onto** aplicar algo sobre. ◇ *vi*: **to ~ at** dar ligeros toques en.

dabble ['dæbl] ◇ *vt* chapotear. ◇ *vi*: **to ~ (in)** pasar el tiempo OR entretenerse (con).

dab hand *n Br*: **to be a ~ (at sthg)** ser un fenómeno OR un hacha (haciendo algo).

Dacca ['dækə] *n* Dacca.

dachshund ['dækshʊnd] *n* perro *m* salchicha.

dad [dæd], **daddy** ['dædɪ] (*pl* -ies) *n inf* papá *m*.

daddy longlegs [-'lɒŋlegz] (*pl inv*) *n* típula *f*.

daffodil ['dæfədɪl] *n* narciso *m*.

daft [dɑːft] *adj Br inf* tonto(ta), baboso(sa) *Amer*.

dagger ['dægə] *n* daga *f*, puñal *m*.

dahlia ['deɪljə] *n* dalia *f*.

daily ['deɪlɪ] (*pl* **-ies**) ◇ *adj* diario(ria); **on a ~ basis** día a día, cada día. ◇ *adv* diariamente; **twice ~** dos veces al día. ◇ *n* **-1.** [newspaper] diario *m*. **-2.** [cleaning woman] asistenta *f*.

daintily ['deɪntɪlɪ] *adv* delicadamente, finamente.

dainty ['deɪntɪ] (*compar* **-ier**, *superl* **-iest**) *adj* delicado(da), fino(na).

dairy ['deərɪ] (*pl* **-ies**) *n* **-1.** [on farm] vaquería *f*. **-2.** [shop] lechería *f*.

dairy cattle *npl* vacas *fpl* lecheras.

dairy farm *n* granja *f* (de productos lácteos).

dairy products *npl* productos *mpl* lácteos.

dais ['deɪɪs] *n* tarima *f*, estrado *m*.

daisy ['deɪzɪ] (*pl* **-ies**) *n* margarita *f*.

daisy wheel *n* margarita *f* (*de máquina de escribir*).

daisy-wheel printer *n* COMPUT impresora *f* de margarita.

Dakar ['dækuː] *n* Dakar.

Dakota [də'kəʊtə] *n* Dakota.

dal [dɑːl] = **dhal**.

dale [deɪl] *n* valle *m*.

dalmatian [dæl'meɪʃn] *n* [dog] dálmata *m*.

dam [dæm] (*pt* & *pp* **-med**, *cont* **-ming**) ◇ *n* [across river] presa *f*. ◇ *vt* represar.

◆ **dam up** *vt sep* [feelings] reprimir.

damage ['dæmɪdʒ] ◇ *n* **-1.** [physical harm]: **~ (to)** daño *m* (a). **-2.** [harmful effect]: **~ (to)** perjuicio *m* (a). ◇ *vt* dañar.

◆ **damages** *npl* JUR daños *mpl* y perjuicios.

damaging ['dæmɪdʒɪŋ] *adj*: **~ (to)** perjudicial (para).

Damascus [də'mæskəs] *n* Damasco.

Dame [deɪm] *n* Br *título honorífico concedido a una mujer*.

damn [dæm] ◇ *adj inf* maldito(ta), puñetero(ra). ◇ *adv inf* tela de, muy. ◇ *n inf*: **I don't give** OR **care a ~ (about it)** me importa un bledo. ◇ *vt* **-1.** RELIG [condemn] condenar. **-2.** *v inf* [curse] maldecir; **~ it!** ¡maldita sea! ◇ *excl v inf* ¡maldita sea!

damnable ['dæmnəbl] *adj dated* [appalling] terrible, detestable.

damnation [dæm'neɪʃn] *n* RELIG condenación *f*.

damned [dæmd] *inf* ◇ *adj* maldito(ta), puñetero(ra), pinche *Amer*; **I'm ~ if ...** que me maten si ...; **well I'll be** OR **I'm ~!** ¡ostras! ◇ *adv* tela de, muy.

damning ['dæmɪŋ] *adj* comprometedor(ra).

damp [dæmp] ◇ *adj* húmedo(da). ◇ *n* humedad *f*. ◇ *vt* [make wet] humedecer.

◆ **damp down** *vt sep* [restrain] aplacar, mitigar.

damp course *n Br* (aislante *m*) hidrófugo *m*.

dampen ['dæmpən] *vt* **-1.** [make wet] humedecer. **-2.** *fig* [emotion] apagar, ahogar.

damper ['dæmpər] *n* **-1.** MUS apagador *m*, sordina *f*. **-2.** [for fire] regulador *m* de tiro. **-3.** *phr*: **to put a ~ on sthg** aguar OR estropear algo.

dampness ['dæmpnɪs] *n* humedad *f*.

damson ['dæmzn] *n* (ciruela *f*) damascena *f*.

dance [dɑːns] ◇ *n* baile *m*. ◇ *vi* **-1.** [to music] bailar. **-2.** [move quickly and lightly] agitarse, moverse.

dance floor *n* pista *f* de baile.

dancer ['dɑːnsər] *n* bailarín *m*, -ina *f*.

dancing ['dɑːnsɪŋ] *n* (U) baile *m*.

D and C (*abbr of* **dilation and curettage**) *n* dilatación *y* legrado.

dandelion ['dændɪlaɪən] *n* diente *m* de león.

dandruff ['dændrʌf] *n* caspa *f*.

dandy ['dændɪ] (*pl* **-ies**) *n* dandy *m*.

Dane [deɪn] *n* danés *m*, -esa *f*.

danger ['deɪndʒər] *n*: **~ (to)** peligro *m* (para); **in/out of ~** en/fuera de peligro; **to be in ~ of doing sthg** correr el riesgo de hacer algo.

danger list *n Br*: **to be on the ~** [building, species, institution] estar en vías de desaparición; [person] estar en estado crítico.

danger money *n* (U) Br plus *m* OR prima *f* de peligrosidad.

dangerous ['deɪndʒərəs] *adj* peligroso(sa).

dangerous driving *n* JUR imprudencia *f* temeraria (al conducir).

dangerously ['deɪndʒərəslɪ] *adv* **-1.** [riskily] peligrosamente. **-2.** MED: **to be ~ ill** estar grave OR en estado crítico.

danger zone *n* zona *f* de peligro.

dangle ['dæŋgl] ◇ *vt* colgar; *fig*: **to ~ sthg before sb** poner los dientes largos a alguien con algo. ◇ *vi* colgar, pender.

Danish ['deɪnɪʃ] ◇ *adj* danés(esa). ◇ *n* **-1.** [language] danés *m*. **-2.** Am = **Danish pastry**. ◇ *npl* [people]: **the ~** los daneses.

Danish blue *n* queso *m* azul danés.

Danish pastry *n* pastel *m* de hojaldre con crema o manzana o almendras etc.

dank [dæŋk] *adj* húmedo(da) e insalubre.

Danube ['dænjuːb] *n*: **the ~** el Danubio.

dapper ['dæpər] *adj* pulcro(cra), atildado(da).

dappled ['dæpld] *adj* **-1.** [light] moteado(da). **-2.** [horse] rodado(da).

Dardanelles [,dɑ:də'nelz] *npl*: **the** ~ los Dardanelos.

dare [deəʳ] ◇ *vt* **-1.** [be brave enough]: **to** ~ **to do sthg** atreverse a hacer algo, osar hacer algo. **-2.** [challenge]: **to** ~ **sb to do sthg** desafiar a alguien a hacer algo. **-3.** *phr*: **I** ~ **say (...)** supongo OR me imagino (que ...). ◇ *vi* atreverse, osar; **how** ~ **you!** ¿cómo te atreves? ◇ *n* desafío *m*, reto *m*.

daredevil ['deə,devl] *n* temerario *m*, -ria *f*.

daren't [deənt] = **dare not**.

Dar es-Salaam [,dɑ:ressə'lɑ:m] *n* Dar es Salam.

daring ['deərɪŋ] ◇ *adj* atrevido(da), audaz. ◇ *n* audacia *f*.

dark [dɑ:k] ◇ *adj* **-1.** [night, colour, hair] oscuro(ra). **-2.** [person, skin] moreno(na), cambujo(ja) *Amer*. **-3.** [thoughts, days, mood] sombrío(a), triste. **-4.** [look, comment, side of character etc] siniestro(tra). ◇ *n* **-1.** [darkness]: **the** ~ la oscuridad; **to be in the** ~ **about sthg** estar a oscuras sobre algo. **-2.** [night]: **before/after** ~ antes/después del anochecer.

Dark Ages *npl*: **the** ~ la Alta Edad Media.

darken ['dɑ:kn] ◇ *vt* oscurecer. ◇ *vi* **-1.** [become darker] oscurecerse. **-2.** [look angry] ensombrecerse.

dark glasses *npl* gafas *fpl* oscuras.

dark horse *n fig* figura *f* OR persona *f* enigmática.

darkness ['dɑ:knɪs] *n* oscuridad *f*.

darkroom ['dɑ:krum] *n* PHOT cuarto *m* oscuro.

darling ['dɑ:lɪŋ] ◇ *adj* **-1.** [dear] querido(da). **-2.** *inf* [cute] adorable, encantador(ra). ◇ *n* **-1.** [loved person] encanto *m*. **-2.** *inf* [addressing any woman] maja *f*. **-3.** [idol] preferido *m*, -da *f*, niño bonito *m*, niña bonita *f*.

darn [dɑ:n] ◇ *adj inf* maldito(ta), condenado(da). ◇ *adv inf* tela de, muy. ◇ *n* zurcido *m*. ◇ *vt* zurcir. ◇ *excl inf* ¡maldita sea!

darning ['dɑ:nɪŋ] *n* (U) [things] ropa *f* para zurcir; [task] zurcido *m*.

darning needle *n* aguja *f* de zurcir.

dart [dɑ:t] ◇ *n* **-1.** [arrow] dardo *m*. **-2.** SEWING pinza *f*. ◇ *vt* lanzar. ◇ *vi* precipitarse.
◆ **darts** *n* (U) [game] dardos *mpl*.

dartboard ['dɑ:tbɔ:d] *n* blanco *m*, diana *f*.

dash [dæʃ] ◇ *n* **-1.** [of liquid, colour] gotas *fpl*, chorrito *m*. **-2.** [in punctuation] guión *m*. **-3.** AUT salpicadero *m*. **-4.** [rush]: **to make a** ~ **for sthg** salir disparado hacia algo. ◇ *vt* **-1.** *literary* [throw] arrojar. **-2.** [hopes] frus-

trar, malograr. ◇ *vi* ir de prisa; **I must** ~! ¡me voy pitando!
◆ **dash off** *vt sep* [write quickly] garrapatear, escribir de prisa.

dashboard ['dæʃbɔ:d] *n* salpicadero *m*.

dashing ['dæʃɪŋ] *adj* gallardo(da), apuesto(ta).

dastardly ['dæstədlɪ] *adj dated* ruin, malvado(da).

DAT [dæt] (*abbr of* **digital audio tape**) *n* DAT *f*.

data ['deɪtə] *n* (U) datos *mpl*.

databank ['deɪtəbæŋk] *n* banco *m* de datos.

database ['deɪtəbeɪs] *n* COMPUT base *f* de datos.

data capture *n* (U) recolección *f* OR recogida *f* de datos.

data processing *n* proceso *m* de datos.

data transmission *n* transmisión *f* de datos.

date [deɪt] ◇ *n* **-1.** [in time] fecha *f*; **to** ~ hasta la fecha. **-2.** [appointment] cita *f*. **-3.** *Am* [person] pareja *f* (*con la que se sale*). **-4.** [fruit] dátil *m*. ◇ *vt* **-1.** [establish the date of] datar. **-2.** [mark with the date] fechar. **-3.** *Am* [go out with] salir con. ◇ *vi* [go out of fashion] pasar de moda, quedarse anticuado.
◆ **date back to, date from** *vt fus* datar de, remontarse a.

dated ['deɪtɪd] *adj* anticuado(da).

date line *n* línea *f* de cambio de fecha.

date of birth *n* fecha *f* de nacimiento.

date stamp *n* **-1.** [device] fechador *m*. **-2.** [mark] sello *m* de fecha.

daub [dɔ:b] *vt*: **to** ~ **sthg with** embadurnar algo con.

daughter ['dɔ:təʳ] *n* hija *f*.

daughter-in-law (*pl* **daughters-in-law**) *n* nuera *f*.

daunt [dɔ:nt] *vt* intimidar, acobardar.

daunting ['dɔ:ntɪŋ] *adj* amedrantador(ra).

dawdle ['dɔ:dl] *vi* remolonear, entretenerse.

dawn [dɔ:n] ◇ *n* **-1.** [of day] amanecer *m*, alba *f*; **at** ~ al amanecer; **from** ~ **to dusk** de sol a sol. **-2.** [of era, period] albores *mpl*, amanecer *m*. ◇ *vi* **-1.** [day] amanecer. **-2.** [era, period] nacer.
◆ **dawn (up)on** *vt fus*: **it** ~**ed on me that** ... caí en la cuenta de que ....

dawn chorus *n* canto *m* de los pájaros al amanecer.

day [deɪ] *n* **-1.** [gen] día *m*; **the** ~ **before/after** el día anterior/siguiente; **the** ~ **before yesterday** anteayer; **the** ~ **after tomorrow** pasado mañana; **any** ~ **now** cualquier día de estos; **one** OR **some** ~, **one of these** ~**s**

uno de estos días; ~ **and night** día y noche; **to call it a** ~ dejarlo por hoy; **to make sb's** ~ dar un alegrón a alguien; **to save sthg for a rainy** ~ guardar algo para cuando haga verdadera falta; **his** ~**s are numbered** tiene los días contados; **it's early** ~**s yet** es aún pronto para hablar, sería prematuro aventurar nada. **-2.** [period in history]: **in my/your** etc ~ en mis/tus etc tiempos; **in the** ~**s of ...** en tiempos de ...; **in those** ~**s** en aquellos tiempos; **in this** ~ **and age** en nuestros días.
◆ **days** adv de día.

dayboy ['deɪbɔɪ] n Br SCH (alumno m) externo m.

daybreak ['deɪbreɪk] n amanecer m, alba f; **at** ~ al amanecer.

day-care centre n guardería f.

daycentre ['deɪsentə] n Br (centro estatal diurno donde se da) acogida y cuidado a niños, ancianos, minusválidos etc.

daydream ['deɪdriːm] ◇ n sueño m, ilusión f. ◇ vi soñar despierto(ta).

daygirl ['deɪgɜːl] n Br SCH (alumna f) externa f.

Day-Glo® ['deɪgləʊ] adj fluorescente.

daylight ['deɪlaɪt] n **-1.** [light] luz f del día. **-2.** [dawn] amanecer m. **-3.** inf phr: **to scare the (living)** ~**s out of sb** dar un susto de muerte a alguien.

daylight robbery n (U) inf: **that's** ~! ¡es un auténtico timo OR robo!

daylight saving time n horario m oficial de verano.

day nursery n guardería f (infantil).

day off (pl days off) n día m libre.

day pupil n Br SCH externo m, -na f.

day release n (U) sistema en que los trabajadores dedican un día de trabajo a la formación profesional en un centro de enseñanza.

day return n Br billete m de ida y vuelta para un día.

dayroom ['deɪruːm] n sala f de estar (en hospital, asilo etc).

day school n externado m.

day shift n turno m de día.

daytime ['deɪtaɪm] ◇ n (U) día m. ◇ comp de día, diurno(na).

day-to-day adj cotidiano(na), diario(ria).

day trip n excursión f (de un día).

day-tripper n Br excursionista m y f.

daze [deɪz] ◇ n: **in a** ~ aturdido(da). ◇ vt lit & fig aturdir.

dazed [deɪzd] adj lit & fig aturdido(da).

dazzle ['dæzl] ◇ n (U) **-1.** [of light] resplandor m. **-2.** [impressiveness] hechizo m, fascinación f. ◇ vt lit & fig deslumbrar.

dazzling ['dæzlɪŋ] adj lit & fig deslumbrante.

DBE (abbr of **Dame Commander of the Order of the British Empire**) n (titular de) distinción honorífica británica para mujeres.

DBS (abbr of **direct broadcasting by satellite**) n emisión vía satélite.

DC ◇ n (abbr of **direct current**) CC f. ◇ abbr of **District of Columbia**.

dd. abbr of **delivered**.

DD (abbr of **Doctor of Divinity**) n (titular de un) doctorado de teología.

D/D abbr of **direct debit**.

D-day ['diːdeɪ] n el día D.

DDS (abbr of **Doctor of Dental Science**) n (titular de un) doctorado de odontología.

DDT (abbr of **dichlorodiphenyltrichloroethane**) n DDT m.

DE abbr of **Delaware**.

DEA (abbr of **Drug Enforcement Administration**) n organismo estadounidense para la lucha contra la droga.

deacon ['diːkn] n diácono m.

deaconess [ˌdiːkə'nes] n diaconisa f.

deactivate [ˌdiːˈæktɪveɪt] vt desactivar.

dead [ded] ◇ adj **-1.** [person, animal, plant] muerto(ta); **to shoot sb** ~ matar a alguien a tiros; **he wouldn't be seen** ~ **doing that** no haría eso por nada del mundo. **-2.** [numb - leg, arm] dormido(da), entumecido(da). **-3.** [telephone] cortado(da); [car battery] descargado(da). **-4.** [silence] absoluto(ta), completo(ta). **-5.** [lifeless - town, party] sin vida.
◇ adv **-1.** [directly, precisely] justo. **-2.** [completely] totalmente, completamente; "~ **slow**" "al paso". **-3.** inf [very] la mar de, muy; **to be** ~ **set against sthg** estar totalmente en contra de algo; **to be** ~ **set on sthg** estar decidido a hacer algo. **-4.** [suddenly]: **to stop** ~ parar en seco.
◇ n [middle, depth]: **at** ~ **of night** en mitad de la noche.
◇ npl: **the** ~ los muertos.

deadbeat ['dedbiːt] n Am inf holgazán m, -ana f.

dead centre n corazón m, centro m mismo.

dead duck n inf fracaso m.

deaden ['dedn] vt atenuar.

dead end n lit & fig callejón m sin salida.

dead-end job n trabajo m sin futuro.

deadhead ['dedhed] vt cortar (flor seca).

dead heat n empate m.

dead letter n fig [rule, law] letra f muerta.

deadline ['dedlaɪn] n plazo m, fecha f tope.

deadlock ['dedlɒk] n punto m muerto.

deadlocked ['dedlɒkt] adj paralizado(da).

dead loss n inf -1. [person] inútil m y f. -2. [thing] inutilidad f.

deadly ['dedlɪ] (compar -ier, superl -iest) ◇ adj -1. [gen] mortal. -2. [accuracy] absoluto(ta). ◇ adv [boring] mortalmente, terriblemente; [serious] totalmente.

deadly nightshade [-'naɪtʃeɪd] n (U) belladona f.

deadpan ['dedpæn] ◇ adj inexpresivo(va), serio(ria). ◇ adv inexpresivamente, seriamente.

Dead Sea n: the ~ el mar Muerto.

dead wood Br, **deadwood** Am ['dedwʊd] n (U) fig [people] gente f que sobra; [in text] paja f.

deaf [def] ◇ adj -1. [unable to hear] sordo(da). -2. [unwilling to hear]: to be ~ to sthg hacer oídos sordos a algo. ◇ npl: the ~ los sordos.

deaf-aid n Br audífono m.

deaf-and-dumb adj sordomudo(da).

deafen ['defn] vt ensordecer.

deafening ['defnɪŋ] adj ensordecedor(ra).

deaf-mute ◇ adj sordomudo(da). ◇ n sordomudo m, -da f.

deafness ['defnɪs] n sordera f.

deal [diːl] (pt & pp dealt) ◇ n -1. [quantity]: a good OR great ~ (of) mucho. -2. [business agreement] trato m, transacción f; to do OR strike a ~ with sb hacer un trato con alguien. -3. inf [treatment] trato m; big ~! ¡vaya cosa! ◇ vt -1. [strike]: to ~ sb/sthg a blow, to ~ a blow to sb/sthg lit & fig asestar un golpe a alguien/algo. -2. [cards] repartir, dar. ◇ vi -1. [in cards] repartir, dar. -2. [in drugs] traficar con droga.
◆ **deal in** vt fus COMM comerciar en, vender.
◆ **deal out** vt sep repartir.
◆ **deal with** vt fus -1. [handle - situation, problem] hacer frente a, resolver; [- customer] tratar con. -2. [be about] tratar de, versar sobre. -3. [be faced with] enfrentarse a.

dealer ['diːlə'] n -1. [trader] comerciante m y f. -2. [in cards] repartidor m, -ra f.

dealership ['diːləʃɪp] n concesionario m.

dealing ['diːlɪŋ] n comercio m.
◆ **dealings** npl [personal] trato m; [in business] tratos mpl.

dealt [delt] pt & pp → deal.

dean [diːn] n -1. [of university] ≃ decano m, -na f. -2. [of church] deán m.

dear [dɪə'] ◇ adj -1. [loved] querido(da); ~ to sb preciado(da) para alguien. -2. [expensive] caro(ra). -3. [in letter]: **Dear Sir** Estimado señor, Muy señor mío; **Dear Madam** Estimada señora. ◇ n querido m, -da f. ◇ excl: oh ~! ¡vaya por Dios!

dearly ['dɪəlɪ] adv [love, wish] profundamente.

dearth [dɜːθ] n carencia f, escasez f.

death [deθ] n muerte f; to be put to ~ ser ejecutado(da); to frighten sb ~ dar un susto de muerte a alguien; to be sick to ~ of sthg/of doing sthg estar hasta las narices de algo/de hacer algo; to starve to ~ morir de hambre; to be at ~'s door estar a las puertas de la muerte.

deathbed ['deθbed] n lecho m de muerte.

death certificate n partida f OR certificado m de defunción.

death duty Br, **death tax** Am n impuesto m de sucesiones.

death knell n fig: to sound the ~ of hacer presagiar el final de.

deathly ['deθlɪ] (compar -ier, superl -iest) ◇ adj sepulcral. ◇ adv: he was ~ pale estaba pálido como un muerto; her hands were ~ cold sus manos estaban frías como la muerte.

death penalty n pena f de muerte.

death rate n índice m OR tasa f de mortalidad.

death row n Am celdas para condenados a muerte.

death sentence n pena f de muerte.

death squad n escuadrón m de la muerte.

death tax Am = death duty.

death toll n número m de víctimas.

death trap n inf trampa f mortal, sitio m peligroso.

Death Valley n la Valle de la Muerte.

deathwatch beetle ['deθwɒtʃ-] n especie de carcoma.

death wish n ganas fpl de morir.

deb [deb] n Br inf = debutante.

débâcle [de'bɑːkl] n debacle f.

debar [diː'bɑː'] (pt & pp -red, cont -ring) vt: to ~ sb from somewhere/from doing sthg privar a alguien del acceso a algún lugar/de hacer algo.

debase [dɪ'beɪs] vt degradar; to ~ o.s. rebajarse.

debasement [dɪ'beɪsmənt] n degradación f.

debatable [dɪ'beɪtəbl] adj discutible.

debate [dɪ'beɪt] ◇ n debate m; that's open to ~ eso está por ver. ◇ vt -1. [issue] discutir, debatir. -2. [what to do]: to ~

(whether to do sthg) pensarse (si hacer algo). ◇ *vi* discutir, debatir.

debating society [dɪˈbeɪtɪŋ-] *n* asociación de debates especialmente universitaria.

debauched [dɪˈbɔːtʃt] *adj* depravado(da), libertino(na).

debauchery [dɪˈbɔːtʃərɪ] *n* depravación *f*, libertinaje *m*.

debenture [dɪˈbentʃər] *n* obligación *f*.

debenture stock *n* (*U*) *Br* obligaciones *fpl*.

debilitate [dɪˈbɪlɪteɪt] *vt* debilitar.

debilitating [dɪˈbɪlɪteɪtɪŋ] *adj* debilitador(ra), debilitante.

debility [dɪˈbɪlətɪ] *n* debilidad *f*.

debit [ˈdebɪt] ◇ *n* debe *m*, débito *m*. ◇ *vt*: **to ~ sb** OR **sb's account with an amount**, **to ~ an amount to sb** adeudar OR cargar una cantidad en la cuenta de alguien.

debit note *n* pagaré *m*.

debonair [ˌdebəˈneər] *adj* apuesto(ta).

debrief [ˌdiːˈbriːf] *vt* pedir un informe completo a.

debriefing [ˌdiːˈbriːfɪŋ] *n* sesión *f* informativa (tras una misión).

debris [ˈdeɪbriː] *n* (*U*) [of building] escombros *mpl*; [of aircraft] restos *mpl*.

debt [det] *n* deuda *f*; **to be in ~ (to sb)** tener una deuda (con alguien); **to be in sb's ~** *fig* estar en deuda con alguien.

debt collector *n* cobrador *m*, -ra *f* de morosos.

debtor [ˈdetər] *n* deudor *m*, -ra *f*.

debug [ˌdiːˈbʌg] (*pt* & *pp* **-ged**, *cont* **-ging**) *vt* **-1.** [room] quitar micrófonos ocultos de. **-2.** COMPUT suprimir fallos de.

debunk [ˌdiːˈbʌŋk] *vt* desmentir, desacreditar.

debut [ˈdeɪbjuː] *n* debut *m*.

debutante [ˈdebjʊtɑːnt] *n* mujer que está siendo presentada en sociedad.

Dec. (*abbr of* **December**) dic.

decade [ˈdekeɪd] *n* década *f*.

decadence [ˈdekədəns] *n* decadencia *f*.

decadent [ˈdekədənt] *adj* decadente.

decaff [ˈdiːkæf] *n inf* descafeinado *m*.

decaffeinated [dɪˈkæfɪneɪtɪd] *adj* descafeinado(da).

decal [ˈdiːkæl] *n Am* calcomanía *f*.

decamp [dɪˈkæmp] *vi inf* escabullirse, esfumarse.

decant [dɪˈkænt] *vt* decantar.

decanter [dɪˈkæntər] *n* licorera *f*.

decapitate [dɪˈkæpɪteɪt] *vt* decapitar.

decathlete [dɪˈkæθliːt] *n* especialista *m* y *f* en decatlón.

decathlon [dɪˈkæθlɒn] *n* decatlón *m*.

decay [dɪˈkeɪ] ◇ *n* (*U*) **-1.** [of tooth] caries *f*; [of body, plant] descomposición *f*. **-2.** *fig* [of building] deterioro *m*; [of society] corrupción *f*, degradación *f*. ◇ *vi* **-1.** [tooth] picarse; [body, plant] pudrirse, descomponerse. **-2.** *fig* [building] deteriorarse; [society] corromperse, degradarse.

deceased [dɪˈsiːst] (*pl inv*) *fml* ◇ *adj* difunto(ta), fallecido(da). ◇ *n*: **the ~** el difunto (la difunta).

deceit [dɪˈsiːt] *n* engaño *m*.

deceitful [dɪˈsiːtfʊl] *adj* [person, smile] embustero(ra); [behaviour] falso(sa).

deceive [dɪˈsiːv] *vt* engañar; **to ~ o.s.** engañarse (a uno mismo).

decelerate [ˌdiːˈseləreɪt] *vi* desacelerar.

December [dɪˈsembər] *n* diciembre *m*; *see also* **September**.

decency [ˈdiːsnsɪ] *n* **-1.** [respectability] decencia *f*. **-2.** [consideration]: **to have the ~ to do sthg** tener la delicadeza de hacer algo.

decent [ˈdiːsnt] *adj* **-1.** [gen] decente. **-2.** [considerate]: **that's very ~ of you** es muy amable de tu parte.

decently [ˈdiːsntlɪ] *adv* [behave, dress] decentemente.

decentralization [diːˌsentrəlaɪˈzeɪʃn] *n* descentralización *f*.

decentralize, **-ise** [ˌdiːˈsentrəlaɪz] *vt* descentralizar.

deception [dɪˈsepʃn] *n* engaño *m*.

deceptive [dɪˈseptɪv] *adj* engañoso(sa).

deceptively [dɪˈseptɪvlɪ] *adv* engañosamente.

decibel [ˈdesɪbel] *n* decibelio *m*.

decide [dɪˈsaɪd] ◇ *vt* **-1.** [gen]: **to ~ (to do sthg)** decidir (hacer algo); **to ~ (that)** decidir que. **-2.** [person] hacer decidirse. **-3.** [issue, case] resolver. ◇ *vi* decidir.

◆ **decide (up)on** *vt fus* decidirse por.

decided [dɪˈsaɪdɪd] *adj* **-1.** [advantage, improvement] indudable. **-2.** [person] decidido(da); [opinion] categórico(ca).

decidedly [dɪˈsaɪdɪdlɪ] *adv* **-1.** [clearly] decididamente, indudablemente. **-2.** [resolutely] con decisión.

deciding [dɪˈsaɪdɪŋ] *adj*: **~ vote** voto *m* decisivo.

deciduous [dɪˈsɪdjʊəs] *adj* de hoja caduca.

decimal [ˈdesɪml] ◇ *adj* decimal. ◇ *n* (número *m*) decimal *m*.

decimal currency *n* moneda *f* de sistema decimal.

decimalize, **-ise** [ˈdesɪməlaɪz] *vt Br* convertir en decimal.

decimal place *n* cifra *f* OR posición *f* decimal.

decimal point *n* coma *f* decimal.

decimate ['desɪmeɪt] *vt* diezmar.

decimation [,desɪ'meɪʃn] *n* práctica destrucción *f*.

decipher [dɪ'saɪfər] *vt* descifrar.

decision [dɪ'sɪʒn] *n* decisión *f*; **to make a ~** tomar una decisión.

decision-making *n* toma *f* de decisiones.

decisive [dɪ'saɪsɪv] *adj* **-1.** [person] decidido(da). **-2.** [factor, event] decisivo(va).

decisively [dɪ'saɪsɪvlɪ] *adv* **-1.** [act, speak] con decisión, decididamente. **-2.** [beaten, superior] claramente.

decisiveness [dɪ'saɪsɪvnɪs] *n* decisión *f*.

deck [dek] ◇ *n* **-1.** [of ship] cubierta *f*; [of bus] piso *m*. **-2.** [of cards] baraja *f*. **-3.** *Am* [of house] entarimado *m* (*junto a una casa*). ◇ *vt*: **to ~ sthg with** engalanar algo con.

◆ **deck out** *vt sep* [place, object] engalanar, adornar; [person] ataviar.

deckchair ['dektʃeər] *n* tumbona *f*.

deckhand ['dekhænd] *n* grumete *m*.

declaration [,deklə'reɪʃn] *n* declaración *f*.

Declaration of Independence *n*: **the ~** *la declaración de independencia estadounidense de 1776*.

declare [dɪ'kleər] *vt* declarar.

declared [dɪ'kleəd] *adj* declarado(da).

declassify [,diː'klæsɪfaɪ] (*pt & pp* **-ied**) *vt* levantar el secreto oficial a.

decline [dɪ'klaɪn] ◇ *n* declive *m*; **in ~** en decadencia; **on the ~** en declive. ◇ *vt* [offer] declinar; [request] denegar; **to ~ to do sthg** rehusar hacer algo. ◇ *vi* **-1.** [deteriorate] decrecer, disminuir. **-2.** [refuse] rehusar, negarse.

declutch [dɪ'klʌtʃ] *vi* AUT desembragar, quitar el embrague.

decode [,diː'kəud] *vt* descodificar.

decoder [,diː'kəudər] *n* descodificador *m*.

decommission [,diːkə'mɪʃn] *vt* desmantelar.

decompose [,diːkəm'pəuz] *vi* descomponerse.

decomposition [,diːkɒmpə'zɪʃn] *n* descomposición *f*.

decompression chamber [,diːkəm'preʃn-] *n* cámara *f* de descompresión.

decompression sickness [,diːkəm'preʃn-] *n* aeroembolismo *m*.

decongestant [,diːkən'dʒestənt] *n* decongestivo *m*.

decontaminate [,diːkən'tæmɪneɪt] *vt* descontaminar.

décor ['deɪkɔːr] *n* decoración *f*.

decorate ['dekəreɪt] *vt* **-1.** [make pretty]: **to ~ sthg (with)** decorar algo (de). **-2.** [with paint] pintar; [with wallpaper] empapelar. **-3.** [with medal] condecorar.

decoration [,dekə'reɪʃn] *n* **-1.** [gen] decoración *f*. **-2.** [ornament] adorno *m*. **-3.** [medal] condecoración *f*.

decorative ['dekərətɪv] *adj* decorativo(va).

decorator ['dekəreɪtər] *n* [painter] pintor *m*, -ra *f*; [paperhanger] empapelador *m*, -ra *f*.

decorous ['dekərəs] *adj fml* decoroso(sa).

decorum [dɪ'kɔːrəm] *n* decoro *m*.

decoy [*n* 'diːkɔɪ, *vb* dɪ'kɔɪ] ◇ *n* señuelo *m*. ◇ *vt* desviar (*mediante señuelo*).

decrease [*n* 'diːkriːs, *vb* dɪ'kriːs] ◇ *n*: **~ (in)** disminución *f* (en), decrecimiento *m* (en). ◇ *vt & vi* disminuir.

decreasing [diː'kriːsɪŋ] *adj* decreciente.

decree [dɪ'kriː] ◇ *n* **-1.** [order, decision] decreto *m*. **-2.** *Am* [judgment] sentencia *f*, fallo *m*. ◇ *vt* decretar.

decree absolute (*pl* **decrees absolute**) *n* *Br* JUR sentencia *f* de divorcio definitiva.

decree nisi [-'naɪsaɪ] (*pl* **decrees nisi**) *n* *Br* JUR sentencia *f* provisional de divorcio.

decrepit [dɪ'krepɪt] *adj* decrépito(ta).

decry [dɪ'kraɪ] (*pt & pp* **-ied**) *vt fml* censurar, deplorar.

dedicate ['dedɪkeɪt] *vt* dedicar; **to ~ o.s. to sthg** consagrarse OR dedicarse a algo.

dedicated ['dedɪkeɪtɪd] *adj* **-1.** [person] dedicado(da). **-2.** [COMPUT - use] dedicado(da); [- message] privilegiado(da).

dedication [,dedɪ'keɪʃn] *n* **-1.** [commitment] dedicación *f*. **-2.** [in book] dedicatoria *f*.

deduce [dɪ'djuːs] *vt*: **to ~ (sthg from sthg)** deducir (algo de algo).

deduct [dɪ'dʌkt] *vt*: **to ~ (from)** deducir (de), descontar (de).

deduction [dɪ'dʌkʃn] *n* deducción *f*.

deed [diːd] *n* **-1.** [action] acción *f*, obra *f*. **-2.** JUR escritura *f*.

deed poll (*pl* **deed polls** OR **deeds poll**) *n* *Br* **to change one's name by ~** cambiarse oficialmente de nombre.

deem [diːm] *vt fml* estimar; **to ~ it wise to do sthg** estimar prudente hacer algo.

deep [diːp] ◇ *adj* **-1.** [gen] profundo(da); **to be 10 feet ~** tener 10 pies de profundidad. **-2.** [sigh, breath] hondo(da). **-3.** [colour] intenso(sa). **-4.** [sound, voice] grave. ◇ *adv* [dig, cut] hondo; **to advance ~ into enemy territory** adentrarse en territorio enemigo; **~ down** OR **inside** por dentro; **to be ~ in thought** estar sumido en sus pensamientos; **to go** OR **run ~** estar muy arraigado.

deepen ['di:pn] ◇ *vt* [hole, channel] ahondar, hacer más profundo(da). ◇ *vi* **-1.** [river, sea] ahondarse, hacerse más profundo(da). **-2.** [crisis, recession] agudizarse; [emotion, darkness] hacerse más intenso(sa).

deepening ['di:pnɪŋ] *adj* [crisis, recession] cada vez más agudo(da).

deep freeze *n* congelador *m*.
◆ **deep-freeze** *vt* congelar.

deep fry *vt* freír (con mucho aceite).

deeply ['di:plɪ] *adv* [gen] profundamente; [dig, breathe, sigh] hondo.

deep-rooted *adj* profundamente arraigado(da).

deep-sea *adj*: ~ **diving** buceo *m* de profundidad; ~ **fishing** pesca *f* de altura.

deep-seated *adj* profundamente arraigado(da).

deep-set *adj* [eyes] hundido(da).

deer [dɪər] (*pl inv*) *n* ciervo *m*.

deerstalker ['dɪə,stɔ:kər] *n especie de gorro con orejeras*.

de-escalate [,di:'eskəleɪt] ◇ *vt* suavizar, paliar. ◇ *vi* suavizarse.

deface [dɪ'feɪs] *vt* pintarrajear.

defamation [,defə'meɪʃn] *n fml* difamación *f*.

defamatory [dɪ'fæmətrɪ] *adj fml* difamatorio(ria).

default [dɪ'fɔ:lt] ◇ *n* **-1.** [on payment, agreement] incumplimiento *m*; [failure to attend] incomparecencia *f*; **by ~** [win] por incomparecencia. **-2.** COMPUT: ~ **(value)** valor *m* de ajuste (por defecto). ◇ *vi* incumplir un compromiso; **to ~ on sthg** incumplir algo.

defaulter [dɪ'fɔ:ltər] *n* [on payment] moroso *m*, -sa *f*.

defeat [dɪ'fi:t] ◇ *n* derrota *f*; **to admit ~** darse por vencido(da). ◇ *vt* [team, opponent] derrotar; [motion] rechazar; [plans] frustrar.

defeatism [dɪ'fi:tɪzm] *n* derrotismo *m*.

defeatist [dɪ'fi:tɪst] ◇ *adj* derrotista. ◇ *n* derrotista *m y f*.

defecate ['defəkeɪt] *vi fml* defecar.

defect [*n* 'di:fekt, *vb* dɪ'fekt] ◇ *n* [fault] defecto *m*. ◇ *vi* POL: **to ~ to the other side** pasarse al otro bando.

defection [dɪ'fekʃn] *n* cambio *m* de bando.

defective [dɪ'fektɪv] *adj* defectuoso(sa).

defector [dɪ'fektər] *n* desertor *m*, -ra *f*.

defence *Br*, **defense** *Am* [dɪ'fens] *n* defensa *f*; **in ~ of** en defensa de.
◆ **defences** *npl* [of country] defensas *fpl*.

defenceless *Br*, **defenseless** *Am* [dɪ'fenslɪs] *adj* indefenso(sa).

defend [dɪ'fend] ◇ *vt* defender; **to ~ o.s.** defenderse. ◇ *vi* SPORT defender.

defendant [dɪ'fendənt] *n* acusado *m*, -da *f*.

defender [dɪ'fendər] *n* **-1.** [gen] defensor *m*, -ra *f*. **-2.** SPORT defensa *m y f*.

defense *Am* = **defence**.

defenseless *Am* = **defenceless**.

defensive [dɪ'fensɪv] ◇ *adj* **-1.** [weapons, tactics] defensivo(va). **-2.** [person] receloso(sa). ◇ *n*: **on the ~** a la defensiva.

defer [dɪ'fɜ:r] (*pt & pp* **-red**, *cont* **-ring**) ◇ *vt* deferir, aplazar. ◇ *vi*: **to ~ to sb** deferir con OR a alguien.

deference ['defərəns] *n* deferencia *f*.

deferential [,defə'renʃl] *adj* deferente, respetuoso(sa).

defiance [dɪ'faɪəns] *n* desafío *m*; **in ~ of** en desafío de, a despecho de.

defiant [dɪ'faɪənt] *adj* desafiante.

defiantly [dɪ'faɪəntlɪ] *adv* de manera desafiante.

deficiency [dɪ'fɪʃnsɪ] (*pl* **-ies**) *n* **-1.** [lack] escasez *f*, insuficiencia *f*. **-2.** [inadequacy] deficiencia *f*, imperfección *f*.

deficient [dɪ'fɪʃnt] *adj* **-1.** [lacking]: **to be ~ in** ser deficitario(ria) en, estar falto(ta) de. **-2.** [inadequate] deficiente.

deficit ['defɪsɪt] *n* déficit *m inv*.

defile [dɪ'faɪl] *vt* [desecrate] profanar; *fig* [mind, purity] corromper.

define [dɪ'faɪn] *vt* definir.

definite ['defɪnɪt] *adj* **-1.** [plan, date, answer] definitivo(va). **-2.** [improvement, difference] indudable, claro(ra). **-3.** [confident - person] tajante, concluyente; **I am quite ~ (about it)** estoy totalmente seguro (de ello).

definitely ['defɪnɪtlɪ] *adv* **-1.** [without doubt] sin duda. **-2.** [for emphasis] desde luego, con (toda) seguridad.

definition [defɪ'nɪʃn] *n* **-1.** [gen] definición *f*; **by ~** por definición. **-2.** [clarity] nitidez *f*.

definitive [dɪ'fɪnɪtɪv] *adj* definitivo(va).

deflate [dɪ'fleɪt] ◇ *vt* **-1.** [balloon] desinflar; *fig* [person] bajar los humos a. **-2.** ECON reducir la inflación en. ◇ *vi* desinflarse.

deflation [dɪ'fleɪʃn] *n* ECON deflación *f*.

deflationary [dɪ'fleɪʃnərɪ] *adj* ECON deflacionario(ria), deflacionista.

deflect [dɪ'flekt] *vt* [gen] desviar; [criticism] soslayar.

deflection [dɪ'flekʃn] *n* desvío *m*.

defog [,di:'fɒg] *vt Am* AUT desempañar.

defogger [,di:'fɒgər] *n Am* AUT dispositivo *m* antivaho, luneta *f* térmica.

deforest [,di:'fɒrɪst] *vt* despoblar (de árboles), deforestar.

deforestation [diːˌfɒrɪ'steɪʃn] *n* despoblación *f* (de árboles), deforestación *f*.

deform [diː'fɔːm] *vt* deformar.

deformed [dɪ'fɔːmd] *adj* deforme.

deformity [dɪ'fɔːmətɪ] (*pl* **-ies**) *n* [in foetus, baby] malformación *f* (congénita); [in adult] deformidad *f*.

defraud [dɪ'frɔːd] *vt* defraudar, estafar.

defray [dɪ'freɪ] *vt* sufragar, correr con.

defrost [ˌdiː'frɒst] ◇ *vt* **-1.** [gen] descongelar. **-2.** *Am* AUT [demist] desempañar. ◇ *vi* descongelarse.

deft [deft] *adj* habilidoso(sa), diestro(tra).

deftly ['deftlɪ] *adv* con destreza, con pericia.

defunct [dɪ'fʌŋkt] *adj* [plan] desechado(da); [body, organization] desaparecido(da).

defuse [ˌdiː'fjuːz] *vt* *Br* **-1.** [bomb] desactivar. **-2.** [situation] neutralizar.

defy [dɪ'faɪ] (*pt* & *pp* **-ied**) *vt* **-1.** [disobey - person, authority] desafiar, desobedecer; [law, rule] violar. **-2.** [challenge]: **to ~ sb to do sthg** retar OR desafiar a alguien a hacer algo. **-3.** [description, analysis] hacer imposible; [attempts, efforts] hacer inútil.

degenerate [*adj* & *n* dɪ'dʒenərət, *vb* dɪ'dʒenəreɪt] ◇ *adj* degenerado(da). ◇ *n* degenerado *m*, -da *f*. ◇ *vi*: **to ~ (into)** degenerar (en).

degradation [ˌdegrə'deɪʃn] *n* degradación *f*.

degrade [dɪ'greɪd] *vt* degradar.

degrading [dɪ'greɪdɪŋ] *adj* denigrante, degradante.

degree [dɪ'griː] *n* **-1.** [unit of measurement, amount] grado *m*; **by ~s** paulatinamente, poco a poco. **-2.** [qualification] título *m* universitario, ≃ licenciatura *f*; **to have/take a ~ (in sthg)** tener/hacer una licenciatura (en algo).

dehumanize, -ise [diː'hjuːmənaɪz] *vt* deshumanizar.

dehydrated [ˌdiːhaɪ'dreɪtɪd] *adj* deshidratado(da).

dehydration [ˌdiːhaɪ'dreɪʃn] *n* deshidratación *f*.

de-ice [diː'aɪs] *vt* descongelar.

de-icer [diː'aɪsəʳ] *n* (producto *m*) descongelante *m*.

deign [deɪn] *vt*: **to ~ to do sthg** dignarse a hacer algo.

deity ['diːɪtɪ] (*pl* **-ies**) *n* deidad *f*, divinidad *f*.

déjà vu [ˌdeʒɑː'vjuː] *n* (sensación *f* de) déjà vu *m*.

dejected [dɪ'dʒektɪd] *adj* abatido(da).

dejection [dɪ'dʒekʃn] *n* abatimiento *m*.

del. (*abbr of* **delete**) [on keyboard] supr.

Del. *abbr of* **Delaware**.

Delaware ['deləweəʳ] *n* Delaware.

delay [dɪ'leɪ] ◇ *n* retraso *m*; **without ~** sin demora. ◇ *vt* retrasar; **to ~ starting sthg** retrasar el comienzo de algo. ◇ *vi*: **to ~ (in doing sthg)** retrasarse (en hacer algo).

delayed [dɪ'leɪd] *adj*: **to be ~** [person] retrasarse; [train] ir con retraso.

delayed-action [dɪ'leɪd-] *adj* de efecto retardado; **~ shutter** PHOT (disparador *m*) automático *m*.

delectable [dɪ'lektəbl] *adj* **-1.** [food] deleitable. **-2.** [person] apetecible.

delegate [*n* 'delɪgət, *vb* 'delɪgeɪt] ◇ *n* delegado *m*, -da *f*. ◇ *vt*: **to ~ sthg (to sb)** delegar algo (en alguien); **to ~ sb to do sthg** delegar a alguien para hacer algo. ◇ *vi* delegar responsabilidades.

delegation [ˌdelɪ'geɪʃn] *n* delegación *f*.

delete [dɪ'liːt] *vt* [gen & COMPUT] borrar.

deletion [dɪ'liːʃn] *n* supresión *f*.

Delhi ['delɪ] *n* Delhi.

deli ['delɪ] *n* *inf abbr of* **delicatessen**.

deliberate [*adj* dɪ'lɪbərət, *vb* dɪ'lɪbəreɪt] ◇ *adj* **-1.** [intentional] deliberado(da). **-2.** [slow] pausado(da). ◇ *vi* *fml* deliberar.

deliberately [dɪ'lɪbərətlɪ] *adv* **-1.** [on purpose] adrede, deliberadamente. **-2.** [slowly] pausadamente.

deliberation [dɪˌlɪbə'reɪʃn] *n* **-1.** [consideration] deliberación *f*. **-2.** [slowness] pausa *f*.
◆ **deliberations** *npl* deliberaciones *fpl*.

delicacy ['delɪkəsɪ] (*pl* **-ies**) *n* **-1.** [gracefulness, tact] delicadeza *f*. **-2.** [food] exquisitez *f*, manjar *m*.

delicate ['delɪkət] *adj* **-1.** [gen] delicado(da). **-2.** [subtle - colour, taste] suave, sutil. **-3.** [tactful] prudente; [instrument] sensible.

delicately ['delɪkətlɪ] *adv* **-1.** [gracefully, tactfully] con delicadeza. **-2.** [subtly] suavemente, sutilmente.

delicatessen [ˌdelɪkə'tesn] *n* ≃ charcutería *f*, ≃ (tienda *f* de) ultramarinos *m inv*.

delicious [dɪ'lɪʃəs] *adj* delicioso(sa).

delight [dɪ'laɪt] ◇ *n* **-1.** [great pleasure] gozo *m*, regocijo *m*; **to take ~ in doing sthg** disfrutar haciendo algo. **-2.** [thing, person] delicia *f*, placer *m*. ◇ *vt* encantar. ◇ *vi*: **to ~ in sthg/in doing sthg** disfrutar con algo/haciendo algo.

delighted [dɪ'laɪtɪd] *adj* encantado(da), muy contento(ta); **~ by** OR **with** encantado con; **to be ~ to do sthg/that** estar encantado de hacer algo/de que; **I'd be ~ (to come)** me encantaría (ir).

delightful [dɪ'laɪtful] *adj* [gen] encantador(ra); [meal] delicioso(sa); [view] muy agradable.

delightfully [dɪ'laɪtfʊlɪ] *adv* deliciosamente.

delimit [diː'lɪmɪt] *vt fml* delimitar.

delineate [dɪ'lɪnɪeɪt] *vt fml* concretar, precisar.

delinquency [dɪ'lɪŋkwənsɪ] *n* delincuencia *f*.

delinquent [dɪ'lɪŋkwənt] ◇ *adj* [behaviour] delictivo(va); [child] delincuente. ◇ *n* delincuente *m y f*.

delirious [dɪ'lɪrɪəs] *adj* [with fever] delirante; *fig* [ecstatic] enfervorizado(da).

delirium [dɪ'lɪrɪəm] *n* delirio *m*, desvarío *m*.

deliver [dɪ'lɪvər] ◇ *vt* -1. [distribute] repartir; [hand over] entregar; **to ~ sthg to sb** entregar algo a alguien. -2. [give - speech, verdict, lecture] pronunciar; [- message] entregar; [- warning, ultimatum] lanzar; [- blow, kick] asestar. -3. [baby] traer al mundo. -4. *fml* [free] liberar, libertar. -5. *Am* POL [votes] captar. ◇ *vi* -1. [take to home, office] hacer reparto. -2. [fulfil promise] cumplir (lo prometido).

deliverance [dɪ'lɪvərəns] *n fml* liberación *f*.

delivery [dɪ'lɪvərɪ] (*pl* -ies) *n* -1. [distribution] reparto *m*; [handing over] entrega *f*. -2. [goods delivered] partida *f*. -3. [way of speaking] (estilo *m* de) discurso *m*. -4. [birth] parto *m*.

delivery note *n* albarán *m*.

delivery van *Br*, **delivery truck** *Am n* furgoneta *f* de reparto.

delphinium [del'fɪnɪəm] (*pl* -s) *n* espuela *f* de caballero.

delta ['deltə] (*pl* -s) *n* delta *m*.

delude [dɪ'luːd] *vt* engañar; **to ~ o.s.** engañarse (a uno mismo).

deluge ['deljuːdʒ] ◇ *n* [flood] diluvio *m*, aluvión *m*; *fig* [huge number] aluvión. ◇ *vt*: **to be ~d with** verse inundado(da) por.

delusion [dɪ'luːʒn] *n* espejismo *m*, engaño *m*; **~s of grandeur** delirios *mpl* de grandeza.

de luxe [də'lʌks] *adj* de lujo.

delve [delv] *vi*: **to ~ (into)** [bag, cupboard] hurgar (en); *fig* [mystery] ahondar (en), profundizar (en).

Dem. *abbr of* Democrat, Democratic.

demagogue ['deməgɒg] *n* demagogo *m*, -ga *f*.

demand [dɪ'mɑːnd] ◇ *n* -1. [claim, firm request] exigencia *f*, reclamación *f*; **on ~** a petición; **wage ~** demanda *f* OR reclamación de aumento salarial. -2. [need]: **~ for** demanda *f* de; **in ~** solicitado(da). ◇ *vt* [gen] exigir; [pay rise] reclamar, demandar; **to ~ to do sthg** exigir hacer algo.

demanding [dɪ'mɑːndɪŋ] *adj* -1. [exhausting] que exige mucho esfuerzo. -2. [not easily satisfied] exigente.

demarcation [ˌdiːmɑː'keɪʃn] *n* demarcación *f*.

demarcation dispute *n* conflicto entre sindicatos sobre las funciones laborales a realizar por sus miembros.

dematerialize, -ise [diːmə'tɪərɪəlaɪz] *vi* inmaterializarse.

demean [dɪ'miːn] *vt* humillar, degradar; **to ~ o.s.** humillarse, rebajarse.

demeaning [dɪ'miːnɪŋ] *adj* humillante, denigrante.

demeanour *Br*, **demeanor** *Am* [dɪ'miːnə] *n* (*U*) *fml* proceder *m*, comportamiento *m*.

demented [dɪ'mentɪd] *adj* demente.

dementia [dɪ'menʃə] *n* demencia *f*.

demerara sugar [ˌdemə'reərə-] *n Br* azúcar *m* moreno.

demigod ['demɪgɒd] *n* semidiós *m*.

demijohn ['demɪdʒɒn] *n* garrafón *f*, damajuana *f*.

demilitarized zone, demilitarised zone [ˌdiːˈmɪlɪtəraɪzd-] *n* zona *f* desmilitarizada.

demise [dɪ'maɪz] *n fml* -1. [death] defunción *f*, fallecimiento *m*. -2. [end] hundimiento *m*.

demist [ˌdiːˈmɪst] *vt Br* desempañar.

demister [ˌdiːˈmɪstər] *n Br* dispositivo *m* antivaho, luneta *f* térmica.

demo ['deməʊ] (*abbr of* demonstration) *n inf* mani *f*.

demobilize, -ise [ˌdiːˈməʊbɪlaɪz] *vt* desmovilizar.

democracy [dɪ'mɒkrəsɪ] (*pl* -ies) *n* democracia *f*.

democrat ['deməkræt] *n* demócrata *m y f*.
◆ **Democrat** *n Am* demócrata *m y f*.

democratic [demə'krætɪk] *adj* democrático(ca).
◆ **Democratic** *adj Am* demócrata.

democratically [ˌdemə'krætɪklɪ] *adv* democráticamente.

Democratic Party *n Am* Partido *m* Demócrata (de Estados Unidos).

democratize, -ise [dɪ'mɒkrətaɪz] *vt* democratizar.

demographic [ˌdemə'græfɪk] *adj* demográfico(ca).

demolish [dɪ'mɒlɪʃ] *vt* -1. [building] demoler; [argument, myth] destrozar. -2. *inf* [eat] zamparse.

demolition [ˌdemə'lɪʃn] *n* [of building] demolición *f*; [of argument, myth] destrucción *f*.

demon ['diːmən] ◇ *n* demonio *m*, diablo *m*. ◇ *comp inf* fenomenal.

demonstrable [dɪ'mɒnstrəbl] *adj* demostrable.

demonstrably [dɪ'mɒnstrəblɪ] *adv* [better, different] decididamente.

demonstrate ['demənstreɪt] ◇ *vt* **-1.** [prove] demostrar. **-2.** [show] hacer una demostración de. ◇ *vi* manifestarse; **to ~ for/against** sthg manifestarse a favor/en contra de algo.

demonstration [demən'streɪʃn] *n* **-1.** [of machine, product] demostración *f.* **-2.** [public meeting] manifestación *f.*

demonstrative [dɪ'mɒnstrətɪv] *adj* efusivo(va), expresivo(va).

demonstrator ['demənstreɪtər] *n* **-1.** [in march] manifestante *m y f.* **-2.** [of machine, product] *persona que hace demostraciones.*

demoralize, -ise [dɪ'mɒrəlaɪz] *vt* desmoralizar.

demoralized [dɪ'mɒrəlaɪzd] *adj* desmoralizado(da).

demote [,diː'məʊt] *vt* descender de categoría.

demotion [,diː'məʊʃn] *n* descenso *m* de categoría.

demotivate [,diː'məʊtɪveɪt] *vt* desmotivar.

demure [dɪ'mjʊər] *adj* recatado(da).

demystify [,diː'mɪstɪfaɪ] (*pt* & *pp* **-ied**) *vt* arrojar luz sobre.

den [den] *n* [lair] guarida *f.*

denationalization ['diː,næʃnəlaɪ'zeɪʃn] *n* privatización *f,* desnacionalización *f.*

denationalize, -ise [,diː'næʃnəlaɪz] *vt* privatizar, desnacionalizar.

denial [dɪ'naɪəl] *n* **-1.** [refutation] negación *f,* rechazo *m.* **-2.** [refusal] denegación *f.*

denier ['denɪə] *n* denier *m.*

denigrate ['denɪgreɪt] *vt fml* desacreditar.

denim ['denɪm] *n* tela *f* vaquera.
◆ **denims** *npl* (pantalones *mpl*) vaqueros *mpl.*

denim jacket *n* cazadora *f* vaquera.

denizen ['denɪzn] *n literary* OR *hum* morador *m,* -ra *f.*

Denmark ['denmɑːk] *n* Dinamarca.

denomination [dɪ,nɒmɪ'neɪʃn] *n* **-1.** [religious group] confesión *f.* **-2.** [of money] valor *m.*

denominator [dɪ'nɒmɪneɪtər] *n* denominador *m.*

denote [dɪ'nəʊt] *vt fml* denotar.

denouement [deɪ'nuːmɒn] *n* desenlace *m.*

denounce [dɪ'naʊns] *vt* denunciar.

dense [dens] *adj* **-1.** [gen] denso(sa); [trees] tupido(da). **-2.** *inf* [stupid] bruto(ta).

densely ['denslɪ] *adv* densamente.

density ['densətɪ] (*pl* **-ies**) *n* densidad *f.*

dent [dent] ◇ *n* [on car] abolladura *f;* [in wall] melladura *f.* ◇ *vt* [car] abollar; [wall] mellar.

dental ['dentl] *adj* dental; **~ surgery** clínica *f* OR consultorio *m* dental.

dental floss *n* hilo *m* OR seda *f* dental.

dental plate *n* [dentures] dentadura *f* postiza.

dental surgeon *n* odontólogo *m,* -ga *f.*

dental treatment *n* cirugía *f* dental.

dented ['dentɪd] *adj* [car] abollado(da); [wall] mellado(da).

dentist ['dentɪst] *n* dentista *m y f;* **to go to the ~'s** ir al dentista.

dentistry ['dentɪstrɪ] *n* odontología *f.*

dentures ['dentʃəz] *npl* dentadura *f* postiza.

denude [dɪ'njuːd] *vt fml:* **to ~ sthg (of)** despojar algo (de).

denunciation [dɪ,nʌnsɪ'eɪʃn] *n* denuncia *f,* condena *f.*

deny [dɪ'naɪ] (*pt* & *pp* **-ied**) *vt* **-1.** [refute] negar, rechazar; **to ~ doing sthg** negar haber hecho algo. **-2.** *fml* [refuse]: **to ~ sb sthg** denegar algo a alguien.

deodorant [diː'əʊdərənt] *n* desodorante *m.*

depart [dɪ'pɑːt] *vi fml* **-1.** [leave]: **~ (from)** salir (de); **this train will ~ from Platform 2** este tren efectuará su salida de la vía 2. **-2.** [differ]: **to ~ from sthg** apartarse de algo.

department [dɪ'pɑːtmənt] *n* **-1.** [gen] departamento *m.* **-2.** [in government] ministerio *m.*

departmental [,diːpɑːt'mentl] *adj* [gen] departamental; [head, secretary] del departamento.

department store *n* grandes almacenes *mpl.*

departure [dɪ'pɑːtʃər] *n* **-1.** [of train, plane] salida *f;* [of person] marcha *f.* **-2.** [change]: **~ (from)** abandono *m* (de); **a new ~** un nuevo enfoque.

departure lounge *n* [in airport] sala *f* de embarque; [in coach station] vestíbulo *m* de salidas.

depend [dɪ'pend] *vi:* **to ~ on** depender de; **you can ~ on me** puedes confiar en mí; **it ~s** depende; **~ing on** según, dependiendo de.

dependable [dɪ'pendəbl] *adj* fiable.

dependant [dɪ'pendənt] *n persona dependiente del cabeza de familia.*

dependence [dɪ'pendəns] *n:* **~ (on)** dependencia *f* (de); **drug ~** drogodependencia *f.*

dependent [dɪ'pendənt] *adj* **-1.** [gen]: **to be ~ (on)** depender (de). **-2.** [addicted] adicto(ta).

depict [dɪ'pɪkt] *vt* **-1.** [in picture] representar, retratar. **-2.** [describe]: **to ~ sthg/sb as sthg** describir algo/a alguien como algo.

depilatory [dɪ'pɪlətrɪ] *adj* depilador(ra), depilatorio(ria).

deplete [dɪ'pliːt] *vt* mermar, reducir.

depletion [dɪ'pliːʃn] *n* merma *f*, reducción *f*.

deplorable [dɪ'plɔːrəbl] *adj* deplorable.

deplore [dɪ'plɔːr] *vt* deplorar.

deploy [dɪ'plɔɪ] *vt* desplegar.

deployment [dɪ'plɔɪmənt] *n* despliegue *m*.

depopulated [ˌdiː'pɒpjʊleɪtɪd] *adj* despoblado(da).

depopulation [diːˌpɒpjʊ'leɪʃn] *n* despoblación *f*.

deport [dɪ'pɔːt] *vt* deportar.

deportation [ˌdiːpɔː'teɪʃn] *n* deportación *f*.

deportation order *n* orden *f* de deportación.

depose [dɪ'pəʊz] *vt* deponer.

deposit [dɪ'pɒzɪt] ◇ *n* **-1.** GEOL yacimiento *m*. **-2.** [sediment] poso *m*, sedimento *m*. **-3.** [payment into bank] ingreso *m*, imposición *f*; **to make a ~** hacer un ingreso. **-4.** [down payment - on house, car] entrada *f*; [- on hotel room] señal *f*, adelanto *m*; [- on hired goods] fianza *f*, enganche *m* Amer; [- on bottle] dinero *m* del envase OR casco. ◇ *vt* **-1.** [put down] depositar. **-2.** [in bank] ingresar.

deposit account *n* Br cuenta *f* de ahorro a plazo fijo.

depositor [də'pɒzɪtər] *n* impositor *m*, -ra *f*, depositante *m* y *f*.

depot ['depəʊ] *n* **-1.** [storage facility] almacén *m*; [for buses] cochera *f*. **-2.** Am [bus or train terminus] terminal *f*, estación *f*.

depraved [dɪ'preɪvd] *adj* depravado(da).

depravity [dɪ'prævətɪ] *n* depravación *f*.

deprecate ['deprɪkeɪt] *vt fml* censurar.

deprecating ['deprɪkeɪtɪŋ] *adj* desaprobatorio(ria).

depreciate [dɪ'priːʃɪeɪt] *vi* depreciarse.

depreciation [dɪˌpriːʃɪ'eɪʃn] *n* depreciación *f*.

depress [dɪ'pres] *vt* **-1.** [person] deprimir. **-2.** [economy] desactivar. **-3.** [price, share value] reducir.

depressant [dɪ'presənt] *n* sedante *m*.

depressed [dɪ'prest] *adj* deprimido(da).

depressing [dɪ'presɪŋ] *adj* deprimente.

depression [dɪ'preʃn] *n* **-1.** [gen & ECON] depresión *f*. **-2.** *fml* [in pillow] hueco *m*.
◆ **Depression** *n* ECON: **the (Great) Depression** la Gran Depresión.

depressive [dɪ'presɪv] *adj* depresivo(va).

deprivation [ˌdeprɪ'veɪʃn] *n* **-1.** [poverty] miseria *f*. **-2.** [lack] privación *f*.

deprive [dɪ'praɪv] *vt*: **to ~ sb of sthg** priva a alguien de algo.

deprived [dɪ'praɪvd] *adj* [children, childhood] necesitado(da); [area] deprimido(da), pobre.

dept. *abbr of* **department**.

depth [depθ] *n* profundidad *f*; **in ~** a fondo; **to be out of one's ~** [in water] perde pie; **he was out of his ~ with that job** ese trabajo le venía grande.
◆ **depths** *npl* **the ~s** [of the sea] las profundidades; **in the ~s of winter** en plenc invierno; **to be in the ~s of despair** esta en un abismo de desesperación.

depth charge *n* carga *f* de profundidad.

deputation [ˌdepjʊ'teɪʃn] *n* delegación *f*, representación *f*.

deputize, -ise ['depjʊtaɪz] *vi*: **to ~ (for)** actuar en representación (de).

deputy ['depjʊtɪ] (*pl* **-ies**) ◇ *adj*: **~ head** subdirector *m*, -ra *f*; **~ chairman/president** vicepresidente *m*. ◇ *n* **-1.** [second-in-command] asistente *m* y *f*, suplente *m* y *f*. **-2.** Am [deputy sheriff] ayudante *m* y *f* de sheriff.

derail [dɪ'reɪl] *vt & vi* [train] descarrilar.

derailment [dɪ'reɪlmənt] *n* descarrilamiento *m*.

deranged [dɪ'reɪndʒd] *adj* perturbado(da) trastornado(da).

derby [Br 'dɑːbɪ, Am 'dɜːbɪ] (*pl* **-ies**) *n* **-1.** [sports event] derby *m* (local). **-2.** Am [hat bombín *m*, sombrero *m* hongo.

deregulate [ˌdiː'regjʊleɪt] *vt* liberalizar.

deregulation [ˌdiːregjʊ'leɪʃn] *n* liberalización *f*.

derelict ['derəlɪkt] *adj* abandonado(da).

deride [dɪ'raɪd] *vt* mofarse de.

derision [dɪ'rɪʒn] *n* mofa *f*, burla *f*.

derisive [dɪ'raɪsɪv] *adj* burlón(ona).

derisory [də'raɪzərɪ] *adj* **-1.** [puny, trivial] irrisorio(ria). **-2.** [derisive] burlón(ona).

derivation [ˌderɪ'veɪʃn] *n* [of word] origen *m*.

derivative [dɪ'rɪvətɪv] ◇ *adj pej* carente de originalidad. ◇ *n* derivado *m*.

derive [dɪ'raɪv] ◇ *vt* **-1.** [draw, gain]: **to ~ sthg from sthg** encontrar algo en algo. **-2.** [come]: **to be ~d from** derivar de. ◇ *vi*: **to ~ from** derivar de.

dermatitis [ˌdɜːmə'taɪtɪs] *n* dermatitis *f inv*.

dermatologist [ˌdɜːmə'tɒlədʒɪst] *n* dermatólogo *m*, -ga *f*.

dermatology [ˌdɜːmə'tɒlədʒɪ] *n* dermatología *f*.

derogatory [dɪ'rɒgətrɪ] *adj* despectivo(va).

derrick ['derɪk] *n* -1. [crane] grúa *f*. -2. [over oil well] torre *f* de perforación.

derv [dɜːv] *n Br* gasóleo *m*, gasoil *m*.

desalination [diːˌsælɪ'neɪʃn] *n* desalinización *f*.

descant ['deskænt] *n* contrapunto *m*.

descend [dɪ'send] ◇ *vt fml* [go down] descender por. ◇ *vi* -1. *fml* [go down] descender. -2. [subj: silence, gloom]: **to ~ (on sthg/sb)** invadir (algo/a alguien). -3. [arrive]: **to ~ on sb** presentarse en casa de alguien. -4. [stoop]: **to ~ to sthg/to doing sthg** rebajarse a algo/a hacer algo.

descendant [dɪ'sendənt] *n* descendiente *m* y *f*.

descended [dɪ'sendɪd] *adj*: **to be ~ from** ser descendiente de, descender de.

descending [dɪ'sendɪŋ] *adj*: **in ~ order** en orden descendiente OR decreciente.

descent [dɪ'sent] *n* -1. [downwards movement] descenso *m*, bajada *f*. -2. [origin] ascendencia *f*.

describe [dɪ'skraɪb] *vt* describir.

description [dɪ'skrɪpʃn] *n* -1. [account] descripción *f*. -2. [type]: **of all ~s** de todas clases.

descriptive [dɪ'skrɪptɪv] *adj* descriptivo(va).

desecrate ['desɪkreɪt] *vt* profanar.

desecration [ˌdesɪ'kreɪʃn] *n* profanación *f*.

desegregate [ˌdiː'segrɪgeɪt] *vt* abolir la segregación racial en.

desegregation [ˌdiːsegrɪ'geɪʃn] *n* abolición *f* de la segregación racial.

deselect [ˌdiːsɪ'lekt] *vt Br* no reelegir como candidato.

desert [*n* 'dezət, *vb & npl* dɪ'zɜːt] ◇ *n* -1. GEOGR desierto *m*. -2. [boring place]: **(cultural) ~** páramo *m* cultural. ◇ *vt* abandonar. ◇ *vi* MIL desertar.

◆ **deserts** *npl*: **to get one's just ~s** llevarse uno su merecido.

deserted [dɪ'zɜːtɪd] *adj* abandonado(da).

deserter [dɪ'zɜːtə'] *n* desertor *m*, -ra *f*.

desertion [dɪ'zɜːʃn] *n* -1. [gen] abandono *m*. -2. MIL deserción *f*.

desert island ['dezət-] *n* isla *f* desierta.

deserve [dɪ'zɜːv] *vt* merecer, ameritar *Amer*; **to ~ to do sthg** merecer hacer algo.

deserved [dɪ'zɜːvd] *adj* merecido(da).

deservedly [dɪ'zɜːvɪdlɪ] *adv* merecidamente.

deserving [dɪ'zɜːvɪŋ] *adj* meritorio(ria), encomiable; **~ of** *fml* merecedor(ra) de.

desiccated ['desɪkeɪtɪd] *adj* desecado(da).

design [dɪ'zaɪn] ◇ *n* -1. [gen] diseño *m*; [of garment] corte *m*. -2. [pattern] dibujo *m*. -3. *fml* [intention] designio *m*, intención *f*; **by ~** adrede; **to have ~s on** tener las miras puestas en. ◇ *vt* -1. [draw plans for] diseñar. -2. [plan, prepare] concebir.

designate [*adj* 'dezɪgnət, *vb* 'dezɪgneɪt] ◇ *adj* designado(da). ◇ *vt* designar, nombrar; **to ~ sb as sthg/to do sthg** designar a alguien algo/para hacer algo.

designation [ˌdezɪg'neɪʃn] *n fml* [name] denominación *f*.

designer [dɪ'zaɪnə'] ◇ *adj* [clothes] de diseño; [glasses] de marca. ◇ *n* [gen] diseñador *m*, -ra *f*; THEATRE escenógrafo *m*, -fa *f*.

desirable [dɪ'zaɪərəbl] *adj* -1. *fml* [appropriate] deseable, conveniente. -2. [attractive] atractivo(va), apetecible.

desire [dɪ'zaɪə'] ◇ *n*: **~ (for sthg/to do sthg)** deseo *m* (de algo/de hacer algo). ◇ *vt* desear; **it leaves a lot to be ~d** deja mucho que desear.

desirous [dɪ'zaɪərəs] *adj fml*: **~ of sthg/of doing sthg** deseoso(sa) de algo/de hacer algo.

desist [dɪ'zɪst] *vi fml*: **to ~ (from doing sthg)** desistir (de hacer algo).

desk [desk] *n* -1. [gen] mesa *f*, escritorio *m*; [in school] pupitre *m*; **cash ~** caja *f*. -2. [service area]: **cash ~** caja *f*; **information ~** (mostrador *m* de) información *f*.

desk clerk *n Am* recepcionista *m* y *f*.

desk lamp *n* flexo *m*, lámpara *f* de mesa.

desktop ['desk,tɒp] *adj* COMPUT: **~ (computer)** ordenador *m* de mesa.

desktop publishing *n* COMPUT autoedición *f* de textos.

desolate ['desələt] *adj* [place, person] desolado(da); [feeling] desolador(ra).

desolation [ˌdesə'leɪʃn] *n* desolación *f*.

despair [dɪ'speə'] ◇ *n* desesperación *f*; **in ~** desesperadamente, con desesperación. ◇ *vi* desesperarse; **to ~ of sb** desesperarse con alguien; **to ~ of sthg/doing sthg** desesperar de algo/hacer algo.

despairing [dɪ'speərɪŋ] *adj* desesperado(da).

despairingly [dɪ'speərɪŋlɪ] *adv* con desesperación.

despatch [dɪ'spætʃ] = **dispatch**.

desperate ['despərət] *adj* desesperado(da); **to be ~ for sthg** necesitar desesperadamente algo.

desperately ['despərətlɪ] *adv* -1. [want, fight, love] desesperadamente. -2. [ill] gravemente; [poor, unhappy, shy] tremendamente.

desperation [ˌdespə'reɪʃn] *n* desesperación *f*; **in ~** con desesperación.

despicable [dɪ'spɪkəbl] *adj* despreciable.

despise [dɪ'spaɪz] *vt* despreciar.

despite [dɪ'spaɪt] *prep* a pesar de, pese a.

despondent [dɪ'spɒndənt] *adj* descorazonado(da).

despot ['despɒt] *n* déspota *m y f*.

despotic [de'spɒtɪk] *adj* despótico(ca).

dessert [dɪ'zɜːt] *n* postre *m*.

dessertspoon [dɪ'zɜːtspuːn] *n* -1. [spoon] cuchara *f* de postre. -2. [spoonful] cucharada *f (de postre)*.

dessert wine *n* vino *m* dulce.

destabilize, -ise [,diː'steɪbɪlaɪz] *vt* desestabilizar.

destination [,destɪ'neɪʃn] *n* destino *m*.

destined ['destɪnd] *adj* -1. [fated, intended]: ~ for sthg/to do sthg destinado(da) a algo/a hacer algo. -2. [bound]: ~ for rumbo a, con destino a.

destiny ['destɪnɪ] *(pl* -ies) *n* destino *m*.

destitute ['destɪtjuːt] *adj* indigente, en la miseria.

destroy [dɪ'strɔɪ] *vt* -1. [ruin] destruir. -2. [put down] matar, sacrificar.

destroyer [dɪ'strɔɪə*ʳ*] *n* -1. [ship] destructor *m*. -2. [person or thing] destructor *m*, -ra *f*.

destruction [dɪ'strʌkʃn] *n* destrucción *f*.

destructive [dɪ'strʌktɪv] *adj* [gen] destructivo(va); [influence] pernicioso(sa).

destructively [dɪ'strʌktɪvlɪ] *adv* destructivamente.

desultory ['desəltrɪ] *adj fml* [conversation] deslabazado(da); [attempt] tímido(da).

Det. *abbr of* **Detective**.

detach [dɪ'tætʃ] *vt* -1. [pull off]: to ~ sthg (from) quitar OR separar algo (de). -2. [disassociate]: to ~ o.s. from sthg distanciarse de algo.

detachable [dɪ'tætʃəbl] *adj* [handle etc] de quita y pon; [collar] postizo(za).

detached [dɪ'tætʃt] *adj* [unemotional] objetivo(va).

detached house *n* casa *f* OR chalet *m* individual.

detachment [dɪ'tætʃmənt] *n* -1. [aloofness] distanciamiento *m*. -2. MIL destacamento *m*.

detail ['diːteɪl] ◇ *n* -1. [small point] detalle *m*, pormenor *m*. -2. (U) [facts, points] detalles *mpl*; to go into ~ entrar en detalles; in ~ detalladamente, con detalle. -3. MIL destacamento *m*. ◇ *vt* [list] detallar.

◆ **details** *npl* [gen] información *f*; [personal] datos *mpl*.

detailed ['diːteɪld] *adj* detallado(da).

detain [dɪ'teɪn] *vt* [gen] retener; [in police station] detener.

detainee [,diːteɪ'niː] *n* preso político *m*, presa política *f*.

detect [dɪ'tekt] *vt* [gen] detectar; [difference] notar, percibir.

detection [dɪ'tekʃn] *n* (U) -1. [gen] detección *f*. -2. [of crime] investigación *f*; [of drugs] descubrimiento *m*.

detective [dɪ'tektɪv] *n* [private] detective *m y f*; [policeman] agente *m y f*.

detective novel *n* novela *f* policíaca.

detector [dɪ'tektə*ʳ*] *n* detector *m*.

détente [deɪ'tɒnt] *n* POL distensión *f*.

detention [dɪ'tenʃn] *n* -1. [of suspect, criminal] detención *f*, arresto *m*; in ~ bajo arresto. -2. [at school] *castigo de permanecer en la escuela después de clase.*

detention centre *n* Br centro *m* de internamiento de delincuentes juveniles.

deter [dɪ'tɜːʳ] *(pt & pp* -red, *cont* -ring) *vt* to ~ sb (from doing sthg) disuadir a alguien (de hacer algo).

detergent [dɪ'tɜːdʒənt] *n* detergente *m*.

deteriorate [dɪ'tɪərɪəreɪt] *vi* [health, economy] deteriorarse; [weather] empeorar.

deterioration [dɪ,tɪərɪə'reɪʃn] *n* [of health, economy] deterioro *m*; [of weather] empeoramiento *m*.

determination [dɪ,tɜːmɪ'neɪʃn] *n* determinación *f*.

determine [dɪ'tɜːmɪn] *vt* determinar; to ~ to do sthg *fml* determinar OR resolver hacer algo.

determined [dɪ'tɜːmɪnd] *adj* decidido(da); ~ to do sthg decidido OR resuelto a hacer algo.

deterrent [dɪ'terənt] ◇ *adj* disuasorio(ria). ◇ *n* fuerza *f* disuasoria; nuclear ~ armas *fpl* nucleares disuasorias.

detest [dɪ'test] *vt* detestar.

detestable [dɪ'testəbl] *adj* detestable.

dethrone [dɪ'θrəʊn] *vt* destronar.

detonate ['detəneɪt] *vt & vi* detonar.

detonator ['detəneɪtə*ʳ*] *n* detonador *m*.

detour ['diː,tʊə*ʳ*] *n* desviación *f*, desvío *m*; to make a ~ dar un rodeo.

detract [dɪ'trækt] *vi*: to ~ from sthg [gen] mermar algo, aminorar algo; [achievement] restar importancia a algo.

detractor [dɪ'træktə*ʳ*] *n* detractor *m*, -ra *f*.

detriment ['detrɪmənt] *n*: to the ~ of en detrimento de.

detrimental [,detrɪ'mentl] *adj* perjudicial.

detritus [dɪ'traɪtəs] *n* (U) desperdicios *mpl*; GEOL detrito *m*, detritus *m inv*.

deuce [djuːs] *n* (U) TENNIS deuce *m*, iguales *mpl* (a cuarenta).

Deutschmark ['dɔɪtʃˌmɑːk] *n* marco *m* alemán.

devaluation [ˌdiːvæljuˈeɪʃn] *n* devaluación *f*.

devalue [ˌdiːˈvæljuː] *vt* **-1.** FIN devaluar. **-2.** [person, achievement] menospreciar, infravalorar.

devastate ['devəsteɪt] *vt* [area, city] devastar, asolar; *fig* [person] desolar.

devastated ['devəsteɪtɪd] *adj* [area, city] devastado(da), asolado(da); *fig* [person] desolado(da).

devastating ['devəsteɪtɪŋ] *adj* **-1.** [destructive - hurricane etc] devastador(ra). **-2.** [effective - remark, argument] abrumador(ra). **-3.** [upsetting - news, experience] desolador(ra). **-4.** [attractive] imponente, irresistible.

devastation [ˌdevəˈsteɪʃn] *n* [destruction] devastación *f*.

develop [dɪˈveləp] ◇ *vt* **-1.** [land] urbanizar. **-2.** [illness] contraer, coger; [habit] adquirir; **to ~ a fault** fallar, estropearse. **-3.** [product] elaborar. **-4.** [idea, argument, resources] desarrollar. **-5.** PHOT revelar. ◇ *vi* **-1.** [grow] desarrollarse. **-2.** [appear] presentarse, darse.

developer [dɪˈveləpəʳ] *n* **-1.** [of land] constructor *m*, -ra *f*. **-2.** [person]: **early/late ~** niño *m*, -ña *f* con desarrollo precoz/tardío. **-3.** PHOT [chemical] líquido *m* de revelado, revelador *m*.

developing country [dɪˈveləpɪŋ-] *n* país *m* en vías de desarrollo.

development [dɪˈveləpmənt] *n* **-1.** (U) [growth] desarrollo *m*. **-2.** [of design, product] elaboración *f*. **-3.** [developed land] urbanización *f*. **-4.** [new event] (nuevo) acontecimiento *m*. **-5.** [advance - in science etc] avance *m*. **-6.** [of illness] contracción *f*; [of fault] aparición *f*.

development area *n* Br ≃ zona de urgente reindustrialización.

deviant ['diːvjənt] ◇ *adj* irregular, anómalo(la); [sexually] pervertido(da). ◇ *n* pervertido *m*, -da *f*.

deviate ['diːvɪeɪt] *vi*: **to ~ from sthg** apartarse OR desviarse de algo.

deviation [ˌdiːvɪˈeɪʃn] *n* desviación *f*.

device [dɪˈvaɪs] *n* dispositivo *m*, mecanismo *m*; **to leave sb to their own ~s** [with nothing to do] dejar a alguien a su aire; [without help] dejar a alguien que se las componga solo.

devil ['devl] *n* diablo *m*, demonio *m*; **little ~** diablillo *m*; **poor ~** pobre diablo; **you lucky ~!** ¡vaya suerte que tienes!; **who/where/why the ~ ...?** ¿quién/dónde/por qué demonios ...?

◆ **Devil** *n* [Satan]: **the Devil** el Diablo, el Demonio.

devilish ['devlɪʃ] *adj* diabólico(ca).

devil-may-care *adj* irresponsable.

devil's advocate *n* abogado *m* del diablo.

devious ['diːvjəs] *adj* **-1.** [person, scheme] malévolo(la), retorcido(da); [means] dudoso(sa). **-2.** [route] sinuoso(sa), tortuoso(sa).

deviousness ['diːvjəsnɪs] *n* [dishonesty] falsedad *f*.

devise [dɪˈvaɪz] *vt* [instrument, system] diseñar; [plan] trazar.

devoid [dɪˈvɔɪd] *adj* fml: **~ of** desprovisto(ta) de.

devolution [ˌdiːvəˈluːʃn] *n* POL ≃ autonomía *f*, ≃ traspaso *m* de competencias.

devolve [dɪˈvɒlv] *vi* fml: **to ~ on** OR **upon** recaer en, transferirse a.

devote [dɪˈvəut] *vt*: **to ~ sthg to** dedicar OR consagrar algo a; **to ~ o.s. to** dedicarse OR consagrarse a.

devoted [dɪˈvəutɪd] *adj* [person] leal; **to be ~ to sb** tener veneración por alguien.

devotee [ˌdevəˈtiː] *n* [fan] devoto *m*, -ta *f*, admirador *m*, -ra *f*.

devotion [dɪˈvəuʃn] *n* (U) **-1.** [commitment]: **~ (to)** dedicación *f* (a). **-2.** RELIG devoción *f*.

devour [dɪˈvauəʳ] *vt* literary lit & fig devorar.

devout [dɪˈvaut] *adj* RELIG devoto(ta), piadoso(sa).

dew [djuː] *n* rocío *m*.

dexterity [dekˈsterətɪ] *n* destreza *f*, habilidad *f*.

dexterous ['dekstrəs] *adj* diestro(tra).

dextrose ['dekstrəus] *n* dextrosa *f*.

dextrous ['dekstrəs] = **dexterous**.

DFE (*abbr of* **Department for Education**) *n ministerio británico de educación,* ≃ MEC *m*.

dhal [dɑːl] *n potaje de legumbres indio muy especiado*.

DHSS (*abbr of* **Department of Health and Social Security**) *n antiguo ministerio británico de la seguridad social*.

diabetes [ˌdaɪəˈbiːtiːz] *n* diabetes *f inv*.

diabetic [ˌdaɪəˈbetɪk] ◇ *adj* **-1.** [person] diabético(ca). **-2.** [jam, chocolate] para diabéticos. ◇ *n* diabético *m*, -ca *f*.

diabolic(al) [ˌdaɪəˈbɒlɪk(l)] *adj* **-1.** [evil] diabólico(ca). **-2.** inf [very bad] demencial, pésimo(ma).

diaeresis Br (*pl* **-eses** [-ɪsiːz]), **dieresis** Am (*pl* **-eses**) [daɪˈerɪsɪs] *n* diéresis *f inv*.

diagnose ['daɪəgnəuz] *vt* MED diagnosticar.

diagnosis [ˌdaɪəgˈnəusɪs] (*pl* **-oses** [-əusiːz])

n MED [verdict] **diagnóstico** *m*; [science, activity] **diagnosis** *f inv.*

diagnostic [,daɪəg'nɒstɪk] *adj* MED diagnóstico(ca).

diagonal [daɪ'ægənl] ◇ *adj* diagonal. ◇ *n* diagonal *f.*

diagonally [daɪ'ægənəlɪ] *adv* diagonalmente, en diagonal.

diagram ['daɪəgræm] *n* diagrama *m*, dibujo *m* esquemático.

diagrammatic [,daɪəgrə'mætɪk] *adj* gráfico(ca), esquemático(ca).

dial ['daɪəl] (*Br pt & pp* **-led**, *cont* **-ling**, *Am pt & pp* **-ed**, *cont* **-ing**) ◇ *n* **-1.** [of watch, clock, meter] esfera *f.* **-2.** [of telephone, radio] dial *m.* ◇ *vt* [number] marcar.

dialect ['daɪəlekt] *n* dialecto *m.*

dialling code ['daɪəlɪŋ-] *n Br* prefijo *m* (telefónico).

dialling tone *Br* ['daɪəlɪŋ-], **dial tone** *Am n* señal *f* de llamada.

dialogue *Br*, **dialog** *Am* ['daɪəlɒg] *n* diálogo *m.*

dial tone *Am* = **dialling tone.**

dialysis [daɪ'ælɪsɪs] *n* diálisis *f inv.*

diamanté [dɪə'mɒnteɪ] *adj* con lentejuelas.

diameter [daɪ'æmɪtər] *n* diámetro *m.*

diametrically [,daɪə'metrɪklɪ] *adv:* ~ **opposed** diametralmente opuesto(ta).

diamond ['daɪəmənd] *n* **-1.** [gem, playing card] diamante *m.* **-2.** [shape] rombo *m.*
◆ **diamonds** *npl* diamantes *mpl.*

diamond wedding *n* bodas *fpl* de diamante.

diaper ['daɪpər] *n Am* pañal *m.*

diaphanous [daɪ'æfənəs] *adj* diáfano(na).

diaphragm ['daɪəfræm] *n* diafragma *m.*

diarrh(o)ea [,daɪə'rɪə] *n* diarrea *f.*

diary ['daɪərɪ] (*pl* **-ies**) *n* **-1.** [appointment book] agenda *f.* **-2.** [journal] diario *m.*

diatribe ['daɪətraɪb] *n* diatriba *f.*

dice [daɪs] (*pl inv*) ◇ *n* dado *m.* ◇ *npl:* **to play** ~ jugar a los dados; **no** ~! *Am inf* ¡qué va! ◇ *vt* cortar en cuadraditos.

dicey ['daɪsɪ] (*compar* **-ier**, *superl* **-iest**) *adj esp Br inf* arriesgado(da).

dichotomy [daɪ'kɒtəmɪ] (*pl* **-ies**) *n fml* dicotomía *f.*

dickens ['dɪkɪnz] *n Br inf dated:* **who/what/where the** ~ ...? ¿quién/qué/dónde demonios ...?

Dictaphone® ['dɪktəfəʊn] *n* dictáfono *m.*

dictate [*vb* dɪk'teɪt, *n* 'dɪkteɪt] ◇ *vt:* **to** ~ **sthg (to sb)** dictar algo (a alguien). ◇ *vi* **-1.** [read out]: **to** ~ **(to sb)** dictar (a alguien). **-2.**

[make demands]: **to** ~ **to sb** dar órdenes a alguien. ◇ *n* [of one's conscience] dictado *m.*

dictation [dɪk'teɪʃn] *n* dictado *m*; **to take** OR **do** ~ escribir al dictado.

dictator [dɪk'teɪtər] *n* dictador *m*, -ra *f.*

dictatorship [dɪk'teɪtəʃɪp] *n* dictadura *f.*

diction ['dɪkʃn] *n* dicción *f.*

dictionary ['dɪkʃənrɪ] (*pl* **-ies**) *n* diccionario *m*; **Japanese** ~ diccionario de japonés.

did [dɪd] *pt* → **do.**

didactic [dɪ'dæktɪk] *adj* didáctico(ca).

diddle ['dɪdl] *vt inf* timar.

didn't ['dɪdnt] = **did not.**

die [daɪ] (*pl sense 2 only* **dice**, *pt & pp* **died**, *cont* **dying**) ◇ *vi* **-1.** [gen] morir, morirse; **to be dying** estar muriéndose OR agonizando; **to be dying for sthg/to do sthg** morirse por algo/por hacer algo. **-2.** *literary* [feeling] extinguirse, disiparse. ◇ *n* **-1.** [for stamping metal] cuño *m*, troquel *m*; [for casting metal] matriz *f.* **-2.** [dice] dado *m.*
◆ **die away** *vi* desvanecerse.
◆ **die down** *vi* [wind] amainar; [sound] apaciguarse; [fire] remitir; [excitement, fuss] calmarse.
◆ **die out** *vi* extinguirse.

diehard ['daɪhɑːd] *n* reaccionario *m*, -ria *f.*

dieresis *Am* = **diaeresis.**

diesel ['diːzl] *n* **-1.** [vehicle] vehículo *m* diesel. **-2.** [fuel] gasóleo *m*, gasoil *m.*

diesel engine *n* AUT motor *m* diesel; RAIL locomotora *f* diesel.

diesel fuel, diesel oil *n* gasóleo *m*, gasoil *m.*

diet ['daɪət] ◇ *n* **-1.** [eating pattern] dieta *f.* **-2.** [to lose weight] régimen *m*; **to be on a** ~ estar a régimen. ◇ *comp* [low-calorie] light (*inv*), bajo(ja) en calorías. ◇ *vi* estar a régimen.

dietary ['daɪətrɪ] *adj* dietético(ca), alimenticio(cia).

dietary fibre *n* (*U*) fibra *f* (alimenticia).

dieter ['daɪətər] *n* persona *f* a régimen.

dietician [,daɪə'tɪʃn] *n* especialista *m y f* en dietética.

differ ['dɪfər] *vi* **-1.** [be different] diferir, ser diferente; **to** ~ **from sthg** distinguirse OR diferir de algo. **-2.** [disagree]: **to** ~ **with sb (about sthg)** disentir OR discrepar de alguien (en algo).

difference ['dɪfrəns] *n* diferencia *f*; **it doesn't make any** ~ da lo mismo; **to make all the** ~ suponer una gran diferencia.

different ['dɪfrənt] *adj:* ~ **(from)** diferente OR distinto(ta) (de).

differential [,dɪfə'renʃl] ◇ *adj* diferencia-

do(da). ◇ *n* **-1.** [between pay scales] diferencia *f* salarial. **-2.** TECH diferencial *m*.

differentiate [,dɪfə'renʃɪeɪt] ◇ *vt*: **to ~ (sthg from sthg)** diferenciar OR distinguir (algo de algo). ◇ *vi*: **to ~ between** diferenciar OR distinguir entre.

differently ['dɪfrəntlɪ] *adv* de forma diferente, de otra forma.

difficult ['dɪfɪkəlt] *adj* difícil.

difficulty ['dɪfɪkəltɪ] (*pl* **-ies**) *n* dificultad *f*; **to have ~ in doing sthg** tener dificultad en OR para hacer algo.

diffidence ['dɪfɪdəns] *n* retraimiento *m*.

diffident ['dɪfɪdənt] *adj* retraído(da).

diffuse [*adj* dɪ'fjuːs, *vb* dɪ'fjuːz] ◇ *adj* **-1.** [gen] difuso(sa). **-2.** [city, company] extenso(sa). ◇ *vt* difundir. ◇ *vi* difundirse.

diffusion [dɪ'fjuːʒn] *n* difusión *f*.

dig [dɪg] (*pt* & *pp* **dug**, *cont* **digging**) ◇ *vt* **-1.** [hole - with spade] cavar; [- with hands, paws] escarbar. **-2.** [garden] cavar en; [mine] excavar. **-3.** [press]: **to ~ sthg into** clavar OR hundir algo en. ◇ *vi* **-1.** [with spade] cavar; [with hands, paws] escarbar. **-2.** [press]: **to ~ into** clavarse OR hundirse en. ◇ *n* **-1.** *fig* [unkind remark] pulla *f*. **-2.** ARCHEOL excavación *f*.

◆ **dig out** *vt sep* **-1.** [rescue] desenterrar, sacar. **-2.** *inf* [find - letter] rescatar, desempolvar; [- information] extraer.

◆ **dig up** *vt sep* [gen] desenterrar; [tree] arrancar.

digest [*n* 'daɪdʒest, *vb* dɪ'dʒest] ◇ *n* compendio *m*. ◇ *vt lit* & *fig* digerir.

digestible [dɪ'dʒestəbl] *adj* digerible.

digestion [dɪ'dʒestʃn] *n* digestión *f*.

digestive [dɪ'dʒestɪv] *adj* digestivo(va); **~ system** aparato *m* digestivo.

digestive biscuit *n Br* galleta hecha con harina integral.

digit ['dɪdʒɪt] *n* **-1.** [figure] dígito *m*. **-2.** [finger, toe] dedo *m*.

digital ['dɪdʒɪtl] *adj* digital.

digital organizer *n* agenda *f* electrónica.

digital recording *n* grabación *f* digital.

digital watch *n* reloj *m* digital.

digitize, -ise ['dɪdʒɪtaɪz] *vt* digitalizar.

dignified ['dɪgnɪfaɪd] *adj* [gen] solemne; [behaviour] ceremonioso(sa).

dignify ['dɪgnɪfaɪ] (*pt* & *pp* **-ied**) *vt* dignificar.

dignitary ['dɪgnɪtrɪ] (*pl* **-ies**) *n* dignatario *m*, -ria *f*.

dignity ['dɪgnətɪ] *n* dignidad *f*.

digress [daɪ'gres] *vi* apartarse del tema; **to ~ from** apartarse OR desviarse de.

digression [daɪ'greʃn] *n* digresión *f*.

digs [dɪgz] *npl Br inf* alojamiento *m*; **to live in ~** vivir de patrona.

dike [daɪk] *n* **-1.** [wall, bank] dique *m*. **-2.** *inf pej* [lesbian] tortillera *f*.

diktat ['dɪktæt] *n* tiranía *f*.

dilapidated [dɪ'læpɪdeɪtɪd] *adj* destartalado(da), derruido(da).

dilate [daɪ'leɪt] ◇ *vt* dilatar. ◇ *vi* dilatarse.

dilated [daɪ'leɪtɪd] *adj* dilatado(da).

dilemma [dɪ'lemə] *n* dilema *m*.

dilettante [,dɪlɪ'tæntɪ] (*pl* **-tes** OR **-ti** [-tɪ]) *n* diletante *m* y *f*.

diligence ['dɪlɪdʒəns] *n* [hard work] diligencia *f*.

diligent ['dɪlɪdʒənt] *adj* diligente.

dill [dɪl] *n* eneldo *m*.

dillydally ['dɪlɪdælɪ] (*pt* & *pp* **-ied**) *vi inf* andar perdiendo el tiempo.

dilute [daɪ'luːt] ◇ *adj* diluido(da). ◇ *vt* diluir; [wine, beer] aguar.

dilution [daɪ'luːʃn] *n* dilución *f*, disolución *f*; [beer, wine] aguado *m*.

dim [dɪm] (*compar* **-mer**, *superl* **-mest**, *pt* & *pp* **-med**, *cont* **-ming**) ◇ *adj* **-1.** [light] mortecino(na), tenue; [room] sombrío(a). **-2.** [outline, figure] difuso(sa), borroso(sa). **-3.** [eyesight] nublado(da). **-4.** [memory] vago(ga). **-5.** *inf* [stupid] tonto(ta), torpe. ◇ *vt* atenuar. ◇ *vi* [light] atenuarse.

dime [daɪm] *n Am* moneda de diez centavos; **they're a ~ a dozen** [common] los hay a porrillo OR mansalva.

dimension [dɪ'menʃn] *n* dimensión *f*.

◆ **dimensions** *npl* dimensiones *fpl*.

-dimensional [dɪ'menʃənl] *suffix*: **one~** unidimensional; **two~** bidimensional.

diminish [dɪ'mɪnɪʃ] *vt* & *vi* disminuir.

diminished [dɪ'mɪnɪʃt] *adj* reducido(da).

diminished responsibility *n* JUR responsabilidad *f* atenuada (por enajenación mental).

diminishing returns [dɪ'mɪnɪʃɪŋ] *npl*: **the law of ~** la ley del rendimiento decreciente.

diminutive [dɪ'mɪnjʊtɪv] *fml* ◇ *adj* diminuto(ta). ◇ *n* GRAMM diminutivo *m*.

dimly ['dɪmlɪ] *adv* [lit] tenuemente; [see] indistintamente; [remember] vagamente.

dimmer ['dɪmər], **dimmer switch** *n* potenciómetro *m*, regulador *m* de intensidad.

dimmers ['dɪməz] *npl Am* [dipped headlights] luces *fpl* cortas OR de cruce; [parking lights] luces de posición OR situación.

dimmer switch = dimmer.

dimple ['dɪmpl] *n* hoyuelo *m*.

dimwit ['dɪmwɪt] n inf bobo m, -ba f.

dim-witted [-'wɪtɪd] adj inf lerdo(da), bobo(ba).

din [dɪn] n inf estrépito m, relajo m Amer.

dine [daɪn] vi fml cenar.

◆ **dine out** vi cenar fuera.

diner ['daɪnəʳ] n -1. [person] comensal m y f (en cena). -2. Am [restaurant - cheap] restaurante m barato; [- on the road] ≃ restaurante m OR parador m de carretera.

dingdong [,dɪŋ'dɒŋ] ◇ adj inf [battle, argument] reñido(da), disputado(da). ◇ n [of bell] din don m.

dinghy ['dɪŋgɪ] (pl -ies) n bote m.

dingo ['dɪŋgəʊ] (pl -es) n dingo m.

dingy ['dɪndʒɪ] (compar -ier, superl -iest) adj [room, street] lóbrego(ga); [clothes, carpet] deslustrado(da).

dining car ['daɪnɪŋ-] n vagón m restaurante.

dining room ['daɪnɪŋ-] n comedor m.

dining table ['daɪnɪŋ-] n mesa f grande (de comedor).

dinner ['dɪnəʳ] n -1. [evening meal] cena f; [midday meal] comida f, almuerzo m. -2. [formal event] cena f de gala, banquete m.

dinner dance n cena f con baile.

dinner jacket n esmoquin m.

dinner party n cena f (de amigos en casa).

dinner service n vajilla f.

dinner table n mesa f (para comer).

dinnertime ['dɪnətaɪm] n [in the evening] la hora de la cena; [at midday] la hora del almuerzo OR de la comida.

dinosaur ['daɪnəsɔːʳ] n [reptile] dinosaurio m.

dint [dɪnt] n fml: by ~ of a base de.

diocese ['daɪəsɪs] n diócesis f inv.

diode ['daɪəʊd] n diodo m.

dip [dɪp] (pt & pp -ped, cont -ping) ◇ n -1. [in road, ground] pendiente f, declive m. -2. [sauce] salsa f. -3. [swim] chapuzón m; to go for/take a ~ ir a darse/darse un chapuzón. ◇ vt -1. [into liquid]: to ~ sthg in OR into sthg mojar algo en algo. -2. Br [headlights]: to ~ one's lights poner las luces de cruce. ◇ vi descender suavemente.

Dip. Br abbr of diploma.

diphtheria [dɪf'θɪərɪə] n difteria f.

diphthong ['dɪfθɒŋ] n diptongo m.

diploma [dɪ'pləʊmə] (pl -s) n diploma m.

diplomacy [dɪ'pləʊməsɪ] n diplomacia f.

diplomat ['dɪpləmæt] n -1. [official] diplomático m, -ca f. -2. [tactful person] persona f diplomática.

diplomatic [,dɪplə'mætɪk] adj diplomático(ca).

diplomatic bag n valija f diplomática.

diplomatic corps n cuerpo m diplomático.

diplomatic immunity n inmunidad f diplomática.

diplomatic relations npl relaciones fpl diplomáticas.

dipsomaniac [,dɪpsə'meɪnɪæk] n dipsomaníaco m, -ca f.

dipstick ['dɪpstɪk] n AUT varilla f (para medir el nivel) del aceite.

dipswitch ['dɪpswɪtʃ] n Br AUT interruptor m de luces de cruce.

dire ['daɪəʳ] adj [consequences] grave; [warning] estremecedor(ra); [need, poverty] extremo(ma).

direct [dɪ'rekt] ◇ adj directo(ta). ◇ vt -1. [gen]: to ~ sthg at sb dirigir algo a alguien. -2. [person to place]: to ~ sb (to) indicar a alguien el camino (a). -3. [order]: to ~ sb to do sthg mandar a alguien hacer algo. ◇ adv directamente.

direct action n acción f directa.

direct current n corriente f continua.

direct debit n Br domiciliación f (de pago).

direct dialling [-'daɪəlɪŋ] n llamada f directa.

direct hit n: to score a ~ dar justo en el blanco.

direction [dɪ'rekʃn] n dirección f; in all ~s en todas direcciones; sense of ~ sentido m de la orientación; under the ~ of bajo la dirección de.

◆ **directions** npl -1. [instructions to place] señas fpl, indicaciones fpl. -2. [instructions for use] instrucciones fpl (de uso), modo m de empleo.

directive [dɪ'rektɪv] n directiva f.

directly [dɪ'rektlɪ] adv -1. [gen] directamente. -2. [immediately] inmediatamente. -3. [very soon] pronto, en breve.

direct mail n propaganda f por correo.

director [dɪ'rektəʳ] n director m, -ra f.

directorate [dɪ'rektərət] n [board of directors] dirección f, (junta f) directiva f.

director-general (pl directors-general OR director-generals) n director general m, directora general f.

Director of Public Prosecutions n Br ≃ fiscal general m y f del estado.

directorship [dɪ'rektəʃɪp] n dirección f.

directory [dɪ'rektərɪ] (pl -ies) n -1. [gen] guía f (alfabética). -2. COMPUT directorio m.

directory enquiries *n* Br (servicio *m* de) información *f* telefónica.

direct rule *n* (sistema *m* de) gobierno *m* central.

direct selling *n* (*U*) venta *f* directa.

direct speech *n* estilo *m* directo.

direct taxation *n* (*U*) impuestos *mpl* directos.

dire straits *npl*: **in** ~ en serios aprietos.

dirge [dɜːdʒ] *n* canto *m* fúnebre.

dirt [dɜːt] *n* (*U*) **-1.** [mud, dust] suciedad *f*. **-2.** [earth] tierra *f*.

dirt cheap *inf* ◇ *adj* tirado(da) de precio. ◇ *adv* a precio de ganga.

dirt track *n* camino *m* de tierra.

dirty ['dɜːtɪ] (*compar* **-ier**, *superl* **-iest**, *pt* & *pp* **-ied**) ◇ *adj* **-1.** [gen] sucio(cia). **-2.** [joke] verde; [film] pornográfico(ca); [book, language] obsceno(na). ◇ *vt* ensuciar.

disability [ˌdɪsə'bɪlətɪ] (*pl* **-ies**) *n* minusvalía *f*.

disable [dɪs'eɪbl] *vt* [injure] dejar inválido(da) OR incapacitado(da).

disabled [dɪs'eɪbld] ◇ *adj* [person] minusválido(da). ◇ *npl*: **the** ~ los minusválidos.

disablement [dɪs'eɪblmənt] *n* incapacitación *f*.

disabuse [ˌdɪsə'bjuːz] *vt* *fml*: **to** ~ **sb (of sthg)** desengañar a alguien (de algo).

disadvantage [ˌdɪsəd'vɑːntɪdʒ] *n* desventaja *f*; **to be at a** ~ estar en desventaja; **to be to one's** ~ ir en perjuicio de uno.

disadvantaged [ˌdɪsəd'vɑːntɪdʒd] *adj* desfavorecido(da).

disadvantageous [ˌdɪsædvɑːn'teɪdʒəs] *adj* desventajoso(sa), desfavorable.

disaffected [ˌdɪsə'fektɪd] *adj* desafecto(ta).

disaffection [ˌdɪsə'fekʃn] *n* desafección *f*.

disagree [ˌdɪsə'griː] *vi* **-1.** [have different opinions]: **to** ~ **(with)** no estar de acuerdo (con). **-2.** [differ] contradecirse, no concordar. **-3.** [subj: food, drink]: **to** ~ **with sb** sentar mal a alguien.

disagreeable [ˌdɪsə'grɪəbl] *adj* desagradable.

disagreement [ˌdɪsə'griːmənt] *n* **-1.** [fact of disagreeing] desacuerdo *m*. **-2.** [argument] discusión *f*. **-3.** [dissimilarity] disconformidad *f*.

disallow [ˌdɪsə'laʊ] *vt* **-1.** *fml* [appeal, claim] rechazar. **-2.** [goal] anular.

disappear [ˌdɪsə'pɪər] *vi* desaparecer.

disappearance [ˌdɪsə'pɪərəns] *n* desaparición *f*.

disappoint [ˌdɪsə'pɔɪnt] *vt* [person] decep-

cionar, desilusionar; [expectations, hopes] defraudar.

disappointed [ˌdɪsə'pɔɪntɪd] *adj* **-1.** [person]: ~ **(in** OR **with sthg)** decepcionado(da) (con algo). **-2.** [expectations, hopes] defraudado(da).

disappointing [ˌdɪsə'pɔɪntɪŋ] *adj* decepcionante.

disappointment [ˌdɪsə'pɔɪntmənt] *n* decepción *f*, desilusión *f*.

disapproval [ˌdɪsə'pruːvl] *n* desaprobación *f*.

disapprove [ˌdɪsə'pruːv] *vi*: **to** ~ **(of sthg/sb)** censurar (algo/a alguien).

disapproving [ˌdɪsə'pruːvɪŋ] *adj* desaprobatorio(ria).

disarm [dɪs'ɑːm] ◇ *vt* *lit* & *fig* desarmar. ◇ *vi* desarmarse.

disarmament [dɪs'ɑːməmənt] *n* desarme *m*.

disarming [dɪs'ɑːmɪŋ] *adj* que hace que uno baje la guardia.

disarray [ˌdɪsə'reɪ] *n*: **in** ~ [clothes, hair] en desorden; [army, political party] sumido(da) en el desconcierto.

disassociate [ˌdɪsə'səʊʃɪeɪt] *vt*: **to** ~ **o.s. from** desasociarse OR disociarse de.

disaster [dɪ'zɑːstər] *n* desastre *m*.

disaster area *n* [after natural disaster] zona *f* catastrófica.

disastrous [dɪ'zɑːstrəs] *adj* desastroso(sa).

disastrously [dɪ'zɑːstrəslɪ] *adv* desastrosamente.

disband [dɪs'bænd] ◇ *vt* disolver, disgregar. ◇ *vi* disolverse, disgregarse.

disbelief [ˌdɪsbɪ'liːf] *n*: **in** OR **with** ~ con incredulidad.

disbelieve [ˌdɪsbɪ'liːv] *vt* dudar de, no creer.

disc Br, **disk** Am [dɪsk] *n* disco *m*.

disc. *abbr of* **discount**.

discard [dɪ'skɑːd] *vt* [old clothes etc] desechar; [possibility] descartar.

discarded [dɪ'skɑːdɪd] *adj* desechado(da).

disc brake *n* freno *m* de disco.

discern [dɪ'sɜːn] *vt* **-1.** [gen] discernir; [improvement] percibir. **-2.** [figure, outline] distinguir.

discernible [dɪ'sɜːnəbl] *adj* **-1.** [visible] distinguible. **-2.** [noticeable] apreciable.

discerning [dɪ'sɜːnɪŋ] *adj* refinado(da); [audience] entendido(da).

discharge [*n* 'dɪstʃɑːdʒ, *vt* dɪs'tʃɑːdʒ] ◇ *n* **-1.** [of patient] alta *f*; [of prisoner, defendant] puesta *f* en libertad; [of soldier] licencia *f*. **-2.** *fml* [of duty etc] cumplimiento *m*, desempeño *m*. **-3.** [of gas, smoke] emisión *f*;

[- of sewage] **vertido** *m*. **-4.** [of debt] **saldo** *m*, **liquidación** *f*. **-5.** [MED - from nose] **mucosidad** *f*; [- from wound] **supuración** *f*. **-6.** ELEC **descarga** *f*.

◇ *vt* **-1.** [patient] **dar de alta**; [prisoner, defendant] **poner en libertad**; [soldier] **licenciar**. **-2.** *fml* [duty etc] **cumplir, desempeñar. -3.** [gas, smoke] **emitir, despedir**; [sewage] **verter**; [cargo] **descargar. -4.** [debt] **saldar, liquidar**.

discharged bankrupt [dɪs'tʃɑːdʒd-] *n* **quebrado** *m* **rehabilitado.**

disciple [dɪ'saɪpl] *n* **-1.** [follower] **discípulo** *m*, -la *f*. **-2.** RELIG **discípulo** *m*.

disciplinarian [ˌdɪsɪplɪ'neərɪən] *n* **amante** *m* y *f* **de la severa disciplina.**

disciplinary [ˈdɪsɪplɪnərɪ] *adj* **disciplinario(ria)**; ~ **action medidas** *fpl* **disciplinarias.**

discipline [ˈdɪsɪplɪn] ◇ *n* **disciplina** *f*. ◇ *vt* **-1.** [control] **disciplinar. -2.** [punish] **castigar.**

disciplined [ˈdɪsɪplɪnd] *adj* **disciplinado(da).**

disc jockey *n* **pinchadiscos** *m* y *f inv*.

disclaim [dɪs'kleɪm] *vt fml* **negar.**

disclaimer [dɪs'kleɪmə*r*] *n* **rectificación** *f*.

disclose [dɪs'kləʊz] *vt* **desvelar, revelar.**

disclosure [dɪs'kləʊʒə*r*] *n* **revelación** *f*.

disco [ˈdɪskəʊ] (*pl* **-s**) (*abbr of* **discotheque**) *n* [place] **discoteca** *f*; [event] **baile** *m*.

discoloration [dɪsˌkʌlə'reɪʃn] *n* [fading, staining] **descoloramiento** *m*.

discolour *Br*, **discolor** *Am* [dɪs'kʌlə*r*] ◇ *vt* **descolorir**. ◇ *vi* **descolorirse.**

discoloured *Br*, **discolored** *Am* [dɪs'kʌləd] *adj* **descolorido(da).**

discomfort [dɪs'kʌmfət] *n* **incomodidad** *f*.

disconcert [ˌdɪskən'sɜːt] *vt* **desconcertar.**

disconcerting [ˌdɪskən'sɜːtɪŋ] *adj* [worrying] **desconcertante**; [embarrassing] **enojoso(sa).**

disconnect [ˌdɪskə'nekt] *vt* **-1.** [detach] **quitar, separar. -2.** [from gas, electricity - appliance] **desconectar**; [- house, subscriber] **cortar el suministro a**; [- supply] **cortar. -3.** [on phone - person] **cortar la línea a**; [- phone] **cortar.**

disconnected [ˌdɪskə'nektɪd] *adj* **inconexo(xa).**

disconsolate [dɪs'kɒnsələt] *adj* **desconsolado(da).**

discontent [ˌdɪskən'tent] *n*: ~ **(with)** **descontento** *m* **(con).**

discontented [ˌdɪskən'tentɪd] *adj* **descontento(ta).**

discontentment [ˌdɪskən'tentmənt] *n*: ~ **(with)** **descontento** *m* **(con).**

discontinue [ˌdɪskən'tɪnjuː] *vt* **interrumpir.**

discontinued line [ˌdɪskən'tɪnjuːd-] *n* COMM **producto** *m* **que ya no se fabrica.**

discord [ˈdɪskɔːd] *n* **-1.** [disagreement] **discordia** *f*. **-2.** MUS **disonancia** *f*.

discordant [dɪ'skɔːdənt] *adj* **-1.** [unpleasant] **discordante. -2.** MUS **disonante.**

discotheque [ˈdɪskəʊtek] *n* **discoteca** *f*.

discount [*n* 'dɪskaʊnt, *vb Br* dɪs'kaʊnt, *Am* 'dɪskaʊnt] ◇ *n* **descuento** *m*. ◇ *vt* [report, claim] **descartar.**

discount house *n* **-1.** FIN *corporación financiera dedicada a negociar con letras de cambio*. **-2.** [store] **tienda** *f* **especializada en rebajas.**

discount rate *n* **tipo** *m* OR **tarifa** *f* **de descuento.**

discount store *n* **tienda** *f* **especializada en rebajas.**

discourage [dɪ'skʌrɪdʒ] *vt* **-1.** [dispirit] **desanimar. -2.** [deter] **desaconsejar**; **to** ~ **sb from doing sthg disuadir a alguien de hacer algo.**

discouraging [dɪ'skʌrɪdʒɪŋ] *adj* **desalentador(ra).**

discourse [ˈdɪskɔːs] *n fml*: ~ **(on)** **discurso** *m* **(sobre).**

discourteous [dɪs'kɜːtjəs] *adj fml* **descortés.**

discourtesy [dɪs'kɜːtɪsɪ] *n* **descortesía** *f*.

discover [dɪ'skʌvə*r*] *vt* **descubrir.**

discoverer [dɪ'skʌvərə*r*] *n* **descubridor** *m*, -ra *f*.

discovery [dɪ'skʌvərɪ] (*pl* **-ies**) *n* **descubrimiento** *m*.

discredit [dɪs'kredɪt] ◇ *n* **descrédito** *m*, **desprestigio** *m*. ◇ *vt* **-1.** [person, organization] **desacreditar, desprestigiar. -2.** [idea, report] **refutar.**

discredited [dɪskredɪtɪd] *adj* **desacreditado(da), desprestigiado(da).**

discreet [dɪ'skriːt] *adj* **discreto(ta).**

discreetly [dɪ'skriːtlɪ] *adv* **discretamente, con discreción.**

discrepancy [dɪ'skrepənsɪ] (*pl* **-ies**) *n*: ~ **(in/between)** **desigualdad** *f* **(en/entre), discrepancia** *f* **(en/entre).**

discrete [dɪs'kriːt] *adj fml* **diferente, independiente.**

discretion [dɪ'skreʃn] *n* (*U*) **-1.** [tact] **discreción** *f*. **-2.** [judgment] **capacidad** *f* **de decisión**; **at the** ~ **of a voluntad de, al arbitrio de.**

discretionary [dɪ'skreʃənərɪ] *adj* **discrecional.**

discriminate [dɪ'skrɪmɪneɪt] *vi* **-1.** [distinguish]: **to** ~ **(between)** **discriminar** OR **distinguir (entre). -2.** [treat unfairly]: **to** ~ **against sb discriminar a alguien.**

discriminating [dɪ'skrɪmɪneɪtɪŋ] *adj* refinado(da); [audience] entendido(da).

discrimination [dɪ,skrɪmɪ'neɪʃn] *n* **-1.** [prejudice]: ~ **(against)** discriminación *f* (hacia). **-2.** [judgment] (buen) gusto *m*.

discus ['dɪskəs] (*pl* **-es**) *n* disco *m* (*en atletismo*).

discuss [dɪ'skʌs] *vt* **-1.** [gen]: **to ~ sthg (with sb)** discutir algo (con alguien). **-2.** [subj: book, lecture] tratar de.

discussion [dɪ'skʌʃn] *n* discusión *f*; **it's under ~** está siendo discutido.

disdain [dɪs'deɪn] *fml* ◇ *n*: ~ **(for)** desdén *m* OR desprecio *m* (hacia). ◇ *vt* desdeñar, despreciar. ◇ *vi*: **to ~ to do sthg** no dignarse (a) hacer algo.

disdainful [dɪs'deɪnfʊl] *adj* desdeñoso(sa).

disease [dɪ'ziːz] *n lit & fig* enfermedad *f*.

diseased [dɪ'ziːzd] *adj lit & fig* enfermo(ma).

disembark [,dɪsɪm'baːk] *vi* desembarcar.

disembarkation [,dɪsɪmbaː'keɪʃn] *n* [of people] desembarco *m*; [of goods] desembarque *m*.

disembodied [,dɪsɪm'bɒdɪd] *adj* incorpóreo(a).

disembowel [,dɪsɪm'baʊəl] (*Br pt & pp* **-led**, *cont* **-ling**, *Am pt & pp* **-ed**, *cont* **-ing**) *vt* destripar, achurar *Amer*.

disenchanted [,dɪsɪn'tʃɑːntɪd] *adj*: ~ **(with)** desencantado(a) (con).

disenchantment [,dɪsɪn'tʃɑːntmənt] *n* desencanto *m*.

disenfranchise [,dɪsɪn'fræntʃaɪz] = **disfranchise**.

disengage [,dɪsɪn'geɪdʒ] *vt* **-1.** [release]: **to ~ sthg (from)** soltar OR desenganchar algo (de); **to ~ o.s. (from)** soltarse OR desengancharse (de). **-2.** TECH [gears] quitar; [clutch] soltar; [mechanism] liberar.

disengagement [,dɪsɪn'geɪdʒmənt] *n* TECH [of clutch] desembrague *m*; [of mechanism] liberación *f*.

disentangle [,dɪsɪn'tæŋgl] *vt*: **to ~ sthg (from)** desenredar algo (de); **to ~ o.s. from** [barbed wire etc] desenredarse de; *fig* [relationship] zafarse de, desembarazarse de.

disfavour *Br*, **disfavor** *Am* [dɪs'feɪvəʳ] *n* **-1.** [disapproval] desaprobación *f*. **-2.** [state of being disapproved of] desgracia *f*; **in ~ with** en desgracia con.

disfigure [dɪs'fɪgəʳ] *vt* desfigurar.

disfranchise [,dɪs'fræntʃaɪz] *vt* privar del derecho al voto.

disgorge [dɪs'gɔːdʒ] *vt* expulsar.

disgrace [dɪs'greɪs] ◇ *n* vergüenza *f*; **he's a ~ to his family** es una deshonra para su familia; **to be in ~** [minister, official] estar desprestigiado(da); [child, pet] estar castigado(da). ◇ *vt* deshonrar; **to ~ o.s.** desprestigiarse.

disgraceful [dɪs'greɪsfʊl] *adj* vergonzoso(sa).

disgruntled [dɪs'grʌntld] *adj* disgustado(da).

disguise [dɪs'gaɪz] ◇ *n* disfraz *m*; **in ~** [policeman, personality] de incógnito. ◇ *vt* disfrazar; **to ~ o.s. as** disfrazarse de.

disgust [dɪs'gʌst] ◇ *n*: ~ **(at)** [physical] asco *m* (hacia); [moral] indignación *f* (ante); **in ~** [physical] lleno de asco; [moral] lleno de indignación. ◇ *vt* [physically] asquear; [morally] indignar.

disgusting [dɪs'gʌstɪŋ] *adj* [physically] asqueroso(sa); [morally] indignante.

dish [dɪʃ] *n* **-1.** [container] fuente *f*. **-2.** [course] plato *m*. **-3.** *Am* [plate] plato *m*.

◆ **dishes** *npl* platos *mpl*; **to do** OR **wash the ~es** fregar (los platos).

◆ **dish out** *vt sep inf* repartir.

◆ **dish up** *vt sep inf* servir.

dish aerial *Br*, **dish antenna** *Am n* (antena *f*) parabólica *f*.

disharmony [,dɪs'haːmənɪ] *n* discordia *f*.

dishcloth ['dɪʃklɒθ] *n* trapo *m* de fregar los platos.

disheartened [dɪs'haːtnd] *adj* descorazonado(da).

disheartening [dɪs'haːtnɪŋ] *adj* descorazonador(ra).

dishevelled *Br*, **disheveled** *Am* [dɪ'ʃevəld] *adj* desastrado(da), desaliñado(da); [hair] despeinado(da).

dishonest [dɪs'ɒnɪst] *adj* deshonesto(ta), nada honrado(da).

dishonesty [dɪs'ɒnɪstɪ] *n* falta *f* de honradez.

dishonorable *Am* = **dishonourable**.

dishonour *Br*, **dishonor** *Am* [dɪs'ɒnəʳ] *fml* ◇ *n* deshonra *f*, deshonor *m*. ◇ *vt* deshonrar.

dishonourable *Br*, **dishonorable** *Am* [dɪs'ɒnərəbl] *adj* deshonroso(sa).

dish soap *n Am* detergente *m* para vajillas.

dish towel *n Am* paño *m* de cocina.

dishwasher ['dɪʃ,wɒʃəʳ] *n* [machine] lavavajillas *m inv*.

dishy ['dɪʃɪ] (*compar* **-ier**, *superl* **-iest**) *adj Br inf*: **to be ~** estar buenísimo(ma).

disillusioned [,dɪsɪ'luːʒnd] *adj* desilusionado(da); **to become ~ (with)** desilusionarse (con).

disillusionment [,dɪsɪ'luːʒnmənt] *n*: ~ **(with)** desilusión *f* (con).

disincentive [ˌdɪsɪn'sentɪv] n freno m, traba f.

disinclined [ˌdɪsɪn'klaɪnd] adj: **to be ~ to do sthg** ser reacio(cia) a hacer algo.

disinfect [ˌdɪsɪn'fekt] vt desinfectar.

disinfectant [ˌdɪsɪn'fektənt] n desinfectante m.

disinformation [ˌdɪsɪnfə'meɪʃn] n desinformación f.

disingenuous [ˌdɪsɪn'dʒenjʊəs] adj falso(sa), poco honrado(da).

disinherit [ˌdɪsɪn'herɪt] vt desheredar.

disintegrate [dɪs'ɪntɪgreɪt] vi lit & fig desintegrarse.

disintegration [dɪsˌɪntɪ'greɪʃn] n desintegración f.

disinterested [ˌdɪs'ɪntrəstɪd] adj **-1.** [objective] desinteresado(da). **-2.** inf [uninterested]: **~ (in)** indiferente (a).

disinvestment [ˌdɪsɪn'vestmənt] n retirada del capital invertido.

disjointed [dɪs'dʒɔɪntɪd] adj deslabazado(da).

disk [dɪsk] n **-1.** COMPUT disquete m. **-2.** Am = disc.

disk drive Br, **diskette drive** Am n COMPUT disquetera f.

diskette [dɪsk'et] n disquete m, disco m flexible.

diskette drive n Am = disk drive.

disk operating system [-ɒpəreɪtɪŋ-] n COMPUT DOS m.

dislike [dɪs'laɪk] ◇ n **-1.** [feeling]: **~ (for)** [things] aversión f (a); [people] antipatía f (por); **to take a ~ to** cogerle manía a. **-2.** [person, thing not liked] fobia f. ◇ vt [thing] tener aversión a; [person] tener antipatía a.

dislocate ['dɪsləkeɪt] vt **-1.** MED dislocar. **-2.** [disrupt] trastocar.

dislodge [dɪs'lɒdʒ] vt: **to ~ sthg/sb (from)** desalojar algo/a alguien (de).

disloyal [ˌdɪs'lɔɪəl] adj: **~ (to)** desleal a.

dismal ['dɪzml] adj **-1.** [weather, future] oscuro(ra), sombrío(a); [place, atmosphere] deprimente. **-2.** [attempt, failure] penoso(sa), lamentable.

dismantle [dɪs'mæntl] vt [machine] desmontar; [organization] desmantelar.

dismay [dɪs'meɪ] ◇ n (U) consternación f; **to my/his** etc **~** para mi/su etc consternación. ◇ vt consternar.

dismember [dɪs'membər] vt desmembrar.

dismiss [dɪs'mɪs] vt **-1.** [refuse to take seriously] desechar. **-2.** [from job]: **to ~ sb (from)** despedir a alguien (de). **-3.** [allow to leave] dar permiso para irse a.

dismissal [dɪs'mɪsl] n **-1.** [from job] despido m, remoción f Amer. **-2.** [refusal to take seriously] rechazo m.

dismissive [dɪs'mɪsɪv] adj: **~ (of)** despreciativo(va) (hacia).

dismount [ˌdɪs'maʊnt] vi: **to ~ (from sthg)** desmontar (de algo).

disobedience [ˌdɪsə'biːdjəns] n desobediencia f.

disobedient [ˌdɪsə'biːdjənt] adj: **~ (to)** desobediente (con).

disobey [ˌdɪsə'beɪ] vt & vi desobedecer.

disorder [dɪs'ɔːdər] n **-1.** [disarray]: **in ~** en desorden. **-2.** (U) [rioting] disturbios mpl. **-3.** MED [physical] afección f, dolencia f; [mental] trastorno m, perturbación f.

disordered [dɪs'ɔːdəd] adj **-1.** [in disarray] desordenado(da). **-2.** MED: **mentally ~** perturbado(da), con trastornos mentales.

disorderly [dɪs'ɔːdəlɪ] adj **-1.** [untidy] desordenado(da). **-2.** [unruly - behaviour] incontrolado(da); [- person] alborotador(ra).

disorderly conduct n JUR conducta f escandalosa.

disorganized, -ised [dɪs'ɔːgənaɪzd] adj desorganizado(da).

disorientated Br [dɪs'ɔːrɪənteɪtɪd], **disoriented** Am [dɪs'ɔːrɪəntɪd] adj desorientado(da).

disown [dɪs'əʊn] vt renegar de, desconocer.

disparage [dɪ'spærɪdʒ] vt menospreciar.

disparaging [dɪ'spærɪdʒɪŋ] adj menospreciativo(va).

disparate ['dɪspərət] adj fml dispar.

disparity [dɪ'spærətɪ] (pl **-ies**) n: **~ (between/in)** disparidad f (entre/en).

dispassionate [dɪs'pæʃnət] adj desapasionado(da).

dispatch [dɪ'spætʃ] ◇ n despacho m. ◇ vt [goods, parcel] expedir; [message, messenger, troops] enviar.

dispatch box n Br POL zona donde dan sus discursos los parlamentarios más importantes en la Cámara de los Comunes.

dispatch rider n MIL correo m; [courier] mensajero m.

dispel [dɪ'spel] (pt & pp **-led**, cont **-ling**) vt disipar.

dispensable [dɪ'spensəbl] adj prescindible.

dispensary [dɪ'spensərɪ] (pl **-ies**) n dispensario m.

dispensation [ˌdɪspen'seɪʃn] n [permission] dispensa f.

dispense [dɪ'spens] vt **-1.** [advice] ofrecer; [justice] administrar. **-2.** [drugs, medicine] despachar, dispensar.

◆ **dispense with** *vt fus* prescindir de.

dispenser [dɪ'spensər] *n* [machine, container] máquina *f* expendedora.

dispensing chemist *Br*, **dispensing pharmacist** *Am* [dɪ'spensɪŋ-] *n* farmacéutico *m*, -ca *f*.

dispersal [dɪ'spɜːsl] *n* dispersión *f*.

disperse [dɪ'spɜːs] ◇ *vt* dispersar. ◇ *vi* dispersarse.

dispirited [dɪ'spɪrɪtɪd] *adj* desanimado(da).

dispiriting [dɪ'spɪrɪtɪŋ] *adj* deprimente.

displace [dɪs'pleɪs] *vt* [supplant] reemplazar, sustituir.

displaced person [dɪs'pleɪst-] *n* [by war, disaster] refugiado *m*, -da *f*; [for political reasons] exiliado *m*, -da *f*.

displacement [dɪs'pleɪsmənt] *n* [of people] desplazamiento *m*.

display [dɪ'spleɪ] ◇ *n* -1. [arrangement - in shop window] escaparate *m*; [- in museum] exposición *f*; [- on stall, pavement] muestrario *m*; **on ~** expuesto(ta). -2. [demonstration, public event] demostración *f*. -3. COMPUT visualización *f*. ◇ *vt* -1. [arrange] exponer. -2. [show] demostrar.

display advertising *n* publicidad *f* a gran escala.

displease [dɪs'pliːz] *vt* [annoy] disgustar; [anger] enfadar.

displeasure [dɪs'pleʒər] *n* [annoyance] disgusto *m*; [anger] enfado *m*.

disposable [dɪ'spəuzəbl] *adj* desechable; **~ income** ingresos *mpl* disponibles.

disposal [dɪ'spəuzl] *n* -1. [removal] eliminación *f*. -2. [availability]: **at sb's ~** a la disposición de alguien.

dispose [dɪ'spəuz]
◆ **dispose of** *vt fus* [rubbish] deshacerse de; [problem] quitarse de encima OR de en medio.

disposed [dɪ'spəuzd] *adj* -1. [willing]: **to be ~ to do sthg** estar dispuesto(ta) a hacer algo. -2. [friendly]: **to be well ~ to** OR **towards sb** tener buena disposición hacia alguien.

disposition [,dɪspə'zɪʃn] *n* -1. [temperament] carácter *m*, disposición *f* de ánimo. -2. [willingness, tendency]: **~ to do sthg** predisposición *f* a hacer algo.

dispossess [,dɪspə'zes] *vt fml*: **to ~ sb of sthg** desposeer a alguien de algo.

disproportion [,dɪsprə'pɔːʃn] *n* desproporción *f*.

disproportionate [,dɪsprə'pɔːʃnət] *adj*: **~ (to)** desproporcionado(da) (a).

disprove [,dɪs'pruːv] *vt* refutar.

dispute [dɪ'spjuːt] ◇ *n* -1. [quarrel] disputa *f*. -2. (*U*) [disagreement] conflicto *m*, desacuerdo *m*; **in ~** [people] en desacuerdo; [matter] en litigio, en entredicho. -3. INDUSTRY conflicto *m* laboral. ◇ *vt* cuestionar.

disqualification [dɪs,kwɒlɪfɪ'keɪʃn] *n* descalificación *f*.

disqualify [,dɪs'kwɒlɪfaɪ] (*pt* & *pp* **-ied**) *vt* -1. [subj: authority, illness etc]: **to ~ sb (from doing sthg)** incapacitar a alguien (para hacer algo). -2. SPORT descalificar. -3. *Br* [from driving] retirar el permiso de conducir a.

disquiet [dɪs'kwaɪət] *n* inquietud *f*, desasosiego *m*.

disregard [,dɪsrɪ'gɑːd] ◇ *n*: **~ (for)** indiferencia *f* (a), despreocupación *f* (por). ◇ *vt* hacer caso omiso de.

disrepair [,dɪsrɪ'peər] *n*: **in a state of ~** en mal estado.

disreputable [dɪs'repjutəbl] *adj* [person, company] de mala fama; [behaviour] vergonzante.

disrepute [,dɪsrɪ'pjuːt] *n*: **to bring sthg into ~** desprestigiar OR desacreditar algo; **to fall into ~** desprestigiarse, desacreditarse.

disrespectful [,dɪsrɪ'spektful] *adj* irrespetuoso(sa).

disrupt [dɪs'rʌpt] *vt* [meeting] interrumpir; [transport system] trastornar, perturbar; [class] revolucionar, enredar en.

disruption [dɪs'rʌpʃn] *n* [of meeting] interrupción *f*; [of transport system] trastorno *m*, desbarajuste *m*.

disruptive [dɪs'rʌptɪv] *adj* [effect] perjudicial, negativo(va); [child, behaviour] revoltoso(sa), travieso(sa).

dissatisfaction ['dɪs,sætɪs'fækʃn] *n* descontento *m*.

dissatisfied [,dɪs'sætɪsfaɪd] *adj*: **~ (with)** insatisfecho(cha) OR descontento(ta) (con).

dissect [dɪ'sekt] *vt* MED disecar; *fig* [study] analizar minuciosamente.

dissection [dɪ'sekʃn] *n* MED disección *f*; *fig* [study] análisis *m inv* minucioso.

disseminate [dɪ'semɪneɪt] *vt* difundir, divulgar.

dissemination [dɪ,semɪ'neɪʃn] *n* difusión *f*, divulgación *f*.

dissension [dɪ'senʃn] *n* disensión *f*.

dissent [dɪ'sent] ◇ *n* [gen] disconformidad *f*, disentimiento *m*; SPORT: **he was booked for ~** le amonestaron por protestar. ◇ *vi*: **to ~ (from)** disentir (de).

dissenter [dɪ'sentər] *n* disidente *m y f*.

dissenting [dɪ'sentɪŋ] *adj* disidente, en desacuerdo.

dissertation [,dɪsə'teɪʃn] *n* tesina *f*.

disservice [,dɪs'sɜːvɪs] *n*: **to do sb a ~** hacer un flaco servicio a alguien.

dissident ['dɪsɪdənt] *n* disidente *m y f*.

dissimilar [,dɪ'sɪmɪləʳ] *adj*: **~ (to)** distinto(ta) (de).

dissipate ['dɪsɪpeɪt] ◇ *vt* **-1.** [heat] disipar. **-2.** [efforts, money] desperdiciar, derrochar. ◇ *vi* disiparse.

dissipated ['dɪsɪpeɪtɪd] *adj* disoluto(ta).

dissociate [dɪ'səʊʃɪeɪt] *vt* disociar, separar; **to ~ o.s. from** disociarse OR desvincularse de.

dissolute ['dɪsəluːt] *adj* disoluto(ta).

dissolution [,dɪsə'luːʃn] *n* disolución *f*.

dissolve [dɪ'zɒlv] ◇ *vt* disolver. ◇ *vi* **-1.** [substance] disolverse. **-2.** *fig* [disappear] desvanecerse, desaparecer.

◆ **dissolve in(to)** *vt fus* deshacerse en.

dissuade [dɪ'sweɪd] *vt*: **to ~ sb (from doing sthg)** disuadir a alguien (de hacer algo).

distance ['dɪstəns] ◇ *n* distancia *f*; **at a ~** a distancia; **from a ~** desde lejos; **in the ~** a lo lejos. ◇ *vt*: **to ~ o.s. from** distanciarse de.

distant ['dɪstənt] *adj* **-1.** [place, time, relative] lejano(na); **~ from** distante de. **-2.** [person, manner] frío(a), distante.

distaste [dɪs'teɪst] *n*: **~ (for)** desagrado *m* (por).

distasteful [dɪs'teɪstful] *adj* desagradable.

Dist. Atty *abbr of* district attorney.

distemper [dɪ'stempəʳ] *n* **-1.** [paint] (pintura *f* al) temple *m*. **-2.** [disease] moquillo *m*.

distended [dɪ'stendɪd] *adj* dilatado(da).

distil *Br* (*pt & pp* **-led**, *cont* **-ling**), **distill** *Am* [dɪ'stɪl] *vt* **-1.** [liquid] destilar. **-2.** [information] extraer.

distiller [dɪ'stɪləʳ] *n* destilador *m*, -ra *f*.

distillery [dɪ'stɪlərɪ] (*pl* **-ies**) *n* destilería *f*.

distinct [dɪ'stɪŋkt] *adj* **-1.** [different]: **~ (from)** distinto(ta) (de); **as ~ from** a diferencia de. **-2.** [clear - improvement] notable, visible; [- possibility] claro(ra).

distinction [dɪ'stɪŋkʃn] *n* **-1.** [difference, excellence] distinción *f*; **to draw** OR **make a ~ between** hacer una distinción entre. **-2.** [in exam result] sobresaliente *m*.

distinctive [dɪ'stɪŋktɪv] *adj* característico(ca), particular.

distinctly [dɪ'stɪŋktlɪ] *adv* **-1.** [see, remember] claramente. **-2.** [improve] notablemente. **-3.** [very]: **it is ~ possible that ...** es muy posible que ...

distinguish [dɪ'stɪŋgwɪʃ] *vt* **-1.** [gen]: **to ~ sthg (from)** distinguir algo (de). **-2.** [perform well]: **to ~ o.s.** distinguirse.

distinguished [dɪ'stɪŋgwɪʃt] *adj* distinguido(da).

distinguishing [dɪ'stɪŋgwɪʃɪŋ] *adj* distintivo(va).

distort [dɪ'stɔːt] *vt* **-1.** [shape, face] deformar; [sound] distorsionar. **-2.** [truth, facts] tergiversar.

distorted [dɪ'stɔːtɪd] *adj* **-1.** [shape, face] deformado(da); [sound] distorsionado(da). **-2.** [account, report] tergiversado(da).

distortion [dɪ'stɔːʃn] *n* **-1.** [of shape, face] deformación *f*; [of sound] distorsión *f*. **-2.** [of truth, facts] tergiversación *f*.

distract [dɪ'strækt] *vt* [person, attention]: **to ~ sb (from)** distraer a alguien (de).

distracted [dɪ'stræktɪd] *adj* distraído(da).

distraction [dɪ'strækʃn] *n* **-1.** [interruption, diversion] distracción *f*. **-2.** [state of mind] confusión *f*; **to drive sb to ~** volver loco a alguien.

distraught [dɪ'strɔːt] *adj* muy turbado(da).

distress [dɪ'stres] ◇ *n* **-1.** [anxiety] angustia *f*; [pain] dolor *m*. **-2.** [danger, difficulty] peligro *m*. ◇ *vt* afligir, apenar.

distressed [dɪ'strest] *adj* angustiado(da), afligido(da).

distressing [dɪ'stresɪŋ] *adj* angustioso(sa), doloroso(sa).

distress signal *n* señal *f* de socorro.

distribute [dɪ'strɪbjuːt] *vt* **-1.** [gen] distribuir, repartir. **-2.** [seeds] diseminar.

distribution [,dɪstrɪ'bjuːʃn] *n* **-1.** [gen] distribución *f*. **-2.** [of seeds] diseminación *f*.

distributor [dɪ'strɪbjutəʳ] *n* **-1.** COMM distribuidor *m*, -ra *f*. **-2.** AUT delco® *m*, distribuidor *m*.

district ['dɪstrɪkt] *n* **-1.** [area - of country] zona *f*, región *f*; [- of town] barrio *m*. **-2.** [administrative area] distrito *m*.

district attorney *n* *Am* fiscal *m y f* (del distrito).

district council *n* *Br* ADMIN ≈ municipio *m*.

district nurse *n* *Br* enfermera encargada de atender a domicilio a los pacientes de una zona.

District of Columbia *n* distrito *m* de Columbia.

distrust [dɪs'trʌst] ◇ *n* desconfianza *f*. ◇ *vt* desconfiar de.

distrustful [dɪs'trʌstful] *adj* desconfiado(da).

disturb [dɪ'stɜːb] *vt* **-1.** [interrupt - person] molestar; [- concentration] perturbar. **-2.** [upset, worry] inquietar. **-3.** [alter - surface, arrangement] alterar; [- papers] desordenar.

disturbance [dɪ'stɜːbəns] *n* **-1.** [fight] tumulto *m*, alboroto *m*. **-2.** JUR: **~ of the peace** alteración *f* del orden público. **-3.**

[interruption] **interrupción** f. **-4.** [of mind, emotions] **trastorno** m.

disturbed [dɪ'stɜːbd] adj **-1.** [upset, ill] **trastornado(da). -2.** [worried] **inquieto(ta).**

disturbing [dɪ'stɜːbɪŋ] adj **inquietante, preocupante.**

disunity [ˌdɪs'juːnətɪ] n **desunión** f.

disuse [ˌdɪs'juːs] n: **to fall into ~** [regulation] **caer en desuso;** [building, mine] **verse paulatinamente abandonado(da).**

disused [ˌdɪs'juːzd] adj **abandonado(da).**

ditch [dɪtʃ] ◇ n [gen] **zanja** f; [by road] **cuneta** f. ◇ vt inf **-1.** [end relationship with] **romper con. -2.** [get rid of] **deshacerse de.**

dither ['dɪðəʳ] vi **vacilar.**

ditto ['dɪtəʊ] adv **ídem, lo mismo.**

diuretic [ˌdaɪjʊ'retɪk] n **diurético** m.

diva ['diːvə] (pl -s) n **diva** f.

divan [dɪ'væn] n **diván** m.

divan bed n **cama** f **turca.**

dive [daɪv] (Br pt & pp **-d**, Am pt **-d** OR **dove**, pp **-d**) ◇ vi **-1.** [into water - person] **zambullirse;** [- submarine, bird, fish] **sumergirse. -2.** [with breathing apparatus] **bucear, clavarse** Amer. **-3.** [through air - person] **lanzarse;** [- plane] **caer en picado. -4.** [into bag, cupboard]: **to ~ into meter la mano en.** ◇ n **-1.** [of person - into water] **zambullida** f. **-2.** [of submarine] **inmersión** f. **-3.** [of person - through air] **salto** m; [- in football etc] **estirada** f. **-4.** [of plane] **picado** m. **-5.** inf pej [bar, restaurant] **garito** m, **antro** m.

dive-bomb vt **bombardear (cayendo en picado).**

diver ['daɪvəʳ] n [underwater] **buceador** m, **-ra** f; [professional] **buzo** m; [from diving board] **saltador** m, **-ra** f (de trampolín).

diverge [daɪ'vɜːdʒ] vi **-1.** [gen]: **to ~ (from) divergir (de). -2.** [disagree] **discrepar.**

divergence [daɪ'vɜːdʒəns] n **divergencia** f.

divergent [daɪ'vɜːdʒənt] adj **divergente.**

diverse [daɪ'vɜːs] adj **diverso(sa).**

diversification [daɪˌvɜːsɪfɪ'keɪʃn] n **diversificación** f.

diversify [daɪ'vɜːsɪfaɪ] (pt & pp **-ied**) ◇ vt **diversificar.** ◇ vi **diversificarse.**

diversion [daɪ'vɜːʃn] n **-1.** [distraction] **distracción** f. **-2.** [of traffic, river, funds] **desvío** m.

diversionary [daɪ'vɜːʃnrɪ] adj **(hecho(cha)) para despistar.**

diversity [daɪ'vɜːsətɪ] n **diversidad** f.

divert [daɪ'vɜːt] vt **-1.** [traffic, river, funds] **desviar. -2.** [person, attention] **distraer.**

divest [daɪ'vest] vt fml: **to ~ sb of sthg des-**

pojar a alguien de algo; **to ~ o.s. of** **despojarse** OR **deshacerse de.**

divide [dɪ'vaɪd] ◇ vt: **to ~ sthg (between** OR **among) dividir algo (entre); to ~ sthg into dividir algo en; to ~ sthg by dividir algo entre** OR **por; ~ 3 into 89 divide 89 entre 3.** ◇ vi **-1.** [river, road, wall] **bifurcarse. -2.** [group] **dividirse.** ◇ n [difference] **división** f.

◆ **divide up** vt sep **-1.** [split up] **dividir. -2.** [share out] **repartir.**

divided [dɪ'vaɪdɪd] adj **dividido(da).**

dividend ['dɪvɪdend] n FIN **dividendo** m; [profit] **beneficio** m; **to pay ~s proporcionar beneficios.**

dividers [dɪ'vaɪdəz] npl **compás** m **de puntas.**

dividing line [dɪ'vaɪdɪŋ-] n **línea** f **divisoria.**

divine [dɪ'vaɪn] ◇ adj **divino(na).** ◇ vt **-1.** [guess] **adivinar. -2.** [find - water] **descubrir (con varilla de zahorí).**

diving ['daɪvɪŋ] n (U) **-1.** [into water] **salto** m. **-2.** [with breathing apparatus] **buceo** m.

divingboard ['daɪvɪŋbɔːd] n **trampolín** m.

diving suit n **traje** m **de buceo, escafandra** f.

divinity [dɪ'vɪnətɪ] (pl **-ies**) n **-1.** [godliness, deity] **divinidad** f. **-2.** [study] **teología** f.

divisible [dɪ'vɪzəbl] adj: **~ (by) divisible (por).**

division [dɪ'vɪʒn] n **-1.** [gen] **división** f. **-2.** [of labour, responsibility] **repartición** f.

division sign n **signo** m **de división.**

divisive [dɪ'vaɪsɪv] adj **divisivo(va).**

divorce [dɪ'vɔːs] ◇ n **divorcio** m. ◇ vt **-1.** [husband, wife] **divorciarse de. -2.** [separate]: **to ~ sthg from separar algo de.**

divorced [dɪ'vɔːst] adj **divorciado(da).**

divorcee [dɪvɔː'siː] n **divorciado** m, **-da** f.

divulge [daɪ'vʌldʒ] vt **divulgar, revelar.**

DIY n abbr of **do-it-yourself.**

dizziness ['dɪzɪnɪs] n [because of heights] **vértigo** m; [because of illness etc] **mareo** m.

dizzy ['dɪzɪ] (compar **-ier**, superl **-iest**) adj **-1.** [because of illness etc] **mareado(da). -2.** [because of heights]: **to feel ~ sentir vértigo. -3.** fig [height] **inimaginable, de vértigo.**

DJ n **-1.** abbr of **disc jockey. -2.** abbr of **dinner jacket.**

Djakarta [dʒə'kɑːtə] → **Jakarta.**

DJIA (abbr of **Dow Jones Industrial Average**) n **índice Dow Jones.**

Djibouti [dʒɪ'buːtɪ] n **Yibuti.**

dl (abbr of **decilitre**) dl.

DLit(t) [ˌdiː'lɪt] (abbr of **Doctor of Letters**) (titular de un) doctorado de letras.

DLO (*abbr of* **dead-letter office**) *n departamento de correos al que van a parar cartas cuyo destinatario ha sido imposible localizar.*

dm (*abbr of* **decimetre**) dm.

DM (*abbr of* **Deutsche Mark**) DM *m.*

DMA (*abbr of* **direct memory access**) *n acceso directo a la memoria.*

DMus [ˌdiːˈmjuːz] (*abbr of* **Doctor of Music**) (*titular de un*) *doctorado de música.*

DMZ *abbr of* **demilitarized zone.**

DNA (*abbr of* **deoxyribonucleic acid**) *n* ADN *m.*

D-notice *n Br petición oficial a la prensa de que cierta información no se haga pública por razones de seguridad nacional.*

do¹ [duː] (*pt* **did**, *pp* **done**, *pl* **dos** OR **do's**)
◇ *aux vb* **-1.** (*in negatives*): **don't leave it there** no lo dejes ahí; **I didn't want to see him** no quería verlo. **-2.** (*in questions*): **what did he want?** ¿qué quería?; ~ **you think she'll come?** ¿crees que vendrá? **-3.** (*referring back to previous verb*): ~ **you think so?** - **yes, I** ~ ¿tú crees? -sí; **she reads more than I** ~ **lee** más que yo; **so** ~ **I/they yo/ellos también. -4.** (*in question tags*): **you know her, don't you?** la conoces ¿no?; **I upset you, didn't I?** te molesté ¿verdad?; **so you think you can dance,** ~ **you?** así que te crees que sabes bailar ¿no? **-5.** (*for emphasis*): **I did tell you but you've forgotten** sí que te lo dije, pero te has olvidado; ~ **come in** ¡pase, por favor!
◇ *vt* **-1.** [gen] hacer; **she does aerobics/ gymnastics** hace aerobic/gimnasia; **to** ~ **the cooking/cleaning** hacer la comida/limpieza; **to** ~ **one's hair** peinarse; **to** ~ **one's teeth** lavarse los dientes; **he did his duty** cumplió con su deber; **what can I** ~ **for you?** ¿en qué puedo servirle?; **what can we** ~? ¿qué le vamos a hacer?; **they** ~ **cheap meals for students** dan OR hacen comidas baratas para estudiantes; **we'll have to** ~ **something about that tree** tendremos que hacer algo con ese árbol. **-2.** [have particular effect] causar, hacer; **to** ~ **more harm than good** fastidiar más las cosas en lugar de arreglarlas. **-3.** [referring to job]: **what** ~ **you** ~? ¿a qué te dedicas?, ¿qué haces? **-4.** [study] hacer; **I did physics at school** hice física en la escuela. **-5.** [travel at a particular speed] ir a; **the car can** ~ **110 mph** el coche puede ir a 110 millas por hora. **-6.** [be good enough for]: **will that** ~ **you?** ¿te vale eso?; **that'll** ~ **me nicely** eso me viene estupendamente.
◇ *vi* **-1.** [gen] hacer; ~ **as she says** haz lo que te dice; **they're** ~**ing really well** les va muy bien; **he could** ~ **better** lo podría hacer mejor; **how did you** ~ **in the exam?** ¿qué tal te salió el examen?; **you would** ~

well to reconsider harías bien en volverlo a pensar. **-2.** [be good enough, sufficient] servir, valer; **this kind of behaviour won't** ~ ese tipo de comportamiento no es aceptable; **that will** ~ **(nicely)** con eso vale; **that will** ~! [showing annoyance] ¡basta ya! **-3.** *phr:* **how** ~ **you** ~ [greeting] ¿cómo está usted?; [answer] mucho gusto.
◇ *n* [party] fiesta *f.*

◆ **dos** *npl:* ~**s and don'ts** normas *fpl* de conducta.

◆ **do away with** *vt fus* [disease, poverty] acabar con; [law, reforms] suprimir.

◆ **do down** *vt sep inf:* **to** ~ **sb down** menospreciar a alguien.

◆ **do for** *vt fus inf:* **these kids will** ~ **for me** estos críos me van a terminar conmigo; **I thought I was done for** me creí morir.

◆ **do in** *vt sep inf* [kill] cargarse, cepillarse.

◆ **do out of** *vt sep:* **to** ~ **sb out of sthg** estafar algo a alguien.

◆ **do up** *vt sep* **-1.** [fasten - shoelaces, tie] atar; [- coat, buttons] abrochar; ~ **your shoes up** átate los zapatos. **-2.** [decorate] renovar, redecorar. **-3.** [wrap up] envolver.

◆ **do with** *vt fus* **-1.** [need]: **I could** ~ **with a drink/new car** no me vendría mal una copa/un coche nuevo. **-2.** [have connection with]: **that has nothing to** ~ **with it** eso no tiene nada que ver (con ello); **it's something to** ~ **with the way he speaks** tiene que ver con su forma de hablar.

◆ **do without** ◇ *vt fus* pasar sin; **I can** ~ **without your sarcasm** podrías ahorrarte tu sarcasmo. ◇ *vi* apañárselas.

do² (*abbr of* **ditto**) íd.

DOA (*abbr of* **dead on arrival**) *adj* ingresó cadáver.

doable [ˈduːəbl] *adj inf* realizable, factible.

dob *abbr of* **date of birth.**

Doberman [ˈdəʊbəmən] (*pl* **-s**) *n:* ~ **(pinscher)** doberman *m.*

docile [*Br* ˈdəʊsaɪl, *Am* ˈdɒsəl] *adj* dócil.

dock [dɒk] ◇ *n* **-1.** [in harbour] dársena *f*, muelle *m.* **-2.** [in court] banquillo *m* (de los acusados). ◇ *vt* [wages] reducir; [money from wages] descontar. ◇ *vi* atracar.

docker [ˈdɒkər] *n* estibador *m.*

docket [ˈdɒkɪt] *n Br* marbete *m.*

docklands [ˈdɒkləndz] *npl Br* muelles *mpl.*

dockworker [ˈdɒkwɜːkər] = **docker.**

dockyard [ˈdɒkjɑːd] *n* astillero *m.*

doctor [ˈdɒktər] ◇ *n* **-1.** [of medicine] médico *m*, -ca *f*; **to go to the** ~**'s** ir al médico. **-2.** [holder of PhD] doctor *m*, -ra *f.* ◇ *vt* **-1.** [results, text] amañar. **-2.** *Br* [cat] castrar. **-3.** [food, drink] adulterar.

doctorate ['dɒktərət], **doctor's degree** n doctorado m.

doctrinaire [,dɒktrɪ'neəʳ] adj doctrinario(ria).

doctrine ['dɒktrɪn] n doctrina f.

docudrama [,dɒkju'drɑːmə] (pl -s) n TV docudrama m.

document [n 'dɒkjʊmənt, vt 'dɒkjʊment] ◇ n documento m. ◇ vt documentar.

documentary [,dɒkju'mentərɪ] (pl -ies) ◇ adj documental. ◇ n documental m.

documentation [,dɒkjʊmen'teɪʃn] n documentación f.

DOD (abbr of **Department of Defense**) n ministerio de defensa estadounidense.

doddering ['dɒdərɪŋ], **doddery** ['dɒdərɪ] adj inf renqueante.

doddle ['dɒdl] n Br inf: it's a ~ está tirado(da) OR chupado(da).

Dodecanese [,dəʊdɪkə'niːz] npl: the ~ el Dodecaneso.

dodge [dɒdʒ] ◇ n inf [fraud] artimaña f, truco m; a tax ~ un truco para pagar menos impuestos. ◇ vt esquivar. ◇ vi echarse a un lado, apartarse.

Dodgems® ['dɒdʒəmz] npl Br coches mpl de choque.

dodgy ['dɒdʒɪ] adj Br inf [business, plan] arriesgado(da), comprometido(da); [chair, brakes] poco fiable.

doe [dəʊ] n -1. [female deer] gama f. -2. [female rabbit] coneja f.

DOE n -1. (abbr of **Department of the Environment**) ministerio de medio ambiente británico. -2. (abbr of **Department of Energy**) ministerio de energía estadounidense.

doer ['duːəʳ] n inf emprendedor m, -ra f, persona f práctica.

does [weak form dəz, strong form dʌz] → do.

doesn't ['dʌznt] = does not.

dog [dɒg] (pt & pp -ged, cont -ging) ◇ n -1. [animal] perro m; it's a ~'s life es una vida de perros; to go to the ~s inf echarse a perder, irse al garete. -2. Am [hot dog] perrito m caliente. ◇ vt -1. [subj: person] seguir. -2. [subj: problems, bad luck] perseguir.

dog biscuit n galleta f de perro.

dog collar n -1. [of dog] collar m de perro. -2. [of priest] alzacuello m.

dog-eared [-ɪəd] adj manoseado(da), sobado(da).

dog-eat-dog adj de todos contra todos, muy competitivo(va).

dog-end n inf colilla f.

dogfight ['dɒgfaɪt] n -1. [between dogs] pe-lea f de perros. -2. [between aircraft] combate m aéreo.

dog food n comida f para perros.

dogged ['dɒgɪd] adj tenaz, obstinado(da).

doggone ['dɒgɒn], **doggoned** ['dɒgɒnd] adj Am inf puñetero(ra).

doggy ['dɒgɪ] (pl -ies) n perrito m, -ta f.

doggy bag n bolsa que da el restaurante para llevarse las sobras a casa.

dogma ['dɒgmə] n dogma m.

dogmatic [dɒg'mætɪk] adj dogmático(ca).

do-gooder [-'gʊdəʳ] n pej persona bien intencionada que sin querer resulta entrometida.

dog paddle n: to do the ~ nadar como los perros.

dogsbody ['dɒgz,bɒdɪ] (pl -ies) n Br inf último mono m, burro m de carga.

dog tag n placa f de identificación (de un soldado).

doing ['duːɪŋ] n: this is all your ~ tú eres responsable por esto.

◆ **doings** npl actividades fpl.

do-it-yourself n bricolaje m.

doldrums ['dɒldrəmz] npl fig: to be in the ~ [trade] estar estancado(da); [person] estar abatido(da).

dole [dəʊl] n (subsidio m de) paro m; to be on the ~ estar parado(da).

◆ **dole out** vt sep distribuir, repartir.

doleful ['dəʊlfʊl] adj triste, lastimero(ra).

doll [dɒl] n [toy] muñeca f.

dollar ['dɒləʳ] n dólar m.

dolled up [dɒld-] adj inf [woman] emperifollada.

dollhouse Am = doll's house.

dollop ['dɒləp] n inf pegote m.

doll's house Br, **dollhouse** Am ['dɒlhaʊs] n casa f de muñecas.

dolly ['dɒlɪ] (pl -ies) n -1. [doll] muñequita f. -2. TECH [for TV or film camera] travelín m, plataforma f móvil.

dolly bird n Br inf dated [woman] muñeca f.

Dolomites ['dɒləmaɪts] npl: the ~ los Dolomitas.

dolphin ['dɒlfɪn] n delfín m.

domain [də'meɪn] n -1. [sphere of interest] campo m, ámbito m. -2. [land] dominios mpl.

dome [dəʊm] n [roof] cúpula f; [ceiling] bóveda f.

domestic [də'mestɪk] ◇ adj -1. [internal policy, flight] nacional. -2. [chores, water supply, animal] doméstico(ca). -3. [home-loving] hogareño(ña), casero(ra). ◇ n doméstico m, -ca f, criado m, -da f.

domestic appliance *n* electrodoméstico *m*.

domesticated [də'mestɪkeɪtɪd] *adj* **-1.** [animal] domesticado(da). **-2.** *hum* [person] hogareño(ña), casero(ra).

domesticity [,dɔʊme'stɪsətɪ] *n* (*U*) vida *f* hogareña.

domicile ['dɒmɪsaɪl] *n fml* domicilio *m*.

dominance ['dɒmɪnəns] *n* (*U*) **-1.** [control, power] dominación *f*, control *m*. **-2.** [importance] predominancia *f*.

dominant ['dɒmɪnənt] *adj* dominante.

dominate ['dɒmɪneɪt] *vt* dominar.

dominating ['dɒmɪneɪtɪŋ] *adj* dominante.

domination [,dɒmɪ'neɪʃn] *n* **-1.** [control, power] dominación *f*. **-2.** [importance] predominancia *f*.

domineering [,dɒmɪ'nɪərɪŋ] *adj* dominante, tiránico(ca).

Dominica [də'mɪnɪkə] *n* Dominica.

Dominican Republic [də'mɪnɪkən-] *n*: the ~ la República Dominicana.

dominion [də'mɪnjən] *n* **-1.** (*U*) [power] dominio *m*. **-2.** [land] dominios *mpl*.

domino ['dɒmɪnəʊ] (*pl* **-es**) *n* dominó *m*.

◆ **dominoes** *npl* dominó *m*.

domino effect *n* reacción *f* en cadena.

don [dɒn] (*pt* & *pp* **-ned**, *cont* **-ning**) ◇ *n Br* UNIV profesor *m*, -ra *f* de universidad. ◇ *vt* ponerse.

donate [də'neɪt] *vt* donar.

donation [də'neɪʃn] *n* **-1.** [act of donating] donación *f*. **-2.** [sum] donativo *m*.

done [dʌn] ◇ *pp* → **do**. ◇ *adj* **-1.** [finished] listo(ta). **-2.** [cooked] hecho(cha); **well-**~ muy hecho. **-3.** [socially acceptable]: **it's not the** ~ **thing** no se hace, está mal visto. ◇ *adv* [to conclude deal]: ~! ¡(trato) hecho!

donkey ['dɒŋkɪ] (*pl* **donkeys**) *n* burro *m*, -rra *f*.

donkey jacket *n chaqueta gruesa que suelen llevar los obreros.*

donkeywork ['dɒŋkɪwɜːk] *n Br inf* parte *f* más pesada del trabajo.

donor ['dəʊnə'] *n* donante *m y f*.

donor card *n* carné *m* de donante.

don't [dəʊnt] = **do not**.

doodle ['duːdl] ◇ *n* garabatos *mpl*. ◇ *vi* garabatear.

doom [duːm] *n* perdición *f*, fatalidad *f*.

doomed [duːmd] *adj* [plan, mission] condenado(da) al fracaso; **to be** ~ **to sthg/to do sthg** estar condenado a algo/a hacer algo.

door [dɔː'] *n* **-1.** [gen] puerta *f*; **to open the** ~ **to** *fig* abrir la puerta a. **-2.** [doorway] entrada *f*.

doorbell ['dɔːbel] *n* timbre *m* (de la puerta).

doorhandle ['dɔːhændl] *n* [gen] tirador *m* (de la puerta); [of car] manija *f*.

doorknob ['dɔːnɒb] *n* pomo *m*.

doorknocker ['dɔː,nɒkə'] *n* aldaba *f*.

doorman ['dɔːmən] (*pl* **-men** [-mən]) *n* portero *m*.

doormat ['dɔːmæt] *n* **-1.** [mat] felpudo *m*. **-2.** *fig* [person]: **he's a** ~ se deja pisar por todo el mundo.

doorstep ['dɔːstep] *n* peldaño *m* de la puerta.

doorstop ['dɔːstɒp] *n* tope *m* (de la puerta).

door-to-door *adj* a domicilio.

doorway ['dɔːweɪ] *n* entrada *f*, portal *m*.

dope [dəʊp] ◇ *n inf* **-1.** *drugs sl* [cannabis] maría *f*, marihuana *f*. **-2.** [for athlete, horse] estimulante *m*. **-3.** [fool] bobo *m*, -ba *f*, tonto *m*, -ta *f*. ◇ *vt* drogar, dopar.

dope test *n. inf* control *m* OR prueba *f* antidoping.

dopey ['dəʊpɪ] (*compar* **-ier**, *superl* **-iest**) *adj inf* **-1.** [groggy] atontado(da), grogui. **-2.** [stupid] imbécil.

dormant ['dɔːmənt] *adj* **-1.** [volcano] inactivo(va). **-2.** [idea, law] (en estado) latente.

dormer (window) ['dɔːmə'-] *n* claraboya *f*, buhardilla *f*.

dormice ['dɔːmaɪs] *pl* → **dormouse**.

dormitory ['dɔːmətrɪ] (*pl* **-ies**) *n* dormitorio *m*.

Dormobile® ['dɔːmə,biːl] *n* combi *m*.

dormouse ['dɔːmaʊs] (*pl* **-mice**) *n* lirón *m*.

Dors (*abbr of* **Dorset**) *condado inglés.*

DOS [dɒs] (*abbr of* **disk operating system**) *n* DOS *m*.

dosage ['dəʊsɪdʒ] *n* dosis *f inv*, dosificación *f*.

dose [dəʊs] ◇ *n lit* & *fig* dosis *f inv*; **a** ~ **of flu** un ataque de gripe. ◇ *vt*: **to** ~ **sb (with)** medicar a alguien (con).

doss [dɒs]

◆ **doss down** *vi Br inf* echarse a dormir.

dosser ['dɒsə'] *n Br inf* gandul *m*, -la *f*, vago *m*, -ga *f*.

dosshouse ['dɒshaʊs, *pl* -haʊzɪz] *n Br inf* pensión *f* de mala muerte.

dossier ['dɒsɪeɪ] *n* expediente *m*, dosier *m*.

dot [dɒt] (*pt* & *pp* **-ted**, *cont* **-ting**) ◇ *n* punto *m*; **on the** ~ en punto. ◇ *vt* salpicar.

DOT (*abbr of* **Department of Transportation**) *n ministerio de transporte estadounidense.*

dotage ['dəʊtɪdʒ] *n*: **to be in one's** ~ chochear.

dote [dəʊt]

◆ **dote (up)on** *vt fus* adorar.

doting ['dəʊtɪŋ] *adj* complaciente.

dot-matrix printer *n* COMPUT impresora *f* matricial de agujas.

dotted line ['dɒtɪd-] *n* línea *f* de puntos; **to sign on the ~** firmar.

dotty ['dɒtɪ] (*compar* **-ier**, *superl* **-iest**) *adj inf* chiflado(da).

double ['dʌbl] ◇ *adj* **-1.** [gen] doble. **-2.** [repeated] repetido(da); **~ three eight two** treinta y tres, ochenta y dos; **written with a ~ "t"** con dos tes.
◇ *adv* **-1.** [twice] doble; **~ the amount** el doble; **to see ~** ver doble. **-2.** [in two - fold] en dos; **to bend ~** doblarse, agacharse.
◇ *n* **-1.** [twice as much] el doble. **-2.** [drink] doble *m*. **-3.** [lookalike] doble *m* y *f*.
◇ *vt* doblar.
◇ *vi* **-1.** [increase twofold] doblarse, duplicarse. **-2.** [have second purpose]: **to ~ as** hacer las veces de.
◆ **doubles** *npl* TENNIS (partido *m* de) dobles *mpl*.
◆ **double up** ◇ *vt sep*: **to be ~d up** doblarse; **to be ~d up with laughter** troncharse de risa. ◇ *vi* doblarse.

double act *n* pareja *f* de cómicos.

double agent *n* agente *m* y *f* doble.

double-barrelled *Br*, **double-barreled** *Am* [-'bærəld] *adj* **-1.** [shotgun] de dos cañones. **-2.** [name] *con dos apellidos unidos con guión*.

double bass [-beɪs] *n* contrabajo *m*.

double bed *n* cama *f* de matrimonio.

double-breasted [-'brestɪd] *adj* cruzado(da).

double-check *vt & vi* verificar dos veces.

double chin *n* papada *f*.

double cream *n* nata *f* enriquecida.

double-cross *vt* traicionar, timar.

double-dealer *n* traicionero *m*, -ra *f*.

double-decker [-'dekə'] *n* autobús *m* de dos pisos.

double-declutch *vi Br* AUT desembragar (*mediante doble embrague*).

double-density *adj* COMPUT de doble densidad.

double-dutch *n Br hum*: **to talk ~** hablar en chino; **it's ~ to me** me suena a chino.

double-edged *adj lit & fig* de doble filo.

double entendre [,duːblɑ̃'tɑ̃ndr] *n* frase *f* ambigua, equívoco *m*.

double figures *npl* dos cifras *fpl*.

double-glazing [-'gleɪzɪŋ] *n* doble acristalamiento *m*.

double-jointed [-'dʒɔɪntɪd] *adj* con articulaciones muy flexibles.

double-park *vi* aparcar en doble fila.

double-quick *inf* ◇ *adj* rapidísimo(ma). ◇ *adv* rapidísimamente.

double room *n* habitación *f* doble.

double-sided *adj* COMPUT [disk] de dos caras.

double standards *npl*: **to have ~** no medir las cosas por el mismo rasero.

double take *n*: **to do a ~** quedarse atónito(ta) OR con la boca abierta.

double-talk *n* (*U*) embustes *mpl*, engañifas *fpl*.

double time *n* paga *f* doble.

double vision *n* vista *f* doble.

double whammy [-'wæmɪ] *n* mazazo *m* por partida doble.

doubly ['dʌblɪ] *adv* doblemente.

doubt [daʊt] ◇ *n* duda *f*; **there is no ~ that** no hay OR cabe duda de que; **without (a) ~** sin duda (alguna); **beyond all ~** fuera de toda duda; **to be in ~ about** sthg estar dudando acerca de algo; **to cast ~ on** poner en duda; **no ~** sin duda. ◇ *vt* **-1.** [not trust] dudar de. **-2.** [consider unlikely] dudar; **to ~ whether** OR **if** dudar que.

doubtful ['daʊtfʊl] *adj* **-1.** [gen] dudoso(sa). **-2.** [unsure] incierto(ta); **to be ~ about** OR **of** tener dudas acerca de.

doubtless ['daʊtlɪs] *adv* sin duda.

dough [dəʊ] *n* (*U*) **-1.** [for baking] masa *f*, pasta *f*. **-2.** *v inf* [money] pasta *f*, lana *f* *Amer*.

doughnut ['dəʊnʌt] *n* [without hole] buñuelo *m*; [with hole] dónut® *m*.

dour [dʊə'] *adj* austero(ra), adusto(ta).

douse [daʊs] *vt* **-1.** [put out] apagar. **-2.** [drench] mojar, empapar.

dove¹ [dʌv] *n* paloma *f*.

dove² [dəʊv] *Am pt* → **dive**.

dovecot(e) ['dʌvkɒt] *n* palomar *m*.

dovetail ['dʌvteɪl] *vt & vi* encajar.

dovetail joint *n* cola *f* de milano.

dowager ['daʊədʒə'] *n literary* viuda *f* rica.

dowdy ['daʊdɪ] (*compar* **-ier**, *superl* **-iest**) *adj* poco elegante.

Dow-Jones average [,daʊ'dʒəʊnz-] *n* índice *m* Dow-Jones.

down [daʊn] ◇ *adv* **-1.** [downwards] (hacia) abajo; **to fall ~** caer; **to bend ~** agacharse; **~ here/there** aquí/allí abajo. **-2.** [along]: **I'm going ~ the pub** voy a acercarme al pub. **-3.** [southwards] hacia el sur; **we're going ~ to Brighton** vamos a bajar a Brighton. **-4.** [lower in amount]: **you must**

keep your weight ~ debes mantenerte bajo de peso; **prices are coming** ~ van bajando los precios. **-5.** [including]: ~ **to the last detail** hasta el último detalle. **-6.** [as deposit]: **to pay £5** ~ pagar 5 libras ahora (y el resto después). **-7.** [in written form]: **to write sthg** ~ apuntar algo.

◇ *prep* **-1.** [downwards]: **they ran** ~ **the hill** corrieron cuesta abajo; **he walked** ~ **the stairs** bajó la escalera; **rain poured** ~ **the window** la lluvia resbalaba por la ventana. **-2.** [along]: **she was walking** ~ **the street** iba andando por la calle.

◇ *adj* **-1.** *inf* [depressed] deprimido(da). **-2.** [behind]: **he's a minute** ~ **on the leader** va un minuto por detrás del líder; **we're three goals** ~ nos sacan tres goles. **-3.** [written] por escrito. **-4.** [not in operation]: **the computer is** ~ **again** el ordenador se ha estropeado otra vez. **-5.** [lower in amount]: **prices are** ~ los precios han bajado.

◇ *n* [feathers] plumón *m*; [hair] pelusa *f*, vello *m*.

◇ *vt* **-1.** [knock over] derribar. **-2.** [swallow] beberse de un trago. **-3.** *phr*: **to** ~ **tools** [go on strike] declararse en huelga.

◆ **downs** *npl* *Br* montes del sur de Inglaterra.
◆ **down with** *excl*: ~ **with the King!** ¡abajo el rey!

down-and-out ◇ *adj* vagabundo(da). ◇ *n* vagabundo *m*, -da *f*.

down-at-heel *adj* desastrado(da).

downbeat ['daʊnbiːt] *adj* *inf* pesimista.

downcast ['daʊnkɑːst] *adj* *fml* **-1.** [sad] alicaído(da), triste. **-2.** [looking downwards] mirando al suelo.

downer ['daʊnəʳ] *n* *inf* **-1.** [drug] tranquilizante *m*. **-2.** [depressing event or person]: **it's a real** ~ es muy deprimente; **to be on a** ~ estar deprimido(da).

downfall ['daʊnfɔːl] *n* (*U*) ruina *f*, caída *f*.

downgrade ['daʊngreɪd] *vt* degradar.

downhearted [ˌdaʊn'hɑːtɪd] *adj* desanimado(da).

downhill [ˌdaʊn'hɪl] ◇ *adj* cuesta abajo. ◇ *adv* **-1.** [downwards] cuesta abajo. **-2.** [worse] en declive. ◇ *n* SKIING descenso *m*.

Downing Street ['daʊnɪŋ-] *n* Downing Street.

DOWNING STREET:
En Downing Street (Londres) se encuentran las residencias oficiales del Primer Ministro, en el nº10, y del ministro de Finanzas, en el nº11. Con frecuencia se utiliza la expresión 'Downing Street' para referirse al gobierno británico

download [ˌdaʊn'ləʊd] *vt* COMPUT cargar por teleproceso.

down-market *adj* barato(ta), de baja calidad.

down payment *n* entrada *f*.

downplay ['daʊnpleɪ] *vt* minimizar.

downpour ['daʊnpɔːʳ] *n* chaparrón *m*, aguacero *m*.

downright ['daʊnraɪt] ◇ *adj* patente, manifiesto(ta). ◇ *adv* completamente.

downside ['daʊnsaɪd] *n* desventaja *f*, inconveniente *m*.

Down's syndrome *n* síndrome *m* de Down, mongolismo *m*.

downstairs [ˌdaʊn'steəz] ◇ *adj* de abajo. ◇ *adv* abajo; **to come/go** ~ bajar (la escalera).

downstream [ˌdaʊn'striːm] *adv* río OR aguas abajo.

downtime ['daʊntaɪm] *n* tiempo *m* de inactividad.

down-to-earth *adj* realista, práctico(ca).

downtown [ˌdaʊn'taʊn] ◇ *adj* céntrico(ca), del centro (de la ciudad). ◇ *adv* [live] en el centro; [go] al centro.

downtrodden ['daʊnˌtrɒdn] *adj* oprimido(da), tiranizado(da).

downturn ['daʊntɜːn] *n*: ~ **(in)** descenso *m* (en).

down under *adv* en/a Australia o Nueva Zelanda.

downward ['daʊnwəd] ◇ *adj* **-1.** [towards ground] hacia abajo. **-2.** [decreasing] descendente. ◇ *adv* *Am* = **downwards**.

downwards ['daʊnwədz] *adv* **-1.** [gen] hacia abajo; **face** ~ boca abajo. **-2.** [in hierarchy]: **everyone, from the president** ~ todos, empezando por el presidente.

downwind [ˌdaʊn'wɪnd] *adv* a favor del viento.

dowry ['daʊərɪ] (*pl* **-ies**) *n* dote *f*.

doz. (*abbr of* **dozen**) doc.

doze [dəʊz] ◇ *n* sueñecito *m*; **to have a** ~ echar una cabezada. ◇ *vi* dormitar.
◆ **doze off** *vi* dormirse, quedarse adormilado(da).

dozen ['dʌzn] ◇ *num adj*: **a** ~ **eggs** una docena de huevos. ◇ *n* docena *f*; **50p a** ~ 50 peniques la docena.
◆ **dozens** *npl* *inf*: ~**s of** montones *mpl* OR miles *mpl* de.

dozy ['dəʊzɪ] (*compar* **-ier**, *superl* **-iest**) *adj* **-1.** [sleepy] soñoliento(ta), amodorrado(da). **-2.** *Br* *inf* [stupid] tonto(ta).

DP (*abbr of* **data processing**) *n* informática *f*.

DPh, **DPhil** [ˌdiːˈfɪl] (*abbr of* **Doctor of Philosophy**) *n* (*titular de un*) *doctorado en el campo de las humanidades.*

DPP *n abbr of* **Director of Public Prosecutions.**

DPT (*abbr of* **diphtheria, pertussis, tetanus**) *n vacuna de la difteria, la tos ferina y el tétano.*

DPW (*abbr of* **Department of Public Works**) *n ministerio estadounidense de obras públicas,* ≃ MOPU *m.*

dr *abbr of* **debtor.**

Dr. -1. (*abbr of* **Drive**) *c/.* **-2.** (*abbr of* **Doctor**) Dr.

drab [dræb] (*compar* **-ber**, *superl* **-best**) *adj* [colour] apagado(da); [building, clothes] sobrio(bria); [lives] monótono(na).

draconian [drəˈkəʊnjən] *adj fml* draconiano(na).

draft [drɑːft] ◇ *n* **-1.** [early version] borrador *m.* **-2.** [money order] letra *f* de cambio, giro *m.* **-3.** *Am* MIL: **the ~** la llamada a filas. **-4.** *Am* = **draught.** ◇ *vt* **-1.** [write] redactar, hacer un borrador de. **-2.** *Am* MIL llamar a filas. **-3.** [transfer - staff etc] transferir.

draft dodger [-dɒdzər] *n Am* prófugo *m.*

draftee [ˌdrɑːfˈtiː] *n Am* recluta *m.*

draftsman *Am* = **draughtsman.**

draftsmanship *Am* = **draughtsmanship.**

drafty *Am* = **draughty.**

drag [dræg] (*pt & pp* **-ged**, *cont* **-ging**) ◇ *vt* **-1.** [gen] arrastrar. **-2.** [lake, river] dragar, rastrear. ◇ *vi* **-1.** [dress, coat] arrastrarse. **-2.** [time, play] ir muy despacio. ◇ *n inf* **-1.** [bore - thing] lata *f*, rollo *m*; [- person] pesado *m*, -da *f.* **-2.** [on cigarette] calada *f*, chupada *f*, pitada *f Amer.* **-3.** [cross-dressing]: **in ~** vestido de mujer. **-4.** [air resistance] resistencia *f* aerodinámica.

◆ **drag down** *vt sep* hundir, deprimir.

◆ **drag into** *vt sep* [person] meter OR involucrar en.

◆ **drag on** *vi* ser interminable.

◆ **drag out** *vt sep* **-1.** [protract] prolongar. **-2.** [extract - fact, information] sacar, obtener.

dragnet [ˈdrægnet] *n* **-1.** [net] red *f* barredera. **-2.** *fig* [to catch criminal] emboscada *f.*

dragon [ˈdrægən] *n* **-1.** [beast] dragón *m.* **-2.** *inf* [woman] bruja *f.*

dragonfly [ˈdrægnflaɪ] (*pl* **-ies**) *n* libélula *f.*

dragoon [drəˈguːn] ◇ *n* dragón *m.* ◇ *vt*: **to ~ sb into** forzar a alguien a.

drag racing *n* (U) carreras *fpl* de coches trucados OR modificados.

dragster [ˈdrægstər] *n* coche *m* trucado OR modificado.

drain [dreɪn] ◇ *n* **-1.** [for water] desagüe *m*; [for sewage] alcantarilla *f*; [grating] sumidero *m*; **to go down the ~** echarse a perder. **-2.** [depletion]: **it's a ~ on my energy** agota todas mis energías. ◇ *vt* **-1.** [marsh, field] drenar; [vegetables] escurrir. **-2.** [energy, resources] agotar. **-3.** [drink, glass] apurar. ◇ *vi* **-1.** [dishes] escurrirse. **-2.** [colour, blood, tension] desaparecer poco a poco.

drainage [ˈdreɪnɪdʒ] *n* **-1.** [pipes, ditches] alcantarillado *m.* **-2.** [of land] drenaje *m.*

draining board *Br* [ˈdreɪnɪŋ-], **drainboard** *Am* [ˈdreɪnbɔːrd] *n* escurridero *m.*

drainpipe [ˈdreɪnpaɪp] *n* tubo *m* de desagüe.

drainpipes, **drainpipe trousers** *npl Br* pantalón *m* de pitillo.

drake [dreɪk] *n* pato *m* (macho).

dram [dræm] *n* trago *m.*

drama [ˈdrɑːmə] ◇ *n* **-1.** [gen] drama *m.* **-2.** [subject] teatro *m.* ◇ *comp* de arte dramático.

dramatic [drəˈmætɪk] *adj* **-1.** [concerned with theatre] dramático(ca). **-2.** [gesture, escape, improvement] espectacular.

dramatically [drəˈmætɪklɪ] *adv* **-1.** [noticeably] espectacularmente. **-2.** [theatrically] dramáticamente.

dramatist [ˈdræmətɪst] *n* dramaturgo *m*, -ga *f.*

dramatization [ˌdræmətaɪˈzeɪʃn] *n* dramatización *f.*

dramatize, **-ise** [ˈdræmətaɪz] *vt* **-1.** [rewrite as play] adaptar, escenificar. **-2.** *pej* [make exciting] dramatizar, exagerar.

drank [dræŋk] *pt* → **drink.**

drape [dreɪp] *vt*: **to ~ sthg over sthg** cubrir algo con algo; **~d with** OR **in** cubierto con.

◆ **drapes** *npl Am* cortinas *fpl.*

draper [ˈdreɪpər] *n* pañero *m*, -ra *f.*

drastic [ˈdræstɪk] *adj* **-1.** [extreme, urgent] drástico(ca). **-2.** [noticeable] importante, radical.

drastically [ˈdræstɪklɪ] *adv* [change, decline] drásticamente.

draught *Br*, **draft** *Am* [drɑːft] *n* **-1.** [air current] corriente *f* de aire. **-2.** *literary* [gulp] trago *m.* **-3.** **on ~** [beer] de barril.

◆ **draughts** *n Br* damas *fpl.*

draught beer *n Br* cerveza *f* de barril.

draughtboard [ˈdrɑːftbɔːd] *n Br* tablero *m* de damas.

draughtsman *Br* (*pl* **-men** [-mən]), **draftsman** *Am* (*pl* **-men** [-mən]) [ˈdrɑːftsmən] *n* delineante *m y f.*

draughtsmanship *Br*, **draftsmanship** *Am* [ˈdrɑːftsmənʃɪp] *n* **-1.** [technique] dibujo *m* lineal. **-2.** [skill] ejecución f de un dibujo lineal.

draughty Br (compar **-ier**, superl **-iest**), **drafty** Am (compar **-ier**, superl **-iest**) ['drɔːftɪ] adj que tiene corrientes de aire.

draw [drɔː] (pt **drew**, pp **drawn**) ◇ vt **-1.** [sketch] dibujar; [line, circle] trazar. **-2.** [pull - cart etc] tirar de; **she drew the comb through her hair** se pasó el peine por el cabello; **he drew her towards him** la atrajo hacia él, tomándola en sus brazos. **-3.** [curtains - open] descorrer; [- close] correr. **-4.** [breathe]: **to ~ breath** respirar. **-5.** [gun, sword] sacar. **-6.** [conclusion] llegar a. **-7.** [distinction, comparison] señalar. **-8.** [attract - criticism, praise, person] atraer; **to ~ sb's attention to sthg** llamar la atención de alguien hacia algo; **to be** OR **feel drawn to** sentirse atraído a OR por.
◇ vi **-1.** [sketch] dibujar. **-2.** [move] moverse; **to ~ away** alejarse; **to ~ closer** acercarse; **to ~ to an end** OR **a close** llegar a su fin. **-3.** SPORT: **to ~ (with)** empatar (con).
◇ n **-1.** SPORT empate m. **-2.** [lottery] sorteo m. **-3.** [attraction] atracción f.
◆ **draw in** vi [days] acortarse.
◆ **draw into** vt sep: **to ~ sb into sthg** involucrar a alguien en algo.
◆ **draw on** vt fus **-1.** [reserves, experience] recurrir a; [statistics, facts] barajar. **-2.** [cigarette] dar una calada a.
◆ **draw out** vt sep **-1.** [encourage to talk] hacer hablar. **-2.** [prolong] prolongar. **-3.** [money] sacar.
◆ **draw up** ◇ vt sep [draft] preparar, redactar. ◇ vi [stop] pararse.
◆ **draw upon** vt fus [reserves, experience] recurrir a; [statistics, facts] barajar.

drawback ['drɔːbæk] n inconveniente m, desventaja f.

drawbridge ['drɔːbrɪdʒ] n puente m levadizo.

drawer [drɔːr] n [in desk, chest] cajón m.

drawing ['drɔːɪŋ] n dibujo m.

drawing board n tablero m de delineante; **back to the ~!** inf ¡a empezar de nuevo!

drawing pin n Br chincheta f.

drawing room n cuarto m de estar, salón m.

drawl [drɔːl] ◇ n manera lenta y poco clara de hablar, alargando las vocales. ◇ vt hablar de manera lenta y poco clara, alargando las vocales.

drawn [drɔːn] ◇ pp → **draw**. ◇ adj **-1.** [curtain, blind] corrido(da), cerrado(da). **-2.** [tired, ill] cansado(da), ojeroso(sa).

drawn-out adj interminable.

drawstring ['drɔːstrɪŋ] n cordón m.

dread [dred] ◇ n terror m, pavor m. ◇ vt: **to ~ (doing sthg)** temer (hacer algo); **I ~ to think** me horroriza (el) pensarlo.

dreaded ['dredɪd] adj terrible.

dreadful ['dredful] adj **-1.** [very unpleasant - pain, weather] terrible, espantoso(sa). **-2.** [poor - play, English] horrible, fatal. **-3.** [for emphasis - waste, bore] espantoso(sa).

dreadfully ['dredfulɪ] adv terriblemente.

dreadlocks ['dredlɒks] npl pelo m al estilo rastafari.

dream [driːm] (pt & pp **-ed** OR **dreamt**) ◇ n lit & fig sueño m; **bad ~** pesadilla f. ◇ adj ideal. ◇ vt: **to ~ that** soñar que; **I never ~ed this would happen** jamás creí OR imaginé que esto pudiera pasar. ◇ vi lit & fig: **to ~ of doing sthg** soñar con hacer algo; **to ~ (of** OR **about)** soñar (con); **I wouldn't ~ of it** ¡ni hablar!, ¡de ninguna manera!
◆ **dream up** vt sep inventar, idear.

dreamer ['driːmər] n soñador m, -ra f.

dreamily ['driːmɪlɪ] adv distraídamente.

dreamlike ['driːmlaɪk] adj de ensueño.

dreamt [dremt] pp → **dream**.

dream world n mundo m de ensueño.

dreamy ['driːmɪ] (compar **-ier**, superl **-iest**) adj **-1.** [distracted] soñador(ra), distraído(da). **-2.** [peaceful, dreamlike] de ensueño.

dreary ['drɪərɪ] (compar **-ier**, superl **-iest**) adj **-1.** [weather, day] triste. **-2.** [job, life] monótono(na), aburrido(da); [persona] gris.

dredge [dredʒ] vt dragar.
◆ **dredge up** vt sep **-1.** [with dredger] extraer (del agua) con draga. **-2.** fig [from past] sacar a (la) luz.

dredger ['dredʒər] n NAUT draga f.

dregs [dregz] npl **-1.** [of liquid] sedimento m. **-2.** fig [of society] hez f.

drench [drentʃ] vt empapar; **~ed to the skin** calado hasta los huesos; **to be ~ed in** OR **with** estar empapado en.

Dresden ['drezdən] n Dresde.

dress [dres] ◇ n **-1.** [woman's garment] vestido m. **-2.** (U) [clothing] traje m. ◇ vt **-1.** [clothe] vestir; **to be ~ed in** ir vestido de; **to be ~ed** estar vestido; **to get ~ed** vestirse. **-2.** [bandage] vendar. **-3.** CULIN aliñar, aderezar. ◇ vi **-1.** [put on clothing] vestirse. **-2.** [wear clothes] vestir; **to ~ well/badly** vestir bien/mal.
◆ **dress up** ◇ vt sep disfrazar. ◇ vi **-1.** [in costume] disfrazarse. **-2.** [in best clothes] engalanarse.

dressage ['dresɑːʒ] n doma f de caballos.

dress circle n piso m principal.

dresser ['dresər] n **-1.** [for dishes] aparador m. **-2.** Am [chest of drawers] cómoda f. **-3.**

[person]: **smart/sloppy** ~ persona elegante/ descuidada (en el vestir).

dressing ['dresɪŋ] n **-1.** [bandage] vendaje m. **-2.** [for salad] aliño m. **-3.** Am [for turkey etc] relleno m.

dressing gown n bata f.

dressing room n THEATRE camerino m; SPORT vestuario m.

dressing table n tocador m.

dressmaker ['dres,meɪkər] n costurero m, -ra f, modisto m, -ta f.

dressmaking ['dres,meɪkɪŋ] n costura f.

dress rehearsal n ensayo m general.

dress shirt n camisa f de vestir.

dressy ['dresɪ] (compar **-ier**, superl **-iest**) adj elegante.

drew [druː] pt → **draw**.

dribble ['drɪbl] ◇ n **-1.** [saliva] baba f. **-2.** [trickle] hilo m. ◇ vt **-1.** SPORT [ball] regatear. **-2.** [liquid]: **to ~ saliva** babear. ◇ vi **-1.** [drool] babear. **-2.** [spill] gotear, caer gota a gota.

dribs [drɪbz] npl: **in ~ and drabs** en cantidades pequeñas.

dried [draɪd] ◇ pp & pt → **dry**. ◇ adj [gen] seco(ca); [milk, eggs] en polvo.

dried fruit n (U) fruta f pasa.

dried-up adj seco(ca).

drier ['draɪər] = **dryer**.

drift [drɪft] ◇ n **-1.** [trend, movement] movimiento m, tendencia f; [of current] flujo m. **-2.** [meaning] significado m, sentido m; **I get your ~** entiendo la idea. **-3.** [mass - of snow] ventisquero m; [- of sand, leaves] montículo m. ◇ vi **-1.** [boat] ir a la deriva. **-2.** [snow, sand, leaves] amontonarse. **-3.** [person] ir sin rumbo; **to ~ into** [job, marriage] dejarse llevar a; **to ~ apart** tener cada vez menos en común.

◆ **drift off** vi [person] dormirse, quedarse dormido(da).

drifter ['drɪftər] n [person] persona que no permanece por mucho tiempo en un sitio o empleo.

driftwood ['drɪftwʊd] n madera f de deriva.

drill [drɪl] ◇ n **-1.** [tool - gen] taladro m; [- bit] broca f; [- dentist's] fresa f; [- in mine, oilfield] perforadora f. **-2.** [exercise - for fire, battle] simulacro m. ◇ vt **-1.** [tooth, wood, oil well] perforar. **-2.** [instruct - people, pupils] adiestrar, entrenar; [- soldiers] instruir; **to ~ sthg into sb** inculcar algo en alguien. ◇ vi: **to ~ into/for** perforar en/en busca de.

drilling platform ['drɪlɪŋ-] n plataforma f de perforación.

drily ['draɪlɪ] = **dryly**.

drink [drɪŋk] (pt **drank**, pp **drunk**) ◇ n **-1.** [gen] bebida f; **a ~ of water** un trago de agua. **-2.** [alcoholic beverage] copa f; **would you like a ~?** ¿quieres tomar algo (de beber)?; **to have a ~** tomar algo, tomar una copa. ◇ vt beber. ◇ vi beber; **to ~ to sb/sb's success** beber a la salud de alguien/por el éxito de alguien.

drinkable ['drɪŋkəbl] adj **-1.** [suitable for drinking] potable. **-2.** [palatable]: **this wine is very ~** este vino no está nada mal.

drink-driving Br, **drunk-driving** Am n conducción f en estado de embriaguez.

drinker ['drɪŋkər] n **-1.** [of alcohol] bebedor m, -ra f. **-2.** [of tea, coffee]: **tea/coffee ~** persona que bebe té/café.

drinking ['drɪŋkɪŋ] ◇ adj: **a ~ man** un bebedor. ◇ n (U) bebida f.

drinking fountain n fuente f (de agua potable).

drinking-up time n Br inf tiempo concedido en los bares para apurar el trago antes de cerrar.

drinking water n agua f potable.

drip [drɪp] (pt & pp **-ped**, cont **-ping**) ◇ n **-1.** [drop] gota f; [drops] goteo m. **-2.** MED gota a gota m inv. **-3.** inf [wimp] soso m, -sa f. ◇ vt dejar caer en gotas. ◇ vi **-1.** [liquid, tap, nose] gotear. **-2.** [person]: **to be dripping with sthg** [sweat, blood] estar chorreando algo; [diamonds, furs] estar cubierto(ta) de algo.

drip-dry adj de lava y pon.

drip-feed ◇ n gota a gota m inv. ◇ vt alimentar gota a gota.

dripping ['drɪpɪŋ] ◇ adj: **~ (wet)** chorreando, empapado(da). ◇ n grasa f (de carne), pringue m y f.

drive [draɪv] (pt **drove**, pp **driven**) ◇ n **-1.** [outing] paseo m (en coche); **to go for a ~** ir a dar una vuelta en coche. **-2.** [journey] viaje m (en coche); **it's a two-hour ~ (away)** está a dos horas en coche. **-3.** [urge] instinto m. **-4.** [campaign] campaña f. **-5.** [energy] vigor m, energía f. **-6.** [road to house] camino m (de entrada). **-7.** SPORT drive m. **-8.** COMPUT unidad f de disco.

◇ vt **-1.** [vehicle] conducir, manejar Amer. **-2.** [passenger] llevar (en coche). **-3.** [fuel, power] impulsar. **-4.** [force to move - gen] arrastrar; [- cattle] arrear; **it drove people from their homes** obligó a la gente a abandonar sus hogares. **-5.** [motivate] motivar. **-6.** [force]: **to ~ sb to do sthg** conducir OR llevar a alguien a hacer algo; **to ~ sb to despair** hacer desesperar a alguien; **to ~ sb mad** OR **crazy** volver loco a alguien. **-7.** [hammer] clavar. **-8.** SPORT [hit hard] golpear con fuerza.

◇ *vi* AUT conducir; **I don't ~** no sé conducir.

◆ **drive at** *vt fus* insinuar, querer decir.

drive-in ◇ *n* **-1.** [restaurant] *restaurante donde se sirve a la clientela en su coche*. **-2.** [cinema] autocine *m*. ◇ *adj*: **~ bank** banco *en el que se puede realizar transacciones desde el coche*.

drivel ['drɪvl] *n inf* (*U*) tonterías *fpl*.

driven ['drɪvn] *pp* → **drive**.

driver ['draɪvər] *n* **-1.** [gen] conductor *m*, -ra *f*; RAIL maquinista *m y f*; [of racing car] piloto *m y f*. **-2.** COMPUT controlador *m*.

driver's license *Am* = **driving licence**.

drive shaft *n* (eje *m* de) transmisión *f*.

driveway ['draɪvweɪ] *n* camino *m* de entrada.

driving ['draɪvɪŋ] ◇ *adj* [rain] torrencial; [wind] huracanado(da). ◇ *n* (*U*) conducción *f*, el conducir.

driving force *n* fuerza *f* motriz.

driving instructor *n* instructor *m*, -ra *f* de conducción.

driving lesson *n* clase *f* de conducir OR conducción.

driving licence *Br*, **driver's license** *Am n* carné *m* OR permiso *m* de conducir.

driving mirror *n* retrovisor *m*.

driving school *n* autoescuela *f*.

driving test *n* examen *m* de conducir.

drizzle ['drɪzl] ◇ *n* llovizna *f*, garúa *f Amer*. ◇ *v impers* lloviznar.

drizzly ['drɪzlɪ] (*compar* **-ier**, *superl* **-iest**) *adj* lloviznoso(sa).

droll [drəʊl] *adj* gracioso(sa).

dromedary ['drɒmədrɪ] (*pl* **-ies**) *n* dromedario *m*.

drone [drəʊn] ◇ *n* **-1.** [hum] zumbido *m*. **-2.** [bee] zángano *m*. ◇ *vi* zumbar.

◆ **drone on** *vi*: **to ~ on (about)** hablar interminablemente y de forma monótona (sobre).

drool [druːl] *vi* **-1.** [dribble] babear. **-2.** *fig* [admire]: **to ~ over** caérsele la baba con.

droop [druːp] *vi* **-1.** [shoulders] encorvarse; [eyelids] cerrarse; [head] inclinarse; [flower] marchitarse. **-2.** [spirits] desanimarse.

drop [drɒp] (*pt & pp* **-ped**, *cont* **-ping**) ◇ *n* **-1.** [of liquid, milk, whisky] gota *f*. **-2.** [sweet] pastilla *f*. **-3.** [decrease]: **~ (in)** [price] caída *f* (de); [temperature] descenso *m* (de); [demand, income] disminución *f* (en). **-4.** [distance down] caída *f*.

◇ *vt* **-1.** [let fall - gen] dejar caer; [- bomb] lanzar; **she dropped a stitch** se le escapó un punto. **-2.** [decrease] reducir. **-3.** [voice] bajar. **-4.** [abandon - subject, course] dejar;

[- charges] retirar; [- person, lover] abandonar; [- player] excluir, no seleccionar. **-5.** [utter - hint, remark] lanzar, soltar; **he's always dropping names** siempre se las está dando de conocer a gente importante. **-6.** SPORT [game, set] perder. **-7.** [write - letter, postcard] poner, escribir. **-8.** [let out of car] dejar.

◇ *vi* **-1.** [fall down] caer; **to ~ to one's knees** arrodillarse; **~ dead!** ¡vete a la porra!; **we walked until we dropped** estuvimos andando hasta no poder más. **-2.** [fall away - ground] ceder. **-3.** [decrease - temperature, price, voice] bajar; [- attendance, demand, unemployment] disminuir; [- wind] calmarse, amainar.

◆ **drops** *npl* MED gotas *fpl*.

◆ **drop by** *vi inf*: **to ~ by (at)** pasarse (por).

◆ **drop in** *vi inf*: **to ~ in on** pasarse por casa de.

◆ **drop off** ◇ *vt sep* [person, letter] dejar. ◇ *vi* **-1.** [fall asleep] quedarse dormido(da), dormirse. **-2.** [grow less] disminuir, bajar.

◆ **drop out** *vi*: **to ~ out (of OR from)** [school, college] dejar de asistir (a); [competition] retirarse (de).

drop-in centre *n centro patrocinado por los servicios sociales, iglesias etc, a donde la gente puede ir a pasar un rato*.

droplet ['drɒplɪt] *n* gotita *f*.

dropout ['drɒpaʊt] *n* [from society] marginado *m*, -da *f*; [from university] persona *f* que ha dejado los estudios.

dropper ['drɒpər] *n* cuentagotas *m inv*.

droppings ['drɒpɪŋz] *npl* excremento *m* (de animales).

drop shot *n* dejada *f*.

dross [drɒs] *n* escoria *f*.

drought [draʊt] *n* sequía *f*.

drove [drəʊv] ◇ *pt* → **drive**. ◇ *n* [of people] multitud *f*.

drown [draʊn] ◇ *vt* **-1.** [kill] ahogar. **-2.** [sound]: **to ~ sb/sthg (out)** ahogar a alguien/algo. ◇ *vi* ahogarse.

drowsy ['draʊzɪ] (*compar* **-ier**, *superl* **-iest**) *adj* [person] somnoliento(ta).

drudge [drʌdʒ] *n* esclavo *m*, -va *f* del trabajo.

drudgery ['drʌdʒərɪ] *n* trabajo pesado y monótono.

drug [drʌg] (*pt & pp* **-ged**, *cont* **-ging**) ◇ *n* **-1.** [medicine] medicamento *m*, medicina *f*. **-2.** [narcotic] droga *f*; **to be on OR take ~s** drogarse. ◇ *vt* **-1.** [person] narcotizar, drogar. **-2.** [food, drink] echar droga a.

drug abuse *n* consumo *m* de drogas.

drug addict *n* drogadicto *m*, -ta *f*, toxicómano *m*, -na *f*.

drug addiction *n* drogadicción *f*, toxicomanía *f*.

druggist ['drʌgɪst] *n Am* farmacéutico *m*, -ca *f*.

drug pedlar *n* traficante *m y f* de drogas al por menor.

drugstore ['drʌgstɔːʳ] *n Am* farmacia *f* (*que también vende productos de perfumería etc*).

druid ['druːɪd] *n* druida *m*.

drum [drʌm] (*pt & pp* **-med**, *cont* **-ming**) ◇ *n* **-1.** [instrument] tambor *m*; **~s** batería *f*. **-2.** [container, cylinder] bidón *m*. ◇ *vt* [fingers] tamborilear con. ◇ *vi* [rain, hoofs] golpetear.

◆ **drum into** *vt sep*: **to ~ sthg into sb** inculcar algo a alguien.

◆ **drum up** *vt sep* intentar conseguir.

drumbeat ['drʌmbiːt] *n* toque *m* de tambor.

drum brake *n* freno *m* de tambor.

drummer ['drʌməʳ] *n* [in orchestra] tambor *m y f*; [in pop group] batería *m y f*.

drumming ['drʌmɪŋ] *n* **-1.** [of fingers, rain] tamborileo *m*. **-2.** [playing drum] el tocar el tambor.

drum roll *n* redoble *m* de tambor.

drumstick ['drʌmstɪk] *n* **-1.** [for drum] palillo *m*. **-2.** [food] muslo *m*.

drunk [drʌŋk] ◇ *pp* → **drink**. ◇ *adj* **-1.** [on alcohol] borracho(cha), bolo(la) *Amer*; **to get ~** emborracharse; **to be ~** estar borracho; **~ and disorderly** borracho y escandaloso. **-2.** *fig* [excited, carried away]: **to be ~ with** OR **on** estar ebrio(bria) de. ◇ *n* borracho *m*, -cha *f*.

drunkard ['drʌŋkəd] *n* borracho *m*, -cha *f*.

drunk-driving *Am* = **drink-driving**.

drunken ['drʌŋkn] *adj* **-1.** [person] borracho(cha). **-2.** [talk, steps, stupor] de borracho(cha).

drunken driving = **drink-driving**.

drunkenness ['drʌŋkənnɪs] *n* embriaguez *f*.

dry [draɪ] (*compar* **-ier**, *superl* **-iest**, *pt & pp* **dried**) ◇ *adj* **-1.** [gen] seco(ca). **-2.** [day] sin lluvia. **-3.** [earth, soil] árido(da). **-4.** [thirsty] sediento(ta); **to feel** OR **be ~** tener sed. **-5.** [dull] aburrido(da). ◇ *vt* [gen] secar; [hands, hair] secar; **to ~ o.s** secarse; **to ~ one's eyes** secarse las lágrimas. ◇ *vi* secarse.

◆ **dry out** ◇ *vt sep* secar. ◇ *vi* secarse.

◆ **dry up** ◇ *vt sep* secar. ◇ *vi* **-1.** [river, well] secarse. **-2.** [stop - supply] agotarse. **-3.** [stop speaking] cortarse. **-4.** [dry dishes] secar.

dry battery *n* pila *f* (seca).

dry-clean *vt* limpiar en seco.

dry cleaner *n*: **~'s** tintorería *f*.

dry-cleaning *n* limpieza *f* en seco.

dry dock *n* dique *m* seco.

dryer ['draɪəʳ] *n* [for clothes] secadora *f*.

dry ginger *n* ginger ale *m*.

dry goods *npl* artículos *mpl* de mercería.

dry ice *n* nieve *f* carbónica.

dry land *n* tierra *f* firme.

dryly ['draɪlɪ] *adv* [wryly] secamente.

dryness ['draɪnɪs] *n* **-1.** [of ground, lecture] aridez *f*. **-2.** [of comment, humour] sequedad *f*.

dry rot *n* putrefacción *f* de la madera.

dry run *n* ensayo *m*.

dry ski slope *n* pista *f* de esquí artificial.

dry-stone wall *n* muro construido con piedras amontonadas y sin mortero.

DSc (*abbr of* **Doctor of Science**) *n* (*titular de un*) *doctorado en el campo de las ciencias*.

DSS (*abbr of* **Department of Social Security**) *n* *ministerio británico de la seguridad social*.

DST (*abbr of* **daylight saving time**) *hora de verano*.

DT *abbr of* **data transmission**.

DTI (*abbr of* **Department of Trade and Industry**) *n* *ministerio británico de comercio e industria*.

DTp (*abbr of* **Department of Transport**) *n* *ministerio británico de transporte*.

DTP (*abbr of* **desktop publishing**) *n* autoed. *f*.

DT's [ˌdiːˈtiːz] (*abbr of* **delirium tremens**) *npl inf*: **to have the ~** tener un delirium tremens.

dual ['djuːəl] *adj* doble.

dual carriageway *n Br* carretera de dos sentidos *y doble vía separados*, ≃ autovía *f*.

dual control *n* doble mando *m*.

dual nationality *n* doble nacionalidad *f*.

dual-purpose *adj* de doble uso.

Dubai [ˌduːˈbaɪ] *n* Dubai.

dubbed [dʌbd] *adj* **-1.** CINEMA doblado(da). **-2.** [nicknamed] apodado(da).

dubious ['djuːbjəs] *adj* **-1.** [questionable - person, deal, reasons] sospechoso(sa); [- honour, distinction] paradójico(ca). **-2.** [uncertain, undecided] dudoso(sa); **to feel** OR **be ~ (about)** tener dudas (sobre).

Dublin ['dʌblɪn] *n* Dublín.

Dubliner ['dʌblɪnəʳ] *n* dublinés *m*, -esa *f*.

duchess ['dʌtʃɪs] *n* duquesa *f*.

duchy ['dʌtʃɪ] (*pl* **-ies**) *n* ducado *m*.

duck [dʌk] ◇ *n* **-1.** [bird] pato *m*, -ta *f*; **to take to sthg like a ~ to water** encontrarse en seguida en su salsa con algo. **-2.** [food] pato *m*. ◇ *vt* **-1.** [lower] agachar, bajar. **-2.** [try to avoid - duty] eludir, esquivar. **-3.** [submerge] sumergir. ◇ *vi* **-1.** [lower head] agacharse. **-2.** [dive]: **to ~ behind/into sthg** esconderse detrás de/en algo.

◆ **duck out** *vi*: **to ~ out (of sthg/of doing sthg)** esquivar (algo/hacer algo).

duckling ['dʌklɪŋ] *n* patito *m*.

duct [dʌkt] *n* conducto *m*.

dud [dʌd] ◇ *adj* [gen] falso(sa); [mine] que no estalla; [cheque] sin fondos. ◇ *n persona o cosa inútil*.

dude [dju:d] *n Am inf* [man] tío *m*.

dude ranch *n Am* rancho *m* para turistas.

due [dju:] ◇ *adj* **-1.** [expected] esperado(da); **it's ~ out in May** saldrá en mayo; **she's ~ back soon** tendría que volver dentro de poco; **the train's ~ in half an hour** el tren debe llegar dentro de media hora. **-2.** [appropriate] oportuno(na), debido(da); **with all ~ respect** sin ganas de ofender; **in ~ course** [at appropriate time] a su debido tiempo; [eventually] al final. **-3.** [owed, owing] pagadero(ra); **I'm ~ a bit of luck** ya sería hora que tuviera un poco de suerte; **how much are you ~?** ¿cuánto te deben?; **to be ~ to** deberse a.

◇ *n* [deserts]: **to give sb their ~** hacer justicia a alguien.

◇ *adv*: **~ north/south** derecho hacia el norte/sur.

◆ **dues** *npl* cuota *f*.

◆ **due to** *prep* debido a.

due date *n* (fecha *f* de) vencimiento *m*.

duel ['dju:əl] (*Br pt & pp* **-led**, *cont* **-ling**, *Am pt & pp* **-ed**, *cont* **-ing**) ◇ *n* duelo *m*. ◇ *vi* batirse en duelo.

duet [dju:'et] *n* dúo *m*.

duff [dʌf] *adj Br inf* inútil.

◆ **duff up** *vt sep Br inf* dar una paliza a.

duffel bag ['dʌfl-] *n* morral *m*.

duffel coat ['dʌfl-] *n* trenca *f*.

duffle bag ['dʌfl-] = **duffel bag**.

duffle coat ['dʌfl-] = **duffel coat**.

dug [dʌg] *pt & pp* → **dig**.

dugout ['dʌgaʊt] *n* **-1.** [canoe] *canoa hecha de un tronco ahuecado*. **-2.** SPORT foso *m*, banquillo *m*.

duke [dju:k] *n* duque *m*.

dull [dʌl] ◇ *adj* **-1.** [boring] aburrido(da). **-2.** [listless] torpe. **-3.** [dim] apagado(da). **-4.** [cloudy] gris, triste. **-5.** [thud, boom, pain] sordo(da). ◇ *vt* **-1.** [senses] embotar, entorpecer; [pain] aliviar; [pleasure, memory] enturbiar. **-2.** [make less bright] deslustrar.

duly ['dju:lɪ] *adv* **-1.** [properly] debidamente. **-2.** [as expected] como era de esperar.

dumb [dʌm] *adj* **-1.** [unable to speak] mudo(da); **to be struck ~** quedarse de una pieza. **-2.** *inf* [stupid] estúpido(da).

dumbbell ['dʌmbel] *n* [weight] pesa *f*.

dumbfound [dʌm'faʊnd] *vt*: **to be ~ed** quedar mudo de asombro.

dumbing down [,dʌmɪŋ-] *n* [of TV, newspapers] empobrecimiento *m* de contenidos OR de la calidad.

dumbstruck ['dʌmstrʌk] *adj* mudo(da) de asombro.

dumbwaiter [,dʌm'weɪtə'] *n* [lift] montaplatos *m inv*.

dumdum (bullet) ['dʌmdʌm-] *n* (bala *f*) dúmdum *f*.

dummy ['dʌmɪ] (*pl* **-ies**) ◇ *adj* falso(sa). ◇ *n* **-1.** [of ventriloquist] muñeco *m*; [in shop window] maniquí *m*. **-2.** [copy] imitación *f*. **-3.** *Br* [for baby] chupete *m*, chupón *m Amer*. **-4.** SPORT amago *m*. ◇ *vt* SPORT amagar.

dummy run *n* ensayo *m*, prueba *f*.

dump [dʌmp] ◇ *n* **-1.** [for rubbish] basurero *m*, vertedero *m*. **-2.** [for ammunition] depósito *m*. **-3.** *inf* [ugly place - house] casucha *f*; [- hotel] hotelucho *m*. ◇ *vt* **-1.** [put down - sand, load] descargar; [- bags, washing] dejar. **-2.** [dispose of] deshacerse de. **-3.** COMPUT volcar. **-4.** *inf* [jilt] deshacerse de.

◆ **dumps** *npl*: **to be (down) in the ~s** tener murria, estar por los suelos.

dumper (truck) *Br* ['dʌmpə'-], **dump truck** *Am n* volquete *m*.

dumping ['dʌmpɪŋ] *n* vertido *m*; **"no ~"** "prohibido verter basura".

dumping ground *n* vertedero *m*.

dumpling ['dʌmplɪŋ] *n bola de masa que se guisa al vapor con carne y verduras*.

dump truck *Am* = **dumper (truck)**.

dumpy ['dʌmpɪ] (*compar* **-ier**, *superl* **-iest**) *adj inf* bajito y regordete (bajita y regordeta).

dunce [dʌns] *n* zoquete *m y f*.

dune [dju:n] *n* duna *f*.

dung [dʌŋ] *n* [of animal] excremento *m*; [used as manure] estiércol *m*.

dungarees [,dʌngə'ri:z] *npl* **-1.** *Br* [for work] mono *m*; [fashion garment] pantalones *mpl* de peto. **-2.** *Am* [heavy jeans] *vaqueros de tela gruesa utilizados para trabajar*.

dungeon ['dʌndʒən] *n* mazmorra *f*, calabozo *m*.

dunk [dʌŋk] *vt inf* mojar.

Dunkirk [dʌn'kɜ:k] *n* Dunkerque.

duo ['dju:əʊ] *n* dúo *m*.

duodenal ulcer ['dju:əʊ'di:nl-] *n* úlcera *f* de duodeno.

dupe [dju:p] ◇ *n* primo *m*, -ma *f*, inocente *m y f*. ◇ *vt*: **to ~ sb (into doing sthg)** embaucar a uno (a que haga algo).

duplex ['djuːpleks] n Am **-1.** [apartment] dúplex m, piso en que las habitaciones están distribuidas entre dos plantas. **-2.** [house] casa f adosada.

duplicate [adj & n 'djuːplɪkət, vb 'djuːplɪkeɪt] ◇ adj duplicado(da). ◇ n copia f, duplicado m; **in** ~ por duplicado. ◇ vt **-1.** [copy] duplicar, hacer una copia de. **-2.** [double, repeat] repetir.

duplication [,djuːplɪ'keɪʃn] n (U) **-1.** [copying] duplicación f, copia f. **-2.** [doubling, repetition] repetición f.

duplicity [djuː'plɪsətɪ] n fml doblez f, duplicidad f.

Dur (abbr of **Durham**) condado inglés.

durability [,djʊərə'bɪlətɪ] n durabilidad f.

durable ['djʊərəbl] adj duradero(ra).

duration [djʊ'reɪʃn] n duración f; **for the** ~ **of** durante.

duress [djʊ'res] n: **under** ~ por coacción f.

Durex® ['djʊəreks] n [condom] preservativo m, condón m.

during ['djʊərɪŋ] prep durante.

dusk [dʌsk] n crepúsculo m, anochecer m.

dusky ['dʌskɪ] (compar **-ier**, superl **-iest**) adj literary moreno(na).

dust [dʌst] ◇ n polvo m; **coal** ~ cisco m; **to gather** ~ [get dusty] cubrirse de polvo; fig [be ignored] quedar arrinconado. ◇ vt **-1.** [clean] quitar el polvo a, limpiar. **-2.** [cover with powder]: **to** ~ **sthg (with)** espolvorear algo (con). ◇ vi quitar el polvo.
◆ **dust off** vt sep lit & fig desempolvar.

dustbin ['dʌstbɪn] n Br cubo m de la basura.

dustbowl ['dʌstbəʊl] n zona f semiárida (que sufre vendavales de polvo).

dustcart ['dʌstkɑːt] n Br camión m de la basura.

dust cover = **dust jacket**.

duster ['dʌstər] n **-1.** [cloth] bayeta f, trapo m (de quitar el polvo). **-2.** Am [overall] guardapolvo m.

dust jacket n sobrecubierta f.

dustman ['dʌstmən] (pl **-men** [-mən]) n Br basurero m.

dustpan ['dʌstpæn] n recogedor m.

dustsheet ['dʌstʃiːt] n Br guardapolvo m (para muebles).

dust storm n vendaval m de polvo.

dustup ['dʌstʌp] n inf reyerta f, riña f.

dusty ['dʌstɪ] (compar **-ier**, superl **-iest**) adj [covered in dust] polvoriento(ta).

Dutch [dʌtʃ] ◇ adj holandés(esa). ◇ n [language] holandés m. ◇ npl: **the** ~ los holandeses.

Dutch auction n Br subasta en la que se va reduciendo el precio de venta hasta encontrar comprador.

Dutch barn n Br granero formado por un armazón con techo.

Dutch cap n Br diafragma m.

Dutch courage n valentía f causada por la embriaguez.

Dutch elm disease n hongo que ataca a los olmos.

Dutchman ['dʌtʃmən] (pl **-men** [-mən]) n holandés m.

Dutchwoman ['dʌtʃ,wʊmən] (pl **-women** [-,wɪmɪn]) n holandesa f.

dutiable ['djuːtjəbl] adj sujeto(ta) a derechos de aduana.

dutiful ['djuːtɪfʊl] adj obediente, sumiso(sa).

duty ['djuːtɪ] (pl **-ies**) n **-1.** (U) [moral, legal responsibility] deber m; **to do one's** ~ cumplir uno con su deber. **-2.** [work] servicio m; **to be on/off** ~ estar/no estar de servicio. **-3.** [tax] impuesto m; **customs** ~ derechos mpl de aduana.
◆ **duties** npl tareas fpl.

duty bound adj: **to be** ~ **(to do sthg)** estar obligado(da) (a hacer algo).

duty-free adj libre de impuestos.

duty-free shop n tienda f libre de impuestos.

duty officer n oficial m y f de guardia.

duvet ['duːveɪ] n Br edredón m.

duvet cover n Br funda f del edredón.

DVLC (abbr of **Driver and Vehicle Licensing Centre**) n organismo británico encargado de la matriculación de coches y la emisión de carnets de conducir, ≃ Dirección f General de Tráfico.

DVM (abbr of **Doctor of Veterinary Medicine**) n (titular de un) doctorado de veterinaria.

dwarf [dwɔːf] (pl **-s** OR **dwarves** [dwɔːvz]) ◇ adj enano(na). ◇ n enano m, -na f. ◇ vt achicar, empequeñecer.

dwell [dwel] (pt & pp **-ed** OR **dwelt**) vi literary morar, habitar.
◆ **dwell on** vt fus darle vueltas a.

-dweller ['dwelər] suffix: **cave**~ habitante m y f de las cavernas; **city**~ habitante m y f de la ciudad.

dwelling ['dwelɪŋ] n literary morada f.

dwelt [dwelt] pt & pp → **dwell**.

dwindle ['dwɪndl] vi ir disminuyendo.

dwindling ['dwɪndlɪŋ] adj decreciente.

dye [daɪ] ◇ n tinte m, colorante m. ◇ vt teñir.

dyed [daɪd] adj teñido(da).

dying ['daɪɪŋ] ◇ cont → **die**. ◇ adj **-1.** [person, animal] moribundo(da). **-2.** [activity, practice] en vías de desaparición. ◇ npl: **the ~** los moribundos.

dyke [daɪk] = **dike**.

dynamic [daɪ'næmɪk] adj dinámico(ca).
◆ **dynamics** npl dinámica f.

dynamism ['daɪnəmɪzm] n dinamismo m.

dynamite ['daɪnəmaɪt] ◇ n lit & fig dinamita f. ◇ vt dinamitar.

dynamo ['daɪnəməʊ] (pl **-s**) n dinamo f.

dynasty [Br 'dɪnəstɪ, Am 'daɪnəstɪ] (pl **-ies**) n dinastía f.

dysentery ['dɪsntrɪ] n disentería f.

dyslexia [dɪs'leksɪə] n dislexia f.

dyslexic [dɪs'leksɪk] adj disléxico(ca).

dyspepsia [dɪs'pepsɪə] n dispepsia f.

dystrophy ['dɪstrəfɪ] n → **muscular dystrophy**.

E

e (pl **e's** OR **es**), **E** (pl **E's** OR **Es**) [iː] n [letter] e f, E f.
◆ **E** n **-1.** MUS mi m. **-2.** (abbr of **east**) E m.

ea. (abbr of **each**) c/u; £3.00 ~ 3 libras cada uno.

each [iːtʃ] ◇ adj cada. ◇ pron cada uno m, una f; **one ~** uno cada uno; **~ of us/the boys** cada uno de nosotros/los niños; **two of ~** dos de cada (uno); **~ other** el uno al otro; **they kissed ~ other** se besaron; **we know ~ other** nos conocemos.

eager ['iːgəʳ] adj [pupil] entusiasta; [smile, expression] de entusiasmo; **to be ~ for sthg/to do sthg** ansiar algo/hacer algo, desear vivamente algo/hacer algo.

eagerly ['iːgəlɪ] adv con entusiasmo.

eagle ['iːgl] n águila f.

eagle-eyed [-'aɪd] adj con ojos de lince.

eaglet ['iːglɪt] n aguilucho m.

E and OE (abbr of **errors and omissions excepted**) s.e.u.o.

ear [ɪəʳ] n **-1.** [of person, animal] oreja f; **to go in one ~ and out the other** inf entrar por un oído y salir por el otro; **to have** OR **keep one's ~ to the ground** inf mantenerse al corriente. **-2.** fig [attention] atención f. **-3.**

fig [talent]: **to have an ~ for** tener oído para. **-4.** [of corn] espiga f. **-5.** MUS: **by ~** de oído; **to play it by ~** fig obrar por instinto OR sobre la marcha.

earache ['ɪəreɪk] n dolor m de oídos.

eardrum ['ɪədrʌm] n tímpano m.

earl [ɜːl] n conde m.

earlier ['ɜːlɪəʳ] ◇ adj anterior. ◇ adv antes; **~ on** antes.

earliest ['ɜːlɪəst] ◇ adj primero(ra). ◇ n: **at the ~** como muy pronto.

early ['ɜːlɪ] (compar **-ier**, superl **-iest**) ◇ adj **-1.** [before expected time, in day] temprano(na); **she was ~** llegó temprano OR con adelanto; **I'll take an ~ lunch** almorzaré pronto OR temprano; **to get up ~** madrugar. **-2.** [at beginning]: **~ morning** la madrugada; **the ~ chapters** los primeros capítulos; **her ~ life** los primeros años de su vida; **in the ~ 1950s** a principios de los años 50.
◇ adv **-1.** [before expected time] temprano, pronto; **we got up ~** nos levantamos temprano; **it arrived ten minutes ~** llegó con diez minutos de adelanto. **-2.** [at beginning]: **as ~ as 1920** ya en 1920; **~ this morning** esta mañana temprano; **~ in the year** a principios de año; **~ in the book** al comienzo del libro; **~ on** temprano.

early retirement n jubilación f anticipada.

early warning system n MIL sistema m de alerta roja.

earmark ['ɪəmɑːk] vt: **to be ~ed for** estar destinado(da) a.

earn [ɜːn] vt **-1.** [be paid] ganar. **-2.** [generate - subj: business, product] generar. **-3.** fig [gain - respect, praise] ganarse.

earned income [ɜːnd-] n rentas fpl del trabajo.

earner ['ɜːnəʳ] n fuente f de ingresos.

earnest ['ɜːnɪst] adj [gen] serio(ria); [wish] sincero(ra).
◆ **in earnest** ◇ adj serio(ria). ◇ adv [seriously] en serio.

earnestly ['ɜːnɪstlɪ] adv [talk] seriamente, con toda seriedad; [wish] sinceramente, de todo corazón.

earnings ['ɜːnɪŋz] npl ingresos mpl.

earnings-related adj proporcional a los ingresos.

ear, nose and throat specialist n otorrinolaringólogo m, -ga f.

earphones ['ɪəfəʊnz] npl auriculares mpl.

earplugs ['ɪəplʌgz] npl tapones mpl para los oídos.

earring ['ɪərɪŋ] *n* pendiente *m*, caravana *f* Amer.

earshot ['ɪəʃɒt] *n*: **within/out of** ~ al alcance/fuera del alcance del oído.

ear-splitting *adj* ensordecedor(ra).

earth [ɜːθ] ◇ *n* **-1.** [gen] tierra *f*; **how/ what/where/why on** ~ ...? ¿cómo/qué/ dónde/por qué demonios ...?; **to cost the** ~ *Br* costar un dineral. **-2.** [in electric plug, appliance] toma *f* de tierra. ◇ *vt Br*: **to be ~ed** estar conectado(da) a tierra.

earthenware ['ɜːθnweə'] ◇ *adj* de loza, de barro. ◇ *n* loza *f*.

earthling ['ɜːθlɪŋ] *n* terrícola *m y f*.

earthly ['ɜːθlɪ] *adj* **-1.** [of material world] terrenal. **-2.** *inf* [possible] posible; **what** ~ **reason could she have for doing it?** ¿a cuento de qué haría lo que hizo?

earthquake ['ɜːθkweɪk] *n* terremoto *m*.

earthshattering ['ɜːθ,ʃætərɪŋ] *adj Br inf* extraordinario(ria).

earth tremor *n* temblor *m* de tierra.

earthward(s) ['ɜːθwəd(z)] *adv* hacia la tierra.

earthworks ['ɜːθwɜːks] *npl* ARCHEOL terraplén *m*.

earthworm ['ɜːθwɜːm] *n* lombriz *f* (de tierra).

earthy ['ɜːθɪ] (*compar* **-ier**, *superl* **-iest**) *adj* **-1.** [rather crude] natural, desinhibido(da). **-2.** [of, like earth] terroso(sa).

earwax ['ɪəwæks] *n* cerumen *m*.

earwig ['ɪəwɪg] *n* tijereta *f*.

ease [iːz] ◇ *n* (*U*) **-1.** [lack of difficulty] facilidad *f*; **with** ~ con facilidad. **-2.** [comfort] comodidad *f*; **at** ~ cómodo(da); **ill at** ~ incómodo(da). ◇ *vt* **-1.** [pain, grief] calmar, aliviar; [problems, tension] atenuar. **-2.** [move carefully]: **to** ~ **sthg open** abrir algo con cuidado; **to** ~ **o.s. out of sthg** levantarse despacio de algo. ◇ *vi* [problem] atenuarse; [pain] calmarse; [rain] amainar; [grip] relajarse, aflojarse.

◆ **ease off** *vi* [problem] atenuarse; [pain] calmarse; [rain] amainar.

◆ **ease up** *vi* **-1.** *inf* [treat less severely]: **to** ~ **up on sb** no ser muy duro(ra) con alguien. **-2.** [rain] aflojar, amainar. **-3.** [relax - person] tomarse las cosas con más calma.

easel ['iːzl] *n* caballete *m*.

easily ['iːzɪlɪ] *adv* **-1.** [without difficulty] fácilmente. **-2.** [without doubt] sin lugar a dudas. **-3.** [in a relaxed manner] tranquilamente, relajadamente.

easiness ['iːzɪnɪs] *n* [lack of difficulty] facilidad *f*.

east [iːst] ◇ *n* **-1.** [direction] este *m*. **-2.** [region]: **the** ~ el este. ◇ *adj* oriental; [wind] del este. ◇ *adv*: ~ **(of)** al este (de).

◆ **East** *n*: **the East** POL el Este; [Asia] el Oriente.

eastbound ['iːstbaʊnd] *adj* con dirección este.

East End *n*: **the** ~ el este de Londres.

Easter ['iːstə'] *n* Semana *f* Santa.

Easter egg *n* huevo *m* de Pascua.

Easter Island *n* la isla de Pascua.

easterly ['iːstəlɪ] *adj* del este; **in an** ~ **direction** hacia el este.

eastern ['iːstən] *adj* del este, oriental.

◆ **Eastern** *adj* [gen & POL] del Este; [from Asia] oriental.

Eastern bloc [-'blɒk] *n*: **the** ~ el bloque del Este.

Easterner ['iːstənə'] *n* habitante del este de los E.E.U.U.

Easter Sunday *n* Domingo *m* de Resurrección.

East German ◇ *adj* de Alemania Oriental. ◇ *n* [person] alemán *m*, -ana *f* oriental.

East Germany *n*: **(the former)** ~ (la antigua) Alemania Oriental.

eastward ['iːstwəd] ◇ *adj* hacia el este. ◇ *adv* = **eastwards**.

eastwards ['iːstwədz] *adv* hacia el este.

easy ['iːzɪ] (*compar* **-ier**, *superl* **-iest**) ◇ *adj* **-1.** [not difficult] fácil. **-2.** [life, time] cómodo(da). **-3.** [manner] natural, relajado(da). ◇ *adv*: **to go** ~ **on sb** *inf* no ser muy duro(ra) con alguien; **to go** ~ **on sthg** *inf* no pasarse con algo, tener cuidado con algo; **to take it** OR **things** ~ tomarse las cosas con calma.

easy-care *adj Br* no delicado(da).

easy chair *n* [armchair] sillón *m*, butaca *f*.

easygoing [,iːzɪ'gəʊɪŋ] *adj* [person] tolerante, tranquilo(la); [manner] relajado(da).

eat [iːt] (*pt* **ate**, *pp* **eaten**) *vt & vi* comer.

◆ **eat away, eat into** *vt sep* **-1.** [corrode] corroer. **-2.** [deplete] mermar.

◆ **eat out** *vi* comer fuera.

◆ **eat up** *vt sep* **-1.** [food] comerse. **-2.** [money, time] consumir un montón de.

eatable ['iːtəbl] *adj* comible, comestible.

eaten ['iːtn] *pp* → **eat**.

eater ['iːtə'] *n*: **I'm not a great fruit** ~ no como mucha fruta.

eatery ['iːtərɪ] *n Am* restaurante *m*.

eating apple ['iːtɪŋ-] *n* manzana *f* (para comer).

eau de cologne [,əʊdəkə'ləʊn] *n* (agua *f* de) colonia *f*.

eaves ['iːvz] *npl* alero *m*.

eavesdrop ['iːvzdrɒp] (*pt* & *pp* **-ped**, *cont* **-ping**) *vi*: **to ~ (on)** escuchar secretamente (a).

ebb [eb] ◇ *n* reflujo *m*; **the ~ and flow of** *fig* los altibajos de; **at a low ~** *fig* de capa caída. ◇ *vi* **-1.** [tide, sea] bajar. **-2.** *literary* [strength, pain, feeling]: **to ~ (away)** decrecer, disminuir.

ebb tide *n* marea *f* baja, bajamar *f*.

ebony ['ebənɪ] ◇ *adj literary* [colour] de color ébano. ◇ *n* ébano *m*.

ebullient [ɪ'bʊljənt] *adj* [person] entusiasta; [wit, manner] exuberante.

EC (*abbr of* **European Community**) *n* CE *f*.

eccentric [ɪk'sentrɪk] ◇ *adj* excéntrico(ca). ◇ *n* excéntrico *m*, -ca *f*.

eccentricity [ˌeksen'trɪsətɪ] (*pl* **-ies**) *n* excentricidad *f*.

ecclesiastic(al) [ɪˌkliːzɪ'æstɪ(l)] *adj* eclesiástico(ca).

ECG (*abbr of* **electrocardiogram**) *n* ECG *m*.

ECGD (*abbr of* **Export Credits Guarantee Department**) *n* organismo para el fomento del comercio exterior.

ECH (*abbr of* **electric central heating**) *Br* cal. cent. eléc.

echelon ['eʃəlɒn] *n fml* [level in organization] escalafón *m*, rango *m*.

echo ['ekəʊ] (*pl* **-es**, *pt* & *pp* **-ed**, *cont* **-ing**) ◇ *n lit* & *fig* eco *m*. ◇ *vt* [words] repetir; [opinion] hacerse eco de. ◇ *vi* resonar.

éclair [eɪ'kleəʳ] *n* eclair *m*, pastelillo relleno de crema.

eclectic [ɪ'klektɪk] *adj* ecléctico(ca).

eclipse [ɪ'klɪps] ◇ *n lit* & *fig* eclipse *m*; **a total/partial ~** un eclipse total/parcial. ◇ *vt* *fig* eclipsar.

ECM (*abbr of* **European Common Market**) *n Am* MCE *m*.

ecological [ˌiːkə'lɒdʒɪkl] *adj* **-1.** [pattern, balance, impact] ecológico(ca). **-2.** [group, movement, person] ecologista.

ecologically [ˌiːkə'lɒdʒɪklɪ] *adv* ecológicamente.

ecologist [ɪ'kɒlədʒɪst] *n* **-1.** [scientist] ecólogo *m*, -ga *f*. **-2.** [conservationist] ecologista *m* y *f*.

ecology [ɪ'kɒlədʒɪ] *n* ecología *f*.

economic [ˌiːkə'nɒmɪk] *adj* **-1.** [of money, industry] económico(ca). **-2.** [profitable] rentable.

economical [ˌiːkə'nɒmɪkl] *adj* económico(ca).

economics [ˌiːkə'nɒmɪks] ◇ *n* (*U*) econo-

mía *f*. ◇ *npl* [of plan, business] aspecto *m* económico.

economist [ɪ'kɒnəmɪst] *n* economista *m* y *f*.

economize, -ise [ɪ'kɒnəmaɪz] *vi*: **to ~ (on)** economizar (en).

economy [ɪ'kɒnəmɪ] (*pl* **-ies**) *n* economía *f*; **economies of scale** economías *fpl* de escala.

economy class *n* clase *f* económica OR turista.

economy drive *n* campaña *f* de ahorro.

economy-size(d) *adj* de tamaño económico.

ecosystem ['iːkəʊˌsɪstəm] *n* ecosistema *m*.

ECSC (*abbr of* **European Coal & Steel Community**) *n* CECA *f*.

ecotourism [ˌiːkəʊ'tʊərɪzm] *n* ecotourismo *m*, turismo *m* verde.

ecstasy ['ekstəsɪ] (*pl* **-ies**) *n* éxtasis *m inv*; **to go into ecstasies about** extasiarse ante.

ecstatic [ek'stætɪk] *adj* extático(ca).

ecstatically [ek'stætɪklɪ] *adv* eufóricamente.

ECT (*abbr of* **electroconvulsive therapy**) *n* terapia de electrochoque.

ectoplasm ['ektəplæzm] *n* ectoplasma *m*.

ECU, Ecu ['ekjuː] (*abbr of* **European Currency Unit**) *n* ECU *m*, ecu *m*.

Ecuador ['ekwədɔːʳ] *n* (el) Ecuador.

Ecuadoran [ˌekwə'dɔːrən], **Ecuadorian** [ˌekwə'dɔːrɪən] ◇ *adj* ecuatoriano(na). ◇ *n* ecuatoriano *m*, -na *f*.

ecumenical [iːkjʊ'menɪkl] *adj* ecuménico(ca).

eczema ['eksɪmə] *n* eccema *m*, eczema *m*.

ed. -1. (*abbr of* **edition**) ed. **-2.** (*abbr of* **editor**) ed.

eddy ['edɪ] (*pl* **-ies**, *pt* & *pp* **-ied**) ◇ *n* remolino *m*. ◇ *vi* arremolinarse.

Eden ['iːdn] *n*: **(the Garden of) ~** (el jardín del) Edén *m*.

edge [edʒ] ◇ *n* **-1.** [of cliff, table, garden] borde *m*; **to be on the ~ of** estar al borde de. **-2.** [of coin] canto *m*; [of knife] filo *m*. **-3.** [advantage]: **to have an ~ over** OR **the ~ on** llevar ventaja a. **-4.** *fig* [of voice] nota *f* de enfado, aspereza *f*. ◇ *vi*: **to ~ towards** ir poco a poco hacia; **to ~ away/closer** ir alejándose/acercándose poco a poco.
◆ **on edge** *adj* con los nervios de punta.

edged [edʒd] *adj*: **~ with** [trees] bordeado(da) de; [lace, gold] ribeteado(da) de.

edgeways ['edʒweɪz], **edgewise** ['edʒwaɪz] *adv* de lado.

edging ['edʒɪŋ] *n* ribete *m*, orla *f*.

edgy ['edʒɪ] (*compar* **-ier**, *superl* **-iest**) *adj* nervioso(sa).

edible ['edɪbl] *adj* comestible.

edict ['iːdɪkt] *n* edicto *m*.

edifice ['edɪfɪs] *n fml* edificio *m* imponente.

edifying ['edɪfaɪɪŋ] *adj fml* edificante.

Edinburgh ['edɪnbrə] *n* Edimburgo.

Edinburgh Festival *n*: the ~ el Festival de Edimburgo.

THE EDINBURGH FESTIVAL:
El Festival internacional de Edimburgo, creado en 1947, es actualmente uno de los festivales de teatro, música y cine más importantes del mundo. Se celebra cada año durante tres semanas entre agosto y septiembre. Un festival paralelo e independiente llamado 'the Fringe' es un gran punto de encuentro para el teatro experimental

---

edit ['edɪt] *vt* **-1.** [correct - text] corregir, revisar. **-2.** [select material for - book] recopilar. **-3.** CINEMA, RADIO & TV montar. **-4.** [run - newspaper, magazine] dirigir.

◆ **edit out** *vt sep* eliminar.

edition [ɪ'dɪʃn] *n* edición *f*.

editor ['edɪtər] *n* **-1.** [of newspaper, magazine] director *m*, -ra *f*. **-2.** [of section of newspaper, programme, text] redactor *m*, -ra *f*. **-3.** [compiler - of book] autor *m*, -ra *f* de la edición. **-4.** CINEMA, RADIO & TV montador *m*, -ra *f*.

editorial [,edɪ'tɔːrɪəl] ◇ *adj* editorial; ~ staff redacción *f*. ◇ *n* editorial *m*.

EDP (*abbr of* **electronic data processing**) *n* TED *m*.

EDT (*abbr of* **Eastern Daylight Time**) *n hora de verano de Nueva York*.

educate ['edʒʊkeɪt] *vt* **-1.** [at school, college] educar. **-2.** [inform] informar.

educated ['edʒʊkeɪtɪd] *adj* culto(ta).

education [,edʒʊ'keɪʃn] *n* (*U*) **-1.** [activity, sector] enseñanza *f*. **-2.** [process or result of teaching] educación *f*, formación *f*.

educational [,edʒʊ'keɪʃənl] *adj* educativo(va); [establishment] docente.

educationalist [,edʒʊ'keɪʃnəlɪst] *n* pedagogo *m*, -ga *f*.

educative ['edʒʊkətɪv] *adj* educativo(va).

educator ['edʒʊkeɪtər] *n fml* educador *m*, educadora *f*.

edutainment [edʒʊ'teɪnmənt] *n* (*U*) juegos *mpl* educativos.

Edwardian [ed'wɔːdɪən] *adj* eduardiano(na).

EEC (*abbr of* **European Economic Community**) *n* CEE *f*.

EEG (*abbr of* **electroencephalogram**) *n* EEG *m*.

eel [iːl] *n* anguila *f*.

EENT (*abbr of* **eye, ear, nose and throat**) *n otorrinolaringología y ojos*.

EEOC (*abbr of* **Equal Employment Opportunity Commission**) *n organismo estadounidense contra la discriminación en el trabajo*.

eerie ['ɪərɪ] *adj* espeluznante.

EET (*abbr of* **Eastern European Time**) *n hora de Europa oriental*.

efface [ɪ'feɪs] *vt* borrar.

effect [ɪ'fekt] ◇ *n* efecto *m*; **to have an ~ on** tener OR surtir efecto en; **to do sthg for ~** hacer algo para causar efecto; **to take ~** [law, rule] entrar en vigor; [drug] hacer efecto; **to put sthg into ~** hacer entrar algo en vigor; **to the ~ that** en el sentido de que, de lo que se deduce que; **to that ~** a tal efecto; **words to that ~** palabras por el estilo. ◇ *vt* efectuar, llevar a cabo.

◆ **effects** *npl*: (**special**) ~**s** efectos *mpl* especiales.

effective [ɪ'fektɪv] *adj* **-1.** [successful] eficaz. **-2.** [actual, real] efectivo(va). **-3.** [law, ceasefire] operativo(va).

effectively [ɪ'fektɪvlɪ] *adv* **-1.** [well, successfully] eficazmente. **-2.** [in fact] de hecho.

effectiveness [ɪ'fektɪvnɪs] *n* eficacia *f*.

effeminate [ɪ'femɪnət] *adj pej* afeminado(da).

effervesce [,efə'ves] *vi* estar en efervescencia.

effervescent [,efə'vesənt] *adj* efervescente.

effete [ɪ'fiːt] *adj pej* [weak, effeminate] afeminado(da).

efficacious [efɪ'keɪʃəs] *adj fml* eficaz.

efficacy ['efɪkəsɪ] *n* eficacia *f*.

efficiency [ɪ'fɪʃənsɪ] *n* [gen] eficiencia *f*; [of machine] rendimiento *m*.

efficient [ɪ'fɪʃənt] *adj* [gen] eficiente; [machine] de buen rendimiento.

efficiently [ɪ'fɪʃəntlɪ] *adv* [competently] con eficiencia, eficientemente.

effigy ['efɪdʒɪ] (*pl* **-ies**) *n* efigie *f*.

effluent ['efluənt] *n* aguas *fpl* residuales.

effort ['efət] *n* **-1.** [gen] esfuerzo *m*; **to be worth the ~** merecer la pena; **with ~** con esfuerzo; **to make the ~ to do sthg** hacer el esfuerzo de hacer algo; **to make an/no ~ to do sthg** hacer un esfuerzo/no hacer ningún esfuerzo por hacer algo. **-2.** *inf* [result of trying] tentativa *f*.

effortless ['efətlɪs] *adj* fácil, sin gran esfuerzo.

effortlessly ['efətlɪslɪ] *adv* sin esfuerzo alguno, fácilmente.

effrontery [ɪ'frʌntərɪ] *n* descaro *m*.

effusive [ɪ'fjuːsɪv] *adj* efusivo(va).

effusively [ɪ'fjuːsɪvlɪ] *adv* efusivamente.

EFL ['efəl, ˌiːef'el] (*abbr of* **English as a foreign language**) *n* inglés para extranjeros.

EFTA ['eftə] (*abbr of* **European Free Trade Association**) *n* EFTA *f*.

e.g. (*abbr of* **exempli gratia**) *adv* p. ej.

EGA (*abbr of* **enhanced graphics adapter**) *n* COMPUT EGA *f*.

egalitarian [ɪˌgælɪ'teərɪən] *adj* igualitario(ria).

egg [eg] *n* **-1.** [gen] huevo *m*, blanquillo *m* Amer. **-2.** [ovum] óvulo *m*.
♦ **egg on** *vt sep* incitar.

eggcup ['egkʌp] *n* huevera *f*.

eggplant ['egplɑːnt] *n Am* berenjena *f*.

eggshell ['egʃel] *n* cáscara *f* de huevo.

egg timer *n* reloj *m* de arena.

egg whisk *n* batidor *m* (de huevos), varilla *f*.

egg white *n* clara *f* (de huevo).

egg yolk *n* yema *f* (de huevo).

ego ['iːgəʊ] (*pl* **-s**) *n* [opinion of self] amor *m* propio, ego *m*.

egocentric [ˌiːgəʊ'sentrɪk] *adj* egocéntrico(ca).

egoism ['iːgəʊɪzm] *n* egoísmo *m*.

egoist ['iːgəʊɪst] *n* egoísta *m y f*.

egoistic [ˌiːgəʊ'ɪstɪk] *adj* egoísta.

egotism ['iːgətɪzm] *n* egotismo *m*.

egotist ['iːgətɪst] *n* egotista *m y f*.

egotistic(al) [ˌiːgə'tɪstɪk(l)] *adj* egotista.

ego trip *n inf*: to be on an ~ estar haciendo algo que hace a uno sentirse el ombligo del mundo.

Egypt ['iːdʒɪpt] *n* Egipto.

Egyptian [ɪ'dʒɪpʃn] ◇ *adj* egipcio(cia). ◇ *n* [person] egipcio *m*, -cia *f*.

eh [eɪ] *excl Br inf* **-1.** [inviting reply, agreement] ¿no?, ¿verdad? **-2.** [asking for repeat] ¿cómo?, ¿qué?

eiderdown ['aɪdədaʊn] *n* edredón *m*.

eight [eɪt] *num* ocho; *see also* **six**.

eighteen [ˌeɪ'tiːn] *num* dieciocho; *see also* **six**.

eighteenth [ˌeɪ'tiːnθ] ◇ *num adj* decimoctavo(va). ◇ *num n* **-1.** [in order] decimoctavo *m*, -va *f*. **-2.** [fraction] decimoctavo *m*; *see also* **sixth**.

eighth [eɪtθ] ◇ *num adj* octavo(va). ◇ *num n* **-1.** [in order] octavo *m*, -va *f*. **-2.** [fraction] octavo *m*; *see also* **sixth**.

eightieth ['eɪtɪɪθ] ◇ *num adj* octogésimo(ma). ◇ *num n* **-1.** [in order] octogésimo *m*, -ma *f*. **-2.** [fraction] octogésimo *m*; *see also* **sixth**.

eighty ['eɪtɪ] (*pl* **-ies**) *num* ochenta; *see also* **sixty**.

Eire ['eərə] *n* Eire.

EIS (*abbr of* **Educational Institute of Scotland**) *n* sindicato escocés de la enseñanza.

either ['aɪðə, 'iːðə] ◇ *adj* **-1.** [one or the other] cualquiera de los dos; she couldn't find ~ **jumper** no podía encontrar ninguno de los dos jerseys; ~ **way** de cualquiera de las formas. **-2.** [each] cada; **on** ~ **side** de ambos lados.
◇ *pron*: ~ **(of them)** cualquiera (de ellos (ellas)); I don't like ~ **(of them)** no me gusta ninguno de ellos (ninguna de ellas).
◇ *adv* (*in negatives*) tampoco; she can't and I can't ~ ella no puede y yo tampoco.
◇ *conj*: ~ ... **or** o ... o; ~ **you or me** o tú o yo; I don't like ~ **him or his wife** no me gusta ni él ni su mujer (tampoco).

ejaculate [ɪ'dʒækjʊleɪt] ◇ *vt* [exclaim] exclamar. ◇ *vi* [have orgasm] eyacular.

eject [ɪ'dʒekt] *vt* **-1.** [object] expulsar, despedir. **-2.** [person]: **to** ~ **sb (from)** expulsar a alguien (de).

ejector seat *Br* [ɪ'dʒektə-], **ejection seat** *Am* [ɪ'dʒekʃn-] *n* asiento *m* eyectable.

eke [iːk]
♦ **eke out** ◇ *vt sep* alargar *fig*, estirar *fig*. ◇ *vt fus*: **to** ~ **out a living** ganarse la vida a duras penas.

EKG (*abbr of* **electrocardiogram**) *n Am* ECG *m*.

el [el] (*abbr of* **elevated railroad**) *n Am inf* paso elevado.

elaborate [*adj* ɪ'læbrət, *vb* ɪ'læbəreɪt] ◇ *adj* [ceremony] complicado(da); [carving] trabajado(da); [explanation, plan] detallado(da). ◇ *vi*: **to** ~ **on sthg** ampliar algo, explicar algo con más detalle.

elaborately [ɪ'læbərətlɪ] *adv* [decorate] laboriosamente, profusamente; [plan] detalladamente.

elapse [ɪ'læps] *vi* transcurrir.

elastic [ɪ'læstɪk] ◇ *adj* **-1.** [gen] elástico(ca). **-2.** *fig* [flexible] flexible. ◇ *n* elástico *m*.

elasticated [ɪ'læstɪkeɪtɪd] *adj* elástico(ca).

elastic band *n Br* gomita *f*, goma *f* (elástica).

elasticity [ˌelæ'stɪsətɪ] *n* [stretchiness] elasticidad *f*.

elated [ɪ'leɪtɪd] *adj* eufórico(ca).

elation [ɪ'leɪʃn] *n* euforia *f*, regocijo *m*.

elbow ['elbəʊ] ◇ *n* **-1.** codo *m*. ◇ *vt*: **to** ~ **sb aside** apartar a alguien a codazos.

elbow grease *n inf*: to use a lot of ~ to do sthg hacer algo a fuerza de puños.

elbowroom ['elbəʊrʊm] *n inf* espacio *m* (libre), sitio *m*.

elder ['eldər] ◇ *adj* mayor. ◇ *n* **-1.** [older person] mayor *m y f*. **-2.** [of tribe, church] anciano *m*. **-3.** ~ **(tree)** saúco *m*.

elderberry ['eldə,berɪ] (*pl* **-ies**) *n* baya *f* del saúco.

elderly ['eldəlɪ] ◇ *adj* mayor, anciano(na). ◇ *npl*: **the** ~ los ancianos.

elder statesman *n* santón *m fig.*

eldest ['eldɪst] *adj* mayor.

Eldorado [,eldɔ'rɑːdəʊ] *n* El Dorado.

elect [ɪ'lekt] ◇ *adj* electo(ta); **the president** ~ el presidente electo. ◇ *vt* **-1.** [by voting] elegir; **to** ~ **sb (as) sthg** elegir a alguien (como) algo. **-2.** *fml* [choose]: **to** ~ **to do sthg** optar por OR decidir hacer algo.

elected [ɪ'lektɪd] *adj* elegido(da).

election [ɪ'lekʃn] *n* elección *f*; **to have** OR **hold an** ~ celebrar (unas) elecciones; **local** ~**s** elecciones *fpl* municipales.

election campaign *n* campaña *f* electoral.

electioneering [ɪ,lekʃə'nɪərɪŋ] *n usu pej* electoralismo *m*.

elective [ɪ'lektɪv] *n Am & Scot* SCH & UNIV materia *f* optativa.

elector [ɪ'lektər] *n* elector *m*, -ra *f*.

electoral [ɪ'lektərəl] *adj* electoral.

electoral college *n cuerpo de compromisarios de un colegio electoral.*

electoral register, electoral roll *n*: **the** ~ el censo electoral.

electorate [ɪ'lektərət] *n*: **the** ~ el electorado.

electric [ɪ'lektrɪk] *adj* **-1.** [gen] eléctrico(ca). **-2.** *fig* [exciting] electrizante.

◆ **electrics** *npl Br inf* sistema *m* eléctrico.

electrical [ɪ'lektrɪkl] *adj* eléctrico(ca).

electrical engineer *n* ingeniero *m*, -ra *f* en electrónica.

electrical engineering *n* ingeniería *f* eléctrica, electrotecnia *f*.

electrically [ɪ'lektrɪklɪ] *adv* por electricidad.

electrical shock *Am* = electric shock.

electric blanket *n* manta *f* eléctrica.

electric chair *n*: **the** ~ la silla eléctrica.

electric cooker *n* cocina *f* eléctrica.

electric current *n* corriente *f* eléctrica.

electric fire *n* estufa *f* eléctrica.

electric guitar *n* guitarra *f* eléctrica.

electrician [,ɪlek'trɪʃn] *n* electricista *m y f*.

electricity [,ɪlek'trɪsətɪ] *n* electricidad *f*.

electric light *n* luz *f* eléctrica.

electric shock *Br*, **electrical shock** *Am n* descarga *f* eléctrica.

electric shock therapy *n* terapia *f* de electrochoque.

electric storm *n* tormenta *f* eléctrica.

electrify [ɪ'lektrɪfaɪ] (*pt & pp* **-ied**) *vt* **-1.** [rail line] electrificar. **-2.** [excite] electrizar.

electrifying [ɪ'lektrɪfaɪŋ] *adj* electrizante.

electro- [ɪ'lektrəʊ] *prefix* electro-.

electrocardiograph [ɪ,lektrəʊ'kɑːdɪəgrɑːf] *n* electrocardiógrafo *m*.

electrocute [ɪ'lektrəkjuːt] *vt*: **to** ~ **o.s., to be** ~**d** electrocutarse.

electrode [ɪ'lektrəʊd] *n* electrodo *m*.

electroencephalograph [ɪ,lektrəʊen'sefələgrɑːf] *n* electroencefalógrafo *m*.

electrolysis [,ɪlek'trɒləsɪs] *n* electrólisis *f inv*.

electromagnet [ɪ,lektrəʊ'mægnɪt] *n* electroimán *m*.

electromagnetic [ɪ,lektrəʊmæg'netɪk] *adj* electromagnético(ca).

electron [ɪ'lektrɒn] *n* electrón *m*.

electronic [,ɪlek'trɒnɪk] *adj* electrónico(ca).

electronic data processing *n* proceso *m* electrónico de datos.

electronic mail *n* COMPUT correo *m* electrónico.

electronic purse *n* monedero *m* electrónico.

electronics [ɪlek'trɒnɪks] ◇ *n* (*U*) [technology] electrónica *f*. ◇ *npl* [equipment] sistema *m* electrónico.

electron microscope *n* microscopio *m* electrónico.

electroplated [ɪ'lektrəʊ,pleɪtɪd] *adj* galvanizado(da).

elegance ['elɪgəns] *n* elegancia *f*.

elegant ['elɪgənt] *adj* elegante, elegantoso(sa) *Amer.*

elegantly ['elɪgəntlɪ] *adv* elegantemente, con elegancia.

elegy ['elɪdʒɪ] (*pl* **-ies**) *n* elegía *f*.

element ['elɪmənt] ◇ *n* **-1.** [gen] elemento *m*. **-2.** [amount, proportion] toque *m*, matiz *m*. **-3.** [in heater, kettle] resistencia *f*. **-4.** *phr*: **to be in one's** ~ estar uno en su elemento.

◆ **elements** *npl* **-1.** [basics] elementos *mpl*. **-2.** [weather]: **the** ~**s** los elementos.

elementary [,elɪ'mentərɪ] *adj* elemental; ~ **education** enseñanza *f* primaria.

elementary school *n Am* escuela *f* primaria.

elephant ['elɪfənt] (*pl inv* OR **-s**) *n* elefante *m*.

elevate ['elɪveɪt] *vt*: **to** ~ **sthg/sb (to** OR **into)** elevar algo/a alguien (a la categoría de).

elevated ['elɪveɪtɪd] *adj fml* elevado(da).

elevation [,elɪ'veɪʃn] n fml **-1.** [promotion] elevación f. **-2.** [height] altura f, altitud f.

elevator ['elɪveɪtər] n Am ascensor m, elevador m Amer.

eleven [ɪ'levn] num once m; see also **six**.

elevenses [ɪ'levnzɪz] n (U) Br tentempié m que se toma sobre las once.

eleventh [ɪ'levnθ] ◇ num adj undécimo(ma). ◇ num n **-1.** [in order] undécimo m, -ma f. **-2.** [fraction] undécimo m; see also **sixth**.

eleventh hour n fig: at the ~ a última hora.

elf [elf] (pl **elves**) n duende m, elfo m.

elicit [ɪ'lɪsɪt] vt fml **-1.** [response, reaction]: to ~ sthg (from sb) provocar algo (en alguien). **-2.** [information]: to ~ sthg (from sb) sacar algo (a alguien).

eligibility [,elɪdʒə'bɪlətɪ] n **-1.** [suitability] elegibilidad f. **-2.** dated [of bachelor] idoneidad f.

eligible ['elɪdʒəbl] adj **-1.** [suitable, qualified] elegible; to be ~ for sthg/to do sthg reunir los requisitos para algo/para hacer algo. **-2.** dated [marriageable]: to be ~ ser un buen partido.

eliminate [ɪ'lɪmɪneɪt] vt eliminar; to be ~d from sthg ser eliminado(da) de algo.

elimination [ɪ,lɪmɪ'neɪʃn] n eliminación f.

elite [ɪ'liːt] ◇ adj selecto(ta). ◇ n élite f.

elitism [ɪ'liːtɪzm] n pej elitismo m.

elitist [ɪ'liːtɪst] pej ◇ adj elitista. ◇ n elitista m y f.

elixir [ɪ'lɪksər] n literary lit & fig elixir m.

Elizabethan [ɪ,lɪzə'biːθn] ◇ adj isabelino(na). ◇ n isabelino m, -na f.

elk [elk] (pl inv OR **-s**) n alce m.

ellipse [ɪ'lɪps] n elipse f.

elliptical [ɪ'lɪptɪkl] adj elíptico(ca).

elm [elm] n: ~ (**tree**) olmo m.

elocution [,elə'kjuːʃn] n dicción f.

elongated ['iːlɒŋgeɪtɪd] adj alargado(da).

elope [ɪ'ləʊp] vi: to ~ (**with**) fugarse (con).

elopement [ɪ'ləʊpmənt] n fuga f.

eloquence ['eləkwəns] n elocuencia f.

eloquent ['eləkwənt] adj elocuente.

eloquently ['eləkwəntlɪ] adv elocuentemente.

El Salvador [,el'sælvədɔːr] n El Salvador.

else [els] adv: anything ~? ¿algo más?; I don't need anything ~ no necesito nada más; everyone ~ todos los demás (todas las demás); everywhere ~ en/a todas las otras partes; little ~ poco más; nothing/nobody ~ nada/nadie más; someone/something ~ otra persona/cosa; some-

where ~ en/a otra parte; who ~? ¿quién si no?; what ~? ¿qué más?; where ~? ¿en/a qué otro sitio?
◆ **or else** conj **-1.** [or if not] si no, de lo contrario. **-2.** [as threat]: you had better watch it, or ~ ándate con cuidado, o verás.

elsewhere [els'weər] adv a/en otra parte.

ELT (abbr of English language teaching) n enseñanza del inglés.

elucidate [ɪ'luːsɪdeɪt] fml ◇ vt elucidar. ◇ vi aclararse.

elude [ɪ'luːd] vt [gen] escaparse de, eludir a; [blow] esquivar; his name ~s me no consigo recordar su nombre.

elusive [ɪ'luːsɪv] adj [person, success] esquivo(va); [quality] difícil de encontrar.

elves [elvz] pl → **elf**.

'em [əm] pron inf = **them**.

emaciated [ɪ'meɪʃɪeɪtɪd] adj demacrado(da).

E-mail (abbr of electronic mail) n COMPUT correo m electrónico.

emanate ['eməneɪt] fml ◇ vt emanar. ◇ vi: to ~ from emanar de.

emancipate [ɪ'mænsɪpeɪt] vt: to ~ sb (from) emancipar a alguien (de).

emancipation [ɪ,mænsɪ'peɪʃn] n: ~ (from) emancipación f (de).

emasculate [ɪ'mæskjʊleɪt] vt fml [weaken] debilitar, minar.

emasculation [ɪ,mæskjʊ'leɪʃn] n fml [weakening] debilitación f.

embalm [ɪm'bɑːm] vt embalsamar.

embankment [ɪm'bæŋkmənt] n **-1.** RAIL terraplén m. **-2.** [of river] dique m.

embargo [em'bɑːgəʊ] (pl **-es**, pt & pp **-ed**, cont **-ing**) ◇ n: ~ (**on**) embargo m OR prohibición f (de). ◇ vt embargar, prohibir.

embark [ɪm'bɑːk] vi: to ~ on lit & fig embarcarse en.

embarkation [,embɑː'keɪʃn] n [gen] embarque m; [of troops] embarco m.

embarkation card n Br tarjeta f de embarque.

embarrass [ɪm'bærəs] vt **-1.** [gen] avergonzar; it ~es me me da vergüenza. **-2.** [financially] poner en un aprieto.

embarrassed [ɪm'bærəst] adj avergonzado(da), violento(ta).

embarrassing [ɪm'bærəsɪŋ] adj embarazoso(sa), violento(ta); how ~! ¡qué vergüenza!

embarrassment [ɪm'bærəsmənt] n **-1.** [feeling] vergüenza f, pena f Amer. **-2.** [embarrassing person or thing]: to be an ~ to sb poner a alguien en una situación de lo más embarazosa.

embassy ['embəsɪ] (*pl* **-ies**) *n* embajada *f*.

embattled [ɪm'bætld] *adj* [troubled] asediado(da), acosado(da).

embedded [ɪm'bedɪd] *adj* **-1.** [buried]: ~ **(in)** incrustado(da) (en). **-2.** [ingrained]: ~ **(in)** arraigado(da) (en).

embellish [ɪm'belɪʃ] *vt*: **to ~ sthg (with)** adornar OR embellecer algo (con).

embers ['embəz] *npl* brasas *fpl*, rescoldos *mpl*.

embezzle [ɪm'bezl] *vt* malversar.

embezzlement [ɪm'bezlmənt] *n* malversación *f*.

embezzler [ɪm'bezlər] *n* malversador *m*, -ra *f*.

embittered [ɪm'bɪtəd] *adj* amargado(da), resentido(da).

emblazoned [ɪm'bleɪznd] *adj* **-1.** [in heraldry]: ~ **(on/with)** blasonado(da) (en/con). **-2.** [shown prominently]: ~ **across** estampado(da) en.

emblem ['embləm] *n* emblema *m*.

embodiment [ɪm'bɒdɪmənt] *n* personificación *f*, encarnación *f*.

embody [ɪm'bɒdɪ] (*pt* & *pp* **-ied**) *vt* personificar, encarnar; **to be embodied in sthg** estar plasmado en algo.

embolism ['embəlɪzm] *n* embolia *f*.

embossed [ɪm'bɒst] *adj* **-1.** [heading, design]: ~ **(on)** [paper] estampado(da) (en); [leather, metal] repujado(da) (en). **-2.** [paper]: ~ **(with)** estampado(da) (con). **-3.** [leather, metal]: ~ **(with)** repujado(da) (con).

embrace [ɪm'breɪs] ◇ *n* abrazo *m*. ◇ *vt* **-1.** [hug] abrazar, dar un abrazo a. **-2.** *fml* [convert to] convertirse a, abrazar. **-3.** *fml* [include] abarcar. ◇ *vi* abrazarse.

embrocation [,embrə'keɪʃn] *n fml* embrocación *f*, ungüento *m*.

embroider [ɪm'brɔɪdər] ◇ *vt* **-1.** SEWING bordar. **-2.** *pej* [embellish] adornar. ◇ *vi* SEWING bordar.

embroidered [ɪm'brɔɪdəd] *adj* SEWING bordado(da).

embroidery [ɪm'brɔɪdərɪ] *n* (*U*) bordado *m*.

embroil [ɪm'brɔɪl] *vt*: **to get/be ~ed (in)** enredarse/estar enredado (en).

embryo ['embrɪəʊ] (*pl* **-s**) *n* embrión *m*; **in ~ fig** en embrión, en estado embrionario.

embryonic [,embrɪ'ɒnɪk] *adj* embrionario(ria).

emcee [,em'siː] (*abbr of* **master of ceremonies**) *n Am inf* presentador *m*, -ra *f*.

emend [ɪ'mend] *vt* enmendar, corregir.

emerald ['emərəld] ◇ *adj* [colour] esmeralda

m inv; ~ **green** verde *m* esmeralda. ◇ *n* [stone] esmeralda *f*.

emerge [ɪ'mɜːdʒ] ◇ *vi* **-1.** [gen]: **to ~ (from)** salir (de). **-2.** [come into existence, become known] surgir, emerger. ◇ *vt*: **it ~d that ...** resultó que ....

emergence [ɪ'mɜːdʒəns] *n* surgimiento *m*, aparición *f*.

emergency [ɪ'mɜːdʒənsɪ] (*pl* **-ies**) ◇ *adj* [case, exit, services] de emergencia; [ward] de urgencia; [supplies] de reserva; [meeting] extraordinario(ria). ◇ *n* emergencia *f*.

emergency exit *n* salida *f* de emergencia.

emergency landing *n* aterrizaje *m* forzoso.

emergency services *npl* servicios *mpl* de urgencia.

emergency stop *n* frenazo *m* en seco.

emergent [ɪ'mɜːdʒənt] *adj* pujante, emergente.

emery board ['emərɪ-] *n* lima *f* de uñas.

emetic [ɪ'metɪk] ◇ *adj* emético(ca). ◇ *n* emético *m*.

emigrant ['emɪgrənt] *n* emigrante *m y f*.

emigrate ['emɪgreɪt] *vi*: **to ~ (to/from)** emigrar (a/de).

emigration [,emɪ'greɪʃn] *n* emigración *f*.

émigré ['emɪgreɪ] *n fml* emigrado político *m*, emigrada política *f*.

eminence ['emɪnəns] *n* (*U*) [prominence] eminencia *f*.

eminent ['emɪnənt] *adj* eminente.

eminently ['emɪnəntlɪ] *adv fml* eminentemente, sumamente.

emir [e'mɪər] *n* emir *m*.

emirate ['emərət] *n* emirato *m*.

emissary ['emɪsərɪ] (*pl* **-ies**) *n fml* emisario *m*, -ria *f*.

emission [ɪ'mɪʃn] *n* emisión *f*.

emit [ɪ'mɪt] (*pt* & *pp* **-ted**, *cont* **-ting**) *vt* [gen] emitir; [smell, smoke] despedir.

emollient [ɪ'mɒlɪənt] *n* MED emoliente *m*.

emolument [ɪ'mɒljumənt] *n fml* emolumento *m*.

emotion [ɪ'məʊʃn] *n* emoción *f*.

emotional [ɪ'məʊʃənl] *adj* **-1.** [gen] emotivo(va). **-2.** [needs, problems] emocional.

emotionally [ɪ'məʊʃnəlɪ] *adv* **-1.** [with strong feeling] emotivamente. **-2.** [psychologically] emocionalmente.

emotionless [ɪ'məʊʃnlɪs] *adj* desapasionado(da).

emotive [ɪ'məʊtɪv] *adj* emotivo(va); [issue] candente.

empathy ['empəθɪ] *n*: ~ **(with)** empatía *f* (con).

emperor ['empərər] *n* emperador *m*.

emphasis ['emfəsɪs] (*pl* **-ases** [-əsiːz]) *n*: ~ **(on)** énfasis *m inv* (en); **to lay** OR **place** ~ **on** poner énfasis en, hacer hincapié en.

emphasize, -ise ['emfəsaɪz] *vt* [word, syllable] acentuar; [point, fact, feature] subrayar, hacer hincapié en; **to** ~ **that** ... poner de relieve OR subrayar que ....

emphatic [ɪm'fætɪk] *adj* [forceful] rotundo(da), categórico(ca).

emphatically [ɪm'fætɪklɪ] *adv* **-1.** [with emphasis] rotundamente, enfáticamente. **-2.** [certainly] ciertamente.

emphysema [,emfɪ'siːmə] *n* enfisema *m*.

empire ['empaɪər] *n* imperio *m*.

empire building *n* construcción *f* de imperios económicos.

empirical [ɪm'pɪrɪkl] *adj* empírico(ca).

empiricism [ɪm'pɪrɪsɪzm] *n* empirismo *m*.

employ [ɪm'plɔɪ] *vt* **-1.** [give work to] emplear; **to be ~ed as** estar empleado de. **-2.** *fml* [use] utilizar, emplear; **to** ~ **sthg as sthg/to do sthg** utilizar algo de algo/para hacer algo.

employable [ɪm'plɔɪəbl] *adj* en situación de trabajar.

employee [ɪm'plɔɪiː] *n* empleado *m*, -da *f*.

employer [ɪm'plɔɪər] *n* patrono *m*, -na *f*, empresario *m*, -ria *f*.

employment [ɪm'plɔɪmənt] *n* empleo *m*; **to be in** ~ tener trabajo.

employment agency *n* agencia *f* de trabajo.

employment office *n* oficina *f* de empleo.

emporium [em'pɔːrɪəm] *n* [shop] almacenes *mpl*, tienda *f* grande.

empower [ɪm'paʊər] *vt fml*: **to be ~ed to do sthg** estar autorizado(da) a OR para hacer algo.

empress ['emprɪs] *n* emperatriz *f*.

emptiness ['emptɪnɪs] *n* (*U*) **-1.** [of place] soledad *f*, vacuidad *f*. **-2.** [feeling] vacío *m*.

empty ['emptɪ] (*compar* **-ier**, *superl* **-iest**, *pt* & *pp* **-ied**, *pl* **-ies**) ◇ *adj* **-1.** [gen] vacío(a); [town] desierto(ta). **-2.** *pej* [words, threat, promise] vano(na). ◇ *vt* vaciar; **to** ~ **sthg into sthg** vaciar algo en algo; **to** ~ **the water out of the bottle** vaciar de agua la botella. ◇ *vi* vaciarse. ◇ *n inf* casco *m*.

empty-handed [-'hændɪd] *adv* con las manos vacías.

empty-headed [-'hedɪd] *adj pej* cabeza hueca, bobo(ba).

EMS (*abbr of* **European Monetary System**) *n* SME *m*.

EMT (*abbr of* **emergency medical technician**) *n* médico ayudante de urgencias.

emu ['iːmjuː] (*pl inv* OR **-s**) *n* emú *m*.

emulate ['emjʊleɪt] *vt* emular.

emulsion [ɪ'mʌlʃn] ◇ *n* **-1.** ~ **(paint)** pintura *f* mate. **-2.** PHOT emulsión *f*. ◇ *vt Br* pintar con pintura mate.

enable [ɪ'neɪbl] *vt*: **to** ~ **sb to do sthg** permitir a alguien hacer algo.

enact [ɪ'nækt] *vt* **-1.** JUR promulgar. **-2.** [act] representar.

enactment [ɪ'næktmənt] *n* JUR promulgación *f*.

enamel [ɪ'næml] *n* **-1.** [gen] esmalte *m*. **-2.** [paint] pintura *f* de esmalte.

enamelled *Br*, **enameled** *Am* [ɪ'næmld] *adj* esmaltado(da).

enamel paint *n* pintura *f* de esmalte.

enamoured *Br*, **enamored** *Am* [ɪ'næməd] *adj*: ~ **of** [thing] entusiasmado(da) con; [person] enamorado(da) de.

en bloc [ã'blɒk] *adv fml* en bloque.

enc. (*abbr of* **enclosure, enclosed**) adj.

encamp [ɪn'kæmp] *vi* acampar.

encampment [ɪn'kæmpmənt] *n* campamento *m*.

encapsulate [ɪn'kæpsjʊleɪt] *vt*: **to** ~ **sthg (in)** sintetizar algo (en).

encase [ɪn'keɪs] *vt*: **~d in** encajonado(da) en.

encash [ɪn'kæʃ] *vt Br* cobrar, hacer efectivo.

enchanted [ɪn'tʃɑːntɪd] *adj*: ~ **(by** OR **with)** encantado(da) (con).

enchanting [ɪn'tʃɑːntɪŋ] *adj* encantador(ra).

encircle [ɪn'sɜːkl] *vt* rodear.

enclave ['enkleɪv] *n* enclave *m*.

enclose [ɪn'kləʊz] *vt* **-1.** [surround, contain] rodear; **~d by** OR **with** rodeado de; **an ~d space** un espacio cerrado. **-2.** [put in envelope] adjuntar; **please find ~d** ... envío adjunto ....

enclosure [ɪn'kləʊʒər] *n* **-1.** [place] recinto *m* (vallado). **-2.** [in letter] anexo *m*, documento *m* adjunto.

encompass [ɪn'kʌmpəs] *vt fml* **-1.** [include] abarcar. **-2.** [surround] rodear.

encore ['ɒŋkɔːr] ◇ *n* bis *m*. ◇ *excl* ¡otra!

encounter [ɪn'kaʊntər] ◇ *n* encuentro *m*. ◇ *vt fml* encontrarse con.

encourage [ɪn'kʌrɪdʒ] *vt* **-1.** [give confidence to]: **to** ~ **sb (to do sthg)** animar a alguien (a hacer algo). **-2.** [foster] fomentar.

encouragement [ɪn'kʌrɪdʒmənt] *n* ánimo *m*, aliento *m*; [of industry] fomento *m*.

encouraging [ɪn'kʌrɪdʒɪŋ] *adj* alentador(ra), esperanzador(ra).

encroach [ɪn'krəʊtʃ] *vi*: **to ~ on** OR **upon** [rights, territory] usurpar; [privacy, time] invadir.

encrusted [ɪn'krʌstɪd] *adj*: ~ **with** incrustado(da) de.

encumber [ɪn'kʌmbər] *vt fml*: **to be ~ed with** tener que cargar con.

encyclop(a)edia [ɪn,saɪklə'piːdjə] *n* enciclopedia *f*.

encyclop(a)edic [ɪn,saɪkləʊ'piːdɪk] *adj* enciclopédico(ca).

end [end] ◇ *n* **-1.** [last part, finish] fin *m*, final *m*; **at the ~ of May/1992** a finales de mayo/1992; **at an ~** terminando; **to bring sthg to an ~** poner fin a algo; **to come to an ~** llegar a su fin, terminarse; **"the ~"** [in films] "FIN"; **to put an ~ to sthg** poner fin a algo; **at the ~ of the day** *fig* a fin de cuentas, al fin y al cabo; **in the ~** [finally] finalmente, por fin. **-2.** [of two-ended thing] extremo *m*, punta *f*; [of phone line] lado *m*; ~ **to ~** extremo con extremo; **to turn sthg on its ~** poner algo boca abajo; **cigarette ~** colilla *f*. **-3.** *fml* [purpose] fin *m*, objetivo *m*; **an ~ in itself** un fin en sí mismo. **-4.** *literary* [death] final *m*.
◇ *vt*: **to ~ sthg (with)** terminar algo (con).
◇ *vi* [finish] acabarse, terminarse; **to ~ in/.with** acabar en/con, terminar en/con.
◆ **no end** *adv inf*: **it cheered me up no ~** no paraba de alegrarme, me alegraba un montón.
◆ **no end of** *prep. inf* la mar de.
◆ **on end** *adv* **-1.** [upright - hair] de punta; [- object] de pie. **-2.** [continuously]: **for days on ~** día tras día.
◆ **end up** *vi* acabar, terminar; **to ~ up doing sthg** acabar por hacer algo/haciendo algo, terminar por hacer algo/haciendo algo; **to ~ up in** ir a parar a.

endanger [ɪn'deɪndʒər] *vt* poner en peligro.

endangered species [ɪn'deɪndʒəd-] *n* especie *f* en peligro de extinción.

endear [ɪn'dɪər] *vt*: **to ~ sb to sb** hacer que alguien congenie con alguien; **to ~ o.s. to sb** hacerse querer por alguien.

endearing [ɪn'dɪərɪŋ] *adj* atrayente, simpático(ca).

endearment [ɪn'dɪəmənt] *n fml* palabra *f* tierna OR cariñosa.

endeavour *Br*, **endeavor** *Am* [ɪn'devər] *fml* ◇ *n* esfuerzo *m*. ◇ *vt*: **to ~ to do sthg** procurar hacer algo.

endemic [en'demɪk] *adj lit* & *fig* endémico(ca).

ending ['endɪŋ] *n* final *m*, desenlace *m*.

endive ['endaɪv] *n* **-1.** [salad vegetable] endibia *f*. **-2.** [chicory] achicoria *f*.

endless ['endlɪs] *adj* [gen] interminable; [patience, resources] inagotable.

endlessly ['endlɪslɪ] *adv* interminablemente; [patient, kind] infinitamente.

endorse [ɪn'dɔːs] *vt* **-1.** [approve] apoyar, respaldar. **-2.** [cheque] endosar. **-3.** *Br* AUT: **to ~ a driving licence** hacer constar una sanción en el carnet de conducir.

endorsement [ɪn'dɔːsmənt] *n* **-1.** [approval] apoyo *m*, respaldo *m*. **-2.** [of cheque] endoso *m*. **-3.** *Br* [on driving licence] nota de sanción que consta en el carnet de conducir.

endow [ɪn'dau] *vt* **-1.** *fml* [equip]: **to be ~ed with** estar dotado(da) de. **-2.** [donate money to] donar fondos a.

endowment [ɪn'daumənt] *n* **-1.** *fml* [ability] dote *f*. **-2.** [gift of money] donación *f*.

endowment insurance *n* seguro *m* de vida.

endowment mortgage *n* hipoteca mixta en la que se pagan los plazos a un seguro de vida y los intereses al acreedor.

end product *n* producto *m* final.

end result *n* resultado *m* final.

endurable [ɪn'djuərəbl] *adj* tolerable.

endurance [ɪn'djuərəns] *n* resistencia *f*.

endurance test *n* prueba *f* de resistencia.

endure [ɪn'djuə] ◇ *vt* soportar, aguantar. ◇ *vi fml* perdurar.

enduring [ɪn'djuərɪŋ] *adj fml* perdurable.

end user *n* COMPUT usuario *m* último OR final.

endways *Br* ['endweɪz], **endwise** *Am* ['endwaɪz] *adv* **-1.** [not sideways] de frente. **-2.** [with ends touching] extremo con extremo.

enema ['enɪmə] *n* enema *m*.

enemy ['enɪmɪ] (*pl* **-ies**) ◇ *n* enemigo *m*, -ga *f*. ◇ *comp* enemigo(ga).

energetic [,enə'dʒetɪk] *adj* **-1.** [lively, physically taxing] enérgico(ca). **-2.** [enthusiastic] activo(va), vigoroso(sa).

energy ['enədʒɪ] (*pl* **-ies**) *n* energía *f*.

energy-saving *adj* ahorrador(ra) de energía.

enervate ['enəveɪt] *vt fml* enervar, debilitar.

enervating ['enəveɪtɪŋ] *adj fml* enervante.

enfold [ɪn'fəʊld] *vt literary*: **to ~ sthg/sb (in)** envolver algo/a alguien (en).

enforce [ɪn'fɔːs] *vt* [law] hacer cumplir, aplicar; [standards] imponer.

enforceable [ɪn'fɔːsəbl] *adj* aplicable.

enforced [ɪn'fɔːst] *adj* inevitable, forzoso(sa).

enforcement [ɪn'fɔːsmənt] *n* aplicación *f*.

enfranchise [ɪnˈfræntʃaɪz] *vt* **-1.** [give vote to] conceder el derecho a votar a. **-2.** [set free] manumitir.

engage [ɪnˈɡeɪdʒ] ◇ *vt* **-1.** [attract] atraer; **to ~ sb in conversation** entablar conversación con alguien. **-2.** [TECH - clutch] pisar; [- gear] meter. **-3.** *fml* [employ] contratar; **to be ~d in** OR **on** dedicarse a, estar ocupado(da) en. ◇ *vi* [be involved]: **to ~ in** [gen] meterse en, dedicarse a; [conversation] entablar.

engaged [ɪnˈɡeɪdʒd] *adj* **-1.** [to be married]: **~ (to)** prometido(da) (con); **to get ~** prometerse. **-2.** [busy, in use] ocupado(da); **~ in sthg** ocupado en algo. **-3.** TELEC comunicando.

engaged tone *n Br* señal *f* de comunicando.

engagement [ɪnˈɡeɪdʒmənt] *n* **-1.** [to be married] compromiso *m*; [period] noviazgo *m*. **-2.** [appointment] cita *f*, compromiso *m*.

engagement ring *n* anillo *m* de compromiso.

engaging [ɪnˈɡeɪdʒɪŋ] *adj* atractivo(va).

engender [ɪnˈdʒendər] *vt fml* engendrar.

engine [ˈendʒɪn] *n* **-1.** [of vehicle] motor *m*. **-2.** RAIL locomotora *f*, máquina *f*.

engine driver *n Br* maquinista *m y f*.

engineer [ˌendʒɪˈnɪər] ◇ *n* **-1.** [gen] ingeniero *m*, -ra *f*. **-2.** *Am* [engine driver] maquinista *m y f*. ◇ *vt* **-1.** [construct] construir. **-2.** [contrive] tramar.

engineering [ˌendʒɪˈnɪərɪŋ] *n* ingeniería *f*.

England [ˈɪŋɡlənd] *n* Inglaterra *f*.

English [ˈɪŋɡlɪʃ] ◇ *adj* inglés(esa). ◇ *n* [language] inglés *m*. ◇ *npl* [people]: **the ~** los ingleses.

English breakfast *n* desayuno *m* inglés.

ENGLISH BREAKFAST:
El desayuno tradicional inglés consiste en un plato caliente (huevos con beicon, por ejemplo), cereales o 'porridge', y tostadas con mermelada de naranja, todo acompañado de café o té; actualmente se tiende a sustituirlo por algo más ligero

English Channel *n*: **the ~** el canal de la Mancha.

Englishman [ˈɪŋɡlɪʃmən] (*pl* **-men** [-mən]) *n* inglés *m*.

English muffin *n Am* ≃ bollo *m*.

Englishwoman [ˈɪŋɡlɪʃˌwʊmən] (*pl* **-women** [-ˌwɪmən]) *n* inglesa *f*.

engrave [ɪnˈɡreɪv] *vt lit & fig*: **to ~ sthg (on)** grabar algo (en).

engraver [ɪnˈɡreɪvər] *n* grabador *m*, -ra *f*.

engraving [ɪnˈɡreɪvɪŋ] *n* grabado *m*.

engrossed [ɪnˈɡrəʊst] *adj*: **to be ~ (in)** estar absorto(ta) (en).

engrossing [ɪnˈɡrəʊsɪŋ] *adj* absorbente.

engulf [ɪnˈɡʌlf] *vt*: **to be ~ed in** [flames etc] verse devorado(da) por; [fear, despair] verse sumido(da) en.

enhance [ɪnˈhɑːns] *vt* [gen] aumentar, acrecentar; [status, position] elevar; [beauty] realzar.

enhancement [ɪnˈhɑːnsmənt] *n* [gen] aumento *m*; [of status, position] elevación *f*; [of beauty] realce *m*.

enigma [ɪˈnɪɡmə] *n* enigma *m*.

enigmatic [ˌenɪɡˈmætɪk] *adj* enigmático(ca).

enjoy [ɪnˈdʒɔɪ] ◇ *vt* **-1.** [like] disfrutar de; **did you ~ the film/book?** ¿te gustó la película/el libro?; **she ~s reading** le gusta leer; **~ your meal!** ¡que aproveche!, ¡buen provecho!; **to ~ o.s.** pasarlo bien, divertirse. **-2.** *fml* [possess] gozar OR disfrutar de. ◇ *vi Am*: **~!** [enjoy yourself] ¡que lo pases bien!; [before meal] ¡que aproveche!

enjoyable [ɪnˈdʒɔɪəbl] *adj* agradable.

enjoyment [ɪnˈdʒɔɪmənt] *n* **-1.** [pleasure] placer *m*. **-2.** [possession] disfrute *m*, posesión *f*.

enlarge [ɪnˈlɑːdʒ] *vt* [gen & PHOT] ampliar.

◆ **enlarge (up)on** *vt fus* ampliar, explicar con detalle.

enlargement [ɪnˈlɑːdʒmənt] *n* [gen & PHOT] ampliación *f*.

enlighten [ɪnˈlaɪtn] *vt fml* aclarar, iluminar.

enlightened [ɪnˈlaɪtnd] *adj* amplio(plia) de miras.

enlightening [ɪnˈlaɪtnɪŋ] *adj* instructivo(va), informativo(va).

enlightenment [ɪnˈlaɪtnmənt] *n* (U) aclaración *f*.

◆ **Enlightenment** *n*: **the Enlightenment** la Ilustración.

enlist [ɪnˈlɪst] ◇ *vt* **-1.** [person] alistar, reclutar. **-2.** [support] obtener. ◇ *vi* MIL: **to ~ (in)** alistarse (en).

enlisted man [ɪnˈlɪstɪd-] *n Am* recluta *m*.

enliven [ɪnˈlaɪvn] *vt* avivar, animar.

en masse [ˌɒnˈmæs] *adv* en masa.

enmeshed [ɪnˈmeʃt] *adj*: **to be ~ in** estar enredado(da) en.

enmity [ˈenmɪtɪ] (*pl* **-ies**) *n* enemistad *f*.

ennoble [ɪˈnəʊbl] *vt* ennoblecer.

enormity [ɪˈnɔːmətɪ] *n* [extent] enormidad *f*.

enormous [ɪˈnɔːməs] *adj* enorme.

enormously [ɪˈnɔːməslɪ] *adv* enormemente.

enough [ɪˈnʌf] ◇ *adj* bastante, suficiente. ◇ *pron* bastante; **more than ~** más que suficiente; **that's ~** [sufficient] ya está bien;

~ **is** ~ ya basta, ya está bien; **that's** ~ **(of that)!** ¡basta ya!; **to have had** ~ **(of)** [expressing annoyance] **estar harto (de).**

◇ *adv* bastante, suficientemente; **I was stupid** ~ **to believe him** fui lo bastante tonto como para creerle; **he was good** ~ **to lend me his car** *fml* tuvo la bondad de dejarme su coche; **strangely** ~ curiosamente.

enquire [ɪn'kwaɪə^r] *vi* [ask for information] informarse, pedir información; **to** ~ **about** sthg informarse de algo; **to** ~ **when/how/whether/if** ... preguntar cuándo/cómo/si ....

♦ **enquire after** *vt fus* preguntar por.

♦ **enquire into** *vt fus* investigar.

enquiry [ɪn'kwaɪərɪ] (*pl* **-ies**) *n* **-1.** [question] pregunta *f;* **"Enquiries"** "Información". **-2.** [investigation] investigación *f.*

enraged [ɪn'reɪdʒd] *adj* enfurecido(da).

enrich [ɪn'rɪtʃ] *vt* enriquecer; [soil] fertilizar.

enrol *Br* (*pt* & *pp* **-led,** *cont* **-ling**), **enroll** *Am* [ɪn'rəʊl] ◇ *vt* matricular. ◇ *vi:* **to** ~ **(on)** matricularse (en).

enrolment *Br,* **enrollment** *Am* [ɪn'rəʊlmənt] *n* (*U*) matrícula *f,* inscripción *f.*

en route [,ɒn'ruːt] *adv:* ~ **(from/to)** en el camino (de/a).

ensconced [ɪn'skɒnst] *adj fml:* ~ **(in)** repantigado(da) OR arrellanado(da) (en).

enshrine [ɪn'ʃraɪn] *vt:* **to be** ~d **in sthg** estar amparado(da) OR salvaguardado(da) por algo.

ensign ['ensaɪn] *n* **-1.** [flag] bandera *f,* enseña *f.* **-2.** *Am* [sailor] ≃ alférez *m* de fragata.

enslave [ɪn'sleɪv] *vt* esclavizar.

ensue [ɪn'sjuː] *vi fml* originarse; [war] sobrevenir.

ensuing [ɪn'sjuːɪŋ] *adj fml* subsiguiente.

ensure [ɪn'ʃɔː^r] *vt:* **to** ~ **(that)** asegurar que.

ENT (*abbr of* **Ear, Nose & Throat**) *n* otorrinolaringología *f.*

entail [ɪn'teɪl] *vt* [involve] conllevar, suponer.

entangled [ɪn'tæŋgld] *adj* **-1.** [gen]: **to be** ~ **(in)** estar enredado(da) (en). **-2.** [emotionally]: **to be** ~ **with sb** tener un lío con alguien.

entanglement [ɪn'tæŋglmənt] *n* [emotional] lío *m.*

enter ['entə^r] ◇ *vt* **-1.** [gen] entrar en. **-2.** [join - profession, parliament] ingresar en; [- university] matricularse en; [- army, navy] alistarse en. **-3.** [become involved in - politics etc] meterse en; [- race, examination etc] presentarse a. **-4.** [register]: **to** ~ **sthg/sb for sthg** inscribir algo/a alguien en algo. **-5.** [write down] anotar, apuntar. **-6.** [appear in]

presentarse OR aparecer en. **-7.** COMPUT meter, dar entrada a.

◇ *vi* **-1.** [come or go in] entrar. **-2.** [participate]: **to** ~ **(for sthg)** presentarse (a algo).

♦ **enter into** *vt fus* entrar en; [agreement] comprometerse a.

enteritis [,entə'raɪtɪs] *n* enteritis *f inv.*

enter key *n* COMPUT tecla *f* de entrada.

enterprise ['entəpraɪz] *n* empresa *f.*

enterprise culture *n* cultura *f* empresarial.

enterprise zone *n zona del Reino Unido donde se fomenta la actividad industrial y empresarial.*

enterprising ['entəpraɪzɪŋ] *adj* emprendedor(ra).

entertain [,entə'teɪn] ◇ *vt* **-1.** [amuse] divertir, entretener. **-2.** [invite] recibir (en casa). **-3.** *fml* [idea, proposal] considerar. **-4.** *fml* [hopes, ambitions] abrigar. ◇ *vi* **-1.** [amuse] divertir, entretener. **-2.** [have guests] recibir.

entertainer [,entə'teɪnə^r] *n* artista *m y f.*

entertaining [,entə'teɪnɪŋ] ◇ *adj* divertido(da), entretenido(da). ◇ *n* (*U*): **she does a lot of** ~ siempre tiene invitados en casa.

entertainment [,entə'teɪnmənt] ◇ *n* **-1.** (*U*) [amusement] diversión *f,* entretenimiento *m,* entretención *f Amer.* **-2.** [show] espectáculo *m.* ◇ *comp* del espectáculo.

entertainment allowance *n* gastos *mpl* de representación.

enthral (*pt* & *pp* **-led,** *cont* **-ling**), **enthrall** *Am* [ɪn'θrɔːl] *vt* cautivar, embelesar.

enthralling [ɪn'θrɔːlɪŋ] *adj* cautivador(ra).

enthrone [ɪn'θrəʊn] *vt fml* entronizar.

enthuse [ɪn'θjuːz] *vi:* **to** ~ **(about)** entusiasmarse (por).

enthusiasm [ɪn'θjuːzɪæzm] *n* **-1.** [passion, eagerness]: ~ **(for)** entusiasmo *m* (por). **-2.** [interest] pasión *f,* interés *m.*

enthusiast [ɪn'θjuːzɪæst] *n* entusiasta *m y f.*

enthusiastic [ɪn,θjuːzɪ'æstɪk] *adj* [person] entusiasta; [cry, response] entusiástico(ca).

enthusiastically [ɪn,θjuːzɪ'æstɪklɪ] *adv* con entusiasmo.

entice [ɪn'taɪs] *vt* seducir, atraer.

enticing [ɪn'taɪsɪŋ] *adj* tentador(ra), atractivo(va).

entire [ɪn'taɪə^r] *adj* entero(ra); **the** ~ **evening** toda la noche.

entirely [ɪn'taɪəlɪ] *adv* enteramente; **I'm not** ~ **sure** no estoy del todo seguro.

entirety [ɪn'taɪrətɪ] *n fml:* **in its** ~ en su totalidad.

entitle [ɪn'taɪtl] *vt* [allow]: **to** ~ **sb to sthg**

dar a alguien derecho a algo; **to ~ sb to do sthg** autorizar a alguien a hacer algo.

entitled [ɪn'taɪtld] *adj* **-1.** [allowed]: **to be ~ to sthg/to do sthg** tener derecho a algo/a hacer algo. **-2.** [having the title] titulado(da).

entitlement [ɪn'taɪtlmənt] *n* derecho *m*.

entity ['entətɪ] (*pl* **-ies**) *n* entidad *f*.

entomology [,entə'mɒlədʒɪ] *n* entomología *f*.

entourage [,ɒntʊ'rɑːʒ] *n* séquito *m*.

entrails ['entreɪlz] *npl* entrañas *fpl*.

entrance [*n* 'entrəns, *vt* ɪn'trɑːns] ◇ *n*: **~ (to)** entrada *f* (a OR de); **to gain ~ to** *fml* [building] lograr acceso a; [society, university] lograr el ingreso en. ◇ *vt* encantar, hechizar.

entrance examination *n* examen *m* de ingreso.

entrance fee *n* (precio *m* de) entrada *f*.

entrancing [ɪn'trɑːnsɪŋ] *adj* encantador(ra), cautivador(ra).

entrant ['entrənt] *n* participante *m* y *f*.

entreat [ɪn'triːt] *vt*: **to ~ sb (to do sthg)** suplicar OR rogar a alguien (que haga algo).

entreaty [ɪn'triːtɪ] (*pl* **-ies**) *n* ruego *m*, súplica *f*.

entrenched [ɪn'trentʃt] *adj* [firm] arraigado(da).

entrepreneur [,ɒntrəprə'nɜːr] *n* empresario *m*, -ria *f*.

entrepreneurial [,ɒntrəprə'nɜːrɪəl] *adj* empresarial.

entrust [ɪn'trʌst] *vt*: **to ~ sthg to sb, to ~ sb with sthg** confiar algo a alguien.

entry ['entrɪ] (*pl* **-ies**) *n* **-1.** [gen]: **~ (into)** entrada *f* (en); **no ~** se prohíbe la entrada, prohibido el paso. **-2.** *fig* [joining - of group, society] ingreso *m*. **-3.** [in competition] participante *m* y *f*. **-4.** [in diary] anotación *f*; [in ledger] partida *f*.

entry fee *n* [for cinema, museum] entrada *f*; [for organization] cuota *f* (de ingreso).

entry form *n* boleto *m* OR impreso *m* de inscripción.

entry phone *n* Br portero *m* automático.

entryway ['entrɪ,weɪ] *n* Am camino *m* de entrada.

entwine [ɪn'twaɪn] ◇ *vt* entrelazar. ◇ *vi* entrelazarse.

E number *n* número *m* E.

enumerate [ɪ'njuːməreɪt] *vt* enumerar.

enunciate [ɪ'nʌnsɪeɪt] ◇ *vt* **-1.** [word] pronunciar. **-2.** [idea, plan] enunciar. ◇ *vi* vocalizar.

envelop [ɪn'veləp] *vt*: **to ~ sthg/sb in** envolver algo/a alguien en.

envelope ['envələʊp] *n* sobre *m*.

enviable ['envɪəbl] *adj* envidiable.

envious ['envɪəs] *adj* [person] envidioso(sa); [look] de envidia.

enviously ['envɪəslɪ] *adv* con envidia.

environment [ɪn'vaɪərənmənt] *n* **-1.** [surroundings] ambiente *m*, entorno *m*. **-2.** [natural world]: **the ~** el medio ambiente; **Department of the Environment** Br ministerio *m* del medio ambiente. **-3.** COMPUT entorno *m*.

environmental [ɪn,vaɪərən'mentl] *adj* medioambiental, ambiental; **~ pollution** contaminación *f* del medio ambiente.

environmentalist [ɪn,vaɪərən'mentəlɪst] *n* ecologista *m* y *f*.

environmentally [ɪn,vaɪərən'mentəlɪ] *adv* ecológicamente; **~ friendly** ecológico(ca), que no daña al medio ambiente.

Environmental Protection Agency *n* Am ministerio *m* del medio ambiente.

environs [ɪn'vaɪərənz] *npl* alrededores *mpl*.

envisage [ɪn'vɪzɪdʒ], **envision** Am [ɪn'vɪʒn] *vt* prever.

envoy ['envɔɪ] *n* enviado *m*, -da *f*.

envy ['envɪ] (*pt* & *pp* **-ied**) ◇ *n* envidia *f*; **to be the ~ of** ser la envidia de; **to be green with ~** estar muerto de envidia. ◇ *vt*: **to ~ (sb sthg)** envidiar (algo a alguien).

enzyme ['enzaɪm] *n* enzima *f*.

EOC *n abbr of* **Equal Opportunities Commission**.

eon Am = **aeon**.

EP (*abbr of* **extended-play**) *n* MUS EP *m*.

EPA *n abbr of* **Environmental Protection Agency**.

epaulet(te) [,epə'let] *n* charretera *f*.

ephemeral [ɪ'femərəl] *adj* efímero(ra).

epic ['epɪk] ◇ *adj* épico(ca). ◇ *n* epopeya *f*.

epicentre Br, **epicenter** Am ['epɪsentər] *n* epicentro *m*.

epidemic [,epɪ'demɪk] *n* epidemia *f*.

epidural [,epɪ'djʊərəl] *n* epidural *f*.

epigram ['epɪɡræm] *n* epigrama *m*.

epilepsy ['epɪlepsɪ] *n* epilepsia *f*.

epileptic [,epɪ'leptɪk] ◇ *adj* epiléptico(ca). ◇ *n* epiléptico *m*, -ca *f*.

epilogue Br, **epilog** Am ['epɪlɒɡ] *n* epílogo *m*.

Epiphany [ɪ'pɪfənɪ] *n* Epifanía *f*.

episcopal [ɪ'pɪskəpl] *adj* [of bishop] episcopal.

episode ['epɪsəʊd] *n* **-1.** [event] episodio *m*. **-2.** [of story, TV series] capítulo *m*.

episodic [,epɪ'sɒdɪk] *adj* episódico(ca).

epistle [ɪ'pɪsl] *n* epístola *f*.

epitaph ['epɪtɑːf] *n* epitafio *m*.

epithet ['epɪθet] *n* epíteto *m*.

epitome [ɪ'pɪtəmɪ] *n*: **the ~ of** [person] la personificación de; [thing] el vivo ejemplo de.

epitomize, -ise [ɪ'pɪtəmaɪz] *vt* [subj: person] personificar; [subj: thing] representar el paradigma de.

epoch ['iːppk] *n* época *f*.

epoch-making *adj* histórico(ca), que hace época.

eponymous [ɪ'ppnɪməs] *adj* epónimo(ma).

EPOS ['iːpps] (*abbr of* **electronic point of sale**) *n punto de venta electrónica.*

equable ['ekwəbl] *adj* [calm, reasonable] ecuánime.

equal ['iːkwəl] (*Br pt & pp* **-led**, *cont* **-ling**, *Am pt & pp* **-ed**, *cont* **-ing**) ◇ *adj* igual; **~ to** [sum] igual a; **~ rights** igualdad de derechos; **on ~ terms** en igualdad de condiciones; **to be ~ to** [task etc] estar a la altura de. ◇ *n* igual *m y f*. ◇ *vt* **-1.** MATH ser igual a. **-2.** [person, quality] igualar.

equality [iː'kwɒlətɪ] *n* igualdad *f*.

equalize, -ise ['iːkwəlaɪz] ◇ *vt* igualar. ◇ *vi* SPORT empatar.

equalizer ['iːkwəlaɪzəʳ] *n* SPORT (gol *m* de la) igualada *f*.

equally ['iːkwəlɪ] *adv* **-1.** [gen] igualmente; **~ important** igual de importante. **-2.** [share, divide] a partes iguales, por igual.

equal opportunities *npl* igualdad *f* de oportunidades.

Equal Opportunities Commission *n organismo gubernamental británico contra la discriminación sexual.*

equal(s) sign *n* signo *m* de igualdad.

equanimity [,ekwə'nɪmətɪ] *n* ecuanimidad *f*.

equate [ɪ'kweɪt] *vt*: **to ~ sthg with** equiparar algo con.

equation [ɪ'kweɪʒn] *n* ecuación *f*.

equator [ɪ'kweɪtəʳ] *n*: **the ~** el ecuador.

equatorial [,ekwə'tɔːrɪəl] *adj* ecuatorial.

Equatorial Guinea *n* Guinea Ecuatorial *f*.

equestrian [ɪ'kwestrɪən] *adj* ecuestre.

equidistant [,iːkwɪ'dɪstənt] *adj*: **~ (from)** equidistante (de).

equilateral triangle [,iːkwɪ'lætərəl-] *n* triángulo *m* equilátero.

equilibrium [,iːkwɪ'lɪbrɪəm] *n* equilibrio *m*.

equine ['ekwaɪn] *adj* equino(na).

equinox ['iːkwɪnɒks] *n* equinoccio *m*.

equip [ɪ'kwɪp] (*pt & pp* **-ped**, *cont* **-ping**) *vt* **-1.** [provide with equipment]: **to ~ sthg (with)** equipar algo (con); **to ~ sb (with)** proveer a alguien (de). **-2.** [prepare]: **to be equipped for** estar bien dotado(da) para.

equipment [ɪ'kwɪpmənt] *n* (*U*) equipo *m*.

equitable ['ekwɪtəbl] *adj* equitativo(va).

equities ['ekwətɪz] *npl* ST EX acciones *fpl* ordinarias.

equivalent [ɪ'kwɪvələnt] ◇ *adj* equivalente; **to be ~ to** equivaler a. ◇ *n* equivalente *m*.

equivocal [ɪ'kwɪvəkl] *adj* equívoco(ca).

equivocate [ɪ'kwɪvəkeɪt] *vi* andarse con ambigüedades.

er [ɜːʳ] *excl* ¡ejem!

ER (*abbr of* **Elizabeth Regina**) *emblema de la reina Isabel.*

era ['ɪərə] (*pl* **-s**) *n* era *f*, época *f*.

ERA ['ɪərə] (*abbr of* **Equal Rights Amendment**) *n ley estadounidense de igualdad de derechos para las mujeres.*

eradicate [ɪ'rædɪkeɪt] *vt* erradicar.

eradication [ɪ,rædɪ'keɪʃn] *n* erradicación *f*.

erase [ɪ'reɪz] *vt lit & fig* borrar.

eraser [ɪ'reɪzəʳ] *n* goma *f* de borrar.

erect [ɪ'rekt] ◇ *adj* **-1.** [person, posture] erguido(da). **-2.** [penis] erecto(ta). ◇ *vt* **-1.** [building, statue] erigir, levantar. **-2.** [tent] montar.

erection [ɪ'rekʃn] *n* **-1.** (*U*) [of building, statue] construcción *f*. **-2.** [erect penis] erección *f*.

ergonomics [,ɜːgə'nɒmɪks] *n* ergonomía *f*.

ERISA [ə'riːsə] (*abbr of* **Employee Retirement Income Security Act**) *n ley estadounidense de pensiones de jubilación.*

Eritrea [,erɪ'treɪə] *n* Eritrea.

Eritrean [,erɪ'treɪən] ◇ *adj* eritreo(a). ◇ *n* eritreo *m*, -a *f*.

ERM (*abbr of* **Exchange Rate Mechanism**) *n mecanismo de tipos de cambio del SME.*

ermine ['ɜːmɪn] *n* armiño *m*.

ERNIE ['ɜːnɪ] (*abbr of* **Electronic Random Number Indicator Equipment**) *n ordenador central que selecciona los números ganadores de los premium bonds en Gran Bretaña.*

erode [ɪ'rəud] ◇ *vt* **-1.** [rock, soil] erosionar; [metal] desgastar. **-2.** [confidence, rights] mermar. ◇ *vi* **-1.** [rock, soil] erosionarse; [metal] desgastarse. **-2.** [confidence, rights] mermarse.

erogenous zone [ɪ'rɒdʒɪnəs-] *n* zona *f* erógena.

erosion [ɪ'rəuʒn] *n* **-1.** [of rock, soil] erosión *f*; [of metal] desgaste *m*. **-2.** [of confidence, rights] merma *f*.

erotic [ɪ'rɒtɪk] *adj* erótico(ca).

eroticism [ɪ'rɒtɪsɪzm] *n* erotismo *m*.

err [ɜːr] *vi* equivocarse, errar; **to ~ is human** equivocarse es de humanos; **to ~ on the side of caution** pecar de prudente.

errand ['erənd] *n* recado *m*, mandado *m*; **to go on** OR **run an ~** hacer un recado.

errand boy *n* recadero *m*, chico *m* de los recados.

erratic [ɪ'rætɪk] *adj* irregular.

erroneous [ɪ'rəʊnjəs] *adj fml* erróneo(a).

error ['erər] *n* error *m*; **spelling ~** falta *f* de ortografía; **~ of judgment** error de cálculo; **in ~** por equivocación.

error message *n* COMPUT mensaje *m* de error.

erstwhile ['ɜːstwaɪl] *adj literary* antiguo(gua).

erudite ['eruːdaɪt] *adj* erudito(ta).

erupt [ɪ'rʌpt] *vi* [volcano] entrar en erupción; *fig* [violence, war] estallar.

eruption [ɪ'rʌpʃn] *n* **-1.** [of volcano] erupción *f*. **-2.** [of violence, war] estallido *m*, explosión *f*.

ESA (*abbr of* European Space Agency) *n* ESA *f*.

escalate ['eskəleɪt] *vi* **-1.** [conflict] intensificarse. **-2.** [costs] ascender, incrementarse.

escalation [,eskə'leɪʃn] *n* **-1.** [of conflict, violence] intensificación *f*, escalada *f*. **-2.** [of costs] ascenso *m*, incremento *m*.

escalator ['eskəleɪtər] *n* escalera *f* mecánica.

escalator clause *n* cláusula *f* de actualización.

escapade [,eskə'peɪd] *n* aventura *f*.

escape [ɪ'skeɪp] ◇ *n* **-1.** [gen] fuga *f*. **-2.** [leakage - of gas, water] escape *m*. ◇ *vt* **-1.** [avoid] escapar a, eludir; **to ~ notice** pasar inadvertido(da). **-2.** [subj: fact, name]: **her name ~s me** ahora mismo no caigo en su nombre. ◇ *vi* **-1.** [gen]: **to ~ (from)** escaparse (de). **-2.** [survive] escapar.

escape clause *n* cláusula *f* de excepción.

escape key *n* COMPUT tecla *f* de escape.

escape route *n* **-1.** [from prison] vía *f* de escape. **-2.** [from fire] salida *f* de emergencia.

escapism [ɪ'skeɪpɪzm] *n* (*U*) escapismo *m*, evasión *f*.

escapist [ɪ'skeɪpɪst] *adj* de evasión.

escapologist [,eskə'pɒlədʒɪst] *n* escapista *m y f*.

escarpment [ɪ'skɑːpmənt] *n* escarpa *f*.

eschew [ɪs'tʃuː] *vt fml* evitar.

escort [*n* 'eskɔːt, *vb* ɪ'skɔːt] ◇ *n* **-1.** [guard] escolta *f*; **under ~** bajo escolta. **-2.** [companion] acompañante *m y f*. ◇ *vt* escol-

tar; **to ~ sb home** acompañar a alguien a casa.

escort agency *n* agencia *f* de acompañantes.

Eskimo ['eskɪməʊ] (*pl* **-s**) ◇ *adj* esquimal. ◇ *n* **-1.** [person] esquimal *m y f*. **-2.** [language] esquimal *m*.

ESL (*abbr of* English as a Second Language) *n* inglés para extranjeros.

esophagus *Am* = oesophagus.

esoteric [,esə'terɪk] *adj* esotérico(ca).

esp. (*abbr of* especially) esp.

ESP *n* **-1.** (*abbr of* extrasensory perception) *percepción extrasensorial*. **-2.** (*abbr of* English for special purposes) *inglés especializado*.

espadrille [,espə'drɪl] *n* alpargata *f*.

especial [ɪ'speʃl] *adj* especial.

especially [ɪ'speʃəlɪ] *adv* **-1.** [in particular] sobre todo. **-2.** [more than usually, specifically] especialmente.

Esperanto [,espə'ræntəʊ] *n* esperanto *m*.

espionage ['espɪə,nɑːʒ] *n* espionaje *m*.

esplanade [,esplə'neɪd] *n* paseo *m* marítimo.

espouse [ɪ'spaʊz] *vt* apoyar.

espresso [e'spresəʊ] (*pl* **-s**) *n* café *m* exprés.

Esq. (*abbr of* esquire) D.; **James Roberts, ~** D. James Roberts.

Esquire [ɪ'skwaɪər] *n* Sr. Don; **B. Jones ~** Sr. Don B. Jones.

essay ['eseɪ] *n* **-1.** SCH redacción *f*, composición *f*; UNIV trabajo *m*. **-2.** LITERATURE ensayo *m*.

essayist ['eseɪɪst] *n* ensayista *m y f*.

essence ['esns] *n* esencia *f*; **in ~** esencialmente.

essential [ɪ'senʃl] *adj* **-1.** [absolutely necessary]: **~ (to** OR **for)** esencial OR indispensable (para). **-2.** [basic] fundamental, esencial.
◆ **essentials** *npl* **-1.** [basic commodities] lo indispensable. **-2.** [most important elements] elementos *mpl* esenciales.

essentially [ɪ'senʃəlɪ] *adv* [basically] esencialmente.

est. -1. *abbr of* established. **-2.** *abbr of* estimated.

EST (*abbr of* Eastern Standard Time) *n hora oficial de Nueva York*.

establish [ɪ'stæblɪʃ] *vt* **-1.** [gen] establecer; **to ~ contact with** establecer contacto con; **to ~ o.s. (as)** establecerse (como). **-2.** [facts, cause] verificar.

established [ɪ'stæblɪʃt] *adj* **-1.** [custom] arraigado(da). **-2.** [company] establecido(da), consolidado(da).

establishment [ɪ'stæblɪʃmənt] *n* establecimiento *m*.
◆ **Establishment** *n*: **the Establishment** el sistema.

estate [ɪ'steɪt] *n* **-1.** [land, property] finca *f*. **-2. (housing)** ~ urbanización *f*. **-3. (industrial)** ~ polígono *m* industrial. **-4.** JUR [inheritance] herencia *f*.

estate agency *n Br* agencia *f* inmobiliaria.

estate agent *n Br* agente inmobiliario *m*, agente inmobiliaria *f*.

estate car *n Br* ranchera *f*, coche *m* familiar.

estd., est'd. *abbr of* **established.**

esteem [ɪ'stiːm] ◇ *n* estima *f*, consideración *f*; **to hold sthg/sb in high** ~ tener en mucha estima algo/a alguien. ◇ *vt* estimar, apreciar.

esthete *etc Am* = **aesthete** *etc.*

estimate [*n* 'estɪmət, *vb* 'estɪmeɪt] ◇ *n* **-1.** [calculation, judgment] cálculo *m*, estimación *f*. **-2.** [written quote] presupuesto *m*. ◇ *vt* estimar. ◇ *vi* COMM: **to** ~ **for** hacer un presupuesto de.

estimated ['estɪmeɪtɪd] *adj* estimado(da), calculado(da).

estimation [,estɪ'meɪʃn] *n* **-1.** [opinion] juicio *m*; **in my** ~ a mi juicio. **-2.** [calculation] cálculo *m*.

Estonia [e'stəʊnɪə] *n* Estonia.

Estonian [e'stəʊnɪən] ◇ *adj* estonio(nia). ◇ *n* **-1.** [person] estonio *m*, -nia *f*. **-2.** [language] estonio *m*.

estranged [ɪ'streɪndʒd] *adj* [husband, wife] separado(da); **his** ~ **son** su hijo con el que no se habla.

estrogen *Am* = **oestrogen**.

estuary ['estjʊərɪ] (*pl* **-ies**) *n* estuario *m*.

ETA (*abbr of* **estimated time of arrival**) *n* hora prevista de llegada.

et al. [,et'æl] (*abbr of* **et alii**) et al.

etc. (*abbr of* **etcetera**) etc.

etcetera [ɪt'setərə] *adv* etcétera.

etch [etʃ] *vt* [engrave] grabar al agua fuerte; *fig* [imprint]: **to be** ~**ed on sb's memory** estar grabado(da) en la memoria de alguien.

etching ['etʃɪŋ] *n* aguafuerte *m o f*.

ETD (*abbr of* **estimated time of departure**) *n* hora prevista de salida.

eternal [ɪ'tɜːnl] *adj* [gen] eterno(na); *fig* [complaints, whining] perpetuo(tua), continuo(nua).

eternally [ɪ'tɜːnəlɪ] *adv* [gen] eternamente; [complain, whine] continuamente.

eternity [ɪ'tɜːnətɪ] *n* eternidad *f*.

eternity ring *n Br* alianza *f* del amor eterno.

ether ['iːθəʳ] *n* éter *m*.

ethereal [ɪ'θɪərɪəl] *adj* etéreo(a).

ethic ['eθɪk] *n* ética *f*.
◆ **ethics** ◇ *n* (U) [study] ética *f*. ◇ *npl* [morals] moralidad *f*.

ethical ['eθɪkl] *adj* ético(ca).

Ethiopia [,iːθɪ'əʊpɪə] *n* Etiopía.

Ethiopian [,iːθɪ'əʊpɪən] ◇ *adj* etíope. ◇ *n* etíope *m y f*.

ethnic ['eθnɪk] *adj* **-1.** [traditions, conflict] étnico(ca). **-2.** [food] *típico de una cultura distinta a la occidental*; ~ **music** música con raíces.

ethnic cleansing [-'klensɪŋ] *n* limpieza *f* étnica.

ethnic minority *n* minoría *f* étnica.

ethnology [eθ'nɒlədʒɪ] *n* etnología *f*.

ethos ['iːθɒs] *n* ética *f*, código *m* de valores.

etiquette ['etɪket] *n* etiqueta *f*.

ETU (*abbr of* **Electrical Trades Union**) *n* sindicato británico de electricistas.

ETV (*abbr of* **educational television**) *n* televisión educativa.

etymology [,etɪ'mɒlədʒɪ] (*pl* **-ies**) *n* etimología *f*.

EU (*abbr of* **European Union**) UE *f*.

eucalyptus [,juːkə'lɪptəs] *n* eucalipto *m*.

eulogize, -ise ['juːlədʒaɪz] *vt* elogiar.

eulogy ['juːlədʒɪ] (*pl* **-ies**) *n* elogio *m*.

eunuch ['juːnək] *n* eunuco *m*.

euphemism ['juːfəmɪzm] *n* eufemismo *m*.

euphemistic [,juːfə'mɪstɪk] *adj* eufemístico(ca).

euphoria [juː'fɔːrɪə] *n* euforia *f*.

euphoric [juː'fɒrɪk] *adj* eufórico(ca).

Eurasia [jʊə'reɪʒə] *n* Eurasia *f*.

Eurasian [jʊə'reɪʒən] ◇ *adj* euroasiático(ca). ◇ *n* euroasiático *m*, -ca *f*.

euro ['jʊərəʊ] *n* [currency] euro *m*.

Euro- ['jʊərəʊ] *prefix* euro-.

Eurocheque ['jʊərəʊ,tʃek] *n* eurocheque *m*.

Eurocrat ['jʊərə,kræt] *n* eurócrata *m y f*.

Eurocurrency ['juːrəʊ,kʌrənsɪ] (*pl* **-ies**) *n* eurodivisa *f*.

Eurodollar ['jʊərəʊ,dɒləʳ] *n* eurodólar *m*.

Euro MP *n* eurodiputado *m*, -da *f*.

Europe ['jʊərəp] *n* Europa *f*.

European [,jʊərə'piːən] ◇ *adj* europeo(a). ◇ *n* europeo *m*, -a *f*.

European Community *n*: **the** ~ la Comunidad Europea.

European Court of Human Rights *n*: **the** ~ el Tribunal Europeo de Derechos Humanos.

European Court of Justice *n*: **the** ~ el Tribunal Europeo de Justicia.

European Currency Unit *n* Unidad *f* Monetaria Europea, ecu *m*.

Europeanism [,juərə'piːənɪzm] *n* europeísmo *m*.

Europeanize, -ise [,juərə'piːənaɪz] *vt* europeizar.

European Monetary System *n*: **the** ~ el Sistema Monetario Europeo.

European Parliament *n*: **the** ~ el Parlamento Europeo.

European Union *n*: **the** ~ la Unión Europea.

euthanasia [,juːθə'neɪzjə] *n* eutanasia *f*.

evacuate [ɪ'vækjʊeɪt] *vt* evacuar.

evacuation [ɪ,vækjʊ'eɪʃn] *n* evacuación *f*.

evacuee [ɪ,vækjuː'iː] *n* evacuado *m*, -da *f*.

evade [ɪ'veɪd] *vt* eludir.

evaluate [ɪ'væljʊeɪt] *vt* evaluar.

evaluation [ɪ,væljʊ'eɪʃn] *n* evaluación *f*.

evangelical [,iːvæn'dʒelɪkl] *adj* evangélico(ca).

evangelism [ɪ'vændʒəlɪzm] *n* evangelismo *m*.

evangelist [ɪ'vændʒəlɪst] *n* evangelizador *m*, -ra *f*.

evangelize, -ise [ɪ'vændʒəlaɪz] *vt* evangelizar.

evaporate [ɪ'væpəreɪt] *vi* [liquid] evaporarse; *fig* [feeling] desvanecerse.

evaporated milk [ɪ'væpəreɪtɪd-] *n* leche *f* evaporada.

evaporation [ɪ,væpə'reɪʃn] *n* evaporación *f*.

evasion [ɪ'veɪʒn] *n* **-1.** [of responsibility, payment etc] evasión *f*. **-2.** [lie] evasiva *f*.

evasive [ɪ'veɪsɪv] *adj* evasivo(va); **to take** ~ **action** quitarse de en medio.

evasiveness [ɪ'veɪsɪvnɪs] *n*: **with** ~ evasivamente.

eve [iːv] *n*: **on the** ~ **of** en la víspera de.

even ['iːvn] ◇ *adj* **-1.** [regular] uniforme, constante. **-2.** [calm] sosegado(da). **-3.** [flat, level] llano(na), liso(sa). **-4.** [equal - contest, teams] igualado(da); [- chance] igual; **to get** ~ **with** ajustarle las cuentas a. **-5.** [number] par. ◇ *adv* **-1.** [gen] incluso, hasta; ~ **now/then** incluso ahora/entonces; **not** ~ ni siquiera. **-2.** [in comparisons] aun; ~ **more** aun más.
◆ **even as** *conj* incluso mientras.
◆ **even if** *conj* aunque, aun cuando, así *Amer.*
◆ **even so** *conj* aun así.
◆ **even though** *conj* aunque.
◆ **even out** ◇ *vt sep* igualar. ◇ *vi* igualarse.

even-handed [-'hændɪd] *adj* imparcial.

evening ['iːvnɪŋ] *n* **-1.** [end of day - early part] tarde *f*; [- later part] noche *f*. **-2.** [event, entertainment] velada *f*.
◆ **evenings** *adv* [early] por la tarde; [late] por la noche.

evening class *n* clase *f* nocturna.

evening dress *n* **-1.** [worn by man] traje *m* de etiqueta. **-2.** [worn by woman] traje *m* de noche.

evening star *n*: **the** ~ el lucero de la tarde.

evenly ['iːvnlɪ] *adv* **-1.** [regularly] de modo uniforme. **-2.** [equally] igualmente, equitativamente. **-3.** [calmly] sosegadamente.

evenness ['iːvnnɪs] *n* **-1.** [regularity] uniformidad *f*. **-2.** [equality] igualdad *f*.

evensong ['iːvnsɒŋ] *n* vísperas *fpl*.

event [ɪ'vent] *n* **-1.** [happening] acontecimiento *m*, suceso *m*; **in the** ~ **of** en caso de; **in the** ~ **that it rains** (en) caso de que llueva. **-2.** SPORT prueba *f*.
◆ **in any event** *adv* en todo caso.
◆ **in the event** *adv Br* al final, llegada la hora.

even-tempered [-'tempəd] *adj* apacible, ecuánime.

eventful [ɪ'ventfʊl] *adj* accidentado(da).

eventide home ['iːvntaɪd-] *n Br euphemism* residencia *f* de ancianos.

eventing [ɪ'ventɪŋ] *n Br* SPORT: **(three-day)** ~ concurso hípico de tres días.

eventual [ɪ'ventʃʊəl] *adj* final.

eventuality [ɪ,ventʃʊ'ælətɪ] (*pl* **-ies**) *n* eventualidad *f*.

eventually [ɪ'ventʃʊəlɪ] *adv* finalmente.

ever ['evəʳ] *adv* **-1.** [at any time] alguna vez; **have you** ~ **done it?** ¿lo has hecho alguna vez?; **hardly** ~ casi nunca; **if** ~ si acaso. [all the time] siempre; **as** ~ como siempre; **for** ~ para siempre. **-3.** [for emphasis]: ~ **so** muy; ~ **such a mess** un lío tan grande; **we had** ~ **such a good time** lo pasamos verdaderamente en grande; **why/how** ~ **did you do it?** ¿por qué/cómo diablos lo hiciste?; **what** ~ **can it be?** ¿qué diablos puede ser?
◆ **ever since** ◇ *adv* desde entonces. ◇ *conj* desde que. ◇ *prep* desde.

Everest ['evərɪst] *n* Everest.

Everglades ['evəˌgleɪdz] *npl*: **the** ~ los Everglades.

evergreen ['evəgriːn] ◇ *adj* de hoja perenne. ◇ *n* árbol *m* de hoja perenne.

everlasting [,evə'lɑːstɪŋ] *adj* eterno(na).

every ['evrɪ] *adj* cada; ~ **day** cada día, todos los días; **there's** ~ **chance he'll win** tiene bastantes posibilidades de ganar.

◆ **every now and then, every so often** *adv* de vez en cuando.

◆ **every other** *adj*: ~ **other day** un día sí y otro no, cada dos días.

◆ **every which way** *adv Am* en todas direcciones, sin orden ni concierto.

everybody ['evrɪ,bɒdɪ] = everyone.

everyday ['evrɪdeɪ] *adj* diario(ria), cotidiano(na).

everyone ['evrɪwʌn] *pron* todo el mundo, todos(das).

everyplace *Am* = everywhere.

everything ['evrɪθɪŋ] *pron* todo; **money isn't ~** el dinero no lo es todo.

everywhere ['evrɪweəʳ], **everyplace** *Am* ['evrɪ,pleɪs] *adv* en OR por todas partes; [with verbs of motion] a todas partes.

evict [ɪ'vɪkt] *vt*: **to ~ sb from** desahuciar a alguien de.

eviction [ɪ'vɪkʃn] *n* desahucio *m*.

eviction notice *n* notificación *f* de desahucio.

evidence ['evɪdəns] *n* (*U*) **-1.** [proof] evidencia *f*, prueba *f*. **-2.** JUR [of witness] declaración *f*, testimonio *m*; **to give ~** dar testimonio, prestar declaración.

◆ **in evidence** *adj* [noticeable]: **to be in ~** hacerse notar.

evident ['evɪdənt] *adj* evidente, manifiesto(ta).

evidently ['evɪdəntlɪ] *adv* **-1.** [seemingly] por lo visto, al parecer. **-2.** [obviously] evidentemente, obviamente.

evil ['iːvl] ◇ *adj* [person] malo(la), malvado(da); [torture, practice] perverso(sa), vil. ◇ *n* **-1.** [evil quality] maldad *f*. **-2.** [evil thing] mal *m*.

evil-minded [-'maɪndɪd] *adj* malintencionado(da).

evince [ɪ'vɪns] *vt fml* mostrar.

evocation [,evəʊ'keɪʃn] *n* evocación *f*.

evocative [ɪ'vɒkətɪv] *adj* evocador(ra), sugerente.

evoke [ɪ'vəʊk] *vt* **-1.** [memory, emotion] evocar. **-2.** [response] producir.

evolution [,iːvə'luːʃn] *n* **-1.** BIOL evolución *f*. **-2.** [development] desarrollo *m*.

evolve [ɪ'vɒlv] ◇ *vt* desarrollar. ◇ *vi* **-1.** BIOL: **to ~ (into/from)** evolucionar (en/de). **-2.** [develop] desarrollarse.

ewe [juː] *n* oveja *f*.

ex- [eks] *prefix* ex-.

exacerbate [ɪg'zæsəbeɪt] *vt* exacerbar.

exact [ɪg'zækt] ◇ *adj* exacto(ta); **to be ~** para ser exacto. ◇ *vt*: **to ~ sthg (from)** exigir algo (de).

exacting [ɪg'zæktɪŋ] *adj* **-1.** [job, work] arduo(dua). **-2.** [standards] severo(ra); [person] exigente.

exactitude [ɪg'zæktɪtjuːd] *n fml* exactitud *f*.

exactly [ɪg'zæktlɪ] ◇ *adv* [precisely] exactamente; **it's ~ ten o'clock** son las diez en punto; **not ~** [not really] no precisamente; [as reply] no exactamente. ◇ *excl* ¡exacto!, ¡exactamente!

exaggerate [ɪg'zædʒəreɪt] *vt & vi* exagerar.

exaggerated [ɪg'zædʒəreɪtɪd] *adj* exagerado(da).

exaggeration [ɪg,zædʒə'reɪʃn] *n* exageración *f*.

exalted [ɪg'zɔːltɪd] *adj* [person, position] elevado(da).

exam [ɪg'zæm] (*abbr of* **examination**) *n* examen *m*; **to take** OR **sit an ~** presentarse a un examen.

examination [ɪg,zæmɪ'neɪʃn] *n* **-1.** = exam. **-2.** [inspection] inspección *f*, examen *m*. **-3.** MED reconocimiento *m*. **-4.** [consideration] estudio *m*.

examination board *n* tribunal *m* examinador.

examination paper *n Br* examen *m*, cuestionario *m* de examen.

examine [ɪg'zæmɪn] *vt* **-1.** [gen] examinar. **-2.** MED reconocer. **-3.** [consider - idea, proposal] estudiar, considerar. **-4.** JUR interrogar.

examiner [ɪg'zæmɪnəʳ] *n* examinador *m*, -ra *f*; **internal ~** *examinador perteneciente al centro*; **external ~** *examinador independiente o externo*.

example [ɪg'zɑːmpl] *n* ejemplo *m*; **for ~** por ejemplo; **to follow sb's ~** seguir el ejemplo de alguien; **to make an ~ of sb** dar un castigo ejemplar a alguien.

exasperate [ɪg'zæspəreɪt] *vt* exasperar, sacar de quicio.

exasperating [ɪg'zæspəreɪtɪŋ] *adj* exasperante, irritante.

exasperation [ɪg,zæspə'reɪʃn] *n* exasperación *f*, irritación *f*.

excavate ['ekskəveɪt] *vt* excavar.

excavation [,ekskə'veɪʃn] *n* excavación *f*.

excavator ['ekskə,veɪtəʳ] *n Br* [machine] excavadora *f*.

exceed [ɪk'siːd] *vt* **-1.** [amount, number] exceder, pasar. **-2.** [limit, expectations] rebasar.

exceedingly [ɪk'siːdɪŋlɪ] *adv* extremadamente.

excel [ɪk'sel] (*pt & pp* **-led**, *cont* **-ling**) *vi*: **to ~ (in** OR **at)** sobresalir (en); **to ~ o.s.** *Br* lucirse.

excellence ['eksələns] *n* excelencia *f*.

Excellency ['eksələnsı] (*pl* **-ies**) *n*: **Your/His** ~ Su Excelencia.

excellent ['eksələnt] *adj* excelente.

except [ık'sept] ◇ *prep & conj*: ~ **(for)** excepto, salvo. ◇ *vt*: **to** ~ **sb** (**from**) exceptuar OR excluir a alguien (de).

excepted [ık'septıd] *adj* exceptuando a, excepto.

excepting [ık'septıŋ] *prep & conj* = **except**.

exception [ık'sepʃn] *n* **-1.** [exclusion]: ~ (**to**) excepción *f* (a); **with the** ~ **of** a excepción de; **without** ~ sin excepción. **-2.** [offence]: **to take** ~ **to** ofenderse por.

exceptional [ık'sepʃənl] *adj* excepcional.

exceptionally [ık'sepʃnəlı] *adv* excepcionalmente.

excerpt ['eksɜ:pt] *n*: ~ (**from**) extracto *m* (de).

excess [ık'ses, *before nouns* 'ekses] ◇ *adj* excedente. ◇ *n* exceso *m*; **in** ~ **of** superior a, por encima de; **to** ~ en exceso.
◆ **excesses** *npl* excesos *mpl*.

excess baggage *n* exceso *m* de equipaje.

excess fare *n Br* suplemento *m*.

excessive [ık'sesıv] *adj* excesivo(va).

excess luggage *n* = **excess baggage**.

exchange [ıks'tʃeındʒ] ◇ *n* **-1.** [gen] intercambio *m*; **in** ~ **(for)** a cambio (de). **-2.** FIN cambio *m*. **-3.** TELEC: (**telephone**) ~ central *f* telefónica. **-4.** *fml* [conversation]: **a heated** ~ una acalorada discusión. ◇ *vt* [swap] intercambiar, cambiar; **to** ~ **sthg for sthg** cambiar algo por algo; **to** ~ **sthg with sb** intercambiar algo con alguien.

exchange rate *n* FIN tipo *m* de cambio.

Exchequer [ıks'tʃekər] *n Br*: **the** ~ ≃ Hacienda.

excise ['eksaız] ◇ *n* (*U*) impuestos *mpl* sobre el consumo interior. ◇ *vt fml* extirpar.

excise duties *npl* derechos *mpl* arancelarios.

excitable [ık'saıtəbl] *adj* excitable.

excite [ık'saıt] *vt* **-1.** [person] emocionar, excitar. **-2.** [suspicion, interest] despertar, suscitar.

excited [ık'saıtıd] *adj* emocionado(da), entusiasmado(da).

excitement [ık'saıtmənt] *n* emoción *f*.

exciting [ık'saıtıŋ] *adj* emocionante, apasionante.

excl. (*abbr of* **excluding**) sin incluir; ~ **taxes** sin incluir impuestos.

exclaim [ık'skleım] ◇ *vt* exclamar. ◇ *vi*: **to** ~ **(at)** exclamar (ante).

exclamation [,eksklə'meıʃn] *n* exclamación *f*.

exclamation mark *Br*, **exclamation point** *Am n* signo *m* de admiración.

exclude [ık'sklu:d] *vt*: **to** ~ **sthg/sb** (**from**) excluir algo/a alguien (de).

excluding [ık'sklu:dıŋ] *prep* excepto, con excepción de.

exclusion [ık'sklu:ʒn] *n*: ~ (**from**) exclusión *f* (de); **to the** ~ **of** con exclusión de.

exclusion clause *n* cláusula *f* de exclusión.

exclusive [ık'sklu:sıv] ◇ *adj* **-1.** [high-class] selecto(ta). **-2.** [sole] exclusivo(va). ◇ *n* [news story] exclusiva *f*.
◆ **exclusive of** *prep* excluyendo.

exclusively [ık'sklu:sıvlı] *adv* exclusivamente.

excommunicate [,ekskə'mju:nıkeıt] *vt* excomulgar.

excommunication ['ekskə,mju:nı'keıʃn] *n fml* excomunión *f*.

excrement ['ekskrımənt] *n* excremento *m*.

excrete [ık'skri:t] *vt fml* excretar.

excruciating [ık'skru:ʃıeıtıŋ] *adj* insoportable.

excursion [ık'skɜ:ʃn] *n* excursión *f*.

excusable [ık'skju:zəbl] *adj* perdonable, excusable.

excuse [*n* ık'skju:s, *vb* ık'skju:z] ◇ *n* excusa *f*; **to make an** ~ dar una excusa, excusarse. ◇ *vt* **-1.** [gen]: **to** ~ **sb** (**for sthg/for doing sthg**) perdonar a alguien (por algo/por haber hecho algo); **to** ~ **o.s.** (**for doing sthg**) excusarse OR disculparse (por haber hecho algo). **-2.** [let off]: **to** ~ **sb** (**from**) dispensar a alguien (de). **-3.** *phr*: ~ **me** [to attract attention] oiga (por favor); [when coming past] ¿me deja pasar?; [apologizing] perdone; *Am* [pardon me?] ¿perdón?, ¿cómo?

ex-directory *adj Br* que no figura en la guía telefónica.

exec [ıg'zek] *abbr of* **executive**.

execrable ['eksıkrəbl] *adj fml* execrable.

execute ['eksıkju:t] *vt* [gen & COMPUT] ejecutar.

execution [,eksı'kju:ʃn] *n* ejecución *f*.

executioner [,eksı'kju:ʃnər] *n* verdugo *m*.

executive [ıg'zekjutıv] ◇ *adj* **-1.** [decision-making] ejecutivo(va). **-2.** [for company executives] **para** OR **de** ejecutivos. ◇ *n* **-1.** [person] ejecutivo *m*, -va *f*. **-2.** [committee] ejecutiva *f*, órgano *m* ejecutivo.

executive director *n* director ejecutivo *m*, directora ejecutiva *f*.

executive toy *n* juego *m* de concentración (para ejecutivos).

executor [ıg'zekjutər] *n* albacea *m*.

exemplary [ɪg'zemplərɪ] *adj* [perfect] ejemplar.

exemplify [ɪg'zemplɪfaɪ] (*pt* & *pp* **-ied**) *vt* ejemplificar.

exempt [ɪg'zempt] ◇ *adj*: ~ **(from)** exento(ta) (de). ◇ *vt*: **to ~ sthg/sb (from)** eximir algo/a alguien (de).

exemption [ɪg'zempʃn] *n* exención *f*.

exercise ['eksəsaɪz] ◇ *n* **-1.** [gen] ejercicio *m*; **an ~ in** un ejercicio de; **to take ~** hacer ejercicio. **-2.** MIL maniobra *f*. ◇ *vt* **-1.** [dog] llevar de paseo; [horse] entrenar. **-2.** *fml* [power, right] ejercer; [caution, restraint] mostrar. **-3.** [trouble]: **to ~ one's mind** preocuparle a uno. ◇ *vi* hacer ejercicio.

exercise bike *n* bicicleta *f* estática.

exercise book *n* cuaderno *m* de ejercicios.

exert [ɪg'zɜːt] *vt* ejercer; **to ~ o.s.** esforzarse.

exertion [ɪg'zɜːʃn] *n* esfuerzo *m*.

ex gratia [eks'greɪʃə] *adj Br* ex gratia.

exhale [eks'heɪl] ◇ *vt* exhalar, despedir. ◇ *vi* espirar.

exhaust [ɪg'zɔːst] ◇ *n* (*U*) [fumes] gases *mpl* de combustión; ~ **(pipe)** tubo *m* de escape. ◇ *vt* agotar.

exhausted [ɪg'zɔːstɪd] *adj* [person] agotado(da).

exhausting [ɪg'zɔːstɪŋ] *adj* agotador(ra).

exhaustion [ɪg'zɔːstʃn] *n* agotamiento *m*.

exhaustive [ɪg'zɔːstɪv] *adj* exhaustivo(va).

exhibit [ɪg'zɪbɪt] ◇ *n* **-1.** ART objeto *m* expuesto. **-2.** JUR prueba *f* (instrumental). ◇ *vt* **-1.** *fml* [feeling] mostrar, manifestar. **-2.** ART exponer. ◇ *vi* ART exponer.

exhibition [ˌeksɪ'bɪʃn] *n* **-1.** ART exposición *f*. **-2.** [of feeling] manifestación *f*, demostración *f*. **-3.** *phr*: **to make an ~ of o.s.** *Br* ponerse en evidencia, hacer el ridículo.

exhibitionist [ˌeksɪ'bɪʃnɪst] *n* exhibicionista *m y f*.

exhibitor [ɪg'zɪbɪtər] *n* expositor *m*, -ra *f*.

exhilarating [ɪg'zɪləreɪtɪŋ] *adj* estimulante.

exhort [ɪg'zɔːt] *vt fml*: **to ~ sb to do sthg** exhortar a alguien a hacer algo.

exhume [eks'hjuːm] *vt fml* exhumar.

exile ['eksaɪl] ◇ *n* **-1.** [condition] exilio *m*; **in ~** en el exilio. **-2.** [person] exiliado *m*, -da *f*. ◇ *vt*: **to ~ sb (from/to)** exiliar a alguien (de/a).

exiled ['eksaɪld] *adj* exiliado(da).

exist [ɪg'zɪst] *vi* existir.

existence [ɪg'zɪstəns] *n* existencia *f*; **to be in ~** existir; **to come into ~** nacer.

existentialism [ˌegzɪ'stenʃəlɪzm] *n* existencialismo *m*.

existentialist [ˌegzɪ'stenʃəlɪst] ◇ *adj* existencialista. ◇ *n* existencialista *m y f*.

existing [ɪg'zɪstɪŋ] *adj* existente, actual.

exit ['eksɪt] ◇ *n* salida *f*. ◇ *vi fml* salir; THEATRE hacer mutis.

exit poll *n Br* sondeo *m* electoral (*a la salida de los colegios electorales*).

exit visa *n* visado *m* de salida.

exodus ['eksədəs] *n* éxodo *m*.

ex officio [eksə'fɪʃɪəʊ] *adj & adv fml* de oficio.

exonerate [ɪg'zɒnəreɪt] *vt*: **to ~ sb (from)** exonerar a alguien (de).

exorbitant [ɪg'zɔːbɪtənt] *adj* [cost] excesivo(va); [demand, price] exorbitante.

exorcist ['eksɔːsɪst] *n* exorcista *m y f*.

exorcize, -ise ['eksɔːsaɪz] *vt* exorcizar.

exotic [ɪg'zɒtɪk] *adj* exótico(ca).

expand [ɪk'spænd] ◇ *vt* extender, ampliar. ◇ *vi* extenderse, ampliarse; [materials, fluids] expandirse, dilatarse.

◆ **expand (up)on** *vt fus* desarrollar.

expanse [ɪk'spæns] *n* extensión *f*.

expansion [ɪk'spænʃn] *n* expansión *f*.

expansion card *n* COMPUT tarjeta *f* de expansión.

expansionism [ɪk'spænʃənɪzm] *n* expansionismo *m*.

expansionist [ɪk'spænʃənɪst] *adj* expansionista.

expansion slot *n* COMPUT ranura *f* de expansión.

expansive [ɪk'spænsɪv] *adj* [relaxed, talkative] expansivo(va).

expatriate [eks'pætrɪət] ◇ *adj* expatriado(da). ◇ *n* expatriado *m*, -da *f*.

expect [ɪk'spekt] ◇ *vt* **-1.** [gen] esperar; **to ~ sb to do sthg** esperar que alguien haga algo; **to ~ sthg (from sb)** esperar algo (de alguien); **as ~ed** como era de esperar. **-2.** [suppose] imaginarse, suponer; **I ~ so** supongo que sí. ◇ *vi* **-1.** [anticipate]: **to do sthg** esperar hacer algo. **-2.** [be pregnant]: **to be ~ing** estar embarazada OR en estado.

expectancy → **life expectancy**.

expectant [ɪk'spektənt] *adj* expectante.

expectantly [ɪk'spektəntlɪ] *adv* con expectación.

expectant mother *n* futura madre *f*, mujer *f* embarazada.

expectation [ˌekspek'teɪʃn] *n* esperanza *f*; **against all ~** OR **~s, contrary to all ~** OR **~s** contrariamente a lo que se esperaba; **to live up to/fall short of sb's ~s** estar/no estar a la altura de lo esperado.

expectorant [ɪk'spektərənt] *n* expectorante *m*.

expedient [ɪk'spiːdjənt] *fml* ◇ *adj* conveniente, oportuno(na). ◇ *n* recurso *m*.

expedite ['ekspɪdaɪt] *vt fml* acelerar.

expedition [,ekspɪ'dɪʃn] *n* -1. [journey] expedición *f*. -2. [outing] salida *f*.

expeditionary force [,ekspɪ'dɪʃnərɪ-] *n* cuerpo *m* expedicionario.

expel [ɪk'spel] (*pt* & *pp* -led, *cont* -ling) *vt* -1. [person]: to ~ sb (from) expulsar a alguien (de). -2. [gas, liquid]: to ~ sthg (from) expeler algo (de).

expend [ɪk'spend] *vt*: to ~ sthg (on) emplear algo (en).

expendable [ɪk'spendəbl] *adj* reemplazable.

expenditure [ɪk'spendɪtʃər] *n* (U) gasto *m*.

expense [ɪk'spens] *n* (U) gasto *m*; **to go to great** ~ **(to do sthg)** incurrir en grandes gastos (para hacer algo); **at the** ~ **of** [sacrificing] a costa de; **at sb's** ~ *lit* & *fig* a costa de alguien.

◆ **expenses** *npl* COMM gastos *mpl*; **on** ~**s** en gastos.

expense account *n* cuenta *f* de gastos.

expensive [ɪk'spensɪv] *adj* caro(ra).

experience [ɪk'spɪərɪəns] ◇ *n* experiencia *f*. ◇ *vt* experimentar.

experienced [ɪk'spɪərɪənst] *adj*: ~ (at OR in) experimentado(da) (en).

experiment [ɪk'sperɪmənt] ◇ *n* experimento *m*; **to carry out an** ~ llevar a cabo un experimento. ◇ *vi*: to ~ (with/on) experimentar (con), hacer experimentos (con).

experimental [ɪk,serɪ'mentl] *adj* experimental.

expert ['eksp3ːt] ◇ *adj*: ~ (at sthg/at doing sthg) experto(ta) (en algo/en hacer algo). ◇ *n* experto *m*, -ta *f*, especialista *m* y *f*.

expertise [,eksp3ː'tiːz] *n* (U) competencia *f*, aptitud *f*.

expert system *n* COMPUT sistema *m* experto.

expiate ['ekspɪeɪt] *vt fml* expiar.

expire [ɪk'spaɪər] *vi* [licence, membership] caducar; [lease] vencer.

expiry [ɪk'spaɪərɪ] *n* [of licence] caducidad *f*; [of lease] vencimiento *m*.

expiry date *n* fecha *f* de caducidad.

explain [ɪk'spleɪn] ◇ *vt*: to ~ sthg (to sb) explicar algo (a alguien). ◇ *vi* explicar; to ~ to sb about sthg explicarle algo a alguien.

◆ **explain away** *vt sep* justificar.

explanation [,eksplə'neɪʃn] *n*: ~ (for) explicación *f* (de).

explanatory [ɪk'splænətrɪ] *adj* explicativo(va), aclaratorio(ria).

expletive [ɪk'spliːtɪv] *n fml* palabrota *f*.

explicit [ɪk'splɪsɪt] *adj* explícito(ta).

explode [ɪk'spləʊd] ◇ *vt* [bomb] hacer explotar; [building etc] volar; *fig* [theory] reventar. ◇ *vi lit* & *fig* estallar, explotar.

exploit [*n* 'eksplɔɪt, *vb* ɪk'splɔɪt] ◇ *n* proeza *f*, hazaña *f*. ◇ *vt* explotar.

exploitation [,eksplɔɪ'teɪʃn] *n* (U) explotación *f*.

exploration [,eksplə'reɪʃn] *n* exploración *f*.

exploratory [ɪk'splɒrətrɪ] *adj* [operation, examination] exploratorio(ria); [talks] preparatorio(ria).

explore [ɪk'splɔːr] *vt* & *vi lit* & *fig* explorar.

explorer [ɪk'splɔːrər] *n* explorador *m*, -ra *f*.

explosion [ɪk'spləʊʒn] *n* explosión *f*.

explosive [ɪk'spləʊsɪv] ◇ *adj* explosivo(va). ◇ *n* explosivo *m*.

explosive device *n fml* artefacto *m* explosivo.

exponent [ɪk'spəʊnənt] *n* -1. [supporter] partidario *m*, -ria *f*. -2. [expert] experto *m*, -ta *f*.

exponential [,ekspə'nenʃl] *adj fml* [growth] vertiginoso(sa).

export [*n* & *comp* 'ekspɔːt, *vb* ɪk'spɔːt] ◇ *n* -1. [act] exportación *f*. -2. [exported product] artículo *m* de exportación. ◇ *comp* de exportación. ◇ *vt lit* & *fig* exportar.

◆ **exports** *npl* exportaciones *fpl*.

exportable [ɪk'spɔːtəbl] *adj* exportable.

exportation [,ekspɔː'teɪʃn] *n* exportación *f*.

exporter [ek'spɔːtər] *n* exportador *m*, -ra *f*.

export licence *n Br* licencia *f* de exportación.

expose [ɪk'spəʊz] *vt lit* & *fig* descubrir; **to be** ~**d to sthg** estar OR verse expuesto a algo.

exposé [eks'pəʊzeɪ] *n* revelación *f*.

exposed [ɪk'spəʊzd] *adj* [land, house, position] expuesto(ta), al descubierto.

exposition [,ekspə'zɪʃn] *n* -1. *fml* [explanation] explicación *f*. -2. [exhibition] feria *f*.

exposure [ɪk'spəʊʒər] *n* -1. [to light, radiation] exposición *f*. -2. MED hipotermia *f*. -3. [unmasking · of person] desenmascaramiento *m*; [- of corruption] revelación *f*. -4. PHOT [time] (tiempo *m* de) exposición *f*; [photograph] foto *f*, fotografía *f*. -5. [publicity] publicidad *f*.

exposure meter *n* fotómetro *m*.

expound [ɪk'spaʊnd] *fml* ◇ *vt* exponer. ◇ *vi*: to ~ on sthg exponer algo.

express [ɪk'spres] ◇ *adj* -1. *Br* [letter, delivery] urgente. -2. [train, coach] expreso(sa).

rápido(da). **-3.** *fml* [specific] **expreso(sa)**, explícito(ta). ◇ *adv* **urgente**. ◇ *n* [train] **expreso** *m*. ◇ *vt* **expresar; to ~ o.s. expresarse**.

expression [ɪk'spreʃn] *n* expresión *f*.

expressionism [ɪk'spreʃənɪzm] *n* expresionismo *m*.

expressionist [ɪk'spreʃənɪst] ◇ *adj* expresionista. ◇ *n* expresionista *m* y *f*.

expressionless [ɪk'spreʃənlɪs] *adj* inexpresivo(va).

expressive [ɪk'spresɪv] *adj* [full of feeling] expresivo(va).

expressively [ɪk'spresɪvlɪ] *adv* de manera expresiva.

expressly [ɪk'spreslɪ] *adv* [specifically] expresamente.

expressway [ɪk'spresweɪ] *n Am* autopista *f*.

expropriate [eks'prəʊprɪeɪt] *vt fml* expropiar.

expropriation [eks,prəʊprɪ'eɪʃn] *n fml* expropiación *f*.

expulsion [ɪk'spʌlʃn] *n*: ~ **(from)** expulsión *f* (de).

exquisite [ɪk'skwɪzɪt] *adj* exquisito(ta).

exquisitely [ɪk'skwɪzɪtlɪ] *adv* [beautifully] de forma exquisita.

ex-serviceman *n Br* excombatiente *m*.

ex-servicewoman *n Br* excombatiente *f*.

ext., extn. (*abbr of* **extension**) ext., extn.; ~ **4174** ext. 4174.

extant [ek'stænt] *adj* existente.

extemporize, -ise [ɪk'stempəraɪz] *vi fml* improvisar.

extend [ɪk'stend] ◇ *vt* **-1.** [gen] **extender**; [house] **ampliar**; [road, railway] **prolongar**; [visa] **prorrogar. -2.** [offer - welcome, help] **brindar**; [- credit] **conceder.** ◇ *vi* **-1.** [become longer] **extenderse. -2.** [include]: **to ~ to sthg incluir algo. -3.** [from surface, object] **sobresalir**.

extendable [ɪk'stendəbl] *adj* [deadline, visa] prorrogable.

extended-play [ɪk'stendɪd-] *adj* [record] de larga duración.

extension [ɪk'stenʃn] *n* **-1.** [gen & TELEC] extensión *f*. **-2.** [to building] ampliación *f*. **-3.** [of visit] prolongación *f*; [of deadline, visa] prórroga *f*. **-4.** COMPUT: **filename ~** extensión *f* del nombre de fichero. **-5.** ELEC: ~ **(lead)** alargador *m*.

extension cable *n* alargador *m*.

extensive [ɪk'stensɪv] *adj* [gen] extenso(sa); [changes] profundo(da); [negotiations] amplio(plia); **to make ~ use of** hacer (un) gran uso de.

extensively [ɪk'stensɪvlɪ] *adv* extensamente.

extent [ɪk'stent] *n* **-1.** [size] extensión *f*. **-2.** [of problem, damage] alcance *m*, extensión *f*. **-3.** [degree]: **to what ~ ...?** ¿hasta qué punto ...?; **to the ~ that** [in that, in so far as] en la medida en que; [to the point where] hasta tal punto que; **to some/a certain ~** hasta cierto punto; **to a large** OR **great ~** en gran medida.

extenuating circumstances [ɪk'stenjʊeɪtɪŋ-] *npl* circunstancias *fpl* atenuantes.

exterior [ɪk'stɪərɪə'] ◇ *adj* exterior. ◇ *n* exterior *m*.

exterminate [ɪk'stɜːmɪneɪt] *vt* exterminar.

extermination [ɪk,stɜːmɪ'neɪʃn] *n* exterminio *m*.

external [ɪk'stɜːnl] *adj* externo(na).

◆ **externals** *npl* aspecto *m* exterior.

externally [ɪk'stɜːnəlɪ] *adv* por fuera; "**to be applied ~**" "de uso tópico".

extinct [ɪk'stɪŋkt] *adj* extinto(ta).

extinction [ɪk'stɪŋkʃn] *n* [of species] extinción *f*.

extinguish [ɪk'stɪŋgwɪʃ] *vt fml* [gen] extinguir; [cigarette] apagar.

extinguisher [ɪk'stɪŋgwɪʃə'] *n* extintor *m*.

extn. = ext.

extol (*pt* & *pp* **-led**, *cont* **-ling**), **extoll** *Am* [ɪk'stəʊl] *vt* [merits, values] ensalzar.

extort [ɪk'stɔːt] *vt*: **to ~ sthg from sb** [confession, promise] arrancar algo a alguien; [money] sacar algo a alguien.

extortion [ɪk'stɔːʃn] *n* extorsión *f*.

extortionate [ɪk'stɔːʃnət] *adj* desorbitado(da), exorbitante.

extra ['ekstrə] ◇ *adj* [additional] **extra** (*inv*), **adicional**; [spare] de más, de sobra; **take ~ care pon sumo cuidado.** ◇ *n* **-1.** [addition] extra *m*. **-2.** [additional charge] suplemento *m*. **-3.** CINEMA & THEATRE extra *m* y *f*. ◇ *adv* extra; **to pay/charge ~** pagar/cobrar un suplemento.

extra- ['ekstrə] *prefix* extra-.

extract [*n* 'ekstrækt, *vb* ɪk'strækt] ◇ *n* **-1.** [from book, piece of music] fragmento *m*. **-2.** CHEM extracto *m*. ◇ *vt*: **to ~ sthg (from)** [gen] extraer algo (de); [confession] arrancar algo (de).

extraction [ɪk'strækʃn] *n* extracción *f*.

extractor (fan) [ɪk'stræktə'-] *n Br* extractor *m* (de humos).

extracurricular [,ekstrəkə'rɪkjʊlə'] *adj* SCH extraescolar.

extradite ['ekstrədaɪt] *vt*: **to ~ sb (from/to)** extraditar OR extradir a alguien (de/a).

extradition [,ekstrə'dɪʃn] ◇ *n* extradición *f*. ◇ *comp* de extradición.

extramarital [ˌekstrə'mærɪtl] *adj* fuera del matrimonio.

extramural [ˌekstrə'mjʊərəl] *adj* UNIV *fuera de la universidad pero organizado por ella.*

extraneous [ɪk'streɪnjəs] *adj* **-1.** [irrelevant] ajeno(na). **-2.** [outside] externo(na).

extraordinary [ɪk'strɔːdnrɪ] *adj* extraordinario(ria).

extraordinary general meeting *n* junta *f* (general) extraordinaria.

extrapolate [ɪk'stræpəleɪt] ◇ *vt* **-1.** MATH: to ~ sthg (from) extrapolar algo (a partir de). **-2.** [deduce]: to ~ sthg (from) deducir algo (a partir de). ◇ *vi* **-1.** MATH: to ~ from extrapolar a partir de. **-2.** [deduce]: to ~ from deducir a partir de.

extrasensory perception [ˌekstrə'sensərɪ-] *n* percepción *f* extrasensorial.

extraterrestrial [ˌekstrətə'restrɪəl] *adj* extraterrestre.

extra time *n* Br FTBL prórroga *f*.

extravagance [ɪk'strævəgəns] *n* **-1.** (*U*) [excessive spending] derroche *m*, despilfarro *m*. **-2.** [luxury] extravagancia *f*.

extravagant [ɪk'strævəgənt] *adj* **-1.** [wasteful] derrochador(ra). **-2.** [expensive] caro(ra). **-3.** [exaggerated] extravagante.

extravaganza [ɪkˌstrævə'gænzə] *n* fastos *mpl*, *espectáculo público de enorme fastuosidad.*

extreme [ɪk'striːm] ◇ *adj* extremo(ma). ◇ *n* [furthest limit] extremo *m*; to go to ~s llegar a grandes extremos; in the ~ en grado sumo, en extremo.

extremely [ɪk'striːmlɪ] *adv* [very] sumamente, extremadamente.

extremism [ɪk'striːmɪzm] *n* extremismo *m*.

extremist [ɪk'striːmɪst] ◇ *adj* extremista. ◇ *n* extremista *m y f*.

extremity [ɪk'stremətɪ] (*pl* **-ies**) *n* **-1.** *fml* [extreme adversity] suma gravedad *f*. **-2.** [extremeness] extremosidad *f*. **-3.** *fml* [end] extremo *m*.

◆ **extremities** *npl* [of body] extremidades *fpl*.

extricate ['ekstrɪkeɪt] *vt*: to ~ sthg from lograr sacar algo de; to ~ o.s. from lograr salirse de.

extrovert ['ekstrəvɜːt] ◇ *adj* extrovertido(da). ◇ *n* extrovertido *m*, -da *f*.

extruded [ɪk'struːdɪd] *adj* [metal, plastic] extrudido(da).

exuberance [ɪg'zjuːbərəns] *n* exuberancia *f*, euforia *f*.

exuberant [ɪg'zjuːbərənt] *adj* exuberante, eufórico(ca).

exude [ɪg'zjuːd] *vt lit* & *fig* rezumar.

exult [ɪg'zʌlt] *vi*: to ~ (at OR in) regocijarse OR alegrarse (por).

exultant [ɪg'zʌltənt] *adj* regocijado(da), jubiloso(sa).

eye [aɪ] (*cont* **eyeing** OR **eying**) ◇ *n* ojo *m*; before my *etc* (very) ~s ante mis *etc* propios ojos; to cast OR run one's ~ over sthg echar un ojo OR un vistazo a algo; to catch one's/sb's ~ llamar la atención de uno/ alguien; to clap OR lay OR set ~s on sb poner la vista en alguien; to cry one's ~s out llorar a moco tendido; to feast one's ~s on sthg regalarse la vista con algo; to have an ~ for sthg tener buen ojo para algo; to have one's ~ on sthg echar el ojo a algo; in my *etc* ~s en mi *etc* entender; in the ~s of the law a (los) ojos de la ley; to keep one's ~s open for, to keep an ~ out for estar atento a; to keep an ~ on sthg echar un ojo a algo, vigilar algo; there is more to this than meets the ~ esto tiene más enjundia de lo que parece; to open sb's ~s (to sthg) abrirle los ojos a alguien (sobre algo); not to see ~ to ~ with sb no ver las cosas de la misma forma que alguien; to close OR shut one's ~s to sthg cerrar los ojos a algo; to turn a blind ~ (to sthg) hacer la vista gorda (a algo); to be up to one's ~s in work Br estar hasta arriba de trabajo. ◇ *vt* mirar.

◆ **eye up** *vt sep* Br comerse con los ojos a.

eyeball ['aɪbɔːl] ◇ *n* globo *m* ocular. ◇ *vt* Am *inf* clavar los ojos en.

eyebath ['aɪbɑːθ] *n* lavaojos *m inv*, baño *m* ocular.

eyebrow ['aɪbraʊ] *n* ceja *f*; to raise one's ~s *fig* arquear las cejas.

eyebrow pencil *n* lápiz *m* de cejas.

eye-catching *adj* llamativo(va).

eye contact *n* cruce *m* de miradas, contacto *m* visual.

eyelash ['aɪlæʃ] *n* pestaña *f*.

eyelet ['aɪlɪt] *n* ojete *m*.

eye-level *adj* a la altura de los ojos.

eyelid ['aɪlɪd] *n* párpado *m*; she didn't bat an ~ *inf* ni siquiera parpadeó.

eyeliner ['aɪˌlaɪnər] *n* lápiz *m* de ojos.

eye-opener *n inf* [revelation] revelación *f*; [surprise] sorpresa *f*.

eyepatch ['aɪpætʃ] *n* parche *m* (en el ojo).

eye shadow *n* sombra *f* de ojos.

eyesight ['aɪsaɪt] *n* vista *f*.

eyesore ['aɪsɔːr] *n* horror *m*, monstruosidad *f*.

eyestrain ['aɪstreɪn] *n* vista *f* cansada.

eyetooth ['aɪtuːθ] (*pl* **-teeth**) *n*: **to give one's eyeteeth for sthg/to do sthg** dar lo que fuera por algo/por hacer algo.

eyewash ['aɪwɒʃ] *n* (*U*) *inf* [nonsense] disparates *mpl*, tonterías *fpl*.

eyewitness [,aɪ'wɪtnɪs] *n* testigo *m* y *f* ocular.

eyrie ['ɪərɪ] *n* aguilera *f*.

f (*pl* **f's** OR **fs**), **F** (*pl* **F's** OR **Fs**) [ef] *n* [letter] f *f*, F *f*.
◆ **F** ◇ *n* MUS fa *m*. ◇ *adj* (*abbr of* **Fahrenheit**) F.

FA (*abbr of* **Football Association**) *n federación británica de fútbol*, ≃ FEF *f*.

FAA (*abbr of* **Federal Aviation Administration**) *n dirección federal estadounidense de aviación civil*.

fable ['feɪbl] *n* [traditional story] fábula *f*.

fabled ['feɪbld] *adj* legendario(ria).

fabric ['fæbrɪk] *n* **-1.** [cloth] tela *f*, tejido *m*. **-2.** [of building, society] estructura *f*.

fabricate ['fæbrɪkeɪt] *vt* **-1.** [invent - story] inventar; [- evidence] falsear. **-2.** [manufacture] fabricar.

fabrication [,fæbrɪ'keɪʃn] *n* **-1.** [lying, lie] invención *f*. **-2.** [manufacture] fabricación *f*.

fabulous ['fæbjʊləs] *adj inf* [excellent] fabuloso(sa).

fabulously ['fæbjʊləslɪ] *adv* fabulosamente, increíblemente.

facade [fə'sɑːd] *n* fachada *f*.

face [feɪs] ◇ *n* **-1.** [of person] cara *f*, rostro *m*; **~ to ~** cara a cara; **to fly in the ~ of sthg** oponerse a algo; **to look sb in the ~** mirar a alguien a la cara; **to lose ~** quedar mal; **to save ~** salvar las apariencias; **to say sthg to sb's ~** decir algo a alguien en su cara; **to show one's ~** dejarse ver. **-2.** [expression] semblante *m*, cara *f*; **to make** OR **pull a ~** hacer muecas; **her ~ fell** puso cara larga. **-3.** [of cliff, mountain, coin] cara *f*; [of building] fachada *f*. **-4.** [of clock, watch] esfera *f*. **-5.** [appearance, nature] aspecto *m*. **-6.** [surface] superficie *f*; **the ~ of the earth** la faz de la tierra; **on the ~ of it** a primera vista.

◇ *vt* **-1.** [point towards] mirar a. **-2.** [confront, accept, deal with] hacer frente a, enfrentarse a. **-3.** *inf* [cope with] aguantar, soportar.
◇ *vi*: **to ~ forwards/south** mirar hacia delante/al sur.
◆ **face down** *adv* boca abajo.
◆ **face up** *adv* boca arriba.
◆ **in the face of** *prep* [in spite of] a pesar de.
◆ **face up to** *vt fus* hacer frente a, enfrentarse a.

facecloth ['feɪsklɒθ] *n Br* toallita *f* (*para lavarse*).

face cream *n* crema *f* facial.

faceless ['feɪslɪs] *adj* anónimo(ma), sin rostro.

face-lift *n* [on face] lifting *m*, estiramiento *m* de piel; *fig* [on building etc] lavado *m* de cara.

face pack *n* mascarilla *f* facial.

face powder *n* (*U*) polvos *mpl* para la cara.

face-saving [-'seɪvɪŋ] *adj* para salvar las apariencias.

facet ['fæsɪt] *n* faceta *f*.

facetious [fə'siːʃəs] *adj* guasón(ona).

facetiously [fə'siːʃəslɪ] *adv* fuera de tono.

face-to-face *adj* cara a cara.

face value *n* [of coin, stamp] valor *m* nominal; **to take sthg at ~** tomarse algo literalmente.

facial ['feɪʃl] ◇ *adj* facial; [expression] de la cara. ◇ *n* limpieza *f* de cutis.

facile [*Br* 'fæsaɪl, *Am* 'fæsl] *adj fml* & *pej* [remark, analysis] superficial; [reply, solution] facilón(ona).

facilitate [fə'sɪlɪteɪt] *vt fml* facilitar.

facility [fə'sɪlətɪ] (*pl* **-ies**) *n* **-1.** [ability]: **to have a ~ for sthg** tener facilidad para algo. **-2.** [feature] dispositivo *m*.
◆ **facilities** *npl* [amenities] instalaciones *fpl*; [services] servicios *mpl*.

facing ['feɪsɪŋ] *adj* opuesto(ta).

facsimile [fæk'sɪmɪlɪ] *n* facsímil *m*.

facsimile machine *fml* = **fax machine**.

fact [fækt] *n* **-1.** [piece of information] dato *m*; [established truth] hecho *m*; **the ~ is el hecho es que**; **the ~ remains that ...** no obstante ...; **to know sthg for a ~** saber algo a ciencia cierta. **-2.** (*U*) [truth] realidad *f*.
◆ **as a matter of fact** *adv* de hecho, en realidad.
◆ **in fact** *conj* & *adv* de hecho, en realidad.

fact-finding [-'faɪndɪŋ] *adj* de investigación.

faction ['fækʃn] *n* [group] facción *f*.

factional ['fækʃənl] *adj* [dispute] entre facciones.

fact of life *n* hecho *m* ineludible.

◆ **facts of life** *npl euphemism*: **to tell sb (about) the facts of life** contar a alguien cómo nacen los niños.

factor ['fæktər] *n* factor *m*.

factory ['fæktərɪ] (*pl* **-ies**) *n* fábrica *f*.

factory farming *n* cría *f* intensiva de animales de granja.

factory ship *n* buque *m* factoría.

factotum [fæk'təʊtəm] (*pl* **-s**) *n* factótum *m*.

fact sheet *n Br* hoja *f* informativa.

factual ['fæktʃʊəl] *adj* basado(da) en hechos reales.

faculty ['fækltɪ] (*pl* **-ies**) *n* **-1.** [gen] facultad *f*. **-2.** *Am* [in college]: **the ~** el profesorado.

FA Cup *n* ≃ Copa *f* del Rey.

fad [fæd] *n* [of person] capricho *m*; [of society] moda *f* pasajera.

faddy ['fædɪ] (*compar* **-ier**, *superl* **-iest**) *adj inf pej* tiquismiquis (*inv*).

fade [feɪd] ◇ *vt* descolorar, desteñir. ◇ *vi* **-1.** [jeans, curtains, paint] descolorarse, desteñirse; [flower] marchitarse. **-2.** [light, sound, smile] irse apagando. **-3.** [memory, feeling, interest] desvanecerse.

◆ **fade away**, **fade out** *vi* desvanecerse.

faded ['feɪdɪd] *adj* descolorido(da), desteñido(da).

faeces *Br*, **feces** *Am* ['fiːsiːz] *npl* heces *fpl*.

Faeroe, **Faroe** ['feərəʊ] *n*: **the ~ Islands**, **the ~s** las islas Faroe.

faff [fæf]
◆ **faff about**, **faff around** *vi Br inf* enredar, perder el tiempo.

fag [fæg] *n inf* **-1.** *Br* [cigarette] pitillo *m*. **-2.** *Br* [chore] lata *f*, rollo *m*. **-3.** *Am pej* [homosexual] marica *m*, maricón *m*.

fag end *n Br inf* colilla *f*.

fagged out [fægd-] *adj Br inf* molido(da), hecho(cha) polvo.

faggot, **fagot** *Am* ['fægət] *n* **-1.** *Br* CULIN *tipo de albóndiga*. **-2.** *Am inf pej* [homosexual] marica *m*, maricón *m*, joto *m Amer*.

Fahrenheit ['færənhaɪt] *adj* Fahrenheit (*inv*).

fail [feɪl] ◇ *vt* **-1.** [exam, test, candidate] suspender. **-2.** [not succeed]: **to ~ to do sthg** no lograr hacer algo. **-3.** [neglect]: **to ~ to do sthg** no hacer algo. **-4.** [let down] fallar. ◇ *vi* **-1.** [not succeed] fracasar. **-2.** [not pass exam] suspender. **-3.** [stop functioning] fallar. **-4.** [weaken] debilitarse.

failed [feɪld] *adj* fracasado(da).

failing ['feɪlɪŋ] ◇ *n* [weakness] fallo *m*. ◇ *prep* a falta de; **~ that** en su defecto.

fail-safe *adj* protegido(da) en caso de fallos.

failure ['feɪljər] *n* **-1.** [lack of success, unsuccessful thing] fracaso *m*. **-2.** [person] fracasado *m*, -da *f*. **-3.** [in exam] suspenso *m*. **-4.** [act of neglecting]: **her ~ to do it** el que no lo hiciera. **-5.** [breakdown, malfunction] avería *f*, fallo *m*. **-6.** [of nerve, courage etc] pérdida *f*.

faint [feɪnt] ◇ *adj* **-1.** [weak, vague] débil, tenue; [outline] impreciso(sa); [memory, longing] vago(ga); [trace, smell] ligero(ra), leve. **-2.** [chance] reducido(da), mínimo(ma). **-3.** [dizzy] mareado(da). ◇ *vi* desmayarse.

faintest ['feɪntəst] *adj*: **I haven't the ~ idea** no tengo ni la más remota idea.

faint-hearted [-'hɑːtɪd] *adj* pusilánime.

faintly ['feɪntlɪ] *adv* **-1.** [smile, shine] débilmente; [recall] vagamente. **-2.** [ludicrous, pathetic] ligeramente.

faintness ['feɪntnɪs] *n* (*U*) **-1.** [dizziness] mareos *mpl*. **-2.** [of image] imprecisión *f*. **-3.** [of memory] vaguedad *f*; [of smell, sound] levedad *f*.

fair [feər] ◇ *adj* **-1.** [just] justo(ta); **it's not ~!** ¡no hay derecho!; **to be ~ ...** para ser justos .... **-2.** [quite large] considerable. **-3.** [quite good] bastante bueno(na); "**~**" SCH "regular". **-4.** [hair] rubio(bia). **-5.** [skin, complexion] blanco(ca), claro(ra). **-6.** [weather] bueno(na). ◇ *n* **-1.** *Br* [funfair] parque *m* de atracciones. **-2.** [trade fair] feria *f*. ◇ *adv* [fairly] limpio.

◆ **fair enough** *adv Br inf* está bien, vale.

fair copy *n* copia *f* en limpio.

fair game *n*: **to be ~ (for)** ser un blanco *m* fácil (para).

fairground ['feəgraʊnd] *n* (recinto *m* del) parque *m* de atracciones.

fair-haired [-'heəd] *adj* rubio(bia).

fairly ['feəlɪ] *adv* **-1.** [moderately] bastante. **-2.** [justly] justamente, equitativamente.

fair-minded [-'maɪndɪd] *adj* justo(ta), equitativo(va).

fairness ['feənɪs] *n* [justness] justicia *f*; **in ~ (to)** para ser justos (con).

fair play *n* juego *m* limpio.

fair trade *n* comercio *m* justo.

fairway ['feəweɪ] *n* calle *f* (*en golf*).

fairy ['feərɪ] (*pl* **-ies**) *n* hada *f*.

fairy lights *npl Br* bombillas *fpl* OR luces *fpl* de colores.

fairy tale *n* cuento *m* de hadas.

fait accompli [,feɪtə'kɒmplɪ] (*pl* **faits ac-**

complis [ˌfeɪtə'kɒmplɪ]) *n* hecho *m* consumado.

faith [feɪθ] *n* fe *f*; **in good/bad** ~ de buena/mala fe.

faithful ['feɪθfʊl] ◇ *adj* fiel. ◇ *npl* RELIG: **the** ~ los fieles.

faithfully ['feɪθfʊlɪ] *adv* fielmente; **Yours** ~ *Br* [in letter] le saluda atentamente.

faithfulness ['feɪθfʊlnɪs] *n* fidelidad *f*.

faith healer *n persona que cura enfermedades mediante la fe religiosa.*

faithless ['feɪθlɪs] *adj* desleal.

fake [feɪk] ◇ *adj* falso(sa). ◇ *n* **-1.** [object, painting] falsificación *f*. **-2.** [person] impostor *m*, -ra *f*. ◇ *vt* **-1.** [results, signature] falsificar. **-2.** [illness, emotions] fingir. ◇ *vi* [pretend] fingir.

falcon ['fɔːlkən] *n* halcón *m*.

Falkland Islands ['fɔːklənd-], **Falklands** ['fɔːkləndz] *npl*: **the** ~ las (Islas) Malvinas.

fall [fɔːl] (*pt* fell, *pp* fallen) ◇ *vi* **-1.** [gen] caer; **he fell off the chair** se cayó de la silla; **to** ~ **to bits** OR **pieces** hacerse pedazos; **to** ~ **flat** *fig* no causar el efecto deseado. **-2.** [decrease] bajar, disminuir. **-3.** [become]: **to** ~ **ill** ponerse enfermo(ma); **to** ~ **asleep** dormirse; **to** ~ **silent** quedarse en silencio; **to** ~ **vacant** quedar libre; **to** ~ **in love** enamorarse, encamotarse *Amer*; **to** ~ **open** caer abierto. **-4.** [belong, be classed]: **to** ~ **into/under** pertenecer a. **-5.** [MIL - city] **to** ~ **(to)** caer (en manos de). **-6.** *Br* POL [constituency]: **to** ~ **to sb/sthg** ir a parar a alguien/algo. **-7.** [cover]: **to** ~ **on** OR **across** [light] iluminar; [shadow] oscurecer. ◇ *n* **-1.** [gen] caída *f*. **-2.** [of snow] nevada *f*. **-3.** [MIL - of city] derrota *f*. **-4.** [decrease]: ~ **(in)** descenso *m* (de). **-5.** *Am* [autumn] otoño *m*.

◆ **falls** *npl* cataratas *fpl*.

◆ **fall about** *vi Br inf*: **to** ~ **about** (laughing) partirse (de risa), troncharse.

◆ **fall apart** *vi* [book, chair] caerse a trozos, romperse; *fig* [country, person] desmoronarse.

◆ **fall away** *vi* **-1.** [land] descender. **-2.** [plaster] desprenderse, caerse.

◆ **fall back** *vi* [person, crowd] echarse atrás, retroceder.

◆ **fall back on** *vt fus* [resort to] recurrir a.

◆ **fall behind** *vi* **-1.** [in race] quedarse atrás. **-2.** [with rent, work] retrasarse.

◆ **fall down** *vi* [fail] fallar.

◆ **fall for** *vt fus* **-1.** *inf* [fall in love with] enamorarse de. **-2.** [trick, lie] tragarse.

◆ **fall in** *vi* **-1.** [roof, ceiling] desplomarse, hundirse. **-2.** MIL formar filas.

◆ **fall in with** *vt fus* [go along with] aceptar.

◆ **fall off** *vi* **-1.** [branch, handle] desprenderse. **-2.** [demand, numbers] disminuir.

◆ **fall on** *vt fus* **-1.** [subj: eyes, gaze] posarse en. **-2.** [attack] caer OR lanzarse sobre.

◆ **fall out** *vi* **-1.** [hair, tooth]: **his hair is** ~ **ing out** se le está cayendo el pelo. **-2.** [friends] pelearse, discutir. **-3.** MIL romper filas.

◆ **fall over** ◇ *vt fus* tropezar con; **to be** ~ **ing over o.s. to do sthg** *inf* desvivirse por hacer algo. ◇ *vi* [person, chair etc] caer, caerse.

◆ **fall through** *vi* [plan, deal] fracasar.

◆ **fall to** *vt fus*: **it fell to me to do it** me tocó a mí hacerlo.

fallacious [fə'leɪʃəs] *adj fml* erróneo(a), falso(sa).

fallacy ['fæləsɪ] (*pl* **-ies**) *n* concepto *m* erróneo, error *m*.

fallen ['fɔːln] *pp* → **fall**.

fall guy *n Am inf* [scapegoat] cabeza *f* de turco.

fallible ['fæləbl] *adj* falible.

falling ['fɔːlɪŋ] *adj* [decreasing] descendente, en descenso.

fallopian tube [fə'ləʊpɪən-] *n* trompa *f* de Falopio.

fallout ['fɔːlaʊt] *n* [radiation] lluvia *f* radiactiva.

fallout shelter *n* refugio *m* atómico.

fallow ['fæləʊ] *adj* en barbecho; **to lie** ~ quedar en barbecho.

false [fɔːls] *adj* [gen] falso(sa); [eyelashes, nose] postizo(za).

false alarm *n* falsa alarma *f*.

falsehood ['fɔːlshʊd] *n fml* falsedad *f*.

falsely ['fɔːlslɪ] *adv* falsamente.

false start *n* [in race] salida *f* nula; *fig* comienzo *m* en falso.

false teeth *npl* dentadura *f* postiza.

falsetto [fɔːl'setəʊ] (*pl* **-s**) ◇ *n* falsete *m*. ◇ *adv* con falsete.

falsify ['fɔːlsɪfaɪ] (*pt* & *pp* **-ied**) *vt* [facts, accounts] falsificar.

falter ['fɔːltər] *vi* vacilar.

faltering ['fɔːltərɪŋ] *adj* [steps, voice] vacilante, titubeante.

fame [feɪm] *n* fama *f*.

familiar [fə'mɪljər] *adj* **-1.** [known] familiar, conocido(da); **to be** ~ **to sb** serle familiar a alguien. **-2.** [conversant]: ~ **with** familiarizado(da) con; **to be on** ~ **terms with sb** tener confianza con alguien. **-3.** *pej* [too informal - person] que se toma muchas confianzas; [- tone, manner] demasiado amistoso(sa).

familiarity [fə,mılı'ærətı] n (U) **-1.** [knowledge]: ~ **with** conocimiento m de. **-2.** [normality] familiaridad f. **-3.** pej [excessive informality] familiaridades fpl, confianzas fpl.

familiarize, -ise [fə'mıljəraız] vt: **to** ~ **o.s./ sb with sthg** familiarizarse/familiarizar a alguien con algo.

family ['fæmlı] (pl **-ies**) ◇ n familia f. ◇ comp **-1.** [belonging to family] familiar. **-2.** [suitable for all ages] para toda la familia.

family business n negocio m familiar.

family credit n (U) Br ≃ prestación f OR ayuda f familiar.

family doctor n médico m de cabecera.

family life n vida f familiar.

family planning n planificación f familiar.

family tree n árbol m genealógico.

famine ['fæmın] n hambruna f.

famished ['fæmıʃt] adj inf [very hungry] muerto(ta) de hambre, famélico(ca).

famous ['feıməs] adj: ~ **(for)** famoso(sa) (por).

famously ['feıməslı] adv dated: **to get on** OR **along** ~ **(with sb)** llevarse de maravilla (con alguien).

fan [fæn] (pt & pp **-ned**, cont **-ning**) ◇ n **-1.** [of paper, silk] abanico m. **-2.** [electric or mechanical] ventilador m. **-3.** [enthusiast] fan m y f, admirador m, -ra f; FTBL hincha m y f. ◇ vt **-1.** [cool] abanicar; **to** ~ **o.s.** abanicarse. **-2.** [stimulate - fire, feelings] avivar.
◆ **fan out** vi desplegarse en abanico.

fanatic [fə'nætık] n fanático m, -ca f.

fanatical [fə'nætıkl] adj fanático(ca).

fanaticism [fə'nætısızm] n fanatismo m.

fan belt n correa f del ventilador.

fanciful ['fænsıful] adj **-1.** [odd] rocambolesco(ca). **-2.** [elaborate] extravagante.

fan club n club m de fans.

fancy ['fænsı] (compar **-ier**, superl **-iest**, pl **-ies**, pt & pp **-ied**) ◇ vt **-1.** inf [feel like]: **I** ~ **a cup of tea/going to the cinema** me apetece una taza de té/ir al cine. **-2.** inf [desire]: **do you** ~ **her?** ¿te gusta?, ¿te mola?; **to** ~ **o.s.** tenérselo creído; **to** ~ **o.s. as sthg** dárselas de algo. **-3.** [imagine]: ~ **meeting you here!** ¡qué casualidad encontrarte por aquí!; ~ **that!** ¡imagínate!, ¡mira por dónde! **-4.** dated [think] creer. ◇ n **-1.** [desire, liking] capricho m; **to take a** ~ **to** encapricharse con. **-2.** [fantasy] fantasía f. ◇ adj **-1.** [elaborate] elaborado(da). **-2.** [expensive] de lujo, caro(ra); [prices] exorbitante.

fancy dress n (U) disfraz m.

fancy-dress party n fiesta f de disfraces.

fancy goods npl artículos mpl de fantasía.

fanfare ['fænfeəʳ] n fanfarria f.

fang [fæŋ] n colmillo m.

fan heater n convector m, estufa f de aire.

fanlight ['fænlaıt] n Br montante m en abanico.

fan mail n (U) cartas fpl de fans.

fanny ['fænı] n Am inf [buttocks] nalgas fpl.

fanny pack n Am riñonera f.

fantasize, -ise ['fæntəsaız] vi fantasear; **to** ~ **about sthg/about doing sthg** soñar con algo/con hacer algo.

fantastic [fæn'tæstık] adj **-1.** [gen] fantástico(ca), chévere Amer. **-2.** [exotic] exótico(ca).

fantastically [fæn'tæstıklı] adv **-1.** [extremely] enormemente. **-2.** [exotically] de manera exótica.

fantasy ['fæntəsı] (pl **-ies**) ◇ n fantasía f. ◇ comp imaginario(ria), de ensueño.

fantasy football n ≃ la liga fantástica®, juego en el que cada participante crea su propio equipo de fútbol imaginario con nombres de jugadores reales y va sumando puntos según la actuación de dichos jugadores en la competición real.

fanzine ['fænziːn] n fanzine m.

fao (abbr of **for the attention of**) a/a.

FAO (abbr of **Food and Agriculture Organization**) n FAO f.

FAQ (abbr of **free alongside quay**) muelle franco.

far [fɑːʳ] (compar **farther** OR **further**, superl **farthest** OR **furthest**) ◇ adv **-1.** [in distance, time] lejos; **is it** ~? ¿está lejos?; **how** ~ **is it?** ¿a qué distancia está?; **how** ~ **is it to Prague?** ¿cuánto hay de aquí a Praga?; ~ **away** OR **off** [a long way away, a long time away] lejos; **as** ~ **back as 1900** ya en 1900; **so** ~ por ahora, hasta ahora; ~ **and wide** por todas partes; **from** ~ **and wide** de todas partes; **as** ~ **as** hasta. **-2.** [in degree or extent]: ~ **more/better/stronger** mucho más/mejor/más fuerte; **I wouldn't trust him very** ~ no me fiaría mucho de él; **how** ~ **have you got?** ¿hasta dónde has llegado?; **he's not** ~ **wrong** OR **out** OR **off** no anda del todo descaminado; **as** ~ **as I know** que yo sepa; **as** ~ **as I'm concerned** por OR en lo que a mí respecta; **as** ~ **as possible** en (la medida de) lo posible; **it's all right as** ~ **as it goes** para lo que es, no está mal; ~ **and away, by** ~ con mucho; ~ **from it** en absoluto, todo lo contrario; **so** ~ hasta un cierto punto; **so** ~ **so good** por OR hasta ahora todo va bien; **to go so** ~ **as to do sthg** llegar incluso a hacer algo; **to go too** ~ ir demasiado lejos.
◇ adj **-1.** [extreme] extremo(ma). **-2.** literary [remote] lejano(na).

faraway ['fɑːrəweɪ] *adj* **-1.** [land etc] lejano(na). **-2.** [look, expression] ausente.

farce [fɑːs] *n lit* & *fig* farsa *f.*

farcical ['fɑːsɪkl] *adj* absurdo(da), grotesco(ca).

fare [feəʳ] ◇ *n* **-1.** [payment] (precio *m* del) billete *m*; [in taxi] tarifa *f.* **-2.** (*U*) *fml* [food] comida *f.* ◇ *vi* [manage]: she ~d well/badly le fue bien/mal.

Far East *n*: the ~ el Extremo Oriente.

fare stage *n Br* [of bus] *parada donde aumenta el precio del billete.*

farewell [,feə'wel] ◇ *n* adiós *m*, despedida *f.* ◇ *excl literary* ¡vaya con Dios!

farfetched [,fɑː'fetʃt] *adj* traído(da) por los pelos, inverosímil.

farm [fɑːm] ◇ *n* granja *f,* chacra *f Amer.* ◇ *vt* [land] cultivar; [livestock] criar. ◇ *vi* [grow crops] cultivar la tierra; [raise livestock] criar ganado.
◆ **farm out** *vt sep* encargar, mandar hacer.

farmer ['fɑːməʳ] *n* agricultor *m,* -ra *f,* granjero *m,* -ra *f,* chacarero *m,* -ra *f Amer.*

farmhand ['fɑːmhænd] *n* peón *m,* labriego *m,* -ga *f.*

farmhouse ['fɑːmhaʊs, *pl* -haʊzɪz] *n* granja *f,* caserío *m.*

farming ['fɑːmɪŋ] *n* (*U*) **-1.** AGR [industry] agricultura *f.* **-2.** [act - of crops] cultivo *m*; [- of animals] cría *f,* crianza *f.*

farm labourer = **farmhand.**

farmland ['fɑːmlænd] *n* (*U*) tierras *fpl* de labranza.

farmstead ['fɑːmsted] *n Am* granja *f.*

farm worker = **farmhand.**

farmyard ['fɑːmjɑːd] *n* corral *m.*

Faroe = **Faeroe.**

far-off *adj* lejano(na), remoto(ta).

far-reaching [-'riːtʃɪŋ] *adj* trascendental.

farsighted [,fɑː'saɪtɪd] *adj* **-1.** [gen] con visión de futuro. **-2.** *Am* [long-sighted] présbita.

fart [fɑːt] *v inf* ◇ *n* **-1.** [flatulence] pedo *m.* **-2.** [person] gilipuertas *m y f inv.* ◇ *vi* tirarse un pedo.

farther ['fɑːðəʳ] *compar* → **far.**

farthest ['fɑːðəst] *superl* → **far.**

FAS (*abbr of* **free alongside ship**) *franco al costado.*

fascia ['feɪʃə] *n* **-1.** [on shop] rótulo *m.* **-2.** AUT salpicadero *m.*

fascinate ['fæsɪneɪt] *vt* fascinar.

fascinating ['fæsɪneɪtɪŋ] *adj* fascinante.

fascination [,fæsɪ'neɪʃn] *n* fascinación *f.*

fascism ['fæʃɪzm] *n* fascismo *m.*

fascist ['fæʃɪst] ◇ *adj* fascista. ◇ *n* fascista *m y f.*

fashion ['fæʃn] ◇ *n* **-1.** [clothing, style, vogue] moda *f*; **in/out of** ~ de/pasado de moda. **-2.** [manner] manera *f*; **after a** ~ más o menos. ◇ *vt fml* elaborar; *fig* forjar.

fashionable ['fæʃnəbl] *adj* de moda.

fashion-conscious *adj* que sigue la moda.

fashion designer *n* diseñador *m,* -ra *f* de modas.

fashion show *n* pase *m* OR desfile *m* de modelos.

fast [fɑːst] ◇ *adj* **-1.** [rapid] rápido(da). **-2.** [clock, watch] que adelanta. **-3.** [dye, colour] sólido(da), que no destiñe. ◇ *adv* **-1.** [rapidly] de prisa, rápidamente. **-2.** [firmly]: **stuck** ~ bien pegado(da); **to hold** ~ **to sthg** [person, object] agarrarse fuerte a algo; [principles] mantenerse fiel a algo; ~ **asleep** profundamente dormido. ◇ *n* ayuno *m.* ◇ *vi* ayunar.

fasten ['fɑːsn] ◇ *vt* **-1.** [gen] sujetar; [clothes, belt] abrochar; **he** ~ed **his coat** se abrochó el abrigo. **-2.** [attach]: **to** ~ **sthg to sthg** fijar algo a algo. **-3.** [hands, teeth] apretar. ◇ *vi*: **to** ~ **on to sb/sthg** aferrarse a alguien/algo.

fastener ['fɑːsnəʳ] *n* cierre *m,* broche *m*; [zip] cremallera *f.*

fastening ['fɑːsnɪŋ] *n* [of door, window] cerrojo *m,* pestillo *m.*

fast food *n* (*U*) comida *f* rápida.

fast-forward ◇ *n* avance *m* rápido. ◇ *vt* & *vi* correr hacia adelante.

fastidious [fə'stɪdɪəs] *adj* [fussy] quisquilloso(sa).

fast lane *n* [on motorway] carril *m* rápido; **to live life in the** ~ *fig* llevar un frenético tren de vida.

fat [fæt] (*compar* **-ter,** *superl* **-test**) ◇ *adj* **-1.** [gen] gordo(da); **to get** ~ engordar. **-2.** [meat] con mucha grasa. **-3.** [book, package] grueso(sa). **-4.** [profit, fee, cheque] abultado(da). **-5.** *iro* [small]: **a** ~ **lot of good** OR **use that was!** ¡pues sí que sirvió de mucho eso! ◇ *n* **-1.** [gen] grasa *f.* **-2.** [for cooking] manteca *f.*

fatal ['feɪtl] *adj* **-1.** [serious] fatal, funesto(ta). **-2.** [mortal] mortal.

fatalism ['feɪtəlɪzm] *n* fatalismo *m.*

fatalistic [,feɪtə'lɪstɪk] *adj* fatalista.

fatality [fə'tælətɪ] (*pl* **-ies**) *n* **-1.** [accident victim] víctima *f* mortal, muerto *m.* **-2.** = **fatalism.**

fatally ['feɪtəlɪ] *adv* **-1.** [seriously] gravemente. **-2.** [mortally] mortalmente.

fate

196

fate [feɪt] *n* **-1.** [destiny] destino *m*; **to tempt ~** tentar a la suerte. **-2.** [result, end] final *m*, suerte *f*.
fated ['feɪtɪd] *adj* predestinado(da); **to be ~ to do sthg** estar predestinado a hacer algo.
fateful ['feɪtfʊl] *adj* fatídico(ca).
fathead ['fæthed] *n inf* majadero *m*, -ra *f*, imbécil *m y f*.
father ['fɑːðər] ◇ *n lit* & *fig* padre *m*. ◇ *vt* engendrar.
◆ **Father** *n* **-1.** [priest] padre *m*. **-2.** [God] Padre *m*.
Father Christmas *n Br* Papá *m* Noel.
fatherhood ['fɑːðəhʊd] *n* paternidad *f*.
father-in-law (*pl* **father-in-laws** OR **fathers-in-law**) *n* suegro *m*.
fatherly ['fɑːðəlɪ] *adj* paternal.
Father's Day *n* día *m* del padre.
fathom ['fæðəm] ◇ *n* braza *f*. ◇ *vt*: **to ~ sthg/sb (out)** llegar a comprender algo/a alguien.
fatigue [fə'tiːg] ◇ *n* fatiga *f*. ◇ *vt* fatigar.
◆ **fatigues** *npl* traje *m* de faena.
fatless ['fætlɪs] *adj* sin grasas.
fatness ['fætnɪs] *n* [of person] gordura *f*.
fatten ['fætn] *vt* engordar.
◆ **fatten up** *vt sep* engordar, cebar.
fattening ['fætnɪŋ] *adj* que engorda.
fatty ['fætɪ] (*compar* -ier, *superl* -iest, *pl* -ies) ◇ *adj* graso(sa). ◇ *n inf pej* gordinflón *m*, -ona *f*.
fatuous ['fætjʊəs] *adj* necio(cia).
fatuously ['fætjʊəslɪ] *adv* neciamente.
faucet ['fɔːsɪt] *n Am* grifo *m*.
fault ['fɔːlt] ◇ *n* **-1.** [responsibility] culpa *f*; **through no ~ of my own** sin que la culpa sea mía; **to be at ~** tener la culpa. **-2.** [mistake, imperfection] defecto *m*; **to find ~ with** encontrar defectos a. **-3.** GEOL falla *f*. **-4.** [in tennis] falta *f*. ◇ *vt*: **to ~ sb (on sthg)** criticar a alguien (en algo).
faultless ['fɔːltlɪs] *adj* perfecto(ta), impecable.
faulty ['fɔːltɪ] (*compar* -ier, *superl* -iest) *adj* [machine, system] defectuoso(sa); [reasoning, logic] imperfecto(ta).
fauna ['fɔːnə] *n* fauna *f*.
faux pas [,fəʊ'pɑː] (*pl inv*) *n* plancha *f*, metedura *f* de pata.
favour *Br*, **favor** *Am* ['feɪvər] ◇ *n* **-1.** [gen] favor *m*, gauchada *f Amer*; **in sb's ~** a favor de alguien; **to be in/out of ~ (with)** ser/dejar de ser popular (con); **to do sb a ~** hacerle un favor a alguien; **to curry ~ with sb** tratar de congraciarse con alguien; **to rule in sb's ~** decidir a favor de alguien.

-2. [favouritism] favoritismo *m*. ◇ *vt* **-1.** [prefer] decantarse por, preferir. **-2.** [treat better, help] favorecer. **-3.** *iro* [honour]: **to ~ sb with sthg** honrar a alguien con algo.
◆ **in favour** *adv* [in agreement] a favor.
◆ **in favour of** *prep* **-1.** [in preference to] en favor de. **-2.** [in agreement with]: **to be in ~ of sthg/of doing sthg** estar a favor de algo/de hacer algo.
favourable *Br*, **favorable** *Am* ['feɪvrəbl] *adj* [positive] favorable.
favourably *Br*, **favorably** *Am* ['feɪvrəblɪ] *adv* favorablemente.
favoured *Br*, **favored** *Am* ['feɪvəd] *adj* [with special advantages] privilegiado(da), favorecido(da).
favourite *Br*, **favorite** *Am* ['feɪvrɪt] ◇ *adj* favorito(ta). ◇ *n* favorito *m*, -ta *f*.
favouritism *Br*, **favoritism** *Am* ['feɪvrɪtɪzm] *n* favoritismo *m*.
fawn [fɔːn] ◇ *adj* pajizo(za), beige (*inv*). ◇ *n* [animal] cervato *m*, cervatillo *m*. ◇ *vi*: **to ~ on sb** adular a alguien.
fax [fæks] ◇ *n* fax *m*. ◇ *vt* **-1.** [send fax to] mandar un fax a. **-2.** [send by fax] enviar por fax.
fax machine *n* fax *m*.
fax modem *n* modem *m* fax.
fax number *n* número *m* de fax.
faze [feɪz] *vt inf* dejar fuera de juego.
FBI (*abbr of* **Federal Bureau of Investigation**) *n* FBI *m*.
FCC (*abbr of* **Federal Communications Commission**) *n* dirección federal estadounidense de medios audiovisuales.
FCO (*abbr of* **Foreign and Commonwealth Office**) *n* ministerio británico de asuntos exteriores y relaciones con la Commonwealth.
FD (*abbr of* **Fire Department**) *n* cuerpo de bomberos en Estados Unidos.
FDA (*abbr of* **Food and Drug Administration**) *n* organismo estadounidense para el control de medicamentos y productos alimentarios.
FE *n abbr of* **Further Education**.
fear [fɪər] ◇ *n* **-1.** [gen] miedo *m*, temor *m*; **for ~ of** por miedo a. **-2.** [risk] peligro *m*. ◇ *vt* **-1.** [be afraid of] temer. **-2.** [anticipate] temerse; **to ~ (that)** ... temerse que .... ◇ *vi* [be afraid]: **to ~ for sb/sthg** temer por alguien/algo.
fearful ['fɪəfʊl] *adj* **-1.** *fml* [frightened] temeroso(sa). **-2.** [frightening] terrible, pavoroso(sa).
fearless ['fɪəlɪs] *adj* valiente, intrépido(da).
fearlessly ['fɪəlɪslɪ] *adv* sin miedo.
fearsome ['fɪəsəm] *adj* terrible, espantoso(sa).

feasibility [ˌfiːzəˈbɪlətɪ] *n* viabilidad *f*.

feasibility study *n* estudio *m* de viabilidad.

feasible [ˈfiːzəbl] *adj* factible, viable.

feast [fiːst] ◇ *n* [meal] banquete *m*, festín *m*. ◇ *vi*: **to ~ on** OR **off sthg** darse un banquete a base de algo.

feat [fiːt] *n* hazaña *f*.

feather [ˈfeðər] *n* pluma *f*.

feather bed *n* colchón *m* de plumas.

featherbrained [ˈfeðəbreɪnd] *adj* [person] atontolinado(da); [idea, scheme] disparatado(da).

featherweight [ˈfeðəweɪt] *n* [boxer] peso *m* pluma.

feature [ˈfiːtʃər] ◇ *n* -1. [characteristic] característica *f*. -2. [of face] rasgo *m*. -3. GEOGR accidente *m* geográfico. -4. [article] artículo *m* de fondo. -5. RADIO & TV [programme] programa *m* especial. -6. CINEMA = **feature film**. ◇ *vt* [subj: film] tener como protagonista a; [subj: exhibition] tener como atracción principal a. ◇ *vi*: **to ~ (in)** aparecer OR figurar (en).

feature film *n* largometraje *m*.

featureless [ˈfiːtʃəlɪs] *adj* anodino(na).

Feb. [feb] (*abbr of* **February**) feb.

February [ˈfebruərɪ] *n* febrero *m*; *see also* **September**.

feces *Am* = **faeces**.

feckless [ˈfeklɪs] *adj* irresponsable.

fed [fed] *pt & pp* → **feed**.

Fed [fed] ◇ *n inf* (*abbr of* **Federal Reserve Board**) *órgano de control del banco central estadounidense*. ◇ -1. *abbr of* **federal**. -2. *abbr of* **federation**.

federal [ˈfedrəl] *adj* federal.

Federal Bureau of Investigation *n* FBI *m*.

federalism [ˈfedrəlɪzm] *n* federalismo *m*.

federation [ˌfedəˈreɪʃn] *n* federación *f*.

fed up *adj*: **~ (with)** harto(ta) (de).

fee [fiː] *n* [to lawyer, doctor etc] honorarios *mpl*; **membership ~** cuota *f* de socio; **entrance ~** entrada *f*; **school ~s** (precio *m* de) matrícula *f*.

feeble [ˈfiːbəl] *adj* -1. [weak] débil. -2. [poor, silly] pobre, flojo(ja).

feebleminded [ˌfiːbəlˈmaɪndɪd] *adj* corto(ta) de entendederas.

feebleness [ˈfiːblnɪs] *n* (*U*) -1. [weakness] debilidad *f*. -2. [of excuse, joke] flojedad *f*.

feebly [ˈfiːblɪ] *adv* -1. [weakly] débilmente. -2. [ineffectively] de modo poco convincente.

feed [fiːd] (*pt & pp* **fed**) ◇ *vt* -1. [gcɪɪ] alimentar; [animal] dar de comer a. -2. [put, insert]: **to ~ sthg into sthg** introducir algo en algo. ◇ *vi* comer; **to ~ on** OR **off sthg** *lit & fig* alimentarse de algo. ◇ *n* -1. [meal] comida *f*. -2. [animal food] pienso *m*.

feedback [ˈfiːdbæk] *n* (*U*) -1. [reaction] respuesta *f*, reacciones *fpl*. -2. COMPUT & ELEC realimentación *f*; [on guitar etc] feedback *m*.

feedbag [ˈfiːdbæg] *n Am* morral *m*.

feeder [ˈfiːdər] ◇ *n* [baby]: **he's a messy ~** se ensucia mucho al comer. ◇ *comp*: **~ road** carretera *f* secundaria.

feeding bottle [ˈfiːdɪŋ-] *n Br* biberón *m*.

feel [fiːl] (*pt & pp* **felt**) ◇ *vt* -1. [touch] tocar. -2. [sense, notice, experience] sentir; **I felt myself blushing** noté que me ponía colorado. -3. [believe] creer; **to ~ (that)** creer OR pensar que. -4. *phr*: **not to ~ o.s.** no encontrarse bien.
◇ *vi* -1. [have sensation]: **to ~ hot/cold/sleepy** tener calor/frío/sueño. -2. [have emotion]: **to ~ safe/happy** sentirse seguro/feliz. -3. [seem] parecer (al tacto). -4. [by touch]: **to ~ for sthg** buscar algo a tientas. -5. [be in mood]: **do you ~ like a drink/eating out?** ¿te apetece beber algo/comer fuera?, ¿te provoca beber algo/comer fuera? *Amer*.
◇ *n* -1. [sensation, touch] tacto *m*, sensación *f*. -2. [atmosphere] atmósfera *f*. -3. *phr*: **to have ▪ ~ for sthg** tener un don especial ▪▪▪.

▪▪▪[ːlər] *n* antena *f*.

▪▪▪[ˈfiːlɪŋ] *n* -1. [emotion] sentimiento ~ resentimiento *m*. -2. [sensation] ▪▪▪ *f*. -3. [intuition] presentimiento *m*; ▪▪▪ OR **get the ~ (that)** ... me da la ▪▪ **n** de que .... -4. [understanding] apreci▪ón *f*, entendimiento *m*; **to have a ~ for sthg** saber apreciar algo.

◆ **feelings** *npl* sentimientos *mpl*; **to hurt sb's ~s** herir los sentimientos de alguien; **no hard ~s?** ¿todo olvidado?

fee-paying [-ˈpeɪɪŋ] *adj Br* de pago.

feet [fiːt] *pl* → **foot**.

feign [feɪn] *vt fml* fingir, aparentar.

feint [feɪnt] ◇ *n* finta *f*. ◇ *vi* fintar.

feisty [ˈfaɪstɪ] (*compar* -**ier**, *superl* -**iest**) *adj inf* con ganas de pelea, combativo(va).

felicitous [fɪˈlɪsɪtəs] *adj fml* afortunado(da).

feline [ˈfiːlaɪn] ◇ *adj* felino(na). ◇ *n fml* felino *m*.

fell [fel] ◇ *pt* → **fall**. ◇ *vt* -1. [tree] talar. -2. [person] derribar.

◆ **fells** *npl* GEOGR monte *m*.

fellow [ˈfeləʊ] ◇ *adj*: **~ students/prisoners** compañeros de clase/celda. ◇ *n* -1. *dated* [man] tipo *m*. -2. [comrade, peer] camarada *m* y f, compañero m, -ra f. **-3.** [of society] miembro m. **-4.** [of college] miembro m del claustro de profesores.

fellowship ['feləʊʃɪp] n **-1.** [comradeship] camaradería f. **-2.** [society] asociación f. **-3.** [of society or college] pertenencia f.

felony ['feləni] (pl **-ies**) n JUR delito m grave.

felt [felt] ◇ pt & pp → **feel**. ◇ n (U) fieltro m.

felt-tip pen n rotulador m.

female ['fi:meɪl] ◇ adj [animal, plant] hembra; [figure, sex] femenino(na). ◇ n **-1.** [female animal] hembra f. **-2.** [woman] mujer f.

feminine ['femɪnɪn] ◇ adj femenino(na). ◇ n GRAMM femenino m.

femininity [femɪ'nɪnəti] n femineidad f.

feminism ['femɪnɪzm] n feminismo m.

feminist ['femɪnɪst] n feminista m y f.

fence [fens] ◇ n valla f; **to sit on the ~** fig nadar entre dos aguas. ◇ vt vallar, cercar.
◆ **fence off** vt sep cerrar con una valla OR cerca.

fencing ['fensɪŋ] n **-1.** SPORT esgrima f. **-2.** [material] material m para cercas.

fend [fend] vi: **to ~ for o.s.** valerse por sí mismo.
◆ **fend off** vt sep [blows] defenderse de, desviar; [questions, reporters] eludir.

fender ['fendər] n **-1.** [round fireplace] pantalla f, guardafuego m. **-2.** [on boat] defensa f. **-3.** Am [on car] guardabarros m inv.

feng shui [feŋ'ʃweɪ] n feng shui m, disciplina china que estudia la correcta colocación del mobiliario y decoración de la casa de acuerdo con unos criterios místicos.

fennel ['fenl] n hinojo m.

fens [fenz] npl Br pantanal m.

feral ['fɪərəl] adj salvaje.

ferment [n 'fɜ:ment, vb fə'ment] ◇ n [unrest] agitación f. ◇ vi fermentar.

fermentation [fɜ:mən'teɪʃn] n fermentación f.

fermented [fə'mentɪd] adj fermentado(da).

fern [fɜ:n] n helecho m.

ferocious [fə'rəʊʃəs] adj feroz.

ferociously [fə'rəʊʃəslɪ] adv ferozmente.

ferocity [fə'rɒsəti] n ferocidad f.

ferret ['ferɪt] n hurón m.
◆ **ferret about**, **ferret around** vi inf rebuscar.
◆ **ferret out** vt sep inf conseguir descubrir.

ferris wheel ['ferɪs-] n noria f.

ferry ['ferɪ] ◇ n [large, for cars] transbordador m, ferry m; [small] barca f. ◇ vt llevar, transportar.

ferryboat ['ferɪbəʊt] n = **ferry**.

ferryman ['ferɪmən] (pl **-men** [-mən]) n barquero m.

fertile ['fɜ:taɪl] adj fértil.

fertility [fə'tɪlətɪ] n fertilidad f.

fertility drug n estimulador m de la ovulación para mujeres estériles.

fertilization [fɜ:tɪlaɪ'zeɪʃn] n **-1.** AGR fertilización f, abono m. **-2.** BIOL fecundación f.

fertilize, -ise ['fɜ:tɪlaɪz] vt **-1.** AGR fertilizar, abonar. **-2.** BIOL fecundar.

fertilizer ['fɜ:tɪlaɪzər] n fertilizante m, abono m.

fervent ['fɜ:vənt] adj ferviente.

fervour Br, **fervor** Am ['fɜ:və'] n fervor m.

fester ['festə'] vi enconarse.

festival ['festəvl] n **-1.** [event, celebration] festival m. **-2.** [holiday] día m festivo.

festive ['festɪv] adj festivo(va).

festive season n: **the ~** las Navidades.

festivities [fes'tɪvətɪz] npl festividades fpl.

festoon [fe'stu:n] vt engalanar.

fetal ['fi:tl] = **foetal**.

fetch [fetʃ] vt **-1.** [go and get] ir a buscar, traer. **-2.** inf [raise - money] venderse por, alcanzar.

fetching ['fetʃɪŋ] adj atractivo(va).

fete, fête [feɪt] ◇ n fiesta f benéfica. ◇ vt festejar, agasajar.

FETE:
Los 'village fetes' en Gran Bretaña son una especie de fiesta al aire libre, generalmente con fines benéficos, en que se venden productos caseros y se celebran competiciones deportivas y juegos para niños

fetid ['fetɪd] adj fétido(da).

fetish ['fetɪʃ] n **-1.** [object of sexual obsession] fetiche m. **-2.** [mania] obsesión f, manía f.

fetlock ['fetlɒk] n espolón m.

fetter ['fetə'] vt encadenar, atar.
◆ **fetters** npl grilletes mpl.

fettle ['fetl] n: **in fine ~** en plena forma.

fetus ['fi:təs] = **foetus**.

feud [fju:d] ◇ n desavenencia f, enfrentamiento m duradero. ◇ vi pelearse.

feudal ['fju:dl] adj feudal.

fever ['fi:və'] n lit & fig fiebre f; **to have a ~** tener fiebre.

fevered ['fi:vəd] adj lit & fig febril.

feverish ['fi:vərɪʃ] adj lit & fig febril.

fever pitch n (U) punto m álgido.

few [fju:] ◇ adj pocos(cas); **a ~** algunos(nas); **a ~ more potatoes** algunas patatas más; **quite a ~**, **a good ~** bastantes; **~**

and far between escasos, contados. ◇ *pron* pocos *mpl*, -cas *fpl*; **a ~ (of them)** algunos *mpl*, -nas *fpl*.

fewer ['fjuːə'] ◇ *adj* menos; **no ~ than** nada menos que. ◇ *pron* menos.

fewest ['fjuːəst] *adj* menos.

FH *Br abbr of* **fire hydrant**.

FHA (*abbr of* **Federal Housing Administration**) *n* organismo estadounidense para la gestión de viviendas sociales.

fiancé [fɪˈɒnseɪ] *n* prometido *m*.

fiancée [fɪˈɒnseɪ] *n* prometida *f*.

fiasco [fɪˈæskəʊ] (*Br pl* **-s**, *Am pl* **-es**) *n* fiasco *m*.

fib [fɪb] (*pt & pp* **-bed**, *cont* **-bing**) *inf* ◇ *n* bola *f*, trola *f*. ◇ *vi* decir bolas OR trolas.

fibber ['fɪbə'] *n inf* bolero *m*, -ra *f*, trolero *m*, -ra *f*.

fibre *Br*, **fiber** *Am* ['faɪbə'] *n* fibra *f*.

fibreboard *Br*, **fiberboard** *Am* ['faɪbəbɔːd] *n* (*U*) conglomerado *m*.

fibreglass *Br*, **fiberglass** *Am* ['faɪbəglɑːs] ◇ *n* (*U*) fibra *f* de vidrio. ◇ *comp* de fibra de vidrio.

fibre optics *n* (*U*) fibra *f* óptica.

fibroid ['faɪbrɔɪd] *n* fibroma *m*.

fibrositis [ˌfaɪbrəˈsaɪtɪs] *n* fibrositis *f inv*.

FICA (*abbr of* **Federal Insurance Contributions Act**) *n* ley estadounidense de cotizaciones sociales.

fickle ['fɪkl] *adj* voluble.

fiction ['fɪkʃn] *n* **-1.** [stories] (literatura *f* de) ficción *f*. **-2.** [fabrication] ficción *f*.

fictional ['fɪkʃənl] *adj* **-1.** [literary] novelesco(ca). **-2.** [invented] ficticio(cia).

fictionalize, **-ise** ['fɪkʃənəlaɪz] *vt* novelar.

fictitious [fɪkˈtɪʃəs] *adj* [false] ficticio(cia).

fiddle ['fɪdl] ◇ *n* **-1.** [violin] violín *m*; **(as) fit as a ~** sano como una manzana; **to play second ~ (to)** estar relegado(da) a un segundo plano (respecto a). **-2.** *Br inf* [fraud] timo *m*, fraude *m*. ◇ *vt Br inf* amañar, falsear. ◇ *vi* [play around]: **to ~ (with sthg)** juguetear (con algo).
◆ **fiddle about**, **fiddle around** *vi* **-1.** [play around]: **to ~ about (with sthg)** juguetear (con algo). **-2.** [waste time] perder el tiempo.

fiddler ['fɪdlə'] *n* violinista *m y f*.

fiddly ['fɪdlɪ] (*compar* **-ier**, *superl* **-iest**) *adj Br* [job] delicado(da); [gadget] intrincado(da).

fidelity [fɪˈdelətɪ] *n* fidelidad *f*.

fidget ['fɪdʒɪt] *vi* moverse sin parar, no estarse quieto(ta).

fidgety ['fɪdʒɪtɪ] *adj inf* nervioso(sa), inquieto(ta).

fiduciary [fɪˈduːʃjərɪ] (*pl* **-ies**) ◇ *adj* fiduciario(ria). ◇ *n* fiduciario *m*, -ria *f*.

field [fiːld] ◇ *n* [gen & COMPUT] campo *m*; **in the ~** sobre el terreno; **~ of vision** campo visual. ◇ *vi* parar y devolver la pelota.

field day *n*: **to have a ~** disfrutar de lo lindo.

fielder ['fiːldə'] *n* jugador *m* del equipo que no batea.

field event *n* prueba *f* atlética de salto/lanzamiento.

field glasses *npl* prismáticos *mpl*, gemelos *mpl*.

field marshal *n* mariscal *m* de campo.

field mouse *n* ratón *m* de campo.

field trip *n* excursión *f* para hacer trabajo de campo.

fieldwork ['fiːldwɜːk] *n* (*U*) trabajo *m* de campo.

fieldworker ['fiːldwɜːkə'] *n* investigador *m*, -ra *f* que hace trabajo de campo.

fiend [fiːnd] *n* **-1.** [cruel person] malvado *m*, -da *f*. **-2.** *inf* [fanatic] fanático *m*, -ca *f*.

fiendish ['fiːndɪʃ] *adj* **-1.** [evil] malévolo(la), diabólico(ca). **-2.** *inf* [very difficult] endiablado(da).

fierce [fɪəs] *adj* [gen] feroz; [temper] endiablado(da); [loyalty] ferviente; [heat] asfixiante.

fiercely ['fɪəslɪ] *adv* **-1.** [aggressively, ferociously] ferozmente. **-2.** [wildly] furiosamente. **-3.** [intensely] encarnizadamente, intensamente.

fiery ['faɪərɪ] (*compar* **-ier**, *superl* **-iest**) *adj* **-1.** [burning] ardiente. **-2.** [volatile - temper] endiablado(da); [- speech] encendido(da), fogoso(sa); [- person] apasionado(da), vehemente. **-3.** [bright red] encendido(da).

FIFA ['fiːfə] (*abbr of* **Fédération Internationale de Football Association**) *n* FIFA *f*.

fifteen [fɪfˈtiːn] *num* quince; *see also* **six**.

fifteenth [ˌfɪfˈtiːnθ] ◇ *num adj* decimoquinto(ta). ◇ *num n* [fraction] decimoquinto *m*; [in order] decimoquinto *m*, -ta *f*; *see also* **sixth**.

fifth [fɪfθ] ◇ *num adj* quinto(ta). ◇ *num n* [fraction] quinto *m*; [in order] quinto *m*, -ta *f*; *see also* **sixth**.

Fifth Amendment *n*: **the ~** *quinta enmienda de la Constitución de los Estados Unidos que garantiza los derechos de las personas inculpadas por un delito*.

fifth column *n* quinta columna *f*.

fiftieth ['fɪftɪəθ] ◇ *num adj* quincuagésimo(ma). ◇ *num n* **-1.** [fraction] quincuagésimo *m*. **-2.** [in order] quincuagésimo *m*, -ma *f*; *see also* **sixth**.

fifty ['fıftı] *num* cincuenta; *see also* **sixty**.

fifty-fifty ◇ *adj* al cincuenta por ciento; **a ~ chance** unas posibilidades del cincuenta por ciento. ◇ *adv*: **to go ~** ir a medias.

fig [fıg] *n* higo *m*.

fight [faıt] (*pt* & *pp* **fought**) ◇ *n* pelea *f*; [fig] lucha *f*; **to have a ~ (with)** pelearse (con); **to put up a ~** oponer resistencia. ◇ *vt* [gen] luchar contra; [battle, campaign] librar; [war] luchar en. ◇ *vi* **-1.** [in punch-up] pelearse; [in war] luchar. **-2.** *fig* [battle, struggle]: **to ~ (for/against)** luchar (por/contra). **-3.** [argue]: **to ~ (about** OR **over)** pelearse OR discutir (por).
◆ **fight back** ◇ *vt fus* reprimir, contener. ◇ *vi* defenderse.
◆ **fight off** *vt sep* **-1.** [deter] rechazar, deshacerse (por la fuerza) de. **-2.** [overcome] ahuyentar, sobreponerse a.
◆ **fight out** *vt sep*: **to ~ it out** verse las caras.

fighter ['faıtər] *n* **-1.** [plane] caza *m*. **-2.** [soldier] combatiente *m y f*. **-3.** [combative person] luchador *m*, -ra *f*.

fighting ['faıtıŋ] *n* (*U*) [punch-up] pelea *f*; [on streets, terraces] peleas *fpl*; [in war] combate *m*.

fighting chance *n*: **to have a ~ (of doing sthg)** tener una remota posibilidad (de hacer algo).

figment ['fıgmənt] *n*: **a ~ of sb's imagination** un producto de la imaginación de alguien.

figurative ['fıgərətıv] *adj* figurado(da).

figuratively ['fıgərətıvlı] *adv* figuradamente.

figure [*Br* 'fıgər, *Am* 'fıgjər] ◇ *n* **-1.** [statistic, number] cifra *f*; **to put a ~ on sthg** dar un número exacto de algo; **to be in single/double ~s** no sobrepasar/sobrepasar la decena. **-2.** [shape of person, personality] figura *f*. **-3.** [diagram] gráfico *m*, diagrama *m*. ◇ *vt* [suppose] figurarse, suponer. ◇ *vi* [feature] figurar.
◆ **figure out** *vt sep* [reason, motives] figurarse; [problem etc] resolver; **to ~ out how to do sthg** dar con la forma de hacer algo.

figurehead ['fıgəhed] *n* **-1.** [on ship] mascarón *m* de proa. **-2.** [leader without real power] testaferro *m*.

figure of eight *Br*, **figure eight** *Am n* forma *f* de ocho.

figure of speech *n* forma *f* de hablar.

figure skating *n* patinaje *m* artístico.

figurine [*Br* 'fıgəri:n, *Am* ˌfıgjə'ri:n] *n* figurín *m*.

Fiji ['fi:dʒi:] *n* Fiyi.

Fijian [ˌfi:'dʒi:ən] ◇ *adj* fiyiano(na). ◇ *n* fiyiano *m*, -na *f*.

filament ['fıləmənt] *n* [in lightbulb] filamento *m*.

filch [fıltʃ] *vt inf* birlar, mangar.

file [faıl] ◇ *n* **-1.** [folder] carpeta *f*, archivador *m*. **-2.** [report] expediente *m*, dossier *m*; **on ~, on the ~s** archivado. **-3.** COMPUT fichero *m*. **-4.** [tool] lima *f*. **-5.** [line]: **in single ~** en fila india. ◇ *vt* **-1.** [put in file] archivar. **-2.** JUR presentar. **-3.** [shape, smoothe] limar. ◇ *vi* **-1.** [walk in single file] ir en fila. **-2.** JUR: **to ~ for divorce** presentar demanda de divorcio.

file clerk *Am* = **filing clerk**.

filename ['faılˌneım] *n* COMPUT nombre *m* de fichero.

filet *Am* = **fillet**.

filibuster ['fılıbʌstər] *vi* POL pronunciar discursos obstruccionistas.

filigree ['fılıgri:] ◇ *adj* de filigrana. ◇ *n* (*U*) filigrana *f*.

filing cabinet ['faılıŋ-] *n* archivo *m*, fichero *m*.

filing clerk ['faılıŋ-] *n Br* archivero *m*, -ra *f* (de oficina).

Filipino [ˌfılı'pi:nəʊ] (*pl* **-s**) ◇ *adj* filipino(na). ◇ *n* filipino *m*, -na *f*.

fill [fıl] ◇ *vt* **-1.** [gen]: **to ~ sthg (with)** llenar algo (de). **-2.** [gap, hole, crack] rellenar; [tooth] empastar, calzar *Amer*. **-3.** [need, vacancy etc] cubrir. ◇ *n*: **to have had one's ~ of sthg** estar hasta la coronilla de algo; **to eat one's ~** comer hasta hartarse.
◆ **fill in** ◇ *vt sep* **-1.** [complete] rellenar. **-2.** [inform]: **to ~ sb in (on)** poner a alguien al corriente (de). ◇ *vt fus*: **to be ~ing in time** estar matando el tiempo. ◇ *vi* [substitute]: **to ~ in (for sb)** sustituir (a alguien).
◆ **fill out** ◇ *vt sep* [complete] rellenar. ◇ *vi* [get fatter] engordar.
◆ **fill up** ◇ *vt sep* llenar (hasta arriba). ◇ *vi* llenarse.

filled [fıld] *adj* **-1.** [roll] relleno(na). **-2.** [with emotion]: **~ with** lleno(na) de.

filler ['fılər] *n* [for cracks] masilla *f*.

filler cap *n Br* tapón *m* del depósito de gasolina.

fillet *Br*, **filet** *Am* ['fılıt] *n* filete *m*.

fillet steak *n* filete *m* (de carne).

fill-in *n inf* [person] sustituto *m*, -ta *f*; [thing] sustitutivo *m*.

filling ['fılıŋ] ◇ *adj* [satisfying] que llena mucho. ◇ *n* **-1.** [in tooth] empaste *m*, calza *f Amer*. **-2.** [in cake, sandwich] relleno *m*.

filling station *n* estación *f* de servicio, gasolinera *f*.

fillip ['fɪlɪp] *n* estímulo *m*, aliciente *m*.

filly ['fɪlɪ] (*pl* **-ies**) *n* potranca *f*.

film [fɪlm] ◇ *n* **-1.** [gen] película *f*. **-2.** (*U*) [footage] escenas *fpl* filmadas. ◇ *vt* & *vi* filmar, rodar.

filming ['fɪlmɪŋ] *n* (*U*) filmación *f*, rodaje *m*.

film star *n* estrella *f* de cine.

filmstrip ['fɪlm,strɪp] *n* serie *f* de diapositivas.

film studio *n* estudio *m* cinematográfico.

Filofax® ['faɪləʊfæks] *n* agenda *f* (de hojas recambiables).

filter ['fɪltə*r*] ◇ *n* filtro *m*. ◇ *vt* [purify] filtrar. ◇ *vi* [people]: **to ~ in/out** ir entrando/saliendo.

◆ **filter out** *vt sep* [remove by filtering] filtrar.

◆ **filter through** *vi* filtrarse.

filter coffee *n* café *m* de filtro.

filter lane *n Br* carril *m* de giro.

filter paper *n* (papel *m* de) filtro *m*.

filter-tipped [-'tɪpt] *adj* con filtro.

filth [fɪlθ] *n* (*U*) **-1.** [dirt] suciedad *f*, porquería *f*. **-2.** [obscenity] basura *f*, obscenidades *fpl*.

filthy ['fɪlθɪ] (*compar* **-ier**, *superl* **-iest**) *adj* **-1.** [very dirty] mugriento(ta), sucísimo(ma). **-2.** [obscene] obsceno(na).

filtration plant [fɪl'treɪʃn-] *n* estación *f* depuradora.

Fimbra ['fɪmbrə] (*abbr of* **Financial Intermediaries, Managers and Brokers Regulatory Association**) *n* asociación *que regula la actividad de intermediarios financieros, managers y corredores de Bolsa*.

fin [fɪn] *n* **-1.** [on fish] aleta *f*. **-2.** *Am* [on swimmer] aleta *f*.

final ['faɪnl] ◇ *adj* **-1.** [last] último(ma). **-2.** [at end] final. **-3.** [definitive] definitivo(va). ◇ *n* final *f*.

◆ **finals** *npl* UNIV exámenes *mpl* finales.

final demand *n* último aviso *m*.

finale [fɪ'nɑːlɪ] *n* final *m*.

finalist ['faɪnəlɪst] *n* finalista *m y f*.

finalize, -ise ['faɪnəlaɪz] *vt* ultimar.

finally ['faɪnəlɪ] *adv* **-1.** [at last] por fin, finalmente. **-2.** [lastly] finalmente, por último.

finance [*n* 'faɪnæns, *vb* faɪ'næns] ◇ *n* (*U*) **-1.** [money] fondos *mpl*. **-2.** [money management] finanzas *fpl*. ◇ *vt* financiar.

◆ **finances** *npl* finanzas *fpl*.

financial [fɪ'nænʃl] *adj* financiero(ra).

financial adviser *n* asesor financiero *m*, asesora financiera *f*.

financially [fɪ'nænʃəlɪ] *adv* económicamente; **to be ~ independent** tener independencia económica.

financial services *npl* servicios *mpl* financieros.

financial year *Br*, **fiscal year** *Am n* ejercicio *m* financiero.

financier [fɪ'nænsɪə*r*] *n Br* financiero *m*, -ra *f*, financista *m y f Amer*.

finch [fɪntʃ] *n* pinzón *m*.

find [faɪnd] (*pt* & *pp* **found**) ◇ *vt* **-1.** [gen] encontrar; **to ~ one's way** encontrar el camino. **-2.** [realize - fact] darse cuenta de, descubrir. **-3.** JUR: **to be found guilty/not guilty (of)** ser declarado(da) culpable/inocente (de). ◇ *n* hallazgo *m*, descubrimiento *m*.

◆ **find out** ◇ *vt fus* [fact] averiguar. ◇ *vt sep* [person] descubrir.

findings ['faɪndɪŋz] *npl* resultados *mpl*, conclusiones *fpl*.

fine [faɪn] ◇ *adj* **-1.** [excellent] magnífico(ca), excelente. **-2.** [perfectly satisfactory]: **it's/that's ~** está bien, perfecto; **how are you?** – **fine thanks** ¿qué tal? – muy bien. **-3.** [weather] bueno(na); **it will be ~ tomorrow** mañana hará buen día. **-4.** [thin, smooth] fino(na). **-5.** [minute - detail, distinction] sutil; [- adjustment, tuning] milimétrico(ca). ◇ *adv* [very well] muy bien. ◇ *n* multa *f*. ◇ *vt* multar.

fine arts *npl* bellas artes *fpl*.

finely ['faɪnlɪ] *adv* **-1.** [thinly, smoothly] fino(na), en trocitos. **-2.** [accurately] con precisión.

fineness ['faɪnnɪs] *n* **-1.** [quality] excelencia *f*. **-2.** [thinness, smoothness] finura *f*. **-3.** [subtlety] sutileza *f*.

finery ['faɪnərɪ] *n* (*U*) galas *fpl*.

finesse [fɪ'nes] *n* finura *f*, delicadeza *f*.

fine-tooth comb *n*: **to go over sthg with a ~** examinar algo minuciosamente.

fine-tune *vt* poner a punto.

finger ['fɪŋgə*r*] ◇ *n* dedo *m*; **she didn't lay a ~ on him** no le tocó un pelo de la ropa; **he didn't lift a ~ to help** no movió un dedo para ayudar; **to keep one's ~s crossed** cruzar los dedos; **to point a** OR **the ~ at sb** señalar a alguien con el dedo; **to put one's ~ on sthg** acertar a identificar algo; **to twist sb round one's little ~** tener a alguien en el bote. ◇ *vt* acariciar con los dedos.

fingermark ['fɪŋgəmɑːk] *n* huella *f* (de dedo), dedada *f*.

fingernail ['fɪŋgəneɪl] *n* uña *f* (*de las manos*).

fingerprint ['fɪŋgəprɪnt] *n* huella *f* dactilar OR digital; **to take sb's ~s** tomar las huellas dactilares OR digitales a alguien.

fingertip ['fɪŋgətɪp] *n* punta *f* OR yema *f* del dedo; **at one's ~s** al alcance de la mano; **to have a subject at one's ~s** saber un tema al dedillo.

finicky ['fɪnɪkɪ] *adj pej* [person] melindroso(sa); [task] minucioso(sa), delicado(da).

finish ['fɪnɪʃ] ◇ *n* -**1**. [end] final *m*. -**2**. [surface texture] acabado *m*. ◇ *vt*: **to ~ sthg/doing sthg** acabar algo/de hacer algo, terminar algo/de hacer algo. ◇ *vi* acabar, terminar.

◆ **finish off** *vt sep* acabar OR terminar del todo.

◆ **finish up** *vi* acabar, terminar.

◆ **finish with** *vt fus* [boyfriend etc] romper con.

finished ['fɪnɪʃt] *adj* -**1**. [ready, over] acabado(da), terminado(da). -**2**. [no longer interested]: **to be ~ with sthg** no querer tener nada que ver con algo. -**3**. *inf* [done for] acabado(da).

finishing line ['fɪnɪʃɪŋ-] *n* línea *f* de meta.

finishing school ['fɪnɪʃɪŋ-] *n colegio privado donde se prepara a las alumnas de clase alta para entrar en sociedad.*

finite ['faɪnaɪt] *adj* -**1**. [limited] finito(ta). -**2**. GRAMM conjugado(da).

Finland ['fɪnlənd] *n* Finlandia *f*.

Finn [fɪn] *n* [person] finlandés *m*, -esa *f*.

Finnish ['fɪnɪʃ] ◇ *adj* finlandés(esa). ◇ *n* [language] finlandés *m*.

fiord [fjɔːd] = **fjord**.

fir [fɜːr] *n* abeto *m*.

fire ['faɪər] ◇ *n* -**1**. [gen] fuego *m*; **on ~** en llamas; **to catch ~** incendiarse; **to open ~ (on sb)** abrir fuego (contra alguien); **to set ~ to** prender fuego a. -**2**. [blaze] incendio *m*. -**3**. *Br* [heater]: **(electric/gas) ~** estufa *f* (eléctrica/de gas). ◇ *vt* -**1**. [shoot] disparar. -**2**. [rap out]: **to ~ questions at sb** acribillar a preguntas a alguien. -**3**. [dismiss] despedir. ◇ *vi*: **to ~ (on** OR **at)** disparar (contra).

fire alarm *n* alarma *f* antiincendios.

firearm ['faɪərɑːm] *n* arma *f* de fuego.

fireball ['faɪəbɔːl] *n* bola *f* de fuego.

firebomb ['faɪəbɒm] ◇ *n* bomba *f* incendiaria. ◇ *vt* lanzar bombas incendiarias a.

firebreak ['faɪəbreɪk] *n* cortafuego *m*.

fire brigade *Br*, **fire department** *Am n* cuerpo *m* de bomberos.

fire chief *Am* = **fire master**.

firecracker ['faɪəˌkrækər] *n* petardo *m*.

fire-damaged *adj* estropeado(da) en un incendio.

fire department *Am* = **fire brigade**.

fire door *n* puerta *f* cortafuegos.

fire drill *n* simulacro *m* de incendio.

fire-eater *n* [performer] tragafuegos *m y f inv*.

fire engine *n* coche *m* de bomberos.

fire escape *n* escalera *f* de incendios.

fire extinguisher *n* extintor *m* (de incendios).

fire fighter *n* bombero *m*, -ra *f*.

fireguard ['faɪəgɑːd] *n* pantalla *f* (de chimenea).

fire hazard *n* peligro *m* de incendio.

fire hydrant [-'haɪdrənt], **fireplug** ['faɪəplʌg] *n* boca *f* de incendio.

firelight ['faɪəlaɪt] *n* luz *f* del fuego.

firelighter ['faɪəlaɪtər] *n* enciende-fuegos *m inv*, tea *f*.

fireman ['faɪəmən] (*pl* **-men** [-mən]) *n* bombero *m*.

fire master *Br*, **fire chief** *Am n* jefe *m*, -fa *f* del cuerpo de bomberos.

fireplace ['faɪəpleɪs] *n* chimenea *f*.

fireplug *Am* = **fire hydrant**.

firepower ['faɪəˌpaʊər] *n* potencia *f* de fuego.

fireproof ['faɪəpruːf] *adj* incombustible, ininflamable.

fire-raiser [-ˌreɪzər] *n Br* pirómano *m*, -na *f*, incendiario *m*, -ria *f*.

fire regulations *npl* normativa *f* sobre incendios.

fire service *n Br* cuerpo *m* de bomberos.

fireside ['faɪəsaɪd] *n*: **by the ~** al calor de la chimenea.

fire station *n* parque *m* de bomberos.

firewood ['faɪəwʊd] *n* leña *f*.

firework ['faɪəwɜːk] *n* fuego *m* de artificio.

◆ **fireworks** *npl* fuegos *mpl* artificiales OR de artificio.

firework display *n* espectáculo *m* pirotécnico.

firing ['faɪərɪŋ] *n* (*U*) MIL disparos *mpl*, tiroteo *m*.

firing squad *n* pelotón *m* de ejecución OR fusilamiento.

firm [fɜːm] ◇ *adj* -**1**. [gen] firme; **to stand ~** mantenerse firme. -**2**. FIN [steady] estable. ◇ *n* firma *f*, empresa *f*.

◆ **firm up** ◇ *vt sep* afianzar. ◇ *vi* afianzarse.

firmly ['fɜːmlɪ] *adv* firmemente.

firmness ['fɜːmnɪs] *n* firmeza *f*.

first [fɜːst] ◇ *adj* primero(ra); **for the ~ time** por primera vez; **~ thing (in the**

morning) a primera hora (de la mañana); ~ **things** ~ lo primero es lo primero; **I don't know the** ~ **thing about it** no tengo ni la más remota idea del asunto. ◇ *adv* **-1.** [gen] primero; ~ **of all** en primer lugar. **-2.** [for the first time] por primera vez. ◇ *n* **-1.** [person] primero *m*, -ra *f*. **-2.** [unprecedented event] acontecimiento *m* sin precedentes. **-3.** *Br* UNIV ≃ sobresaliente *m*.

◆ **at first** *adv* al principio.

◆ **at first hand** *adv* de primera mano.

first aid *n* (*U*) primeros auxilios *mpl*.

first-aider [-'eɪdə'] *n* socorrista *m y f*.

first-aid kit *n* botiquín *m* de primeros auxilios.

first-class *adj* **-1.** [excellent] de primera, clase *Amer*. **-2.** *Br* UNIV: ~ **degree** ≃ sobresaliente *m*. **-3.** [letter, ticket] de primera clase.

first-class mail *n* ≃ correo *m* urgente.

first cousin *n* primo *m*, -ma *f* carnal.

first day cover *n* *sobre timbrado en el primer día de emisión de sus sellos*.

first-degree *adj* **-1.** MED: ~ **burn** quemadura *f* de primer grado. **-2.** *Am* JUR: ~ **murder** homicidio *m* en primer grado.

first floor *n* **-1.** *Br* [above ground level] primer piso *m*. **-2.** *Am* [at ground level] planta *f* baja.

firsthand [,fɜːst'hænd] ◇ *adj* de primera mano. ◇ *adv* directamente.

first lady *n* primera dama *f*.

first language *n* lengua *f* materna.

first lieutenant *n* ≃ teniente *m y f*.

firstly ['fɜːstlɪ] *adv* en primer lugar.

first mate *n* segundo *m* de a bordo.

first name *n* nombre *m* de pila.

◆ **first-name** *adj*: **to be on first-name terms (with)** ≃ tutearse (con).

first night *n* noche *f* del estreno.

first offender *n* delincuente *m y f* sin antecedentes penales.

first officer = **first mate**.

first-past-the-post system *n* *Br* sistema *m* de mayoría simple.

first-rate *adj* de primera.

first refusal *n* primera opción *f* de compra.

First World War *n*: **the** ~ la Primera Guerra Mundial.

firtree ['fɜːtriː] = **fir**.

FIS (*abbr of* **Family Income Supplement**) *n* *antigua asignación familiar en Gran Bretaña*.

fiscal ['fɪskl] *adj* fiscal.

fiscal year *Am* = **financial year**.

fish [fɪʃ] (*pl inv*) ◇ *n* **-1.** [animal] pez *m*. **-2.** (*U*) [food] pescado *m*. ◇ *vt* pescar en. ◇ *vi* **-1.** [for fish]: **to** ~ **(for sthg)** pescar (algo). **-2.** [for compliments etc]: **to** ~ **for sthg** buscar algo.

◆ **fish out** *vt sep inf* [bring out] sacar.

fish and chips *npl* pescado *m* frito con patatas fritas.

fish and chip shop *n* *Br* tienda *f* de pescado frito con patatas fritas.

fishbowl ['fɪʃbəʊl] *n* pecera *f*.

fishcake ['fɪʃkeɪk] *n* pastelillo *m* de pescado.

fisherman ['fɪʃəmən] (*pl* **-men** [-mən]) *n* pescador *m*.

fishery ['fɪʃərɪ] (*pl* **-ies**) *n* caladero *m*.

fish-eye lens *n* objetivo *m* de ojo de pez.

fish factory *n* fábrica *f* de pescado.

fish farm *n* piscifactoría *f*.

fish fingers *Br*, **fish sticks** *Am npl* palitos *mpl* de pescado.

fishhook ['fɪʃ,hʊk] *n* anzuelo *m*.

fishing ['fɪʃɪŋ] *n* pesca *f*; **to go** ~ ir de pesca.

fishing boat *n* barco *m* pesquero.

fishing line *n* sedal *m*.

fishing rod *n* caña *f* de pescar.

fishmonger ['fɪʃ,mʌŋgə'] *n* pescadero *m*, -ra *f*; ~**'s (shop)** pescadería *f*.

fishnet ['fɪʃnet] *n*: ~ **tights** medias *fpl* de malla.

fish slice *n* *Br* paleta *f*, espátula *f*.

fish sticks *Am* = **fish fingers**.

fishwife ['fɪʃwaɪf] (*pl* **-wives** [-waɪvz]) *n pej* verdulera *f*.

fishy ['fɪʃɪ] (*compar* **-ier**, *superl* **-iest**) *adj* **-1.** [smell, taste] a pescado. **-2.** [suspicious] sospechoso(sa).

fission ['fɪʃn] *n* fisión *f*.

fissure ['fɪʃə'] *n* fisura *f*.

fist [fɪst] *n* puño *m*.

fit [fɪt] (*pt & pp* **-ted**, *cont* **-ting**) ◇ *adj* **-1.** [suitable]: ~ **(for sthg/to do sthg)** apto(ta) (para algo/para hacer algo); **to see** OR **think** ~ **to do sthg** creer conveniente hacer algo; **do as you think** ~ haz lo que te parezca conveniente. **-2.** [healthy] en forma; **to keep** ~ mantenerse en forma.

◇ *n* **-1.** [of clothes, shoes etc]: **it's a good** ~ le/te *etc* sienta OR va bien; **it's a tight fit** le/te *etc* va justo. **-2.** [bout, seizure] ataque *m*; **he had a** ~ *lit & fig* le dio un ataque; **in** ~**s and starts** a trompicones.

◇ *vt* **-1.** [be correct size for] sentar bien a, ir bien a. **-2.** [place]: **to** ~ **sthg into** encajar algo en. **-3.** [provide]: **to** ~ **sthg with** equi-

par algo con; **to have an alarm fitted** poner una alarma. **-4.** [be suitable for] adecuarse a, corresponder a. **-5.** [for clothes]: **to be fitted for sthg** probarse algo.
◇ *vi* **-1.** [clothes, shoes] estar bien de talla. **-2.** [part - when assembling etc] **this bit ~s in here** esta pieza encaja aquí. **-3.** [have enough room] **caber.**
◆ **fit in** ◇ *vt sep* [accommodate] hacer un hueco a. ◇ *vi* **-1.** [subj: person]: **to ~ in (with)** adaptarse (a). **-2.** [be compatible]: **it doesn't ~ in with our plans** no encaja con nuestros planes.

fitful ['fɪtful] *adj* irregular, intermitente.

fitment ['fɪtmənt] *n* mueble *m*.

fitness ['fɪtnɪs] *n* (U) **-1.** [health] buen estado *m* físico. **-2.** [suitability]: **~ (for)** idoneidad *f* (para).

fitted ['fɪtəd] *adj* **-1.** [suited]: **~ (for OR to)** idóneo(a) (para); **to be ~ to do sthg** ser idóneo para hacer algo. **-2.** [tailored] a medida. **-3.** *Br* [built-in] empotrado(da).

fitted kitchen *n Br* cocina *f* de módulos.

fitter ['fɪtə*r*] *n* [mechanic] (mecánico *m*) ajustador *m*.

fitting ['fɪtɪŋ] ◇ *adj fml* conveniente, adecuado(da). ◇ *n* **-1.** [part] accesorio *m*. **-2.** [for clothing] prueba *f*.
◆ **fittings** *npl* accesorios *mpl*.

fitting room *n* probador *m*.

five [faɪv] *num* cinco; *see also* **six**.

five-day week *n* semana *f* inglesa.

fiver ['faɪvə*r*] *n Br inf* (billete de) cinco libras.

five-star *adj* [hotel] de cinco estrellas; [treatment] de primera.

fix [fɪks] ◇ *vt* **-1.** [gen] fijar; **to ~ sthg (to)** fijar algo (a). **-2.** [repair] arreglar, refaccionar *Amer*. **-3.** *inf* [rig] amañar. **-4.** [prepare - food, drink] preparar. ◇ *n* **-1.** *inf* [difficult situation]: **to be in a ~** estar en un aprieto. **-2.** *drugs sl* dosis *f inv*.
◆ **fix up** *vt sep* **-1.** [provide]: **to ~ sb up with** proveer a alguien de. **-2.** [arrange] organizar, preparar.

fixation [fɪk'seɪʃn] *n*: **~ (on OR about)** fijación *f* (con).

fixed [fɪkst] *adj* fijo(ja).

fixed assets *npl* activo *m* inmovilizado.

fixture ['fɪkstʃə*r*] *n* **-1.** [furniture] instalación *f* fija. **-2.** [permanent feature] rasgo *m* característico. **-3.** [sports event] encuentro *m*.

fizz [fɪz] ◇ *vi* burbujear. ◇ *n* [sound] burbujeo *m*.

fizzle ['fɪzl]
◆ **fizzle out** *vi* [firework, fire] apagarse; *fig* disiparse.

fizzy ['fɪzi] (*compar* **-ier**, *superl* **-iest**) *adj* gaseoso(sa).

fjord [fjɔːd] *n* fiordo *m*.

FL *abbr of* **Florida**.

flab [flæb] *n* (U) grasa *f*, michelines *mpl*.

flabbergasted ['flæbəgɑːstɪd] *adj* pasmado(da), boquiabierto(ta).

flabby ['flæbɪ] (*compar* **-ier**, *superl* **-iest**) *adj* fofo(fa), gordo(da).

flaccid ['flæsɪd] *adj* fláccido(da).

flag [flæg] (*pt* & *pp* **-ged**, *cont* **-ging**) ◇ *n* [banner] bandera *f*. ◇ *vi* decaer.
◆ **flag down** *vt sep*: **to ~ sb down** hacer señales a alguien para que se detenga.

Flag Day *n* [in the US] 14 de junio, día de la bandera en Estados Unidos.

flag of convenience *n* pabellón *m* de conveniencia.

flagon ['flægən] *n* **-1.** [bottle] botellón *m*. **-2.** [jug] jarro *m*.

flagpole ['flægpəʊl] *n* asta *f* (de bandera).

flagrant ['fleɪgrənt] *adj* flagrante.

flagship ['flægʃɪp] *n* **-1.** [ship] buque *m* insignia. **-2.** [main asset] modelo *m*, paradigma *m*.

flagstone ['flægstəʊn] *n* losa *f*.

flail [fleɪl] ◇ *vt* sacudir, agitar con violencia. ◇ *vi* agitarse con violencia.

flair [fleə*r*] *n* don *m*; **to have a ~ for sthg** tener un don para algo.

flak [flæk] *n* (U) **-1.** [gunfire] fuego *m* antiaéreo. **-2.** *inf* [criticism] críticas *fpl*.

flake [fleɪk] ◇ *n* [of skin] escama *f*; [of snow] copo *m*; [of paint] desconchón *m*. ◇ *vi* [skin] descamarse; [paint, plaster] descascarillarse, desconcharse.
◆ **flake out** *vi inf* caer rendido(da).

flaky ['fleɪkɪ] (*compar* **-ier**, *superl* **-iest**) *adj* **-1.** [skin] con escamas; [paintwork] desconchado(da). **-2.** *Am inf* [person] extravagante.

flaky pastry *n* hojaldre *m*.

flambé ['flɑːmbeɪ] (*pt* & *pp* **-ed**, *cont* **-ing**) ◇ *adj* flameado(da). ◇ *vt* flamear.

flamboyant [flæm'bɔɪənt] *adj* **-1.** [person, behaviour] extravagante. **-2.** [clothes, design] vistoso(sa), llamativo(va).

flame [fleɪm] ◇ *n* llama *f*; **in ~s** en llamas; **to burst into ~s** estallar en llamas; **an old ~** un antiguo amor. ◇ *vi* **-1.** [be on fire] llamear. **-2.** [redden] encenderse.

flameproof ['fleɪmpruːf] *adj* ignífugo(ga).

flame-retardant [-rɪ'tɑːdənt] *adj* resistente al fuego.

flame-thrower [-'θrəʊə*r*] *n* lanzallamas *m inv*.

flaming ['fleımıŋ] *adj* **-1.** [fire-coloured] llameante. **-2.** *Br* [very angry] acalorado(da). **-3.** *Br inf* [expressing annoyance] maldito(ta).

flamingo [flə'mıŋgəʊ] (*pl* **-s** OR **-es**) *n* flamenco *m*.

flammable ['flæməbl] *adj* inflamable.

flan [flæn] *n* tarta *f* (*de fruta etc*).

Flanders ['flɑːndəz] *n* Flandes.

flange [flændʒ] *n* pestaña *f*, reborde *m*.

flank [flæŋk] ◇ *n* **-1.** [of animal] costado *m*, ijada *f*. **-2.** [of army] flanco *m*. ◇ *vt*: **to be ~ed by** estar flanqueado(da) por.

flannel ['flænl] *n* **-1.** [fabric] franela *f*. **-2.** *Br* [facecloth] toallita *f* (de baño para lavarse).
◆ **flannels** *npl* pantalones *mpl* de franela.

flannelette [flænə'let] *n* muletón *m*.

flap [flæp] (*pt* & *pp* **-ped**, *cont* **-ping**) ◇ *n* **-1.** [of skin] colgajo *m*; [of pocket, book, envelope] solapa *f*. **-2.** *inf* [panic]: **to be in a ~** estar histérico(ca). ◇ *vt* agitar; [wings] batir. ◇ *vi* [flag, skirt] ondear; [wings] aletear.

flapjack ['flæpdʒæk] *n* **-1.** *Br* [biscuit] torta *f* de avena. **-2.** *Am* [pancake] torta *f*, crepe *f*.

flare [fleəʳ] ◇ *n* [signal] bengala *f*. ◇ *vi* **-1.** [burn brightly]: **to ~ (up)** llamear. **-2.** [intensify]: **to ~ (up)** estallar. **-3.** [widen] acampanarse.
◆ **flares** *npl Br* pantalones *mpl* de campana.

flared [fleəd] *adj* acampanado(da).

flash [flæʃ] ◇ *adj* **-1.** PHOT del flash; [photography] con flash. **-2.** *inf* [expensive-looking] chulo(la); *pej* ostentoso(sa).
◇ *n* **-1.** [of light] destello *m*; [of lightning] relámpago *m*, refucilo *m Amer*. **-2.** PHOT flash *m*. **-3.** [of genius, inspiration etc] momento *m*; [of anger] acceso *m*; **in a ~** en un instante; **quick as a ~** como un relámpago.
◇ *vt* **-1.** [shine in specified direction] dirigir; [switch on briefly] encender intermitentemente. **-2.** [send out] lanzar. **-3.** [show - picture, image] mostrar; [- information, news] emitir.
◇ *vi* **-1.** [light] destellar. **-2.** [eyes] brillar. **-3.** [rush]: **to ~ by** OR **past** pasar como un rayo. **-4.** [appear]: **it ~ed across his mind that ...** de pronto se le ocurrió que ....

flashback ['flæʃbæk] *n* escena *f* retrospectiva, flashback *m*.

flashbulb ['flæʃbʌlb] *n* flash *m*.

flash card *n* tarjeta en la que aparece una palabra o dibujo y que se emplea como material didáctico.

flashcube ['flæʃkjuːb] *n* flash *m* (en forma) de cubo.

flasher ['flæʃəʳ] *n* **-1.** [light] indicador *m*. **-2.** *Br inf* [man] exhibicionista *m*.

flash flood *n* inundación *f* repentina.

flashgun ['flæʃgʌn] *n* disparador *m* de flash.

flashlight ['flæʃlaɪt] *n* [torch] linterna *f* eléctrica.

flash point *n* **-1.** [moment] punto *m* álgido. **-2.** [place] punto *m* conflictivo.

flashy ['flæʃi] (*compar* **-ier**, *superl* **-iest**) *adj inf* chulo(la); *pej* ostentoso(sa).

flask [flɑːsk] *n* **-1.** [thermos flask] termo *m*. **-2.** [used in chemistry] matraz *m*. **-3.** [hip flask] petaca *f*.

flat [flæt] (*compar* **-ter**, *superl* **-test**) ◇ *adj* **-1.** [surface, ground] llano(na); [feet] plano. **-2.** [shoes] bajo(ja). **-3.** [tyre] desinflado(da). **-4.** [refusal, denial] rotundo(da). **-5.** [business, trade] flojo(ja); [voice, tone] monótono(na); [colour] soso(sa); [performance, writing] desangelado(da). **-6.** MUS [lower than correct note] desafinado(da); [lower than stated note] bemol (*inv*). **-7.** [fare, price] único(ca). **-8.** [beer, lemonade] muerto(ta), sin fuerza. **-9.** [battery] descargado(da).
◇ *adv* **-1.** [level]: **to lie ~** estar totalmente extendido; **to fall ~** [person] caerse de bruces. **-2.** [absolutely]: **~ broke** sin un duro. **-3.** [of time]: **in five minutes ~** en cinco minutos justos. **-4.** MUS: **to sing/play ~** desafinar.
◇ *n* **-1.** *Br* [apartment] piso *m*, apartamento *m*. **-2.** MUS bemol *m*.
◆ **flat out** *adv* a toda velocidad.

flat cap *n Br* gorra *f* de tela.

flat-chested [-'tʃestɪd] *adj* de poco pecho, liso(sa).

flatfish ['flætfɪʃ] (*pl inv*) *n* pez *m* plano (*lenguado etc*).

flat-footed [-'fʊtɪd] *adj* [with flat feet] de pies planos.

flatlet ['flætlɪt] *n Br* pisito *m*.

flatly ['flætlɪ] *adv* **-1.** [refuse, deny] de plano, terminantemente. **-2.** [speak, perform] monótonamente.

flatmate ['flætmeɪt] *n Br* compañero *m*, -ra *f* de piso.

flat racing *n* (*U*) carreras *fpl* de caballos sin obstáculos.

flat rate *n* tarifa *f* única.

flatten ['flætn] *vt* **-1.** [surface, paper, bumps] allanar, aplanar; [paper] alisar; **to ~ o.s. against sthg** pegarse a algo. **-2.** [building, city] arrasar. **-3.** *inf* [person, boxer] aplastar.
◆ **flatten out** ◇ *vi* allanarse, nivelarse. ◇ *vt sep* allanar.

flatter ['flætəʳ] *vt* **-1.** [subj: person, report] adular, halagar; **to ~ o.s. (that)** congratularse de que, felicitarse de que. **-2.** [subj: clothes, colour, photograph] favorecer.

flatterer ['flætərə'] *n* adulador *m*, -ra *f*.

flattering ['flætərɪŋ] *adj* **-1.** [remark, interest] halagador(ra). **-2.** [clothes, colour, photograph] favorecedor(ra).

flattery ['flætərɪ] *n* (*U*) halagos *mpl*, adulación *f*.

flatulence ['flætjʊləns] *n* flatulencia *f*.

flatware ['flætweə'] *n* (*U*) *Am* cubiertos *mpl*.

flaunt [flɔːnt] *vt* ostentar, hacer gala de.

flautist *Br* ['flaʊtɪst], **flutist** *Am* ['fluːtɪst] *n* flautista *m y f*.

flavour *Br*, **flavor** *Am* ['fleɪvə'] ◇ *n* **-1.** [taste] sabor *m*. **-2.** *fig* [atmosphere] aire *m*, toque *m*. ◇ *vt* condimentar.

flavouring *Br*, **flavoring** *Am* ['fleɪvərɪŋ] *n* (*U*) condimento *m*.

flaw [flɔː] *n* [fault] desperfecto *m*, imperfección *f*.

flawed [flɔːd] *adj* imperfecto(ta), defectuoso(sa).

flawless ['flɔːlɪs] *adj* impecable.

flax [flæks] *n* lino *m*.

flay [fleɪ] *vt lit & fig* desollar.

flea [fliː] *n* pulga *f*; **to send sb away with a ~ in his/her ear** echar una regañina a alguien.

flea market *n* rastro *m*.

fleck [flek] ◇ *n* mota *f*. ◇ *vt*: ~ed with salpicado(da) de.

fled [fled] *pt & pp* → flee.

fledg(e)ling ['fledʒlɪŋ] ◇ *adj* [new, young] novato(ta). ◇ *n* pajarito *m*.

flee [fliː] (*pt & pp* **fled**) ◇ *vt* huir de. ◇ *vi*: to ~ (**from/to**) huir (de/a).

fleece [fliːs] ◇ *n* vellón *m*. ◇ *vt inf* [cheat] desplumar.

fleet [fliːt] *n* **-1.** [of ships] flota *f*. **-2.** [of cars, buses] parque *m* (móvil).

fleeting ['fliːtɪŋ] *adj* fugaz.

Fleet Street *n* Fleet Street.

FLEET STREET:

Esta calle, que se encuentra en la City londinense, fue antiguamente el centro de la prensa inglesa. Aunque hoy día muchos periódicos se han trasladado a otros barrios, especialmente a los 'Docklands', se sigue utilizan- do el término 'Fleet Street' para referirse a la prensa en general

Fleming ['flemɪŋ] *n* flamenco *m*, -ca *f*.

Flemish ['flemɪʃ] ◇ *adj* flamenco(ca). ◇ *n*

[language] flamenco *m*. ◇ *npl*: **the ~** los flamencos.

flesh [fleʃ] *n* **-1.** [of body] carne *f*; **to be one's (own) ~ and blood** [family] ser de la misma (carne y) sangre que uno; **in the ~** en persona. **-2.** [of fruit, vegetable] pulpa *f*.
◆ **flesh out** *vt sep* desarrollar.

flesh wound *n* herida *f* superficial.

fleshy ['fleʃɪ] (*compar* **-ier**, *superl* **-iest**) *adj* [fat] gordo(da).

flew [fluː] *pt* → fly.

flex [fleks] ◇ *n* ELEC cable *m*, cordón *m*. ◇ *vt* flexionar.

flexibility [,fleksə'bɪlətɪ] *n* flexibilidad *f*.

flexible ['fleksəbl] *adj* flexible.

flexitime ['fleksɪtaɪm] *n* (*U*) horario *m* flexible.

flick [flɪk] ◇ *n* **-1.** [of whip, towel] golpe *m* rápido. **-2.** [with finger] toba *f*. ◇ *vt* **-1.** [whip, towel] dar un golpe seco con. **-2.** [with finger] dar una toba a. **-3.** [switch] apretar, pulsar.
◆ **flicks** *npl inf*: **the ~s** el cine.
◆ **flick through** *vt fus* hojear rápidamente.

flicker ['flɪkə'] ◇ *n* parpadeo *m*; *fig*: **a ~ of hope** un rayo de esperanza; **a ~ of interest** un atisbo de interés. ◇ *vi* [eyes] parpadear; [flame] vacilar.

flick knife *n Br* navaja *f* automática.

flier ['flaɪə'] *n* **-1.** [pilot] aviador *m*, -ra *f*. **-2.** [advertising leaflet] folleto *m* publicitario.

flight [flaɪt] *n* **-1.** [gen] vuelo *m*; **~ of fancy** OR **of the imagination** vuelo de la imaginación. **-2.** [of steps, stairs] tramo *m*. **-3.** [of birds] bandada *f*. **-4.** [escape] huida *f*, fuga *f*.

flight attendant *n* auxiliar *m* de vuelo, azafata *f*.

flight crew *n* tripulación *f* de vuelo.

flight deck *n* **-1.** [of aircraft carrier] cubierta *f* de vuelo. **-2.** [of plane] cabina *f* del piloto.

flight path *n* trayectoria *f* de vuelo.

flight recorder *n* registrador *m* de vuelo.

flighty ['flaɪtɪ] (*compar* **-ier**, *superl* **-iest**) *adj* frívolo(la), veleidoso(sa).

flimsy ['flɪmzɪ] (*compar* **-ier**, *superl* **-iest**) *adj* **-1.** [dress, material] muy ligero(ra). **-2.** [structure] débil, poco sólido(da). **-3.** [excuse] flojo(ja).

flinch [flɪntʃ] *vi* **-1.** [shudder] estremecerse; **without ~ing** sin pestañear. **-2.** [be reluctant]: **to ~ (from sthg/from doing sthg)** retroceder (ante algo/ante hacer algo); **without ~ing** sin inmutarse.

fling [flɪŋ] (*pt & pp* **flung**) ◇ *n* **-1.** [irresponsible adventure]: **to have a ~** echar una cana al aire. **-2.** [affair] aventura *f* amorosa.

◇ *vt* arrojar; **he flung himself to the ground** se arrojó al suelo.

flint [flɪnt] *n* **-1.** [rock] sílex *m*. **-2.** [in lighter] piedra *f*.

flip [flɪp] (*pt* & *pp* **-ped**, *cont* **-ping**) ◇ *vt* **-1.** [turn] dar la vuelta a; **to ~ sthg open** abrir algo de golpe. **-2.** [switch] pulsar. **-3.** [send through air] lanzar al aire. ◇ *vi inf* [become angry] mosquearse, ponerse hecho(cha) una furia. ◇ *n* **-1.** [of coin] toba *f*, papirotazo *m*. **-2.** [somersault] salto *m* mortal.
◆ **flip through** *vt fus* hojear.

flip-flop *n* [shoe] chancleta *f*.

flippant ['flɪpənt] *adj* frívolo(la), poco serio(ria).

flippantly ['flɪpəntlɪ] *adv* frívolamente, con poca seriedad.

flipper ['flɪpə'] *n* aleta *f*.

flipping ['flɪpɪŋ] *Br inf* ◇ *adj* condenado(da), maldito(ta). ◇ *adv* absolutamente, sencillamente.

flip side *n* [of record] cara *f* B.

flirt [flɜːt] ◇ *n* coqueto *m*, -ta *f*. ◇ *vi* **-1.** [with person]: **to ~ (with)** flirtear OR coquetear (con). **-2.** [with idea]: **to ~ with** acariciar, contemplar.

flirtation [flɜːˈteɪʃn] *n* **-1.** [flirting] flirteo *m*, coqueteo *m*. **-2.** [love affair] amorío *m*, aventura *f*. **-3.** [brief interest]: **I had a brief ~ with the idea of going abroad** me pasó por la cabeza la idea de ir al extranjero.

flirtatious [flɜːˈteɪʃəs] *adj* coqueto(ta).

flit [flɪt] (*pt* & *pp* **-ted**, *cont* **-ting**) *vi* **-1.** [bird] revolotear. **-2.** [expression, idea]: **to ~ through** pasar rápidamente por, cruzar.

float [fləʊt] ◇ *n* **-1.** [for fishing line] corcho *m*. **-2.** [buoyant object] flotador *m*. **-3.** [in procession] carroza *f*. **-4.** [supply of change] cambio *m*. ◇ *vt* **-1.** [on water] hacer flotar. **-2.** [idea, project] plantear, lanzar. ◇ *vi* flotar.

floating ['fləʊtɪŋ] *adj* flotante.

floating voter *n Br* votante indeciso *m*, votante indecisa *f*.

flock [flɒk] ◇ *n* **-1.** [of sheep] rebaño *m*; [of birds] bandada *f*. **-2.** *fig* [of people] multitud *f*, tropel *m*. **-3.** RELIG grey *f*. ◇ *vi*: **to ~ to** acudir en masa OR tropel a.

floe [fləʊ] *n* témpano *m*.

flog [flɒg] (*pt* & *pp* **-ged**, *cont* **-ging**) *vt* **-1.** [whip] azotar. **-2.** *Br inf* [sell] vender.

flood [flʌd] ◇ *n* **-1.** [of water] inundación *f*. **-2.** [of letters, people] aluvión *m*, riada *f*. ◇ *vt lit* & *fig*: **to ~ sthg (with)** inundar algo (de). ◇ *vi* **-1.** [river] desbordarse. **-2.** [street, land] inundarse, anegarse. **-3.** [arrive in masses]: **to ~ in** [letters etc] llegar a montones; [people] entrar a raudales; **the memories came flooding back** los recuerdos le embargaron de pronto.
◆ **floods** *npl fig*: **to be in ~s of tears** llorar a mares.

floodgates ['flʌdgeɪts] *npl*: **to open the ~ to** abrir paso a.

flooding ['flʌdɪŋ] *n* (*U*) inundación *f*.

floodlight ['flʌdlaɪt] *n* foco *m*.

floodlit ['flʌdlɪt] *adj* iluminado(da) con focos.

flood tide *n* pleamar *f*, marea *f* alta.

floor [flɔː'] ◇ *n* **-1.** [of room, forest] suelo *m*; [of club, disco] pista *f*. **-2.** [of sea, valley] fondo *m*. **-3.** [of building] piso *m*, planta *f*. **-4.** [at meeting, debate]: **to give/have the ~** dar/tener la palabra. **-5.** [of stock exchange] patio *m*, parqué *m*. ◇ *vt* **-1.** [knock down] derribar. **-2.** [baffle] desconcertar, dejar perplejo(ja).

floorboard ['flɔːbɔːd] *n* tabla *f* (del suelo).

floor cloth *n Br* trapo *m* del suelo.

flooring ['flɔːrɪŋ] *n* solería *f*, suelo *m*.

floor lamp *n Am* lámpara *f* de pie.

floor show *n* espectáculo *m* de cabaret.

floorwalker ['flɔːˌwɔːkə'] *n* jefe *m*, -fa *f* de sección (*en tiendas*).

floozy ['fluːzɪ] (*pl* **-ies**) *n dated* & *pej* pelandusca *f*.

flop [flɒp] (*pt* & *pp* **-ped**, *cont* **-ping**) *inf* ◇ *n* [failure] fracaso *m*. ◇ *vi* **-1.** [fail] fracasar. **-2.** [fall] desplomarse.

floppy ['flɒpɪ] (*compar* **-ier**, *superl* **-iest**) *adj* caído(da), flojo(ja).

floppy (disk) *n* disco *m* flexible, disquete *m*.

flora ['flɔːrə] *n* flora *f*; **~ and fauna** flora y fauna.

floral ['flɔːrəl] *adj* **-1.** [made of flowers] floral. **-2.** [patterned with flowers] de flores.

Florence ['flɒrəns] *n* Florencia.

floret ['flɒrɪt] *n* brote *m*, grumo *m*.

florid ['flɒrɪd] *adj* **-1.** [red] rojizo(za). **-2.** [extravagant] florido(da).

Florida ['flɒrɪdə] *n* Florida.

florist ['flɒrɪst] *n* florista *m y f*; **~'s (shop)** floristería *f*.

floss [flɒs] ◇ *n* (*U*) **-1.** [silk] seda *f* floja. **-2.** [dental floss] (hilo *m* de) seda *f* dental. ◇ *vt*: **to ~ one's teeth** limpiarse los dientes con seda dental.

flotation [fləʊˈteɪʃn] *n* COMM [of shares] emisión *f*; [of company] lanzamiento *m*.

flotilla [fləˈtɪlə] *n* flotilla *f*.

flotsam ['flɒtsəm] *n* (*U*): **~ and jetsam** restos *mpl* del naufragio; *fig* desechos *mpl* de la humanidad.

flounce [flauns] ◇ *n* **-1.** [movement] desplante *m*, bufido *m*. **-2.** SEWING volante *m*. ◇ *vi* moverse con aire de indignación; **to ~ out** salir airadamente.

flounder ['flaundər] (*pl inv* OR **-s**) ◇ *n* platija *f*. ◇ *vi* **-1.** [move with difficulty] debatirse, forcejear. **-2.** [when speaking] titubear.

flour ['flauər] *n* harina *f*.

flourish ['flʌrɪʃ] ◇ *vi* florecer. ◇ *vt* agitar. ◇ *n*: **to do sthg with a ~** hacer algo con una floritura.

flourishing ['flʌrɪʃɪŋ] *adj* floreciente.

flout [flaut] *vt* incumplir, no obedecer.

flow [fləu] ◇ *n* [gen] flujo *m*; [of opinion] corriente *f*. ◇ *vi* **-1.** [gen] fluir, correr. **-2.** [tide] subir, crecer. **-3.** [hair, clothes] ondear. **-4.** [result]: **to ~ from** emanar de.

flow chart, flow diagram *n* organigrama *m*, cuadro *m* sinóptico.

flower ['flauər] ◇ *n lit* & *fig* flor *f*. ◇ *comp* de flores. ◇ *vi lit* & *fig* florecer.

flowerbed ['flauəbed] *n* arriate *m*, parterre *m*, cantero *m Amer*.

flowered ['flauəd] *adj* de flores, floreado(da).

flowering ['flauərɪŋ] ◇ *adj* floreciente. ◇ *n* florecimiento *m*.

flowerpot ['flauəpɒt] *n* maceta *f*, tiesto *m*.

flowery ['flauərɪ] (*compar* **-ier**, *superl* **-iest**) *adj* **-1.** [patterned] de flores, floreado(da). **-2.** *pej* [elaborate] florido(da). **-3.** [sweet-smelling] con olor a flores.

flowing ['fləuɪŋ] *adj* [movement, writing, style] fluido(da); [water] corriente; [hair, clothes] suelto(ta).

flown [fləun] *pp* → **fly**.

fl. oz. *abbr of* **fluid ounce**.

flu [fluː] *n* gripe *f*, gripa *f Amer*; **to have ~** tener la gripe.

fluctuate ['flʌktʃueɪt] *vi* fluctuar.

fluctuation [ˌflʌktʃuˈeɪʃn] *n* fluctuación *f*.

flue [fluː] *n* humero *m*.

fluency ['fluːənsɪ] *n* soltura *f*, fluidez *f*; **~ in French** dominio *m* del francés.

fluent ['fluːənt] *adj* **-1.** [in foreign language]: **to be ~ in French, to speak ~ French** dominar el francés. **-2.** [style] elocuente, fluido(da).

fluently ['fluːəntlɪ] *adv* con soltura; **to speak French ~** dominar el francés.

fluff [flʌf] ◇ *n* pelusa *f*. ◇ *vt inf* [action, task] hacer mal; [words, lines] decir mal.

◆ **fluff up** *vt sep* [cushion, hair] ahuecar; [feathers] encrespar.

fluffy ['flʌfɪ] (*compar* **-ier**, *superl* **-iest**) *adj* [jumper] de pelusa; [toy] de peluche.

fluid ['fluːɪd] ◇ *n* fluido *m*, líquido *m*. ◇ *adj* **-1.** [flowing] fluido(da). **-2.** [situation, opinion] incierto(ta).

fluid ounce *n* = 0,03 litre, onza *f* líquida.

fluke [fluːk] *n inf* chiripa *f*; **by a ~** por OR de chiripa.

flummox ['flʌməks] *vt Br inf* desconcertar, confundir.

flung [flʌŋ] *pt* & *pp* → **fling**.

flunk [flʌŋk] *vt* & *vi inf* catear.

fluorescent [fluəˈresnt] *adj* fluorescente.

fluorescent light *n* luz *f* fluorescente.

fluoridate ['fluərɪdeɪt] *vt* añadir fluoruro a.

fluoride ['fluəraɪd] *n* fluoruro *m*.

fluorine ['fluəriːn] *n* flúor *m*.

flurry ['flʌrɪ] (*pl* **-ies**) *n* **-1.** [shower] ráfaga *f*. **-2.** [burst] frenesí *m*.

flush [flʌʃ] ◇ *adj* **-1.** [level]: **~ with** nivelado(da) con. **-2.** *inf* [with plenty of money]: **to be ~** estar forrado(da). ◇ *n* **-1.** [of lavatory] cadena *f*. **-2.** [blush] rubor *m*. **-3.** [sudden feeling] arrebato *m*; **in the first ~ of youth** *literary* en la primera juventud. ◇ *vt* **-1.** [toilet] tirar de la cadena de. **-2.** [down toilet]: **to ~ sthg away** tirar algo al water. **-3.** [force out of hiding]: **to ~ sb out** hacer salir a alguien. ◇ *vi* [blush] ruborizarse.

flushed [flʌʃt] *adj* **-1.** [red-faced] encendido(da). **-2.** [excited]: **~ (with)** enardecido(da) (por).

fluster ['flʌstər] ◇ *n*: **to get in a ~**. aturullarse. ◇ *vt* aturullar.

flustered ['flʌstəd] *adj* aturullado(da).

flute [fluːt] *n* MUS flauta *f*.

fluted ['fluːtɪd] *adj* acanalado(da).

flutist *Am* = **flautist**.

flutter ['flʌtər] ◇ *n* **-1.** [of wings] aleteo *m*; [of eyelashes] pestañeo *m*. **-2.** [of heart] palpitación *f*. **-3.** *inf* [of excitement] arranque *m*. ◇ *vt* agitar; **to ~ one's eyelashes** parpadear. ◇ *vi* **-1.** [bird] aletear. **-2.** [flag, dress] ondear. **-3.** [heart] palpitar.

flux [flʌks] *n* [change]: **to be in a state of ~** cambiar constantemente.

fly [flaɪ] (*pt* **flew**, *pp* **flown**, *pl* **flies**) ◇ *n* **-1.** [insect] mosca *f*; **a ~ in the ointment** una pega. **-2.** [in trousers] bragueta *f*. ◇ *vt* **-1.** [plane] pilotar; [kite, model aircraft] hacer volar. **-2.** [passengers, supplies] transportar en avión. **-3.** [flag] ondear. ◇ *vi* **-1.** [bird, plane, person] volar; **time flies** el tiempo vuela; **I must ~!** ¡me voy volando!; **to go ~** *inf* caer aparatosamente; **to send sthg/sb ~ing, to knock sthg/sb ~ing** *inf* mandar algo/a alguien por los aires. **-2.** [pilot a plane] pilotar. **-3.** [travel by plane] ir en avión. **-4.** [rumours, stories] abundar. **-5.** [attack]: **to ~ at sb** arremeter contra alguien. **-6.** [flag] ondear.

◆ **fly away** *vi* irse volando.

◆ **fly in** ◇ *vt sep* traer (en avión). ◇ *vi* [person] llegar (en avión); [plane] aterrizar.

◆ **fly into** *vt fus*: **to ~ into a rage** OR **a temper** montar en cólera.

◆ **fly out** ◇ *vt sep* llevarse (en avión). ◇ *vi* irse (en avión).

flyby *Am* = flypast.

fly-fishing *n* pesca *f* con mosca.

fly half *n Br* (medio *m*) apertura *m*.

flying ['flaɪɪŋ] ◇ *adj* **-1.** [able to fly] volador(ra), volante. **-2.** [running]: **a ~ leap** OR **jump** un salto con carrerilla. ◇ *n*: **I hate/love ~** odio/me encanta ir en avión; **her hobby is ~** es aficionada a la aviación.

flying colours *npl*: **to pass (sthg) with ~** salir airoso(sa) (de algo).

flying doctor *n* médico que utiliza el avión para visitar a sus pacientes en zonas alejadas.

flying officer *n Br* ≃ teniente *m* de aviación.

flying picket *n* piquete de apoyo proveniente de otra fábrica o sindicato.

flying saucer *n* platillo *m* volante.

flying squad *n* brigada *f* volante.

flying start *n*: **to get off to a ~** empezar con muy buen pie.

flying visit *n* visita *f* relámpago.

flyleaf ['flaɪliːf] (*pl* **-leaves**) *n* (hoja *f* de) guarda *f*.

flyover ['flaɪ,əʊvə'] *n Br* paso *m* elevado.

flypast *Br* ['flaɪ,pɑːst], **flyby** *Am* ['flaɪ,baɪ] desfile *m* aéreo.

flysheet ['flaɪfiːt] *n* doble techo *m*.

fly spray *n* matamoscas *m inv* (en aerosol).

flyweight ['flaɪweɪt] *n* peso *m* mosca.

flywheel ['flaɪwiːl] *n* volante *m* (de motor).

FM -1. (*abbr of* **frequency modulation**) FM *f*. **-2.** *abbr of* **field marshal**.

FMB (*abbr of* **Federal Maritime Board**) *n* organismo estadounidense federal de la marina mercante.

FMCS (*abbr of* **Federal Mediation and Conciliation Services**) *n* organismo estadounidense de arbitraje en conflictos laborales, ≃ IMAC *m*.

FO *n abbr of* **Foreign Office**.

foal [fəʊl] *n* potro *m*.

foam [fəʊm] ◇ *n* **-1.** [bubbles] espuma *f*. **-2. ~ (rubber)** gomaespuma *f*. ◇ *vi* hacer espuma; **to ~ at the mouth** echar espuma por la boca.

foamy ['fəʊmɪ] (*compar* **-ier**, *superl* **-iest**) *adj* espumoso(sa).

fob [fɒb] (*pt & pp* **-bed**, *cont* **-bing**)

◆ **fob off** *vt sep*: **to ~ sb off (with sthg)** dar largas a alguien (con algo); **to ~ sthg off on sb** endosar a alguien algo.

FOB, **f.o.b.** (*abbr of* **free on board**) f.a.b.

fob watch *n* reloj *m* de bolsillo.

foc (*abbr of* **free of charge**) fco.

focal ['fəʊkl] *adj* [important] clave (*inv*).

focal point *n* punto *m* focal OR central.

focus ['fəʊkəs] (*pl* **-cuses** OR **-ci** [-saɪ]) ◇ *n* [gen] foco *m*; **in ~** enfocado; **out of ~** desenfocado; **~ of attention** centro *m* de atención. ◇ *vt* **-1.** [eyes, lens, rays] enfocar. **-2.** [attention] fijar, centrar. ◇ *vi* **-1.** [eyes, lens]: **to ~ (on sthg)** enfocar (algo). **-2.** [attention]: **to ~ on sthg** centrarse en algo.

fodder ['fɒdə'] *n* forraje *m*.

foe [fəʊ] *n literary* enemigo *m*, -ga *f*.

FOE *n* **-1.** (*abbr of* **Friends of the Earth**) AT *mpl*. **-2.** (*abbr of* **Fraternal Order of Eagles**) organización benéfica estadounidense.

foetal ['fiːtl] *adj* fetal.

foetus ['fiːtəs] *n* feto *m*.

fog [fɒg] *n* niebla *f*.

fogbound ['fɒgbaʊnd] *adj* inmovilizado(da) por la niebla.

fogey ['fəʊgɪ] = fogy.

foggiest ['fɒgɪəst] *n inf*: **I haven't the ~** no tengo la menor idea.

foggy ['fɒgɪ] (*compar* **-ier**, *superl* **-iest**) *adj* [misty] brumoso(sa); [day] de niebla.

foghorn ['fɒghɔːn] *n* sirena *f* (de niebla).

fog lamp *n* faro *m* antiniebla.

fogy ['fəʊgɪ] (*pl* **-ies**) *n inf* carroza *m y f*, carca *m y f*.

foible ['fɔɪbl] *n* manía *f*.

foil [fɔɪl] ◇ *n* **-1.** (*U*) [metal sheet] papel *m* aluminio OR de plata. **-2.** [contrast]: **a ~ to** OR **for** un contraste con. ◇ *vt* frustrar.

foist [fɔɪst] *vt*: **to ~ sthg on sb** endosar algo a alguien.

fold [fəʊld] ◇ *vt* [sheet, blanket] doblar; [chair, pram] plegar; **to ~ one's arms** cruzar los brazos. ◇ *vi* **-1.** [table, chair etc] plegarse. **-2.** *inf* [collapse] venirse abajo. ◇ *n* **-1.** [in material, paper] pliegue *m*, doblez *m*. **-2.** [for animals] aprisco *m*, redil *m*. **-3.** *fig* [spiritual home]: **the ~** el redil.

◆ **fold up** ◇ *vt sep* **-1.** [bend] doblar. **-2.** [close up] plegar. ◇ *vi* **-1.** [bend] doblarse. **-2.** [close up] plegarse. **-3.** [collapse] venirse abajo.

foldaway ['fəʊldə,weɪ] *adj* plegable.

folder ['fəʊldər] *n* -1. [gen] carpeta *f*. -2. COMPUT carpeta *f*, directorio *m*.

folding ['fəʊldɪŋ] *adj* plegable; [ladder] de tijera.

foliage ['fəʊlɪɪdʒ] *n* follaje *m*.

folk [fəʊk] ◇ *adj* popular. ◇ *n* -1. [people] gente *f*. -2. = folk music.
◆ **folks** *npl inf* -1. [relatives] familia *f*. -2. [everyone] chicos *mpl*, -cas *fpl*.

folklore ['fəʊklɔːr] *n* folklore *m*.

folk music *n* música *f* folklórica OR popular.

folk singer *n* cantante *m y f* folk OR de música popular.

folk song *n* canción *f* popular.

folksy ['fəʊksɪ] (*compar* -ier, *superl* -iest) *adj* *Am inf* [friendly] campechano(na).

follicle ['fɒlɪkl] *n* folículo *m*.

follow ['fɒləʊ] ◇ *vt* -1. [gen] seguir. -2. [understand] comprender. ◇ *vi* -1. [gen] seguir; **as ~s** como sigue. -2. [be logical] ser lógico(ca); **it ~s that** se deduce que. -3. [understand] comprender.
◆ **follow up** *vt sep* examinar en más detalle; **to ~ sthg up with** proseguir algo con.

follower ['fɒləʊər] *n* partidario *m*, -ria *f*, seguidor *m*, -ra *f*.

following ['fɒləʊɪŋ] ◇ *adj* siguiente. ◇ *n* partidarios *mpl*; [of team] afición *f*. ◇ *prep* tras.

follow-up ◇ *adj* complementario(ria), de seguimiento. ◇ *n* -1. [service] seguimiento *m*. -2. [continuation] continuación *f*.

folly ['fɒlɪ] *n* (*U*) [foolishness] locura *f*.

foment [fəʊ'ment] *vt fml* fomentar.

fond [fɒnd] *adj* -1. [affectionate] afectuoso(sa), cariñoso(sa). -2. [having a liking]: **to be ~ of sb** tener cariño a alguien; **to be ~ of sthg/of doing sthg** ser aficionado(da) a algo/a hacer algo. -3. *fml* [naive, unrealistic] inocente.

fondle ['fɒndl] *vt* acariciar.

fondly ['fɒndlɪ] *adv* -1. [affectionately] afectuosamente, con cariño. -2. [naively] inocentemente.

fondness ['fɒndnɪs] *n* -1. [affection]: ~ (for) cariño *m* (a). -2. [liking]: ~ for afición *f* a.

fondue ['fɒndjuː] *n* fondue *f*.

font [fɒnt] *n* -1. [in church] pila *f* bautismal. -2. COMPUT: **hard/printer/screen ~** grupo *m* de caracteres impreso/de impresora/de pantalla.

food [fuːd] *n* comida *f*; ~ **for thought** algo en qué pensar.

food chain *n* cadena *f* alimentaria.

food mixer *n* batidora *f* eléctrica.

food poisoning [-'pɔɪznɪŋ] *n* intoxicación *f* alimenticia.

food processor *n* robot *m* de cocina.

food stamp *n Am* cupón *estatal canjeable por comida.*

foodstuffs ['fuːdstʌfs] *npl* comestibles *mpl*.

fool [fuːl] ◇ *n* -1. [idiot] tonto *m*, -ta *f*, imbécil *m y f*; **to make a ~ of sb/of o.s.** poner a alguien/ponerse en ridículo; **to act** OR **play the ~** hacer el tonto. -2. *Br* [dessert] *mousse de fruta con nata.* ◇ *vt* [deceive] engañar; [joke with] tomar el pelo a; **to ~ sb into doing sthg** embaucar a alguien para que haga algo. ◇ *vi* bromear.
◆ **fool about**, **fool around** *vi* -1. [behave foolishly]: **to ~ about (with sthg)** hacer el tonto (con algo). -2. [be unfaithful]: **to ~ about (with sb)** tontear (con alguien).

foolhardy ['fuːl,hɑːdɪ] *adj* temerario(ria).

foolish ['fuːlɪʃ] *adj* tonto(ta), estúpido(da).

foolishly ['fuːlɪʃlɪ] *adv* tontamente, estúpidamente.

foolishness ['fuːlɪʃnɪs] *n* (*U*) necedad *f*.

foolproof ['fuːlpruːf] *adj* infalible.

foolscap ['fuːlzkæp] *n* (*U*) ≃ pliego *m*.

foot [fʊt] (*pl sense 1* feet, *pl sense 2 inv* OR feet) ◇ *n* -1. [gen] pie *m*; [of bird, animal] pata *f*; **to be on one's feet** estar de pie; **to get to one's feet** levantarse; **on ~** a pie, andando; **to be back on one's feet** haberse recuperado; **to be rushed off one's feet** andar muy atareado; **to have itchy feet** tener ganas de viajar; **to put one's ~ down** *fig* ponerse firme; **to put one's ~ in it** meter la pata; **to put one's feet up** descansar (con los pies en alto); **to set ~ in** poner los pies en; **to stand on one's two feet** valerse por sí mismo. -2. [unit of measurement] = 30,48 *cm*, pie *m*. ◇ *vt inf*: **to ~ the bill (for sthg)** pagar la cuenta (de algo).

footage ['fʊtɪdʒ] *n* (*U*) secuencias *fpl*.

foot-and-mouth disease *n* fiebre *f* aftosa, glosopeda *f*.

football ['fʊtbɔːl] *n* -1. [game - soccer] fútbol *m*; [- American football] fútbol *m* americano. -2. [ball] balón *m*.

football club *n Br* club *m* de fútbol.

footballer ['fʊtbɔːlər] *n Br* futbolista *m y f*.

football field *n Am* campo *m* de fútbol americano.

football game *n Am* partido *m* de fútbol americano.

football ground *n Br* campo *m* de fútbol.

football match *n Br* partido *m* de fútbol.

football player = footballer.

football pools *npl Br* quinielas *fpl*.

football supporter *n Br* hincha *m y f*.

footbrake ['fʊtbreɪk] *n* freno *m* de pedal.

footbridge ['fʊtbrɪdʒ] *n* paso *m* elevado, pasarela *f*.

foot fault *n* falta *f* de saque.

foothills ['fʊthɪlz] *npl* estribaciones *fpl*.

foothold ['fʊthəʊld] *n* punto *m* de apoyo para el pie; **to get a ~** [on mountain, rockface] encontrar un punto de apoyo; [in organization, company] afianzarse.

footing ['fʊtɪŋ] *n* **-1.** [foothold] equilibrio *m*; **to lose one's ~** perder el equilibrio. **-2.** [basis] nivel *m*; **on an equal ~ (with)** en pie de igualdad (con).

footlights ['fʊtlaɪts] *npl* candilejas *fpl*.

footling ['fuːtlɪŋ] *adj* dated & *pej* nimio(mia).

footman ['fʊtmən] (*pl* **-men** [-mən]) *n* lacayo *m*.

footmark ['fʊtmɑːk] *n* pisada *f*.

footmen ['fʊtmən] *pl* → **footman**.

footnote ['fʊtnəʊt] *n* nota *f* a pie de página.

footpath ['fʊtpɑːθ, *pl* -pɑːðz] *n* senda *f*, camino *m*.

footprint ['fʊtprɪnt] *n* huella *f*, pisada *f*.

footsore ['fʊtsɔːr] *adj* con los pies doloridos.

footstep ['fʊtstep] *n* **-1.** [sound] paso *m*. **-2.** [footprint] pisada *f*; **to follow in sb's ~s** seguir los pasos de alguien.

footwear ['fʊtweər] *n* calzado *m*.

footwork ['fʊtwɜːk] *n* (*U*) juego *m* de piernas.

for [fɔːr] *prep* **-1.** [indicating intention, destination, purpose] para; **this is ~ you** esto es para ti; **I'm going ~ the paper** voy (a) por el periódico; **the plane ~ Paris** [gen] el avión para OR de París; [in airport announcements] el avión con destino a París; **it's time ~ bed** es hora de irse a la cama; **we did it ~ a laugh** OR **~ fun** lo hicimos de broma OR por divertirnos; **to wait ~ a bus** esperar al autobús; **to go ~ a walk** ir a dar un paseo; **what's it ~?** ¿para qué es OR sirve? **-2.** [representing, on behalf of] por; **the MP ~ Barnsley** el diputado por Barnsley; **let me do it ~ you** deja que lo haga por ti; **he plays ~ England** juega en la selección inglesa; **to work ~** trabajar para. **-3.** [because of] por; **~ various reasons** por varias razones; **a prize ~ bravery** un premio a la valentía; **to jump ~ joy** dar saltos de alegría; **~ fear of failing** por miedo a fracasar. **-4.** [with regard to] para; **to be ready ~ sthg** estar listo para algo; **it's not ~ me to say** no me toca a mí decidir; **he looks young ~ his age** aparenta ser más joven de lo que

es; **to feel sorry/glad ~ sb** sentirlo/alegrarse por alguien. **-5.** [indicating amount of time, space] para; **there's no time/room ~ it** no hay tiempo/sitio para eso. **-6.** [indicating period of time - during] durante; [- by, in time for] para; **she cried ~ two hours** estuvo llorando durante dos horas; **I've lived here ~ three years** llevo tres años viviendo aquí, he vivido aquí (durante) tres años; **I've worked here ~ years** trabajo aquí desde hace años; **I'll do it ~ tomorrow** lo tendré hecho para mañana. **-7.** [indicating distance] en; **there were roadworks ~ 50 miles** había obras en 50 millas; **we walked ~ miles** andamos millas y millas. **-8.** [indicating particular occasion] para; **I got it ~ my birthday** me lo regalaron para OR por mi cumpleaños; **it's scheduled ~ the 30th** está programado para el día 30; **~ the first time** por vez primera. **-9.** [indicating amount of money, price] por; **I bought/sold it ~ £10** lo compré/vendí por 10 libras; **they're 50p ~ ten** son a 50 peniques cada diez. **-10.** [in favour of, in support of] a favor de; **is she ~ or against it?** ¿está a favor o en contra?; **to vote ~ sthg/sb** votar por algo/a alguien; **to be all ~ sthg** estar completamente a favor de algo. **-11.** [in ratios] por. **-12.** [indicating meaning]: **green is ~ go** el verde quiere decir adelante; **P ~ Peter** P de Pedro; **what's the Greek ~ "mother"?** ¿cómo se dice "madre" en griego?

◆ **for all** ◇ *prep* **-1.** [in spite of] a pesar de, pese a; **~ all your moaning** a pesar de lo mucho que te quejas. **-2.** [considering how little] para; **~ all the good it has done me** para lo que me ha servido. ◇ *conj*: **~ all he promised to do it, he never actually did** con todo lo que prometió que lo haría, al final nada; **~ all I care, she could be dead** por mí, como si se muere; **~ all I know** por lo que yo sé, que yo sepa; **~ all I know, he could be dead** no tengo ni idea; podría hasta haber muerto.

FOR (*abbr of* **free on rail**) *franco en ferrocarril*.

forage ['fɒrɪdʒ] *vi* [search]: **to ~ (for sthg)** buscar (algo).

foray ['fɒreɪ] *n lit* & *fig*: **~ (into)** incursión *f* (en).

forbad [fə'bæd], **forbade** [fə'beɪd] *pt* → **forbid**.

forbearing [fɔː'beərɪŋ] *adj* indulgente.

forbid [fə'bɪd] (*pt* **-bade** OR **-bad**, *pp* **forbid** OR **-bidden**, *cont* **-bidding**) *vt*: **to ~ sb (to do sthg)** prohibir a alguien (hacer algo); **God** OR **Heaven ~!** ¡no quiera Dios!

forbidden [fə'bɪdn] *adj* prohibido(da).

forbidding [fə'bɪdɪŋ] *adj* [building, landscape]

inhóspito(ta); [person, expression] severo(ra), austero(ra).

force [fɔːs] ◇ *n* fuerza *f*; **a ~ to be reckoned with** alguien/algo a tener en cuenta; **a powerful ~ for change** una dinámica de cambio; **~ of habit** la fuerza de la costumbre; **sales ~** personal *m* de ventas; **security ~s** fuerzas *fpl* de seguridad; **by ~** a la fuerza; **to be in/come into ~** estar/entrar en vigor; **in ~** [in large numbers] en masa, en gran número. ◇ *vt* forzar; **to ~ sb to do sthg** [gen] forzar a alguien a hacer algo; [subj: event, circumstances] obligar a alguien a hacer algo; **to ~ open** forzar, abrir a la fuerza; **to ~ one's way through/into** abrirse paso a la fuerza a través de/para entrar en.

◆ **forces** *npl*: **the ~s** las fuerzas armadas; **to join ~s (with)** unirse (con).

◆ **by force of** *prep* a fuerza de.

◆ **force back** *vt sep* [crowd, enemy] hacer retroceder; [emotion, tears] contener, reprimir.

◆ **force down** *vt sep* **-1.** [food, drink] tragar a la fuerza. **-2.** [aircraft] obligar a aterrizar.

forced [fɔːst] *adj* forzado(da).

forced landing *n* aterrizaje *m* forzoso.

force-feed *vt* alimentar a la fuerza.

forceful ['fɔːsful] *adj* [person, impression] fuerte; [support, recommendation] enérgico(ca); [speech, idea, argument] contundente.

forcefully ['fɔːsfuli] *adv* enérgicamente.

forcemeat ['fɔːsmiːt] *n* (picadillo *m* de) relleno *m*.

forceps ['fɔːseps] *npl* fórceps *m inv*.

forcible ['fɔːsəbl] *adj* **-1.** [using physical force] por la fuerza. **-2.** [reminder, example, lesson] vivo(va); [recommendation, argument] enérgico(ca).

forcibly ['fɔːsəbli] *adv* **-1.** [using physical force] por la fuerza. **-2.** [remind] vivamente; [express, argue, recommend] enérgicamente.

ford [fɔːd] ◇ *n* vado *m*. ◇ *vt* vadear.

fore [fɔːr] ◇ *adj* NAUT de proa. ◇ *n*: **to come to the ~** empezar a destacar, emerger.

forearm ['fɔːrɑːm] *n* antebrazo *m*.

forebears ['fɔːbeəz] *npl fml* antepasados *mpl*.

foreboding [fɔː'bəudiŋ] *n* **-1.** [presentiment] presagio *m*. **-2.** [apprehension] miedo *m*.

forecast ['fɔːkɑːst] (*pt & pp* forecast OR **-ed**) ◇ *n* [prediction] predicción *f*, previsión *f*; [of weather] pronóstico *m*. ◇ *vt* [predict] predecir; [weather] pronosticar.

forecaster ['fɔːkɑːstər] *n* analista *m y f*, pronosticador *m*, -ra *f*; [of weather] meteorólogo *m*, -ga *f*.

foreclose [fɔː'kləuz] ◇ *vi*: **to ~ on sb** privar a alguien del derecho a redimir su hipoteca. ◇ *vt* ejecutar.

foreclosure [fɔː'kləuʒər] *n* privación *f* del derecho a redimir una hipoteca.

forecourt ['fɔːkɔːt] *n* patio *m*.

forefathers ['fɔː,fɑːðəz] = **forebears**.

forefinger ['fɔː,fiŋgər] *n* (dedo *m*) índice *m*.

forefront ['fɔːfrʌnt] *n*: **in** OR **at the ~ of** en OR a la vanguardia de.

forego [fɔː'gəu] = **forgo**.

foregoing [fɔː'gəuiŋ] ◇ *adj* anterior, precedente. ◇ *n fml*: **the ~** lo anteriormente dicho.

foregone conclusion ['fɔːgɒn-] *n*: **it's a ~** es un resultado inevitable.

foreground ['fɔːgraund] *n* primer plano *m*; **in the ~** en primer plano.

forehand ['fɔːhænd] *n* [stroke] golpe *m* natural, drive *m*.

forehead ['fɔːhed] *n* frente *f*.

foreign ['fɒrən] *adj* **-1.** [from abroad] extranjero(ra). **-2.** [external - policy] exterior; [- correspondent, holiday] en el extranjero. **-3.** [unwanted, harmful] extraño(ña). **-4.** [alien, untypical]: **~ (to sb/sthg)** ajeno(na) (a alguien/algo).

foreign affairs *npl* asuntos *mpl* exteriores.

foreign aid *n* ayuda *f* extranjera.

foreign body *n* cuerpo *m* extraño.

foreign competition *n* competencia *f* extranjera.

foreign currency *n* (*U*) divisa *f*.

foreigner ['fɒrənər] *n* extranjero *m*, -ra *f*.

foreign exchange *n* (*U*) divisas *fpl*; **~ markets/rates** mercados *mpl*/cambio *m* de divisas.

foreign investment *n* (*U*) inversión *f* extranjera.

foreign minister *n* ministro *m*, -tra *f* de asuntos exteriores.

Foreign Office *n Br*: **the ~** el Ministerio de Asuntos Exteriores británico.

Foreign Secretary *n Br* Ministro *m*, -tra *f* de Asuntos Exteriores.

foreleg ['fɔːleg] *n* pata *f* delantera.

foreman ['fɔːmən] (*pl* **-men** [-mən]) *n* **-1.** [of workers] capataz *m*. **-2.** [of jury] presidente *m*.

foremost ['fɔːməust] ◇ *adj* primero(ra). ◇ *adv*: **first and ~** ante todo, por encima de todo.

forename ['fɔːneim] *n* nombre *m* (de pila).

forensic [fə'rensik] *adj* forense.

forensic medicine *n* medicina *f* forense.

forensic science *n* ciencia *f* forense.

forerunner ['fɔːˌrʌnəʳ] *n* [precursor] precursor *m*, -ra *f*.

foresee [fɔː'siː] (*pt* **-saw** [-'sɔː], *pp* **-seen**) *vt* prever.

foreseeable [fɔː'siːəbl] *adj* previsible; **for/in the ~ future** en un futuro próximo.

foreseen [fɔː'siːn] *pp* → **foresee**.

foreshadow [fɔː'ʃædəu] *vt* presagiar.

foreshortened [fɔː'ʃɔːtnd] *adj* en escorzo, escorzado(da).

foresight ['fɔːsaɪt] *n* (*U*) previsión *f*.

foreskin ['fɔːskɪn] *n* prepucio *m*.

forest ['fɒrɪst] *n* bosque *m*.

forestall [fɔː'stɔːl] *vt* anticiparse a.

forestry ['fɒrɪstrɪ] *n* silvicultura *f*.

Forestry Commission *n Br*: **the ~** la comisión británica del patrimonio forestal.

foretaste ['fɔːteɪst] *n* anticipo *m*, adelanto *m*.

foretell [fɔː'tel] (*pt & pp* **-told**) *vt* predecir.

forethought ['fɔːθɔːt] *n* previsión *f*.

foretold [fɔː'təuld] *pt & pp* → **foretell**.

forever [fə'revəʳ] *adv* **-1.** [eternally] para siempre. **-2.** *inf* [incessantly] siempre, continuamente. **-3.** *inf* [a long time]: **it took (us) ~** nos llevó una eternidad.

forewarn [fɔː'wɔːn] *vt* prevenir, advertir.

foreword ['fɔːwɜːd] *n* prefacio *m*.

forfeit ['fɔːfɪt] ⋄ *n* precio *m*; [in game] prenda *f*. ⋄ *vt* renunciar a, perder.

forgave [fə'geɪv] *pt* → **forgive**.

forge [fɔːdʒ] ⋄ *n* fragua *f*, forja *f*. ⋄ *vt* **-1.** [gen] forjar, fraguar. **-2.** [falsify] falsificar.

◆ **forge ahead** *vi* hacer grandes progresos.

forger ['fɔːdʒəʳ] *n* falsificador *m*, -ra *f*.

forgery ['fɔːdʒərɪ] (*pl* **-ies**) *n* falsificación *f*.

forget [fə'get] (*pt* **-got**, *pp* **-gotten**, *cont* **-getting**) ⋄ *vt*: **to ~ (to do sthg)** olvidar (hacer algo); **to ~ o.s.** dejarse llevar por un impulso. ⋄ *vi*: **to ~ (about sthg)** olvidarse (de algo).

forgetful [fə'getful] *adj* olvidadizo(za), desmemoriado(da).

forgetfulness [fə'getfulnɪs] *n* olvido *m*, falta *f* de memoria.

forget-me-not *n* nomeolvides *m inv*.

forgive [fə'gɪv] (*pt* **-gave**, *pp* **-given**) *vt*: **to ~ sb (for sthg/for doing sthg)** perdonar a alguien (algo/por haber hecho algo).

forgiveness [fə'gɪvnɪs] *n* perdón *m*.

forgiving [fə'gɪvɪŋ] *adj* indulgente.

forgo [fɔː'gəu] (*pt* **-went**, *pp* **-gone** [-'gɒn]) *vt* sacrificar, renunciar a.

forgot [fə'gɒt] *pt* → **forget**.

forgotten [fə'gɒtn] *pp* → **forget**.

fork [fɔːk] ⋄ *n* **-1.** [for food] tenedor *m*. **-2.** [for gardening] horca *f*. **-3.** [in road etc] bifurcación *f*. ⋄ *vi* bifurcarse.

◆ **fork out** *inf* ⋄ *vt fus*: **to ~ out money on** OR **for sthg** soltar pelas para algo. ⋄ *vi*: **to ~ out for sthg** soltar pelas para algo.

forklift truck ['fɔːklɪft-] *n* carretilla *f* elevadora.

forlorn [fə'lɔːn] *adj* **-1.** [person, expression] consternado(da). **-2.** [place, landscape] desolado(da). **-3.** [hope, attempt] desesperado(da).

form [fɔːm] ⋄ *n* **-1.** [shape, type] forma *f*; **in the ~ of** en forma de; **to take the ~ of** consistir en. **-2.** [fitness]: **on ~** *Br*, **in ~** *Am* en forma; **off ~** en baja forma. **-3.** [document] impreso *m*, formulario *m*, planilla *f* *Amer*. **-4.** [figure - of person] figura *f*. **-5.** *Br* [class] clase *f*. **-6.** [usual behaviour]: **true to ~** como era de esperar. ⋄ *vt* formar; [plan] concebir; [impression, idea] formarse. ⋄ *vi* formarse.

formal ['fɔːml] *adj* **-1.** [gen] formal; [education] convencional. **-2.** [clothes, wedding, party] de etiqueta.

formality [fɔː'mælətɪ] (*pl* **-ies**) *n* formalidad *f*.

formalize, -ise ['fɔːməlaɪz] *vt* formalizar.

formally ['fɔːməlɪ] *adv* formalmente; [dressed] de etiqueta.

format ['fɔːmæt] (*pt & pp* **-ted**, *cont* **-ting**) ⋄ *n* [gen & COMPUT] formato *m*; [of meeting] plan *m*. ⋄ *vt* COMPUT formatear.

formation [fɔː'meɪʃn] *n* formación *f*; [of ideas, plans] creación *f*.

formative ['fɔːmətɪv] *adj* formativo(va).

former ['fɔːməʳ] ⋄ *adj* **-1.** [previous] antiguo(gua); **in ~ times** antiguamente. **-2.** [first of two] primero(ra). ⋄ *n*: **the ~** el primero (la primera)/los primeros (las primeras).

formerly ['fɔːməlɪ] *adv* antes, antiguamente.

form feed *n* salto *m* de página.

Formica® [fɔː'maɪkə] *n* formica® *f*.

formidable ['fɔːmɪdəbl] *adj* **-1.** [frightening] imponente, temible. **-2.** [impressive] formidable.

formless ['fɔːmlɪs] *adj* sin forma, informe.

Formosa [fɔː'məusə] *n* Formosa.

formula ['fɔːmjulə] (*pl* **-as** OR **-ae** [-iː]) *n* fórmula *f*.

formulate ['fɔːmjuleɪt] *vt* formular.

formulation [ˌfɔːmjʊ'leɪʃn] *n* formulación *f*.
fornicate ['fɔːnɪkeɪt] *vi fml* fornicar.
forsake [fə'seɪk] (*pt* **forsook**, *pp* **forsaken**) *vt literary* abandonar.
forsaken [fə'seɪkn] *adj* abandonado(da).
forsook [fə'sʊk] *pt* → **forsake**.
forsythia [fɔː'saɪθjə] *n* forsitia *f*.
fort [fɔːt] *n* fuerte *m*, fortaleza *f*; **to hold the ~ (for sb)** quedarse al cargo (en lugar de alguien).
forte ['fɔːtɪ] *n* fuerte *m*.
forth [fɔːθ] *adv literary* **-1.** [outwards, onwards] hacia adelante. **-2.** [into future]: **from that day ~** desde aquel día en adelante.
forthcoming [fɔːθ'kʌmɪŋ] *adj* **-1.** [election, book, events] próximo(ma). **-2.** [help, information, answer] disponible; **no reply was ~** no hubo respuesta. **-3.** [person] abierto(ta), amable.
forthright ['fɔːθraɪt] *adj* [person, manner, opinions] directo(ta), franco(ca); [opposition] rotundo(da).
forthwith [ˌfɔːθ'wɪθ] *adv fml* inmediatamente.
fortieth ['fɔːtɪθ] ◇ *num adj* cuadragésimo(ma). ◇ *num n* **-1.** [in order] cuadragésimo *m*, -ma *f*. **-2.** [fraction] cuarentavo *m*; *see also* **sixth**.
fortification [ˌfɔːtɪfɪ'keɪʃn] *n* fortificación *f*.
fortified wine ['fɔːtɪfaɪd-] *n* vino *m* licoroso.
fortify ['fɔːtɪfaɪ] (*pt & pp* **-ied**) *vt* **-1.** MIL fortificar. **-2.** [person, resolve] fortalecer.
fortitude ['fɔːtɪtjuːd] *n* fortaleza *f*, valor *m*.
fortnight ['fɔːtnaɪt] *n* quincena *f*.
fortnightly ['fɔːtˌnaɪtlɪ] ◇ *adj* quincenal. ◇ *adv* quincenalmente.
fortress ['fɔːtrɪs] *n* fortaleza *f*.
fortuitous [fɔː'tjuːɪtəs] *adj fml* fortuito(ta).
fortunate ['fɔːtʃnət] *adj* afortunado(da).
fortunately ['fɔːtʃnətlɪ] *adv* afortunadamente.
fortune ['fɔːtʃuːn] *n* **-1.** [money, luck] fortuna *f*. **-2.** [future]: **to tell sb's ~** decir a alguien la buenaventura.
◆ **fortunes** *npl* [vicissitudes] vicisitudes *fpl*; [luck] suerte *f*.
fortune-teller *n* adivino *m*, -na *f*.
forty ['fɔːtɪ] *num* cuarenta; *see also* **sixty**.
forum ['fɔːrəm] (*pl* **-s**) *n* **-1.** *lit & fig* foro *m*. **-2.** COMPUT [on Internet] foro *m* OR grupo *m* de discusión.
forward ['fɔːwəd] ◇ *adj* **-1.** [towards front - movement] hacia adelante; [near front - position etc] delantero(ra). **-2.** [towards future]: **~ planning** planificación *f* anticipada. **-3.** [advanced]: **we're (no) further ~** (no) hemos

adelantado (nada). **-4.** [impudent] atrevido(da). ◇ *adv* **-1.** [ahead] hacia adelante; **to go** OR **move ~** avanzar. **-2.** [in time]: **to bring sthg ~** adelantar algo; **to put a clock ~ (by 30 minutes)** adelantar un reloj (30 minutos). ◇ *n* SPORT delantero *m*, -ra *f*. ◇ *vt* **-1.** [send on] remitir, reenviar; **"please ~"** "remítase al destinatario". **-2.** *fml* [further] promover.
forwarding address ['fɔːwədɪŋ-] *n* nueva dirección *f* para reenvío de correo.
forward-looking [-'lʊkɪŋ] *adj* progresista.
forwardness ['fɔːwədnɪs] *n* [boldness] atrevimiento *m*.
forwards ['fɔːwədz] *adv* = **forward**.
forwent [fɔː'went] *pt* → **forgo**.
fossil ['fɒsl] *n* fósil *m*.
fossil fuel *n* combustible *m* fósil.
fossilized, **-ised** ['fɒsɪlaɪzd] *adj* fosilizado(da).
foster ['fɒstə'] ◇ *adj* adoptivo(va). ◇ *vt* **-1.** [child] acoger. **-2.** [idea, arts, relations] promover. ◇ *vi* acoger a un niño dentro de la familia de uno.
foster child *n* menor *m y f* en régimen de acogimiento familiar.
foster parents *npl* familia *f* de acogida.
fought [fɔːt] *pt & pp* → **fight**.
foul [faʊl] ◇ *adj* **-1.** [unclean - smell] fétido(da); [- taste] asqueroso(sa); [- water, language] sucio(cia). **-2.** [very unpleasant] horrible; **to fall ~ of sb** ponerse a mal con alguien. ◇ *n* falta *f*. ◇ *vt* **-1.** [make dirty] ensuciar. **-2.** SPORT cometer una falta contra. **-3.** [obstruct] enmarañarse en.
◆ **foul up** *vt sep inf* fastidiar, echar a perder.
foul-mouthed [-'maʊðd] *adj pej* malhablado(da).
foul play *n* (*U*) **-1.** SPORT juego *m* sucio. **-2.** [criminal acts] actos *mpl* criminales.
found [faʊnd] ◇ *pt & pp* → **find**. ◇ *vt*: **to ~ sthg (on)** fundar algo (en).
foundation [faʊn'deɪʃn] *n* **-1.** [organization, act of establishing] fundación *f*. **-2.** [basis] fundamento *m*, base *f*. **-3.** [make-up]: **~ (cream)** crema *f* base.
◆ **foundations** *npl* CONSTR cimientos *mpl*.
foundation stone *n* primera piedra *f*.
founder ['faʊndə'] ◇ *n* fundador *m*, -ra *f*. ◇ *vi lit & fig* hundirse, irse a pique.
founder member *n* miembro fundador *m*, miembro fundadora *f*.
founding ['faʊndɪŋ] *n* fundación *f*.
founding father *n* fundador *m*.
foundry ['faʊndrɪ] (*pl* **-ies**) *n* fundición *f*.
fount [faʊnt] *n* [origin] fuente *f*.

fraternize

fountain ['faʊntɪn] n **-1.** [structure] fuente f. **-2.** [jet] chorro m.

fountain pen n (pluma f) estilográfica f.

four [fɔːr] num cuatro; **on all ~s** a gatas; see also **six.**

four-leaved clover [-liːvd-] n trébol m de cuatro hojas.

four-letter word n palabrota f, taco m.

four-poster (bed) n cama f de columnas.

foursome ['fɔːsəm] n grupo m de cuatro personas.

four-star adj de cuatro estrellas.

fourteen [,fɔːˈtiːn] num catorce; see also **six.**

fourteenth [,fɔːˈtiːnθ] ◇ num adj decimocuarto(ta). ◇ num n **-1.** [in order] decimocuarto m, -ta f. **-2.** [fraction] catorceavo m; see also **sixth.**

fourth [fɔːθ] ◇ num adj cuarto(ta). ◇ num n [in order] cuarto m, -ta f; see also **sixth.**

Fourth of July n: the ~ el cuatro de julio, día de la independencia estadounidense.

four-way stop n Am cruce m (de cuatro estops).

four-wheel drive n tracción f a cuatro ruedas.

fowl [faʊl] (pl inv OR **-s**) n ave f de corral.

fox [fɒks] ◇ n zorro m, -rra f. ◇ vt [perplex] dejar perplejo(ja).

foxglove ['fɒksglʌv] n digital f, dedalera f.

foxhole ['fɒkshəʊl] n hoyo m para atrincherarse.

foxhound ['fɒkshaʊnd] n perro m raposero OR zorrero.

foxhunt ['fɒkshʌnt] n cacería f de zorros.

foxhunting ['fɒks,hʌntɪŋ] n caza f de zorros.

foxy ['fɒksɪ] adj inf [sexy] cañón (inv), sexy.

foyer ['fɔɪeɪ] n vestíbulo m.

FP n **-1.** (abbr of **former pupil**) AA m y f. **-2.** abbr of **fireplug.**

FPA (abbr of **Family Planning Association**) n asociación para la planificación familiar.

fr. (abbr of **franc**) fr.

Fr. (abbr of **father**) P.

fracas ['frækɑː, Am 'freɪkəs] (Br pl inv, Am pl **fracases**) n fml riña f, gresca f.

fraction ['frækʃn] n **-1.** MATH quebrado m, fracción f. **-2.** [small part] fracción f; **can you lift it up a ~?** ¿puedes levantarlo un poquito?

fractionally ['frækʃnəlɪ] adv ligeramente.

fractious ['frækʃəs] adj desapacible, irritable.

fracture ['fræktʃər] ◇ n fractura f. ◇ vt fracturar.

fragile ['frædʒaɪl] adj frágil.

fragility [frəˈdʒɪlətɪ] n fragilidad f.

fragment [n 'frægmənt, vb fræg'ment] ◇ n **-1.** [of glass, text] fragmento m; [of paper, plastic] trozo m. **-2.** [of truth] atisbo m. ◇ vi fragmentarse.

fragmentary ['frægməntrɪ] adj fragmentario(ria).

fragmented [fræg'mentɪd] adj fragmentado(da).

fragrance ['freɪgrəns] n fragancia f.

fragrant ['freɪgrənt] adj fragante.

frail [freɪl] adj frágil.

frailty ['freɪltɪ] (pl **-ies**) n **-1.** fragilidad f. **-2.** [imperfection] flaqueza f, defecto m.

frame [freɪm] ◇ n **-1.** [of picture, door] marco m; [of glasses] montura f; [of chair, bed] armadura f; [of bicycle] cuadro m; [of boat] armazón m o f. **-2.** [physique] cuerpo m. ◇ vt **-1.** [put in a frame] enmarcar. **-2.** [express] formular, expresar. **-3.** inf [set up] tender una trampa a, amañar la culpabilidad de.

frame of mind n estado m de ánimo, humor m.

framework ['freɪmwɜːk] n **-1.** [physical structure] armazón m o f, esqueleto m. **-2.** [basis] marco m.

France [frɑːns] n Francia f.

franchise ['fræntʃaɪz] n **-1.** POL sufragio m, derecho m de voto. **-2.** COMM concesión f, licencia f exclusiva.

franchisee [,fræntʃaɪˈziː] n concesionario m, -ria f.

franchisor ['fræntʃaɪzər] n entidad f adjudicatoria de una concesión.

frank [fræŋk] ◇ adj franco(ca). ◇ vt franquear.

Frankfurt ['fræŋkfət] n: ~ **(Am Main)** Francfort (del Meno).

frankfurter ['fræŋkfɜːtər] n salchicha f de Francfort.

frankincense ['fræŋkɪnsens] n incienso m.

franking machine ['fræŋkɪŋ-] n máquina f de franquear.

frankly ['fræŋklɪ] adv francamente.

frankness ['fræŋknɪs] n franqueza f.

frantic ['fræntɪk] adj frenético(ca).

frantically ['fræntɪklɪ] adv frenéticamente.

fraternal [frəˈtɜːnl] adj fraternal, fraterno(na).

fraternity [frəˈtɜːnətɪ] (pl **-ies**) n **-1.** fml [community] gremio m, cofradía f. **-2.** [in American university] club m de estudiantes. **-3.** (U) fml [friendship] fraternidad f.

fraternize, -ise ['frætənaɪz] vi: **to ~ (with)** fraternizar (con).

fraud [frɔːd] n **-1.** (U) [deceit] fraude m. **-2.** pej [impostor] farsante m y f.

fraudulent ['frɔːdjʊlənt] adj fraudulento(ta).

fraught [frɔːt] adj **-1.** [full]: ~ **with** lleno(na) OR cargado(da) de. **-2.** Br [frantic] tenso(sa).

fray [freɪ] ◇ vt fig [temper, nerves] crispar, poner de punta. ◇ vi **-1.** [sleeve, cuff] deshilacharse. **-2.** fig [temper, nerves] crisparse. ◇ n literary: **to enter the** ~ saltar a la palestra.

frayed [freɪd] adj [sleeve, cuff] deshilachado(da).

frazzled ['fræzld] adj inf rendido(da).

FRB (abbr of **Federal Reserve Board**) n órgano de control del banco central estadounidense.

FRCP (abbr of **Fellow of the Royal College of Physicians**) miembro del Royal College of Physicians, colegio británico de médicos.

FRCS (abbr of **Fellow of the Royal College of Surgeons**) miembro del Royal College of Surgeons, colegio británico de cirujanos.

freak [friːk] ◇ adj imprevisible, inesperado(da). ◇ n **-1.** [strange creature - in appearance] fenómeno m, monstruo m; [- in behaviour] estrafalario m, -ria f. **-2.** [unusual event] anormalidad f. **-3.** inf [fanatic]: **film/fitness** ~ fanático m, -ca f del cine/ejercicio.
◆ **freak out** inf ◇ vi flipar, alucinar. ◇ vt sep flipar, alucinar.

freakish ['friːkɪʃ] adj anormal, extraño(ña).

freckle ['frekl] n peca f.

free [friː] (compar **freer**, superl **freest**, pt & pp **freed**) ◇ adj **-1.** [gen]: ~ **(from** OR **of)** libre (de); **to be** ~ **to do sthg** ser libre de hacer algo; **feel** ~! ¡adelante!, ¡cómo no!; **to set** ~ liberar. **-2.** [not paid for] gratis (inv), gratuito(ta); ~ **of charge** gratis (inv). **-3.** [unattached] suelto(ta). **-4.** [generous]: **to be** ~ **with sthg** no regatear algo. ◇ adv **-1.** [without payment]: **(for)** ~ gratis. **-2.** [unrestricted] libremente. **-3.** [loose]: **to pull/cut sthg** ~ soltar algo tirando/cortando. ◇ vt **-1.** [release] liberar, libertar; **to** ~ **sb of sthg** librar a alguien de algo. **-2.** [make available] dejar libre. **-3.** [extricate - person] rescatar; [- one's arm, oneself] soltar.

-free [friː] suffix: **lead**~ sin plomo.

freebie ['friːbɪ] n inf regalito m.

freedom ['friːdəm] n libertad f; ~ **from** indemnidad f ante OR de.

freedom fighter n luchador m, -ra f por la libertad.

free enterprise n libre empresa f.

free-fall n (U) caída f libre.

freefone ['friːfəʊn] n (U) Br teléfono m OR número m gratuito.

free-for-all n refriega f.

free gift n obsequio m.

freehand [,friː'hænd] adj & adv a pulso.

freehold ['friːhəʊld] ◇ adv en propiedad absoluta. ◇ n propiedad f absoluta.

freeholder ['friːhəʊldər] n propietario absoluto m, propietaria absoluta f.

free house n bar no controlado por una compañía cervecera.

free kick n tiro m libre.

freelance ['friːlɑːns] ◇ adj autónomo(ma). ◇ adv autónomamente, por libre. ◇ n (trabajador m, -ra f) autónomo m, -ma f. ◇ vi trabajar por libre OR por cuenta propia.

freeloader ['friːləʊdər] n inf gorrón m, -ona f.

freely ['friːlɪ] adv **-1.** [readily - admit, confess] sin reparos; [- available] fácilmente. **-2.** [openly] abiertamente, francamente. **-3.** [without restrictions] libremente. **-4.** [generously] liberalmente.

freeman ['friːmən] (pl **-men**) n ciudadano m honorífico, ciudadana f honorífica.

free-market economy n economía f de libre mercado.

Freemason ['friː,meɪsn] n francmasón m, -ona f.

Freemasonry ['friː,meɪsnrɪ] n francmasonería f, masonería f.

freemen ['friːmən] pl → freeman.

freephone ['friːfəʊn] = freefone.

freepost ['friːpəʊst] n franqueo m pagado.

free-range adj de granja.

free sample n muestra f (gratuita).

freesia ['friːzjə] n fresia f.

free speech n libertad f de expresión.

freestanding [,friː'stændɪŋ] adj independiente.

freestyle ['friːstaɪl] n [in swimming] estilo m libre.

freethinker [,friː'θɪŋkər] n librepensador m, -ra f.

Freetown ['friːtaʊn] n Freetown.

free trade n libre cambio m.

freeway ['friːweɪ] n Am autopista f.

freewheel [,friː'wiːl] vi [on bicycle] andar sin pedalear; [in car] ir en punto muerto.

freewheeling [,friː'wiːlɪŋ] adj inf informal.

free will n libre albedrío m; **to do sthg of one's own** ~ hacer algo por voluntad propia.

free world n: **the** ~ el mundo libre.

freeze [friːz] (pt **froze**, pp **frozen**) ◇ vt **-1.** [gen] helar. **-2.** [food, wages, prices] congelar. **-3.** [assets] bloquear. ◇ vi **-1.** [gen] helarse. **-2.** [food, wages, prices] congelarse. ◇ v im-

pers METEOR **helar.** ◇ *n* **-1.** [cold weather] helada *f*. **-2.** [of wages, prices] congelación *f*.
◆ **freeze over** *vi* helarse.
◆ **freeze up** *vi* helarse.

freeze-dried [-'draɪd] *adj* liofilizado(da).

freeze frame *n* **-1.** [photograph] fotograma *m*. **-2.** [on video] imagen *f* congelada.

freezer ['friːzər] *n* congelador *m*.

freezing ['friːzɪŋ] ◇ *adj* helado(da); **it's ~ in here** hace un frío espantoso aquí. ◇ *n* = **freezing point.**

freezing point *n* punto *m* de congelación.

freight [freɪt] *n* (U) [goods] mercancías *fpl*, flete *m*.

freight train *n* (tren *m* de) mercancías *m inv*.

French [frentʃ] ◇ *adj* francés(esa). ◇ *n* [language] francés *m*. ◇ *npl*: **the ~** los franceses.

French bean *n* judía *f* verde.

French bread *n* (U) pan *m* de barra.

French Canadian ◇ *adj* francocanadiense. ◇ *n* francocanadiense *m* y *f*.

French chalk *n* (U) jaboncillo *m*, jabón *m* de sastre.

French dressing *n* [in UK] [vinaigrette] vinagreta *f*; [in US] ≃ salsa *f* rosa.

French fries *npl* patatas *fpl* fritas.

Frenchman ['frentʃmən] (*pl* **-men** [-mən]) *n* francés *m*.

French polish *n* laca *f*.

French Riviera *n*: **the ~** la Riviera francesa.

French stick *n Br* barra *f* de pan.

French toast *n* torrija *f*.

French windows *npl* puertaventanas *fpl*.

Frenchwoman ['frentʃ,wumən] (*pl* **-women** [-,wɪmɪn]) *n* francesa *f*.

frenetic [frə'netɪk] *adj* frenético(ca).

frenzied ['frenzɪd] *adj* [haste, activity] frenético(ca).

frenzy ['frenzɪ] (*pl* **-ies**) *n* frenesí *m*; **a ~ of activity** una actividad febril.

frequency ['friːkwənsɪ] (*pl* **-ies**) *n* frecuencia *f*.

frequency modulation *n* modulación *f* de frecuencia.

frequent [*adj* 'friːkwənt, *vb* frɪ'kwent] ◇ *adj* frecuente. ◇ *vt* frecuentar.

frequently ['friːkwəntlɪ] *adv* a menudo, con frecuencia.

fresco ['freskəʊ] (*pl* **-es** OR **-s**) *n* fresco *m*.

fresh [freʃ] ◇ *adj* **-1.** [gen] fresco(ca); [flavour, taste] refrescante; **~ from** OR **recién salido(da) de. -2.** [bread] del día. **-3.** [not canned] natural. **-4.** [water] dulce. **-5.** [pot of tea, fighting, approach] nuevo(va); **to make a ~ start** empezar de nuevo. **-6.** [bright and pleasant] alegre. ◇ *adv* recién; **to be ~ out of sthg** *inf* haberse quedado sin algo.

freshen ['freʃn] ◇ *vt* [air] refrescar. ◇ *vi* [wind] soplar más fuerte.
◆ **freshen up** ◇ *vt sep* **-1.** [wash]: **to ~ o.s up** refrescarse. **-2.** [smarten up] arreglar. ◇ *vi* [person] refrescarse, lavarse.

fresher ['freʃər] *n Br inf* estudiante *m* y *f* de primer año.

freshly ['freʃlɪ] *adv* recién.

freshman ['freʃmən] (*pl* **-men** [-mən]) *n* estudiante *m* y *f* de primer año.

freshness ['freʃnɪs] *n* (U) **-1.** [of food] buen estado *m*. **-2.** [originality] novedad *f*, originalidad *f*. **-3.** [brightness] pulcritud *f*. **-4.** [refreshing quality] frescor *m*. **-5.** [energy] vigor *m*.

freshwater ['freʃ,wɔːtər] *adj* de agua dulce.

fret [fret] (*pt* & *pp* **-ted**, *cont* **-ting**) *vi* preocuparse.

fretful ['fretful] *adj* [baby] quejoso(sa); [night, sleep] agitado(da), inquieto(ta).

fretsaw ['fretsɔː] *n* segueta *f*, sierra *f* de calar.

Freudian slip ['frɔɪdɪən-] *n* desliz *m*, lapsus *m inv*.

FRG (*abbr of* **Federal Republic of Germany**) *n* RFA *f*.

Fri. (*abbr of* **Friday**) viern.

friar ['fraɪər] *n* fraile *m*.

friction ['frɪkʃn] *n* fricción *f*.

Friday ['fraɪdɪ] *n* viernes *m inv*; *see also* **Saturday**.

fridge [frɪdʒ] *n* nevera *f*.

fridge-freezer *n Br* nevera *f* congeladora.

fried [fraɪd] *adj* frito(ta).

friend [frend] *n* **-1.** [close acquaintance] amigo *m*, -ga *f*, cuate *m* y *f inv Amer*; **to be ~s with sb** ser amigo de alguien; **to make ~s (with)** hacerse amigo (de), trabar amistad (con). **-2.** [supporter · of cause] partidario *m*, -ria *f*; [· of country] aliado *m*, -da *f*.

friendless ['frendlɪs] *adj* sin amigos.

friendly ['frendlɪ] (*compar* **-ier**, *superl* **-iest**, *pl* **-ies**) ◇ *adj* **-1.** [person] amable, simpático(ca); [attitude, manner, welcome] amistoso(sa); **to be ~ with sb** ser amigo de alguien. **-2.** [nation] amigo(ga), aliado(da). **-3.** [argument, game] amistoso(sa). ◇ *n* partido *m* amistoso.

friendly society *n Br* mutua *f*, mutualidad *f*.

friendship ['frendʃɪp] *n* amistad *f*.

fries [fraɪz] = **french fries.**

Friesian (cow) ['friːzjən-] *n* vaca *f* lechera.

frieze [friːz] *n* friso *m*.

frigate ['frɪɡət] *n* fragata *f*.

fright [fraɪt] *n* **-1.** [fear] miedo *m*; **to take ~** espantarse, asustarse. **-2.** [shock] susto *m*; **to give sb a ~** darle un susto a alguien.

frighten ['fraɪtn] *vt* asustar; **to ~ sb into doing sthg** atemorizar a alguien para que haga algo.
◆ **frighten away, frighten off** *vt sep* espantar, ahuyentar.

frightened ['fraɪtnd] *adj* asustado(da); **to be ~ of sthg/of doing sthg** tener miedo a algo/a hacer algo.

frightening ['fraɪtnɪŋ] *adj* aterrador(ra), espantoso(sa).

frightful ['fraɪtfʊl] *adj dated* terrible, espantoso(sa).

frigid ['frɪdʒɪd] *adj* [sexually] frígido(da).

frill [frɪl] *n* **-1.** [decoration] volante *m*. **-2.** *inf* [extra] adorno *m*.

frilly ['frɪlɪ] (*compar* **-ier**, *superl* **-iest**) *adj* con volantes.

fringe ['frɪndʒ] (*cont* **fringeing**) ◇ *n* **-1.** [decoration] flecos *mpl*. **-2.** *Br* [of hair] flequillo *m*, cerquillo *m Amer*. **-3.** [edge] periferia *f*. **-4.** [extreme] margen *m*. ◇ *vt* [edge] bordear.

fringe benefit *n* beneficio *m* complementario.

fringe group *n* grupo *m* marginal.

fringe theatre *n Br* teatro *m* experimental.

Frisbee® ['frɪzbɪ] *n* frisbee® *m*, plato *m* volador.

Frisian Islands ['frɪʒən-] *npl*: **the ~** las islas Frisias.

frisk [frɪsk] ◇ *vt* cachear, registrar. ◇ *vi* retozar, brincar.

frisky ['frɪskɪ] (*compar* **-ier**, *superl* **-iest**) *adj inf* retozón(ona), juguetón(ona).

fritter ['frɪtər] *n* buñuelo *m*.
◆ **fritter away** *vt sep*: **to ~ money/time away on sthg** malgastar dinero/tiempo en algo.

frivolity [frɪ'vɒlətɪ] (*pl* **-ies**) *n* frivolidad *f*.

frivolous ['frɪvələs] *adj* frívolo(la).

frizzy ['frɪzɪ] (*compar* **-ier**, *superl* **-iest**) *adj* crespo(pa), ensortijado(da).

fro [frəʊ] *adv*: **to and ~** de un lado a otro, de aquí para allá.

frock [frɒk] *n dated* vestido *m*.

frog [frɒɡ] *n* [animal] rana *f*; **to have a ~ in one's throat** tener carraspera.

frogman ['frɒɡmən] (*pl* **-men**) *n* hombre-rana *m*.

frogmarch ['frɒɡmɑːtʃ] *vt* llevar por la fuerza.

frogmen ['frɒɡmən] *pl* → **frogman**.

frogspawn ['frɒɡspɔːn] *n* (*U*) huevos *mpl* de rana.

frolic ['frɒlɪk] (*pt* & *pp* **-ked**, *cont* **-king**) ◇ *n* juego *m* alegre. ◇ *vi* retozar, triscar.

from [*weak form* frəm, *strong form* frɒm] *prep* **-1.** [indicating source, origin, removal] de; **where are you ~?** ¿de dónde eres?; **I got a letter ~ her today** hoy me ha llegado una carta suya; **a flight ~ Paris** un vuelo de París; **to translate ~ Spanish into English** traducir del español al inglés; **he took a notebook ~ his pocket** sacó un cuaderno del bolsillo; **he's not back ~ work yet** no ha vuelto del trabajo aún; **to take sthg away ~ sb** quitarle algo a alguien. **-2.** [indicating a deduction]: **take 15 (away) ~ 19** quita 15 a 19; **to deduct sthg ~ sthg** deducir OR descontar algo de algo. **-3.** [indicating escape, separation] de; **he ran away ~ home** huyó de casa. **-4.** [indicating position] desde; **seen ~ above/below** visto desde arriba/abajo; **a light bulb hung ~ the ceiling** una bombilla colgaba del techo. **-5.** [indicating distance] de; **it's 60 km ~ here** está a 60 kms. de aquí; **how far is London ~ here?** ¿a cuánto está Londres de aquí? **-6.** [indicating material object is made out of] de; **it's made ~ wood/plastic** está hecho de madera/plástico. **-7.** [starting at a particular time] desde; **closed ~ 1 pm to 2 pm** cerrado de 13h a 14h; **~ birth** desde el nacimiento; **~ the moment I saw him** desde el momento en que lo vi. **-8.** [indicating difference, change] de; **to be different ~** ser diferente de; **~ ... to** de ... a; **the price went up ~ £100 to £150** el precio subió de 100 a 150 libras. **-9.** [because of, as a result of] de; **to die ~ cold** morir de frío; **to suffer ~ cold/hunger** padecer frío/hambre. **-10.** [on the evidence of] por; **to speak ~ personal experience** hablar por propia experiencia; **I could see ~ her face she was angry** por la cara que tenía vi que estaba enfadada. **-11.** [indicating lowest amount]: **prices range ~ £5 to £500** los precios oscilan entre 5 y 500 libras; **prices start ~ £50** los precios empiezan desde 50 libras; **it could take anything ~ 15 to 20 weeks** podría llevar de 15 a 20 semanas.

frond [frɒnd] *n* fronda *f*.

front [frʌnt] ◇ *n* **-1.** [gen] parte *f* delantera; [- of house] fachada *f*. **-2.** METEOR, MIL & POL frente *m*. **-3.** [issue, area] terreno *m*; **on the domestic/employment ~** a nivel nacional/de empleo. **-4.** [on coast]: **(sea) ~** paseo *m* marítimo. **-5.** [outward appearance] fachada

f; **to put on a ~** ponerse una máscara. ◇ *adj* [gen] delantero(ra); [page] primero(ra). ◇ *vt* **-1.** [be opposite] dar a. **-2.** [lead] dirigir. ◇ *vi*: **to ~ onto** dar a.
◆ **in front** *adv* **-1.** [further forward] delante. **-2.** [winning] en cabeza.
◆ **in front of** *prep* delante de.

frontage ['frʌntɪdʒ] *n* fachada *f*.

frontal ['frʌntl] *adj* frontal.

frontbench [,frʌnt'bentʃ] *n* *Br* en la Cámara de los Comunes, cada una de las dos filas de escaños ocupadas respectivamente por los ministros del Gobierno y los principales líderes de la oposición mayoritaria.

front desk *n* recepción *f*.

front door *n* puerta *f* principal.

frontier ['frʌn,tɪə', *Am* frʌn'tɪər] *n* *lit* & *fig* frontera *f*.

frontispiece ['frʌntɪspiːs] *n* frontispicio *m*.

front line *n*: **the ~** la primera línea.

front man *n* **-1.** [of group] portavoz *m* y *f*. **-2.** [of programme] presentador *m*.

front-page *adj* de primera página OR plana.

front room *n* sala *f* de estar.

front-runner *n* favorito *m*, -ta *f*.

front-wheel drive *n* [vehicle] vehículo *m* de tracción delantera.

frost [frɒst] ◇ *n* **-1.** [layer of ice] escarcha *f*. **-2.** [weather] helada *f*. ◇ *vi*: **to ~ over** OR **up** cubrirse de escarcha.

frostbite ['frɒstbaɪt] *n* (*U*) congelación *f* MED.

frostbitten ['frɒst,bɪtn] *adj* congelado(da) MED.

frosted ['frɒstɪd] *adj* **-1.** [glass] esmerilado(da). **-2.** *Am* CULIN escarchado(da).

frosting ['frɒstɪŋ] *n* *Am* azúcar *m* glaseado.

frosty ['frɒstɪ] (*compar* **-ier**, *superl* **-iest**) *adj* **-1.** [very cold] de helada. **-2.** [covered with frost] escarchado(da). **-3.** *fig* [unfriendly] glacial.

froth [frɒθ] ◇ *n* espuma *f*. ◇ *vi* hacer espuma.

frothy ['frɒθɪ] (*compar* **-ier**, *superl* **-iest**) *adj* espumoso(sa).

frown [fraun] ◇ *n* ceño *m*. ◇ *vi* fruncir el ceño.
◆ **frown (up)on** *vt fus* desaprobar.

froze [frəuz] *pt* → **freeze**.

frozen [frəuzn] ◇ *pp* → **freeze**. ◇ *adj* **-1.** [gen] helado(da). **-2.** [preserved] congelado(da). **-3.** *fig* [rigid]: **~ (with)** tieso(sa) (de).

FRS *n* **-1.** (*abbr of* **Fellow of the Royal Society**) miembro de la *Royal Society*, organización británica para la investigación científica. **-2.**

(*abbr of* **Federal Reserve System**) *banco central estadounidense.*

frugal ['fruːgl] *adj* frugal.

fruit [fruːt] (*pl inv* OR **fruits**) ◇ *n* **-1.** [food] fruta *f*. **-2.** [result] fruto *m*; **to bear ~** dar fruto. ◇ *comp* [made with fruit] de frutas; [producing fruit] frutal; **~ bowl** frutero *m*. ◇ *vi* dar fruto.

fruitcake ['fruːtkeɪk] *n* pastel *m* de frutas.

fruiterer ['fruːtərə'] *n* *Br* frutero *m*, -ra *f*; **~'s (shop)** frutería *f*.

fruitful ['fruːtfʊl] *adj* [successful] fructífero(ra).

fruition [fruː'ɪʃn] *n*: **to come to ~** [plan] realizarse; [hope] cumplirse.

fruit juice *n* zumo *m* de fruta.

fruitless ['fruːtlɪs] *adj* infructuoso(sa).

fruit machine *n* *Br* máquina *f* tragaperras.

fruit salad *n* macedonia *f* (de frutas).

frumpy ['frʌmpɪ] (*compar* **-ier**, *superl* **-iest**) *adj* chapado(da) a la antigua.

frustrate [frʌ'streɪt] *vt* frustrar.

frustrated [frʌ'streɪtɪd] *adj* frustrado(da).

frustrating [frʌ'streɪtɪŋ] *adj* frustrante.

frustration [frʌ'streɪʃn] *n* frustración *f*.

fry [fraɪ] (*pt* & *pp* **fried**) ◇ *vt* [food] freír. ◇ *vi* [food] freírse.

frying pan ['fraɪɪŋ-] *n* sartén *f*, paila *f* *Amer*; **to jump out of the ~ into the fire** salir de Guatemala y meterse en Guatepeor.

ft. *abbr of* **foot, feet.**

FT (*abbr of* **Financial Times**) *n* diario británico de información económica; **the ~ index** el índice bursátil del *Financial Times*.

FTC (*abbr of* **Federal Trade Commission**) *n* organismo estadounidense encargado de hacer respetar la legislación sobre monopolios.

fuchsia ['fjuːʃə] *n* fucsia *f*.

fuck [fʌk] *vulg* ◇ *vt* & *vi* joder, follar, chingar *Amer*. ◇ *excl* ¡joder!
◆ **fuck off** *vi vulg*: **~ off!** ¡vete a tomar por culo!

fucking ['fʌkɪŋ] *adj vulg* **-1.** [to show anger]: **you ~ idiot!** ¡idiota de los cojones! **-2.** [for emphasis]: **where are my ~ keys?** ¿dónde coño están mis llaves?; **you must be ~ stupid** hay que ser gilipollas.

fuddled ['fʌdld] *adj* aturdido(da).

fuddy-duddy ['fʌdɪ,dʌdɪ] (*pl* **fuddy-duddies**) *n* *inf* carcamal *m* y *f*.

fudge [fʌdʒ] ◇ *n* (*U*) [sweet] dulce de azúcar, leche y mantequilla. ◇ *vt* *inf* esquivar, eludir.

fuel [fjʊəl] (*Br pt* & *pp* **-led**, *cont* **-ling**, *Am pt* & *pp* **-ed**, *cont* **-ing**) ◇ *n* combustible *m*; **to add ~ to the fire** OR **the flames** echar leña al fuego. ◇ *vt* **-1.** [supply with fuel] abastecer de combustible, alimentar. **-2.** [increase] exacerbar, agravar.

fuel pump *n* bomba *f* de combustible.

fuel tank *n* depósito *m* de gasolina.

fugitive ['fju:dʒətɪv] *n* fugitivo *m*, -va *f*.

fugue [fju:g] *n* fuga *f*.

fulcrum ['fʊlkrəm] (*pl* **-crums** OR **-cra** [-krə]) *n* fulcro *m*, punto *m* de apoyo.

fulfil (*pt* & *pp* **-led**, *cont* **-ling**), **fulfill** *Am* [fʊl'fɪl] *vt* [promise, duty, threat] cumplir; [hope, ambition] realizar, satisfacer; [obligation] cumplir con; [role] desempeñar; [requirement] satisfacer; **to ~ o.s.** realizarse.

fulfilling [fʊl'fɪlɪŋ] *adj* gratificante.

fulfilment, **fulfillment** *Am* [fʊl'fɪlmənt] *n* **-1.** [satisfaction] satisfacción *f*, realización *f* (de uno mismo). **-2.** [of promise, duty, threat] cumplimiento *m*; [of hope, ambition] realización *f*; [of role] desempeño *m*; [of requirement] satisfacción *f*.

full [fʊl] ◇ *adj* **-1.** [filled]: **~ (of)** lleno(na) (de); **I'm ~!** [after meal] ¡no puedo más! **-2.** [complete - recovery, employment, control] pleno(na); [- name, price, fare] completo(ta); [- explanation, information] detallado(da); [- member, professor] numerario(ria). **-3.** [maximum - volume, power etc] máximo(ma). **-4.** [sound, flavour] rico(ca). **-5.** [plump] grueso(sa). **-6.** [wide] holgado(da), amplio(plia). ◇ *adv* **-1.** [directly] justo, de lleno. **-2.** [very]: **to know sthg ~ well** saber algo perfectamente. **-3.** [at maximum] al máximo. ◇ *n*: **in ~** íntegramente; **to the ~** al máximo, completamente; **to live life to the ~** disfrutar de la vida al máximo.

fullback ['fʊlbæk] *n* (defensa *m* y *f*) lateral *m* y *f*.

full-blooded [-'blʌdɪd] *adj* **-1.** [pure-blooded] de pura raza. **-2.** [strong, complete] vigoroso(sa).

full-blown [-'bləʊn] *adj* [gen] auténtico(ca); [AIDS] desarrollado(da).

full board *n* pensión *f* completa.

full-bodied [-'bɒdɪd] *adj* de mucho cuerpo.

full dress *n* (U) [of soldiers etc] uniforme *m* de gala.

full-face *adj* de frente.

full-fashioned *Am* = fully fashioned.

full-fledged *Am* = fully fledged.

full-frontal *adj*: **a ~ picture** un desnudo frontal.

full-grown [-'grəʊn] *adj* adulto(ta).

full house *n* [at show, event] lleno *m*.

full-length ◇ *adj* **-1.** [portrait, mirror] de cuerpo entero. **-2.** [dress] largo(ga). **-3.** [novel] extenso(sa); [film] de largo metraje. ◇ *adv* a lo largo, completamente.

full moon *n* luna *f* llena.

fullness ['fʊlnɪs] *n* [of voice] riqueza *f*; [of life] plenitud *f*; **in the ~ of time** a su debido tiempo.

full-page *adj* a toda plana.

full-scale *adj* **-1.** [life-size] de tamaño natural. **-2.** [complete] a gran escala.

full-size(d) *adj* **-1.** [life - size] de tamaño natural. **-2.** [adult] adulto(ta). **-3.** *Am* AUT: **~ car** turismo *m*.

full stop ◇ *n* punto *m*. ◇ *adv* *Br* punto.

full time *n* *Br* SPORT final *m* del (tiempo reglamentario del) partido.

◆ **full-time** ◇ *adj* de jornada completa. ◇ *adv* a tiempo completo.

full up *adj* lleno(na).

fully ['fʊlɪ] *adv* **-1.** [completely] completamente. **-2.** [thoroughly] detalladamente.

fully-fashioned *Br*, **full-fashioned** *Am* [-'fæʃnd] *adj* ajustado(da).

fully-fledged *Br*, **full-fledged** *Am* [-'fledʒd] *adj* *fig* hecho(cha) y derecho(cha); [member] de pleno derecho.

fulness ['fʊlnɪs] = fullness.

fulsome ['fʊlsəm] *adj* exagerado(da), excesivo(va); **to be ~ in one's praise** (of sb/ sthg) colmar de elogios (a alguien/algo).

fumble ['fʌmbl] ◇ *vt* perder, no agarrar bien. ◇ *vi* hurgar; **to ~ for sthg** [for key, light switch] buscar algo a tientas; [for words] buscar algo titubeando.

fume [fju:m] *vi* [with anger] echar humo, rabiar.

◆ **fumes** *npl* humo *m*.

fumigate ['fju:mɪgeɪt] *vt* fumigar.

fun [fʌn] *n* (U) **-1.** [pleasure, amusement] diversión *f*; **my uncle/parachuting is great ~** mi tío/el paracaidismo es muy divertido; **to have ~** divertirse, pasarlo bien; **have ~!** ¡que te diviertas!; **for ~, for the ~ of it** por diversión. **-2.** [playfulness]: **he's full of ~** le encanta todo lo que sea diversión. **-3.** [at sb else's expense]: **to make ~ of sb, to poke ~ at sb** reírse OR burlarse de alguien. ◇ *adj* *inf* divertido(da).

function ['fʌŋkʃn] ◇ *n* **-1.** [gen & MATH] función *f*. **-2.** [way of working] funcionamiento *m*. **-3.** [formal social event] acto *m*, ceremonia *f*. ◇ *vi* funcionar; **to ~ as** hacer de, actuar como.

functional ['fʌŋkʃnəl] *adj* **-1.** [practical] funcional. **-2.** [operational] en funcionamiento.

functionary ['fʌŋkʃnərɪ] (*pl* **-ies**) *n* funcionario *m*, -ria *f*.

function key *n* COMPUT tecla *f* de función.

fund [fʌnd] ◇ *n* fondo *m*. ◇ *vt* financiar.

◆ **funds** *npl* fondos *mpl*.

fundamental [ˌfʌndə'mentl] *adj*: ~ **(to)** fundamental (para).
◆ **fundamentals** *npl* fundamentos *mpl*.
fundamentalism [ˌfʌndə'mentəlɪzm] *n* fundamentalismo *m*.
fundamentally [ˌfʌndə'mentəlɪ] *adv* fundamentalmente.
funding ['fʌndɪŋ] *n* financiación *f*.
fund-raising [-ˌreɪzɪŋ] ◇ *n* recolección *f* de fondos. ◇ *comp* de OR para recolección de fondos.
funeral ['fjuːnərəl] *n* funeral *m*.
funeral director *n* director *m* de funeraria.
funeral parlour *n* funeraria *f*.
funeral service *n* honras *fpl* fúnebres, exequias *fpl*.
funereal [fjuː'nɪərɪəl] *adj* fúnebre.
funfair ['fʌnfeə'] *n* parque *m* de atracciones.
fungus ['fʌŋgəs] (*pl* -**gi** [-gaɪ] OR -**guses**) *n* hongo *m*.
funk [fʌŋk] *n* (*U*) -**1.** MUS (música *f*) funky *m*. -**2.** *dated* [fear] canguis *m*, mieditis *f*.
funky ['fʌŋkɪ] (*compar* -**ier**, *superl* -**iest**) *adj* MUS funky (*inv*).
funnel ['fʌnl] (*Br pt* & *pp* -**led**, *cont* -**ling**, *Am pt* & *pp* -**ed**, *cont* -**ing**) ◇ *n* -**1.** [for pouring] embudo *m*. -**2.** [on ship] chimenea *f*. ◇ *vt* [liquid] pasar por un embudo; [money, food] canalizar. ◇ *vi* pasar.
funnily ['fʌnɪlɪ] *adv* [strangely] de manera rara; ~ **enough** curiosamente.
funny ['fʌnɪ] (*compar* -**ier**, *superl* -**iest**) *adj* -**1.** [amusing] divertido(da), gracioso(sa). -**2.** [odd] raro(ra). -**3.** [ill] pachucho(cha).
funny bone *n* hueso *m* de la risa.
funny farm *n* Am *inf hum* casa *f* de los locos.
fun run *n* carrera atlética de fondo con fines benéficos.
fur [fɜː'] *n* -**1.** [on animal] pelaje *m*, pelo *m*. -**2.** [garment] (prenda *f* de) piel *f*.
fur coat *n* abrigo *m* de piel OR pieles.
furious ['fjʊərɪəs] *adj* -**1.** [very angry] furioso(sa). -**2.** [frantic] frenético(ca).
furiously ['fjʊərɪəslɪ] *adv* -**1.** [angrily] con furia. -**2.** [frantically] frenéticamente.
furled [fɜːld] *adj* plegado(da).
furlong ['fɜːlɒŋ] *n* = 201,17 *metros*.
furnace ['fɜːnɪs] *n* horno *m*.
furnish ['fɜːnɪʃ] *vt* -**1.** [fit out] amueblar. -**2.** *fml* [provide · goods, explanation] proveer, suministrar; [- proof] aducir; **to** ~ **sb with sthg** proporcionar algo a alguien.
furnished ['fɜːnɪʃt] *adj* amueblado(da).
furnishings ['fɜːnɪʃɪŋz] *npl* mobiliario *m*.

furniture ['fɜːnɪtʃə'] *n* (*U*) muebles *mpl*, mobiliario *m*; **a piece of** ~ un mueble.
furniture polish *n* cera *f* para muebles.
furore *Br* [fjʊ'rɔːrɪ], **furor** *Am* ['fjʊrɔːr] *n* escándalo *m*.
furrier ['fʌrɪə'] *n* peletero *m*, -ra *f*.
furrow ['fʌrəʊ] *n lit* & *fig* surco *m*.
furrowed ['fʌrəʊd] *adj* -**1.** [field, land] arado(da). -**2.** [brow] arrugado(da).
furry ['fɜːrɪ] (*compar* -**ier**, *superl* -**iest**) *adj* peludo(da).
further ['fɜːðə'] ◇ *compar* → **far**. ◇ *adv* -**1.** [in distance] más lejos; **how much** ~ **is it?** ¿cuánto queda (de camino)?; ~ **on** más adelante. -**2.** [to a more advanced point]: **they decided not to take the matter any** ~ decidieron no seguir adelante con el asunto; **this mustn't go any** ~ esto debe quedar entre nosotros. -**3.** [in degree, extent, time] más; ~ **on/back** más adelante/atrás. -**4.** [in addition] además. ◇ *adj* otro(tra); **until** ~ **notice** hasta nuevo aviso. ◇ *vt* promover, fomentar.
◆ **further to** *prep fml* con relación a.
further education *n Br* estudios postescolares no universitarios.
furthermore [ˌfɜːðə'mɔːr] *adv* lo que es más.
furthermost ['fɜːðəməʊst] *adj* más lejano(na).
furthest ['fɜːðɪst] ◇ *superl* → **far**. ◇ *adj* -**1.** [in distance] más lejano(na). -**2.** [greatest - in degree, extent] extremo(ma). ◇ *adv* -**1.** [in distance] más lejos. -**2.** [to greatest degree, extent] más.
furtive ['fɜːtɪv] *adj* furtivo(va).
furtively ['fɜːtɪvlɪ] *adv* furtivamente.
fury ['fjʊərɪ] *n* furia *f*; **in a** ~ furioso(sa).
fuse *esp Br*, **fuze** *Am* [fjuːz] ◇ *n* -**1.** ELEC fusible *m*, plomo *m*. -**2.** [of bomb, firework] mecha *f*, espoleta *f*. ◇ *vt* fundir. ◇ *vi* -**1.** [gen & ELEC] fundirse. -**2.** [companies] fusionarse.
fuse-box *n* caja *f* de fusibles.
fused [fjuːzd] *adj* [fitted with a fuse] con fusible.
fuselage ['fjuːzəlɑːʒ] *n* fuselaje *m*.
fuse wire *n* alambre *m* de fusibles.
fusillade [ˌfjuːzə'leɪd] *n* descarga *f* de fusilería.
fusion ['fjuːʒn] *n* fusión *f*.
fuss [fʌs] ◇ *n* (*U*) -**1.** [excitement, anxiety] jaleo *m*, alboroto *m*; **to make a** ~ armar un escándalo. -**2.** [complaints] protestas *fpl*. -**3.** *phr*: **to make a** ~ **of sb** *Br* hacer fiestas a alguien. ◇ *vi* apurarse, angustiarse.
◆ **fuss over** *vt fus* deshacerse por, mimar.
fusspot ['fʌspɒt] *n inf* quisquilloso *m*, -sa *f*.

fussy ['fʌsɪ] (*compar* -**ier**, *superl* -**iest**) *adj* -**1.** [fastidious] delicado(da), quisquilloso(sa). -**2.** [over-decorated] recargado(da), aparatoso(sa).

fusty ['fʌstɪ] (*compar* -**ier**, *superl* -**iest**) *adj* -**1.** [not fresh] con olor a cerrado. -**2.** [old-fashioned] anticuado(da), rancio(cia).

futile ['fjuːtaɪl] *adj* inútil, vano(na).

futility [fjuː'tɪlətɪ] *n* inutilidad *f*.

futon ['fuːtɒn] *n* futón *m*.

future ['fjuːtʃə'] ◇ *n* futuro *m*; **in ~ de** ahora en adelante; **in the ~** en el futuro; **~ (tense)** futuro *m*. ◇ *adj* futuro(ra).

◆ **futures** *npl* COMM futuros *mpl*.

futuristic [ˌfjuːtʃə'rɪstɪk] *adj* futurista.

fuze *Am* = **fuse**.

fuzz [fʌz] *n* -**1.** [hair] vello *m*. -**2.** *inf* [police]: **the ~** la poli.

fuzzy ['fʌzɪ] (*compar* -**ier**, *superl* -**iest**) *adj* -**1.** [hair] rizado(da), ensortijado(da). -**2.** [photo, image] borroso(sa). -**3.** [thoughts, mind] confuso(sa).

fwd. *abbr of* **forward**.

fwy *abbr of* **freeway**.

FY *n abbr of* **fiscal year**.

FYI *abbr of* **for your information**.

G

g¹ (*pl* **g's** OR **gs**), **G** (*pl* **G's** OR **Gs**) [dʒiː] *n* [letter] g *f*, G *f*.

◆ **G** *n* -**1.** MUS sol *m*. -**2.** (*abbr of* **good**) B. -**3.** *Am* CINEMA (*abbr of* **general (audience)**) para todos los públicos.

g² *n* -**1.** (*abbr of* **gram**) g. *m*. -**2.** (*abbr of* **gravity**) g. *f*.

GA *abbr of* **Georgia**.

gab [gæb] *n* → **gift**.

gabardine [ˌgæbə'diːn] *n* gabardina *f*.

gabble ['gæbl] ◇ *vt & vi* farfullar, balbucir. ◇ *n* farfulleo *m*.

gable ['geɪbl] *n* aguilón *m*.

Gabon [gæ'bɒn] *n* (el) Gabón.

Gabonese [ˌgæbɒ'niːz] ◇ *adj* gabonés(esa). ◇ *n* gabonés *m*, -esa *f*. ◇ *npl*: **the ~** los gaboneses.

gad [gæd] (*pt & pp* -**ded**, *cont* -**ding**)

◆ **gad about** *vi inf* andar por ahí holgazaneando.

gadget ['gædʒɪt] *n* artilugio *m*, chisme *m*.

gadgetry ['gædʒɪtrɪ] *n* (*U*) artilugios *mpl*.

Gaelic ['geɪlɪk] ◇ *adj* gaélico(ca). ◇ *n* [language] gaélico *m*.

gaffe [gæf] *n* metedura *f* de pata, patinazo *m*.

gaffer ['gæfə'] *n Br inf* [boss] mandamás *m*.

gag [gæg] (*pt & pp* -**ged**, *cont* -**ging**) ◇ *n* -**1.** [for mouth] mordaza *f*. -**2.** *inf* [joke] chiste *m*. ◇ *vt* amordazar. ◇ *vi* [retch] tener arcadas.

gage *Am* = **gauge**.

gaiety ['geɪətɪ] *n* alegría *f*, regocijo *m*.

gaily ['geɪlɪ] *adv* alegremente.

gain [geɪn] ◇ *n* -**1.** [profit] beneficio *m*, ganancia *f*. -**2.** [improvement] mejora *f*. ◇ *vt* -**1.** [gen] ganar. -**2.** [subj: watch, clock] adelantarse. ◇ *vi* -**1.** [advance]: **to ~ in sthg** ganar algo. -**2.** [benefit]: **to ~ (from** OR **by)** beneficiarse (de). -**3.** [watch, clock] adelantarse.

◆ **gain on** *vt fus* ganar terreno a, adelantar.

gainful ['geɪnful] *adj fml*: **~ employment** trabajo *m* remunerado.

gainfully ['geɪnfulɪ] *adv fml* provechosamente.

gainsay [ˌgeɪn'seɪ] (*pt & pp* -**said**) *vt fml* negar, contradecir.

gait [geɪt] *n* andares *mpl*, forma *f* de andar.

gaiters ['geɪtəz] *npl* polainas *fpl*.

gal. *abbr of* **gallon**.

gala ['gɑːlə] ◇ *n* [celebration] fiesta *f*, celebración *f*. ◇ *comp* de gala.

Galapagos Islands [gə'læpəgəs-] *npl*: **the ~** las islas Galápagos.

galaxy ['gæləksɪ] (*pl* -**ies**) *n* galaxia *f*.

gale [geɪl] *n* vendaval *m*.

Galicia [gə'lɪʃɪə] *n* Galicia *f*.

gall [gɔːl] ◇ *n* [nerve]: **to have the ~ to do sthg** tener el descaro de hacer algo. ◇ *vt* soliviantar, indignar.

gall. *abbr of* **gallon**.

gallant [sense 1 'gælənt, sense 2 gə'lænt, 'gælənt] *adj* -**1.** [courageous] valiente, valeroso(sa). -**2.** [polite to women] galante.

gallantry ['gæləntrɪ] *n* -**1.** [courage] valentía *f*, heroísmo *m*. -**2.** [politeness to women] galantería *f*.

gall bladder *n* vesícula *f* biliar.

galleon ['gælɪən] *n* galeón *m*.

gallery ['gælərɪ] (*pl* -**ies**) *n* -**1.** [for art] galería *f*. -**2.** [in courtroom, parliament] tribuna *f*. -**3.** [in theatre] gallinero *m*, paraíso *m*.

galley ['gælɪ] (*pl* **galleys**) *n* **-1.** [ship] galera *f.* **-2.** [kitchen] cocina *f.*

Gallic ['gælɪk] *adj* galo(la).

galling ['gɔːlɪŋ] *adj* indignante.

gallivant [,gælɪ'vænt] *vi inf* andar por ahí holgazaneando.

gallon ['gælən] *n* = 4,546 *litros*, galón *m.*

gallop ['gæləp] ◇ *n* galope *m.* ◇ *vi lit* & *fig* galopar.

galloping ['gæləpɪŋ] *adj* [soaring] galopante.

gallows ['gæləʊz] (*pl inv*) *n* horca *f*, patíbulo *m.*

gallstone ['gɔːlstəʊn] *n* cálculo *m* biliar.

Gallup poll ['gæləp-] *n Br* sondeo *m* de opinión.

galore [gə'lɔːr] *adj* en abundancia, a troche y moche.

galoshes [gə'lɒʃɪz] *npl* chanclos *mpl.*

galvanize, -ise ['gælvənaɪz] *vt* **-1.** TECH galvanizar. **-2.** [impel]: **to ~ sb into action** impulsar a alguien a la acción.

Gambia ['gæmbɪə] *n*: **(the) ~** Gambia.

Gambian ['gæmbɪən] ◇ *adj* gambiano(na). ◇ *n* gambiano *m*, -na *f.*

gambit ['gæmbɪt] *n* táctica *f.*

gamble ['gæmbl] ◇ *n* [calculated risk] riesgo *m*, empresa *f* arriesgada; **to take a ~** arriesgarse. ◇ *vi* **-1.** [bet] jugar; **to ~ on** [race etc] apostar a; [stock exchange] jugar a. **-2.** [take risk]: **to ~ on** contar de antemano con que.

gambler ['gæmblər] *n* jugador *m*, -ra *f.*

gambling ['gæmblɪŋ] *n* (*U*) juego *m.*

gambol ['gæmbl] (*Br pt* & *pp* **-led**, *cont* **-ling**, *Am pt* & *pp* **-ed**, *cont* **-ing**) *vi* triscar, retozar.

game [geɪm] ◇ *n* **-1.** [gen] juego *m.* **-2.** [of football, rugby etc] partido *m*; [of snooker, chess, cards] partida *f.* **-3.** [hunted animals] caza *f.* **-4.** *phr*: **to beat sb at their own ~** ganar a alguien la partida en su propio terreno; **the ~'s up** se acabó el juego; **to give the ~ away** dejar ver OR enseñar las cartas. ◇ *adj* **-1.** [brave] valiente. **-2.** [willing]: **~ (for sthg/to do sthg)** dispuesto(ta) (a algo/a hacer algo).

◆ **games** ◇ *n* (*U*) [at school] deportes *mpl.* ◇ *npl* [sporting contest] juegos *mpl.*

gamekeeper ['geɪm,kiːpər] *n* guarda *m* de caza.

gamely ['geɪmlɪ] *adv* **-1.** [bravely] con determinación. **-2.** [willingly] de buena gana.

game reserve *n* coto *m* de caza.

gamesmanship ['geɪmzmənʃɪp] *n* falta *f* de deportividad.

gamma rays ['gæmə-] *npl* rayos *mpl* gamma.

gammon ['gæmən] *n* jamón *m.*

gammy ['gæmɪ] (*compar* **-ier**, *superl* **-iest**) *adj Br inf* fastidiado(da).

gamut ['gæmət] *n* gama *f*; **to run the ~ of sthg** recorrer toda la gama de algo.

gander ['gændər] *n* [male goose] ganso *m* (macho).

gang [gæŋ] *n* **-1.** [of criminals] banda *f.* **-2.** [of young people] pandilla *f.*

◆ **gang up** *vi inf*: **to ~ up (on sb)** confabularse (contra alguien).

Ganges ['gændʒiːz] *n*: **the (River) ~** el (río) Ganges.

gangland ['gæŋlænd] *n* (*U*) bajos fondos *mpl*, mundo *m* del hampa.

gangling ['gæŋglɪŋ], **gangly** ['gæŋglɪ] (*compar* **-ier**, *superl* **-iest**) *adj* larguirucho(cha), desgarbado(da).

gangplank ['gæŋplæŋk] *n* pasarela *f*, plancha *f.*

gangrene ['gæŋgriːn] *n* gangrena *f.*

gangrenous ['gæŋgrɪnəs] *adj* gangrenoso(sa).

gangster ['gæŋstər] *n* gángster *m.*

gangway ['gæŋweɪ] *n* **-1.** *Br* [aisle] pasillo *m.* **-2.** = **gangplank**.

gannet ['gænɪt] (*pl inv* OR **-s**) *n* [bird] alcatraz *m.*

gantry ['gæntrɪ] (*pl* **-ies**) *n* pórtico *m* (*para grúas*).

GAO (*abbr of* **General Accounting Office**) *n* oficina estadounidense de contabilidad.

gaol [dʒeɪl] *Br* = **jail**.

gap [gæp] *n* **-1.** [empty space] hueco *m*; [in traffic, trees, clouds] claro *m*; [in text] espacio *m* en blanco. **-2.** [interval] intervalo *m.* **-3.** *fig* [in knowledge, report] laguna *f.* **-4.** *fig* [great difference] desfase *m.*

gape [geɪp] *vi* **-1.** [person] mirar boquiabierto(ta). **-2.** [hole, wound] estar muy abierto(ta).

gaping ['geɪpɪŋ] *adj* **-1.** [open-mouthed] boquiabierto(ta). **-2.** [wide-open] abierto(ta).

garage [*Br* 'gærɑːʒ, 'gærɪdʒ, *Am* gə'rɑːʒ] *n* **-1.** [for keeping car] garaje *m.* **-2.** *Br* [for fuel] gasolinera *f.* **-3.** [for car repair] taller *m.* **-4.** *Br* [for selling cars] concesionario *m* de automóviles.

garb [gɑːb] *n fml* atuendo *m.*

garbage ['gɑːbɪdʒ] *n* (*U*) **-1.** [refuse] basura *f.* **-2.** *inf* [nonsense] chorradas *fpl*, tonterías *fpl.*

garbage can *n Am* cubo *m* de la basura.

garbage collector *n Am* basurero *m*, -ra *f.*

garbage truck *n Am* camión *m* de la basura.

garbled ['gɑːbld] *adj* confuso(sa).

garden ['gɑːdn] ◇ *n* jardín *m*. ◇ *comp* de jardín. ◇ *vi* trabajar en el jardín.

◆ **gardens** *npl* jardines *mpl*.

garden centre *n* centro *m* de jardinería.

garden city *n Br* ciudad *f* jardín.

gardener ['gɑːdnə'] *n* jardinero *m*, -ra *f*.

gardenia [gɑː'diːnjə] *n* gardenia *f*.

gardening ['gɑːdnɪŋ] ◇ *n* jardinería *f*. ◇ *comp* de jardinería.

garden party *n* recepción *f* al aire libre.

gargantuan [gɑː'gæntjʊən] *adj* pantagruélico(ca).

gargle ['gɑːgl] *vi* hacer gárgaras.

gargoyle ['gɑːgɔɪl] *n* gárgola *f*.

garish ['geərɪʃ] *adj* chillón(ona), llamativo(va).

garland ['gɑːlənd] *n* guirnalda *f*.

garlic ['gɑːlɪk] *n* ajo *m*.

garlic bread *n* pan *m* de ajo.

garlicky ['gɑːlɪkɪ] *adj inf* [food] con mucho ajo; [breath] con olor a ajo.

garment ['gɑːmənt] *n* prenda *f* (de vestir).

garner ['gɑːnə'] *vt fml* hacer acopio de.

garnet ['gɑːnɪt] *n* granate *m*.

garnish ['gɑːnɪʃ] ◇ *n* guarnición *f*. ◇ *vt* guarnecer.

garret ['gærət] *n* desván *m*, buhardilla *f*.

garrison ['gærɪsn] ◇ *n* guarnición *f*. ◇ *vt* guarnecer, proteger.

garrulous ['gærələs] *adj* parlanchín(ina), gárrulo(la).

garter ['gɑːtə'] *n* -1. [band round leg] liga *f*. -2. *Am* [suspender] portaligas *m inv*, liguero *m*.

gas [gæs] (*pl* -es OR -ses, *pt* & *pp* -sed, *cont* -sing) ◇ *n* -1. CHEM gas *m*. -2. *Am* [petrol] gasolina *f*. ◇ *vt* asfixiar con gas.

gas chamber *n* cámara *f* de gas.

gas cooker *n Br* cocina *f* de gas.

gas cylinder *n* bombona *f* de gas.

gas fire *n Br* estufa *f* de gas.

gas fitter *n* técnico *m* (de la compañía de gas).

gas gauge *n Am* indicador *m* del nivel de gasolina.

gash [gæʃ] ◇ *n* raja *f*, corte *m*. ◇ *vt* rajar, cortar.

gasket ['gæskɪt] *n* junta *f*.

gasman ['gæsmæn] (*pl* -men [-men]) *n* hombre *m* del gas.

gas mask *n* máscara *f* antigás.

gas meter *n* contador *m* del gas.

gasoline ['gæsəliːn] *n Am* gasolina *f*.

gasometer [gæ'sɒmɪtə'] *n* gasómetro *m*.

gas oven *n* -1. [for cooking] horno *m* de gas. -2. [gas chamber] cámara *f* de gas.

gasp [gɑːsp] ◇ *n* resuello *m*, jadeo *m*. ◇ *vi* -1. [breathe quickly] resollar, jadear. -2. [in shock, surprise] ahogar un grito.

gas pedal *n Am* acelerador *m*.

gasping ['gɑːspɪŋ] *adj Br inf*: to be ~ (for a drink) estar muerto(ta) de sed.

gas station *n Am* gasolinera *f*, grifo *m* Amer.

gas stove = gas cooker.

gassy ['gæsɪ] (*compar* -ier, *superl* -iest) *adj pej* con mucho gas.

gas tank *n Am* depósito *m* de gasolina.

gas tap *n* llave *f* del gas.

gastric ['gæstrɪk] *adj* gástrico(ca).

gastric ulcer *n* úlcera *f* gástrica.

gastritis [gæs'traɪtɪs] *n* gastritis *f inv*.

gastroenteritis ['gæstrəʊ,entə'raɪtɪs] *n* gastroenteritis *f inv*.

gastronomic [,gæstrə'nɒmɪk] *adj* gastronómico(ca).

gastronomy [gæs'trɒnəmɪ] *n* gastronomía *f*.

gasworks ['gæswɜːks] (*pl inv*) *n* fábrica *f* de gas.

gate [geɪt] *n* -1. [gen] puerta *f*; [metal] verja *f*. -2. SPORT [takings] taquilla *f*; [attendance] entrada *f*.

gâteau ['gætəʊ] (*pl* -x [-z]) *n Br* tarta *f* (con nata).

gatecrash ['geɪtkræʃ] *inf* ◇ *vt* colarse de gorra en. ◇ *vi* colarse de gorra.

gatecrasher ['geɪt,kræʃə'] *n inf* intruso *m*, -sa *f*.

gatehouse ['geɪthaʊs, *pl* -haʊzɪz] *n* casa *f* del guarda/portero.

gatekeeper ['geɪt,kiːpə'] *n* portero *m*, -ra *f*.

gatepost ['geɪtpəʊst] *n* poste *m*.

gateway ['geɪtweɪ] *n* -1. [entrance] puerta *f*, pórtico *m*. -2. [means of access]: the Pyrenees, ~ to the Iberian Peninsula los Pirineos, antesala de la Península Ibérica.

gather ['gæðə'] ◇ *vt* -1. [collect] recoger; to ~ together reunir. -2. [increase - speed, strength] ganar, cobrar. -3. [understand]: to ~ (that) sacar en conclusión que. -4. [cloth] fruncir. ◇ *vi* [people, animals] reunirse; [clouds] acumularse.

◆ **gather up** *vt sep* recoger.

gathering ['gæðərɪŋ] *n* [meeting] reunión *f*.

GATT [gæt] (*abbr of* General Agreement on Tariffs and Trade) *n* GATT *m*.

gauche [gəʊʃ] *adj* torpe.

gaudy ['gɔːdɪ] (*compar* -ier, *superl* -iest) *adj* chillón(ona), llamativo(va).

gauge, gage *Am* [geɪdʒ] ◇ *n* **-1.** [for fuel, temperature] indicador *m*; [for width of tube, wire] calibrador *m*. **-2.** [calibre] calibre *m*. **-3.** RAIL ancho *m* de vía. ◇ *vt lit & fig* calibrar.

Gaul [gɔːl] *n* **-1.** [country] la Galia. **-2.** [person] galo *m*, -la *f*.

gaunt [gɔːnt] *adj* **-1.** [person, face] enjuto(ta), enteco(ca). **-2.** [building, landscape] adusto(ta).

gauntlet ['gɔːntlɪt] *n* guante *m*; **to run the ~ of** sthg exponerse a algo; **to throw down the ~ (to** sb) arrojar el guante (a alguien).

gauze [gɔːz] *n* gasa *f*.

gave [geɪv] *pt* → **give**.

gawky ['gɔːkɪ] (*compar* **-ier**, *superl* **-iest**) *adj* desgarbado(da).

gawp [gɔːp] *vi*: **to ~ (at** sthg/sb) mirar boquiabierto(ta) (algo/a alguien).

gay [geɪ] ◇ *adj* **-1.** [homosexual] gay, homosexual. **-2.** [cheerful, lively, bright] alegre. ◇ *n* gay *m* y *f*.

Gaza Strip ['gɑːzə-] *n*: **the ~** la franja de Gaza.

gaze [geɪz] ◇ *n* mirada *f* fija. ◇ *vi*: **to ~ (at** sthg/sb) mirar fijamente (algo/a alguien).

gazebo [gə'ziːbəʊ] (*pl* **-s**) *n* belvedere *m*.

gazelle [gə'zel] (*pl inv* OR **-s**) *n* gacela *f*.

gazette [gə'zet] *n* [newspaper] gaceta *f*.

gazetteer [ˌgæzɪ'tɪəʳ] *n* índice *m* geográfico.

gazump [gə'zʌmp] *vt Br inf*: **to ~ sb** acordar vender una casa a alguien y luego vendérsela a otro a un precio más alto.

GB (*abbr of* **Great Britain**) *n* GB *f*.

GBH *n abbr of* **grievous bodily harm**.

GC (*abbr of* **George Cross**) *n (titular de la) segunda condecoración británica en importancia*.

GCE (*abbr of* **General Certificate of Education**) *n* **-1.** [O level] *antiguo examen final de enseñanza secundaria en Gran Bretaña para alumnos de buen rendimiento escolar*. **-2.** = **A level**.

GCH *Br* (*abbr of* **gas central heating**) cal. cent. por gas.

GCHQ (*abbr of* **Government Communications Headquarters**) *n centro de recogida de información de los servicios secretos británicos*.

GCSE (*abbr of* **General Certificate of Secondary Education**) *n examen final de enseñanza secundaria en Gran Bretaña*.

Gdns. *abbr of* **Gardens**.

GDP (*abbr of* **gross domestic product**) *n* PIB *m*.

GDR (*abbr of* **German Democratic Republic**) *n* RDA *f*.

gear [gɪəʳ] ◇ *n* **-1.** [mechanism] engranaje *m*. **-2.** [speed - of car, bicycle] marcha *f*; **in ~** con una marcha metida; **out of ~** en punto muerto. **-3.** (*U*) [equipment, clothes] equipo *m*. ◇ *vt*: **to ~ sthg to** orientar OR encaminar algo hacia.
♦ **gear up** *vi*: **to ~ up for** sthg/**to do** sthg hacer preparativos para algo/para hacer algo.

gearbox ['gɪəbɒks] *n* caja *f* de cambios.

gearing ['gɪərɪŋ] *n* [assembly of gears] engranaje *m*.

gear lever, gear stick *Br*, **gear shift** *Am n* palanca *f* de cambios.

gear wheel *n* rueda *f* dentada.

gee [dʒiː] *excl* **-1.** [to horse]: **~ up!** ¡arre! **-2.** *Am inf* [expressing surprise, excitement]: **~ (whiz)!** ¡caramba!, ¡jolines!

geese [giːs] *pl* → **goose**.

Geiger counter ['gaɪgəʳ-] *n* contador *m* Geiger.

geisha (girl) ['geɪʃə-] *n* geisha *f*.

gel [dʒel] (*pt & pp* **-led**, *cont* **-ling**) ◇ *n* [for shower] gel *m*; [for hair] gomina *f*. ◇ *vi* **-1.** [thicken] aglutinarse. **-2.** [plan] cuajar; [idea, thought] tomar forma.

gelatin ['dʒelətɪn], **gelatine** [ˌdʒelə'tiːn] *n* gelatina *f*.

gelding ['geldɪŋ] *n* caballo *m* castrado.

gelignite ['dʒelɪgnaɪt] *n* gelignita *f*.

gem [dʒem] *n lit & fig* joya *f*.

Gemini ['dʒemɪnaɪ] *n* Géminis *m inv*; **to be (a) ~** ser Géminis.

gemstone ['dʒemstəʊn] *n* piedra *f* preciosa.

gen [dʒen] (*pt & pp* **-ned**, *cont* **-ning**) *Br inf n* (*U*) información *f*, detalles *mpl*.
♦ **gen up** *vi Br inf*: **to ~ up (on** sthg) informarse (sobre algo).

gen. **-1.** (*abbr of* **general**) gral. **-2.** (*abbr of* **generally**) grlte.

Gen. (*abbr of* **General**) *rango militar*, ≈ Gen.

gender ['dʒendəʳ] *n* género *m*.

gene [dʒiːn] *n* gene *m*, gen *m*.

genealogist [ˌdʒiːnɪ'ælədʒɪst] *n* genealogista *m* y *f*.

genealogy [ˌdʒiːnɪ'ælədʒɪ] (*pl* **-ies**) *n* genealogía *f*.

genera ['dʒenərə] *pl* → **genus**.

general ['dʒenərəl] ◇ *adj* general. ◇ *n* general *m*.
♦ **in general** *adv* **-1.** [as a whole] en general. **-2.** [usually] por lo general.

general anaesthetic *n* anestesia *f* general.

general delivery *n Am* lista *f* de correos.

general election *n* elecciones *fpl* generales.

generality [,dʒenəˈrælətɪ] (*pl* **-ies**) *n* generalidad *f*.

generalization [,dʒenərəlaɪˈzeɪʃn] *n* generalización *f*.

generalize, -ise [ˈdʒenərəlaɪz] *vi*: **to** ~ (**about**) generalizar (sobre).

general knowledge *n* cultura *f* general.

generally [ˈdʒenərəlɪ] *adv* en general.

general manager *n* administrador *m*, -ra *f* general.

general practice *n* **-1.** [work] medicina *f* general. **-2.** [clinic] consulta *f*.

general practitioner *n* médico *m*, -ca *f* de cabecera.

general public *n*: **the** ~ el gran público.

general-purpose *adj* de uso general.

general strike *n* huelga *f* general.

generate [ˈdʒenəreɪt] *vt* generar.

generation [,dʒenəˈreɪʃn] *n* generación *f*; **first/second** ~ de primera/segunda generación.

generation gap *n* barrera *f* generacional.

generator [ˈdʒenəreɪtə] *n* generador *m*.

generic [dʒɪˈnerɪk] *adj* genérico(ca).

generosity [,dʒenəˈrɒsətɪ] *n* generosidad *f*.

generous [ˈdʒenərəs] *adj* generoso(sa); [cut of clothes] amplio(plia).

generously [ˈdʒenərəslɪ] *adv* generosamente.

genesis [ˈdʒenəsɪs] (*pl* **-eses** [-əsiːz]) *n* génesis *f inv*.

genetic [dʒɪˈnetɪk] *adj* genético(ca).

genetic engineering *n* ingeniería *f* genética.

genetic fingerprinting [-ˈfɪŋɡəprɪntɪŋ] *n* identificación *f* genética.

genetics [dʒɪˈnetɪks] *n* (U) genética *f*.

Geneva [dʒəˈniːvə] *n* Ginebra.

Geneva convention *n*: **the** ~ la Convención de Ginebra.

genial [ˈdʒiːnjəl] *adj* cordial, afable.

genie [ˈdʒiːnɪ] (*pl* **genies** OR **genii** [ˈdʒiːnɪaɪ]) *n* genio *m*, duende *m*.

genitals [ˈdʒenɪtlz] *npl* genitales *mpl*.

genius [ˈdʒiːnjəs] (*pl* **-es**) *n* genio *m*; ~ **for sthg/for doing sthg** don *m* para algo/para hacer algo.

Genoa [dʒəˈnəʊə] *n* Génova.

genocide [ˈdʒenəsaɪd] *n* genocidio *m*.

genre [ˈʒɑ̃rə] *n* género *m*.

gent [dʒent] *n* *inf* caballero *m*.
◆ **gents** *n* *Br* [toilets] servicio *m* de caballeros.

genteel [dʒenˈtiːl] *adj* fino(na), refinado(da).

gentile [ˈdʒentaɪl] ◇ *adj* gentil, no judío(a). ◇ *n* gentil *m y f*.

gentle [ˈdʒentl] *adj* **-1.** [kind] tierno(na), dulce. **-2.** [breeze, movement, slope] suave. **-3.** [scolding] ligero(ra); [hint] sutil.

gentleman [ˈdʒentlmən] (*pl* **-men** [-mən]) *n* **-1.** [well-behaved man] caballero *m*; ~'s **agreement** pacto *m* de caballeros. **-2.** [man] señor *m*, caballero *m*.

gentlemanly [ˈdʒentlmənlɪ] *adj* caballeroso(sa).

gentleness [ˈdʒentlnɪs] *n* **-1.** [kindness] ternura *f*, dulzura *f*. **-2.** [softness] suavidad *f*.

gently [ˈdʒentlɪ] *adv* **-1.** [kindly] dulcemente, tiernamente. **-2.** [softly, smoothly] suavemente. **-3.** [carefully] con cuidado.

gentry [ˈdʒentrɪ] *n* alta burguesía *f*.

genuflect [ˈdʒenjuːflekt] *vi* *fml* hacer una genuflexión.

genuine [ˈdʒenjuːɪn] *adj* **-1.** [real] auténtico(ca), genuino(na). **-2.** [sincere] sincero(ra).

genuinely [ˈdʒenjuːɪnlɪ] *adv* **-1.** [really] auténticamente. **-2.** [sincerely] sinceramente.

genus [ˈdʒiːnəs] (*pl* **genera**) *n* género *m*.

geographer [dʒɪˈɒɡrəfə] *n* geógrafo *m*, -fa *f*.

geographical [,dʒɪəˈɡræfɪkl] *adj* geográfico(ca).

geography [dʒɪˈɒɡrəfɪ] *n* geografía *f*.

geological [,dʒɪəˈlɒdʒɪkl] *adj* geológico(ca).

geologist [dʒɪˈɒlədʒɪst] *n* geólogo *m*, -ga *f*.

geology [dʒɪˈɒlədʒɪ] *n* geología *f*.

geometric(al) [,dʒɪəˈmetrɪk(l)] *adj* geométrico(ca).

geometry [dʒɪˈɒmətrɪ] *n* geometría *f*.

geophysics [,dʒiːəʊˈfɪzɪks] *n* geofísica *f*.

Geordie [ˈdʒɔːdɪ] ◇ *adj* de o relativo a Tyneside. ◇ *n* [person] natural o habitante de Tyneside.

George Cross [dʒɔːˈdʒ-] *n* *Br* ≃ medalla *f* al mérito civil.

Georgia [ˈdʒɔːdʒə] *n* [in US, in CIS] Georgia.

Georgian [ˈdʒɔːdʒən] *adj* GEOGR & HISTORY georgiano(na).

geranium [dʒɪˈreɪnjəm] (*pl* **-s**) *n* geranio *m*.

gerbil [ˈdʒɜːbɪl] *n* jerbo *m*, gerbo *m*.

geriatric [,dʒerɪˈætrɪk] *adj* **-1.** [of old people] geriátrico(ca). **-2.** *pej* [very old, inefficient] anticuado(da).

germ [dʒɜːm] *n* BIOL & *fig* germen *m*; MED microbio *m*.

German [ˈdʒɜːmən] ◇ *adj* alemán(ana). ◇ *n* **-1.** [person] alemán *m*, -ana *f*. **-2.** [language] alemán *m*.

Germanic [dʒɜːˈmænɪk] *adj* germánico(ca).

German measles *n* rubéola *f*.

German shepherd (dog) *n* pastor *m* alemán.

Germany ['dʒɜːmənɪ] (*pl* **-ies**) *n* Alemania.

germicide ['dʒɜːmɪsaɪd] *n* germicida *f*, bactericida *f*.

germinate ['dʒɜːmɪneɪt] *vt & vi lit & fig* germinar.

germination [,dʒɜːmɪ'neɪʃn] *n lit & fig* germinación *f*.

germ warfare *n* guerra *f* bacteriológica.

Gerona [dʒə'rəunə] *n* Gerona.

gerrymandering ['dʒerɪmændərɪŋ] *n división de una zona electoral de forma que se da ventaja a un partido frente a otros.*

gerund ['dʒerənd] *n* gerundio *m*.

gestation [dʒe'steɪʃn] *n* gestación *f*.

gestation period *n lit & fig* periodo *m* de gestación.

gesticulate [dʒes'tɪkjʊleɪt] *vi* gesticular.

gesticulation [dʒe,stɪkjʊ'leɪʃn] *n* gesticulación *f*.

gesture ['dʒestʃə'] ◇ *n* gesto *m*. ◇ *vi*: **to ~ to** OR **towards sb** hacer gestos a alguien.

get (*Br pt & pp* **got**, *cont* **-ting**, *Am pt* **got**, *pp* **gotten**, *cont* **-ting**) ◇ *vt* **-1.** [cause to do]: **to ~ sb to do sthg** hacer que alguien haga algo; **I'll ~ my sister to help** le pediré a mi hermana que ayude. **-2.** [cause to be done]: **to ~ sthg done** mandar hacer algo; **have you got the car fixed yet?** ¿te han arreglado ya el coche? **-3.** [cause to become]: **to ~ sthg ready** preparar algo; **to ~ sb pregnant** dejar a alguien preñada; **to ~ things going** poner las cosas en marcha. **-4.** [cause to move]: **can you ~ it through the gap?** ¿puedes meterlo por el hueco?; **to ~ sthg/sb out of sthg** conseguir sacar algo/a alguien de algo. **-5.** [bring, fetch] traer; **can I ~ you something to eat/drink?** ¿te traigo algo de comer/beber?; **I'll ~ my coat** voy a por el abrigo; **could you ~ me the boss, please?** [when phoning] póngame con el jefe. **-6.** [obtain] conseguir; **she got top marks** sacó las mejores notas. **-7.** [receive] recibir; **when did you ~ the news?** ¿cuándo recibiste la noticia?; **what did you ~ for your birthday?** ¿qué te regalaron para tu cumpleaños?; **she ~s a good salary** gana un buen sueldo. **-8.** [experience - a sensation]: **do you ~ the feeling he doesn't like us?** ¿no te da la sensación de que no le gustamos?; **I got the impression she was unhappy** me dio la impresión de que era infeliz; **I ~ a thrill out of driving fast** encuentro emocionante lo de conducir deprisa. **-9.** [catch - bus, criminal, illness] coger, agarrar *Amer*; **I've got a cold** estoy resfriado; **he got cancer** contrajo cáncer. **-10.** [understand] entender; **I don't**

~ it *inf* no me aclaro, no lo entiendo; **he didn't seem to ~ the point** no pareció captar el sentido. **-11.** *inf* [annoy] poner negro(gra); **what really ~s me is his smugness** lo que me pone negro es lo engreído que es. **-12.** [find]: **you ~ a lot of artists here** hay mucho artista por aquí; *see also* **have**.

◇ *vi* **-1.** [become] ponerse; **to ~ angry/pale** ponerse furioso/pálido; **to ~ ready** prepararse; **to ~ dressed** vestirse; **I'm getting cold/bored** me estoy enfriando/aburriendo; **it's getting late** se está haciendo tarde. **-2.** [arrive] llegar; **how do I ~ there?** ¿cómo se llega (allí)?; **I only got back yesterday** regresé justo ayer. **-3.** [eventually succeed]: **to ~ to do sthg** llegar a hacer algo; **I never got to know him/visit Moscow** nunca llegué a conocerle/visitar Moscú; **she got to enjoy the classes** llegaron a gustarle las clases; **did you ~ to see him?** ¿conseguiste verlo? **-4.** [progress] llegar; **how far have you got?** ¿cuánto llevas?, ¿hasta dónde has llegado?; **we only got as far as buying the paint** no llegamos más que a comprar la pintura; **I got to the point where I didn't care any more** llegó un punto en el que ya nada me importaba; **now we're getting somewhere** ahora sí que vamos por buen camino; **we're getting nowhere** así no llegamos a ninguna parte.

◇ *aux vb*: **to ~ excited** emocionarse; **someone could ~ hurt** alguien podría resultar herido; **I got beaten up** me zurraron; **let's ~ going** OR **moving** vamos a ponernos en marcha.

◆ **get about, get around** *vi* **-1.** [move from place to place] salir a menudo. **-2.** [circulate - news etc] difundirse; *see also* **get around**.

◆ **get across** *vt sep*: **to ~ sthg across to sb** hacerle comprender algo a alguien; **to ~ a message across** transmitir un mensaje.

◆ **get ahead** *vi* [in life] abrirse camino.

◆ **get along** *vi* **-1.** [manage] arreglárselas, apañárselas. **-2.** [progress]: **how are you getting along?** ¿cómo te va? **-3.** [have a good relationship]: **to ~ along (with sb)** llevarse bien (con alguien).

◆ **get around, get round** ◇ *vt fus* [overcome - problem] solventar; [- obstacle] sortear. ◇ *vi* **-1.** [circulate - news etc] difundirse. **-2.** [eventually do]: **to ~ around to (doing) sthg** sacar tiempo para (hacer) algo; *see also* **get about**.

◆ **get at** *vt fus* **-1.** [reach] llegar a, alcanzar; **he's determined to ~ at the truth** está decidido a descubrir la verdad. **-2.** [imply] referirse a; **what are you getting at?** ¿qué quieres decir con eso? **-3.** *inf* [criticize]: **stop get-**

ting at me! ¡deja ya de meterte conmigo!

◆ **get away** *vi* **-1.** [leave] salir, irse. **-2.** [go on holiday]: **I really need to ~ away** necesito unas buenas vacaciones; **to ~ away from it all** escaparse de todo. **-3.** [escape] escaparse.

◆ **get away with** *vt fus* salir impune de; **she lets him ~ away with everything** ella se lo consiente todo.

◆ **get back** ◇ *vt sep* [recover, regain] recuperar. ◇ *vi* [move away] echarse atrás, apartarse.

◆ **get back to** *vt fus* **-1.** [return to previous state, activity] volver a; **to ~ back to sleep/normal** volver a dormirse/a la normalidad; **to ~ back to work** volver a trabajar OR al trabajo. **-2.** *inf* [phone back]: **I'll ~ back to you later** te llamo de vuelta más tarde.

◆ **get by** *vi* apañárselas, apañarse.

◆ **get down** *vt sep* **-1.** [depress] deprimir. **-2.** [fetch from higher level] bajar.

◆ **get down to** *vt fus*: **to ~ down to doing sthg** ponerse a hacer algo; **to ~ down to work** ponerse manos a la obra.

◆ **get in** ◇ *vi* **-1.** [enter] entrar. **-2.** [arrive] llegar. **-3.** [be elected] salir elegido(da). ◇ *vt sep* **-1.** [bring in - washing] meter dentro; [- harvest] recoger; [- provisions] aprovisionarse de. **-2.** [interject]: **to ~ a word in** decir algo.

◆ **get in on** *vt fus* apuntarse a.

◆ **get into** *vt fus* **-1.** [car] subir a. **-2.** [become involved in] meterse en; **to ~ into an argument (with)** meterse en una discusión (con). **-3.** [enter into a particular situation, state]: **to get into a panic** OR **state** ponerse nerviosísimo; **to ~ into trouble** meterse en líos; **to ~ into the habit of doing sthg** adquirir el hábito OR coger la costumbre de hacer algo. **-4.** [be accepted as a student at]: **she managed to ~ into Oxford** consiguió entrar en Oxford. **-5.** *inf* [affect]: **what's got into you?** ¿qué mosca te ha picado?

◆ **get off** ◇ *vt sep* [remove] quitar. ◇ *vt fus* **-1.** [go away from] irse OR salirse de; **~ off my land!** ¡fuera de mis tierras! **-2.** [train, bus, etc] bajarse de. ◇ *vi* **-1.** [leave bus, train] bajarse, desembarcarse *Amer*. **-2.** [escape punishment] escaparse; **he got off lightly** salió bien librado. **-3.** [depart] irse, salir.

◆ **get off with** *vt fus Br inf* ligar con.

◆ **get on** ◇ *vt sep* [put on] ponerse. ◇ *vt fus* [bus, train, horse] subirse a, montarse en. ◇ *vi* **-1.** [enter bus, train] subirse, montarse. **-2.** [have good relationship] llevarse bien. **-3.** [progress]: **how are you getting on?** ¿cómo te va? **-4.** [proceed]: **to ~ on with sthg** seguir OR continuar con algo. **-5.** [be successful professionally] triunfar. **-6.** [grow old]: **he's getting on a bit** se está haciendo mayor.

◆ **get on for** *vt fus inf* [be approximately]: **it's getting on for five o'clock** casi son las cinco; **she's getting on for 65** ronda los 65.

◆ **get on to** *vt fus* **-1.** [begin talking about] ponerse a hablar de. **-2.** [contact] ponerse en contacto con.

◆ **get out** ◇ *vt sep* [remove - object, prisoner] sacar; [- stain etc] quitar; **she got a pen out of her bag** sacó un bolígrafo del bolso. ◇ *vi* **-1.** [leave car, bus, train] bajarse. **-2.** [become known - news] difundirse, filtrarse.

◆ **get out of** ◇ *vt fus* **-1.** [car etc] bajar de. **-2.** [escape from] escapar OR huir de. **-3.** [avoid] librarse de, eludir; **to ~ out of (doing) sthg** librarse de (hacer) algo. ◇ *vt sep* [cause to escape from]: **to ~ sb out of jail** ayudar a alguien a escapar de la cárcel.

◆ **get over** *vt fus* **-1.** [recover from] recuperarse de, reponerse de; **you'll ~ over it** ya se te pasará. **-2.** [overcome] superar. **-3.** [communicate] hacer comprender.

◆ **get over with** *vt sep*: **to ~ sthg over with** terminar con algo.

◆ **get round** = **get around**.

◆ **get through** ◇ *vt fus* **-1.** [job, task] terminar, acabar. **-2.** [exam] pasar, aprobar. **-3.** [food, drink] consumir. **-4.** [unpleasant situation] sobrevivir a, aguantar. ◇ *vi* **-1.** [make oneself understood]: **to ~ through (to sb)** hacerse comprender (por alguien). **-2.** TELEC conseguir comunicar.

◆ **get to** *vt fus inf* [annoy] fastidiar, molestar.

◆ **get together** ◇ *vt sep* [organize - project, demonstration] organizar, montar; [- team] juntar; [- report] preparar. ◇ *vi* juntarse, reunirse.

◆ **get up** ◇ *vi* levantarse. ◇ *vt fus* [organize - petition etc] preparar, organizar.

◆ **get up to** *vt fus inf* hacer, montar; **I wonder what they're getting up to me** pregunto qué demonios estarán haciendo.

getaway ['getəweɪ] *n* fuga *f*, huida *f*; **to make one's ~** darse a la fuga.

getaway car *n* coche en que huyen los criminales de la escena del crimen.

get-together *n inf* reunión *f*.

getup ['getʌp] *n inf* indumentaria *f*, atuendo *m*.

get-up-and-go *n inf* brío *m*.

get-well card *n* tarjeta que se envía a una persona enferma deseándole que se mejore pronto.

geyser ['giːzəʳ] *n* **-1.** [hot spring] géiser *m*. **-2.** *Br* [water heater] calentador *m* de agua.

Ghana ['gɑːnə] *n* Ghana.

Ghanaian [gɑː'neɪən] ◇ adj ghanés(esa). ◇ n ghanés m, -esa f.

ghastly ['gɑːstlɪ] (compar -ier, superl -iest) adj -1. inf [very bad, unpleasant] horrible, espantoso(sa). -2. [horrifying] horripilante. -3. [ill] fatal.

gherkin ['gɜːkɪn] n pepinillo m.

ghetto ['getəʊ] (pl -s OR -es) n gueto m.

ghetto blaster [-'blɑːstəʳ] n inf radiocasete portátil de gran tamaño y potencia.

ghost [gəʊst] ◇ n [spirit] fantasma m; **he doesn't have a ~ of a chance** no tiene ni la más remota posibilidad. ◇ vt = **ghostwrite**.

ghostly ['gəʊstlɪ] (compar -ier, superl -iest) adj fantasmal.

ghost town n pueblo m fantasma OR abandonado.

ghostwrite ['gəʊstraɪt] (pt -wrote, pp -written) vt escribir anónimamente para otras personas.

ghostwriter ['gəʊst,raɪtəʳ] n escritor anónimo que escribe un libro en lugar de su autor oficial.

ghostwritten ['gəʊst,rɪtn] pp → ghostwrite.

ghostwrote ['gəʊstrəʊt] pp → ghostwrite.

ghoul [guːl] n -1. [spirit] espíritu m del mal. -2. pej [ghoulish person] persona f macabra.

ghoulish ['guːlɪʃ] adj macabro(bra).

GHQ (abbr of general headquarters) n cuartel general.

GI (abbr of government issue) n soldado raso estadounidense.

giant ['dʒaɪənt] ◇ adj gigantesco(ca). ◇ n gigante m.

giant-size(d) adj de tamaño gigante.

gibber ['dʒɪbəʳ] vi farfullar.

gibberish ['dʒɪbərɪʃ] n galimatías m inv.

gibbon ['gɪbən] n gibón m.

gibe [dʒaɪb] ◇ n pulla f, sarcasmo m. ◇ vi: **to ~ (at)** mofarse (de).

giblets ['dʒɪblɪts] npl menudillos mpl.

Gibraltar [dʒɪ'brɔːltəʳ] n Gibraltar; **the Rock of ~** el Peñón.

giddy ['gɪdɪ] (compar -ier, superl -iest) adj [dizzy] mareado(da).

gift [gɪft] n -1. [present] regalo m, obsequio m. -2. [talent] don m; **to have a ~ for sthg/ for doing sthg** tener un don especial para algo/para hacer algo; **to have the ~ of the gab** tener un pico de oro.

GIFT [gɪft] (abbr of gamete in fallopian transfer) n técnica de inseminación artificial.

gift certificate Am = gift token.

gifted ['gɪftɪd] adj -1. [talented] dotado(da), de talento. -2. [extremely intelligent] superdotado(da).

gift token, **gift voucher** n Br vale m OR cupón m para regalo.

gift-wrapped [-ræpt] adj envuelto(ta) para regalo.

gig [gɪg] n inf [concert] actuación f, concierto m.

gigabyte ['gaɪgəbaɪt] n COMPUT gigaocteto m.

gigantic [dʒaɪ'gæntɪk] adj gigantesco(ca).

giggle ['gɪgl] ◇ n -1. [laugh] risita f, risa f tonta. -2. Br inf [fun]: **it's a real ~** es la mar de divertido; **to do sthg for a ~** hacer algo por puro cachondeo. ◇ vi [laugh] tener la risa tonta.

giggly ['gɪglɪ] (compar -ier, superl -iest) adj con la risa tonta.

GIGO ['gaɪgəʊ] (abbr of garbage in, garbage out) información errónea genera resultados erróneos.

gigolo ['ʒɪgələʊ] (pl -s) n pej gigoló m.

gigot ['ʒiːgəʊ] n pierna f de cordero.

gilded ['gɪldɪd] = gilt.

gill [dʒɪl] n [unit of measurement] = 0,142 litros.

gills [gɪlz] npl [of fish] agallas fpl.

gilt [gɪlt] ◇ adj dorado(da). ◇ n dorado m. ◆ **gilts** npl FIN valores mpl de máxima garantía.

gilt-edged adj FIN de máxima garantía.

gimme ['gɪmɪ] inf = give me.

gimmick ['gɪmɪk] n pej artilugio m innecesario; **advertising ~** reclamo m publicitario.

gin [dʒɪn] n ginebra f; **~ and tonic** gin-tonic m.

ginger ['dʒɪndʒəʳ] ◇ adj Br [hair] bermejo(ja); [cat] de color bermejo. ◇ n jengibre m.

ginger ale n [mixer] ginger-ale m.

ginger beer n [slightly alcoholic] refresco m de jengibre.

gingerbread ['dʒɪndʒəbred] n -1. [cake] pan m de jengibre. -2. [biscuit] galleta f de jengibre.

ginger group n Br grupo m de presión.

ginger-haired [-'heəd] adj pelirrojo(ja).

gingerly ['dʒɪndʒəlɪ] adv con mucho tiento.

gingham ['gɪŋəm] n guinga f.

gingivitis [,dʒɪndʒɪ'vaɪtɪs] n gingivitis f inv.

ginseng ['dʒɪnseŋ] n ginseng m.

gipsy ['dʒɪpsɪ] (pl -ies) ◇ adj gitano(na). ◇ n Br gitano m, -na f.

giraffe [dʒɪ'rɑːf] (pl inv OR -s) n jirafa f.

gird [gɜːd] (pt & pp -ed OR girt) vt → loin.

girder ['gɜːdəʳ] n viga f.

girdle ['gɜːdl] n [corset] faja f.

girl [gɜːl] *n* **-1.** [child] niña *f*. **-2.** [young woman] chica *f*, muchacha *f*. **-3.** [daughter] niña *f*, chica *f*. **-4.** *inf* [female friend]: **the ~s** las amigas, las chicas.

girl Friday *n* secretaria *f*.

girlfriend ['gɜːlfrend] *n* **-1.** [female lover] novia *f*. **-2.** [female friend] amiga *f*.

girl guide *Br*, **girl scout** *Am n* [individual] exploradora *f*.
◆ **Girl Guides** *n* [organization]: **the Girl Guides** las exploradoras.

girlie magazine ['gɜːlɪ-] *n inf* revista *f* de desnudos.

girlish ['gɜːlɪʃ] *adj* de niña.

girl scout *Am* = **girl guide**.

giro ['dʒaɪrəʊ] *n Br* **-1.** (*U*) [system] giro *m*. **-2.** ~ **(cheque)** cheque *m* para giro bancario.

girt [gɜːt] *pt & pp* → **gird**.

girth [gɜːθ] *n* **-1.** [circumference] circunferencia *f*. **-2.** [of horse] cincha *f*.

GIS (*abbr of* **geographic information system**) *n sistema de información geográfica.*

gist [dʒɪst] *n*: **the ~ of** lo esencial de; **to get the ~ (of sthg)** entender el sentido (de algo).

give [gɪv] (*pt* **gave**, *pp* **given**) ◇ *vt* **-1.** [gen] dar; [time, effort] dedicar; [attention] prestar; **to ~ sb/sthg sthg**, **to ~ sthg to sb/sthg** dar algo a alguien/algo; **to ~ a shrug** encogerse de hombros. **-2.** [as present]: **to ~ sb sthg**, **to ~ sthg to sb** regalar algo a alguien. **-3.** [hand over]: **to ~ sb sthg**, **to ~ sthg to sb** entregar OR dar algo a alguien. **-4.** *inf* [pay]: **to ~ sthg (for sthg)** dar OR pagar algo (por algo). **-5.** *phr*: **I am given to believe** OR **understand that ...** *fml* tengo entendido que ...; **I'd ~ anything** OR **my right arm to do that** daría cualquier cosa por hacer eso. ◇ *vi* [collapse, break] romperse, ceder. ◇ *n* [elasticity] elasticidad *f*.
◆ **give or take** *prep* más o menos; **in half an hour ~ or take five minutes** en más o menos media hora.
◆ **give away** *vt sep* **-1.** [as present] regalar. **-2.** [reveal] revelar, descubrir.
◆ **give back** *vt sep* [return] devolver, regresar *Amer*.
◆ **give in** *vi* **-1.** [admit defeat] rendirse, darse por vencido(da), transar *Amer*. **-2.** [agree unwillingly]: **to ~ in to sthg** ceder ante algo.
◆ **give off** *vt fus* [produce, emit] despedir.
◆ **give out** ◇ *vt sep* [distribute] repartir, distribuir. ◇ *vi* [supply, strength] agotarse, acabarse; [legs, machine] fallar.
◆ **give over** ◇ *vt sep* [dedicate]: **to be given over to sthg** dedicarse a algo. ◇ *vi Br inf* [stop]: ~ **over!** ¡basta OR vale ya!

◆ **give up** ◇ *vt sep* **-1.** [stop] abandonar; **to ~ up chocolate** dejar de comer chocolate. **-2.** [job] dimitir de, renunciar a. **-3.** [surrender]: **to ~ o.s. up (to sb)** rendirse (a alguien). ◇ *vi* rendirse, darse por vencido (da).
◆ **give up on** *vt fus* [abandon] dejar por imposible.

give-and-take *n* toma y daca *m*.

giveaway ['gɪvə,weɪ] ◇ *adj* **-1.** [tell-tale] revelador(ra). **-2.** [very cheap] de regalo. ◇ *n* [tell-tale sign] indicio *m*, signo *m* revelador.

given ['gɪvn] ◇ *pp* → **give**. ◇ *adj* **-1.** [set, fixed] dado(da); **at any ~ time** en un momento dado. **-2.** [prone]: **to be ~ to sthg/to doing sthg** ser dado(da) a algo/a hacer algo. ◇ *prep* [taking into account] dado(da); ~ **that** dado que.

given name *n* nombre *m* de pila.

giver ['gɪvə'] *n* donante *m y f*.

glacé cherry ['glæseɪ-] *n* cereza *f* escarchada OR confitada.

glacial ['gleɪsjəl] *adj lit & fig* glacial.

glacier ['glæsjə'] *n* glaciar *m*.

glad [glæd] (*compar* **-der**, *superl* **-dest**) *adj* **-1.** [happy, pleased] alegre, contento(ta); **to be ~ about/that** alegrarse de/de que. **-2.** [willing]: **to be ~ to do sthg** tener gusto en hacer algo. **-3.** [grateful]: **to be ~ of sthg** agradecer algo.

gladden ['glædn] *vt literary* regocijar, llenar de gozo.

glade [gleɪd] *n literary* claro *m*.

gladiator ['glædɪeɪtə'] *n* gladiador *m*.

gladioli [,glædɪ'əʊlaɪ] *npl* gladiolos *mpl*.

gladly ['glædlɪ] *adv* **-1.** [happily, eagerly] alegremente. **-2.** [willingly] con mucho gusto.

glamor *Am* = **glamour**.

glamorize, -ise ['glæmə raɪz] *vt* hacer más atractivo(va).

glamorous ['glæmərəs] *adj* atractivo(va), lleno(na) de encanto.

glamour *Br*, **glamor** *Am* ['glæmə'] *n* encanto *m*, atractivo *m*.

glance [glɑːns] ◇ *n* [quick look] mirada *f*, vistazo *m*; **to cast** OR **take a ~ at sthg** echar un vistazo a algo; **at a ~** de un vistazo; **at first ~** a primera vista. ◇ *vi* [look quickly]: **to ~ at sb** lanzar una mirada a alguien; **to ~ at sthg** echar una ojeada OR un vistazo a algo; **to ~ at** OR **through sthg** hojear algo.
◆ **glance off** *vt fus* rebotar en.

glancing ['glɑːnsɪŋ] *adj* oblicuo(cua).

gland [glænd] *n* glándula *f*.

glandular fever ['glændjʊlə'-] *n* mononucleosis *f inv* infecciosa.

glare [gleə^r] ◇ *n* **-1.** [scowl] mirada *f* asesina. **-2.** [blaze, dazzle] destello *m*, deslumbramiento *m*. **-3.** (*U*) *fig* [of publicity] foco *m*. ◇ *vi* **-1.** [scowl]: **to ~ (at sthg/sb)** mirar con furia (algo/a alguien). **-2.** [blaze, dazzle] deslumbrar.

glaring ['gleərɪŋ] *adj* **-1.** [very obvious] evidente. **-2.** [blazing, dazzling] deslumbrante.

glasnost ['glæznɒst] *n* glasnost *f*.

glass [glɑːs] ◇ *n* **-1.** [material] vidrio *m*, cristal *m*. **-2.** [drinking vessel, glassful] vaso *m*; [with stem] copa *f*. **-3.** (*U*) [glassware] cristalería *f*. ◇ *comp* de vidrio, de cristal.
◆ **glasses** *npl* [spectacles] gafas *fpl*.

glassblowing ['glɑːs,bləʊɪŋ] *n* soplado *m* de vidrio.

glass fibre *n* (*U*) *Br* fibra *f* de vidrio.

glasshouse ['glɑːshaʊs, *pl* -haʊzɪz] *n* *Br* [greenhouse] invernadero *m*.

glassware ['glɑːsweə^r] *n* (*U*) cristalería *f*.

glassy ['glɑːsɪ] (*compar* -ier, *superl* -iest) *adj* **-1.** [smooth, shiny] cristalino(na). **-2.** [blank, lifeless] vidrioso(sa).

Glaswegian [glæz'wiːdʒən] ◇ *adj* de o relativo a Glasgow. ◇ *n* [person] natural o habitante de Glasgow.

glaucoma [glɔː'kəʊmə] *n* glaucoma *m*.

glaze [gleɪz] ◇ *n* [on pottery] vidriado *m*; [on food] glaseado *m*. ◇ *vt* [pottery] vidriar; [food] glasear.
◆ **glaze over** *vi* apagarse.

glazed [gleɪzd] *adj* **-1.** [dull, bored] vidrioso(sa). **-2.** [pottery] vidriado(da); [food] glaseado(da). **-3.** [door, window] acristalado(da).

glazier ['gleɪzjə^r] *n* vidriero *m*, -ra *f*.

GLC (*abbr of* **Greater London Council**) *n* antiguo ayuntamiento de Londres.

gleam [gliːm] ◇ *n* destello *m*; [of hope] rayo *m*. ◇ *vi* relucir.

gleaming ['gliːmɪŋ] *adj* reluciente.

glean [gliːn] *vt* [gather] recoger.

glee [gliː] *n* (*U*) [joy, delight] alegría *f*, regocijo *m*.

gleeful ['gliːfʊl] *adj* alegre, jubiloso(sa).

glen [glen] *n* *Scot* cañada *f*.

glib [glɪb] (*compar* -ber, *superl* -best) *adj* *pej* de mucha labia.

glibly ['glɪblɪ] *adv* *pej* con mucha labia.

glide [glaɪd] *vi* **-1.** [move smoothly] deslizarse. **-2.** [fly] planear.

glider ['glaɪdə^r] *n* [plane] planeador *m*.

gliding ['glaɪdɪŋ] *n* [sport] vuelo *m* sin motor.

glimmer ['glɪmə^r] ◇ *n* **-1.** [faint light] luz *f*

tenue. **-2.** *fig* [trace, sign] atisbo *m*; [of hope] rayo *m*. ◇ *vi* brillar tenuemente.

glimpse [glɪmps] ◇ *n* **-1.** [look, sight] vislumbre *f*; **to catch a ~ of sthg/sb** entrever algo/a alguien. **-2.** [idea, perception] asomo *m*, atisbo *m*. ◇ *vt* entrever, vislumbrar.

glint [glɪnt] ◇ *n* **-1.** [flash] destello *m*. **-2.** [in eyes] fulgor *m*. ◇ *vi* destellar.

glisten ['glɪsn] *vi* relucir, brillar.

glitch [glɪtʃ] *n* *Am inf* pequeño fallo *m* técnico.

glitter ['glɪtə^r] ◇ *n* brillo *m*. ◇ *vi* relucir, brillar.

glittering ['glɪtərɪŋ] *adj* brillante, reluciente.

glitzy ['glɪtsɪ] (*compar* -ier, *superl* -iest) *adj* *inf* [glamorous] deslumbrante.

gloat [gləʊt] *vi*: **to ~ (over sthg)** regodearse (con algo).

global ['gləʊbl] *adj* [worldwide] mundial.

globally ['gləʊbəlɪ] *adv* **-1.** [overall] en términos globales. **-2.** [worldwide] mundialmente.

global warming [-'wɔːmɪŋ] *n* calentamiento *m* mundial, cambio *m* climático.

globe [gləʊb] *n* **-1.** [gen] globo *m*. **-2.** [spherical map] globo *m* (terráqueo).

globetrotter ['gləʊb,trɒtə^r] *n* *inf* trotamundos *m* y *f inv*.

globule ['glɒbjuːl] *n* glóbulo *m*.

gloom [gluːm] *n* (*U*) **-1.** [darkness] penumbra *f*. **-2.** [unhappiness] pesimismo *m*, melancolía *f*.

gloomy ['gluːmɪ] (*compar* -ier, *superl* -iest) *adj* **-1.** [dark, cloudy] oscuro(ra). **-2.** [unhappy] triste, melancólico(ca). **-3.** [without hope - report, forecast] pesimista; [- situation, prospects] desalentador(ra).

glorification [,glɔːrɪfɪ'keɪʃn] *n* glorificación *f*.

glorified ['glɔːrɪfaɪd] *adj* *pej* [jumped-up] venido(da) a más.

glorify ['glɔːrɪfaɪ] (*pt* & *pp* -ied) *vt* [overpraise] ensalzar.

glorious ['glɔːrɪəs] *adj* magnífico(ca), espléndido(da).

glory ['glɔːrɪ] (*pl* -ies) *n* **-1.** [gen] gloria *f*. **-2.** [beauty, splendour] esplendor *m*.
◆ **glories** *npl* [triumphs] éxitos *mpl*, triunfos *mpl*.
◆ **glory in** *vt fus* [relish] disfrutar de, regocijarse con.

Glos (*abbr of* **Gloucestershire**) *condado inglés*.

gloss [glɒs] *n* **-1.** [shine] lustre *m*, brillo *m*. **-2.** **~ (paint)** pintura *f* esmalte.
◆ **gloss over** *vt fus* tocar muy por encima.

glossary ['glɒsərɪ] (*pl* -ies) *n* glosario *m*.

glossy ['glɒsɪ] (*compar* **-ier**, *superl* **-iest**) *adj*
-1. [smooth, shiny] brillante, lustroso(sa). **-2.**
[on shiny paper] de papel satinado.

glossy magazine *n* revista *f* lujosa a todo
color.

glove [glʌv] *n* guante *m*.

glove compartment *n* guantera *f*.

glove puppet *n Br* guiñol *m* (*marioneta*).

glow [gləu] ◇ *n* **-1.** [light] brillo *m*, fulgor
m. **-2.** [flush] rubor *m*. **-3.** [feeling] calor *m*,
ardor *m*. ◇ *vi* **-1.** [gen] brillar. **-2.** [flush]: **to
~ (with)** [embarrassment] sonrojarse (de);
[happiness, pleasure etc] estar rebosante (de).

glower ['glauər] *vi*: **to ~ (at sthg/sb)** mirar
con furia (algo/a alguien).

glowing ['gləuɪŋ] *adj* [very favourable] entusiasta.

glow-worm *n* luciérnaga *f*.

glucose ['glu:kəus] *n* glucosa *f*.

glue [glu:] (*cont* **glueing** OR **gluing**) ◇ *n*
[paste] pegamento *m*; [for glueing wood, metal
etc] cola *f*. ◇ *vt* [paste] pegar (con pegamento); [wood, metal etc] encolar; **to be ~d to**
sthg [absorbed by] estar pegado a algo.

glue-sniffing [-,snɪfɪŋ] *n* inhalación *f* de
pegamento.

glum [glʌm] (*compar* **-mer**, *superl* **-mest**) *adj*
[unhappy] sombrío(a).

glut [glʌt] *n* exceso *m*, superabundancia *f*.

gluten ['glu:tən] *n* gluten *m*.

glutinous ['glu:tɪnəs] *adj* pegajoso(sa), glu-
tinoso(sa).

glutton ['glʌtn] *n* [greedy person] glotón *m*,
-ona *f*; **to be a ~ for punishment** ser un
masoquista.

gluttony ['glʌtənɪ] *n* glotonería *f*, gula *f*.

glycerin ['glɪsərɪn], **glycerine** ['glɪsəri:n] *n*
glicerina *f*.

gm (*abbr of* **gram**) gr.

GMAT (*abbr of* **Graduate Management Admissions Test**) *n examen de admisión al segundo ciclo de enseñanza superior en Estados
Unidos.*

GMB *n importante sindicato de obreros británicos.*

GMT (*abbr of* **Greenwich Mean Time**) *hora
GMT del meridiano de Greenwich.*

gnarled [nɑ:ld] *adj* nudoso(sa).

gnash [næʃ] *vt*: **to ~ one's teeth** hacer rechinar los dientes.

gnat [næt] *n* mosquito *m*.

gnaw [nɔ:] *vt* **-1.** [chew] roer; **to ~ (away)
at sb** corroer a alguien.

gnome [nəum] *n* gnomo *m*.

GNP (*abbr of* **gross national product**) *n*
PNB *m*.

gnu [nu:] (*pl inv* OR **-s**) *n* ñu *m*.

go [gəu] (*pt* **went**, *pp* **gone**, *pl* **goes**) ◇ *vi*
-1. [move, travel, attend] ir; **where are you
~ing?** ¿dónde vas?; **he's gone to Portugal**
se ha ido a Portugal; **we went by bus/train**
fuimos en autobús/tren; **to ~ and do sthg**
ir a hacer algo; **where does this path ~?** ¿a
dónde lleva este camino?; **to ~ swim-
ming/shopping** ir a nadar/de compras; **to ~
for a walk/run** ir a dar un paseo/a correr;
to ~ to church/school ir a misa/la escuela;
to ~ to work ir a trabajar; **where do we ~
from here?** ¿y ahora qué? **-2.** [depart - per-
son] irse, marcharse; [- bus] irse, salir; **I
must ~, I have to ~** tengo que irme; **what
time does the bus ~?** ¿a qué hora sale OR
se va el autobús?; **it's time we went** es
hora de irse OR marcharse; **let's ~!** ¡vámonos! **-3.** [pass - time] pasar; **the time went
slowly/quickly** el tiempo pasaba lenta-
mente/rápido. **-4.** [progress] ir; **to ~ well/
badly** ir bien/mal; **how's it ~ing?** *inf* [how
are you?] ¿qué tal? **-5.** [belong, fit] ir; **the
plates ~ in the cupboard** los platos van en
el armario; **it won't ~ into the suitcase** no
cabe en la maleta. **-6.** [become] ponerse; **to
~ grey** ponerse gris; **to ~ mad** volverse
loco; **to ~ blind** quedarse ciego. **-7.** [be or
remain in a particular state]: **to ~ naked** andar
desnudo; **to ~ hungry** pasar hambre; **we
went in fear of our lives** temíamos por
nuestras vidas; **to ~ unpunished** salir impune. **-8.** [indicating intention, certainty, ex-
pectation]: **to be ~ing to do sthg** ir a hacer
algo; **what are you ~ing to do now?** ¿qué
vas a hacer ahora?; **he said he was ~ing to
be late** dijo que llegaría tarde; **it's ~ing to
rain/snow** va a llover/nevar; **I feel like I'm
~ing to be sick** me parece que voy a devolver; **she's ~ing to have a baby** va a tener un niño. **-9.** [match, be compatible]: **to ~
(with)** ir bien (con); **this blouse goes well
with the skirt** esta blusa va muy bien OR
hace juego con la falda; **those colours
don't really ~** la verdad es que esos colores no combinan bien. **-10.** [function, work]
funcionar; **is the tape recorder still ~ing?**
[still in working order] ¿funciona todavía el
casete?; [still on] ¿está todavía encendido el
casete? **-11.** [bell, alarm] sonar. **-12.** [when
referring to saying, story or song] decir; **as the
saying goes** como dice el refrán; **how does
that song ~?** ¿cómo es OR dice esa canción? **-13.** [stop working] estropearse; **the
fuse must have gone** han debido de saltar
los plomos. **-14.** [deteriorate]: **her sight/
hearing is ~ing** está perdiendo la vista/el
oído. **-15.** [be spent]: **to ~ on** ir a parar a,
gastarse en; **all my money goes on food**

and **rent** todo el dinero se me va en comida y alquiler. **-16.** [be given]: **the prize/contract went to B. Jones** el premio/contrato le fue concedido a B. Jones. **-17.** [be disposed of]: **he'll have to ~** habrá que despedirle; **everything must ~!** ¡gran liquidación! **-18.** *inf* [with negative - in giving advice]: **now, don't ~ catching cold y** cuidado no cojas frío ¿eh? **-19.** *inf* [expressing irritation, surprise]: **now what's he gone and done?** ¿qué leches ha hecho ahora?; **she's gone and bought a new car!** ¡ha ido y se ha comprado un coche nuevo!; **you've gone and done it now!** ¡ya la has liado! **-20.** [in division]: **three into two won't ~** dos entre tres no cabe. **-21.** *phr:* **it just goes to show (that) ...** eso demuestra OR prueba que ....
◇ *vt* [make noise of] hacer; **the dog went "woof"** el perro hizo "¡guau!".
◇ *n* **-1.** [turn] turno *m*; **it's my ~** me toca a mí. **-2.** *inf* [attempt]: **to have a ~ at sthg** intentar OR probar algo; **have a ~!** ¡prueba!, ¡inténtalo! **-3.** *inf* [success]: **to make a ~ of sthg** tener éxito con OR en algo. **-4.** *phr:* **to have a ~ at sb** *inf* echar una bronca a alguien; **to be on the ~** *inf* no parar, estar muy liado.

◆ **to go** *adv* **-1.** [remaining]: **there are only three days to ~** sólo quedan tres días. **-2.** [to take away] para llevar.

◆ **go about** ◇ *vt fus* **-1.** [perform] hacer, realizar; **to ~ about one's business** ocuparse uno de sus asuntos. **-2.** [tackle]: **to ~ about doing sthg** apañárselas para hacer algo; **how do you intend** ◇ **ing about it?** ¿cómo piensas hacerlo? ◇ *vi* = **go around**.

◆ **go after** *vt fus* ir a por OR detrás de.

◆ **go against** *vt fus* **-1.** [conflict with, be unfavourable to] ir en contra de. **-2.** [act contrary to] actuar en contra de.

◆ **go ahead** *vi* **-1.** [begin]: **to ~ ahead (with sthg)** seguir adelante (con algo); **~ ahead!** ¡adelante! **-2.** [take place] celebrarse.

◆ **go along** *vi* [proceed]: **as you ~ along** a medida que lo vayas haciendo; **he made it up as he went along** se lo inventaba sobre la marcha.

◆ **go along with** *vt fus* estar de acuerdo con; **he agreed to ~ along with our ideas** aceptó nuestras ideas sin demasiado entusiasmo.

◆ **go around** *vi* **-1.** *inf* [behave in a certain way]: **to ~ around doing sthg** ir por ahí haciendo algo. **-2.** [associate]: **to ~ around with sb** juntarse con alguien. **-3.** [joke, illness, story] correr (por ahí); **there's a rumour ~ing around about her** corren rumores acerca de ella.

◆ **go back on** *vt fus* [promise] faltar a.

◆ **go back to** *vt fus* **-1.** [return to activity] continuar OR seguir con; **to ~ back to sleep** volver a dormir. **-2.** [return to previous topic] volver a. **-3.** [date from] datar de, remontarse a.

◆ **go before** *vi* [precede] preceder; **we wanted to forget what had gone before** queríamos olvidar lo ocurrido.

◆ **go by** ◇ *vi* [time] pasar. ◇ *vt fus* **-1.** [be guided by] guiarse por. **-2.** [judge from]: **~ing by her voice, I'd say she was French** a juzgar por su voz yo diría que es francesa.

◆ **go down** ◇ *vi* **-1.** [get lower - prices etc] bajar. **-2.** [be accepted]: **to ~ down well/badly** tener una buena/mala acogida. **-3.** [sun] ponerse. **-4.** [tyre, balloon] deshincharse. ◇ *vt fus* bajar.

◆ **go down with** *vt fus inf* [illness] coger, pillar, agarrar *Amer*.

◆ **go for** *vt fus* **-1.** [choose] decidirse por, escoger. **-2.** [be attracted to]: **I don't really ~ for men like him** no me gustan mucho los hombres como él. **-3.** [attack] lanzarse sobre, atacar. **-4.** [try to obtain - record, job] ir a por. **-5.** [be valid] valer para; **does that ~ for me too?** ¿eso va por mí también?

◆ **go in** *vi* entrar.

◆ **go in for** *vt fus* **-1.** [competition, exam] presentarse a. **-2.** [take up as a profession] dedicarse a. **-3.** *inf* [enjoy]: **he goes in for sports in a big way** hace un montón de deporte; **I don't really ~ in for classical music** no me va la música clásica.

◆ **go into** *vt fus* **-1.** [discuss, describe in detail] entrar en; **to ~ into details** entrar en detalles. **-2.** [investigate] investigar. **-3.** [take up as a profession] dedicarse a. **-4.** [be put into - subj: effort, money] invertirse; [- subj: work] emplearse; **a lot of hard work went into that book** se dedicó mucho trabajo a ese libro. **-5.** [begin]: **to ~ into a rage** ponerse frenético; **to ~ into a dive** empezar a caer en picado.

◆ **go off** ◇ *vi* **-1.** [explode - bomb] estallar; [- gun] dispararse. **-2.** [alarm] saltar, sonar. **-3.** [go bad - food] echarse a perder, estropearse; [- milk] cortarse. **-4.** [lights, heating] apagarse. **-5.** [happen]: **to ~ off (well/badly)** salir (bien/mal). ◇ *vt fus inf* [lose interest in] perder el gusto a OR el interés en.

◆ **go off with** *vt fus inf:* **he went off with his best friend's wife** se largó con la mujer de su mejor amigo.

◆ **go on** ◇ *vi* **-1.** [take place] pasar, ocurrir. **-2.** [continue]: **to ~ on (doing sthg)** seguir (haciendo algo); **I can't ~ on!** ¡no puedo más!; **shall I tell you? - ~ on** ¿te lo cuento? - vale. **-3.** [proceed to further activity]: **to ~ on to sthg/to do sthg** pasar a algo/a hacer algo. **-4.** [proceed to another place]: **we went**

on to a nightclub afterwards después nos fuimos a una discoteca. **-5.** [pass - time] pasar. **-6.** [go in advance]: **you ~ on, I'll wait here** tú continúa, yo te espero aquí. **-7.** [heating etc] encenderse. **-8.** [talk for too long]: **to ~ on (about)** no parar de hablar (de); **don't ~ on about it** déjalo ya, no sigas con eso.
◇ *vt fus* [be guided by] guiarse por.
◇ *excl* ¡venga!, ¡vamos!; **~ on, treat yourself** ¡venga, hombre! ¡date el gusto!
◆ **go on at** *vt fus* [nag] dar la lata a.
◆ **go out** ◇ *vi* **-1.** [leave house] salir; **to ~ out for a meal** cenar fuera. **-2.** [as friends or lovers]: **to ~ out (with sb)** salir (con alguien), pololear (con alguien) *Amer.* **-3.** [light, fire, cigarette] apagarse. **-4.** [stop being fashionable] pasarse de moda.
◆ **go over** *vt fus* **-1.** [examine] repasar. **-2.** [repeat] repetir.
◆ **go over to** *vt fus* **-1.** [change to] cambiar OR pasar a. **-2.** [change sides to] pasarse a; **to ~ over to the other side** pasarse al otro bando. **-3.** RADIO & TV conectar con.
◆ **go round** *vi* **-1.** [be enough for everyone]: **there's just enough to ~ round** hay lo justo para que alcance para todos. **-2.** [revolve] girar, dar vueltas; *see also* **go around.**
◆ **go through** ◇ *vt fus* **-1.** [experience] pasar por, experimentar. **-2.** [spend] gastarse. **-3.** [study, search through] registrar; **she went through his pockets** le miró en los bolsillos. **-4.** [read] examinar leyendo; [say out loud] enumerar, decir en alto; **I'll ~ through it again** lo voy a repetir. ◇ *vi* [bill, divorce etc] aprobarse.
◆ **go through with** *vt fus* llevar a cabo.
◆ **go towards** *vt fus* contribuir a.
◆ **go under** *vi lit & fig* hundirse.
◆ **go up** ◇ *vi* **-1.** [rise - prices, temperature, balloon] subir. **-2.** [be built] levantarse, construirse. **-3.** [explode] explotar, saltar por los aires. **-4.** [burst into flames]: **to ~ up (in flames)** ser pasto de las llamas. **-5.** [be uttered]: **a shout went up from amongst the crowd** unos gritos surgieron de entre la multitud. ◇ *vt fus* subir; **we went up the Eiffel Tower** subimos a la torre Eiffel.
◆ **go with** *vt fus* [be included with] ir con.
◆ **go without** ◇ *vt fus* prescindir de. ◇ *vi* apañárselas.

goad [gəʊd] *vt* [provoke] aguijonear, incitar; **to ~ sb into doing sthg** incitar a alguien a hacer algo.

go-ahead ◇ *adj* [dynamic] emprendedor(ra), dinámico(ca). ◇ *n* (U) [permission] luz *f* verde; **to give sb the ~ (for)** darle a alguien luz verde (para).

goal [gəʊl] *n* **-1.** SPORT [area between goalposts] portería *f*, meta *f*, arco *m Amer*; [point scored] gol *m*; **to score a ~** marcar un gol. **-2.** [aim] objetivo *m*, meta *f*.

goalie ['gəʊlɪ] *n inf* portero *m*, -ra *f*.

goalkeeper ['gəʊl,kiːpəʳ] *n* portero *m*, -ra *f*, guardameta *m y f*, arquero *m*, -ra *f Amer.*

goalless ['gəʊllɪs] *adj*: **~ draw** empate *m* a cero.

goalmouth ['gəʊlmaʊθ, *pl* -maʊðz] *n* portería *f*, meta *f*.

goalpost ['gəʊlpəʊst] *n* poste *m* (de la portería).

goat [gəʊt] *n* [animal] cabra *f*; **to act the ~** *Br* hacer el ganso OR oso.

gob [gɒb] (*pt & pp* **-bed**, *cont* **-bing**) *v inf* ◇ *n Br* [mouth] pico *m*. ◇ *vi* [spit] escupir.

gobble ['gɒbl] *vt* [food] engullir, tragar.
◆ **gobble down, gobble up** *vt sep* engullir, tragar.

gobbledygook ['gɒbldɪguːk] *n* (U) **-1.** [incomprehensible language] jerga *f* incomprensible, jerigonza *f*. **-2.** *inf* [nonsense] tonterías *fpl*.

go-between *n* intermediario *m*, -ria *f*.

Gobi ['gəʊbɪ] *n*: **the ~ Desert** el desierto de Gobi.

goblet ['gɒblɪt] *n* copa *f*.

goblin ['gɒblɪn] *n* duende *m*.

gobsmacked ['gɒbsmækt] *adj Br inf* alucinado(da), flipado(da).

go-cart = **go-kart.**

god [gɒd] *n* dios *m*.
◆ **God** ◇ *n* Dios *m*; **God knows** sabe Dios; **for God's sake** ¡por el amor de Dios!; **thank God** ¡gracias a Dios! ◇ *excl*: **(my) God!** ¡Dios (mío)!
◆ **gods** *npl Br inf*: **the ~s** THEATRE el gallinero.

godchild ['gɒdtʃaɪld] (*pl* **-children** [-,tʃɪldrən]) *n* ahijado *m*, -da *f*.

goddam(n) ['gɒdæm] ◇ *adj* maldito(ta). ◇ *excl* ¡maldita sea!

goddaughter ['gɒd,dɔːtəʳ] *n* ahijada *f*.

goddess ['gɒdɪs] *n* diosa *f*.

godfather ['gɒd,fɑːðəʳ] *n* padrino *m*.

godforsaken ['gɒdfə,seɪkn] *adj* dejado(da) de la mano de Dios.

godmother ['gɒd,mʌðəʳ] *n* madrina *f*.

godparents ['gɒd,peərənts] *npl* padrinos *mpl*.

godsend ['gɒdsend] *n*: **to be a ~** venir como agua de mayo.

godson ['gɒdsʌn] *n* ahijado *m*.

goes [gəʊz] → **go.**

gofer ['gəʊfəʳ] *n Am inf* recadero *m*, -ra *f*.

go-getter [-'getər] *n* persona *f* emprendedora y ambiciosa.

goggle ['gɒgl] *vi*: **to ~ (at sthg/sb)** mirar con ojos desorbitados (algo/a alguien).

◆ **goggles** *npl* [for swimming] gafas *fpl* submarinas; [for skiing] gafas de esquí; [for welding] gafas de protección.

go-go dancer *n* (chica *f*) gogó *f*.

going ['gəʊɪŋ] ◇ *adj* **-1.** *Br* [available] disponible; **is there any beer ~?** ¿no habrá una cervecita para mí?; **you have a lot ~ for you** *inf* tienes mucho futuro. **-2.** [rate] actual. ◇ *n* (*U*) **-1.** [rate of advance] marcha *f*; **that's** OR **that was good ~** ¡qué rápido! **-2.** [conditions] condiciones *fpl*; **to be rough** OR **heavy ~** hacerse pesado; **to be easy ~** ser fácil.

going concern *n* empresa *f* rentable y en marcha.

goings-on *npl inf* tejemanejes *mpl*.

go-kart [-kɑːt] *n* kart *m*.

Golan Heights ['gəʊ,læn-] *npl*: **the ~** los altos del Golán.

gold [gəʊld] ◇ *adj* [gold-coloured] dorado(da). ◇ *n* **-1.** [gen] oro *m*; **to be as good as ~** ser más bueno que el pan. **-2.** [medal] medalla *f* de oro. ◇ *comp* [made of gold] de oro.

golden ['gəʊldən] *adj* **-1.** [made of gold] de oro. **-2.** [gold-coloured] dorado(da).

golden age *n* edad *f* de oro.

◆ **Golden Age** *n* [in Spanish history] Siglo *m* de Oro.

golden eagle *n* águila *f* real.

golden handshake *n* gratificación cuantiosa al jubilarse.

golden opportunity *n* ocasión *f* de oro.

golden retriever *n* tipo de perdiguero.

golden rule *n* regla *f* de oro.

golden wedding *n* bodas *fpl* de oro.

goldfish ['gəʊldfɪʃ] (*pl inv*) *n* pez *m* de colores.

goldfish bowl *n* pecera *f*.

gold leaf *n* pan *m* de oro.

gold medal *n* medalla *f* de oro.

goldmine ['gəʊldmaɪn] *n lit* & *fig* mina *f* de oro.

gold-plated [-'pleɪtɪd] *adj* chapado(da) en oro.

goldsmith ['gəʊldsmɪθ] *n* orfebre *m* y *f*.

gold standard *n*: **the ~** el patrón oro.

golf [gɒlf] *n* golf *m*.

golf ball *n* **-1.** [for golf] pelota *f* de golf. **-2.** [for typewriter] esfera *f* impresora.

golf club *n* **-1.** [society, place] club *m* de golf. **-2.** [stick] palo *m* de golf.

golf course *n* campo *m* de golf.

golfer ['gɒlfər] *n* golfista *m* y *f*.

golly ['gɒlɪ] *excl inf dated* ¡caray!, ¡cáspita!

gondola ['gɒndələ] *n* [boat] góndola *f*.

gondolier [,gɒndə'lɪər] *n* gondolero *m*, -ra *f*.

gone [gɒn] ◇ *pp* → **go**. ◇ *adj*: **those days are ~** esos tiempos ya pasaron. ◇ *prep* [past]: **it was ~ six already** ya eran las seis pasadas.

gong [gɒŋ] *n* gong *m*.

gonna ['gɒnə] *inf* = **going to**.

gonorrh(o)ea [,gɒnə'rɪə] *n* gonorrea *f*.

goo [guː] *n inf* pegajosidad *f*.

good [gʊd] (*compar* **better**, *superl* **best**) ◇ *adj* **-1.** [gen] bueno(na); **it's ~ to see you** me alegro de verte; **she's ~ at it** se le da bien; **to be ~ with** saber manejárselas con; **she's ~ with her hands** es muy mañosa; **it's ~ for you** es bueno, es beneficioso; **to feel ~** sentirse fenomenal; **that feels ~!** ¡qué gusto!; **it's ~ that ...** está bien que ...; **to look ~** [attractive] estar muy guapo; [appetizing, promising] tener buena pinta; **it looks ~** atractivo *m*; **be ~!** ¡sé bueno!, ¡pórtate bien!; **~!** ¡muy bien!, ¡estupendo! **-2.** [kind] amable; **to be ~ to sb** ser amable con alguien; **to be ~ enough to do sthg** ser tan amable de hacer algo. **-3.** *phr*: **it's a ~ job** OR **thing (that) ...** menos mal que ...; **~ for you!** ¡muy bien!, ¡bien hecho!; **to give as ~ as one gets** devolver todos los golpes; **to make sthg ~** reparar OR enmendar algo. ◇ *n* **-1.** (*U*) [benefit] bien *m*; **for the ~ of** por el bien de; **for your own ~** por tu propio bien; **it will do him ~** le hará bien. **-2.** [use] beneficio *m*, provecho *m*; **what's the ~ of ...?** ¿de OR para qué sirve ...?; **it's no ~** no sirve para nada; **will this be any ~?** ¿servirá esto para algo? **-3.** [morally correct behaviour] el bien; **to be up to no ~** estar tramando algo malo.

◆ **goods** *npl* **-1.** [COM - for sale] productos *mpl*, artículos *mpl*; [- when transported] mercancías *fpl*; **to come up with** OR **deliver the ~s** *Br inf* cumplir (lo prometido). **-2.** ECON bienes *mpl*.

◆ **as good as** *adv* casi, prácticamente; **it's as ~ as new** está como nuevo.

◆ **for good** *adv* [forever] para siempre.

◆ **good afternoon** *excl* ¡buenas tardes!

◆ **good day** *excl dated* or *Austr* ¡buenas!, ¡buenos días!

◆ **good evening** *excl* [in the evening] ¡buenas tardes!; [at night] ¡buenas noches!

◆ **good morning** *excl* ¡buenos días!, ¡buen día! *Amer*.

◆ **good night** *excl* ¡buenas noches!

goodbye [ˌgʊdˈbaɪ] ◇ *excl* ¡adiós! ◇ *n* adiós *m*.

good-for-nothing ◇ *adj* inútil. ◇ *n* inútil *m y f*.

Good Friday *n* Viernes *m* Santo.

good-humoured [-ˈhjuːməd] *adj* jovial.

good-looking [-ˈlʊkɪŋ] *adj* [person] guapo(pa).

good-natured [-ˈneɪtʃəd] *adj* bondadoso(sa).

goodness [ˈgʊdnɪs] ◇ *n* (U) **-1.** [kindness] bondad *f*. **-2.** [nutritive quality] alimento *m*. ◇ *excl*: **(my) ~!** ¡Dios mío!; **for ~'s sake!** ¡por Dios!; **thank ~** ¡gracias a Dios!

goods train *n Br* mercancías *m inv*.

good-tempered [-ˈtempəd] *adj* afable.

good turn *n*: **to do sb a ~** hacer un favor a alguien.

goodwill [ˌgʊdˈwɪl] *n* **-1.** [kind feelings] buena voluntad *f*. **-2.** COMM fondo *m* de comercio.

goody [ˈgʊdɪ] (*pl* **-ies**) *inf* ◇ *n* bueno *m*, -na *f*. ◇ *excl* ¡qué chupi!

◆ **goodies** *npl inf* **-1.** [delicious food] golosinas *fpl*. **-2.** [desirable objects] cosas *fpl* apetecibles.

gooey [ˈguːɪ] (*compar* **gooier**, *superl* **gooiest**) *adj inf* [sticky] pegajoso(sa); [cake, dessert] empalagoso(sa).

goof [guːf] *Am inf* ◇ *n* [mistake] metedura *f* de pata. ◇ *vi* meter la pata.

◆ **goof off** *vi Am inf* escaquearse.

goofy [ˈguːfɪ] (*compar* **-ier**, *superl* **-iest**) *adj inf* [silly] bobo(ba), tonto(ta).

goose [guːs] (*pl* **geese**) *n* [bird] ganso *m*, oca *f*.

gooseberry [ˈgʊzbərɪ] (*pl* **-ies**) *n* **-1.** [fruit] grosella *f* silvestre, uva *f* espina. **-2.** *inf* [third person]: **to play ~** hacer de carabina.

gooseflesh [ˈguːsfleʃ] *n*, **goose pimples** *Br*, **goosebumps** *Am* [ˈguːsbʌmps] *npl* carne *f* de gallina.

goosestep [ˈguːsˌstep] (*pt & pp* **-ped**, *cont* **-ping**) ◇ *n* paso *m* de ganso. ◇ *vi* marchar a paso de ganso.

GOP (*abbr of* **Grand Old Party**) *n Am partido republicano estadounidense*.

gopher [ˈgəʊfəʳ] *n* taltuza *f*.

gore [gɔːʳ] ◇ *n literary* [blood] sangre *f* (derramada). ◇ *vt* dar una cornada a, cornear.

gorge [gɔːdʒ] ◇ *n* cañón *m*, garganta *f*. ◇ *vt*: **to ~ o.s. on** OR **with** atracarse de. ◇ *vi* hartarse, saciarse.

gorgeous [ˈgɔːdʒəs] *adj* **-1.** [lovely] magnífico(ca), esplénd(ida). **-2.** *inf* [good-looking]: **to be ~** estar como un tren.

gorilla [gəˈrɪlə] *n* gorila *m y f*.

gormless [ˈgɔːmlɪs] *adj Br inf* memo(ma), lerdo(da).

gorse [gɔːs] *n* (U) tojo *m*.

gory [ˈgɔːrɪ] (*compar* **-ier**, *superl* **-iest**) *adj* [death, scene] sangriento(ta); [details, film] escabroso(sa).

gosh [gɒʃ] *excl inf* ¡joroba!, ¡caray!

go-slow *n Br* huelga *f* de celo.

gospel [ˈgɒspl] ◇ *n* **-1.** [doctrine] evangelio *m*. **-2.** **~ (truth)** la pura verdad. ◇ *comp* espiritual negro, gospel (*inv*).

◆ **Gospel** *n* [in Bible] Evangelio *m*.

gossamer [ˈgɒsəməʳ] *n* (U) **-1.** [spider's thread] telaraña *f*. **-2.** [material] gasa *f*.

gossip [ˈgɒsɪp] ◇ *n* **-1.** [conversation] cotilleo *m*. **-2.** [person] cotilla *m y f*, chismoso *m*, -sa *f*. ◇ *vi* cotillear.

gossip column *n* ecos *mpl* de sociedad.

got [gɒt] *pt & pp* → **get**.

Gothic [ˈgɒθɪk] *adj* gótico(ca).

gotta [ˈgɒtə] *inf* = **got to**.

gotten [ˈgɒtn] *pp Am* → **get**.

gouge [gaʊdʒ]

◆ **gouge out** *vt sep* [hole] excavar; [eyes] arrancar.

goulash [ˈguːlæʃ] *n* gulasch *m*.

gourd [gʊəd] *n* calabaza *f*.

gourmet [ˈgʊəmeɪ] ◇ *n* gastrónomo *m*, -ma *f*, gourmet *m y f*. ◇ *comp* para/de gastrónomos.

gout [gaʊt] *n* gota *f*.

govern [ˈgʌvən] ◇ *vt* **-1.** POL gobernar. **-2.** [control] dictar, guiar. ◇ *vi* POL gobernar.

governable [ˈgʌvnəbl] *adj* gobernable.

governess [ˈgʌvənɪs] *n* institutriz *f*.

governing [ˈgʌvənɪŋ] *adj* gobernante.

governing body *n* organismo *m* rector.

government [ˈgʌvnmənt] ◇ *n* gobierno *m*. ◇ *comp* gubernamental.

governmental [ˌgʌvnˈmentl] *adj* gubernamental.

government stock *n* (U) bonos *mpl* del estado.

governor [ˈgʌvənəʳ] *n* **-1.** POL gobernador *m*, -ra *f*. **-2.** [of school, bank, prison] director *m*, -ra *f*.

governor-general (*pl* **governor-generals** OR **governors-general**) *n* gobernador *m*, -ra *f* general.

govt (*abbr of* **government**) gob.

gown [gaʊn] *n* **-1.** [dress] vestido *m*, traje *m*. **-2.** [of judge etc] toga *f*.

GP (*abbr of* **general practitioner**) *n médico de cabecera*.

GPMU (*abbr of* **Graphical, Paper and**

Media Union) *n sindicato británico de trabajadores de la industria del libro.*

GPO (*abbr of* **General Post Office**) *n* **-1.** [in UK] *antiguo servicio de correos británico.* **-2.** [in US] *servicio de correos estadounidense.*

gr. *abbr of* **gross.**

grab [græb] (*pt & pp* **-bed,** *cont* **-bing**) ◇ *vt* **-1.** [snatch away] arrebatar; [grip] agarrar, asir. **-2.** *inf* [sandwich, lunch] pillar, coger. **-3.** *inf* [appeal to] seducir. ◇ *vi*: **to ~ at sthg** intentar agarrar algo. ◇ *n*: **to make a ~ at** OR **for sthg** intentar arrebatar/agarrar algo.

grace [greɪs] ◇ *n* **-1.** (U) [elegance] elegancia *f*, gracia *f*. **-2.** [graciousness]: **to do sthg with good ~** hacer algo de buena gana; **to have the ~ to do sthg** tener la delicadeza de hacer algo. **-3.** (U) [delay] prórroga *f*. **-4.** [prayer] bendición *f* de la mesa; **to say ~** bendecir la mesa. ◇ *vt fml* **-1.** [honour] honrar. **-2.** [decorate] adornar, embellecer.

graceful ['greɪsfʊl] *adj* **-1.** [beautiful] elegante. **-2.** [gracious] cortés.

graceless ['greɪslɪs] *adj* **-1.** [ugly] desagradable, feo(a). **-2.** [ill-mannered] descortés.

gracious ['greɪʃəs] ◇ *adj* **-1.** [polite] cortés. **-2.** [elegant] elegante. ◇ *excl*: **(good) ~!** ¡Dios mío!

graciously ['greɪʃəslɪ] *adv* **-1.** [politely] cortésmente. **-2.** [elegantly] elegantemente.

gradation [grə'deɪʃn] *n* gradación *f*.

grade [greɪd] ◇ *n* **-1.** [level, quality] clase *f*, calidad *f*; **to make the ~** triunfar, tener éxito. **-2.** *Am* [class] curso *m*, clase *f*. **-3.** [mark] nota *f*. ◇ *vt* **-1.** [classify] clasificar. **-2.** [mark, assess] calificar.

grade crossing *n Am* paso *m* a nivel.

grade school *n Am* escuela *f* primaria.

gradient ['greɪdjənt] *n* pendiente *f*.

gradual ['grædʒʊəl] *adj* gradual.

gradually ['grædʒʊəlɪ] *adv* gradualmente.

graduate [*n* 'grædʒʊət, *vb* 'grædʒʊeɪt] ◇ *n* **-1.** [person with a degree] licenciado *m*, -da *f*, egresado *m*, -da *f Amer.* **-2.** *Am* [of high school] ≃ bachiller *m* y *f*. ◇ *comp Am* [postgraduate] posgraduado(da). ◇ *vi* **-1.** [with a degree]: **to ~ (from)** licenciarse (por), egresar (de) *Amer.* **-2.** *Am* [from high school]: **to ~ (from)** ≃ obtener el título de bachiller (en). **-3.** [progress]: **to ~ from sthg (to)** pasar de algo (a).

graduated ['grædʒʊeɪtɪd] *adj* graduado(da).

graduate school *n Am* escuela *f* de posgraduados.

graduation [ˌgrædʒʊ'eɪʃn] *n* graduación *f*, egreso *m Amer.*

graffiti [grə'fiːtɪ] *n* (U) pintadas *fpl*.

graft [grɑːft] ◇ *n* **-1.** BOT & MED injerto *m*. **-2.** *Br inf* [hard work] curro *m* muy duro. **-3.** *Am inf* [corruption] chanchullos *mpl*, corruptela *f*. ◇ *vt* **-1.** BOT & MED: **to ~ sthg (onto sthg)** injertar algo (en algo). **-2.** [idea, system]: **to ~ sthg (onto sthg)** implantar algo (en algo).

grain [greɪn] *n* **-1.** [seed, granule] grano *m*. **-2.** (U) [crop] cereales *mpl*. **-3.** *fig* [small amount] pizca *f*. **-4.** [pattern] veta *f*; **to go against the ~** ir a contrapelo.

gram [græm] *n* gramo *m*.

grammar ['græmər] *n* gramática *f*.

grammar school *n* [in UK] *centro de enseñanza media*; [in US] escuela *f* primaria.

GRAMMAR SCHOOL:

En Gran Bretaña el término 'grammar school' designa colegios privados o con subvención estatal para mayores de 11 años. Estos colegios preparan a los alumnos para la enseñanza superior y son famosos por impartir una educación tradicional y de alta calidad. Para acceder a un 'grammar school' es necesario haber aprobado unas pruebas de acceso o haber obtenido muy buenas notas previamente. Estos colegios acogen a menos del 5% de los alumnos británicos

grammatical [grə'mætɪkl] *adj* **-1.** [of grammar] gramatical. **-2.** [correct] (gramaticalmente) correcto(ta).

gramme [græm] *Br* = **gram.**

gramophone ['græməfəʊn] *dated* ◇ *n* gramófono *m*. ◇ *comp* de gramófono.

gran [græn] *n Br inf* abuelita *f*, yaya *f*.

Granada [grə'nɑːdə] *n* Granada.

granary ['grænərɪ] (*pl* **-ies**) *n* granero *m*.

grand [grænd] ◇ *adj* **-1.** [impressive] grandioso(sa), monumental. **-2.** [ambitious] ambicioso(sa). **-3.** [important] distinguido(da). **-4.** *inf dated* [excellent] fenomenal. ◇ *n inf* [thousand pounds or dollars]: **a ~** mil libras/dólares; **five ~** cinco mil libras/dólares.

Grand Canyon *n*: **the ~** el Gran Cañón.

grandchild ['græntʃaɪld] (*pl* **-children** [-ˌtʃɪldrən]) *n* nieto *m*, -ta *f*.

grand(d)ad ['grændæd] *n inf* abuelito *m*, yayo *m*.

granddaughter ['grænˌdɔːtər] *n* nieta *f*.

grand duke *n* gran duque *m*.

grandeur ['grændʒər] *n* **-1.** [splendour] grandiosidad *f*, magnificencia *f*. **-2.** [status] grandeza *f*.

grandfather ['grændˌfɑːðər] *n* abuelo *m*.

grandfather clock *n* reloj *m* de caja, reloj *m* con carillón.

grandiose ['grændɪəuz] *adj pej* [building, design] fastuoso(sa), ostentoso(sa); [plan] ambicioso(sa).

grand jury *n Am* jurado *m* de acusación.

grandma ['grænmɑː] *n inf* abuelita *f*, yaya *f*, mamá *f* grande *Amer*.

grand master *n* gran maestro *m*.

grandmother ['græn,mʌðə'] *n* abuela *f*.

Grand National *n*: **the ~** *importante carrera anual de caballos que se celebra en Aintree*.

grandpa ['grænpɑː] *n inf* abuelito *m*, yayo *m*, papá *m* grande *Amer*.

grandparents ['græn,peərnts] *npl* abuelos *mpl*.

grand piano *n* piano *m* de cola.

grand prix [,grɒn'priː] (*pl* **grands prix** [,grɒn'priː]) *n* gran premio *m*, grand prix *m*.

grand slam *n* SPORT [in tennis] gran slam *m*; [in rugby] gran chelem *f*.

grandson ['grænsʌn] *n* nieto *m*.

grandstand ['grændstænd] *n* tribuna *f*.

grand total *n* [total number] cantidad *f* total; [total sum, cost] importe *m* total.

granite ['grænɪt] *n* granito *m*.

granny ['grænɪ] (*pl* **-ies**) *n inf* abuelita *f*, yaya *f*.

granny flat *n Br* *alojamiento independiente que forma parte de una vivienda (concebido para un familiar anciano)*.

granola [grə'nəulə] *n Am* muesli *m*.

grant [grɑːnt] ◇ *n* subvención *f*; [for study] beca *f*. ◇ *vt fml* **-1.** [gen] conceder; **to take** sthg/sb for ~ed no apreciar algo/a alguien en lo que vale; **it is taken for ~ed that ...** se da por sentado que .... **-2.** [admit - truth, logic] admitir, aceptar; **I ~ (that) ...** admito que ....

granulated sugar ['grænjuleɪtɪd-] *n* azúcar *m* granulado.

granule ['grænjuːl] *n* gránulo *m*.

grape [greɪp] *n* uva *f*; **a bunch of ~s** un racimo de uvas.

grapefruit ['greɪpfruːt] (*pl inv* OR **-s**) *n* pomelo *m*.

grape picking [-'pɪkɪŋ] *n* (*U*) vendimia *f*.

grapevine ['greɪpvaɪn] *n* **-1.** [plant] vid *f*; [against wall] parra *f*. **-2.** [information channel]: **I heard on the ~ that ...** me ha dicho un pajarito que ....

graph [grɑːf] *n* gráfica *f*.

graphic ['græfɪk] *adj lit* & *fig* gráfico(ca).
◆ **graphics** *npl* [pictures] ilustraciones *fpl*; **computer ~s** gráficos *mpl*.

graphic design *n* diseño *m* gráfico.

graphic designer *n* grafista *m* y *f*, diseñador gráfico *m*, diseñadora gráfica *f*.

graphic equalizer *n* ecualizador *m*.

graphics card *n* COMPUT tarjeta *f* gráfica.

graphite ['græfaɪt] *n* grafito *m*.

graphology [græ'fɒlədʒɪ] *n* grafología *f*.

graph paper *n* (*U*) papel *m* cuadriculado.

grapple ['græpl]
◆ **grapple with** *vt fus* **-1.** [person] forcejear con. **-2.** [problem] esforzarse por resolver.

grappling iron ['græplɪŋ-] *n* garfio *m*.

grasp [grɑːsp] ◇ *n* **-1.** [grip] agarre *m*, asimiento *m*. **-2.** [power to achieve]: **in** OR **within sb's ~** al alcance de alguien. **-3.** [understanding] comprensión *f*; **to have a good ~ of sthg** dominar algo. ◇ *vt* **-1.** [grip, seize] agarrar, asir. **-2.** [understand] comprender. **-3.** [opportunity] aprovechar.

grasping ['grɑːspɪŋ] *adj pej* avaro(ra), codicioso(sa).

grass [grɑːs] ◇ *n* **-1.** [plant] hierba *f*; [lawn] césped *m*; [pasture] pasto *m*; **"keep off the ~"** "prohibido pisar el césped". **-2.** *drugs sl* [marijuana] hierba *f*, maría *f*. ◇ *vi Br crime sl*: **to ~ (on sb)** chivarse (de alguien).

grasshopper ['grɑːs,hɒpə'] *n* saltamontes *m inv*.

grassland ['grɑːslænd] *n* pastos *mpl*, pastizal *m*.

grass roots ◇ *npl* bases *fpl*. ◇ *comp* de base.

grass snake *n* culebra *f*.

grassy ['grɑːsɪ] (*compar* **-ier**, *superl* **-iest**) *adj* cubierto(ta) de hierba.

grate [greɪt] ◇ *n* parrilla *f*, rejilla *f*. ◇ *vt* rallar. ◇ *vi* rechinar, chirriar; **to ~ on sb's nerves** poner a alguien los nervios de punta.

grateful ['greɪtful] *adj* [gen] agradecido(da); [smile, letter] de agradecimiento; **to be ~ to sb (for sthg)** estar agradecido a alguien (por algo); **I'm very ~ to you** te lo agradezco mucho.

gratefully ['greɪtfulɪ] *adv* con agradecimiento.

grater ['greɪtə'] *n* rallador *m*.

gratification [,grætɪfɪ'keɪʃn] *n* satisfacción *f*.

gratify ['grætɪfaɪ] (*pt* & *pp* **-ied**) *vt* **-1.** [please - person]: **to be gratified** estar satisfecho. **-2.** [satisfy - wish] satisfacer.

gratifying ['grætɪfaɪɪŋ] *adj* satisfactorio(ria), gratificante.

grating ['greɪtɪŋ] ◇ *adj* chirriante. ◇ *n* [grille] reja *f*, enrejado *m*.

gratitude ['grætɪtjuːd] *n* (*U*): **~ (to sb for)** agradecimiento *m* OR gratitud *f* (a alguien por).

gratuitous [grə'tjuːɪtəs] *adj fml* gratuito(ta).

gratuity [grə'tjuːɪtɪ] (*pl* **-ies**) *n fml* [tip] propina *f*.

grave[1] [greɪv] ◇ *adj* grave. ◇ *n* sepultura *f*, tumba *f*; **he must be turning in his ~!** ¡si levantara la cabeza!

grave[2] [grɑːv] *adj* LING: **e ~ e** grave.

grave accent *n* acento *m* grave.

gravedigger ['greɪv,dɪgə'] *n* sepulturero *m*, -ra *f*.

gravel ['grævl] ◇ *n* grava *f*, gravilla *f*, pedregullo *m* *Amer*. ◇ *comp* de grava OR gravilla.

gravelled *Br*, **graveled** *Am* ['grævld] *adj* cubierto(ta) de grava OR gravilla.

gravestone ['greɪvstəun] *n* lápida *f* (sepulcral).

graveyard ['greɪvjɑːd] *n* cementerio *m*.

gravitate ['grævɪteɪt] *vi*: **to ~ towards** [be attracted] verse atraído(da) por.

gravity ['grævətɪ] *n* gravedad *f*.

gravy ['greɪvɪ] *n* **-1.** (*U*) [meat juice] salsa *f* OR jugo *m* de carne. **-2.** *Am* *v inf* [easy money] pasta *f* fácil.

gravy boat *n* salsera *f*.

gravy train *n inf*: **the ~** el chollo del siglo.

gray *Am* = **grey**.

graze [greɪz] ◇ *vt* **-1.** [feed on] pacer OR pastar en. **-2.** [cause to feed] apacentar. **-3.** [skin, knee etc] rasguñar. **-4.** [touch lightly] rozar. ◇ *vi* pacer, pastar. ◇ *n* rasguño *m*.

grease [griːs] ◇ *n* grasa *f*. ◇ *vt* engrasar.

grease gun *n* pistola *f* engrasadora.

greasepaint ['griːspeɪnt] *n* maquillaje *m* (de actores).

greaseproof paper ['griːspruːf-] *n* (*U*) *Br* papel *m* de cera (para envolver).

greasy ['griːzɪ] (*compar* **-ier**, *superl* **-iest**) *adj* grasiento(ta); [inherently] graso(sa).

great [greɪt] ◇ *adj* **-1.** [gen] grande; [heat] intenso(sa); **~ big** enorme; **you ~ big coward!** ¡pero qué cobardica eres! **-2.** *inf* [splendid] estupendo(da), fenomenal, chévere *Amer*; **we had a ~ time** lo pasamos en grande; **~!** ¡estupendo! ◇ *n* grande *m y f*.

Great Barrier Reef *n*: **the ~** la Gran Barrera de Coral.

Great Bear *n*: **the ~** la Osa Mayor.

Great Britain *n* Gran Bretaña.

greatcoat ['greɪtkəut] *n* gabán *m*.

Great Dane *n* gran danés *m*.

Greater ['greɪtə'] *adj*: **~ London/Manchester** área metropolitana de Londres/ Manchester.

great-grandchild *n* bisnieto *m*, -ta *f*.

great-grandfather *n* bisabuelo *m*.

great-grandmother *n* bisabuela *f*.

Great Lakes *npl*: **the ~** los grandes Lagos.

greatly ['greɪtlɪ] *adv* enormemente.

greatness ['greɪtnɪs] *n* grandeza *f*.

Great Wall of China *n*: **the ~** la muralla china.

Great War *n*: **the ~** la Gran Guerra, la Primera Guerra Mundial.

Grecian ['griːʃn] *adj* griego(ga).

Greece [griːs] *n* Grecia.

greed [griːd] *n* (*U*): **~ (for)** [food] glotonería *f* (con); [money] codicia *f* (de); [power] ambición *f* (de).

greedily ['griːdɪlɪ] *adv* con avidez.

greedy ['griːdɪ] (*compar* **-ier**, *superl* **-iest**) *adj* **-1.** [for food] glotón(ona). **-2.** [for money, power]: **~ for** codicioso(sa) OR ávido(da) de.

Greek [griːk] ◇ *adj* griego(ga); **the ~ Islands** las islas griegas. ◇ *n* **-1.** [person] griego *m*, -ga *f*. **-2.** [language] griego *m*.

green [griːn] ◇ *adj* **-1.** [gen] verde. **-2.** *inf* [pale] pálido(da). **-3.** *inf* [inexperienced] novato(ta). **-4.** *inf* [jealous]: **~ (with envy)** muerto(ta) de envidia. ◇ *n* **-1.** [colour] verde *m*; **in ~** de verde. **-2.** [in village] terreno *m* comunal; [in golf] green *m*.

◆ **Green** *n* POL verde *m y f*, ecologista *m y f*; **the Greens** los verdes.

◆ **greens** *npl* [vegetables] verduras *fpl*.

greenback ['griːnbæk] *n* *Am inf* billete de banco americano.

green bean *n* judía *f* verde, ejote *m* *Amer*.

green belt *n* *Br* cinturón *m* verde.

Green Beret *n* *Am inf*: **the ~s** el comando (de asalto).

green card *n* **-1.** *Br* [for vehicle] seguro que cubre a conductores en el extranjero. **-2.** *Am* [work permit] permiso *m* de trabajo (*en Estados Unidos*).

Green Cross Code *n* en Gran Bretaña, código de circulación básico para niños.

greenery ['griːnərɪ] *n* follaje *m*, vegetación *f*.

greenfinch ['griːnfɪntʃ] *n* verderón *m*.

green fingers *npl* *Br*: **to have ~** tener dotes para la jardinería.

greenfly ['griːnflaɪ] (*pl inv* OR **-ies**) *n* pulgón *m*.

greengage ['griːngeɪdʒ] *n* ciruela *f* claudia.

greengrocer ['griːn,grəusə'] *n* verdulero *m*, -ra *f*; **~'s (shop)** verdulería *f*.

greenhorn ['griːnhɔːn] *n* *Am* **-1.** [newcomer] recién llegado *m*, recién llegada *f*. **-2.** [novice] novato *m*, -ta *f*.

greenhouse ['griːnhaus, *pl* -hauzɪz] *n* invernadero *m*.

greenhouse effect *n*: the ~ el efecto invernadero.

greenish ['griːnɪʃ] *adj* verdoso(sa).

greenkeeper ['griːnˌkiːpər] *n persona encargada del cuidado de un campo de golf*.

Greenland ['griːnlənd] *n* Groenlandia.

Greenlander ['griːnləndər] *n* groenlandés *m*, -esa *f*.

green light *n fig*: the ~ la luz verde.

green paper *n* POL libro *m* verde.

Green Party *n*: the ~ los verdes, el partido verde.

green salad *n* ensalada *f* verde.

green thumb *n Am*: to have a ~ tener dotes para la jardinería.

greet [griːt] *vt* -1. [say hello to] saludar. -2. [receive] recibir. -3. [subj: sight, smell]: he was ~ed by total chaos se encontró con un auténtico caos.

greeting ['griːtɪŋ] *n* saludo *m*; [welcome] recibimiento *m*.
  ◆ **greetings** *npl*: **Christmas/birthday** ~**s!** ¡feliz navidad/cumpleaños!; ~**s from ...** recuerdos de ....

greetings card *Br*, **greeting card** *Am n* tarjeta *f* de felicitación.

gregarious [grɪ'geərɪəs] *adj* gregario(ria).

gremlin ['gremlɪn] *n inf* duende *m*.

Grenada [grə'neɪdə] *n* Granada.

grenade [grə'neɪd] *n*: **(hand)** ~ granada *f* (de mano).

Grenadian [grə'neɪdjən] ◇ *adj* granadino(na). ◇ *n* granadino *m*, -na *f*.

grenadier [ˌgrenə'dɪər] *n* granadero *m*.

grenadine ['grenədiːn] *n* granadina *f*.

grew [gruː] *pt* → **grow**.

grey *Br*, **gray** *Am* [greɪ] ◇ *adj lit & fig* gris; **to go** ~ [grey-haired] echar canas, encanecer. ◇ *n* gris *m*; **in** ~ de gris.

grey area *n* tema *m* oscuro, área *f* difusa.

grey-haired [-'heəd] *adj* canoso(sa).

greyhound ['greɪhaʊnd] *n* galgo *m*, -ga *f*.

greying *Br*, **graying** *Am* ['greɪɪŋ] *adj* canoso(sa).

grey matter *n* (*U*) -1. MED materia *f* gris. -2. *inf* [brain power] cerebro *m*.

greyscale *Br*, **grayscale** *Am* ['greɪskeɪl] *n* COMPUT escala *f* de grises.

grey squirrel *n* ardilla *f* gris.

grid [grɪd] *n* -1. [grating] reja *f*, enrejado *m*. -2. [system of squares] cuadrícula *f*.

griddle ['grɪdl] *n* plancha *f*.

gridiron ['grɪdˌaɪən] *n* -1. [in cooking] parrilla *f*. -2. *Am* [game] fútbol *m* americano; [field] *campo de fútbol americano*.

gridlock ['grɪdlɒk] *n Am* embotellamiento *m*, atasco *m*.

grief [griːf] *n* (*U*) -1. [sorrow] dolor *m*, pesar *m*. -2. *inf* [trouble] problemas *mpl*. -3. *phr*: **to come to** ~ [person] sufrir un percance; [plans] irse al traste; **good** ~! ¡madre mía!

grief-stricken *adj* desconsolado(da), apesadumbrado(da).

grievance ['griːvns] *n* (motivo *m* de) queja *f*.

grieve [griːv] ◇ *vt*: **it** ~**s me to say it** *fml* me apena decirlo. ◇ *vi*: **to** ~ **(for)** llorar (por).

grieving ['griːvɪŋ] *n* (*U*) aflicción *f*.

grievous ['griːvəs] *adj fml* grave.

grievous bodily harm *n* (*U*) lesiones *fpl* graves.

grievously ['griːvəslɪ] *adv fml* gravemente.

grill [grɪl] ◇ *n* -1. [of cooker] parrilla *f*. -2. [food] parrillada *f*. ◇ *vt* -1. CULIN asar a la parrilla. -2. *inf* [interrogate] someter a un duro interrogatorio.

grille [grɪl] *n* [on radiator, machine] rejilla *f*; [on window, door] reja *f*.

grim [grɪm] (*compar* **-mer**, *superl* **-mest**) *adj* -1. [expression] adusto(ta); [determination] inexorable. -2. [place, facts, prospects] descorazonador(ra), lúgubre.

grimace [grɪ'meɪs] ◇ *n* mueca *f*. ◇ *vi* hacer una mueca.

grime [graɪm] *n* mugre *f*.

grimly ['grɪmlɪ] *adv* -1. [resolutely] inexorablemente. -2. [mirthlessly] lúgubremente.

grimy ['graɪmɪ] (*compar* **-ier**, *superl* **-iest**) *adj* mugriento(ta).

grin [grɪn] (*pt & pp* **-ned**, *cont* **-ning**) ◇ *n* sonrisa *f* (abierta). ◇ *vi*: **to** ~ **(at)** sonreír (a); **to** ~ **and bear it** poner al mal tiempo buena cara.

grind [graɪnd] (*pt & pp* **ground**) ◇ *vt* -1. [crush] moler. -2. [press]: **to** ~ **sthg into sthg** aplastar algo contra algo. ◇ *vi* [scrape] rechinar, chirriar. ◇ *n* -1. [hard, boring work] rutina *f*; **what a** ~! ¡qué lata! -2. *Am inf* [hard worker] currante *m y f*.
  ◆ **grind down** *vt sep* [oppress] oprimir, acogotar.
  ◆ **grind up** *vt sep* pulverizar, hacer polvo.

grinder ['graɪndər] *n* molinillo *m*.

grinding ['graɪndɪŋ] *adj* oprimente, agobiante.

grinning ['grɪnɪŋ] *adj* sonriente.

grip [grɪp] (*pt & pp* **-ped**, *cont* **-ping**) ◇ *n* -1. [grasp, hold]: **to have a** ~ **(on sthg/sb)** tener (algo/a alguien) bien agarrado. -2. [control, domination]: ~ **on** control *m* de, dominio *m* de; **in the** ~ **of sthg** en las garras de algo, dominado por algo; **to get to ~s with** llegar a controlar; **to get a ~ on o.s.** calmarse, controlarse; **to lose one's ~** *fig* perder el control. **-3.** [adhesion] sujeción *f*, adherencia *f*. **-4.** [handle] asidero *m*. **-5.** [bag] bolsa *f* de viaje. ◇ *vt* **-1.** [grasp] agarrar, asir; [hand] apretar; [weapon] empuñar. **-2.** [seize] apoderarse de.

gripe [graɪp] *inf* ◇ *n* [complaint] queja *f*. ◇ *vi*: **to ~ (about)** quejarse (de).

gripping ['grɪpɪŋ] *adj* apasionante.

grisly ['grɪzlɪ] (*compar* **-ier**, *superl* **-iest**) *adj* [horrible, macabre] espeluznante, horripilante.

grist [grɪst] *n*: **it's all ~ to the mill** todo vale OR sirve.

gristle ['grɪsl] *n* cartílago *m*, ternilla *f*.

gristly ['grɪslɪ] (*compar* **-ier**, *superl* **-iest**) *adj* cartilaginoso(sa).

grit [grɪt] (*pt* & *pp* **-ted**, *cont* **-ting**) ◇ *n* **-1.** [stones] grava *f*; [sand, dust] arena *f*. **-2.** *inf* [courage] valor *m*. ◇ *vt* cubrir de arena (*las calles*).
♦ **grits** *npl Am* granos *mpl* de maíz molidos.

gritter ['grɪtər] *n* vehículo que cubre de arena o gravilla las carreteras en tiempos de heladas.

gritty ['grɪtɪ] (*compar* **-ier**, *superl* **-iest**) *adj* **-1.** [stony] arenoso(sa). **-2.** *inf* [brave] valiente.

grizzled ['grɪzld] *adj* canoso(sa).

grizzly ['grɪzlɪ] (*pl* **-ies**) *n*: **~ (bear)** oso *m* pardo.

groan [grəʊn] ◇ *n* gemido *m*, quejido *m*. ◇ *vi* **-1.** [moan] gemir. **-2.** [creak] crujir.

grocer ['grəʊsər] *n* tendero *m*, -ra *f*, abarrotero *m*, -ra *f Amer*; **~'s (shop)** tienda *f* de comestibles OR ultramarinos, abarrotería *f Amer*.

groceries ['grəʊsərɪz] *npl* [foods] comestibles *mpl*, abarrotes *mpl Amer*.

grocery ['grəʊsərɪ] (*pl* **-ies**) *n* [shop] tienda *f* de comestibles OR ultramarinos, abarrotería *f Amer*.

groggy ['grɒgɪ] (*compar* **-ier**, *superl* **-iest**) *adj* atontado(da), mareado(da).

groin [grɔɪn] *n* ingle *f*.

groom [gruːm] ◇ *n* **-1.** [of horses] mozo *m* de cuadra. **-2.** [bridegroom] novio *m*. ◇ *vt* **-1.** [brush] cepillar, almohazar. **-2.** [prepare]: **to ~ sb (for sthg)** preparar a alguien (para algo).

groove [gruːv] *n* [deep line] ranura *f*; [in record] surco *m*.

grope [grəʊp] ◇ *vt* **-1.** [fondle] toquetear, meter mano a. **-2.** [try to find]: **to ~ one's way** andar a tientas. ◇ *vi*: **to ~ (about) for**

sthg [object] buscar algo a tientas; [solution, remedy] buscar algo a ciegas.

gross [grəʊs] (*pl inv* OR **-es**) ◇ *adj* **-1.** [total] bruto(ta). **-2.** *fml* [serious, inexcusable] grave, intolerable. **-3.** [coarse, vulgar] basto(ta), vulgar. **-4.** *inf* [obese] obeso(sa). ◇ *n* gruesa *f*. ◇ *vt* ganar en bruto.

gross domestic product *n* producto *m* interior bruto.

grossly ['grəʊslɪ] *adv* [seriously] enormemente.

gross national product *n* producto *m* nacional bruto.

gross profit *n* beneficio *m* bruto.

grotesque [grəʊ'tesk] *adj* grotesco(ca).

grotto ['grɒtəʊ] (*pl* **-es** OR **-s**) *n* gruta *f*.

grotty ['grɒtɪ] (*compar* **-ier**, *superl* **-iest**) *adj Br inf* asqueroso(sa), cochambroso(sa).

grouchy ['graʊtʃɪ] (*compar* **-ier**, *superl* **-iest**) *adj inf* refunfuñón(ona).

ground [graʊnd] ◇ *pt* & *pp* → **grind**.
◇ *n* **-1.** [surface of earth] suelo *m*, tierra *f*; **above/below ~** sobre/bajo tierra; **on the ~** en el suelo; **to be thin on the ~** ser escaso; **to get sthg off the ~** *fig* poner algo en marcha. **-2.** [area of land] terreno *m*; SPORT campo *m*, terreno *m* de juego. **-3.** [subject area] campo *m*; **to break fresh** OR **new ~** abrir nuevas fronteras. **-4.** [advantage]: **to gain/lose ~** ganar/perder terreno. **-5.** *phr*: **to cut the ~ from under sb's feet** pisar el terreno a alguien; **to go to ~** esconderse, refugiarse; **to run sthg/sb to ~** encontrar algo/a alguien (finalmente); **to stand one's ~** permanecer firme.
◇ *vt* **-1.** [base]: **to be ~ed on** OR **in sthg** basarse en algo. **-2.** [aircraft, pilot] hacer permanecer en tierra. **-3.** *Am inf* [child] castigar sin salir. **-4.** *Am* ELEC: **to be ~ed** estar conectado(da) a tierra.
♦ **grounds** *npl* **-1.** [reason]: **~s (for sthg/for doing sthg)** motivos *mpl* (para algo/para hacer algo); **on the ~s of** por motivos de; **on the ~s that** aduciendo que, debido a que. **-2.** [around building] jardines *mpl*. **-3.** [area] zona *f*.

ground control *n* control *m* de tierra.

ground cover *n* maleza *f*.

ground crew *n* personal *m* de tierra.

ground floor *n* planta *f* baja; **~ flat** (piso *m*) bajo *m*.

ground-in *adj* incrustado(da), adherido(da).

grounding ['graʊndɪŋ] *n*: **~ (in)** base *f* (de), conocimientos *mpl* básicos (de).

groundless ['graʊndlɪs] *adj* infundado(da), sin fundamento.

ground level *n*: at ~ a nivel del suelo.

groundnut ['graʊndnʌt] *n* cacahuete *m*.

ground plan *n* [of building] planta *f*.

ground rent *n alquiler pagado al propietario de un terreno durante largo tiempo con el fin de edificar.*

ground rules *npl* reglas *fpl* básicas.

groundsheet ['graʊndʃiːt] *n* lona *f* impermeable (*para camping etc*).

groundsman ['graʊndzmən] (*pl* -men [-mən]) *n Br* cuidador *m* del campo OR terreno de juego.

ground staff *n* -1. [at sports ground] personal *m* al cargo de las instalaciones. -2. *Br* = ground crew.

groundswell ['graʊndswel] *n* [of opinion etc] oleada *f*, ola *f*.

groundwork ['graʊndwɜːk] *n* (*U*) trabajo *m* preliminar.

group [gruːp] ◇ *n* grupo *m*. ◇ *vt* agrupar. ◇ *vi*: **to ~ (together)** agruparse.

group captain *n Br* ≃ coronel *m* (de aviación).

groupie ['gruːpɪ] *n inf* groupie *f*, *fan que persigue a su grupo de rock favorito en las giras intentando entablar relación con ellos.*

group practice *n* gabinete *m* médico.

group therapy *n* terapia *f* de grupo.

grouse [graʊs] ◇ *n* -1. [bird] urogallo *m*. -2. *inf* [complaint] queja *f*. ◇ *vi inf* quejarse.

grove [grəʊv] *n* [of trees] arboleda *f*; **lemon ~** limonar *m*.
◆ **Grove** *n* [in street names] *nombre de ciertas calles británicas.*

grovel ['grɒvl] (*Br pt & pp* -led, *cont* -ling, *Am pt & pp* -ed, *cont* -ing) *vi lit & fig*: **to ~ (to)** arrastrarse (ante).

grow [grəʊ] (*pt* grew, *pp* grown) ◇ *vi* -1. [gen] crecer. -2. [become] volverse, ponerse; **to ~ dark** oscurecer; **to ~ old** envejecer. -3. [come]: **to ~ to do sthg** llegar a hacer algo. ◇ *vt* -1. [plants] cultivar. -2. [hair, beard] dejarse crecer.
◆ **grow apart** *vi* distanciarse.
◆ **grow into** *vt fus* -1. [clothes, shoes] crecer lo suficiente para poder llevar. -2. [become, turn into] hacerse, convertirse en.
◆ **grow on** *vt fus inf* gustar cada vez más.
◆ **grow out** *vi* [perm, dye] irse, desaparecer.
◆ **grow out of** *vt fus* -1. [become too big for]: **he has grown out of his clothes** se le ha quedado pequeña la ropa. -2. [lose - habit etc] perder.
◆ **grow up** *vi* crecer; **~ up!** ¡no seas niño!

grower ['grəʊə'] *n* cultivador *m*, -ra *f*.

growl [graʊl] ◇ *n* [of dog, person] gruñido *m*; [of engine, lion] rugido *m*. ◇ *vi* [dog, person] gruñir; [lion, engine] rugir.

grown [grəʊn] ◇ *pp* → **grow**. ◇ *adj* crecido(da), adulto(ta).

grown-up ◇ *adj* adulto(ta). ◇ *n* persona *f* mayor.

growth [grəʊθ] *n* -1. [gen]: ~ (**of** OR **in**) crecimiento *m* (de). -2. MED tumor *m*.

growth rate *n* tasa *f* de crecimiento.

GRSM (*abbr of* Graduate of the Royal Schools of Music) (*titular de un*) *diploma de las Royal Schools of Music, conservatorios británicos de música.*

grub [grʌb] *n* -1. [insect] larva *f*, gusano *m*. -2. *inf* [food] manduca *f*, papeo *m*.

grubby ['grʌbɪ] (*compar* -ier, *superl* -iest) *adj* sucio(cia), mugriento(ta).

grudge [grʌdʒ] ◇ *n* rencor *m*; **to bear sb a ~, to bear a ~ against sb** guardar rencor a alguien. ◇ *vt*: **to ~ sb sthg** conceder algo a alguien a regañadientes; **to ~ doing sthg** hacer algo a regañadientes.

grudging ['grʌdʒɪŋ] *adj* concedido(da) a regañadientes.

grudgingly ['grʌdʒɪŋlɪ] *adv* a regañadientes, de mala gana.

gruelling *Br*, **grueling** *Am* ['grʊəlɪŋ] *adj* agotador(ra).

gruesome ['gruːsəm] *adj* espantoso(sa), horripilante.

gruff [grʌf] *adj* -1. [hoarse] bronco(ca). -2. [rough, unfriendly] hosco(ca), brusco(ca).

grumble ['grʌmbl] ◇ *n* -1. [complaint] queja *f*. -2. [of stomach] gruñido *m* (de tripas). ◇ *vi* -1. [complain] quejarse, refunfuñar; **to ~ about sthg** quejarse de algo, refunfuñar por algo. -2. [stomach] gruñir, hacer ruido.

grumbling ['grʌmblɪŋ] *n* (*U*) -1. [complaining] refunfuñeo *m*, quejas *fpl*. -2. [of stomach] gruñidos *mpl* (de las tripas).

grumpy ['grʌmpɪ] (*compar* -ier, *superl* -iest) *adj inf* gruñón(ona).

grunt [grʌnt] ◇ *n* gruñido *m*. ◇ *vi* gruñir.

G-string *n* taparrabos *m inv*, tanga *m*.

GU *abbr of* Guam.

Guadeloupe [ˌgwɑːdəˈluːp] *n* Guadalupe.

guarantee [ˌgærənˈtiː] ◇ *n* garantía *f*; **under ~** en periodo de garantía. ◇ *vt* garantizar.

guarantor [ˌgærənˈtɔːr] *n* garante *m* y *f*.

guard [gɑːd] ◇ *n* -1. [person] guardia *m* y *f*, rondín *m* Amer. -2. [group of guards, operation] guardia *f*; **to be on/stand ~** estar de/hacer guardia; **to be on (one's) ~ (against)** estar en guardia OR alerta (contra); **to catch sb off ~** coger a alguien desprevenido. -3.

Br RAIL **jefe** *m* de tren. **-4.** [protective device - for body] **defensa** *f*, protector *m*; [- for machine] **cubierta** *f* **protectora.** ◇ *vt* **-1.** [protect, hide] **guardar. -2.** [prevent from escaping] **vigilar.**

◆ **guard against** *vt fus* protegerse de OR contra.

guard dog *n* perro *m* guardián.

guarded ['gɑːdɪd] *adj* cauteloso(sa), discreto(ta).

guardian ['gɑːdjən] *n* **-1.** [of child] tutor *m*, -ra *f*. **-2.** [protector] guardián *m*, -ana *f*, protector *m*, -ra *f*.

guardian angel *n* ángel *m* de la guarda, ángel custodio.

guardianship ['gɑːdjənʃɪp] *n* tutela *f*.

guardrail ['gɑːdreɪl] *n Am* [on road] pretil *m*.

guardsman ['gɑːdzmən] (*pl* **-men** [-mən]) *n* [in UK] guardia *m* (de la guardia real).

guard's van *n Br* furgón *m* de cola.

Guatemala [,gwɑːtə'mɑːlə] *n* Guatemala.

Guatemalan [,gwɑːtə'mɑːlən] ◇ *adj* guatemalteco(ca). ◇ *n* guatemalteco *m*, -ca *f*.

guava ['gwɑːvə] *n* guayaba *f*.

guerilla [gə'rɪlə] = **guerrilla.**

Guernsey ['gɜːnzɪ] *n* **-1.** [place] Guernsey. **-2.** [sweater] jersey *m* grueso de lana. **-3.** [cow] *tipo de vaca.*

guerrilla [gə'rɪlə] *n* guerrillero *m*, -ra *f*; **urban** ~ guerrillero de ciudad.

guerrilla warfare *n* (*U*) guerra *f* de guerrillas.

guess [ges] ◇ *n* suposición *f*, conjetura *f*; **to take a** ~ intentar adivinar; **it's anybody's** ~ vete a saber, ¿quién sabe? ◇ *vt* adivinar; ~ **what?** ¿sabes qué? ◇ *vi* **-1.** [conjecture] suponer, conjeturar; **to** ~ **at sthg** tratar de adivinar algo; **to keep sb** ~**ing** tener a alguien en la incertidumbre. **-2.** [suppose] **I** ~ **(so)** supongo OR me imagino que sí.

guesstimate ['gestɪmət] *n inf* cálculo *m* a bulto.

guesswork ['geswɜːk] *n* (*U*) conjeturas *fpl*, suposiciones *fpl*.

guest [gest] *n* **-1.** [at home] invitado *m*, -da *f*. **-2.** [at hotel] huésped *m* y *f*. **-3.** *phr*: **be my** ~! ¡pues claro!

guesthouse ['gesthaʊs, *pl* -haʊzɪz] *n* casa *f* de huéspedes.

guest of honour *n* invitado *m*, -da *f* de honor.

guestroom ['gestrʊm] *n* cuarto *m* de los huéspedes.

guest star *n* estrella *f* invitada.

guffaw [gʌ'fɔː] ◇ *n* risotada *f*, carcajada *f*. ◇ *vi* dar risotadas, reírse a carcajadas.

Guiana [gaɪ'ænə] *n* (la) Guayana.

guidance ['gaɪdəns] *n* (*U*) **-1.** [help] orientación *f*, consejos *mpl*. **-2.** [leadership] dirección *f*; **under the** ~ **of** bajo la dirección de.

guide [gaɪd] ◇ *n* **-1.** [person] guía *m* y *f*. **-2.** [book] guía *f*. ◇ *vt* **-1.** [show by leading] guiar. **-2.** [control] conducir, dirigir. **-3.** [influence]: **to be** ~**d by** guiarse por.

◆ **Guide** *n* = **Girl Guide.**

guide book *n* guía *f*.

guided missile ['gaɪdɪd-] *n* misil *m* teledirigido.

guide dog *n* perro *m* lazarillo, perro *m* guía.

guidelines ['gaɪdlaɪnz] *npl* directrices *fpl*.

guiding ['gaɪdɪŋ] *adj* [principle] rector(ra).

guild [gɪld] *n* **-1.** HISTORY gremio *m*. **-2.** [association] corporación *f*.

guildhall ['gɪldhɔːl] *n* sede *de una corporación.*

guile [gaɪl] *n* (*U*) *literary* astucia *f*.

guileless ['gaɪllɪs] *adj literary* inocente, candoroso(sa).

guillemot ['gɪlɪmɒt] *n* arao *m* común.

guillotine ['gɪlə,tiːn] ◇ *n* **-1.** [gen] guillotina *f*. **-2.** *Br* POL *estipulación de un tiempo determinado para debatir un proyecto de ley.* ◇ *vt* guillotinar.

guilt [gɪlt] *n* **-1.** [remorse] culpa *f*. **-2.** JUR culpabilidad *f*.

guiltily ['gɪltɪlɪ] *adv* con aire de culpabilidad.

guilty ['gɪltɪ] (*compar* **-ier**, *superl* **-iest**) *adj* **-1.** [gen]: ~ **(of)** culpable (de); **to be found** ~**/not** ~ ser declarado culpable/inocente; **to have a** ~ **conscience** sentirse culpable. **-2.** [secret, thought] que causa remordimiento.

guinea ['gɪnɪ] *n* guinea *f*.

Guinea ['gɪnɪ] *n* Guinea.

Guinea-Bissau [-bɪ'saʊ] *n* Guinea-Bissau.

guinea fowl *n* gallina *f* de Guinea.

guinea pig *n lit* & *fig* conejillo *m* de Indias.

guise [gaɪz] *n fml* apariencia *f*.

guitar [gɪ'tɑːr] *n* guitarra *f*.

guitarist [gɪ'tɑːrɪst] *n* guitarrista *m* y *f*.

gulch [gʌltʃ] *n Am* barranco *m*.

gulf [gʌlf] *n* **-1.** [sea] golfo *m*. **-2.** [chasm] sima *f*, abismo *m*. **-3.** [big difference]: ~ **(between)** abismo *m* (entre).

◆ **Gulf** *n*: **the Gulf** el Golfo.

Gulf States *npl*: **the** ~ los países del Golfo.

Gulf Stream *n*: **the** ~ la corriente del Golfo.

gull [gʌl] *n* gaviota *f*.

gullet ['gʌlɪt] *n* esófago *m*.

gullible ['gʌləbl] *adj* crédulo(la).

gully ['gʌlɪ] (*pl* **-ies**) *n* barranco *m*.

gulp [gʌlp] ◇ *n* trago *m*. ◇ *vt* [liquid] tragarse; [food] engullir. ◇ *vi* tragar saliva.
◆ **gulp down** *vt sep* [liquid] tragarse; [food] engullir.

gum [gʌm] (*pt & pp* **-med**, *cont* **-ming**) ◇ *n* **-1.** [chewing gum] chicle *m*. **-2.** [adhesive] cola *f*, pegamento *m*. **-3.** ANAT encía *f*. ◇ *vt* pegar, engomar.

gumboil ['gʌmbɔɪl] *n* flemón *m*.

gumboots ['gʌmbuːts] *npl Br* botas *fpl* de agua OR de goma.

gumption ['gʌmpʃn] *n* (*U*) *inf* **-1.** [common sense] seso *m*, sentido *m* común. **-2.** [determination] agallas *fpl*, coraje *m*.

gumshoe ['gʌmʃuː] *n Am crime sl* sabueso *m*, polizonte *m y f*.

gun [gʌn] (*pt & pp* **-ned**, *cont* **-ning**) *n* **-1.** [pistol] pistola *f*; [rifle] escopeta *f*, fusil *m*; **to stick to one's ~s** mantenerse en sus trece; **to jump the ~** adelantarse a los acontecimientos. **-2.** [tool] pistola *f*.
◆ **gun down** *vt sep* abatir (a tiros).

gunboat ['gʌnbəʊt] *n* lancha *f* cañonera, cañonero *m*.

gundog ['gʌndɒg] *n* perro *m* de caza.

gunfire ['gʌnfaɪəʳ] *n* (*U*) disparos *mpl*, tiroteo *m*.

gunge [gʌndʒ] *n* (*U*) *Br inf* porquería *f*, guarrería *f*.

gung-ho [,gʌŋ'həʊ] *adj Br inf* demasiado confiado en uno mismo.

gunk [gʌŋk] *n inf* porquería *f*, guarrería *f*.

gunman ['gʌnmən] (*pl* **-men** [-mən]) *n* pistolero *m*.

gunner ['gʌnəʳ] *n* artillero *m*.

gunpoint ['gʌnpɔɪnt] *n*: **at ~** a punta de pistola.

gunpowder ['gʌn,paʊdəʳ] *n* pólvora *f*.

gunrunning ['gʌn,rʌnɪŋ] *n* tráfico *m* de armas.

gunshot ['gʌnʃɒt] *n* tiro *m*, disparo *m*.

gunsmith ['gʌnsmɪθ] *n* armero *m*.

gurgle ['gɜːgl] ◇ *vi* **-1.** [water] gorgotear. **-2.** [baby] gorjear. ◇ *n* **-1.** [of water] gorgoteo *m*. **-2.** [of baby] gorjeo *m*.

guru ['gʊruː] *n lit & fig* gurú *m*.

gush [gʌʃ] ◇ *n* chorro *m*. ◇ *vt* chorrear. ◇ *vi* **-1.** [flow out] chorrear, manar. **-2.** *pej* [enthuse] ser muy efusivo(va).

gushing ['gʌʃɪŋ] *adj pej* efusivo(va).

gusset ['gʌsɪt] *n* escudete *m*.

gust [gʌst] ◇ *n* ráfaga *f*, racha *f*. ◇ *vi* [wind] soplar racheado(da).

gusto ['gʌstəʊ] *n*: **with ~** con deleite.

gusty ['gʌstɪ] (*compar* **-ier**, *superl* **-iest**) *adj* [day] ventoso(sa); [wind] racheado(da).

gut [gʌt] (*pt & pp* **-ted**, *cont* **-ting**) ◇ *n* **-1.** MED intestino *m*. **-2.** [strong thread] sedal *m*. ◇ *vt* **-1.** [animal] destripar. **-2.** [building etc] destruir el interior de.
◆ **guts** *npl inf* **-1.** [intestines] tripas *fpl*; **to hate sb's ~s** odiar a alguien a muerte. **-2.** [courage] agallas *fpl*.

gut reaction *n* primer impulso *m*.

gutter ['gʌtəʳ] *n* **-1.** [ditch] cuneta *f*. **-2.** [on roof] canalón *m*.

guttering ['gʌtərɪŋ] *n* (*U*) canalones *mpl*.

gutter press *n pej* prensa *f* amarilla OR sensacionalista.

guttural ['gʌtərəl] *adj* gutural.

guv [gʌv] *n Br inf* jefe *m*.

guy [gaɪ] *n* **-1.** *inf* [man] tipo *m*, tío *m*, chavo *m Amer*. **-2.** *Br* [dummy] *muñeco que se quema en Gran Bretaña la noche de Guy Fawkes*.

Guyana [gaɪˈænə] *n* Guyana.

Guy Fawkes' Night *n* la noche de Guy Fawkes.

GUY FAWKES' NIGHT:

Festejo británico que se celebra la noche del 5 de noviembre y que conmemora un complot católico encabezado por Guy Fawkes en 1605 para volar las casas del parlamento. En esta noche se encienden hogueras en las que se quema una efigie de Guy Fawkes y se lanzan fuegos artificiales; por eso esta noche también se llama 'Fireworks Night' o 'Bonfire Night'

---

guy rope *n* viento *m*, cuerda *f* (*de tienda de campaña*).

guzzle ['gʌzl] ◇ *vt* zamparse. ◇ *vi* zampar.

gym [dʒɪm] *n inf* **-1.** [gymnasium] gimnasio *m*. **-2.** [exercises] gimnasia *f*.

gymkhana [dʒɪmˈkɑːnə] *n* gincana *f*.

gymnasium [dʒɪmˈneɪzjəm] (*pl* **-siums** OR **-sia** [-zjə]) *n* gimnasio *m*.

gymnast ['dʒɪmnæst] *n* gimnasta *m y f*.

gymnastics [dʒɪmˈnæstɪks] *n* (*U*) gimnasia *f*.

gym shoes *npl* zapatillas *fpl* de gimnasia.

gymslip ['dʒɪm,slɪp] *n Br* bata *f* de colegio.

gynaecological *Br*, **gynecological** *Am* [,gaɪnəkəˈlɒdʒɪkl] *adj* ginecológico(ca).

gynaecologist *Br*, **gynecologist** *Am* [,gaɪnəˈkɒlədʒɪst] *n* ginecólogo *m*, -ga *f*.

gynaecology *Br*, **gynecology** *Am* [,gaɪnəˈkɒlədʒɪ] *n* ginecología *f*.

gyp [dʒɪp] *Am* ◇ *vt* timar, estafar. ◇ *n* tramposo *m*, -sa *f*.

gypsy ['dʒɪpsɪ] (*pl* **-ies**) = **gipsy**.

gyrate [dʒaɪ'reɪt] *vi* girar.

gyration [dʒaɪ'reɪʃn] *n* giro *m*, rotación *f*.

gyroscope ['dʒaɪrəskəʊp] *n* giroscopio *m*.

h (*pl* **h's** OR **hs**), **H** (*pl* **H's** OR **Hs**) [eɪtʃ] *n* [letter] h *f*, H *f*.

ha [hɑː] *excl* ¡ah!

habeas corpus [,heɪbjəs'kɔːpəs] *n* hábeas corpus *m*.

haberdashery ['hæbədæʃərɪ] (*pl* **-ies**) *n* mercería *f*.

habit ['hæbɪt] *n* **-1.** [custom] costumbre *f*, hábito *m*; **to be in the ~ of doing sthg** tener la costumbre de hacer algo; **to make a ~ of sthg** tomar algo por costumbre; **to make a ~ of doing sthg** tener por costumbre hacer algo. **-2.** [garment] hábito *m*.

habitable ['hæbɪtəbl] *adj* habitable.

habitat ['hæbɪtæt] *n* hábitat *m*.

habitation [hæbɪ'teɪʃn] *n* **-1.** [occupation] ocupación *f*, habitación *f*. **-2.** [house] morada *f*.

habit-forming [-,fɔːmɪŋ] *adj* que crea hábito.

habitual [hə'bɪtʃʊəl] *adj* **-1.** [usual] habitual, acostumbrado(da). **-2.** [smoker, gambler] empedernido(da).

habitually [hə'bɪtʃʊəlɪ] *adv* por costumbre, habitualmente.

hack [hæk] ◇ *n* **-1.** *pej* [writer] escritorzuelo *m*, -la *f*; [journalist] gacetillero *m*, -ra *f*. **-2.** *Am inf* [taxi] taxi *m*. ◇ *vt* **-1.** [cut] cortar en tajos, acuchillar. **-2.** COMPUT piratear. ◇ *vi* [cut] dar tajos OR hachazos.
◆ **hack into** *vt fus* piratear.
◆ **hack through** *vt fus* [cut]: **to ~ (one's way) through sthg** abrirse paso por algo a hachazos.

hacker ['hækər] *n*: **(computer) ~** pirata *m y f* informático.

hackie ['hækɪ] *n Am inf* taxista *m y f*.

hacking ['hækɪŋ] *n* COMPUT piratería *f* (informática).

hacking cough *n* tos *f* seca.

hackles ['hæklz] *npl* pelo o plumas del cuello de un animal; **to make sb's ~ rise** poner negro a alguien.

hackney cab, **hackney carriage** ['hæknɪ-] *n fml* [taxi] taxi *m*.

hackneyed ['hæknɪd] *adj pej* trillado(da), gastado(da).

hacksaw ['hæksɔː] *n* sierra *f* para metales.

had [*weak form* həd, *strong form* hæd] *pt & pp* → **have**.

haddock ['hædək] (*pl inv*) *n* eglefino *m*.

hadn't ['hædnt] = **had not**.

haematology [,hiːmə'tɒlədʒɪ] = **hematology**.

haemoglobin [,hiːmə'gləʊbɪn] = **hemoglobin**.

haemophilia [,hiːmə'fɪlɪə] = **hemophilia**.

haemophiliac [,hiːmə'fɪlɪæk] = **hemophiliac**.

haemorrhage ['hemərɪdʒ] = **hemorrhage**.

haemorrhoids ['hemərɔɪdz] = **hemorrhoids**.

hag [hæg] *n pej* bruja *f*, arpía *f*.

haggard ['hægəd] *adj* ojeroso(sa).

haggis ['hægɪs] *n plato típico escocés hecho con las asaduras del cordero*.

haggle ['hægl] *vi*: **to ~ (with sb over** OR **about sthg)** regatear (algo con alguien).

haggling ['hæglɪŋ] *n* regateo *m*.

Hague [heɪg] *n*: **The ~** La Haya.

hail [heɪl] ◇ *n* **-1.** METEOR granizo *m*, pedrisco *m*. **-2.** *fig* [large number] lluvia *f*. ◇ *vt* **-1.** [call] llamar. **-2.** [acclaim]: **to ~ sb as sthg** aclamar a alguien algo; **to ~ sthg as sthg** ensalzar algo catalogándolo de algo. ◇ *v impers* granizar.

hailstone ['heɪlstəʊn] *n* granizo *m*, piedra *f*.

hair [heər] ◇ *n* **-1.** (*U*) [gen] pelo *m*; **to do one's ~** arreglarse el pelo; **to let one's ~ down** [fig] soltarse el pelo, desmadrarse; **to make sb's ~ stand on end** ponerle a alguien los pelos de punta; **to split ~s** hilar muy fino, rizar el rizo. **-2.** [on person's skin] vello *m*. ◇ *comp* para el pelo.

hairbrush ['heəbrʌʃ] *n* cepillo *m* para el pelo.

haircut ['heəkʌt] *n* corte *m* de pelo.

hairdo ['heəduː] (*pl* **-s**) *n inf* peinado *m*.

hairdresser ['heə,dresər] *n* peluquero *m*, -ra *f*; **~'s (salon)** peluquería *f*.

hairdressing ['heə,dresɪŋ] ◇ *n* peluquería *f*. ◇ *comp* de peluquería.

hairdryer ['heə,draɪər] *n* secador *m* (de pelo).

hair gel *n* gomina *f*.

hairgrip ['heəgrɪp] *n Br* horquilla *f*.

hairline ['heəlaɪn] *n* nacimiento *m* del pelo.

hairline fracture *n* fractura *f* muy fina.

hairnet ['heənet] *n* redecilla *f*.

hairpiece ['heəpiːs] *n* peluquín *m*, postizo *m*.

hairpin ['heəpɪn] *n* horquilla *f* de moño.

hairpin bend *n* curva *f* muy cerrada.

hair-raising [-,reɪzɪŋ] *adj* espeluznante.

hair remover *n* crema *f* depilatoria, depilatorio *m*.

hair-restorer *n* crecepelo *m*, loción *f* capilar.

hair's breadth *n*: **by a** ~ por un pelo.

hair slide *n Br* pasador *m*.

hair-splitting *n* (*U*) *pej* sutilezas *fpl*.

hairspray ['heəspreɪ] *n* laca *f* (para el pelo).

hairstyle ['heəstaɪl] *n* peinado *m*.

hairstylist ['heə,staɪlɪst] *n* peluquero *m*, -ra *f*.

hairy ['heərɪ] (*compar* **-ier**, *superl* **-iest**) *adj* **-1.** [covered in hair] peludo(da). **-2.** *inf* [scary] espeluznante, espantoso(sa).

Haiti ['heɪtɪ] *n* Haití.

Haitian ['heɪʃn] ◇ *adj* haitiano(na). ◇ *n* haitiano *m*, -na *f*.

hake [heɪk] (*pl inv* OR **-s**) *n* merluza *f*.

halal [hə'lɑːl] ◇ *adj* [meat] *que ha sido matado de acuerdo con la ley musulmana*. ◇ *n carne de animal matado de acuerdo con la ley musulmana*.

halcyon days ['hælsɪən-] *npl literary* días *mpl* idílicos.

hale [heɪl] *adj*: ~ **and hearty** sano y fuerte (sana y fuerte).

half [*Br* hɑːf, *Am* hæf] (*pl senses 1 and 3* **halves**, *pl senses 2 and 4* **halves** OR **halfs**) ◇ *adj* medio(dia); ~ **a dozen/mile** media docena/milla; ~ **an hour** media hora. ◇ *adv* **-1.** [gen]: ~ **full/open** lleno/abierto por la mitad; ~ **and** ~ mitad y mitad; **not** ~! *Br inf* ¡y cómo! **-2.** [by half]: ~ **as big (as)** la mitad de grande (que). **-3.** [in telling the time]: ~ **past nine,** ~ **after nine** *Am* las nueve y media; **it's** ~ **past** son y media. ◇ *n* **-1.** [one of two parts] mitad *f*; ~ **(of)** the group la mitad del grupo; **a pound/mile and a** ~ una libra/milla y media; **by** ~ en un cincuenta por ciento; **in** ~ por la mitad, en dos; **he doesn't do things by halves** no hace las cosas a medias; **to be too clever by** ~ pasarse de listo; **to go halves (with sb)** ir a medias (con alguien). **-2.** [fraction, halfback, child's ticket] medio *m*. **-3.** [of sports match] tiempo *m*, mitad *f*. **-4.** [of beer] media pinta *f*. ◇ *pron* la mitad; ~ **of it/them** la mitad.

halfback ['hɑːfbæk] *n* medio *m*.

half-baked [-'beɪkt] *adj* descabalado(da).

half board *n* media pensión *f*.

half-breed ◇ *adj* mestizo(za). ◇ *n* mestizo *m*, -za *f* (*atención: el término "half-breed" se considera racista*).

half-brother *n* hermanastro *m*.

half-caste ◇ *adj* mestizo(za). ◇ *n* mestizo *m*, -za *f* (*atención: el término "half-caste" se considera racista*).

half cock *n*: **to go off (at)** ~ fracasar por falta de preparación.

half-day *n* media jornada *f*.

half-hearted [-'hɑːtɪd] *adj* poco entusiasta.

half-heartedly [-'hɑːtɪdlɪ] *adv* sin entusiasmo.

half hour *n* media hora *f*.

◆ **half-hour** *adj* = **half-hourly**.

half-hourly *adj* de media hora.

half-length *adj* de medio cuerpo.

half-light *n* media luz *f*.

half-mast *n*: **at** ~ [flag] a media asta.

half measures *npl* medias tintas *fpl*.

half moon *n* media luna *f*.

half note *n Am* MUS blanca *f*.

halfpenny ['heɪpnɪ] (*pl* **-pennies** OR **-pence**) *n* medio penique *m*.

half-price *adj* a mitad de precio.

◆ **half price** *adv* a mitad de precio.

half-sister *n* hermanastra *f*.

half step *n Am* MUS semitono *m*.

half term *n Br breves vacaciones escolares a mitad de trimestre*.

half time *n* (*U*) descanso *m*.

half tone *n Am* MUS semitono *m*.

half-truth *n* verdad *f* a medias.

halfway [hɑːf'weɪ] ◇ *adj* intermedio(dia). ◇ *adv* **-1.** [in space]: **I was** ~ **down the street** llevaba la mitad de la calle andada. **-2.** [in time]: **the film was** ~ **through** la película iba por la mitad. **-3.** *phr*: **to meet sb** ~ llegar a un acuerdo con alguien (*cediendo ambas partes*).

half-wit *n* imbécil *m y f*.

half-yearly *adj* semestral.

◆ **half yearly** *adv* semestralmente.

halibut ['hælɪbət] (*pl inv* OR **-s**) *n* halibut *m*.

halitosis [,hælɪ'təʊsɪs] *n* halitosis *f inv*.

hall [hɔːl] *n* **-1.** [in house] vestíbulo *m*. **-2.** [public building] sala *f*. **-3.** *Br* UNIV residencia *f* universitaria, colegio *m* mayor; **to live in** ~**s** vivir en una residencia universitaria. **-4.** [country house] mansión *f*, casa *f* solariega.

halleluja [,hælɪ'luːjə] *excl* ¡aleluya!

hallmark ['hɔːlmɑːk] n -1. [typical feature] sello m distintivo. -2. [on metal] contraste m.

hallo [hə'ləʊ] = hello.

hall of residence (pl halls of residence) n Br residencia f universitaria, colegio m mayor.

hallowed ['hæləʊd] adj [respected] santificado(da), santo(ta).

Hallowe'en [,hæləʊ'iːn] n fiesta celebrada la noche del 31 de octubre.

HALLOWE'EN:
Fiesta celebrada la noche del 31 de octubre en que los niños, disfrazados de brujas, fantasmas etc, van de puerta en puerta pidiendo golosinas a cambio de no asustar a la gente

hallucinate [hə'luːsɪneɪt] vi alucinar.

hallucination [,həluːsɪ'neɪʃn] n alucinación f.

hallucinogenic [hə,luːsɪnə'dʒenɪk] adj alucinógeno(na).

hallway ['hɔːlweɪ] n entrada f, vestíbulo m.

halo ['heɪləʊ] (pl -es OR -s) n halo m, aureola f.

halogen ['hælədʒen] ◇ n halógeno m. ◇ comp halógeno(na).

halt [hɔːlt] ◇ n [stop]: to come to a ~ [vehicle] pararse; [activity] interrumpirse; to grind to a ~ [vehicle] ir parando lentamente; [process] paralizarse; to call a ~ to poner fin a. ◇ vt [person] parar, detener; [development, activity] interrumpir. ◇ vi [person, train] pararse, detenerse; [development, activity] interrumpirse.

halter ['hɔːltə'] n [for horse] ronzal m, cabestro m, bozal m Amer.

halterneck ['hɔːltənek] adj escotado(da) por detrás.

halting ['hɔːltɪŋ] adj vacilante.

halve [Br hɑːv, Am hæv] vt -1. [reduce by half] reducir a la mitad. -2. [divide] partir en dos, partir por la mitad.

halves [Br hɑːvz, Am hævz] pl → half.

ham [hæm] (pt & pp -med, cont -ming) ◇ n -1. [meat] jamón m. -2. pej [actor] histrión m, comicastro m. -3. [radio fanatic]: (radio) ~ radioaficionado m, -da f. ◇ comp de jamón. ◇ vt: to ~ it up sobreactuar.

Hamburg ['hæmbɜːg] n Hamburgo.

hamburger ['hæmbɜːgə'] n -1. [burger] hamburguesa f. -2. (U) Am [mince] carne f picada.

ham-fisted [-'fɪstɪd] adj torpe, desmañado(da).

hamlet ['hæmlɪt] n aldea f.

hammer ['hæmə'] ◇ n [gen & SPORT] martillo m. ◇ vt -1. [with tool] martillear. -2. [with fist] aporrear. -3. inf [defeat] dar una paliza a. ◇ vi -1. [with tool] martillear. -2. [with fist]: to ~ (on sthg) aporrear (algo). -3. phr: to ~ away at sthg [task] trabajar con ahínco en algo; [problem, subject] machacar algo.
◆ **hammer in** vt sep: to ~ sthg into sb meter algo en la cabeza a alguien.
◆ **hammer out** ◇ vt fus [solution, agreement] alcanzar con esfuerzo. ◇ vt sep [dent] quitar a martillo.

hammock ['hæmək] n hamaca f, chinchorro m Amer.

hammy ['hæmɪ] (compar -ier, superl -iest) adj inf histriónico(ca), exagerado(da).

hamper ['hæmpə'] ◇ n -1. [for food] cesta f, canasta f. -2. Am [for laundry] cesto m de la ropa sucia. ◇ vt obstaculizar.

hamster ['hæmstə'] n hámster m.

hamstring ['hæmstrɪŋ] ◇ n tendón m de la corva. ◇ vt paralizar.

hand [hænd] ◇ n -1. [gen] mano f; ~s up! ¡manos arriba!; to hold ~s ir cogidos de la mano; ~ in ~ [people] cogidos de la mano; by ~ a mano; at the ~s of a manos de; in ~ [problem, situation] bajo control; in the ~s of en manos de; to have sthg on one's ~s tener uno algo en sus manos; to change ~s cambiar de manos OR de dueño; to force sb's ~ apretarle las tuercas a alguien; to get OR lay one's ~s on sthg hacerse con algo; to get OR lay one's ~s on sb pillar a alguien; to get out of ~ [situation] hacerse incontrolable; [person] desmandarse; to give sb a free ~ dar carta blanca a alguien; to give OR lend sb a ~ (with) echar una mano a alguien (con); to go ~ in ~ [things] ir de la mano; to have one's ~s full estar muy ocupado; to have time in ~ tener tiempo de sobra; to overplay one's ~ fig extralimitarse; to take sb in ~ hacerse cargo OR ocuparse de alguien; to try one's ~ at sthg intentar hacer algo; to wait on sb ~ and foot traérselo todo en bandeja a alguien; to wash one's ~s of sthg lavarse las manos con respecto a algo; with his bare ~s con sus propias manos. -2. [influence] intervención f, influencia f; to have a ~ in sthg/in doing sthg intervenir en algo/al hacer algo. -3. [worker - on farm] bracero m, peón m; [- on ship] tripulante m. -4. [of clock, watch] manecilla f, aguja f. -5. [handwriting] letra f.
◇ vt: to ~ sthg to sb, to ~ sb sthg dar OR entregar algo a alguien.
◆ **(close) at hand** adv cerca.

◆ **on hand** *adv* al alcance de la mano.
◆ **on the other hand** *conj* por otra parte.
◆ **out of hand** *adv* [completely] terminantemente.
◆ **to hand** *adv* a mano.
◆ **hand down** *vt sep* [heirloom] pasar en herencia; [knowledge] transmitir.
◆ **hand in** *vt sep* entregar.
◆ **hand on** *vt sep* pasar, hacer circular.
◆ **hand out** *vt sep* repartir, distribuir.
◆ **hand over** ◇ *vt sep* **-1.** [baton, money] entregar. **-2.** [responsibility, power] ceder. ◇ *vi*: **to ~ over (to)** dar paso (a).

handbag ['hændbæg] *n* bolso *m*.

handball ['hændbɔ:l] *n* balonmano *m*.

handbill ['hændbɪl] *n* panfleto *m*.

handbook ['hændbʊk] *n* manual *m*.

handbrake ['hændbreɪk] *n* freno *m* de mano.

handclap ['hændklæp] *n*: **slow ~** *aplauso lento y rítmico de protesta*.

handcrafted ['hænd,krɑ:ftɪd] *adj* hecho(cha) a mano, de artesanía.

handcuff ['hændkʌf] *vt* esposar.
◆ **handcuffs** *npl* esposas *fpl*.

handful ['hændfʊl] *n* **-1.** [gen] puñado *m*. **-2.** *inf* [uncontrollable person]: **to be a ~** ser un demonio.

handgun ['hændgʌn] *n* pistola *f*.

handicap ['hændɪkæp] (*pt & pp* **-ped**, *cont* **-ping**) ◇ *n* **-1.** [disability] incapacidad *f*, minusvalía *f*. **-2.** [disadvantage] desventaja *f*, obstáculo *m*. **-3.** SPORT hándicap *m*. ◇ *vt* estorbar, obstaculizar.

handicapped ['hændɪkæpt] ◇ *adj* minusválido(da). ◇ *npl*: **the ~** los minusválidos.

handicraft ['hændɪkrɑ:ft] *n* [skill] trabajos *mpl* manuales, artesanía *f*.

handiwork ['hændɪwɜːk] *n* (*U*) [doing, work] obra *f*.

handkerchief ['hæŋkətʃɪf] (*pl* **-chiefs** OR **-chieves** [-tʃiːvz]) *n* pañuelo *m*.

handle ['hændl] ◇ *n* [of door, window] pomo *m*; [of tool] mango *m*; [of suitcase, cup, jug] asa *f*; **to fly off the ~** perder los estribos. ◇ *vt* [gen] manejar; [order, complaint, application] encargarse de; [negotiations, takeover] conducir; [people] tratar.

handlebars ['hændlbɑ:z] *npl* manillar *m*.

handler ['hændlə^r] *n* **-1.** [of animal] guardián *m*, -ana *f*. **-2.** [at airport]: **(baggage) ~** mozo *m* de equipajes.

handling charges ['hændlɪŋ-] *npl* [at bank] gastos *mpl* de tramitación.

hand lotion *n* crema *f* para las manos.

hand luggage *n Br* equipaje *m* de mano.

handmade [,hænd'meɪd] *adj* hecho(cha) a mano.

hand-me-down *n inf* prenda *f* usada.

handout ['hændaʊt] *n* **-1.** [gift] donativo *m*. **-2.** [leaflet] hojas *fpl* (informativas).

handover ['hændəʊvə^r] *n* [of power] cesión *f*, transferencia *f*; [of prisoners, baton] entrega *f*.

handpicked [,hænd'pɪkt] *adj* cuidadosamente escogido(da).

handrail ['hændreɪl] *n* pasamano *m*, barandilla *f*.

handset ['hændset] *n* auricular *m* (*de teléfono*); **to lift/replace the ~** descolgar/colgar (el teléfono).

handshake ['hændʃeɪk] *n* apretón *m* de manos.

hands-off *adj* de no intervención.

handsome ['hænsəm] *adj* **-1.** [man] guapo, atractivo. **-2.** [literary] [woman] bella. **-3.** [reward, profit] considerable.

handsomely ['hænsəmlɪ] *adv* generosamente.

hands-on *adj* práctico(ca).

handstand ['hændstænd] *n* pino *m*.

hand-to-mouth *adj* precario(ria).
◆ **hand to mouth** *adv* precariamente.

handwriting ['hænd,raɪtɪŋ] *n* letra *f*, caligrafía *f*.

handwritten ['hænd,rɪtn] *adj* escrito(ta) a mano.

handy ['hændɪ] (*compar* **-ier**, *superl* **-iest**) *adj inf* **-1.** [useful] práctico(ca); **to come in ~** venir bien. **-2.** [skilful] mañoso(sa). **-3.** [near] a mano, cerca; **to keep sthg ~** tener algo a mano.

handyman ['hændɪmæn] (*pl* **-men** [-men]) *n*: **a good ~** un manitas.

hang [hæŋ] (*pt & pp sense 1* **hung**, *pt & pp sense 2* **hung** OR **hanged**) ◇ *vt* **-1.** [fasten] colgar. **-2.** [execute] ahorcar. ◇ *vi* **-1.** [be fastened] colgar, pender. **-2.** [be executed] ser ahorcado(da). ◇ *n*: **to get the ~ of sthg** *inf* coger el tranquillo a algo.
◆ **hang about, hang around** *vi* pasar el rato; **they didn't ~ about** se pusieron en marcha sin perder un minuto.
◆ **hang on** ◇ *vt fus* [depend on] depender de. ◇ *vi* **-1.** [keep hold]: **to ~ on (to)** agarrarse (a). **-2.** *inf* [continue waiting] esperar, aguardar. **-3.** [persevere] resistir.
◆ **hang onto** *vt fus* **-1.** [keep hold of] agarrarse a. **-2.** [keep] quedarse con; [power] aferrarse a.
◆ **hang out** ◇ *vt sep* [washing] tender. ◇ *vi inf* [spend time] moverse, pasar el rato.
◆ **hang round** = hang about.

◆ **hang together** *vi* [alibi, argument] sostenerse, tenerse en pie.

◆ **hang up** ◇ *vt sep* colgar. ◇ *vi* colgar.

◆ **hang up on** *vt fus* colgar.

hangar ['hæŋəʳ] *n* hangar *m*.

hangdog ['hæŋdɒg] *adj* avergonzado(da).

hanger ['hæŋəʳ] *n* percha *f*.

hanger-on (*pl* **hangers-on**) *n* lapa *f*, moscón *m*, -ona *f*.

hang glider *n* [apparatus] ala *f* delta.

hang gliding *n* vuelo *m* con ala delta.

hanging ['hæŋɪŋ] *n* **-1.** (*U*) [form of punish-
ment] horca *f*. **-2.** [execution] ahorcamiento
m. **-3.** [drapery] colgadura *f*.

hangman ['hæŋmən] (*pl* **-men** [-mən]) *n*
verdugo *m*.

hangover ['hæŋˌəʊvəʳ] *n* **-1.** [from drinking]
resaca *f*. **-2.** [from past]: ~ **(from)** vestigio *m*
(de).

hang-up *n inf* complejo *m*.

hank [hæŋk] *n* madeja *f*.

hanker ['hæŋkəʳ]

◆ **hanker after**, **hanker for** *vt fus* anhelar.

hankering ['hæŋkərɪŋ] *n*: ~ **after** OR **for**
anhelo *m* de.

hankie, **hanky** ['hæŋkɪ] (*pl* **-ies**) (*abbr of*
handkerchief) *n inf* pañuelo *m*.

Hanoi [hæ'nɔɪ] *n* Hanoi.

Hansard ['hænsɑːd] *n* actas oficiales de los debates del Parlamento británico.

Hants [hænts] (*abbr of* **Hampshire**) *condado
inglés*.

haphazard [ˌhæp'hæzəd] *adj* desordena-
do(da), caótico(ca).

haphazardly [ˌhæp'hæzədlɪ] *adv* desordenadamente, de cualquier manera.

hapless ['hæplɪs] *adj literary* desventura-
do(da), desgraciado(da).

happen ['hæpən] *vi* **-1.** [occur] pasar, ocurrir; **to ~ to sb** pasarle OR sucederle a alguien. **-2.** [chance]: **I ~ed to be looking out
of the window ...** dio la casualidad de que
estaba mirando por la ventana ...; **do you
~ to have a pen on you?** ¿no tendrás un
boli acaso OR por casualidad?; **as it ~s ...**
da la casualidad de que ....

happening ['hæpənɪŋ] *n* suceso *m*, acontecimiento *m*.

happily ['hæpɪlɪ] *adv* **-1.** [with pleasure] alegremente, felizmente. **-2.** [fortunately] afortunadamente.

happiness ['hæpɪnɪs] *n* [state] felicidad *f*;
[feeling] alegría *f*.

happy ['hæpɪ] (*compar* **-ier**, *superl* **-iest**) *adj*
-1. [gen] feliz, contento(ta); ~ **Christmas/**

birthday! ¡Feliz Navidad/cumpleaños!; **to
be ~ with/about sthg** estar contento con
algo. **-2.** [causing contentment] feliz, alegre.
-3. [fortunate] feliz, oportuno(na). **-4.** [will-
ing]: **to be ~ to do sthg** estar más que dis-
puesto(ta) a hacer algo; **I'd be ~ to do it**
yo lo haría con gusto.

happy event *n*: **when's the ~?** ¿cuándo
nacerá el niño?

happy-go-lucky *adj* despreocupado(da).

happy hour *n inf espacio de tiempo durante
el cual se venden las bebidas a precio reducido
en un bar.*

happy medium *n* término *m* medio.

harangue [həˈræŋ] ◇ *n* arenga *f*. ◇ *vt* arengar.

Harare [həˈrɑːrɪ] *n* Harare.

harass ['hærəs] *vt* acosar.

harassed ['hærəst] *adj* agobiado(da).

harassment ['hærəsmənt] *n* acoso *m*.

harbinger ['hɑːbɪndʒəʳ] *n literary* precursor
m, heraldo *m*.

harbour *Br*, **harbor** *Am* ['hɑːbəʳ] ◇ *n* puerto *m*. ◇ *vt* **-1.** [feeling] abrigar. **-2.** [person]
dar refugio a, encubrir.

harbour master *n* capitán *m* de puerto.

hard [hɑːd] ◇ *adj* **-1.** [gen] duro(ra); [frost]
fuerte; **to be ~ on sb/sthg** [subj: person] ser
duro con alguien/algo; [subj: work, strain]
perjudicar a alguien/algo; [subj: result] ser
inmerecido para alguien/algo. **-2.** [difficult]
difícil. **-3.** [forceful - push, kick etc] fuerte. **-4.**
[fact, news] concreto(ta). **-5.** *Br* [extreme]: ~
left/right extrema izquierda/derecha. ◇ *adv*
-1. [try] mucho; [work, rain] intensamente;
[listen] atentamente. **-2.** [push, kick] fuerte,
con fuerza. **-3.** *phr*: **to be ~ pushed** OR **put**
OR **pressed to do sthg** vérselas y deseárselas para hacer algo; **to feel ~ done by** sentirse tratado injustamente.

hard-and-fast *adj* estricto(ta), fijo(ja).

hardback ['hɑːdbæk] ◇ *adj* de pasta dura.
◇ *n* edición *f* en pasta dura OR en tela.

hard-bitten *adj* duro(ra), curtido(da).

hardboard ['hɑːdbɔːd] *n* madera *f* conglo-
merada.

hard-boiled *adj lit & fig* duro(ra).

hard cash *n* dinero *m* contante y sonante.

hard cider *n Am* sidra *f*.

hard copy *n* COMPUT copia *f* impresa.

hard-core *adj* **-1.** [support] acérrimo(ma);
[criminal] incorregible. **-2.** [pornography]
duro(ra).

◆ **hard core** *n* [of group] núcleo *m*.

hard court *n* pista *f* de cemento, pista de
superficie dura.

hard currency *n* divisa *f* fuerte.

hard disk *n* COMPUT disco *m* duro.

hard drugs *npl* drogas *fpl* duras.

harden ['hɑːdn] ◇ *vt* **-1.** [gen] endurecer. **-2.** [resolve, opinion] reforzar. ◇ *vi* **-1.** [gen] endurecerse. **-2.** [resolve, opinion] reforzarse.

hardened ['hɑːdnd] *adj* [criminal] habitual.

hardening ['hɑːdnɪŋ] *n* endurecimiento *m*.

hard hat *n* casco *m* (de protección).

hard-headed [-'hedɪd] *adj* práctico(ca), realista.

hard-hearted [-'hɑːtɪd] *adj* insensible, sin corazón.

hard-hitting [-'hɪtɪŋ] *adj* impactante.

hard labour *n* (*U*) trabajos *mpl* forzados.

hard line *n*: to take a ~ on sthg seguir una tendencia de mano dura con algo.

◆ **hard-line** *adj* de línea dura.

◆ **hard lines** *npl Br*: ~s! ¡mala suerte!

hard-liner *n* partidario *m*, -ria *f* de la línea dura.

hardly ['hɑːdlɪ] *adv* apenas; ~ **ever/ anything** casi nunca/nada; **I'm ~ a communist, am I?** ¡pues sí que tengo yo mucho que ver con el comunismo!

hardness ['hɑːdnɪs] *n* **-1.** [firmness] dureza *f*. **-2.** [difficulty] dificultad *f*.

hard-nosed [-'nəʊzd] *adj* contundente, decidido(da).

hard sell *n* venta *f* agresiva.

hardship ['hɑːdʃɪp] *n* **-1.** (*U*) [difficult conditions] privaciones *fpl*, penurias *fpl*. **-2.** [difficult circumstance] infortunio *m*.

hard shoulder *n Br* AUT arcén *m*.

hard up *adj inf* sin blanca, sin un duro; to be ~ for sthg andar escaso de algo.

hardware ['hɑːdweəʳ] *n* (*U*) **-1.** [tools, equipment] artículos *mpl* de ferretería. **-2.** COMPUT hardware *m*, soporte *m* físico.

hardware shop *n* ferretería *f*.

hardwearing [,hɑːd'weərɪŋ] *adj Br* resistente, duradero(ra).

hardwood ['hɑːdwʊd] *n* madera *f* brava.

hardworking [,hɑːd'wɜːkɪŋ] *adj* trabajador(ra).

hardy ['hɑːdɪ] (*compar* **-ier**, *superl* **-iest**) *adj* **-1.** [person, animal] fuerte, robusto(ta). **-2.** [plant] resistente.

hare [heəʳ] ◇ *n* liebre *f*. ◇ *vi Br inf*: to ~ **off** echar a correr a toda pastilla.

harebrained ['heə,breɪnd] *adj inf* atolondrado(da).

harelip [,heə'lɪp] *n* labio *m* leporino.

harem [*Br* hɑː'riːm, *Am* 'hærəm] *n* harén *m*.

haricot (bean) ['hærɪkəʊ-] *n* judía *f*, alubia *f*.

hark [hɑːk]

◆ **hark back** *vi*: to ~ back to sthg volver a OR rememorar algo.

harlequin ['hɑːləkwɪn] ◇ *n* arlequín *m*. ◇ *comp* de arlequín, arlequinesco(ca).

Harley Street ['hɑːlɪ-] *n calle londinense famosa por sus médicos especialistas.*

harm [hɑːm] ◇ *n* daño *m*; to do ~ to sthg/sb, to do sthg/sb ~ [physically] hacer daño a algo/alguien; *fig* perjudicar algo/a alguien; to mean no ~ (by sthg) no tener mala intención (al hacer algo); there's no ~ in it no hay nada malo en ello; there's no ~ in trying/asking no pasa nada por intentarlo/preguntar; to be out of ~'s way estar a salvo; to come to no ~ [person] salir sano y salvo; [thing] no dañarse. ◇ *vt* [gen] hacer daño a, dañar; [reputation, chances, interests] dañar.

harmful ['hɑːmfʊl] *adj*: ~ **(to)** perjudicial OR dañino(na) (para).

harmless ['hɑːmlɪs] *adj* inofensivo(va).

harmlessly ['hɑːmlɪslɪ] *adv* sin causar daño.

harmonic [hɑː'mɒnɪk] *adj* armónico(ca).

harmonica [hɑː'mɒnɪkə] *n* armónica *f*.

harmonious [hɑː'məʊnjəs] *adj* armonioso(sa).

harmonium [hɑː'məʊnjəm] (*pl* **-s**) *n* armonio *m*.

harmonize, -ise ['hɑːmənaɪz] ◇ *vi*: to ~ **(with)** armonizar (con). ◇ *vt* armonizar.

harmony ['hɑːmənɪ] (*pl* **-ies**) *n* armonía *f*; in ~ with en armonía con.

harness ['hɑːnɪs] ◇ *n* **-1.** [for horse] arreos *mpl*, guarniciones *fpl*. **-2.** [for child] andadores *mpl*; [for climbing etc] correaje *m*. ◇ *vt* **-1.** [horse] enjaezar, poner los arreos a. **-2.** [use] aprovechar.

harp [hɑːp] *n* arpa *f*.

◆ **harp on** *vi*: to ~ **on (about sthg)** dar la matraca (con algo).

harpist ['hɑːpɪst] *n* arpista *m y f*.

harpoon [hɑː'puːn] ◇ *n* arpón *m*. ◇ *vt* arponear.

harpsichord ['hɑːpsɪkɔːd] *n* clavicordio *m*.

harrowing ['hærəʊɪŋ] *adj* horroroso(sa), pavoroso(sa).

harry ['hærɪ] (*pt* & *pp* **-ied**) *vt* **-1.** [badger]: to ~ **sb (for sthg)** acosar a alguien (para obtener algo). **-2.** MIL hostigar.

harsh [hɑːʃ] *adj* **-1.** [life, conditions, winter] duro(ra). **-2.** [punishment, decision, person] severo(ra). **-3.** [texture, taste, voice] áspero(ra); [light, sound] violento(ta).

harshly ['hɑːʃlɪ] *adv* **-1.** [punish, criticize, treat] severamente, duramente. **-2.** [grate] ásperamente; [shine] violentamente.

harshness ['hɑːʃnɪs] *n* **-1.** [of life, conditions, winter] dureza *f*. **-2.** [of punishment, decision, person] severidad *f*. **-3.** [of texture, taste, voice] aspereza *f*; [of light, sound] violencia *f*.

harvest ['hɑːvɪst] ◇ *n* [gen] cosecha *f*, pizca *f Amer*; [of grapes] vendimia *f*. ◇ *vt* cosechar.

harvest festival *n* festividad religiosa para celebrar la recogida de la cosecha.

has [weak form həz, strong form hæz] 3rd person sg → **have**.

has-been *n inf pej* vieja gloria *f*.

hash [hæʃ] *n*. **-1.** [meat] picadillo *m* (de carne). **-2.** *inf* [mess]: **to make a ~ of sthg** hacer algo fatal. **-3.** *drugs sl* [hashish] hachís *m*, chocolate *m*.

◆ **hash up** *vt sep Br inf* [make a mess of] fastidiar, estropear.

hash browns *npl Am* patatas cortadas en cuadraditos, fritas y servidas en forma de croqueta.

hashish ['hæʃiːʃ] *n* hachís *m*.

hasn't ['hæznt] = **has not**.

hassle ['hæsl] *inf* ◇ *n* (*U*) [annoyance] rollo *m*, lío *m*; **it's a real ~** es una lata. ◇ *vt* dar la lata a.

haste [heɪst] *n* prisa *f*; **to do sthg in ~** hacer algo de prisa y corriendo; **to make ~** *dated* darse prisa, apresurarse.

hasten ['heɪsn] *fml* ◇ *vt* acelerar. ◇ *vi*: **to ~ (to do sthg)** apresurarse (a hacer algo).

hastily ['heɪstɪlɪ] *adv* **-1.** [quickly] de prisa, precipitadamente. **-2.** [rashly] a la ligera, sin reflexionar.

hasty ['heɪstɪ] (*compar* **-ier**, *superl* **-iest**) *adj* **-1.** [quick] apresurado(da), precipitado(da). **-2.** [rash] irreflexivo(va).

hat [hæt] *n* sombrero *m*; **keep it under your ~** de esto ni palabra a nadie; **to be talking through one's ~** no decir más que pamplinas; **that's old ~** eso está más visto que el tebeo.

hatbox ['hæt,bɒks] *n* sombrerera *f*.

hatch [hætʃ] ◇ *vi* **-1.** [chick] romper el cascarón, salir del huevo. **-2.** [egg] romperse. ◇ *vt* **-1.** [chick, egg] empollar, incubar. **-2.** *fig* [scheme, plot] idear, tramar. ◇ *n* [for serving food] ventanilla *f*.

hatchback ['hætʃ,bæk] *n* coche *m* con puerta trasera.

hatchet ['hætʃɪt] *n* hacha *f*; **to bury the ~** hacer las paces.

hatchet job *n inf*: **to do a ~ on sb** despellejar a alguien.

hatchway ['hætʃ,weɪ] *n* escotilla *f*.

hate [heɪt] ◇ *n* odio *m*. ◇ *vt* odiar; **to ~ doing sthg** odiar hacer algo; **I ~ to seem**

pernickety, but ... no es que quiera ser quisquillosa, pero ....

hateful ['heɪtful] *adj* odioso(sa).

hatred ['heɪtrɪd] *n* odio *m*.

hat trick *n* SPORT *tres tantos marcados por un jugador en el mismo partido.*

haughty ['hɔːtɪ] (*compar* **-ier**, *superl* **-iest**) *adj* altanero(ra), altivo(va).

haul [hɔːl] ◇ *n* **-1.** [of stolen goods] botín *m*; [of drugs] alijo *m*. **-2.** [distance]: **long ~** largo camino *m*, largo trayecto *m*. ◇ *vt* **-1.** [pull] tirar, arrastrar. **-2.** [by lorry] transportar.

haulage ['hɔːlɪdʒ] *n* transporte *m*.

haulage contractor *n* transportista *m y f*, contratista *m y f* de transportes.

haulier *Br* ['hɔːlɪər], **hauler** *Am* ['hɔːlər] *n* transportista *m y f*, contratista *m y f* de transportes.

haunch [hɔːntʃ] *n* **-1.** [of person] asentaderas *fpl*; **to squat on one's ~es** ponerse en cuclillas. **-2.** [of animal] pernil *m*.

haunt [hɔːnt] ◇ *n* sitio *m* favorito, lugar *m* predilecto. ◇ *vt* **-1.** [subj: ghost] aparecer en. **-2.** [subj: memory, fear, problem] atormentar, obsesionar.

haunted ['hɔːntɪd] *adj* **-1.** [house, castle] encantado(da). **-2.** [look] atormentado(da).

haunting ['hɔːntɪŋ] *adj* obsesionante.

Havana [hə'vænə] *n* La Habana.

have [hæv] (*pt & pp* **had**) ◇ *aux vb* (*to form perfect tenses*) haber; **to ~ eaten** haber comido; **I've been on holiday** he estado de vacaciones; **we've never met before** no nos conocemos; **he hasn't gone yet, has he?** no se habrá ido ya ¿no?; **no, he hasn't (done it)** no, no lo ha hecho; **yes, he has (done it)** sí, lo ha hecho; **I was out of breath, having run all the way** estaba sin aliento después de haber corrido todo el camino.

◇ *vt* **-1.** [possess, receive]: **to ~ (got)** tener; **I ~ no money, I haven't got any money** no tengo dinero; **he has big hands** tiene las manos grandes; **I've got things to do** tengo cosas que hacer; **I had a letter from her** tuve carta de ella; **she's got loads of imagination** tiene mucha imaginación; **do you ~ a car?, ~ you got a car?** ¿tienes coche? **-2.** [experience, suffer] tener; **I had an accident** tuve un accidente; **I had a nasty surprise** me llevé una desagradable sorpresa; **to ~ a cold** tener un resfriado; **to ~ a good time** pasarlo bien. **-3.** (*referring to an action, instead of another verb*): **it will ~ no effect** no tendrá ningún efecto; **to ~ a look** mirar, echar una mirada; **to ~ a walk** dar un paseo; **to ~ a swim** darse un baño, nadar; **to ~ breakfast** desayunar; **to ~ lunch** comer; **to ~ dinner** cenar; **to ~ a cigarette** fumarse un cigarro; **to ~ an operation** operarse. **-4.** [give birth to]: **to ~ a baby** tener un niño. **-5.** [cause to be done]: **to ~ sb do sthg** hacer que alguien haga algo; **she had me clean my teeth again** me hizo lavarme los dientes otra vez; **to ~ sthg done** hacer que se haga algo; **I'm having the house decorated** voy a contratar a alguien para que me decore la casa; **to ~ one's hair cut** (ir a) cortarse el pelo. **-6.** [be treated in a certain way]: **I had my car stolen** me robaron el coche. **-7.** *inf* [cheat]: **you've been had** te han timado. **-8.** *phr*: **to ~ it in for sb** tenerla tomada con alguien; **to ~ had it** [car, machine] estar para el arrastre; **these clothes ~ had it** esta ropa está para tirarla; **I've had it!** [expressing exhaustion] ¡no puedo más!

◇ *modal vb* [be obliged]: **to ~ (got) to do sthg** tener que hacer algo; **do you ~ to go?, ~ you got to go?** ¿tienes que irte?; **I've got to go to work** tengo que ir a trabajar.

◆ **haves** *npl*: **the ~s and ~ nots** los privilegiados y los desposeídos.

◆ **have on** *vt sep* **-1.** [be wearing] llevar (puesto); **to ~ nothing on** no llevar nada encima OR puesto. **-2.** [tease] vacilar, tomar el pelo a. **-3.** [have to do]: **to ~ (got) a lot on** tener mucho que hacer; **~ you got anything on on Friday?** ¿estás libre OR haces algo el viernes?

◆ **have out** *vt sep* **-1.** [have removed]: **to ~ one's tonsils out** operarse de las amígdalas; **to ~ a tooth out** sacarse un diente. **-2.** [discuss frankly]: **to ~ it out with sb** poner las cuentas claras con alguien.

◆ **have up** *vt sep inf Br*: **to ~ sb up for sthg** meterle un puro OR llevar al juzgado a alguien por algo.

haven ['heɪvn] *n fig* refugio *m*, asilo *m*.

haven't ['hævnt] = **have not**.

haversack ['hævəsæk] *n* mochila *f*, zurrón *m*.

havoc ['hævək] *n* (*U*) caos *m*, estragos *mpl*; **to play ~ with sthg** causar estragos en algo.

Hawaii [hə'waɪiː] *n* Hawai.

Hawaiian [hə'waɪjən] ◇ *adj* hawaiano(na). ◇ *n* hawaiano *m*, -na *f*.

hawk [hɔːk] ◇ *n* halcón *m*; **to watch sb like a ~** observar a alguien con ojos de lince. ◇ *vt* vender por las calles.

hawker ['hɔːkər] *n* vendedor *m*, -ra *f* ambulante, abonero *m*, -ra *f Amer*.

hawthorn ['hɔːθɔːn] *n* majuelo *m*, espino *m*.

hay [heɪ] *n* heno *m*.

hay fever *n* (*U*) fiebre *f* del heno.

haymaking ['heɪ,meɪkɪŋ] *n* siega *f* del heno.

haystack ['heɪ,stæk] *n* almiar *m*.

haywire ['heɪ,waɪər] *adj inf*: **to go ~** [person] volverse majara; [plan] liarse, embrollarse; [computer, TV etc] changarse.

hazard ['hæzəd] ◇ *n* riesgo *m*, peligro *m*. ◇ *vt* [guess, suggestion] aventurar, atreverse a hacer.

hazardous ['hæzədəs] *adj* arriesgado(da), peligroso(sa).

hazard warning lights *npl Br* luces *fpl* de emergencia.

haze [heɪz] *n* neblina *f*.

hazel ['heɪzl] ◇ *adj* color avellana (*inv*). ◇ *n* [tree] avellano *m*.

hazelnut ['heɪzl,nʌt] *n* avellana *f*.

hazy ['heɪzɪ] (*compar* **-ier**, *superl* **-iest**) *adj* **-1.** [misty] neblinoso(sa). **-2.** [vague] vago(ga), confuso(sa).

H-bomb *n* bomba *f* H.

h & c (*abbr of* **hot and cold (water)**) c & f.

he [hiː] ◇ *pers pron* él; **~'s tall/happy** es alto/feliz; **~ loves fish** le encanta el pescado; **HE can't do it** ÉL no puede hacerlo; **there ~ is** allí está; **~ who** *fml* aquel que, el que. ◇ *n inf*: **it's a ~** [animal] es macho; [baby] es (un) niño. ◇ *comp*: **~-goat** macho cabrío *m*; **~-bear** oso *m* macho.

HE -1. *abbr of* **high explosive. -2.** (*abbr of* **His/Her Excellency**) S. Exc., S.E.

head [hed] ◇ *n* **-1.** ANAT & COMPUT cabeza *f*; **a ~ per ~** por cabeza, por persona; **off the top of one's ~** así de repente; **I couldn't make ~ nor tail of it** aquello no tenía ni pies ni cabeza; **on your own ~ be it** tú verás lo que haces, la responsabilidad es tuya; **to be banging one's ~ against a brick wall** predicar en el desierto; **to be soft in the ~** estar mal de la sesera; **to bite** OR **snap sb's ~ off** soltar un bufido a alguien sin motivo; **to be off one's ~** *Br*, **to be out of one's ~** *Am* estar como una cabra; **we put our ~s together** tratamos de resolverlo juntos; **it went to her ~** se le subió a la cabeza; **to keep/lose one's ~** no perder/perder la cabeza; **to laugh one's ~ off** reír a mandíbula batiente; **to sing/shout one's ~ off** cantar/gritar a todo pulmón. **-2.** [mind, brain] talento *m*, aptitud *f*; **she has a ~ for figures** se le dan bien las cuentas. **-3.** [top - gen] cabeza *f*; [- of bed] cabecera *f*. **-4.** [of flower] cabezuela *f*; [of cabbage] cogollo *m*. **-5.** [leader] jefe *m*, -fa *f*. **-6.** [head teacher] director *m*, -ra *f* (de colegio). **-7.** *phr*: **to come to a ~** llegar a un punto crítico.

◇ vt **-1.** [procession, convoy, list] encabezar. **-2.** [organization, delegation] dirigir. **-3.** FTBL cabecear.

◇ vi: **to ~ north/for home** dirigirse hacia el norte/a casa.

◆ **heads** npl [on coin] cara f; **~s or tails?** ¿cara o cruz?

◆ **head for** vt fus **-1.** [place] dirigirse a. **-2.** fig [trouble, disaster] ir camino a.

◆ **head off** vt sep **-1.** [intercept] interceptar. **-2.** fig [forestall] anticiparse a.

headache ['hedeɪk] n **-1.** MED dolor m de cabeza. **-2.** fig [problem] quebradero m de cabeza.

headband ['hedbænd] n cinta f, banda f (para el pelo).

headboard ['hed,bɔːd] n cabecero m.

head boy n Br [at school] alumno delegado principal que suele representar a sus condiscípulos en actos escolares.

head cold n resfriado que provoca dolor de cabeza pero no tos.

head count n recuento m (de los asistentes).

headdress ['hed,dres] n tocado m.

header ['hedə'] n FTBL cabezazo m.

headfirst [,hed'fɜːst] adv de cabeza.

headgear ['hed,gɪə'] n (U) tocado m.

head girl n Br [in school] alumna delegada principal que suele representar a sus condiscípulas en actos escolares.

headhunt ['hedhʌnt] vt contratar (nuevos talentos).

headhunter ['hed,hʌntə'] n cazatalentos m y f inv.

heading ['hedɪŋ] n encabezamiento m.

headlamp ['hedlæmp] n Br faro m.

headland ['hedlənd] n cabo m, promontorio m.

headlight ['hedlaɪt] n faro m.

headline ['hedlaɪn] n titular m.

headlong ['hedlɒŋ] ◇ adv **-1.** [headfirst] de cabeza. **-2.** [quickly, unthinkingly] precipitadamente. ◇ adj [unthinking] precipitado(da).

headmaster [,hed'mɑːstə'] n director m (de colegio).

headmistress [,hed'mɪstrɪs] n directora f (de colegio).

head office n oficina f central.

head-on ◇ adj de frente, frontal. ◇ adv de frente.

headphones ['hedfəʊnz] npl auriculares mpl.

headquarters [,hed'kwɔːtəz] npl (oficina f) central f, sede f; MIL cuartel m general.

headrest ['hedrest] n reposacabezas m inv.

headroom ['hedrʊm] n (U) [in car] espacio m entre la cabeza y el techo; [below bridge] altura f libre, gálibo m.

headscarf ['hedskɑːf] (pl **-scarves** [-skɑːvz] OR **-scarfs**) n pañuelo m (para la cabeza).

headset ['hedset] n auriculares mpl con micrófono.

headship ['hedʃɪp] n EDUC dirección f (de colegio).

headstand ['hedstænd] n puntal m.

head start n: **~ (on OR over)** ventaja f (con respecto a).

headstone ['hedstəʊn] n lápida f mortuoria.

headstrong ['hedstrɒŋ] adj obstinado(da).

head teacher n director m, -ra f (de colegio).

head waiter n jefe m de rango OR de camareros.

headway ['hedweɪ] n: **to make ~** avanzar, hacer progresos.

headwind ['hedwɪnd] n viento m de proa.

heady ['hedɪ] (compar **-ier**, superl **-iest**) adj **-1.** [exciting] excitante, emocionante. **-2.** [causing giddiness] embriagador(ra).

heal [hiːl] ◇ vt **-1.** [person] curar, sanar; [wound] cicatrizar. **-2.** fig [troubles, discord] remediar. ◇ vi cicatrizar.

◆ **heal up** vi cicatrizarse.

healing ['hiːlɪŋ] ◇ adj curativo(va). ◇ n curación f.

health [helθ] n **-1.** [gen] salud f; **to be in good/poor ~** estar bien/mal de salud; **to drink (to) sb's ~** brindar por alguien. **-2.** fig [of country, organization] buen estado m.

health centre n ambulatorio m, centro m sanitario.

health-conscious adj consciente de los problemas relacionados con la salud.

health farm n centro m de salud.

health food n comida f dietética.

health food shop n tienda f de dietética.

health hazard n riesgo m para la salud.

health service n servicio m sanitario de la Seguridad Social, ≃ INSALUD m.

health visitor n Br enfermero m, -ra f visitante.

healthy ['helθɪ] (compar **-ier**, superl **-iest**) adj **-1.** [gen] sano(na), saludable. **-2.** [profit] pingüe. **-3.** [attitude, respect] natural, sano(na).

heap [hiːp] ◇ n montón m, pila f, ruma f Amer; **in a ~** amontonado. ◇ vt **-1.** [pile up]: **to ~ sthg (on OR onto sthg)** amontonar algo (sobre algo). **-2.** [give]: **to ~ sthg on sb** colmar a alguien de algo.

◆ **heaps** npl inf montones fpl, mogollón m.

hear [hɪəʳ] (*pt* & *pp* **heard** [hɜːd]) ◇ *vt* **-1.** [gen] oír; **I ~ (that)** me dicen que. **-2.** JUR ver. ◇ *vi* **-1.** [gen] oír; **did you ~ about her husband?** ¿te enteraste de lo de su marido?; **have you heard about that job yet?** ¿sabes algo del trabajo ese?; **to ~ from sb** tener noticias de alguien. **-2.** *phr:* **to have heard of** haber oído hablar de; **I won't ~ of it!** ¡de eso ni hablar!

◆ **hear out** *vt sep* escuchar (sin interrumpir).

hearing ['hɪərɪŋ] *n* **-1.** [sense] oído *m*; **in** OR **within sb's ~** al alcance del oído de alguien; **hard of ~** duro de oído. **-2.** JUR vista *f*; **to give sb a fair ~** *fig* dar a alguien la oportunidad de que se exprese.

hearing aid *n* audífono *m*.

hearsay ['hɪəseɪ] *n* (*U*) habladurías *fpl*.

hearse [hɜːs] *n* coche *m* fúnebre.

heart [hɑːt] *n* **-1.** [gen] corazón *m*; **from the ~** con toda sinceridad; **my ~ leapt** me dio un vuelco el corazón; **my ~ sank** me llevé una gran desilusión; **it's a subject close to my ~** es un tema que me apasiona; **from the bottom of my ~** de (todo) corazón; **his ~ isn't in it** no pone el corazón en ello; **in my ~ of ~s** en lo más profundo de mi corazón; **to do sthg to one's ~'s content** hacer algo cuanto uno quiera; **to break sb's ~** romper OR partir el corazón a alguien; **to set one's ~ on sthg/on doing sthg** estar muy ilusionado con algo/con hacer algo; **to take sthg to ~** tomarse algo a pecho; **to have a ~ of gold** tener un corazón de oro. **-2.** [courage]: **I didn't have the ~ to tell her** no tuve valor para decírselo; **to lose ~** descorazonarse. **-3.** [centre - of issue, problem] quid *m*; [- of city etc] centro *m*; [- of lettuce] cogollo *m*.

◆ **hearts** *npl* corazones *mpl*; **the six of ~s** el seis de corazones.

◆ **at heart** *adv* en el fondo.

◆ **by heart** *adv* de memoria.

heartache ['hɑːteɪk] *n* congoja *f*.

heart attack *n* infarto *m*, ataque *m* cardíaco.

heartbeat ['hɑːtbiːt] *n* latido *m*.

heartbreaking ['hɑːt,breɪkɪŋ] *adj* desolador(ra).

heartbroken ['hɑːt,brəʊkn] *adj* desolado(da), abatido(da).

heartburn ['hɑːtbɜːn] *n* ardor *m* de estómago.

heart disease *n* enfermedades *fpl* cardíacas OR del corazón.

heartening ['hɑːtnɪŋ] *adj* alentador(ra).

heart failure *n* paro *m* cardíaco.

heartfelt ['hɑːtfelt] *adj* sincero(ra), de todo corazón.

hearth [hɑːθ] *n* hogar *m*.

heartland ['hɑːtlænd] *n* *fig* núcleo *m*, corazón *m*.

heartless ['hɑːtlɪs] *adj* cruel, inhumano(na).

heartrending ['hɑːt,rendɪŋ] *adj* desgarrador(ra).

heart-searching *n* examen *m* de conciencia.

heartthrob ['hɑːtθrɒb] *n* ídolo *m*.

heart-to-heart ◇ *n* charla *f* íntima. ◇ *adj* íntimo(ma).

heart transplant *n* transplante *m* de corazón.

heartwarming ['hɑːt,wɔːmɪŋ] *adj* gratificante, grato(ta).

hearty ['hɑːtɪ] (*compar* **-ier**, *superl* **-iest**) *adj* **-1.** [laughter] bonachón(ona) [welcome, congratulations, thanks] cordial; [person] fuerte(ta). **-2.** [meal] abundante; [appetite] bueno(na). **-3.** [dislike, distrust] profundo(da).

heat [hiːt] ◇ *n* **-1.** [gen] calor *m*. **-2.** [specific temperature] temperatura *f*. **-3.** *fig* [pressure] tensión *f*; **in the ~ of the moment** en el calor del momento. **-4.** [eliminating round] serie *f*, prueba *f* eliminatoria. **-5.** ZOOL: **on** Br OR **in ~** en celo *m*. ◇ *vt* calentar.

◆ **heat up** ◇ *vt sep* calentar. ◇ *vi* calentarse.

heated ['hiːtɪd] *adj* acalorado(da).

heater ['hiːtəʳ] *n* calentador *m*.

heath [hiːθ] *n* [place] brezal *m*.

heathen ['hiːðn] ◇ *adj* pagano(na). ◇ *n* pagano *m*, -na *f*.

heather ['heðəʳ] *n* brezo *m*.

heating ['hiːtɪŋ] *n* calefacción *f*.

heat rash *n* sarpullido *m* (*por el calor*).

heat-resistant *adj* refractario(ria), resistente al calor.

heat-seeking [-,siːkɪŋ] *adj* buscador(ra) de calor.

heatstroke ['hiːtstrəʊk] *n* (*U*) insolación *f*.

heat wave *n* ola *f* de calor.

heave [hiːv] ◇ *vt* **-1.** [pull] tirar de, arrastrar; [push] empujar. **-2.** *inf* [throw] tirar, lanzar. ◇ *vi* **-1.** [pull] tirar. **-2.** [rise and fall - waves] ondular; [- chest] palpitar. **-3.** [retch]: **my stomach ~d** tuve náuseas. ◇ *n* [pull] tirón *m*; [push] empujón *m*.

heaven ['hevn] *n* **-1.** [Paradise] cielo *m*; **~ (alone) knows!** ¡sabe Dios! **-2.** [delightful thing] encanto *m*, delicia *f*.

◆ **heavens** *npl*: **the ~s** *literary* los cielos; **(good) ~s!** ¡cielos!

heavenly ['hevnlı] *adj* **-1.** *inf dated* [delightful] **divino(na). -2.** *literary* [of the skies] celestial.

heavily ['hevılı] *adv* **-1.** [smoke, drink] mucho; [rain] con fuerza; **~ in debt** con muchas deudas. **-2.** [solidly] **~ built** corpulento(ta). **-3.** [breathe, sigh] **profundamente. -4.** [sit, move, fall] **pesadamente. -5.** [speak] pesarosamente.

heaviness ['hevınıs] *n* **-1.** [of fighting, traffic] **intensidad** *f*; [of casualties] **gran número** *m*. **-2.** [of soil, mixture] **densidad** *f*. **-3.** [of movement, breathing] **pesadez** *f*; [of blow] **dureza** *f*.

heavy ['hevı] (*compar* **-ier**, *superl* **-iest**) *adj* **-1.** [gen] **pesado(da);** [solid] **sólido(da); ~ build corpulencia** *f*; **how ~ is it?** ¿cuánto pesa? **-2.** [traffic, rain, fighting] **intenso(sa); to be a ~ sleeper** tener el sueño muy profundo; **to be a ~ smoker/drinker** ser un fumador/bebedor empedernido. **-3.** [soil, mixture] **denso(sa). -4.** [blow] **duro(ra). -5.** [busy - schedule, day] **apretado(da). -6.** [work] **duro(ra). -7.** [weather, air, day] **cargado(da). -8.** [sad]: **with a ~ heart** con pesar. **-9.** [laden]: **~ with** *literary* cargado(da) de.

heavy cream *n Am* nata *f* para montar.

heavy-duty *adj* [materials] **resistente;** [machinery] **sólido(da), para grandes cargas.**

heavy goods vehicle *n Br* vehículo *m* (de transporte) pesado.

heavy-handed [-'hændıd] *adj* torpe, poco sutil.

heavy industry *n* industria *f* pesada.

heavy metal *n* MUS música *f* heavy, heavy metal *m*.

heavyweight ['hevıweıt] SPORT ◇ *adj* de los pesos pesados. ◇ *n* peso *m* pesado.

Hebrew ['hi:bru:] ◇ *adj* hebreo(a). ◇ *n* **-1.** [person] hebreo *m*, -a *f*. **-2.** [language] hebreo *m*.

Hebrides ['hebrıdi:z] *npl*: **the ~ las Hébridas.**

heck [hek] *excl*: **what/where/why the ~ ...?** ¿qué/dónde/por qué demonios ...?; **a ~ of a lot** of la mar de.

heckle ['hekl] *vt & vi* interrumpir con exabruptos.

heckler ['heklər] *n* persona que interrumpe a un orador, cómico etc.

hectare ['hekteər] *n* hectárea *f*.

hectic ['hektık] *adj* muy agitado(da), ajetreado(da).

hector ['hektər] ◇ *vt* intimidar con fanfarronadas. ◇ *vi* fanfarronear.

he'd [hi:d] = **he had, he would.**

hedge [hedʒ] ◇ *n* seto *m*. ◇ *vi* [prevaricate] contestar con evasivas.

hedgehog ['hedʒhɒg] *n* erizo *m*.

hedgerow ['hedʒrəu] *n* seto *m* (*en el campo*).

hedonism ['hi:dənızm] *n* hedonismo *m*.

hedonist ['hi:dənıst] *n* hedonista *m y f*.

heed [hi:d] ◇ *n*: **to pay ~ to sb** hacer caso a alguien; **to take ~ of sthg** tener algo en cuenta. ◇ *vt fml* tener en cuenta.

heedless ['hi:dlıs] *adj*: **to be ~ of sthg** no hacer caso de algo.

heel [hi:l] *n* **-1.** [of foot] **talón** *m*; **to dig one's ~s in** plantarse, mantenerse en sus trece; **to follow hard on the ~s (of)** ir inmediatamente a continuación (de); **to take to one's ~s** poner pies en polvorosa; **to turn on one's ~** dar media vuelta. **-2.** [of shoe] **tacón** *m*, **taco** *m Amer*.

hefty ['heftı] (*compar* **-ier**, *superl* **-iest**) *adj inf* **-1.** [person] **fornido(da). -2.** [salary, fee, fine] **considerable, importante.**

heifer ['hefər] *n* vaquilla *f*.

height [haıt] *n* **-1.** [gen] **altura** *f*; [of person] **estatura** *f*; **5 metres in ~** 5 metros de altura; **what ~ is it/are you?** ¿cuánto mide/mides?; **to gain/lose ~** ganar/perder altura. **-2.** [zenith]: **the ~ of** [gen] el punto álgido de; [ignorance, bad taste] el colmo de.
   ◆ **heights** *npl* [high places] **alturas** *fpl*; **to be afraid of ~s** tener vértigo.

heighten ['haıtn] ◇ *vt* intensificar, aumentar. ◇ *vi* intensificarse, aumentar.

heinous ['heınəs] *adj fml* execrable, atroz.

heir [eər] *n* heredero *m*.

heir apparent (*pl* **heirs apparent**) *n* heredero *m* forzoso.

heiress ['eərıs] *n* heredera *f*.

heirloom ['eəlu:m] *n* reliquia *f* de familia.

heist [haıst] *n inf* golpe *m*, robo *m*.

held [held] *pt & pp* → **hold.**

helices ['helısi:z] *pl* → **helix.**

helicopter ['helıkɒptər] *n* helicóptero *m*.

heliport ['helıpɔ:t] *n* helipuerto *m*.

helium ['hi:lıəm] *n* helio *m*.

helix ['hi:lıks] (*pl* **-es** OR **helices**) *n* [spiral] hélice *f*.

hell [hel] ◇ *n* infierno *m*; **what/where/why the ~ ...?** *inf* ¿qué/dónde/por qué demonios ...?; **one** OR **a ~ of a mess** *inf* un lío de mil demonios; **one** OR **a ~ of a nice guy** *inf* un tipo estupendo; **like ~** [a lot] una barbaridad; [not at all so] ¡qué va!; **to get the ~ out (of)** *inf* salir echando leches (de); **all ~ broke loose** *inf* se armó la gorda; **to do sthg for the ~ of it** *inf* hacer algo porque sí; **to give sb ~** *inf* hacérselas pasar canutas a alguien; **go to ~!** *v inf* ¡vete al infierno!; **to play ~ with sthg** *inf* causar estragos en algo; **to ~ with ... inf** ¡a la porra (con) ...! ◇ *excl inf* ¡hostias!

he'll [hiːl] = **he will.**

hell-bent *adj*: **to be ~ on sthg/on doing sthg** estar totalmente decidido(da) a hacer algo.

hellish ['helɪʃ] *adj inf* diabólico(ca), infernal.

hello [hə'ləʊ] *excl* **-1.** [as greeting] ¡hola!; [on phone - when answering] ¡diga!, ¡bueno! *Amer*; [- when calling] ¡oiga! **-2.** [to attract attention] ¡oiga!

helm [helm] *n lit* & *fig* timón *m*; **at the ~** al timón.

helmet ['helmɪt] *n* casco *m*.

helmsman ['helmzmən] (*pl* **-men** [-mən]) *n* NAUT timonel *m*.

help [help] ◇ *n* **-1.** [gen] ayuda *f*; **with the ~ of** con la ayuda de; **to be a ~** ser una ayuda; **to be of ~** ayudar. **-2.** (*U*) [emergency aid] socorro *m*, ayuda *f*. ◇ *vt* **-1.** [assist]: **to ~ sb ((to) do sthg/with sthg)** ayudar a alguien (a hacer algo/con algo); **can I ~ you?** [in shop, bank] ¿en qué puedo servirle? **-2.** [avoid]: **I can't ~ it/feeling sad** no puedo evitarlo/evitar que me dé pena. **-3.** [with food, drink]: **to ~ o.s. (to sthg)** servirse (algo). ◇ *vi*: **to ~ (with)** ayudar (con). ◇ *excl* ¡socorro!, ¡auxilio!
◆ **help out** ◇ *vt sep* echar una mano a. ◇ *vi* echar una mano.

helper ['helpə'] *n* **-1.** [gen] ayudante *m y f*. **-2.** *Am* [to do housework] mujer *f* OR señora *f* de la limpieza.

helpful ['helpfʊl] *adj* **-1.** [willing to help] servicial, atento(ta). **-2.** [providing assistance] útil.

helping ['helpɪŋ] *n* ración *f*; **would you like a second ~?** ¿quiere repetir?

helping hand *n* ayuda *f*.

helpless ['helplɪs] *adj* [child] indefenso(sa); [look, gesture] impotente.

helplessly ['helplɪslɪ] *adv* **-1.** [unable to stop] sin poder parar. **-2.** [in a helpless manner] impotentemente.

helpline ['helplaɪn] *n* servicio *m* telefónico de ayuda.

Helsinki ['helsɪŋkɪ] *n* Helsinki.

helter-skelter [,heltə'skeltə'] *Br* ◇ *n* tobogán *m* gigante. ◇ *adv* atropelladamente.

hem [hem] (*pt* & *pp* **-med**, *cont* **-ming**) ◇ *n* dobladillo *m*. ◇ *vt* hacerle el dobladillo a.
◆ **hem in** *vt sep* rodear, cercar.

he-man *n inf hum* tiarrón *m*.

hematology [,hiːmə'tɒlədʒɪ] *n* hematología *f*.

hemisphere ['hemɪ,sfɪə'] *n* [of earth] hemisferio *m*.

hemline ['hemlaɪn] *n* bajo *m* (*de falda etc*).

hemoglobin [,hiːmə'gləʊbɪn] *n* hemoglobina *f*.

hemophilia [,hiːmə'fɪlɪə] *n* hemofilia *f*.

hemophiliac [,hiːmə'fɪlɪæk] *n* hemofílico *m*, -ca *f*.

hemorrhage ['hemərɪdʒ] ◇ *n* hemorragia *f*. ◇ *vi* tener una hemorragia.

hemorrhoids ['hemərɔɪdz] *npl* hemorroides *fpl*.

hemp [hemp] *n* cáñamo *m*.

hen [hen] *n* **-1.** [female chicken] gallina *f*. **-2.** [female bird] hembra *f*.

hence [hens] *adv fml* **-1.** [therefore] por lo tanto, así pues. **-2.** [from now]: **five years ~** de aquí a cinco años.

henceforth [,hens'fɔːθ] *adv fml* de ahora en adelante, en lo sucesivo.

henchman ['hentʃmən] (*pl* **-men** [-mən]) *n pej* esbirro *m*.

henna ['henə] ◇ *n* henna *f*. ◇ *vt* teñir con henna.

hen party *n inf* despedida *f* de soltera.

henpecked ['henpekt] *adj pej* calzonazos (*inv*).

hepatitis [,hepə'taɪtɪs] *n* hepatitis *f inv*.

her [hɜː'] ◇ *pers pron* **-1.** (*direct - unstressed*) la; (*- stressed*) ella; [- referring to ship, car etc] lo; **I know ~** la conozco; **I like ~** me gusta; **it's ~** es ella; **if I were** OR **was ~** si (yo) fuera ella; **you can't expect** HER **to do it** no esperarás que ELLA lo haga; **fill ~ up!** AUT ¡llénemelo!, ¡lléneme el depósito! **-2.** (*indirect - gen*) le; (*- with other third person pronouns*) se; **he sent ~ a letter** le mandó una carta; **we spoke to ~** hablamos con ella; **I gave it to ~** se lo di. **-3.** (*after prep, in comparisons etc*) ella; **I'm shorter than ~** yo soy más bajo que ella.
◇ *poss adj* su, sus (*pl*); **~ coat** su abrigo; **~ children** sus niños; **~ name is Sarah** se llama Sarah; **it wasn't** HER **fault** no fue culpa suya OR su culpa; **she washed ~ hair** se lavó el pelo.

herald ['herəld] ◇ *vt fml* **-1.** [signify, usher in] anunciar. **-2.** [proclaim] proclamar. ◇ *n* **-1.** [messenger] heraldo *m*. **-2.** [sign] anuncio *m*.

heraldry ['herəldrɪ] *n* heráldica *f*.

herb [hɜːb] *n* hierba *f* (*aromática o medicinal*).

herbaceous [hɜː'beɪʃəs] *adj* herbáceo(a).

herbal ['hɜːbl] *adj* a base de hierbas.

herbicide ['hɜːbɪsaɪd] *n* herbicida *m*.

herbivore ['hɜːbɪvɔːʳ] *n* herbívoro *m*, -ra *f*.

herb tea *n* infusión *f*.

herd [hɜːd] ◇ *n* manada *f*, rebaño *m*. ◇ *vt* **-1.** [drive] llevar en manada. **-2.** *fig* [push] conducir (en grupo) bruscamente.

herdsman ['hɜːdzmən] (*pl* **-men** [-mən]) *n* [of cattle] vaquero *m*.

here [hɪəʳ] *adv* aquí; ~ **he is/they are** aquí está/están; ~ **it is** aquí está; ~ **is the book** aquí tienes el libro; ~ **and there** aquí y allá; ~ **are the keys** aquí tienes las llaves; ~**'s to** [in toast] brindemos por.

hereabouts *Br* ['hɪərə,baʊts], **hereabout** *Am* [,hɪərə'baʊt] *adv* por aquí.

hereafter [,hɪər'ɑːftəʳ] ◇ *adv fml* [from now on] a partir de ahora, de ahora en adelante; [later on] más tarde. ◇ *n*: **the** ~ el más allá, la otra vida.

hereby [,hɪə'baɪ] *adv fml* **-1.** [in documents] por la presente. **-2.** [when speaking]: **I** ~ **declare you the winner** desde este momento te declaro vencedor.

hereditary [hɪ'redɪtrɪ] *adj* hereditario(ria).

heredity [hɪ'redətɪ] *n* herencia *f*.

heresy ['herəsɪ] (*pl* **-ies**) *n* RELIG & *fig* herejía *f*.

heretic ['herətɪk] *n* RELIG hereje *m y f*; *fig* [unorthodox thinker] rebelde *m y f*, iconoclasta *m y f*.

herewith [,hɪə'wɪð] *adv fml* [with letter]: **please find** ~ ... le mando adjunto ....

heritage ['herɪtɪdʒ] *n* patrimonio *m*.

heritage centre *n* edificio o museo en un lugar de interés histórico.

hermaphrodite [hɜː'mæfrədaɪt] ZOOL ◇ *adj* hermafrodita. ◇ *n* hermafrodita *m y f*.

hermetic [hɜː'metɪk] *adj* hermético(ca).

hermetically [hɜː'metɪkəlɪ] *adv*: ~ **sealed** cerrado(da) herméticamente.

hermit ['hɜːmɪt] *n* ermitaño *m*, -ña *f*.

hernia ['hɜːnjə] *n* hernia *f* de hiato OR hiatal.

hero ['hɪərəʊ] (*pl* **-es**) *n* **-1.** [gen] héroe *m*. **-2.** [idol] ídolo *m*.

heroic [hɪ'rəʊɪk] *adj* heroico(ca).

heroin ['herəʊɪn] *n* heroína *f (droga)*.

heroine ['herəʊɪn] *n* heroína *f*.

heroism ['herəʊɪzm] *n* heroísmo *m*.

heron ['herən] (*pl inv* OR **-s**) *n* garza *f* real.

hero worship *n* veneración *f*.

herpes ['hɜːpiːz] *n* herpes *m inv*.

herring ['herɪŋ] (*pl inv* OR **-s**) *n* arenque *m*.

herringbone ['herɪŋbəʊn] *n* [pattern] espiga *f*, espiguilla *f*.

hers [hɜːz] *poss pron* suyo (suya); **that money is** ~ ese dinero es suyo; **those keys are** ~ esas llaves son suyas; **it wasn't his fault, it was** HERS no fue culpa de él sino de ella; **a friend of** ~ un amigo suyo, un amigo de ella; **mine is good, but** ~ **is bad** el mío es bueno pero el suyo es malo.

herself [hɜː'self] *pron* **-1.** (*reflexive*) se; (*after prep*) sí misma; **with** ~ consigo misma. **-2.** (*for emphasis*) ella misma; **she did it** ~ lo hizo ella sola.

Herts. [hɑːts] (*abbr of* **Hertfordshire**) *condado inglés*.

he's [hiːz] = **he is**, **he has**.

hesitant ['hezɪtənt] *adj* **-1.** [unsure of oneself] indeciso(sa), inseguro(ra). **-2.** [faltering, slow to appear] vacilante.

hesitate ['hezɪteɪt] *vi* vacilar, dudar; **to** ~ **to do sthg** dudar en hacer algo.

hesitation [,hezɪ'teɪʃn] *n* vacilación *f*; **without** ~ sin vacilar; **to have no** ~ **in doing sthg** no dudar en hacer algo.

hessian ['hesɪən] *n Br* arpillera *f*.

heterogeneous [,hetərə'dʒiːnjəs] *adj fml* heterogéneo(a).

heterosexual [,hetərəʊ'sekʃʊəl] ◇ *adj* heterosexual. ◇ *n* heterosexual *m y f*.

het up [het-] *adj inf* nervioso(sa), hecho(cha) un manojo de nervios.

hew [hjuː] (*pt* **-ed**, *pp* **-ed** OR **-n**) *vt literary* [tree, branch] talar; [figure, statue] tallar.

HEW (*abbr of* **(Department of) Health, Education and Welfare**) *n ministerio estadounidense de educación y sanidad pública*.

hex [heks] *n* [curse] maleficio *m*, maldición *f*.

hexagon ['heksəgən] *n* hexágono *m*.

hexagonal [hek'sægənl] *adj* hexagonal.

hey [heɪ] *excl* ¡eh!, ¡oye!, ¡che! *Amer*.

heyday ['heɪdeɪ] *n* apogeo *m*, auge *m*.

hey presto [-'prestəʊ] *excl* ¡tachaán!

HF (*abbr of* **high frequency**) AF *f*.

HGV *n abbr of* **heavy goods vehicle**; **an** ~ **licence** un carnet de vehículo de gran tonelaje.

hi [haɪ] *excl inf* [hello] ¡hola!

HI *abbr of* **Hawaii**.

hiatus [haɪ'eɪtəs] (*pl* **-es**) *n fml* [pause] pausa *f*.

hiatus hernia *n* hernia *f* de hiato.

hibernate ['haɪbəneɪt] *vi* hibernar.

hibernation [,haɪbə'neɪʃn] *n* hibernación *f*.

hiccough, **hiccup** ['hɪkʌp] (*pt* & *pp* **-ped**, *cont* **-ping**) ◇ *n* **-1.** [caused by wind] hipo *m*;

to have ~s tener hipo. **-2.** *fig* [difficulty] contratiempo *m.* ◇ *vi* hipar.

hick [hɪk] *n inf pej* paleto *m*, -ta *f*, palurdo *m*, -da *f.*

hid [hɪd] *pt* → **hide.**

hidden ['hɪdn] ◇ *pp* → **hide.** ◇ *adj* oculto(ta).

hide [haɪd] (*pt* **hid**, *pp* **hidden**) ◇ *vt* **-1.** [conceal] esconder, ocultar; **to ~ sthg (from sb)** esconder OR ocultar algo (a alguien). **-2.** [cover] tapar, ocultar. ◇ *vi* esconderse, ocultarse. ◇ *n* **-1.** [animal skin] piel *f.* **-2.** [for watching birds, animals] puesto *m.*

hide-and-seek *n* escondite *m.*

hideaway ['haɪdəweɪ] *n inf* escondite *m.*

hidebound ['haɪdbaʊnd] *adj pej* de miras estrechas.

hideous ['hɪdɪəs] *adj* horrible, espantoso(sa).

hideout ['haɪdaʊt] *n* guarida *f*, escondrijo *m.*

hiding ['haɪdɪŋ] *n* **-1.** [concealment]: **in ~** escondido(da). **-2.** *inf* [beating]: **to give sb/get a (good) ~** darle a alguien/recibir una (buena) paliza.

hiding place *n* escondite *m.*

hierarchical [ˌhaɪə'rɑːkɪkl] *adj* jerárquico(ca).

hierarchy ['haɪərɑːkɪ] (*pl* **-ies**) *n* jerarquía *f.*

hieroglyphics [ˌhaɪərə'glɪfɪks] *npl* jeroglíficos *mpl.*

hi-fi ['haɪfaɪ] *n* equipo *m* de alta fidelidad.

higgledy-piggledy [ˌhɪgldɪ'pɪgldɪ] *inf* ◇ *adj* desordenado(da). ◇ *adv* de cualquier manera, a la buena de Dios.

high [haɪ] ◇ *adj* **-1.** [gen] alto(ta); [wind] fuerte; [altitude] grande; **it's 6 metres ~** tiene 6 metros de alto OR altura; **how ~ is it?** ¿cuánto mide?; **temperatures in the ~ 20s** temperaturas cercanas a los 30 grados; **to have a ~ opinion of** tener muy buen concepto de. **-2.** [ideals, principles, tone] elevado(da). **-3.** [high-pitched] agudo(da). **-4.** *drug sl* flipado(da), puesto(ta). ◇ *adv* alto; **he threw the ball ~ in the air** lanzó la bola muy alto. ◇ *n* [highest point] punto *m* álgido; **to reach a new ~** alcanzar un nuevo récord.

highball ['haɪbɔːl] *n Am* highball *m.*

highbrow ['haɪbraʊ] *adj* culto(ta), intelectual.

high chair *n* trona *f.*

high-class *adj* [superior] de (alta) categoría.

high command *n* alto mando *m.*

high commissioner *n* alto comisario *m*, alta comisaria *f.*

High Court *n Br* tribunal *m* supremo.

high-density *adj* COMPUT de alta densidad.

higher ['haɪə^r] *adj* [exam, qualification] superior.

◆ **Higher** *n*: **Higher (Grade)** *en Escocia, examen realizado al final de la enseñanza secundaria.*

higher education *n* enseñanza *f* superior.

high explosive *n* explosivo *m* de gran potencia.

high-fidelity *adj* de alta fidelidad.

high-flier *n persona ambiciosa y con un prometedor futuro.*

high-flying *adj* [ambitious] ambicioso y prometedor (ambiciosa y prometedora).

high-handed [-'hændɪd] *adj* despótico(ca), arbitrario(ria).

high-heeled [-'hiːld] *adj* de tacón alto.

high horse *n inf*: **to get on one's ~** querer sentar cátedra.

high jump *n* salto *m* de altura; **you're** OR **you'll be for the ~** *Br inf* te la vas a cargar.

Highland Games ['haɪlənd-] *npl fiesta de deportes escoceses.*

HIGHLAND GAMES:
En Escocia, especie de fiesta local al aire libre durante la cual se celebran de manera simultánea todo tipo de concursos (de baile, gaita etc) y pruebas deportivas (carreras, lanzamiento de martillo y también 'tossing the caber', 'tug o'war' etc). En algunas de estas pruebas sólo puede participar la población local mientras que otras están abiertas a la participación del público en general

Highlands ['haɪləndz] *npl*: **the ~** [of Scotland] las Tierras Altas del Norte (de Escocia).

high-level *adj* de alto nivel.

high life *n*: **the ~** la buena vida.

highlight ['haɪlaɪt] ◇ *n* [of event, occasion] punto *m* culminante. ◇ *vt* **-1.** [visually] subrayar, marcar. **-2.** [emphasize] destacar, resaltar.

◆ **highlights** *npl* [in hair] reflejos *mpl.*

highlighter (pen) ['haɪlaɪtə^r-] *n* rotulador *m*, marcador *m.*

highly ['haɪlɪ] *adv* **-1.** [very, extremely] muy, enormemente. **-2.** [in important position]: **~ placed** en un puesto importante. **-3.** [favourably]: **to speak ~ of sb** hablar muy bien de alguien; **to think ~ of sb** tener a alguien en mucha estima.

highly-strung *adj* tenso(sa), muy nervioso(sa).

high mass *n* misa *f* mayor.

high-minded [-'maɪndɪd] *adj* de moral elevada en exceso.

Highness ['haɪnɪs] *n*: **His/Her/Your (Royal)** ~ Su Alteza *f* (Real); **their (Royal)** ~**es** Sus Altezas (Reales).

high-octane *adj* súper (*inv*), de calidad superior.

high-pitched *adj* agudo(da).

high point *n* [of occasion] momento *m* OR punto *m* culminante.

high-powered [-'pəʊəd] *adj* **-1.** [powerful] de gran potencia. **-2.** [prestigious - activity, place] prestigioso(sa); [- person] de altos vuelos.

high-pressure *adj* **-1.** [cylinder, gas etc] a alta presión. **-2.** METEOR [zone, area] de altas presiones. **-3.** [persuasive] perseverante.

high priest *n* RELIG sumo sacerdote *m*.

high-ranking *adj* [in army etc] de alta graduación; [in government]: ~ **official** alto cargo *m*.

high resolution *adj* COMPUT de alta resolución.

high-rise *adj*: ~ **building** edificio de muchos pisos.

high-risk *adj* de alto riesgo.

high school *n* ≈ instituto *m* de bachillerato.

high seas *npl*: **the** ~ alta mar.

high season *n* temporada *f* alta.

high-speed *adj* de alta velocidad.

high-spirited *adj* [person] animado(da).

high spot *n* punto *m* culminante.

high street *n* Br calle *f* mayor OR principal.

hightail ['haɪteɪl] *vt* inf: **to** ~ **it** pirárselas.

high tea *n* Br merienda *f* cena.

high tech [-,tek] *adj* de alta tecnología.

high technology *n* alta tecnología *f*.

high-tension *adj* de alta tensión.

high tide *n* [of sea] marea *f* alta.

high treason *n* alta traición *f*.

high water *n* (*U*) marea *f* alta.

highway ['haɪweɪ] *n* **-1.** Am [main road between cities] autopista *f*. **-2.** Br [any main road] carretera *f*.

Highway Code *n* Br: **the** ~ el código de la circulación.

high wire *n* alambre *m*, cuerda *f* floja.

hijack ['haɪdʒæk] ◇ *n* [of aircraft] secuestro *m* aéreo. ◇ *vt* [aircraft] secuestrar.

hijacker ['haɪdʒækə'] *n* secuestrador *m*, -ra *f* (*de un avión*).

hike [haɪk] ◇ *n* [long walk] excursión *f*, caminata *f*; **to go for** OR **on a** ~ ir de excursión. ◇ *vi* [go for walk] ir de excursión.

hiker ['haɪkə'] *n* excursionista *m* y *f*.

hiking ['haɪkɪŋ] *n* excursionismo *m*; **to go** ~ ir de excursión.

hilarious [hɪ'leərɪəs] *adj* desternillante.

hilarity [hɪ'lærətɪ] *n* fml hilaridad *f*.

hill [hɪl] *n* **-1.** [mound] colina *f*. **-2.** [slope] cuesta *f*.

hillbilly ['hɪl,bɪlɪ] (*pl* **-ies**) *n* Am pej palurdo *m*, -da *f* de las montañas.

hillock ['hɪlək] *n* altozano *m*, collado *m*.

hillside ['hɪlsaɪd] *n* ladera *f*.

hill start *n* arranque *m* en una cuesta.

hilltop ['hɪltɒp] ◇ *adj* en la cumbre de una colina. ◇ *n* cumbre *f* de una colina.

hilly ['hɪlɪ] (*compar* **-ier**, *superl* **-iest**) *adj* montañoso(sa).

hilt [hɪlt] *n* puño *m*, empuñadura *f*; **to support/defend sb to the** ~ apoyar/ defender a alguien sin reservas; **to be mortgaged to the** ~ tener una hipoteca enorme.

him [hɪm] *pers pron* **-1.** (*direct - unstressed*) lo, le; (*- stressed*) él; **I know** ~ lo OR le conozco; **I like** ~ me gusta; **it's** ~ es él; **if I were** OR **was** ~ si (yo) fuera él; **you can't expect** HIM **to do it** no esperarás que ÉL lo haga. **-2.** (*indirect - gen*) le; (*- with other third person pronouns*) se; **she sent** ~ **a letter** le mandó una carta; **we spoke to** ~ hablamos con él; **I gave it to** ~ se lo di. **-3.** (*after prep, in comparisons etc*) él; **I'm shorter than** ~ yo soy más bajo que él.

Himalayan [,hɪmə'leɪən] *adj* himalayo(ya).

Himalayas [,hɪmə'leɪəz] *npl*: **the** ~ el Himalaya.

himself [hɪm'self] *pron* **-1.** (*reflexive*) se; (*after prep*) sí mismo; **with** ~ consigo mismo. **-2.** (*for emphasis*) él mismo; **he did it** ~ lo hizo él solo.

hind [haɪnd] (*pl inv* OR **-s**) ◇ *adj* trasero(ra), posterior. ◇ *n* cierva *f*.

hinder ['hɪndə'] *vt* [gen] estorbar; [progress, talks, attempts] entorpecer, dificultar.

Hindi ['hɪndɪ] *n* [language] hindi *m*.

hindmost ['haɪndməʊst] *adj* postrero(ra).

hindquarters ['haɪndkwɔːtəz] *npl* cuartos *mpl* traseros.

hindrance ['hɪndrəns] *n* **-1.** [obstacle] obstáculo *m*, impedimento *m*; [person] estorbo *m*. **-2.** (*U*) [delay] interrupciones *fpl*, retrasos *mpl*.

hindsight ['haɪndsaɪt] *n*: **with the benefit of** ~ ahora que se sabe lo que pasó.

Hindu ['hɪnduː] (*pl* **-s**) ◇ *adj* hindú. ◇ *n* hindú *m* y *f*.

Hinduism ['hɪnduːɪzm] *n* hinduismo *m*.

hinge [hɪndʒ] (*cont* **hingeing**) *n* [on door, window] bisagra *f*.

◆ **hinge (up)on** *vt fus* [depend on] depender de.

hint [hɪnt] ◇ *n* **-1.** [indication] indirecta *f*; **to drop a** ~ lanzar una indirecta; **to take the** ~ darse por aludido(da). **-2.** [piece of advice] consejo *m*. **-3.** [small amount, suggestion] atisbo *m*, asomo *m*; [of colour] pizca *f*. ◇ *vi*: **to** ~ **at sthg** insinuar algo. ◇ *vt*: **to** ~ **that** insinuar que.

hinterland ['hɪntəlænd] *n* [area around coast, river] interior *m*.

hip [hɪp] *n* ANAT cadera *f*.

hipbath ['hɪpbɑːθ] *n* baño *m* de asiento.

hipbone ['hɪpbəʊn] *n* hueso *m* de la cadera.

hip flask *n* petaca *f*.

hip-hop *n* MUS hip hop *m*.

hippie ['hɪpɪ] *n* hippy *m* y *f*.

hippo ['hɪpəʊ] (*pl* **-s**) *n inf* hipopótamo *m*.

hippopotamus [,hɪpə'pɒtəməs] (*pl* **-muses** OR **-mi** [-maɪ]) *n* hipopótamo *m*.

hippy ['hɪpɪ] (*pl* **-ies**) *n* = **hippie**.

hire ['haɪəʳ] ◇ *n* (*U*) [of car, equipment] alquiler *m*; **for** ~ [taxi] libre; **boats for** ~ se alquilan barcos; **on** ~ de alquiler. ◇ *vt* **-1.** [rent] alquilar. **-2.** [employ] contratar.

◆ **hire out** *vt sep* [car, equipment] alquilar; [one's services] ofrecer.

hire car *n Br* coche *m* de alquiler.

hire purchase *n* (*U*) *Br* compra *f* a plazos; **to buy sthg on** ~ comprar algo a plazos.

his [hɪz] ◇ *poss adj* su, sus (*pl*); ~ **house** su casa; ~ **children** sus niños; ~ **name is Joe** se llama Joe; **it wasn't** HIS **fault** no fue culpa suya OR su culpa; **he washed** ~ **hair** se lavó el pelo. ◇ *poss pron* suyo (suya); **that money is** ~ ese dinero es suyo; **those keys are** ~ esas llaves son suyas; **it wasn't her fault, it was** HIS no fue culpa de ella sino de él; **a friend of** ~ un amigo suyo, un amigo de él; **mine is good, but** ~ **is bad** el mío es bueno pero el suyo es malo.

Hispanic [hɪ'spænɪk] ◇ *adj* hispánico(ca). ◇ *n* hispano *m*, -na *f*.

hiss [hɪs] ◇ *n* **-1.** [of person] bisbiseo *m*, siseo *m*. **-2.** [of steam, gas, snake] silbido *m*. ◇ *vt* [performance] ≃ silbar, ≃ pitar. ◇ *vi* **-1.** [person] bisbisear, sisear; [to express disapproval] ≃ silbar, ≃ pitar. **-2.** [steam, gas, snake] silbar.

histogram ['hɪstəgræm] *n* histograma *m*.

historian [hɪ'stɔːrɪən] *n* historiador *m*, -ra *f*.

historic [hɪ'stɒrɪk] *adj* [significant] histórico(ca).

historical [hɪ'stɒrɪkəl] *adj* histórico(ca).

history ['hɪstərɪ] (*pl* **-ies**) *n* **-1.** [gen] historia *f*; **to go down in** ~ pasar a la historia; **to make** ~ hacer historia. **-2.** [past record] historial *m*.

histrionics [hɪstrɪ'ɒnɪks] *npl pej* teatro *m*, teatralidad *f*.

hit [hɪt] (*pt* & *pp* **hit**, *cont* **-ting**) ◇ *n* **-1.** [blow] golpe *m*. **-2.** [successful strike] impacto *m*; **to score a direct** ~ dar de lleno en el blanco. **-3.** [success] éxito *m*. ◇ *comp* de éxito. ◇ *vt* **-1.** [subj: person] pegar, golpear. **-2.** [crash into] chocar contra OR con. **-3.** [reach] alcanzar, llegar a; [bull's-eye] dar en. **-4.** [affect badly] afectar. **-5.** *phr*: **to** ~ **it off (with sb)** hacer buenas migas (con alguien).

◆ **hit back** *vi*: **to** ~ **back (at sb)** devolver la pelota (a alguien); **to** ~ **back (at sthg)** responder (a algo).

◆ **hit on** *vt fus* **-1.** = **hit upon. -2.** *Am inf* [chat up] ligar con.

◆ **hit out** *vi*: **to** ~ **out at** [physically] tratar de golpear; [criticize] condenar.

◆ **hit upon** *vt fus* [think of] dar con.

hit-and-miss = **hit-or-miss**.

hit-and-run *adj* [driver] que se da a la fuga después de causar un accidente.

hitch [hɪtʃ] ◇ *n* [problem, snag] obstáculo *m*, pega *f*. ◇ *vt* **-1.** [catch]: **to** ~ **a lift** conseguir que le lleven en coche a uno. **-2.** [fasten]: **to** ~ **sthg on** OR **onto sthg** enganchar algo a algo. ◇ *vi* [hitchhike] hacer autoestop.

◆ **hitch up** *vt sep* [clothes] subirse.

hitchhike ['hɪtʃhaɪk] *vi* hacer autoestop.

hitchhiker ['hɪtʃhaɪkəʳ] *n* autoestopista *m* y *f*.

hi-tech [,haɪ'tek] = **high tech**.

hither ['hɪðəʳ] *adv literary* hasta aquí, acá; ~ **and thither** acá y acullá.

hitherto [,hɪðə'tuː] *adv fml* hasta ahora.

hit list *n* lista *f* negra, lista *f* de futuras víctimas.

hit man *n* asesino *m* a sueldo.

hit-or-miss *adj* azaroso(sa), a la buena de Dios.

hit parade *n dated* lista *f* de éxitos.

HIV (*abbr of* **human immunodeficiency virus**) *n* VIH *m*, HIV *m*; **to be** ~**-positive** ser seropositivo.

hive [haɪv] *n* [for bees] colmena *f*; **a** ~ **of activity** un enjambre, un centro de actividad.

◆ **hive off** *vt sep* [separate] transferir.

hl (*abbr of* **hectolitre**) hl.

HM (*abbr of* **His (or Her) Majesty**) SM.

HMG (*abbr of* **His (or Her) Majesty's Government**) *expresión utilizada en documentos oficiales en Gran Bretaña.*

HMI (*abbr of* **His (or Her) Majesty's Inspector**) *n* inspector de enseñanza en Gran Bretaña.

HMO (*abbr of* **health maintenance organization**) *n* organismo estadounidense de salud pública.

HMS (*abbr of* **His (or Her) Majesty's Ship**) *buque de guerra británico*.

HMSO (*abbr of* **His (or Her) Majesty's Stationery Office**) *n* servicio oficial de publicaciones en Gran Bretaña, ≃ Imprenta *f* Nacional.

HNC (*abbr of* **Higher National Certificate**) *n* diploma técnico en Gran Bretaña.

HND (*abbr of* **Higher National Diploma**) *n* diploma técnico superior en Gran Bretaña.

hoard [hɔ:d] ◇ *n* [store] acumulación *f*, acopio *m*. ◇ *vt* [collect, save] acumular; [food] acaparar.

hoarding ['hɔ:dɪŋ] *n Br* [for advertisements, posters] valla *f* publicitaria.

hoarfrost [,hɔ:'frɒst] *n* escarcha *f*.

hoarse [hɔ:s] *adj* **-1.** [voice] ronco(ca). **-2.** [person] afónico(ca).

hoax [həʊks] *n* engaño *m*; ~ **call** falsa alarma telefónica.

hoaxer ['həʊksər] *n* bromista *m y f*.

hob [hɒb] *n Br* [on cooker] encimera *f*.

hobble ['hɒbl] *vi* [limp] cojear.

hobby ['hɒbɪ] (*pl* **-ies**) *n* [leisure activity] hobby *m*, distracción *f* favorita.

hobbyhorse ['hɒbɪhɔːs] *n* **-1.** [toy] caballo *m* de juguete. **-2.** [favourite topic] caballo *m* de batalla, tema *m* favorito.

hobnob ['hɒbnɒb] (*pt & pp* **-bed**, *cont* **-bing**) *vi*: **to ~ with sb** codearse con alguien.

hobo ['həʊbəʊ] (*pl* **-es** OR **-s**) *n Am* [tramp] vagabundo *m*, -da *f*.

Ho Chi Minh City ['həʊ,tʃiː'mɪn-] *n* Ho Chi Minh.

hock [hɒk] *n* [wine] vino *m* blanco del Rin.

hockey ['hɒkɪ] *n* **-1.** [on grass] hockey *m* sobre hierba. **-2.** *Am* [ice hockey] hockey *m* sobre hielo.

hocus-pocus [,həʊkəs'pəʊkəs] *n* (*U*) [trickery] camelo *m*, engaño *m*.

hod [hɒd] *n* [for bricks] artesa *f*, gaveta *f*.

hodgepodge *Am* = **hotchpotch**.

hoe [həʊ] ◇ *n* azada *f*, azadón *m*. ◇ *vt* azadonar.

hog [hɒg] (*pt & pp* **-ged**, *cont* **-ging**) ◇ *n* cerdo *m*; **to go the whole ~** *fig* ir a por todas. ◇ *vt* *inf* [monopolize] acaparar.

Hogmanay ['hɒgmənei] *n denominación escocesa de la Nochevieja*.

hoist [hɔɪst] ◇ *n* [pulley, crane] grúa *f*; [lift] montacargas *m inv*. ◇ *vt* izar.

hokum ['həʊkəm] *n Am inf* palabrería *f*.

hold [həʊld] (*pt & pp* **held**) ◇ *vt* **-1.** [have hold of] tener cogido(da). **-2.** [embrace] abrazar. **-3.** [keep in position, sustain, support] sostener, aguantar. **-4.** [as prisoner] detener; **to ~ sb prisoner/hostage** tener a alguien como prisionero/rehén. **-5.** [have, possess] poseer. **-6.** [contain - gen] contener; [- fears, promise etc] guardar; [- number of people] tener cabida para. **-7.** [conduct, stage - event] celebrar; [- conversation] mantener. **-8.** *fml* [consider] considerar; **to ~ (that)** mantener OR sostener que; **to ~ sb responsible for sthg** considerar a alguien responsable de algo; **to ~ sthg dear** apreciar mucho algo. **-9.** [on telephone]: **please ~ the line** no cuelgue por favor. **-10.** [maintain - interest etc] mantener. **-11.** MIL ocupar, tener. **-12.** *phr*: **~ it** OR **everything!** ¡para!, ¡espera!; **to ~ one's own** defenderse.

◇ *vi* **-1.** [luck, weather] continuar así; [promise, offer] seguir en pie; **to ~ still** OR **steady** estarse quieto. **-2.** [on phone] esperar.

◇ *n* **-1.** [grasp, grip]: **to have a firm ~ on sthg** tener algo bien agarrado; **to take** OR **lay ~ of sthg** agarrar algo; **to get ~ of sthg** [obtain] hacerse con algo; **to get ~ of sb** [find] localizar a alguien. **-2.** [of ship, aircraft] bodega *f*. **-3.** [control, influence] dominio *m*, control *m*; **to take ~** [fire] prender.

◆ **hold against** *vt sep*: **to ~ sthg against sb** *fig* tomarle a alguien algo en cuenta.

◆ **hold back** ◇ *vi* [hesitate] vacilar; **to ~ back from doing sthg** abstenerse de hacer algo. ◇ *vt sep* **-1.** [tears, anger] contener, reprimir. **-2.** [secret] ocultar, no revelar. **-3.** [person]: **to ~ sb back from doing sthg** impedir a alguien hacer algo.

◆ **hold down** *vt sep* [job] conservar.

◆ **hold off** ◇ *vt sep* [fend off] mantener a distancia. ◇ *vi* no darse, no producirse.

◆ **hold on** *vi* **-1.** [wait] esperar; [on phone] no colgar. **-2.** [grip]: **to ~ on (to sthg)** agarrarse (a algo).

◆ **hold onto** *vt fus* retener.

◆ **hold out** ◇ *vt sep* [hand, arms] extender, tender. ◇ *vi* **-1.** [last] durar. **-2.** [resist]: **to ~ out (against sthg/sb)** resistir (ante algo/a alguien).

◆ **hold out for** *vt fus* insistir en.

◆ **hold up** *vt sep* **-1.** [raise] levantar, alzar. **-2.** [delay] retrasar. **-3.** *inf* [rob] atracar, asaltar.

◆ **hold with** *vt fus* [approve of] estar de acuerdo con, aprobar.

holdall ['həʊldɔ:l] *n Br* bolsa *f* de viaje.

holder ['həʊldə'] n **-1.** [container] soporte m; [for candle] candelero m; [for cigarette] boquilla f. **-2.** [owner] titular m y f; [of ticket, record, title] poseedor m, -ra f.

holding ['həʊldɪŋ] ◇ n **-1.** [investment] participación f, acciones fpl. **-2.** [farm] propiedad f, terreno m de cultivo. ◇ adj [action, operation] de mantenimiento.

holding company n holding m.

holdup ['həʊldʌp] n **-1.** [robbery] atraco m a mano armada. **-2.** [delay] retraso m.

hole [həʊl] n **-1.** [gen] agujero m; [in ground, road etc] hoyo m; **to pick ~s in sthg** [criticize] encontrar defectos en algo. **-2.** [in golf] hoyo m; **~ in one** hoyo en uno. **-3.** [horrible place] cuchitril m, madriguera f. **-4.** inf [predicament] apuro m, aprieto m.

◆ **hole up** vi [hide, take shelter] esconderse, refugiarse.

holiday ['hɒlɪdeɪ] n **-1.** [vacation] vacaciones fpl; **to be/go on ~** estar/ir de vacaciones. **-2.** [public holiday] fiesta f, día m festivo.

holiday camp n Br colonia f veraniega.

holidaymaker ['hɒlɪdeɪˌmeɪkə'] n Br turista m y f.

holiday pay n Br sueldo m de vacaciones.

holiday resort n Br lugar m de veraneo.

holiday season n temporada f turística OR de vacaciones.

holiness ['həʊlɪnɪs] n santidad f.

◆ **Holiness** n [in titles]: **His/Your Holiness** Su Santidad.

holistic [həʊ'lɪstɪk] adj holístico(ca).

Holland ['hɒlənd] n Holanda.

hollandaise sauce [ˌhɒlən'deɪz-] n salsa f holandesa.

holler ['hɒlə'] vt & vi inf gritar.

hollow ['hɒləʊ] ◇ adj **-1.** [not solid] hueco(ca). **-2.** [cheeks, eyes] hundido(da). **-3.** [resonant] sonoro(ra), resonante. **-4.** [false, meaningless] vano(na); [laugh] falso(sa). ◇ n hueco m; [in ground] depresión f, hondonada f.

◆ **hollow out** vt sep **-1.** [make hollow] dejar hueco. **-2.** [make by hollowing] hacer ahuecando.

holly ['hɒlɪ] n acebo m.

Hollywood ['hɒlɪwʊd] ◇ n [film industry] Hollywood m. ◇ comp de Hollywood.

holocaust ['hɒləkɔːst] n holocausto m.

◆ **Holocaust** n: **the Holocaust** el Holocausto.

hologram ['hɒləgræm] n holograma m.

hols [hɒlz] (abbr of **holidays**) npl Br inf vacas fpl, vacaciones fpl.

holster ['həʊlstə'] n pistolera f, funda f (de pistola).

holy ['həʊlɪ] (compar **-ier**, superl **-iest**) adj **-1.** [sacred] sagrado(da); [water] bendito(ta). **-2.** [pure and good] santo(ta).

Holy Communion n Sagrada Comunión f.

Holy Ghost n Espíritu m Santo.

Holy Grail [-'greɪl] n: **the ~** el Santo Grial.

Holy Land n: **the ~** Tierra Santa.

holy orders npl sagradas órdenes fpl; **take ~** ordenarse (sacerdote).

Holy See n: **the ~** la Santa Sede.

Holy Spirit n: **the ~** el Espíritu Santo.

homage ['hɒmɪdʒ] n (U) fml homenaje m; **to pay ~ to** rendir homenaje a.

home [həʊm] ◇ n **-1.** [house, flat] casa f; **to make one's ~ somewhere** establecerse en algún sitio; **it's a ~ from ~** Br OR **~ away from ~** Am para mí es como mi propia casa. **-2.** [own country] tierra f; [own city] ciudad f natal. **-3.** [family] hogar m; **to leave ~** independizarse, irse de casa. **-4.** [place of origin] cuna f. **-5.** [institution] asilo m.

◇ adj **-1.** [not foreign] nacional. **-2.** [in one's own home - cooking] casero(ra); [- life] familiar; [- improvements] en la casa. **-3.** SPORT de casa.

◇ adv **-1.** [to one's house] a casa; [at one's house] en casa. **-2.** phr: **to bring sthg ~ to sb** hacer que alguien se dé cuenta de algo; **to drive** OR **hammer sthg ~ to sb** hacer que alguien se dé perfecta cuenta de algo.

◆ **at home** adv **-1.** [in one's house, flat] en casa. **-2.** [comfortable]: **at ~ (with)** a gusto (con); **to make o.s. at ~** acomodarse. **-3.** [in one's own country] en mi país. **-4.** SPORT: **to play at ~** jugar en casa.

◆ **home in** vi: **to ~ in on sthg** dirigirse hacia algo; fig centrarse en algo.

home address n domicilio m particular.

home banking n (U) home banking m, sistema computerizado para recibir información o realizar transferencias bancarias desde casa o la oficina.

home brew n (U) [beer] cerveza f casera.

homecoming ['həʊmˌkʌmɪŋ] n **-1.** [return] regreso m a casa. **-2.** Am SCH & UNIV recepción f para ex-alumnos.

home computer n ordenador m personal.

Home Counties npl: **the ~** los condados de los alrededores de Londres.

home economics n (U) economía f doméstica.

home fries npl Am patatas fpl salteadas.

home ground n **-1.** [familiar place]: **to be on ~** estar en territorio conocido. **-2.** [familiar subject]: **to be on ~** estar en su terreno. **-3.** SPORT campo m propio.

homegrown [ˌhəʊm'grəʊn] *adj* [grown in one's garden] **de cosecha propia**; [not imported] **de la tierra, local**.

home help *n Br* asistente empleado por el ayuntamiento para ayudar en las tareas domésticas a enfermos y ancianos.

homeland ['həʊmlænd] *n* **-1.** [country of birth] **tierra** *f* **natal, patria** *f*. **-2.** [in South Africa] territorio donde se confina a la población negra.

homeless ['həʊmlɪs] ◇ *adj* **sin hogar**. ◇ *npl*: **the ~ las personas sin hogar**.

homelessness ['həʊmlɪsnəs] *n* (fenómeno *m* de la) **carencia** *f* **de hogar**.

home loan *n* **crédito** *m* **para reforma de vivienda**.

homely ['həʊmlɪ] *adj* **-1.** [simple] **sencillo(lla)**. **-2.** [unattractive] **feúcho(cha)**.

homemade [ˌhəʊm'meɪd] *adj* [clothes] **de fabricación casera**; [food] **casero(ra)**.

home movie *n* **película** *f* **casera**.

Home Office *n Br*: **the ~ el Ministerio del Interior británico**.

homeopathic [ˌhəʊmɪəʊ'pæθɪk] *adj* **homeopático(ca)**.

homeopathy [ˌhəʊmɪ'ɒpəθɪ] *n* **homeopatía** *f*.

homeowner ['həʊmˌəʊnəʳ] *n* **propietario** *m*, **-ria** *f* **de vivienda**.

home page *n* COMPUT **página** *f* **inicial** OR **de inicio**.

home rule *n* **autonomía** *f*.

home run *n Am inf* **home run** *m*.

Home Secretary *n Br*: **the ~ el Ministro** *m* **del Interior británico**.

homesick ['həʊmsɪk] *adj* **nostálgico(ca)**; **to be ~ tener morriña**.

homesickness ['həʊmˌsɪknɪs] *n* **morriña** *f*.

homespun ['həʊmspʌn] *adj fig* [unsophisticated] **pedestre, corriente**.

homestead ['həʊmsted] *n* **granja** *f*.

home straight *n*: **the ~ la recta final**.

hometown ['həʊmtaʊn] *n* **pueblo** *m*/**ciudad** *f* **natal**.

home truth *n*: **to tell sb a few ~s soltarle a alguien cuatro verdades** OR **frescas**.

homeward ['həʊmwəd] ◇ *adj* **de regreso** OR **vuelta (a casa)**. ◇ *adv* = **homewards**.

homewards ['həʊmwədz] *adv* **hacia casa**.

homework ['həʊmwɜːk] *n* (U) **deberes** *mpl*.

homey, homy ['həʊmɪ] *adj Am* **confortable, agradable**.

homicidal [ˌhɒmɪsaɪdl] *adj* **homicida**.

homicide ['hɒmɪsaɪd] *n fml* **homicidio** *m*.

homily ['hɒmɪlɪ] (*pl* **-ies**) *n* [lecture] **sermón** *m*.

homing ['həʊmɪŋ] *adj*: **~ instinct querencia** *f*; **~ device** [on missile] **sistema** *m* **de guiado pasivo**.

homing pigeon *n* **paloma** *f* **mensajera**.

homoeopathy *etc* [ˌhəʊmɪ'ɒpəθɪ] = **homeopathy** *etc*.

homogeneous [ˌhɒmə'dʒiːnjəs] *adj* **homogéneo(a)**.

homogenize, -ise [hə'mɒdʒənaɪz] *vt Br* **homogeneizar**.

homosexual [ˌhɒmə'sekʃʊəl] ◇ *adj* **homosexual**. ◇ *n* **homosexual** *m* y *f*.

homosexuality [ˌhɒmə,sekʃʊ'ælətɪ] *n* **homosexualidad** *f*.

homy = **homey**.

Hon. **-1.** *abbr of* **Honourable**. **-2.** *abbr of* **Honorary**.

Honduran [hɒn'djʊərən] ◇ *adj* **hondureño(ña)**. ◇ *n* **hondureño** *m*, **-ña** *f*.

Honduras [hɒn'djʊərəs] *n* **Honduras**.

hone [həʊn] *vt* **-1.** [sharpen] **afilar**. **-2.** [develop, refine] **afinar**.

honest ['ɒnɪst] ◇ *adj* **-1.** [trustworthy, legal] **honrado(da)**. **-2.** [frank] **franco(ca)**, **sincero(ra)**; **to be ~ ... si he de serte franco ....** ◇ *adv inf* = **honestly 2**.

honestly ['ɒnɪstlɪ] ◇ *adv* **-1.** [truthfully] **honradamente**. **-2.** [expressing sincerity] **de verdad, en serio**. ◇ *excl* [expressing impatience, disapproval] **¡será posible!**

honesty ['ɒnɪstɪ] *n* **honradez** *f*.

honey ['hʌnɪ] *n* **-1.** [food] **miel** *f*. **-2.** [form of address] **cielo** *m*, **mi vida** *f*.

honeybee ['hʌnɪbiː] *n* **abeja** *f* (**obrera**).

honeycomb ['hʌnɪkəʊm] *n* **panal** *m*.

honeymoon ['hʌnɪmuːn] ◇ *n* **luna** *f* **de miel**; *fig* **periodo** *m* **idílico**. ◇ *vi* **pasar la luna de miel**.

honeysuckle ['hʌnɪ,sʌkl] *n* **madreselva** *f*.

Hong Kong [ˌhɒŋ'kɒŋ] *n* **Hong Kong**.

honk [hɒŋk] ◇ *vi* **-1.** [motorist] **tocar el claxon**. **-2.** [goose] **graznar**. ◇ *vt* **tocar**. ◇ *n* **-1.** [of horn] **bocinazo** *m*. **-2.** [of goose] **graznido** *m*.

honky ['hɒŋkɪ] (*pl* **-ies**) *n Am v inf* término peyorativo que designa a un blanco.

Honolulu [ˌhɒnə'luːluː] *n* **Honolulú**.

honor *etc Am* = **honour** *etc*.

honorary [*Br* 'ɒnərərɪ, *Am* ɒnə'reərɪ] *adj* **-1.** [given as an honour] **honorario(ria)**. **-2.** [unpaid] **honorífico(ca)**.

honor roll *n Am* **lista** *f* **de honor**.

honour *Br*, **honor** *Am* ['ɒnəʳ] ◇ *n* **-1.** [gen] **honor** *m*, **honra** *f*; **in ~ of en honor de**. **-2.** [source of pride - person] **honra** *f*. ◇ *vt* **-1.** [promise, agreement] **cumplir**; [debt] **satisfa-**

cer; [cheque] pagar, aceptar. **-2.** *fml* [bring honour to] honrar.
◆ **Honour** *n* [in titles]: **His/Her/Your Honour** Su Señoría.
◆ **honours** *npl* **-1.** [tokens of respect] honores *mpl.* **-2.** *Br* UNIV: ~**s degree** *licenciatura de cuatro años necesaria para acceder a un máster.* **-3.** *phr:* **to do the** ~**s** hacer los honores de la casa.

honourable *Br*, **honorable** *Am* ['ɒnrəbl] *adj* **-1.** [proper] honroso(sa). **-2.** [morally upright] honorable.
◆ **Honourable** *adj* [in titles] Honorable; **the Honourable gentleman/lady** Su Señoría el señor diputado/la señora diputada.

honourably *Br*, **honorably** *Am* ['ɒnərəblɪ] *adv* [properly] honrosamente.

honour bound *adj:* **to be** ~ **to do sthg** estar obligado(da) moralmente a hacer algo.

honours list *n Br* lista de personas que reciben un título nobiliario de manos de la corona británica.

Hons. *abbr of* **honours degree.**

hooch [huːtʃ] *n Am inf* priva *f.*

hood [hʊd] *n* **-1.** [on cloak, jacket] capucha *f.* **-2.** [of pram, convertible car] capota *f;* [of cooker] campana *f.* **-3.** *Am* [car bonnet] capó *m.*

hooded ['hʊdɪd] *adj* **-1.** [wearing a hood] encapuchado(da). **-2.** [eyes] de grandes párpados.

hoodlum ['huːdləm] *n Am inf* matón *m.*

hoodwink ['hʊdwɪŋk] *vt* engañar, burlar.

hooey ['huːɪ] *n* (U) *Am inf* tonterías *fpl,* bobadas *fpl.*

hoof [huːf, hʊf] (*pl* **-s** OR **hooves**) *n* [of horse] casco *m;* [of cow etc] pezuña *f.*

hook [hʊk] ◇ *n* **-1.** [gen] gancho *m;* **off the** ~ [phone] descolgado(da). **-2.** [for catching fish] anzuelo *m.* **-3.** [fastener] corchete *m.* **-4.** *phr:* **to get sb off the** ~ sacar a alguien de un apuro. ◇ *vt* **-1.** [attach with hook] enganchar. **-2.** [fish] pescar, coger. **-3.** [arm, leg]: **he** ~**ed his leg around the chair** enganchó la silla con el pie.
◆ **hook up** *vt sep:* **to** ~ **sthg up to sthg** conectar algo a algo.

hook and eye (*pl* **hooks and eyes**) *n* corchete *m.*

hooked [hʊkt] *adj* **-1.** [nose] aguileño(ña), ganchudo(da). **-2.** *inf* [addicted]: **to be** ~ **(on)** estar enganchado(da) (a).

hooker ['hʊkər] *n Am inf* puta *f.*

hook(e)y ['hʊkɪ] *n Am inf:* **to play** ~ hacer pellas OR novillos.

hooligan ['huːlɪgən] *n* gamberro *m.*

hooliganism ['huːlɪgənɪzm] *n* gamberrismo *m.*

hoop [huːp] *n* aro *m.*

hoop-la ['huːplɑː] *n* (U) [game] *juego de feria en que se intentan colar aros en los premios.*

hooray [hʊ'reɪ] = **hurray.**

hoot [huːt] ◇ *n* **-1.** [of owl] grito *m,* ululato *m.* **-2.** [of horn] bocinazo *m.* **-3.** [of laughter] risotada *f,* carcajada *f.* **-4.** *Br inf* [amusing thing]: **she's/it was a** ~ es/fue la monda. ◇ *vi* **-1.** [owl] ulular. **-2.** [horn] sonar. **-3.** *inf* [laugh] carcajearse, reírse a carcajadas. ◇ *vt* tocar.

hooter ['huːtər] *n* **-1.** [horn] claxon *m,* bocina *f.* **-2.** *Br inf* [nose] napias *fpl.*

Hoover® ['huːvər] *n Br* aspiradora *f.*
◆ **hoover** ◇ *vt* pasar la aspiradora por. ◇ *vi* pasar la aspiradora.

hooves [huːvz] *pl* → **hoof.**

hop [hɒp] (*pt* & *pp* **-ped,** *cont* **-ping**) ◇ *n* **-1.** [of person] salto *m* a la pata coja. **-2.** [of bird etc] saltito *m.* **-3.** *inf* [trip] viaje *m.* ◇ *vi* **-1.** [person] saltar a la pata coja. **-2.** [bird etc] dar saltitos. **-3.** *inf* [move nimbly] ponerse de un brinco. ◇ *vt Am inf* [bus, train] subirse a.
◆ **hops** *npl* lúpulo *m.*

hope [həʊp] ◇ *vi:* **to** ~ **(for sthg)** esperar (algo); **I** ~ **so/not** espero que sí/no; **to** ~ **for the best** esperar que todo vaya bien. ◇ *vt:* **to** ~ **(that)** esperar que; **to** ~ **to do sthg** esperar hacer algo. ◇ *n* esperanza *f;* **to be beyond** ~ ser un caso desesperado; **in the** ~ **of** con la esperanza de; **to pin one's** ~**s on sthg** poner una todas sus esperanzas en algo; **I don't hold out much** ~ no tengo muchas esperanzas; **to raise sb's** ~**s** dar esperanzas a alguien.

hope chest *n Am* ajuar *m.*

hopeful ['həʊpfʊl] ◇ *adj* **-1.** [optimistic] optimista; **to be** ~ **of sthg/of doing sthg** tener esperanzas de algo/hacer algo. **-2.** [promising] prometedor(ra), esperanzador(ra). ◇ *n* aspirante *m y f.*

hopefully ['həʊpfəlɪ] *adv* **-1.** [in a hopeful way] esperanzadamente. **-2.** [with luck] con suerte.

hopeless ['həʊplɪs] *adj* **-1.** [despairing] desesperado(da). **-2.** [impossible] imposible. **-3.** *inf* [useless] inútil.

hopelessly ['həʊplɪslɪ] *adv* **-1.** [despairingly] desesperadamente. **-2.** [completely] totalmente.

hopper ['hɒpər] *n* [funnel] tolva *f.*

hopping ['hɒpɪŋ] *adv:* **to be** ~ **mad** estar echando chispas.

hopscotch ['hɒpskɒtʃ] *n* tejo *m,* rayuela *f Amer.*

horde [hɔːd] *n* horda *f.*

◆ **hordes** *npl* multitud *f.*

horizon [hə'raɪzn] *n* [of sky] horizonte *m*; **on the ~** *lit* en el horizonte; *fig* a la vuelta de la esquina.

◆ **horizons** *npl* horizontes *mpl.*

horizontal [ˌhɒrɪ'zɒntl] ◇ *adj* horizontal. ◇ *n*: **the ~** la horizontal.

hormone ['hɔːməʊn] *n* hormona *f.*

hormone replacement therapy *n* terapia *f* de sustitución hormonal.

horn [hɔːn] *n* **-1.** [of animal] cuerno *m*, cacho *m* *Amer.* **-2.** MUS [instrument] trompa *f.* **-3.** [on car] claxon *m*, bocina *f*; [on ship] sirena *f.*

hornet ['hɔːnɪt] *n* avispón *m.*

horn-rimmed [-'rɪmd] *adj* con montura de concha.

horny ['hɔːnɪ] (*compar* **-ier**, *superl* **-iest**) *adj* **-1.** [scale, body, armour] córneo(a); [hand] calloso(sa). **-2.** *v inf* [sexually excited] cachondo(da), caliente.

horoscope ['hɒrəskəʊp] *n* horóscopo *m.*

horrendous [hɒ'rendəs] *adj* horrendo(da).

horrible ['hɒrəbl] *adj* horrible.

horribly ['hɒrəblɪ] *adv* **-1.** [horrifically] horriblemente. **-2.** *inf* [very] terriblemente, tremendamente.

horrid ['hɒrɪd] *adj* [person] antipático(ca); [idea, place] horroroso(sa).

horrific [hɒ'rɪfɪk] *adj* horrendo(da).

horrify ['hɒrɪfaɪ] (*pt* & *pp* **-ied**) *vt* horrorizar.

horrifying ['hɒrɪfaɪɪŋ] *adj* horroroso(sa), horripilante.

horror ['hɒrə*] *n* horror *m*; **to my/his ~** para mi/su horror; **to have a ~ of sthg** tener horror a algo.

horror film *n* película *f* de terror OR de miedo.

horror-struck *adj* horrorizado(da).

hors d'oeuvre [ɔː'dɜːvr] (*pl* **hors d'oeuvres** [ɔː'dɜːvr]) *n* entremeses *mpl.*

horse [hɔːs] *n* [animal] caballo *m.*

horseback ['hɔːsbæk] ◇ *adj*: **~ riding** equitación *f.* ◇ *n*: **on ~** a caballo.

horsebox *Br* ['hɔːsbɒks], **horsecar** *Am* ['hɔːskɑːr] *n* furgón *m* para el transporte de caballos.

horse chestnut *n* [nut] castaña *f* de Indias; **~ (tree)** castaño *m* de Indias.

horse-drawn *adj* tirado(da) por caballos.

horsefly ['hɔːsflaɪ] (*pl* **-flies**) *n* tábano *m.*

horsehair ['hɔːsheə*] *n* crin *f.*

horseman ['hɔːsmən] (*pl* **-men** [-mən]) *n* jinete *m.*

horse opera *n* *Am* *hum* western *m*, película *f* del oeste.

horseplay ['hɔːspleɪ] *n* pelea *f* en broma.

horsepower ['hɔːs,paʊə*] *n* (U) caballos *mpl* de vapor.

horse racing *n* (U) carreras *fpl* de caballos.

horseradish ['hɔːs,rædɪʃ] *n* rábano *m* silvestre.

horse riding *n* equitación *f*; **to go ~** montar a caballo.

horseshoe ['hɔːsʃuː] *n* herradura *f.*

horse show *n* concurso *m* hípico.

horse-trading *n* *fig* & *pej* negociación *f*, regateo *m.*

horse trials *npl* concurso *m* hípico.

horsewhip ['hɔːswɪp] (*pt* & *pp* **-ped**, *cont* **-ping**) *vt* azotar.

horsewoman ['hɔːs,wʊmən] (*pl* **-women** [-,wɪmɪn]) *n* amazona *f.*

horticultural [ˌhɔːtɪ'kʌltʃərəl] *adj* hortícola.

horticulture ['hɔːtɪkʌltʃə*] *n* horticultura *f.*

hose [həʊz] ◇ *n* [hosepipe] manguera *f.* ◇ *vt* [irrigate] regar con manguera; [wash] limpiar con manguera.

◆ **hose down** *vt sep* limpiar con manguera.

hosepipe ['həʊzpaɪp] *n* = **hose**.

hosiery ['həʊzɪərɪ] *n* (U) medias *fpl* y calcetines.

hospice ['hɒspɪs] *n* hospicio *m.*

hospitable [hɒ'spɪtəbl] *adj* hospitalario(ria).

hospital ['hɒspɪtl] *n* hospital *m*, nosocomio *m* *Amer.*

hospitality [ˌhɒspɪ'tælətɪ] *n* hospitalidad *f.*

hospitality suite *n* bar *m* con barra libre (*en conferencias etc*).

hospitalize, -ise ['hɒspɪtəlaɪz] *vt* hospitalizar.

host [həʊst] ◇ *n* **-1.** [person, place, organization] anfitrión *m*, -ona *f*; **~ country** país *m* anfitrión OR organizador. **-2.** [compere] presentador *m*, -ra *f.* **-3.** *literary* [large number]: **a ~ of** una multitud de. **-4.** RELIG hostia *f.* ◇ *vt* [show] presentar; [event] ser el anfitrión de.

hostage ['hɒstɪdʒ] *n* rehén *m*; **to be taken/held ~** ser cogido(da)/mantenido(da) como rehén.

hostel ['hɒstl] *n* albergue *m.*

hostelry ['hɒstəlrɪ] (*pl* **-ries**) *n* *hum* [pub] bar *m.*

hostess ['həʊstes] *n* **-1.** [at party] anfitriona *f.* **-2.** [in club etc] chica *f* de alterne.

hostile [*Br* 'hɒstaɪl, *Am* 'hɒstl] *adj* **-1.** [antagonistic, enemy]: ~ **(to)** hostil (hacia). **-2.** [unfavourable] adverso(sa), desfavorable.

hostility [hɒsˈtɪlətɪ] *n* [antagonism] hostilidad *f*.

◆ **hostilities** *npl* hostilidades *fpl*.

hot [hɒt] (*compar* **-ter**, *superl* **-test**, *pt* & *pp* **-ted**, *cont* **-ting**) *adj* **-1.** [gen] caliente; **I'm** ~ tengo calor. **-2.** [weather, climate] caluroso(sa); **it's (very)** ~ hace (mucho) calor. **-3.** [spicy] picante, picoso(sa) *Amer.* **-4.** *inf* [expert]: ~ **on** OR **at** experto(ta) en. **-5.** [recent] caliente, último(ma). **-6.** [temper] vivo(va).

◆ **hot up** *vi inf* animarse, calentarse.

hot-air balloon *n* aeróstato *m*, globo *m*.

hotbed [ˈhɒtbed] *n* semillero *m*.

hotchpotch *Br* [ˈhɒtʃpɒtʃ], **hodgepodge** *Am* [ˈhɒdʒpɒdʒ] *n inf* revoltijo *m*, batiburrillo *m*.

hot-cross bun *n* bollo a base de especias y pasas con una cruz dibujada en una cara que se come en Semana Santa.

hot dog *n* perrito *m* caliente.

hotel [həʊˈtel] ◇ *n* hotel *m*. ◇ *comp* [gen] de hotel; [industry] hotelero(ra).

hotelier [həʊˈtelɪə'] *n* hotelero *m*, -ra *f*.

hot flush *Br*, **hot flash** *Am* *n* sofoco *m*.

hotfoot [ˈhɒt,fʊt] *adv literary* presto, raudamente.

hotheaded [,hɒtˈhedɪd] *adj* irreflexivo(va).

hothouse [ˈhɒthaʊs, *pl* -haʊzɪz] ◇ *n* [greenhouse] invernadero *m*. ◇ *comp* de invernadero.

hot line *n* teléfono *m* rojo, línea *f* de emergencia.

hotly [ˈhɒtlɪ] *adv* **-1.** [passionately] acaloradamente. **-2.** [closely]: **we were** ~ **pursued** nos pisaban los talones.

hotplate [ˈhɒtpleɪt] *n* calentador *m*, fuego *m*.

hotpot [ˈhɒtpɒt] *n Br* estofado de cabrito típico de Lancashire.

hot potato *n inf fig* tema *m* espinoso.

hot rod *n* AUT bólido *m*.

hot seat *n inf*: **to be in the** ~ ser quien tiene que sacar las castañas del fuego.

hot spot *n* **-1.** [exciting place] lugar *m* de moda. **-2.** POL zona *f* conflictiva, polvorín *m*.

hot-tempered *adj* iracundo(da).

hot water *n fig*: **to get into/be in** ~ meterse/estar en un berenjenal.

hot-water bottle *n* bolsa *f* de agua caliente.

hot-wire *vt inf*: **to** ~ **a car** poner un coche en marcha haciendo un puente.

hound [haʊnd] ◇ *n* [dog] perro *m* de caza, sabueso *m*. ◇ *vt* **-1.** [persecute] acosar. **-2.** [drive]: **to** ~ **sb out (of somewhere)** conseguir echar a alguien (de algún sitio) acosándolo.

hour [ˈaʊə'] *n* **-1.** [gen] hora *f*; **half an** ~ media hora; **70 miles per** OR **an** ~ 70 millas por hora; **on the** ~ a la hora en punto cada hora; **in the small** ~s a altas horas de la madrugada. **-2.** *literary* [important time] momento *m*.

◆ **hours** *npl* **-1.** [of business] horas *fpl*; **after** ~s fuera de horas. **-2.** [of person - routine] horario *m*; **to keep late** ~s acostarse siempre tarde.

hourly [ˈaʊəlɪ] ◇ *adj* **-1.** [happening every hour] de hora en hora, cada hora. **-2.** [per hour] por hora. ◇ *adv* **-1.** [every hour] cada hora. **-2.** [per hour] por hora. **-3.** *fig* [constantly] continuamente.

house [*n* & *adj* haʊs, *pl* ˈhaʊzɪz, *vb* haʊz] ◇ *n* **-1.** [gen] casa *f*; **it's on the** ~ la casa invita, es cortesía de la casa; **to put** OR **set one's** ~ **in order** poner las cosas en orden. **-2.** POL cámara *f*. **-3.** [in theatre] audiencia *f*; **to bring the** ~ **down** *inf* ser un exitazo, ser muy aplaudido. **-4.** [in debates]: **this** ~ ... los participantes en este debate .... ◇ *vt* [person, family] alojar; [department, library, office] albergar. ◇ *adj* **-1.** [within business] de la empresa. **-2.** [wine] de la casa.

house arrest *n*: **under** ~ bajo arresto domiciliario.

houseboat [ˈhaʊsbəʊt] *n* casa *f* flotante.

housebound [ˈhaʊsbaʊnd] *adj* confinado(da) en casa.

housebreaking [ˈhaʊs,breɪkɪŋ] *n* allanamiento *m* de morada.

housebroken [ˈhaʊs,brəʊkn] *adj Am* [pet] bien enseñado(da).

housecoat [ˈhaʊskəʊt] *n* bata *f*.

household [ˈhaʊshəʊld] ◇ *adj* **-1.** [domestic] doméstico(ca), de la casa. **-2.** [word, name] conocido(da) por todos. ◇ *n* hogar *m*, casa *f*.

householder [ˈhaʊs,həʊldə'] *n* [owner] dueño *m*, -ña *f*; [tenant] inquilino *m*, -na *f*.

househunting [ˈhaʊs,hʌntɪŋ] *n* búsqueda *f* de vivienda.

house husband *n* hombre encargado de las tareas domésticas.

housekeeper [ˈhaʊs,kiːpə'] *n* ama *f* de llaves.

housekeeping [ˈhaʊs,kiːpɪŋ] *n* (U) **-1.** [work] quehaceres *mpl* domésticos, tareas *fpl* domésticas. **-2.** ~ **(money)** dinero *m* para los gastos de la casa.

houseman ['haʊsmən] (*pl* **-men** [-mən]) *n* Br interno *m*, -na *f*.

house music *n* música *f* ácida OR house.

House of Commons *n Br*: **the ~** la Cámara de los Comunes.

HOUSE OF COMMONS:
La Cámara de los Comunes está compuesta por 650 diputados, elegidos para un periodo de 5 años, que se reúnen unos 175 días al año

---

House of Lords *n Br*: **the ~** la Cámara de los Lores.

HOUSE OF LORDS:
La Cámara de los Lores está compuesta por personas con título nobiliario y clérigos. Es el tribunal de última instancia para todo el Reino Unido menos Escocia. La Cámara de los Lores puede enmendar determinados proyectos de ley aprobados por la Cámara de los Comunes

---

House of Representatives *n Am*: **the ~** la Cámara de los Representantes.

HOUSE OF REPRESENTATIVES:
Junto con el Senado, la Cámara de los Representantes constituye el cuerpo legislativo de los Estados Unidos. Los diputados son elegidos a través de un sistema proporcional basado en la población de cada estado

---

house-owner *n* propietario *m*, -ria *f* (de vivienda).

houseplant ['haʊsplɑːnt] *n* planta *f* interior.

house-proud *adj* muy ama de su casa.

Houses of Parliament *n*: **the ~** el Parlamento británico.

house-to-house *adj* de casa en casa.

house-train *vt Br* enseñar dónde hacer sus necesidades a (*perro, gato*).

housewarming (party) ['haʊs,wɔːmɪŋ-] *n* fiesta *f* de inauguración de una casa.

housewife ['haʊswaɪf] (*pl* **-wives** [-waɪvz]) *n* ama *f* de casa.

housework ['haʊswɜːk] *n* (*U*) quehaceres *mpl* domésticos.

housing ['haʊzɪŋ] ◇ *n* **-1.** [houses] vivienda *f*; [act of accommodating] alojamiento *m*. **-2.** [covering] cubierta *f* protectora; AUT cárter *m*. ◇ *comp* de la vivienda.

housing association *n Br* cooperativa *f* de viviendas.

housing benefit *n* (*U*) *subsidio estatal para ayudar con el pago del alquiler y otros gastos.*

housing development *n* urbanización *f*.

housing estate *Br*, **housing project** *Am n* *urbanización generalmente de protección oficial,* ≈ fraccionamiento *m Amer*.

hovel ['hɒvl] *n* casucha *f*, tugurio *m*.

hover ['hɒvəʳ] *vi* **-1.** [fly] cernerse. **-2.** [linger] merodear. **-3.** [hesitate] debatirse, vacilar.

hovercraft ['hɒvəkrɑːft] (*pl inv* OR **-s**) *n* aerodeslizador *m*.

hoverport ['hɒvəpɔːt] *n* puerto *m* para aerodeslizadores.

how [haʊ] *adv* **-1.** [gen] cómo; **~ do you do it?** ¿cómo se hace?; **I found out ~ he did it** averigüé cómo lo hizo; **~ are you?** ¿cómo estás?; **~ do you do?** mucho gusto. **-2.** [referring to degree, amount]: **~ high is it?** ¿cuánto mide de alto OR de altura?; **he asked ~ high it was** preguntó cuánto media de alto; **~ expensive is it?** ¿cómo de caro es?, ¿es muy caro?; **~ long have you been waiting?** ¿cuánto llevas esperando?; **~ many people came?** ¿cuánta gente vino?; **~ old are you?** ¿qué edad OR cuántos años tienes? **-3.** [in exclamations] qué; **~ nice/awful!** ¡qué bonito/horrible!; **~ I hate doing it!** ¡cómo OR cuánto odio tener que hacerlo!; **~ can you say that?** ¿cómo puedes decir eso?

◆ **how about** *adv*: **~ about a drink?** ¿qué tal una copa?; **~ about you?** ¿qué te parece?, ¿y tú?

◆ **how much** ◇ *pron* cuánto(ta); **~ much does it cost?** ¿cuánto cuesta? ◇ *adj* cuánto(ta); **~ much bread?** ¿cuánto pan?

howdy ['haʊdɪ] *excl Am inf* ¡hola!

however [haʊ'evəʳ] ◇ *adv* **-1.** [nevertheless] sin embargo, no obstante. **-2.** [no matter how]: **~ difficult it may be** por (muy) difícil que sea; **~ many times** OR **much I told her** por mucho que se lo dijera. **-3.** [how] cómo. ◇ *conj* comoquiera que; **~ you want** como quieras.

howl [haʊl] ◇ *n* **-1.** [of animal] aullido *m*. **-2.** [of person - in pain, anger] alarido *m*, grito *m*; [- in laughter] carcajada *f*. ◇ *vi* **-1.** [animal] aullar. **-2.** [person - in pain, anger] gritar; [- in laughter] reírse a carcajadas. **-3.** [wind] bramar.

howler ['haʊləʳ] *n inf* error *m* garrafal.

howling ['haʊlɪŋ] *adj inf* [success] clamoroso(sa).

hp (*abbr of* **horsepower**) CV *m*, cv *m*.

HP *n* **-1.** *Br abbr of* **hire purchase**; **to buy sthg on ~** comprar algo a plazos. **-2.** = **hp**.

HQ *n abbr of* **headquarters**.

hr (*abbr of* **hour**) h.

HRH (*abbr of* **His/Her Royal Highness**) S.A.R. *m y f.*

HS (*abbr of* **high school**) Inst. *m.*

HST (*abbr of* **Hawaiian Standard Time**) *hora oficial de Hawai.*

ht *abbr of* **height**.

HT (*abbr of* **high tension**) AT *f.*

HTML (*abbr of* **hypertext markup language**) *n* COMPUT HTML *m.*

hub [hʌb] *n* **-1.** [of wheel] cubo *m.* **-2.** [of activity] centro *m*, eje *m.*

hub airport *n Am* aeropuerto *m* principal.

hubbub ['hʌbʌb] *n* alboroto *m*, barullo *m.*

hubcap ['hʌbkæp] *n* tapacubos *m inv.*

HUD (*abbr of* **Department of Housing and Urban Development**) *n antiguo ministerio estadounidense de vivienda y desarrollo urbanístico.*

huddle ['hʌdl] ◇ *vi* **-1.** [crouch, curl up] acurrucarse. **-2.** [cluster] apretarse unos contra otros, apiñarse. ◇ *n* piña *f*, grupo *m.*

hue [hju:] *n* [colour] tono *m*, matiz *m.*

huff [hʌf] ◇ *n*: **in a ~** enojado(da). ◇ *vi*: **to ~ and puff** bufar, resoplar.

huffy ['hʌfɪ] (*compar* **-ier**, *superl* **-iest**) *adj inf* **-1.** [offended] enojado(da), ofendido(da). **-2.** [touchy] susceptible, enfadadizo(za).

hug [hʌg] (*pt & pp* **-ged**, *cont* **-ging**) ◇ *n* abrazo *m*; **to give sb a ~** abrazar a alguien, dar un abrazo a alguien. ◇ *vt* **-1.** [embrace, hold] abrazar; **to ~ sthg to o.s.** abrazar algo fuertemente. **-2.** [stay close to] ceñirse a.

huge [hju:dʒ] *adj* enorme.

huh [hʌ] *excl* **-1.** [after questions] ¿eh? **-2.** [expressing surprise, asking to repeat] ¿eh?, ¿qué? **-3.** [expressing scorn] ¡ja!

hulk [hʌlk] *n* **-1.** [of ship] casco *m* abandonado. **-2.** [person] tiarrón *m*, -ona *f.*

hulking ['hʌlkɪŋ] *adj* gigantesco(ca).

hull [hʌl] *n* casco *m.*

hullabaloo [,hʌləbə'lu:] *n inf* conmoción *f.*

hullo [hə'ləʊ] = **hello**.

hum [hʌm] (*pt & pp* **-med**, *cont* **-ming**) ◇ *vi* **-1.** [buzz] zumbar. **-2.** [sing] canturrear, tararear. **-3.** [be busy] bullir, hervir. **-4.** *phr*: **to ~ and haw** titubear, vacilar. ◇ *vt* tararear, canturrear. ◇ *n* (*U*) zumbido *m*; [of conversation] murmullo *m.*

human ['hju:mən] ◇ *adj* humano(na). ◇ *n*: **~ (being)** (ser *m*) humano *m.*

humane [hju:'meɪn] *adj* humano(na), humanitario(ria).

humanely [hju:'meɪnlɪ] *adv* humanamente.

human error *n* error *m* humano.

humanist ['hju:mənɪst] *n* humanista *m y f.*

humanitarian [hju:,mænɪ'teərɪən] ◇ *adj* humanitario(ria). ◇ *n* luchador *m*, -ra *f* por la justicia social.

humanity [hju:'mænətɪ] *n* humanidad *f.*
◆ **humanities** *npl*: **the humanities** las humanidades.

humanly ['hju:mənlɪ] *adv*: **~ possible** humanamente posible.

human nature *n* la naturaleza humana.

human race *n*: **the ~** la raza humana.

human resources *npl* recursos *mpl* humanos.

human rights *npl* derechos *mpl* humanos.

humble ['hʌmbl] ◇ *adj* humilde. ◇ *vt fml* humillar; **to ~ o.s.** humillarse.

humbly ['hʌmblɪ] *adv* humildemente.

humbug ['hʌmbʌg] *n* **-1.** *dated* [hypocrisy] farsa *f*, hipocresía *f.* **-2.** *Br* [sweet] caramelo *m* de menta.

humdrum ['hʌmdrʌm] *adj* rutinario(ria), aburrido(da).

humid ['hju:mɪd] *adj* húmedo(da).

humidity [hju:'mɪdətɪ] *n* humedad *f.*

humiliate [hju:'mɪlɪeɪt] *vt* humillar.

humiliating [hju:'mɪlɪeɪtɪŋ] *adj* humillante.

humiliation [hju:,mɪlɪ'eɪʃn] *n* humillación *f.*

humility [hju:'mɪlətɪ] *n* humildad *f.*

hummingbird ['hʌmɪŋbɜ:d] *n* colibrí *m.*

humor *Am* = **humour**.

humorist ['hju:mərɪst] *n* humorista *m y f.*

humorous ['hju:mərəs] *adj* humorístico(ca).

humour *Br*, **humor** *Am* ['hju:mə] ◇ *n* **-1.** [sense of fun, mood] humor *m*; **in good/bad ~** de buen/mal humor. **-2.** [funny side] gracia *f.* ◇ *vt* complacer, seguir la corriente a.

hump [hʌmp] ◇ *n* **-1.** [hill] montículo *m.* **-2.** [on back] joroba *f*, giba *f*, curca *f Amer.* ◇ *vt inf* [carry] acarrear, cargar con.

humpbacked bridge ['hʌmpbækt-] *n* puente *m* peraltado.

humus ['hju:məs] *n* humus *m inv.*

hunch [hʌntʃ] ◇ *n inf* presentimiento *m*, corazonada *f.* ◇ *vt* encorvar. ◇ *vi* encorvarse.

hunchback ['hʌntʃbæk] *n* jorobado *m*, -da *f.*

hunched [hʌntʃt] *adj* encorvado(da).

hundred ['hʌndrəd] *num* cien; **a** OR **one ~** cien; **a** OR **one ~ and eighty** ciento ochenta; *see also* **six**.
◆ **hundreds** *npl* cientos *mpl*, centenares *mpl.*

hundredth ['hʌndrətθ] ◇ *num adj* centésimo(ma). ◇ *num n* **-1.** [in order] centésimo *m*, -ma *f.* **-2.** [fraction] centésimo *m*; **a ~ of a second** una centésima; *see also* **sixth**.

hundredweight ['hʌndrədweɪt] *n* [in UK] = *50,8 kg*; [in US] = *45,3 kg*.

hung [hʌŋ] ◇ *pt & pp* → **hang**. ◇ *adj* POL sin mayoría.

Hungarian [hʌŋ'geərɪən] ◇ *adj* húngaro(ra). ◇ *n* **-1.** [person] húngaro *m*, -ra *f*. **-2.** [language] húngaro *m*.

Hungary ['hʌŋgərɪ] *n* Hungría.

hunger ['hʌŋgə'] *n* **-1.** [for food] hambre *f*. **-2.** *literary* [for change, knowledge etc] sed *f*.
◆ **hunger after**, **hunger for** *vt fus literary* anhelar, ansiar.

hunger strike *n* huelga *f* de hambre.

hung over *adj inf*: to be ~ tener resaca.

hungry ['hʌŋgrɪ] (*compar* **-ier**, *superl* **-iest**) *adj* **-1.** [for food] hambriento(ta); to be/go ~ tener/pasar hambre. **-2.** [eager]: to be ~ for estar ávido(da) de.

hung up *adj inf*: to be ~ (on OR about) estar neura (por culpa de).

hunk [hʌŋk] *n* **-1.** [large piece] pedazo *m*, trozo *m*. **-2.** *inf* [attractive man] tío *m* bueno, macizo *m*.

hunky-dory [,hʌŋkɪ'dɔːrɪ] *adj inf*: to be ~ ir de perlas.

hunt [hʌnt] ◇ *n* **-1.** [of animals, birds] caza *f*, cacería *f*. **-2.** [for person, clue etc] busca *f*, búsqueda *f*. ◇ *vi* **-1.** [for animals, birds] cazar. **-2.** [for person, clue etc]: to ~ (for sthg) buscar (algo). ◇ *vt* **-1.** [animals, birds] cazar. **-2.** [person] perseguir.
◆ **hunt down** *vt sep* atrapar.

hunter ['hʌntə'] *n* **-1.** [of animals, birds] cazador *m*, -ra *f*. **-2.** [of things]: bargain/autograph ~ *persona que anda a la caza de gangas/autógrafos*.

hunting ['hʌntɪŋ] ◇ *n* **-1.** [of animals] caza *f*; to go ~ ir de caza OR cacería. **-2.** *Br* [of foxes] caza *f* del zorro. ◇ *comp* de caza.

huntsman ['hʌntsmən] (*pl* **-men** [-mən]) *n* cazador *m*.

hurdle ['hɜːdl] ◇ *n* **-1.** [in race] valla *f*. **-2.** [obstacle] obstáculo *m*. ◇ *vt* saltar.

hurl [hɜːl] *vt* **-1.** [throw] lanzar, arrojar. **-2.** [shout] proferir, soltar.

hurrah [hʊ'rɑː] *excl dated* ¡hurra!

hurray [hʊ'reɪ] *excl* ¡hurra!

hurricane ['hʌrɪkən] *n* huracán *m*.

hurried ['hʌrɪd] *adj* [hasty] apresurado(da), precipitado(da).

hurriedly ['hʌrɪdlɪ] *adv* apresuradamente, precipitadamente.

hurry ['hʌrɪ] (*pt & pp* **-ied**) ◇ *vt* [person] meter prisa a; [work, speech] apresurar. ◇ *vi*: to ~ (to do sthg) apresurarse (a hacer algo), darse prisa (en hacer algo). ◇ *n* prisa *f*; to be in a ~ tener prisa; to do sthg in a ~ hacer algo de prisa OR apresuradamente; to be in no ~ to do sthg [unwilling] no tener ningunas ganas de hacer algo.
◆ **hurry up** ◇ *vi* darse prisa. ◇ *vt sep* meter prisa a.

hurt [hɜːt] (*pt & pp* **hurt**) ◇ *vt* **-1.** [physically - person] hacer daño a; [- one's leg, arm] hacerse daño en. **-2.** [emotionally] herir. **-3.** [harm] perjudicar. ◇ *vi* **-1.** [gen] doler; my head ~s me duele la cabeza. **-2.** [cause physical pain, do harm] hacer daño. ◇ *adj* **-1.** [injured] herido(da). **-2.** [offended] dolido(da), ofendido(da). ◇ *n* (U) [emotional pain] dolor *m*.

hurtful ['hɜːtfʊl] *adj* hiriente.

hurtle ['hɜːtl] *vi*: to ~ past pasar como un rayo; to ~ over precipitarse por.

husband ['hʌzbənd] *n* marido *m*.

husbandry ['hʌzbəndrɪ] *n fml* [of animals] cría *f*.

hush [hʌʃ] ◇ *n* silencio *m*. ◇ *excl* ¡silencio!, ¡a callar!
◆ **hush up** *vt* echar tierra a.

hush money *n* (U) *inf* soborno *m* (*para pagar el silencio de alguien*).

husk [hʌsk] *n* [of seed, grain] cáscara *f*, cascarilla *f*.

husky ['hʌskɪ] (*compar* **-ier**, *superl* **-iest**) ◇ *adj* [hoarse] ronco(ca). ◇ *n* (perro *m*) samoyedo *m*, perro *m* esquimal.

hustings ['hʌstɪŋz] *npl Br* campaña *f* electoral.

hustle ['hʌsl] ◇ *vt* **-1.** [hurry] meter prisa a. **-2.** *Am* [persuade]: to ~ sb into doing sthg presionar a alguien para que haga algo. ◇ *n*: ~ (and bustle) bullicio *m*, ajetreo *m*.

hut [hʌt] *n* **-1.** [rough house] cabaña *f*, choza *f*, jacal *m Amer*. **-2.** [shed] cobertizo *m*.

hutch [hʌtʃ] *n* conejera *f*.

hyacinth ['haɪəsɪnθ] *n* jacinto *m*.

hybrid ['haɪbrɪd] ◇ *adj* híbrido(da). ◇ *n* híbrido *m*.

hydrangea [haɪ'dreɪndʒə] *n* hortensia *f*.

hydrant ['haɪdrənt] *n* boca *f* de riego; [for fire] boca *f* de incendio.

hydraulic [haɪ'drɔːlɪk] *adj* hidráulico(ca).
◆ **hydraulics** *n* (U) hidráulica *f*.

hydrocarbon [,haɪdrə'kɑːbən] *n* hidrocarburo *m*.

hydrochloric acid [,haɪdrə'klɔːrɪk-] *n* ácido *m* clorhídrico.

hydroelectric [,haɪdrəʊ'lektrɪk] *adj* hidroeléctrico(ca).

hydroelectricity [,haɪdrəʊlek'trɪsətɪ] *n* hidroelectricidad *f*.

hydrofoil ['haɪdrəfɔɪl] *n* embarcación *f* con hidroala.

hydrogen ['haɪdrədʒən] *n* hidrógeno *m*.
hydrogen bomb *n* bomba *f* de hidrógeno.
hydrophobia [,haɪdrə'fəʊbjə] *n* *fml* [rabies] hidrofobia *f*.
hydroplane ['haɪdrəpleɪn] *n* **-1.** [speedboat] hidroplano *m*. **-2.** [hydrofoil] embarcación *f* con hidroala.
hyena [haɪ'iːnə] *n* hiena *f*.
hygiene ['haɪdʒiːn] *n* higiene *f*.
hygienic [haɪ'dʒiːnɪk] *adj* higiénico(ca).
hygienist [haɪ'dʒiːnɪst] *n* higienista *m* y *f* dental.
hymn [hɪm] *n* himno *m*.
hymn book *n* himnario *m*.
hype [haɪp] *inf* ◇ *n* bombo *m*, publicidad *f* exagerada. ◇ *vt* dar mucho bombo a.
hyped up [haɪpd-] *adj* *inf* [person] hecho(cha) un manojo de nervios.
hyper ['haɪpər] *adj* *inf* nervioso(sa).
hyperactive [,haɪpər'æktɪv] *adj* hiperactivo(va).
hyperbole [haɪ'pɜːbəlɪ] *n* hipérbole *f*.
hyperinflation [,haɪpərɪn'fleɪʃn] *n* hiperinflación *f*.
hypermarket ['haɪpə,mɑːkɪt] *n* hipermercado *m*.
hypersensitive [,haɪpə'sensɪtɪv] *adj* hipersensible.
hypertension [,haɪpə'tenʃn] *n* hipertensión *f*.
hypertext ['haɪpətekst] COMPUT ◇ *n* hipertexto *m* ◇ *comp*: ~ **link** enlace *m* hipertextual OR de hipertexto.
hyperventilate [,haɪpə'ventɪleɪt] *vi* hiperventilar.
hyphen ['haɪfn] *n* guión *m*.
hyphenate ['haɪfəneɪt] *vt* separar con guión.
hypnosis [hɪp'nəʊsɪs] *n* hipnosis *f* *inv*; **under** ~ bajo los efectos de la hipnosis.
hypnotic [hɪp'nɒtɪk] *adj* hipnótico(ca).
hypnotism ['hɪpnətɪzm] *n* hipnotismo *m*.
hypnotist ['hɪpnətɪst] *n* hipnotizador *m*, -ra *f*.
hypnotize, -ise ['hɪpnətaɪz] *vt* hipnotizar.
hypoallergenic ['haɪpəʊ,ælə'dʒenɪk] *adj* hipoalergénico(ca).
hypochondriac [,haɪpə'kɒndrɪæk] *n* hipocondríaco *m*, -ca *f*.
hypocrisy [hɪ'pɒkrəsɪ] *n* hipocresía *f*.
hypocrite ['hɪpəkrɪt] *n* hipócrita *m* y *f*.
hypocritical [,hɪpə'krɪtɪkl] *adj* hipócrita, falluto(ta) *Amer*.
hypodermic needle [,haɪpə'dɜːmɪk-] *n* aguja *f* hipodérmica.

hypodermic syringe [,haɪpə'dɜːmɪk-] *n* jeringuilla *f* hipodérmica.
hypothermia [,haɪpəʊ'θɜːmɪə] *n* hipotermia *f*.
hypothesis [haɪ'pɒθɪsɪs] (*pl* **-theses** [-θɪsiːz]) *n* hipótesis *f* *inv*.
hypothesize, -ise [haɪ'pɒθɪsaɪz] ◇ *vt* hacer hipótesis sobre. ◇ *vi* hacer hipótesis.
hypothetical [,haɪpə'θetɪkl] *adj* hipotético(ca).
hysterectomy [,hɪstə'rektəmɪ] (*pl* **-ies**) *n* histerectomía *f*.
hysteria [hɪs'tɪərɪə] *n* histeria *f*.
hysterical [hɪs'terɪkl] *adj* **-1.** [frantic] histérico(ca). **-2.** *inf* [very funny] tronchante, desternillante.
hysterics [hɪs'terɪks] *npl* **-1.** [panic, excitement] histeria *f*, histerismo *m*. **-2.** *inf* [fits of laughter]: **to be in** ~ troncharse OR partirse de risa.
HZ (*abbr of* **hertz**) Hz.

I

i (*pl* **i's** OR **is**), **I** (*pl* **I's** OR **Is**) [aɪ] *n* [letter] i *f*, I *f*.
I[1] [aɪ] *pers pron* yo; **I'm happy** soy feliz; **I'm leaving** me voy; **she and** ~ **were at college together** ella y yo fuimos juntos a la universidad; **it is** ~ *fml* soy yo; **I can't do it** yo no puedo hacer esto.
I[2] *abbr of* **Island, Isle**.
IA *abbr of* **Iowa**.
IAEA (*abbr of* **International Atomic Energy Agency**) *n* AIEA *f*.
IBA (*abbr of* **Independent Broadcasting Authority**) *n* organismo británico de regulación de las cadenas privadas de radio y televisión.
Iberian ◇ *adj* ibérico(ca). ◇ *n* ibero *m*, -ra *f*.
Iberian peninsula *n*: **the** ~ la Península Ibérica.
ibid (*abbr of* **ibidem**) ibid.
i/c *abbr of* **in charge**.
ICA (*abbr of* **Institute of Contemporary Art**) *n* centro londinense de arte moderno.
ICBM (*abbr of* **intercontinental ballistic missile**) *n* ICBM *m*.

ICC *n* **-1.** *(abbr of* **International Chamber of Commerce)** CCI *f.* **-2.** *(abbr of* **Interstate Commerce Commission)** *comité federal regulador del comercio interestatal en Estados Unidos.*

ice [aɪs] ◇ *n* **-1.** [frozen water] hielo *m*; **to break the ~** *fig* romper el hielo. **-2.** *Br* [ice cream] helado *m.* ◇ *vt* glasear, alcorzar.
◆ **ice over, ice up** *vi* helarse.

ice age *n* era *f* glaciar.

iceberg ['aɪsbɜːɡ] *n* iceberg *m.*

iceberg lettuce *n* lechuga *f* iceberg.

icebox ['aɪsbɒks] *n* **-1.** *Br* [in refrigerator] congelador *m.* **-2.** *Am* [refrigerator] refrigerador *m.*

icebreaker ['aɪsˌbreɪkəʳ] *n* [ship] rompehielos *m inv.*

ice bucket *n* cubo *m* del hielo.

ice cap *n* casquete *m* polar.

ice-cold *adj* helado(da).

ice cream *n* helado *m.*

ice cream van *n Br* furgoneta de venta de helados.

ICE CREAM VAN:
Con el buen tiempo las calles británicas saludan la llegada del vendedor ambulante de helados. Con una furgoneta de vivos colores e inconfundible campanilleo hace su entrada en el barrio, donde chicos y grandes salen a la calle para hacer cola frente a su mostrador

---

ice cube *n* cubito *m* de hielo.

iced [aɪst] *adj* **-1.** [cooled with ice] con hielo. **-2.** [covered in icing] glaseado(da).

ice floe *n* témpano *m* de hielo.

ice hockey *n* hockey *m* sobre hielo.

Iceland ['aɪslənd] *n* Islandia.

Icelander ['aɪsləndəʳ] *n* islandés *m*, -esa *f.*

Icelandic [aɪs'lændɪk] ◇ *adj* islandés(esa). ◇ *n* [language] islandés *m.*

ice lolly *n Br* polo *m.*

ice pick *n* pico *m* para el hielo.

ice rink *n* pista *f* de (patinaje sobre) hielo.

ice skate *n* patín *m* de cuchilla.
◆ **ice-skate** *vi* patinar sobre hielo.

ice-skater *n* patinador *m*, -ra *f* sobre hielo.

ice-skating *n* patinaje *m* sobre hielo.

icicle ['aɪsɪkl] *n* carámbano *m.*

icily ['aɪsɪlɪ] *adv* [in unfriendly way] glacialmente, con mucha frialdad.

icing ['aɪsɪŋ] *n* glaseado *m*; **the ~ on the cake** *fig* la guinda.

icing sugar *n Br* azúcar *m o f* glas.

ICJ *(abbr of* **International Court of Justice)** *n* TIJ *m.*

icon ['aɪkɒn] *n* COMPUT & RELIG icono *m.*

iconoclast [aɪ'kɒnəklæst] *n* iconoclasta *m y f.*

ICR *(abbr of* **Institute for Cancer Research)** *n* instituto estadounidense de investigación del cáncer.

ICU *(abbr of* **intensive care unit)** *n* UCI *f.*

icy ['aɪsɪ] *(compar* **-ier**, *superl* **-iest)** *adj* **-1.** [gen] helado(da). **-2.** *fig* [unfriendly] glacial.

id [ɪd] *n* ello *m*, id *m.*

I'd [aɪd] = **I would, I had.**

ID ◇ *n* (U) *(abbr of* **identification)** ≃ DNI *m.* ◇ *abbr of* **Idaho.**

Idaho ['aɪdəˌhəʊ] *n* Idaho.

ID card = **identity card.**

IDD *(abbr of* **international direct dialling)** *sistema de llamadas telefónicas internacionales directas.*

idea [aɪ'dɪə] *n* **-1.** [gen] idea *f*; **to have an ~ of sthg** tener (alguna) idea de algo; **to have no ~** no tener ni idea; **to get the ~** *inf* captar la idea, hacerse una idea; **to get the ~ (that)** tener la impresión de que; **the ~ is to ...** la idea es .... **-2.** [intuition, feeling] sensación *f*, impresión *f*; **to have an ~ (that) ...** tener la sensación de que ....

ideal [aɪ'dɪəl] ◇ *adj:* **~ (for)** ideal (para). ◇ *n* ideal *m.*

idealism [aɪ'dɪəlɪzm] *n* idealismo *m.*

idealist [aɪ'dɪəlɪst] *n* idealista *m y f.*

idealize, -ise [aɪ'dɪəlaɪz] *vt* idealizar.

ideally [aɪ'dɪəlɪ] *adv* **-1.** [perfectly] idealmente; [suited] perfectamente. **-2.** [preferably] preferiblemente, a ser posible.

identical [aɪ'dentɪkl] *adj* idéntico(ca).

identical twins *npl* gemelos *mpl* idénticos.

identifiable [aɪ'dentɪfaɪəbl] *adj* identificable.

identification [aɪˌdentɪfɪ'keɪʃn] *n* **-1.** [gen]: **~ (with)** identificación *f* (con). **-2.** [documentation] documentación *f.*

identify [aɪ'dentɪfaɪ] *(pt & pp* **-ied)** ◇ *vt* identificar; **to ~ sb with sthg** relacionar a alguien con algo. ◇ *vi:* **to ~ with sb/sthg** identificarse con alguien/algo.

Identikit picture® [aɪ'dentɪkɪt-] *n* fotorrobot *f.*

identity [aɪ'dentətɪ] *(pl* **-ies)** *n* identidad *f.*

identity card *n* carné *m* OR documento *m* de identidad, cédula *f Amer.*

identity parade *n* rueda *f* de identificación.

ideological [ˌaɪdɪə'lɒdʒɪkl] *adj* ideológico(ca).

ideology [ˌaɪdɪ'ɒlədʒɪ] *(pl* **-ies)** *n* ideología *f.*

idiom ['ɪdɪəm] *n* **-1.** [phrase] locución *f*, modismo *m.* **-2.** *fml* [style] lenguaje *m.*

idiomatic [ˌɪdɪə'mætɪk] *adj* idiomático(ca).

idiosyncrasy [ˌɪdɪə'sɪŋkrəsɪ] (*pl* **-ies**) *n* rareza *f*, manía *f*.

idiot ['ɪdɪət] *n* [fool] idiota *m y f*, boludo *m*, -da *f Amer.*

idiotic [ˌɪdɪ'ɒtɪk] *adj* idiota.

idle ['aɪdl] ◇ *adj* **-1.** [lazy] perezoso(sa), vago(ga). **-2.** [not working - machine, factory] parado(da); [- person] desocupado(da), sin trabajo. **-3.** [rumour] infundado(da); [threat, boast] vano(na); [curiosity] que no viene a cuento. ◇ *vi* estar en punto muerto.

◆ **idle away** *vt sep* perder, desperdiciar.

idleness ['aɪdlnɪs] *n* [laziness] pereza *f*, holgazanería *f*.

idler ['aɪdləʳ] *n* vago *m*, -ga *f*, holgazán *m*, -ana *f*.

idly ['aɪdlɪ] *adv* **-1.** [lazily] sin hacer nada, haciendo el vago. **-2.** [without purpose] distraídamente.

idol ['aɪdl] *n* ídolo *m*.

idolize, -ise ['aɪdəlaɪz] *vt* idolatrar.

idyl(l) ['ɪdɪl] *n* idilio *m*.

idyllic [ɪ'dɪlɪk] *adj* idílico(ca).

i.e. (*abbr of* **id est**) i.e.

if [ɪf] ◇ *conj* **-1.** [gen] si; ~ **I were you** yo que tú, yo en tu lugar. **-2.** [though] aunque. ◇ *n*: ~**s and buts** peros *mpl*, pegas *fpl*.

◆ **if not** *conj* por no decir.

◆ **if only** ◇ *conj* **-1.** [naming a reason] aunque sólo sea. **-2.** [expressing regret] si; ~ **only I'd been quicker!** ¡ojalá hubiera sido más rápido! ◇ *excl* ¡ojalá!

iffy ['ɪfɪ] (*compar* **-ier**, *superl* **-iest**) *adj inf* dudoso(sa).

igloo ['ɪgluː] (*pl* **-s**) *n* iglú *m*.

ignite [ɪg'naɪt] ◇ *vt* encender. ◇ *vi* encenderse.

ignition [ɪg'nɪʃn] *n* **-1.** [act of igniting] ignición *f*. **-2.** [in car] encendido *m*.

ignition key *n* llave *f* de contacto.

ignoble [ɪg'nəʊbl] *adj fml* innoble.

ignominious [ˌɪgnə'mɪnɪəs] *adj fml* ignominioso(sa).

ignominy ['ɪgnəmɪnɪ] *n* (*U*) *fml* ignominia *f*.

ignoramus [ˌɪgnə'reɪməs] (*pl* **-es**) *n* ignorante *m y f*.

ignorance ['ɪgnərəns] *n* ignorancia *f*.

ignorant ['ɪgnərənt] *adj* **-1.** [uneducated, rude] ignorante. **-2.** *fml* [unaware]: **to be ~ of sthg** ignorar algo.

ignore [ɪg'nɔːʳ] *vt* [take no notice of] no hacer caso de, ignorar.

iguana [ɪ'gwɑːnə] (*pl inv* OR **-s**) *n* iguana *f*.

ikon ['aɪkɒn] = **icon**.

IL *abbr of* **Illinois**.

ILEA (*abbr of* **Inner London Education Authority**) *n* antiguo organismo responsable de educación en Londres.

ileum ['ɪlɪəm] (*pl* **ilea** ['ɪlɪə]) *n* íleon *m*.

ilk [ɪlk] *n*: **of that** ~ [of that sort] de ese tipo.

ill [ɪl] ◇ *adj* **-1.** [unwell] enfermo(ma); **to feel** ~ encontrarse mal; **to be taken** OR **to fall** ~ caer OR ponerse enfermo. **-2.** [bad] malo(la). ◇ *adv* **-1.** [badly] mal. **-2.** *fml* [unfavourably]: **to speak/think** ~ **of sb** hablar/pensar mal de alguien.

◆ **ills** *npl* desgracias *fpl*, infortunios *mpl*.

ill. *abbr of* **illustration**.

I'll [aɪl] = **I will**, **I shall**.

ill-advised [-əd'vaɪzd] *adj* [action] poco aconsejable; [person] imprudente, insensato(ta); **to be** ~ **to do sthg** cometer una imprudencia al hacer algo.

ill at ease *adj* incómodo(da), violento(ta).

ill-bred *adj* maleducado(da).

ill-considered *adj* poco meditado(da).

ill-disposed *adj*: **to be** ~ **towards** tener una actitud poco propicia hacia.

illegal [ɪ'liːgl] *adj* ilegal.

illegally [ɪ'liːgəlɪ] *adv* ilegalmente.

illegible [ɪ'ledʒəbl] *adj* ilegible.

illegitimate [ˌɪlɪ'dʒɪtɪmət] *adj* ilegítimo(ma).

ill-equipped *adj*: **to be** ~ **to do sthg** estar mal preparado(da) para hacer algo.

ill-fated *adj* desafortunado(da).

ill feeling *n* resentimiento *m*.

ill-founded [-'faʊndɪd] *adj* sin fundamento, infundado(da).

ill-gotten gains [-'gɒtən-] *npl fml* ganancias *fpl* ilícitas.

ill health *n* mala salud *f*.

illicit [ɪ'lɪsɪt] *adj* ilícito(ta).

illicitly [ɪ'lɪsɪtlɪ] *adv* de manera ilícita.

ill-informed *adj* mal informado(da).

Illinois [ˌɪlɪ'nɔɪs] *n* Illinois.

illiteracy [ɪ'lɪtərəsɪ] *n* analfabetismo *m*.

illiterate [ɪ'lɪtərət] ◇ *adj* analfabeto(ta). ◇ *n* analfabeto *m*, -ta *f*.

ill-mannered *adj* grosero(ra), descortés.

illness ['ɪlnɪs] *n* enfermedad *f*.

illogical [ɪ'lɒdʒɪkl] *adj* ilógico(ca).

ill-suited *adj*: ~ **(for)** poco adecuado(da) (para).

ill-tempered *adj* malhumorado(da).

ill-timed [-'taɪmd] *adj* inoportuno(na).

ill-treat *vt* maltratar.

ill-treatment *n* (*U*) malos tratos *mpl*.

illuminate [ɪ'luːmɪneɪt] *vt* **-1.** [light up] iluminar. **-2.** [explain] ilustrar, aclarar.

illuminated [ɪˈluːmɪneɪtɪd] *adj* iluminado(da).

illuminating [ɪˈluːmɪneɪtɪŋ] *adj* esclarecedor(ra).

illumination [ɪˌluːmɪˈneɪʃn] *n* [lighting] alumbrado *m*, iluminación *f.*

◆ **illuminations** *npl* Br iluminaciones *fpl*, alumbrado *m* decorativo.

illusion [ɪˈluːʒn] *n* **-1.** [gen] ilusión *f*; **to have no ~s about** no hacerse ilusiones sobre; **to be under the ~ that** creer equivocadamente que. **-2.** [magic trick] truco *m* de ilusionismo.

illusionist [ɪˈluːʒənɪst] *n* ilusionista *m y f.*

illusory [ɪˈluːsərɪ] *adj fml* ilusorio(ria).

illustrate [ˈɪləstreɪt] *vt* ilustrar.

illustration [ˌɪləˈstreɪʃn] *n* ilustración *f.*

illustrator [ˈɪləstreɪtər] *n* ilustrador *m*, -ra *f.*

illustrious [ɪˈlʌstrɪəs] *adj fml* ilustre.

ill will *n* rencor *m*, animadversión *f.*

ill wind [-wɪnd] *n*: **it's an ~ (that blows nobody any good)** *proverb* no hay mal que por bien no venga *proverb.*

ILO (*abbr of* International Labour Organization) *n* OIT *f.*

ILWU (*abbr of* International Longshoremen's and Warehousemen's Union) *n sindicato internacional de trabajadores del sector portuario y de almacenes.*

I'm [aɪm] = **I am.**

image [ˈɪmɪdʒ] *n* imagen *f*; **to be the ~ of sb** [exactly like] ser el vivo retrato de alguien.

imagery [ˈɪmɪdʒrɪ] *n* (*U*) imágenes *fpl.*

imaginable [ɪˈmædʒɪnəbl] *adj* imaginable.

imaginary [ɪˈmædʒɪnrɪ] *adj* imaginario(ria).

imagination [ɪˌmædʒɪˈneɪʃn] *n* imaginación *f.*

imaginative [ɪˈmædʒɪnətɪv] *adj* imaginativo(va).

imagine [ɪˈmædʒɪn] *vt* **-1.** [gen] imaginar; **~ never having to work!** ¡imagina que nunca tuvieras que trabajar!; **~ (that)!** ¡imagínate! **-2.** [suppose]: **to ~ (that)** imaginarse que.

imaginings [ɪˈmædʒɪnɪŋz] *npl literary* imaginaciones *fpl.*

imbalance [ˌɪmˈbæləns] *n* desequilibrio *m.*

imbecile [ˈɪmbɪsiːl] *n* imbécil *m y f.*

imbue [ɪmˈbjuː] *vt*: **to be ~d with** imbuirse de.

IMF (*abbr of* International Monetary Fund) *n* FMI *m.*

imitate [ˈɪmɪteɪt] *vt* imitar.

imitation [ˌɪmɪˈteɪʃn] ◇ *n* imitación *f.* ◇ *adj* de imitación.

imitator [ˈɪmɪteɪtər] *n* imitador *m*, -ra *f.*

immaculate [ɪˈmækjʊlət] *adj* **-1.** [clean and tidy] inmaculado(da); [taste] exquisito(ta). **-2.** [impeccable] impecable, perfecto(ta).

immaculately [ɪˈmækjʊlətlɪ] *adv* **-1.** [cleanly, tidily] de manera inmaculada. **-2.** [impeccably] impecablemente, a la perfección.

immaterial [ˌɪməˈtɪərɪəl] *adj* [irrelevant, unimportant] irrelevante.

immature [ˌɪməˈtjʊər] *adj* inmaduro(ra); [animal] joven.

immaturity [ˌɪməˈtjʊərətɪ] *n* **-1.** [lack of judgment] inmadurez *f.* **-2.** [youth] juventud *f.*

immeasurable [ɪˈmeʒrəbl] *adj* inmenso(sa), inconmensurable.

immediacy [ɪˈmiːdjəsɪ] *n* inmediatez *f.*

immediate [ɪˈmiːdjət] *adj* **-1.** [gen] inmediato(ta); **in the ~ future** en el futuro más cercano. **-2.** [family] directo(ta).

immediately [ɪˈmiːdjətlɪ] ◇ *adv* **-1.** [at once] inmediatamente. **-2.** [directly] directamente. ◇ *conj* en cuanto, tan pronto como.

immemorial [ˌɪmɪˈmɔːrɪəl] *adj* inmemorial; **from time ~** desde tiempos inmemoriales.

immense [ɪˈmens] *adj* inmenso(sa).

immensely [ɪˈmenslɪ] *adv* inmensamente.

immensity [ɪˈmensətɪ] *n* inmensidad *f.*

immerse [ɪˈmɜːs] *vt* **-1.** [plunge]: **to ~ sthg in sthg** sumergir algo en algo. **-2.** [involve]: **to ~ o.s. in sthg** enfrascarse en algo.

immersion heater [ɪˈmɜːʃn-] *n* calentador *m* de inmersión.

immigrant [ˈɪmɪgrənt] ◇ *n* inmigrante *m y f.* ◇ *comp* inmigrante.

immigration [ˌɪmɪˈgreɪʃn] ◇ *n* inmigración *f.* ◇ *comp* de inmigración.

imminence [ˈɪmɪnəns] *n fml* inminencia *f.*

imminent [ˈɪmɪnənt] *adj* inminente.

immobile [ɪˈməʊbaɪl] *adj* inmóvil.

immobilization [ɪˌməʊbɪlaɪˈzeɪʃn] *n* inmovilización *f.*

immobilize, -ise [ɪˈməʊbɪlaɪz] *vt* inmovilizar.

immobilizer [ɪˈməʊbɪlaɪzər] *n* cortacorriente *m*, dispositivo *m* antirrobo.

immodest [ɪˈmɒdɪst] *adj* **-1.** [vain] vanidoso(sa), inmodesto(ta). **-2.** [indecent] indecente, indecoroso(sa).

immoral [ɪˈmɒrəl] *adj* inmoral.

immorality [ˌɪməˈrælətɪ] *n* inmoralidad *f.*

immortal [ɪˈmɔːtl] ◇ *adj* inmortal. ◇ *n* **-1.** [god] dios *m* OR divinidad *f* inmortal. **-2.** [hero] inmortal *m y f.*

immortality [ˌɪmɔːˈtælətɪ] *n* inmortalidad *f.*

immortalize, -ise [ɪˈmɔːtəlaɪz] *vt* inmortalizar.

immovable [ɪ'muːvəbl] *adj* **-1.** [fixed] fijo(ja), inamovible. **-2.** [determined, decided] inconmovible, inflexible.

immune [ɪ'mjuːn] *adj* **-1.** [gen & MED]: ~ **(to)** inmune (a). **-2.** [exempt]: ~ **(from)** exento(ta) (de).

immune system *n* sistema *m* inmunológico.

immunity [ɪ'mjuːnətɪ] *n* **-1.** [gen & MED]: ~ **(to)** inmunidad *f* (a). **-2.** [exemption]: ~ **(from)** exención *f* (de).

immunization [ˌɪmjuːnaɪ'zeɪʃn] *n* inmunización *f*.

immunize, -ise ['ɪmjuːnaɪz] *vt*: **to** ~ **sb (against sthg)** inmunizar a alguien (contra algo).

immunodeficiency [ˌɪmjuːnəʊdɪ'fɪʃənsɪ] *n* inmunodeficiencia *f*.

immunology [ˌɪmjuːn'ɒlədʒɪ] *n* inmunología *f*.

immutable [ɪ'mjuːtəbl] *adj fml* inmutable.

imp [ɪmp] *n* **-1.** [creature] duendecillo *m*. **-2.** [naughty child] diablillo *m*.

impact [*n* 'ɪmpækt, *vb* ɪm'pækt] ⋄ *n* impacto *m*; **on** ~ **al** chocar OR estrellarse; **to make an** ~ **on** OR **upon** causar impacto en. ⋄ *vt* **-1.** [collide with] chocar con. **-2.** [influence] influenciar.

impair [ɪm'peəʳ] *vt* [sight, hearing] dañar, debilitar; [ability, efficiency] mermar; [movement] entorpecer.

impaired [ɪm'peəd] *adj* dañado(da), debilitado(da).

impale [ɪm'peɪl] *vt*: **to be** ~**d on sthg** quedar atravesado(da) en algo.

impart [ɪm'pɑːt] *vt fml* **-1.** [information]: **to** ~ **sthg (to sb)** comunicar algo (a alguien). **-2.** [feeling, quality]: **to** ~ **sthg (to sthg)** conferir algo (a algo).

impartial [ɪm'pɑːʃl] *adj* imparcial.

impartiality [ɪm,pɑːʃɪ'ælətɪ] *n* imparcialidad *f*.

impassable [ɪm'pɑːsəbl] *adj* intransitable, impracticable.

impasse [æm'pɑːs] *n* impasse *m*, callejón *m* sin salida.

impassioned [ɪm'pæʃnd] *adj* apasionado(da).

impassive [ɪm'pæsɪv] *adj* impasible.

impatience [ɪm'peɪʃns] *n* impaciencia *f*.

impatient [ɪm'peɪʃnt] *adj* impaciente; **to be** ~ **to do sthg** estar impaciente por hacer algo; **to be** ~ **for sthg** esperar algo con impaciencia.

impatiently [ɪm'peɪʃntlɪ] *adv* impacientemente, con impaciencia.

impeach [ɪm'piːtʃ] *vt* [president, official] destituir (por prevaricación).

impeachment [ɪm'piːtʃmənt] *n* [of president, official] destitución *f* (por prevaricación).

impeccable [ɪm'pekəbl] *adj* impecable.

impeccably [ɪm'pekəblɪ] *adv* impecablemente.

impecunious [ˌɪmpɪ'kjuːnjəs] *adj fml* indigente, menesteroso(sa).

impede [ɪm'piːd] *vt* dificultar, entorpecer.

impediment [ɪm'pedɪmənt] *n* **-1.** [obstacle] impedimento *m*, obstáculo *m*. **-2.** [disability] defecto *m*.

impel [ɪm'pel] (*pt & pp* **-led,** *cont* **-ling**) *vt*: **to** ~ **sb to do sthg** impulsar OR impeler a alguien a hacer algo.

impending [ɪm'pendɪŋ] *adj* inminente.

impenetrable [ɪm'penɪtrəbl] *adj* **-1.** [impossible to penetrate] impenetrable. **-2.** [impossible to understand] incomprensible.

imperative [ɪm'perətɪv] ⋄ *adj* [essential] apremiante, imperativo(va). ⋄ *n* imperativo *m*.

imperceptible [ˌɪmpə'septəbl] *adj* imperceptible.

imperfect [ɪm'pɜːfɪkt] ⋄ *adj* [not perfect] imperfecto(ta). ⋄ *n* GRAMM: ~ **(tense)** (pretérito *m*) imperfecto *m*.

imperfection [ˌɪmpə'fekʃn] *n* imperfección *f*.

imperial [ɪm'pɪərɪəl] *adj* **-1.** [of an empire or emperor] imperial. **-2.** [system of measurement]: ~ **system** sistema anglosajón de medidas.

imperialism [ɪm'pɪərɪəlɪzm] *n* imperialismo *m*.

imperialist [ɪm'pɪərɪəlɪst] ⋄ *adj* imperialista. ⋄ *n* imperialista *m y f*.

imperil [ɪm'perɪl] (*Br pt & pp* **-led,** *cont* **-ling,** *Am pt & pp* **-ed,** *cont* **-ing**) *vt fml* poner en peligro.

imperious [ɪm'pɪərɪəs] *adj* imperioso(sa).

impersonal [ɪm'pɜːsnl] *adj* impersonal.

impersonate [ɪm'pɜːsəneɪt] *vt* [gen] hacerse pasar por; THEATRE imitar.

impersonation [ɪm,pɜːsə'neɪʃn] *n* **-1.** [pretending to be]: **charged with** ~ **of a policeman** acusado de hacerse pasar por policía. **-2.** [impression] imitación *f*; **to do** ~**s (of)** imitar a, hacer imitaciones de.

impersonator [ɪm'pɜːsəneɪtəʳ] *n* imitador *m*, -ra *f*.

impertinence [ɪm'pɜːtɪnəns] *n* impertinencia *f*, insolencia *f*.

impertinent [ɪm'pɜːtɪnənt] *adj* impertinente, insolente.

imperturbable [,ɪmpə'tɜːbəbl] *adj* imperturbable.

impervious [ɪm'pɜːvjəs] *adj* [not influenced]: ~ **to** insensible a.

impetuous [ɪm'petʃʊəs] *adj* impetuoso(sa), irreflexivo(va).

impetus ['ɪmpɪtəs] *n* (*U*) **-1.** [momentum] ímpetu *m*. **-2.** [stimulus] incentivo *m*, impulso *m*.

impinge [ɪm'pɪndʒ] *vi*: **to** ~ **on sthg/sb** afectar algo/a alguien.

impish ['ɪmpɪʃ] *adj* travieso(sa).

implacable [ɪm'plækəbl] *adj* implacable.

implant [*n* 'ɪmplɑːnt, *vb* ɪm'plɑːnt] ◇ *n* injerto *m*. ◇ *vt* **-1.** [fix - idea etc] **to** ~ **sthg in** OR **into** inculcar algo en. **-2.** MED: **to** ~ **sthg in** OR **into** implantar algo en.

implausible [ɪm'plɔːzəbl] *adj* inverosímil.

implement [*n* 'ɪmplɪmənt, *vt* 'ɪmplɪment] ◇ *n* herramienta *f*. ◇ *vt* llevar a cabo, poner en práctica.

implementation [,ɪmplɪmen'teɪʃn] *n* puesta *f* en práctica, ejecución *f*.

implicate ['ɪmplɪkeɪt] *vt*: **to** ~ **sb in** implicar OR involucrar a alguien en.

implication [,ɪmplɪ'keɪʃn] *n* **-1.** [involvement] implicación *f*, complicidad *f*. **-2.** [inference] consecuencia *f*; **by** ~ de forma indirecta.

implicit [ɪm'plɪsɪt] *adj* **-1.** [gen]: ~ **(in)** implícito(ta) (en). **-2.** [complete - belief] absoluto(ta); [- faith] incondicional.

implicitly [ɪm'plɪsɪtlɪ] *adv* **-1.** [by inference] implícitamente. **-2.** [completely] incondicionalmente, ciegamente.

implied [ɪm'plaɪd] *adj* implícito(ta).

implode [ɪm'pləʊd] *vi* implosionar.

implore [ɪm'plɔːʳ] *vt*: **to** ~ **sb (to do sthg)** suplicar a alguien (que haga algo).

imply [ɪm'plaɪ] (*pt* & *pp* **-ied**) *vt* **-1.** [suggest] insinuar, dar a entender. **-2.** [involve] implicar, suponer.

impolite [,ɪmpə'laɪt] *adj* maleducado(da), descortés.

imponderable [ɪm'pɒndrəbl] *adj* imponderable, inestimable.

◆ **imponderables** *mpl* imponderables *mpl*.

import [*n* 'ɪmpɔːt, *vt* ɪm'pɔːt] ◇ *n* **-1.** [act of importing, product] importación *f*. **-2.** *fml* [meaning] sentido *m*, significado *m*. **-3.** *fml* [importance] trascendencia *f*, importancia *f*. ◇ *vt* *lit* & *fig* importar.

importance [ɪm'pɔːtns] *n* importancia *f*.

important [ɪm'pɔːtnt] *adj*: ~ **(to)** importante (para); **it's not** ~ no importa.

importantly [ɪm'pɔːtntlɪ] *adv*: **more** ~ lo que es aún más importante.

importation [,ɪmpɔː'teɪʃn] *n* importación *f*.

imported [ɪm'pɔːtɪd] *adj* importado(da), de importación.

importer [ɪm'pɔːtəʳ] *n* importador *m*, -ra *f*.

impose [ɪm'pəʊz] ◇ *vt*: **to** ~ **sthg (on)** imponer algo (a). ◇ *vi*: **to** ~ **(on)** abusar (de), molestar (a).

imposing [ɪm'pəʊzɪŋ] *adj* imponente, impresionante.

imposition [,ɪmpə'zɪʃn] *n* **-1.** [enforcement] imposición *f*. **-2.** [cause of trouble] molestia *f*.

impossibility [ɪm,pɒsə'bɪlətɪ] (*pl* **-ies**) *n* imposibilidad *f*.

impossible [ɪm'pɒsəbl] ◇ *adj* **-1.** [gen] imposible. **-2.** [person, behaviour] inaguantable, insufrible. ◇ *n*: **to do the** ~ hacer lo imposible.

impostor, imposter *Am* [ɪm'pɒstəʳ] *n* impostor *m*, -ra *f*.

impotence ['ɪmpətəns] *n* impotencia *f*.

impotent ['ɪmpətənt] *adj* impotente.

impound [ɪm'paʊnd] *vt* confiscar, incautarse.

impoverished [ɪm'pɒvərɪʃt] *adj* [country, people, imagination] empobrecido(da).

impracticable [ɪm'præktɪkəbl] *adj* impracticable, irrealizable.

impractical [ɪm'præktɪkl] *adj* poco práctico(ca).

imprecation [,ɪmprɪ'keɪʃn] *n* imprecación *f*.

imprecise [ɪmprɪ'saɪs] *adj* impreciso(sa).

impregnable [ɪm'pregnəbl] *adj* *lit* & *fig* inexpugnable, impenetrable.

impregnate ['ɪmpregneɪt] *vt* **-1.** [introduce substance into]: **to** ~ **sthg (with)** impregnar OR empapar algo (de). **-2.** *fml* [fertilize] fecundar.

impresario [,ɪmprɪ'sɑːrɪəʊ] (*pl* **-s**) *n* empresario *m*, -ria *f* (de espectáculos).

impress [ɪm'pres] *vt* **-1.** [produce admiration in] impresionar, causar impresión a. **-2.** [stress]: **to** ~ **sthg on sb** hacer comprender a alguien la importancia de algo.

impression [ɪm'preʃn] *n* **-1.** [gen] impresión *f*; **to make an** ~ impresionar; **to make a good/bad** ~ causar una buena/mala impresión; **to be under the** ~ **that** tener la impresión de que. **-2.** [imitation] imitación *f*.

impressionable [ɪm'preʃnəbl] *adj* impresionable.

Impressionism [ɪm'preʃənɪzm] *n* impresionismo *m*.

impressionist [ɪm'preʃənɪst] *n* imitador *m*, -ra *f*.

◆ **Impressionist** ◇ *adj* impresionista. ◇ *n* impresionista *m y f*.

impressive [ɪmˈpresɪv] *adj* impresionante.

imprint [ˈɪmprɪnt] *n* **-1.** [mark] huella *f*, impresión *f*. **-2.** [publisher's name] pie *m* de imprenta.

imprinted [ɪmˈprɪntɪd] *adj* **-1.** [marked] marcado(da). **-2.** *fig* [on mind, memory]: ~ **on** impreso(sa) OR grabado(da) en.

imprison [ɪmˈprɪzn] *vt* encarcelar.

imprisonment [ɪmˈprɪznmənt] *n* encarcelamiento *m*.

improbable [ɪmˈprɒbəbl] *adj* [event] improbable; [story, excuse] inverosímil; [clothes, hat] estrafalario(ria); [contraption] extraño(ña).

impromptu [ɪmˈprɒmptjuː] *adj* improvisado(da).

improper [ɪmˈprɒpər] *adj* **-1.** [unsuitable] impropio(pia). **-2.** [incorrect, illegal] indebido(da). **-3.** [rude] indecente, indecoroso(sa).

impropriety [ˌɪmprəˈpraɪətɪ] *n* **-1.** [unsuitability] impropiedad *f*. **-2.** [rudeness] indecencia *f*.

improve [ɪmˈpruːv] ◇ *vi* mejorar, mejorarse; **to** ~ **on** OR **upon sthg** mejorar algo. ◇ *vt* mejorar.

improved [ɪmˈpruːvd] *adj* mejorado(da).

improvement [ɪmˈpruːvmənt] *n* **-1.** [gen]: ~ **(in/on)** mejora *f* (en/con respecto a). **-2.** [to home] reforma *f*.

improvisation [ˌɪmprəvaɪˈzeɪʃn] *n* improvisación *f*.

improvise [ˈɪmprəvaɪz] *vt & vi* improvisar.

imprudent [ɪmˈpruːdənt] *adj* imprudente.

impudent [ˈɪmpjʊdənt] *adj* insolente, descarado(da).

impugn [ɪmˈpjuːn] *vt fml* impugnar.

impulse [ˈɪmpʌls] *n* impulso *m*; **on** ~ sin pensar.

impulse buying [-ˈbaɪɪŋ] *n* (U) compra *f* impulsiva OR irreflexiva.

impulsive [ɪmˈpʌlsɪv] *adj* impulsivo(va), irreflexivo(va).

impunity [ɪmˈpjuːnətɪ] *n*: **with** ~ impunemente.

impure [ɪmˈpjʊər] *adj lit & fig* impuro(ra).

impurity [ɪmˈpjʊərətɪ] (*pl* **-ies**) *n* impureza *f*.

IMRO [ˈɪmrəʊ] (*abbr of* **Investment Management Regulatory Organization**) *n organismo regulador de inversiones*.

in [ɪn] ◇ *prep* **-1.** [indicating place, position] en; ~ **a box/the garden/the lake** en una caja/el jardín/el lago; ~ **Paris/Belgium/the country** en París/Bélgica/el campo; **that coat** ~ **the window** el abrigo del escaparate; **to be** ~ **hospital/prison** estar en el hospital/la cárcel; ~ **here/there** aquí/allí

dentro. **-2.** [wearing] con; **she was still** ~ **her nightclothes** todavía llevaba su vestido de noche; **he was dressed** ~ **a suit** llevaba un traje. **-3.** [appearing in, included in] en; **there's a mistake** ~ **this paragraph** hay un error en este párrafo; **she's** ~ **today's Guardian** sale en el Guardian de hoy. **-4.** [at a particular time]: **at four o'clock** ~ **the morning/afternoon** a las cuatro de la mañana/tarde; ~ **the morning** por la mañana; ~ **1992/May/the spring** en 1992/mayo/primavera. **-5.** [within] en; **he learned to type** ~ **two weeks** aprendió a escribir a máquina en dos semanas; **I'll be ready** ~ **five minutes** estoy listo en cinco minutos. **-6.** [during] desde hace; **it's my first decent meal** ~ **weeks** es lo primero decente que como desde hace OR en semanas. **-7.** [indicating situation, circumstances]: ~ **these circumstances** en estas circunstancias; **to live/die** ~ **poverty** vivir/morir en la pobreza; ~ **danger/difficulty** en peligro/dificultades; ~ **the sun** al sol; ~ **the rain** bajo la lluvia; **don't go out** ~ **this weather** no salgas con este tiempo; **a rise** ~ **prices** un aumento de los precios. **-8.** [indicating manner, condition] en; ~ **a loud/soft voice** en voz alta/baja; ~ **pencil/ink** a lápiz/bolígrafo. **-9.** [indicating emotional state] con; ~ **anger/joy** con enfado/alegría; ~ **my excitement I forgot the keys** con la emoción se me olvidaron las llaves. **-10.** [specifying area of activity]: **advances** ~ **medicine** avances en la medicina; **he's** ~ **computers** está metido en informática. **-11.** [with numbers - showing quantity, age]: ~ **large/small quantities** en grandes/pequeñas cantidades; ~ **(their) thousands** a OR por millares; **she's** ~ **her sixties** andará por los sesenta. **-12.** [describing arrangement]: ~ **a line/circle** en línea/círculo; **to stand** ~ **twos** estar en pares OR parejas. **-13.** [as regards] en; ~ **these matters** en estos temas; **two metres** ~ **length/width** dos metros de largo/ancho; **a change** ~ **direction** un cambio de dirección. **-14.** [in ratios]: **one** ~ **ten** uno de cada diez; **five pence** ~ **the pound** cinco peniques por libra. **-15.** (*after superl*) de; **the best** ~ **the world** el mejor del mundo. **-16.** (*+ present participle*): ~ **doing sthg** al hacer algo.

◇ *adv* **-1.** [inside] dentro; **put the clothes** ~ mete la ropa (dentro); **to jump** ~ saltar adentro; **do come** ~ pasa por favor. **-2.** [at home, work]: **is Judith** ~? ¿está Judith?; **I'm staying** ~ **tonight** esta noche no salgo. **-3.** [of train, boat, plane]: **is the train** ~ **yet?** ¿ha llegado el tren? **-4.** [of tide]: **the tide's** ~ la marea está alta. **-5.** *phr*: **you're** ~ **for a surprise** te vas a llevar una sorpresa; **we're**

~ **for some bad weather** nos espera mal tiempo; **to be ~ on it** estar en el ajo; **to have it ~ for sb** tenerla tomada con alguien.
◇ *adj inf* de moda; **short skirts are ~ this year** las faldas cortas se llevan este año.
◆ **ins** *npl*: **the ~s and outs** los detalles, los pormenores.
◆ **in that** *conj* dado que, ya que.

in. *abbr of* **inch**.

IN *abbr of* **Indiana**.

inability [,ɪnə'bɪlətɪ] *n*: ~ **(to do sthg)** incapacidad *f* (de hacer algo).

inaccessible [,ɪnək'sesəbl] *adj* inaccesible.

inaccuracy [ɪn'ækjʊrəsɪ] (*pl* **-ies**) *n* **-1.** (*U*) [quality of being inaccurate] inexactitud *f*. **-2.** [imprecise statement] incorrección *f*, error *m*.

inaccurate [ɪn'ækjʊrət] *adj* incorrecto(ta), inexacto(ta).

inaction [ɪn'ækʃn] *n* pasividad *f*, inacción *f*.

inactive [ɪn'æktɪv] *adj* inactivo(va).

inactivity [,ɪnæk'tɪvətɪ] *n* inactividad *f*.

inadequacy [ɪn'ædɪkwəsɪ] (*pl* **-ies**) *n* [of thing, system] insuficiencia *f*; [of person] incapacidad *f*.

inadequate [ɪn'ædɪkwət] *adj* **-1.** [insufficient] insuficiente. **-2.** [person] incapaz.

inadmissible [,ɪnəd'mɪsəbl] *adj* improcedente.

inadvertent [,ɪnəd'vɜːtnt] *adj* accidental, fortuito(ta).

inadvertently [,ɪnəd'vɜːtəntlɪ] *adv* sin querer, accidentalmente.

inadvisable [,ɪnəd'vaɪzəbl] *adj* desaconsejable, poco aconsejable.

inalienable [ɪn'eɪljənəbl] *adj fml* inalienable.

inane [ɪ'neɪn] *adj* necio(cia).

inanely [ɪ'neɪnlɪ] *adv* neciamente.

inanimate [ɪn'ænɪmət] *adj* inanimado(da).

inanity [ɪ'nænətɪ] *n* necedad *f*.

inapplicable [,ɪnə'plɪkəbl] *adj* inaplicable.

inappropriate [,ɪnə'prəʊprɪət] *adj* [remark, clothing] impropio(pia); [time] inoportuno(na).

inarticulate [,ɪnɑː'tɪkjʊlət] *adj* [person] incapaz de expresarse; [speech, explanation] mal pronunciado(da) OR expresado(da).

inasmuch [,ɪnəz'mʌtʃ]
◆ **inasmuch as** *conj* en la medida en que.

inattention [,ɪnə'tenʃn] *n*: ~ **(to)** falta *f* de atención (a), desatención *f* (a).

inattentive [,ɪnə'tentɪv] *adj*: ~ **(to)** desatento(ta) (a).

inaudible [ɪ'nɔːdɪbl] *adj* inaudible.

inaugural [ɪ'nɔːgjʊrəl] *adj* inaugural.

inaugurate [ɪ'nɔːgjʊreɪt] *vt* **-1.** [leader, president] investir. **-2.** [building, system] inaugurar.

inauguration [ɪ,nɔːgjʊ'reɪʃn] *n* **-1.** [of leader, president] investidura *f*. **-2.** [of building, system] inauguración *f*.

inauspicious [,ɪnɔː'spɪʃəs] *adj* desfavorable, poco propicio(cia).

in-between *adj* intermedio(dia).

inboard ['ɪnbɔːd] *adj* interior.

inborn [,ɪn'bɔːn] *adj* innato(ta).

inbound ['ɪnbaʊnd] *adj Am* que se aproxima.

inbred [,ɪn'bred] *adj* **-1.** [closely related] consanguíneo(a), endogámico(ca). **-2.** [inborn] innato(ta).

inbreeding ['ɪn,briːdɪŋ] *n* relaciones *fpl* de consanguinidad.

inbuilt [,ɪn'bɪlt] *adj* [in person] innato(ta); [in thing] inherente.

inc. (*abbr of* **inclusive**) inclus.; **12th-15th April** ~ 12-15 de abril inclus.

Inc. [ɪŋk] (*abbr of* **incorporated**) ≃ S.A.

Inca ['ɪŋkə] *n* inca *m y f*.

incalculable [ɪn'kælkjʊləbl] *adj* [very great] incalculable.

incandescent [,ɪnkæn'desnt] *adj* incandescente.

incantation [,ɪnkæn'teɪʃn] *n* conjuro *m*, ensalmo *m*.

incapable [ɪn'keɪpəbl] *adj* **-1.** [unable]: **to be ~ of sthg/of doing sthg** ser incapaz de algo/de hacer algo. **-2.** [useless] incompetente.

incapacitate [,ɪnkə'pæsɪteɪt] *vt* incapacitar.

incapacitated [,ɪnkə'pæsɪteɪtɪd] *adj* incapacitado(da).

incapacity [,ɪnkə'pæsətɪ] *n*: ~ **(for)** incapacidad *f* (para).

incarcerate [ɪn'kɑːsəreɪt] *vt fml* encarcelar.

incarceration [ɪn,kɑːsə'reɪʃn] *n fml* encarcelamiento *m*.

incarnate [ɪn'kɑːneɪt] *adj*: **she's generosity ~** es la generosidad personificada.

incarnation [,ɪnkɑː'neɪʃn] *n* **-1.** [personification] personificación *f*. **-2.** [existence] encarnación *f*.

incendiary device [ɪn'sendjərɪ-] *n* artefacto *m* incendiario.

incense [*n* 'ɪnsens, *vt* ɪn'sens] ◇ *n* incienso *m*. ◇ *vt* sulfurar, indignar.

incentive [ɪn'sentɪv] *n* incentivo *m*.

incentive scheme *n* plan *m* de incentivos.

inception [ɪn'sepʃn] *n fml* inicio *m*, origen *m*.

incessant [ɪn'sesnt] *adj* incesante, constante.

incessantly [ɪn'sesntlɪ] *adv* incesantemente, constantemente.

incest ['ɪnsest] *n* incesto *m*.

incestuous [ɪn'sestjʊəs] *adj* -1. [sexual] incestuoso(sa). -2. *fig* [too close] cerrado en sí mismo, cerrada en sí misma.

inch [ɪntʃ] ◇ *n* = 2,5 *cm*, pulgada *f*. ◇ *vi* avanzar poco a poco.

incidence ['ɪnsɪdəns] *n* [of disease, theft] índice *m*.

incident ['ɪnsɪdənt] *n* incidente *m*, suceso *m*.

incidental [,ɪnsɪ'dentl] *adj* accesorio(ria), secundario(ria).

incidentally [,ɪnsɪ'dentəlɪ] *adv* por cierto, a propósito.

incidental music *n* música *f* de fondo.

incinerate [ɪn'sɪnəreɪt] *vt* incinerar, quemar.

incinerator [ɪn'sɪnəreɪtə'] *n* incinerador *m*.

incipient [ɪn'sɪpɪənt] *adj fml* incipiente.

incision [ɪn'sɪʒn] *n fml* incisión *f*.

incisive [ɪn'saɪsɪv] *adj* [comment, person] incisivo(va); [mind] penetrante.

incisor [ɪn'saɪzə'] *n* incisivo *m*.

incite [ɪn'saɪt] *vt* incitar, provocar; **to ~ sb to do sthg** incitar a alguien a que haga algo.

incitement [ɪn'saɪtmənt] *n* (*U*): **~ (to sthg/ to do sthg)** instigación *f* (a algo/a hacer algo).

incl. *abbr of* **including, inclusive.**

inclement [ɪn'klemənt] *adj fml* inclemente.

inclination [,ɪnklɪ'neɪʃn] *n* -1. (*U*) [liking, preference] inclinación *f*, propensión *f*. -2. [tendency]: **~ to do sthg** tendencia *f* a hacer algo.

incline [*n* 'ɪnklaɪn, *vb* ɪn'klaɪn] ◇ *n* pendiente *f*, cuesta *f*. ◇ *vt* [head] inclinar, ladear.

inclined [ɪn'klaɪnd] *adj* -1. [tending]: **to be ~ to sthg** ser propenso OR tener tendencia a algo; **to be ~ to do sthg** tener tendencia a hacer algo. -2. *fml* [wanting]: **to be ~ to do sthg** estar dispuesto a hacer algo. -3. [sloping] inclinado(da).

include [ɪn'kluːd] *vt* -1. [gen] incluir. -2. [with letter] adjuntar.

included [ɪn'kluːdɪd] *adj* incluido(da).

including [ɪn'kluːdɪŋ] *prep* inclusive; **six died, ~ a child** seis murieron, incluido un niño.

inclusion [ɪn'kluːʒn] *n* inclusión *f*.

inclusive [ɪn'kluːsɪv] *adj* -1. [including everything] inclusivo(va); **one to nine ~** uno a nueve inclusive. -2. [including all costs]: **~ of VAT** con el IVA incluido; **£150 ~** 150 libras todo incluido.

incognito [,ɪnkɒg'niːtəʊ] *adv* de incógnito.

incoherent [,ɪnkəʊ'hɪərənt] *adj* incoherente, ininteligible.

income ['ɪŋkʌm] *n* [gen] ingresos *mpl*; [from property] renta *f*; [from investment] réditos *mpl*.

incomes policy *n Br* política *f* de rentas.

income support *n Br subsidio para personas con muy bajos ingresos o desempleados sin derecho a subsidio de paro*, ≃ salario *m* social.

income tax *n* impuesto *m* sobre la renta.

incoming ['ɪn,kʌmɪŋ] *adj* -1. [tide, wave] ascendente. -2. [plane] de llegada. -3. [government] entrante. -4. [mail, report] que llega de fuera; **~ phone call** llamada de fuera OR del exterior.

incommunicado [,ɪnkəmjuːnɪ'kɑːdəʊ] *adv* en aislamiento, incomunicado(da).

incomparable [ɪn'kɒmpərəbl] *adj* incomparable, sin par.

incompatible [,ɪnkəm'pætɪbl] *adj*: **~ (with)** incompatible (con).

incompetence [ɪn'kɒmpɪtəns] *n* incompetencia *f*, incapacidad *f*.

incompetent [ɪn'kɒmpɪtənt] *adj* incompetente, incapaz.

incomplete [,ɪnkəm'pliːt] *adj* incompleto(ta).

incomprehensible [ɪn,kɒmprɪ'hensəbl] *adj* incomprensible.

inconceivable [,ɪnkən'siːvəbl] *adj* inconcebible.

inconclusive [,ɪnkən'kluːsɪv] *adj* [evidence, argument] poco convincente; [meeting, outcome] sin conclusión clara.

incongruous [ɪn'kɒŋgrʊəs] *adj* incongruente.

inconsequential [,ɪnkɒnsɪ'kwenʃl] *adj* intranscendente, de poca importancia.

inconsiderable [,ɪnkən'sɪdərəbl] *adj*: **not ~** nada insignificante OR despreciable.

inconsiderate [,ɪnkən'sɪdərət] *adj* desconsiderado(da).

inconsistency [,ɪnkən'sɪstənsɪ] (*pl* -ies) *n* -1. [between theory and practice] inconsecuencia *f*; [between statements etc] falta *f* de correspondencia. -2. [contradictory point] contradicción *f*.

inconsistent [,ɪnkən'sɪstənt] *adj* -1. [translation, statement]: **~ (with)** falto(ta) de correspondencia (con); [group, government, person] inconsecuente. -2. [erratic] irregular, desigual.

inconsolable [,ɪnkən'səʊləbl] *adj* inconsolable.

inconspicuous [ˌɪnkən'spɪkjʊəs] *adj* discreto(ta).

incontinence [ɪn'kɒntɪnəns] *n* incontinencia *f*.

incontinent [ɪn'kɒntɪnənt] *adj* incontinente.

incontrovertible [ˌɪnkɒntrə'vɜːtəbl] *adj* incontrovertible.

inconvenience [ˌɪnkən'viːnjəns] ◇ *n* **-1.** [difficulty, discomfort] molestia *f*, incomodidad *f*. **-2.** [inconvenient thing] inconveniente *m*. ◇ *vt* incomodar, molestar.

inconvenient [ˌɪnkən'viːnjənt] *adj* [time] inoportuno(na); [position] incómodo(da); **that date is ~** esa fecha no me viene bien.

incorporate [ɪn'kɔːpəreɪt] *vt* **-1.** [integrate]: **to ~ sthg/sb (in), to ~ sthg/sb (into)** incorporar algo/a alguien (en). **-2.** [include] incluir, comprender.

incorporated [ɪn'kɔːpəreɪtɪd] *adj* COMM: **~ company** sociedad *f* anónima.

incorporation [ɪnˌkɔːpə'reɪʃn] *n* **-1.** [integration] incorporación *f*. **-2.** COMM [of company] constitución *f* en sociedad anónima.

incorrect [ˌɪnkə'rekt] *adj* incorrecto(ta), erróneo(a).

incorrigible [ɪn'kɒrɪdʒəbl] *adj* incorregible.

incorruptible [ˌɪnkə'rʌptəbl] *adj* incorruptible.

increase [*n* 'ɪnkriːs, *vb* ɪn'kriːs] ◇ *n:* **~ (in)** [gen] aumento *m* (de); [in price] subida *f* (de); **to be on the ~** ir en aumento. ◇ *vt* aumentar, incrementar. ◇ *vi* [gen] aumentar, aumentarse; [price] subir.

increased [ɪn'kriːst] *adj* aumentado(da).

increasing [ɪn'kriːsɪŋ] *adj* creciente.

increasingly [ɪn'kriːsɪŋlɪ] *adv* cada vez más, más y más.

incredible [ɪn'kredəbl] *adj* increíble.

incredulous [ɪn'kredjʊləs] *adj* incrédulo(la).

increment ['ɪnkrɪmənt] *n* incremento *m*, aumento *m*.

incriminate [ɪn'krɪmɪneɪt] *vt* incriminar; **to ~ o.s.** incriminarse a sí mismo.

incriminating [ɪn'krɪmɪneɪtɪŋ] *adj* incriminatorio(ria).

incrust [ɪn'krʌst] = **encrust**.

incubate ['ɪnkjʊbeɪt] ◇ *vt* [egg] incubar, empollar. ◇ *vi* **-1.** [egg] incubarse. **-2.** [infection] incubar.

incubation [ˌɪnkjʊ'beɪʃn] *n* incubación *f*.

incubator ['ɪnkjʊbeɪtə'] *n* [for baby] incubadora *f*.

inculcate ['ɪnkʌlkeɪt] *vt fml:* **to ~ sthg in** OR **into** inculcar algo en.

incumbent [ɪn'kʌmbənt] *fml* ◇ *adj:* **to be ~**

on OR **upon sb to do sthg** incumbir a alguien hacer algo. ◇ *n* titular *m* y *f*.

incur [ɪn'kɜːʳ] (*pt* & *pp* **-red**, *cont* **-ring**) *vt* [wrath, criticism] incurrir en, atraerse; [loss] contraer; [expenses] incurrir en.

incurable [ɪn'kjʊərəbl] *adj lit* & *fig* incurable.

incursion [*Br* ɪn'kɜːʃn, *Am* ɪn'kɜːʒn] *n* incursión *f*.

indebted [ɪn'detɪd] *adj* **-1.** [grateful]: **~ (to)** agradecido(da) (a). **-2.** [owing money]: **~ (to)** en deuda (con).

indecency [ɪn'diːsnsɪ] *n* indecencia *f*.

indecent [ɪn'diːsnt] *adj* **-1.** [improper] indecente. **-2.** [unreasonable, excessive] desmedido(da).

indecent assault *n* atentado *m* contra el pudor.

indecent exposure *n* exhibicionismo *m*.

indecipherable [ˌɪndɪ'saɪfərəbl] *adj* indescifrable.

indecision [ˌɪndɪ'sɪʒn] *n* indecisión *f*, irresolución *f*.

indecisive [ˌɪndɪ'saɪsɪv] *adj* **-1.** [person] indeciso(sa), irresoluto(ta). **-2.** [result] no decisivo(va).

indeed [ɪn'diːd] *adv* **-1.** [certainly] ciertamente, realmente; **are you coming? - ~ I am** ¿vienes tú? - por supuesto que sí. **-2.** [in fact] de hecho. **-3.** [for emphasis] realmente; **very big ~** grandísimo; **very few ~** poquísimos. **-4.** [to express surprise, disbelief]: **~?** ¿ah sí?

indefatigable [ˌɪndɪ'fætɪgəbl] *adj* infatigable, incansable.

indefensible [ˌɪndɪ'fensəbl] *adj* [position, view] insostenible, indefendible; [behaviour] inexcusable.

indefinable [ˌɪndɪ'faɪnəbl] *adj* indefinible.

indefinite [ɪn'defɪnɪt] *adj* **-1.** [time, number] indefinido(da). **-2.** [answer, opinion] impreciso(sa).

indefinitely [ɪn'defɪnətlɪ] *adv* **-1.** [for unfixed period] indefinidamente. **-2.** [imprecisely] de forma imprecisa.

indelible [ɪn'deləbl] *adj* indeleble.

indelicate [ɪn'delɪkət] *adj* poco delicado(da).

indemnify [ɪn'demnɪfaɪ] (*pt* & *pp* **-ied**) *vt:* **to ~ sb for** OR **against** indemnizar a alguien de OR por.

indemnity [ɪn'demnətɪ] *n* **-1.** [insurance] indemnidad *f*. **-2.** [compensation] indemnización *f*, compensación *f*.

indent [ɪn'dent] *vt* **-1.** [dent] mellar. **-2.** [text] sangrar.

indentation [ˌɪndenˈteɪʃn] n -1. [dent] mella f, muesca f. -2. [in text] sangría f.

indenture [ɪnˈdentʃəʳ] n contrato m de aprendizaje.

independence [ˌɪndɪˈpendəns] n independencia f.

Independence Day n fiesta del 4 de julio en Estados Unidos en conmemoración de la Declaración de Independencia de este país en 1776.

independent [ˌɪndɪˈpendənt] adj: ~ (of) independiente (de).

independently [ˌɪndɪˈpendəntlɪ] adv independientemente; ~ of aparte de.

independent school n Br colegio m privado.

in-depth adj a fondo, exhaustivo(va).

indescribable [ˌɪndɪˈskraɪbəbl] adj indescriptible.

indestructible [ˌɪndɪˈstrʌktəbl] adj indestructible.

indeterminate [ˌɪndɪˈtɜːmɪnət] adj indeterminado(da).

index [ˈɪndeks] (pl -es OR indices) ◇ n índice m. ◇ vt poner índice a.

index card n ficha f.

index finger n (dedo m) índice m.

index-linked adj ligado(da) al coste de la vida.

India [ˈɪndjə] n (la) India.

India ink Am = Indian ink.

Indian [ˈɪndjən] ◇ adj -1. [from India] hindú, indio(dia). -2. [from the Americas] indio(dia). ◇ n -1. [from India] hindú m y f, indio m, -dia f. -2. [from the Americas] indio m, -dia f, china f Amer.

Indiana [ˌɪndɪˈænə] n Indiana.

Indian ink Br, **India ink** Am n tinta f china.

Indian Ocean n: the ~ el océano Índico.

Indian summer n veranillo m de San Martín.

india rubber n [material] caucho m; [eraser] goma f de borrar.

indicate [ˈɪndɪkeɪt] ◇ vt indicar. ◇ vi [when driving]: to ~ left/right indicar a la izquierda/derecha.

indication [ˌɪndɪˈkeɪʃn] n -1. [suggestion, idea] indicación f. -2. [sign] indicio m, señal f.

indicative [ɪnˈdɪkətɪv] ◇ adj: ~ of sthg indicativo(va) de algo. ◇ n GRAMM indicativo m.

indicator [ˈɪndɪkeɪtəʳ] n -1. [sign] indicador m. -2. [on car] intermitente m.

indices [ˈɪndɪsiːz] pl → index.

indict [ɪnˈdaɪt] vt: to ~ sb (for) acusar a alguien (de).

indictable [ɪnˈdaɪtəbl] adj procesable.

indictment [ɪnˈdaɪtmənt] n -1. JUR acusación f. -2. [criticism] crítica f severa.

indie [ˈɪndɪ] adj Br inf independiente.

indifference [ɪnˈdɪfrəns] n indiferencia f.

indifferent [ɪnˈdɪfrənt] adj -1. [uninterested]: ~ (to) indiferente (a). -2. [mediocre] ordinario(ria), mediocre.

indigenous [ɪnˈdɪdʒɪnəs] adj indígena.

indigestible [ˌɪndɪˈdʒestəbl] adj lit & fig indigesto(ta), indigestible.

indigestion [ˌɪndɪˈdʒestʃn] n (U) indigestión f.

indignant [ɪnˈdɪgnənt] adj: ~ (at) indignado(da) (por).

indignantly [ɪnˈdɪgnəntlɪ] adv con indignación.

indignation [ˌɪndɪgˈneɪʃn] n indignación f.

indignity [ɪnˈdɪgnətɪ] (pl -ies) n indignidad f.

indigo [ˈɪndɪgəu] ◇ adj (color) añil. ◇ n añil m.

indirect [ˌɪndɪˈrekt] adj indirecto(ta).

indirect costs npl gastos mpl generales OR indirectos.

indirect lighting n luz f OR iluminación f indirecta.

indirectly [ˌɪndɪˈrektlɪ] adv indirectamente.

indirect speech n estilo m indirecto.

indirect taxation n (U) impuestos mpl indirectos.

indiscreet [ˌɪndɪˈskriːt] adj indiscreto(ta), imprudente.

indiscretion [ˌɪndɪˈskreʃn] n indiscreción f.

indiscriminate [ˌɪndɪˈskrɪmɪnət] adj indiscriminado(da).

indiscriminately [ˌɪndɪˈskrɪmɪnətlɪ] adv indiscriminadamente.

indispensable [ˌɪndɪˈspensəbl] adj indispensable, imprescindible.

indisposed [ˌɪndɪˈspəuzd] adj fml [unwell] indispuesto(ta).

indisputable [ˌɪndɪˈspjuːtəbl] adj incuestionable.

indistinct [ˌɪndɪˈstɪŋkt] adj [memory] confuso(sa); [words] imperceptible, indistinto(ta); [picture, marking] borroso(sa), indistinto(ta).

indistinguishable [ˌɪndɪˈstɪŋgwɪʃəbl] adj: ~ (from) indistinguible (de).

individual [ˌɪndɪˈvɪdʒuəl] ◇ adj -1. [gen] individual. -2. [tuition] particular. -3. [approach, style] personal. ◇ n individuo m.

individualist [ˌɪndɪˈvɪdʒuəlɪst] n individualista m y f.

individualistic ['ındı,vıdʒʊə'lıstık] *adj* individualista.

individuality ['ındı,vıdʒʊ'ælətı] *n* individualidad *f*, personalidad *f*.

individually [,ındı'vıdʒʊəlı] *adv* [separately] individualmente, por separado.

indivisible [,ındı'vızəbl] *adj* indivisible.

Indochina [,ındəʊ'tʃaınə] *n* Indochina.

indoctrinate [ın'dɒktrıneıt] *vt* adoctrinar.

indoctrination [ın,dɒktrı'neıʃn] *n* adoctrinamiento *m*.

indolent ['ındələnt] *adj* indolente, perezoso(sa).

indomitable [ın'dɒmıtəbl] *adj* indómito(ta), indomable.

Indonesia [,ındə'niːzjə] *n* Indonesia.

Indonesian [,ındə'niːzjən] ◇ *adj* indonesio(sia). ◇ *n* **-1.** [person] indonesio *m*, -sia *f*. **-2.** [language] indonesio *m*.

indoor ['ındɔːʳ] *adj* [gen] interior; [shoes] de andar por casa; [plant] de interior; [sports] en pista cubierta; ~ **swimming pool** piscina *f* cubierta.

indoors [,ın'dɔːz] *adv* [gen] dentro; [at home] en casa.

indubitably [ın'djuːbıtəblı] *adv* indudablemente, sin duda.

induce [ın'djuːs] *vt* **-1.** [persuade]: **to ~ sb to do sthg** inducir OR persuadir a alguien a que haga algo. **-2.** [labour, sleep, anger] provocar.

inducement [ın'djuːsmənt] *n* [incentive] incentivo *m*, aliciente *m*.

induction [ın'dʌkʃn] *n* **-1.** [into official position]: ~ **into** introducción *f* OR inducción *f* a. **-2.** ELEC & MED inducción *f*. **-3.** [introduction to job] introducción *f*.

induction course *n* cursillo *m* introductorio, curso *m* de iniciación.

indulge [ın'dʌldʒ] ◇ *vt* **-1.** [whim, passion] satisfacer. **-2.** [child, person] consentir; **to ~ o.s.** darse un gusto, permitirse un lujo. ◇ *vi*: **to ~ in sthg** permitirse algo.

indulgence [ın'dʌldʒəns] *n* **-1.** [act of indulging] indulgencia *f*. **-2.** [special treat] gratificación *f*, vicio *m*.

indulgent [ın'dʌldʒənt] *adj* indulgente.

Indus ['ındəs] *n*: **the (River) ~** el (río) Indus.

industrial [ın'dʌstrıəl] *adj* industrial.

industrial action *n* huelga *f*; **to take ~** declararse en huelga.

industrial estate *Br*, **industrial park** *Am* *n* polígono *m* industrial.

industrial injury *n* accidente *m* laboral.

industrialist [ın'dʌstrıəlıst] *n* industrial *m* y *f*.

industrialization [ın,dʌstrıəlaı'zeıʃn] *n* industrialización *f*.

industrialize, -ise [ın'dʌstrıəlaız] ◇ *vt* industrializar. ◇ *vi* industrializarse.

industrial park *Am* = **industrial estate**.

industrial relations *npl* relaciones *fpl* laborales.

industrial revolution *n* revolución *f* industrial.

industrial tribunal *n* magistratura *f* del trabajo.

industrious [ın'dʌstrıəs] *adj* diligente, trabajador(ra).

industry ['ındəstrı] (*pl* **-ies**) *n* **-1.** [gen] industria *f*. **-2.** [hard work] laboriosidad *f*.

inebriated [ı'niːbrıeıtıd] *adj fml* ebrio (ebria).

inedible [ın'edıbl] *adj* no comestible.

ineffective [,ını'fektıv] *adj* ineficaz, inútil.

ineffectual [,ını'fektʃʊəl] *adj* ineficaz, inútil.

inefficiency [,ını'fıʃnsı] *n* ineficacia *f*.

inefficient [,ını'fıʃnt] *adj* ineficaz, ineficiente.

inelegant [ın'elıgənt] *adj* poco elegante.

ineligible [ın'elıdʒəbl] *adj*: ~ **(for)** inelegible (para).

inept [ı'nept] *adj* inepto(ta); ~ **at** incapaz para.

ineptitude [ı'neptıtjuːd] *n* ineptitud *f*, incompetencia *f*.

inequality [,ını'kwɒlətı] (*pl* **-ies**) *n* desigualdad *f*.

inequitable [ın'ekwıtəbl] *adj fml* injusto(ta).

ineradicable [,ını'rædıkəbl] *adj fml* inextirpable.

inert [ı'nɜːt] *adj* inerte.

inertia [ı'nɜːʃə] *n* inercia *f*.

inertia-reel seat belt *n* cinturón *m* de seguridad autotensable OR con retensor.

inescapable [,ını'skeıpəbl] *adj* ineludible.

inessential [,ını'senʃl] *adj*: ~ **(to)** innecesario(ria) (para).

inestimable [ın'estıməbl] *adj fml* inestimable.

inevitable [ın'evıtəbl] ◇ *adj* inevitable. ◇ *n*: **the ~** lo inevitable.

inevitably [ın'evıtəblı] *adv* inevitablemente.

inexact [,ınıg'zækt] *adj* inexacto(ta).

inexcusable [,ınık'skjuːzəbl] *adj* inexcusable, imperdonable.

inexhaustible [,ınıg'zɔːstəbl] *adj* inagotable.

inexorable [ɪn'eksərəbl] *adj fml* [unpreventable] inexorable.

inexorably [ɪn'eksərəblɪ] *adv* inexorablemente.

inexpensive [,ɪnɪk'spensɪv] *adj* barato(ta), económico(ca).

inexperience [,ɪnɪk'spɪərɪəns] *n* inexperiencia *f*.

inexperienced [,ɪnɪk'spɪərɪənst] *adj* inexperto(ta).

inexpert [ɪn'eksp3ːt] *adj* inexperto(ta).

inexplicable [,ɪnɪk'splɪkəbl] *adj* inexplicable.

inexplicably [,ɪnɪk'splɪkəblɪ] *adv* inexplicablemente.

inextricably [,ɪnɪk'strɪkəblɪ] *adv* indisolublemente, inseparablemente.

infallible [ɪn'fæləbl] *adj* infalible.

infamous ['ɪnfəməs] *adj* infame.

infamy ['ɪnfəmɪ] *n fml* infamia *f*.

infancy ['ɪnfənsɪ] *n* primera infancia *f*; **to be in its ~** *fig* dar sus primeros pasos.

infant ['ɪnfənt] *n* **-1.** [baby] bebé *m*. **-2.** [young child] niño pequeño *m*, niña pequeña *f*.

infantile ['ɪnfəntaɪl] *adj* infantil.

infant mortality *n* mortalidad *f* infantil.

infantry ['ɪnfəntrɪ] *n* infantería *f*.

infantryman ['ɪnfəntrɪmən] (*pl* **-men** [-mən]) *n* soldado *m* de infantería.

infant school *n Br* colegio *m* preescolar.

infatuated [ɪn'fætjʊeɪtɪd] *adj*: **~ (with)** encaprichado(da) (con).

infatuation [ɪn,fætjʊ'eɪʃn] *n*: **~ (with)** encaprichamiento *m* (con).

infect [ɪn'fekt] *vt* **-1.** [wound] infectar; [person]: **to ~ sb (with sthg)** contagiar a alguien (algo). **-2.** *fig* [spread to] contagiar.

infected [ɪn'fektɪd] *adj*: **~ (with)** [wound] infectado(da) (de); [patient] contagiado(da) (de).

infection [ɪn'fekʃn] *n* **-1.** [disease] infección *f*. **-2.** [spreading of germs] contagio *m*.

infectious [ɪn'fekʃəs] *adj lit* & *fig* contagioso(sa).

infer [ɪn'f3ː] (*pt* & *pp* **-red**, *cont* **-ring**) *vt* **-1.** [deduce]: **to ~ (that)** deducir OR inferir que; **to ~ sthg (from sthg)** deducir OR inferir algo (de algo). **-2.** *inf* [imply] insinuar, sugerir.

inference ['ɪnfrəns] *n* **-1.** [conclusion] conclusión *f*. **-2.** [deduction]: **by ~** por deducción.

inferior [ɪn'fɪərɪə] ◇ *adj*: **~ (to)** inferior (a). ◇ *n* [in status] inferior *m* y *f*.

inferiority [ɪn,fɪərɪ'ɒrətɪ] *n* inferioridad *f*.

inferiority complex *n* complejo *m* de inferioridad.

infernal [ɪn'f3ːnl] *adj inf dated* infernal.

inferno [ɪn'f3ːnəʊ] (*pl* **-s**) *n* infierno *m*.

infertile [ɪn'f3ːtaɪl] *adj* estéril.

infertility [,ɪnfə'tɪlətɪ] *n* esterilidad *f*.

infestation [,ɪnfe'steɪʃn] *n* plaga *f*.

infested [ɪn'festɪd] *adj*: **~ with** infestado(da) de.

infidelity [,ɪnfɪ'delətɪ] *n* [of partner] infidelidad *f*.

infighting ['ɪn,faɪtɪŋ] *n* (*U*) disputas *fpl* internas.

infiltrate ['ɪnfɪltreɪt] ◇ *vt* infiltrar. ◇ *vi*: **to ~ into sthg** infiltrarse en algo.

infinite ['ɪnfɪnət] *adj* infinito(ta).

infinitely ['ɪnfɪnətlɪ] *adv* infinitamente.

infinitesimal [,ɪnfɪnɪ'tesɪml] *adj* infinitesimal.

infinitive [ɪn'fɪnɪtɪv] *n* infinitivo *m*.

infinity [ɪn'fɪnətɪ] *n* **-1.** MATH infinito *m*. **-2.** [incalculable number]: **an ~ (of)** infinidad *f* (de).

infirm [ɪn'f3ːm] ◇ *adj* achacoso(sa). ◇ *npl*: **the ~** los enfermos.

infirmary [ɪn'f3ːmərɪ] (*pl* **-ies**) *n* **-1.** [hospital] hospital *m*. **-2.** [room] enfermería *f*.

infirmity [ɪn'f3ːmətɪ] (*pl* **-ies**) *n* **-1.** [illness] dolencia *f*. **-2.** [state] enfermedad *f*.

inflamed [ɪn'fleɪmd] *adj* MED inflamado(da).

inflammable [ɪn'flæməbl] *adj* [burning easily] inflamable.

inflammation [,ɪnflə'meɪʃn] *n* MED inflamación *f*.

inflammatory [ɪn'flæmətrɪ] *adj* incendiario(ria).

inflatable [ɪn'fleɪtəbl] *adj* inflable, hinchable.

inflate [ɪn'fleɪt] *vt* **-1.** [gen] inflar, hinchar. **-2.** ECON inflar, aumentar.

inflated [ɪn'fleɪtɪd] *adj* **-1.** [gen] inflado(da), hinchado(da). **-2.** ECON [prices] inflacionístico(ca).

inflation [ɪn'fleɪʃn] *n* ECON inflación *f*.

inflationary [ɪn'fleɪʃnrɪ] *adj* ECON inflacionario(ria), inflacionista.

inflationary spiral *n* espiral *f* inflacionaria.

inflation-proof *adj* que no se ve afectado(da) por la inflación.

inflexible [ɪn'fleksəbl] *adj* **-1.** [material, person, attitude] inflexible. **-2.** [decision, arrangement] fijo(ja).

inflict [ɪn'flɪkt] *vt*: **to ~ sthg on sb** infligir algo a alguien.

in-flight *adj* durante el vuelo.

inflow ['ɪnfləʊ] *n* afluencia *f*.

influence ['ɪnfluəns] ◇ *n*: ~ **(on** OR **over sb)** influencia *f* (sobre alguien); ~ **(on sthg)** influencia (en algo); **under the** ~ **of** [person, group] bajo la influencia de; [alcohol, drugs] bajo los efectos de. ◇ *vt* influenciar.

influential [ˌɪnfluˈenʃl] *adj* influyente.

influenza [ˌɪnfluˈenzə] *n fml* gripe *f*.

influx ['ɪnflʌks] *n* afluencia *f*.

info ['ɪnfəʊ] *n* (U) *inf* información *f*.

inform [ɪnˈfɔːm] *vt*: **to** ~ **sb (of/about sthg)** informar a alguien (de/sobre algo).

◆ **inform on** *vt fus* delatar.

informal [ɪnˈfɔːml] *adj* informal; [language] familiar.

informally [ɪnˈfɔːməlɪ] *adv* de manera informal.

informant [ɪnˈfɔːmənt] *n* **-1.** [informer] confidente *m y f*, delator *m*, -ra *f*. **-2.** [of researcher] fuente *f* de información (*persona*).

information [ˌɪnfəˈmeɪʃn] *n* (U): ~ **(on** OR **about)** información *f* OR datos *mpl* (sobre); **a piece of** ~ un dato; **for your** ~ para tu información.

information desk *n* (mostrador *m* de) información *f*.

information office *n* oficina *f* de información.

information retrieval *n* recuperación *f* OR búsqueda *f* de información.

information technology *n* informática *f*.

informative [ɪnˈfɔːmətɪv] *adj* informativo(va).

informed [ɪnˈfɔːmd] *adj* informado(da); ~ **guess** conjetura *f* bien fundada.

informer [ɪnˈfɔːməʳ] *n* confidente *m y f*, delator *m*, -ra *f*.

infra dig [ˌɪnfrə-] *adj* degradante.

infrared [ˌɪnfrəˈred] *adj* infrarrojo(ja).

infrastructure ['ɪnfrəˌstrʌktʃəʳ] *n* infraestructura *f*.

infrequent [ɪnˈfriːkwənt] *adj* infrecuente.

infringe [ɪnˈfrɪndʒ] (*cont* **infringeing**) ◇ *vt* infringir, vulnerar. ◇ *vi*: **to** ~ **on sthg** infringir OR vulnerar algo.

infringement [ɪnˈfrɪndʒmənt] *n* violación *f*, transgresión *f*.

infuriate [ɪnˈfjʊərɪeɪt] *vt* enfurecer, exasperar.

infuriating [ɪnˈfjʊərɪeɪtɪŋ] *adj* exasperante.

infuse [ɪnˈfjuːz] ◇ *vt*: **to** ~ **sb with sthg** infundir algo a alguien. ◇ *vi* reposar (*una infusión*).

infusion [ɪnˈfjuːʒn] *n* infusión *f*.

ingenious [ɪnˈdʒiːnjəs] *adj* ingenioso(sa), inventivo(va).

ingenuity [ˌɪndʒɪˈnjuːətɪ] *n* ingenio *m*, inventiva *f*.

ingenuous [ɪnˈdʒenjʊəs] *adj fml* ingenuo(nua).

ingest [ɪnˈdʒest] *vt fml* ingerir.

ingot ['ɪŋgət] *n* lingote *m*.

ingrained [ˌɪnˈgreɪnd] *adj* **-1.** [ground in] incrustado(da). **-2.** [deeply rooted] arraigado(da).

ingratiate [ɪnˈgreɪʃɪeɪt] *vt*: **to** ~ **o.s. with sb** congraciarse con alguien.

ingratiating [ɪnˈgreɪʃɪeɪtɪŋ] *adj* obsequioso(sa), lisonjero(ra).

ingratitude [ɪnˈgrætɪtjuːd] *n* ingratitud *f*.

ingredient [ɪnˈgriːdjənt] *n* ingrediente *m*.

ingrowing ['ɪnˌgrəʊɪŋ], **ingrown** ['ɪnˌgrəʊn] *adj* encarnado(da).

inhabit [ɪnˈhæbɪt] *vt* habitar.

inhabitant [ɪnˈhæbɪtənt] *n* habitante *m y f*.

inhalation [ˌɪnhəˈleɪʃn] *n* inhalación *f*.

inhale [ɪnˈheɪl] ◇ *vt* inhalar. ◇ *vi* [gen] inspirar; [smoker] tragarse el humo.

inhaler [ɪnˈheɪləʳ] *n* MED inhalador *m*.

inherent [ɪnˈhɪərənt, ɪnˈherənt] *adj*: ~ **(in)** inherente (a).

inherently [ɪnˈhɪərəntlɪ, ɪnˈherəntlɪ] *adv* intrínsecamente.

inherit [ɪnˈherɪt] ◇ *vt*: **to** ~ **sthg (from sb)** heredar algo (de alguien). ◇ *vi* heredar.

inheritance [ɪnˈherɪtəns] *n* herencia *f*.

inheritor [ɪnˈherɪtəʳ] *n* heredero *m*, -ra *f*.

inhibit [ɪnˈhɪbɪt] *vt* [restrict] impedir.

inhibited [ɪnˈhɪbɪtɪd] *adj* [repressed, reserved] cohibido(da), inhibido(da).

inhibition [ˌɪnhɪˈbɪʃn] *n* inhibición *f*.

inhospitable [ˌɪnhɒˈspɪtəbl] *adj* **-1.** [unwelcoming] inhospitalario(ria). **-2.** [harsh] inhóspito(ta).

in-house ◇ *adj* [journal, report] de circulación interna; [staff] de plantilla. ◇ *adv* en la oficina.

inhuman [ɪnˈhjuːmən] *adj* **-1.** [cruel] inhumano(na). **-2.** [not human] infrahumano(na).

inhumane [ˌɪnhjuːˈmeɪn] *adj* inhumano(na).

inimitable [ɪˈnɪmɪtəbl] *adj* inimitable.

iniquitous [ɪˈnɪkwɪtəs] *adj fml* inicuo(cua).

iniquity [ɪˈnɪkwətɪ] (*pl* **-ies**) *n* iniquidad *f*.

initial [ɪˈnɪʃl] (*Br pt & pp* **-led**, *cont* **-ling**, *Am pt & pp* **-ed**, *cont* **-ing**) ◇ *adj* inicial. ◇ *vt* poner las iniciales a.

◆ **initials** *npl* [of person] iniciales *fpl*.

initialize, -ise [ɪˈnɪʃəlaɪz] *vt* COMPUT inicializar.

initially [ɪˈnɪʃəlɪ] *adv* inicialmente.

initiate [ɪ'nɪʃɪeɪt] ◇ *vt* iniciar; **to ~ sb into sthg** iniciar a alguien en algo. ◇ *n* iniciado *m*, -da *f*.

initiation [ɪ,nɪʃɪ'eɪʃn] *n* iniciación *f*.

initiative [ɪ'nɪʃətɪv] *n* iniciativa *f*; **to have/take the ~** llevar/tomar la iniciativa; **to use one's ~** hacer (uno) uso de su propia iniciativa; **on one's own ~** por iniciativa propia.

inject [ɪn'dʒekt] *vt* -**1.** MED: **to ~ sb with sthg, to ~ sthg into sb** inyectarle algo a alguien. -**2.** [life, excitement etc]: **to ~ sthg into sthg** infundir algo a algo. -**3.** [funds, capital]: **to ~ sthg into sthg** inyectar algo en OR a algo.

injection [ɪn'dʒekʃn] *n* inyección *f*.

injudicious [,ɪndʒuː'dɪʃəs] *adj fml* imprudente, poco juicioso(sa).

injunction [ɪn'dʒʌŋkʃn] *n* interdicto *m*, requerimiento *m* judicial.

injure ['ɪndʒəʳ] *vt* [gen] herir; [reputation] dañar; [chances] perjudicar; **to ~ o.s.** lesionarse, hacerse daño.

injured ['ɪndʒəd] ◇ *adj* [gen] herido(da); [reputation] dañado(da). ◇ *npl*: **the ~** los heridos.

injurious [ɪn'dʒʊərɪəs] *adj fml*: **~ (to)** pernicioso(sa) (para).

injury ['ɪndʒərɪ] (*pl* -**ies**) *n* -**1.** (*U*) [physical harm] lesiones *fpl*. -**2.** [wound] lesión *f*; **to do o.s. an ~** hacerse daño. -**3.** [to pride, reputation] agravio *m*.

injury time *n* (*U*) (tiempo *m* de) descuento *m*.

injustice [ɪn'dʒʌstɪs] *n* injusticia *f*; **to do sb an ~** no hacerle justicia a alguien.

ink [ɪŋk] ◇ *n* tinta *f*. ◇ *comp* de tinta.
◆ **ink in** *vt sep* repasar con tinta.

ink-jet printer *n* COMPUT impresora *f* de chorro de tinta.

inkling ['ɪŋklɪŋ] *n*: **to have an ~ of sthg** tener una vaga idea de algo; **to have an ~ that** tener la vaga idea de que.

inkpad ['ɪŋkpæd] *n* tampón *m*, almohadilla *f*.

inkwell ['ɪŋkwel] *n* tintero *m*.

inlaid [,ɪn'leɪd] *adj* incrustado(da); **~ with** [jewels] con incrustaciones de.

inland [*adj* 'ɪnlənd, *adv* ɪn'lænd] ◇ *adj* interior. ◇ *adv* hacia el interior.

Inland Revenue *n Br*: **the ~** ≃ Hacienda *f*.

in-laws *npl inf* suegros *mpl*.

inlet ['ɪnlet] *n* -**1.** [stretch of water] entrante *m*. -**2.** [way in] entrada *f*, admisión *f*.

inmate ['ɪnmeɪt] *n* [of prison] preso *m*, -sa *f*; [of mental hospital] interno *m*, -na *f*.

inmost ['ɪnməʊst] *adj literary* [deepest] más íntimo(ma), más profundo(da).

inn [ɪn] *n* fonda *f*; [pub] *pub decorado a la vieja usanza*.

innards ['ɪnədz] *npl* tripas *fpl*.

innate [,ɪ'neɪt] *adj* innato(ta).

inner ['ɪnəʳ] *adj* -**1.** [gen] interior. -**2.** [feelings] íntimo(ma); [fears, doubts, meaning] interno(na).

inner city ◇ *n* núcleo *m* urbano deprimido. ◇ *comp* de los núcleos urbanos deprimidos.

innermost ['ɪnəməʊst] = **inmost**.

inner tube *n* cámara *f* (de aire).

innings ['ɪnɪŋz] (*pl inv*) *n Br* [in cricket] entrada *f*, turno *m*; **to have had a good ~** *fig* haber tenido una vida larga y provechosa.

innocence ['ɪnəsəns] *n* inocencia *f*.

innocent ['ɪnəsənt] ◇ *adj*: **~ (of)** inocente (de). ◇ *n* [naive person] inocente *m y f*.

innocuous [ɪ'nɒkjʊəs] *adj* inocuo(cua), inofensivo(va).

innovation [,ɪnə'veɪʃn] *n* innovación *f*.

innovative ['ɪnəvətɪv] *adj* innovador(ra).

innovator ['ɪnəveɪtəʳ] *n* innovador *m*, -ra *f*.

innuendo [,ɪnjuː'endəʊ] (*pl* -**es** OR -**s**) *n* -**1.** [individual remark] insinuación *f*, indirecta *f*. -**2.** (*U*) [style of speaking] insinuaciones *fpl*, indirectas *fpl*.

innumerable [ɪ'njuːmərəbl] *adj* innumerable.

inoculate [ɪ'nɒkjʊleɪt] *vt*: **to ~ sb (against sthg)** inocular a alguien (contra algo); **to ~ sb with sthg** inocular algo a alguien.

inoculation [ɪ,nɒkjʊ'leɪʃn] *n* inoculación *f*.

inoffensive [,ɪnə'fensɪv] *adj* inofensivo(va).

inoperable [ɪn'ɒprəbl] *adj* -**1.** MED inoperable. -**2.** *fml* [unworkable] impracticable.

inoperative [ɪn'ɒprətɪv] *adj* -**1.** [rule, tax etc] en suspenso. -**2.** [machine] que no funciona.

inopportune [ɪn'ɒpətjuːn] *adj fml* inoportuno(na).

inordinate [ɪ'nɔːdɪnət] *adj fml* desmesurado(da), desmedido(da).

inordinately [ɪ'nɔːdɪnətlɪ] *adv fml* desmesuradamente, de forma desmedida.

inorganic [,ɪnɔː'gænɪk] *adj* inorgánico(ca).

in-patient *n* paciente interno *m*, paciente interna *f*.

input ['ɪnpʊt] (*pt & pp* input OR -**ted**, *cont* -**ting**) ◇ *n* -**1.** [contribution] aportación *f*, contribución *f*. -**2.** COMPUT entrada *f*. ◇ *vt* COMPUT entrar.

input/output *n* COMPUT entrada/salida *f*.

inquest ['ɪnkwest] *n* investigación *f* judicial.

inquire [ɪnˈkwaɪəʳ] ◇ *vi* [ask for information] informarse, pedir información; **to ~ about** sthg informarse de algo. ◇ *vt*: **to ~ when/ if/how ...** preguntar cuándo/si/cómo ....
◆ **inquire after** *vt fus* preguntar por.
◆ **inquire into** *vt fus* investigar.

inquiring [ɪnˈkwaɪərɪŋ] *adj* **-1.** [mind] inquieto(ta), lleno(na) de curiosidad. **-2.** [look, tone] inquisitivo(va).

inquiry [*Br* ɪnˈkwaɪərɪ, *Am* ˈɪnkwərɪ] (*pl* **-ies**) *n* **-1.** [question] pregunta *f*; **"Inquiries"** "Información". **-2.** [investigation] investigación *f*; **to hold an ~ (into)** emprender una investigación (sobre).

inquiry desk *n* (mostrador *m* de) información *f*.

inquisition [ˌɪnkwɪˈzɪʃn] *n* interrogatorio *m*.
◆ **Inquisition** *n*: **the Inquisition** la Inquisición.

inquisitive [ɪnˈkwɪzətɪv] *adj* curioso(sa).

inroads [ˈɪnrəʊdz] *npl*: **to make ~ into** [savings, supplies] mermar; [market, enemy territory] abrirse paso en.

insane [ɪnˈseɪn] ◇ *adj* [mad] demente; *fig* [jealousy, person] loco(ca). ◇ *npl*: **the ~** los enfermos mentales.

insanitary [ɪnˈsænɪtrɪ] *adj* insalubre, antihigiénico(ca).

insanity [ɪnˈsænətɪ] *n* [madness] demencia *f*; *fig* locura *f*.

insatiable [ɪnˈseɪʃəbl] *adj* insaciable.

inscribe [ɪnˈskraɪb] *vt* **-1.** [engrave]: **to ~ sthg (on sthg)** inscribir algo (en algo); **she ~d the book with her name** inscribió su nombre en el libro. **-2.** [write]: **to ~ sthg in sthg** escribir algo en algo a modo de dedicatoria.

inscription [ɪnˈskrɪpʃn] *n* **-1.** [engraved] inscripción *f*. **-2.** [written] dedicatoria *f*.

inscrutable [ɪnˈskruːtəbl] *adj* inescrutable.

insect [ˈɪnsekt] *n* insecto *m*.

insect bite *n* picadura *f* de insecto.

insecticide [ɪnˈsektɪsaɪd] *n* insecticida *m*.

insect repellent *n* loción *f* antiinsectos.

insecure [ˌɪnsɪˈkjʊəʳ] *adj* **-1.** [not confident] inseguro(ra). **-2.** [not safe] poco seguro(ra).

insecurity [ˌɪnsɪˈkjʊərətɪ] *n* inseguridad *f*.

insensible [ɪnˈsensəbl] *adj* **-1.** [unconscious] inconsciente. **-2.** [unaware]: **to be ~ of sthg** no ser consciente de algo. **-3.** [unable to feel]: **to be ~ to sthg** ser insensible a algo.

insensitive [ɪnˈsensətɪv] *adj*: **~ (to)** insensible (a).

insensitivity [ɪnˌsensəˈtɪvətɪ] *n*: **~ (to)** insensibilidad *f* (a).

inseparable [ɪnˈseprəbl] *adj*: **~ (from)** inseparable (de).

insert [*vb* ɪnˈsɜːt, *n* ˈɪnsɜːt] ◇ *vt*: **to ~ sthg (in OR into)** [hole] introducir algo (en); [text] insertar algo (en). ◇ *n* PRESS encarte *m*.

insertion [ɪnˈsɜːʃn] *n* inserción *f*.

in-service training *n Br* formación *f* en horas de trabajo.

inset [ˈɪnset] *n* recuadro *m* (*insertado en la esquina de otro de mayor tamaño*).

inshore [*adj* ˈɪnʃɔːr, *adv* ɪnˈʃɔːr] ◇ *adj* costero(ra). ◇ *adv* hacia la orilla OR la costa.

inside [ɪnˈsaɪd] ◇ *prep* dentro de; **~ three months** en menos de tres meses. ◇ *adv* **-1.** [be, remain] dentro; [go, move etc] hacia dentro; *fig* [feel, hurt etc] interiormente; **come ~!** ¡metéos dentro! **-2.** *prison sl* en chirona, en la cárcel. ◇ *adj* interior. ◇ *n* interior *m*; **from the ~** desde dentro; **to overtake on the ~** [of road] adelantar por dentro; **~ out** [wrong way] al revés; **to know sthg ~ out** conocer algo de arriba abajo OR al dedillo.
◆ **insides** *npl inf* tripas *fpl*.
◆ **inside of** *prep Am* [building, object] dentro de.

inside information *n* (*U*) información *f* confidencial.

inside job *n inf* robo cometido con la ayuda de un empleado de la empresa o local allanados.

inside lane *n* AUT carril *m* de dentro.

insider [ˌɪnˈsaɪdəʳ] *n* persona *f* bien informada (*dentro de una organización*).

insider dealing, **insider trading** *n* (*U*) en bolsa, uso indebido de información privilegiada.

inside story *n* historia *f* íntima.

insidious [ɪnˈsɪdɪəs] *adj* insidioso(sa).

insight [ˈɪnsaɪt] *n* **-1.** (*U*) [power of understanding] perspicacia *f*, capacidad *f* de penetración. **-2.** [understanding] idea *f*.

insignia [ɪnˈsɪgnɪə] (*pl inv*) *n* insignias *fpl*.

insignificance [ˌɪnsɪgˈnɪfɪkəns] *n* insignificancia *f*.

insignificant [ˌɪnsɪgˈnɪfɪkənt] *adj* insignificante.

insincere [ˌɪnsɪnˈsɪəʳ] *adj* insincero(ra).

insincerity [ˌɪnsɪnˈserətɪ] *n* insinceridad *f*.

insinuate [ɪnˈsɪnjʊeɪt] *pej vt*: **to ~ (that)** insinuar (que).

insinuation [ɪnˌsɪnjʊˈeɪʃn] *n pej* insinuación *f*.

insipid [ɪnˈsɪpɪd] *adj pej* soso(sa), insípido(da).

insist [ɪnˈsɪst] ◇ *vt*: **to ~ that** insistir en que. ◇ *vi*: **to ~ on sthg** exigir algo; **to ~ (on doing sthg)** insistir (en hacer algo).

insistence [ɪnˈsɪstəns] *n* insistencia *f*; **~ on**

sthg/on doing sthg empeño *m* en algo/en hacer algo.

insistent [ɪnˈsɪstənt] *adj* **-1.** [determined] insistente; **to be ~ on sthg** insistir en algo. **-2.** [continual] persistente.

in situ [ˌɪnˈsɪtjuː] *adv* [repairs etc] a domicilio.

insofar [ˌɪnsəʊˈfɑːr]
◆ **insofar as** *conj* en la medida en que.

insole [ˈɪnsəʊl] *n* plantilla *f*.

insolence [ˈɪnsələns] *n* insolencia *f*.

insolent [ˈɪnsələnt] *adj* insolente.

insoluble *Br* [ɪnˈsɒljʊbl], **insolvable** *Am* [ɪnˈsɒlvəbl] *adj* insoluble.

insolvency [ɪnˈsɒlvənsɪ] *n* insolvencia *f*.

insolvent [ɪnˈsɒlvənt] *adj* insolvente.

insomnia [ɪnˈsɒmnɪə] *n* insomnio *m*.

insomniac [ɪnˈsɒmnɪæk] *n* insomne *m* y *f*.

insomuch [ˌɪnsəʊˈmʌtʃ]
◆ **insomuch as** *conj* en la medida en que.

inspect [ɪnˈspekt] *vt* inspeccionar; [troops] pasar revista a.

inspection [ɪnˈspekʃn] *n* inspección *f*.

inspector [ɪnˈspektər] *n* inspector *m*, -ra *f*; [on bus, train] revisor *m*, -ra *f*.

inspector of taxes *n* ≃ inspector *m*, -ra *f* de Hacienda.

inspiration [ˌɪnspəˈreɪʃn] *n* **-1.** [gen] inspiración *f*. **-2.** [source of inspiration]: ~ **(for)** fuente *f* de inspiración (para).

inspire [ɪnˈspaɪər] *vt* **-1.** [stimulate, encourage]: **to ~ sb (to do sthg)** alentar OR animar a alguien (a hacer algo). **-2.** [fill]: **to ~ sb with sthg, to ~ sthg in sb** inspirar algo a alguien.

inspired [ɪnˈspaɪəd] *adj* inspirado(da).

inspiring [ɪnˈspaɪərɪŋ] *adj* [stimulating, exciting] inspirador(ra).

inst. [ɪnst] *(abbr of* **instant)** cte.; **on the 4th ~** el 4 del cte.

instability [ˌɪnstəˈbɪlətɪ] *n* inestabilidad *f*.

install *Br*, **instal** *Am* [ɪnˈstɔːl] *vt* **-1.** [gen & COMPUT] instalar. **-2.** [appoint]: **to ~ sb (as)** investir a alguien (con el cargo de). **-3.** [settle]: **to ~ o.s. in front of the fire** instalarse frente al fuego.

installation [ˌɪnstəˈleɪʃn] *n* [gen & COMPUT] instalación *f*.

installment *Am* = **instalment.**

installment plan *n Am* compra *f* a plazos.

instalment *Br*, **installment** *Am* [ɪnˈstɔːlmənt] *n* **-1.** [payment] plazo *m*, abono *m Amer*; **in ~s** a plazos. **-2.** TV & RADIO episodio *m*; [of novel] entrega *f*.

instance [ˈɪnstəns] *n* [example, case] ejemplo

m; **for ~** por ejemplo; **in the first ~** *fml* en primer lugar; **in this ~** en este caso.

instant [ˈɪnstənt] ◇ *adj* instantáneo(a). ◇ *n* [moment] instante *m*; **at that** OR **the same ~** en aquel mismo instante; **the ~ (that)** ... en cuanto ...; **this ~** ahora mismo.

instantaneous [ˌɪnstənˈteɪnjəs] *adj* instantáneo(a).

instantly [ˈɪnstəntlɪ] *adv* en el acto.

instead [ɪnˈsted] *adv* en cambio.
◆ **instead of** *prep* en lugar de, en vez de.

instep [ˈɪnstep] *n* [of foot] empeine *m*.

instigate [ˈɪnstɪgeɪt] *vt* iniciar; **to ~ sb to do sthg** instigar a alguien a hacer algo.

instigation [ˌɪnstɪˈgeɪʃn] *n*: **at the ~ of** a instancias de.

instigator [ˈɪnstɪgeɪtər] *n* instigador *m*, -ra *f*.

instil *Br* (*pt* & *pp* **-led,** *cont* **-ling), instill** *Am* (*pt* & *pp* **-ed,** *cont* **-ing)** [ɪnˈstɪl] *vt*: **to ~ sthg in** OR **into sb** inculcar OR infundir algo a alguien.

instinct [ˈɪnstɪŋkt] *n* instinto *m*; **my first ~ was** ... mi primer impulso fue ....

instinctive [ɪnˈstɪŋktɪv] *adj* instintivo(va).

instinctively [ɪnˈstɪŋktɪvlɪ] *adv* instintivamente.

institute [ˈɪnstɪtjuːt] ◇ *n* instituto *m*. ◇ *vt* [proceedings] iniciar, entablar; [system] instituir.

institution [ˌɪnstɪˈtjuːʃn] *n* **-1.** [gen] institución *f*. **-2.** [home - for children, old people] asilo *m*; [- for mentally-handicapped] hospital *m* psiquiátrico.

institutional [ˌɪnstɪˈtjuːʃənl] *adj* **-1.** [of organization] institucional. **-2.** [food, life etc] típico(ca) de una institución benéfica.

institutionalized, -ised [ˌɪnstɪˈtjuːʃnə,laɪzd] *adj* **-1.** *pej* [influenced by institutional life] acostumbrado a la vida hospitalaria, carcelaria *etc*. **-2.** [established] institucionalizado(da).

instruct [ɪnˈstrʌkt] *vt* **-1.** [tell, order]: **to ~ sb to do sthg** mandar OR ordenar a alguien que haga algo. **-2.** [teach]: **to ~ sb (in sthg)** instruir a alguien (en algo).

instruction [ɪnˈstrʌkʃn] *n* instrucción *f*.
◆ **instructions** *npl* [for use] instrucciones *fpl*.

instruction manual *n* manual *m* de instrucciones.

instructive [ɪnˈstrʌktɪv] *adj* instructivo(va).

instructor [ɪnˈstrʌktər] *n* **-1.** [gen] instructor *m*. **-2.** [in skiing] monitor *m*. **-3.** [in driving] profesor *m*. **-4.** *Am* SCH profesor *m*, -ra *f*.

instructress [ɪnˈstrʌktrɪs] *n* instructora *f*; [in skiing] monitora *f*; [in driving] profesora *f*.

instrument [ˈɪnstrʊmənt] *n* instrumento *m*.

instrumental [ˌɪnstrʊˈmentl] ◇ *adj* **-1.** [important, helpful]: **to be ~ in sthg** jugar un papel fundamental en algo. **-2.** MUS instrumental. ◇ *n* pieza *f* instrumental.

instrumentalist [ˌɪnstrʊˈmentəlɪst] *n* instrumentista *m y f*.

instrument panel *n* tablero *m* de instrumentos.

insubordinate [ˌɪnsəˈbɔːdɪnət] *adj fml* insubordinado(da).

insubordination [ˈɪnsəˌbɔːdɪˈneɪʃn] *n fml* insubordinación *f*.

insubstantial [ˌɪnsəbˈstænʃl] *adj* [frame, structure] endeble; [meal] poco sustancioso(sa).

insufferable [ɪnˈsʌfərəbl] *adj* insufrible.

insufficient [ˌɪnsəˈfɪʃnt] *adj*: **~ (for)** insuficiente (para).

insular [ˈɪnsjʊləʳ] *adj* estrecho(cha) de miras.

insulate [ˈɪnsjʊleɪt] *vt* aislar; **to ~ sb against** OR **from sthg** aislar a alguien de algo.

insulating tape [ˈɪnsjʊleɪtɪŋ-] *n Br* cinta *f* aislante.

insulation [ˌɪnsjʊˈleɪʃn] *n* [material, substance] aislamiento *m*.

insulin [ˈɪnsjʊlɪn] *n* insulina *f*.

insult [*vt* ɪnˈsʌlt, *n* ˈɪnsʌlt] ◇ *vt* [with words] insultar; [with actions] ofender. ◇ *n* [remark] insulto *m*; [action] ofensa *f*; **to add ~ to injury** para colmo, para más inri.

insulting [ɪnˈsʌltɪŋ] *adj* [remark] insultante; [behaviour] ofensivo(va), insultante.

insuperable [ɪnˈsuːprəbl] *adj fml* insalvable, insuperable.

insurance [ɪnˈʃɔːrəns] ◇ *n* **-1.** [against fire, accident, theft]: **~ (against)** seguro *m* (contra). **-2.** *fig* [safeguard, protection]: **~ (against)** prevención *f* (contra). ◇ *comp* de seguros; **~ company** compañía *f* de seguros.

insurance broker *n* agente *m y f* de seguros.

insurance policy *n* póliza *f* de seguros.

insurance premium *n* prima *f* (del seguro).

insure [ɪnˈʃɔːʳ] ◇ *vt* **-1.** [against fire, accident, theft]: **to ~ sthg/sb (against)** asegurar algo/a alguien (contra). **-2.** *Am* [make certain] asegurar. ◇ *vi* [prevent]: **to ~ (against)** prevenir OR prevenirse (contra).

insured [ɪnˈʃɔːd] ◇ *adj* **-1.** [against fire, accident, theft]: **~ (against** OR **for)** asegurado(da) (contra). **-2.** *Am* [certain] asegurado(da). ◇ *n*: **the ~** el asegurado (la asegurada).

insurer [ɪnˈʃɔːrəʳ] *n* asegurador *m*, -ra *f*.

insurgent [ɪnˈsɜːdʒənt] *n* insurgente *m y f*.

insurmountable [ˌɪnsəˈmaʊntəbl] *adj fml* infranqueable, insuperable.

insurrection [ˌɪnsəˈrekʃn] *n* insurrección *f*.

intact [ɪnˈtækt] *adj* intacto(ta).

intake [ˈɪnteɪk] *n* **-1.** [of food, drink] ingestión *f*; [of air] inspiración *f*. **-2.** [in army] reclutamiento *m*; [in organization] número *m* de ingresos. **-3.** TECH [inlet] toma *f*.

intangible [ɪnˈtændʒəbl] *adj* intangible; **~ assets** bienes *mpl* inmateriales.

integral [ˈɪntɪɡrəl] *adj* integrante, intrínseco(ca); **to be ~ to** ser parte integrante de.

integrate [ˈɪntɪɡreɪt] ◇ *vi*: **to ~ (with** OR **into)** integrarse (en). ◇ *vt*: **to ~ sthg/sb with sthg, to ~ sthg/sb into sthg** integrar algo/a alguien en algo.

integrated [ˈɪntɪɡreɪtɪd] *adj* [mixed] integrado(da).

integrated circuit *n* circuito *m* integrado.

integration [ˌɪntɪˈɡreɪʃn] *n*: **~ (with** OR **into)** integración *f* (en).

integrity [ɪnˈteɡrətɪ] *n* integridad *f*.

intellect [ˈɪntəlekt] *n* **-1.** [mind, cleverness] intelecto *m*, inteligencia *f*.

intellectual [ˌɪntəˈlektjʊəl] ◇ *adj* intelectual. ◇ *n* intelectual *m y f*.

intellectualize, -ise [ˌɪntəˈlektjʊəlaɪz] *vt* intelectualizar, dar tono intelectual a.

intelligence [ɪnˈtelɪdʒəns] *n* (U) **-1.** [ability to think] inteligencia *f*. **-2.** [information service] servicio *m* secreto OR de espionaje. **-3.** [information] información *f* secreta.

intelligence quotient *n* coeficiente *m* de inteligencia.

intelligence test *n* test *m* de inteligencia.

intelligent [ɪnˈtelɪdʒənt] *adj* [clever] inteligente.

intelligent card *n* tarjeta *f* inteligente, tarjeta con chip.

intelligently [ɪnˈtelɪdʒəntlɪ] *adv* inteligentemente.

intelligentsia [ɪnˌtelɪˈdʒentsɪə] *n*: **the ~** la intelectualidad.

intelligible [ɪnˈtelɪdʒəbl] *adj* inteligible.

intemperate [ɪnˈtempərət] *adj fml* [remarks, climate] destemplado(da); [behaviour] inmoderado(da).

intend [ɪnˈtend] *vt* pretender, proponerse; **to be ~ed for/as sthg** [project, book] estar pensado para/como algo; **to ~ doing** OR **to do sthg** tener la intención de OR pretender hacer algo; **later than I had ~ed** más tarde de lo que había pensado.

intended [ɪnˈtendɪd] *adj* pretendido(da).

intense [ɪnˈtens] *adj* **-1.** [extreme, profound]

intenso(sa). -2. [serious - person] **muy se-rio(ria).**

intensely [ɪn'tenslɪ] *adv* **-1.** [very - boring, ir-ritating] **enormemente. -2.** [very much - suf-fer] **intensamente;** [- dislike] **profundamente.**

intensify [ɪn'tensɪfaɪ] (*pt* & *pp* **-ied**) ◇ *vt* **intensificar.** ◇ *vi* **intensificarse.**

intensity [ɪn'tensətɪ] *n* **intensidad** *f*.

intensive [ɪn'tensɪv] *adj* [concentrated] **inten-sivo(va).**

intensive care *n* (*U*): **(in) ~ (bajo) cuida-dos** *mpl* **intensivos.**

intensive care unit *n* **unidad** *f* **de cuida-dos intensivos** OR **de vigilancia intensiva.**

intent [ɪn'tent] ◇ *adj* **-1.** [absorbed] **aten-to(ta). -2.** [determined]: **to be ~ on** OR **upon doing sthg estar empeñado(da) en hacer algo.** ◇ *n fml* **intención** *f*; **to all ~s and purposes para todos los efectos.**

intention [ɪn'tenʃn] *n* **intención** *f*.

intentional [ɪn'tenʃənl] *adj* **deliberado(da), intencionado(da).**

intentionally [ɪn'tenʃənəlɪ] *adv* **deliberada-mente, intencionadamente.**

intently [ɪn'tentlɪ] *adv* **atentamente.**

inter [ɪn'tɜːʳ] (*pt* & *pp* **-red**, *cont* **-ring**) *vt fml* **sepultar.**

interact [ˌɪntər'ækt] *vi* **-1.** [communicate, work together]: **to ~ (with sb) comunicarse (con alguien). -2.** [react]: **to ~ (with sthg) interaccionar (con algo).**

interaction [ˌɪntər'ækʃn] *n* **interacción** *f*.

interactive [ˌɪntər'æktɪv] *adj* COMPUT **inte-ractivo(va).**

intercede [ˌɪntə'siːd] *vi fml*: **to ~ (with/for) interceder (ante/por).**

intercept [ˌɪntə'sept] *vt* **interceptar.**

interception [ˌɪntə'sepʃn] *n* **interceptación** *f*.

interchange [*n* 'ɪntətʃeɪndʒ, *vb* ˌɪntə-'tʃeɪndʒ] ◇ *n* **-1.** [exchange] **intercambio** *m*. **-2.** [on motorway] **cruce** *m*. ◇ *vt* **intercam-biar.**

interchangeable [ˌɪntə'tʃeɪndʒəbl] *adj*: **~ (with) intercambiable (con).**

intercity [ˌɪntə'sɪtɪ] ◇ *adj Br* **interurba-no(na), de largo recorrido.** ◇ *n* **red de trenes rápidos que conecta las principales ciudades bri-tánicas; Intercity 125® tren británico de alta velocidad.**

intercom ['ɪntəkɒm] *n* [for block of flats] **por-tero** *m* **automático;** [within a building] **inter-fono** *m*.

interconnect [ˌɪntəkə'nekt] *vi*: **to ~ (with) interconectarse (con).**

intercontinental ['ɪntəˌkɒntɪ'nentl] *adj* **in-tercontinental.**

intercontinental ballistic missile *n* **misil** *m* **balístico intercontinental.**

intercourse ['ɪntəkɔːs] *n* (*U*): **sexual ~ re-laciones** *fpl* **sexuales, coito** *m*.

interdenominational ['ɪntədɪˌnɒmɪ'neɪʃənl] *adj* **interconfesional.**

interdepartmental ['ɪntəˌdiːpɑːt'mentl] *adj* **interdepartamental.**

interdependent [ˌɪntədɪ'pendənt] *adj* **inter-dependiente.**

interdict ['ɪntədɪkt] *n* JUR & RELIG **interdicto** *m*.

interest ['ɪntrəst] ◇ *n* **-1.** [gen & FIN]: **~ (in) interés** *m* **(en** OR **por); that's of no ~ eso no tiene interés; in the ~** OR **~s of** [in order to benefit] **en interés de;** [in order to achieve] **en pro de. -2.** [hobby] **afición** *f*. ◇ *vt* **intere-sar; to ~ sb in sthg/in doing sthg interesar a alguien en algo/en hacer algo.**

interested ['ɪntrəstɪd] *adj* **interesado(da); to be ~ in sthg/in doing sthg estar interesado en algo/en hacer algo.**

interest-free *adj* **libre de interés.**

interesting ['ɪntrəstɪŋ] *adj* **interesante.**

interest rate *n* **tipo** *m* **de interés.**

interface [*n* 'ɪntəfeɪs, *vb* ˌɪntə'feɪs] ◇ *n* **-1.** COMPUT **interfaz** *f*. **-2.** [junction, boundary] **zona** *f* **de interacción.** ◇ *vt* COMPUT **conec-tar mediante interfaz.**

interfere [ˌɪntə'fɪəʳ] *vi* **-1.** [meddle]: **to ~ (with** OR **in sthg) entrometerse** OR **interferir (en algo). -2.** [damage] **interferir; to ~ with sthg** [career, routine] **interferir en algo;** [work, performance] **interrumpir algo.**

interference [ˌɪntə'fɪərəns] *n* (*U*) **-1.** [med-dling]: **~ (with** OR **in) intromisión** *f* OR **in-terferencia** *f* **(en). -2.** [on radio, TV, tele-phone] **interferencia** *f*.

interfering [ˌɪntə'fɪərɪŋ] *adj pej* **entrometi-do(da).**

intergalactic [ˌɪntəgə'læktɪk] *adj* **intergalác-tico(ca).**

interim ['ɪntərɪm] ◇ *adj* [report] **parcial;** [measure] **provisional;** [government] **interi-no(na).** ◇ *n*: **in the ~ entre tanto.**

interior [ɪn'tɪərɪəʳ] ◇ *adj* **-1.** [inner] **interior. -2.** POL [minister, department] **del Interior.** ◇ *n* **interior** *m*.

interior decorator, interior designer *n* **diseñador** *m*, **-ra** *f* **de interiores.**

interject *fml* [ˌɪntə'dʒekt] ◇ *vt* [add, inter-rupt] **intercalar.** ◇ *vi* **interponer.**

interjection [ˌɪntə'dʒekʃn] *n* **-1.** [remark] **in-terrupción** *f*. **-2.** GRAMM **interjección** *f*.

interleave [ˌɪntə'liːv] *vt*: **to ~ sthg (with) interfoliar algo (con).**

interlock [ˌɪntəˈlɒk] ◇ *vi* [fingers] entrelazarse; [cogs] engranar. ◇ *vt*: **to ~ sthg (with)** [fingers] entrelazar algo (con); [cogs] engranar algo (con).

interloper [ˈɪntələʊpəʳ] *n* intruso *m*, -sa *f*.

interlude [ˈɪntəluːd] *n* **-1.** [pause] intervalo *m*. **-2.** [interval] descanso *m*, intermedio *m*.

intermarry [ˌɪntəˈmærɪ] (*pt & pp* **-ied**) *vi*: **to ~ (with)** casarse (con) (*parientes o personas de distinta raza, religión etc*).

intermediary [ˌɪntəˈmiːdjərɪ] (*pl* **-ies**) *n* intermediario *m*, -ria *f*, mediador *m*, -ra *f*.

intermediate [ˌɪntəˈmiːdjət] *adj* intermedio(dia).

interminable [ɪnˈtɜːmɪnəbl] *adj* interminable.

intermingle [ˌɪntəˈmɪŋgl] *vi*: **to ~ (with)** entremezclarse (con).

intermission [ˌɪntəˈmɪʃn] *n* [of film] descanso *m*; [of play, opera, ballet] entreacto *m*.

intermittent [ˌɪntəˈmɪtənt] *adj* intermitente.

intern [*vb* ɪnˈtɜːn, *n* ˈɪntɜːn] ◇ *vt* recluir, internar. ◇ *n* médico *m* interno residente.

internal [ɪnˈtɜːnl] *adj* **-1.** [gen] interno(na). **-2.** [within a country] interior, nacional; **~ flight** vuelo *m* nacional.

internal-combustion engine *n* motor *m* de combustión interna.

internally [ɪnˈtɜːnəlɪ] *adv* **-1.** [gen] internamente. **-2.** [within a country] a nivel nacional, en el interior.

Internal Revenue *n Am*: **the ~** ≃ Hacienda *f*.

international [ˌɪntəˈnæʃənl] ◇ *adj* internacional. ◇ *n Br* SPORT **-1.** [match] encuentro *m* internacional. **-2.** [player] internacional *m* y *f*.

international date line *n*: **the ~** la línea de cambio de fecha en el Pacífico.

internationally [ˌɪntəˈnæʃnəlɪ] *adv* internacionalmente.

International Monetary Fund *n*: **the ~** el Fondo Monetario Internacional.

international relations *npl* relaciones *fpl* internacionales.

internecine [*Br* ˌɪntəˈniːsaɪn, *Am* ˌɪntərˈniːsn] *adj fml* intestino(na).

internee [ˌɪntɜːˈniː] *n* recluso *m*, -sa *f*, internado *m*, -da *f*.

Internet [ˈɪntənet] *n*: **the ~** Internet *f*.

internment [ɪnˈtɜːnmənt] *n* reclusión *f*, internamiento *m*.

interpersonal [ˌɪntəˈpɜːsənl] *adj* interpersonal.

interplay [ˈɪntəpleɪ] *n* (*U*): **~ (of/between)** interacción *f* (de/entre).

Interpol [ˈɪntəpɒl] *n* Interpol *f*.

interpolate [ɪnˈtɜːpəleɪt] *vt fml*: **to ~ sthg (into)** interpolar algo (en).

interpose [ˌɪntəˈpəʊz] *vt fml* interponer; **to ~ o.s.** interponerse.

interpret [ɪnˈtɜːprɪt] ◇ *vt* interpretar. ◇ *vi* hacer de intérprete.

interpretation [ɪnˌtɜːprɪˈteɪʃn] *n* interpretación *f*.

interpreted language [ɪnˈtɜːprɪtɪd-] *n* COMPUT lenguaje *m* de programación interpretado.

interpreter [ɪnˈtɜːprɪtəʳ] *n* [person] intérprete *m* y *f*.

interpreting [ɪnˈtɜːprɪtɪŋ] *n* [occupation] interpretación *f*.

interracial [ˌɪntəˈreɪʃl] *adj* interracial.

interrelate [ˌɪntərɪˈleɪt] ◇ *vt* interrelacionar. ◇ *vi*: **to ~(with)** interrelacionarse (con).

interrogate [ɪnˈterəgeɪt] *vt* [gen & COMPUT] interrogar.

interrogation [ɪnˌterəˈgeɪʃn] *n* interrogatorio *m*.

interrogation mark *n Am* signo *m* de interrogación.

interrogative [ˌɪntəˈrɒgətɪv] ◇ *adj* interrogativo(va). ◇ *n* **-1.** [form]: **the ~** la forma interrogativa. **-2.** [word] interrogativo *m*.

interrogator [ɪnˈterəgeɪtəʳ] *n* interrogador *m*, -ra *f*.

interrupt [ˌɪntəˈrʌpt] *vt & vi* interrumpir.

interruption [ˌɪntəˈrʌpʃn] *n* interrupción *f*.

intersect [ˌɪntəˈsekt] ◇ *vi* cruzarse, cortarse. ◇ *vt* cruzar, cortar.

intersection [ˌɪntəˈsekʃn] *n* [junction] intersección *f*, cruce *m*.

intersperse [ˌɪntəˈspɜːs] *vt*: **to be ~d with** OR **by** estar entremezclado con.

interstate (highway) [ˈɪntəsteɪt-] *n* autopista *f* interestatal.

interval [ˈɪntəvl] *n* **-1.** [gen & MUS]: **~ (between)** intervalo *m* (entre); **at ~s** [now and again] a ratos; [regularly] a intervalos; **at monthly/yearly ~s** a intervalos de un mes/un año. **-2.** *Br* [at play, concert] intermedio *m*, descanso *m*.

intervene [ˌɪntəˈviːn] *vi* **-1.** [gen]: **to ~ (in)** intervenir (en). **-2.** [prevent thing from happening] interponerse. **-3.** [pass] transcurrir.

intervening [ˌɪntəˈviːnɪŋ] *adj* [time] transcurrido(da); [space] intermedio(dia).

intervention [ˌɪntəˈvenʃn] *n* intervención *f*.

interventionist [ˌɪntəˈvenʃənɪst] ◇ *adj* intervencionista. ◇ *n* intervencionista *m* y *f*.

interview [ˈɪntəvjuː] ◇ *n* entrevista *f*. ◇ *vt* entrevistar.

interviewee [ˌɪntəvjuːˈiː] *n* entrevistado *m*, -da *f*.

interviewer [ˈɪntəvjuːəʳ] *n* entrevistador *m*, -ra *f*.

interweave [ˌɪntəˈwiːv] (*pt* -wove, *pp* -woven) *fig* ◇ *vt* entretejer. ◇ *vi* entretejerse.

intestate [ɪnˈtesteɪt] *adj*: **to die** ~ morir intestado(da).

intestine [ɪnˈtestɪn] *n* intestino *m*.
◆ **intestines** *npl* tripa *f*, intestinos *mpl*.

intimacy [ˈɪntɪməsɪ] (*pl* -ies) *n*: ~ **(between/with)** intimidad *f* (entre/con).

intimate [*adj & n* ˈɪntɪmət, *vb* ˈɪntɪmeɪt] ◇ *adj* -1. [gen] íntimo(ma). -2. *fml* [sexually]: **to be** ~ **with sb** tener relaciones íntimas con alguien. -3. [knowledge] profundo(da). ◇ *n fml* amigo íntimo *m*, amiga íntima *f*. ◇ *vt fml*: **to** ~ **(that)** dar a entender (que).

intimately [ˈɪntɪmətlɪ] *adv* -1. [very closely] íntimamente. -2. [as close friends] en la intimidad. -3. [in detail] en profundidad, a fondo.

intimation [ˌɪntɪˈmeɪʃn] *n fml* señal *f*, indicio *m*.

intimidate [ɪnˈtɪmɪdeɪt] *vt* intimidar.

intimidation [ɪnˌtɪmɪˈdeɪʃn] *n* intimidación *f*.

into [ˈɪntʊ] *prep* -1. [inside] en; **to put sthg** ~ **sthg** meter algo en algo; **to get** ~ **a car** subir a un coche. -2. [against] con; **to bump/crash** ~ tropezar/chocar con. -3. [referring to change in condition etc]: **to turn** OR **develop** ~ convertirse en; **to translate sthg** ~ **Spanish** traducir algo al español. -4. [concerning] en relación con; **research** ~ **electronics** investigación en torno a la electrónica. -5. MATH: **to divide 4** ~ **8** dividir 8 entre 4. -6. *inf* [interested in]: **I'm** ~ **classical music** me va OR me mola la música clásica.

intolerable [ɪnˈtɒlrəbl] *adj fml* [position, conditions] intolerable; [boredom, pain] inaguantable.

intolerance [ɪnˈtɒlərəns] *n* intolerancia *f*.

intolerant [ɪnˈtɒlərənt] *adj* intolerante; **to be** ~ **of** ser intolerante con.

intonation [ˌɪntəˈneɪʃn] *n* entonación *f*.

intone [ɪnˈtəʊn] *vt literary* salmodiar.

intoxicated [ɪnˈtɒksɪkeɪtɪd] *adj* -1. [drunk] embriagado(da), ebrio (ebria). -2. *fig* [excited]: ~ **(by** OR **with)** ebrio (ebria) (de).

intoxicating [ɪnˈtɒksɪkeɪtɪŋ] *adj* embriagador(ra).

intoxication [ɪnˌtɒksɪˈkeɪʃn] *n* embriaguez *f*.

intractable [ɪnˈtræktəbl] *adj fml* -1. [stub-

born] intratable. -2. [insoluble] inextricable, insoluble.

intransigent [ɪnˈtrænzɪdʒənt] *adj fml* intransigente.

intransitive [ɪnˈtrænzətɪv] *adj* intransitivo(va).

intrauterine device [ˌɪntrəˈjuːtəraɪn-] *n* dispositivo *m* intrauterino.

intravenous [ˌɪntrəˈviːnəs] *adj* intravenoso(sa).

in-tray *n* bandeja para cartas y documentos recién llegados a la oficina.

intrepid [ɪnˈtrepɪd] *adj literary* intrépido(da).

intricacy [ˈɪntrɪkəsɪ] (*pl* -ies) *n* -1. [complexity] complejidad *f*, intrincamiento *m*. -2. [detail] entresijo *m*.

intricate [ˈɪntrɪkət] *adj* intrincado(da), enrevesado(da).

intrigue [ɪnˈtriːg] ◇ *n* intriga *f*. ◇ *vt* intrigar. ◇ *vi*: **to** ~ **(against sb)** intrigar (contra alguien).

intriguing [ɪnˈtriːgɪŋ] *adj* intrigante.

intrinsic [ɪnˈtrɪnsɪk] *adj* intrínseco(ca).

intro [ˈɪntrəʊ] (*pl* -s) *n inf* [of song] primeros compases *mpl*.

introduce [ˌɪntrəˈdjuːs] *vt* -1. [present - person, programme] presentar; **to** ~ **sb (to sb)** presentar a alguien (a alguien); **to** ~ **o.s.** presentarse. -2. [bring in]: **to** ~ **sthg (to** OR **into)** introducir algo (en). -3. [show for first time]: **to** ~ **sb to sthg** iniciar a alguien en algo. -4. [signal beginning of] preludiar.

introduction [ˌɪntrəˈdʌkʃn] *n* -1. [gen]: ~ **(to sthg)** introducción *f* (a algo). -2. [of people]: ~ **(to sb)** presentación *f* (a alguien).

introductory [ˌɪntrəˈdʌktrɪ] *adj* [chapter] introductorio(ria); [remarks] preliminar.

introspective [ˌɪntrəˈspektɪv] *adj* introspectivo(va).

introvert [ˈɪntrəvɜːt] *n* introvertido *m*, -da *f*.

introverted [ˈɪntrəvɜːtɪd] *adj* introvertido(da).

intrude [ɪnˈtruːd] *vi*: **to** ~ **(on** OR **upon sb)** inmiscuirse (en los asuntos de alguien); **to** ~ **(on** OR **upon sthg)** inmiscuirse (en algo).

intruder [ɪnˈtruːdəʳ] *n* intruso *m*, -sa *f*.

intrusion [ɪnˈtruːʒn] *n* [into sb's business] intromisión *f*; [into a place] intrusión *f*.

intrusive [ɪnˈtruːsɪv] *adj* [person] entrometido(da); [presence] indeseado(da).

intuition [ˌɪntjuːˈɪʃn] *n* intuición *f*.

intuitive [ɪnˈtjuːɪtɪv] *adj* intuitivo(va).

Inuit [ˈɪnʊɪt] ◇ *adj* inuit (*inv*). ◇ *n* inuit *m y f inv*.

inundate ['ɪnʌndeɪt] *vt* **-1.** *fml* [flood] inundar. **-2.** [overwhelm] desbordar; **to be ~d with** verse desbordado por.

inured [ɪ'njʊəd] *adj fml*: **to be/become ~ to** sthg estar habituado(da)/habituarse a algo.

invade [ɪn'veɪd] *vt* invadir.

invader [ɪn'veɪdə'] *n* invasor *m*, -ra *f*.

invading [ɪn'veɪdɪŋ] *adj* invasor(ra).

invalid [*adj* ɪn'vælɪd, *n* & *vb* 'ɪnvəlɪd] ◇ *adj* **-1.** [marriage, vote, ticket] nulo(la). **-2.** [argument, result] que no es válido(da). ◇ *n* inválido *m*, -da *f*.
◆ **invalid out** *vt sep*: **to be ~ed out (of)** ser licenciado(da) por invalidez (de).

invalidate [ɪn'vælɪdeɪt] *vt* [theory] refutar; [rule] invalidar; [marriage, election] anular, invalidar.

invalid chair ['ɪnvəlɪd-] *n* silla *f* de ruedas.

invaluable [ɪn'væljʊəbl] *adj*: **~ (to)** [information, advice] inestimable (para); [person] valiosísimo(ma) (para).

invariable [ɪn'veərɪəbl] *adj* invariable.

invariably [ɪn'veərɪəblɪ] *adv* siempre, invariablemente.

invasion [ɪn'veɪʒn] *n* invasión *f*.

invective [ɪn'vektɪv] *n* (U) *fml* invectivas *fpl*.

inveigle [ɪn'veɪgl] *vt*: **to ~ sb into doing sthg** embaucar a alguien para que haga algo.

invent [ɪn'vent] *vt* inventar.

invention [ɪn'venʃn] *n* **-1.** [gen] invención *f*. **-2.** [ability to invent] inventiva *f*.

inventive [ɪn'ventɪv] *adj* [person, mind] inventivo(va); [solution] ingenioso(sa).

inventor [ɪn'ventə'] *n* inventor *m*, -ra *f*.

inventory ['ɪnvəntrɪ] (*pl* **-ies**) *n* **-1.** [list] inventario *m*. **-2.** *Am* [goods] existencias *fpl*.

inventory control *n* control *m* de inventario.

inverse [ɪn'vɜːs] ◇ *adj* [proportion, relation] inverso(sa). ◇ *n fml* antítesis *f inv*.

invert [ɪn'vɜːt] *vt fml* invertir.

invertebrate [ɪn'vɜːtɪbreɪt] *n* invertebrado *m*.

inverted commas [ɪn'vɜːtɪd-] *npl Br* comillas *fpl*; **in ~** entre comillas.

inverted snob [ɪn'vɜːtɪd-] *n persona que finge que no le gustan las cosas caras o de buena calidad.*

invest [ɪn'vest] ◇ *vt* **-1.** [money, time, energy]: **to ~ sthg (in)** invertir algo (en). **-2.** *fml* [endow]: **to ~ sb with** investir a alguien de. ◇ *vi lit* & *fig*: **to ~ (in)** invertir (en).

investigate [ɪn'vestɪgeɪt] *vt* & *vi* investigar.

investigation [ɪn,vestɪ'geɪʃn] *n* [enquiry, examination]: **~ (into)** investigación *f* (en).

investigative [ɪn'vestɪgətɪv] *adj* de investigación.

investigator [ɪn'vestɪgeɪtə'] *n* investigador *m*, -ra *f*.

investiture [ɪn'vestɪtʃə'] *n* investidura *f*.

investment [ɪn'vestmənt] *n* inversión *f*.

investment analyst *n* analista financiero *m*, analista financiera *f*.

investment trust *n* fondo *m* de inversiones.

investor [ɪn'vestə'] *n* inversor *m*, -ra *f*.

inveterate [ɪn'vetərət] *adj* [liar] incorregible; [reader, smoker] empedernido(da).

invidious [ɪn'vɪdɪəs] *adj* [task, role] desagradable; [comparison] odioso(sa).

invigilate [ɪn'vɪdʒɪleɪt] *vt* & *vi Br* vigilar (*en un examen*).

invigilator [ɪn'vɪdʒɪleɪtə'] *n Br* vigilante *m* y *f* (*en un examen*).

invigorating [ɪn'vɪgəreɪtɪŋ] *adj* [bath, walk] vigorizante; [experience] estimulante.

invincible [ɪn'vɪnsɪbl] *adj* **-1.** [unbeatable] invencible. **-2.** [unchangeable] inalterable, inamovible.

inviolate [ɪn'vaɪələt] *adj literary* inviolado(da).

invisible [ɪn'vɪzɪbl] *adj* invisible.

invisible assets *npl* activo *m* inmaterial.

invisible earnings *npl* ingresos *mpl* invisibles.

invisible ink *n* tinta *f* simpática.

invitation [,ɪnvɪ'teɪʃn] *n* invitación *f*; **an ~ to sthg/to do sthg** una invitación a algo/a hacer algo.

invite [ɪn'vaɪt] *vt*: **to ~ sb (to sthg/to do sthg)** invitar a alguien (a algo/a hacer algo).

inviting [ɪn'vaɪtɪŋ] *adj* tentador(ra).

in vitro fertilization [,ɪn'viːtrəʊ-] *n* fertilización *f* in vitro.

invoice ['ɪnvɔɪs] ◇ *n* factura *f*. ◇ *vt* **-1.** [send invoice to] mandar la factura a. **-2.** [prepare invoice for] facturar.

invoke [ɪn'vəʊk] *vt* **-1.** *fml* [quote as justification] invocar, acogerse a. **-2.** [cause] suscitar.

involuntary [ɪn'vɒləntrɪ] *adj* involuntario(ria).

involve [ɪn'vɒlv] *vt* **-1.** [entail, require]: **to ~ sthg/doing sthg** conllevar algo/hacer algo; **it ~s working weekends** supone OR implica trabajar los fines de semana. **-2.** [concern, affect] afectar a; **to be ~d in sthg** [accident, crash] verse envuelto en algo. **-3.** [make part of sthg]: **to ~ sb (in)** involucrar a alguien (en); **to ~ o.s. in** meterse en.

involved [ɪnˈvɒlvd] *adj* **-1.** [complex] enrevesado(da), complicado(da). **-2.** [participating]: **to be ~ in** estar metido(da) en. **-3.** [in a relationship]: **to be/get ~ with sb** estar liado(da)/liarse con alguien.

involvement [ɪnˈvɒlvmənt] *n* **-1.** ~ **(in)** [crime] implicación *f* (en); [running sthg] participación *f* (en). **-2.** [concern, enthusiasm]: ~ **(in)** compromiso *m* (con).

invulnerable [ɪnˈvʌlnərəbl] *adj*: **to be ~ (to)** ser invulnerable (a).

inward [ˈɪnwəd] ◇ *adj* **-1.** [inner] interno(na). **-2.** [towards the inside] hacia el interior. ◇ *adv Am* = **inwards**.

inwardly [ˈɪnwədlɪ] *adv* por dentro.

inwards [ˈɪnwədz] *adv* hacia dentro.

IOC (*abbr of* **International Olympic Committee**) *n* COI *m*.

iodine [*Br* ˈaɪədiːn, *Am* ˈaɪədaɪn] *n* yodo *m*.

IOM *abbr of* **Isle of Man**.

ion [ˈaɪən] *n* ión *m*.

Ionian Sea [aɪˈəʊnjən-] *n*: **the ~** el mar Jónico.

iota [aɪˈəʊtə] *n* pizca *f*, ápice *m*.

IOU (*abbr of* **I owe you**) *n* pag. *m*.

IOW *abbr of* **Isle of Wight**.

Iowa [ˈaɪəʊə] *n* Iowa.

IPA (*abbr of* **International Phonetic Alphabet**) *n* AFI *m*.

IQ (*abbr of* **intelligence quotient**) *n* C.I. *m*.

IRA *n* **-1.** (*abbr of* **Irish Republican Army**) IRA *m*. **-2.** (*abbr of* **individual retirement account**) *cuenta personal de jubilación*.

Iran [ɪˈrɑːn] *n* (el) Irán.

Iranian [ɪˈreɪnjən] ◇ *adj* iraní. ◇ *n* [person] iraní *m y f*.

Iraq [ɪˈrɑːk] *n* (el) Irak.

Iraqi [ɪˈrɑːkɪ] ◇ *adj* iraquí. ◇ *n* [person] iraquí *m y f*.

irascible [ɪˈræsəbl] *adj* irascible.

irate [aɪˈreɪt] *adj* iracundo(da), airado(da).

Ireland [ˈaɪələnd] *n* Irlanda; **the Republic of ~** la República de Irlanda.

iridescent [ˌɪrɪˈdesənt] *adj* iridiscente.

iris [ˈaɪərɪs] (*pl* **-es**) *n* **-1.** [flower] lirio *m*. **-2.** [of eye] iris *m inv*.

Irish [ˈaɪrɪʃ] ◇ *adj* irlandés(esa). ◇ *n* [language] irlandés *m*. ◇ *npl* [people]: **the ~** los irlandeses.

Irish coffee *n* café *m* irlandés.

Irishman [ˈaɪrɪʃmən] (*pl* **-men** [-mən]) *n* irlandés *m*.

Irish Sea *n*: **the ~** el mar de Irlanda.

Irish stew *n* estofado de carne y verdura.

Irishwoman [ˈaɪrɪʃˌwʊmən] (*pl* **-women** [-ˌwɪmɪn]) *n* irlandesa *f*.

irk [ɜːk] *vt* fastidiar.

irksome [ˈɜːksəm] *adj* fastidioso(sa).

IRN (*abbr of* **Independent Radio News**) *n* agencia británica de noticias para emisoras de radio privadas.

IRO (*abbr of* **International Refuge Organization**) *n* organización humanitaria estadounidense para refugiados.

iron [ˈaɪən] ◇ *adj lit* & *fig* de hierro. ◇ *n* **-1.** [metal] hierro *m*, fierro *m Amer*. **-2.** [for clothes] plancha *f*. **-3.** [golf club] hierro *m*. ◇ *vt* planchar.

◆ **iron out** *vt sep fig* [overcome] resolver.

Iron Age ◇ *n*: **the ~** la Edad del Hierro. ◇ *comp* de la Edad del Hierro.

Iron Curtain *n*: **the ~** el telón de acero.

ironic(al) [aɪˈrɒnɪk(l)] *adj* irónico(ca); **how ~!** ¡qué ironía!

ironically [aɪˈrɒnɪklɪ] *adv* irónicamente.

ironing [ˈaɪənɪŋ] *n* **-1.** [work] planchado *m*; **to do the ~** planchar la ropa. **-2.** [clothes to be ironed] ropa *f* para planchar.

ironing board *n* tabla *f* de planchar.

iron lung *n* pulmón *m* de acero OR artificial.

ironmonger [ˈaɪənˌmʌŋgər] *n Br* ferretero *m*, -ra *f*; ~**'s (shop)** ferretería *f*, tlapalería *f Amer*.

ironworks [ˈaɪənwɜːks] (*pl inv*) *n* [where iron smelted] fundición *f*; [where iron cast] herrería *f*.

irony [ˈaɪrənɪ] (*pl* **-ies**) *n* ironía *f*; **the ~ of it is that ...** lo curioso del caso es que ....

irradiate [ɪˈreɪdɪeɪt] *vt* irradiar.

irrational [ɪˈræʃənl] *adj* irracional.

irreconcilable [ɪˈrekənsaɪləbl] *adj* [completely different] irreconciliable.

irredeemable [ˌɪrɪˈdiːməbl] *adj fml* **-1.** [irreplaceable] irrecuperable. **-2.** [hopeless] irreparable, insalvable.

irrefutable [ˌɪrɪˈfjuːtəbl] *adj fml* irrefutable.

irregular [ɪˈregjʊlər] *adj* [gen & GRAMM] irregular.

irregularity [ɪˌregjʊˈlærətɪ] (*pl* **-ies**) *n* irregularidad *f*.

irregularly [ɪˈregjʊləlɪ] *adv* [at uneven intervals] de forma irregular.

irrelevance [ɪˈreləvəns], **irrelevancy** [ɪˈreləvənsɪ] (*pl* **-ies**) *n* **-1.** [state of being irrelevant] irrelevancia *f*, falta *f* de pertinencia. **-2.** [something irrelevant]: **to be an ~** ser algo sin importancia.

irrelevant [ɪˈreləvənt] *adj* irrelevante, que no viene al caso.

irreligious [,ɪrɪ'lɪdʒəs] *adj* irreligioso(sa).

irremediable [,ɪrɪ'miːdjəbl] *adj fml* irremediable, irreparable.

irreparable [ɪ'repərəbl] *adj* irreparable, irremediable.

irreplaceable [,ɪrɪ'pleɪsəbl] *adj* irreemplazable, insustituible.

irrepressible [,ɪrɪ'presəbl] *adj* [enthusiasm] irreprimible; [person] imparable.

irreproachable [,ɪrɪ'prəʊtʃəbl] *adj* irreprochable.

irresistible [,ɪrɪ'zɪstəbl] *adj* irresistible.

irresolute [ɪ'rezəluːt] *adj fml* irresoluto(ta).

irrespective [,ɪrɪ'spektɪv]
◆ **irrespective of** *prep* con independencia de.

irresponsible [,ɪrɪ'spɒnsəbl] *adj* irresponsable.

irretrievable [,ɪrɪ'triːvəbl] *adj* irreparable.

irreverent [ɪ'revərənt] *adj* irreverente, irrespetuoso(sa).

irreversible [,ɪrɪ'vɜːsəbl] *adj* [judgment] irrevocable; [change] irreversible.

irrevocable [ɪ'revəkəbl] *adj* irrevocable.

irrigate ['ɪrɪgeɪt] *vt* regar, irrigar.

irrigation [,ɪrɪ'geɪʃn] ◇ *n* riego *m*, irrigación *f*. ◇ *comp* de riego.

irritable ['ɪrɪtəbl] *adj* irritable.

irritant ['ɪrɪtənt] ◇ *adj* irritante. ◇ *n* **-1.** [irritating situation] motivo *m* de irritación. **-2.** [substance] sustancia *f* irritante.

irritate ['ɪrɪteɪt] *vt* irritar.

irritating ['ɪrɪteɪtɪŋ] *adj* irritante.

irritation [ɪrɪ'teɪʃn] *n* **-1.** [anger, soreness] irritación *f*. **-2.** [cause of anger] motivo *m* de irritación.

IRS (*abbr of* **Internal Revenue Service**) *n Am*: the ~ ≃ Hacienda *f*.

is [ɪz] → **be**.

ISBN (*abbr of* **International Standard Book Number**) *n* ISBN *m*.

Islam ['ɪzlɑːm] *n* [religion] islam *m*, islamismo *m*.

Islamabad [ɪz'lɑːməbæd] *n* Islamabad.

Islamic [ɪz'læmɪk] *adj* islámico(ca).

island ['aɪlənd] *n* **-1.** [in water] isla *f*. **-2.** [in traffic] isleta *f*, refugio *m*.

islander ['aɪləndər] *n* isleño *m*, -ña *f*.

isle [aɪl] *n* [as part of name] isla *f*; *literary* [island] ínsula *f*.

Isle of Man *n*: the ~ la isla de Man.

Isle of Wight [-waɪt] *n*: the ~ la isla de Wight.

isn't ['ɪznt] = **is not**.

ISO (*abbr of* **International Standards Organization**) *n* ISO *f*, *organización internacional de normalización*.

isobar ['aɪsəbɑːr] *n* isobara *f*.

isolate ['aɪsəleɪt] *vt* **-1.** to ~ sb (from) [physically] aislar a alguien (de); [socially] marginar a alguien (de). **-2.** MED: to ~ sb poner a alguien en cuarentena. **-3.** CHEM & ELEC: to ~ sthg (from) aislar algo (de).

isolated ['aɪsəleɪtɪd] *adj* aislado(da).

isolation [aɪsə'leɪʃn] *n* [solitariness] aislamiento *m*; **in** ~ [alone] en soledad; [separately] aisladamente.

isolationism [,aɪsə'leɪʃənɪzm] *n* aislacionismo *m*.

isosceles triangle [aɪ'sɒsɪliːz-] *n* triángulo *m* isósceles.

isotope ['aɪsətəʊp] *n* isótopo *m*.

Israel ['ɪzreɪəl] *n* Israel.

Israeli [ɪz'reɪlɪ] ◇ *adj* israelí. ◇ *n* israelí *m y f*.

Israelite ['ɪzrəlaɪt] ◇ *adj* israelita. ◇ *n* israelita *m y f*.

issue ['ɪʃuː] ◇ *n* **-1.** [important subject] cuestión *f*, tema *m*; **at** ~ en cuestión, a tratar; **to make an** ~ **of sthg** darle demasiada importancia a algo. **-2.** [of newspaper, magazine] número *m*, edición *f*. **-3.** [of stamps, shares, banknotes] emisión *f*. ◇ *vt* **-1.** [decree] promulgar; [statement, warning] hacer público(ca). **-2.** [stamps, shares, banknotes] emitir, poner en circulación. **-3.** [passport, document]: **to** ~ **sthg to sb, to** ~ **sb with sthg** expedir algo a alguien. ◇ *vi fml*: **to** ~ (**from**) surgir (de).

Istanbul [,ɪstæn'bʊl] *n* Estambul.

ISTC (*abbr of* **Iron and Steels Confederation**) *n sindicato británico de obreros de la siderurgia*.

isthmus ['ɪsməs] *n* istmo *m*.

it [ɪt] *pron* **-1.** [referring to specific thing or person - subj] él *m*, ella *f*; [- direct object] lo *m*, la *f*; [- indirect object] le; ~ **is in my hand** está en mi mano; ~ **broke** se rompió; **did you find** ~? ¿lo encontraste?; **give** ~ **to me** dámelo; **I like** ~ me gusta; **he gave** ~ **a kick** le dio una patada. **-2.** (*with prepositions*) él *m*, ella *f*; [- meaning "this matter" etc] ello; **as if his life depended on** ~ como si le fuera la vida en ello; **in** ~ dentro; **give this bone to** ~ dale este hueso; **have you been to** ~ **before?** ¿has estado antes?; **he's good at** ~ se le da bien; **on** ~ encima; **to talk about** ~ hablar de él/ella/ello; **under/beneath** ~ debajo; **beside** ~ al lado; **from/of** ~ de él/ella/ello; **over** ~ por encima. **-3.** (*impersonal use*): ~ **was raining** llovía; ~ **is cold today** hace frío hoy; ~'**s two o'clock** son las dos;

who is ~? - it's Mary/me ¿quién es? - soy Mary/yo; **what day is** ~? ¿a qué (día) estamos hoy?; ~'**s the children who worry me most** son los niños lo que más me preocupa.

IT n abbr of **Information Technology**.

Italian [ɪ'tæljən] ◇ adj italiano(na). ◇ n **-1.** [person] italiano m, -na f. **-2.** [language] italiano m.

italic [ɪ'tælɪk] adj cursiva.
◆ **italics** npl cursiva f.

Italy ['ɪtəlɪ] n Italia.

itch [ɪtʃ] ◇ n picor m, picazón f. ◇ vi **-1.** [be itchy - person] tener picazón; [- arm, leg etc] picar. **-2.** fig [be impatient]: **to be ~ing to do sthg** estar deseando hacer algo.

itchy ['ɪtʃɪ] (compar **-ier**, superl **-iest**) adj que pica.

it'd ['ɪtəd] = **it would, it had**.

item ['aɪtəm] n **-1.** [in collection] artículo m; [on list, agenda] asunto m, punto m. **-2.** [article in newspaper] artículo m; **news ~** noticia f.

itemize, -ise ['aɪtəmaɪz] vt detallar.

itemized bill ['aɪtəmaɪzd-] n factura f detallada.

itinerant [ɪ'tɪnərənt] adj itinerante, ambulante.

itinerary [aɪ'tɪnərərɪ] (pl **-ies**) n itinerario m.

it'll [ɪtl] = **it will**.

ITN (abbr of **Independent Television News**) n agencia de noticias para los canales de la Independent Broadcasting Authority.

its [ɪts] poss adj su, sus (pl); **the dog broke ~ leg** el perro se rompió la pata.

it's [ɪts] = **it is, it has**.

itself [ɪt'self] pron **-1.** (reflexive) se; (after prep) sí mismo(ma); **with ~** consigo mismo(ma). **-2.** (for emphasis): **the town ~ is lovely** el pueblo en sí es bonito; **in ~** en sí.

ITV (abbr of **Independent Television**) n ITV f, canal privado de televisión en Gran Bretaña.

IUCD (abbr of **intrauterine contraceptive device**) n DIU m.

IUD (abbr of **intrauterine device**) n DIU m.

I've [aɪv] = **I have**.

IVF (abbr of **in vitro fertilization**) n fertilización in vitro.

ivory ['aɪvərɪ] ◇ adj [ivory-coloured] de color marfil, marfileño(ña). ◇ n marfil m. ◇ comp de marfil.

Ivory Coast n: **the ~** la Costa de Marfil.

ivory tower n torre f de marfil.

ivy ['aɪvɪ] n hiedra f.

Ivy League n Am grupo de ocho prestigiosas universidades del este de los EEUU.

j (pl **j's** OR **js**), **J** (pl **J's** OR **Js**) [dʒeɪ] n [letter] j f, J f.

JA (abbr of **judge advocate**) auditor de guerra.

J/A abbr of **joint account**.

jab [dʒæb] (pt & pp **-bed**, cont **-bing**) ◇ n Br inf [injection] pinchazo m. ◇ vt: **to ~ sthg into** clavar algo en; **to ~ sthg at** apuntarle algo a. ◇ vi: **to ~ at sthg/sb** intentar golpear algo/a alguien.

jabber ['dʒæbər] ◇ vt farfullar. ◇ vi charlotear.

jack [dʒæk] n **-1.** [device] gato m. **-2.** [playing card] ≃ sota f.
◆ **jack in** vt sep Br inf mandar a paseo.
◆ **jack up** vt sep **-1.** [lift with a jack] levantar con gato. **-2.** [force up] subir.

jackal ['dʒækəl] n chacal m.

jackdaw [dʒækdɔː] n grajilla f.

jacket ['dʒækɪt] n **-1.** [garment] chaqueta f, americana f, saco m Amer. **-2.** [potato skin] piel f. **-3.** [book cover] sobrecubierta f. **-4.** Am [of record] cubierta f.

jacket potato n patata f asada con piel.

jackhammer ['dʒæk,hæmər] n Am martillo m neumático.

jack-in-the-box n caja f sorpresa.

jack knife n navaja f.
◆ **jack-knife** vi derrapar la parte delantera.

jack-of-all-trades (pl **jacks-of-all-trades**) n persona que sabe un poco de todo.

jack plug n (enchufe m de) clavija f.

jackpot ['dʒækpɒt] n (premio m) gordo m.

Jacobean [,dʒækə'bɪən] adj de la época de Jacobo I.

Jacobite ['dʒækəbaɪt] ◇ adj jacobita. ◇ n jacobita m y f.

Jacuzzi® [dʒə'kuːzɪ] n jacuzzi® m.

jade [dʒeɪd] ◇ adj [jade-coloured] jade (inv). ◇ comp de jade. ◇ n **-1.** [stone] jade m. **-2.** [colour] color m jade.

jaded ['dʒeɪdɪd] adj [tired] agotado(da); [bored] hastiado(da).

JAG (*abbr of* **Judge Advocate General**) *auditor general del ejército.*

jagged ['dʒægɪd] *adj* dentado(da).

jaguar ['dʒægjʊəʳ] *n* jaguar *m*.

jail [dʒeɪl] ◇ *n* cárcel *f*. ◇ *vt* encarcelar.

jailbird ['dʒeɪlbɜːd] *n inf* preso *m*, -sa *f* reincidente.

jailbreak ['dʒeɪlbreɪk] *n* fuga *f*, evasión *f*.

jailer ['dʒeɪləʳ] *n* carcelero *m*, -ra *f*.

Jakarta [dʒəˈkɑːtə] *n* Djakarta.

jam [dʒæm] (*pt & pp* **-med**, *cont* **-ming**) ◇ *n* **-1.** [preserve] mermelada *f*. **-2.** [of traffic] embotellamiento *m*, atasco *m*. **-3.** *inf* [difficult situation]: **to get into/be in a ~** meterse/estar en un apuro. ◇ *vt* **-1.** [place roughly] meter a la fuerza. **-2.** [fix] sujetar; **~ the door shut** atranca la puerta. **-3.** [pack tightly] apiñar. **-4.** [fill] abarrotar, atestar. **-5.** TELEC bloquear. **-6.** [cause to stick] atascar. **-7.** RADIO interferir. ◇ *vi* [stick] atascarse.

Jamaica [dʒəˈmeɪkə] *n* Jamaica.

Jamaican [dʒəˈmeɪkn] ◇ *adj* jamaicano(na). ◇ *n* jamaicano *m*, -na *f*.

jamb [dʒæm] *n* jamba *f*.

jamboree [ˌdʒæmbəˈriː] *n* **-1.** [celebration] juerga *f*. **-2.** [gathering of scouts] reunión *f* de niños exploradores.

jamming ['dʒæmɪŋ] *n* RADIO interferencia *f*.

jam-packed [-ˈpækt] *adj inf* a tope, atestado(da).

jam session *n* sesión improvisada de jazz o rock.

Jan. [dʒæn] (*abbr of* **January**) ene. *m*.

jangle ['dʒæŋgl] ◇ *n* tintineo *m*. ◇ *vt* hacer tintinear. ◇ *vi* tintinear.

janitor ['dʒænɪtəʳ] *n Am & Scot* conserje *m*, portero *m*.

January ['dʒænjʊərɪ] *n* enero *m*; *see also* **September**.

Japan [dʒəˈpæn] *n* (el) Japón.

Japanese [ˌdʒæpəˈniːz] (*pl inv*) ◇ *adj* japonés(esa). ◇ *n* [language] japonés *m*. ◇ *npl*: **the ~** los japoneses.

jape [dʒeɪp] *n dated* broma *f*.

jar [dʒɑːʳ] (*pt & pp* **-red**, *cont* **-ring**) ◇ *n* tarro *m*. ◇ *vt* [shake] sacudir. ◇ *vi* **-1.** [upset]: **to ~ (on sb)** poner los nervios de punta (a alguien). **-2.** [clash - opinions] discordar; [- colours] desentonar.

jargon ['dʒɑːgən] *n* jerga *f*.

jarring ['dʒɑːrɪŋ] *adj* **-1.** [upsetting] crispante. **-2.** [clashing - opinions] discordante; [- colours] que desentonan.

Jas. *abbr of* **James**.

jasmine ['dʒæzmɪn] *n* jazmín *m*.

jaundice ['dʒɔːndɪs] *n* ictericia *f*.

jaundiced ['dʒɔːndɪst] *adj fig* [attitude, view] desencantado(da).

jaunt [dʒɔːnt] *n* excursión *f*.

jaunty ['dʒɔːntɪ] (*compar* **-ier**, *superl* **-iest**) *adj* [hat, wave] airoso(sa); [person] vivaz, desenvuelto(ta).

Java ['dʒɑːvə] *n* Java.

javelin ['dʒævlɪn] *n* jabalina *f*.

jaw [dʒɔː] ◇ *n* [of person] mandíbula *f*; [of animal] quijada *f*. ◇ *vi inf* cotorrear.

jawbone ['dʒɔːbəʊn] *n* [of person] mandíbula *f*, maxilar *m*; [of animal] quijada *f*.

jay [dʒeɪ] *n* arrendajo *m*.

jaywalk ['dʒeɪwɔːk] *vi* cruzar la calle descuidadamente.

jaywalker ['dʒeɪwɔːkəʳ] *n* peatón *m* imprudente.

jazz [dʒæz] *n* **-1.** MUS jazz *m*. **-2.** *Am inf* [insincere talk] palabrería *f*.

◆ **jazz up** *vt sep inf* alegrar, avivar.

jazz band *n* conjunto *m* OR banda *f* de jazz.

jazz singer *n* cantante *m y f* de jazz.

jazzy ['dʒæzɪ] (*compar* **-ier**, *superl* **-iest**) *adj* [bright] llamativo(va).

JCR (*abbr of* **junior common room**) *n cuarto de estudiantes.*

JCS *n* (*abbr of* **Joint Chiefs of Staff**) ≃ Jemad *f*.

JD (*abbr of* **Justice Department**) *n ministerio de justicia estadounidense.*

jealous ['dʒeləs] *adj* **-1.** [envious]: **to be ~ (of)** tener celos OR estar celoso(sa) (de). **-2.** [possessive]: **to be ~ (of)** ser celoso(sa) (de).

jealously ['dʒeləslɪ] *adv* celosamente.

jealousy ['dʒeləsɪ] *n* (*U*) celos *mpl*.

jeans [dʒiːnz] *npl* vaqueros *mpl*, tejanos *mpl*, bluyínes *mpl Amer*.

Jedda ['dʒedə] *n* Yedda.

jeep [dʒiːp] *n* jeep *m*, campero *m Amer*.

jeer [dʒɪəʳ] ◇ *vt* [boo] abuchear; [mock] mofarse de. ◇ *vi*: **to ~ (at sb)** [boo] abuchear (a alguien); [mock] mofarse (de alguien).

◆ **jeers** *npl* [booing] abucheo *m*; [mocking] burlas *fpl*.

jeering ['dʒɪərɪŋ] *adj* burlón(ona).

Jehovah's Witness [dʒɪˈhəʊvəz-] *n* testigo *m y f* de Jehová.

Jello® ['dʒeləʊ] *n Am* jalea *f*, gelatina *f*.

jelly ['dʒelɪ] (*pl* **-ies**) *n* **-1.** [dessert] jalea *f*, gelatina *f*. **-2.** [jam] mermelada *f*.

jelly baby *n Br* caramelo en forma de muñeco.

jelly bean *n* gominola *f*.

jellyfish ['dʒelɪfɪʃ] (*pl inv* OR **-es**) *n* medusa *f*.

jelly roll *n Am* brazo *m* de gitano.

jemmy *Br* ['dʒemɪ], **jimmy** *Am* ['dʒɪmɪ] (*pl* **-ies**) *n* palanqueta *f*.

jeopardize, -ise ['dʒepədaɪz] *vt* poner en peligro, arriesgar.

jeopardy ['dʒepədɪ] *n*: **in** ~ en peligro.

jerk [dʒɜːk] ◇ *n* **-1.** [of head] movimiento *m* brusco; [of arm] tirón *m*; [of vehicle] sacudida *f*. **-2.** *v inf* [fool] idiota *m y f*, majadero *m*, -ra *f*. ◇ *vt* tirar bruscamente de; **he ~ed his head round** giró la cabeza bruscamente. ◇ *vi* [person] saltar; [vehicle] dar sacudidas.

jerkily ['dʒɜːkɪlɪ] *adv* [person] a trompicones; [vehicle] a tirones, a sacudidas.

jerkin ['dʒɜːkɪn] *n* jubón *m*.

jerky ['dʒɜːkɪ] (*compar* **-ier**, *superl* **-iest**) *adj* brusco(ca), espasmódico(ca).

jerry-built ['dʒerɪ-] *adj* mal construido(da).

jersey ['dʒɜːzɪ] (*pl* **jerseys**) *n* **-1.** [sweater] jersey *m*. **-2.** [cloth] tejido *m* de punto.

Jersey ['dʒɜːzɪ] *n* Jersey.

Jerusalem [dʒə'ruːsələm] *n* Jerusalén.

jest [dʒest] *n*: **in** ~ en broma *f*.

jester ['dʒestə'] *n* bufón *m*.

Jesuit ['dʒezjʊɪt] ◇ *adj* jesuita. ◇ *n* jesuita *m*.

Jesus (Christ) ['dʒiːzəs-] *n* Jesús *m*, Jesucristo *m*.

jet [dʒet] (*pt & pp* **-ted**, *cont* **-ting**) ◇ *n* **-1.** [aircraft] reactor *m*, jet *m*. **-2.** [stream] chorro *m*. **-3.** [nozzle, outlet] boca *f*, boquilla *f*. ◇ *vi* [travel by jet] volar en reactor.

jet-black *adj* negro(gra) azabache.

jet engine *n* reactor *m*.

jetfoil ['dʒetfɔɪl] *n* hidroplano *m*.

jet lag *n* aturdimiento tras un largo viaje en avión.

jet-propelled [-prə'peld] *adj* de propulsión a chorro.

jetsam ['dʒetsəm] → **flotsam**.

jet set *n*: **the** ~ la jet-set.

jettison ['dʒetɪsən] *vt* [cargo] deshacerse de; *fig* [ideas] desechar.

jetty ['dʒetɪ] (*pl* **-ies**) *n* embarcadero *m*, malecón *m*.

Jew [dʒuː] *n* judío *m*, -a *f*.

jewel ['dʒuːəl] ◇ *n* **-1.** [gemstone] piedra *f* preciosa. **-2.** [jewellery] joya *f*. **-3.** [in watch] rubí *m*. ◇ *comp* de joyas.

jeweller *Br*, **jeweler** *Am* ['dʒuːələ'] *n* joyero *m*, -ra *f*; ~**'s (shop)** joyería *f*.

jewellery *Br*, **jewelry** *Am* ['dʒuːəlrɪ] *n* (*U*) joyas *fpl*, alhajas *fpl*.

Jewess ['dʒuːɪs] *n* judía *f*.

Jewish ['dʒuːɪʃ] *adj* judío(a).

JFK *abbr of* **John Fitzgerald Kennedy International Airport**.

jib [dʒɪb] (*pt & pp* **-bed**, *cont* **-bing**) ◇ *n* **-1.** [beam] aguilón *m*. **-2.** [sail] foque *m*. ◇ *vi*: **to** ~ **at doing sthg** vacilar en hacer algo.

jibe [dʒaɪb] *n* pulla *f*, burla *f*.

Jidda ['dʒɪdə] = **Jedda**.

jiffy ['dʒɪfɪ] *n inf*: **in a** ~ en un santiamén.

Jiffy bag® *n* sobre *m* acolchado.

jig [dʒɪg] (*pt & pp* **-ged**, *cont* **-ging**) ◇ *n* giga *f*. ◇ *vi* danzar dando brincos.

jiggle ['dʒɪgl] *vt* menear.

jigsaw (puzzle) ['dʒɪgsɔː-] *n* rompecabezas *m inv*, puzzle *m*.

jihad [dʒɪ'hɑːd] *n* yihad *f*, guerra *f* santa.

jilt [dʒɪlt] *vt* dejar plantado(da).

jimmy *Am* = **jemmy**.

jingle ['dʒɪŋgl] ◇ *n* **-1.** [sound] tintineo *m*. **-2.** [song] *sintonía de anuncio publicitario*. ◇ *vi* tintinear.

jingoism ['dʒɪŋgəʊɪzm] *n* patriotería *f*.

jinx [dʒɪŋks] *n* gafe *m*.

jinxed ['dʒɪŋkst] *adj* gafado(da).

jitters ['dʒɪtəz] *npl inf*: **to have the** ~ estar como un flan.

jittery ['dʒɪtərɪ] *adj inf*: **to be** ~ estar como un flan.

jive [dʒaɪv] ◇ *n* **-1.** [dance] swing *m*. **-2.** *Am inf* [glib talk] palabrería *f*. ◇ *vi* bailar el swing.

job [dʒɒb] *n* **-1.** [paid employment] trabajo *m*, empleo *m*. **-2.** [task] trabajo *m*; **to do a good** ~ hacer un buen trabajo; **to make a good** ~ **of sthg** hacer un buen trabajo con algo. **-3.** [difficult task]: **we had a** ~ **doing it** nos costó trabajo hacerlo. **-4.** [function] cometido *m*, deber *m*. **-5.** *inf* [plastic surgery]: **she's had a nose** ~ se ha hecho la cirugía en la nariz. **-6.** *phr*: **that's just the** ~ *Br inf* eso me viene de perilla.

jobbing ['dʒɒbɪŋ] *adj Br* (que trabaja) a destajo.

job centre *n Br* oficina *f* de empleo.

job creation scheme *n* proyecto *m* de creación de empleo.

job description *n* descripción *f* de trabajo.

jobless ['dʒɒblɪs] ◇ *adj* desempleado(da). ◇ *npl*: **the** ~ los desempleados.

job lot *n* saldo *m*.

job satisfaction *n* satisfacción *f* en el trabajo.

job security *n* seguridad *f* OR garantía *f* en el trabajo.

jobsharing ['dʒɒbʃeərɪŋ] *n* (*U*) empleo *m* compartido.

Joburg ['dʒəubɜːg] *n inf* Johanesburgo.

jockey ['dʒɒkɪ] (*pl* -s) ◇ *n* jockey *m*, jinete *m*. ◇ *vi*: **to ~ for position** competir por colocarse en mejor posición.

jockstrap ['dʒɒkstræp] *n* suspensorio *m*.

jocular ['dʒɒkjʊləʳ] *adj* -1. [cheerful] bromista. -2. [funny] jocoso(sa).

jodhpurs ['dʒɒdpəz] *npl* pantalón *m* de montar.

Joe Public [dʒəʊ-] *n* el hombre de la calle.

jog [dʒɒg] (*pt* & *pp* -ged, *cont* -ging) ◇ *n* trote *m*; **to go for a ~** hacer footing. ◇ *vt* golpear ligeramente; **to ~ sb's memory** refrescar la memoria a alguien. ◇ *vi* hacer footing.

jogger ['dʒɒgəʳ] *n* persona *f* que hace footing.

jogging ['dʒɒgɪŋ] *n* footing *m*.

joggle ['dʒɒgl] *vt* menear.

Johannesburg [dʒəʊ'hænɪsbɜːg] *n* Johanesburgo.

john [dʒɒn] *n Am inf* [toilet] wáter *m*.

John Hancock [-'hænkɒk] *n Am inf* [signature] firma *f*.

join [dʒɔɪn] ◇ *n* juntura *f*. ◇ *vt* -1. [unite] unir, juntar, empatar *Amer*. -2. [get together with] reunirse con; **I'll ~ you for lunch** os acompaño a almorzar. -3. [become a member of - political party] afiliarse a; [- club] hacerse socio de; [- army] alistarse en. -4. [take part in] unirse a; **to ~ a queue** *Br*, **to ~ a line** *Am* meterse en la cola. ◇ *vi* -1. [rivers] confluir; [edges, pieces] unirse, juntarse. -2. [become a member - of political party] afiliarse; [- of club] hacerse socio; [- of army] alistarse.

◆ **join in** ◇ *vt fus* participar en, tomar parte en. ◇ *vi* participar, tomar parte.

◆ **join up** *vi* MIL alistarse.

joiner ['dʒɔɪnəʳ] *n* carpintero *m*.

joinery ['dʒɔɪnərɪ] *n* carpintería *f*.

joint [dʒɔɪnt] ◇ *adj* [responsibility] compartido(da); [effort] conjunto(ta); **~ owner** copropietario *m*, -ria *f*. ◇ *n* -1. ANAT articulación *f*. -2. [place where things are joined] juntura *f*, junta *f*, empate *m Amer*. -3. *Br* [of meat - uncooked] corte *m* para asar; [- cooked] asado *m*. -4. *inf pej* [place] antro *m*, garito *m*. -5. *drugs sl* porro *m*.

joint account *n* cuenta *f* conjunta.

Joint Chiefs of Staff *npl*: **the ~** la Junta de Jefes de Estado Mayor.

jointed ['dʒɔɪntɪd] *adj* articulado(da).

jointly ['dʒɔɪntlɪ] *adv* conjuntamente, en común.

joint ownership *n* copropiedad *f*.

joint-stock company *n* ≃ sociedad *f* anónima.

joint venture *n* empresa *f* colectiva OR conjunta.

joist [dʒɔɪst] *n* vigueta *f*.

jojoba [hə'həʊbə] *n* jojoba *f*.

joke [dʒəʊk] ◇ *n* -1. [funny story] chiste *m*; [funny action] broma *f*; **to go beyond a ~** pasarse de castaño oscuro; **to play a ~ on sb** gastarle una broma a alguien; **to be a ~** [person] ser un hazmerreír; [situation] ser una broma; **it's no ~** [not easy] no es (nada) fácil. ◇ *vi* bromear; **you're joking** estás de broma; **to ~ about sthg/with sb** bromear acerca de algo/con alguien.

joker ['dʒəʊkəʳ] *n* -1. [person] bromista *m y f*. -2. [playing card] comodín *m*.

jollity ['dʒɒlətɪ] *n* alegría *f*.

jolly ['dʒɒlɪ] (*compar* -ier, *superl* -iest) ◇ *adj* [person, laugh] alegre; [time] divertido(da). ◇ *adv Br inf* muy; **~ good!** ¡genial!

jolt [dʒəʊlt] ◇ *n lit* & *fig* sacudida *f*. ◇ *vt* -1. [jerk] sacudir, zarandear. -2. [shock] sacudir; **to ~ sb into doing sthg** acabar convenciendo a alguien de hacer algo. ◇ *vi* traquetear.

Joneses ['dʒəʊnzɪz] *npl*: **to keep up with the ~** no ser menos que el vecino.

Jordan ['dʒɔːdən] *n* Jordania; **the (River) ~** el (río) Jordán.

Jordanian [dʒɔː'deɪnjən] ◇ *adj* jordano(na). ◇ *n* jordano *m*, -na *f*.

joss stick [dʒɒs-] *n* varita *f* de incienso.

jostle ['dʒɒsl] ◇ *vt* empujar, dar empujones a. ◇ *vi* empujar, dar empujones.

jot [dʒɒt] (*pt* & *pp* -ted, *cont* -ting) *n* pizca *f*; **I don't care a ~** no me importa en lo más mínimo.

◆ **jot down** *vt sep* apuntar, anotar.

jotter ['dʒɒtəʳ] *n* bloc *m*.

jottings ['dʒɒtɪŋz] *npl* apuntes *mpl*, notas *fpl*.

journal ['dʒɜːnl] *n* -1. [magazine] revista *f*, boletín *m*. -2. [diary] diario *m*.

journalese [,dʒɜːnə'liːz] *n pej* jerga *f* periodística.

journalism ['dʒɜːnəlɪzm] *n* periodismo *m*.

journalist ['dʒɜːnəlɪst] *n* periodista *m y f*.

journey ['dʒɜːnɪ] (*pl* -s) *n* viaje *m*.

joust [dʒaʊst] *vi* justar.

jovial ['dʒəʊvjəl] *adj* jovial.

jowls [dʒaʊlz] *npl* carrillo *m*.

joy [dʒɔɪ] *n* -1. [happiness] alegría *f*, regocijo *m*. -2. [cause of joy] placer *m*, deleite *m*.

joyful ['dʒɔɪfʊl] *adj* alegre.

joyfully ['dʒɔɪfʊlɪ] *adv* alegremente, con júbilo.

joyous ['dʒɔɪəs] *adj* jubiloso(sa).

joyously ['dʒɔɪəslɪ] *adv* jubilosamente.

joyride ['dʒɔɪraɪd] (*pt* **-rode**, *pp* **-ridden**) *vi* darse una vuelta en un coche robado.

joyrider ['dʒɔɪraɪdə'] *n persona que se da una vuelta en un coche robado.*

joyrode ['dʒɔɪrəʊd] *pt →* **joyride.**

joystick ['dʒɔɪstɪk] *n* [of aircraft] palanca *f* de mando; [for video games, computers] joystick *m.*

JP *n abbr of* **justice of the peace.**

Jr. *Am (abbr of* **Junior)** jr.

JTPA (*abbr of* **Job Training Partnership Act**) *n programa gubernamental de formación profesional en Estados Unidos.*

jubilant ['dʒuːbɪlənt] *adj* [person] jubiloso(sa); [shout] alborozado(da).

jubilation [,dʒuːbɪ'leɪʃn] *n* júbilo *m*, alborozo *m.*

jubilee ['dʒuːbɪliː] *n* aniversario *m.*

Judaism ['dʒuː'deɪɪzm] *n* judaísmo *m.*

judder ['dʒʌdə'] *vi Br* vibrar.

judge [dʒʌdʒ] ◇ *n* [gen & JUR] juez *m y f.* ◇ *vt* **-1.** [gen & JUR] juzgar. **-2.** [age, distance] calcular. ◇ *vi* juzgar; **to ~ from** OR **by, judging from** OR **by** a juzgar por.

judg(e)ment ['dʒʌdʒmənt] *n* **-1.** JUR fallo *m*, sentencia *f*; **to pass ~ (on sb)** pronunciar sentencia (sobre alguien). **-2.** [opinion] juicio *m*; **to pass ~ (on sb/sthg)** pronunciarse (sobre alguien/algo). **-3.** [ability to form opinion] juicio *m*; **against my better ~** en contra de lo que me dicta el juicio. **-4.** [punishment] castigo *m.*

judg(e)mental [dʒʌdʒ'mentl] *adj pej* crítico(ca).

judicial [dʒuː'dɪʃl] *adj* judicial.

judiciary [dʒuː'dɪʃərɪ] *n*: **the ~** el poder judicial.

judicious [dʒuː'dɪʃəs] *adj* juicioso(sa).

judo ['dʒuːdəʊ] *n* judo *m.*

jug [dʒʌg] *n* jarra *f.*

juggernaut ['dʒʌgənɔːt] *n* camión *m* grande.

juggle ['dʒʌgl] ◇ *vt* **-1.** [throw] hacer juegos malabares con. **-2.** [rearrange] jugar con. ◇ *vi* hacer juegos malabares.

juggler ['dʒʌglə'] *n* malabarista *m y f.*

jugular (vein) ['dʒʌgjʊlə'-] *n* yugular *f.*

juice [dʒuːs] *n* **-1.** [from fruit, vegetables] zumo *m*, jugo *m.* **-2.** [from meat] jugo *m.*
♦ **juices** *npl* [in stomach] jugos *mpl* gástricos.

juicy ['dʒuːsɪ] (*compar* **-ier,** *superl* **-iest**) *adj* **-1.** [gen] jugoso(sa). **-2.** *inf* [scandalous] sabroso(sa), picante.

jujitsu [dʒuː'dʒɪtsuː] *n* jiu-jitsu *m.*

jukebox ['dʒuːkbɒks] *n* máquina *f* de discos.

Jul. (*abbr of* **July**) jul. *m.*

July [dʒuː'laɪ] *n* julio *m*; *see also* **September.**

jumble ['dʒʌmbl] ◇ *n* [mixture] revoltijo *m.* ◇ *vt*: **to ~ (up)** revolver.

jumble sale *n Br* rastrillo *m* benéfico.

jumbo jet [,dʒʌmbəʊ-] *n* jumbo *m.*

jumbo-sized *adj* gigante, de tamaño familiar.

jump [dʒʌmp] ◇ *n* **-1.** [act of jumping] salto *m.* **-2.** [fence in horsejumping] obstáculo *m.* **-3.** [rapid increase] incremento *m*, salto *m.* **-4.** *phr*: **to keep one ~ ahead of sb** mantener la delantera con respecto a alguien. ◇ *vt* **-1.** [cross by jumping] saltar. **-2.** *inf* [attack] asaltar. **-3.** *Am* [train, bus] colarse en. ◇ *vi* **-1.** [spring] saltar. **-2.** [make a sudden movement] sobresaltarse; **his heart ~ed** le dio un vuelco el corazón. **-3.** [increase rapidly] dar un salto, aumentar de golpe.
♦ **jump at** *vt fus* no dejar escapar.

jumped-up ['dʒʌmpt-] *adj Br inf pej* creído(da), presuntuoso(sa).

jumper ['dʒʌmpə'] *n* **-1.** *Br* [pullover] jersey *m*, chomba *f Amer.* **-2.** *Am* [dress] pichi *m.*

jump jet *n* avión *m* de despegue vertical.

jump leads *npl* cables *mpl* de empalme (*de batería*).

jump-start *vt* arrancar empujando.

jumpsuit ['dʒʌmpsuːt] *n* mono *m.*

jumpy ['dʒʌmpɪ] (*compar* **-ier,** *superl* **-iest**) *adj* inquieto(ta).

Jun, Jun. *abbr of* **June** jun. *m.*

Jun., Junr *Am (abbr of* **Junior**) jr.

junction ['dʒʌŋkʃn] *n* [of roads] cruce *m*; [of railway lines] empalme *m.*

junction box *n* caja *f* de empalmes.

juncture ['dʒʌŋktʃə'] *n fml*: **at this ~** en esta coyuntura.

June [dʒuːn] *n* junio *m*; *see also* **September.**

jungle ['dʒʌŋgl] *n lit & fig* selva *f.*

jungle gym *n Am barras de metal para que trepen los niños.*

junior ['dʒuːnjə'] ◇ *adj* **-1.** [officer] subalterno(na); [partner, member] de menor antigüedad, júnior (*inv*). **-2.** *Am* [after name] júnior (*inv*), hijo(ja). ◇ *n* **-1.** [person of lower rank] subalterno *m*, -na *f.* **-2.** [younger person]: **he's my ~** soy mayor que él. **-3.** *Am* SCH & UNIV *alumno de penúltimo año.*

junior college *n Am* colegio universitario para los dos primeros años.

junior doctor *n* médico que lleva poco ejerciendo.

junior high school *n Am* ≃ instituto *m* de bachillerato (*13-15 años*).

junior minister *n Br* subsecretario *m*, -ria *f*.

junior school *n Br* ≃ escuela *f* primaria.

juniper ['dʒuːnɪpəʳ] *n* enebro *m*.

junk [dʒʌŋk] *inf* ◇ *n* (*U*) [unwanted things] trastos *mpl*. ◇ *vt inf* tirar a la basura.

junket ['dʒʌŋkɪt] *n* **-1.** [pudding] dulce *m* de leche cuajada. **-2.** *inf pej* [trip] viaje lujoso pagado con dinero del estado.

junk food *n* (*U*) *pej* comida preparada poco nutritiva o saludable.

junkie ['dʒʌŋkɪ] *n drugs sl* yonqui *m y f*.

junk mail *n* (*U*) *pej* propaganda *f* (*por correo*).

junk shop *n* tienda *f* de objetos usados, cambalache *m Amer*.

Junr = Jun.

junta [*Br* 'dʒʌntə, *Am* 'hʊntə] *n* junta *f* militar.

Jupiter ['dʒuːpɪtəʳ] *n* Júpiter *m*.

jurisdiction [,dʒʊərɪs'dɪkʃn] *n* jurisdicción *f*.

jurisprudence [,dʒʊərɪs'pruːdəns] *n* jurisprudencia *f*.

juror ['dʒʊərəʳ] *n* jurado *m*.

jury ['dʒʊərɪ] (*pl* **-ies**) *n* jurado *m*.

jury box *n* tribuna *f* del jurado.

jury service *n* servicio realizado como miembro de un jurado.

just [dʒʌst] ◇ *adv* **-1.** [recently]: **he has ~ left/moved** acaba de salir/mudarse. **-2.** [at that moment]: **we were ~ leaving when ...** justo íbamos a salir cuando ...; **I'm ~ about to do it** voy a hacerlo ahora; **I couldn't do it ~ then** no lo podía hacer en aquel momento; **~ as I was leaving** justo en el momento en que me salía. **-3.** [only, simply] sólo, solamente; "**~ add water**" "añada un poco de agua"; **~ a minute** OR **moment** OR **second** un momento. **-4.** [almost not] apenas; **I (only) ~ did it** conseguí hacerlo por muy poco. **-5.** [for emphasis]: **I ~ know it!** ¡estoy seguro!; **~ look what you've done!** ¡mira lo que has hecho! **-6.** [exactly, precisely] exactamente, precisamente; **~ what I need** justo lo que necesito; **~ here/ there** aquí/allí mismo. **-7.** [in requests]: **could you ~ open your mouth?** ¿podrías abrir la boca un momento, por favor? ◇ *adj* justo(ta).
◆ **just about** *adv* casi.

◆ **just as** *adv*: **~ as ... as** tan ... como, igual de ... que.

◆ **just now** *adv* **-1.** [a short time ago] hace un momento. **-2.** [at this moment] justo ahora, ahora mismo.

justice ['dʒʌstɪs] *n* justicia *f*; **to bring sb to ~** llevar a alguien ante los tribunales; **to do ~ to sthg** [to a job] estar a la altura de algo; [to a meal] hacerle los honores a algo.

Justice of the Peace (*pl* **Justices of the Peace**) *n* juez *m y f* de paz.

justifiable ['dʒʌstɪfaɪəbl] *adj* justificable.

justifiable homicide *n* ≃ homocidio *m* con eximente de defensa propia.

justifiably ['dʒʌstɪfaɪəblɪ] *adv* justificadamente.

justification [,dʒʌstɪfɪ'keɪʃn] *n* justificación *f*.

justify ['dʒʌstɪfaɪ] (*pt* & *pp* **-ied**) *vt*: **to ~ (sthg/doing sthg)** justificar (algo/el haber hecho algo).

justly ['dʒʌstlɪ] *adv* justamente.

justness ['dʒʌstnɪs] *n* justicia *f*.

jut [dʒʌt] (*pt* & *pp* **-ted**, *cont* **-ting**) *vi*: **to ~ (out)** sobresalir.

jute [dʒuːt] *n* yute *m*.

juvenile ['dʒuːvənaɪl] ◇ *adj* **-1.** JUR juvenil. **-2.** [childish] infantil. ◇ *n* JUR menor *m y f* (de edad).

juvenile court *n* tribunal *m* (tutelar) de menores.

juvenile delinquent *n* delincuente *m y f* juvenil.

juxtapose [,dʒʌkstə'pəʊz] *vt*: **to ~ sthg (with)** yuxtaponer algo (a).

juxtaposition [,dʒʌkstəpə'zɪʃn] *n* yuxtaposición *f*.

K

k (*pl* **k's** OR **ks**), **K** (*pl* **K's** OR **Ks**) [keɪ] *n* [letter] k *f*, K *f*.
◆ **K -1.** (*abbr of* **kilobyte(s)**) K. **-2.** *abbr of* **Knight**. **-3.** *abbr of* **thousand**.

Kabul ['kɑːbʊl] *n* Kabul.

kaftan ['kæftæn] *n* caftán *m*.

Kalahari Desert [,kæləˈhɑːrɪ-] *n*: **the** ~ el desierto de Kalahari.

kale [keɪl] *n* col *f* rizada.

kaleidoscope [kəˈlaɪdəskəʊp] *n lit* & *fig* caleidoscopio *m*, calidoscopio *m*.

kamikaze [,kæmɪˈkɑːzɪ] *n* kamikaze *m*.

Kampala [kæmˈpɑːlə] *n* Kampala.

Kampuchea [,kæmpuˈtʃɪə] *n* Kampuchea.

Kampuchean [,kæmpuˈtʃɪən] ◇ *adj* camboyano(na). ◇ *n* camboyano *m*, -na *f*.

kangaroo [,kæŋgəˈruː] *n* canguro *m*.

Kansas ['kænzəs] *n* Kansas.

kaolin ['keɪəlɪn] *n* caolín *m*.

kaput [kəˈpʊt] *adj inf* escacharrado(da).

karat ['kærət] *n Am* quilate *m*.

karate [kəˈrɑːtɪ] *n* kárate *m*.

Kashmir [kæʃˈmɪə] *n* Cachemira.

Katar = **Qatar**.

Katmandu [,kætmænˈduː] *n* Katmandú.

kayak ['kaɪæk] *n* kayac *m*.

Kazakhstan [,kæzækˈstɑːn] *n* (el) Kazajstán.

KB *n abbr of* **kilobyte**.

KC (*abbr of* **King's Counsel**) abogado del Estado.

kcal (*abbr of* **kilocalorie**) kcal.

kd (*abbr of* **knocked down**) derribado.

kebab [kɪˈbæb] *n* pincho *m* moruno, brocheta *f*.

kedgeree ['kedʒəriː] *n Br* (U) plato de arroz, pescado y huevo duro.

keel [kiːl] *n* quilla *f*; **on an even** ~ en equilibrio estable.
◆ **keel over** *vi* [ship] zozobrar; [person] desplomarse.

keen [kiːn] *adj* **-1.** [enthusiastic] entusiasta; **to be** ~ **on sthg** ser aficionado(da) a algo; **she is** ~ **on you** tú le gustas; **to be** ~ **to do** OR **on doing sthg** tener ganas de hacer algo. **-2.** [intense - interest, desire] profundo(da); [- competition] reñido(da). **-3.** [sharp - sense of smell, hearing, vision] agudo(da); [- eye, ear] fino(na); [- mind] agudo, penetrante.

keenly ['kiːnlɪ] *adv* **-1.** [intensely - interested] vivamente; [- contested] reñidamente. **-2.** [intently] atentamente.

keenness ['kiːnnɪs] *n* **-1.** [enthusiasm] entusiasmo *m*. **-2.** [of interest] intensidad *f*, viveza *f*; [of competition] porfía *f*, lo reñido. **-3.** [sharpness] agudeza *f*.

keep [kiːp] (*pt* & *pp* **kept**) ◇ *vt* **-1.** [maintain in a particular place or state or position] mantener; **to** ~ **sb waiting/awake** tener a alguien esperando/despierto. **-2.** [retain] quedarse con; ~ **the change** quédese con la vuelta. **-3.** [put aside, store] guardar. **-4.** [prevent]: **to** ~ **sb/sthg from doing sthg** impedir a alguien/algo hacer algo. **-5.** [detain] detener; **what kept you?** ¿por qué llegas tan tarde?; **to** ~ **sb waiting** hacer esperar a alguien. **-6.** [fulfil, observe - appointment] acudir a; [- promise, vow] cumplir, guardar. **-7.** [not disclose]: **to** ~ **sthg from sb** ocultar algo a alguien; **to** ~ **sthg to o.s.** no contarle algo a nadie. **-8.** [in writing - record, account] llevar; [- diary] escribir; [- note] tomar. **-9.** [own - animals] criar; [- shop] tener. **-10.** *phr*: **they** ~ **themselves to themselves** no tienen mucho trato con nadie.
◇ *vi* **-1.** [remain] mantenerse; **to** ~ **quiet** callarse. **-2.** [continue]: **to** ~ **doing sthg** [repeatedly] no dejar de hacer algo; [without stopping] continuar OR seguir haciendo algo; **to** ~ **going** seguir adelante. **-3.** [continue in a particular direction] continuar, seguir; **to** ~ **left/right** circular por la izquierda/derecha; **to** ~ **north/south** seguir hacia el norte/el sur. **-4.** [food] conservarse. **-5.** *Br* [be in a particular state of health] estar, andar; **how are you** ~**ing?** ¿qué tal estás?
◇ *n* [food, board etc] manutención *f*, sustento *m*; **to earn one's** ~ ganarse el pan.
◆ **keeps** *n*: **for** ~ para siempre.
◆ **keep at** *vt fus*: **to** ~ **at it** perseverar.
◆ **keep back** *vt sep* [information] ocultar; [money, salary] retener.
◆ **keep down** *vt sep* contener.
◆ **keep off** *vt fus*: "~ **off the grass**" "no pisar la hierba".
◆ **keep on** *vi* **-1.** [continue]: **to** ~ **on doing sthg** [continue to do] continuar OR seguir haciendo algo; [do repeatedly] no dejar de hacer algo. **-2.** [talk incessantly]: **to** ~ **on (about)** seguir dale que te pego (con).
◆ **keep on at** *vt fus Br* seguir dando la lata a.

◆ **keep out** ◇ *vt sep* no dejar pasar. ◇ *vi*: "~ **out**" "prohibida la entrada".

◆ **keep to** ◇ *vt fus* [follow] ceñirse a. ◇ *vt sep* [limit] limitar a.

◆ **keep up** ◇ *vt sep* mantener; **to ~ up appearances** guardar las apariencias. ◇ *vi* **-1.** [maintain pace, level etc] mantener el ritmo; **to ~ up with sb/sthg** seguir el ritmo de alguien/algo. **-2.** [stay in contact]: **to ~ up with sb** mantener contacto con alguien.

keeper ['ki:pər] *n* guarda *m y f*.

keep-fit *Br* ◇ *n* (U) ejercicios *mpl* de mantenimiento. ◇ *comp* [class, exercises] de mantenimiento; [enthusiast] de ejercicios de mantenimiento.

keeping ['ki:pɪŋ] *n* **-1.** [care]: **in sb's ~** al cuidado de alguien; **in safe ~** en lugar seguro. **-2.** [conformity, harmony]: **in/out of ~ (with)** en armonía/desacuerdo (con).

keepsake ['ki:pseɪk] *n* recuerdo *m*.

keg [keg] *n* barrilete *m*.

kelp [kelp] *n* varec *m*, alga *f* marina.

ken [ken] *n*: **to be beyond one's ~** resultar del todo incomprensible para uno.

kennel ['kenl] *n* **-1.** [for dog] caseta *f* del perro. **-2.** *Am* = **kennels**.

◆ **kennels** *npl Br* residencia *f* para perros.

Kentucky [ken'tʌkɪ] *n* Kentucky.

Kenya ['kenjə] *n* Kenia.

Kenyan ['kenjən] ◇ *adj* keniano(na). ◇ *n* keniano *m*, -na *f*.

kept [kept] *pt & pp* → **keep**.

kerb [kɜ:b] *n Br* bordillo *m*, cordón *m Amer*.

kerb crawler [-,krɔ:lər] *n Br conductor que busca prostitutas desde el coche*.

kerbstone ['kɜ:bstəʊn] *n Br* piedra *f* de bordillo.

kerfuffle [kə'fʌfl] *n Br inf* follón *m*.

kernel ['kɜ:nl] *n* [of nut, fruit] pepita *f*.

kerosene ['kerəsi:n] *n* queroseno *m*.

kestrel ['kestrəl] *n* cernícalo *m*.

ketch [ketʃ] *n* queche *m*.

ketchup ['ketʃəp] *n* ketchup *m*, catsup *m*.

kettle ['ketl] *n* tetera *f* para hervir, hervidor *m*.

kettledrum ['ketldrʌm] *n* timbal *m*.

key [ki:] ◇ *n* **-1.** [for lock] llave *f*. **-2.** [of typewriter, computer, piano] tecla *f*. **-3.** [explanatory list] clave *f*. **-4.** [solution, answer]: **the ~ (to)** la clave (de). **-5.** MUS [scale of notes] tono *m*. ◇ *adj* clave (*inv*).

◆ **key in** *vt sep* teclear.

keyboard ['ki:bɔ:d] ◇ *n* teclado *m*. ◇ *vt* teclear.

keyboarder ['ki:bɔ:dər] *n* teclista *m y f* (de ordenadores).

keyed up [ki:d-] *adj* nervioso(sa).

keyhole ['ki:həʊl] *n* ojo *m* de la cerradura.

keynote ['ki:nəʊt] ◇ *n* núcleo *m* fundamental. ◇ *comp*: ~ **speech** discurso *m* que marca la tónica.

keypad ['ki:pæd] *n* teclado *m* (*de teléfono, fax etc*).

keypunch ['ki:pʌntʃ] *n Am* perforadora *f*.

key ring *n* llavero *m*.

keystone ['ki:stəʊn] *n* **-1.** [stone] clave *f*. **-2.** [essential idea] piedra *f* angular.

keystroke ['ki:strəʊk] *n* pulsación *f* (*de tecla*).

kg (*abbr of* **kilogram**) kg *m*.

KGB *n* KGB *m*.

khaki ['kɑ:kɪ] ◇ *adj* caqui. ◇ *n* caqui *m*.

Khmer [kə'meər] ◇ *adj* jemer. ◇ *n* **-1.** [person] jemer *m y f*; ~ **Rouge** Jemer Rojo. **-2.** [language] jemer *m*.

kibbutz [kɪ'bʊts] (*pl* **kibbutzim** [,kɪbʊt'si:m] OR **-es**) *n* kibutz *m*.

kick [kɪk] ◇ *n* **-1.** [from person] patada *f*, puntapié *m*; [from animal] coz *f*. **-2.** *inf* [excitement]: **to do sthg for ~s** hacer algo para divertirse; **to get a ~ from sthg** disfrutar con algo. **-3.** *inf* [of drink]: **to have a ~** estar cantidad de fuerte. ◇ *vt* **-1.** [hit with foot] dar una patada OR un puntapié a. **-2.** *fig* [be angry with]: **I could have ~ed myself** estaba que me tiraba de los pelos. **-3.** *inf* [give up] dejar. ◇ *vi* [person] dar patadas; [animal] dar coces, cocear.

◆ **kick about**, **kick around** *vi Br inf* andar rondando por ahí.

◆ **kick off** *vi* **-1.** [football] hacer el saque inicial. **-2.** *inf* [start activity] empezar.

◆ **kick out** *vt sep inf* echar, poner de patitas en la calle.

◆ **kick up** *vt fus inf* armar.

kickoff ['kɪkɒf] *n* saque *m* inicial.

kick-start *vt* arrancar.

kid [kɪd] (*pt & pp* **-ded**, *cont* **-ding**) ◇ *n* **-1.** *inf* [child] crío *m*, -a *f*, chavalín *m*, -ina *f*. **-2.** *inf* [young person] chico *m*, -ca *f*, chaval *m*, -la *f*, pibe *m*, -ba *f Amer*. **-3.** [young goat] cabrito *m*. **-4.** [leather] cabritilla *f*. ◇ *comp inf* [brother, sister] menor, pequeño(ña). ◇ *vt inf* **-1.** [tease] tomar el pelo a. **-2.** [delude]: **to ~ o.s.** hacerse ilusiones. ◇ *vi inf*: **to be kidding** estar de broma; **no kidding!** [honestly] ¡en serio!; [really] ¡no me digas!

kiddie, **kiddy** ['kɪdɪ] (*pl* **-ies**) *n inf* crío *m*, -a *f*.

kid gloves *npl*: **to treat** OR **handle sb with ~** tratar a alguien con guante blanco.

kidnap ['kɪdnæp] (*Br pt & pp* **-ped**, *cont*

-ping, *Am pt* & *pp* -ed, *cont* -ing) *vt* secuestrar, raptar, plagiar *Amer*.

kidnapper *Br*, **kidnaper** *Am* ['kɪdnæpə'] *n* secuestrador *m*, -ra *f*, raptor *m*, -ra *f*, plagiario *m*, -ria *f Amer*.

kidnapping *Br*, **kidnaping** *Am* ['kɪdnæpɪŋ] *n* secuestro *m*, rapto *m*, plagio *m Amer*.

kidney ['kɪdnɪ] (*pl* **kidneys**) *n* ANAT & CULIN riñón *m*.

kidney bean *n* judía *f* pinta.

kidney machine *n* riñón *m* artificial.

Kilimanjaro [ˌkɪlɪmən'dʒɑːrəʊ] *n* Kilimanjaro.

kill [kɪl] ◇ *vt* -1. [gen] matar, ultimar *Amer*; my feet are ~ing me! ¡cómo me duelen los pies!; **to ~ time** matar el tiempo. -2. *fig* [cause to end, fail] poner fin a. -3. [occupy]: **to ~ time** matar el tiempo. ◇ *vi* matar. ◇ *n* -1. [killing] matanza *f*. -2. [dead animal] pieza *f*, presa *f*.
◆ **kill off** *vt sep* -1. [cause death of] exterminar. -2. *fig* [cause to end, fail] poner fin a.

killer ['kɪlə'] *n* -1. [person, animal] asesino *m*, -na *f*. -2. [disease] enfermedad *f* mortal.

killer whale *n* orca *f*.

killing ['kɪlɪŋ] ◇ *adj inf* [very funny] matador(ra). ◇ *n* asesinato *m*; **to make a ~** *inf* hacer su agosto, forrarse.

killjoy ['kɪldʒɔɪ] *n* aguafiestas *m inv* y *f inv*.

kiln [kɪln] *n* horno *m*.

kilo ['kiːləʊ] (*pl* -s) (*abbr of* **kilogram**) *n* kilo *m*.

kilo- [kɪlə] *prefix* kilo-.

kilobyte ['kɪləbaɪt] *n* kilobyte *m*.

kilocalorie ['kɪlə,kælərɪ] *n* kilocaloría *f*.

kilogram(me) ['kɪləgræm] *n* kilogramo *m*.

kilohertz ['kɪləhɜːtz] (*pl inv*) *n* kilohercio *m*.

kilojoule ['kɪlədʒuːl] *n* kilojulio *m*.

kilometre *Br* ['kɪlə,miːtə'], **kilometer** *Am* [kɪ'lɒmɪtə'] *n* kilómetro *m*.

kilowatt ['kɪləwɒt] *n* kilovatio *m*.

kilt [kɪlt] *n* falda *f* escocesa.

kimono [kɪ'məʊnəʊ] (*pl* -s) *n* kimono *m*.

kin [kɪn] → **kith**.

kind [kaɪnd] ◇ *adj* [person, gesture] amable; [thought] considerado(da); **would you be so ~ as to ...?** ¿sería usted tan amable de ...? ◇ *n* tipo *m*, clase *f*; **a ~ of** una especie de; **~ of** *Am inf* un poco; **coffee of a ~** un tipo de café que no es gran cosa; **they're two of a ~** son tal para cual; **in ~** [payment] en especie.

kindergarten ['kɪndə,gɑːtn] *n* jardín *m* de infancia.

kind-hearted [-'hɑːtɪd] *adj* bondadoso(sa).

kindle ['kɪndl] *vt* -1. [fire] encender. -2. *fig* [idea, feeling] despertar.

kindling ['kɪndlɪŋ] *n* (*U*) leña *f* menuda, astillas *fpl*.

kindly ['kaɪndlɪ] (*compar* -ier, *superl* -iest) ◇ *adj* amable, bondadoso(sa). ◇ *adv* -1. [gently, favourably] amablemente; **to look ~ on sthg/sb** mirar algo/a alguien con buenos ojos. -2. [please]: **will you ~ ...?** ¿sería tan amable de ...? -3. *phr*: **not to take ~ to sthg** no tomarse algo bien.

kindness ['kaɪndnɪs] *n* -1. [gentleness] amabilidad *f*. -2. [helpful act] favor *m*.

kindred ['kɪndrɪd] *adj* [similar] afín; **~ spirit** alma *f* gemela.

kinetic [kɪ'netɪk] *adj* cinético(ca).

kinfolk(s) ['kɪnfəʊk(s)] *Am* = **kinsfolk**.

king [kɪŋ] *n* rey *m*.

kingdom ['kɪŋdəm] *n* reino *m*.

kingfisher ['kɪŋ,fɪʃə'] *n* martín *m* pescador.

kingpin ['kɪŋpɪn] *n* -1. TECH clavija *f* maestra. -2. *fig* [person] persona *f* clave.

king-size(d) *adj* [cigarette] extra largo; [bed, pack] gigante.

kink [kɪŋk] *n* [in rope] retorcimiento *m*; [in hair] rizo *m*.

kinky ['kɪŋkɪ] (*compar* -ier, *superl* -iest) *adj inf* morboso(sa), pervertido(da).

kinsfolk ['kɪnzfəʊk] *npl* parientes *mpl*.

kinship ['kɪnʃɪp] *n* -1. [family relationship] parentesco *m*. -2. [closeness] afinidad *f*.

kiosk ['kiːɒsk] *n* -1. [small shop] kiosco *m*, quiosco *m*. -2. *Br* [telephone box] cabina *f* telefónica.

kip [kɪp] (*pt* & *pp* -ped, *cont* -ping) *Br inf* ◇ *n* cabezadita *f*, sueñecito *m*. ◇ *vi* sobar, dormir.

kipper ['kɪpə'] *n* arenque *m* ahumado.

Kirk [kɜːk] *n Scot*: **the ~** la Iglesia de Escocia.

kirsch [kɪəʃ] *n* kirsch *m*.

kiss [kɪs] ◇ *n* beso *m*. ◇ *vt* besar; **to ~ sb goodbye** dar un beso de despedida a alguien. ◇ *vi* besarse.

kissagram ['kɪsəgræm] *n forma de felicitar a alguien contratando a una persona para que le bese.*

kiss curl *n Br* caracol *m* (*rizo*).

kiss of life *n* [to resuscitate sb]: **the ~** la respiración boca a boca.

kit [kɪt] (*pt* & *pp* -ted, *cont* -ting) *n* -1. [set] utensilios *mpl*, equipo *m*. -2. *Br* [clothes] equipo *m*. -3. [to be assembled] modelo *m* para armar, kit *m*.
◆ **kit out** *vt sep Br* equipar.

kit bag *n* macuto *m*, petate *m*.

kitchen ['kɪtʃɪn] *n* cocina *f*.

kitchenette [,kɪtʃɪ'net] *n* cocina *f* pequeña.

kitchen garden *n* huerto *m*.

kitchen sink *n* fregadero *m*.

kitchen unit *n* módulo *m* OR armario *m* de cocina.

kitchenware ['kɪtʃɪnweəʳ] *n* (*U*) batería *f* de cocina.

kite [kaɪt] *n* **-1.** [toy] cometa *f*, papalote *m* Amer. **-2.** [bird] milano *m*.

Kite mark *n* Br marchamo oficial de calidad.

kith [kɪθ] *n*: ~ **and kin** parientes *mpl* y amigos.

kitsch [kɪtʃ] *n* kitsch *m*, cursilería *f*.

kitten ['kɪtn] *n* gatito *m*.

kitty ['kɪtɪ] (*pl* **-ies**) *n* [for bills, drinks] fondo *m* común; [in card games] bote *m*, puesta *f*.

kiwi ['kiːwiː] *n* **-1.** [bird] kiwi *m*. **-2.** *inf* [New Zealander] persona *f* de Nueva Zelanda.

kiwi fruit *n* kiwi *m*.

KKK *abbr of* **Ku Klux Klan**.

klaxon ['klæksn] *n* bocina *f*, claxon *m*.

Kleenex® ['kliːneks] *n* kleenex® *m*, pañuelo *m* de papel.

kleptomaniac [,kleptə'meɪnɪæk] *n* cleptómano *m*, -na *f*.

km (*abbr of* **kilometre**) km.

km/h (*abbr of* **kilometres per hour**) km/h.

knack [næk] *n*: **it's easy once you've got the** ~ es fácil cuando le coges el tranquillo; **he has the** ~ **of appearing at the right moment** tiene el don de aparecer en el momento adecuado.

knacker ['nækəʳ] Br ◇ *n* [horse slaughterer] matarife *m*. ◇ *vt* *inf* dejar hecho(cha) polvo.

knackered ['nækəd] *adj* Br *inf* hecho(cha) polvo.

knapsack ['næpsæk] *n* mochila *f*.

knave [neɪv] *n* [playing card - in British pack] jota *f*; [- in Spanish pack] sota *f*.

knead [niːd] *vt* amasar.

knee [niː] *n* rodilla *f*; **to be on one's ~s** [kneeling] estar de rodillas; **to bring sb to their ~s** *fig* hacer hincar la rodilla a alguien.

kneecap ['niːkæp] *n* rótula *f*.

knee-deep *adj* [snow, water] que cubre hasta las rodillas; [person]: ~ **in water** con el agua hasta las rodillas.

knee-high *adj* que llega hasta las rodillas.

kneel [niːl] (Br *pt* & *pp* **knelt**, Am *pt* & *pp* **-ed** OR **knelt**) *vi* arrodillarse.

◆ **kneel down** *vi* arrodillarse.

knee-length *adj* hasta las rodillas.

knees-up *n* Br *inf* jolgorio *m*, juerga *f*.

knell [nel] *n* toque *m* de difuntos.

knelt [nelt] *pt* & *pp* → **kneel**.

knew [njuː] *pt* → **know**.

knickers ['nɪkəz] *npl* **-1.** Br [underwear] bragas *fpl*, calzonarios *mpl* Amer. **-2.** Am [knickerbockers] bombachos *mpl*.

knick-knack ['nɪknæk] *n* chuchería *f*, baratija *f*.

knife [naɪf] (*pl* **knives**) ◇ *n* cuchillo *m*. ◇ *vt* acuchillar.

knifing ['naɪfɪŋ] *n* apuñalamiento *m*.

knight [naɪt] ◇ *n* **-1.** HIST caballero *m*. **-2.** [knighted man] *hombre con el título de "Sir"*. **-3.** [in chess] caballo *m*. ◇ *vt* *conceder el título de "Sir" a*.

knighthood ['naɪthʊd] *n* **-1.** [present-day title] título *m* de "Sir". **-2.** HIST título *m* de caballero.

knit [nɪt] (*pt* & *pp* **knit** OR **-ted**, *cont* **-ting**) ◇ *adj*: **closely** OR **tightly** ~ muy unido(da). ◇ *vt* [make with wool] tejer, tricotar. ◇ *vi* **-1.** [with wool] hacer punto, tricotar. **-2.** [join] soldarse.

knitted ['nɪtɪd] *adj* de punto.

knitting ['nɪtɪŋ] *n* (*U*) **-1.** [activity] labor *f* de punto. **-2.** [work produced] punto *m*, calceta *f*.

knitting machine *n* máquina *f* de tricotar, tricotosa *f*.

knitting needle *n* aguja *f* de hacer punto.

knitting pattern *n* patrón *m* de punto.

knitwear ['nɪtweəʳ] *n* (*U*) género *m* OR ropa *f* de punto.

knives [naɪvz] *pl* → **knife**.

knob [nɒb] *n* **-1.** [on door, drawer, bedstead] pomo *m*. **-2.** [on TV, radio etc] botón *m*.

knobbly Br ['nɒblɪ] (*compar* **-ier**, *superl* **-iest**), **knobby** Am ['nɒbɪ] (*compar* **-ier**, *superl* **-iest**) *adj* nudoso(sa), con bultos.

knock [nɒk] ◇ *n* **-1.** [hit] golpe *m*. **-2.** *inf* [piece of bad luck] revés *m*. ◇ *vt* **-1.** [hit hard] golpear; **to** ~ **a nail into a wall** clavar un clavo en una pared; **to** ~ **one's head** darse en la cabeza; **to** ~ **sb over** [gen] hacer caer a alguien; AUT atropellar a alguien; **to** ~ **sthg over** tirar OR volcar algo, voltear algo Amer. **-2.** [make by hitting] hacer, abrir; **to** ~ **a hole in a wall** abrir un agujero en una pared. **-3.** *inf* [criticize] cargarse, poner por los suelos. ◇ *vi* **-1.** [on door]: **to** ~ (**at** OR **on**) llamar (a). **-2.** [car engine] traquetear.

◆ **knock about, knock around** *inf* ◇ *vt sep* [beat up] zurrar. ◇ *vi* **-1.** [travel a lot] rodar. **-2.** [spend time]: **to** ~ **about with sb** andar con alguien.

◆ **knock back** *vt sep inf* pimplarse.

◆ **knock down** *vt sep* **-1.** [subj: car, driver] atropellar. **-2.** [building] derribar. **-3.** [price] rebajar.

◆ **knock off** ◇ *vt sep* **-1.** [lower price by]: I'll ~ £5 off it lo rebajaré en cinco libras. **-2.** *Br inf* [steal] mangar, birlar. ◇ *vi inf* [stop working] parar de currar.

◆ **knock out** *vt sep* **-1.** [subj: person, punch] dejar sin conocimiento; [subj: drug] dejar dormido a. **-2.** [eliminate from competition] eliminar.

◆ **knock up** ◇ *vt sep* [make hurriedly] hacer de prisa. ◇ *vi* TENNIS pelotear.

knocker ['nɒkə'] *n* [on door] aldaba *f*.

knocking ['nɒkɪŋ] *n* **-1.** (*U*) [on door etc] golpes *mpl*. **-2.** *inf* [criticism] palos *mpl*, críticas *fpl*.

knock-kneed [-'niːd] *adj* patizambo(ba).

knock-on effect *n Br* reacción *f* en cadena.

knockout ['nɒkaʊt] *n* K.O. *m*.

knockout competition *n Br* competición *f* por el sistema de eliminación.

knock-up *n* TENNIS peloteo *m*.

knot [nɒt] (*pt & pp* **-ted**, *cont* **-ting**) ◇ *n* **-1.** [gen] nudo *m*; **to tie/untie a ~** hacer/deshacer un nudo. **-2.** [of people] corrillo *m*. ◇ *vt* anudar.

knotted ['nɒtɪd] *adj* anudado(da).

knotty ['nɒtɪ] (*compar* **-ier**, *superl* **-iest**) *adj* intrincado(da).

know [nəʊ] (*pt* **knew**, *pp* **known**) ◇ *vt* **-1.** [gen]: **to ~ (that)** saber (que); [language] saber hablar; **to ~ how to do sthg** saber hacer algo; **to get to ~ sthg** enterarse de algo; **to let sb ~ (about)** avisar a alguien (de). **-2.** [be familiar with - person, place] conocer; **to get to ~ sb** llegar a conocer a alguien. ◇ *vi* **-1.** [have knowledge] saber; **to ~ of** OR **about sthg** saber algo, estar enterado(da) de algo; **you ~** [to emphasize] ¿sabes?; [to remind] ¡ya sabes!, ¡sí hombre!; **God** OR **Heaven ~s!** ¡sabe Dios!; **there is no ~ing ...** no hay modo de saber ...; **to ~ sthg backwards** saberse algo al dedillo; **I ~ better** a mí no me engaña; **not to ~ when one is well off** no saber la suerte que uno tiene. **-2.** [be knowledgeable]: **to ~ about sthg** saber de algo. ◇ *n*: **to be in the ~** estar enterado(da).

know-all *n Br* sabelotodo *m y f*, sabihondo *m*, -da *f*.

know-how *n* conocimientos *mpl*.

knowing ['nəʊɪŋ] *adj* cómplice.

knowingly ['nəʊɪŋlɪ] *adv* **-1.** [in knowing manner] con complicidad. **-2.** [intentionally] adrede.

know-it-all = **know-all**.

knowledge ['nɒlɪdʒ] *n* (*U*) conocimiento *m*; **it's common ~ that** es de dominio común que; **to my ~** que yo sepa, según tengo entendido; **to the best of my ~** por lo que yo sé.

knowledgeable ['nɒlɪdʒəbl] *adj* entendido(da).

known [nəʊn] ◇ *pp* → **know**. ◇ *adj* conocido(da).

knuckle ['nʌkl] *n* **-1.** ANAT nudillo *m*. **-2.** [of meat] jarrete *m*.

◆ **knuckle down** *vi* ponerse seriamente a trabajar; **to ~ down to sthg/to doing sthg** dedicarse seriamente a algo/a hacer algo.

◆ **knuckle under** *vi* pasar por el aro.

knuckle-duster *n* puño *m* americano.

KO (*abbr of* **knock-out**) K.O. *m*.

koala (bear) [kəʊ'ɑːlə-] *n* koala *m*.

kook [kuːk] *n Am inf* majara *m y f*, majareta *m y f*.

kooky ['kuːkɪ] (*compar* **-ier**, *superl* **-iest**) *adj Am inf* majara, majareta.

Koran [kɒ'rɑːn] *n*: **the ~** el Corán.

Korea [kə'rɪə] *n* Corea.

Korean [kə'rɪən] ◇ *adj* coreano(na). ◇ *n* **-1.** [person] coreano *m*, -na *f*. **-2.** [language] coreano *m*.

kosher ['kəʊʃə'] *adj* **-1.** [meat] *permitido por la religión judía*. **-2.** *inf* [reputable] limpio(pia), legal.

Kowait → **Kuwait**.

kowtow [,kaʊ'taʊ] *vi*: **to ~ (to)** arrastrarse OR rebajarse (ante).

Krakow ['krækaʊ] = **Crakow**.

Kremlin ['kremlɪn] *n*: **the ~** el Kremlin.

KS *abbr of* **Kansas**.

KT *abbr of* **Knight**.

Kuala Lumpur [,kwɑːlə'lʊmpə'] *n* Kuala Lumpur.

kudos ['kjuːdɒs] *n* prestigio *m*, gloria *f*.

Ku Klux Klan [kuːklʌks'klæn] *n*: **the ~** el Ku-Klux-Klan.

kumquat ['kʌmkwɒt] *n tipo de naranja china*.

kung fu [,kʌŋ'fuː] *n* kung-fu *m*.

Kurd [kɜːd] *n* kurdo *m*, -da *f*.

Kurdish ['kɜːdɪʃ] *adj* kurdo(da).

Kurdistan [kɜːdɪ'stɑːn] *n* (el) Kurdistán.

Kuwait [kjuː'weɪt] *n* Kuwait.

Kuwaiti [kjuː'weɪtɪ] ◇ *adj* kuwaití. ◇ *n* kuwaití *m y f*.

kW (*abbr of* **kilowatt**) kw.

KY *abbr of* **Kentucky**.

L

l¹ (*pl* **l's** OR **ls**), **L** (*pl* **L's** OR **Ls**) [el] *n* [letter]
l *f*, L *f*.
◆ **L -1.** *abbr of* **lake. -2.** (*abbr of* **large**) G.
-3. (*abbr of* **left**) izq. **-4.** (*abbr of* **learner**) L.

L:
En Gran Bretaña, la letra "L" pegada a la
parte trasera de un vehículo indica que el
conductor todavía no tiene carné de conducir pero que va acompañado por alguien
que sí lo tiene

---

l² (*abbr of* **litre**) l.

la [lɑː] *n* MUS la *f*.

La *abbr of* **Louisiana**.

LA -1. *abbr of* **Los Angeles. -2.** *abbr of*
Louisiana.

L.A. (*abbr of* **Los Angeles**) *n* Los Ángeles.

lab [læb] *inf* = **laboratory**.

label ['leɪbl] (*Br pt* & *pp* **-led,** *cont* **-ling,** *Am
pt* & *pp* **-ed,** *cont* **-ing**) ◇ *n* **-1.** [identification]
etiqueta *f*. **-2.** [of record] sello *m* discográfico, casa *f* discográfica. ◇ *vt* **-1.** [fix label to]
etiquetar. **-2.** *usu pej* [describe]: **to ~ sb (as)**
calificar OR etiquetar a alguien (de).

labor *etc Am* = **labour** *etc*.

laboratory [*Br* lə'bɒrətrɪ, *Am* 'læbrə,tɔːrɪ] (*pl
-ies) ◇ *n* laboratorio *m*. ◇ *comp* de laboratorio.

Labor Day *n Am* Día *m* del Trabajador (*1
de septiembre*).

laborious [lə'bɔːrɪəs] *adj* laborioso(sa).

labor union *n Am* sindicato *m*.

labour *Br*, **labor** *Am* ['leɪbər] ◇ *n* **-1.** [hard
work] trabajo *m*. **-2.** [piece of work] esfuerzo
m. **-3.** [workers, work carried out] mano *f* de
obra. **-4.** [giving birth] parto *m*; **in ~** de parto. ◇ *vt* insistir sobre. ◇ *vi* **-1.** [work hard]
trabajar (duro). **-2.** [work with difficulty]: **to
~ at** OR **over** trabajar duro en. **-3.** [persist]:
to ~ under a delusion ser víctima de una
ilusión.
◆ **Labour** POL ◇ *adj* laborista. ◇ *n Br* (U)
los laboristas.

labour camp *n* campo *m* de trabajo.

labour costs *npl* coste *m* de mano de
obra.

laboured *Br*, **labored** *Am* ['leɪbəd] *adj*
[style] trabajoso(sa); [gait, breathing] peno-
so(sa), fatigoso(sa).

labourer *Br*, **laborer** *Am* ['leɪbərər] *n* obrero *m*, -ra *f*.

labour force *n* mano *f* de obra.

labour-intensive *adj* que emplea mucha
mano de obra.

labour market *n* mercado *m* de trabajo.

labour of love *n* trabajo *m* hecho por
amor al arte.

labour pains *npl* dolores *mpl* del parto.

Labour Party *n Br*: **the ~** el partido Laborista.

labour relations *npl* relaciones *fpl* laborales.

laboursaving *Br*, **laborsaving** *Am* ['leɪbə,
seɪvɪŋ] *adj* que ahorra trabajo.

Labrador ['læbrədɔːr] *n* **-1.** [dog] (perro *m*
de) terranova *m*, labrador *m*. **-2.** GEOGR Labrador.

labyrinth ['læbərɪnθ] *n* laberinto *m*.

lace [leɪs] ◇ *n* **-1.** [fabric] encaje *m*. **-2.**
[shoelace] cordón *m*. ◇ *comp* de encaje. ◇ *vt*
-1. [shoe, boot] atar. **-2.** [drink, food]: **coffee
~d with brandy** café con unas gotas de co-
ñac.
◆ **lace up** *vt sep* atar.

lacemaking ['leɪs,meɪkɪŋ] *n* labor *f* de encaje.

laceration [,læsə'reɪʃn] *n fml* laceración *f*.

lace-up ◇ *adj* de cordón. ◇ *n Br* zapato *m*
de cordón.

lack [læk] ◇ *n* falta *f*, carencia *f*; **for** OR
through ~ of por falta de; **no ~ of** abundancia de. ◇ *vt* carecer de. ◇ *vi*: **to be
~ing in** carecer de; **to be ~ing** faltar.

lackadaisical [,lækə'deɪzɪkl] *adj pej* apáti-
co(ca), desganado(da).

lackey ['lækɪ] (*pl* **lackeys**) *n pej* lacayo *m*.

lacklustre *Br*, **lackluster** *Am* ['læk,lʌstər]
adj pej soso(sa), apagado(da).

laconic [lə'kɒnɪk] *adj* lacónico(ca).

lacquer ['lækər] ◇ *n* laca *f*. ◇ *vt* **-1.** [wood,
metal] laquear, dar laca a. **-2.** [hair] poner
laca en.

lacrosse [lə'krɒs] *n* lacrosse *m*.

lactic acid ['læktɪk-] *n* ácido *m* láctico.

lacy ['leɪsɪ] (*compar* **-ier,** *superl* **-iest**) *adj* de
encaje.

lad [læd] *n* **-1.** *inf* [boy] chaval *m*, chavalo *m*
Amer. **-2.** *Br* [stable boy] mozo *m* de cuadra.

ladder ['lædər] ◇ *n* **-1.** [for climbing] escalera *f*. **-2.** *Br* [in tights] carrera *f*. ◇ *vt Br*

[tights] hacerse una carrera en. ◇ *vi Br*
[tights] tener una carrera.

laden ['leɪdn] *adj*: ~ **(with)** cargado(da)
(de).

la-di-da [,lɑːdɪ'dɑː] *adj inf pej* cursi, afecta-
do(da).

ladies *Br* ['leɪdɪz], **ladies' room** *Am n* lavabo *m* de señoras.

lading ['leɪdɪŋ] → bill.

ladle ['leɪdl] ◇ *n* cucharón *m*. ◇ *vt* servir
con cucharón.

lady ['leɪdɪ] (*pl* -ies) ◇ *n* -1. [woman] señora *f*. -2. [woman of high status] dama *f*. -3.
Am inf [to address woman] señora *f*. ◇ *comp*
mujer; ~ **doctor** doctora *f*.
◆ **Lady** *n* -1. [woman of noble rank] lady *f*.
-2. RELIG: **Our Lady** Nuestra Señora *f*.

ladybird *Br* ['leɪdɪbɜːd], **ladybug** *Am*
['leɪdɪbʌg] *n* mariquita *f*.

lady-in-waiting [-'weɪtɪŋ] (*pl* **ladies-in-
waiting**) *n* dama *f* de honor.

lady-killer *n inf* tenorio *m*, castigador *m*.

ladylike ['leɪdɪlaɪk] *adj* distinguido(da), elegante.

Ladyship ['leɪdɪʃɪp] *n*: **her/your** ~ su señoría *f*.

lag [læg] (*pt & pp* -ged, *cont* -ging) ◇ *vi* -1.
[move more slowly]: **to** ~ **(behind)** rezagarse.
-2. [develop more slowly]: **to** ~ **(behind)** andar a la zaga. ◇ *vt* revestir. ◇ *n* [timelag]
retraso *m*, demora *f*.

lager ['lɑːgəʳ] *n* cerveza *f* rubia.

lager lout *n Br* ≈ gamberro *m* de litrona.

lagging ['lægɪŋ] *n* revestimiento *m*.

lagoon [lə'guːn] *n* laguna *f*.

Lagos ['leɪgɒs] *n* Lagos.

lah-di-dah [,lɑːdɪ'dɑː] = la-di-da.

laid [leɪd] *pt & pp* → lay.

laid-back *adj inf* relajado(da), cachazu-
do(da).

lain [leɪn] *pp* → lie.

lair [leəʳ] *n* guarida *f*.

laissez-faire [,leɪseɪ'feəʳ] ◇ *adj* no intervencionista. ◇ *n* política *f* económica de
no intervencionismo.

laity ['leɪətɪ] *n* RELIG: **the** ~ los seglares, los
legos.

lake [leɪk] *n* lago *m*.

Lake District *n*: **the** ~ el Distrito de los Lagos al noroeste de Inglaterra.

Lake Geneva *n* lago *m* Leman.

lakeside ['leɪksaɪd] *adj* a orillas del lago.

lama ['lɑːmə] (*pl* -s) *n* lama *m*.

lamb [læm] *n* cordero *m*.

lambast [læm'bæst], **lambaste** [læm'beɪst]
vt vapulear.

lamb chop *n* chuleta *f* de cordero.

lambing ['læmɪŋ] *n* época del parto de las ove-
jas.

lambskin ['læmskɪn] *n* piel *f* de cordero.

lambswool ['læmzwʊl] ◇ *n* lana *f* de cordero. ◇ *comp* de lana de cordero.

lame [leɪm] *adj* -1. [person, horse] cojo(ja).
-2. [excuse, argument] pobre.

lamé ['lɑːmeɪ] *n* lamé *m*.

lame duck *n* -1. *fig* [person] inútil *m y f*;
[business] fracaso *m*. -2. *Am* [President] presidente *m* saliente.

lamely ['leɪmlɪ] *adv* poco convincentemen-
te.

lament [lə'ment] ◇ *n* lamento *m*. ◇ *vt* lamentar.

lamentable ['læməntəbl] *adj* lamentable.

laminated ['læmɪneɪtɪd] *adj* laminado(da).

lamp [læmp] *n* lámpara *f*.

lamplight ['læmplaɪt] *n* luz *f* de la lámpara.

lampoon [læm'puːn] ◇ *n* pasquín *m*, sátira
f. ◇ *vt* satirizar.

lamppost ['læmppəʊst] *n* farola *f*, farol
m.

lampshade ['læmpʃeɪd] *n* pantalla *f*.

lance [lɑːns] ◇ *n* lanza *f*. ◇ *vt* abrir con
lanceta.

lance corporal *n* cabo *m* interino, soldado
m de primero.

lancet ['lɑːnsɪt] *n* lanceta *f*.

Lancs. (*abbr of* Lancashire) *condado inglés*.

land [lænd] *n* -1. [gen] tierra *f*. -2. [prop-
erty] tierras *fpl*, finca *f*. ◇ *vt* -1. [unload] desembarcar. -2. [catch - fish] pescar. -3. *inf*
[obtain] conseguir, pillar. -4. [plane] hacer
aterrizar. -5. *inf* [place]: **to** ~ **sb in sthg** meter a alguien en algo; **to** ~ **sb with sth/sthg**
cargar a alguien con alguien/algo. ◇ *vi* -1.
[by plane] aterrizar, tomar tierra. -2. [fall]
caer. -3. [from ship] desembarcar.
◆ **land up** *vi inf*: **to** ~ **up (in)** acabar (en).

landed gentry ['lændɪd-] *npl*: **the** ~ los te-
rratenientes.

landing ['lændɪŋ] *n* -1. [of stairs] rellano *m*,
descansillo *m*. -2. [of aeroplane] aterrizaje *m*.
-3. [of person] desembarco *m*.

landing card *n* tarjeta *f* de desembarque.

landing craft *n* lancha *f* de desembarco.

landing gear *n* (U) tren *m* de aterrizaje.

landing stage *n* desembarcadero *m*.

landing strip *n* pista *f* de aterrizaje.

landlady ['lænd,leɪdɪ] (*pl* -ies) *n* casera *f*,
patrona *f*.

landlocked ['lændlɒkt] *adj* sin acceso al
mar.

landlord ['lændlɔːd] *n* **-1.** [of rented room or building] dueño *m*, casero *m*. **-2.** [of pub] patrón *m*.

landmark ['lændmɑːk] *n* **-1.** [prominent feature] punto *m* de referencia. **-2.** *fig* [in history] hito *m*, acontecimiento *m* decisivo.

landmine ['lændmaɪn] *n* mina *f* de tierra.

landowner ['lænd,əʊnəʳ] *n* terrateniente *m* y *f*.

Land Rover® [-,rəʊvəʳ] *n* todo-terreno *m*, Land Rover® *m*.

landscape ['lændskeɪʃ] ◇ *n* paisaje *m*. ◇ *vt* ajardinar.

landscape gardener *n* (jardinero *m*) paisajista *m*, (jardinera *f*) paisajista.

landslide ['lændslaɪd] ◇ *n* **-1.** [of earth, rocks] desprendimiento *m* de tierras. **-2.** POL victoria *f* arrolladora OR aplastante.

landslip ['lændslɪp] *n* pequeño desprendimiento *m* de tierras.

lane [leɪn] *n* **-1.** [road in country] camino *m*. **-2.** [road in town] callejuela *f*, callejón *m*. **-3.** [for traffic] carril *m*; *"keep in ~"* cartel que prohíbe el cambio de carril. **-4.** [in swimming pool, race track] calle *f*. **-5.** [for shipping, aircraft] ruta *f*.

language ['læŋgwɪdʒ] *n* **-1.** [gen] lengua *f*, idioma *m*. **-2.** [faculty or style of communication] lenguaje *m*.

language laboratory *n* laboratorio *m* de idiomas.

languid ['læŋgwɪd] *adj* lánguido(da).

languish ['læŋgwɪʃ] *vi* [in misery] languidecer; [in prison] pudrirse.

languorous ['læŋgərəs] *adj literary* lánguido(da).

lank [læŋk] *adj* lacio(cia).

lanky ['læŋkɪ] (*compar* **-ier**, *superl* **-iest**) *adj* larguirucho(cha), desgarbado(da).

lanolin(e) ['lænəlɪn] *n* lanolina *f*.

lantern ['læntən] *n* farol *m*.

Laos [laʊs] *n* Laos.

Laotian ['laʊʃən] ◇ *adj* laosiano(na). ◇ *n* **-1.** [person] laosiano *m*, -na *f*. **-2.** [language] laosiano *m*.

lap [læp] (*pt* & *pp* **-ped**, *cont* **-ping**) ◇ *n* **-1.** [of person] regazo *m*. **-2.** [of race] vuelta *f*. ◇ *vt* **-1.** [subj: animal] beber a lengüetadas. **-2.** [overtake in race] doblar. ◇ *vi* [water, waves] romper con suavidad.

◆ **lap up** *vt sep* **-1.** [drink] beber a lengüetadas. **-2.** *fig* [compliments, lies] tragarse; [information] asimilar con avidez.

laparoscopy [,læpə'rɒskəpɪ] (*pl* **-ies**) *n* laparoscopia *f*.

La Paz [læ'pæz] *n* La Paz.

lapdog ['læpdɒg] *n* [dog] perro *m* faldero.

lapel [lə'pel] *n* solapa *f*.

Lapland ['læplænd] *n* Laponia.

Lapp [læp] ◇ *adj* lapón(ona). ◇ *n* **-1.** [person] lapón *m*, -ona *f*. **-2.** [language] lapón *m*.

lapse [læps] ◇ *n* **-1.** [failing] fallo *m*, lapsus *m inv*. **-2.** [in behaviour] desliz *m*. **-3.** [of time] lapso *m*, período *m*. ◇ *vi* **-1.** [membership] caducar; [treatment, agreement] cumplir, expirar. **-2.** [standards, quality] bajar momentáneamente; [tradition] extinguirse, desaparecer. **-3.** [subj: person]: **to ~ into** terminar cayendo en.

lapsed [læpst] *adj* no practicante.

lap-top (computer) *n* COMPUT (pequeño) ordenador *m* portátil.

larceny ['lɑːsənɪ] *n* (*U*) hurto *m*, latrocinio *m*.

larch [lɑːtʃ] *n* alerce *m*.

lard [lɑːd] *n* manteca *f* de cerdo.

larder ['lɑːdəʳ] *n* despensa *f*.

large [lɑːdʒ] *adj* [gen] grande; [family] numeroso(sa); [sum] importante.

◆ **at large** *adv* **-1.** [as a whole] en general. **-2.** [escaped prisoner, animal] suelto(ta).

◆ **by and large** *adv* en general, por lo general.

largely ['lɑːdʒlɪ] *adv* [mostly] en gran parte; [chiefly] principalmente.

larger-than-life ['lɑːdʒəʳ-] *adj* exageradamente arquetípico(ca).

large-scale *adj* a gran escala.

largesse, **largess** *Am* [lɑː'dʒes] *n* generosidad *f*.

lark [lɑːk] *n* **-1.** [bird] alondra *f*. **-2.** *inf* [joke] broma *f*; **for a ~** para divertirse.

◆ **lark about** *vi* hacer el gamberro.

larva ['lɑːvə] (*pl* **-vae** [-viː]) *n* larva *f*.

laryngitis [,lærɪn'dʒaɪtɪs] *n* (*U*) laringitis *f inv*.

larynx ['lærɪŋks] (*pl* **larynxes**) *n* laringe *f*.

lasagna, **lasagne** [lə'zænjə] *n* (*U*) lasaña *f*.

lascivious [lə'sɪvɪəs] *adj* lascivo(va), lujurioso(sa).

laser ['leɪzəʳ] *n* láser *m*.

laser beam *n* rayo *m* láser.

laser printer *n* COMPUT impresora *f* láser.

laser show *n* juego *m* de luces láser.

lash [læʃ] ◇ *n* **-1.** [eyelash] pestaña *f*. **-2.** [blow with whip] latigazo *m*. ◇ *vt* **-1.** *lit* & *fig* [whip] azotar. **-2.** [tie]: **to ~ sthg (to)** amarrar algo (a).

◆ **lash out** *vi* **-1.** [physically]: **to ~ out (at** OR **against sb)** soltar un golpe (a alguien). **-2.** *Br inf* [spend money]: **to ~ out (on sthg)** derrochar el dinero (en algo).

lass [læs] *n* chavala *f*, muchacha *f*.

lasso [læ'su:] (*pl* **-s**, *pt* & *pp* **-ed**, *cont* **-ing**) ◇ *n* lazo *m*. ◇ *vt* coger con lazo, lazar.

last [lɑ:st] ◇ *adj* último(ma); ~ **month**/**Tuesday** el mes/martes pasado; ~ **but one** penúltimo(ma); ~ **but two** antepenúltimo(ma); ~ **night** anoche; **down to the** ~ **detail** hasta el último detalle. ◇ *adv* **-1.** [most recently] por última vez. **-2.** [finally, in final position] en último lugar; **he arrived** ~ llegó el último. ◇ *pron*: **the year**/**Saturday before** ~ no el año/sábado pasado, sino el anterior; **the** ~ **but one** el penúltimo (la penúltima); **the night before** ~ anteanoche; **the time before** ~ la vez anterior a la pasada; **to leave sthg till** ~ dejar algo para lo último. ◇ *n*: **the** ~ **I saw**/**heard of him** la última vez que lo vi/que oí de él. ◇ *vi* durar; [food] conservarse. ◆ **at (long) last** *adv* por fin.

last-ditch *adj* último(ma), desesperado(da).

lasting ['lɑ:stɪŋ] *adj* [peace, effect] duradero(ra); [mistrust] profundo(da).

lastly ['lɑ:stlɪ] *adv* **-1.** [to conclude] por último, para finalizar. **-2.** [at the end] al final.

last-minute *adj* de última hora.

last name *n* apellido *m*.

last post *n Br* **-1.** [postal collection] última recogida *f*. **-2.** MIL (toque *m* de) retreta *f*.

last rites *npl* últimos sacramentos *mpl*.

last straw *n*: **it was the** ~ fue la gota que colmó el vaso.

Last Supper *n*: **the** ~ la Última Cena.

last word *n*: **to have the** ~ tener la última palabra.

Las Vegas [ˌlæs'veɪgəs] *n* Las Vegas.

latch [lætʃ] ◇ *n* pestillo *m*; **the door is on the** ~ la puerta no tiene echado el pestillo. ◇ *vt* echar el pestillo a. ◆ **latch onto** *vt fus inf* [person] pegarse OR engancharse a; [idea] pillar, coger el tranquillo a.

latchkey ['lætʃki:] (*pl* **latchkeys**) *n* llavín *m*.

late [leɪt] ◇ *adj* **-1.** [not on time] con retraso; **to be** ~ **(for)** llegar tarde (a). **-2.** [near end of]: **in the** ~ **afternoon** al final de la tarde; **in** ~ **December** a finales de diciembre. **-3.** [later than normal] tardío(a); **we had a** ~ **breakfast** desayunamos tarde. **-4.** [former]: **the** ~ **president** el ex-presidente. **-5.** [dead] difunto(ta). ◇ *adv* **-1.** [gen] tarde. **-2.** [near end of period]: ~ **in the day** al final del día; ~ **in August** a finales de agosto. ◆ **of late** *adv* últimamente, recientemente.

latecomer ['leɪtˌkʌmər] *n* persona *f* que llega tarde.

lately ['leɪtlɪ] *adv* últimamente, recientemente.

lateness ['leɪtnɪs] *n* (*U*) retraso *m*.

late-night *adj* [late evening] nocturno(na), de noche; [after midnight] de madrugada; ~ **chemist's** farmacia *f* de guardia.

latent ['leɪtənt] *adj* latente.

later ['leɪtər] ◇ *adj* **-1.** [date, edition] posterior. **-2.** [near end of]: **in** ~ **life** al final de su vida; **in the** ~ **15th century** a finales del siglo XV. ◇ *adv* [at a later time]: ~ **(on)** más tarde.

lateral ['lætərəl] *adj* lateral.

latest ['leɪtɪst] ◇ *adj* [most recent] último(ma). ◇ *n*: **at the** ~ a más tardar, como muy tarde.

latex ['leɪteks] ◇ *n* látex *m*. ◇ *comp* de látex.

lath [lɑ:θ] *n* listón *m*.

lathe [leɪð] *n* torno *m*.

lather ['lɑ:ðər] ◇ *n* espuma *f* (de jabón). ◇ *vt* enjabonar. ◇ *vi* hacer espuma.

Latin ['lætɪn] ◇ *adj* **-1.** [temperament, blood] latino(na). **-2.** [studies] de latín. ◇ *n* [language] latín *m*.

Latin America *n* América *f* Latina, Latinoamérica *f*.

Latin American ◇ *adj* latinoamericano(na). ◇ *n* [person] latinoamericano *m*, -na *f*.

latitude ['lætɪtju:d] *n* **-1.** GEOGR latitud *f*. **-2.** *fml* [freedom] libertad *f*.

latrine [lə'tri:n] *n* letrina *f*.

latte ['læteɪ] *n* café *m* con leche (de máquina).

latter ['lætər] ◇ *adj* **-1.** [near to end] último(ma). **-2.** [second] segundo(da). ◇ *n*: **the** ~ éste, -ta *f*.

latter-day *adj* moderno(na).

latterly ['lætəlɪ] *adv* últimamente, recientemente.

lattice ['lætɪs] *n* enrejado *m*, celosía *f*.

lattice window *n* ventana *f* de celosía.

Latvia ['lætvɪə] *n* Letonia.

Latvian ['lætvɪən] ◇ *adj* letón(ona). ◇ *n* **-1.** [person] letón *m*, -ona *f*. **-2.** [language] letón *m*.

laudable ['lɔ:dəbl] *adj* loable.

laugh [lɑ:f] ◇ *n* **-1.** [sound] risa *f*; **to have the last** ~ ser el último en reírse. **-2.** *inf* [fun, joke]: **to have a** ~ reírse un rato; **he's a good** ~ es un cachondo; **to do sthg for** ~**s** OR **a** ~ hacer algo para divertirse OR en cachondeo. ◇ *vi* reírse. ◆ **laugh at** *vt fus* [mock] reírse de.

◆ **laugh off** *vt sep* [dismiss] restar importancia a, tomarse a risa.

laughable ['lɑːfəbl] *adj pej* [absurd] ridículo(la), risible.

laughing gas ['lɑːfɪŋ-] *n* gas *m* hilarante.

laughingstock ['lɑːfɪŋstɒk] *n* hazmerreír *m*.

laughter ['lɑːftər] *n* (*U*) risa *f*.

launch [lɔːntʃ] ◇ *n* -1. [of boat, ship] botadura *f*. -2. [of rocket, missile, product] lanzamiento *m*; [of book] publicación *f*. -3. [boat] lancha *f*. ◇ *vt* -1. [boat, ship] botar. -2. [missile, attack, product] lanzar; [book] publicar, sacar. -3. [strike] convocar; [company] fundar.

◆ **launch into** *vt fus* [attack] emprender; [lecture, explanation] enfrascarse en.

launching ['lɔːntʃɪŋ] *n* -1. [of boat, ship] botadura *f*. -2. [of rocket, missile, product] lanzamiento *m*; [of book] publicación *f*.

launch(ing) pad *n* plataforma *f* de lanzamiento.

launder ['lɔːndər] *vt* -1. [wash] lavar. -2. *inf* [money] blanquear.

laund(e)rette [lɔːn'dret], **Laundromat**® *Am* ['lɔːndrəmæt] *n* lavandería *f* (automática).

laundry ['lɔːndrɪ] (*pl* **-ies**) *n* -1. [clothes - about to be washed] colada *f*, ropa *f* sucia; [- newly washed] ropa *f* limpia. -2. [business, room] lavandería *f*.

laundry basket *n* cesto *m* de la ropa sucia.

laureate ['lɔːrɪət] → **poet laureate**.

laurels ['lɒrəlz] *npl*: **to rest on one's ~** dormirse en los laureles.

Lautro ['lɑːutrəu] (*abbr of* **Life Assurance and Unit Trust Regulatory Organization**) *n organismo británico que regula las compañías de seguros de vida y los fondos de inversión mobiliaria.*

lava ['lɑːvə] *n* lava *f*.

lavatory ['lævətrɪ] (*pl* **-ies**) *n* -1. [receptacle] wáter *m*. -2. [room] servicio *m*.

lavatory paper *n Br* papel *m* higiénico.

lavender ['lævəndər] ◇ *adj* [colour] de color lavanda. ◇ *n* -1. [plant] lavanda *f*, espliego *m*. -2. [colour] color *m* lavanda.

lavish ['lævɪʃ] ◇ *adj* -1. [person] pródigo(ga); [gifts, portions] muy generoso(sa); **to be ~ with** [praise, attention] ser pródigo en; [money] ser desprendido(da) con. -2. [sumptuous] espléndido(da), suntuoso(sa). ◇ *vt*: **to ~ sthg on** [praise, care] prodigar algo a; [time, money] gastar algo en.

lavishly ['lævɪʃlɪ] *adv* -1. [generously] gene-

rosamente. -2. [sumptuously] suntuosamente.

law [lɔː] ◇ *n* -1. [gen] ley *f*; **against the ~** contra la ley; **to break the ~** infringir OR violar la ley; **~ and order** el orden público; **the ~ of the jungle** la ley de la selva. -2. [set of rules, study, profession] derecho *m*. -3. *inf* [police]: **the ~** la poli. -4. *phr*: **to lay down the ~** imponer OR dictar la ley. ◇ *comp* [degree] en derecho; [student] de derecho; [firm] jurídico(ca).

law-abiding *adj* observante de la ley.

law-breaker *n* infractor *m*, -ra *f* de la ley.

law court *n* tribunal *m* de justicia.

lawful ['lɔːful] *adj fml* legal, lícito(ta).

lawfully ['lɔːfulɪ] *adv fml* legalmente, lícitamente.

lawless ['lɔːlɪs] *adj* -1. *fml* [illegal] ilegal, ilícito(ta). -2. [without laws] anárquico(ca).

Law Lords *npl Br* JUR: **the ~** los miembros de la Cámara de los Lores que forman el Tribunal Supremo.

lawmaker ['lɔːˌmeɪkər] *n* legislador *m*, -ra *f*.

lawn [lɔːn] *n* [grass] césped *m*.

lawnmower ['lɔːnˌməuər] *n* cortacésped *m* o *f*.

lawn party *n Am* recepción *f* al aire libre.

lawn tennis *n* tenis *m* sobre hierba.

law school *n* facultad *f* de derecho.

lawsuit ['lɔːsuːt] *n* pleito *m*.

lawyer ['lɔːjər] *n* abogado *m*, -da *f*.

lax [læks] *adj* [discipline, morals] relajado(da); [person] negligente.

laxative ['læksətɪv] *n* laxante *m*.

laxity ['læksətɪ], **laxness** ['læksnɪs] *n* [of discipline] relajamiento *m*, relajación *f*; [of person] negligencia *f*.

lay [leɪ] (*pt* & *pp* **laid**) ◇ *pt* → **lie**. ◇ *vt* -1. [put, place] colocar, poner. -2. [prepare - plans] hacer; **to ~ the table** poner la mesa. -3. [put in position - bricks] poner; [- cable, trap] tender; [- foundations] echar. -4. [egg] poner. -5. [blame, curse] echar. ◇ *adj* -1. [not clerical] laico(ca), seglar. -2. [untrained, unqualified] profano(na), lego(ga).

◆ **lay aside** *vt sep* -1. [store for future - food] guardar; [- money] ahorrar. -2. [put away] dejar a un lado.

◆ **lay before** *vt sep* [present] exponer, presentar.

◆ **lay down** *vt sep* -1. [set out] imponer, dictar. -2. [put down - arms] deponer, entregar; [- tools] dejar.

◆ **lay into** *vt fus inf* arremeter contra.

◆ **lay off** ◇ *vt sep* [make redundant] despedir. ◇ *vt fus inf* -1. [leave in peace] dejar en

paz. -2. [stop, give up]: **to ~ off (doing sthg)** dejar (de hacer algo).

◆ **lay on** *vt sep Br* [provide, supply] proveer.

◆ **lay out** *vt sep* **-1.** [arrange, spread out] disponer. **-2.** [plan, design] diseñar el trazado de.

◆ **lay over** *vi Am* hacer noche.

layabout ['leɪəbaʊt] *n Br inf* holgazán *m*, -ana *f*, gandul *m*, -la *f*, atorrante *m* y *f Amer*.

lay-by (*pl* **lay-bys**) *n Br* área *f* de descanso.

lay days *npl* plazo estipulado para la carga o descarga de un barco.

layer ['leɪə'] *n* **-1.** [of substance, material] capa *f*. **-2.** *fig* [level] nivel *m*.

layette [leɪ'et] *n* ajuar *m* (del bebé).

layman ['leɪmən] (*pl* **-men** [-mən]) *n* **-1.** [untrained, unqualified person] profano *m*, -na *f*, lego *m*, -ga *f*. **-2.** RELIG laico *m*, -ca *f*, seglar *m* y *f*.

lay-off *n* [redundancy] despido *m*.

layout ['leɪaʊt] *n* [of building, garden] trazado *m*, diseño *m*; [of text] presentación *f*, composición *f*.

layover ['leɪəʊvə'] *n Am* [gen] parada *f*; [of plane] escala *f*.

laze [leɪz] *vi*: **to ~ (about OR around)** gandulear, holgazanear.

lazily ['leɪzɪlɪ] *adv* perezosamente.

laziness ['leɪzɪnɪs] *n* [idleness] pereza *f*.

lazy ['leɪzɪ] (*compar* **-ier**, *superl* **-iest**) *adj* **-1.** [person] perezoso(sa), vago(ga), atorrante *Amer*. **-2.** [stroll, gesture] lento(ta); [afternoon] ocioso(sa).

lazybones ['leɪzɪbəʊnz] (*pl inv*) *n* gandul *m*, -la *f*, holgazán *m*, -ana *f*.

lb (*abbr of* **pound**) lb.

LB *abbr of* **Labrador**.

lbw (*abbr of* **leg before wicket**) *protección ilegal de los palos con la pierna en cricket*.

lc (*abbr of* **lower case**) cb.

LC (*abbr of* **Library of Congress**) *n biblioteca del Congreso de Estados Unidos*.

L/C *abbr of* **letter of credit**.

LCD *n abbr of* **liquid crystal display**.

Ld *abbr of* **Lord**.

L-driver *n Br conductor que lleva la L*.

LDS (*abbr of* **Licentiate in Dental Surgery**) *(titular de una) licenciatura superior de cirugía dental*.

LEA (*abbr of* **local education authority**) *n organismo responsable de educación en un área determinada de Gran Bretaña*.

lead¹ [liːd] (*pt* & *pp* **led**) ◇ *n* **-1.** [winning position] delantera *f*; **to be in OR have the ~** llevar la delantera, ir en cabeza. **-2.**

[amount ahead]: **to have a ~ of ...** llevar una ventaja de .... **-3.** [initiative, example] iniciativa *f*, ejemplo *m*; **to take the ~** [do sthg first] tomar la delantera. **-4.** THEATRE: **(to play) the ~** (hacer) el papel principal. **-5.** [clue] pista *f*. **-6.** [for dog] correa *f*. **-7.** [wire, cable] cable *m*.

◇ *adj* [singer, actor] principal; [story in newspaper] más destacado(da).

◇ *vt* **-1.** [be in front of] encabezar. **-2.** [take, guide, direct] conducir. **-3.** [be in charge of, take the lead in] estar al frente de, dirigir; **to ~ the way** enseñar el camino. **-4.** [life] llevar. **-5.** [cause]: **to ~ sb to do sthg** llevar a alguien a hacer algo.

◇ *vi* **-1.** [go]: **to ~ (to)** conducir OR llevar (a). **-2.** [give access to]: **to ~ (to OR into)** dar (a). **-3.** [be winning] ir en cabeza. **-4.** [result in]: **to ~ to** conducir a.

◆ **lead off** ◇ *vt fus* [subj: door, room] comunicar con. ◇ *vi* [road, corridor]: **to ~ off (from)** salir (de); [in card game, discussion] empezar.

◆ **lead up to** *vt fus* **-1.** [build up to] conducir a, preceder. **-2.** [plan to introduce] apuntar a.

lead² [led] ◇ *n* **-1.** [metal] plomo *m*. **-2.** [in pencil] mina *f*. ◇ *comp* [made of or with lead] de plomo.

leaded ['ledɪd] *adj* **-1.** [petrol] con plomo. **-2.** [window] emplomado(da).

leaden ['ledn] *adj* **-1.** *literary* [dark grey] plomizo(za). **-2.** *literary* [heavy] pesado(da). **-3.** [very dull] muy soso(sa), muy aburrido(da).

leader ['liːdə'] *n* **-1.** [of party etc, in competition] líder *m* y *f*. **-2.** *Br* [in newspaper] editorial *m*, artículo *m* de fondo.

leadership ['liːdəʃɪp] *n* (U) **-1.** [people in charge]: **the ~** los líderes, los dirigentes. **-2.** [position of leader] liderazgo *m*, mando *m*. **-3.** [qualities of leader] autoridad *f*, dotes *fpl* de mando.

lead-free [led-] *adj* sin plomo.

leading ['liːdɪŋ] *adj* **-1.** [major - athlete, writer] destacado(da). **-2.** [main - part] principal. **-3.** [at front] que va en cabeza.

leading article *n Br* editorial *m*, artículo *m* de fondo.

leading lady *n* primera actriz *f*.

leading light *n* cerebro *m*, cabeza *f* pensante.

leading man *n* primer actor *m*.

leading question *n* pregunta formulada de tal manera que sugiere una respuesta determinada.

lead pencil [led-] *n* lápiz *m* de mina.

lead poisoning [led-] *n* saturnismo *m*.

lectern

lead time [li:d-] *n* COMM·plazo *m* de entrega.

leaf [li:f] (*pl* **leaves**) *n* -1. [of tree, book] hoja *f*. -2. [of table] hoja *f* abatible.

◆ **leaf through** *vt fus* hojear.

leaflet ['li:flɪt] ◇ *n* [small brochure] folleto *m*; [piece of paper] octavilla *f*. ◇ *vt* repartir folletos en.

leafy ['li:fɪ] (*compar* -**ier**, *superl* -**iest**) *adj* frondoso(sa).

league [li:g] *n* [gen & SPORT] liga *f*; **to be in ~ with** [work with] estar confabulado con.

league table *n* clasificación *f*.

leak [li:k] ◇ *n* -1. [hole - in tank, bucket] agujero *m*; [- in roof] gotera *f*. -2. [escape] escape *m*, fuga *f*. -3. [disclosure] filtración *f*. ◇ *vt* [make known] filtrar. ◇ *vi* -1. [bucket] tener un agujero; [roof] tener goteras. -2. [water, gas] salirse, escaparse; **to ~ (out) from** salirse de.

◆ **leak out** *vi* -1. [liquid] salirse, escaparse. -2. *fig* [secret, information] trascender, filtrarse.

leakage ['li:kɪdʒ] *n* fuga *f*, escape *m*.

leaky ['li:kɪ] (*compar* -**ier**, *superl* -**iest**) *adj* [tank, bucket] con agujeros; [roof] con goteras.

lean [li:n] (*pt & pp* **leant** OR -**ed**) ◇ *adj* -1. [person] delgado(da). -2. [meat] magro(gra), sin grasa. -3. [winter, year] de escasez. ◇ *vt* [support, prop]: **to ~ sthg against** apoyar algo contra. ◇ *vi* -1. [bend, slope] inclinarse. -2. [rest]: **to ~ on/against** apoyarse en/contra.

leaning ['li:nɪŋ] *n*: ~ **(towards)** inclinación *f* (hacia OR por).

leant [lent] *pt & pp* → **lean**.

lean-to (*pl* **lean-tos**) *n* cobertizo *m*.

leap [li:p] (*pt & pp* **leapt** OR -**ed**) ◇ *n* salto *m*. ◇ *vi* [gen] saltar; [prices] dispararse.

◆ **leap at** *vt fus* no dejar escapar.

leapfrog ['li:pfrɒg] (*pt & pp* -**ged**, *cont* -**ging**) ◇ *n* pídola *f*. ◇ *vi* saltar.

leapt [lept] *pt & pp* → **leap**.

leap year *n* año *m* bisiesto.

learn [lɜ:n] (*pt & pp* -**ed** OR **learnt**) ◇ *vt* -1. [acquire knowledge of, memorize] aprender; **to ~ (how) to do sthg** aprender a hacer algo. -2. [hear]: **to ~ (that)** enterarse de (que). ◇ *vi* -1. [acquire knowledge] aprender. -2. [hear]: **to ~ (of** OR **about)** enterarse (de).

learned ['lɜ:nɪd] *adj* erudito(ta).

learner ['lɜ:nər] *n* principiante *m y f*.

learner (driver) *n* conductor *m* principiante OR en prácticas.

learning ['lɜ:nɪŋ] *n* saber *m*, erudición *f*.

learning curve *n* ritmo *m* de aprendizaje.

learnt [lɜ:nt] *pt & pp* → **learn**.

lease [li:s] ◇ *n* JUR contrato *m* de arrendamiento, arriendo *m*; **to give sb a new ~ of life** *Br* OR **on life** *Am* darle nueva vida a alguien. ◇ *vt* arrendar; **to ~ sthg from/to sb** arrendar algo de/a alguien.

leaseback ['li:sbæk] *n* arreglo por el que el comprador alquila lo comprado al vendedor.

leasehold ['li:shəʊld] ◇ *adj* arrendado(da). ◇ *adv* en arriendo.

leaseholder ['li:s,həʊldər] *n* arrendatario *m*, -ria *f*.

leash [li:ʃ] *n* [for dog] correa *f*.

least [li:st] (*superl of* **little**) ◇ *adj* [smallest in amount, degree] menor; **he earns the ~ money** es el que menos dinero gana. ◇ *pron* [smallest amount]: **the ~** lo menos; **it's the ~ (that) he can do** es lo menos que puede hacer; **not in the ~** en absoluto; **to say the ~** por no decir otra cosa. ◇ *adv* [to the smallest amount, degree] menos.

◆ **at least** *adv* por lo menos, al menos.

◆ **least of all** *adv* y menos (todavía).

◆ **not least** *adv fml* en especial.

leather ['leðər] ◇ *n* cuero *m*, piel *f*. ◇ *comp* [jacket, trousers] de cuero; [shoes, bag] de piel.

leatherette [,leðə'ret] *n* polipiel *f*, skay *m*.

leave [li:v] (*pt & pp* **left**) ◇ *vt* -1. [gen] dejar; **he left it to her to decide** dejó que ella decidiera; **to ~ sb alone** dejar a alguien en paz; **it ~s me cold** me da igual, me trae al fresco. -2. [go away from - house, room] salir de; [- wife, home] abandonar. -3. [do not take, forget] dejarse. -4. [bequeath]: **to ~ sb sthg, to ~ sthg to sb** dejarle algo a alguien. ◇ *vi* [bus, train, plane] salir; [person] irse, marcharse. ◇ *n* [time off] permiso *m*; **to be on ~** estar de permiso.

◆ **leave behind** *vt sep* -1. [abandon] dejar. -2. [forget] dejarse.

◆ **leave off** ◇ *vt sep* -1. [omit] no incluir en. -2. [stop]: **to ~ off (doing sthg)** dejar (de hacer algo). ◇ *vi*: **to carry on from where one left off** continuar desde donde uno lo había dejado.

◆ **leave out** *vt sep* excluir; **to feel left out** sentirse ignorado(da) OR excluido(da).

leave of absence *n* excedencia *f*.

leaves [li:vz] *pl* → **leaf**.

Lebanese [,lebə'ni:z] (*pl inv*) ◇ *adj* libanés(esa). ◇ *n* [person] libanés *m*, -esa *f*.

Lebanon ['lebənən] *n*: **(the) ~** (el) Líbano.

lecherous ['letʃərəs] *adj* lascivo(va), lujurioso(sa).

lechery ['letʃərɪ] *n* lascivia *f*, lujuria *f*.

lectern ['lektən] *n* atril *m*.

lecture ['lektʃər] ◇ n -1. [talk - at university] clase f; [- at conference] conferencia f; to give a ~ (on) [at university] dar una clase (sobre); [at conference] dar una conferencia (sobre). -2. [criticism, reprimand] sermón m. ◇ vt [scold] echar un sermón a. ◇ vi [give talk]: to ~ (on/in) [at university] dar una clase (de/en); [at conference] dar una conferencia (sobre/en).

lecture hall n [at university] aula f; [in conference centre] sala f de conferencias.

lecturer ['lektʃərər] n profesor m, -ra f de universidad.

lecture theatre n [at university] aula f; [in conference centre] sala f de conferencias.

led [led] pt & pp → lead[1].

LED (abbr of light-emitting diode) n LED m.

ledge [ledʒ] n -1. [of window] alféizar m, antepecho m. -2. [of mountain] saliente m.

ledger ['ledʒər] n libro m mayor.

lee [liː] n [shelter]: in the ~ of al abrigo de.

leech [liːtʃ] n lit & fig sanguijuela f.

leek [liːk] n puerro m.

leer [lɪər] ◇ n mirada f lasciva. ◇ vi: to ~ at sb mirar lascivamente a alguien.

Leeward Islands ['liːwəd-] npl: the ~ las islas de Sotavento.

leeway ['liːweɪ] n -1. [room to manoeuvre] libertad f (de acción OR movimientos). -2. [time lost]: to make up ~ recuperar el tiempo perdido.

left [left] ◇ adj -1. [remaining]: there's no wine ~ no queda vino. -2. [not right] izquierdo(da). ◇ adv a la izquierda. ◇ n: on OR to the ~ a la izquierda; keep to the ~! [on road signs] ¡circulen por la izquierda! ◆ **Left** n POL: the Left la izquierda.

left-hand adj de la izquierda, izquierdo(da); the ~ side el lado izquierdo, la izquierda.

left-hand drive ◇ adj con el volante a la izquierda. ◇ n vehículo que tiene el volante a la izquierda.

left-handed [-'hændɪd] ◇ adj -1. [person] zurdo(da). -2. [implement] para zurdos. -3. Am [compliment] con doble sentido. ◇ adv con la (mano) izquierda.

left-hander [-'hændər] n zurdo m, -da f.

Leftist POL ◇ adj izquierdista, de izquierdas. ◇ n izquierdista m y f.

left luggage (office) n Br consigna f.

leftover ['leftəʊvər] adj sobrante. ◆ **leftovers** npl sobras fpl.

left wing POL n izquierda f. ◆ **left-wing** adj de izquierdas, izquierdista.

left-winger n POL izquierdista m y f.

lefty ['leftɪ] (pl -ies) n -1. Br inf pej & POL izquierdoso m, -sa f. -2. Am [left-handed person] zurdo m, -da f.

leg [leg] n -1. [of person] pierna f, canilla f Amer; to be on one's last ~s estar en las últimas; you don't have a ~ to stand on no tienes en qué basarte; to pull sb's ~ tomarle el pelo a alguien. -2. [of animal] pata f. -3. [of trousers] pernera f, pierna f. -4. CULIN [of lamb, pork] pierna f; [of chicken] muslo m. -5. [of furniture] pata f. -6. [of journey] etapa f; [of tournament] fase f, manga f.

legacy ['legəsɪ] (pl -ies) n lit & fig legado m.

legal ['liːgl] adj -1. [concerning the law] jurídico(ca), legal. -2. [lawful] legal, lícito(ta).

legal action n pleito m, demanda f; to take ~ against sb presentar una demanda contra alguien.

legal aid n asistencia f de un abogado de oficio.

legality [liː'gælətɪ] n legalidad f.

legalize, -ise ['liːgəlaɪz] vt legalizar.

legally ['liːgəlɪ] adv legalmente; ~ responsible responsable ante la ley; ~ binding con fuerza de ley.

legal tender n moneda f de curso legal.

legation [lɪ'geɪʃn] n legación f.

legend ['ledʒənd] n lit & fig leyenda f.

legendary ['ledʒəndrɪ] adj legendario(ria).

leggings ['legɪŋz] npl mallas fpl.

leggy ['legɪ] (compar -ier, superl -iest) adj [woman] de largas y bonitas piernas.

legible ['ledʒəbl] adj legible.

legibly ['ledʒəblɪ] adv de manera legible.

legion ['liːdʒən] ◇ n lit & fig legión f. ◇ adj fml: to be ~ ser múltiples.

legionnaire's disease [,liːdʒə'neəz-] n legionella f.

legislate ['ledʒɪsleɪt] vi legislar; to ~ for/against dictar una ley a favor de/en contra de.

legislation [,ledʒɪs'leɪʃn] n legislación f.

legislative ['ledʒɪslətɪv] adj legislativo(va).

legislator ['ledʒɪsleɪtər] n legislador m, -ra f.

legislature ['ledʒɪsleɪtʃər] n legislatura f.

legitimacy [lɪ'dʒɪtɪməsɪ] n legitimidad f.

legitimate [lɪ'dʒɪtɪmət] adj legítimo(ma).

legitimately [lɪ'dʒɪtɪmətlɪ] adv legítimamente.

legitimize, -ise [lɪ'dʒɪtəmaɪz] vt legitimar.

legless ['leglɪs] adj Br inf [drunk] trompa, como una cuba.

legroom ['legrʊm] n (U) sitio m para las piernas.

leg-warmers [-,wɔːməz] npl calentadores mpl.

legwork ['legwɜːk] *n* (U): **to do the** ~ encargarse del trabajo de campo.

Leics (*abbr of* **Leicestershire**) *condado inglés.*

Leipzig ['laɪpzɪg] *n* Leipzig.

leisure [*Br* 'leʒər, *Am* 'liːʒər] *n* ocio *m*, tiempo *m* libre; **do it at your** ~ hazlo cuando tengas tiempo.

leisure centre *n* centro *m* deportivo y cultural.

leisurely [*Br* 'leʒəlɪ, *Am* 'liːʒərlɪ].◇ *adj* lento(ta). ◇ *adv* con calma, sin prisa.

leisure time *n* tiempo *m* libre, ocio *m*.

lemming ['lemɪŋ] *n* [animal] lemming *m*.

lemon ['lemən] *n* [fruit] limón *m*.

lemonade [ˌlemə'neɪd] *n* **-1.** *Br* [fizzy drink] gaseosa *f*. **-2.** [made with fresh lemons] limonada *f*.

lemon curd *n Br* crema *f* OR cuajada *f* de limón.

lemon juice *n* zumo *m* de limón.

lemon sole *n* platija *f*.

lemon squash *n Br* limonada *f*.

lemon squeezer *n* exprimidor *m*, exprimelimones *m inv*.

lemon tea *n* té *m* con limón.

lend [lend] (*pt & pp* **lent**) *vt* **-1.** [loan] prestar, dejar; **to** ~ **sb sthg, to** ~ **sthg to sb** prestarle algo a alguien. **-2.** [offer]: **to** ~ **sthg (to sb)** prestar algo (a alguien); **to** ~ **itself to sthg** prestarse a algo. **-3.** [add]: **to** ~ **sthg to** prestar algo a.

lender ['lendər] *n* prestamista *m y f*.

lending library ['lendɪŋ-] *n* biblioteca *f* pública.

lending rate ['lendɪŋ-] *n* tipo *m* de interés (en un crédito).

length [leŋθ] *n* **-1.** [measurement] longitud *f*, largo *m*; **what** ~ **is it?** ¿cuánto mide de largo?; **in** ~ de largo. **-2.** [whole distance, size] extensión *f*; **throughout the** ~ **and breadth of** a lo largo y ancho de. **-3.** [of swimming pool] largo *m*. **-4.** [piece - of string, wood] trozo *m* alargado; [- of cloth] largo *m*. **-5.** [duration] duración *f*. **-6.** *phr*: **to go to great** ~**s to do sthg** hacer lo imposible para hacer algo.
◆ **at length** *adv* **-1.** [eventually] por fin. **-2.** [in detail - speak] largo y tendido; [- discuss] con detenimiento.

lengthen ['leŋθən] ◇ *vt* alargar. ◇ *vi* alargarse.

lengthways ['leŋθweɪz] *adv* a lo largo.

lengthy ['leŋθɪ] (*compar* **-ier**, *superl* **-iest**) *adj* [stay, visit] extenso(sa); [discussions, speech] prolijo(ja), prolongado(da).

leniency ['liːnjənsɪ] *n* indulgencia *f*.

lenient ['liːnjənt] *adj* indulgente.

Leningrad ['lenɪngræd] *n* Leningrado.

lens [lenz] *n* **-1.** [in glasses] lente *f*; [in camera] objetivo *m*. **-2.** [contact lens] lentilla *f*, lente *f* de contacto.

lent [lent] *pt & pp* → **lend**.

Lent [lent] *n* Cuaresma *f*.

lentil ['lentɪl] *n* lenteja *f*.

Leo ['liːəʊ] *n* Leo *m*; **to be (a)** ~ ser Leo.

leopard ['lepəd] *n* leopardo *m*.

leopardess ['lepədɪs] *n* leopardo *m* hembra.

leotard ['liːətɑːd] *n* malla *f*.

leper ['lepər] *n* leproso *m*, -sa *f*.

leprechaun ['leprəkɔːn] *n* gnomo *m*, duende *m*.

leprosy ['leprəsɪ] *n* lepra *f*.

lesbian ['lezbɪən] ◇ *adj* lesbiano(na). ◇ *n* lesbiana *f*.

lesbianism ['lezbɪənɪzm] *n* lesbianismo *m*.

lesion ['liːʒn] *n* lesión *f*.

Lesotho [lə'səʊtəʊ] *n* Lesoto.

less [les] (*compar of* **little**) ◇ *adj* menos; ~ ... **than** menos ... que; ~ **and** ~ cada vez menos. ◇ *pron* menos; **the** ~ **you work, the** ~ **you earn** cuanto menos trabajas, menos ganas; **it costs** ~ **than you think** cuesta menos de lo que piensas; **no** ~ **than** nada menos que. ◇ *adv* menos; ~ **than five** menos de cinco; ~ **and** ~ cada vez menos. ◇ *prep* [minus] menos.

lessee [le'siː] *n fml* [of land, business premises] arrendatario *m*, -ria *f*; [of house, flat] inquilino *m*, -na *f*.

lessen ['lesn] ◇ *vt* aminorar, reducir. ◇ *vi* aminorarse, reducirse.

lesser [lesər] *adj* menor; **to a** ~ **extent** OR **degree** en menor grado.

lesson ['lesn] *n* **-1.** [class] clase *f*; **to give/take** ~**s (in)** dar/recibir clases (de). **-2.** [warning experience] lección *f*; **to teach sb a** ~ darle una buena lección a alguien.

lessor [le'sɔːr] *n fml* arrendador *m*, -ra *f*.

lest [lest] *conj fml* para que no; ~ **we forget** no sea que nos olvidemos.

let [let] (*pt & pp* **let**, *cont* **-ting**) *vt* **-1.** [allow]: **to** ~ **sb do sthg** dejar a alguien hacer algo; **to** ~ **sthg happen** dejar que algo ocurra; **she** ~ **her hair grow** se dejó crecer el pelo; **to** ~ **sb know sthg** avisar a alguien de algo; **to** ~ **go of sthg/sb** soltar algo/a alguien; **to** ~ **sthg/sb go** [release] liberar a algo/alguien, soltar a algo/alguien. **-2.** [in verb forms]: ~**'s go!** ¡vamos!; ~**'s see** veamos; ~ **him wait!** ¡déjale que espere! **-3.** [rent out - house, room] alquilar; [- land] arrendar; "**to** ~" "se alquila".
◆ **let alone** *adv* ni mucho menos.

◆ **let down** *vt sep* **-1.** [deflate] desinflar. **-2.** [disappoint] fallar, defraudar.

◆ **let in** *vt sep* **-1.** [admit] dejar entrar. **-2.** [leak] dejar pasar.

◆ **let in for** *vt sep*: to ~ o.s. in for sthg meterse en algo.

◆ **let in on** *vt sep*: to ~ sb in on sthg confiar OR revelar a alguien algo.

◆ **let off** *vt sep* **-1.** [excuse]: to ~ sb off sthg eximir a alguien de algo. **-2.** [not punish] perdonar. **-3.** [cause to explode - bomb] hacer estallar; [- gun] disparar.

◆ **let on** *vi*: don't ~ on! ¡no cuentes nada!

◆ **let out** *vt sep* **-1.** [allow to go out] dejar salir. **-2.** [emit - sound] soltar.

◆ **let up** *vi* **-1.** [heat, rain] cesar. **-2.** [person] parar.

letdown ['letdaʊn] *n inf* chasco *m*, decepción *f*.

lethal ['liːθl] *adj* letal, mortífero(ra).

lethargic [ləˈθɑːdʒɪk] *adj* [mood] letárgico(ca); [person] aletargado(da).

lethargy ['leθədʒɪ] *n* letargo *m*.

Letraset® ['letrəset] *n* letraset® *m*.

let's [lets] = **let us**.

letter ['letəʳ] *n* **-1.** [written message] carta *f*. **-2.** [of alphabet] letra *f*.

letter bomb *n* carta *f* bomba.

letterbox ['letəbɒks] *n Br* buzón *m*.

letterhead ['letəhed] *n* membrete *m*.

lettering ['letərɪŋ] *n* (*U*) [writing] letra *f*.

letter of credit *n* carta *f* de crédito.

letter opener *n* abrecartas *m inv*.

letter-perfect *adj Am* impecable.

letter quality *n* COMPUT calidad *f* de impresión alta.

letters patent *npl* patente *f*.

lettuce ['letɪs] *n* lechuga *f*.

letup ['letʌp] *n* tregua *f*, respiro *m*.

leuk(a)emia [luːˈkiːmɪə] *n* leucemia *f*.

levee ['levɪ] *n Am* [embankment] dique *m*.

level ['levl] (*Br pt & pp* -led, *cont* -ling, *Am pt & pp* -ed, *cont* -ing) ◇ *adj* **-1.** [equal in speed, score] igualado(da); [equal in height] nivelado(da); to be ~ (with sthg) estar al mismo nivel (que algo). **-2.** [flat - floor, field] liso(sa), llano(na); [- spoonful] raso(sa).
◇ *adv*: ~ (with) al mismo nivel OR altura (que); to fly ~ with the ground volar a ras de suelo; to draw ~ with sb llegar a la altura de alguien.
◇ *n* **-1.** [gen] nivel *m*; to be on a ~ (with) estar al mismo nivel (que). **-2.** *phr*: to be on the ~ *inf* ir en serio. **-3.** *Am* [spirit level] nivel *m* de burbuja de aire.
◇ *vt* **-1.** [make flat] allanar, alisar. **-2.** [demolish - building] derribar; [- forest] arrasar.

-3. [weapon]: to ~ sthg at apuntar (con) algo a. **-4.** [accusation, criticism]: to ~ sthg at OR against sb dirigir algo a alguien.

◆ **level off, level out** *vi* **-1.** [stabilize, slow down] estabilizarse. **-2.** [ground] nivelarse; [plane] enderezarse.

◆ **level with** *vt fus inf* ser sincero(ra) con.

level crossing *n Br* paso *m* a nivel.

level-headed [-ˈhedɪd] *adj* sensato(ta), equilibrado(da).

level pegging [-ˈpegɪŋ] *adj Br* to be ~ estar igualado(da).

lever [*Br* 'liːvəʳ, *Am* 'levəʳ] *n* **-1.** [handle, bar] palanca *f*. **-2.** *fig* [tactic] resorte *m*.

leverage [*Br* 'liːvərɪdʒ, *Am* 'levərɪdʒ] *n* (*U*) **-1.** [force] fuerza *f* de apalanque. **-2.** *fig* [influence] influencia *f*.

leviathan [lɪˈvaɪəθn] *n* leviatán *m*.

levitation [ˌlevɪˈteɪʃn] *n* levitación *f*.

levity ['levətɪ] *n* ligereza *f*.

levy ['levɪ] (*pt & pp* -ied) ◇ *n*: ~ (on) [financial contribution] contribución *f* (a OR para); [tax] recaudación *f* OR impuesto *m* (sobre). ◇ *vt* recaudar.

lewd [ljuːd] *adj* [person, look] lascivo(va); [behaviour, song] obsceno(na); [joke] verde.

lexical ['leksɪkl] *adj* léxico(ca).

LI *abbr of* **Long Island**.

liability [ˌlaɪəˈbɪlətɪ] (*pl* -ies) *n* **-1.** [hindrance] estorbo *m*. **-2.** [legal responsibility]: ~ (for) responsabilidad *f* (de OR por).

◆ **liabilities** *npl* FIN pasivo *m*, deudas *fpl*.

liable ['laɪəbl] *adj* **-1.** [likely]: that's ~ to happen eso pueda que ocurra. **-2.** [prone]: to be ~ to ser propenso(sa) a. **-3.** [legally responsible]: to be ~ (for) ser responsable (de).

liaise [lɪˈeɪz] *vi*: to ~ (with) estar en contacto (con); to ~ (between) servir de enlace (entre).

liaison [lɪˈeɪzɒn] *n* **-1.** [contact, co-operation]: ~ (with/between) relación *f* (con/entre), enlace *m* (con/entre). **-2.** [affair, relationship]: ~ (with/between) amorío *m* (con/entre).

liar ['laɪəʳ] *n* mentiroso *m*, -sa *f*, embustero *m*, -ra *f*.

Lib. *abbr of* **Liberal**.

libel ['laɪbl] (*Br pt & pp* -led, *cont* -ling, *Am pt & pp* -ed, *cont* -ing) ◇ *n* libelo *m*. ◇ *vt* publicar un libelo contra.

libellous *Br*, **libelous** *Am* ['laɪbələs] *adj* difamatorio(ria).

liberal ['lɪbərəl] ◇ *adj* **-1.** [tolerant] liberal. **-2.** [generous] generoso(sa). ◇ *n* liberal *m* y *f*.

◆ **Liberal** POL ◇ *adj* liberal. ◇ *n* (miembro *m* del partido) liberal *m* y *f*.

liberal arts *npl* letras *fpl*.
Liberal Democrat ◇ *adj* demócrata liberal. ◇ *n* (miembro *m* del partido) demócrata liberal *m* y *f*.
liberalize, -ise ['lɪbərəlaɪz] *vt* liberalizar.
liberal-minded [-'maɪndɪd] *adj* liberal.
Liberal Party *n*: **the ~** el partido Liberal.
liberate ['lɪbəreɪt] *vt* liberar.
liberation [,lɪbə'reɪʃn] *n* liberación *f*.
liberator ['lɪbəreɪtə'] *n* libertador *m*, -ra *f*.
Liberia [laɪ'bɪərɪə] *n* Liberia.
Liberian [laɪ'bɪərɪən] ◇ *adj* liberiano(na). ◇ *n* liberiano *m*, -na *f*.
libertine ['lɪbətiːn] *n* libertino *m*, -na *f*.
liberty ['lɪbətɪ] (*pl* **-ies**) *n* libertad *f*; **at ~** en libertad; **to be at ~ to do sthg** ser libre de hacer algo; **to take liberties (with sb)** tomarse demasiadas libertades (con alguien).
libido [lɪ'biːdəʊ] (*pl* **-s**) *n* libido *f*.
Libra ['liːbrə] *n* Libra *f*; **to be (a) ~** ser Libra.
librarian [laɪ'breərɪən] *n* bibliotecario *m*, -ria *f*.
librarianship [laɪ'breərɪənʃɪp] *n* biblioteconomía *f*.
library ['laɪbrərɪ] (*pl* **-ies**) *n* **-1.** [public institution] biblioteca *f*. **-2.** [private collection] colección *f*.
library book *n* libro *m* de biblioteca.
libretto [lɪ'bretəʊ] (*pl* **-s**) *n* libreto *m*.
Libya ['lɪbɪə] *n* Libia.
Libyan ['lɪbɪən] ◇ *adj* libio(bia). ◇ *n* libio *m*, -bia *f*.
lice [laɪs] *pl* → **louse**.
licence ['laɪsəns] ◇ *n* permiso *m*, licencia *f*; **under ~** con autorización OR permiso oficial. ◇ *vt Am* = **license**.
license ['laɪsəns] ◇ *vt* [person, organization] dar licencia a; [activity] autorizar. ◇ *n Am* = **licence**.
licensed ['laɪsənst] *adj* **-1.** [person]: **to be ~ to do sthg** estar autorizado(da) para hacer algo. **-2.** [object] registrado(da), con licencia. **-3.** *Br* [premises] autorizado(da) a vender alcohol.
licensee [,laɪsən'siː] *n* concesionario *m*, -ria *f*.
license plate *n Am* (placa *f* de) matrícula *f*.
licensing hours ['laɪsənsɪŋ-] *npl Br* horas en que un *pub* está autorizado a servir alcohol.

LICENSING HOURS:
Tradicionalmente, los horarios comerciales de los *pubs* están sujetos a una reglamentación muy estricta (ligada a la legislación sobre la venta de bebidas alcohólicas), aunque

ésta se volvió más flexible a partir de 1988. En lugar de abrir únicamente de las 11h 30 a las 14h 30 y de las 18h a las 23h, desde ese año los *pubs* pueden abrir de las 11h a las 23h excepto el domingo (de 11h a 15h y de 19h a 22h 30). En Escocia esta reglamentación no es tan estricta

licensing laws ['laɪsənsɪŋ-] *npl Br* leyes que controlan la venta de bebidas alcohólicas.
licentious [laɪ'senʃəs] *adj fml & pej* licencioso(sa).
lichen ['laɪkən] *n* liquen *m*.
lick [lɪk] ◇ *n* **-1.** [act of licking] lametón *m*, lametada *f*. **-2.** *inf* [small amount]: **a ~ of paint** una mano de pintura. ◇ *vt* **-1.** *lit & fig* lamer, lamber *Amer*; **to ~ one's lips** relamerse (los labios). **-2.** *inf* [defeat] dar una paliza a.
licorice ['lɪkərɪs] = **liquorice**.
lid [lɪd] *n* **-1.** [cover] tapa *f*, tapadera *f*. **-2.** [eyelid] párpado *m*.
lido ['liːdəʊ] (*pl* **-es**) *n* **-1.** *Br* [swimming pool] piscina *f* (al aire libre). **-2.** [beach] playa *f*.
lie [laɪ] (*pt sense 1* **lied**, *pt senses 2-5* **lay**, *pp sense 1* **lied**, *pp senses 2-5* **lain**, *cont all senses* **lying**) ◇ *n* mentira *f*; **to tell ~s** contar mentiras, mentir. ◇ *vi* **-1.** [tell lie] mentir; **to ~ to sb** mentirle a alguien. **-2.** [be horizontal] tumbarse, echarse; [be buried] yacer; **to be lying** estar tumbado(da). **-3.** [be situated] hallarse. **-4.** [be - solution, attraction] hallarse, encontrarse. **-5.** *phr*: **to ~ low** permanecer escondido(da).
◆ **lie about, lie around** *vi* estar OR andar tirado(da).
◆ **lie down** *vi* tumbarse, echarse; **to take sthg lying down** aceptar algo sin rechistar.
◆ **lie in** *vi Br* quedarse en la cama hasta tarde.
Liechtenstein ['lɪktən,staɪn] *n* Liechtenstein.
lie detector *n* detector *m* de mentiras.
lie-down *n Br* siesta *f*.
lie-in *n Br*: **to have a ~** quedarse en la cama hasta tarde.
lieu [ljuː, luː]
◆ **in lieu** *adv* a cambio; **in ~ of** en lugar de.
Lieut. (*abbr of* **lieutenant**) ≃ Tte.
lieutenant [*Br* lef'tenənt, *Am* luː'tenənt] *n* teniente *m*.
lieutenant colonel *n* teniente *m* coronel.
life [laɪf] (*pl* **lives**) ◇ *n* **-1.** [gen] vida *f*; **that's ~!** ¡así es la vida!; **for ~** de por vida, para toda la vida; **for the ~ of me** *inf* por

mucho que lo intento; **to breathe ~ into sthg** infundir una nueva vida a algo; **to come to ~** [thing] cobrar. vida; [person] reanimarse de pronto; **to lay down one's ~** entregar (uno) su vida; **to risk ~ and limb** jugarse el pellejo; **to scare the ~ out of sb** pegarle a alguien un susto de muerte; **to take sb's ~** acabar con la vida de alguien; **to take one's own ~** quitarse la vida. **-2.** *inf* [life imprisonment] cadena *f* perpetua. ◇ *comp* [member etc] vitalicio(cia).

life-and-death *adj* [situation] de vida o muerte; [struggle] a vida o muerte.

life annuity *n* renta *f* OR pensión *f* anual vitalicia.

life assurance = **life insurance**.

life belt *n* flotador *m*, salvavidas *m inv*.

lifeblood ['laɪfblʌd] *n* [source of strength] alma *f*, sustento *m*.

lifeboat ['laɪfbəʊt] *n* [on a ship] bote *m* salvavidas; [on shore] lancha *f* de salvamento.

lifeboatman ['laɪfbəʊtmən] (*pl* **-men** [-mən]) *n* socorrista *m y f* de la lancha de salvamento.

life buoy *n* flotador *m*, salvavidas *m inv*.

life expectancy [-ɪk'spektənsɪ] *n* expectativa *f* de vida.

lifeguard ['laɪfgʊːd] *n* socorrista *m y f*.

life imprisonment *n* cadena *f* perpetua.

life insurance *n* seguro *m* de vida.

life jacket *n* chaleco *m* salvavidas.

lifeless ['laɪflɪs] *adj* **-1.** [dead] sin vida. **-2.** [listless] insulso(sa).

lifelike ['laɪflaɪk] *adj* realista, natural.

lifeline ['laɪflaɪn] *n* **-1.** [rope] cuerda *f* OR cable *m* (de salvamento). **-2.** [something vital for survival] cordón *m* umbilical.

lifelong ['laɪflɒŋ] *adj* de toda la vida, de siempre.

life peer *n Br* noble británico con título no hereditario.

life preserver [-prɪˌzɜːvəʳ] *n Am* salvavidas *m inv*.

life raft *n* balsa *f* salvavidas.

lifesaver ['laɪfˌseɪvəʳ] *n* **-1.** [person] socorrista *m y f*. **-2.** *fig* [relief, help]: **it was a real ~** me salvó la vida, me sacó de un gran apuro.

life sentence *n* (condena *f* a) cadena *f* perpetua.

life-size(d) *adj* (de) tamaño natural.

lifespan ['laɪfspæn] *n* **-1.** [of person, animal, plant] vida *f*. **-2.** [of product, machine] vida *f*, duración *f*.

lifestyle ['laɪfstaɪl] *n* estilo *m* OR modo *m* de vida.

life-support system *n* aparato *m* de respiración artificial.

lifetime ['laɪftaɪm] *n* vida *f*.

lift [lɪft] ◇ *n* **-1.** [ride - in car etc] **to give sb a ~ (somewhere)** acercar OR llevar a alguien (a algún sitio). **-2.** *Br* [elevator] ascensor *m*, elevador *m Amer*. ◇ *vt* **-1.** [gen] levantar; **to ~ sthg down** bajar algo. **-2.** [plagiarize] copiar. ◇ *vi* **-1.** [be able to be lifted] levantarse, alzarse. **-2.** [disappear - mist] despejarse, levantarse.

lift-off *n* despegue *m*.

ligament ['lɪgəmənt] *n* ligamento *m*.

light [laɪt] (*pt & pp* **lit** OR **-ed**) ◇ *adj* **-1.** [gen] ligero(ra); [rain] fino(na); [traffic] escaso(sa). **-2.** [not strenuous - duties, responsibilities] simple; [- work] suave; [- punishment] leve. **-3.** [bright] luminoso(sa), lleno(na) de luz; **it's growing ~** se hace de día. **-4.** [pale - colour] claro(ra).

◇ *n* **-1.** [brightness, source of light] luz *f*. **-2.** [for cigarette, pipe] fuego *m*, lumbre *f*; **have you got a ~?** ¿tienes fuego? **-3.** [perspective]: **in the ~ of** *Br*, **in ~ of** *Am* a la luz de; **to see sthg/sb in a different ~** ver algo/a alguien de otra manera distinta. **-4.** *literary* [look in eyes] brillo *m*. **-5.** *phr*: **to come to ~** salir a la luz (pública); **to set ~ to** prender fuego a; **to see the ~** verlo claro; **to throw** OR **cast** OR **shed ~ on** arrojar luz sobre.

◇ *vt* **-1.** [ignite] encender. **-2.** [illuminate] iluminar.

◇ *adv* con poco equipaje.

◆ **light out** *vi Am inf* irse a escape.

◆ **light up** ◇ *vt sep* **-1.** [illuminate] iluminar. **-2.** [start smoking] encender. ◇ *vi* **-1.** [look happy] iluminarse, encenderse. **-2.** *inf* [start smoking] ponerse a fumar.

light aircraft (*pl inv*) *n* avión *m* de hélice.

light ale *n Br* tipo suave de cerveza rubia.

light bulb *n* bombilla *f*, foco *m Amer*.

light cream *n Am* nata *f* líquida.

lighted ['laɪtɪd] *adj* **-1.** [illuminated] iluminado(da). **-2.** [on fire] encendido(da).

light-emitting diode [-ɪ'mɪtɪŋ-] *n* diodo *m* emisor de luz.

lighten ['laɪtn] ◇ *vt* **-1.** [make brighter - room] iluminar; [- hair] aclarar. **-2.** [make less heavy] aligerar. ◇ *vi* **-1.** [brighten] aclararse. **-2.** [become happier, more relaxed] alegrarse.

lighter ['laɪtəʳ] *n* [cigarette lighter] encendedor *m*, mechero *m*.

light-fingered [-'fɪŋgəd] *adj inf* largo(ga) de uñas.

light-headed [-'hedɪd] *adj* mareado(da).

light-hearted [-'hɑːtɪd] *adj* **-1.** [cheerful] alegre. **-2.** [amusing] frívolo(la).

lighthouse ['laɪthaʊs, *pl* -haʊzɪz] *n* faro *m*.

light industry *n* industria *f* ligera.

lighting ['laɪtɪŋ] *n* iluminación *f*; **street ~** alumbrado *m* público.

lighting-up time *n* hora *f* de encendida del alumbrado público.

lightly ['laɪtlɪ] *adv* **-1.** [gently] suavemente. **-2.** [slightly] ligeramente. **-3.** [frivolously] a la ligera.

light meter *n* fotómetro *m*.

lightning ['laɪtnɪŋ] *n* (*U*) relámpago *m*.

lightning conductor *Br*, **lightning rod** *Am n* pararrayos *m inv*.

lightning strike *n Br* huelga *f* salvaje.

light opera *n* opereta *f*.

light pen *n* lápiz *m* óptico.

lightship ['laɪtʃɪp] *n* buque *m* faro.

lights-out *n* hora en que se apagan las luces.

lightweight ['laɪtweɪt] ◇ *adj* **-1.** [object] ligero(ra). **-2.** *fig* [person] de poca monta. ◇ *n* **-1.** [boxer] peso *m* ligero. **-2.** *fig* [person] figura *f* menor.

light year *n* año *m* luz.

likable ['laɪkəbl] *adj* simpático(ca).

like [laɪk] ◇ *prep* **-1.** [gen] como; (*in questions or indirect questions*) cómo; **what did it taste ~?** ¿a qué sabía?; **what did it look ~?** ¿cómo era?; **tell me what it's ~** dime cómo es; **something ~ £100** algo así como cien libras; **something ~ that** algo así, algo por el estilo. **-2.** [in the same way as] como, igual que; **~ this/that** así. **-3.** [typical of] propio(pia) OR típico(ca) de. ◇ *vt* **-1.** [find pleasant, approve of]: **I ~ cheese** me gusta el queso; **I ~ it/them** me gusta/gustan; **he ~s doing** OR **to do sthg** (a él) le gusta hacer algo. **-2.** [want] querer; **I don't ~ to bother her** no quiero molestarla; **would you ~ some more?** ¿quieres un poco más?; **I'd ~ to come tomorrow** querría OR me gustaría venir mañana; **I'd ~ you to come to dinner** me gustaría que vinieras a cenar; [in shops, restaurants]: **I'd ~ a kilo of apples/the soup** póngame un kilo de manzanas/la sopa. ◇ *adj* [similar] semejante; [the same] igual. ◇ *n*: **the ~ of sb/sthg** alguien/algo del estilo; **and the ~** y similares, y cosas por el estilo; **I've never seen the ~ (of it)** nunca he visto nada igual.
◆ **likes** *npl* [things one likes] gustos *mpl*, preferencias *fpl*.

likeable ['laɪkəbl] = **likable**.

likelihood ['laɪklɪhʊd] *n* (*U*) probabilidad *f*; **in all ~** con toda probabilidad.

likely ['laɪklɪ] *adj* **-1.** [probable] probable; **rain is ~** es probable que llueva; **he's ~ to**

come es probable que venga; **a ~ story!** *iron* ¡puro cuento! **-2.** [suitable] indicado(da).

like-minded [-'maɪndɪd] *adj* de igual parecer.

liken ['laɪkn] *vt*: **to ~ sthg/sb to** comparar algo/a alguien con.

likeness ['laɪknɪs] *n* **-1.** [resemblance]: **~ (to)** parecido *m* (con). **-2.** [portrait] retrato *m*.

likewise ['laɪkwaɪz] *adv* [similarly] de la misma forma; **to do ~** hacer lo mismo.

liking ['laɪkɪŋ] *n*: **to have a ~ for sthg** tener afición *f* por OR a algo; **to take a ~ to sb** tomar OR coger cariño *m* a alguien; **to be to sb's ~** ser del gusto de alguien; **for my/his** *etc* **~** para mi/su *etc* gusto.

lilac ['laɪlək] ◇ *adj* [colour] lila. ◇ *n* **-1.** [tree] lila *f*. **-2.** [colour] lila *m*.

Lilo® ['laɪləʊ] (*pl* -s) *n Br* colchoneta *f*, colchón *m* hinchable.

lilt [lɪlt] *n* entonación *f*, deje *m*.

lilting ['lɪltɪŋ] *adj* melodioso(sa).

lily ['lɪlɪ] (*pl* -ies) *n* lirio *m*, azucena *f*.

lily of the valley (*pl* **lilies of the valley**) *n* lirio *m* de los valles.

Lima ['liːmə] *n* Lima.

limb [lɪm] *n* **-1.** [of body] miembro *m*, extremidad *f*. **-2.** [of tree] rama *f*. **-3.** *phr*: **to be out on a ~** estar aislado(da).

limber ['lɪmbə']
◆ **limber up** *vi* calentar, desentumecerse.

limbo ['lɪmbəʊ] (*pl* -s) *n* **-1.** (*U*) [uncertain state]: **to be in ~** estar en un estado de incertidumbre. **-2.** [dance]: **the ~** *danza caribeña en la que se pasa por debajo de una barra con el cuerpo inclinado hacia atrás*.

lime [laɪm] *n* **-1.** [fruit] lima *f*. **-2.** [drink]: **~ (juice)** lima *f*. **-3.** [linden tree] tilo *m*. **-4.** CHEM cal *f*.

lime cordial *n refresco de lima*.

lime-green *adj* (de color) verde lima.

limelight ['laɪmlaɪt] *n*: **in the ~** en (el) candelero.

limerick ['lɪmərɪk] *n copla humorística de cinco versos*.

limestone ['laɪmstəʊn] *n* (*U*) (piedra *f*) caliza *f*.

limey ['laɪmɪ] (*pl* **limeys**) *n Am inf término peyorativo que designa a un inglés*.

limit ['lɪmɪt] ◇ *n* **-1.** [gen] límite *m*. **-2.** [test of patience]: **you're the ~!** *inf* ¡eres el colmo! **-3.** *phr*: **off ~s** en zona prohibida; **within ~s** dentro de un límite. ◇ *vt* limitar, restringir; **to ~ o.s. to** limitarse a.

limitation [,lɪmɪ'teɪʃn] *n* limitación *f*.

limited ['lɪmɪtɪd] *adj* [restricted] limitado(da); **to be ~ to** estar limitado a.

limited edition *n* edición *f* limitada.

limited (liability) company *n* sociedad *f* limitada.

limitless ['lɪmɪtlɪs] *adj* ilimitado(da).

limo ['lɪməʊ] *n inf abbr of* **limousine**.

limousine ['lɪməziːn] *n* limusina *f*.

limp [lɪmp] ◇ *adj* flojo(ja). ◇ *n* cojera *f*. ◇ *vi* cojear.

limpet ['lɪmpɪt] *n* lapa *f*.

limpid ['lɪmpɪd] *adj literary* límpido(da).

limply ['lɪmplɪ] *adv* lánguidamente.

linchpin ['lɪntʃpɪn] *n fig* eje *m*.

Lincs. [lɪŋks] (*abbr of* **Lincolnshire**) *condado inglés*.

linctus ['lɪŋktəs] *n Br* jarabe *m* para la tos.

line [laɪn] ◇ *n* **-1.** [gen] línea *f*. **-2.** [row] fila *f*. **-3.** [queue] cola *f*; **to stand** OR **wait in ~** hacer cola; **to be in ~ for promotion** estar camino de un ascenso. **-4.** [course · direction] línea *f*; [- of action] camino *m*; **to walk in a straight ~** andar en línea recta; **what's his ~ of business?** ¿a qué negocios se dedica?; **to follow the party ~** seguir las directrices del partido; **along the same ~s** por el estilo. **-5.** [length · of rope] cuerda *f*; [- for fishing] sedal *m*; [- of wire] hilo *m*, cable *m*. **-6.** TELEC: **(telephone) ~** línea *f* (telefónica); **hold the ~, please** no cuelgue, por favor; **the ~ is busy** está comunicando; **it's a bad ~** hay interferencias. **-7.** [on page] línea *f*, renglón *m*; [of poem, song] verso *m*; [letter]: **to drop sb a ~** *inf* mandar unas letras a alguien. **-8.** [system of transport]: **(railway) ~** [track] vía *f* (férrea); [route] línea *f* (férrea); **shipping ~** [company] compañía *f* naviera; [route] ruta *f* marítima. **-9.** [wrinkle] arruga *f*. **-10.** [succession of kings etc] sucesión *f*. **-11.** [borderline] límite *m*, frontera *f*. **-12.** COMM línea *f*. **-13.** *phr*: **to be on the right ~s** estar en el buen camino; **to draw the ~ at sthg** no pasar por algo, negarse a algo; **to read between the ~s** leer entre líneas; **to step out of ~** saltarse las reglas.
◇ *vt* **-1.** [form rows along] alinearse a lo largo de; **crowds ~d the street** la gente se apiñaba a los lados de la calle. **-2.** [coat, curtains] forrar; [drawer] cubrir el interior de.
◆ **lines** *npl* **-1.** SCH *castigo consistente en escribir la misma frase gran número de veces.* **-2.** THEATRE papel *m*.
◆ **on the line** *adv*: **to be on the ~** estar en juego.
◆ **out of line** *adv*: **to be out of ~** estar fuera de lugar.
◆ **line up** ◇ *vt sep* **-1.** [make into a row or queue] alinear. **-2.** [arrange] programar, orga-

nizar. ◇ *vi* [form a queue] alinearse, ponerse en fila.

lineage ['lɪnɪɪdʒ] *n fml* linaje *m*.

linear ['lɪnɪəʳ] *adj* lineal.

lined [laɪnd] *adj* **-1.** [of paper] reglado(da), de rayos. **-2.** [wrinkled] arrugado(da).

line drawing *n* dibujo *m* lineal.

line feed *n* cambio *m* de renglón.

linen ['lɪnɪn] ◇ *n* **-1.** [cloth] lino *m*. **-2.** [tablecloths, sheets] ropa *f* blanca OR de hilo; **bed ~** ropa *f* de cama. ◇ *comp* **-1.** [suit, napkins] de hilo. **-2.** [cupboard, drawer] de la ropa.

linen basket *n* cesta *f* de la ropa (sucia).

line printer *n* impresora *f* de línea.

liner ['laɪnəʳ] *n* [ship] transatlántico *m*.

linesman ['laɪnzmən] (*pl* **-men** [-mən]) *n* juez *m y f* de línea.

lineup ['laɪnʌp] *n* **-1.** [of players, competitors] alineación *f*. **-2.** *Am* [identification parade] rueda *f* de identificación.

linger ['lɪŋgəʳ] *vi* **-1.** [remain · over activity] entretenerse; [- in a place] rezagarse. **-2.** [persist] persistir.

lingerie ['lænʒərɪ] *n* ropa *f* interior femenina.

lingering ['lɪŋgrɪŋ] *adj* [illness, hopes] persistente; [death] lento(ta); [kiss] largo(ga).

lingo ['lɪŋgəʊ] (*pl* **-es**) *n inf* [foreign language] idioma *m*; [jargon] jerga *f*.

linguist ['lɪŋgwɪst] *n* **-1.** [someone good at languages] persona *f* con facilidad para las lenguas. **-2.** [student or teacher of linguistics] lingüista *m y f*.

linguistic [lɪŋ'gwɪstɪk] *adj* lingüístico(ca).

linguistics [lɪŋ'gwɪstɪks] *n* (*U*) lingüística *f*.

liniment ['lɪnɪmənt] *n* linimento *m*.

lining ['laɪnɪŋ] *n* **-1.** [gen & AUT] forro *m*. **-2.** [of stomach, nose] paredes *fpl* interiores.

link [lɪŋk] ◇ *n* **-1.** [of chain] eslabón *m*. **-2.** [connection] conexión *f*, enlace *m*; **rail ~** enlace ferroviario; **telephone ~** conexión OR línea *f* telefónica; **~s (between/with)** lazos *mpl* (entre/con), vínculos *mpl* (entre/con). ◇ *vt* **-1.** [connect · cities] comunicar, enlazar; [- computers] conectar; [- facts] relacionar, asociar; **to ~ sthg with** OR **to** relacionar OR asociar algo con. **-2.** [join · arms] enlazar.
◆ **link up** *vt sep*: **to ~ sthg up (with)** conectar algo (con).

linkage ['lɪŋkɪdʒ] *n* (*U*) [relationships] conexión *f*, nexo *m* de unión.

linked [lɪŋkt] *adj* **-1.** [connected · cities] unido(da); [- computers] conectado(da); [- facts] relacionado(da). **-2.** [joined · arms] enlazado(da).

links [lɪŋks] (*pl inv*) *n* campo *m* de golf.

linkup ['lɪŋkʌp] *n* [of TV channels] conexión *f*; [of spaceships] acoplamiento *m*.

lino ['laɪnəu], **linoleum** [lɪ'nəuljəm] *n* linóleo *m*.

linseed oil ['lɪnsiːd-] *n* aceite *m* de linaza.

lint [lɪnt] *n* (*U*) **-1.** [dressing] hilas *fpl*. **-2.** *Am* [fluff] pelusa *f*.

lintel ['lɪntl] *n* dintel *m*.

lion ['laɪən] *n* león *m*.

lion cub *n* cachorro *m* de león.

lioness ['laɪənes] *n* leona *f*.

lionize, -ise ['laɪənaɪz] *vt* encumbrar.

lip [lɪp] *n* **-1.** [of mouth] labio *m*; **my ~s are sealed** soy una tumba; **to keep a stiff upper ~** mantener el tipo. **-2.** [of cup] borde *m*; [of jug] pico *m*.

lip-read *vi* leer en los labios.

lip-reading *n* lectura *f* de labios.

lip salve *n Br* vaselina® *f*, cacao *m*.

lip service *n*: **to pay ~ to sthg** hablar en favor de algo sin hacer nada al respeto.

lipstick ['lɪpstɪk] *n* **-1.** [container] lápiz *m* OR barra *f* de labios. **-2.** [substance] carmín *m*, lápiz *m* de labios.

liquefy ['lɪkwɪfaɪ] (*pt & pp* **-ied**) ◇ *vt* licuar. ◇ *vi* licuarse.

liqueur [lɪ'kjʊər] *n* licor *m*.

liquid ['lɪkwɪd] ◇ *adj* líquido(da). ◇ *n* líquido *m*.

liquid assets *npl* activo *m* disponible.

liquidate ['lɪkwɪdeɪt] *vt* liquidar.

liquidation [,lɪkwɪ'deɪʃn] *n* liquidación *f*.

liquidator ['lɪkwɪdeɪtər] *n* liquidador *m*, -ra *f*.

liquid crystal display *n* pantalla *f* de cristal líquido.

liquidity [lɪ'kwɪdətɪ] *n* **-1.** [having money] liquidez *f*. **-2.** [being liquid] condición *f* de líquido.

liquidize, -ise ['lɪkwɪdaɪz] *vt Br* licuar.

liquidizer ['lɪkwɪdaɪzər] *n Br* licuadora *f*.

liquor ['lɪkər] *n* (*U*) alcohol *m*, bebida *f* alcohólica.

liquorice ['lɪkərɪs] *n* (*U*) regaliz *m*.

liquor store *n Am tienda donde se venden bebidas alcohólicas para llevar*.

lira ['lɪərə] *n* lira *f*.

Lisbon ['lɪzbən] *n* Lisboa.

lisp [lɪsp] ◇ *n* ceceo *m*. ◇ *vi* cecear.

lissom(e) ['lɪsəm] *adj literary* grácil, esbelto(ta).

list [lɪst] ◇ *n* lista *f*. ◇ *vt* **-1.** [in writing] hacer una lista de. **-2.** [in speech] enumerar. ◇ *vi* NAUT escorar.

listed building [,lɪstɪd-] *n Br edificio declarado de interés histórico y artístico*.

listed company [,lɪstɪd-] *n Br* sociedad *f* que se cotiza en bolsa.

listen ['lɪsn] *vi* **-1.** [give attention]: **to ~ (to sthg/sb)** escuchar (algo/a alguien); **to ~ for** estar atento a. **-2.** [heed advice]: **to ~ (to sb/sthg)** hacer caso (a alguien/de algo); **to ~ to reason** atender a razones.
◆ **listen in** *vi* **-1.** RADIO: **to ~ in (to a programme)** escuchar OR sintonizar (un programa en) una emisora. **-2.** [eavesdrop]: **to ~ in (on sthg)** escuchar (algo) a hurtadillas.
◆ **listen up** *vi Am inf* escuchar.

listener ['lɪsnər] *n* **-1.** [person listening] oyente *m y f*. **-2.** [to radio] radioyente *m y f*.

listing ['lɪstɪŋ] *n* listado *m*.
◆ **listings** *npl* cartelera *f*.

listless ['lɪstlɪs] *adj* apático(ca).

list price *n* precio *m* de catálogo.

lit [lɪt] *pt & pp* → **light**.

litany ['lɪtənɪ] (*pl* **-ies**) *n lit & fig* letanía *f*.

liter *Am* = **litre**.

literacy ['lɪtərəsɪ] *n* alfabetización *f*.

literal ['lɪtərəl] *adj* literal.

literally ['lɪtərəlɪ] *adv* literalmente; **to take sthg ~** tomarse algo al pie de la letra.

literary ['lɪtərərɪ] *adj* **-1.** [gen] literario(ria). **-2.** [person] literato(ta).

literate ['lɪtərət] *adj* **-1.** [able to read and write] alfabetizado(da). **-2.** [well-read] culto(ta), instruido(da).

literature ['lɪtrətʃər] *n* **-1.** [novels, plays, poetry] literatura *f*. **-2.** [books on a particular subject] publicaciones *fpl*, bibliografía *f*. **-3.** [printed information] documentación *f*, información *f*.

lithe [laɪð] *adj* ágil.

lithograph ['lɪθəɡrɑːf] *n* litografía *f*.

lithography [lɪ'θɒɡrəfɪ] *n* litografía *f*.

Lithuania [,lɪθjʊ'eɪnɪə] *n* Lituania.

Lithuanian [,lɪθjʊ'eɪnjən] ◇ *adj* lituano(na). ◇ *n* **-1.** [person] lituano *m*, -na *f*. **-2.** [language] lituano *m*.

litigant ['lɪtɪɡənt] *n fml* litigante *m y f*, pleiteante *m y f*.

litigate ['lɪtɪɡeɪt] *vi fml* litigar, pleitear.

litigation [,lɪtɪ'ɡeɪʃn] *n fml* litigio *m*, pleito *m*.

litmus paper ['lɪtməs-] *n* papel *m* de tornasol.

litre *Br*, **liter** *Am* ['liːtər] *n* litro *m*.

litter ['lɪtər] ◇ *n* **-1.** [waste material] basura *f*. **-2.** [newborn animals] camada *f*. ◇ *vt*: **to ~ sthg (with)** ensuciar algo (de); **papers ~ed**

the floor los papeles estaban esparcidos por el suelo.

litterbin ['lɪtəbɪn] n Br papelera f.

litterlout Br ['lɪtəlaʊt], **litterbug** ['lɪtəbʌg] n persona que ensucia la vía pública.

litter tray n recipiente para los excrementos del gato.

little ['lɪtl] (compar sense 3 **less**, superl sense 3 **least**) ◇ adj **-1.** [small in size, younger] pequeño(ña). **-2.** [short in length] corto(ta); a ~ **while** un ratito. **-3.** [not much] poco(ca); he speaks ~ **English** habla poco inglés; he speaks a ~ **English** habla un poco de inglés. ◇ pron: **I understood very** ~ entendí muy poco; a ~ un poco; a ~ **(bit)** un poco; **give me a** ~ **(bit)** dame un poco. ◇ adv poco; ~ **by** ~ poco a poco.

little finger n dedo m meñique.

little-known adj poco conocido(da).

liturgy ['lɪtədʒɪ] (pl **-ies**) n [form of worship] liturgia f.

live¹ [lɪv] ◇ vi **-1.** [gen] vivir. **-2.** [continue to be alive] seguir viviendo, vivir; **long** ~ **the Queen!** ¡viva la reina! ◇ vt llevar; **to** ~ **a quiet life** llevar una vida tranquila; **to** ~ **it up** inf pegarse la gran vida.
◆ **live down** vt sep lograr hacer olvidar.
◆ **live for** vt fus vivir para.
◆ **live in** vi [student] ser interno(na); [servant, nanny] residir OR vivir en la casa.
◆ **live off** vt fus [savings, land] vivir de; [people] vivir a costa de.
◆ **live on** ◇ vt fus **-1.** [survive on] vivir con OR de. **-2.** [eat] vivir de, alimentarse de. ◇ vi [memory, feeling] permanecer, perdurar.
◆ **live out** ◇ vt fus [life] acabar; **he won't** ~ **out the month** no va a vivir hasta finales de mes. ◇ vi [student] residir OR vivir fuera.
◆ **live together** vi vivir juntos.
◆ **live up to** vt fus estar a la altura de.
◆ **live with** vt fus **-1.** [live in same house as] vivir con. **-2.** [accept - situation, problem] aceptar.

live² [laɪv] ◇ adj **-1.** [living] vivo(va). **-2.** [burning] encendido(da). **-3.** [unexploded] sin explotar. **-4.** ELEC cargado(da). **-5.** [performance] en directo. ◇ adv [broadcast, perform] en directo, en vivo.

live-in [lɪv-] adj inf [housekeeper] residente; **Jane's** ~ **lover** el amante de Jane instalado en su casa.

livelihood ['laɪvlɪhʊd] n sustento m, medio m de vida.

liveliness ['laɪvlɪnɪs] n [of person] vivacidad f, viveza f; [of mind] sagacidad f, agudeza f; [of debate] animación f.

lively ['laɪvlɪ] (compar **-ier**, superl **-iest**) adj **-1.** [person, debate, time] animado(da). **-2.**

[mind] agudo(da), perspicaz. **-3.** [colours] vivo(va), llamativo(va).

liven ['laɪvn]
◆ **liven up** ◇ vt sep animar. ◇ vi animarse.

liver ['lɪvə'] n hígado m.

Liverpudlian [,lɪvə'pʌdlɪən] ◇ adj de o relativo a Liverpool. ◇ n natural o habitante de Liverpool.

liver sausage Br, **liverwurst** Am ['lɪvəwɜːst] n paté m de hígado en embutido.

livery ['lɪvərɪ] (pl **-ies**) n [of servant] librea f; [of company] uniforme m.

lives [laɪvz] pl → **life**.

livestock ['laɪvstɒk] n ganado m.

live wire [laɪv-] n **-1.** [wire] cable m cargado OR con corriente. **-2.** inf [person] puro nervio m y f.

livid ['lɪvɪd] adj **-1.** [angry] furioso(sa). **-2.** [blue-grey] lívido(da).

living ['lɪvɪŋ] ◇ adj [relatives, language] vivo(va); [artist etc] contemporáneo(a). ◇ n **-1.** [means of earning money] medio m de vida; **what do you do for a** ~? ¿cómo te ganas la vida? **-2.** [lifestyle] vida f.

living conditions npl condiciones fpl de vida.

living expenses npl gastos mpl de mantenimiento.

living room n cuarto m de estar, salón m.

living standards npl nivel m de vida.

living wage n salario m OR sueldo m mínimo.

lizard ['lɪzəd] n [small] lagartija f; [big] lagarto m.

llama ['lɑːmə] (pl inv OR **-s**) n llama f.

LLB (abbr of **Bachelor of Laws**) n (titular de una) licenciatura de derecho.

LLD (abbr of **Doctor of Laws**) n (titular de un) doctorado de derecho.

LMT (abbr of **Local Mean Time**) hora local.

lo [ləʊ] excl: ~ **and behold** ¡he aquí!

load [ləʊd] ◇ n **-1.** [something carried] carga f. **-2.** [amount of work]: **a heavy/light** ~ mucho/poco trabajo. **-3.** [large amount]: ~**s of** inf montones OR un montón de; **it was a** ~ **of rubbish** inf fue una porquería. ◇ vt **-1.** [gen & COMPUT]: **to** ~ **sthg/sb (with)** cargar algo/a alguien con (de). **-2.** [camera, video recorder]: **he** ~**ed the camera with a film** cargó la cámara con una película.
◆ **load up** vt sep & vi cargar.

loaded ['ləʊdɪd] adj **-1.** [question, statement] con doble sentido OR intención. **-2.** inf [rich] forrado(da).

loading bay ['ləʊdɪŋ-] *n* zona *f* de carga y descarga.

loaf [ləʊf] (*pl* **loaves**) *n* [of bread] (barra *f* de) pan *m*.

loafer ['ləʊfər] *n* [shoe] mocasín *m*.

loam [ləʊm] *n* marga *f*.

loan [ləʊn] ◇ *n* [something lent] préstamo *m*; **on ~** prestado(da). ◇ *vt* prestar; **to ~ sthg to sb, to ~ sb sthg** prestar algo a alguien.

loan account *n* cuenta *f* de crédito.

loan capital *n* capital *m* en préstamo.

loan shark *n* *inf* *pej* usurero *m*, -ra *f*.

loath [ləʊθ] *adj*: **to be ~ to do sthg** ser reacio(cia) a hacer algo.

loathe [ləʊð] *vt*: **to ~ (doing sthg)** aborrecer OR detestar (hacer algo).

loathing ['ləʊðɪŋ] *n* aborrecimiento *m*, odio *m*.

loathsome ['ləʊðsəm] *adj* [smell] repugnante; [person, behaviour] odioso(sa), detestable.

loaves [ləʊvz] *pl* → **loaf**.

lob [lɒb] (*pt* & *pp* **-bed**, *cont* **-bing**) ◇ *n* TENNIS lob *m*. ◇ *vt* **-1.** [throw] lanzar. **-2.** TENNIS [ball] hacer un lob con, bombear; [opponent] hacer un lob a.

lobby ['lɒbɪ] (*pl* **-ies**, *pt* & *pp* **-ied**) ◇ *n* **-1.** [hall] vestíbulo *m*. **-2.** [pressure group] grupo *m* de presión, lobby *m*. ◇ *vt* ejercer presión (política) sobre.

lobbyist ['lɒbɪɪst] *n* miembro *m* y *f* de un lobby.

lobe [ləʊb] *n* lóbulo *m*.

lobelia [lə'biːljə] *n* lobelia *f*.

lobotomy [lə'bɒtəmɪ] (*pl* **-ies**) *n* lobotomía *f*.

lobster ['lɒbstər] *n* langosta *f*.

local ['ləʊkl] ◇ *adj* local. ◇ *n* *inf* **-1.** [person]: **the ~s** [in village] los lugareños; [in town] los vecinos del lugar. **-2.** *Br* [pub] bar *m* del barrio. **-3.** *Am* [bus, train] omnibús *m*.

local anaesthetic *n* anestesia *f* local.

local area network *n* COMPUT red *f* de área local.

local authority *n* *Br* autoridad *f* local.

local call *n* llamada *f* local.

local colour *n* ambientación *f*.

local derby *n* *Br* partido *m* entre dos equipos locales.

locale [ləʊ'kɑːl] *n* *fml* lugar *m*, emplazamiento *m*.

local government *n* gobierno *m* municipal.

locality [lə'kælətɪ] (*pl* **-ies**) *n* localidad *f*.

localized, -ised ['ləʊkəlaɪzd] *adj* localizado(da).

locally ['ləʊkəlɪ] *adv* **-1.** [on local basis] localmente, en el lugar. **-2.** [nearby] cerca, por la zona.

local time *n* hora *f* local.

locate [*Br* ləʊ'keɪt, *Am* 'ləʊkeɪt] ◇ *vt* **-1.** [find] localizar. **-2.** [situate] ubicar. ◇ *vi* *Am* [settle] establecerse.

location [ləʊ'keɪʃn] *n* **-1.** [place] localización *f*, situación *f*. **-2.** CINEMA: **on ~** en exteriores.

loc. cit. (*abbr of* **loco citato**) loc. cit.

loch [lɒk] *n* *Scot* lago *m*.

lock [lɒk] ◇ *n* **-1.** [of door] cerradura *f*, chapa *f* *Amer*; [of bicycle] candado *m*; **under ~ and key** bajo siete llaves, bajo llave. **-2.** [on canal] esclusa *f*. **-3.** AUT [steering lock] ángulo *m* de giro. **-4.** *literary* [of hair] mechón *m*. **-5.** *phr*: **~, stock and barrel** por completo. ◇ *vt* **-1.** [with key] cerrar con llave; [with padlock] cerrar con candado. **-2.** [keep safely] poner bajo llave. **-3.** [immobilize] bloquear. **-4.** [hold firmly]: **to be ~ed in an embrace** estar abrazados(das) fuertemente; **to be ~ed in combat** estar enzarzados(das) en una lucha. ◇ *vi* **-1.** [with key] cerrarse con llave; [with padlock] cerrarse con candado. **-2.** [become immobilized] bloquearse.
◆ **locks** *npl* *literary* cabellos *mpl*.
◆ **lock in** *vt* *sep* encerrar.
◆ **lock out** *vt* *sep* **-1.** [accidentally] dejar fuera al cerrar accidentalmente la puerta; **to ~ o.s. out** quedarse fuera (*por olvidarse la llave dentro*). **-2.** [deliberately] dejar fuera a.
◆ **lock up** ◇ *vt* *sep* **-1.** [person - in prison] encerrar; [- in asylum] internar. **-2.** [house] cerrar (con llave). **-3.** [valuables] guardar bajo llave. ◇ *vi* cerrar (con llave).

lockable ['lɒkəbl] *adj* bloqueable.

locker ['lɒkər] *n* taquilla *f*, armario *m*.

locker room *n* *Am* vestuario *m* con taquillas.

locket ['lɒkɪt] *n* guardapelo *m*.

lockjaw ['lɒkdʒɔː] *n* tétanos *m*.

lockout ['lɒkaʊt] *n* cierre *m* patronal, lockout *m*.

locksmith ['lɒksmɪθ] *n* cerrajero *m*, -ra *f*.

lockup ['lɒkʌp] *n* **-1.** [prison] calabozo *m*, prisión *f*. **-2.** *Br* [garage] garaje *m*.

loco ['ləʊkəʊ] (*pl* **-s**) *inf* ◇ *adj* *Am* loco(ca). ◇ *n* *Br* [locomotive] locomotora *f*.

locomotive ['ləʊkə,məʊtɪv] *n* locomotora *f*.

locum ['ləʊkəm] (*pl* **-s**) *n* interino *m*, -na *f*.

locust ['ləʊkəst] *n* langosta *f*.

lodge [lɒdʒ] ◇ *n* **-1.** [caretaker's etc room] portería *f*. **-2.** [of manor house] casa *f* del guarda. **-3.** [of freemasons] logia *f*. **-4.** [for hunting] refugio *m* de caza. ◇ *vi* **-1.** [stay]:

to ~ (with sb) alojarse (con alguien). **-2.** [become stuck] alojarse. **-3.** *fig* [in mind] grabarse (en la mente). ◇ *vt fml* [register] presentar.

lodger ['lɒdʒə'] *n* huésped *m* y *f*.

lodging ['lɒdʒɪŋ] → **board**.
◆ **lodgings** *npl* habitación *f* (alquilada).

loft [lɒft] *n* [in house] desván *m*, entretecho *m* Amer; [for hay] pajar *m*.

lofty ['lɒftɪ] (*compar* **-ier**, *superl* **-iest**) *adj* **-1.** [noble] noble, elevado(da). **-2.** *pej* [haughty] arrogante, altanero(ra). **-3.** *literary* [high] elevado(da), alto(ta).

log [lɒg] (*pt* & *pp* **-ged**, *cont* **-ging**) ◇ *n* **-1.** [of wood] tronco *m*. **-2.** [written record - of ship] diario *m* de a bordo; [- of plane] diario *m* de vuelo. ◇ *vt* anotar.
◆ **log in** *vi* COMPUT entrar (en el sistema).
◆ **log out** *vi* COMPUT salir (del sistema).

loganberry ['lɒugənbərɪ] (*pl* **-ies**) *n* zarza *f* frambuesa.

logarithm ['lɒgərɪðm] *n* logaritmo *m*.

logbook ['lɒgbuk] *n* **-1.** [of ship] diario *m* de a bordo; [of plane] diario *m* de vuelo. **-2.** [of car] documentación *f*.

log cabin *n* cabaña *f*.

log fire *n* fuego *m* (de leña).

loggerheads ['lɒgəhedz] *n*: **to be at ~** estar a matar.

logic ['lɒdʒɪk] *n* lógica *f*.

logical ['lɒdʒɪkl] *adj* lógico(ca).

logically ['lɒdʒɪklɪ] *adv* **-1.** [gen] lógicamente. **-2.** [reasonably, sensibly] razonablemente, sensatamente.

logistical [lə'dʒɪstɪkl] *adj* logístico(ca).

logistics [lə'dʒɪstɪks] ◇ *n* (U) logística *f*. ◇ *npl* logística *f*.

logjam ['lɒgdʒæm] *n* atolladero *m*.

logo ['lɒugəu] (*pl* **-s**) *n* logo *m*, logotipo *m*.

logrolling ['lɒgrəulɪŋ] *n* (U) Am acción de alabar o respaldar el trabajo de alguien para recibir después el mismo trato.

logy ['lɒugɪ] *adj* Am *inf* atontado(da), mareado(da).

loin [lɒɪn] *n* lomo *m*.
◆ **loins** *npl* ijada *f*, ijar *m*; **to gird one's ~s** prepararse para la batalla.

loincloth ['lɒɪnklɒθ] *n* taparrabos *m inv*.

loiter ['lɒɪtə'] *vi* [for bad purpose] merodear; [hang around] vagar.

loll [lɒl] *vi* **-1.** [sit, lie about] repantigarse. **-2.** [hang down] colgar; **his head was ~ing** cabeceaba.

lollipop ['lɒlɪpɒp] *n* pirulí *m*.

lollipop lady *n* Br *mujer encargada de parar el tráfico en un paso de cebra para que crucen los niños*.

lollipop man *n* Br *hombre encargado de parar el tráfico en un paso de cebra para que crucen los niños*.

lolly ['lɒlɪ] (*pl* **-ies**) *n* *inf* **-1.** [lollipop] pirulí *m*. **-2.** Br [ice cream] polo *m*. **-3.** Br [money] pasta *f*.

London ['lʌndən] *n* Londres.

Londoner ['lʌndənə'] *n* londinense *m* y *f*.

lone [ləun] *adj* solitario(ria).

loneliness ['ləunlɪnɪs] *n* soledad *f*.

lonely ['ləunlɪ] (*compar* **-ier**, *superl* **-iest**) *adj* **-1.** [person] solo(la). **-2.** [time, childhood] solitario(ria). **-3.** [place] solitario(ria), aislado(da).

lone parent *n* Br [man] padre *m* soltero; [woman] madre *f* soltera.

loner ['ləunə'] *n* solitario *m*, -ria *f*.

lonesome ['ləunsəm] *adj* Am *inf* **-1.** [person] solo(la). **-2.** [place] solitario(ria).

long [lɒŋ] ◇ *adj* largo(ga); **two days ~** de dos días de duración; **the table is 5m ~** la mesa mide OR tiene 5m de largo; **the journey is 50km ~** el viaje es de 50 km; **the book is 500 pages ~** el libro tiene 500 páginas. ◇ *adv* mucho tiempo; **how ~ will it take?** ¿cuánto se tarda?; **how ~ will you be?** ¿cuánto tardarás?; **how ~ have you been waiting?** ¿cuánto tiempo llevas esperando?; **how ~ is the journey?** ¿cuánto hay de viaje?; **I'm no ~er young** ya no soy joven; **I can't wait any ~er** no puedo esperar más; **so ~** *inf* hasta luego OR pronto; **before ~** pronto; **for ~** mucho tiempo.
◇ *n*: **the ~ and the short of it is that ...** en pocas palabras lo que pasa es que ....
◇ *vt*: **to ~ to do sthg** desear ardientemente hacer algo.
◆ **as long as**, **so long as** *conj* mientras; **as ~ as you do it, so will I** siempre y cuando tú lo hagas, yo también lo haré.
◆ **long for** *vt fus* desear ardientemente.

long. (*abbr of* **longitude**) long.

long-awaited [-ə'weɪtɪd] *adj* tan esperado (tan esperada).

long-distance *adj* [runner] de fondo; [lorry driver] para distancias grandes.

long-distance call *n* conferencia *f* (telefónica).

long division *n* división *f* no abreviada.

long-drawn-out *adj* interminable.

long drink *n* bebida que resulta de la mezcla de alcohol y un refresco, tipo cuba libre.

longevity [lɒn'dʒevətɪ] *n* longevidad *f*.

longhaired [ˌlɒŋ'heəd] *adj* de pelo largo.
longhand ['lɒŋhænd] *n* escritura *f* a mano.
long-haul *adj* de larga distancia.
longing ['lɒŋɪŋ] ◇ *adj* anhelante. ◇ *n* **-1.** [desire] anhelo *m*, deseo *m*; [nostalgia] nostalgia *f*, añoranza *f*. **-2.** [strong wish]: **(a)** ~ **(for)** (un) ansia *f* (de).
longingly ['lɒŋɪŋlɪ] *adv* de manera anhelante.
Long Island *n* Long Island.
longitude ['lɒndʒɪtjuːd] *n* longitud *f*.
long johns *npl* calzones *mpl* largos.
long jump *n* salto *m* de longitud.
long-lasting *adj* duradero(ra).
long-life *adj* de larga duración.
long-lost *adj* desaparecido(da) hace tiempo.
long-playing record [-'pleɪɪŋ-] *n* disco *m* de larga duración.
long-range *adj* **-1.** [missile, bomber] de largo alcance. **-2.** [plan, forecast] a largo plazo.
long-running *adj* [TV programme] en antena mucho tiempo; [play] en cartelera mucho tiempo; [dispute] que dura desde tiempo inmemorial.
longshoreman ['lɒŋʃɔːmən] (*pl* **-men** [-mən]) *n Am* estibador *m*.
long shot *n* posibilidad *f* remota.
longsighted [ˌlɒŋ'saɪtɪd] *adj* présbita.
long-standing *adj* antiguo(gua).
longsuffering [ˌlɒŋ'sʌfərɪŋ] *adj* sufrido(da).
long term *n*: **in the** ~ a largo plazo.
◆ **long-term** *adj* a largo plazo.
long vacation *n Br* vacaciones *fpl* de verano.
long wave *n* (*U*) onda *f* larga.
longways ['lɒŋweɪz] *adv* a lo largo, longitudinalmente.
longwearing [ˌlɒŋ'weərɪŋ] *adj Am* resistente, duradero(ra).
long weekend *n* fin *m* de semana largo, puente *m*.
longwinded [ˌlɒŋ'wɪndɪd] *adj* prolijo(ja).
loo [luː] (*pl* **-s**) *n Br inf* retrete *m*, wáter *m*.
loofa(h) ['luːfə] *n* esponja *f* vegetal.
look [lʊk] ◇ *n* **-1.** [with eyes] mirada *f*; **to take** OR **have a** ~ **(at sthg)** echar una ojeada (a algo). **-2.** [search]: **to have a** ~ **(for sthg)** buscar (algo). **-3.** [glance] ojeada *f*; **to give sb a** ~ dirigir la mirada hacia OR a alguien. **-4.** [appearance] aspecto *m*; **by the** ~ OR ~**s of it, it has been here for ages** parece que hace años que está aquí.
◇ *vi* **-1.** [with eyes]: **to** ~ **(at sthg/sb)** mirar (algo/a alguien). **-2.** [search]: **to** ~ **(for sthg/sb)** buscar (algo/a alguien). **-3.** [build-

ing, window]: **to** ~ **(out) onto** dar a. **-4.** [have stated appearance] verse; [seem] parecer; **he** ~**s as if he hasn't slept** tiene pinta de no haber dormido; **it** ~**s like rain** OR **as if it will rain** parece que va a llover; **she** ~**s like her mother** se parece a su madre.
◇ *vt* **-1.** [look at] mirar. **-2.** [appear]: **to** ~ **one's age** representar la edad que se tiene; **to** ~ **one's best** vestir elegantemente.
◇ *excl*: ~**!**, ~ **here!** ¡mira!, ¡oye!
◆ **looks** *npl* belleza *f*.
◆ **look after** *vt fus* **-1.** [take care of] cuidar. **-2.** [be responsible for] encargarse de.
◆ **look at** *vt fus* **-1.** [see, glance at] mirar, aguaitar *Amer*; [examine] examinar. **-2.** [judge] estudiar.
◆ **look back** *vi* [reminisce] recordar; **she's never** ~**ed back** no ha dejado de prosperar.
◆ **look down on** *vt fus* [condescend to] despreciar.
◆ **look for** *vt fus* buscar.
◆ **look forward to** *vt fus* esperar (ansiosamente).
◆ **look into** *vt fus* [problem, possibility] estudiar; [issue] investigar.
◆ **look on** ◇ *vt fus* = **look upon.** ◇ *vi* mirar, observar.
◆ **look out** *vi* tener cuidado; ~ **out!** ¡cuidado!
◆ **look out for** *vt fus* estar atento(ta) a.
◆ **look round** ◇ *vt fus* [shop] echar un vistazo; [castle, town] visitar. ◇ *vi* volver la cabeza.
◆ **look through** *vt fus* **-1.** [look at briefly - book, paper] hojear; [- collection, pile] echar un vistazo a. **-2.** [check] revisar.
◆ **look to** *vt fus* **-1.** [depend on] recurrir a. **-2.** [think about] pensar en.
◆ **look up** ◇ *vt sep* **-1.** [in book] buscar. **-2.** [visit - person] ir a ver OR visitar. ◇ *vi* [improve] mejorar.
◆ **look upon** *vt fus*: **to** ~ **upon sthg/sb as** considerar algo/a alguien como.
◆ **look up to** *vt fus* respetar, admirar.
look-alike *n* sosia *m*.
look-in *n Br inf*: **to get a** ~ [chance to win] tener la posibilidad (de ganar); [chance to participate] tener la oportunidad (de participar).
lookout ['lʊkaʊt] *n* **-1.** [place] puesto *m* de observación, atalaya *f*. **-2.** [person] guardia *m y f*, centinela *m y f*. **-3.** [search]: **to be on the** ~ **for** estar al acecho de.
look-up table *n* COMPUT tabla *f* de consulta.
loom [luːm] ◇ *n* telar *m*. ◇ *vi* **-1.** [rise up] surgir OR aparecer amenazante. **-2.** *fig* [be imminent] cernerse, ser inminente; **to** ~ **large** ser agobiante.

◆ **loom up** *vi* divisarse sombríamente.

LOOM (*abbr of* **Loyal Order of the Moose**) *n organización benéfica estadounidense.*

looming ['luːmɪŋ] *adj* inminente.

loony ['luːnɪ] (*compar* **-ier**, *superl* **-iest**, *pl* **-ies**) *inf* ◇ *adj* majara, chiflado(da). ◇ *n* majara *m y f*, chiflado *m*, -da *f*.

loop [luːp] ◇ *n* **-1.** [shape] lazo *m*. **-2.** [contraceptive] esterilete *m*. **-3.** COMPUT bucle *m*. ◇ *vt*: **to ~ sthg round sthg** pasar algo alrededor de algo. ◇ *vi* hacer un lazo.

loophole ['luːphəʊl] *n* laguna *f*.

loo roll *n Br inf* rollo *m* de papel higiénico.

loose [luːs] ◇ *adj* **-1.** [not firmly fixed] flojo(ja). **-2.** [unattached - paper, sweets, hair] suelto(ta). **-3.** [clothes, fit] holgado(da). **-4.** *dated* [promiscuous] promiscuo(cua). **-5.** [inexact - translation] poco exacto (poco exacta), impreciso(sa). **-6.** [association] no muy estrecho (no muy estrecha). **-7.** *Am inf* [relaxed]: **to stay ~** seguir tranqui. ◇ *n* (*U*): **to be on the ~** andar suelto(ta).

loose change *n* (dinero *m*) suelto *m*, sencillo *m Amer.*

loose end *n* cabo *m* suelto; **to be at a ~** *Br*, **to be at ~s** *Am* estar desocupado(da).

loose-fitting *adj* amplio(plia), holgado(da).

loose-leaf binder *n* carpeta *f* de hojas sueltas.

loosely ['luːslɪ] *adv* **-1.** [not firmly] holgadamente, sin apretar. **-2.** [inexactly] vagamente.

loosen ['luːsn] ◇ *vt* aflojar. ◇ *vi* aflojarse.

◆ **loosen up** *vi* **-1.** [before game, race] desentumecerse. **-2.** *inf* [relax] relajarse.

loot [luːt] ◇ *n* botín *m*. ◇ *vt* saquear.

looter ['luːtər] *n* saqueador *m*, -ra *f*.

looting ['luːtɪŋ] *n* saqueo *m*.

lop [lɒp] (*pt & pp* **-ped**, *cont* **-ping**) *vt* podar.

◆ **lop off** *vt sep* cortar.

lope [ləʊp] *vi* andar con paso largo y ligero.

lop-sided [-'saɪdɪd] *adj* **-1.** [uneven] ladeado(da), torcido(da). **-2.** *fig* [biased] desequilibrado(da).

lord [lɔːd] *n Br* [man of noble rank] noble *m*.

◆ **Lord** *n* **-1.** RELIG: **the Lord** [God] el Señor; **good Lord!** *Br* ¡Dios mío! **-2.** [in titles] lord *m*; [as form of address]: **my Lord** [bishop] su Ilustrísima; [judge] su Señoría.

◆ **Lords** *npl Br* POL: **the Lords** la Cámara de los Lores.

Lord Chancellor *n Br presidente de la Cámara de los Lores y responsable de Justicia en Inglaterra y Gales.*

lordly ['lɔːdlɪ] (*compar* **-ier**, *superl* **-iest**) *adj* **-1.** [noble] señorial, noble. **-2.** *pej* [arrogant] arrogante, altivo(va).

Lord Mayor *n Br* alcalde *m*.

Lordship ['lɔːdʃɪp] *n*: **your/his ~** su Señoría *f*.

Lord's Prayer *n*: **the ~** el Padrenuestro.

lore [lɔːr] *n* (*U*) saber *m* OR tradición *f* popular.

lorry ['lɒrɪ] (*pl* **-ies**) *n Br* camión *m*.

lorry driver *n Br* camionero *m*, -ra *f*.

lose [luːz] (*pt & pp* **lost**) ◇ *vt* [gen] perder; [subj: clock, watch] atrasarse; **to ~ sight of sthg/sb** & *fig* perder de vista algo/a alguien; **to ~ one's way** perderse. ◇ *vi* **-1.** [fail to win] perder. **-2.** [clock] atrasarse.

◆ **lose out** *vi* salir perdiendo; **to ~ out on sthg** salir perdiendo en algo.

loser ['luːzər] *n* **-1.** [of competition] perdedor *m*, -ra *f*; **to be a good/bad ~** saber/no saber perder. **-2.** *inf pej* [unsuccessful person] desgraciado *m*, -da *f*.

losing ['luːzɪŋ] *adj* vencido(da), derrotado(da).

loss [lɒs] *n* **-1.** [gen] pérdida *f*; **~ of life** muertes *fpl*; **to make a ~** sufrir pérdidas, perder. **-2.** [failure to win] derrota *f*. **-3.** **a dead ~** *inf* una birria. **-4.** *phr*: **to be at a ~ to explain sthg** no saber cómo explicar algo; **to cut one's ~es** ahorrarse problemas cortando por lo sano.

loss adjuster [-ə'dʒʌstər] *n* perito *m* tasador de seguros.

loss leader *n* COMM artículo *m* de reclamo.

lost [lɒst] ◇ *pt & pp* → **lose**. ◇ *adj* **-1.** [unable to find way] perdido(da); **to get ~** perderse; **get ~!** *inf* ¡vete a la porra! **-2.** [that cannot be found] extraviado(da), perdido(da). **-3.** [ineffective]: **to be ~ on sb** no surtir efecto en alguien. **-4.** [opportunity] desaprovechado(da).

lost-and-found office *n Am* oficina *f* de objetos perdidos.

lost cause *n* causa *f* perdida.

lost property *n* (*U*) objetos *mpl* perdidos.

lost property office *n Br* oficina *f* de objetos perdidos.

lot [lɒt] *n* **-1.** [large amount]: **a ~ of**, **~s of** mucho(cha); **a ~ of people** mucha gente, muchas personas; **a ~ of problems** muchos problemas; **the ~** todo. **-2.** [group, set] grupo *m*. **-3.** *inf* [group of people] panda *f*, pandilla *f*. **-4.** [destiny] destino *m*, suerte *f*. **-5.** *Am* [of land] terreno *m*; [car park] aparcamiento *m*. **-6.** [at auction] partida *f*, lote *m*. **-7.** *phr*: **to draw ~s** echar a suerte.

◆ **a lot** *adv* mucho.

loth [ləʊθ] = **loath**.

lotion ['ləʊʃn] *n* loción *f*.

lottery ['lɒtəri] (*pl* **-ies**) *n* lotería *f*.

lotus position ['ləʊtəs-] *n* posición *f* de loto.

loud [laʊd] ◇ *adj* **-1.** [voice, music] alto(ta); [bang] fuerte; [person] ruidoso(sa). **-2.** [emphatic]: **to be ~ in one's criticism of** ser enérgico(ca) en la crítica de. **-3.** [too bright] chillón(ona), llamativo(va). ◇ *adv* alto, fuerte; **~ and clear** alto y claro; **out ~** en voz alta.

loudhailer [,laʊd'heɪlər] *n Br* megáfono *m*.

loudly ['laʊdlɪ] *adv* **-1.** [shout] a voz en grito; [talk] en voz alta. **-2.** [gaudily] con colores chillones OR llamativos.

loudmouth ['laʊdmaʊθ, *pl* -maʊðz] *n inf* bocazas *m y f inv*.

loudness ['laʊdnɪs] *n* fuerza *f*, intensidad *f*.

loudspeaker [,laʊd'spiːkər] *n* altavoz *m*, altoparlante *m Amer*.

Louisiana [luː,iːzɪ'ænə] *n* Luisiana.

lounge [laʊndʒ] (*cont* **loungeing**) ◇ *n* **-1.** [in house] salón *m*. **-2.** [in airport] sala *f* de espera. **-3.** *Br* [lounge bar] salón-bar *m*. ◇ *vi* repantigarse.

◆ **lounge about, lounge around** *vi* holgazanear.

lounge bar *n Br* salón-bar *m*.

lounge suit *n Br* traje *m*.

louse [laʊs] (*pl sense 1* **lice**, *pl sense 2* **-s**) *n* **-1.** [insect] piojo *m*. **-2.** *inf pej* [person] canalla *m y f*.

◆ **louse up** *Am vt sep v inf* jorobar, fastidiar.

lousy ['laʊzɪ] (*compar* **-ier**, *superl* **-iest**) *adj inf* **-1.** [poor quality] fatal, pésimo(ma). **-2.** [ill]: **to feel ~** sentirse fatal.

lout [laʊt] *n* gamberro *m*.

louvre *Br*, **louver** *Am* ['luːvər] *n* persiana *f*.

lovable ['lʌvəbl] *adj* encantador(ra), adorable.

love [lʌv] ◇ *n* **-1.** [gen] amor *m*; **give her my ~** dale un abrazo de mi parte; **~ from** [at end of letter] un abrazo de; **a ~-hate relationship** una relación de amor y odio; **to be in ~ (with)** estar enamorado(da) (de); **to fall in ~** enamorarse; **to make ~** hacer el amor. **-2.** [liking, interest] pasión *f*; **a ~ of** OR **for** una pasión por. **-3.** *inf* [form of address] cariño *m y f*. **-4.** TENNIS: **30 ~ 30** a nada. ◇ *vt* **-1.** [feel affection for] amar, querer. **-2.** [like]: **I ~ football** me encanta el fútbol; **I ~ going to** OR **to go to the theatre** me encanta ir al teatro.

love affair *n* aventura *f* amorosa.

lovebite ['lʌvbaɪt] *n* moratón *m*, mordisco *m* (*por un beso*).

loveless ['lʌvlɪs] *adj* sin amor.

love letter *n* carta *f* de amor.

love life *n* vida *f* amorosa.

lovely ['lʌvlɪ] (*compar* **-ier**, *superl* **-iest**) *adj* **-1.** [beautiful - person] encantador(ra); [- dress, place] precioso(sa). **-2.** [pleasant] estupendo(da).

lovemaking ['lʌv,meɪkɪŋ] *n* (*U*) relaciones *fpl* sexuales.

lover ['lʌvər] *n* **-1.** [sexual partner] amante *m y f*. **-2.** [enthusiast] amante *m y f*, apasionado *m*, -da *f*.

lovesick ['lʌvsɪk] *adj* enfermo(ma) de amor (no correspondido).

love song *n* canción *f* de amor.

love story *n* historia *f* de amor.

loving ['lʌvɪŋ] *adj* cariñoso(sa), afectuoso(sa).

lovingly ['lʌvɪŋlɪ] *adv* cariñosamente, afectuosamente.

low [ləʊ] ◇ *adj* **-1.** [gen] bajo(ja); **cook on a ~ heat** cocinar a fuego lento; **in the ~ twenties** 20 y algo; **a ~ trick** una mala jugada. **-2.** [little remaining] escaso(sa); **to be ~ on sthg** andar escaso de algo. **-3.** [unfavourable - opinion] malo(la); [- esteem] poco(ca). **-4.** [dim] tenue. **-5.** [dress, neckline] escotado(da). **-6.** [depressed] deprimido(da). ◇ *adv* **-1.** [gen] bajo; **morale is very ~** la moral está por los suelos; **~ paid** mal pagado. **-2.** [speak] en voz baja. ◇ *n* **-1.** [low point] punto *m* más bajo. **-2.** METEOR área *f* de bajas presiones.

low-alcohol *adj* bajo(ja) en alcohol.

lowbrow ['ləʊbraʊ] *adj* PRESS & TV para las masas.

low-calorie *adj* light (*inv*), bajo(ja) en calorías.

Low Church *n* corriente evangélica de la iglesia anglicana.

Low Countries *npl*: **the ~** los Países Bajos.

low-cut *adj* escotado(da).

low-down *inf* ◇ *adj* bajo(ja), sucio(cia). ◇ *n*: **to give sb the ~ (on sthg)** dar los detalles concretos (sobre algo) a alguien.

lower[1] ['ləʊər] ◇ *adj* inferior. ◇ *vt* **-1.** [gen] bajar; **to ~ one's eyes** bajar la mirada; [flag] arriar. **-2.** [reduce] reducir.

lower[2] ['laʊər] *vi* **-1.** [be dark] estar oscuro(ra). **-2.** [frown]: **to ~ at sb** fruncir el ceño a alguien.

Lower Chamber [,ləʊər-] *n* POL Cámara *f* Baja.

lower class [ˌləʊəˈ-] *n*: **the** ~ OR ~**es** las clases bajas.

Lower House [ˌləʊəˈ-] *n* Cámara *f* Baja.

lowest common denominator [ˈləʊɪst-] *n* mínimo común denominador *m*.

low-fat *adj* bajo(ja) en grasas.

low-flying *adj* de vuelo bajo OR rasante.

low frequency *n* baja frecuencia *f*.

low gear *n Am* primera *f* (*velocidad*).

low-key *adj* discreto(ta).

Lowlands [ˈləʊləndz] *npl*: **the** ~ [of Scotland] las Tierras Bajas (de Escocia).

low-level language *n* COMPUT lenguaje *m* de bajo nivel.

low-loader [-ˈləʊdəʳ] *n Br* vehículo con plataforma de carga baja.

lowly [ˈləʊlɪ] (*compar* **-ier**, *superl* **-iest**) *adj* humilde.

low-lying *adj* bajo(ja).

Low Mass *n* misa *f* hablada.

low-necked [-ˈnekt] *adj* escotado(da).

low-paid *adj* mal pagado (mal pagada).

low-rise *adj* bajo(ja), de planta y piso.

low season *n* temporada *f* baja.

low tide *n* marea *f* baja.

loyal [ˈlɔɪəl] *adj* leal, fiel.

loyalist [ˈlɔɪəlɪst] *n* leal *m y f* (al gobierno).

loyalty [ˈlɔɪəltɪ] (*pl* **-ies**) *n* lealtad *f*, fidelidad *f*.

lozenge [ˈlɒzɪndʒ] *n* **-1.** [tablet] tableta *f*, pastilla *f*. **-2.** [shape] rombo *m*.

LP (*abbr of* **long-playing record**) *n* LP *m*.

L-plate *n Br* placa *f* L (de prácticas).

LPN (*abbr of* **licensed practical nurse**) *n* ≈ ATS *m y f*.

LRAM (*abbr of* **Licentiate of the Royal Academy of Music**) *n* (*titular de un*) *diploma de la Royal Academy of Music*.

LSAT (*abbr of* **Law School Admissions Test**) *n examen de acceso a los estudios de derecho en Estados Unidos.*

LSD (*abbr of* **lysergic acid diethylamide**) *n* LSD *m*.

LSD, L.S.D., £.s.d., l.s.d. (*abbr of* **pounds, shillings and pence - librae, solidi, denarii**) *sistema monetario usado en Gran Bretaña hasta 1971.*

LSE (*abbr of* **London School of Economics**) *n escuela londinense de ciencias políticas y económicas.*

LSO (*abbr of* **London Symphony Orchestra**) *n* Orquesta Sinfónica de Londres.

Lt. (*abbr of* **lieutenant**) ≈ Tte.

LT (*abbr of* **low tension**) *n* BT.

Ltd, ltd (*abbr of* **limited**) S.L., SL.

lubricant [ˈluːbrɪkənt] *n* lubricante *m*.

lubricate [ˈluːbrɪkeɪt] *vt* lubricar, engrasar.

lubrication [ˌluːbrɪˈkeɪʃn] *n* lubricación *f*, engrase *m*.

lucid [ˈluːsɪd] *adj* **-1.** [clear] claro(ra). **-2.** [not confused] lúcido(da).

lucidly [ˈluːsɪdlɪ] *adv* claramente, lúcidamente.

luck [lʌk] *n* suerte *f*, bolada *f Amer*; **good/bad** ~ [good, bad fortune] buena/mala suerte; **good** ~! [said to express best wishes] ¡buena suerte!; **bad** OR **hard** ~! ¡mala suerte!; **to be in** ~ estar de suerte; **to try one's** ~ **at** sthg probar suerte a OR con algo; **with (any)** ~ con un poco de suerte.

◆ **luck out** *vi Am inf* tener potra.

luckily [ˈlʌkɪlɪ] *adv* afortunadamente.

luckless [ˈlʌklɪs] *adj* desafortunado(da), sin suerte.

lucky [ˈlʌkɪ] (*compar* **-ier**, *superl* **-iest**) *adj* **-1.** [fortunate - person] afortunado(da), con suerte; [- event] oportuno(na). **-2.** [bringing good luck] que trae buena suerte; ~ **number** número *m* de la buena suerte.

lucky dip *n Br* caja *f* de las sorpresas.

lucrative [ˈluːkrətɪv] *adj* lucrativo(va).

ludicrous [ˈluːdɪkrəs] *adj* absurdo(da), ridículo(la).

ludo [ˈluːdəʊ] *n Br* parchís *m*.

lug [lʌg] (*pt & pp* **-ged**, *cont* **-ging**) *vt inf* arrastrar, tirar con dificultad.

luggage [ˈlʌgɪdʒ] *n Br* equipaje *m*.

luggage rack *n Br* [of car] baca *f*, portaequipajes *m inv*; [in train] redecilla *f*.

luggage van *n Br* furgón *m* de equipajes.

lugubrious [luˈguːbrɪəs] *adj fml* lúgubre.

lukewarm [ˈluːkwɔːm] *adj* **-1.** [tepid] tibio(bia), templado(da). **-2.** [unenthusiastic] indiferente, desapasionado(da).

lull [lʌl] ◇ *n*: ~ **(in)** [activity] respiro *m* OR pausa *f* (en); [fighting] tregua *f* (en); **the** ~ **before the storm** *fig* la calma antes de la tormenta. ◇ *vt*: **to** ~ **sb into a false sense of security** infundir una sensación de falsa seguridad a alguien; **to** ~ **sb to sleep** adormecer OR hacer dormir a alguien.

lullaby [ˈlʌləbaɪ] (*pl* **-ies**) *n* nana *f*, canción *f* de cuna.

lumbago [lʌmˈbeɪgəʊ] *n* (U) lumbago *m*.

lumber [ˈlʌmbəʳ] ◇ *n* (U) **-1.** *Am* [timber] maderos *mpl*. **-2.** *Br* [bric-a-brac] trastos *mpl*. ◇ *vi* moverse pesadamente.

◆ **lumber with** *vt sep Br inf*: **to** ~ **sb with** sthg cargar a alguien con algo.

lumbering [ˈlʌmbərɪŋ] *adj* torpe, pesado(da).

lumberjack ['lʌmbədʒæk] *n* leñador *m*, -ra *f*.

lumbermill ['lʌmbə‚mɪl] *n Am* aserradero *m*, serrería *f*.

lumber-room *n Br* cuarto *m* trastero.

lumberyard ['lʌmbəjɑːd] *n* almacén *m* de madera.

luminous ['luːmɪnəs] *adj* luminoso(sa).

lump [lʌmp] ◇ *n* **-1.** [of coal, earth] trozo *m*; [of sugar] terrón *m*; [in sauce] grumo *m*. **-2.** [on body] bulto *m*. **-3.** *fig* [in throat] nudo *m*. ◇ *vt*: **to ~ sthg together** [things] amontonar algo; [people, beliefs] agrupar OR juntar algo; **to ~ it** *inf* aguantarse.

lumpectomy [‚lʌm'pektəmɪ] (*pl* **-ies**) *n* extirpación *f* de un tumor de pecho.

lump sum *n* suma *f* OR cantidad *f* global.

lumpy ['lʌmpɪ] (*compar* **-ier**, *superl* **-iest**) *adj* [sauce] grumoso(sa); [mattress] lleno(na) de bultos.

lunacy ['luːnəsɪ] *n* locura *f*.

lunar ['luːnəʳ] *adj* lunar.

lunatic ['luːnətɪk] ◇ *adj pej* demencial. ◇ *n* **-1.** *pej* [fool] idiota *m y f*. **-2.** [insane person] loco *m*, -ca *f*.

lunatic asylum *n* manicomio *m*.

lunatic fringe *n* grupúsculo *m* extremista.

lunch [lʌntʃ] ◇ *n* comida *f*, almuerzo *m*. ◇ *vi* almorzar, comer.

luncheon ['lʌntʃən] *n fml* comida *f*, almuerzo *m*.

luncheonette [‚lʌntʃə'net] *n Am* cafetería *f*.

luncheon meat *n* carne de cerdo en lata troceada.

luncheon voucher *n Br* vale *m* del almuerzo.

lunch hour *n* hora *f* del almuerzo.

lunchtime ['lʌntʃtaɪm] *n* hora *f* del almuerzo.

lung [lʌŋ] *n* pulmón *m*.

lung cancer *n* cáncer *m* de pulmón.

lunge [lʌndʒ] (*cont* **lungeing**) *vi* lanzarse, abalanzarse; **to ~ at sb** arremeter contra alguien.

lupin *Br* ['luːpɪn], **lupine** *Am* ['luːpaɪn] *n* altramuz *m*, lupino *m*.

lurch [lɜːtʃ] ◇ *n* [of boat] bandazo *m*; [of person] tumbo *m*; **to leave sb in the ~** dejar a alguien en la estacada. ◇ *vi* [boat] dar bandazos; [person] tambalearse.

lure [ljʊəʳ] ◇ *n* fascinación *f*, atracción *f*. ◇ *vt* atraer OR convencer con engaños.

lurid ['ljʊərɪd] *adj* **-1.** [brightly coloured] chillón(ona). **-2.** [shockingly unpleasant] espeluznante.

lurk [lɜːk] *vi* **-1.** [person] estar al acecho. **-2.** [memory, danger, fear] ocultarse.

lurking ['lɜːkɪŋ] *adj* que sigue rondando.

Lusaka [luː'sɑːkə] *n* Lusaka.

luscious ['lʌʃəs] *adj lit* & *fig* apetitoso(sa).

lush [lʌʃ] ◇ *adj* **-1.** [luxuriant] exuberante. **-2.** *inf* [rich] lujoso(sa). ◇ *n Am inf* [drunkard] borracho *m*, -cha *f*.

lust [lʌst] *n* **-1.** [sexual desire] lujuria *f*. **-2.** [strong desire]: **~ for sthg** ansia *f* de algo. ◆ **lust after**, **lust for** *vt fus* **-1.** [desire - wealth, success] codiciar. **-2.** [desire sexually] desear.

luster *Am* = **lustre**.

lustful ['lʌstfʊl] *adj* lascivo(va).

lustre *Br*, **luster** *Am* ['lʌstəʳ] *n* [brightness] lustre *m*.

lusty ['lʌstɪ] (*compar* **-ier**, *superl* **-iest**) *adj* vigoroso(sa), fuerte.

lute [luːt] *n* laúd *m*.

luv [lʌv] *n Br inf* rey *m*, reina *f*; **what do you want, ~?** ¿qué quieres, rey?

luvvie ['lʌvɪ] *n inf* figurón *m*, actor *m*, -triz *f* pedante.

Luxembourg ['lʌksəm‚bɜːg] *n* Luxemburgo.

luxuriant [lʌg'ʒʊərɪənt] *adj* exuberante, abundante.

luxuriate [lʌg'ʒʊərɪeɪt] *vi*: **to ~ (in)** deleitarse (con).

luxurious [lʌg'ʒʊərɪəs] *adj* **-1.** [expensive] lujoso(sa). **-2.** [pleasurable] voluptuoso(sa).

luxury ['lʌkʃərɪ] (*pl* **-ies**) ◇ *n* lujo *m*. ◇ *comp* de lujo.

luxury goods *npl* artículos *mpl* de lujo.

LV *abbr of* **luncheon voucher**.

LW (*abbr of* **long wave**) *n* OL *f*.

lychee [‚laɪ'tʃiː] *n* lichi *m*.

Lycra® ['laɪkrə] ◇ *n* lycra® *f*. ◇ *comp* de lycra.

lying ['laɪɪŋ] ◇ *adj* mentiroso(sa), falso(sa). ◇ *n* (*U*) mentira *f*.

lymph gland [lɪmf-] *n* glándula *f* linfática.

lynch [lɪntʃ] *vt* linchar.

lynx [lɪŋks] (*pl inv* OR **-es**) *n* lince *m*.

lyre ['laɪəʳ] *n* lira *f*.

lyric ['lɪrɪk] *adj* lírico(ca).

lyrical ['lɪrɪkl] *adj* **-1.** [poetic] lírico(ca). **-2.** [enthusiastic] entusiasmado(da).

lyrics ['lɪrɪks] *npl* letra *f*.

m¹ (*pl* **m's** OR **ms**), **M** (*pl* **M's** OR **Ms**) [em] *n* [letter] m *f*, M *f*.
◆ **M** -**1.** *abbr of* **motorway**. -**2.** (*abbr of* **medium**) M.

m² -**1.** (*abbr of* **metre**) m. -**2.** (*abbr of* **million**) m. -**3.** *abbr of* **mile**.

ma [mɑː] *n inf* mamá *f*.

MA ◇ *n* -**1.** *abbr of* **Master of Arts**. -**2.** (*abbr of* **military academy**) *academia militar.* ◇ *abbr of* **Massachusetts**.

ma'am [mæm] *n* señora *f*.

mac [mæk] (*abbr of* **mackintosh**) *n Br inf* [coat] impermeable *m*.

macabre [məˈkɑːbrə] *adj* macabro(bra).

Macao [məˈkaʊ] *n* Macao.

macaroni [ˌmækəˈrəʊnɪ] *n* (*U*) macarrones *mpl*.

macaroni cheese *n* macarrones *mpl* al gratén.

macaroon [ˌmækəˈruːn] *n* mostachón *m*, macarrón *m*.

mace [meɪs] *n* -**1.** [ornamental rod] maza *f*. -**2.** [spice] macis *f inv*.

Macedonia [ˌmæsɪˈdəʊnɪə] *n* Macedonia.

Macedonian [ˌmæsɪˈdəʊnɪən] ◇ *adj* macedonio(nia). ◇ *n* macedonio *m*, -nia *f*.

machete [məˈʃetɪ] *n* machete *m*.

Machiavellian [ˌmækɪəˈvelɪən] *adj* maquiavélico(ca).

machinations [ˌmækɪˈneɪʃnz] *npl* maquinaciones *fpl*.

machine [məˈʃiːn] ◇ *n* -**1.** [power-driven device] máquina *f*. -**2.** [organization] aparato *m*. ◇ *vt* -**1.** SEWING coser a máquina. -**2.** TECH hacer con una máquina.

machine code *n* COMPUT código *m* máquina.

machinegun [məˈʃiːngʌn] (*pt* & *pp* **-ned**, *cont* **-ning**) ◇ *n* ametralladora *f*. ◇ *vt* ametrallar.

machine language *n* COMPUT lenguaje *m* máquina.

machine-readable *adj* COMPUT legible por máquina.

machinery [məˈʃiːnərɪ] *n lit* & *fig* maquinaria *f*.

machine shop *n* taller *m* de máquinas.

machine tool *n* máquina *f* herramienta.

machine-washable *adj* lavable a máquina.

machinist [məˈʃiːnɪst] *n* operario *m*, -ria *f* (de máquina).

machismo [məˈtʃɪzməʊ] *n* machismo *m*.

macho [ˈmætʃəʊ] *adj inf* macho.

mackerel [ˈmækrəl] (*pl inv* OR **-s**) *n* caballa *f*.

mackintosh [ˈmækɪntɒʃ] *n Br* impermeable *m*.

macramé [məˈkrɑːmɪ] *n* macramé *m*.

macro [ˈmækrəʊ] (*abbr of* **macroinstruction**) *n* COMPUT macro *f*.

macrobiotic [ˌmækrəʊbaɪˈɒtɪk] *adj* macrobiótico(ca).

macrocosm [ˈmækrəʊkɒzm] *n* macrocosmo *m*.

macroeconomics [ˈmækrəʊˌiːkəˈnɒmɪks] *n* (*U*) macroeconomía *f*.

mad [mæd] (*compar* **-der**, *superl* **-dest**) *adj* -**1.** [gen] loco(ca); [attempt, idea] disparatado(da), descabellado(da); **to be ~ about** sb/sthg estar loco(ca) por alguien/algo; **to go ~** volverse loco. -**2.** [furious] furioso(sa), enloquecido(da). -**3.** [hectic] desenfrenado(da); **like ~** como loco.

Madagascan [ˌmædəˈgæskən] ◇ *adj* malgache. ◇ *n* -**1.** [person] malgache *m y f*. -**2.** [language] malgache *m*.

Madagascar [ˌmædəˈgæskəʳ] *n* Madagascar.

madam [ˈmædəm] *n* señora *f*.

madcap [ˈmædkæp] *adj* descabellado(da), disparatado(da).

madden [ˈmædn] *vt* volver loco(ca), exasperar.

maddening [ˈmædnɪŋ] *adj* enloquecedor.

made [meɪd] *pt* & *pp* → **make**.

-made [meɪd] *suffix*: **French~** fabricado(da) en Francia.

Madeira [məˈdɪərə] *n* -**1.** [wine] madeira *m*, madera *m*. -**2.** GEOGR Madeira.

made-to-measure *adj* hecho(cha) a la medida.

made-up *adj* -**1.** [with make-up - face, person] maquillado(da); [- lips, eyes] pintado(da). -**2.** [prepared] (ya) preparado(da). -**3.** [invented] inventado(da).

madhouse [ˈmædhaʊs, *pl* -haʊzɪz] *n* manicomio *m*.

madly [ˈmædlɪ] *adv* [frantically] enloquecidamente; **~ in love** locamente enamorado.

madman ['mædmən] (*pl* **-men** [-mən]) *n* loco *m*.

madness ['mædnıs] *n* locura *f*.

Madonna [mə'dɒnə] *n* **-1.** RELIG: **the** ~ la Virgen. **-2.** ART madona *f*.

Madrid [mə'drıd] *n* Madrid.

madrigal ['mædrıgl] *n* madrigal *m*.

madwoman ['mæd,wʊmən] (*pl* **-women** [-,wımın]) *n* loca *f*.

maestro ['maıstrəʊ] (*pl* **-tros** OR **-tri** [-trı]) *n* maestro *m*.

Mafia ['mæfıə] *n*: **the** ~ la mafia.

mag [mæg] (*abbr of* **magazine**) *n inf* revista *f*.

magazine [,mægə'ziːn] *n* **-1.** [periodical] revista *f*. **-2.** [news programme] magazín *m*. **-3.** [on a gun] recámara *f*.

magenta [mə'dʒentə] ◇ *adj* magenta. ◇ *n* magenta *m*.

maggot ['mægət] *n* gusano *m*, cresa *f*.

Maghreb ['mʌgreb] *n*: **the** ~ el Magreb.

magic ['mædʒık] ◇ *adj* **-1.** [gen] mágico(ca); ~ **spell** hechizo *m*. **-2.** [referring to conjuring] de magia. ◇ *n* magia *f*.

magical ['mædʒıkl] *adj lit* & *fig* mágico(ca).

magic carpet *n* alfombra *f* mágica.

magic eye *n Br* célula *f* fotoeléctrica.

magician [mə'dʒıʃn] *n* **-1.** [conjuror] ilusionista *m y f*, prestidigitador *m*, -ra *f*. **-2.** [wizard] mago *m*.

magic wand *n* varita *f* mágica.

magisterial [,mædʒı'stıərıəl] *adj* **-1.** *fml* [authoritative] magistral. **-2.** JUR de magistrado(da).

magistrate ['mædʒıstreıt] *n* magistrado *m*, -da *f*.

magistrates' court *n Br* juzgado *m* de primera instancia.

Magna Carta [,mægnə'kɑːtə] *n*: **the** ~ la Carta Magna.

magnanimous [mæg'nænıməs] *adj* magnánimo(ma).

magnate ['mægneıt] *n* magnate *m*.

magnesium [mæg'niːzıəm] *n* magnesio *m*.

magnet ['mægnıt] *n* imán *m*.

magnetic [mæg'netık] *adj* **-1.** [attracting iron] magnético(ca). **-2.** *fig* [appealingly forceful] atrayente, carismático(ca).

magnetic disk *n* disco *m* magnético.

magnetic field *n* campo *m* magnético.

magnetic tape *n* cinta *f* magnetofónica.

magnetism ['mægnıtızm] *n lit* & *fig* magnetismo *m*.

magnification [,mægnıfı'keıʃn] *n* **-1.** [process] ampliación *f*. **-2.** [degree of enlargement] aumento *m*.

magnificence [mæg'nıfısəns] *n* grandiosidad *f*, esplendor *m*.

magnificent [mæg'nıfısənt] *adj* [building, splendour] grandioso(sa); [idea, book, game] magnífico(ca).

magnify ['mægnıfaı] (*pt* & *pp* **-ied**) *vt* **-1.** [in vision] aumentar. **-2.** [in the mind] exagerar.

magnifying glass ['mægnıfaıŋ-] *n* lupa *f*, lente *f* de aumento.

magnitude ['mægnıtjuːd] *n* magnitud *f*.

magnolia [mæg'nəʊljə] *n* **-1.** [tree] magnolio *m*. **-2.** [flower] magnolia *f*.

magnum ['mægnəm] (*pl* **-s**) *n* botella *de 1,5 litros de capacidad*.

magpie ['mægpaı] *n* urraca *f*.

maharaja(h) [,mɑːhə'rɑːdʒə] *n* maharajá *m*.

mahogany [mə'hɒgənı] *n* [wood] caoba *f*; [colour] caoba *m*.

maid [meıd] *n* [in hotel] camarera *f*, recamarera *f Amer*; [domestic] criada *f*, china *f Amer*.

maiden ['meıdn] ◇ *adj* inaugural. ◇ *n literary* doncella *f*.

maiden aunt *n* tía *f* soltera.

maiden name *n* nombre *m* de soltera.

maiden speech *n* POL discurso *m* inaugural.

mail [meıl] ◇ *n* **-1.** [letters, parcels received] correspondencia *f*. **-2.** [system] correo *m*; **by** ~ por correo. ◇ *vt* [send] mandar por correo; [put in mail box] echar al buzón.

mailbag ['meılbæg] *n* saca *f* de correspondencia.

mailbox ['meılbɒks] *n Am* buzón *m*.

mailing list ['meılıŋ-] *n* lista *f* de distribución de publicidad OR información.

mailman ['meılmən] (*pl* **-men** [-mən]) *n Am* cartero *m*.

mail order *n* pedido *m* por correo.

mailshot ['meılʃɒt] *n* folleto *m* de publicidad (por correo).

mail train *n* tren *m* correo.

mail truck *n Am* furgoneta *f* postal.

mail van *n Br* **-1.** AUT furgoneta *f* postal. **-2.** RAIL vagón *m* postal.

maim [meım] *vt* mutilar.

main [meın] ◇ *adj* principal. ◇ *n* [pipe] tubería *f* principal; [wire] cable *m* principal.
◆ **mains** *npl*: **the** ~**s** [gas, water] la tubería principal; [electricity] la red eléctrica.
◆ **in the main** *adv* por lo general.

main course *n* plato *m* fuerte.

Maine [meın] *n* Maine.

mainframe (computer) ['meınfreım-] *n* unidad *f* central, procesador *m* central.

mainland ['meɪnlənd] ◇ *adj* continental; ~ Spain la Península. ◇ *n*: **the** ~ el continente.

main line *n* RAIL línea *f* principal.

◆ **mainline** ◇ *adj* de una línea principal. ◇ *vt & vi drugs sl* chutarse, pincharse.

mainly ['meɪnlɪ] *adv* principalmente.

main road *n* carretera *f* principal.

mainsail ['meɪnseɪl, 'meɪnsəl] *n* vela *f* mayor.

mainstay ['meɪnsteɪ] *n* fundamento *m*, base *f*.

mainstream ['meɪnstriːm] ◇ *adj* [gen] predominante; [taste] corriente; [political party] convencional. ◇ *n*: **the** ~ la tendencia general.

maintain [meɪn'teɪn] *vt* -1. [gen] mantener. -2. [support, provide for] sostener, sustentar. -3. [assert]: **to** ~ **(that)** sostener que.

maintenance ['meɪntənəns] *n* -1. [gen] mantenimiento *m*. -2. [money] pensión *f* alimenticia.

maintenance order *n Br* JUR orden *m* de pensión alimenticia.

maisonette [,meɪzə'net] *n* dúplex *m inv*.

maize [meɪz] *n* maíz *m*.

Maj. (*abbr of* **Major**) ≃ Cte.

majestic [mə'dʒestɪk] *adj* majestuoso(sa).

majestically [mə'dʒestɪklɪ] *adv* majestuosamente.

majesty ['mædʒəstɪ] (*pl* -ies) *n* [grandeur] majestad *f*.

◆ **Majesty** *n*: **His/Her/Your Majesty** Su Majestad.

major ['meɪdʒər] ◇ *adj* -1. [important] principal. -2. MUS mayor. -3 *n* MIL comandante *m*. ◇ *vi*: **to** ~ **in** especializarse en.

Majorca [mə'jɔːkə, mə'dʒɔːkə] *n* Mallorca.

Majorcan [mə'jɔːkən, mə'dʒɔːkən] ◇ *adj* mallorquín(ina). ◇ *n* mallorquín *m*, -ina *f*.

majorette [,meɪdʒə'ret] *n* majorette *f*.

major general *n* general *m* de división.

majority [mə'dʒɒrətɪ] (*pl* -ies) *n* mayoría *f*; **in a** OR **the** ~ en una OR la mayoría.

majority shareholder *n* accionista *m y f* principal.

make [meɪk] (*pt & pp* **made**) ◇ *vt* -1. [produce] hacer; **it made a lot of noise** hizo mucho ruido; **she ~s her own clothes** se hace su propia ropa. -2. [perform - action] hacer; **to** ~ **a speech** pronunciar OR dar un discurso; **to** ~ **a decision** tomar una decisión; **to** ~ **a mistake** cometer un error. -3. [cause to be, cause to do] hacer; **it ~s me seem fatter** me hace parecer más gordo; **it ~s me sick** me pone enfermo; **it made him angry** hizo que se enfadara; **you made me jump!** ¡vaya

susto que me has dado!; **we were made to wait in the hall** nos hicieron esperar en el vestíbulo; **to** ~ **sb happy** hacer a alguien feliz; **to** ~ **sb sad** entristecer a alguien; **to** ~ **o.s. heard** hacerse oír; **don't** ~ **me laugh!** ¡no me hagas reír! **-4.** [force]: **to** ~ **sb do sthg** hacer que alguien haga algo, obligar a alguien a hacer algo; **they made the hostages lie on the ground** hicieron tumbarse en el suelo a los rehenes. **-5.** [construct]: **to be made of sthg** estar hecho(cha) de algo; **it's made of wood/metal** está hecho de madera/metal; **made in Spain** fabricado en España; **what's it made of?** ¿de qué está hecho? **-6.** [add up to] hacer, ser; **2 and 2** ~ **4** 2 y 2 hacen OR son 4. **-7.** [calculate] calcular; **I** ~ **it 50/six o'clock** calculo que serán 50/las seis; **what time do you** ~ **it?** ¿qué hora es? **-8.** [earn] ganar; **she ~s £20,000 a year** gana 20.000 libras al año; **to** ~ **a profit** obtener beneficios; **to** ~ **a loss** sufrir pérdidas. **-9.** [have the right qualities for] ser; **she'd** ~ **a good doctor** seguro que sería una buena doctora; **books** ~ **excellent presents** los libros son un regalo excelente. **-10.** [reach] llegar a. **-11.** [cause to be a success]: **she really ~s the play** ella es la que de verdad levanta la obra. **-12.** [gain - friend, enemy] hacer; **to** ~ **friends with sb** hacerse amigo de alguien. **-13.** *phr*: **to** ~ **it** [arrive in time] conseguir llegar a tiempo; [be a success] alcanzar el éxito; [be able to attend] venir/ir; **to have it made** tenerlo hecho, tener el éxito asegurado; **to** ~ **do with sthg** apañarse OR arreglarse con algo. ◇ *n* -1. [brand] marca; **what** ~ **is your car?** ¿de qué marca es tu coche? -2. *v inf pej*: **to be on the** ~ [act dishonestly, selfishly] barrer siempre para dentro.

◆ **make for** *vt fus* -1. [move towards] dirigirse a OR hacia. -2. [contribute to] posibilitar, contribuir a.

◆ **make of** *vt sep* -1. [understand] entender; **what do you** ~ **of this word?** ¿qué entiendes tú por esta palabra? -2. [have opinion of] opinar de.

◆ **make off** *vi* darse a la fuga.

◆ **make off with** *vt fus inf* birlar.

◆ **make out** ◇ *vt sep* -1. *inf* [see] distinguir; [hear] entender, oír. -2. *inf* [understand - word, number] descifrar; [- person, attitude] comprender. -3. [fill out - form] rellenar, cumplimentar; [- cheque, receipt] extender; [- list] hacer. ◇ *vt fus inf* [pretend] fingir, pretender; **she ~s out she's tough** se las da de dura.

◆ **make up** ◇ *vt sep* -1. [compose, constitute] componer, constituir. -2. [invent] inventar. -3. [apply cosmetics to] maquillar; **to** ~ **o.s. up** maquillarse. -4. [prepare - parcel, prescription, bed] **preparar, hacer. -5.** [make complete - amount] **completar;** [- difference] **cubrir. -6.** [resolve - quarrel]: **to ~ it up (with sb)** hacer las paces (con alguien). ◇ *vi* [become friends again]: **to ~ up (with sb)** hacer las paces (con alguien).

◆ **make up for** *vt fus* compensar; **to ~ up for** lost time recuperar el tiempo perdido.

◆ **make up to** *vt sep*: **to ~ it up to sb (for sthg)** recompensar a alguien (por algo).

make-believe *n* invención *f*.

maker ['meɪkə'] *n* [of film, programme] creador *m*, -ra *f*; [of product] fabricante *m y f*.

makeshift ['meɪkʃɪft] *adj* [temporary] provisional; [improvized] **improvisado(da).**

make-up *n* **-1.** [cosmetics] maquillaje *m*; **~ bag** neceser *m*; **~ remover** loción *f* OR crema *f* OR leche *f* desmaquilladora. **-2.** [person's character] carácter *m*. **-3.** [structure] estructura *f*; [of team] composición *f*.

makeweight ['meɪkweɪt] *n lit* & *fig* contrapeso *m*.

making ['meɪkɪŋ] *n* [of product] fabricación *f*; [of film] rodaje *m*; [of decision] toma *f*; **this is history in the ~** esto pasará a la historia; **your problems are of your own ~** tus problemas te los has buscado tú mismo; **to be the ~ of sb/sthg** ser la causa del éxito de alguien/algo; **to have the ~s of** tener madera de.

maladjusted [,mælə'dʒʌstɪd] *adj* **inadaptado(da).**

malaise [mæ'leɪz] *n fml* malestar *m*.

malaria [mə'leərɪə] *n* malaria *f*.

Malawi [mə'lɑːwɪ] *n* Malaui.

Malawian [mə'lɑːwɪən] ◇ *adj* malauita. ◇ *n* malauita *m y f*.

Malay [mə'leɪ] ◇ *adj* malayo(ya). ◇ *n* **-1.** [person] malayo *m*, -ya *f*. **-2.** [language] malayo *m*.

Malaya [mə'leɪə] *n* Malaya.

Malayan [mə'leɪən] ◇ *adj* malayo(ya). ◇ *n* malayo *m*, -ya *f*.

Malaysia [mə'leɪzɪə] *n* Malaisia.

Malaysian [mə'leɪzɪən] ◇ *adj* malaisio(sia). ◇ *n* malaisio *m*, -sia *f*.

malcontent ['mælkən,tent] *n* malcontento *m*, -ta *f*.

Maldives ['mɔːldaɪvz] *npl*: **the ~** las Maldivas.

male [meɪl] ◇ *adj* **-1.** [animal] macho. **-2.** [human] masculino(na), varón. **-3.** [concerning men] masculino(na), del hombre. ◇ *n* **-1.** [animal] macho *m*. **-2.** [human] varón *m*.

male chauvinist (pig) *n* machista *m*.

male nurse *n* enfermero *m*.

malevolent [mə'levələnt] *adj* malévolo(la).

malformed [mæl'fɔːmd] *adj* malformado(da).

malfunction [mæl'fʌŋkʃn] ◇ *n* funcionamiento *m* defectuoso. ◇ *vi* funcionar mal.

Mali ['mɑːlɪ] *n* Malí.

malice ['mælɪs] *n* malicia *f*.

malicious [mə'lɪʃəs] *adj* malicioso(sa), malévolo(la).

malign [mə'laɪn] ◇ *adj* maligno(na), perjudicial. ◇ *vt fml* difamar, hablar mal de.

malignant [mə'lɪgnənt] *adj* **-1.** *fml* [full of hate] malvado(da). **-2.** MED maligno(na).

malinger [mə'lɪŋgə'] *vi pej* fingirse enfermo(ma).

malingerer [mə'lɪŋgərə'] *n pej* enfermo fingido *m*, enferma fingida *f*.

mall [mɔːl] *n*: **(shopping) ~** centro *m* comercial peatonal.

malleable ['mælɪəbl] *adj lit* & *fig* maleable.

mallet ['mælɪt] *n* mazo *m*.

malnourished [,mæl'nʌrɪʃt] *adj* malnutrido(da).

malnutrition [,mælnjuː'trɪʃn] *n* malnutrición *f*.

malpractice [,mæl'præktɪs] *n* (U) JUR negligencia *f*.

malt [mɔːlt] *n* **-1.** [grain] malta *f*. **-2.** [whisky] whisky *m* de malta.

Malta ['mɔːltə] *n* Malta.

Maltese [,mɔːl'tiːz] (*pl inv*) ◇ *adj* maltés(esa). ◇ *n* **-1.** [person] maltés *m*, -esa *f*. **-2.** [language] maltés *m*.

maltreat [,mæl'triːt] *vt* maltratar.

maltreatment [,mæl'triːtmənt] *n* malos tratos *mpl*.

malt whisky *n* whisky *m* de malta.

mammal ['mæml] *n* mamífero *m*.

Mammon ['mæmən] *n* becerro *m* de oro.

mammoth ['mæməθ] ◇ *adj* descomunal, gigante. ◇ *n* mamut *m*.

man [mæn] (*pl* **men**, *pt* & *pp* **-ned**, *cont* **-ning**) ◇ *n* hombre *m*; **the ~ in the street** el hombre de la calle, el ciudadano de a pie; **to talk ~ to ~** hablar de hombre a hombre; **to be ~ enough to do sthg** ser lo suficientemente hombre para hacer algo. ◇ *vt* [gen] manejar; [ship, plane] tripular; **manned 24 hours a day** [telephone] en servicio las 24 horas del día.

manacles ['mænəklz] *npl* esposas *fpl*, grilletes *mpl*.

manage ['mænɪdʒ] ◇ *vi* **-1.** [cope] poder; **can you ~ with that box?** ¿puedes con la caja? **-2.** [survive] arreglárselas, apañárselas. ◇ *vt* **-1.** [succeed]: **to ~ to do sthg** conseguir hacer algo. **-2.** [company] dirigir, llevar;

[money] administrar, manejar; [pop star] re-presentar; [time] organizar. **-3.** [be available for]: **I can only ~ an hour tonight** sólo dispongo de una hora esta noche.

manageable ['mænɪdʒəbl] *adj* [task] factible, posible; [children] dominable; [inflation, rate] controlable.

management ['mænɪdʒmənt] *n* **-1.** [control, running] gestión *f*. **-2.** [people in control] dirección *f*.

management consultant *n* asesor *m*, -ra *f* en gestión de empresas.

manager ['mænɪdʒəʳ] *n* **-1.** [of company] director *m*, -ra *f*; [of shop] jefe *m*, -fa *f*; [of pop star] manager *m* y *f*. **-2.** SPORT ≈ entrenador *m*, -ra *f*.

manageress [ˌmænɪdʒəˈres] *n Br* [of company] directora *f*; [of shop] jefa *f*.

managerial [ˌmænɪˈdʒɪərɪəl] *adj* directivo(va).

managing director ['mænɪdʒɪŋ-] *n* director *m*, -ra *f* gerente.

Managua [məˈnægwə] *n* Managua.

Mancunian [mænˈkjuːnjən] ◇ *adj* de o relativo a Manchester. ◇ *n* natural o habitante de Manchester.

mandarin ['mændərɪn] *n* **-1.** [fruit] mandarina *f*. **-2.** [civil servant] mandarín *m*, -ina *f*, persona *f* demasiado influyente.

mandate ['mændeɪt] *n* **-1.** [elected right or authority] mandato *m*. **-2.** [task] misión *f*.

mandatory ['mændətrɪ] *adj* obligatorio(ria).

mandolin [mændəˈlɪn] *n* mandolina *f*.

mane [meɪn] *n* [of horse] crin *f*; [of lion] melena *f*.

man-eating [-ˌiːtɪŋ] *adj* que come carne humana.

maneuver *Am* = **manoeuvre**.

manfully ['mænfʊlɪ] *adv* valientemente.

manganese ['mæŋgəniːz] *n* manganeso *m*.

mange [meɪndʒ] *n* sarna *f*.

manger ['meɪndʒəʳ] *n* pesebre *m*.

mangetout (pea) [ˌmãʒ'tuː-] *n Br* guisante *m* mollar.

mangle ['mæŋgl] *vt* [crush] aplastar; [tear to pieces] despedazar.

mango ['mæŋgəʊ] (*pl* **-es** OR **-s**) *n* mango *m*.

mangrove ['mæŋgrəʊv] *n* mangle *m*.

mangy ['meɪndʒɪ] (*compar* **-ier**, *superl* **-iest**) *adj* sarnoso(sa).

manhandle ['mænˌhændl] *vt* [person] maltratar.

manhole ['mænhəʊl] *n* boca *f* (del alcantarillado).

manhood ['mænhʊd] *n* **-1.** [state] madurez *f*, virilidad *f*. **-2.** [time] edad *f* viril OR adulta.

manhour ['mæn,aʊəʳ] *n* hora *f* de trabajo (realizada por una persona).

manhunt ['mænhʌnt] *n* búsqueda *f* (de un delincuente).

mania ['meɪnjə] *n* **-1.** [excessive liking]: ~ **(for)** manía *f* (por). **-2.** PSYCH manía *f*.

maniac ['meɪnɪæk] *n* **-1.** [madman] maníaco *m*, -ca *f*. **-2.** [fanatic] fanático *m*, -ca *f*.

manic ['mænɪk] *adj* maníaco(ca).

manic-depressive ◇ *adj* maníacodepresivo(va). ◇ *n* maníacodepresivo *m*, -va *f*.

manicure ['mænɪˌkjʊəʳ] ◇ *n* manicura *f*. ◇ *vt*: **to ~ sb** hacerle la manicura a alguien; **to ~ one's nails** arreglarse las uñas.

manifest ['mænɪfest] *fml* ◇ *adj* manifiesto(ta), evidente. ◇ *vt* manifestar.

manifestation [ˌmænɪfesˈteɪʃn] *n fml* manifestación *f*.

manifestly ['mænɪfestlɪ] *adv fml* evidentemente, claramente.

manifesto [ˌmænɪˈfestəʊ] (*pl* **-s** OR **-es**) *n* manifiesto *m*.

manifold ['mænɪfəʊld] ◇ *adj literary* múltiple. ◇ *n* AUT colector *m*.

manil(l)a [məˈnɪlə] *adj* manila (*inv*).

Manila [məˈnɪlə] *n* Manila.

manipulate [məˈnɪpjʊleɪt] *vt* **-1.** [control for personal benefit] manipular. **-2.** [machine] manejar; [controls, lever] accionar.

manipulation [məˌnɪpjʊˈleɪʃn] *n* **-1.** [control for personal benefit] manipulación *f*. **-2.** [machine] manejo *m*, operación *f*; [of controls, lever] accionamiento *m*.

manipulative [məˈnɪpjʊlətɪv] *adj* manipulador(ra).

Manitoba [ˌmænɪˈtəʊbə] *n* Manitoba.

mankind [mænˈkaɪnd] *n* la humanidad, el género humano.

manly ['mænlɪ] (*compar* **-ier**, *superl* **-iest**) *adj* varonil, viril.

man-made *adj* [environment, problem, disaster] producido(da) por el hombre; [fibre] artificial.

manna ['mænə] *n* maná *m*.

manned [mænd] *adj* tripulado(da).

mannequin ['mænɪkɪn] *n dated* maniquí *m* y *f*.

manner ['mænəʳ] *n* **-1.** [method] manera *f*, forma *f*; **in a ~ of speaking** por así decirlo. **-2.** [bearing, attitude] comportamiento *m*. **-3.**

esp literary [type, sort] tipo *m*, clase *f*; **all ~ of** toda clase OR todo tipo de.

◆ **manners** *npl* modales *mpl*; **it's good/bad ~s to do sthg** es de buena/mala educación hacer algo.

mannered ['mænəd] *adj fml* afectado(da), amanerado(da).

mannerism ['mænərɪzm] *n* costumbre *f* (típica de uno).

mannish ['mænɪʃ] *adj* [woman] hombruno(na).

manoeuvrable *Br*, **maneuverable** *Am* [mə'nuːvrəbl] *adj* manejable.

manoeuvre *Br*, **maneuver** *Am* [mə'nuːvəʳ] ◇ *n lit* & *fig* maniobra *f*. ◇ *vt* maniobrar, manejar. ◇ *vi* maniobrar.

◆ **manoeuvres** *npl* MIL maniobras *fpl*.

manor ['mænəʳ] *n* [house] casa *f* solariega.

manpower ['mæn,paʊəʳ] *n* [manual workers] mano *f* de obra; [white-collar workers] personal *m*.

manservant ['mænsɜːvənt] (*pl* **menservants**) *n dated* criado *m*, sirviente *m*, mucamo *m Amer*.

mansion ['mænʃn] *n* [manor] casa *f* solariega; [big house] casa grande.

man-size(d) *adj* de tamaño extra-largo, muy grande.

manslaughter ['mæn,slɔːtəʳ] *n* homicidio *m* involuntario.

mantelpiece ['mæntlpiːs] *n* repisa *f* (de la chimenea).

mantle ['mæntl] *n* **-1.** [layer, covering] capa *f*. **-2.** [of leadership, high office] manto *m*.

man-to-man *adj* de hombre a hombre.

manual ['mænjʊəl] ◇ *adj* manual. ◇ *n* manual *m*.

manually ['mænjʊəlɪ] *adv* manualmente, a mano.

manual worker *n* obrero *m*, -ra *f*.

manufacture [,mænjʊ'fæktʃəʳ] ◇ *n* manufacturación *f*, fabricación *f*. ◇ *vt* **-1.** [make] manufacturar, fabricar. **-2.** [invent] inventar.

manufacturer [,mænjʊ'fæktʃərəʳ] *n* fabricante *m* y *f*.

manufacturing [,mænjʊ'fæktʃərɪŋ] *n* manufacturación *f*, fabricación *f*.

manufacturing industries *npl* industrias *fpl* manufactureras.

manure [mə'njʊəʳ] *n* estiércol *m*, abono *m*.

manuscript ['mænjʊskrɪpt] *n* **-1.** [gen] manuscrito *m*. **-2.** [in exam] hoja *f* de examen.

Manx [mæŋks] ◇ *adj* de o relativo a la Isla de Man. ◇ *n* [language] lengua de la Isla de Man.

many ['menɪ] (*compar* **more**, *superl* **most**) ◇ *adj* muchos(chas); **~ people** muchas personas, mucha gente; **how ~?** ¿cuántos(tas)?; **I wonder how ~ people went** me pregunto cuánta gente fue; **too ~** demasiados(das); **there weren't too ~ students** no había muchos estudiantes; **as ~ ... as** tantos(tas) ... como; **so ~** tantos(tas); **I've never seen so ~ people** nunca había visto tanta gente; **a good** OR **great ~** muchísimos(mas). ◇ *pron* muchos(chas).

Maori ['maʊrɪ] ◇ *adj* maorí. ◇ *n* maorí *m* y *f*.

map [mæp] (*pt* & *pp* **-ped**, *cont* **-ping**) *n* mapa *m*.

◆ **map out** *vt sep* planear, planificar.

maple ['meɪpl] *n* arce *m*.

maple leaf *n* hoja *f* de arce.

maple syrup *n* jarabe *m* de arce.

Maputo [mə'puːtəʊ] *n* Maputo.

mar [maːʳ] (*pt* & *pp* **-red**, *cont* **-ring**) *vt* deslucir.

Mar. (*abbr of* **March**) mar.

marathon ['mærəθn] ◇ *adj* maratoniano(na). ◇ *n* maratón *m*.

marathon runner *n* corredor *m*, -ra *f* de maratón.

marauder [mə'rɔːdəʳ] *n* merodeador *m*, -ra *f*.

marauding [mə'rɔːdɪŋ] *adj* **-1.** [human] merodeador(ra). **-2.** [animal] depredador(ra).

marble ['maːbl] *n* **-1.** [stone] mármol *m*. **-2.** [for game] canica *f*, bolita *f Amer*.

◆ **marbles** *n* (*U*) [game] canicas *fpl*.

march [maːtʃ] ◇ *n* **-1.** MIL marcha *f*. **-2.** [of demonstrators] manifestación *f*. **-3.** [steady progress] avance *m*, progreso *m*. ◇ *vi* **-1.** [in formation] marchar. **-2.** [in protest] hacer una manifestación, manifestarse. **-3.** [speedily]: **to ~ out** salir enfadado(da); **to ~ up to sb** abordar a alguien decididamente. ◇ *vt* llevar por la fuerza.

March [maːtʃ] *n* marzo *m*; *see also* **September**.

marcher ['maːtʃəʳ] *n* [protester] manifestante *m* y *f*.

marching orders ['maːtʃɪŋ-] *npl*: **to give sb his/her ~** expulsar a alguien.

marchioness ['maːʃənes] *n* marquesa *f*.

march-past *n* desfile *m*.

Mardi Gras [,maːdɪ'graː] *n* Martes *m* de Carnaval.

mare [meəʳ] *n* yegua *f*.

marg. *n inf abbr of* **margarine**.

margarine [,maːdʒə'riːn, ,maːgə'riːn] *n* margarina *f*.

marge [maːdʒ] *n inf* margarina *f*.

margin ['mɑːdʒɪn] *n* -1. [gen] margen *m*. -2. [of desert, forest] límite *m*, lindero *m*.

marginal ['mɑːdʒɪnl] *adj* -1. [unimportant] marginal. -2. *Br* POL: ~ **seat** OR **constituency** escaño vulnerable a ser perdido en las elecciones por tener una mayoría escasa.

marginally ['mɑːdʒɪnəlɪ] *adv* ligeramente.

marigold ['mærɪɡəʊld] *n* caléndula *f*.

marihuana, **marijuana** [,mærɪ'wɑːnə] *n* marihuana *f*.

marina [mə'riːnə] *n* puerto *m* deportivo.

marinade [,mærɪ'neɪd] ◇ *n* [of fish] marinada *f*; [of meat] adobo *m*. ◇ *vt & vi* [fish] marinar.

marinate ['mærɪneɪt] *vt & vi* [fish] marinar; [meat] adobar.

marine [mə'riːn] ◇ *adj* marino(na). ◇ *n* soldado *m* de infantería de marina.

marionette [,mærɪə'net] *n* marioneta *f*, títere *m*.

marital ['mærɪtl] *adj* marital, matrimonial.

marital status *n* estado *m* civil.

maritime ['mærɪtaɪm] *adj* marítimo(ma).

Maritime Provinces, **Maritimes** *npl*: the ~ las Provincias Marítimas.

marjoram ['mɑːdʒərəm] *n* mejorana *f*.

mark [mɑːk] ◇ *n* -1. [stain] mancha *f*. -2. [written symbol - on paper] marca *f*; [- in the sand] señal *f*. -3. [in exam] nota *f*; **to get good** ~s sacar buenas notas. -4. [stage, level]: **once past the halfway** ~ una vez llegado a medio camino; **above the billion** ~ por encima del billón. -5. [sign - of respect] señal *f*; [- of illness, old age] huella *f*. -6. [currency] marco *m*. -7. *phr*: **to make one's** ~ dejar huella, distinguirse; **to be quick/slow off the** ~ reaccionar rápido/tarde; **wide of the** ~ lejos de la verdad.
◇ *vt* -1. [stain] manchar. -2. [label - with initials etc] señalar. -3. [exam, essay] puntuar, calificar. -4. [identify - place] señalar; [- beginning, end] marcar. -5. [commemorate] conmemorar, celebrar. -6. [characterize] caracterizar.

◆ **mark down** *vt sep* -1. COMM [price] rebajar; [goods] bajar el precio de. -2. [downgrade] bajar la nota a.

◆ **mark off** *vt sep* [cross off] tachar.

◆ **mark up** *vt sep* COMM [price] subir; [goods] subir el precio de.

marked [mɑːkt] *adj* [improvement] notable, apreciable; [difference] marcado(da), acusado(da).

markedly ['mɑːkɪdlɪ] *adv* [better] sensiblemente; [worse] acusadamente; [different] marcadamente.

marker ['mɑːkəʳ] *n* [sign] señal *f*.

marker pen *n* rotulador *m*.

market ['mɑːkɪt] ◇ *n* mercado *m*; **on the** ~ a la venta. ◇ *vt* comercializar. ◇ *vi* *Am* [shop]: **to go** ~**ing** ir a hacer la compra.

marketable ['mɑːkɪtəbl] *adj* vendible, comerciable.

market analysis *n* análisis *m* de mercado.

market day *n* (día *m* de) mercado *m*.

market forces *npl* tendencias *fpl* de mercado.

market garden *n* [small] huerto *m*; [large] huerta *f*.

marketing ['mɑːkɪtɪŋ] *n* marketing *m*, estudio *m* de mercados.

marketplace ['mɑːkɪtpleɪs] *n* *lit & fig* mercado *m*.

market price *n* precio *m* corriente OR de mercado.

market research *n* estudio *m* de mercados.

market town *n* población *f* con mercado.

market value *n* valor *m* actual OR en venta.

marking ['mɑːkɪŋ] *n* [of exams etc] corrección *f*.

◆ **markings** *npl* [of flower, animal] pintas *fpl*, manchas *fpl*; [on road] señales *fpl*.

marksman ['mɑːksmən] (*pl* **-men** [-mən]) *n* tirador *m*.

marksmanship ['mɑːksmənʃɪp] *n* puntería *f*.

markup ['mɑːkʌp] *n* subida *f*, aumento *m*.

marmalade ['mɑːməleɪd] *n* mermelada *f* (*de cítricos*).

maroon [mə'ruːn] *adj* granate.

marooned [mə'ruːnd] *adj* incomunicado(da), aislado(da).

marquee [mɑː'kiː] *n* carpa *f*, toldo *m* grande.

marquess ['mɑːkwɪs] = **marquis**.

marquetry ['mɑːkɪtrɪ] *n* marquetería *f*.

marquis ['mɑːkwɪs] *n* marqués *m*.

marriage ['mærɪdʒ] *n* -1. [act] boda *f*. -2. [state, institution] matrimonio *m*.

marriage bureau *n* *Br* agencia *f* matrimonial.

marriage certificate *n* certificado *m* de matrimonio.

marriage guidance *n* asesoría *f* matrimonial.

marriage guidance counsellor *n* consejero *m*, -ra *f* matrimonial.

married ['mærɪd] *adj* -1. [wedded] casado(da). -2. [of marriage] matrimonial, de casado(da).

marrow ['mærəu] *n* **-1.** *Br* [vegetable] calabacín *m* grande. **-2.** [in bones] médula *f*.

marry ['mærɪ] (*pt* & *pp* **-ied**) ◇ *vt* casar; **to get married** casarse. ◇ *vi* casarse.

Mars [mɑːz] *n* Marte *m*.

Marseilles [mɑːˈseɪlz] *n* Marsella.

marsh [mɑːʃ] *n* **-1.** [area of land] zona *f* pantanosa. **-2.** [type of land] pantano *m*.

marshal ['mɑːʃl] (*Br pt* & *pp* **-led**, *cont* **-ling**, *Am pt* & *pp* **-ed**, *cont* **-ing**) ◇ *n* **-1.** MIL mariscal *m*. **-2.** [steward] oficial *m* y *f*, miembro *m* y *f* del servicio de orden. **-3.** *Am* [officer] jefe *m*, **-fa** *f* de policía. ◇ *vt* [people] dirigir, conducir; [thoughts] ordenar.

marshalling yard ['mɑːʃlɪŋ-] *n* estación *f* de clasificación de trenes.

marshland ['mɑːʃlænd] *n* tierra *f* pantanosa.

marshmallow [*Br* ,mɑːʃˈmæləu, *Am* 'mɑːrʃ-,meləu] *n* **-1.** [sweet] esponja *f*, golosina de merengue blando. **-2.** [substance] malvavisco *m*.

marshy ['mɑːʃɪ] (*compar* **-ier**, *superl* **-iest**) *adj* pantanoso(sa).

marsupial [mɑːˈsuːpjəl] *n* marsupial *m*.

martial ['mɑːʃl] *adj* [music, discipline] militar.

martial arts *npl* artes *fpl* marciales.

martial law *n* ley *f* marcial.

Martian ['mɑːʃn] ◇ *adj* marciano(na). ◇ *n* marciano *m*, **-na** *f*.

martin ['mɑːtɪn] *n* avión *m*.

martini [mɑːˈtiːnɪ] *n* martini *m*.

Martinique [,mɑːtɪˈniːk] *n* (la) Martinica.

martyr ['mɑːtər] *n* mártir *m* y *f*.

martyrdom ['mɑːtədəm] *n* martirio *m*.

martyred ['mɑːtəd] *adj* de mártir.

marvel ['mɑːvl] (*Br pt* & *pp* **-led**, *cont* **-ling**, *Am pt* & *pp* **-ed**, *cont* **-ing**) ◇ *n* maravilla *f*; **it's a ~ he managed** es un milagro que haya podido. ◇ *vt* maravillarse, sorprenderse. ◇ *vi*: **to ~ (at)** maravillarse OR asombrarse (ante).

marvellous *Br*, **marvelous** *Am* ['mɑːvələs] *adj* maravilloso(sa).

Marxism ['mɑːksɪzm] *n* marxismo *m*.

Marxist ['mɑːksɪst] ◇ *adj* marxista. ◇ *n* marxista *m* y *f*.

Maryland ['meərɪlænd] *n* Maryland.

marzipan ['mɑːzɪpæn] *n* mazapán *m*.

mascara [mæsˈkɑːrə] *n* rímel *m*.

mascot ['mæskət] *n* mascota *f*.

masculine ['mæskjulɪn] *adj* [gen] masculino(na); [woman, appearance] hombruno(na).

masculinity [,mæskjuˈlɪnətɪ] *n* masculinidad *f*.

mash [mæʃ] *vt* triturar.

MASH [mæʃ] (*abbr of* **mobile army surgical hospital**) *n* hospital militar estadounidense de campaña.

mashed potatoes [mæʃt-] *npl* puré *m* de patatas.

mask [mɑːsk] ◇ *n* lit & fig máscara *f*. ◇ *vt* **-1.** [to hide] enmascarar. **-2.** [cover up] ocultar, disfrazar.

masked [mɑːskt] *adj* enmascarado(da).

masking tape ['mɑːskɪŋ-] *n* cinta *f* adhesiva.

masochism ['mæsəkɪzm] *n* masoquismo *m*.

masochist ['mæsəkɪst] *n* masoquista *m* y *f*.

masochistic [,mæsəˈkɪstɪk] *adj* masoquista.

mason ['meɪsn] *n* **-1.** [stonemason] cantero *m*. **-2.** [freemason] masón *m*.

masonic [məˈsɒnɪk] *adj* masónico(ca).

masonry ['meɪsnrɪ] *n* [stones] albañilería *f*.

masquerade [,mæskəˈreɪd] *vi*: **to ~ as** hacerse pasar por; **he ~d under the name of ...** se identificó baja el nombre de ....

mass [mæs] ◇ *n* **-1.** [gen] masa *f*. **-2.** [large amount] cantidad *f*, montón *m*. ◇ *adj* [unemployment] masivo(va), multitudinario(ria); [communication] de masas. ◇ *vt* agrupar, concentrar. ◇ *vi* agruparse, concentrarse.

◆ **Mass** *n* [religious ceremony] misa *f*.

◆ **masses** *npl* **-1.** *inf* [lots] montones *mpl*. **-2.** [workers]: **the ~es** las masas.

Massachusetts [,mæsəˈtʃuːsɪts] *n* Massachusetts.

massacre ['mæsəkər] ◇ *n* matanza *f*, masacre *f*. ◇ *vt* asesinar en masa, masacrar.

massage [*Br* 'mæsɑːʒ, *Am* məˈsɑːʒ] ◇ *n* masaje *m*. ◇ *vt* dar masajes a.

massage parlour *n* **-1.** [for massage] salón *m* de masajes. **-2.** *euphemism* [brothel] burdel *m*.

masseur [mæˈsɜːr] *n* masajista *m*.

masseuse [mæˈsɜːz] *n* masajista *f*.

massive ['mæsɪv] *adj* [gen] enorme; [majority] aplastante.

massively ['mæsɪvlɪ] *adv* enormemente.

mass-market *adj* para un mercado masivo.

mass media *n*: **the ~** los medios de comunicación de masas.

mass-produce *vt* producir OR fabricar en serie.

mass production *n* producción *f* OR fabricación *f* en serie.

mast [mɑːst] *n* **-1.** [on boat] mástil *m*. **-2.** RADIO & TV poste *m*, torre *f*.

mastectomy [mæs'tektəmɪ] (*pl* **-ies**) *n* mastectomía *f*.

master [mɑːstər] ◇ *n* **-1.** [of people, animals] amo *m*, dueño *m*; [of house] señor *m*. **-2.** *fig* [of situation] dueño *m*, -ña *f*. **-3.** *Br* [teacher - primary school] maestro *m*; [- secondary school] profesor *m*. ◇ *adj* maestro(tra). ◇ *vt* **-1.** [situation] dominar, controlar; [difficulty] vencer, superar. **-2.** [technique etc] dominar.

master bedroom *n* dormitorio *m* principal.

master disk *n* COMPUT disco *m* maestro.

masterful ['mɑːstəful] *adj* autoritario(ria), dominante.

master key *n* llave *f* maestra.

masterly ['mɑːstəlɪ] *adj* magistral.

mastermind ['mɑːstəmaɪnd] ◇ *n* cerebro *m*. ◇ *vt* ser el cerebro de, dirigir.

Master of Arts (*pl* **Masters of Arts**) *n* **-1.** [degree] maestría *f* OR máster *m* en Letras. **-2.** [person] licenciado *m*, -da *f* con maestría en Letras.

master of ceremonies (*pl* **masters of ceremonies**) *n* maestro *m* de ceremonias.

Master of Science (*pl* **Masters of Science**) *n* **-1.** [degree] maestría *f* OR máster *m* en Ciencias. **-2.** [person] licenciado *m*, -da *f* con maestría en Ciencias.

masterpiece ['mɑːstəpiːs] *n* *lit* & *fig* obra *f* maestra.

master plan *n* plan *m* maestro.

master's degree *n* maestría *f*, máster *m*.

masterstroke ['mɑːstəstrəuk] *n* golpe *m* maestro.

master switch *n* interruptor *m* general.

masterwork ['mɑːstəwɜːk] *n* obra *f* maestra.

mastery ['mɑːstərɪ] *n* dominio *m*.

mastic ['mæstɪk] *n* masilla *f*.

masticate ['mæstɪkeɪt] *fml vt* & *vi* masticar.

mastiff ['mæstɪf] *n* mastín *m*.

masturbate ['mæstəbeɪt] *vi* masturbarse.

masturbation [,mæstə'beɪʃn] *n* masturbación *f*.

mat [mæt] *n* **-1.** [beer mat] posavasos *m inv*; [tablemat] salvamanteles *m inv*. **-2.** [doormat] felpudo *m*; [rug] alfombrilla *f*.

matador ['mætədɔːr] *n* matador *m*.

match [mætʃ] ◇ *n* **-1.** [game] partido *m*. **-2.** [for lighting] cerilla *f*, cerillo *m Amer*. **-3.** [equal]: **to be no ~ for** no poder competir con. ◇ *vt* **-1.** [be the same as] coincidir con. **-2.** [pair off]: **to ~ sthg (to)** emparejar algo (con). **-3.** [be equal with] competir con, rivalizar con. **-4.** [go well with] hacer juego con.

◇ *vi* **-1.** [be the same] coincidir. **-2.** [go together well] hacer juego.

matchbox ['mætʃbɒks] *n* caja *f* de cerillas.

matched [mætʃt] *adj*: **to be well ~** [well suited] hacer buena pareja; [equal in strength] estar igualado(da).

matching ['mætʃɪŋ] *adj* a juego, que combina bien.

matchless ['mætʃlɪs] *adj literary* incomparable, sin par.

matchmaker ['mætʃ,meɪkər] *n* casamentero *m*, -ra *f*, celestina *f*.

match play *n* GOLF *partido de golf entre 2 equipos*.

match point *n* TENNIS pelota *f* OR punto *m* de partido.

matchstick ['mætʃstɪk] *n* cerilla *f*.

mate [meɪt] ◇ *n* **-1.** *inf* [friend] amigo *m*, -ga *f*, compañero *m*, -ra *f*, compa *m* y *f Amer*. **-2.** *Br inf* [term of address] colega *m* y *f*. **-3.** [of animal] macho *m*, hembra *f*. **-4.** NAUT: **(first) ~ (primer)** oficial *m*. ◇ *vi* [animals]: **to ~ (with)** aparearse (con).

material [mə'tɪərɪəl] ◇ *adj* **-1.** [physical] material. **-2.** [important] sustancial. ◇ *n* **-1.** [substance] material *m*. **-2.** [type of substance] materia *f*. **-3.** [fabric] tela *f*, tejido *m*. **-4.** [type of fabric] tejido *m*. **-5.** (*U*) [ideas, information] información *f*, documentación *f*.

◆ **materials** *npl*: **building ~s** materiales *mpl* de construcción; **writing ~s** objetos *mpl* de escritorio; **cleaning ~s** productos *mpl* de limpieza.

materialism [mə'tɪərɪəlɪzm] *n* materialismo *m*.

materialist [mə'tɪərɪəlɪst] *n* materialista *m* y *f*.

materialistic [mə,tɪərɪə'lɪstɪk] *adj* materialista.

materialize, -ise [mə'tɪərɪəlaɪz] *vi* **-1.** [happen] materializarse, producirse. **-2.** [appear] aparecer, presentarse.

materially [mə'tɪərɪəlɪ] *adv* **-1.** [physically] materialmente. **-2.** [significantly, importantly] esencialmente.

maternal [mə'tɜːnl] *adj* [gen] maternal; [grandparent] materno(na).

maternity [mə'tɜːnətɪ] *n* maternidad *f*.

maternity benefit *n* (*U*) subsidio *m* de maternidad.

maternity dress *n* vestido *m* premamá.

maternity hospital *n* hospital *m* de maternidad.

math *Am* = **maths**.

mathematical [,mæθə'mætɪkl] *adj* matemático(ca); **he's very ~** es muy dotado para las matemáticas.

mathematician [,mæθəmə'tɪʃn] *n* matemático *m*, -ca *f*.

mathematics [,mæθə'mætɪks] *n* (*U*) matemáticas *fpl*.

maths *Br* [mæθs], **math** *Am* [mæθ] (*abbr of* **mathematics**) *inf* ◇ *n* (*U*) mates *fpl*. ◇ *comp* de matemáticas.

maths coprocessor [-,kəʊ'prəʊsesəʳ] *n* COMPUT coprocesador *m* matemático.

matinée ['mætɪneɪ] *n* [at cinema] primera sesión *f*; [at theatre] función *f* de tarde, vermú *f Amer*.

matinée jacket *n Br* abrigo *m* corto de niño.

mating call ['meɪtɪŋ-] *n* reclamo *m*.

mating season ['meɪtɪŋ-] *n* época *f* de celo.

matriarch ['meɪtrɪɑːk] *n* matriarca *f*.

matrices ['meɪtrɪsiːz] *pl* → **matrix**.

matriculate [mə'trɪkjʊleɪt] *vi* matricularse.

matriculation [me,trɪkjʊ'leɪʃn] *n* matrícula *f*.

matrimonial [,mætrɪ'məʊnjəl] *adj* matrimonial.

matrimony ['mætrɪmənɪ] *n* (*U*) matrimonio *m*.

matrix ['meɪtrɪks] (*pl* **matrices** OR **-es**) *n* matriz *f*.

matron ['meɪtrən] *n* **-1.** *Br* [in hospital] enfermera *f* jefa. **-2.** [in school] ama *f* de llaves. **-3.** *Am* [in prison] funcionaria *f* de prisiones, carcelera *f*.

matronly ['meɪtrənlɪ] *adj euphemism* corpulenta y de edad madura.

matt *Br*, **matte** *Am* [mæt] *adj* mate.

matted ['mætɪd] *adj* enmarañado(da).

matter ['mætəʳ] ◇ *n* **-1.** [question, situation] asunto *m*; **a ~ of life and death** un asunto de vida o muerte; **the fact** OR **truth of the ~ is (that)** ... la verdad es que ...; **that's another** OR **a different ~** es otra cuestión OR cosa; **as a ~ of course** automáticamente; **to make ~s worse** para colmo de desgracias; **as a ~ of principle** por principio; **within a ~ of hours** en cuestión de horas; **a ~ of opinion** una cuestión de opiniones; **it's a ~ of time** es cuestión de tiempo. **-2.** [trouble, cause of pain]: **what's the ~ (with it/her)?** ¿qué (le) pasa?; **something's the ~ with my car** algo le pasa a mi coche. **-3.** PHYSICS materia *f*. **-4.** (*U*) [material] material *m*; **printed ~** impresos *mpl*.
◇ *vi* [be important] importar; **it doesn't ~** no importa.
◆ **no matter** *adv*: **no ~ how hard I try** por mucho que lo intente; **no ~ what he does** haga lo que haga; **we must win, no ~ what** tenemos que ganar como sea.

◆ **as a matter of fact** *adv* en realidad.
◆ **for that matter** *adv* de hecho.

Matterhorn ['mætə,hɔːn] *n*: **the ~** el monte Cervino.

matter-of-fact *adj* pragmático(ca).

matting ['mætɪŋ] *n* estera *f*.

mattress ['mætrɪs] *n* colchón *m*.

mature [mə'tjʊəʳ] ◇ *adj* [person, wine] maduro(ra); [cheese] curado(da). ◇ *vi* madurar.

mature student *n Br* UNIV estudiante *m y f* en edad adulta.

maturity [mə'tjʊərətɪ] *n* madurez *f*.

maudlin ['mɔːdlɪn] *adj* [tearful] llorón(ona); [sentimental] sensiblero(ra).

maul [mɔːl] *vt* [savage] herir gravemente.

Mauritania [,mɒrɪ'teɪnɪə] *n* Mauritania.

Mauritanian [,mɒrɪ'teɪnɪən] ◇ *adj* mauritano(na). ◇ *n* mauritano *m*, -na *f*.

Mauritian [mə'rɪʃən] ◇ *adj* mauriciano(na). ◇ *n* mauriciano *m*, -na *f*.

Mauritius [mə'rɪʃəs] *n* (la) isla Mauricio.

mausoleum [,mɔːsə'lɪəm] (*pl* **-s**) *n* mausoleo *m*.

mauve [məʊv] ◇ *adj* malva. ◇ *n* malva *m*.

maverick ['mævərɪk] *n* inconformista *m y f*.

mawkish ['mɔːkɪʃ] *adj* sensiblero(ra).

max. [mæks] (*abbr of* **maximum**) máx.

maxim ['mæksɪm] (*pl* **-s**) *n* máxima *f*.

maxima ['mæksɪmə] *pl* → **maximum**.

maximize, -ise ['mæksɪmaɪz] *vt* maximizar.

maximum ['mæksɪməm] (*pl* **maxima** OR **-s**) ◇ *adj* máximo(ma). ◇ *n* máximo *m*.

may [meɪ] *modal vb* poder; **the coast ~ be seen** se puede ver la costa; **you ~ like it** puede OR es posible que te guste; **I ~ come, I ~ not** puede que venga, puede que no; **it ~ be done in two different ways** puede hacerse de dos maneras (distintas); **~ I come in?** ¿se puede (pasar)?; **~ I?** ¿me permite?; **it ~ be cheap, but it's good** puede que sea barato, pero es bueno; **~ all your dreams come true!** ¡que todos tus sueños se hagan realidad!; **be that as it ~** aunque así sea; **come what ~** pase lo que pase; *see also* **might**.

May [meɪ] *n* mayo *m*; *see also* **September**.

Maya ['maɪə] *n*: **the ~** los mayas.

Mayan ['maɪən] *adj* maya.

maybe ['meɪbiː] *adv* **-1.** [perhaps] quizás, tal vez; **~ she'll come** tal vez venga. **-2.** [approximately] más o menos.

mayday ['meɪdeɪ] *n* s.o.s. *m*, señal *f* de socorro.

May Day *n* Primero *m* de Mayo.

mayfly ['meɪflaɪ] (*pl* **-flies**) *n* cachipolla *f*, efímera *f*.

mayhem ['meɪhem] *n* alboroto *m*, jaleo *m*.

mayn't [meɪnt] = **may not**.

mayonnaise [,meɪə'neɪz] *n* mayonesa *f*.

mayor [meə'] *n* alcalde *m*, -esa *f*.

mayoress ['meərɪs] *n* alcaldesa *f*.

maypole ['meɪpəʊl] *n* mayo *m*.

may've ['meɪəv] = **may have**.

maze [meɪz] *n lit* & *fig* laberinto *m*.

MB -1. (*abbr of* **megabyte**) MB *m*. **-2.** *abbr of* **Manitoba**.

MBA (*abbr of* **Master of Business Administration**) *n* (*titular de un*) *título postuniversitario de empresariales de unos dos años de duración*.

MBBS (*abbr of* **Bachelor of Medicine and Surgery**) *n* (*titular de una*) *licenciatura de medicina y cirugía*.

MBE (*abbr of* **Member of the Order of the British Empire**) *n* (*titular de*) *distinción honorífica británica*.

MC *n abbr of* **master of ceremonies**.

MCAT (*abbr of* **Medical College Admissions Test**) *n examen de acceso a los estudios de medicina en Estados Unidos*.

MCC (*abbr of* **Marylebone Cricket Club**) *n famoso club londinense de cricket*.

McCarthyism macartismo *m*, *movimiento anticomunista de los años cuarenta y cincuenta que desencadenó una caza de brujas entre personajes de la vida pública estadounidense*.

McCoy [mə'kɔɪ] *n inf*: **it's the real ~** es auténtico(ca).

MCP *n inf abbr of* **male chauvinist pig**.

MD ◇ *n* **-1.** *abbr of* **Doctor of Medicine**. **-2.** *abbr of* **managing director**. ◇ *abbr of* **Maryland**.

MDT (*abbr of* **Mountain Daylight Time**) *hora de verano de los Estados de las montañas Rocosas*.

me [miː] *pers pron* **-1.** (*direct, indirect*) me; **can you see/hear ~?** ¿me ves/oyes?; **it's ~** soy yo; **they spoke to ~** hablaron conmigo; **she gave it to ~** me lo dio; **give it to ~!** ¡dámelo! **-2.** (*stressed*): **you can't expect** ME **to do it** no esperarás que YO lo haga. **-3.** (*after prep*) mí; **they went with/without ~** fueron conmigo/sin mí. **-4.** (*in comparisons*) yo; **she's shorter than ~** (ella) es más baja que yo.

ME ◇ *n* **-1.** (*abbr of* **myalgic encephalomyelitis**) encefalomielitis miálgica. **-2.** (*abbr of* **medical examiner**) médico forense. ◇ *abbr of* **Maine**.

meadow ['medəʊ] *n* prado *m*, pradera *f*.

meagre *Br*, **meager** *Am* ['miːgə'] *adj* miserable, escaso(sa).

meal [miːl] *n* comida *f*; **to make a ~ of sthg** *Br fig* & *pej* recrearse en algo.

meals on wheels *npl Br* servicio domiciliario de comidas preparadas para ancianos y necesitados.

mealtime ['miːltaɪm] *n* hora *f* de la comida; **at ~s** en la hora de la comida.

mealy-mouthed [,miːlɪ'maʊðd] *adj pej* evasivo(va).

mean [miːn] (*pt* & *pp* **meant**) ◇ *vt* **-1.** [signify] significar, querer decir; **it ~s nothing to me** no significa nada para mí. **-2.** [have in mind] querer decir, referirse a; **what do you ~?** ¿qué quieres decir?; **to ~ to do sthg** tener la intención de OR querer hacer algo; **I meant to phone you earlier** iba a llamarte antes; **to be meant for** estar destinado(da) a; **they were meant for each other** estaban hechos el uno para el otro; **to be meant to do sthg** deber hacer algo; **that's not meant to be there** esto no debería estar allí; **it was meant to be a joke** era solamente una broma; **to ~ well** tener buenas intenciones. **-3.** [be serious about]: **I ~ it** hablo OR lo digo en serio. **-4.** [be important, matter] significar, suponer. **-5.** [entail] suponer, implicar. **-6.** *phr*: **I ~** quiero decir, o sea.
◇ *adj* **-1.** [miserly] tacaño(ña), amarrete (*inv*) *Amer*; **to be ~ with** ser tacaño con. **-2.** [unkind] mezquino(na), malo(la); **to be ~ to sb** ser malo con alguien. **-3.** [average] medio(dia). **-4.** *iro*: **he's no ~ singer** [excellent] es un cantante de primera; **it's no ~ task** [difficult, challenging] es una tarea muy difícil.
◇ *n* [average] promedio *m*, media *f*; *see also* **means**.

meander [mɪ'ændə'] *vi* **-1.** [river, road] serpentear. **-2.** [walk aimlessly] vagar; [write, speak aimlessly] divagar.

meaning ['miːnɪŋ] *n* **-1.** [sense - of a word etc] significado *m*. **-2.** [significance] intención *f*, sentido *m*. **-3.** [purpose, point] propósito *m*, razón *f* de ser.

meaningful ['miːnɪŋfʊl] *adj* **-1.** [expressive] significativo(va). **-2.** [profound] profundo(da).

meaningless ['miːnɪŋlɪs] *adj* **-1.** [without meaning, purpose] sin sentido. **-2.** [irrelevant, unimportant] irrelevante.

meanness ['miːnnɪs] *n* **-1.** [stinginess] tacañería *f*. **-2.** [unkindness] mezquindad *f*.

means [miːnz] ◇ *n* [method, way] medio *m*; **we have no ~ of doing it** no tenemos manera de hacerlo; **a ~ to an end** un medio para alcanzar un objetivo; **by ~ of** por medio de. ◇ *npl* [money] recursos *mpl*, medios *mpl*.

◆ **by all means** *adv* por supuesto.

◆ **by no means** *adv fml* en absoluto, de ningún modo.

means test *n* evaluación *f* sobre los ingresos económicos.

meant [ment] *pt & pp* → **mean**.

meantime ['miːn,taɪm] *n*: **in the** ~ mientras tanto.

meanwhile ['miːn,waɪl] *adv* mientras tanto, entre tanto.

measles ['miːzlz] *n*: **(the)** ~ sarampión *m*.

measly ['miːzlɪ] (*compar* **-ier**, *superl* **-iest**) *adj inf* raquítico(ca).

measurable ['meʒərəbl] *adj* [significant] notable, sensible.

measurably ['meʒərəblɪ] *adv* notablemente, sensiblemente.

measure ['meʒə] ◇ *n* **-1.** [step, action] medida *f*. **-2.** [degree]: **a** ~ **of** cierto grado de; **and for good** ~ y encima, y además. **-3.** [of alcohol] medida *f*. **-4.** [indication, sign]: **a** ~ **of** una muestra de. ◇ *vt* [object] medir; [damage, impact etc] determinar, juzgar. ◇ *vi* medir.
◆ **measure up** *vi* dar la talla; **to** ~ **up to** estar a la altura de.

measured ['meʒəd] *adj* [tone] moderado(da); [step] contado(da).

measurement ['meʒəmənt] *n* medida *f*.

measuring tape ['meʒərɪŋ-] *n* cinta *f* métrica, metro *m*.

meat [miːt] *n* carne *f*; **cold** ~ fiambre *m*.

meatball ['miːtbɔːl] *n* albóndiga *f*.

meat pie *n Br* pastel *m* de carne.

meaty ['miːtɪ] (*compar* **-ier**, *superl* **-iest**) *adj fig* sustancioso(sa).

Mecca ['mekə] *n* GEOGR La Meca; *fig* meca *f*.

mechanic [mɪ'kænɪk] *n* mecánico *m*, -ca *f*.
◆ **mechanics** ◇ *n* (U) [study] mecánica *f*. ◇ *npl fig* mecanismos *mpl*.

mechanical [mɪ'kænɪkl] *adj* **-1.** [worked by machinery, routine] mecánico(ca). **-2.** [good at mechanics] dotado(da) por la mecánica.

mechanical engineering *n* ingeniería *f* mecánica, mecánica *f* industrial.

mechanism ['mekənɪzm] *n lit & fig* mecanismo *m*.

mechanization [,mekənaɪ'zeɪʃn] *n* mecanización *f*.

mechanize, -ise ['mekənaɪz] ◇ *vt* mecanizar. ◇ *vi* mecanizarse.

MEd [,em'ed] (*abbr of* **Master of Education**) *n* (titular de un) título postuniversitario de pedagogía de unos dos años de duración.

medal ['medl] *n* medalla *f*.

medallion [mɪ'dæljən] *n* medallón *m*.

medallist *Br*, **medalist** *Am* ['medəlɪst] *n* ganador *m*, -ra *f* de una medalla.

meddle ['medl] *vi*: **to** ~ **(in)** entrometerse OR interferir (en); **to** ~ **with sthg** manosear algo.

meddlesome ['medlsəm] *adj* entrometido(da), metete *Amer*.

media ['miːdjə] ◇ *pl* → **medium**. ◇ *n or npl*: **the** ~ los medios de comunicación.

mediaeval [,medɪ'iːvl] = **medieval**.

media event *n* montaje de los medios de difusión.

median ['miːdjən] ◇ *adj* mediano(na). ◇ *n Am* [of road] mediana *f*.

mediate ['miːdɪeɪt] ◇ *vt* negociar. ◇ *vi*: **to** ~ **(for/between)** mediar (por/entre).

mediation [,miːdɪ'eɪʃn] *n* mediación *f*.

mediator ['miːdɪeɪtə] *n* mediador *m*, -ra *f*.

medic ['medɪk] *n inf* **-1.** [medical student] estudiante *m y f* de medicina. **-2.** [doctor] médico *m*, -ca *f*.

Medicaid ['medɪkeɪd] *n Am* sistema estatal de ayuda médica.

medical ['medɪkl] ◇ *adj* médico(ca). ◇ *n* reconocimiento *m* médico, chequeo *m*.

medical certificate *n* **-1.** [result of medical exam] certificado *m* médico. **-2.** [for sickness] parte *m* OR notificación *f* de baja médica.

medical insurance *n* seguro *m* médico.

medical student *n* estudiante *m y f* de medicina.

medicament ['medɪkəmənt] *n fml* medicamento *m*.

Medicare ['medɪkeə] *n Am* ayuda médica estatal para ancianos.

medicated ['medɪkeɪtɪd] *adj* medicinal.

medication [,medɪ'keɪʃn] *n* medicación *f*.

medicinal [me'dɪsɪnl] *adj* medicinal.

medicine ['medsɪn] *n* **-1.** [treatment of illness] medicina *f*; **Doctor of Medicine** UNIV doctor *m*, -ra *f* en medicina. **-2.** [substance] medicina *f*, medicamento *m*.

medicine man *n* chamán *m*, hechichero *m*.

medieval [,medɪ'iːvl] *adj* medieval.

mediocre [,miːdɪ'əukə] *adj* mediocre.

mediocrity [,miːdɪ'ɒkrətɪ] *n* mediocridad *f*.

meditate ['medɪteɪt] *vi*: **to** ~ **(on** OR **upon)** meditar OR reflexionar (sobre).

meditation [,medɪ'teɪʃn] *n* meditación *f*.

Mediterranean [,medɪtə'reɪnjən] ◇ *n* **-1.** [sea]: **the** ~ **(Sea)** el (mar) Mediterráneo. **-2.** [person] mediterráneo *m*, -a *f*. ◇ *adj* mediterráneo(a).

medium ['miːdjəm] (*pl sense 1* **media**, *pl sense 2* **mediums**) ◇ *adj* mediano(na). ◇ *n*

-1. [way of communicating] medio *m*. **-2.** [spiritualist] médium *m* y *f*.

medium-dry *adj* semiseco(ca).

medium-sized *adj* de tamaño mediano.

medium wave *n* onda *f* media.

medley ['medlı] (*pl* **medleys**) *n* **-1.** [mixture] mezcla *f*, amalgama *f*. **-2.** [selection of music] popurrí *m*.

meek [miːk] *adj* sumiso(sa), dócil.

meekly ['miːklı] *adv* sumisamente, dócilmente.

meet [miːt] (*pt* & *pp* **met**) ◇ *vt* **-1.** [by chance] encontrarse con; [for first time, come across] conocer; [by arrangement, for a purpose] reunirse con. **-2.** [go to meet - person] ir/venir a buscar; [- train, bus]: **I met the eight o'clock train to pick up my son** fui a buscar a mi hijo en el tren de las ocho. **-3.** [need, demand] satisfacer. **-4.** [deal with - problem, challenge] hacer frente a. **-5.** [costs, debts] pagar. **-6.** [experience - problem, situation] encontrarse con. **-7.** [hit, touch] darse OR chocar contra. **-8.** [face]: **her eyes met his** sus ojos se encontraron con los de él. **-9.** [join] juntarse OR unirse con.
◇ *vi* **-1.** [by chance] encontrarse; [by arrangement] verse; [for a purpose] reunirse. **-2.** [get to know sb] conocerse. **-3.** [hit in collision] chocar; [touch] tocar. **-4.** [eyes] cruzarse. **-5.** [join - roads etc] juntarse. ◇ *n Am* [meeting] encuentro *m*.
◆ **meet up** *vi*: **to ~ up (with sb)** quedarse en verse (con alguien).
◆ **meet with** *vt fus* **-1.** [refusal, disappointment] recibir; **to ~ with success** tener éxito; **to ~ with failure** fracasar. **-2.** *Am* [by arrangement] reunirse con.

meeting ['miːtɪŋ] *n* **-1.** [for discussions, business] reunión *f*. **-2.** [by chance, in sport] encuentro *m*; [by arrangement] cita *f*; [formal] entrevista *f*. **-3.** [people at meeting]: **the ~** la asamblea.

meeting place *n* lugar *m* de reunión.

mega- [megə] *prefix* **-1.** [in measurements] mega-. **-2.** *inf* [very big] super-.

megabit ['megəbɪt] *n* COMPUT megabit *m*.

megabyte ['megəbaɪt] *n* COMPUT megaocteto *m*.

megahertz ['megəhɜːts] *n* megahercio *m*.

megalomania [,megələ'meɪnjə] *n* megalomanía *f*.

megalomaniac [,megələ'meɪnɪæk] *n* megalómano *m*, -na *f*.

megaphone ['megəfəun] *n* megáfono *m*.

megaton ['megətʌn] *n* megatón *m*.

megawatt ['megəwɒt] *n* megavatio *m*.

melamine ['meləmiːn] *n* melamina *f*.

melancholy ['melənkəlı] ◇ *adj* melancólico(ca). ◇ *n* melancolía *f*.

mellow ['meləu] ◇ *adj* **-1.** [sound, colour, light] suave; [wine] añejo(ja). **-2.** [fruit] maduro(ra). ◇ *vt*: **to be ~ed by** [age] estar apaciguado(da) por; [alcohol] sentirse relajado(da) por. ◇ *vi* suavizarse; [person] ablandarse.

melodic [mɪ'lɒdɪk] *adj* melódico(ca).

melodious [mɪ'ləudjəs] *adj* melodioso(sa).

melodrama ['melədrɑːmə] *n* melodrama *m*.

melodramatic [,melədrə'mætɪk] *adj* melodramático(ca).

melody ['melədı] (*pl* **-ies**) *n* melodía *f*.

melon ['melən] *n* melón *m*.

melt [melt] ◇ *vt* **-1.** [make liquid] derretir. **-2.** *fig* [soften] ablandar. ◇ *vi* **-1.** [become liquid] derretirse. **-2.** *fig* [soften] ablandarse. **-3.** [disappear]: **to ~ into the crowd** desaparecer entre la multitud; **to ~ away** [savings] esfumarse; [anger] desvanecerse.
◆ **melt down** *vt sep* fundir.

meltdown ['meltdaun] *n* **-1.** [act of melting] fusión *f*. **-2.** [incident] fuga *f* radiactiva.

melting point ['meltɪŋ-] *n* punto *m* de fusión.

melting pot ['meltɪŋ-] *n fig* crisol *m*.

member ['membər] ◇ *n* **-1.** [of social group] miembro *m* y *f*. **-2.** [of party, union] afiliado *m*, -da *f*, miembro *m* y *f*; [of organization, club] socio *m*, -cia *f*. ◇ *comp* miembro.

Member of Congress (*pl* **Members of Congress**) *n* miembro *m* y *f* del Congreso (*de los Estados Unidos*).

Member of Parliament (*pl* **Members of Parliament**) *n Br* diputado *m*, -da *f* (*del parlamento británico*).

membership ['membəʃɪp] *n* **-1.** [of party, union] afiliación *f*; [of club] calidad *f* de miembro OR socio. **-2.** [number of members] número *m* de socios. **-3.** [people themselves]: **the ~** [of organization] los miembros; [of club] los socios.

membership card *n* carnet *m* de socio, -cia *f*.

membrane ['membreɪn] *n* membrana *f*.

memento [mɪ'mentəu] (*pl* **-s**) *n* recuerdo *m*.

memo ['meməu] (*pl* **-s**) *n* memorándum *m*.

memoirs ['memwɑːz] *npl* memorias *fpl*.

memo pad *n* bloc *m* para notas.

memorabilia [,memərə'bɪlɪə] *npl* objetos personales de una celebridad.

memorable ['memərəbl] *adj* memorable.

memorandum [,memə'rændəm] (*pl* **-da** [-də] OR **-dums**) *n fml* memorándum *m*.

memorial [mɪ'mɔːrɪəl] ◇ adj conmemorativo(va). ◇ n monumento m conmemorativo.

memorize, -ise ['meməraɪz] vt memorizar, aprender de memoria.

memory ['meməri] (pl -ies) n -1. [faculty, of computer] memoria f. -2. [thing or things remembered] recuerdo m; **from ~ de memoria; within living ~ que se recuerda; to lose one's ~ perder la memoria; to keep sb's ~ alive** mantener vivo el recuerdo de alguien; **to search one's ~** intentar recordar; **in ~ of** en memoria de.

memory card n COMPUT tarjeta f de expansión de memoria.

men [men] pl → **man.**

menace ['menəs] ◇ n -1. [threat] amenaza f; [danger] peligro m. -2. [threatening quality]: **with ~ de** modo amenazador. -3. inf [nuisance, pest] pesadez f, lata f. ◇ vt amenazar.

menacing ['menəsɪŋ] adj amenazador(ra).

menacingly ['menəsɪŋlɪ] adv amenazadoramente.

menagerie [mɪ'nædʒərɪ] n reserva f particular de animales.

mend [mend] ◇ n inf: **to be on the ~** sentirse mejor, ir recuperándose. ◇ vt [shoes, toy] arreglar; [socks] zurcir; [clothes] remendar; **to ~ one's ways** enmendarse.

mending ['mendɪŋ] n: **to do the ~** zurcir OR remendar la ropa.

menfolk ['menfəʊk] npl hombres mpl.

menial ['miːnjəl] adj servil, bajo(ja).

meningitis [,menɪn'dʒaɪtɪs] n (U) meningitis f.

menopause ['menəpɔːz] n: **the ~ la** menopausia.

menservants ['mensɜːvənts] pl → **manservant.**

men's room n Am: **the ~ los** servicios de caballeros.

menstrual ['menstrʊəl] adj menstrual.

menstruate ['menstrʊeɪt] vi menstruar, tener la menstruación.

menstruation [,menstrʊ'eɪʃn] n menstruación f.

menswear ['menzweəʳ] n ropa f de caballeros.

mental ['mentl] adj mental.

mental age n edad f mental.

mental block n: **to have a ~ about** tener bloqueo mental respecto a.

mental hospital n hospital m psiquiátrico, loquería f Amer.

mentality [men'tælətɪ] n mentalidad f.

mentally ['mentəlɪ] adv mentalmente; **to be ~ ill/retarded** ser un enfermo/retrasado mental.

mentally handicapped npl: **the ~ los** disminuidos psíquicos.

◆ **mentally-handicapped** adj disminuido psíquico (disminuida psíquica).

mental note n: **to make a ~ to do sthg** tomar nota mentalmente de hacer algo.

menthol ['menθɒl] n mentol m.

mentholated ['menθəleɪtɪd] adj mentolado(da).

mention ['menʃn] ◇ vt: **to ~ sthg (to)** mencionar algo (a); **not to ~ sin** mencionar, además de; **don't ~ it! ¡de** nada!, ¡no hay de qué! ◇ n mención f.

mentor ['mentɔːʳ] n fml mentor m, -ra f.

menu ['menjuː] n -1. [in restaurant] carta f. -2. COMPUT menú m.

menu bar n COMPUT barra f de menús.

menu-driven adj COMPUT guiado(da) por menús.

meow Am = **miaow.**

MEP (abbr of Member of the European Parliament) n eurodiputado m, -da f.

mercantile ['mɜːkəntaɪl] adj mercantil.

mercenary ['mɜːsɪnrɪ] (pl -ies) ◇ adj mercenario(ria). ◇ n mercenario m, -ria f.

merchandise ['mɜːtʃəndaɪz] n (U) mercancías fpl, géneros mpl.

merchant ['mɜːtʃənt] ◇ adj [seaman, ship] mercante. ◇ n comerciante m y f, negociante m y f.

merchant bank n Br banco m comercial.

merchant navy Br, **merchant marine** Am n marina f mercante.

merciful ['mɜːsɪfʊl] adj -1. [showing mercy] compasivo(va), misericordioso(sa). -2. [fortunate] afortunado(da).

mercifully ['mɜːsɪfʊlɪ] adv [fortunately] afortunadamente, por suerte.

merciless ['mɜːsɪlɪs] adj implacable, despiadado(da).

mercilessly ['mɜːsɪlɪslɪ] adv implacablemente, despiadadamente.

mercurial [mɜː'kjʊərɪəl] adj literary variable.

mercury ['mɜːkjʊrɪ] n mercurio m.

Mercury ['mɜːkjʊrɪ] n Mercurio m.

mercy ['mɜːsɪ] (pl -ies) n -1. [kindness, pity] compasión f, misericordia f; **at the ~ of** fig a merced de. -2. [blessing] suerte f.

mercy killing n eutanasia f.

mere [mɪəʳ] adj simple, mero(ra); **she's a ~ child** no es más que una niña.

merely ['mɪəlɪ] *adv* simplemente, sólamente.

meretricious [,merɪ'trɪʃəs] *adj fml* ilusorio(ria).

merge [mɜːdʒ] ◇ *vt* **-1.** [gen] mezclar. **-2.** COMM & COMPUT fusionar. ◇ *vi* **-1.** [join, combine]: **to ~ (with)** [company] fusionarse (con); [roads, branches] unirse OR convergir (con). **-2.** [blend - colours] fundirse, mezclarse; **to ~ into** confundirse con. ◇ *n* COMPUT fusión *f*.

merger ['mɜːdʒər] *n* fusión *f*.

meridian [mə'rɪdɪən] *n* meridiano *m*.

meringue [mə'ræŋ] *n* merengue *m*.

merino [mə'riːnəʊ] *adj* [wool] merino(na); [jumper, scarf] de lana merina.

merit ['merɪt] ◇ *n* mérito *m*. ◇ *vt* merecer, ser digno(na) de.
◆ **merits** *npl* ventajas *fpl*; **to discuss the ~s of** sopesar las ventajas de; **to judge sthg on its ~s** evaluar OR juzgar algo según sus méritos.

meritocracy [,merɪ'tɒkrəsɪ] (*pl* **-ies**) *n* meritocracia *f*.

mermaid ['mɜːmeɪd] *n* sirena *f*.

merrily ['merɪlɪ] *adv* **-1.** [gen] alegremente. **-2.** *literary* [burn, sparkle] resplandeciente.

merriment ['merɪmənt] *n literary* alegría *f*, diversión *f*.

merry ['merɪ] (*compar* **-ier**, *superl* **-iest**) *adj* **-1.** *literary* [gen] alegre. **-2.** [party] animado(da). **Merry Christmas!** ¡feliz Navidad! **-3.** *inf* [tipsy] alegre, achispado(da).

merry-go-round *n* tiovivo *m*, calesita *f* Amer.

merrymaking ['merɪ,meɪkɪŋ] *n* (*U*) *literary* diversión *f*, juerga *f*.

mesh [meʃ] ◇ *n* malla *f*. ◇ *vi* encajar.

mesmerize, -ise ['mezməraɪz] *vt*: **to be ~d (by)** estar fascinado(da) (por).

mess [mes] *n* **-1.** [untidy state] desorden *m*, entrevero *m* Amer; **to be (in) a ~** estar en desorden. **-2.** [muddle, problematic situation] lío *m*. **-3.** MIL [room] comedor *m*; [food] rancho.
◆ **mess about, mess around** *inf* ◇ *vt sep* fastidiar. ◇ *vi* **-1.** [waste time] pasar el rato, matar el tiempo; [fool around] hacer el tonto. **-2.** [interfere]: **to ~ about with sthg** manosear algo.
◆ **mess up** *vt sep inf* **-1.** [clothes] ensuciar; [room] desordenar. **-2.** [plan, evening] echar a perder.
◆ **mess with** *vt fus inf* meterse con.

message ['mesɪdʒ] *n* **-1.** [piece of information] recado *m*, mensaje *m*. **-2.** [of book etc] mensaje *m*. **-3.** *phr*: **to get the ~** *inf* entender.

messenger ['mesɪndʒər] *n* mensajero *m*, -ra *f*; **by ~** por mensajero.

Messiah [mɪ'saɪə] *n*: **the ~** el Mesías.

Messrs, Messrs. ['mesəz] (*abbr of* **messieurs**) Sres.

messy ['mesɪ] (*compar* **-ier**, *superl* **-iest**) *adj* **-1.** [dirty] sucio(cia), desordenado(da). **-2.** *inf* [complicated, confused] complicado(da), enredado(da).

met [met] *pt & pp* → **meet**.

Met [met] (*abbr of* **Metropolitan Opera**) *n*: **the ~** el (teatro de la ópera) Metropolitan de Nueva York.

metabolism [mə'tæbəlɪzm] *n* metabolismo *m*.

metal ['metl] ◇ *n* metal *m*. ◇ *comp* de metal, metálico(ca).

metallic [mɪ'tælɪk] *adj* **-1.** [gen] metálico(ca). **-2.** [paint, finish] metalizado(da).

metallurgist [mə'tælədʒɪst] *n* metalúrgico *m*, -ca *f*.

metallurgy [mə'tælədʒɪ] *n* metalurgia *f*.

metalwork ['metlwɜːk] *n* [craft] metalistería *f*.

metalworker ['metəl,wɜːkər] *n* metalista *m*.

metamorphose [,metə'mɔːfəʊz] *vi fml*: **to ~ (into)** transformarse (en).

metamorphosis [,metə'mɔːfəsɪs, ,metəmɔː'fəʊsɪs] (*pl* **-phoses** [-siːz]) *n lit & fig* metamorfosis *f*.

metaphor ['metəfər] *n* metáfora *f*.

metaphorical [,metə'fɒrɪkl] *adj* metafórico(ca).

metaphysical [,metə'fɪzɪkl] *adj* [in philosophy] metafísico(ca).

metaphysics [,metə'fɪzɪks] *n* metafísica *f*.

mete [miːt]
◆ **mete out** *vt sep*: **to ~ sthg out to sb** imponer algo a alguien.

meteor ['miːtɪər] *n* bólido *m*.

meteoric [,miːtɪ'ɒrɪk] *adj fig* meteórico(ca), vertiginoso(sa).

meteorite ['miːtjəraɪt] *n* meteorito *m*.

meteorological [,miːtjərə'lɒdʒɪkl] *adj* meteorológico(ca).

meteorologist [,miːtjə'rɒlədʒɪst] *n* meteorólogo(ga).

meteorology [,miːtjə'rɒlədʒɪ] *n* meteorología *f*.

meter ['miːtər] ◇ *n* **-1.** [device] contador *m*. **-2.** *Am* = **metre**. ◇ *vt* [measure] medir.

methadone ['meθədəʊn] *n* metadona *f*.

methane ['miːθeɪn] *n* metano *m*.

method ['meθəd] *n* método *m*.

methodical [mɪ'θɒdɪkl] *adj* metódico(ca).

methodically [mɪ'θɒdɪklɪ] *adv* metódicamente.

Methodist ['meθədɪst] ◇ *adj* metodista. ◇ *n* metodista *m* y *f*.

methodology [ˌmeθə'dɒlədʒɪ] (*pl* -ies) *n* *fml* & GRAMM metodología *f*.

meths [meθs] *n* *Br* *inf* alcohol *m* metilado OR desnaturalizado.

methylated spirits ['meθɪleɪtɪd-] *n* alcohol *m* metilado OR desnaturalizado.

meticulous [mɪ'tɪkjʊləs] *adj* meticuloso(sa), minucioso(sa).

meticulously [mɪ'tɪkjʊləslɪ] *adv* meticulosamente, minuciosamente.

Met Office (*abbr of* Meteorological Office) *n* instituto británico de meteorología.

metre *Br*, **meter** *Am* ['miːtə'] *n* metro *m*.

metric ['metrɪk] *adj* métrico(ca).

metrication [ˌmetrɪ'keɪʃn] *n* *Br* adopción *f* del sistema métrico decimal.

metric system *n*: **the ~** el sistema métrico.

metric ton *n* tonelada *f* métrica.

metro ['metrəʊ] (*pl* -s) *n* metro *m* (*esp de París*).

metronome ['metrənəʊm] *n* metrónomo *m*.

metropolis [mɪ'trɒpəlɪs] (*pl* -es) *n* metrópoli *f*.

metropolitan [ˌmetrə'pɒlɪtn] *adj* [of a metropolis] metropolitano(na).

Metropolitan Police *npl* policía de Londres.

mettle ['metl] *n*: **to be on one's ~** estar dispuesto(ta) a hacer lo mejor posible; **to show** OR **prove one's ~** mostrar el valor de uno.

mew [mjuː] = miaow.

mews [mjuːz] (*pl inv*) *n* *Br* callejuela de antiguas caballerizas convertidas en viviendas de lujo.

Mexican ['meksɪkn] ◇ *adj* mejicano(na). ◇ *n* mejicano *m*, -na *f*.

Mexico ['meksɪkəʊ] *n* Méjico.

Mexico City *n* Méjico DF.

mezzanine ['metsəniːn] *n* **-1.** [floor] entresuelo *m*. **-2.** *Am* [in theatre] primer palco *m* OR piso *m*.

MFA (*abbr of* Master of Fine Arts) *n* (*titular de un*) *título postuniversitario de bellas artes de unos dos años de duración.*

mfr *abbr of* manufacturer.

mg (*abbr of* milligram) mg *m*.

Mgr -1. (*abbr of* Monseigneur, Monsignor) Mons. **-2.** *abbr of* manager.

MHR *n* *abbr of* Member of the House of Representatives.

MHz (*abbr of* megahertz) MHz.

MI *abbr of* Michigan.

MI5 (*abbr of* Military Intelligence 5) *n* organismo británico de contraespionaje.

MI6 (*abbr of* Military Intelligence 6) *n* organismo británico de espionaje.

MIA (*abbr of* missing in action) *desaparecido en combate.*

miaow *Br* [miːˈaʊ], **meow** *Am* [mɪˈaʊ] ◇ *n* maullido *m*. ◇ *vi* maullar.

mice [maɪs] *pl* → mouse.

Mich. *abbr of* Michigan.

Michigan ['mɪʃɪgən] *n* Michigan.

mickey ['mɪkɪ] *n*: **to take the ~ out of sb** *Br* *inf* tomar el pelo a alguien.

micro ['maɪkrəʊ] (*pl* -s) *n* microordenador *m*, microcomputadora *f*.

micro- ['maɪkrəʊ] *prefix* micro-.

microbe ['maɪkrəʊb] *n* microbio *m*.

microbiologist [ˌmaɪkrəʊbaɪˈɒlədʒɪst] *n* microbiólogo *m*, -ga *f*.

microbiology [ˌmaɪkrəʊbaɪˈɒlədʒɪ] *n* microbiología *f*.

microchip ['maɪkrəʊtʃɪp] *n* COMPUT microchip *m*.

microcircuit ['maɪkrəʊˌsɜːkɪt] *n* microcircuito *m*.

microcomputer [ˌmaɪkrəʊkəmˈpjuːtə'] *n* microordenador *m*.

microcosm ['maɪkrəkɒzm] *n* microcosmos *m*.

microfiche ['maɪkrəʊfiːʃ] (*pl inv* OR -s) *n* microficha *f*.

microfilm ['maɪkrəʊfɪlm] *n* microfilm *m*.

microlight ['maɪkrəlaɪt] *n* ultraligero *m*.

micromesh ['maɪkrəʊmeʃ] *n* malla *f* (para medias).

micron ['maɪkrɒn] *n* micra *f*, micrón *m*.

microorganism [ˌmaɪkrəʊˈɔːgənɪzm] *n* microorganismo *m*.

microphone ['mɪkrəfəʊn] *n* micrófono *m*.

microprocessor ['maɪkrəʊˌprəʊsesə'] *n* COMPUT microprocesador *m*.

microscope ['maɪkrəskəʊp] *n* microscopio *m*.

microscopic [ˌmaɪkrə'skɒpɪk] *adj* *lit* & *fig* microscópico(ca).

microsecond ['maɪkrəʊˌsekənd] *n* microsegundo *m*.

microsurgery [ˌmaɪkrə'sɜːdʒərɪ] *n* microcirugía *f*.

microwave (oven) ['maɪkrəweɪv-] *n* (horno *m*) microondas *m inv*.

mid- [mɪd] *prefix* medio(dia); **(in) midmorning** a media mañana; **(in) ~August** a mediados de agosto; **(in) midwinter** en pleno invierno; **she's in her ~twenties** tiene unos 25 años.

midair [mɪd'eəʳ] ◇ *adj* en el aire. ◇ *n*: **in ~** en el aire.

midday ['mɪddeɪ] *n* mediodía *m*.

middle ['mɪdl] ◇ *adj* **-1.** [gen] del medio. **-2.** [in time]: **she's in her ~ twenties** tiene unos 25 años. ◇ *n* **-1.** [of room, town etc] medio *m*, centro *m*; **in the ~ (of)** en el medio *m* OR centro (de); **in the ~ of the month/ the 19th century** a mediados del mes/del siglo XIX; **to be in the ~ of doing sthg** estar haciendo algo; **in the ~ of the night** en plena noche; **in the ~ of nowhere** en el quinto pino. **-2.** [waist] cintura *f*.

middle age *n* mediana edad *f*.

middle-aged *adj* de mediana edad.

Middle Ages *npl*: **the ~** la Edad Media.

middle-class *adj* de clase media.

middle classes *npl*: **the ~** la clase media.

middle distance *n*: **in the ~** en segundo plano OR término.

Middle East *n*: **the ~** el Oriente Medio.

Middle Eastern *adj* del Oriente Medio.

middleman ['mɪdlmæn] (*pl* **-men** [-men]) *n* intermediario *m*.

middle management *n* (*U*) cuadros *mpl* OR mandos *mpl* intermedios.

middle name *n* segundo nombre *m* (*en un nombre compuesto*).

middle-of-the-road *adj* moderado(da).

middle school *n* Br *escuela para niños de 9 a 13 años*.

middleweight ['mɪdlweɪt] *n* peso *m* medio.

middling ['mɪdlɪŋ] *adj* regular, mediano(na).

Middx (*abbr of* **Middlesex**) *antiguo condado inglés*.

Mideast [,mɪd'iːst] *n* Am: **the ~** el Oriente Medio.

midfield [,mɪd'fiːld] *n* FTBL medio campo *m*.

midge ['mɪdʒ] *n* (tipo *m* de) mosquito *m*.

midget ['mɪdʒɪt] *n* enano *m*, -na *f*.

midi system ['mɪdɪ-] *n* minicadena *f*.

Midlands ['mɪdləndz] *npl*: **the ~** *la región central de Inglaterra*.

midnight ['mɪdnaɪt] ◇ *n* medianoche *f*. ◇ *comp* de medianoche.

midriff ['mɪdrɪf] *n* diafragma *m*.

midst [mɪdst] *n* **-1.** [in space]: **in the ~ of** *literary* en medio de; **in our ~** entre nosotros. **-2.** [in time]: **in the ~ of** en medio de.

midstream [mɪd'striːm] *n* **-1.** [of river]: **in ~** en medio de la corriente. **-2.** *fig* [when talking]: **in ~** en medio de la conversación.

midsummer ['mɪd,sʌməʳ] *n* pleno verano *m*.

Midsummer Day *n* Día *m* de San Juan (*24 de junio*).

midway [,mɪd'weɪ] *adv* **-1.** [in space]: **~ (between)** a medio camino (entre). **-2.** [in time]: **~ (through)** a la mitad (de).

midweek [*adj* mɪd'wiːk, *adv* 'mɪdwiːk] ◇ *adj* de entre semana. ◇ *adv* entre semana.

Midwest [,mɪd'west] *n*: **the ~** *la llanura central de los Estados Unidos*.

Midwestern [,mɪd'westən] *adj* de o relativo a *la llanura central de los Estados Unidos*.

midwife ['mɪdwaɪf] (*pl* **-wives** [-waɪvz]) *n* comadrona *f*.

midwifery ['mɪd,wɪfərɪ] *n* obstetricia *f*.

miffed [mɪft] *adj* *inf* molesto(ta), fastidiado(da).

might [maɪt] ◇ *modal vb* **-1.** [expressing possibility]: **he ~ be armed** podría estar armado; **I ~ do it** puede que OR quizás lo haga; **we ~ have been killed, had we not been careful** si no hubiéramos tenido cuidado, podríamos haber muerto. **-2.** [expressing suggestion]: **you ~ have told me!** ¡podrías habérmelo dicho!; **it ~ be better to wait** quizás sea mejor esperar. **-3.** *fml* [asking permission]: **he asked if he ~ leave the room** pidió permiso para salir. **-4.** [expressing concession]: **you ~ well be right, but ...** puede que tengas razón, pero .... **-5.** *phr*: **I ~ have known** OR **guessed** podría haberlo sospechado. ◇ *n* (*U*) fuerza *f*, poder *m*.

mightn't ['maɪtənt] = **might not**.

might've ['maɪtəv] = **might have**.

mighty ['maɪtɪ] (*compar* **-ier**, *superl* **-iest**) ◇ *adj* **-1.** [strong] fuerte; [powerful] poderoso(sa). **-2.** [very large] enorme. ◇ *adv* muy.

migraine ['miːgreɪn, 'maɪgreɪn] *n* jaqueca *f*, migraña *f*.

migrant ['maɪgrənt] ◇ *adj* **-1.** [bird, animal] migratorio(ria). **-2.** [workers] emigrante. ◇ *n* **-1.** [bird, animal] migratorio *m*, -ria *f*. **-2.** [person] emigrante *m* y *f*.

migrate [Br maɪ'greɪt, Am 'maɪgreɪt] *vi* emigrar.

migration [maɪ'greɪʃn] *n* emigración *f*.

migratory ['maɪgrətrɪ] *adj* migratorio(ria).

mike [maɪk] (*abbr of* **microphone**) *n* *inf* micro *m*.

mild [maɪld] ◇ *adj* **-1.** [taste, disinfectant, wind] suave; [effect, surprise, illness] leve. **-2.** [person, nature] apacible, sosegado(da); [tone of voice] sereno(na). **-3.** [climate] templado(da). ◇ *n tipo de cerveza ligera*.

mildew ['mɪldjuː] *n* [gen] moho *m*; [on plants] añublo *m*.

mildly ['maɪldlɪ] *adv* **-1.** [gen] ligeramente, levemente; **to put it ~** por no decir más. **-2.** [talk] suavemente.

mild-mannered *adj* apacible, sosegado(da).

mildness ['maɪldnɪs] *n* [of voice, manner, person] suavidad *f*, serenidad *f*; [of reproach, illness] levedad *f*.

mile [maɪl] *n* milla *f*; **we could see for ~s** la vista nos alcanzaba a ver mucho; **we had walked for ~s** habíamos andado muchísimo; **this is ~s better** esto es muchísimo mejor; **to be ~s away** *fig* estar en la luna.

mileage ['maɪlɪdʒ] *n* distancia *f* en millas.

mileage allowance *n* pago *m* por millas recorridas.

mileometer [maɪ'lɒmɪtər] *n* cuentamillas *m inv*, ≃ cuentakilómetros *m inv*.

milestone ['maɪlstəʊn] *n* **-1.** [marker stone] mojón *m*, hito *m*. **-2.** *fig* [event] hito *m*.

milieu [*Br* 'miːljɜː, *Am* miːl'juː] (*pl* **-s** OR **-x**) *n* entorno *m*, (medio) ambiente *m*.

militant ['mɪlɪtənt] ◇ *adj* militante. ◇ *n* militante *m y f*.

militarism ['mɪlɪtərɪzm] *n* militarismo *m*.

militarist ['mɪlɪtərɪst] *n* militarista *m y f*.

militarized zone, **militarised zone** ['mɪlɪtəraɪzd-] *n* zona *f* militar.

military ['mɪlɪtrɪ] ◇ *adj* militar. ◇ *n*: **the ~** los militares, las fuerzas armadas.

military police *n* policía *f* militar.

militate ['mɪlɪteɪt] *vi fml*: **to ~ against sthg** militar en contra de algo.

militia [mɪ'lɪʃə] *n* milicia *f*.

milk [mɪlk] ◇ *n* leche *f*. ◇ *vt* **-1.** [cow etc] ordeñar. **-2.** [use to own ends] sacar todo el jugo a; **they ~ed him for every penny he had** le chuparon hasta el último centavo.

milk chocolate ◇ *n* chocolate *m* con leche. ◇ *comp* de chocolate con leche.

milk float *Br*, **milk truck** *Am n* vehículo distribuidor de leche.

milking ['mɪlkɪŋ] *n* ordeño *m*.

milkman ['mɪlkmən] (*pl* **-men** [-mən]) *n* lechero *m*.

milk round *n Br* [by milkman] recorrido *m* del lechero.

milk shake *n* batido *m*.

milk tooth *n* diente *m* de leche.

milk truck *Am* = **milk float**.

milky ['mɪlkɪ] (*compar* **-ier**, *superl* **-iest**) *adj* **-1.** *Br* [with milk] con mucha leche. **-2.** [pale white] lechoso(sa), pálido(da).

Milky Way *n*: **the ~** la Vía Láctea.

mill [mɪl] ◇ *n* **-1.** [flour-mill] molino *m*. **-2.** [factory] fábrica *f*. **-3.** [grinder] molinillo *m*. ◇ *vt* moler.

◆ **mill about**, **mill around** *vi* arremolinarse.

millennium [mɪ'lenɪəm] (*pl* **-nnia** [-nɪə]) *n* milenio *m*.

miller ['mɪlər] *n* molinero *m*, -ra *f*.

millet ['mɪlɪt] *n* mijo *m*.

milli- ['mɪlɪ] *prefix* mili-.

millibar ['mɪlɪbɑːr] *n* milibar *m*.

milligram(me) ['mɪlɪgræm] *n* miligramo *m*.

millilitre *Br*, **milliliter** *Am* ['mɪlɪˌliːtər] *n* mililitro *m*.

millimetre *Br*, **millimeter** *Am* ['mɪlɪˌmiːtər] *n* milímetro *m*.

millinery ['mɪlɪnrɪ] *n* sombrerería *f* (de señoras).

million ['mɪljən] *n* millón *m*; **a ~**, **~s of** *fig* millones de.

millionaire [ˌmɪljə'neər] *n* millonario *m*.

millionairess [ˌmɪljə'neərɪs] *n* millonaria *f*.

millipede ['mɪlɪpiːd] *n* miriápodo *m*.

millisecond ['mɪlɪˌsekənd] *n* milésima *f* de segundo.

millstone ['mɪlstəʊn] *n* piedra *f* de molino, muela *f*; **a ~ round one's neck** una cruz.

millwheel ['mɪlwiːl] *n* rueda *f* de molino.

milometer [maɪ'lɒmɪtər] = **mileometer**.

mime [maɪm] ◇ *n* **-1.** [acting] mímica *f*, pantomima *f*. **-2.** [act] imitación *f* a base de gestos. ◇ *vt* describir con gestos. ◇ *vi* hacer mímica.

mimic ['mɪmɪk] (*pt* & *pp* **-ked**, *cont* **-king**) ◇ *n* imitador *m*, -ra *f*. ◇ *vt* imitar.

mimicry ['mɪmɪkrɪ] *n* imitación *f*.

mimosa [mɪ'məʊzə] *n* mimosa *f*.

min [mɪn] (*abbr of* **minimum**) mín.

min. (*abbr of* **minute**) min.

Min. *abbr of* **ministry**.

mince [mɪns] ◇ *n Br* carne *f* picada. ◇ *vt* picar. ◇ *vi* andar dando pasitos.

mincemeat ['mɪnsmiːt] *n* **-1.** [fruit] *mezcla de fruta confitada y especias*. **-2.** *Am* [minced meat] carne *f* picada.

mince pie *n* pastelillo *m* de fruta confitada.

mincer ['mɪnsər] *n* máquina *f* de picar carne.

mind [maɪnd] ◇ *n* **-1.** [gen] mente *f*; **state of ~** estado *m* de ánimo; **to come into** OR **to cross sb's ~** pasársele a alguien por la cabeza; **to concentrate one's ~** hacer que uno se concentre; **to have sthg on one's ~** estar preocupado por algo; **to keep an open ~** tener una actitud abierta; **to put** OR

set sb's ~ at rest tranquilizar a alguien; it slipped my ~ se me olvidó; to take sb's ~ off sthg hacer olvidar algo a alguien; that was a load OR weight off my ~ me quité un peso de encima; great ~s think alike! ¡ves! ahí estamos de acuerdo; to broaden one's ~ ampliar los horizontes de uno; to make one's ~ up decidirse. **-2.** [attention] atención f; to put one's ~ to sthg poner empeño en algo. **-3.** [opinion]: to change one's ~ cambiar de opinión f; to my ~ en mi opinión; to be in two ~s about sthg no estar seguro(ra) de algo; to speak one's ~ hablar sin rodeos. **-4.** [memory] memoria f; to bear sthg in ~ tener presente algo; to call sthg to ~ recordar algo; to cast one's ~ back echar la mente OR mirada atrás. **-5.** [intention]: to have sthg in ~ tener algo en mente; to have a ~ to do sthg estar pensando en hacer algo.
◇ vi **-1.** [be bothered]: do you ~? ¿te importa?; I don't ~ ... no me importa ...; never ~ [don't worry] no te preocupes; [it's not important] no importa. **-2.** [be careful]: ~ out! Br ¡cuidado!
◇ vt **-1.** [be bothered about, dislike]: do you ~ if I leave? ¿te molesta si me voy?; I don't ~ waiting no me importa esperar; I wouldn't ~ a ... no me vendría mal un .... **-2.** [pay attention to] tener cuidado con. **-3.** [take care of] cuidar.
◆ **mind you** adv: he's a bit deaf; ~ you, he is old está un poco sordo; te advierto que es ya mayor.

mind-bending [-,bendɪŋ] adj inf embrollado(da).

minder ['maɪndəʳ] n Br inf [bodyguard] guardaespaldas m y f.

mindful ['maɪndfʊl] adj: ~ of consciente de.

mindless ['maɪndlɪs] adj **-1.** [stupid] absurdo(da), sin sentido. **-2.** [not requiring thought] aburrido(da).

mind reader n persona f que adivina los pensamientos.

mindset ['maɪndset] n predisposición f.

mind's eye n: in one's ~ en la mente (de uno).

mine¹ [maɪn] poss pron mío (mía); that money is ~ ese dinero es mío; his car hit ~ su coche chocó contra el mío; it wasn't your fault, it was MINE la culpa no fue tuya sino MÍA; a friend of ~ un amigo mío.

mine² [maɪn] ◇ n mina f; a ~ of information una mina de información. ◇ vt **-1.** [excavate - coal] extraer. **-2.** [lay mines in] minar.

mine detector n detector m de minas.

minefield ['maɪnfiːld] n lit & fig campo m de minas.

minelayer ['maɪn,leɪəʳ] n minador m.

miner ['maɪnəʳ] n minero m, -ra f.

mineral ['mɪnərəl] ◇ adj mineral. ◇ n mineral m.

mineralogy [,mɪnə'rælədʒɪ] n mineralogía f.

mineral water n agua f mineral.

minestrone [,mɪnɪ'strəʊnɪ] n (sopa f) minestrone f.

minesweeper ['maɪn,swiːpəʳ] n dragaminas m inv.

mingle ['mɪŋgl] ◇ vt: to ~ sthg with mezclar algo con. ◇ vi **-1.** [combine]: to ~ (with) mezclarse (con). **-2.** [socially]: to ~ (with) alternar (con).

mini ['mɪnɪ] n minifalda f.

miniature ['mɪnətʃəʳ] ◇ adj en miniatura. ◇ n **-1.** [painting] miniatura f. **-2.** [of alcohol] botellín de licor en miniatura. **-3.** [small scale]: in ~ en miniatura.

minibus ['mɪnɪbʌs] (pl -es) n microbús m, micro m Amer.

minicab ['mɪnɪkæb] n Br taxi que se puede pedir por teléfono, pero no se puede parar en la calle.

minicomputer [,mɪnɪkəm'pjuːtəʳ] n miniordenador m.

minim ['mɪnɪm] n blanca f.

minima ['mɪnɪmə] pl → minimum.

minimal ['mɪnɪml] adj mínimo(ma).

minimize, -ise ['mɪnɪmaɪz] vt minimizar.

minimum ['mɪnɪməm] (pl -mums OR -ma) ◇ adj mínimo(ma). ◇ n mínimo m.

minimum lending rate [-'lendɪŋ-] n tipo m de descuento oficial.

minimum wage n salario m mínimo.

mining ['maɪnɪŋ] ◇ n minería f. ◇ adj minero(ra); ~ engineer ingeniero m, -ra f de minas.

minion ['mɪnjən] n hum or pej lacayo m.

miniseries ['mɪnɪsɪərɪz] (pl inv) n miniserie f.

miniskirt ['mɪnɪskɜːt] n minifalda f.

minister ['mɪnɪstəʳ] n **-1.** POL: ~ (for) ministro m, -tra f (de). **-2.** RELIG pastor m, -ra f.
◆ **minister to** vt fus atender a.

ministerial [,mɪnɪ'stɪərɪəl] adj ministerial.

minister of state n: ~ (for) ministro m, -tra f de estado (para).

ministry ['mɪnɪstrɪ] (pl -ies) n **-1.** POL ministerio m; **Ministry of Defence** Ministerio de Defensa. **-2.** RELIG: **the ~** el clero, el sacerdocio.

mink [mɪŋk] (*pl inv*) *n* visón *m*.

mink coat *n* abrigo *m* de visón.

Minnesota [ˌmɪnɪˈsəʊtə] *n* Minnesota.

minnow [ˈmɪnəʊ] *n* pececillo *m* (de agua dulce).

minor [ˈmaɪnəʳ] ◇ *adj* menor. ◇ *n* menor *m y f* (de edad).

Minorca [mɪˈnɔːkə] *n* Menorca.

minority [maɪˈnɒrətɪ] (*pl* **-ies**) *n* minoría *f*; **to be in a** OR **the ~** estar en la minoría, ser minoría.

minority government *n* gobierno *m* minoritario.

minster [ˈmɪnstəʳ] *n* catedral *f*.

minstrel [ˈmɪnstrəl] *n* juglar *m*.

mint [mɪnt] ◇ *n* **-1.** [herb] menta *f*, hierbabuena *f*. **-2.** [peppermint] pastilla *f* de menta. **-3.** [for coins]: **the ~** la Casa de la Moneda; **in ~ condition** en perfecto estado, como nuevo(va). ◇ *vt* acuñar.

mint sauce *n* salsa *f* de menta.

minuet [ˌmɪnjʊˈet] *n* minué *m*.

minus [ˈmaɪnəs] (*pl* **-es**) ◇ *prep* **-1.** MATH [less]: **4 ~ 2 is 2** 4 menos 2 es 2. **-2.** [in temperatures]: **it's ~ 5°C** estamos a 5° bajo cero. ◇ *adj* MATH [less than zero] negativo(va). ◇ *n* **-1.** MATH signo *m* (de) menos. **-2.** [disadvantage] pega *f*, desventaja *f*.

minuscule [ˈmɪnəskjuːl] *adj* minúsculo(la).

minus sign *n* signo *m* (de) menos.

minute[1] [ˈmɪnɪt] *n* minuto *m*; **at any ~** en cualquier momento; **at the last ~** en el último minuto; **this ~** ahora mismo; **up to the ~** [news] de última hora; [technology] punta (*inv*); **wait a ~** espera un momento. ◆ **minutes** *npl* acta *f*; **to take ~s** levantar OR tomar acta.

minute[2] [maɪˈnjuːt] *adj* diminuto(ta).

minutiae [maɪˈnjuːʃɪaɪ] *npl* minucias *fpl*.

miracle [ˈmɪrəkl] *n lit & fig* milagro *m*.

miraculous [mɪˈrækjʊləs] *adj* milagroso(sa).

miraculously [mɪˈrækjʊləslɪ] *adv* milagrosamente.

mirage [mɪˈrɑːʒ] *n lit & fig* espejismo *m*.

mire [maɪəʳ] *n* fango *m*, lodo *m*.

mirror [ˈmɪrəʳ] ◇ *n* espejo *m*. ◇ *vt* reflejar.

mirror image *n* reflejo *m* a la inversa.

mirth [mɜːθ] *n* risa *f*.

misadventure [ˌmɪsədˈventʃəʳ] *n* desgracia *f*, desventura *f*; **death by ~** JUR muerte *f* accidental.

misanthropist [mɪsˈænθrəpɪst] *n* misántropo *m*, -pa *f*.

misapplication [ˈmɪsˌæplɪˈkeɪʃn] *n* abuso *m*, mala aplicación *f*.

misapprehension [ˈmɪsˌæprɪˈhenʃn] *n* **-1.** [misunderstanding] malentendido *m*. **-2.** [mistaken belief] creencia *f* errónea.

misappropriate [ˌmɪsəˈprəʊprɪeɪt] *vt* malversar.

misappropriation [ˈmɪsəˌprəʊprɪˈeɪʃn] *n*: **~ (of)** malversación *f* (de).

misbehave [ˌmɪsbɪˈheɪv] *vi* portarse mal.

misbehaviour *Br*, **misbehavior** *Am* [ˌmɪsbɪˈheɪvjəʳ] *n* mal comportamiento *m*, mala conducta *f*.

misc *abbr of* **miscellaneous**.

miscalculate [ˌmɪsˈkælkjʊleɪt] *vt & vi* calcular mal.

miscalculation [ˌmɪskælkjʊˈleɪʃn] *n* **-1.** (*U*) [poor judgment] cálculos *mpl* erróneos. **-2.** [mistake] error *m* de cálculo.

miscarriage [ˌmɪsˈkærɪdʒ] *n* [at birth] aborto *m* (natural).

miscarriage of justice *n* error *m* judicial.

miscarry [ˌmɪsˈkærɪ] (*pt & pp* **-ied**) *vi* **-1.** [woman] tener un aborto (natural). **-2.** [plan] fracasar.

miscellaneous [ˌmɪsəˈleɪnjəs] *adj* diverso(sa).

miscellany [*Br* mɪˈselənɪ, *Am* ˈmɪsəleɪnɪ] (*pl* **-ies**) *n* miscelánea *f*.

mischance [ˌmɪsˈtʃɑːns] *n* **-1.** [piece of bad luck] infortunio *m*, desgracia *f*. **-2.** [bad luck] mala suerte *f*; **by ~** por desgracia.

mischief [ˈmɪstʃɪf] *n* (*U*) **-1.** [playfulness] picardía *f*. **-2.** [naughty behaviour] travesuras *fpl*, diabluras *fpl*. **-3.** [harm] daño *m*.

mischievous [ˈmɪstʃɪvəs] *adj* **-1.** [playful] lleno(na) de picardía. **-2.** [naughty] travieso(sa).

misconceived [ˌmɪskənˈsiːvd] *adj* mal concebido(da).

misconception [ˌmɪskənˈsepʃn] *n* concepto *m* erróneo, idea *f* falsa.

misconduct [ˌmɪsˈkɒndʌkt] *n* mala conducta *f*.

misconstrue [ˌmɪskənˈstruː] *vt fml* malinterpretar.

miscount [ˌmɪsˈkaʊnt] *vt & vi* contar mal.

misdeed [ˌmɪsˈdiːd] *n literary* fechoría *f*, delito *m*.

misdemeanour *Br*, **misdemeanor** *Am* [ˌmɪsdɪˈmiːnəʳ] *n fml* delito *m* menor, infracción *f*.

misdirected [ˌmɪsdɪˈrektɪd] *adj* [efforts] mal encaminado(da); [letter] con la dirección equivocada.

miser [ˈmaɪzəʳ] *n* avaro *m*, -ra *f*.

miserable ['mɪzrəbl] *adj* -1. [unhappy] infeliz, triste. -2. [wretched, poor] miserable. -3. [weather] horrible. -4. [pathetic] lamentable.

miserably ['mɪzrəblɪ] *adv* -1. [unhappily] tristemente. -2. [wretchedly, poorly] miserablemente. -3. [pathetically] lamentablemente.

miserly ['maɪzəlɪ] *adj* miserable, mezquino(na).

misery ['mɪzərɪ] (*pl* **-ies**) *n* -1. [unhappiness] desdicha *f*, tristeza *f*. -2. [wretchedness] miseria *f*.

misfire [,mɪs'faɪəʳ] *vi* -1. [gun] encasquillarse. -2. [car engine] no arrancar. -3. [plan] fracasar.

misfit ['mɪsfɪt] *n* inadaptado *m*, -da *f*.

misfortune [mɪs'fɔːtʃuːn] *n* -1. [bad luck] mala suerte *f*. -2. [piece of bad luck] desgracia *f*, infortunio *m*.

misgivings [mɪs'gɪvɪŋz] *npl* recelo *m*, recelos *mpl*.

misguided [,mɪs'gaɪdɪd] *adj* [person] descaminado(da); [attempt] equivocado(da).

mishandle [,mɪs'hændl] *vt* -1. [person, animal] maltratar. -2. [affair] llevar mal.

mishap ['mɪshæp] *n* percance *m*, contratiempo *m*; **without** ~ sin problemas.

mishear [,mɪs'hɪəʳ] (*pt & pp* **-heard** [-'hɜːd]) *vt & vi* oír mal.

mishmash ['mɪʃmæʃ] *n inf* revoltijo *m*, batiburrillo *m*.

misinform [,mɪsɪn'fɔːm] *vt* malinformar, desinformar.

misinformation [,mɪsɪnfə'meɪʃn] *n* información *f* errónea, desinformación *f*.

misinterpret [,mɪsɪn'tɜːprɪt] *vt* malinterpretar.

misjudge [,mɪs'dʒʌdʒ] *vt* -1. [guess wrongly] calcular mal. -2. [appraise wrongly] juzgar mal.

misjudg(e)ment [,mɪs'dʒʌdʒmənt] *n* -1. [poor judgment] estimación *f* equivocada. -2. [error of judgment] error *m* de juicio.

mislay [,mɪs'leɪ] (*pt & pp* **-laid**) *vt* extraviar, perder.

mislead [,mɪs'liːd] (*pt & pp* **-led**) *vt* engañar.

misleading [,mɪs'liːdɪŋ] *adj* engañoso(sa).

misled [,mɪs'led] *pt & pp* → **mislead**.

mismanage [,mɪs'mænɪdʒ] *vt* manejar OR llevar mal.

mismanagement [,mɪs'mænɪdʒmənt] *n* mala administración *f*.

mismatch [,mɪs'mætʃ] *vt*: **to be ~ed** emparejar mal.

misnomer [,mɪs'nəʊməʳ] *n* término *m* equivocado.

misogynist [mɪ'sɒdʒɪnɪst] *n* misógino *m*, -na *f*.

misplace [,mɪs'pleɪs] *vt* extraviar, perder.

misplaced [,mɪs'pleɪst] *adj* mal encaminado(da), fuera de lugar.

misprint ['mɪsprɪnt] *n* errata *f*, error *m* de imprenta.

mispronounce [,mɪsprə'naʊns] *vt* pronunciar mal.

misquote [,mɪs'kwəʊt] *vt* citar incorrectamente.

misread [,mɪs'riːd] (*pt & pp* **-read**) *vt* -1. [read wrongly] leer mal. -2. [misinterpret] malinterpretar.

misrepresent ['mɪs,reprɪ'zent] *vt* [person] dar una imagen equivocada de; [words] tergiversar.

misrepresentation ['mɪs,reprɪzen'teɪʃn] *n* -1. (*U*) [wrong interpretation] mala interpretación *f*. -2. [false account] tergiversación *f*.

misrule [,mɪs'ruːl] *n* mal gobierno *m*.

miss [mɪs] ◇ *vt* -1. [fail to see - TV programme, film] perderse; [- error, person in crowd] no ver. -2. [shot] fallar; [ball] no dar a; **to** ~ **the target** no dar en el blanco. -3. [feel absence of] echar de menos OR en falta. -4. [opportunity] perder, dejar pasar; [turning] pasarse. -5. [train, bus] perder. -6. [appointment] faltar a, no asistir a. -7. [avoid] evitar; **I just** ~**ed being run over** no me atropellaron por muy poco. ◇ *vi* fallar. ◇ *n*: **to give sthg a** ~ *inf* pasar de algo.
◆ **miss out** ◇ *vt sep* pasar por alto. ◇ *vi*: **to** ~ **out (on sthg)** perderse (algo).

Miss [mɪs] *n* señorita *f*.

misshapen [,mɪs'ʃeɪpn] *adj* deformado(da), deforme.

missile [*Br* 'mɪsaɪl, *Am* 'mɪsəl] *n* -1. [weapon] misil *m*. -2. [thrown object] proyectil *m*.

missile launcher [-,lɔːntʃəʳ] *n* lanzamisiles *m inv*.

missing ['mɪsɪŋ] *adj* -1. [lost] perdido(da), extraviado(da). -2. [not present] que falta; **to be** ~ faltar.

missing link *n* eslabón *m* perdido.

missing person *n* desaparecido *m*, -da *f*.

mission ['mɪʃn] *n* misión *f*.

missionary ['mɪʃənrɪ] (*pl* **-ies**) *n* misionero *m*, -ra *f*.

Mississippi [,mɪsɪ'sɪpɪ] -1. [river]: **the** ~ (**River**) el (río) Misisipí. -2. [state] Misisipí.

missive ['mɪsɪv] *n* misiva *f*.

Missouri [mɪ'zʊərɪ] *n* Misuri.

misspell [,mɪs'spel] (*pt & pp* **-spelt** OR

-spelled) *vt* escribir con faltas de ortografía.

misspelling [,mɪsˈspelɪŋ] *n* falta *f* de ortografía.

misspelt [,mɪsˈspelt] *pt & pp* → **misspell**.

misspend [,mɪsˈspend] (*pt & pp* **-spent**) *vt* malgastar.

mist [mɪst] *n* [gen] neblina *f*; [at sea] bruma *f*.

◆ **mist over, mist up** *vi* [windows, spectacles] empañarse; [eyes] llenarse de lágrimas.

mistake [mɪˈsteɪk] (*pt* **-took**, *pp* **-taken**) ◇ *n* error *m*; **to make a ~** equivocarse, cometer un error; **by ~** por error. ◇ *vt* **-1.** [misunderstand] entender mal. **-2.** [fail to recognize]: **to ~ sthg/sb for** confundir algo/a alguien con; **there's no mistaking ... ...** es inconfundible.

mistaken [mɪˈsteɪkn] ◇ *pp* → **mistake**. ◇ *adj* equivocado(da); **to be ~ about sb/sthg** estar equivocado respecto a alguien/algo.

mistaken identity *n*: **a case of ~** un caso de identificación *f* errónea.

mistakenly [mɪsˈteɪknlɪ] *adv* equivocadamente.

mister [ˈmɪstər] *n inf* amigo *m*.

◆ **Mister** *n* señor *m*.

mistime [,mɪsˈtaɪm] *vt* hacer a destiempo, calcular mal.

mistletoe [ˈmɪsltəʊ] *n* muérdago *m*.

mistook [mɪˈstʊk] *pt* → **mistake**.

mistranslation [,mɪstrænsˈleɪʃn] *n* traducción *f* equivocada.

mistreat [,mɪsˈtriːt] *vt* maltratar.

mistreatment [mɪsˈtriːtmənt] *n* (*U*) malos tratos *mpl*.

mistress [ˈmɪstrɪs] *n* **-1.** [woman in control] señora *f*; **~ of the situation** dueña *f* de la situación. **-2.** [female lover] amante *f*, querida *f*. **-3.** *Br* [school teacher - primary] maestra *f*, señorita *f*; [- secondary] profesora *f*.

mistrial [ˈmɪstraɪəl] *n* juicio *m* nulo.

mistrust [,mɪsˈtrʌst] ◇ *n* desconfianza *f*, recelo *m*. ◇ *vt* desconfiar de.

mistrustful [,mɪsˈtrʌstfʊl] *adj* desconfiado(da), receloso(sa); **to be ~ of** desconfiar de.

misty [ˈmɪstɪ] (*compar* **-ier**, *superl* **-iest**) *adj* [gen] neblinoso(sa); [at sea] brumoso(sa).

misunderstand [,mɪsʌndəˈstænd] (*pt & pp* **-stood**) *vt & vi* entender OR comprender mal.

misunderstanding [,mɪsʌndəˈstændɪŋ] *n* malentendido *m*.

misunderstood [,mɪsʌndəˈstʊd] *pt & pp* → **misunderstand**.

misuse [*n* ,mɪsˈjuːs, *vb* ,mɪsˈjuːz] ◇ *n* uso *m* indebido. ◇ *vt* hacer uso indebido de.

MIT (*abbr of* **Massachusetts Institute of Technology**) *n* principal instituto de investigación tecnológica en Estados Unidos.

mite [maɪt] *n* **-1.** [insect] ácaro *m*, insecto *m* diminuto. **-2.** *inf* [small amount]: **a ~** un pelín, una pizca. **-3.** [small child] criatura *f*.

miter *Am* = **mitre**.

mitigate [ˈmɪtɪgeɪt] *vt fml* mitigar, atenuar.

mitigating [ˈmɪtɪgeɪtɪŋ] *adj fml*: **~ circumstances** circunstancias *fpl* atenuantes.

mitigation [,mɪtɪˈgeɪʃn] *n fml* descargo *m*, atenuante *m*.

mitre *Br*, **miter** *Am* [ˈmaɪtər] *n* **-1.** [hat] mitra *f*. **-2.** [joint] inglete *m*.

mitt [mɪt] *n* manopla *f*.

mitten [ˈmɪtn] *n* manopla *f*.

mix [mɪks] ◇ *vt*: **to ~ sthg (with)** mezclar algo (con). ◇ *vi* **-1.** [substances] mezclarse; [activities] ir bien juntos(tas). **-2.** [socially]: **to ~ with** alternar OR salir con. ◇ *n* mezcla *f*.

◆ **mix up** *vt sep* **-1.** [confuse] confundir. **-2.** [disorder] mezclar.

mixed [mɪkst] *adj* **-1.** [of different kinds] surtido(da), variado(da); **to have ~ feelings about** tener sentimientos encontrados acerca de, no estar seguro de; **~ salad** ensalada *f* mixta. **-2.** [of different sexes] mixto(ta).

mixed-ability *adj Br* de varios niveles.

mixed blessing *n* bendición *f* a medias.

mixed doubles *n* (*U*) dobles *mpl* mixtos.

mixed economy *n* economía *f* mixta.

mixed grill *n* parrillada *f* mixta.

mixed marriage *n* matrimonio *m* mixto.

mixed up *adj* **-1.** [confused] confuso(sa). **-2.** [involved]: **~ in** [fight, crime] involucrado(da) en.

mixer [ˈmɪksər] *n* **-1.** [for food] batidora *f*; [for cement] hormigonera *f*. **-2.** [non-alcoholic drink] *bebida no alcohólica para mezclar con bebidas alcohólicas.*

mixer tap *n Br* grifo *m* único (para agua fría y caliente).

mixing bowl [ˈmɪksɪŋ-] *n* cuenco *m* (para mezclar).

mixture [ˈmɪkstʃər] *n* [gen] mezcla *f*; [of sweets] surtido *m*.

mix-up *n inf* lío *m*, confusión *f*.

MK, **mk** *abbr of* **mark**.

mkt *abbr of* **market**.

MLitt [,emˈlɪt] (*abbr of* **Master of Literature, Master of Letters**) *n* (*titular de un*) *título postuniversitario de unos dos años de duración en el campo de las humanidades.*

MLR *n abbr of* **minimum lending rate**.

mm (*abbr of* **millimetre**) mm.

MN ◇ *n abbr of* **Merchant Navy**. ◇ *abbr of* **Minnesota**.

mnemonic [nɪ'mɒnɪk] *n* frase *f* mnemotécnica.

m.o. *abbr of* **money order**.

MO ◇ *n* **-1.** (*abbr of* **medical officer**) *oficial médico*. **-2.** (*abbr of* **modus operandi**) *modus operandi*. ◇ *abbr of* **Missouri**.

moan [məʊn] ◇ *n* **-1.** [of pain, sadness] gemido *m*. **-2.** *inf* [complaint] queja *f*. ◇ *vi* **-1.** [in pain, sadness] gemir. **-2.** *inf* [complain]: **to ~ (about)** quejarse (de).

moaning ['məʊnɪŋ] *n* (*U*) [complaining] quejas *fpl*.

moat [məʊt] *n* foso *m*.

mob [mɒb] (*pt & pp* **-bed**, *cont* **-bing**) ◇ *n* muchedumbre *f*, turba *f*. ◇ *vt* agolparse en torno de, asediar.

mobile ['məʊbaɪl] ◇ *adj* **-1.** [able to move] móvil. **-2.** [able to travel]: **to be ~** poder viajar. ◇ *n* móvil *m*.

mobile home *n* caravana *f*.

mobile library *n* biblioteca *f* móvil OR ambulante.

mobile phone *n* teléfono *m* portátil.

mobile shop *n* tienda *f* ambulante (*camión*).

mobility [məˈbɪlətɪ] *n* movilidad *f*.

mobility allowance *n Br ayuda económica que reciben los minusválidos para poder viajar.*

mobilization [ˌməʊbɪlaɪˈzeɪʃn] *n* movilización *f*.

mobilize, -ise ['məʊbɪlaɪz] ◇ *vt* movilizar. ◇ *vi* movilizarse.

moccasin ['mɒkəsɪn] *n* mocasín *m*.

mock [mɒk] ◇ *adj* fingido(da); **~ (exam)** simulacro *m* de examen. ◇ *vt* burlarse de. ◇ *vi* burlarse.

mockery ['mɒkərɪ] *n* burla *f*; **to make a ~ of sthg** poner en ridículo algo.

mocking ['mɒkɪŋ] *adj* burlón(ona).

mockingbird ['mɒkɪŋbɜːd] *n* sinsonte *m*.

mock-up *n* maqueta *f* de tamaño natural.

mod [mɒd] *n Br* mod *m* y *f*, *aficionado a la música soul inglesa de los años 60.*

MOD *n abbr of* **Ministry of Defence**.

mod cons (*abbr of* **modern conveniences**) *npl Br inf*: **all ~** con todas las comodidades.

mode [məʊd] *n* modo *m*.

model ['mɒdl] (*Br pt & pp* **-led**, *cont* **-ling**, *Am pt & pp* **-ed**, *cont* **-ing**) ◇ *n* **-1.** [gen] modelo *m*. **-2.** [small copy] maqueta *f*. **-3.** [for painter, in fashion] modelo *m* y *f*. ◇ *adj* **-1.** [exemplary] modelo (*inv*). **-2.** [reduced-

scale] en miniatura. ◇ *vt* **-1.** [shape] modelar. **-2.** [wear] lucir (*en pase de modelos*). **-3.** [copy]: **to ~ o.s. on sb** tener a alguien como modelo. ◇ *vi* trabajar de modelo.

modem ['məʊdem] *n* COMPUT módem *m*.

moderate [*adj & n* 'mɒdərət, *vb* 'mɒdəreɪt] ◇ *adj* moderado(da). ◇ *n* POL moderado *m*, -da *f*. ◇ *vt* moderar. ◇ *vi* moderarse.

moderately ['mɒdərətlɪ] *adv* moderadamente.

moderation [ˌmɒdəˈreɪʃn] *n* moderación *f*; **in ~** con moderación.

moderator ['mɒdəreɪtər] *n* [of exam] moderador *m*, -ra *f*.

modern ['mɒdən] *adj* moderno(na).

modern-day *adj* de nuestros días.

modernism ['mɒdənɪzm] *n* modernismo *m*.

modernization [ˌmɒdənaɪˈzeɪʃn] *n* modernización *f*.

modernize, -ise ['mɒdənaɪz] ◇ *vt* modernizar. ◇ *vi* modernizarse.

modern languages *npl* lenguas *fpl* modernas.

modest ['mɒdɪst] *adj* **-1.** [gen] modesto(ta). **-2.** [improvement] ligero(ra); [price] módico(ca).

modestly ['mɒdɪstlɪ] *adv* [gen] modestamente; [improve] ligeramente.

modesty ['mɒdɪstɪ] *n* modestia *f*.

modicum ['mɒdɪkəm] *n fml*: **a ~ of** un mínimo de.

modification [ˌmɒdɪfɪˈkeɪʃn] *n* modificación *f*.

modify ['mɒdɪfaɪ] (*pt & pp* **-ied**) *vt* modificar.

modular ['mɒdjʊlər] *adj* modular.

modulated ['mɒdjʊleɪtɪd] *adj* modulado(da).

modulation [ˌmɒdjʊˈleɪʃn] *n* modulación *f*.

module ['mɒdjuːl] *n* módulo *m*.

Mogadishu [ˌmɒgəˈdɪʃuː] *n* Mogadiscio.

moggy ['mɒgɪ] (*pl* **-ies**) *n Br inf* minino *m*.

mogul ['məʊgl] *n* magnate *m* y *f*.

MOH (*abbr of* **Medical Officer of Health**) *n jefe de sanidad municipal.*

mohair ['məʊheər] ◇ *n* mohair *m*. ◇ *comp* de mohair.

Mohammedan [məˈhæmɪdn] ◇ *adj* mahometano(na). ◇ *n* mahometano *m*, -na *f*.

Mohican [məʊˈhiːkən] *n* mohicano *m*, -na *f*.

moist [mɔɪst] *adj* húmedo(da).

moisten ['mɔɪsn] *vt* humedecer.

moisture ['mɔɪstʃər] *n* humedad *f*.

moisturize, -ise ['mɔɪstʃəraɪz] *vt* hidratar.

moisturizer ['mɔɪstʃəraɪzəʳ] *n* (crema *f*) hidratante *m*.

molar ['məʊləʳ] *n* muela *f*.

molasses [mə'læsɪz] *n* (*U*) melaza *f*.

mold *etc Am* = **mould**.

Moldavia [mɒl'deɪvɪə] *n* Moldavia.

mole [məʊl] *n* -1. [animal, spy] topo *m*. -2. [spot] lunar *m*.

molecular [mə'lekjʊləʳ] *adj* molecular.

molecule ['mɒlɪkjuːl] *n* molécula *f*.

molehill ['məʊlhɪl] *n* topera *f*.

molest [mə'lest] *vt* -1. [attack sexually] acosar sexualmente. -2. [attack] atacar.

molester [mə'lestəʳ] *n*: **child** ~ pervertidor *m*, -ra *f* de menores.

mollify ['mɒlɪfaɪ] (*pt* & *pp* **-ied**) *vt fml* apaciguar.

mollusc, mollusk *Am* ['mɒləsk] *n* molusco *m*.

mollycoddle ['mɒlɪˌkɒdl] *vt inf* mimar.

Molotov cocktail ['mɒlətɒf-] *n* cóctel *m* molotov.

molt *Am* = **moult**.

molten ['məʊltn] *adj* fundido(da), derretido(da).

mom [mɒm] *n Am inf* mamá *f*.

moment ['məʊmənt] *n* momento *m*; ~ **of truth** momento de la verdad; **at any** ~ de un momento a otro; **at the** ~ en este momento; **at the last** ~ en el último momento; **for the** ~ de momento; **for one** ~ por un momento.

momentarily ['məʊməntərɪlɪ] *adv* -1. [for a short time] momentáneamente. -2. *Am* [soon] pronto, de un momento a otro.

momentary ['məʊməntrɪ] *adj* momentáneo(a).

momentous [mə'mentəs] *adj* trascendental.

momentum [mə'mentəm] *n* (*U*) -1. PHYSICS momento *m*. -2. *fig* [speed, force] ímpetu *m*, impulso *m*; **to gather** ~ cobrar intensidad.

momma ['mɒmə], **mommy** ['mɒmɪ] *n Am* mamá *f*.

Mon. (*abbr of* **Monday**) lun.

Monaco ['mɒnəkəʊ] *n* Mónaco.

monarch ['mɒnək] *n* monarca *m* y *f*.

monarchist ['mɒnəkɪst] *n* monárquico *m*, -ca *f*.

monarchy ['mɒnəkɪ] (*pl* **-ies**) *n* -1. [gen] monarquía *f*. -2. [royal family]: **the** ~ la familia real.

monastery ['mɒnəstrɪ] (*pl* **-ies**) *n* monasterio *m*.

monastic [mə'næstɪk] *adj* monástico(ca).

Monday ['mʌndɪ] *n* lunes *m*; *see also* **Saturday**.

monetarism ['mʌnɪtərɪzm] *n* monetarismo *m*.

monetarist ['mʌnɪtərɪst] *n* monetarista *m* y *f*.

monetary ['mʌnɪtrɪ] *adj* monetario(ria).

money ['mʌnɪ] *n* dinero *m*, plata *f Amer*; **to make** ~ hacer dinero; **to get one's** ~'s **worth** sacarle provecho al dinero de uno.

moneybox ['mʌnɪbɒks] *n* hucha *f*.

moneyed ['mʌnɪd] *adj fml* adinerado(da).

moneylender ['mʌnɪˌlendəʳ] *n* prestamista *m* y *f*.

moneymaker ['mʌnɪˌmeɪkəʳ] *n* mina *f* (de dinero).

moneymaking ['mʌnɪˌmeɪkɪŋ] *adj* para hacer dinero.

money market *n* mercado *m* monetario.

money order *n* giro *m* postal.

money-spinner *n inf* mina *f* (de dinero).

money supply *n* volumen *m* de moneda.

mongol ['mɒŋgəl] *dated* & *offensive* ◇ *adj* mongólico(ca). ◇ *n* mongólico *m*, -ca *f*.

◆ **Mongol** = **Mongolian**.

Mongolia [mɒŋ'gəʊlɪə] *n* Mongolia.

Mongolian [mɒŋ'gəʊlɪən] ◇ *adj* mongol(la). ◇ *n* -1. [person] mongol *m*, -la *f*. -2. [language] mongol *m*.

mongoose ['mɒŋguːs] (*pl* **-s**) *n* mangosta *f*.

mongrel ['mʌŋgrəl] *n* perro *m* cruzado OR sin pedigrí.

monitor ['mɒnɪtəʳ] ◇ *n* [gen & COMPUT] monitor *m*. ◇ *vt* -1. [check] controlar, hacer un seguimiento de. -2. [listen in to] escuchar.

monk [mʌŋk] *n* monje *m*.

monkey ['mʌŋkɪ] (*pl* **monkeys**) *n* mono *m*.

monkey nut *n* cacahuete *m*.

monkey wrench *n* llave *f* inglesa.

mono ['mɒnəʊ] ◇ *adj* monoaural, mono (*inv*). ◇ *n* -1. [sound] *inf* sonido *m* monoaural. -2. *Am inf* [glandular fever] mononucleosis *f inv* infecciosa.

monochrome ['mɒnəkrəʊm] *adj* monocromo(ma).

monocle ['mɒnəkl] *n* monóculo *m*.

monogamous [mɒ'nɒgəməs] *adj* monógamo(ma).

monogamy [mɒ'nɒgəmɪ] *n* monogamia *f*.

monogrammed ['mɒnəgræmd] *adj* bordado(da) con iniciales.

monolingual [ˌmɒnə'lɪŋgwəl] *adj* monolingüe.

monolithic [ˌmɒnə'lɪθɪk] *adj* monolítico(ca).

monologue, monolog *Am* ['mɒnəlɒg] *n* monólogo *m*.

mononucleosis ['mɒnəʊˌnjuːklɪ'əʊsɪs] *n Am* mononucleosis *f inv* infecciosa.

monoplane ['mɒnəpleɪn] *n* monoplano *m*.

monopolize, -ise [mə'nɒpəlaɪz] *vt* monopolizar.

monopoly [mə'nɒpəlɪ] (*pl* **-ies**) *n*: ~ (**on** OR **of**) monopolio *m* (de); **the Monopolies and Mergers Commission** *Br la organización que investiga la posible conversión en monopolio de ciertas empresas.*

monorail ['mɒnəreɪl] *n* monorraíl *m*.

monosodium glutamate [,mɒnə'səʊdjəm-'gluːtəmeɪt] *n* glutamato *m* monosódico.

monosyllabic [,mɒnəsɪ'læbɪk] *adj* monosilábico(ca).

monosyllable ['mɒnə,sɪləbl] *n* monosílabo *m*.

monotone ['mɒnətəʊn] *n*: **in a** ~ con voz *f* monótona.

monotonous [mə'nɒtənəs] *adj* monótono(na).

monotonously [mə'nɒtənəslɪ] *adv* de forma monótona.

monotony [mə'nɒtənɪ] *n* monotonía *f*.

monoxide [mɒ'nɒksaɪd] *n* monóxido *m*.

Monrovia [mɒn'rəʊvɪə] *n* Monrovia.

Monsignor [,mɒn'siːnjə] *n* monseñor *m*.

monsoon [mɒn'suːn] *n* lluvias *fpl* monzónicas, monzón *m*.

monster ['mɒnstə'] ◇ *n* **-1.** [imaginary creature, cruel person] monstruo *m*. **-2.** [very large thing] mastodonte *m*. ◇ *adj* gigantesco(ca), enorme.

monstrosity [mɒn'strɒsətɪ] (*pl* **-ies**) *n* monstruosidad *f*.

monstrous ['mɒnstrəs] *adj* **-1.** [very unfair, frightening, ugly] monstruoso(sa). **-2.** [very large] gigantesco(ca).

montage ['mɒntɑːʒ] *n* montaje *m*.

Montana [mɒn'tænə] *n* Montana.

Mont Blanc [mɔ̃blɑ̃] *n* Mont Blanc.

Montenegro [,mɒntɪ'niːgrəʊ] *n* Montenegro.

Montevideo [,mɒntɪvɪ'deɪəʊ] *n* Montevideo.

month [mʌnθ] *n* mes *m*.

monthly ['mʌnθlɪ] (*pl* **-ies**) ◇ *adj* mensual. ◇ *adv* mensualmente. ◇ *n* revista *f* mensual.

Montreal [mɒntrɪ'ɔːl] *n* Montreal.

monument ['mɒnjʊmənt] *n* monumento *m*.

monumental [,mɒnjʊ'mentl] *adj* **-1.** [gen] monumental. **-2.** [error] descomunal.

moo [muː] (*pl* **-s**) ◇ *n* mugido *m*. ◇ *vi* mugir.

mooch [muːtʃ]
◆ **mooch about, mooch around** *vi inf* deambular.

mood [muːd] *n* [of individual] humor *m*; [of public, voters] disposición *f*; **in a (bad)** ~ de mal humor; **in a good** ~ de buen humor.

moody ['muːdɪ] (*compar* **-ier**, *superl* **-iest**) *adj pej* **-1.** [changeable] de humor variable. **-2.** [bad-tempered] malhumorado(da), irritable.

moon [muːn] *n* luna *f*; **to be over the** ~ *inf* estar dando saltos de alegría.

moonbeam ['muːnbiːm] *n* rayo *m* de luna.

moonlight ['muːnlaɪt] (*pt* & *pp* **-ed**) ◇ *n* luz *f* de la luna; **in the** ~ a la luz de la luna. ◇ *vi inf* estar pluriempleado(da).

moonlighting ['muːnlaɪtɪŋ] *n* pluriempleo *m*.

moonlit ['muːnlɪt] *adj* [night] de luna; [landscape] iluminado(da) por la luna.

moonscape ['muːnskeɪp] *n* paisaje *m* lunar.

moon shot *n* viaje *m* a la luna.

moonstone ['muːnstəʊn] *n* labradorita *f*, piedra *f* de la luna.

moonstruck ['muːnstrʌk] *adj inf* chiflado(da), chalado(da).

moony ['muːnɪ] (*compar* **-ier**, *superl* **-iest**) *adj Br inf* en la luna.

moor [mɔː'] ◇ *n* páramo *m*, brezal *m*. ◇ *vt* amarrar. ◇ *vi* echar las amarras.

Moor [mɔː'] *n* moro *m*, -ra *f*.

moorings ['mɔːrɪŋz] *npl* [ropes, chains] amarras *fpl*; [place] amarradero *m*.

Moorish ['mɔːrɪʃ] *adj* moro(ra), morisco(ca).

moorland ['mɔːlənd] *n* páramo *m*, brezal *m*.

moose [muːs] (*pl inv*) *n* [North American] alce *m*.

moot [muːt] *vt* proponer.

moot point *n* cuestión *f* discutible.

mop [mɒp] (*pt* & *pp* **-ped**, *cont* **-ping**) ◇ *n* **-1.** [for cleaning] fregona *f*. **-2.** *inf* [of hair] pelambrera *f*, chasca *f Amer*. ◇ *vt* **-1.** [clean with mop] fregar, pasar la fregona por. **-2.** [dry with cloth - sweat] enjugar.
◆ **mop up** *vt sep* [clean up] limpiar.

mope [məʊp] *vi pej* estar deprimido(da).
◆ **mope about, mope around** *vi pej* vagar como un alma en pena.

moped ['məʊped] *n* ciclomotor *m*, motoneta *f Amer*.

moral ['mɒrəl] ◇ *adj* moral; ~ **support** apoyo *m* moral. ◇ *n* [lesson] moraleja *f*.
◆ **morals** *npl* [principles] moral *f*.

morale [mə'rɑːl] *n* (*U*) moral *f*.

moralistic [,mɒrə'lɪstɪk] *adj pej* moralista.

morality [mə'rælətɪ] (*pl* **-ies**) *n* **-1.** [gen]

moralidad *f.* **-2.** [system of principles] moral *f.*

moralize, -ise ['mɒrəlaɪz] *vi pej*: **to ~ (about** OR **on)** moralizar (sobre).

morally ['mɒrəlɪ] *adv* moralmente.

Moral Majority *n grupo de presión ultraconservador apoyado por las iglesias fundamentalistas en Estados Unidos.*

morass [mə'ræs] *n* cenagal *m.*

moratorium [,mɒrə'tɔːrɪəm] (*pl* **-ria** [-rɪə]) *n fml*: **~ (on)** moratoria *f* (para).

morbid ['mɔːbɪd] *adj* morboso(sa).

more [mɔːʳ] ◇ *adv* **-1.** (*with adjectives and adverbs*) más; **~ important (than)** más importante (que); **~ quickly/often (than)** más rápido/a menudo (que). **-2.** [to a greater degree] más; **she's ~ like a mother to me than a sister** para mí ella es más una madre que una hermana; **we were ~ hurt than angry** más que enfadados estábamos heridos. **-3.** [another time]: **once/twice ~** una vez/dos veces más.
◇ *adj* más; **there are ~ trains in the morning** hay más trenes por la mañana; **~ food than drink** más comida que bebida; **~ than 70 people died** más de 70 personas murieron; **have some ~ tea** toma un poco más de té; **I finished two ~ chapters today** acabé otros dos capítulos hoy.
◇ *pron* más; **~ than five** más de cinco; **he's got ~ than I have** él tiene más que yo; **there's ~ if you want it** hay más si quieres; **there's no ~ (left)** no queda nada (más); **what ~ do you want?** ¿qué más quieres?; **(and) what's ~** (y lo que) es más.
◆ **any more** *adv*: **not ... any ~** ya no ....
◆ **more and more** ◇ *adv* cada vez más; **I became ~ and ~ depressed** estaba cada vez más deprimido. ◇ *adj* cada vez más; **there are ~ and ~ cars on the roads** hay cada vez más coches en las carreteras. ◇ *pron* cada vez más; **we spend ~ and ~ on petrol** cada vez gastamos más en gasolina.
◆ **more or less** *adv* más o menos; **she ~ or less suggested I had stolen it** lo que vino a decir es que yo lo había robado.

moreover [mɔː'rəʊvəʳ] *adv fml* además, es más.

morgue [mɔːg] *n* depósito *m* de cadáveres.

MORI ['mɔːrɪ] (*abbr of* **Market & Opinion Research Institute**) *n empresa británica especializada en encuestas de opinión.*

moribund ['mɒrɪbʌnd] *adj fml* agonizante *fig.*

Mormon ['mɔːmən] *n* mormón *m*, -ona *f.*

morning ['mɔːnɪŋ] *n* **-1.** [first part of day] mañana *f*; **in the ~** por la mañana; **six o'clock in the ~** las seis de la mañana. **-2.**
[between midnight and dawn] madrugada *f.* **-3.** [tomorrow morning]: **in the ~** mañana por la mañana.
◆ **mornings** *adv Am* por la mañana.

morning-after pill *n* píldora *f* abortiva.

morning dress *n* traje *m* de etiqueta.

morning sickness *n* (U) náuseas *fpl* del embarazo.

Moroccan [mə'rɒkən] ◇ *adj* marroquí. ◇ *n* marroquí *m y f.*

Morocco [mə'rɒkəʊ] *n* Marruecos.

moron ['mɔːrɒn] *n inf* imbécil *m y f*, idiota *m y f.*

moronic [mə'rɒnɪk] *adj* imbécil, idiota.

morose [mə'rəʊs] *adj* malhumorado(da).

morphine ['mɔːfiːn] *n* morfina *f.*

morris dancing ['mɒrɪs-] *n* (U) *baile regional inglés cuyos bailarines llevan campanillas cosidas a la ropa.*

Morse (code) [mɔːs-] *n* (alfabeto *m*) Morse *m.*

morsel ['mɔːsl] *n* bocado *m.*

mortal ['mɔːtl] ◇ *adj* **-1.** [gen] mortal. **-2.** [fear] horrible, espantoso(sa). ◇ *n* mortal *m y f.*

mortality [mɔː'tælətɪ] *n* mortalidad *f.*

mortality rate *n* tasa *f* de mortalidad.

mortally ['mɔːtəlɪ] *adv* **-1.** [fatally] mortalmente, de muerte. **-2.** [deeply] profundamente.

mortar ['mɔːtəʳ] *n* **-1.** [cement mixture] argamasa *f.* **-2.** [gun, bowl] mortero *m*, molcajete *m Amer.*

mortarboard ['mɔːtəbɔːd] *n* birrete *m.*

mortgage ['mɔːgɪdʒ] ◇ *n* hipoteca *f.* ◇ *vt* hipotecar.

mortgagee [,mɔːgɪ'dʒiː] *n* acreedor hipotecario *m*, acreedora hipotecaria *f.*

mortgagor [,mɔːgɪ'dʒɔːʳ] *n* deudor hipotecario *m*, deudora hipotecaria *f.*

mortician [mɔː'tɪʃn] *n Am* director *m*, -ra *f* de funeraria.

mortified ['mɔːtɪfaɪd] *adj* muerto(ta) de vergüenza.

mortise lock ['mɔːtɪs-] *n* cerradura *f* embutida.

mortuary ['mɔːtʃʊərɪ] (*pl* **-ies**) *n* depósito *m* de cadáveres, tanatorio *m.*

mosaic [mə'zeɪɪk] *n* mosaico *m.*

Moscow ['mɒskəʊ] *n* Moscú.

Moslem ['mɒzləm] = **Muslim.**

mosque [mɒsk] *n* mezquita *f.*

mosquito [mə'skiːtəʊ] (*pl* **-es** OR **-s**) *n* mosquito *m*, zancudo *m Amer.*

mosquito net *n* mosquitera *f.*

moss [mɒs] *n* musgo *m.*

mossy ['mɒsɪ] (*compar* **-ier**, *superl* **-iest**) *adj* cubierto(ta) de musgo.

most [məʊst] (*superl of* **many**) ◇ *adj* **-1.** [the majority of] la mayoría de; ~ **people** la mayoría de la gente. **-2.** [largest amount of]: **(the)** ~ más; **who has got (the)** ~ **money?** ¿quién es el que tiene más dinero? ◇ *pron* **-1.** [the majority]: ~ **(of)** la mayoría (de); ~ **of the time** la mayor parte del tiempo. **-2.** [largest amount]: **(the)** ~ lo más, lo máximo; **at** ~ como mucho, todo lo más. **-3.** *phr*: **to make the** ~ **of sthg** sacarle el mayor partido a algo. ◇ *adv* **-1.** [to the greatest extent]: **(the)** ~ el/la/lo más; **what I like** ~ lo que más me gusta. **-2.** *fml* [very] muy; ~ **certainly** con toda seguridad. **-3.** *Am* [almost] casi.

mostly ['məʊstlɪ] *adv* [in the main part] principalmente, mayoritariamente; [usually] normalmente.

MOT (*abbr of* **Ministry of Transport test**) *n* ≃ ITV *f*; **to have one's car ~'d** ≃ pasar la ITV.

motel [məʊ'tel] *n* motel *m*.

moth [mɒθ] *n* polilla *f*.

mothball ['mɒθbɔːl] *n* bola *f* de naftalina.

moth-eaten *adj* apolillado(da).

mother ['mʌðəʳ] ◇ *n* madre *f*. ◇ *vt usu pej* [spoil] mimar.

motherboard ['mʌðə,bɔːd] *n* COMPUT placa *f* de base, placa *f* de expansión.

motherhood ['mʌðəhʊd] *n* maternidad *f*.

Mothering Sunday ['mʌðərɪŋ-] *n* día *m* de la madre.

mother-in-law (*pl* **mothers-in-law** OR **mother-in-laws**) *n* suegra *f*.

motherland ['mʌðəlænd] *n* madre *f* patria.

motherless ['mʌðəlɪs] *adj* sin madre, huérfano(na) de madre.

motherly ['mʌðəlɪ] *adj* maternal.

Mother Nature *n* madre *f* naturaleza.

mother-of-pearl ◇ *n* nácar *m*. ◇ *comp* de nácar.

Mother's day *n* día *m* de la madre.

mother ship *n* buque *m* nodriza.

mother superior *n* madre *f* superiora.

mother-to-be (*pl* **mothers-to-be**) *n* futura madre *f*.

mother tongue *n* lengua *f* materna.

motif [məʊ'tiːf] *n* ART & MUS motivo *m*.

motion ['məʊʃn] ◇ *n* **-1.** [gen] movimiento *m*; **to set sthg in** ~ poner algo en marcha; **to go through the** ~**s (of doing sthg)** (hacer algo para) cubrir el expediente. **-2.** [proposal] moción *f*. ◇ *vt*: **to** ~ **sb to do sthg** indicar a alguien con un gesto que haga algo.

◇ *vi*: **to** ~ **to sb** hacer una señal (con la mano) a alguien.

motionless ['məʊʃənlɪs] *adj* inmóvil.

motion picture *n Am* película *f*.

motivate ['məʊtɪveɪt] *vt* motivar.

motivated ['məʊtɪveɪtɪd] *adj* motivado(da).

motivation [,məʊtɪ'veɪʃn] *n* motivación *f*.

motive ['məʊtɪv] *n* [gen] motivo *m*; [for crime] móvil *m*.

motley ['mɒtlɪ] *adj pej* variopinto(ta), abigarrado(da).

motocross ['məʊtəkrɒs] *n* motocross *m*.

motor ['məʊtəʳ] ◇ *adj Br* [industry, accident] automovilístico(ca); [mechanic] de automóviles. ◇ *n* motor *m*. ◇ *vi dated* viajar en coche.

Motorail® ['məʊtəreɪl] *n Br* servicio *m* ferroviario de transporte de coches.

motorbike ['məʊtəbaɪk] *n inf* moto *f*.

motorboat ['məʊtəbəʊt] *n* lancha *f* motora.

motorcade ['məʊtəkeɪd] *n* caravana *f* de coches.

motorcar ['məʊtəkɑːʳ] *n* automóvil *m*.

motorcycle ['məʊtə,saɪkl] *n* motocicleta *f*.

motorcyclist ['məʊtə,saɪklɪst] *n* motociclista *m y f*.

motoring ['məʊtərɪŋ] ◇ *adj Br* automovilístico(ca); ~ **offence** infracción *f* de tráfico. ◇ *n dated* automovilismo *m*.

motorist ['məʊtərɪst] *n* automovilista *m y f*, conductor *m*, -ra *f*.

motorize, -ise ['məʊtəraɪz] *vt* motorizar.

motor lodge *n Am* motel *m*.

motor racing *n* automovilismo *m* deportivo.

motor scooter *n* Vespa® *f*, escúter *m*.

motor vehicle *n* vehículo *m* de motor.

motorway ['məʊtəweɪ] *Br* ◇ *n* autopista *f*. ◇ *comp* de autopista.

mottled ['mɒtld] *adj* con manchas, moteado(da).

motto ['mɒtəʊ] (*pl* **-s** OR **-es**) *n* lema *m*.

mould, mold *Am* [məʊld] ◇ *n* **-1.** [growth] moho *m*. **-2.** [shape] molde *m*. ◇ *vt lit* & *fig* moldear.

moulding, molding *Am* ['məʊldɪŋ] *n* **-1.** [decoration] moldura *f*. **-2.** [moulded object] objeto *m* sacado de un molde.

mouldy (*compar* **-ier**, *superl* **-iest**), **moldy** *Am* (*compar* **-ier**, *superl* **-iest**) ['məʊldɪ] *adj* mohoso(sa).

moult, molt *Am* [məʊlt] ◇ *vt* mudar. ◇ *vi* [bird] mudar la pluma; [dog] mudar el pelo.

mound [maʊnd] *n* **-1.** [small hill] montículo *m*. **-2.** [untidy pile] montón *m*.

mount [maunt] ⋄ n **-1.** [gen] montura f; [for photograph] marco m; [for jewel] engaste m. **-2.** [mountain] monte m. ⋄ vt **-1.** [horse, bike] subirse a, montar en. **-2.** [hill, steps] subir. **-3.** [attack] lanzar; to ~ **guard over sthg/sb** montar guardia para vigilar algo/a alguien. **-4.** [exhibition] montar. **-5.** [jewel] engastar; [photograph] enmarcar. ⋄ vi **-1.** [increase] aumentar. **-2.** [climb on horse] montar.

mountain ['mauntɪn] n lit & fig montaña f; **to make a ~ out of a molehill** hacer una montaña de un grano de arena.

mountain bike n bicicleta f de montaña.

mountaineer [,mauntɪ'nɪər] n montañero m, -ra f, andinista m y f Amer.

mountaineering [,mauntɪ'nɪərɪŋ] n montañismo m, andinismo m Amer.

mountainous ['mauntɪnəs] adj montañoso(sa).

mountain range n cordillera f, cadena f montañosa.

mountain rescue n rescate m de montaña.

mounted ['mauntɪd] adj montado(da).

Mountie ['mauntɪ] n inf miembro de la policía montada del Canadá.

mourn [mɔːn] ⋄ vt [person] llorar por; [thing] lamentarse de. ⋄ vi afligirse; to ~ **for sb** llorar la muerte de alguien.

mourner ['mɔːnər] n doliente m y f.

mournful ['mɔːnful] adj [face, voice] afligido(da), lúgubre; [sound] lastimero(ra).

mourning ['mɔːnɪŋ] n luto m; **in ~** de luto.

mouse [maus] (pl **mice**) n ZOOL & COMPUT ratón m.

mouse mat n COMPUT alfombrilla f (del ratón).

mousetrap ['maustræp] n ratonera f.

moussaka [muː'sɑːkə] n moussaka f, plato griego a base de berenjenas y carne picada.

mousse [muːs] n **-1.** [food] mousse m. **-2.** [for hair] espuma f.

moustache Br [mə'stɑːʃ], **mustache** Am ['mʌstæʃ] n bigote m.

mouth [n mauθ, vt mauð] ⋄ n [gen] boca f; [of river] desembocadura f; **to keep one's ~ shut** inf callarse, no abrir la boca. ⋄ vt articular con los labios (sin hablar).

mouthful ['mauθful] n **-1.** [of food] bocado m; [of drink] trago m. **-2.** inf [difficult word] trabalenguas m inv.

mouthorgan ['mauθ,ɔːgən] n armónica f, rondín m Amer.

mouthpiece ['mauθpiːs] n **-1.** [of telephone] micrófono m. **-2.** [of musical instrument] boquilla f. **-3.** [spokesperson] portavoz m y f.

mouth-to-mouth adj: ~ **resuscitation** (respiración f) boca a boca m.

mouthwash ['mauθwɒʃ] n elixir m bucal.

mouth-watering [-,wɔːtərɪŋ] adj muy apetitoso(sa).

movable ['muːvəbl] adj movible.

move [muːv] ⋄ n **-1.** [movement] movimiento m; **a ~ towards** un paso hacia; **a ~ away from** un alejamiento de; **on the ~** [travelling around] viajando; [beginning to move] en marcha; **to get a ~ on** inf espabilarse, darse prisa. **-2.** [change - of house] mudanza f; [- of job] cambio m. **-3.** [in board game] jugada f; **it's your ~** mueves tú. **-4.** [course of action] medida f.

⋄ vt **-1.** [shift] mover. **-2.** [change - house] mudarse de; [- job] cambiar de. **-3.** [affect] conmover. **-4.** [in debate - motion] proponer. **-5.** [cause]: **to ~ sb to do sthg** mover OR llevar a alguien a hacer algo.

⋄ vi **-1.** [gen] moverse; [events] cambiar. **-2.** [change house] mudarse.

◆ **move about** vi **-1.** [fidget] ir de aquí para allá. **-2.** [travel] viajar.

◆ **move along** vt sep hacer circular. ⋄ vi **-1.** [move towards front or back] hacerse a un lado, correrse. **-2.** [move away – crowd, car] circular.

◆ **move around** = move about.

◆ **move away** vi [leave] marcharse.

◆ **move in** ⋄ vt sep [troops] mandar. ⋄ vi **-1.** [to new house] instalarse. **-2.** [take control, attack] prepararse para el ataque.

◆ **move off** vi salir, ponerse en marcha.

◆ **move on** ⋄ vt sep hacer circular. ⋄ vi **-1.** [go away] reanudar la marcha. **-2.** [progress] avanzar, cambiar; **to ~ on (to a different subject)** pasar a otro tema.

◆ **move out** ⋄ vt sep [troops] retirar. ⋄ vi mudarse.

◆ **move over** vi hacer sitio, correrse.

◆ **move up** vi [on bench etc] hacer sitio, correrse.

moveable = movable.

movement ['muːvmənt] n **-1.** [gen] movimiento m. **-2.** [transportation] transporte m.

movie ['muːvɪ] n película f.

movie camera n cámara f cinematográfica.

moviegoer ['muːvɪ,gəuər] n Am persona f que va mucho al cine.

movie star n Am estrella f de cine.

movie theater n Am cine m.

moving ['muːvɪŋ] adj **-1.** [touching] conmovedor(ra). **-2.** [not fixed] móvil.

moving staircase n escalera f mecánica.

mow [məu] (pt **-ed**, pp **-ed** OR **mown**) vt [grass, lawn] cortar; [corn] segar.

◆ **mow down** vt sep acribillar.

mower ['məʊəʳ] n cortacésped m o f.

mown [məʊn] pp → mow.

Mozambican [,məʊzəm'biːkən] ◇ adj mozambiqueño(ña). ◇ n mozambiqueño m, -ña f.

Mozambique [,məʊzəm'biːk] n Mozambique.

MP n -1. (abbr of **Military Police**) PM f. -2. Br abbr of **Member of Parliament**. -3. (abbr of **Mounted Police**) la policía montada del Canadá.

mpg (abbr of **miles per gallon**) millas/galón; it does 35 ~ consume 35 millas/galón.

mph (abbr of **miles per hour**) mph.

MPhil [,em'fɪl] (abbr of **Master of Philosophy**) n (titular de un) título universitario de unos dos años de duración en el campo de la medicina.

MPS (abbr of **Member of the Pharmaceutical Society**) n miembro de la Pharmaceutical Society, sociedad británica de farmacéuticos.

Mr ['mɪstəʳ] n Sr.; ~ **Jones** el Sr. Jones.

MRC (abbr of **Medical Research Council**) n principal organismo gubernamental para la investigación en el campo de las humanidades.

MRCP (abbr of **Member of the Royal College of Physicians**) n miembro del Royal College of Physicians, colegio británico de médicos.

MRCS (abbr of **Member of the Royal College of Surgeons**) n miembro del Royal College of Surgeons, colegio británico de cirujanos.

MRCVS (abbr of **Member of the Royal College of Veterinary Surgeons**) n miembro del Royal College of Veterinary Surgeons, colegio británico de veterinarios.

Mrs ['mɪsɪz] n Sra.; ~ **Jones** la Sra. Jones.

ms. (abbr of **manuscript**) n ms.

Ms [mɪz] n abreviatura utilizada delante de un apellido de mujer cuando no se quiere especificar si está casada o no.

MS ◇ n -1. (abbr of **manuscript**) Ms. -2. (abbr of **Master of Science**) (titular de un) título postuniversitario de unos dos años de duración en el campo de las ciencias. ◇ abbr of **Mississippi**.

MS, ms n abbr of **multiple sclerosis**.

MSA (abbr of **Master of Science in Agriculture**) n (titular de un) título postuniversitario de agricultura de unos dos años de duración.

MSc (abbr of **Master of Science**) n (titular de un) título postuniversitario de unos dos años de duración en el campo de las ciencias.

MSC (abbr of **Manpower Services Commission**) n antiguo organismo gubernamental de empleo en Gran Bretaña.

MSF (abbr of **Manufacturing Science and Finance**) n confederación sindical británica.

MSG n abbr of **monosodium glutamate**.

Msgr (abbr of **Monsignor**) Msr.

MST (abbr of **Mountain Standard Time**) hora oficial de los Estados de las montañas Rocosas.

MSW (abbr of **Master of Social Work**) n (titular de un) título postuniversitario de trabajo social de unos dos años de duración.

Mt (abbr of **mount**) mte.

MT ◇ n (abbr of **machine translation**) traducción automática. ◇ abbr of **Montana**.

much [mʌtʃ] (compar **more**, superl **most**) ◇ adj mucho(cha); **there isn't ~ rice left** no queda mucho arroz; **as ~ time as** ... tanto tiempo como ...; **how ~ money?** ¿cuánto dinero?; **so ~** tanto(ta); **too ~** demasiado(da); **how ~ ...?** ¿cuánto(ta) ...?; **how ~ time?** ¿cuánto tiempo?
◇ pron: **have you got ~?** ¿tienes mucho?; **I don't see ~ of him** no lo veo mucho; **I don't think ~ of it** no me parece gran cosa; **as ~ as** tanto como; **too ~** demasiado; **how ~?** ¿cuánto?; **this isn't ~ of a party** esta fiesta no es nada del otro mundo; **so ~ for** tanto con; **I thought as ~** ya me lo imaginaba; **it's not up to ~** inf no es precisamente una maravilla.
◇ adv mucho; **I don't go out ~** no salgo mucho; **~ too cold** demasiado frío; **so ~** tanto; **thank you very ~** muchas gracias; **as ~ as** tanto como; **he is not so ~ stupid as** lazy más que tonto es vago; **too ~** demasiado; **without so ~ as** ... sin siquiera ...
◆ **much as** conj: ~ **as (I like him)** por mucho OR más que (me guste).

muchness ['mʌtʃnɪs] n: **to be much of a ~** venir a ser lo mismo.

muck [mʌk] n inf (U) -1. [dirt] mugre f, porquería f. -2. [manure] estiércol m.
◆ **muck about, muck around** Br inf ◇ vt sep hacer perder el tiempo. ◇ vi hacer el indio OR tonto.
◆ **muck in** vi Br inf arrimar el hombro.
◆ **muck out** vt sep limpiar.
◆ **muck up** vt sep inf Br fastidiar.

muckraking ['mʌkreɪkɪŋ] fig n sensacionalismo m, periodismo m del cotilleo.

mucky ['mʌkɪ] (compar **-ier**, superl **-iest**) adj guarro(rra).

mucus ['mjuːkəs] n mucosidad f.

mud [mʌd] n barro m, lodo m.

muddle ['mʌdl] ◇ n -1. [disorder] desorden m; **to be in a ~** estar en desorden. -2. [confusion] lío m, confusión f; **to be in a ~** estar hecho un lío. ◇ vt -1. [put into disorder] desordenar. -2. [confuse] liar, confundir.
◆ **muddle along** vi apañárselas más o menos.

◆ **muddle through** *vi* arreglárselas.

◆ **muddle up** *vt sep* [put into disorder] desordenar; [confuse] liar, confundir.

muddle-headed [-,hedɪd] *adj* [plan] confuso(sa); [person] incapaz de pensar con claridad.

muddy ['mʌdɪ] (*compar* **-ier**, *superl* **-iest**, *pt* & *pp* **-ied**) ◇ *adj* **-1.** [gen] embarrado(da), lleno(na) de barro; [river] cenagoso(sa). **-2.** [in colour] marrón. ◇ *vt fig* embrollar.

mudflap ['mʌdflæp] *n* alfombra *f* salpicadero.

mudflat ['mʌdflæt] *n* marisma *f*.

mudguard ['mʌdgɑːd] *n* guardabarros *m inv*, tapabarro *m Amer*.

mudpack ['mʌdpæk] *n* mascarilla *f* facial (de barro).

mudslinging ['mʌd,slɪŋɪŋ] *n* (*U*) *fig* insultos *mpl*, improperios *mpl*.

muesli ['mjuːzlɪ] *n Br* muesli *m*.

muff [mʌf] ◇ *n* manguito *m*. ◇ *vt inf* [catch] fallar; [chance] dejar escapar.

muffin ['mʌfɪn] *n* **-1.** *Br* [bread roll] panecillo *m*. **-2.** *Am* [cake] *especie de magdalena que se come caliente*.

muffle ['mʌfl] *vt* [sound] amortiguar.

muffled ['mʌfld] *adj* **-1.** [sound] apagado(da). **-2.** [wrapped up warmly]: ~ **(up)** abrigado(da), tapado(da).

muffler ['mʌflə'] *n Am* [for car] silenciador *m*.

mug [mʌg] (*pt* & *pp* **-ged**, *cont* **-ging**) ◇ *n* **-1.** [cup] taza *f* (alta). **-2.** *inf* [fool] primo *m*, -ma *f*. ◇ *vt* asaltar, atracar.

mugger ['mʌgə'] *n* atracador *m*, -ra *f*.

mugging ['mʌgɪŋ] *n* [single attack] atraco *m*; [series of attacks] atracos *mpl*.

muggy ['mʌgɪ] (*compar* **-ier**, *superl* **-iest**) *adj* bochornoso(sa).

mugshot ['mʌgʃɒt] *n inf* foto *f* (hecha por la policía).

mujaheddin [,muːdʒəhe'diːn] *npl* muyahedin *mpl*, muyahidin *mpl*.

mulatto [mjuː'lætəʊ] (*pl* **-s** OR **-es**) *n* mulato *m*, -ta *f*.

mulberry ['mʌlbərɪ] (*pl* **-ies**) *n* **-1.** [tree] morera *f*, moral *m*. **-2.** [fruit] mora *f*.

mule [mjuːl] *n* mula *f*.

mull [mʌl]

◆ **mull over** *vt sep* reflexionar sobre.

mullah ['mʌlə] *n* mulá *m*.

mulled [mʌld] *adj*: ~ **wine** vino caliente con azúcar y especias.

mullet ['mʌlɪt] (*pl inv* OR **-s**) *n*: **grey** ~ mújol *m*; **red** ~ salmonete *m*.

mulligatawny [,mʌlɪgə'tɔːnɪ] *n* sopa con especias.

mullioned ['mʌlɪənd] *adj* dividido(da) con parteluces.

multi- ['mʌltɪ] *prefix* multi-.

multicoloured *Br*, **multicolored** *Am* [,mʌltɪ'kʌləd] *adj* multicolor.

multicultural [,mʌltɪ'kʌltʃərəl] *adj* multicultural.

multifarious [,mʌltɪ'feərɪəs] *adj* múltiple.

multigym ['mʌltɪdʒɪm] *n* multiestación *f* (de musculación).

multilateral [,mʌltɪ'lætərəl] *adj* multilateral.

multimedia [,mʌltɪ'miːdjə] *adj* COMPUT multimedia (*inv*), de multidifusión.

multimillionaire ['mʌltɪ,mɪljə'neə'] *n* multimillonario *m*, -ria *f*.

multinational [,mʌltɪ'næʃənl] ◇ *adj* multinacional. ◇ *n* multinacional *f*.

multiple ['mʌltɪpl] ◇ *adj* múltiple. ◇ *n* múltiplo *m*.

multiple-choice *adj* tipo test (*inv*).

multiple crash *n* colisión *f* múltiple OR en cadena.

multiple injuries *npl* heridas *fpl* múltiples.

multiple sclerosis [-sklɪ'rəʊsɪs] *n* esclerosis *f inv* múltiple.

multiplex cinema ['mʌltɪpleks-] (cine *m*) multisalas *m inv*.

multiplication [,mʌltɪplɪ'keɪʃn] *n* multiplicación *f*.

multiplication sign *n* signo *m* de multiplicación.

multiplication table *n* tabla *f* de multiplicar.

multiplicity [,mʌltɪ'plɪsətɪ] *n* multiplicidad *f*.

multiply ['mʌltɪplaɪ] (*pt* & *pp* **-ied**) ◇ *vt* multiplicar. ◇ *vi* **-1.** MATH multiplicar. **-2.** [increase, breed] multiplicarse.

multipurpose [,mʌltɪ'pɜːpəs] *adj* multiuso (*inv*).

multiracial [,mʌltɪ'reɪʃl] *adj* multirracial.

multistorey *Br*, **multistory** *Am* [,mʌltɪ'stɔːrɪ] ◇ *adj* de varias plantas. ◇ *n* aparcamiento *m* de varias plantas.

multitude ['mʌltɪtjuːd] *n* multitud *f*.

mum [mʌm] *Br inf* ◇ *n* mamá *f*. ◇ *adj*: **to keep** ~ no decir ni pío, mantener la boca cerrada.

mumble ['mʌmbl] ◇ *vt* mascullar, decir entre dientes. ◇ *vi* musitar, hablar entre dientes.

mumbo jumbo ['mʌmbəʊ'dʒʌmbəʊ] *n pej* galimatías *m inv*.

mummify ['mʌmɪfaɪ] (*pt* & *pp* **-ied**) *vt* momificar.

mummy ['mʌmɪ] (*pl* **-ies**) *n* **-1.** *Br inf* [mother] mamá *f*, mami *f*. **-2.** [preserved body] momia *f*.

mumps [mʌmps] *n* (*U*) paperas *fpl*.

munch [mʌntʃ] *vt & vi* masticar.

mundane [mʌn'deɪn] *adj* trivial.

mung bean [mʌŋ-] *n* tipo de legumbre procedente de Asia.

municipal [mju:'nɪsɪpl] *adj* municipal.

municipality [mju:,nɪsɪ'pælətɪ] (*pl* **-ies**) *n* municipio *m*.

munificent [mju:'nɪfɪsənt] *adj fml* munífico(ca), dadivoso(sa).

munitions [mju:'nɪʃnz] *npl* municiones *fpl*.

mural ['mjuːərəl] *n* mural *m*.

murder ['mɜːdər] ◇ *n* asesinato *m*; **to get away with ~** hacer lo que a uno le viene en gana. ◇ *vt* asesinar.

murderer ['mɜːdərər] *n* asesino *m*.

murderess ['mɜːdərɪs] *n* asesina *f*.

murderous ['mɜːdərəs] *adj* asesino(na), homicida.

murky ['mɜːkɪ] (*compar* **-ier**, *superl* **-iest**) *adj* **-1.** [water, past] turbio(bia). **-2.** [night, street] sombrío(a), lúgubre.

murmur ['mɜːmər] ◇ *n* **-1.** [low sound] murmullo *m*. **-2.** MED [of heart] soplo *m*. ◇ *vt & vi* murmurar.

MusB [,mju:z'bi:], **MusBac** [,mju:z'bæk] *abbr of* **Bachelor of Music**.

muscle ['mʌsl] *n* **-1.** MED músculo *m*. **-2.** *fig* [power] poder *m*.
◆ **muscle in** *vi* entrometerse.

muscleman ['mʌslmən] (*pl* **-men** [-mən]) *n* forzudo *m*.

Muscovite ['mʌskəvaɪt] ◇ *adj* moscovita. ◇ *n* moscovita *m y f*.

muscular ['mʌskjʊlər] *adj* **-1.** [of muscles] muscular. **-2.** [strong] musculoso(sa).

muscular dystrophy [-'dɪstrəfɪ] *n* distrofia *f* muscular.

MusD [,mju:z'di:], **MusDoc** [,mju:z'dɒk] *abbr of* **Doctor of Music**.

muse [mju:z] ◇ *n* musa *f*. ◇ *vi* meditar, reflexionar.

museum [mju:'zi:əm] *n* museo *m*.

mush [mʌʃ] *n inf* **-1.** [gunge] pasta *f*, masa *f* blandengue. **-2.** [drivel] sensiblería *f*.

mushroom ['mʌʃrʊm] ◇ *n* [button] champiñón *m*; [field] seta *f*; BOT hongo *m*, callampa *f Amer*. ◇ *vi* extenderse rápidamente.

mushroom cloud *n* hongo *m* nuclear.

mushy ['mʌʃɪ] (*compar* **-ier**, *superl* **-iest**) *adj* **-1.** [very soft] blandengue. **-2.** [oversentimental] sensiblero(ra).

music ['mju:zɪk] *n* música *f*.

musical ['mju:zɪkl] ◇ *adj* **-1.** [gen] musical. **-2.** [talented in music] con talento para la música. ◇ *n* musical *m*.

musical box *Br*, **music box** *Am n* caja *f* de música.

musical chairs *n* (*U*) juego *m* de las sillas.

musical instrument *n* instrumento *m* musical.

music box *Am* = **musical box**.

music centre *n* cadena *f* (musical), equipo *m* (de música).

music hall *n Br* teatro *m* de variedades OR de revista.

musician [mju:'zɪʃn] *n* músico *m*, -ca *f*.

music stand *n* atril *m*.

musk [mʌsk] *n* almizcle *m*.

musket ['mʌskɪt] *n* mosquete *m*.

muskrat ['mʌskræt] *n* rata *f* almizclada.

Muslim ['mʊzlɪm] ◇ *adj* musulmán(ana). ◇ *n* musulmán *m*, -ana *f*.

muslin ['mʌzlɪn] *n* muselina *f*.

musquash ['mʌskwɒʃ] *n* **-1.** [animal] rata *f* almizclada. **-2.** [fur] piel *f* de rata almizclada.

muss [mʌs] *vt Am*: **to ~ sthg (up)** [hair] despeinar; [clothes] arrugar.

mussel ['mʌsl] *n* mejillón *m*, choro *m Amer*.

must [mʌst] ◇ *aux vb* **-1.** [have to, intend to] deber, tener que; **I ~ go** tengo que OR debo irme. **-2.** [as suggestion] tener que; **you ~ come and see us** tienes que venir a vernos. **-3.** [to express likelihood] deber (de); **it ~ be true** debe (de) ser verdad; **they ~ have known** deben de haberlo sabido. ◇ *n inf*: **a ~** algo imprescindible; **the film is a ~** no puedes perderte esta película.

mustache *Am* = **moustache**.

mustard ['mʌstəd] *n* mostaza *f*; **~ and cress** *Br* brotes *mpl* de mostaza y berro.

mustard gas *n* gas *m* mostaza.

muster ['mʌstər] ◇ *vt* reunir; **to ~ the courage to do sthg** armarse de valor para hacer algo. ◇ *vi* [subj: soldiers] formar; [subj: volunteers] reunirse.
◆ **muster up** *vt fus* [strength, support] reunir; [courage] armarse de.

mustn't ['mʌsnt] = **must not**.

must've ['mʌstəv] = **must have**.

musty ['mʌstɪ] (*compar* **-ier**, *superl* **-iest**) *adj* [room] que huele a cerrado; [book] que huele a viejo.

mutant ['mju:tənt] ◇ *adj* mutante. ◇ *n* mutante *m y f*.

mutate [mju:'teɪt] *vi*: **to ~ (into)** mutarse (en).

mutation [mju:'teɪʃn] *n* mutación *f*.

mute [mjuːt] ◇ adj mudo(da). ◇ n mudo m, -da f. ◇ vt amortiguar.

muted ['mjuːtɪd] adj **-1.** [not bright] apagado(da). **-2.** [subdued] contenido(da).

mutilate ['mjuːtɪleɪt] vt mutilar.

mutilation [ˌmjuːtɪ'leɪʃn] n mutilación f.

mutineer [ˌmjuːtɪ'nɪəʳ] n amotinado m, -da f.

mutinous ['mjuːtɪnəs] adj rebelde.

mutiny ['mjuːtɪnɪ] (pl **-ies**, pt & pp **-ied**) ◇ n motín m. ◇ vi amotinarse.

mutt [mʌt] n inf **-1.** [fool] tonto m, -ta f, bobo m, -ba f. **-2.** Am [dog] chucho m.

mutter ['mʌtəʳ] ◇ vt musitar, mascullar. ◇ vi murmurar; **to ~ to sb** gruñirle a alguien; **to ~ to o.s.** refunfuñar.

muttering ['mʌtərɪŋ] n murmullo m.

mutton ['mʌtn] n (carne f de) carnero m; **~ dressed as lamb** Br lobo m con piel de cordero, mujer madura vestida de jovencita.

mutual ['mjuːtʃʊəl] adj **-1.** [reciprocal] mutuo(tua). **-2.** [common] común.

mutual fund n Am sociedad f de inversión colectiva.

mutually ['mjuːtʃʊəlɪ] adv mutuamente; **~ exclusive** que se anulan entre sí.

Muzak® ['mjuːzæk] n ≃ hilo m musical®.

muzzle ['mʌzl] ◇ n **-1.** [animal's nose and jaws] hocico m, morro m. **-2.** [wire guard] bozal m. **-3.** [of gun] boca f. ◇ vt **-1.** [put muzzle on] poner bozal a. **-2.** fig [silence] amordazar, silenciar.

muzzy ['mʌzɪ] (compar **-ier**, superl **-iest**) adj [head] embotado(da); [memory] borroso(sa).

MVP (abbr of **most valuable player**) jugador más valioso.

MW (abbr of **medium wave**) OM f.

my [maɪ] poss adj **-1.** [gen] mi, mis (pl); **~ house/sister** mi casa/hermana; **~ children** mis hijos; **~ name is Sarah** me llamo Sarah; **it wasn't** MY **fault** no fue culpa mía OR mi culpa; **I washed ~ hair** me lavé el pelo. **-2.** [in titles]: **~ Lord** milord; **~ Lady** milady.

mynah (bird) ['maɪnə-] n minae m.

myopic [maɪ'ɒpɪk] adj miope.

myriad ['mɪrɪəd] literary ◇ adj innumerables. ◇ n miríada f.

myrrh [mɜːʳ] n mirra f.

myrtle ['mɜːtl] n mirto m, arrayán m.

myself [maɪ'self] pron **-1.** (reflexive) me; (after prep) mí mismo(ma); **with ~** conmigo mismo. **-2.** (for emphasis) yo mismo(ma); **I did it ~** lo hice yo solo(la).

mysterious [mɪ'stɪərɪəs] adj misterioso(sa);

to be ~ about sthg andarse con misterios sobre algo.

mysteriously [mɪ'stɪərɪəslɪ] adv misteriosamente.

mystery ['mɪstərɪ] (pl **-ies**) ◇ adj misterioso(sa). ◇ n misterio m.

mystery story n historia f policiaca, novela f de intriga.

mystery tour n viaje m sorpresa.

mystic ['mɪstɪk] ◇ adj místico(ca). ◇ n místico m, -ca f.

mystical ['mɪstɪkl] adj místico(ca).

mysticism ['mɪstɪsɪzm] n misticismo m.

mystified ['mɪstɪfaɪd] adj desconcertado(da), perplejo(ja).

mystifying ['mɪstɪfaɪɪŋ] adj desconcertante.

mystique [mɪ'stiːk] n misterio m.

myth [mɪθ] n mito m.

mythic ['mɪθɪk] adj [like a myth] mítico(ca).

mythical ['mɪθɪkl] adj **-1.** [imaginary] mítico(ca). **-2.** [untrue] falso(sa).

mythological [ˌmɪθə'lɒdʒɪkl] adj mitológico(ca).

mythology [mɪ'θɒlədʒɪ] (pl **-ies**) n **-1.** [collection of myths] mitología f. **-2.** [set of false beliefs] mito m.

myxomatosis [ˌmɪksəmə'təʊsɪs] n mixomatosis f inv.

n (pl **n's** OR **ns**), **N** (pl **N's** OR **Ns**) [en] n [letter] n f, N f.
◆ **N** (abbr of **north**) N.

n/a, **N/A** (abbr of **not applicable**) no interesa.

NA (abbr of **Narcotics Anonymous**) n organización estadounidense de ayuda a los toxicómanos.

NAACP (abbr of **National Association for the Advancement of Colored People**) n organización estadounidense de ayuda a la gente de color.

NAAFI ['næfɪ] (abbr of **Navy, Army & Air Force Institute**) n organización gubernamental encargada del aprovisionamiento de las fuerzas armadas británicas.

nab [næb] (pt & pp **-bed**, cont **-bing**) vt inf

-1. [arrest] pillar, echar el guante a. **-2.** [get quickly] coger.

NACU (*abbr of* **National Association of Colleges and Universities**) *n* asociación estadounidense de centros de enseñanza superior.

nadir ['neɪ,dɪə'] *n* **-1.** ASTRON nadir *m*. **-2.** *fig* [low point] punto *m* más bajo.

naff [næf] *adj Br inf* [behaviour] tonto(ta); [film, story] hortera.

nag [næg] (*pt & pp* **-ged**, *cont* **-ging**) ◇ *vt* dar la lata a. ◇ *vi* **-1.** [person]: **to ~ (at sb)** dar la lata OR fastidiar (a alguien). **-2.** [thought, doubt]: **to ~ at sb** consumir OR corroer a alguien. ◇ *n inf* **-1.** [person] quejica *m y f*. **-2.** [horse] jamelgo *m*, rocín *m*.

nagging ['nægɪŋ] *adj* **-1.** [thought, doubt] incesante, persistente. **-2.** [person] gruñón(ona).

nail [neɪl] ◇ *n* **-1.** [for fastening] clavo *m*; **to hit the ~ on the head** dar en el clavo. **-2.** [of finger, toe] uña *f*. ◇ *vt*: **to ~ sthg to sthg** clavar algo en OR a algo.

◆ **nail down** *vt sep* **-1.** [fasten] clavar. **-2.** [person]: **I couldn't ~ him down** no pude hacerle concretar.

◆ **nail up** *vt sep* clavar.

nail-biting *adj* emocionantísimo(ma), lleno(na) de suspense.

nailbrush ['neɪlbrʌʃ] *n* cepillo *m* de uñas.

nail file *n* lima *f* de uñas.

nail polish *n* esmalte *m* para las uñas.

nail scissors *npl* tijeras *fpl* para las uñas.

nail varnish *n* esmalte *m* para las uñas.

nail varnish remover *n* quitaesmaltes *m inv*.

Nairobi [naɪ'rəʊbɪ] *n* Nairobi.

naive, **naïve** ['naɪiːv] *adj* ingenuo(nua).

naivety, **naïvety** [naɪ'iːvtɪ] *n* ingenuidad *f*.

naked ['neɪkɪd] *adj* **-1.** [gen] desnudo(da), calato(ta) *Amer*; **~ flame** llama *f* sin protección. **-2.** [blatant - hostility, greed] abierto(ta); [- facts] sin tapujos. **-3.** [unaided]: **with the ~ eye** a simple vista.

NALGO ['nælgəʊ] (*abbr of* **National and Local Government Officers' Association**) *n* antiguo sindicato de funcionarios británicos.

Nam [næm] (*abbr of* **Vietnam**) *n Am* Vietnam *m*.

NAM (*abbr of* **National Association of Manufacturers**) *n* organización de empresarios estadounidenses.

name [neɪm] ◇ *n* [gen] nombre *m*; [surname] apellido *m*; **what's your ~?** ¿cómo te llamas?; **my ~ is John** me llamo John; **by ~** por el nombre; **is there anyone by the ~ of ...** ¿hay alguien que se llame ...?; **in sb's ~** a nombre de alguien; **in the ~ of** en nombre de; **in ~ only** sólo de nombre; **to call sb ~s** llamar de todo a alguien; **to make a ~ for o.s.** hacerse un nombre. ◇ *vt* **-1.** [christen] poner nombre a; **to ~ sb after sb** *Br*, **to ~ sb for sb** *Am* poner a alguien el nombre de alguien. **-2.** [identify] nombrar. **-3.** [date, price] poner, decir. **-4.** [appoint] nombrar.

namedropping ['neɪmdrɒpɪŋ] *n*: **he loves ~** le encanta alardear mencionando nombres de gente que conoce o a la que ha leído.

nameless ['neɪmlɪs] *adj* **-1.** [unknown - person, author] anónimo(ma); [- disease] desconocido(da). **-2.** [indescribable] indescriptible.

namely ['neɪmlɪ] *adv* a saber.

nameplate ['neɪmpleɪt] *n* placa *f* con el nombre.

namesake ['neɪmseɪk] *n* tocayo *m*, -ya *f*.

Namibia [nɑː'mɪbɪə] *n* Namibia.

Namibian [nɑː'mɪbɪən] ◇ *adj* namibio(bia). ◇ *n* namibio *m*, -bia *f*.

nan(a) [næn(ə)] *n inf Br* yaya *f*, abuelita *f*.

nan bread [næn-] *n* (*U*) pan indio sin levadura.

nanny ['nænɪ] (*pl* **-ies**) *n* niñera *f*.

nanny goat *n* cabra *f*.

nap [næp] (*pt & pp* **-ped**, *cont* **-ping**) ◇ *n* siesta *f*; **to take** OR **have a ~** echarse la siesta. ◇ *vi* dormir la siesta; **we were caught napping** *inf* nos pilló desprevenidos.

NAPA (*abbr of* **National Association of Performing Artists**) *n* sindicato estadounidense de gente del mundo del espectáculo.

napalm ['neɪpɑːm] *n* napalm *m*.

nape [neɪp] *n*: **~ of the neck** nuca *f*.

napkin ['næpkɪn] *n* servilleta *f*.

nappy ['næpɪ] (*pl* **-ies**) *n Br* pañal *m*.

nappy liner *n* parte desechable de un pañal de gasa.

narcissi [nɑː'sɪsaɪ] *pl* → **narcissus**.

narcissism ['nɑːsɪsɪzm] *n* narcisismo *m*.

narcissistic [,nɑːsɪ'sɪstɪk] *adj* narcisista.

narcissus [nɑː'sɪsəs] (*pl* **-cissuses** OR **-cissi**) *n* narciso *m*.

narcotic [nɑː'kɒtɪk] *n* narcótico *m*.

nark [nɑːk] *Br inf* ◇ *n* [police informer] soplón *m*, -ona *f*. ◇ *vt* cabrear.

narky ['nɑːkɪ] (*compar* **-ier**, *superl* **-iest**) *adj Br inf* de mala uva.

narrate [*Br* nə'reɪt, *Am* 'næreɪt] *vt* narrar.

narration [*Br* nə'reɪʃn, *Am* næ'reɪʃn] *n* narración *f*.

narrative ['nærətɪv] ◇ *adj* narrativo(va). ◇ *n* **-1.** [account] narración *f*. **-2.** [art of narrating] narrativa *f*.

narrator [Br nə'reɪtə', Am 'næreɪtər] n narrador m, -ra f.

narrow ['nærəʊ] ◇ adj **-1.** [not wide] estrecho(cha). **-2.** [limited] estrecho(cha) de miras. **-3.** [victory, defeat] por un estrecho margen; [escape, miss] por muy poco, por los pelos. ◇ vt **-1.** [eyes] entornar. **-2.** [gap, choice] reducir. ◇ vi **-1.** [become less wide] estrecharse. **-2.** [eyes] entornarse. **-3.** [gap] acortarse, reducirse.

◆ **narrow down** vt sep reducir.

narrow-gauge adj RAIL de vía estrecha.

narrowly ['nærəʊlɪ] adv [barely] por muy poco.

narrow-minded [-'maɪndɪd] adj estrecho(cha) de miras.

NAS (abbr of **National Academy of Sciences**) n organismo estadounidense que fomenta la investigación científica.

NASA ['næsə] (abbr of **National Aeronautics and Space Administration**) n NASA f.

nasal ['neɪzl] adj nasal.

nascent ['neɪsənt] adj fml naciente.

nastily ['nɑːstɪlɪ] adv **-1.** [unkindly] con mala intención. **-2.** [painfully]: **he fell** ~ tuvo una caída muy mala.

nastiness ['nɑːstɪnɪs] n **-1.** [unkindness] mala intención f. **-2.** [painfulness]: **the** ~ (of) lo doloroso (de).

nasturtium [nəs'tɜːʃəm] (pl **-s**) n capuchina f.

nasty ['nɑːstɪ] (compar **-ier**, superl **-iest**) adj **-1.** [unkind] malintencionado(da). **-2.** [smell, taste, feeling] desagradable; [weather] horrible; **cheap and** ~ barato(ta) y de mal gusto. **-3.** [problem, decision] peliagudo(da), que se las trae. **-4.** [injury, disease] doloroso(sa); [fall] malo(la).

NAS/UWT (abbr of **National Association of Schoolmasters/Union of Women Teachers**) n sindicato británico de profesores.

Natal [nə'tæl] n Natal.

nation ['neɪʃn] n nación f.

national ['næʃənl] ◇ adj nacional. ◇ n súbdito m, -ta f.

national anthem n himno m nacional.

national debt n deuda f pública.

national dress n traje m típico (de un país).

National Front n: **the** ~ partido político minoritario de extrema derecha en Gran Bretaña.

national grid n Br red nacional de tendido eléctrico.

National Guard n Am: **the** ~ la Guardia Nacional estadounidense.

National Health Service n Br: **the** ~ organismo gestor de la salud pública, ≈ el Insalud.

National Heritage Minister n ministro de cultura y deportes británico.

National Insurance n Br ≈ Seguridad f Social.

nationalism ['næʃnəlɪzm] n nacionalismo m.

nationalist ['næʃnəlɪst] ◇ adj nacionalista. ◇ n nacionalista m y f.

nationality [,næʃə'nælətɪ] (pl **-ies**) n nacionalidad f.

nationalization [,næʃnəlaɪ'zeɪʃn] n nacionalización f.

nationalize, -ise ['næʃnəlaɪz] vt nacionalizar.

nationalized ['næʃnəlaɪzd] adj nacionalizado(da).

national park n parque m nacional.

national service n Br MIL servicio m militar.

National Trust n Br the ~ organización británica encargada de la preservación de edificios históricos y lugares de interés, ≈ el Patrimonio Nacional.

nation state n estado m nación.

nationwide ['neɪʃənwaɪd] ◇ adj a escala nacional, por todo el país. ◇ adv [travel] por todo el país; [be broadcast] a todo el país.

native ['neɪtɪv] ◇ adj **-1.** [country, area] natal. **-2.** [speaker] nativo(va); ~ **language** lengua f materna. **-3.** [plant, animal]: ~ **(to)** originario(ria) (de). ◇ n natural m y f, nativo m, -va f.

Native American n indio americano m, india americana f.

Nativity [nə'tɪvətɪ] n: **the** ~ la Natividad.

nativity play n obra teatral sobre la Natividad.

NATO ['neɪtəʊ] (abbr of **North Atlantic Treaty Organization**) n OTAN f.

natter Br ['nætə'] inf ◇ n: **to have a** ~ charlar. ◇ vi charlar.

natty ['nætɪ] (compar **-ier**, superl **-iest**) adj inf [smart] chulo(la), elegante.

natural ['nætʃrəl] ◇ adj **-1.** [gen] natural. **-2.** [comedian, musician] nato(ta); **to die of** ~ **causes** morir por causas naturales. ◇ n: **to be a** ~ tener talento natural.

natural childbirth n parto m natural.

natural gas n gas m natural.

natural history n historia f natural.

naturalist ['nætʃrəlɪst] n naturalista m y f.

naturalize, -ise ['nætʃrəlaɪz] vt naturalizar; **to be** ~**d** naturalizarse.

naturally ['nætʃrəlɪ] adv **-1.** [as expected, understandably] naturalmente. **-2.** [unaffectedly] con naturalidad. **-3.** [instinctively] por naturaleza; **to come ~ to sb** ser innato en alguien. **-4.** [in nature] de forma natural, en la naturaleza.

naturalness ['nætʃrəlnɪs] *n* naturalidad *f*.

natural resources *npl* recursos *mpl* naturales.

natural science *n* ciencias *fpl* naturales.

natural wastage *n* (U) reducción de plantilla por jubilación escalonada.

nature ['neɪtʃəʳ] *n* **-1.** [gen] naturaleza *f*. **-2.** [disposition] modo *m* de ser, carácter *m*; **by ~** por naturaleza.

nature reserve *n* reserva *f* natural.

nature trail *n* senda especialmente señalizada para la observación del entorno natural.

naturist ['neɪtʃərɪst] *n* naturista *m y f*.

naughty ['nɔːtɪ] (*compar* **-ier**, *superl* **-iest**) *adj* **-1.** [badly behaved] travieso(sa), malo(la). **-2.** [rude] verde, atrevido(da).

nausea ['nɔːsjə] *n* náusea *f*.

nauseam ['nɔːzɪæm] → **ad nauseam**.

nauseate ['nɔːsɪeɪt] *vt lit* & *fig* dar náuseas a.

nauseating ['nɔːsɪeɪtɪŋ] *adj lit* & *fig* nauseabundo(da).

nauseous ['nɔːsjəs] *adj* **-1.** [sick]: **to feel ~** sentir náuseas. **-2.** *fig* [revolting] nauseabundo(da).

nautical ['nɔːtɪkl] *adj* náutico(ca), marítimo(ma).

nautical mile *n* milla *f* marina.

naval ['neɪvl] *adj* naval.

naval officer *n* oficial *m y f* de marina.

nave [neɪv] *n* nave *f*.

navel ['neɪvl] *n* ombligo *m*.

navigable ['nævɪgəbl] *adj* navegable.

navigate ['nævɪgeɪt] ◇ *vt* **-1.** [steer] pilotar, gobernar. **-2.** [travel safely across] surcar, navegar por. ◇ *vi* [in plane, ship] dirigir, gobernar; [in car] guiar, dirigir.

navigation [ˌnævɪ'geɪʃn] *n* gobierno *m*.

navigator ['nævɪgeɪtəʳ] *n* oficial *m y f* de navegación, navegante *m y f*.

navvy ['nævɪ] (*pl* **-ies**) *n Br inf* peón *m* caminero.

navy ['neɪvɪ] (*pl* **-ies**) ◇ *n* armada *f*. ◇ *adj* [in colour] azul marino (*inv*).

navy blue ◇ *adj* azul marino (*inv*). ◇ *n* azul *m* marino.

Nazi ['nɑːtsɪ] (*pl* **-s**) ◇ *adj* nazi. ◇ *n* nazi *m y f*.

NB -1. (*abbr of* **nota bene**) N.B. **-2.** *abbr of* **New Brunswick**.

NBA *n* **-1.** (*abbr of* **National Basketball Association**) NBA *f*. **-2.** (*abbr of* **National Box-** **ing Association**) *federación de boxeo estadounidense*.

NBC (*abbr of* **National Broadcasting Company**) *n* NBC *f, cadena de televisión estadounidense*.

NBS (*abbr of* **National Bureau of Standards**) *n organismo estadounidense de normalización de unidades de medida*.

NC -1. (*abbr of* **no charge**) gratis. **-2.** *abbr of* **North Carolina**.

NCC (*abbr of* **Nature Conservancy Council**) *n instituto británico para la conservación de la naturaleza*, ≃ Icona *m*.

NCCL (*abbr of* **National Council for Civil Liberties**) *n organización independiente británica para la defensa de los derechos del ciudadano*.

NCO *n abbr of* **noncommissioned officer**.

NCU (*abbr of* **National Communications Union**) *n sindicato británico de trabajadores del sector de telecomunicaciones*.

ND *abbr of* **North Dakota**.

NE -1. *abbr of* **Nebraska**. **-2.** *abbr of* **New England**. **-3.** (*abbr of* **north-east**) NE.

Neanderthal [nɪ'ændətɑːl] ◇ *adj* de Neanderthal. ◇ *n* (hombre *m* de) Neanderthal *m*.

neap tide [niːp-] *n* marea *f* muerta.

near [nɪəʳ] ◇ *adj* **-1.** [close in distance, time] cerca; **in the ~ future** en un futuro próximo. **-2.** [related] cercano(na), próximo(ma); **the ~est thing to ...** lo más parecido a .... **-3.** [almost happened]: **it was ~ chaos** fue casi un caos; **it was a ~ thing** poco le faltó. ◇ *adv* **-1.** [close in distance, time] cerca; **nowhere ~** ni de lejos, ni mucho menos; **to draw** OR **come ~** acercarse. **-2.** [almost] casi. ◇ *prep* **-1.** [close in position]: **~ (to)** cerca de. **-2.** [close in time]: **~ (to)** casi; **~ the end** casi al final; **~er the time** cuando se acerque la fecha. **-3.** [on the point of]: **~ (to)** al borde de. **-4.** [similar to]: **~ (to)** cerca de; **it's ~ (to) the truth** se acerca a la verdad. ◇ *vt* acercarse OR aproximarse a. ◇ *vi* acercarse, aproximarse.

nearby [nɪə'baɪ] ◇ *adj* cercano(na). ◇ *adv* cerca.

Near East *n*: **the ~** el Oriente Próximo.

nearly ['nɪəlɪ] *adv* casi; **I ~ fell** por poco me caigo; **not ~** ni con mucho, ni mucho menos.

near miss *n* **-1.** [nearly a hit]: **to be a ~** fallar por poco. **-2.** [nearly a collision] incidente *m* aéreo (sin colisión).

nearness ['nɪənɪs] *n* proximidad *f*, cercanía *f*.

nearside ['nɪəsaɪd] ◇ *adj* [right-hand drive] del lado izquierdo; [left-hand drive] del lado derecho. ◇ *n* [right-hand drive] lado izquierdo; [left-hand drive] lado derecho.

nearsighted [,nɪə'saɪtɪd] *adj Am* miope, corto(ta) de vista.

neat [niːt] *adj* **-1.** [tidy, precise - gen] pulcro(cra); [- room, house] arreglado(da); [- handwriting] esmerado(da). **-2.** [smart] arreglado(da), pulcro(cra). **-3.** [skilful] hábil. **-4.** [undiluted] solo(la). **-5.** *Am inf* [very good] guay, de buten (*inv*).

neatly ['niːtlɪ] *adv* **-1.** [tidily, smartly] con pulcritud. **-2.** [skilfully] hábilmente.

neatness ['niːtnɪs] *n* pulcritud *f*.

Nebraska [nɪ'bræskə] *n* Nebraska.

nebulous ['nebjʊləs] *adj fml* nebuloso(sa).

NEC (*abbr of* **National Exhibition Centre**) *n* gran complejo para ferias y exposiciones de Birmingham, Gran Bretaña.

necessarily ['nesəsrəlɪ] *adv* necesariamente, por fuerza; **not** ~ no necesariamente.

necessary ['nesəsrɪ] *adj* **-1.** [required] necesario(ria). **-2.** [inevitable] inevitable.

necessitate [nɪ'sesɪteɪt] *vt fml* requerir, exigir.

necessity [nɪ'sesətɪ] (*pl* **-ies**) *n* necesidad *f*; **of** ~ por fuerza, por necesidad.

◆ **necessities** *n pl* artículos *mpl* de primera necesidad.

neck [nek] ◇ *n* [of person] cuello *m*; [of animal] pescuezo *m*, cuello; **to be up to one's** ~ **(in sthg)** estar hasta el cuello (de algo); **to breathe down sb's** ~ estar encima de alguien; **to stick one's** ~ **out** jugarse el tipo. ◇ *vi inf* pegarse el lote.

neckerchief ['nekətʃɪf] (*pl* **-chiefs** OR **-chieves** [-tʃiːvz]) *n* pañuelo *m* de cuello.

necklace ['neklɪs] *n* collar *m*.

neckline ['neklaɪn] *n* escote *m*.

necktie ['nektaɪ] *n Am* corbata *f*.

nectar ['nektə^r] *n* néctar *m*.

nectarine ['nektərɪn] *n* nectarina *f*.

NEDC (*abbr of* **National Economic Development Council**) *n* antigua organización gubernamental británica que fomentaba los contactos con sindicatos y organizaciones empresariales.

Neddy ['nedɪ] *n inf nombre con el que se conocía popularmente al NEDC.*

née [neɪ] *adj* de soltera.

need [niːd] ◇ *n*: ~ **(for sthg/to do sthg)** necesidad *f* (de algo/de hacer algo); **to be in** OR **to have** ~ **of sthg** necesitar algo; **he was in** ~ **of rest** le hacía falta descansar; **to have no** ~ of no necesitar; **there's no** ~ **for you to cry** no hace falta que llores; **if** ~ **be** si hace falta; **in** ~ necesitado(da). ◇ *vt* **-1.**

[require] necesitar; **I** ~ **a haircut** me hace falta un corte de pelo. **-2.** [be obliged]: **to** ~ **to do sthg** tener que hacer algo. ◇ *modal vb*: **to** ~ **to do sthg** necesitar hacer algo; ~ **we go?** ¿tenemos que irnos?; **it** ~ **not happen** no tiene por qué ser así.

◆ **needs** *adv*: **if** ~**s must** si es menester.

needle ['niːdl] ◇ *n* aguja *f*; **it's like looking for a** ~ **in a haystack** es como buscar una aguja en un pajar. ◇ *vt inf* pinchar.

needlecord ['niːdlkɔːd] *n* pana *f* fina.

needlepoint ['niːdlpɔɪnt] *n* encaje *m* de aguja.

needless ['niːdlɪs] *adj* innecesario(ria); ~ **to say** ... está de más decir que ....

needlessly ['niːdlɪslɪ] *adv* innecesariamente.

needlework ['niːdlwɜːk] *n* **-1.** [embroidery] bordado *m*. **-2.** (*U*) [activity] costura *f*.

needn't ['niːdnt] = **need not.**

needy ['niːdɪ] (*compar* **-ier**, *superl* **-iest**) ◇ *adj* necesitado(da). ◇ *npl*: **the** ~ los necesitados.

nefarious [nɪ'feərɪəs] *adj fml* execrable, infame.

negate [nɪ'geɪt] *vt fml* anular, invalidar.

negation [nɪ'geɪʃn] *n fml* invalidación *f*, anulación *f*.

negative ['negətɪv] ◇ *adj* negativo(va). ◇ *n* **-1.** PHOT negativo *m*. **-2.** LING partícula *f* negativa, negación *f*; **to answer in the** ~ decir que no.

neglect [nɪ'glekt] ◇ *n* [of garden, work] descuido *m*, desatención *f*; [of duty] incumplimiento *m*; **a state of** ~ un estado de abandono. ◇ *vt* **-1.** [ignore] desatender. **-2.** [duty, work] no cumplir con; **to** ~ **to do sthg** dejar de hacer algo.

neglected [nɪ'glektɪd] *adj* desatendido(da).

neglectful [nɪ'glektfʊl] *adj* descuidado(da), negligente; **to be** ~ **of sthg/sb** desatender algo/a alguien.

negligee ['neglɪʒeɪ] *n* salto *m* de cama.

negligence ['neglɪdʒəns] *n* negligencia *f*.

negligent ['neglɪdʒənt] *adj* negligente.

negligently ['neglɪdʒəntlɪ] *adv* con negligencia.

negligible ['neglɪdʒəbl] *adj* insignificante.

negotiable [nɪ'gəʊʃjəbl] *adj* negociable.

negotiate [nɪ'gəʊʃɪeɪt] ◇ *vt* **-1.** [obtain through negotiation] negociar. **-2.** [obstacle] salvar, franquear; [hill] superar, remontar; [bend] tomar. ◇ *vi*: **to** ~ **(with sb for sthg)** negociar (con alguien algo).

negotiation [nɪ,gəʊʃɪ'eɪʃn] *n* negociación *f*.

◆ **negotiations** *npl* negociaciones *fpl*.

negotiator [nɪ'gəʊʃieɪtə'] *n* negociador *m*, -ra *f*.

Negress ['niːgrɪs] *n* negra *f*.

Negro ['niːgrəʊ] (*pl* **-es**) ◇ *adj* negro(gra). ◇ *n* negro *m*, -gra *f*.

neigh [neɪ] *vi* relinchar.

neighbour *Br*, **neighbor** *Am* ['neɪbə'] *n* vecino *m*, -na *f*.

neighbourhood *Br*, **neighborhood** *Am* ['neɪbəhʊd] *n* **-1.** [of town] barrio *m*, vecindad *f*; **in the ~ (of)** en la zona (de). **-2.** [approximate figure]: **in the ~ of** alrededor de.

neighbourhood watch *n Br* patrulla *f* de vecinos.

neighbouring *Br*, **neighboring** *Am* ['neɪbərɪŋ] *adj* vecino(na).

neighbourly *Br*, **neighborly** *Am* ['neɪbəlɪ] *adj* de buen vecino; **to be ~** ser un buen vecino.

neither ['naɪðə', 'niːðə'] ◇ *adv*: **I don't drink – me ~** no bebo – yo tampoco; **the food was ~ good nor bad** la comida no era ni buena ni mala; **to be ~ here nor there** no tener nada que ver. ◇ *pron* ninguno(na); **~ of us/them** ninguno de nosotros/ellos. ◇ *adj*: **~ cup is blue** ninguna de las dos tazas es azul. ◇ *conj*: **~ ... nor ...** ni ... ni ...; **she could ~ eat nor sleep** no podía ni comer ni dormir.

neo- ['niːəʊ] *prefix* neo-.

neoclassical [,niːəʊ'klæsɪkl] *adj* neoclásico(ca).

neolithic [,niːəʊ'lɪθɪk] *adj* neolítico(ca).

neologism [niː'ɒlədʒɪzm] *n* neologismo *m*.

neon ['niːɒn] *n* neón *m*.

neon light *n* lámpara *f* OR luz *f* de neón.

neon sign *n* letrero *m* de neón.

Nepal [nɪ'pɔːl] *n* (el) Nepal.

Nepalese [,nepə'liːz] (*pl inv*) ◇ *adj* nepalés(esa). ◇ *n* [person] nepalés *m*, -esa *f*.

Nepali [nɪ'pɔːlɪ] *n* [language] nepalés *m*, nepalí *m*.

nephew ['nefjuː] *n* sobrino *m*.

nepotism ['nepətɪzm] *n* nepotismo *m*.

Neptune ['neptjuːn] *n* Neptuno *m*.

nerve [nɜːv] *n* **-1.** ANAT nervio *m*. **-2.** [courage] valor *m*; **to lose one's ~** echarse atrás, perder el valor. **-3.** [cheek] cara *f*; **to have the ~ to do sthg** tener la cara de hacer algo. ◆ **nerves** *npl* nervios *mpl*; **to get on sb's ~s** sacar de quicio OR poner los nervios de punta a alguien.

nerve centre *n* **-1.** ANAT centro *m* nervioso. **-2.** *fig* [headquarters] punto *m* OR centro *m* neurálgico.

nerve gas *n* gas *m* nervioso.

nerve-racking [-,rækɪŋ] *adj* crispante, angustioso(sa).

nervous ['nɜːvəs] *adj* **-1.** ANAT & PSYCH nervioso(sa). **-2.** [apprehensive] inquieto(ta), aprensivo(va); **to be ~ of sthg/of doing sthg** tener miedo a algo/a hacer algo; **to be ~ about sthg** estar inquieto por algo.

nervous breakdown *n* crisis *f inv* nerviosa.

nervously ['nɜːvəslɪ] *adv* con nerviosismo, nerviosamente.

nervousness ['nɜːvəsnɪs] *n* nerviosismo *m*.

nervous system *n* sistema *m* nervioso.

nervous wreck *n* manojo *m* de nervios.

nervy ['nɜːvɪ] (*compar* **-ier**, *superl* **-iest**) *adj* **-1.** *inf* [nervous] nervioso(sa). **-2.** *Am* [cheeky] descarado(da).

nest [nest] ◇ *n* nido *m*; **ant's ~** hormiguero *m*; **wasps' ~** avispero *m*; **~ of tables** mesas *fpl* nido. ◇ *vi* anidar.

nest egg *n* ahorros *mpl*.

nestle ['nesl] *vi* **-1.** [settle snugly - in chair] arrellanarse; [- in bed] acurrucarse. **-2.** [be situated] estar situado(da) OR emplazado(da).

nestling ['neslɪŋ] *n* pajarito *m*.

net [net] (*pt & pp* **-ted**, *cont* **-ting**) ◇ *adj* **-1.** [weight, price, loss] neto(ta). **-2.** [final] final. ◇ *n* red *f*. ◇ *vt* **-1.** [catch] coger con red. **-2.** [acquire] embolsarse. **-3.** [gain as profit - subj: person] obtener un beneficio neto de; [- subj: deal] reportar un beneficio neto de.

Net [net] *n* COMPUT: **the ~** la Red; **to surf the ~** navegar por la Red.

netball ['netbɔːl] *n deporte parecido al baloncesto femenino*.

net curtains *npl* visillos *mpl*.

Netherlands ['neðələndz] *npl*: **the ~** los Países Bajos.

nethermost ['neðəməʊst] *adj literary* más bajo (más baja).

net profit *n* beneficio *m* neto.

nett [net] *adj* = **net**.

netting ['netɪŋ] *n* red *f*, malla *f*.

nettle ['netl] ◇ *n* ortiga *f*. ◇ *vt* irritar, molestar.

network ['netwɜːk] ◇ *n* **-1.** [gen & COMPUT] red *f*. **-2.** RADIO & TV [station] cadena *f*. ◇ *vt* **-1.** RADIO & TV [broadcast] emitir en toda la cadena. **-2.** COMPUT conectar a la red.

neuralgia [njʊə'rældʒə] *n* neuralgia *f*.

neurological [,njʊərə'lɒdʒɪkl] *adj* neurológico(ca).

neurologist [,njʊə'rɒlədʒɪst] *n* neurólogo *m*, -ga *f*.

neurology [,njʊə'rɒlədʒɪ] *n* neurología *f*.

neurosis [ˌnjʊəˈrəʊsɪs] (*pl* **-ses** [-siːz]) *n* neurosis *f inv*.

neurosurgery [ˌnjʊərəʊˈsɜːdʒərɪ] *n* neurocirugía *f*.

neurotic [ˌnjʊəˈrɒtɪk] ◇ *adj* neurótico(ca). ◇ *n* neurótico *m*, -ca *f*.

neuter [ˈnjuːtər] ◇ *adj* neutro(tra). ◇ *vt* castrar.

neutral [ˈnjuːtrəl] ◇ *adj* **-1.** [gen] neutro(tra); [shoe cream] incoloro(ra). **-2.** [nonallied] neutral. **-3.** [unexpressive] inexpresivo(va). ◇ *n* **-1.** AUT punto *m* muerto. **-2.** [country] país *m* neutral; [person] persona *f* neutral.

neutrality [njuːˈtrælətɪ] *n* neutralidad *f*.

neutralize, -ise [ˈnjuːtrəlaɪz] *vt* neutralizar.

neutron [ˈnjuːtrɒn] *n* neutrón *m*.

neutron bomb *n* bomba *f* de neutrones.

Nevada [nɪˈvɑːdə] *n* Nevada.

never [ˈnevər] *adv* **-1.** [at no time] nunca, jamás; ~ ever nunca jamás, nunca en la vida; **well I** ~! ¡vaya!, ¡caramba! **-2.** *inf* [as negative] no; **you** ~ **did!** ¡no (me digas)!

never-ending *adj* interminable, inacababable.

nevertheless [ˌnevəðəˈles] *adv* sin embargo, no obstante.

new [*adj* njuː, *n* njuːz] *adj* nuevo(va); [baby] recién nacido (recién nacida); **to be** ~ **to sthg** ser nuevo(va) en algo; **as good as** ~ como nuevo.
◆ **news** *n* (*U*) noticias *fpl*; **a piece of** ~ una noticia; **the** ~ las noticias; **that's** ~ **to me** me coge de nuevas; **to break the** ~ **to sb** dar la noticia a alguien.

New Age *n* movimiento que gira en torno a las ciencias ocultas, medicinas alternativas, religiones orientales etc.

new blood *n fig* sangre *f* OR savia *f* nueva.

newborn [ˈnjuːbɔːn] *adj* recién nacido (recién nacida).

New Brunswick [-ˈbrʌnzwɪk] *n* New Brunswick.

New Caledonia [-ˌkælɪˈdəʊnjə] *n* Nueva Caledonia.

New Caledonian [-ˌkælɪˈdəʊnjən] ◇ *adj* neocaledonio(nia). ◇ *n* neocaledonio *m*, -nia *f*.

newcomer [ˈnjuːˌkʌmər] *n*: ~ **(to)** recién llegado *m*, recién llegada *f* (a).

New Delhi *n* Nueva Delhi.

New England *n* Nueva Inglaterra.

newfangled [ˌnjuːˈfæŋgld] *adj inf pej* novedoso(sa).

new-found *adj* [gen] recién descubierto (recién descubierta); [friend] reciente.

Newfoundland [ˈnjuːfəndlənd] *n* Terranova.

New Guinea *n* Nueva Guinea.

New Hampshire [-ˈhæmpʃər] *n* New Hampshire.

New Hebrides *npl*: **the** ~ las Nuevas Hébridas.

New Jersey *n* Nueva Jersey.

newly [ˈnjuːlɪ] *adv* recién.

newlyweds [ˈnjuːlɪwedz] *npl* recién casados *mpl*.

New Mexico *n* Nuevo Méjico.

new moon *n* luna *f* nueva.

New Orleans [-ˈɔːlɪənz] *n* Nueva Orleans.

New Quebec *n* New Quebec.

news agency *n* agencia *f* de noticias.

newsagent *Br* [ˈnjuːzeɪdʒənt], **newsdealer** *Am* [ˈnjuːzdiːlər] *n* [person] vendedor *m*, -ra *f* de periódicos; ~**'s (shop)** ≃ quiosco *m* de periódicos.

news bulletin *n* boletín *m* de noticias.

newscast [ˈnjuːzkɑːst] *n* TV telediario *m*; RADIO noticiario *m*, diario *m* hablado.

newscaster [ˈnjuːzkɑːstər] *n* presentador *m*, -ra *f*, locutor *m*, -ra *f*.

news conference *n* conferencia *f* de prensa.

newsdealer *Am* = newsagent.

newsflash [ˈnjuːzflæʃ] *n* flash *m* informativo, noticia *f* de última hora.

newsgroup [ˈnjuːzgruːp] *n* COMPUT grupo *m* de notícias.

newshound [ˈnjuːzhaʊnd] *n* sabueso *m* de la prensa.

newsletter [ˈnjuːzˌletər] *n* boletín *m*, hoja *f* informativa.

newsman [ˈnjuːzmæn] (*pl* **-men** [-men]) *n* periodista *m*, reportero *m*.

New South Wales *n* Nueva Gales del Sur.

newspaper [ˈnjuːzˌpeɪpər] *n* **-1.** [publication, company] periódico *m*, diario *m*. **-2.** [paper] papel *m* de periódico.

newspaperman [ˈnjuːzˌpeɪpəmæn] (*pl* **-men** [-men]) *n* periodista *m y f*.

newsprint [ˈnjuːzprɪnt] *n* papel *m* de periódico.

newsreader [ˈnjuːzˌriːdər] *n* presentador *m*, -ra *f*, locutor *m*, -ra *f*.

newsreel [ˈnjuːzriːl] *n* noticiario *m* cinematográfico.

newsroom [ˈnjuːzrʊm] *n* (sala *f* de) redacción *f*.

newssheet [ˈnjuːzˌʃiːt] *n* boletín *m*, hoja *f* informativa.

newsstand [ˈnjuːzstænd] *n* puesto *m* de periódicos.

newsworthy ['njuːz,wɜːðɪ] *adj* de interés periodístico.

newt [njuːt] *n* tritón *m*.

new technology *n* nueva tecnología *f*.

New Testament *n*: **the** ~ el Nuevo Testamento.

new town *n Br ciudad nueva construida por el gobierno*.

new wave *n* nueva ola *f*.

New World *n*: **the** ~ el Nuevo Mundo.

New Year *n* Año *m* Nuevo; **Happy** ~! ¡Feliz Año Nuevo!

New Year's Day *n* día *m* de Año Nuevo.

New Year's Eve *n* Nochevieja *f*.

New York *n* -1. [city]: ~ (**City**) Nueva York. -2. [state]: ~ (**State**) (el estado de) Nueva York.

New Yorker [-'jɔːkəʳ] *n* neoyorquino *m*, -na *f*.

New Zealand [-'ziːlənd] *n* Nueva Zelanda.

New Zealander [-'ziːləndəʳ] *n* neozelandés *m*, -esa *f*.

next [nekst] ◇ *adj* -1. [in time] próximo(ma); **the** ~ **day** el día siguiente; ~ **Tuesday/year** el martes/el año que viene; ~ **week** la semana próxima OR que viene; **the** ~ **week** los próximos siete días. -2. [in space - page etc] siguiente; [- room] de al lado. ◇ *pron* el siguiente (la siguiente); **the day after** ~ pasado mañana; **the week after** ~ la semana que viene no, la otra. ◇ *adv* -1. [afterwards] después. -2. [again] de nuevo. -3. [with superlatives]: ~ **best/biggest** *etc* el segundo mejor/más grande *etc*. ◇ *prep Am* al lado de, junto a.
◆ **next to** *prep* al lado de, junto a; ~ **to nothing** casi nada.

next door *adv* (en la casa de) al lado.
◆ **next-door** *adj*: **next-door neighbour** vecino *m*, -na *f* de al lado.

next of kin *n* pariente más cercano *m*, pariente más cercana *f*.

NF ◇ *n abbr of* **National Front**. ◇ *abbr of* Newfoundland.

NFL (*abbr of* **National Football League**) *n* federación estadounidense de fútbol americano.

NFU (*abbr of* **National Farmers' Union**) *n* asociación británica de agricultores.

NG *abbr of* **National Guard**.

NGO (*abbr of* **non-governmental organization**) *n* organización no gubernamental.

NH *abbr of* **New Hampshire**.

NHL (*abbr of* **National Hockey League**) *n* federación estadounidense de hockey sobre hielo.

NHS *n abbr of* **National Health Service**.

NI ◇ *n abbr of* **National Insurance**. ◇ *abbr of* **Northern Ireland**.

Niagara [naɪ'ægrə] *n*: ~ **Falls** las cataratas del Niágara.

nib [nɪb] *n* plumilla *f*.

nibble ['nɪbl] ◇ *n* mordisquito *m*. ◇ *vt* mordisquear. ◇ *vi*: **to** ~ **at sthg** mordisquear algo.

Nicaragua [,nɪkə'rægjuə] *n* Nicaragua.

Nicaraguan [,nɪkə'rægjuən] ◇ *adj* nicaragüense. ◇ *n* nicaragüense *m* y *f*.

nice [naɪs] *adj* -1. [attractive] bonito(ta); [good] bueno(na). -2. [kind] amable; [pleasant, friendly] agradable, simpático(ca), dije *Amer*; **to be** ~ **to sb** ser agradable con alguien.

nice-looking [-'lʊkɪŋ] *adj* [person] atractivo(va), guapo(pa); [car, room] bonito(ta).

nicely ['naɪslɪ] *adv* -1. [well, attractively] bien. -2. [politely] educadamente, con educación. -3. [satisfactorily] bien; **that will do** ~ esto irá de perlas.

nicety ['naɪsətɪ] (*pl* -ies) *n* detalle *m*.

niche [niːʃ] *n* -1. [in wall] nicho *m*, hornacina *f*. -2. [in life] buena posición *f*.

nick [nɪk] ◇ *n* -1. [cut] cortecito *m*; [notch] muesca *f*. -2. *Br inf* [jail]: **the** ~ el trullo, la trena. -3. [condition]: **in good/bad** ~ *Br inf* en buenas/malas condiciones. -4. *phr*: **in the** ~ **of time** justo a tiempo. ◇ *vt* -1. [cut] cortar; [make notch in] mellar. -2. *Br inf* [steal] birlar, mangar. -3. *Br inf* [arrest] trincar, pillar.

nickel ['nɪkl] *n* -1. [metal] níquel *m*. -2. *Am* [coin] moneda *f* de cinco centavos.

nickname ['nɪkneɪm] ◇ *n* apodo *m*. ◇ *vt* apodar.

Nicosia [,nɪkə'siːə] *n* Nicosia.

nicotine ['nɪkətiːn] *n* nicotina *f*.

niece [niːs] *n* sobrina *f*.

nifty ['nɪftɪ] (*compar* -ier, *superl* -iest) *adj inf* apañado(da).

Niger ['naɪdʒəʳ] *n* -1. [country] Níger. -2. [river]: **the (River)** ~ el (río) Níger.

Nigeria [naɪ'dʒɪərɪə] *n* Nigeria.

Nigerian [naɪ'dʒɪərɪən] ◇ *adj* nigeriano(na). ◇ *n* nigeriano *m*, -na *f*.

Nigerien [naɪ'dʒɪərɪən] ◇ *adj* nigerino(na). ◇ *n* nigerino *m*, -na *f*.

niggardly ['nɪgədlɪ] *adj* [person] avaro(ra), tacaño(ña); [gift, amount] miserable.

niggle ['nɪgl] ◇ *n* [worry] duda *f* (insignificante). ◇ *vt Br* -1. [worry] inquietar. -2. [criticize] meterse con, criticar. ◇ *vi* -1. [worry]: **it** ~**d at me all day** le di vueltas todo el día. -2. [criticize] criticar, quejarse.

nigh [naɪ] *adv literary* [near] cerca; **well ~** [almost] casi.

night [naɪt] *n* noche *f*; [evening] tarde *f*; **last ~** anoche, ayer por la noche; **at ~** por la noche, de noche; **~ and day, day and ~** noche y día, día y noche; **to have an early/a late ~** irse a dormir pronto/tarde. ◆ **nights** *adv* **-1.** *Am* [at night] por las noches. **-2.** *Br* [nightshift]: **to work ~s** hacer el turno de noche.

nightcap ['naɪtkæp] *n* **-1.** [drink] *bebida que se toma antes de ir a dormir.* **-2.** [hat] gorro *m* de dormir.

nightclothes ['naɪtkləʊðz] *npl* ropa *f* de dormir.

nightclub ['naɪtklʌb] *n* club *m* nocturno.

nightdress ['naɪtdres] *n* camisón *m*, dormilona *f Amer.*

nightfall ['naɪtfɔːl] *n* anochecer *m*.

nightgown ['naɪtɡaʊn] *n* camisón *m*, dormilona *f Amer.*

nightie ['naɪtɪ] *n inf* camisón *m*.

nightingale ['naɪtɪŋɡeɪl] *n* ruiseñor *m*.

nightlife ['naɪtlaɪf] *n* vida *f* nocturna.

nightlight ['naɪtlaɪt] *n* lucecita *f* (*que se deja encendida durante la noche*).

nightly ['naɪtlɪ] ◇ *adj* nocturno(na), de cada noche. ◇ *adv* cada noche, todas las noches.

nightmare ['naɪtmeəʳ] *n lit & fig* pesadilla *f*.

nightmarish ['naɪtmeərɪʃ] *adj* horripilante, de pesadilla.

night owl *n fig* noctámbulo *m*, -la *f*.

night porter *n* recepcionista *m y f* del turno de noche.

night safe *n* caja *f* fuerte (*en la pared exterior de un banco*).

night school *n* (*U*) escuela *f* nocturna.

night shift *n* turno *m* de noche.

nightshirt ['naɪtʃɜːt] *n* camisa *f* de dormir (masculina).

nightspot ['naɪtspɒt] *n* club *m* nocturno.

nightstick ['naɪtstɪk] *n Am* porra *f*.

nighttime ['naɪttaɪm] *n* noche *f*.

night watchman *n* vigilante *m* nocturno, nochero *m Amer.*

nightwear ['naɪtweəʳ] *n* ropa *f* de dormir.

nihilism ['naɪəlɪzm] *n* nihilismo *m*.

nil [nɪl] *n* **-1.** [nothing] nada *f*. **-2.** *Br* SPORT cero *m*.

Nile [naɪl] *n*: **the ~** el Nilo.

nimble ['nɪmbl] *adj* **-1.** [person, fingers] ágil. **-2.** [mind] rápido(da).

nimbly ['nɪmblɪ] *adv* con agilidad.

nine [naɪn] *num* nueve; *see also* **six**.

nineteen [ˌnaɪn'tiːn] *num* diecinueve; *see also* **six**.

nineteenth [naɪn'tiːnθ] ◇ *num adj* decimonoveno(na). ◇ *num n* **-1.** [fraction] decimonoveno *m*. **-2.** [in order] decimonoveno *m*, -na *f*; *see also* **sixth**.

ninetieth ['naɪntɪəθ] ◇ *num adj* nonagésimo(ma). ◇ *num n* **-1.** [fraction] noventa *m*. **-2.** [in order] nonagésimo *m*, -ma *f*; *see also* **sixth**.

ninety ['naɪntɪ] *num* noventa; *see also* **six**.

ninny ['nɪnɪ] (*pl* **-ies**) *n inf* tonto *m*, -ta *f*, bobo *m*, -ba *f*.

ninth [naɪnθ] ◇ *num adj* noveno(na). ◇ *num n* **-1.** [fraction] noveno *m*. **-2.** [in order] noveno *m*, -na *f*; *see also* **sixth**.

nip [nɪp] (*pt & pp* **-ped**, *cont* **-ping**) ◇ *n* **-1.** [pinch] pellizco *m*; [bite] mordisco *m*. **-2.** [drink] trago *m*. ◇ *vt* [pinch] pellizcar; [bite] mordisquear. ◇ *vi inf* [dash]: **to ~ out** salir un momento.

nipper ['nɪpəʳ] *n Br inf* chiquillo *m*, chaval *m*, chigüín *m Amer.*

nipple ['nɪpl] *n* **-1.** [of woman] pezón *m*. **-2.** [of baby's bottle, man] tetilla *f*.

nippy ['nɪpɪ] (*compar* **-ier**, *superl* **-iest**) *adj* **-1.** [cold] fresco(ca); **it's a bit ~ this morning** hace fresquito esta mañana. **-2.** [quick] rápido(da).

Nissen hut ['nɪsn-] *n* refugio *m* militar.

nit [nɪt] *n* **-1.** [in hair] liendre *f*. **-2.** *Br inf* [idiot] idiota *m y f*, imbécil *m y f*.

nitpicking ['nɪtpɪkɪŋ] *inf* ◇ *adj* puñetero(ra). ◇ *n* (*U*) nimiedades *fpl*.

nitrate ['naɪtreɪt] *n* nitrato *m*.

nitric acid ['naɪtrɪk-] *n* ácido *m* nítrico.

nitrogen ['naɪtrədʒən] *n* nitrógeno *m*.

nitroglycerin(e) [ˌnaɪtrəʊ'ɡlɪsərɪːn] *n* nitroglicerina *f*.

nitty-gritty [ˌnɪtɪ'ɡrɪtɪ] *n inf*: **to get down to the ~** ir al grano.

nitwit ['nɪtwɪt] *n inf* idiota *m y f*, imbécil *m y f*.

nix [nɪks] *Am* ◇ *n* [nothing] nada *f*. ◇ *adv* no. ◇ *vt* [say no to] decir (que) no a.

NJ *abbr of* **New Jersey**.

NLF (*abbr of* **National Liberation Front**) *n* FLN *m*.

NLQ (*abbr of* **near letter quality**) *de calidad correspondencia*.

NLRB (*abbr of* **National Labor Relations Board**) *n organismo estadounidense para arbitraje laboral,* ≃ IMAC *m*.

NM *abbr of* **New Mexico**.

no [nəʊ] (*pl* **-es**) ◇ *adv* [gen] no; **you're ~ better than me** tú no eres mejor que yo.

adj no; **I have ~ time** no tengo tiempo; **that's ~ excuse** esa no es excusa que valga; **there are ~ taxis** no hay taxis; **he's ~ fool** no es ningún tonto; **she's ~ friend of mine** no es amiga mía; **"~ smoking/parking/cameras"** "prohibido fumar/aparcar/hacer fotos". ⬦ *n* no *m*; **he/she won't take ~ for an answer** no acepta una respuesta negativa.

No., no. (*abbr of* **number**) n.º.

Noah's ark ['nəʊəz-] *n* el arca *f* de Noé.

nobble ['nɒbl] *vt Br inf* **-1.** [racehorse] drogar. **-2.** [bribe] sobornar. **-3.** [detain - person] coger por banda y dar la lata a.

Nobel prize [nəʊ'bel-] *n* premio *m* Nobel.

nobility [nə'bɪlətɪ] *n* nobleza *f*.

noble ['nəʊbl] ⬦ *adj* noble. ⬦ *n* noble *m* y *f*.

nobleman ['nəʊblmən] (*pl* **-men** [-mən]) *n* noble *m*.

noblewoman ['nəʊbl,wʊmən] (*pl* **-women** [-,wɪmɪn]) *n* noble *f*.

nobly ['nəʊblɪ] *adv* noblemente, con generosidad.

nobody ['nəʊbədɪ] (*pl* **-ies**) ⬦ *pron* nadie. ⬦ *n pej* don nadie *m*.

no-claim bonus *n* bonificación *f* por ausencia de siniestralidad.

nocturnal [nɒk'tɜːnl] *adj* nocturno(na).

nod [nɒd] (*pt & pp* **-ded**, *cont* **-ding**) ⬦ *n* inclinación *f* de cabeza. ⬦ *vt*: **to ~ one's head** [in agreement] asentir con la cabeza; [as greeting] saludar con la cabeza. ⬦ *vi* **-1.** [in agreement] asentir con la cabeza. **-2.** [to indicate sthg] indicar con la cabeza. **-3.** [as greeting] saludar con la cabeza.
◆ **nod off** *vi* dar cabezadas.

node [nəʊd] *n* nudo *m*.

nodule ['nɒdjuːl] *n* nódulo *m*.

no-go area *n Br* zona *f* (de entrada) prohibida.

noise [nɔɪz] *n* ruido *m*; **to make a ~** armar OR hacer ruido.

noiseless ['nɔɪzlɪs] *adj* silencioso(sa).

noiselessly ['nɔɪzlɪslɪ] *adv* silenciosamente, sin hacer ruido.

noisily ['nɔɪzɪlɪ] *adv* ruidosamente, haciendo ruido.

noisy ['nɔɪzɪ] (*compar* **-ier**, *superl* **-iest**) *adj* ruidoso(sa).

nomad ['nəʊmæd] *n* nómada *m* y *f*.

nomadic [nə'mædɪk] *adj* nómada.

no-man's-land *n* tierra *f* de nadie.

nominal ['nɒmɪnl] *adj* nominal.

nominally ['nɒmɪnəlɪ] *adv* nominalmente.

nominate ['nɒmɪneɪt] *vt* **-1.** [propose]: **to ~ sb (for** OR **as)** proponer a alguien (por OR como). **-2.** [appoint]: **to ~ sb (to sthg)** nombrar a alguien (algo).

nomination [,nɒmɪ'neɪʃn] *n* **-1.** [proposal] nominación *f*. **-2.** [appointment]: **~ (to sthg)** nombramiento *m* (a algo).

nominee [,nɒmɪ'niː] *n* nominado *m*, **-da** *f*.

non- [nɒn] *prefix* no.

nonaddictive [,nɒnə'dɪktɪv] *adj* que no crea adicción.

nonaggression [,nɒnə'greʃn] *n* no agresión *f*.

nonalcoholic [,nɒnælkə'hɒlɪk] *adj* sin alcohol.

nonaligned [,nɒnə'laɪnd] *adj* no alineado(da).

nonbeliever [,nɒnbɪ'liːvəʳ] *n* no creyente *m* y *f*.

nonchalant [*Br* 'nɒnʃələnt, *Am* ,nɒnʃə'lɑːnt] *adj* indiferente, despreocupado(da).

nonchalantly [*Br* 'nɒnʃələntlɪ, *Am* ,nɒnʃə'lɑːntlɪ] *adv* con indiferencia.

noncombatant [*Br* ,nɒn'kɒmbətənt, *Am* ,nɒnkəm'bætənt] *n* no combatiente *m* y *f*.

noncommissioned officer [,nɒnkə-'mɪʃənd-] *n* suboficial *m* y *f*.

noncommittal [,nɒnkə'mɪtl] *adj* que no compromete a nada, evasivo(va).

noncompetitive [,nɒnkəm'petɪtɪv] *adj* no competitivo(va).

non compos mentis [-,kɒmpəs'mentɪs] *adj* que no está en posesión de sus facultades mentales.

nonconformist [,nɒnkən'fɔːmɪst] ⬦ *adj* inconformista. ⬦ *n* inconformista *m* y *f*.

nonconformity [,nɒnkən'fɔːmətɪ] *n* inconformismo *m*.

noncontributory [,nɒnkən'trɪbjʊtərɪ] *adj* no contributivo (no contributiva).

noncooperation ['nɒnkəʊ,ɒpə'reɪʃn] *n* no cooperación *f*.

nondescript [*Br* 'nɒndɪskrɪpt, *Am* ,nɒndɪ'skrɪpt] *adj* anodino(na), soso(sa).

nondrinker [,nɒn'drɪŋkəʳ] *n* persona *f* que no bebe (alcohol).

nondrip [,nɒn'drɪp] *adj* que no gotea.

nondriver [,nɒn'draɪvəʳ] *n* persona *f* que no sabe conducir.

none [nʌn] ⬦ *pron* **-1.** [not any] nada; **there is ~ left** no queda nada; **it's ~ of your business** no es asunto tuyo; **I'll have ~ of your nonsense** no voy a aguantar tus tonterías. **-2.** [not one - object, person] ninguno(na); **~ of us/the books** ninguno de nosotros/de los libros; **I had ~** no tenía ninguno. ⬦ *adv*: **I'm ~ the worse/better** no me ha perjudicado/ayudado en nada; **I'm ~ the wiser** no he entendido nada.

◆ **none too** *adv* no demasiado.

nonentity [nɒ'nentəti] (*pl* **-ies**) *n* cero *m* a la izquierda.

nonessential [ˌnɒnɪ'senʃl] *adj* no esencial.

nonetheless [ˌnʌnðə'les] *adv* sin embargo, no obstante.

non-event *n* fracaso *m*.

nonexecutive director [ˌnɒn'ɪgsekjətɪv-] *n* director no ejecutivo *m*, directora no ejecutiva *f*.

nonexistent [ˌnɒnɪg'zɪstənt] *adj* inexistente.

nonfattening [ˌnɒn'fætnɪŋ] *adj* que no engorda.

nonfiction [ˌnɒn'fɪkʃn] *n* no ficción *f*.

nonflammable [ˌnɒn'flæməbl] *adj* ininflamable.

noninfectious [ˌnɒnɪn'fekʃəs] *adj* no infeccioso(sa).

noninflammable [ˌnɒnɪn'flæməbl] *adj* ininflamable.

noninterference [ˌnɒnɪntə'fɪərəns], **nonintervention** [ˌnɒnɪntə'venʃn] *n* no intervención *f*.

non-iron *adj* que no necesita plancha.

nonmalignant [ˌnɒnmə'lɪgnənt] *adj* no maligno (no maligna).

non-member *n* no miembro *m*, no socio *m*.

non-negotiable *adj* no negociable.

no-no *n* *inf*: **it's a ~** ¡nones!

no-nonsense *adj* práctico(ca).

nonoperational [ˌnɒnɒpə'reɪʃənl] *adj* [machine, factory] que no es operativo (que no es operativa); [forces] no operacional.

nonparticipation [ˌnɒnpuːtɪsə'peɪʃən] *n* no participación *f*.

nonpayment [ˌnɒn'peɪmənt] *n* impago *m*.

nonplussed, **nonplused** *Am* [ˌnɒn'plʌst] *adj* perplejo(ja).

non-profit-making *Br*, **non-profit** *Am* *adj* sin fines lucrativos.

nonproliferation ['nɒnprə,lɪfə'reɪʃn] *n* no proliferación *f*.

nonrenewable [ˌnɒnrɪ'njuːəbl] *adj* [natural resources] no renovable; [contract] no prorrogable.

nonresident [ˌnɒn'rezɪdənt] *n* **-1.** [of country] no residente *m* y *f*. **-2.** [of hotel]: **open to ~s** abierto al público.

nonreturnable [ˌnɒnrɪ'tɜːnəbl] *adj* no retornable, sin retorno.

nonsense ['nɒnsəns] ◇ *n* (U) **-1.** [gen] tonterías *fpl*, bobadas *fpl*; **it is ~ to suggest that ...** es absurdo sugerir que ...; **stop this ~ at once!** ¡dejaros de tonterías ahora mismo!; **to make (a) ~ of sthg** dar al traste con algo. **-2.** [incomprehensible words] galimatías *m* inv; **it's ~ to me** me es incomprensible. ◇ *excl* ¡tonterías!, ¡bobadas!

nonsensical [nɒn'sensɪkl] *adj* disparatado(da), absurdo(da).

non sequitur [-'sekwɪtər] *n* incoherencia *f*, incongruencia *f*.

nonshrink [ˌnɒn'ʃrɪŋk] *adj* que no encoge.

nonslip [ˌnɒn'slɪp] *adj* antideslizante.

nonsmoker [ˌnɒn'sməʊkər] *n* no fumador *m*, no fumadora *f*.

nonstarter [ˌnɒn'stɑːtər] *n* *Br* **-1.** [plan]: **to be a ~** *inf* estar condenado(da) al fracaso. **-2.** [in race] *caballo participante en una carrera que no toma la salida*.

nonstick [ˌnɒn'stɪk] *adj* antiadherente.

nonstop [ˌnɒn'stɒp] ◇ *adj* [activity, rain] continuo(nua), incesante; [flight] sin escalas. ◇ *adv* sin parar.

nontaxable [ˌnɒn'tæksəbl] *adj* no imponible.

nontoxic [ˌnɒn'tɒksɪk] *adj* no tóxico(ca).

nontransferable [ˌnɒntrænz'fɜːrəbl] *adj* intransferible.

non-U *adj* *Br dated* poco refinado(da).

nonviolence [ˌnɒn'vaɪələns] *n* no violencia *f*.

nonvoter [ˌnɒn'vəʊtər] *n* persona *f* que no vota.

nonvoting [ˌnɒn'vəʊtɪŋ] *adj* **-1.** [person] sin voto. **-2.** FIN [shares] sin derecho a voto.

nonwhite [ˌnɒn'waɪt] ◇ *adj* que no es de raza blanca. ◇ *n* persona *f* que no es de raza blanca.

noodles ['nuːdlz] *npl* fideos *mpl*.

nook [nʊk] *n* [of room] rincón *m*, recoveco *m*; **every ~ and cranny** todos los recovecos.

noon [nuːn] *n* mediodía *m*.

noonday ['nuːndeɪ] ◇ *n* mediodía *m*. ◇ *comp* de mediodía.

no one *pron* = **nobody.**

noose [nuːs] *n* [loop] nudo *m* corredizo; [for hanging] soga *f*.

no-place *Am* = **nowhere.**

nor [nɔːr] *conj* **-1.** → **neither.** **-2.** [and not] ni; **I don't smoke - ~ do I** no fumo - yo tampoco; **I don't know, ~ do I care** ni lo sé, ni me importa.

Nordic ['nɔːdɪk] *adj* nórdico(ca).

Norf (*abbr of* **Norfolk**) *condado inglés*.

norm [nɔːm] *n* norma *f*; **the ~** lo normal.

normal ['nɔːml] *adj* normal.

normality [nɔː'mælɪtɪ], **normalcy** *Am*
['nɔːmlsɪ] *n* normalidad *f*.
normalize, -ise ['nɔːməlaɪz] ◇ *vt* normalizar. ◇ *vi* normalizarse.
normally ['nɔːməlɪ] *adv* normalmente.
Normandy ['nɔːməndɪ] *n* Normandía.
Norse [nɔːs] *adj* nórdico(ca).
north [nɔːθ] ◇ *n* **-1.** [direction] norte *m*. **-2.**
[region]: **the North** el norte. ◇ *adj* del norte; **North London** el norte de Londres. ◇
adv: ~ **(of)** al norte (de).
North Africa *n* África del Norte.
North America *n* Norteamérica.
North American ◇ *adj* norteamerica-
no(na). ◇ *n* norteamericano *m*, -na *f*.
Northants [nɔː'θænts] (*abbr of* **Northamp-
tonshire**) *condado inglés*.
northbound ['nɔːθbaʊnd] *adj* (con) dirección (al) norte.
North Carolina [-,kærə'laɪnə] *n* Carolina
del Norte.
Northd (*abbr of* **Northumberland**) *condado
inglés*.
North Dakota [-də'kəʊtə] *n* Dakota del
Norte.
northeast [,nɔːθ'iːst] ◇ *n* **-1.** [direction] nordeste *m*. **-2.** [region]: **the Northeast** el nordeste. ◇ *adj* del nordeste. ◇ *adv*: ~ **(of)** al
nordeste (de).
northeasterly [,nɔːθ'iːstəlɪ] *adj* del nordeste; **in a** ~ **direction** hacia el nordeste.
northerly ['nɔːðəlɪ] *adj* del norte; **in a** ~
direction hacia el norte.
northern ['nɔːðən] *adj* del norte, norte-
ño(ña).
Northerner ['nɔːðənəʳ] *n* norteño *m*, -ña *f*.
Northern Ireland *n* Irlanda del Norte.
Northern Lights *npl*: **the** ~ la aurora boreal.
northernmost ['nɔːðənməʊst] *adj* más septentrional OR al norte.
Northern Territory *n* (el) Territorio del
Norte.
North Korea *n* Corea del Norte.
North Korean ◇ *adj* norcoreano(na). ◇ *n*
norcoreano *m*, -na *f*.
North Pole *n*: **the** ~ el Polo Norte.
North Sea ◇ *n*: **the** ~ el Mar del Norte.
◇ *comp* [fishing] en el Mar del Norte; [oil,
oilrig] del Mar del Norte.
North Star *n*: **the** ~ la estrella Polar.
North Vietnam *n* Vietnam del Norte.
North Vietnamese ◇ *adj* norvietnamita.
◇ *n* norvietnamita *m y f*.
northward ['nɔːθwəd] ◇ *adj* hacia el nor-
te. ◇ *adv* = **northwards**.

northwards ['nɔːθwədz] *adv* hacia el norte.
northwest [,nɔːθ'west] ◇ *n* **-1.** [direction]
noroeste *m*. **-2.** [region]: **the Northwest** el
noroeste. ◇ *adj* del noroeste. ◇ *adv*: ~
(of) al noroeste (de).
northwesterly [,nɔːθ'westəlɪ] *adj* del noroeste; **in a** ~ **direction** hacia el noroeste.
Northwest Territories *npl Can*: **the** ~ los
territorios del Noroeste.
North Yemen *n* (el) Yemen del Norte.
Norway ['nɔːweɪ] *n* Noruega.
Norwegian [nɔː'wiːdʒən] ◇ *adj* norue-
go(ga). ◇ *n* **-1.** [person] noruego *m*, -ga *f*.
-2. [language] noruego *m*.
Nos., nos. (*abbr of* **numbers**) n.ᵒˢ.
nose [nəʊz] *n* [of person] nariz *f*; [of animal]
hocico *m*; [of plane, car] morro *m*; **under
one's** ~ delante de las narices de uno; **to
cut off one's** ~ **to spite one's face** *salir uno
perjudicado al intentar perjudicar a otro*; **to
have a** ~ **for sthg** tener olfato para algo; **he
gets up my** ~ *inf* me saca de quicio; **to
keep one's** ~ **out of sthg** no meter las narices en algo; **to look down one's** ~ **at sb/
sthg** mirar por encima del hombro a
alguien/algo; **to pay through the** ~ pagar
un dineral; **to poke** OR **stick one's** ~ **in** *inf*
meter las narices; **to turn up one's** ~ **at
sthg** hacerle ascos a algo.
◆ **nose about, nose around** *vi* curiosear.
nosebag ['nəʊzbæg] *n* morral *m*.
nosebleed ['nəʊzbliːd] *n* hemorragia *f* nasal.
nosecone ['nəʊzkəʊn] *n* morro *m*.
nosedive ['nəʊzdaɪv] ◇ *n* [of plane] picado
m. ◇ *vi lit & fig* bajar en picado.
nosey ['nəʊzɪ] = **nosy**.
nosh [nɒʃ] *n Br inf* papeo *m*.
nosh-up *n Br inf* comilona *f*.
nostalgia [nɒ'stældʒə] *n*: ~ **(for)** nostalgia *f*
(de).
nostalgic [nɒ'stældʒɪk] *adj* nostálgico(ca).
nostril ['nɒstrəl] *n* ventana *f* de la nariz.
nosy ['nəʊzɪ] (*compar* **-ier**, *superl* **-iest**) *adj*
fisgón(ona), curioso(sa).
not [nɒt] *adv* no; **this is** ~ **the first time** no
es la primera vez; **it's green, isn't it?** es
verde, ¿no?; **I hope/think** ~ espero/creo
que no; ~ **a chance** de ninguna manera; ~
even a ... ni siquiera un (una) ...; ~ **all** OR
every no todos(das); ~ **always** no siempre;
~ **that** ... no es que ...; ~ **at all** [no] en absoluto; [to acknowledge thanks] de nada.
notable ['nəʊtəbl] ◇ *adj* notable; **to be** ~
for sthg destacar por algo. ◇ *n* notable *m y
f*, personaje *m*.

notably ['nəutəblɪ] *adv* **-1.** [in particular] especialmente. **-2.** [noticeably] notablemente, marcadamente.

notary ['nəutərɪ] (*pl* **-ies**) *n*: ~ **(public)** notario *m*, -ria *f*.

notation [nəu'teɪʃn] *n* notación *f*.

notch [nɒtʃ] *n* **-1.** [cut] muesca *f*. **-2.** *fig* [on scale] punto *m*.

◆ **notch up** *vt fus* apuntarse.

note [nəut] ◇ *n* **-1.** [gen] nota *f*; **to take** ~ **of sthg** tener algo presente; **to compare** ~**s** cambiar impresiones. **-2.** [paper money] billete *m*. **-3.** [tone] tono *m*. **-4.** [importance]: **of** ~ de importancia, notable. ◇ *vt* **-1.** [observe] notar. **-2.** [mention] mencionar.

◆ **notes** *npl* [written record] apuntes *mpl*; **to take** ~**s** tomar apuntes; [in book] notas *fpl*.

◆ **note down** *vt sep* anotar, apuntar.

notebook ['nəutbuk] *n* **-1.** [for taking notes] libreta *f*, cuaderno *m*. **-2.** COMPUT: ~ **(computer)** ordenador *m* portátil.

noted ['nəutɪd] *adj* señalado(da), destacado(da); **to be** ~ **for** distinguirse por.

notepad ['nəutpæd] *n* bloc *m* de notas.

notepaper ['nəutpeɪpə'] *n* papel *m* de escribir OR de cartas.

noteworthy ['nəut,wɜːðɪ] (*compar* **-ier**, *superl* **-iest**) *adj* digno(na) de mención, significativo(va).

nothing ['nʌθɪŋ] ◇ *pron* nada; **I've got** ~ **to do** no tengo nada que hacer; **there's** ~ **in it** [it's untrue] es falso; **there's** ~ **to it** es facilísimo; **for** ~ [free] gratis; [for no purpose] en vano, en balde; **he's** ~ **if not generous** otra cosa no será pero desde luego generoso sí que es; ~ **but** tan sólo; **there's** ~ **for it (but to do sthg)** *Br* no hay más remedio (que hacer algo). ◇ *adv*: **to be** ~ **like sb/sthg** no parecerse en nada a alguien/algo; **I'm** ~ **like finished** no he terminado ni mucho menos.

nothingness ['nʌθɪŋnɪs] *n* nada *f*.

notice ['nəutɪs] ◇ *n* **-1.** [on wall, door] letrero *m*, cartel *m*; [in newspaper] anuncio *m*. **-2.** [attention] atención *f*; **to come to one's** ~ llegar al conocimiento de uno; **to escape one's** ~ pasarle inadvertido OR escapársele a uno; **to take** ~ **(of)** hacer caso (de), prestar atención (a); **to take no** ~ **(of)** no hacer caso (de); **he/she** *etc* **didn't take a blind bit of** ~ no hizo ni el más mínimo caso. **-3.** [warning] aviso *m*; **at short** ~ casi sin previo aviso; **until further** ~ hasta nuevo aviso. **-4.** [at work]: **to be given one's** ~ ser despedido(da); **to hand in one's** ~ presentar la dimisión.

◇ *vt* [sense, smell] notar; [see] fijarse en, ver;

to ~ **sb doing sthg** fijarse en alguien que está haciendo algo.

noticeable ['nəutɪsəbl] *adj* notable.

noticeably ['nəutɪsəblɪ] *adv* notablemente.

notice board *n* tablón *m* de anuncios.

notification [,nəutɪfɪ'keɪʃn] *n* notificación *f*.

notify ['nəutɪfaɪ] (*pt* & *pp* **-ied**) *vt*: **to** ~ **sb (of sthg)** notificar OR comunicar (algo) a alguien.

notion ['nəuʃn] *n* noción *f*.

◆ **notions** *npl* *Am* artículos *mpl* de mercería.

notional ['nəuʃənl] *adj* hipotético(ca).

notoriety [,nəutə'raɪətɪ] *n* mala fama *f*.

notorious [nəu'tɔːrɪəs] *adj* notorio(ria), célebre; **to be** ~ **for sthg** ser muy conocido(da) por algo.

notoriously [nəu'tɔːrɪəslɪ] *adv* notoriamente.

Notts [nɒts] (*abbr of* **Nottinghamshire**) *condado inglés*.

notwithstanding [,nɒtwɪθ'stændɪŋ] *fml* ◇ *prep* a pesar de. ◇ *adv* sin embargo, no obstante.

nougat ['nuːgɑː] *n* *dulce hecho a base de nueces y frutas*.

nought [nɔːt] *num* cero; ~**s and crosses** tres *fpl* en raya.

noun [naun] *n* nombre *m*, sustantivo *m*.

nourish ['nʌrɪʃ] *vt* **-1.** [feed] nutrir, alimentar. **-2.** [entertain] alimentar, albergar.

nourishing ['nʌrɪʃɪŋ] *adj* nutritivo(va), rico(ca).

nourishment ['nʌrɪʃmənt] *n* alimento *m*, sustento *m*.

Nov. (*abbr of* **November**) nov.

Nova Scotia [,nəuvə'skəuʃə] *n* Nueva Escocia.

Nova Scotian [,nəuvə'skəuʃn] ◇ *adj* neoescocés(esa). ◇ *n* neoescocés *m*, -esa *f*.

novel ['nɒvl] ◇ *adj* original. ◇ *n* novela *f*.

novelist ['nɒvəlɪst] *n* novelista *m* *y* *f*.

novelty ['nɒvltɪ] (*pl* **-ies**) *n* **-1.** [gen] novedad *f*. **-2.** [cheap object] baratija *f* (poco útil).

November [nə'vembə'] *n* noviembre *m*; *see also* **September**.

novice ['nɒvɪs] *n* **-1.** [inexperienced person] principiante *m* *y* *f*. **-2.** RELIG novicio(cia).

Novocaine® ['nəuvəkeɪn] *n* novocaína® *f*.

now [nau] ◇ *adv* **-1.** [at this time, at once] ahora; **do it** ~ hazlo ahora; **he's been away for two weeks** ~ lleva dos semanas fuera; **any day** ~ cualquier día de éstos; **any time** ~ en cualquier momento; **for** ~ por ahora, por el momento; ~ **and then** OR **again** de vez en cuando. **-2.** [at a particular time in the past] entonces. **-3.** [to introduce statement] vamos a ver. ◇ *conj:* ~ **(that)** ahora que, ya que. ◇ *n* ahora; **from** ~ **on** a partir de ahora; **they should be here by** ~ ya deberían estar aquí; **up until** ~ hasta ahora.

NOW [nau] (*abbr of* **National Organization for Women**) *n principal organización estadounidense contra la discriminación sexual.*

nowadays ['nauədeɪz] *adv* hoy en día, actualmente.

nowhere *Br* ['nəuweər], **no-place** *Am adv* en ninguna parte; ~ **else** en ninguna otra parte; **to appear out of** OR **from** ~ salir de la nada; **to be getting** ~ no estar avanzando nada, no ir a ninguna parte; **(to be)** ~ **near (as ... as ...)** (no ser) ni mucho menos (tan ... como ...); **this is getting us** ~ esto no nos lleva a nada.

no-win situation *n situación en la que se haga lo que se haga se sale perdiendo.*

noxious ['nɒkʃəs] *adj* nocivo(va).

nozzle ['nɒzl] *n* boquilla *f.*

NP *n abbr of* **notary public.**

NS *abbr of* **Nova Scotia.**

NSC (*abbr of* **National Security Council**) *n consejo federal estadounidense para la coordinación de la política exterior y de defensa.*

NSF ◇ *n* (*abbr of* **National Science Foundation**) *fundación estadounidense para la investigación científica.* ◇ *abbr of* **not sufficient funds.**

NSPCC (*abbr of* **National Society for the Prevention of Cruelty to Children**) *n organización benéfica para la prevención de malos tratos a los niños.*

NSU (*abbr of* **nonspecific urethritis**) *n uretritis sin manifestar.*

NSW *abbr of* **New South Wales.**

NT *n* **-1.** (*abbr of* **New Testament**) N.T. *m.* **-2.** *abbr of* **National Trust.**

nth [enθ] *adj inf:* **to the** ~ **degree** al máximo; **for the** ~ **time** por enésima vez.

nuance [njuː'ɑːns] *n* matiz *m.*

nub [nʌb] *n:* **the** ~ el quid, la clave.

Nubian Desert ['njuːbɪən-] *n:* **the** ~ el desierto de Nubia.

nubile [*Br* 'njuːbaɪl, *Am* 'nuːbəl] *adj fml or hum* núbil.

nuclear ['njuːklɪər] *adj* nuclear.

nuclear bomb *n* bomba *f* atómica.

nuclear disarmament *n* desarme *m* nuclear.

nuclear energy *n* energía *f* nuclear.

nuclear family *n* familia *f* nuclear.

nuclear fission *n* fisión *f* nuclear.

nuclear-free zone *n* zona *f* libre de energía nuclear.

nuclear fusion *n* fusión *f* nuclear.

nuclear physics *n* física *f* nuclear.

nuclear power *n* energía *f* nuclear.

nuclear reactor *n* reactor *m* nuclear.

nuclear winter *n* invierno *m* nuclear.

nucleus ['njuːklɪəs] (*pl* **-lei** [-lɪaɪ]) *n lit* & *fig* núcleo *m.*

NUCPS (*abbr of* **National Union of Civil and Public Servants**) *n sindicato británico de funcionarios.*

nude [njuːd] ◇ *adj* desnudo(da). ◇ *n* ART desnudo *m;* **in the** ~ desnudo(da), en cueros.

nudge [nʌdʒ] ◇ *n* **-1.** [with elbow] codazo *m.* **-2.** *fig* [to encourage] empujón *m.* ◇ *vt* **-1.** [with elbow] dar un codazo a. **-2.** *fig* [to encourage] empujar, impulsar.

nudist ['njuːdɪst] ◇ *adj* nudista. ◇ *n* nudista *m y f.*

nudity ['njuːdətɪ] *n* desnudez *f.*

nugget ['nʌgɪt] *n* **-1.** [of gold] pepita *f.* **-2.** *fig* [valuable piece]: ~**s of wisdom** gotas *fpl* de sabiduría.

nuisance ['njuːsns] *n* [thing] fastidio *m,* molestia *f;* [person] pesado *m;* **to make a** ~ **of o.s.** dar la lata.

NUJ (*abbr of* **National Union of Journalists**) *n sindicato británico de periodistas.*

nuke [njuːk] *inf* ◇ *n* bomba *f* atómica. ◇ *vt* atacar con arma nuclear.

null [nʌl] *adj:* ~ **and void** nulo(la) y sin efecto.

nullify ['nʌlɪfaɪ] (*pt* & *pp* **-ied**) *vt* anular.

NUM (*abbr of* **National Union of Mineworkers**) *n sindicato británico de mineros.*

numb [nʌm] ◇ *adj* [gen] entumecido(da), insensible; [leg, hand] dormido(da); **to be** ~ **with cold** estar helado(da) de frío; **to be** ~ **with fear** estar paralizado(da) de miedo. ◇ *vt* entumecer.

number ['nʌmbər] ◇ *n* **-1.** [gen] número *m;* **a** ~ **of** varios(rias); **any** ~ **of** la mar de. **-2.** [of car] matrícula *f.* ◇ *vt* **-1.** [amount to] ascender a. **-2.** [give a number to] numerar. **-3.** [include]: **to be** ~**ed among** figurar entre.

number-crunching [-,krʌntʃɪŋ] *n inf* cálculo *m* a gran escala.

numberless ['nʌmbəlɪs] *adj* incontables, innumerables.

number one ◇ *adj* principal, número uno. ◇ *n* **-1.** [priority] lo más importante. **-2.** *inf* [oneself] uno mismo (una misma).

numberplate ['nʌmbəpleɪt] *n* matrícula *f* (de vehículo).

Number Ten *n* el número 10 de *Downing Street, residencia oficial del primer ministro británico.*

numbness ['nʌmnɪs] *n* **-1.** [with cold] entumecimiento *m*. **-2.** *fig* [with shock, fear] parálisis *f inv*.

numbskull ['nʌmskʌl] = **numskull**.

numeracy ['nju:mərəsɪ] *n Br* conocimiento *m* básico de aritmética.

numeral ['nju:mərəl] *n* número *m*, cifra *f*.

numerate ['nju:mərət] *adj Br* competente en aritmética.

numerical [nju:'merɪkl] *adj* numérico(ca).

numeric keypad [nju:'merɪk-] *n* COMPUT teclado *m* numérico.

numerous ['nju:mərəs] *adj* numeroso(sa).

numskull ['nʌmskʌl] *n inf* imbécil *m y f*, mentecato *m*, -ta *f*.

nun [nʌn] *n* monja *f*.

NUPE ['nju:pɪ] (*abbr of* **National Union of Public Employees**) *n antiguo sindicato británico que acogía principalmente a empleados de las administraciones locales.*

nuptial ['nʌpʃl] *adj fml* nupcial.

NURMTW (*abbr of* **National Union of Rail, Maritime and Transport Workers**) *n sindicato británico del sector de transporte.*

nurse ['nɜːs] ◇ *n* MED enfermero *m*, -ra *f*; [nanny] niñera *f*. ◇ *vt* **-1.** [care for] cuidar, atender. **-2.** [try to cure - a cold] curarse. **-3.** [nourish] abrigar. **-4.** [subj: mother] criar, amamantar.

nursemaid ['nɜːsmeɪd] *n* niñera *f*.

nursery ['nɜːsərɪ] (*pl* **-ies**) ◇ *adj* preescolar. ◇ *n* **-1.** [at home] cuarto *m* de los niños; [away from home] guardería *f*. **-2.** [for plants] semillero *m*, vivero *m*.

nursery nurse *n Br* [at school] niñera *f*; [in hospital] enfermera *f* puericultora.

nursery rhyme *n* poema *m* OR canción *f* infantil.

nursery school *n* parvulario *m*, escuela *f* de párvulos.

nursery slopes *npl* pista *f* para principiantes.

nursing ['nɜːsɪŋ] *n* [profession] profesión *f* de enfermero; [of patient] asistencia *f*, cuidado *m*.

nursing home *n* [for old people] clínica *f* de reposo (privada); [for childbirth] clínica *f* (privada) de maternidad.

nurture ['nɜːtʃər] *vt* **-1.** [child, plant] criar. **-2.** [plan, feelings] alimentar.

NUS (*abbr of* **National Union of Students**) *n sindicato nacional de estudiantes en Gran Bretaña.*

nut [nʌt] *n* **-1.** [to eat] nuez *f*. **-2.** [of metal] tuerca *f*; **the ~s and bolts** *fig* lo esencial, lo básico. **-3.** *inf* [mad person] chiflado *m*, -da *f*, loco *m*, -ca *f*. **-4.** *inf* [enthusiast] maniático *m*, -ca *f*. **-5.** *inf* [head]: **she's off her ~** *Br* está mal del coco.
◆ **nuts** *inf* ◇ *adj*: **to be ~s** estar chalado(da). ◇ *excl Am* ¡maldita sea!

NUT (*abbr of* **National Union of Teachers**) *n sindicato británico de profesores.*

nutcase ['nʌtkeɪs] *n inf* pirado *m*, -da *f*, loco *m*, -ca *f*.

nutcrackers ['nʌt,krækəz] *npl* cascanueces *m inv*.

nutmeg ['nʌtmeg] *n* nuez *f* moscada.

nutrient ['nju:trɪənt] *n* elemento *m* nutritivo.

nutrition [nju:'trɪʃn] *n* nutrición *f*, alimentación *f*.

nutritional [nju:'trɪʃənl] *adj* nutritivo(va).

nutritionist [nju:'trɪʃənɪst] *n* dietista *m y f*.

nutritious [nju:'trɪʃəs] *adj* nutritivo(va), rico(ca).

nutshell ['nʌtʃel] *n*: **in a ~** en una palabra.

nutter ['nʌtər] *n Br inf* chiflado *m*, -da *f*, loco *m*, -ca *f*.

nuzzle ['nʌzl] ◇ *vt* rozar con el hocico. ◇ *vi*: **to ~ (up) against** arrimarse a.

NV *abbr of* **Nevada**.

NW (*abbr of* **north-west**) NO.

NWT *abbr of* **Northwest Territories**.

NY *abbr of* **New York**.

NYC *abbr of* **New York City**.

nylon ['naɪlɒn] ◇ *n* nylon *m*. ◇ *comp* de nylon.
◆ **nylons** *npl dated* medias *fpl* de nylon.

nymph [nɪmf] *n* ninfa *f*.

nymphomaniac [,nɪmfə'meɪnɪæk] *n* ninfómana *f*.

NYSE (*abbr of* **New York Stock Exchange**) *n la Bolsa de Nueva York.*

NZ *abbr of* **New Zealand**.

o (*pl* **o's** OR **os**), **O** (*pl* **O's** OR **Os**) [əʊ] *n*
-1. [letter] o *f*, O *f*. **-2.** [zero] cero *m*.

oaf [əʊf] *n* zoquete *m* y *f*, lerdo *m*, **-da** *f*.

oak [əʊk] ⋄ *n* roble *m*. ⋄ *comp* de roble.

OAP *n abbr of* **old age pensioner.**

oar [ɔːʳ] *n* remo *m*; **to put** OR **stick one's** ~
in entrometerse.

oarlock ['ɔːlɒk] *n Am* [rowlock] escálamo *m*,
tolete *m*.

oarsman ['ɔːzmən] (*pl* **-men** [-mən]) *n* remero *m*.

oarswoman ['ɔːz,wʊmən] (*pl* **-women**
[-,wɪmɪn]) *n* remera *f*.

OAS (*abbr of* **Organization of American
States**) *n* OEA *f*.

oasis [əʊ'eɪsɪs] (*pl* **oases** [əʊ'eɪsiːz]) *n lit* &
fig oasis *m inv*.

oatcake ['əʊtkeɪk] *n* galleta *f* de avena.

oath [əʊθ] *n* **-1.** [promise] juramento *m*; **on**
OR **under** ~ bajo juramento. **-2.** [swearword]
palabrota *f*.

oatmeal ['əʊtmiːl] ⋄ *n* harina *f* de avena.
⋄ *comp* de avena.

oats [əʊts] *npl* [grain] avena *f*.

OAU (*abbr of* **Organization of African
Unity**) *n* OUA *f*.

OB *abbr of* **outside broadcast.**

obdurate ['ɒbdjʊrət] *adj fml* obstinado(da).

OBE (*abbr of* **Order of the British Empire**) *n*
(titular de) distinción honorífica británica.

obedience [ə'biːdjəns] *n:* ~ **(to sb)** obediencia *f* (a alguien).

obedient [ə'biːdjənt] *adj* obediente.

obediently [ə'biːdjəntlɪ] *adv* obedientemen-
te.

obelisk ['ɒbəlɪsk] *n* obelisco *m*.

obese [əʊ'biːs] *adj fml* obeso(sa).

obesity [əʊ'biːsətɪ] *n* obesidad *f*.

obey [ə'beɪ] *vt* & *vi* obedecer.

obfuscate ['ɒbfʌskeɪt] *vt fml* oscurecer.

obituary [ə'bɪtʃʊərɪ] (*pl* **-ies**) *n* nota *f* ne-
crológica, necrología *f*.

object [*n* 'ɒbdʒɪkt, *vb* ɒb'dʒekt] ⋄ *n* **-1.** [gen]
objeto *m*. **-2.** [aim] objeto *m*, propósito *m*.
-3. GRAMM complemento *m*. ⋄ *vt* objetar.

⋄ *vi:* **to** ~ **(to sthg/to doing sthg)** oponerse
(a algo/a hacer algo).

objection [əb'dʒekʃn] *n* objeción *f*, reparo
m; **to have no** ~ **(to sthg/to doing sthg)** no
tener inconveniente (en algo/en hacer
algo).

objectionable [əb'dʒekʃənəbl] *adj* [person]
desagradable; [behaviour] censurable.

objective [əb'dʒektɪv] ⋄ *adj* objetivo(va).
⋄ *n* objetivo *m*.

objectively [əb'dʒektɪvlɪ] *adv* objetivamen-
te.

objectivity [,ɒbdʒek'tɪvətɪ] *n* objetividad *f*.

object lesson ['ɒbdʒɪkt-] *n:* **an** ~ **in sthg** un
perfecto ejemplo de algo.

objector [əb'dʒektəʳ] *n* objetante *m* y *f*.

obligate ['ɒblɪgeɪt] *vt fml:* **to** ~ **sb to do
sthg** obligar a alguien a hacer algo.

obligation [,ɒblɪ'geɪʃn] *n* **-1.** [compulsion]
obligación *f*; **to be under an** ~ **to do sthg**
tener la obligación de hacer algo. **-2.** [duty]
deber *m*.

obligatory [ə'blɪgətrɪ] *adj* obligatorio(ria).

oblige [ə'blaɪdʒ] ⋄ *vt* **-1.** [force]: **to** ~ **sb to
do sthg** obligar a alguien a hacer algo. **-2.**
fml [do a favour to] hacer un favor a. ⋄ *vi*
hacer el favor.

obliging [ə'blaɪdʒɪŋ] *adj* servicial, aten-
to(ta).

oblique [ə'bliːk] ⋄ *adj* **-1.** [indirect - refer-
ence] indirecto(ta). **-2.** [slanting] obli-
cuo(cua). ⋄ *n* TYPO barra *f*.

obliquely [ə'bliːklɪ] *adv* indirectamente.

obliterate [ə'blɪtəreɪt] *vt* arrasar.

obliteration [ə,blɪtə'reɪʃn] *n* arrasamiento
m.

oblivion [ə'blɪvɪən] *n* olvido *m*.

oblivious [ə'blɪvɪəs] *adj* inconsciente; **to be**
~ **to** OR **of sthg** no ser consciente de algo.

oblong ['ɒblɒŋ] ⋄ *adj* rectangular, oblon-
go(ga). ⋄ *n* rectángulo *m*.

obnoxious [əb'nɒkʃəs] *adj* repugnante, detestable.

o.b.o. (*abbr of* **or best offer**) *o la mejor oferta.*

oboe ['əʊbəʊ] *n* oboe *m*.

oboist ['əʊbəʊɪst] *n* oboe *m*, oboísta *m* y *f*.

obscene [əb'siːn] *adj* obsceno(na), indecente.

obscenity [əb'senətɪ] (*pl* **-ies**) *n* obscenidad
f.

obscure [əb'skjʊəʳ] ⋄ *adj lit* & *fig* oscu-
ro(ra). ⋄ *vt* **-1.** [make difficult to understand]
oscurecer. **-2.** [hide] esconder.

obscurity [əb'skjʊərətɪ] *n lit* & *fig* oscuridad
f.

obsequious [əb'siːkwɪəs] *adj fml* & *pej* servil.

observable [əb'zɜːvəbl] *adj* visible, observable.

observably [əb'zɜːvəblɪ] *adv* visiblemente.

observance [əb'zɜːvəns] *n* observancia *f*, cumplimiento *m*.

observant [əb'zɜːvnt] *adj* observador(ra).

observation [ˌɒbzə'veɪʃn] *n* **-1.** [by police] vigilancia *f*; [by doctor] observación *f*. **-2.** [comment] observación *f*, comentario *m*.

observation post *n* puesto *m* de observación.

observatory [əb'zɜːvətrɪ] (*pl* **-ies**) *n* observatorio *m*.

observe [əb'zɜːv] *vt* **-1.** [gen] observar. **-2.** [obey] cumplir con, observar.

observer [əb'zɜːvəʳ] *n* observador *m*, -ra *f*.

obsess [əb'ses] *vt* obsesionar; **to be ~ed by** OR **with** estar obsesionado con.

obsession [əb'seʃn] *n* obsesión *f*, idea *f* fija.

obsessional [əb'seʃənl] *adj* obsesivo(va).

obsessive [əb'sesɪv] *adj* obsesivo(va).

obsolescence [ˌɒbsə'lesns] *n* obsolescencia *f*, caída *f* en desuso.

obsolescent [ˌɒbsə'lesnt] *adj* obsolescente, que está cayendo en desuso.

obsolete ['ɒbsəliːt] *adj* obsoleto(ta).

obstacle ['ɒbstəkl] *n* **-1.** [object] obstáculo *m*. **-2.** [difficulty] estorbo *m*, impedimento *m*.

obstacle race *n* carrera *f* de obstáculos.

obstetrician [ˌɒbstə'trɪʃn] *n* tocólogo *m*, -ga *f*, obstetra *m* y *f*.

obstetrics [ɒb'stetrɪks] *n* obstetricia *f*.

obstinacy ['ɒbstɪnəsɪ] *n* terquedad *f*, obstinación *f*.

obstinate ['ɒbstənət] *adj* **-1.** [stubborn] obstinado(da), terco(ca). **-2.** [persistent] tenaz.

obstinately ['ɒbstənətlɪ] *adv* obstinadamente, tercamente.

obstreperous [əb'strepərəs] *adj fml or hum* [unruly] desmandado(da).

obstruct [əb'strʌkt] *vt* **-1.** [block] obstruir, bloquear. **-2.** [hinder] estorbar, entorpecer.

obstruction [əb'strʌkʃn] *n* [gen] obstrucción *f*; [in road] obstáculo *m*.

obstructive [əb'strʌktɪv] *adj* obstructor(ra).

obtain [əb'teɪn] *vt* obtener, conseguir.

obtainable [əb'teɪnəbl] *adj* que se puede conseguir, asequible.

obtrusive [əb'truːsɪv] *adj* [smell] penetrante; [colour] chillón(ona); [person] entrometido(da).

obtrusively [əb'truːsɪvlɪ] *adv* entrometidamente, indiscretamente.

obtuse [əb'tjuːs] *adj lit* & *fig* obtuso(sa).

obverse ['ɒbvɜːs] *n* **-1.** [front side] anverso *m*. **-2.** [opposite]: **the ~ of** la otra cara de.

obviate ['ɒbvɪeɪt] *vt fml* evitar, obviar.

obvious ['ɒbvɪəs] ◇ *adj* obvio(via), evidente. ◇ *n*: **to state the ~** afirmar lo obvio OR lo evidente.

obviously ['ɒbvɪəslɪ] *adv* **-1.** [of course] evidentemente, obviamente; **~ not** claro que no. **-2.** [clearly] claramente, obviamente; **he's ~ lying** está claro que miente.

obviousness ['ɒbvɪəsnɪs] *n* obviedad *f*, lo evidente.

OCAS (*abbr of* **Organization of Central American States**) *n* ODECA *f*.

occasion [ə'keɪʒn] ◇ *n* **-1.** [time] vez *f*, ocasión *f*; **on one ~** una vez, en una ocasión; **on several ~s** varias veces, en varias ocasiones; **on ~** *fml* de vez en cuando. **-2.** [important event] acontecimiento *m*; **to rise to the ~** ponerse a la altura de las circunstancias. **-3.** *fml* [opportunity] ocasión *f*. ◇ *vt fml* [cause] ocasionar, causar.

occasional [ə'keɪʒənl] *adj* [trip, drink] poco frecuente, esporádico(ca); [showers] ocasional.

occasionally [ə'keɪʒnəlɪ] *adv* de vez en cuando.

occasional table *n* mesita *f* (auxiliar).

occluded front [ə'kluːdɪd-] *n* oclusión *f* METEOR.

occult [ɒ'kʌlt] ◇ *adj* oculto(ta). ◇ *n*: **the ~** lo oculto.

occupancy ['ɒkjʊpənsɪ] *n* ocupación *f*.

occupant ['ɒkjʊpənt] *n* **-1.** [of building, room] inquilino *m*, -na *f*. **-2.** [of chair, vehicle] ocupante *m* y *f*.

occupation [ˌɒkjʊ'peɪʃn] *n* **-1.** [job] empleo *m*, ocupación *f*. **-2.** [pastime] pasatiempo *m*. **-3.** MIL [of country, building] ocupación *f*.

occupational [ˌɒkjuː'peɪʃənl] *adj* laboral.

occupational hazard *n*: **~s** gajes *mpl* del oficio.

occupational therapist *n* terapeuta *m* y *f* ocupacional.

occupational therapy *n* terapia *f* ocupacional.

occupied ['ɒkjʊpaɪd] *adj* ocupado(da).

occupier ['ɒkjʊpaɪəʳ] *n* inquilino *m*, -na *f*.

occupy ['ɒkjʊpaɪ] (*pt* & *pp* **-ied**) *vt* **-1.** [gen] ocupar. **-2.** [live in] habitar. **-3.** [entertain]: **to ~ o.s.** entretenerse.

occur [ə'kɜːʳ] (*pt* & *pp* **-red**, *cont* **-ring**) *vi* **-1.** [happen] ocurrir, suceder. **-2.** [be present] encontrarse, existir. **-3.** [thought, idea]: **to ~ to sb** ocurrírsele a alguien; **it ~s to me that ...** se me ocurre que ....

occurrence [ə'kʌrəns] *n* **-1.** [event] acontecimiento *m*. **-2.** [coming about] existencia *f*, aparición *f*.

ocean ['əʊʃn] *n* océano *m*; *Am* [sea] mar *m* o *f*.

oceangoing ['əʊʃn,gəʊɪŋ] *adj* de alta mar.

Oceania [,əʊʃɪ'ɑːnɪə] *n* Oceanía.

Oceanian [,əʊʃɪ'ɑːnɪən] ◇ *adj* oceánico(ca). ◇ *n* oceánico *m*, -ca *f*.

ochre *Br*, **ocher** *Am* ['əʊkəʳ] *adj* ocre.

o'clock [ə'klɒk] *adv*: **it's one** ~ es la una; **it's two/three** ~ son las dos/las tres; **at one/two** ~ a la una/las dos.

OCR *n* COMPUT **-1.** (*abbr of* **optical character reader**) LOC *m*. **-2.** (*abbr of* **optical character recognition**) ROC *m*.

Oct. (*abbr of* **October**) oct.

octagon ['ɒktəgən] *n* octágono *m*.

octagonal [ɒk'tægənl] *adj* octagonal.

octane ['ɒkteɪn] *n* octano *m*.

octane number, **octane rating** *n* octanaje *m*.

octave ['ɒktɪv] *n* octava *f*.

octet [ɒk'tet] *n* octeto *m*.

October [ɒk'təʊbəʳ] *n* octubre *m*; *see also* **September**.

octogenarian [,ɒktəʊdʒɪ'neərɪən] *n* octogenario *m*, -ria *f*.

octopus ['ɒktəpəs] (*pl* **-puses** OR **-pi** [-paɪ]) *n* pulpo *m*.

OD -1. *abbr of* **overdose**. **-2.** *abbr of* **overdrawn**.

odd [ɒd] *adj* **-1.** [strange] raro(ra), extraño(ña). **-2.** [not part of pair] sin pareja, suelto(ta). **-3.** [number] impar. **-4.** *inf* [leftover] sobrante. **-5.** *inf* [occasional]: **I play the** ~ **game** juego alguna que otra vez. **-6.** *inf* [approximately]: **30** ~ **years** 30 y tantos OR y pico años.

◆ **odds** *npl* **-1. the** ~**s** [probability] las probabilidades; [in betting] las apuestas; **the** ~**s are that ...** lo más probable es que ...; **against all** ~**s** contra viento y marea; **against the** ~**s** contra (todo) pronóstico. **-2.** [bits]: ~**s and ends** chismes *mpl*, cosillas *fpl*. **-3.** *phr*: **to be at** ~**s with sthg** no concordar con algo; **to be at** ~**s with sb** estar reñido con alguien.

oddball ['ɒdbɔːl] *n inf* chiflado *m*, -da *f*, chalado *m*, -da *f*.

oddity ['ɒdɪtɪ] (*pl* **-ies**) *n* rareza *f*.

odd-job man *Br*, **odd jobber** *Am* *n* hombre *m* que hace chapuzas.

odd jobs *npl* chapuzas *fpl*.

oddly ['ɒdlɪ] *adv* extrañamente; ~ **enough** aunque parezca mentira.

oddments ['ɒdmənts] *npl* retales *mpl*.

odds-on ['ɒdz-] *adj inf*: **the** ~ **favourite** el favorito indiscutible; **it's** ~ **that ... fijo que** ....

ode [əʊd] *n* oda *f*.

odious ['əʊdjəs] *adj* odioso(sa), detestable.

odometer [əʊ'dɒmɪtəʳ] *n* cuentakilómetros *m inv*.

odorless *Am* = **odourless**.

odour *Br*, **odor** *Am* ['əʊdəʳ] *n* [gen] olor *m*; [of perfume] fragancia *f*.

odourless *Br*, **odorless** *Am* ['əʊdəlɪs] *adj* inodoro(ra).

odyssey ['ɒdɪsɪ] (*pl* **odysseys**) *n literary* odisea *f*.

OECD (*abbr of* **Organization for Economic Cooperation and Development**) *n* OCDE *f*.

oesophagus *Br*, **esophagus** *Am* [ɪ'sɒfəgəs] *n* esófago *m*.

oestrogen *Br*, **estrogen** *Am* [iːstrədʒən] *n* estrógeno *m*.

of [*unstressed* əv, *stressed* ɒv] *prep* **-1.** [gen] de; **the cover** ~ **a book** la portada de un libro; **the King** ~ **England** el rey de Inglaterra; **both** ~ **us** nosotros dos; **to die** ~ **sthg** morir de algo. **-2.** [expressing quantity, referring to container] de; **thousands** ~ **people** miles de personas; **a litre** ~ **petrol** un litro de gasolina; **a cup** ~ **coffee** un café, una taza de café. **-3.** [indicating amount, age, time] de; **a child** ~ **five** un niño de cinco (años); **an increase** ~ **6%** un incremento del 6%; **the 12th** ~ **February** el 12 de febrero; **the night** ~ **the disaster** la noche del desastre. **-4.** [made from] de; **a dress** ~ **silk** un vestido de seda; **to be made** ~ **sthg** estar hecho de algo. **-5.** [with emotions, opinions]: **fear** ~ **ghosts** miedo a los fantasmas; **love** ~ **good food** amor por la buena mesa; **it was very kind** ~ **you** fue muy amable de OR por tu parte.

off [ɒf] ◇ *adv* **-1.** [away]: **to drive** ~ alejarse conduciendo; **to turn** ~ **(the road)** salir de la carretera; **I'm** ~! ¡me voy! **-2.** [at a distance - in time] **it's two days** ~ quedan dos días; **that's a long time** ~ aún queda mucho para eso; [- in space] **it's ten miles** ~ está a diez millas; **far** ~ lejos. **-3.** [so as to remove]: **to take** ~ [gen] quitar; [one's clothes] quitarse; **to cut** ~ cortar; **could you help me** ~ **with my coat?** ¿me ayudas a quitarme el abrigo? **-4.** [so as to complete]: **to finish** ~ terminar, acabar; **to kill** ~ rematar. **-5.** [not at work] libre, de vacaciones; **a day** ~ un día libre; **time** ~ tiempo *m* libre. **-6.** [so as to separate]: **to fence** ~ vallar; **to wall** ~ tapiar. **-7.** [discounted]: **£10** ~ 10 libras de descuento. **-8.** [having money]: **to**

be well/badly ~ andar bien/mal de dinero. ◇ *prep* **-1.** [away from]: **to get ~ sthg** bajarse de algo; **to keep ~ sthg** mantenerse alejado de algo; "**keep ~ the grass**" "prohibido pisar el césped". **-2.** [close to]: **just ~ the coast** muy cerca de la costa; **it's ~ Oxford Street** está al lado de Oxford Street. **-3.** [removed from]: **to cut a slice ~ sthg** cortar un pedazo de algo; **take your hands ~ me!** ¡quítame las manos de encima! **-4.** [not attending]: **to be ~ work/duty** no estar trabajando/de servicio. **-5.** *inf* [no longer liking]: **she's ~ coffee/her food** no le apetece café/comer. **-6.** [deducted from]: **there's 10% ~ the price** hay un 10% de rebaja sobre el precio. **-7.** *inf* [from]: **I bought it ~ him** se lo compré a él.
◇ *adj* **-1.** [gone bad · meat, cheese] pasado(da), estropeado(da); [- milk] cortado(da). **-2.** [not operating] apagado(da). **-3.** [cancelled] suspendido(da). **-4.** *inf* [offhand] brusco(ca), descortés. **-5.** [not being served]: **ice cream's ~ today** no hay helado hoy.

offal ['ɒfl] *n* (*U*) asaduras *fpl*.

off-balance *adv* **-1.** [not standing firmly] en equilibrio precario; **to throw** OR **push sb ~** hacer perder el equilibrio a alguien. **-2.** [unprepared] desprevenido(da).

offbeat ['ɒfbiːt] *adj inf* original, poco convencional.

off-centre ◇ *adj* descentrado(da). ◇ *adv* a un lado, cerca del centro.

off-chance *n*: **on the ~** por si acaso.

off colour *adj* indispuesto(ta).

offcut ['ɒfkʌt] *n* [of fabric] retazo *m*; [of wood] trozo *m* suelto.

off-day *n inf* mal día *m*.

off duty *adj* fuera de servicio.

offence *Br*, **offense** *Am* [ə'fens] *n* **-1.** [crime] delito *m*. **-2.** [cause of upset] ofensa *f*; **to take ~** ofenderse.

offend [ə'fend] ◇ *vt* ofender. ◇ *vi* **-1.** [contravene]: **to ~ against sthg** infringir algo. **-2.** [commit a crime] cometer un delito.

offended [ə'fendɪd] *adj* ofendido(da).

offender [ə'fendər] *n* **-1.** [criminal] delincuente *m y f*. **-2.** [culprit] culpable *m y f*.

offending [ə'fendɪŋ] *adj* [object] enojoso(sa); [word, statement] ofensivo(va).

offense *Am* [*sense* 2 'ɒfens] *n* **-1.** = **offence**. **-2.** SPORT ataque *m*.

offensive [ə'fensɪv] ◇ *adj* **-1.** [remark, behaviour] ofensivo(va); [smell] repugnante. **-2.** [aggressive] atacante. ◇ *n* **-1.** MIL ofensiva *f*. **-2.** *fig* [attack]: **to go on** OR **take the ~** tomar la ofensiva.

offensiveness [ə'fensɪvnɪs] *n*: **the ~ of** lo ofensivo de.

offer ['ɒfər] ◇ *n* oferta *f*; **on ~** [available] disponible; [at a special price] en oferta. ◇ *vt* ofrecer; **to ~ sthg to sb, to ~ sb sthg** ofrecer algo a alguien; [be willing]: **to ~ to do sthg** ofrecerse a hacer algo. ◇ *vi* ofrecerse.

OFFER ['ɒfər] (*abbr of* Office of Electricity Regulation) *n organismo británico regulador de las compañías regionales de electricidad*.

offering ['ɒfərɪŋ] *n* **-1.** [thing offered] ofrecimiento *m*; [gift] regalo *m*. **-2.** [sacrifice] ofrenda *f*.

off-guard *adj* desprevenido(da).

offhand [ˌɒf'hænd] ◇ *adj* brusco(ca), descortés. ◇ *adv* de improviso.

office ['ɒfɪs] *n* **-1.** [gen] oficina *f*. **-2.** [room] despacho *m*, oficina *f*. **-3.** [position of authority] cargo *m*; **in ~** [political party] en el poder; [person] en el cargo; **to take ~** [political party] subir al poder; [person] asumir el cargo.

office automation *n* ofimática *f*.

office block *n* bloque *m* de oficinas.

office boy *n* chico *m* de los recados, ordenanza *m*.

officeholder ['ɒfɪsˌhəʊldər] *n* alto cargo *m* gubernamental.

office hours *npl* horas *fpl* de oficina.

office junior *n Br* subalterno *m*, -na *f*.

Office of Fair Trading *n organismo gubernamental regulador de la competencia en Gran Bretaña*.

officer ['ɒfɪsər] *n* **-1.** MIL oficial *m y f*. **-2.** [in organization] director *m*, -ra *f*. **-3.** [in police force] agente *m y f* de policía.

office work *n* trabajo *m* de oficina.

office worker *n* oficinista *m y f*.

official [ə'fɪʃl] ◇ *adj* oficial. ◇ *n* [of union] delegado *m*, -da *f*; [of government] funcionario *m*, -ria *f*.

officialdom [ə'fɪʃəldəm] *n* burocracia *f*.

officially [ə'fɪʃəlɪ] *adv* oficialmente.

official receiver *n* síndico *m*, depositario *m*, -ria *f* judicial.

officiate [ə'fɪʃɪeɪt] *vi*: **to ~ (at)** oficiar (en).

officious [ə'fɪʃəs] *adj pej que se excede en cumplir su deber*.

offing ['ɒfɪŋ] *n*: **to be in the ~** estar al caer OR a la vista.

off-key ◇ *adj* desafinado(da). ◇ *adv* desafinadamente.

off-licence *n Br tienda donde se venden bebidas alcohólicas para llevar*.

off limits *adj* prohibido(da).

off-line *adj* COMPUT desconectado(da).

offload [ɒf'ləʊd] *vt inf*: to ~ sthg onto sb echarle a alguien algo encima.

off-peak ◇ *adj* [electricity, phone call, travel] de tarifa reducida; [period] económico(ca). ◇ *adv* en las horas de tarifa reducida.

off-putting [-ˌpʊtɪŋ] *adj* repelente, chocante.

off sales *npl Br* venta de bebidas alcohólicas para llevar.

off season *n*: the ~ la temporada baja.
◆ **off-season** *adj* de temporada baja.

offset ['ɒfset] (*pt & pp* offset, *cont* -ting) *vt* compensar, contrarrestar.

offshoot ['ɒfʃuːt] *n* vástago *m*, retoño *m*.

offshore ['ɒfʃɔːr] ◇ *adj* [wind] costero(ra); [fishing] de bajura; [oil rig] marítimo(ma); [banking] en bancos extranjeros. ◇ *adv* mar adentro, cerca de la costa; **two miles** ~ a dos millas de la costa.

offside [*adj & adv* ˌɒf'saɪd, *n* 'ɒfsaɪd] ◇ *adj* **-1.** [part of vehicle - right-hand drive] izquierdo(da); [- left-hand drive] derecho(cha). **-2.** SPORT fuera de juego. ◇ *adv* SPORT fuera de juego. ◇ *n* [of vehicle - right-hand drive] lado *m* izquierdo; [- left-hand drive] lado *m* derecho.

offspring ['ɒfsprɪŋ] (*pl inv*) *n* **-1.** [of people - child] *fml or hum* descendiente *m y f*; [- children] descendencia *f*, prole *f*. **-2.** [of animals] crías *fpl*.

offstage [ˌɒf'steɪdʒ] *adj & adv* entre bastidores.

off-the-cuff ◇ *adj* improvisado(da). ◇ *adv* improvisadamente.

off-the-peg *adj Br* confeccionado(da).

off-the-record ◇ *adj* extraoficial, oficioso(sa). ◇ *adv* extraoficialmente, oficiosamente.

off-the-wall *adj* descabelado(da), extravagante.

off-white *adj* blancuzco(ca).

OFGAS ['ɒfgæs] (*abbr of* Office of Gas Supply) *n organismo británico regulador del suministro de gas.*

OFT *n abbr of* Office of Fair Trading.

OFTEL ['ɒftel] (*abbr of* Office of Telecommunications) *n organismo gubernamental británico para la supervisión de los servicios de telecomunicaciones.*

often ['ɒfn, 'ɒftn] *adv* [many times] a menudo, con frecuencia; **how** ~ **do you go?** ¿cada cuánto OR con qué frecuencia vas?; **I don't** ~ **see him** no lo veo mucho.
◆ **as often as** *adv* con frecuencia, muchas veces.
◆ **every so often** *adv* cada cierto tiempo.

◆ **more often than not** *adv* la mayoría de las veces.

OFWAT ['ɒfwɒt] (*abbr of* Office of Water Supply) *n organismo gubernamental británico para la supervisión del suministro de agua.*

ogle ['əʊgl] *vt pej* comerse con los ojos.

ogre ['əʊgər] *n* [in fairy tales] ogro *m*.

oh [əʊ] *excl* **-1.** [to introduce comment] ¡ah!; ~ **really?** ¿de verdad? **-2.** [expressing hesitation] mmm .... **-3.** [expressing joy, surprise, fear] ¡oh!; **oh no!** ¡no!

OH *abbr of* Ohio.

Ohio [əʊ'haɪəʊ] *n* Ohio.

ohm [əʊm] *n* ohmio *m*.

OHMS (*abbr of* On His/Her Majesty's Service) *expresión que indica el carácter oficial de un documento en Gran Bretaña.*

oil [ɔɪl] ◇ *n* **-1.** [gen] aceite *m*. **-2.** [petroleum] petróleo *m*. ◇ *vt* engrasar, lubricar.
◆ **oils** *npl* ART: **to paint in** ~**s** pintar al óleo.

oilcan ['ɔɪlkæn] *n* aceitera *f*.

oil change *n* cambio *m* de aceite.

oilcloth ['ɔɪlklɒθ] *n* hule *m*.

oilfield ['ɔɪlfiːld] *n* yacimiento *m* petrolífero.

oil filter *n* filtro *m* del aceite.

oil-fired [-ˌfaɪəd] *adj* de fuel-oil.

oil industry *n*: the ~ la industria petrolífera.

oilman ['ɔɪlmən] (*pl* -men [-mən]) *n* [businessman] magnate *m* del petróleo; [worker] trabajador *m* (del sector) petrolero.

oil paint *n* pintura *f* al óleo.

oil painting *n* (pintura *f* al) óleo *m*.

oilrig ['ɔɪlrɪg] *n* plataforma *f* petrolífera.

oilskins ['ɔɪlskɪnz] *npl* [gen] prenda *f* de hule; [coat] impermeable *m*, chubasquero *m*.

oil slick *n* marea *f* negra.

oil tanker *n* **-1.** [ship] petrolero *m*. **-2.** [lorry] camión *m* cisterna.

oil well *n* pozo *m* petrolífero OR de petróleo.

oily ['ɔɪlɪ] (*compar* -ier, *superl* -iest) *adj* **-1.** [food] aceitoso(sa); [rag, cloth] grasiento(ta). **-2.** *pej* [smarmy] pegajoso(sa), empalagoso(sa).

ointment ['ɔɪntmənt] *n* pomada *f*, ungüento *m*.

oiro (*abbr of* offers in the region of): ~ £100 ofertas en torno a las 100 libras.

OK¹ (*pl* OKs, *pt & pp* OKed, *cont* OKing), **okay** [ˌəʊ'keɪ] *inf* ◇ *adj*: **is it** ~ **with you?** ¿te parece bien? ◇ *n*: **to give (sb) the** ~ dar el visto bueno (a alguien). ◇ *excl* **-1.** [gen]

vale, de acuerdo. **-2.** [to introduce new topic] bien, vale. ◇ *vt* aprobar, dar el visto bueno a.

OK² *abbr of* **Oklahoma**.

Oklahoma [,əʊkləˈhəʊmə] *n* Oklahoma.

okra [ˈəʊkrə] *n* quingombó *m*.

old [əʊld] ◇ *adj* **-1.** [gen] viejo(ja); **how ~ are you?** ¿cuántos años tienes?, ¿qué edad tienes?; **I'm 20 years ~** tengo 20 años. **-2.** [former] antiguo(gua); **in the ~ days** antiguamente, en el pasado. **-3.** *inf* [as intensifier]: **any ~ thing** cualquier cosa. ◇ *npl*: **the ~** los ancianos.

old age *n* vejez *f*.

old age pension *n Br* jubilación *f*, pensión *f*.

old age pensioner *n Br* pensionista *m* y *f*, jubilado *m*, -da *f*.

Old Bailey [-ˈbeɪlɪ] *n*: **the ~** *juzgado criminal central de Inglaterra*.

olden [ˈəʊldn] *adj*: **in the ~ days** antaño.

old-fashioned [ˈfæʃnd] *adj* **-1.** [outmoded] pasado(da) de moda, anticuado(da). **-2.** [traditional] anticuado(da), tradicional.

old flame *n* antiguo amor *m*.

old hat *adj inf pej*: **to be ~** ser pasado(da) de moda OR anticuado(da).

old maid *n pej* [spinster] solterona *f*.

old master *n* **-1.** [painter] antiguo maestro *m* de la pintura. **-2.** [painting] antigua obra *f* maestra de la pintura.

old people's home *n* residencia *f* OR hogar *m* de ancianos.

Old Testament *n*: **the ~** el Antiguo Testamento.

old-time *adj* de antaño, antiguo(gua).

old-timer *n* **-1.** [veteran] veterano *m*, -na *f*. **-2.** [old man] viejo *m*, -ja *f*.

old wives' tale *n* cuento *m* de viejas.

Old World *n*: **the ~** el Viejo Mundo, el mundo antiguo.

O level *n Br* ≃ Bachillerato *m*, ≃ BUP *m*.

oligarchy [ˈɒlɪgɑːkɪ] (*pl* **-ies**) *n* oligarquía *f*.

olive [ˈɒlɪv] ◇ *adj* verde oliva. ◇ *n* [fruit] aceituna *f*, oliva *f*; **~ (tree)** olivo *m*.

olive green *adj* verde oliva.

olive oil *n* aceite *m* de oliva.

Olympic [əˈlɪmpɪk] *adj* olímpico(ca).
◆ **Olympics** *npl*: **the ~s** los Juegos Olímpicos.

Olympic Games *npl*: **the ~** los Juegos Olímpicos.

OM (*abbr of* **Order of Merit**) *n* (*titular de*) *distinción honorífica británica*.

O & M (*abbr of* **organisation and method**) *n organización y método*.

Oman [əʊˈmɑːn] *n* Omán.

OMB (*abbr of* **Office of Management and Budget**) *n organismo estadounidense de asesoramiento al presidente en materia presupuestaria*.

ombudsman [ˈɒmbʊdzmən] (*pl* **-men** [-mən]) *n* ≃ Defensor *m* del Pueblo.

omelet(te) [ˈɒmlɪt] *n* tortilla *f*.

omen [ˈəʊmen] *n* presagio *m*, agüero *m*.

ominous [ˈɒmɪnəs] *adj* siniestro(tra), de mal agüero.

ominously [ˈɒmɪnəslɪ] *adv* siniestramente, amenazadoramente.

omission [əˈmɪʃn] *n* **-1.** [thing left out] olvido *m*, descuido *m*. **-2.** [act of omitting] omisión *f*.

omit [əˈmɪt] (*pt* & *pp* **-ted**, *cont* **-ting**) *vt* omitir; [name - from list] pasar por alto; **to ~ to do sthg** olvidar hacer algo.

omnibus [ˈɒmnɪbəs] *n* **-1.** [book] antología *f*. **-2.** *Br* RADIO & TV *programa que emite varios capítulos seguidos*.

omnipotence [ɒmˈnɪpətəns] *n fml* omnipotencia *f*.

omnipotent [ɒmˈnɪpətənt] *adj fml* omnipotente.

omnipresent [,ɒmnɪˈprezənt] *adj fml* omnipresente.

omniscient [ɒmˈnɪsɪənt] *adj fml* omnisciente.

omnivorous [ɒmˈnɪvərəs] *adj* omnívoro(ra).

on [ɒn] ◇ *prep* **-1.** [indicating position - gen] en; [- on top of] sobre, en; **~ a chair** en OR sobre una silla; **~ the wall/ground** en la pared/el suelo; **to stand ~ one leg** ponerse a la pata coja; **he was lying ~ his side/back** estaba tumbado de costado/de espaldas; **she had a strange look ~ her face** su rostro tenía un extraño aspecto; **~ the left/right** la izquierda/derecha; **I haven't got any money ~ me** no llevo nada de dinero encima. **-2.** [indicating means]: **it runs ~ diesel** funciona con diesel; **~ TV/the radio** en la tele/la radio; **she's ~ the telephone** está al teléfono; **he lives ~ fruit** vive (a base) de fruta; **to hurt o.s. ~ sthg** hacerse daño con algo. **-3.** [indicating mode of transport]: **to travel ~ a bus/train/ship** viajar en autobús/tren/barco; **I was ~ the bus** iba en el autobús; **to get ~ a bus/train/ship** subirse a un autobús/tren/barco; **~ foot** a pie. **-4.** [indicating time, activity]: **~ Thursday** el jueves; **~ my birthday** el día de mi cumpleaños; **~ the 10th of February** el 10 de febrero; **~ my return**, **~ returning** al volver; **~ business/holiday** de negocios/vacaciones; **~ nightshift** en turno de noche. **-5.** [concerning] sobre, acerca de; **a book ~ astronomy** un libro acerca de OR sobre astrono-

mía. **-6.** [indicating membership]: **to be ~ a committee** estar en un comité. **-7.** [indicating influence] en, sobre; **the impact ~ the environment** el impacto en OR sobre el medio ambiente. **-8.** [using, supported by]: **to be ~ social security** cobrar dinero de la seguridad social; **he's ~ tranquillizers** está tomando tranquilizantes; **to be ~ drugs** [addicted] drogarse. **-9.** [earning]: **she's ~ £25,000 a year** gana 25.000 libras al año; **to be ~ a low income** tener bajos ingresos. **-10.** [obtained from]: **interest ~ investments** intereses de OR por inversiones; **a tax ~ alcohol** un impuesto sobre el alcohol. **-11.** [referring to musical instrument] con; **~ the violin** con el violín; **~ the piano** al piano. **-12.** *inf* [paid by]: **the drinks are ~ me** yo pago las copas, a las copas invito yo.
◇ *adv* **-1.** [indicating covering, clothing]: **put the lid ~** pon la tapa; **what did she have ~?** ¿qué llevaba encima OR puesto?; **put your coat ~** ponte el abrigo. **-2.** [taking place]: **when the war was ~** cuando la guerra. **-3.** [being shown]: **what's ~ at the cinema?** ¿qué echan OR ponen en el cine? **-4.** [working - machine] funcionando; [- radio. TV, light] encendido(da); [- tap] abierto(ta); [- brakes] puesto(ta); **turn ~ the power** pulse el botón de encendido. **-5.** [indicating continuing action]: **we talked/worked ~ into the night** seguimos hablando/trabajando hasta bien entrada la noche; **he kept ~ walking** siguió caminando. **-6.** [forward]: **send my mail ~ (to me)** reenvíame el correo; **later ~** más tarde, después; **earlier ~** con anterioridad, antes. **-7.** [of transport]: **the train stopped and we all got ~** paró el tren y todos nos subimos. **-8.** *inf* [referring to behaviour]: **it's just not ~!** ¡es una pasada! **-9.** *inf*: **to be** OR **go ~ at sb (to do sthg)** darle la tabarra a alguien (para que haga algo).
◆ **from ... on** *adv*: **from now ~** de ahora en adelante; **from that moment/time ~** desde aquel momento/aquella vez.
◆ **on about** *adv inf*: **to go ~ about sthg** dar la tabarra con algo.
◆ **on and on** *adv*: **to go ~ and ~** seguir sin parar; **she chattered ~ and ~** no paraba de charlar.
◆ **on and off** *adv* de vez en cuando.
◆ **on to, onto** *prep* (*only written as* **onto** *for senses* 4 *and* 5) **-1.** [to a position on top of] encima de, sobre; **she jumped ~ to the chair** salto encima de OR sobre la silla. **-2.** [to a position on a vehicle]: **to get ~ to a bus/train/plane** subirse a un autobús/tren/avión. **-3.** [to a position attached to]: **stick the photo ~ to the page** pega la foto a la hoja. **-4.** [aware of wrongdoing]: **to be onto**

sb andar detrás de alguien. **-5.** [into contact with]: **get onto the factory** ponte en contacto con la fábrica.

ON *abbr of* **Ontario**.

ONC (*abbr of* **Ordinary National Certificate**) *n* titulación técnica de enseñanza secundaria en Gran Bretaña.

once [wʌns] ◇ *adv* **-1.** [on one occasion] una vez; **~ a week** una vez a la semana; **~ again** OR **more** otra vez; **for ~** por una vez; **~ and for all** de una vez por todas; **~ or twice** alguna que otra vez; **~ in a while** de vez en cuando. **-2.** [previously] en otro tiempo, antiguamente; **~ upon a time** érase una vez. ◇ *conj* una vez que; **~ you have done it** una vez que lo hayas hecho.
◆ **at once** *adv* **-1.** [immediately] en seguida, inmediatamente. **-2.** [at the same time] a la vez, al mismo tiempo; **all at ~** de repente, de golpe.

once-over *n inf*: **to give sthg the ~** echar un vistazo a algo.

oncoming ['ɒn,kʌmɪŋ] *adj* [traffic] que viene en dirección contraria; [danger, event] venidero(ra).

OND (*abbr of* **Ordinary National Diploma**) *n* titulación superior que se obtiene tras dos años de formación técnica en Gran Bretaña.

one [wʌn] ◇ *num* [the number 1] un (una); **I only want ~** sólo quiero uno; **~ hundred** cien; **~ thousand** mil; **~ fifth** un quinto, una quinta parte; **~ of my friends** uno de mis amigos; **on page a hundred and ~** en la página ciento uno; **(number) ~** el uno; **to arrive in ~s and twos** llegar poco a poco OR con cuentagotas.
◇ *adj* **-1.** [only] único(ca); **it's her ~ ambition** es su única ambición. **-2.** [indefinite]: **~ day we went to Athens** un día fuimos a Atenas; **~ of these days** uno de éstos. **-3.** *inf* [a]: **~ hell of a bang/racket** una explosión/un jaleo de la leche.
◇ *pron* **-1.** [referring to a particular thing or person] uno (una); **I want the red ~** yo quiero el rojo; **the ~ with the blond hair** la del pelo rubio; **which ~ do you want?** ¿cuál quieres?; **this ~** éste (ésta); **that ~** ése (ésa); **she's the ~ I told you about** es (ésa) de la que te hablé; **I'm not** OR **I've never been ~ to gossip but ...** yo no soy de ésos que van por ahí cotilleando, pero .... **-2.** *fml* [you, anyone] uno (una); **to do ~'s duty** cumplir uno con su deber. **-3.** *inf* [blow] tortazo *m*, galleta *f*; **she really thumped him ~** le dio un galletón que no veas.
◆ **at one** *adv*: **to be at ~ with** estar completamente de acuerdo con.

◆ **for one** *adv* por lo menos, por mi/tu *etc* parte; **I for ~ remain unconvinced** yo, por lo menos OR por mi parte, sigo poco convencido.

◆ **one up on** *adv*: **to be** OR **have ~ up on sb** aventajar a alguien.

one-armed bandit *n* (máquina *f*) tragaperras *f inv*.

one-liner *n* chiste *m* breve.

one-man *adj* individual, en solitario.

one-man band *n* **-1.** [musician] hombre *m* orquesta. **-2.** [business, operation] aventura *f* en solitario.

oneness ['wʌnnɪs] *n* (*U*) unidad *f*.

one-night stand *n* **-1.** [performance] representación *f* única. **-2.** *inf* [sexual relationship] ligue *m* de una noche.

one-off *inf* ◇ *adj* único(ca). ◇ *n* caso *m* excepcional.

one-on-one *Am* = one-to-one.

one-parent family *n* familia *f* monoparental.

one-piece *adj* de una pieza.

onerous ['əʊnərəs] *adj* oneroso(sa), pesado(da).

oneself [wʌn'self] *pron* **-1.** (*reflexive, after prep*) uno mismo (una misma); **to buy presents for ~** hacerse regalos a sí mismo. **-2.** (*for emphasis*): **by ~** [without help] solo(la).

one-sided [-'saɪdɪd] *adj* **-1.** [unequal] desigual. **-2.** [biased] parcial.

onetime ['wʌntaɪm] *adj* [former] antiguo(gua).

one-to-one *Br*, **one-on-one** *Am adj* [relationship, discussion] entre dos; [tuition] individual.

one-upmanship [,wʌn'ʌpmənʃɪp] *n habilidad para ganar ventaja sin hacer trampas*.

one-way *adj* **-1.** [street] de dirección única, de sentido único. **-2.** [ticket] de ida.

ongoing ['ɒn,gəʊɪŋ] *adj* actual, en curso.

onion ['ʌnjən] *n* cebolla *f*.

online ['ɒnlaɪn] *adj & adv* COMPUT en línea.

onlooker ['ɒn,lʊkə‍ʳ] *n* espectador *m*, -ra *f*.

only ['əʊnlɪ] ◇ *adj* único(ca); **an ~ child** hijo único. ◇ *adv* [exclusively] sólo, solamente; **I was ~ too willing to help** estaba encantado de poder ayudar; **I ~ wish I could!** ¡ojalá pudiera!; **it's ~ natural** es completamente normal; **not ~ ... but** no sólo ... sino; **~ just** apenas. ◇ *conj* sólo OR solamente que; **I would go, ~ I'm too tired** iría, lo que pasa es que estoy muy cansado.

o.n.o., **ono** (*abbr of* **or near(est) offer**) *o la oferta más cercana a dicha cantidad*.

onrush ['ɒnrʌʃ] *n* avalancha *f*.

on-screen *adj & adv* COMPUT en pantalla.

onset ['ɒnset] *n* comienzo *m*.

onshore ['ɒnʃɔːʳ] ◇ *adj* [wind] procedente del mar; [oil production] en tierra firme. ◇ *adv* [blow] hacia la tierra; [produce oil] en tierra firme.

onside [ɒn'saɪd] *adj & adv* SPORT en posición legal OR correcta.

onslaught ['ɒnslɔːt] *n lit & fig* acometida *f*, embestida *f*.

Ont. *abbr of* **Ontario**.

Ontario [ɒn'teərɪəʊ] *n* Ontario.

on-the-job *adj* en el trabajo, práctico(ca).

on-the-spot *adj* en el acto.

onto ['ɒntuː] = **on to**.

onus ['əʊnəs] *n* responsabilidad *f*; **the ~ is on you** en tí recae la responsabilidad.

onward ['ɒnwəd] ◇ *adj* [in time] progresivo(va); [in space] hacia delante. ◇ *adv* = onwards.

onwards ['ɒnwədz] *adv* [in space] adelante, hacia delante; [in time]: **from now/then ~** de ahora/allí en adelante.

onyx ['ɒnɪks] *n* ónice *m*.

oodles ['uːdlz] *npl inf* montones *mpl*.

oof [ʊf] *excl inf* ¡ay!

ooh [uː] *excl inf* ¡oh!

oops [ʊps, uːps] *excl inf* ¡uy!, ¡ay!

ooze [uːz] ◇ *vt fig* rebosar. ◇ *vi*: **to ~ (from** OR **out of)** rezumar (de); **to ~ with sthg** *fig* rebosar OR irradiar algo. ◇ *n* cieno *m*.

opacity [ə'pæsətɪ] *n* **-1.** [non-transparency] opacidad *f*. **-2.** *fig* [obscurity] obscuridad *f*.

opal ['əʊpl] *n* ópalo *m*.

opaque [əʊ'peɪk] *adj* **-1.** [not transparent] opaco(ca). **-2.** *fig* [obscure] oscuro(ra).

OPEC ['əʊpek] (*abbr of* **Organization of Petroleum Exporting Countries**) *n* OPEP *f*.

open ['əʊpn] ◇ *adj* **-1.** [gen] abierto(ta); [curtains] descorrido(da); [view, road] despejado(da). **-2.** [receptive]: **to be ~ to** [ideas, suggestions] estar abierto a; [blame, criticism, question] prestarse a; **to lay o.s. ~ to criticism** quedar expuesto a las críticas. **-3.** [frank] sincero(ra), franco(ca). **-4.** [uncovered - car] descubierto(ta); **~ fire** chimenea *f*. **-5.** [available - subj: choice, chance]: **to be ~ to sb** estar disponible para alguien. ◇ *n*: **in the ~** [fresh air] al aire libre; **to bring sthg out into the ~** sacar a luz algo. ◇ *vt* **-1.** [gen] abrir; **to ~ fire** abrir fuego. **-2.** [inaugurate - public area, event] inaugurar. ◇ *vi* **-1.** [door, flower] abrirse. **-2.** [shop, office] abrir. **-3.** [event, play] dar comienzo.

◆ **open on to** *vt fus* dar a.

◆ **open out** *vi* extenderse.

◆ **open up** ◇ *vt sep* abrir. ◇ *vi* **-1.** [become available] surgir. **-2.** [unlock door] abrir.

open-air *adj* al aire libre.

open-and-shut *adj* obvio(via).

opencast ['əʊpnkɑːst] *adj* a cielo abierto.

open day *n* día en que un colegio, universidad etc puede ser visitado por cualquiera.

open-ended [-'endɪd] *adj* abierto(ta).

opener ['əʊpnə'] *n* abridor *m*; [for tins] abrelatas *m inv*; [for bottles] abrebotellas *m inv*.

open-handed [-'hændɪd] *adj* generoso(sa).

openhearted [ˌəʊpn'hɑːtɪd] *adj* franco(ca), sincero(ra).

open-heart surgery *n* cirugía *f* a corazón abierto.

opening ['əʊpnɪŋ] ◇ *adj* inicial. ◇ *n* **-1.** [beginning] comienzo *m*, principio *m*. **-2.** [gap - in fence] abertura *f*; [- in clouds] claro *m*. **-3.** [opportunity] oportunidad *f*, ocasión *f*; ~ **for** oportunidad para. **-4.** [job vacancy] puesto *m* vacante.

opening hours *npl* horario *m* (de apertura).

opening night *n* noche *f* del estreno.

opening time *n Br* hora *f* de abrir.

open letter *n* carta *f* abierta.

openly ['əʊpənlɪ] *adv* abiertamente.

open market *n* mercado *m* abierto.

open marriage *n* matrimonio *m* abierto, pareja *f* abierta.

open-minded [-'maɪndɪd] *adj* sin prejuicios.

open-mouthed [-'maʊðd] ◇ *adj* boquiabierto(ta). ◇ *adv*: **to look** ~ mirar boquiabierto(ta).

open-necked [-'nekt] *adj* con el cuello abierto.

openness ['əʊpənnɪs] *n* [frankness] franqueza *f*.

open-plan *adj* de plan abierto, sin tabiques.

open prison *n* prisión *f* de régimen abierto.

open sandwich *n* bocadillo con sólo un trozo de pan.

open season *n* temporada *f* (abierta).

open shop *n* lugar de trabajo donde los empleados no necesitan pertenecer a un sindicato obrero.

Open University *n Br*: **the** ~ ≃ la Universidad Nacional de Educación a Distancia.

open verdict *n JUR* fallo en que no se da la causa de la muerte.

opera ['ɒpərə] *n* ópera *f*.

opera glasses *npl* gemelos *mpl* (de teatro).

opera house *n* teatro *m* de la ópera.

opera singer *n* cantante *m y f* de ópera.

operate ['ɒpəreɪt] ◇ *vt* **-1.** [machine] hacer funcionar. **-2.** [business, system] dirigir. ◇ *vi* **-1.** [carry out trade, business] operar, actuar. **-2.** [function] funcionar. **-3.** MED: **to** ~ **(on sb/sthg)** operar (a alguien/de algo).

operatic [ˌɒpə'rætɪk] *adj* de ópera, operístico(ca).

operating room ['ɒpəreɪtɪŋ-] *Am* = operating theatre.

operating system ['ɒpəreɪtɪŋ-] *n* COMPUT sistema *m* operativo.

operating theatre ['ɒpəreɪtɪŋ-] *Br*, **operating room** ['ɒpəreɪtɪŋ-] *Am n* quirófano *m*, sala *f* de operaciones.

operation [ˌɒpə'reɪʃn] *n* **-1.** [planned activity - police, rescue, business] operación *f*; [- military] maniobra *f*. **-2.** [running - of business] administración *f*. **-3.** [functioning - of machine] funcionamiento *m*; **to be in** ~ [machine] funcionar; [law, system] estar en vigor. **-4.** MED operación *f*, intervención *f* quirúrgica; **to have an** ~ **(for/on)** operarse (de).

operational [ˌɒpə'reɪʃənl] *adj* **-1.** [ready for use] operacional, en estado de funcionamiento. **-2.** [concerning an operation] de operaciones.

operative ['ɒprətɪv] ◇ *adj* en vigor, vigente. ◇ *n* operario *m*, -ria *f*.

operator ['ɒpəreɪtə'] *n* **-1.** TELEC operador *m*, -ra *f*, telefonista *m y f*. **-2.** [employee] operario *m*, -ria *f*. **-3.** [person in charge - of business] encargado *m*, -da *f*.

operetta [ˌɒpə'retə] *n* opereta *f*.

ophthalmic optician [ɒfˈθælmɪk-] *n* óptico *m*, -ca *f*, oculista *m y f*.

ophthalmologist [ˌɒfθæl'mɒlədʒɪst] *n* oftalmólogo *m*, -ga *f*, oculista *m y f*.

opinion [ə'pɪnjən] *n* opinión *f*; **to be of the** ~ **that** opinar OR creer que; **in my** ~ a mi juicio, en mi opinión.

opinionated [ə'pɪnjəneɪtɪd] *adj pej* terco(ca).

opinion poll *n* sondeo *m*, encuesta *f*.

opium ['əʊpjəm] *n* opio *m*.

opponent [ə'pəʊnənt] *n* **-1.** POL adversario *m*, -ria *f*. **-2.** SPORT contrincante *m y f*, adversario *m*, -ria *f*.

opportune ['ɒpətjuːn] *adj* oportuno(na).

opportunism [ˌɒpə'tjuːnɪzm] *n* oportunismo *m*.

opportunist [ˌɒpə'tjuːnɪst] *n* oportunista *m y f*.

opportunity [ˌɒpə'tjuːnətɪ] (*pl* **-ies**) *n* oportunidad *f*, ocasión *f*, chance *f Amer*; **to take**

the ~ to do OR of doing sthg aprovechar la ocasión de OR para hacer algo.

oppose [ə'pəʊz] *vt* oponerse a.

opposed [ə'pəʊzd] *adj* opuesto(ta); **to be ~ to** oponerse a; **as ~ to** en vez de, en lugar de; **I like beer as ~ to wine** me gusta la cerveza y no el vino.

opposing [ə'pəʊzɪŋ] *adj* opuesto(ta), contrario(ria).

opposite ['ɒpəzɪt] ⋄ *adj* **-1.** [facing - side, house] de enfrente. **-2.** [very different]: ~ **(to)** opuesto(ta) OR contrario(ria) (a). ⋄ *adv* enfrente. ⋄ *prep* enfrente de. ⋄ *n* contrario *m*; **Janet and John are complete ~s** Janet y John son totalmente diferentes.

opposite number *n* homólogo *m*, -ga *f*, equivalente *m* y *f*.

opposite sex *n*: **the ~** el sexo opuesto.

opposition [ˌɒpə'zɪʃn] *n* **-1.** [gen] oposición *f*. **-2.** [opposing team] oponentes *mpl* y *fpl*.

◆ **Opposition** *n Br* POL: **the Opposition** la oposición.

oppress [ə'pres] *vt* **-1.** [persecute] oprimir. **-2.** [depress] agobiar, deprimir.

oppressed [ə'prest] ⋄ *adj* oprimido(da). ⋄ *npl*: **the ~** los oprimidos.

oppression [ə'preʃn] *n* opresión *f*.

oppressive [ə'presɪv] *adj* **-1.** [unjust] tiránico(ca), opresivo(va). **-2.** [stifling] agobiante, sofocante. **-3.** [causing unease] opresivo(va), agobiante.

oppressor [ə'presər] *n* opresor *m*, -ra *f*.

opprobrium [ə'prəʊbrɪəm] *n fml* oprobio *m*.

opt [ɒpt] ⋄ *vt*: **to ~ to do sthg** optar por OR elegir hacer algo. ⋄ *vi*: **to ~ for sthg** optar por OR elegir algo.

◆ **opt in** *vi*: **to ~ in (to sthg)** optar por participar (en algo).

◆ **opt out** *vi*: **to ~ out (of sthg)** decidir no tomar parte (en algo).

optic ['ɒptɪk] *adj* óptico(ca).

optical ['ɒptɪkl] *adj* óptico(ca).

optical character reader *n* COMPUT lector *m* óptico de caracteres.

optical character recognition *n* COMPUT reconocimiento *m* óptico de caracteres.

optical fibre *n* fibra *f* óptica.

optical illusion *n* ilusión *f* óptica.

optician [ɒp'tɪʃn] *n* óptico *m*, -ca *f*; ~**'s (shop)** óptica *f*.

optics ['ɒptɪks] *n* (U) óptica *f*.

optimism ['ɒptɪmɪzm] *n* optimismo *m*.

optimist ['ɒptɪmɪst] *n* optimista *m* y *f*.

optimistic [ˌɒptɪ'mɪstɪk] *adj* optimista; **to be ~ about** ser optimista respecto a.

optimize, -ise ['ɒptɪmaɪz] *vt* optimizar.

optimum ['ɒptɪməm] *adj* óptimo(ma).

option ['ɒpʃn] *n* opción *f*; **to have the ~ to do** OR **of doing sthg** tener la opción OR la posibilidad de hacer algo.

optional ['ɒpʃənl] *adj* facultativo(va), optativo(va); ~ **extra** extra *m* opcional.

opulence ['ɒpjʊləns] *n* opulencia *f*.

opulent ['ɒpjʊlənt] *adj* opulento(ta).

opus ['əʊpəs] (*pl* **-es** OR **opera**) *n* MUS opus *m inv*, obra *f*.

or [ɔːr] *conj* **-1.** [gen] o (*before "o" or "ho"*) u; ~ **(else)** o de lo contrario, si no; **he must be okay** ~ **he wouldn't be eating** debe estar bien, si no no comería. **-2.** (*after negative*): **he cannot read** ~ **write** no sabe ni leer ni escribir.

OR *abbr of* **Oregon**.

oracle ['ɒrəkl] *n* oráculo *m*.

oral ['ɔːrəl] ⋄ *adj* **-1.** [spoken] oral. **-2.** [relating to the mouth] bucal. ⋄ *n* examen *m* oral.

orally ['ɔːrəlɪ] *adv* **-1.** [in spoken form] oralmente. **-2.** [via the mouth] por vía oral.

orange ['ɒrɪndʒ] ⋄ *adj* naranja *inv*. ⋄ *n* **-1.** [fruit] naranja *f*; ~ **tree** naranjo *m*. **-2.** [colour] color *m* naranja.

orangeade [ˌɒrɪndʒ'eɪd] *n* naranjada *f*.

orange blossom *n* (U) azahar *m*.

Orangeman ['ɒrɪndʒmən] (*pl* **-men** [-mən]) *n Br* orangista *m*.

orangutang [ɔːˌræŋuː'tæŋ] *n* orangután *m*.

oration [ɔː'reɪʃn] *n fml* discurso *m*.

orator ['ɒrətər] *n* orador *m*, -ra *f*.

oratorio [ˌɒrə'tɔːrɪəʊ] (*pl* **-s**) *n* oratorio *m*.

oratory ['ɒrətrɪ] *n* oratoria *f*.

orb [ɔːb] *n* esfera *f*.

orbit ['ɔːbɪt] ⋄ *n* órbita *f*; **to be in/go into** ~ **(around)** estar/entrar en órbita (alrededor de); **to put sthg into** ~ **(around)** poner algo en órbita (alrededor de). ⋄ *vt* girar alrededor de.

orchard ['ɔːtʃəd] *n* huerto *m*.

orchestra ['ɔːkɪstrə] *n* orquesta *f*.

orchestral [ɔː'kestrəl] *adj* orquestal.

orchestra pit *n* foso *m* (de la orquesta).

orchestrate ['ɔːkɪstreɪt] *vt* MUS & *fig* orquestar.

orchestration [ˌɔːke'streɪʃn] *n* MUS & *fig* orquestación *f*.

orchid ['ɔːkɪd] *n* orquídea *f*.

ordain [ɔː'deɪn] *vt* **-1.** *fml* [decree] decretar, ordenar. **-2.** RELIG: **to be ~ed** ordenarse (sacerdote).

ordeal [ɔː'diːl] *n* calvario *m*, experiencia *f* terrible.

order ['ɔːdəʳ] ◇ *n* **-1.** [instruction] orden *f*; **to be under ~s to do sthg** tener órdenes de hacer algo. **-2.** COMM [request] pedido *m*; **to be on ~** estar pedido; **to ~** por encargo. **-3.** [sequence, discipline, system] orden *m*; **in ~** en orden; **in ~ of importance** por orden de importancia; **to keep ~** mantener el orden. **-4.** [fitness for use]: **in working ~** en funcionamiento; "**out of ~**" "no funciona"; **to be out of ~** [not working] estar estropeado(da); [incorrect behaviour] ser improcedente; **in ~** [correct] en regla. **-5.** RELIG orden *f*. **-6.** *Am* [portion] ración *f*.
◇ *vt* **-1.** [command]: **to ~ sb (to do sthg)** ordenar a alguien (que haga algo); **to ~ that** ordenar que. **-2.** [request - drink, taxi] pedir. **-3.** COM encargar.
◇ *vi* pedir.
◆ **orders** *npl* RELIG: **(holy) ~s** órdenes *fpl* sagradas.
◆ **in the order of** *Br*, **on the order of** *Am prep* del orden de.
◆ **in order that** *conj* para que.
◆ **in order to** *conj* para.
◆ **order about**, **order around** *vt sep* mangonear.

order book *n* libro *m* de pedidos.

order form *n* hoja *f* de pedido.

orderly ['ɔːdəlɪ] (*pl* **-ies**) ◇ *adj* [person, crowd] obediente, pacífico(ca); [room] ordenado(da), en orden. ◇ *n* [in hospital] auxiliar *m y f* sanitario.

order number *n* número *m* de pedido.

ordinal ['ɔːdɪnl] ◇ *adj* ordinal. ◇ *n* ordinal *m*.

ordinarily ['ɔːdənrəlɪ] *adv* de ordinario, generalmente.

ordinary ['ɔːdənrɪ] ◇ *adj* **-1.** [normal] corriente, normal. **-2.** *pej* [unexceptional] mediocre, ordinario(ria). ◇ *n*: **out of the ~** fuera de lo común.

ordinary level *n Br* ≃ Bachillerato *m*, ≃ BUP *m*.

ordinary seaman *n Br* marinero *m*.

ordinary shares *npl Br* FIN acciones *fpl* ordinarias.

ordination [,ɔːdɪ'neɪʃn] *n* ordenación *f*.

ordnance ['ɔːdnəns] *n* (*U*) **-1.** [military supplies] pertrechos *mpl* de guerra. **-2.** [artillery] artillería *f*.

Ordnance Survey *n Br*: **the ~** servicio oficial de topografía y cartografía.

ore [ɔːʳ] *n* mineral *m*.

oregano [,ɒrɪ'guːnəʊ] *n* orégano *m*.

Oregon ['ɒrɪɡən] *n* Oregón *m*.

organ ['ɔːɡən] *n* órgano *m*.

organic [ɔː'ɡænɪk] *adj* orgánico(ca).

organically [ɔː'ɡænɪklɪ] *adv* orgánicamente.

organic chemistry *n* química *f* orgánica.

organism ['ɔːɡənɪzm] *n* organismo *m*.

organist ['ɔːɡənɪst] *n* organista *m y f*.

organization [,ɔːɡənaɪ'zeɪʃn] *n* organización *f*.

organizational [,ɔːɡənaɪ'zeɪʃnl] *adj* organizativo(va).

organization chart *n* organigrama *m*.

organize, -ise ['ɔːɡənaɪz] ◇ *vt* organizar. ◇ *vi* organizarse, sindicarse.

organized ['ɔːɡənaɪzd] *adj* organizado(da).

organized crime *n* crimen *m* organizado.

organized labour *n* obreros *mpl* sindicados.

organizer ['ɔːɡənaɪzəʳ] *n* organizador *m*, -ra *f*.

organza [ɔː'ɡænzə] *n* organza *f*.

orgasm ['ɔːɡæzm] *n* orgasmo *m*.

orgy ['ɔːdʒɪ] (*pl* **-ies**) *n lit* & *fig* orgía *f*.

orient ['ɔːrɪənt] = **orientate**.

Orient ['ɔːrɪənt] *n*: **the ~** el Oriente.

oriental [,ɔːrɪ'entl] ◇ *adj* oriental. ◇ *n* oriental *m y f* (*atención: el término "oriental" se considera racista*).

orientate ['ɔːrɪenteɪt] *vt* orientar; **to ~ o.s.** orientarse.

orientation [,ɔːrɪen'teɪʃn] *n* orientación *f*.

orienteering [,ɔːrɪən'tɪərɪŋ] *n* deporte *m* de orientación, orienteering *m*.

orifice ['ɒrɪfɪs] *n* orificio *m*.

origami [,ɒrɪ'ɡuːmɪ] *n* papiroflexia *f*.

origin ['ɒrɪdʒɪn] *n* origen *m*; **country of ~** país *m* de origen.
◆ **origins** *npl* origen *m*.

original [ə'rɪdʒənl] ◇ *adj* original; **the ~ owner** el primer propietario. ◇ *n* original *m*.

originality [ə,rɪdʒə'nælətɪ] *n* originalidad *f*.

originally [ə'rɪdʒənəlɪ] *adv* [at first] originariamente; [with originality] originalmente.

original sin *n* pecado *m* original.

originate [ə'rɪdʒəneɪt] ◇ *vt* originar, producir. ◇ *vi*: **to ~ (in)** nacer OR surgir (de); **to ~ from** nacer OR surgir de.

origination [ə,rɪdʒə'neɪʃn] *n* (*U*) origen *m*, creación *f*.

originator [ə'rɪdʒəneɪtəʳ] *n* autor *m*, -ra *f*, inventor *m*, -ra *f*.

Orinoco [,ɒrɪ'nəʊkəʊ] *n*: **the (River) ~** el (río) Orinoco.

Orkney Islands ['ɔːknɪ-], **Orkneys** ['ɔːknɪz] *npl*: **the ~** las Orcadas.

ornament ['ɔːnəmənt] *n* adorno *m*.

ornamental [ˌɔːnə'mentl] *adj* ornamental, decorativo(va).

ornamentation [ˌɔːnəmen'teɪʃn] *n* ornamentación *f*, adorno *m*.

ornate [ɔː'neɪt] *adj* [style] recargado(da); [decoration, vase] muy vistoso(sa).

ornately [ɔː'neɪtlɪ] *adv* vistosamente, ornadamente.

ornery ['ɔːnərɪ] *adj Am inf* borde.

ornithologist [ˌɔːnɪ'θɒlədʒɪst] *n* ornitólogo *m*, -ga *f*.

ornithology [ˌɔːnɪ'θɒlədʒɪ] *n* ornitología *f*.

orphan ['ɔːfn] ◇ *n* huérfano *m*, -na *f*. ◇ *vt*: to be ~ed quedarse huérfano.

orphanage ['ɔːfənɪdʒ] *n* orfelinato *m*, orfanato *m*.

orthodontist [ˌɔːθə'dɒntɪst] *n* ortodontista *m y f*.

orthodox ['ɔːθədɒks] *adj* ortodoxo(xa).

Orthodox Church *n*: the ~ la Iglesia Ortodoxa.

orthodoxy ['ɔːθədɒksɪ] *n* ortodoxia *f*.

orthopaedic [ˌɔːθə'piːdɪk] *adj* ortopédico(ca).

orthopaedics [ˌɔːθə'piːdɪks] *n* (U) ortopedia *f*.

orthopaedist [ˌɔːθə'piːdɪst] *n* ortopedista *m y f*.

orthopedic *etc* [ˌɔːθə'piːdɪk] = **orthopaedic** *etc*.

OS ◇ *n abbr of* **Ordnance Survey**. ◇ *abbr of* **outsize**.

O/S *abbr of* **out of stock**.

Oscar ['ɒskə'] *n* CINEMA Oscar *m*.

oscillate ['ɒsɪleɪt] *vi lit* & *fig*: to ~ (between) oscilar (entre).

oscilloscope [ɒ'sɪləskəʊp] *n* osciloscopio *m*.

OSD (*abbr of* **optical scanning device**) *n* LO *m*.

OSHA (*abbr of* **Occupational Safety and Health Administration**) *n organismo estadounidense de seguridad e higiene laborales*.

Oslo ['ɒzləʊ] *n* Oslo.

osmosis [ɒz'məʊsɪs] *n* osmosis *f inv*.

osprey ['ɒspri] (*pl* **ospreys**) *n* quebrantahuesos *m inv*.

Ostend [ɒs'tend] *n* Ostende.

ostensible [ɒ'stensəbl] *adj* aparente.

ostensibly [ɒ'stensəblɪ] *adv* aparentemente.

ostentation [ˌɒstən'teɪʃn] *n* ostentación *f*.

ostentatious [ˌɒstən'teɪʃəs] *adj* **-1.** [lifestyle, wealth] ostentoso(sa). **-2.** [person] ostentativo(va). **-3.** [behaviour] ostensible.

osteoarthritis [ˌɒstɪəʊɑː'θraɪtɪs] *n* osteoartritis *f inv*.

osteopath ['ɒstɪəpæθ] *n* osteópata *m y f*.

osteopathy [ˌɒstɪ'ɒpəθɪ] *n* osteopatía *f*.

ostracize, -ise ['ɒstrəsaɪz] *vt* [colleague etc] marginar, hacer el vacío a; POL condenar al ostracismo.

ostrich ['ɒstrɪtʃ] *n* avestruz *m*.

OT *n* **-1.** (*abbr of* **Old Testament**) A.T. *m*. **-2.** *abbr of* **occupational therapy**.

OTC (*abbr of* **Officer Training Corps**) *n unidad de formación de oficiales del ejército británico*.

OTE (*abbr of* **on target earnings**) *n beneficios según objetivos*.

other ['ʌðə'] ◇ *adj* otro(tra); **the ~ one** el otro (la otra); **the ~ day** el otro día. ◇ *pron* **-1.** [different one]: ~s otros *mpl*, otras *fpl*. **-2.** [remaining, alternative one]: **the ~** el otro (la otra); **the ~s** los otros (las otras), los demás (las demás); **one after the ~** uno tras otro; **one or ~** uno u otro; **to be none ~ than** no ser otro(tra) sino.

◆ **something or other** *pron* una cosa u otra.

◆ **somehow or other** *adv* de una u otra forma.

◆ **other than** *conj* excepto, salvo.

otherwise ['ʌðəwaɪz] ◇ *adv* **-1.** [or else] si no. **-2.** [apart from that] por lo demás. **-3.** [differently] de otra manera; **deliberately or ~** adrede o no. ◇ *conj* sino, de lo contrario.

other world *n*: the ~ el otro mundo, el más allá.

otherworldly [ˌʌðə'wɜːldlɪ] *adj* espiritual, poco realista.

OTT (*abbr of* **over the top**) *adj Br inf*: **it's a bit ~** eso es pasarse un poco de la raya.

Ottawa ['ɒtəwə] *n* Ottawa.

otter ['ɒtə'] *n* nutria *f*.

OU *n abbr of* **Open University**.

ouch [aʊtʃ] *excl* ¡ay!

ought [ɔːt] *aux vb* deber; **you ~ to go/be nicer** deberías irte/ser más amable; **she ~ to pass the exam** tiene probabilidades de aprobar el examen.

oughtn't ['ɔːtnt] = **ought not**.

Ouija board® ['wiːdʒə-] *n tablero de la ouija para hacer espiritismo*.

ounce [aʊns] *n* **-1.** [unit of measurement] = 28,35g, ≃ onza *f*. **-2.** *fig* [small amount] pizca *f*.

our ['aʊə'] *poss adj* nuestro(tra), nuestros(tras) (*pl*); ~ **money** nuestro dinero; ~ **house** nuestra casa; ~ **children** nuestros hijos; **it wasn't OUR fault** no fue culpa nuestra OR nuestra culpa; **we washed ~ hair** nos lavamos el pelo.

ours ['auəz] *poss pron* nuestro (nuestra); **that money is** ~ ese dinero es nuestro; **those keys are** ~ esas llaves son nuestras; **it wasn't their fault, it was OURS** no fue culpa de ellos sino de nosotros; **a friend of** ~ un amigo nuestro; **their car hit** ~ suyo coche chocó contra el nuestro.

ourselves [auə'selvz] *pron pl* **-1.** (*reflexive*) nos *mpl y fpl*; (*after prep*) nosotros *mpl*, nosotras *fpl*. **-2.** (*for emphasis*) nosotros *mpl* mismos, nosotras *fpl* mismas; **we did it by** ~ lo hicimos nosotros solos.

oust [aust] *vt fml*: **to** ~ **sb (from)** [job] desbancar a alguien (de); [land] desalojar a alguien (de).

ouster ['austər] *n Am* [from country] expulsión *f*; [from office] destitución *f*.

out [aut] *adv* **-1.** [not inside, out of doors] fuera; **we all went** ~ todos salimos fuera; **I'm going** ~ **for a walk** voy a salir a dar un paseo; **they ran** ~ salieron corriendo; **he poured the water** ~ sirvió el agua; ~ **here/there** aquí/allí fuera; ~ **you go!** ¡hala, afuera! **-2.** [away from home, office] fuera; **John's** ~ **at the moment** John está fuera ahora mismo; **don't stay** ~ **too late** no estés fuera hasta muy tarde; **an afternoon** ~ una tarde fuera. **-3.** [extinguished] apagado(da); **the fire went** ~ el fuego se apagó. **-4.** [of tides]: **the tide had gone** ~ la marea estaba baja. **-5.** [out of fashion] pasado(da) de moda. **-6.** [published, released - book] publicado(da); **they've a new record** ~ han sacado un nuevo disco. **-7.** [in flower] en flor; **the blossom's** ~ **already** ya ha florecido. **-8.** [visible]: **the moon's** ~ ha salido la luna. **-9.** *inf* [on strike] en huelga. **-10.** [not possible]: **sorry, that's** ~ lo siento, pero eso no se puede hacer. **-11.** [determined]: **to be** ~ **to do sthg** estar decidido(da) a hacer algo.
◆ **out of** *prep* **-1.** [away from, outside] fuera de; **I was** ~ **of the country** estaba fuera del país; **to go** ~ **of the room** salir de la habitación. **-2.** [indicating cause] por; ~ **of spite/love** por rencor/amor. **-3.** [indicating origin, source] de; **a page** ~ **of a book** una página de un libro; **to drink** ~ **of a glass** beber del vaso; **to get information** ~ **of sb** sacar información a alguien. **-4.** [without] sin; **we're** ~ **of sugar** estamos sin azúcar, se nos ha acabado el azúcar. **-5.** [made from] de; **it's made** ~ **of plastic** está hecho de plástico. **-6.** [using] de; **we can pay for it** ~ **of petty cash** podemos pagarlo con el dinero efectivo para gastos. **-7.** [sheltered from] a resguardo de; **we're** ~ **of the wind here** aquí estamos resguardados del viento. **-8.** [to indicate proportion]: **one** ~ **of ten people** una de cada diez personas; **ten** ~ **of ten** [mark] diez de OR sobre diez.

out-and-out *adj* [disgrace, lie] infame; [liar, crook] redomado(da).

outback ['autbæk] *n*: **the** ~ los llanos del interior de Australia.

outbid [,aut'bɪd] (*pt & pp* **outbid**, *cont* **-ding**) *vt*: **to** ~ **sb (for)** pujar más alto que alguien (por).

outboard (motor) ['autbɔːd-] *n* (motor *m*) fueraborda *m*.

outbound ['autbaund] *adj* [train, flight] de ida; [traffic] de salida.

outbreak ['autbreɪk] *n* [of war] comienzo *m*; [of crime] ola *f*, oleada *f*; [of illness] epidemia *f*; [of spots] erupción *f*.

outbuildings ['autbɪldɪŋz] *npl* dependencias *fpl*.

outburst ['autbɜːst] *n* **-1.** [sudden expression of emotion] explosión *f*, arranque *m*. **-2.** [sudden occurrence] estallido *m*.

outcast ['autkɑːst] *n* marginado *m*, -da *f*, paria *m y f*.

outclass [,aut'klɑːs] *vt* aventajar en OR con mucho.

outcome ['autkʌm] *n* resultado *m*.

outcrop ['autkrɒp] *n* afloramiento *m*.

outcry ['autkraɪ] (*pl* **-ies**) *n* protestas *fpl*.

outdated [,aut'deɪtɪd] *adj* anticuado(da), pasado(da) de moda.

outdid [,aut'dɪd] *pt* → **outdo**.

outdistance [,aut'dɪstəns] *vt lit & fig* dejar atrás.

outdo [,aut'duː] (*pt* **-did**, *pp* **-done** [-dʌn]) *vt* aventajar, superar.

outdoor ['autdɔːr] *adj* [life, swimming pool] al aire libre; [clothes] de calle.

outdoors [aut'dɔːz] *adv* al aire libre; **let's eat** ~ vamos a comer fuera.

outer ['autər] *adj* exterior, externo(na); **Outer London** las afueras de Londres.

Outer Mongolia *n* Mongolia Exterior.

outermost ['autəməust] *adj* [layer] más exterior; [place, planet] más remoto(ta).

outer space *n* espacio *m* exterior.

outfit ['autfɪt] *n* **-1.** [clothes] conjunto *m*, traje *m*. **-2.** *inf* [organization] grupo *m*, equipo *m*.

outfitters ['aut,fɪtəz] *n dated* tienda *f* de confección.

outflank [,aut'flæŋk] *vt* **-1.** MIL sorprender por la retaguardia. **-2.** *fig* [in argument, business] superar.

outgoing ['aʊt,gəʊɪŋ] *adj* **-1.** [chairman] saliente. **-2.** [train] de salida. **-3.** [sociable] extrovertido(da), abierto(ta).
◆ **outgoings** *npl Br* gastos *mpl*.

outgrow [,aʊt'grəʊ] (*pt* **-grew**, *pp* **-grown**) *vt* **-1.** [grow too big for]: **he has outgrown his shirts** las camisas se le han quedado pequeñas. **-2.** [grow too old for] ser demasiado mayor para.

outhouse ['aʊthaʊs, *pl* -haʊzɪz] *n* dependencia *f*.

outing ['aʊtɪŋ] *n* **-1.** [trip] excursión *f*. **-2.** [of homosexuals] *revelación de la condición homosexual de un personaje célebre*.

outlandish [aʊt'lændɪʃ] *adj* extravagante, estrafalario(ria).

outlast [aʊt'lɑːst] *vt* sobrevivir a, durar más tiempo que.

outlaw ['aʊtlɔː] ◇ *n* proscrito *m*, -ta *f*. ◇ *vt* **-1.** [make illegal] ilegalizar. **-2.** [declare an outlaw] proscribir, declarar fuera de la ley.

outlay ['aʊtleɪ] *n* desembolso *m*, inversión *f*.

outlet ['aʊtlet] *n* **-1.** [for emotions] salida *f*, desahogo *m*. **-2.** [for water] desagüe *m*; [for gas] salida *f*. **-3.** [shop] punto *m* de venta. **-4.** *Am* ELEC toma *f* de corriente.

outline ['aʊtlaɪn] ◇ *n* **-1.** [brief description] esbozo *m*, resumen *m*; **in ~** en líneas generales. **-2.** [silhouette] contorno *m*. ◇ *vt* **-1.** [describe briefly] esbozar, resumir. **-2.** [silhouette]: **to be ~d against** perfilarse contra.

outlive [,aʊt'lɪv] *vt* **-1.** [subj: person] sobrevivir a. **-2.** [subj: idea, object] durar más tiempo que.

outlook ['aʊtlʊk] *n* **-1.** [attitude, disposition] enfoque *m*, actitud *f*. **-2.** [prospect] perspectiva *f* (de futuro).

outlying ['aʊt,laɪɪŋ] *adj* [remote] lejano(na), remoto(ta); [on edge of town] periférico(ca).

outmanoeuvre *Br*, **outmaneuver** *Am* [,aʊtmə'nuːvə'] *vt* superar estratégicamente.

outmoded [,aʊt'məʊdəd] *adj* anticuado(da), pasado(da) de moda.

outnumber [,aʊt'nʌmbə'] *vt* exceder en número.

out-of-date *adj* **-1.** [clothes, belief] anticuado(da), pasado(da) de moda. **-2.** [passport, season ticket] caducado(da).

out of doors *adv* al aire libre.

out-of-the-way *adj* [far away] remoto(ta), aislado(da); [unusual] poco común.

outpace [,aʊt'peɪs] *vt lit* & *fig* dejar atrás.

outpatient ['aʊt,peɪʃnt] *n* paciente externo *m*, paciente externa *f*.

outplay [,aʊt'pleɪ] *vt* superar, jugar mejor que.

outpost ['aʊtpəʊst] *n* puesto *m* avanzado.

outpouring ['aʊt,pɔːrɪŋ] *n literary* efusión *f*.

output ['aʊtpʊt] ◇ *n* **-1.** [production] producción *f*, rendimiento *m*. **-2.** [COMPUT - printing out] salida *f*; [- printout] impresión *f*. ◇ *vt* COMPUT imprimir.

outrage ['aʊtreɪdʒ] ◇ *n* **-1.** [anger] indignación *f*. **-2.** [atrocity] atrocidad *f*, escándalo *m*. ◇ *vt* ultrajar, atropellar.

outraged ['aʊtreɪdʒd] *adj* indignado(da).

outrageous [aʊt'reɪdʒəs] *adj* **-1.** [offensive, shocking] indignante, escandaloso(sa). **-2.** [very unusual] extravagante.

outran [,aʊt'ræn] *pt* → **outrun**.

outrank [,aʊt'ræŋk] *vt* ser de categoría superior a.

outrider ['aʊt,raɪdə'] *n* [on motorcycle] escolta *m* en moto; [on horse] escolta a caballo.

outright [*adj* 'aʊtraɪt, *adv* ,aʊt'raɪt] ◇ *adj* **-1.** [categoric] categórico(ca). **-2.** [total - disaster] completo(ta); [- victory, winner] indiscutible. ◇ *adv* **-1.** [ask] abiertamente, francamente; [deny] categóricamente. **-2.** [win, ban] totalmente, completamente; [be killed] en el acto.

outrun [,aʊt'rʌn] (*pt* **-ran**, *pp* **-run**, *cont* **-ning**) *vt* correr más que.

outsell [,aʊt'sel] (*pt* & *pp* **-sold**) *vt* vender más que.

outset ['aʊtset] *n*: **at the ~** al principio; **from the ~** desde el principio.

outshine [,aʊt'ʃaɪn] (*pt* & *pp* **-shone** [-ʃɒn]) *vt fig* eclipsar.

outside [*adv* ,aʊt'saɪd, *adj*, *prep* & *n* 'aʊtsaɪd] ◇ *adj* **-1.** [gen] exterior. **-2.** [opinion, criticism] independiente. **-3.** [chance] remoto(ta). ◇ *adv* fuera; **to go/run/look ~** ir/correr/mirar fuera. ◇ *prep* fuera de; **we live half an hour ~ London** vivimos a media hora de Londres. ◇ *n* **-1.** [exterior] exterior *m*. **-2.** [limit]: **at the ~** a lo sumo.
◆ **outside of** *prep Am* [apart from] aparte de.

outside broadcast *n Br* RADIO & TV emisión *f* desde exteriores.

outside lane *n* carril *m* de adelantamiento.

outside line *n* línea *f* exterior.

outsider [,aʊt'saɪdə'] *n* **-1.** [stranger] forastero *m*, -ra *f*, desconocido *m*, -da *f*. **-2.** [in horse race] *caballo que no es uno de los favoritos*.

outsize ['aʊtsaɪz] *adj* **-1.** [bigger than usual] enorme. **-2.** [clothes] de talla muy grande.

outsized ['aʊtsaɪzd] *adj* enorme.

outskirts ['aʊtskɜːts] *npl*: **the ~** las afueras.

outsmart [,aʊt'smɑːt] *vt* ser más listo(ta) que.

outsold [ˌaʊt'səʊld] *pt & pp* → **outsell**.

outspoken [ˌaʊt'spəʊkn] *adj* abierto(ta), franco(ca).

outspread [ˌaʊt'spred] *adj* extendido(da), desplegado(da).

outstanding [ˌaʊt'stændɪŋ] *adj* **-1.** [excellent] destacado(da). **-2.** [not paid, unfinished] pendiente.

outstay [ˌaʊt'steɪ] *vt*: **to ~ one's welcome** quedarse más tiempo de lo debido.

outstretched [ˌaʊt'stretʃt] *adj* extendido(da).

outstrip [ˌaʊt'strɪp] (*pt & pp* **-ped**, *cont* **-ping**) *vt lit & fig* aventajar, dejar atrás.

out-take *n* CINEMA & TV descarte *m*.

out-tray *n cubeta o bandeja de asuntos ya resueltos.*

outvote [ˌaʊt'vəʊt] *vt*: **to be ~d** perder en una votación.

outward ['aʊtwəd] ◇ *adj* **-1.** [journey] de ida. **-2.** [composure, sympathy] aparente. **-3.** [sign, proof] visible, exterior. ◇ *adv Am* = **outwards.**

outwardly ['aʊtwədlɪ] *adv* [apparently] aparentemente, de cara al exterior.

outwards *Br* ['aʊtwədz], **outward** *Am adv* hacia fuera.

outweigh [ˌaʊt'weɪ] *vt* pesar más que.

outwit [ˌaʊt'wɪt] (*pt & pp* **-ted**, *cont* **-ting**) *vt* ser más listo(ta) que.

outworker ['aʊtˌwɜːkər] *n* colaborador externo *m*, colaboradora externa *f*.

oval ['əʊvl] ◇ *adj* oval, ovalado(da). ◇ *n* óvalo *m*.

Oval Office *n*: **the ~** el Despacho Oval, *oficina que tiene el presidente de Estados Unidos en la Casa Blanca.*

ovarian [əʊ'veərɪən] *adj* [gen] ovárico(ca); [cancer] de ovario.

ovary ['əʊvərɪ] (*pl* **-ies**) *n* ovario *m*.

ovation [əʊ'veɪʃn] *n* ovación *f*; **a standing ~** una ovación de gala (con el público en pie).

oven ['ʌvn] *n* horno *m*.

oven glove *n* guante *m* para el horno.

ovenproof ['ʌvnpruːf] *adj* refractario(ria).

oven-ready *adj* listo(ta) para meter al horno.

ovenware ['ʌvnweər] *n* (*U*) utensilios *mpl* para el horno.

over ['əʊvər] ◇ *prep* **-1.** [directly above, on top of] encima de; **a fog hung ~ the river** una espesa niebla flotaba sobre el río; **put your coat ~ the chair** pon el abrigo encima de la silla. **-2.** [to cover] sobre; **she wore a veil ~ her face** un velo le cubría el rostro.

-3. [on other side of] al otro lado de; **he lives ~ the road** vive enfrente. **-4.** [across surface of] por encima de; **they sailed ~ the ocean** cruzaron el océano en barco. **-5.** [more than] más de; **~ and above** además de. **-6.** [senior to] por encima de. **-7.** [with regard to] por; **a fight ~ a woman** una pelea por una mujer. **-8.** [during] durante; **~ the weekend** (en) el fin de semana.
◇ *adv* **-1.** [short distance away]: **~ here** aquí; **~ there** allí. **-2.** [across]: **to cross ~** cruzar; **to go ~** ir. **-3.** [down]: **to fall ~** caerse; **to push ~** empujar, tirar. **-4.** [round]: **to turn sthg ~** dar la vuelta a algo; **to roll ~** darse la vuelta. **-5.** [more] más. **-6.** [remaining]: **to be (left) ~** quedar, sobrar. **-7.** [at sb's house]: **~ at Mum's** en casa de mamá; **invite them ~** invítalos a casa. **-8.** RADIO: **(and out)!** ¡cambio (y cierro)! **-9.** [involving repetitions]: **(all) ~ again** otra vez desde el principio; **~ and ~ (again)** una y otra vez.
◇ *adj* [finished] terminado(da).
◇ *n en críquet, serie de seis lanzamientos de un mismo jugador.*

◆ **all over** ◇ *prep* por todo(da). ◇ *adv* [everywhere] por todas partes. ◇ *adj* [finished] terminado(da), acabado(da).

over- ['əʊvər] *prefix* sobre-, super-.

overabundance [ˌəʊvərə'bʌndəns] *n* superabundancia *f*.

overact [ˌəʊvər'ækt] *vi pej* [in play] sobreactuar, exagerar.

overactive [ˌəʊvər'æktɪv] *adj* demasiado activo(va).

overall [*adj & n* 'əʊvərɔːl, *adv* ˌəʊvər'ɔːl] ◇ *adj* [general] global, total. ◇ *adv* en conjunto, en general. ◇ *n* **-1.** [gen] guardapolvo *m*, bata *f*. **-2.** *Am* [for work] mono *m*.

◆ **overalls** *npl* **-1.** [for work] mono *m*. **-2.** *Am* [dungarees] pantalones *mpl* de peto.

overambitious [ˌəʊvəræm'bɪʃəs] *adj* demasiado ambicioso(sa).

overanxious [ˌəʊvər'æŋkʃəs] *adj* demasiado preocupado(da).

overarm ['əʊvərɑːm] *adj & adv* por encima del hombro.

overate [ˌəʊvər'et] *pt* → **overeat**.

overawe [ˌəʊvər'ɔː] *vt* intimidar.

overbalance [ˌəʊvə'bæləns] *vi* perder el equilibrio.

overbearing [ˌəʊvə'beərɪŋ] *adj pej* déspótico(ca).

overblown [ˌəʊvə'bləʊn] *adj pej* exagerado(da).

overboard ['əʊvəbɔːd] *adv*: **to fall ~** caer al agua OR por la borda; **to go ~ (about sb/sthg)** *inf* [be over-enthusiastic about] ponerse como loco(ca) (con alguien/algo).

overbook [,əʊvə'bʊk] *vi* hacer overbooking.

overburden [,əʊvə'bɜːdn] *vt*: to be ~ed with sthg estar sobrecargado(da) de algo.

overcame [,əʊvə'keɪm] *pt* → overcome.

overcapitalize, -ise [,əʊvə'kæpɪtəlaɪz] FIN *vt & vi* sobrecapitalizar.

overcast ['əʊvəkɑːst] *adj* cubierto(ta), nublado(da).

overcharge [,əʊvə'tʃɑːdʒ] ◇ *vt*: to ~ sb (for sthg) cobrar a alguien en exceso (por algo). ◇ *vi*: to ~ (for sthg) cobrar en exceso (por algo).

overcoat ['əʊvəkəʊt] *n* abrigo *m*.

overcome [,əʊvə'kʌm] (*pt* -came, *pp* -come) *vt* -1. [deal with] vencer, superar. -2. [overwhelm]: to be ~ (by OR with) [fear, grief, emotion] estar abrumado(da) (por); [smoke, fumes] estar asfixiado(da) (por).

overcompensate [,əʊvə'kɒmpənseɪt] *vi*: to ~ (for sthg) compensar en exceso (por algo).

overconfident [,əʊvə'kɒnfɪdənt] *adj* demasiado confiado(da).

overcook [,əʊvə'kʊk] *vt* hacer demasiado.

overcrowded [,əʊvə'kraʊdɪd] *adj* [room] atestado(da) de gente; [country] superpoblado(da).

overcrowding [,əʊvə'kraʊdɪŋ] *n* [of country] superpoblación *f*; [of prison] hacinamiento *m*.

overdeveloped [,əʊvədə'veləpt] *adj* -1. PHOT sobreprocesado(da). -2. [too high, too big] excesivo(va).

overdo [,əʊvə'duː] (*pt* -did [-dɪd], *pp* -done) *vt* -1. *pej* [exaggerate] exagerar. -2. [do too much]: to ~ one's work/the walking trabajar/andar demasiado; to ~ it pasarse. -3. [overcook] hacer demasiado.

overdone [,əʊvə'dʌn] ◇ *pp* → overdo. ◇ *adj* muy hecho(cha).

overdose [*n* 'əʊvədəʊs, *vb* ,əʊvə'dəʊs] ◇ *n* sobredosis *f inv*. ◇ *vi*: to ~ on tomar una sobredosis de.

overdraft ['əʊvədrɑːft] *n* [sum owed] saldo *m* deudor; [loan arranged] (giro *m* OR crédito *m* en) descubierto *m*.

overdrawn [,əʊvə'drɔːn] *adj*: to be ~ tener un saldo deudor.

overdress [,əʊvə'dres] *vi* trajearse.

overdrive ['əʊvədraɪv] *n fig*: to go into ~ ir a marchas forzadas.

overdue [,əʊvə'djuː] *adj* -1. [late]: to be ~ [train] ir con retraso; [library book] estar con el plazo de préstamo caducado; I'm ~ (for) a bit of luck va siendo hora de tener un poco de suerte. -2. [awaited]: (long) ~ (lar-

gamente) esperado(da), ansiado(da). -3. [unpaid] vencido(da) y sin pagar.

overeager [,əʊvər'iːgəʳ] *adj* demasiado ansioso(sa).

overeat [,əʊvər'iːt] (*pt* -ate, *pp* -eaten) *vi* comer con exceso, atracarse.

overemphasize, -ise [,əʊvər'emfəsaɪz] *vt* poner demasiado énfasis en.

overenthusiastic ['əʊvərɪn,θjuːzɪ'æstɪk] *adj* demasiado entusiasta.

overestimate [,əʊvər'estɪmeɪt] *vt* sobreestimar.

overexcited [,əʊvərɪk'saɪtɪd] *adj* sobreexcitado(da).

overexpose [,əʊvərɪk'spəʊz] *vt* PHOT sobreexponer.

overfeed [,əʊvə'fiːd] (*pt & pp* -fed [-fed]) *vt* sobrealimentar.

overfill [,əʊvə'fɪl] *vt* llenar demasiado.

overflow [*vb* ,əʊvə'fləʊ, *n* 'əʊvəfləʊ] ◇ *vi* -1. [spill over] rebosar; [river] desbordarse. -2. [go beyond limits]: to ~ (into) rebosar (hacia). -3. [be very full]: to be ~ing (with) rebosar (de); full to ~ing lleno a rebosar. ◇ *vt* desbordarse de, salir de. ◇ *n* [pipe] cañería *f* de desagüe.

overgrown [,əʊvə'grəʊn] *adj* cubierto(ta) de matojos.

overhang [*n* 'əʊvəhæŋ, *vb* ,əʊvə'hæŋ] (*pt & pp* -hung) ◇ *n* saliente *m*. ◇ *vt* sobresalir por encima de. ◇ *vi* sobresalir.

overhaul [*n* 'əʊvəhɔːl, *vb* ,əʊvə'hɔːl] ◇ *n* -1. [of car, machine] revisión *f*. -2. [of method, system] repaso *m* general. ◇ *vt* revisar.

overhead [*adv* ,əʊvə'hed, *adj & n* 'əʊvəhed] ◇ *adj* aéreo(a). ◇ *adv* por lo alto, por encima. ◇ *n Am* (U) gastos *mpl* generales.

◆ **overheads** *npl* gastos *mpl* generales.

overhead projector *n* retroproyector *m*.

overhear [,əʊvə'hɪəʳ] (*pt & pp* -heard [-hɜːd]) *vt* oír por casualidad.

overheat [,əʊvə'hiːt] ◇ *vt* recalentar. ◇ *vi* recalentarse.

overhung [,əʊvə'hʌŋ] *pt & pp* → overhang.

overindulge [,əʊvərɪn'dʌldʒ] ◇ *vt* mimar excesivamente. ◇ *vi*: to ~ (in sthg) abusar (de algo).

overjoyed [,əʊvə'dʒɔɪd] *adj*: to be ~ (at sthg) estar encantado(da) (con algo).

overkill ['əʊvəkɪl] *n* exageración *f*, exceso *m*.

overladen [,əʊvə'leɪdn] ◇ *pp* → overload. ◇ *adj* sobrecargado(da).

overlaid [,əʊvə'leɪd] *pt & pp* → overlay.

overland ['əʊvəlænd] ◇ *adj* terrestre. ◇ *adv* por tierra.

overlap [*n* 'əʊvəlæp, *vb* ˌəʊvə'læp] (*pt & pp* -**ped**, *cont* -**ping**) ◇ *n* -**1.** [similarity] coincidencia *f.* -**2.** [overlapping part, amount] superposición *f.* ◇ *vt* -**1.** [cover] superponerse a. -**2.** [be similar to] coincidir en parte con. ◇ *vi* -**1.** [cover each other] superponerse. -**2.** [be similar]: **to ~ (with sthg)** coincidir en parte (en algo).

overlay [ˌəʊvə'leɪ] (*pt & pp* -**laid**) *vt*: **to be overlaid with** estar revestido(da) de.

overleaf [ˌəʊvə'liːf] *adv* al dorso, a la vuelta.

overload [ˌəʊvə'ləʊd] (*pp* -**loaded** OR -**laden**) *vt* sobrecargar; **to be ~ed (with sthg)** estar sobrecargado (de algo).

overlong [ˌəʊvə'lɒŋ] ◇ *adj* demasiado largo(ga). ◇ *adv* demasiado tiempo.

overlook [ˌəʊvə'lʊk] *vt* -**1.** [look over] mirar OR dar a. -**2.** [disregard, miss] pasar por alto, no considerar. -**3.** [forgive] perdonar.

overlord ['əʊvəlɔːd] *n fml* señor *m*.

overly ['əʊvəlɪ] *adv* demasiado.

overmanning [ˌəʊvə'mænɪŋ] *n* exceso *m* de mano de obra.

overnight [*adj* 'əʊvənaɪt, *adv* ˌəʊvə'naɪt] ◇ *adj* -**1.** [for all of night] de noche, nocturno(na). -**2.** [for a night's stay - clothes] para una noche; **~ bag** bolso *m* de viaje. -**3.** [very sudden] súbito(ta), de la noche a la mañana. ◇ *adv* -**1.** [for all of night] durante la noche. -**2.** [very suddenly] de la noche a la mañana.

overpaid [ˌəʊvə'peɪd] ◇ *pt & pp* → **overpay.** ◇ *adj* pagado(da) en exceso.

overpass ['əʊvəpɑːs] *n Am* paso *m* elevado.

overpay [ˌəʊvə'peɪ] (*pt & pp* -**paid**) *vt* pagar en exceso.

overplay [ˌəʊvə'pleɪ] *vt* exagerar.

overpopulated [ˌəʊvə'pɒpjʊleɪtɪd] *adj* superpoblado(da).

overpower [ˌəʊvə'paʊə'] *vt* -**1.** [in fight] vencer, subyugar. -**2.** *fig* [overwhelm] sobreponerse a, vencer.

overpowering [ˌəʊvə'paʊərɪŋ] *adj* arrollador(ra), abrumador(ra).

overpriced [ˌəʊvə'praɪst] *adj* de precio excesivo.

overproduction [ˌəʊvəprə'dʌkʃn] *n* exceso *m* de producción, superproducción *f.*

overprotective [ˌəʊvəprə'tektɪv] *adj* que protege excesivamente.

overran [ˌəʊvə'ræn] *pt* → **overrun.**

overrated [ˌəʊvə'reɪtɪd] *adj* sobreestimado(da).

overreach [ˌəʊvə'riːtʃ] *vt*: **to ~ o.s.** extralimitarse, ir demasiado lejos.

overreact [ˌəʊvərɪ'ækt] *vi*: **to ~ (to sthg)** reaccionar demasiado (a algo).

override [ˌəʊvə'raɪd] (*pt* -**rode**, *pp* -**ridden**) *vt* -**1.** [be more important than] predominar sobre. -**2.** [overrule] desautorizar.

overriding [ˌəʊvə'raɪdɪŋ] *adj* predominante.

overripe [ˌəʊvə'raɪp] *adj* pasado(da), demasiado maduro(ra).

overrode [ˌəʊvə'rəʊd] *pt* → **override.**

overrule [ˌəʊvə'ruːl] *vt* [person] desautorizar; [decision] anular; [request] denegar.

overrun [ˌəʊvə'rʌn] (*pt* -**ran**, *pp* -**run**, *cont* -**running**) ◇ *vt* -**1.** MIL [enemy, army] apabullar, arrasar; [country] ocupar, invadir. -**2.** *fig* [cover]: **to be ~ with** estar invadido(da) de. ◇ *vi* rebasar el tiempo previsto.

oversaw [ˌəʊvə'sɔː] *pt* → **oversee.**

overseas [*adj* 'əʊvəsiːz, *adv* ˌəʊvə'siːz] ◇ *adj* -**1.** [in or to foreign countries - market] exterior; [- sales, aid] al extranjero; [- network, branches] en el extranjero. -**2.** [from abroad] extranjero(ra). ◇ *adv* [go, travel] al extranjero; [study, live] en el extranjero.

oversee [ˌəʊvə'siː] (*pt* -**saw**, *pp* -**seen** [-'siːn]) *vt* supervisar.

overseer ['əʊvəˌsiːə'] *n* supervisor *m*, -ra *f.*

overshadow [ˌəʊvə'ʃædəʊ] *vt* -**1.** [be taller than] ensombrecer, eclipsar. -**2.** [be more important than]: **to be ~ed by** ser eclipsado(da) por. -**3.** [mar]: **to be ~ed by sthg** ser ensombrecido(da) por algo.

overshoot [ˌəʊvə'ʃuːt] (*pt & pp* -**shot**) *vt* [go past] pasarse.

oversight ['əʊvəsaɪt] *n* descuido *m.*

oversimplification ['əʊvəˌsɪmplɪfɪ'keɪʃn] *n* simplificación *f* excesiva.

oversimplify [ˌəʊvə'sɪmplɪfaɪ] (*pt & pp* -**ied**) *vt & vi* simplificar demasiado.

oversleep [ˌəʊvə'sliːp] (*pt & pp* -**slept** [-'slept]) *vi* no despertarse a tiempo, quedarse dormido(da).

overspend [ˌəʊvə'spend] (*pt & pp* -**spent** [-'spent]) *vi* gastar más de la cuenta.

overspill ['əʊvəspɪl] *n* exceso *m* de población.

overstaffed [ˌəʊvə'stɑːft] *adj* con exceso de empleados.

overstate [ˌəʊvə'steɪt] *vt* exagerar.

overstay [ˌəʊvə'steɪ] *vt*: **to ~ one's welcome** quedarse más tiempo de lo debido.

overstep [ˌəʊvə'step] (*pt & pp* -**ped**, *cont* -**ping**) *vt* pasar de; **to ~ the mark** pasarse de la raya.

overstock [ˌəʊvə'stɒk] *vt* abarrotar.

overstrike ['əʊvəstraɪk] (*pt & pp* -**struck**) COMPUT ◇ *n* superposición *f.* ◇ *vt* superponer.

oversubscribed [,əʊvəsʌb'skraɪbd] *adj* suscrito(ta) en exceso.

overt ['əʊvɜːt] *adj* abierto(ta), evidente.

overtake [,əʊvə'teɪk] (*pt* -**took**, *pp* -**taken** [-'teɪkn]) ◇ *vt* -**1.** AUT adelantar. -**2.** [subj: event] sorprender, coger de improviso. -**3.** [subj: emotion] abrumar, apabullar. ◇ *vi* AUT adelantar.

overtaking [,əʊvə'teɪkɪŋ] *n* adelantamiento *m*; "no ~" "prohibido adelantar".

overthrow [*n* 'əʊvəθrəʊ, *vb* ,əʊvə'θrəʊ] (*pt* -**threw**, *pp* -**thrown**) ◇ *n* [of government] derrocamiento *m*, derrumbamiento *m*. ◇ *vt* -**1.** [oust] derrocar. -**2.** [idea, standard] echar abajo.

overtime ['əʊvətaɪm] ◇ *n* (U) -**1.** [extra work] horas *fpl* extra. -**2.** *Am* SPORT (tiempo *m* de) descuento *m*. ◇ *adv*: **to work** ~ trabajar horas extra.

overtly ['əʊvɜːtlɪ] *adv* abiertamente, públicamente.

overtones ['əʊvətəʊnz] *npl* tono *m*, matiz *m*.

overtook [,əʊvə'tʊk] *pt* → **overtake**.

overture ['əʊvə,tjʊər] *n* MUS obertura *f*.
◆ **overtures** *npl*: **to make** ~**s to sb** hacer una propuesta a alguien.

overturn [,əʊvə'tɜːn] ◇ *vt* -**1.** [turn over] volcar. -**2.** [overrule] rechazar. -**3.** [overthrow] derrocar, derrumbar. ◇ *vi* [vehicle] volcar; [boat] zozobrar.

overuse [,əʊvə'juːz] *vt* usar demasiado.

overview ['əʊvəvjuː] *n* visión *f* general OR de conjunto.

overweening [,əʊvə'wiːnɪŋ] *adj* desmesurado(da).

overweight [,əʊvə'weɪt] *adj* grueso(sa), gordo(da).

overwhelm [,əʊvə'welm] *vt* -**1.** [make helpless] abrumar. -**2.** [defeat] aplastar, arrollar.

overwhelming [,əʊvə'welmɪŋ] *adj* -**1.** [despair, kindness] abrumador(ra). -**2.** [defeat, majority] contundente, aplastante.

overwhelmingly [,əʊvə'welmɪŋlɪ] *adv* abrumadoramente.

overwork [,əʊvə'wɜːk] ◇ *n* trabajo *m* excesivo. ◇ *vt* -**1.** [give too much work to] hacer trabajar demasiado. -**2.** [overuse] usar demasiado. ◇ *vi* trabajar demasiado.

overwrought [,əʊvə'rɔːt] *adj fml* nerviosísimo(ma), sobreexcitado(da).

ovulate ['ɒvjʊleɪt] *vi* ovular.

ovulation [,ɒvjʊ'leɪʃn] *n* ovulación *f*.

ow [aʊ] *excl* ¡ay!

owe [əʊ] *vt*: **to** ~ **sthg to sb**, **to** ~ **sb sthg** deber algo a alguien.

owing ['əʊɪŋ] *adj* que se debe.

◆ **owing to** *prep* debido a, por causa de.

owl [aʊl] *n* búho *m*, lechuza *f*, tecolote *m* *Amer*.

own [əʊn] ◇ *adj*: **my/your/his** *etc* ~ **car** mi/tu/su *etc* propio coche. ◇ *pron*: **my** ~ **el** mío (la mía); **his/her** ~ **el** suyo (la suya); **a house of my/his** ~ mi/su propia casa; **on one's** ~ solo(la); **to get one's** ~ **back** *inf* tomarse la revancha, desquitarse. ◇ *vt* poseer, tener.
◆ **own up** *vi*: **to** ~ **up (to sthg)** confesar (algo).

own brand *n* COMM marca *f* propia (del comerciante).

owner ['əʊnər] *n* propietario *m*, -ria *f*.

owner-occupier *n persona que ha comprado la vivienda en la que habita.*

ownership ['əʊnəʃɪp] *n* propiedad *f*.

own goal *n* -**1.** FTBL gol *m* en propia meta, autogol *m*. -**2.** *Br fig* [foolish mistake] metedura *f* de pata.

ox [ɒks] (*pl* **oxen**) *n* buey *m*.

Oxbridge ['ɒksbrɪdʒ] *n* (U) *las universidades de Oxford y Cambridge.*

oxen ['ɒksn] *pl* → **ox**.

Oxfam ['ɒksfæm] *n sociedad benéfica de ayuda a países subdesarrollados.*

oxide ['ɒksaɪd] *n* óxido *m*.

oxidize, -ise ['ɒksɪdaɪz] *vi* oxidarse.

Oxon (*abbr of* **Oxfordshire**) *condado inglés.*

Oxon. (*abbr of* **Oxoniensis**) *de o relativo a Oxford, esp su universidad.*

oxtail soup ['ɒksteɪl-] *n* sopa *f* de rabo de buey.

ox tongue *n* lengua *f* de buey.

oxyacetylene [,ɒksɪə'setɪliːn] ◇ *n* oxiacetileno *m*. ◇ *comp* oxiacetilénico(ca).

oxygen ['ɒksɪdʒən] *n* oxígeno *m*.

oxygenate ['ɒksɪdʒəneɪt] *vt* oxigenar.

oxygen mask *n* máscara *f* de oxígeno.

oxygen tent *n* tienda *f* de oxígeno.

oyster ['ɔɪstər] *n* ostra *f*.

oz. *abbr of* **ounce**.

ozone ['əʊzəʊn] *n* ozono *m*.

ozone-friendly *adj* que no daña a la capa de ozono.

ozone layer *n* capa *f* de ozono.

P

p¹ (*pl* **p's** OR **ps**), **P** (*pl* **P's** OR **Ps**) [piː] *n* [letter] p *f*, P *f*.
◆ **P** **-1.** *abbr of* **president**. **-2.** (*abbr of* **prince**) P.

p² **-1.** (*abbr of* **page**) p. **-2.** *abbr of* **penny**, **pence**.

pa [pɑː] *n inf* papá *m*.

p.a. (*abbr of* **per annum**) p.a.

PA ◇ *n* **-1.** *Br abbr of* **personal assistant**. **-2.** *abbr of* **public-address system**. **-3.** (*abbr of* **Press Association**) *agencia de noticias británica dedicada a información nacional.* ◇ *abbr of* **Pennsylvania**.

PABX (*abbr of* **private automatic branch exchange**) *n centralita automática.*

PAC (*abbr of* **political action committee**) *n comité estadounidense de acción política.*

pace [peɪs] ◇ *n* paso *m*, ritmo *m*; **at one's own ~** al ritmo de uno; **to keep ~ (with sthg)** [change, events] mantenerse al corriente (de algo); **to keep ~ (with sb)** llevar el mismo paso (que alguien). ◇ *vt* pasearse por. ◇ *vi*: **to ~ (up and down)** pasearse de un lado a otro.

pacemaker ['peɪsˌmeɪkəʳ] *n* **-1.** MED marcapasos *m inv.* **-2.** [in race] liebre *f*.

pacesetter ['peɪsˌsetəʳ] *n Am* liebre *f*.

pachyderm ['pækɪdɜːm] *n* paquidermo *m*.

Pacific [pə'sɪfɪk] ◇ *adj* del Pacífico. ◇ *n*: **the ~ (Ocean)** el (océano) Pacífico.

pacification [ˌpæsɪfɪ'keɪʃn] *n fml* **-1.** [calming] apaciguamiento *m*. **-2.** [bringing of peace] pacificación *f*.

pacifier ['pæsɪfaɪəʳ] *n Am* [for child] chupete *m*.

pacifism ['pæsɪfɪzm] *n* pacifismo *m*.

pacifist ['pæsɪfɪst] *n* pacifista *m y f*.

pacify ['pæsɪfaɪ] (*pt & pp* **-ied**) *vt* **-1.** [person, mob] calmar, apaciguar. **-2.** [country, area] pacificar.

pack [pæk] ◇ *n* **-1.** [bundle] lío *m*, fardo *m*; [rucksack] mochila *f*. **-2.** [packet] paquete *m*. **-3.** [of cards] baraja *f*. **-4.** [of dogs] jauría *f*; [of wolves] manada *f*; *pej* [of people] banda *f*. **-5.** RUGBY delanteros *mpl*. ◇ *vt* **-1.** [for journey - bags, suitcase] hacer; [- clothes, etc] meter (en la maleta). **-2.** [put in parcel] empaquetar; [put in container] envasar. **-3.** [fill] llenar, abarrotar; **to be ~ed into** estar apretujados dentro de. ◇ *vi* hacer las maletas, hacer el equipaje.
◆ **pack in** *inf* ◇ *vt sep Br* [stop] dejar; **~ it in!** ¡déjalo!, ¡ya basta! ◇ *vi* parar.
◆ **pack off** *vt sep inf* enviar, mandar.
◆ **pack up** ◇ *vt sep* **-1.** [for journey] meter en la maleta. **-2.** *Br inf* [stop] dejar. ◇ *vi* **-1.** [for journey] hacer las maletas. **-2.** *inf* [finish work] terminar de currar. **-3.** *Br inf* [break down] escacharrarse. **-4.** *inf* [stop] parar.

package ['pækɪdʒ] ◇ *n* [gen & COMPUT] paquete *m*. ◇ *vt* [wrap up] envasar.

package deal *n* convenio *m* OR acuerdo *m* global.

package holiday *n* paquete *m* turístico, vacaciones *fpl* con todo incluido.

packager ['pækɪdʒəʳ] *n* **-1.** [person packaging] empaquetador *m*, -ra *f*. **-2.** COMM productora *f* independiente.

package tour *n* paquete *m* turístico, vacaciones *fpl* con todo incluido.

packaging ['pækɪdʒɪŋ] *n* [wrapping] envasado *m*.

packed [pækt] *adj*: **~ (with)** repleto(ta) (de).

packed lunch *n Br* almuerzo *preparado de antemano que se lleva uno al colegio, la oficina etc.*

packed-out *adj Br inf* a tope, de bote en bote.

packet ['pækɪt] *n* **-1.** [gen] paquete *m*; [of crisps, sweets] bolsa *f*. **-2.** *Br inf* [lot of money] dineral *m*.

packhorse ['pækhɔːs] *n* caballo *m* de carga.

pack ice *n* (U) banco *m* de hielo.

packing ['pækɪŋ] *n* **-1.** [protective material] embalaje *m*. **-2.** [for journey]: **to do the ~** hacer el equipaje.

packing case *n* cajón *m* de embalaje.

pact [pækt] *n* pacto *m*.

pad [pæd] (*pt & pp* **-ded**, *cont* **-ding**) ◇ *n* **-1.** [of material] almohadillado *m*; **shin ~** espinillera *f*; **shoulder ~** hombrera *f*. **-2.** [of paper] bloc *m*, cuaderno *m*. **-3.** SPACE: **(launch) ~** plataforma *f* (de lanzamiento). **-4.** [of cat, dog] almohadilla *f*. **-5.** *inf dated* [home] casa *f*. ◇ *vt* acolchar, rellenar. ◇ *vi* [walk softly] andar con suavidad.
◆ **pad out** *vt sep* [fill out] meter paja en.

padded ['pædɪd] *adj* [shoulders] con hombreras; [chair] acolchado(da).

padded cell *n* celda *f* acolchada.

padding ['pædɪŋ] *n* (U) **-1.** [in jacket, chair] relleno *m*. **-2.** [in speech] paja *f*.

paddle ['pædl] ◇ *n* **-1.** [for canoe, dinghy] pala *f*, canalete *m*. **-2.** [walk in sea] paseo *m* por la orilla. ◇ *vt* remar. ◇ *vi* **-1.** [in canoe] remar. **-2.** [duck] chapotear. **-3.** [person - in sea] pasear por la orilla.

paddle boat, **paddle steamer** *n* vapor *m* de paletas OR ruedas.

paddling pool ['pædlɪŋ-] *n Br* **-1.** [in park] piscina *f* infantil, estanque *m* para chapotear. **-2.** [inflatable] piscina *f* inflable.

paddock ['pædək] *n* **-1.** [small field] potrero *m*, corral *m*. **-2.** [at racecourse] explanada *f* de ensillado, paddock *m*.

paddy field ['pædɪ-] *n* arrozal *m*.

paddy wagon ['pædɪ-] *n Am* [Black Maria] coche *m* celular, furgón *m* policial.

padlock ['pædlɒk] ◇ *n* candado *m*. ◇ *vt* cerrar con candado.

paederast ['pedəræst] = **pederast**.

paediatric [,pi:dɪ'ætrɪk] = **pediatric**.

paediatrician [,pi:dɪə'trɪʃn] = **pediatrician**.

paediatrics [,pi:dɪ'ætrɪks] = **pediatrics**.

paedophile ['pi:dəfaɪl] = **pedophile**.

paella [paɪ'elə] *n* paella *f*.

paeony ['pi:ənɪ] = **peony**.

pagan ['peɪgən] ◇ *adj* pagano(na). ◇ *n* pagano *m*, -na *f*.

paganism ['peɪgənɪzm] *n* paganismo *m*.

page [peɪdʒ] ◇ *n* página *f*. ◇ *vt* [in hotel, airport] llamar por megafonía.

pageant ['pædʒənt] *n* procesión *f*, desfile *m*.

pageantry ['pædʒəntrɪ] *n* boato *m*, pompa *f*.

page boy *n* **-1.** *Br* [at wedding] paje *m*. **-2.** [hairstyle] peinado *m* estilo paje.

pager ['peɪdʒə'] *n* busca *m*, buscapersonas *m inv*.

pagination [,pædʒɪ'neɪʃn] *n* paginación *f*.

pagoda [pə'gəʊdə] *n* pagoda *f*.

paid [peɪd] ◇ *pt & pp* → **pay**. ◇ *adj* [holiday, leave] pagado(da); [work, staff] remunerado(da); **badly/well** ~ mal/bien pagado.

paid-up *adj Br* que ha pagado cuota.

pail [peɪl] *n* cubo *m*.

pain [peɪn] ◇ *n* **-1.** [ache] dolor *m*; **to be in** ~ dolerse, sufrir dolor. **-2.** [mental suffering] pena *f*, sufrimiento *m*. **-3.** *inf* [annoyance - person] pesado *m*, -da *f*; [- thing] pesadez *f*; **a** ~ **in the neck** [person] un pesado (una pesada); [thing] una lata, un latazo. ◇ *vt fml*: **to** ~ **sb (to do sthg)** dolerle a alguien (hacer algo).

◆ **pains** *npl* [effort, care] esfuerzos *mpl*; **to be at** ~**s to do sthg** afanarse por hacer algo; **to take** ~**s to do sthg** esforzarse en hacer algo; **he got absolutely nothing for his** ~**s** tantas molestias y no obtuvo nada de nada.

pained [peɪnd] *adj* apenado(da).

painful ['peɪnfʊl] *adj* [back, eyes] dolorido(da); [injury, exercise, memory] doloroso(sa); **my shoes are** ~ los zapatos me hacen daño.

painfully ['peɪnfʊlɪ] *adv* **-1.** [causing pain] dolorosamente. **-2.** [extremely] terriblemente.

painkiller ['peɪn,kɪlə'] *n* calmante *m*.

painless ['peɪnlɪs] *adj* **-1.** [physically] indoloro(ra). **-2.** [emotionally] sencillo(lla), sin complicaciones.

painlessly ['peɪnlɪslɪ] *adv* **-1.** [without physical pain] sin dolor. **-2.** [without emotional pain] sin complicaciones.

painstaking ['peɪnz,teɪkɪŋ] *adj* meticuloso(sa), minucioso(sa).

painstakingly ['peɪnz,teɪkɪŋlɪ] *adv* meticulosamente, minuciosamente.

paint [peɪnt] ◇ *n* pintura *f*. ◇ *vt* pintar; **to** ~ **the ceiling white** pintar el techo de blanco; **to** ~ **one's lips** pintarse los labios.

paintbox ['peɪntbɒks] *n* ART caja *f* de acuarelas.

paintbrush ['peɪntbrʌʃ] *n* **-1.** ART pincel *m*. **-2.** [of decorator] brocha *f*.

painted ['peɪntɪd] *adj* pintado(da).

painter ['peɪntə'] *n* pintor *m*, -ra *f*.

painting ['peɪntɪŋ] *n* **-1.** [picture] cuadro *m*, pintura *f*. **-2.** (U) [art form, trade] pintura *f*.

paint stripper *n* quitapinturas *f inv*.

paintwork ['peɪntwɜ:k] *n* (U) pintura *f*.

pair [peə'] *n* **-1.** [of shoes, socks, wings] par *m*; [of aces] pareja *f*. **-2.** [two-part object]: **a** ~ **of scissors** unas tijeras; **a** ~ **of trousers** unos pantalones; **a** ~ **of compasses** un compás. **-3.** [couple - of people] pareja *f*.

◆ **pair off** ◇ *vt sep* emparejar. ◇ *vi* emparejarse.

paisley (pattern) ['peɪzlɪ-] ◇ *n* (U) cachemira *f* (*dibujo de una tela*). ◇ *comp* de cachemira.

pajamas [pə'dʒɑːməz] = **pyjamas**.

Paki ['pækɪ] *n Br v inf* término racista que designa a un *paquistaní*.

Pakistan [*Br* ,pɑːkɪ'stɑːn, *Am* ,pækɪ'stæn] *n* (el) Paquistán.

Pakistani [*Br* ,pɑːkɪ'stɑːnɪ, *Am* ,pækɪ'stænɪ] ◇ *adj* paquistaní. ◇ *n* paquistaní *m y f*.

pal [pæl] *n inf* **-1.** [friend] amiguete *m*, -ta *f*, colega *m y f*. **-2.** [as term of address] tío *m*, -a *f*.

PAL (*abbr of* **phase alternation line**) *n* PAL *f*.

palace ['pælɪs] *n* palacio *m*.

palaeontology *Br*, **paleontology** *Am* [,pælɪɒn'tɒlədʒɪ] *n* paleontología *f*.

palatable ['pælətəbl] *adj* **-1.** [pleasant to taste] sabroso(sa). **-2.** [acceptable] aceptable, admisible.

palate ['pælət] *n* paladar *m*.

palatial [pə'leɪʃl] *adj* señorial, fastuoso(sa).

palaver [pə'lɑːvə'] *n inf* **-1.** [talk] palabrería *f*. **-2.** [fuss] follón *m*, lío *m*.

pale [peɪl] ◇ *adj* **-1.** [colour, clothes, paint] claro(ra); [light] tenue. **-2.** [person] pálido(da). ◇ *vi* palidecer.

pale ale *n Br* tipo de cerveza rubia.

paleness ['peɪlnɪs] *n* [lack of brightness] palidez *f*.

Palestine ['pælɪ,staɪn] *n* Palestina.

Palestinian [,pælə'stɪnɪən] ◇ *adj* palestino(na). ◇ *n* [person] palestino *m*, -na *f*.

palette ['pælət] *n* paleta *f*.

palette knife *n* espátula *f*.

palimony ['pælɪmənɪ] *n pensión alimenticia pagada al ex-amante*.

palindrome ['pælɪndrəʊm] *n* palindromo *m*.

palings ['peɪlɪŋz] *npl* cerca *f*, empalizada *f*.

pall [pɔːl] ◇ *n* **-1.** [of smoke] nube *f*, cortina *f*. **-2.** *Am* [coffin] féretro *m*. ◇ *vi* cansar, hacerse pesado(da).

pallbearer ['pɔːl,beərə'] *n* portador *m*, -ra *f* del féretro.

pallet ['pælɪt] *n* plataforma *f* de carga.

palliative ['pælɪətɪv] *n fml* paliativo *m*.

pallid ['pælɪd] *adj literary* pálido(da).

pallor ['pælə'] *n literary* palidez *f*.

palm [pɑːm] *n* **-1.** [tree] palmera *f*. **-2.** [of hand] palma *f*; **to read sb's ~** leerle la mano a alguien.

◆ **palm off** *vt sep inf*: **to ~ sthg off on sb** endosar OR encasquetar algo a alguien; **to ~ sb off with** despachar a alguien con; **to ~ sthg off as** hacer pasar algo por.

palmistry ['pɑːmɪstrɪ] *n* quiromancia *f*.

palm oil *n* aceite *m* de palma.

Palm Sunday *n* Domingo *m* de Ramos.

palm tree *n* palmera *f*.

palomino [,pælə'miːnəʊ] (*pl* **-s**) *n* palomino *m*.

palpable ['pælpəbl] *adj* palpable.

palpably ['pælpəblɪ] *adv* evidentemente.

palpitate ['pælpɪteɪt] *vi* **-1.** [beat quickly] palpitar. **-2.** *fml* [tremble]: **to ~ (with)** estremecerse (de).

palpitations [,pælpɪ'teɪʃənz] *npl* palpitaciones *fpl*.

palsy ['pɔːlzɪ] *n* perlesía *f*.

paltry ['pɔːltrɪ] (*compar* **-ier**, *superl* **-iest**) *adj* mísero(ra).

pampas ['pæmpəz] *n*: **the ~** la Pampa.

pampas grass *n* cortadera *f*.

pamper ['pæmpə'] *vt* mimar.

pamphlet ['pæmflɪt] ◇ *n* [political] panfleto *m*; [publicity, information] folleto *m*. ◇ *vi* repartir panfletos.

pamphleteer [,pæmflə'tɪə'] *n* POL panfletista *m y f*.

pan [pæn] (*pt & pp* **-ned**, *cont* **-ning**) ◇ *n* **-1.** [saucepan] cazuela *f*, cacerola *f*; [frying pan] sartén *f*. **-2.** *Am* [for bread, cakes etc] molde *m*. ◇ *vt inf* [criticize] poner por los suelos. ◇ *vi* **-1.** [for gold] cribar. **-2.** CINEMA tomar vistas panorámicas.

panacea [,pænə'sɪə] *n*: **a ~ (for)** la panacea (de).

panache [pə'næʃ] *n* garbo *m*, donaire *m*.

Panama [,pænə'mɑː] *n* Panamá.

Panama Canal *n*: **the ~** el canal de Panamá.

Panama City *n* Ciudad de Panamá.

panama (hat) *n* panamá *m*.

Panamanian [,pænə'meɪnɪən] ◇ *adj* panameño(ña). ◇ *n* panameño *m*, -ña *f*.

pan-American *adj* panamericano(na).

pancake ['pænkeɪk] *n* torta *f*, crepe *f*.

Pancake Day *n Br* ≃ Martes *m inv* de Carnaval.

pancake roll *n* rollito *m* de primavera.

Pancake Tuesday = Pancake Day.

pancreas ['pæŋkrɪəs] *n* pancreas *m inv*.

panda ['pændə] (*pl inv* OR **-s**) *n* panda *m*.

Panda car *n Br* coche *m* patrulla.

pandemonium [,pændɪ'məʊnjəm] *n* pandemónium *m*, jaleo *m*.

pander ['pændə'] *vi*: **to ~ to** complacer a.

pane [peɪn] *n* (hoja *f* de) cristal *m*.

panel ['pænl] *n* **-1.** [group of people] equipo *m*. **-2.** [of a material] panel *m*. **-3.** [of a machine] tablero *m*, panel *m*.

panel game *n Br* programa *m* concurso de equipos.

panelling *Br*, **paneling** *Am* ['pænəlɪŋ] *n* (U) [on a ceiling] artesonado *m*; [on a wall] paneles *mpl*.

panellist *Br*, **panelist** *Am* ['pænəlɪst] *n* integrante *m y f* (de un equipo).

panel pin *n Br* puntilla *f*, espiga *f* (*clavo*).

pang [pæŋ] *n* punzada *f*.

panic ['pænɪk] (*pt & pp* **-ked**, *cont* **-king**) ◇ *n* pánico *m*. ◇ *vi* aterrarse, aterrorizarse.

panicky ['pænɪkɪ] *adj* [person] aterrado(da), nervioso(sa); [feeling] aterrador(ra), de pánico.

panic stations *n inf*: it was ~ fue una verdadera locura.

panic-stricken *adj* preso(sa) OR víctima del pánico.

pannier ['pænɪəʳ] *n* [on horse] alforja *f*; [on bicycle, sb's back] cesta *f*.

panoply ['pænəplɪ] *n fml* pompa *f*.

panorama [ˌpænə'rɑːmə] *n* panorama *m*, vista *f*.

panoramic [ˌpænə'ræmɪk] *adj* panorámico(ca).

pansy ['pænzɪ] (*pl* **-ies**) *n* **-1.** [flower] pensamiento *m*. **-2.** *pej inf* [man] marica *m*.

pant [pænt] *vi* jadear.

panther ['pænθəʳ] (*pl inv* OR **-s**) *n* pantera *f*.

panties ['pæntɪz] *npl inf* bragas *fpl*.

pantihose ['pæntɪhəʊz] = **panty hose**.

panto ['pæntəʊ] (*pl* **-s**) *n Br inf* = **pantomime**.

pantomime ['pæntəmaɪm] *n Br obra musical humorística para niños celebrada en Navidad.*

PANTOMIME:

El género teatral típicamente británico de la 'pantomime' posee una serie de convenciones, tales como personajes-tipo ('pantomime dame', 'principal boy') y frases concretas ('look behind you!', 'Oh yes he is! - Oh no he isn't!'), que se repiten en todas las obras. Estas obras, que se representan durante las fiestas navideñas, se inspiran generalmente en los cuentos de hadas

pantry ['pæntrɪ] (*pl* **-ies**) *n* despensa *f*.

pants [pænts] *npl* **-1.** *Br* [underpants] calzoncillos *mpl*. **-2.** *Am* [trousers] pantalones *mpl*.

panty hose ['pæntɪ-] *npl Am* medias *fpl*.

papa [*Br* pə'pɑː, *Am* 'pæpə] *n* papá *m*.

papacy ['peɪpəsɪ] (*pl* **-ies**) *n* papado *m*, pontificado *m*.

papal ['peɪpl] *adj* papal, pontificio(cia).

paparazzi [ˌpæpə'rætsɪ] *npl usu pej* paparazzi *mpl*, *periodistas que asedian a los famosos*.

papaya [pə'paɪə] *n* papaya *f*.

paper ['peɪpəʳ] ◇ *n* **-1.** (*U*) [material] papel *m*; **piece of** ~ [sheet] hoja *f* de papel; [scrap] trozo *m* de papel; **on** ~ [written down] por escrito; [in theory] sobre el papel. **-2.** [newspaper] periódico *m*. **-3.** [in exam] examen *m*. **-4.** [essay - gen] estudio *m*, ensayo *m*; [- for conference] ponencia *f*. ◇ *adj* **-1.** [made of paper] de papel. **-2.** *fig* [hypothetical] teórico(ca). ◇ *vt* empapelar.

◆ **papers** *npl* **-1.** [official documents] documentación *f*. **-2.** [collected information] documentos *mpl*.

◆ **paper over** *vt fus fig* disimular.

paperback ['peɪpəbæk] ◇ *n* libro *m* en rústica; **in** ~ en rústica. ◇ *comp*: ~ **(book)** libro *m* en rústica.

paperboy ['peɪpəbɔɪ] *n* repartidor *m* de periódicos.

paper clip *n* clip *m*.

papergirl ['peɪpəgɜːl] *n* repartidora *f* de periódicos.

paper handkerchief *n* pañuelo *m* de papel, klínex® *m inv*.

paper knife *n* abrecartas *m inv*, cortapapeles *m inv*.

paper money *n* (*U*) papel *m* moneda.

paper shop *n Br* quiosco *m* de periódicos.

paperweight ['peɪpəweɪt] *n* pisapapeles *m inv*.

paperwork ['peɪpəwɜːk] *n* papeleo *m*.

papier-mâché [ˌpæpjeɪ'mæʃeɪ] ◇ *n* cartón *m* piedra. ◇ *comp* de cartón piedra.

papist ['peɪpɪst] *n pej* papista *m y f*.

paprika ['pæprɪkə] *n* pimentón *m*.

Papua ['pæpjʊə] *n* Papúa.

Papuan ['pæpjʊən] ◇ *adj* papú, papúa. ◇ *n* papú *m y f*, papúa *m y f*.

Papua New Guinea *n* Papúa Nueva Guinea.

par [pɑːʳ] *n* **-1.** [parity]: **on a** ~ **with** al mismo nivel que. **-2.** GOLF par *m*; **under/over** ~ bajo/sobre par. **-3.** [good health]: **below** OR **under** ~ pachucho(cha).

para ['pærə] *n Br* paracaidista *m y f* (*del ejército*).

parable ['pærəbl] *n* parábola *f*.

parabola [pə'ræbələ] *n* parábola *f*.

paracetamol [ˌpærə'siːtəmɒl] *n* paracetamol *m*.

parachute ['pærəʃuːt] ◇ *n* paracaídas *m inv*. ◇ *vi* saltar en paracaídas.

parade [pə'reɪd] ◇ *n* **-1.** [procession] desfile *m*; **on** ~ MIL pasando revista. **-2.** *Br* [street of shops] *zona de tiendas*. ◇ *vt* **-1.** [soldiers] hacer desfilar; [criminals, captives] pasear. **-2.** [trophy, medal] pasear. **-3.** *fig* [flaunt] exhibir, hacer alarde de. ◇ *vi* desfilar.

parade ground *n* plaza *f* de armas.

paradigm ['pærədaɪm] *n* paradigma *m*.

paradigmatic [ˌpærədɪg'mætɪk] *adj* paradigmático(ca).

paradise ['pærədaɪs] *n fig* paraíso *m*.

◆ **Paradise** *n* [Heaven] el Paraíso.

paradox ['pærədɒks] *n* paradoja *f*.

paradoxical [ˌpærə'dɒksɪkl] *adj* paradójico(ca).

paradoxically [ˌpærə'dɒksɪklɪ] *adv* paradójicamente.

paraffin ['pærəfɪn] *n* parafina *f*.

paraffin wax *n* parafina *f*.

paragon ['pærəgən] *n* dechado *m*.

paragraph ['pærəgrɑːf] *n* párrafo *m*, acápite *m Amer*.

Paraguay ['pærəgwaɪ] *n* (el) Paraguay.

Paraguayan [,pærə'gwaɪən] ◇ *adj* paraguayo(ya). ◇ *n* paraguayo *m*, -ya *f*.

parakeet ['pærəkiːt] *n* periquito *m*.

parallel ['pærəlel] ◇ *adj*: ~ (**to** OR **with**) paralelo(la) (a). ◇ *n* **-1.** [parallel line, surface] paralela *f*. **-2.** [something, someone similar]: **to have no** ~ no tener precedente. **-3.** [similarity] semejanza *f*, paralelo *m*. **-4.** GEOGR paralelo *m*. ◇ *vt* ser equiparable a.

parallel bars *npl* paralelas *fpl*.

paralyse *Br*, **-yze** *Am* ['pærəlaɪz] *vt lit & fig* paralizar.

paralysed *Br*, **paralyzed** *Am* ['pærəlaɪzd] *adj lit & fig* paralizado(da).

paralysis [pə'rælɪsɪs] (*pl* **-lyses** [-lɪsiːz]) *n* parálisis *f inv*.

paralytic [,pærə'lɪtɪk] ◇ *adj* **-1.** MED paralítico(ca). **-2.** *Br inf* [drunk]: **to be** ~ estar como una cuba. ◇ *n* paralítico *m*, -ca *f*.

paramedic [,pærə'medɪk] *n* auxiliar sanitario *m*, auxiliar sanitaria *f*.

paramedical [,pærə'medɪkl] *adj* de auxiliar sanitario.

parameter [pə'ræmɪtəʳ] *n* parámetro *m*.

paramilitary [,pærə'mɪlɪtrɪ] *adj* paramilitar.

paramount ['pærəmaunt] *adj* vital, fundamental; **of** ~ **importance** de suma importancia.

paranoia [,pærə'nɔɪə] *n* paranoia *f*.

paranoiac [,pærə'nɔɪæk] ◇ *adj* paranoico(ca). ◇ *n* paranoico *m*, -ca *f*.

paranoid ['pærənɔɪd] *adj* paranoico(ca).

paranormal [,pærə'nɔːml] *adj* paranormal.

parapet ['pærəpɪt] *n* parapeto *m*.

paraphernalia [,pærəfə'neɪljə] *n* parafernalia *f*.

paraphrase ['pærəfreɪz] ◇ *n* paráfrasis *f inv*. ◇ *vt* parafrasear.

paraplegia [,pærə'pliːdʒə] *n* paraplejía *f*.

paraplegic [,pærə'pliːdʒɪk] ◇ *adj* parapléjico(ca). ◇ *n* parapléjico *m*, -ca *f*.

parapsychology [,pærəsaɪ'kɒlədʒɪ] *n* parapsicología *f*.

Paraquat® ['pærəkwɒt] *n tipo de herbicida*.

parasite ['pærəsaɪt] *n* parásito *m*, -ta *f*.

parasitic [,pærə'sɪtɪk] *adj* parásito(ta).

parasol ['pærəsɒl] *n* sombrilla *f*.

paratrooper ['pærətruːpəʳ] *n* paracaidista *m y f* (*del ejército*).

parboil ['pɑːbɔɪl] *vt* cocer a medias.

parcel ['pɑːsl] (*Br pt & pp* **-led**, *cont* **-ling**, *Am pt & pp* **-ed**, *cont* **-ing**) *n* paquete *m*, encomienda *f Amer*.

◆ **parcel up** *vt sep* empaquetar.

parcel post *n* (servicio *m* de) paquete *m* postal.

parched [pɑːtʃt] *adj* **-1.** [land] abrasado(da); [plant] agostado(da). **-2.** [throat, mouth] seco(ca); [lips] quemado(da). **-3.** *inf* [very thirsty] seco(ca).

parchment ['pɑːtʃmənt] *n* [paper] pergamino *m*.

pardon ['pɑːdn] ◇ *n* **-1.** JUR perdón *m*, indulto *m*. **-2.** [forgiveness] perdón *m*; **I beg your** ~? [showing surprise, asking for repetition] ¿perdón?, ¿cómo (dice)?; **I beg your** ~ [to apologize] le ruego me disculpe, perdón. ◇ *vt* **-1.** [forgive]: **to** ~ **sb** (**for sthg**) perdonar a alguien (por algo); ~? ¿perdón?, ¿cómo (dice)?; ~ **me** [touching sb accidentally, belching] discúlpeme, perdón; [excuse me] con permiso. **-2.** JUR indultar.

pardonable ['pɑːdnəbl] *adj* perdonable.

pare [peəʳ] *vt* [apple] pelar; [fingernails] cortar.

◆ **pare down** *vt sep* recortar.

parent ['peərənt] *n* [father] padre *m*; [mother] madre *f*.

◆ **parents** *npl* padres *mpl*.

parentage ['peərəntɪdʒ] *n* (*U*) origen *m*, ascendencia *f*.

parental [pə'rentl] *adj* [paternal] paterno(na); [maternal] materno(na).

parent company *n* compañía *f* OR casa *f* matriz.

parenthesis [pə'renθɪsɪs] (*pl* **-theses** [-θɪsiːz]) *n* paréntesis *m inv*.

parenthetical [,pærən'θetɪkl] *adj* parentético(ca), al margen.

parenthood ['peərənthud] *n* [fatherhood] paternidad *f*; [motherhood] maternidad *f*.

parenting ['peərəntɪŋ] *n* crianza *f*.

parent-teacher association *n asociación de padres y maestros*.

par excellence *adj* por excelencia.

pariah [pə'raɪə] *n pej* marginado *m*, -da *f*, paria *m y f*.

Paris ['pærɪs] *n* París.

parish ['pærɪʃ] *n* **-1.** [of church] parroquia *f*. **-2.** *Br* [area of local government] municipio *m*.

parish council *n Br* ≃ consejo *m* parroquial OR municipal.

parishioner [pə'rɪʃənəʳ] *n* parroquiano *m*, -na *f*.

Parisian [pə'rɪzjən] ◇ *adj* parisino(na). ◇ *n* parisino *m*, -na *f*.

parity ['pærətɪ] *n*: ~ **(with/between)** igualdad *f* (con/entre).

park [pɑːk] ◇ *n* parque *m*. ◇ *vt & vi* aparcar, parquear *Amer*.

parka ['pɑːkə] *n* parka *f*.

parking ['pɑːkɪŋ] *n* aparcamiento *m*; **"no ~"** "prohibido aparcar".

parking garage *n Am* aparcamiento *m* (*en edificio*).

parking light *n Am* luz *f* de estacionamiento.

parking lot *n Am* aparcamiento *m* (al aire libre).

parking meter *n* parquímetro *m*.

parking place *n* aparcamiento *m*.

parking ticket *n* multa *f* por aparcamiento indebido.

Parkinson's disease ['pɑːkɪnsnz-] *n* enfermedad *f* de Parkinson.

park keeper *n Br* guarda *m y f* del parque.

parkland ['pɑːklænd] *n* (*U*) parque *m*.

parkway ['pɑːkweɪ] *n Am* avenida *f*.

parky ['pɑːkɪ] (*compar* **-ier**, *superl* **-iest**) *adj Br inf* fresco(ca).

parlance ['pɑːləns] *n*: **in common/legal** *etc* ~ en el habla común/legal *etc*, en el lenguaje común/legal *etc*.

parliament ['pɑːləmənt] *n* **-1.** [assembly, institution] parlamento *m*. **-2.** [session] legislatura *f*.

parliamentarian [,pɑːləmen'teərɪən] parlamentario *m*, -ria *f*.

parliamentary [,pɑːlə'mentərɪ] *adj* parlamentario(ria).

parlour *Br*, **parlor** *Am* ['pɑːləʳ] *n dated* salón *m*.

parlour game *n* juego *m* de salón.

parlous ['pɑːləs] *adj fml* precario(ria).

Parmesan (cheese) [,pɑːmɪ'zæn-] *n* (queso *m*) parmesano *m*.

parochial [pə'rəʊkjəl] *adj pej* de miras estrechas.

parody ['pærədɪ] (*pl* **-ies**, *pt & pp* **-ied**) ◇ *n* parodia *f*. ◇ *vt* parodiar.

parole [pə'rəʊl] ◇ *n* libertad *f* condicional (bajo palabra); **on** ~ en libertad condicional. ◇ *vt* poner en libertad condicional.

paroxysm ['pærəksɪzm] *n* **-1.** [of anger, laughter] acceso *m*. **-2.** MED ataque *m*.

parquet ['pɑːkeɪ] *n* parqué *m*.

parrot ['pærət] *n* loro *m*, papagayo *m*.

parrot fashion *adv* como un loro.

parry ['pærɪ] (*pt & pp* **-ied**) *vt* **-1.** [blow] parar; [attack] desviar. **-2.** [question] eludir.

parsimonious [,pɑːsɪ'məʊnjəs] *adj fml & pej* mezquino(na), tacaño(ña).

parsley ['pɑːslɪ] *n* perejil *m*.

parsnip ['pɑːsnɪp] *n* chirivía *f*, pastinaca *f*.

parson ['pɑːsn] *n* párroco *m*.

parson's nose *n Br* rabadilla *f* (del pollo).

part [pɑːt] ◇ *n* **-1.** [gen] parte *f*; **in** ~ en parte; **the best** OR **better** ~ **of** la mayor parte de; **for the most** ~ en su mayoría; ~ **and parcel of** parte integrante de. **-2.** [component] pieza *f*. **-3.** THEATRE papel *m*. **-4.** [involvement]: ~ **(in)** participación *f* (en); **to play an important** ~ **(in)** desempeñar OR jugar un papel importante (en); **to take** ~ **(in)** tomar parte (en); **to want no** ~ **in** no querer tener nada que ver con; **for my/his** ~ por mi/su parte; **on my/his** ~ por mi/su parte. **-5.** *Am* [hair parting] raya *f*. ◇ *adv* en parte; **it's** ~ **black and** ~ **white** es blanco y negro. ◇ *vt* **-1.** [lips, curtains] abrir. **-2.** [hair] peinar con raya. ◇ *vi* **-1.** [leave one another] separarse. **-2.** [separate - lips, curtains] abrirse.

◆ **parts** *npl* [place] tierras *fpl*, pagos *mpl*.

◆ **part with** *vt fus* desprenderse de, separarse de.

partake [pɑː'teɪk] (*pt* **-took**, *pp* **-taken**) *vi fml*: **to** ~ **of** [wine] beber; [food] comer.

part exchange *n* sistema de pagar parte de algo con un artículo usado; **in** ~ como parte del pago.

partial ['pɑːʃl] *adj* **-1.** [incomplete, biased] parcial. **-2.** [fond]: ~ **to** amigo(ga) de, aficionado(da) a.

partiality [,pɑːʃɪ'ælətɪ] *n* **-1.** [bias] parcialidad *f*. **-2.** [fondness]: ~ **for** afición *f* a.

partially ['pɑːʃəlɪ] *adv* parcialmente, en parte.

participant [pɑː'tɪsɪpənt] *n* participante *m y f*.

participate [pɑː'tɪsɪpeɪt] *vi*: **to** ~ **(in)** participar (en).

participation [pɑː,tɪsɪ'peɪʃn] *n* participación *f*.

participle ['pɑːtɪsɪpl] *n* participio *m*.

particle ['pɑːtɪkl] *n* partícula *f*.

particular [pə'tɪkjʊləʳ] *adj* **-1.** [specific, unique] especial, en concreto OR particular. **-2.** [extra, greater] especial. **-3.** [difficult] exigente.

◆ **particulars** *npl* [of person] datos *mpl*; [of thing] detalles *mpl*.

◆ **in particular** *adv* en particular, en especial.

particularity [pə,tɪkjʊ'lærətɪ] (*pl* **-ies**) *n fml* **-1.** [fussiness] escrupulosidad *f*. **-2.** [detail] pormenor *m*, detalle *m*.

particularly [pə'tɪkjʊləlɪ] *adv* especialmente.

parting ['pɑːtɪŋ] *n* -1. [separation] despedida *f*. -2. *Br* [in hair] raya *f*.

parting shot *n*: to deliver a ~ lanzar un último comentario antes de marcharse.

partisan [ˌpɑːtɪ'zæn] ◇ *adj* partidista. ◇ *n* [freedom fighter] partisano *m*, -na *f*.

partition [pɑː'tɪʃn] ◇ *n* -1. [wall] tabique *m*; [screen] separación *f*. -2. [of a country] división *f*. ◇ *vt* -1. [room] dividir con tabiques. -2. [country] dividir.

partly ['pɑːtlɪ] *adv* en parte.

partner ['pɑːtnər] ◇ *n* -1. [spouse, lover] pareja *f*. -2. [in an activity] compañero *m*, -ra *f*. -3. [in a business] socio *m*, -cia *f*. -4. [ally] colega *m y f*. ◇ *vt* ir de pareja de OR con.

partnership ['pɑːtnəʃɪp] *n* -1. [relationship] asociación *f*; to go into ~ (with) asociarse (con). -2. [business] sociedad *f*.

partook [pɑː'tʊk] *pt* → partake.

partridge ['pɑːtrɪdʒ] *n* perdiz *f*.

part-time ◇ *adj* a tiempo parcial, de media jornada. ◇ *adv* a tiempo parcial.

part-timer *n* trabajador *m*, -ra *f* a tiempo parcial.

party ['pɑːtɪ] (*pl* -ies) ◇ *n* -1. POL partido *m*. -2. [social gathering] fiesta *f*. -3. [group] grupo *m*. -4. JUR parte *f*. -5. [involved person]: to be a ~ to participar en. ◇ *vi inf* irse de juerga.

party line *n* -1. POL línea *f* (política) del partido. -2. TELEC línea *f* (telefónica) compartida.

party piece *n inf número favorito que alguien suele ejecutar siempre para entretener a la gente en fiestas etc.*

party political broadcast *n Br* espacio *m* electoral.

party politics *n* (*U*) política *f* del partidismo.

party wall *n* pared *f* medianera.

parvenu ['pɑːvənjuː] *n* advenedizo *m*.

parvenue ['pɑːvənjuː] *n* advenediza *f*.

pass [pɑːs] ◇ *n* -1. SPORT pase *m*. -2. [document, permit] pase *m*; travel ~ tarjeta *f* OR abono *m* de transportes. -3. *Br* [successful result] aprobado *m*. -4. [route between mountains] vía *f*, desfiladero *m*. -5. *phr*: to make a ~ at sb intentar ligar con alguien.
◇ *vt* -1. [gen] pasar; to ~ sthg (to sb), to ~ (sb) sthg pasar OR pasarle algo (a alguien); ~ the string through the hole pase la cuerda por el agujero. -2. [move past - thing] pasar por (delante de); [- person] pasar delante de; to ~ sb in the street cruzarse con alguien. -3. AUT adelantar. -4. [exceed] sobrepasar. -5. [exam, candidate, law] aprobar; to ~ sthg fit (for) dar algo por bueno (para). -6. [opinion, judgement] formular; [sentence] dictar.
◇ *vi* -1. [gen] pasar. -2. AUT adelantar. -3. [in exam] pasar, aprobar. -4. [occur] transcurrir; to ~ unnoticed pasar desapercibido.

◆ **pass around** = pass round.

◆ **pass as** *vt fus* pasar por.

◆ **pass away** *vi* fallecer, pasar a mejor vida.

◆ **pass by** ◇ *vt sep* [subj: people] hacer caso omiso a; [subj: events, life] pasar desapercibido(da) a. ◇ *vi* pasar cerca.

◆ **pass for** = pass as.

◆ **pass off** *vt sep*: to ~ sthg/sb off as sthg hacer pasar algo/a alguien por algo.

◆ **pass on** ◇ *vt sep*: to ~ sthg on (to) pasar algo (a). ◇ *vi* -1. [move on] continuar; to ~ on to the next subject pasar al siguiente tema. -2. = pass away.

◆ **pass out** *vi* -1. [faint] desmayarse. -2. *Br* MIL graduarse.

◆ **pass over** *vt fus* hacer caso omiso de, pasar por alto.

◆ **pass round** *vt sep* ir pasando, pasar.

◆ **pass to** *vt fus* [be left to] pasar a.

◆ **pass up** *vt sep* dejar pasar OR escapar.

passable ['pɑːsəbl] *adj* -1. [satisfactory] pasable, aceptable. -2. [not blocked] transitable.

passably ['pɑːsəblɪ] *adv* aceptablemente.

passage ['pæsɪdʒ] *n* -1. [corridor - between houses] pasadizo *m*, pasaje *m*; [- between rooms] pasillo *m*. -2. [clear path] paso *m*, hueco *m*. -3. MED conducto *m*, tubo *m*. -4. [of music, speech] pasaje *m*. -5. *fml* [of vehicle, person, time] paso *m*. -6. [sea journey] travesía *f*.

passageway ['pæsɪdʒweɪ] *n* [between houses] pasadizo *m*, pasaje *m*; [between rooms] pasillo *m*.

passbook ['pɑːsbʊk] *n* ≈ cartilla *f* OR libreta *f* de banco.

passé [pæ'seɪ] *adj pej* pasado(da) de moda, desfasado(da).

passenger ['pæsɪndʒər] *n* pasajero *m*, -ra *f*.

passerby [ˌpɑːsə'baɪ] (*pl* passersby [ˌpɑːsəz'baɪ]) *n* transeúnte *m y f*.

passing ['pɑːsɪŋ] ◇ *adj* [fad] pasajero(ra); [remark] de pasada. ◇ *n* paso *m*, transcurso *m*.

◆ **in passing** *adv* de pasada.

passion ['pæʃn] *n*: ~ (for) pasión *f* (por).

◆ **Passion** *n*: the Passion la Pasión.

passionate ['pæʃənət] *adj* apasionado(da).

passionately ['pæʃənətlɪ] *adv* apasionadamente.

passionfruit ['pæʃənfruːt] *n* granadilla *f*.

passive ['pæsɪv] ◇ *adj* pasivo(va). ◇ *n*: **the** ~ la pasiva.

passively ['pæsɪvlɪ] *adv* con pasividad.

passive resistance *n* resistencia *f* pasiva.

passive smoker *n* fumador *m* pasivo.

passivity [pæ'sɪvətɪ] *n* pasividad *f*.

passkey ['pɑːskiː] *n* **-1.** [particular] llave *f*. **-2.** [universal] llave *f* maestra.

Passover ['pɑːsˌəʊvəʳ] *n*: **(the)** ~ **(la)** Pascua judía.

passport ['pɑːspɔːt] *n* pasaporte *m*; *fig*: ~ **to sthg** pasaporte a algo.

passport control *n* control *m* de pasaportes.

password ['pɑːswɜːd] *n* [gen & COMPUT] contraseña *f*.

past [pɑːst] ◇ *adj* **-1.** [former] anterior. **-2.** [most recent] pasado(da); **over the** ~ **week** durante la última semana. **-3.** [finished] terminado(da); **our problems are** ~ se han acabado los problemas.
◇ *adv* **-1.** [telling the time]: **it's ten** ~ son y diez. **-2.** [beyond, in front] por delante; **to walk/run** ~ pasar andando/corriendo.
◇ *n* **-1.** [time]: **the** ~ el pasado. **-2.** [personal history] pasado *m*.
◇ *prep* **-1.** [telling the time]: **it's five/half/a quarter** ~ **ten** son las diez y cinco/media/cuarto. **-2.** [alongside, in front of] por delante de. **-3.** [beyond] más allá de; **it's** ~ **the bank** está pasado el banco; **to be** ~ **it** *inf* estar para el arrastre; **I wouldn't put it** ~ **him** *inf* tratándose de él no me extrañaría un pelo.

pasta ['pæstə] *n* (*U*) pasta *f*.

paste [peɪst] ◇ *n* **-1.** [smooth mixture] pasta *f*. **-2.** [food] paté *m*, pasta *f*. **-3.** [glue] engrudo *m*. **-4.** [jewellery] bisutería *f*. ◇ *vt* [labels, stamps] pegar; [surface] engomar, engrudar.

pastel ['pæstl] ◇ *adj* pastel (*inv*). ◇ *n* **-1.** [colour] color *m* pastel. **-2.** ART [crayon] pastel *m*.

paste-up *n* TYPO maqueta *f*.

pasteurize, -ise ['pɑːstʃəraɪz] *vt* pasteurizar.

pastiche [pæ'stiːʃ] *n* **-1.** [imitation] imitación *f*. **-2.** [mixture] pastiche *m*.

pastille ['pæstɪl] *n* pastilla *f*.

pastime ['pɑːstaɪm] *n* pasatiempo *m*, afición *f*.

pasting ['peɪstɪŋ] *n* *inf* paliza *f*.

pastor ['pɑːstəʳ] *n* pastor *m* RELIG.

pastoral ['pɑːstərəl] *adj* **-1.** RELIG pastoral. **-2.** [of the country] pastoril, bucólico(ca).

past participle *n* participio *m* pasado.

pastrami [pə'strɑːmɪ] *n* embutido *de ternera ahumada.*

pastry ['peɪstrɪ] (*pl* **-ies**) *n* **-1.** [mixture] pasta *f*. **-2.** [cake] pastel *m*.

past tense *n*: **the** ~ el pasado.

pasture ['pɑːstʃəʳ] *n* pastó *m*.

pastureland ['pɑːstʃəlænd] *n* pasto *m*, prado *m*.

pasty¹ ['peɪstɪ] (*compar* **-ier**, *superl* **-iest**) *adj* pálido(da).

pasty² ['pæstɪ] (*pl* **-ies**) *n* *Br* empanada *f*.

pasty-faced ['peɪstɪ-] *adj* pálido(da).

pat [pæt] (*compar* **-ter**, *superl* **-test**, *pt* & *pp* **-ted**, *cont* **-ting**) ◇ *adj* preparado(da), ensayado(da). ◇ *n* **-1.** [gen] golpecito *m*; [to dog] caricia *f*; [on back, hand] palmadita *f*. **-2.** [of butter etc] porción *f*. ◇ *vt* [gen] golpear ligeramente; [dog] acariciar; [back, hand] dar palmaditas a.

Patagonia [ˌpætə'gəʊnɪə] *n* (la) Patagonia.

Patagonian [ˌpætə'gəʊnɪən] ◇ *adj* patagónico(ca). ◇ *n* patagón *m*, -ona *f*.

patch [pætʃ] ◇ *n* **-1.** [for mending] remiendo *m*; [to cover eye] parche *m*. **-2.** [part of surface] área *f*. **-3.** [area of land] bancal *m*, parcela *f*. **-4.** [period of time] período *m*. **-5.** *phr*: **not to be a** ~ **on** *inf* no igualar ni con mucho a. ◇ *vt* remendar.

◆ **patch together** *vt sep* [government, team] formar a duras penas; [agreement, solution] alcanzar a duras penas.

◆ **patch up** *vt sep* **-1.** [mend] reparar. **-2.** [resolve - quarrel] resolver; [- relationship] salvar.

patchwork ['pætʃwɜːk] ◇ *adj* de *trozos de distintos colores y formas.* ◇ *n* *fig* [of fields] mosaico *m*.

patchy ['pætʃɪ] (*compar* **-ier**, *superl* **-iest**) *adj* **-1.** [uneven - fog, sunshine] irregular; [- colour] desigual. **-2.** [incomplete] deficiente, incompleto(ta). **-3.** [good in parts] irregular.

pâté ['pæteɪ] *n* paté *m*.

patent [*Br* 'peɪtənt, *Am* 'pætənt] ◇ *adj* [obvious] patente, evidente. ◇ *n* patente *f*. ◇ *vt* patentar.

patented [*Br* 'peɪtəntɪd, *Am* 'pætəntɪd] *adj* patentado(da).

patentee [*Br* ˌpeɪtən'tiː, *Am* ˌpætən'tiː] *n* poseedor *m*, -ra *f* de una patente.

patent leather *n* charol *m*.

patently [*Br* 'peɪtəntlɪ, *Am* 'pætəntlɪ] *adv* evidentemente, patentemente.

Patent Office *n*: **the** ~ ≃ el Registro de Patentes y Marcas.

paternal [pə'tɜːnl] *adj* [love, attitude] paternal; [grandmother, grandfather] paterno(na).

paternalistic [pəˌtɜːnə'lɪstɪk] *adj* *pej* paternalista.

paternity [pə'tɜːnətɪ] *n* paternidad *f*.

paternity leave *n* permiso *m* por paternidad.

paternity suit *n* litigio *m* de paternidad.

path [pɑːθ, *pl* pɑːðz] *n* -1. [track, way ahead] camino *m*; **our ~s had crossed before** nuestros caminos se habían cruzado anteriormente. -2. [trajectory - of bullet] trayectoria *f*; [- of flight] rumbo *m*. -3. [course of action] curso *m*.

pathetic [pə'θetɪk] *adj* -1. [causing pity] patético(ca), lastimoso(sa). -2. [attempt, person] inútil, infeliz; [actor, film] malísimo(ma).

pathetically [pə'θetɪklɪ] *adv* -1. [causing pity] patéticamente. -2. [uselessly] lastimosamente.

pathological [ˌpæθə'lɒdʒɪkl] *adj* patológico(ca).

pathologist [pə'θɒlədʒɪst] *n* patólogo *m*, -ga *f*.

pathology [pə'θɒlədʒɪ] *n* patología *f*.

pathos ['peɪθɒs] *n* patetismo *m*.

pathway ['pɑːθweɪ] *n* camino *m*, sendero *m*.

patience ['peɪʃns] *n* -1. [quality] paciencia *f*; **to try sb's ~** poner a prueba la paciencia de alguien. -2. [card game] solitario *m*.

patient ['peɪʃnt] ◇ *adj* paciente. ◇ *n* paciente *m y f*.

patiently ['peɪʃntlɪ] *adv* pacientemente.

patina ['pætɪnə] *n* pátina *f*.

patio ['pætɪəʊ] (*pl* -s) *n* patio *m*.

patio doors *npl* puertas de cristal que dan a un patio.

patisserie [pə'tiːsərɪ] *n* pastelería *f*.

Patna rice ['pætnə-] *n* tipo de arroz largo procedente de la India.

patois ['pætwɑː] (*pl inv*) *n* dialecto *m*.

patriarch ['peɪtrɪɑːk] *n* [head of family] patriarca *m*.

patriarchy ['peɪtrɪɑːkɪ] (*pl* -ies) *n* patriarcado *m*.

patrimony [*Br* 'pætrɪmənɪ, *Am* 'pætrɪməʊnɪ] *n fml* patrimonio *m*.

patriot [*Br* 'pætrɪət, *Am* 'peɪtrɪət] *n* patriota *m y f*.

patriotic [*Br* ˌpætrɪ'ɒtɪk, *Am* ˌpeɪtrɪ'ɒtɪk] *adj* patriótico(ca).

patriotism [*Br* 'pætrɪətɪzm, *Am* 'peɪtrɪətɪzm] *n* patriotismo *m*.

patrol [pə'trəʊl] (*pt & pp* -led, *cont* -ling) ◇ *n* patrulla *f*; **on ~** de patrulla. ◇ *vt* patrullar.

patrol car *n* coche *m* patrulla.

patrolman [pə'trəʊlmən] (*pl* -men [-mən]) *n* *Am* policía *m*, guardia *m*.

patrol wagon *n* *Am* coche *m* celular.

patrolwoman [pə'trəʊlˌwʊmən] (*pl* -women [-ˌwɪmɪn]) *n* (mujer *f*) policía *f*, guardia *f*.

patron ['peɪtrən] *n* -1. [of arts] mecenas *m y f inv*. -2. *Br* [of charity, campaign] patrocinador *m*, -ra *f*. -3. *fml* [customer] cliente *m y f*.

patronage ['peɪtrənɪdʒ] *n* patrocinio *m*.

patronize, -ise ['pætrənaɪz] *vt* -1. *pej* [talk down to] tratar con aire paternalista OR condescendiente. -2. *fml* [back financially] patrocinar.

patronizing ['pætrənaɪzɪŋ] *adj pej* paternalista, condescendiente.

patron saint *n* santo patrón *m*, santa patrona *f*.

patter ['pætə'] ◇ *n* -1. [of raindrops] repiqueteo *m*, golpeteo *m*; [of feet] pasitos *mpl*. -2. [sales talk] charlatanería *f*. ◇ *vi* [dog, feet] corretear; [rain] repiquetear.

pattern ['pætən] *n* -1. [design] dibujo *m*, diseño *m*. -2. [of life, work] estructura *f*; [of illness, events] desarrollo *m*, evolución *f*. -3. [for sewing, knitting] patrón *m*. -4. [model] modelo *m*.

patterned ['pætənd] *adj* estampado(da).

patty ['pætɪ] (*pl* -ies) *n* empanada *f*.

paucity ['pɔːsətɪ] *n fml* escasez *f*.

paunch [pɔːntʃ] *n* barriga *f*, panza *f*.

paunchy ['pɔːntʃɪ] (*compar* -ier, *superl* -iest) *adj* barrigón(ona).

pauper ['pɔːpə'] *n* pobre *m y f*, indigente *m y f*.

pause [pɔːz] ◇ *n* pausa *f*. ◇ *vi* -1. [stop speaking] hacer una pausa. -2. [stop moving, doing sthg] detenerse.

pave [peɪv] *vt* pavimentar; **to ~ the way for** preparar el terreno para.

paved [peɪvd] *adj* pavimentado(da).

pavement ['peɪvmənt] *n* -1. *Br* [at side of road] acera *f*, andén *m* *Amer*. -2. *Am* [roadway] calzada *f*.

pavement artist *n* *Br* artista callejero que dibuja en las aceras.

pavilion [pə'vɪljən] *n* -1. *Br* [at sports field] vestuarios *mpl*. -2. [at exhibition] pabellón *m*.

paving ['peɪvɪŋ] *n* (U) pavimento *m*.

paving stone *n* losa *f*.

paw [pɔː] ◇ *n* [foot] pata *f*; [claw] zarpa *f*, garra *f*. ◇ *vt* -1. [subj: animal] dar zarpazos a; **to ~ the ground** piafar. -2. *pej* [subj: person] manosear, sobar.

pawn [pɔːn] ◇ *n* -1. [chesspiece] peón *m*. -2. [unimportant person] marioneta *f*. ◇ *vt* empeñar.

pawnbroker ['pɔːn‚brəukəʳ] *n* prestamista *m y f*.

pawnshop ['pɔːnʃɒp] *n* casa *f* de empeños, monte *m* de piedad.

pay [peɪ] (*pt* & *pp* **paid**) ◇ *vt* **-1.** [gen] pagar; **to ~ sb for sthg** pagar a alguien por algo; **he paid £20 for it** pagó 20 libras por ello; **to ~ one's way** costearse uno sus propios gastos. **-2.** *Br* [put into bank account]: **to ~ sthg into** ingresar algo en; **he paid in his wages** ingresó su sueldo. **-3.** [be profitable to] ser rentable a. **-4.** [be advantageous to] ser provechoso(sa) a; **it will ~ you not to say anything** más te vale no decir nada. **-5.** [compliment, visit] hacer; [respects] ofrecer; [attention] prestar; [homage] rendir.
◇ *vi* **-1.** [gen] pagar; **to ~ dearly for sthg** pagar caro (por) algo. **-2.** [be profitable] ser rentable.
◇ *n* paga *f*.
◆ **pay back** *vt sep* **-1.** [money] devolver, reembolsar. **-2.** [revenge oneself]: **to ~ sb back (for sthg)** hacer pagar a alguien (por algo).
◆ **pay off** ◇ *vt sep* **-1.** [repay - debt] liquidar, saldar. **-2.** [dismiss] despedir con indemnización. **-3.** [bribe] comprar, pagar. ◇ *vi* salir bien, tener éxito.
◆ **pay out** ◇ *vt sep* **-1.** [spend] pagar, desembolsar. **-2.** [rope] soltar. ◇ *vi* [spend money] pagar.
◆ **pay up** *vi* pagar.

payable ['peɪəbl] *adj* **-1.** [to be paid] pagadero(ra). **-2.** [on cheque]: **~ to** a favor de.

paybed ['peɪbed] *n Br* cama utilizada por un paciente de pago en un hospital público.

paycheck ['peɪtʃek] *n Am* paga *f*.

payday ['peɪdeɪ] *n* día *m* de paga.

PAYE (*abbr of* **pay as you earn**) *n* en el Reino Unido, sistema de retención fiscal de parte del sueldo del trabajador por la empresa.

payee [peɪ'iː] *n* beneficiario *m*, -ria *f*.

pay envelope *n Am* sobre *m* de paga.

payer ['peɪəʳ] *n* pagador *m*, -ra *f*.

paying guest ['peɪɪŋ-] *n* huésped *m y f* de pago.

paying-in ['peɪɪŋ-] *adj*: **~ slip** hoja *f* de ingreso.

payload ['peɪləud] *n* **-1.** [gen] carga *f* útil. **-2.** [explosive in missile] carga *f* explosiva.

paymaster ['peɪ‚mɑːstəʳ] *n* (oficial *m*) pagador *m*.

paymaster general *n* ministro encargado de pagar a los empleados de la Administración.

payment ['peɪmənt] *n* pago *m*.

payoff ['peɪɒf] *n* **-1.** [result] resultado *m*. **-2.**

Br [redundancy payment] indemnización *f* (por despido).

payola [peɪ'əulə] *n inf* soborno *m*.

payout ['peɪaut] *n inf* reparto *m* de dinero.

pay packet *n Br* **-1.** [envelope] sobre *m* de paga. **-2.** [wages] paga *f*.

pay phone, **pay station** *Am n* teléfono *m* público.

payroll ['peɪrəul] *n* nómina *f*.

payslip ['peɪslɪp] *n Br* hoja *f* de paga.

pay station *Am* = **pay phone**.

pay TV *n* televisión *f* a la carta.

PBS (*abbr of* **Public Broadcasting Service**) *n* organismo americano de producción audiovisual.

PBX (*abbr of* **private branch exchange**) *n* centralita.

pc ◇ *n abbr of* **postcard**. ◇ (*abbr of* **per cent**) p.c.

p/c *abbr of* **petty cash**.

PC ◇ *n* **-1.** (*abbr of* **personal computer**) PC *m*. **-2.** (*abbr of* **police constable**). **-3.** (*abbr of* **privy councillor**) *miembro del Privy Council*. ◇ *adj abbr of* **politically correct**.

PCB (*abbr of* **printed circuit board**) *n* PCB *m*.

PCV (*abbr of* **passenger carrying vehicle**) *n* VSP *m*.

pd *abbr of* **paid**.

PD *abbr of* **police department**.

pdq (*abbr of* **pretty damn quick**) *adv inf* superrápido.

PDSA (*abbr of* **People's Dispensary for Sick Animals**) *n* organización benéfica que ofrece tratamiento veterinario gratuito.

PDT (*abbr of* **Pacific Daylight Time**) *hora de verano de la costa oeste de Estados Unidos*.

PE (*abbr of* **physical education**) *n* EF *f*.

pea [piː] *n* guisante *m*, arveja *f Amer*.

peace [piːs] *n* **-1.** [gen] paz *f*; **to be at ~ (with)** estar en paz (con). **-2.** [quiet] calma *f*, tranquilidad *f*; **~ of mind** tranquilidad de espíritu. **-3.** [freedom from disagreement] orden *m*; **to make (one's) ~ (with)** hacer las paces (con).

peaceable ['piːsəbl] *adj* [not aggressive] pacífico(ca).

peaceably ['piːsəblɪ] *adv* [agree] pacíficamente; [live] en paz.

Peace Corps *n* organización estadounidense para la cooperación con los países en vías de desarrollo.

peaceful ['piːsful] *adj* **-1.** [quiet, calm] tranquilo(la). **-2.** [not aggressive] pacífico(ca).

peacefully ['piːsfulɪ] *adv* **-1.** [quietly, calmly] tranquilamente. **-2.** [without aggression] pacíficamente.

peacefulness ['piːsfʊlnɪs] *n* **-1.** [quietness] tranquilidad *f*. **-2.** [calmness] sosiego *m*, paz *f*.

peacckeeping force ['piːs,kiːpɪŋ-] *n* fuerzas *fpl* de pacificación.

peacemaker ['piːs,meɪkə'] *n* pacificador *m*, -ra *f*, conciliador *m*, -ra *f*.

peace offering *n* *inf* ofrenda *f* de paz.

peacetime ['piːstaɪm] *n* (*U*) tiempos *mpl* de paz.

peach [piːtʃ] ◇ *adj* [in colour] de color melocotón. ◇ *n* **-1.** [fruit] melocotón *m*. **-2.** [colour] color *m* melocotón. ◇ *comp* de melocotón.

Peach Melba [-'melbə] *n* melocotón servido con helado y zumo de frambuesa.

peacock ['piːkɒk] *n* pavo *m* real.

peahen ['piːhen] *n* pava *f* real.

peak [piːk] ◇ *n* **-1.** [mountain top] pico *m*, cima *f*. **-2.** [highest point] apogeo *m*. **-3.** [of cap] visera *f*. ◇ *adj* [season] alto(ta); [condition] perfecto(ta). ◇ *vi* alcanzar el máximo.

peaked [piːkt] *adj* con visera.

peak hour *n* hora *f* punta.

peak period *n* [of electricity etc] periodo *m* de tarifa máxima; [of traffic] horas *fpl* punta.

peak rate *n* tarifa *f* máxima.

peaky ['piːkɪ] (*compar* **-ier**, *superl* **-iest**) *adj* *Br inf* pachucho(cha).

peal [piːl] ◇ *n* [of bells] repique *m*; ~ **(of laughter)** carcajada *f*; ~ **(of thunder)** trueno *m*. ◇ *vi* repicar.

peanut ['piːnʌt] *n* cacahuete *m*, maní *m* Amer.

peanut butter *n* manteca *f* de cacahuete.

pear [peə'] *n* pera *f*.

pearl [pɜːl] *n* perla *f*.

pearly ['pɜːlɪ] (*compar* **-ier**, *superl* **-iest**) *adj* nacarado(da).

peasant ['peznt] *n* **-1.** [in countryside] campesino *m*, -na *f*, guajiro *m*, -ra *f* Amer. **-2.** *pej* [ignorant person] paleto *m*, palurdo *m*.

peasantry ['pezntrɪ] *n*: **the** ~ los campesinos.

peashooter ['piː,ʃuːtə'] *n* cerbatana *f*.

peat [piːt] *n* turba *f*.

peaty ['piːtɪ] (*compar* **-ier**, *superl* **-iest**) *adj* turboso(sa).

pebble ['pebl] *n* guijarro *m*.

pebbledash ['pebl,dæʃ] *n* *Br* enguijarrado *m*.

pecan (nut) [pɪ'kæn-] *n* pacana *f*.

peck [pek] ◇ *n* **-1.** [with beak] picotazo *m*. **-2.** [kiss] besito *m*. ◇ *vt* **-1.** [with beak] picotear. **-2.** [kiss] dar un besito a. ◇ *vi* picotear.

pecking order ['pekɪŋ-] *n* jerarquía *f*.

peckish ['pekɪʃ] *adj* *Br inf*: **to feel** ~ estar algo hambriento(ta).

pectin ['pektɪn] *n* pectina *f*.

pectoral ['pektərəl] *adj* pectoral.

peculiar [pɪ'kjuːljə'] *adj* **-1.** [odd] singular, extraño(ña). **-2.** [slightly ill] raro(ra), indispuesto(ta). **-3.** [characteristic]: **to be** ~ **to** ser propio(pia) de.

peculiarity [pɪ,kjuːlɪ'ærətɪ] (*pl* **-ies**) *n* **-1.** [eccentricity] extravagancia *f*, manía *f*. **-2.** [characteristic] peculiaridad *f*. **-3.** [oddness] rareza *f*.

peculiarly [pɪ'kjuːljəlɪ] *adv* **-1.** [especially] particularmente. **-2.** [oddly] de una manera extraña. **-3.** [characteristically] peculiarmente, característicamente.

pecuniary [pɪ'kjuːnjərɪ] *adj* pecuniario(ria).

pedagogy ['pedəgɒdʒɪ] *n* pedagogía *f*.

pedal ['pedl] (*Br pt* & *pp* **-led**, *cont* **-ling**, *Am pt* & *pp* **-ed**, *cont* **-ing**) ◇ *n* pedal *m*. ◇ *vi* pedalear.

pedal bin *n* cubo *m* de basura con pedal.

pedalo ['pedələʊ] *n* *Br* patín *m*.

pedant ['pedənt] *n* *pej* puntilloso *m*, -sa *f*.

pedantic [pɪ'dæntɪk] *adj* *pej* puntilloso(sa).

pedantry ['pedəntrɪ] *n* *pej* excesiva minuciosidad *f*.

peddle ['pedl] *vt* **-1.** [drugs] traficar con; [wares] vender de puerta en puerta. **-2.** [rumours] divulgar, difundir.

peddler ['pedlə'] *n* **-1.** [drug dealer] traficante *m y f* (de drogas). **-2.** *Am* = **pedlar**.

pederast ['pedəræst] *n* pederasta *m*.

pedestal ['pedɪstl] *n* pedestal *m*; **to put sb on a** ~ poner a alguien en un pedestal.

pedestrian [pɪ'destrɪən] ◇ *adj* *pej* mediocre. ◇ *n* peatón *m*.

pedestrian crossing *n* *Br* paso *m* de peatones.

pedestrianize, -ise [pɪ'destrɪənaɪz] *vt* peatonizar, convertir en zona peatonal.

pedestrian precinct *Br*, **pedestrian zone** *Am n* zona *f* peatonal.

pediatric [,piːdɪ'ætrɪk] *adj* pediátrico(ca).

pediatrician [,piːdɪə'trɪʃn] *n* pediatra *m y f*.

pediatrics [,piːdɪ'ætrɪks] *n* pediatría *f*.

pedicure ['pedɪ,kjʊə'] *n* pedicura *f*.

pedigree ['pedɪgriː] ◇ *adj* de raza. ◇ *n* **-1.** [of animal] pedigrí *m*. **-2.** [of person] linaje *m*.

pedlar *Br*, **peddler** *Am* ['pedlə'] *n* vendedor *m*, -ra *f* ambulante.

pedophile ['piːdəfaɪl] *n* paidófilo *m*, -la *f*.

pee [piː] *inf* ◇ *n* pis *m*; **to go for a** ~ ir a hacer un pis. ◇ *vi* mear, hacer pis.

peek [piːk] *inf* ◇ *n* mirada *f*, ojeada *f*. ◇ *vi* mirar a hurtadillas.

peel [piːl] ◇ *n* [gen] piel *f*; [of orange, lemon] corteza *f*; [once removed] mondaduras *fpl*. ◇ *vt* pelar, mondar. ◇ *vi* [walls, paint] desconcharse; [wallpaper] despegarse, desprenderse; [skin, nose] pelarse, despellejarse.
◆ **peel off** *vt sep* **-1.** [label] despegar; [cover] quitar. **-2.** [clothes] quitarse.

peeler ['piːləʳ] *n* mondador *m*.

peelings ['piːlɪŋz] *npl* peladuras *fpl*.

peep [piːp] ◇ *n* **-1.** [look] mirada *f* furtiva, ojeada *f*. **-2.** *inf* [sound] pío *m*. ◇ *vi* [look] mirar furtivamente.
◆ **peep out** *vi* asomar.

peephole ['piːphəʊl] *n* mirilla *f*.

peeping Tom [ˌpiːpɪŋ'tɒm] *n* mirón *m*.

peep show *n* mundonuevo *m*, cosmorama *m*.

peer [pɪəʳ] ◇ *n* **-1.** [noble] par *m*. **-2.** [equal] igual *m*. ◇ *vi* mirar con atención.

peerage ['pɪərɪdʒ] *n* **-1.** [rank] rango *m* de par. **-2.** [group]: **the** ~ la nobleza.

peeress ['pɪərɪs] *n* paresa *f*.

peer group *n* grupo generacional o social.

peer pressure *n* presión ejercida por el grupo generacional o social al que uno pertenece.

peeved [piːvd] *adj inf* fastidiado(da), disgustado(da).

peevish ['piːvɪʃ] *adj* malhumorado(da).

peg [peg] (*pt & pp* **-ged**, *cont* **-ging**) ◇ *n* **-1.** [hook] gancho *m*. **-2.** [for washing line] pinza *f*. **-3.** [on tent] estaca *f*. ◇ *vt* [prices] fijar, estabilizar.
◆ **peg out** *vi Br inf* estirar la pata.

pegboard ['pegbɔːd] *n* tablero vertical con agujeros donde se depositan clavijas.

PEI *n abbr of* Prince Edward Island.

pejorative [prɪ'dʒɒrətɪv] *adj* peyorativo(va), despectivo(va).

pekinese [ˌpiːkə'niːz], **pekingese** [ˌpiːkɪŋ'iːz] (*pl inv* OR **-s**) *n* [dog] pequinés *m*.
◆ **Pekinese, Pekingese** ◇ *adj* pequinés(esa). ◇ *n* [person] pequinés *m*, -esa *f*.

Peking [piː'kɪŋ] *n* Pekín.

pekingese = pekinese.

pelican ['pelɪkən] (*pl inv* OR **-s**) *n* pelícano *m*.

pelican crossing *n Br* paso de peatones con semáforo accionado por el usuario.

pellet ['pelɪt] *n* **-1.** [small ball] bolita *f*. **-2.** [for gun] perdigón *m*.

pell-mell [ˌpel'mel] *adv* atropelladamente.

pelmet ['pelmɪt] *n Br* galería *f*.

Peloponnese [ˌpeləpə'niːz] *npl*: **the** ~ el Peloponeso.

pelt [pelt] ◇ *n* **-1.** [animal skin] piel *f*. **-2.** [speed]: **(at) full** ~ a toda pastilla, a todo meter. ◇ *vt*: **to** ~ **sb with sthg** acribillar a alguien con algo, arrojar algo a alguien. ◇ *vi* **-1.** [rain] llover a cántaros. **-2.** [run very fast] correr a toda pastilla.

pelvic ['pelvɪk] *adj* pélvico(ca).

pelvis ['pelvɪs] (*pl* **-vises** OR **-ves** [-viːz]) *n* pelvis *f*.

pen [pen] (*pt & pp* **-ned**, *cont* **-ning**) ◇ *n* **-1.** [ballpoint] bolígrafo *m*, lapicera *f* Amer; [fountain pen] pluma *f*; [felt-tip] rotulador *m*. **-2.** [enclosure] redil *m*, corral *m*. ◇ *vt* **-1.** *literary* [write] escribir. **-2.** [enclose] encerrar.
◆ **pen in** *vt sep* encerrar.

penal ['piːnl] *adj* penal.

penalize, -ise ['piːnəlaɪz] *vt* **-1.** [gen] penalizar; SPORT penalizar, castigar. **-2.** [JUR - with fine] multar; [- with imprisonment] condenar. **-3.** [put at a disadvantage] perjudicar.

penal settlement *n* colonia *f* penal.

penalty ['penltɪ] (*pl* **-ies**) *n* **-1.** [punishment] pena *f*; **to pay the** ~ **(for sthg)** *fig* pagar las consecuencias (de algo). **-2.** [fine] multa *f*. **-3.** SPORT penalty *m*; ~ (**kick**) FTBL penalty *m*; RUGBY golpe *m* de castigo.

penalty area, **penalty box** *n Br* FTBL área *f* de castigo.

penalty clause *n* cláusula *f* penal.

penalty goal *n* RUGBY gol *m* de penalty.

penalty kick = penalty.

penance ['penəns] *n* *fig & RELIG* penitencia *f*.

pen-and-ink *adj* a pluma.

pence [pens] *Br pl* → **penny**.

penchant [*Br* pɑ̃ʃɑ̃, *Am* 'pentʃənt] *n*: **to have a** ~ **for** tener debilidad por.

pencil ['pensl] (*Br pt & pp* **-led**, *cont* **-ling**; *Am pt & pp* **-ed**, *cont* **-ing**) ◇ *n* lápiz *m*, lapicero *m*; **in** ~ a lápiz. ◇ *vt* escribir a lápiz.

pencil case *n* estuche *m*, plumero *m*.

pencil sharpener *n* sacapuntas *m inv*.

pendant ['pendənt] *n* [jewel on chain] colgante *m*.

pending ['pendɪŋ] *fml* ◇ *adj* **-1.** [about to happen] inminente. **-2.** [waiting to be dealt with] pendiente. ◇ *prep* a la espera de.

pending tray *n Br* bandeja *f* OR cajón *m* de asuntos pendientes.

pendulum ['pendjʊləm] (*pl* **-s**) *n* [of clock] péndulo *m*.

penetrate ['penɪtreɪt] ◇ *vt* **-1.** [barrier] salvar, atravesar; [jungle, crowd] adentrarse en, introducirse en; [subj: wind, rain, sharp object] penetrar en. **-2.** [infiltrate - organization] infiltrarse en. ◇ *vi inf* [be understood] hacer mella.

penetrating ['penitreitiŋ] *adj* **-1.** [gen] penetrante. **-2.** [sound] penetrante, agudo(da).
penetration [,peni'treiʃn] *n* **-1.** [act of penetrating] penetración *f.* **-2.** *fml* [insight] agudeza *f*, perspicacia *f.*
pen friend *n* amigo *m*, -ga *f* por correspondencia.
penguin ['peŋgwin] *n* pingüino *m.*
penicillin [,peni'silin] *n* penicilina *f.*
peninsula [pə'ninsjulə] (*pl* -s) *n* península *f*; **the Iberian Peninsula** la Península Ibérica.
penis ['pi:nis] (*pl* **penises** ['pi:nisiz]) *n* pene *m.*
penitent ['penitənt] *adj fml* penitente.
penitentiary [,peni'tenʃəri] (*pl* -ies) *n Am* penitenciaría *f.*
penknife ['pennaif] (*pl* -knives [-naivz]) *n* navaja *f*, chaveta *f Amer.*
pen name *n* seudónimo *m.*
pennant ['penənt] *n* banderín *m.*
penniless ['penilis] *adj* sin dinero.
Pennines ['penainz] *npl*: **the ~** los Peninos.
Pennsylvania [,pensil'veiniə] *n* Pensilvania.
penny ['peni] (*pl sense 1* -ies, *pl sense 2* **pence**) *n* **-1.** [coin] *Br* penique *m; Am* centavo *m.* **-2.** *Br* [value] penique *m.* **-3.** *phr*: **a ~ for your thoughts** ¿en qué estás pensando?; **as I listened, the ~ dropped** *Br inf* mientras la escuchaba, caí en la cuenta; **to spend a ~** *Br inf* ir al váter; **two** OR **ten a ~** *Br inf* a porrillo.
penny-pinching [-,pintʃiŋ] ◇ *adj* tacaño(ña), mezquino(na). ◇ *n* tacañería *f.*
pen pal *n inf* amigo *m*, -ga *f* por correspondencia.
pension ['penʃn] *n* **-1.** *Br* [gen] pensión *f.* **-2.** [disability pension] subsidio *m.*
◆ **pension off** *vt sep* jubilar.
pensionable ['penʃənəbl] *adj* [age] de jubilación; [job] con derecho a pensión.
pension book *n Br* libreta *f* de pensiones.
pensioner ['penʃənə'] *n Br*: **(old-age) ~** pensionista *m y f.*
pension fund *n* fondo *m* de pensiones.
pension plan, **pension scheme** *n* plan *m* de pensiones.
pensive ['pensiv] *adj* pensativo(va).
pentagon ['pentəgən] *n* pentágono *m.*
◆ **Pentagon** *n Am*: **the Pentagon** el Pentágono.

PENTAGON:

El Pentágono, un inmenso edificio con cinco fachadas situado en Washington, alberga el ministerio de Defensa estadounidense; de manera más general, este nombre se utiliza para referirse al poder militar estadounidense

pentathlon [pen'tæθlən] (*pl* -s) *n* pentatlón *m.*
Pentecost ['pentikɒst] *n* Pentecostés *m.*
penthouse ['penthaus, *pl* -hauziz] *n* ático *m.*
Pentium® **processor** [,pentiəm-] *n* procesador *m* Pentium® *m.*
pent up ['pent-] *adj* reprimido(da).
penultimate [pe'nʌltimət] *adj* penúltimo(ma).
penury ['penjuri] *n fml* miseria *f*, pobreza *f.*
peony ['piəni] (*pl* -ies) *n* peonía *f.*
people ['pi:pl] ◇ *n* [nation, race] pueblo *m.* ◇ *npl* **-1.** [gen] gente *f*; [individuals] personas *fpl*; **a table for eight ~** una mesa para ocho personas; **~ say that ...** dice la gente que .... **-2.** [inhabitants] habitantes *mpl.* **-3.** POL: **the ~** el pueblo. ◇ *vt*: **to be ~d by** OR **with** estar poblado(da) de.
pep [pep] (*pt & pp* -ped, *cont* -ping) *n inf* vitalidad *f.*
◆ **pep up** *vt sep* animar.
PEP (*abbr of* **personal equity plan**) *n plan personal de inversión.*
pepper ['pepə'] *n* **-1.** [spice] pimienta *f*; **black/white ~** pimienta negra/blanca. **-2.** [vegetable] pimiento *m*; **red/green ~** pimiento rojo/verde.
pepperbox *Am* = **pepper pot.**
peppercorn ['pepəkɔ:n] *n* grano *m* de pimienta.
peppered ['pepəd] *adj* **-1.** [with mistakes, statistics]: **~ (with)** salpicado(da) (de). **-2.** [with bullets]: **~ (with)** acribillado(da) (de).
pepper mill *n* molinillo *m* de pimienta.
peppermint ['pepəmint] *n* **-1.** [sweet] pastilla *f* de menta. **-2.** [herb] menta *f.*
pepper pot *Br*, **pepperbox** *Am* ['pepəbɒks] *n* pimentero *m.*
peppery ['pepəri] *adj* [spicy] picante.
pep talk *n inf* palabras *fpl* de ánimo.
peptic ulcer ['peptik-] *n* úlcera *f* estomacal.
per [pɜ:'] *prep* [expressing rate, ratio] por; **~ hour/kilo/person** por hora/kilo/persona; **~ day** al día; **as ~ instructions** de acuerdo con OR según las instrucciones.
per annum *adv* al OR por año.
P-E ratio (*abbr of* **price-earnings ratio**) *n* índice *m* de beneficio.
per capita [pə'kæpitə] ◇ *adj* per cápita. ◇ *adv* por cabeza.
perceive [pə'si:v] *vt* **-1.** [notice] percibir, apreciar. **-2.** [understand, realize] advertir,

apreciar. **-3.** [see]: **to ~ sthg/sb as** ver algo/ a alguien como.

per cent *adv* por ciento.

percentage [pə'sentɪdʒ] *n* porcentaje *m*.

perceptible [pə'septəbl] *adj* perceptible, apreciable.

perception [pə'sepʃn] *n* **-1.** [act of seeing] percepción *f*. **-2.** [insight] perspicacia *f*. **-3.** [opinion] idea *f*.

perceptive [pə'septɪv] *adj* perspicaz.

perceptively [pə'septɪvlɪ] *adv* sagazmente.

perch [pɜːtʃ] (*pl sense 3 only inv* OR **-es**) ◇ *n* **-1.** [for bird] percha *f*, vara *f*. **-2.** [high position] posición *f* elevada. **-3.** [fish] perca *f*. ◇ *vi*: **to ~ (on)** [bird] posarse (en); [person] sentarse (en).

percolate ['pɜːkəleɪt] *vi lit* & *fig* filtrarse.

percolator ['pɜːkəleɪtər] *n* percolador *m*.

percussion [pə'kʌʃn] *n* MUS percusión *f*; **the ~** la percusión.

percussionist [pə'kʌʃənɪst] *n* percusionista *m y f*.

peremptory [pə'remptərɪ] *adj* perentorio(ria).

perennial [pə'renjəl] ◇ *adj* [gen & BOT] perenne. ◇ *n* BOT planta *f* perenne.

perestroika [ˌperə'strɔɪkə] *n* perestroika *f*.

perfect [*adj* & *n* 'pɜːfɪkt, *vb* pə'fekt] ◇ *adj* perfecto(ta); **he's a ~ stranger to me** me es completamente desconocido; **it makes ~ sense** es totalmente lógico. ◇ *n* GRAMM: **the ~ (tense)** el perfecto. ◇ *vt* perfeccionar.

perfect competition ['pɜːfɪkt-] *n* ECON competencia *f* perfecta.

perfection [pə'fekʃn] *n* perfección *f*; **to ~ a** la perfección.

perfectionist [pə'fekʃənɪst] *n* perfeccionista *m y f*.

perfectly ['pɜːfɪktlɪ] *adv* **-1.** [for emphasis] absolutamente; **~ well** perfectamente bien. **-2.** [to perfection] perfectamente.

perforate ['pɜːfəreɪt] *vt* perforar.

perforation [ˌpɜːfə'reɪʃn] *n* [in paper] perforación *f*.

perform [pə'fɔːm] ◇ *vt* **-1.** [carry out] llevar a cabo, realizar. **-2.** [music, dance] interpretar; [play] representar. ◇ *vi* **-1.** [function - car, machine] funcionar; [- person, team] desenvolverse. **-2.** [in front of audience] actuar.

performance [pə'fɔːməns] *n* **-1.** [carrying out] realización *f*, ejecución *f*. **-2.** [show] representación *f*. **-3.** [of actor, singer etc] interpretación *f*, actuación *f*. **-4.** [of car, engine] rendimiento *m*.

performance art *n* arte *m* teatral.

performance car *n* coche *m* de máximo rendimiento.

performer [pə'fɔːmər] *n* [actor, singer etc] intérprete *m y f*.

performing arts [pə'fɔːmɪŋ-] *npl*: **the ~** las artes teatrales.

perfume ['pɜːfjuːm] *n* perfume *m*.

perfumed [*Br* 'pɜːfjuːmd, *Am* pər'fjuːmd] *adj* perfumado(da).

perfunctory [pə'fʌŋktərɪ] *adj* superficial, hecho(cha) a la ligera.

perhaps [pə'hæps] *adv* **-1.** [maybe] quizás, quizá; **~ she'll do it** quizás ella lo haga; **~ so/not** tal vez sí/no. **-2.** [in polite requests, suggestions, remarks]: **~ you could help?** ¿te importaría ayudar?; **~ you should start again** ¿por qué no empiezas de nuevo?

peril ['perɪl] *n literary* peligro *m*; **at one's ~** a su propio riesgo.

perilous ['perələs] *adj literary* peligroso(sa).

perilously ['perələslɪ] *adv* peligrosamente.

perimeter [pə'rɪmɪtər] *n* perímetro *m*; **~ fence** OR **wall** cerca *f*.

period ['pɪərɪəd] ◇ *n* **-1.** [of time] período *m*, periodo *m*. **-2.** HISTORY época *f*. **-3.** SCH clase *f*, hora *f*. **-4.** [menstruation] período *m*. **-5.** *Am* [full stop] punto *m*. ◇ *comp* de época.

periodic [ˌpɪərɪ'ɒdɪk] *adj* periódico(ca).

periodical [ˌpɪərɪ'ɒdɪkl] ◇ *adj* = **periodic**. ◇ *n* [magazine] revista *f*, publicación *f* periódica.

periodic table *n* cuadro *m* de elementos.

period pains *npl* dolores *mpl* menstruales.

period piece *n* obra *f* de época.

peripatetic [ˌperɪpə'tetɪk] *adj* ambulante, itinerante.

peripheral [pə'rɪfərəl] ◇ *adj* **-1.** [of little importance] marginal. **-2.** [at edge] periférico(ca). ◇ *n* COMPUT periférico *m*.

periphery [pə'rɪfərɪ] (*pl* **-ies**) *n* **-1.** [edge] periferia *f*. **-2.** [unimportant area] márgenes *mpl*.

periscope ['perɪskəup] *n* periscopio *m*.

perish ['perɪʃ] *vi* **-1.** [die] perecer. **-2.** [decay] deteriorarse.

perishable ['perɪʃəbl] *adj* perecedero(ra).

◆ **perishables** *npl* productos *mpl* perecederos.

perishing ['perɪʃɪŋ] *adj Br inf* **-1.** [cold]: **it's ~ (cold)** hace un frío que pela. **-2.** [damn] condenado(da).

peritonitis [ˌperɪtə'naɪtɪs] *n* (*U*) peritonitis *f*.

perjure ['pɜːdʒər] *vt* JUR: **to ~ o.s.** perjurarse.

perjury ['pɜːdʒərɪ] *n* JUR perjurio *m*.

perk [pɜːk] *n inf* extra *m*, beneficio *m* adicional.

◆ **perk up** *vi* animarse.

perky ['pɜːkɪ] (*compar* -ier, *superl* -iest) *adj inf* alegre, animado(da).

perm [pɜːm] ◇ *n* permanente *f*. ◇ *vt*: **to have one's hair ~ed** hacerse la permanente.

permanence ['pɜːmənəns] *n* permanencia *f*.

permanent ['pɜːmənənt] ◇ *adj* **-1.** [gen] permanente; [job, address] fijo(ja). **-2.** [continuous, constant] constante. ◇ *n Am* [perm] permanente *f*.

permanently ['pɜːmənəntlɪ] *adv* permanentemente.

permeable ['pɜːmjəbl] *adj* permeable.

permeate ['pɜːmɪeɪt] *vt* impregnar.

permissible [pəˈmɪsəbl] *adj* permisible.

permission [pəˈmɪʃn] *n*: ~ (**to do sthg**) permiso *m* (para hacer algo).

permissive [pəˈmɪsɪv] *adj* permisivo(va).

permissiveness [pəˈmɪsɪvnɪs] *n* permisividad *f*.

permit [*vb* pəˈmɪt, *n* ˈpɜːmɪt] (*pt & pp* -ted, *cont* -ting) ◇ *vt* permitir; **to ~ sb sthg/to do sthg** permitir a alguien algo/hacer algo; **weather permitting** si el tiempo lo permite. ◇ *n* permiso *m*.

permutation [,pɜːmjuːˈteɪʃn] *n* permutación *f*.

pernicious [pəˈnɪʃəs] *adj fml* pernicioso(sa).

pernickety [pəˈnɪkətɪ] *adj inf* quisquilloso(sa).

peroxide [pəˈrɒksaɪd] *n* peróxido *m*.

peroxide blonde *n* rubia *f* teñida.

perpendicular [,pɜːpənˈdɪkjʊlər] ◇ *adj* **-1.** MATH: ~ (**to**) perpendicular (a). **-2.** [upright] vertical. ◇ *n* MATH perpendicular *f*.

perpetrate ['pɜːpɪtreɪt] *vt fml* perpetrar.

perpetration [,pɜːpɪˈtreɪʃn] *n fml* perpetración *f*.

perpetrator ['pɜːpɪtreɪtər] *n fml* perpetrador *m*, -ra *f*, autor *m*, -ra *f*.

perpetual [pəˈpetʃʊəl] *adj* **-1.** *pej* [constant] constante. **-2.** [everlasting] perpetuo(tua).

perpetually [pəˈpetʃʊəlɪ] *adv* **-1.** *pej* [constantly] continuamente, constantemente. **-2.** [for ever] perpetuamente.

perpetual motion *n* movimiento *m* continuo.

perpetuate [pəˈpetʃʊeɪt] *vt* perpetuar.

perpetuation [pə,petʃʊˈeɪʃn] *n* perpetuación *f*.

perpetuity [,pɜːpɪˈtjuːətɪ] *n*: **in ~** *fml* a perpetuidad.

perplex [pəˈpleks] *vt* confundir, dejar perplejo(ja).

perplexed [pəˈplekst] *adj* perplejo(ja).

perplexing [pəˈpleksɪŋ] *adj* desconcertante.

perplexity [pəˈpleksətɪ] *n* perplejidad *f*.

perquisite ['pɜːkwɪzɪt] *n fml* beneficio *m* adicional.

per se [pɜːˈseɪ] *adv* en sí.

persecute ['pɜːsɪkjuːt] *vt* perseguir.

persecution [,pɜːsɪˈkjuːʃn] *n* persecución *f*.

persecutor ['pɜːsɪkjuːtər] *n* perseguidor *m*, -ra *f*.

perseverance [,pɜːsɪˈvɪərəns] *n* perseverancia *f*.

persevere [,pɜːsɪˈvɪər] *vi*: **to ~ (with sthg/in doing sthg)** perseverar (en algo/en hacer algo).

Persia ['pɜːʃə] *n* Persia.

Persian ['pɜːʃn] ◇ *adj* persa. ◇ *n* [language] persa *m*.

Persian cat *n* gato *m* persa.

Persian Gulf *n*: **the ~** el Golfo Pérsico.

persist [pəˈsɪst] *vi* **-1.** [problem, rain] persistir. **-2.** [person]: **to ~ in doing sthg** empeñarse en hacer algo.

persistence [pəˈsɪstəns] *n* **-1.** [continuation] persistencia *f*. **-2.** [determination] perseverancia *f*.

persistent [pəˈsɪstənt] *adj* **-1.** [constant] continuo(nua). **-2.** [determined] persistente.

persistently [pəˈsɪstəntlɪ] *adv* **-1.** [constantly] continuamente. **-2.** [determinedly] con persistencia, persistentemente.

persnickety [pəˈsnɪkɪtɪ] *adj Am* quisquilloso(sa).

person ['pɜːsn] (*pl* **people** OR **persons** *fml*) *n* **-1.** [man, woman] persona *f*; **in ~** en persona; **in the ~ of** en la persona de. **-2.** [body]: **about one's ~** en su cuerpo.

persona [pəˈsəʊnə] (*pl* -s OR -ae [-iː]) *n* imagen *f*.

personable ['pɜːsnəbl] *adj* agradable.

personage ['pɜːsənɪdʒ] *n fml* personaje *m*.

personal ['pɜːsənl] ◇ *adj* **-1.** [gen] personal. **-2.** [private - life, problem] privado(da). **-3.** *pej* [rude] ofensivo(va); **to be ~** hacer alusiones personales. ◇ *n Am* anuncio *m* personal (por palabras).

personal account *n* cuenta *f* personal.

personal allowance *n* [regular payment] renta *f* personal; [in tax] desgravación *f* personal.

personal assistant *n* asistente *m*, -ta *f* personal.

personal call *n* llamada *f* personal.

personal column *n* sección *f* de asuntos personales.

personal computer *n* ordenador *m* personal.

personal estate *n* patrimonio *m* personal.

personal hygiene *n* higiene *f* personal.

personality [,pɜːsə'næləti] (*pl* **-ies**) *n* personalidad *f*.

personalize, -ise ['pɜːsənəlaɪz] *vt* personalizar.

personalized ['pɜːsənəlaɪzd] *adj* personalizado(da).

personally ['pɜːsnəlɪ] *adv* personalmente; **to take sthg ~** tomarse algo como algo personal.

personal organizer *n* agenda *f* (personal).

personal pension plan *n* plan *m* de jubilación personalizado.

personal pronoun *n* pronombre *m* personal.

personal property *n* (*U*) bienes *mpl* muebles.

personal stereo *n* walkman® *m inv*.

persona non grata [-'grɑːtə] (*pl* **personae non gratae** [-'grɑːtiː]) *n* persona *f* no grata.

personify [pə'sɒnɪfaɪ] (*pt & pp* **-ied**) *vt* personificar.

personnel [,pɜːsə'nel] ◇ *n* (*U*) [department] personal *m*. ◇ *npl* [staff] personal *m*.

personnel department *n* departamento *m* de personal.

personnel officer *n* jefe *m*, -fa *f* de personal.

person-to-person *adj* de persona a persona.

perspective [pə'spektɪv] *n* perspectiva *f*; **to get sthg in ~** *fig* poner algo en perspectiva.

Perspex® ['pɜːspeks] *n Br* ≃ plexiglás® *m*.

perspicacious [,pɜːspɪ'keɪʃəs] *adj fml* perspicaz.

perspiration [,pɜːspə'reɪʃn] *n* transpiración *f*.

perspire [pə'spaɪəʳ] *vi* transpirar.

persuade [pə'sweɪd] *vt*: **to ~ sb (of sthg/to do sthg)** persuadir a alguien (de algo/a hacer algo); **to ~ sb that** convencer a alguien (de) que.

persuasion [pə'sweɪʒn] *n* **-1.** [act of persuading] persuasión *f*. **-2.** [belief] creencia *f*.

persuasive [pə'sweɪsɪv] *adj* persuasivo(va).

persuasively [pə'sweɪsɪvlɪ] *adv* de modo persuasivo.

pert [pɜːt] *adj* vivaracho(cha).

pertain [pə'teɪn] *vi fml*: **~ing to** relacionado(da) con.

pertinence ['pɜːtɪnəns] *n* pertinencia *f*, relevancia *f*.

pertinent ['pɜːtɪnənt] *adj* pertinente, relevante.

perturb [pə'tɜːb] *vt fml* perturbar, inquietar.

perturbed [pə'tɜːbd] *adj fml* perturbado(da), inquieto(ta).

Peru [pə'ruː] *n* (el) Perú.

perusal [pə'ruːzl] *n* [careful reading] lectura *f* detenida; [brief reading] lectura por encima.

peruse [pə'ruːz] *vt* [read carefully] leer detenidamente; [browse through] leer por encima.

Peruvian [pə'ruːvjən] ◇ *adj* peruano(na). ◇ *n* [person] peruano *m*, -na *f*.

pervade [pə'veɪd] *vt* impregnar.

pervasive [pə'veɪsɪv] *adj* dominante, penetrante.

perverse [pə'vɜːs] *adj* [delight, enjoyment] perverso(sa); [contrary] puñetero(ra).

perversely [pə'vɜːslɪ] *adv* [contrarily, ironically] paradójicamente, irónicamente.

perversion [*Br* pə'vɜːʃn, *Am* pə'vɜːrʒn] *n* **-1.** [sexual deviation] perversión *f*. **-2.** [of justice, truth] tergiversación *f*.

perversity [pə'vɜːsətɪ] *n* [contrariness] puñetería *f*.

pervert [*n* 'pɜːvɜːt, *vb* pə'vɜːt] ◇ *n* pervertido *m*, -da *f*. ◇ *vt* **-1.** [course of justice] tergiversar. **-2.** [sexually corrupt] pervertir.

perverted [pə'vɜːtɪd] *adj* **-1.** [sexually deviant] pervertido(da). **-2.** [twisted] torcido(da).

peseta [pə'seɪtə] *n* peseta *f*.

peso ['peɪsəʊ] (*pl* **-s**) *n* peso *m*.

pessary ['pesərɪ] (*pl* **-ies**) *n* pesario *m*.

pessimism ['pesɪmɪzm] *n* pesimismo *m*.

pessimist ['pesɪmɪst] *n* pesimista *m y f*.

pessimistic [,pesɪ'mɪstɪk] *adj* pesimista.

pest [pest] *n* **-1.** [insect] insecto *m* nocivo; [animal] animal *m* nocivo. **-2.** *inf* [annoying person] pesado *m*, -da *f*; [annoying thing] lata *f*.

pester ['pestəʳ] *vt* dar la lata a, cargosear *Amer*.

pesticide ['pestɪsaɪd] *n* pesticida *m*.

pestle ['pesl] *n* mano *f* (de mortero).

pet [pet] (*pt & pp* **-ted**, *cont* **-ting**) ◇ *adj* [subject, theory] preferido(da); **~ hate** gran fobia *f*. ◇ *n* **-1.** [domestic animal] animal *m* doméstico. **-2.** [favourite person] preferido *m*, -da *f*, favorito *m*, -ta *f*. ◇ *vt* acariciar. ◇ *vi* besuquearse.

petal ['petl] *n* pétalo *m*.

peter ['pi:tə']
◆ **peter out** *vi* [supplies, interest] agotarse; [path] desaparecer.

pethidine ['peθɪdi:n] *n* tipo de analgésico.

petit bourgeois [pə,ti:'bʊəʒwɑ:] (*pl* **petits bourgeois** [pə,ti:'bʊəʒwɑ:]) ◇ *adj* pequeño burgués (pequeña burguesa). ◇ *n* pequeño burgués *m*, pequeña burguesa *f*.

petite [pə'ti:t] *adj* [woman] chiquita.

petit four [,peti-] (*pl* **petits fours** [,peti-]) *n* dulce de bizcocho cubierto de alcorza.

petition [pɪ'tɪʃn] ◇ *n* petición *f*. ◇ *vt* presentar una petición a. ◇ *vi* **-1.** [campaign]: to ~ for sthg solicitar algo; to ~ against sthg presentar una petición contra algo. **-2.** JUR: to ~ for divorce pedir el divorcio.

petitioner [pɪ'tɪʃnə'] *n* solicitante *m y f*.

pet name *n* nombre *m* cariñoso.

petrified ['petrɪfaɪd] *adj* [terrified] petrificado(da).

petrify ['petrɪfaɪ] (*pt & pp* **-ied**) *vt* [terrify] petrificar.

petrochemical [,petrəʊ'kemɪkl] *adj* petroquímico(ca).

petrodollar ['petrəʊ,dɒlə'] *n* petrodólar *m*.

petrol ['petrəl] *n Br* gasolina *f*, nafta *f Amer*.

petrolatum [,petrə'leɪtəm] *n Am* vaselina *f*.

petrol bomb *n Br* bomba *f* de gasolina.

petrol can *n Br* lata *f* de gasolina.

petroleum [pɪ'trəʊljəm] *n* petróleo *m*.

petroleum jelly *n Br* vaselina *f*.

petrol pump *n Br* surtidor *m* de gasolina, bomba *f Amer*.

petrol station *n Br* gasolinera *f*, grifo *m Amer*.

petrol tank *n Br* depósito *m* de gasolina.

petticoat ['petɪkəʊt] *n* [underskirt] enaguas *fpl*, enagua *f*, fustán *m Amer*; [full-length] combinación *f*.

pettiness ['petɪnɪs] *n* [small-mindedness] mezquindad *f*.

petty ['peti] (*compar* **-ier**, *superl* **-iest**) *adj* **-1.** [small-minded] mezquino(na). **-2.** [trivial] insignificante.

petty cash *n* dinero *m* para gastos menores.

petty officer *n* sargento *m* de la marina.

petulant ['petjʊlənt] *adj* cascarrabias (*inv*).

pew [pju:] *n* banco *m*.

pewter ['pju:tə'] *n* peltre *m*.

PG (*abbr of* **parental guidance**) para menores acompañados.

PGA (*abbr of* **Professional Golfers' Association**) *n* asociación de golfistas profesionales.

p & h (*abbr of* **postage and handling**) *n Am* gastos *mpl* de envío.

PH ◇ *n* (*abbr of* **Purple Heart**) (*titular de*) distinción honorífica que otorga el gobierno estadounidense a soldados heridos en combate. ◇ (*abbr of* **potential of hydrogen**) PH.

PHA (*abbr of* **Public Housing Administration**) *n* organismo estadounidense encargado de proveer alojamiento para personas necesitadas.

phallic ['fælɪk] *adj* fálico(ca); ~ symbol símbolo *m* fálico.

phallus ['fæləs] (*pl* **-es** OR **phalli** ['fælaɪ]) *n* falo *m*.

phantom ['fæntəm] ◇ *adj* ilusorio(ria). ◇ *n* [ghost] fantasma *m*.

phantom pregnancy *n* embarazo *m* psicológico.

pharaoh ['feərəʊ] *n* faraón *m*.

Pharisee ['færɪsi:] *n* fariseo *m*, -a *f*.

pharmaceutical [,fɑ:mə'sju:tɪkl] *adj* farmacéutico(ca).
◆ **pharmaceuticals** *npl* productos *mpl* farmacéuticos.

pharmacist ['fɑ:məsɪst] *n* farmacéutico *m*, -ca *f*.

pharmacology [,fɑ:mə'kɒlədʒɪ] *n* farmacología *f*.

pharmacy ['fɑ:məsɪ] (*pl* **-ies**) *n* [shop] farmacia *f*.

phase [feɪz] ◇ *n* fase *f*. ◇ *vt* escalonar.
◆ **phase in** *vt sep* introducir progresivamente.
◆ **phase out** *vt sep* retirar progresivamente.

PhD (*abbr of* **Doctor of Philosophy**) *n* (*titular de un*) doctorado en el campo de las humanidades.

pheasant ['feznt] (*pl inv* OR **-s**) *n* faisán *m*.

phenobarbitone *Br* [,fi:nəʊ'bɑ:bɪtəʊn], **phenobarbitol** *Am* [,fi:nəʊ'bɑ:bɪtl] *n* fenobarbital *m*.

phenomena [fɪ'nɒmɪnə] *pl* → **phenomenon**.

phenomenal [fɪ'nɒmɪnl] *adj* fenomenal.

phenomenon [fɪ'nɒmɪnən] (*pl* **-mena**) *n lit & fig* fenómeno *m*.

phew [fju:] *excl* ¡puf!

phial ['faɪəl] *n* frasco *m* (pequeño).

Philadelphia [,fɪlə'delfɪə] *n* Filadelfia.

philanderer [fɪ'lændərə'] *n* tenorio *m*.

philanthropic [,fɪlən'θrɒpɪk] *adj* filantrópico(ca).

philanthropist [fɪ'lænθrəpɪst] *n* filantrópico *m*, -ca *f*.

philately [fɪ'lætəlɪ] *n* filatelia *f*.

philharmonic [,fɪlɑ:'mɒnɪk] *adj* filarmónico(ca).

Philippine ['fɪlɪpiːn] *adj* filipino(na); **the ~ Islands** las Filipinas.

◆ **Philippines** *npl*: **the ~s** las Filipinas.

philistine [*Br* 'fɪlɪstaɪn, *Am* 'fɪlɪstiːn] *n* filisteo *m*, -a *f*.

Phillips® ['fɪlɪps] *comp*: ~ **screw** tornillo *m* de cabeza en cruz; ~ **screwdriver** destornillador *m* de cabeza en cruz.

philosopher [fɪ'lɒsəfə'] *n* filósofo *m*, -fa *f*.

philosophical [,fɪlə'sɒfɪkl] *adj* filosófico(ca).

philosophize, -ise [fɪ'lɒsəfaɪz] *vi* filosofar.

philosophy [fɪ'lɒsəfɪ] (*pl* **-ies**) *n* filosofía *f*.

phlegm [flem] *n* [mucus] flema *f*.

phlegmatic [fleg'mætɪk] *adj* flemático(ca).

Phnom Penh [,nɒm'pen] *n* Phnom Penh.

phobia ['fəʊbjə] *n* fobia *f*; **to have a ~ about sthg** tener fobia a algo.

phoenix ['fiːnɪks] *n* fénix *m*.

phone [fəʊn] ◇ *n* teléfono *m*; **to be on the ~** [speaking] estar al teléfono; *Br* [connected to network] tener teléfono. ◇ *comp* telefónico(ca). ◇ *vt & vi* telefonear, llamar.

◆ **phone up** *vt sep & vi* llamar.

phone book *n* guía *f* telefónica.

phone booth *n* teléfono *m* público.

phone box *n Br* cabina *f* telefónica.

phone call *n* llamada *f* telefónica; **to make a ~** hacer una llamada.

phonecard ['fəʊnkɑːd] *n* tarjeta *f* telefónica.

phone-in *n* RADIO & TV programa *m* a micrófono abierto.

phone line *n* **-1.** [wire] cable *m* de teléfonos. **-2.** [connection] línea *f* telefónica.

phone number *n* número *m* de teléfono.

phone-tapping [-,tæpɪŋ] *n* interceptación *f* telefónica.

phonetics [fə'netɪks] *n* (*U*) fonética *f*.

phoney *Br*, **phony** *Am* ['fəʊnɪ] (*compar* **-ier**, *superl* **-iest**, *pl* **-ies**) *adj inf* falso(sa) ◇ *n* farsante *m* y *f*.

phoney war *n* estado de guerra sin confrontación armada.

phony *Am* = **phoney**.

phosphate ['fɒsfeɪt] *n* fosfato *m*.

phosphorus ['fɒsfərəs] *n* fósforo *m*.

photo ['fəʊtəʊ] *n* foto *f*; **to take a ~ (of)** sacar una foto (de).

photocall ['fəʊtəʊkɔːl] *n* cita de una persona famosa con la prensa para que le saquen fotos.

photocopier [,fəʊtəʊ'kɒpɪə'] *n* fotocopiadora *f*.

photocopy ['fəʊtəʊ,kɒpɪ] (*pl* **-ies**, *pt & pp* **-ied**) ◇ *n* fotocopia *f*. ◇ *vt* fotocopiar.

photoelectric cell [,fəʊtəʊɪ'lektrɪk-] *n* célula *f* fotoeléctrica.

photo finish *n* SPORT foto-finish *f*, *final de carrera reñido decidido por foto.*

Photofit® ['fəʊtəʊfɪt] *n*: ~ **(picture)** fotorrobot *f*.

photogenic [,fəʊtəʊ'dʒenɪk] *adj* fotogénico(ca).

photograph ['fəʊtəɡrɑːf] ◇ *n* fotografía *f*; **to take a ~ (of)** sacar una fotografía (de). ◇ *vt* fotografiar.

photographer [fə'tɒɡrəfə'] *n* fotógrafo *m*, -fa *f*.

photographic [,fəʊtə'ɡræfɪk] *adj* fotográfico(ca).

photographic memory *n* memoria *f* fotográfica.

photography [fə'tɒɡrəfɪ] *n* fotografía *f*.

photojournalism [,fəʊtəʊ'dʒɜːnəlɪzm] *n* periodismo *m* fotográfico.

photon ['fəʊtɒn] *n* fotón *m*.

photo opportunity *n oportunidad de ofrecer una imagen favorable mediante una foto.*

photosensitive [,fəʊtəʊ'sensɪtɪv] *adj* fotosensible.

Photostat® ['fəʊtəstæt] (*pt & pp* **-ted**, *cont* **-ting**) *n* fotostato *m*.

◆ **photostat** *vt* fotocopiar.

photosynthesis [,fəʊtəʊ'sɪnθəsɪs] *n* fotosíntesis *f*.

phrasal verb ['freɪzl-] *n* verbo *m* con preposición.

phrase [freɪz] ◇ *n* **-1.** [group of words] locución *f*, frase *f*. **-2.** [expression] expresión *f*. ◇ *vt* [apology, refusal] expresar; [letter] redactar.

phrasebook ['freɪzbʊk] *n* libro *m* de frases.

phraseology [,freɪzɪ'ɒlədʒɪ] *n* fraseología *f*.

physical ['fɪzɪkl] ◇ *adj* físico(ca). ◇ *n* [examination] examen *m* médico.

physical chemistry *n* fisicoquímica *f*.

physical education *n* educación *f* física.

physical examination *n* examen *m* médico.

physical geography *n* geografía *f* física.

physical jerks *npl Br hum* gimnasia *f*, ejercicios *mpl* físicos.

physically ['fɪzɪklɪ] *adv* físicamente.

physically handicapped ◇ *adj* minusválido(da). ◇ *npl*: **the ~** los minusválidos.

physical science *n* (*U*) ciencias *fpl* físicas.

physical training *n* preparación *f* física.

physician [fɪ'zɪʃn] *n* médico *m* y *f*.

physicist ['fɪzɪsɪst] *n* físico *m*, -ca *f*.

physics ['fɪzɪks] *n* (*U*) física *f*.

physio ['fɪzɪəʊ] (*pl* **-s**) *n Br inf* **-1.** (*abbr of* **physiotherapist**) fisioterapeuta *m* y *f*. **-2.** (*abbr of* **physiotherapy**) fisioterapia *f*.

physiognomy [ˌfɪzɪ'ɒnəmɪ] (*pl* **-ies**) *n fml* fisionomía *f*.

physiology [ˌfɪzɪ'ɒlədʒɪ] *n* fisiología *f*.

physiotherapist [ˌfɪzɪəʊ'θerəpɪst] *n* fisioterapeuta *m y f*.

physiotherapy [ˌfɪzɪəʊ'θerəpɪ] *n* fisioterapia *f*.

physique [fɪ'ziːk] *n* físico *m*.

pianist ['pɪənɪst] *n* pianista *m y f*.

piano [pɪ'ænəʊ] (*pl* **-s**) *n* [instrument] piano *m*.

piano accordion *n* acordeón-piano *m*.

Picardy ['pɪkədɪ] *n* Picardía.

piccalilli [ˌpɪkə'lɪlɪ] *n* salsa amarilla picante con coliflor etc.

piccolo ['pɪkələʊ] (*pl* **-s**) *n* flautín *m*.

pick [pɪk] ◇ *n* **-1.** [tool] piqueta *f*. **-2.** [selection]: **take your** ~ escoge el que quieras. **-3.** [best]: **the** ~ **of** lo mejor de. ◇ *vt* **-1.** [team, winner] seleccionar; [time, book, dress] elegir; **to** ~ **one's way across** OR **through** andar con tiento por. **-2.** [fruit, flowers] coger. **-3.** [remove - hairs etc]: **to** ~ **sthg off sthg** quitar algo de algo. **-4.** [nose] hurgarse; [teeth] mondarse. **-5.** [provoke]: **to** ~ **a fight/quarrel (with)** buscar pelea/bronca (con). **-6.** [open - lock] forzar (con ganzúa). ◇ *vi*: **he can afford to** ~ **and choose** tiene donde elegir.
◆ **pick at** *vt fus* picar, picotear.
◆ **pick on** *vt fus* meterse con.
◆ **pick out** *vt sep* **-1.** [recognize] reconocer, identificar. **-2.** [select] escoger, elegir.
◆ **pick up** ◇ *vt sep* **-1.** [gen] recoger; **to** ~ **up the pieces** *fig* volver a la normalidad. **-2.** [buy, acquire] adquirir; **to** ~ **up speed** [car] acelerar. **-3.** [learn - tips, language] aprender. **-4.** [subj: police]: **to** ~ **sb up for sthg** coger a alguien por algo. **-5.** *inf* [approach] ligar con. **-6.** RADIO & TELEC captar, recibir. **-7.** [start again] reanudar. ◇ *vi* **-1.** [improve] mejorar. **-2.** [start again] proseguir.

pickaxe *Br*, **pickax** *Am* ['pɪkæks] *n* piqueta *f*.

picker ['pɪkə'] *n* recolector *m*, -ra *f*.

picket ['pɪkɪt] ◇ *n* piquete *m*. ◇ *vt* formar piquetes en.

picketing ['pɪkətɪŋ] *n* (*U*) piquetes *mpl*.

picket line *n* piquete *m* (de huelga).

pickings ['pɪkɪŋz] *npl*: **easy/rich** ~ dinero *m* fácil/a raudales.

pickle ['pɪkl] ◇ *n* **-1.** [vinegar preserve] encurtido *m*; [sweet vegetable sauce] salsa espesa agridulce con trozos de cebolla etc. **-2.** *inf* [difficult situation]: **to be in a** ~ estar en un lío. ◇ *vt* encurtir.

pickled ['pɪkld] *adj* **-1.** [food] encurtido(da). **-2.** *inf* [drunk] bebido(da).

pick-me-up *n inf* tónico *m*, reconstituyente *m*.

pickpocket ['pɪkˌpɒkɪt] *n* carterista *m y f*.

pick-up *n* **-1.** [of record player] fonocaptor *m*. **-2.** [truck] camioneta *f*, furgoneta *f*.

pick-up truck *n* camioneta *f*, furgoneta *f*.

picky ['pɪkɪ] (*compar* **-ier**, *superl* **-iest**) *adj* quisquilloso(sa).

picnic ['pɪknɪk] (*pt* & *pp* **-ked**, *cont* **-king**) ◇ *n* comida *f* campestre, picnic *m*. ◇ *vi* ir de merienda al campo.

picnicker ['pɪknɪkə'] *n* excursionista *m y f*.

Pict [pɪkt] *n*: **the** ~**s** los Pictos.

pictorial [pɪk'tɔːrɪəl] *adj* ilustrado(da).

picture ['pɪktʃə'] ◇ *n* **-1.** [painting] cuadro *m*; [drawing] dibujo *m*. **-2.** [photograph] foto *f*. **-3.** [on TV] imagen *f*. **-4.** [cinema film] película *f*. **-5.** [in mind] idea *f*, imagen *f*. **-6.** [situation] situación *f*. **-7.** [epitome]: **the** ~ **of** la imagen de. **-8.** *phr*: **to get the** ~ *inf* entenderlo; **to put sb in the** ~ poner a alguien al corriente; **to be in/out of the** ~ estar/no estar en el ajo. ◇ *vt* **-1.** [imagine] imaginarse. **-2.** [in media]: **to be** ~**d** aparecer en la foto. **-3.** [in painting] pintar; [in drawing] dibujar.
◆ **pictures** *npl* *Br*: **the** ~**s** el cine.

picture book *n* libro *m* ilustrado.

picture rail *n* moldura *f* para colgar cuadros.

picturesque [ˌpɪktʃə'resk] *adj* pintoresco(ca).

picture window *n* ventanal *m*.

piddling ['pɪdlɪŋ] *adj* *inf* *pej* de poca monta.

pidgin ['pɪdʒɪn] ◇ *n* lengua *f* macarrónica. ◇ *comp* macarrónico(ca).

pie [paɪ] *n* [sweet] tarta *f* (cubierta de hojaldre); [savoury] empanada *f*, pastel *m*; ~ **in the sky** castillos en el aire.

piebald ['paɪbɔːld] *adj* pío(a).

piece [piːs] *n* **-1.** [individual part or portion] trozo *m*, pedazo *m*; **to come to** ~**s** deshacerse; **to be smashed to** ~**s** ser destrozado; **to take sthg to** ~**s** desmontar algo; **in** ~**s** en pedazos; **in one** ~ [intact] intacto(ta); [unharmed] sano y salvo (sana y salva); **to go to** ~**s** *fig* venirse abajo. **-2.** (with *uncountable noun*) [individual object]: ~ **of furniture** mueble *m*; ~ **of clothing** prenda *f* de vestir; ~ **of advice** consejo *m*; ~ **of news** noticia *f*; ~ **of luck** golpe *m* de suerte; ~ **of work** [object] pieza *f*; [nasty person] *inf* elemento *m*. **-3.** [in board game] pieza *f*. **-4.** [valuable or interesting object, composition,

play] pieza *f*. **-5.** [of journalism] artículo *m*.
-6. [coin] moneda *f*.
◆ **piece together** *vt sep* [discover] componer.

pièce de résistance [ˌpjesdərezıs'tɑ̃ːs] (*pl* **pièces de résistance** [ˌpjesdərezıs'tɑ̃ːs]) *n* plato *m* principal.

piecemeal ['piːsmiːl] ◇ *adj* poco sistemático(ca). ◇ *adv* gradualmente, por etapas.

piecework ['piːswɜːk] *n* (*U*) trabajo *m* a destajo.

pie chart *n* gráfico *m* circular OR de sectores.

pied-a-terre [ˌpɪeɪdæ'teəʳ] (*pl* **pieds-a-terre** [ˌpɪeɪdæ'teəʳ]) *n* apeadero *m* (*casa*).

pie-eyed [-'aɪd] *adj inf* como una cuba.

pie plate *n* Am tortera *f*, molde *m* de pastelería.

pier [pɪəʳ] *n* [at seaside] *paseo marítimo en un malecón*.

pierce [pɪəs] *vt* **-1.** [subj: bullet, needle] perforar; **to have one's ears ~d** hacerse agujeros en las orejas. **-2.** [subj: voice, scream] romper.

pierced [pɪəst] *adj* perforado(da).

piercing ['pɪəsɪŋ] *adj* **-1.** [scream] desgarrador(ra); [sound, voice] agudo(da). **-2.** [wind] cortante. **-3.** [look, eyes] penetrante.

piety ['paɪətɪ] *n* piedad *f*.

piffle ['pɪfl] *n* (*U*) *inf* tonterías *fpl*, disparates *mpl*.

piffling ['pɪflɪŋ] *adj inf* ridículo(la).

pig [pɪg] (*pt & pp* **-ged**, *cont* **-ging**) *n* **-1.** [animal] cerdo *m*, puerco *m*, chancho *m* Amer. **-2.** *inf pej* [greedy eater] tragón *m*, -ona *f*, comilón *m*, -ona *f*; **to make a ~ of o.s.** darse un atracón. **-3.** *inf pej* [unkind person] cerdo *m*, -da *f*.
◆ **pig out** *vi inf* darse un atracón.

pigeon ['pɪdʒɪn] (*pl inv* OR **-s**) *n* paloma *f*.

pigeon-chested [-ˌtʃestɪd] *adj* de pecho salido.

pigeonhole ['pɪdʒɪnhəʊl] ◇ *n* [compartment] casilla *f*. ◇ *vt* [classify] encasillar.

pigeon-toed [-ˌtəʊd] *adj* patituerto(ta).

piggish ['pɪgɪʃ] *adj inf* [dirty] cochino(na); [eating too much] cerdo(da).

piggy ['pɪgɪ] (*compar* **-ier**, *superl* **-iest**, *pl* **-ies**) ◇ *adj* de cerdito. ◇ *n inf* cerdito *m*.

piggyback ['pɪgɪbæk] *n*: **to give sb a ~** llevar a alguien a cuestas.

piggybank ['pɪgɪbæŋk] *n* hucha *f* con forma de cerdito.

pigheaded [ˌpɪg'hedɪd] *adj* cabezota.

piglet ['pɪglɪt] *n* cerdito *m*, cochinillo *m*.

pigment ['pɪgmənt] *n* pigmento *m*.

pigmentation [ˌpɪgmən'teɪʃn] *n* pigmentación *f*.

pigmy = **pygmy**.

pigpen Am = **pigsty**.

pigskin ['pɪgskɪn] ◇ *n* piel *f* de cerdo. ◇ *comp* de piel de cerdo.

pigsty ['pɪgstaɪ] (*pl* **-ies**), **pigpen** Am ['pɪgpen] *n lit & fig* pocilga *f*.

pigswill ['pɪgswɪl] *n* bazofia *f*.

pigtail ['pɪgteɪl] *n* [girl's] trenza *f*; [Chinese, bullfighter's] coleta *f*.

pike [paɪk] (*pl sense 1 only inv* OR **-s**) *n* **-1.** [fish] lucio *m*. **-2.** [weapon] pica *f*.

pikestaff ['paɪkstɑːf] *n*: **to be as plain as a ~** estar más claro que el agua.

pilaster [pɪ'læstəʳ] *n* pilastra *f*.

pilchard ['pɪltʃəd] *n* sardina *f*.

pile [paɪl] ◇ *n* **-1.** [heap] montón *m*, ruma *f* Amer; **a ~** OR **~s of** un montón de. **-2.** [neat stack] pila *f*. **-3.** [of carpet, fabric] pelo *m*. ◇ *vt* apilar, amontonar; **a plate ~d with food** un plato colmado de comida.
◆ **piles** *npl* MED almorranas *fpl*.
◆ **pile in** *vi inf* entrar en tropel.
◆ **pile into** *vt fus inf* amontonarse OR meterse en.
◆ **pile out** *vi inf*: **to ~ out (of)** salir en tropel (de).
◆ **pile up** ◇ *vt sep* apilar, amontonar. ◇ *vi* **-1.** [form a heap] apilarse, amontonarse. **-2.** [mount up] acumularse.

pile driver *n* martinete *m*.

pileup ['paɪlʌp] *n* accidente *m* en cadena.

pilfer ['pɪlfəʳ] ◇ *vt* sisar. ◇ *vi*: **to ~ (from)** sisar (de).

pilgrim ['pɪlgrɪm] *n* peregrino *m*, -na *f*.

pilgrimage ['pɪlgrɪmɪdʒ] *n* peregrinación *f*.

pill [pɪl] *n* **-1.** MED píldora *f*, pastilla *f*. **-2.** [contraceptive]: **the ~** la píldora (anticonceptiva); **to be on the ~** tomar la píldora.

pillage ['pɪlɪdʒ] ◇ *n* pillaje *m*, saqueo *m*. ◇ *vt* saquear, pillar.

pillar ['pɪləʳ] *n lit & fig* pilar *m*; **to be a ~ of strength** mostrar gran fortaleza.

pillar box *n Br* buzón *m*.

pillbox ['pɪlbɒks] *n* **-1.** [box for pills] cajita *f* para pastillas. **-2.** MIL fortín *m*.

pillion ['pɪljən] *n* asiento *m* trasero; **to ride ~** ir en el asiento trasero (*de una moto*).

pillock ['pɪlək] *n Br inf* gilipollas *m y f inv*.

pillory ['pɪlərɪ] (*pl* **-ies**, *pt & pp* **-ied**) ◇ *n* picota *f*. ◇ *vt* poner en ridículo.

pillow ['pɪləʊ] *n* **-1.** [for bed] almohada *f*. **-2.** Am [on sofa, chair] cojín *m*.

pillowcase ['pɪləʊkeɪs], **pillowslip** ['pɪləʊslɪp] *n* funda *f* de almohada.

pilot ['paɪlət] ◇ n -1. AERON & NAUT piloto m. -2. TV programa m piloto. ◇ comp piloto (inv), de prueba. ◇ vt -1. AERON & NAUT pilotar. -2. [person] conducir, guiar; [scheme, plan] llevar personalmente a la práctica.

pilot burner, pilot light n piloto m, luz f indicadora.

pilot scheme n proyecto m piloto.

pilot study n estudio m piloto.

pimento [pɪ'mentəʊ] (pl inv OR -s) n pimiento m morrón.

pimp [pɪmp] n inf chulo m, padrote m Amer.

pimple ['pɪmpl] n grano m.

pimply ['pɪmplɪ] (compar -ier, superl -iest) adj cubierto(ta) de granos.

pin [pɪn] (pt & pp -ned, cont -ning) ◇ n -1. [for sewing] alfiler m; ~s and needles hormigueo m. -2. [drawing pin] chincheta f. -3. [safety pin] imperdible m. -4. [of plug] polo m. -5. TECH clavija f. -6. [in grenade] percutor m.
◇ vt -1. [fasten]: to ~ sthg to OR on [notice] clavar con alfileres algo en; [medal, piece of cloth] prender algo en. -2. [trap]: to ~ sb against OR to inmovilizar a alguien contra. -3. [apportion]: to ~ sthg on OR upon sb endosar algo a alguien.
◆ **pin down** vt sep -1. [identify] determinar, identificar. -2. [force to make a decision]: to ~ sb down (to) obligar a alguien a comprometerse (a).
◆ **pin up** vt sep -1. [fasten with pins] clavar. -2. [raise with pins] prender con alfileres.

PIN [pɪn] (abbr of personal identification number) n código m personal.

pinafore ['pɪnəfɔːr] n -1. [apron] delantal m. -2. Br [dress] pichi m.

pinball ['pɪnbɔːl] n millón m, flíper m.

pinball machine n máquina f de millón OR flíper.

pincer movement ['pɪnsər-] n movimiento m de tenazas.

pincers ['pɪnsəz] npl -1. [tool] tenazas fpl. -2. [front claws] pinzas fpl.

pinch [pɪntʃ] ◇ n -1. [nip] pellizco m; to feel the ~ tener que apretarse el cinturón. -2. [small quantity] pizca f. ◇ vt -1. [nip] pellizcar; [subj: shoes] apretar. -2. inf [steal] mangar.
◆ **at a pinch** Br, **in a pinch** Am adv si no hay más remedio.

pinched [pɪntʃt] adj -1. [thin, pale] demacrado(da); ~ with [cold] aterido(da) de; [hunger] muerto(ta) de; ~ for [time, money] escaso(sa) de.

pincushion ['pɪn,kʊʃn] n acerico m.

pine [paɪn] ◇ n pino m. ◇ comp de pino. ◇ vi: to ~ for suspirar por.
◆ **pine away** vi morirse de pena.

pineapple ['paɪn,æpl] n piña f, ananá m Amer.

pinecone ['paɪnkəʊn] n piña f.

pine needle n aguja f de pino.

pinetree ['paɪntriː] n pino m.

pinewood ['paɪnwʊd] n -1. [forest] pinar m. -2. [material] madera f de pino.

ping [pɪŋ] ◇ n [of bell] tilín m; [of metal] sonido m metálico. ◇ vi producir un sonido metálico.

Ping-Pong® [-pɒŋ] n ping-pong® m.

pinhole ['pɪnhəʊl] n agujero m de alfiler.

pinion ['pɪnjən] ◇ n TECH piñón m. ◇ vt [tie up] maniatar; [hold down] inmovilizar.

pink [pɪŋk] ◇ adj rosa. ◇ n -1. [colour] rosa m. -2. [flower] clavel m.

pink gin n Br ginebra f con angostura.

pinkie ['pɪŋkɪ] n Am & Scot dedo m meñique.

pinking ['pɪŋkɪŋ] n Br AUT picado m.

pinking scissors, pinking shears npl tijeras fpl dentadas.

pin money n dinero adicional para gastos menores.

pinnacle ['pɪnəkl] n -1. [high point] cumbre f, cúspide f. -2. [mountain peak, spire] pináculo m, cima f.

pinny ['pɪnɪ] (pl -ies) n inf delantal m.

pinpoint ['pɪnpɔɪnt] vt determinar, identificar.

pinprick ['pɪnprɪk] n -1. [mark, hole] marca f de pinchazo. -2. [slight irritation] pequeña molestia f.

pin-striped [-,straɪpt] adj a rayas.

pint [paɪnt] n -1. [unit of measurement] = 0,568 litros Br, = 0,473 litros Am, ≃ pinta f. -2. Br [beer]: to go for a ~ salir tomar una caña; they went out for a ~ salieron a tomar una caña.

pintable ['pɪnteɪbl] n Br máquina f de millón OR flíper.

pinto ['pɪntəʊ] (pl -s OR -es) Am ◇ adj pinto(ta). ◇ n caballo m pío.

pint-size(d) adj inf enano(na), muy pequeño(ña).

pinup ['pɪnʌp] n [of model] (póster de) mujer medio desnuda; [of film star etc] (póster de) una atractiva estrella del pop, del cine etc.

pioneer [,paɪə'nɪər] ◇ n pionero m, -ra f. ◇ vt iniciar, introducir.

pioneering [,paɪə'nɪərɪŋ] adj pionero(ra), innovador(ra).

pious ['paɪəs] *adj* **-1.** [religious] piadoso(sa). **-2.** *pej* [sanctimonious] mojigato(ta).

piously ['paɪəslɪ] *adv pej* piadosamente, devotamente.

pip [pɪp] *n* **-1.** [seed] pepita *f.* **-2.** *Br* [bleep] señal *f.*

pipe [paɪp] ◇ *n* **-1.** [for gas, water] tubería *f.* **-2.** [for smoking] pipa *f.* ◇ *vt* **-1.** [transport via pipes] conducir por tuberías. **-2.** [say] decir con voz de pito.
◆ **pipes** *npl* MUS gaita *f.*
◆ **pipe down** *vi inf* cerrar la boca.
◆ **pipe up** *vi inf:* to ~ up with a suggestion saltar con una sugerencia.

pipe cleaner *n* limpiapipas *m inv.*

piped music [paɪpt-] *n Br* hilo *m* musical®.

pipe dream *n* sueño *m* imposible, castillos *mpl* en al aire.

pipeline ['paɪplaɪn] *n* [for gas] gasoducto *m;* [for oil] oleoducto *m;* [for water] tuberías *fpl;* to be in the ~ *fig* estar en trámites.

piper ['paɪpə'] *n* gaitero *m,* -ra *f.*

piping hot ['paɪpɪŋ-] *adj* humeante, calentito(ta).

pipsqueak ['pɪpskwiːk] *n pej* fantoche *m y f,* mequetrefe *m y f.*

piquant ['piːkənt] *adj* **-1.** [food] picante. **-2.** [story] intrigante; [situation] que suscita un placer mordaz.

pique [piːk] *n* resentimiento *m;* a fit of ~ un arrebato de despecho.

piracy ['paɪrəsɪ] *n* **-1.** [at sea] piratería *f.* **-2.** [illegal copying] reproducción *f* pirata.

piranha [pɪ'rɑːnə] *n* piraña *f.*

pirate ['paɪrət] ◇ *adj* [gen & COMPUT] pirata. ◇ *n* **-1.** [sailor] pirata *m y f.* **-2.** [illegal copy] edición *f* pirata. ◇ *vt* piratear, hacer una edición pirata de.

pirate radio *n Br* radio *f* pirata.

pirouette [,pɪru'et] ◇ *n* pirueta *f.* ◇ *vi* hacer piruetas.

Pisces ['paɪsiːz] *n* Piscis *m inv;* to be (a) ~ ser Piscis.

piss [pɪs] *vulg* ◇ *n* **-1.** [urine] meada *f;* to take the ~ out of vacilar a. **-2.** [urination]: to have a ~ mear. ◇ *vi* mear.
◆ **piss down** *vi Br* llover a cántaros.
◆ **piss off** ◇ *vt sep* cabrear. ◇ *vi Br* irse a la mierda.

pissed [pɪst] *adj vulg* **-1.** *Br* [drunk] pedo (*inv*), cocido(da). **-2.** *Am* [annoyed] molesto(ta), irritado(da).

pissed off *adj vulg:* to be OR to feel ~ estar cabreado(da).

pistachio [pɪ'stɑːʃɪəʊ] (*pl* **-s**) *n* pistacho *m.*

piste [piːst] *n* pista *f* de esquí.

pistol ['pɪstl] *n* pistola *f.*

pistol-whip *vt Am* golpear con la culata de una pistola.

piston ['pɪstən] *n* pistón *m,* émbolo *m.*

pit [pɪt] (*pt* & *pp* **-ted,** *cont* **-ting**) ◇ *n* **-1.** [large hole] hoyo *m.* **-2.** [small hole - in metal, glass] señal *f,* marca *f;* [- on face] picadura *f.* **-3.** [for orchestra] foso *m* de la orquesta. **-4.** [mine] mina *f.* **-5.** [quarry] cantera *f.* **-6.** *Am* [of fruit] hueso *m.* **-7.** *phr:* the ~ of one's stomach las entrañas. ◇ *vt:* to be pitted against ser enfrentado(da) con; to ~ one's wits against medirse con.
◆ **pits** *npl* **-1.** [in motor racing]: the ~s el box. **-2.** *inf* [awful]: it's the ~s está fatal.

pitch [pɪtʃ] ◇ *n* **-1.** SPORT campo *m.* **-2.** MUS tono *m.* **-3.** [level, degree] grado *m,* punto *m.* **-4.** [selling place] puesto *m.* **-5.** *inf* [sales talk] labia *f* de comerciante. **-6.** [motion - of ship, plane] tumbo *m,* bandazo *m.* ◇ *vt* **-1.** [throw] lanzar, arrojar; to be ~ed into a situation encontrarse de la noche a la mañana en una situación. **-2.** [speech] dar un tono a; [price] establecer un precio para. **-3.** [tent] montar, poner. ◇ *vi* **-1.** [ball] tocar el suelo; to ~ forwards [person] precipitarse hacia delante. **-2.** [ship, plane] dar un bandazo.
◆ **pitch in** *vi* ponerse manos a la obra.

pitch-black *adj* negro(gra) como boca de lobo.

pitched [pɪtʃt] *adj* [sloping] inclinado(da), pendiente.

pitched battle *n* HISTORY batalla *f* campal; *fig* [bitter struggle] lucha *f* encarnizada.

pitcher ['pɪtʃə'] *n Am* **-1.** [jug] cántaro *m,* jarro *m.* **-2.** [in baseball] lanzador *m,* pitcher *m.*

pitchfork ['pɪtʃfɔːk] *n* horca *f.*

piteous ['pɪtɪəs] *adj* lastimero(ra).

piteously ['pɪtɪəslɪ] *adv* lastimeramente.

pitfall ['pɪtfɔːl] *n* peligro *m,* escollo *m.*

pith [pɪθ] *n* parte blanca de la piel de una fruta.

pithead ['pɪthed] *n* bocamina *f.*

pith helmet *n* salacot *m.*

pithy ['pɪθɪ] (*compar* **-ier,** *superl* **-iest**) *adj* conciso(sa) y contundente.

pitiable ['pɪtɪəbl] *adj* lastimoso(sa).

pitiful ['pɪtɪfʊl] *adj* [condition, excuse, effort] lamentable; [person, appearance] lastimoso(sa).

pitifully ['pɪtɪfʊlɪ] *adv:* she looks ~ thin está tan delgada que da pena; a ~ poor excuse una excusa lamentable.

pitiless ['pɪtɪlɪs] *adj* [person] despiadado(da), cruel; [weather] deplorable.

pitman ['pɪtmən] (*pl* **-men** [-mən]) *n* minero *m*.

pit pony *n Br tipo de poni que antiguamente hacía de animal de carga en las minas británicas.*

pit prop *n* puntal *m*.

pit stop *n* [in motor racing] parada *f* en boxes.

pitta bread ['pɪtə-] *n tipo de pan sin levadura en el que se pone carne, ensalada etc.*

pittance ['pɪtəns] *n* miseria *f*.

pitted ['pɪtɪd] *adj*: ~ **with** picado(da) de.

pitter-patter ['pɪtə,pætər] *n* golpeteo *m*.

pituitary [pɪ'tjuɪtrɪ] (*pl* **-ies**) *n*: ~ **(gland)** glándula *f* pituitaria.

pity ['pɪtɪ] (*pt & pp* **-ied**) ◇ *n* [compassion] compasión *f*; [shame] pena *f*, lástima *f*; **what a ~!** ¡qué pena!; **to take** OR **have ~ on** compadecerse de. ◇ *vt* compadecerse de, sentir pena por.

pitying ['pɪtɪɪŋ] *adj* compasivo(va).

pivot ['pɪvət] ◇ *n* pivote *m*, eje *m*; *fig* eje *m*. ◇ *vi*: **to ~ (on)** girar (sobre).

pixel ['pɪksl] *n* COMPUT & TV punto *m* luminoso, elemento *m* de imagen digital.

pixie, pixy ['pɪksɪ] (*pl* **-ies**) *n* duendecillo *m*.

pizza ['piːtsə] *n* pizza *f*.

pizzazz [pɪ'zæz] *n inf* vitalidad *f*, energía *f*.

Pl. *abbr of* **Place**.

P & L (*abbr of* **profit and loss**) *n* ganancias y pérdidas *fpl*.

placard ['plækɑːd] *n* pancarta *f*.

placate [plə'keɪt] *vt* aplacar, apaciguar.

placatory [plə'keɪtərɪ] *adj* apaciguador(ra).

place [pleɪs] ◇ *n* **-1.** [gen] lugar *m*, sitio *m*; ~ **of birth** lugar de nacimiento. **-2.** [proper position] sitio *m*; **to fall into** ~ encajar; **to put sb in their** ~ poner a alguien en su sitio. **-3.** [suitable occasion, time] momento *m*. **-4.** [home] casa *f*. **-5.** [specific seat] asiento *m*; THEATRE localidad *f*. **-6.** [setting at table] cubierto *m*. **-7.** [on course, at university] plaza *f*. **-8.** [on committee, in team] puesto *m*. **-9.** [role, function] papel *m*; **to have an important** ~ in desempeñar un papel importante en; **it's not my** ~ **to question it** no es de mi incumbencia cuestionarlo. **-10.** [rank] lugar *m*, posición *f*. **-11.** [in book] página *f*; [in speech] momento *m*; **to lose one's** ~ no saber (uno) dónde estaba. **-12.** MATH: **decimal** ~ **punto** *m* decimal. **-13.** [instance]: **in the first** ~ [from the start] desde el principio; **in the first** ~ ... **and in the second** ~ ... [firstly, secondly] en primer lugar ... y en segundo lugar .... **-14.** *phr*: **to take** ~ tener lugar; **to take the** ~ **of** sustituir a.

◇ *vt* **-1.** [position, put] colocar, poner; **to be well** ~**d to do sthg** estar en buena posición para hacer algo. **-2.** [lay, apportion]: **to** ~ **the blame on** echar la culpa a; **to** ~ **pressure on** ejercer presión sobre. **-3.** [identify]: **I recognize the face, but I can't** ~ **her** me suena su cara, pero no sé de qué. **-4.** [bet, order etc] hacer. **-5.** [in horse racing]: **to be** ~**d** llegar entre los tres primeros.

♦ **all over the place** *adv* por todas partes.

♦ **in place** *adv* **-1.** [in proper position] en su sitio. **-2.** [established, set up] en marcha OR funcionamiento.

♦ **in place of** *prep* en lugar de, en vez de.

♦ **out of place** *adv* **-1.** [in wrong position]: **to be out of** ~ no estar en su sitio. **-2.** [inappropriate, unsuitable] fuera de lugar.

placebo [plə'siːbəʊ] (*pl* **-s** OR **-es**) *n* placebo *m*.

place card *n* tarjeta *f* (de colocación de los invitados).

placed [pleɪst] *adj* situado(da).

placekick ['pleɪskɪk] *n* tiro *m* libre.

place mat *n* mantel *m* individual.

placement ['pleɪsmənt] *n* colocación *f*.

placenta [plə'sentə] (*pl* **-s** OR **-tae** [-tiː]) *n* placenta *f*.

place setting *n* cubierto *m*.

placid ['plæsɪd] *adj* **-1.** [even-tempered] apacible, afable. **-2.** [peaceful] tranquilo(la).

placidly ['plæsɪdlɪ] *adv* apaciblemente, afablemente.

plagiarism ['pleɪdʒjərɪzm] *n* plagio *m*.

plagiarist ['pleɪdʒjərɪst] *n* plagiario *m*, -ria *f*.

plagiarize, -ise ['pleɪdʒjəraɪz] *vt* plagiar.

plague [pleɪg] ◇ *n* **-1.** [attack of disease] peste *f*. **-2.** [disease]: **(the)** ~ la peste; **to avoid sb/sthg like the** ~ huir de alguien/algo como de la peste. **-3.** [of rats, insects] plaga *f*. ◇ *vt*: **to** ~ **sb with** [complaints, requests] acosar a alguien con; [questions] coser a alguien; **to be** ~**d by** [ill health] estar acosado de; [doubts] estar atormentado de.

plaice [pleɪs] (*pl inv*) *n* platija *f*.

plaid [plæd] *n* tejido *m* escocés.

Plaid Cymru [,plaɪd'kʌmrɪ] *n Br* POL *partido nacionalista galés*.

plain [pleɪn] ◇ *adj* **-1.** [not patterned] liso(sa). **-2.** [simple - gen] sencillo(lla); [- yoghurt] natural. **-3.** [clear] evidente, claro(ra); **to make sthg** ~ **to sb** dejar algo bien claro a alguien. **-4.** [speaking, statement] franco(ca). **-5.** [absolute - madness etc] total, auténtico(ca). **-6.** [not pretty] sin atractivo. ◇ *adv inf* completamente. ◇ *n* GEOGR llanura *f*, planicie *f*.

plain chocolate *n Br* chocolate *m* amargo.

plain-clothes *adj* vestido(da) de paisano.

plain flour *n Br* harina *f* (sin levadura).

plainly ['pleɪnlɪ] *adv* **-1.** [upset, angry] evidentemente. **-2.** [visible, audible] claramente. **-3.** [frankly] francamente. **-4.** [simply] sencillamente.

plain sailing *n*: it's ~ es coser y cantar.

plainspoken [ˌpleɪn'spəʊkən] *adj* franco(ca).

plaintiff ['pleɪntɪf] *n* demandante *m y f*, querellante *m y f*.

plaintive ['pleɪntɪv] *adj* quejumbroso(sa), lastimero(ra).

plait [plæt] ◇ *n* trenza *f*. ◇ *vt* trenzar.

plan [plæn] (*pt & pp* **-ned**, *cont* **-ning**) ◇ *n* **-1.** [strategy] plan *m*, proyecto *m*; **to go according to** ~ salir según lo previsto. **-2.** [of story, essay] esquema *m*. **-3.** [of building etc] plano *m*.
◇ *vt* **-1.** [organize] planear, organizar. **-2.** [career, future] planificar; **to** ~ **to do sthg** tener la intención de hacer algo; **it wasn't planned** no estaba previsto. **-3.** [design, devise] trazar un esquema OR boceto de.
◇ *vi* hacer planes OR proyectos; **to** ~ **for sthg** prever algo.
◆ **plans** *npl* planes *mpl*; **to have ~s for** tener planes para.

◆ **plan on** *vt fus*: **to** ~ **on doing sthg** pensar hacer algo.

◆ **plan out** *vt sep* planear.

plane [pleɪn] ◇ *adj* plano(na). ◇ *n* **-1.** [aircraft] avión *m*. **-2.** GEOM [flat surface] plano *m*. **-3.** *fig* [level - intellectual] nivel *m*, plano *m*. **-4.** [tool] cepillo *m*. **-5.** [tree] plátano *m*.
◇ *vt* cepillar.

planet ['plænɪt] *n* planeta *m*.

planetarium [ˌplænɪ'teərɪəm] (*pl* **-riums** OR **-ria** [-rɪə]) *n* planetario *m*.

planetary ['plænɪtrɪ] *adj* planetario(ria).

plane tree *n* plátano *m*.

plangent ['plændʒənt] *adj literary* plañidero(ra).

plank [plæŋk] *n* **-1.** [piece of wood] tablón *m*, tabla *f*. **-2.** POL [main policy] punto *m* fundamental.

plankton ['plæŋktən] *n* plancton *m*.

planned [plænd] *adj* [crime] planeado(da); [economy] planificado(da).

planner ['plænər] *n* planificador *m*, -ra *f*; **town** ~ urbanista *m y f*.

planning ['plænɪŋ] *n* [gen] planificación *f*; **town** ~ urbanismo *m*.

planning permission *n* permiso *m* de construcción OR de obras.

plan of action *n* plan *m* de acción.

plant [plɑːnt] ◇ *n* **-1.** BOT planta *f*. **-2.** [factory] planta *f*, fábrica *f*. **-3.** [heavy machinery] maquinaria *f*. ◇ *vt* **-1.** [seed, tree, vegetable]: **to** ~ **sthg (in)** plantar algo (en). **-2.** [field, garden]: **to** ~ **sthg with** sembrar algo de. **-3.** [kiss, chair] colocar. **-4.** [bomb, bug] colocar secretamente; **to** ~ **sthg on sb** [drugs, weapon] endosar algo a alguien.

◆ **plant out** *vt sep* trasplantar.

plantain ['plæntɪn] *n* llantén *m*.

plantation [plæn'teɪʃn] *n* plantación *f*.

planter ['plɑːntər] *n* **-1.** [farmer] plantador *m*, -ra *f*. **-2.** [container] macetero *m*.

plant pot *n* maceta *f*, tiesto *m*.

plaque [plɑːk] *n* placa *f*.

plasma ['plæzmə] *n* plasma *m*.

plaster ['plɑːstər] ◇ *n* **-1.** [for wall, ceiling] yeso *m*. **-2.** [for broken bones] escayola *f*; **in** ~ escayolado(da). **-3.** *Br* [bandage] tirita® *f*, esparadrapo *m*. ◇ *vt* **-1.** [put plaster on] enyesar. **-2.** [cover]: **to** ~ **sthg (with)** cubrir algo (de).

plasterboard ['plɑːstəbɔːd] *n* cartón *m* yeso.

plaster cast *n* **-1.** [for broken bones] escayola *f*. **-2.** [model, statue] vaciado *m* en yeso.

plastered ['plɑːstəd] *adj inf* [drunk] cocido(da).

plasterer ['plɑːstərər] *n* yesero *m*, -ra *f*.

plastering ['plɑːstərɪŋ] *n* enyesado *m*.

plaster of Paris *n* yeso *m* mate.

plastic ['plæstɪk] ◇ *adj* [made from plastic] de plástico. ◇ *n* plástico *m*.

plastic bullet *n* bala *f* de goma.

plastic explosive *n* (explosivo *m*) plástico *m*.

Plasticine® ['plæstɪsiːn] *n Br* ≃ plastilina® *f*.

plasticize, -ise ['plæstɪsaɪz] *vt* plastificar.

plastic money *n* (U) tarjetas *fpl* de crédito.

plastic surgeon *n* cirujano plástico *m*, cirujana plástica *f*.

plastic surgery *n* cirugía *f* plástica.

plate [pleɪt] ◇ *n* **-1.** [dish, plateful] plato *m*; **to have a lot on one's** ~ [be busy] estar hasta el cuello de trabajo; **to hand sthg on a** ~ **to sb** ponerle algo a alguien en bandeja de plata. **-2.** [on machinery, wall, door] placa *f*. **-3.** (U) [metal covering]: **gold/silver** ~ chapa *f* de oro/plata. **-4.** [photograph] lámina *f*. **-5.** [in dentistry] dentadura *f* postiza. ◇ *vt*: **to be** ~**d (with)** estar chapado(da) (en OR de).

Plate [pleɪt] *n*: **the River** ~ el río de la Plata.

plateau ['plætəʊ] (*pl* **-s** OR **-x** [-z]) *n* **-1.** [high, flat land] meseta *f*. **-2.** *fig* [steady level] estado *m* estacionario.

plateful ['pleɪtful] *n* plato *m*.

plate glass *n* vidrio *m* cilindrado.

plate rack *n* escurreplatos *m inv.*

platform ['plætfɔːm] *n* **-1.** [gen] plataforma *f*; [stage] estrado *m*; [at meeting] tribuna *f*. **-2.** RAIL andén *m*. **-3.** POL programa *m* electoral. **-4.** [of bus] *en los autobuses londinenses, parte trasera abierta por donde entran y salen los pasajeros.*

platform ticket *n Br* billete *m* de andén.

plating ['pleɪtɪŋ] *n* chapeado *m*.

platinum ['plætɪnəm] ◇ *adj* [colour] platino (*inv*). ◇ *n* platino *m*. ◇ *comp* [made of platinum] de platino.

platinum blonde *n* rubia *f* platino.

platitude ['plætɪtjuːd] *n* tópico *m*, cliché *m*.

platonic [plə'tɒnɪk] *adj* platónico(ca).

platoon [plə'tuːn] *n* pelotón *m*.

platter ['plætər] *n* [dish] fuente *f*.

platypus ['plætɪpəs] (*pl* **-es**) *n* ornitorrinco *m*.

plaudits ['plɔːdɪts] *npl* aplausos *mpl*.

plausible ['plɔːzəbl] *adj* plausible, admisible.

plausibly ['plɔːzəblɪ] *adv* plausiblemente.

play [pleɪ] ◇ *n* **-1.** (*U*) [amusement] juego *m*. **-2.** [piece of drama] obra *f*. **-3.** SPORT: **out of/in** ~ fuera de/en juego. **-4.** [consideration]: **to come into** ~ entrar en juego. **-5.** [game]: ~ **on words** juego *m* de palabras. **-6.** TECH juego *m*. ◇ *vt* **-1.** [game, sport] jugar a. **-2.** [play game against]: **to** ~ **sb (at sthg)** jugar contra alguien (a algo). **-3.** [perform for amusement]: **to** ~ **a joke on** gastar una broma a; **to** ~ **a dirty trick on** jugar una mala pasada a. **-4.** [act - part, character] representar; **to** ~ **a part** OR **role in** *fig* desempeñar un papel en; **to** ~ **the fool** hacer OR hacerse el tonto. **-5.** [instrument, tune] tocar; [record, cassette] poner. **-6.** *phr*: **to** ~ **it safe** actuar sobre seguro; **to** ~ **it cool** comportarse con calma. ◇ *vi* **-1.** [gen]: **to** ~ **(with/against)** jugar (con/contra); **to** ~ **for sb/a team** jugar para alguien/con un equipo. **-2.** [act]: **to** ~ **in** sthg actuar en algo. **-3.** [MUS - person] tocar; [- music] sonar. **-4.** *literary* [flicker - light, sunshine] rielar.

◆ **play along** *vi*: **to** ~ **along (with)** seguir la corriente (a).

◆ **play at** *vt fus* jugar a.

◆ **play back** *vt sep* volver a poner.

◆ **play down** *vt sep* quitar importancia a.

◆ **play off** ◇ *vt sep*: **to** ~ **sthg/sb off against** oponer algo/a alguien contra. ◇ *vi* jugar un partido de desempate.

◆ **play (up)on** *vt fus* aprovecharse de.

◆ **play up** ◇ *vt sep* [emphasize] hacer resaltar, realzar. ◇ *vi* [machine, part of body, child] dar guerra.

playable ['pleɪəbl] *adj* en condiciones para que se juegue (un partido).

play-act *vi* fingir, hacer comedia.

playbill ['pleɪbɪl] *n* cartel *m* anunciador.

playboy ['pleɪbɔɪ] *n* playboy *m*, fifí *m Amer*.

play dough *n* ≃ plastilina® *f*.

player ['pleɪər] *n* **-1.** [of sport, game] jugador *m*, -ra *f*. **-2.** MUS músico *m* y *f*, intérprete *m* y *f*. **-3.** THEATRE actor *m*, actriz *f*.

playfellow ['pleɪˌfeləʊ] *n* compañero *m*, -ra *f* de juego.

playful ['pleɪful] *adj* juguetón(ona).

playfully ['pleɪfulɪ] *adv* de manera juguetona.

playgoer ['pleɪˌgəʊər] *n* aficionado *m*, -da *f* al teatro.

playground ['pleɪgraʊnd] *n* patio *m* de recreo.

playgroup ['pleɪgruːp] *n* jardín *m* de infancia, guardería *f*.

playhouse ['pleɪhaʊs, *pl* -haʊzɪz] *n Am* casita de juguete del tamaño de un niño.

playing card ['pleɪɪŋ-] *n* naipe *m*, carta *f*.

playing field ['pleɪɪŋ-] *n* campo *m* de juego.

playlist ['pleɪlɪst] *n Br* lista de éxitos que pone un disc-jockey en la radio.

playmate ['pleɪmeɪt] *n* compañero *m*, -ra *f* de juego.

play-off *n* partido *m* de desempate.

playpen ['pleɪpen] *n* parque *m* (de niños) (*tipo cuna*).

playroom ['pleɪrʊm] *n* cuarto *m* de los juguetes.

playschool ['pleɪskuːl] *n* jardín *m* de infancia, guardería *f*.

plaything ['pleɪθɪŋ] *n lit* & *fig* juguete *m*.

playtime ['pleɪtaɪm] *n* recreo *m*.

playwright ['pleɪraɪt] *n* autor *m*, -ra *f* de teatro, dramaturgo *m*, -ga *f*.

plaza ['plɑːzə] *n* **-1.** [public square] plaza *f*. **-2.** [building complex] complejo *m* comercial.

plc *abbr of* **public limited company**.

plea [pliː] *n* **-1.** [appeal] súplica *f*, petición *f*. **-2.** JUR declaración por parte del acusado de culpabilidad o inocencia.

plea bargaining *n sistema por el cual el acusado se declara culpable de un delito menos grave quedándole anulada la imputación de otro mayor.*

plead [pliːd] (*pt* & *pp* **-ed** OR **pled**) ◇ *vt* **-1.** JUR [one's cause] defender; **to** ~ **guilty/not guilty** declararse culpable/inocente; **to** ~

insanity alegar desequilibrio mental. **-2.** [give as excuse] pretender. ◇ *vi* **-1.** [beg]: to ~ **(with sb to do sthg)** rogar OR implorar (a alguien que haga algo); **to ~ for sthg** pedir algo. **-2.** JUR declarar.

pleading ['pliːdɪŋ] ◇ *adj* de súplica, implorante. ◇ *n* (*U*) súplicas *fpl*.

pleasant ['pleznt] *adj* **-1.** [smell, taste, view] agradable; [surprise, news] grato(ta). **-2.** [person, smile, face] simpático(ca), dije *Amer*.

pleasantly ['plezntlɪ] *adv* [smile, say] agradablemente; [be surprised] gratamente.

pleasantry ['plezntrɪ] (*pl* **-ies**) *n*: to exchange pleasantries intercambiar cumplidos.

please [pliːz] ◇ *vt* complacer, agradar; **he always ~s himself** él siempre hace lo que le da la gana; **~ yourself!** ¡como quieras! ◇ *vi* **-1.** [give satisfaction] satisfacer, agradar. **-2.** [think appropriate]: **to do as one ~s** hacer como a uno le parezca; **if you ~** si no le importa. ◇ *adv* por favor.

pleased [pliːzd] *adj*: to be ~ **(about/with)** estar contento(ta) (por/con); ~ **to meet you!** ¡encantado(da) de conocerle!, ¡mucho gusto!

pleasing ['pliːzɪŋ] *adj* agradable, grato(ta).

pleasingly ['pliːzɪŋlɪ] *adv* agradablemente.

pleasurable ['pleʒərəbl] *adj* agradable, grato(ta).

pleasure ['pleʒəʳ] *n* **-1.** [feeling of happiness] gusto *m*; **to take ~ in sthg** disfrutar haciendo algo; **with ~** con gusto. **-2.** [enjoyment] diversión *f*. **-3.** [delight] placer *m*; **it's a ~ to talk to him** da gusto hablar con él; **it's a ~, my ~** no hay de qué.

pleat [pliːt] ◇ *n* pliegue *m*. ◇ *vt* plisar, hacer pliegues en.

pleated ['pliːtɪd] *adj* plisado(da).

plebiscite ['plebɪsaɪt] *n* plebiscito *m*.

plectrum ['plektrəm] (*pl* **-s**) *n* púa *f*, plectro *m*.

pled [pled] *pt & pp* → **plead**.

pledge [pledʒ] ◇ *n* **-1.** [promise] promesa *f*. **-2.** [token] señal *f*, prenda *f*. ◇ *vt* **-1.** [promise] prometer. **-2.** [make promise]: **to ~ sb to sthg** hacer jurar a alguien algo; **to ~ o.s. to** comprometerse a. **-3.** [pawn] empeñar.

plenary session ['pliːnərɪ-] *n* sesión *f* plenaria.

plenitude ['plenɪtjuːd] *n fml* plenitud *f*.

plentiful ['plentɪfʊl] *adj* abundante.

plenty ['plentɪ] ◇ *n* (*U*) abundancia *f*. ◇ *pron*: **we've got ~** tenemos de sobra; ~ **of** mucho(cha); ~ **of reasons** muchas razones; ~ **of time** tiempo de sobra. ◇ *adv Am* [very] muy.

plethora ['pleθərə] *n* plétora *f*.

pleurisy ['plʊərəsɪ] *n* pleuresía *f*.

Plexiglas® ['pleksɪɡlɑːs] *n Am* plexiglás® *m*.

pliable ['plaɪəbl], **pliant** ['plaɪənt] *adj* flexible.

pliers ['plaɪəz] *npl* tenazas *fpl*, alicates *mpl*.

plight [plaɪt] *n* grave situación *f*.

plimsoll ['plɪmsəl] *n Br* playera *f*, zapato *m* de tenis.

Plimsoll line *n* línea *f* de máxima carga.

plinth [plɪnθ] *n* [for statue] peana *f*; [for pillar] plinto *m*.

PLO (*abbr of* **Palestine Liberation Organization**) *n* OLP *f*.

plod [plɒd] (*pt & pp* **-ded**, *cont* **-ding**) *vi* **-1.** [walk slowly] caminar con paso cansino. **-2.** [work slowly] llevar a cabo un trabajo pesado.

plodder ['plɒdəʳ] *n pej* persona *f* mediocre pero voluntariosa (en el trabajo).

plonk [plɒŋk] *n* (*U*) *Br inf* [wine] vino *m* peleón.

◆ **plonk down** *vt sep inf* dejar caer.

plop [plɒp] (*pt & pp* **-ped**, *cont* **-ping**) ◇ *n* paf *m*. ◇ *vi* hacer paf.

plot [plɒt] (*pt & pp* **-ted**, *cont* **-ting**) ◇ *n* **-1.** [plan] complot *m*, conspiración *f*. **-2.** [story] argumento *m*, trama *f*. **-3.** [of land] parcela *f*. **-4.** *Am* [house plan] plano *m* básico, plano *m* inicial. ◇ *vt* **-1.** [plan] tramar, urdir. **-2.** [on map, graph] trazar. ◇ *vi*: **to ~ (to do sthg)** tramar (hacer algo); **to ~ against** conspirar contra.

plotter ['plɒtəʳ] *n* [schemer] conspirador *m*, -ra *f*.

plough *Br*, **plow** *Am* [plaʊ] ◇ *n* arado *m*. ◇ *vt* arar.

◆ **plough into** ◇ *vt sep* [invest] invertir. ◇ *vt fus* [hit] chocar contra.

◆ **plough on** *vi* continuar trabajosamente.

◆ **plough up** *vt sep* arar.

ploughman's ['plaʊmənz] (*pl inv*) *n Br*: ~ **(lunch)** *queso, cebolletas y ensalada con pan*.

ploughshare *Br*, **plowshare** *Am* ['plaʊʃeəʳ] *n* reja *f* del arado.

plow *etc Am* = **plough** *etc*.

ploy [plɔɪ] *n* táctica *f*, estratagema *f*.

PLR (*abbr of* **Public Lending Right**) *n derechos de autor en concepto de las obras prestadas por las bibliotecas.*

pluck [plʌk] ◇ *vt* **-1.** [fruit, flower] coger. **-2.** [pull sharply] arrancar. **-3.** [bird] desplumar. **-4.** [eyebrows] depilar. **-5.** [instrument] puntear. ◇ *n dated* valor *m*, ánimo *m*.

◆ **pluck up** *vt fus*: **to ~ up the courage to do sthg** armarse de valor para hacer algo.

plucky ['plʌkɪ] (*compar* **-ier**, *superl* **-iest**) *adj* dated valiente.

plug [plʌg] (*pt* & *pp* **-ged**, *cont* **-ging**) ◇ *n* **-1.** ELEC enchufe *m*, clavija *f*. **-2.** [for bath or sink] tapón *m*. **-3.** *inf* [favourable mention] publicidad *f*. ◇ *vt* **-1.** [hole, leak] tapar, taponar. **-2.** *inf* [mention favourably] dar publicidad a.

♦ **plug in** *vt sep* enchufar.

plughole ['plʌghəʊl] *n* desagüe *m*.

plum [plʌm] ◇ *adj* **-1.** [colour] de color ciruela. **-2.** [choice]: ∼ **job** chollo *m*. ◇ *n* [fruit] ciruela *f*.

plumage ['pluːmɪdʒ] *n* plumaje *m*.

plumb [plʌm] ◇ *adv* **-1.** *Br* [exactly]: ∼ **in the middle** justo en medio. **-2.** *Am* [completely] completamente, por completo. ◇ *vt*: **to** ∼ **the depths of** alcanzar las cotas más bajas de.

♦ **plumb in** *vt sep Br* instalar.

plumber ['plʌmər] *n* fontanero *m*, -ra *f*, gásfiter *m Amer*.

plumbing ['plʌmɪŋ] *n* (*U*) **-1.** [fittings] tubería *f*. **-2.** [work] fontanería *f*.

plumb line *n* (hilo *m* de) plomada *f*.

plume [pluːm] *n* **-1.** [feather] pluma *f*. **-2.** [decoration, of smoke] penacho *m*.

plummet ['plʌmɪt] *vi* caer en picado.

plummy ['plʌmɪ] (*compar* **-ier**, *superl* **-iest**) *adj Br inf pej* [posh] afectado(da).

plump [plʌmp] *adj* regordete(ta), rollizo(za).

♦ **plump for** *vt fus* optar OR decidirse por.

♦ **plump up** *vt sep* ahuecar.

plumpness ['plʌmpnɪs] *n* gordura *f*.

plum pudding *n* budín navideño con pasas.

plunder ['plʌndər] ◇ *n* **-1.** [stealing, raiding] saqueo *m*, pillaje *m*. **-2.** [stolen goods] botín *m*. ◇ *vt* saquear.

plunge [plʌndʒ] ◇ *n* **-1.** [decrease] caída *f* vertiginosa. **-2.** [fall, dive] chapuzón *m*, zambullida *f*; **to take the** ∼ dar el paso decisivo. ◇ *vt* **-1.** [knife etc]: **to** ∼ **sthg into** hundir algo en. **-2.** [into darkness, water]: **to** ∼ **sthg into** sumergir algo en. ◇ *vi* **-1.** [fall, dive] hundirse, zambullirse. **-2.** [decrease] bajar vertiginosamente.

plunger ['plʌndʒər] *n* [for blocked pipes] desatascador *m*.

plunging ['plʌndʒɪŋ] *adj* escotado(da).

pluperfect [,pluː'pɜːfɪkt] *n*: ∼ **(tense)** (pretérito *m*) pluscuamperfecto *m*.

plural ['plʊərəl] ◇ *adj* [gen] plural. ◇ *n* plural *m*.

pluralistic [,plʊərə'lɪstɪk] *adj* pluralista.

plurality [plʊ'rælətɪ] *n* **-1.** [large number] pluralidad *f*. **-2.** *Am* [majority] mayoría *f*.

plus [plʌs] (*pl* **-es** OR **-ses**) ◇ *adj* **-1.** [or more]: **35-**∼ 35 o más. **-2.** [in marks]: **B-**∼ ≈ notable *m* alto. ◇ *n* **-1.** MATH [sign] signo *m* más. **-2.** *inf* [bonus] ventaja *f*. ◇ *prep* más. ◇ *conj* además.

plus fours *npl* (pantalones *mpl*) bombachos *mpl*.

plush [plʌʃ] *adj* lujoso(sa).

plus sign *n* signo *m* más.

Pluto ['pluːtəʊ] *n* [planet] Plutón *m*.

plutocrat ['pluːtəkræt] *n* plutócrata *m y f*.

plutonium [pluː'təʊnɪəm] *n* plutonio *m*.

ply [plaɪ] (*pt* & *pp* **plied**) ◇ *n* [of wood] número *m* de capas; [of wool, rope] número de cabos. ◇ *vt* **-1.** [trade] ejercer. **-2.** [supply, provide]: **to** ∼ **sb with sthg** [questions] acosar a alguien con algo; [food, drink] no parar de ofrecer a alguien algo. ◇ *vi* navegar.

plywood ['plaɪwʊd] *n* contrachapado *m*.

p.m., pm (*abbr of* **post meridiem**): **at 3** ∼ a las tres de la tarde.

PM *n abbr of* **prime minister**.

PMT, PMS (*abbr of* **premenstrual tension, premenstrual syndrome**) *n* SPM *m*.

pneumatic [njuː'mætɪk] *adj* **-1.** [pump, lift] de aire comprimido. **-2.** [tyre, chair] neumático(ca).

pneumatic drill *n* martillo *m* neumático.

pneumonia [njuː'məʊnjə] *n* (*U*) pulmonía *f*.

Po [pəʊ] *n*: **the (River)** ∼ el (río) Po.

PO *n abbr of* **Post Office**.

PO, po *n abbr of* **postal order**.

POA (*abbr of* **Prison Officers' Association**) *n* sindicato británico de empleados de prisiones.

poach [pəʊtʃ] ◇ *vt* **-1.** [game] cazar en vedado; [fish] pescar en vedado. **-2.** [copy] plagiar. **-3.** CULIN [salmon] hervir; [egg] escalfar. ◇ *vi* [for game] cazar 'en vedado;' [for fish] pescar en vedado.

poacher ['pəʊtʃər] *n* [hunter] cazador furtivo *m*, cazadora furtiva *f*; [fisherman] pescador furtivo *m*, pescadora furtiva *f*.

poaching ['pəʊtʃɪŋ] *n* [for game] caza *f* furtiva; [for fish] pesca *f* furtiva.

PO Box (*abbr of* **Post Office Box**) *n* apdo. *m*.

pocket ['pɒkɪt] ◇ *n* **-1.** [in clothes] bolsillo *m*; **to live in each other's** ∼**s** vivir continuamente pegado el uno al otro; **to be £10 out of** ∼ salir perdiendo 10 libras; **to pick sb's** ∼ vaciar a alguien el bolsillo. **-2.** [in car door etc] bolsa *f*, bolsillo *m*. **-3.** [of resistance] foco *m*; [of air] bolsa *f*. ◇ *vt* **-1.** [place in pocket] meterse en el bolsillo. **-2.** [steal] birlar. ◇ *adj* de bolsillo.

pocketbook ['pɒkɪtbʊk] *n* **-1.** [notebook] libreta *f*. **-2.** *Am* [handbag] bolso *m*.

pocket calculator n calculadora f de bolsillo.

pocketful ['pɒkɪtfʊl] n bolsillo m.

pocket-handkerchief n pañuelo m.

pocketknife ['pɒkɪtnaɪf] (pl -knives [-naɪvz]) n navaja f (de bolsillo).

pocket money n propina f, dinero m para gastar.

pocket-sized adj de bolsillo.

pockmark ['pɒkmɑːk] n marca f OR señal f (en la cara).

pod [pɒd] n -1. [of plants] vaina f. -2. [of spacecraft] módulo m espacial.

podgy ['pɒdʒɪ] (compar -ier, superl -iest) adj inf gordinflón(ona).

podiatrist [pə'daɪətrɪst] n Am podólogo m, -ga f, pedicuro m, -ra f.

podium ['pəʊdɪəm] (pl -diums OR -dia [-dɪə]) n podio m.

POE (abbr of port of entry) n puerto de entrada.

poem ['pəʊɪm] n poema m, poesía f.

poet ['pəʊɪt] n poeta m y f.

poetic [pəʊ'etɪk] adj poético(ca).

poetic justice n: it was ~ that he was sacked too se llevó su merecido con el despido.

poet laureate n poeta m laureado.

poetry ['pəʊɪtrɪ] n poesía f.

pogo stick n palo provisto de un muelle para dar saltos.

pogrom ['pɒgrəm] n pogromo m.

poignancy ['pɔɪnjənsɪ] n patetismo m.

poignant ['pɔɪnjənt] adj patético(ca), conmovedor(ra).

poinsettia [pɔɪn'setɪə] n flor f de Pascua.

point [pɔɪnt] ◇ n -1. [gen] punto m; at that ~ en aquel momento; ~ of no return punto de no retorno; a sore ~ fig un asunto espinoso OR delicado. -2. [tip] punta f. -3. [detail, argument]: to make a ~ hacer una observación; to make one's ~ explicar la postura de uno; to have a ~ tener razón. -4. [main idea]: the ~ is ... lo fundamental OR más importante es ...; to miss the ~ of no coger la idea de; to get OR come to the ~ ir al grano; it's beside the ~ no viene al caso; to the ~ relevante, concreto(ta). -5. [feature] cualidad f; weak/strong ~ punto m débil/fuerte. -6. [purpose] sentido m; what's the ~? ¿para qué?; there's no ~ in it no tiene sentido. -7. [decimal point] coma f; two ~ six dos coma seis. -8. Br ELEC toma f de corriente. -9. phr: to make a ~ of doing sthg poner empeño en hacer algo.
◇ vi: to ~ a gun at sthg/sb apuntar a algo/alguien con una pistola; to ~ one's finger at sthg/sb señalar algo/a alguien con el dedo.
◇ vi -1. [indicate with finger]: to ~ at sthg/sb, to ~ to sthg/sb señalar algo/a alguien con el dedo. -2. [hands of clock etc]: to ~ north/to ten o'clock indicar el norte/las diez. -3. fig [suggest]: everything ~s to her guilt todo indica que ella es la culpable.
◆ **points** npl Br RAIL agujas fpl.
◆ **up to a point** adv hasta cierto punto.
◆ **on the point of** prep: to be on the ~ of doing sthg estar a punto de hacer algo.
◆ **point out** vt sep [person, object, fact] señalar, indicar; [mistake] hacer notar.

point-blank ◇ adj -1. [refusal etc] categórico(ca). -2. [close-range] a quemarropa. ◇ adv -1. [refuse, deny] categóricamente. -2. [at close range] a quemarropa, a bocajarro.

point duty n Br control m de tráfico en un cruce.

pointed ['pɔɪntɪd] adj -1. [sharp, angular] en punta, puntiagudo(da). -2. [cutting, incisive] intencionado(da).

pointedly ['pɔɪntɪdlɪ] adv intencionadamente.

pointer ['pɔɪntə'] n -1. [piece of advice] consejo m. -2. [needle] aguja f. -3. [for map, blackboard] puntero m. -4. COMPUT puntero m.

pointing ['pɔɪntɪŋ] n [on wall] rejuntado m.

pointless ['pɔɪntlɪs] adj sin sentido, inútil.

point of order (pl points of order) n: to raise a ~ hacer una moción sobre el acatamiento de las normas.

point of sale (pl points of sale) n punto m de venta.

point of view (pl points of view) n -1. [opinion] punto m de vista. -2. [aspect, perspective] perspectiva f.

point-to-point n Br carrera de caballos por el campo señalizada con banderines.

poise [pɔɪz] n [self-assurance] aplomo m, serenidad f; [elegance] elegancia f.

poised [pɔɪzd] adj -1. [ready]: to be ~ to do sthg estar listo(ta) para hacer algo; to be ~ for sthg estar preparado(da) para algo. -2. [calm and dignified] sereno(na).

poison ['pɔɪzn] ◇ n veneno m. ◇ vt -1. [gen - intentionally] envenenar; [- unintentionally] intoxicar. -2. [environment] contaminar. -3. fig [spoil, corrupt] corromper.

poisoning ['pɔɪznɪŋ] n -1. [intentional] envenenamiento m; [unintentional] intoxicación f. -2. [of environment] contaminación f.

poisonous ['pɔɪznəs] adj -1. [substance, gas] tóxico(ca). -2. [snake] venenoso(sa). -3. fig [influence] pernicioso(sa); [rumours] malintencionado(da).

poison-pen letter *n* anónimo *m* ofensivo.
poke [pəʊk] ◇ *n* [blow] golpe *m*; [push] empujón *m*; [with elbow] codazo *m*. ◇ *vt* **-1.** [with finger, stick] empujar; [with elbow] dar un codazo a; [fire] atizar; **to ~ sb in the eye** meter el dedo en el ojo de alguien. **-2.** [push, stuff]: **to ~ sthg into** meter algo en. **-3.** [stretch]: **he ~d his head round the door** asomó la cabeza por la puerta. ◇ *vi* **-1.** [protrude]: **to ~ out of sthg** sobresalir por algo. **-2.** [prod]: **his elbow was poking into my back** me estaba clavando el codo en la espalda.
◆ **poke about, poke around** *vi inf* fisgonear, hurgar.
◆ **poke at** *vt fus* dar golpecitos a.
poker ['pəʊkəʳ] *n* **-1.** [game] póker *m.* **-2.** [for fire] atizador *m.*
poker-faced [-,feɪst] *adj* con cara inexpresiva.
poky ['pəʊkɪ] (*comp* **-ier,** *superl* **-iest**) *adj pej*: **a ~ little room** un cuartucho.
Poland ['pəʊlənd] *n* Polonia.
polar ['pəʊləʳ] *adj* polar.
polar bear *n* oso *m* polar.
polarity [pəʊ'lærətɪ] *n* polaridad *f.*
polarization [,pəʊləraɪ'zeɪʃn] *n* polarización *f.*
polarize, -ise ['pəʊləraɪz] *vt* polarizar.
Polaroid® ['pəʊlərɔɪd] *n* **-1.** [camera] polaroid® *f.* **-2.** [photograph] fotografía *f* polaroid.
Polaroids® ['pəʊlərɔɪdz] *npl* gafas *fpl* de sol (de polaroid).
pole [pəʊl] *n* **-1.** [rod, post] palo *m*; **telegraph ~** poste *m* telegráfico. **-2.** ELEC & GEOGR polo *m*; **to be ~s apart** *fig* ser polos opuestos.
Pole [pəʊl] *n* polaco *m*, -ca *f.*
poleaxed ['pəʊlækst] *adj* atolondrado(da).
polecat ['pəʊlkæt] *n* turón *m.*
polemic [pə'lemɪk] *n fml* polémica *f.*
pole position *n* posición *f* de cabeza.
Pole Star *n*: **the ~** la estrella polar.
pole vault *n*: **the ~** el salto con pértiga.
◆ **pole-vault** *vi* saltar con pértiga.
pole-vaulter [-,vɔːltəʳ] *n* saltador *m*, -ra *f* con pértiga.
police [pə'liːs] ◇ *npl* **-1.** [police force]: **the ~** la policía. **-2.** [policemen, policewomen] policías *mpl y fpl*. ◇ *vt* mantener el orden en, vigilar.
police car *n* coche *m* patrulla.
police constable *n* Br policía *m y f.*
police department *n* Am jefatura *f* de policía.

police dog *n* perro *m* policía.
police force *n* cuerpo *m* de policía.
policeman [pə'liːsmən] (*pl* **-men** [-mən]) *n* policía *m.*
police officer *n* agente *m y f* de la policía.
police record *n*: **(to have a) ~** (tener) antecedentes *mpl* policiales.
police state *n* estado *m* policial.
police station *n* comisaría *f* (de policía).
policewoman [pə'liːs,wʊmən] (*pl* **-women** [-,wɪmɪn]) *n* (mujer *f*) policía *f.*
policy ['pɒləsɪ] (*pl* **-ies**) *n* **-1.** [plan, practice] política *f*; **it's not our ~ to do this** no tenemos por norma hacer esto. **-2.** [document, agreement] póliza *f.*
policy-holder *n* asegurado *m*, -da *f.*
polio ['pəʊlɪəʊ] *n* polio *f.*
polish ['pɒlɪʃ] ◇ *n* **-1.** [for floor] cera *f*; [for shoes] betún *m*; [for window] limpiacristales *m inv*; [for nails] esmalte *m*. **-2.** [shine] brillo *m*, lustre *m*. **-3.** *fig* [refinement] refinamiento *m*. ◇ *vt* **-1.** [floor] encerar; [shoes, window, car] limpiar; [cutlery, silver, glasses] sacar brillo a.
◆ **polish off** *vt sep inf* [food] zamparse; [job] despachar.
Polish ['pəʊlɪʃ] ◇ *adj* polaco(ca). ◇ *n* [language] polaco *m*. ◇ *npl*: **the ~** los polacos *mpl.*
polished ['pɒlɪʃt] *adj* **-1.** [person, manner] refinado(da). **-2.** [performance, speech] esmerado(da).
polite [pə'laɪt] *adj* educado(da), cortés; **~ society** gente *f* educada.
politely [pə'laɪtlɪ] *adv* educadamente, con cortesía.
politeness [pə'laɪtnɪs] *n* educación *f*, cortesía *f.*
politic ['pɒlətɪk] *adj fml* oportuno(na), conveniente.
political [pə'lɪtɪkl] *adj* **-1.** [concerning politics] político(ca). **-2.** [interested in politics] interesado(da) en política.
political asylum *n* asilo *m* político.
political football *n* tema *m* candente, arma *f* arrojadiza (*con fines partidistas*).
political geography *n* geografía *f* política.
politically [pə'lɪtɪklɪ] *adv* políticamente.
politically correct *adj* políticamente correcto(ta), *conforme a la ética del movimiento* 'PC'.

POLITICALLY CORRECT:
Se aplica 'politically correct' a personas, actitudes y términos nacidos de un movimiento, principalmente americano, llamado 'PC'. Este movimiento intenta sustituir términos

que pueden resultar insultantes (racistas, sexistas etc) por otros considerados aceptables, por ejemplo: 'American Indian' por 'Native American', 'short' por 'vertically challenged', 'Disabled' por 'Differently Abled'

political prisoner *n* preso político *m*, presa política *f*.

political science *n* (*U*) ciencia *f* política.

politician [,pɒlɪ'tɪʃn] *n* político *m*, -ca *f*.

politicize, -ise [pə'lɪtɪsaɪz] *vt* politizar.

politics ['pɒlətɪks] ◇ *n* (*U*) **-1.** [gen] política *f*. **-2.** [field of study] ciencias *fpl* políticas. ◇ *npl* **-1.** [personal beliefs] ideas *fpl* políticas. **-2.** [of a group, area] política *f*.

polka ['pɒlkə] *n* polca *f*.

polka dot *n* lunar *m* (*en un vestido*).

poll [pəʊl] ◇ *n* [vote] votación *f*; [of opinion] encuesta *f*. ◇ *vt* **-1.** [people] sondear. **-2.** [votes] obtener.
 ◆ **polls** *npl*: the ~s las elecciones, los comicios; **to go to the ~s** acudir a las urnas.

pollen ['pɒlən] *n* polen *m*.

pollen count *n* índice *m* de polen en el aire.

pollinate ['pɒləneɪt] *vt* polinizar.

pollination [,pɒlɪ'neɪʃn] *n* polinización *f*.

polling ['pəʊlɪŋ] *n* (*U*) [votes] votación *f*.

polling booth *n* cabina *f* electoral.

polling day *n Br* día *m* de elecciones.

polling station *n* mesa *f* OR centro *m* electoral.

pollster ['pəʊlstər] *n* encuestador *m*, -ra *f*, entrevistador *m*, -ra *f*.

poll tax *n impuesto sobre las personas adultas*.
 ◆ **Poll Tax** *n Br*: **the Poll Tax** ≃ ·la contribución urbana.

pollutant [pə'luːtnt] *n* contaminante *m*.

pollute [pə'luːt] *vt* contaminar.

pollution [pə'luːʃn] *n* (*U*) **-1.** [process of polluting] contaminación *f*. **-2.** [impurities] substancias *fpl* contaminantes.

polo ['pəʊləʊ] *n* polo *m*.

polo neck *Br n* **-1.** [neck] cuello *m* alto. **-2.** [jumper] jersey *m* de cuello alto.
 ◆ **polo-neck** *adj* de cuello alto.

polo shirt *n* polo *m*.

poltergeist ['pɒltəgaɪst] *n espíritu que habita una casa, produciendo ruidos y moviendo objetos*.

poly ['pɒlɪ] (*pl* **polys**) *n Br inf abbr of* **polytechnic**.

polyanthus [,pɒlɪ'ænθəs] (*pl* **-thuses** OR **-thi** [-θaɪ]) *n* prímula *f*.

poly bag *n Br inf* bolsa *f* de plástico.

polyester [,pɒlɪ'estər] *n* poliéster *m*.

polyethylene *n Am* = **polythene**.

polygamist [pə'lɪgəmɪst] *n* polígamo *m*, -ma *f*.

polygamy [pə'lɪgəmɪ] *n* poligamia *f*.

polygon ['pɒlɪgɒn] *n* polígono *m*.

polygraph ['pɒlɪgrɑːf] *n* detector *m* de mentiras.

polymer ['pɒlɪmər] *n* polímero *m*.

Polynesia [,pɒlɪ'niːʒə] *n* Polinesia; **French ~** la Polinesia francesa.

Polynesian [,pɒlɪ'niːʒən] ◇ *adj* polinesio(sia). ◇ *n* **-1.** [person] polinesio *m*, -sia *f*. **-2.** [language] polinesio *m*.

polyp ['pɒlɪp] *n* MED pólipo *m*.

polyphony [pə'lɪfənɪ] *n fml* polifonía *f*.

polystyrene [,pɒlɪ'staɪriːn] *n* poliestireno *m*.

polysyllabic [,pɒlɪsɪ'læbɪk] *adj* polisílabo(ba).

polytechnic [,pɒlɪ'teknɪk] *n Br* politécnico *m*, escuela *f* politécnica.

polythene *Br* ['pɒlɪθiːn], **polyethylene** *Am* ['pɒlɪ'eθiliːn] *n* polietileno *m*, politeno *m*.

polythene bag *n Br* bolsa *f* de plástico.

polyunsaturated [,pɒlɪʌn'sætʃəreɪtɪd] *adj* poliinsaturado(da).

polyurethane [,pɒlɪ'jʊərəθeɪn] *n* poliuretano *m*.

pom [pɒm] *n Austr inf término peyorativo que designa a un británico*.

pomander [pə'mændər] *n* bola *f* de loza perfumada.

pomegranate ['pɒmɪ,grænɪt] *n* granada *f*.

pommel ['pɒml] *n* **-1.** [on saddle] perilla *f*. **-2.** [on sword] pomo *m*.

pomp [pɒmp] *n* pompa *f*; **~ and circumstance** pompa *f*, boato *m*.

pompom ['pɒmpɒm] *n* borla *f*, pompón *m*.

pompous ['pɒmpəs] *adj* **-1.** [self-important] presumido(da), pretencioso(sa). **-2.** [style] pomposo(sa); [building] ostentoso(sa).

pompously ['pɒmpəslɪ] *adv* con pretenciosidad, de manera pretenciosa.

ponce [pɒns] *n Br v inf pej* **-1.** [effeminate man] afeminado *m*, maricón *m*. **-2.** [pimp] chulo *m*, macarra *m*.

poncey ['pɒnsɪ] *adj Br v inf pej* mariquita, afeminado(da).

poncho ['pɒntʃəʊ] (*pl* **-s**) *n* poncho *m*, ruana *f Amer*.

pond [pɒnd] *n* estanque *m*.

ponder ['pɒndər] ◇ *vt* considerar. ◇ *vi*: **to ~ (on** OR **over)** reflexionar OR meditar (sobre).

ponderous ['pɒndərəs] *adj* **-1.** [speech, book] pesado(da). **-2.** [building] aparatoso(sa). **-3.** [action, walk] lento(ta) y torpe.

pong [pɒŋ] *Br inf* ◇ *n* (olor *m* a) peste *f.* ◇ *vi* apestar.

pontiff ['pɒntɪf] *n* pontífice *m.*

pontificate [pɒn'tɪfɪkeɪt] *vi pej:* **to ~** (about OR **on**) pontificar (sobre).

pontoon [pɒn'tuːn] *n* **-1.** [bridge] pontón *m.* **-2.** *Br* [game] veintiuna *f.*

pony ['pəʊnɪ] (*pl* **-ies**) *n* poni *m.*

ponytail ['pəʊnɪteɪl] *n* coleta *f* (de caballo).

pony-trekking [-,trekɪŋ] *n* excursión *f* en poni.

poodle ['puːdl] *n* caniche *m.*

poof [pʊf] *n Br v inf pej* maricón *m.*

pooh [puː] *excl* [said in scorn] ¡bah!; [said in disgust] ¡puaj!

pooh-pooh *vt inf* despreciar, desdeñar.

pool [puːl] ◇ *n* **-1.** [of water, blood, ink] charco *m*; [pond] estanque *m.* **-2.** [swimming pool] piscina *f.* **-3.** [of light] foco *m.* **-4.** COMM [fund] fondos *mpl* comunes. **-5.** [of people, things]: **typing ~** servicio *m* de mecanografía; **car ~** parque *m* de automóviles. **-6.** [game] billar *m* americano. ◇ *vt* [resources, funds] juntar; [knowledge] poner en común.
◆ **pools** *npl Br:* **the ~s** las quinielas.

poor [pɔːr] ◇ *adj* **-1.** [gen] pobre; **~ old John!** ¡el pobre de John! **-2.** [quality, result] malo(la); **to be in ~ health** estar enfermo(ma). ◇ *npl:* **the ~** los pobres.

poorhouse ['pɔːhaʊs, *pl* -hauzɪz] *n* asilo *m* para pobres.

poorly ['pɔːlɪ] ◇ *adj Br* pachucho(cha). ◇ *adv* mal.

poorness ['pɔːnɪs] *n* [inadequacy, inferiority] inferioridad *f.*

poor relation *n fig* pariente *m* pobre.

pop [pɒp] (*pt* & *pp* **-ped**, *cont* **-ping**) ◇ *n* **-1.** [music] (música *f*) pop *m.* **-2.** (U) *inf* [fizzy drink] gaseosa *f.* **-3.** *inf* [father] papá *m.* **-4.** [sound] pequeña explosión *f.*
◇ *vt* **-1.** [balloon, bubble] pinchar. **-2.** [put quickly]: **to ~ sthg into** meter algo en; **he popped his head round the door** asomó la cabeza por la puerta.
◇ *vi* **-1.** [balloon] explotar, reventar; [cork, button] saltar. **-2.** [eyes] saltarse, salirse de las órbitas. **-3.** [go quickly]: **I'm just popping round to the shop** voy un momento a la tienda.
◆ **pop in** *vi* entrar un momento.
◆ **pop up** *vi* aparecer de repente.

popadum ['pɒpədəm] *n tipo de pan indio muy delgado y frito en aceite.*

pop art *n* pop art *m.*

pop concert *n* concierto *m* de música pop.

popcorn ['pɒpkɔːn] *n* palomitas *fpl* (de maíz).

pope [pəʊp] *n* papa *m.*

pop group *n* grupo *m* (de música) pop.

poplar ['pɒplər] *n* álamo *m.*

poplin ['pɒplɪn] *n* popelina *f.*

popper ['pɒpər] *n Br* [on clothes] corchete *m.*

poppy ['pɒpɪ] (*pl* **-ies**) *n* amapola *f.*

poppycock ['pɒpɪkɒk] *n* (U) *inf pej* bobadas *fpl*, tonterías *fpl.*

Poppy Day *n Br día en conmemoración de los caídos de las guerras mundiales.*

POPPY DAY:
Jornada de conmemoración durante la cual la gente lleva una amapola de papel en la solapa como recuerdo de los soldados británicos muertos en las guerras mundiales

Popsicle® ['pɒpsɪkl] *n Am* polo *m.*

pop singer *n* cantante *m* y *f* pop.

populace ['pɒpjʊləs] *n:* **the ~** [masses] el populacho; [people] el pueblo.

popular ['pɒpjʊlər] *adj* **-1.** [gen] popular; [person] estimado(da). **-2.** [belief, attitude, dis-content] generalizado(da), común. **-3.** [newspaper, politics] para las masas.

popularity [,pɒpjʊ'lærətɪ] *n* popularidad *f.*

popularize, -ise ['pɒpjʊləraɪz] *vt* **-1.** [make popular] popularizar. **-2.** [simplify] vulgarizar.

popularly ['pɒpjʊləlɪ] *adv* **-1.** [unofficially]: **~ known as** conocido(da) popularmente como. **-2.** [believed] generalmente.

populate ['pɒpjʊleɪt] *vt* poblar.

populated ['pɒpjʊleɪtɪd] *adj* poblado(da).

population [,pɒpjʊ'leɪʃn] *n* población *f.*

population explosion *n* explosión *f* demográfica.

populist ['pɒpjʊlɪst] *n* populista *m* y *f.*

pop-up *adj* **-1.** [toaster] automático(ca). **-2.** [book] desplegable.

porcelain ['pɔːsəlɪn] *n* porcelana *f.*

porch [pɔːtʃ] *n* **-1.** [entrance] porche *m*, pórtico *m.* **-2.** *Am* [verandah] terraza *f.*

porcupine ['pɔːkjʊpaɪn] *n* puerco *m* espín.

pore [pɔːr] *n* poro *m.*
◆ **pore over** *vt fus* estudiar esmeradamente.

pork [pɔːk] *n* carne *f* de cerdo.

pork chop *n* chuleta *f* de cerdo.

pork pie *n* empanada *f* de carne de cerdo.

porn [pɔːn] (*abbr of* **pornography**) *n inf* porno *m*; **hard/soft ~** porno duro/blando.

pornographic [ˌpɔːnəˈgræfɪk] *adj* pornográfico(ca).

pornography [pɔːˈnɒgrəfɪ] *n* pornografía *f*.

porous [ˈpɔːrəs] *adj* poroso(sa).

porpoise [ˈpɔːpəs] *n* marsopa *f*.

porridge [ˈpɒrɪdʒ] *n* papilla *f* OR gachas *fpl* de avena.

port [pɔːt] ◇ *n* **-1.** [coastal town, harbour] puerto *m*. **-2.** NAUT [left-hand side] babor *m*; **to ~ a** babor. **-3.** [drink] oporto *m*. **-4.** COMPUT conexión *f*. ◇ *comp* **-1.** [relating to a port] portuario(ria). **-2.** NAUT [right-hand] a babor.

portable [ˈpɔːtəbl] *adj* portátil.

Portacrib® [ˈpɔːtəˌkrɪb] *n Am* moisés *m*, cuco *m*.

portal [ˈpɔːtl] *n literary* pórtico *m*.

Port-au-Prince [ˌpɔːtəʊˈprɪns] *n* Puerto Príncipe.

portcullis [ˌpɔːtˈkʌlɪs] *n* rastrillo *m*.

portend [pɔːˈtend] *vt literary* presagiar, augurar.

portent [ˈpɔːtənt] *n literary* presagio *m*, augurio *m*.

porter [ˈpɔːtəʳ] *n* **-1.** *Br* [in block of flats] portero *m*, -ra *f*; [in public building, hotel] conserje *m y f*. **-2.** [for luggage] mozo *m*. **-3.** *Am* [on train] empleado *m*, -da *f* de coche cama.

portfolio [ˌpɔːtˈfəʊljəʊ] (*pl* **-s**) *n* **-1.** ART, FIN & POL cartera *f*. **-2.** [sample of work] carpeta *f*.

porthole [ˈpɔːthəʊl] *n* portilla *f*.

portion [ˈpɔːʃn] *n* **-1.** [part, section] porción *f*. **-2.** [of chips, vegetables etc] ración *f*.

portly [ˈpɔːtlɪ] (*compar* **-ier**, *superl* **-iest**) *adj* corpulento(ta).

port of call *n* **-1.** NAUT puerto *m* de escala. **-2.** *fig* [on journey] escala *f*, parada *f*.

Port of Spain *n* Puerto España.

portrait [ˈpɔːtreɪt] *n* retrato *m*.

portraitist [ˈpɔːtreɪtɪst] *n* retratista *m y f*.

portray [pɔːˈtreɪ] *vt* **-1.** [represent - in a play, film] representar. **-2.** [describe] describir. **-3.** [paint] retratar.

portrayal [pɔːˈtreɪəl] *n* **-1.** [representation - in a play, film] representación *f*. **-2.** [painting, photograph] retrato *m*. **-3.** [description] descripción *f*.

Portugal [ˈpɔːtʃʊgl] *n* Portugal.

Portuguese [ˌpɔːtʃʊˈgiːz] ◇ *adj* portugués(esa). ◇ *n* [language] portugués *m*. ◇ *npl*: **the ~** los portugueses.

Portuguese man-of-war *n* medusa *f* venenosa.

pose [pəʊz] ◇ *n* **-1.** [position, stance] postura *f*. **-2.** *pej* [pretence, affectation] pose *f*. ◇ *vt*

-1. [problem, threat] presentar. **-2.** [question] formular. ◇ *vi* **-1.** [model] posar. **-2.** *pej* [behave affectedly] adoptar una pose. **-3.** [pretend to be]: **to ~ as sb/sthg** fingir ser alguien/algo.

poser [ˈpəʊzəʳ] *n* **-1.** *pej* [person] presumido *m*, -da *f*. **-2.** *inf* [hard question] pregunta *f* difícil.

poseur [pəʊˈzɜːʳ] *n pej* presumido *m*, -da *f*.

posh [pɒʃ] *adj inf* **-1.** [hotel, area etc] de lujo, elegante. **-2.** *Br* [person, accent] afectado(da).

posit [ˈpɒzɪt] *vt fml* proponer.

position [pəˈzɪʃn] ◇ *n* **-1.** [gen] posición *f*. **-2.** [right place] sitio *m*, lugar *m*; **in ~** en su sitio. **-3.** [status] rango *m*. **-4.** [job] puesto *m*. **-5.** [in a race, competition] lugar *m*. **-6.** [state, situation] situación *f*; **to be in a/no ~ to do sthg** estar/no estar en condiciones de hacer algo. **-7.** [stance, opinion]: **~ on** opinión *f* respecto a. ◇ *vt* colocar; **to ~ o.s.** colocarse.

positive [ˈpɒzətɪv] *adj* **-1.** [gen] positivo(va). **-2.** [sure]: **to be ~ (about)** estar seguro(ra) (de). **-3.** [optimistic, confident]: **to be ~ (about)** ser optimista (respecto a). **-4.** [definite - action] decisivo(va); [- decision] categórico(ca). **-5.** [irrefutable - evidence, fact] irrefutable, evidente; [- proof] concluyente. **-6.** [for emphasis - delight, nuisance] auténtico(ca), total.

positive discrimination *n* discriminación *f* positiva.

positively [ˈpɒzətɪvlɪ] *adv* **-1.** [optimistically - think etc] positivamente. **-2.** [definitely - act] decisivamente. **-3.** [favourably - react, reply] favorablemente. **-4.** [irrefutably - prove] irrefutablemente. **-5.** [for emphasis - rude, unbearable] realmente.

positive vetting *n Br investigación completa a la que es sometido un aspirante a un cargo público relacionado con la seguridad nacional.*

positivism [ˈpɒzɪtɪvɪzm] *n* positivismo *m*.

posse [ˈpɒsɪ] *n Am* **-1.** [to pursue criminal] grupo *m* de hombres a caballo. **-2.** [group] grupo *m*.

possess [pəˈzes] *vt* **-1.** [gen] poseer. **-2.** [subj: emotion] adueñarse de; **what ~ed him to do it?** ¿qué le empujó a hacerlo?

possessed [pəˈzest] *adj* [mad] poseso(sa), poseído(da).

possession [pəˈzeʃn] *n* posesión *f*; **to have sthg in one's ~, to be in ~ of sthg** tener (posesión de) algo.
◆ **possessions** *npl* bienes *mpl*.

possessive [pəˈzesɪv] ◇ *adj* **-1.** [gen] posesivo(va). **-2.** *pej* [selfish] egoísta. ◇ *n* GRAMM posesivo *m*.

possessively [pə'zesɪvlɪ] *adv* -1. [clingingly] posesivamente. -2. [selfishly] egoísticamente.

possessor [pə'zesəʳ] *n fml* poseedor *m*, -ra *f*.

possibility [,pɒsə'bɪlətɪ] (*pl* -ies) *n* posibilidad *f*.

possible ['pɒsəbl] ◇ *adj* -1. [gen] posible; **as soon as** ~ cuanto antes; **as much as** ~ todo lo posible; **it's** ~ **that she'll come** es posible que venga. -2. [viable · plan etc] viable, factible. ◇ *n* candidato *m*, -ta *f*.

possibly ['pɒsəblɪ] *adv* -1. [perhaps] posiblemente, quizás. -2. [within one's power]: **I'll do all I** ~ **can** haré todo lo que pueda; **could you** ~ **help me?** ¿te importaría ayudarme? -3. [to show surprise]: **how could he** ~ **do that?** ¿cómo demonios pudo hacer eso? -4. [for emphasis]: **I can't** ~ **do it** no puedo hacerlo de ninguna manera.

possum ['pɒsəm] (*pl inv* OR **-s**) *n Am* zarigüeya *f*.

post [pəʊst] ◇ *n* -1. [service]: **the** ~ el correo; **by** ~ por correo; **in the** ~ en el correo. -2. (*U*) [letters etc] cartas *fpl*. -3. [delivery] reparto *m*. -4. *Br* [collection] colecta *f*. -5. [pole] poste *m*. -6. [position, job] puesto *m*. -7. MIL puesto *m*. -8. *phr*: **to pip sb at the** ~ ganar a alguien por los pelos. ◇ *vt* -1. [by mail] echar al correo. -2. [transfer] enviar, destinar. -3. *phr*: **to keep sb** ~**ed** mantener a alguien al tanto.

post- [pəʊst] *prefix* pos-.

postage ['pəʊstɪdʒ] *n* franqueo *m*, porte *m*; ~ **and packing** gastos *mpl* de envío.

postage stamp *n fml* sello *m*.

postal ['pəʊstl] *adj* postal.

postal order *n* giro *m* postal.

postbag ['pəʊstbæg] *n* -1. *Br* [bag] saco *m* postal. -2. *inf* [letters received] cartas *fpl*.

postbox ['pəʊstbɒks] *n Br* buzón *m*.

postcard ['pəʊstkɑːd] *n* postal *f*.

postcode ['pəʊstkəʊd] *n Br* código *m* postal.

postdate [,pəʊst'deɪt] *vt* poner posfecha a.

poster ['pəʊstəʳ] *n* cartel *m*, póster *m*.

poste restante [,pəʊst'restɑːnt] *n* lista *f* de correos.

posterior [pɒ'stɪərɪəʳ] ◇ *adj* posterior, trasero(ra). ◇ *n hum* trasero *m*.

posterity [pɒ'sterətɪ] *n* posteridad *f*.

poster paint *n* aguada *f*.

post-free *adj* libre de gastos de envío, porte pagado (*inv*).

postgraduate [,pəʊst'grædʒʊət] ◇ *adj* posgraduado(da). ◇ *n* posgraduado *m*, -da *f*.

posthaste [,pəʊst'heɪst] *adv dated* rápidamente, a toda prisa.

posthumous ['pɒstjʊməs] *adj* póstumo(ma).

posthumously ['pɒstjʊməslɪ] *adv* póstumamente.

post-industrial *adj* postindustrial.

posting ['pəʊstɪŋ] *n* destino *m*.

postman ['pəʊstmən] (*pl* **-men** [-mən]) *n* cartero *m*.

postmark ['pəʊstmɑːk] ◇ *n* matasellos *m inv*. ◇ *vt* matasellar.

postmaster ['pəʊst,mɑːstəʳ] *n* administrador *m* de correos.

Postmaster General (*pl* **Postmasters General**) *n* ≃ director *m* general de correos.

postmistress ['pəʊst,mɪstrɪs] *n* administradora *f* de correos.

postmortem [,pəʊst'mɔːtəm] ◇ *adj* postmórtem (*inv*). ◇ *n* -1. [autopsy] autopsia *f*. -2. *fig* [analysis] reflexión *f* autocrítica retrospectiva.

postnatal [,pəʊst'neɪtl] *adj* posnatal, posparto.

post office *n* -1. [organization]: **the Post Office** ≃ Correos *m inv*. -2. [building] oficina *f* de correos.

post office box *n* apartado *m* de correos, casilla *f* de correos *Amer*.

postoperative [,pəʊst'ɒpərətɪv] *adj* postoperatorio(ria).

postpaid [,pəʊst'peɪd] *adj* libre de gastos de envío, porte pagado (*inv*).

postpone [,pəʊst'pəʊn] *vt* posponer.

postponement [,pəʊst'pəʊnmənt] *n* aplazamiento *m*.

postscript ['pəʊstskrɪpt] *n* [additional message] posdata *f*, postdata *f*; *fig* [additional information] nota *f* final.

postulate [*n* 'pɒstjʊlət, *vb* 'pɒstjʊleɪt] *fml* ◇ *n* postulado *m*. ◇ *vt* postular.

posture ['pɒstʃəʳ] ◇ *n lit* & *fig* postura *f*; ~ **on sthg** postura hacia algo. ◇ *vi* adoptar poses.

posturing ['pɒstʃərɪŋ] *n* fingimiento *m*.

postviral syndrome [,pəʊst'vaɪərl-] *n* síndrome *m* postviral.

postwar [,pəʊst'wɔːʳ] *adj* de (la) posguerra.

posy ['pəʊsɪ] (*pl* -ies) *n* ramillete *m*.

pot [pɒt] (*pt* & *pp* **-ted**, *cont* **-ting**) ◇ *n* -1. [for cooking] olla *f*. -2. [for tea] tetera *f*; [for coffee] cafetera *f*. -3. [for paint] bote *m*; [for jam] tarro *m*. -4. [flowerpot] tiesto *m*, maceta *f*. -5. (*U*) *inf* [cannabis] maría *f*, hierba *f*. -6.

phr: **to go to** ~ ir al traste. ◇ *vt* plantar (en un tiesto).

potash ['pɒtæʃ] *n* potasa *f*.

potassium [pə'tæsɪəm] *n* potasio *m*.

potato [pə'teɪtəʊ] (*pl* **-es**) *n* patata *f*.

potato crisps *Br*, **potato chips** *Am n* patatas *fpl* fritas (*de bolsa*).

potato peeler *n* pelapatatas *m inv*.

pot-bellied [-,belɪd] *adj* **-1.** [from overeating] barrigón(ona), barrigudo(da), guatón(ona) *Amer*. **-2.** [from malnutrition] con el vientre hinchado.

potboiler ['pɒt,bɔɪlə'] *n* obra *f* con fin comercial (de escaso valor artístico).

potbound ['pɒtbaʊnd] *adj* con muchas raíces.

potency ['pəʊtənsɪ] *n* [gen] potencia *f*; [of argument] fuerza *f*.

potent ['pəʊtənt] *adj* **-1.** [powerful, influential] poderoso(sa). **-2.** [drink, drug] fuerte. **-3.** [sexually capable] potente.

potentate ['pəʊtənteɪt] *n* potentado *m*, -da *f*.

potential [pə'tenʃl] ◇ *adj* potencial, posible. ◇ *n* (*U*) potencial *m*; **to have** ~ tener ~posibilidades, prometer.

potentially [pə'tenʃəlɪ] *adv* en potencia.

pothole ['pɒthəʊl] *n* **-1.** [in road] bache *m*. **-2.** [underground] cueva *f*.

potholer ['pɒt,həʊlə'] *n Br* espeleólogo *m*, -ga *f*.

potholing ['pɒt,həʊlɪŋ] *n Br* espeleología *f*.

potion ['pəʊʃn] *n* poción *f*.

potluck [,pɒt'lʌk] *n*: **to take** ~ [gen] elegir a ojo; [at meal] conformarse con lo que haya.

pot plant *n* planta *f* de interior.

potpourri [,pəʊ'pʊərɪ] *n* (*U*) [dried flowers] popurrí *m* (*aromático*).

pot roast *n* estofado *m* de carne.

potshot ['pɒt,ʃɒt] *n*: **to take a** ~ (**at sthg/ sb**) disparar (a algo/alguien) sin apuntar.

potted ['pɒtɪd] *adj* **-1.** [plant] en tiesto. **-2.** [meat, fish] en conserva. **-3.** *Br fig* [biography, history] resumido(da).

potter ['pɒtə'] *n* alfarero *m*, -ra *f*, ceramista *m y f*.

◆ **potter about, potter around** *vi Br* entretenerse.

Potteries ['pɒtərɪz] *npl*: **the** ~ *parte de Staffordshire conocida por su industria alfarera*.

potter's wheel *n* torno *m* de alfarero.

pottery ['pɒtərɪ] (*pl* **-ies**) *n* **-1.** [gen] cerámica *f*, alfarería *f*. **-2.** [factory] fábrica *f* de cerámica.

potting compost ['pɒtɪŋ-] *n* abono *m* para plantas interiores.

potty ['pɒtɪ] (*compar* **-ier**, *superl* **-iest**, *pl* **-ies**) *Br inf* ◇ *adj* [person] chalado(da); **to be** ~ **about** estar chalado por. ◇ *n* orinal *m*.

potty-trained [-,treɪnd] *adj* que ya no lleva pañales.

pouch [paʊtʃ] *n* **-1.** [small bag] bolsa *f* pequeña; [for tobacco] petaca *f*. **-2.** [on animal's body] bolsa *f* (abdominal).

pouffe [puːf] *n Br* [seat] puf *m*.

poultice ['pəʊltɪs] *n* cataplasma *f*, emplasto *m*.

poultry ['pəʊltrɪ] ◇ *n* [meat] carne *f* de pollería. ◇ *npl* [birds] aves *fpl* de corral.

pounce [paʊns] *vi* **-1.** [leap]: **to** ~ (**on** OR **upon**) abalanzarse (sobre). **-2.** *fig* [comment immediately]: **he's quick to** ~ **on** OR **upon the slightest error** siempre está a la que salta con el más mínimo error.

pound [paʊnd] ◇ *n* **-1.** [unit of money, weight] libra *f*; **the** ~ la libra (esterlina). **-2.** [for cars] depósito *m* (de coches); [for dogs] perrera *f*. ◇ *vt* **-1.** [hammer on] golpear, aporrear. **-2.** [pulverize] machacar. ◇ *vi* **-1.** [hammer]: **to** ~ **on sthg** golpear OR aporrear algo. **-2.** [beat, throb] palpitar.

pounding ['paʊndɪŋ] *n* **-1.** (*U*) [hammering] golpes *mpl*, aporreamiento *m*. **-2.** (*U*) [beating, throbbing] palpitación *f*. **-3.** *fig*: **to get** OR **take a** ~ [team] recibir una soberana paliza; [city] verse sometido a un feroz bombardeo.

pound sterling *n* libra *f* esterlina.

pour [pɔː'] ◇ *vt* **-1.** [cause to flow]: **to** ~ **sthg** (**into**) echar OR verter algo (en); **to** ~ **sb a drink, to** ~ **a drink for sb** servirle una copa a alguien. **-2.** *fig*: **to** ~ **money into sthg** invertir mucho dinero en algo. ◇ *vi* **-1.** [liquid] chorrear; [smoke] salir a borbotones. **-2.** *fig* [rush]: **to** ~ **in/out** entrar/salir en manada. ◇ *v impers* [rain hard] llover a cántaros.

◆ **pour in** *vi* llegar a raudales.

◆ **pour out** *vt sep* **-1.** [empty] echar, vaciar. **-2.** [serve] servir. **-3.** *fig* [reveal]: **to** ~ **out one's feelings** OR **heart (to sb)** desahogarse (con alguien).

pouring ['pɔːrɪŋ] *adj* [rain] torrencial.

pout [paʊt] ◇ *n* [showing displeasure] puchero *m*, mohín *m*; [being provocative] gesto *m* provocador (de los labios). ◇ *vi* [showing displeasure] hacer pucheros; [being provocative] hacer un gesto provocador con los labios.

poverty ['pɒvətɪ] *n lit & fig* pobreza *f*.

poverty line *n* umbral *m* de pobreza.

poverty-stricken *adj* necesitado(da).

poverty trap *n Br* situación del que gana menos trabajando que en el paro, porque sus ingre-

sos superan por poco el nivel mínimo de contri-bución fiscal.

pow [paʊ] *excl inf* ¡pum!, ¡pumba!

POW *n abbr of* **prisoner of war**.

powder ['paʊdər] ◇ *n* polvo *m*; [make-up] polvos *mpl*. ◇ *vt* poner polvos en; **to ~ o.s.** darse polvos, empolvarse.

powder compact *n* polvera *f*.

powdered ['paʊdəd] *adj* **-1.** [in powder form] en polvo. **-2.** [covered in powder] em-polvado(da).

powder puff *n* borla *f*.

powder room *n* servicios *mpl* de señoras, tocador *m*.

powdery ['paʊdəri] *adj* [snow] en polvo; [cake etc] harinoso(sa).

power ['paʊər] ◇ *n* **-1.** (*U*) [authority, con-trol] poder *m*; **to have ~ over sb** tener po-der sobre alguien; **to come to/take ~** llegar al/hacerse con el poder; **to be in ~** estar en el poder. **-2.** [ability] facultad *f*; **it isn't within my ~** to do it no está dentro de mis posibilidades hacerlo. **-3.** [legal authority] autoridad *f*, competencia *f*; **to have the ~ to do sthg** tener autoridad para hacer algo. **-4.** [physical strength] fuerza *f*. **-5.** [energy -solar, steam etc] energía *f*. **-6.** [electricity] corriente *f*; **to turn the ~ on/off** dar/cortar la corriente. **-7.** [powerful nation, person, group] potencia *f*; **the ~s that be** el orden estable-cido. ◇ *vt* propulsar, impulsar.

power base *n* zona *f* de mayor respaldo político.

powerboat ['paʊəbəʊt] *n* motora *f*.

power broker *n* fuerza *f* política influyen-te.

power cut *n* apagón *m*, corte *m* de co-rriente.

power failure *n* corte *m* de corriente.

powerful ['paʊəfʊl] *adj* **-1.** [gen] podero-so(sa). **-2.** [blow, voice, drug] potente. **-3.** [speech, film] conmovedor(ra).

powerhouse ['paʊəhaʊs, *pl* -haʊzɪz] *n* fig fuente *f* generadora.

powerless ['paʊəlɪs] *adj* **-1.** [helpless] impo-tente. **-2.** [unable]: **to be ~ to do sthg** no poder hacer algo.

power line *n* cable *m* del tendido eléctri-co.

power of attorney *n* poder *m*, procura-ción *f*.

power plant *n* central *f* eléctrica.

power point *n Br* toma *f* (de corriente).

power-sharing [-,ʃeərɪŋ] *n* repartición *f* de poder.

power station *n* central *f* eléctrica.

power steering *n* dirección *f* asistida.

power worker *n* trabajador *m*, -ra *f* de una central eléctrica.

pp (*abbr of* **per procurationem**) p.p.

p & p *abbr of* **postage and packing**.

PPE *n abbr of* **philosophy, politics and eco-nomics**.

ppm (*abbr of* **parts per million**) *npl* p.p.m.

PPS ◇ *n* (*abbr of* **parliamentary private secretary**) *diputado británico que ejerce de ase-sor personal de un ministro.* ◇ (*abbr of* **post postscriptum**) PPD.

PQ *abbr of* **Province of Quebec**.

Pr. (*abbr of* **Prince**) P.

PR ◇ *n* **-1.** *abbr of* **proportional represen-tation**. **-2.** *abbr of* **public relations**. ◇ *abbr of* **Puerto Rico**.

practicable ['præktɪkəbl] *adj* viable, facti-ble.

practical ['præktɪkl] ◇ *adj* **-1.** [gen] prácti-co(ca). **-2.** [skilled with hands] hábil, maño-so(sa). ◇ *n* práctica *f*.

practicality [,præktɪ'kælətɪ] *n* viabilidad *f*.
◆ **practicalities** *npl* aspectos *mpl* prácti-cos.

practical joke *n* broma *f* pesada.

practically ['præktɪklɪ] *adv* **-1.** [in a practical way] de manera práctica. **-2.** [almost] prácti-camente, casi.

practice, practise *Am* ['præktɪs] *n* **-1.** [training, training session] práctica *f*; SPORT en-trenamiento *m*; MUS ensayo *m*; **I'm out of ~** me falta práctica. **-2.** [reality]: **to put sthg into ~** llevar algo a la práctica; **in ~** [in fact] en la práctica. **-3.** [habit, regular activity] cos-tumbre *f*. **-4.** [of profession] ejercicio *m*. **-5.** [business - of doctor] consulta *f*; [- of lawyer] bufete *m*, despacho *m*.

practiced *Am* = **practised**.

practicing *Am* = **practising**.

practise, practice *Am* ['præktɪs] ◇ *vt* **-1.** SPORT entrenar; MUS & THEATRE ensayar. **-2.** [religion, economy, safe sex] practicar; **to ~ what one preaches** predicar con el ejem-plo. **-3.** [medicine, law] ejercer. ◇ *vi* **-1.** [train - gen] practicar; [- SPORT] entrenarse. **-2.** [as doctor] practicar; [as lawyer] ejercer.

practised, practiced *Am* ['præktɪst] *adj* ex-perto(ta); **to be ~ at doing sthg** ser un ex-perto en hacer algo.

practising, practicing *Am* ['præktɪsɪŋ] *adj* **-1.** [Catholic, Jew etc] practicante. **-2.** [doctor, lawyer] en ejercicio. **-3.** [homosexual] acti-vo(va).

practitioner [præk'tɪʃnər] *n*: **general ~** mé-dico *m*, -ca *f* de cabecera; **medical ~** médi-co *m*, -ca *f*.

pragmatic [præg'mætɪk] *adj* pragmático(ca).

pragmatism ['prægmətɪzm] *n* pragmatismo *m*.

pragmatist ['prægmətɪst] *n* pragmatista *m y f*.

Prague [prɑːg] *n* Praga.

prairie ['preərɪ] *n* pradera *f*, prado *m*.

praise [preɪz] ◇ *n* (U) elogio *m*, alabanza *f*; **to sing sb's ~s** cantar alabanzas de alguien. ◇ *vt* elogiar, alabar.

praiseworthy ['preɪz,wɜːðɪ] *adj* digno(na) de elogio, encomiable.

praline ['prɑːliːn] *n* praliné *m*.

pram [præm] *n* cochecito *m* de niño.

PRAM [præm] (*abbr of* **programmable random access memory**) *n* RAM *f* programable.

prance [prɑːns] *vi* **-1.** [person] ir dando brincos. **-2.** [horse] hacer cabriolas.

prang [præŋ] *Br inf dated* ◇ *n* leñazo *m*, galleta *f*. ◇ *vt* estrellar.

prank [præŋk] *n* diablura *f*, travesura *f*; **to play a ~ on sb** gastarle una broma pesada a alguien.

prat [præt] *n Br inf* gilipuertas *m y f inv*.

prattle ['prætl] *pej* ◇ *n* cháchara *f*. ◇ *vi* estar de cháchara; **to ~ on about sthg** rajar sobre algo.

prawn [prɔːn] *n* gamba *f*.

prawn cocktail *n* cóctel *m* de gambas.

prawn cracker *n* pan *m* de gambas.

pray [preɪ] *vi* rezar, orar; **to ~ to sb** rogar a alguien; **to ~ for sthg/for sthg to happen** *lit & fig* rogar algo/que pase algo.

prayer [preər] *n* **-1.** RELIG oración *f*; **to say one's ~s** decir uno sus oraciones. **-2.** *fig* [strong hope] ruego *m*, súplica *f*.

◆ **prayers** *npl* [service] oraciones *fpl*.

prayer book *n* devocionario *m*, misal *m*.

prayer meeting *n reunión de fieles para rezar*.

pre- [priː] *prefix* pre-.

preach [priːtʃ] ◇ *vt* [gen] predicar; [sermon] dar. ◇ *vi* **-1.** RELIG: **to ~ (to)** predicar (a). **-2.** *pej* [pontificate]: **to ~ (at)** sermonear (a).

preacher ['priːtʃər] *n* predicador *m*, -ra *f*.

preamble [priː'æmbl] *n* preámbulo *m*.

prearrange [,priːə'reɪndʒ] *vt* organizar de antemano.

precarious [prɪ'keərɪəs] *adj* precario(ria).

precariously [prɪ'keərɪəslɪ] *adv* precariamente.

precast [,priː'kɑːst] *adj*: **~ concrete** hormigón *m* en bloques.

precaution [prɪ'kɔːʃn] *n* precaución *f*; **as a ~ (against)** como precaución (contra).

precautionary [prɪ'kɔːʃənərɪ] *adj* preventivo(va).

precede [prɪ'siːd] *vt* preceder.

precedence ['presɪdəns] *n*: **to take ~ over** tener prioridad sobre.

precedent ['presɪdənt] *n* precedente *m*.

preceding [prɪ'siːdɪŋ] *adj* anterior, precedente.

precept ['priːsept] *n* precepto *m*.

precinct ['priːsɪŋkt] *n* **-1.** *Br* [shopping area] zona *f* comercial. **-2.** *Am* [district] distrito *m*.

◆ **precincts** *npl* recinto *m*.

precious ['preʃəs] *adj* **-1.** [gen] precioso(sa); **~ little** muy poco. **-2.** [memories, possessions] preciado(da). **-3.** [affected] afectado(da).

precious metal *n* metal *m* precioso.

precious stone *n* piedra *f* preciosa.

precipice ['presɪpɪs] *n lit & fig* precipicio *m*.

precipitate [*adj* prɪ'sɪpɪtət, *vb* prɪ'sɪpɪteɪt] *fml* ◇ *adj* precipitado(da). ◇ *vt* precipitar.

precipitation [prɪ,sɪpɪ'teɪʃn] *n* precipitación *f*.

precipitous [prɪ'sɪpɪtəs] *adj* **-1.** [very steep] escarpado(da). **-2.** [hasty] precipitado(da).

précis [*Br* 'preɪsiː, *Am* 'preɪsiː] *n* resumen *m*.

precise [prɪ'saɪs] *adj* preciso(sa), exacto(ta); **to be ~** para ser preciso.

precisely [prɪ'saɪslɪ] *adv* **-1.** [with accuracy] exactamente. **-2.** [exactly, literally] precisamente. **-3.** [as confirmation]: **~!** ¡eso es!, ¡exactamente!

precision [prɪ'sɪʒn] ◇ *n* precisión *f*. ◇ *comp* de precisión.

preclude [prɪ'kluːd] *vt fml* evitar, impedir; [possibility] excluir; **to ~ sthg/sb from doing sthg** impedir que algo/alguien haga algo.

precocious [prɪ'kəʊʃəs] *adj* precoz.

precocity [prɪ'kɒsətɪ] *n* precocidad *f*.

precognition [,priːkɒg'nɪʃn] *n* precognición *f*.

preconceived [,priːkən'siːvd] *adj* preconcebido(da).

preconception [,priːkən'sepʃn] *n* idea *f* preconcebida.

precondition [,priːkən'dɪʃn] *n fml*: **~ (for)** requisito *m* previo (para).

precooked [,priː'kʊkt] *adj* precocinado(da).

precursor [,priː'kɜːsər] *n fml* precursor *m*, -ra *f*; **to be a ~ of** OR **to sthg** ser el precursor de algo.

predate [,priː'deɪt] *vt* preceder.

predator ['predətər] *n* depredador *m*, -ra *f*; *fig* buitre *m y f*.

predatory ['predətrɪ] *adj* depredador(ra); *fig* rapaz, rapiñero(ra).

predecease [,priːdɪ'siːs] *vt fml* morir antes que.

predecessor ['priːdɪsesəʳ] *n* antecesor *m*, -ra *f*.

predestination [priː,destɪ'neɪʃn] *n* predestinación *f*.

predestine [,priː'destɪn] *vt*: **to be ~d to sthg/to do sthg** estar predestinado(da) a algo/a hacer algo.

predetermine [,priːdɪ'tɜːmɪn] *vt* predeterminar.

predetermined [,priːdɪ'tɜːmɪnd] *adj* predeterminado(da).

predicament [prɪ'dɪkəmənt] *n* apuro *m*, aprieto *m*.

predict [prɪ'dɪkt] *vt* predecir, pronosticar.

predictable [prɪ'dɪktəbl] *adj* **-1.** [result etc] previsible. **-2.** [film, book, person] poco original.

predictably [prɪ'dɪktəblɪ] *adv* como era de esperar.

prediction [prɪ'dɪkʃn] *n* predicción *f*, pronóstico *m*.

predictor [prɪ'dɪktəʳ] *n* indicador *m*.

predigest [,priːdaɪ'dʒest] *vt fig* simplificar.

predilection [,priːdɪ'lekʃn] *n*: **~ (for)** predilección *f* (por).

predispose [,priːdɪs'pəuz] *vt*: **to be ~d to sthg/to do sthg** [by nature] estar predispuesto(ta) a algo/a hacer algo.

predisposition ['priː,dɪspə'zɪʃn] *n*: **~ to** OR **towards sthg** predisposición *f* hacia OR propensión *f* a algo; **~ to do sthg** tendencia *f* a hacer algo.

predominance [prɪ'dɒmɪnəns] *n* predominio *m*.

predominant [prɪ'dɒmɪnənt] *adj* predominante.

predominantly [prɪ'dɒmɪnəntlɪ] *adv* fundamentalmente.

predominate [prɪ'dɒmɪneɪt] *vi* predominar.

preeminent [priː'emɪnənt] *adj* preeminente.

preempt [,priː'empt] *vt* **-1.** [make ineffective] adelantarse a. **-2.** [acquire] apropiarse de.

preemptive [,priː'emptɪv] *adj* preventivo(va).

preemptive strike *n* ataque *m* preventivo.

preen [priːn] *vt* **-1.** [subj: bird] arreglar (con el pico). **-2.** *fig* [subj: person]: **to ~ o.s.** acicalarse.

preexist [,priːɪg'zɪst] *vi* existir antes.

prefab ['priːfæb] *n inf* casa *f* prefabricada.

prefabricate [,priː'fæbrɪkeɪt] *vt* prefabricar.

preface ['prefɪs] ◇ *n*: **~ (to)** prólogo *m* OR prefacio *m* (a). ◇ *vt*: **to ~ sthg with sthg/by**

doing sthg introducir algo con algo/haciendo algo.

prefect ['priːfekt] *n Br* [pupil] delegado *m*, -da *f* de curso.

prefer [prɪ'fɜːʳ] (*pt* & *pp* **-red**, *cont* **-ring**) *vt*: **to ~ sthg (to)** preferir algo (a); **to ~ to do sthg** preferir hacer algo.

preferable ['prefrəbl] *adj*: **to be ~ (to)** ser preferible (a).

preferably ['prefrəblɪ] *adv* preferentemente.

preference ['prefərəns] *n*: **~ (for)** preferencia *f* (por); **to give sb ~, to give ~ to sb** dar preferencia a alguien.

preference shares *Br npl*, **preferred stock** *Am n* (U) acciones *fpl* preferentes.

preferential [,prefə'renʃl] *adj* preferente.

preferment [prɪ'fɜːmənt] *n fml* ascenso *m*.

preferred [prɪ'fɜːd] *adj* preferido(da).

preferred stock *Am* = **preference shares**.

prefigure [priː'fɪgəʳ] *vt fml* anunciar, prefigurar.

prefix ['priːfɪks] *n* prefijo *m*.

pregnancy ['pregnənsɪ] (*pl* **-ies**) *n* embarazo *m*.

pregnancy test *n* prueba *f* del embarazo.

pregnant ['pregnənt] *adj* **-1.** [carrying unborn baby] embarazada. **-2.** *fig* [significant] significativo(va); **~ with** cargado de.

preheated [,priː'hiːtɪd] *adj* precalentado(da).

prehistoric [,priːhɪ'stɒrɪk] *adj* prehistórico(ca).

prehistory [,priː'hɪstərɪ] *n* prehistoria *f*.

pre-industrial *adj* preindustrial.

prejudge [,priː'dʒʌdʒ] *vt* prejuzgar, juzgar de antemano.

prejudice ['predʒudɪs] ◇ *n*: **~ (against)** prejuicio *m* (contra); **~ in favour of** predisposición *f* a favor de. ◇ *vt* **-1.** [bias]: **to ~ sb (in favour of/against)** predisponer a alguien (a favor de/en contra de). **-2.** [harm] perjudicar.

prejudiced ['predʒudɪst] *adj* parcial; **to be ~ in favour of/against** estar predispuesto a favor de/en contra de.

prejudicial [,predʒu'dɪʃl] *adj*: **~ (to)** perjudicial (para).

prelate ['prelɪt] *n* prelado *m*.

preliminary [prɪ'lɪmɪnərɪ] (*pl* **-ies**) *adj* preliminar.

◆ **preliminaries** *npl* preliminares *mpl*.

prelims ['priːlɪmz] *npl Br* [exams] exámenes *mpl* preliminares.

prelude ['preljuːd] *n* [event]: **~ (to)** preludio *m* (a).

premarital [,pri:'mærɪtl] *adj* prematrimonial.

premature ['premə,tjʊəʳ] *adj* prematuro(ra).

prematurely [,premə'tjʊəlɪ] *adv* antes de tiempo.

premeditated [,pri:'medɪteɪtɪd] *adj* premeditado(da).

premenstrual syndrome, premenstrual tension [pri:'menstrʊəl-] *n* síndrome *m* premenstrual.

premier ['premjəʳ] ◇ *adj* primero(ra). ◇ *n* primer ministro *m*, primera ministra *f*.

premiere ['premɪeəʳ] *n* estreno *m*.

Premier League *n* Br FTBL *en Inglaterra, máxima división futbolística administrativamente independiente de las demás.*

premiership ['premɪəʃɪp] *n* presidencia *f* del gobierno.

premise ['premɪs] *n* premisa *f*; **on the ~ that** con la idea de que.

◆ **premises** *npl* local *m*; **on the ~s** en el local.

premium ['pri:mjəm] *n* prima *f*; **at a ~** [above usual value] por encima de su valor; [in great demand] muy solicitado(da); **to put** OR **place a high ~ on sthg** dar gran importancia a algo.

premium bond *n* Br *boleto numerado emitido por el Estado que autoriza a participar en sorteos mensuales de dinero hasta su amortización.*

premonition [,premə'nɪʃn] *n* premonición *f*.

prenatal [,pri:'neɪtl] *adj* Am prenatal.

preoccupation [pri:,ɒkjʊ'peɪʃn] *n*: **~ (with)** preocupación *f* (por).

preoccupied [pri:'ɒkjʊpaɪd] *adj*: **~ (with)** preocupado(da) (por).

preoccupy [pri:'ɒkjʊpaɪ] (*pt & pp* -**ied**) *vt* preocupar.

preordain [,pri:ɔ:'deɪn] *vt* predeterminar; **to be ~ed to do sthg** estar predestinado a hacer algo.

prep [prep] (*abbr of* **preparation**) *n* (*U*) Br *inf* tarea *f*, deberes *mpl*; **to do one's ~** hacer los deberes.

prepacked [,pri:'pækt] *adj* empaquetado(da).

prepaid ['pri:peɪd] *adj* [post paid] porte pagado.

preparation [,prepə'reɪʃn] *n* -**1.** [act of preparing] preparación *f*; **in ~ for** en preparación para. -**2.** [prepared mixture] preparado *m*.

◆ **preparations** *npl* preparativos *mpl*; **to make ~s for** hacer los preparativos para.

preparatory [prɪ'pærətrɪ] *adj* preparatorio(ria), preliminar.

preparatory school *n* [in UK] *colegio de pago para niños de 7 a 12 años*; [in US] *colegio privado que prepara a sus alumnos para estudios superiores.*

prepare [prɪ'peəʳ] ◇ *vt* preparar. ◇ *vi*: **to ~ for sthg/to do sthg** prepararse para algo/para hacer algo.

prepared [prɪ'peəd] *adj* -**1.** [gen] preparado(da); **to be ~ for sthg** estar preparado para algo. -**2.** [willing]: **to be ~ to do sthg** estar dispuesto(ta) a hacer algo.

preponderance [prɪ'pɒndərəns] *n* predominio *m*.

preponderantly [prɪ'pɒndərəntlɪ] *adv* mayoritariamente.

preposition [,prepə'zɪʃn] *n* preposición *f*.

prepossessing [,pri:pə'zesɪŋ] *adj fml* atractivo(va), agradable.

preposterous [prɪ'pɒstərəs] *adj* absurdo(da).

preppy ['prepɪ] (*pl* -**ies**) Am *inf* ◇ *adj* pijo(ja). ◇ *n* niño *m*, -ña *f* bien.

prep school *n* *inf abbr of* **preparatory school.**

Pre-Raphaelite [,pri:'ræfəlaɪt] ◇ *adj* prerrafaelista. ◇ *n* prerrafaelista *m* y *f*.

prerecorded [,pri:rɪ'kɔ:dɪd] *adj* pregrabado(da).

prerequisite [,pri:'rekwɪzɪt] *n*: **~ (for)** requisito *m* (para).

prerogative [prɪ'rɒgətɪv] *n* prerrogativa *f*.

presage ['presɪdʒ] *vt fml* presagiar.

Presbyterian [,prezbɪ'tɪərɪən] ◇ *adj* presbiteriano(na). ◇ *n* presbiteriano *m*, -na *f*.

presbytery ['prezbɪtrɪ] *n* [residence] presbiterio *m*.

preschool [,pri:'sku:l] ◇ *adj* preescolar. ◇ *n* Am parvulario *m*, escuela *f* de párvulos.

prescient ['presɪənt] *adj fml* presciente.

prescribe [prɪ'skraɪb] *vt* -**1.** MED recetar. -**2.** [order] ordenar, mandar.

prescription [prɪ'skrɪpʃn] *n* receta *f*; **on ~** con receta médica.

prescription charge *n* Br *precio fijo por el coste de los medicamentos recetados por médicos de la seguridad social.*

prescriptive [prɪ'skrɪptɪv] *adj* preceptivo(va).

presence ['prezns] *n* presencia *f*; **to be in sb's ~** OR **in the ~ of sb** estar en presencia de alguien; **to have ~** tener presencia.

presence of mind *n* presencia *f* de ánimo, aplomo *m*.

present [*adj & n* 'preznt, *vb* prɪ'zent] ◇ *adj* -**1.** [current] actual; **at the ~ time** actualmente. -**2.** [in attendance] presente; **to be ~**

at sthg asistir a algo, estar presente en algo.
◇ *n* **-1.** [current time]: **the ~** el presente; **at ~** actualmente; **for the ~** de momento, por ahora. **-2.** LING: **~ (tense)** (tiempo *m*) presente *m*. **-3.** [gift] regalo *m*.
◇ *vt* **-1.** [gen] presentar; **to ~ sb with sthg, to ~ sthg to sb** [challenge, opportunity] representar algo para alguien; **to ~ sb to sb** presentar a alguien a alguien; **to ~ o.s.** [arrive] presentarse. **-2.** [give]: **to ~ sb with sthg, to ~ sthg to sb** [as present] obsequiar algo a alguien; [at ceremony] entregar algo a alguien. **-3.** [play etc] representar.

presentable [prɪ'zentəbl] *adj* presentable; **to make o.s. ~** arreglarse.

presentation [,prezn'teɪʃn] *n* **-1.** [gen] presentación *f*. **-2.** [ceremony] entrega *f*. **-3.** [performance] representación *f*.

presentation copy *n* ejemplar *m* gratuito.

present day *n*: **the ~** el presente.

◆ **present-day** *adj* actual, de hoy en día.

presenter [prɪ'zentəʳ] *n Br* presentador *m*, -ra *f*.

presentiment [prɪ'zentɪmənt] *n fml* presentimiento *m*.

presently ['prezntlɪ] *adv* **-1.** [soon] dentro de poco. **-2.** [now] actualmente, ahora.

preservation [,prezə'veɪʃn] *n* preservación *f*, conservación *f*.

preservation order *n* orden *f* de protección.

preservative [prɪ'zɜːvətɪv] *n* conservante *m*.

preserve [prɪ'zɜːv] ◇ *vt* conservar. ◇ *n* [jam] mermelada *f*.

◆ **preserves** *npl* [jam] mermelada *f*; [vegetables] conserva *f*.

preserved [prɪ'zɜːvd] *adj* conservado(da).

preset [,priː'set] (*pt* & *pp* **preset**, *cont* **-ting**) *vt* programar.

preshrunk [,priː'ʃrʌŋk] *adj* lavado(da) de antemano.

preside [prɪ'zaɪd] *vi*: **to ~ (over OR at sthg)** presidir (algo).

presidency ['prezɪdənsɪ] (*pl* **-ies**) *n* presidencia *f*.

president ['prezɪdənt] *n* presidente *m*, -ta *f*.

President-elect *n* el presidente electo (la presidenta electa).

presidential [,prezɪ'denʃl] *adj* presidencial.

press [pres] ◇ *n* **-1.** [push]: **to give sthg a ~** apretar algo. **-2.** [newspapers, reporters]: **the ~** la prensa; **to get a good/bad ~** tener buena/mala prensa. **-3.** [machine] prensa *f*.
◇ *vt* **-1.** [gen] apretar; **to ~ sthg against sthg** apretar algo contra algo. **-2.** [grapes,

flowers] prensar. **-3.** [iron] planchar. **-4.** [urge]: **to ~ sb (to do sthg OR into doing sthg)** presionar a alguien (para que haga algo); **to ~ sb for sthg** presionar a alguien en busca de algo. **-5.** [force]: **to ~ sthg on OR upon sb** obligar a alguien a aceptar algo. **-6.** [pursue · claim] insistir en; **to ~ charges against sb** JUR demandar a alguien.
◇ *vi* **-1.** [gen]: **to ~ (on sthg)** apretar (algo). **-2.** [crowd]: **to ~ forward** empujar hacia adelante.

◆ **press for** *vt fus* exigir, reclamar.
◆ **press on** *vi* [continue] proseguir, continuar; **to ~ on (with)** proseguir (con).

press agency *n* agencia *f* de prensa.

press agent *n* agente *m* y *f* de prensa.

press baron *n Br* magnate *m* de la prensa.

press box *n* cabina *f* de prensa.

press conference *n* rueda *f* de prensa.

press corps *n Am*: **the ~** la prensa.

press cutting *n Br* recorte *m* de prensa.

pressed [prest] *adj*: **to be ~ (for time/money)** andar escaso(sa) (de tiempo/de dinero).

press fastener *n Br* automático *m*.

press gallery *n* tribuna *f* de prensa.

pressgang ['presgæŋ] ◇ *n* grupo de hombres que antiguamente obligaban a otros a enrolarse en la marina. ◇ *vt Br*: **to ~ sb into doing sthg** obligar a alguien a hacer algo.

pressing ['presɪŋ] *adj* apremiante, urgente.

pressman ['presmæn] (*pl* **-men** [-men]) *n Br* periodista *m*.

press officer *n* jefe *m*, -fa *f* de prensa.

press release *n* comunicado *m* de prensa.

press-stud *n Br* automático *m*.

press-up *n Br* flexión *f*.

pressure ['preʃəʳ] ◇ *n* presión *f*; **to put ~ on sb (to do sthg)** presionar a alguien (para que haga algo); **to be under ~** estar OR verse presionado. ◇ *vt*: **to ~ sb to do OR into doing sthg** presionar a alguien para que haga algo.

pressure cooker *n* olla *f* a presión.

pressure gauge *n* manómetro *m*.

pressure group *n* grupo *m* de presión.

pressurize, -ise ['preʃəraɪz] *vt* **-1.** TECH presurizar. **-2.** *Br* [force]: **to ~ sb to do OR into doing sthg** presionar a alguien para que haga algo.

Prestel® ['prestel] *n Br servicio público de videotexto ofrecido por el servicio postal británico.*

prestige [pre'stiːʒ] ◇ *n* prestigio *m*. ◇ *comp* de prestigio.

prestigious [pre'stɪdʒəs] *adj* prestigioso(sa).

prestressed concrete [ˌpriːˈstrest-] *n* hormigón *m* pretensado.

presumably [prɪˈzjuːməblɪ] *adv*: ~ **you've** read it supongo que los has leído.

presume [prɪˈzjuːm] *vt* suponer; **he is ~d dead** se supone que está muerto; **to ~ that** suponer que, imaginar que.

presumption [prɪˈzʌmpʃn] *n* **-1.** [assumption] suposición *f*; [of innocence] presunción *f*. **-2.** (U) [audacity] presunción *f*, osadía *f*.

presumptuous [prɪˈzʌmptʃʊəs] *adj* presuntuoso(sa).

presuppose [ˌpriːsəˈpəʊz] *vt* presuponer.

pretax [ˌpriːˈtæks] *adj* bruto(ta).

pretence, pretense *Am* [prɪˈtens] *n* fingimiento *m*, simulación *f*; **to make a ~ of doing sthg** fingir hacer algo; **under false ~s** con engaños, con falsos pretextos.

pretend [prɪˈtend] ◇ *vt*: **to ~ to do sthg** fingir hacer algo. ◇ *vi* fingir, simular.

pretense *Am* = **pretence**.

pretension [prɪˈtenʃn] *n* pretensión *f*; **to have ~s to sthg** tener pretensiones de algo.

pretentious [prɪˈtenʃəs] *adj* pretencioso(sa).

pretentiously [prɪˈtenʃəslɪ] *adv* de forma pretenciosa.

pretentiousness [prɪˈtenʃəsnɪs] *n* pretenciosidad *f*.

preterite [ˈpretərət] *n* pretérito *m*.

pretext [ˈpriːtekst] *n* pretexto *m*; **on** OR **under the ~ that .../of doing sthg** con el pretexto de que .../de estar haciendo algo.

Pretoria [prɪˈtɔːrɪə] *n* Pretoria.

prettify [ˈprɪtɪfaɪ] (*pt & pp* **-ied**) *vt* embellecer.

prettily [ˈprɪtɪlɪ] *adv* de una forma bonita.

prettiness [ˈprɪtɪnɪs] *n* belleza *f*.

pretty [ˈprɪtɪ] (*compar* **-ier**, *superl* **-iest**) ◇ *adj* bonito(ta). ◇ *adv* bastante; ~ **much** más o menos; ~ **well** [almost] casi.

pretzel [ˈpretsl] *n* galleta *f* salada.

prevail [prɪˈveɪl] *vi* **-1.** [be widespread] predominar, imperar. **-2.** [triumph]: **to ~ (over)** prevalecer (sobre). **-3.** [persuade]: **to ~ on** OR **upon sb to do sthg** persuadir a alguien para que haga algo.

prevailing [prɪˈveɪlɪŋ] *adj* predominante.

prevalence [ˈprevələns] *n* predominio *m*.

prevalent [ˈprevələnt] *adj* predominante, imperante.

prevaricate [prɪˈværɪkeɪt] *vi* andarse con evasivas.

prevent [prɪˈvent] *vt* impedir; **to ~ sthg (from) happening** impedir OR evitar que algo pase; **to ~ sb (from) doing sthg** impe-

dir a alguien que haga algo; [event, illness, accident] evitar.

preventable [prɪˈventəbl] *adj* evitable.

preventative [prɪˈventətɪv] = **preventive**.

prevention [prɪˈvenʃn] *n* prevención *f*.

preventive [prɪˈventɪv] *adj* preventivo(va).

preview [ˈpriːvjuː] *n* [of film, exhibition] preestreno *m*.

previous [ˈpriːvjəs] *adj* previo(via), anterior; **the ~ week/president** la semana/el presidente anterior; ~ **convictions** antecedentes *mpl* penales.

previously [ˈpriːvjəslɪ] *adv* **-1.** [formerly] anteriormente. **-2.** [before]: **two years ~** dos años antes.

prewar [ˌpriːˈwɔːr] *adj* de preguerra.

prey [preɪ] *n* presa *f*, víctima *f*; **to fall ~ to** ser víctima de.

◆ **prey on** *vt fus* **-1.** [live off] cazar, alimentarse de. **-2.** [trouble]: **to ~ on sb's mind** atormentar a alguien.

price [praɪs] ◇ *n* *lit & fig* precio *m*; **to go up/down in ~** subir/bajar de precio; **to pay the ~ for sthg** pagar el precio de algo; **at any ~** a toda costa, a cualquier precio; **at a ~** a un alto precio; **to pay a high ~ for sthg** pagar algo caro. ◇ *vt* poner precio a.

price-cutting *n* (U) reducción *f* de precios.

price-fixing [-ˌfɪksɪŋ] *n* (U) fijación *f* de precios.

priceless [ˈpraɪslɪs] *adj* *lit & fig* que no tiene precio, inestimable.

price list *n* lista *f* OR tarifa *f* de precios.

price tag *n* [label] etiqueta *f* (del precio).

price war *n* guerra *f* de precios.

pricey [ˈpraɪsɪ] (*compar* **-ier**, *superl* **-iest**) *adj* caro(ra).

prick [prɪk] ◇ *n* **-1.** [wound] pinchazo *m*. **-2.** *vulg* [penis] polla *f*, pinga *f* *Amer*. **-3.** *vulg* [stupid person] gilipollas *m y f inv*. ◇ *vt* **-1.** [gen] pinchar. **-2.** [sting] picar.

◆ **prick up** *vt fus*: **to ~ up one's ears** [subj: animal] levantar las orejas; [subj: person] aguzar el oído.

prickle [ˈprɪkl] ◇ *n* **-1.** [thorn] espina *f*, pincho *m*. **-2.** [sensation] comezón *f*. ◇ *vi* picar.

prickly [ˈprɪklɪ] (*compar* **-ier**, *superl* **-iest**) *adj* **-1.** [thorny] espinoso(sa). **-2.** *fig* [touchy] susceptible, enojadizo(za).

prickly heat *n* (U) sarpullido *por causa del calor*.

pride [praɪd] ◇ *n* orgullo *m*; **to take ~ in sthg/in doing sthg** enorgullecerse de algo/de hacer algo; ~ **and joy** orgullo; **to have ~ of place** ocupar el lugar de honor; **to swal-**

low one's ~ tragarse el orgullo. ◇ *vt*: **to ~ o.s. on sthg** enorgullecerse de algo.

priest [priːst] *n* sacerdote *m*.

priestess ['priːstɪs] *n* sacerdotisa *f*.

priesthood ['priːsthʊd] *n* **-1.** [position, office]: **the ~** el sacerdocio. **-2.** [priests collectively]: **the ~** el clero.

prig [prɪg] *n* mojigato *m*, -ta *f*.

prim [prɪm] (*compar* **-mer**, *superl* **-mest**) *adj* remilgado(da).

primacy ['praɪməsɪ] *n* prioridad *f*, primacía *f*.

prima donna [ˌpriːmə'dɒnə] (*pl* **-s**) *n* **-1.** [female singer] prima donna *f*. **-2.** *pej* [self-important person]: **to be a ~** ir de estrella.

primaeval [praɪ'miːvəl] = **primeval**.

prima facie [ˌpraɪmə'feɪʃiː] *adj* a primera vista.

primal ['praɪml] *adj* **-1.** [original] primario(ria). **-2.** [most important] primordial.

primarily ['praɪmərɪlɪ] *adv* principalmente.

primary ['praɪmərɪ] (*pl* **-ies**) ◇ *adj* **-1.** [main] principal. **-2.** SCH primario(ria). ◇ *n* *Am* POL primaria *f*.

PRIMARIES:

Las primarias estadounidenses son unas elecciones (directas o indirectas según los estados) mediante las cuales se selecciona a los candidatos que representarán a los dos partidos nacionales en las elecciones presidenciales

primary colour *n* color *m* primario.

primary election *n* *Am* primaria *f*.

primary school *n* escuela *f* primaria.

primate ['praɪmeɪt] *n* **-1.** ZOOL primate *m*. **-2.** RELIG primado *m*.

prime [praɪm] ◇ *adj* **-1.** [main] primero(ra), principal. **-2.** [excellent] excelente; [quality] primero(ra). ◇ *n*: **in one's ~** en la flor de la vida. ◇ *vt* **-1.** [inform]: **to ~ sb about sthg** preparar a alguien a fondo para algo. **-2.** [surface] preparar. **-3.** [gun, pump] cebar.

prime minister *n* primer ministro *m*, primera ministra *f*.

prime mover [-'muːvər] *n* fuerza *f* motriz.

prime number *n* número *m* primo.

primer ['praɪmər] *n* **-1.** [paint] imprimación *f*. **-2.** [textbook] cartilla *f*.

prime time *n* (*U*) hora *f* de mayor audiencia.

◆ **prime-time** *adj* de mayor audiencia.

primeval [praɪ'miːvl] *adj* [ancient] primitivo(va); **~ forest** bosque *m* virgen.

primitive ['prɪmɪtɪv] *adj* [tribe, species etc]

primitivo(va); [accommodation, sense of humour] rudimentario(ria).

primordial [praɪ'mɔːdjəl] *adj* *fml* primordial.

primrose ['prɪmrəʊz] *n* primavera *f*, prímula *f*.

Primus stove® ['praɪməs-] *n* hornillo *m* de camping.

prince [prɪns] *n* príncipe *m*.

◆ **Prince** *n*: **Prince of Wales** Príncipe de Gales.

Prince Charming *n* *hum* príncipe *m* azul.

Prince Edward Island [-'edwəd-] *n* isla Príncipe Eduardo.

princely ['prɪnslɪ] (*compar* **-ier**, *superl* **-iest**) *adj* **-1.** [of a prince] principesco(ca). **-2.** [magnificent] magnífico(ca).

princess [prɪn'ses] *n* princesa *f*.

◆ **Princess** *n*: **Princess Royal** Princesa Real.

principal ['prɪnsəpl] ◇ *adj* principal. ◇ *n* SCH director *m*, -ra *f*.

principality [ˌprɪnsɪ'pælətɪ] (*pl* **-ies**) *n* principado *m*.

principally ['prɪnsəplɪ] *adv* principalmente, sobre todo.

principle ['prɪnsəpl] *n* **-1.** [gen] principio *m*. **-2.** (*U*) [integrity] principios *mpl*; **(to do sthg) on ~** OR **as a matter of ~** (hacer algo) por principio.

◆ **in principle** *adv* en principio.

principled ['prɪnsəpld] *adj* de principios.

print [prɪnt] ◇ *n* **-1.** (*U*) [type] caracteres *mpl* (de imprenta); **in ~** [available] disponible; [in printed characters] en letra impresa; **to be out of ~** estar agotado. **-2.** [piece of artwork] grabado *m*. **-3.** [reproduction] reproducción *f*. **-4.** [photograph] fotografía *f*. **-5.** [fabric] estampado *m*. **-6.** [mark - of foot etc] huella *f*.

◇ *vt* **-1.** TYPO imprimir. **-2.** [produce by printing - book, newspaper] tirar. **-3.** [publish] publicar. **-4.** [decorate - cloth etc] estampar. **-5.** [write in block letters] escribir con letra de imprenta.

◇ *vi* imprimir.

◆ **print out** *vt sep* COMPUT imprimir.

printed circuit ['prɪntɪd-] *n* circuito *m* impreso.

printed matter ['prɪntɪd-] *n* (*U*) impresos *mpl*.

printer ['prɪntər] *n* **-1.** [person] impresor *m*, -ra *f*; [firm] imprenta *f*. **-2.** [machine] impresora *f*.

printing ['prɪntɪŋ] *n* **-1.** (*U*) [act of printing] impresión *f*. **-2.** [trade] imprenta *f*.

printing press *n* prensa *f* (*máquina*).

printout ['prɪntaut] *n* COMPUT salida *f* de impresora.

prior ['praɪəʳ] ◇ *adj* **-1.** [previous] anterior, previo(via). **-2.** [more important] preferente. ◇ *n* [monk] prior *m*.

◆ **prior to** *prep* antes de.

prioritize, -ise [praɪ'ɒrɪtaɪz] *vt* dar prioridad a.

priority [praɪ'ɒrətɪ] (*pl* **-ies**) ◇ *adj* prioritario(ria). ◇ *n* prioridad *f*; **to have** OR **take ~ (over)** tener prioridad (sobre).

◆ **priorities** *npl* prioridades *fpl*.

priory ['praɪərɪ] (*pl* **-ies**) *n* priorato *m*.

prise [praɪz] *vt*: **to ~ sthg open/away** abrir/separar algo haciendo palanca.

prism ['prɪzm] *n* prisma *m*.

prison ['prɪzn] *n* cárcel *f*, prisión *f*.

prison camp *n* campamento *m* de prisioneros.

prisoner ['prɪznəʳ] *n* **-1.** [convict] preso *m*, -sa *f*. **-2.** [captive] prisionero *m*, -ra *f*; **to be taken ~** ser hecho prisionero.

prisoner of war (*pl* **prisoners of war**) *n* prisionero *m*, -ra *f* de guerra.

prissy ['prɪsɪ] (*compar* **-ier**, *superl* **-iest**) *adj* remilgado(da).

pristine ['prɪstiːn] *adj* prístino(na).

privacy [*Br* 'prɪvəsɪ, *Am* 'praɪvəsɪ] *n* intimidad *f*.

private ['praɪvɪt] ◇ *adj* **-1.** [gen] privado(da); [class] particular; [telephone call, belongings] **personal. -2.** [thoughts, plans] secreto(ta). **-3.** [secluded] retirado(da). **-4.** [unsociable · person] reservado(da). ◇ *n* **-1.** [soldier] soldado *m* raso. **-2. (to do sthg) in ~** [in secret] (hacer algo) en privado.

◆ **privates** *npl inf* partes *fpl* (pudendas).

private company *n* empresa *f* privada.

private detective *n* detective privado *m*, -da *f*.

private enterprise *n* (*U*) empresa *f* privada.

private eye *n* detective privado *m*, -da *f*.

private income *n Br* renta *f* personal.

private investigator *n* detective privado *m*, -da *f*.

privately ['praɪvɪtlɪ] *adv* **-1.** [not by the state] de forma privada; **~ owned** de propiedad privada. **-2.** [confidentially] en privado. **-3.** [secretly] en el fuero interno de uno.

private member's bill *n Br proyecto de ley presentado por un diputado sin cargo en el gobierno.*

private parts *npl inf* partes *fpl* (íntimas).

private practice *n Br* ejercicio *m* privado de la medicina.

private property *n* propiedad *f* privada.

private school *n* escuela *f* privada, colegio *m* privado.

private sector *n*: **the ~** el sector privado.

privation [praɪ'veɪʃn] *n* privación *f*.

privatization [ˌpraɪvətaɪ'zeɪʃn] *n* privatización *f*.

privatize, -ise ['praɪvɪtaɪz] *vt* privatizar.

privet ['prɪvɪt] *n* alheña *f*.

privilege ['prɪvɪlɪdʒ] *n* privilegio *m*.

privileged ['prɪvɪlɪdʒd] *adj* privilegiado(da).

privy ['prɪvɪ] *adj*: **to be ~ to sthg** estar enterado(da) de algo.

Privy Council *n Br*: **the ~** *en Gran Bretaña, consejo privado que asesora al monarca.*

PRIVY COUNCIL:

Forman parte del 'Privy Council' todos los ministros del gobierno así como otras personalidades de la Commonwealth. Este organismo es un consejo real que consta de unos 400 miembros que sólo se reúnen en pleno en circunstancias excepcionales

---

Privy Purse *n*: **the ~** *presupuesto aprobado por el Parlamento de Gran Bretaña y destinado a cubrir los gastos del monarca.*

prize [praɪz] ◇ *adj* de primera. ◇ *n* premio *m*. ◇ *vt*: **to be ~d** ser apreciado(da).

prize day *n Br* (día *m* de la) entrega *f* de premios.

prizefight ['praɪzfaɪt] *n* combate *m* de boxeo profesional.

prize-giving [-ˌgɪvɪŋ] *n Br* entrega *f* de premios.

prizewinner ['praɪzˌwɪnəʳ] *n* premiado *m*, -da *f*.

pro [prəʊ] (*pl* **-s**) *n* **-1.** *inf* [professional] profesional *m y f*. **-2.** [advantage]: **the ~s and cons** los pros y los contras.

pro- [prəʊ] *prefix* pro-.

PRO (*abbr of* **public relations officer**) *n jefe de relaciones públicas.*

pro-am [ˌprəʊ'æm] ◇ *adj* de profesionales y amateurs. ◇ *n competición mixta de profesionales y amateurs.*

probability [ˌprɒbə'bɪlətɪ] (*pl* **-ies**) *n* probabilidad *f*; **in all ~ they'll win** es muy probable que ganen.

probable ['prɒbəbl] *adj* probable.

probably ['prɒbəblɪ] *adv* probablemente.

probate ['prəʊbeɪt] ◇ *n* JUR legalización *f* de un testamento. ◇ *vt Am* legalizar (*un testamento*).

probation [prə'beɪʃn] *n* **-1.** [of prisoner] libertad *f* condicional; **to put sb on** ~ poner a alguien en libertad condicional. **-2.** [trial period] periodo *m* de prueba; **to be on** ~ estar en periodo de prueba.

probationary [prə'beɪʃnrɪ] *adj* **-1.** [teacher, nurse] en periodo de prueba. **-2.** [period] de prueba.

probationer [prə'beɪʃnəʳ] *n* **-1.** [employee] empleado *m*, -da *f* a prueba. **-2.** [offender] persona *f* en libertad condicional.

probation officer *n encargado de vigilar a los que están en libertad condicional.*

probe [prəʊb] ◇ *n* **-1.** [investigation]: ~ **(into)** investigación (sobre). **-2.** MED & SPACE sonda *f*. ◇ *vt* **-1.** [investigate] investigar. **-2.** [with tool] sondar; [with finger, stick] hurgar en. ◇ *vi*: **to** ~ **for sthg** investigar para encontrar algo; **to** ~ **into sthg** explorar algo.

probing ['prəʊbɪŋ] *adj* inquisitivo(va).

probity ['prəʊbətɪ] *n fml* probidad *f*.

problem ['prɒbləm] ◇ *n* problema *m*; **no** ~! *inf* ¡por supuesto!, ¡desde luego! ◇ *comp* problemático(ca), difícil.

problematic(al) [,prɒblə'mætɪk(l)] *adj* problemático(ca), difícil.

procedural [prə'siːdʒərəl] *adj* de procedimiento.

procedure [prə'siːdʒəʳ] *n* procedimiento *m*.

proceed [prə'siːd] *vi* **-1.** [do subsequently]: **to** ~ **to do sthg** proceder a hacer algo. **-2.** [continue]: **to** ~ **(with sthg)** proseguir (con algo). **-3.** *fml* [advance] avanzar.

◆ **proceeds** *npl* ganancias *fpl*, beneficios *mpl*.

proceedings [prə'siːdɪŋz] *npl* **-1.** [series of events] acto *m*. **-2.** [legal action] proceso *m*; **to start** ~ **against sb** entablar proceso contra alguien.

process ['prəʊses] ◇ *n* proceso *m*; **in the** ~ en el intento; **to be in the** ~ **of doing sthg** estar en vías de hacer algo. ◇ *vt* **-1.** [gen & COMPUT] procesar. **-2.** [application] tramitar.

processed cheese ['prəʊsest-] *n* queso *m* en lonchas OR para sandwiches.

processing ['prəʊsesɪŋ] *n* **-1.** [gen & COMPUT] procesamiento *m*. **-2.** [of applications etc] tramitación *f*.

procession [prə'seʃn] *n* desfile *m*; [religious] procesión *f*.

processor ['prəʊsesəʳ] *n* **-1.** COMPUT unidad *f* central (de procesamiento). **-2.** CULIN procesador *m*.

pro-choice *adj* en favor del derecho de la mujer a decidir en materia de aborto.

proclaim [prə'kleɪm] *vt* [gen] proclamar; [law] promulgar.

proclamation [,prɒklə'meɪʃn] *n* [gen] proclamación *f*; [of law] promulgación *f*.

proclivity [prə'klɪvətɪ] (*pl* **-ies**) *n fml*: ~ **(to** OR **towards)** propensión *f* OR tendencia *f* (a).

procrastinate [prə'kræstɪneɪt] *vi* andarse con dilaciones.

procrastination [prə,kræstɪ'neɪʃn] *n* (*U*) dilaciones *fpl*.

procreate ['prəʊkrɪeɪt] *vi* procrear.

procreation [,prəʊkrɪ'eɪʃn] *n* procreación *f*.

procurator fiscal ['prɒkjʊreɪtəʳ-] *n Scot* ≈ fiscal *m* y *f*.

procure [prə'kjʊəʳ] *vt* [obtain] obtener, conseguir.

procurement [prə'kjʊəmənt] *n* obtención *f*.

prod [prɒd] (*pt* & *pp* **-ded**, *cont* **-ding**) ◇ *n* **-1.** [push, poke] golpecito *m*, empujoncito *m*. **-2.** *fig* [reminder] toque *m*, aviso *m*. ◇ *vt* **-1.** [push, poke] dar golpecitos a. **-2.** [remind, prompt]: **to** ~ **sb (into doing sthg)** darle un toque a alguien (para que haga algo).

prodigal ['prɒdɪgl] *adj* [son, daughter] pródigo(ga).

prodigious [prə'dɪdʒəs] *adj* prodigioso(sa).

prodigy ['prɒdɪdʒɪ] (*pl* **-ies**) *n* [person] prodigio *m*.

produce [*n* 'prɒdjuːs, *vb* prə'djuːs] ◇ *n* (*U*) productos *mpl* agrícolas; **"~ of France"** "producto de Francia". ◇ *vt* **-1.** [gen] producir; [offspring, flowers] engendrar. **-2.** [evidence, argument] presentar. **-3.** [bring out] mostrar, enseñar. **-4.** THEATRE poner en escena.

producer [prə'djuːsəʳ] *n* **-1.** [gen] productor *m*, -ra *f*. **-2.** THEATRE director *m*, -ra *f* de escena.

product ['prɒdʌkt] *n* producto *m*; **to be a** ~ **of** ser el resultado OR producto de.

production [prə'dʌkʃn] *n* **-1.** [gen] producción *f*; **to put/go into** ~ empezar a fabricar/fabricarse. **-2.** (*U*) THEATRE puesta *f* en escena.

production line *n* cadena *f* de producción.

production manager *n* **-1.** THEATRE director *m*, -ra *f* de producción. **-2.** [in factory] jefe *m*, -fa *f* de producción.

productive [prə'dʌktɪv] *adj* **-1.** [efficient] productivo(va). **-2.** [rewarding] provechoso(sa).

productively [prə'dʌktɪvlɪ] *adv* **-1.** [efficiently] de manera productiva. **-2.** [rewardingly] de manera provechosa.

productivity [,prɒdʌk'tɪvətɪ] *n* productividad *f*.

productivity deal *n* acuerdo *m* sobre la productividad.

Prof. [prɒf] (*abbr of* **Professor**) Catedr.

profane [prəˈfeɪn] *adj* [disrespectful] obsceno(na).

profanity [prəˈfænɪtɪ] (*pl* **-ies**) *n* **-1.** [of language, behaviour] obscenidad *f*, indecencia *f*. **-2.** [word] palabrota *f*, taco *m*.

profess [prəˈfes] *vt* **-1.** [claim]: **to ~ (to do sthg)** pretender (hacer algo). **-2.** [declare] declarar.

professed [prəˈfest] *adj* **-1.** [avowed] declarado(da). **-2.** [supposed] pretendido(da).

profession [prəˈfeʃn] *n* profesión *f*; **by ~** de profesión.

professional [prəˈfeʃənl] ◇ *adj* profesional. ◇ *n* profesional *m y f*, profesionista *m y f Amer*.

professional foul *n* falta *f* profesional.

professionalism [prəˈfeʃnəlɪzm] *n* profesionalismo *m*.

professionally [prəˈfeʃnəlɪ] *adv* **-1.** [for a profession]: **to be ~ trained/qualified** tener una formación/un título profesional. **-2.** [not as amateur] profesionalmente. **-3.** [skilfully] de manera profesional.

professor [prəˈfesəʳ] *n* **-1.** *Br* [head of department] catedrático *m*, -ca *f*. **-2.** *Am & Can* [lecturer] profesor *m*, -ra *f* (de universidad).

professorship [prəˈfesəʃɪp] *n* **-1.** *Br* [position of head of department] cátedra *f*. **-2.** *Am & Can* [lectureship] cargo *de profesor de universidad*.

proffer [ˈprɒfəʳ] *vt*: **to ~ sthg (to)** ofrecer algo (a).

proficiency [prəˈfɪʃənsɪ] *n*: **~ (in)** competencia *f* (en).

proficient [prəˈfɪʃənt] *adj*: **~ (in OR at)** competente (en).

profile [ˈprəʊfaɪl] *n* perfil *m*; **high ~** notoriedad *f*; **in ~** de perfil; **to keep a low ~** mantenerse en segundo plano.

profit [ˈprɒfɪt] ◇ *n* **-1.** [financial gain] beneficio *m*, ganancia *f*; **to make a ~** sacar un beneficio; **to sell sthg at a ~** vender algo con beneficios. **-2.** [advantage] provecho *m*. ◇ *vi*: **to ~ (from OR by)** sacar provecho (de).

profitability [ˌprɒfɪtəˈbɪlətɪ] *n* rentabilidad *f*.

profitable [ˈprɒfɪtəbl] *adj* **-1.** [making a profit] rentable. **-2.** [beneficial] provechoso(sa).

profitably [ˈprɒfɪtəblɪ] *adv* **-1.** [at a profit] con beneficios. **-2.** [spend time] de manera provechosa.

profiteering [ˌprɒfɪˈtɪərɪŋ] *n* especulación *f*.

profit-making ◇ *adj* con fines lucrativos. ◇ *n* obtención *f* de beneficios.

profit margin *n* margen *m* de beneficios.

profit sharing [-ˌʃeərɪŋ] *n* participación *f* en los beneficios.

profligate [ˈprɒflɪgɪt] *adj* **-1.** [extravagant] derrochador(ra). **-2.** [immoral] libertino(na).

pro forma [-ˈfɔːmə] *adj* proforma.

profound [prəˈfaʊnd] *adj* profundo(da).

profoundly [prəˈfaʊndlɪ] *adv* profundamente.

profuse [prəˈfjuːs] *adj* profuso(sa).

profusely [prəˈfjuːslɪ] *adv* profusamente.

profusion [prəˈfjuːʒn] *n* profusión *f*.

progeny [ˈprɒdʒənɪ] (*pl* **-ies**) *n* progenie *f*.

progesterone [prəˈdʒestərəʊn] *n* progesterona *f*.

prognosis [prɒgˈnəʊsɪs] (*pl* **-noses** [-ˈnəʊsiːz]) *n* pronóstico *m*.

prognostication [prɒgˌnɒstɪˈkeɪʃn] *n* pronóstico *m*.

program [ˈprəʊgræm] (*pt & pp* **-med** OR **-ed**, *cont* **-ming** OR **-ing**) ◇ *n* **-1.** COMPUT programa *m*. **-2.** *Am* = **programme**. ◇ *vt* **-1.** COMPUT programar. **-2.** *Am* = **programme**. ◇ *vi* COMPUT programar.

programer *Am* = **programmer**.

programmable [prəʊˈgræməbl] *adj* programable.

programme *Br*, **program** *Am* [ˈprəʊgræm] ◇ *n* programa *m*. ◇ *vt*: **to ~ sthg (to do sthg)** programar algo (para que haga algo).

programmer *Br*, **programer** *Am* [ˈprəʊgræməʳ] *n* COMPUT programador *m*, -ra *f*.

programming [ˈprəʊgræmɪŋ] *n* programación *f*.

programming language *n* lenguaje *m* de programación.

progress [*n* ˈprəʊgres, *vb* prəʊˈgres] ◇ *n* **-1.** [gen] progreso *m*; **in ~** en curso; **to make ~** hacer progresos. **-2.** [forward movement] avance *m*. ◇ *vi* **-1.** [gen] progresar; [pupil etc] hacer progresos. **-2.** [move forward] avanzar. **-3.** [move on]: **to ~ to sthg** pasar a algo.

progression [prəˈgreʃn] *n* **-1.** [development] evolución *f*. **-2.** [series] sucesión *f*.

progressive [prəˈgresɪv] *adj* **-1.** [enlightened] progresista. **-2.** [gradual] progresivo(va).

progressively [prəˈgresɪvlɪ] *adv* progresivamente.

progress report *n* [on work, project] informe *m* sobre el desarrollo del trabajo.

prohibit [prəˈhɪbɪt] *vt* prohibir; **to ~ sb**

from doing sthg prohibirle a alguien hacer algo.

prohibition [ˌprəʊɪˈbɪʃn] n prohibición f.

prohibitive [prəˈhɪbətɪv] adj prohibitivo(va).

project [n ˈprɒdʒekt, vb prəˈdʒekt] ◇ n -1. [plan, idea] proyecto m. -2. SCH: ~ **(on)** estudio m OR trabajo m (sobre). ◇ vt -1. [gen] proyectar. -2. [estimate - statistic, costs] estimar. -3. [company, person] dar una imagen de; [image] proyectar. ◇ vi proyectarse.

projectile [prəˈdʒektaɪl] n proyectil m.

projection [prəˈdʒekʃn] n -1. [gen] proyección f. -2. [protrusion] saliente m.

projectionist [prəˈdʒekʃənɪst] n operador m, -ra f, proyeccionista m y f.

projection room n cabina f de proyecciones.

projector [prəˈdʒektər] n proyector m.

proletarian [ˌprəʊlɪˈteərɪən] adj proletario(ria).

proletariat [ˌprəʊlɪˈteərɪət] n proletariado m.

pro-life adj pro-vida.

proliferate [prəˈlɪfəreɪt] vi proliferar.

prolific [prəˈlɪfɪk] adj prolífico(ca).

prologue, prolog Am [ˈprəʊlɒg] n prólogo m; **to be the** OR **a ~ to sthg** fig ser el prólogo a algo.

prolong [prəˈlɒŋ] vt prolongar.

prom [prɒm] n -1. abbr of **promenade concert**. -2. (abbr of **promenade**) Br inf [road by sea] paseo m marítimo. -3. Am [ball] baile m de gala (en la escuela).

promenade [ˌprɒməˈnɑːd] n Br [by sea] paseo m marítimo.

promenade concert n Br concierto sinfónico en donde parte del público está de pie.

prominence [ˈprɒmɪnəns] n -1. [importance] importancia f. -2. [conspicuousness] prominencia f.

prominent [ˈprɒmɪnənt] adj -1. [important] destacado(da), importante. -2. [noticeable] prominente.

prominently [ˈprɒmɪnəntlɪ] adv de forma destacada.

promiscuity [ˌprɒmɪsˈkjuːətɪ] n promiscuidad f.

promiscuous [prɒˈmɪskjʊəs] adj promiscuo(cua).

promise [ˈprɒmɪs] ◇ n promesa f; **to make (sb) a ~** hacer una promesa (a alguien); **to show ~** prometer, ser prometedor. ◇ vt: **to ~ (to do sthg)** prometer (hacer algo); **to ~ sb sthg** prometer a alguien algo. ◇ vi: **I ~** te lo prometo.

promising [ˈprɒmɪsɪŋ] adj prometedor(ra).

promissory note [ˈprɒmɪsərɪ-] n pagaré m.

promo [ˈprəʊməʊ] (pl -s) (abbr of **promotion**) n inf film m promocional.

promontory [ˈprɒməntrɪ] (pl -ies) n promontorio m.

promote [prəˈməʊt] vt -1. [foster] fomentar, promover. -2. [push, advertise] promocionar. -3. [in job]: **to ~ sb (to sthg)** ascender a alguien (a algo); SPORT: **to be ~d** subir.

promoter [prəˈməʊtər] n -1. [organizer] organizador m, -ra f. -2. [supporter] promotor m, -ra f.

promotion [prəˈməʊʃn] n -1. [in job] ascenso m; **to get** OR **be given ~** conseguir un ascenso. -2. [advertising] promoción f. -3. [campaign] campaña f de promoción.

prompt [prɒmpt] ◇ adj rápido(da), inmediato(ta). ◇ adv en punto. ◇ vt -1. [motivate]: **to ~ sb (to do sthg)** inducir OR impulsar a alguien (a hacer algo). -2. [encourage]: **to ~ sb (to do sthg)** animar a alguien (a hacer algo). -3. THEATRE apuntar. ◇ n THEATRE [line] apunte m.

prompter [ˈprɒmptər] n apuntador m, -ra f.

promptly [ˈprɒmptlɪ] adv -1. [reply, react, pay] inmediatamente, rápidamente. -2. [arrive, leave] puntualmente.

promptness [ˈprɒmptnɪs] n -1. [of reply, reaction, payment] rapidez f. -2. [of arrival, departure] puntualidad f.

promulgate [ˈprɒmlgeɪt] vt promulgar.

prone [prəʊn] adj -1. [susceptible]: **to be ~ to sthg/to do sthg** ser propenso(sa) a algo/a hacer algo. -2. [lying flat] boca abajo.

prong [prɒŋ] n diente m, punta f.

pronoun [ˈprəʊnaʊn] n pronombre m.

pronounce [prəˈnaʊns] ◇ vt -1. [gen] pronunciar. -2. [declare] declarar. ◇ vi: **to ~ on sthg** pronunciarse sobre algo.

pronounced [prəˈnaʊnst] adj pronunciado(da), marcado(da).

pronouncement [prəˈnaʊnsmənt] n declaración f.

pronunciation [prəˌnʌnsɪˈeɪʃn] n pronunciación f.

proof [pruːf] ◇ n -1. [gen & TYPO] prueba f. -2. [of alcohol]: **to be 10% ~** tener 10 grados. ◇ adj [secure]: **~ against** a prueba de.

proofread [ˈpruːfriːd] (pt & pp -read [-red]) vt corregir las pruebas (de imprenta) de.

proofreader [ˈpruːfˌriːdər] n corrector m, -ra f de pruebas.

prop [prɒp] (pt & pp -ped, cont -ping) ◇ n -1. [physical support] puntal m, apoyo m. -2. fig [supporting thing, person] sostén m. -3.

RUGBY pilar *m.* ◇ *vt*: **to ~ sthg on/against sthg** apoyar algo contra algo.

◆ **props** *npl* accesorios *mpl.*

◆ **prop up** *vt sep* **-1.** [physically support] apuntalar. **-2.** *fig* [sustain] apoyar, sostener.

Prop. *abbr of* **proprietor**.

propaganda [ˌprɒpə'gændə] *n* propaganda *f.*

propagate ['prɒpəgeɪt] ◇ *vt* propagar. ◇ *vi* propagarse.

propagation [ˌprɒpə'geɪʃn] *n* propagación *f.*

propane ['prəʊpeɪn] *n* propano *m.*

propel [prə'pel] (*pt & pp* **-led**, *cont* **-ling**) *vt* propulsar, impulsar.

propeller [prə'pelər] *n* hélice *f.*

propelling pencil [prə'pelɪŋ-] *n Br* portaminas *m inv.*

propensity [prə'pensətɪ] (*pl* **-ies**) *n fml*: **~ (for OR to sthg)** propensión *f* (a algo); **to have a ~ to do sthg** tener una propensión a hacer algo.

proper ['prɒpər] *adj* **-1.** [real] de verdad. **-2.** [correct - gen] correcto(ta); [- time, place, equipment] adecuado(da). **-3.** [as emphasis]: **a ~ idiot** *inf* un perfecto idiota.

properly ['prɒpəlɪ] *adv* **-1.** [satisfactorily, correctly] bien. **-2.** [decently] correctamente.

proper noun *n* nombre *m* propio.

property ['prɒpətɪ] (*pl* **-ies**) *n* **-1.** [gen] propiedad *f.* **-2.** [estate] finca *f.* **-3.** *fml* [house] inmueble *m.*

property developer *n* empresa *f* constructora.

property owner *n* propietario *m*, -ria *f* de un inmueble.

property tax *n* impuesto *m* sobre los bienes raíces.

prophecy ['prɒfɪsɪ] (*pl* **-ies**) *n* profecía *f.*

prophesy ['prɒfɪsaɪ] (*pt & pp* **-ied**) *vt* profetizar.

prophet ['prɒfɪt] *n* profeta *m y f.*

prophetic [prə'fetɪk] *adj* profético(ca).

propitious [prə'pɪʃəs] *adj fml* propicio(cia).

proponent [prə'pəʊnənt] *n* partidario *m*, -ria *f*, defensor *m*, -ra *f.*

proportion [prə'pɔːʃn] *n* **-1.** [part] parte *f.* **-2.** [ratio, comparison] proporción *f*; **in ~ to** en proporción a; **out of all ~ (to)** totalmente desproporcionado (con relación a). **-3.** [correct relationship]: **in ~** en proporción; **out of ~** desproporcionado(da); **to get things out of ~** *fig* sacar las cosas fuera de quicio; **sense of ~** *fig* sentido *m* de la medida.

proportional [prə'pɔːʃənl] *adj*: **~ (to)** proporcional (a), en proporción (a).

proportional representation *n* representación *f* proporcional.

proportionate [prə'pɔːʃnət] *adj*: **~ (to)** proporcional (a).

proposal [prə'pəʊzl] *n* **-1.** [plan, suggestion] propuesta *f.* **-2.** [offer of marriage] proposición *f.*

propose [prə'pəʊz] ◇ *vt* **-1.** [suggest] proponer; [motion] presentar. **-2.** [intend]: **to ~ doing OR to do sthg** tener la intención de hacer algo. ◇ *vi* [make offer of marriage] declararse; **to ~ to sb** pedir la mano de alguien.

proposed [prə'pəʊzd] *adj* propuesto(ta).

proposition [ˌprɒpə'zɪʃn] ◇ *n* **-1.** [statement of theory] proposición *f.* **-2.** [suggestion] propuesta *f*; **to make sb a ~** hacer una propuesta a alguien. ◇ *vt fml* hacer proposiciones a.

propound [prə'paʊnd] *vt fml* exponer, plantear.

proprietary [prə'praɪətrɪ] *adj fml* **-1.** [brand name] registrado(da). **-2.** [possessive] posesivo(va).

proprietor [prə'praɪətər] *n* propietario *m*, -ria *f.*

propriety [prə'praɪətɪ] *n* (*U*) *fml* **-1.** [moral correctness] propiedad *f.* **-2.** [rightness] conveniencia *f*, oportunidad *f.*

propulsion [prə'pʌlʃn] *n* propulsión *f.*

pro rata [-'rɑːtə] *adj & adv* a prorrata.

prosaic [prəʊ'zeɪɪk] *adj* prosaico(ca).

Pros. Atty *abbr of* **prosecuting attorney**.

proscenium [prə'siːnjəm] (*pl* **-nia** [njə] OR **-niums**) *n*: **~ (arch)** proscenio *m.*

proscribe [prəʊ'skraɪb] *vt fml* proscribir.

prose [prəʊz] ◇ *n* **-1.** (*U*) LITERATURE prosa *f.* **-2.** SCH traducción *f* inversa. ◇ *comp* en prosa.

prosecute ['prɒsɪkjuːt] ◇ *vt* procesar, enjuiciar; **to be ~d for** ser procesado(da) por. ◇ *vi* **-1.** [bring a charge] entablar una acción judicial. **-2.** [represent in court] representar al demandante.

prosecution [ˌprɒsɪ'kjuːʃn] *n* **-1.** [gen] procesamiento *m.* **-2.** [lawyers]: **the ~** la acusación.

prosecutor ['prɒsɪkjuːtər] *n* fiscal *m y f.*

prospect [*n* 'prɒspekt, *vb* prə'spekt] ◇ *n* **-1.** [gen] perspectiva *f.* **-2.** [possibility] posibilidad *f*; **there's little ~ of that happening** hay pocas posibilidades de que eso ocurra. ◇ *vi*: **to ~ (for)** hacer prospecciones (de).

◆ **prospects** *npl*: **~s (for)** perspectivas *fpl* (de).

prospecting [prə'spektɪŋ] *n* (*U*) prospecciones *fpl.*

prospective [prə'spektɪv] *adj* posible.

prospector [prə'spektəʳ] *n* prospector *m*, -ra *f*.

prospectus [prə'spektəs] (*pl* -es) *n* prospecto *m*, folleto *m* informativo.

prosper ['prɒspəʳ] *vi* prosperar.

prosperity [prɒ'sperətɪ] *n* prosperidad *f*.

prosperous ['prɒspərəs] *adj* próspero(ra).

prostate (gland) ['prɒsteɪt-] *n* próstata *f*.

prosthesis [prɒs'θiːsɪs] (*pl* -theses ['θiːsiːz]) *n* prótesis *f inv*.

prostitute ['prɒstɪtjuːt] *n* prostituta *f*; **male ~** prostituto *m*.

prostitution [,prɒstɪ'tjuːʃn] *n* prostitución *f*.

prostrate [*adj* 'prɒstreɪt, *vb* prɒ'streɪt] ◇ *adj* postrado(da). ◇ *vt*: **to ~ o.s. (before sb)** postrarse (ante alguien).

protagonist [prə'tægənɪst] *n* -1. *fml* [supporter] partidario *m*, -ria *f*, defensor *m*, -ra *f*. -2. [main character] protagonista *m y f*.

protect [prə'tekt] *vt*: **to ~ sthg/sb (against/ from)** proteger algo/a alguien (contra/de).

protection [prə'tekʃn] *n*: **~ (against/from)** protección *f* (contra/de).

protectionism [prə'tekʃənɪzm] *n* proteccionismo *m*.

protectionist [prə'tekʃənɪst] *adj* proteccionista.

protection money *n* dinero *m* pagado a cambio de protección.

protective [prə'tektɪv] *adj* protector(ra); **to feel ~ towards sb** tener sentimientos protectores hacia alguien.

protective custody *n* detención *f* preventiva.

protectiveness [prə'tektɪvnɪs] *n* sentimiento *m* protector.

protector [prə'tektəʳ] *n* protector *m*, -ra *f*.

protectorate [prə'tektərət] *n* protectorado *m*.

protégé ['prɒteʒeɪ] *n* protegido *m*.

protégée ['prɒteʒeɪ] *n* protegida *f*.

protein ['prəʊtiːn] *n* proteína *f*.

protest [*n* 'prəʊtest, *vb* prə'test] ◇ *n* protesta *f*. ◇ *vt* -1. [state] manifestar, aseverar. -2. *Am* [oppose] protestar en contra de. ◇ *vi*: **to ~ (about/against/at)** protestar (por/en contra de/por).

Protestant ['prɒtɪstənt] ◇ *adj* protestante. ◇ *n* protestante *m y f*.

Protestantism ['prɒtɪstəntɪzm] *n* protestantismo *m*.

protestation [,prəʊte'steɪʃn] *n fml* proclamación *f*.

protester [prə'testəʳ] *n* manifestante *m y f*.

protest march *n* manifestación *f*.

protocol ['prəʊtəkɒl] *n* protocolo *m*.

proton ['prəʊtɒn] *n* protón *m*.

prototype ['prəʊtətaɪp] *n* prototipo *m*.

protracted [prə'træktɪd] *adj* prolongado(da).

protractor [prə'træktəʳ] *n* transportador *m*.

protrude [prə'truːd] *vi*: **to ~ (from)** sobresalir (de).

protrusion [prə'truːʒn] *n* saliente *m*.

protuberance [prə'tjuːbərəns] *n* protuberancia *f*.

proud [praʊd] *adj* -1. [gen]: **~ (of)** orgulloso(sa) (de); **to be ~ to do sthg** tener el honor de hacer algo. -2. *pej* [arrogant] soberbio(bia), arrogante.

proudly ['praʊdlɪ] *adv* -1. [with satisfaction] orgullosamente. -2. *pej* [arrogantly] arrogantemente.

provable ['pruːvəbl] *adj* demostrable.

prove [pruːv] (*pp* -d OR **proven**) *vt* -1. [show to be true] probar, demostrar; **events ~d her right** los acontecimientos le dieron la razón. -2. [show oneself to be]: **to ~ (to be) sthg** demostrar ser algo; **to ~ o.s. to be sthg** resultar ser algo; **to ~ o.s.** demostrar (uno) sus cualidades.

proven ['pruːvn, 'prəʊvn] ◇ *pp* → **prove**. ◇ *adj* probado(da).

Provençal [,prɒvɒn'sɑːl] ◇ *adj* provenzal. ◇ *n* -1. [person] provenzal *m y f*. -2. [language] provenzal *m*.

Provence [prɒ'vɒns] *n* Provenza.

proverb ['prɒvɜːb] *n* refrán *m*, proverbio *m*.

proverbial [prə'vɜːbjəl] *adj* proverbial.

provide [prə'vaɪd] *vt* proporcionar, proveer; **to ~ sb with sthg** proporcionar a alguien algo; **to ~ sthg for sb** ofrecer algo a alguien.

◆ **provide for** *vt fus* -1. [support] mantener. -2. *fml* [make arrangements for] prevenir, tomar medidas para.

provided [prə'vaɪdɪd]

◆ **provided (that)** *conj* con tal que, a condición de que.

providence ['prɒvɪdəns] *n* providencia *f*.

providential [,prɒvɪ'denʃl] *adj fml* providencial.

provider [prə'vaɪdəʳ] *n* proveedor *m*, -ra *f*.

providing [prə'vaɪdɪŋ]

◆ **providing (that)** *conj* = **provided**.

province ['prɒvɪns] *n* -1. [part of country] provincia *f*. -2. [speciality] campo *m*, competencia *f*.

◆ **provinces** *npl*: **in the ~s** en provincias.

provincial [prə'vɪnʃl] *adj* -1. [of a province] provincial. -2. *pej* [narrow-minded] provinciano(na).

provision [prə'vɪʒn] *n* -1. [gen] suministro *m*. -2. (*U*) [arrangement]: **to make ~ for** [eventuality, future] tomar medidas para; [one's family] asegurar el porvenir de. -3. [in agreement, law] disposición *f*.
◆ **provisions** *npl* [supplies] provisiones *fpl*, víveres *mpl*.

provisional [prə'vɪʒənl] *adj* provisional.

Provisional IRA *n*: **the ~** el IRA Provisional.

provisional licence *n Br* carné *m* de conducir provisional.

provisionally [prə'vɪʒnəlɪ] *adv* provisionalmente.

proviso [prə'vaɪzəʊ] (*pl* -**s**) *n* condición *f*; **with the ~ that ...** con la condición de que ....

Provo ['prəʊvəʊ] (*pl* -**s**) (*abbr of* **Provisional**) *n inf*: **the ~s** los provisionales del IRA.

provocation [,prɒvə'keɪʃn] *n* provocación *f*.

provocative [prə'vɒkətɪv] *adj* -1. [controversial] provocador(ra). -2. [sexy] provocativo(va).

provocatively [prə'vɒkətɪvlɪ] *adv* -1. [controversially] provocadoramente. -2. [sexily] provocativamente.

provoke [prə'vəʊk] *vt* provocar; **to ~ sb to do sthg** provocar a alguien a que haga algo.

provoking [prə'vəʊkɪŋ] *adj* provocador(ra).

provost ['prɒvəst] *n* -1. *Br* [head of college] rector *m*, -ra *f*. -2. *Scot* [head of town council] ≃ alcalde *m*, -desa *f*.

prow [praʊ] *n* proa *f*.

prowess ['praʊɪs] *n fml* proezas *fpl*.

prowl [praʊl] ◇ *n*: **on the ~** merodeando. ◇ *vt* merodear por. ◇ *vi* merodear.

prowl car *n Am* coche *m* patrulla.

prowler ['praʊlə'] *n* merodeador *m*, -ra *f*.

proximity [prɒk'sɪmətɪ] *n fml* proximidad *f*; **in close ~ to** muy cerca de; **in the ~ of** en las proximidades de.

proxy ['prɒksɪ] (*pl* -**ies**) *n*: **by ~** por poderes.

prude [pruːd] *n* mojigato *m*, -ta *f*.

prudence ['pruːdns] *n fml* prudencia *f*.

prudent ['pruːdnt] *adj* prudente.

prudently ['pruːdntlɪ] *adv* prudentemente.

prudish ['pruːdɪʃ] *adj* mojigato(ta).

prune [pruːn] ◇ *n* [fruit] ciruela *f* pasa. ◇ *vt* podar.

prurient ['prʊərɪənt] *adj fml* lascivo(va).

Prussian ['prʌʃn] ◇ *adj* prusiano(na). ◇ *n* prusiano *m*, -na *f*.

pry [praɪ] (*pt & pp* **pried**) *vi* fisgonear, curiosear; **to ~ into sthg** entrometerse en algo.

PS (*abbr of* **postscript**) *n* PD.

psalm [sɑːm] *n* salmo *m*.

PSBR (*abbr of* **public sector borrowing requirement**) *n* deuda *f* pública.

pseud [sjuːd] *n Br inf* intelectualoide *m y f*.

pseudo- [,sjuːdəʊ] *prefix* pseudo-, seudo-.

pseudonym ['sjuːdənɪm] *n* seudónimo *m*.

psi (*abbr of* **pounds per square inch**) *libras por pulgada cuadrada*.

psoriasis [sɒ'raɪəsɪs] *n* soriasis *f inv*.

psst [pst] *excl* ¡pss!

PST (*abbr of* **Pacific Standard Time**) *hora oficial de la costa oeste de Estados Unidos*.

psych [saɪk].
◆ **psych up** *vt sep inf* mentalizar; **to ~ o.s. up** mentalizarse.

psyche ['saɪkɪ] *n* psique *f*.

psychedelic [,saɪkɪ'delɪk] *adj* psicodélico(ca).

psychiatric [,saɪkɪ'ætrɪk] *adj* psiquiátrico(ca).

psychiatric nurse *n* enfermero psiquiátrico *m*, enfermera psiquiátrica *f*.

psychiatrist [saɪ'kaɪətrɪst] *n* psiquiatra *m y f*.

psychiatry [saɪ'kaɪətrɪ] *n* psiquiatría *f*.

psychic ['saɪkɪk] ◇ *adj* -1. [clairvoyant] clarividente. -2. [mental] psíquico(ca). ◇ *n* médium *m y f*.

psychoanalyse, -yze *Am* [,saɪkəʊ'ænəlaɪz] *vt* psicoanalizar.

psychoanalysis [,saɪkəʊə'næləsɪs] *n* psicoanálisis *m inv*.

psychoanalyst [,saɪkəʊ'ænəlɪst] *n* psicoanalista *m y f*.

psychological [,saɪkə'lɒdʒɪkl] *adj* psicológico(ca).

psychological warfare *n* (*U*) guerra *f* psicológica.

psychologist [saɪ'kɒlədʒɪst] *n* psicólogo *m*, -ga *f*.

psychology [saɪ'kɒlədʒɪ] *n* psicología *f*.

psychopath ['saɪkəpæθ] *n* psicópata *m y f*.

psychosis [saɪ'kəʊsɪs] (*pl* -**choses** ['kəʊsiːz]) *n* psicosis *f inv*.

psychosomatic [,saɪkəʊsə'mætɪk] *adj* psicosomático(ca).

psychotherapy [,saɪkəʊ'θerəpɪ] *n* psicoterapia *f*.

psychotic [saɪk'ɒtɪk] ◇ *adj* psicótico(ca). ◇ *n* psicótico *m*, -ca *f*.

pt -1. *abbr of* **pint**. -2. *abbr of* **point**.

Pt. (*abbr of* **Point**) [on map] Pta.

PT n abbr of **physical training.**

PTA (abbr of **parent-teacher association**) n ≃ APA f.

Pte. abbr of **Private.**

PTO ◇ n Am (abbr of **parent-teacher organization**) asociación de padres de alumnos, ≃ APA. ◇ (abbr of **please turn over**) sigue.

PTV -1. (abbr of **pay television**) televisión de pago. -2. (abbr of **public television**) televisión pública.

pub [pʌb] (abbr of **public house**) n pub m (británico).

PUB:
En el conjunto de las Islas Británicas el 'pub' es uno de los grandes centros de vida local, pero su importancia varía según las zonas (Inglaterra, Escocia, Irlanda, Gales) y según se encuentre en una ciudad o un pueblo. Estos establecimientos - de acceso prohibido para los menores de 16 años que no vayan acompañados - eran conocidos por sus estrictos horarios, aunque desde hace poco éstos son mucho más flexibles (ver 'licensing hours'). Los 'pubs' suelen ofrecer una amplia gama de cervezas y los licores se sirven de acuerdo con estrictas medidas. Tradicionalmente en los 'pubs' lo típico era comer patatas fritas de bolsa pero hoy en día muchos sirven comidas ligeras también

pub. abbr of **published.**

pub-crawl n Br: **to go on a** ~ ir de bar en bar.

puberty ['pjuːbətɪ] n pubertad f.

pubescent [pjuː'besnt] adj pubescente.

pubic ['pjuːbɪk] adj púbico(ca).

public ['pʌblɪk] ◇ adj público(ca); **to be** ~ **knowledge** ser del dominio público; **to make sthg** ~ hacer público algo; **to go** ~ COMM constituirse en sociedad anónima (con cotización en Bolsa). ◇ n público m; **in** ~ en público; **the** ~ el gran público.

public-address system n sistema m de megafonía.

publican ['pʌblɪkən] n Br patrón m, -ona f de un "pub".

publication [,pʌblɪ'keɪʃn] n publicación f.

public bar n Br en ciertos pubs y hoteles, bar de sencilla decoración con precios más bajos que los del "saloon bar".

public company n sociedad f anónima (con cotización en Bolsa).

public convenience n Br aseos mpl públicos.

public domain software n software m de gran consumo.

public holiday n fiesta f nacional.

public house n Br fml pub m (británico).

publicist ['pʌblɪsɪst] n publicista m y f.

publicity [pʌb'lɪsɪtɪ] ◇ n publicidad f. ◇ comp publicitario(ria).

publicity stunt n truco m publicitario.

publicize, -ise ['pʌblɪsaɪz] vt divulgar.

public limited company n sociedad f anónima (con cotización en Bolsa).

publicly ['pʌblɪklɪ] adv públicamente.

public office n cargo m público.

public opinion n (U) opinión f pública.

public ownership n propiedad f del estado.

public prosecutor n fiscal m y f del Estado.

public relations ◇ n (U) relaciones fpl públicas. ◇ npl relaciones fpl públicas.

public relations officer n agente m y f de relaciones públicas.

public school n -1. Br [private school] colegio m privado. -2. Am [state school] escuela f pública.

PUBLIC SCHOOL:
En Inglaterra y Gales una 'public school' es una escuela privada tradicional; algunas de estas escuelas (Eton y Harrow, por ejemplo) gozan de gran fama y están muy solicitadas. Se considera que las 'public schools' forman a la élite de la nación. En los Estados Unidos y en algunos casos en Escocia, el término designa las escuelas públicas

public sector n sector m estatal.

public servant n funcionario m, -ria f.

public service vehicle n Br vehículo m de servicio público.

public-spirited adj con sentido cívico.

public transport n transporte m público.

public utility n servicio m público.

public works npl obras fpl públicas.

publish ['pʌblɪʃ] ◇ vt -1. [gen] publicar. -2. [make known] hacer público(ca). ◇ vi publicar.

publisher ['pʌblɪʃər] n [person] editor m, -ra f; [firm] editorial f.

publishing ['pʌblɪʃɪŋ] n (U) industria f editorial.

publishing company, publishing house n (casa f) editorial f.

pub lunch n almuerzo servido en un "pub".

puce [pjuːs] adj de color morado oscuro.

puck [pʌk] n disco m (en hockey sobre hielo).

pucker ['pʌkər] ◇ vt fruncir. ◇ vi fruncirse.

pudding ['pudɪŋ] n **-1.** [sweet] pudín m; [savoury] pastel m. **-2.** (U) Br [course] postre m.

puddle ['pʌdl] n charco m.

pudgy ['pʌdʒɪ] = podgy.

puerile ['pjuəraɪl] adj fml pueril.

Puerto Rican [,pwɜːtəu'riːkən] ◇ adj puertorriqueño(ña). ◇ n puertorriqueño m, -ña f.

Puerto Rico [,pwɜːtəu'riːkəu] n Puerto Rico.

puff [pʌf] ◇ n **-1.** [of cigarette, pipe] calada f, pitada f Amer. **-2.** [gasp] jadeo m. **-3.** [of air] soplo m; [of smoke] bocanada f. ◇ vt dar caladas a, pitar Amer. ◇ vi **-1.** [smoke]: **to ~ at** OR **on** dar caladas a. **-2.** [pant] jadear, resoplar.

◆ **puff out** vt sep [cheeks, chest] hinchar; [feathers] ahuecar.

◆ **puff up** vi hincharse.

puffed [pʌft] adj **-1.** [swollen]: ~ **(up)** hinchado(da). **-2.** Br inf [out of breath]: ~ **(out)** jadeante.

puffed sleeve n manga f ablusada.

puffin ['pʌfɪn] n frailecillo m.

puffiness ['pʌfɪnɪs] n hinchazón f.

puff pastry, **puff paste** Am n hojaldre m.

puffy ['pʌfɪ] (compar **-ier**, superl **-iest**) adj hinchado(da).

pug [pʌg] n doguillo m.

pugnacious [pʌg'neɪʃəs] adj fml pugnaz, belicoso(sa).

puke [pjuːk] vi v inf devolver, echar la papilla.

pull [pul] ◇ vt **-1.** [gen] tirar de; [trigger] apretar. **-2.** [tooth, cork] sacar, extraer. **-3.** [muscle] sufrir un tirón en. **-4.** [attract] atraer. **-5.** [gun] sacar y apuntar. ◇ vi tirar. ◇ n **-1.** [tug with hand] tirón m. **-2.** (U) [influence] influencia f.

◆ **pull ahead** vi: **to ~ ahead (of)** adelantar (a).

◆ **pull apart** vt sep [machine etc] desmontar.

◆ **pull at** vt fus dar tirones de.

◆ **pull away** vi **-1.** [from roadside] alejarse (de la acera). **-2.** [in race] despegarse.

◆ **pull back** vi retroceder, retirarse.

◆ **pull down** vt sep [building] derribar.

◆ **pull in** vi [train] pararse (en el andén).

◆ **pull off** vt sep **-1.** [clothes] quitarse rápidamente. **-2.** [succeed in] conseguir llevar a cabo.

◆ **pull on** vt sep [clothes] ponerse rápidamente.

◆ **pull out** ◇ vt sep retirar. ◇ vi **-1.** [vehicle] alejarse (de la acera). **-2.** [withdraw] retirarse.

◆ **pull over** vi AUT hacerse a un lado.

◆ **pull through** ◇ vi recobrarse, reponerse. ◇ vt sep ayudar a salir de.

◆ **pull together** ◇ vt sep: **to ~ o.s. together** calmarse, serenarse. ◇ vi fig cooperar, aunar fuerzas.

◆ **pull up** ◇ vt sep **-1.** [move closer] acercar. **-2.** [stop]: **to ~ sb up short** parar a alguien en seco. ◇ vi parar, detenerse.

pull-down menu n COMPUT menú m desplegable.

pulley ['pulɪ] (pl **pulleys**) n polea f.

pullout ['pulaut] n suplemento m.

pullover ['pul,əuvər] n jersey m.

pulp [pʌlp] ◇ adj [novel etc] de pacotilla. ◇ n **-1.** [soft mass] papilla f. **-2.** [of fruit] pulpa f. **-3.** [of wood] pasta f de papel. ◇ vt [books] reducir a pasta de papel.

pulpit ['pulpɪt] n púlpito m.

pulsar ['pʌlsɑːr] n púlsar m.

pulsate [pʌl'seɪt] vi palpitar.

pulse [pʌls] ◇ n **-1.** [in body] pulso m; **to take sb's ~** tomarle el pulso a alguien. **-2.** TECH impulso m. ◇ vi latir.

◆ **pulses** npl [food] legumbres fpl.

pulverize, **-ise** ['pʌlvəraɪz] vt lit & fig pulverizar.

puma ['pjuːmə] (pl inv OR **-s**) n puma m.

pumice (stone) ['pʌmɪs-] n piedra f pómez.

pummel ['pʌml] (Br pt & pp **-led**, cont **-ling**, Am pt & pp **-ed**, cont **-ing**) vt aporrear.

pump [pʌmp] ◇ n **-1.** [machine] bomba f. **-2.** [for petrol] surtidor m. ◇ vt **-1.** [convey by pumping] bombear. **-2.** inf [invest]: **to ~ sthg into sthg** inyectar algo en algo. **-3.** inf [interrogate] sonsacar. ◇ vi latir.

◆ **pumps** npl [shoes] zapatillas fpl de tenis.

pumpernickel ['pʌmpənɪkl] n pan m integral de centeno.

pumpkin ['pʌmpkɪn] n calabaza f.

pumpkin pie n pastel de calabaza que constituye el postre tradicional de la cena de acción de gracias en Estados Unidos.

pun [pʌn] n juego m de palabras.

punch [pʌntʃ] ◇ n **-1.** [blow] puñetazo m. **-2.** [tool - for leather etc] punzón m; [- for tickets] máquina f para picar billetes. **-3.** [drink] ponche m. ◇ vt **-1.** [hit] dar un puñetazo a, trompear Amer. **-2.** [ticket] picar. **-3.** [hole] perforar.

◆ **punch in** vi Am fichar (a la entrada).

◆ **punch out** vi Am fichar (a la salida).

Punch-and-Judy show [-'dʒuːdɪ-] n teatro de guiñol para niños con personajes arquetípicos y representado normalmente en la playa.

punch bag, **punch ball**, **punching bag** *Am* ['pʌntʃɪŋ-] *n* punching ball *m*.

punch bowl *n* ponchera *f*.

punch-drunk *adj* grogui, aturdido(da).

punch(ed) card [pʌntʃ(t)-] *n* tarjeta *f* perforada.

punching bag *Am* = punch bag.

punch line *n* remate *m* (*de un chiste*).

punch-up *n Br inf* pelea *f*.

punchy ['pʌntʃɪ] (*compar* -ier, *superl* -iest) *adj inf* efectista, resultón(ona).

punctilious [pʌŋk'tɪlɪəs] *adj fml* puntilloso(sa).

punctual ['pʌŋktʃʊəl] *adj* puntual.

punctually ['pʌŋktʃʊəlɪ] *adv* puntualmente.

punctuate ['pʌŋktʃʊeɪt] *vt* -1. GRAMM puntuar. -2. [interrupt]: **to be ~d by** OR **with** ser interrumpido(da) por.

punctuation [,pʌŋktʃʊ'eɪʃn] *n* puntuación *f*.

punctuation mark *n* signo *m* de puntuación.

puncture ['pʌŋktʃər] ◇ *n* pinchazo *m*; [in skin] punción *f*. ◇ *vt* pinchar, ponchar *Amer*.

pundit ['pʌndɪt] *n* lumbrera *f*, experto *m*, -ta *f*.

pungent ['pʌndʒənt] *adj* -1. [strong-smelling] penetrante, fuerte. -2. *fig* [biting] mordaz.

punish ['pʌnɪʃ] *vt*: **to ~ sb (for sthg/for doing sthg)** castigar a alguien (por algo/por haber hecho algo).

punishable ['pʌnɪʃəbl] *adj* castigable, sancionable.

punishing ['pʌnɪʃɪŋ] *adj* trabajoso(sa), penoso(sa).

punishment ['pʌnɪʃmənt] *n* -1. [for crime] castigo *m*. -2. [severe treatment]: **to take a lot of ~** sufrir estragos.

punitive ['pjuːnətɪv] *adj* punitivo(va).

Punjab [,pʌn'dʒɑːb] *n*: **the ~** el Punjab.

Punjabi [,pʌn'dʒɑːbɪ] ◇ *adj* punjabí. ◇ *n* -1. [person] punjabí *m y f*. -2. [language] punjabí *m*.

punk [pʌŋk] ◇ *adj* punk. ◇ *n* -1. [music]: ~ **(rock)** punk *m*. -2. [person]: ~ **(rocker)** punki *m y f*. -3. *Am inf* [lout] gamberro *m*.

punnet ['pʌnɪt] *n Br* cajita *f* (*para fresas etc*).

punt [pʌnt] ◇ *n* batea *f*. ◇ *vi* navegar en batea.

punter ['pʌntər] *n Br* -1. [better] apostante *m y f*. -2. *inf* [customer] cliente *m*, -ta *f*, parroquiano *m*, -na *f*.

puny ['pjuːnɪ] (*compar* -ier, *superl* -iest) *adj* [person, limbs] enclenque, raquítico(ca); [effort] penoso(sa), lamentable.

pup [pʌp] *n* -1. [young dog] cachorro *m*. -2. [young seal, otter] cría *f*.

pupil ['pjuːpl] *n* -1. [student] alumno *m*, -na *f*. -2. [follower] pupilo *m*, -la *f*. -3. [of eye] pupila *f*.

puppet ['pʌpɪt] *n lit* & *fig* títere *m*.

puppet government *n* gobierno *m* títere.

puppet show *n* teatro *m* de títeres.

puppy ['pʌpɪ] (*pl* -ies) *n* cachorro *m*, perrito *m*.

puppy fat *n inf* gordura *f* infantil.

purchase ['pɜːtʃəs] *fml* ◇ *n* compra *f*, adquisición *f*. ◇ *vt* comprar, adquirir.

purchase order *n* orden *f* de compra.

purchase price *n* precio *m* de compra.

purchaser ['pɜːtʃəsər] *n* comprador *m*, -ra *f*.

purchase tax *n Br* impuesto *m* sobre la venta.

purchasing power ['pɜːtʃəsɪŋ-] *n* poder *m* adquisitivo.

purdah ['pɜːdə] *n* práctica musulmana de mantener a las mujeres alejadas del contacto con los hombres.

pure [pjʊər] *adj* puro(ra).

purebred ['pjʊəbred] *adj* de pura sangre.

purée ['pjʊəreɪ] ◇ *n* puré *m*. ◇ *vt* hacer puré.

purely ['pjʊəlɪ] *adv* puramente.

pureness ['pjʊənɪs] *n* pureza *f*.

purgative ['pɜːgətɪv] *n* purgante *m*.

purgatory ['pɜːgətrɪ] *n* (*U*) *hum* [suffering] purgatorio *m*.

♦ **Purgatory** *n* [place] Purgatorio *m*.

purge [pɜːdʒ] ◇ *n* POL purga *f*. ◇ *vt*: **to ~ sthg (of)** purgar algo (de).

purification [,pjʊərɪfɪ'keɪʃn] *n* purificación *f*.

purifier ['pjʊərɪfaɪər] *n* depurador *m*.

purify ['pjʊərɪfaɪ] (*pt* & *pp* -ied) *vt* purificar.

purist ['pjʊərɪst] *n* purista *m y f*.

puritan ['pjʊərɪtən] ◇ *adj* puritano(na). ◇ *n* puritano *m*, -na *f*.

puritanical [,pjʊərɪ'tænɪkl] *adj pej* puritano(na).

purity ['pjʊərətɪ] *n* pureza *f*.

purl [pɜːl] ◇ *n* (*U*) punto *m* del revés. ◇ *vt* & *vi* tejer con punto del revés.

purloin [pɜː'lɔɪn] *vt fml* & *hum* hurtar.

purple ['pɜːpl] ◇ *adj* morado(da). ◇ *n* (color *m*) morado *m*.

purport [pə'pɔːt] *vi fml*: **to ~ to do/be sthg** pretender hacer/ser algo.

purpose ['pɜːpəs] *n* -1. [gen] propósito *m*; **for tax ~s** a efectos fiscales; **it serves no ~**

carece de sentido; **to no** ~ en vano. **-2.** [determination] resolución *f.*

◆ **on purpose** *adv* a propósito, adrede.

purpose-built *adj* especialmente construido(da).

purposeful ['pɜːpəsful] *adj* resuelto(ta).

purposely ['pɜːpəslɪ] *adv* adrede, intencionadamente.

purr [pɜːʳ] ◇ *n* **-1.** [of cat] ronroneo *m.* **-2.** [of engine] zumbido *m.* ◇ *vi* **-1.** [cat, person] ronronear. **-2.** [engine, machine] zumbar.

purse [pɜːs] ◇ *n* **-1.** [for money] monedero *m.* **-2.** *Am* [handbag] bolso *m.* ◇ *vt* fruncir (con desagrado).

purser ['pɜːsəʳ] *n* contador *m*, -ra *f.*

purse snatcher [-,snætʃəʳ] *n Am* ladrón *m* que roba dando el tirón.

purse strings *npl*: **to hold the** ~ administrar el dinero.

pursue [pəˈsjuː] *vt* **-1.** [follow] perseguir. **-2.** *fml* [policy] llevar a cabo; [aim, pleasure etc] ir en pos de, buscar; [topic, question] profundizar en; [hobby, studies] dedicarse a.

pursuer [pəˈsjuːəʳ] *n* perseguidor *m*, -ra *f.*

pursuit [pəˈsjuːt] *n* **-1.** (*U*) *fml* [attempt to achieve] búsqueda *f.* **-2.** [chase, in cycling] persecución *f*; **in** ~ **of** en persecución de; **in hot** ~ **(of)** pisando los talones (a). **-3.** [occupation, activity] ocupación *f*; **leisure** ~ pasatiempo *m.*

purveyor [pəˈveɪəʳ] *n fml* proveedor *m*, -ra *f.*

pus [pʌs] *n* pus *m.*

push [puʃ] ◇ *vt* **-1.** [shove] empujar; **to** ~ **sthg into sthg** meter algo en algo; **to** ~ **sthg open/shut** abrir/cerrar algo empujándolo. **-2.** [press - button] apretar, pulsar. **-3.** [encourage]: **to** ~ **sb (to do sthg)** empujar a alguien (a hacer algo). **-4.** [force]: **to** ~ **sb (into doing sthg)** obligar a alguien (a hacer algo). **-5.** *inf* [promote] promocionar. **-6.** *drugs sl* pasar, vender. ◇ *vi* **-1.** [press forward] empujar; [on button] apretar, pulsar. **-2.** [move past]: **to** ~ **through** abrirse paso (a empujones) entre. ◇ *n lit* & *fig* empujón *m*; **to give sb the** ~ *inf* [end relationship] dar calabazas a alguien; [from job] dar la patada a alguien.

◆ **push ahead** *vi*: **to** ~ **ahead (with sthg)** seguir adelante sin parar (con algo).

◆ **push around** *vt sep inf* mandonear.

◆ **push for** *vt fus* [demand] reclamar.

◆ **push in** *vi* [in queue] colarse.

◆ **push off** *vi inf* largarse.

◆ **push on** *vi* seguir adelante sin parar.

◆ **push over** *vt sep* volcar.

◆ **push through** *vt sep* [law etc] conseguir que se apruebe.

pushbike ['puʃbaɪk] *n Br inf* bici *f.*

push-button *adj* de botón.

pushcart ['puʃkɑːt] *n* carrito *m.*

pushchair ['puʃtʃeəʳ] *n Br* silla *f* (de paseo).

pushed [puʃt] *adj inf*: **to be** ~ **for sthg** andar corto(ta) de algo; **to be hard** ~ **to do sthg** tenerlo difícil para hacer algo.

pusher ['puʃəʳ] *n inf* camello *m.*

pushing ['puʃɪŋ] *prep inf* alrededor de.

pushover ['puʃ,əʊvəʳ] *n inf*: **it's a** ~ está chupado.

push-start *vt* arrancar empujando.

push-up *n* flexión *f.*

pushy ['puʃɪ] (*compar* **-ier**, *superl* **-iest**) *adj pej* agresivo(va), insistente.

puss [pus], **pussy (cat)** ['pusɪ-] *n inf* gatito *m*, minino *m.*

pussy willow ['pusɪ-] *n* sauce *m* blanco.

put [put] (*pt* & *pp* put, *cont* **-ting**) *vt* **-1.** [gen] poner; **to** ~ **sthg into sthg** meter algo en algo. **-2.** [place exactly] colocar. **-3.** [send - to prison etc] meter; **to** ~ **the children to bed** acostar a los niños. **-4.** [express] expresar, formular. **-5.** [ask - question] hacer; **to** ~ **it to sb that ...** sugerir OR insinuar a alguien que .... **-6.** [estimate]: **to** ~ **sthg at** calcular algo en. **-7.** [invest]: **to** ~ **sthg into sthg** poner algo en algo, dedicar algo a algo. **-8.** [apply]: **to** ~ **pressure on** presionar a; **that** ~**s a great responsibility on us** eso nos supone una gran responsabilidad.

◆ **put across** *vt sep* transmitir.

◆ **put aside** *vt sep* **-1.** [money] ahorrar. **-2.** [book, work, differences] dejar a un lado.

◆ **put away** *vt sep* **-1.** [tidy away] poner en su sitio, guardar. **-2.** *inf* [lock up] encerrar.

◆ **put back** *vt sep* **-1.** [replace] volver a poner en su sitio. **-2.** [postpone] aplazar. **-3.** [clock, watch] atrasar.

◆ **put by** *vt sep* [money] ahorrar.

◆ **put down** *vt sep* **-1.** [lay down] dejar (*encima de algún sitio*). **-2.** [quell] sofocar, reprimir. **-3.** *inf* [criticize]: **to** ~ **sb down** poner mal a alguien. **-4.** *Br* [animal] matar (*a un animal que es viejo o está enfermo*). **-5.** [write down] apuntar.

◆ **put down to** *vt sep* achacar a.

◆ **put forward** *vt sep* **-1.** [plan, theory, name] proponer, presentar; [proposal] someter. **-2.** [clock, meeting, event] adelantar.

◆ **put in** *vt sep* **-1.** [spend - time] dedicar. **-2.** [submit] presentar.

◆ **put off** *vt sep* **-1.** [postpone] posponer, aplazar. **-2.** [cause to wait] hacer esperar. **-3.** [discourage] disuadir, desanimar. **-4.** [cause to dislike]: **to** ~ **sb off sthg** hacerle pasar a alguien las ganas de algo.

◆ **put on** *vt sep* **-1.** [wear] ponerse. **-2.** [show, play] representar; [exhibition] hacer. **-3.** [gain]: **to ~ on weight** engordar; **I've ~ on 10 kilos** he engordado 10 kilos. **-4.** [radio, light] poner, encender; **to ~ on the brakes** poner el freno, frenar. **-5.** [record, tape] poner. **-6.** [start cooking] empezar a hacer OR cocinar. **-7.** [bet] apostar por. **-8.** [add] añadir. **-9.** [feign - air, accent] fingir. **-10.** *inf* [tease]: **to ~ sb on** tomar el pelo a alguien.

◆ **put onto** *vt sep* [tell about]: **to ~ sb onto sthg/sb** dirigir a alguien a algo/alguien.

◆ **put out** *vt sep* **-1.** [place outside] sacar. **-2.** [issue - statement] hacer público. **-3.** [extinguish] apagar. **-4.** [switch off] quitar, apagar. **-5.** [prepare for use - clothes] sacar. **-6.** [extend - hand, leg] extender; [- tongue] sacar. **-7.** *inf* [injure] dislocar. **-8.** [upset]: **to be ~ out** estar enfadado(da). **-9.** [inconvenience] causar molestias a; **to ~ o.s. out** molestarse.

◆ **put over** = **put across**.

◆ **put through** *vt sep* **-1.** TELEC [call] poner; **to ~ sb through to sb** poner a alguien con alguien. **-2.** [cause to suffer]: **to ~ sb through sthg** hacer pasar a alguien por algo.

◆ **put together** *vt sep* **-1.** [machine, tool] ensamblar; [team] reunir; [report] elaborar. **-2.** [combine] mezclar. **-3.** [organize - event] organizar.

◆ **put up** ◇ *vt sep* **-1.** [build] construir. **-2.** [umbrella] abrir; [flag] izar. **-3.** [poster] fijar, pegar; [painting] colgar. **-4.** [provide - money] poner. **-5.** [propose - candidate] proponer. **-6.** [increase] subir, aumentar. **-7.** [provide accommodation for] alojar, hospedar. ◇ *vt fus* [resistance] ofrecer; **to ~ up a fight** resistir.

◆ **put upon** *vt fus Br* molestar.

◆ **put up to** *vt sep*: **to ~ sb up to sthg** incitar a alguien a hacer algo.

◆ **put up with** *vt fus* aguantar, soportar.

putative ['pjuːtətɪv] *adj fml* putativo(va).

put-down *n inf* desaire *m*, corte *m*.

putrefaction [ˌpjuːtrɪ'fækʃn] *n* putrefacción *f*.

putrefy ['pjuːtrɪfaɪ] (*pt & pp* **-ied**) *vi fml* pudrirse.

putrid ['pjuːtrɪd] *adj fml* putrefacto(ta).

putsch [pʊtʃ] *n* golpe *m* de estado.

putt [pʌt] ◇ *n* putt *m*, tiro *m* al hoyo. ◇ *vt & vi* tirar al hoyo.

putter ['pʌtər] *n* [club] putt *m*, *palo de golf para golpes cortos*.

◆ **putter about**, **putter around** *Am* entretenerse haciendo algo.

putting green ['pʌtɪŋ-] *n* minigolf *m* (*sin obstáculos*).

putty ['pʌtɪ] *n* masilla *f*.

put-up job *n inf* amaño *m*.

put-upon *adj inf* utilizado(da).

puzzle ['pʌzl] ◇ *n* **-1.** [toy, game] rompecabezas *m inv*. **-2.** [mystery] misterio *m*, enigma *m*. ◇ *vt* dejar perplejo, desconcertar. ◇ *vi*: **to ~ over sthg** romperse la cabeza con algo.

◆ **puzzle out** *vt sep* descifrar, resolver.

puzzled ['pʌzld] *adj* desconcertado(da), perplejo(ja).

puzzling ['pʌzlɪŋ] *adj* desconcertante.

PVC (*abbr of* **polyvinyl chloride**) *n* PVC *m*.

Pvt. (*abbr of* **Private**) soldado *m* raso.

pw (*abbr of* **per week**) a la semana.

PWR (*abbr of* **pressurized-water reactor**) *n* reactor de agua a presión.

PX (*abbr of* **post exchange**) *n Am* economato militar.

pygmy ['pɪgmɪ] (*pl* **-ies**) ◇ *adj* pigmeo(a). ◇ *n* pigmeo *m*, -a *f*.

pyjama [pə'dʒɑːmə] *comp* del pijama.

◆ **pyjamas** *npl* pijama *m*.

pylon ['paɪlən] *n* torre *f* (*de conducción eléctrica*).

pyramid ['pɪrəmɪd] *n* **-1.** [structure] pirámide *f*. **-2.** [pile] montón *m*, pila *f*.

pyramid selling *n* estructura *f* de ventas piramidal.

pyre ['paɪər] *n* pira *f*.

Pyrenean [ˌpɪrə'niːən] *adj* pirenaico(ca).

Pyrenees [ˌpɪrə'niːz] *npl*: **the ~** los Pirineos.

Pyrex® ['paɪreks] ◇ *n* pírex® *m*. ◇ *comp* de pírex.

pyromaniac [ˌpaɪrə'meɪnɪæk] *n* pirómano *m*, -na *f*.

pyrotechnics [ˌpaɪrəʊ'teknɪks] ◇ *n* [skill] demostración *f* de habilidad extraordinaria. ◇ *npl* [show] fuegos *mpl* artificiales.

python ['paɪθn] (*pl inv* OR **-s**) *n* pitón *m*.

q (*pl* **q's** OR **qs**), **Q** (*pl* **Q's** OR **Qs**) [kjuː] *n* [letter] q *f*, Q *f*.

Qatar [kæ'tɑːr] *n* Qatar.

QC *n abbr of* **Queen's Counsel**.

QED (*abbr of* **quod erat demonstrandum**) Q.E.D.

QM *n abbr of* **quartermaster**.

q.t., **QT** (*abbr of* **quiet**) *inf*: **I did it on the ~** lo hice en secreto.

qty (*abbr of* **quantity**) cdad.

quack [kwæk] ◇ *n* **-1.** [noise] graznido (*de pato*). **-2.** *inf* [doctor] matasanos *m inv.* ◇ *vi* graznar (*el pato*).

quad [kwɒd] *n abbr of* **quadrangle**.

quadrangle ['kwɒdræŋgl] *n* **-1.** [figure] cuadrángulo *m*. **-2.** [courtyard] patio *m*.

quadrant ['kwɒdrənt] *n* cuadrante *m*.

quadraphonic [,kwɒdrə'fɒnɪk] *adj* cuadrafónico(ca).

quadrilateral [,kwɒdrɪ'lætərəl] ◇ *adj* cuadrilátero(ra). ◇ *n* cuadrilátero *m*.

quadruped ['kwɒdruped] *n* cuadrúpedo *m*.

quadruple [kwɒ'druːpl] ◇ *adj* cuatro veces mayor. ◇ *vt* cuadruplicar. ◇ *vi* cuadruplicarse.

quadruplets [kwɒ'druplɪts] *npl* cuatrillizos *mpl*, -zas *fpl*.

quads [kwɒdz] *npl inf* cuatrillizos *mpl*, -zas *fpl*.

quaff [kwɒf] *vt dated* echarse al coleto.

quagmire ['kwægmaɪər] *n* lodazal *m*, cenagal *m*.

quail [kweɪl] (*pl inv* OR **-s**) ◇ *n* codorniz *f*. ◇ *vi fml* amedrentarse, acobardarse.

quaint [kweɪnt] *adj* pintoresco(ca).

quaintness ['kweɪntnɪs] *n* lo pintoresco.

quake [kweɪk] ◇ *n inf* terremoto *m*. ◇ *vi* temblar, estremecerse.

Quaker ['kweɪkər] *n* cuáquero *m*, -ra *f*.

qualification [,kwɒlɪfɪ'keɪʃn] *n* **-1.** [examination, certificate] título *m*. **-2.** [ability, skill] aptitud *f*. **-3.** [qualifying statement] modificación *f*. **-4.** [becoming qualified] obtención *f* del título.

qualified ['kwɒlɪfaɪd] *adj* **-1.** [trained] cualificado(da); **to be ~ to do sthg** estar cualificado para hacer algo. **-2.** [limited] limitado(da).

qualify ['kwɒlɪfaɪ] (*pt & pp* **-ied**) ◇ *vt* **-1.** [modify] modificar. **-2.** [entitle]: **to ~ sb to do sthg** capacitar a alguien para hacer algo. ◇ *vi* **-1.** [pass exams] sacar el título. **-2.** [be entitled]: **to ~ (for)** tener derecho (a). **-3.** SPORT clasificarse.

qualifying ['kwɒlɪfaɪɪŋ] *adj* **-1.** [modifying] calificativo(va). **-2.** [in sport, exam] eliminatorio(ria); **~ round** eliminatoria *f*.

qualitative ['kwɒlɪtətɪv] *adj* cualitativo(va).

quality ['kwɒlətɪ] (*pl* **-ies**) ◇ *n* **-1.** [standard] calidad *f*. **-2.** [characteristic] cualidad *f*. ◇ *comp* de calidad.

quality control *n* control *m* de calidad.

quality press *n Br*: **the ~** la prensa de calidad.

qualms ['kwɑːmz] *npl* remordimientos *mpl*, escrúpulos *mpl*.

quandary ['kwɒndərɪ] (*pl* **-ies**) *n*: **to be in a ~ about** OR **over sthg** estar en un dilema sobre algo.

quango ['kwæŋgəʊ] (*pl* **-s**) (*abbr of* **quasi-autonomous non-governmental organization**) *n Br usu pej* organismo autónomo de la *Administración*.

quantifiable [kwɒntɪ'faɪəbl] *adj* cuantificable.

quantify ['kwɒntɪfaɪ] (*pt & pp* **-ied**) *vt* cuantificar.

quantitative ['kwɒntɪtətɪv] *adj* cuantitativo(va).

quantity ['kwɒntətɪ] (*pl* **-ies**) *n* cantidad *f*; **in ~** en cantidad; **unknown ~** incógnita *f*.

quantity surveyor *n* aparejador *m*, -ra *f*.

quantum leap ['kwɒntəm-] *n fml* enorme salto *m* adelante.

quantum theory ['kwɒntəm-] *n*: **the ~** la (teoría) cuántica.

quarantine ['kwɒrəntiːn] ◇ *n* cuarentena *f*; **to be in ~** estar en cuarentena. ◇ *vt* poner en cuarentena.

quark [kwɑːk] *n* **-1.** PHYSICS cuark *m*. **-2.** CULIN *tipo de queso blando bajo en grasas*.

quarrel ['kwɒrəl] (*Br pt & pp* **-led**, *cont* **-ling**, *Am pt & pp* **-ed**, *cont* **-ing**) ◇ *n* pelea *f*, disputa *f*; **to have no ~ with sb/sthg** no tener nada en contra de alguien/algo. ◇ *vi* pelearse, reñir; **to ~ with sb** pelearse con alguien; **to ~ with sthg** no estar de acuerdo con algo.

quarrelsome ['kwɒrəlsəm] *adj* pendenciero(ra).

quarry ['kwɒrɪ] (*pl* **-ies**, *pt* & *pp* **-ied**) ◇ *n*
-1. [place] cantera *f*. **-2.** [prey] presa *f*. ◇ *vt*
extraer.

quarry tile *n* baldosa *f* mate.

quart [kwɔːt] *n* cuarto *m* de galón.

quarter ['kwɔːtəʳ] *n* **-1.** [fraction] cuarto *m*.
-2. [in telling time]: ~ **past two** *Br* , ~ **after**
two *Am* las dos y cuarto; ~ **to two** *Br* , ~
of two *Am* las dos menos cuarto. **-3.** [of
year] trimestre *m*. **-4.** *Am* [coin] cuarto *m* de
dólar, moneda *f* de 25 centavos. **-5.** [four
ounces] cuatro onzas *fpl*, cuarto *m* de libra.
-6. [area in town] barrio *m*. **-7.** [group of
people] lugar *m*, parte *f*; **in some ~s this is**
seen as lying algunos ven eso como una
mentira.
◆ **quarters** *npl* [rooms] residencia *f*, alojamiento *m*.
◆ **at close quarters** *adv* muy de cerca.

quarterback ['kwɔːtəbæk] *n* *Am* jugador *de*
fútbol americano que lanza la pelota en las juga-
das ofensivas.

quarterdeck ['kwɔːtədek] *n* alcázar *m*.

quarterfinal [,kwɔːtə'faɪnl] *n* cuarto *m* de
final.

quarter-hour *adj* cada cuarto de hora.

quarter light *n* *Br* ventanilla *f* de un coche (para ventilación).

quarterly ['kwɔːtəlɪ] (*pl* **-ies**) ◇ *adj* trimestral. ◇ *adv* trimestralmente. ◇ *n* trimestral
f.

quartermaster ['kwɔːtə,mɑːstəʳ] *n* oficial *m*
de intendencia.

quarter note *n* *Am* MUS negra *f*.

quarter sessions *npl* audiencia *f* trimestral.

quartet [kwɔː'tet] *n* cuarteto *m*.

quarto ['kwɔːtəʊ] (*pl* **-s**) *n* cuarto *m*.

quartz [kwɔːts] *n* cuarzo *m*.

quartz watch *n* reloj *m* de cuarzo.

quasar ['kweɪzɑːʳ] *n* quasar *m*.

quash [kwɒʃ] *vt* **-1.** [reject] anular, invalidar. **-2.** [quell] reprimir, sofocar.

quasi- ['kweɪzaɪ] *prefix* cuasi-.

quaver ['kweɪvəʳ] ◇ *n* **-1.** MUS corchea *f*.
-2. [in voice] trémolo *m*. ◇ *vi* temblar.

quavering ['kweɪvərɪŋ] *adj* trémulo(la).

quay [kiː] *n* muelle *m*.

quayside ['kiːsaɪd] *n* muelle *m*.

queasy ['kwiːzɪ] (*compar* **-ier**, *superl* **-iest**)
adj mareado(da).

Quebec [kwɪ'bek] *n* Quebec.

Quebecer, Quebecker [kwɪ'bekəʳ] *n* que-
bequés *m*, -esa *f*.

queen [kwiːn] *n* **-1.** [gen] reina *f*. **-2.** [play-
ing card] dama *f*.

Queen Mother *n*: the ~ la reina madre.

Queen's Counsel *n* *Br* abogado inglés de
alto rango.

Queen's English *n* *Br*: the ~ el inglés ha-
blado con mayor corrección en Gran Bretaña.

queen's evidence *n* *Br*: to turn ~ *testificar*
un delincuente ante un tribunal en contra de
otros a cambio de una reducción de condena.

queer [kwɪəʳ] ◇ *adj* [odd] raro(ra), extra-
ño(ña). ◇ *n* *inf pej* marica *m*, maricón *m*,
joto *m* *Amer*.

quell [kwel] *vt* **-1.** [rebellion] sofocar, reprimir. **-2.** [feelings] dominar, contener.

quench [kwentʃ] *vt* apagar.

querulous ['kwerʊləs] *adj* *fml* quejumbro-
so(sa).

query ['kwɪərɪ] (*pl* **-ies**, *pt* & *pp* **-ied**) ◇ *n*
pregunta *f*, duda *f*. ◇ *vt* poner en duda.

quest [kwest] *n* *literary*: ~ **(for)** búsqueda *f*
(de).

question ['kwestʃn] ◇ *n* **-1.** [query, problem
in exam] pregunta *f*; **to ask (sb) a** ~ hacer
una pregunta (a alguien). **-2.** [doubt] duda *f*;
to bring sthg into ~ hacer reflexionar sobre algo; **to call sthg into** ~ poner algo en
duda; **without** ~ sin duda; **beyond** ~ fuera
de toda duda; **open to** ~ debatible. **-3.** [is-
sue, matter] cuestión *f*, asunto *m*. **-4.** *phr*:
there's no ~ **of ...** es imposible que ....
◇ *vt* **-1.** [interrogate] interrogar. **-2.** [express
doubt about] cuestionar.
◆ **in question** *adv*: the matter in ~ el
asunto en cuestión.
◆ **out of the question** *adv* imposible.

questionable ['kwestʃənəbl] *adj* [gen] cuestionable; [taste] dudoso(sa).

questioner ['kwestʃənəʳ] *n* interrogador *m*,
-ra *f*.

questioning ['kwestʃənɪŋ] ◇ *adj* de interrogación, interrogativo(va). ◇ *n* interrogatorio *m*.

question mark *n* (signo *m* de) interrogación *f*.

question master, quizmaster ['kwɪz-
,mɑːstəʳ] *n* presentador *m*, -ra *f* de un concurso.

questionnaire [,kwestʃə'neəʳ] *n* cuestionario *m*.

question time *n* *Br* POL ruegos *mpl* y preguntas (*en el parlamento*).

queue [kjuː] *Br* ◇ *n* cola *f*; **to jump the** ~
colarse. ◇ *vi*: **to** ~ **(up for sthg)** hacer cola
(para algo).

queue-jump *vi* *Br* colarse.

quibble ['kwɪbl] *pej* ◇ *n* queja *f* OR pega *f*
insignificante. ◇ *vi* quejarse por tonterías;

to ~ **over** OR **about** quejarse tontamente por OR de.

quiche [kiːʃ] *n* quiche *f.*

quick [kwɪk] ◇ *adj* **-1.** [gen] rápido(da); **be ~!** ¡date prisa! **-2.** [clever - person] espabilado(da); [- wit] agudo(da). **-3.** [irritable]: **a ~ temper** un genio vivo; **to be ~ to take offence** ofenderse por nada. ◇ *adv* rápidamente.

quicken ['kwɪkn] ◇ *vt* apretar, acelerar. ◇ *vi* acelerarse, apresurarse.

quickly ['kwɪklɪ] *adv* **-1.** [rapidly] rápidamente, de prisa. **-2.** [without delay] rápidamente, en seguida.

quickness ['kwɪknɪs] *n* **-1.** [gen] rapidez *f.* **-2.** [cleverness - of person] inteligencia *f* viva; [- of wit] agudeza *f.* **-3.** [of temper] viveza *f.*

quicksand ['kwɪksænd] *n* arenas *fpl* movedizas.

quicksilver ['kwɪk,sɪlvər] *n* argento *m* vivo, mercurio *m.*

quickstep ['kwɪkstep] *n*: **the ~** baile de salón de pasos rápidos.

quick-tempered *adj* de genio vivo.

quick-witted [-'wɪtɪd] *adj* agudo(da).

quid [kwɪd] (*pl inv*) *n* Br *inf* libra *f* (esterlina).

quid pro quo [-'kwəʊ] (*pl* **quid pro quos**) *n* compensación *f.*

quiescent [kwaɪ'esnt] *adj* fml inactivo(va), en reposo.

quiet ['kwaɪət] ◇ *adj* **-1.** [silent - gen] silencioso(sa); [- room, place] tranquilo(la); **in a ~ voice** en voz baja; **to keep ~ about sthg** guardar silencio sobre algo. **-2.** [not talkative] callado(da). **-3.** [tranquil, uneventful] tranquilo(la); **business is ~** el negocio está un poco apagado. **-4.** [unpublicized - wedding etc] privado(da), íntimo(ma). **-5.** [colours] apagado(da). ◇ *n* tranquilidad *f*, silencio *m*; **on the ~** a escondidas. ◇ *vt* Am tranquilizar, calmar.

◆ **quiet down** ◇ *vt sep* calmar, tranquilizar. ◇ *vi* calmarse, tranquilizarse.

quieten ['kwaɪətn] *vt* calmar, tranquilizar.

◆ **quieten down** ◇ *vt sep* calmar, tranquilizar. ◇ *vi* calmarse, tranquilizarse.

quietly ['kwaɪətlɪ] *adv* **-1.** [without noise] silenciosamente, sin hacer ruido; **to speak ~** hablar en voz baja. **-2.** [without moving] sin moverse. **-3.** [without excitement] tranquilamente. **-4.** [without fuss] discretamente.

quietness ['kwaɪətnɪs] *n* **-1.** [lack of noise] silencio *m.* **-2.** [lack of movement] quietud *f*, tranquilidad *f.*

quiff [kwɪf] *n* Br copete *m*, tupé *m.*

quill (pen) [kwɪl-] *n* pluma *f.*

quilt [kwɪlt] *n* edredón *m.*

quilted ['kwɪltɪd] *adj* acolchado(da).

quince [kwɪns] *n* membrillo *m.*

quinine [kwɪ'niːn] *n* quinina *f.*

quins Br [kwɪnz], **quints** Am [kwɪnts] *npl inf* quintillizos *mpl*, -zas *fpl.*

quintessential [kwɪntə'senʃl] *adj* puro(ra).

quintet [kwɪn'tet] *n* quinteto *m.*

quints Am = **quins**.

quintuplets [kwɪn'tjuːplɪts] *npl* quintillizos *mpl*, -zas *fpl.*

quip [kwɪp] (*pt & pp* **-ped**, *cont* **-ping**) ◇ *n* ocurrencia *f*, salida *f.* ◇ *vi* bromear.

quire ['kwaɪər] *n* mano *f* de papel (*conjunto de cinco cuadernillos*).

quirk [kwɜːk] *n* **-1.** [habit] manía *f*, rareza *f.* **-2.** [strange event] extraña coincidencia *f*; **~ of fate** capricho del destino.

quirky ['kwɜːkɪ] (*compar* **-ier**, *superl* **-iest**) *adj* peculiar, idiosincrásico(ca).

quit [kwɪt] (Br *pt & pp* **quit** OR **-ted**, *cont* **-ting**, Am *pt & pp* **quit**, *cont* **-ting**) ◇ *vt* **-1.** [resign from] dejar, abandonar. **-2.** [stop]: **to ~ doing sthg** dejar de hacer algo. ◇ *vi* [resign] dimitir.

quite [kwaɪt] *adv* **-1.** [completely] totalmente, completamente. **-2.** [fairly] bastante; **~ a lot of people** bastante gente. **-3.** [after negative]: **it's not ~ big enough** no es todo lo grande que tendría que ser; **I don't understand/know** no entiendo/sé muy bien. **-4.** [to emphasize]: **~ a ...** todo un (toda una) .... **-5.** [to express agreement]: **~ (so)!** ¡efectivamente!, ¡desde luego!

Quito ['kiːtəʊ] *n* Quito.

quits [kwɪts] *adj inf*: **to be ~ (with sb)** estar en paz (con alguien); **to call it ~** quedar en paz.

quitter ['kwɪtər] *n inf pej*: **she's not a ~** no es de las que abandonan.

quiver ['kwɪvər] ◇ *n* **-1.** [shiver] temblor *m*, estremecimiento *m.* **-2.** [for arrows] carcaj *m*, aljaba *f.* ◇ *vi* temblar, estremecerse.

quivering ['kwɪvərɪŋ] *adj* tembloroso(sa).

quixotic [kwɪk'sɒtɪk] *adj literary* quijotesco(ca).

quiz [kwɪz] (*pl* **-zes**, *pt & pp* **-zed**, *cont* **-zing**) ◇ *n* **-1.** [gen] concurso *m.* **-2.** Am SCH control *m.* ◇ *comp*: **~ programme** concurso *m.* ◇ *vt*: **to ~ sb (about)** interrogar a alguien (sobre).

quizmaster = **question master**.

quizzical ['kwɪzɪkl] *adj* [smile] burlón(ona); [look, glance] interrogativo(va).

quoits [kwɔɪts] *n* juego *m* de los aros.

Quonset hut ['kwɒnsɪt-] *n Am* refugio *m* militar.

quorate ['kwɔːreɪt] *adj Br* donde hay quórum.

quorum ['kwɔːrəm] *n* quórum *m*.

quota ['kwəʊtə] *n* cuota *f*.

quotation [kwəʊ'teɪʃn] *n* -1. [citation] cita *f*. -2. COMM presupuesto *m*.

quotation marks *npl* comillas *fpl*.

quote [kwəʊt] ◇ *n inf* -1. [citation] cita *f*. -2. COMM presupuesto *m*. ◇ *vt* -1. [cite] citar. -2. [figures, example, price] dar; **he ~d** £100 fijó un precio de 100 libras. ◇ *vi* -1. [cite]: **to ~ (from)** citar (de). -2. COMM: **to ~ for** dar un presupuesto por.

◆ **quotes** *npl inf* comillas *fpl*.

quoted company ['kwəʊtɪd-] *n Br* compañía *f* cotizada en la Bolsa.

quotient ['kwəʊʃnt] *n* cociente *m*.

qv (*abbr of* **quod vide**) *v*.

qwerty keyboard ['kwɜːtɪ-] *n Br teclado estándar inglés para una máquina de escribir o un ordenador.*

R

r (*pl* **r's** OR **rs**), **R** (*pl* **R's** OR **Rs**) [ɑːr] *n* [letter] r *f*, R *f*.

◆ **R** -1. (*abbr of* **right**) dcha. -2. *abbr of* **River**. -3. (*abbr of* **Réaumur**) R. -4. *Am* (*abbr of* **restricted**) no recomendada para menores. -5. *Am abbr of* **Republican**. -6. *Br* (*abbr of* **Rex**) *Rex*. -7. *Br* (*abbr of* **Regina**) *Regina*.

RA (*abbr of* **Royal Academy**) *n academia británica de bellas artes.*

RAAF (*abbr of* **Royal Australian Air Force**) *n fuerzas aéreas australianas.*

Rabat [rə'bɑːt] *n* Rabat.

rabbi ['ræbaɪ] *n* rabino *m*.

rabbit ['ræbɪt] *n* conejo *m*.

rabbit hole *n* madriguera *f* de conejos.

rabbit hutch *n* conejera *f*.

rabbit warren *n* madriguera *f* de conejos.

rabble ['ræbl] *n* chusma *f*, populacho *m*.

rabble-rousing *adj* que agita a las masas.

rabid ['ræbɪd, 'reɪbɪd] *adj* -1. [infected with rabies] rabioso(sa). -2. *pej* [fanatical] fanático(ca).

rabies ['reɪbiːz] *n* rabia *f*.

RAC (*abbr of* **Royal Automobile Club**) *n asociación británica del automóvil*, ≃ RACE *m*.

raccoon [rə'kuːn] *n* mapache *m*.

race [reɪs] ◇ *n* -1. *lit & fig* [competition] carrera *f*. -2. [people, descent] raza *f*. ◇ *vt* -1. [compete against] competir con (*corriendo*); **they ~d each other to the door** echaron una carrera hasta la puerta. -2. [cars, pigeons] hacer carreras de; [horses] hacer correr. ◇ *vi* -1. [rush] ir corriendo. -2. [beat fast] acelerarse.

race car *Am* = **racing car**.

racecourse ['reɪskɔːs] *n* hipódromo *m*.

race driver *Am* = **racing driver**.

racehorse ['reɪshɔːs] *n* caballo *m* de carreras.

race meeting *n* concurso *m* hípico.

race relations *npl* relaciones *fpl* entre distintas razas.

race riot *n* disturbio *m* racial.

racetrack ['reɪstræk] *n* [for horses] hipódromo *m*; [for cars] autódromo *m*, pista *f* (de carreras); [for runners] pista *f* (de carreras).

racial discrimination ['reɪʃl-] *n* discriminación *f* racial.

racialism *etc* ['reɪʃəlɪzm] = **racism** *etc*.

racing ['reɪsɪŋ] *n* carreras *fpl*; **motor ~** carreras de coches.

racing car *Br*, **race car** *Am n* coche *m* de carreras.

racing driver *Br*, **race driver** *Am n* piloto *m* y *f* de carreras.

racism ['reɪsɪzm] *n* racismo *m*.

racist ['reɪsɪst] ◇ *adj* racista. ◇ *n* racista *m* y *f*.

rack [ræk] ◇ *n* -1. [for plates] escurreplatos *m inv*; [for clothes] percha *f*; [for magazines] revistero *m*; [for bottles] botellero *m*. -2. [for luggage] portaequipajes *m inv*. ◇ *vt*: **to be ~ed by** OR **with** *literary* estar transido(da) de; **to ~** *Br* OR **cudgel** *Am* **one's brains** devanarse los sesos.

racket ['rækɪt] *n* -1. [noise] jaleo *m*, alboroto *m*, guachafita *f Amer*. -2. [swindle] timo *m*. -3. [illegal activity] negocio *m* sucio. -4. SPORT raqueta *f*.

racketeering [,rækə'tɪərɪŋ] *n pej* estafa *f*, timo *m*.

raconteur [,rækɒn'tɜːr] *n persona que sabe contar anécdotas.*

racquet ['rækɪt] *n* SPORT = **racket**.

racy ['reɪsɪ] (*compar* **-ier**, *superl* **-iest**) *adj* entretenido(da) y picante.

RADA ['rɑːdə] (*abbr of* **Royal Academy of**

Dramatic Art) *n academia británica de arte dramático*.

radar ['reɪdɑːr] *n* radar *m*.

radar trap *n* radar *m* para controlar la velocidad de los automóviles.

radial (tyre) ['reɪdjəl-] *n* neumático *m* radial.

radian ['reɪdjən] *n* radián *f*.

radiance ['reɪdjəns] *n* **-1.** [of face, smile] lo radiante. **-2.** *literary* [brilliance] resplandor *m*.

radiant ['reɪdjənt] *adj* **-1.** [happy] radiante. **-2.** *literary* [brilliant] resplandeciente. **-3.** TECH por radiación.

radiate ['reɪdɪeɪt] ◇ *vt* lit & *fig* irradiar. ◇ *vi* **-1.** [be emitted] ser irradiado(da). **-2.** [spread from centre] salir, extenderse.

radiation [,reɪdɪ'eɪʃn] *n* radiación *f*.

radiation sickness *n* enfermedad *f* causada por la radiación.

radiator ['reɪdɪeɪtər] *n* radiador *m*.

radiator grille *n* calandra *f*.

radical ['rædɪkl] ◇ *adj* radical. ◇ *n* POL radical *m* y *f*.

radically ['rædɪklɪ] *adv* radicalmente.

radii ['reɪdɪaɪ] *pl* → radius.

radio ['reɪdɪəʊ] (*pl* **-s**) ◇ *n* radio *f*, radio *m* Amer. ◇ *comp* de radio, radiofónico(ca). ◇ *vt* mandar un mensaje por radio a.

radioactive [,reɪdɪəʊ'æktɪv] *adj* radiactivo(va).

radioactive waste *n* (*U*) residuos *mpl* radiactivos.

radioactivity [,reɪdɪəʊæk'tɪvətɪ] *n* radiactividad *f*.

radio alarm *n* radiodespertador *m*.

radio-controlled *adj* teledirigido(da).

radio frequency *n* radiofrecuencia *f*.

radiogram ['reɪdɪəʊ,græm] *n* [apparatus] radiogramola *f*.

radiographer [,reɪdɪ'ɒgrəfər] *n* radiógrafo *m*, -fa *f*.

radiography [,reɪdɪ'ɒgrəfɪ] *n* radiografía *f*.

radiology [,reɪdɪ'ɒlədʒɪ] *n* radiología *f*.

radiopaging ['reɪdɪəʊ,peɪdʒɪŋ] *n* localización *f* por busca.

radiotelephone [,reɪdɪəʊ'telɪfəʊn] *n* radioteléfono *m*.

radiotherapist [,reɪdɪəʊ'θerəpɪst] *n* radioterapeuta *m* y *f*.

radiotherapy [,reɪdɪəʊ'θerəpɪ] *n* radioterapia *f*.

radish ['rædɪʃ] *n* rábano *m*.

radium ['reɪdɪəm] *n* radio *m*.

radius ['reɪdɪəs] (*pl* **radii**) *n* [gen & ANAT] radio *m*.

radon ['reɪdɒn] *n* radón *m*.

RAF [ɑːreɪ'ef, ræf] *n abbr of* **Royal Air Force**.

raffia ['ræfɪə] *n* rafia *f*.

raffish ['ræfɪʃ] *adj* disoluto(ta) pero con encanto.

raffle ['ræfl] ◇ *n* rifa *f*, sorteo *m*. ◇ *comp*: ~ **ticket** boleto *m*. ◇ *vt* rifar, sortear.

raft [rɑːft] *n* **-1.** [craft] balsa *f*. **-2.** [large number]: **a** ~ **of policies** POL un montón de disposiciones.

rafter ['rɑːftər] *n* par *m* (*de armadura de tejado*).

rag [ræg] *n* **-1.** [piece of cloth] trapo *m*, harapo *m*; **it was like a red** ~ **to a bull** era una provocación total. **-2.** *pej* [newspaper] periodicucho *m*.

◆ **rags** *npl* [clothes] trapos *mpl*; **from** ~**s to riches** de la pobreza a la riqueza.

ragamuffin ['rægə,mʌfɪn] *n* golfillo *m*, galopín *m*.

rag-and-bone man *n* trapero *m*.

ragbag ['rægbæg] *n pej* batiburrillo *m*.

rag doll *n* muñeca *f* de trapo.

rage [reɪdʒ] ◇ *n* **-1.** [fury] rabia *f*, ira *f*; **to fly into a** ~ montar en cólera. **-2.** *inf* [fashion]: **the** ~ la moda; **it's all the** ~ es la última moda. ◇ *vi* **-1.** [behave angrily] estar furioso(sa). **-2.** [subj: storm, sea] enfurecerse; [subj: disease] hacer estragos; [subj: argument, controversy] continuar con violencia.

ragged ['rægɪd] *adj* **-1.** [wearing torn clothes] andrajoso(sa), harapiento(ta). **-2.** [torn] hecho(cha) jirones. **-3.** [uneven, poor-quality] desigual.

raging ['reɪdʒɪŋ] *adj* terrible.

ragout ['ræguː] *n* ragú *m*.

ragtime ['rægtaɪm] *n* ragtime *m*.

rag trade *n inf*: **the** ~ la industria del vestir.

rag week *n Br* semana en que los universitarios organizan actividades divertidas con fines benéficos.

raid [reɪd] ◇ *n* **-1.** [attack] incursión *f*. **-2.** [forced entry - by robbers] asalto *m*; [- by police] redada *f*. ◇ *vt* **-1.** [attack] atacar por sorpresa. **-2.** [subj: robbers] asaltar; [subj: police] hacer una redada en.

raider ['reɪdər] *n* **-1.** [attacker] invasor *m*, -ra *f*. **-2.** [thief] ladrón *m*, -ona *f*, asaltante *m* y *f*.

rail [reɪl] ◇ *n* **-1.** [on staircase] baranda *f*, barandilla *f*. **-2.** [bar] barra *f*; **towel** ~ toallero *m*. **-3.** [of railway line] carril *m*, riel *m*. **-4.** [form of transport] ferrocarril *m*; **by** ~ por ferrocarril. ◇ *comp* ferroviario(ria).

railcard ['reɪlkɑːd] *n Br* tarjeta que permite algunos descuentos al viajar en tren.

railing ['reɪlɪŋ] *n* reja *f*.

railway *Br* ['reɪlweɪ], **railroad** *Am* ['reɪlrəʊd] *n* **-1.** [company] ferrocarril *m*. **-2.** [route] línea *f* de ferrocarril.

railway engine *n* locomotora *f*.

railway line *n* línea *f* de ferrocarril.

railwayman ['reɪlweɪmən] (*pl* **-men** [-mən]) *n Br* ferroviario *m*.

railway station *n* estación *f* de ferrocarril.

railway track *n* vía *f* férrea.

rain [reɪn] ◇ *n* lluvia *f*. ◇ *v impers* METEOR llover. ◇ *vi* caer.

◆ **rain down** *vi* llover.

◆ **rain off** *Br*, **rain out** *Am vt sep* interrumpir a causa de la lluvia.

rainbow ['reɪnbəʊ] *n* arco *m* iris.

rain check *n Am*: **I'll take a ~ (on that)** no lo quiero ahora, pero igual me apunto la próxima vez.

raincoat ['reɪnkəʊt] *n* impermeable *m*.

raindrop ['reɪndrɒp] *n* gota *f* de lluvia.

rainfall ['reɪnfɔːl] *n* pluviosidad *f*.

rain forest *n* bosque *m* tropical.

rain gauge *n* pluviómetro *m*.

rainproof ['reɪnpruːf] *adj* impermeable.

rainstorm ['reɪnstɔːm] *n* temporal *m* de lluvia.

rainwater ['reɪn,wɔːtəʳ] *n* agua *f* de lluvia.

rainy ['reɪnɪ] (*compar* **-ier**, *superl* **-iest**) *adj* lluvioso(sa).

raise [reɪz] ◇ *vt* **-1.** [lift up] levantar; **to ~ o.s.** levantarse. **-2.** [increase - level] aumentar; **to ~ one's voice** levantar la voz. **-3.** [improve] elevar. **-4.** [obtain - from donations] recaudar; [- by selling, borrowing] conseguir. **-5.** [memory, thoughts] traer, evocar; [doubts] levantar. **-6.** [bring up, breed] criar. **-7.** [crops] cultivar. **-8.** [mention] plantear. **-9.** [build] construir, erigir. ◇ *n Am* aumento *m*, subida *f*.

raisin ['reɪzn] *n* pasa *f*.

Raj [rɑːdʒ] *n*: **the ~** el imperio británico en la India (*antes de 1947*).

rajah ['rɑːdʒə] *n* rajá *m*.

rake [reɪk] ◇ *n* **-1.** [implement] rastrillo *m*. **-2.** *dated* & *literary* [immoral man] libertino *m*, calavera *m*. ◇ *vt* **-1.** [smooth] rastrillar. **-2.** [gather] recoger con el rastrillo.

◆ **rake in** *vt sep inf* amasar.

◆ **rake up** *vt sep* sacar a relucir.

rake-off *n inf* tajada *f*.

rakish ['reɪkɪʃ] *adj* **-1.** [dissolute] libertino(na), disoluto(ta). **-2.** [jaunty] ladeado(da).

rally ['rælɪ] (*pl* **-ies**, *pt* & *pp* **-ied**) ◇ *n* **-1.** [meeting] mitin *m*, reunión *f*. **-2.** [car race]

rally *m*. **-3.** [in tennis etc] peloteo *m*. ◇ *vt* reunir. ◇ *vi* **-1.** [come together] reunirse. **-2.** [recover] recuperarse.

◆ **rally round** ◇ *vt fus* formar una piña con. ◇ *vi inf* formar una piña.

rallycross ['rælɪkrɒs] *n* autocross *m*.

rallying ['rælɪɪŋ] *n* rally *m*.

rallying cry *n* grito *m* de guerra.

rallying point *n* punto *m* de encuentro.

ram [ræm] (*pt* & *pp* **-med**, *cont* **-ming**) ◇ *n* carnero *m*. ◇ *vt* **-1.** [crash into] chocar con OR contra. **-2.** [force] embutir. **-3.** *phr*: **to ~ sthg home** dejar algo bien claro.

RAM [ræm] (*abbr of* **random access memory**) *n* COMPUT RAM *f*.

Ramadan [,ræmə'dæn] *n* ramadán *m*.

ramble ['ræmbl] ◇ *n* paseo *m* por el campo. ◇ *vi* **-1.** [walk] pasear. **-2.** [talk] divagar.

◆ **ramble on** *vi* divagar sin parar.

rambler ['ræmbləʳ] *n* [walker] excursionista *m y f*.

rambling ['ræmblɪŋ] *adj* **-1.** [building, house] laberíntico(ca); [town] desparramado(da). **-2.** [speech, writing] confuso(sa), incoherente.

RAMC (*abbr of* **Royal Army Medical Corps**) *n cuerpo médico de las fuerzas armadas británicas*.

ramekin ['ræmɪkɪn] *n* recipiente *m* individual para el horno.

ramification [,ræmɪfɪ'keɪʃn] *n* ramificación *f*.

ramp [ræmp] *n* **-1.** [slope] rampa *f*. **-2.** AUT [in road] rompecoches *m inv*.

rampage [ræm'peɪdʒ] ◇ *n*: **to go on the ~** desbandarse, salir a la desbanda. ◇ *vi* desbandarse, salir a la desbanda.

rampant ['ræmpənt] *adj* desenfrenado(da).

ramparts ['ræmpɑːts] *npl* murallas *fpl*.

ramshackle ['ræm,ʃækl] *adj* destartalado(da).

ran [ræn] *pt* → **run**.

RAN (*abbr of* **Royal Australian Navy**) *n armada australiana*.

ranch [rɑːntʃ] *n* rancho *m*.

rancher ['rɑːntʃəʳ] *n* ranchero *m*, -ra *f*.

ranch house *n Am* **-1.** [house on ranch] hacienda *f*, estancia *f*. **-2.** [ranch-style house] rancho *m*.

rancid ['rænsɪd] *adj* rancio(cia).

rancour *Br*, **rancor** *Am* ['ræŋkəʳ] *n* rencor *m*.

random ['rændəm] ◇ *adj* fortuito(ta), hecho(cha) al azar. ◇ *n*: **at ~** al azar.

random access memory *n* COMPUT memoria *f* de acceso aleatorio.

rasp

randomly ['rændəmlɪ] *adv* al azar.

randomness ['rændəmnɪs] *n* lo fortuito.

R and R (*abbr of* **rest and recreation**) *n Am* permiso militar.

randy ['rændɪ] (*compar* **-ier**, *superl* **-iest**) *adj inf* cachondo(da), caliente.

rang [ræŋ] *pt* → **ring**.

range [reɪndʒ] (*cont* **rangeing**) ◇ *n* **-1.** [of missile, telescope] alcance *m*; [of ship, plane] autonomía *f*; **to be out of/within ~** estar fuera del/al alcance; **at close ~** de cerca. **-2.** [variety] variedad *f*, gama *f*. **-3.** [of prices, salaries] escala *f*. **-4.** [of mountains] sierra *f*, cordillera *f*. **-5.** [shooting area] campo *m* de tiro. **-6.** [of voice] registro *m*.
◇ *vt* alinear.
◇ *vi* **-1.** [vary]: **to ~ from ... to ...**, **to ~ between ... and ...** oscilar OR fluctuar entre ... y .... **-2.** [deal with, include]: **to ~ over sthg** comprender algo.

ranger ['reɪndʒəʳ] *n* guardabosques *m y f inv*.

Rangoon [ræŋ'guːn] *n* Rangún.

rangy ['reɪndʒɪ] (*compar* **-ier**, *superl* **-iest**) *adj* zancudo(da).

rank [ræŋk] ◇ *adj* **-1.** [utter, absolute - bad luck, outsider] absoluto(ta); [- disgrace, injustice] flagrante. **-2.** [foul] pestilente.
◇ *n* **-1.** [position, grade] grado *m*, graduación *f*; **to pull ~** abusar de su autoridad. **-2.** [social class] clase *f*, categoría *f*; **the ~ and file** las bases (del partido). **-3.** [row] fila *f*, hilera *f*; **to close ~s** cerrar filas.
◇ *vt* **-1.** [class]: **to be ~ed** estar clasificado(da). **-2.** *Am* [outrank] ser de más alta graduación que.
◇ *vi*: **to ~ as** estar considerado(da) (como); **to ~ among** encontrarse entre.
◆ **ranks** *npl* **-1.** MIL: **the ~s** los soldados rasos. **-2.** *fig* [members] filas *fpl*.

ranking ['ræŋkɪŋ] ◇ *n* clasificación *f*. ◇ *adj Am* de alta graduación.

rankle ['ræŋkl] *vi* amargar, doler.

ransack ['rænsæk] *vt* [search] registrar a fondo; [plunder] saquear.

ransom ['rænsəm] *n* rescate *m*; **to hold sb to ~** [keep prisoner] pedir rescate por alguien; *fig* hacer chantaje a alguien.

rant [rænt] *vi* despotricar.

ranting ['ræntɪŋ] *n* despotrique *m*.

rap [ræp] (*pt & pp* **-ped**, *cont* **-ping**) ◇ *n* **-1.** [knock] golpecito *m*. **-2.** [type of music] rap *m*. **-3.** *phr*: **to take the ~** pagar el pato. ◇ *vt* dar golpecitos en. ◇ *vi* **-1.** [knock]: **to ~ on sthg** dar golpecitos en algo. **-2.** [sing rap music] cantar rap.

rapacious [rə'peɪʃəs] *adj fml* [greedy] rapaz, codicioso(sa).

rapacity [rə'pæsətɪ] *n fml* rapacidad *f*, codicia *f*.

rape [reɪp] ◇ *n* **-1.** [crime] violación *f*. **-2.** [of countryside etc] destrucción *f*. **-3.** BOT colza *f*. ◇ *vt* violar.

rapeseed ['reɪpsiːd] *n* semilla *f* de colza.

rapid ['ræpɪd] *adj* rápido(da).
◆ **rapids** *npl* rápidos *mpl*.

rapid-fire *adj* **-1.** MIL [gun] de tiro rápido. **-2.** *fig* [spoken quickly] lanzado uno tras otro (lanzada una tras otra).

rapidity [rə'pɪdətɪ] *n* rapidez *f*.

rapidly ['ræpɪdlɪ] *adv* rápidamente.

rapidness ['ræpɪdnɪs] = **rapidity**.

rapist ['reɪpɪst] *n* violador *m*, -ra *f*.

rapper ['ræpəʳ] *n* rápper *m y f*, intérprete *m y f* de rap.

rapport [ræ'pɔːʳ] *n* compenetración *f*; **to have a ~ with sb** compenetrarse con alguien.

rapprochement [ræ'prɒʃmɑ̃] *n* acercamiento *m*.

rapt [ræpt] *adj* absorto(ta), ensimismado(da).

rapture ['ræptʃəʳ] *n* arrebato *m*, arrobamiento *m*; **to go into ~s over** OR **about** deshacerse en elogios a.

rapturous ['ræptʃərəs] *adj* muy entusiasta.

rare [reəʳ] *adj* **-1.** [scarce] poco común, raro(ra). **-2.** [infrequent] poco frecuente, raro(ra). **-3.** [exceptional] raro(ra), excepcional. **-4.** CULIN poco hecho(cha).

rarefied ['reərɪfaɪd] *adj* **-1.** [exalted] exclusivo(va), elevado(da). **-2.** [lacking in oxygen] enrarecido(da).

rarely ['reəlɪ] *adv* raras veces.

rareness ['reənɪs] *n* **-1.** [scarcity] rareza *f*. **-2.** [infrequency] infrecuencia *f*.

raring ['reərɪŋ] *adj*: **to be ~ to go** estar ansioso(sa) por empezar.

rarity ['reərətɪ] (*pl* **-ies**) *n* rareza *f*.

rascal ['rɑːskl] *n* pícaro *m*, -ra *f*, tunante *m*, -ta *f*.

rash [ræʃ] ◇ *adj* precipitado(da). ◇ *n* **-1.** MED erupción *f* (cutánea), sarpullido *m*, jiote *m Amer*. **-2.** [spate] aluvión *m*.

rasher ['ræʃəʳ] *n* loncha *f*.

rashly ['ræʃlɪ] *adv* precipitadamente.

rashness ['ræʃnɪs] *n* precipitación *f*, impetuosidad *f*.

rasp [rɑːsp] ◇ *n* [harsh sound] chirrido *m*. ◇ *vi* [subj: person] hablar con voz áspera y estridente; [subj: voice] tener un sonido áspero y estridente.

raspberry ['rɑːzbərɪ] (*pl* **-ies**) *n* **-1.** [fruit] frambuesa *f*. **-2.** [rude sound] pedorreta *f*.

rasping ['rɑːspɪŋ] *adj* áspero(ra) y estridente.

rasta ['ræstə] *n inf* rasta *m* y *f*.

rastafarian [,ræstə'feərɪən] *n* rastafari *m* y *f*.

rat [ræt] *n* **-1.** [animal] rata *f*; **to smell a ~** olerse que hay gato encerrado. **-2.** *pej* [person] canalla *m* y *f*.

ratbag ['rætbæg] *n Br pej* granuja *m* y *f*.

ratchet ['rætʃɪt] *n* trinquete *m*.

rate [reɪt] ◇ *n* **-1.** [speed] velocidad *f*; **at this ~** a este paso. **-2.** [of birth, death] índice *m*; [of unemployment, inflation] tasa *f*. **-3.** [price] precio *m*, tarifa *f*; [of interest] tipo *m*. ◇ *vt* **-1.** [consider]: **to ~ sthg/sb (as/among)** considerar algo/a alguien (como/entre). **-2.** [deserve] merecer.
◆ **rates** *npl Br* ≃ contribución *f* urbana.
◆ **at any rate** *adv* **-1.** [at least] al menos. **-2.** [anyway] de todos modos.

rateable value ['reɪtəbl-] *n Br* valor *m* catastral.

rate of exchange *n* (tipo *m* de) cambio *m*.

ratepayer ['reɪt,peɪər] *n Br* contribuyente *m* y *f*.

rather ['rɑːðər] *adv* **-1.** [to quite a large extent] bastante; **I ~ thought so** eso es lo que pensaba. **-2.** [to a limited extent] algo; **he's ~ like you** se parece (en) algo a ti. **-3.** [as preference]: **I would ~ wait** preferiría esperar; **I'd ~ not** mejor que no. **-4.** [more exactly]: **or ~ ...** o más bien ..., o mejor dicho .... **-5.** [on the contrary]: **(but) ~ ...** (sino) más bien OR por el contrario ....
◆ **rather than** *conj* antes que.

ratification [,rætɪfɪ'keɪʃn] *n* ratificación *f*.

ratify ['rætɪfaɪ] (*pt & pp* **-ied**) *vt* ratificar.

rating ['reɪtɪŋ] *n* **-1.** [standing] clasificación *f*, posición *f*. **-2.** *Br* [sailor] marinero *m*.
◆ **ratings** *npl* índices *mpl* de audiencia.

ratio ['reɪʃɪəʊ] (*pl* **-s**) *n* proporción *f*, relación *f*.

ration ['ræʃn] ◇ *n* ración *f*. ◇ *vt* racionar.
◆ **rations** *npl* víveres *mpl*.

rational ['ræʃənl] *adj* racional.

rationale [,ræʃə'nɑːl] *n* lógica *f*, razones *fpl*.

rationalization [,ræʃənəlaɪ'zeɪʃn] *n* racionalización *f*.

rationalize, -ise ['ræʃənəlaɪz] *vt* racionalizar.

rationing ['ræʃənɪŋ] *n* racionamiento *m*.

rat race *n* mundo despiadadamente competitivo de los negocios.

rattle ['rætl] ◇ *n* **-1.** [of engine, metal] ruido *m*, traqueteo *m*; [of glass] tintineo *m*; [of typewriter] repiqueteo *m*. **-2.** [toy] sonajero

m. ◇ *vt* **-1.** [make rattle] hacer sonar. **-2.** [unsettle] desconcertar. ◇ *vi* golpetear; [gunfire] tabletear.
◆ **rattle off** *vt sep* decir de corrido.
◆ **rattle on** *vi*: **to ~ on (about)** hablar sin parar (sobre).
◆ **rattle through** *vt fus* acabar en un santiamén.

rattlesnake ['rætlsneɪk], **rattler** *Am* ['rætlər] *n* serpiente *f* de cascabel.

ratty ['rætɪ] (*compar* **-ier**, *superl* **-iest**) *adj inf* **-1.** *Br* [in bad mood] picajoso(sa), irritable. **-2.** *Am* [in bad condition - person] desastrado(da); [- thing] destartalado(da).

raucous ['rɔːkəs] *adj* ronco(ca) y estridente.

raunchy ['rɔːntʃɪ] (*compar* **-ier**, *superl* **-iest**) *adj* sexy (*inv*).

ravage ['rævɪdʒ] *vt* estragar, asolar.
◆ **ravages** *npl* estragos *mpl*.

rave [reɪv] ◇ *adj* muy entusiasta. ◇ *n Br inf* [party] juerga *f*. ◇ *vt inf*: **to ~ it up** divertirse de lo lindo. ◇ *vi* **-1.** [talk angrily]: **to ~ at sb** increpar a alguien; **to ~ against sb/sthg** despotricar contra alguien/algo. **-2.** [talk enthusiastically]: **to ~ about sthg** deshacerse en alabanzas sobre algo.

raven ['reɪvn] ◇ *adj* negro azabache. ◇ *n* cuervo *m*.

ravenous ['rævənəs] *adj* [person, animal] famélico(ca), hambriento(ta); [appetite] voraz.

raver ['reɪvər] *n Br inf* juergista *m* y *f*, parrandero *m*, -ra *f*.

rave-up *n Br inf* juerga *f*.

ravine [rə'viːn] *n* barranco *m*.

raving ['reɪvɪŋ] *adj* [lunatic] de atar; [fantasy] delirante.
◆ **ravings** *npl* desvaríos *mpl*.

ravioli [,rævɪ'əʊlɪ] *n* (*U*) raviolis *mpl*.

ravish ['rævɪʃ] *vt* embelesar.

ravishing ['rævɪʃɪŋ] *adj* [sight, beauty] de ensueño; [person] bellísimo(ma).

raw [rɔː] *adj* **-1.** [uncooked] crudo(da). **-2.** [untreated] en bruto, sin refinar. **-3.** [painful - wound] en carne viva. **-4.** [inexperienced] novato(ta), inexperto(ta). **-5.** [cold] crudo(da), frío(a).

raw deal *n*: **to get a ~** recibir un trato injusto.

raw material *n* materia *f* prima.

ray [reɪ] *n* rayo *m*; **~ of hope** resquicio *m* de esperanza.

rayon ['reɪɒn] *n* rayón *m*.

raze [reɪz] *vt* destruir por completo, arrasar.

razor ['reɪzər] *n* [wet shaver] navaja *f*; [electric machine] maquinilla *f* de afeitar.

razor blade *n* hoja *f* de afeitar.

razor-sharp *adj* -1. [very sharp] muy afilado(da). -2. *fig* [very quick] muy agudo(da).

razzle ['ræzl] *n Br inf*: **to go on the** ~ irse de juerga.

razzmatazz ['ræzəmətæz] *n inf* revuelo *m*.

R & B *n abbr of* **rhythm and blues**.

RC *abbr of* **Roman Catholic**.

RCA (*abbr of* **Royal College of Art**) *n escuela londinense de bellas artes*.

RCAF (*abbr of* **Royal Canadian Air Force**) *n fuerzas aéreas canadienses*.

RCMP (*abbr of* **Royal Canadian Mounted Police**) *n policía montada de Canadá*.

RCN *n* -1. (*abbr of* **Royal College of Nursing**) *sindicato británico de enfermeras*. -2. (*abbr of* **Royal Canadian Navy**) *armada canadiense*.

Rd *abbr of* **road**.

R & D (*abbr of* **research and development**) *n* I & D.

RDC (*abbr of* **rural district council**) *n ayuntamiento de un municipio rural en Gran Bretaña*.

re [riː] *prep* Ref.

RE *n* -1. (*abbr of* **religious education**) *religión f*. -2. (*abbr of* **Royal Engineers**) *unidad del ejército británico encargada de la construcción de fortificaciones, puentes y otras obras de ingeniería*.

reach [riːtʃ] ◇ *n* alcance *m*; **he has a long** ~ tiene los brazos largos; **within (sb's)** ~ [easily touched] al alcance (de alguien); [easily travelled to] a poco distancia (de alguien); **out of** OR **beyond sb's** ~ fuera del alcance de alguien.
◇ *vt* -1. [gen] alcanzar, llegar a; **to** ~ **an agreement/a decision** llegar a un acuerdo/una decisión; **to** ~ **an objective** alcanzar un objetivo. -2. [arrive at - place etc] llegar a. -3. [get by stretching - object, shelf] alcanzar. -4. [contact] localizar, contactar con.
◇ *vi*: **to** ~ **out/across** alargar la mano; **to** ~ **down** agacharse.
◆ **reaches** *npl* [of river] tramo *m* recto; **upper lower** ~**es** parte *f* alta/baja.

reachable ['riːtʃəbl] *adj* -1. [place] accesible. -2. [person, organization] localizable; **he's** ~ **by phone** se le puede contactar por teléfono.

react [rɪ'ækt] *vi* -1. [respond]: **to** ~ **(to)** reaccionar (a OR ante). -2. [rebel]: **to** ~ **against** reaccionar en contra de. -3. CHEM: **to** ~ **with** reaccionar con. -4. MED: **to** ~ **to sthg** sufrir una reacción por algo.

reaction [rɪ'ækʃn] *n*: ~ **(to/against)** reacción *f* (a/contra).

reactionary [rɪ'ækʃənrɪ] ◇ *adj* reaccionario(ria). ◇ *n* reaccionario *m*, -ria *f*.

reactivate [rɪ'æktɪveɪt] *vt* reactivar.

reactor [rɪ'æktər] *n* reactor *m*.

read [riːd] (*pt* & *pp* **read** [red]) ◇ *vt* -1. [gen] leer. -2. [subj: sign, words] poner, decir. -3. [interpret] interpretar. -4. [subj: thermometer, meter etc] marcar. -5. *Br* UNIV estudiar. ◇ *vi* -1. [person] leer. -2. [read aloud]: **to** ~ **(to sb)** leerle (a alguien). -3. [piece of writing] leerse. ◇ *n*: **to be a good** ~ ser una lectura amena.
◆ **read into** *vt sep*: **I wouldn't** ~ **too much into it** no le des demasiada importancia.
◆ **read out** *vt sep* leer en voz alta.
◆ **read up on** *vt fus* leer OR documentarse sobre.

readable ['riːdəbl] *adj* ameno(na), que se lee con agrado.

readdress [ˌriːə'dres] *vt* reexpedir.

reader ['riːdər] *n* [person who reads] lector *m*, -ra *f*.

readership ['riːdəʃɪp] *n* [total number of readers] lectores *mpl*.

readily ['redɪlɪ] *adv* -1. [willingly] de buena gana, de buen grado. -2. [easily] en seguida.

readiness ['redɪnɪs] *n* -1. [preparation]: **to be in a state of** ~ estar preparado(da). -2. [willingness]: ~ **(to do sthg)** buena disposición *f* (para hacer algo).

reading ['riːdɪŋ] *n* -1. [gen] lectura *f*. -2. [recital] recital *m*.

reading lamp *n* flexo *m*.

reading room *n* sala *f* de lectura.

readjust [ˌriːə'dʒʌst] ◇ *vt* reajustar, ajustar. ◇ *vi*: **to** ~ **(to)** volverse a adaptar (a).

readmit [ˌriːəd'mɪt] *vt* readmitir.

readout ['riːdaʊt] *n* COMPUT texto *m* en pantalla.

read-through [riːd-] *n* leída *f*.

ready ['redɪ] (*pt* & *pp* **-ied**) ◇ *adj* -1. [prepared] listo(ta), preparado(da); **to be** ~ **for sthg/to do sthg** estar listo para algo/para hacer algo. -2. [willing]: **to be** ~ **to do sthg** estar dispuesto(ta) a hacer algo. -3. [in need of]: **to be** ~ **for sthg** necesitar algo. -4. [likely]: **to be** ~ **to do sthg** estar a punto de hacer algo. -5. [cash] contante; [smile] pronto(ta). ◇ *vt* preparar.

ready cash *n* dinero *m* contante.

ready-made *adj* -1. [products] hecho(cha); [clothes] confeccionado(da). -2. *fig* [excuse etc] a la medida.

ready money *n* dinero *m* contante.

ready-to-wear *adj* confeccionado(da).

reaffirm [ˌriːə'fɜːm] *vt* reafirmar.

reafforest [ˌriːə'fɒrɪst] *vt* repoblar con árboles.

reafforestation ['riːəˌfɒrɪ'steɪʃn] *n* repoblación *f* forestal.

real ['rɪəl] ◇ *adj* **-1.** [not imagined, actual] real; **the ~ thing** lo auténtico; **this isn't a joke, it's the ~ thing** esto no va en broma, va en serio; **for ~** de verdad; **in ~ terms** en términos reales. **-2.** [genuine, proper] auténtico(ca). ◇ *adv Am* muy.

real ale *n Br* cerveza *f* hecha a la manera tradicional.

real estate *n* propiedad *f* inmobiliaria.

realign [,ri:ə'laɪn] *vt* volver a alinear.

realignment [,ri:ə'laɪnmənt] *n* nueva alineación *f*.

realism ['rɪəlɪzm] *n* realismo *m*.

realist ['rɪəlɪst] *n* realista *m y f*.

realistic [,rɪə'lɪstɪk] *adj* realista; **to be ~ about** ser realista acerca de.

realistically [,rɪə'lɪstɪklɪ] *adv* **-1.** [reasonably] de manera realista. **-2.** [accurately] con realismo.

reality [rɪ'ælətɪ] (*pl* **-ies**) *n* realidad *f*; **in ~** en realidad.

realization [,rɪəlaɪ'zeɪʃn] *n* **-1.** [recognition] comprensión *f*. **-2.** [achievement] consecución *f*.

realize, -ise ['rɪəlaɪz] *vt* **-1.** [become aware of] darse cuenta de. **-2.** [produce, achieve, make profit of] realizar.

reallocate [,ri:'æləkeɪt] *vt* redistribuir.

really ['rɪəlɪ] ◇ *adv* **-1.** [for emphasis] de verdad; **~ good** buenísimo; **~ bad** malísimo. **-2.** [actually, honestly] realmente, en realidad. **-3.** [to sound less negative] en realidad. ◇ *excl* **-1.** [expressing doubt]: **~?** [in affirmatives] ¿ah sí?; [in negatives] ¿ah no? **-2.** [expressing surprise, disbelief]: **~?** ¿de verdad?, ¿seguro? **-3.** [expressing anger]: **~!** ¡hay que ver!

realm [relm] *n* **-1.** [field] campo *m*, esfera *f*. **-2.** [kingdom] reino *m*.

real-time *adj* COMPUT en tiempo real.

realtor ['rɪəltər] *n Am* agente inmobiliario *m*, agente inmobiliaria *f*.

ream [ri:m] *n* resma *f*.
◆ **reams** *npl* montones *mpl*.

reap ['ri:p] *vt lit & fig* cosechar.

reappear [,ri:ə'pɪər] *vi* reaparecer.

reappearance [,ri:ə'pɪərəns] *n* reaparición *f*.

reapply [,ri:ə'plaɪ] (*pt & pp* **-ied**) *vi*: **to ~ (for)** volver a presentar una solicitud (para).

reappraisal [,ri:ə'preɪzl] *n* revaluación *f*.

reappraise [,ri:ə'preɪz] *vt* replantear, reexaminar.

rear [rɪər] ◇ *adj* trasero(ra), de atrás. ◇ *n* **-1.** [back] parte *f* de atrás; **to be at the ~** estar al final; **to bring up the ~** cerrar la marcha. **-2.** *inf* [bottom] trasero *m*. ◇ *vt* criar. ◇ *vi*: **to ~ (up)** encabritarse.

rear admiral *n* contraalmirante *m*.

rearguard action ['rɪəgɑ:d-] *n*: **to fight a ~** MIL atacar desde la retaguardia; *fig* emprender una última tentativa.

rear light *n* luz *f* trasera, calavera *f Amer*.

rearm [ri:'ɑ:m] ◇ *vt* rearmar. ◇ *vi* rearmarse.

rearmament [rɪ'ɑ:məmənt] *n* rearme *m*.

rearmost ['rɪəməust] *adj* último(ma).

rearrange [,ri:ə'reɪndʒ] *vt* **-1.** [room, furniture] colocar de otro modo; [system, plans] reorganizar. **-2.** [meeting] volver a concertar.

rearrangement [,ri:ə'reɪndʒmənt] *n* **-1.** [reorganization] reorganización *f*. **-2.** [rescheduling] nueva concertación *f*.

rearview mirror ['rɪəvju:-] *n* espejo *m* retrovisor.

reason ['ri:zn] ◇ *n* **-1.** [cause]: **~ (for)** razón *f* (para); **by ~ of** a causa de; **for some ~** por alguna razón. **-2.** [justification]: **to have ~ to do sthg** tener motivo para hacer algo. **-3.** [rationality] razón *f*, sensatez *f*; **it stands to ~** es razonable; **to listen to ~** avenirse a razones. ◇ *vt & vi* razonar.
◆ **reason with** *vt fus* razonar con.

reasonable ['ri:znəbl] *adj* razonable.

reasonably ['ri:znəblɪ] *adv* razonablemente.

reasoned ['ri:znd] *adj* razonado(da).

reasoning ['ri:znɪŋ] *n* razonamiento *m*.

reassemble [,ri:ə'sembl] ◇ *vt* **-1.** [reconstruct] volver a montar. **-2.** [regroup] reagrupar. ◇ *vi* reagruparse, volver a reunirse.

reassess [,ri:ə'ses] *vt* revaluar, reconsiderar.

reassessment [,ri:ə'sesmənt] *n* revaluación *f*.

reassurance [,ri:ə'ʃɔ:rəns] *n* **-1.** (*U*) [comfort] palabras *fpl* tranquilizadoras. **-2.** [promise] promesa *f*, compromiso *m*.

reassure [,ri:ə'ʃɔ:r] *vt* tranquilizar.

reassuring [,ri:ə'ʃɔ:rɪŋ] *adj* tranquilizador(ra).

reawaken [,ri:ə'weɪkn] *vt* volver a despertar.

rebate ['ri:beɪt] *n* devolución *f*, bonificación *f*.

rebel [*n* 'rebl, *vb* rɪ'bel] (*pt & pp* **-led**, *cont* **-ling**) ◇ *n* rebelde *m y f*. ◇ *vi*: **to ~ (against)** rebelarse (contra), alebrestarse (contra) *Amer*.

rebellion [rɪ'beljən] *n* rebelión *f*.

rebellious [rɪ'beljəs] *adj* rebelde.

rebirth [,ri:'bɜ:θ] *n* renacimiento *m*.

rebound [*n* 'riːbaʊnd, *vb* ˌrɪ'baʊnd] ◇ *n*: **on the ~** [ball] de rebote *m*; **to marry on the ~** casarse por despecho. ◇ *vi* **-1.** [bounce back] rebotar. **-2.** [harm]: **to ~ on** OR **upon sb** volverse contra alguien.

rebuff [rɪ'bʌf] ◇ *n* desaire *m*, negativa *f*. ◇ *vt* desairar, rechazar.

rebuild [ˌriː'bɪld] *vt* reconstruir.

rebuke [rɪ'bjuːk] ◇ *n* reprimenda *f*, reprobación *f*. ◇ *vt*: **to ~ sb (for)** reprender a alguien (por).

rebut [riː'bʌt] (*pt* & *pp* **-ted**, *cont* **-ting**) *vt* rebatir, refutar.

rebuttal [riː'bʌtl] *n* refutación *f*.

rec. *abbr of* **received**.

recalcitrant [rɪ'kælsɪtrənt] *adj* recalcitrante.

recall [rɪ'kɔːl] ◇ *n* **-1.** [memory] memoria *f*. **-2.** [change]: **beyond ~** inalterable. ◇ *vt* **-1.** [remember] recordar, acordarse de. **-2.** [ambassador] retirar, hacer volver.

recant [rɪ'kænt] ◇ *vt* [statement, opinion] retractarse de; [religion] renegar de. ◇ *vi* [deny statement] retractarse; [deny religion] renegar de la fe.

recap ['riːkæp] (*pt* & *pp* **-ped**, *cont* **-ping**) *inf* ◇ *n* resumen *m*, recapitulación *f*. ◇ *vt* **-1.** [summarize] recapitular, resumir. **-2.** *Am* [tyre] recauchutar. ◇ *vi* recapitular, resumir.

recapitulate [ˌriːkə'pɪtjʊleɪt] *vt* & *vi* recapitular, resumir.

recapture [ˌriː'kæptʃəʳ] ◇ *n* reconquista *f*. ◇ *vt* **-1.** [experience again] revivir, volver a experimentar. **-2.** MIL [regain] reconquistar, volver a tomar. **-3.** [catch again] volver a capturar.

recd, **rec'd** *abbr of* **received**.

recede [riː'siːd] *vi* **-1.** [person, car] alejarse; [coastline] retroceder. **-2.** [light] apagarse; [colour] difuminarse. **-3.** *fig* [disappear] esfumarse. **-4.** [hair]: **his hair is receding** empieza a tener entradas.

receding [rɪ'siːdɪŋ] *adj* [chin] medida hacia dentro; [forehead] hundida; **~ hairline** entradas *fpl*.

receipt [rɪ'siːt] *n* recibo *m*; **to acknowledge ~** acusar recibo.

◆ **receipts** *npl* recaudación *f*.

receivable [rɪ'siːvəbl] *adj* **-1.** [able to be received] admisible. **-2.** [liable for payment] por cobrar.

receive [rɪ'siːv] ◇ *vt* **-1.** [gen] recibir. **-2.** [reaction] tener; [injury, setback] sufrir. **-3.** [greet]: **to be well/badly ~d** tener una buena/mala acogida. ◇ *vi* [in tennis etc] restar.

receiver [rɪ'siːvəʳ] *n* **-1.** [of telephone] auricular *m*. **-2.** [radio, TV set] receptor *m*. **-3.**

[criminal] perista *m* y *f*, receptador *m*, -ra *f*. **-4.** FIN síndico *m*, -ca *f*.

receivership [rɪ'siːvəʃɪp] *n* bancarrota *f*.

receiving end [rɪ'siːvɪŋ-] *n*: **to be on the ~ (of)** ser la víctima (de).

recent ['riːsnt] *adj* reciente.

recently ['riːsntlɪ] *adv* recientemente.

receptacle [rɪ'septəkl] *n* receptáculo *m*.

reception [rɪ'sepʃn] *n* recepción *f*.

reception centre *n* centro *m* de acogida.

reception class *n* *Br* primer curso *m* de primaria.

reception desk *n* recepción *f*.

receptionist [rɪ'sepʃənɪst] *n* recepcionista *m* y *f*.

reception room *n* sala *f* de estar, salón *m*.

receptive [rɪ'septɪv] *adj* receptivo(va); **to be ~ to sthg** estar abierto a algo.

receptiveness [rɪ'septɪvnɪs] *n* receptividad *f*.

recess ['riːses, *Br* rɪ'ses] *n* **-1.** [vacation] período *m* vacacional; **to be in ~** estar clausurado(da); **to go into ~** suspender las sesiones. **-2.** [alcove] nicho *m*, hueco *m*. **-3.** *Am* SCH recreo *m*.

◆ **recesses** *npl* [of mind, heart] recovecos *mpl*; [of building] escondrijos *mpl*.

recessed ['riːsest, *Br* rɪ'sest] *adj* empotrado(da).

recession [rɪ'seʃn] *n* recesión *f*.

recessionary [rɪ'seʃənrɪ] *adj* recesivo(va).

recessive [rɪ'sesɪv] *adj* BIOL recesivo(va).

recharge [ˌriː'tʃɑːdʒ] *vt* recargar.

rechargeable [ˌriː'tʃɑːdʒəbl] *adj* recargable.

recipe ['resɪpɪ] *n* CULIN & *fig* receta *f*.

recipient [rɪ'sɪpɪənt] *n* [of letter, cheque] destinatario *m*, -ria *f*.

reciprocal [rɪ'sɪprəkl] *adj* recíproco(ca).

reciprocate [rɪ'sɪprəkeɪt] ◇ *vt* corresponder a. ◇ *vi* corresponder.

recital [rɪ'saɪtl] *n* recital *m*.

recitation [ˌresɪ'teɪʃn] *n* recitación *f*.

recite [rɪ'saɪt] *vt* **-1.** [poem] recitar. **-2.** [list] enumerar.

reckless ['reklɪs] *adj* imprudente, temerario(ria).

recklessness ['reklɪsnɪs] *n* imprudencia *f*, temeridad *f*.

reckon ['rekn] *vt* **-1.** *inf* [think]: **to ~ (that)** pensar que, suponer que. **-2.** [consider, judge]: **to be ~ed to be sthg** ser considerado(da) algo. **-3.** [expect]: **to ~ to do sthg** esperar hacer algo. **-4.** [calculate] calcular.

◆ **reckon on** *vt fus* contar con.

◆ **reckon with** *vt fus* **-1.** [expect] contar con. **-2.** [face, deal with]: **he/she** *etc* **is a** force to be ~ed with es alguien a tener muy en cuenta.

◆ **reckon without** *vt fus* no contar con.

reckoning ['rekənɪŋ] *n* [calculation] cálculo *m*; **by my ~** según mis cálculos.

reclaim [rɪ'kleɪm] *vt* **-1.** [claim back] reclamar. **-2.** [recover]: **to ~ land from the sea** ganarle tierra al mar.

reclamation [,reklə'meɪʃn] *n* conversión *f* en terreno utilizable.

recline [rɪ'klaɪn] *vi* reclinarse.

reclining [rɪ'klaɪnɪŋ] *adj* reclinable.

recluse [rɪ'kluːs] *n* solitario *m*, -ria *f*.

reclusive [rɪ'kluːsɪv] *adj* solitario(ria), retraído(da).

recognition [,rekəg'nɪʃn] *n* reconocimiento *m*; **beyond** OR **out of all ~** de modo irreconocible; **in ~ of** en reconocimiento a.

recognizable ['rekəgnaɪzəbl] *adj* reconocible.

recognize, -ise ['rekəgnaɪz] *vt* reconocer.

recoil [*vb* rɪ'kɔɪl, *n* 'riːkɔɪl] ◇ *vi* **-1.** [draw back] retroceder, echarse atrás. **-2.** *fig* [shrink from]: **to ~ from** OR **at sthg** [truth, bad news] esquivar OR rehuir algo; [idea, suggestion] estremecerse ante algo. ◇ *n* [of gun] retroceso *m*, culatazo *m*.

recollect [,rekə'lekt] *vt* recordar.

recollection [,rekə'lekʃn] *n* recuerdo *m*; **I have no ~ of** it no lo recuerdo.

recommence [,riːkə'mens] ◇ *vt & vi* volver a empezar, recomenzar.

recommend [,rekə'mend] *vt* recomendar.

recommendation [,rekəmen'deɪʃn] *n* recomendación *f*.

recommended retail price [,rekə'mendɪd-] *n* precio *m* recomendado.

recompense ['rekəmpens] ◇ *n*: **~ (for)** compensación *f* OR indemnización *f* (por). ◇ *vt*: **to ~ sb (for)** recompensar a alguien (por).

reconcile ['rekənsaɪl] *vt* **-1.** [find agreement between] conciliar; **to ~ sthg with** hacer compatible algo con. **-2.** [make friendly again] reconciliar; **to be ~d with sb** reconciliarse con alguien. **-3.** [accept]: **to ~ o.s. to** resignarse a.

reconciliation [,rekənsɪlɪ'eɪʃn] *n* **-1.** [accommodation] conciliación *f*. **-2.** [forgiveness] reconciliación *f*.

recondite ['rekəndaɪt] *adj fml* abstruso(sa).

reconditioned [,riːkən'dɪʃnd] *adj* revisado(da), reparado(da).

reconnaissance [rɪ'kɒnɪsəns] *n* reconocimiento *m*.

reconnect [,riːkə'nekt] *vt* volver a conectar.

reconnoitre *Br*, **reconnoiter** *Am* [,rekə'nɔɪtə*r*] ◇ *vt* reconocer. ◇ *vi* hacer un reconocimiento.

reconsider [,riːkən'sɪdə*r*] *vt & vi* reconsiderar.

reconstitute [,riː'kɒnstɪtjuːt] *vt* **-1.** [re-form] reconstituir. **-2.** [dried food] poner en remojo.

reconstruct [,riːkən'strʌkt] *vt* **-1.** [building, crime] reconstruir. **-2.** [system, policy] rehacer.

reconstruction [,riːkən'strʌkʃn] *n* reconstrucción *f*.

reconvene [,riːkən'viːn] *vt* convocar de nuevo.

record [*n & adj* 'rekɔːd, *vb* rɪ'kɔːd] ◇ *n* **-1.** [of event, piece of information] registro *m*, anotación *f*; [of meeting] actas *fpl*; **on ~** [on file] archivado; [ever recorded] de que se tiene constancia; **to go/be on ~ as saying that ...** declarar/haber declarado públicamente que ...; **off the ~** confidencial. **-2.** [vinyl disc] disco *m*. **-3.** [best achievement] récord *m*. **-4.** [history] historial *m*; **criminal ~** antecedentes *mpl* penales; **school ~** expediente *m* académico. **-5.** *phr*: **to set** OR **put the ~ straight** dejar las cosas bien claras.
◇ *vt* **-1.** [write down] anotar, tomar nota de. **-2.** [put on tape] grabar.
◇ *adj* récord (*inv*).

record-breaker *n* plusmarquista *m y f*.

record-breaking *adj* que rompe todos los récords.

recorded delivery [rɪ'kɔːdɪd-] *n* correo *m* certificado.

recorder [rɪ'kɔːdə*r*] *n* **-1.** [machine] grabadora *f*. **-2.** [musical instrument] flauta *f*.

record holder *n* plusmarquista *m y f*.

recording [rɪ'kɔːdɪŋ] *n* grabación *f*.

recording studio *n* estudio *m* de grabación.

record library *n* fonoteca *f*, discoteca *f*.

record player *n* tocadiscos *m inv*.

recount [*n* 'riːkaʊnt, *vt sense 1* rɪ'kaʊnt, *sense 2* ,riː'kaʊnt] ◇ *n* recuento *m*. ◇ *vt* **-1.** [narrate] narrar. **-2.** [count again] volver a contar.

recoup [rɪ'kuːp] *vt* recuperar.

recourse [rɪ'kɔːs] *n fml*: **to have ~ to** recurrir a.

recover [rɪ'kʌvə*r*] ◇ *vt* **-1.** [retrieve, recoup] recuperar. **-2.** [regain - calm etc] recobrar; **to ~ o.s.** reponerse. ◇ *vi*: **to ~ (from)** recuperarse (de).

recoverable [rɪ'kʌvrəbl] *adj* FIN recuperable.

recovery [rɪ'kʌvərɪ] (*pl* **-ies**) *n* recuperación *f*.

recovery vehicle *n* *Br* vehículo *m* de asistencia en carretera.

recreate [ˌriː'krɪəɪt] *vt* [reproduce] recrear.

recreation [ˌrekrɪ'eɪʃn] *n* [leisure] esparcimiento *m*, recreo *m*.

recreational [ˌrekrɪ'eɪʃənl] *adj* de recreo.

recreation room *n* **-1.** [in public building] sala *f* de recreo. **-2.** *Am* [in house] sala *f* de juegos.

recrimination [rɪˌkrɪmɪ'neɪʃn] *n* recriminación *f*.

recrudescence [ˌriːkruː'desns] *n* *fml* recrudecimiento *m*.

recruit [rɪ'kruːt] ◇ *n* recluta *m* y *f*. ◇ *vt* **-1.** [gen] reclutar; **to ~ sb (for sthg/to do sthg)** reclutar a alguien (para algo/para hacer algo). **-2.** [find, employ] contratar. ◇ *vi* buscar empleados nuevos.

recruitment [rɪ'kruːtmənt] *n* [gen] reclutamiento *m*; [of staff] contratación *f*.

rectangle ['rek.tæŋgl] *n* rectángulo *m*.

rectangular [rek'tæŋgjʊlə] *adj* rectangular.

rectification [ˌrektɪfɪ'keɪʃn] *n* *fml* rectificación *f*.

rectify ['rektɪfaɪ] (*pt* & *pp* **-ied**) *vt* *fml* rectificar.

rectitude ['rektɪtjuːd] *n* *fml* rectitud *f*.

rector ['rektə] *n* **-1.** [priest] párroco *m*. **-2.** *Scot* [head - of school] director *m*, -ra *f*; [- of college, university] rector *m*, -ra *f*.

rectory ['rektərɪ] (*pl* **-ies**) *n* rectoría *f*.

rectum ['rektəm] (*pl* **-s**) *n* recto *m*.

recuperate [rɪ'kuːpəreɪt] *vi* *fml*: **to ~ (from)** recuperarse (de).

recuperation [rɪˌkuːpə'reɪʃn] *n* recuperación *f*.

recur [rɪ'kɜːr] (*pt* & *pp* **-red**, *cont* **-ring**) *vi* repetirse, volver a producirse.

recurrence [rɪ'kʌrəns] *n* *fml* repetición *f*.

recurrent [rɪ'kʌrənt] *adj* que se repite, periódico(ca).

recurring [rɪ'kɜːrɪŋ] *adj* **-1.** [often repeated] que se repite, periódico(ca). **-2.** MATH: **3.3 ~** 3,3 periódico.

recyclable [ˌriː'saɪkləbl] *adj* reciclable.

recycle [ˌriː'saɪkl] *vt* reciclar.

red [red] (*compar* **-der**, *superl* **-dest**) ◇ *adj* rojo(ja); [hair] pelirrojo(ja). ◇ *n* [colour] rojo *m*; **to be in the ~** *inf* estar en números rojos; **to see ~** ponerse hecho(cha) una furia. ◆ **Red** *pej* POL ◇ *adj* rojo(ja). ◇ *n* rojo *m*, -ja *f*.

red alert *n*: **(to be on) ~** (estar en) alerta *f* roja.

red blood cell *n* glóbulo *m* rojo.

red-blooded [-'blʌdɪd] *adj* *hum* viril.

red-brick *Br* *adj* [building] de ladrillo rojo.

◆ **redbrick** *adj* *Br* UNIV: **the redbrick universities** *las universidades británicas de provincias construidas a finales del siglo XIX*.

red card *n* FTBL: **to show sb the ~** mostrarle a alguien (la) tarjeta roja.

red carpet *n*: **to roll out the ~ for sb** recibir a alguien con todos los honores. ◆ **red-carpet** *adj*: **to give sb the red-carpet treatment** dispensar a alguien un gran recibimiento.

Red Crescent *n*: **the ~** la Media Luna Roja.

Red Cross *n*: **the ~** la Cruz Roja.

redcurrant ['redkʌrənt] *n* **-1.** [fruit] grosella *f*. **-2.** [bush] grosellero *m*.

red deer *n* ciervo *m*.

redden ['redn] ◇ *vt* [make red] teñir de rojo. ◇ *vi* [flush] enrojecer.

redecorate [ˌriː'dekəreɪt] *vt* & *vi* volver a pintar (*o empapelar*).

redeem [rɪ'diːm] *vt* **-1.** [save, rescue] salvar, rescatar; **he ~ed himself for his mistake** reparó su error. **-2.** *fml* [at pawnbroker's] desempeñar.

redeeming [rɪ'diːmɪŋ] *adj*: **his only ~ feature** lo único que le salva.

redefine [ˌriːdɪ'faɪn] *vt* volver a definir.

redemption [rɪ'dempʃn] *n* RELIG redención *f*; **beyond** OR **past ~** *fig* que no tiene remedio, irremediable.

redeploy [ˌriːdɪ'plɔɪ] *vt* reorganizar.

redeployment [ˌriːdɪ'plɔɪmənt] *n* reorganización *f*, redistribución *f*.

redesign [ˌriːdɪ'zaɪn] *vt* **-1.** [replan, redraw] diseñar de nuevo. **-2.** [rethink] elaborar de nuevo.

redevelop [ˌriːdɪ'veləp] *vt* reconstruir, volver a urbanizar.

redevelopment [ˌriːdɪ'veləpmənt] *n* reconstrucción *f*.

red-faced [-'feɪst] *adj* **-1.** [flushed] rojo(ja), colorado(da). **-2.** [with embarrassment] rojo(ja) de vergüenza.

red-haired [-'heəd] *adj* pelirrojo(ja).

red-handed [-'hændɪd] *adj*: **to catch sb ~** coger a alguien con las manos en la masa.

redhead ['redhed] *n* pelirrojo *m*, -ja *f*.

red herring *n* *fig* [unhelpful clue] pista *f* falsa; [means of distracting attention] ardid *m* para distraer la atención.

red-hot *adj* [metal, person, passion] al rojo (vivo); [zeal] ardiente, fervoroso(sa).

redid [ˌriː'dɪd] *pt* → redo.

Red Indian ◇ *adj* piel roja. ◇ *n* piel roja

m y f (atención: el término 'Red Indian' se considera racista).

redirect [ˌriːdɪˈrekt] *vt vt* **-1.** [retarget] redirigir. **-2.** [send elsewhere] enviar a otro lugar. **-3.** [forward] reexpedir.

rediscover [ˌriːdɪˈskʌvəʳ] *vt* **-1.** [re-experience] volver a descubrir. **-2.** [make popular, famous again]: **to be ~ed** ser descubierto(ta) de nuevo.

redistribute [ˌriːdɪˈstrɪbjuːt] *vt* redistribuir.

red-letter day *n* día *m* señalado.

red light *n* [traffic signal] semáforo *m* rojo.

red-light district *n* barrio *m* chino, barrios *mpl* bajos.

red meat *n* carne *f* roja.

redness [ˈrednɪs] *n* rojez *f*.

redo [ˌriːˈduː] (*pt* **-did**, *pp* **-done**) *vt* **-1.** [do again] volver a hacer. **-2.** *inf* [redecorate] volver a pintar (*o empapelar*).

redolent [ˈredələnt] *adj literary* **-1.** [reminiscent]: **~ of** evocador(ra) de. **-2.** [smelling]: **~ of** que huele a, con olor a.

redouble [ˌriːˈdʌbl] *vt*: **to ~ one's efforts (to do sthg)** redoblar esfuerzos (para hacer algo).

redoubtable [rɪˈdautəbl] *adj fml* imponente.

redraft [ˌriːˈdrɑːft] *vt* volver a redactar.

redraw [ˌriːˈdrɔː] (*pt* **-drew**, *pp* **-drawn** [-ˈdrɔːn]) *vt* volver a dibujar.

redress [rɪˈdres] *fml ⋄ n* (U) reparación *f*, desagravio *m*. *⋄ vt*: **to ~ the balance (between)** equilibrar la balanza (entre).

redrew [ˌriːˈdruː] *pt →* **redraw**.

Red Sea *n*: **the ~** el mar Rojo.

Red Square *n* la plaza Roja.

red squirrel *n* ardilla *f* roja.

red tape *n fig* papeleo *m*.

reduce [rɪˈdjuːs] *⋄ vt* reducir; **to be ~d to doing sthg** verse rebajado OR forzado a hacer algo; **to be ~d to** verse sumido OR hundido en. *⋄ vi Am* [diet] (intentar) adelgazar.

reduced [rɪˈdjuːst] *adj* **-1.** [smaller] reducido(da). **-2.** [poorer]: **in ~ circumstances** venido(da) a menos.

reduction [rɪˈdʌkʃn] *n* **-1.** [gen]: **~ (in)** reducción *f* (de). **-2.** COMM: **~ (of)** descuento *m* (de).

redundancy [rɪˈdʌndənsɪ] (*pl* **-ies**) *n* **-1.** *Br* [job loss] despido *m*. **-2.** [unemployment] desempleo *m*.

redundancy payment *n Br* indemnización *f* (por despido).

redundant [rɪˈdʌndənt] *adj* **-1.** *Br* [jobless]: **to be made ~** perder el empleo. **-2.** [not required - equipment, factory] innecesario(ria); [- comment] redundante.

redwood [ˈredwʊd] *n*: **~ (tree)** secoya *f*.

reecho [ˌriːˈekəʊ] *⋄ vt* repetir. *⋄ vi* resonar.

reed [riːd] *⋄ n* **-1.** [plant] carrizo *m*, cañavera *f*. **-2.** [of musical instrument] lengüeta *f*. *⋄ comp* de carrizo.

reeducate [ˌriːˈedjʊkeɪt] *vt* reeducar.

reedy [ˈriːdɪ] (*compar* **-ier**, *superl* **-iest**) *adj* [voice] agudo(da), chillón(ona).

reef [riːf] *n* arrecife *m*.

reek [riːk] *⋄ n* hedor *m*. *⋄ vi*: **to ~ (of)** apestar (a).

reel [riːl] *⋄ n* [of cotton, film, on fishing rod] carrete *m*. *⋄ vi* **-1.** [stagger] tambalearse, hacer eses. **-2.** [whirl - mind] dar vueltas. **-3.** [be stunned]: **to ~ from sthg** quedarse atónito(ta) por algo.

◆ **reel in** *vt sep* sacar enrollando el carrete (*en pesca*).

◆ **reel off** *vt sep* recitar al corrido.

reelect [ˌriːɪˈlekt] *vt*: **to ~ sb (as)** reelegir a alguien (como).

reelection [ˌriːɪˈlekʃn] *n* reelección *f*.

reemphasize [ˌriːˈemfəsaɪz] *vt* recalcar OR subrayar de nuevo.

reenact [ˌriːɪˈnækt] *vt* representar de nuevo.

reenter [ˌriːˈentəʳ] *vt* volver a entrar en.

reentry [ˌriːˈentrɪ] *n* reingreso *m*, nueva entrada *f*.

reexamine [ˌriːɪgˈzæmɪn] *vt* examinar de nuevo, reexaminar.

reexport [ˌriːˈekspɔːt] COMM *⋄ n* **-1.** [act of exporting] reexportación *f*. **-2.** [goods exported] mercancía *f* reexportada. *⋄ vt* reexportar.

ref [ref] *n* **-1.** (*abbr of* **referee**) *inf* SPORT árbitro *m*. **-2.** (*abbr of* **reference**) ADMIN ref.

refectory [rɪˈfektərɪ] (*pl* **-ies**) *n* refectorio *m*.

refer [rɪˈfɜːʳ] (*pt & pp* **-red**, *cont* **-ring**) *vt* **-1.** [send, direct]: **to ~ sb to** [to place] enviar a alguien a; [to source of information] remitir a alguien a. **-2.** [report, submit]: **to ~ sthg to** remitir algo a.

◆ **refer to** *vt fus* **-1.** [mention, speak about] referirse a. **-2.** [consult] consultar.

referee [ˌrefəˈriː] *⋄ n* **-1.** SPORT árbitro *m*. **-2.** *Br* [for job application] *persona que recomienda a alguien para un trabajo.* *⋄ vt & vi* SPORT arbitrar.

reference [ˈrefrəns] *n* **-1.** [mention, reference number]: **to make ~ to** hacer referencia a; **with ~ to** *fml* con referencia a. **-2.** (U) [for advice, information]: **~ (to)** consulta *f* (a); **for future ~** para consultas futuras. **-3.** [for job - letter] referencias *fpl*; [- person] *persona que recomienda a alguien para un trabajo.*

reference book *n* libro *m* de consulta.

reference library *n* biblioteca *f* de consulta.

reference number *n* número *m* de referencia.

referendum [,refə'rendəm] (*pl* -s OR -da [-də]) *n* referéndum *m*.

referral [rɪ'fɜːrəl] *n* (*U*) *fml* remisión *f*.

refill [*n* 'riːfɪl, *vb* ,riː'fɪl] ◇ *n inf*: **would you like a ~?** ¿te apetece otra copa? ◇ *vt* volver a llenar.

refillable [,riː'fɪləbl] *adj* [bottle] rellenable; [pen] recargable.

refine [rɪ'faɪn] *vt* -1. [oil, food] refinar. -2. [plan, speech] pulir.

refined [rɪ'faɪnd] *adj* -1. [oil, food, person] refinado(da). -2. [equipment, theory] perfeccionado(da).

refinement [rɪ'faɪnmənt] *n* -1. [improvement]: **~ (on)** mejora *f* (de). -2. (*U*) [gentility] refinamiento *m*.

refinery [rɪ'faɪnərɪ] (*pl* -ies) *n* refinería *f*.

refit [*n* 'riːfɪt, *vb* ,riː'fɪt] (*pt* & *pp* -ted, *cont* -ting) ◇ *n* [of ship] reacondicionamiento *m*. ◇ *vt* [ship] reacondicionar.

reflate [,riː'fleɪt] ECON ◇ *vt* reflacionar. ◇ *vi* reflacionarse.

reflation [,riː'fleɪʃn] *n* ECON reflación *f*.

reflationary [riː'fleɪʃənrɪ] *adj* ECON reflacionario(ria).

reflect [rɪ'flekt] ◇ *vt* -1. [gen] reflejar; **to be ~ed in** reflejarse en. -2. [think, consider]: **to ~ that ...** considerar que .... ◇ *vi*: **to ~ (on** OR **upon)** reflexionar (sobre).

reflection [rɪ'flekʃn] *n* -1. [gen] reflejo *m*. -2. [criticism]: **~ on** crítica *f* de. -3. [thinking] reflexión *f*; **on ~** pensándolo bien. -4. [thought]: **~s (on)** reflexiones *fpl* (sobre).

reflective [rɪ'flektɪv] *adj* -1. [thoughtful] reflexivo(va). -2. [shiny] reflectante.

reflector [rɪ'flektər] *n* reflector *m*.

reflex ['riːfleks] *n*: **~ (action)** (acto *m*) reflejo *m*.
◆ **reflexes** *npl* reflejos *mpl*.

reflex camera *n* cámara *f* réflex.

reflexive [rɪ'fleksɪv] *adj* GRAMM reflexivo(va).

reflexology [,riːflek'sɒlədʒɪ] *n* reflexoterapia *f*.

reforest [,riː'fɒrɪst] = **reafforest**.

reforestation [riː,fɒrɪ'steɪʃn] = **reafforestation**.

reform [rɪ'fɔːm] ◇ *n* reforma *f*. ◇ *vt* reformar. ◇ *vi* reformarse.

reformat [,riː'fɔːmæt] (*pt* & *pp* -ted, *cont* -ting) *vt* COMPUT formatear de nuevo.

Reformation [,refə'meɪʃn] *n*: **the ~** la Reforma.

reformatory [rɪ'fɔːmətrɪ] *n Am* reformatorio *m*, centro *m* de menores.

reformed [rɪ'fɔːmd] *adj* [better behaved] reformado(da).

reformer [rɪ'fɔːmər] *n* reformador *m*, -ra *f*.

reformist [rɪ'fɔːmɪst] ◇ *adj* reformista. ◇ *n* reformista *m y f*.

refract [rɪ'frækt] ◇ *vt* refractar. ◇ *vi* refractarse.

refrain [rɪ'freɪn] ◇ *n* [chorus] estribillo *m*. ◇ *vi fml*: **to ~ from doing sthg** abstenerse de hacer algo.

refresh [rɪ'freʃ] *vt* refrescar; **to ~ sb's memory** refrescarle la memoria a alguien.

refreshed [rɪ'freʃt] *adj* descansado(da), vigorizado(da).

refresher course [rɪ'freʃər-] *n* cursillo *m* de reciclaje.

refreshing [rɪ'freʃɪŋ] *adj* [change, honesty, drink] refrescante; [sleep] vigorizante.

refreshments [rɪ'freʃmənts] *npl* refrigerio *m*.

refrigerate [rɪ'frɪdʒəreɪt] *vt* refrigerar.

refrigeration [rɪ,frɪdʒə'reɪʃn] *n* refrigeración *f*.

refrigerator [rɪ'frɪdʒəreɪtər] *n* refrigerador *m*.

refuel [,riː'fjʊəl] (*Br pt* & *pp* -led, *cont* -ling, *Am pt* & *pp* -ed, *cont* -ing) ◇ *vt* llenar de carburante. ◇ *vi* repostar.

refuge ['refjuːdʒ] *n* refugio *m*; **to seek** OR **take ~ (in)** *fig* buscar refugio (en).

refugee [,refjʊ'dʒiː] *n* refugiado *m*, -da *f*.

refugee camp *n* campamento *m* de refugiados.

refund [*n* 'riːfʌnd, *vb* rɪ'fʌnd] ◇ *n* reembolso *m*. ◇ *vt*: **to ~ sthg to sb**, **to ~ sb sthg** reembolsar algo a alguien.

refurbish [,riː'fɜːbɪʃ] *vt* [building] restaurar; [office, shop] renovar.

refurbishment [,riː'fɜːbɪʃmənt] *n* [of building] restauración *f*; [of office, shop] renovación *f*.

refurnish [,riː'fɜːnɪʃ] *vt* volver a amueblar.

refusal [rɪ'fjuːzl] *n* -1. [disagreement, saying no]: **~ (to do sthg)** negativa *f* (a hacer algo). -2. [withholding, denial] denegación *f*. -3. [non-acceptance]: **to meet with ~** ser rechazado(da).

refuse[1] [rɪ'fjuːz] ◇ *vt* -1. [withold, deny]: **to ~ sb sthg**, **to ~ sthg to sb** denegar a alguien algo. -2. [decline, reject] rechazar. -3. [not agree, be completely unwilling]: **to ~ to do sthg** negarse a hacer algo. ◇ *vi* negarse, decir que no.

refuse² ['refjuːs] *n* [rubbish] basura *f*.

refuse collection ['refjuːs-] *n* recogida *f* de basuras.

refuse collector ['refjuːs-] *n* basurero *m*, -ra *f*.

refuse dump ['refjuːs-] *n* vertedero *m* (de basuras).

refute [rɪ'fjuːt] *vt fml* refutar.

reg., regd. *(abbr of* registered): ~ **trademark** marca *f* registrada.

regain [rɪ'geɪn] *vt* [leadership, first place] recuperar; [health, composure] recobrar.

regal ['riːgl] *adj* regio(gia).

regale [rɪ'geɪl] *vt*: **to ~ sb with** entretener a alguien con.

regalia [rɪ'geɪljə] *n* (U) *fml* ropaje *m*, vestiduras *fpl*.

regard [rɪ'gɑːd] ◇ *n* -**1.** *fml* [respect, esteem]: ~ **(for)** estima *f* OR respeto *m* (por); **to hold sthg/sb in high ~** tener algo/a alguien en gran estima. -**2.** [aspect]: **in this/that ~** a este/ese respecto. ◇ *vt* -**1.** [consider]: **to ~ o.s. as sthg** considerarse algo; **to ~ sthg/sb as** considerar algo/a alguien como. -**2.** [look at, view]: **to ~ sb/sthg with** ver a alguien/algo con; **to be highly ~ed** estar muy bien considerado.
◆ **regards** *npl* [in greetings] recuerdos *mpl*.
◆ **as regards** *prep* en cuanto a, por lo que se refiere a.
◆ **in regard to, with regard to** *prep* respecto a, en cuanto a.

regarding [rɪ'gɑːdɪŋ] *prep* respecto a, en cuanto a.

regardless [rɪ'gɑːdlɪs] *adv* a pesar de todo.
◆ **regardless of** *prep* sin tener en cuenta; ~ **of the cost** cueste lo que cueste.

regatta [rɪ'gætə] *n* regata *f*.

Regency ['riːdʒənsɪ] *adj* del estilo regencia.

regenerate [rɪ'dʒenəreɪt] *vt* regenerar.

regeneration [rɪ,dʒenə'reɪʃn] *n* regeneración *f*.

regent ['riːdʒənt] ◇ *adj* regente. ◇ *n* regente *m y f*.

reggae ['regeɪ] *n* reggae *m*.

regime [reɪ'ʒiːm] *n* régimen *m*.

regiment ['redʒɪmənt] *n* MIL regimiento *m*.

regimental [,redʒɪ'mentl] *adj* MIL del regimiento.

regimented ['redʒɪmentɪd] *adj pej* [life, workers] estrictamente controlado(da); [garden, rows] ordenado(da) en filas.

region ['riːdʒən] *n* región *f*; **in the ~ of** alrededor de.

regional ['riːdʒənl] *adj* regional.

register ['redʒɪstə'] ◇ *n* [of electors etc] registro *m*; [at school] lista *f*. ◇ *vt* -**1.** [record - gen] registrar; [- car] matricular. -**2.** [express] mostrar, reflejar. ◇ *vi* -**1.** [be put on official list]: **to ~ (as/for)** inscribirse (como/para). -**2.** [book in - at hotel] registrarse; [- at conference] inscribirse. -**3.** *inf* [be noticed]: **I told him but it didn't seem to ~** se lo dije, pero no pareció que lo captara.

registered ['redʒɪstəd] *adj* -**1.** [officially listed] inscrito(ta) oficialmente. -**2.** [letter, parcel] certificado(da).

registered nurse *n* enfermera *f* diplomada.

registered post *Br*, **registered mail** *Am n* correo *m* certificado.

registered trademark *n* marca *f* registrada.

registrar [,redʒɪ'strɑː'] *n* -**1.** [keeper of records] registrador *m*, -ra *f* oficial. -**2.** UNIV secretario *m*, -ria *f* general. -**3.** [doctor] médico *m*, -ca *f* de hospital.

registration [,redʒɪ'streɪʃn] *n* -**1.** [gen] registro *m*. -**2.** AUT = **registration number**.

registration document *n* documentos *mpl* de matriculación.

registration number *n* número *m* de matrícula.

registry ['redʒɪstrɪ] *(pl* -**ies)** *n* registro *m*.

registry office *n* registro *m* civil.

regress [rɪ'gres] *vi fml*: **to ~ (to)** sufrir un retroceso (a).

regression [rɪ'greʃn] *n fml* regresión *f*.

regressive [rɪ'gresɪv] *adj fml* regresivo(va).

regret [rɪ'gret] *(pt & pp* -**ted,** *cont* -**ting)** ◇ *n* -**1.** *fml* [sorrow] pesar *m*. -**2.** [sad feeling]: **I've no ~s about it** no lo lamento en absoluto; **he sends his ~s** manda sus excusas. ◇ *vt* [be sorry about]: **to ~ sthg/doing sthg** lamentar algo/haber hecho algo; **we ~ to announce ...** lamentamos comunicar ....

regretful [rɪ'gretful] *adj* [person] pesaroso(sa); [smile, look] de arrepentimiento.

regretfully [rɪ'gretfulɪ] *adv* con pesar; ~, **we have to announce ...** lamentamos tener que anunciar ...

regrettable [rɪ'gretəbl] *adj fml* lamentable.

regrettably [rɪ'gretəblɪ] *adv* lamentablemente.

regroup [,riː'gruːp] *vi* reagruparse.

regt *(abbr of* regiment) regto.

regular ['regjulə'] ◇ *adj* -**1.** [gen] regular. -**2.** [customer] habitual, asiduo(dua). -**3.** [time, place] acostumbrado(da); [problem] usual, normal. -**4.** *Am* [pleasant] legal. ◇ *n* cliente *m* habitual.

regular army *n* ejército *m* regular.

regularity [ˌregjʊˈlærətɪ] n regularidad f.

regularly [ˈregjʊlǝlɪ] adv -1. [gen] con regularidad. -2. [equally spaced] de manera uniforme.

regulate [ˈregjʊleɪt] vt regular.

regulation [ˌregjʊˈleɪʃn] ◇ adj [standard] reglamentario(ria). ◇ n -1. [rule] regla f, norma f. -2. (U) [control] regulación f.

regurgitate [rɪˈgɜːdʒɪteɪt] vt -1. [bring up] regurgitar. -2. fig & pej [repeat] repetir maquinalmente.

rehabilitate [ˌriːǝˈbɪlɪteɪt] vt rehabilitar.

rehabilitation [ˈriːǝˌbɪlɪˈteɪʃn] n rehabilitación f.

rehash [ˌriːˈhæʃ] vt inf pej hacer un refrito de.

rehearsal [rɪˈhɜːsl] n ensayo m.

rehearse [rɪˈhɜːs] ◇ vt ensayar. ◇ vi: to ~ (for) ensayar (para).

rehouse [ˌriːˈhaʊz] vt dar una nueva vivienda a, realojar.

reign [reɪn] lit & fig ◇ n reinado m. ◇ vi: to ~ (over) reinar (sobre).

reigning [ˈreɪnɪŋ] adj actual.

reimburse [ˌriːɪmˈbɜːs] vt: to ~ sb (for sthg) reembolsar a alguien (algo).

reimbursement [ˌriːɪmˈbɜːsmǝnt] n fml: ~ (for) reembolso m (de OR por).

rein [reɪn] n fig: to give (a) free ~ to sb, to give sb free ~ dar rienda suelta a alguien; to keep a tight ~ on sb/sthg tener muy controlado(da) a alguien/algo.

◆ **reins** npl -1. [for horse] riendas fpl. -2. [for child] andadores mpl.

◆ **rein in** vt sep [horse] refrenar.

reincarnation [ˌriːɪnkɑːˈneɪʃn] n reencarnación f.

reindeer [ˈreɪnˌdɪǝ] (pl inv) n reno m.

reinforce [ˌriːɪnˈfɔːs] vt reforzar.

reinforced concrete [ˌriːɪnˈfɔːst-] n cemento m OR hormigón m armado.

reinforcement [ˌriːɪnˈfɔːsmǝnt] n refuerzo m.

◆ **reinforcements** npl refuerzos mpl.

reinstate [ˌriːɪnˈsteɪt] vt -1. [give job back to] restituir OR reintegrar en su puesto a. -2. [bring back] restablecer.

reinstatement [ˌriːɪnˈsteɪtmǝnt] n [of worker] rehabilitación f (laboral).

reinterpret [ˌriːɪnˈtɜːprɪt] vt interpretar de nuevo, reinterpretar.

reintroduce [ˈriːˌɪntrǝˈdjuːs] vt reintroducir.

reintroduction [riːˌɪntrǝˈdʌkʃn] n reintroducción f.

reissue [riːˈɪʃuː] ◇ n reedición f, reimpre-

sión f. ◇ vt [gen] reeditar, reimprimir; [film] reestrenar, reponer.

reiterate [riːˈɪtǝreɪt] vt fml reiterar.

reiteration [riːˌɪtǝˈreɪʃn] n fml reiteración f.

reject [n ˈriːdʒekt, vb rɪˈdʒekt] ◇ n desecho m; ~s artículos mpl defectuosos. ◇ vt rechazar.

rejection [rɪˈdʒekʃn] n rechazo m.

rejig [ˌriːˈdʒɪg] (pt & pp -ged, cont -ging) vt Br inf modificar OR alterar un poco.

rejoice [rɪˈdʒɔɪs] vi: to ~ (at OR in) alegrarse OR regocijarse (con).

rejoicing [rɪˈdʒɔɪsɪŋ] n: ~ (at OR over) regocijo m (por).

rejoin[1] [ˌriːˈdʒɔɪn] vt -1. [go back to] volver (a encontrarse) con. -2. [club] volver a hacerse socio(cia) de; [army] volver a alistarse en.

rejoin[2] [rɪˈdʒɔɪn] vt [reply] replicar.

rejoinder [rɪˈdʒɔɪndǝ] n réplica f.

rejuvenate [rɪˈdʒuːvǝneɪt] vt rejuvenecer.

rejuvenation [rɪˌdʒuːvǝˈneɪʃn] n renovación f.

rekindle [ˌriːˈkɪndl] vt fig reavivar.

relapse [rɪˈlæps] ◇ n recaída f; to have a ~ tener una recaída. ◇ vi: to ~ into volver a caer en.

relate [rɪˈleɪt] ◇ vt -1. [connect]: to ~ sthg (to) relacionar algo (con). -2. [tell] contar, relatar. ◇ vi -1. [be connected]: to ~ to estar relacionado(da) con. -2. [concern]: to ~ to referirse a. -3. [empathize]: to ~ (to sb) tener mucho en común (con alguien).

◆ **relating to** prep concerniente OR referente a.

related [rɪˈleɪtɪd] adj -1. [in same family] emparentado(da); to be ~ to sb ser pariente de alguien. -2. [connected] relacionado(da).

relation [rɪˈleɪʃn] n -1. [connection]: ~ (to/between) relación f (con/entre); to bear no ~ to no tener nada que ver con; in ~ to [state, size] en relación a; [position] respecto a. -2. [family member] pariente m y f, familiar m y f.

◆ **relations** npl [family, race, industrial] relaciones fpl.

relational [rɪˈleɪʃǝnl] adj COMPUT relacional.

relational database n COMPUT base f de datos relacional.

relationship [rɪˈleɪʃnʃɪp] n relación f; a good ~ buenas relaciones.

relative [ˈrelǝtɪv] ◇ adj relativo(va). ◇ n pariente m y f, familiar m y f.

◆ **relative to** prep fml con relación a.

relatively [ˈrelǝtɪvlɪ] adv relativamente.

relativity [ˌrelǝˈtɪvǝtɪ] n relatividad f.

relax [rɪˈlæks] ◇ *vt* **-1.** [gen] relajar. **-2.** [loosen - grip] aflojar. ◇ *vi* **-1.** [gen] relajarse. **-2.** [loosen] aflojarse.

relaxation [ˌriːlækˈseɪʃn] *n* **-1.** [recreation] relajación *f*, esparcimiento *m*. **-2.** [slackening - of discipline] relajación *f*, relajamiento *m*.

relaxed [rɪˈlækst] *adj* [gen] relajado(da); [person] tranquilo(la); [atmosphere] desenfadado(da).

relaxing [rɪˈlæksɪŋ] *adj* relajante.

relay [ˈriːleɪ] (*pt & pp senses 1 & 2* -ed, *pt & pp sense 3* relaid) ◇ *n* **-1.** SPORT: ~ (race) carrera *f* de relevos; **in** ~s *fig* por turnos. **-2.** RADIO & TV retransmisión *f*. ◇ *vt* **-1.** [broadcast] retransmitir. **-2.** [repeat]: **to ~ sthg (to)** transmitir algo (a). **-3.** [lay again] volver a poner.

release [rɪˈliːs] ◇ *n* **-1.** [setting free] puesta *f* en libertad, liberación *f*. **-2.** [relief] liberación *f*. **-3.** [statement] comunicado *m*. **-4.** [emitting - of gas] escape *m*; [- of heat, pressure] emisión *f*. **-5.** [thing issued - of film] estreno *m*; [- of record] grabación *f*; **on** ~ en pantalla.
◇ *vt* **-1.** [set free]: **to ~ sb (from)** liberar a alguien (de); **to be ~d** ser puesto en libertad. **-2.** [lift restriction on]: **to ~ sb from** descargar OR liberar a alguien de. **-3.** [make available - funds, resources] entregar. **-4.** [let go - rope, reins, person] soltar; [- grip] aflojar; [- brake, lever] soltar; [- mechanism, trigger] disparar. **-5.** [emit - gas, heat] despedir, emitir. **-6.** [issue - film] estrenar; [- record] sacar; [- statement] hacer público.

relegate [ˈrelɪgeɪt] *vt* **-1.** [demote]: **to ~ sthg/sb (to)** relegar algo/a·alguien (a). **-2.** *Br* FTBL: **to be ~d** descender (*a una división inferior*).

relegation [ˌrelɪˈgeɪʃn] *n* **-1.** [demotion]: ~ **(to)** relegación *f* (a). **-2.** *Br* FTBL: ~ **(to)** descenso *m* (a).

relent [rɪˈlent] *vi* [person] ablandarse; [wind, storm] remitir, aminorar.

relentless [rɪˈlentlɪs] *adj* implacable, despiadado(da).

relentlessly [rɪˈlentlɪslɪ] *adv* implacablemente, despiadadamente.

relevance [ˈreləvəns] *n*: ~ **(to** OR **for)** relevancia *f* (para).

relevant [ˈreləvənt] *adj* **-1.** [connected]: ~ **(to)** relacionado(da) (con), pertinente (a). **-2.** [important]: ~ **(to)** importante OR relevante (para). **-3.** [appropriate] pertinente, oportuno(na).

reliability [rɪˌlaɪəˈbɪlətɪ] *n* fiabilidad *f*.

reliable [rɪˈlaɪəbl] *adj* **-1.** [dependable] de fiar, fiable. **-2.** [information] fidedigno(na).

reliably [rɪˈlaɪəblɪ] *adv* **-1.** [dependably] sin fallar. **-2.** [correctly]: **to be ~ informed about sthg** saber algo de fuentes fidedignas.

reliance [rɪˈlaɪəns] *n*: ~ **(on)** dependencia *f* (de OR respecto de).

reliant [rɪˈlaɪənt] *adj*: **to be ~ on sb/sthg** depender de alguien/de algo.

relic [ˈrelɪk] *n* **-1.** [gen] reliquia *f*. **-2.** [custom still in use] vestigio *m*.

relief [rɪˈliːf] *n* **-1.** [comfort] alivio *m*; **she sighed with ~** suspiró aliviada. **-2.** [for poor, refugees] ayuda *f* (benéfica). **-3.** *Am* [social security] subsidio *m*.

relief map *n* mapa *m* en relieve.

relief road *n* desvío *m*.

relieve [rɪˈliːv] *vt* **-1.** [ease, lessen] aliviar. **-2.** [take away from]: **to ~ sb of sthg** liberar a alguien de algo.

relieved [rɪˈliːvd] *adj* aliviado(da).

religion [rɪˈlɪdʒn] *n* religión *f*.

religious [rɪˈlɪdʒəs] *adj* religioso(sa).

reline [ˌriːˈlaɪn] *vt* [cupboard, skirt] volver a forrar; [brakes] cambiar el forro de.

relinquish [rɪˈlɪŋkwɪʃ] *vt* [power, claim] renunciar a; [hold] soltar.

relish [ˈrelɪʃ] ◇ *n* **-1.** [enjoyment]: **with (great)** ~ con (gran) deleite. **-2.** [pickle] *salsa rojiza agridulce con pepinillo etc.* ◇ *vt* disfrutar con; **to ~ the thought** OR **idea** OR **prospect of doing sthg** disfrutar de antemano con la idea de hacer algo.

relive [ˌriːˈlɪv] *vt* revivir.

relocate [ˌriːləʊˈkeɪt] ◇ *vt* trasladar. ◇ *vi* trasladarse, establecerse en otro lugar.

relocation [ˌriːləʊˈkeɪʃn] *n* traslado *m*.

relocation expenses *npl* gastos *mpl* de traslado.

reluctance [rɪˈlʌktəns] *n* desgana *f*; **with** ~ de (muy) mala gana.

reluctant [rɪˈlʌktənt] *adj* reacio(cia); **to be ~ to do sthg** estar poco·dispuesto a hacer algo.

reluctantly [rɪˈlʌktəntlɪ] *adv* con desgana.

rely [rɪˈlaɪ] (*pt & pp* -ied)
◆ **rely on** *vt fus* **-1.** [count on] contar con; **to ~ on sb/sthg to do sthg** estar seguro de que alguien/algo hará algo. **-2.** [be dependent on]: **to ~ on sb/sthg for sthg** depender de alguien/algo para algo.

REM (*abbr of* **rapid eye movement**) *n* REM *m*.

remain [rɪˈmeɪn] ◇ *vt* continuar como; **to ~ the same** continuar siendo igual. ◇ *vi* **-1.** [stay] quedarse, permanecer. **-2.** [survive - custom, problem] quedar, continuar. **-3.** [be left]: **to ~ to be done/proved** quedar por

hacer/probar; **it** ~**s to be seen** ... eso hay que verlo.
◆ **remains** *npl* restos *mpl*.

remainder [rɪ'meɪndəʳ] *n* **-1.** [rest]: **the** ~ el resto. **-2.** MATH resto *m*.

remaining [rɪ'meɪnɪŋ] *adj* que queda, restante.

remake [*n* 'riːmeɪk, *vb* ˌriː'meɪk] CINEMA ◇ *n* nueva versión *f*. ◇ *vt* hacer una nueva versión de.

remand [rɪ'mɑːnd] JUR ◇ *n*: **on** ~ detenido(da) en espera de juicio. ◇ *vt* remitir; **to be** ~**ed in custody** estar bajo custodia.

remand centre *n Br* centro *m* de prisión preventiva.

remark [rɪ'mɑːk] ◇ *n* [comment] comentario *m*. ◇ *vt*: **to** ~ **(that)** comentar que. ◇ *vi*: **to** ~ **on** hacer comentarios OR una observación sobre.

remarkable [rɪ'mɑːkəbl] *adj* excepcional, extraordinario(ria).

remarkably [rɪ'mɑːkəblɪ] *adv* [extremely] excepcionalmente, extraordinariamente; [surprisingly] sorprendentemente.

remarry [ˌriː'mærɪ] (*pt* & *pp* **-ied**) *vi* volverse a casar.

remedial [rɪ'miːdjəl] *adj* **-1.** SCH [class, teacher] de refuerzo; [pupil] atrasado(da). **-2.** [corrective] correctivo(va).

remedy ['remədɪ] (*pl* **-ies**, *pt* & *pp* **-ied**) ◇ *n lit* & *fig*: ~ **(for)** remedio *m* (para). ◇ *vt* remediar, poner remedio a.

remember [rɪ'membəʳ] ◇ *vt* **-1.** [gen] recordar, acordarse de; ~ **that his eyesight is poor** ten presente que tiene la vista mal; **to** ~ **to do sthg** acordarse de hacer algo; **to** ~ **doing sthg** recordar OR acordarse de haber hecho algo. **-2.** [as greeting]: **to** ~ **sb to sb** dar recuerdos a alguien de parte de alguien. ◇ *vi* **-1.** [gen] recordar, acordarse. **-2.** [not forget] acordarse.

remembrance [rɪ'membrəns] *n fml*: **in** ~ **of** en conmemoración de.

Remembrance Day *n* en *Gran Bretaña, día en conmemoración por los caídos en las dos guerras mundiales.*

remind [rɪ'maɪnd] *vt*: **to** ~ **sb (about sthg/to do sthg)** recordar a alguien (algo/que haga algo); **she** ~**s me of my sister** me recuerda a mi hermana.

reminder [rɪ'maɪndəʳ] *n* **-1.** [to jog memory] recordatorio *m*, recuerdo *m*. **-2.** [letter, note] notificación *f*, aviso *m*.

reminisce [ˌremɪ'nɪs] *vi*: **to** ~ **(about sthg)** rememorar (algo).

reminiscences [ˌremɪ'nɪsənsɪz] *npl* reminiscencias *fpl*.

reminiscent [ˌremɪ'nɪsnt] *adj* [similar to]: ~ **of** evocador(ra) de, que recuerda a.

remiss [rɪ'mɪs] *adj* negligente, remiso(sa); **it was** ~ **of me** fue una negligencia por mi parte.

remission [rɪ'mɪʃn] *n* (*U*) **-1.** JUR reducción *f* de condena. **-2.** MED remisión *f*.

remit[1] [rɪ'mɪt] (*pt* & *pp* **-ted**, *cont* **-ting**) *vt* [money] remitir.

remit[2] ['riːmɪt] *n* [responsibility] misión *f*.

remittance [rɪ'mɪtns] *n* giro *m*.

remnant ['remnənt] *n* **-1.** [remaining part] resto *m*. **-2.** [of cloth] retal *m*.

remodel [ˌriː'mɒdl] (*Br pt* & *pp* **-led**, *cont* **-ling**, *Am pt* & *pp* **-ed**, *cont* **-ing**) *vt* remodelar, reformar.

remold *n* & *vt Am* = **remould**.

remonstrate ['remənstreɪt] *vi fml*: **to** ~ **(with sb about sthg)** censurar (a alguien algo).

remorse [rɪ'mɔːs] *n* (*U*) remordimiento *m*.

remorseful [rɪ'mɔːsfʊl] *adj* lleno(na) de remordimiento.

remorseless [rɪ'mɔːslɪs] *adj* **-1.** [pitiless] despiadado(da). **-2.** [unstoppable] implacable.

remorselessly [rɪ'mɔːslɪslɪ] *adv* **-1.** [pitilessly] de forma despiadada. **-2.** [unstoppably] implacablemente.

remote [rɪ'məʊt] *adj* **-1.** [place, time possibility] remoto(ta). **-2.** [from reality etc]: ~ **(from)** apartado(da) OR alejado(da) (de).

remote control *n* mando *m* a distancia.

remote-controlled [-kən'trəʊld] *adj* teledirigido(da).

remotely [rɪ'məʊtlɪ] *adv* **-1.** [in the slightest]: **not** ~ ni remotamente, en lo más mínimo. **-2.** [far off] en un lugar remoto, muy lejos.

remoteness [rɪ'məʊtnɪs] *n* **-1.** [of place] lejanía *f*. **-2.** [of person] distanciamiento *m*. **-3.** [of subject] obscuridad *f*.

remould *Br*, **remold** *Am* ['riːməʊld] *n* neumático *m* recauchutado.

removable [rɪ'muːvəbl] *adj* **-1.** [stain] que se puede quitar. **-2.** [detachable] separable.

removal [rɪ'muːvl] *n* **-1.** (*U*) [act of removing] separación *f*, extracción *f*; [of threat, clause] supresión *f*. **-2.** *Br* [change of house] mudanza *f*.

removal man *n Br* encargado *m* de mudanzas.

removal van *n Br* camión *m* de mudanzas.

remove [rɪ'muːv] *vt* **-1.** [take away, clean away]: **to** ~ **sthg (from)** quitar algo (de). **-2.** [take off] quitarse, sacarse. **-3.** [from a job, post]: **to** ~ **sb (from)** destituir a alguien (de). **-4.** [problem] eliminar, resolver; [suspicion] disipar.

removed [rɪ'muːvd] *adj*: **to be far ~ from** estar bien lejos de.

remover [rɪ'muːvər] *n*: **stain ~** quitamanchas *m inv*; **paint ~** quitapinturas *m inv*.

remuneration [rɪ,mjuːnə'reɪʃn] *n fml* remuneración *f*.

Renaissance [rə'neɪsɒns] ◇ *n*: **the ~** el Renacimiento. ◇ *comp* renacentista.

rename [,riː'neɪm] *vt* poner un nombre nuevo a.

rend [rend] (*pt & pp* **rent**) *vt lit & fig* desgarrar.

render ['rendər] *vt* **-1.** [make]: **to ~ sthg useless** hacer OR volver algo inútil; **to ~ sb speechless** dejar a alguien boquiabierto. **-2.** [give help] prestar, dar; **to ~ an account** pasar factura.

rendering ['rendərɪŋ] *n* interpretación *f*.

rendezvous ['rɒndɪvuː] (*pl inv*) *n* **-1.** [meeting] cita *f*. **-2.** [place] lugar *m* (*de una cita*).

rendition [ren'dɪʃn] *n* interpretación *f*.

renegade ['renɪgeɪd] ◇ *adj* renegado(da). ◇ *n* renegado *m*, -da *f*.

renege [rɪ'niːg] *vi fml*: **to ~ on sthg** incumplir algo.

renegotiate [,riːnɪ'gəʊʃɪeɪt] ◇ *vt* renegociar. ◇ *vi* reiniciar las negociaciones.

renew [rɪ'njuː] *vt* **-1.** [attempt, attack] reemprender. **-2.** [relationship] reanudar, renovar. **-3.** [licence, contract] renovar. **-4.** [strength, interest] reavivar.

renewable [rɪ'njuːəbl] *adj* renovable.

renewal [rɪ'njuːəl] *n* **-1.** [of an activity] reanudación *f*. **-2.** [of a contract, licence etc] renovación *f*.

rennet ['renɪt] *n* cuajo *m*.

renounce [rɪ'naʊns] *vt* renunciar a.

renovate ['renəveɪt] *vt* reformar, renovar.

renovation [,renə'veɪʃn] *n* reforma *f*, renovación *f*.

renown [rɪ'naʊn] *n* renombre *m*.

renowned [rɪ'naʊnd] *adj*: **~ (for)** célebre (por).

rent [rent] ◇ *pt & pp* → **rend**. ◇ *n* alquiler *m*. ◇ *vt* alquilar, rentar *Amer*.

◆ **rent out** *vt sep* alquilar.

rental ['rentl] ◇ *adj* de alquiler. ◇ *n* alquiler *m*.

rent book *n* libro que registra la fecha y el pago de alquiler por parte de un inquilino.

rent boy *n Br inf* chapero *m*.

rented ['rentɪd] *adj* alquilado(da).

rent-free ◇ *adj* exento(ta) de alquiler. ◇ *adv* sin pagar alquiler.

renumber [,riː'nʌmbər] *vt* volver a numerar.

renunciation [rɪ,nʌnsɪ'eɪʃn] *n* renuncia *f*.

reoccurrence [,riːə'kʌrəns] *n* repetición *f*.

reopen [,riː'əʊpn] ◇ *vt* **-1.** [gen] volver a abrir. **-2.** [court case] rever. ◇ *vi* **-1.** [gen] volver a abrir. **-2.** [start again] volverse a iniciar. **-3.** [wound] volverse a abrir.

reorganization ['riː,ɔːgənaɪ'zeɪʃn] *n* reorganización *f*.

reorganize, -ise [,riː'ɔːgənaɪz] ◇ *vt* reorganizar. ◇ *vi* reorganizarse.

rep [rep] *n* **-1.** *abbr of* **representative**. **-2.** *abbr of* **repertory**. **-3.** *abbr of* **repertory company**.

Rep. *Am* **-1.** *abbr of* **Representative**. **-2.** *abbr of* **Republican**.

repaid [riː'peɪd] *pt & pp* → **repay**.

repaint [,riː'peɪnt] *vt* repintar.

repair [rɪ'peər] ◇ *n* reparación *f*, refacción *f Amer*; **in good/bad ~** en buen/mal estado; **it's beyond ~** no tiene arreglo. ◇ *vt* reparar, refaccionar *Amer*.

repair kit *n* caja de herramientas de una bicicleta.

repaper [,riː'peɪpər] *vt* volver a empapelar.

reparations [,repə'reɪʃnz] *npl* indemnizaciones *fpl*.

repartee [,repɑː'tiː] *n* intercambio *m* de réplicas ingeniosas.

repatriate [,riː'pætrɪeɪt] *vt* repatriar.

repay [riː'peɪ] (*pt & pp* **repaid**) *vt* devolver; **to ~ sb sthg**, **to ~ sthg to sb** devolver a alguien algo.

repayment [riː'peɪmənt] *n* **-1.** [act of paying back] devolución *f*, reembolso *m*. **-2.** [sum] pago *m*.

repeal [rɪ'piːl] ◇ *n* revocación *f*, abrogación *f*. ◇ *vt* revocar, abrogar.

repeat [rɪ'piːt] ◇ *vt* **-1.** [gen] repetir; **to ~ o.s.** repetirse. **-2.** [TV, radio programme] volver a emitir. ◇ *n* reposición *f*.

repeated [rɪ'piːtɪd] *adj* repetido(da).

repeatedly [rɪ'piːtɪdlɪ] *adv* repetidamente.

repel [rɪ'pel] (*pt & pp* **-led**, *cont* **-ling**) *vt* [disgust] repeler.

repellent [rɪ'pelənt] ◇ *adj* repelente. ◇ *n* espray *m* anti-insectos.

repent [rɪ'pent] ◇ *vt* arrepentirse de. ◇ *vi*: **to ~ of** arrepentirse de.

repentance [rɪ'pentəns] *n* arrepentimiento *m*.

repentant [rɪ'pentənt] *adj* [person] arrepentido(da); [smile] de arrepentimiento.

repercussions [,riːpə'kʌʃnz] *npl* repercusiones *fpl*.

repertoire ['repətwɑːʳ] *n* repertorio *m*.

repertory ['repətrɪ] *n* repertorio *m*.

repertory company *n* compañía *f* de repertorio.

repetition [,repɪ'tɪʃn] *n* repetición *f*.

repetitious [,repɪ'tɪʃəs], **repetitive** [rɪ'petɪtɪv] *adj* repetitivo(va).

rephrase [,riː'freɪz] *vt* [question] hacer con otras palabras; [statement] decir con otras palabras.

replace [rɪ'pleɪs] *vt* **-1.** [take the place of] sustituir. **-2.** [change for something else]: **to ~ sthg (with)** cambiar algo (por). **-3.** [change for somebody else]: **to ~ sb (with)** sustituir a alguien (por). **-4.** [supply another]: **to ~ sthg** dar otro(tra). **-5.** [put back] poner en su sitio.

replacement [rɪ'pleɪsmənt] *n* **-1.** [act of replacing] sustitución *f*. **-2.** [something new]: ~ **(for)** sustituto *m*, -ta *f* (para). **-3.** [somebody new]: ~ **(for)** sustituto *m*, -ta *f* OR suplente *m* y *f* (de).

replacement part *n* pieza *f* de recambio.

replay [*n* 'riːpleɪ, *vb* ,riː'pleɪ] ◇ *n* repetición *f* (*de un partido*). ◇ *vt* **-1.** [match, game] volver a jugar. **-2.** [film, tape] volver a poner.

replenish [rɪ'plenɪʃ] *vt fml*: **to ~ sthg (with)** reaprovisionar OR reponer algo (de).

replete [rɪ'pliːt] *adj fml* repleto(ta).

replica ['replɪkə] *n* réplica *f*.

replicate ['replɪkeɪt] *vt fml* reproducir exactamente.

replication [,replɪ'keɪʃn] *n fml* **-1.** [process] reproducción *f* exacta. **-2.** [copy] réplica *f*.

reply [rɪ'plaɪ] (*pl* **-ies**, *pt* & *pp* **-ied**) ◇ *n*: ~ **(to)** respuesta *f* (a); **in ~ (to)** en respuesta (a). ◇ *vt* responder, contestar. ◇ *vi*: **to ~ (to sb/sthg)** responder (a alguien/algo).

reply coupon *n* cupón *m* de respuesta.

reply-paid *adj* con porte pagado.

report [rɪ'pɔːt] ◇ *n* **-1.** [gen] informe *m*, reporte *m Amer*; PRESS & TV reportaje *m*. **-2.** *Br* SCH boletín *m* de evaluación.
◇ *vt* **-1.** [say, make known]: **to ~ that** informar que, reportar que *Amer*; **to ~ sthg (to)** informar de algo (a). **-2.** [complain about]: **to ~ sb (to sb for sthg)** denunciar a alguien (a alguien por algo), reportar a alguien (a alguien por algo) *Amer*.
◇ *vi* **-1.** [give account]: **to ~ on** informar sobre. **-2.** [present oneself]: **to ~ to sb/for sthg** presentarse a alguien/para algo, reportarse a alguien/para algo *Amer*.
◆ **report back** *vi*: **to ~ back (to sb)** informar (a alguien) de regreso.

reportage [,repɔː'tɑːʒ] *n* (*U*) reportaje *m*.

report card *n* boletín *m* de evaluación.

reportedly [rɪ'pɔːtɪdlɪ] *adv* según se afirma.

reported speech [rɪ'pɔːtɪd-] *n* estilo *m* indirecto.

reporter [rɪ'pɔːtəʳ] *n* reportero *m*, -ra *f*.

repose [rɪ'pəʊz] *n literary* reposo *m*.

repository [rɪ'pɒzɪtrɪ] (*pl* **-ies**) *n* [store] depósito *m*, almacén *m*.

repossess [,riːpə'zes] *vt* requisar la posesión de.

repossession [,riːpə'zeʃn] *n* lanzamiento *m*.

repossession order *n* orden *f* de requisición.

reprehensible [,reprɪ'hensəbl] *adj fml* reprensible.

represent [,reprɪ'zent] *vt* **-1.** [gen] representar; [person, country] representar a; **to be well** OR **strongly ~ed** estar bien representado(da). **-2.** [describe]: **to ~ sthg/sb as** describir algo/a alguien como.

representation [,reprɪzen'teɪʃn] *n* representación *f*.
◆ **representations** *npl fml*: **to make ~s to** presentar una queja a.

representative [,reprɪ'zentətɪv] ◇ *adj*: ~ **(of)** representativo(va) (de). ◇ *n* representante *m* y *f*.

repress [rɪ'pres] *vt* reprimir.

repressed [rɪ'prest] *adj* reprimido(da).

repression [rɪ'preʃn] *n* represión *f*.

repressive [rɪ'presɪv] *adj* represivo(va).

repressiveness [rɪ'presɪvnɪs] *n* represión *f*, lo represivo.

reprieve [rɪ'priːv] ◇ *n* **-1.** [delay] tregua *f*. **-2.** [of death sentence] indulto *m*. ◇ *vt* [prisoner] indultar.

reprimand ['reprɪmɑːnd] ◇ *n* reprensión *f*. ◇ *vt* reprender.

reprint [*n* 'riːprɪnt, *vb* ,riː'prɪnt] ◇ *n* reimpresión *f*. ◇ *vt* reimprimir.

reprisal [rɪ'praɪzl] *n* represalia *f*.

reproach [rɪ'prəʊtʃ] ◇ *n* reproche *m*. ◇ *vt*: **to ~ sb (for** OR **with sthg)** reprochar a alguien (algo).

reproachful [rɪ'prəʊtʃfʊl] *adj* de reproche.

reprobate ['reprəbeɪt] *n hum* libertino *m*, -na *f*.

reproduce [,riːprə'djuːs] ◇ *vt* reproducir. ◇ *vi* BIOL reproducirse.

reproduction [,riːprə'dʌkʃn] *n* reproducción *f*.

reproductive [,riːprə'dʌktɪv] *adj* reproductor(ra).

reprogram [,riː'prəʊgræm] (*pt* & *pp* **-ed** OR **-med**, *cont* **-ing** OR **-ming**) *vt* volver a programar.

reproof [rɪ'pruːf] *n* **-1.** [words of blame] reprobación *f.* **-2.** [disapproval] reproche *m.*

reprove [rɪ'pruːv] *vt*: **to ~ sb (for)** reprobar a alguien (por).

reproving [rɪ'pruːvɪŋ] *adj* de reprobación, reprobatorio(ria).

reptile ['reptaɪl] *n* reptil *m.*

Repub. *Am abbr of* **Republican.**

republic [rɪ'pʌblɪk] *n* república *f.*

republican [rɪ'pʌblɪkən] ◇ *adj* republicano(na). ◇ *n* republicano *m,* -na *f.*
◆ **Republican** ◇ *adj* **-1.** [in US] republicano(na); **the Republican Party** el partido republicano. **-2.** [in Northern Ireland] independentista. ◇ *n* **-1.** [in US] republicano *m,* -na *f.* **-2.** [in Northern Ireland] independentista *m* y *f.*

repudiate [rɪ'pjuːdɪeɪt] *vt fml* repudiar.

repudiation [rɪ,pjuːdɪ'eɪʃn] *n fml* repulsa *f.*

repugnant [rɪ'pʌgnənt] *adj fml*: **to be ~ (to sb)** repugnar (a alguien).

repulse [rɪ'pʌls] *vt* rechazar.

repulsion [rɪ'pʌlʃn] *n* repulsión *f.*

repulsive [rɪ'pʌlsɪv] *adj* repulsivo(va).

reputable ['repjʊtəbl] *adj* de buena fama OR reputación.

reputation [,repjʊ'teɪʃn] *n* reputación *f;* **to have a ~ for sthg/for being sthg** tener fama de algo/de ser algo.

repute [rɪ'pjuːt] *n fml*: **of good/ill ~** de buena/mala fama; **of ~** de reputación.

reputed [rɪ'pjuːtɪd] *adj* reputado(da); **to be ~ to be/do sthg** tener fama de ser/hacer algo.

reputedly [rɪ'pjuːtɪdlɪ] *adv* según se dice.

reqd *abbr of* **required.**

request [rɪ'kwest] ◇ *n*: **~ (for)** petición *f* (de); **on ~** a petición del interesado; **at sb's ~** a petición de alguien. ◇ *vt* solicitar, pedir; **to ~ sb to do sthg** rogar a alguien que haga algo.

request stop *n Br* parada *f* discrecional.

requiem (mass) ['rekwɪəm-] *n* (misa *f* de) réquiem *m.*

require [rɪ'kwaɪər] *vt* necesitar, requerir; **to ~ sb to do sthg** exigir a alguien que haga algo.

required [rɪ'kwaɪəd] *adj* necesario(ria).

requirement [rɪ'kwaɪəmənt] *n* requisito *m.*

requisite ['rekwɪzɪt] *adj fml* que se requiere, preciso(sa).

requisition [,rekwɪ'zɪʃn] *vt* requisar.

reran [,riː'ræn] *pt* → **rerun.**

reread [,riː'riːd] (*pt & pp* **reread** [,riː'red]) *vt* releer.

rerecord [,riːrɪ'kɔːd] *vt* volver a grabar.

reroof [,riː'ruːf] *vt* volver a techar, poner un nuevo techo a.

reroute [,riː'ruːt] *vt* desviar.

rerun [*n* 'riːrʌn, *vb* ,riː'rʌn] (*pt* **-ran,** *pp* **-run,** *cont* **-ning**) ◇ *n* **-1.** [film, programme] reposición *f.* **-2.** [repeated situation] repetición *f.* ◇ *vt* **-1.** [race] volver a correr. **-2.** [film, programme] reponer. **-3.** [tape] volver a poner.

resale price maintenance ['riːseɪl-] *n Br* FIN mantenimiento *m* del precio de reventa.

resat [,riː'sæt] *pt & pp* → **resit.**

reschedule [*Br* ,riː'ʃedjʊl, *Am* ,riː'skedʒʊl] *vt* FIN reprogramar.

rescind [rɪ'sɪnd] *vt* JUR [contract] rescindir; [law] revocar.

rescue ['reskjuː] ◇ *n* rescate *m;* **to go** OR **come to sb's ~** ir OR acudir al rescate de alguien. ◇ *vt*: **to ~ sb/sthg (from)** rescatar a alguien/algo (de).

rescue operation *n* operación *f* de rescate OR salvamento.

rescuer ['reskjʊər] *n* rescatador *m,* -ra *f.*

reseal [,riː'siːl] *vt* volver a cerrar.

resealable [,riː'siːləbl] *adj* que se puede volver a cerrar.

research [,riː'sɜːtʃ] ◇ *n* (U): **~ (on** OR **into)** investigación *f* (de OR sobre); **~ and development** investigación y desarrollo. ◇ *vt* investigar, hacer una investigación sobre. ◇ *vi*: **to ~ (into)** hacer una investigación (sobre).

researcher [rɪ'sɜːtʃər] *n* investigador *m,* -ra *f.*

research work *n* (U) investigaciones *fpl,* trabajos *mpl* de investigación.

resell [,riː'sel] (*pt & pp* **resold**) *vt* volver a vender.

resemblance [rɪ'zembləns] *n* parecido *m,* semejanza *f;* **to bear a strong ~ to** tener un gran parecido con.

resemble [rɪ'zembl] *vt* parecerse a, asemejarse a.

resent [rɪ'zent] *vt* resentirse de, tomarse a mal.

resentful [rɪ'zentfʊl] *adj* resentido(da).

resentfully [rɪ'zentfʊlɪ] *adv* con resentimiento.

resentment [rɪ'zentmənt] *n* resentimiento *m.*

reservation [,rezə'veɪʃn] *n* **-1.** [booking] reserva *f.* **-2.** [uncertainty]: **without ~** sin reserva. **-3.** *Am* [for Native Americans] reserva *f.*
◆ **reservations** *npl* [doubts] reservas *fpl.*

reserve [rɪ'zɜːv] ◇ *n* **-1.** [gen] reserva *f;* **in ~** en reserva. **-2.** SPORT reserva *m* y *f,* suplente *m* *y* *f*. ◇ *vt* **-1.** [save, book] reservar. **-2.** [retain]: **to ~ the right to do sthg** reservarse el derecho a hacer algo.

reserve bank *n* *banco de reserva federal estadounidense*.

reserve currency *n* (*U*) divisas *fpl* de reserva.

reserved [rɪ'zɜːvd] *adj* reservado(da).

reserve price *n* *Br* precio *m* mínimo.

reserve team *n* *Br* equipo *m* de reserva OR suplente.

reservist [rɪ'zɜːvɪst] *n* reservista *m* *y* *f*.

reservoir ['rezəvwɑːr] *n* **-1.** [lake] pantano *m*, embalse *m*. **-2.** [large supply] cantera *f*.

reset [,riː'set] (*pt* & *pp* **reset**, *cont* **-ting**) ◇ *vt* **-1.** [clock] poner en hora; [meter, controls, computer] reinicializar. **-2.** [bone] (volver a) encajar. ◇ *vi* COMPUT reinicializar.

resettle [,riː'setl] ◇ *vt* reasentar, volver a establecer. ◇ *vi* reasentarse, volver a establecerse.

resettlement [,riː'setlmənt] *n* **-1.** [of land] repoblación *f*, nueva colonización *f*. **-2.** [of people] reasentamiento *m*.

reshape [,riː'ʃeɪp] *vt* [policy, thinking] reformar, rehacer.

reshuffle [,riː'ʃʌfl] ◇ *n* remodelación *f*; **cabinet ~** remodelación del gabinete. ◇ *vt* remodelar.

reside [rɪ'zaɪd] *vi* *fml* **-1.** [live] residir. **-2.** [be found]: **to ~ in** residir en.

residence ['rezɪdəns] *n* **-1.** [house] residencia *f*. **-2.** [state of residing]: **to be in ~ (at)** residir (a); **to take up ~** instalarse.

residence permit *n* permiso *m* de residencia.

resident ['rezɪdənt] ◇ *adj* **-1.** [settled, living] residente. **-2.** [on-site, live-in] que vive en su lugar de trabajo. ◇ *n* residente *m* *y* *f*.

residential [,rezɪ'denʃl] *adj* [live-in] en régimen de internado.

residential area *n* zona *f* residencial.

residents' association *n* ≃ asociación *f* de vecinos.

residual [rɪ'zɪdjuəl] *adj* residual.

residue ['rezɪdjuː] *n* residuo *m*.

resign [rɪ'zaɪn] ◇ *vt* **-1.** [give up] dimitir de, renunciar a. **-2.** [accept calmly]: **to ~ o.s. to sthg** resignarse a algo. ◇ *vi* [quit]: **to ~ (from)** dimitir (de).

resignation [,rezɪg'neɪʃn] *n* **-1.** [from job] dimisión *f*. **-2.** [calm acceptance] resignación *f*.

resigned [rɪ'zaɪnd] *adj*: **~ (to)** resignado(da) (a).

resilience [rɪ'zɪlɪəns] *n* capacidad *f* de recuperación.

resilient [rɪ'zɪlɪənt] *adj* [person] resistente, fuerte; [rubber] elástico(ca).

resin ['rezɪn] *n* resina *f*.

resist [rɪ'zɪst] *vt* **-1.** [refuse to accept] resistir, oponerse a. **-2.** [fight against] resistir a. **-3.** [refuse to give in to - temptation] resistir.

resistance [rɪ'zɪstəns] *n*: **~ (to)** resistencia *f* (a).

resistant [rɪ'zɪstənt] *adj* **-1.** [opposed]: **~ to sthg** que se resiste a algo. **-2.** [immune]: **~ (to sthg)** resistente (a algo).

resistor [rɪ'zɪstər] *n* ELEC reóstato *m*.

resit [*n* 'riːsɪt, *vb* ,riː'sɪt] (*pt* & *pp* **-sat**, *cont* **-ting**) *Br* ◇ *n* (examen *m* de) repesca *f*. ◇ *vt* volver a presentarse a.

resold [,riː'səʊld] *pt* & *pp* → **resell**.

resolute ['rezəluːt] *adj* resuelto(ta), determinado(da).

resolutely ['rezəluːtlɪ] *adv* con resolución, resueltamente.

resolution [,rezə'luːʃn] *n* **-1.** [gen] resolución *f*. **-2.** [vow, promise] propósito *m*.

resolve [rɪ'zɒlv] ◇ *n* (*U*) resolución *f*. ◇ *vt* **-1.** [vow, promise]: **to ~ that** resolver que; **to ~ to do sthg** resolver hacer algo. **-2.** [solve] resolver.

resonance ['rezənəns] *n* resonancia *f*.

resonant ['rezənənt] *adj* resonante.

resonate ['rezəneɪt] *vi* resonar.

resort [rɪ'zɔːt] *n* **-1.** [for holidays] lugar *m* de vacaciones. **-2.** [solution]: **as a** OR **in the last ~** como último recurso.

◆ **resort to** *vt fus* recurrir a.

resound [rɪ'zaʊnd] *vi* **-1.** [noise] resonar, retumbar. **-2.** [place]: **the room ~ed with laughter** la risa resonaba por la habitación.

resounding [rɪ'zaʊndɪŋ] *adj* **-1.** [loud - noise, knock] retumbante; [- crash] estruendoso(sa). **-2.** [very great] clamoroso(sa), resonante.

resource [rɪ'sɔːs] *n* recurso *m*.

resourceful [rɪ'sɔːsful] *adj* de recursos.

resourcefulness [rɪ'sɔːsfulnɪs] *n* (*U*) recursos *mpl*, inventiva *f*.

respect [rɪ'spekt] ◇ *n* **-1.** [gen]: **~ (for)** respeto *m* (por); **with ~** con respeto. **-2.** [aspect] aspecto *m*; **in this ~** a este respecto; **in that ~** en cuanto a esto. ◇ *vt* [admire] respetar; **to ~ sb for sthg** respetar a alguien por algo.

◆ **respects** *npl*: **to pay one's ~s (to)** presentar uno sus respetos (a); **to pay one's last ~s (to)** rendir el último homenaje (a).

◆ **with respect to** *prep* con respecto a.

respectability [rɪ,spektə'bɪlətɪ] *n* respetabilidad *f*.

respectable [rɪ'spektəbl] *adj* respetable.

respectably [rɪ'spektəblɪ] *adv* [correctly] de manera respetable.

respectful [rɪ'spektfʊl] *adj* respetuoso(sa).

respectfully [rɪ'spektfʊlɪ] *adv* respetuosamente.

respective [rɪ'spektɪv] *adj* respectivo(va).

respectively [rɪ'spektɪvlɪ] *adv* respectivamente.

respiration [,respə'reɪʃn] *n* respiración *f*.

respirator ['respəreɪtə] *n* careta *f* antigás.

respiratory [Br rɪ'spɪrətrɪ, Am 'respərətɔːrɪ] *adj* respiratorio(ria).

respire [rɪ'spaɪə] *vi* respirar.

respite ['respaɪt] *n* **-1.** [lull] respiro *m*. **-2.** [delay] aplazamiento *m*.

resplendent [rɪ'splendənt] *adj literary* resplandeciente.

respond [rɪ'spɒnd] ◇ *vt* responder. ◇ *vi*: to ~ **(to)** responder (a); **to ~ by doing sthg** responder haciendo algo.

response [rɪ'spɒns] *n* respuesta *f*; **in ~** en respuesta.

responsibility [rɪ,spɒnsə'bɪlətɪ] (*pl* **-ies**) *n*: ~ **(for)** responsabilidad *f* (de); **to have a ~ to sb** ser responsable ante alguien.

responsible [rɪ'spɒnsəbl] *adj* **-1.** [gen] responsable; ~ **(for)** responsable (de). **-2.** [answerable]: ~ **to sb** responsable ante alguien. **-3.** [job, position] de responsabilidad.

responsibly [rɪ'spɒnsəblɪ] *adv* de manera responsable.

responsive [rɪ'spɒnsɪv] *adj* **-1.** [quick to react] que responde muy bien. **-2.** [aware]: ~ **(to)** sensible OR perceptivo(va) (a).

respray [*n* 'riːspreɪ, *vb* ,riː'spreɪ] ◇ *n*: **to give sthg a ~** volver a pintar algo. ◇ *vt* volver a pintar (*con pistola*).

rest [rest] ◇ *n* **-1.** [remainder]: **the ~ (of)** el resto (de). **-2.** [relaxation, break] descanso *m*; **to have a ~** descansar. **-3.** [support - for feet] descanso *m*; [- for head] respaldo *m*; [- for snooker cue] *utensilio para reposar el taco de billar en los tiros largos*. **-4.** *phr*: **to come to ~** pararse.
◇ *vt* **-1.** [relax - eyes, feet] descansar. **-2.** [support] apoyar, descansar.
◇ *vi* **-1.** [relax, be still] descansar. **-2.** [depend]: **to ~ on** OR **upon** depender de. **-3.** [duty, responsibility]: **to ~ with sb** pesar sobre alguien. **-4.** [be supported] apoyarse, descansar. **-5.** *literary* [eyes]: **to ~ on** pararse OR clavarse en. **-6.** *phr*: ~ **assured that** ... tenga la seguridad de que ....

rest area *n Am* & *Austr* área *f* de descanso (*en la autopista*).

restart [*n* 'riːstɑːt, *vb* ,riː'stɑːt] ◇ *n* nuevo comienzo *m*. ◇ *vt* [vehicle] (volver a) poner en marcha. ◇ *vi* **-1.** [play, film] empezar de nuevo. **-2.** [vehicle] (volver a) arrancar.

restate [,riː'steɪt] *vt* volver a exponer.

restaurant ['restərɒnt] *n* restaurante *m*.

restaurant car *n Br* coche *m* OR vagón *m* restaurante.

rest cure *n* cura *f* de reposo.

rested ['restɪd] *adj* descansado(da).

restful ['restfʊl] *adj* tranquilo(la), apacible.

rest home *n* [for the elderly] asilo *m* de ancianos; [for the sick] casa *f* de reposo.

resting place ['restɪŋ-] *n* última morada *f*.

restitution [,restɪ'tjuːʃn] *n fml* restitución *f*.

restive ['restɪv] *adj* intranquilo(la), inquieto(ta).

restless ['restlɪs] *adj* **-1.** [bored, dissatisfied] impaciente, desasosegado(da). **-2.** [fidgety] inquieto(ta), agitado(da). **-3.** [sleepless] en blanco, agitado(da).

restlessly ['restlɪslɪ] *adv* con impaciencia, con desasosiego.

restock [,riː'stɒk] ◇ *vt* [shop, cupboard] reabastecer, reaprovisionar; [lake, river] repoblar. ◇ *vi* reponer las existencias.

restoration [,restə'reɪʃn] *n* restauración *f*.

restorative [rɪ'stɒrətɪv] *adj fml* reconstituyente.

restore [rɪ'stɔː] *vt* **-1.** [reestablish] restablecer. **-2.** [to a previous position or condition]: **to ~ sb to sthg** restaurar a alguien en algo; **to ~ sthg to sthg** volver a poner algo en algo. **-3.** [renovate] restaurar. **-4.** [give back] devolver.

restorer [rɪ'stɔːrə] *n* **-1.** [person] restaurador *m*, -ra *f*. **-2.** [substance]: **hair ~** crecepelo *m*.

restrain [rɪ'streɪn] *vt* controlar; **to ~ o.s. from doing sthg** contenerse para no hacer algo.

restrained [rɪ'streɪnd] *adj* comedido(da).

restraint [rɪ'streɪnt] *n* **-1.** [rule, check] restricción *f*, limitación *f*. **-2.** [control] (*U*) control *m*.

restrict [rɪ'strɪkt] *vt* [limit] restringir, limitar; **to ~ sthg/sb to** restringir algo/a alguien a; **to ~ o.s. to sthg** limitarse a algo.

restricted [rɪ'strɪktɪd] *adj* **-1.** [limited, small] restringido(da), limitado(da); ~ **area** zona *f* de velocidad limitada. **-2.** [classified, not public] secreto(ta).

restriction [rɪ'strɪkʃn] *n* restricción *f*; ~**s on** restricciones en OR de.

restrictive [rɪ'strɪktɪv] *adj* restrictivo(va).

restrictive practices *npl* prácticas *fpl* restrictivas.

rest room *n Am* servicios *mpl*, aseos *mpl*.

restructure [,riː'strʌktʃər] *vt* reestructurar.

result [rɪ'zʌlt] ◇ *n* resultado *m*; **as a ~** como resultado. ◇ *vi* **-1.** [cause]: **to ~ (in sthg)** tener como resultado (algo). **-2.** [be caused]: **to ~ (from)** resultar (de).

resultant [rɪ'zʌltənt] *adj fml* resultante.

resume [rɪ'zjuːm] ◇ *vt* **-1.** [start again] reanudar. **-2.** *fml* [return to] volver a. ◇ *vi* volver a empezar, continuar.

résumé ['rezjuːmeɪ] *n* **-1.** [summary] resumen *m*. **-2.** *Am* [of career, qualifications] currículum *m* (vitae), currículo *m*.

resumption [rɪ'zʌmpʃn] *n* reanudación *f*.

resurface [,riː'sɜːfɪs] ◇ *vt* pavimentar de nuevo. ◇ *vi* volver a salir en la superficie.

resurgence [rɪ'sɜːdʒəns] *n* resurgimiento *m*.

resurrect [,rezə'rekt] *vt* resucitar.

resurrection [,rezə'rekʃn] *n* resurrección *f*.
◆ **Resurrection** *n*: **the Resurrection** la Resurrección.

resuscitate [rɪ'sʌsɪteɪt] *vt* resucitar, revivir.

resuscitation [rɪ,sʌsɪ'teɪʃn] *n* resucitación *f*.

retail ['riːteɪl] ◇ *n* venta *f* al por menor OR al detalle. ◇ *adv* al por menor, al detalle.

retailer ['riːteɪlər] *n* minorista *m y f*, detallista *m y f*.

retail outlet *n* punto *m* de venta.

retail price *n* precio *m* de venta al público.

retail price index *n Br* índice *m* de precios al consumo.

retain [rɪ'teɪn] *vt* retener.

retainer [rɪ'teɪnər] *n* **-1.** [fee] anticipo *m*. **-2.** [servant] criado *m*, -da *f* (*con muchos años de servicio en una familia*).

retaining wall [rɪ'teɪnɪŋ-] *n* muro *m* de contención.

retaliate [rɪ'tælɪeɪt] *vi* desquitarse, tomar represalias.

retaliation [rɪ,tælɪ'eɪʃn] *n* (*U*) represalias *fpl*.

retarded [rɪ'tɑːdɪd] *adj* retrasado(da).

retch [retʃ] *vi* tener náuseas.

retention [rɪ'tenʃn] *n* retención *f*.

retentive [rɪ'tentɪv] *adj* retentivo(va).

rethink [*n* 'riːθɪŋk, *vb* ,riː'θɪŋk] (*pt & pp* **-thought** [-'θɔːt]) ◇ *n*: **to have a ~** volver a pensar, reconsiderar. ◇ *vt & vi* volver a pensar, reconsiderar.

reticence ['retɪsəns] *n* reticencia *f*.

reticent ['retɪsənt] *adj* reticente, reservado(da).

retina ['retɪnə] (*pl* **-nas** OR **-nae** [-niː]) *n* retina *f*.

retinue ['retɪnjuː] *n* séquito *m*, comitiva *f*.

retire [rɪ'taɪər] *vi* **-1.** [from work] jubilarse. **-2.** *fml* [to another place, to bed] retirarse.

retired [rɪ'taɪəd] *adj* jubilado(da).

retirement [rɪ'taɪəmənt] *n* jubilación *f*, retiro *m*.

retirement age *n* edad *f* de jubilación.

retirement pension *n* pensión *f* de jubilación.

retiring [rɪ'taɪərɪŋ] *adj* **-1.** [shy] retraído(da), tímido(da). **-2.** [about to retire from work] que está a punto de jubilarse.

retort [rɪ'tɔːt] ◇ *n* [sharp reply] réplica *f*. ◇ *vt*: **to ~ (that)** replicar (que).

retouch [,riː'tʌtʃ] *vt* retocar.

retrace [rɪ'treɪs] *vt*: **to ~ one's steps** desandar lo andado.

retract [rɪ'trækt] ◇ *vt* **-1.** [withdraw, take back] retractarse de. **-2.** [pull in - claws] meter, retraer. ◇ *vi* [subj: claws] meterse, retraerse; [subj: wheels] replegarse.

retractable [rɪ'træktəbl] *adj* [pencil] retráctil; [wheels] replegable.

retraction [rɪ'trækʃn] *n* [of statement] retractación *f*.

retrain [,riː'treɪn] ◇ *vt* reciclar. ◇ *vi* reciclarse.

retraining [,riː'treɪnɪŋ] *n* reciclaje *m*.

retread ['riːtred] *n* neumático *m* recauchutado.

retreat [rɪ'triːt] ◇ *n* **-1.** MIL: **~ (from)** retirada *f* (de); **to beat a (hasty) ~** marcharse a toda prisa. **-2.** [backing down]: **~ (from)** abandono *m* (de). **-3.** [peaceful place] refugio *m*. ◇ *vi* [move away]: **to ~ (from)** [gen] retirarse (de); [from a person] apartarse (de).

retrenchment [riː'trentʃmənt] *n fml* reducción *f* de gastos.

retrial [,riː'traɪəl] *n* nuevo juicio *m*.

retribution [,retrɪ'bjuːʃn] *n* castigo *m* merecido.

retrieval [rɪ'triːvl] *n* COMPUT recuperación *f*.

retrieve [rɪ'triːv] *vt* **-1.** [get back] recobrar. **-2.** COMPUT recuperar. **-3.** [rescue - situation] salvar.

retriever [rɪ'triːvər] *n* perro *m* cobrador.

retroactive [,retrəʊ'æktɪv] *adj fml* retroactivo(va).

retrograde ['retrəgreɪd] *adj fml* [gen] retrógrado(da); [step] hacia atrás.

retrogressive [,retrə'gresɪv] *adj fml & pej* retrógrado(da).

retrospect ['retrəspekt] *n*: **in ~** retrospectivamente, mirando hacia atrás.

retrospective [ˌretrə'spektɪv] ◇ *adj* **-1.** *fml* [gen] retrospectivo(va). **-2.** [law, pay rise] con efecto retroactivo. ◇ *n* exposición *f* retrospectiva.

retrospectively [ˌretrə'spektɪvlɪ] *adv* **-1.** *fml* [gen] retrospectivamente. **-2.** [introduce law, pay rise] de forma retroactiva.

return [rɪ'tɜːn] ◇ *n* **-1.** (U) [arrival back] vuelta *f*, regreso *m*; ~ **to** vuelta a. **-2.** [in tennis] resto *m*. **-3.** *Br* [ticket] billete *m* de ida y vuelta. **-4.** [profit] ganancia *f*, rédito *m*.
◇ *comp* [journey] de vuelta, de regreso.
◇ *vt* **-1.** [book, visit, compliment] devolver. **-2.** [reciprocate] corresponder a. **-3.** [replace] volver a poner en su sitio. **-4.** JUR [verdict] pronunciar. **-5.** POL [candidate] elegir.
◇ *vi*: **to** ~ **(from/to)** volver (de/a), regresar (de/a).
◆ **returns** *npl* **-1.** COMM rendimiento *m*, réditos *mpl*. **-2.** *phr*: **many happy** ~**s (of the day)!** ¡y que cumplas muchos más!
◆ **in return** *adv* en recompensa.
◆ **in return for** *prep* en recompensa por.

returnable [rɪ'tɜːnəbl] *adj* retornable.

returning officer [rɪ'tɜːnɪŋ-] *n Br* oficial *m* encargado de organizar las elecciones al Parlamento en su distrito electoral y que anuncia oficialmente los resultados de éstas.

return (key) *n* COMPUT tecla *f* de retorno de carro.

return match *n* partido *m* de vuelta.

return ticket *n Br* billete *m* de ida y vuelta.

reunification [ˌriːjuːnɪfɪ'keɪʃn] *n* reunificación *f*.

reunion [ˌriː'juːnjən] *n* reunión *f*.

Reunion [ˌriː'juːnjən] *n*: ~ **(Island)** isla *f* Reunión.

reunite [ˌriːjuː'naɪt] *vt* [people]: **to be** ~**d with** volver a encontrarse OR verse con; [factions, parts] reunir.

reupholster [ˌriːʌp'həʊlstər] *vt* tapizar de nuevo.

reusable [riː'juːzəbl] *adj* reutilizable.

reuse [*n* ˌriː'juːs, *vb* ˌriː'juːz] ◇ *n* reutilización *f*. ◇ *vt* reutilizar.

rev [rev] (*pt* & *pp* **-ved**, *cont* **-ving**) *inf* ◇ *n* (*abbr of* **revolution**) revolución *f* (motriz). ◇ *vt*: **to** ~ **sthg (up)** acelerar algo. ◇ *vi*: **to** ~ **(up)** acelerar el motor.

Rev [rev] (*abbr of* **Reverend**) *n* R., Revdo.

revalue [ˌriː'væljuː] *vt* revalorizar.

revamp [ˌriː'væmp] *vt* *inf* renovar.

rev counter *n* contador *m* de revoluciones.

Revd (*abbr of* **Reverend**) *n* R., Revdo.

reveal [rɪ'viːl] *vt* revelar.

revealing [rɪ'viːlɪŋ] *adj* revelador(ra).

reveille [*Br* rɪ'vælɪ, *Am* 'revəlɪ] *n* toque *m* de diana.

revel ['revl] (*Br* *pt* & *pp* **-led**, *cont* **-ling**, *Am* *pt* & *pp* **-ed**, *cont* **-ing**) *vi*: **to** ~ **in** deleitarse en.

revelation [ˌrevə'leɪʃn] *n* revelación *f*.

reveller *Br*, **reveler** *Am* ['revələr] *n* juergista *m* y *f*.

revelry ['revlrɪ] *n* (U) juerga *f*.

revenge [rɪ'vendʒ] ◇ *n* venganza *f*; **to take** ~ **(on sb)** vengarse (en alguien). ◇ *comp* por venganza. ◇ *vt* vengar; **to** ~ **o.s. on sb/sthg** vengarse uno en alguien/en algo.

revenue ['revənjuː] *n* ingresos *mpl*.

reverberate [rɪ'vɜːbəreɪt] *vi* **-1.** [reecho] resonar, retumbar. **-2.** [have repercussions] repercutir.

reverberations [rɪˌvɜːbə'reɪʃnz] *npl* **-1.** [echoes] reverberación *f*. **-2.** [repercussions] repercusiones *fpl*.

revere [rɪ'vɪər] *vt* *fml* venerar, reverenciar.

reverence ['revərəns] *n* *fml* reverencia *f*.

Reverend ['revərənd] *n* reverendo *m*.

Reverend Mother *n* reverenda madre *f*.

reverent ['revərənt] *adj* reverente.

reverential [ˌrevə'renʃl] *adj* *fml* reverencial.

reverie ['revərɪ] *n* *fml* ensueño *m*.

revers [rɪ'vɪə] (*pl inv*) *n* solapa *f*.

reversal [rɪ'vɜːsl] *n* **-1.** [turning around] cambio *m* total. **-2.** [ill fortune] contratiempo *m*, revés *m*.

reverse [rɪ'vɜːs] ◇ *adj* inverso(sa). ◇ *n* **-1.** AUT: ~ **(gear)** marcha *f* atrás; **to be in** ~ tener puesta la marcha atrás; **to go into** ~ ir a la baja. **-2.** [opposite]: **the** ~ lo contrario. **-3.** [opposite side, back]: **the** ~ [gen] el revés; [of coin] el reverso; [of piece of paper] el dorso.
◇ *vt* **-1.** AUT dar marcha atrás a. **-2.** [change usual order] invertir. **-3.** [change to opposite] cambiar completamente. **-4.** *Br* TELEC: **to** ~ **the charges** llamar a cobro revertido.
◇ *vi* AUT dar marcha atrás.

reverse-charge call *n Br* llamada *f* a cobro revertido.

reversible [rɪ'vɜːsəbl] *adj* reversible.

reversing light [rɪ'vɜːsɪŋ-] *n Br* luz *f* de marcha atrás.

reversion [rɪ'vɜːʃn] *n* reversión *f*.

revert [rɪ'vɜːt] *vi*: **to** ~ **to** volver a.

review [rɪ'vjuː] ◇ *n* **-1.** [examination] revisión *f*, repaso *m*; **to come under** ~ ser revisado; **under** ~ bajo revisión. **-2.** [critique] reseña *f*. ◇ *vt* **-1.** [reexamine] revisar. **-2.**

[consider] **reconsiderar. -3.** [write an article on] **reseñar. -4.** *Am* [study again] **repasar.**

reviewer [rɪ'vjuːəʳ] *n* crítico *m*, -ca *f*, reseñador *m*, -ra *f*.

revile [rɪ'vaɪl] *vt literary* injuriar.

revise [rɪ'vaɪz] ◇ *vt* **-1.** [reconsider] revisar. **-2.** [rewrite] modificar, corregir. **-3.** *Br* [study] repasar. ◇ *vi Br*: **to ~ (for sthg)** repasar (para algo).

revised [rɪ'vaɪzd] *adj* revisado(da).

revision [rɪ'vɪʒn] *n* **-1.** [alteration] corrección *f*, modificación *f*. **-2.** *Br* [study] repaso *m*.

revisionist [rɪ'vɪʒnɪst] ◇ *adj* revisionista. ◇ *n* revisionista *m y f*.

revisit [ˌriː'vɪzɪt] *vt* volver a visitar.

revitalize, -ise [ˌriː'vaɪtəlaɪz] *vt* revivificar.

revival [rɪ'vaɪvl] *n* reactivación *f*.

revive [rɪ'vaɪv] ◇ *vt* **-1.** [person, plant] resucitar; [economy] reactivar. **-2.** [tradition, play, memories] restablecer. ◇ *vi* reponerse.

revoke [rɪ'vəʊk] *vt fml* revocar.

revolt [rɪ'vəʊlt] ◇ *n* rebelión *f*, sublevación *f*. ◇ *vt* repugnar. ◇ *vi*: **to ~ (against)** rebelarse OR sublevarse (contra).

revolting [rɪ'vəʊltɪŋ] *adj* repugnante, asqueroso(sa).

revolution [ˌrevə'luːʃn] *n* revolución *f*; **~ in** sthg revolución en OR de algo.

revolutionary [ˌrevə'luːʃnərɪ] (*pl* **-ies**) ◇ *adj* revolucionario(ria). ◇ *n* revolucionario *m*, -ria *f*.

revolutionize, -ise [ˌrevə'luːʃənaɪz] *vt* revolucionar.

revolve [rɪ'vɒlv] *vi* [go round] dar vueltas, girar; **to ~ around** OR **round** *lit* & *fig* girar en torno a.

revolver [rɪ'vɒlvəʳ] *n* revólver *m*.

revolving [rɪ'vɒlvɪŋ] *adj* giratorio(ria).

revolving door *n* puerta *f* giratoria.

revue [rɪ'vjuː] *n* revista *f* (teatral).

revulsion [rɪ'vʌlʃn] *n* asco *m*, repugnancia *f*.

reward [rɪ'wɔːd] ◇ *n* recompensa *f*, premio *m*. ◇ *vt*: **to ~ sb (for/with)** recompensar a alguien (por/con).

rewarding [rɪ'wɔːdɪŋ] *adj* gratificador(ra).

rewind [ˌriː'waɪnd] (*pt* & *pp* **rewound**) *vt* rebobinar.

rewire [ˌriː'waɪəʳ] *vt* cambiar la instalación eléctrica de.

reword [ˌriː'wɜːd] *vt* expresar de otra forma.

rework [ˌriː'wɜːk] *vt* rehacer.

rewound [ˌriː'waʊnd] *pt* & *pp* → **rewind**.

rewrite [ˌriː'raɪt] (*pt* **rewrote** [ˌriː'rəʊt], *pp*

rewritten [ˌriː'rɪtn]) *vt* volver a escribir, rehacer.

REX (*abbr of* **real-time executive routine**) *n* *programa en tiempo real.*

Reykjavik ['rekjəvɪk] *n* Reykjavik.

RFC (*abbr of* **Rugby Football Club**) *n* *club de rugby.*

RGN (*abbr of* **registered general nurse**) *n Br* enfermero diplomado *m*, enfermera diplomada *f*.

Rh (*abbr of* **rhesus**) Rh.

rhapsody ['ræpsədɪ] (*pl* **-ies**) *n* **-1.** MUS rapsodia *f*. **-2.** [strong approval] entusiasmo *m*.

Rhesus ['riːsəs] *n*: **~ positive/negative** Rhesus positivo/negativo.

rhetoric ['retərɪk] *n* retórica *f*.

rhetorical question [rɪ'tɒrɪkl-] *n* pregunta *f* retórica (*a la que no se espera contestación*).

rheumatic [ruː'mætɪk] *adj* reumático(ca).

rheumatism ['ruːmətɪzm] *n* reumatismo *m*.

rheumatoid arthritis ['ruːmətɔɪd-] *n* reuma *m* articular.

Rhine [raɪn] *n*: **the ~** el Rin.

Rhineland ['raɪnlænd] *n* Renania *f*.

rhinestone ['raɪnstəʊn] *n* diamante *m* falso.

rhino ['raɪnəʊ] (*pl inv* OR **-s**), **rhinoceros** [raɪ'nɒsərəs] (*pl inv* OR **-es**) *n* rinoceronte *m*.

Rhode Island [rəʊd-] *n* Rhode Island.

Rhodes [rəʊdz] *n* Rodas.

Rhodesia [rəʊ'diːʃə] *n* Rodesia.

Rhodesian [rəʊ'diːʃn] ◇ *adj* rodesio(sia). ◇ *n* rodesio *m*, -sia *f*.

rhododendron [ˌrəʊdə'dendrən] *n* rododendro *m*.

Rhône [rəʊn] *n*: **the (River) ~** el (río) Ródano.

rhubarb ['ruːbɑːb] *n* ruibarbo *m*.

rhyme [raɪm] ◇ *n* **-1.** [gen] rima *f*. **-2.** [poem] poesía *f*, versos *mpl*; **in ~** en verso. ◇ *vi*: **to ~ (with)** rimar (con).

rhyming slang ['raɪmɪŋ-] *n Br* rasgo del argot del este de Londres, que consiste en rimar dos palabras que dan el significado de una tercera.

rhythm ['rɪðm] *n* ritmo *m*.

rhythm and blues *n* rhythm *m* and blues.

rhythmic(al) ['rɪðmɪk(l)] *adj* rítmico(ca).

RI ◇ *n* (*abbr of* **religious instruction**) religión. ◇ *abbr of* **Rhode Island.**

rib [rɪb] *n* **-1.** ANAT costilla *f*. **-2.** [of umbrella] varilla *f*.

ribald ['rɪbəld] *adj* escabroso(sa), verde.

ribbed [rɪbd] *adj* de canalé.

ribbon ['rɪbən] *n* cinta *f*.

rib cage *n* caja *f* torácica.

rice [raɪs] *n* arroz *m*.

rice field n arrozal m.

rice paper n papel m de arroz.

rice pudding n arroz m con leche.

rich [rɪtʃ] ◇ adj -1. [gen] rico(ca). -2. [full]: **to be ~ in** abundar en. -3. [fertile] fértil. -4. [indigestible] pesado(da). -5. [vibrant - sound] sonoro(ra); [- colour] brillante. -6. [sumptuous] suntuoso(sa). ◇ npl: **the ~** los ricos.

◆ **riches** npl -1. [natural resources] riquezas fpl. -2. [wealth] riqueza f.

richly ['rɪtʃlɪ] adv -1. [well - rewarded] ricamente; **~ deserved** bien merecido. -2. [plentifully] copiosamente, abundantemente. -3. [sumptuously] suntuosamente.

richness ['rɪtʃnɪs] n -1. [gen] riqueza f. -2. [fertility] fertilidad f. -3. [indigestibility] pesadez f. -4. [vibrancy - of sound] sonoridad f; [- of colour] brillantez f. -5. [sumptuousness] suntuosidad f.

Richter scale ['rɪktə-] n: **the ~** la escala Richter.

rickets ['rɪkɪts] n raquitismo m.

rickety ['rɪkətɪ] adj tambaleante, desvencijado(da).

rickshaw ['rɪkʃɔː] n jinrikisha f.

ricochet ['rɪkəʃeɪ] (pt & pp -ed OR -ted, cont -ing OR -ting) ◇ n rebote m. ◇ vi: **to ~ (off)** rebotar (de).

rid [rɪd] (pt rid OR -ded, pp rid, cont -ding) ◇ adj: **to be ~ of** estar libre de. ◇ vt: **to ~ sthg/sb of** librar algo/a alguien de; **to ~ o.s. of** librarse uno de; **to get ~ of** deshacerse de.

riddance ['rɪdəns] n inf: **good ~!** ¡adiós y viento fresco!

ridden ['rɪdn] pp → ride.

riddle ['rɪdl] n -1. [verbal puzzle] acertijo m, adivinanza f. -2. [mystery] enigma m.

riddled ['rɪdld] adj: **to be ~ with** estar plagado(da) de.

ride [raɪd] (pt rode, pp ridden) ◇ n paseo m; **to go for a ~** [on horseback] darse un paseo a caballo; [on bike] darse un paseo en bicicleta; [in car] darse una vuelta en coche; **to take sb for a ~** inf fig embaucar a alguien.
◇ vt -1. [horse] montar a. -2. [bicycle, motorbike] montar en; **he rode his bike to the station** fue a la estación en bici. -3. Am [bus, train] ir en; [elevator] subir/bajar en. -4. [distance] recorrer.
◇ vi -1. [on horseback] montar a caballo; **she rode over to see me** vino a verme a caballo. -2. [on bicycle] ir en bici; [on motorbike] ir en moto. -3. [in car]: **we rode to London in a jeep** fuimos a Londres en jeep.

◆ **ride up** vi subirse.

rider ['raɪdə-] n -1. [on horseback] jinete m, amazona f. -2. [on bicycle] ciclista m y f; [on motorbike] motorista m y f.

ridge [rɪdʒ] n -1. [on mountain] cresta f. -2. [on flat surface] rugosidad f.

ridicule ['rɪdɪkjuːl] ◇ n (U) burlas fpl. ◇ vt ridiculizar.

ridiculous [rɪ'dɪkjʊləs] adj ridículo(la), absurdo(da).

ridiculously [rɪ'dɪkjʊləslɪ] adv ridículosamente.

riding ['raɪdɪŋ] ◇ n equitación f. ◇ comp de equitación.

riding crop n fusta f.

riding habit n traje m de montar.

riding school n escuela f de equitación.

rife [raɪf] adj extendido(da); **to be ~ with** estar lleno de.

riffraff ['rɪfræf] n gentuza f.

rifle ['raɪfl] ◇ n rifle m, fusil m. ◇ vt desvalijar.

◆ **rifle through** vt fus revolver.

rifle range n campo m de tiro.

rift [rɪft] n -1. GEOL hendedura f, grieta f. -2. [quarrel] desavenencia f. -3. POL: **~ between/in** escisión f entre/en.

Rift Valley n: **the ~** el Rift Valley.

rig [rɪg] (pt & pp -ged, cont -ging) ◇ n: **(oil) ~** [onshore] torre f de perforación; [offshore] plataforma f petrolífera. ◇ vt [falsify] amañar, falsificar.

◆ **rig up** vt sep construir, armar.

rigging ['rɪgɪŋ] n cordaje m.

right [raɪt] ◇ adj -1. [correct] correcto(ta), bueno(na); **have you got the ~ time?** ¿tienes la hora buena?; **to be ~ (about)** tener razón (respecto a); **he never gets anything ~** nunca le salen las cosas bien; **get it ~!** ¡hazlo bien! -2. [satisfactory] bien. -3. [morally correct, socially acceptable] apropiado(da); **to be ~ to do sthg** hacer bien en hacer algo. -4. [uppermost]: **~ side** cara f anterior OR de arriba. -5. [on right-hand side] derecho(cha). -6. Br inf [complete - mess, idiot] puro(ra), perfecto(ta).
◇ n -1. (U) [moral correctness] bien m; **to be in the ~** tener razón. -2. [entitlement, claim] derecho m; **by ~s** en justicia; **in one's own ~** por propio derecho. -3. [right-hand side] derecha f.
◇ adv -1. [correctly] bien, correctamente. -2. [to right-hand side] a la derecha. -3. [emphatic use]: **~ here** aquí mismo; **~ at the top** arriba del todo; **~ in the middle** justo en el medio. -4. [immediately]: **I'll be ~ back** ahora mismo vuelvo; **~ before/after (sthg)** justo antes/después (de algo); **~ now**

ahora mismo, ahorita *Amer*; ~ **away** en seguida, luego *Amer*.
◇ *vt* **-1.** [correct] corregir, rectificar. **-2.** [make upright] enderezar.
◇ *excl* ¡bien!
◆ **Right** *n* POL: **the Right** la derecha.

right angle *n* ángulo *m* recto; **at ~s (to)** en ángulo recto (con).

righteous ['raɪtʃəs] *adj* [anger] justo(ta); [person] honrado(da).

righteousness ['raɪtʃəsnɪs] *n* honradez *f*, rectitud *f*.

rightful ['raɪtful] *adj* justo(ta), legítimo(ma).

rightfully ['raɪtfulɪ] *adv* legítimamente, justamente.

right-hand *adj* derecho(cha); **the ~ side** el lado derecho, la derecha.

right-hand drive *adj* que se conduce por la derecha.

right-handed [-'hændɪd] *adj* diestro(tra).

right-hand man *n* brazo *m* derecho.

rightly ['raɪtlɪ] *adv* **-1.** [correctly] correctamente. **-2.** [appropriately] debidamente, bien. **-3.** [morally] justamente, con razón.

right-minded [-'maɪndɪd] *adj* honrado(da).

rightness ['raɪtnɪs] *n* corrección *f*.

righto ['raɪtəʊ] *excl inf* ¡vale!

right of way *n* **-1.** AUT prioridad *f*. **-2.** [access] derecho *m* de paso.

right-on *adj inf* esnob.

rights issue *n* emisión *f* de derechos de suscripción.

right-thinking [-'θɪŋkɪŋ] *adj* juicioso(sa), sensato(ta).

right wing *n*: **the ~** la derecha.
◆ **right-wing** *adj* de derechas, derechista.

right-winger *n* derechista *m y f*.

rigid ['rɪdʒɪd] *adj* **-1.** [stiff] rígido(da). **-2.** [harsh, unbending] inflexible.

rigidity [rɪ'dʒɪdətɪ] *n* **-1.** [stiffness] rigidez *f*. **-2.** [harshness] severidad *f*, inflexibilidad *f*.

rigidly ['rɪdʒɪdlɪ] *adv* **-1.** [without moving] rígidamente. **-2.** [inflexibly] inflexiblemente, severamente.

rigmarole ['rɪgmərəʊl] *n inf pej* **-1.** [process] ritual *m*. **-2.** [story] galimatías *m inv*.

rigor *Am* = **rigour**.

rigor mortis [-'mɔːtɪs] *n* rigor *m* mortis.

rigorous ['rɪgərəs] *adj* riguroso(sa).

rigorously ['rɪgərəslɪ] *adv* rigurosamente.

rigour *Br*, **rigor** *Am* ['rɪgər] *n* [firmness] rigor *m*, severidad *f*.
◆ **rigours** *npl* [severe conditions] dureza *f*, rigor *m*.

rig-out *n Br inf* atuendo *m*.

rile [raɪl] *vt* irritar, sacar de quicio.

rim [rɪm] *n* **-1.** [of container] borde *m*. **-2.** [of spectacles] montura *f*.

rind [raɪnd] *n* corteza *f*.

ring [rɪŋ] (*pt* **rang**, *pp* **rung** *vt senses 1 & 2 & vi*, *pt & pp* **ringed** *vt senses 3 & 4 only*) ◇ *n* **-1.** [telephone call]: **to give sb a ~** llamar a alguien (por teléfono). **-2.** [sound of doorbell] timbrazo *m*, llamada *f*. **-3.** [quality]: **it has a familiar ~** me suena (familiar). **-4.** [metal hoop] aro *m*; [for curtains] anilla *f*. **-5.** [on finger] anillo *m*. **-6.** [circle - of trees] círculo *m*; [- of people] corro *m*. **-7.** [for boxing] cuadrilátero *m*. **-8.** [illegal group] cartel *m*.
◇ *vt* **-1.** *Br* [phone] llamar por teléfono, telefonear. **-2.** [bell] tocar. **-3.** [draw a circle round] señalar con un círculo. **-4.** [surround] cercar, rodear; **to be ~ed with** estar rodeado de.
◇ *vi* **-1.** *Br* [phone] llamar por teléfono, telefonear. **-2.** [bell] sonar. **-3.** [to attract attention]: **to ~ (for)** llamar (para). **-4.** [resound]: **to ~ with** resonar con. **-5.** *phr*: **to ~ true** sonar a ser cierto.
◆ **ring back** *vt sep & vi Br* volver a llamar.
◆ **ring off** *vi Br* colgar.
◆ **ring out** *vi* **-1.** [sound] sonar. **-2.** *Br* TELEC llamar.
◆ **ring up** *vt sep Br* llamar (por teléfono).

ring binder *n* carpeta *f* de anillas.

ringer ['rɪŋər] *n*: **to be a dead ~ for sb** ser el vivo retrato de alguien.

ring finger *n* (dedo *m*) anular *m*.

ringing ['rɪŋɪŋ] ◇ *adj* resonante, sonoro(ra). ◇ *n* [of bell] repique *m*, tañido *m*; [in ears] zumbido *m*.

ringing tone *n* tono *m* de llamada.

ringleader ['rɪŋˌliːdər] *n* cabecilla *m y f*.

ringlet ['rɪŋlɪt] *n* rizo *m*, tirabuzón *m*.

ringmaster ['rɪŋˌmɑːstər] *n* director *m* de circo, jefe *m* de pista.

ring road *n Br* carretera *f* de circunvalación.

ringside ['rɪŋsaɪd] ◇ *n*: **the ~** *espacio inmediato al cuadrilátero o a la pista de circo*. ◇ *comp* de primera fila.

ringway ['rɪŋweɪ] *n Br* carretera *f* de circunvalación.

ringworm ['rɪŋwɜːm] *n* tiña *f*.

rink [rɪŋk] *n* pista *f*.

rinse [rɪns] ◇ *n* [of dishes, vegetables] enjuague *m*; [of clothes] aclarado *m*. ◇ *vt* **-1.** [dishes, vegetables] enjuagar; [clothes] aclarar. **-2.** [wash out]: **to ~ one's mouth out** enjuagarse la boca.

Rio (de Janeiro) [ˌriːəʊ(dədʒəˈnɪərəʊ)] *n* Río (de Janeiro).

Rio Grande [ˌriːəʊ'grændɪ] *n*: the ~ el río Bravo.

Rio Negro [ˌriːəʊ'neɪgrəʊ] *n*: the ~ el río Negro.

riot ['raɪət] ◇ *n* disturbio *m*; to run ~ desbocarse. ◇ *vi* amotinarse.

rioter ['raɪətər] *n* amotinado *m*, -da *f*.

rioting ['raɪətɪŋ] *n* (*U*) disturbios *mpl*.

riotous ['raɪətəs] *adj* ruidoso(sa).

riot police *npl* brigada *f* antidisturbios.

riot shield *n* escudo *m* antidisturbios.

rip [rɪp] (*pt & pp* **-ped**, *cont* **-ping**) ◇ *n* rasgón *m*. ◇ *vt* **-1.** [tear] rasgar, desgarrar. **-2.** [remove violently] quitar de un tirón. ◇ *vi* rasgarse, romperse.

◆ **rip off** *vt sep inf* **-1.** [person] timar. **-2.** [product, idea] copiar.

◆ **rip up** *vt sep* hacer pedazos.

RIP (*abbr of* **rest in peace**) RIP.

ripcord ['rɪpkɔːd] *n* cabo *m* de desgarre.

ripe [raɪp] *adj* maduro(ra); to be ~ (for sthg) estar listo (para algo).

ripen ['raɪpn] *vt & vi* madurar.

ripeness ['raɪpnɪs] *n* madurez *f*.

rip-off *n inf* estafa *f*.

ripple ['rɪpl] ◇ *n* **-1.** [in water] onda *f*, rizo *m*. **-2.** [of laughter, applause] murmullo *m*. ◇ *vt* rizar.

rip-roaring *adj inf* [party] bullicioso(sa); [success] apoteósico(ca).

rise [raɪz] (*pt* **rose**, *pp* **risen** ['rɪzn]) ◇ *n* **-1.** [increase] ascenso *m*, subida *f*. **-2.** *Br* [increase in salary] aumento *m*. **-3.** [to fame etc] subida *f*. **-4.** *phr*: to give ~ to sthg dar origen a algo.
◇ *vi* **-1.** [gen] elevarse. **-2.** [sun, moon] salir. **-3.** [price, wage, temperature] subir. **-4.** [stand up, get out of bed] levantarse. **-5.** [street, ground] subir. **-6.** [respond]: to ~ to reaccionar ante; to ~ to a challenge aceptar un reto. **-7.** [rebel] sublevarse. **-8.** [move up in status] ascender; to ~ to power/fame ascender al poder/a la gloria.

◆ **rise above** *vt fus* superar, mostrarse superior a.

riser ['raɪzər] *n*: early ~ madrugador *m*, -ra *f*; late ~ persona que se levanta tarde.

risible ['rɪzəbl] *adj fml* risible.

rising ['raɪzɪŋ] ◇ *adj* **-1.** [sloping upwards] ascendente. **-2.** [increasing] creciente. **-3.** [increasingly successful] prometedor(ra). ◇ *n* rebelión *f*.

rising damp *n* humedad *f*.

risk [rɪsk] ◇ *n* [gen] riesgo *m*; [danger] peligro *m*; to run the ~ of sthg/of doing sthg correr el riesgo de algo/de hacer algo; to take a ~ arriesgarse; at your own ~ bajo tu cuenta y riesgo; at ~ en peligro; at the ~ of a riesgo de. ◇ *vt* **-1.** [put in danger] arriesgar. **-2.** [take the chance of]: to ~ doing sthg exponerse a hacer algo.

risk capital *n* capital *m* de riesgo.

risk-taking *n* toma *f* de riesgos.

risky ['rɪskɪ] (*compar* **-ier**, *superl* **-iest**) *adj* peligroso(sa), arriesgado(da).

risotto [rɪ'zɒtəʊ] (*pl* **-s**) *n arroz guisado con pollo o verduras etc.*

risqué ['riːskeɪ] *adj* verde, subido(da) de tono.

rissole ['rɪsəʊl] *n Br especie de albóndiga de carne o verduras.*

rite [raɪt] *n* rito *m*.

ritual ['rɪtʃʊəl] ◇ *adj* ritual. ◇ *n* ritual *m*.

rival ['raɪvl] (*Br pt & pp* **-led**, *cont* **-ling**, *Am pt & pp* **-ed**, *cont* **-ing**) ◇ *adj* rival, opuesto(ta). ◇ *n* rival *m* y *f*, competidor *m*, -ra *f*. ◇ *vt* rivalizar OR competir con.

rivalry ['raɪvlrɪ] *n* rivalidad *f*, competencia *f*.

river ['rɪvər] *n* río *m*.

river bank *n* orilla *f* OR margen *f* del río.

riverbed ['rɪvəbed] *n* cauce *m* OR lecho *m* del río.

riverside ['rɪvəsaɪd] *n*: the ~ la ribera OR orilla del río.

rivet ['rɪvɪt] ◇ *n* remache *m*. ◇ *vt* **-1.** [fasten] remachar. **-2.** *fig*: to be ~ed by sthg estar fascinado(da) con algo.

riveting ['rɪvɪtɪŋ] *adj* fascinante.

Riviera [ˌrɪvɪ'eərə] *n*: the French ~ la Riviera francesa; the Italian ~ la Riviera italiana.

Riyadh ['riːæd] *n* Riad.

RMSD (*abbr of* **Royal Mail Special Delivery**) *sección del servicio de correos británico encargada de entregas especiales.*

RN *n* **-1.** *abbr of* **Royal Navy**. **-2.** *abbr of* **registered nurse**.

RNA (*abbr of* **ribonucleic acid**) *n* ARN *m*.

RNLI (*abbr of* **Royal National Lifeboat Institution**) *n organización de voluntarios que ofrece un servicio de rescate marítimo en Gran Bretaña e Irlanda.*

RNZAF (*abbr of* **Royal New Zealand Air Force**) *n fuerzas aéreas neozelandesas.*

RNZN (*abbr of* **Royal New Zealand Navy**) *n armada neozelandesa.*

roach [rəʊtʃ] *n Am* [cockroach] cucaracha *f*.

road [rəʊd] *n* [minor] camino *m*; [major] carretera *f*; [street] calle *f*; to be on the ~ to *fig* estar en camino de; on the ~ en camino.

road atlas *n* guía *f* de carreteras.

roadblock ['rəʊdblɒk] *n* control *m*.

road-fund licence *n Br* ≃ impuesto *m* de circulación.

road hog *n inf pej* conductor rápido y negligente.

roadholding ['rəʊd,həʊldɪŋ] *n* agarre *m*.

roadie ['rəʊdɪ] *n inf* encargado del transporte y montaje de un equipo musical en gira.

road map *n* mapa *m* de carreteras.

road rage *n* arrebato de ira de un automovilista que puede conducirle en ocasiones a cometer una agresión.

road roller *n* apisonadora *f*.

road safety *n* seguridad *f* en carretera.

road sense *n* buen instinto *m* en la carretera.

roadshow ['rəʊdʃəʊ] *n* programa radiofónico transmitido en directo desde un lugar de veraneo por un disc-jockey en gira.

roadside ['rəʊdsaɪd] ◇ *n*: **the** ~ el borde de la carretera. ◇ *comp* al borde de la carretera.

road sign *n* señal *f* de carretera.

roadsweeper ['rəʊd,swiːpəʳ] *n* camión *m* limpiacarreteras.

road tax *n* impuesto *m* de circulación.

road test *n* prueba *f* en carretera.

◆ **road-test** *vt* probar en carretera.

road transport *n* transporte *m* por carretera.

roadway ['rəʊdweɪ] *n* calzada *f*.

road works *npl* obras *fpl* de carretera.

roadworthy ['rəʊd,wɜːðɪ] *adj* apto(ta) para circular.

roam [rəʊm] ◇ *vt* vagar por. ◇ *vi* vagar.

roar [rɔːʳ] ◇ *vi* [make a loud noise] rugir, bramar; **to** ~ **with laughter** reírse a carcajadas. ◇ *vt* rugir, decir a voces. ◇ *n* **-1.** [of traffic] fragor *m*, estruendo *m*. **-2.** [of lion, person] rugido *m*.

roaring ['rɔːrɪŋ] *adj* **-1.** [loud] clamoroso(sa), fragoroso(sa). **-2.** [blazing] espectacular. **-3.** [as emphasis]: **a** ~ **success** un éxito clamoroso; **to do a** ~ **trade** hacer un gran negocio.

roast [rəʊst] ◇ *adj* asado(da). ◇ *n* asado *m*. ◇ *vt* **-1.** [potatoes, meat] asar. **-2.** [nuts, coffee beans] tostar.

roast beef *n* rosbif *m*.

roasting ['rəʊstɪŋ] *adj inf* achicharrante.

roasting tin *n* bandeja *f* de asar.

rob [rɒb] (*pt* & *pp* **-bed,** *cont* **-bing**) *vt* robar; **to** ~ **sb of sthg** robar a alguien algo.

robber ['rɒbəʳ] *n* ladrón *m*, -ona *f*.

robbery ['rɒbərɪ] (*pl* **-ies**) *n* robo *m*.

robe [rəʊb] *n* **-1.** [towelling] albornoz *m*. **-2.**

[of student] toga *f*. **-3.** [of priest] sotana *f*. **-4.** *Am* [dressing gown] bata *f*.

robin ['rɒbɪn] *n* petirrojo *m*.

robot ['rəʊbɒt] *n* robot *m*.

robotics [rəʊ'bɒtɪks] *n* (*U*) robótica *f*.

robust [rəʊ'bʌst] *adj* robusto(ta), fuerte.

robustly [rəʊ'bʌstlɪ] *adv* robustamente, fuertemente.

rock [rɒk] ◇ *n* **-1.** (*U*) [substance] roca *f*. **-2.** [boulder] peñasco *m*. **-3.** *Am* [pebble] guijarro *m*. **-4.** [music] rock *m*. **-5.** *Br* [sweet] palo *m* de caramelo. ◇ *comp* de rock. ◇ *vt* **-1.** [cause to move] mecer, balancear. **-2.** [shock] sacudir. ◇ *vi* mecerse, balancearse.

◆ **Rock** *n inf* [Gibraltar]: **the Rock** el Peñón.

◆ **on the rocks** *adv* **-1.** [drink] con hielo. **-2.** [marriage, relationship] que va mal.

rock and roll *n* rock and roll *m*.

rock bottom *n* el fondo; **to hit** ~ tocar fondo.

◆ **rock-bottom** *adj*: **rock-bottom prices** precios muy bajos.

rock cake *n Br* bizcocho con frutos secos.

rock climber *n* escalador *m*, -ra *f* (de rocas).

rock-climbing *n* escalada *f* (de rocas).

rock dash *n Am* enguijarrado *m*.

rocker ['rɒkəʳ] *n* [chair] mecedora *f*; **he's off his** ~ *inf* le falta un tornillo.

rockery ['rɒkərɪ] (*pl* **-ies**) *n* jardín *m* de rocas.

rocket ['rɒkɪt] ◇ *n* cohete *m*. ◇ *vi* subir rápidamente.

rocket launcher [-,lɔːntʃəʳ] *n* lanzacohetes *m inv*.

rock face *n* pared *f* de roca.

rockfall ['rɒkfɔːl] *n* deslizamiento *m* de montaña.

rock-hard *adj* duro(ra) como una piedra.

Rockies ['rɒkɪz] *npl*: **the** ~ las Rocosas.

rocking chair ['rɒkɪŋ-] *n* mecedora *f*.

rocking horse ['rɒkɪŋ-] *n* caballo *m* de balancín.

rock music *n* música *f* rock.

rock'n'roll [,rɒkən'rəʊl] = **rock and roll**.

rock pool *n* charca *f* entre las rocas en la playa.

rock salt *n* sal *f* gema.

rocky ['rɒkɪ] (*compar* **-ier,** *superl* **-iest**) *adj* **-1.** [full of rocks] rocoso(sa). **-2.** [unsteady] inestable.

Rocky Mountains *npl*: **the** ~ las montañas Rocosas.

rococo [rə'kəʊkəʊ] *adj* rococó.

rod [rɒd] *n* [wooden] vara *f*; [metal] barra *f*; [for fishing] caña *f*.

rode [rəʊd] *pt* → ride.

rodent ['rəʊdənt] *n* roedor *m*.

rodeo ['rəʊdɪəʊ] (*pl* -s) *n* rodeo *m*.

roe [rəʊ] *n* hueva *f*.

roe deer *n* corzo *m*.

rogue [rəʊg] ◇ *adj* -1. [animal] solitario y peligroso (solitaria y peligrosa). -2. *fig* [person] rebelde. ◇ *n* -1. [likeable rascal] picaruelo *m*, -la *f*. -2. *dated* [dishonest person] bellaco *m*, -ca *f*.

roguish ['rəʊgɪʃ] *adj* picaruelo(la), travieso(sa).

role [rəʊl] *n* THEATRE & *fig* papel *m*.

roll [rəʊl] ◇ *n* -1. [gen] rollo *m*; [of paper, banknotes] fajo *m*; [of cloth] pieza *f*. -2. [of bread] panecillo *m*. -3. [list] lista *f*; [payroll] nómina *f*. -4. [of drums] redoble *m*; [of thunder] retumbo *m*. ◇ *vt* -1. [turn over] hacer rodar; **to ~ one's eyes** poner los ojos en blanco. -2. [roll up] enrollar; **~ed into one** todo en uno. -3. [cigarette] liar. ◇ *vi* -1. [ball, barrel] rodar. -2. [vehicle] ir, avanzar. -3. [ship] balancearse. -4. [thunder] retumbar; [drum] redoblar.
  ◆ **roll about, roll around** *vi*: **to ~ about** OR **around (on)** rodar (por).
  ◆ **roll back** *vt sep Am* [prices] bajar.
  ◆ **roll in** *vi inf* llegar a raudales.
  ◆ **roll over** *vi* darse la vuelta.
  ◆ **roll up** ◇ *vt sep* -1. [make into roll] enrollar. -2. [sleeves] remangarse. ◇ *vi* -1. [vehicle] llegar. -2. *inf* [person] presentarse, aparecer.

roll bar *n* barra *f* antivolcamiento.

roll call *n*: **to take a ~** pasar lista.

rolled gold [rəʊld-] *n* oro *m* laminado.

roller ['rəʊlə^r] *n* -1. [cylinder] rodillo *m*. -2. [curler] rulo *m*.

roller blind *n* persiana *f* enrollable.

roller coaster *n* montaña *f* rusa.

roller skate *n* patín *m* de ruedas.
  ◆ **roller-skate** *vi* ir en patines.

roller towel *n* toalla *f* de rodillo.

rollicking ['rɒlɪkɪŋ] *adj*: **we had a ~ good time** lo pasamos en grande.

rolling ['rəʊlɪŋ] *adj* -1. [undulating] ondulante. -2. *phr*: **to be ~ in it** *inf* nadar en la abundancia.

rolling mill *n* taller *m* de laminación.

rolling pin *n* rodillo *m* (de cocina).

rolling stock *n* material *m* rodante.

rollneck ['rəʊlnek] *adj* de cuello de cisne.

roll of honour *n* lista *f* de honor.

roll-on *adj* [deodorant etc] de bola.

roll-on roll-off *adj Br* de carga OR transbordo horizontal.

roly-poly [,rəʊlɪ'pəʊlɪ] (*pl* -ies) *n Br*: ~ **(pudding)** *dulce compuesto de mermelada y masa pastelera enrolladas y que se hace al horno o hierve.*

ROM [rɒm] (*abbr of* read only memory) *n* ROM *f*.

romaine lettuce [rəʊ'meɪn-] *n Am* lechuga *f* (*de hoja larga*).

Roman ['rəʊmən] ◇ *adj* romano(na). ◇ *n* romano *m*, -na *f*.

Roman candle *n tipo de fuego artificial.*

Roman Catholic ◇ *adj* católico (romano) (católica (romana)). ◇ *n* católico (romano) *m*, católica (romana) *f*.

romance [rəʊ'mæns] *n* -1. [romantic quality] lo romántico. -2. [love affair] amorío *m*. -3. [in fiction - modern] novela *f* romántica; [- medieval] libro *m* de caballerías, romance *m*.

Romanesque [,rəʊmə'nesk] *adj* románico(ca).

Romani = Romany.

Romania [ruː'meɪnjə] *n* Rumanía.

Romanian [ruː'meɪnjən] ◇ *adj* rumano(na). ◇ *n* -1. [person] rumano *m*, -na *f*. -2. [language] rumano *m*.

Roman numerals *npl* números *mpl* romanos.

romantic [rəʊ'mæntɪk] *adj* romántico(ca).

romanticism [rəʊ'mæntɪsɪzm] *n* romanticismo *m*.

romanticize, -ise [rəʊ'mæntɪsaɪz] ◇ *vt* poner una nota romántica en. ◇ *vi* soñar despierto, fantasear.

Romany, Romani ['rəʊmənɪ] (*pl* -ies) ◇ *adj* gitano(na), romaní. ◇ *n* -1. [person] romaní *m* y *f*, gitano *m*, -na *f*. -2. [language - gen] lengua *f* gitana; [- in Spain] caló *m*.

Rome [rəʊm] *n* Roma.

romp [rɒmp] ◇ *n* retozo *m*, jugueteo *m*. ◇ *vi* retozar, juguetear.

rompers ['rɒmpəz] *npl*, **romper suit** ['rɒmpə-] *n* pelele *m*.

roof [ruːf] *n* -1. [of building] tejado *m*; [of vehicle] techo *m*; **under the same ~** bajo el mismo techo; **under one's ~** en la casa de uno; **to have a ~ over one's head** tener cobijo; **to go through** OR **hit the ~** [person] subirse por las paredes. -2. [of mouth] paladar *m*.

roof garden *n* azotea o terraza con flores y plantas.

roofing ['ruːfɪŋ] *n* materiales *mpl* para techar, techumbre *f*.

roof rack *n* baca *f*, portaequipajes *m inv*, parrilla *f Amer*.

rooftop ['ruːftɒp] *n* tejado *m*.

rook [rʊk] *n* **-1.** [bird] grajo *m*. **-2.** [chess piece] torre *f*.

rookie ['rʊkɪ] *n Am inf* novato *m*, -ta *f*.

room [ruːm, rʊm] *n* **-1.** [in house, building] habitación *f*. **-2.** [for conferences etc] sala *f*. **-3.** [bedroom] habitación *f*, cuarto *m*, ambiente *m Amer*. **-4.** (*U*) [space] sitio *m*, espacio *m*. **-5.** [opportunity, possibility]: ~ **for improvement** posibilidad de mejora; ~ **to** OR **for manoeuvre** espacio para maniobrar.

rooming house ['ruːmɪŋ-] *n Am* casa *f* de huéspedes, pensión *f*.

roommate ['ruːmmeɪt] *n* compañero *m*, -ra *f* de habitación.

room service *n* servicio *m* de habitación.

room temperature *n* temperatura *f* ambiente.

roomy ['ruːmɪ] (*compar* **-ier**, *superl* **-iest**) *adj* espacioso(sa), amplio(plia).

roost [ruːst] ◇ *n* percha *f*, palo *m*; **to rule the** ~ llevar el cotarro. ◇ *vi* dormir (en una percha).

rooster ['ruːstə^r] *n* gallo *m*.

root [ruːt] ◇ *adj* [fundamental] de raíz. ◇ *n lit* & *fig* raíz *f*; **to take** ~ *lit* & *fig* arraigar; **to put down** ~**s** [person] echar raíces, radicarse. ◇ *vi* [pig etc] hozar; [person] hurgar, escarbar.

◆ **roots** *npl* [origins] raíces *fpl*.

◆ **root for** *vt fus Am inf* apoyar a.

◆ **root out** *vt sep* [eradicate] desarraigar, arrancar de raíz.

root beer *n Am cerveza sin alcohol hecha de raíces*.

root crop *n* tubérculos *mpl*.

rooted ['ruːtɪd] *adj*: **to be** ~ **to the spot** quedar inmóvil.

rootless ['ruːtlɪs] *adj* desarraigado(da).

root vegetable *n* tubérculo *m*.

rope [rəʊp] ◇ *n* [thin] cuerda *f*, cabuya *f Amer*; [thick] soga *f*; NAUT maroma *f*, cable *m*; **to know the** ~**s** saber de qué va el asunto. ◇ *vt* atar con cuerda.

◆ **rope in** *vt sep inf* arrastrar OR enganchar a.

◆ **rope off** *vt sep* acordonar.

rop(e)y ['rəʊpɪ] (*compar* **-ier**, *superl* **-iest**) *adj Br inf* **-1.** [poor-quality] malo(la). **-2.** [unwell] malucho(cha).

rosary ['rəʊzərɪ] (*pl* **-ies**) *n* rosario *m*.

rose [rəʊz] ◇ *pt* → **rise**. ◇ *adj* [pink] rosa, color de rosa. ◇ *n* [flower] rosa *f*.

rosé ['rəʊzeɪ] *n* rosado *m*.

rosebed ['rəʊzbed] *n* rosaleda *f*.

rosebud ['rəʊzbʌd] *n* capullo *m* de rosa.

rose bush *n* rosal *m*.

rose hip *n* escaramujo *m*.

rosemary ['rəʊzmərɪ] *n* romero *m*.

rosette [rəʊ'zet] *n* [of clothing] escarapela *f*; [of building] rosetón *m*.

rosewater ['rəʊz‚wɔːtə^r] *n* agua *f* de rosas.

rosewood ['rəʊzwʊd] *n* palisandro *m*.

ROSPA ['rɒspə] (*abbr of* **Royal Society for the Prevention of Accidents**) *n organización británica para la prevención de accidentes*.

roster ['rɒstə^r] *n* lista *f*.

rostrum ['rɒstrəm] (*pl* **-trums** OR **-tra** [-trə]) *n* tribuna *f*.

rosy ['rəʊzɪ] (*compar* **-ier**, *superl* **-iest**) *adj* **-1.** [pink] sonrosado(da). **-2.** [hopeful] prometedor(ra).

rot [rɒt] (*pt* & *pp* **-ted**, *cont* **-ting**) ◇ *n* (*U*) **-1.** [of wood, food] podredumbre *f*, putrefacción *f*; [in society, organization] decadencia *f*. **-2.** *Br dated* [nonsense] tonterías *fpl*, bobadas *fpl*. ◇ *vt* pudrir, corromper. ◇ *vi* pudrirse, corromperse.

rota ['rəʊtə] *n* lista *f* (de turnos).

rotary ['rəʊtərɪ] ◇ *adj* giratorio(ria), rotativo(va). ◇ *n Am* [roundabout] glorieta *f*, cruce *m* de circulación giratoria.

Rotary Club *n*: **the** ~ la Sociedad Rotaria.

rotate [rəʊ'teɪt] ◇ *vt* **-1.** [turn] hacer girar, dar vueltas a. **-2.** [jobs] alternar; [crops] cultivar en rotación. ◇ *vi* **-1.** [turn] girar, dar vueltas. **-2.** [jobs] alternarse; [crops] cultivarse en rotación.

rotation [rəʊ'teɪʃn] *n* **-1.** [gen] rotación *f*. **-2.** [of jobs] turno *m*; **in** ~ por turno OR turnos.

rote [rəʊt] *n*: **by** ~ de memoria.

rote learning *n* aprendizaje *m* de memoria.

rotor ['rəʊtə^r] *n* rotor *m*.

rotten ['rɒtn] *adj* **-1.** [decayed] podrido(da). **-2.** *inf* [poor-quality] malísimo(ma), fatal. **-3.** *inf* [unpleasant] despreciable. **-4.** *inf* [unwell]: **to feel** ~ sentirse fatal OR muy mal. **-5.** [unhappy]: **to feel** ~ **(about)** sentirse mal (por).

rotund [rəʊ'tʌnd] *adj fml* regordete(ta).

rouble ['ruːbl] *n* rublo *m*.

rouge [ruːʒ] *n* colorete *m*.

rough [rʌf] ◇ *adj* **-1.** [not smooth - surface, skin] áspero(ra); [- ground, road] desigual. **-2.** [not gentle, brutal] bruto(ta). **-3.** [crude, not refined - person, manner] grosero(ra), liso(sa) *Amer*, tosco(ca); [- shelter] precario(ria); [- food, living conditions] simple. **-4.** [approximate - plan, sketch] a grandes rasgos; [- estimate, translation] aproximado(da). **-5.** [unpleasant] duro(ra), difícil. **-6.** [wind] violento(ta); [sea] picado(da), embravecido(da); [weather, day] tormentoso(sa), borrascoso(sa). **-7.** [harsh - wine, voice] áspero(ra). **-8.** [violent - area] peligroso(sa); [- person] violento(ta). **-9.** [tired, ill]: **to look/feel ~** tener un aspecto/sentirse fatal.

◇ *adv*: **to sleep ~** dormir al raso.

◇ *n* **-1.** GOLF: **the ~** el rough. **-2.** [undetailed form]: **in ~** en borrador.

◇ *vt phr*: **to ~ it** vivir sin comodidades.

◆ **rough out** *vt sep* esbozar, bosquejar.

roughage ['rʌfɪdʒ] *n* (*U*) fibra *f*.

rough and ready *adj* tosco(ca).

rough-and-tumble *n* (*U*) riña *f*.

roughcast ['rʌfkɑːst] *n* mortero *m* grueso.

rough diamond *n Br fig* diamante *m* en bruto.

roughen ['rʌfn] *vt* poner áspero(ra).

rough justice *n* injusticia *f*.

roughly ['rʌflɪ] *adv* **-1.** [approximately] más o menos. **-2.** [not gently] brutalmente. **-3.** [crudely] toscamente.

roughneck ['rʌfnek] *n* **-1.** [oilworker] *trabajador en una explotación petrolífera*. **-2.** *Am inf* [ruffian] matón *m*, duro *m*.

roughness ['rʌfnɪs] *n* **-1.** [lack of smoothness] aspereza *f*. **-2.** [lack of gentleness] brutalidad *f*.

roughshod ['rʌfʃɒd] *adv*: **to ride ~ over sthg/sb** tratar algo/a alguien sin contemplaciones.

roulette [ruː'let] *n* ruleta *f*.

round [raʊnd] ◇ *adj* redondo(da).

◇ *prep* **-1.** [surrounding] alrededor de. **-2.** [near] cerca de; **~ here** por aquí. **-3.** [all over - the world etc] por todo(da). **-4.** [in circular movement]: **~ (and ~)** alrededor de. **-5.** [in measurements]: **she's 30 inches ~ the waist** mide 30 pulgadas de cintura. **-6.** [at or to the other side of]: **they were waiting ~ the corner** esperaban a la vuelta de la esquina; **to drive ~ the corner** doblar la esquina; **to go ~ sthg** rodear algo. **-7.** [so as to avoid]: **he drove ~ the pothole** condujo esquivando el bache.

◇ *adv* **-1.** [on all sides]: **all ~** por todos lados; **to sit ~ in a circle** sentarse formando un círculo. **-2.** [near]: **~ about** alrededor, en las proximidades. **-3.** [all over]: **to travel ~** viajar por ahí. **-4.** [in circular movement]: **~ (and ~)** en redondo; **to go** OR **spin ~** girar. **-5.** [in measurements] en redondo. **-6.** [to the other side] al otro lado; **to go ~** dar un rodeo. **-7.** [at or to nearby place]: **he came ~ to see us** vino a vernos; **I'm going ~ to the shop** voy un momento a la tienda.

◇ *n* **-1.** [of talks, drinks] ronda *f*; **a ~ of applause** una salva de aplausos. **-2.** [in championship] vuelta *f*. **-3.** [of doctor] visita *f*; [of milkman, postman] recorrido *m*. **-4.** [of ammunition] cartucho *m*. **-5.** [in boxing] asalto *m*. **-6.** [in golf] vuelta *f*, round *m*.

◇ *vt* doblar.

◆ **rounds** *npl* [of doctor] visitas *fpl*; [of postman] recorrido *m*; **to do** OR **go the ~s** [joke, rumour] divulgarse; [illness] estar rodando.

◆ **round off** *vt sep* terminar.

◆ **round up** *vt sep* **-1.** [gather together] reunir. **-2.** MATH redondear.

roundabout ['raʊndəbaʊt] ◇ *adj* indirecto(ta). ◇ *n Br* **-1.** [on road] glorieta *f*, cruce *m* de circulación giratoria. **-2.** [at fairground] tiovivo *m*, caballitos *mpl*. **-3.** [at playground] *plataforma giratoria para que los niños la empujen y monten en ella*.

rounded ['raʊndɪd] *adj* redondeado(da).

rounders ['raʊndəz] *n Br juego parecido al béisbol*.

Roundhead ['raʊndhed] *n seguidor de Oliver Cromwell en la guerra civil inglesa del siglo XVII*.

roundly ['raʊndlɪ] *adv* rotundamente, terminantemente.

round-shouldered [-'ʃəʊldəd] *adj* cargado(da) de espaldas.

round-table *adj* en igualdad de condiciones.

round the clock *adv* (durante) las 24 horas del día.

◆ **round-the-clock** *adj* continuo(nua), 24 horas al día.

round trip ◇ *adj Am* de ida y vuelta. ◇ *n* viaje *m* de ida y vuelta.

roundup ['raʊndʌp] *n* [summary] resumen *m*.

rouse [raʊz] *vt* **-1.** *fml* [wake up] despertar. **-2.** [impel]: **to ~ sb/o.s. to do sthg** animar a alguien/animarse a hacer algo. **-3.** [excite] excitar. **-4.** [give rise to] suscitar.

rousing ['raʊzɪŋ] *adj* [speech] conmovedor(ra); [cheer] entusiasta.

rout [raʊt] ◇ *n* derrota *f* aplastante. ◇ *vt* derrotar, aplastar.

route [ruːt] ◇ *n* **-1.** [gen] ruta *f*; [of bus] línea *f*, recorrido *m*; [of ship] rumbo *m*. ◇ *vt* [gen] dirigir; [goods] enviar.

route map *n* plano *m* (del camino).

route march *n* marcha *f* de entrenamiento.

routine [ruː'tiːn] ◇ *adj* rutinario(ria). ◇ *n* rutina *f*.

routinely [ruː'tiːnlɪ] *adv* rutinariamente.

rove [rəʊv] *literary* ◇ *vt* vagar por. ◇ *vi*: **to ~ around** vagar.

roving ['rəʊvɪŋ] *adj* volante, itinerante.

row¹ [rəʊ] ◇ *n* **-1.** [line] fila *f*, hilera *f*. **-2.** [succession] serie *f*; **three in a ~** tres seguidos. ◇ *vt* **-1.** [boat] remar. **-2.** [people, things] llevar en bote. ◇ *vi* remar.

row² [raʊ] ◇ *n* **-1.** [quarrel] pelea *f*, bronca *f*. **-2.** *inf* [noise] estruendo *m*, ruido *m*. ◇ *vi* [quarrel] reñir, pelearse.

rowboat ['rəʊbəʊt] *n Am* bote *m* de remos.

rowdiness ['raʊdɪnɪs] *n* alboroto *m*, ruido *m*.

rowdy ['raʊdɪ] (*compar* **-ier**, *superl* **-iest**) *adj* [noisy] ruidoso(sa); [quarrelsome] pendenciero(ra).

rower ['rəʊəʳ] *n* remero *m*, -ra *f*.

row house [rəʊ-] *n Am* casa *f* adosada.

rowing ['rəʊɪŋ] *n* remo *m*.

rowing boat *n* bote *m* de remo.

rowing machine *n* máquina *f* de remar.

rowlock ['rɒlək] *n Br* escálamo *m*, tolete *m*.

royal ['rɔɪəl] ◇ *adj* real. ◇ *n inf* miembro *m* de la familia real; **the Royals** la realeza.

Royal Air Force *n*: **the ~** las Fuerzas Aéreas de Gran Bretaña.

royal blue *adj* azul marino.

royal family *n* familia *f* real.

royalist ['rɔɪəlɪst] *n* monárquico *m*, -ca *f*.

royal jelly *n* jalea *f* real.

Royal Mail *n Br*: **the ~** ≃ Correos *m*.

Royal Marines *npl Br*: **the ~** la Infantería de Marina de Gran Bretaña.

Royal Navy *n*: **the ~** la Armada de Gran Bretaña.

royalty ['rɔɪəltɪ] *n* realeza *f*.

◆ **royalties** *npl* derechos *mpl* de autor, royalties *mpl*.

RP (*abbr of* **received pronunciation**) *n* pronunciación estándar del inglés.

RPI (*abbr of* **retail price index**) *n* IPC *m*.

rpm (*abbr of* **revolutions per minute**) r.p.m. *fpl*.

RR (*abbr of* **railroad**) FC.

RRP *n abbr of* **recommended retail price**.

RSA (*abbr of* **Royal Society of Arts**) *n* sociedad británica para el fomento de las artes, la producción industrial y el comercio.

RSC (*abbr of* **Royal Shakespeare Company**) *n* compañía de teatro británica.

RSI (*abbr of* **repetitive strain injury**) *n* lesión muscular producida por ejemplo por el trabajo continuado tecleando en un ordenador.

RSPB (*abbr of* **Royal Society for the Protection of Birds**) *n* sociedad británica para la pro-

tección de las aves en su medio ambiente natural.

RSPCA (*abbr of* **Royal Society for the Prevention of Cruelty to Animals**) *n* sociedad británica protectora de animales, ≃ SPA *f*.

RST (*abbr of* **Royal Shakespeare Theatre**) *n* teatro británico especializado en la obra de Shakespeare.

RSVP (*abbr of* **répondez s'il vous plaît**) s.r.c.

Rt Hon (*abbr of* **Right Honourable**) su Sría.

Rt Rev (*abbr of* **Right Reverend**) muy Rdo.

rub [rʌb] (*pt & pp* **-bed**, *cont* **-bing**) ◇ *vt*: **to ~ sthg** (**against** OR **on**) frotar algo (en OR contra); **to ~ sthg on** OR **onto** frotar algo en; **to ~ sthg in** OR **into** frotar algo en; **to ~ it in** *inf* insistir, machacar; **to ~ sb up the wrong way** *Br*, **to ~ sb the wrong way** *Am* sacar a alguien de quicio. ◇ *vi*: **to ~** (**against**) rozar; **to ~** (**together**) rozarse.

◆ **rub off on** *vt fus* [subj: quality] influir en.

◆ **rub out** *vt sep* [erase] borrar.

rubber ['rʌbəʳ] ◇ *adj* de goma, de caucho. ◇ *n* **-1.** [substance] goma *f*, caucho *m*. **-2.** *Br* [eraser] goma *f* de borrar. **-3.** *Am inf* [condom] goma *f*. **-4.** [in bridge] partida *f*. **-5.** *Am* [overshoe] chanclo *m*.

rubber band *n* gomita *f*, goma *f*.

rubber boot *n Am* bota *f* de agua.

rubber dinghy *n* lancha *f* neumática.

rubberize, -ise ['rʌbəraɪz] *vt* encauchar.

rubberneck ['rʌbənek] *vi Am inf* curiosear.

rubber ring *n* flotador *m*.

rubber stamp *n* estampilla *f*.

◆ **rubber-stamp** *vt* aprobar oficialmente.

rubber tree *n* árbol *m* de caucho, árbol gomero.

rubbery ['rʌbərɪ] *adj* elástico(ca), que parece de goma.

rubbing ['rʌbɪŋ] *n* dibujo o impresión que se obtiene al frotar un papel, que cubre una superficie labrada, con carbón, ceras etc.

rubbish ['rʌbɪʃ] ◇ *n* (U) **-1.** [refuse] basura *f*. **-2.** *inf fig* [worthless matter] porquería *f*; **it was** ~ fue una porquería. **-3.** *inf* [nonsense] tonterías *fpl*, babosadas *fpl Amer*. ◇ *vt inf* poner por los suelos.

rubbish bin *n Br* cubo *m* de la basura.

rubbish dump *n Br* vertedero *m*, basurero *m*.

rubbishy ['rʌbɪʃɪ] *adj inf* de mala calidad.

rubble ['rʌbl] *n* (U) escombros *mpl*.

rubella [ruː'belə] *n* rubéola *f*.

ruby ['ruːbɪ] (*pl* **-ies**) *n* rubí *m*.

RUC (*abbr of* **Royal Ulster Constabulary**) *n*

fuerzas de seguridad del gobierno británico en Irlanda del Norte.

ruched [ruːʃt] *adj* fruncido(da).

ruck [rʌk] *n* **-1.** *inf* [fight] trifulca *f*, cisco *m*. **-2.** RUGBY melé *f* espontánea.

rucksack ['rʌksæk] *n* mochila *f*.

ructions ['rʌkʃnz] *npl inf* bronca *f*, lío *m*.

rudder ['rʌdər] *n* timón *m*.

ruddy ['rʌdɪ] (*compar* **-ier**, *superl* **-iest**) *adj* **-1.** [reddish] rojizo(za). **-2.** *Br dated* [for emphasis] condenado(da), maldito(ta).

rude [ruːd] *adj* **-1.** [impolite - person, manners, word] grosero(ra), liso(sa) *Amer*; [- joke] verde. **-2.** [shocking] violento(ta), brusco(ca). **-3.** *literary* [rough-and-ready] tosco(ca).

rudely ['ruːdlɪ] *adv* **-1.** [impolitely] groseramente. **-2.** [shockingly] bruscamente, violentamente.

rudeness ['ruːdnɪs] *n* grosería *f*.

rudimentary [,ruːdɪ'mentərɪ] *adj* rudimentario(ria).

rudiments ['ruːdɪmənts] *npl* rudimentos *mpl*, nociones *fpl* básicas.

rue [ruː] *vt* lamentar, arrepentirse de.

rueful ['ruːful] *adj* arrepentido(da).

ruff [rʌf] *n* [on clothes] gola *f*; [of animal] collarín *m*.

ruffian ['rʌfjən] *n* rufián *m*.

ruffle ['rʌfl] *vt* **-1.** [hair] revolver, despeinar; [water] perturbar, agitar; [feathers] encrespar. **-2.** [composure, nerves] enervar, encrespar.

rug [rʌg] *n* **-1.** [carpet] alfombra *f*. **-2.** [blanket] manta *f* de viaje.

rugby ['rʌgbɪ] *n* rugby *m*.

Rugby League *n tipo de rugby con equipos de 13 jugadores profesionales.*

Rugby Union *n tipo de rugby con equipos de 15 jugadores aficionados.*

rugged ['rʌgɪd] *adj* **-1.** [wild, inhospitable] escabroso(sa), accidentado(da). **-2.** [sturdy] fuerte. **-3.** [roughly handsome] duro y atractivo (dura y atractiva).

ruggedness ['rʌgɪdnɪs] *n* escabrosidad *f*.

rugger ['rʌgər] *n Br inf* rugby *m*.

ruin ['ruːɪn] ◇ *n* ruina *f*. ◇ *vt* **-1.** [destroy] arruinar, estropear. **-2.** [bankrupt] arruinar.
◆ **in ruin(s)** *adv* en ruinas.

ruination [ruːɪ'neɪʃn] *n* ruina *f*.

ruinous ['ruːɪnəs] *adj* [expensive] ruinoso(sa).

rule [ruːl] ◇ *n* **-1.** [regulation, guideline] regla *f*, norma *f*; **to bend the ~s** hacer una pequeña excepción (con las normas). **-2.** [norm]: **the ~** la regla, la norma; **as a ~** por regla general. **-3.** [government] dominio *m*.

-4. [ruler] regla *f*. ◇ *vt* **-1.** *fml* [control] regir. **-2.** [govern] gobernar. **-3.** [decide]: **to ~ that** decidir OR ordenar que. ◇ *vi* **-1.** [give decision] decidir, fallar. **-2.** *fml* [be paramount] regir, ser primordial. **-3.** [govern] gobernar.
◆ **rule out** *vt sep* descartar.

rulebook ['ruːlbʊk] *n* [set of rules]: **the ~** el libro de reglamento.

ruled [ruːld] *adj* rayado(da).

ruler ['ruːlər] *n* **-1.** [for measurement] regla *f*. **-2.** [monarch] soberano *m*, -na *f*.

ruling ['ruːlɪŋ] ◇ *adj* en el poder. ◇ *n* fallo *m*, decisión *f*.

rum [rʌm] (*compar* **-mer**, *superl* **-mest**) ◇ *n* ron *m*. ◇ *adj Br dated* extraño(ña), raro(ra).

Rumania [ruː'meɪnjə] = **Romania**.

Rumanian [ruː'meɪnjən] = **Romanian**.

rumba ['rʌmbə] *n* rumba *f*.

rumble ['rʌmbl] ◇ *n* **-1.** [gen] estruendo *m*; [of stomach] ruido *m*. **-2.** *Am inf* [fight] riña *f* callejera. ◇ *vt Br inf dated* calar. ◇ *vi* [gen] retumbar; [stomach] hacer ruido.

rumbustious [rʌm'bʌstʃəs] *adj Br* bullicioso(sa).

ruminate ['ruːmɪneɪt] *vi fml*: **to ~ (about** OR **on sthg)** rumiar (algo).

rummage ['rʌmɪdʒ] *vi* hurgar, rebuscar.

rummage sale *n Am venta de objetos usados con fines benéficos.*

rummy ['rʌmɪ] *n* rum *m*.

rumour *Br*, **rumor** *Am* ['ruːmər] *n* rumor *m*.

rumoured *Br*, **rumored** *Am* ['ruːməd] *adj*: **to be ~** rumorearse; **she is ~ to be very rich** se rumorea que es muy rica.

rump [rʌmp] *n* **-1.** [of animal] grupa *f*, ancas *fpl*. **-2.** *inf* [of person] trasero *m*, culo *m*. **-3.** [of organisation, political party] los incondicionales *mpl*.

rumple ['rʌmpl] *vt* [clothes] arrugar; [hair] desordenar.

rump steak *n* filete *m* de lomo.

rumpus ['rʌmpəs] *n inf* lío *m*, jaleo *m*, despiole *m Amer*.

rumpus room *n Am* cuarto *m* de juegos.

run [rʌn] (*pt* **ran**, *pp* **run**, *cont* **-ning**) ◇ *n* **-1.** [on foot] carrera *f*; **to go for a ~** ir a correr; **on the ~** en fuga; **to make a ~ for it** tratar de fugarse. **-2.** [journey - in car] paseo *m* OR **vuelta** *f* (en coche); [- in plane, ship] viaje *m*. **-3.** [series - of wins, disasters] serie *f*; [- of luck] racha *f*. **-4.** THEATRE: **the play had a 6-week ~** la obra estuvo en cartelera 6 semanas. **-5.** [great demand]: **~ on sthg** gran demanda de algo. **-6.** [in tights] carrera *f*. **-7.** [in cricket, baseball] carrera *f*. **-8.** [for skiing etc] **pista** f. **-9.** [term]: **in the short/long ~** a corto/largo plazo.

◇ vt **-1.** [on foot] **correr. -2.** [manage - business] **dirigir, administrar;** [- life, event] **organizar. -3.** [operate - computer program, machine, film] **poner;** [- experiment] **montar. -4.** [have and use - car etc] **hacer funcionar; it's cheap to ~** es barato de mantener; **it ~s on diesel/off the mains** funciona con diesel/electricidad. **-5.** [open - tap] **abrir; to ~ a bath** llenar la bañera. **-6.** [publish] **publicar. -7.** inf [transport by car] **llevar. -8.** [move]: **to ~ sthg along** OR **over** pasar algo por.

◇ vi **-1.** [on foot] **correr; to ~ for it** echar a correr. **-2.** [follow a direction] **seguir. -3.** [in election]: **to ~ (for)** presentarse como candidato(ta) (a). **-4.** [factory, machine] **funcionar;** [engine] **estar encendido(da); to ~ on** OR **off sthg** funcionar con algo; **to ~ smoothly** ir bien. **-5.** [bus, train] **ir. -6.** [flow] **correr; to ~ dry** secarse, quedarse sin agua. **-7.** [tap] **gotear;** [nose] **moquear;** [eyes] **llorar. -8.** [colour] **desteñir. -9.** [pass - gen] **pasar. -10.** [continue to be] **seguir. -11.** [remain valid] **ser válido(da). -12.** phr: **feelings were running high** la gente estaba indignada; **to be running late** ir con retraso.

◆ **run across** vt fus [meet] **encontrarse con.**

◆ **run along** vi dated: **~ along now!** ¡vete!, ¡anda ya!

◆ **run away** vi **-1.** [flee]: **to ~ away (from)** huir OR fugarse (de). **-2.** fig [avoid]: **to ~ away from** [responsibility, subject] **evadir;** [thought] **evitar.**

◆ **run away with** vt fus: **he lets his enthusiasm ~ away with him** se deja llevar por el entusiasmo.

◆ **run down** ◇ vt sep **-1.** [run over] **atropellar. -2.** [criticize] **hablar mal de. -3.** [allow to decline] **debilitar.** ◇ vi [battery] **acabarse;** [clock] **pararse;** [project, business] **debilitarse, perder energía.**

◆ **run into** vt fus **-1.** [problem] **encontrar;** [person] **tropezarse con; to ~ into debt** endeudarse. **-2.** [in vehicle] **chocar con. -3.** [blend with]: **to ~ into each other** mezclarse. **-4.** [amount to] **ascender a.**

◆ **run off** ◇ vt sep **imprimir.** ◇ vi: **to ~ off (with)** fugarse (con).

◆ **run on** vi [continue] **continuar.**

◆ **run out** vi **-1.** [become used up] **acabarse. -2.** [expire] **caducar.**

◆ **run out of** vt fus **quedarse sin; we've ~ out of food** se nos ha acabado la comida.

◆ **run over** vt sep **atropellar.**

◆ **run through** vt fus **-1.** [be present in] **recorrer, atravesar. -2.** [practise] **ensayar, practicar. -3.** [read through] **echar un** vistazo a.

◆ **run to** vt fus **-1.** [amount to] **ascender a. -2.** [be able to afford] **permitirse.**

◆ **run up** vt fus [amass] **incurrir en, contraer.**

◆ **run up against** vt fus **tropezar con.**

run-around n inf: **to give sb the ~** traerle a alguien al retortero.

runaway ['rʌnəweɪ] ◇ adj **-1.** [gen] **fugitivo(va);** [horse] **desbocado(da);** [train] **fuera de control;** [inflation] **desenfrenado(da). -2.** [victory] **fácil.** ◇ n **fugitivo** m, **-va** f.

rundown ['rʌndaʊn] n **-1.** [report] **informe** m, **resumen** m. **-2.** [decline] **desmantelamiento** m **gradual.**

◆ **run-down** adj **-1.** [dilapidated] **en ruinas, en decadencia. -2.** [tired] **agotado(da).**

rung [rʌŋ] ◇ pp → **ring.** ◇ n lit & fig **peldaño** m.

run-in n inf **altercado** m, **disputa** f.

runnel ['rʌnl] n **arroyuelo** m.

runner ['rʌnəʳ] n **-1.** [athlete] **corredor** m, **-ra** f. **-2.** [smuggler] **traficante** m y f, **contrabandista** m y f. **-3.** [on skate] **cuchilla** f; [on sledge] **carril** m; [of drawer, sliding seat] **carro** m.

runner bean n Br **judía** f **escarlata.**

runner-up (pl **runners-up**) n **subcampeón** m, **-ona** f.

running ['rʌnɪŋ] ◇ adj **-1.** [continuous] **continuo(nua). -2.** [consecutive] **seguidos(das). -3.** [water] **corriente.** ◇ n **-1.** [act of running] **el correr; to go ~** hacer footing. **-2.** SPORT **carreras** fpl. **-3.** [management] **dirección** f, **organización** f. **-4.** [operation] **funcionamiento** m. **-5.** phr: **to make the ~** ir en cabeza; **to be in/out of the ~ (for sthg)** tener/no tener posibilidades (de algo). ◇ comp **de correr.**

running commentary n **comentario** m **en directo.**

running costs npl **gastos** mpl **corrientes (de mantenimiento).**

running mate n Am **candidato** m, **-ta** f a **vice-presidente.**

running repairs npl **reparación** f **temporal.**

runny ['rʌnɪ] (compar **-ier,** superl **-iest**) adj **-1.** [food] **derretido(da). -2.** [nose] **que moquea;** [eyes] **llorosos(as).**

run-of-the-mill adj **normal y corriente.**

runt [rʌnt] n **-1.** [animal] **cría** f **más pequeña y débil. -2.** pej [person] **renacuajo** m.

run-through n **ensayo** m.

run-up n **-1.** [preceding time] **periodo** m **previo. -2.** SPORT **carrerilla** f.

runway ['rʌnweɪ] n **pista** f.

rupture ['rʌptʃər] n -1. MED hernia f. -2. [of relationship] ruptura f.

rural ['rʊərəl] adj rural.

ruse [ruːz] n ardid m.

rush [rʌʃ] ◇ n -1. [hurry] prisa f; **to be in a ~** tener prisa; **there's no ~** no hay prisa. **-2.** [burst of activity]: **~ (for OR on sthg)** avalancha f (en busca de algo); **there was a ~ to stock up on sugar** hubo una fiebre repentina por almacenar azúcar. **-3.** [busy period] hora f punta. **-4.** [surge - of air] ráfaga f; [- of water] torrente m; [- mental] arrebato m; **to make a ~ for sthg** ir en desbandada hacia algo.
◇ vt **-1.** [hurry] acelerar, apresurar; **don't ~ me!** ¡no me metas prisa!; **to ~ sb into doing sthg** apresurar a alguien para que haga algo. **-2.** [send quickly] llevar rápidamente. **-3.** [attack suddenly] atacar repentinamente.
◇ vi **-1.** [hurry] ir de prisa, correr; **to ~ into sthg** meterse de cabeza en algo. **-2.** [surge] correr, precipitarse.
◆ **rushes** npl **-1.** BOT juncos mpl. **-2.** CINEMA primeras pruebas fpl.

rushed [rʌʃt] adj atareado(da).

rush hour n hora f punta.

rush job n trabajo m precipitado.

rusk [rʌsk] n galleta que se da a los niños pequeños para que se acostumbren a masticar.

russet ['rʌsɪt] adj rojizo(za).

Russia ['rʌʃə] n Rusia.

Russian ['rʌʃn] ◇ adj ruso(sa). ◇ n **-1.** [person] ruso m, -sa f. **-2.** [language] ruso m.

Russian roulette n ruleta f rusa.

rust [rʌst] ◇ n moho m, óxido m. ◇ vi oxidarse.

rustic ['rʌstɪk] adj rústico(ca).

rustle ['rʌsl] ◇ n [of wind, leaves] susurro m; [of paper] crujido m. ◇ vt **-1.** [paper] hacer crujir. **-2.** Am [cattle] robar. ◇ vi [wind, leaves] susurrar; [paper] crujir.

rustproof ['rʌstpruːf] adj inoxidable.

rusty ['rʌstɪ] (compar **-ier**, superl **-iest**) adj lit & fig oxidado(da).

rut [rʌt] n [track] rodada f; **to get into/be in a ~** fig caer/estar metido en una rutina.

rutabaga [ˌruːtə'beɪgə] n Am nabo m sueco.

ruthless ['ruːθlɪs] adj despiadado(da).

ruthlessly ['ruːθlɪslɪ] adv despiadadamente.

ruthlessness ['ruːθlɪsnɪs] n crueldad f.

RV n **-1.** (abbr of **revised version**) traducción al inglés de la Biblia de finales del siglo XIX. **-2.** Am (abbr of **recreational vehicle**) casa-remolque f.

Rwanda [rʊ'ændə] n Ruanda.

Rwandan [rʊ'ændən] ◇ adj ruandés(esa). ◇ n ruandés m, -esa f.

rye [raɪ] n **-1.** [grain] centeno m. **-2.** [bread] pan m de centeno.

rye bread n pan m de centeno.

rye grass n ballico m.

rye whiskey n whisky m de centeno.

S

s (pl **ss** OR **s's**), **S** (pl **Ss** OR **S's**) [es] n [letter] s f, S f.
◆ **S** (abbr of **south**) S.

SA -1. abbr of **South Africa**. **-2.** abbr of **South America**.

Sabbath ['sæbəθ] n: **the ~** [for Christians] el domingo; [for Jews] el sábado.

sabbatical [sə'bætɪkl] n sabático m; **on ~** de sabático.

saber Am = sabre.

sabotage ['sæbətɑːʒ] ◇ n sabotaje m. ◇ vt sabotear.

saboteur [ˌsæbə'tɜːr] n saboteador m, -ra f.

sabre Br, **saber** Am ['seɪbər] n sable m.

saccharin(e) ['sækərɪn] n sacarina f.

sachet ['sæʃeɪ] n bolsita f.

sack [sæk] ◇ n **-1.** [bag] saco m. **-2.** Br inf [dismissal]: **to get** OR **be given the ~** ser despedido(da). ◇ vt Br inf despedir, remover Amer.

sackful ['sækfʊl] n saco m.

sacking ['sækɪŋ] n [fabric] harpillera f.

sacrament ['sækrəmənt] n sacramento m.

sacred ['seɪkrɪd] adj lit & fig sagrado(da).

sacrifice ['sækrɪfaɪs] RELIG & fig ◇ n sacrificio m. ◇ vt sacrificar.

sacrilege ['sækrɪlɪdʒ] n RELIG & fig sacrilegio m.

sacrilegious [ˌsækrɪ'lɪdʒəs] adj sacrílego(ga).

sacrosanct ['sækrəʊsæŋkt] adj sacrosanto(ta).

sad [sæd] (compar **-der**, superl **-dest**) adj triste.

sadden ['sædn] vt entristecer.

saddle ['sædl] ◇ n **-1.** [for horse] silla f (de montar). **-2.** [of bicycle, motorcycle] sillín m, asiento m. ◇ vt **-1.** [horse] ensillar. **-2.** fig [burden]: **to ~ sb with sthg** cargar a alguien con algo.

◆ **saddle up** vt fus & vi ensillar.

saddlebag ['sædlbæg] n alforja f.

saddler ['sædlə^r] n talabartero m, -ra f.

sadism ['seɪdɪzm] n sadismo m.

sadist ['seɪdɪst] n sádico m, -ca f.

sadistic [sə'dɪstɪk] adj sádico(ca).

sadly ['sædlɪ] adv tristemente.

sadness ['sædnɪs] n tristeza f.

s.a.e., sae n abbr of **stamped addressed envelope**.

safari [sə'fɑːrɪ] n safari m; **to go on ~** ir de safari.

safari park n safari m, reserva f de animales.

safe [seɪf] ◇ adj **-1.** [gen] seguro(ra); **~ and sound** sano y salvo (sana y salva). **-2.** [without harm] feliz, sin contratiempos. **-3.** [not causing disagreement]: **it's ~ to say that ...** se puede afirmar con seguridad que ...; **to be on the ~ side** por mayor seguridad. **-4.** [reliable] digno(na) de confianza; **in ~ hands** en buenas manos. ◇ n caja f (de caudales).

safebreaker ['seɪf,breɪkə^r] n ladrón m, -ona f de cajas.

safe-conduct n salvoconducto m.

safe-deposit box n caja f de seguridad.

safeguard ['seɪfgɑːd] ◇ n salvaguardia f, protección f; **~ against sthg** protección contra algo. ◇ vt: **to ~ sthg/sb (against sthg)** salvaguardar OR proteger algo/a alguien (contra algo).

safe house n piso m franco.

safekeeping [,seɪf'kiːpɪŋ] n protección f.

safely ['seɪflɪ] adv **-1.** [with no danger] sin peligro, con seguridad. **-2.** [not in danger] seguramente. **-3.** [unharmed] sin novedad. **-4.** [for certain]: **I can ~ say that** puedo decir con toda confianza que.

safe sex n sexo m sin riesgo.

safety ['seɪftɪ] ◇ n seguridad f. ◇ comp de seguridad.

safety belt n cinturón m de seguridad.

safety catch n seguro m.

safety curtain n telón m de seguridad.

safety-deposit box = **safe-deposit box**.

safety island n Am refugio m.

safety match n cerilla f de seguridad.

safety net n **-1.** [in circus] red f de seguridad. **-2.** fig [means of protection] protección f.

safety pin n imperdible m, seguro m Amer.

safety valve n **-1.** TECH válvula f de seguri-

dad. **-2.** fig [for emotions] válvula f de escape.

saffron ['sæfrən] n **-1.** [spice] azafrán m. **-2.** [colour] color m azafrán.

sag [sæg] (pt & pp **-ged**, cont **-ging**) vi **-1.** [sink downwards] hundirse, combarse. **-2.** fig [lessen] bajar.

saga ['sɑːgə] n **-1.** LITERATURE saga f. **-2.** pej [drawn-out account] historia f.

sage [seɪdʒ] ◇ adj sabio(bia). ◇ n **-1.** [herb] salvia f. **-2.** [wise man] sabio m.

saggy ['sægɪ] (compar **-gier**, superl **-giest**) adj [bed] hundido(da); [breasts] caído(da).

Sagittarius [,sædʒɪ'teərɪəs] n Sagitario m; **to be (a) ~** ser Sagitario.

Sahara [sə'hɑːrə] n: **the ~ (Desert)** el (desierto del) Sáhara.

Saharan [sə'hɑːrən] ◇ n saharaui m y f. ◇ adj saharaui, sahariano(na).

said [sed] pt & pp → **say**.

sail [seɪl] ◇ n **-1.** [of boat] vela f; **to set ~** zarpar. **-2.** [journey by boat] paseo m en barco de vela. ◇ vt **-1.** [boat, ship] gobernar. **-2.** [sea] cruzar. ◇ vi **-1.** [travel by boat] navegar. **-2.** [move - boat]: **the ship ~ed across the ocean** el barco cruzó el océano. **-3.** [leave by boat] zarpar. **-4.** [move quickly] volar.

◆ **sail through** vt fus hacer con facilidad.

sailboard ['seɪlbɔːd] n tabla f de windsurf.

sailboat Am = **sailing boat**.

sailcloth ['seɪlklɒθ] n lona f.

sailing ['seɪlɪŋ] n **-1.** (U) SPORT vela f; **plain ~** coser y cantar. **-2.** [trip by ship] travesía f.

sailing boat Br, **sailboat** Am ['seɪlbəʊt] n barco m de vela.

sailing ship n (buque m) velero m.

sailor ['seɪlə^r] n marinero m, -ra f, marino m, -na f; **to be a good ~** no marearse.

saint [seɪnt] n RELIG & fig santo m, -ta f.

Saint Helena [-ɪ'liːnə] n Santa Elena.

Saint Lawrence [-'lɒrəns] n: **the ~ (River)** el (río) San Lorenzo.

Saint Lucia [-'luːʃə] n Santa Lucía.

saintly ['seɪntlɪ] (compar **-ier**, superl **-iest**) adj santo(ta), piadoso(sa).

sake [seɪk] n: **for the ~ of** por (el bien de); **to argue for its own ~** discutir por discutir; **for God's** OR **heaven's ~** ¡por el amor de Dios!

salad ['sæləd] n ensalada f.

salad bowl n ensaladera f.

salad cream n Br salsa parecida a la mahonesa para aderezar la ensalada.

salad dressing n aliño m (para la ensalada).

salad oil *n* aceite *m* (para ensaladas).

salamander ['sælə‚mændəʳ] *n* salamandra *f*.

salami [sə'lɑːmɪ] *n* salami *m*.

salaried ['sælərɪd] *adj* [person] asalariado(da); [job] de sueldo fijo.

salary ['sælərɪ] (*pl* **-ies**) *n* sueldo *m*.

salary scale *n* banda *f* salarial.

sale [seɪl] *n* **-1.** [gen] venta *f*; **on** ~ en venta; **(up) for** ~ en venta; **"for** ~**"** "se vende". **-2.** [at reduced prices] liquidación *f*, saldo *m*.
◆ **sales** ◇ *npl* **-1.** ECON ventas *fpl*. **-2.** [at reduced prices]: **the** ~**s** las rebajas. ◇ *comp* de ventas.

saleroom *Br* ['seɪlrʊm], **salesroom** *Am* ['seɪlzrʊm] *n* sala *f* de subastas.

sales assistant, **salesclerk** *Am* ['seɪlzklɜːrk] *n* dependiente *m*, -ta *f*.

sales conference *n* conferencia *f* de ventas.

sales drive *n* promoción *f* de ventas.

sales force *n* personal *m* de ventas.

salesman ['seɪlzmən] (*pl* **-men** [-mən]) *n* [in shop] dependiente *m*, vendedor *m*; [travelling] viajante *m*.

sales pitch *n* cháchara *f* publicitaria.

sales rep *n* *inf* representante *m* y *f*.

sales representative *n* representante *m* y *f*.

salesroom *Am* = saleroom.

sales slip *n* *Am* [receipt] recibo *m*.

sales tax *n* impuesto *m* de venta.

sales team *n* personal *m* de ventas.

saleswoman ['seɪlz‚wʊmən] (*pl* **-women** [-‚wɪmɪn]) *n* [in shop] dependienta *f*, vendedora *f*; [travelling] viajante *f*.

salient ['seɪljənt] *adj* *fml* sobresaliente.

saline ['seɪlaɪn] *adj* salino(na).

saliva [sə'laɪvə] *n* saliva *f*.

salivate ['sælɪveɪt] *vi* salivar.

sallow ['sæləʊ] *adj* cetrino(na), amarillento(ta).

sally ['sælɪ] (*pl* **-ies**, *pt* & *pp* **-ied**) *n* [clever remark] salida *f*.
◆ **sally forth** *vi* *hum or literary* salir resueltamente.

salmon ['sæmən] (*pl* *inv* OR **-s**) *n* salmón *m*.

salmonella [‚sælmə'nelə] *n* salmonelosis *f* *inv*.

salmon pink ◇ *adj* rosa salmón. ◇ *n* color *m* rosa salmón.

salon ['sælɒn] *n* salón *m*.

saloon [sə'luːn] *n* **-1.** *Br* [car] (coche *m*) utilitario *m*. **-2.** *Am* [bar] bar *m*. **-3.** *Br* [in pub]: ~ **(bar)** en ciertos pubs y hoteles, bar elegante con precios más altos que los del 'public bar'. **-4.** [in ship] salón *m*.

salopettes [‚sælə'pets] *npl* pantalones *mpl* de peto para esquiar.

salt [sɔːlt, sɒlt] ◇ *n* sal *f*; **the** ~ **of the earth** la sal de la tierra; **to rub** ~ **into the wounds, he said ...** por si fuera poco, encima dijo ...; **to take sthg with a pinch of** ~ considerar algo con cierta reserva. ◇ *comp* salado(da). ◇ *vt* [food] salar; [roads] echar sal en (*las carreteras etc para evitar que se hielen*).
◆ **salt away** *vt sep* *inf* ahorrar, guardar.

SALT [sɔːlt] (*abbr of* Strategic Arms Limitation Talks/Treaty) *n* SALT *fpl*.

salt cellar *Br*, **salt shaker** *Am* [-‚ʃeɪkəʳ] *n* salero *m*.

salted ['sɔːltɪd] *adj* salado(da), con sal.

saltpetre *Br*, **saltpeter** *Am* [‚sɔːlt'piːtəʳ] *n* salitre *m*.

salt shaker *Am* = salt cellar.

saltwater ['sɔːlt‚wɔːtəʳ] ◇ *n* agua *f* de mar, agua salada. ◇ *adj* de agua salada.

salty ['sɔːltɪ] (*compar* **-ier**, *superl* **-iest**) *adj* salado(da), salobre.

salubrious [sə'luːbrɪəs] *adj* salubre, sano(na).

salutary ['sæljʊtrɪ] *adj* saludable.

salute [sə'luːt] ◇ *n* **-1.** [with hand] saludo *m*. **-2.** MIL [firing of guns] salva *f*, saludo *m*. **-3.** [formal acknowledgement] homenaje *m*. ◇ *vt* **-1.** MIL [with hand] saludar. **-2.** [acknowledge formally] reconocer. ◇ *vi* saludar.

Salvadorean, **Salvadorian** [‚sælvə'dɔːrɪən] ◇ *adj* salvadoreño(ña). ◇ *n* salvadoreño *m*, -ña *f*.

salvage ['sælvɪdʒ] ◇ *n* (*U*) **-1.** [rescue of ship] salvamento *m*. **-2.** [property rescued] objetos *mpl* recuperados OR rescatados. ◇ *vt* *lit* & *fig*: **to** ~ **sthg (from)** salvar algo (de).

salvage vessel *n* nave *f* de salvamento.

salvation [sæl'veɪʃn] *n* salvación *f*.

Salvation Army *n*: **the** ~ el Ejército de Salvación.

salve [sælv] *vt*: **to** ~ **one's conscience (by doing sthg)** apaciguar a la conciencia (haciendo algo).

salver ['sælvəʳ] *n* bandeja *f* (metálica).

salvo ['sælvəʊ] (*pl* **-s** OR **-es**) *n* [of guns, missiles] salva *f*.

Samaritan [sə'mærɪtn] *n*: **good** ~ buen alma *f*, buena persona *f*.

samba ['sæmbə] *n* samba *f*.

same [seɪm] ◇ *adj* mismo(ma); **the** ~ **colour as his** el mismo color que el suyo; **at the** ~ **time** [simultaneously] al mismo tiempo; [yet] aún así; **one and the** ~ el mismo (la misma).

◇ *pron*: **the** ~ el mismo (la misma); **she did the** ~ hizo lo mismo; **the ingredients are the** ~ los ingredientes son iguales OR mismos; **I'll have the** ~ **(again)** tomaré lo mismo (que antes); **all** OR **just the** ~ [nevertheless, anyway] de todos modos; **it's all the** ~ **to me** me da igual; **it's not the** ~ no es lo mismo.
◇ *adv*: **the** ~ lo mismo.

sameness ['seɪmnɪs] *n* uniformidad *f*.

Samoa [sə'məʊə] *n* Samoa; **American** ~ Samoa Oriental.

Samoan [sə'məʊən] ◇ *adj* samoano(na). ◇ *n* samoano *m*, -na *f*.

samosa [sə'məʊsə] *n especie de empanadilla rellena de carne, verdura etc típica de la cocina india.*

sample ['sɑːmpl] ◇ *n* muestra *f*. ◇ *vt* **-1.** [food, wine, attractions] probar. **-2.** MUS samplear.

sampler ['sɑːmplə*r*] *n* SEWING dechado *m*.

sanatorium (*pl* **-riums** OR **-ria** [-rɪə]), **sanitorium** *Am* (*pl* **-riums** OR **-ria** [-rɪə]) [,sænə'tɔːrɪəm] *n* sanatorio *m*.

sanctify ['sæŋktɪfaɪ] (*pt* & *pp* **-ied**) *vt* **-1.** RELIG santificar. **-2.** [approve] aprobar.

sanctimonious [,sæŋktɪ'məʊnjəs] *adj pej* santurrón(ona).

sanction ['sæŋkʃn] ◇ *n* sanción *f*. ◇ *vt* sancionar.

◆ **sanctions** *npl* sanciones *fpl*.

sanctity ['sæŋktətɪ] *n* santidad *f*.

sanctuary ['sæŋktʃʊərɪ] (*pl* **-ies**) *n* **-1.** [for birds, wildlife] reserva *f*. **-2.** [refuge] refugio *m*. **-3.** [holy place] santuario *m*.

sanctum ['sæŋktəm] (*pl* **-s**) *n* [private place] lugar *m* sagrado, espacio *m* privado.

sand [sænd] ◇ *n* arena *f*. ◇ *vt* lijar.

◆ **sands** *npl* arenas *fpl*.

sandal ['sændl] *n* sandalia *f*.

sandalwood ['sændlwʊd] *n* sándalo *m*.

sandbag ['sændbæg] *n* saco *m* de arena.

sandbank ['sændbæŋk] *n* banco *m* de arena.

sandblast ['sændblɑːst] *vt* limpiar con chorro de arena.

sandbox *Am* = **sandpit**.

sandcastle ['sænd,kɑːsl] *n* castillo *m* de arena.

sand dune *n* duna *f*.

sander ['sændə*r*] *n* lijadora *f*.

sandpaper ['sænd,peɪpə*r*] ◇ *n* papel *m* de lija. ◇ *vt* lijar.

sandpit *Br* ['sændpɪt], **sandbox** *Am* ['sændbɒks] *n* cuadro *m* de arena.

sandstone ['sændstəʊn] *n* piedra *f* arenisca.

sandstorm ['sændstɔːm] *n* tormenta *f* de arena.

sand trap *n Am* GOLF bunker *m*.

sandwich ['sænwɪdʒ] ◇ *n* [made with roll etc] bocadillo *m*; [made with sliced bread] sandwich *m* frío. ◇ *vt fig* apretujar.

sandwich board *n* cartelón *m* (de hombre-anuncio).

sandwich course *n Br curso universitario que incluye un cierto tiempo de experiencia profesional.*

sandy ['sændɪ] (*compar* **-ier**, *superl* **-iest**) *adj* **-1.** [covered in sand] arenoso(sa). **-2.** [sand-coloured] rojizo(za).

sane [seɪn] *adj* **-1.** [not mad] cuerdo(da). **-2.** [sensible] prudente, sensato(ta).

sang [sæŋ] *pt* → **sing**.

sanguine ['sæŋgwɪn] *adj* optimista.

sanitary ['sænɪtrɪ] *adj* **-1.** [connected with health] sanitario(ria). **-2.** [clean, hygienic] higiénico(ca).

sanitary towel, **sanitary napkin** *Am n* [disposable] compresa *f* (higiénica); [made of cloth] paño *m* (higiénico).

sanitation [,sænɪ'teɪʃn] *n* sanidad *f*, higiene *f*.

sanitation worker *n Am* basurero *m*, -ra *f*.

sanitize, -ise ['sænɪtaɪz] *vt* descafeinar *fig*.

sanitorium *Am* = **sanatorium**.

sanity ['sænətɪ] *n* **-1.** [saneness] cordura *f*. **-2.** [good sense] sensatez *f*, prudencia *f*.

sank [sæŋk] *pt* → **sink**.

San Marino [,sænmə'riːnəʊ] *n* San Marino.

San Salvador [,sæn'sælvədɔː*r*] *n* San Salvador.

San Sebastian [,sænsə'bæstɪən] *n* San Sebastián.

Sanskrit ['sænskrɪt] *n* sánscrito *m*.

Santa (Claus) ['sæntə(,klaʊz)] *n* Papá Noel.

Sao Paulo [,saʊ'paʊləʊ] *n* Sao Paulo.

sap [sæp] (*pt* & *pp* **-ped**, *cont* **-ping**) ◇ *n* **-1.** [of plant] savia *f*. **-2.** *Am inf* [gullible person] primo *m*, -ma *f*. ◇ *vt* [weaken] minar, agotar.

sapling ['sæplɪŋ] *n* árbol *m* nuevo, arbolito *m*.

sapphire ['sæfaɪə*r*] *n* zafiro *m*.

Saragossa [,særə'gɒsə] *n* Zaragoza.

Sarajevo [,særə'jeɪvəʊ] *n* Sarajevo.

sarcasm ['sɑːkæzm] *n* sarcasmo *m*.

sarcastic [sɑː'kæstɪk] *adj* sarcástico(ca).

sarcophagus [sɑː'kɒfəgəs] (*pl* **-gi** [-gaɪ] OR **-es**) *n* sarcófago *m*.

sardine [sɑː'diːn] *n* sardina *f*.

Sardinia [sɑː'dɪnjə] *n* Cerdeña.

sardonic [sɑː'dɒnɪk] *adj* sardónico(ca).

Sargasso Sea [sɑː'gæsəʊ-] *n*: **the ~** el mar de los Sargazos.

sari ['sɑːrɪ] *n* sari *m*.

sarong [sə'rɒŋ] *n* *prenda de vestir malaya que se lleva como falda anudada a la cintura o bajo los brazos.*

sarsaparilla [ˌsɑːspə'rɪlə] *n* zarzaparrilla *f*.

sartorial [sɑː'tɔːrɪəl] *adj fml* en el vestir.

SAS (*abbr of* **Special Air Service**) *n unidad especial del ejército británico encargada de operaciones de sabotaje.*

SASE *n abbr of* **self-addressed stamped envelope**.

sash [sæʃ] *n* faja *f*.

sash window *n* ventana *f* de guillotina.

Saskatchewan [ˌsæs'kætʃɪ,wən] *n* Saskatchewan.

sassy ['sæsɪ] *adj Am inf* descarado(da), fresco(ca).

sat [sæt] *pt & pp* → **sit**.

Sat. (*abbr of* **Saturday**) sáb.

SAT [sæt] *n* **-1.** (*abbr of* **Standard Assessment Test**) *examen de aptitud que se realiza a los siete, once y catorce años en Inglaterra y Gales.* **-2.** (*abbr of* **Scholastic Aptitude Test**) *examen de ingreso a la universidad en Estados Unidos.*

Satan ['seɪtn] *n* Satanás *m*, Satán *m*.

satanic [sə'tænɪk] *adj* satánico(ca).

satchel ['sætʃəl] *n* cartera *f*.

sated ['seɪtɪd] *adj fml*: ~ **(with)** saciado(da) (de).

satellite ['sætəlaɪt] ◇ *n lit & fig* satélite *m*. ◇ *comp* **-1.** [link, broadcast] por satélite. **-2.** [dependent] satélite.

satellite TV *n* televisión *f* por satélite.

satiate ['seɪʃɪeɪt] *vt fml* saciar, hartar.

satin ['sætɪn] ◇ *n* satén *m*, raso *m*. ◇ *comp* de satén, de raso.

satire ['sætaɪə*r*] *n* sátira *f*.

satirical [sə'tɪrɪkl] *adj* satírico(ca).

satirist ['sætərɪst] *n* escritor satírico *m*, escritora satírica *f*.

satirize, -ise ['sætəraɪz] *vt* satirizar.

satisfaction [ˌsætɪs'fækʃn] *n* satisfacción *f*; **to do sthg to sb's ~** hacer algo a la satisfacción OR al gusto de alguien.

satisfactory [ˌsætɪs'fæktərɪ] *adj* satisfactorio(ria).

satisfied ['sætɪsfaɪd] *adj* satisfecho(cha); **to be ~ with sthg** estar satisfecho con algo; **to be ~ that** estar convencido (de) que.

satisfy ['sætɪsfaɪ] (*pt & pp* **-ied**) *vt* **-1.** [gen] satisfacer. **-2.** [convince] convencer; **to ~ sb**

that convencer a alguien (de) que; **to ~ o.s. that** convencerse (de) que.

satisfying ['sætɪsfaɪɪŋ] *adj* agradable, satisfactorio(ria).

satsuma [ˌsæt'suːmə] *n* satsuma *f*, *tipo de mandarina.*

saturate ['sætʃəreɪt] *vt* **-1.** [drench]: **to ~ sthg (with)** empapar algo (de). **-2.** [fill completely]: **to ~ sthg (with)** saturar algo (de).

saturated fat ['sætʃəreɪtɪd-] *n* grasa *f* saturada.

saturation [ˌsætʃə'reɪʃn] ◇ *n* saturación *f*. ◇ *comp* [bombing] por saturación; TV: ~ **coverage** cobertura exhaustiva.

saturation point *n*: **to reach ~** llegar al punto de saturación.

Saturday ['sætədɪ] ◇ *n* sábado *m*; **what day is it? - it's ~** ¿a qué estamos hoy? - estamos a sábado; **on ~** el sábado; **are you going ~?** *inf* ¿te vas el sábado?; **see you ~!** *inf* ¡hasta el sábado!; **on ~s** los sábados; **last ~** el sábado pasado; **this ~** este sábado, el sábado que viene; **next ~** el sábado de la semana que viene; **every ~** todos los sábados; **every other ~** cada dos sábados, un sábado sí y otro no; **the ~ before** el sábado anterior; **the ~ after next** no este sábado sino el siguiente; **the ~ before last** hace dos sábados; **~ week, a week on ~** del sábado en ocho días; **to work ~s** trabajar los sábados.
◇ *comp* del sábado; **~ morning/afternoon/evening/night** la mañana/tarde/noche del sábado; **a ~ job** un trabajo los sábados.

Saturn ['sætən] *n* Saturno *m*.

sauce [sɔːs] *n* **-1.** CULIN salsa *f*. **-2.** *Br inf* [cheek] frescura *f*, descaro *m*.

sauce boat *n* salsera *f*.

saucepan ['sɔːspən] *n* [with two handles] cacerola *f*; [with one long handle] cazo *m*.

saucer ['sɔːsə*r*] *n* platillo *m*.

saucy ['sɔːsɪ] (*compar* **-ier**, *superl* **-iest**) *adj inf* descarado(da), fresco(ca).

Saudi Arabia ['saʊdɪ-] *n* Arabia Saudí.

Saudi (Arabian) ['saʊdɪ-] ◇ *adj* saudí, saudita. ◇ *n* [person] saudí *m y f*, saudita *m y f*.

sauna ['sɔːnə] *n* sauna *f*.

saunter ['sɔːntə*r*] *vi* pasearse (tranquilamente).

sausage ['sɒsɪdʒ] *n* salchicha *f*.

sausage roll *n Br* *salchicha envuelta en masa como de empanadilla.*

sauté [*Br* 'səʊteɪ, *Am* səʊ'teɪ] (*pt & pp* **sautéed** OR **sautéd**) ◇ *adj* salteado(da). ◇ *vt* saltear.

savage ['sævɪdʒ] ◇ *adj* [cruel, fierce] feroz, salvaje. ◇ *n pej* salvaje *m y f*. ◇ *vt* **-1.** [subj:

animal] embestir, atacar. **-2.** [subj: person] atacar con ferocidad.

savageness ['sævɪdʒnɪs], **savagery** ['sævɪdʒrɪ] *n* salvajismo *m*, ferocidad *f*.

savanna(h) [sə'vænə] *n* sabana *f*.

save [seɪv] ◇ *vt* **-1.** [rescue] salvar, rescatar; **to ~ sb from sthg** salvar a alguien de algo. **-2.** [prevent waste of - time, money, energy] ahorrar; [- food, strength] guardar, reservar. **-3.** [set aside - money] ahorrar; [- food, strength] guardar, reservar. **-4.** [avoid] evitar; **to ~ sb from doing sthg** evitar a alguien (el) hacer algo. **-5.** SPORT parar. **-6.** COMPUT guardar. ◇ *vi* ahorrar. ◇ *n* SPORT parada *f*. ◇ *prep fml:* **~ (for)** excepto.
◆ **save up** *vi* ahorrar.

save-as-you-earn *n Br* forma de ahorro en que la contribución mensual origina rédito libre de impuestos.

saveloy ['sævəlɔɪ] *n Br* salchicha ahumada muy sazonada.

saver ['seɪvəʳ] *n* **-1.** [thing that prevents wastage]: **a time ~** algo que ahorra tiempo. **-2.** FIN ahorrador *m*, -ra *f*.

saving grace ['seɪvɪŋ-] *n* lo único positivo.

savings ['seɪvɪŋz] *npl* ahorros *mpl*.

savings account *n Am* cuenta *f* de ahorros.

savings and loan association *n* sociedad *f* de préstamos inmobiliarios.

savings bank *n* ≃ caja *f* de ahorros.

saviour *Br*, **savior** *Am* ['seɪvjəʳ] *n* salvador *m*, -ra *f*.
◆ **Saviour** *n:* **the Saviour** el Salvador.

savoir-faire [sævwɑː'feəʳ] *n* tacto *m*, don *m* de gentes.

savour *Br*, **savor** *Am* ['seɪvəʳ] *vt lit & fig* saborear.

savoury *Br* (*pl* **-ies**), **savory** (*pl* **-ies**) *Am* ['seɪvərɪ] ◇ *adj* **-1.** [not sweet] salado(da). **-2.** [respectable, pleasant] respetable, agradable. ◇ *n* comida *f* de aperitivo.

saw [sɔː] (*Br pt* **-ed**, *pp* **sawn**, *Am pt & pp* **-ed**) ◇ *pt* → **see**. ◇ *n* sierra *f*. ◇ *vt* serrar.

sawdust ['sɔːdʌst] *n* serrín *m*.

sawed-off shotgun *Am* = **sawn-off shotgun**.

sawmill ['sɔːmɪl] *n* aserradero *m*.

sawn [sɔːn] *pp Br* → **saw**.

sawn-off shotgun *Br*, **sawed-off shotgun** *Am* [sɔːd-] *n* arma *f* de cañones recortados.

sax [sæks] *n inf* saxo *m*.

Saxon ['sæksn] ◇ *adj* sajón(ona). ◇ *n* sajón *m*, -ona *f*.

saxophone ['sæksəfəʊn] *n* saxofón *m*.

saxophonist [*Br* ˌsæks'ɒfənɪst, *Am* 'sæksəfəʊnɪst] *n* saxofón *m y f*.

say [seɪ] (*pt & pp* **said**) ◇ *vt* **-1.** [gen] decir; **to ~ sthg again** repetir algo; **to ~ to o.s.** decirse a uno mismo; **to ~ yes** decir que sí; **he's said to be good** se dice que es bueno; **let's ~ you were to win** pongamos que ganaras; **to ~ nothing of** sin mencionar; **that goes without ~ing** ni que decir tiene; **I'll ~ this for him/her ...** hay que decir OR admitir que él/ella ...; **it has a lot to be said for it** tiene muy buenos puntos en su favor; **she didn't have much to ~ for herself** *inf* era muy reservada. **-2.** [indicate - clock, meter] marcar.
◇ *n:* **to have a/no ~ in sthg** tener/no tener voz y voto en algo; **let me have my ~** déjame decir lo que pienso.
◆ **that is to say** *adv* es decir.

SAYE *n abbr of* **save as you earn**.

saying ['seɪɪŋ] *n* dicho *m*.

say-so *n inf* **-1.** [unproven statement]: **it's only ~** es algo que se dice, solamente. **-2.** [permission] aprobación *f*.

SBA (*abbr of* **Small Business Administration**) *n* organismo gubernamental estadounidense de ayuda a la pequeña empresa.

s/c *abbr of* **self-contained**.

SC ◇ *n abbr of* **supreme court**. ◇ *abbr of* **South Carolina**.

scab [skæb] *n* **-1.** MED costra *f*. **-2.** *pej* [non-striker] esquirol *m*.

scabby ['skæbɪ] (*compar* **-ier**, *superl* **-iest**) *adj* costroso(sa).

scabies ['skeɪbiːz] *n* (*U*) sarna *f*.

scaffold ['skæfəʊld] *n* **-1.** [around building] andamio *m*. **-2.** [for execution] cadalso *m*, patíbulo *m*.

scaffolding ['skæfəldɪŋ] *n* (*U*) andamios *mpl*, andamiaje *m*.

scalawag *Am* = **scallywag**.

scald [skɔːld] ◇ *n* escaldadura *f*. ◇ *vt* escaldar.

scalding ['skɔːldɪŋ] *adj* hirviendo.

scale [skeɪl] ◇ *n* **-1.** [gen] escala *f*. **-2.** [size, extent] tamaño *m*, escala *f*; **to ~** a escala. **-3.** [of fish, snake] escama *f*. **-4.** *Am* = **scales**. ◇ *vt* **-1.** [climb] escalar. **-2.** [remove scales from] escamar.
◆ **scales** *npl* **-1.** [for weighing food] balanza *f*. **-2.** [for weighing person] báscula *f*.
◆ **scale down** *vt fus* reducir.

scale diagram *n* diagrama *m* en escala.

scale model *n* maqueta *f*.

scallion ['skæljən] *n Am* cebolleta *f*.

scallop ['skɒləp] ◇ *n* ZOOL vieira *f*. ◇ *vt* [decorate edge of] festonear.

scallywag *Br* ['skælɪwæg], **scalawag** *Am* ['skæləwæg] *n inf* bribón *m*, -ona *f*, tunante *m*, -ta *f*.

scalp [skælp] ◇ *n* cuero *m* cabelludo. ◇ *vt* escalpar.

scalpel ['skælpəl] *n* bisturí *m*.

scalper ['skælpər] *n Am* [tout] revendedor *m*, -ra *f*.

scam [skæm] *n inf* estratagema *f*.

scamp [skæmp] *n inf* bribón *m*, -ona *f*, tunante *m*, -ta *f*.

scamper ['skæmpər] *vi* corretear.

scampi ['skæmpɪ] *n* (*U*): (**breaded**) ~ gambas *fpl* a la gabardina.

scan [skæn] (*pt* & *pp* -ned, *cont* -ning) ◇ *n* exploración *f* ultrasónica. ◇ *vt* -**1.** [examine carefully] examinar. -**2.** [glance at] dar un vistazo a. -**3.** ELECTRON & TV registrar. -**4.** COMPUT hacer un escáner de. ◇ *vi* -**1.** LITERATURE estar bien medido(da). -**2.** COMPUT hacer un escáner.

scandal ['skændl] *n* -**1.** [scandalous event, outrage] escándalo *m*. -**2.** [scandalous talk] habladurías *fpl*.

scandalize, -ise ['skændəlaɪz] *vt* escandalizar.

scandalous ['skændələs] *adj* escandaloso(sa).

Scandinavia [,skændɪ'neɪvjə] *n* Escandinavia.

Scandinavian [,skændɪ'neɪvjən] ◇ *adj* escandinavo(va). ◇ *n* [person] escandinavo *m*, -va *f*.

scanner ['skænər] *n* COMPUT & MED escáner *m*.

scant [skænt] *adj* escaso(sa).

scanty ['skæntɪ] (*compar* -ier, *superl* -iest) *adj* [amount, resources] escaso(sa); [dress] ligero(ra); [meal] insuficiente.

scapegoat ['skeɪpɡəut] *n* cabeza *f* de turco.

scar [skɑːr] (*pt* & *pp* -red, *cont* -ring) ◇ *n* -**1.** [physical] cicatriz *f*. -**2.** *fig* [mental] señal *f*. ◇ *vt* -**1.** [physically] dejar una cicatriz en. -**2.** *fig* [mentally] marcar.

scarce [skeəs] *adj* escaso(sa); **to make o.s.** ~ esfumarse, quitarse de en medio.

scarcely ['skeəslɪ] *adv* apenas; ~ **anyone/ever** casi nadie/nunca.

scarcity ['skeəsətɪ] *n* escasez *f*.

scare [skeər] ◇ *n* -**1.** [sudden fear] susto *m*, sobresalto *m*. -**2.** [public fear] temor *m*. ◇ *vt* asustar, sobresaltar.

◆ **scare away, scare off** *vt sep* ahuyentar.

scarecrow ['skeəkrəu] *n* espantapájaros *m inv*.

scared ['skeəd] *adj* -**1.** [frightened] asustado(da); **to be** ~ **stiff** OR **to death** estar muerto de miedo. -**2.** [worried]: **to be** ~ **that** tener miedo que.

scarey ['skeərɪ] = **scary**.

scarf [skɑːf] (*pl* -**s** OR **scarves**) *n* [for neck] bufanda *f*; [for head] pañuelo *m* de cabeza.

scarlet ['skɑːlət] ◇ *adj* color escarlata. ◇ *n* escarlata *f*.

scarlet fever *n* escarlatina *f*.

scarves [skɑːvz] *pl* → **scarf**.

scary ['skeərɪ] (*compar* -ier, *superl* -iest) *adj inf* espeluznante.

scathing ['skeɪðɪŋ] *adj* mordaz; **to be** ~ **about sthg/sb** criticar duramente algo/a alguien.

scatter ['skætər] ◇ *vt* esparcir, desparramar. ◇ *vi* dispersarse.

scatterbrained ['skætəbreɪnd] *adj inf* atolondrado(da).

scattered ['skætəd] *adj* disperso(sa).

scattering ['skætərɪŋ] *n*: **a** ~ **of snow** un poco de nieve; **a** ~ **of phone calls** unas cuantas llamadas.

scatty ['skætɪ] (*compar* -ier, *superl* -iest) *adj Br inf* atolondrado(da).

scavenge ['skævɪndʒ] ◇ *vt* -**1.** [subj: animal]: **to** ~ **food** buscar carroña. -**2.** [subj: person] rebuscar entre las basuras. ◇ *vi* -**1.** [animal]: **to** ~ **for food** buscar carroña. -**2.** [person]: **to** ~ **for sthg** rebuscar algo.

scavenger ['skævɪndʒər] *n* -**1.** [animal] carroñero *m*, -ra *f*. -**2.** [person] persona *f* que rebusca en las basuras.

SCE (*abbr of* **Scottish Certificate of Education**) *n título de enseñanza secundaria en Escocia*.

scenario [sɪ'nɑːrɪəu] (*pl* -**s**) *n* -**1.** [possible situation] situación *f* hipotética. -**2.** [of film, play] resumen *m* del argumento.

scene [siːn] *n* -**1.** [gen] escena *f*; **behind the** ~**s** entre bastidores. -**2.** [painting of place] panorama *m*, paisaje *m*. -**3.** [location] sitio *m*; **on the** ~ en el sitio; **a change of** ~ un cambio de ambiente OR de aires; **it's not my** ~ no es lo mío. -**4.** [show of emotion] jaleo *m*, escándalo *m*; **to make a** ~ montar una escena. -**5.** *phr*: **to set the** ~ [for person] describir la escena; [for event] crear el ambiente propicio.

scenery ['siːnərɪ] *n* (*U*) -**1.** [of countryside] paisaje *m*. -**2.** THEATRE decorado *m*.

scenic ['siːnɪk] *adj* [view] pintoresco(ca); [tour] turístico(ca).

scenic route *n* ruta *f* turística.

scent [sent] ◇ *n* -**1.** [smell - of flowers] fragancia *f*; [- of animal] rastro *m*. -**2.** *fig* [track]

pista *f.* **-3.** [perfume] perfume *m.* ◇ *vt* **-1.** [subj: animal] olfatear, husmear. **-2.** *fig* [subj: person] percibir.

scented ['sentɪd] *adj* perfumado(da).

scepter *Am* = sceptre.

sceptic *Br*, **skeptic** *Am* ['skeptɪk] *n* escéptico *m*, -ca *f.*

sceptical *Br*, **skeptical** *Am* ['skeptɪkl] *adj* escéptico(ca); **to be ~ about** tener muchas dudas acerca de.

scepticism *Br*, **skepticism** *Am* ['skeptɪsɪzm] *n* escepticismo *m.*

sceptre *Br*, **scepter** *Am* ['septər] *n* cetro *m.*

SCF (*abbr of* **Save the Children Fund**) *n* organización caritativa internacional que trabaja por el bienestar de los niños.

schedule [*Br* 'ʃedjʊl, *Am* 'skedʒʊl] ◇ *n* **-1.** [plan] programa *m*, plan *m*; **(according) to ~** según lo previsto; **on ~** sin retraso; **ahead of ~** con adelanto; **behind ~** con retraso. **-2.** [of prices, contents] lista *f*; [of times] horario *m.* ◇ *vt*: **to ~ sthg (for)** fijar algo (para).

scheduled flight [*Br* 'ʃedjʊld-, *Am* 'skedʒʊld-] *n* vuelo *m* regular.

schematic [skɪ'mætɪk] *adj* esquemático(ca).

scheme [skiːm] ◇ *n* **-1.** [plan] plano *m*, proyecto *m.* **-2.** *pej* [dishonest plan] intriga *f*, treta *f.* **-3.** [arrangement, decoration - of room] disposición *f*; [- of colours] combinación *f.* **-4.** *phr*: **the ~ of things** el orden de las cosas. ◇ *vi pej*: **to ~ (to do sthg)** intrigar (para hacer algo).

scheming ['skiːmɪŋ] *adj* intrigante.

schism ['sɪzm, 'skɪzm] *n* cisma *f.*

schizophrenia [,skɪtsə'friːnjə] *n* esquizofrenia *f.*

schizophrenic [,skɪtsə'frenɪk] ◇ *adj* esquizofrénico(ca). ◇ *n* esquizofrénico *m*, -ca *f.*

schlepp [ʃlep] *Am inf* ◇ *vt* arrastrar. ◇ *vi*: **to ~ (around)** arrastrarse de un sitio a otro.

schmal(t)z [ʃmɔːlts] *n inf* sensiblería *f.*

schmuck [ʃmʌk] *n Am inf* tonto *m*, -ta *f.*

scholar ['skɒlər] *n* **-1.** [expert] erudito *m*, -ta *f.* **-2.** *dated* [student] alumno *m*, -na *f.* **-3.** [holder of scholarship] becario *m*, -ria *f.*

scholarship ['skɒləʃɪp] *n* **-1.** [grant] beca *f.* **-2.** [learning] erudición *f.*

scholastic [skə'læstɪk] *adj fml* escolar.

school [skuːl] *n* **-1.** [gen] colegio *m*, escuela *f*; [for driving, art] escuela *f*; [for medicine, law] facultad *f.* **-2.** *Am* [university] universidad *f.* **-3.** [group of fish, dolphins] banco *m.*

school age *n* edad *f* escolar.

schoolbook ['skuːlbʊk] *n* libro *m* de texto.

schoolboy ['skuːlbɔɪ] *n* colegial *m*, escolar *m.*

schoolchild ['skuːltʃaɪld] (*pl* **-children** [-tʃɪldrən]) *n* colegial *m*, -la *f*, alumno *m*, -na *f.*

schooldays ['skuːldeɪz] *npl* años *mpl* de colegio.

school dinner *n* comida *f* del colegio.

school district *n Am* autoridad local de Estados Unidos con competencias en materia de educación primaria y secundaria.

school friend *n* amigo *m*, -ga *f* de colegio.

schoolgirl ['skuːlgɜːl] *n* colegiala *f*, escolar *f.*

schooling ['skuːlɪŋ] *n* educación *f* escolar.

schoolkid ['skuːlkɪd] *n inf* colegial *m*, -la *f*, alumno *m*, -na *f.*

school-leaver [-,liːvər] *n Br* joven que ha terminado la enseñanza obligatoria.

school-leaving age [-'liːvɪŋ-] *n* edad de finalización de la enseñanza obligatoria.

schoolmarm ['skuːlmɑːm] *n Am* maestra *f* rural.

schoolmaster ['skuːl,mɑːstər] *n dated* [at primary school] maestro *m*; [at secondary school] profesor *m.*

schoolmistress ['skuːl,mɪstrɪs] *n dated* [at primary school] maestra *f*; [at secondary school] profesora *f.*

school of thought *n* corriente *f* de opinión.

school report *n* informe *m* escolar.

schoolroom ['skuːlrʊm] *n dated* clase *f*, aula *f.*

schoolteacher ['skuːl,tiːtʃər] *n* [primary] maestro *m*, -tra *f*; [secondary] profesor *m*, -ra *f.*

school uniform *n* uniforme *m* escolar.

schoolwork ['skuːlwɜːk] *n* (*U*) trabajo *m* escolar.

school year *n* año *m* escolar.

schooner ['skuːnər] *n* **-1.** [ship] goleta *f.* **-2.** *Br* [sherry glass] copa *f* larga (para jerez).

sciatica [saɪ'ætɪkə] *n* ciática *f.*

science ['saɪəns] ◇ *n* ciencia *f.* ◇ *comp* de ciencias.

science fiction *n* ciencia *f* ficción.

science park *n* área de investigación científica promovida por empresas.

scientific [,saɪən'tɪfɪk] *adj* científico(ca).

scientist ['saɪəntɪst] *n* científico *m*, -ca *f.*

sci-fi [,saɪ'faɪ] (*abbr of* **science fiction**) *n inf* ciencia *f* ficción.

Scilly Isles ['sɪlɪ-], **Scillies** ['sɪlɪz] *npl*: **the ~** las islas Sorlinga.

scintillating ['sɪntɪleɪtɪŋ] *adj* brillante, chispeante.

scissors ['sɪzəz] *npl* tijeras *fpl*; **a pair of** ~ unas tijeras.

sclerosis → **multiple sclerosis**.

scoff [skɒf] ◇ *vt Br inf* zamparse, tragarse. ◇ *vi*: **to** ~ **(at sb/sthg)** mofarse OR burlarse (de alguien/de algo).

scold [skəʊld] *vt* regañar, reñir.

scone [skɒn] *n* bollo tomado con té a la hora de la merienda.

scoop [skuːp] ◇ *n* **-1.** [utensil - for sugar] cucharita *f* plana; [- for ice cream] pinzas *fpl* (*de helado*); [- for flour] paleta *f*. **-2.** [amount - of sugar] cucharilla *f*; [- of ice cream] bola *f*. **-3.** PRESS exclusiva *f*. ◇ *vt* **-1.** [with hands] recoger. **-2.** [with utensil] recoger con cucharilla.
◆ **scoop out** *vt sep* sacar con cuchara.

scoot [skuːt] *vi inf* ir pitando.

scooter ['skuːtər] *n* **-1.** [toy] patinete *m*. **-2.** [motorcycle] escúter *m*, Vespa® *f*, motoneta *f Amer*.

scope [skəʊp] *n* (*U*) **-1.** [opportunity] posibilidades *fpl*. **-2.** [range] alcance *m*.

scorch [skɔːtʃ] ◇ *vt* **-1.** [dress, meat] chamuscar; [face, skin] quemar. **-2.** [dry out] secar. ◇ *vi* [burn - dress, meat] chamuscarse; [face, skin] quemarse.

scorched earth policy [skɔːtʃt-] *n* política *f* de tierra quemada.

scorcher ['skɔːtʃər] *n inf* día *m* abrasador.

scorching ['skɔːtʃɪŋ] *adj inf* abrasador(ra).

score [skɔːr] ◇ *n* **-1.** [in test] calificación *f*, nota *f*; [in competition] puntuación *f*. **-2.** SPORT resultado *m*; **what's the** ~? ¿cómo van? **-3.** *dated* [twenty] veintena *f*. **-4.** MUS partitura *f*. **-5.** [subject]: **on that** ~ a ese respecto, por lo que se refiere a eso. ◇ *vt* **-1.** SPORT marcar. **-2.** [achieve - success, victory] obtener. **-3.** [win in an argument - point] marcar, apuntarse. **-4.** [cut] grabar. ◇ *vi* **-1.** SPORT marcar. **-2.** [in test etc] obtener una puntuación. **-3.** [win in an argument]: **to** ~ **over sb** aventajar a alguien.
◆ **scores** *npl* [large number]: ~s **(of)** montones *mpl* (de).
◆ **score out** *vt sep Br* tachar.

scoreboard ['skɔːbɔːd] *n* tanteador *m*, marcador *m*.

scorecard ['skɔːkɑːd] *n* GOLF tarjeta *f* (*para los resultados*).

scorer ['skɔːrər] *n* **-1.** [official] tanteador *m*, -ra *f*. **-2.** [player - in football] goleador *m*, -ra *f*; [- in other sports] marcador *m*, -ra *f*.

scorn [skɔːn] ◇ *n* menosprecio *m*, desdén

m; **to pour** ~ **on sthg/sb** despreciar algo/a alguien. ◇ *vt* menospreciar, desdeñar.

scornful ['skɔːnfʊl] *adj* despectivo(va), de desdén; **to be** ~ **of sthg** desdeñar algo.

Scorpio ['skɔːpɪəʊ] (*pl* **-s**) *n* Escorpión *m*; **to be (a)** ~ ser Escorpión.

scorpion ['skɔːpjən] *n* escorpión *m*, alacrán *m*.

Scot [skɒt] *n* escocés *m*, -esa *f*.

scotch [skɒtʃ] *vt* [rumour] poner fin a, desmentir; [idea] desechar.

Scotch [skɒtʃ] ◇ *adj* escocés(esa). ◇ *n* whisky *m* escocés.

Scotch egg *n Br* bola *f* de fiambre de salchicha rebozada y con huevo duro en el centro.

Scotch (tape)® *n Am* cinta *f* adhesiva, ≃ celo® *m*.

scot-free *adj inf*: **to get off** ~ salir impune.

Scotland ['skɒtlənd] *n* Escocia.

Scotland Yard *n* sede central de la policía londinense. Por extensión, ésta última.

Scots [skɒts] ◇ *adj* escocés(esa). ◇ *n* [dialect] escocés *m*..

Scotsman ['skɒtsmən] (*pl* **-men** [-mən]) *n* escocés *m*.

Scotswoman ['skɒtswʊmən] (*pl* **-women** [-,wɪmɪn]) *n* escocesa *f*.

Scottish ['skɒtɪʃ] *adj* escocés(esa).

Scottish National Party *n*: **the** ~ el Partido Nacionalista Escocés.

scoundrel ['skaʊndrəl] *n dated* sinvergüenza *m*, canalla *m*.

scour [skaʊər] *vt* **-1.** [clean] fregar, restregar. **-2.** [search] registrar, batir.

scourer ['skaʊrər] *n* estropajo *m*.

scourge [skɜːdʒ] *n* **-1.** [cause of suffering] azote *m*. **-2.** [critic] castigador *m*, -ra *f*.

Scouse [skaʊs] *n inf* **-1.** [person] persona procedente de Liverpool. **-2.** [accent] dialecto de las personas procedentes de Liverpool.

scout [skaʊt] *n* MIL explorador *m*.
◆ **Scout** *n* [boy scout] explorador *m*.

scout around *vi*: **to** ~ **around (for)** explorar el terreno (en busca de).

scoutmaster ['skaʊt,mɑːstər] *n* jefe *m* de exploradores.

scowl [skaʊl] ◇ *n* ceño *m* fruncido. ◇ *vi* fruncir el ceño; **to** ~ **at sb** mirar con ceño a alguien.

SCR (*abbr of* **senior common room**) *n Br* sala de profesores.

scrabble ['skræbl] *vi* **-1.** [scramble, scrape] escarbar; **to** ~ **up/down** subir/bajar escarbando. **-2.** [feel around] palpar en busca de algo; **to** ~ **around for sthg** hurgar en busca de algo.

Scrabble® ['skræbl] *n* Scrabble® *m*.

scraggy ['skrægɪ] (*compar* **-ier**, *superl* **-iest**) *adj inf* flaco(ca).

scram [skræm] (*pt* & *pp* **-med**, *cont* **-ming**) *vi inf* largarse.

scramble ['skræmbl] ◇ *n* [rush] pelea *f*. ◇ *vi* **-1.** [climb] trepar. **-2.** [move clumsily]: **to ~ to one's feet** levantarse rápidamente y tambaleándose; **to ~ out of the way** apartarse atropelladamente.

scrambled eggs ['skræmbld-] *npl* huevos *mpl* revueltos.

scrambler ['skræmblər] *n* COMPUT distorsionador *m* (de frecuencias).

scrap [skræp] (*pt* & *pp* **-ped**, *cont* **-ping**) ◇ *n* **-1.** [small piece] trozo *m*, pedazo *m*; **it won't make a ~ of difference** no lo cambiará en lo más mínimo. **-2.** [metal] chatarra *f*. **-3.** *inf* [fight, quarrel] pelotera *f*. ◇ *vt* desechar, descartar.

♦ **scraps** *npl* [food] sobras *fpl*.

scrapbook ['skræpbʊk] *n* álbum *m* de recortes.

scrap dealer *n* chatarrero *m*, -ra *f*.

scrape [skreɪp] ◇ *n* **-1.** [noise] chirrido *m*. **-2.** *dated* [difficult situation] apuro *m*, lío *m*. ◇ *vt* **-1.** [remove]: **to ~ sthg off sthg** raspar algo de algo. **-2.** [vegetables] raspar. **-3.** [car, bumper, glass] rayar; [knee, elbow, skin] rasguñar, arañar. ◇ *vi* **-1.** [rub]: **to ~ against/on sthg** rozar contra/en algo. **-2.** [save money] economizar.

♦ **scrape through** *vt fus* aprobar por los pelos.

♦ **scrape together**, **scrape up** *vt sep* juntar (a duras penas).

scraper ['skreɪpər] *n* raspador *m*.

scrap heap *n* montón *m* de chatarra; **to end up on the ~** [idea] ir a parar al cubo de basura; [person] quedar arrinconado.

scrapings ['skreɪpɪŋz] *npl* raspaduras *fpl*.

scrap merchant *n Br* chatarrero *m*, -ra *f*.

scrap metal *n* chatarra *f*.

scrap paper *Br*, **scratch paper** *Am n* (U) papel *m* usado.

scrappy ['skræpɪ] (*compar* **-ier**, *superl* **-iest**) *adj pej* deshilvanado(da), fragmentario(ria).

scrapyard ['skræpjɑːd] *n* [gen] depósito *m* de chatarra; [for cars] cementerio *m* de coches.

scratch [skrætʃ] ◇ *n* **-1.** [wound] arañazo *m*, rasguño *m*. **-2.** [mark] raya *f*, surco *m*. **-3.** *phr*: **to do sthg from ~** hacer algo partiendo desde el principio; **to be up to ~** estar a la altura requerida. ◇ *vt* **-1.** [wound] arañar, rasguñar. **-2.** [mark] rayar. **-3.** [rub - head, leg] rascar; **to ~ o.s.** rascarse. ◇ *vi* **-1.**

[make mark]: **to ~ at/against sthg** arañar algo. **-2.** [rub] rascarse.

scratch card *n* tarjeta con una zona que hay que rascar para ver si contiene premio.

scratchpad ['skrætʃpæd] *n Am* bloc *m* de notas.

scratch paper *Am* = **scrap paper**.

scratchy ['skrætʃɪ] (*compar* **-ier**, *superl* **-iest**) *adj* **-1.** [record] rayado(da). **-2.** [material] áspero(ra); [pen] que raspea.

scrawl [skrɔːl] ◇ *n* garabatos *mpl*. ◇ *vt* garabatear.

scrawny ['skrɔːnɪ] (*compar* **-ier**, *superl* **-iest**) *adj* flaco(ca).

scream [skriːm] ◇ *n* **-1.** [cry, shout] grito *m*, chillido *m*; **~s of laughter** carcajadas *fpl*. **-2.** [noise] chirrido *m*. **-3.** *inf* [funny person]: **she's a ~** ella es la monda. ◇ *vt* vociferar. ◇ *vi* **-1.** [person] gritar, chillar. **-2.** [tyres] chirriar; [jet] silbar.

scree [skriː] *n* montón *de piedras desprendidas de la ladera de una montaña.*

screech [skriːtʃ] ◇ *n* **-1.** [of person] chillido *m*; [of bird] chirrido *m*. **-2.** [of car, tyres] chirrido *m*, rechinar *m*. ◇ *vt* gritar. ◇ *vi* **-1.** [person, bird] chillar. **-2.** [car, tyres] chirriar, rechinar.

screen [skriːn] ◇ *n* **-1.** TV, CINEMA & COMPUT pantalla *f*. **-2.** [panel] biombo *m*. ◇ *vt* **-1.** [show in cinema] proyectar. **-2.** [broadcast on TV] emitir. **-3.** [shield]: **to ~ sthg/sb (from)** proteger algo/a alguien (de). **-4.** [candidate, patient] examinar; **to ~ sb for sthg** hacer un chequeo a alguien para algo.

♦ **screen off** *vt sep* separar mediante un biombo.

screen door *n* puerta *f* de tela metálica.

screen dump *n* COMPUT volcado *m* de pantalla.

screening ['skriːnɪŋ] *n* **-1.** [of film] proyección *f*. **-2.** [of TV programme] emisión *f*. **-3.** [for security] examen *m*, investigación *f*. **-4.** MED [examination] chequeo *m*.

screenplay ['skriːnpleɪ] *n* guión *m*.

screen print *n* serigrafía *f*.

screen saver *n* COMPUT sistema *para proteger la pantalla*.

screen test *n* prueba *f* cinematográfica.

screenwriter ['skriːnˌraɪtər] *n* guionista *m* y *f*.

screw [skruː] ◇ *n* [for fastening] tornillo *m*. ◇ *vt* **-1.** [fix]: **to ~ sthg to** atornillar algo a. **-2.** [twist] enroscar. **-3.** *vulg* [woman] follar, coger *Amer*. ◇ *vi* enroscarse.

♦ **screw up** *vt sep* **-1.** [sheet of paper etc] arrugar. **-2.** [eyes] entornar; [face] arrugar. **-3.** *v inf* [ruin] jorobar.

screwball ['skruːbɔːl] *n Am* [person] cabeza *m y f* loca.

screwdriver ['skruːˌdraɪvəʳ] *n* destornillador *m*, desarmador *m Amer*.

screwtop jar ['skruːtɒp-] *n* tarro *m* con tapa de rosca.

screwy ['skruːɪ] *adj Am inf* pirado(da).

scribble ['skrɪbl] ◇ *n* garabato *m*. ◇ *vt & vi* garabatear.

scribe [skraɪb] *n fml* amanuense *m y f*, scriba *f*.

scrimp [skrɪmp] *vi*: **to ~ and save (to do sthg)** apretarse el cinturón (para hacer algo).

script [skrɪpt] *n* **-1.** [of play, film etc] guión *m*. **-2.** [system of writing] escritura *f*. **-3.** [handwriting] letra *f*.

scripted ['skrɪptɪd] *adj* con guión.

Scriptures ['skrɪptʃəz] *npl*: **the ~** las Sagradas Escrituras.

scriptwriter ['skrɪptˌraɪtəʳ] *n* guionista *m y f*.

scroll [skrəʊl] ◇ *n* rollo *m* de pergamino/papel. ◇ *vt* COMPUT desplazar.

◆ **scroll down** *vi* COMPUT desplazarse hacia abajo.

◆ **scroll up** *vi* COMPUT desplazarse hacia arriba.

scroll bar *n* COMPUT barra *f* de desplazamiento.

scrooge [skruːdʒ] *n inf pej* ruin *m y f*, tacaño *m*, -ña *f*.

scrotum ['skrəʊtəm] (*pl* **-ta** [-tə] OR **-tums**) *n* escroto *m*.

scrounge [skraʊndʒ] *inf* ◇ *vt* gorrear, gorronear. ◇ *vi*: **to ~ (off sb)** *Br* gorrear OR gorronear (de alguien).

scrounger ['skraʊndʒəʳ] *n inf* gorrón *m*, -ona *f*.

scrub [skrʌb] (*pt & pp* **-bed**, *cont* **-bing**) ◇ *n* **-1.** [rub] restregón *m*, fregado *m*. **-2.** [undergrowth] maleza *f*. ◇ *vt* restregar.

scrubbing brush *Br* ['skrʌbɪŋ-], **scrub brush** *Am n* cepillo *m* de fregar.

scruff [skrʌf] *n*: **by the ~ of the neck** por el pescuezo.

scruffy ['skrʌfɪ] (*compar* **-ier**, *superl* **-iest**) *adj* [person] dejado(da); [clothes] andrajoso(sa); [room] desordenado(da).

scrum(mage) ['skrʌm(ɪdʒ)] *n* RUGBY melé *f*.

scrumptious ['skrʌmpʃəs] *adj inf* riquísimo(ma).

scrunch [skrʌntʃ] *inf* ◇ *vt* estrujar. ◇ *vi* crujir.

scruples ['skruːplz] *npl* escrúpulos *mpl*.

scrupulous ['skruːpjʊləs] *adj* escrupuloso(sa).

scrupulously ['skruːpjʊləslɪ] *adv* **-1.** [fairly] escrupulosamente. **-2.** [thoroughly] completamente, totalmente.

scrutinize, -ise ['skruːtɪnaɪz] *vt* escudriñar.

scrutiny ['skruːtɪnɪ] *n* (*U*) escrutinio *m*, examen *m*.

scuba diving ['skuːbə-] *n* buceo *m* con botellas de oxígeno.

scud [skʌd] (*pt & pp* **-ded**, *cont* **-ding**) *vi literary* deslizarse rápidamente.

scuff [skʌf] *vt* **-1.** [drag] arrastrar. **-2.** [damage - shoes] pelar; [- furniture, floor] rayar.

scuffle ['skʌfl] ◇ *n* refriega *f*, reyerta *f*. ◇ *vi*: **to ~ (with sb)** pelearse (con alguien).

scull [skʌl] ◇ *n* [oar] remo *m*. ◇ *vi* remar.

scullery ['skʌlərɪ] (*pl* **-ies**) *n* trascocina *f*, fregadero *m*.

sculpt [skʌlpt] *vt* esculpir.

sculptor ['skʌlptəʳ] *n* escultor *m*, -ra *f*.

sculpture ['skʌlptʃəʳ] ◇ *n* escultura *f*. ◇ *vt* esculpir.

scum [skʌm] *n* **-1.** [froth] espuma *f*. **-2.** *v inf pej* [worthless person] escoria *f*.

scupper ['skʌpəʳ] *vt* NAUT & *fig* hundir.

scurf [skɜːf] *n* caspa *f*.

scurrilous ['skʌrələs] *adj fml* injurioso(sa), difamatorio(ria).

scurry ['skʌrɪ] (*pt & pp* **-ied**) *vi*: **to ~ off** OR **away** escabullirse.

scurvy ['skɜːvɪ] *n* escorbuto *m*.

scuttle ['skʌtl] ◇ *n* cubo *m* del carbón, carbonera *f*. ◇ *vi* [rush]: **to ~ off** OR **away** escabullirse.

scythe [saɪð] ◇ *n* guadaña *f*. ◇ *vt* guadañar, segar.

SD *abbr of* **South Dakota**.

SDI (*abbr of* **Strategic Defense Initiative**) *n* IDE *f*.

SDLP (*abbr of* **Social Democratic and Labour Party**) *n partido político norirlandés que defiende la integración pacífica en la república de Irlanda*.

SDP (*abbr of* **Social Democratic Party**) *n partido político británico formado como escisión centrista del partido laborista*.

SE (*abbr of* **south-east**) SE.

sea [siː] ◇ *n* **-1.** [not land] mar *m o f*; **at ~** en el mar; **by ~** en barco; **by the ~** a orillas del mar; **out to ~** [away from shore] mar adentro; [across the water] hacia el mar. **-2.** [not ocean] mar *m*. **-3.** *fig* [large number] mar *m*. **-4.** *phr*: **to be all at ~** estar totalmente perdido(da). ◇ *comp* de mar.

◆ **seas** *npl*: **the ~s** los mares.

sea air *n* aire *m* del mar.

sea anemone *n* anémona *f* de mar.

seabed ['si:bed] *n*: **the ~** el lecho marino.

seabird ['si:bɜːd] *n* ave *f* marina.

seaboard ['si:bɔːd] *n fml* litoral *m*.

sea breeze *n* brisa *f* marina.

seafaring ['si:,feərɪŋ] *adj* marinero(ra).

seafood ['si:fuːd] *n* (*U*) mariscos *mpl*.

seafront ['si:frʌnt] *n* paseo *m* marítimo.

seagoing ['si:,gəʊɪŋ] *adj* de alta mar.

seagull ['si:gʌl] *n* gaviota *f*.

seahorse ['si:hɔːs] *n* caballo *m* de mar.

seal [si:l] (*pl inv* OR **-s**) ◇ *n* **-1.** [animal] foca *f*. **-2.** [official mark] sello *m*; **~ of approval** aprobación *f*, visto *m* bueno; **to put** OR **set the ~ on sthg** sellar algo. **-3.** [on bottle, meter] precinto *m*; [on letter] sello *m*. **-4.** TECH sello *m*. ◇ *vt* **-1.** [envelope] sellar, cerrar. **-2.** [opening, tube, crack] tapar, cerrar.
◆ **seal off** *vt sep* [entrance, exit] cerrar; [area] acordonar.

sealable ['si:lɪbl] *adj* precintable.

sea lane *n* ruta *f* marítima.

sealant ['si:lənt] *n* [of document, bottle] sello *m*; [for leaks, wood] aislante *m*.

sea level *n* nivel *m* del mar.

sealing wax ['si:lɪŋ-] *n* lacre *m*.

sea lion (*pl inv* OR **-s**) *n* león *m* marítimo.

sealskin ['si:lskɪn] *n* piel *f* de foca.

seam [si:m] *n* **-1.** SEWING costura *f*; **to be bursting at the ~s** estar a tope. **-2.** [of coal] veta *f*.

seaman ['si:mən] (*pl* **-men** [-mən]) *n* marinero *m*.

seamanship ['si:mənʃɪp] *n* náutica *f*.

sea mist *n* bruma *f*.

seamless ['si:mlɪs] *adj* **-1.** SEWING sin costura. **-2.** *fig* [faultless] perfecto(ta).

seamstress ['semstrɪs] *n* costurera *f*.

seamy ['si:mɪ] (*compar* **-ier**, *superl* **-iest**) *adj* sórdido(da).

séance ['seɪɒns] *n* sesión *f* de espiritismo.

seaplane ['si:pleɪn] *n* hidroavión *m*.

seaport ['si:pɔːt] *n* puerto *m* de mar.

search [sɜːtʃ] ◇ *n* [gen] búsqueda *f*; [of room, drawer] registro *m*; [of person] cacheo *m*; **~ for sthg** búsqueda de algo; **in ~ of** en busca de. ◇ *vt* [gen] registrar; [one's mind] escudriñar; **to ~ sthg for sthg** buscar algo en algo. ◇ *vi*: **to ~ (for sthg/sb)** buscar (algo/a alguien).
◆ **search out** *vt sep* encontrar, descubrir.

searcher ['sɜːtʃəʳ] *n* buscador *m*, -ra *f*.

searching ['sɜːtʃɪŋ] *adj* [question] agudo(da); [look] penetrante.

searchlight ['sɜːtʃlaɪt] *n* reflector *m*, proyector *m*.

search party *n* equipo *m* de búsqueda.

search warrant *n* mandamiento *m* de registro.

searing ['sɪərɪŋ] *adj* **-1.** [pain] punzante; [heat] abrasador(ra). **-2.** [criticism] acerado(da).

sea salt *n* sal *f* marina.

seashell ['si:ʃel] *n* concha *f* (marina).

seashore ['si:ʃɔːʳ] *n*: **the ~** la orilla del mar.

seasick ['si:sɪk] *adj* mareado(da).

seaside ['si:saɪd] *n*: **the ~** la playa.

seaside resort *n* lugar *m* de veraneo (en la playa).

season ['si:zn] ◇ *n* **-1.** [of year] estación *f*. **-2.** [particular period] época *f*, período *m*. **-3.** [of holiday] temporada *f*; **out of ~** fuera de temporada. **-4.** [of food]: **out of/in ~** fuera de/en sazón. **-5.** [of talks, films] temporada *f*. ◇ *vt* sazonar, condimentar.

seasonal ['si:zənl] *adj* [work] temporal; [change] estacional.

seasoned ['si:znd] *adj* veterano(na).

seasoning ['si:znɪŋ] *n* condimento *m*.

season ticket *n* abono *m*.

seat [si:t] ◇ *n* **-1.** [gen] asiento *m*. **-2.** [of trousers, skirt] trasero *m*. **-3.** POL [in parliament] escaño *m*. ◇ *vt* **-1.** [sit down] sentar; **be ~ed!** ¡siéntese!; **to ~ o.s.** sentarse. **-2.** [subj: building, vehicle] tener cabida para.

seat belt *n* cinturón *m* de seguridad.

seated ['si:tɪd] *adj* sentado(da).

-seater ['si:təʳ] *suffix*: **a two~** car un coche de dos plazas.

seating ['si:tɪŋ] ◇ *n* (*U*) [capacity] asientos *mpl*. ◇ *comp*: **~ capacity** cabida *f*; **~ plan** distribución *f* de asientos.

SEATO ['si:təʊ] (*abbr of* **Southeast Asia Treaty Organization**) *n* OTSEA *f*.

sea urchin *n* erizo *m* de mar.

seawall ['si:wɔːl] *n* dique *m*.

seawater ['si:,wɔːtəʳ] *n* agua *f* de mar.

seaweed ['si:wi:d] *n* (*U*) alga *f* marina, huiro *m* Amer.

seaworthy ['si:,wɜːðɪ] *adj* en condiciones de navegar.

sebaceous [sɪ'beɪʃəs] *adj* sebáceo(a).

sec. (*abbr of* **second**) seg.

SEC (*abbr of* **Securities and Exchange Commission**) *n organismo gubernamental estadounidense que regula las transacciones bursátiles.*

secateurs [,sekə'tɜːz] *npl Br* podadera *f*.

secede [sɪ'si:d] *vi fml*: **to ~ (from sthg)** separarse (de algo).

secession [sɪ'seʃn] *n fml* secesión *f.*

secluded [sɪ'kluːdɪd] *adj* apartado(da).

seclusion [sɪ'kluːʒn] *n* aislamiento *m.*

second[1] ['sekənd] ◇ *n* -1. [gen] segundo *m.* -2. *Br* UNIV ≃ licenciatura *f* con notable. ◇ *num adj* segundo(da); ~ **only to** después de. ◇ *num n* -1. [in order] segundo *m,* -da *f.* -2. [in dates]: **the ~ (of May)** el dos (de mayo); *see also* **sixth.** ◇ *vt* secundar.

◆ **seconds** *npl* -1. COMM artículos *mpl* defectuosos. -2. [of food]: **to have ~s** repetir (*en una comida*).

second[2] [sɪ'kɒnd] *vt Br* [employee] trasladar temporalmente.

secondary ['sekəndrɪ] *adj* -1. [SCH · school] secundario(ria); [- education] medio(dia); [- teacher] de enseñanza media. -2. [less important]: **to be ~ to** ser secundario(ria) a.

secondary modern *n Br* escuela de formación profesional.

secondary picketing *n* (*U*) piquetes *mpl* de solidaridad.

secondary school *n* escuela *f* de enseñanza media.

second best ['sekənd-] *adj* segundo(da) (mejor).

second-class ['sekənd-] *adj* -1. [gen] de segunda clase. -2. *Br* UNIV *nota global de licenciatura equivalente a un notable o un aprobado alto.*

second cousin ['sekənd-] *n* primo segundo *m,* prima segunda *f.*

second-degree burn ['sekənd-] *n* quemadura *f* de segundo grado.

seconder ['sekəndə'] *n* persona *f* que secunda una moción.

second floor ['sekənd-] *n Br* segundo piso *m; Am* primer piso *m.*

second-guess ['sekənd-] *vt inf* juzgar a posteriori.

second hand ['sekənd-] *n* [of clock] segundero *m.*

second-hand ['sekənd-] ◇ *adj* -1. [goods, information] de segunda mano. -2. [shop] de artículos de segunda mano. ◇ *adv* -1. [not new] de segunda mano. -2. *fig* [indirectly]: **to hear sthg ~** oír algo de segunda mano.

second-in-command ['sekənd-] *n* segundo *m* en jefe.

secondly ['sekəndlɪ] *adv* en segundo lugar.

secondment [sɪ'kɒndmənt] *n Br* traslado *m* temporal.

second nature ['sekənd-] *n* (*U*) hábito muy arraigado en una persona.

second-rate ['sekənd-] *adj pej* de segunda categoría, mediocre.

second thought ['sekənd-] *n*: **to have ~s about sthg** tener dudas acerca de algo; **on ~s** *Br,* **on ~** *Am* pensándolo bien.

secrecy ['siːkrəsɪ] *n* (*U*) secreto *m.*

secret ['siːkrɪt] ◇ *adj* secreto(ta). ◇ *n* secreto *m;* **in ~** en secreto.

secret agent *n* agente secreto *m,* agente secreta *f.*

secretarial [,sekrə'teərɪəl] *adj* [course, training] de secretariado; [staff] de secretaría, administrativo(va).

secretariat [,sekrə'teərɪət] *n* secretariado *m.*

secretary [*Br* 'sekrətrɪ, *Am* 'sekrə,terɪ] (*pl* -ies) *n* -1. [gen] secretario *m,* -ria *f.* -2. POL [minister] ministro *m.*

secretary-general (*pl* **secretaries-general**) *n* secretario *m,* -ria *f* general.

Secretary of State *n* -1. *Br:* ~ **(for)** ministro *m* (de). -2. *Am* ministro *m* estadounidense de Asuntos Exteriores.

secrete [sɪ'kriːt] *vt* -1. [produce] secretar, segregar. -2. *fml* [hide] esconder, ocultar.

secretion [sɪ'kriːʃn] *n* secreción *f.*

secretive ['siːkrətɪv] *adj* [person] reservado(da); [organization] secreto(ta).

secretly ['siːkrɪtlɪ] *adv* [hope, think] secretamente; [tell] en secreto.

secret police *n* policía *f* secreta.

secret service *n* [in UK] servicio *m* secreto; [in US] *departamento del gobierno de Estados Unidos que se encarga de la protección del presidente y vicepresidente del país y de sus familias.*

sect [sekt] *n* secta *f.*

sectarian [sek'teərɪən] *adj* sectario(ria).

section ['sekʃn] ◇ *n* sección *f.* ◇ *vt* seccionar.

sector ['sektə'] *n* sector *m.*

secular ['sekjʊlə'] *adj* [education, life] laico(ca), secular; [music] profano(na).

secure [sɪ'kjʊə'] ◇ *adj* -1. [gen] seguro(ra). -2. [house, building] protegido(da), seguro(ra). ◇ *vt* -1. [obtain] conseguir, obtener. -2. [make safe] proteger. -3. [fasten] cerrar bien.

securely [sɪ'kjʊəlɪ] *adv* [fixed, locked] firmemente.

security [sɪ'kjʊərətɪ] (*pl* -ies) ◇ *n* -1. seguridad *f.* -2. [legal protection]: ~ **of tenure** cargo *m* vitalicio. -3. [for loan] garantía *f.* ◇ *comp* de seguridad.

◆ **securities** *npl* FIN valores *mpl,* títulos *mpl.*

security blanket *n* manta u otro objeto por el cual un niño se siente protegido.

Security Council *n*: **the ~** el Consejo de Seguridad.

security forces *npl* fuerzas *fpl* de seguridad.

security guard *n* guardia *m* jurado OR de seguridad.

security risk *n* persona *f* de dudosa lealtad.

secy (*abbr of* **secretary**) sec.

sedan [sɪ'dæn] *n Am* (coche *m*) utilitario *m*.

sedan chair *n* silla *f* de manos.

sedate [sɪ'deɪt] ◇ *adj* sosegado(da). ◇ *vt* sedar.

sedation [sɪ'deɪʃn] *n* (*U*) sedación *f*.

sedative ['sedətɪv] ◇ *adj* sedante. ◇ *n* sedante *m*, calmante *m*.

sedentary ['sedntrɪ] *adj* sedentario(ria).

sediment ['sedɪmənt] *n* sedimento *m*.

sedition [sɪ'dɪʃn] *n* sedición *f*.

seditious [sɪ'dɪʃəs] *adj* sedicioso(sa).

seduce [sɪ'djuːs] *vt*: **to ~ sb (into doing sthg)** seducir a alguien (a hacer algo).

seduction [sɪ'dʌkʃn] *n* seducción *f*.

seductive [sɪ'dʌktɪv] *adj* seductor(ra).

see [siː] (*pt* **saw**, *pp* **seen**) ◇ *vt* **-1.** [gen] ver. **-2.** [visit - friend, doctor] ir a ver, visitar; **~ you soon/later/tomorrow** *etc*! ¡hasta pronto/luego/mañana *etc*!; **~ you!** ¡hasta luego!, ¡chau! *Amer*; **as I ~ it** tal y como yo lo veo; **~ below/p 10** véase más abajo/pág. 10. **-3.** [accompany - to door etc] acompañar. **-4.** [make sure]: **to ~ (to it) that ...** encargarse de que .... ◇ *vi* [gen] ver; **to ~ if one can do sthg** ver si uno puede hacer algo; **let's ~, let me ~** vamos a ver, veamos; **you ~ ...** verás, es que ...; **I ~** ya veo.
◆ **seeing as, seeing that** *conj inf* como.
◆ **see about** *vt fus* **-1.** [arrange] encargarse de. **-2.** [consider further]: **we'll ~ about that** ya veremos.
◆ **see off** *vt sep* **-1.** [say goodbye to] despedir. **-2.** *Br* [chase away] ahuyentar.
◆ **see through** *vt fus* [person] ver claramente las intenciones de.
◆ **see to** *vt fus* ocuparse de.

seed [siːd] *n* [of plant] semilla *f*.
◆ **seeds** *npl fig* [of doubt] semilla *f*; [of idea] germen *m*.

seedless ['siːdlɪs] *adj* sin pepitas.

seedling ['siːdlɪŋ] *n* plantón *m*.

seedy ['siːdɪ] (*compar* **-ier**, *superl* **-iest**) *adj* [room, area] sórdido(da); [person] desaliñado(da).

seek [siːk] (*pt* & *pp* **sought**) *fml* ◇ *vt* **-1.** [look for, try to obtain] buscar. **-2.** [ask for] solicitar. **-3.** [try]: **to ~ to do sthg** procurar hacer algo. ◇ *vi* **-1.** [look for]: **to ~ for sthg**

buscar algo. **-2.** [ask for]: **to ~ for sthg** solicitar algo.
◆ **seek out** *vt sep* buscar.

seem [siːm] ◇ *vi* parecer; **it ~s (to be) good** parece (que es) bueno; **I can't ~ to do it** no puedo hacerlo (por mucho que lo intente); **I ~ to remember that ...** creo recordar que .... ◇ *v impers*: **it ~s that** parece que.

seeming ['siːmɪŋ] *adj fml* aparente.

seemingly ['siːmɪŋlɪ] *adv* aparentemente.

seemly ['siːmlɪ] (*compar* **-ier**, *superl* **-iest**) *adj dated* & *literary* decoroso(sa).

seen [siːn] *pp* → **see**.

seep [siːp] *vi* rezumar, filtrarse.

seersucker ['sɪə,sʌkə'] *n* sirsaca *f*.

seesaw ['siːsɔː] *n* balancín *m*, subibaja *m*.

seethe [siːð] *vi* **-1.** [person] rabiar. **-2.** [place]: **to be seething with** estar a rebosar de.

seething ['siːðɪŋ] *adj* rabioso(sa).

see-through *adj* transparente.

segment ['segmənt] *n* **-1.** [proportion, section] segmento *m*. **-2.** [of fruit] gajo *m*.

segregate ['segrɪgeɪt] *vt* segregar.

segregation [,segrɪ'geɪʃn] *n* segregación *f*.

Seine [seɪn] *n*: **the (River) ~** el (río) Sena.

seismic ['saɪzmɪk] *adj* sísmico(ca).

seize [siːz] *vt* **-1.** [grab] agarrar, coger. **-2.** [capture - control, power, town] tomar, hacerse con. **-3.** [arrest] detener. **-4.** [take advantage of] aprovechar.
◆ **seize (up)on** *vt fus* valerse de.
◆ **seize up** *vi* agarrotarse.

seizure ['siːʒə'] *n* **-1.** MED ataque *m*. **-2.** [taking, capturing] toma *f*.

seldom ['seldəm] *adv* raramente.

select [sɪ'lekt] ◇ *adj* selecto(ta). ◇ *vt* [gen] elegir, escoger; [team] seleccionar.

select committee *n* comité *m* de investigación.

selected [sɪ'lektɪd] *adj* escogido(da).

selection [sɪ'lekʃn] *n* **-1.** [gen] selección *f*. **-2.** [fact of being selected] elección *f*. **-3.** [in shop] surtido *m*.

selective [sɪ'lektɪv] *adj* selectivo(va).

selector [sɪ'lektə'] *n* seleccionador *m*, -ra *f*.

self [self] (*pl* **selves**) *n* uno mismo (una misma); **he's his old ~ again** vuelve a ser el mismo de antes; **the ~** el yo.

self- [self] *prefix* auto-.

self-addressed envelope [-ə'drest-] *n* sobre con la dirección de uno mismo.

self-addressed stamped envelope [-ə'dreststæmpt-] *n Am* sobre con sus señas y franqueo.

self-adhesive *adj* autoadhesivo(va).

self-appointed [-ə'pɔɪntɪd] *adj pej* por nombramiento propio.

self-assembly *adj Br* desmontable.

self-assertive *adj* que se impone ante los demás.

self-assurance *n* confianza *f* en sí mismo (sí misma).

self-assured *adj* seguro de sí mismo (segura de sí misma).

self-catering *adj* sin pensión.

self-centred [-'sentəd] *adj* egocéntrico(ca).

self-cleaning *adj* autolimpiable.

self-coloured *adj Br* unicolor.

self-confessed [-kən'fest] *adj* confeso(sa).

self-confidence *n* confianza *f* en sí mismo, -ma *f*.

self-confident *adj* [person] seguro de sí mismo (segura de sí misma); [attitude, remark] lleno(na) de seguridad.

self-conscious *adj* cohibido(da).

self-contained *adj* autosuficiente.

self-control *n* control *m* de sí mismo (sí misma).

self-controlled *adj* sereno(na).

self-defence *n* defensa *f* propia, autodefensa *f*; **in ~** en defensa propia.

self-denial *n* abnegación *f*.

self-destruct [-dɪs'trʌkt] ◇ *adj* autodestructor(ra). ◇ *vi* autodestruirse.

self-determination *n* autodeterminación *f*.

self-discipline *n* autodisciplina *f*.

self-doubt *n* inseguridad *f*, falta *f* de confianza en uno mismo (una misma).

self-drive *adj Br* alquilado(da) sin chófer.

self-educated *adj* autodidacta.

self-effacing [-ɪ'feɪsɪŋ] *adj* humilde.

self-employed [-ɪm'plɔɪd] *adj* autónomo(ma), que trabaja por cuenta propia.

self-esteem *n* amor *m* propio.

self-evident *adj* evidente, patente.

self-explanatory *adj* evidente, que queda muy claro(ra).

self-expression *n* autoexpresión *f*.

self-focusing [-'fəʊkəsɪŋ] *adj* con enfoque automático.

self-government *n* autogobierno *m*.

self-help *n* (*U*) ayuda *f* propia.

self-important *adj pej* engreído(da).

self-imposed [-ɪm'pəʊzd] *adj* autoimpuesto(ta).

self-indulgent *adj pej* que se permite excesos.

self-inflicted [-ɪn'flɪktɪd] *adj* autoinfligido(da).

self-interest *n pej* (*U*) interés *m* propio.

selfish ['selfɪʃ] *adj* egoísta.

selfishness ['selfɪʃnɪs] *n* egoísmo *m*.

selfless ['selflɪs] *adj* desinteresado(da).

self-locking [-'lɒkɪŋ] *adj* de cierre automático.

self-made *adj* que ha triunfado por su propio esfuerzo.

self-opinionated *adj pej* que siempre tiene que decir la suya.

self-perpetuating [-pə'petʃʊeɪtɪŋ] *adj* que se perpetúa a sí mismo (sí misma).

self-pity *n pej* lástima *f* de uno mismo.

self-portrait *n* autorretrato *m*.

self-possessed *adj* dueño de sí mismo (dueña de sí misma).

self-proclaimed [-prə'kleɪmd] *adj pej* autodenominado(da), supuesto(ta).

self-raising flour *Br* [-,reɪzɪŋ-], **self-rising flour** *Am n* harina *f* con levadura.

self-regard *n* (*U*) **-1.** *pej* [self-interest] interés *m* propio. **-2.** [self-respect] propia estima *f*.

self-regulating [-'regjʊleɪtɪŋ] *adj* autorregulador(ra).

self-reliant *adj* independiente.

self-respect *n* amor *m* propio.

self-respecting [-rɪs'pektɪŋ] *adj* que se precie, digno(na).

self-restraint *n* dominio *m* de sí mismo.

self-righteous *adj pej* santurrón(ona).

self-rising flour *Am* = self-raising flour.

self-rule *n* autogobierno *m*.

self-sacrifice *n* abnegación *f*.

selfsame ['selfseɪm] *adj* mismísimo(ma).

self-satisfied *adj pej* [person] satisfecho de sí mismo (satisfecha de sí misma); [smile] lleno(na) de suficiencia.

self-sealing [-'siːlɪŋ] *adj* [envelope] autoadhesivo(va).

self-seeking [-'siːkɪŋ] *pej* ◇ *adj* interesado(da), egoísta. ◇ *n* propio interés *m*, egoísmo *m*.

self-service ◇ *n* autoservicio *m*. ◇ *comp* de autoservicio.

self-starter *n* **-1.** AUT arranque *m* automático. **-2.** [person] emprendedor *m*, -ra *f*.

self-styled [-'staɪld] *adj pej* autodenominado(da), supuesto(ta).

self-sufficient *adj*: **~ (in)** autosuficiente (en).

self-supporting [-sə'pɔːtɪŋ] *adj* [business, industry] económicamente independiente.

self-taught *adj* autodidacta.

self-test *vi* COMPUT self-test *m*.

self-will *n pej* obstinación *f*.

sell [sel] (*pt & pp* **sold**) ◇ *vt* **-1.** [gen] vender; **to ~ sthg to sb, to ~ sb sthg** vender algo a alguien; **to ~ sthg for** vender algo por. **-2.** [encourage sale of] hacer vender. **-3.** *fig* [make acceptable, desirable]: **I'm not really sold on it** no estoy convencido(da) de ello; **to ~ o.s.** venderse. ◇ *vi* **-1.** [exchange for money] venderse. **-2.** [be bought]: **to ~ (for** OR **at)** venderse (a).
◆ **sell off** *vt sep* liquidar.
◆ **sell out** ◇ *vt sep* [performance]: **to be sold out** estar agotado(da). ◇ *vi* **-1.** [shop]: **to ~ out (of sthg)** agotar las existencias (de algo). **-2.** [be disloyal, unprincipled] venderse.
◆ **sell up** *vi* venderlo todo.

sell-by date *n Br* fecha *f* de caducidad.

seller ['selǝʳ] *n* vendedor *m*, -ra *f*.

seller's market *n* mercado *m* de demanda OR favorable al vendedor.

selling ['selɪŋ] *n* (*U*) venta *f*.

selling price *n* precio *m* de venta.

Sellotape® ['selǝteɪp] *n Br* ≃ celo® *m*, cinta *f* adhesiva.
◆ **sellotape** *vt* pegar con cinta adhesiva.

sell-out *n* [performance, match] lleno *m*.

seltzer ['seltsǝʳ] *n Am* agua *f* de seltz.

selves [selvz] *pl* → **self**.

semantic [sɪ'mæntɪk] *adj* semántico(ca).

semantics [sɪ'mæntɪks] *n* (*U*) semántica *f*.

semaphore ['semǝfɔːʳ] *n* (*U*) semáforo *m*.

semblance ['semblǝns] *n fml* apariencia *f*.

semen ['siːmen] *n* semen *m*.

semester [sɪ'mestǝʳ] *n* semestre *m*.

semi ['semɪ] *n* **-1.** *Br inf* (*abbr of* **semidetached house**) casa *f* adosada (a otra). **-2.** *Am abbr of* **semitrailer**.

semi- ['semɪ] *prefix* semi-.

semiautomatic [,semɪ,ɔːtǝ'mætɪk] *adj* semiautomático(ca).

semicircle ['semɪ,sɜːkl] *n* semicírculo *m*.

semicircular [,semɪ'sɜːkjʊlǝʳ] *adj* semicircular.

semicolon [,semɪ'kǝʊlǝn] *n* punto *m* y coma.

semiconscious [,semɪ'kɒnʃǝs] *adj* semiconsciente.

semidetached [,semɪdɪ'tætʃt] ◇ *adj* adosado(da). ◇ *n Br* casa *f* adosada (a otra).

semifinal [,semɪ'faɪnl] *n* semifinal *f*.

semifinalist [,semɪ'faɪnǝlɪst] *n* semifinalista *m* y *f*.

seminal ['semɪnl] *adj* **-1.** [of semen] seminal. **-2.** [influential] muy influyente.

seminar ['semɪnɑːʳ] *n* seminario *m*.

seminary ['semɪnǝrɪ] (*pl* **-ies**) *n* RELIG seminario *m*.

semiotics [,semɪ'ɒtɪks] *n* (*U*) semiótica *f*.

semiprecious ['semɪ,preʃǝs] *adj* semiprecioso(sa).

semiskilled [,semɪ'skɪld] *adj* semicualificado(da).

semi-skimmed [-'skɪmd] *adj* semidesnatado(da).

semitrailer [,semɪ'treɪlǝʳ] *n* **-1.** [trailer] remolque *m*. **-2.** *Am* [lorry] camión *m* articulado.

semolina [,semǝ'liːnǝ] *n* sémola *f*.

Sen. -1. *abbr of* **senator**. **-2.** *abbr of* **Senior**.

SEN (*abbr of* **State Enrolled Nurse**) *n enfermero diplomado*.

Senate ['senɪt] *n* POL: **the (United States) ~** el Senado (de los Estados Unidos).

SENATE:

El Senado es, junto con la Cámara de Representantes, el órgano legislativo estadounidense; formado por 100 miembros (dos por Estado), tiene la prerrogativa del derecho de 'impeachment'

senator ['senǝtǝʳ] *n* senador *m*, -ra *f*.

send [send] (*pt & pp* **sent**) *vt* **-1.** [gen] mandar; **to ~ sb sthg, to ~ sthg to sb** mandar a alguien algo. **-2.** [tell to go, arrange for attendance]: **to ~ sb (to)** enviar OR mandar a alguien (a). **-3.** [subj: explosion, blow] lanzar.
◆ **send down** *vt sep* [send to prison] encarcelar.
◆ **send for** *vt fus* **-1.** [person] mandar llamar a. **-2.** [goods, information] pedir, encargar.
◆ **send in** *vt sep* mandar, enviar.
◆ **send off** *vt sep* **-1.** [by post] mandar (por correo). **-2.** SPORT expulsar.
◆ **send off for** *vt fus* [goods, information] pedir, encargar.
◆ **send up** *vt sep inf* **-1.** *Br* [imitate] parodiar, satirizar. **-2.** *Am* [send to prison] encarcelar.

sender ['sendǝʳ] *n* remitente *m* y *f*.

send-off *n* despedida *f*.

send-up *n Br inf* parodia *f*, sátira *f*.

Senegal [,senɪ'gɔːl] *n* (el) Senegal.

Senegalese [,senɪgǝ'liːz] ◇ *adj* senegalés(esa). ◇ *npl*: **the ~** los senegaleses.

senile ['siːnaɪl] *adj* senil.

senile dementia *n* demencia *f* senil.

senility [sɪ'nɪlǝtɪ] *n* senilidad *f*.

senior ['siːnjər] ◇ *adj* **-1.** [highest-ranking] superior, de rango superior. **-2.** [higher-ranking]: ~ **to sb** superior a alguien. **-3.** SCH [pupil] mayor; [class, common room] de los mayores; ~ **year** *Am* último curso de la enseñanza secundaria y de la universidad en Estados Unidos. ◇ *n* **-1.** [older person]: **I'm five years his** ~ le llevo cinco años; **she's my** ~ **es** mayor que yo. **-2.** SCH mayor *m y f*.

senior citizen *n* ciudadano *m*, -na *f* de la tercera edad.

senior high school *n Am* ≃ instituto *m* de bachillerato (16-18 años).

seniority [ˌsiːnɪ'ɒrəti] *n* [degree of importance] categoría *f*.

sensation [sen'seɪʃn] *n* sensación *f*.

sensational [sen'seɪʃənl] *adj* **-1.** [gen] sensacional. **-2.** [sensationalist] sensacionalista.

sensationalist [sen'seɪʃnəlɪst] *adj pej* sensacionalista.

sense [sens] ◇ *n* **-1.** [faculty, meaning] sentido *m*; **to make** ~ [have meaning] tener sentido; **to make** ~ **of sthg** entender algo. **-2.** [feeling - of guilt, terror] sentimiento *m*; [- of urgency] sensación *f*; [- of honour, duty] sentido *m*. **-3.** [natural ability]: **business** ~ talento *m* para los negocios; **dress** ~ gusto *m* en el vestir; ~ **of humour/style** sentido *m* del humor/estilo. **-4.** [wisdom, reason] juicio *m*, sentido *m* común; **to make** ~ [be sensible] ser sensato; **to talk** ~ hablar con sentido común; **there's no** OR **little** ~ **in arguing** no tiene sentido discutir. **-5.** *phr*: **to come to one's** ~**s** [see reason] entrar en razón. ◇ *vt*: **to** ~ **(that)** percibir OR sentir que.

◆ **in a sense** *adv* en cierto sentido.

senseless ['senslɪs] *adj* **-1.** [stupid] sin sentido. **-2.** [unconscious] inconsciente.

sensibilities [ˌsensɪ'bɪlətɪz] *npl* [delicate feelings] sensibilidad *f*.

sensible ['sensəbl] *adj* [person, decision] sensato(ta), razonable; [clothes] práctico(ca).

sensibly ['sensəblɪ] *adv* sensatamente.

sensitive ['sensɪtɪv] *adj* **-1.** [understanding]: ~ **(to)** comprensivo(va) (hacia). **-2.** [easily hurt, touchy]: ~ **(to/about)** susceptible (a/ acerca de). **-3.** [controversial] delicado(da). **-4.** [easily damaged, tender]: ~ **(to)** sensible (a). **-5.** [responsive - instrument] sensible.

sensitivity [ˌsensɪ'tɪvətɪ] *n* **-1.** [understanding] comprensión *f*. **-2.** [tenderness - of eyes, skin] sensibilidad *f*.

sensor ['sensər] *n* sensor *m*.

sensual ['sensjʊəl] *adj* sensual.

sensuous ['sensjʊəs] *adj* sensual.

sent [sent] *pt & pp* → **send**.

sentence ['sentəns] ◇ *n* **-1.** [group of words] frase *f*, oración *f*. **-2.** JUR sentencia *f*. ◇ *vt*: **to** ~ **sb (to)** condenar a alguien (a).

sententious [sen'tenʃəs] *adj pej* sentencioso(sa).

sentiment ['sentɪmənt] *n* **-1.** [feeling] sentimiento *m*. **-2.** [opinion] opinión *f*. **-3.** *pej* [emotion, tenderness] sentimentalismo *m*.

sentimental [ˌsentɪ'mentl] *adj* sentimental.

sentimentality [ˌsentɪmen'tælətɪ] *n pej* sentimentalismo *m*.

sentinel ['sentɪnl] *n* HISTORY centinela *m*.

sentry ['sentrɪ] (*pl* **-ies**) *n* centinela *m*.

Seoul [səʊl] *n* Seúl.

separable ['seprəbl] *adj*: ~ **(from)** separable (de).

separate [*adj & n* 'seprət, *vb* 'sepəreɪt] ◇ *adj* **-1.** [not joined, apart]: ~ **(from)** separado(da) (de). **-2.** [individual, distinct] distinto(ta). ◇ *vt* **-1.** [keep or move apart]: **to** ~ **sthg/sb (from)** separar algo/a alguien (de). **-2.** [distinguish]: **to** ~ **sthg/sb from** diferenciar algo/a alguien de. **-3.** [divide]: **to** ~ **sthg/sb into** dividir algo/a alguien en. ◇ *vi* **-1.** [gen]: **to** ~ **(from)** separarse (de). **-2.** [divide]: **to** ~ **(into)** dividirse (en).

◆ **separates** *npl Br* piezas *fpl* (*de vestir que combinan*).

separated ['sepəreɪtɪd] *adj* separado(da).

separately ['seprətlɪ] *adv* **-1.** [on one's own] independientemente. **-2.** [one by one] separadamente, por separado.

separation [ˌsepə'reɪʃn] *n* separación *f*.

separatist ['seprətɪst] *n* separatista *m y f*.

sepia ['siːpjə] *adj* sepia, de color sepia.

Sept. (*abbr of* **September**) sep.

September [sep'tembər] ◇ *n* septiembre *m*, setiembre *m*; **when are you going? -** ~ ¿cuándo te vas? - en septiembre; **one of the hottest** ~**s on record** uno de los septiembres más calurosos que se recuerdan; **1 - 1992** [in letters etc] 1 de septiembre de 1992; **by/in** ~ para/en septiembre; **last/ this/next** ~ en septiembre del año pasado/ de este año/del año que viene; **every** ~ todos los años en septiembre; **during** ~ en septiembre, durante el mes de septiembre; **at the beginning/end of** ~ a principios/ finales de septiembre; **in the middle of** ~ a mediados de septiembre.

◇ *comp* de septiembre; **I've got a** ~ **birthday** cumplo los años en septiembre.

septet [sep'tet] *n* septeto *m*.

septic ['septɪk] *adj* séptico(ca); **to go** ~ infectarse.

septicaemia *Br*, **septicemia** *Am* [ˌseptɪ'siːmɪə] *n* septicemia *f*.

septic tank *n* fosa *f* séptica.

sepulchre *Br* ['sepəlkəʳ], **sepulcher** *Am* ['sepʌlkər] *n literary* sepulcro *m*.

sequel ['siːkwəl] *n* **-1.** [book, film]: ~ **(to)** continuación *f* (de). **-2.** [consequence]: ~ **(to)** secuela *f* (de).

sequence ['siːkwəns] *n* **-1.** [series] sucesión *f*. **-2.** [order, of film] secuencia *f*; **in** ~ en secuencia.

sequester [sɪ'kwestəʳ], **sequestrate** [sɪ'kwestreɪt] *vt* JUR embargar, secuestrar.

sequin ['siːkwɪn] *n* lentejuela *f*.

sera ['sɪərə] *pl* → **serum**.

Serb = **Serbian**.

Serbia ['sɜːbjə] *n* Serbia.

Serbian ['sɜːbjən], **Serb** [sɜːb] ◇ *adj* serbio(bia). ◇ *n* **-1.** [person] serbio *m*, -bia *f*. **-2.** [dialect] serbio *m*.

Serbo-Croat [,sɜːbəʊ'krəʊaet], **Serbo-Croatian** [,sɜːbəʊkrəʊ'eɪʃn] ◇ *adj* serbocroata. ◇ *n* [language] serbocroata *m*.

serenade [,serə'neɪd] ◇ *n* serenata *f*. ◇ *vt* dar una serenata a.

serene [sɪ'riːn] *adj* sereno(na).

serenely [sɪ'riːnlɪ] *adv* serenamente.

serenity [sɪ'renətɪ] *n* serenidad *f*.

serf [sɜːf] *n* HISTORY siervo *m*, -va *f*.

serge [sɜːdʒ] *n* sarga *f*.

sergeant ['sɑːdʒənt] *n* **-1.** MIL sargento *m*. **-2.** [in police] ≈ subinspector *m* de policía.

sergeant major *n* sargento *m* mayor.

serial ['sɪərɪəl] *n* serial *m*.

serialize, -ise ['sɪərɪəlaɪz] *vt* publicar por entregas.

serial killer *n* asesino que asesina en serie.

serial number *n* número *m* de serie.

series ['sɪəriːz] (*pl inv*) *n* serie *f*.

serious ['sɪərɪəs] *adj* **-1.** [gen] serio(ria); **are you** ~? ¿hablas en serio? **-2.** [very bad] grave.

seriously ['sɪərɪəslɪ] *adv* **-1.** [honestly] en serio. **-2.** [very badly] gravemente. **-3.** [in a considered, earnest, solemn manner] seriamente. **-4.** *phr*: **to take sthg/sb** ~ tomar algo/a alguien en serio.

seriousness ['sɪərɪəsnɪs] *n* **-1.** [gravity] gravedad *f*. **-2.** [honesty]: **in all** ~ seriamente. **-3.** [solemnity] seriedad *f*.

sermon ['sɜːmən] *n* RELIG & *pej* sermón *m*.

serpent ['sɜːpənt] *n literary* serpiente *f*, sierpe *f*.

serrated [sɪ'reɪtɪd] *adj* serrado(da), dentado(da).

serum ['sɪərəm] (*pl* **serums** OR **sera**) *n* suero *m*.

servant ['sɜːvənt] *n* sirviente *m*, -ta *f*.

serve [sɜːv] ◇ *vt* **-1.** [work for] servir. **-2.** [have effect]: **to** ~ **to do sthg** servir para hacer algo. **-3.** [fulfil]: **to** ~ **a purpose** cumplir un propósito. **-4.** [provide for] abastecer; **the town is** ~**d by three motorways** la ciudad tiene tres autopistas. **-5.** [food, drink]: **to** ~ **sthg to sb, to** ~ **sb sthg** servir algo a alguien. **-6.** [in shop, bar etc] despachar, servir. **-7.** JUR: **to** ~ **sb with sthg, to** ~ **sthg on sb** entregar a alguien algo. **-8.** [prison sentence] cumplir; [apprenticeship] hacer; [term of office] ejercer. **-9.** SPORT servir, sacar. **-10.** *phr*: **that** ~**s you right!** ¡bien merecido lo tienes!
◇ *vi* **-1.** [work, give food or drink] servir. **-2.** [function]: **to** ~ **as** servir de. **-3.** [in shop, bar etc] despachar. **-4.** SPORT sacar.
◇ *n* saque *m*.

◆ **serve out, serve up** *vt sep* servir.

server ['sɜːvəʳ] *n* COMPUT servidor *m*.

service ['sɜːvɪs] ◇ *n* **-1.** [gen] servicio *m*; **in** ~ en funcionamiento; **out of** ~ fuera de servicio. **-2.** [mechanical check] revisión *f*. **-3.** RELIG oficio *m*, servicio *m*. **-4.** [set - of plates etc] servicio *m*, juego *m*. **-5.** SPORT saque *m*. **-6.** [use]: **to be of** ~ **(to sb)** servir (a alguien). ◇ *vt* **-1.** [car, machine] revisar. **-2.** FIN [debt] pagar los intereses de.

◆ **services** ◇ *npl* **-1.** [on motorway] área *f* de servicios. **-2.** [armed forces]: **the** ~**s** las fuerzas armadas. **-3.** [efforts, work] servicios *mpl*.

serviceable ['sɜːvɪsəbl] *adj* útil, práctico(ca).

service area *n* área *f* de servicios.

service charge *n* servicio *m*.

service industries *npl* industrias *fpl* de servicios.

serviceman ['sɜːvɪsmən] (*pl* **-men** [-mən]) *n* militar *m*.

service station *n* estación *f* de servicio.

servicewoman ['sɜːvɪs,wʊmən] (*pl* **-women** [-,wɪmɪn]) *n* militar *f*.

serviette [,sɜːvɪ'et] *n* servilleta *f*.

servile ['sɜːvaɪl] *adj* servil.

servility [sɜː'vɪlətɪ] *n* servilismo *m*.

serving ['sɜːvɪŋ] ◇ *adj* de servir. ◇ *n* porción *f*.

sesame ['sesəmɪ] *n* sésamo *m*.

session ['seʃn] *n* **-1.** [gen] sesión *f*; **in** ~ en sesión. **-2.** *Am* [school term] trimestre *m*.

set [set] (*pt* & *pp* set, *cont* -ting) ◇ *adj* **-1.** [fixed - expression, amount] fijo(ja); [- pattern, method] establecido(da); ~ **phrase** frase hecha. **-2.** *Br* SCH [text etc] asignado(da). **-3.** [ready, prepared]: ~ **(for sthg/to do sthg)** listo(ta) (para algo/para hacer algo). **-4.** [determined]: **to be** ~ **on sthg/doing sthg** estar empeñado(da) en algo/hacer algo. **-5.** *phr*: **to be ~ in one's ways** tener costumbres muy arraigadas.

◇ *n* **-1.** [collection - gen] juego *m*; [- of stamps] serie *f*. **-2.** [TV, radio] aparato *m*. **-3.** THEATRE decorado *m*; CINEMA plató *m*. **-4.** TENNIS set *m*.

◇ *vt* **-1.** [position, place] poner, colocar. **-2.** [fix, insert]: **to ~ sthg in** OR **into** montar algo en. **-3.** [cause to be or start]: **to ~ free** poner en libertad; **to ~ fire to** prender fuego a; **to ~ sthg in motion** poner algo en marcha; **to ~ sb's mind at rest** tranquilizar a alguien; **to ~ sb thinking** hacer pensar a alguien. **-4.** [trap, table, essay] poner. **-5.** [alarm, meter] poner. **-6.** [time, wage] fijar. **-7.** [example] dar; [precedent] sentar; [trend] imponer, dictar. **-8.** [target] fijar. **-9.** [face] compungir; [jaw] apretar. **-10.** MED [bones, leg] componer. **-11.** [arrange]: **to ~ sthg to music** poner música a algo. **-12.** [book, play, film] situar, ambientar.

◇ *vi* **-1.** [sun] ponerse. **-2.** [jelly] cuajarse; [glue, cement] secarse, solidificarse.

◆ **set about** *vt fus* [start - task] comenzar; [- problem] atacar; **to ~ about doing sthg** ponerse a hacer algo.

◆ **set against** *vt sep* **-1.** [lessen effect of] contrarrestar con. **-2.** [cause to oppose] enemistar con.

◆ **set ahead** *vt sep Am* [clock] adelantar.

◆ **set apart** *vt sep*: **to ~ sthg/sb apart from** distinguir algo/a alguien de.

◆ **set aside** *vt sep* **-1.** [keep, save] reservar. **-2.** [dismiss - enmity, differences] dejar de lado.

◆ **set back** *vt sep* **-1.** [delay] retrasar. **-2.** *inf* [cost]: **this book ~ me back £10** este libro me costó 10 libras.

◆ **set down** *vt sep* **-1.** [write down] poner por escrito. **-2.** [drop off] dejar.

◆ **set in** *vi* [depression] afianzarse; [winter, infection] comenzar.

◆ **set off** ◇ *vt sep* **-1.** [initiate, cause] provocar. **-2.** [ignite - bomb] hacer estallar. ◇ *vi* ponerse en camino.

◆ **set on** *vt sep* arremeter contra.

◆ **set out** ◇ *vt sep* **-1.** [arrange] disponer. **-2.** [explain] exponer. ◇ *vi* **-1.** [on journey] ponerse en camino. **-2.** [intend]: **to ~ out to do sthg** proponerse a hacer algo.

◆ **set up** ◇ *vt sep* **-1.** [business] poner, montar; [committee, organization] crear; [procedure] establecer; [interview, meeting] organizar; **to ~ o.s. up** establecerse; **to ~ up house** OR **home** instalarse. **-2.** [statue, roadblock] levantar. **-3.** [cause, produce] provocar. **-4.** [prepare for use] preparar. **-5.** *inf* [frame] tender una trampa a. ◇ *vi* [establish o.s.] establecerse.

setback ['setbæk] *n* revés *m*, contratiempo *m*.

set menu *n* menú *m* del día.

set piece *n* ART & LITERATURE obra *f* de tema clásico.

setsquare ['setskweər] *n Br* escuadra *f*, cartabón *m*.

settee [se'tiː] *n* sofá *m*.

setter ['setər] *n* [dog] setter *m*.

setting ['setɪŋ] *n* **-1.** [surroundings] escenario *m*. **-2.** [of dial, control] posición *f*.

settle ['setl] ◇ *vt* **-1.** [conclude, decide] resolver. **-2.** [pay] ajustar, saldar. **-3.** [make o.s. comfortable]: **to ~ o.s.** acomodarse, sentarse cómodamente. **-4.** [calm - nerves] tranquilizar. ◇ *vi* **-1.** [stop travelling] instalarse. **-2.** [make o.s. comfortable] acomodarse. **-3.** [dust, sediment] depositarse, posarse. **-4.** [calm down] calmarse. **-5.** [bird]: **to ~ on** posarse en.

◆ **settle down** *vi* **-1.** [concentrate on]: **to ~ down to doing sthg** ponerse a hacer algo; **to ~ down to sthg** concentrarse en algo; **to ~ down (for sthg)** prepararse (para algo). **-2.** [become respectable] sentar la cabeza. **-3.** [calm oneself] calmarse.

◆ **settle for** *vt fus* conformarse con.

◆ **settle in** *vi* [in new home] instalarse; [in new job] adaptarse.

◆ **settle on** *vt fus* [choose] decidirse por.

◆ **settle up** *vi*: **to ~ up (with sb)** ajustar las cuentas (con alguien).

settled ['setld] *adj* [unchanging] estable.

settlement ['setlmənt] *n* **-1.** [agreement] acuerdo *m*. **-2.** [village] poblado *m*.

settler ['setlər] *n* colono *m*.

set-to *n inf* pelea *f*.

set-up *n inf* **-1.** [system, organization] sistema *m*. **-2.** [frame, trap] trampa *f*, lazo *m*.

seven ['sevn] *num* siete; *see also* **six**.

seventeen [ˌsevn'tiːn] *num* diecisiete; *see also* **six**.

seventeenth [ˌsevn'tiːnθ] *num* decimoséptimo(ma); *see also* **sixth**.

seventh ['sevnθ] ◇ *num adj* séptimo(ma). ◇ *num n* **-1.** [fraction] séptimo *m*. **-2.** [in order] séptimo *m*, -ma *f*; *see also* **sixth**.

seventh heaven *n*: **to be in (one's) ~** estar en el séptimo cielo.

seventieth ['sevntjəθ] ◇ *num adj* septuagésimo(ma). ◇ *num n* **-1.** [fraction] septuagésimo *m*. **-2.** [in order] septuagésimo *m*, -ma *f*; *see also* **sixth**.

seventy ['sevntɪ] *num* setenta; *see also* **sixty**.

sever ['sevər] *vt* **-1.** [cut through] cortar. **-2.** [finish completely] romper.

several ['sevrəl] ◇ *adj* varios(rias). ◇ *pron* varios *mpl*, -rias *fpl*.

severance ['sevrəns] *n fml* ruptura *f*.

severance pay *n* despido *m*.

severe [sɪ'vɪəʳ] *adj* [gen] severo(ra); [pain] fuerte, agudo(da).

severely [sɪ'vɪəlɪ] *adv* **-1.** [badly] gravemente. **-2.** [sternly] severamente, con severidad.

severity [sɪ'verətɪ] *n* [gen] gravedad *f*; [of shortage, problem] severidad *f*.

Seville [sə'vɪl] *n* Sevilla.

sew [səʊ] (*Br pp* **sewn**, *Am pp* **sewed** OR **sewn**) *vt* & *vi* coser.

◆ **sew up** *vt sep* **-1.** [cloth] coser. **-2.** *inf* [arrange, fix]: **to have sthg sewn up** [deal, election etc] tener algo atado y bien atado; [market] tener algo controlado(da).

sewage ['suːɪdʒ] *n* (*U*) aguas *fpl* residuales.

sewage farm *n* estación *f* depuradora.

sewer ['suəʳ] *n* alcantarilla *f*, cloaca *f*.

sewerage ['suərɪdʒ] *n* alcantarillado *m*.

sewing ['səʊɪŋ] *n* (*U*) **-1.** [activity] labor *f* de costura. **-2.** [items] costura *f*.

sewing machine *n* máquina *f* de coser.

sewn [səʊn] *pp* → **sew**.

sex [seks] *n* sexo *m*; **to have ~** tener relaciones sexuales.

sex appeal *n* atractivo *m*, sex appeal *m*.

sex education *n* educación *f* sexual.

sexism ['seksɪzm] *n* sexismo *m*.

sexist ['seksɪst] ◇ *adj* sexista. ◇ *n* sexista *m* y *f*.

sex life *n* vida *f* sexual.

sex object *n* objeto *m* sexual.

sex shop *n* sex shop *m*.

sextet [seks'tet] *n* sexteto *m*.

sextuplet [seks'tjuːplɪt] *n* sextillizo *m*, -za *f*.

sexual ['sekʃʊəl] *adj* sexual.

sexual assault *n* atentado *m* sexual.

sexual harassment *n* acoso *m* sexual.

sexual intercourse *n* (*U*) relaciones *fpl* sexuales.

sexuality [,sekʃʊ'ælətɪ] *n* sexualidad *f*.

sexy ['seksɪ] (*compar* **-ier**, *superl* **-iest**) *adj inf* sexi (*inv*).

Seychelles [seɪ'ʃelz] *npl*: **the ~** las islas Seychelles.

SF, sf *n abbr of* **science fiction**.

SFO (*abbr of* **Serious Fraud Office**) *n departamento de policía que investiga delitos económicos.*

SG (*abbr of* **Surgeon General**) *n responsable de sanidad pública en Estados Unidos.*

Sgt (*abbr of* **sergeant**) ≃ sarg.

sh [ʃ] *excl* ¡chis!, ¡chitón!

shabby ['ʃæbɪ] (*compar* **-ier**, *superl* **-iest**) *adj* **-1.** [clothes, briefcase] desastrado(da); [street]

de aspecto abandonado. **-2.** [person] andrajoso(sa). **-3.** [treatment etc] mezquino(na).

shack [ʃæk] *n* chabola *f*.

shackle ['ʃækl] *vt* **-1.** [enchain] poner grilletes a. **-2.** *literary* [restrict] restringir.

◆ **shackles** *npl* **-1.** [metal rings] grilletes *mpl*, grillos *mpl*. **-2.** *literary* [restrictions] trabas *fpl*.

shade [ʃeɪd] ◇ *n* **-1.** (*U*) [shadow] sombra *f*. **-2.** [lampshade] pantalla *f*. **-3.** [of colour, meaning] matiz *m*. ◇ *vt* [from light] sombrear, dar sombra a; **to ~ one's eyes** protegerse del sol con la mano. ◇ *vi*: **to ~ into** sthg fundirse con algo.

◆ **shades** *npl inf* [sunglasses] gafas *fpl* de sol.

shading ['ʃeɪdɪŋ] *n* sombreado *m*.

shadow ['ʃædəʊ] ◇ *adj Br* POL en la sombra. ◇ *n* **-1.** [dark shape, form] sombra *f*. **-2.** [darkness] oscuridad *f*. **-3.** *phr*: **to be a ~ of one's former self** ser una sombra de lo que uno era; **there's not a ~** OR **the ~ of a doubt** no hay la menor duda.

shadow cabinet *n* gobierno *m* en la sombra, *directiva del principal partido de la oposición en Gran Bretaña.*

shadowy ['ʃædəʊɪ] *adj* **-1.** [dark] sombrío(a). **-2.** [hard to see] vago(ga). **-3.** [unknown, sinister] oscuro(ra).

shady ['ʃeɪdɪ] (*compar* **-ier**, *superl* **-iest**) *adj* **-1.** [sheltered from sun] sombreado(da). **-2.** [providing shade] que da sombra. **-3.** *inf* [dishonest - businessman] dudoso(sa), sospechoso(sa); [- deal] turbio(bia).

shaft [ʃɑːft] ◇ *n* **-1.** [vertical passage] pozo *m*. **-2.** [rod - of propellor etc] eje *m*. **-3.** [of light] rayo *m*. ◇ *vt v inf* **-1.** [dupe] engañar, timar. **-2.** *Am* [treat unfairly] tratar a palos.

shaggy ['ʃægɪ] (*compar* **-ier**, *superl* **-iest**) *adj* [dog] peludo(da).

shaggy-dog story *n chiste largo y pesado.*

shake [ʃeɪk] (*pt* **shook**, *pp* **shaken** ['ʃeɪkən]) ◇ *vt* **-1.** [move vigorously] sacudir, remecer *Amer*; **to ~ sb's hand** dar OR estrechar la mano a alguien; **to ~ hands** darse OR estrecharse la mano; **to ~ one's head** [in refusal] negar con la cabeza; [in disbelief] mover la cabeza mostrando incredulidad. **-2.** [shock] trastornar, conmocionar. **-3.** [undermine] quebrantar, hacer flaquear.

◇ *vi* temblar.

◇ *n* [of bottle etc] sacudida *f*; [of head in disbelief] movimiento *m* de la cabeza mostrando incredulidad; [of head in disagreement] negación *f* con la cabeza.

◆ **shake down** *Am vt sep inf* **-1.** [rob] chantajear, hacer chantaje a. **-2.** [search] registrar.

◆ **shake off** *vt sep* [pursuer] deshacerse de; [cold] quitarse de encima; [illness] superar.

shakedown ['ʃeɪkdaʊn] *Am inf n* **-1.** [extortion] chantaje *m*, extorsión *f*. **-2.** [search] registro *m*.

shaken ['ʃeɪkn] *pp* → **shake**.

shakeout ['ʃeɪkaʊt] *n* FIN ligera recesión *f*.

Shakespearean [ʃeɪk'spɪərɪən] *adj* shakesperiano(na).

shake-up *n inf* restructuración *f*, reorganización *f*.

shaky ['ʃeɪkɪ] (*compar* **-ier**, *superl* **-iest**) *adj* **-1.** [weak, nervous] tembloroso(sa). **-2.** [unconfident, insecure - start] incierto(ta); [- argument] poco sólido(da); [- finances] precario(ria).

shale [ʃeɪl] *n* esquisto *m*.

shall [weak form ʃəl, strong form ʃæl] *aux vb* **-1.** (*1st person sg & 1st person pl*) [to express future tense]: **we ~ be there tomorrow** mañana estaremos ahí; **I shan't be home till ten** no estaré en casa hasta las diez. **-2.** (*esp 1st person sg & 1st person pl*) [in questions]: **~ we go for a walk?** ¿vamos a dar una vuelta?; **~ I give her a ring?** ¿la llamo?; **I'll do that, ~ I?** hago esto, ¿vale? **-3.** [will definitely]: **we ~ overcome!** ¡venceremos! **-4.** [in orders]: **you ~ do as I tell you!** ¡harás lo que yo te diga!; **no one ~ leave until I say so** que nadie salga hasta que yo lo diga.

shallot [ʃə'lɒt] *n* chalote *m*.

shallow ['ʃæləʊ] *adj* **-1.** [in size] poco profundo(da). **-2.** *pej* [superficial] superficial.

◆ **shallows** *npl* bajío *m*, bajos *mpl*.

sham [ʃæm] (*pt & pp* **-med**, *cont* **-ming**) ◇ *adj* fingido(da), simulado(da). ◇ *n* farsa *f*. ◇ *vi* fingir, simular.

shambles ['ʃæmblz] *n* desbarajuste *m*, follón *m*; **in a ~** patas arriba.

shame [ʃeɪm] ◇ *n* **-1.** (*U*) [remorse] vergüenza *f*, pena *f Amer*. **-2.** [dishonour]: **to bring ~ on** OR **upon sb** deshonrar a alguien. **-3.** [pity]: **what a ~!** ¡qué pena OR lástima!; **it's a ~** es una pena OR lástima. ◇ *vt* **-1.** [fill with shame] avergonzar. **-2.** [force by making ashamed]: **to ~ sb into doing sthg** conseguir que alguien haga algo avergonzándole.

shamefaced [,ʃeɪm'feɪst] *adj* avergonzado(da).

shameful ['ʃeɪmfʊl] *adj* vergonzoso(sa).

shameless ['ʃeɪmlɪs] *adj* desvergonzado(da).

shammy ['ʃæmɪ] (*pl* **-ies**) *n inf* gamuza *f*.

shampoo [ʃæm'puː] (*pl* **-s**, *pt & pp* **-ed**, *cont* **-ing**) ◇ *n* **-1.** [liquid] champú *m*. **-2.** [act of shampooing] lavado *m* (con champú). ◇ *vt* lavar (con champú).

shamrock ['ʃæmrɒk] *n* trébol *m*.

shandy ['ʃændɪ] (*pl* **-ies**) *n* cerveza *f* con gaseosa, clara *f*.

shan't [ʃɑːnt] = **shall not**.

shantytown ['ʃæntɪtaʊn] *n* barrio *m* de chabolas, cantegril *m Amer*.

shape [ʃeɪp] ◇ *n* **-1.** [outer form] forma *f*. **-2.** [definite form, silhouette] figura *f*. **-3.** [structure] configuración *f*; **to take ~** tomar forma. **-4.** [guise]: **in the ~ of** en forma de; **in any ~ or form** de ninguna manera. **-5.** [form, health]: **to be in good/bad ~** [person] estar/no estar en forma; [business etc] estar en buen/mal estado; **to lick** OR **knock sb into ~** poner a alguien a punto. ◇ *vt* **-1.** [mould]: **to ~ sthg (into)** dar a algo forma (de). **-2.** [cause to develop] desarrollar.

◆ **shape up** *vi* [develop] desarrollarse.

SHAPE [ʃeɪp] (*abbr of* **Supreme Headquarters Allied Powers, Europe**) *n* cuartel general de las potencias aliadas en Europa.

-shaped ['ʃeɪpt] *suffix*: **egg/star~** en forma de huevo/estrella.

shapeless ['ʃeɪplɪs] *adj* sin forma.

shapely ['ʃeɪplɪ] (*compar* **-ier**, *superl* **-iest**) *adj* bien hecho(cha).

shard [ʃɑːd] *n* [of glass] esquirla *f*; [of cup, vase] fragmento *m*.

share [ʃeəʳ] ◇ *n* **-1.** [portion]: **~ (of** OR **in)** parte *f* (de). **-2.** [contribution, quota]: **to have/do one's ~ of sthg** tener/hacer la parte que a uno le toca de algo. ◇ *vt* **-1.** [gen]: **to ~ sthg (with)** compartir algo (con). **-2.** [reveal]: **to ~ sthg (with)** revelar algo (a). ◇ *vi* compartir.

◆ **shares** *npl* acciones *fpl*.

◆ **share out** *vt sep* repartir, distribuir.

share capital *n* capital *m* social.

share certificate *n* certificado *m* de acciones.

shareholder ['ʃeə,həʊldəʳ] *n* accionista *m y f*.

share index *n* índice *m* de cotización.

share-out *n* reparto *m*.

shareware ['ʃeə,weəʳ] *n* COMPUT shareware *m*.

shark [ʃɑːk] (*pl inv* OR **-s**) *n* tiburón *m*; *fig* estafador *m*, -ra *f*.

sharp [ʃɑːp] ◇ *adj* **-1.** [not blunt] afilado(da). **-2.** [well-defined - outline] definido(da); [- photograph] nítido(da); [- contrast] marcado(da). **-3.** [intelligent, keen - person] listo(ta), filoso(sa) *Amer*; [- eyesight] penetrante; [- hearing] fino(na); [- intelligence] vivo(va). **-4.** [abrupt, sudden] brusco(ca), re-

pentino(na). **-5.** [quick, firm - blow] seco(ca). **-6.** [angry, severe] cortante. **-7.** [piercing, acute - sound, cry, pain] agudo(da); [- cold, wind] penetrante. **-8.** [bitter] ácido(da). **-9.** MUS en tono demasiado alto, desafinado(da).
◇ *adv* **-1.** [punctually] en punto. **-2.** [quickly, suddenly] bruscamente. **-3.** MUS demasiado alto, desafinadamente.
◇ *n* MUS sostenido *m*.

sharpen ['ʃɑːpn] ◇ *vt* **-1.** [make sharp] afilar; [pencil] sacar punta a. **-2.** [make keener, quicker, greater] agudizar. **-3.** [make angrier - voice]: **to ~ one's voice** hablar con tono de enfado. ◇ *vi* **-1.** [gen] agudizarse. **-2.** [become angrier]: **his voice ~ed** se le notaba el enfado en la voz.

sharp end *n Br fig:* **to be at the ~ of sthg** llevar a las espaldas todo el peso de algo.

sharpener ['ʃɑːpnə*ʳ*] *n* [for pencils] sacapuntas *m inv*; [for knives] afilador *m*.

sharp-eyed [-'aɪd] *adj* perspicaz.

sharply ['ʃɑːplɪ] *adv* **-1.** [distinctly] claramente. **-2.** [suddenly] repentinamente. **-3.** [harshly] duramente.

sharpness ['ʃɑːpnɪs] *n* **-1.** [of point, edge] lo afilado, agudeza *f*. **-2.** [fine definition] nitidez *f*. **-3.** [of intelligence, eyesight, hearing] agudeza *f*. **-4.** [harshness, severity] dureza *f*, aspereza *f*. **-5.** [loudness, painfulness] agudeza *f*. **-6.** [of pain, cold] intensidad *f*. **-7.** [bitterness] acritud *f*.

sharpshooter ['ʃɑːpˌʃuːtə*ʳ*] *n* tirador *m*, -ra *f* de primera.

sharp-tongued [-'tʌŋd] *adj* de lengua afilada.

sharp-witted [-'wɪtɪd] *adj* agudo(da).

shat [ʃæt] *pt & pp →* shit.

shatter ['ʃætə*ʳ*] ◇ *vt* **-1.** [smash] hacer añicos. **-2.** [hopes etc] destruir, echar por tierra. **-3.** [shock, upset]: **to be ~ed (by)** quedar destrozado(da) (por). ◇ *vi* hacerse añicos, romperse en pedazos.

shattered ['ʃætəd] *adj* **-1.** [shocked, upset] destrozado(da). **-2.** *Br inf* [very tired] hecho(cha) polvo.

shattering ['ʃætərɪŋ] *adj* **-1.** [shocking, upsetting] terrible. **-2.** *Br* [tiring] agotador(ra).

shatterproof ['ʃætəpruːf] *adj* inastillable.

shave [ʃeɪv] ◇ *n* afeitado *m*; **to have a ~** afeitarse; **it was a close ~** nos salvamos por los pelos. ◇ *vt* **-1.** [face, body] afeitar. **-2.** [cut pieces off] raspar. ◇ *vi* afeitar.
◆ **shave off** *vt sep* afeitar.

shaven ['ʃeɪvn] *adj* rapado(da).

shaver ['ʃeɪvə*ʳ*] *n* maquinilla *f* (de afeitar) eléctrica.

shaving brush ['ʃeɪvɪŋ-] *n* brocha *f* de afeitar.

shaving cream ['ʃeɪvɪŋ-] *n* crema *f* de afeitar.

shaving foam ['ʃeɪvɪŋ-] *n* espuma *f* de afeitar.

shavings ['ʃeɪvɪŋz] *npl* virutas *fpl*.

shaving soap ['ʃeɪvɪŋ-] *n* jabón *m* de afeitar.

shawl [ʃɔːl] *n* chal *m*.

she [ʃiː] ◇ *pers pron* **-1.** [referring to woman, girl, animal] ella; **~'s tall** es alta; **~ loves fish** le encanta el pescado; SHE **can't do it** ella no puede hacerlo; **there ~ is** allí está; **if I were** OR **was ~** *fml* si (yo) fuera ella. **-2.** [referring to boat, car, country]: **~'s a fine ship** es un buen barco. ◇ *n*: **it's a ~** [animal] es hembra; [baby] es (una) niña. ◇ *comp*: **~-elephant** elefanta *f*; **~ bear** osa *f*.

sheaf [ʃiːf] (*pl* sheaves) *n* **-1.** [of papers, letters] fajo *m*. **-2.** [of corn, grain] gavilla *f*.

shear [ʃɪə*ʳ*] (*pt* **-ed**, *pp* **-ed** OR **shorn**) *vt* [sheep] esquilar.
◆ **shears** *npl* **-1.** [for garden] tijeras *fpl* de podar. **-2.** [for dressmaking] tijeras *fpl*.
◆ **shear off** ◇ *vt fus* romper. ◇ *vi* romperse.

sheath [ʃiːθ] (*pl* **-s**) *n* **-1.** [covering for knife] funda *f*, vaina *f*. **-2.** *Br* [condom] preservativo *m*, condón *m*.

sheathe [ʃiːð] *vt* **-1.** [put away] envainar, enfundar. **-2.** [cover]: **to ~ sthg in** envolver algo en.

sheath knife *n* cuchillo *m* de monte.

sheaves [ʃiːvz] *pl →* sheaf.

shed [ʃed] (*pt & pp* **shed**, *cont* **-ding**) ◇ *n* cobertizo *m*, galpón *m Amer*. ◇ *vt* **-1.** [skin] mudar de; [leaves] despojarse de. **-2.** [discard] deshacerse de. **-3.** [accidentally lose - load] perder. **-4.** [tears] derramar; **to ~ blood** derramar sangre.

she'd [*weak form* ʃɪd, *strong form* ʃiːd] = **she had, she would**.

sheen [ʃiːn] *n* brillo *m*, lustre *m*.

sheep [ʃiːp] (*pl inv*) *n* [animal] oveja *f*; *fig* [person] borrego *m*, cordero *m*.

sheepdog ['ʃiːpdɒg] *n* perro *m* pastor.

sheepfold ['ʃiːpfəʊld] *n* aprisco *m*, redil *m*.

sheepish ['ʃiːpɪʃ] *adj* avergonzado(da).

sheepishly ['ʃiːpɪʃlɪ] *adv* tímidamente.

sheepskin ['ʃiːpskɪn] *n* piel *f* de carnero.

sheepskin jacket *n* zamarra *f*, pelliza *f*.

sheepskin rug *n* alfombra *f* de piel de carnero.

sheer [ʃɪə*ʳ*] *adj* **-1.** [absolute] puro(ra). **-2.** [very steep - cliff] escarpado(da); [- drop] vertical. **-3.** [delicate] diáfano(na).

sheet [ʃiːt] *n* **-1.** [for bed] sábana *f*; **as white as a ~** blanco como el papel. **-2.** [of paper] hoja *f*. **-3.** [of glass, metal, wood] lámina *f*.

sheet feed *n* COMPUT alimentador *m* automático de papel.

sheet ice *n* capa *f* de hielo.

sheeting ['ʃiːtɪŋ] *n* (U) chapas *fpl*.

sheet lightning *n* (U) fucilazo *m*, relámpago *m*.

sheet metal *n* (U) chapa *f* de metal.

sheet music *n* (U) partituras *fpl* sueltas.

sheik(h) [ʃeɪk] *n* jeque *m*.

shelf [ʃelf] (*pl* **shelves**) *n* estante *m*.

shelf life *n* periodo *m* de conservación.

shell [ʃel] ◇ *n* **-1.** [of egg, nut] cáscara *f*. **-2.** [of tortoise, crab] caparazón *m*; [of snail, mussels] concha *f*. **-3.** [on beach] concha *f*. **-4.** [of building] esqueleto *m*; [of boat] casco *m*; [of car] armazón *m*, chasis *m inv*. **-5.** MIL [missile] proyectil *m*. ◇ *vt* **-1.** [peas] desvainar; [nuts, eggs] quitar la cáscara a. **-2.** MIL [fire shells at] bombardear.

◆ **shell out** *inf* ◇ *vt sep* aflojar, soltar. ◇ *vi*: **to ~ out for** aflojar la pasta para.

she'll [ʃiːl] = **she will, she shall.**

shellfish ['ʃelfɪʃ] (*pl inv*) *n* **-1.** [creature] crustáceo *m*. **-2.** (U) [food] mariscos *mpl*.

shelling ['ʃelɪŋ] *n* MIL bombardeo *m*.

shellshock ['ʃelʃɒk] *n* (U) trauma *m* de guerra.

shell suit *n Br* chandal *m* (de nailon).

shelter ['ʃeltər] ◇ *n* **-1.** [building, protection] refugio *m*. **-2.** [place to live] techo *m*. ◇ *vt* **-1.** [protect]: **to be ~ed by/from** estar protegido(da) por/de. **-2.** [provide place to live for] dar asilo OR cobijo a. **-3.** [hide] proteger, esconder. ◇ *vi*: **to ~ from/in** resguardarse de/en, protegerse de/en.

sheltered ['ʃeltəd] *adj* **-1.** [place, existence] protegido(da). **-2.** [accommodation, housing]: **~ housing** *conjunto de viviendas especialmente diseñado para ancianos o minusválidos.*

shelve [ʃelv] ◇ *vt* dar carpetazo a. ◇ *vi* descender en pendiente.

shelves [ʃelvz] *pl* → **shelf.**

shelving ['ʃelvɪŋ] *n* (U) estantería *f*.

shenanigans [ʃɪ'nænɪɡənz] *npl inf* **-1.** [trickery] tejemanejes *mpl*. **-2.** [mischief] travesuras *fpl*.

shepherd ['ʃepəd] ◇ *n* pastor *m*. ◇ *vt fig* acompañar.

shepherd's pie ['ʃepədz-] *n carne picada cubierta de puré de patatas.*

sherbet ['ʃɜːbət] *n* **-1.** *Br* [sweet powder] sidral *m*. **-2.** *Am* [sorbet] sorbete *m*.

sheriff ['ʃerɪf] *n Am* sheriff *m*.

sherry ['ʃerɪ] (*pl* **sherries**) *n* jerez *m*.

she's [ʃiːz] = **she is, she has.**

Shetland ['ʃetlənd] *n*: **(the) ~ (Islands)** las islas Shetland.

sh(h) [ʃ] *excl* ¡chis!, ¡chitón!

shield [ʃiːld] ◇ *n* **-1.** [armour, sports trophy] escudo *m*. **-2.** [protection]: **~ against** protección *f* contra. ◇ *vt*: **to ~ sb (from)** proteger a alguien (de); **to ~ o.s. (from)** protegerse (de).

shift [ʃɪft] ◇ *n* **-1.** [slight change] cambio *m*. **-2.** [period of work, workers] turno *m*. ◇ *vt* **-1.** [furniture etc] cambiar de sitio, mover. **-2.** [attitude, belief] cambiar de. **-3.** [transfer]: **to ~ the blame (on to sb)** echar la culpa (a alguien). ◇ *vi* **-1.** [person] moverse; [wind, opinion] cambiar. **-2.** *Am* AUT cambiar de marcha.

shift key *n* tecla *f* de mayúsculas.

shiftless ['ʃɪftlɪs] *adj* vago(ga), remolón(ona).

shift stick *n Am* cambio *m* de marchas.

shifty ['ʃɪftɪ] (*compar* **-ier**, *superl* **-iest**) *adj inf* [person] con pinta deshonesta; [behaviour] sospechoso(sa); [look] huidizo(za).

Shiite ['ʃiːaɪt] ◇ *adj* chiíta. ◇ *n* chiíta *m y f*.

shilling ['ʃɪlɪŋ] *n* chelín *m*.

shilly-shally ['ʃɪlɪ,ʃælɪ] (*pt & pp* **-ied**) *vi* titubear, vacilar.

shimmer ['ʃɪmər] ◇ *n* resplandor *m* trémulo. ◇ *vi* rielar, brillar con luz trémula.

shin [ʃɪn] (*pt & pp* **-ned**, *cont* **-ning**) *n* espinilla *f*.

◆ **shin up** *Br*, **shinny up** *Am vt fus* trepar.

shinbone ['ʃɪnbəʊn] *n* espinilla *f*.

shine [ʃaɪn] (*pt & pp* **shone**) ◇ *n* brillo *m*. ◇ *vt* [torch, lamp] dirigir. ◇ *vi* **-1.** [gen] brillar. **-2.** [excel]: **to ~ at** despuntar en.

shingle ['ʃɪŋɡl] *n* (U) [on beach] guijarros *mpl*.

◆ **shingles** *n* (U) herpes *m inv*.

shining ['ʃaɪnɪŋ] *adj* **-1.** [gleaming] brillante, brilloso(sa) *Amer*. **-2.** [outstanding] excepcional.

shinny ['ʃɪnɪ] *Am*

◆ **shinny up** = **shin up.**

shiny ['ʃaɪnɪ] (*compar* **-ier**, *superl* **-iest**) *adj* brillante.

ship [ʃɪp] (*pt & pp* **-ped**, *cont* **-ping**) ◇ *n* barco *m*, buque *m*. ◇ *vt* enviar por barco.

shipbuilder ['ʃɪp,bɪldər] *n* constructor *m*, -ra *f* de naves.

shipbuilding ['ʃɪp,bɪldɪŋ] *n* construcción *f* naval.

ship canal *n* canal *m* de navegación.

shipment ['ʃɪpmənt] *n* envío *m*.

shipper ['ʃɪpər] *n* compañía *f* naviera.

shipping ['ʃɪpɪŋ] *n* (U) **-1.** [transport] envío *m*, transporte *m*. **-2.** [ships] barcos *mpl*, buques *mpl*.

shipping agent *n* agente marítimo *m*, agente marítima *f*.

shipping company *n* compañía *f* naviera.

shipping forecast *n* predicción *f* del estado de la mar.

shipping lane *n* ruta *f* marítima.

shipshape ['ʃɪpʃeɪp] *adj* en orden.

shipwreck ['ʃɪprek] ◇ *n* **-1.** [destruction of ship] naufragio *m*. **-2.** [wrecked ship] barco *m* náufrago. ◇ *vt*: **to be** ~**ed** naufragar.

shipwrecked ['ʃɪprekt] *adj* náufrago(ga).

shipyard ['ʃɪpjɑːd] *n* astillero *m*.

shire [ʃaɪər] *n* [county] condado *m*.
 ◆ **Shire** *n*: **the Shires** *los condados centrales de Inglaterra*.

shire horse *n* percherón *m*, caballo *m* de tiro.

shirk [ʃɜːk] *vt* eludir.

shirker ['ʃɜːkər] *n* vago *m*, -ga *f*.

shirt [ʃɜːt] *n* camisa *f*.

shirtsleeves ['ʃɜːtsliːvz] *npl*: **to be in (one's)** ~ ir en mangas de camisa.

shirttail ['ʃɜːtteɪl] *n* faldón *m*.

shirty ['ʃɜːtɪ] (*compar* **-ier**, *superl* **-iest**) *adj* *Br inf* de mala uva.

shit [ʃɪt] (*pt & pp* **shit** OR **-ted** OR **shat**, *cont* **-ting**) *vulg* ◇ *n* **-1.** [excrement] mierda *f*. **-2.** (U) [nonsense] gilipolleces *fpl*. **-3.** [person] hijo *m*, -ja *f* de puta. ◇ *vi* cagar. ◇ *excl* ¡mierda!

shiver ['ʃɪvər] ◇ *n* escalofrío *m*, estremecimiento *m*; **to give sb the** ~**s** dar escalofríos a alguien. ◇ *vi*: **to** ~ **(with)** [fear] temblar OR estremecerse (de); [cold] tiritar (de).

shoal [ʃəʊl] *n* banco *m*.

shock [ʃɒk] ◇ *n* **-1.** [unpleasant surprise, reaction, emotional state] susto *m*; **I got a real** ~ me dio un vuelco de corazón; **it came as a** ~ fue un duro golpe. **-2.** (U) MED: **to be suffering from** ~ estar en un estado de choque. **-3.** [impact] choque *m*. **-4.** [electric shock] descarga *f* OR sacudida *f* (eléctrica). **-5.** [thick mass] mata *f*. ◇ *vt* **-1.** [upset] conmocionar. **-2.** [offend] escandalizar. ◇ *vi* escandalizar.

shock absorber [-əb,zɔːbər] *n* amortiguador *m*.

shocked [ʃɒkt] *adj* **-1.** [upset] horrorizado(da). **-2.** [offended] escandalizado(da), ofendido(da).

shocking ['ʃɒkɪŋ] *adj* **-1.** [very bad] pésimo(ma). **-2.** [behaviour, film] escandaloso(sa); [price] de escándalo.

shockproof ['ʃɒkpruːf] *adj* a prueba de choques.

shock tactics *npl* MIL & *fig* táctica *f* de choque.

shock therapy, **shock treatment** *n* tratamiento *m* a base de electrochoques.

shock troops *npl* tropas *fpl* de asalto.

shock wave *n* [intense heat, pressure] onda *f* expansiva; *fig* oleada *f* de turbación.

shod [ʃɒd] ◇ *pt & pp* → **shoe**. ◇ *adj* calzado(da).

shoddy ['ʃɒdɪ] (*compar* **-ier**, *superl* **-iest**) *adj* [work] chapucero(ra); [goods] de pacotilla; *fig* [treatment] vil, despreciable.

shoe [ʃuː] (*pt & pp* **shod** OR **shoed**, *cont* **shoeing**) ◇ *n* zapato *m*. ◇ *vt* herrar.

shoebrush ['ʃuːbrʌʃ] *n* cepillo *m* para los zapatos.

shoe cleaner *n* betún *m* líquido.

shoehorn ['ʃuːhɔːn] *n* calzador *m*.

shoelace ['ʃuːleɪs] *n* cordón *m* del zapato, pasador *m* Amer.

shoemaker ['ʃuː,meɪkər] *n* zapatero *m*, -ra *f*.

shoe polish *n* betún *m*.

shoe repairer [-rɪ,peərər] *n* zapatero (remendón) *m*, zapatera (remendona) *f*.

shoe shop *n* zapatería *f*.

shoestring ['ʃuːstrɪŋ] ◇ *adj* muy reducido(da). ◇ *n fig*: **on a** ~ con cuatro cuartos, con muy poco dinero.

shoetree ['ʃuːtriː] *n* horma *f*.

shone [ʃɒn] *pt & pp* → **shine**.

shoo [ʃuː] ◇ *vt* [animal] espantar, ahuyentar; [person] mandar a otra parte. ◇ *excl* ¡fuera!

shook [ʃʊk] *pt* → **shake**.

shoot [ʃuːt] (*pt & pp* **shot**) ◇ *n* **-1.** *Br* [hunting expedition] cacería *f*. **-2.** [new growth] brote *m*, retoño *m*.
◇ *vt* **-1.** [fire gun at] disparar contra, abalear *Amer*; [injure] herir a tiros; [kill] matar a tiros; **to** ~ **o.s.** pegarse un tiro. **-2.** *Br* [hunt] cazar. **-3.** [arrow] disparar. **-4.** [direct - glance] lanzar, echar; [- question] disparar. **-5.** CINEMA rodar, filmar. **-6.** *Am* [play]: **to** ~ **pool** jugar al billar americano.
◇ *vi* **-1.** [fire gun]: **to** ~ **(at)** disparar (contra). **-2.** *Br* [hunt] cazar. **-3.** [move quickly]: **to** ~ **in/out/past** entrar/salir/pasar disparado(da). **-4.** CINEMA rodar, filmar. **-5.** SPORT chutar.
◇ *excl Am inf* **-1.** [go ahead] ¡venga!, ¡vamos! **-2.** [damn] ¡ostras!
 ◆ **shoot down** *vt sep* **-1.** [plane] derribar. **-2.** [person] matar a tiros. **-3.** *fig* [reject] echar por tierra.

◆ **shoot up** *vi* **-1.** [child, plant] crecer rápidamente. **-2.** [prices] dispararse. **-3.** *drugs sl* [take drugs] chutarse.

shooting ['ʃuːtɪŋ] *n* **-1.** [killing] asesinato *m* (*a tiros*). **-2.** (*U*) [hunting] caza *f*, cacería *f*.

shooting range *n* campo *m* de tiro.

shooting star *n* estrella *f* fugaz.

shooting stick *n* bastón que sirve de asiento.

shoot-out *n* tiroteo *m*.

shop [ʃɒp] (*pt & pp* **-ped**, *cont* **-ping**) ◇ *n* **-1.** [store] tienda *f*; **to talk** ~ hablar del trabajo. **-2.** [workshop] taller *m*. ◇ *vi* comprar; **to go shopping** ir de compras.

◆ **shop around** *vi* comparar precios.

shop assistant *n Br* dependiente *m*, -ta *f*.

shop floor *n*: **the** ~ el personal, los obreros.

shopkeeper ['ʃɒp,kiːpəʳ] *n* tendero *m*, -ra *f*.

shoplifter ['ʃɒp,lɪftəʳ] *n* ladrón *m*, -ona *f* en una tienda.

shoplifting ['ʃɒp,lɪftɪŋ] *n* (*U*) robo *m* en una tienda.

shopper ['ʃɒpəʳ] *n* comprador *m*, -ra *f*.

shopping ['ʃɒpɪŋ] *n* (*U*) **-1.** [purchases] compras *fpl*. **-2.** [act of shopping] compra *f*.

shopping bag *n* bolsa *f* de la compra.

shopping centre *Br*, **shopping mall** *Am*, **shopping plaza** *Am n* centro *m* comercial.

shopping list *n* lista *f* de la compra.

shopping mall *Am*, **shopping plaza** *Am* = **shopping centre**.

shopsoiled *Br* ['ʃɒpsɔɪld], **shopworn** *Am* ['ʃɒpwɔːn] *adj* deteriorado(da).

shop steward *n* enlace *m* y *f* sindical.

shopwalker [,ʃɒp'wɔːkəʳ] *n Br* persona encargada de supervisar al personal y atender a los clientes.

shopwindow [,ʃɒp'wɪndəʊ] *n* escaparate *m*.

shopworn *Am* = **shopsoiled**.

shore [ʃɔːʳ] *n* **-1.** [of sea, lake, river] orilla *f*. **-2.** [land]: **on** ~ en tierra.

◆ **shore up** *vt sep* apuntalar.

shore leave *n* permiso *m* para bajar a tierra.

shoreline ['ʃɔːlaɪn] *n* orilla *f*.

shorn [ʃɔːn] ◇ *pp* → **shear**. ◇ *adj* [grass, hair] corto(ta); [head] rapado(da).

short [ʃɔːt] ◇ *adj* **-1.** [gen] corto(ta). **-2.** [not tall] bajo(ja). **-3.** [curt]: **to be** ~ (**with sb**) ser seco(ca) (con alguien). **-4.** [lacking] escaso(sa); **to be** ~ **on sthg** no andar sobrado de algo; **to be** ~ **of** estar OR andar mal de; **we're a chair/pound** ~ nos falta una silla/libra; **to be** ~ **of breath** estar sin aliento. **-5.** [be shorter form]: **to be** ~ **for** ser el diminutivo de.

◇ *adv* **-1.** [out of]: **we are running** ~ **of water** se nos está acabando el agua. **-2.** [suddenly, abruptly]: **to cut sthg** ~ interrumpir algo antes de acabar; **to stop** ~ parar en seco OR de repente; **to bring** OR **pull sb up** ~ hacer a alguien parar en seco.

◇ *n* **-1.** *Br* [alcoholic drink] licor *m*. **-2.** [film] cortometraje *m*.

◆ **shorts** *npl* **-1.** [gen] pantalones *mpl* cortos, shorts *mpl*. **-2.** *Am* [underwear] calzoncillos *mpl*.

◆ **for short** *adv* para abreviar.

◆ **in short** *adv* en resumen, en pocas palabras.

◆ **nothing short of** *prep*: **it was nothing** ~ **of madness/a disgrace** fue una auténtica locura/vergüenza.

◆ **short of** *prep* **-1.** [just before] cerca de; **just** ~ **of the cliff** casi al borde del precipicio. **-2.** [without]: ~ **of asking, I can't see how you'll find out** salvo que preguntes, no sé cómo lo vas a averiguar.

shortage ['ʃɔːtɪdʒ] *n* falta *f*, escasez *f*.

short back and sides *n Br* pelo *m* corto a los lados y en la nuca.

shortbread ['ʃɔːtbred] *n* especie de torta hecha de azúcar, harina y mantequilla.

short-change *vt* [in shop] dar mal el cambio a; *fig* [reward unfairly] estafar, engañar.

short circuit *n* cortocircuito *m*.

◆ **short-circuit** ◇ *vt* provocar un cortocircuito en. ◇ *vi* tener un cortocircuito.

shortcomings [,ʃɔːt'kʌmɪŋz] *npl* defectos *mpl*.

shortcrust pastry ['ʃɔːtkrʌst-] *n* pasta *f* quebrada.

short cut *n* **-1.** [quick way] atajo *m*. **-2.** [quick method] método *m* rápido.

shorten ['ʃɔːtn] ◇ *vt* acortar. ◇ *vi* acortarse.

shortening ['ʃɔːtnɪŋ] *n* CULIN grasa vegetal o animal utilizada para hacer masas pasteleras.

shortfall ['ʃɔːtfɔːl] *n*: ~ (**in** OR **of**) déficit *m* (de).

shorthand ['ʃɔːthænd] *n* **-1.** [writing system] taquigrafía *f*. **-2.** [short form]: ~ (**for**) una forma breve (de decir).

shorthanded [,ʃɔːt'hændɪd] *adj*: **to be** ~ estar falto(ta) de personal.

shorthand typist *n Br* taquimecanógrafo *m*, -fa *f*.

short-haul *adj* que cubre distancias cortas.

short list *n Br* [for job] lista *f* de candidatos seleccionados; [for prize] relación *f* de finalistas.

◆ **short-list** *vt*: **to be short-listed (for)** [job] estar entre los candidatos (para); [prize] estar entre los finalistas (a).

short-lived [-'lɪvd] *adj* efímero(ra).

shortly ['ʃɔːtlɪ] *adv* **-1.** [soon] dentro de poco; ~ **before/after** poco antes/después de. **-2.** [curtly] secamente, bruscamente.

shortness ['ʃɔːtnɪs] *n* **-1.** [in time] brevedad *f*. **-2.** [in height] baja estatura *f*; [in length] cortedad *f*.

short-range *adj* [aircraft] de corto radio de acción; [missile] de corto alcance; [weather forecast] a corto plazo.

short shrift [-'ʃrɪft] *n*: **to give sb** ~ prestar poca atención a alguien.

shortsighted [ˌʃɔːt'saɪtɪd] *adj* [myopic] miope, corto(ta) de vista; *fig* [lacking foresight] corto de miras.

short-staffed [-'stɑːft] *adj*: **to be** ~ estar falto(ta) de personal.

short story *n* cuento *m*.

short-tempered [-'tempəd] *adj* de mal genio, de genio vivo.

short-term *adj* a corto plazo.

short time *n Br*: **to be on** ~ trabajar con jornada reducida.

short wave *n* (U) onda *f* corta.

shot [ʃɒt] ◇ *pt & pp* → **shoot**. ◇ *n* **-1.** [gunshot] tiro *m*, disparo *m*; **like a** ~ [quickly] en el acto. **-2.** [marksman] tirador *m*, -ra *f*. **-3.** [in football] chut *m*, tiro *m*; [in golf, tennis] golpe *m*. **-4.** [photograph] foto *f*. **-5.** CINEMA plano *m*, toma *f*. **-6.** *inf* [try, go] intento *m*. **-7.** [injection] inyección *f*. **-8.** [of alcohol] trago *m*.

shotgun ['ʃɒtɡʌn] *n* escopeta *f*.

shot put *n*: **the** ~ el lanzamiento de peso.

should [ʃʊd] *aux vb* **-1.** [be desirable]: **we** ~ **leave now** deberíamos irnos ya OR ahora. **-2.** [seeking advice, permission]: ~ **I go too?** ¿voy yo también? **-3.** [as suggestion]: **I** ~ **deny everything** yo lo negaría todo. **-4.** [indicating probability]: **she** ~ **be home soon** tiene que llegar a casa pronto. **-5.** [have been expected]: **they** ~ **have won the match** tendrían que OR deberían haber ganado el partido. **-6.** [indicating intention, wish]: **I** ~ **like to come with you** me gustaría ir contigo. **-7.** (*as conditional*): **you** ~ **go, if you were invited** tendrías que OR deberías ir si te han invitado. **-8.** (*in 'that' clauses*): **we decided that you** ~ **do it** decidimos que lo hicieras tú. **-9.** [expressing uncertain opinion]: **I** ~ **think he's about 50 (years old)** yo diría que tiene unos 50 (años).

shoulder ['ʃəʊldər] ◇ *n* **-1.** [part of body, clothing] hombro *m*; **to look over one's** ~ mirar hacia atrás; **a** ~ **to cry on** un paño de lágrimas; **to rub** ~**s with** codearse con. **-2.** CULIN espaldilla *f*. ◇ *vt* **-1.** [carry - load] echarse al hombro. **-2.** [accept - responsibility] cargar con.

shoulder bag *n* bolso *m* de bandolera.

shoulder blade *n* omóplato *m*.

shoulder-length *adj* que llega hasta los hombros.

shoulder strap *n* **-1.** [on dress] tirante *m*. **-2.** [on bag] correa *f*, bandolera *f*.

shouldn't ['ʃʊdnt] = should not.

should've ['ʃʊdəv] = should have.

shout [ʃaʊt] ◇ *n* grito *m*. ◇ *vt* gritar. ◇ *vi*: **to** ~ **(at)** gritar (a).

◆ **shout down** *vt sep* acallar a gritos.

◆ **shout out** *vt sep* gritar.

shouting ['ʃaʊtɪŋ] *n* (U) gritos *mpl*.

shove [ʃʌv] ◇ *n*: **(to give sthg/sb) a** ~ (dar a algo/a alguien) un empujón. ◇ *vt* empujar; **to** ~ **sthg/sb in** meter algo/a alguien a empujones; **to** ~ **sthg/sb out** sacar algo/a alguien a empujones; **to** ~ **sthg/sb about** empujar algo/a alguien.

◆ **shove off** *vi* **-1.** [in boat] alejarse del muelle, la orilla etc. **-2.** *inf* [go away] largarse.

shovel ['ʃʌvl] (*Br pt & pp* **-led**, *cont* **-ling**, *Am pt & pp* **-ed**, *cont* **-ing**) ◇ *n* pala *f*. ◇ *vt* remover con la pala OR a paletadas; **to** ~ **food into one's mouth** *fig* zamparse la comida.

show [ʃəʊ] (*pt* **-ed**, *pp* **shown** OR **-ed**) ◇ *n* **-1.** [display, demonstration] demostración *f*. **-2.** [piece of entertainment - at theatre] espectáculo *m*; [- on radio, TV] programa *m*. **-3.** [performance] función *f*. **-4.** [of dogs, flowers, art] exposición *f*; **on** ~ expuesto; **for** ~ para impresionar.

◇ *vt* **-1.** [gen] mostrar; **to** ~ **sb sthg, to** ~ **sthg to sb** enseñar OR mostrar a alguien algo; **to** ~ **sb how to do sthg** enseñar OR mostrar a alguien cómo hacer algo; **he has nothing to** ~ **for all his efforts** todos sus esfuerzos han sido en balde. **-2.** [escort]: **to** ~ **sb to sthg** llevar OR acompañar a alguien hasta algo. **-3.** [make visible, reveal] dejar ver; **to** ~ **o.s.** dejarse ver. **-4.** [indicate - increase, profit, loss] arrojar, registrar; **it just goes to** ~ **that ...** viene a demostrar que .... **-5.** [broadcast - film] proyectar; [- TV programme] emitir.

◇ *vi* **-1.** [indicate, make clear] indicar, mostrar. **-2.** [be visible] verse, notarse. **-3.** [film] proyectarse.

◆ **show around** = show round.

◆ **show off** ◇ *vt sep* lucir, presumir de. ◇ *vi* presumir.

◆ **show round** *vt sep*: **to ~ sb round the flat** enseñarle a alguien el piso nuevo.

◆ **show up** ◇ *vt sep* poner en evidencia. ◇ *vi* **-1.** [stand out] resaltar. **-2.** [turn up] aparecer.

showbiz ['ʃəubɪz] *n inf* mundo *m* del espectáculo.

show business *n* (*U*) mundo *m* del espectáculo.

showcase ['ʃəukeɪs] *n* **-1.** [glass case] vitrina *f*. **-2.** *fig* [advantageous setting] escaparate *m*, plataforma *f*.

showdown ['ʃəudaun] *n*: **to have a ~ with** enfrentarse abiertamente a OR con.

shower ['ʃauər] ◇ *n* **-1.** [device] ducha *f*, regadera *f Amer*. **-2.** [wash]: **to have OR take a ~** ducharse. **-3.** [of rain] chubasco *m*, chaparrón *m*. **-4.** [stream] lluvia *f*. **-5.** *Am* [party] *fiesta con regalos organizada en honor de una mujer por sus amigas*. ◇ *vt* **-1.** [sprinkle] rociar. **-2.** [bestow]: **to ~ sb with sthg, to ~ sthg on** OR **upon sb** [present, compliments] colmar a alguien de algo; [insults] acribillar a alguien a algo. ◇ *vi* ducharse.

shower cap *n* gorro *m* de baño.

showerproof ['ʃauəpruːf] *adj* impermeable.

showery ['ʃauərɪ] *adj* lluvioso(sa).

showing ['ʃəuɪŋ] *n* [of film] pase *m*, proyección *f*; [of paintings] exposición *f*.

show jumping [-ˌdʒʌmpɪŋ] *n* concurso *m* hípico de salto.

showman ['ʃəumən] (*pl* **-men** [-mən]) *n* **-1.** [at fair, circus] empresario *m*. **-2.** *fig* [publicity-seeker] showman *m*.

showmanship ['ʃəumənʃɪp] *n* teatralidad *f*, talento *m* teatral.

shown [ʃəun] *pp* → **show**.

show-off *n inf* presumido *m*, -da *f*.

show of hands *n*: **to have a ~** votar a mano alzada.

showpiece ['ʃəupiːs] *n* pieza *f* de mayor interés.

showroom ['ʃəurum] *n* salón *m* OR sala *f* de exposición.

showy ['ʃəuɪ] (*compar* **-ier**, *superl* **-iest**) *adj* [person] ostentoso(sa); [clothes, colour] llamativo(va).

shrank [ʃræŋk] *pt* → **shrink**.

shrapnel ['ʃræpnl] *n* metralla *f*.

shred [ʃred] (*pt* & *pp* **-ded**, *cont* **-ding**) ◇ *n* [small piece - of material] jirón *m*; [- of paper] trocito *m*, pedacito *m*; *fig* [scrap] ápice *m*, pizca *f*. ◇ *vt* [paper] hacer trizas; [food] rallar.

shredder ['ʃredər] *n* [for paper] destructora *f*; [for food] rallador *m*.

shrew [ʃruː] *n* ZOOL musaraña *f*.

shrewd [ʃruːd] *adj* astuto(ta), abusado(da) *Amer*.

shrewdness ['ʃruːdnɪs] *n* astucia *f*.

shriek [ʃriːk] ◇ *n* chillido *m*, grito *m*. ◇ *vt* chillar, gritar. ◇ *vi*: **to ~ (with** OR **in)** chillar (de).

shrill [ʃrɪl] *adj* [high-pitched] estridente, agudo(da).

shrimp [ʃrɪmp] *n* camarón *m*, quisquilla *f*.

shrine [ʃraɪn] *n* santuario *m*.

shrink [ʃrɪŋk] (*pt* **shrank**, *pp* **shrunk**) ◇ *vt* encoger. ◇ *vi* **-1.** [become smaller] encoger. **-2.** *fig* [contract, diminish] disminuir. **-3.** [recoil]: **to ~ away from** retroceder OR arredrarse ante. **-4.** [be reluctant]: **to ~ from** sthg eludir algo.

shrinkage ['ʃrɪŋkɪdʒ] *n* [loss in size] encogimiento *m*; *fig* [contraction] reducción *f*.

shrink-wrap *vt* precintar o envasar con plástico termoretráctil.

shrivel ['ʃrɪvl] (*Br pt* & *pp* **-led**, *cont* **-ling**; *Am pt* & *pp* **-ed**, *cont* **-ing**) ◇ *vt*: **to ~ (up)** secar, marchitar. ◇ *vi*: **to ~ (up)** secarse, marchitarse.

shroud [ʃraud] ◇ *n* [cloth] mortaja *f*, sudario *m*. ◇ *vt*: **to be ~ed in sthg** estar envuelto(ta) en.

Shrove Tuesday ['ʃrəuv-] *n* martes *m* de carnaval.

shrub [ʃrʌb] *n* arbusto *m*.

shrubbery ['ʃrʌbərɪ] *n* arbustos *mpl*.

shrug [ʃrʌg] (*pt* & *pp* **-ged**, *cont* **-ging**) ◇ *n* encogimiento *m* de hombros. ◇ *vt*: **to ~ one's shoulders** encogerse de hombros. ◇ *vi* encogerse de hombros.

◆ **shrug off** *vt sep* quitar importancia a.

shrunk [ʃrʌŋk] *pp* → **shrink**.

shrunken ['ʃrʌŋkn] *adj* [person] encogido(da); [fruit] seco(ca).

shucks [ʃʌks] *excl Am inf* **-1.** [it was nothing] ¡no es nada! **-2.** [damn] ¡ostras!

shudder ['ʃʌdər] ◇ *n* escalofrío *m*, estremecimiento *m*. ◇ *vi* **-1.** [tremble]: **to ~ (with)** estremecerse (de); **I ~ to think** me entran escalofríos sólo con pensar. **-2.** [shake] temblar, dar sacudidas.

shuffle ['ʃʌfl] ◇ *n* **-1.** [of feet]: **to walk with a ~** andar arrastrando los pies. **-2.** [of cards]: **to give the cards a ~** barajar las cartas. ◇ *vt* **-1.** [feet] arrastrar. **-2.** [cards] barajar. ◇ *vi* **-1.** [walk by dragging feet]: **to ~ in/out/along** entrar/salir/andar arrastrando los pies. **-2.** [fidget] moverse nerviosamente.

shun [ʃʌn] (*pt* & *pp* **-ned**, *cont* **-ning**) *vt* rehuir, esquivar.

shunt [ʃʌnt] *vt* RAIL cambiar de vía; *fig* [move] llevar (de un sitio a otro).

shunter ['ʃʌntər] n RAIL [engine] guardagujas m y f inv.

shush [ʃʊʃ] excl ¡chis!, ¡chitón!

shut [ʃʌt] (pt & pp **shut**, cont **-ting**) ◇ adj cerrado(da). ◇ vt cerrar; ~ **your mouth** OR **face!** v inf ¡cierra el pico! ◇ vi **-1.** [close] cerrarse. **-2.** [close for business] cerrar.
◆ **shut away** vt sep guardar bajo llave; **to** ~ **o.s. away** encerrarse.
◆ **shut down** vt sep & vi cerrar.
◆ **shut in** vt sep encerrar; **to** ~ **o.s. in** encerrarse.
◆ **shut out** vt sep **-1.** [person, cat] dejar fuera a; [light, noise] no dejar que entre. **-2.** [thought, feeling] bloquear.
◆ **shut up** inf ◇ vt sep [silence] hacer callar. ◇ vi callarse.

shutdown ['ʃʌtdaʊn] n cierre m.

shutter ['ʃʌtər] n **-1.** [on window] postigo m, contraventana f. **-2.** [in camera] obturador m.

shuttle ['ʃʌtl] ◇ adj: ~ **service** [of planes] puente m aéreo; [of buses, trains] servicio m regular. ◇ n [plane] avión m (de puente aéreo). ◇ vi ir y venir.

shuttlecock ['ʃʌtlkɒk] n volante m.

shy [ʃaɪ] (pt & pp **shied**) ◇ adj **-1.** [timid] tímido(da). **-2.** [wary]: **to be** ~ **of doing sthg** no atreverse a hacer algo. ◇ vi asustarse, espantarse.
◆ **shy away from** vt fus: **to** ~ **away from sthg** huir de algo; **to** ~ **away from doing sthg** negarse a hacer algo.

shyly ['ʃaɪlɪ] adv tímidamente, con timidez.

shyness ['ʃaɪnɪs] n timidez f.

Siam [ˌsaɪˈæm] n Siam.

Siamese [ˌsaɪəˈmiːz] (pl inv) ◇ adj siamés(esa). ◇ n **-1.** [person] siamés m, -esa f. **-2.** ZOOL: ~ **(cat)** (gato m) siamés m.

Siamese twins npl hermanos mpl siameses.

SIB (abbr of **Securities and Investment Board**) n organismo regulador de inversiones bursátiles.

Siberia [saɪˈbɪərɪə] n Siberia.

Siberian [saɪˈbɪərɪən] ◇ adj siberiano(na). ◇ n siberiano m, -na f.

sibling ['sɪblɪŋ] n hermano m, -na f.

Sicilian [sɪˈsɪljən] ◇ adj siciliano(na). ◇ n [person] siciliano m, -na f.

Sicily ['sɪsɪlɪ] n Sicilia.

sick [sɪk] adj **-1.** [ill] enfermo(ma). **-2.** [nauseous]: **to feel** ~ marearse. **-3.** [vomiting]: **to be** ~ Br devolver, vomitar. **-4.** [fed up]: **to be** ~ **of sthg/of doing sthg** estar harto(ta) de algo/de hacer algo. **-5.** [angry, disgusted]:

to make sb ~ fig poner enfermo(ma) a alguien. **-6.** [offensive] de mal gusto.

sickbay ['sɪkbeɪ] n enfermería f.

sickbed ['sɪkbed] n cama f (donde yace un enfermo).

sicken ['sɪkn] ◇ vt poner enfermo(ma), asquear. ◇ vi Br: **to be** ~**ing for sthg** estar cogiendo algo.

sickening ['sɪknɪŋ] adj **-1.** [disgusting] asqueroso(sa), repugnante. **-2.** [infuriating] exasperante.

sickle ['sɪkl] n hoz f.

sick leave n (U) baja f por enfermedad.

sickly ['sɪklɪ] (compar **-ier**, superl **-iest**) adj **-1.** [unhealthy] enfermizo(za). **-2.** [unpleasant] nauseabundo(da).

sickness ['sɪknɪs] n **-1.** [illness] enfermedad f. **-2.** Br (U) [nausea, vomiting] mareo m.

sickness benefit n (U) subsidio m por enfermedad.

sick pay n (U) paga f por enfermedad.

sickroom ['sɪkrʊm] n habitación f de un enfermo.

side [saɪd] ◇ n **-1.** [gen] lado m; **at** OR **by one's** ~ al lado de uno; **on every** ~, **on all** ~**s** por todos los lados; **from** ~ **to** ~ de un lado a otro; ~ **by** ~ juntos, uno al lado de otro; **to put sthg to** OR **on one** ~ poner algo a un lado. **-2.** [of person] costado m; [of animal] ijada f. **-3.** [edge] lado m, borde m. **-4.** [of hill, valley] falda f, ladera f. **-5.** [bank] orilla f. **-6.** [page] cara f. **-7.** [participant - in war, game] lado m, parte f; [- in sports match] equipo m. **-8.** [viewpoint] punto m de vista; **to take sb's** ~ ponerse del lado OR de parte de alguien; **to be on sb's** ~ estar del lado OR de parte de alguien. **-9.** [line of parentage]: **on my father's** ~ por parte de mi padre. **-10.** [aspect] aspecto m; **to be on the safe** ~ para estar seguro. **-11.** phr: **on the large/small** ~ algo grande/pequeño; **to do sthg on the** ~ hacer algo para sacarse un dinero extra; **to keep** OR **stay on the right** ~ **of sb** no llevarle la contraria a alguien. ◇ adj lateral.
◆ **side with** vt fus ponerse de parte de.

sideboard ['saɪdbɔːd] n aparador m.

sideboards Br ['saɪdbɔːdz], **sideburns** Am ['saɪdbɜːnz] npl patillas fpl.

sidecar ['saɪdkɑːr] n sidecar m.

side dish n acompañamiento m, guarnición f.

side effect n MED & fig efecto m secundario.

sidekick ['saɪdkɪk] n inf compinche m y f, secuaz m y f.

sidelight ['saɪdlaɪt] n luz f lateral.

sideline ['saɪdlaɪn] *n* **-1.** [extra business] negocio *m* suplementario. **-2.** [on tennis court] línea *f* lateral; [on football pitch] línea de banda. **-3.** [periphery]: **on the ~s al margen.**

sidelong ['saɪdlɒŋ] *adj & adv* de reojo OR soslayo.

side-on ◇ *adj* lateral. ◇ *adv* de lado.

side plate *n* platillo *m* de pan.

side road *n* calle *f* lateral.

sidesaddle ['saɪd,sædl] *adv*: **to ride ~** montar a sentadillas OR mujeriegas.

sideshow ['saɪdʃəʊ] *n* barraca *f* OR caseta *f* de feria.

sidestep ['saɪdstep] (*pt & pp* **-ped**, *cont* **-ping**) *vt* **-1.** [in football, rugby] regatear. **-2.** *fig* [problem, question] esquivar.

side street *n* calle *f* lateral.

sidetrack ['saɪdtræk] *vt*: **to be ~ed** desviarse OR salirse del tema.

sidewalk ['saɪdwɔːk] *n Am* acera *f*.

sideways ['saɪdweɪz] ◇ *adj* [movement] de lado, hacia un lado; [glance] de soslayo. ◇ *adv* [move] de lado; [look] de reojo.

siding ['saɪdɪŋ] *n* apartadero *m*, vía *f* muerta.

sidle ['saɪdl]
◆ **sidle up** *vi*: **to ~ up to** acercarse furtivamente a.

SIDS (*abbr of* **sudden infant death syndrome**) *n* muerte súbita del recién nacido.

siege [siːdʒ] *n* **-1.** [by army] sitio *m*, cerco *m*. **-2.** [by police] cerco *m* policial.

Sierra Leone [sɪˈerəlɪˈəʊn] *n* Sierra Leona.

Sierra Leonean [sɪˈerə lɪˈəʊnjən] ◇ *adj* sierraleonés(esa). ◇ *n* sierraleonés *m*, -esa *f*.

sieve [sɪv] ◇ *n* [utensil] colador *m*; **to have a head** OR **memory like a ~** tener muy mala memoria. ◇ *vt* [soup] colar; [flour, sugar] tamizar, cerner.

sift [sɪft] ◇ *vt* **-1.** [sieve] tamizar, cerner. **-2.** *fig* [examine carefully] examinar cuidadosamente. ◇ *vi*: **to ~ through sthg** examinar cuidadosamente algo.

sigh [saɪ] ◇ *n* suspiro *m*; **to heave a ~ of relief** respirar aliviado. ◇ *vi* suspirar.

sight [saɪt] ◇ *n* **-1.** [vision] vista *f*. **-2.** [act of seeing]: **her first ~ of the sea** la primera vez que vio el mar; **in ~** a la vista; **to disappear out of ~** perderse de vista; **to catch ~ of sthg/sb** alcanzar a ver algo/a alguien; **to know sb by ~** conocer a alguien de vista; **to lose ~ of** *lit & fig* perder de vista; **to shoot on ~** disparar sin esperar; **at first ~** a primera vista. **-3.** [something seen] imagen *f*; **a beautiful ~** una vista preciosa. **-4.** [on gun] mira *f*; **to set one's ~s on sthg** echarle

el ojo a algo. **-5.** [small amount]: **a ~ better/worse** mucho mejor/peor.
◇ *vt* divisar, avistar.
◆ **sights** *npl* atracciones *fpl* turísticas; **to see the ~s** ir a ver la ciudad.

sighting ['saɪtɪŋ] *n*: **there had been only two ~s of the bird** el pájaro sólo se había visto dos veces.

sightseeing ['saɪt,siːɪŋ] *n* recorrido *m* turístico.

sightseer ['saɪt,siːə'] *n* turista *m y f*.

sign [saɪn] ◇ *n* **-1.** [written symbol] signo *m*. **-2.** [gesture] señal *f*. **-3.** [of pub, shop] letrero *m*; [on road] señal *f*; [notice] cartel *m*. **-4.** [indication] señal *f*, indicio *m*; **there's no ~ of him** no se le ve por ninguna parte. ◇ *vt* firmar.
◆ **sign away** *vt sep* ceder.
◆ **sign for** *vt fus* **-1.** [sign receipt for] firmar acusando recibo de. **-2.** [sign contract for - football team] fichar por.
◆ **sign in** *vi* firmar en el registro.
◆ **sign on** *vi* **-1.** [enrol, register]: **to ~ on (for)** [army] alistarse (en); [job] firmar el contrato (de); [course] matricularse (en). **-2.** [register as unemployed] firmar para cobrar el paro.
◆ **sign out** *vi* firmar al marcharse (de un hotel o club).
◆ **sign up** ◇ *vt sep* [employee] contratar; [recruit] alistar. ◇ *vi*: **to ~ up (for)** [army] alistarse (en); [job] firmar el contrato (de); [course] matricularse (en).

signal ['sɪgnl] (*Br pp & pt* **-led**, *cont* **-ling**, *Am pp & pt* **-ed**, *cont* **-ing**) ◇ *n* señal *f*. ◇ *vt* **-1.** [indicate] indicar. **-2.** [tell]: **to ~ sb (to do sthg)** hacer señas a alguien (para que haga algo). **-3.** *fig* [change, event] señalar. ◇ *adj* *fml* [triumph] señalado(da); [failure] estrepitoso(sa). ◇ *vi* **-1.** AUT señalizar. **-2.** [indicate]: **to ~ sb (to do sthg)** hacer señas a alguien (para que haga algo); **to ~ for sthg** pedir algo por señas.

signal box *Br*, **signal tower** *Am n* puesto *m* de mando.

signally ['sɪgnəlɪ] *adv fml* [fail] estrepitosamente.

signalman ['sɪgnlmən] (*pl* **-men** [-mən]) *n* RAIL guardavía *m*.

signal tower *Am* = **signal box**.

signatory ['sɪgnətrɪ] (*pl* **-ies**) *n* signatario *m*, -ria *f*, firmante *m y f*.

signature ['sɪgnətʃə'] *n* firma *f*.

signature tune *n* sintonía *f*.

signet ring ['sɪgnɪt-] *n* (anillo *m* de) sello *m*.

significance [sɪgˈnɪfɪkəns] *n* trascendencia *f*, importancia *f*.

significant [sɪg'nɪfɪkənt] *adj* **-1.** [considerable, meaningful] **significativo(va). -2.** [important] **trascendente.**

significantly [sɪg'nɪfɪkəntlɪ] *adv* **-1.** [considerably, meaningfully] **de manera significativa. -2.** [importantly]: **~, he was absent** fue significativo el hecho de su ausencia.

signify ['sɪgnɪfaɪ] (*pt* & *pp* **-ied**) *vt* significar.

signing ['saɪnɪŋ] *n Br* SPORT fichaje *m*.

sign language *n* lenguaje *m* por señas.

signpost ['saɪnpəʊst] *n* letrero *m* indicador.

Sikh [siːk] ◇ *adj* sij. ◇ *n* [person] sij *m* y *f*.

Sikhism ['siːkɪzm] *n* sijismo *m*.

silage ['saɪlɪdʒ] *n* ensilaje *m*.

silence ['saɪləns] ◇ *n* silencio *m*. ◇ *vt* [person, critic] acallar, hacer callar; [gun] silenciar.

silencer ['saɪlənsə] *n* silenciador *m*.

silent ['saɪlənt] *adj* **-1.** [gen] silencioso(sa). **-2.** [not revealing anything]: **to be ~ about** quedar en silencio respecto a. **-3.** CINEMA & LING mudo(da).

silently ['saɪləntlɪ] *adv* **-1.** [without speaking] en silencio. **-2.** [noiselessly] silenciosamente.

silent partner *n Am* socio comanditario *m*, socia comanditaria *f*.

silhouette [,sɪluː'et] ◇ *n* silueta *f*. ◇ *vt*: **to be ~d against** perfilarse OR destacarse sobre.

silicon ['sɪlɪkən] *n* silicio *m*.

silicon chip *n* chip *m* de silicio.

silicone ['sɪlɪkəʊn] *n* silicona *f*.

Silicon Valley *zona industrial californiana en la que se concentra la producción electrónica estadounidense.*

silk [sɪlk] ◇ *n* seda *f*. ◇ *comp* de seda.

silk screen printing *n* serigrafía *f*.

silkworm ['sɪlkwɜːm] *n* gusano *m* de seda.

silky ['sɪlkɪ] (*compar* **-ier**, *superl* **-iest**) *adj* [hair, dress, skin] sedoso(sa); [voice] aterciopelado(da).

sill [sɪl] *n* [of window] alféizar *m*.

silliness ['sɪlɪnɪs] *n* (*U*) estupidez *f*.

silly ['sɪlɪ] (*compar* **-ier**, *superl* **-iest**) *adj* estúpido(da), sonso(sa) *Amer*.

silo ['saɪləʊ] (*pl* **-s**) *n* silo *m*.

silt [sɪlt] *n* cieno *m*, légamo *m*.

◆ **silt up** *vi* cegarse.

silver ['sɪlvə] ◇ *adj* [of colour] plateado(da). ◇ *n* (*U*) **-1.** [metal, silverware] plata *f*. **-2.** [coins] monedas *fpl* plateadas. ◇ *comp* de plata.

silver foil, silver paper *n* papel *m* de plata.

silver-plated [-'pleɪtɪd] *adj* bañado(da) de plata, plateado(da).

silver screen *n inf*: **the ~** el cine, las películas.

silversmith ['sɪlvəsmɪθ] *n* platero *m*, -ra *f*.

silverware ['sɪlvəweə] *n* (*U*) **-1.** [dishes etc] plata *f*. **-2.** *Am* [cutlery] cubertería *f* de plata.

silver wedding *n* bodas *fpl* de plata.

similar ['sɪmɪlə] *adj*: **~ (to)** parecido(da) OR similar (a).

similarity [,sɪmɪ'lærətɪ] (*pl* **-ies**) *n*: **~ (between/to)** parecido *m* OR semejanza *f* (entre/con).

similarly ['sɪmɪləlɪ] *adv* [likewise] asimismo; [equally] igualmente.

simile ['sɪmɪlɪ] *n* símil *m*.

simmer ['sɪmə] *vt* & *vi* hervir a fuego lento.

◆ **simmer down** *vi inf* calmarse.

simper ['sɪmpə] ◇ *n* sonrisa *f* boba. ◇ *vi* sonreír con cara de tonto(ta).

simpering ['sɪmpərɪŋ] *adj* [person] que sonríe con cara de tonto(ta); [smile] bobo(ba).

simple ['sɪmpl] *adj* **-1.** [gen] sencillo(lla). **-2.** *dated* [mentally retarded] simple. **-3.** [plainfact] mero(ra); [- truth] puro(ra).

simple-minded [-'maɪndɪd] *adj* simple.

simpleton ['sɪmpltən] *n dated* simplón *m*, -ona *f*.

simplicity [sɪm'plɪsətɪ] *n* sencillez *f*.

simplification [,sɪmplɪfɪ'keɪʃn] *n* simplificación *f*.

simplify ['sɪmplɪfaɪ] (*pt* & *pp* **-ied**) *vt* simplificar.

simplistic [sɪm'plɪstɪk] *adj* simplista.

simply ['sɪmplɪ] *adv* **-1.** [merely] sencillamente, simplemente. **-2.** [for emphasis]: **you ~ must go and see it!** ¡no puedes perdértelo!; **~ dreadful/wonderful** francamente terrible/maravilloso; **I ~ can't believe it!** ¡no me lo puedo creer! **-3.** [in a simple way] de manera sencilla.

simulate ['sɪmjʊleɪt] *vt* simular.

simulation [,sɪmjʊ'leɪʃn] *n* **-1.** [gen & COMPUT] simulación *f*. **-2.** [feigning] simulacro *m*.

simulator ['sɪmjʊleɪtə] *n* simulador *m*.

simultaneous [*Br* ,sɪmʊl'teɪnjəs, *Am* ,saɪməl'teɪnjəs] *adj* simultáneo(a).

simultaneously [*Br* ,sɪmʊl'teɪnjəslɪ, *Am* ,saɪməl'teɪnjəslɪ] *adv* simultáneamente.

sin [sɪn] (*pt* & *pp* **-ned**, *cont* **-ning**) ◇ *n* pecado *m*; **to live in ~** vivir en pecado. ◇ *vi*: **to ~ (against)** pecar (contra).

sin bin *n inf* ICE HOCKEY banquillo *m* para los expulsados.

since [sɪns] ◇ *adv* desde entonces; **long ~** hace mucho tiempo. ◇ *prep* desde; **he has worked here ~ 1975** trabaja aquí desde 1975. ◇ *conj* **-1.** [in time] desde que; **it's ages ~ I saw you** hace siglos que no te veo. **-2.** [because] ya que, puesto que.

sincere [sɪn'sɪəʳ] *adj* sincero(ra).

sincerely [sɪn'sɪəlɪ] *adv* sinceramente; **Yours ~** [at end of letter] atentamente.

sincerity [sɪn'serətɪ] *n* sinceridad *f*.

sinecure ['saɪnɪˌkjʊəʳ] *n* sinecura *f*.

sinew ['sɪnjuː] *n* tendón *m*.

sinewy ['sɪnjuːɪ] *adj*: **a ~ man** un hombre que es pura fibra.

sinful ['sɪnfʊl] *adj* **-1.** [person] pecador(ra). **-2.** [thought, act] pecaminoso(sa).

sing [sɪŋ] (*pt* **sang**, *pp* **sung**) *vt & vi* cantar.

Singapore [ˌsɪŋə'pɔːʳ] *n* Singapur.

Singaporean [ˌsɪŋə'pɔːrɪən] ◇ *adj* singapurense. ◇ *n* [person] singapurense *m y f*.

singe [sɪndʒ] (*cont* **singeing**) ◇ *n* chamusco *m*. ◇ *vt* chamuscar.

singer ['sɪŋəʳ] *n* cantante *m y f*.

Singhalese [ˌsɪŋə'liːz] ◇ *adj* cingalés(esa). ◇ *n* **-1.** [person] cingalés *m*, -esa *f*. **-2.** [language] cingalés *m*.

singing ['sɪŋɪŋ] ◇ *adj* de canto. ◇ *n* (*U*) canto *m*.

singing telegram *n* telegrama *m* cantado.

single ['sɪŋgl] ◇ *adj* **-1.** [only one] único(ca); **not one ~ time** ni una sola vez. **-2.** [individual]: **every ~ penny** todos y cada uno de los peniques. **-3.** [unmarried] soltero(ra). **-4.** *Br* [one-way] de ida. ◇ *n* **-1.** *Br* [one-way ticket] billete *m* de ida. **-2.** MUS [record] sencillo *m*, single *m*.
◆ **singles** *npl* TENNIS (partido *m*) individual *m*.
◆ **single out** *vt sep*: **to ~ sb out (for)** escoger a alguien (para).

single bed *n* cama *f* individual.

single-breasted [-'brestɪd] *adj* recto(ta), sin cruzar.

single cream *n Br* crema *f* de leche, nata *f* líquida.

single-decker (bus) [-'dekəʳ-] *n Br* autobús *m* de un piso.

Single European Market *n*: **the ~** el Mercado Único Europeo.

single file *n*: **in ~** en fila india.

single-handed [-'hændɪd] *adv* sin ayuda.

single-minded [-'maɪndɪd] *adj* resuelto(ta); **to be ~ about** tener un objetivo muy claro respecto a.

single-parent family *n* familia *f* en la que falta uno de los padres.

single quotes *npl* comillas *fpl* simples.

single room *n* habitación *f* individual.

singles bar *n bar de encuentro para solteros*.

singlet ['sɪŋglɪt] *n Br* camiseta *f* sin mangas.

single ticket *n Br* billete *m* de ida.

singsong ['sɪŋsɒŋ] *inf* ◇ *adj* cantarín(ina). ◇ *n Br* reunión *f* para cantar.

singular ['sɪŋgjʊləʳ] ◇ *adj* singular. ◇ *n* singular *m*.

singularly ['sɪŋgjʊləlɪ] *adv* singularmente.

Sinhalese ['sɪnhəliːz] = **Singhalese**.

sinister ['sɪnɪstəʳ] *adj* siniestro(tra).

sink [sɪŋk] (*pt* **sank**, *pp* **sunk**) ◇ *n* **-1.** [in kitchen] fregadero *m*. **-2.** [in bathroom] lavabo *m*. ◇ *vt* **-1.** [cause to go under water] hundir. **-2.** [cause to penetrate]: **to ~ sthg into** [knife, claws] clavar algo en; [teeth] hincar algo en. ◇ *vi* **-1.** [go down - ship, sun] hundirse. **-2.** [slump - person] hundirse; **to ~ to one's knees** caer de rodillas. **-3.** [decrease] bajar. **-4.** [become quieter]: **her voice sank** bajó la voz. **-5.** *fig* [into poverty, despair]: **to ~ into** hundirse en. **-6.** [become depressed]: **his heart** OR **spirits sank** se le cayó el alma a los pies.
◆ **sink in** *vi* hacer mella.

sink board *n Am* escurridero *m*.

sinking ['sɪŋkɪŋ] *n* hundimiento *m*.

sinking fund *n* fondo *m* de amortización.

sink unit *n* fregadero *m* (con mueble debajo).

sinner ['sɪnəʳ] *n* pecador *m*, -ra *f*.

Sinn Féin [ˌʃɪn'feɪn] *n* Sinn Fein *m*, *rama política del IRA*.

sinuous ['sɪnjʊəs] *adj* sinuoso(sa).

sinus ['saɪnəs] (*pl* **-es**) *n* seno *m*.

sip [sɪp] (*pt & pp* **-ped**, *cont* **-ping**) ◇ *n* sorbo *m*. ◇ *vt* beber a sorbos.

siphon ['saɪfn] ◇ *n* sifón *m*. ◇ *vt* **-1.** [liquid] sacar con sifón. **-2.** *fig* [funds] desviar.
◆ **siphon off** *vt sep* **-1.** [liquid] sacar con sifón. **-2.** *fig* [funds] desviar.

sir [sɜːʳ] *n* **-1.** [form of address] señor *m*. **-2.** [in titles]: **Sir Philip Holden** Sir Philip Holden.

siren ['saɪərən] *n* [alarm] sirena *f*.

sirloin (steak) ['sɜːlɔɪn] *n* solomillo *m*.

sissy ['sɪsɪ] (*pl* **-ies**) *inf n* mariquita *m*.

sister ['sɪstəʳ] ◇ *adj* [organization, newspaper] hermano(na); [ship] gemelo(la). ◇ *n* **-1.** [gen] hermana *f*. **-2.** *Br* [senior nurse] enfermera *f* jefe.

sisterhood ['sɪstəhʊd] *n* hermandad *f* (entre mujeres).

sister-in-law (*pl* **sisters-in-law** OR **sister-in-laws**) *n* cuñada *f*.

sisterly ['sɪstəlɪ] *adj* de buena hermana.

sit [sɪt] (*pt* & *pp* **sat**, *cont* **-ting**) ◇ *vi* **-1.** [be seated, sit down] sentarse. **-2.** [be member]: **to ~ on** ser miembro de. **-3.** [be in session] reunirse, celebrar sesión. **-4.** [be situated] estar emplazado(da). **-5.** *phr*: **to ~ tight** quedarse quieto(ta). ◇ *vt Br* [exam] presentarse a.
◆ **sit about**, **sit around** *vi* estar sentado(da) sin hacer nada.
◆ **sit back** *vi* cruzarse de brazos.
◆ **sit down** ◇ *vt sep* sentar. ◇ *vi* sentarse.
◆ **sit in on** *vt fus* estar presente en (*sin tomar parte*).
◆ **sit out** *vt sep* **-1.** [tolerate] aguantar (hasta el final). **-2.** [not participate in] no tomar parte en.
◆ **sit through** *vt fus* aguantar (hasta el final).
◆ **sit up** *vi* **-1.** [sit upright] incorporarse. **-2.** [stay up] quedarse levantado(da).

sitcom ['sɪtkɒm] *n inf* comedia *f* de situación.

sit-down ◇ *adj* [meal] con los comensales sentados a la mesa; **~ strike** huelga *f* de brazos caídos. ◇ *n Br*: **to have a ~** sentarse un rato.

site [saɪt] ◇ *n* [place] sitio *m*, lugar *m*; [of construction work] obra *f*. ◇ *vt* situar.

sit-in *n* sentada *f*.

sitter ['sɪtər] *n* **-1.** ART modelo *m* y *f*. **-2.** [babysitter] canguro *m* y *f*.

sitting ['sɪtɪŋ] *n* **-1.** [serving of meal] turno *m* (para comer). **-2.** [session] sesión *f*.

sitting duck *n inf* blanco *m* fácil.

sitting room *n* sala *f* de estar.

sitting tenant *n Br* inquilino *m*, -na *f* legal.

situate ['sɪtjʊeɪt] *vt* **-1.** [locate] situar, emplazar. **-2.** [put in context] poner en contexto.

situated ['sɪtjʊeɪtɪd] *adj* [located]: **to be ~** estar situado(da).

situation [ˌsɪtjʊ'eɪʃn] *n* **-1.** [gen] situación *f*. **-2.** [job] colocación *f*, empleo *m*; "Situations Vacant" *Br* "Ofertas de trabajo".

situation comedy *n* comedia *f* de situación.

sit-up *n* abdominal *m*.

six [sɪks] ◇ *num adj* seis (*inv*); **she's ~ (years old)** tiene seis años.
◇ *num n* **-1.** [the number six] seis *m inv*; **two hundred and ~** doscientos seis; **~ comes before seven** el seis va antes que el siete; **my favourite number is ~** mi número favorito es el seis. **-2.** [in times]: **it's ~ (thirty)**

son las seis (y media); **we arrived at ~** llegamos a las seis. **-3.** [in temperatures]: **it's ~ below** hace seis grados bajo cero. **-4.** [in addresses]: **~ Peyton Place** Peyton Place número seis, el seis de Peyton Place. **-5.** [referring to group of six] seis *m inv*; **we sell them in ~es** se venden de seis en seis; **to form into ~es** formar en grupos de (a) seis. **-6.** [in scores]: **~-nil** seis a cero. **-7.** [in cards] seis *m*; **to lay** OR **play a ~** jugar un seis.
◇ *num pron* seis *m* y *f*; **I want ~** quiero seis; **~ of us** seis de nosotros; **there are ~ of us** somos seis; **groups of ~** grupos de seis.

six-shooter [-'ʃuːtər] *n Am* revólver *m* de seis tiros.

sixteen [sɪks'tiːn] *num* dieciséis; *see also* **six**.

sixteenth [sɪks'tiːnθ] *num* decimosexto(ta); *see also* **sixth**.

sixth [sɪksθ] ◇ *num adj* sexto(ta). ◇ *num adv* sexto(ta). ◇ *num pron* sexto *m*, -ta *f*. ◇ *n* **-1.** [fraction]: **a ~** OR **one ~ of** un sexto de, la sexta parte de. **-2.** [in dates]: **the ~** el (día) seis; **the ~ of September** el seis de septiembre.

sixth form *n Br* SCH *curso optativo de dos años de enseñanza secundaria con vistas al examen de ingreso a la universidad*, ≃ COU *m*.

sixth form college *n Br centro público para alumnos de 16 a 18 años donde se preparan para los 'A levels' o para exámenes de formación profesional.*

sixth sense *n* sexto sentido *m*.

sixtieth ['sɪkstɪəθ] *num* sexagésimo(ma); *see also* **sixth**.

sixty ['sɪkstɪ] (*pl* **-ies**) *num* sesenta; *see also* **six**.
◆ **sixties** *npl* **-1.** [decade]: **the sixties** los años sesenta. **-2.** [in ages]: **to be in one's sixties** tener más de sesenta años. **-3.** [in temperatures]: **the temperature was in the sixties** hacía más de sesenta grados (Fahrenheit).

size [saɪz] *n* **-1.** [gen] tamaño *m*. **-2.** [of clothes] talla *f*; [of shoes] número *m*. **-3.** *phr*: **to cut sb down to ~** bajarle los humos a alguien.
◆ **size up** *vt sep* [situation] evaluar; [person] juzgar.

sizeable ['saɪzəbl] *adj* considerable.

-sized [saɪzd] *suffix*: **...~** de tamaño ....

sizzle ['sɪzl] *vi* chisporrotear.

SK *abbr of* **Saskatchewan**.

skate [skeɪt] (*pl sense 2 only inv* OR **-s**) ◇ *n* **-1.** [ice skate, roller skate] patín *m*. **-2.** [fish] raya *f*. ◇ *vi* [on skates] patinar.
◆ **skate over**, **skate round** *vt fus* [problem] eludir.

skateboard ['skeɪtbɔːd] *n* monopatín *m*.

skateboarder ['skeɪtbɔːdər] *n persona que monta un monopatín.*

skater ['skeɪtər] *n* patinador *m*, -ra *f.*

skating ['skeɪtɪŋ] *n* patinaje *m.*

skating rink *n* pista *f* de patinaje.

skein [skeɪn] *n* madeja *f.*

skeletal ['skelɪtl] *adj* [emaciated] esquelético(ca).

skeleton ['skelɪtn] ◇ *adj* mínimo(ma). ◇ *n* ANAT esqueleto *m*; **to have a ~ in the cupboard** *fig* guardar un secreto vergonzante.

skeleton key *n* llave *f* maestra.

skeleton staff *n* personal *m* mínimo.

skeptic *etc Am* = **sceptic** *etc.*

sketch [sketʃ] ◇ *n* **-1.** [drawing, brief outline] esbozo *m*, bosquejo *m*. **-2.** [humorous scene] sketch *m*. ◇ *vt* esbozar. ◇ *vi* hacer esbozos OR bosquejos.

◆ **sketch in** *vt sep* dar una idea rápida de.

◆ **sketch out** *vt sep* dar una idea rápida de.

sketchbook ['sketʃbʊk] *n* cuaderno *m* de dibujo.

sketchpad ['sketʃpæd] *n* bloc *m* de dibujo.

sketchy ['sketʃɪ] (*compar* **-ier**, *superl* **-iest**) *adj* incompleto(ta), poco detallado(da).

skew [skjuː] ◇ *n Br*: **on the ~** torcido(da). ◇ *vt* torcer. ◇ *vi* [vehicle] desviar OR virar bruscamente.

skewer ['skjʊər] ◇ *n* brocheta *f*, broqueta *f.* ◇ *vt* ensartar en una brocheta.

skew-whiff [,skjuː'wɪf] *adj Br inf* torcido(da).

ski [skiː] (*pt & pp* **skied**, *cont* **skiing**) ◇ *n* esquí *m.* ◇ *comp* de esquí, de esquiar. ◇ *vi* esquiar.

ski boots *npl* botas *fpl* de esquí.

skid [skɪd] (*pt & pp* **-ded**, *cont* **-ding**) ◇ *n* patinazo *m*, derrape *m.* ◇ *vi* patinar, derrapar.

skid mark *n* huella *f* de un derrape.

skid row [-rəʊ] *n Am inf* barrio *m* bajo.

skier ['skiːər] *n* esquiador *m*, -ra *f.*

skies [skaɪz] *pl* → **sky**.

skiing ['skiːɪŋ] ◇ *n* (*U*) esquí *m.* ◇ *comp* [holiday, accident] de esquí; [enthusiast] del esquí.

ski instructor *n* monitor *m*, -ra *f* de esquí.

ski jump *n* **-1.** [slope] pista *f* para saltos de esquí. **-2.** [event] saltos *mpl* de esquí.

skilful, skillful *Am* ['skɪlfʊl] *adj* hábil.

skilfully, skillfully *Am* ['skɪlfʊlɪ] *adv* hábilmente, con habilidad.

ski lift *n* telesilla *m.*

skill [skɪl] *n* **-1.** (*U*) [expertise] habilidad *f*, destreza *f.* **-2.** [craft, technique] técnica *f.*

skilled [skɪld] *adj* **-1.** [skilful] habilidoso(sa); **to be ~ (in** OR **at doing sthg)** ser experto(ta) (en hacer algo). **-2.** [trained] cualificado(da), especializado(da).

skillet ['skɪlɪt] *n Am* sartén *f.*

skillful *etc Am* = **skilful** *etc.*

skim [skɪm] (*pt & pp* **-med**, *cont* **-ming**) ◇ *vt* **-1.** [remove - cream] desnatar, sacar la nata a; [- grease] espumar. **-2.** [fly above] volar rozando. **-3.** [glance through] hojear, leer por encima. ◇ *vi*: **to ~ through sthg** hojear algo, leer algo por encima.

skim(med) milk [skɪm(d)-] *n* leche *f* desnatada.

skimp [skɪmp] ◇ *vt* [gen] escatimar; [work] hacer de prisa y corriendo. ◇ *vi*: **to ~ on sthg** [gen] escatimar algo; [work] hacer algo de prisa y corriendo.

skimpy ['skɪmpɪ] (*compar* **-ier**, *superl* **-iest**) *adj* [clothes] muy corto y estrecho (muy corta y estrecha); [meal, facts] escaso(sa).

skin [skɪn] (*pt & pp* **-ned**, *cont* **-ning**) ◇ *n* **-1.** [gen] piel *f*; [on face] cutis *m*; **to do sthg by the ~ of one's teeth** hacerse algo por los pelos; **to jump out of one's ~** *Br* llevarse un susto de muerte; **it makes my ~ crawl** me da escalofríos; **to save** OR **protect one's own ~** salvar el pellejo. **-2.** [on milk, pudding] nata *f*; [on paint] capa *f*, película *f.* ◇ *vt* **-1.** [animal] despellejar, desollar. **-2.** [knee, elbow etc] rasguñarse.

skin-deep *adj* superficial.

skin diver *n* submarinista *m y f.*

skin diving *n* buceo *m*, submarinismo *m* (sin traje ni escafandra).

skinflint ['skɪnflɪnt] *n* agarrado *m*, -da *f*, roñoso *m*, -sa *f.*

skin graft *n* injerto *m* de piel.

skinhead ['skɪnhed] *n Br* cabeza *m* rapada, skinhead *m.*

skinny ['skɪnɪ] (*compar* **-ier**, *superl* **-iest**) *adj inf* flaco(ca).

skint [skɪnt] *adj Br v inf* pelado(da), sin un duro.

skin test *n* cutirreacción *f*, dermorreacción *f.*

skin-tight *adj* muy ajustado(da).

skip [skɪp] (*pt & pp* **-ped**, *cont* **-ping**) ◇ *n* **-1.** [little jump] brinco *m*, saltito *m*. **-2.** *Br* [large container] contenedor *m*, container *m.* ◇ *vt* saltarse. ◇ *vi* **-1.** [move in little jumps] ir dando brincos. **-2.** *Br* [jump over rope] saltar a la comba.

ski pants *npl* pantalones *mpl* de esquí.

ski pole *n* bastón *m* para esquiar.

skipper ['skɪpər] *n* NAUT & SPORT capitán *m*, -ana *f.*

skipping ['skɪpɪŋ] *n Br* el saltar a la comba.

skipping rope *n Br* comba *f*, cuerda *f* de saltar.

ski resort *n* estación *f* de esquí.

skirmish ['skɜːmɪʃ] ◇ *n lit & fig* escaramuza *f*. ◇ *vi* MIL sostener una escaramuza; *fig* [argue] tener una agarrada.

skirt [skɜːt] ◇ *n* falda *f*, pollera *f Amer*. ◇ *vt* **-1.** [border] rodear, bordear. **-2.** [go round - obstacle] sortear; [- person, group] esquivar. **-3.** [avoid dealing with] evitar, eludir.

◆ **skirt round** *vt fus* **-1.** [obstacle] sortear. **-2.** [issue, problem] evitar, eludir.

skirting board ['skɜːtɪŋ-] *n Br* zócalo *m*, rodapié *m*.

ski stick *n* bastón *m* para esquiar.

skit [skɪt] *n*: ~ **(on)** parodia *f* (de).

skittish ['skɪtɪʃ] *adj* **-1.** [person] frívolo(la). **-2.** [animal] asustadizo(za).

skittle ['skɪtl] *n Br* bolo *m*.

◆ **skittles** *n* (*U*) bolos *mpl*.

skive [skaɪv] *vi Br inf*: **to** ~ **(off)** escaquearse.

skivvy ['skɪvɪ] (*pl* **-ies**, *pt & pp* **-ied**) *Br inf* ◇ *n* fregona *f*. ◇ *vi*: **to** ~ **(for sb)** sacar la porquería (a alguien).

skulduggery [skʌl'dʌgərɪ] *n* (*U*) chanchullos *mpl*.

skulk [skʌlk] *vi* esconderse.

skull [skʌl] *n* [gen] calavera *f*; ANAT cráneo *m*.

skullcap ['skʌlkæp] *n* [of priest] solideo *m*; [of Jew] casquete *m*.

skunk [skʌŋk] *n* mofeta *f*.

sky [skaɪ] (*pl* **skies**) *n* cielo *m*.

skycap ['skaɪkæp] *n Am* mozo *m* de equipaje (*en un aeropuerto*).

skydiver ['skaɪ,daɪvər] *n* paracaidista *m y f* de estilo.

skydiving ['skaɪ,daɪvɪŋ] *n* paracaidismo *m* de estilo.

sky-high *inf* ◇ *adj* por las nubes. ◇ *adv*: **to blow sthg** ~ [blow up] volar algo; [destroy] echar por tierra algo; **to go** ~ ponerse por las nubes.

skylark ['skaɪlɑːk] *n* alondra *f*.

skylight ['skaɪlaɪt] *n* claraboya *f*, tragaluz *m*.

skyline ['skaɪlaɪn] *n* perfil *m* de la ciudad.

skyscraper ['skaɪ,skreɪpər] *n* rascacielos *m inv*.

slab [slæb] *n* [of stone] losa *f*; [of cheese] trozo *m*, pedazo *m*; [of chocolate] tableta *f*.

slack [slæk] ◇ *adj* **-1.** [rope, cable] flojo(ja). **-2.** [business] inactivo(va). **-3.** [person - care-

less] descuidado(da). ◇ *n* [in rope] parte *f* floja.

◆ **slacks** *npl dated* pantalones *mpl* (de esport).

slacken ['slækn] ◇ *vt* [speed, pace] reducir; [rope] aflojar. ◇ *vi* [speed, pace] reducirse.

slag [slæg] *n* [waste material] escoria *f*.

slagheap ['slæghiːp] *n* escorial *m*.

slain [sleɪn] *pp* → **slay**.

slalom ['slɑːləm] *n* eslálom *m*.

slam [slæm] (*pt & pp* **-med**, *cont* **-ming**) ◇ *vt* **-1.** [shut] cerrar de golpe. **-2.** [criticize] vapulear, descuerar *Amer*. **-3.** [place with force]: **to** ~ **sthg on** OR **onto sthg** dar un golpe con algo contra algo violentamente. ◇ *vi* [shut] cerrarse de golpe.

slander ['slɑːndər] ◇ *n* calumnia *f*, difamación *f*. ◇ *vt* calumniar, difamar.

slanderous ['slɑːndrəs] *adj* calumnioso(sa), difamatorio(ria).

slang [slæŋ] ◇ *adj* de argot. ◇ *n* argot *m*, jerga *f*.

slant [slɑːnt] ◇ *n* **-1.** [diagonal angle] inclinación *f*; **on** OR **at a** ~ inclinado(da), ladeado(da). **-2.** [perspective] enfoque *m*. ◇ *vt* [bias] dar un enfoque a. ◇ *vi* inclinarse.

slanting ['slɑːntɪŋ] *adj* inclinado(da).

slap [slæp] (*pt & pp* **-ped**, *cont* **-ping**) ◇ *n* [in face] bofetada *f*; [on back] palmada *f*; **a** ~ **in the face** *fig* una bofetada. ◇ *vt* **-1.** [person, face] abofetear; [back] dar una palmada a. **-2.** [place with force]: **to** ~ **sthg on** OR **onto** dar un golpe con algo contra. ◇ *adv inf* [directly] de narices; ~ **in the middle of** ... justo en medio de ....

slapdash ['slæpdæʃ], **slaphappy** ['slæp,hæpɪ] *adj inf* chapucero(ra).

slapstick ['slæpstɪk] *n* (*U*) payasadas *fpl*.

slap-up *adj Br inf*: ~ **meal** comilona *f*.

slash [slæʃ] ◇ *n* **-1.** [long cut] raja *f*, tajo *m*. **-2.** [oblique stroke] barra *f* oblicua. ◇ *vt* **-1.** [material] rasgar; [wrists] cortar. **-2.** *inf* [prices etc] recortar drásticamente.

slat [slæt] *n* tablilla *f*.

slate [sleɪt] ◇ *n* pizarra *f*. ◇ *vt* [criticize] poner por los suelos.

slatted ['slætɪd] *adj* de tablillas.

slaughter ['slɔːtər] ◇ *n lit & fig* matanza *f*. ◇ *vt* matar, carnear *Amer*.

slaughterhouse ['slɔːtəhaʊs, *pl* **-haʊzɪz**] *n* matadero *m*.

Slav [slɑːv] ◇ *adj* eslavo(va). ◇ *n* eslavo *m*, -va *f*.

slave [sleɪv] ◇ *n* esclavo *m*, -va *f*; **a** ~ **to** *fig* un esclavo de. ◇ *vi* [work hard]: **to** ~ **(over)** trabajar como un negro (en).

slaver ['slævər] *vi* [salivate] babear.

slavery ['sleɪvərɪ] *n lit* & *fig* esclavitud *f*.

slave trade *n*: **the ~** el comercio OR tráfico de esclavos.

Slavic ['slɑːvɪk] ◇ *adj* eslavo(va). ◇ *n* HISTORY eslavo *m*, -va *f*.

slavish ['sleɪvɪʃ] *adj pej* [imitation, person] servil; [obedience, devotion] ciego(ga).

Slavonic [slə'vɒnɪk] = **Slavic**.

slay [sleɪ] (*pt* **slew**, *pp* **slain**) *vt literary* asesinar, matar.

sleazy ['sliːzɪ] (*compar* **-ier**, *superl* **-iest**) *adj* [disreputable] de mala muerte.

sledge [sledʒ], **sled** *Am* [sled] *n* trineo *m*.

sledgehammer ['sledʒ,hæmər] *n* almádena *f*.

sleek [sliːk] *adj* **-1.** [hair] suave y brillante; [fur] lustroso(sa). **-2.** [shape] de línea depurada.

sleep [sliːp] (*pt* & *pp* **slept**) ◇ *n* sueño *m*; **to go to ~** [doze off] dormirse; **my foot has gone to ~** [become numb] se me ha dormido el pie; **to put to ~** [animal] matar (*a un animal que es viejo o está enfermo*). ◇ *vi* dormir.

◆ **sleep around** *vi inf pej* acostarse con medio mundo.

◆ **sleep in** *vi* dormir hasta tarde, levantarse tarde.

◆ **sleep off** *vt sep*: **to ~ off a hangover** dormir la borrachera.

◆ **sleep through** *vt fus* no despertarse con.

◆ **sleep together** *vi* acostarse, tener relaciones sexuales.

◆ **sleep with** *vt fus euphemism* acostarse con.

sleeper ['sliːpər] *n* **-1.** [person]: **to be a heavy/light ~** tener el sueño profundo/ligero. **-2.** [sleeping compartment] coche-cama *m*. **-3.** [train] tren *m* nocturno (con literas). **-4.** *Br* [on railway track] traviesa *f*.

sleepily ['sliːpɪlɪ] *adv* soñolientamente.

sleeping bag ['sliːpɪŋ-] *n* saco *m* de dormir, bolsa *f Amer*.

sleeping car ['sliːpɪŋ-] *n* coche-cama *m*.

sleeping partner ['sliːpɪŋ-] *n Br* socio comanditario *m*, socia comanditaria *f*.

sleeping pill ['sliːpɪŋ-] *n* pastilla *f* para dormir.

sleeping policeman ['sliːpɪŋ-] *n Br inf* rompecoches *m inv*.

sleeping tablet ['sliːpɪŋ-] *n* pastilla *f* para dormir.

sleepless ['sliːplɪs] *adj* en blanco, sin dormir.

sleeplessness ['sliːplɪsnɪs] *n* insomnio *m*.

sleepwalk ['sliːpwɔːk] *vi* [be a sleepwalker] ser somnámbulo(la); [walk in one's sleep] andar mientras uno duerme.

sleepy ['sliːpɪ] (*compar* **-ier**, *superl* **-iest**) *adj* **-1.** [person] soñoliento(ta). **-2.** [place] muerto(ta), poco animado(da).

sleet [sliːt] ◇ *n* aguanieve *f*. ◇ *v impers*: **it's ~ing** cae aguanieve.

sleeve [sliːv] *n* **-1.** [of garment] manga *f*; **to have sthg up one's ~** guardar una carta en la manga. **-2.** [for record] cubierta *f*.

sleeveless ['sliːvlɪs] *adj* sin mangas.

sleigh [sleɪ] *n* trineo *m*.

sleight of hand [,slaɪt-] *n* (*U*) *lit* & *fig* juego *m* de manos.

slender ['slendər] *adj* **-1.** [thin] esbelto(ta). **-2.** [scarce] escaso(sa).

slept [slept] *pt* & *pp* → **sleep**.

sleuth [sluːθ] *n inf hum* sabueso *m*, detective *m y f*.

slew [sluː] ◇ *pt* → **slay**. ◇ *vi* girar bruscamente.

slice [slaɪs] ◇ *n* **-1.** [of bread] rebanada *f*; [of cheese] loncha *f*; [of sausage] raja *f*; [of lemon] rodaja *f*; [of meat] tajada *f*. **-2.** [of market, glory] parte *f*. **-3.** TENNIS golpe *m* con efecto bajo. ◇ *vt* [gen] cortar; [bread] rebanar. ◇ *vi*: **to ~ through** OR **into sthg** cortar algo.

sliced bread [slaɪst-] *n* (*U*) pan *m* de molde rebanado.

slick [slɪk] *adj* **-1.** [smooth, skilful] logrado(da). **-2.** *pej* [superficial - talk] aparentemente brillante; [- person] de labia fácil.

slicker ['slɪkər] *n Am* [raincoat] impermeable *m*.

slide [slaɪd] (*pt* & *pp* **slid** [slɪd]) ◇ *n* **-1.** [decline] descenso *m*. **-2.** PHOT diapositiva *f*. **-3.** [in playground] tobogán *m*. **-4.** [for microscope] portaobjeto *m*. **-5.** *Br* [for hair] pasador *m*. ◇ *vt* deslizar. ◇ *vi* **-1.** [slip] resbalar. **-2.** [glide] deslizarse. **-3.** [decline gradually] caer; **to let things ~** dejar que las cosas empeoren.

slide projector *n* proyector *m* de diapositivas.

slide rule *n* regla *f* de cálculo.

sliding door [slaɪdɪŋ-] *n* puerta *f* corredera.

sliding scale ['slaɪdɪŋ-] *n* escala *f* móvil.

slight [slaɪt] ◇ *adj* **-1.** [improvement, hesitation etc] ligero(ra); [wound] superficial; **not in the ~est** *fml* en absoluto. **-2.** [slender] menudo(da), de aspecto frágil. ◇ *n* desaire *m*. ◇ *vt* menospreciar, desairar.

slightly ['slaɪtlɪ] *adv* **-1.** [to small extent] ligeramente. **-2.** [slenderly]: **~ built** menudo(da).

slim [slɪm] (*compar* **-mer**, *superl* **-mest**, *pt* & *pp* **-med**, *cont* **-ming**) ◇ *adj* **-1.** [person, object] delgado(da). **-2.** [chance, possibility] remoto(ta). ◇ *vi* (intentar) adelgazar.

slime [slaɪm] *n* [in pond etc] lodo *m*, cieno *m*; [of snail, slug] baba *f*.

slimmer ['slɪmər] *n* persona *f* que intenta adelgazar.

slimming ['slɪmɪŋ] *n* adelgazamiento *m*.

slimness ['slɪmnɪs] *n* delgadez *f*, esbeltez *f*.

slimy ['slaɪmɪ] (*compar* **-ier**, *superl* **-iest**) *adj* **-1.** [pond etc] fangoso(sa); [snail] baboso(sa). **-2.** *pej* [servile] empalagoso(sa), zalamero(ra).

sling [slɪŋ] (*pt* & *pp* **slung**) ◇ *n* **-1.** [for injured arm] cabestrillo *m*. **-2.** [for carrying things] braga *f*, honda *f*. ◇ *vt* **-1.** [hang roughly] colgar descuidadamente. **-2.** *inf* [throw] tirar. **-3.** [hang by both ends] colgar.

slingback ['slɪŋbæk] *n* zapato abierto en la parte del tacón.

slingshot ['slɪŋʃɒt] *n Am* tirachinas *m inv*.

slink [slɪŋk] (*pt* & *pp* **slunk**) *vi*: **to ~ (away** OR **off)** escabullirse.

slip [slɪp] (*pt* & *pp* **-ped**, *cont* **-ping**) ◇ *n* **-1.** [mistake] descuido *m*, desliz *m*; **a ~ of the pen/tongue** un lapsus. **-2.** [of paper - gen] papelito *m*; [- form] hoja *f*. **-3.** [underskirt] enaguas *fpl*. **-4.** *phr*: **to give sb the ~** *inf* dar esquinazo a alguien.

◇ *vt*: **to ~ sthg into** meter algo rápidamente en; **to ~ into sthg, to ~ sthg on** [clothes] ponerse rápidamente algo.

◇ *vi* **-1.** [lose one's balance] resbalar, patinar. **-2.** [slide] escurrirse, resbalar. **-3.** [decline] empeorar; **to let things ~** dejar que las cosas empeoren. **-4.** *phr*: **to let sthg ~** decir algo sin querer.

◆ **slip up** *vi* cometer un error (poco importante).

slip-on *adj* sin cordones.

◆ **slip-ons** *npl* zapatos *mpl* sin cordones.

slippage ['slɪpɪdʒ] *n* bajón *m*.

slipped disc [ˌslɪpt-] *n* hernia *f* discal.

slipper ['slɪpər] *n* zapatilla *f*.

slippery ['slɪpərɪ] *adj* resbaladizo(za).

slip road *n Br* [for joining motorway] acceso *m*; [for leaving motorway] salida *f*.

slipshod ['slɪpʃɒd] *adj* descuidado(da), chapucero(ra).

slipstream ['slɪpstriːm] *n* estela *f*.

slip-up *n inf* fallo *m* poco importante.

slipway ['slɪpweɪ] *n* grada *f*.

slit [slɪt] (*pt* & *pp* **slit**, *cont* **-ting**) ◇ *n* ranura *f*, hendidura *f*. ◇ *vt* abrir, cortar (a lo largo).

slither ['slɪðər] *vi* deslizarse.

sliver ['slɪvər] *n* [of glass] esquirla *f*; [of wood] astilla *f*; [of cheese, ham] tajada *f* muy fina.

slob [slɒb] *n inf* guarro *m*, -rra *f*.

slobber ['slɒbər] *vi* babear.

slog [slɒg] (*pt* & *pp* **-ged**, *cont* **-ging**) *inf* ◇ *n* **-1.** [work] curro *m*, trabajo *m* pesado. **-2.** [journey] viaje *m* pesado. ◇ *vi* **-1.** [work]: **to ~ (away) at** trabajar sin descanso en. **-2.** [move] caminar con dificultad.

slogan ['sləʊgən] *n* eslogan *m*.

sloop [sluːp] *n* balandro *m*.

slop [slɒp] (*pt* & *pp* **-ped**, *cont* **-ping**) ◇ *vt* derramar. ◇ *vi* derramarse.

slope [sləʊp] ◇ *n* cuesta *f*, pendiente *f*; **to be on a slippery ~** estar en un callejón sin salida. ◇ *vi* inclinarse.

sloping ['sləʊpɪŋ] *adj* [gen] inclinado(da); [ground] en pendiente.

sloppy ['slɒpɪ] (*compar* **-ier**, *superl* **-iest**) *adj* **-1.** [person] descuidado(da); [work] chapucero(ra); [appearance] dejado(da). **-2.** *inf* [sentimental] sensiblero(ra).

slosh [slɒʃ] ◇ *vt* agitar. ◇ *vi* chapotear.

sloshed [slɒʃt] *adj inf* como una cuba..

slot [slɒt] (*pt* & *pp* **-ted**, *cont* **-ting**) *n* **-1.** [opening - gen & COMPUT] ranura *f*. **-2.** [groove] muesca *f*. **-3.** [place in schedule] espacio *m*.

◆ **slot in** ◇ *vt sep* [into slot] introducir en la ranura; [into timetable etc] hacer un hueco a. ◇ *vi* [fit neatly] encajar.

sloth [sləʊθ] *n* **-1.** [animal] perezoso *m*. **-2.** *literary* [laziness] pereza *f*.

slot machine *n* **-1.** [vending machine] máquina *f* automática (*de bebidas, cigarrillos etc*). **-2.** [arcade machine] máquina *f* tragaperras.

slot meter *n Br* contador *m* que funciona con monedas.

slouch [slaʊtʃ] ◇ *n*: **to walk with a ~** andar con los hombros caídos. ◇ *vi* ir con los hombros caídos.

slough [slaʊ]

◆ **slough off** *vt sep* [shed] mudar; *fig* [get rid of] deshacerse de.

Slovak ['sləʊvæk] ◇ *adj* eslovaco(ca). ◇ *n* **-1.** [person] eslovaco *m*, -ca *f*. **-2.** [language] eslovaco *m*.

Slovakia [slə'vækɪə] *n* Eslovaquia.

Slovakian [slə'vækɪən] ◇ *adj* eslovaco(ca). ◇ *n* eslovaco *m*, -ca *f*.

Slovenia [slə'viːnjə] *n* Eslovenia.

Slovenian [slə'viːnjən] ◇ *adj* esloveno(na). ◇ *n* esloveno *m*, -na *f*.

slovenly ['slʌvnlɪ] *adj* [unkempt] desaliñado(da); [careless] descuidado(da).

slow [sləʊ] ◇ *adj* **-1.** [not fast] lento(ta). **-2.** [not prompt]: **to be ~ to do sthg** tardar en hacer algo. **-3.** [clock etc] atrasado(da). **-4.** [not busy - business, place] poco activo(va). **-5.** [not intelligent] corto(ta) (de alcances). ◇ *vt* aminorar, ralentizar. ◇ *vi* ir más despacio.

◆ **slow down, slow up** ◇ *vt sep* [growth] retrasar; [car] reducir la velocidad de. ◇ *vi* [walker] ir más despacio; [car] reducir la velocidad.

slow-acting *adj* de efectos retardados.

slowcoach ['sləʊkəʊtʃ], **slow-poke** *Am n inf* cachazudo *m*, -da *f*, parsimonioso *m*, -sa *f*.

slowdown ['sləʊdaʊn] *n* ralentización *f*.

slow handclap *n* aplauso lento y rítmico de protesta.

slowly ['sləʊlɪ] *adv* despacio, lentamente; ~ but surely lento pero seguro.

slow motion *n* cámara *f* lenta.

◆ **slow-motion** *adj* a cámara lenta.

slow-poke *Am* = **slowcoach**.

SLR (*abbr of* **single-lens reflex**) *n* réflex de un objetivo.

sludge [slʌdʒ] *n* (U) [mud] fango *m*, lodo *m*; [sewage] aguas *fpl* residuales.

slug [slʌg] (*pt & pp* **-ged**, *cont* **-ging**) ◇ *n* **-1.** [animal] babosa *f*. **-2.** *inf* [of alcohol] lingotazo *m*. **-3.** *Am inf* [bullet] bala *f*. ◇ *vt inf* pegar un puñetazo a.

sluggish ['slʌgɪʃ] *adj* [movement, activity] lento(ta); [feeling] aturdido(da).

sluice [sluːs] ◇ *n* [passage] canal *m* de desagüe; [gate] compuerta *f*. ◇ *vt* [rinse]: **to ~ sthg down** OR **out** lavar algo con mucha agua.

slum [slʌm] (*pt & pp* **-med**, *cont* **-ming**) ◇ *n* [area] barrio *m* bajo. ◇ *vt*: **to ~ it** *inf* instalarse de cualquier manera provisionalmente.

slumber ['slʌmbəʳ] *literary* ◇ *n* sueño *m*. ◇ *vi* dormir.

slump [slʌmp] ◇ *n* **-1.** [decline]: ~ **(in)** bajón *m* (en). **-2.** ECON crisis *f* económica. ◇ *vi* **-1.** [fall in value] dar un bajón. **-2.** [fall heavily - person] desplomarse, dejarse caer.

slung [slʌŋ] *pt & pp* → **sling**.

slunk [slʌŋk] *pt & pp* → **slink**.

slur [slɜːʳ] (*pt & pp* **-red**, *cont* **-ring**) ◇ *n* [insult] agravio *m*, afrenta *f*. ◇ *vt* mascullar.

slurp [slɜːp] *vt* sorber ruidosamente.

slurred [slɜːd] *adj* indistinto(ta).

slurry ['slʌrɪ] *n* [manure] mezcla *f* de estiércol y agua.

slush [slʌʃ] *n* nieve *f* medio derretida.

slush fund, slush money *Am n* fondos utilizados para actividades corruptas.

slut [slʌt] *n* **-1.** *inf* [dirty or untidy woman] marrana *f*. **-2.** *v inf* [sexually immoral woman] ramera *f*.

sly [slaɪ] (*compar* **slyer** OR **slier**, *superl* **slyest** OR **sliest**) ◇ *adj* **-1.** [look, smile] furtivo(va). **-2.** [person] astuto(ta), ladino(na). ◇ *n*: **on the ~** a escondidas.

slyness ['slaɪnɪs] *n* (U) [of person] astucia *f*.

S & M (*abbr of* **sadism and masochism**) *n* sado-maso *m*.

smack [smæk] ◇ *n* **-1.** [slap] cachete *m*, cachetada *f* Amer. **-2.** [impact] golpe *m*. ◇ *vt* **-1.** [slap] pegar, dar un cachete a. **-2.** [place violently] tirar de golpe. **-3.** *phr*: **to ~ one's lips** relamerse. ◇ *adv inf* [directly]: ~ **in the middle** justo en medio.

small [smɔːl] ◇ *adj* [gen] pequeño(ña); [person] bajo(ja); [matter, attention] de poca importancia; [importance] poco(ca); **in a ~ way** a pequeña escala. ◇ *n*: **the ~ of the back** la zona lumbar.

◆ **smalls** *npl* Br *inf dated* paños *mpl* menores.

small ads *npl* Br anuncios *mpl* clasificados.

small arms *npl* armas *fpl* portátiles OR de mano.

small change *n* cambio *m*, suelto *m*.

small fry *n* gente *f* de poco monta.

smallholder ['smɔːl,həʊldəʳ] *n* Br minifundista *m y f*.

smallholding ['smɔːl,həʊldɪŋ] *n* minifundio *m*.

small hours *npl* primeras horas *fpl* de la madrugada.

smallness ['smɔːlnɪs] *n* [gen] pequeñez *f*; [of rise, amount] escasez *f*.

smallpox ['smɔːlpɒks] *n* viruela *f*.

small print *n*: **the ~** la letra pequeña.

small-scale *adj* en pequeña escala.

small talk *n* (U) conversación *f* trivial.

small-time *adj* de poca monta.

smarmy ['smɑːmɪ] (*compar* **-ier**, *superl* **-iest**) *adj* cobista.

smart [smɑːt] ◇ *adj* **-1.** [neat, stylish] elegante. **-2.** [clever] inteligente. **-3.** [fashionable, exclusive] distinguido(da), elegante. **-4.** [quick, sharp] rápido(da). ◇ *vi* **-1.** [eyes, wound] escocer. **-2.** [person] sentir resquemor.

smart card *n* tarjeta *f* inteligente, tarjeta *f* con chip.

smarten ['smɑːtn]

◆ **smarten up** *vt sep* arreglar.

smash [smæʃ] ◇ *n* **-1.** [sound] estrépito *m*. **-2.** *inf* [car crash] accidente *m*. **-3.** *inf* [suc-

cess] éxito m. **-4.** TENNIS mate m, smash m.
◇ vt **-1.** [break into pieces] romper, hacer pedazos. **-2.** [hit, crash]: **to ~ one's fist into sth** dar un puñetazo en algo. **-3.** fig [defeat] aplastar.
◇ vi **-1.** [break into pieces] romperse, hacerse pedazos. **-2.** [crash, collide]: **to ~ through sth** romper algo atravesándolo; **to ~ into sth** chocar violentamente con algo.
♦ **smash up** vt sep hacer pedazos.

smash-and-grab (raid) Br n robo rápido después de romper un escaparate.

smashed [smæʃt] adj inf [drunk] cocido(da).

smash hit n gran éxito m.

smashing ['smæʃɪŋ] adj inf fenomenal, estupendo(da).

smash-up n choque m violento, colisión f.

smattering ['smætərɪŋ] n nociones fpl; **he has a ~ of Spanish** habla cuatro palabras de español.

SME (abbr of **small and medium-sized enterprise**) n PYME f.

smear [smɪəʳ] ◇ n **-1.** [dirty mark] mancha f. **-2.** MED frotis m. **-3.** [slander] calumnia f, difamación f. ◇ vt **-1.** [smudge] manchar. **-2.** [spread]: **to ~ sth onto sth** untar algo con algo. **-3.** [slander] calumniar, difamar.

smear campaign n campaña f difamatoria.

smear test n citología f.

smell [smel] (pt & pp **-ed** OR **smelt**) ◇ n **-1.** [odour] olor m. **-2.** [sense of smell] olfato m. ◇ vt lit & fig oler. ◇ vi **-1.** [gen] oler; **to ~ of/like** oler a/como; **to ~ good/bad** oler bien/mal. **-2.** [smell unpleasantly] apestar.

smelly ['smelɪ] (compar **-ier**, superl **-iest**) adj maloliente, apestoso(sa).

smelt [smelt] ◇ pt & pp → **smell**. ◇ vt fundir.

smile [smaɪl] ◇ n sonrisa f. ◇ vi sonreír. ◇ vt mostrar con una sonrisa.

smiling ['smaɪlɪŋ] adj sonriente.

smirk [smɜːk] ◇ n sonrisa f desdeñosa. ◇ vi sonreír desdeñosamente.

smith [smɪθ] n herrero m, -ra f.

smithereens [ˌsmɪðə'riːnz] npl inf: **to be smashed to ~** hacerse añicos.

smithy ['smɪðɪ] (pl **-ies**) n herrería f.

smitten ['smɪtn] adj inf hum: **to be ~ (with sb)** estar colado(da) (por alguien); **to be ~ (with sth)** estar entusiasmado(da) (con algo).

smock [smɒk] n blusón m.

smog [smɒg] n niebla f baja, smog m.

smoke [sməʊk] ◇ n **-1.** [gen] humo m. **-2.** [act of smoking]: **to have a ~** fumar. ◇ vt **-1.** [cigarette, cigar] fumar. **-2.** [fish, meat, cheese]

ahumar. ◇ vi **-1.** [smoke tobacco] fumar. **-2.** [give off smoke] echar humo.

smoked [sməʊkt] adj ahumado(da).

smokeless fuel ['sməʊklɪs-] n combustible m que no hecha humo.

smokeless zone ['sməʊklɪs-] n zona en la que se prohibe el uso de combustible que eche humo.

smoker ['sməʊkəʳ] n **-1.** [person] fumador m, -ra f. **-2.** RAIL [compartment] compartimiento m de fumadores.

smokescreen ['sməʊkskriːn] n fig cortina f de humo.

smoke shop n Am estanco m.

smokestack ['sməʊkstæk] n chimenea f.

smokestack industry n Am industria f pesada.

smoking ['sməʊkɪŋ] n: **~ is bad for you** fumar es malo; **"no ~"** "prohibido fumar".

smoking compartment Br, **smoking car** Am n compartimiento m de fumadores.

smoky ['sməʊkɪ] (compar **-ier**, superl **-iest**) adj **-1.** [full of smoke] lleno(na) de humo. **-2.** [taste, colour] ahumado(da).

smolder Am = **smoulder**.

smooch [smuːtʃ] vi inf besuquearse.

smooth [smuːð] ◇ adj **-1.** [surface] liso(sa); [skin] terso(sa). **-2.** [mixture] sin grumos. **-3.** [movement, taste] suave. **-4.** [flight, ride] tranquilo(la). **-5.** pej [person, manner] meloso(sa). **-6.** [trouble-free] sin problemas. ◇ vt alisar; **to ~ the way** allanar el camino.
♦ **smooth out** vt sep alisar.
♦ **smooth over** vt fus: **to ~ things over** limar asperezas.

smoothie ['smuːðɪ] n bebida a base de yogur y zumo de frutas.

smoothly ['smuːðlɪ] adv **-1.** [evenly] suavemente. **-2.** [suavely] sin alterarse. **-3.** [without problems] sin problemas.

smoothness ['smuːðnɪs] n **-1.** [of surface] lisura f. **-2.** [of movement, mixture] suavidad f. **-3.** [comfort] tranquilidad f. **-4.** pej [of person] melosidad f.

smooth-talking adj que tiene mucha labia.

smother ['smʌðəʳ] vt **-1.** [cover thickly]: **to ~ sth in** OR **with** cubrir algo de. **-2.** [kill] asfixiar. **-3.** [extinguish] sofocar, apagar. **-4.** fig [control] controlar, contener. **-5.** [suffocate with love] abrumar de afecto.

smoulder Br, **smolder** Am ['sməʊldəʳ] vi **-1.** [fire] arder sin llama. **-2.** fig [person, feelings] arder.

smudge [smʌdʒ] ◇ n [dirty mark] mancha f;

[ink blot] **borrón** m. ◇ vt [by blurring] **embo-rronar**; [by dirtying] **manchar**.

smug [smʌg] (compar **-ger**, superl **-gest**) adj pej pagado OR satisfecho de sí mismo (pagada OR satisfecha de sí misma).

smuggle ['smʌgl] vt **-1.** [across frontiers] pasar de contrabando. **-2.** [against rules]: **to ~ sthg in/out** pasar/sacar algo.

smuggler ['smʌglər] n contrabandista m y f.

smuggling ['smʌglɪŋ] n (U) contrabando m.

smugness ['smʌgnɪs] n pej presunción f.

smut [smʌt] n **-1.** [dirty mark] tiznón m, tiznadura f. **-2.** (U) inf pej [lewd matter] guarrerías fpl.

smutty ['smʌtɪ] (compar **-ier**, superl **-iest**) adj inf pej guarro(rra).

snack [snæk] ◇ n bocado m, piscolabis m inv, botana f Amer. ◇ vi Am picar.

snack bar n bar m, cafetería f.

snag [snæg] (pt & pp **-ged**, cont **-ging**) ◇ n [problem] pega f. ◇ vt engancharse. ◇ vi: **to ~ (on)** engancharse (en).

snail [sneɪl] n caracol m.

snake [sneɪk] ◇ n [large] serpiente f; [small] culebra f. ◇ vi serpentear.

snap [snæp] (pt & pp **-ped**, cont **-ping**) ◇ adj repentino(na).
◇ n **-1.** [act or sound] crujido m, chasquido m. **-2.** inf [photograph] foto f. **-3.** [card game] ≃ guerrilla f.
◇ vt **-1.** [break] partir (en dos). **-2.** [move with a snap]: **to ~ sthg open** abrir algo de golpe. **-3.** [speak sharply] decir bruscamente OR de mala manera.
◇ vi **-1.** [break] partirse (en dos). **-2.** [move with a snap]: **to ~ into place** colocarse con un golpe seco. **-3.** [attempt to bite]: **to ~ at sthg/sb** intentar morder algo/a alguien. **-4.** [speak sharply]: **to ~ (at sb)** contestar bruscamente OR de mala manera a alguien. **-5.** phr: **to ~ out of it** animarse de repente.
◆ **snap up** vt sep no dejar escapar.

snap fastener n cierre m (en la ropa etc).

snappish ['snæpɪʃ] adj irritable.

snappy ['snæpɪ] (compar **-ier**, superl **-iest**) adj inf **-1.** [stylish] con estilo. **-2.** [quick] rápido(da); **make it ~!** ¡date prisa!

snapshot ['snæpʃɒt] n foto f.

snare [sneər] ◇ n trampa f. ◇ vt [animal] cazar con trampa; [person] hacer caer en la trampa.

snarl [snɑːl] ◇ n gruñido m. ◇ vi gruñir.

snarl-up n [gen] embrollo m; [of traffic] atasco m.

snatch [snætʃ] ◇ n [of conversation, song] fragmento m. ◇ vt **-1.** [grab] agarrar; **to ~ sthg from sb** arrancarle OR arrebatarle algo

a alguien. **-2.** [take as time allows]: **to ~ some sleep** sacar tiempo para dormir; **to ~ an opportunity/a few moments** aprovechar una oportunidad/unos minutos. ◇ vi: **to ~ at sthg** intentar agarrar algo.

snazzy ['snæzɪ] (compar **-ier**, superl **-iest**) adj inf [stylish] **chulo(la)**; [showy] llamativo(va).

sneak [sniːk] (Am pt **snuck**) ◇ n Br inf acusica m y f, chivato m, -ta f. ◇ vt colar, pasar a escondidas; **to ~ a look at** echar una mirada furtiva a. ◇ vi: **to ~ in/out** entrar/salir a escondidas.

sneakers ['sniːkəz] npl Am zapatos mpl de lona.

sneaking ['sniːkɪŋ] adj secreto(ta).

sneak preview n pase m privado (de una película aún no estrenada).

sneaky ['sniːkɪ] (compar **-ier**, superl **-iest**) adj inf solapado(da).

sneer [snɪər] ◇ n mueca f de desprecio. ◇ vi **-1.** [smile unpleasantly] sonreír con desprecio. **-2.** [ridicule]: **to ~ (at)** burlarse (de).

sneeze [sniːz] ◇ n estornudo m. ◇ vi estornudar; **it's not to be ~d at** inf no es de despreciar.

snicker ['snɪkər] vi Am reírse por lo bajo.

snide [snaɪd] adj sarcástico(ca).

sniff [snɪf] ◇ n: **to give a ~** sorber por la nariz. ◇ vt **-1.** [smell] oler. **-2.** [drug] esnifar. ◇ vi **-1.** [to clear nose] sorber por la nariz. **-2.** [to show disapproval]: **to ~ at sthg** desdeñar algo.
◆ **sniff out** vt sep **-1.** [detect by sniffing] olfatear. **-2.** inf [seek out] descubrir.

sniffer dog ['snɪfər-] n perro entrenado para descubrir drogas o explosivos.

sniffle ['snɪfl] vi [during a cold] sorberse los mocos; [when crying] sorberse las lágrimas.

snigger ['snɪgər] ◇ n risa f disimulada. ◇ vi reírse por lo bajo.

snip [snɪp] (pt & pp **-ped**, cont **-ping**) ◇ n inf [bargain] ganga f. ◇ vt cortar con tijeras.

snipe [snaɪp] vi **-1.** [shoot]: **to ~ (at)** disparar (sobre). **-2.** [criticize]: **to ~ at sb** criticar a alguien.

sniper ['snaɪpər] n francotirador m, -ra f.

snippet ['snɪpɪt] n retazo m, fragmento m.

snivel ['snɪvl] (Br pt & pp **-led**, cont **-ling**, Am pt & pp **-ed**, cont **-ing**) vi lloriquear.

snob [snɒb] n esnob m y f.

snobbery ['snɒbərɪ] n esnobismo m.

snobbish ['snɒbɪʃ], **snobby** ['snɒbɪ] (compar **-ier**, super **-iest**) adj esnob.

snooker ['snuːkər] ◇ n snooker m, juego parecido al billar. ◇ vt Br inf: **to be ~ed** estar con las manos atadas.

snoop [snuːp] *vi inf* fisgonear.

snooper ['snuːpəʳ] *n inf* fisgón *m*, -ona *f*.

snooty ['snuːtɪ] (*compar* -ier, *superl* -iest) *adj* engreído(da).

snooze [snuːz] ◇ *n* cabezada *f*. ◇ *vi* dormitar.

snore [snɔːʳ] ◇ *n* ronquido *m*. ◇ *vi* roncar.

snoring ['snɔːrɪŋ] *n* (*U*) ronquidos *mpl*.

snorkel ['snɔːkl] *n* tubo *m* respiratorio.

snorkelling *Br*, **snorkeling** *Am* ['snɔːklɪŋ] *n* buceo *m* con tubo.

snort [snɔːt] ◇ *n* resoplido *m*. ◇ *vi* resoplar. ◇ *vt drugs sl* esnifar.

snotty ['snɒtɪ] (*compar* -ier, *superl* -iest) *adj inf* [snooty] altivo(va).

snout [snaʊt] *n* hocico *m*.

snow [snəʊ] ◇ *n* nieve *f*. ◇ *v impers* nevar.

◆ **snow in** *vt sep*: **to be ~ed in** estar bloqueado(da) por la nieve.

◆ **snow under** *vt sep*: **to be ~ed under (with)** estar inundado(da) (de).

snowball ['snəʊbɔːl] ◇ *n* bola *f* de nieve. ◇ *vi fig* aumentar rápidamente.

snow blindness *n* ceguera *f* de la nieve.

snowbound ['snəʊbaʊnd] *adj* bloqueado(da) por la nieve.

snow-capped [-,kæpt] *adj* con el pico cubierto de nieve.

snowdrift ['snəʊdrɪft] *n* montón *m* de nieve.

snowdrop ['snəʊdrɒp] *n* campanilla *f* blanca.

snowfall ['snəʊfɔːl] *n* nevada *f*.

snowflake ['snəʊfleɪk] *n* copo *m* de nieve.

snowman ['snəʊmæn] (*pl* -men [-men]) *n* muñeco *m* de nieve.

snow pea *n Am* guisante *m* mollar.

snowplough *Br*, **snowplow** *Am* ['snəʊplaʊ] *n* quitanieves *m inv*.

snowshoe ['snəʊʃuː] *n* raqueta *f* de nieve.

snowstorm ['snəʊstɔːm] *n* tormenta *f* de nieve.

snowy ['snəʊɪ] (*compar* -ier, *superl* -iest) *adj* de mucha nieve.

SNP *n abbr of* **Scottish National Party**.

Snr, **snr** (*abbr of* **senior**) sén.

snub [snʌb] (*pt* & *pp* -bed, *cont* -bing) ◇ *n* desaire *m*. ◇ *vt* desairar.

snuck [snʌk] *pt* → **sneak**.

snuff [snʌf] *n* [tobacco] rapé *m*.

snuffle ['snʌfl] *vi* [during a cold] sorberse los mocos; [when crying] sorberse las lágrimas.

snuff movie *n* película *porno* con un asesinato como desenlace.

snug [snʌg] (*compar* -ger, *superl* -gest) *adj* **-1.** [person] cómodo y calentito (cómoda y calentita); [feeling] de bienestar. **-2.** [place] acogedor(ra). **-3.** [close-fitting] ajustado(da), ceñido(da).

snuggle ['snʌgl] *vi*: **to ~ up to sb** arrimarse a alguien acurrucándose; **to ~ down** acurrucarse.

so [səʊ] ◇ *adv* **-1.** [to such a degree] tan; **~ difficult (that)** tan difícil (que); **don't be ~ stupid!** ¡no seas bobo!; **I've never seen ~ much money/many cars** en mi vida he visto tanto dinero/tantos coches; **he's not ~ stupid as he looks** no es tan bobo como parece; **we're ~ glad you could come** estamos tan contentos de que pudieras venir. **-2.** [in referring back to previous statement, event etc]: **~ what's the point then?** entonces ¿qué sentido tiene?; **~ you knew already?** ¿así que ya lo sabías?; **I don't think ~** no creo, me parece que no; **I'm afraid ~** me temo que sí; **if ~** si es así, de ser así; **is that ~?** ¿es cierto?, ¿es así? **-3.** [also] también; **~ can I** y yo (también puedo); **~ do I** y yo (también); **she speaks French and ~ does her husband** ella habla francés y su marido también; **as with children ~ with adults** igual que con los niños, también con los adultos; **just as some people like family holidays ~ others prefer to holiday alone** igual que hay gente a la que le gustan las vacaciones familiares, otros las prefieren pasar solos. **-4.** [in such a way]: **(like) ~** así, de esta forma; **it was ~ arranged as to look impressive** estaba dispuesto de tal manera que pareciera impresionante. **-5.** [in expressing agreement]: **~ there is!** ¡pues (sí que) es verdad!, ¡sí que lo hay, sí!; **~ I see** ya lo veo. **-6.** [unspecified amount, limit]: **they pay us ~ much a week** nos pagan tanto a la semana; **it's not ~ much the money as the time involved** no es tanto el dinero como el tiempo que conlleva; **or ~** o así; **a year/week or ~ ago** hace un año/una semana o así.

◇ *conj* **-1.** [with the result that, therefore] así que, por lo tanto; **he said yes and ~ we got married** dijo que sí, así que nos casamos. **-2.** [to introduce a statement] (bueno) pues; **~ what have you been up to?** bueno, ¿y qué has estado haciendo?; **~ that's who she is!** ¡anda! ¡o sea que ella!; **~ what?** *inf* ¿y qué?; **~ there** *inf* ¡(y si no te gusta,) te chinchas!

◆ **and so on, and so forth** *adv* y cosas por el estilo.

◆ **so as** *conj* para; **we didn't knock ~ as not to disturb them** no llamamos para no molestarlos.

◆ **so that** *conj* para que; **he lied ~ that she would go free** mintió para que ella saliera en libertad.

SO *abbr of* **standing order**.

soak [səʊk] ◇ *vt* **-1.** [leave immersed] poner en remojo. **-2.** [wet thoroughly] empapar, ensopar *Amer*; **to be ~ed with** estar empapado de. ◇ *vi* **-1.** [become thoroughly wet]: **to leave sthg to ~, to let sthg ~** dejar algo en remojo. **-2.** [spread]: **to ~ into** OR **through sthg** calar algo.

◆ **soak up** *vt sep* [liquid] empapar, absorber.

soaked [səʊkt] *adj* empapado(da); **to be ~ through** estar empapado hasta los huesos.

soaking ['səʊkɪŋ] *adj* empapado(da).

so-and-so *n inf* **-1.** [to replace a name] fulano *m*, -na *f* de tal. **-2.** [annoying person] hijo *m*, -ja *f* de tal.

soap [səʊp] ◇ *n* **-1.** (U) [for washing] jabón *m*. **-2.** TV culebrón *m*. ◇ *vt* enjabonar.

soap bubble *n* pompa *f* de jabón.

soap flakes *npl* escamas *fpl* de jabón.

soap opera *n* culebrón *m*.

soap powder *n* jabón *m* en polvo.

soapsuds ['səʊpsʌdz] *npl* espuma *f* de jabón, jabonaduras *fpl*.

soapy ['səʊpɪ] (*compar* **-ier**, *superl* **-iest**) *adj* **-1.** [full of soap] jabonoso(sa). **-2.** [taste] a jabón; [texture] de jabón.

soar [sɔːr] *vi* **-1.** [bird] remontar el vuelo. **-2.** [rise into the sky] elevarse. **-3.** [increase rapidly] alcanzar cotas muy altas. **-4.** *literary* [be impressively high] elevarse. **-5.** [rise in volume or pitch] subir de volumen.

soaring ['sɔːrɪŋ] *adj* **-1.** [rapidly increasing, rising] cada vez más alto(ta). **-2.** [impressively high] altísimo(ma).

sob [sɒb] (*pt* & *pp* **-bed**, *cont* **-bing**) ◇ *n* sollozo *m*. ◇ *vt* decir sollozando. ◇ *vi* sollozar.

sobbing ['sɒbɪŋ] *n* (U) sollozos *mpl*.

sober ['səʊbər] *adj* **-1.** [gen] sobrio(bria). **-2.** [serious] serio(ria).

◆ **sober up** *vi* pasársele a uno la borrachera.

sobering ['səʊbərɪŋ] *adj* que hace reflexionar.

sobriety [səʊ'braɪətɪ] *n fml* sobriedad *f*.

Soc. *abbr of* **Society**.

so-called [-kɔːld] *adj* **-1.** [misleadingly named] mal llamado(da), supuesto(ta). **-2.** [widely known as] así llamado(da).

soccer ['sɒkər] *n* (U) fútbol *m*.

sociable ['səʊʃəbl] *adj* sociable.

social ['səʊʃl] *adj* social.

social climber *n pej* arribista *m y f*.

social club *n* local *m* social de una empresa.

social conscience *n* conciencia *f* social.

social democracy *n* social democracia *f*.

social event *n* **-1.** [at work etc] acto *m* social. **-2.** [in village etc] acontecimiento *m* social.

social fund *n en Gran Bretaña, fondo de prestaciones en casos de extrema necesidad*.

socialism ['səʊʃəlɪzm] *n* socialismo *m*.

socialist ['səʊʃəlɪst] ◇ *adj* socialista. ◇ *n* socialista *m y f*.

socialite ['səʊʃəlaɪt] *n* persona *f* que frecuenta fiestas.

socialize, -ise ['səʊʃəlaɪz] *vi*: **to ~ (with)** alternar (con).

socialized medicine ['səʊʃəlaɪzd-] *n Am asistencia médica estatal financiada mediante impuestos*.

social life *n* vida *f* social.

socially ['səʊʃəlɪ] *adv* **-1.** [towards society] socialmente. **-2.** [outside business] fuera del trabajo.

social order *n* orden *m* social.

social science *n* **-1.** (U) [in general] ciencias *fpl* sociales. **-2.** [individual science] ciencia *f* social.

social security *n* seguridad *f* social.

social services *npl* servicios *mpl* sociales.

social studies *npl* estudios *mpl* sociales.

social work *n* (U) trabajo *m* social.

social worker *n* asistente *m*, -ta *f* social.

society [sə'saɪətɪ] (*pl* **-ies**) *n* **-1.** [gen] sociedad *f*. **-2.** [club, organization] sociedad *f*, asociación *f*.

socioeconomic ['səʊsɪəʊ,iːkə'nɒmɪk] *adj* socioeconómico(ca).

sociological [,səʊsjə'lɒdʒɪkl] *adj* sociológico(ca).

sociologist [,səʊsɪ'ɒlədʒɪst] *n* sociólogo *m*, -ga *f*.

sociology [,səʊsɪ'ɒlədʒɪ] *n* sociología *f*.

sock [sɒk] *n* calcetín *m*; **to pull one's ~s up** *inf* hacer un esfuerzo.

socket ['sɒkɪt] *n* **-1.** ELEC enchufe *m*. **-2.** [of eye] cuenca *f*; [of joint] glena *f*.

sod [sɒd] *n* **-1.** [of turf] tepe *m*. **-2.** *v inf* [person] cabroncete *m*.

soda ['səʊdə] *n* **-1.** [gen] soda *f*. **-2.** *Am* [fizzy drink] gaseosa *f*.

soda syphon *n* sifón *m*.

soda water *n* soda *f*.

sodden ['sɒdn] *adj* empapado(da).

sodium ['səʊdɪəm] *n* sodio *m*.

sofa ['səʊfə] *n* sofá *m*.

sofa bed *n* sofá cama *m*.

Sofia ['səʊfjə] *n* Sofía.

soft [sɒft] *adj* **-1.** [pliable, not stiff, not strict] blando(da). **-2.** [smooth, gentle, not bright] suave. **-3.** [caring - person] de buen corazón.

soft-boiled *adj* pasado(da) por agua.

soft drink *n* refresco *m*.

soft drugs *npl* drogas *fpl* blandas.

soften ['sɒfn] ◇ *vt* suavizar. ◇ *vi* **-1.** [substance] ablandarse. **-2.** [expression] suavizarse, dulcificarse.

◆ **soften up** *vt sep inf* ablandar.

softener ['sɒfnər] *n* suavizante *m*.

soft focus *n* difuminado *m*; **in ~** en difuminado.

soft furnishings *npl Br* (tela *f* para) tapicería *f*.

softhearted [,sɒft'hɑ:tɪd] *adj* de buen corazón.

softly ['sɒftlɪ] *adv* **-1.** [gently] con delicadeza. **-2.** [quietly, not brightly] suavemente. **-3.** [leniently] con indulgencia.

softness ['sɒftnɪs] *n* **-1.** [gen] suavidad *f*. **-2.** [pliability] blandura *f*. **-3.** [lenience] indulgencia *f*.

soft-pedal *vi inf*: **to ~ on sthg** quitar importancia a algo.

soft sell *n inf sistema de venta en el que no se presiona al posible comprador*.

soft-spoken *adj* de voz suave.

soft toy *n* muñeco *m* de peluche.

software ['sɒftweər] *n* COMPUT software *m*.

software package *n* COMPUT paquete *m* de software.

softwood ['sɒftwʊd] *n* [wood] madera *f* blanda; [tree] árbol *m* de madera blanca.

softy ['sɒftɪ] (*pl* **-ies**) *n inf* **-1.** *pej* [weak person] blandengue *m y f*. **-2.** [sensitive person] blando *m*, -da *f*.

soggy ['sɒgɪ] (*compar* **-ier**, *superl* **-iest**) *adj inf* empapado(da).

soil [sɔɪl] ◇ *n* **-1.** [earth] tierra *f*, suelo *m*. **-2.** *fig* [territory] territorio *m*. ◇ *vt* ensuciar.

soiled [sɔɪld] *adj* sucio(cia).

solace ['sɒləs] *n literary* consuelo *m*.

solar ['səʊlər] *adj* solar.

solarium [sə'leərɪəm] (*pl* **-riums** OR **-ria** [-rɪə]) *n* solarium *m*.

solar panel *n* panel *m* solar.

solar plexus [-'pleksəs] *n*: **the ~** el plexo solar.

solar system *n*: **the Solar System** el sistema solar.

sold [səʊld] *pt & pp* → **sell**.

solder ['səʊldər] ◇ *n* (U) soldadura *f*. ◇ *vt* soldar.

soldering iron ['səʊldərɪŋ-] *n* soldador *m*.

soldier ['səʊldʒər] *n* soldado *m*.

◆ **soldier on** *vi Br* seguir adelante a pesar de las dificultades.

sold-out *adj* agotado(da); **the theatre was ~** se agotaron las localidades.

sole [səʊl] (*pl sense 2 only inv* OR **-s**) ◇ *adj* **-1.** [only] único(ca). **-2.** [exclusive] exclusivo(va). ◇ *n* **-1.** [of foot] planta *f*; [of shoe] suela *f*. **-2.** [fish] lenguado *m*.

solely ['səʊllɪ] *adv* únicamente.

solemn ['sɒləm] *adj* solemne.

solemnly ['sɒləmlɪ] *adv* solemnemente, con solemnidad.

sole-trader *n Br* comercio *m* individual.

solicit [sə'lɪsɪt] ◇ *vt fml* [request] solicitar. ◇ *vi* [prostitute] ofrecer sus servicios.

solicitor [sə'lɪsɪtər] *n Br* JUR *abogado que lleva casos administrativos y legales, pero que no acude a los tribunales superiores*.

solicitous [sə'lɪsɪtəs] *adj fml* solícito(ta); **~ about** OR **of** OR **for** preocupado(da) por.

solid ['sɒlɪd] ◇ *adj* **-1.** [gen] sólido(da). **-2.** [rock, wood, gold] macizo(za). **-3.** [reliable, respectable] serio(ria), formal. **-4.** [without interruption] sin interrupción. ◇ *n* sólido *m*.

solidarity [,sɒlɪ'dærətɪ] *n* solidaridad *f*.

solid fuel *n* combustible *m* sólido.

solidify [sə'lɪdɪfaɪ] (*pt & pp* **-ied**) *vi* solidificarse.

solidly ['sɒlɪdlɪ] *adv* **-1.** [sturdily] sólidamente. **-2.** [completely, definitely] enteramente. **-3.** [without interruption] sin interrupción.

soliloquy [sə'lɪləkwɪ] (*pl* **-ies**) *n* soliloquio *m*.

solitaire [,sɒlɪ'teər] *n* **-1.** [jewel, board game] solitario *m*. **-2.** *Am* [card game] solitario *m*.

solitary ['sɒlɪtrɪ] *adj* solitario(ria).

solitary confinement *n*: **to be in ~** estar incomunicado(da) (en la cárcel).

solitude ['sɒlɪtjuːd] *n* soledad *f*.

solo ['səʊləʊ] (*pl* **-s**) ◇ *adj & adv* a solas. ◇ *n* solo *m*.

soloist ['səʊləʊɪst] *n* solista *m y f*.

Solomon Islands ['sɒləmən-] *npl*: **the ~** las islas Salomón.

solstice ['sɒlstɪs] *n* solsticio *m*.

soluble ['sɒljʊbl] *adj* soluble.

solution [sə'luːʃn] *n*: **~ (to)** solución *f* (a).

solve [sɒlv] *vt* resolver.

solvency ['sɒlvənsɪ] *n* FIN solvencia *f*.

solvent ['sɒlvənt] ◇ *adj* FIN solvente. ◇ *n* disolvente *m*.

solvent abuse [-ə'bjuːs] *n* aspiración por la nariz de gomas o colas.

Som. (*abbr of* **Somerset**) *condado inglés.*

Somali [sə'mɑːlɪ] ◇ *adj* somalí. ◇ *n* **-1.** [person] somalí *m y f.* **-2.** [language] somalí *m.*

Somalia [sə'mɑːlɪə] *n* Somalia.

sombre *Br,* **somber** *Am* ['sɒmbəʳ] *adj* sombrío(a).

some [sʌm] ◇ *adj* **-1.** [a certain amount, number of]: **would you like ~ coffee?** ¿quieres café?; **give me ~ money** dame algo de dinero; **there are ~ good articles in it** tiene algunos artículos buenos; **I bought ~ socks** [one pair] me compré unos calcetines; [more than one pair] me compré calcetines. **-2.** [fairly large number or quantity of]: **I've known him for ~ years** lo conozco desde hace bastantes años; **we still have ~ way to go** nos queda un buen trecho todavía; **I had ~ difficulty getting here** me costó lo mío llegar aquí. **-3.** (*contrastive use*) [certain] algunos(as), ciertos(as); **~ jobs are better paid than others** algunos trabajos están mejor pagados que otros; **~ people say that ...** los hay que dicen que .... **-4.** [in imprecise statements] algún(una); **there must be ~ mistake** debe haber un OR algún error; **she married ~ writer or other** se casó con no sé qué escritor. **-5.** *inf* [very good] menudo(da); **that's ~ car he's got** ¡menudo coche tiene!; *iro:* **~ help you are!** [not very good] ¡menuda OR valiente ayuda me das! ◇ *pron* **-1.** [a certain amount]: **can I have ~?** [money, milk, coffee etc] ¿puedo coger un poco?; **I've already had ~** ya he tomado; **~ of** parte de. **-2.** [a certain number] algunos(as); **can I have ~?** [books, potatoes etc] ¿puedo coger algunos?; **~ (of them) left early** algunos se fueron temprano; **~ say he lied** hay quien dice que mintió. ◇ *adv* unos(as); **there were ~ 7,000 people there** había unas 7.000 personas.

somebody ['sʌmbədɪ] ◇ *pron* alguien. ◇ *n:* **he thinks he's ~** se cree que es alguien.

someday ['sʌmdeɪ] *adv* algún día.

somehow ['sʌmhaʊ], **someway** *Am* ['sʌmweɪ] *adv* **-1.** [by some action] de alguna manera. **-2.** [for some reason] por alguna razón.

someone ['sʌmwʌn] *pron* alguien; **~ or other** alguien, no sé quien.

someplace *Am inf* = **somewhere**.

somersault ['sʌməsɔːlt] ◇ *n* [in air] salto *m* mortal; [on ground] voltereta *f.* ◇ *vi* [in air] dar un salto mortal; [on ground] dar una voltereta.

something ['sʌmθɪŋ] ◇ *pron* algo; **or ~** *inf* o algo así; **that's ~** [at least] ya es algo; **to be really ~** ser de lo que no hay, ser increíble; **she's ~ of a poet** ella es un poco poeta; **it came as ~ of a surprise to me** me pilló un poco por sorpresa. ◇ *adv:* **~ like, ~ in the region of** algo así como.

sometime ['sʌmtaɪm] ◇ *adj* antiguo(gua). ◇ *adv* en algún momento; **~ next week** durante la semana que viene.

sometimes ['sʌmtaɪmz] *adv* a veces.

someway *Am* = **somehow**.

somewhat ['sʌmwɒt] *adv fml* algo.

somewhere *Br* ['sʌmweəʳ], **someplace** *Am* ['sʌmpleɪs] *adv* **-1.** [unknown place - with verbs of position] en alguna parte; [- with verbs of movement] a alguna parte; **it's ~ else** está en otra parte; **shall we go ~ else?** ¿nos vamos a otra parte? **-2.** [in approximations]: **~ between five and ten** entre cinco y diez; **~ around 20** alrededor de 20. **-3.** *phr:* **to be getting ~** avanzar, ir a alguna parte.

son [sʌn] *n* hijo *m.*

sonar ['səʊnɑːʳ] *n* sonar *m.*

sonata [sə'nɑːtə] *n* sonata *f.*

song [sɒŋ] *n* **-1.** [gen] canción *f;* **they burst into ~** se pusieron a cantar; **to make a ~ and dance about sthg** *inf* armar la de Dios es Cristo sobre algo. **-2.** [of bird] canto *m.* **-3.** *phr:* **for a ~** *inf* [cheaply] por cuatro cuartos.

songbook ['sɒŋbʊk] *n* cancionero *m.*

sonic ['sɒnɪk] *adj* sónico(ca).

sonic boom *n* estampido *m* OR boom *m* sónico.

son-in-law (*pl* **sons-in-law** OR **son-in-laws**) *n* yerno *m.*

sonnet ['sɒnɪt] *n* soneto *m.*

sonny ['sʌnɪ] (*pl* **-ies**) *n inf* hijo *m,* chico *m.*

soon [suːn] *adv* pronto; **how ~ will it be ready?** ¿para cuándo estará listo?; **~ after** poco después; **as ~ as** tan pronto como; **as ~ as possible** cuanto antes; **I'd just as ~ ...** igual me daría ... , no me importaría ....

sooner ['suːnəʳ] *adv* **-1.** [in time] antes; **no ~ did he arrive than ...** apenas había llegado cuando ...; **~ or later** (más) tarde o (más) temprano; **the ~ the better** cuanto antes mejor. **-2.** [expressing preference]: **I'd ~ ...** preferiría ....

soot [sʊt] *n* hollín *m.*

soothe [suːð] *vt* **-1.** [pain] aliviar. **-2.** [nerves etc] calmar.

soothing ['suːðɪŋ] *adj* **-1.** [pain-relieving] calmante. **-2.** [calming] sedante, relajante.

525

sooty ['sʊtɪ] (*compar* **-ier**, *superl* **-iest**) *adj* cubierto(ta) de hollín.

sop [sɒp] *n pej*: ~ **(to)** compensación *f* de poca monta (para).

SOP (*abbr of* **standard operating procedure**) *n procedimiento habitual*.

sophisticated [sə'fɪstɪkeɪtɪd] *adj* **-1.** [gen] sofisticado(da). **-2.** [intelligent] inteligente.

sophistication [sə,fɪstɪ'keɪʃn] *n* **-1.** [gen] sofisticación *f*. **-2.** [intelligence] inteligencia *f*.

sophomore ['sɒfəmɔːʳ] *n Am* estudiante *m* y *f* del segundo curso.

soporific [,sɒpə'rɪfɪk] *adj* soporífico(ca).

sopping ['sɒpɪŋ] *adj*: ~ **(wet)** chorreando.

soppy ['sɒpɪ] (*compar* **-ier**, *superl* **-iest**) *adj inf pej* sentimentaloide.

soprano [sə'prɑːnəʊ] (*pl* **-s**) *n* soprano *f*.

sorbet ['sɔːbeɪ] *n* sorbete *m*.

sorcerer ['sɔːsərəʳ] *n* mago *m*, **-ga** *f*, brujo *m*, **-ja** *f*.

sordid ['sɔːdɪd] **-1.** [immoral] obsceno(na). **-2.** [dirty, unpleasant] sórdido(da).

sore [sɔːʳ] ◇ *adj* **-1.** [painful] dolorido(da); **to have a** ~ **throat** tener dolor de garganta. **-2.** *Am* [upset] enfadado(da). **-3.** *literary* [dire, great] enorme. ◇ *n* llaga *f*, úlcera *f*.

sorely ['sɔːlɪ] *adv literary* enormemente.

sorority [sə'rɒrətɪ] *n Am club de estudiantes universitarias*.

sorrel ['sɒrəl] *n* acedera *f*.

sorrow ['sɒrəʊ] *n* pesar *m*, pena *f*.

sorrowful ['sɒrəfʊl] *adj* apesadumbrado(da), apenado(da).

sorry ['sɒrɪ] (*compar* **-ier**, *superl* **-iest**) ◇ *adj* **-1.** [expressing apology]: **to be** ~ **about sthg** sentir OR lamentar algo; **I'm** ~ **for what I did** siento lo que hice; **I'm** ~ lo siento; **I'm** ~ **if I'm disturbing you** OR **to disturb you** siento molestarte. **-2.** [expressing shame, disappointment]: **to be** ~ **that** sentir que; **we were** ~ **about his resignation** sentimos que dimitiera; **to be** ~ **for** arrepentirse de; **we're** ~ **to see you go** sentimos que te vayas. **-3.** [expressing regret]: **I'm** ~ **to have to say that ...** siento tener que decir que .... **-4.** [expressing pity]: **to be** OR **feel** ~ **for sb** sentir lástima por alguien; **to be** OR **feel** ~ **for o.s.** sentir lástima de uno mismo (una misma). **-5.** [expressing polite disagreement]: **I'm** ~, **but ...** perdón, pero .... **-6.** [poor, pitiable] lamentable, penoso(sa). ◇ *interj* **-1.** [pardon]: ~? ¿perdón? **-2.** [to correct oneself]: **a girl,** ~, **a woman** una chica, perdón, una mujer.

sort [sɔːt] ◇ *n* tipo *m*, clase *f*; **all** ~**s of** todo tipo de; ~ **of** más o menos, así así; **a** ~ **of** una especie de. ◇ *vt* clasificar.

◆ **sorts** *npl*: **a lawyer of** ~**s** una especie de abogado; **to be out of** ~**s** estar bajo(ja) de tono.

◆ **sort out** *vt sep* **-1.** [classify] clasificar. **-2.** [solve] solucionar, resolver.

sortie ['sɔːtiː] *n* salida *f*.

sorting office ['sɔːtɪŋ-] *n* oficina de clasificación del correo.

sort-out *n Br inf* limpieza *f* a fondo.

SOS (*abbr of* **save our souls**) *n* SOS *m*.

so-so *adj & adv inf* así así.

soufflé ['suːfleɪ] *n* suflé *m*.

sought [sɔːt] *pt & pp* → **seek**.

sought-after *adj* solicitado(da), buscado(da).

soul [səʊl] *n* **-1.** [gen] alma *f*; **she's a good** ~ es buena persona; **poor** ~! ¡pobrecito! **-2.** [of nation etc] espíritu *m*. **-3.** [music] música *f* soul.

soul-destroying [-dɪ,strɔɪɪŋ] *adj* desmoralizador(ra).

soulful ['səʊlfʊl] *adj* lleno(na) de sentimiento.

soulless ['səʊllɪs] *adj* desangelado(da).

soul mate *n* alma *f* gemela.

soul music *n* música *f* soul.

soul-searching *n* (U) examen *f* de conciencia.

sound [saʊnd] ◇ *adj* **-1.** [healthy] sano(na). **-2.** [sturdy] sólido(da). **-3.** [reliable] fiable, seguro(ra). ◇ *adv*: **to be** ~ **asleep** estar profundamente dormido(da). ◇ *n* **-1.** [gen] sonido *m*. **-2.** [particular noise] ruido *m*. **-3.** [impression]: **I don't like the** ~ **of it** no me gusta nada; **by the** ~ **of it** por lo que parece. ◇ *vt* [bell etc] hacer sonar, tocar. ◇ *vi* **-1.** [gen] sonar. **-2.** [give impression]: **it** ~**s like fun** suena divertido; **he** ~**s like a nice man** parece un hombre simpático.

◆ **sound out** *vt sep*: **to** ~ **sb out (on** OR **about)** sondear a alguien (sobre).

sound barrier *n* barrera *f* del sonido.

sound bite *n* frase *f* lapidaria (*pronunciada por políticos etc en los medios de comunicación con intenciones efectistas*).

sound effects *npl* efectos *mpl* sonoros.

sounding ['saʊndɪŋ] *n* NAUT sondeo *m* marino.

◆ **soundings** *npl fig* [investigations] sondeos *mpl*.

sounding board *n lit & fig* caja *f* de resonancia.

soundly ['saʊndlɪ] *adv* **-1.** [severely - beat] totalmente. **-2.** [deeply] profundamente.

soundness ['saʊndnɪs] *n* [reliability] solidez *f*.

soundproof ['saʊndpruːf] *adj* insonoriza-do(da).

soundtrack ['saʊndtræk] *n* banda *f* sonora.

sound wave *n* onda *f* sonora.

soup [suːp] *n* [thick] sopa *f*; [clear] caldo *m*, consomé *m*.
◆ **soup up** *vt sep inf* **-1.** [car] trucar. **-2.** [book etc] emperifollar.

soup kitchen *n* comedor *m* de beneficiencia.

soup plate *n* plato *m* hondo OR sopero.

soup spoon *n* cuchara *f* sopera.

sour [saʊəʳ] ◇ *adj* **-1.** [acidic] ácido(da). **-2.** [milk, person, reply] agrio(gria). **-3.** *phr*: **to go** OR **turn** ~ *fig* [evening, plans] irse al traste; [relationship] agriarse. ◇ *vt* agriar. ◇ *vi* agriarse.

source [sɔːs] *n* **-1.** [gen] fuente *f*. **-2.** [cause] origen *m*. **-3.** [of river] nacimiento *m*.

sour cream *n* nata *f* agria.

sour grapes *n* (*U*) *inf*: **it's** ~! ¡están verdes!

sourness ['saʊənɪs] *n* **-1.** [acidity] acidez *f*. **-2.** [of milk] agrura *f*. **-3.** [of persons, relations] acritud *f*.

south [saʊθ] ◇ *n* **-1.** [direction] sur *m*. **-2.** [region]: **the South** el sur. ◇ *adj* del sur. ◇ *adv*: ~ **(of)** al sur (de).

South Africa *n*: **(the Republic of)** ~ (la república de) Suráfrica.

South African ◇ *adj* surafricano(na). ◇ *n* [person] surafricano *m*, -na *f*.

South America *n* Sudamérica.

South American ◇ *adj* sudamericano(na). ◇ *n* [person] sudamericano *m*, -na *f*.

southbound ['saʊθbaʊnd] *adj* con rumbo al sur.

South Carolina [-ˌkærəˈlaɪnə] *n* Carolina del Sur.

South Dakota *n* Dakota del Sur.

southeast [ˌsaʊθˈiːst] ◇ *n* **-1.** [direction] sudeste *m*. **-2.** [region]: **the Southeast** el sudeste. ◇ *adj* del sudeste. ◇ *adv*: ~ **(of)** hacia el sudeste (de).

Southeast Asia *n* el sureste asiático.

southeasterly [ˌsaʊθˈiːstəlɪ] *adj* del sudeste; **in a** ~ **direction** hacia el sudeste.

southeastern [ˌsaʊθˈiːstən] *adj* del sudeste.

southerly ['sʌðəlɪ] *adj* del sur; **in a** ~ **direction** hacia el sur.

southern ['sʌðən] *adj* del sur, sureño(ña).

Southern Africa *n* África austral.

Southerner ['sʌðənəʳ] *n* sureño *m*, -ña *f*, meridional *m y f*.

South Korea *n* Corea del Sur.

South Korean ◇ *adj* surcoreano(na). ◇ *n* surcoreano *m*, -na *f*.

South Pole *n*: **the** ~ el polo Sur.

South Vietnam *n* (el) Vietnam del Sur.

South Vietnamese ◇ *adj* survietnamita. ◇ *n* survietnamita *m y f*.

southward ['saʊθwəd] ◇ *adj* sur. ◇ *adv* = **southwards**.

southwards ['saʊθwədz] *adv* hacia el sur.

southwest [ˌsaʊθˈwest] ◇ *n* **-1.** [direction] suroeste *m*. **-2.** [region]: **the Southwest** el suroeste. ◇ *adj* del suroeste. ◇ *adv*: ~ **(of)** hacia el suroeste (de).

southwesterly [ˌsaʊθˈwestəlɪ] ◇ *adj* del suroeste; **in a** ~ **direction** hacia el suroeste.

southwestern [ˌsaʊθˈwestən] *adj* del suroeste.

South Yemen *n* (el) Yemen del Sur.

souvenir [ˌsuːvəˈnɪəʳ] *n* recuerdo *m*.

sou'wester [saʊˈwestəʳ] *n* [hat] sueste *m*.

sovereign ['sɒvrɪn] ◇ *adj* soberano(na). ◇ *n* **-1.** [ruler] soberano *m*, -na *f*. **-2.** [coin] soberano *m*.

sovereignty ['sɒvrɪntɪ] *n* soberanía *f*.

soviet ['səʊvɪət] *n* soviet *m*.
◆ **Soviet** ◇ *adj* soviético(ca). ◇ *n* [person] soviético *m*, -ca *f*.

Soviet Union *n*: **the (former)** ~ la (antigua) Unión Soviética.

sow[1] [səʊ] (*pt* **-ed**, *pp* **sown** OR **-ed**) *vt lit* & *fig* sembrar.

sow[2] [saʊ] *n* cerda *f*, puerca *f*.

sown [səʊn] *pp* → **sow**[1].

sox [sɒks] → **bobby sox**.

soya ['sɔɪə] *n* soja *f*.

soy(a) bean ['sɔɪ(ə)-] *n* semilla *f* de soja.

soy sauce [sɔɪ-] *n* salsa *f* de soja.

sozzled ['sɒzld] *adj Br inf* trompa, mamado(da).

spa [spɑː] *n* balneario *m*.

space [speɪs] ◇ *n* espacio *m*; **to stare into** ~ tener la mirada perdida. ◇ *comp* espacial. ◇ *vt* espaciar.
◆ **space out** *vt sep* [arrange with spaces between] espaciar.

space age *n*: **the** ~ la era espacial.
◆ **space-age** *adj inf* de la era espacial.

space bar *n* [on computer, typewriter] espaciador *m*.

space capsule *n* cápsula *f* espacial.

spacecraft ['speɪskrɑːft] (*pl inv*) *n* nave *f* espacial, astronave *f*.

spaceman ['speɪsmæn] (*pl* **-men** [-men]) *n* astronauta *m*.

space probe *n* sonda *f* espacial.

spaceship ['speɪsʃɪp] *n* nave *f* espacial, astronave *f*.

space shuttle *n* transbordador *m* espacial.

space station *n* estación *f* espacial.

spacesuit ['speɪssuːt] *n* traje *m* espacial.

spacewoman ['speɪsˌwʊmən] (*pl* **-women** [-ˌwɪmɪn]) *n* astronauta *f*.

spacing ['speɪsɪŋ] *n* TYPO espacio *m*.

spacious ['speɪʃəs] *adj* espacioso(sa).

spade [speɪd] *n* **-1.** [tool] pala *f*. **-2.** [playing card] pica *f*.
◆ **spades** *npl* picas *fpl*; **the six of** ~**s** el seis de picas.

spadework ['speɪdwɜːk] *n inf* trabajo *m* previo.

spaghetti [spə'getɪ] *n* (*U*) espaguetis *mpl*.

Spain [speɪn] *n* España.

span [spæn] (*pt* & *pp* **-ned**, *cont* **-ning**) ◇ *pt* → **spin**. ◇ *n* **-1.** [in time] lapso *m*, período *m*. **-2.** [range] gama *f*. **-3.** [of wings] envergadura *f*. **-4.** [of bridge, arch] ojo *m*. ◇ *vt* **-1.** [in time] abarcar. **-2.** [subj: bridge etc] cruzar, atravesar.

spandex ['spændeks] *n Am* fibra *f* de poliuretano.

spangled ['spæŋgld] *adj literary*: ~ **(with)** adornado(da) (con).

Spaniard ['spænjəd] *n* español *m*, -la *f*.

spaniel ['spænjəl] *n* perro *m* de aguas.

Spanish ['spænɪʃ] ◇ *adj* español(la). ◇ *n* [language] español *m*, castellano *m*. ◇ *npl* [people]: **the** ~ los españoles.

Spanish America *n* Hispanoamérica.

Spanish American ◇ *adj* **-1.** [in US] hispano(na). **-2.** [in Latin America] hispanoamericano(na). ◇ *n* **-1.** [in US] hispano *m*, -na *f*. **-2.** [in Latin America] hispanoamericano *m*, -na *f*.

spank [spæŋk] ◇ *n* azote *m*, guantazo *m* (*en las nalgas*). ◇ *vt* dar unos azotes a, zurrar.

spanner ['spænər] *n* llave *f* inglesa.

spar [spaːr] (*pt* & *pp* **-red**, *cont* **-ring**) ◇ *n* palo *m*, verga *f*. ◇ *vi* **-1.** BOXING: **to** ~ **(with)** entrenarse (con). **-2.** [verbally]: **to** ~ **(with)** discutir amistosamente (con).

spare [speər] ◇ *adj* **-1.** [surplus] de sobra. **-2.** [free - chair, time] libre.
◇ *n* **-1.** [spare object] (pieza *f* de) recambio *m*, repuesto *m*. **-2.** *inf* [tyre] neumático *m* de recambio. **-3.** *inf* [part] pieza *f* de recambio OR repuesto.
◇ *vt* **-1.** [time] conceder; [money] dejar; **we can't** ~ **any time/money** no tenemos

tiempo/dinero; **to** ~ **de sobra. -2.** [not harm - person, life] perdonar; [- company, city] salvar. **-3.** [not use, not take]: **to** ~ **no expense/effort** no escatimar gastos/esfuerzos. **-4.** [save from]: **to** ~ **sb sthg** ahorrarle a alguien algo.

spare part *n* AUT pieza *f* de recambio OR repuesto, refacción *f Amer*.

spare room *n* habitación *f* de invitados.

spare time *n* tiempo *m* libre.

spare tyre *n* **-1.** AUT neumático *m* de recambio. **-2.** *hum* [fat waist] michelines *mpl*.

spare wheel *n* rueda *f* de recambio.

sparing ['speərɪŋ] *adj*: ~ **with** OR **of** parco(ca) en.

sparingly ['speərɪŋlɪ] *adv* con moderación.

spark [spaːk] ◇ *n lit* & *fig* chispa *f*. ◇ *vt* provocar.

sparking plug *Br* ['spaːkɪŋ-] = **spark plug**.

sparkle ['spaːkl] ◇ *n* (*U*) **-1.** [of diamond] destello *m*; [of eyes] brillo *m*. **-2.** [style] brillo *m*, estilo *m*. ◇ *vi* **-1.** [star, jewels] centellear; [eyes] brillar. **-2.** *fig* [person, work] brillar, ser brillante.

sparkler ['spaːklər] *n* [firework] bengala *f*.

sparkling wine ['spaːklɪŋ-] *n* vino *m* espumoso.

spark plug *n* bujía *f*.

sparrow ['spærəʊ] *n* gorrión *m*.

sparse ['spaːs] *adj* escaso(sa).

spartan ['spaːtn] *adj* espartano(na).

spasm ['spæzm] *n* **-1.** MED [state] espasmo *m*. **-2.** MED [attack] acceso *m*. **-3.** [of emotion] ataque *m*.

spasmodic [spæz'mɒdɪk] *adj* espasmódico(ca).

spastic ['spæstɪk] MED ◇ *adj* espástico(ca). ◇ *n* espástico *m*, -ca *f*.

spat [spæt] *pt* & *pp* → **spit**.

spate [speɪt] *n* cadena *f*, serie *f*.

spatial ['speɪʃl] *adj fml* espacial.

spatter ['spætər] ◇ *vt* salpicar. ◇ *vi*: **to** ~ **on sthg** salpicar algo.

spatula ['spætjʊlə] *n* espátula *f*.

spawn [spɔːn] ◇ *n* (*U*) huevas *fpl*. ◇ *vt fig* engendrar. ◇ *vi* desovar, frezar.

spay [speɪ] *vt* sacar los ovarios a (*un animal*).

SPCA (*abbr of* **Society for the Prevention of Cruelty to Animals**) *n* sociedad estadounidense protectora de animales, ≃ SPA *f*.

SPCC (*abbr of* **Society for the Prevention of Cruelty to Children**) *n* organización estadounidense para la prevención de malos tratos a los niños.

speak [spiːk] (*pt* **spoke**, *pp* **spoken**) ◇ *vt* **-1.** [say] decir; **to ~ ill of** hablar mal de. **-2.** [language] hablar. ◇ *vi* hablar; **to ~ to** OR **with** hablar con; **to ~ to sb (about)** hablar con alguien (de); **to ~ about** hablar de; **to ~ to sb (on sthg)** [give speech] hablar ante alguien (sobre algo); **to ~ well** OR **highly of** hablar bien de; **nobody/nothing to ~ of** nadie/nada especial.

◆ **so to speak** *adv* como quien dice, por así decirlo.

◆ **speak for** *vt fus* [represent] hablar en nombre de; **~ for yourself!** ¡eso lo dirás tú!; **it ~s for itself** es evidente.

◆ **speak out** *vi*: **to ~ out (against/in favour of)** hablar claro (en contra de/a favor de).

◆ **speak up** *vi* **-1.** [speak out]: **to ~ up for** salir en defensa de. **-2.** [speak louder] hablar más alto.

speaker ['spiːkəʳ] *n* **-1.** [person talking] persona *f* que habla. **-2.** [person making a speech - at meal etc] orador *m*, -ra *f*; [- at conference] conferenciante *m y f*. **-3.** [of a language] hablante *m y f*. **-4.** [of radio] altavoz *m*.

speaking ['spiːkɪŋ] ◇ *adv*: **generally/legally ~** desde una perspectiva general/legal; **~ as** [in the position of] hablando como; **~ of** [on the subject of] hablando de. ◇ *n* oratoria *f*.

speaking clock *n Br* información *f* horaria.

spear [spɪəʳ] ◇ *n* [gen] lanza *f*; [for hunting] jabalina *f*. ◇ *vt* [animal] atravesar; [piece of food] pinchar.

spearhead ['spɪəhed] ◇ *n* punta *f* de lanza, abanderado *m*, -da *f*. ◇ *vt* encabezar.

spec [spek] *n Br inf*: **to buy on ~** comprar sin garantías; **to go on ~** ir sin haber reservado con anterioridad.

special ['speʃl] ◇ *adj* **-1.** [gen] especial. **-2.** [particular, individual] particular. ◇ *n* **-1.** [on menu]: **today's ~** plato *m* del día. **-2.** [TV programme] programa *m* especial.

special agent *n* agente *m y f* especial.

special constable *n Br* guardia *m y f* auxiliar.

special correspondent *n* enviado *m*, -da *f* especial.

special delivery *n* correo *m* urgente.

special effects *npl* efectos *mpl* especiales.

specialist ['speʃəlɪst] ◇ *adj* [doctor] especialista; [literature] especializado(da). ◇ *n* especialista *m y f*.

speciality [ˌspeʃɪ'ælətɪ] (*pl* **-ies**), **specialty** *Am* ['speʃltɪ] (*pl* **-ies**) *n* especialidad *f*.

specialize, -ise ['speʃəlaɪz] *vi*: **to ~ (in)** especializarse (en).

specially ['speʃəlɪ] *adv* especialmente.

special offer *n* oferta *f* especial.

special school *n* escuela *f* especial (*para disminuidos físicos o psíquicos*).

specialty *Am* = **speciality**.

species ['spiːʃiːz] (*pl inv*) *n* especie *f*.

specific [spə'sɪfɪk] *adj* **-1.** [particular] determinado(da). **-2.** [precise] específico(ca). **-3.** [unique]: **~ to** específico(ca) de.

◆ **specifics** *npl* datos *mpl* específicos.

specifically [spə'sɪfɪklɪ] *adv* **-1.** [particularly] expresamente. **-2.** [precisely] específicamente.

specification [ˌspesɪfɪ'keɪʃn] *n* [plan] especificación *f*.

◆ **specifications** *npl* [of machine etc] datos *mpl* técnicos, descripción *f* técnica.

specify ['spesɪfaɪ] (*pt & pp* **-ied**) *vt*: **to ~ (that)** especificar (que).

specimen ['spesɪmən] *n* **-1.** [example] espécimen *m*, ejemplar *m*. **-2.** [sample] muestra *f*.

specimen copy *n* ejemplar *m* de muestra.

specimen signature *n* muestra *f* de firma.

speck [spek] *n* **-1.** [small stain] manchita *f*. **-2.** [small particle] mota *f*.

speckled ['spekld] *adj*: **~ (with)** moteado(da) (de), con manchas (de).

specs [speks] *npl Br inf* [glasses] gafas *fpl*.

spectacle ['spektəkl] *n* **-1.** [gen] espectáculo *m*. **-2.** [person] facha *f*.

◆ **spectacles** *npl Br* gafas *fpl*.

spectacular [spek'tækjʊləʳ] ◇ *adj* espectacular. ◇ *n* espectáculo *m*.

spectate [spek'teɪt] *vi* asistir como espectador.

spectator [spek'teɪtəʳ] *n* espectador *m*, -ra *f*.

spectator sport *n* deporte *m* de masas.

spectre *Br*, **specter** *Am* ['spektəʳ] *n lit & fig* fantasma *m*.

spectrum ['spektrəm] (*pl* **-tra** [-trə]) *n* **-1.** [gen] espectro *m*. **-2.** *fig* [variety] gama *f*, abanico *m*.

speculate ['spekjʊleɪt] *vi* especular.

speculation [spekjʊ'leɪʃn] *n* especulación *f*.

speculative ['spekjʊlətɪv] *adj* especulativo(va).

speculator ['spekjʊleɪtəʳ] *n* FIN especulador *m*, -ra *f*.

sped [sped] *pt & pp* → **speed**.

speech [spiːtʃ] *n* **-1.** [gen] habla *f*. **-2.** [formal talk] discurso *m*; **to give** OR **make a ~ (on sthg to sb)** pronunciar un discurso (sobre algo a alguien). **-3.** THEATRE parlamento *m*. **-4.** [manner of speaking] manera *f* de hablar. **-5.** [dialect] dialecto *m*, habla *f*.

speech day *n Br* día *m* de la entrega de premios.

speech impediment *n* defecto *m* en el habla.

speechless ['spiːtʃlɪs] *adj*: **to be ~ (with)** enmudecer (de).

speech processing *n* tratamiento *m* de voz.

speech therapist *n* logopeda *m y f*.

speech therapy *n* logopedia *f*.

speed [spiːd] (*pt & pp* **-ed** OR **sped**) ◇ *n* **-1.** [rate of movement] velocidad *f*; **at ~ a** gran velocidad; **at top ~** a toda velocidad. **-2.** [rapidity] rapidez *f*. **-3.** [gear] marcha *f*. ◇ *vi* **-1.** [move fast]: **to ~ (along/away/by)** ir/alejarse/pasar a toda velocidad. **-2.** AUT [go too fast] conducir con exceso de velocidad.

◆ **speed up** ◇ *vt sep* [gen] acelerar; [person] meter prisa a. ◇ *vi* [gen] acelerarse; [person] darse prisa.

speedboat ['spiːdbəʊt] *n* lancha *f* motora.

speeding ['spiːdɪŋ] *n* (*U*) exceso *m* de velocidad.

speed limit *n* límite *m* de velocidad.

speedo ['spiːdəʊ] (*pl* **-s**) *n Br inf* velocímetro *m*.

speedometer [spɪ'dɒmɪtər] *n* velocímetro *m*.

speed trap *n* control *m* policial de velocidad.

speedway ['spiːdweɪ] *n* **-1.** (*U*) SPORT carreras *fpl* de moto. **-2.** *Am* [road] autopista *f*.

speedy ['spiːdɪ] (*compar* **-ier**, *superl* **-iest**) *adj* rápido(da).

speleology [ˌspiːlɪ'ɒlədʒɪ] *n fml* espeleología *f*.

spell [spel] (*Br pt & pp* **spelt** OR **-ed**, *Am pt & pp* **-ed**) ◇ *n* **-1.** [of time] temporada *f*; [of weather] racha *f*; **to go through a good/bad ~** pasar una buena/mala racha. **-2.** [enchantment] hechizo *m*; **to cast** OR **put a ~ on sb** hechizar a alguien. **-3.** [magic words] conjuro *m*. ◇ *vt* **-1.** [form by writing] deletrear. **-2.** *fig* [signify] significar. ◇ *vi* escribir correctamente.

◆ **spell out** *vt sep* **-1.** [read aloud] deletrear. **-2.** [explain]: **to ~ sthg out (for** OR **to sb)** decir algo por las claras (a alguien).

spellbound ['spelbaʊnd] *adj* hechizado(da), embelesado(da).

spelling ['spelɪŋ] *n* ortografía *f*; **~ mistake** falta *f* de ortografía.

spelt [spelt] *Br pt & pp* → **spell**.

spend [spend] (*pt & pp* **spent**) *vt* **-1.** [gen] gastar; **to ~ sthg on** gastar algo en. **-2.** [time, life] pasar.

spender ['spendər] *n* gastador *m*, -ra *f*.

spending ['spendɪŋ] *n* (*U*) gasto *m*, gastos *mpl*.

spending money *n* dinero *m* para pequeños gastos.

spending power *n* poder *m* adquisitivo.

spendthrift ['spendθrɪft] *n* derrochador *m*, -ra *f*, despilfarrador *m*, -ra *f*.

spent [spent] ◇ *pt & pp* → **spend**. ◇ *adj* [matches, ammunition] usado(da); [patience] agotado(da).

sperm [spɜːm] (*pl inv* OR **-s**) *n* esperma *m*.

spermicidal cream [ˌspɜːmɪ'saɪdl-] *n* crema *f* espermicida.

sperm whale *n* cachalote *m*.

spew [spjuː] ◇ *vt* arrojar, escupir. ◇ *vi*: **flames ~ed out of the volcano** el volcán arrojaba llamas.

sphere [sfɪər] *n* **-1.** [gen] esfera *f*. **-2.** [of people] círculo *m*.

spherical ['sferɪkl] *adj* esférico(ca).

sphincter ['sfɪŋktər] *n* esfínter *m*.

sphinx [sfɪŋks] (*pl* **-es**) *n* esfinge *f*.

spice [spaɪs] ◇ *n* **-1.** CULIN especia *f*. **-2.** *fig* [excitement] sabor *m*. ◇ *vt* **-1.** CULIN: **to ~ sthg (with)** condimentar algo (con). **-2.** *fig* [add excitement to]: **to ~ sthg (up)** dar sabor a algo.

spick-and-span [ˌspɪkən'spæn] *adj* inmaculado(da).

spicy ['spaɪsɪ] (*compar* **-ier**, *superl* **-iest**) *adj* CULIN & *fig* picante, picoso(sa) *Amer*.

spider ['spaɪdər] *n* araña *f*.

spider's web, **spiderweb** *Am* ['spaɪdəweb] *n* telaraña *f*.

spidery ['spaɪdərɪ] *adj* [handwriting] de rasgos largos y finos.

spiel [ʃpiːl] *n* rollo *m*.

spike [spaɪk] *n* **-1.** [on railing etc] punta *f*; [- on wall] clavo *m*. **-2.** [on plant] pincho *m*; [of hair] pelo *m* de punta.

◆ **spikes** *npl Br* zapatillas *fpl* con clavos.

spiky ['spaɪkɪ] (*compar* **-ier**, *superl* **-iest**) *adj* puntiagudo(da); [hair] erizado(da), en punta.

spill [spɪl] (*Br pt & pp* **spilt** OR **-ed**, *Am pt & pp* **-ed**) ◇ *vt* derramar, verter. ◇ *vi* **-1.** [flow] derramarse, verterse. **-2.** [flood out]: **to ~ out of** salir en masa de.

spillage ['spɪlɪdʒ] *n* derrame *m*.

spilt [spɪlt] *Br pt & pp* → **spill**.

spin [spɪn] (*pt* **span** OR **spun**, *pp* **spun**, *cont* **spinning**) ◇ *n* **-1.** [turn] vuelta *f*. **-2.** AERON barrena *f*. **-3.** *inf* [in car] vuelta *f*. ◇ *vt* **-1.** [cause to rotate] girar, dar vueltas a. **-2.** [clothes, washing] centrifugar. **-3.** [wool, yarn] hilar. ◇ *vi* **-1.** [rotate] girar, dar vueltas. **-2.** [feel dizzy]: **my head is spinning** me da vueltas la cabeza. **-3.** [make thread, wool, cloth] hilar.

◆ **spin out** *vt sep* [story] alargar, prolongar; [money] estirar.

spina bifida [ˌspaɪnəˈbɪfɪdə] *n* espina *f* bífida.

spinach [ˈspɪnɪdʒ] *n* (U) espinacas *fpl*.

spinal column [ˈspaɪnl-] *n* columna *f* vertebral.

spinal cord [ˈspaɪnl-] *n* médula *f* espinal.

spindle [ˈspɪndl] *n* **-1.** [machine, rod] eje *m*. **-2.** [for spinning] huso *m*.

spindly [ˈspɪndlɪ] (*compar* **-ier**, *superl* **-iest**) *adj* larguirucho(cha).

spin doctor *n pej persona encargada de las relaciones con la prensa y de manipular y filtrar la información que se le proporciona.*

spin-dry *vt Br* centrifugar.

spin-dryer *n Br* centrifugadora *f*.

spine [spaɪn] *n* **-1.** ANAT espina *f* dorsal. **-2.** [of book] lomo *m*. **-3.** [spike, prickle] espina *f*, púa *f*.

spine-chilling *adj* escalofriante, espeluznante.

spineless [ˈspaɪnlɪs] *adj* [feeble] pobre de espíritu.

spinner [ˈspɪnər] *n* [person] hilandera *f*.

spinning [ˈspɪnɪŋ] *n* hilado *m*.

spinning top *n* peonza *f*.

spin-off *n* [by-product] resultado *m* OR efecto *m* indirecto.

spinster [ˈspɪnstər] *n* soltera *f*.

spiral [ˈspaɪərəl] (*Br pt* & *pp* **-led**, *cont* **-ling**, *Am pt* & *pp* **-ed**, *cont* **-ing**) ◇ *adj* en espiral. ◇ *n* **-1.** [curve] espiral *f*. **-2.** [increase] escalada *f*. **-3.** [decrease] descenso *m* rápido. ◇ *vi* **-1.** [move in spiral curve] moverse en espiral. **-2.** [increase rapidly] subir vertiginosamente. **-3.** [decrease rapidly]: **to ~ downwards** bajar vertiginosamente.

spiral staircase *n* escalera *f* de caracol.

spire [spaɪər] *n* aguja *f*.

spirit [ˈspɪrɪt] ◇ *n* **-1.** [gen] espíritu *m*; **to enter into the ~ of** entrar OR meterse en el ambiente de. **-2.** [vigour] vigor *m*, valor *m*. ◇ *vt*: **to ~ sb in/out** meter/sacar a alguien a escondidas.

◆ **spirits** *npl* **-1.** [mood] humor *m*; **to be in high/low ~s** estar exultante/alicaído. **-2.** [alcohol] licores *mpl*.

spirited [ˈspɪrɪtɪd] *adj* animado(da), enérgico(ca).

spirit level *n* nivel *m* de burbuja de aire.

spiritual [ˈspɪrɪtʃʊəl] *adj* espiritual.

spiritualism [ˈspɪrɪtʃʊəlɪzm] *n* espiritismo *m*.

spiritualist [ˈspɪrɪtʃʊəlɪst] *n* espiritista *m y f*.

spit [spɪt] (*Br pt* & *pp* **spat**, *cont* **-ting**, *Am pt* & *pp* **spit**, *cont* **-ting**) ◇ *n* **-1.** [saliva] saliva *f*. **-2.** [skewer] asador *m*. ◇ *vi* escupir. ◇ *v impers Br* [rain lightly]: **it's spitting** está chispeando.

◆ **spit out** *vt sep lit* & *fig* escupir.

spite [spaɪt] ◇ *n* rencor *m*; **to do sthg out of/from ~** hacer algo por despecho. ◇ *vt* fastidiar, molestar.

◆ **in spite of** *prep* a pesar de; **I did it in ~ of myself** [unintentionally] lo hice muy a pesar mío.

spiteful [ˈspaɪtful] *adj* [person, behaviour] rencoroso(sa); [action, remark] malintencionado(da).

spitting image [ˈspɪtɪŋ-] *n*: **to be the ~ of** ser el vivo retrato de.

spittle [ˈspɪtl] *n* saliva *f*.

splash [splæʃ] ◇ *n* **-1.** [sound] chapoteo *m*. **-2.** [small quantity]: **a ~ of lemonade** un chorrito de limonada. **-3.** [of colour, light] mancha *f*. ◇ *vt* salpicar. ◇ *vi* **-1.** [person]: **to ~ about** OR **around** chapotear. **-2.** [water, liquid]: **to ~ on** OR **against sthg** salpicar algo.

◆ **splash out** *inf* ◇ *vt sep*: **to ~ sthg out on** gastar algo en. ◇ *vi*: **to ~ out (on sthg)** gastar un dineral (en algo).

splashdown [ˈsplæʃdaʊn] *n* amerizaje *m*.

splashguard [ˈsplæʃgɑːd] *n Am* alfombra *f* salpicadero.

splay [spleɪ] ◇ *vt* extender, estirar. ◇ *vi*: **to ~ (out)** extenderse, estirarse.

spleen [spliːn] *n* ANAT bazo *m*; *fig* [anger] cólera *f*.

splendid [ˈsplendɪd] *adj* **-1.** [marvellous] espléndido(da). **-2.** [magnificent, beautiful] magnífico(ca).

splendidly [ˈsplendɪdlɪ] *adv* **-1.** [marvellously] maravillosamente. **-2.** [magnificently] magníficamente.

splendour *Br*, **splendor** *Am* [ˈsplendər] *n* esplendor *m*.

splice [splaɪs] *vt* [rope] empalmar; [tape, film] montar.

splint [splɪnt] *n* tablilla *f*.

splinter [ˈsplɪntər] ◇ *n* [of wood] astilla *f*; [of glass, metal] fragmento *m*. ◇ *vt*: **to be ~ed** [wood] estar astillado(da); [glass, metal] estar fragmentado(da). ◇ *vi* astillarse.

splinter group *n* grupo *m* disidente.

split [splɪt] (*pt* & *pp* **split**, *cont* **-ting**) ◇ *n* **-1.** [crack - in wood] grieta *f*; [- in garment] desgarrón *m*. **-2.** [division]: **~ (in)** escisión *f* (en). **-3.** [difference]: ~ **(between)** diferencia f (entre).

◇ vt **-1.** [tear] desgarrar, rasgar; [crack] agrietar. **-2.** [break in two] partir, romper. **-3.** [party, organization] escindir. **-4.** [share] repartir, dividir; **to ~ the difference** partir la diferencia.

◇ vi **-1.** [break up - road] bifurcarse; [- object] partirse, romperse. **-2.** [party, organization] escindirse. **-3.** [wood] partirse, agrietarse; [fabric] desgarrarse, rasgarse. **-4.** Am inf [leave] largarse.

◆ **splits** npl: **to do the ~s** hacer el spagat, caer al suelo con las piernas abiertas.

◆ **split off** ◇ vt sep [break off]: **to ~ sthg off (from)** separar algo (de). ◇ vi [break off]: **to ~ off (from)** desprenderse (de).

◆ **split up** ◇ vt sep: **to ~ sthg up (into)** dividir algo (en). ◇ vi separarse.

split ends npl puntas fpl rotas.

split-level adj de dos niveles.

split pea n guisante m seco.

split personality n desdoblamiento m de personalidad.

split screen n COMPUT pantalla f partida.

split second n fracción f de segundo.

splitting ['splıtıŋ] adj [headache] insoportable.

splutter ['splʌtər] ◇ n [of person] balbuceo m. ◇ vi **-1.** [person] balbucear, farfullar. **-2.** [fire, oil] chisporrotear.

spoil [spɔɪl] (pt & pp **-ed** OR **spoilt**) vt **-1.** [ruin] estropear, echar a perder. **-2.** [child etc] mimar, regalonear Amer; **to ~ o.s.** darse un capricho.

◆ **spoils** npl botín m.

spoiled [spɔɪld] = **spoilt**.

spoilsport ['spɔɪlspɔːt] n aguafiestas m y f inv.

spoilt [spɔɪlt] ◇ pt & pp → **spoil**. ◇ adj mimado(da), consentido(da).

spoke [spəʊk] ◇ pt → **speak**. ◇ n radio m.

spoken ['spəʊkn] pp → **speak**.

spokesman ['spəʊksmən] (pl **-men** [-mən]) n portavoz m.

spokesperson ['spəʊks,pɜːsn] n portavoz m y f.

spokeswoman ['spəʊks,wʊmən] (pl **-women** [-,wɪmɪn]) n portavoz f.

sponge [spʌndʒ] (cont **spongeing** Br, **sponging** Am) ◇ n **-1.** [for cleaning, washing] esponja f. **-2.** [cake] bizcocho m. ◇ vt limpiar con una esponja. ◇ vi inf: **to ~ off** vivir a costa de.

sponge bag n Br neceser m.

sponge cake n bizcocho m.

sponge pudding n Br pudín de bizcocho hecho al baño maría.

sponger ['spʌndʒər] n inf pej gorrón m, -ona f.

spongy ['spʌndʒɪ] (compar **-ier**, superl **-iest**) adj esponjoso(sa).

sponsor ['spɒnsər] ◇ n patrocinador m, -ra f. ◇ vt **-1.** [gen] patrocinar. **-2.** [support] respaldar.

sponsored walk [,spɒnsəd-] n marcha f benéfica.

SPONSORED WALK:

Los 'sponsored walks' son marchas a pie que sirven para recaudar fondos. En ellas cada marchador dispone de una lista de personas que han aceptado donar una cierta suma de dinero por kilómetro recorrido. El término 'sponsored' se aplica también a otras actividades, deportivas o no: 'sponsored swim', 'sponsored parachute jump', etc

sponsorship ['spɒnsəʃɪp] n patrocinio m.

spontaneity [,spɒntə'neɪətɪ] n espontaneidad f.

spontaneous [spɒn'teɪnjəs] adj espontáneo(a).

spontaneously [spɒn'teɪnjəslɪ] adv espontáneamente.

spoof [spuːf] n: ~ **(of** OR **on)** parodia f (de).

spook [spuːk] vt Am asustar.

spooky ['spuːkɪ] (compar **-ier**, superl **-iest**) adj inf escalofriante, estremecedor(ra).

spool [spuːl] ◇ n [gen & COMPUT] bobina f. ◇ vi COMPUT tratar en diferido.

spoon [spuːn] ◇ n **-1.** [piece of cutlery] cuchara f. **-2.** [spoonful] cucharada f. ◇ vt: **to ~ sthg onto** OR **into** poner una cucharada de algo en.

spoon-feed vt **-1.** [feed with spoon] dar de comer con cuchara a. **-2.** fig [present in simple form] dar masticado.

spoonful ['spuːnfʊl] (pl **-s** OR **spoonsful** ['spuːnzfʊl]) n cucharada f.

sporadic [spə'rædɪk] adj esporádico(ca).

sport [spɔːt] ◇ n **-1.** [game] deporte m. **-2.** dated [cheerful person] persona f amable. ◇ vt lucir, llevar.

◆ **sports** ◇ npl Br [sports day] día m dedicado a los deportes. ◇ comp deportivo(va).

sporting ['spɔːtɪŋ] adj lit & fig deportivo(va); **to give sb a ~ chance** dar a alguien la oportunidad de ganar.

sports car n coche m deportivo.

sports day n Br día m dedicado a los deportes.

sports jacket n chaqueta f de esport.

sportsman ['spɔːtsmən] (*pl* **-men** [-mən]) *n* deportista *m*.

sportsmanship ['spɔːtsmənʃip] *n* deportividad *f*.

sports pages *npl* sección *f* OR páginas *fpl* de deportes.

sports personality *n* personalidad *f* de los deportes.

sportswear ['spɔːtsweəʳ] *n* ropa *f* deportiva.

sportswoman ['spɔːts,wumən] (*pl* **-women** [-,wɪmɪn]) *n* deportista *f*.

sporty ['spɔːtɪ] (*compar* **-ier**, *superl* **-iest**) *adj inf* **-1.** [fond of sports] aficionado(da) a los deportes. **-2.** [flashy] llamativo(va).

spot [spɒt] (*pt* & *pp* **-ted**, *cont* **-ting**) ◇ *n* **-1.** [stain] mancha *f*, mota *f*; [dot] punto *m*. **-2.** [pimple] grano *m*. **-3.** [drop] gota *f*. **-4.** *inf* [bit, small amount] pizca *f*, miaja *f*. **-5.** [place] lugar *m*; on the ~ en el lugar; to do sthg on the ~ hacer algo en el acto. **-6.** RADIO & TV espacio *m*. **-7.** *phr*: to have a soft ~ for sb tener debilidad por alguien; to put sb on the ~ poner a alguien en un aprieto OR contra las cuerdas.
◇ *vt* [notice] notar, ver.

spot check *n* control *m* aleatorio.

spotless ['spɒtlɪs] *adj* [thing] inmaculado(da); [reputation] intachable.

spotlight ['spɒtlaɪt] *n* [of car] faro *m* auxiliar; [in theatre, home] foco *m*, reflector *m* de luz; to be in the ~ *fig* ser el centro de atención.

spot-on *adj Br inf* exacto(ta), preciso(sa).

spot price *n* precio *m* por entrega inmediata.

spotted ['spɒtɪd] *adj* de lunares, moteado(da).

spotty ['spɒtɪ] (*compar* **-ier**, *superl* **-iest**) *adj* **-1.** *Br* [skin] con granos. **-2.** *Am* [patchy] irregular.

spouse [spaus] *n* cónyuge *m* y *f*.

spout [spaut] ◇ *n* [of kettle, teapot] pitorro *m*; [of jug] pico *m*; [of pipe] caño *m*. ◇ *vt pej* [churn out] soltar. ◇ *vi*: to ~ **from** OR **out of** [liquid] salir a chorros de; [smoke, flames] salir incesantemente de.

sprain [spreɪn] ◇ *n* torcedura *f*. ◇ *vt* torcerse.

sprang [spræŋ] *pt* → **spring**.

sprat [spræt] *n* espadín *m*.

sprawl [sprɔːl] ◇ *n* (*U*): **urban ~** desorganización *f* urbana. ◇ *vi* **-1.** [sit] repantigarse, arrellanarse; [lie] echarse, tumbarse. **-2.** [cover large area] extenderse.

sprawling ['sprɔːlɪŋ] *adj* de urbanización caótica.

spray [spreɪ] ◇ *n* **-1.** [small drops - of liquid] rociada *f*; [- of sea] espuma *f*; [- of aerosol] pulverización *f*. **-2.** [pressurized liquid] líquido *m* pulverizado, espray *m*. **-3.** [can, container - gen] atomizador *m*; [- for garden] pulverizador *m*. **-4.** [of flowers] ramo *m*. ◇ *vt* rociar, vaporizar. ◇ *vi*: **water ~ed all over the room** el agua salpicó toda la habitación.

spray can *n* aerosol *m*, espray *m*.

spray paint *n* pintura *f* en aerosol.

spread [spred] (*pt* & *pp* **spread**) ◇ *n* **-1.** [soft food] pasta *f* para untar. **-2.** [of fire, disease] propagación *f*. **-3.** [of ideas, interests] variedad *f*; [of products] gama *f*, surtido *m*. **-4.** PRESS: **two-page ~** doble página *f*.
◇ *vt* **-1.** [rug, tablecloth] extender; [map] desplegar. **-2.** [legs, fingers etc] estirar. **-3.** [butter, jam] untar; [glue] repartir; to ~ sthg over sthg extender algo por algo. **-4.** [disease] propagar; [news] difundir, diseminar. **-5.** [in time]: to be ~ over tener una duración de. **-6.** [wealth, work] repartir equitativamente.
◇ *vi* **-1.** [disease, fire, news] extenderse, propagarse. **-2.** [gas, cloud] esparcirse.
◆ **spread out** ◇ *vt sep* **-1.** to be ~ out [far apart] estar diseminado(da); [sprawling] extenderse. **-2.** [rug, tablecloth, legs] extender; [map] desplegar. ◇ *vi* diseminarse, dispersarse.

spread-eagled [-,iːgld] *adj* despatarrado(da).

spreadsheet ['spredʃiːt] *n* COMPUT hoja *f* de cálculo electrónica.

spree [spriː] *n* jarana *f*.

sprig [sprɪg] *n* ramita *f*.

sprightly ['spraɪtlɪ] (*compar* **-ier**, *superl* **-iest**) *adj* animado(da).

spring [sprɪŋ] (*pt* **sprang**, *pp* **sprung**) ◇ *n* **-1.** [season] primavera *f*; **in ~** en primavera. **-2.** [coil] muelle *m*. **-3.** [jump] salto *m*. **-4.** [water source] manantial *m*, vertiente *f* Amer. ◇ *comp* primaveral.
◇ *vt* **-1.** [make known suddenly]: to ~ sthg on sb soltar OR decir de repente algo a alguien. **-2.** [develop]: to ~ a leak empezar a hacer agua.
◇ *vi* **-1.** [jump] saltar. **-2.** [move suddenly] moverse de repente; **she sprang to her feet** se levantó de un salto; to ~ **into action** OR to life ponerse en marcha. **-3.** [originate]: to ~ **from** derivar de.
◆ **spring up** *vi* surgir de repente.

springboard ['sprɪŋbɔːd] *n lit* & *fig* trampolín *m*.

spring-clean ◇ *vt* limpiar a fondo. ◇ *vi* hacer una limpieza general.

spring onion *n Br* cebolleta *f*.

spring roll *n Br* rollito *m* de primavera.

spring tide *n* marea *f* viva.

springtime ['sprɪŋtaɪm] *n*: **in (the)** ~ en primavera.

springy ['sprɪŋɪ] (*compar* **-ier**, *superl* **-iest**) *adj* [carpet, mattress, grass] mullido(da); [rubber] elástico(ca).

sprinkle ['sprɪŋkl] *vt* rociar, salpicar; **to ~ sthg over** OR **on sthg, to ~ sthg with sthg** rociar algo sobre algo.

sprinkler ['sprɪŋklər] *n* aspersor *m*.

sprinkling ['sprɪŋklɪŋ] *n* [of water, sand] pizca *f*; **a ~ of people** unas cuantas personas.

sprint [sprɪnt] ◇ *n* **-1.** SPORT esprint *m*. **-2.** [fast run] carrera *f*. ◇ *vi* SPORT esprintar; [run fast] correr a toda velocidad.

sprinter ['sprɪntər] *n* corredor *m*, -ra *f* de velocidad, esprínter *m y f*.

sprite [spraɪt] *n* hada *f*.

spritzer ['sprɪtsər] *n* vino *m* con gaseosa.

sprocket ['sprɒkɪt] *n* [wheel] rueda *f* dentada.

sprout [spraʊt] ◇ *n* **-1.** **(Brussels)** ~**s** coles *fpl* de Bruselas. **-2.** [shoot] brote *m*, retoño *m*. ◇ *vt* **-1.** [subj: plant] echar. **-2.** [subj: person, animal] **he has ~ed a beard** le ha salido barba. ◇ *vi* **-1.** [plants, vegetables] crecer. **-2.** [leaves, shoots] brotar. **-3.** [hairs, feathers, horns] salir. **-4.** [appear]: **to ~ (up)** aparecer rápidamente.

spruce [spruːs] ◇ *adj* pulcro(cra). ◇ *n* picea *f*.
◆ **spruce up** *vt sep* arreglar; **to ~ o.s. up** arreglarse.

sprung [sprʌŋ] *pp* → **spring**.

spry [spraɪ] (*compar* **-ier**, *superl* **-iest**) *adj* ágil, activo(va).

SPUC [spʌk] (*abbr of* **Society for the Protection of the Unborn Child**) *n* asociación contra el aborto.

spud [spʌd] *n inf* papa *f*, patata *f*.

spun [spʌn] *pt & pp* → **spin**.

spunk [spʌŋk] *n* (*U*) *inf* [courage] agallas *fpl*.

spur [spɜːr] (*pt & pp* **-red**, *cont* **-ring**) ◇ *n* **-1.** [incentive]: ~ **(to sthg)** estímulo *m* (para conseguir algo). **-2.** [on rider's boot] espuela *f*. ◇ *vt* **-1.** [encourage]: **to ~ sb to do sthg** animar a alguien a hacer algo. **-2.** [bring about] impulsar.
◆ **on the spur of the moment** *adv* sin pensarlo dos veces.
◆ **spur on** *vt sep*: **to ~ sb on** animar a alguien.

spurious ['spʊərɪəs] *adj* falso(sa).

spurn [spɜːn] *vt* rechazar.

spurt [spɜːt] ◇ *n* **-1.** [of water] chorro *m*; [of flame] llamarada *f*. **-2.** [of activity, effort] arranque *m*. **-3.** [of speed] acelerón *m*; **to put on a ~** acelerar. ◇ *vi* **-1.** [gush]: **to ~ (out of** OR **from)** [liquid] salir a chorros de; [flame] salir incesantemente de. **-2.** [run] acelerar.

sputter ['spʌtər] *vi* [engine] renquear; [fire, oil] chisporrotear.

spy [spaɪ] (*pl* **spies**, *pt & pp* **-ied**) ◇ *n* espía *m y f*. ◇ *vt inf* divisar. ◇ *vi*: **to ~ (on)** espiar (a), aguaitar (a) *Amer*.

spying ['spaɪɪŋ] *n* espionaje *m*.

spy satellite *n* satélite *m* espía.

Sq., sq. *abbr of* **square**.

squabble ['skwɒbl] ◇ *n* riña *f*. ◇ *vi*: **to ~ (about** OR **over)** reñir (por).

squad [skwɒd] *n* **-1.** [of police] brigada *f*. **-2.** MIL pelotón *m*. **-3.** [SPORT - of club] plantilla *f*, equipo *m* completo; [- of national team] seleccionado *m*.

squad car *n* coche *m* patrulla.

squadron ['skwɒdrən] *n* [of planes] escuadrilla *f*; [of warships] escuadra *f*; [of soldiers] escuadrón *m*.

squadron leader *n Br* ≃ comandante *m* de aviación.

squalid ['skwɒlɪd] *adj* **-1.** [filthy] miserable, sórdido(da). **-2.** [dishonest] despreciable, ruin.

squall [skwɔːl] *n* [storm] turbión *m*.

squalor ['skwɒlər] *n* (*U*) miseria *f*.

squander ['skwɒndər] *vt* [opportunity] desaprovechar; [money] despilfarrar; [resources] malgastar.

square [skweər] ◇ *adj* **-1.** [gen] cuadrado(da). **-2.** [not owing money]: **we're ~ now** ya estamos en paz. ◇ *n* **-1.** [shape] cuadrado *m*. **-2.** [in town, city] plaza *f*. **-3.** *inf* [unfashionable person] carroza *m y f*. **-4.** *phr*: **to be back to ~ one** haber vuelto al punto de partida. ◇ *vt* **-1.** MATH elevar al cuadrado. **-2.** [balance, reconcile]: **how can you ~ that with your principles?** ¿cómo encajas esto con tus principios?; **it doesn't ~ with the facts** no cuadra con los hechos.
◆ **square up** *vi* [settle up]: **to ~ up with** saldar cuentas con. **-2.** **to ~ up to** [confront] hacer frente a.

squared [skweəd] *adj* cuadriculado(da).

square dance *n* baile *m* de figuras.

square deal *n* trato *m* justo.

squarely ['skweəlɪ] *adv* **-1.** [directly] justo, exactamente. **-2.** [honestly] abiertamente, honradamente.

square meal *n* comida *f* satisfactoria.

square root *n* raíz *f* cuadrada.

squash [skwɒʃ] ◇ *n* **-1.** [game] squash *m*. **-2.** *Br* [drink] zumo *m*. **-3.** *Am* [vegetable] cucurbitácea *f*. ◇ *vt* [squeeze, flatten] aplastar.

squat [skwɒt] (*compar* **-ter**, *superl* **-test**, *pt* & *pp* **-ted**, *cont* **-ting**) ◇ *adj* achaparrado(da). ◇ *n Br* [building] vivienda *f* ocupada. ◇ *vi* **-1.** [crouch]: **to ~ (down)** agacharse, ponerse en cuclillas. **-2.** [be a squatter] vivir en una casa ocupada.

squatter ['skwɒtər] *n Br* ocupante *m y f* ilegal, squatter *m y f*.

squawk [skwɔːk] ◇ *n* [of bird] graznido *m*, chillido *m*. ◇ *vi* [of bird] graznar, chillar.

squeak [skwiːk] ◇ *n* **-1.** [of animal] chillido *m*. **-2.** [of hinge] chirrido *m*. ◇ *vi* **-1.** [animal] chillar. **-2.** [hinge] chirriar.

squeaky ['skwiːkɪ] (*compar* **-ier**, *superl* **-iest**) *adj* [voice] chillón(ona); [hinge] chirriante.

squeal [skwiːl] ◇ *n* **-1.** [of person, animal] chillido *m*, grito *m*. **-2.** [of brakes, tyres] chirrido *m*. ◇ *vi* **-1.** [person, animal] chillar, gritar. **-2.** [brakes] chirriar.

squeamish ['skwiːmɪʃ] *adj* aprensivo(va).

squeeze [skwiːz] ◇ *n* **-1.** [pressure] apretón *m*. **-2.** *inf* [squash]: **it was a real ~** estábamos totalmente apiñados.
◇ *vt* **-1.** [press firmly] apretar. **-2.** [force out - toothpaste] sacar (estrujando); [- juice] exprimir. **-3.** [cram]: **to ~ sthg into sthg** [into place] conseguir meter algo en algo; [into time] arreglárselas para hacer algo en algo. **-4.** *fig*: **to ~ sthg out of sb** [extract] arrancar algo a alguien.
◇ *vi*: **to ~ into/through** conseguir meterse en/por.

squeezebox ['skwiːzbɒks] *n Br* acordeón *m*.

squeezer ['skwiːzər] *n* exprimidor *m*.

squelch [skweltʃ] *vi*: **to ~ through mud** cruzar el barro chapoteando.

squib [skwɪb] *n* [firework] petardo *m*; **to be a damp ~** *fig* ser un chasco.

squid [skwɪd] (*pl inv* OR **-s**) *n* **-1.** ZOOL calamar *m* **-2.** (*U*) [food] calamares *mpl*.

squiffy ['skwɪfɪ] (*compar* **-ier**, *superl* **-iest**) *adj Br inf dated* achispado(da).

squiggle ['skwɪgl] *n* garabato *m*.

squint [skwɪnt] ◇ *n* estrabismo *m*, bizquera *f* ◇ *vi*: **to ~ at** mirar con los ojos entrecerrados.

squire ['skwaɪər] *n* [landowner] terrateniente *m y f*.

squirm [skwɜːm] *vi* **-1.** [wriggle] retorcerse. **-2.** [wince]: **to ~ (with)** sentirse violento(ta) (por).

squirrel [*Br* 'skwɪrəl, *Am* 'skwɜːrəl] *n* ardilla *f*.

squirt [skwɜːt] ◇ *vt* **-1.** [force out] sacar a chorro de. **-2.** [cover with liquid]: **to ~ the plants with water** echar agua en las plantas. ◇ *vi*: **to ~ out of** salir a chorro.

Sr -1. *abbr of* **senior**. **-2.** *abbr of* **sister**.

SRC *n* **-1.** (*abbr of* **Students' Representative Council**) *consejo estudiantil*. **-2.** (*abbr of* **Science Research Council**) *consejo británico de investigación científica*.

Sri Lanka [ˌsriː'læŋkə] *n* Sri Lanka.

Sri Lankan [ˌsriː'læŋkn] ◇ *adj* esrilanqués(esa). ◇ *n* [person] esrilanqués *m*, -esa *f*.

SRN (*abbr of* **State Registered Nurse**) *n Br* enfermero diplomado *m*, enfermera diplomada *f*.

SS (*abbr of* **steamship**) *barco de vapor*.

SSA (*abbr of* **Social Security Administration**) *n organismo estadounidense de la seguridad social*.

ssh [ʃ] *excl* ¡chiss!

SSSI (*abbr of* **site of special scientific interest**) *n en Gran Bretaña, lugar de especial interés científico*.

St -1. (*abbr of* **saint**) Sto., Sta. **-2.** (*abbr of* **Street**) c/.

ST (*abbr of* **Standard Time**) *hora oficial*.

stab [stæb] (*pt* & *pp* **-bed**, *cont* **-bing**) ◇ *n* **-1.** [with knife] puñalada *f*. **-2.** *inf* [attempt]: **to have a ~ (at sthg)** probar (a hacer algo). **-3.** [twinge] punzada *f*. ◇ *vt* **-1.** [with knife] apuñalar. **-2.** [jab] pinchar. ◇ *vi*: **to ~ at sthg** señalar algo con movimientos bruscos del dedo índice.

stabbing ['stæbɪŋ] ◇ *adj* punzante. ◇ *n* apuñalamiento *m*.

stability [stə'bɪlətɪ] *n* estabilidad *f*.

stabilize, **-ise** ['steɪbəlaɪz] ◇ *vt* estabilizar. ◇ *vi* estabilizarse.

stabilizer ['steɪbəlaɪzər] *n* estabilizador *m*.

stable ['steɪbl] ◇ *adj* **-1.** [unchanging] estable. **-2.** [not moving] fijo(ja). **-3.** MED [condition] estacionario(ria); [mental health] equilibrado(da). ◇ *n* [building] cuadra *f*.

stable lad *n* mozo *m* de cuadra.

staccato [stə'kɑːtəʊ] *adj* entrecortado(da).

stack [stæk] ◇ *n* **-1.** [pile] pila *m*. **-2.** *inf* [a lot, lots]: **~s** OR **a ~ of** montones OR un montón de. ◇ *vt* **-1.** [pile up] apilar. **-2.** [fill]: **to be ~ed with** estar amontonado(da) de.

◆ **stack up** *vi Am inf* compararse.

stadium ['steɪdjəm] (*pl* **-diums** OR **-dia** [-djə]) *n* estadio *m*.

staff [stɑːf] ◇ *n* [employees] empleados *mpl*, personal *m*. ◇ *vt*: **the shop is ~ed by women** la tienda está llevada por una plantilla de mujeres.

staffing ['stɑːfɪŋ] n contratación f de personal.

staff nurse n Br enfermero titulado m, enfermera titulada f.

staff room n sala f de profesores.

Staffs [stæfs] (abbr of **Staffordshire**) condado inglés.

stag [stæg] (pl inv OR -s) n ciervo m, venado m.

stage [steɪdʒ] ◇ n -1. [part of process, phase] etapa f. -2. [in theatre, hall] escenario m, escena f; **on ~** en escena; **to set the ~ for** preparar el terreno para. -3. [acting profession]: **the ~** el teatro. ◇ vt -1. THEATRE representar. -2. [event, strike] organizar.

stagecoach ['steɪdʒkəʊtʃ] n diligencia f.

stage door n entrada f de artistas.

stage fright n miedo m al público.

stagehand ['steɪdʒhænd] n tramoyista m y f.

stage-manage vt -1. THEATRE dirigir. -2. fig [orchestrate] urdir, maquinar.

stage name n nombre m artístico.

stagflation [stæg'fleɪʃn] n estanflación f.

stagger ['stægər] ◇ vt -1. [astound] dejar atónito(ta). -2. [arrange at different times] escalonar. ◇ vi tambalearse.

staggering ['stægərɪŋ] adj asombroso(sa).

staging ['steɪdʒɪŋ] n -1. THEATRE puesta f en escena. -2. [of event] organización f.

stagnant ['stægnənt] adj lit & fig estancado(da).

stagnate [stæg'neɪt] vi estancarse, paralizarse.

stagnation [stæg'neɪʃn] n estancamiento m, paralización f.

stag party n despedida f de soltero.

staid [steɪd] adj recatado y conservador (recatada y conservadora).

stain [steɪn] ◇ n mancha f. ◇ vt manchar.

stained [steɪnd] adj -1. [marked] manchado(da). -2. [coloured - wood] teñido(da).

stained glass n (U) vidrio m de color.

stainless steel ['steɪnlɪs-] n acero m inoxidable.

stain remover n quitamanchas m inv.

stair [steər] n peldaño m, escalón m.

◆ **stairs** npl escaleras fpl, escalera f.

staircase ['steəkeɪs] n escalera f.

stairway ['steəweɪ] n escalera f.

stairwell ['steəwel] n hueco m OR caja f de la escalera.

stake [steɪk] ◇ n -1. [share]: **to have a ~ in** tener intereses en. -2. [wooden post] estaca f. -3. [in gambling] apuesta f. ◇ vt -1. [risk]: **to ~ sthg (on** OR **upon)** arriesgar OR jugarse algo (en). -2. [in gambling] apostar. -3. [state]: **to ~ a claim to sthg** reivindicar algo.

◆ **stakes** npl -1. [prize] premio m. -2. [contest] contienda f.

◆ **at stake** adv: **to be at ~** estar en juego.

stakeout ['steɪkaʊt] n [police surveillance] vigilancia f.

stalactite ['stæləktaɪt] n estalactita f.

stalagmite ['stæləgmaɪt] n estalagmita f.

stale [steɪl] adj -1. [bread] duro(ra); [food] rancio(cia), pasado(da); [air] viciado(da). -2. [athlete] agotado(da); [artist etc] falto(ta) de ideas.

stalemate ['steɪlmeɪt] n -1. [deadlock] punto m muerto. -2. CHESS tablas fpl.

staleness ['steɪlnɪs] n [of bread] dureza f; [of food] rancidez f, deterioro m; [of air] lo viciado.

stalk [stɔːk] ◇ n -1. [of flower, plant] tallo m. -2. [of leaf, fruit] pecíolo m, rabillo m. ◇ vt [hunt] acechar, seguir sigilosamente. ◇ vi: **to ~ in/out** entrar/salir con paso airado.

stall [stɔːl] ◇ n [in market, at exhibition] puesto m, caseta f. ◇ vt -1. AUT calar. -2. [delay - event] retrasar, retardar; [- person] retener. ◇ vi -1. AUT calarse. -2. [delay] andar con evasivas.

◆ **stalls** npl Br platea f.

stallholder ['stɔːl,həʊldər] n Br propietario m, -ria f de un puesto (en un mercado).

stallion ['stæljən] n semental m.

stalwart ['stɔːlwət] ◇ adj [loyal] leal, incondicional. ◇ n partidario m, -ria f incondicional.

stamen ['steɪmən] n estambre m.

stamina ['stæmɪnə] n resistencia f.

stammer ['stæmər] ◇ n tartamudeo m. ◇ vi tartamudear.

stamp [stæmp] ◇ n -1. [gen] sello m, estampilla f Amer. -2. [tool] tampón m. ◇ vt -1. [mark by stamping] timbrar. -2. [stomp]: **to ~ one's feet** patear. -3. [stick stamp on] sellar, poner un sello en. -4. fig [identify, mark]: **to ~ sthg/sb as** identificar algo/a alguien como. ◇ vi -1. [stomp] patalear, dar patadas. -2. [tread heavily]: **to ~ on sthg** pisotear OR pisar algo.

◆ **stamp out** vt sep [custom] erradicar; [fire, revolution] sofocar.

stamp album n álbum m de sellos.

stamp-collecting n filatelia f.

stamp collector n coleccionista m y f de sellos.

stamp duty n Br póliza f, impuesto m del timbre.

stamped addressed envelope ['stæmptə,drest-] n Br sobre con sus señas y franqueo.

stampede [stæm'piːd] ◇ *n lit* & *fig* estampida *f*, desbandada *f*. ◇ *vi* salir de estampida.

stamp machine *n* máquina *f* expendedora de sellos.

stance [stæns] *n* **-1.** [way of standing] postura *f*. **-2.** [attitude]: ~ **(on)** postura *f* (ante).

stand [stænd] (*pt* & *pp* **stood**) ◇ *n* **-1.** [stall] puesto *m*; [selling newspapers] quiosco *m*. **-2.** [supporting object] soporte *m*; **coat** ~ perchero *m*; **music** ~ atril *m*. **-3.** SPORT tribuna *f*. **-4.** [act of defence]: **to make a** ~ resistir al enemigo. **-5.** [publicly stated view] postura *f*; **to take a** ~ **on sthg** adoptar una postura ante OR hacia algo. **-6.** *Am* JUR estrado *m*; **to take the** ~ subir al estrado.
◇ *vt* **-1.** [place upright] colocar (verticalmente). **-2.** [withstand, tolerate] soportar. **-3.** [treat]: **to** ~ **sb sthg** invitar a alguien a algo. **-4.** JUR: **to** ~ **trial** ser procesado(da).
◇ *vi* **-1.** [be upright - person] estar de pie; [- object] estar (*en posición vertical*). **-2.** [get to one's feet] ponerse de pie, levantarse. **-3.** [liquid] reposar. **-4.** [still be valid] seguir vigente OR en pie. **-5.** [be in particular state]: **unemployment** ~**s at three million** la cifra de desempleados es de tres millones; **as things** ~ tal como están las cosas. **-6.** [have attitude]: **where do you** ~ **on ...?** ¿cúal es tu postura ante ...? **-7.** [be likely]: **I** ~ **to win/lose** es probable que gane/pierda. **-8.** *Br* POL [be a candidate] presentarse; **to** ~ **for Parliament** presentarse para las elecciones al Parlamento. **-9.** *Am* AUT: **"no** ~**ing"** "prohibido aparcar".
◆ **stand aside** *vi* hacerse a un lado.
◆ **stand back** *vi* echarse para atrás.
◆ **stand by** ◇ *vt fus* **-1.** [person] seguir al lado de. **-2.** [promise, decision] mantener. ◇ *vi* **-1.** [in readiness]: **to** ~ **by (for sthg/to do sthg)** estar preparado(da) (para algo/para hacer algo). **-2.** [remain inactive] quedarse sin hacer nada.
◆ **stand down** *vi* [resign] retirarse.
◆ **stand for** *vt fus* **-1.** [signify] significar. **-2.** [support - policy, ideas] defender. **-3.** [tolerate] aguantar, tolerar.
◆ **stand in** *vi*: **to** ~ **in for sb** sustituir a alguien.
◆ **stand out** *vi* sobresalir, destacarse.
◆ **stand up** ◇ *vt sep inf* [boyfriend etc] dejar plantado(da). ◇ *vi* **-1.** [rise from seat] levantarse, pararse *Amer*. **-2.** [claim, evidence] ser convincente.
◆ **stand up for** *vt fus* salir en defensa de.
◆ **stand up to** *vt fus* **-1.** [weather, heat etc] resistir. **-2.** [person] hacer frente a.

standard ['stændəd] ◇ *adj* **-1.** [normal] corriente, estándar. **-2.** [accepted] estableci-

do(da). **-3.** [basic] clave, fundamental. ◇ *n* **-1.** [acceptable level] nivel *m*. **-2.** [point of reference - moral] criterio *m*; [- technical] norma *f*. **-3.** [flag] bandera *f*, estandarte *m*.
◆ **standards** *npl* [principles] valores *mpl* morales.

standard-bearer *n fig* portaestandarte *m* y *f*, abanderado *m*, -da *f*.

standardize, -ise ['stændədaɪz] *vt* normalizar, estandarizar.

standard lamp *n Br* lámpara *f* de pie.

standard of living (*pl* **standards of living**) *n* nivel *m* de vida.

standard time *n* hora *f* oficial.

standby ['stændbaɪ] (*pl* **standbys**) ◇ *n* recurso *m*; **on** ~ preparado(da). ◇ *comp*: ~ **ticket** billete *m* en lista de espera.

stand-in *n* [stuntman] doble *m* y *f*; [temporary replacement] sustituto *m*, -ta *f*.

standing ['stændɪŋ] ◇ *adj* [permanent] permanente; **a** ~ **joke** la broma de siempre; ~ **invitation** invitación abierta. ◇ *n* **-1.** [reputation] reputación *f*. **-2.** [duration] duración *f*; **friends of 20 years'** ~ amigos desde hace 20 años.

standing committee *n* comité *m* permanente.

standing order *n* domiciliación *f* de pago.

standing ovation *n* ovación *f* calurosa en pie.

standing room *n* (U) [on bus] sitio *m* para estar de pie; [at theatre, sports ground] localidades *fpl* de pie.

standoffish [ˌstændˈɒfɪʃ] *adj* distante.

standpipe ['stændpaɪp] *n* tubo *m* vertical.

standpoint ['stændpɔɪnt] *n* punto *m* de vista.

standstill ['stændstɪl] *n*: **at a** ~ [not moving] parado(da); *fig* [not active] en un punto muerto, estancado(da); **to come to a** ~ [stop moving] pararse; *fig* [cease] llegar a un punto muerto, estancarse.

stank [stæŋk] *pt* → **stink**.

stanza ['stænzə] *n* estrofa *f*.

staple ['steɪpl] ◇ *adj* [principal] básico(ca), de primera necesidad. ◇ *n* **-1.** [item of stationery] grapa *f*, corchete *m* *Amer*. **-2.** [principal commodity] producto *m* básico OR de primera necesidad. ◇ *vt* grapar.

staple diet *n* dieta *f* básica.

staple gun *n* grapadora *f* industrial.

stapler ['steɪplər] *n* grapadora *f*, corchetera *f* *Amer*.

star [stɑːr] (*pt* & *pp* **-red**, *cont* **-ring**) ◇ *n* **-1.** [gen] estrella *f*. **-2.** [asterisk] asterisco *m*. ◇ *comp* estelar. ◇ *vt*: **the film** ~**s Kevin Costner** la película está protagonizada por

Kevin Costner. ◇ *vi*: **to ~ (in)** hacer de protagonista en.

◆ **stars** *npl* horóscopo *m*.

star attraction *n* atracción *f* principal.

starboard ['stɑːbəd] ◇ *adj* de estribor. ◇ *n*: **to ~** a estribor.

starch [stɑːtʃ] *n* **-1.** [gen] almidón *m*. **-2.** [in potatoes etc] fécula *f*.

starched [stɑːtʃt] *adj* almidonado(da).

starchy ['stɑːtʃɪ] (*compar* **-ier**, *superl* **-iest**) *adj* [foods] feculento(ta).

stardom ['stɑːdəm] *n* estrellato *m*.

stare [steəʳ] ◇ *n* mirada *f* fija. ◇ *vi*: **to ~ (at sthg/sb)** mirar fijamente (algo/a alguien).

starfish ['stɑːfɪʃ] (*pl inv* OR **-es**) *n* estrella *f* de mar.

stark [stɑːk] ◇ *adj* **-1.** [bleak - landscape] desierto(ta); [- decoration, room] austero(ra). **-2.** [harsh - reality] crudo(da); [- fact] sin tapujos. ◇ *adv*: ~ **naked** en cueros.

starlight ['stɑːlaɪt] *n* luz *f* de las estrellas.

starling ['stɑːlɪŋ] *n* estornino *m*.

starlit ['stɑːlɪt] *adj* iluminado(da) por las estrellas.

starry ['stɑːrɪ] (*compar* **-ier**, *superl* **-iest**) *adj* estrellado(da), lleno(na) de estrellas.

starry-eyed [-'aɪd] *adj* [optimism etc] iluso(sa); [lovers] encandilado(da).

Stars and Stripes *n*: **the ~** la bandera de las barras y estrellas.

star sign *n* signo *m* del horóscopo.

star-studded *adj*: ~ **cast** reparto *m* estelar.

start [stɑːt] ◇ *n* **-1.** [beginning] principio *m*, comienzo *m*; **at the ~ of the year** a principios de año; **to make a good/bad ~** tener un buen/mal comienzo; **for a ~** para empezar. **-2.** [jerk, jump] sobresalto *m*, susto *m*. **-3.** [starting place] salida *f*. **-4.** [time advantage] ventaja *f*; **to have a ~ on sb** llevar ventaja a alguien.

◇ *vt* **-1.** [begin] empezar, comenzar; **to ~ doing** OR **to do sthg** empezar a hacer algo. **-2.** [turn on - machine, engine] poner en marcha; [- vehicle] arrancar. **-3.** [set up] formar, crear; [business] montar.

◇ *vi* **-1.** [begin] empezar, comenzar; **to ~ with sb/sthg** empezar por alguien/algo. **-2.** [machine, tape] ponerse en marcha; [vehicle] arrancar. **-3.** [begin journey] salir, ponerse en camino. **-4.** [jerk, jump] asustarse, sobresaltarse. **-5.** *inf* [be annoying]: **don't ~!** ¡no empieces!

◆ **start off** ◇ *vt sep* [discussion, rumour] desencadenar; [meeting] empezar; [person]: **this should be enough to ~ you off** con esto tienes suficiente trabajo para empe-

zar. ◇ *vi* **-1.** [begin] empezar, comenzar; **to ~ off by doing sthg** empezar por hacer algo; **I ~ed off as a clerk** empecé de oficinista. **-2.** [leave on journey] salir, ponerse en camino.

◆ **start on** *vt fus* empezar con.

◆ **start out** *vi* **-1.** [originally be] empezar, comenzar. **-2.** [leave on journey] salir, ponerse en camino.

◆ **start up** ◇ *vt sep* **-1.** [business] montar, establecer; [shop] poner; [association] crear, formar. **-2.** [car, engine] arrancar, poner en marcha. ◇ *vi* **-1.** [begin] empezar. **-2.** [car, engine] arrancar, ponerse en marcha.

starter ['stɑːtəʳ] *n* **-1.** *Br* [of meal] primer plato *m*, entrada *f*. **-2.** AUT (motor *m* de) arranque *m*. **-3.** [person participating in race] participante *m y f*, competidor *m*, -ra *f*.

starter motor *n* (motor *m* de) arranque *m*.

starter pack *n* paquete *m* de iniciación.

starting block ['stɑːtɪŋ-] *n* puesto *m* de salida.

starting point ['stɑːtɪŋ-] *n lit & fig* punto *m* de partida.

starting price ['stɑːtɪŋ-] *n precio al que se pagan las apuestas al comienzo de una carrera*.

startle ['stɑːtl] *vt* asustar.

startling ['stɑːtlɪŋ] *adj* sorprendente, asombroso(sa).

starvation [stɑːˈveɪʃn] *n* hambre *f*, inanición *f*.

starve [stɑːv] ◇ *vt* **-1.** [deprive of food] privar de comida, no dar de comer a. **-2.** [deprive]: **to ~ sb of sthg** privar a alguien de algo. ◇ *vi* **-1.** [have no food] pasar hambre. **-2.** *inf* [be hungry]: **I'm starving!** ¡me muero de hambre!

Star Wars *n* guerra *f* de las galaxias (*programa espacial militar estadounidense*).

state [steɪt] ◇ *n* estado *m*; **not to be in a fit ~ to do sthg** no estar en condiciones de hacer algo; **to be in a ~** tener los nervios de punta. ◇ *comp* [ceremony] oficial, de Estado; [control, ownership] estatal. ◇ *vt* **-1.** [gen] indicar; [reason, policy] plantear; [case] exponer. **-2.** [time, date, amount] fijar.

◆ **State** *n*: **the State** el Estado.

◆ **States** *npl*: **the States** los Estados Unidos.

state-controlled *adj* controlado(da) por el Estado.

State Department *n Am* ≃ Ministerio *m* de Asuntos Exteriores.

state education *n Br* enseñanza *f* pública.

stateless ['steɪtlɪs] *adj* apátrida.

stately ['steɪtlɪ] (*compar* **-ier**, *superl* **-iest**) *adj* majestuoso(sa).

stately home n Br casa grande de campo abierta al público.

statement ['steɪtmənt] n **-1.** [gen] declaración f. **-2.** [from bank] extracto m OR estado m de cuenta.

state of affairs n situación f.

state of emergency n estado m de emergencia.

state of mind (pl states of mind) n estado m de ánimo.

state-of-the-art adj vanguardista.

state-owned [-'əʊnd] adj estatal.

state school n escuela f pública.

state secret n secreto m de estado.

state's evidence n Am: **to turn** ~ testificar un delincuente ante un tribunal en contra de otros a cambio de una reducción de condena.

stateside ['steɪtsaɪd] Am ◇ adj estadounidense. ◇ adv [travel] hacia Estados Unidos; [live] en Estados Unidos.

statesman ['steɪtsmən] (pl -men [-mən]) n estadista m, hombre m de Estado.

statesmanship ['steɪtsmənʃɪp] n arte m OR habilidad f de gobernar.

static ['stætɪk] ◇ adj estático(ca). ◇ n (U) interferencias fpl, parásitos mpl.

static electricity n electricidad f estática.

station ['steɪʃn] ◇ n **-1.** [gen] estación f. **-2.** RADIO emisora f. **-3.** [centre of activity] centro m, puesto m. **-4.** fml [rank] rango m. ◇ vt **-1.** [position] situar, colocar. **-2.** MIL estacionar, apostar.

stationary ['steɪʃnərɪ] adj inmóvil.

stationer ['steɪʃnə'] n papelero m, -ra f; ~'s (shop) papelería f.

stationery ['steɪʃnərɪ] n (U) objetos mpl de escritorio.

station house n Am comisaría f (de policía).

stationmaster ['steɪʃn,mɑːstə'] n jefe m de estación.

station wagon n Am ranchera f.

statistic [stə'tɪstɪk] n estadística f.
◆ **statistics** n (U) estadística f.

statistical [stə'tɪstɪkl] adj estadístico(ca).

statistician [,stætɪ'stɪʃn] n estadístico m, -ca f.

statue ['stætʃuː] n estatua f.

statuesque [,stætʃu'esk] adj escultural.

statuette [,stætʃu'et] n figurilla f.

stature ['stætʃə'] n **-1.** [height] estatura f, talla f. **-2.** [importance] talla f, categoría f.

status ['steɪtəs] n (U) **-1.** [position, condition] condición f, estado m. **-2.** [prestige] prestigio m, estatus m inv.

status quo [-'kwəʊ] n: **the** ~ el statu quo.

status symbol n símbolo m de posición social.

statute ['stætjuːt] n estatuto m.

statute book n: **the** ~ el código de leyes.

statutory ['stætjʊtrɪ] adj reglamentario(ria).

staunch [stɔːntʃ] ◇ adj fiel, leal. ◇ vt restañar.

stave [steɪv] (pt & pp -d OR stove) n MUS pentagrama m.
◆ **stave off** vt sep [disaster, defeat] retrasar; [hunger, illness] aplacar temporalmente.

stay [steɪ] ◇ vi **-1.** [not move away] quedarse, permanecer; **to** ~ **put** permanecer en el mismo sitio; ~ **put!** ¡no te muevas! **-2.** [as visitor] alojarse, estar. **-3.** [continue, remain] permanecer; **to** ~ **away from sb/somewhere** no acercarse a alguien/algún sitio; **to** ~ **out of sthg** mantenerse al margen de algo. **-4.** Scot [reside] vivir. ◇ n estancia f, permanencia f.
◆ **stay in** vi quedarse en casa.
◆ **stay on** vi permanecer, quedarse.
◆ **stay out** vi **-1.** [from home] quedarse fuera, no volver a casa. **-2.** [strikers] permanecer en huelga.
◆ **stay up** vi quedarse levantado(da).

stayer ['steɪə'] n Br [horse] caballo m resistente; [person] persona f resistente.

staying power ['steɪɪŋ-] n resistencia f.

St Bernard [Br -'bɜːnəd, Am -bər'nɑːrd] n (perro m) San Bernardo m.

STD n **-1.** (abbr of subscriber trunk dialling) sistema de llamadas telefónicas directas de larga distancia. **-2.** (abbr of sexually transmitted disease) ETS f.

stead [sted] n: **to stand sb in good** ~ servir de mucho a alguien.

steadfast ['stedfɑːst] adj [supporter] fiel, leal; [gaze] fijo(ja), imperturbable; [resolve] inquebrantable.

steadily ['stedɪlɪ] adv **-1.** [gradually] constantemente. **-2.** [regularly - breathe, move] normalmente. **-3.** [calmly - look] fijamente; [- speak] con tranquilidad.

steady ['stedɪ] (compar -ier, superl -iest, pt & pp -ied) ◇ adj **-1.** [gradual] gradual. **-2.** [regular, constant] constante, continuo(nua). **-3.** [not shaking] firme. **-4.** [voice] sereno(na); [stare] fijo(ja). **-5.** [relationship] estable, serio(ria); [boyfriend, girlfriend] formal; **a** ~ **job** un trabajo fijo. **-6.** [reliable, sensible] sensato(ta).
◇ vt **-1.** [stop from shaking] mantener firme; **he steadied his hand** dejó de temblar; **to** ~ **o.s.** dejar de temblar. **-2.** [nerves, voice] dominar, controlar; **to** ~ **o.s.** controlar los nervios.

steak [steɪk] n **-1.** (U) [meat] bistec m, filete

m, bife *m* *Amer*. **-2.** [piece of meat, fish] filete *m*.

steakhouse ['steɪkhaʊs, *pl* -haʊzɪz] *n* restaurante *m* especializado en bistecs.

steal [stiːl] (*pt* **stole**, *pp* **stolen**) ◇ *vt* **-1.** [gen] robar; [idea] apropiarse de; **to ~ sthg from sb** robar algo a alguien; **to ~ a glance at** echar una mirada furtiva a. ◇ *vi* **-1.** [take illegally] robar, hurtar. **-2.** [move secretly] moverse sigilosamente.

stealing ['stiːlɪŋ] *n* (*U*) robo *m*.

stealth [stelθ] *n* cautela *f*, sigilo *m*.

stealthy ['stelθɪ] (*compar* **-ier**, *superl* **-iest**) *adj* cauteloso(sa), sigiloso(sa).

steam [stiːm] ◇ *n* (*U*) vapor *m*, vaho *m*; **to let off ~** desfogarse; **to run out of ~** quemarse, quedarse sin fuerzas. ◇ *comp* de vapor. ◇ *vt* CULIN cocer al vapor. ◇ *vi* **-1.** [water, food] echar vapor. **-2.** [train, ship] moverse echando vapor.

◆ **steam up** ◇ *vt sep* **-1.** [mist up] empañar. **-2.** *fig* [get angry]: **to get ~ed up about sthg** mosquearse por algo. ◇ *vi* empañarse.

steamboat ['stiːmbəʊt] *n* buque *m* de vapor.

steam engine *n* máquina *f* de vapor.

steamer ['stiːmə'] *n* **-1.** [ship] buque *m* de vapor. **-2.** CULIN *tipo de colador para hacer verduras etc al vapor.*

steam iron *n* plancha *f* de vapor.

steamroller ['stiːm,rəʊlə'] *n* apisonadora *f*.

steam shovel *n* *Am* excavadora *f*.

steamy ['stiːmɪ] (*compar* **-ier**, *superl* **-iest**) *adj* **-1.** [full of steam] lleno(na) de vaho. **-2.** *inf* [erotic] caliente.

steel [stiːl] ◇ *n* acero *m*. ◇ *comp* de acero. ◇ *vt*: **to ~ o.s. (for sthg)** armarse de valor (para algo).

steel industry *n* industria *f* del acero.

steel wool *n* estropajo *m* de acero.

steelworker ['stiːl,wɜːkə'] *n* obrero *m*, -ra *f* de la siderurgia.

steelworks ['stiːlwɜːks] (*pl inv*) *n* fundición *f* de acero.

steely ['stiːlɪ] (*compar* **-ier**, *superl* **-iest**) *adj* **-1.** [steel-coloured] acerado(da). **-2.** [strong, determined] inflexible, duro(ra).

steep [stiːp] ◇ *adj* **-1.** [hill, road] empinado(da). **-2.** [considerable - increase, fall] importante, considerable. **-3.** *inf* [expensive] muy caro(ra), abusivo(va). ◇ *vt* remojar.

steeped [stiːpt] *adj* *fig*: **~ in sthg** empapado(da) OR sumido(da) en algo.

steeple ['stiːpl] *n* aguja *f* (*de un campanario*).

steeplechase ['stiːpltʃeɪs] *n* carrera *f* de obstáculos.

steeplejack ['stiːpldʒæk] *n* reparador *m*, -ra *f* de campanarios y chimeneas.

steeply ['stiːplɪ] *adv* *lit* & *fig* vertiginosamente.

steer ['stɪə'] ◇ *n* buey *m*. ◇ *vt* **-1.** [vehicle] conducir. **-2.** [person, discussion etc] dirigir. ◇ *vi*: **the car ~s well** el coche se conduce bien; **the bus ~ed into a ditch** el autobús se desvió y fue a parar en la cuneta; **to ~ clear of sthg/sb** evitar algo/a alguien.

steering ['stɪərɪŋ] *n* (*U*) dirección *f*.

steering column *n* columna *f* de dirección.

steering committee *n* comité *m* de dirección.

steering lock *n* capacidad *f* de giro.

steering wheel *n* volante *m*, timón *m* *Amer*.

stellar ['stelə'] *adj* estelar.

stem [stem] (*pt* & *pp* **-med**, *cont* **-ming**) ◇ *n* **-1.** [of plant] tallo *m*. **-2.** [of glass] pie *m*. **-3.** [of pipe] tubo *m*. **-4.** GRAMM raíz *f*. ◇ *vt* [flow] contener, detener; [blood] restañar.

◆ **stem from** *vt fus* derivarse de, ser el resultado de.

stench [stentʃ] *n* hedor *m*.

stencil ['stensl] (*Br* *pt* & *pp* **-led**, *cont* **-ling**, *Am* *pt* & *pp* **-ed**, *cont* **-ing**) ◇ *n* plantilla *f*. ◇ *vt* estarcir.

stenographer [stə'nɒgrəfə'] *n* *Am* taquígrafo *m*, -fa *f*.

stenography [stə'nɒgrəfɪ] *n* *Am* taquigrafía *f*.

step [step] (*pt* & *pp* **-ped**, *cont* **-ping**) ◇ *n* **-1.** [gen] paso *m*; **~ by ~** paso a paso; **to be in/out of ~** *lit* llevar/no llevar el paso; *fig* estar/no estar al tanto; **to watch one's ~** mirar por donde pisa uno; *fig* andarse con cuidado. **-2.** [action] medida *f*. **-3.** [stair, rung] peldaño *m*. **-4.** *Am* MUS tono *m*.

◇ *vi* **-1.** [move foot] dar un paso; **watch where you ~!** ¡mira dónde pisas!; **he stepped off the bus** se bajó del autobús. **-2.** [tread]: **to ~ on sthg** pisar algo; **to ~ in sthg** meter el pie en algo.

◆ **steps** *npl* **-1.** [stairs - indoors] escaleras *fpl*; [- outside] escalinata *f*. **-2.** *Br* [stepladder] escalera *f* de tijera.

◆ **step aside** *vi* **-1.** [move away] apartarse, hacerse a un lado. **-2.** [leave job] renunciar.

◆ **step back** *vi* [pause to reflect] detenerse a pensar.

◆ **step down** *vi* [leave job] renunciar.

◆ **step in** *vi* intervenir.

◆ **step up** *vt sep* aumentar.

stepbrother ['step,brʌðə'] *n* hermanastro *m*.

stepchild ['steptʃaɪld] (*pl* **-children** [-,tʃɪldrən]) *n* hijastro *m*, -tra *f*.

stepdaughter ['step,dɔːtəʳ] *n* hijastra *f*.

stepfather ['step,fɑːðəʳ] *n* padrastro *m*.

stepladder ['step,lædəʳ] *n* escalera *f* de tijera.

stepmother ['step,mʌðəʳ] *n* madrastra *f*.

stepping-stone ['stepɪŋ-] *n* **-1.** [in river] pasadera *f*. **-2.** *fig* [to success] trampolín *m*.

stepsister ['step,sɪstəʳ] *n* hermanastra *f*.

stepson ['stepsʌn] *n* hijastro *m*.

stereo ['steriəʊ] (*pl* **-s**) ◇ *adj* estereofónico(ca). ◇ *n* **-1.** [record player] equipo *m* estereofónico. **-2.** [stereo sound] estéreo *m*.

stereophonic [,steriə'fɒnɪk] *adj fml* estereofónico(ca).

stereotype ['steriətaɪp] ◇ *n* estereotipo *m*. ◇ *vt* estereotipar.

sterile ['steraɪl] *adj* **-1.** [germ-free] esterilizado(da). **-2.** [unable to produce offspring] estéril. **-3.** *pej* [unimaginative] improductivo(va).

sterility [ste'rɪlətɪ] *n* **-1.** [gen] esterilidad *f*. **-2.** *pej* [lack of imagination] improductividad *f*.

sterilization [,steralaɪ'zeɪʃn] *n* esterilización *f*.

sterilize, -ise ['steralaɪz] *vt* esterilizar.

sterilized milk ['steralaɪzd-] *n* leche *f* esterilizada.

sterling ['stɜːlɪŋ] ◇ *adj* **-1.** [of British money] esterlina. **-2.** [excellent] excelente. ◇ *n* (*U*) libra *f* esterlina. ◇ *comp* en libras esterlinas.

sterling silver *n* plata *f* de ley.

stern [stɜːn] ◇ *adj* severo(ra). ◇ *n* popa *f*.

sternly ['stɜːnlɪ] *adv* reprobadoramente.

steroid ['stɪərɔɪd] *n* esteroide *m*.

stethoscope ['steθəskəʊp] *n* estetoscopio *m*.

stetson ['stetsn] *n* sombrero *m* de vaquero.

stevedore ['stiːvədɔːʳ] *n* estibador *m*, -ra *f*.

stew [stjuː] ◇ *n* estofado *m*, guisado *m*. ◇ *vt* [meat, vegetables] estofar, guisar; [fruit] hacer una compota de. ◇ *vi*: **to let sb ~** *fig* hacer sufrir a alguien.

steward ['stjʊəd] *n* **-1.** [on plane] auxiliar *m* de vuelo; [on ship, train] camarero *m*. **-2.** *Br* [organizer] ayudante *m y f* de organización.

stewardess ['stjʊədɪs] *n* auxiliar *f* de vuelo, azafata *f*.

stewing steak *Br* ['stjuːɪŋ-], **stewbeef** *Am* ['stjuːbiːf] *n* carne *f* para guisar OR estofar.

stg *abbr of* **sterling**.

stick [stɪk] (*pt & pp* **stuck**) ◇ *n* **-1.** [of wood, for playing sport] palo *m*. **-2.** [of dynamite] cartucho *m*; [of liquorice, rock] barra *f*.

-3. [walking stick] bastón *m*. **-4.** *phr*: **to get the wrong end of the ~** entender al revés. ◇ *vt* **-1.** [push]: **to ~ sthg in** OR **into sthg** [knife, pin] clavar algo en algo; [finger] meter algo en algo; **to ~ sthg through sthg** atravesar algo con algo. **-2.** [make adhere]: **to ~ sthg (on** OR **to sthg)** pegar algo (en algo). **-3.** *inf* [put] meter. **-4.** *Br inf* [tolerate] soportar, aguantar; **to ~ it** aguantarlo, soportarlo. ◇ *vi* **-1.** [adhere]: **to ~ (to)** pegarse (a). **-2.** [jam] atrancarse. **-3.** [remain]: **to ~ in one's mind** permanecer en la mente de uno.

◆ **stick around** *vi inf* quedarse.

◆ **stick at** *vt fus* perseverar en.

◆ **stick by** *vt fus* [person] ser fiel a; [what one has said] reafirmarse en.

◆ **stick out** ◇ *vt sep* **-1.** [make protrude] sacar. **-2.** [endure] aguantar. ◇ *vi* **-1.** [protrude] sobresalir. **-2.** *inf* [be noticeable] llamar la atención, cantar.

◆ **stick out for** *vt fus Br* insistir hasta conseguir.

◆ **stick to** *vt fus* **-1.** [follow closely] seguir. **-2.** [principles] ser fiel a; [promise, agreement] cumplir con; [decision] atenerse a; **if I were you, I'd ~ to French** yo que tú, me limitaría al francés.

◆ **stick together** *vi* [friends etc] apoyarse mutuamente.

◆ **stick up** ◇ *vt sep* **-1.** [attach] pegar OR poner en la pared. **-2.** [with gun] robar a mano armada. ◇ *vi* salir, sobresalir.

◆ **stick up for** *vt fus* defender.

◆ **stick with** *vt fus* **-1.** [not change from] seguir con. **-2.** [follow closely] seguir.

sticker ['stɪkəʳ] *n* [piece of paper] pegatina *f*.

sticking plaster ['stɪkɪŋ-] *n* esparadrapo *m*, curita *f Amer*.

stick insect *n* insecto *m* palo.

stick-in-the-mud *n inf* carroza *m y f*.

stickleback ['stɪklbæk] *n* espinoso *m*.

stickler ['stɪkləʳ] *n*: **~ for sthg** maniático *m*, -ca *f* de algo.

stick-on *adj* adhesivo(va).

stickpin ['stɪkpɪn] *n Am* alfiler *m* de corbata.

stick shift *n Am* palanca *f* de cambios.

stick-up *n inf* atraco *m* a mano armada.

sticky ['stɪkɪ] (*compar* **-ier**, *superl* **-iest**) *adj* **-1.** [tacky] pegajoso(sa). **-2.** [adhesive] adhesivo(va). **-3.** *inf* [awkward] engorroso(sa). **-4.** [humid] bochornoso(sa).

stiff [stɪf] ◇ *adj* **-1.** [inflexible] rígido(da). **-2.** [door, drawer] atascado(da). **-3.** [aching] agarrotado(da); **to be ~** tener agujetas. **-4.** [formal - person, manner] estirado(da); [- smile] rígido(da). **-5.** [severe, intense] severo(ra). **-6.**

[difficult - task] duro(ra). **-7.** *inf* [strong in alcohol] cargado(da). **-8.** [breeze] fuerte. ◇ *adv inf*: **bored/frozen** ~ muerto(ta) de aburrimiento/frío.

stiffen ['stɪfn] ◇ *vt* **-1.** [make inflexible - gen] poner rígido(da); [- clothes] almidonar. **-2.** [make more severe, intense] reforzar, intensificar. ◇ *vi* **-1.** [become inflexible] endurecerse. **-2.** [bones] entumecerse; [muscles] agarrotarse. **-3.** [become more severe, intense] intensificarse, endurecerse. **-4.** [wind] volverse más fuerte.

stiffener ['stɪfnəʳ] *n* contrafuerte *m*.

stiffness ['stɪfnɪs] *n* (*U*) **-1.** [inflexibility - of material, person] rigidez *f*. **-2.** [inability to move freely] atasco *m*. **-3.** [aching] entumecimiento *m*. **-4.** [severeness, intensity] endurecimiento *m*. **-5.** [difficulty] dureza *f*, dificultad *f*.

stifle ['staɪfl] ◇ *vt* **-1.** [prevent from breathing] ahogar, sofocar. **-2.** [prevent from happening] reprimir. ◇ *vi* ahogarse, sofocarse.

stifling ['staɪflɪŋ] *adj* agobiante, sofocante.

stigma ['stɪgmə] *n* estigma *m*.

stigmatize, -ise ['stɪgmətaɪz] *vt* estigmatizar.

stile [staɪl] *n* escalones *mpl* para pasar una valla.

stiletto heel [stɪ'letəʊ-] *n Br* tacón *m* fino OR de aguja.

still [stɪl] ◇ *adv* **-1.** [up to now, up to then, even now] todavía. **-2.** [to emphasize remaining amount] aún; **I've** ~ **got two left** aún me quedan dos. **-3.** [nevertheless, however] sin embargo, no obstante. **-4.** [with comparatives] aún; ~ **bigger** aún más grande. **-5.** [motionless] **sin moverse; sit** ~**!** ¡siéntate y no te muevas! ◇ *adj* **-1.** [not moving] inmóvil. **-2.** [calm, quiet] tranquilo(la), sosegado(da). **-3.** [not windy] apacible. **-4.** [not fizzy] sin gas. ◇ *n* **-1.** PHOT vista *f* fija. **-2.** [for making alcohol] alambique *m*.

stillborn ['stɪlbɔːn] *adj* nacido muerto (nacida muerta).

still life (*pl* **-s**) *n* bodegón *m*, naturaleza *f* muerta.

stillness ['stɪlnɪs] *n* quietud *f*.

stilted ['stɪltɪd] *adj* forzado(da).

stilts [stɪlts] *npl* **-1.** [for person] zancos *mpl*. **-2.** [for building] pilotes *mpl*.

stimulant ['stɪmjʊlənt] *n* estimulante *m*.

stimulate ['stɪmjʊleɪt] *vt* [gen] estimular; [interest] excitar.

stimulating ['stɪmjʊleɪtɪŋ] *adj* [physically] estimulante; [mentally] interesante.

stimulation [ˌstɪmjʊ'leɪʃn] *n* estímulo *m*.

stimulus ['stɪmjʊləs] (*pl* **-li** [-laɪ]) *n* estímulo *m*.

sting [stɪŋ] (*pt* & *pp* **stung**) ◇ *n* **-1.** [by bee] picadura *f*. **-2.** [of bee] aguijón *m*. **-3.** [sharp pain] escozor *m*; **to take the** ~ **out of sthg** suavizar algo. ◇ *vt* **-1.** [subj: bee, nettle] picar. **-2.** [cause sharp pain to] escocer. **-3.** *fig* [subj: criticism] herir. ◇ *vi* picar.

stinging nettle ['stɪŋɪŋ-] *n Br* ortiga *f*.

stingray ['stɪŋreɪ] *n* pastinaca *f*.

stingy ['stɪndʒɪ] (*compar* **-ier**, *superl* **-iest**) *adj inf* tacaño(ña), roñoso(sa).

stink [stɪŋk] (*pt* **stank** OR **stunk**, *pp* **stunk**) ◇ *n* peste *f*, hedor *m*. ◇ *vi* **-1.** [have unpleasant smell] apestar, heder. **-2.** *inf fig* [be worthless] no valer nada.

stink-bomb *n* bomba *f* fétida.

stinking ['stɪŋkɪŋ] ◇ *adj inf fig* asqueroso(sa). ◇ *adv* increíblemente; **they're** ~ **rich** están podridos de dinero.

stint [stɪnt] ◇ *n* período *m*. ◇ *vi*: **to** ~ **on sthg** escatimar algo.

stipend ['staɪpend] *n* estipendio *m*, remuneración *f*.

stipulate ['stɪpjʊleɪt] *vt* estipular.

stipulation [ˌstɪpjʊ'leɪʃn] *n* **-1.** [stating of conditions] estipulación *f*. **-2.** [condition] condición *f*.

stir [stɜːʳ] (*pt* & *pp* **-red**, *cont* **-ring**) ◇ *n* **-1.** [act of stirring] **to give sthg a** ~ remover algo. **-2.** [public excitement] revuelo *m*, sensación *f*. ◇ *vt* **-1.** [mix] remover. **-2.** [move gently] agitar, mover. **-3.** [move emotionally] impresionar, conmover. **-4.** [move]: **to** ~ **o.s.** moverse. ◇ *vi* **-1.** [move gently] moverse, agitarse. **-2.** [feeling, idea] despertar el interés.
◆ **stir up** *vt sep* **-1.** [cause to rise] levantar. **-2.** [cause] provocar.

stir-fry *vt* freír *rápidamente en aceite muy caliente y removiendo constantemente*.

stirring ['stɜːrɪŋ] ◇ *adj* conmovedor(ra). ◇ *n* indicio *m*.

stirrup ['stɪrəp] *n* estribo *m*.

stitch [stɪtʃ] ◇ *n* **-1.** SEWING puntada *f*. **-2.** [in knitting] punto *m*. **-3.** MED punto *m* (de sutura). **-4.** [stomach pain]: **to have a** ~ sentir pinchazos (en el estómago). **-5.** *phr*: **to be in** ~**es** partirse de risa. ◇ *vt* **-1.** SEWING coser. **-2.** MED suturar, poner puntos.

stitching ['stɪtʃɪŋ] *n* costura *f*.

stoat [stəʊt] *n* armiño *m*.

stock [stɒk] ◇ *n* **-1.** [supply] reserva *f*. **-2.** (*U*) COMM [reserves] existencias *fpl*; [selection] surtido *m*; **in** ~ en existencia, en almacén; **out of** ~ agotado(da). **-3.** FIN [of company] capital *m*; **government** ~ papel *m* del esta-

do; ~s and shares acciones *fpl*, valores *mpl*. **-4.** [ancestry] linaje *m*, estirpe *f*. **-5.** CULIN caldo *m*. **-6.** [livestock] ganado *m*, ganadería *f*. **-7.** *phr*: to take ~ (of sthg) evaluar (algo). ◇ *adj* estereotipado(da).
◇ *vt* **-1.** COMM abastecer de, tener en el almacén. **-2.** [shelves] llenar; [lake] repoblar.
◆ **stock up** *vi*: to ~ up (with) abastecerse (de).

stockade [stɒ'keɪd] *n* estacada *f*, empalizada *f*.

stockbroker ['stɒk,brəʊkəʳ] *n* corredor *m*, -ra *f* de bolsa.

stockbroking ['stɒk,brəʊkɪŋ] *n* corretaje *m* de bolsa.

stockcar ['stɒkkɑːʳ] *n* stock-car *m* (*coche adaptado para carrera de obstáculos*).

stock company *n Am* ≃ sociedad *f* anónima.

stock control *n* control *m* de existencias.

stock cube *n Br* pastilla *f* de caldo.

stock exchange *n* bolsa *f*.

stockholder ['stɒk,həʊldəʳ] *n Am* accionista *m y f*.

Stockholm ['stɒkhəʊm] *n* Estocolmo.

stocking ['stɒkɪŋ] *n* [for woman] media *f*.

stock-in-trade *n* [thing important for work] *cosa o cualidad indispensable para el trabajo*.

stockist ['stɒkɪst] *n Br* distribuidor *m*, -ra *f*.

stock market *n* bolsa *f*, mercado *m* de valores.

stock phrase *n* frase *f* estereotipada.

stockpile ['stɒkpaɪl] ◇ *n* reservas *fpl*. ◇ *vt* almacenar, acumular.

stockroom ['stɒkrʊm] *n* almacén *m*.

stock-still *adv* inmóvil.

stocktaking ['stɒk,teɪkɪŋ] *n* (U) inventario *m*, balance *m*.

stocky ['stɒkɪ] (*compar* **-ier**, *superl* **-iest**) *adj* corpulento(ta), robusto(ta).

stodgy ['stɒdʒɪ] (*compar* **-ier**, *superl* **-iest**) *adj* **-1.** [indigestible] indigesto(ta). **-2.** *pej* [uninteresting] pesado(da).

stoic ['stəʊɪk] ◇ *adj* estoico(ca). ◇ *n* estoico *m*, -ca *f*.

stoical ['stəʊɪkl] *adj* estoico(ca).

stoicism ['stəʊɪsɪzm] *n* estoicismo *m*.

stoke [stəʊk] *vt* [fire] avivar, alimentar.

stole [stəʊl] ◇ *pt* → **steal**. ◇ *n* estola *f*.

stolen ['stəʊln] *pp* → **steal**.

stolid ['stɒlɪd] *adj* impasible, imperturbable.

stomach ['stʌmək] ◇ *n* **-1.** [organ] estómago *m*. **-2.** [abdomen] vientre *m*. ◇ *vt* tragar, aguantar.

stomachache ['stʌməkeɪk] *n* dolor *m* de estómago.

stomach pump *n* bomba *f* estomacal.

stomach ulcer *n* úlcera *f* de estómago.

stomach upset [-'ʌpset] *n* trastorno *m* gástrico.

stomp [stɒmp] *vi*: to ~ in/out entrar/salir pisando fuerte.

stone [stəʊn] (*pl sense 4 only inv* OR **-s**) ◇ *n* **-1.** [mineral] piedra *f*; a ~'s throw from a tiro de piedra de. **-2.** [jewel] piedra *f* preciosa. **-3.** [seed] hueso *m*, carozo *m Amer*. **-4.** *Br* [unit of measurement] = 6,35 kilos. ◇ *comp* de piedra. ◇ *vt* apedrear.

Stone Age *n*: the ~ la Edad de Piedra.

stone-cold *adj* helado(da).

stoned [stəʊnd] *adj v inf* **-1.** [drunk] mamado(da). **-2.** [affected by drugs] colocado(da), puesto(ta).

stonemason ['stəʊn,meɪsn] *n* abañil *m*.

stonewall [,stəʊn'wɔːl] *vi* andarse con evasivas.

stoneware ['stəʊnweəʳ] *n* cerámica *f* de gres.

stonewashed ['stəʊnwɒʃt] *adj* lavado(da) a la piedra.

stonework ['stəʊnwɜːk] *n* mampostería *f*.

stony ['stəʊnɪ] (*compar* **-ier**, *superl* **-iest**) *adj* **-1.** [covered with stones] pedregoso(sa). **-2.** [unfriendly] muy frío(a), glacial.

stood [stʊd] *pt & pp* → **stand**.

stooge [stuːdʒ] *n* **-1.** *inf* [manipulated person] monigote *m y f*. **-2.** [in comedy act] comparsa *f*.

stool [stuːl] *n* [seat] taburete *m*.

stoop [stuːp] ◇ *n* **-1.** [bent back]: to walk with a ~ caminar encorvado(da). **-2.** *Am* [of house] umbral *m* con escaleras. ◇ *vi* **-1.** [bend] inclinarse, agacharse. **-2.** [hunch shoulders] encorvarse. **-3.** *fig* [debase oneself]: to ~ to sthg rebajarse a algo.

stop [stɒp] (*pt & pp* **-ped**, *cont* **-ping**) ◇ *n* **-1.** [gen] parada *f*; to come to a ~ pararse; *fig* detenerse, paralizarse; to put a ~ to sthg poner fin a algo. **-2.** [full stop] punto *m*. ◇ *vt* **-1.** [gen] parar; to ~ doing sthg dejar de hacer algo. **-2.** [prevent] impedir; to ~ sb/sthg from doing sthg impedir que alguien/algo haga algo. **-3.** [cause to stop moving] detener. **-4.** [not pay - wages] suspender; [- cheque] anular, invalidar. **-5.** [block - pipe] tapar, taponar. ◇ *vi* [gen] pararse; [rain, music] cesar; to ~ at nothing (to do sthg) no reparar en nada (para hacer algo).
◆ **stop off** *vi* hacer una parada.
◆ **stop over** *vi* pasar la noche.

◆ **stop up** ◇ *vt sep* [block] taponar, tapar. ◇ *vi Br inf* quedarse levantado(da).

stopcock ['stɒpkɒk] *n* llave *f* de paso.

stopgap ['stɒpgæp] *n* [thing] recurso *m* provisional; [person] sustituto *m*, -ta *f*.

stopover ['stɒp,əʊvər] *n* [gen] parada *f*; [of plane] escala *f*.

stoppage ['stɒpɪdʒ] *n* **-1.** [strike] paro *m*, huelga *f*. **-2.** *Br* [deduction] retención *f*.

stopper ['stɒpər] *n* tapón *m*.

stopping ['stɒpɪŋ] *adj Br*: ~ **train** tren con parada en todas las estaciones, ≃ tren *m* tranvía.

stop press *n* noticias *fpl* de última hora.

stopwatch ['stɒpwɒtʃ] *n* cronómetro *m*.

storage ['stɔːrɪdʒ] *n* almacenamiento *m*.

storage heater *n Br* calentador por almacenamiento térmico.

store [stɔːr] ◇ *n* **-1.** [shop] tienda *f*. **-2.** [supply] provisión *f*, reserva *f*. **-3.** [place of storage] almacén *m*. **-4.** *phr*: to set great ~ by OR on sthg valorar mucho algo. ◇ *vt* **-1.** [gen & COMPUT] almacenar. **-2.** [keep] guardar.

◆ **in store** *adv*: there's a surprise in ~ for you te espera una sorpresa.

◆ **store up** *vt sep* [provisions, goods] almacenar; [information] acumular.

store detective *n* guardia *m y f* de seguridad.

storehouse ['stɔːhaʊs, *pl* -haʊzɪz] *n* **-1.** [warehouse] almacén *m*, depósito *m*. **-2.** *fig* [mine] mina *f*.

storekeeper ['stɔː,kiːpər] *n Am* tendero *m*, -ra *f*.

storeroom ['stɔːrʊm] *n* [gen] almacén *m*; [for food] despensa *f*.

storey *Br* (*pl* **storeys**), **story** *Am* ['stɔːrɪ] (*pl* **-ies**) *n* planta *f*.

stork [stɔːk] *n* cigüeña *f*.

storm [stɔːm] ◇ *n* **-1.** [bad weather] tormenta *f*; a ~ in a teacup una tormenta en un vaso de agua. **-2.** [violent reaction] torrente *m*. ◇ *vt* MIL asaltar. ◇ *vi* **-1.** [go angrily]: to ~ out salir echando pestes. **-2.** [say angrily] vociferar.

storm cloud *n lit* nubarrón *m*.

storming ['stɔːmɪŋ] *n* asalto *m*; the ~ of the Bastille la toma de la Bastilla.

stormy ['stɔːmɪ] (*compar* **-ier**, *superl* **-iest**) *adj* **-1.** [weather] tormentoso(sa). **-2.** [meeting] acalorado(da); [relationship] tempestuoso(sa).

story ['stɔːrɪ] (*pl* **-ies**) *n* **-1.** [tale] cuento *m*, relato *m*; it's the (same) old ~ es la misma historia de siempre; to cut a long ~ short en resumidas cuentas, para abreviar. **-2.**

[history] historia *f*. **-3.** [news article] artículo *m*. **-4.** *euphemism* [lie] cuento *m*. **-5.** *Am* = storey.

storybook ['stɔːrɪbʊk] *adj* de novela, de cuento.

storyteller ['stɔːrɪ,telər] *n* **-1.** [teller of story] narrador *m*, -ra *f*, cuentista *m y f*. **-2.** *euphemism* [liar] cuentista *m y f*.

stout [staʊt] ◇ *adj* **-1.** [rather fat] corpulento(ta), gordo(da). **-2.** [strong, solid] fuerte, sólido(da). **-3.** [resolute] firme. ◇ *n* (U) cerveza *f* negra.

stoutness ['staʊtnɪs] *n* [portliness] corpulencia *f*.

stove [stəʊv] ◇ *pt & pp* → stave. ◇ *n* [for heating] estufa *f*; [for cooking] cocina *f*.

stow [stəʊ] *vt*: to ~ sthg (away) guardar algo.

◆ **stow away** *vi* viajar de polizón.

stowaway ['stəʊəweɪ] *n* polizón *m*.

straddle ['strædl] *vt* **-1.** [subj: person] sentarse a horcajadas sobre. **-2.** [subj: bridge, town] atravesar, cruzar.

strafe [strɑːf] *vt* MIL bombardear.

straggle ['strægl] *vi* **-1.** [sprawl] desparramarse. **-2.** [dawdle] rezagarse.

straggler ['stræglər] *n* rezagado *m*, -da *f*.

straggly ['stræglɪ] (*compar* **-ier**, *superl* **-iest**) *adj* desordenado(da).

straight [streɪt] ◇ *adj* **-1.** [not bent] recto(ta). **-2.** [hair] liso(sa). **-3.** [honest, frank] franco(ca), sincero(ra). **-4.** [tidy] arreglado(da). **-5.** [choice, swap] simple, fácil. **-6.** [alcoholic drink] solo(la), sin mezclar. **-7.** *inf* [conventional] ordinario(ria). **-8.** *gay sl* [heterosexual] heterosexual.

◇ *adv* **-1.** [in a straight line - horizontally] directamente; [- vertically] recto(ta); ~ ahead todo recto; I couldn't see ~ no veía bien. **-2.** [directly] directamente; [immediately] inmediatamente. **-3.** [frankly] francamente. **-4.** [tidy] en orden. **-5.** [undiluted] solo(la). **-6.** *phr*: let's get things ~ vamos a aclarar las cosas; to go ~ [criminal] dejar la mala vida.

◇ *n* [of race track]: the ~ la recta final.

◆ **straight off** *adv* en el acto.

◆ **straight out** *adv* sin tapujos.

straightaway [,streɪtə'weɪ] *adv* en seguida.

straighten ['streɪtn] ◇ *vt* **-1.** [tidy - room] ordenar; [- hair, dress] poner bien. **-2.** [make straight - horizontally] poner recto(ta); [- vertically] enderezar. ◇ *vi*: to ~ (up) enderezarse, ponerse recto(ta).

◆ **straighten out** *vt sep* [mess] arreglar; [problem] resolver.

straight face *n*: to keep a ~ aguantar la risa.

straightforward [ˌstreɪt'fɔːwəd] *adj* **-1.** [easy] sencillo(lla). **-2.** [frank - answer] directo(ta); [- person] abierto(ta), sincero(ra).

strain [streɪn] ◇ *n* **-1.** [weight] peso *m*; [pressure] presión *f*. **-2.** [mental stress] tensión *f* nerviosa. **-3.** [physical injury] distensión *f*, torcedura *f*; **eye ~** vista *f* cansada. **-4.** [worry, difficulty] esfuerzo *m*. **-5.** [variety] tipo *m*, variedad *f*.
◇ *vt* **-1.** [overtax - budget] estirar; [- ceiling] forzar; [- enthusiasm] agotar. **-2.** [use hard]: **to ~ one's eyes/ears** aguzar la vista/el oído. **-3.** [injure - eyes] cansar; [- muscle, back] distender, torcerse. **-4.** [drain] colar.
◇ *vi*: **to ~ to do sthg** esforzarse por hacer algo.
◆ **strains** *npl literary* [of music] acordes *mpl*, compases *mpl*.

strained [streɪnd] *adj* **-1.** [worried] preocupado(da). **-2.** [unfriendly] tirante, tenso(sa). **-3.** [insincere] forzado(da).

strainer ['streɪnər] *n* colador *m*.

strait [streɪt] *n* estrecho *m*.
◆ **straits** *npl*: **in dire** OR **desperate ~s** en un serio aprieto.

straitened ['streɪtnd] *adj fml*: **in ~ circumstances** en circunstancias apuradas.

straitjacket ['streɪtˌdʒækɪt] *n* [garment] camisa *f* de fuerza.

straitlaced [ˌstreɪt'leɪst] *adj pej* mojigato(ta), estrecho(cha).

Strait of Gibraltar *n*: **the ~** el estrecho de Gibraltar.

Strait of Hormuz [-hɔː'muːz], **Strait of Ormuz** [-ɔː'muːz] *n*: **the ~** el estrecho de Ormuz.

strand [strænd] *n* **-1.** [thin piece] hebra *f*; **a ~ of hair** un pelo del cabello. **-2.** [theme, element] cabo *m*.

stranded [strændɪd] *adj* [ship] varado(da), encallado(da); [person] colgado(da).

strange [streɪndʒ] *adj* **-1.** [unusual] raro(ra), extraño(ña). **-2.** [unfamiliar] extraño(ña), desconocido(da).

strangely ['streɪndʒlɪ] *adv* **-1.** [in an odd manner] de manera extraña. **-2.** [unexpectedly] inesperadamente. **-3.** [surprisingly]: **~ (enough)** aunque parezca extraño.

stranger ['streɪndʒər] *n* **-1.** [unfamiliar person] extraño *m*, -ña *f*, desconocido *m*, -da *f*; **to be a/no ~ to sthg** no estar/estar familiarizado con algo. **-2.** [outsider] forastero *m*, -ra *f*.

strangle ['stræŋgl] *vt* **-1.** [kill] estrangular. **-2.** *fig* [stifle] ahogar, reprimir.

stranglehold ['stræŋglhəʊld] *n* **-1.** [round neck] collar *m* de fuerza. **-2.** *fig* [strong influence] dominio *m* absoluto.

strangulation [ˌstræŋgjʊ'leɪʃn] *n* estrangulamiento *m*.

strap [stræp] ◇ (*pt* & *pp* **-ped**, *cont* **-ping**) ◇ *n* **-1.** [of handbag, rifle] bandolera *f*. **-2.** [of watch, case] correa *f*; [of dress, bra] tirante *m*. ◇ *vt* [fasten] atar con correa.

strapless ['stræplɪs] *adj* sin tirantes.

strapping ['stræpɪŋ] *adj* robusto(ta).

Strasbourg ['stræzbɜːg] *n* Estrasburgo.

strata ['strɑːtə] *pl* → **stratum**.

stratagem ['strætədʒəm] *n* estratagema *f*.

strategic [strə'tiːdʒɪk] *adj* estratégico(ca).

strategist ['strætɪdʒɪst] *n* estratega *m y f*.

strategy ['strætɪdʒɪ] (*pl* **-ies**) *n* estrategia *f*.

stratified ['strætɪfaɪd] *adj lit* & *fig* estratificado(da).

stratosphere ['strætəˌsfɪər] *n*: **the ~** la estratosfera.

stratum ['strɑːtəm] (*pl* **-ta**) *n lit* & *fig* estrato *m*.

straw [strɔː] ◇ *n* **-1.** AGR paja *f*. **-2.** [for drinking] pajita *f*, paja *f*, pitillo *m Amer*. **-3.** *phr*: **to clutch at ~s** agarrarse a un clavo ardiendo; **the last ~** el colmo. ◇ *comp* de paja.

strawberry ['strɔːbərɪ] (*pl* **-ies**) ◇ *n* fresa *f*, frutilla *f Amer*. ◇ *comp* de fresa.

straw poll *n* sondeo *m* de opinión.

stray [streɪ] ◇ *adj* **-1.** [animal - without owner] callejero(ra); [- lost] extraviado(da). **-2.** [bullet] perdido(da); [example] aislado(da). ◇ *n* [animal] animal *m* callejero. ◇ *vi* **-1.** [from path] desviarse; [from group] extraviarse. **-2.** [thoughts, mind] perderse; **to ~ from the point** desviarse del tema, divagar.

streak [striːk] ◇ *n* **-1.** [of hair] mechón *m*; [of lightning] rayo *m*; [of grease] raya *f*. **-2.** [in character] vena *f*. **-3.** [period]: **a lucky ~** una racha de (buena) suerte. ◇ *vi* [move quickly] ir como un rayo.

streaked [striːkt] *adj* [marked]: **~ with** [colour] veteado(da) de; [grease, dirt] manchado(da) de.

streaky ['striːkɪ] (*compar* **-ier**, *superl* **-iest**) *adj* rayado(da), veteado(da).

streaky bacon *n Br* bacon *m* entreverado.

stream [striːm] ◇ *n* **-1.** [small river] riachuelo *m*, río *m*, quebrada *f Amer*. **-2.** [of liquid, gas] chorro *m*; [of gas, light] raudal *m*. **-3.** [current] corriente *f*. **-4.** [of people, cars] torrente *m*. **-5.** [continuous series] sarta *f*, serie *f*. **-6.** *Br* SCH grupo *m*.
◇ *vi* **-1.** [liquid, gas, light]: **to ~ into** entrar a raudales en; **to ~ out of** brotar de. **-2.** [people, cars]: **to ~ into** entrar atropelladamente en; **to ~ out of** salir atropelladamente de.

◇ *vt Br* SCH agrupar de acuerdo con el rendimiento escolar.

streamer ['striːməʳ] *n* [for party] serpentina *f*.

streamline ['striːmlaɪn] *vt* **-1.** [make aerodynamic] dar línea aerodinámica a. **-2.** [make efficient] racionalizar.

streamlined ['striːmlaɪnd] *adj* **-1.** [aerodynamic] aerodinámico(ca). **-2.** [efficient] racional.

street [striːt] *n* calle *f*, jirón *m Amer*; **to be right up one's ~** *Br inf* ser justo lo que a uno le interesa; **to be ~s ahead of sb** *Br* estar muy por delante de alguien.

streetcar ['striːtkɑːʳ] *n Am* tranvía *m*.

street-credibility *n* (*U*) *inf* imagen *f*, aceptación *f* (*entre la gente joven*).

street lamp, street light *n* farola *f*.

street lighting *n* alumbrado *m* público.

street map *n* plano *m* (de la ciudad).

street market *n* mercado *m* al aire libre.

street plan *n* plano *m* (de la ciudad).

street value *n* precio *m* OR valor *m* en la calle.

streetwise ['striːtwaɪz] *adj inf* espabilado(da).

strength [streŋθ] *n* **-1.** [physical or mental power] fuerza *f*. **-2.** [power, influence] poder *m*; **to go from ~ to ~** tener cada vez más éxito, prosperar. **-3.** [quality] punto *m* fuerte. **-4.** [solidity - of material structure] solidez *f*. **-5.** [intensity - of feeling, smell, wind] intensidad *f*; [- of accent, wine] fuerza *f*; [- of drug] potencia *f*. **-6.** [credibility, weight] peso *m*, fuerza *f*; **on the ~ of** a partir de, en base a. **-7.** (*U*) [in numbers - gen] número *m*; [- army] efectivos *mpl*; **in ~** en gran número; **to be at/below full ~** estar/no estar al completo. **-8.** [of currency] valor *m*.

strengthen ['streŋθn] ◇ *vt* **-1.** [gen] fortalecer. **-2.** [reinforce - argument, bridge] reforzar. **-3.** [intensify] acentuar, intensificar. **-4.** [make closer] estrechar. ◇ *vi* **-1.** [improve - sales, currency] fortalecerse. **-2.** [intensify] acentuarse, intensificarse. **-3.** [become closer] estrecharse.

strenuous ['strenjʊəs] *adj* agotador(ra), extenuante.

stress [stres] ◇ *n* **-1.** [emphasis]: **~ (on)** hincapié *m* OR énfasis *m inv* (en). **-2.** [tension, anxiety] estrés *m*, tensión *f* nerviosa; **to be under ~** estar estresado. **-3.** [physical pressure]: **~ (on)** presión *f* (en). **-4.** LING [on word, syllable] acento *m*. ◇ *vt* **-1.** [emphasize] recalcar, subrayar. **-2.** LING [word, syllable] acentuar.

stressed [strest] *adj* [anxious] estresado(da).

stressful ['stresful] *adj* estresante.

stretch [stretʃ] ◇ *adj* elástico(ca). ◇ *n* **-1.** [of land, water] extensión *f*; [of road, river] tramo *m*, trecho *m*. **-2.** [of time] período *m*. **-3.** [effort]: **by no ~ of the imagination** ni por asomo. ◇ *vt* **-1.** [gen] estirar. **-2.** [overtax - person] extender. **-3.** [challenge] hacer rendir al máximo. ◇ *vi* **-1.** [area]: **to ~ over/from ... to** extenderse por/desde ... hasta. **-2.** [person, animal] estirarse. **-3.** [be pulled taut] dar de sí.

◆ **at a stretch** *adv* de un tirón, sin interrupción.

◆ **stretch out** ◇ *vt sep* [foot, leg] estirar; [hand, arm] alargar. ◇ *vi* **-1.** [lie down] tumbarse. **-2.** [reach out] estirarse.

stretcher ['stretʃəʳ] *n* camilla *f*.

stretcher party *n* camilleros *mpl*.

stretchmarks ['stretʃmɑːks] *npl* estrías *fpl*.

stretchy ['stretʃɪ] (*compar* **-ier,** *superl* **-iest**) *adj* elástico(ca).

strew [struː] (*pt* **-ed,** *pp* **strewn** [struːn] OR **-ed**) *vt*: **to be strewn on/over** estar esparcido(da) sobre/por; **to be strewn with** estar cubierto(ta) de.

stricken ['strɪkn] *adj*: **to be ~ by** OR **with** [illness] estar aquejado(da) de; [grief] estar afligido(da) por; [doubts, horror] estar atenazado(da) por.

strict [strɪkt] *adj* **-1.** [gen] estricto(ta). **-2.** [precise] exacto(ta), estricto(ta). **-3.** [faithful, disciplined] riguroso(sa).

strictly ['strɪktlɪ] *adv* **-1.** [severely] severamente. **-2.** [absolutely - prohibited] terminantemente; [- confidential] absolutamente, totalmente. **-3.** [exactly] exactamente; **~ speaking** en el sentido estricto de la palabra. **-4.** [exclusively] exclusivamente.

strictness ['strɪktnɪs] *n* [severity, rigidity] severidad *f*.

stride [straɪd] (*pt* **strode,** *pp* **stridden** ['strɪdn]) ◇ *n* zancada *f*; **to take sthg in one's ~** tomarse algo con calma. ◇ *vi* andar a zancadas.

◆ **strides** *npl*: **to make ~s** hacer progresos.

strident ['straɪdnt] *adj* **-1.** [harsh] estridente. **-2.** [vociferous] exaltado(da).

strife [straɪf] *n* (*U*) *fml* conflictos *mpl*.

strike [straɪk] (*pt* & *pp* **struck**) ◇ *n* **-1.** [refusal to work etc] huelga *f*; **to be (out) on ~** estar en huelga; **to go on ~** declararse en huelga. **-2.** MIL. ataque *m*. **-3.** [find] descubrimiento *m*.

◇ *comp* de huelga.

◇ *vt* **-1.** *fml* [hit - deliberately] golpear, pegar; [- accidentally] chocar contra. **-2.** [subj: disaster, earthquake] asolar; [subj: lightning]

fulminar, alcanzar. **-3.** [subj: thought, idea]. ocurrírsele a. **-4.** [give impression]: **to ~ sb as sthg** parecer a alguien algo. **-5.** [impress]: **to be struck by** OR **with sthg** estar impresionado(da) por OR ante algo. **-6.** [deal, bargain] cerrar. **-7.** [match] encender. **-8.** [find] encontrar; **to ~ a balance (between)** llegar a un punto medio (entre); **to ~ a serious note** tener un tono de seriedad. **-9.** *phr*: **to be struck blind/dumb** quedarse ciego(ga)/mudo(da); **to ~ fear** OR **terror into sb** infundir temor en alguien; **to ~ (it) lucky** tener suerte; **to ~ it rich** hacerse rico(ca). ◇ *vi* **-1.** [stop working] estar en huelga. **-2.** *fml* [hit accidentally]: **to ~ against** chocar contra. **-3.** [hurricane, disaster] sobrevenir; [lightning] caer. **-4.** *fml* [attack] atacar. **-5.** [chime] dar la hora; **the clock struck six** el reloj dio las seis.
◆ **strike back** *vi* devolver el golpe.
◆ **strike down** *vt sep* fulminar.
◆ **strike off** *vt sep*: **to be struck off** ser inhabilitado(da).
◆ **strike out** ◇ *vt sep* tachar. ◇ *vi* **-1.** [head out] partir, ponerse en camino. **-2.** [do something different] hacer algo diferente; **to ~ out on one's own** establecerse uno por su cuenta.
◆ **strike up** ◇ *vt fus* **-1.** [friendship] trabar; [conversation] entablar. **-2.** [tune] empezar a tocar. ◇ *vi* empezar a tocar.

strikebound ['straɪkbaʊnd] *adj* paralizado(da) por la huelga.

strikebreaker ['straɪk,breɪkə'] *n* esquirol *m* y *f*.

strike pay *n* (*U*) subsidio *m* de huelga.

striker ['straɪkə'] *n* **-1.** [person on strike] huelguista *m* y *f*. **-2.** FTBL delantero *m*, -ra *f*.

striking ['straɪkɪŋ] *adj* **-1.** [noticeable, unusual] chocante, sorprendente. **-2.** [attractive] llamativo(va), atractivo(va).

striking distance *n*: **to be within ~ (of)** estar a corta distancia (de).

string [strɪŋ] (*pt & pp* **strung**) ◇ *n* **-1.** [thin rope] cuerda *f*, piolín *m Amer*; **a (piece of) ~** un cordón; **(with) no ~s attached** sin ninguna condición OR ningún compromiso; **to pull ~s** utilizar uno sus influencias. **-2.** [of beads, pearls] sarta *f*. **-3.** [series] serie *f*, sucesión *f*. **-4.** [of musical instrument] cuerda *f*. ◇ *comp* de cuerda.
◆ **strings** *npl* MUS: **the ~s** los instrumentos de cuerda.
◆ **string along** *vt sep inf* [deceive] dar falsas esperanzas a.
◆ **string out** *vt fus*: **to be strung out** alinearse.
◆ **string together** *vt sep* enlazar, unir.

◆ **string up** *vt sep inf* [kill by hanging] colgar.

string bean *n* judía *f* verde.

stringed instrument ['strɪŋd-] *n* instrumento *m* de cuerda.

stringent ['strɪndʒənt] *adj* estricto(ta), severo(ra).

string quartet *n* cuarteto *m* de cuerda.

strip [strɪp] (*pt & pp* **-ped**, *cont* **-ping**) ◇ *n* **-1.** [narrow piece] tira *f*; **to tear a ~ off sb, to tear sb off a ~** *Br* echarle una bronca a alguien. **-2.** [narrow area] franja *f*. **-3.** *Br* SPORT camiseta *f*, colores *mpl*. ◇ *vt* **-1.** [undress] desnudar. **-2.** [paint, wallpaper] quitar. **-3.** [take away from]: **to ~ sb of sthg** despojar a alguien de algo. ◇ *vi* **-1.** [undress] desnudarse. **-2.** [do a striptease] hacer un striptease.
◆ **strip off** ◇ *vt sep* quitarse. ◇ *vi* desnudarse.

strip cartoon *n Br* historieta *f*, tira *f* cómica.

stripe [straɪp] *n* **-1.** [band of colour] raya *f*, franja *f*. **-2.** [sign of rank] galón *m*.

striped [straɪpt] *adj* a rayas.

strip lighting *n* alumbrado *m* fluorescente.

stripper ['strɪpə'] *n* **-1.** [performer of striptease] artista *m* y *f* de striptease. **-2.** [for paint] disolvente *m*.

strip-search ◇ *n* registro policial de una persona haciéndole desnudarse. ◇ *vt* registrar a alguien haciéndole desnudarse.

strip show *n* espectáculo *m* de striptease.

striptease ['striptiːz] *n* striptease *m*.

stripy ['straɪpɪ] (*compar* **-ier**, *superl* **-iest**) *adj* a rayas, de rayas.

strive [straɪv] (*pt* **strove**, *pp* **striven** ['strɪvn]) *vi fml*: **to ~ for sthg** luchar por algo; **to ~ to do sthg** esforzarse por hacer algo.

strobe (light) ['strəʊb-] *n* luz *f* de discoteca, luz estroboscópica.

strode [strəʊd] *pt* → **stride**.

stroke [strəʊk] ◇ *n* **-1.** MED apoplejía *f*, derrame *m* cerebral. **-2.** [of pen] trazo *m*; [of brush] pincelada *f*. **-3.** [in swimming] brazada *f*; [in rowing] palada *f*. **-4.** [style of swimming] estilo *m*. **-5.** [in tennis, golf etc] golpe *m*. **-6.** [of clock] campanada *f*. **-7.** *Br* TYPO [oblique] barra *f*. **-8.** [piece]: **a ~ of genius** una genialidad; **a ~ of luck** un golpe de suerte; **not to do a ~ of work** no dar (ni) golpe; **at a ~** de una vez, de golpe. ◇ *vt* acariciar.

stroll [strəʊl] ◇ *n* paseo *m*. ◇ *vi* pasear.

stroller ['strəʊlə'] *n Am* [for baby] sillita *f* (de niño).

strong [strɒŋ] *adj* **-1.** [gen] fuerte; **to be still going ~** [person] conservarse bien; [group]

seguir en la brecha; [object] funcionar bien. **-2.** [material, structure] sólido(da), resistente. **-3.** [feeling, belief] profundo(da); [opposition, denial] firme; [support] acérrimo(ma); [accent] marcado(da). **-4.** [discipline, policy] estricto(ta). **-5.** [argument] convincente. **-6.** [in numbers]: **the crowd was 2,000 ~** la multitud constaba de 2.000 personas. **-7.** [good, gifted]: **I've never been ~ at sums** las sumas nunca han sido mi fuerte; **one's ~ point** el punto fuerte de uno. **-8.** [concentrated] concentrado(da).

strongarm ['strɒŋɑ:m] *adj*: **to use ~ tactics** recurrir a la mano dura.

strongbox ['strɒŋbɒks] *n* caja *f* fuerte.

stronghold ['strɒŋhəʊld] *n fig* [bastion] bastión *m*, baluarte *m*.

strong language *n* (*U*) *euphemism* lenguaje *m* fuerte.

strongly ['strɒŋlɪ] *adv* **-1.** [sturdily] fuertemente. **-2.** [in degree] intensamente. **-3.** [fervently]: **to support/oppose sthg ~** apoyar/oponerse a algo totalmente.

strong man *n* forzudo *m*, hércules *m inv*.

strong-minded [-'maɪndɪd] *adj* firme, decidido(da).

strong room *n* cámara *f* acorazada.

strong-willed [-'wɪld] *adj* tozudo(da).

stroppy ['strɒpɪ] (*compar* **-ier**, *superl* **-iest**) *adj Br inf* con mala uva; **to get ~** cabrearse.

strove ['strəʊv] *pt* → **strive**.

struck [strʌk] *pt & pp* → **strike**.

structural ['strʌktʃərəl] *adj* estructural.

structurally ['strʌktʃərəlɪ] *adv* estructuralmente.

structure ['strʌktʃə'] ◇ *n* **-1.** [arrangement] estructura *f*. **-2.** [building] construcción *f*. ◇ *vt* estructurar.

struggle ['strʌgl] ◇ *n* **-1.** [great effort]: **~ (for sthg/to do sthg)** lucha *f* (por algo/por hacer algo). **-2.** [fight, tussle] forcejeo *m*. **-3.** [difficult task]: **it will be a ~ to do it** hacerlo supondrá un gran esfuerzo.
◇ *vi* **-1.** [make great effort]: **to ~ (for sthg/to do sthg)** luchar (por algo/por hacer algo). **-2.** [to free o.s.]: **to ~ free** forcejear para soltarse. **-3.** [fight]: **to ~ (with sb)** pelearse (con alguien). **-4.** [move with difficulty]: **to ~ with sthg** llevar algo con dificultad; **to ~ to one's feet** lograr levantarse a duras penas.
◆ **struggle on** *vi*: **to ~ on (with sthg)** continuar a duras penas (con algo).

struggling ['strʌglɪŋ] *adj* [likely to lose, fail] con dificultades.

strum [strʌm] (*pt & pp* **-med**, *cont* **-ming**) *vt & vi* rasguear.

strung [strʌŋ] *pt & pp* → **string**.

strut [strʌt] (*pt & pp* **-ted**, *cont* **-ting**) ◇ *n* **-1.** CONSTR puntal *m*. **-2.** AERON montante *m*. ◇ *vi* andar pavoneándose.

strychnine ['strɪkni:n] *n* estricnina *f*.

stub [stʌb] (*pt & pp* **-bed**, *cont* **-bing**) ◇ *n* **-1.** [of cigarette] colilla *f*; [of pencil] cabo *m*. **-2.** [of ticket] resguardo *m*; [of cheque] matriz *f*. ◇ *vt*: **to ~ one's toe on** darse con el pie en.
◆ **stub out** *vt sep* apagar.

stubble ['stʌbl] *n* (*U*) **-1.** [in field] rastrojo *m*. **-2.** [on chin] barba *f* incipiente OR de tres días.

stubborn ['stʌbən] *adj* **-1.** [person] terco(ca), testarudo(da). **-2.** [stain] rebelde, difícil.

stubbornly ['stʌbənlɪ] *adv* tercamente, obstinadamente.

stubby ['stʌbɪ] (*compar* **-ier**, *superl* **-iest**) *adj* rechoncho(cha).

stucco ['stʌkəʊ] *n* estuco *m*.

stuck [stʌk] ◇ *pt & pp* → **stick**. ◇ *adj* **-1.** [jammed - lid, window] atascado(da); [- finger] pillado(da). **-2.** [unable to progress] atascado(da). **-3.** [stranded] colgado(da). **-4.** [in a meeting, at home] encerrado(da).

stuck-up *adj inf pej* engreído(da), que se lo tiene creído.

stud [stʌd] *n* **-1.** [metal decoration] tachón *m*. **-2.** [earring] pendiente *m*. **-3.** *Br* [on boot, shoe] taco *m*. **-4.** [horse] semental *m*; **to be put out to ~** ser utilizado como semental.

studded ['stʌdɪd] *adj*: **~ (with)** tachonado(da) (con).

student ['stju:dnt] ◇ *n* **-1.** [at college, university] estudiante *m* y *f*. **-2.** [scholar] estudioso *m*, **-sa** *f*. ◇ *comp* estudiantil.

students' union *n* **-1.** [organization] sindicato *m* de estudiantes. **-2.** [building] *lugar donde se reúnen los estudiantes*.

stud farm *n* cuadra *f*.

studied ['stʌdɪd] *adj* [look, smile] estudiado(da); [answer] premeditado(da).

studio ['stju:dɪəʊ] (*pl* **-s**) *n* estudio *m*.

studio apartment *Am* = **studio flat**.

studio audience *n* público *m* invitado (al estudio).

studio flat *Br*, **studio apartment** *Am n* estudio *m*.

studious ['stju:djəs] *adj* estudioso(sa).

studiously ['stju:djəslɪ] *adv* cuidadosamente.

study ['stʌdɪ] (*pl* **-ies**, *pt & pp* **-ied**) ◇ *n* [gen] estudio *m*; [piece of research] investigación *f*. ◇ *vt* **-1.** [learn] estudiar. **-2.** [examine - report, sb's face] examinar, estudiar. ◇ *vi* estudiar.

stuff [stʌf] ◇ n (U) inf **-1.** [things, belongings] cosas fpl; **to know one's ~** saber uno lo que se hace; **and all that ~** y todo eso. **-2.** [substance]: **what's that ~ in your pocket?** ¿qué es eso que llevas en el bolsillo?; **this whisky is good ~** este whisky es del bueno.
◇ vt **-1.** [push, put] meter. **-2.** [fill, cram]: **to ~ sthg (with)** [box, room] llenar algo (de); [pillow, doll] rellenar algo (de). **-3.** [with food]: **to ~ o.s. (with** OR **on)** inf atiborrarse OR hartarse (de). **-4.** CULIN rellenar.

stuffed [stʌft] adj **-1.** [filled, crammed]: **~ with** atestado(da) de. **-2.** inf [subj: person - with food] lleno(na), inflado(da). **-3.** CULIN relleno(na). **-4.** [preserved - animal] disecado(da). **-5.** phr: **get ~!** Br v inf ¡vete al cuerno!

stuffing ['stʌfɪŋ] n (U) relleno m.

stuffy ['stʌfɪ] (compar **-ier**, superl **-iest**) adj **-1.** [atmosphere] cargado(da); [room] mal ventilado(da). **-2.** [old-fashioned] retrógrado(da), carca.

stumble ['stʌmbl] vi **-1.** [trip] tropezar. **-2.** [make mistake in speech] equivocarse; **to ~ at** OR **over sthg** trabársele la lengua con algo; **to ~ through sthg** decir algo sin parar de equivocarse.
◆ **stumble across, stumble on** vt fus [thing] dar con; [person] encontrarse con.

stumbling block ['stʌmblɪŋ-] n obstáculo m, escollo m.

stump [stʌmp] ◇ n [of tree] tocón m; [of limb] muñón m. ◇ vt [subj: question, problem] dejar perplejo(ja). ◇ vi caminar con paso fuerte.
◆ **stumps** npl CRICKET estacas fpl.
◆ **stump up** vt fus Br inf apoquinar.

stun [stʌn] (pt & pp **-ned**, cont **-ning**) vt lit & fig aturdir.

stung [stʌŋ] pt & pp → **sting**.

stun grenade n granada f de estampida.

stunk [stʌŋk] pt & pp → **stink**.

stunning ['stʌnɪŋ] adj **-1.** [very beautiful] imponente. **-2.** [shocking] pasmoso(sa).

stunt [stʌnt] ◇ n **-1.** [for publicity] truco m publicitario. **-2.** CINEMA escena f arriesgada OR peligrosa. ◇ vt atrofiar.

stunted ['stʌntɪd] adj esmirriado(da).

stunt man n especialista m, doble m.

stupefy ['stju:pɪfaɪ] (pt & pp **-ied**) vt **-1.** [tire, bore] aturdir, atontar. **-2.** [surprise] dejar estupefacto(ta).

stupendous [stju:'pendəs] adj inf [wonderful] estupendo(da); [very large] enorme.

stupid ['stju:pɪd] adj **-1.** [foolish] estúpi-

do(da), baboso(sa) Amer. **-2.** inf [annoying] puñetero(ra).

stupidity [stju:'pɪdətɪ] n (U) estupidez f.

stupidly ['stju:pɪdlɪ] adv estúpidamente, tontamente.

stupor ['stju:pə'] n estupor m, atontamiento m.

sturdy ['stɜːdɪ] (compar **-ier**, superl **-iest**) adj [person, shoulders] fuerte; [furniture, bridge] firme, sólido(da).

sturgeon ['stɜːdʒən] (pl inv) n esturión m.

stutter ['stʌtə'] ◇ n tartamudeo m. ◇ vi tartamudear.

sty [staɪ] (pl **sties**) n [pigsty] pocilga f.

stye [staɪ] n orzuelo m.

style [staɪl] ◇ n **-1.** [characteristic manner] estilo m; **in the ~ of** al estilo de. **-2.** (U) [smartness, elegance] clase f. **-3.** [design] modelo m. ◇ vt [hair] peinar.

styling mousse ['staɪlɪŋ-] n espuma f (moldeadora).

stylish ['staɪlɪʃ] adj elegante, con estilo.

stylist ['staɪlɪst] n [hairdresser] peluquero m, -ra f.

stylized, -ised ['staɪlaɪzd] adj estilizado(da).

stylus ['staɪləs] (pl **-es**) n [on record player] aguja f.

stymie ['staɪmɪ] vt inf [plan] fastidiar; [person] desconcertar.

styrofoam® ['staɪrəfəʊm] n Am poliestireno m.

suave [swɑːv] adj [well-mannered] afable, amable; [obsequious] zalamero(ra).

sub [sʌb] n inf **-1.** SPORT (abbr of **substitute**) reserva m y f. **-2.** (abbr of **submarine**) submarino m. **-3.** Br (abbr of **subscription**) subscripción f. **-4.** Am [sandwich] bocadillo largo y con relleno variado.

sub- [sʌb] prefix sub-.

subcommittee ['sʌbkə,mɪtɪ] n [gen] subcomité m; POL subcomisión f.

subconscious [,sʌb'kɒnʃəs] ◇ adj subconsciente. ◇ n: **the ~** el subconsciente.

subconsciously [,sʌb'kɒnʃəslɪ] adj de forma subconsciente.

subcontinent [,sʌb'kɒntɪnənt] n subcontinente m.

subcontract [,sʌbkən'trækt] vt subcontratar.

subculture ['sʌb,kʌltʃə'] n subcultura f.

subdivide [,sʌbdɪ'vaɪd] vt subdividir.

subdue [səb'dju:] vt **-1.** [enemy, nation] someter, sojuzgar. **-2.** [feelings] contener, dominar. **-3.** [light, colour] atenuar, suavizar.

subdued [səb'djuːd] *adj* **-1.** [person] apagado(da). **-2.** [emotion] ligero(ra). **-3.** [colour, light] tenue.

subeditor [ˌsʌb'edɪtəʳ] *n* redactor *m*, -ra *f*.

subgroup ['sʌbgruːp] *n* subgrupo *m*.

subheading ['sʌbˌhedɪŋ] *n* subtítulo *m*.

subhuman [ˌsʌb'hjuːmən] *adj pej* infrahumano(na).

subject [*adj, n & prep* 'sʌbdʒekt, *vt* səb'dʒekt] ◇ *adj* **-1.** [not independent] subyugado(da). **-2.** [affected]: ~ **to** sthg [taxes, changes, law] sujeto(ta) a; [illness] proclive a. ◇ *n* **-1.** [topic] tema *m*. **-2.** GRAMM sujeto *m*. **-3.** SCH & UNIV asignatura *f*. **-4.** [citizen] súbdito *m*, -ta *f*. ◇ *vt* **-1.** [bring under control] someter, dominar. **-2.** [force to experience]: **to ~ sb to sthg** someter a alguien a algo. ◆ **subject to** *prep* dependiendo de; ~ **to approval** previa aprobación.

subjection [səb'dʒekʃn] *n* sometimiento *m*, dominación *f*.

subjective [səb'dʒektɪv] *adj* subjetivo(va).

subjectively [səb'dʒektɪvlɪ] *adv* de forma subjetiva.

subject matter ['sʌbdʒekt-] *n* (*U*) tema *m*, contenido *m*.

sub judice [-'dʒuːdɪsɪ] *adj* JUR sub júdice.

subjugate ['sʌbdʒʊgeɪt] *vt fml* **-1.** [conquer] subyugar, sojuzgar. **-2.** [treat as less important] supeditar.

subjunctive [səb'dʒʌŋktɪv] *n* GRAMM: **(mood)** (modo *m*) subjuntivo *m*.

sublet [ˌsʌb'let] (*pt & pp* **sublet**, *cont* **-ting**) *vt & vi* subarrendar.

sublime [sə'blaɪm] *adj* [wonderful] sublime; **from the ~ to the ridiculous** de lo sublime a lo ridículo.

sublimely [sə'blaɪmlɪ] *adv* absolutamente, completamente.

subliminal [ˌsʌb'lɪmɪnl] *adj* subliminal.

submachine gun [ˌsʌbmə'ʃiːn-] *n* metralleta *f*, ametralladora *f*.

submarine [ˌsʌbmə'riːn] *n* submarino *m*.

submerge [səb'mɜːdʒ] ◇ *vt* **-1.** [in water] sumergir. **-2.** *fig* [in activity]: **to ~ o.s. in sthg** dedicarse de lleno a algo. ◇ *vi* sumergirse.

submission [səb'mɪʃn] *n* **-1.** [capitulation] sumisión *f*. **-2.** [presentation] presentación *f*.

submissive [səb'mɪsɪv] *adj* sumiso(sa).

submit [səb'mɪt] (*pt & pp* **-ted**, *cont* **-ting**) ◇ *vt* presentar. ◇ *vi*: **to ~ (to sb)** rendirse (a alguien); **to ~ (to sthg)** someterse (a algo).

subnormal [ˌsʌb'nɔːml] *adj* subnormal.

subordinate [*adj & n* sə'bɔːdɪnət, *vt* sə-'bɔːdɪneɪt] ◇ *adj fml* [less important]: ~ **(to)** subordinado(da) (a). ◇ *n* subordinado *m*, -da *f*. ◇ *vt fml* subordinar.

subordinate clause [sə'bɔːdɪnət-] *n* oración *f* subordinada.

subordination [sə,bɔːdɪ'neɪʃn] *n*: ~ **(of sthg to sthg)** subordinación *f* (de algo a algo).

subpoena [səb'piːnə] (*pt & pp* **-ed**) JUR ◇ *n* citación *f*. ◇ *vt* citar.

sub-post office *n Br* estafeta de correos semiprivada.

subroutine ['sʌbruːˌtiːn] *n* COMPUT subrutina *f*.

subscribe [səb'skraɪb] ◇ *vi* **-1.** [to magazine, newspaper]: **to ~ (to)** suscribirse (a). **-2.** [to belief]: **to ~ to** estar de acuerdo con. ◇ *vt* donar.

subscriber [səb'skraɪbəʳ] *n* **-1.** [to magazine, newspaper] suscriptor *m*, -ra *f*. **-2.** [to service] abonado *m*, -da *f*. **-3.** [to charity] donante *m* y *f*.

subscription [səb'skrɪpʃn] *n* [to magazine] suscripción *f*; [to service] abono *m*; [to society, club] cuota *f*.

subsection ['sʌbˌsekʃn] *n* apartado *m*.

subsequent ['sʌbsɪkwənt] *adj* subsiguiente, posterior.

subsequently ['sʌbsɪkwəntlɪ] *adv* posteriormente.

subservient [səb'sɜːvjənt] *adj* **-1.** [servile]: ~ **(to sb)** servil (ante alguien). **-2.** [less important]: ~ **(to sthg)** subordinado(da) (a algo).

subset ['sʌbset] *n* MATH subconjunto *m*.

subside [səb'saɪd] *vi* **-1.** [anger] apaciguarse; [pain] calmarse; [grief] pasarse; [storm, wind] amainar. **-2.** [noise] apagarse. **-3.** [river] bajar, descender; [building, ground] hundirse.

subsidence [səb'saɪdns, 'sʌbsɪdns] *n* CONSTR hundimiento *m*.

subsidiarity [səbsɪdɪ'ærɪtɪ] *n* subsidiariedad *f*.

subsidiary [səb'sɪdjərɪ] (*pl* **-ies**) ◇ *adj* secundario(ria). ◇ *n*: ~ **(company)** filial *f*.

subsidize, -ise ['sʌbsɪdaɪz] *vt* subvencionar.

subsidy ['sʌbsɪdɪ] (*pl* **-ies**) *n* subvención *f*.

subsist [səb'sɪst] *vi*: **to ~ (on sthg)** subsistir (a base de algo).

subsistence [səb'sɪstəns] *n* subsistencia *f*.

subsistence allowance *n* (*U*) *Br* dietas *fpl*.

subsistence farming *n* agricultura *f* de autoabastecimiento.

subsistence level *n* nivel *m* mínimo de subsistencia.

substance ['sʌbstəns] *n* **-1.** [gen] sustancia *f*. **-2.** [essence] esencia *f*.

substandard [ˌsʌb'stændəd] *adj* deficiente.

substantial [səb'stænʃl] *adj* -1. [large, considerable] sustancial, considerable; [meal] abundante. -2. [solid] sólido(da).

substantially [səb'stænʃəlɪ] *adv* -1. [quite a lot] sustancialmente, considerablemente. -2. [fundamentally] esencialmente; [for the most part] en gran parte.

substantiate [səb'stænʃɪeɪt] *vt fml* justificar.

substantive [sʌb'stæntɪv] *adj fml* [meaningful] sustancial, sustancioso(sa).

substitute ['sʌbstɪtjuːt] ◇ *n* -1. [replacement]: ~ **(for)** sustituto *m*, -ta *f* (de); **to be no ~ (for)** ser un pobre remedio (de). -2. SPORT suplente *m* y *f*, reserva *m* y *f*. ◇ *vt*: **to ~ sthg/sb for** sustituir algo/a alguien por. ◇ *vi*: **to ~ for sb/sthg** sustituir a alguien/algo.

substitute teacher *n Am* profesor *m*, -ra *f* suplente.

substitution [ˌsʌbstɪ'tjuːʃn] *n* sustitución *f*.

subterfuge ['sʌbtəfjuːdʒ] *n* -1. [art of deception] engaño *m*. -2. [trick] subterfugio *m*.

subterranean [ˌsʌbtə'reɪnjən] *adj* subterráneo(a).

subtitle ['sʌbˌtaɪtl] *n* subtítulo *m*.

subtle ['sʌtl] *adj* -1. [gen] sutil; [taste, smell] delicado(da). -2. [plan, behaviour] ingenioso(sa).

subtlety ['sʌtltɪ] *n* sutileza *f*; [of taste, smell] delicadeza *f*; [of plan, behaviour] ingenio *m*.

subtly ['sʌtlɪ] *adv* -1. [not obviously] sútilmente. -2. [cleverly] ingeniosamente.

subtotal ['sʌbˌtəʊtl] *n* subtotal *m*.

subtract [səb'trækt] *vt*: **to ~ sthg (from)** restar algo (de).

subtraction [səb'trækʃn] *n* resta *f*.

subtropical [ˌsʌb'trɒpɪkl] *adj* subtropical.

suburb ['sʌbɜːb] *n* barrio *m* residencial.
◆ **suburbs** *npl*: **the ~s** las afueras.

suburban [sə'bɜːbn] *adj* -1. [of suburbs] de los barrios residenciales. -2. *pej* [boring] convencional, burgués(esa).

suburbia [sə'bɜːbɪə] *n* (*U*) barrios *mpl* residenciales.

subversion [səb'vɜːʃn] *n* subversión *f*.

subversive [səb'vɜːsɪv] ◇ *adj* subversivo(va). ◇ *n* subversivo *m*, -va *f*.

subvert [səb'vɜːt] *vt* subvertir.

subway ['sʌbweɪ] *n* -1. *Br* [underground walkway] paso *m* subterráneo. -2. *Am* [underground railway] metro *m*.

sub-zero *adj* bajo cero.

succeed [sək'siːd] ◇ *vt* suceder a. ◇ *vi* -1. [gen] tener éxito. -2. [achieve desired result]: **to ~ in sthg/in doing sthg** conseguir algo/

hacer algo. -3. [plan, tactic] dar (buen) resultado, salir bien. -4. [go far in life] triunfar.

succeeding [sək'siːdɪŋ] *adj fml* siguiente, sucesivo(va).

success [sək'ses] *n* -1. [gen] éxito *m*; **to be a ~** tener éxito. -2. [in career, life] triunfo *m*.

successful [sək'sesfʊl] *adj* [gen] de éxito; [attempt] logrado(da), próspero(ra); [politician] popular.

successfully [sək'sesfʊlɪ] *adv* con éxito.

succession [sək'seʃn] *n* sucesión *f*; **to follow in quick** OR **close ~** sucederse rápidamente.

successive [sək'sesɪv] *adj* sucesivo(va), consecutivo(va).

successor [sək'sesəʳ] *n* sucesor *m*, -ra *f*.

success story *n* éxito *m*.

succinct [sək'sɪŋkt] *adj* sucinto(ta).

succinctly [sək'sɪŋktlɪ] *adv* sucintamente.

succour *Br*, **succor** *Am* ['sʌkəʳ] *n literary* socorro *m*, auxilio *m*.

succulent ['sʌkjʊlənt] *adj* suculento(ta).

succumb [sə'kʌm] *vi*: **to ~ (to)** sucumbir (a).

such [sʌtʃ] ◇ *adj* -1. [like that] semejante, tal; ~ **stupidity** tal OR semejante estupidez. -2. [like this]: **have you got ~ a thing as a tin opener?** ¿tendrías acaso un abrelatas?; ~ **words as "duty" and "honour"** palabras (tales) como "deber" y "honor". -3. [whatever]: **I've spent ~ money as I had** he gastado el poco dinero que tenía. -4. [so great, so serious]: **there are ~ differences that ...** las diferencias son tales que ...; ~ **... that** tal ... que.
◇ *adv* tan; ~ **a lot of books** tantos libros; ~ **nice people** una gente tan amable; ~ **a good car** un coche tan bueno; ~ **a long time** tanto tiempo.
◇ *pron*: **and ~ (like)** y otros similares OR por el estilo; **this is my car, ~ as it is** este es mi coche, aunque no sea gran cosa; **have some wine, ~ as there is** sírvete vino, si es que aún queda.
◆ **as such** *pron* propiamente dicho(cha).
◆ **such and such** *adj*: **at ~ and ~ a time** a tal hora.

suchlike ['sʌtʃlaɪk] ◇ *adj* de este tipo, por el estilo. ◇ *pron* [things] cosas por el estilo; [people] gente de este tipo.

suck [sʌk] *vt* -1. [by mouth] chupar. -2. [subj: machine] aspirar. -3. *fig* [involve]: **to be ~ed into sthg** verse envuelto(ta) en algo.
◆ **suck up** *vi inf*: **to ~ up (to)** hacer la pelota (a).

sucker ['sʌkəʳ] *n* -1. [of animal] ventosa *f*.

-2. inf [gullible person] primo m, -ma f, ingenuo m, -nua f.

suckle ['sʌkl] ◇ vt amamantar. ◇ vi mamar.

sucrose ['suːkrəʊz] n sacarosa f.

suction ['sʌkʃn] n [gen] succión f; [by machine] aspiración f.

suction pump n bomba f de aspiración.

Sudan [suːˈdɑːn] n (el) Sudán.

Sudanese [ˌsuːdəˈniːz] ◇ adj sudanés(esa). ◇ n sudanés m, -esa f. ◇ npl: **the ~** los sudaneses.

sudden ['sʌdn] adj [quick] repentino(na); [unforeseen] inesperado(da); **all of a ~** de repente.

sudden death n SPORT muerte f súbita.

suddenly ['sʌdnlɪ] adv de repente, de pronto.

suddenness ['sʌdnɪs] n [quickness] lo repentino; [unexpectedness] lo inesperado.

suds [sʌdz] npl espuma f del jabón.

sue [suː] vt: **to ~ sb (for)** demandar a alguien (por).

suede [sweɪd] ◇ n [for jacket, shoes] ante m; [for gloves] cabritilla f. ◇ comp [jacket, shoes] de ante; [gloves] de cabritilla.

suet ['suɪt] n sebo m.

Suez ['suɪz] n Suez.

Suez Canal n: **the ~** el canal de Suez.

suffer ['sʌfər] ◇ vt sufrir. ◇ vi **-1.** [gen] sufrir. **-2.** [experience negative effects] salir perjudicado(da). **-3.** MED: **to ~ from** [illness] sufrir OR padecer de.

sufferance ['sʌfrəns] n: **on ~** por tolerancia.

sufferer ['sʌfrər] n enfermo m, -ma f.

suffering ['sʌfrɪŋ] n [gen] sufrimiento m; [pain] dolor m.

suffice [səˈfaɪs] vi fml ser suficiente, bastar.

sufficient [səˈfɪʃnt] adj fml suficiente, bastante.

sufficiently [səˈfɪʃntlɪ] adv fml suficientemente, bastante.

suffix ['sʌfɪks] n sufijo m.

suffocate ['sʌfəkeɪt] ◇ vt asfixiar, ahogar. ◇ vi asfixiarse, ahogarse.

suffocation [ˌsʌfəˈkeɪʃn] n asfixia f, ahogo m.

suffrage ['sʌfrɪdʒ] n sufragio m.

suffuse [səˈfjuːz] vt: **~d with** bañado de.

sugar ['ʃʊgər] ◇ n azúcar m o f. ◇ vt echar azúcar a.

sugar beet n remolacha f (azucarera).

sugar bowl n azucarero m.

sugarcane ['ʃʊgəkeɪn] n (U) caña f de azúcar.

sugar-coated [-ˈkəʊtɪd] adj [sweets] cubierto(ta) de azúcar; [almonds] garrapiñado(da).

sugared ['ʃʊgəd] adj azucarado(da), con azúcar.

sugar lump n terrón m de azúcar.

sugar refinery n refinería f de azúcar.

sugary ['ʃʊgərɪ] adj **-1.** [high in sugar] azucarado(da), dulce. **-2.** pej [sentimental] sensiblero(ra).

suggest [səˈdʒest] vt **-1.** [propose] sugerir, proponer; **to ~ that sb do sthg** sugerir que alguien haga algo. **-2.** [imply] insinuar; **his work ~s a lack of care** su trabajo hace pensar que no se preocupa lo suficiente.

suggestion [səˈdʒestʃn] n **-1.** [proposal] sugerencia f. **-2.** [implication] insinuación f. **-3.** PSYCH sugestión f.

suggestive [səˈdʒestɪv] adj **-1.** [implying sexual connotation] provocativo(va), insinuante. **-2.** [implying a certain conclusion]: **~ (of)** indicativo(va) (de). **-3.** [reminiscent]: **~ of** evocador(ra) (de).

suicidal [sʊɪˈsaɪdl] adj lit & fig suicida.

suicide ['sʊɪsaɪd] n lit & fig suicidio m; **to commit ~** suicidarse.

suicide attempt n intento m de suicidio.

suit [suːt] ◇ n **-1.** [clothes - for men] traje m, tenida f Amer; [- for women] traje m de chaqueta. **-2.** [in cards] palo m. **-3.** JUR pleito m. **-4.** phr: **to follow ~** fig seguir el ejemplo, hacer lo mismo.
◇ vt **-1.** [look attractive on] favorecer, sentar bien a, embonar Amer. **-2.** [be convenient or agreeable to] convenir, venir bien a; **~ yourself!** ¡como quieras! **-3.** [be appropriate to] ser adecuado(da) para; **that job ~s you perfectly** ese trabajo te va de perlas.
◇ vi: **does that ~?** ¿te va bien?

suitability [ˌsuːtəˈbɪlətɪ] n [aptness] idoneidad f; [convenience] conveniencia f.

suitable ['suːtəbl] adj adecuado(da); **the most ~ person** la persona más indicada.

suitably ['suːtəblɪ] adv adecuadamente; **I was ~ impressed** como era de esperar, estaba impresionado.

suitcase ['suːtkeɪs] n maleta f, petaca f Amer.

suite [swiːt] n **-1.** [of rooms] suite f. **-2.** [of furniture] juego m; **dining-room ~** comedor m.

suited ['suːtɪd] adj: **~ to/for** adecuado(da) para; **the couple are ideally ~** forman una pareja perfecta.

suitor ['suːtər] n dated pretendiente m.

sulfate Am = **sulphate**.

sulfur Am = **sulphur**.

sulfuric acid Am = **sulphuric acid**.

sulk [sʌlk] ◇ *n*: he went into a ~ le entró un arrebato de mal humor. ◇ *vi* estar de mal humor, enfurruñarse.

sulky ['sʌlkɪ] (*compar* -ier, *superl* -iest) *adj* malhumorado(da).

sullen ['sʌlən] *adj* hosco(ca), antipático(ca).

sulphate *Br*, **sulfate** *Am* ['sʌlfeɪt] *n* sulfato *m*.

sulphur *Br*, **sulfur** *Am* ['sʌlfər] *n* azufre *m*.

sulphuric acid *Br*, **sulfuric acid** *Am* [sʌl'fjuərɪk-] *n* ácido *m* sulfúrico.

sultan ['sʌltən] *n* sultán *m*.

sultana [səl'tɑːnə] *n Br* [dried grape] pasa *f* de Esmirna.

sultry ['sʌltrɪ] (*compar* -ier, *superl* -iest) *adj* **-1.** [hot] bochornoso(sa), sofocante. **-2.** [sexual] sensual.

sum [sʌm] (*pt & pp* -med, *cont* -ming) *n* suma *f*.
◆ **sum up** *vt sep & vi* [summarize] resumir.

Sumatra [sʊ'mɑːtrə] *n* Sumatra.

Sumatran [sʊ'mɑːtrən] ◇ *adj* sumatrino(na). ◇ *n* sumatrino *m*, -na *f*.

summarily ['sʌmərəlɪ] *adv* sumariamente.

summarize, -ise ['sʌməraɪz] *vt & vi* resumir.

summary ['sʌmərɪ] (*pl* -ies) ◇ *adj fml* sumario(ria). ◇ *n* resumen *m*.

summation [sʌ'meɪʃn] *n* [sum] suma *f*; [summary] resumen *m*.

summer ['sʌmər] ◇ *n* verano *m*; in ~ en verano. ◇ *comp* de verano.

summer camp *n Am* colonia *f* de verano.

summerhouse ['sʌməhaʊs, *pl* -haʊzɪz] *n* cenador *m*.

summer school *n* escuela *f* de verano.

summertime ['sʌmətaɪm] ◇ *adj* veraniego(ga), de verano. ◇ *n*: **(the)** ~ (el) verano.

Summer Time *n Br* hora *f* de verano.

summery ['sʌmərɪ] *adj* veraniego(ga), estival.

summing-up [,sʌmɪŋ-] (*pl* summings-up) *n* JUR resumen *m*.

summit ['sʌmɪt] *n* **-1.** [mountain-top] cima *f*, cumbre *f*. **-2.** [meeting] cumbre *f*.

summon ['sʌmən] *vt* [person] llamar; [meeting] convocar.
◆ **summon up** *vt sep* [courage] armarse de; to ~ up one's strength reunir fuerzas.

summons ['sʌmənz] (*pl* summonses) JUR ◇ *n* citación *f*. ◇ *vt* citar.

sumo (wrestling) ['suːməʊ-] *n* sumo *m*.

sump [sʌmp] *n* cárter *m*.

sumptuous ['sʌmptʊəs] *adj* suntuoso(sa).

sum total *n* suma *f* total.

sun [sʌn] (*pt & pp* -ned, *cont* -ning) ◇ *n* sol *m*; **in the** ~ al sol. ◇ *vt*: **to** ~ **o.s.** tomar el sol.

Sun. (*abbr of* **Sunday**) dom.

sunbathe ['sʌnbeɪð] *vi* tomar el sol.

sunbeam ['sʌnbiːm] *n* rayo *m* de sol.

sunbed ['sʌnbed] *n* camilla *f* de rayos ultravioletas.

sunburn ['sʌnbɜːn] *n* (*U*) quemadura *f* de sol.

sunburned ['sʌnbɜːnd], **sunburnt** ['sʌnbɜːnt] *adj* quemado(da) por el sol.

sun cream *n* crema *f* para el sol.

sundae ['sʌndeɪ] *n* helado con fruta y nueces.

Sunday ['sʌndɪ] *n* domingo *m*; ~ **lunch** comida del domingo que generalmente consiste en rosbif, patatas asadas etc; see also **Saturday**.

Sunday paper *n Br* (periódico *m*) dominical *m*.

SUNDAY PAPERS:

Los principales periódicos británicos que aparecen el domingo son:
The Independent on Sunday (tendencia centrista)
The Mail on Sunday (tendencia derechista)
The News of the World (tendencia derechista)
The Observer (tendencia centroizquierda)
The People (tendencia derechista)
The Sunday Express (tendencia derechista)
The Sunday Mirror (tendencia centroizquierda)
The Sunday Telegraph (tendencia derechista)
The Sunday Times (tendencia centroderecha)

Sunday school *n* catequesis *f inv*.

sundial ['sʌndaɪəl] *n* reloj *m* de sol.

sundown ['sʌndaʊn] *n* anochecer *m*.

sundries ['sʌndrɪz] *npl fml* [gen] artículos *mpl* diversos; FIN gastos *mpl* diversos.

sundry ['sʌndrɪ] *adj fml* diversos(sas); **all and** ~ todos sin excepción.

sunflower ['sʌn,flaʊər] *n* girasol *m*.

sung [sʌŋ] *pp* → **sing**.

sunglasses ['sʌn,glɑːsɪz] *npl* gafas *fpl* de sol.

sunhat ['sʌnhæt] *n* pamela *f*.

sunk [sʌŋk] *pp* → **sink**.

sunken ['sʌŋkən] *adj* hundido(da).

sunlamp ['sʌnlæmp] *n* lámpara *f* de rayos ultravioletas.

sunlight ['sʌnlaɪt] *n* luz *f* del sol.

sunlit ['sʌnlɪt] *adj* iluminado(da) por el sol.

Sunni ['sʊnɪ] (*pl* **-s**) *n* [doctrine] sunna *f*.

sunny ['sʌnɪ] (*compar* **-ier**, *superl* **-iest**) *adj* **-1.** [day] de sol; [room] soleado(da). **-2.** [cheerful] alegre. **-3.** *phr*: ~ **side up** *Am* [egg] frito.

sunray ['sʌnreɪ] *adj* de rayos ultravioletas.

sunray lamp *n* lámpara *f* de rayos ultravioletas.

sunrise ['sʌnraɪz] *n* **-1.** (*U*) [time of day] amanecer *m*. **-2.** [event] salida *f* del sol.

sunroof ['sʌnruːf] *n* [on car] techo *m* corredizo; [on building] azotea *f*.

sunset ['sʌnset] *n* **-1.** (*U*) [time of day] anochecer *m*. **-2.** [event] puesta *f* del sol.

sunshade ['sʌnʃeɪd] *n* sombrilla *f*.

sunshine ['sʌnʃaɪn] *n* (luz *f* del) sol *m*.

sunspot ['sʌnspɒt] *n* ASTRON mancha *f* solar.

sunstroke ['sʌnstrəʊk] *n* (*U*) insolación *f*.

suntan ['sʌntæn] ◇ *n* bronceado *m*. ◇ *comp* bronceador(ra).

suntanned ['sʌntænd] *adj* bronceado(da).

suntrap ['sʌntræp] *n* lugar *m* muy soleado.

sunup ['sʌnʌp] *n* (*U*) *Am inf* salida *f* del sol.

super ['suːpər] ◇ *adj* **-1.** *inf* [wonderful] estupendo(da), fenomenal. **-2.** [better than normal - size etc] superior.

superabundance [,suːpərə'bʌndəns] *n* superabundancia *f*.

superannuation ['suːpə,rænjʊ'eɪʃn] *n* (*U*) jubilación *f*, pensión *f*.

superb [suː'pɜːb] *adj* excelente, magnífico(ca).

superbly [suː'pɜːblɪ] *adv* de manera excelente.

Super Bowl *n Am*: **the** ~ *la final del campeonato estadounidense de fútbol americano.*

supercilious [,suːpə'sɪlɪəs] *adj* altanero(ra).

superficial [,suːpə'fɪʃl] *adj* superficial.

superfluous [suː'pɜːfluəs] *adj* superfluo(flua).

superglue ['suːpəgluː] *n* cola *f* de contacto.

superhuman [,suːpə'hjuːmən] *adj* sobrehumano(na).

superimpose [,suːpərɪm'pəʊz] *vt*: **to** ~ **sthg on** superponer OR sobreponer algo a.

superintend [,suːpərɪn'tend] *vt* supervisar.

superintendent [,suːpərɪn'tendənt] *n* **-1.** *Br* [of police] ≃ subjefe *m*, -fa *f* (de policía). **-2.** *fml* [of department] supervisor *m*, -ra *f*.

superior [suː'pɪərɪər] ◇ *adj* **-1.** [gen]: ~ **(to)** superior (a). **-2.** *pej* [arrogant] altanero(ra), arrogante. ◇ *n* superior *m* y *f*.

superiority [suː,pɪərɪ'ɒrətɪ] *n* **-1.** [gen] superioridad *f*. **-2.** *pej* [arrogance] altanería *f*, arrogancia *f*.

superlative [suː'pɜːlətɪv] ◇ *adj* [of the highest quality] supremo(ma). ◇ *n* GRAMM superlativo *m*.

supermarket ['suːpə,mɑːkɪt] *n* supermercado *m*.

supernatural [,suːpə'nætʃrəl] ◇ *adj* sobrenatural. ◇ *n*: **the** ~ lo sobrenatural.

superpower ['suːpə,paʊər] *n* superpotencia *f*.

superscript ['suːpəskrɪpt] *adj* volado(da).

supersede [,suːpə'siːd] *vt* suplantar.

supersonic [,suːpə'sɒnɪk] *adj* supersónico(ca).

superstar ['suːpəstɑːr] *n* superestrella *f*.

superstition [,suːpə'stɪʃn] *n* superstición *f*.

superstitious [,suːpə'stɪʃəs] *adj* supersticioso(sa).

superstore ['suːpəstɔːr] *n* hipermercado *m*.

superstructure ['suːpə,strʌktʃər] *n* superestructura *f*.

supertanker ['suːpə,tæŋkər] *n* superpetrolero *m*.

supertax ['suːpətæks] *n* impuesto *m* adicional.

supervise ['suːpəvaɪz] *vt* [person] vigilar; [activity] supervisar.

supervision [,suːpə'vɪʒn] *n* supervisión *f*.

supervisor ['suːpəvaɪzər] *n* [gen] supervisor *m*, -ra *f*; [of thesis] director *m*, -ra *f*.

supper ['sʌpər] *n* **-1.** [evening meal] cena *f*. **-2.** [before bedtime] *tentempié tomado antes de acostarse.*

supplant [sə'plɑːnt] *vt fml* suplantar, reemplazar.

supple ['sʌpl] *adj* flexible.

supplement [*n* 'sʌplɪmənt, *vb* 'sʌplɪment] ◇ *n* suplemento *m*. ◇ *vt* complementar.

supplementary [,sʌplɪ'mentərɪ] *adj* suplementario(ria).

supplementary benefit *n Br* subsidio *m* social.

supplier [sə'plaɪər] *n* proveedor *m*, -ra *f*, suministrador *m*, -ra *f*.

supply [sə'plaɪ] ◇ *n* **-1.** [gen] suministro *m*; [of jokes etc] surtido *m*; **water/electricity** ~ suministro de agua/electricidad; **to be in short** ~ escasear. **-2.** (*U*) ECON oferta *f*. ◇ *vt*: **to** ~ **sthg (to)** suministrar OR proveer algo (a); **to** ~ **sb (with)** proveer a alguien (de); **to** ~ **sthg with sthg** suministrar a algo de algo.

◆ **supplies** *npl* MIL pertrechos *mpl*; [food] provisiones *fpl*; [for office etc] material *m*.

supply teacher *n Br* profesor *m*, -ra *f* suplente.

support [sə'pɔːt] ◇ *n* **-1.** (*U*) [physical, moral, emotional] apoyo *m*. **-2.** (*U*) [financial] ayuda *f*. **-3.** (*U*) [intellectual] respaldo *m*. **-4.** TECH soporte *m*. ◇ *vt* **-1.** [physically] sostener. **-2.** [emotionally, morally, intellectually] apoyar. **-3.** [financially - oneself, one's family] mantener; [- company, organization] financiar. **-4.** SPORT seguir.

supporter [sə'pɔːtər] *n* **-1.** [gen] partidario *m*, -ria *f*. **-2.** SPORT hincha *m y f*, seguidor *m*, -ra *f*.

supportive [sə'pɔːtɪv] *adj* comprensivo(va).

suppose [sə'pəʊz] ◇ *vt* suponer; I don't ~ you could help me [in polite request] ¿crees que podrías ayudarme, por favor?; you don't ~ she's ill, do you? [asking opinion] no estará enferma, ¿verdad? ◇ *vi* suponer; I ~ (so) supongo (que sí); I ~ not supongo que no; I ~ you're right supongo que tienes razón. ◇ *conj* si; ~ your father found out? ¿y si se entera tu padre?

supposed [sə'pəʊzd] *adj* **-1.** [doubtful] supuesto(ta). **-2.** [intended]: he was ~ to be here at eight debería haber estado aquí a las ocho. **-3.** [reputed]: it's ~ to be very good se supone OR se dice que es muy bueno.

supposedly [sə'pəʊzɪdlɪ] *adv* según cabe suponer.

supposing [sə'pəʊzɪŋ] *conj*: ~ your father found out? ¿y si se entera tu padre?

supposition [ˌsʌpə'zɪʃn] *n* suposición *f*.

suppository [sə'pɒzɪtrɪ] (*pl* **-ies**) *n* supositorio *m*.

suppress [sə'pres] *vt* **-1.** [uprising] reprimir. **-2.** [information] ocultar. **-3.** [emotions] contener.

suppression [sə'preʃn] *n* **-1.** [gen] represión *f*. **-2.** [of information] ocultación *f*.

suppressor [sə'presər] *n* ELEC supresor *m*.

supranational [ˌsuːprə'næʃənl] *adj* supranacional.

supremacy [sʊ'preməsɪ] *n* supremacía *f*.

supreme [sʊ'priːm] *adj* supremo(ma).

Supreme Court *n*: the ~ [in US] el Tribunal Supremo (de los Estados Unidos).

SUPREME COURT:
El Tribunal Supremo es el máximo órgano de la administración de justicia en Estados Unidos y está formado por miembros nombrados por el presidente; este tribunal ostenta el poder de decisión final, así como el derecho a interpretar la Constitución

supremely [sʊ'priːmlɪ] *adv* sumamente.

supremo [sʊ'priːməʊ] (*pl* **-s**) *n* Br inf jefe supremo *m*, jefa suprema *f*.

Supt. *abbr of* **superintendent**.

surcharge ['sɜːtʃɑːdʒ] ◇ *n*: ~ (on) recargo *m* (en). ◇ *vt*: to ~ sb (on) cobrar un recargo a alguien (en).

sure [ʃʊər] ◇ *adj* **-1.** [gen] seguro(ra); I'm ~ I know him estoy seguro de que lo conozco. **-2.** [certain - of outcome]: to be ~ of poder estar seguro(ra) de; it's ~ to happen (es) seguro que pasará; make ~ (that) you do it asegúrate de que lo haces. **-3.** [confident]: to be ~ of o.s. estar seguro(ra) de uno mismo. **-4.** *phr*: be ~ to lock the door! ¡no te olvides de cerrar la puerta! ◇ *adv* **-1.** *inf* [yes] por supuesto, pues claro. **-2.** *Am* [really] realmente.

◆ **for sure** *adv* con seguridad, a ciencia cierta.

◆ **sure enough** *adv* efectivamente.

surefire ['ʃʊəfaɪər] *adj* *inf* seguro(ra).

surefooted [ˌʃʊə'fʊtɪd] *adj* [steady on one's feet] de pie firme.

surely ['ʃʊəlɪ] *adv* sin duda; ~ you remember him? ¡no me digas que no te acuerdas de él!; ~ not! ¡no puede ser!

sure thing *excl Am inf* por supuesto, claro.

surety ['ʃʊərətɪ] *n* (*U*) fianza *f*.

surf [sɜːf] ◇ *n* espuma *f* (*de las olas*). ◇ *vi* hacer surf.

surface ['sɜːfɪs] ◇ *n* **-1.** [gen] superficie *f*. **-2.** *fig* [immediately visible part]: on the ~ a primera vista; below OR beneath the ~ debajo de las apariencias. **-3.** *phr*: to scratch the ~ of sthg tocar algo por encima. ◇ *vi* **-1.** [gen] salir a la superficie. **-2.** *inf hum* [person] aparecer.

surface mail *n* correo *m* por vía terrestre/marítima.

surface-to-air *adj* tierra-aire (*inv*).

surfboard ['sɜːfbɔːd] *n* plancha *f* OR tabla *f* de surf.

surfeit ['sɜːfɪt] *n* *fml* exceso *m*.

surfer ['sɜːfər] *n* surfista *m y f*.

surfing ['sɜːfɪŋ] *n* surf *m*.

surge [sɜːdʒ] ◇ *n* **-1.** [of waves, people] oleada *f*; [of electricity] sobrecarga *f* momentánea. **-2.** [of emotion] arranque *m*, arrebato *m*. **-3.** [of interest, support, sales] aumento *m* súbito. ◇ *vi* **-1.** [people, vehicles] avanzar en masa; [sea] encresparse; the blood ~d to his head la sangre se le subió a la cabeza. **-2.** [emotion]: anger ~d inside him la rabia se apoderó de él. **-3.** [prices, current] aumentar súbitamente.

surgeon ['sɜːdʒən] *n* cirujano *m*, -na *f*.

surgery ['sɜːdʒərɪ] (*pl* **-ies**) *n* **-1.** (*U*) MED [performing operations] cirugía *f.* **-2.** *Br* MED [place] consultorio *m*; [consulting period] consulta *f.* **-3.** *Br* POL *consultorio de un diputado para atender los problemas de los vecinos.*

surgical ['sɜːdʒɪkl] *adj* **-1.** [gen] quirúrgico(ca). **-2.** [stocking, boot etc] ortopédico(ca).

surgical spirit *n Br* alcohol *m* de 90°.

Surinam [ˌsʊərɪ'næm] *n* Surinam.

surly ['sɜːlɪ] (*compar* **-ier**, *superl* **-iest**) *adj* hosco(ca), malhumorado(da).

surmise [sɜː'maɪz] *vt fml* conjeturar.

surmount [sɜː'maʊnt] *vt* **-1.** [overcome] superar, vencer. **-2.** *fml* [top] coronar.

surname ['sɜːneɪm] *n* apellido *m.*

surpass [sə'pɑːs] *vt fml* [exceed] superar, sobrepasar.

surplus ['sɜːpləs] ◇ *adj* excedente, sobrante; **you are ~ to requirements** ya no requerimos tus servicios. ◇ *n* [gen] excedente *m*, sobrante *m*; [in budget] superávit *m.*

surprise [sə'praɪz] ◇ *n* sorpresa *f*; **to take sb by ~** coger a alguien desprevenido. ◇ *vt* sorprender.

surprised [sə'praɪzd] *adj* [person, expression] asombrado(da); **I wouldn't be ~ if she came** no me extrañaría que viniera.

surprising [sə'praɪzɪŋ] *adj* sorprendente.

surprisingly [sə'praɪzɪŋlɪ] *adv* sorprendentemente.

surreal [sə'rɪəl] *adj* surrealista.

surrealism [sə'rɪəlɪzm] *n* surrealismo *m.*

surrealist [sə'rɪəlɪst] ◇ *adj* surrealista. ◇ *n* surrealista *m y f.*

surrender [sə'rendə'] ◇ *n* rendición *f.* ◇ *vt fml* [weapons, passport] rendir, entregar; [claim, right] renunciar a. ◇ *vi lit & fig*: **to ~ (to)** rendirse OR entregarse (a).

surreptitious [ˌsʌrəp'tɪʃəs] *adj* subrepticio(cia).

surrogate ['sʌrəgeɪt] ◇ *adj* sustitutorio(ria). ◇ *n* sustituto *m*, -ta *f.*

surrogate mother *n* madre *f* de alquiler.

surround [sə'raʊnd] ◇ *n* borde *m.* ◇ *vt lit & fig* rodear.

surrounding [sə'raʊndɪŋ] *adj* **-1.** [area, countryside] circundante. **-2.** [controversy, debate] relacionado(da).

surroundings [sə'raʊndɪŋz] *npl* [physical] alrededores *mpl*; [social] entorno *m.*

surtax ['sɜːtæks] *n* recargo *m* (*en los impuestos*).

surveillance [sɜː'veɪləns] *n* vigilancia *f.*

survey [*n* 'sɜːveɪ, *vb* sə'veɪ] ◇ *n* **-1.** [of public opinion, population] encuesta *f*, estudio *m.* **-2.** [of land] medición *f*; [of building] inspec-

ción *f*, reconocimiento *m.* ◇ *vt* **-1.** [contemplate] contemplar. **-2.** [investigate statistically] hacer un estudio de. **-3.** [examine - land] medir; [- building] inspeccionar.

surveyor [sə'veɪə'] *n* [of property] perito *m* tasador de la propiedad; [of land] agrimensor *m*, -ra *f.*

survival [sə'vaɪvl] *n* **-1.** [gen] supervivencia *f.* **-2.** [relic] reliquia *f*, vestigio *m.*

survive [sə'vaɪv] ◇ *vt* sobrevivir a. ◇ *vi* **-1.** [person] sobrevivir; [custom, project] perdurar. **-2.** *inf* [cope successfully]: **how will you ~?** ¿cómo te las arreglarás?
◆ **survive on** *vt fus* ir tirando con.

survivor [sə'vaɪvə'] *n* **-1.** [person who escapes death] superviviente *m y f.* **-2.** [resilient person] persona *f* que siempre sale adelante.

susceptible [sə'septəbl] *adj* **-1.** [to pressure, flattery]: **~ (to)** sensible (a). **-2.** MED: **~ (to)** propenso(sa) (a).

suspect [*adj & n* 'sʌspekt, *vb* sə'spekt] ◇ *adj* sospechoso(sa). ◇ *n* sospechoso *m*, -sa *f.* ◇ *vt* **-1.** [distrust] sospechar. **-2.** [think likely] imaginar. **-3.** [consider guilty]: **to ~ sb (of)** considerar a alguien sospechoso(sa) (de).

suspend [sə'spend] *vt* [gen] suspender; [payments, work] interrumpir; [schoolchild] expulsar temporalmente.

suspended animation [sə'spendɪd-] *n* muerte *f* aparente.

suspended sentence [sə'spendɪd-] *n* condena *f* condicional.

suspender belt [sə'spendə'-] *n Br* liguero *m.*

suspenders [sə'spendəz] *npl* **-1.** *Br* [for stockings] ligas *fpl.* **-2.** *Am* [for trousers] tirantes *mpl.*

suspense [sə'spens] *n* [gen] incertidumbre *f*; CINEMA suspense *m*; **to keep sb in ~** mantener a alguien en vilo.

suspension [sə'spenʃn] *n* **-1.** [gen & AUT] suspensión *f.* **-2.** [from job, school] expulsión *f* temporal.

suspension bridge *n* puente *m* colgante.

suspicion [sə'spɪʃn] *n* **-1.** [gen] sospecha *f*; [distrust] recelo *m*; **under ~** bajo sospecha. **-2.** [small amount] pizca *f.*

suspicious [sə'spɪʃəs] *adj* **-1.** [having suspicions] receloso(sa). **-2.** [causing suspicion] sospechoso(sa).

suspiciously [sə'spɪʃəslɪ] *adv* **-1.** [behave] sospechosamente. **-2.** [ask, look at] con recelo.

suss [sʌs]
◆ **suss out** *Br inf vt sep* [person] calar; [thing] pillar el tranquillo a; **to ~ out how to do sthg** descubrir cómo hacer algo.

sustain [sə'steɪn] vt -1. [gen] sostener. -2. [subj: food, drink] sustentar. -3. *fml* [injury, damage] sufrir.

sustenance ['sʌstɪnəns] n (U) *fml* sustento m.

suture ['suːtʃər] n sutura f.

svelte [svelt] adj esbelto(ta).

SW -1. (abbr of **short wave**) OC. **-2.** (abbr of **south-west**) SO.

swab [swɒb] n (trozo m de) algodón m.

swagger ['swægər] ◇ n pavoneo m. ◇ vi pavonearse.

Swahili [swɑːˈhiːlɪ] ◇ adj suahili. ◇ n [language] suahili m.

SWALK [swɔːlk] (abbr of **sealed with a loving kiss**) *inf* expresión utilizada en cartas de amor que indica que la carta está sellada con un beso.

swallow ['swɒləʊ] ◇ n -1. [bird] golondrina f. -2. [of food] bocado m; [of drink] trago m. ◇ vt -1. [food, drink] tragar. -2. *fig* [accept, hold back] tragarse. ◇ vi tragar.

swam [swæm] pt → swim.

swamp [swɒmp] ◇ n pantano m, ciénaga f. ◇ vt -1. [flood - boat] hundir; [- land] inundar. -2. [overwhelm]: **to ~ sthg (with)** [office] inundar algo de (de); **to ~ sb (with)** agobiar a alguien (con).

swan [swɒn] n cisne m.

swap [swɒp] (pt & pp **-ped**, cont **-ping**) ◇ n cambio m, intercambio m. ◇ vt -1. [of one thing]: **to ~ sthg (for/with)** cambiar algo (por/con). -2. [of two things]: **to ~ sthg (over OR round)** [hats, chairs] cambiarse algo; [stories, experiences] intercambiar algo; **to ~ places** cambiarse de sitio. ◇ vi hacer un intercambio.

swap meet n Am mercadillo m de segunda mano.

SWAPO ['swɑːpəʊ] (abbr of **South West Africa People's Organization**) n SWAPO f.

swarm [swɔːm] ◇ n [of bees] enjambre m; *fig* [of people] multitud f, tropel m. ◇ vi -1. [bees] enjambrar. -2. *fig* [people] ir en tropel. -3. *fig* [place]: **to be ~ing (with)** estar abarrotado(da) (de).

swarthy ['swɔːðɪ] (compar **-ier**, superl **-iest**) adj moreno(na).

swashbuckling ['swɒʃˌbʌklɪŋ] adj [person] intrépido(da); [film] de aventuras.

swastika ['swɒstɪkə] n esvástica f cruz f gamada.

swat [swɒt] (pt & pp **-ted**, cont **-ting**) vt aplastar.

swatch [swɒtʃ] n muestra f.

swathe [sweɪð] ◇ n [large area] extensión f.

◇ vt esp literary [gen] envolver; [in bandages] vendar.

swathed [sweɪðd] adj esp literary: **~ (in)** envuelto(ta) (en).

swatter ['swɒtər] n matamoscas m inv.

sway [sweɪ] ◇ vt -1. [cause to sway] balancear. -2. [influence] convencer, persuadir. ◇ vi balancearse. ◇ n *fml*: **to hold ~ (over** sthg/sb) dominar (algo/a alguien); **to come under the ~ of** estar bajo el dominio de.

Swazi ['swɑːzɪ] n suazi m y f.

Swaziland ['swɑːzɪlænd] n Suazilandia.

swear [sweər] (pt **swore**, pp **sworn**) ◇ vt: **to ~ (to do sthg)** jurar (hacer algo); **to ~ an oath** prestar juramento. ◇ vi -1. [state emphatically] jurar. -2. [use swearwords] decir tacos, jurar.

◆ **swear by** vt fus *inf* [method, remedy] confiar totalmente en.

◆ **swear in** vt sep JUR tomar juramento a.

swearword ['sweəwɜːd] n palabrota f, taco m.

sweat [swet] ◇ n -1. [perspiration] sudor m. -2. (U) *inf* [hard work] trabajo m duro. -3. *inf* [state of anxiety]: **to be in a ~ about sthg** tener una neura con algo; **to be in a cold ~** sentir un sudor frío. ◇ vi -1. [perspire] sudar. -2. *inf* [worry] estar aneurado(da).

sweatband ['swetbænd] n [for head] banda f; [for wrist] muñequera f.

sweater ['swetər] n suéter m, jersey m, chompa f Amer.

sweatshirt ['swetʃɜːt] n sudadera f.

sweatshop ['swetʃɒp] n fábrica donde se explota al obrero.

sweaty ['swetɪ] (compar **-ier**, superl **-iest**) adj -1. [skin] sudoroso(sa); [clothes] sudado(da). -2. [room, atmosphere] cargado(da); [activity] agotador(ra).

swede [swiːd] n Br nabo m sueco.

Swede [swiːd] n sueco m, -ca f.

Sweden ['swiːdn] n Suecia.

Swedish ['swiːdɪʃ] ◇ adj sueco(ca). ◇ n [language] sueco m. ◇ npl: **the ~** los suecos.

sweep [swiːp] (pt & pp **swept**) ◇ n -1. [movement - of broom] barrido m; [- of arm, hand] movimiento m OR gesto m amplio. -2. [by police] redada f. -3. [chimney sweep] deshollinador m, -ra f. ◇ vt -1. [with brush] barrer. -2. [with light-beam] rastrear; [with eyes] recorrer. -3. [move rapidly through - subj: ideas, disease] extenderse rápidamente por. -4. [for bugs or bombs] registrar. -5. [subj: sea, wave] arrastrar. -6. [push]: **she swept the papers off her desk** apartó los papeles de su escritorio.

◇ *vi* **-1.** [wind, rain]: **to ~ over** OR **across** sthg azotar algo; [vehicle]: **to ~ along** ir a toda marcha. **-2.** [emotion, laughter, rumour]: **to ~ through** sthg extenderse por algo. **-3.** [person]: **to ~ past** pasar como un rayo.

◆ **sweep aside** *vt sep* [objections] rechazar.

◆ **sweep away** *vt sep* [destroy] destruir completamente.

◆ **sweep up** *vt sep & vi* barrer.

sweeper ['swiːpə^r] *n* FTBL líbero *m*.

sweeping ['swiːpɪŋ] *adj* **-1.** [effect, change] radical. **-2.** [statement] demasiado general. **-3.** [curve] amplio(plia).

sweepstake ['swiːpsteɪk] *n* lotería basada en carreras de caballos.

sweet [swiːt] ◇ *adj* **-1.** [gen] dulce; [sugary] azucarado(da). **-2.** [feelings] placentero(ra). **-3.** [smell - of flowers, air] fragante, perfumado(da). **-4.** [sound] melodioso(sa). **-5.** [character, person] amable. ◇ *n Br* **-1.** [candy] caramelo *m*, golosina *f*. **-2.** [dessert] postre *m*.

sweet-and-sour *adj* agridulce.

sweet corn *n* maíz *m*.

sweeten ['swiːtn] *vt* endulzar.

sweetener ['swiːtnə^r] *n* **-1.** [substance] edulcorante *m*. **-2.** *inf* [bribe] especie *f* de soborno.

sweetheart ['swiːthɑːt] *n* **-1.** [term of endearment] cariño *m*. **-2.** [boyfriend or girlfriend] amor *m*, novio *m*, -via *f*.

sweetness ['swiːtnɪs] *n* **-1.** [gen] dulzura *f*. **-2.** [of taste] dulzor *m*. **-3.** [of smell] fragancia *f*. **-4.** [of sound] melodía *f*.

sweet pea *n* guisante *m* de olor.

sweet potato *n* batata *f*.

sweet shop *n Br* confitería *f*.

sweet tooth *n inf*: **to have a ~** ser goloso(sa).

swell [swel] (*pt* **-ed**, *pp* **swollen** OR **-ed**) ◇ *vi* **-1.** [become larger] hincharse. **-2.** [balloon, sails] inflarse. **-3.** [population, sound] aumentar. ◇ *vt* [numbers etc] aumentar. ◇ *n* [of sea] oleaje *m*. ◇ *adj Am inf* estupendo(da), fenomenal.

swelling ['swelɪŋ] *n* hinchazón *f*.

sweltering ['sweltərɪŋ] *adj* **-1.** [weather] abrasador(ra), sofocante. **-2.** [person] achicharrado(da).

swept [swept] *pt & pp* → **sweep**.

swerve [swɜːv] *vi* virar bruscamente.

swift [swɪft] ◇ *adj* **-1.** [fast] rápido(da). **-2.** [prompt] pronto(ta). ◇ *n* [bird] vencejo *m*.

swiftly ['swɪftlɪ] *adj* **-1.** [quickly] rápidamente. **-2.** [promptly] prontamente, con prontitud.

swiftness ['swɪftnɪs] *n* **-1.** [quickness] rapi-

dez *f*, ligereza *f*. **-2.** [promptness] prontitud *f*.

swig [swɪg] (*pt & pp* **-ged**, *cont* **-ging**) *inf* ◇ *vt* beber a grandes tragos. ◇ *n* trago *m*.

swill [swɪl] ◇ *n* [pig food] bazofia *f*. ◇ *vt Br* [wash] enjuagar.

swim [swɪm] (*pt* **swam**, *pp* **swum**, *cont* **-ming**) ◇ *n* baño *m*; **to go for a ~** ir a nadar OR a darse un baño. ◇ *vi* **-1.** [in water] nadar. **-2.** [head, room] dar vueltas.

swimmer ['swɪmə^r] *n* nadador *m*, -ra *f*.

swimming ['swɪmɪŋ] ◇ *n* natación *f*. ◇ *comp* [club, gala] de natación; [cap] de baño.

swimming baths *npl Br* piscina *f* municipal.

swimming cap *n* gorro *m* de baño.

swimming costume *n Br* bañador *m*, traje *m* de baño.

swimming pool *n* piscina *f*, alberca *f* Amer.

swimming trunks *npl* bañador *m*.

swimsuit ['swɪmsuːt] *n* bañador *m*, traje *m* de baño.

swindle ['swɪndl] ◇ *n* estafa *f*, timo *m*, calote *m* Amer. ◇ *vt* estafar, timar; **to ~ sb out of** sthg estafar a alguien algo.

swine [swaɪn] *n inf pej* [person] cerdo *m*, -da *f*, canalla *m y f*.

swing [swɪŋ] (*pt & pp* **swung**) ◇ *n* **-1.** [child's toy] columpio *m*. **-2.** [change] viraje *m*, cambio *m* brusco. **-3.** [sway] meneo *m*, balanceo *m*. **-4.** *inf* [blow]: **to take a ~ at sb** intentar golpear a alguien. **-5.** *phr*: **to be in full ~** estar en plena marcha; **to get into the ~ of** cogerle la marcha a.

◇ *vt* **-1.** [move back and forth] balancear. **-2.** [move in a curve - car etc] hacer virar bruscamente.

◇ *vi* **-1.** [move back and forth] balancearse, oscilar. **-2.** [move in a curve] girar; **to ~ open** abrirse. **-3.** [turn]: **to ~ (round)** volverse, girarse. **-4.** [hit out]: **to ~ at sb** intentar golpear a alguien. **-5.** [change] virar, cambiar.

swing bridge *n* puente *m* giratorio.

swing door *n* puerta *f* oscilante.

swingeing ['swɪndʒɪŋ] *adj* severo(ra).

swinging ['swɪŋɪŋ] *adj inf* **-1.** [lively] alegre. **-2.** [uninhibited] liberal.

swipe [swaɪp] ◇ *n*: **to take a ~ at sthg** intentar golpear algo. ◇ *vt inf* [steal] birlar. ◇ *vi*: **to ~ at sthg** intentar golpear algo.

swirl [swɜːl] ◇ *n* remolino *m*. ◇ *vt* dar vueltas a. ◇ *vi* arremolinarse.

swish [swɪʃ] ◇ *n* [of curtains, dress] crujido *m*; [of tail] meneo *m*; [of whip] chasquido *m*.

◇ *vt* [tail] **agitar, menear.** ◇ *vi* [curtains, dress] **crujir;** [whip] **dar un chasquido.**

Swiss [swɪs] ◇ *adj* **suizo(za).** ◇ *n* [person] **suizo** *m*, **-za** *f*. ◇ *npl*: **the ~ los suizos.**

swiss roll *n Br* **brazo** *m* **de gitano.**

switch [swɪtʃ] ◇ *n* **-1.** [control device] **interruptor** *m*, **suiche** *m Amer*. **-2.** [change] **cambio** *m* **completo, viraje** *m*. **-3.** *Am* RAIL **aguja** *f*. ◇ *vt* **-1.** [change] **cambiar de; to ~ one's attention to sthg dirigir la atención a** OR **hacia algo. -2.** [swap] **intercambiar.** ◇ *vi*: **to ~ (to/from) cambiar (a/de).**
◆ **switch off** ◇ *vt sep* [light, radio etc] **apagar;** [engine] **parar.** ◇ *vi inf* **desconectar, dejar de prestar atención.**
◆ **switch on** *vt sep* [light, radio etc] **encender;** [engine] **poner en marcha.**

switchblade ['swɪtʃbleɪd] *n Am* **navaja** *f* **automática.**

switchboard ['swɪtʃbɔːd] *n* **centralita** *f*, **conmutador** *m Amer*.

switchboard operator *n* **telefonista** *m y f*.

switched-on ['swɪtʃt-] *adj inf* **al día, a la última.**

Switzerland ['swɪtsələnd] *n* **Suiza.**

swivel ['swɪvl] (*Br pt & pp* **-led**, *cont* **-ling**, *Am pt & pp* **-ed**, *cont* **-ing**) ◇ *vt* **hacer girar.** ◇ *vi* **girar.**

swivel chair *n* **silla** *f* **giratoria.**

swollen ['swəʊln] ◇ *pp* → **swell.** ◇ *adj* [ankle, leg etc] **hinchado(da);** [river] **crecido(da).**

swoon [swuːn] *vi literary or hum* **deshacerse.**

swoop [swuːp] ◇ *n* **-1.** [of bird] **calada** *f*; [of plane] **descenso** *m* **en picado; in one fell ~ de un golpe. -2.** [raid] **redada** *f*. ◇ *vi* **-1.** [move downwards] **caer en picado. -2.** [move quickly] **atacar por sorpresa.**

swop [swɒp] = **swap.**

sword [sɔːd] *n* **espada** *f*; **to cross ~s (with) habérselas (con).**

swordfish ['sɔːdfɪʃ] (*pl inv* OR **-es**) *n* **pez** *m* **espada.**

swordsman ['sɔːdzmən] (*pl* **-men** [-mən]) *n* **espadachín** *m*.

swore [swɔːr] *pt* → **swear.**

sworn [swɔːn] ◇ *pp* → **swear.** ◇ *adj* **-1.** [committed]: **to be ~ enemies ser enemigos implacables. -2.** JUR **jurado(da).**

swot [swɒt] (*pt & pp* **-ted**, *cont* **-ting**) *Br inf* ◇ *n pej* **empollón** *m*, **-ona** *f*. ◇ *vi*: **to ~ (for) empollar (para).**
◆ **swot up** *inf* ◇ *vt sep* **empollar.** ◇ *vi*: **~ up (on sthg) empollar (algo).**

swum [swʌm] *pp* → **swim.**

swung [swʌŋ] *pt & pp* → **swing.**

sycamore ['sɪkəmɔːr] *n* **sicomoro** *m*.

sycophant ['sɪkəfænt] *n* **adulador** *m*, **-ra** *f*.

Sydney ['sɪdnɪ] *n* **Sidney.**

syllable ['sɪləbl] *n* **sílaba** *f*.

syllabub ['sɪləbʌb] *n* **postre de nata o leche y claras de huevo.**

syllabus ['sɪləbəs] (*pl* **-buses** OR **-bi** [-baɪ]) *n* **programa** *m* **(de estudios).**

symbol ['sɪmbl] *n* **símbolo** *m*.

symbolic [sɪm'bɒlɪk] *adj* **simbólico(ca); to be ~ of ser un símbolo de.**

symbolism ['sɪmbəlɪzm] *n* **simbolismo** *m*.

symbolize, -ise ['sɪmbəlaɪz] *vt* **simbolizar.**

symmetrical [sɪ'metrɪkl] *adj* **simétrico(ca).**

symmetry ['sɪmətrɪ] *n* **simetría** *f*.

sympathetic [ˌsɪmpə'θetɪk] *adj* **-1.** [understanding] **comprensivo(va). -2.** [willing to support] **favorable; ~ to bien dispuesto(ta) hacia. -3.** [likable] **agradable.**

sympathize, -ise ['sɪmpəθaɪz] *vi* **-1.** [feel sorry]: **to ~ (with) compadecerse (de). -2.** [understand]: **to ~ (with sthg) comprender (algo). -3.** [support]: **to ~ with sthg apoyar algo.**

sympathizer, -iser ['sɪmpəθaɪzər] *n* **simpatizante** *m y f*.

sympathy ['sɪmpəθɪ] *n* **-1.** [understanding]: **~ (for) comprensión** *f* **(hacia);** [compassion] **compasión** *f* **(por). -2.** [agreement] **solidaridad** *f*; **in ~ (with) de acuerdo (con). -3.** [support]: **in ~ (with) en solidaridad (con).**
◆ **sympathies** *npl* **-1.** [support] **simpatías** *fpl*. **-2.** [to bereaved person] **pésame** *m*.

symphonic [sɪm'fɒnɪk] *adj* **sinfónico(ca).**

symphony ['sɪmfənɪ] (*pl* **-ies**) *n* **sinfonía** *f*.

symphony orchestra *n* **orquesta** *f* **sinfónica.**

symposium [sɪm'pəʊzjəm] (*pl* **-siums** OR **-sia** [sɪm'pəʊzjə]) *n fml* **simposio** *m*.

symptom ['sɪmptəm] *n lit & fig* **síntoma** *m*.

symptomatic [ˌsɪmptə'mætɪk] *adj fml*: **~ of sthg sintomático(ca) (de).**

synagogue ['sɪnəgɒg] *n* **sinagoga** *f*.

sync [sɪŋk] *n inf*: **out of ~ desincronizado(da); in ~ sincronizado(da).**

synchromesh gearbox ['sɪŋkrəʊmeʃ-] *n* **caja** *f* **de cambios sincronizada.**

synchronize, -ise ['sɪŋkrənaɪz] ◇ *vt*: **to ~ sthg (with) sincronizar algo (con).** ◇ *vi* **ser sincrónico.**

synchronized swimming ['sɪŋkrənaɪzd-] *n* **ballet** *m* **acuático.**

syncopated ['sɪŋkəpeɪtɪd] *adj* **sincopado(da).**

syncopation [ˌsɪŋkə'peɪʃn] *n* **síncopa** *f*.

syndicate [*n* 'sɪndɪkət, *vb* 'sɪndɪkeɪt] ◇ *n* sindicato *m*. ◇ *vt* sindicar.

syndrome ['sɪndrəum] *n* síndrome *m*.

synod ['sɪnəd] *n* sínodo *m*.

synonym ['sɪnənɪm] *n*: ~ **(for** OR **of)** sinónimo *m* (de).

synonymous [sɪ'nɒnɪməs] *adj*: ~ **(with)** sinónimo(ma) (de).

synopsis [sɪ'nɒpsɪs] (*pl* **-ses** [-siːz]) *n* sinopsis *f inv*.

syntax ['sɪntæks] *n* sintaxis *f inv*.

synthesis ['sɪnθəsɪs] (*pl* **-ses** [-siːz]) *n* síntesis *f inv*.

synthesize, -ise ['sɪnθəsaɪz] *vt* sintetizar.

synthesizer ['sɪnθəsaɪzəʳ] *n* sintetizador *m*.

synthetic [sɪn'θetɪk] *adj* **-1.** [man-made] sintético(ca). **-2.** *pej* [insincere] artificial.

syphilis ['sɪfɪlɪs] *n* sífilis *f inv*.

syphon ['saɪfn] = **siphon**.

Syria ['sɪrɪə] *n* Siria.

Syrian ['sɪrɪən] ◇ *adj* sirio(ria). ◇ *n* [person] sirio *m*, -ria *f*.

syringe [sɪ'rɪndʒ] (*cont* **syringeing**) ◇ *n* jeringa *f*, jeringuilla *f*. ◇ *vt* jeringar.

syrup ['sɪrəp] *n* (*U*) **-1.** CULIN almíbar *m*. **-2.** MED jarabe *m*.

system ['sɪstəm] *n* [gen] sistema *m*; [of central heating etc] instalación *f*; **digestive** ~ aparato *m* digestivo; **transport** ~ red *f* de transportes; **to get sthg out of one's** ~ *inf* sacarse algo de encima.

systematic [ˌsɪstə'mætɪk] *adj* sistemático(ca).

systematize, -ise ['sɪstəmətaɪz] *vt* sistematizar.

system disk *n* COMPUT disco *m* del sistema.

systems analyst ['sɪstəmz-] *n* COMPUT analista *m* y *f* de sistemas.

systems engineer ['sɪstəmz-] *n* COMPUT ingeniero *m*, -ra *f* de sistemas.

system software *n* COMPUT software *m* del sistema.

T

t (*pl* **t's** OR **ts**), **T** (*pl* **T's** OR **Ts**) [tiː] *n* [letter] t *f*, T *f*.

ta [taː] *excl Br inf* ¡gracias!

TA *n abbr of* **Territorial Army**.

tab [tæb] *n* **-1.** [of cloth] etiqueta *f*. **-2.** [of metal, card etc] lengüeta *f*. **-3.** *Am* [bill] cuenta *f*. **-4.** COMPUT (*abbr of* **tabulator**) tab. **-5.** *phr*: **to keep** ~**s on sb** vigilar de cerca a alguien.

Tabasco sauce® [tə'bæskəu-] *n* tabasco® *m*.

tabby ['tæbɪ] (*pl* **-ies**) *n*: ~ **(cat)** gato *m* atigrado.

tabernacle ['tæbənækl] *n* tabernáculo *m*.

tab key *n* COMPUT (tecla *f* del) tabulador *m*.

table ['teɪbl] ◇ *n* **-1.** [piece of furniture] mesa *f*; [small] mesilla *f*. **-2.** [diagram] tabla *f*. **-3.** *phr*: **to turn the** ~**s on** volver las tornas a. ◇ *vt* **-1.** *Br* [propose] presentar. **-2.** *Am* [postpone] aplazar, posponer.

tableau ['tæbləu] (*pl* **-x** ['tæbləuz] OR **-s**) *n* cuadro *m* vivente.

tablecloth ['teɪblklɒθ] *n* mantel *m*.

table d'hôte ['taːbl,dəut] *n*: **the** ~ el menú.

table lamp *n* lámpara *f* de mesa.

table licence *n* licencia para la venta de bebidas alcohólicas sólo con la comida.

table linen *n* mantelería *f*.

table manners *npl* modales *mpl* en la mesa.

tablemat ['teɪblmæt] *n* salvamanteles *m inv*.

table salt *n* sal *f* de mesa.

tablespoon ['teɪblspuːn] *n* **-1.** [spoon] cuchara *f* grande (*para servir*). **-2.** [spoonful] cucharada *f* (grande).

tablet ['tæblɪt] *n* **-1.** [pill, piece of soap] pastilla *f*. **-2.** [piece of stone] lápida *f*.

table tennis *n* tenis *m* de mesa.

tableware ['teɪblweəʳ] *n* servicio *m* de mesa, vajilla *f*.

table wine *n* vino *m* de mesa.

tabloid ['tæblɔɪd] *n*: **the** ~**s** los periódicos sensacionalistas; ~ **(newspaper)** tabloide *m*.

TABLOID:
En los países anglosajones, el formato pequeño es característico de la prensa sensacionalista. Los periódicos británicos de este tipo son: Daily Express, Daily Mail, Daily Mirror, The Star, The Sun y Today

taboo [tə'buː] (*pl* **-s**) ◇ *adj* tabú. ◇ *n* tabú *m*.

tabulate ['tæbjʊleɪt] *vt* tabular.

tachograph ['tækəɡrɑːf] *n* tacógrafo *m*.

tachometer [tæ'kɒmɪtər] *n* tacómetro *m*.

tacit ['tæsɪt] *adj fml* tácito(ta).

taciturn ['tæsɪtɜːn] *adj fml* taciturno(na).

tack [tæk] ◇ *n* **-1.** [nail] tachuela *f*. **-2.** NAUT bordada *f*. **-3.** *fig* [course of action] táctica *f*, **to change** ~ cambiar de táctica. ◇ *vt* **-1.** [fasten with nail] fijar con tachuelas. **-2.** SEWING hilvanar. ◇ *vi* NAUT virar.
◆ **tack on** *vt sep inf* añadir.

tackle ['tækl] ◇ *n* **-1.** FTBL entrada *f*. **-2.** RUGBY placaje *m*. **-3.** (*U*) [equipment] equipo *m*, aparejos *mpl*. **-4.** [for lifting] aparejo *m*. ◇ *vt* **-1.** [deal with - job] emprender; [- problem] abordar. **-2.** FTBL entrar a, hacer una entrada a. **-3.** RUGBY placar a. **-4.** [attack] atacar, arremeter. **-5.** [talk to]: **to** ~ **sb about** OR **on sthg** discutir algo con alguien.

tacky ['tækɪ] (*compar* **-ier**, *superl* **-iest**) *adj* **-1.** *inf* [cheap and nasty] cutre; [ostentatious and vulgar] hortera. **-2.** [sticky] pegajoso(sa).

taco ['tækəʊ] (*pl* **-s**) *n* taco *m*.

tact [tækt] *n* (*U*) tacto *m*, discreción *f*.

tactful ['tæktfʊl] *adj* discreto(ta).

tactfully ['tæktfʊlɪ] *adv* discretamente.

tactic ['tæktɪk] *n* táctica *f*.
◆ **tactics** *n* (*U*) MIL táctica *f*.

tactical ['tæktɪkl] *adj* estratégico(ca); [weapons] táctico(ca).

tactical voting *n Br* votación *f* táctica.

tactless ['tæktlɪs] *adj* indiscreto(ta), falto(ta) de tacto.

tactlessly ['tæktlɪslɪ] *adv* indiscretamente.

tadpole ['tædpəʊl] *n* renacuajo *m*.

Tadzhikistan [tɑːˌdʒɪkɪ'stɑːn] *n* (el) Tayikistán.

taffeta ['tæfɪtə] *n* tafetán *m*.

taffy ['tæfɪ] (*pl* **-ies**) *n Am* caramelo *m* de melaza.

tag [tæɡ] (*pt & pp* **-ged**, *cont* **-ging**) ◇ *n* **-1.** [of cloth, paper] etiqueta *f*. **-2.** [game] pillapilla *m*. **-3.** COMPUT código *m*, etiqueta *f*. ◇ *vt* etiquetar.
◆ **tag along** *vi inf* pegarse, engancharse.

Tagus ['teɪɡəs] *n*: **the** ~ el Tajo.

Tahiti [tɑː'hiːtɪ] *n* Tahití.

Tahitian [tɑː'hiːʃn] ◇ *adj* tahitiano(na). ◇ *n* tahitiano *m*, -na *f*.

tail [teɪl] ◇ *n* [gen] cola *f*; [of coat, shirt] faldón *m*; **with one's** ~ **between one's legs** [person] con el rabo entre las piernas. ◇ *comp* trasero(ra). ◇ *vt inf* [follow] seguir de cerca.
◆ **tails** *npl* **-1.** [formal dress] frac *m*. **-2.** [side of coin] cruz *f*.
◆ **tail off** *vi* **-1.** [voice] ir debilitándose; [sound] ir disminuyendo. **-2.** [interest, sales etc] ir descendiendo.

tailback ['teɪlbæk] *n Br* cola *f*.

tailcoat [ˌteɪl'kəʊt] *n* frac *m*.

tail end *n* parte *f* final.

tailgate ['teɪlɡeɪt] *n* [of hatchback car] portón *m*.

taillight ['teɪllaɪt] *n* luz *f* trasera, piloto *m*.

tailor ['teɪlər] ◇ *n* sastre *m*. ◇ *vt* adaptar.

tailored ['teɪləd] *adj* entallado(da).

tailor-made *adj* (hecho(cha)) a la medida.

tail pipe *n Am* tubo *m* de escape.

tailplane ['teɪlpleɪn] *n* plano *m* fijo de cola.

tailwind ['teɪlwɪnd] *n* viento *m* de cola.

taint [teɪnt] *fml* ◇ *n* mancha *f*. ◇ *vt* viciar.

tainted ['teɪntɪd] *adj* **-1.** [reputation] manchado(da). **-2.** *Am* [food] estropeado(da).

Taiwan [ˌtaɪ'wɑːn] *n* Taiwán.

Taiwanese [ˌtaɪwə'niːz] ◇ *adj* taiwanés(esa). ◇ *n* taiwanés *m*, -esa *f*.

take [teɪk] (*pt* **took**, *pp* **taken**) ◇ *vt* **-1.** [gen] tomar; ~ **a seat!** ¡siéntate!; **to** ~ **control/command** tomar control/el mando; **to** ~ **a photo** hacer OR tomar una foto; **to** ~ **a walk** dar un paseo; **to** ~ **a bath** bañarse; **to** ~ **a test** hacer un examen; **to** ~ **sthg seriously/badly** tomarse algo en serio/a mal; **to** ~ **pity on sb** compadecerse de alguien; **to** ~ **offence** ofenderse. **-2.** [bring, carry, accompany] llevar. **-3.** [steal] quitar, robar. **-4.** [buy] coger, quedarse con; [rent] alquilar. **-5.** [receive] recibir. **-6.** [take hold of] coger; **let me** ~ **your coat** déjeme que le coja el abrigo; **to** ~ **sb prisoner** capturar a alguien. **-7.** [accept - offer, cheque, criticism] aceptar; [- advice] seguir; [- responsibility, blame] asumir; **the machine only** ~**s 50p pieces** la máquina sólo admite monedas de 50 peniques; ~ **my word for it** créeme. **-8.** [have room for - passengers, goods] tener cabida para. **-9.** [bear - pain etc] soportar, aguantar. **-10.** [require - time, courage] requerir; [- money] costar; **it will** ~ **a week/three hours** llevará una semana/tres horas. **-11.** [travel by - means of transport, route] tomar, coger. **-12.** [wear - shoes] calzar; [- clothes] usar. **-13.** [consider] considerar. **-14.** [assume]: **I ~ it (that) ...** supongo que .... ◇ *vi* [dye] coger; [vaccine, fire] prender. ◇ *n* CINEMA toma *f*.

◆ **take aback** *vt fus* dejar atónito(ta); **to be taken aback** estar atónito.

◆ **take after** *vt fus* parecerse a.

◆ **take apart** *vt sep* [dismantle] desmontar.

◆ **take away** *vt sep* **-1.** [remove] quitar. **-2.** [deduct] restar, sustraer.

◆ **take back** *vt sep* **-1.** [return] devolver. **-2.** [accept - faulty goods] aceptar la devolución de. **-3.** [admit as wrong] retirar.

◆ **take down** *vt sep* **-1.** [dismantle] desmontar. **-2.** [write down] escribir, tomar nota de. **-3.** [lower - trousers] bajarse; [- picture] bajar.

◆ **take in** *vt sep* **-1.** [deceive] engañar. **-2.** [understand] comprender, asimilar. **-3.** [include] incluir, abarcar. **-4.** [provide accommodation for] acoger.

◆ **take off** ◇ *vt sep* **-1.** [clothes, glasses] quitarse. **-2.** [have as holiday] tomarse; **to ~ time off** tomarse tiempo libre. **-3.** *Br inf* [imitate] imitar. **-4.** *inf* [go away suddenly]: **to ~ o.s. off** irse, marcharse. ◇ *vi* **-1.** [plane] despegar, decolar *Amer*. **-2.** [go away suddenly] irse, marcharse. **-3.** [career] consolidarse; [idea, fashion] cuajar.

◆ **take on** ◇ *vt sep* **-1.** [accept - work, job] aceptar; [- responsibility] asumir. **-2.** [employ] emplear, coger. **-3.** [confront] desafiar. ◇ *vt fus* [assume] tomar.

◆ **take out** *vt sep* **-1.** [from container, pocket] sacar. **-2.** [delete] suprimir. **-3.** [go out with]: **to ~ sb out** invitar a salir a alguien; **to ~ it** OR **a lot out of one** *inf* agotar a uno.

◆ **take out on** *vt sep* [feelings, anger] descargar contra; **don't ~ it out on me** ¡no la tomes conmigo!

◆ **take over** ◇ *vt sep* **-1.** [company, business] absorber, adquirir; [country, government] apoderarse de. **-2.** [job] tomar, asumir. ◇ *vi* **-1.** [take control] tomar el poder. **-2.** [in job] entrar en funciones.

◆ **take to** *vt fus* **-1.** [feel a liking for - person] coger cariño a; [- activity] aficionarse a. **-2.** [begin]: **to ~ to doing sthg** empezar a hacer algo.

◆ **take up** *vt sep* **-1.** [begin]: **to ~ up singing** dedicarse a cantar; [job] aceptar, tomar. **-2.** [continue] reanudar. **-3.** [discuss] discutir. **-4.** [time, space] ocupar; [effort] requerir.

◆ **take upon** *vt sep*: **to ~ it upon o.s. to do sthg** permitirse hacer algo.

◆ **take up on** *vt sep* **-1.** [accept]: **to ~ sb up on an offer** aceptar una oferta de alguien. **-2.** [ask to explain]: **to ~ sb up on sthg** pedir que alguien se explique acerca de algo.

takeaway *Br* ['teɪkə,weɪ], **takeout** *Am* ['teɪkaʊt] *n* **-1.** [shop] *establecimiento donde se vende comida preparada para llevar*. **-2.** [food] *comida f para llevar*.

take-home pay *n* sueldo *m* neto.

taken ['teɪkn] ◇ *pp* → **take**. ◇ *adj*: **~ with** atraído(da) por.

takeoff ['teɪkɒf] *n* [of plane] despegue *m*, decolaje *m Amer*.

takeout *Am* = **takeaway**.

takeover ['teɪk,əʊvə*] *n* **-1.** [of company] adquisición *f*. **-2.** [of government] toma *f* del poder.

takeover bid *n* OPA *f*, oferta *f* pública de adquisición de acciones.

taker ['teɪkə*] *n* persona *f* interesada (*en comprar algo etc*).

takeup ['teɪkʌp] *n* grado *m* de aceptación, respuesta *f*.

taking ['teɪkɪŋ] *adj dated* atractivo(va).

◆ **takings** *npl* [of shop] venta *f*; [of show] recaudación *f*.

talc [tælk], **talcum (powder)** ['tælkəm-] *n* talco *m*.

tale [teɪl] *n* **-1.** [fictional story] cuento *m*. **-2.** [anecdote] anécdota *f*.

talent ['tælənt] *n*: **~ (for sthg)** talento *m* (para algo).

talented ['tæləntɪd] *adj* con talento.

talent scout *n* cazatalentos *m y f inv*.

talisman ['tælɪzmən] (*pl* **-s**) *n* talismán *m*.

talk [tɔːk] ◇ *n* **-1.** [conversation] conversación *f*. **-2.** (*U*) [gossip] habladurías *fpl*. **-3.** [lecture] charla *f*, conferencia *f*. ◇ *vi* **-1.** [gen] hablar; **to ~ to/of** hablar con/de; **to ~ on** OR **about** hablar acerca de OR sobre; **to ~ big** fanfarronear, farolear. **-2.** [gossip] chismorrear. ◇ *vt* hablar de.

◆ **talks** *npl* conversaciones *fpl*.

◆ **talk down to** *vt fus* hablar con aires de suficiencia a.

◆ **talk into** *vt sep*: **to ~ sb into doing sthg** convencer a alguien para que haga algo.

◆ **talk out of** *vt sep*: **to ~ sb out of doing sthg** disuadir a alguien de que haga algo.

◆ **talk over** *vt sep* discutir, hablar de.

talkative ['tɔːkətɪv] *adj* hablador(ra).

talker ['tɔːkə*] *n* hablador *m*, -ra *f*.

talking point ['tɔːkɪŋ-] *n* tema *m* de conversación.

talking-to ['tɔːkɪŋ-] *n inf* bronca *f*.

talk show *Am* ◇ *n* programa *m* de entrevistas. ◇ *comp* de programa de entrevistas.

tall [tɔːl] *adj* alto(ta); **she's 2 metres ~** mide 2 metros.

tallboy ['tɔːlbɔɪ] *n* cómoda *f* alta.

tall order *n*: **it's a ~** es mucho pedir.

tall story *n* cuento *m* (increíble).

tally ['tælɪ] (*pl* **-ies**, *pt* & *pp* **-ied**) ◇ *n* cuenta *f*; **to keep a ~** llevar la cuenta. ◇ *vi* concordar, casar.

talon ['tælən] *n* garra *f*.

tambourine [,tæmbə'riːn] *n* pandereta *f*.

tame [teɪm] ◇ *adj* **-1.** [domesticated] doméstico(ca). **-2.** *pej* [obedient] dócil. **-3.** *pej* [unexciting] soso(sa), aburrido(da). ◇ *vt* **-1.** [domesticate] domesticar. **-2.** [bring under control] dominar.

tamely ['teɪmlɪ] *adv* dócilmente, sumisamente.

tamer ['teɪməʳ] *n* domador *m*, -ra *f*.

Tamil ['tæmɪl] ◇ *adj* tamil. ◇ *n* **-1.** [person] tamil *m* y *f*. **-2.** [language] tamil *m*.

tamper ['tæmpəʳ]
◆ **tamper with** *vt fus* [lock] intentar forzar; [records, file] falsear; [machine] manipular.

tampon ['tæmpɒn] *n* tampón *m*.

tan [tæn] (*pt* & *pp* **-ned**, *cont* **-ning**) ◇ *adj* de color marrón claro. ◇ *n* bronceado *m*. ◇ *vi* broncearse.

tandem ['tændəm] *n* [bicycle] tándem *m*; **in ~** conjuntamente, en colaboración.

tandoori [tæn'dʊərɪ] ◇ *n* [cooking method] *método indio de asar la carne en un horno de barro.* ◇ *comp asado al estilo indio en un horno de barro.*

tang [tæŋ] *n* [smell] olor *m* fuerte; [taste] sabor *m* fuerte.

tangent ['tændʒənt] *n* GEOM tangente *f*; **to go off at a ~** salirse por la tangente.

tangerine [,tæn'dʒəriːn] *n* mandarina *f*.

tangible ['tændʒəbl] *adj* tangible.

Tangier [tæn'dʒɪəʳ] *n* Tánger.

tangle ['tæŋgl] ◇ *n* [mass] maraña *f*; *fig* [mess] enredo *m*, embrollo *m*, entrevero *m* *Amer.* ◇ *vi* enredarse, enmarañarse; **to get ~d (up)** enredarse.
◆ **tangle with** *vt fus inf* meterse con.

tangled ['tæŋgld] *adj lit* & *fig* enredado(da).

tango ['tæŋgəʊ] (*pl* **-es**) ◇ *n* tango *m*. ◇ *vi* bailar el tango.

tangy ['tæŋɪ] (*compar* **-ier**, *superl* **-iest**) *adj* fuerte.

tank [tæŋk] *n* **-1.** [container] depósito *m*, tanque *m*. **-2.** MIL tanque *m*, carro *m* de combate.

tankard ['tæŋkəd] *n* bock *m*.

tanker ['tæŋkəʳ] *n* **-1.** [ship · gen] barco *m* cisterna, tanque *m*; [- for oil] petrolero *m*. **-2.** [truck] camión *m* cisterna. **-3.** [train] tren *m* cisterna.

tankful ['tæŋkfʊl] *n* depósito *m* lleno; **give me a ~** lléneme el depósito.

tanned [tænd] *adj* bronceado(da).

tannin ['tænɪn] *n* tanino *m*.

Tannoy® ['tænɔɪ] *n* (sistema *m* de) altavoces *mpl*.

tantalize, -ise ['tæntəlaɪz] *vt* atormentar.

tantalizing ['tæntəlaɪzɪŋ] *adj* tentador(ra).

tantamount ['tæntəmaʊnt] *adj*: **~ to** equivalente a.

tantrum ['tæntrəm] (*pl* **-s**) *n* rabieta *f*.

Tanzania [,tænzə'nɪə] *n* Tanzania.

Tanzanian [,tænzə'nɪən] ◇ *adj* tanzano(na). ◇ *n* tanzano *m*, -na *f*.

tap [tæp] (*pt* & *pp* **-ped**, *cont* **-ping**) ◇ *n* **-1.** [device] grifo *m*. **-2.** [light blow] golpecito *m*. ◇ *vt* **-1.** [hit] golpear ligeramente; **he tapped his fingers on the table** golpeaba ligeramente la mesa con los dedos. **-2.** [strength, resources] utilizar. **-3.** [phone] intervenir. ◇ *vi* dar un golpecito.

tap dance *n* claqué *m*.

tap dancer *n* bailarín *m*, -ina *f* de claqué.

tape [teɪp] ◇ *n* **-1.** [cassette, magnetic tape, strip of cloth] cinta *f*. **-2.** SPORT [at finishing line] cinta *f* de llegada. **-3.** [adhesive plastic] cinta *f* adhesiva. ◇ *vt* **-1.** [on tape recorder, video recorder] grabar. **-2.** [with adhesive tape] pegar con cinta adhesiva. **-3.** *Am* [bandage] vendar.

tape deck *n* pletina *f* del magnetófono.

tape measure *n* cinta *f* métrica.

taper ['teɪpəʳ] ◇ *n* [candle] vela *f*. ◇ *vi* afilarse.
◆ **taper off** *vi* ir disminuyendo.

tape-record [-rɪ,kɔːd] *vt* grabar (en cinta).

tape recorder *n* magnetófono *m*.

tape recording *n* grabación *f* en cinta.

tapered ['teɪpəd] *adj* ahusado(da).

tapestry ['tæpɪstrɪ] (*pl* **-ies**) *n* **-1.** [piece of work] tapiz *m*. **-2.** [craft] tapicería *f*. **-3.** *literary* [pattern] cuadro *m*.

tapeworm ['teɪpwɜːm] *n* tenia *f*, solitaria *f*.

tapioca [,tæpɪ'əʊkə] *n* tapioca *f*.

tapir ['teɪpəʳ] (*pl inv* OR **-s**) *n* tapir *m*.

tappet ['tæpɪt] *n* excéntrica *f*.

tar [tɑːʳ] *n* alquitrán *m*.

tarantula [tə'ræntjʊlə] *n* tarántula *f*.

target ['tɑːgɪt] ◇ *n* **-1.** [of missile, goal, aim] objetivo *m*. **-2.** [in archery, shooting, of criticism] blanco *m*; **to be on ~ to do sthg** llevar el ritmo adecuado para hacer algo. ◇ *vt* **-1.** [aim weapon at] apuntar a. **-2.** [channel]: **to ~ funds on** destinar fondos a.

tariff ['tærɪf] *n* tarifa *f*.

Tarmac® ['tɑːmæk] *n* [material] alquitrán *m*.

◆ **tarmac** *n* AERON: **the tarmac** la pista.

tarnish ['tɑːnɪʃ] ◇ *vt* [make dull] deslustrar; *fig* [damage] empañar, manchar. ◇ *vi* [become dull] deslustrarse.

tarnished ['tɑːnɪʃt] *adj* [dull] deslustrado(da); *fig* [damaged] manchado(da), empañado(da).

tarot ['tærəʊ] *n*: **the ~** el tarot.

tarot card *n* carta *f* de tarot.

tarpaulin [tɑːˈpɔːlɪn] *n* lona *f* alquitranada.

tarragon ['tærəgən] *n* estragón *m*.

tart [tɑːt] ◇ *adj* -**1.** [bitter] agrio (agria). -**2.** [sarcastic] mordaz. ◇ *n* -**1.** [sweet pastry] tarta *f*. -**2.** *v inf* [prostitute] furcia *f*, fulana *f*, cuero *m Amer*.

◆ **tart up** *vt sep Br inf pej* emperejilar; **to ~ o.s. up** emperifollarse.

tartan ['tɑːtn] ◇ *n* tartán *m*. ◇ *comp* de tartán.

tartar(e) sauce ['tɑːtə-] *n* salsa *f* tártara.

tartness ['tɑːtnɪs] *n* -**1.** [of taste] acidez *f*. -**2.** [of comment] mordacidad *f*, acritud *f*.

task [tɑːsk] *n* tarea *f*.

task force *n* MIL destacamento *m* de fuerzas.

taskmaster ['tɑːsk,mɑːstə'] *n*: **a hard ~** un tirano.

Tasmania [tæzˈmeɪnjə] *n* Tasmania.

Tasmanian [tæzˈmeɪnjən] ◇ *adj* tasmanio(nia). ◇ *n* tasmanio *m*, -nia *f*.

tassel ['tæsl] *n* borla *f*.

taste [teɪst] ◇ *n* -**1.** [physical sense, discernment] gusto *m*; **in bad/good ~** de mal/buen gusto. -**2.** [flavour] sabor *m*. -**3.** [try]: **have a ~** pruébalo. -**4.** *fig* [for success, fast cars etc]: **~ (for)** afición *f* (a), gusto *m* (por). -**5.** *fig* [experience] experiencia *f*. ◇ *vt* -**1.** [food] notar un sabor a. -**2.** [test, try] probar. -**3.** *fig* [experience] conocer. ◇ *vi* saber; **to ~ of** OR **like** saber a.

taste bud *n* papila *f* gustativa.

tasteful ['teɪstful] *adj* elegante, de buen gusto.

tastefully ['teɪstfulɪ] *adv* elegantemente, con gusto.

tasteless ['teɪstlɪs] *adj* -**1.** [offensive, cheap and unattractive] de mal gusto. -**2.** [without flavour] insípido(da), soso(sa).

taster ['teɪstə'] *n* catador *m*, -ra *f*.

tasty ['teɪstɪ] (*compar* -**ier**, *superl* -**iest**) *adj* sabroso(sa).

tat [tæt] *n* (*U*) *Br inf pej* baratijas *fpl*.

tattered ['tætəd] *adj* [clothes] andrajoso(sa); [paper] desgastado(da).

tatters ['tætəz] *npl*: **in ~** [clothes] andrajo-

so(sa); *fig* [confidence, reputation] por los suelos.

tattoo [təˈtuː] (*pl* -**s**) ◇ *n* -**1.** [design] tatuaje *m*. -**2.** [rhythmic beating] repiqueteo *m* de tambores. -**3.** *Br* [military display] desfile *m* militar. ◇ *vt* tatuar.

tattooist [təˈtuːɪst] *n* tatuador *m*, -ra *f*.

tatty ['tætɪ] (*compar* -**ier**, *superl* -**iest**) *adj Br inf pej* desastrado(da).

taught [tɔːt] *pt & pp* → **teach**.

taunt [tɔːnt] ◇ *vt* zaherir a. ◇ *n* pulla *f*.

Taurus ['tɔːrəs] *n* Tauro *m*; **to be (a) ~** ser Tauro.

taut [tɔːt] *adj* tenso(sa).

tauten ['tɔːtn] ◇ *vt* tensar. ◇ *vi* tensarse.

tautology [tɔːˈtɒlədʒɪ] *n* tautología *f*.

tavern ['tævn] *n dated* taberna *f*.

tawdry ['tɔːdrɪ] (*compar* -**ier**, *superl* -**iest**) *adj pej* de oropel.

tawny ['tɔːnɪ] *adj* leonado(da).

tax [tæks] ◇ *n* impuesto *m*, contribución *f*. ◇ *vt* -**1.** [goods, profits] gravar. -**2.** [business, person] imponer contribuciones a. -**3.** [strain, test] poner a prueba.

taxable ['tæksəbl] *adj* imponible.

tax allowance *n* desgravación *f* fiscal.

taxation [tækˈseɪʃn] *n* (*U*) -**1.** [system] sistema *m* tributario. -**2.** [amount] impuestos *mpl*, contribuciones *fpl*.

tax avoidance [-əˈvɔɪdəns] *n* evasión *f* fiscal.

tax collector *n* recaudador *m*, -ra *f* de impuestos.

tax cut *n* reducción *f* tributaria.

tax-deductible [-dɪˈdʌktəbl] *adj* desgravable.

tax disc *n Br* pegatina *del impuesto de circulación*.

tax evasion *n* fraude *m* fiscal, evasión *f* de impuestos.

tax-exempt *Am* = **tax-free**.

tax exemption *n* exención *f* de impuestos.

tax exile *n Br* [person] *persona que vive en el extranjero, para evitar los impuestos*.

tax-free *Br*, **tax-exempt** *Am adj* exento(ta) de impuestos.

tax haven *n* paraíso *m* fiscal.

taxi ['tæksɪ] ◇ *n* taxi *m*. ◇ *vi* [plane] rodar por la pista.

taxicab ['tæksɪkæb] *n* taxi *m*.

taxidermist ['tæksɪdɜːmɪst] *n* taxidermista *m y f*.

taxi driver *n* taxista *m y f*.

taximeter ['tæksɪˌmiːtə'] *n* taxímetro *m*.

taxing ['tæksɪŋ] *adj* [gen] agotador(ra); [problem, exam] **abrumador(ra).**

tax inspector *n* ≃ inspector *m*, -ra *f* de Hacienda.

taxi rank *Br*, **taxi stand** *n* parada *f* de taxis.

taxman ['tæksmæn] (*pl* **-men** [-men]) *n* **-1.** [tax collector] recaudador *m*, -ra *f* de impuestos. **-2.** *inf* [tax office]: **the ~** ≃ Hacienda *f*, ≃ el Fisco.

taxpayer ['tæks,peɪə'] *n* contribuyente *m* y *f*.

tax relief *n* (*U*) desgravación *f* fiscal.

tax return *n* declaración *f* de renta.

tax year *n* año *m* fiscal.

TB *n* *abbr of* **tuberculosis**.

T-bone steak *n* bistec con hueso en forma de T.

tbs., tbsp. (*abbr of* **tablespoon(ful)**) *cuchara-da grande*.

TD *n* **-1.** (*abbr of* **Treasury Department**) *ministerio estadounidense de economía y hacienda*. **-2.** *abbr of* **touchdown**.

tea [ti:] *n* **-1.** [drink, leaves] té *m*. **-2.** *Br* [afternoon snack] té *m*, merienda *f*. **-3.** *Br* [evening meal] merienda cena *f*.

teabag ['ti:bæg] *n* bolsita *f* de té.

tea ball *n* *Am* bola de metal perforada que se llena de hojas de té para preparar té.

tea break *n* *Br* descanso *m* (*durante la jornada laboral*).

tea caddy [-,kædɪ] *n* bote *m* del té.

teacake ['ti:keɪk] *n* *Br* bollito *m*.

teach [ti:tʃ] (*pt* & *pp* **taught**) ◇ *vt* **-1.** [give lessons to] dar clases a; **to ~ sb sthg** enseñar algo a alguien; **to ~ sb to do sthg** enseñar a alguien a hacer algo; **to ~ (sb) that** inculcar a alguien que. **-2.** [give lessons in] dar clases de. **-3.** [advocate, state] preconizar; **to ~ sb sthg, to ~ sthg to sb** predicar a alguien algo. ◇ *vi* ser profesor(ra), dar clases.

teacher ['ti:tʃə'] *n* [at primary school] maestro *m*, -tra *f*; [at secondary school] profesor *m*, -ra *f*.

teachers college *Am* = **teacher training college**.

teacher's pet *n* *pej* enchufado *m*, - *f* de la clase.

teacher training college *Br*, **teachers college** *Am* *n* escuela *f* normal.

teaching ['ti:tʃɪŋ] *n* enseñanza *f*; **I've got ten hours of teaching** tengo diez horas de clases.

teaching aids *npl* materiales *mpl* pedagógicos.

teaching hospital *n* *Br* *hospital en el que hacen las prácticas los estudiantes de medicina*.

teaching practice *n* (*U*) prácticas *fpl* de magisterio.

teaching staff *npl* personal *m* docente, profesorado *m*.

tea cloth *n* *Br* **-1.** [tablecloth] mantel *m*. **-2.** [tea towel] paño *m* de cocina.

teacup ['ti:kʌp] *n* taza *f* de té.

teak [ti:k] ◇ *n* teca *f*. ◇ *comp* de teca.

tea leaves *npl* hojas *fpl* de té.

team [ti:m] *n* equipo *m*.
◆ **team up** *vi*: **to ~ up (with)** formar equipo (con).

team games *npl* juegos *mpl* de equipos.

teammate ['ti:mmeɪt] *n* compañero *m*, -ra *f* de equipo.

team spirit *n* espíritu *m* de equipo.

teamster ['ti:mstə'] *n* *Am* camionero *m*.

teamwork ['ti:mwɜ:k] *n* (*U*) trabajo *m* en equipo.

tea party *n* reunión *f* para tomar el té.

teapot ['ti:pɒt] *n* tetera *f*.

tear[1] [tɪə'] *n* lágrima *f*; **in ~s** llorando.

tear[2] [teə'] (*pt* **tore**, *pp* **torn**) ◇ *vt* **-1.** [rip] rasgar, romper; **to ~ sthg open** abrir algo rasgándolo; **to ~ sthg to pieces** *fig* poner algo por los suelos. **-2.** [remove roughly] arrancar. **-3.** *phr*: **to be torn between** vacilar entre. ◇ *vi* **-1.** [rip] romperse, rasgarse. **-2.** *inf* [move quickly] ir a toda pastilla. **-3.** *phr*: **to ~ loose** soltarse de un tirón. ◇ *n* rasgón *m*, desgarrón *m*.
◆ **tear apart** *vt sep* **-1.** [rip up] despedazar. **-2.** *fig* [disrupt greatly] desintegrar. **-3.** [upset greatly] desgarrar.
◆ **tear at** *vt fus* tirar de.
◆ **tear away** *vt sep*: **to ~ o.s. away from** separarse de.
◆ **tear down** *vt sep* echar abajo.
◆ **tear off** *vt sep* [clothes] quitarse precipitadamente.
◆ **tear up** *vt sep* hacer pedazos.

tearaway ['teərə,weɪ] *n* *Br* *inf* alborotador *m*, -ra *f*.

teardrop ['tɪədrɒp] *n* lágrima *f*.

tearful ['tɪəfʊl] *adj* **-1.** [person] lloroso(sa). **-2.** [event] lacrimoso(sa).

tear gas [tɪə'-] *n* (*U*) gas *m* lacrimógeno.

tearing ['teərɪŋ] *adj* *inf*: **at a ~ pace** como una bala; **to be in a ~ hurry** tener mucha prisa.

tearjerker ['tɪə,dʒɜːkə'] *n* *hum* dramón *m*.

tearoom ['ti:rʊm] *n* salón *m* de té.

tease [tiːz] ◇ *n inf* puñetero *m*, -ra *f*. ◇ *vt* [mock]: **to ~ sb (about)** tomar el pelo a alguien (acerca de).

tea service, **tea set** *n* servicio *m* OR juego *m* de té.

tea shop *n* salón *m* de té.

teasing ['tiːzɪŋ] *adj* guasón(ona), burlón(ona).

Teasmaid® ['tiːzmeɪd] *n Br máquina de hacer el té automática.*

teaspoon ['tiːspuːn] *n* **-1.** [utensil] cucharilla *f*. **-2.** [amount] cucharadita *f*.

tea strainer *n* colador *m* de té.

teat [tiːt] *n* **-1.** [of animal] tetilla *f*. **-2.** [of bottle] tetina *f*.

teatime ['tiːtaɪm] *n Br* hora *f* del té.

tea towel *n* paño *m* de cocina, repasador *m Amer*.

tea urn *n cilindro o barril con grifo para servir té en grandes cantidades.*

technical ['teknɪkl] *adj* técnico(ca).

technical college *n Br* ≃ centro *m* de formación profesional.

technical drawing *n* (*U*) dibujo *m* técnico.

technicality [ˌteknɪ'kælətɪ] (*pl* **-ies**) *n* detalle *m* técnico.

technically ['teknɪklɪ] *adv* **-1.** [gen] técnicamente. **-2.** [theoretically] teóricamente, en teoría.

technician [tek'nɪʃn] *n* técnico *m*, -ca *f*.

Technicolor® ['teknɪˌkʌlər] *n* tecnicolor® *m*.

technique [tek'niːk] *n* técnica *f*.

technocrat ['teknəkræt] *n* tecnócrata *m y f*.

technological [ˌteknə'lɒdʒɪkl] *adj* tecnológico(ca).

technologist [tek'nɒlədʒɪst] *n* tecnólogo *m*, -ga *f*.

technology [tek'nɒlədʒɪ] (*pl* **-ies**) *n* tecnología *f*.

teddy ['tedɪ] (*pl* **-ies**) *n*: **~ (bear)** oso *m* de peluche.

tedious ['tiːdjəs] *adj* tedioso(sa).

tedium ['tiːdjəm] *n fml* tedio *m*.

tee [tiː] *n* tee *m*.
◆ **tee off** *vi* GOLF golpear desde el tee.

teem [tiːm] *vi* **-1.** [rain] llover a cántaros. **-2.** [be busy]: **to be ~ing with** estar inundado(da) de.

teen [tiːn] *adj inf* adolescente.

teenage ['tiːneɪdʒ] *adj* adolescente.

teenager ['tiːnˌeɪdʒər] *n* adolescente *m y f*, quinceañero *m*, -ra *f*.

teens [tiːnz] *npl* adolescencia *f*.

teeny (**weeny**) [ˌtiːnɪ('wiːnɪ)], **teensy** (**weensy**) [ˌtiːnzɪ('wiːnzɪ)] *adj inf* pequeñito(ta), chiquitín(ina).

tee shirt *n* camiseta *f*.

teeter ['tiːtər] *vi lit* & *fig* tambalearse.

teeter-totter *n Am* balancín *m*, subibaja *m*.

teeth [tiːθ] *npl* **-1.** → **tooth**. **-2.** *fig* [power] poder *m*.

teethe [tiːð] *vi* echar los dientes.

teething ring ['tiːðɪŋ-] *n* chupador *m*.

teething troubles ['tiːðɪŋ-] *npl fig* problemas *mpl* iniciales.

teetotal [tiː'təʊtl] *adj* abstemio(mia).

teetotaller *Br*, **teetotaler** *Am* [tiː'təʊtlər] *n* abstemio *m*, -mia *f*.

TEFL ['tefl] (*abbr of* **teaching of English as a foreign language**) *n* enseñanza *f* de inglés para extranjeros.

Teflon® ['teflɒn] ◇ *n* teflón® *m*. ◇ *comp* de teflón®.

Tehran, **Teheran** [ˌteə'rɑːn] *n* Teherán *m*.

tel. (*abbr of* **telephone**) tfno.

Tel-Aviv [ˌtelə'viːv] *n*: **~(-Jaffa)** Tel Aviv.

tele- ['telɪ] *prefix* tele-.

telecast ['telɪkɑːst] *n* emisión *f* televisiva.

telecom ['telɪkɒm] *n*, **telecoms** ['telɪkɒmz] *npl Br inf* telecomunicaciones *fpl*.

telecommunications ['telɪkəˌmjuːnɪ'keɪʃnz] *npl* telecomunicaciones *fpl*.

telegram ['telɪgræm] *n* telegrama *m*.

telegraph ['telɪgrɑːf] ◇ *n* telégrafo *m*. ◇ *vt* telegrafiar.

telegraph pole, **telegraph post** *Br n* poste *m* de telégrafos.

telepathic [ˌtelɪ'pæθɪk] *adj* telepático(ca).

telepathy [tɪ'lepəθɪ] *n* telepatía *f*.

telephone ['telɪfəʊn] ◇ *n* teléfono *m*; **to be on the ~** *Br* [connected to network] tener teléfono; [speaking] estar al teléfono. ◇ *vt* & *vi* telefonear.

telephone book *n* guía *f* telefónica.

telephone booth *n* teléfono *m* público.

telephone box *n Br* cabina *f* (telefónica).

telephone call *n* llamada *f* telefónica.

telephone directory *n* guía *f* telefónica.

telephone exchange *n* central *f* telefónica.

telephone kiosk *n Br* cabina *f* (telefónica).

telephone number *n* número *m* de teléfono.

telephone operator *n* operador *m*, -ra *f*, telefonista *m y f*.

telephone tapping [-'tæpɪŋ] *n* (*U*) intervención *f* telefónica.

telephonist [tɪ'lefənɪst] *n Br* telefonista *m y f.*

telephoto lens [ˌtelɪ'fəʊtəʊ-] *n* teleobjetivo *m.*

teleprinter ['telɪˌprɪntəʳ], **teletypewriter** *Am* [ˌtelɪ'taɪpˌraɪtəʳ] *n* teletipo *m*, teleimpresor *m.*

Teleprompter® [ˌtelɪ'prɒmptəʳ] *n* tele-apuntador *m.*

telesales ['telɪseɪlz] *npl* ventas *fpl* por teléfono.

telescope ['telɪskəʊp] *n* telescopio *m.*

telescopic [ˌtelɪ'skɒpɪk] *adj* **-1.** [magnifying] telescópico(ca). **-2.** [contracting] plegable.

teletext ['telɪtekst] *n* teletexto *m.*

telethon ['teliθɒn] *n programa televisivo de larga duración destinado a recaudar fondos para una obra benéfica.*

teletypewriter *Am* = **teleprinter.**

televise ['telɪvaɪz] *vt* televisar.

television ['telɪˌvɪʒn] *n* televisión *f;* **on ~** en televisión.

television licence *n Br documento que prueba el pago del impuesto que da derecho al uso de un televisor.*

television programme *n* programa *m* de televisión.

television set *n* televisor *m*, (aparato *m* de) televisión *f.*

teleworking ['telɪˌwɜːkɪŋ] *n* teletrabajo *m.*

telex ['teleks] ◇ *n* télex *m.* ◇ *vt* [message] transmitir por télex; [person] mandar un télex a.

tell [tel] (*pt* & *pp* **told**) ◇ *vt* **-1.** [gen] decir; **to ~ sb (that)** decir a alguien que; **to ~ sb sthg, to ~ sthg to sb** decir a alguien algo; **to ~ sb to do sthg** decir a alguien que haga algo; **I told you so!** ¡ya te lo dije! **-2.** [joke, story] contar. **-3.** [judge, recognize]: **to ~ what sb is thinking** saber en qué está pensando alguien; **to ~ the time** decir la hora; **there's no telling ...** es imposible saber .... ◇ *vi* [have effect] surtir efecto.

◆ **tell apart** *vt sep* distinguir, diferenciar.

◆ **tell off** *vt sep* reñir, reprender.

teller ['teləʳ] *n* **-1.** [of votes] escrutador *m*, -ra *f.* **-2.** [in bank] cajero *m*, -ra *f.*

telling ['telɪŋ] *adj* **-1.** [speech, argument] efectivo(va). **-2.** [remark] revelador(ra).

telling-off (*pl* **tellings-off**) *n* bronca *f.*

telltale ['telteɪl] ◇ *adj* revelador(ra). ◇ *n* chivato *m*, -ta *f*, acusica *m y f.*

telly ['telɪ] (*pl* **-ies**) (*abbr of* **television**) *n Br inf* tele *f;* **on ~** en la tele.

temerity [tɪ'merətɪ] *n fml* temeridad *f.*

temp [temp] ◇ *n inf Br* (*abbr of* **temporary (employee)**) secretario *m* eventual, secreta-

ria *f* eventual (por horas). ◇ *vi:* **she's ~ing** está de secretaria eventual.

temp. (*abbr of* **temperature**) temp.

temper ['tempəʳ] ◇ *n* **-1.** [state of mind, mood] humor *m;* **to lose one's ~** enfadarse, perder la paciencia; **to have a short ~** tener genio. **-2.** [angry state]: **to be in a ~** estar de mal humor. **-3.** [temperament] temperamento *m.* ◇ *vt fml* templar, suavizar.

temperament ['tempərəmənt] *n* temperamento *m.*

temperamental [ˌtempərə'mentl] *adj* [volatile] temperamental.

temperance ['tempərəns] *n* templanza *f.*

temperate ['tempərət] *adj* templado(da).

temperature ['temprətʃəʳ] *n* temperatura *f;* **to take sb's ~** tomarle a alguien la temperatura; **to have a ~** tener fiebre.

tempered ['tempəd] *adj* templado(da).

tempest ['tempɪst] *n literary* tempestad *f.*

tempestuous [tem'pestjʊəs] *adj lit* & *fig* tempestuoso(sa).

tempi ['tempiː] *pl* → **tempo.**

template ['templɪt] *n* plantilla *f.*

temple ['templ] *n* **-1.** RELIG templo *m.* **-2.** ANAT sien *f.*

templet ['templɪt] = **template.**

tempo ['tempəʊ] (*pl* **-pos** OR **-pi**) *n* **-1.** MUS ritmo *m.* **-2.** [of an event] tempo *m.*

temporarily [ˌtempə'rerəlɪ] *adv* temporalmente, provisionalmente.

temporary ['tempərərɪ] *adj* [gen] temporal, provisional; [improvement, problem] pasajero(ra).

tempt [tempt] *vt* [entice]: **to ~ sb (to do sthg)** tentar a alguien (a hacer algo); **to be** OR **feel ~ed to do sthg** estar OR sentirse tentado de hacer algo.

temptation [temp'teɪʃn] *n* tentación *f.*

tempting ['temptɪŋ] *adj* tentador(ra).

ten [ten] *num* diez; *see also* **six.**

tenable ['tenəbl] *adj* **-1.** [reasonable, credible] sostenible. **-2.** [job, post]: **the post is ~ for one year** el puesto tendrá una duración de un año.

tenacious [tɪ'neɪʃəs] *adj* tenaz.

tenacity [tɪ'næsətɪ] *n* tenacidad *f.*

tenancy ['tenənsɪ] (*pl* **-ies**) *n* **-1.** [period - of house] alquiler *m;* [- of land] arrendamiento *m.* **-2.** [possession] ocupación *f.*

tenant ['tenənt] *n* [of house] inquilino *m*, -na *f;* [of pub] arrendatario *m*, -ria *f.*

Ten Commandments *npl:* **the ~** los Diez Mandamientos.

tend [tend] *vt* **-1.** [have tendency]: **to ~ to do sthg** soler hacer algo, tender a hacer algo; **I**

~ **to think** ... me inclino a pensar .... **-2.** [look after] cuidar.

tendency ['tendənsı] (*pl* **-ies**) *n* **-1.** [trend]: ~ **(for sb/sthg to do sthg)** tendencia *f* (de alguien/algo a hacer algo); ~ **towards** tendencia hacia. **-2.** [leaning, inclination] inclinación *f*.

tender ['tendər] ◇ *adj* [gen] tierno(na); [sore] dolorido(da); **at a** ~ **age** a una edad tierna. ◇ *n* COMM propuesta *f*, oferta *f*. ◇ *vt fml* [resignation] presentar; [apology, suggestion] ofrecer.

tenderize, -ise ['tendəraız] *vt* ablandar.

tenderly ['tendəlı] *adv* [caringly] tiernamente, cariñosamente.

tenderness ['tendənıs] *n* (*U*) **-1.** [care, compassion] ternura *f*, dulzura *f*. **-2.** [soreness] sensibilidad *f*.

tendon ['tendən] *n* tendón *m*.

tendril ['tendrəl] *n* zarcillo *m*.

tenement ['tenəmənt] *n bloque de viviendas modestas.*

Tenerife [,tenə'riːf] *n* Tenerife.

tenet ['tenɪt] *n fml* principio *m*, dogma *m*.

tenner ['tenər] *n Br inf* **-1.** [amount] diez libras *fpl*. **-2.** [note] billete *m* de diez libras.

Tennessee [,tenə'siː] *n* Tennessee.

tennis ['tenɪs] ◇ *n* tenis *m*. ◇ *comp* de tenis; ~ **player** tenista *m y f.*

tennis ball *n* pelota *f* de tenis.

tennis court *n* pista *f* de tenis.

tennis racket *n* raqueta *f* de tenis.

tenor ['tenər] ◇ *adj* de tenor. ◇ *n* **-1.** [singer] tenor. **-2.** *fml* [meaning, mood] tono *m*.

tenpin bowling *Br* ['tenpɪn-], **tenpins** *Am* ['tenpɪnz] *n* (*U*) bolos *mpl*.

tense [tens] ◇ *adj* tenso(sa). ◇ *n* tiempo *m*. ◇ *vt* tensar. ◇ *vi* tensarse, ponerse tenso(sa).

tensed up [tenst-] *adj* tenso(sa), nervioso(sa).

tension ['tenʃn] *n* tensión *f.*

ten-spot *n Am* billete *m* de diez dólares.

tent [tent] *n* tienda *f* (de campaña).

tentacle ['tentəkl] *n* tentáculo *m*.

tentative ['tentətɪv] *adj* **-1.** [person] indeciso(sa); [step, handshake] vacilante. **-2.** [suggestion, conclusion etc] provisional.

tentatively ['tentətɪvlɪ] *adv* **-1.** [hesitantly] con vacilación. **-2.** [not finally] provisionalmente.

tenterhooks ['tentəhʊks] *npl*: **to be on** ~ estar sobre ascuas.

tenth [tenθ] ◇ *num adj* décimo(ma). ◇ *num*

n **-1.** [in order] décimo *m*, -ma *f.* **-2.** [fraction] décimo *m; see also* **sixth.**

tent peg *n* estaca *f.*

tent pole *n* mástil *m* de tienda.

tenuous ['tenjʊəs] *adj* [argument] flojo(ja), poco convincente; [evidence, connection] débil, insignificante; [hold] ligero(ra).

tenuously ['tenjʊəslɪ] *adv* ligeramente.

tenure ['tenjər] *n* (*U*) *fml* **-1.** [of property] arrendamiento *m.* **-2.** [of job] ocupación *f,* ejercicio *m.*

tepee ['tiːpiː] *n* tipi *m*, tienda *f* india.

tepid ['tepɪd] *adj* **-1.** [liquid] tibio(bia). **-2.** *pej* [welcome] poco caluroso(sa); [performance, speech] poco vehemente.

tequila [tɪ'kiːlə] *n* tequila *m.*

Ter., Terr. *abbr of* **Terrace.**

term [tɜːm] ◇ *n* **-1.** [word, expression] término *m.* **-2.** SCH & UNIV trimestre *m.* **-3.** POL mandato *m.* **-4.** [period of time] período *m*; **in the long/short** ~ a largo/corto plazo. ◇ *vt*: **to** ~ **sthg sthg** calificar algo de algo.

◆ **terms** *npl* **-1.** [of contract, agreement] condiciones *fpl.* **-2.** [basis]: **in international/real** ~**s** en términos internacionales/reales; **on equal** OR **the same** ~**s** en condiciones de igualdad; **to be on good** ~**s (with sb)** mantener buenas relaciones (con alguien); **to be on speaking** ~**s (with sb)** hablarse (con alguien); **to come to** ~**s with sthg** aceptar algo. **-3.** *phr*: **to think in** ~**s of doing sthg** pensar hacer algo.

◆ **in terms of** *prep* por lo que se refiere a.

terminal ['tɜːmɪnl] ◇ *adj* MED incurable, terminal. ◇ *n* **-1.** [transport] terminal *f.* **-2.** COMPUT terminal *m.*

terminally ['tɜːmɪnəlɪ] *adv*: **to be** ~ **ill** ser enfermo terminal.

terminate ['tɜːmɪneɪt] ◇ *vt fml* [gen] poner fin a; [pregnancy] interrumpir. ◇ *vi* **-1.** [bus, train] finalizar el trayecto. **-2.** [contract] terminarse.

termination [,tɜːmɪ'neɪʃn] *n* **-1.** *fml* [ending] terminación *f.* **-2.** [abortion]: ~ **(of pregnancy)** interrupción *f* del embarazo.

termini ['tɜːmɪnaɪ] *pl* → **terminus.**

terminology [,tɜːmɪ'nɒlədʒɪ] *n* terminología *f.*

terminus ['tɜːmɪnəs] (*pl* **-ni** OR **-nuses**) (estación *f*) terminal *f.*

termite ['tɜːmaɪt] *n* termita *f.*

Terr. = **Ter.**

terrace ['terəs] *n* **-1.** [gen] terraza *f.* **-2.** *Br* [of houses] hilera *f* de casas adosadas.

◆ **terraces** *npl* FTBL: **the** ~**s** las gradas.

terraced ['terəst] *adj* **-1.** [hillside] a terrazas. **-2.** [house, housing] adosado(da).

terraced house *n Br* casa *f* adosada, chalet *m* adosado.

terracotta [ˌterə'kɒtə] *n* terracota *f*.

terrain [te'reɪn] *n* terreno *m*.

terrapin ['terəpɪn] (*pl inv* OR **-s**) *n* tortuga *f* acuática.

terrestrial [tə'restrɪəl] *adj fml* terrestre.

terrible ['terəbl] *adj* **-1.** [crash, mess, shame] terrible, espantoso(sa). **-2.** [unwell, unhappy, very bad] fatal.

terribly ['terəblɪ] *adv* [sing, play, write] malísimamente, horriblemente; [injured, sorry, expensive] terriblemente.

terrier ['terɪər] *n* terrier *m*.

terrific [tə'rɪfɪk] *adj* **-1.** [wonderful] fabuloso(sa), estupendo(da). **-2.** [enormous] enorme, tremendo(da).

terrified ['terɪfaɪd] *adj* aterrorizado(da); **to be ~ (of)** tener terror a.

terrify ['terɪfaɪ] (*pt* & *pp* **-ied**) *vt* aterrorizar.

terrifying ['terɪfaɪɪŋ] *adj* aterrador(ra), espantoso(sa).

terrine [te'riːn] *n* [paté] tarrina *f*.

territorial [ˌterɪ'tɔːrɪəl] *adj* territorial.

Territorial Army *n Br*: **the ~** *el ejército voluntario de Gran Bretaña*.

territorial waters *npl* aguas *fpl* territoriales, aguas jurisdiccionales.

territory ['terətrɪ] (*pl* **-ies**) *n* **-1.** [political area] territorio *m*. **-2.** [terrain] terreno *m*. **-3.** [area of knowledge] esfera *f*, campo *m*.

terror ['terər] *n* **-1.** [fear] terror *m*. **-2.** *inf* [rascal] demonio *m*.

terrorism ['terərɪzm] *n* terrorismo *m*.

terrorist ['terərɪst] *n* terrorista *m y f*.

terrorize, -ise ['terəraɪz] *vt* aterrorizar, aterrar.

terror-stricken *adj* aterrorizado(da), aterrado(da).

terry(cloth) ['terɪ(klɒθ)] *n* toalla *f* de rizo.

terse [tɜːs] *adj* seco(ca).

tersely ['tɜːslɪ] *adv* secamente.

tertiary ['tɜːʃərɪ] *adj fml* terciario(ria).

tertiary education *n* (*U*) estudios *mpl* superiores.

Terylene® ['terəliːn] *n* terylene® *m*.

TESL ['tesl] (*abbr of* **teaching of English as a second language**) *n* enseñanza de inglés para extranjeros.

TESSA ['tesə] (*abbr of* **tax-exempt special savings account**) *n* plan de ahorro que ofrece exención de impuestos sobre el interés del capital depositado a plazo fijo.

test [test] ◇ *n* **-1.** [trial] prueba *f*; **to put sthg to the ~** poner algo a prueba. **-2.** [ex-

amination] examen *m*, prueba *f*. **-3.** MED [of blood, urine] análisis *m inv*; [of eyes] revisión *f*. ◇ *vt* **-1.** [try out] probar, poner a prueba. **-2.** [examine] examinar; **to ~ sb on** examinar a alguien de.

testament ['testəmənt] *n* **-1.** [will] testamento *m*. **-2.** [proof]: **~ to** testimonio *m* de.

test ban *n* suspensión *f* de pruebas nucleares.

test card *n Br* carta *f* de ajuste.

test case *n* JUR juicio *m* que sienta jurisprudencia.

test-drive *vt* someter a prueba de carretera.

tester ['testər] *n* **-1.** [person testing] probador *m*, -ra *f*. **-2.** [sample] muestra *f* (*de perfume etc*).

test flight *n* vuelo *m* de prueba.

testicles ['testɪklz] *npl* testículos *mpl*.

testify ['testɪfaɪ] (*pt* & *pp* **-ied**) ◇ *vi* **-1.** JUR prestar declaración. **-2.** [be proof]: **to ~ to sthg** dar fe de OR atestiguar algo. ◇ *vt*: **to ~ that** declarar que.

testimonial [ˌtestɪ'məʊnjəl] *n* [letter] carta *f* de recomendación.

testimony ['testəməʊnɪ] *n* **-1.** JUR testimonio *m*, declaración *f*. **-2.** [proof, demonstration]: **~ to** testimonio *m* de.

testing ['testɪŋ] *adj* duro(ra).

testing ground *n* zona *f* de pruebas.

test match *n Br* partido *m* internacional.

test paper *n* **-1.** SCH examen *m*, test *m*. **-2.** CHEM papel *m* reactivo.

test pattern *n Am* carta *f* de ajuste.

test pilot *n* piloto *m y f* de pruebas.

test tube *n* probeta *f*.

test-tube baby *n* bebé *m y f* probeta.

testy ['testɪ] (*compar* **-ier**, *superl* **-iest**) *adj* **-1.** [person] irritable, irascible. **-2.** [remark, comment] acre, agresivo(va).

tetanus ['tetənəs] *n* tétanos *m inv*.

tetchy ['tetʃɪ] (*compar* **-ier**, *superl* **-iest**) *adj* irritable.

tête-à-tête [ˌteɪtɑː'teɪt] *n* conversación *f* confidencial (*entre dos personas*).

tether ['teðər] ◇ *vt* atar. ◇ *n*: **to be at the end of one's ~** estar uno que ya no puede más.

Texan ['teksn] *n* ◇ *adj* tejano(na). ◇ *n* tejano *m*, -na *f*.

Texas ['teksəs] *n* Tejas *m*.

Tex-Mex [ˌteks'meks] *adj* mejicano(na) de Texas.

text [tekst] *n* **-1.** [gen] texto *m*. **-2.** [textbook] libro *m* de texto.

textbook ['tekstbʊk] *n* libro *m* de texto.

textile ['tekstaɪl] ◇ *n* textil *m*, tejido *m*. ◇ *comp* téxtil.
◆ **textiles** *npl* industria *f* textil.

texture ['tekstʃəʳ] *n* textura *f*.

TGIF (*abbr of* **thank God it's Friday!**) *inf* *¡por fin es viernes!*

TGWU (*abbr of* **Transport and General Workers' Union**) *n sindicato británico de mayor afiliación que acoge a trabajadores de diversos sectores industriales.*

Thai [taɪ] ◇ *adj* tailandés(esa). ◇ *n* **-1.** [person] tailandés *m*, -esa *f*. **-2.** [language] tailandés *m*.

Thailand ['taɪlænd] *n* Tailandia.

thalidomide [θə'lɪdəmaɪd] *n* talidomida *f*.

Thames [temz] *n*: **the ~** el Támesis.

than [*weak form* ðən, *strong form* ðæn] ◇ *prep* que; **you're older ~ me** eres mayor que yo; **you're older ~ I thought** eres mayor de lo que pensaba. ◇ *conj* que; **I'd sooner read ~ sleep** prefiero leer que dormir; **no sooner did he arrive ~ she left** tan pronto llegó él, ella se fue; **more ~ three/once** más de tres/de una vez; **rather ~ stay, he chose to go** en vez de quedarse, prefirió irse.

thank [θæŋk] ◇ *vt*: **to ~ sb (for sthg)** dar las gracias a alguien (por algo), agradecer a alguien (algo); **~ God** OR **goodness** OR **heavens!** ¡gracias a Dios!, ¡menos mal!
◆ **thanks** ◇ *npl* agradecimiento *m*. ◇ *excl* ¡gracias!
◆ **thanks to** *prep* gracias a.

thankful ['θæŋkfʊl] *adj* **-1.** [relieved] aliviado(da). **-2.** [grateful]: **~ (for)** agradecido(da) (por).

thankfully ['θæŋkfʊlɪ] *adv* **-1.** [with gratitude] con agradecimiento. **-2.** [thank goodness] gracias a Dios.

thankless ['θæŋklɪs] *adj* ingrato(ta).

thanksgiving ['θæŋks,gɪvɪŋ] *n* acción *f* de gracias.
◆ **Thanksgiving (Day)** *n* Día *m* de Acción de Gracias.

THANKSGIVING:

La fiesta de 'Thanksgiving', el cuarto jueves de noviembre, conmemora el establecimiento de los primeros colonos en América. La cena en familia que generalmente se celebra ese día consiste en un pavo con arándanos, con una guarnición de patatas dulces, y para terminar un pastel de calabaza

thank you *excl* ¡gracias!; **~ for** gracias por.
◆ **thankyou** *n* agradecimiento *m*.

that [ðæt, *weak form of pron and conj* ðət] (*pl* **those**) ◇ *pron* **-1.** (*demonstrative use: pl* *'those')* ése *m*, ésa *f*, ésos *mpl*, ésas *fpl*; (*indefinite*) eso; **~ sounds familiar** eso me resulta familiar; **who's ~?** [who is it?] ¿quién es?; **what's ~?** ¿qué es eso?; **~'s a shame** es una pena; **is ~ Maureen?** [asking someone else] ¿es ésa Maureen?; [asking person in question] ¿eres Maureen?; **do you like these or those?** ¿te gustan éstos o ésos? **-2.** [further away in distance, time] aquél *m*, aquélla *f*, aquéllos *mpl*, aquéllas *fpl*; (*indefinite*) aquello; **~ was the life!** ¡aquello sí que era vida!; **all those who helped me** todos aquellos que me ayudaron. **-3.** (*to introduce relative clauses*) que; **a path ~ led into the woods** un sendero que conducía a los bosque; **everything ~ I have done** todo lo que he hecho; **the room ~ I sleep in** el cuarto donde OR en (el) que duermo; **the day ~ he arrived** el día en que llegó; **the firm ~ he's applying to** la empresa a la que solicita trabajo.
◇ *adj* (*demonstrative: pl* *'those')* ese (esa), esos (esas) (*pl*); [further away in distance, time] aquel (aquella), aquellos (aquellas) (*pl*); **those chocolates are delicious** esos bombones están exquisitos; **I'll have ~ book at the back** yo cogeré aquel libro del fondo; **later ~ day** más tarde ese/aquel mismo día.
◇ *adv* tan; **it wasn't ~ bad** no estuvo tan mal; **it doesn't cost ~ much** no cuesta tanto; **it was ~ big** fue así de grande.
◇ *conj* que; **he recommended ~ I phone you** aconsejó que te telefoneara; **it's time ~ we were leaving** deberíamos irnos ya, ya va siendo hora de irse.
◆ **at that** *prep*: **she's an artist, and a good one at ~** es artista, y además de las buenas.
◆ **that is** *adv* es decir.
◆ **that's it** *adv*: **~'s it, there's no more** ¡ya está!, ¡ya no quedan más!; **~'s it, I'm leaving!** ¡se acabó!, ¡me marcho!
◆ **that's that** *adv* punto, se acabó.

thatched [θætʃt] *adj* con techo de paja.

Thatcherism ['θætʃərɪzm] *n* thatcherismo *m*.

that's [ðæts] = **that is**.

thaw [θɔː] ◇ *vt* [snow, ice] derretir; [frozen food] descongelar. ◇ *vi* [snow, ice] derretirse; [frozen food] descongelarse; *fig* [people, relations] distenderse. ◇ *n* deshielo *m*.

the [*weak form* ðə, *before vowel* ðɪ, *strong form* ðiː] *def art* **-1.** [gen] el (la), (*pl*) los (las) (*before feminine nouns beginning with stressed "a" or "ha" = "el"; "a" + "el" = "al"; "de" + "el" = "del"*); **~ boat** el barco; **~ Queen** la reina; **~ men** los hombres; **~ women** las mujeres; **~ (cold) water** el agua (fría); **to ~**

end of ~ **world** al fin del mundo; ~ **highest mountain in** ~ **world** la montaña más alta del mundo; ~ **monkey is a primate** el mono es un primate; **to play** ~ **piano** tocar el piano; **Joneses are coming to supper** los Jones vienen a cenar; **you're not** THE **John Major, are you?** ¿no será usted John Major el político, verdad?; **it's** THE **place to go to in Paris** es EL sitio al que hay que ir en París. **-2.** (*with an adjective to form a noun*): ~ **old/young** los viejos/jóvenes; ~ **impossible** lo imposible. **-3.** [in dates]: ~ **twelfth of May** el doce de mayo; ~ **forties** los cuarenta. **-4.** (*in comparisons*): ~ **more I see her,** ~ **less I like her** cuanto más la veo, menos me gusta; ~ **sooner** ~ **better** cuanto antes mejor. **-5.** [in titles]: **Catherine** ~ **Great** Catalina la Grande; **George** ~ **First** Jorge Primero.

theatre, theater *Am* ['θɪətər] *n* **-1.** [for plays etc] teatro *m*. **-2.** *Br* [in hospital] quirófano *m*, sala *f* de operaciones. **-3.** *Am* [cinema] cine *m*.

theatregoer, theatergoer *Am* ['θɪətə,gəʊər] *n* aficionado *m*, -da *f* al teatro.

theatrical [θɪ'ætrɪkl] *adj lit* & *fig* teatral.

theft [θeft] *n* [more serious] robo *m*; [less serious] hurto *m*.

their [ðeər] *poss adj* su, sus (*pl*); ~ **house** su casa; ~ **children** sus hijos; **it wasn't** THEIR **fault** no fue culpa suya OR su culpa; **they washed** ~ **hair** se lavaron el pelo.

theirs [ðeəz] *poss pron* suyo (suya); **that money is** ~ ese dinero es suyo; **our car hit** ~ nuestro coche chocó contra el suyo; **it wasn't our fault, it was** THEIRS no fue culpa nuestra sino suya OR de ellos; **a friend of** ~ un amigo suyo OR de ellos.

them [weak form ðəm, strong form ðem] *pers pron pl* **-1.** (*direct*) los *mpl*, las *fpl*; **I know** ~ los conozco; **I like** ~ me gustan; **if I were** OR **was** ~ si (yo) fuera ellos. **-2.** (*indirect - gen*) les *mpl* y *fpl*; (- *with other third person prons*) se *mpl* y *fpl*; **she sent** ~ **a letter** les mandó una carta; **we spoke to** ~ hablamos con ellos; **I gave it to** ~ se lo di (a ellos). **-3.** (*stressed, after prep, in comparisons etc*) ellos *mpl*, ellas *fpl*; **you can't expect** THEM **to do it** no esperarás que ELLOS lo hagan; **with/without** ~ con/sin ellos; **we're not as wealthy as** ~ no somos tan ricos como ellos.

thematic [θɪ'mætɪk] *adj* temático(ca).

theme [θiːm] *n* **-1.** [gen] tema *m*. **-2.** [signature tune] sintonía *f*.

theme park *n parque de atracciones que gira alrededor de un tema.*

theme song *n* tema *m* musical.

theme tune *n* tema *m* musical.

themselves [ðem'selvz] *pron* **-1.** (*reflexive*) se; (*after prep*) sí; **they enjoyed** ~ se divirtieron. **-2.** (*for emphasis*) ellos mismos *mpl*, ellas mismas *fpl*; **they did it** ~ lo hicieron ellos mismos. **-3.** [alone] solos(las); **they organised it (by)** ~ lo organizaron ellas solas.

then [ðen] *adv* **-1.** [not now] entonces; **"it starts at 8"** "**I'll see you** ~" "empieza a las 8" "hasta las 8, entonces". **-2.** [next, afterwards] luego, después. **-3.** [in that case] entonces; **all right** ~ de acuerdo, pues. **-4.** [therefore] entonces, por lo tanto. **-5.** [furthermore, also] además.

thence [ðens] *adv dated* [from that place] desde allí.

theologian [θɪə'ləʊdʒən] *n* teólogo *m*, -ga *f*.

theology [θɪ'ɒlədʒɪ] *n* teología *f*.

theorem ['θɪərəm] *n* teorema *m*.

theoretical [θɪə'retɪkl] *adj* teórico(ca).

theoretically [θɪə'retɪklɪ] *adv* en teoría.

theorist ['θɪərɪst] *n* teórico *m*, -ca *f*.

theorize, -ise ['θɪəraɪz] *vi*: **to** ~ **(about sthg)** teorizar (sobre algo).

theory ['θɪərɪ] (*pl* **-ies**) *n* teoría *f*; **in** ~ en teoría.

therapeutic [,θerə'pjuːtɪk] *adj* terapéutico(ca).

therapist ['θerəpɪst] *n* terapeuta *m* y *f*.

therapy ['θerəpɪ] *n* terapia *f*.

there [ðeər] ◇ *pron* **-1.** [indicating existence] ~ **is/are** hay; ~**'s someone at the door** hay alguien en la puerta; ~ **must be some mistake** debe (de) haber un error; ~ **are five of us** somos cinco. **-2.** *fml* (*with vb*): ~ **followed an ominous silence** a continuación hubo un silencio amenazador.
◇ *adv* **-1.** [in existence, available] ahí; **is anybody** ~? ¿hay alguien ahí?; **is John** ~, **please?** [when telephoning] ¿está John? **-2.** [referring to place - near speaker] ahí; [- further away] allí, allá; **I'm going** ~ **next week** voy para allá OR allí la semana que viene; ~ **it is** ahí está; **over** ~ por allí; **it's six miles** ~ **and back** hay seis millas entre ir y volver. **-3.** [point - in conversation, activity] ahí; **I can't agree with you** ~ ahí no estoy de acuerdo contigo; **we're getting** ~ estamos ya casi. **-4.** *inf phr*: **all/not all** ~ bien/no muy bien de la cabeza.
◇ *interj*: ~, **I knew he'd turn up** ¡mira!, sabía que aparecería; ~, ~ **(don't cry)** ¡venga, venga (no llores)!

◆ **there and then, then and there** *adv* en el acto.

◆ **there you are** *adv* **-1.** [handing over something] ahí tienes/tenéis *etc.* **-2.** [emphasizing that one is right] ahí está, ahí lo tienes; ~ **you are, what did I tell you!** ahí lo tienes, ¿qué te dije? **-3.** [expressing reluctant acceptance]: **it's not ideal, but ~ you are** no es lo ideal, pero ¿qué le vamos a hacer?

thereabouts [ˈðeərəbauts], **thereabout** *Am* [ˈðeərəbaut] *adv*: **or ~** o por ahí.

thereafter [ˌðeərˈɑːftər] *adv fml* después, a partir de entonces.

thereby [ˌðeərˈbaɪ] *adv fml* de ese modo.

therefore [ˈðeəfɔːr] *adv* por lo tanto, por consiguiente.

therein [ˌðeərˈɪn] *adv fml* **-1.** [in that place] allí dentro. **-2.** [in that matter]: ~ **lies the problem** ahí radica el problema.

there's [ðeəz] = **there is**.

thereupon [ˌðeərəˈpɒn] *adv fml* acto seguido.

thermal [ˈθɜːml] *adj* térmico(ca).

thermal reactor *n* reactor *m* térmico.

thermal underwear *n* ropa *f* interior térmica.

thermodynamics [ˌθɜːməudaɪˈnæmɪks] *n* (*U*) termodinámica *f*.

thermoelectric [ˌθɜːməuˈlektrɪk] *adj* termoeléctrico(ca).

thermometer [θəˈmɒmɪtər] *n* termómetro *m*.

thermonuclear [ˌθɜːməuˈnjuːkliər] *adj* termonuclear.

thermoplastic [ˌθɜːməuˈplæstɪk] ◇ *adj* termoplástico(ca). ◇ *n* termoplástico *m*.

Thermos (flask)® [ˈθɜːməs-] *n* termo *m*.

thermostat [ˈθɜːməstæt] *n* termostato *m*.

thesaurus [θɪˈsɔːrəs] (*pl* **-es**) *n* diccionario *m* de sinónimos y voces afines.

these [ðiːz] *pl* → **this**.

thesis [ˈθiːsɪs] (*pl* **theses** [ˈθiːsiːz]) *n* tesis *f inv*.

they [ðeɪ] *pers pron pl* **-1.** [gen] ellos *mpl*, ellas *fpl*; ~**'re pleased** (ellos) están satisfechos; ~**'re pretty earrings** son unos pendientes bonitos; ~ **love fish** les encanta el pescado; THEY **can't do it** ELLOS no pueden hacerlo; **there ~ are** allí están. **-2.** [unspecified people]: ~ **say it's going to snow** dicen que va a nevar; ~**'re going to put petrol up** van a subir la gasolina.

they'd [ðeɪd] = **they had, they would**.

they'll [ðeɪl] = **they shall, they will**.

they're [ðeər] = **they are**.

they've [ðeɪv] = **they have**.

thick [θɪk] ◇ *adj* **-1.** [not thin] grueso(sa); **it's 3 cm ~** tiene 3 cm de grueso; **how ~ is it?** ¿qué espesor tiene? **-2.** [dense - hair, liquid, fog] espeso(sa). **-3.** *inf* [stupid] corto(ta), necio(cia). **-4.** [indistinct]: **a voice ~ with emotion** una voz velada por la emoción. **-5.** [full, covered]: **to be ~ with** estar lleno(na) de. ◇ *n*: **to be in the ~ of** estar en el centro OR meollo de.

◆ **thick and fast** *adv*: **questions came ~ and fast** llovían preguntas de todos los lados.

◆ **through thick and thin** *adv* a las duras y a las maduras.

thicken [ˈθɪkn] ◇ *vt* espesar. ◇ *vi* **-1.** [gen] espesarse. **-2.** [forest, crowd] hacerse más denso(sa). **-3.** *phr*: **the plot ~s** la cosa se complica.

thickening [ˈθɪknɪŋ] *n* espesante *m*.

thicket [ˈθɪkɪt] *n* matorral *m*.

thickly [ˈθɪklɪ] *adv* **-1.** [cut bread] a rebanadas guesas; [spread]: **he spread the butter ~** untó una buena capa de mantequilla. **-2.** [densely] densamente. **-3.** [indistinctly] con voz poco clara.

thickness [ˈθɪknɪs] *n* espesor *m*.

thickset [ˌθɪkˈset] *adj* fornido(da), robusto(ta).

thick-skinned [-ˈskɪnd] *adj* insensible.

thief [θiːf] (*pl* **thieves**) *n* ladrón *m*, -ona *f*.

thieve [θiːv] *vt & vi* robar, hurtar.

thieves [θiːvz] *pl* → **thief**.

thieving [ˈθiːvɪŋ] ◇ *adj* ladrón(ona). ◇ *n* (*U*) robo *m*, hurto *m*.

thigh [θaɪ] *n* muslo *m*.

thighbone [ˈθaɪbəun] *n* fémur *m*.

thimble [ˈθɪmbl] *n* dedal *m*.

thin [θɪn] (*compar* **-ner**, *superl* **-nest**, *pt & pp* **-ned**, *cont* **-ning**) ◇ *adj* **-1.** [not thick] delgado(da), fino(na). **-2.** [skinny] delgado(da), flaco(ca). **-3.** [watery] claro(ra), aguado(da). **-4.** [sparse - crowd, vegetation, mist] poco denso (poco densa); [- hair] ralo(la); **to be ~ on top** estar quedándose calvo.
◇ *adv*: **to be wearing ~** [joke, story] estar perdiendo interés; **my patience is wearing ~** se me está acabando la paciencia.
◇ *vi*: **his hair is thinning** se le está empezando a caer el pelo.

◆ **thin down** *vt sep* aclarar.

thin air *n*: **to appear out of ~** aparecer de la nada; **to disappear into ~** esfumarse.

thing [θɪŋ] *n* **-1.** [gen] cosa *f*; **the next ~ on the list** lo siguiente de la lista; **(the best) to do would be ...** lo mejor sería ...; **for one ~** en primer lugar; **(what) with one ~ and another** entre unas cosas y otras; **the ~ is**

... el caso es que ...; **it's just one of those ~s** *inf* son cosas que pasan; **I have a ~ about ...** *inf* [like] me gusta muchísimo ...; [dislike] no puedo sufrir ...; **to make a ~ (out) of sthg** *inf* exagerar algo. **-2.** [anything]: **not a ~** nada. **-3.** [person]: **poor ~!** ¡pobrecito *m*, -ta *f* ! **-4.** *inf* [fashion]: **the ~** lo último, lo que está de moda.
◆ **things** *npl* **-1.** [clothes, possessions] cosas *fpl*, corotos *mpl* *Amer.* **-2.** *inf* [life]: **how are ~s?** ¿qué tal (van las cosas)?

thingamabob ['θɪŋəmə,bɒb], **thingamajig** ['θɪŋəmədʒɪg], **thingummy (jig)** *Br* ['θɪŋəmɪ-], **thingie** *Br*, **thingy** *Br* ['θɪŋɪ] *n* [thing] chisme *m*; [person] ése *m*, ésa *f*, fulano *m*, -na *f*.

think [θɪŋk] (*pt* & *pp* **thought**) ◇ *vt* **-1.** [believe]: **to ~ (that)** creer OR pensar que; **I ~ so/not** creo que sí/no. **-2.** [have in mind] pensar; **what are you ~ing?** ¿en qué piensas? **-3.** [imagine] entender, hacerse una idea de; **I thought so** ya me lo imaginaba. **-4.** [remember] recordar. **-5.** [in polite requests] creer; **do you ~ you could help me?** ¿cree que podría ayudarme?
◇ *vi* **-1.** [use mind] pensar; **let me ~** vamos a ver. **-2.** [have stated opinion]: **what do you ~ of** OR **about his new film?** ¿qué piensas de su nueva película?; **to ~ a lot of sthg/sb** tener en mucha estima algo/a alguien. **-3.** *phr*: **to ~ better of sthg/doing sthg** pensarse mejor algo/lo de hacer algo; **he ~s nothing of doing it** para él es pan comido hacerlo; **to ~ twice** pensárselo dos veces.
◇ *n* *inf*: **to have a ~ (about sthg)** pensarse (algo).
◆ **think about** *vt fus* pensar en; **I'll have to ~ about it** tendré que pensarlo; **to ~ about doing sthg** pensar en hacer algo.
◆ **think back** *vi* volver la mente atrás; **~ back to your childhood** vuelve la mente a tu infancia.
◆ **think of** *vt fus* **-1.** [consider]: **to ~ of doing sthg** pensar en hacer algo. **-2.** [remember] acordarse de. **-3.** [conceive] pensar en; **how did you ~ of (doing) that?** ¿cómo se te ocurrió (hacer) esto? **-4.** [show consideration for]: **it was kind of you to ~ of me** fue muy amable de tu parte que te acordaras de mí.
◆ **think out, think through** *vt sep* [plan] elaborar; [problem] examinar.
◆ **think over** *vt sep* pensarse, meditar.
◆ **think up** *vt sep* idear.

thinker ['θɪŋkə] *n* pensador *m*, -ra *f*.

thinking ['θɪŋkɪŋ] ◇ *adj*: **the ~ man** el hombre que piensa. ◇ *n* (*U*) opinión *f*; **I'll**

have to do some ~ tendré que pensármelo; **to my way of ~** en mi opinión.

think tank *n* grupo de expertos convocados por una organización para aconsejar sobre un tema determinado.

thinly ['θɪnlɪ] *adv* **-1.** [slice food] a rebanadas finas; [spread]: **he spread the butter ~** untó una ligera capa de mantequilla. **-2.** [sparsely - forested] escasamente; [- populated] poco.

thinner ['θɪnə] *n* disolvente *m*.

thinness ['θɪnnɪs] *n* delgadez *f*.

thin-skinned [-'skɪnd] *adj* susceptible.

third [θɜːd] ◇ *num adj* tercer(ra). ◇ *num n* **-1.** [fraction] tercio *m*. **-2.** [in order] tercero *m*, -ra *f*. **-3.** UNIV ≃ aprobado *m* (*en un título universitario*); *see also* **sixth**.

third-class *adj* *Br* UNIV ≃ aprobado(da).

third-degree burns *npl* quemaduras *fpl* de tercer grado.

thirdly ['θɜːdlɪ] *adv* en tercer lugar.

third party *n* tercero *m*.

third party insurance *n* seguro *m* a terceros.

third-rate *adj pej* de poca categoría.

Third World *n*: **the ~** el Tercer Mundo.

thirst [θɜːst] *n lit* & *fig*: **~ (for)** sed *f* (de).

thirsty ['θɜːstɪ] (*compar* **-ier**, *superl* **-iest**) *adj* **-1.** [parched]: **to be** OR **feel ~** tener sed. **-2.** [causing thirst] que da sed.

thirteen [,θɜː'tiːn] *num* trece; *see also* **six**.

thirteenth [,θɜː'tiːnθ] ◇ *num adj* decimotercero(ra). ◇ *num n* **-1.** [fraction] treceavo *m*. **-2.** [in order] decimotercero *m*, -ra *f*; *see also* **sixth**.

thirtieth ['θɜːtɪəθ] ◇ *num adj* trigésimo(ma). ◇ *num n* **-1.** [fraction] trigésimo *m*. **-2.** [in order] trigésimo *m*, -ma *f*; *see also* **sixth**.

thirty ['θɜːtɪ] (*pl* **-ies**) *num* treinta; *see also* **sixty**.

thirty-something *adj* típico de ciertas personas que sobrepasan la treintena y viven desahogadamente.

this [ðɪs] (*pl* **these**) ◇ *pron* [gen] éste *m*, ésta *f*, éstos *mpl*, éstas *fpl*; (*indefinite*) esto; **~ is/these are for you** esto es/éstos son para tí; **~ can't be true** esto no puede ser cierto; **do you prefer these or those?** ¿prefieres éstos o aquéllos?; **~ is Daphne Logan** [introducing another person] ésta es OR te presento a Daphne Logan; [introducing oneself on phone] soy Daphne Logan; **what's ~?** ¿qué es eso?; **~ and that** esto y lo otro.
◇ *adj* **-1.** [gen] este (esta), estos (estas) (*pl*); **~ country** este país; **these thoughts** estos pensamientos; **I prefer ~ one** prefiero éste;

~ **morning/week** esta mañana/semana; ~ **Sunday/summer** este domingo/verano. **-2.** *inf* [a certain] un (una); **there's** ~ **woman I know** hay una tía que conozco. ◇ *adv*: **it was** ~ **big** era así de grande; **you'll need about** ~ **much** te hará falta un tanto así.

thistle ['θɪsl] *n* cardo *m*.

thither ['ðɪðər] *adv* → **hither**.

tho' [ðəʊ] = **though**.

thong [θɒŋ] *n* **-1.** [of leather] correa *f*. **-2.** *Am* [flip-flop] chancleta *f*.

thorn [θɔːn] *n* **-1.** [prickle] espina *f*; **to be a** ~ **in one's flesh** OR **side** ser un engorro para alguien. **-2.** [bush, tree] espino *m*.

thorny ['θɔːnɪ] (*compar* **-ier**, *superl* **-iest**) *adj lit* & *fig* espinoso(sa).

thorough ['θʌrə] *adj* **-1.** [investigation etc] exhaustivo(va), completo(ta). **-2.** [person, work] minucioso(sa), concienzudo(da). **-3.** [idiot, waste] completo(ta).

thoroughbred ['θʌrəbred] *n* pura sangre *m* y *f*.

thoroughfare ['θʌrəfeər] *n fml* calle *f* mayor, avenida *f* principal.

thoroughly ['θʌrəlɪ] *adv* **-1.** [fully, in detail] a fondo, exhaustivamente. **-2.** [completely, utterly] completamente, totalmente.

thoroughness ['θʌrənɪs] *n* (*U*) **-1.** [exhaustiveness] exhaustividad *f*. **-2.** [meticulousness] minuciosidad *f*.

those [ðəʊz] *pl* → **that**.

though [ðəʊ] ◇ *conj* aunque; **difficult** ~ **it may be** aunque sea difícil; **even** ~ aunque; **as** ~ como si. ◇ *adv* sin embargo.

thought [θɔːt] ◇ *pt* & *pp* → **think**. ◇ *n* **-1.** [notion, idea] idea *f*. **-2.** [act of thinking]: **after much** ~ después de pensarlo mucho. **-3.** [philosophy, thinking] pensamiento *m*. **-4.** [gesture] detalle *m*.

◆ **thoughts** *npl* **-1.** [reflections] reflexiones *fpl*; **she keeps her** ~**s to herself** no expresa lo que piensa; **to collect one's** ~**s** orientarse, concentrarse. **-2.** [views] ideas *fpl*, opiniones *fpl*.

thoughtful ['θɔːtfʊl] *adj* **-1.** [pensive] pensativo(va). **-2.** [considerate] considerado(da), atento(ta).

thoughtfulness ['θɔːtfʊlnɪs] *n* (*U*) **-1.** [pensiveness] aire *m* pensativo. **-2.** [considerateness] consideración *f*.

thoughtless ['θɔːtlɪs] *adj* desconsiderado(da).

thoughtlessness ['θɔːtlɪsnɪs] *n* desconsideración *f*.

thousand ['θaʊznd] *num* mil; **a** OR **one** ~

mil; **two** ~ dos mil; ~**s of miles de**; *see also* **six**.

thousandth ['θaʊznθ] ◇ *num adj* milésimo(ma). ◇ *num n* **-1.** [fraction] milésima *f*. **-2.** [in order] milésimo *m*, **-ma** *f*; *see also* **sixth**.

thrash [θræʃ] *vt lit* & *fig* dar una paliza a.

◆ **thrash about**, **thrash around** *vi* agitarse violentamente.

◆ **thrash out** *vt sep* darle vueltas a, discutir.

thrashing ['θræʃɪŋ] *n lit* & *fig* paliza *f*.

thread [θred] ◇ *n* **-1.** [of cotton, argument] hilo *m*. **-2.** [of screw] rosca *f*, filete *m*. ◇ *vt* **-1.** [needle] enhebrar. **-2.** [move]: **to** ~ **one's way through** colarse por entre.

threadbare ['θredbeər] *adj* raído(da), gastado(da).

threat [θret] *n*: ~ (**to/of**) amenaza *f* (para/de).

threaten ['θretn] ◇ *vt* amenazar; **to** ~ **sb** (**with**) amenazar a alguien (con); **to** ~ **to do sthg** amenazar con hacer algo. ◇ *vi* amenazar.

threatening ['θretnɪŋ] *adj* amenazador(ra).

three [θriː] *num* tres; *see also* **six**.

three-D *adj* tridimensional.

three-day event *n concurso hípico que dura tres días.*

three-dimensional *adj* tridimensional.

threefold ['θriːfəʊld] ◇ *adj* triple. ◇ *adv* tres veces; **to increase** ~ triplicarse.

three-legged race [-'legɪd-] *n carrera por parejas en la que cada corredor tiene una pierna atada a la de su compañero.*

three-piece *adj* de tres piezas; ~ **suite** tresillo *m*.

three-ply *adj* [wood] de tres capas; [rope, wool] de tres hebras.

three-point turn *n Br* AUT: **to do a** ~ hacer la ele.

three-quarters *npl* tres cuartos *mpl*, tres cuartas partes *fpl*.

threesome ['θriːsəm] *n* trío *m*.

three-star *adj* de tres estrellas.

three-wheeler [-'wiːlər] *n* coche *m* de tres ruedas.

thresh [θreʃ] *vt* trillar.

threshing machine ['θreʃɪŋ-] *n* trilladora *f*.

threshold ['θreʃhəʊld] *n* **-1.** [doorway] umbral *m*. **-2.** [level] límite *m*. **-3.** *fig* [verge]: **to be on the** ~ **of** estar en los umbrales OR a las puertas de.

threshold agreement *n acuerdo concertado para compensar una subida inesperada de la inflación.*

threw [θruː] *pt* → throw.

thrift [θrɪft] *n* **-1.** [gen] (*U*) frugalidad *f*, economía *f*. **-2.** *Am* [savings bank] = **thrift institution.**

thrift institution *n* ≃ caja *f* de ahorros.

thrifty ['θrɪftɪ] (*compar* **-ier**, *superl* **-iest**) *adj* [person] ahorrativo(va); [meal] frugal.

thrill [θrɪl] ◇ *n* **-1.** [sudden feeling] estremecimiento *m*. **-2.** [exciting experience]: **it was a ~ to see** it fue emocionante verlo. ◇ *vt* entusiasmar. ◇ *vi*: **to ~** to entusiasmarse con.

thrilled [θrɪld] *adj*: ~ **(with sthg/to do sthg)** encantado(da) (de algo/de hacer algo).

thriller ['θrɪlə'] *n* novela *f*/película *f*/obra *f* de suspense.

thrilling ['θrɪlɪŋ] *adj* emocionante.

thrive [θraɪv] (*pt* **-d** OR **throve**, *pp* **-d**) *vi* [plant] crecer mucho; [person] rebosar de salud; [business] prosperar.

thriving ['θraɪvɪŋ] *adj* [plant] que crece bien.

throat [θrəut] *n* garganta *f*; **to ram** OR **force sthg down sb's ~** *fig* hacerle tragar algo a alguien; **to stick in sb's ~** *fig* atragantársele a alguien; **to be at each other's ~s** tirarse los platos a la cabeza.

throaty ['θrəutɪ] (*compar* **-ier**, *superl* **-iest**) *adj* ronco(ca).

throb [θrɒb] (*pt* & *pp* **-bed**, *cont* **-bing**) ◇ *n* [of heart] latido *m*; [of pulse] palpitación *f*; [of engine, music] vibración *f*. ◇ *vi* **-1.** [heart, pulse] latir; [head] palpitar. **-2.** [engine, music] vibrar, resonar.

throes [θrəuz] *npl*: **to be in the ~ of** estar en medio de.

thrombosis [θrɒm'bəusɪs] (*pl* **-boses** [-siːz]) *n* trombosis *f inv*.

throne [θrəun] *n* trono *m*; **the ~** el trono.

throng [θrɒŋ] ◇ *n* multitud *f*. ◇ *vt* llegar en tropel a. ◇ *vi* llegar en tropel.

throttle ['θrɒtl] ◇ *n* válvula *f* reguladora. ◇ *vt* [strangle] estrangular.

through [θruː] ◇ *adj* [finished]: **to be ~ with sthg** haber terminado algo.
◇ *adv* **-1.** [in place] de parte a parte, de un lado a otro; **they let us ~** nos dejaron pasar; **I read it ~** lo leí hasta el final. **-2.** [in time] hasta el final; **we stayed ~ till Friday** nos quedamos hasta el viernes.
◇ *prep* **-1.** [relating to place, position] a través de; **to cut/travel ~ sthg** cortar/viajar por algo. **-2.** [during] durante; **to go ~ an experience** pasar por una experiencia. **-3.** [because of] a causa de, por. **-4.** [by means of] gracias a, por medio de; **I got it ~ a friend** lo conseguí a través de un amigo. **-5.** *Am* [up to and including]: **Monday ~ Friday** de lunes a viernes.

◆ **through and through** *adv* de pies a cabeza; **to know sthg ~ and ~** conocer algo de arriba abajo.

throughout [θruː'aut] ◇ *prep* **-1.** [during] a lo largo de, durante todo (durante toda). **-2.** [everywhere in] por todo(da). ◇ *adv* **-1.** [all the time] todo el tiempo. **-2.** [everywhere] por todas partes.

throve [θrəuv] *pt* → thrive.

throw [θrəu] (*pt* **threw**, *pp* **thrown**) ◇ *vt* **-1.** [gen] tirar, aventar *Amer*; [ball, hammer, javelin] lanzar; **to ~ one's arms around sb** abrazarse a alguien; **to ~ o.s.** tirarse, echarse; **to ~ o.s. into sthg** *fig* meterse de lleno en algo. **-2.** [subj: horse] derribar, desmontar. **-3.** *fig* [put]: **we were thrown into confusion** quedamos desconcertados; **they threw him into the job at short notice** le cargaron con el trabajo sin apenas avisarle. **-4.** [cast - light, shadow] **to ~ sthg on** proyectar algo sobre. **-5.** [have suddenly]: **to ~ a tantrum/fit** tener una rabieta/un ataque. **-6.** *fig* [confuse] desconcertar.
◇ *n* lanzamiento *m*, tiro *m*.

◆ **throw away** *vt sep* [discard] tirar, botar *Amer*; *fig* [waste] desperdiciar.

◆ **throw in** *vt sep* [extra item] incluir.

◆ **throw out** *vt sep* **-1.** [discard] tirar. **-2.** *fig* [reject] rechazar. **-3.** [force to leave] echar.

◆ **throw up** ◇ *vt sep* [dust] levantar. ◇ *vi inf* [vomit] vomitar, arrojar.

throwaway ['θrəuə,weɪ] *adj* **-1.** [bottle, product] desechable. **-2.** [remark, gesture] hecho(cha) como quien no quiere la cosa.

throwback ['θrəubæk] *n*: ~ **(to)** retroceso *m* (a).

throw-in *n Br* FTBL saque *m* de banda.

thrown [θrəun] *pp* → throw.

thru [θruː] *Am inf* = through.

thrush [θrʌʃ] *n* **-1.** [bird] tordo *m*. **-2.** MED [vaginal] hongos *mpl* (vaginales).

thrust [θrʌst] ◇ *n* **-1.** [of sword] estocada *f*; [of knife] cuchillada *f*; [of troops] arremetida *f*. **-2.** TECH (fuerza *f* de) propulsión *f*. **-3.** [main meaning] esencia *f*. ◇ *vt* **-1.** [shove]: **he ~ the knife into his enemy** hundió el cuchillo en el cuerpo de su enemigo; **he ~ the book at me** me dio el libro con un movimiento brusco. **-2.** [jostle]: **to ~ one's way** abrirse paso a empujones.

◆ **thrust upon** *vt sep*: **to ~ sthg upon sb** imponer algo a alguien.

thrusting ['θrʌstɪŋ] *adj* [aggressive] agresivo(va).

thruway ['θruːweɪ] *n Am* autopista *f*.

thud [θʌd] (*pt* & *pp* **-ded**, *cont* **-ding**) ◇ *n* ruido *m* sordo. ◇ *vi* dar un golpe seco.

thug [θʌg] *n* matón *m*.

thumb [θʌm] ◇ *n* [of hand] pulgar *m*; **to twiddle one's ~s** dar vueltas a los dedos pulgares; *fig* tocarse OR rascarse la barriga. ◇ *vt inf* [hitch]: **to ~ a lift** hacer dedo.
◆ **thumb through** *vt fus* hojear.

thumb index *n* uñeros *mpl* (*de libro*).

thumbnail ['θʌmneɪl] ◇ *adj* breve. ◇ *n* uña *f* del pulgar.

thumbnail sketch *n* descripción *f* breve.

thumbs down *n*: **to get** OR **be given the ~** [plan] ser rechazado(da); [play] ser recibido(da) con descontento.

thumbs up *n*: **we got** OR **were given the ~** nos dieron luz verde OR el visto bueno.

thumbtack ['θʌmtæk] *n Am* chincheta *f*.

thump [θʌmp] ◇ *n* **-1.** [blow] puñetazo *m*, porrazo *m*. **-2.** [thud] golpe *m* seco. ◇ *vt* **-1.** [punch] dar un puñetazo a. **-2.** [place heavily]: **he ~ed the book down on the table** dio un golpe contundente con el libro sobre la mesa. ◇ *vi* **-1.** [person]: **to ~ in/out** entrar/salir con pasos pesados. **-2.** [heart, head] latir con fuerza.

thunder ['θʌndər] ◇ *n* (*U*) **-1.** METEOR truenos *mpl*. **-2.** *fig* [loud sound] estruendo *m*, estrépito *m*. ◇ *vt* vociferar. ◇ *v impers* METEOR tronar. ◇ *vi* [make loud sound] retumbar.

thunderbolt ['θʌndəbəʊlt] *n* rayo *m*.

thunderclap ['θʌndəklæp] *n* trueno *m*.

thundercloud ['θʌndəklaʊd] *n* nube *f* de tormenta.

thundering ['θʌndərɪŋ] *adj* enorme, descomunal.

thunderous ['θʌndərəs] *adj* atronador(ra), ensordecedor(ra).

thunderstorm ['θʌndəstɔːm] *n* tormenta *f*, tempestad *f*.

thunderstruck ['θʌndəstrʌk] *adj fig* atónito(ta).

thundery ['θʌndərɪ] *adj* tormentoso(sa).

Thur, **Thurs** (*abbr of* **Thursday**) juev.

Thursday ['θɜːzdɪ] *n* jueves *m inv*; *see also* Saturday.

thus [ðʌs] *adv fml* **-1.** [therefore] por consiguiente, así que. **-2.** [in this way] así, de esta manera.

thwart [θwɔːt] *vt* frustrar.

thyme [taɪm] *n* tomillo *m*.

thyroid ['θaɪrɔɪd] *n* tiroides *m inv*.

tiara [tɪ'ɑːrə] *n* tiara *f*.

Tiber ['taɪbər] *n*: **the (River) ~** el (río) Tíber.

Tibet [tɪ'bet] *n* (el) Tibet.

Tibetan [tɪ'betn] ◇ *adj* tibetano(na). ◇ *n* **-1.** [person] tibetano *m*, -na *f*. **-2.** [language] tibetano *m*.

tibia ['tɪbɪə] (*pl* **-biae** [-bɪiː] OR **-s**) *n* tibia *f*.

tic [tɪk] *n* tic *m*.

tick [tɪk] ◇ *n* **-1.** [written mark] marca *f* OR señal *f* de visto bueno. **-2.** [sound] tictac *m*. ◇ *vt* marcar (con una señal). ◇ *vi* **-1.** [make ticking sound] hacer tictac. **-2.** *fig* [behave in a certain way]: **what makes her ~?** ¿qué es lo que le mueve?
◆ **tick away**, **tick by** *vi* pasar.
◆ **tick off** *vt sep* **-1.** [mark off] marcar (con una señal de visto bueno). **-2.** [tell off]: **to ~ sb off (for sthg)** echar una bronca a alguien (por algo).
◆ **tick over** *vi* funcionar al ralentí.

ticked [tɪkd] *adj Am* enfadado(da), afectado(da).

tickertape ['tɪkəteɪp] *n* (*U*) cinta de papel que lleva impresa información bursátil.

ticket ['tɪkɪt] *n* **-1.** [for bus, train etc] billete *m*, boleto *m Amer*; [for cinema, football match] entrada *f*. **-2.** [for traffic offence] multa *f*. **-3.** POL lista *f* de candidatos.

ticket agency *n* agencia de venta de entradas o billetes de tren, avión etc.

ticket collector *n Br* revisor *m*, -ra *f*.

ticket holder *n* poseedor *m*, -ra *f* de billete OR de entrada.

ticket inspector *n Br* revisor *m*, -ra *f*.

ticket machine *n* máquina *f* automática para la venta de billetes.

ticket office *n* taquilla *f*, boletería *f Amer*.

ticking off ['tɪkɪŋ-] (*pl* **tickings off**) *n*: **to give sb a ~** echar una bronca a alguien; **to get a ~ (from sb)** recibir una bronca (de alguien).

tickle ['tɪkl] ◇ *vt* **-1.** [touch lightly] hacer cosquillas a. **-2.** *fig* [amuse] divertir. ◇ *vi*: **my feet are tickling** tengo cosquillas en los pies.

ticklish ['tɪklɪʃ] *adj* **-1.** [sensitive to touch]: **to be ~** tener cosquillas. **-2.** *fig* [delicate] delicado(da), peliagudo(da).

tick-tack-toe *n Am* tres *fpl* en raya.

tidal ['taɪdl] *adj* de la marea.

tidal wave *n* maremoto *m*.

tidbit *Am* = **titbit**.

tiddler ['tɪdlər] *n Br* [fish] pececillo *m*.

tiddly ['tɪdlɪ] (*compar* **-ier**, *superl* **-iest**) *adj Br inf* **-1.** [tipsy] piripi. **-2.** [tiny] pequeñito(ta).

tiddlywinks ['tɪdlɪwɪŋks], **tiddledywinks** *Am* ['tɪdldɪwɪŋks] *n* juego *m* de la pulga.

tide [taɪd] *n* **-1.** [of sea] marea *f*. **-2.** *fig* [of opinion, history] corriente *f*. **-3.** *fig* [of protest, feeling] oleada *f*.

◆ **tide over** *vt sep* sacar del bache OR de un apuro.

tidemark ['taɪdmɑːk] *n* **-1.** [of sea] línea *f* de la marea alta. **-2.** *Br* [round bath, neck] cerco *m* de suciedad.

tidily ['taɪdɪlɪ] *adv* ordenadamente.

tidiness ['taɪdɪnɪs] *n* (*U*) [of room, desk] orden *m*; [of appearance] pulcritud *f*.

tidings ['taɪdɪŋz] *npl literary* noticias *fpl*.

tidy ['taɪdɪ] (*compar* **-ier**, *superl* **-iest**, *pt* & *pp* **-ied**) ◇ *adj* **-1.** [room, desk etc] ordenado(da). **-2.** [person, dress, hair] arreglado(da). **-3.** *inf* [sum] considerable. ◇ *vt* ordenar, arreglar.

◆ **tidy away** *vt sep* poner en su sitio.

◆ **tidy up** ◇ *vt sep* ordenar, arreglar. ◇ *vi* ordenar las cosas, recoger.

tie [taɪ] (*pt* & *pp* **tied**, *cont* **tying**) ◇ *n* **-1.** [necktie] corbata *f*. **-2.** [string, cord] atadura *f*. **-3.** [bond, link] vínculo *m*, lazo *m*. **-4.** SPORT [draw] empate *m*. **-5.** *Am* RAIL traviesa *f*.
◇ *vt* **-1.** [attach, fasten]: **to ~ sthg (to** OR **onto sthg)** atar algo (a algo); **to ~ sthg round/with sthg** atar algo a/con algo. **-2.** [do up - shoelaces] atar; [- knot] hacer. **-3.** *fig* [link]: **to be ~d to** estar ligado(da) a. **-4.** *fig* [limited, restricted]: **to be ~d to** estar atado(da) a.
◇ *vi* [draw]: **to ~ (with)** empatar (con).

◆ **tie down** *vt sep fig* atar.

◆ **tie in with** *vt fus* concordar con.

◆ **tie up** *vt sep* **-1.** [gen] atar. **-2.** *fig* [money, resources] inmovilizar. **-3.** *fig* [link]: **to be ~d up with** estar ligado(da) a a.

tiebreak(er) ['taɪbreɪk(ə)] *n* **-1.** TENNIS muerte *f* súbita, tiebreak *m*. **-2.** [in game, competition] *pregunta adicional para romper un empate*.

tied [taɪd] *adj* SPORT [drawn] empatado(da).

tied cottage *n Br casa que un agricultor alquila a uno de sus trabajadores mientras éste permanezca a su servicio.*

tied up *adj* [busy] ocupado(da).

tie-dye *vt hacerle nudos a una prenda antes de teñirla para lograr un reparto desigual del color.*

tie-in *n* **-1.** [link]: **~ between** OR **with** relación *f* entre. **-2.** [product] *libro, disco etc. relacionado con una nueva película, serie televisiva etc.*

tiepin ['taɪpɪn] *n* alfiler *m* de corbata.

tier [tɪə] *n* [of seats] hilera *f*; [of cake] piso *m*.

Tierra del Fuego [tɪˌerədel'fweɪgəʊ] *n* Tierra del Fuego.

tie-up *n* **-1.** [link]: **~ between** OR **with** relación *f* estrecha entre. **-2.** *Am* [interruption - in work] interrupción *f* breve; [- in traffic]

embotellamiento *m*, atasco *m*.

tiff [tɪf] *n* pelea *f* (*de poca importancia*).

tiger ['taɪgə] *n* tigre *m*.

tiger cub *n* cachorro *m* de tigre.

tight [taɪt] ◇ *adj* **-1.** [gen] apretado(da); [shoes] estrecho(cha); **it's a ~ fit** queda muy justo. **-2.** [string, skin] tirante. **-3.** [painful]: **my chest feels ~** siento una opresión en el pecho. **-4.** [budget] ajustado(da). **-5.** [rules, restrictions] riguroso(sa). **-6.** [corner, bend] cerrado(da). **-7.** [match, finish] reñido(da). **-8.** *inf* [drunk] cocido(da). **-9.** *inf* [miserly] agarrado(da).
◇ *adv* **-1.** [hold, squeeze] con fuerza; **to hold ~** agarrarse (fuerte); **to shut** OR **close sthg ~** cerrar algo bien. **-2.** [pull, stretch] de modo tirante.

◆ **tights** *npl* medias *fpl*.

tighten ['taɪtn] ◇ *vt* **-1.** [hold, grip]: **to ~ one's hold** OR **grip on sthg** coger con más fuerza algo. **-2.** [rope, chain] tensar. **-3.** [knot] apretar; [belt] apretarse. **-4.** [rules, system] intensificar. ◇ *vi* [rope, chain] tensarse.

◆ **tighten up** *vt sep* **-1.** [screw, fastening] apretar; [belt] apretarse. **-2.** [rules, system] intensificar.

tightfisted [ˌtaɪt'fɪstɪd] *adj inf pej* agarrado(da).

tightknit [ˌtaɪt'nɪt] *adj* muy unido (muy unida).

tight-lipped [-'lɪpt] *adj* **-1.** [with lips pressed together] con los labios apretados. **-2.** [silent] callado(da).

tightly ['taɪtlɪ] *adv* **-1.** [fit]: **the dress fitted her ~** el vestido le iba muy apretado. **-2.** [hold, squeeze] con fuerza; [fasten] bien. **-3.** [pull, stretch] de modo tirante. **-4.** [pack] apretadamente.

tightness ['taɪtnɪs] *n* **-1.** [gen] estrechez *f*. **-2.** [of budget] lo ajustado. **-3.** [of chest, stomach] opresión *f*. **-4.** [of rules, system] rigor *m*.

tightrope ['taɪtrəʊp] *n* cuerda *f* floja, alambre *m*; **to be on** OR **walking a ~** andar OR bailar en la cuerda floja.

tightrope walker *n* funámbulo *m*, -la *f*.

Tigré ['tiːgreɪ] *n* Tigre.

tigress ['taɪgrɪs] *n* tigresa *f*.

Tigris ['taɪgrɪs] *n*: **the (River) ~** el (río) Tigris.

tilde ['tɪldə] *n* tilde *f*.

tile [taɪl] *n* **-1.** [on roof] teja *f*. **-2.** [on floor] baldosa *f*; [on wall] azulejo *m*, baldosín *m*.

tiled [taɪld] *adj* [roof] tejado(da); [floor] embaldosado(da); [wall] alicatado(da).

tiling ['taɪlɪŋ] *n* **-1.** [act of tiling] colocación *f* de tejas/baldosas/azulejos. **-2.** [tiled surface -

of roof] tejas *fpl*; [- of floor] baldosas *fpl*; [- of wall] azulejos *mpl*, baldosines *mpl*.

till [tɪl] ◇ *prep* hasta; ~ **now/then** hasta ahora/entonces. ◇ *conj* hasta que; **wait** ~ **he arrives** espera hasta que llegue. ◇ *n* caja *f* (registradora).

tiller ['tɪlər] *n* NAUT caña *f* del timón.

tilt [tɪlt] ◇ *n* inclinación *f*, ladeo *m*. ◇ *vt* inclinar, ladear. ◇ *vi* inclinarse, ladearse.

timber ['tɪmbər] *n* **-1.** (*U*) [wood] madera *f* (*para la construcción*). **-2.** [beam - of ship] cuaderna *f*; [- of house] viga *f*.

timbered ['tɪmbəd] *adj* enmaderado(da).

time [taɪm] ◇ *n* **-1.** [gen] tiempo *m*; **a good** ~ **to go** un buen momento de irnos; **ahead of** ~ temprano; **in good** ~ con tiempo; **on** ~ puntualmente; **to take** ~ llevar tiempo; **it's (about)** ~ **to ...** ya es hora de ...; **to get the** ~ **to do sthg** coger el tiempo para hacer algo; **it's high** ~ **...** ya va siendo hora de ...; **to get** ~ **and a half** recibir el pago establecido más la mitad de éste; **to have no** ~ **for** no poder con, no aguantar; **to make good** ~ ir bien de tiempo; **to pass the** ~ pasar el rato; **to play for** ~ intentar ganar tiempo; **to take one's** ~ **(doing sthg)** tomarse uno mucho tiempo (para hacer algo); **take your** ~! ¡tómatelo con calma! **-2.** [as measured by clock] hora *f*; **what** ~ **is it?, what's the** ~? ¿qué hora es?; **the** ~ **is three o'clock** son las tres; **in a week's/year's** ~ dentro de una semana/un año; **to keep** ~ ir a la hora; **to lose** ~ atrasar. **-3.** [length of time] rato *m*; **it was a long** ~ **before he came** pasó mucho tiempo antes de que viniera; **for a** ~ durante un tiempo. **-4.** [point in time in past, era] época *f*; **at that** ~ en aquella época; **in ancient** ~s en la antigüedad; **to be ahead of one's** ~ adelantarse a su tiempo; **before my** ~ antes de que yo naciera. **-5.** [occasion] vez *f*; **three** ~s **a week** tres veces a la semana; **from** ~ **to** ~ de vez en cuando; ~ **after** ~, ~ **and again** una y otra vez; **I don't like children at the best of** ~s ya de entrada no me gustan los niños. **-6.** [experience]: **we had a good/bad** ~ lo pasamos bien/mal; **I had a hard** ~ **making myself understood** me costó mucho hacer que me entendieran. **-7.** MUS compás *m*.
◇ *vt* **-1.** [schedule] programar. **-2.** [race, runner] cronometrar. **-3.** [arrival, remark] elegir el momento oportuno para.
◆ **times** ◇ *n*: **four** ~s **as much as me** cuatro veces más que yo. ◇ *prep* MATH: **4** ~s **5** 4 por 5.
◆ **about time** *adv*: **it's about** ~ ya va siendo hora.

◆ **at a time** *adv*: **for months at a** ~ durante meses seguidos; **one at a** ~ de uno en uno.
◆ **at (any) one time** *adv* en cualquier momento.
◆ **at times** *adv* a veces.
◆ **at the same time** *adv* al mismo tiempo.
◆ **for the time being** *adv* de momento.
◆ **in time** *adv* **-1.** [not late]: **in** ~ **(for)** a tiempo (para). **-2.** [eventually] con el tiempo.

time-and-motion study *n* estudio de métodos para mejorar el rendimiento laboral.

time bomb *n* [bomb] bomba *f* de relojería; *fig* [dangerous situation] bomba *f*.

time-consuming [-kən,sjuːmɪŋ] *adj* que requiere mucho tiempo.

timed [taɪmd] *adj* cronometrado(da); **well-timed** oportuno(na); **badly-timed** poco oportuno.

time difference *n* diferencia *f* horaria.

time-honoured *adj* consagrado(da).

timekeeping ['taɪm,kiːpɪŋ] *n* [punctuality] puntualidad *f*.

time lag *n* intervalo *m*.

time-lapse *adj* PHOT: ~ **photography** montaje cinematográfico para mostrar procesos lentos como el crecimiento de una planta en poco tiempo.

timeless ['taɪmlɪs] *adj* eterno(na).

time limit *n* límite *m* de tiempo, plazo *m*.

timely ['taɪmlɪ] (*compar* **-ier**, *superl* **-iest**) *adj* oportuno(na).

time machine *n* máquina *f* del tiempo.

time off *n* tiempo *m* libre; **I'm owed** ~ **(from) work** me deben algunos días en el trabajo.

time out *n* **-1.** *Am* SPORT tiempo *m* muerto. **-2.** [break]: **to take** ~ **to do sthg** tomarse tiempo libre para hacer algo.

timepiece ['taɪmpiːs] *n dated* reloj *m*.

timer ['taɪmər] *n* temporizador *m*.

timesaving ['taɪm,seɪvɪŋ] *adj* para ahorrar tiempo.

time scale *n* tiempo *m* de ejecución.

time-share *n Br* multipropiedad *f*.

time sheet *n* ficha *f* (de asistencia al trabajo).

time signal *n* señal *f* horaria.

time switch *n* interruptor *m* de reloj.

timetable ['taɪm,teɪbl] *n* **-1.** [of buses, trains, school] horario *m*. **-2.** [schedule of events] programa *m*.

time zone *n* huso *m* horario.

timid ['tɪmɪd] *adj* tímido(da).

timidly ['tɪmɪdlɪ] *adv* tímidamente.

timing ['taɪmɪŋ] *n* (*U*) **-1.** [judgment]: **she made her comment with perfect ~** su comentario fue hecho en el momento más oportuno. **-2.** [scheduling]: **the ~ of the election is crucial** es crucial que las elecciones se celebren en el momento oportuno. **-3.** [measuring] cronometraje *m*.

timing device *n* dispositivo *m* de detonación retardada.

timpani ['tɪmpənɪ] *npl* timbales *mpl*, tímpanos *mpl*.

tin [tɪn] ◇ *n* **-1.** [metal] estaño *m*; **~ plate** hojalata *f*. **-2.** *Br* [can, container] lata *f*. ◇ *comp* [of tin] de estaño; [of tinplate] de hojalata.

tin can *n* lata *f*.

tinder ['tɪndər] *n* yesca *f*.

tinfoil ['tɪnfɔɪl] *n* (*U*) papel *m* de aluminio.

tinge [tɪndʒ] *n* **-1.** [of colour] matiz *m*, toque *m*. **-2.** [of feeling] ligera sensación *f*.

tinged [tɪndʒd] *adj*: **~ with** con un toque de.

tingle ['tɪŋgl] *vi*: **my feet are tingling** siento hormigueo en los pies; **to ~ with** estremecerse de.

tingling ['tɪŋglɪŋ] *n* cosquilleo *m*, hormigueo *m*.

tinker ['tɪŋkər] ◇ *n Br* **-1.** *pej* [gypsy] gitano *m*, -na *f*. **-2.** [rascal] diablillo *m*, granujilla *m* y *f*. ◇ *vi* hacer chapuzas; **to ~ with** enredar con.

tinkle ['tɪŋkl] ◇ *n* **-1.** [sound] tintineo *m*. **-2.** *Br inf* [phone call]: **to give sb a ~** llamar a alguien (por teléfono). ◇ *vi* [ring] tintinear.

tin mine *n* mina *f* de estaño.

tinned [tɪnd] *adj Br* enlatado(da), en conserva.

tinnitus [tɪ'naɪtəs] *n* (*U*) zumbidos *mpl* (en los oídos).

tinny ['tɪnɪ] (*compar* **-ier**, *superl* **-iest**) *adj* **-1.** [sound] metálico(ca). **-2.** *inf pej* [badly made] poco sólido (poco sólida).

tin opener *n Br* abrelatas *m inv*.

tin-pot *adj Br pej* [country] de mala muerte; [politician, general] de pacotilla.

tinsel ['tɪnsl] *n* (*U*) oropel *m*.

tint [tɪnt] ◇ *n* tinte *m*, matiz *m*. ◇ *vt* [hair] teñir; [windows, glass] ahumar.

tinted ['tɪntɪd] *adj* [glasses, windows] tintado(da), ahumado(da).

tiny ['taɪnɪ] (*compar* **-ier**, *superl* **-iest**) *adj* diminuto(ta), pequeñito(ta).

tip [tɪp] (*pt & pp* **-ped**, *cont* **-ping**) ◇ *n* **-1.** [end] punta *f*; **it's on the ~ of my tongue** lo tengo en la punta de la lengua. **-2.** *Br* [dump] vertedero *m*. **-3.** [gratuity] propina *f*.

-4. [piece of advice] consejo *m*. ◇ *vt* **-1.** [tilt] inclinar, ladear. **-2.** [spill, pour] vaciar, verter. **-3.** [give a gratuity to] dar una propina a. ◇ *vi* **-1.** [tilt] inclinarse, ladearse. **-2.** [spill] derramarse. **-3.** [give a gratuity] dar propina.

◆ **tip off** *vt sep* informar (confidencialmente).

◆ **tip over** ◇ *vt sep* volcar. ◇ *vi* volcarse.

tip-off *n* información *f* (confidencial).

tipped [tɪpt] *adj* **-1.** [cigarette] con filtro, emboquillado. **-2.** [spear etc]: **~ with stone/gold** con punta de piedra/oro.

Tipp-Ex® ['tɪpeks] *Br* ◇ *n* Tipp-Ex® *m*. ◇ *vt* corregir con Tipp-Ex®.

tipple ['tɪpl] *n inf* copa *f*, bebida *f* alcohólica.

tipsy ['tɪpsɪ] (*compar* **-ier**, *superl* **-iest**) *adj inf dated* piripi.

tiptoe ['tɪptəʊ] ◇ *n*: **on ~** de puntillas. ◇ *vi* ir de puntillas.

tip-top *adj inf dated* de primera.

TIR (*abbr of* **Transports Internationaux Routiers**) TIR *m*.

tirade [taɪ'reɪd] *n* diatriba *f*.

Tirana, Tiranë [tɪ'rɑːnə] *n* Tirana.

tire ['taɪər] ◇ *n Am* = **tyre**. ◇ *vt* cansar. ◇ *vi*: **to ~ (of)** cansarse (de).

◆ **tire out** *vt sep* agotar.

tired ['taɪəd] *adj*: **~ (of sthg/of doing sthg)** cansado(da) (de algo/de hacer algo).

tiredness ['taɪədnɪs] *n* cansancio *m*.

tireless ['taɪəlɪs] *adj* incansable.

tiresome ['taɪəsəm] *adj* pesado(da).

tiring ['taɪərɪŋ] *adj* cansado(da).

Tirol = **Tyrol**.

tissue ['tɪʃuː] *n* **-1.** [paper handkerchief] pañuelo *m* de papel. **-2.** (*U*) BIOL tejido *m*. **-3.** [paper] papel *m* de seda. **-4.** *phr*: **a ~ of lies** una sarta de mentiras.

tissue paper *n* (*U*) papel *m* de seda.

tit [tɪt] *n* **-1.** [bird] herrerillo *m*. **-2.** *vulg* [breast] teta *f*.

titbit *Br* ['tɪtbɪt], **tidbit** *Am* ['tɪdbɪt] *n* **-1.** [of food] golosina *f*. **-2.** *fig* [of news] noticia *f* breve e interesante.

tit for tat *n*: **it's ~** donde las dan las toman.

titillate ['tɪtɪleɪt] *vt & vi* excitar.

titivate ['tɪtɪveɪt] *vt*: **to ~ o.s.** emperifollarse, ponerse guapo(pa).

title ['taɪtl] *n* título *m*.

titled ['taɪtld] *adj* con título de nobleza.

title deed *n* título *m* de propiedad.

titleholder ['taɪtl,həʊldər] *n* SPORT campeón *m*, -ona *f*.

title page *n* portada *f*.

title role *n* papel *m* principal.

titter ['tɪtə'] *vi* reírse por lo bajo.

tittle-tattle ['tɪtl,tatl] *n* (*U*) *inf pej* cotilleo *m*, chismes *mpl*.

titular ['tɪtjʊlə'] *adj* nominal.

T-junction *n* bifurcación *f* en forma de T.

TLS (*abbr of* **Times Literary Supplement**) *n* suplemento literario semanal del Times que se vende por separado.

TM ◇ *n* (*abbr of* **transcendental medita-tion**) *meditación trascendental*. ◇ *abbr of* **trademark**.

TN *abbr of* **Tennessee**.

TNT (*abbr of* **trinitrotoluene**) *n* TNT *m*.

to [*unstressed before consonant* tə, *unstressed before vowel* tʊ, *stressed* tuː] ◇ *prep* **-1.** [indica-ting place, direction] a; **to go ~ Liverpool/ Spain/school** ir a Liverpool/España/la es-cuela; **to go ~ the doctor's/John's** ir al médico/a casa de John; **the road ~ Glas-gow** la carretera de Glasgow; **~ the left/ right** a la izquierda/derecha; **~ the east/ west** hacia el este/oeste. **-2.** (*to express indi-rect object*) a; **to give sthg ~ sb** darle algo a alguien; **to talk ~ sb** hablar con alguien; **a threat ~ sb** una amenaza para alguien; **we were listening ~ the radio** escuchábamos la radio. **-3.** [as far as] hasta a; **to count ~ ten** contar hasta diez; **we work from nine ~ five** trabajamos de nueve a cinco. **-4.** [in expressions of time]: **it's ten/a quarter ~ three** son las tres menos diez/cuarto. **-5.** [per] por; **40 miles ~ the gallon** un galón (por) cada 40 millas. **-6.** [of] de; [for] para; **the key ~ the car** la llave del coche; **a let-ter ~ my daughter** una carta para OR a mi hija. **-7.** [indicating reaction, effect]: **~ my surprise** para sorpresa mía; **to be ~ one's advantage** ir en beneficio de uno; **to be ~ sb's liking** ser del gusto de alguien. **-8.** [in stating opinion]: **~ me, he's lying** para mí que miente; **it seemed quite unnecessary ~ me/him** *etc* para mí/él *etc* aquello parecía del todo innecesario. **-9.** [indicating state, process]: **to drive sb ~ drink** llevar a al-guien a la bebida; **to shoot ~ fame** verse catapultado a la fama; **to lead ~ trouble** traer problemas. **-10.** [accompanied by]: **we danced ~ the sound of guitars** bailábamos al son de las guitarras.
◇ *adv* [shut]: **push the door ~** cierra la puerta.
◇ *with infinitive* **-1.** (*forming simple infinitive*): **~ walk** andar. **-2.** (*following another verb*): **to begin ~ do sthg** empezar a hacer algo; **to try/want ~ do sthg** intentar/querer hacer algo; **to hate ~ do sthg** odiar tener que ha-cer algo. **-3.** (*following an adjective*): **difficult ~ do** difícil de hacer; **ready ~ go** listos para marchar. **-4.** (*indicating purpose*) para;

I'm doing it ~ help you lo hago para ayu-darte; **he came ~ see me** vino a verme. **-5.** (*substituting for a relative clause*): **I have a lot ~ do** tengo mucho que hacer; **he told me ~ leave** me dijo que me fuera. **-6.** (*to avoid repetition of infinitive*): **I meant to call him but I forgot ~** tenía intención de llamarle pero se me olvidó. **-7.** [in comments]: **~ be honest ...** para ser honesto ...; **~ sum up ...** para resumir ..., resumiendo ....
◆ **to and fro** *adv* de un lado para otro.

toad [təʊd] *n* sapo *m*.

toadstool ['təʊdstuːl] *n* seta *f* venenosa.

toady ['təʊdɪ] (*pl* **-ies**, *pt* & *pp* **-ied**) *pej* ◇ *n* pelota *m y f*, cobista *m y f*. ◇ *vi*: **to ~ (to)** hacer la pelota OR dar coba (a).

to-and-fro *adj* de vaivén OR balanceo.
◆ **to and fro** *adv* de aquí para allá.

toast [təʊst] ◇ *n* **-1.** (*U*) [bread] pan *m* tos-tado; **a slice of ~** una tostada. **-2.** [drink] brindis *m*; **to drink a ~ to** hacer un brindis por. **-3.** [person]: **the ~ of the town** el hé-roe de la ciudad. ◇ *vt* **-1.** [bread] tostar. **-2.** [person] brindar por.

toasted sandwich ['təʊstɪd-] *n* sándwich *m* tostado.

toaster ['təʊstə'] *n* tostador *m*, -ra *f*.

toast rack *n* soporte *m* para tostadas.

tobacco [tə'bækəʊ] *n* tabaco *m*.

tobacconist [tə'bækənɪst] *n* estanquero *m*, -ra *f*; **~'s (shop)** estanco *m*.

Tobago [tə'beɪgəʊ] → **Trinidad and Tobago**.

toboggan [tə'bɒgən] ◇ *n* tobogán *m*, trineo *m*. ◇ *vi* deslizarse en tobogán.

today [tə'deɪ] ◇ *n* **-1.** [this day] hoy *m*. **-2.** [nowadays] hoy (en día). ◇ *adv* **-1.** [this day] hoy. **-2.** [nowadays] hoy (en día).

toddle ['tɒdl] *vi* dar los primeros pasos.

toddler ['tɒdlə'] *n* niño pequeño *m*, niña pequeña *f* (que empieza a andar).

toddy ['tɒdɪ] (*pl* **-ies**) *n* ponche *m*.

to-do [tə'duː] (*pl* **-s**) *n* *inf dated* jaleo *m*, fo-llón *m*.

toe [təʊ] ◇ *n* **-1.** [of foot] dedo *m* (del pie). **-2.** [of sock] punta *f*; [of shoe] puntera *f*. ◇ *vt*: **to ~ the line** acatar las normas.

toehold ['təʊhəʊld] *n* [in rock] punto *m* de apoyo; *fig* [in market]: **to gain a ~ in** ganar-se un hueco en.

toenail ['təʊneɪl] *n* uña *f* del dedo del pie.

toffee ['tɒfɪ] *n* caramelo *m*.

toffee apple *n* *Br* manzana *f* acaramelada.

tofu ['təʊfuː] *n* tofu *m*, *especie de queso hecho de leche de soja*.

toga ['təʊgə] *n* toga *f*.

together [tə'geðəʳ] ◇ *adv* **-1.** [gen] juntos(tas); **all ~** todos juntos; **to stick ~** pegar; **to join ~** unir; **to go (well) ~** combinar bien. **-2.** [at the same time] a la vez, juntos(tas). ◇ *adj inf* organizado(da).
♦ **together with** *prep* junto con.

togetherness [tə'geðənɪs] *n* (U) unión *f*, camaradería *f*.

toggle ['tɒgl] *n* botón *m* de una trenca.

toggle switch *n* COMPUT & ELECTRON conmutador *m* de palanca.

Togo ['təʊgəʊ] *n* Togo.

Togolese [,təʊgə'liːz] ◇ *adj* togolés(esa). ◇ *n* togolés *m*, -esa *f*.

togs [tɒgz] *npl inf* ropa *f*.

toil [tɔɪl] *fml* ◇ *n* trabajo *m* duro. ◇ *vi* trabajar sin descanso.
♦ **toil away** *vi*: **to ~ away (at)** trabajar sin descanso (en).

toilet ['tɔɪlɪt] *n* [at home] wáter *m*, lavabo *m*; [in public place] servicios *mpl*, lavabo *m*; **to go to the ~** ir al wáter.

toilet bag *n* neceser *m*.

toilet paper *n* (U) papel *m* higiénico.

toiletries ['tɔɪlɪtrɪz] *npl* artículos *mpl* de tocador.

toilet roll *n* **-1.** [paper] papel *m* higiénico. **-2.** [roll] rollo *m* de papel higiénico.

toilet soap *n* jabón *m* de tocador.

toilet tissue *n* (U) papel *m* higiénico.

toilet-trained [-,treɪnd] *adj* [child] *que sabe ir solo al wáter.*

toilet water *n* (agua *f* de) colonia *f*.

to-ing and fro-ing [,tuːɪŋən'frəʊɪŋ] (*pl* to-ings and fro-ings) *n* (U) idas *fpl* y venidas.

token ['təʊkn] ◇ *adj* simbólico(ca). ◇ *n* **-1.** [voucher] vale *m*; [disk] ficha *f*. **-2.** [symbol] muestra *f*, símbolo *m*.
♦ **by the same token** *adv* del mismo modo.

Tokyo ['təʊkjəʊ] *n* Tokio.

told [təʊld] *pt & pp* → **tell.**

tolerable ['tɒlərəbl] *adj* tolerable, pasable.

tolerably ['tɒlərəblɪ] *adv* medio.

tolerance ['tɒlərəns] *n* tolerancia *f*.

tolerant ['tɒlərənt] *adj* tolerante.

tolerate ['tɒləreɪt] *vt* **-1.** [put up with] soportar, tolerar. **-2.** [permit] tolerar.

toleration [,tɒlə'reɪʃn] *n* (U) tolerancia *f*.

toll [təʊl] ◇ *n* **-1.** [number]: **death ~** número *m* de víctimas. **-2.** [fee] peaje *m*. **-3.** *phr*: **to take its ~** hacer mella. ◇ *vt* tañer, tocar. ◇ *vi* tocar, doblar.

tollbooth ['təʊlbuːθ] *n* cabina donde se paga el peaje.

toll bridge *n* puente *m* de peaje.

toll-free *Am* ◇ *adj* gratuito(ta). ◇ *adv*: **to call a number ~** llamar a un número gratis.

tomato [*Br* tə'mɑːtəʊ, *Am* tə'meɪtəʊ] (*pl* **-es**) *n* tomate *m*.

tomb [tuːm] *n* tumba *f*, sepulcro *m*.

tombola [tɒm'bəʊlə] *n* tómbola *f*.

tomboy ['tɒmbɔɪ] *n* niña *f* poco feminina.

tombstone ['tuːmstəʊn] *n* lápida *f*.

tomcat ['tɒmkæt] *n* gato *m* (macho).

tomfoolery [tɒm'fuːlərɪ] *n* comportamiento *m* tonto.

tomorrow [tə'mɒrəʊ] ◇ *n* *lit* & *fig* mañana *f*; **the day after ~** pasado mañana; **~ night** mañana por la noche. ◇ *adv* mañana.

ton [tʌn] (*pl inv* OR **-s**) *n* **-1.** [imperial] = 1016 kg *Br*, = 907,2 kg *Am*, ≃ tonelada *f*. **-2.** [metric] = 1000 kg, tonelada *f*. **-3.** *phr*: **to weigh a ~** *inf* pesar una tonelada; **to come down on sb like a ~ of bricks** [speak angrily] echar la gran bronca a alguien; [punish severely] dar un buen escarmiento a alguien.
♦ **tons** *npl inf*: **~s (of)** un montón (de).

tonal ['təʊnl] *adj* tonal.

tone [təʊn] *n* **-1.** [gen] tono *m*. **-2.** [on phone] señal *f*. **-3.** *phr*: **to lower the ~ of** dar mal tono a.
♦ **tone down** *vt sep* suavizar, moderar.
♦ **tone in** *vi*: **to ~ in (with)** ir bien OR armonizar (con).
♦ **tone up** *vt sep* poner en forma.

tone-deaf *adj* que no tiene (buen) oído.

toner ['təʊnə] *n* **-1.** [for photocopier, printer] virador *m*. **-2.** [cosmetic] tónico *m*.

Tonga ['tɒŋgə] *n* Tonga.

tongs [tɒŋz] *npl* [for coal] tenazas *fpl*; [for sugar] pinzas *fpl*, tenacillas *fpl*.

tongue [tʌŋ] *n* **-1.** [gen] lengua *f*; **to have one's ~ in one's cheek** *inf* no ir en serio; **to hold one's ~** *fig* quedarse callado(da); **~s will wag** seguro que la gente murmurará. **-2.** [of shoe] lengüeta *f*.

tongue-in-cheek *adj*: **it was only ~** no iba en serio.

tongue-tied [-,taɪd] *adj* incapaz de hablar (*por timidez o nervios*).

tongue twister [-,twɪstə] *n* trabalenguas *m inv*.

tonic ['tɒnɪk] *n* **-1.** [gen] tónico *m*. **-2.** [tonic water] tónica *f*.

tonic water *n* agua *f* tónica.

tonight [tə'naɪt] *n* esta noche *f*. ◇ *adv* esta noche.

tonnage ['tʌnɪdʒ] *n* tonelaje *m*.

tonne [tʌn] (*pl inv* OR **-s**) *n* tonelada *f* métrica.

tonsil ['tɒnsl] *n* amígdala *f*.

tonsil(l)itis [ˌtɒnsɪ'laɪtɪs] *n* (U) amigdalitis *f inv*.

too [tuː] *adv* **-1.** [also] también. **-2.** [excessively] demasiado; ~ **much** demasiado; ~ **many things** demasiadas cosas; **it finished all** OR **only** ~ **soon** terminó demasiado pronto; **I'd be only** ~ **happy to help** me encantaría ayudarte; **not** ~ no muy.

took [tʊk] *pt* → **take**.

tool [tuːl] *n* **-1.** [implement] herramienta *f*; **garden** ~**s** útiles *mpl* del jardín; **to down** ~**s** *Br* dejar de trabajar como protesta. **-2.** *fig* [means] instrumento *m*; **the** ~**s of one's trade** los instrumentos de trabajo de uno.
◆ **tool around** *vi Am inf* perder el tiempo, entretenerse.

tool bar *n* COMPUT barra *f* de herramientas.

tool box *n* caja *f* de herramientas.

tool kit *n* juego *m* de herramientas.

toot [tuːt] ◇ *n* bocinazo *m*. ◇ *vt* tocar. ◇ *vi* tocar la bocina.

tooth [tuːθ] (*pl* **teeth**) *n* **-1.** [in mouth, of saw, gear wheel] diente *m*; **to be (a bit) long in the** ~ **for sthg** *Br pej* ser ya (un poco) mayorcito para algo; **to be fed up to the back teeth with sthg** *Br inf* estar hasta la coronilla de algo; **to grit one's teeth** apretar los dientes; **to lie through one's teeth** mentir como un bellaco. **-2.** [of comb] púa *f*.

toothache ['tuːθeɪk] *n* dolor *m* de muelas.

toothbrush ['tuːθbrʌʃ] *n* cepillo *m* de dientes.

toothless ['tuːθlɪs] *adj* desdentado(da).

toothpaste ['tuːθpeɪst] *n* pasta *f* de dientes.

toothpick ['tuːθpɪk] *n* palillo *m*.

tooth powder *n* polvos *mpl* dentífricos.

tootle ['tuːtl] *vi inf* [move unhurriedly]: **to** ~ **off** irse sin prisas.

top [tɒp] (*pt* & *pp* **-ped**, *cont* **-ping**) ◇ *adj* **-1.** [highest - step, floor] de arriba; [- object on pile] de encima. **-2.** [most important, successful] importante; **she got the** ~ **mark** sacó la mejor nota. **-3.** [maximum] máximo(ma).
◇ *n* **-1.** [highest point] parte *f* superior OR de arriba; [of list] cabeza *f*, principio *m*; [of tree] copa *f*; [of hill, mountain] cumbre *f*, cima *f*; **on** ~ encima; **to go over the** ~ *Br* pasarse (de la raya); **at the** ~ **of one's voice** a voz en grito. **-2.** [lid, cap - of jar, box] tapa *f*; [- of bottle, tube] tapón *m*; [- of pen] capuchón *m*. **-3.** [upper side] superficie *f*. **-4.** [blouse] blusa *f*; [T-shirt] camiseta *f*; [of pyjamas] parte *f* de arriba. **-5.** [toy] peonza *f*. **-6.** [most important level] cúpula *f*. **-7.** [of league, table, scale] cabeza *f*.
◇ *vt* **-1.** [be first in] estar a la cabeza de. **-2.** [better] superar. **-3.** [exceed] exceder.

◆ **on top of** *prep* **-1.** [in space] encima de. **-2.** [in addition to] además de; **on** ~ **of that** por si fuera poco. **-3.** [in control of]: **to be on** ~ **of sthg** tener algo bajo control. **-4.** *phr*: **to get on** ~ **of sb** abrumar a alguien.

◆ **top up** *Br*, **top off** *Am vt sep* volver a llenar.

topaz ['təʊpæz] *n* topacio *m*.

top brass *n* (U) *inf*: **the** ~ los altos cargos, los mandamases.

topcoat ['tɒpkəʊt] *n* **-1.** [item of clothing] abrigo *m*. **-2.** [paint] última mano *f* (de pintura).

top dog *n inf* mandamás *m y f*.

top-flight *adj inf* de altos vuelos.

top floor *n* último piso *m*.

top gear *n* directa *f*.

top hat *n* chistera *f*, sombrero *m* de copa.

top-heavy *adj* demasiado pesado(da) en la parte de arriba.

topic ['tɒpɪk] *n* tema *m*, asunto *m*.

topical ['tɒpɪkl] *adj* de actualidad, actual.

topknot ['tɒpnɒt] *n* [in hair] moño *m*.

topless ['tɒplɪs] *adj* en topless.

top-level *adj* de alto nivel.

topmost ['tɒpməʊst] *adj* más alto(ta).

top-notch *adj inf* de primera.

topographer [tə'pɒɡrəfə˞] *n* topógrafo *m*, -fa *f*.

topography [tə'pɒɡrəfɪ] *n* topografía *f*.

topped [tɒpt] *adj*: ~ **by** OR **with sthg** con algo encima.

topping ['tɒpɪŋ] *n* capa *f*; **with a** ~ **of cream** cubierto de nata.

topple ['tɒpl] ◇ *vt* [government, pile] derribar; [president] derrocar. ◇ *vi* venirse abajo.
◆ **topple over** *vi* venirse abajo.

top-ranking [-'ræŋkɪŋ] *adj* de alto nivel.

TOPS [tɒps] (*abbr of* **Training Opportunities Scheme**) *n* programa de formación profesional del gobierno británico.

top-secret *adj* sumamente secreto (sumamente secreta).

top-security *adj* de máxima seguridad.

topsoil ['tɒpsɔɪl] *n* capa *f* superficial del suelo.

topspin ['tɒpspɪn] *n* TENNIS liftado *m*.

topsy-turvy [ˌtɒpsɪ'tɜːvɪ] ◇ *adj* **-1.** [messy] patas arriba. **-2.** [haywire] loco(ca). ◇ *adv* [messily] en desorden, de cualquier manera.

tor [tɔː˞] *n* [hill] *colina alta y rocosa típica del suroeste de Inglaterra*.

torch [tɔːtʃ] *n* **-1.** *Br* [electric] linterna *f*. **-2.** [burning] antorcha *f*.

tore [tɔː˞] *pt* → **tear²**.

torment [*n* 'tɔːment, *vb* tɔː'ment] ◇ *n* tormento *m*. ◇ *vt* **-1.** [worry greatly] atormentar. **-2.** [annoy] fastidiar.

tormentor [tɔː'mentər] *n* hostigador *m*, -ra *f*.

torn [tɔːn] *pp* → tear².

tornado [tɔː'neɪdəʊ] (*pl* **-es** OR **-s**) *n* tornado *m*.

Toronto [tə'rɒntəʊ] *n* Toronto.

torpedo [tɔː'piːdəʊ] (*pl* **-es**) ◇ *n* torpedo *m*. ◇ *vt* torpedear.

torpedo boat *n* torpedero *m*.

torpor ['tɔːpə*ʳ*] *n* apatía *f*.

torque [tɔːk] *n* par *m* de torsión.

torrent ['tɒrənt] *n* torrente *m*.

torrential [tə'renʃl] *adj* torrencial.

torrid ['tɒrɪd] *adj* [hot] tórrido(da); *fig* [passionate] apasionado(da).

torso ['tɔːsəʊ] (*pl* **-s**) *n* torso *m*.

tortoise ['tɔːtəs] *n* tortuga *f* (de tierra).

tortoiseshell ['tɔːtəʃel] ◇ *adj*: ~ **cat** gato *m* pardo atigrado. ◇ *n* (*U*) [material] carey *m*, concha *f*. ◇ *comp* de carey OR concha.

tortuous ['tɔːtʃʊəs] *adj* **-1.** [twisting] tortuoso(sa). **-2.** [over-complicated] enrevesado(da), retorcido(da).

torture ['tɔːtʃə*ʳ*] ◇ *n* tortura *f*. ◇ *vt* torturar.

torturer ['tɔːtʃərə*ʳ*] *n* torturador *m*, -ra *f*.

Tory ['tɔːrɪ] (*pl* **-ies**) ◇ *adj* tory, del partido conservador (británico). ◇ *n* tory *m* y *f*, miembro *m* del partido conservador (británico).

toss [tɒs] ◇ *vt* **-1.** [throw carelessly] tirar. **-2.** [move from side to side - head, boat] sacudir. **-3.** [salad] remover; [pancake] darle la vuelta en el aire. **-4.** [coin]: **to ~ a coin** echar a cara o cruz. ◇ *vi* **-1.** [with coin] echar a cara o cruz. **-2.** [move rapidly]: **to ~ and turn** dar vueltas (en la cama). ◇ *n* **-1.** [of coin] tirada *f*. **-2.** [of head] sacudida *f*.

◆ **toss up** *vi* jugar a cara o cruz.

toss-up *n inf*: it's a ~ whether they win or lose igual ganan que pierden.

tot [tɒt] (*pt* & *pp* **-ted**, *cont* **-ting**) *n* **-1.** *inf* [small child] nene *m*, nena *f*. **-2.** [of drink] trago *m*.

◆ **tot up** *vt sep inf* sumar.

total ['təʊtl] (*Br pt* & *pp* **-led**, *cont* **-ling**, *Am pt* & *pp* **-ed**, *cont* **-ing**) ◇ *adj* total. ◇ *n* total *m*; **in ~** en total. ◇ *vt* **-1.** [add up] sumar. **-2.** *Am inf* [wreck] dejar hecho una ruina. ◇ *vi* [amount to] ascender a.

totalitarian [,təʊtælɪ'teərɪən] *adj* totalitario(ria).

totality [təʊ'tælətɪ] *n* totalidad *f*.

totally ['təʊtəlɪ] *adv* [entirely] totalmente.

tote bag [təʊt-] *n Am* bolsa *f* (de la compra).

totem pole ['təʊtəm-] *n* tótem *m*.

toto ['təʊtəʊ]

◆ **in toto** *adv fml* totalmente.

totter ['tɒtə*ʳ*] *vi lit* & *fig* tambalearse.

toucan ['tuːkən] *n* tucán *m*.

touch [tʌtʃ] ◇ *n* **-1.** [sense, act of feeling] tacto *m*. **-2.** [detail, skill, knack] toque *m*; **to put the finishing ~es to sthg** dar el último toque a algo. **-3.** [contact]: **to get/keep in ~ (with)** ponerse/mantenerse en contacto (con); **to lose ~ (with)** perder el contacto (con); **to be out of ~ with** no estar al tanto de. **-4.** SPORT: **in ~** fuera de banda. **-5.** [small amount]: **a ~** un poquito. **-6.** *phr*: **to be ~ and go** ser dudoso OR poco seguro; **to be a soft ~** no saber decir que no. ◇ *vt* **-1.** [gen] tocar. **-2.** [emotionally] conmover. ◇ *vi* **-1.** [with fingers etc] tocar. **-2.** [be in contact] tocarse.

◆ **a touch** *adv* [rather] un poco.

◆ **touch down** *vi* [plane] aterrizar, tomar tierra.

◆ **touch on** *vt fus* tocar, tratar por encima.

touch-and-go *adj* dudoso(sa), poco seguro (poco segura).

touchdown ['tʌtʃdaʊn] *n* **-1.** [of plane] aterrizaje *m*. **-2.** [in American football] ensayo *m*.

touched [tʌtʃt] *adj* **-1.** [grateful] emocionado(da). **-2.** *inf* [slightly mad] tocado(da).

touching ['tʌtʃɪŋ] *adj* conmovedor(ra).

touch judge *n* RUGBY juez *m* de línea.

touchline ['tʌtʃlaɪn] *n* línea *f* de banda.

touchpaper ['tʌtʃ,peɪpə*ʳ*] *n* mecha *f* (*de fuego artificial*).

touch-type *vi* mecanografiar al tacto.

touchy ['tʌtʃɪ] (*compar* **-ier**, *superl* **-iest**) *adj* **-1.** [person]: ~ **(about)** susceptible (con). **-2.** [subject, question] delicado(da).

tough [tʌf] *adj* **-1.** [resilient] fuerte. **-2.** [hard-wearing] resistente. **-3.** [meat, regulations, policies] duro(ra). **-4.** [difficult to deal with] difícil. **-5.** [rough - area] peligroso(sa). **-6.** *inf* [unfortunate] injusto(ta); ~ **luck** mala suerte.

toughen ['tʌfn] *vt* endurecer.

toughened ['tʌfnd] *adj* endurecido(da).

toughness ['tʌfnɪs] *n* (*U*) **-1.** [of character, material] resistencia *f*. **-2.** [of meat, regulations, policies] dureza *f*. **-3.** [of problem, decision] dificultad *f*.

toupee ['tuːpeɪ] *n* peluquín *m*.

tour [tʊə*ʳ*] ◇ *n* **-1.** [long journey] viaje *m* largo. **-2.** [of pop group etc] gira *f*. **-3.** [for sightseeing] recorrido *m*, visita *f*. ◇ *vt* [museum] visitar; [country] recorrer, viajar por. ◇ *vi* estar de gira; **to ~ round sthg** viajar por OR recorrer algo.

tourer ['tʊərəʳ] *n* coche *m* grande descapotable.

touring ['tʊərɪŋ] ◇ *adj* [exhibition] itinerante; [theatre, music group] que va de gira. ◇ *n* viajes *mpl* turísticos; **to go ~** hacer turismo.

tourism ['tʊərɪzm] *n* turismo *m*.

tourist ['tʊərɪst] *n* turista *m* y *f*.

tourist class *n* clase *f* turista.

tourist (information) office *n* oficina *f* de turismo.

touristy ['tʊərɪstɪ] *adj pej* demasiado turístico(ca).

tournament ['tɔːnəmənt] *n* torneo *m*.

tourniquet ['tʊənɪkeɪ] *n* torniquete *m*.

tour operator *n* touroperador *m*, operador *m* turístico.

tousle ['taʊzl] *vt* despeinar, alborotar.

tout [taʊt] ◇ *n* revendedor *m*, -ra *f*. ◇ *vt* revender. ◇ *vi*: **to ~ for sthg** solicitar algo.

tow [təʊ] ◇ *n*: **to give sb a ~** remolcar a alguien; **on ~** *Br* [car] a remolque; **in ~ with sb** acompañado de alguien. ◇ *vt* remolcar.

towards *Br* [tə'wɔːdz], **toward** *Am* [tə'wɔːd] *prep* **-1.** [gen] hacia. **-2.** [for the purpose or benefit of] para; **efforts ~ peace** esfuerzos encaminados hacia la paz; **£20 ~ the blind** 20 libras para los ciegos.

towaway zone ['təʊəweɪ-] *n* *Am* ≃ zona *f* de estacionamiento prohibido.

towbar ['təʊbɑː] *n* barra *f* de remolque.

towel ['taʊəl] *n* toalla *f*.

towelling *Br*, **toweling** *Am* ['taʊəlɪŋ] ◇ *n* (*U*) (tejido *m* de) toalla *f*. ◇ *comp* de toalla.

towel rail *n* toallero *m*.

tower ['taʊəʳ] ◇ *n* torre *f*; **a ~ of strength** *Br* un firme apoyo OR pilar. ◇ *vi*: **to ~ (over sthg)** elevarse (por encima de algo); **to ~ over sb** ser mucho más alto(ta) que alguien.

tower block *n* *Br* bloque *m* (*de pisos u oficinas*).

towering ['taʊərɪŋ] *adj* altísimo(ma).

town [taʊn] *n* **-1.** [gen] ciudad *f*; [smaller] pueblo *m*. **-2.** [centre of town, city] centro *m* de la ciudad; **to go out on the ~** irse de juerga; **to go to ~** *fig* [to put in a lot of effort] emplearse a fondo; [spend a lot of money] tirar la casa por la ventana.

town centre *n* centro *m* (de la ciudad).

town clerk *n* secretario del ayuntamiento *m*, secretaria del ayuntamiento *f*.

town council *n* ayuntamiento *m*.

town hall *n* ayuntamiento *m*.

town house *n* [fashionable house] casa *f* lujosa (*de un barrio alto*).

town plan *n* plano *m* de la ciudad.

town planner *n* urbanista *m* y *f*.

town planning *n* **-1.** [study] urbanismo *m*. **-2.** [practice] planificación *f* urbanística.

townsfolk ['taʊnzfəʊk], **townspeople** ['taʊnz,piːpl] *npl*: **the ~** los habitantes (*de una ciudad*), los ciudadanos.

township ['taʊnʃɪp] *n* **-1.** [in South Africa] zona urbana asignada por el gobierno para la población negra. **-2.** [in US] ≃ municipio *m*.

towpath ['təʊpɑːθ, *pl* -pɑːðz] *n* camino *m* de sirga.

towrope ['təʊrəʊp] *n* cable *m* de remolque.

tow truck *n* *Am* (coche *m*) grúa *f*.

toxic ['tɒksɪk] *adj* tóxico(ca).

toxin ['tɒksɪn] *n* toxina *f*.

toy [tɔɪ] *n* juguete *m*.
◆ **toy with** *vt fus* [idea] acariciar; [food, coin etc] jugetear con.

toy boy *n* *inf* joven amante de una mujer mucho mayor que él.

toy shop *n* juguetería *f*.

trace [treɪs] ◇ *n* **-1.** [evidence, remains] rastro *m*, huella *f*; **without ~** sin dejar rastro. **-2.** [small amount] pizca *f*. ◇ *vt* **-1.** [find] localizar, encontrar. **-2.** [follow progress of] describir. **-3.** [on paper] calcar.

trace element *n* CHEM oligoelemento *m*.

tracer bullet ['treɪsəʳ-] *n* bala *f* trazadora.

tracing ['treɪsɪŋ] *n* [on paper] calco *m*.

tracing paper *n* (*U*) papel *m* de calcar.

track [træk] ◇ *n* **-1.** [path] sendero *m*; **off the beaten ~** apartado(da), aislado(da). **-2.** SPORT pista *f*. **-3.** RAIL vía *f*. **-4.** [mark, trace] rastro *m*, huella *f*; **to hide** OR **cover one's ~s** no dejar rastro; **to stop dead in one's ~s** pararse en seco. **-5.** [on record, tape] canción *f*. **-6.** *phr*: **to keep/lose ~ of sb** no perder/perder la pista a alguien; **to lose/keep ~ of events** perder el hilo de/seguir los acontecimientos; **to be on the right/wrong ~** ir por el buen/mal camino.
◇ *vt* **-1.** [follow tracks of] rastrear, seguir la pista de. **-2.** [with radar] seguir la trayectoria de.
◇ *vi* [camera etc] hacer un travelling.
◆ **track down** *vt sep* localizar.

trackball ['trækbɔːl] *n* COMPUT trackball *m*, esfera *f* de arrastre OR de desplazamiento.

tracker dog ['trækəʳ-] *n* perro *m* rastreador.

track event *n* prueba *f* de atletismo (en pista).

tracking station ['trækɪŋ-] *n* estación *f* de seguimiento.

track record *n* historial *m*.

track shoes *npl* zapatillas *fpl* de atletismo.

tracksuit ['træksuːt] *n* chandal *m*.

tract [trækt] *n* **-1.** [pamphlet] artículo *m* breve. **-2.** [of land, forest] extensión *f*. **-3.** MED: digestive ~ aparato *m* digestivo.

traction ['trækʃn] *n* tracción *f*; **to have one's leg in** ~ tener la pierna escayolada en alto.

traction engine *n* locomotora *f* de tracción.

tractor ['træktə*r*] *n* tractor *m*.

tractor-trailer *n Am* camión *m* articulado.

trade [treɪd] ◇ *n* **-1.** (*U*) [commerce] comercio *m*. **-2.** [job] oficio *m*; **by** ~ de oficio. ◇ *vt* [exchange]: **to** ~ **sthg (for)** cambiar algo (por). ◇ *vi* **-1.** COMM: **to** ~ **(with)** comerciar (con). **-2.** *Am* [shop]: **to** ~ **at** OR **with** hacer sus compras en.

◆ **trade in** *vt sep* [exchange] dar como entrada.

trade barrier *n* barrera *f* comercial.

trade deficit *n* déficit *m* (en la balanza) comercial.

trade discount *n* descuento *m* comercial.

trade fair *n* feria *f* de muestras.

trade gap *n* déficit *m* (en la balanza) comercial.

trade-in *n* artículo usado que se entrega como entrada al comprar un artículo nuevo.

trademark ['treɪdmɑːk] *n* **-1.** COMM marca *f* comercial. **-2.** *fig* [characteristic] rasgo *m* característico.

trade name *n* COMM nombre *m* comercial.

trade-off *n* equilibrio *m*.

trade price *n* precio *m* al por mayor.

trader ['treɪdə*r*] *n* comerciante *m y f*.

trade route *n* ruta *f* comercial.

trade secret *n* secreto *m* comercial.

tradesman ['treɪdzmən] (*pl* **-men** [-mən]) *n* [trader] comerciante *m*; [shopkeeper] tendero *m*.

tradespeople ['treɪdz,piːpl] *npl* comerciantes *mpl y fpl*.

trade(s) union *n Br* sindicato *m*.

Trades Union Congress *n Br*: **the** ~ *la asociación británica de sindicatos*.

trade(s) unionist *n Br* sindicalista *m y f*.

trade wind *n* NAUT viento *m* alisio.

trading ['treɪdɪŋ] *n* (*U*) comercio *m*.

trading estate *n Br* polígono *m* industrial.

trading stamp *n* cupón *m* del ahorro.

tradition [trə'dɪʃn] *n* tradición *f*.

traditional [trə'dɪʃənl] *adj* tradicional.

traditionally [trə'dɪʃnəlɪ] *adv* tradicionalmente.

traffic ['træfɪk] (*pt* & *pp* **-ked**, *cont* **-king**) ◇ *n* **-1.** [vehicles] tráfico *m*. **-2.** [illegal trade]: ~ **(in)** tráfico *m* (de). ◇ *vi*: **to** ~ **in** traficar con.

traffic circle *n Am* glorieta *f*.

traffic island *n* refugio *m*.

traffic jam *n* embotellamiento *m*, atasco *m*.

trafficker ['træfɪkə*r*] *n*: ~ **(in)** traficante *m y f* (de).

traffic lights *npl* semáforos *mpl*.

traffic offence *Br*, **traffic violation** *Am n* infracción *f* de tráfico.

traffic sign *n* señal *f* de tráfico.

traffic violation *Am* = **traffic offence**.

traffic warden *n Br* ≃ guardia *m y f* de tráfico.

tragedy ['trædʒədɪ] (*pl* **-ies**) *n* tragedia *f*.

tragic ['trædʒɪk] *adj* trágico(ca).

tragically ['trædʒɪklɪ] *adv* trágicamente.

trail [treɪl] ◇ *n* **-1.** [path] sendero *m*, camino *m*; **to blaze a** ~ *fig* marcar la pauta. **-2.** [trace, track] rastro *m*, huellas *fpl*; **on the** ~ **of sb/sthg** seguir la pista de alguien/algo. ◇ *vt* **-1.** [drag] arrastrar. **-2.** [lose to] ir por detrás de. ◇ *vi* **-1.** [drag] arrastrarse. **-2.** [move slowly] andar con desgana. **-3.** [lose] ir perdiendo.

◆ **trail away**, **trail off** *vi* apagarse.

trailblazing ['treɪl,bleɪzɪŋ] *adj* pionero(ra).

trailer ['treɪlə*r*] *n* **-1.** [vehicle for luggage] remolque *m*. **-2.** [for living in] roulotte *m*, caravana *f*. **-3.** CINEMA trailer *m*.

trailer park *n Am* camping *m* para roulottes OR caravanas.

train [treɪn] ◇ *n* **-1.** RAIL tren *m*. **-2.** [of dress] cola *f*.
◇ *vt* **-1.** [teach]: **to** ~ **sb (to do sthg)** enseñar a alguien (a hacer algo); **to** ~ **sb in sthg** preparar a alguien para algo. **-2.** [for job]: **to** ~ **sb (as sthg)** formar OR preparar a alguien (como algo). **-3.** SPORT: **to** ~ **sb (for)** entrenar a alguien (para). **-4.** [direct growth of] guiar. **-5.** [aim - gun] apuntar; [- camera] enfocar.
◇ *vi* **-1.** [for job] estudiar, prepararse; **to** ~ **as** formarse OR prepararse como; **to** ~ **as a doctor** estudiar medicina. **-2.** SPORT: **to** ~ **(for)** entrenarse (para).

trained [treɪnd] *adj* cualificado(da).

trainee [treɪ'niː] ◇ *adj* en período de prácticas. ◇ *n* aprendiz *m*, -za *f*, persona *f* que está en período de prácticas.

trainer ['treɪnəʳ] n -**1.** [of animals] amaestrador m, -ra f. -**2.** SPORT entrenador m, -ra f.
◆ **trainers** npl Br zapatillas fpl de deporte.

training ['treɪnɪŋ] n (U) -**1.** [for job]: ~ (in) formación f OR preparación f (para). -**2.** SPORT entrenamiento m.

training college n Br [gen] centro m de formación especializada; [for teachers] escuela f normal.

training course n cursillo m de formación.

training shoes npl Br zapatillas fpl de deporte.

train of thought n hilo m del razonamiento.

train set n tren m eléctrico de juguete.

train spotter [-,spɒtəʳ] n aficionado a los trenes que en una estación apunta el número de las locomotoras al pasar.

train station n Am estación f de ferrocarril.

traipse [treɪps] vi andar con desgana.

trait [treɪt] n rasgo m, característica f.

traitor ['treɪtəʳ] n: ~ (to) traidor m, -ra f (a).

trajectory [trə'dʒektərɪ] (pl -ies) n trayectoria f.

tram [træm], **tramcar** ['træmkɑːʳ] n Br tranvía m.

tramlines ['træmlaɪnz] npl Br -**1.** [for trams] vías fpl de tranvía. -**2.** TENNIS líneas fpl de banda.

tramp [træmp] ◇ n -**1.** [homeless person] vagabundo m, -da f. -**2.** Am inf [woman] fulana f. ◇ vt recorrer pesadamente. ◇ vi andar pesadamente.

trample ['træmpl] ◇ vt pisar, pisotear. ◇ vi -**1.** [tread]: to ~ on sthg pisar algo. -**2.** fig [act cruelly]: to ~ on sb pisar OR pisotear a alguien.

trampoline ['træmpəliːn] n cama f elástica.

trance [trɑːns] n trance m; in a ~ en trance.

tranquil ['træŋkwɪl] adj literary tranquilo(la), apacible.

tranquility Am = tranquillity.

tranquilize Am = tranquillize.

tranquilizer Am = tranquillizer.

tranquillity Br, **tranquility** Am [træŋ'kwɪlətɪ] n tranquilidad f.

tranquillize, **-ise** Br, **tranquilize** Am ['træŋkwɪlaɪz] vt tranquilizar.

tranquillizer Br, **tranquilizer** Am ['træŋkwɪlaɪzəʳ] n tranquilizante m.

transact [træn'zækt] vt fml hacer, llevar a cabo.

transaction [træn'zækʃn] n transacción f.

transatlantic [,trænzət'læntɪk] adj transatlántico(ca).

transceiver [træn'siːvəʳ] n transmisor-receptor m de radio.

transcend [træn'send] vt fml ir más allá de, superar.

transcendental meditation [,trænsen-'dentl-] n meditación f transcendental.

transcribe [træn'skraɪb] vt transcribir.

transcript ['trænskrɪpt] n transcripción f.

transept ['trænsept] n crucero m.

transfer [n 'trænsfɜːʳ, vb træns'fɜːʳ] (pt & pp -red, cont -ring) ◇ n -**1.** [gen] transferencia f. -**2.** [for job] traslado m. -**3.** SPORT traspaso m. -**4.** [design] calcomanía f. -**5.** Am [ticket] billete válido para transbordar a otro autobús, tren etc.
◇ vt -**1.** [from one place to another] trasladar. -**2.** [from one person to another] transferir. -**3.** SPORT traspasar.
◇ vi -**1.** [to different job etc]: **he transferred to a different department** lo trasladaron a otro departamento. -**2.** SPORT: **he transferred to Spurs** fichó por el Spurs.

transferable [træns'fɜːrəbl] adj transferible.

transference ['trænsfərəns] n fml transferencia f.

transfer fee n Br SPORT traspaso m.

transfigure [træns'fɪgəʳ] vt literary transfigurar.

transfix [træns'fɪks] vt [immobilize] paralizar.

transform [træns'fɔːm] vt: **to ~ sthg/sb (into)** transformar algo/a alguien (en).

transformation [,trænsfə'meɪʃn] n transformación f.

transformer [træns'fɔːməʳ] n ELEC transformador m.

transfusion [træns'fuːʒn] n transfusión f.

transgress [træns'gres] fml ◇ vt [limit] traspasar; [law, rules] transgredir. ◇ vi cometer una transgresión.

transgression [træns'greʃn] n fml transgresión f.

transient ['trænzɪənt] ◇ adj fml [fleeting] transitorio(ria), pasajero(ra). ◇ n Am [person] viajero m, -ra f de paso.

transistor [træn'zɪstəʳ] n transistor m.

transistor radio n dated transistor m.

transit ['trænsɪt] n: in ~ de tránsito.

transit camp n campamento m provisional.

transition [træn'zɪʃn] n: ~ (from sthg to sthg) transición f (de algo a algo); in ~ en transición.

transitional [træn'zɪʃənl] adj de transición.

transitive ['trænzɪtɪv] *adj* GRAMM transitivo(va).

transit lounge *n* sala *f* de tránsitos.

transitory ['trænzɪtrɪ] *adj* transitorio(ria).

translate [træns'leɪt] ◇ *vt* **-1.** [languages] traducir. **-2.** [transform]: **to ~ sthg into** convertir OR transformar algo en. ◇ *vi*: **it doesn't ~** no se puede traducir; **to ~ from sthg into** traducir de algo a.

translation [træns'leɪʃn] *n* traducción *f*.

translator [træns'leɪtə'] *n* traductor *m*, -ra *f*.

translucent [trænz'luːsnt] *adj literary* translúcido(da).

transmission [trænz'mɪʃn] *n* transmisión *f*.

transmit [trænz'mɪt] (*pt* & *pp* **-ted**, *cont* **-ting**) *vt* transmitir.

transmitter [trænz'mɪtə'] *n* ELECTRON transmisor *m*.

transparency [trans'pærənsɪ] (*pl* **-ies**) *n* transparencia *f*.

transparent [træns'pærənt] *adj* **-1.** [seethrough] transparente. **-2.** [obvious] claro(ra); **that's a ~ excuse** es claramente una excusa.

transpire [træn'spaɪə'] *fml* ◇ *vt*: **it ~s that** ... resulta que .... ◇ *vi* [happen] ocurrir, pasar.

transplant [*n* 'trænsplɑːnt, *vb* træns'plɑːnt] ◇ *n* trasplante *m*. ◇ *vt* **-1.** [organ, seedlings] trasplantar. **-2.** [headquarters, workers] trasladar.

transport [*n* 'trænspɔːt, *vb* træn'spɔːt] ◇ *n* transporte *m*. ◇ *vt* transportar.

transportable [træn'spɔːtəbl] *adj* transportable.

transportation [,trænspɔː'teɪʃn] *n* transporte *m*.

transport cafe ['trænspɔːt-] *n Br* bar *m* de camioneros.

transporter [træn'spɔːtə'] *n* camión *m* para el transporte de vehículos.

transpose [træns'pəʊz] *vt* [change round] invertir.

transsexual [træns'sekʃʊəl] *n* transexual *m* y *f*.

transvestite [trænz'vestaɪt] *n* travestido *m*, -da *f*, travestí *m* y *f*.

trap [træp] (*pt* & *pp* **-ped**, *cont* **-ping**) ◇ *n* trampa *f*. ◇ *vt* **-1.** [catch - animals, birds] coger con trampa. **-2.** [trick] atrapar, engañar. **-3.** [in place, unpleasant situation]: **to be trapped in** estar atrapado(da) en. **-4.** [energy, heat] almacenar.

trapdoor [,træp'dɔːr] *n* [gen] trampilla *f*, trampa; THEATRE escotillón *m*.

trapeze [trə'piːz] *n* trapecio *m*.

trapper ['træpə'] *n* trampero *m*, -ra *f*.

trappings ['træpɪŋz] *npl* atributos *mpl*.

trash [træʃ] *n Am lit* & *fig* basura *f*.

trashcan ['træʃkæn] *n Am* cubo *m* de la basura.

trashy ['træʃɪ] (*compar* **-ier**, *superl* **-iest**) *adj inf* malísimo(ma), infame.

trauma ['trɔːmə] *n* trauma *m*.

traumatic [trɔː'mætɪk] *adj* traumático(ca).

traumatize, -ise ['trɔːmətaɪz], *vt* [shock] traumatizar.

travel ['trævl] (*Br pt* & *pp* **-led**, *cont* **-ling**, *Am pt* & *pp* **-ed**, *cont* **-ing**) ◇ *n* (*U*) viajes *mpl*; **I'm keen on ~** me gusta viajar. ◇ *vt* [place] viajar por; [distance] recorrer. ◇ *vi* viajar.

◆ **travels** *npl* viajes *mpl*.

travel agency *n* agencia *f* de viajes.

travel agent *n* empleado *m*, -da *f* de una agencia de viajes; **~'s** agencia *f* de viajes.

travel brochure *n* catálogo *m* turístico.

traveler *etc Am* = **traveller** *etc*.

travelled *Br*, **traveled** *Am* ['trævld] *adj* **-1.** [person] que ha viajado mucho. **-2.** [road, route] muy recorrido (muy recorrida).

traveller *Br*, **traveler** *Am* ['trævlə'] *n* **-1.** [person on journey] viajero *m*, -ra *f*. **-2.** [sales representative] viajante *m* y *f* (de comercio).

traveller's cheque *n* cheque *m* de viajero.

travelling *Br*, **traveling** *Am* ['trævlɪŋ] *adj* **-1.** [theatre, showman] ambulante. **-2.** [clock, time, allowance] de viaje.

travelling expenses *npl* gastos *mpl* OR dietas *fpl* de viaje.

travelling salesman *n* viajante *m* y *f* (de comercio).

travelogue, travelog *Am* ['trævəlɒg] *n* **-1.** [talk] conferencia *f* sobre un viaje. **-2.** [film] documental *m* sobre viajes.

travelsick ['trævəlsɪk] *adj* que se marea al viajar.

traverse ['trævəs, ,træ'vɜːs] *vt fml* atravesar.

travesty ['trævəstɪ] (*pl* **-ies**) *n* burda parodia *f*.

trawl [trɔːl] ◇ *n* [fishing net] red *f* barredera. ◇ *vt*: **to ~ sthg (for)** [fish] rastrear algo (en busca de). ◇ *vi*: **to ~ for** [fish] pescar al arrastre en busca de.

trawler ['trɔːlə'] *n* trainera *f*.

tray [treɪ] *n* bandeja *f*, charola *f Amer*.

treacherous ['tretʃərəs] *adj* **-1.** [plan, action] traicionero(ra); [person] traidor(ra). **-2.** [dangerous] peligroso(sa).

treachery ['tretʃərɪ] *n* traición *f*.

treacle ['triːkl] *n Br* melaza *f*.

tread [tred] (*pt* **trod,** *pp* **trodden**) ◇ *n* **-1.** [on tyre, shoe] banda *f*. **-2.** [sound of walking] pasos *mpl*, pisadas *fpl*; [way of walking] modo *m* de andar. ◇ *vt* [crush]: **to ~ sthg into** pisotear algo en. ◇ *vi* **-1.** [step]: **to ~ on sthg** pisar algo. **-2.** [walk] andar; **to ~ carefully** *fig* andar con pies de plomo.

treadle ['tredl] *n* pedal *m*.

treadmill ['tredmɪl] *n* **-1.** [wheel] rueda *f* de molino. **-2.** *fig* [dull routine] rutina *f*.

treas. *abbr of* **treasurer**.

treason ['triːzn] *n* traición *f*.

treasure ['treʒəʳ] ◇ *n lit* & *fig* tesoro *m*. ◇ *vt* guardar como oro en paño.

treasure hunt *n* juego *m* de la caza del tesoro.

treasurer ['treʒərəʳ] *n* tesorero *m*, -ra *f*.

treasure trove *n* JUR tesoro *m* escondido OR oculto.

treasury ['treʒərɪ] (*pl* **-ies**) *n* [room] *habitación donde se guarda el tesoro de un castillo, de una catedral etc.*
◆ **Treasury** *n*: **the Treasury** ≃ el Ministerio de Hacienda.

treasury bill *n* bono *m* del Tesoro.

treat [triːt] ◇ *vt* **-1.** [gen] tratar; **to ~ sb as/like** tratar a alguien como; **to ~ sthg as a joke** tomarse algo como si fuera broma. **-2.** [give sthg special]: **to ~ sb (to)** invitar a alguien (a). ◇ *n* [something special] regalo *m*; **he took me out to dinner as a ~** me invitó a cenar.

treatise ['triːtɪz] *n fml*: **~ (on)** tratado *m* (sobre).

treatment ['triːtmənt] *n* **-1.** MED tratamiento *m*. **-2.** [manner of dealing] trato *m*.

treaty ['triːtɪ] (*pl* **-ies**) *n* tratado *m*.

treble ['trebl] ◇ *adj* **-1.** MUS de tiple. **-2.** [with numbers] triple. ◇ *n* MUS [range, singer] tiple *m*. ◇ *vt* triplicar. ◇ *vi* triplicarse.

treble clef *n* clave *f* de sol.

tree [triː] *n* BOT & COMPUT árbol *m*; **to be barking up the wrong ~** equivocarse de medio a medio.

tree-lined *adj* bordeado(da) de árboles.

tree surgeon *n especialista en el cuidado de los árboles.*

treetop ['triːtɒp] *n* copa *f* (de árbol).

tree-trunk *n* tronco *m* (de árbol).

trek [trek] (*pt* & *pp* **-ked,** *cont* **-king**) ◇ *n* viaje *m* largo y difícil; **it's quite a ~** es toda una caminata. ◇ *vi*: **we trekked round the museums** nos pateamos los museos.

trellis ['trelɪs] *n* enrejado *m*, espaldera *f*.

tremble ['trembl] *vi* temblar.

tremendous [trɪ'mendəs] *adj* **-1.** [impressive, large] enorme, tremendo(da). **-2.** *inf* [really good] estupendo(da), magnífico(ca).

tremendously [trɪ'mendəslɪ] *adv* [impressively, hugely] enormemente.

tremor ['treməʳ] *n* **-1.** [of person, body, voice] estremecimiento *m*. **-2.** [small earthquake] temblor *m*, remezón *m Amer*.

tremulous ['tremjʊləs] *adj literary* [voice] trémulo(la); [smile] tímido(da).

trench [trentʃ] *n* **-1.** [narrow channel] zanja *f*. **-2.** MIL trinchera *f*.

trenchant ['trentʃənt] *adj fml* mordaz.

trench coat *n* trinchera *f*.

trench warfare *n* (*U*) guerra *f* de trincheras.

trend [trend] *n* [tendency] tendencia *f*; [fashion] moda *f*.

trendsetter ['trend,setəʳ] *n* iniciador *m*, -ra *f* de modas.

trendy ['trendɪ] (*compar* **-ier,** *superl* **-iest,** *pl* **-ies**) *inf* ◇ *adj* [person] moderno(na); [clothes] de moda. ◇ *n* moderno *m*, -na *f*.

trepidation [,trepɪ'deɪʃn] *n fml*: **in** OR **with ~** con ansiedad OR agitación.

trespass ['trespəs] *vi* entrar ilegalmente; "**no ~ing**" "prohibido el paso".

trespasser ['trespəsəʳ] *n* intruso *m*, -sa *f*; "**~s will be prosecuted**" "los intrusos serán sancionados por la ley".

trestle ['tresl] *n* caballete *m*.

trestle table *n* mesa *f* de caballete.

trial ['traɪəl] *n* **-1.** JUR juicio *m*, proceso *m*; **to be on ~ (for)** ser procesado(da) (por). **-2.** [test, experiment] prueba *f*; **on ~** de prueba; **by ~ and error** a base de probar. **-3.** [unpleasant experience] suplicio *m*, fastidio *m*; **~s and tribulations** tribulaciones *fpl*.

trial basis *n*: **on a ~** en período de prueba.

trial period *n* período *m* de prueba.

trial run *n* ensayo *m*.

trial-size(d) *adj* en tamaño de muestra.

triangle ['traɪæŋgl] *n* **-1.** GEOM & MUS triángulo *m*. **-2.** *Am* [set square] escuadra *f*, cartabón *m*.

triangular [traɪ'æŋgjʊləʳ] *adj* triangular.

triathlon [traɪ'æθlɒn] (*pl* **-s**) *n* triatlón *m*.

tribal ['traɪbl] *adj* tribal.

tribe [traɪb] *n* tribu *f*.

tribulation [,trɪbjʊ'leɪʃn] *n* → **trial**.

tribunal [traɪ'bjuːnl] *n* tribunal *m*.

tribune ['trɪbjuːn] *n* tribuno *m*.

tributary ['trɪbjʊtrɪ] (*pl* **-ies**) *n* afluente *m*.

tribute ['trɪbjuːt] *n* **-1.** [credit] tributo *m*; **to be a ~ to** hacer honor a; **to pay a ~ (to)**

hacer un homenaje (a). **-2.** (*U*) [respect, admiration]: **to pay ~ (to)** rendir homenaje (a).

trice [traɪs] *n*: **in a ~** en un dos por tres.

triceps ['traɪseps] (*pl inv* OR **-cepses**) *n* tríceps *m*.

trick [trɪk] ◇ *n* **-1.** [to deceive] truco *m*; [to trap] trampa *f*; [joke] broma *f*; **to play a ~ on sb** gastarle una broma a alguien. **-2.** [in magic] juego *m* (de manos). **-3.** [knack] truco *m*; **that should do the ~** eso es lo que necesitamos. ◇ *vt* engañar, timar; **to ~ sb into doing sthg** engañar a alguien para que haga algo. ◇ *comp* [joke] de broma.

trickery ['trɪkərɪ] *n* (*U*) engaño *m*, fraude *m*.

trickle ['trɪkl] ◇ *n* **-1.** [of liquid] hilo *m*. **-2.** [of people, things] sarta *f*, rosario *m*. ◇ *vi* **-1.** [liquid] resbalar (*formando un hilo*). **-2.** [people, things]: **to ~ in/out** llegar/salir poco a poco.

trick or treat *n* *costumbre infantil de ir de puerta en puerta la víspera de Todos los Santos en busca de golosinas.*

trick question *n* pega *f*, pregunta *f* capciosa.

tricky ['trɪkɪ] (*compar* **-ier**, *superl* **-iest**) *adj* [difficult] difícil, embromado(da) *Amer*.

tricycle ['traɪsɪkl] *n* triciclo *m*.

trident ['traɪdnt] *n* tridente *m*.

tried [traɪd] ◇ *pt & pp* → **try.** ◇ *adj*: **~ and tested** probado(da).

trier ['traɪər] *n*: **she's a ~** se esfuerza al máximo.

trifle ['traɪfl] ◇ *n* **-1.** *Br* CULIN *postre de bizcocho con gelatina, crema, frutas y nata.* **-2.** [unimportant thing] pequeñez *f*, nadería *f*.
◆ **a trifle** *adv fml* un poco, ligeramente.
◆ **trifle with** *vt fus* tratar sin respeto.

trifling ['traɪflɪŋ] *adj pej* trivial, insignificante.

trigger ['trɪgər] ◇ *n* [on gun] gatillo *m*. ◇ *vt* desencadenar, provocar.
◆ **trigger off** *vt sep* desencadenar, provocar.

trigonometry [,trɪgə'nɒmətrɪ] *n* trigonometría *f*.

trilby ['trɪlbɪ] (*pl* **-ies**) *n* *Br* sombrero *m* flexible OR de fieltro.

trill [trɪl] ◇ *n* trino *m*. ◇ *vi* [bird] trinar, gorjear; [woman] decir con voz cantarina.

trillions ['trɪljənz] *npl inf*: **~ (of)** montones *mpl* (de).

trilogy ['trɪlədʒɪ] (*pl* **-ies**) *n* trilogía *f*.

trim [trɪm] (*compar* **-mer**, *superl* **-mest**, *pt & pp* **-med**, *cont* **-ming**) ◇ *adj* **-1.** [neat and tidy] limpio y arreglado (limpia y arregla-

da). **-2.** [slim] esbelto(ta). ◇ *n* **-1.** [hair] recorte *m*; [- hedge] poda *f*. **-2.** [decoration] adorno *m*. ◇ *vt* **-1.** [nails, moustache] recortar, cortar. **-2.** [decorate]: **to ~ sthg (with)** adornar algo (con).
◆ **trim away, trim off** *vt sep* cortar.

trimmed [trɪmd] *adj*: **~ with** adornado(da) con.

trimmings ['trɪmɪŋz] *npl* **-1.** [on clothing] adornos *mpl*. **-2.** [with food] guarnición *f*.

Trinidad and Tobago ['trɪnɪdæd-] *n* Trinidad y Tobago.

Trinidadian [,trɪnɪ'dædɪən] ◇ *adj* de o relativo a Trinidad. ◇ *n* natural o habitante de Trinidad.

Trinity ['trɪnətɪ] *n* RELIG: **the ~** la Trinidad.

trinket ['trɪŋkɪt] *n* baratija *f*.

trio ['triːəʊ] (*pl* **-s**) *n* trío *m*.

trip [trɪp] (*pt & pp* **-ped**, *cont* **-ping**) ◇ *n* [gen & drugs sl] viaje *m*. ◇ *vt* [make stumble] hacer la zancadilla a. ◇ *vi* [stumble] tropezar, dar un tropezón; **to ~ over sthg** tropezar con algo.
◆ **trip up** *vt sep* **-1.** [make stumble] hacer la zancadilla a. **-2.** [catch out] coger a, pillar a.

tripartite [,traɪ'pɑːtaɪt] *adj fml* tripartito(ta).

tripe [traɪp] *n* (*U*) **-1.** CULIN callos *mpl*. **-2.** *inf* [nonsense] tonterías *fpl*, idioteces *fpl*.

triple ['trɪpl] ◇ *adj* triple. ◇ *vt* triplicar. ◇ *vi* triplicarse.

triple jump *n*: **the ~** el triple salto.

triplets ['trɪplɪts] *npl* trillizos *mpl*, **-zas** *fpl*, triates *mpl Amer*.

triplicate ['trɪplɪkət] ◇ *adj fml* triplicado(da). ◇ *n*: **in ~** por triplicado.

tripod ['traɪpɒd] *n* trípode *m*.

Tripoli ['trɪpəlɪ] *n* Trípoli.

tripper ['trɪpər] *n Br* excursionista *m y f*, turista *m y f*.

tripwire ['trɪpwaɪər] *n* cable *m* trampa.

trite [traɪt] *adj pej* trillado(da), manido(da).

triumph ['traɪəmf] ◇ *n* triunfo *m*. ◇ *vi*: **to ~ (over)** triunfar (sobre).

triumphal [traɪ'ʌmfl] *adj fml* triunfal.

triumphant [traɪ'ʌmfənt] *adj* [exultant] triunfante.

triumphantly [traɪ'ʌmfəntlɪ] *adv* triunfalmente.

triumvirate [traɪ'ʌmvɪrət] *n* HISTORY triunvirato *m*.

trivet ['trɪvɪt] *n* **-1.** [over fire] trébedes *fpl*. **-2.** [to protect table] salvamanteles *m inv*.

trivia ['trɪvɪə] *n* (*U*) trivialidades *fpl*.

trivial ['trɪvɪəl] *adj pej* trivial.

triviality [,trɪvɪ'ælətɪ] (*pl* **-ies**) *n* trivialidad *f*.

trivialize, -ise ['trɪvɪəlaɪz] *vt* trivializar.

trod [trɒd] *pt* → tread.

trodden ['trɒdn] ◇ *pp* → tread. ◇ *adj* hollado(da), pisado(da).

Trojan ['trəʊdʒən] ◇ *adj* HISTORY troyano(na). ◇ *n* HISTORY troyano *m*, -na *f*; **to work like a ~** *fig* trabajar como un negro.

troll [trəʊl] *n* gnomo *m*, duende *m*.

trolley ['trɒlɪ] (*pl* **trolleys**) *n* **-1.** *Br* [for shopping, food, drinks] carrito *m*. **-2.** *Am* [tram] tranvía *m*.

trolleybus ['trɒlɪbʌs] *n* trolebús *m*.

trombone [trɒm'bəʊn] *n* trombón *m*.

troop [truːp] ◇ *n* [of people] grupo *m*, bandada *f*; [of animals] manada *f*. ◇ *vi* ir en grupo.
◆ **troops** *npl* tropas *fpl*.

trooper ['truːpər] *n* **-1.** MIL soldado *m* de caballería. **-2.** *Am* [policeman] *miembro de la policía estatal*.

troopship ['truːpʃɪp] *n* buque *m* de transporte militar.

trophy ['trəʊfɪ] (*pl* **-ies**) *n* SPORT trofeo *m*.

tropical ['trɒpɪkl] *adj* tropical.

Tropic of Cancer ['trɒpɪk-] *n*: **the ~** el trópico de Cáncer.

Tropic of Capricorn ['trɒpɪk-] *n*: **the ~** el trópico de Capricornio.

tropics ['trɒpɪks] *npl*: **the ~** el trópico.

trot [trɒt] (*pt* & *pp* **-ted**, *cont* **-ting**) ◇ *n* **-1.** [of horse] trote *m*. **-2.** [of person] paso *m* rápido. ◇ *vi* **-1.** [horse] trotar. **-2.** [person] andar con pasos rápidos.
◆ **on the trot** *adv inf*: **three times on the ~** tres veces seguidas.
◆ **trot out** *vt sep pej*: **he trotted out the same old excuses** repitió las mismas excusas manidas.

Trotskyism ['trɒtskɪɪzm] *n* trotskismo *m*.

trotter ['trɒtər] *n* [pig's foot] pie *m* de cerdo.

trouble ['trʌbl] ◇ *n* (*U*) **-1.** [bother] molestia *f*; [difficulty, main problem] problema *m*; **would it be too much ~ to ask you to ...?** ¿tendría inconveniente en ...?; **to be in ~** tener problemas; **to take the ~ to do sthg** tomarse la molestia de hacer algo; **the ~ with sb/sthg is ...** lo malo de alguien/algo es ...; **to be asking for ~** estar buscándose problemas. **-2.** (*U*) [pain] dolor *m*; [illness] enfermedad *f*. **-3.** (*U*) [violence, unpleasantness] problemas *mpl*.
◇ *vt* **-1.** [worry, upset] preocupar. **-2.** [disturb, give pain to] molestar.
◆ **troubles** *npl* **-1.** [problems, worries] problemas *mpl*, preocupaciones *fpl*. **-2.** POL conflicto *m*.

troubled ['trʌbld] *adj* **-1.** [worried, upset] preocupado(da). **-2.** [disturbed, problematic] agitado(da), turbulento(ta).

trouble-free *adj* sin problemas.

troublemaker ['trʌbl,meɪkər] *n* alborotador *m*, -ra *f*.

troubleshooter ['trʌbl,ʃuːtər] *n* [for machines] *especialista en la localización y reparación de averías*; [in organizations] *persona contratada para resolver problemas*.

troublesome ['trʌblsəm] *adj* molesto(ta), fregado(da) *Amer*.

trouble spot *n* lugar *m* OR punto *m* conflictivo.

trough [trɒf] *n* **-1.** [for drinking] abrevadero *m*; [for eating] comedero *m*. **-2.** [low point] punto *m* más bajo.

trounce [traʊns] *vt inf* dar una paliza a.

troupe [truːp] *n* compañía *f*.

trouser press ['traʊzər-] *n* prensa *f* para pantalones.

trousers ['traʊzəz] *npl* pantalones *mpl*.

trouser suit ['traʊzər-] *n* *Br* traje *m* pantalón.

trousseau ['truːsəʊ] (*pl* **-x** [-z] OR **-s**) *n* ajuar *m*.

trout [traʊt] (*pl inv* OR **-s**) *n* trucha *f*.

trove [trəʊv] → treasure trove.

trowel ['traʊəl] *n* **-1.** [for the garden] desplantador *m*. **-2.** [for cement, plaster] paleta *f*, palustre *m*.

truancy ['truːənsɪ] *n* el hacer novillos.

truant ['truːənt] *n* [child] alumno *m*, -na *f* que hace novillos; **to play ~** hacer novillos.

truce [truːs] *n*: **~ (between)** tregua *f* (entre).

truck [trʌk] ◇ *n* **-1.** [lorry] camión *m*. **-2.** RAIL vagón *m* de mercancías. ◇ *vt* *Am* transportar en camión.

truck driver *n* camionero *m*, -ra *f*.

trucker ['trʌkər] *n* *Am* camionero *m*, -ra *f*.

truck farm *n* *Am* *puesto de verduras y frutas para la venta*.

trucking ['trʌkɪŋ] *n* *Am* transporte *m* por camión.

truck stop *n* *Am* restaurante *m* de carretera.

truculent ['trʌkjʊlənt] *adj* agresivo(va), pendenciero(ra).

trudge [trʌdʒ] ◇ *n* caminata *f* pesada. ◇ *vi* caminar con dificultad.

true ['truː] *adj* **-1.** [gen] verdadero(ra); **it's ~** es verdad; **to come ~** hacerse realidad. **-2.** [genuine] auténtico(ca); [friend] de verdad. **-3.** [exact] exacto(ta). **-4.** [TECH - wheel] centrado(da); [- window-frame] nivelado(da).

true-life *adj* basado(da) en la realidad.

truffle ['trʌfl] *n* trufa *f*.

truism ['truːɪzm] *n* truismo *m*.

truly ['truːlɪ] *adv* verdaderamente; **yours** ~ le saluda atentamente.

trump [trʌmp] ◇ *n* triunfo *m* (*en cartas*). ◇ *vt* fallar.

trump card *n fig* baza *f*.

trumped-up ['trʌmpt-] *adj pej* inventado(da).

trumpet ['trʌmpɪt] ◇ *n* trompeta *f*. ◇ *vi* [elephant] barritar.

trumpeter ['trʌmpɪtər] *n* trompetista *m y f*, trompeta *m y f*.

truncate [trʌŋ'keɪt] *vt fml* truncar.

truncheon ['trʌntʃən] *n* porra *f*.

trundle ['trʌndl] ◇ *vt* empujar lentamente. ◇ *vi* rodar lentamente.

trunk [trʌŋk] *n* **-1.** [of tree, person] tronco *m*. **-2.** [of elephant] trompa *f*. **-3.** [box] baúl *m*. **-4.** *Am* [of car] maletero *m*, portaequipaje *m*, cajuela *f Amer*.

◆ **trunks** *npl* bañador *m* (de hombre).

trunk call *n Br* conferencia *f*, llamada *f* interurbana.

trunk road *n* ≃ carretera *f* nacional.

truss [trʌs] *n* **-1.** MED braguero *m*. **-2.** CONSTR armazón *m o f*.

trust [trʌst] ◇ *vt* **-1.** [believe in] confiar en. **-2.** [have confidence in]: **to** ~ **sb to do sthg** confiar en alguien para que haga algo. **-3.** [entrust]: **to** ~ **sb with sthg** confiar algo a alguien. **-4.** *fml* [hope] esperar. **-5.** [accept as safe, reliable] fiarse de. ◇ *n* **-1.** (*U*) [faith, responsibility]: ~ **(in)** confianza *f* (en); **to take sthg on** ~ creer algo sin cuestionarlo; **to put** OR **place one's** ~ **in** confiar en. **-2.** FIN trust *m*; **in** ~ en fideicomiso.

trust company *n* banco *m* fideicomisario.

trusted ['trʌstɪd] *adj* de confianza.

trustee [trʌs'tiː] *n* FIN & JUR fideicomisario *m*, -ria *f*.

trusteeship [,trʌs'tiːʃɪp] *n* fideicomiso *m*, administración *f* fiduciaria.

trust fund *n* fondo *m* de fideicomiso.

trusting ['trʌstɪŋ] *adj* confiado(da).

trustworthy ['trʌst,wɜːðɪ] *adj* digno(na) de confianza.

trusty ['trʌstɪ] (*compar* **-ier**, *superl* **-iest**) *adj hum* fiel.

truth [truːθ] *n* verdad *f*; **the** ~ la verdad; **in (all)** ~ en verdad, verdaderamente.

truth drug *n* suero *m* de la verdad.

truthful ['truːθfʊl] *adj* **-1.** [person] sincero(ra), honesto(ta). **-2.** [story] verídico(ca).

try [traɪ] (*pt & pp* **-ied**, *pl* **-ies**) ◇ *vt* **-1.** [attempt] intentar; **to** ~ **to do sthg** tratar de OR intentar hacer algo. **-2.** [sample, test] probar. **-3.** JUR [case] ver; [criminal] juzgar, procesar. **-4.** [put to the test - person] acabar con la paciencia de; [- patience] acabar con.
◇ *vi* intentar; **to** ~ **for sthg** tratar de conseguir algo.
◇ *n* **-1.** [attempt] intento *m*, tentativa *f*; **to have a** ~ **at sthg** intentar hacer algo. **-2.** [sample, test]: **to give sthg a** ~ probar algo. **-3.** RUGBY ensayo *m*.

◆ **try on** *vt sep* probarse.

◆ **try out** *vt sep* [car, machine] probar; [plan] poner a prueba.

trying ['traɪɪŋ] *adj* difícil, pesado(da).

try-out *n inf* prueba *f*.

tsar [zɑːr] *n* zar *m*.

T-shirt *n* camiseta *f*.

tsp. *abbr of* **teaspoon**.

T-square *n* escuadra *f* en forma de T.

TT *adj abbr of* **teetotal**.

Tuareg ['twɑːreg] *n* **-1.** [person] tuareg *m y f*. **-2.** [language] tuareg *m*.

tub [tʌb] *n* **-1.** [container - small] bote *m*; [- large] tina *f*. **-2.** *inf* [bath] bañera *f*.

tuba ['tjuːbə] *n* tuba *f*.

tubby ['tʌbɪ] (*compar* **-ier**, *superl* **-iest**) *adj inf* regordete(ta), rechoncho(cha).

tube [tjuːb] *n* **-1.** [cylinder, container] tubo *m*. **-2.** ANAT conducto *m*. **-3.** *Br* RAIL metro *m*; **by** ~ en metro.

tubeless ['tjuːblɪs] *adj* sin cámara.

tuber ['tjuːbər] *n* tubérculo *m*.

tuberculosis [tjuː,bɜːkjʊ'ləʊsɪs] *n* tuberculosis *f*.

tube station *n Br* estación *f* de metro.

tubing ['tjuːbɪŋ] *n* (*U*) tubos *mpl*.

tubular ['tjuːbjʊlər] *adj* tubular.

TUC *n abbr of* **Trades Union Congress**.

tuck [tʌk] ◇ *n* SEWING pliegue *m*. ◇ *vt* [place neatly] meter.

◆ **tuck away** *vt sep* **-1.** [money etc] guardar. **-2.** [village, house]: **to be ~ed away** estar escondido(da).

◆ **tuck in** ◇ *vt sep* **-1.** [person - in bed] arropar. **-2.** [clothes] meterse. ◇ *vi inf* comer con apetito.

◆ **tuck up** *vt sep* arropar.

tuck shop *n Br* confitería *f* (*emplazada cerca de un colegio*).

Tudor ['tjuːdər] ◇ *adj* **-1.** HISTORY de la dinastía Tudor. **-2.** ARCHIT de estilo Tudor. ◇ *n* Tudor *m y f*.

Tue., Tues. (*abbr of* **Tuesday**) mart.

Tuesday ['tjuːzdɪ] *n* martes *m inv*; *see also* **Saturday**.

tuft [tʌft] *n* [of hair] mechón *m*; [of grass] manojo *m*.

tug [tʌg] (*pt* & *pp* **-ged**, *cont* **-ging**) ◇ *n* **-1.** [pull] tirón *m*. **-2.** [boat] remolcador *m*. ◇ *vt* tirar de, dar un tirón a. ◇ *vi*: **to ~ (at)** tirar (de).

tugboat ['tʌgbəʊt] *n* remolcador *m*.

tug-of-love *n Br inf* lucha por la custodia de un niño.

tug-of-war *n* juego *m* de la cuerda (*en el que dos equipos compiten tirando de ella*).

tuition [tjuː'ɪʃn] *n* enseñanza *f*; **private ~** clases *fpl* particulares.

tulip ['tjuːlɪp] *n* tulipán *m*.

tulle [tjuːl] *n* tul *m*.

tumble ['tʌmbl] ◇ *vi* **-1.** [person] caerse (rodando). **-2.** [water] caer a borbotones. **-3.** *fig* [prices] caer en picado. **-4.** *inf fig* [become involved]: **to ~ into sthg** meterse de cabeza en algo. ◇ *n* caída *f*.

◆ **tumble to** *vt fus Br inf* caerse en la cuenta de, percatarse de.

tumbledown ['tʌmbldaʊn] *adj* ruinoso(sa).

tumble-dry *vt* secar en secadora.

tumble-dryer [-,draɪə^r] *n* secadora *f*.

tumbler ['tʌmblə^r] *n* [glass] vaso *m*.

tummy ['tʌmɪ] (*pl* **-ies**) *n inf* barriga *f*.

tumour *Br*, **tumor** *Am* ['tjuːmə^r] *n* tumor *m*.

tumult ['tjuːmʌlt] *n fml* tumulto *m*.

tumultuous ['tjuːmʌltjʊəs] *adj fml* tumultuoso(sa).

tuna [*Br* 'tjuːnə, *Am* 'tuːnə] (*pl inv* OR **-s**) *n* atún *m*.

tundra ['tʌndrə] *n* tundra *f*.

tune [tjuːn] ◇ *n* **-1.** [song, melody] melodía *f*. **-2.** [harmony]: **in ~** MUS afinado(da); **out of ~** MUS desafinado(da); **to be out of/in ~ (with sb/sthg)** *fig* no avenirse/avenirse (con alguien/algo); **to the ~ of** *fig* por la friolera de; **to change one's ~** *inf* cambiar de opinión. ◇ *vt* **-1.** MUS afinar. **-2.** RADIO & TV sintonizar; **~ the TV to BBC1** pon la BBC1 (en la tele). **-3.** [engine] poner a punto. ◇ *vi* RADIO & TV: **to ~ to sthg** sintonizar algo.

◆ **tune in** *vi* RADIO & TV: **to ~ in (to sthg)** sintonizar (algo).

◆ **tune up** *vi* MUS concertar OR afinar los instrumentos.

tuneful ['tjuːnfʊl] *adj* melodioso(sa).

tuneless ['tjuːnlɪs] *adj* poco melodioso(sa).

tuner ['tjuːnə^r] *n* **-1.** RADIO & TV sintonizador *m*. **-2.** MUS afinador *m*, -ra *f*.

tuner amplifier *n* amplificador *m* de audio.

tungsten ['tʌŋstən] ◇ *n* tungsteno *m*. ◇ *comp* de tungsteno.

tunic ['tjuːnɪk] *n* túnica *f*.

tuning fork ['tjuːnɪŋ-] *n* diapasón *m*.

Tunis ['tjuːnɪs] *n* Túnez (capital).

Tunisia [tjuː'nɪzɪə] *n* Túnez.

Tunisian [tjuː'nɪzɪən] ◇ *adj* tunecino(na). ◇ *n* [person] tunecino *m*, -na *f*.

tunnel ['tʌnl] (*Br pt* & *pp* **-led**, *cont* **-ling**, *Am pt* & *pp* **-ed**, *cont* **-ing**) ◇ *n* túnel *m*. ◇ *vi* hacer un túnel.

tunnel vision *n* MED visión *f* de túnel; *fig* & *pej* [narrow-mindedness] estrechez *f* de miras.

tunny ['tʌnɪ] (*pl inv* OR **-ies**) *n* [fish] atún *m*.

tuppence ['tʌpəns] *n Br dated* (moneda *f* de) dos peniques *mpl*.

turban ['tɜːbən] *n* turbante *m*.

turbid ['tɜːbɪd] *adj* [water] turbio(bia); [clouds] denso(sa).

turbine ['tɜːbaɪn] *n* turbina *f*.

turbo ['tɜːbəʊ] (*pl* **-s**) *n* turbina *f*.

turbocharged ['tɜːbəʊtʃɑːdʒd] *adj* provisto(ta) de turbina; [car] turbo (*inv*).

turbojet [,tɜːbəʊ'dʒet] *n* turborreactor *m*.

turboprop [,tɜːbəʊ'prɒp] *n* **-1.** [engine] turbopropulsor *m*. **-2.** [plane] avión *m* turbopropulsado.

turbot ['tɜːbət] (*pl inv* OR **-s**) *n* rodaballo *m*.

turbulence ['tɜːbjʊləns] *n* (*U*) *lit* & *fig* turbulencia *f*.

turbulent ['tɜːbjʊlənt] *adj lit* & *fig* turbulento(ta).

tureen [tə'riːn] *n* sopera *f*.

turf [tɜːf] (*pl* **-s** OR **turves**) ◇ *n* **-1.** [grass surface] césped *m*. **-2.** [clod] tepe *m*. ◇ *vt* encespedar, cubrir con césped.

◆ **turf out** *vt sep Br inf* [person] dar la patada a, echar; [old clothes] tirar.

turf accountant *n Br fml* corredor *m*, -ra *f* de apuestas.

turgid ['tɜːdʒɪd] *adj fml* [over-solemn] ampuloso(sa).

Turk [tɜːk] *n* turco *m*, -ca *f*.

Turkestan, Turkistan [,tɜːkɪ'stɑːn] *n* (el) Turquestán.

turkey ['tɜːkɪ] (*pl* **turkeys**) *n* pavo *m*.

Turkey ['tɜːkɪ] *n* Turquía *f*.

Turkish ['tɜːkɪʃ] ◇ *adj* turco(ca). ◇ *n* [language] turco *m*. ◇ *npl* [people]: **the ~** los turcos.

Turkish bath *n* baño *m* turco.

Turkish delight *n* dulce de una sustancia gelatinosa, cubierto de azúcar glas o chocolate.

Turkistan = Turkestan.

Turkmenian [,tɜːk'menɪən] *adj* turcomano(na).

Turkmenistan [,tɜːkmenɪ'stɑːn] *n* Turkmenistán.

turmeric ['tɜːmərɪk] *n* cúrcuma *f*.

turmoil ['tɜːmɔɪl] *n* confusión *f*, alboroto *m*.

turn ['tɜːn] ◇ *n* -1. [in road, river] curva *f*. -2. [of knob, wheel] vuelta *f*. -3. [change] cambio *m*; **to take a ~ for the worse** empeorar. -4. [in game] turno *m*; **it's my ~** me toca a mí; **in ~** sucesivamente, uno tras otro; **to take (it in) ~s (to do sthg)** turnarse (en hacer algo). -5. [of year, decade etc] fin *m*. -6. [performance] número *m*. -7. MED ataque *m*. -8. *phr*: **to do sb a good ~** hacerle un favor a alguien.
◇ *vt* -1. [chair, page, omelette] dar la vuelta a. -2. [knob, wheel] girar. -3. [corner] doblar. -4. [thoughts, attention]: **to ~ sthg to** dirigir algo hacia. -5. [change]: **to ~ sthg into** convertir OR transformar algo en. -6. [cause to become]: **the cold ~ed his fingers blue** se le pusieron los dedos azules por el frío; **to ~ sthg inside out** volver algo del revés. -7. [become]: **it ~ed black** se volvió negro; **the demonstration ~ed nasty** la manifestación se puso violenta. -8. [milk] cortar, agriar.
◇ *vi* -1. [car] girar; [road] torcer; [person] volverse, darse la vuelta. -2. [wheel] dar vueltas. -3. [turn page over]: **~ to page two** pasen a la página dos. -4. [thoughts, attention]: **to ~** dirigirse hacia. -5. [seek consolation]: **to ~ to sb/sthg** buscar consuelo en alguien/algo. -6. [change]: **to ~ into** convertirse OR transformarse en. -7. [go sour] cortarse, agriarse.
◆ **turn against** *vt fus* poner en contra de.
◆ **turn around** = **turn round**.
◆ **turn away** *vt sep* [refuse entry to] no dejar entrar.
◆ **turn back** ◇ *vt sep* [person, vehicle] hacer volver. ◇ *vi* volver, volverse.
◆ **turn down** *vt sep* -1. [offer, person] rechazar. -2. [volume etc] bajar.
◆ **turn in** *vi inf* [go to bed] irse a dormir.
◆ **turn off** ◇ *vt fus* [road, path] desviarse de, salir de. ◇ *vt sep* [radio, heater] apagar; [engine] parar; [gas, tap] cerrar. ◇ *vi* [leave road] desviarse, salir.
◆ **turn on** ◇ *vt sep* -1. [radio, TV, engine] encender; [gas, tap] abrir. -2. *inf* [excite sexually] poner cachondo(da), excitar. ◇ *vt fus* [attack] atacar.
◆ **turn out** ◇ *vt. sep* -1. [extinguish] apagar. -2. *inf* [produce] producir. -3. [eject] echar. -4. [empty - pockets, bag] vaciar. ◇ *vt fus*: **to ~ out to be** *inf* resultar ser; **it ~s out that ... resulta que ....** ◇ *vi* -1. [end up] salir. -2. [arrive]: **to ~ out (for)** venir OR presentarse (a).

◆ **turn over** ◇ *vt sep* -1. [consider] darle vueltas a. -2. *Br* RADIO & TV cambiar. -3. [hand over]: **to ~ sthg/sb over (to)** entregar algo/a alguien (a). ◇ *vi Br* RADIO & TV cambiar de canal.
◆ **turn round** ◇ *vt sep* -1. [gen] dar la vuelta a. -2. [knob, key] hacer girar. ◇ *vi* [person] darse la vuelta, volverse.
◆ **turn up** ◇ *vt sep* [volume, heating] subir. ◇ *vi inf* aparecer.

turnabout ['tɜːnəbaʊt] *n* cambio *m* radical.

turnaround *Am* = **turnround**.

turncoat ['tɜːnkəʊt] *n pej* chaquetero *m*, -ra *f*.

turning ['tɜːnɪŋ] *n* [road] bocacalle *f*.

turning circle *n* diámetro *m* OR ángulo *m* de giro.

turning point *n* momento *m* decisivo.

turnip ['tɜːnɪp] *n* nabo *m*.

turnout ['tɜːnaʊt] *n* número *m* de asistentes, asistencia *f*.

turnover ['tɜːn,əʊvəʳ] *n* (*U*) -1. [of personnel] movimiento *m* de personal. -2. FIN volumen *m* de ventas, facturación *f*.

turnpike ['tɜːnpaɪk] *n Am* autopista *f* de peaje.

turnround *Br* ['tɜːnraʊnd], **turnaround** *Am* ['tɜːnəraʊnd] *n* -1. COMM tiempo *m* de carga y descarga (*de un barco, avión etc*). -2. [change] cambio *m* radical.

turn signal lever *n Am* intermitente *m*.

turnstile ['tɜːnstaɪl] *n* torno *m*, torniquete *m*.

turntable ['tɜːn,teɪbl] *n* plato *m* giratorio.

turn-up *n Br* [on trousers] vuelta *f*; **a ~ for the books** *inf* una auténtica sorpresa.

turpentine ['tɜːpəntaɪn] *n* trementina *f*.

turps [tɜːps] (*abbr of* **turpentine**) *n Br inf* trementina *f*.

turquoise ['tɜːkwɔɪz] ◇ *adj* turquesa. ◇ *n* -1. [mineral, gem] turquesa *f*. -2. [colour] turquesa *m*.

turret ['tʌrɪt] *n* torreta *f*, torrecilla *f*.

turtle ['tɜːtl] (*pl inv* OR **-s**) *n* tortuga *f* (marina).

turtledove ['tɜːtldʌv] *n* tórtola *f*.

turtleneck ['tɜːtlnek] *n* cuello *m* (de) cisne.

turves [tɜːvz] *Br pl* → **turf**.

tusk [tʌsk] *n* colmillo *m*.

tussle ['tʌsl] ◇ *n* lucha *f*, pelea *f*. ◇ *vi*: **to ~ (over)** pelearse (por).

tut [tʌt] *excl* ¡vaya!

tutor ['tjuːtəʳ] ◇ *n* -1. [private] profesor particular *m*, profesora particular *f*, tutor *m*, -ra *f*. -2. UNIV profesor universitario *m*, profesora universitaria *f* (*de un grupo pequeño*). ◇

vt: **to ~ sb in sthg** dar clases particulares de algo a alguien. ◇ *vi* dar clases particulares.

tutorial [tjuː'tɔːrɪəl] ◇ *adj*: **~ group** *grupo reducido de estudiantes que asiste a una clase.* ◇ *n* tutoría *f*, clase *f* con grupo reducido.

tutu ['tuːtuː] *n* tutú *m*.

tux [tʌks] (*abbr of* **tuxedo**) *n inf* esmoquin *m*.

tuxedo [tʌk'siːdəʊ] (*pl* **-s**) *n* esmoquin *m*.

TV (*abbr of* **television**) ◇ *n* televisión *f*; **on ~** en la televisión. ◇ *comp* de televisión.

TV dinner *n comida completa precocinada y lista para el horno.*

twaddle ['twɒdl] *n* (U) *inf pej* tonterías *fpl*, huevada *f Amer*.

twang [twæŋ] ◇ *n* **-1.** [of guitar] tañido *m*; [of string, elastic] sonido *m* vibrante. **-2.** [accent] gangueo *m*, acento *m* nasal. ◇ *vt* [guitar] tañer; [wire, string] hacer vibrar (tirando y soltando). ◇ *vi* producir un sonido vibrante.

tweak [twiːk] *vt inf* [nose, ear] pellizcar, dar un tironcito a.

twee [twiː] *adj Br pej* cursi, siútico(ca) *Amer*.

tweed [twiːd] ◇ *n* tweed *m*. ◇ *comp* de tweed.

tweet [twiːt] *vi inf* piar, hacer pío pío.

tweezers ['twiːzəz] *npl* pinzas *fpl*.

twelfth [twelfθ] ◇ *num adj* duodécimo(ma). ◇ *num n* **-1.** [fraction] duodécimo *m*. **-2.** [in order] duodécimo *m*, -ma *f*; *see also* **sixth**.

Twelfth Night *n* Noche *f* de Reyes.

twelve [twelv] *num* doce; *see also* **six**.

twentieth ['twentɪəθ] ◇ *num adj* vigésimo(ma). ◇ *num n* **-1.** [fraction] vigésimo *m*. **-2.** [in order] vigésimo *m*, -ma *f*; *see also* **sixth**.

twenty ['twentɪ] (*pl* **-ies**) *num* veinte; *see also* **sixty**.

twenty-twenty vision *n* vista *f* perfecta.

twerp [twɜːp] *n inf* imbécil *m* y *f*.

twice [twaɪs] ◇ *num adv* dos veces; **~ a week** dos veces por semana; **it costs ~ as much** cuesta el doble. ◇ *num adj* dos veces; **~ as big** el doble de grande.

twiddle ['twɪdl] ◇ *vt* dar vueltas a. ◇ *vi*: **to ~ with** juguetear con.

twig [twɪg] *n* ramita *f*.

twilight ['twaɪlaɪt] *n* crepúsculo *m*, ocaso *m*.

twill [twɪl] *n* sarga *f*.

twin [twɪn] ◇ *adj* gemelo(la), morocho(cha) *Amer*. ◇ *n* gemelo *m*, -la *f*, morocho *m*, -cha *f Amer*.

twin-bedded [-'bedɪd] *adj* de dos camas.

twin carburettor *n* motor *m* de dos carburadores.

twine [twaɪn] ◇ *n* (U) bramante *m*. ◇ *vt*: **to ~ sthg round sthg** enrollar algo en algo.

twin-engined [-'endʒɪnd] *adj* bimotor.

twinge [twɪndʒ] *n* [of pain] punzada *f*; [of guilt] remordimiento *m*.

twinkie ['twɪŋkɪ] *n Am* [cake] *pastel (relleno de) crema.*

twinkle ['twɪŋkl] ◇ *n* brillo *m*. ◇ *vi* **-1.** [star] centellear, parpadear. **-2.** [eyes] brillar.

twin room *n* habitación *f* con dos camas.

twin set *n Br* conjunto *m* de jersey y rebeca.

twin town *n* ciudad *f* hermanada.

twin tub *n* lavadora *f* de doble tambor.

twirl [twɜːl] ◇ *vt* dar vueltas a. ◇ *vi* dar vueltas rápidamente.

twist [twɪst] ◇ *n* **-1.** [in road] vuelta *f*, recodo *m*; [in river] meandro *m*. **-2.** [of head, lid, knob] giro *m*. **-3.** [shape] espiral *f*. **-4.** *fig* [in plot] giro *m* imprevisto.
◇ *vt* **-1.** [cloth, rope] retorcer; [hair] enroscar. **-2.** [face etc] torcer. **-3.** [dial, lid] dar vueltas a; [head] volver. **-4.** [ankle, knee etc] torcerse. **-5.** [misquote] tergiversar.
◇ *vi* **-1.** [person] retorcerse, contorsionarse; [road, river] serpentear, dar vueltas. **-2.** [face] contorsionarse; [frame, rail] torcerse. **-3.** [turn - head, hand] volverse.

twisted ['twɪstɪd] *adj pej* retorcido(da).

twister ['twɪstər] *n Am* tornado *m*.

twisty ['twɪstɪ] (*compar* **-ier**, *superl* **-iest**) *adj inf* lleno(na) de curvas.

twit [twɪt] *n Br inf* imbécil *m* y *f*, gil *m* y *f Amer*.

twitch [twɪtʃ] ◇ *n* contorsión *f*; **nervous ~ tic** *m* (nervioso). ◇ *vt* mover nerviosamente. ◇ *vi* contorsionarse.

twitter ['twɪtər] *vi* **-1.** [bird] gorjear. **-2.** *pej* [person] parlotear, cotorrear.

two [tuː] *num* dos; **in ~** en dos; *see also* **six**.

two-bit *adj Am pej* de tres al cuarto.

two-dimensional *adj* en dos dimensiones.

two-door *adj* [car] de dos puertas.

twofaced [ˌtuː'feɪst] *adj pej* hipócrita.

twofold ['tuːfəʊld] ◇ *adj* doble; **a ~ increase** un incremento del doble. ◇ *adv*: **to increase ~** duplicarse.

two-handed [-'hændɪd] *adj* [sword, axe] que se usa con las dos manos; [backhand] de dos manos.

two-piece *adj* [suit] de dos piezas.

two-ply *adj* de dos capas.

two-seater [-'siːtər] *n* biplaza *m*.

twosome ['tuːsəm] *n inf* pareja *f*.

two-stroke ◇ *adj* [engine] de dos tiempos; [oil] para motor de dos tiempos. ◇ *n* motor *m* de dos tiempos.

two-time *vt inf* engañar, poner los cuernos a.

two-tone *adj* bicolor.

two-way *adj* **-1.** [traffic] en ambas direcciones; [agreement; cooperation] mutuo(tua). **-2.** TELEC: ~ **radio** aparato *m* emisor y receptor.

TX *abbr of* **Texas**.

tycoon [taɪ'kuːn] *n* magnate *m*.

type [taɪp] ◇ *n* **-1.** [gen] tipo *m*; **he's/she's not my** ~ *inf* no es mi tipo. **-2.** (*U*) TYPO tipo *m*, letra *f*; **in bold/italic** ~ en negrita/cursiva. ◇ *vt* **-1.** [on typewriter] escribir a máquina, mecanografiar. **-2.** [on computer] escribir en el ordenador; **to** ~ **sthg into sthg** entrar algo en algo. ◇ *vi* escribir a máquina.

◆ **type up** *vt sep* escribir a máquina, mecanografiar.

typecast ['taɪpkɑːst] (*pt & pp* **typecast**) *vt*: **to** ~ **sb (as)** encasillar a alguien (como).

typeface ['taɪpfeɪs] *n* tipo *m*, letra *f*.

typescript ['taɪpskrɪpt] *n* copia *f* mecanografiada.

typeset ['taɪpset] (*pt & pp* **typeset**, *cont* **-ting**) *vt* componer.

typewriter ['taɪp,raɪtə'] *n* máquina *f* de escribir.

typhoid (fever) ['taɪfɔɪd-] *n* fiebre *f* tifoidea.

typhoon [taɪ'fuːn] *n* tifón *m*.

typhus ['taɪfəs] *n* tifus *m*.

typical ['tɪpɪkl] *adj*: ~ **(of)** típico(ca) (de).

typically ['tɪpɪklɪ] *adv* **-1.** [usually] normalmente. **-2.** [characteristically] típicamente.

typify ['tɪpɪfaɪ] (*pt & pp* **-ied**) *vt* tipificar.

typing ['taɪpɪŋ] *n* mecanografía *f*.

typing error *n* error *m* mecanográfico.

typing pool *n* servicio *m* de mecanografía (*en una empresa*).

typist ['taɪpɪst] *n* mecanógrafo *m*, -fa *f*.

typo ['taɪpəʊ] *n inf* error *m* tipográfico.

typographic(al) error [,taɪpə'græfɪk(l)-] *n* error *m* tipográfico.

typography [taɪ'pɒgrəfɪ] *n* **-1.** [process, job] tipografía *f*. **-2.** [format] composición *f* tipográfica.

tyrannical [tɪ'rænɪkl] *adj* tiránico(ca).

tyranny ['tɪrənɪ] *n* tiranía *f*.

tyrant ['taɪrənt] *n* tirano *m*, -na *f*.

tyre *Br*, **tire** *Am* ['taɪə'] *n* neumático *m*.

tyre pressure *n* presión *f* de los neumáticos.

Tyrol, Tirol [tɪ'rəʊl] *n*: **the** ~ el Tirol.

Tyrolean [tɪrə'liːən], **Tyrolese** [,tɪrə'liːz] ◇ *adj* tirolés(esa). ◇ *n* tirolés *m*, -esa *f*.

Tyrrhenian Sea [tɪ'riːnɪən-] *n*: **the** ~ el mar Tirreno.

tzar [zɑːr] = **tsar**.

u (*pl* **u's** OR **us**), **U** (*pl* **U's** OR **Us**) [juː] *n* [letter] u *f*, U *f*.

◆ **U** (*abbr of* **universal**) *Br* CINEMA para todos los públicos.

UAW (*abbr of* **United Automobile Workers**) *n* sindicato estadounidense de la industria automovilística.

UB40 (*abbr of* **unemployment benefit form 40**) *n* carnet de paro en Gran Bretaña.

U-bend *n* sifón *m*.

ubiquitous [juː'bɪkwɪtəs] *adj fml* omnipresente, ubicuo(cua).

UCATT ['juːkæt] (*abbr of* **Union of Construction, Allied Trades and Technicians**) *n* sindicato británico de trabajadores de la construcción.

UCCA ['ʌkə] (*abbr of* **Universities Central Council on Admissions**) *n* organismo central encargado de gestionar las solicitudes de ingreso en las universidades británicas.

UCL (*abbr of* **University College, London**) *n* universidad londinense.

UCNW (*abbr of* **University College of North Wales**) *n* universidad galesa.

UCW (*abbr of* **The Union of Communication Workers**) *n* sindicato británico de trabajadores de telecomunicaciones.

UDA (*abbr of* **Ulster Defence Association**) *n* organización paramilitar protestante que defiende la permanencia de Irlanda del Norte en el Reino Unido.

UDC (*abbr of* **Urban District Council**) *n* ayuntamiento de un municipio urbano en Gran Bretaña.

udder ['ʌdə'] *n* ubre *f*.

UDI (*abbr of* **unilateral declaration of independence**) *n* declaración unilateral de independencia.

UDR (*abbr of* **Ulster Defence Regiment**) *n* fuerzas de seguridad de Irlanda del Norte.

UEFA [juːˈeɪfə] (*abbr of* **Union of European Football Associations**) *n* UEFA *f*.

UFC (*abbr of* **Universities Funding Council**) *n organismo británico gestor de las becas universitarias*.

UFO (*abbr of* **unidentified flying object**) *n* OVNI *m*.

Uganda [juːˈgændə] *n* Uganda.

Ugandan [juːˈgændən] ◇ *adj* ugandés(esa). ◇ *n* [person] ugandés *m*, -esa *f*.

ugh [ʌg] *excl* ¡puf!

ugliness [ˈʌglɪnɪs] *n* (*U*) **-1.** [unattractiveness] fealdad *f*. **-2.** *fig* [unpleasantness] lo desagradable.

ugly [ˈʌglɪ] (*compar* **-ier**, *superl* **-iest**) *adj* **-1.** [unattractive] feo(a). **-2.** *fig* [unpleasant] desagradable.

UHF (*abbr of* **ultra-high frequency**) UHF.

UHT (*abbr of* **ultra-heat treated**) UHT.

UK (*abbr of* **United Kingdom**) *n* RU *m*; **the ~** el Reino Unido.

Ukraine [juːˈkreɪn] *n*: **the ~** Ucrania.

Ukrainian [juːˈkreɪnjən] ◇ *adj* ucraniano(na). ◇ *n* **-1.** [person] ucraniano *m*, -na *f*. **-2.** [language] ucraniano *m*.

ukulele [ˌjuːkəˈleɪlɪ] *n* ukelele *m*.

Ulan Bator [ʊˈlɑːnˈbɑːtə] *n* Ulan Bator.

ulcer [ˈʌlsər] *n* úlcera *f*.

ulcerated [ˈʌlsəreɪtɪd] *adj* ulceroso(sa).

Ulster [ˈʌlstər] *n* (el) Úlster.

Ulsterman [ˈʌlstəmən] (*pl* **-men** [-mən]) *n natural o habitante del Úlster*.

Ulster Unionist Party *n partido político norirlandés que defiende la permanencia de Irlanda del Norte en el Reino Unido*.

ulterior [ʌlˈtɪərɪər] *adj*: **~ motive** motivo *m* oculto.

ultimata [ˌʌltɪˈmeɪtə] *pl* → **ultimatum**.

ultimate [ˈʌltɪmət] ◇ *adj* **-1.** [final, long-term] final, definitivo(va). **-2.** [most powerful] máximo(ma). ◇ *n*: **the ~ in** el colmo de.

ultimately [ˈʌltɪmətlɪ] *adv* finalmente, a la larga.

ultimatum [ˌʌltɪˈmeɪtəm] (*pl* **-s** OR **-ta**) *n* ultimátum *m*.

ultra- [ˈʌltrə] *prefix* ultra-.

ultramarine [ˌʌltrəməˈriːn] *adj* azul de ultramar OR ultramarino (*inv*).

ultrasonic [ˌʌltrəˈsɒnɪk] *adj* ultrasónico(ca).

ultrasound [ˌʌltrəsaʊnd] *n* ultrasonido *m*.

ultraviolet [ˌʌltrəˈvaɪələt] *adj* ultravioleta.

um [ʌm] *excl* ¡humm!, ¡mm!

umbilical cord [ʌmˈbɪlɪkl-] *n* cordón *m* umbilical.

umbrage [ˈʌmbrɪdʒ] *n*: **to take ~ (at)** ofenderse (por).

umbrella [ʌmˈbrelə] ◇ *n* **-1.** [for rain] paraguas *m inv*. **-2.** [on beach] parasol *m*. ◇ *adj* que engloba a otros (otras).

UMIST [ˈjuːmɪst] (*abbr of* **University of Manchester Institute of Science and Technology**) *n instituto de ciencia y tecnología de la Universidad de Manchester*.

umpire [ˈʌmpaɪər] ◇ *n* árbitro *m*. ◇ *vt & vi* arbitrar.

umpteen [ˌʌmpˈtiːn] *num adj inf*: **~ times** la tira de veces.

umpteenth [ˌʌmpˈtiːnθ] *num adj inf* enésimo(ma); **for the ~ time** por enésima vez.

UMW (*abbr of* **United Mineworkers of America**) *n sindicato estadounidense de mineros*.

UN (*abbr of* **United Nations**) *n*: **the ~** la ONU.

unabashed [ˌʌnəˈbæʃt] *adj* imperturbable; **to be ~** no avergonzarse.

unabated [ˌʌnəˈbeɪtɪd] *adj* incesante.

unable [ʌnˈeɪbl] *adj*: **to be ~ to do sthg** no poder hacer algo.

unabridged [ˌʌnəˈbrɪdʒd] *adj* íntegro(gra).

unacceptable [ˌʌnəkˈseptəbl] *adj* inaceptable.

unaccompanied [ˌʌnəˈkʌmpənɪd] *adj* **-1.** [child] solo(la), que no va acompañado(da); [luggage] desatendido(da), abandonado(da). **-2.** [song] sin acompañamiento.

unaccountable [ˌʌnəˈkaʊntəbl] *adj* **-1.** [inexplicable] inexplicable. **-2.** [not responsible]: **~ (for/to)** que no es responsable (de/ante).

unaccountably [ˌʌnəˈkaʊntəblɪ] *adv* inexplicablemente.

unaccounted [ˌʌnəˈkaʊntɪd] *adj*: **12 people are ~ for** hay 12 personas aún sin localizar; **£30 are ~ for** hay 30 libras que no aparecen.

unaccustomed [ˌʌnəˈkʌstəmd] *adj* **-1.** [unused]: **to be ~ to** no estar acostumbrado(da) a. **-2.** *fml* [not usual] desacostumbrado(da), inusual.

unacquainted [ˌʌnəˈkweɪntɪd] *adj*: **to be ~ with sthg** no conocer algo.

unadulterated [ˌʌnəˈdʌltəreɪtɪd] *adj* **-1.** [unspoilt] sin adulterar. **-2.** [absolute] completo(ta), absoluto(ta).

unadventurous [ˌʌnədˈventʃərəs] *adj* poco atrevido(da).

unaffected [ˌʌnəˈfektɪd] *adj* **-1.** [unchanged]: **to be ~ (by)** no verse afectado(da) (por). **-2.** [natural] nada afectado(da), natural.

unafraid [ˌʌnəˈfreɪd] *adj* sin miedo.

unaided [ˌʌnˈeɪdɪd] *adj & adv* sin ayuda.

unambiguous [ˌʌnæmˈbɪgjʊəs] *adj* inequívoco(ca).

un-American [ˈʌn-] *adj* antiamericano(na).

unanimity [ˌjuːnəˈnɪmətɪ] *n fml* unanimidad *f*.

unanimous [juːˈnænɪməs] *adj* unánime.

unanimously [juːˈnænɪməslɪ] *adv* unánimemente.

unannounced [ˌʌnəˈnaʊnst] ◇ *adj* no anunciado(da). ◇ *adv* sin anunciarlo.

unanswered [ˌʌnˈɑːnsəd] *adj* sin contestar.

unappealing [ˌʌnəˈpiːlɪŋ] *adj* desagradable.

unappetizing, -ising [ˌʌnˈæpɪtaɪzɪŋ] *adj* poco apetitoso(sa).

unappreciated [ˌʌnəˈpriːʃɪeɪtɪd] *adj* poco apreciado(da).

unappreciative [ˌʌnəˈpriːʃɪətɪv] *adj* poco apreciativo(va); **to be ~ of sthg** no apreciar algo.

unapproachable [ˌʌnəˈprəʊtʃəbl] *adj* inaccesible.

unarmed [ˌʌnˈɑːmd] ◇ *adj* desarmado(da). ◇ *adv* a brazo partido.

unarmed combat *n* lucha *f* OR combate *m* a brazo partido.

unashamed [ˌʌnəˈʃeɪmd] *adj* descarado(da).

unassisted [ˌʌnəˈsɪstɪd] *adj* sin ayuda.

unassuming [ˌʌnəˈsjuːmɪŋ] *adj* sin pretensiones.

unattached [ˌʌnəˈtætʃt] *adj* **-1.** [not fastened, linked] independiente; **~ to** que no está ligado a. **-2.** [without partner] libre, sin compromiso.

unattainable [ˌʌnəˈteɪnəbl] *adj* inalcanzable, inasequible.

unattended [ˌʌnəˈtendɪd] *adj* desatendido(da).

unattractive [ˌʌnəˈtræktɪv] *adj* poco atractivo(va).

unauthorized, -ised [ˌʌnˈɔːθəraɪzd] *adj* no autorizado(da).

unavailable [ˌʌnəˈveɪləbl] *adj* que no está disponible.

unavoidable [ˌʌnəˈvɔɪdəbl] *adj* inevitable, ineludible.

unavoidably [ˌʌnəˈvɔɪdəblɪ] *adv* inevitablemente, ineludiblemente.

unaware [ˌʌnəˈweəʳ] *adj* inconsciente; **to be ~ of** no ser consciente de.

unawares [ˌʌnəˈweəz] *adv*: **to catch** OR **take sb ~** coger a alguien desprevenido(da).

unbalanced [ˌʌnˈbælənst] *adj* desequilibrado(da).

unbearable [ʌnˈbeərəbl] *adj* insoportable, inaguantable.

unbearably [ʌnˈbeərəblɪ] *adv* insoportablemente, inaguantablemente.

unbeatable [ˌʌnˈbiːtəbl] *adj* [gen] insuperable; [prices, value] inmejorable.

unbecoming [ˌʌnbɪˈkʌmɪŋ] *adj fml* [unattractive] poco favorecedor(ra).

unbeknown(st) [ˌʌnbɪˈnəʊn(st)] *adv*: **~ to** sin conocimiento de.

unbelievable [ˌʌnbɪˈliːvəbl] *adj* increíble.

unbelievably [ˌʌnbɪˈliːvəblɪ] *adv* [extremely] increíblemente.

unbend [ˌʌnˈbend] (*pt* & *pp* **unbent**) *vi* [relax] relajarse.

unbending [ˌʌnˈbendɪŋ] *adj* resoluto(ta).

unbent [ˌʌnˈbent] *pt* & *pp* → **unbend**.

unbia(s)sed [ˌʌnˈbaɪəst] *adj* imparcial.

unblemished [ˌʌnˈblemɪʃt] *adj fig* intachable, impecable.

unblock [ˌʌnˈblɒk] *vt* [pipe] desobstruir, desatascar; [road, tunnel] desbloquear, abrir.

unbolt [ˌʌnˈbəʊlt] *vt* [door] abrir el cerrojo de.

unborn [ˌʌnˈbɔːn] *adj* [child] no nacido(da) aún.

unbreakable [ˌʌnˈbreɪkəbl] *adj* irrompible.

unbridled [ˌʌnˈbraɪdld] *adj* desmesurado(da), desenfrenado(da).

unbuckle [ˌʌnˈbʌkl] *vt* deshebillar.

unbutton [ˌʌnˈbʌtn] *vt* desabrochar, desabotonar.

uncalled-for [ˌʌnˈkɔːld-] *adj* injusto(ta), inmerecido(da).

uncanny [ʌnˈkænɪ] (*compar* **-ier**, *superl* **-iest**) *adj* extraño(ña).

uncared-for [ˌʌnˈkeəd-] *adj* abandonado(da), desamparado(da).

uncaring [ˌʌnˈkeərɪŋ] *adj* insensible, falto(ta) de sentimientos.

unceasing [ˌʌnˈsiːsɪŋ] *adj fml* incesante.

unceremonious [ˈʌnˌserɪˈməʊnjəs] *adj* **-1.** [curt] brusco(ca). **-2.** [informal] poco ceremonioso(sa).

unceremoniously [ˈʌnˌserɪˈməʊnjəslɪ] *adj* sin contemplaciones, sin ceremonias.

uncertain [ʌnˈsɜːtn] *adj* [gen] incierto(ta); [undecided, hesitant] indeciso(sa); **in no ~ terms** de forma vehemente.

unchain [ˌʌnˈtʃeɪn] *vt* quitar la cadena a, desencadenar.

unchallenged [ˌʌnˈtʃælɪndʒd] *adj* sin cuestionar.

unchanged [ˌʌnˈtʃeɪndʒd] *adj* sin alterar.

unchanging [ˌʌnˈtʃeɪndʒɪŋ] *adj* imutable, inalterable.

uncharacteristic [ˈʌnˌkærəktəˈrɪstɪk] *adj* inusual, insólito(ta).

uncharitable [ˌʌnˈtʃærɪtəbl] *adj* mezquino(na).

uncharted [ˌʌn'tʃɑːtɪd] *adj lit* & *fig* desconocido(da).

unchecked [ˌʌn'tʃekt] ◇ *adj* [unrestrained] desenfrenado(da). ◇ *adv* [unrestrained] libremente, sin restricciones.

uncivilized, -ised [ˌʌn'sɪvɪlaɪzd] *adj* [society] incivilizado(da); [person] inculto(ta).

unclassified [ˌʌn'klæsɪfaɪd] *adj* no confidencial.

uncle ['ʌŋkl] *n* tío *m*.

unclean [ˌʌn'kliːn] *adj* **-1.** [dirty] sucio(cia). **-2.** RELIG impuro(ra).

unclear [ˌʌn'klɪəʳ] *adj* poco claro(ra); **to be ~ about** sthg no tener claro algo.

Uncle Sam [-sæm] *n inf* el Tío Sam.

unclothed [ˌʌn'kləʊðd] *adj fml* desnudo(da).

uncomfortable [ˌʌn'kʌmftəbl] *adj* **-1.** [gen] incómodo(da). **-2.** *fig* [fact, truth] inquietante, desagradable.

uncomfortably [ˌʌn'kʌmftəblɪ] *adv* **-1.** [in physical discomfort] incómodamente. **-2.** *fig* [uneasily] inquietantemente.

uncommitted [ˌʌnkə'mɪtɪd] *adj* no comprometido(da).

uncommon [ʌn'kɒmən] *adj* **-1.** [rare] poco común, raro(ra). **-2.** *fml* [extreme] sumo(ma).

uncommonly [ʌn'kɒmənlɪ] *adv fml* extraordinariamente.

uncommunicative [ˌʌnkə'mjuːnɪkətɪv] *adj* poco comunicativo(va), reservado(da).

uncomplicated [ˌʌn'kɒmplɪkeɪtɪd] *adj* sencillo(lla), sin complicaciones.

uncomprehending ['ʌnˌkɒmprɪ'hendɪŋ] *adj* incomprensivo(va).

uncompromising [ˌʌn'kɒmprəmaɪzɪŋ] *adj* inflexible, intransigente.

unconcerned [ˌʌnkən'sɜːnd] *adj* [not anxious] indiferente.

unconditional [ˌʌnkən'dɪʃənl] *adj* incondicional.

uncongenial [ˌʌnkən'dʒiːnjəl] *adj fml* [place] desagradable; [person] antipático(ca).

unconnected [ˌʌnkə'nektɪd] *adj* inconexo(xa), sin relación.

unconquered [ˌʌn'kɒŋkəd] *adj* [area, country] no conquistado(da); [people] invicto(ta).

unconscious [ʌn'kɒnʃəs] ◇ *adj* inconsciente; **to be ~ of** sthg ser inconsciente de OR ignorar algo. ◇ *n* inconsciente *m*.

unconsciously [ʌn'kɒnʃəslɪ] *adv* inconscientemente.

unconstitutional ['ʌnˌkɒnstɪ'tjuːʃənl] *adj* inconstitucional.

uncontested [ˌʌnkən'testɪd] *adj* [decision,

judgment] incontestado(da); [seat, election] ganado(da) sin oposición.

uncontrollable [ˌʌnkən'trəʊləbl] *adj* [gen] incontrolable; [desire, hatred] irrefrenable; [laughter] incontenible.

uncontrolled [ˌʌnkən'trəʊld] *adj* [emotion] desenfrenado(da); [trend] incontrolado(da).

unconventional [ˌʌnkən'venʃənl] *adj* poco convencional.

unconvinced [ˌʌnkən'vɪnst] *adj*: **to remain ~** seguir sin convencerse.

unconvincing [ˌʌnkən'vɪnsɪŋ] *adj* poco convincente.

uncooked [ˌʌn'kʊkt] *adj* crudo(da), sin guisar.

uncooperative [ˌʌnkəʊ'ɒpərətɪv] *adj* nada servicial, no dispuesto(ta) a ayudar.

uncork [ˌʌn'kɔːk] *vt* descorchar.

uncorroborated [ˌʌnkə'rɒbəreɪtɪd] *adj* sin corroborar.

uncouth [ʌn'kuːθ] *adj* grosero(ra).

uncover [ʌn'kʌvəʳ] *vt* [gen] descubrir; [jar, tin etc] destapar.

uncurl [ˌʌn'kɜːl] *vi* **-1.** [hair] desrizarse; [wire] desenrollarse. **-2.** [animal] desovillarse, desenroscarse.

uncut [ˌʌn'kʌt] *adj* **-1.** [film] sin cortes. **-2.** [jewel] sin tallar, en bruto.

undamaged [ˌʌn'dæmɪdʒd] *adj* [gen] intacto(ta); [goods] sin disperfectos.

undaunted [ˌʌn'dɔːntɪd] *adj* impávido(da), imperférrito(ta).

undecided [ˌʌndɪ'saɪdɪd] *adj* **-1.** [person] indeciso(sa). **-2.** [issue] pendiente, sin resolver.

undemanding [ˌʌndɪ'mɑːndɪŋ] *adj* **-1.** [task] poco absorbente, que requiere poco esfuerzo. **-2.** [person] poco exigente.

undemonstrative [ˌʌndɪ'mɒnstrətɪv] *adj* poco expresivo(va), reservado(da).

undeniable [ˌʌndɪ'naɪəbl] *adj* innegable.

under ['ʌndəʳ] ◇ *prep* **-1.** [beneath] debajo de. **-2.** [with movement] bajo; **they walked ~ the bridge** pasaron por debajo del puente. **-3.** [subject to, undergoing, controlled by] bajo; **~ the circumstances** dadas las circunstancias; **~ discussion** en proceso de discusión; **he has 20 men ~ him** tiene 20 hombres a su cargo. **-4.** [less than] menos de. **-5.** [according to] según, conforme a. **-6.** [in headings, classifications]: **he filed it ~ "D"** lo archivó en la "D". **-7.** [name, title]: **~ an alias** bajo nombre supuesto.
◇ *adv* **-1.** [gen] debajo; **to go ~** [business] irse a pique. **-2.** [less]: **children of 12 years and ~** niños menores de 13 años.

under- ['ʌndəʳ] *prefix* **-1.** [beneath] inferior, bajo. **-2.** [lower in rank] sub-, segundo(da). **-3.** [insufficiently] insuficientemente.

underachiever [,ʌndərə'tʃiːvəʳ] *n estudiante que no rinde todo lo que puede.*

underage [ʌndər'eɪdʒ] *adj* [person] menor de edad; [sex, drinking] en menores de edad.

underarm ['ʌndərɑːm] ◇ *adj* [deodorant] corporal, para las axilas. ◇ *adv* por debajo del hombro.

underbrush ['ʌndəbrʌʃ] *n* (U) *Am* maleza *f*, monte *m* bajo.

undercarriage ['ʌndə,kærɪdʒ] *n* tren *m* de aterrizaje.

undercharge [,ʌndə'tʃɑːdʒ] *vt* cobrar menos del precio estipulado a.

underclothes ['ʌndəkləʊðz] *npl* ropa *f* interior.

undercoat ['ʌndəkəʊt] *n* [of paint] primera mano *f* OR capa *f*.

undercook [,ʌndə'kʊk] *vt* no guisar suficientemente.

undercover ['ʌndə,kʌvəʳ] ◇ *adj* secreto(ta). ◇ *adv* en la clandestinidad; **to go ~** pasar a la clandestinidad.

undercurrent ['ʌndə,kʌrənt] *n fig* sentimiento *m* oculto.

undercut [,ʌndə'kʌt] (*pt & pp* **undercut**, *cont* **-ting**) *vt* [in price] vender más barato que.

underdeveloped [,ʌndədɪ'veləpt] *adj* subdesarrollado(da).

underdog ['ʌndədɒg] *n*: **the ~** el que lleva las de perder.

underdone [,ʌndə'dʌn] *adj* poco hecho(cha).

underemployment [,ʌndərɪm'plɔɪmənt] *n* subempleo *m*.

underestimate [*n* ,ʌndər'estɪmət, *vb* ,ʌndər'estɪmeɪt] ◇ *n* infravaloración *f*. ◇ *vt* subestimar, infravalorar.

underexposed [,ʌndərɪk'spəʊzd] *adj* PHOT subexpuesto(ta).

underfinanced [,ʌndə'faɪnænst] *adj* insuficientemente financiado(da).

underfoot [,ʌndə'fʊt] *adv* debajo de los pies; **it's wet ~** el suelo está mojado.

undergo [,ʌndə'gəʊ] (*pt* **-went**, *pp* **-gone** [-gɒn]) *vt* [pain, change, difficulties] sufrir, experimentar; [operation, examination] someterse a.

undergraduate [,ʌndə'grædʒʊət] ◇ *adj* [course, studies] de licenciatura; [gown, prospectus] para estudiantes no licenciados. ◇ *n* estudiante universitario no licenciado *m*, estudiante universitaria no licenciada *f*.

underground [*adj & n* 'ʌndəgraʊnd, *adv* ,ʌndə'graʊnd] ◇ *adj* **-1.** [below the ground] subterráneo(a). **-2.** *fig* [secret, illegal] clandestino(na). ◇ *adv*: **to go ~** pasar a la clandestinidad; **to be forced ~** tener que pasar a la clandestinidad. ◇ *n* **-1.** *Br* [railway system] metro *m*. **-2.** [activist movement] resistencia *f*, movimiento *m* clandestino.

undergrowth ['ʌndəgrəʊθ] *n* (U) maleza *f*, monte *m* bajo.

underhand [,ʌndə'hænd] *adj* turbio(bia), poco limpio(pia).

underinsured [,ʌndərɪn'ʃʊəd] *adj* que no está asegurado por una cantidad suficiente.

underlay ['ʌndəleɪ] *n* refuerzo *m*.

underline [,ʌndə'laɪn] *vt* subrayar.

underlying [,ʌndə'laɪɪŋ] *adj* subyacente.

undermanned [,ʌndə'mænd] *adj* sin suficiente personal.

undermentioned [,ʌndə'menʃnd] *adj fml* abajo citado(da).

undermine [,ʌndə'maɪn] *vt fig* minar, socavar.

underneath [,ʌndə'niːθ] ◇ *prep* **-1.** [beneath] debajo de. **-2.** [with movement] bajo. ◇ *adv* **-1.** [under, below] debajo. **-2.** *fig* [fundamentally] por dentro, en el fondo. ◇ *adj inf* inferior, de abajo. ◇ *n* **-1.** [underside]: **the ~** la superficie inferior. **-2.** *fig* [true personality]: **on the ~** en el fondo.

undernourished [,ʌndə'nʌrɪʃt] *adj* desnutrido(da).

underpaid [*pt & pp* ,ʌndə'peɪd, *adj* 'ʌndəpeɪd] ◇ *pt & pp* → **underpay**. ◇ *adj* mal pagado(da).

underpants ['ʌndəpænts] *npl* calzoncillos *mpl*.

underpass ['ʌndəpɑːs] *n* paso *m* subterráneo.

underpay [,ʌndə'peɪ] (*pt & pp* **-paid**) *vt* pagar mal.

underpin [,ʌndə'pɪn] (*pt & pp* **-ned**, *cont* **-ning**) ◇ *vt* apoyar, sostener.

underplay [,ʌndə'pleɪ] *vt* [minimize the importance of] minimizar.

underprice [,ʌndə'praɪs] *vt* marcar con un precio muy por debajo del valor real.

underprivileged [,ʌndə'prɪvɪlɪdʒd] *adj* desvalido(da), desamparado(da).

underproduction [,ʌndəprə'dʌkʃn] *n* producción *f* insuficiente.

underrated [,ʌndə'reɪtɪd] *adj* subestimado(da), infravalorado(da).

underscore [,ʌndə'skɔːʳ] *vt lit & fig* subrayar.

undersea ['ʌndəsiː] *adj* submarino(na).

undersecretary [ˌʌndə'sekrətərɪ] (pl -ies) n subsecretario m, -ria f.

undersell [ˌʌndə'sel] (pt & pp -sold) vt -1. [sell at lower prices than] vender a precio más bajo que. -2. fig [underemphasize] no hacer suficiente hincapié en.

undershirt ['ʌndəʃɜːt] n Am camiseta f.

underside ['ʌndəsaɪd] n: the ~ la superficie inferior.

undersigned ['ʌndəsaɪnd] n fml: the ~ el/la abajo firmante.

undersize(d) [ˌʌndə'saɪz(d)] adj más peque-ño(ña) de lo normal.

underskirt ['ʌndəskɜːt] n enaguas fpl.

undersold [ˌʌndə'səʊld] pt & pp → under-sell.

understaffed [ˌʌndə'stɑːft] adj falto(ta) de personal.

understand [ˌʌndə'stænd] (pt & pp -stood) ◇ vt -1. [gen] comprender, entender; do you ~ French? ¿entiendes francés?; to make o.s. understood hacerse entender. -2. [know all about] entender de. -3. fml [to be informed]: to ~ that tener entendido(da) que. ◇ vi comprender, entender.

understandable [ˌʌndə'stændəbl] adj com-prensible.

understandably [ˌʌndə'stændəblɪ] adv na-turalmente, comprensiblemente.

understanding [ˌʌndə'stændɪŋ] ◇ n -1. [knowledge] entendimiento m, comprensión f. -2. [sympathy] comprensión f mutua. -3. [interpretation]: it is my ~ that tengo la im-presión de que. -4. [informal agreement] acuerdo m, arreglo m; on the ~ that a con-dición de que. ◇ adj comprensivo(va).

understate [ˌʌndə'steɪt] vt minimizar, ate-nuar.

understatement [ˌʌndə'steɪtmənt] n -1. [in-adequate statement] atenuación f; it's an ~ to say he's fat decir que es gordo es quedarse corto. -2. (U) [quality of understating]: he's a master of ~ puede quitarle importancia a cualquier cosa.

understood [ˌʌndə'stʊd] pt & pp → under-stand.

understudy ['ʌndəˌstʌdɪ] (pl -ies) n suplen-te m y f.

undertake [ˌʌndə'teɪk] (pt -took, pp -ta-ken) vt -1. [task] emprender, tomar. -2. [responsibility, control] asumir, tomar. -2. [promise]: to ~ to do sthg comprometerse a hacer algo.

undertaker ['ʌndəˌteɪkə'] n director m, -ra f de pompas fúnebres.

undertaking [ˌʌndə'teɪkɪŋ] n -1. [task] tarea f, empresa f. -2. [promise] promesa f.

undertone ['ʌndətəʊn] n -1. [quiet voice] voz f baja. -2. [vague feeling] matiz m.

undertook [ˌʌndə'tʊk] pt → undertake.

undertow ['ʌndətəʊ] n resaca f (marítima).

undervalue [ˌʌndə'væljuː] vt [person] subes-timar, menospreciar; [house] subvalorar.

underwater [ˌʌndə'wɔːtə'] ◇ adj submari-no(na). ◇ adv bajo el agua.

underwear ['ʌndəweə'] n ropa f interior.

underweight [ˌʌndə'weɪt] adj flaco(ca), que no pesa lo suficiente.

underwent [ˌʌndə'went] pt → undergo.

underworld ['ʌndəˌwɜːld] n [criminal socie-ty]: the ~ el hampa, los bajos fondos.

underwrite ['ʌndəraɪt] (pt -wrote, pp -written) vt -1. fml [guarantee] suscribir. -2. [in insurance] asegurar.

underwriter ['ʌndəˌraɪtə'] n asegurador m, -ra f.

underwritten ['ʌndəˌrɪtn] pp → under-write.

underwrote ['ʌndərəʊt] pt → underwrite.

undeserved [ˌʌndɪ'zɜːvd] adj inmereci-do(da).

undesirable [ˌʌndɪ'zaɪərəbl] adj indeseable.

undeveloped [ˌʌndɪ'veləpt] adj [country] subdesarrollado(da).

undid [ˌʌn'dɪd] pt → undo.

undies ['ʌndɪz] npl inf paños mpl menores, calzonarios mpl Amer.

undignified [ʌn'dɪgnɪfaɪd] adj indecoro-so(sa).

undiluted [ˌʌndaɪ'ljuːtɪd] adj -1. [joy etc] puro(ra). -2. [liquid] sin diluir.

undiplomatic [ˌʌndɪplə'mætɪk] adj poco di-plomático(ca), indiscreto(ta).

undischarged [ˌʌndɪs'tʃɑːdʒd] adj -1. [debt] sin liquidar. -2. [person]: ~ bankrupt perso-na en quiebra no rehabilitada.

undisciplined [ʌn'dɪsɪplɪnd] adj indiscipli-nado(da).

undiscovered [ˌʌndɪ'skʌvəd] adj no descu-bierto(ta).

undisputed [ˌʌndɪ'spjuːtɪd] adj indiscutible.

undistinguished [ˌʌndɪ'stɪŋgwɪʃt] adj me-diocre.

undivided [ˌʌndɪ'vaɪdɪd] adj entero(ra), ín-tegro(gra); his ~ attention toda su aten-ción.

undo [ˌʌn'duː] (pt -did, pp -done) vt -1. [unfasten - knot] desatar, desanudar; [- but-ton, clasp] desabrochar; [- parcel] abrir. -2. [nullify] anular, deshacer.

undoing [ˌʌn'duːɪŋ] n (U) fml ruina f, perdi-ción f.

undone [ˌʌn'dʌn] ◇ *pp* → **undo**. ◇ *adj* **-1.** [coat] desabrochado(da); [shoes] desatado(da). **-2.** *fml* [not done] por hacer.

undoubted [ʌn'daʊtɪd] *adj* indudable.

undoubtedly [ʌn'daʊtɪdlɪ] *adv fml* indudablemente, sin duda (alguna).

undreamed-of [ʌn'driːmdɒv], **undreamt-of** [ʌn'dremtɒv] *adj* inimaginable.

undress [ˌʌn'dres] ◇ *vt* desnudar. ◇ *vi* desnudarse.

undressed [ˌʌn'drest] *adj* desnudo(da); **to get ~** desnudarse.

undrinkable [ˌʌn'drɪŋkəbl] *adj* **-1.** [unfit to drink] no potable. **-2.** [disgusting] imbebible.

undue [ˌʌn'djuː] *adj fml* indebido(da), excesivo(va).

undulate ['ʌndjʊleɪt] *vi fml* ondular.

unduly [ˌʌn'djuːlɪ] *adv fml* indebidamente, excesivamente.

undying [ʌn'daɪɪŋ] *adj literary* imperecedero(ra).

unearned income [ˌʌn'ɜːnd-] *n* (U) renta *f* (no salarial).

unearth [ˌʌn'ɜːθ] *vt* [dig up] desenterrar; *fig* [discover] descubrir.

unearthly [ʌn'ɜːθlɪ] *adj* **-1.** [ghostly] sobrenatural, misterioso(sa). **-2.** *inf* [hour] intempestivo(va).

unease [ʌn'iːz] *n* malestar *m*.

uneasy [ʌn'iːzɪ] (*compar* **-ier**, *superl* **-iest**) *adj* **-1.** [person, feeling] intranquilo(la). **-2.** [peace] inseguro(ra).

uneatable [ˌʌn'iːtəbl] *adj* incomible.

uneaten [ˌʌn'iːtn] *adj* sin comer.

uneconomic ['ʌnˌiːkə'nɒmɪk] *adj* poco rentable.

uneducated [ˌʌn'edjʊkeɪtɪd] *adj* ignorante, inculto(ta).

unemotional [ˌʌnɪ'məʊʃənl] *adj* [person, voice] impasible; [statement, report] objetivo(va).

unemployable [ˌʌnɪm'plɔɪəbl] *adj* que difícilmente puede encontrar trabajo.

unemployed [ˌʌnɪm'plɔɪd] ◇ *adj* parado(da), desempleado(da). ◇ *npl*: **the ~** los parados.

unemployment [ˌʌnɪm'plɔɪmənt] *n* desempleo *m*, paro *m*.

unemployment benefit *Br*, **unemployment compensation** *Am n* subsidio *m* de desempleo OR paro.

unenviable [ˌʌn'envɪəbl] *adj* poco envidiable.

unequal [ˌʌn'iːkwəl] *adj* desigual.

unequalled *Br*, **unequaled** *Am* [ˌʌn'iːkwəld] *adj* sin par, inigualado(da).

unequivocal [ˌʌnɪ'kwɪvəkl] *adj fml* inequívoco(ca).

unerring [ˌʌn'ɜːrɪŋ] *adj* infalible.

UNESCO [juː'neskəʊ] (*abbr of* **United Nations Educational, Scientific and Cultural Organization**) *n* UNESCO *f*.

unethical [ʌn'eθɪkl] *adj* poco ético(ca).

uneven [ˌʌn'iːvn] *adj* **-1.** [not flat - road] lleno(na) de baches; [- land] escabroso(sa). **-2.** [inconsistent, unfair] desigual.

uneventful [ˌʌnɪ'ventfʊl] *adj* tranquilo(la), sin incidentes.

unexceptional [ˌʌnɪk'sepʃənl] *adj* normal, corriente.

unexpected [ˌʌnɪk'spektɪd] *adj* inesperado(da).

unexpectedly [ˌʌnɪk'spektɪdlɪ] *adv* inesperadamente.

unexplained [ˌʌnɪk'spleɪnd] *adj* inexplicado(da).

unexploded [ˌʌnɪk'spləʊdɪd] *adj* [bomb] sin explotar.

unexpurgated [ˌʌn'ekspəgeɪtɪd] *adj* sin expurgar, íntegro(gra).

unfailing [ʌn'feɪlɪŋ] *adj* indefectible.

unfair [ˌʌn'feə] *adj* injusto(ta).

unfair dismissal *n* despido *m* improcedente.

unfairness [ˌʌn'feənɪs] *n* injusticia *f*.

unfaithful [ˌʌn'feɪθfʊl] *adj* [sexually] infiel.

unfamiliar [ˌʌnfə'mɪljə] *adj* **-1.** [not well-known] desconocido(da), nuevo(va). **-2.** [not acquainted]: **to be ~ with** sthg/sb desconocer algo/a alguien.

unfashionable [ˌʌn'fæʃnəbl] *adj* [clothes, ideas] pasado(da) de moda; [area of town] poco popular.

unfasten [ˌʌn'fɑːsn] *vt* [garment, buttons] desabrochar; [rope, tie] desatar, soltar; [door] abrir.

unfavourable *Br*, **unfavorable** *Am* [ˌʌn'feɪvrəbl] *adj* desfavorable.

unfeeling [ʌn'fiːlɪŋ] *adj* insensible.

unfinished [ˌʌn'fɪnɪʃt] *adj* sin terminar.

unfit [ˌʌn'fɪt] *adj* **-1.** [injured] lesionado(da); [in poor shape] que no está en forma. **-2.** [not suitable - thing] impropio(pia); [- person] **~ to** incapaz de; **~ for** no apto para.

unflagging [ˌʌn'flægɪŋ] *adj* incansable.

unflappable [ˌʌn'flæpəbl] *adj* imperturbable.

unflattering [ˌʌn'flætərɪŋ] *adj* poco favorecedor(ra).

unflinching [ʌn'flɪntʃɪŋ] *adj* impávido(da).

unfold [ʌn'fəʊld] ◇ *vt* **-1.** [open out] desple-

gar, desdoblar. -2. [explain] **exponer, revelar.** ◇ *vi* [become clear] **revelarse.**

unforeseeable [ˌʌnfɔːˈsiːəbl] *adj* **imprevisible.**

unforeseen [ˌʌnfɔːˈsiːn] *adj* **imprevisto(ta).**

unforgettable [ˌʌnfəˈgetəbl] *adj* **inolvidable.**

unforgivable [ˌʌnfəˈgɪvəbl] *adj* **imperdonable.**

unformatted [ˌʌnˈfɔːmætɪd] *adj* COMPUT **sin formato.**

unfortunate [ʌnˈfɔːtʃnət] *adj* **-1.** [unlucky] **desgraciado(da), desdichado(da), salado(da)** *Amer.* **-2.** [regrettable] **inoportuno(na).**

unfortunately [ʌnˈfɔːtʃnətlɪ] *adv* **desgraciadamente, desafortunadamente.**

unfounded [ˌʌnˈfaundɪd] *adj* **infundado(da).**

unfriendly [ˌʌnˈfrendlɪ] (*compar* **-ier,** *superl* **-iest**) *adj* **poco amistoso(sa).**

unfulfilled [ˌʌnfulˈfɪld] *adj* **-1.** [not yet realized] **incumplido(da), sin realizar. -2.** [unsatisfied] **insatisfecho(cha).**

unfurl [ˌʌnˈfɜːl] *vt* **desplegar.**

unfurnished [ˌʌnˈfɜːnɪʃt] *adj* **sin muebles, desamueblado(da).**

ungainly [ʌnˈgeɪnlɪ] *adj* **torpe, desgarbado(da).**

ungenerous [ˌʌnˈdʒenərəs] *adj* **-1.** [parsimonious - person] **poco generoso(sa);** [- amount] **miserable. -2.** [uncharitable] **poco caritativo(va).**

ungodly [ˌʌnˈgɒdlɪ] *adj* **-1.** [irreligious] **impío(a). -2.** *inf* [hour] **intempestivo(va).**

ungrateful [ʌnˈgreɪtful] *adj* **desagradecido(da), ingrato(ta).**

ungratefulness [ʌnˈgreɪtfulnɪs] *n* **ingratitud** *f.*

unguarded [ˌʌnˈgɑːdɪd] *adj* **-1.** [not guarded] **sin protección. -2.** [careless]: **in an ~ moment en un momento de descuido.**

unhappily [ʌnˈhæpɪlɪ] *adv* **-1.** [sadly] **tristemente. -2.** *fml* [unfortunately] **lamentablemente, desafortunadamente.**

unhappiness [ʌnˈhæpɪnɪs] *n* (*U*) **tristeza** *f,* **desdicha** *f.*

unhappy [ʌnˈhæpɪ] (*compar* **-ier,** *superl* **-iest**) *adj* **-1.** [sad] **triste;** [wretched] **desdichado(da), infeliz. -2.** [uneasy]: **to be ~ (with** OR **about) estar inquieto(ta) (por). -3.** *fml* [unfortunate] **desafortunado(da).**

unharmed [ˌʌnˈhɑːmd] *adj* [person] **ileso(sa);** [thing] **indemne.**

UNHCR (*abbr of* **United Nations High Commission for Refugees**) *n* **ACNUR** *m.*

unhealthy [ʌnˈhelθɪ] (*compar* **-ier,** *superl* **-iest**) *adj* **-1.** [in bad health] **enfermizo(za). -2.** [causing bad health] **insalubre. -3.** *fig* [interest etc] **morboso(sa).**

unheard [ˌʌnˈhɜːd] *adj*: **to be** OR **go ~ pasar sin ser oído(da).**

unheard-of *adj* **-1.** [unknown, completely absent] **inaudito(ta). -2.** [unprecedented] **sin precedente.**

unheeded [ˌʌnˈhiːdɪd] *adj*: **her warning went ~ nadie hizo caso de su advertencia.**

unhelpful [ˌʌnˈhelpful] *adj* **-1.** [unwilling to help] **poco servicial. -2.** [not useful] **inútil.**

unhindered [ʌnˈhɪndəd] *adj*: **~ (by) no estorbado(da) (por).**

unhook [ˌʌnˈhuk] *vt* **-1.** [unfasten hooks of] **desabrochar. -2.** [remove from hook] **descolgar, desenganchar.**

unhurt [ˌʌnˈhɜːt] *adj* **ileso(sa).**

unhygienic [ˌʌnhaɪˈdʒiːnɪk] *adj* **antihigiénico(ca).**

UNICEF [ˈjuːnɪˌsef] (*abbr of* **United Nations International Children's Emergency Fund**) *n* **UNICEF** *f.*

unicorn [ˈjuːnɪkɔːn] *n* **unicornio** *m.*

unicycle [ˈjuːnɪsaɪkl] *n* **monociclo** *m.*

unidentified [ˌʌnaɪˈdentɪfaɪd] *adj* **sin identificar, no identificado(da).**

unidentified flying object *n* **objeto** *m* **volador no identificado.**

unification [ˌjuːnɪfɪˈkeɪʃn] *n* **unificación** *f.*

uniform [ˈjuːnɪfɔːm] ◇ *adj* **uniforme, constante.** ◇ *n* **uniforme** *m.*

uniformity [ˌjuːnɪˈfɔːmətɪ] *n* **uniformidad** *f.*

uniformly [ˈjuːnɪfɔːmlɪ] *adv* **de modo uniforme.**

unify [ˈjuːnɪfaɪ] (*pt* & *pp* **-ied**) *vt* **unificar, unir.**

unifying [ˈjuːnɪfaɪɪŋ] *adj* **unificador(ra).**

unilateral [ˌjuːnɪˈlætərəl] *adj* **unilateral.**

unimaginable [ˌʌnɪˈmædʒɪnəbl] *adj* **inimaginable, inconcebible.**

unimaginative [ˌʌnɪˈmædʒɪnətɪv] *adj* **poco imaginativo(va).**

unimpaired [ˌʌnɪmˈpeəd] *adj* [gen] **intacto(ta);** [health] **inalterado(da).**

unimpeded [ˌʌnɪmˈpiːdɪd] *adj* **sin estorbos, libre.**

unimportant [ˌʌnɪmˈpɔːtənt] *adj* **sin importancia, insignificante.**

unimpressed [ˌʌnɪmˈprest] *adj* **no impresionado(da).**

uninhabited [ˌʌnɪnˈhæbɪtɪd] *adj* **deshabitado(da), desierto(ta).**

uninhibited [ˌʌnɪnˈhɪbɪtɪd] *adj* **desinhibido(da).**

uninitiated [ˌʌnɪˈnɪʃɪeɪtɪd] *npl*: **the ~ los no iniciados.**

uninjured [ˌʌnˈɪndʒəd] *adj* **ileso(sa).**

uninspiring [ˌʌnɪn'spaɪrɪŋ] *adj* nada inspirador(ra).

unintelligent [ˌʌnɪn'telɪdʒənt] *adj* poco inteligente.

unintentional [ˌʌnɪn'tenʃənl] *adj* involuntario(ria).

uninterested [ˌʌn'ɪntrəstɪd] *adj* no interesado(da).

uninterrupted ['ʌnˌɪntə'rʌptɪd] *adj* ininterrumpido(da).

uninvited [ˌʌnɪn'vaɪtɪd] *adj* no invitado(da).

union ['juːnjən] ◇ *n* **-1.** [trade union] sindicato *m*. **-2.** [alliance] unión *f*, alianza *f*. ◇ *comp* sindical.

Unionist ['juːnjənɪst] *n Br* POL unionista *m y f* (*partidario de que Irlanda del Norte siga siendo parte del Reino Unido*).

unionize, -ise ['juːnjənaɪz] *vt* sindicar.

Union Jack *n*: the ~ *la bandera del Reino Unido*.

union shop *n Am taller, fábrica etc donde todos los empleados tienen que pertenecer a un sindicato.*

unique [juː'niːk] *adj* **-1.** [gen] único(ca). **-2.** *fml* [peculiar, exclusive]: ~ **to** peculiar de.

uniquely [juː'niːklɪ] *adv* **-1.** *fml* [exclusively] exclusivamente. **-2.** [exceptionally] excepcionalmente.

unisex ['juːnɪseks] *adj* unisex (*inv*).

unison ['juːnɪzn] *n* unísono *m*; in ~ [simultaneously] al unísono.

UNISON ['juːnɪzn] *n sindicato grande que acoge a la gran mayoría de los funcionarios británicos.*

unit ['juːnɪt] *n* **-1.** [gen] unidad *f*. **-2.** [piece of furniture] módulo *m*, elemento *m*.

unit cost *n* costo *m* unitario.

unite [juː'naɪt] ◇ *vt* [gen] unir; [country] unificar. ◇ *vi* unirse, juntarse.

united [juː'naɪtɪd] *adj* unido(da); **to be ~ in** estar todos(das) de acuerdo en.

United Arab Emirates *npl*: the ~ los Emiratos Árabes Unidos.

united front *n*: to present a ~ (on) hacer frente común (ante).

United Kingdom *n*: the ~ el Reino Unido.

United Nations *n*: the ~ las Naciones Unidas.

United States *n*: the ~ (los) Estados Unidos *mpl*; the ~ of America los Estados Unidos de América.

unit price *n* precio *m* unitario.

unit trust *n Br* fondo *m* de inversión mobiliaria.

unity ['juːnətɪ] *n* (*U*) unidad *f*, unión *f*.

Univ. *abbr of* **University**.

universal [ˌjuːnɪ'vɜːsl] *adj* universal.

universal joint *n* junta *f* universal.

universe ['juːnɪvɜːs] *n*: the ~ el universo.

university [ˌjuːnɪ'vɜːsətɪ] (*pl* **-ies**) ◇ *n* universidad *f*. ◇ *comp* universitario(ria); ~ **student** (estudiante) universitario *m*, (estudiante) universitaria *f*.

unjust [ˌʌn'dʒʌst] *adj* injusto(ta).

unjustifiable [ʌn'dʒʌstɪˌfaɪəbl] *adj* injustificable.

unjustified [ʌn'dʒʌstɪfaɪd] *adj* injustificado(da).

unkempt [ˌʌn'kempt] *adj* [person] desaseado(da); [hair] despeinado(da); [clothes] descuidado(da).

unkind [ʌn'kaɪnd] *adj* **-1.** [uncharitable] poco amable, cruel. **-2.** *fig* [inhospitable] riguroso(sa).

unkindly [ʌn'kaɪndlɪ] *adv* cruelmente.

unknown [ˌʌn'nəʊn] ◇ *adj* desconocido(da). ◇ *n* **-1.** [thing]: the ~ lo desconocido. **-2.** [person] desconocido *m*, -da *f*.

unlace [ˌʌn'leɪs] *vt* [clothes] desenlazar; [shoes] desatar los cordones de.

unladen [ˌʌn'leɪdn] *adj* vacío(a), sin carga.

unlawful [ˌʌn'lɔːful] *adj* ilegal, ilícito(ta).

unleaded [ˌʌn'ledɪd] *adj* sin plomo.

unleash [ˌʌn'liːʃ] *vt literary* desatar, desencadenar.

unleavened [ˌʌn'levnd] *adj* ázimo, sin levadura.

unless [ən'les] *conj* a menos que; ~ **I say so** a menos que yo lo diga; ~ **I'm mistaken** si no me equivoco.

unlicensed, unlicenced *Am* [ˌʌn'laɪsənst] *adj* **-1.** [without a licence - person, vehicle] sin permiso; [- activity] sin licencia. **-2.** [not licensed to sell alcohol] no autorizado(da).

unlike [ˌʌn'laɪk] *prep* **-1.** [different from] distinto(ta) a, diferente a. **-2.** [differently from] a diferencia de. **-3.** [not typical of] impropio(pia) de, poco característico(ca) de.

unlikely [ʌn'laɪklɪ] *adj* **-1.** [not probable] improbable, poco probable. **-2.** [bizarre] inverosímil.

unlimited [ʌn'lɪmɪtɪd] *adj* ilimitado(da), sin límites.

unlisted [ʌn'lɪstɪd] *adj Am* [phone number] que no figura en la guía telefónica.

unlit [ˌʌn'lɪt] *adj* **-1.** [not burning] sin encender. **-2.** [dark] no iluminado(da).

unload [ˌʌn'ləʊd] *vt* **-1.** [goods, car] descargar. **-2.** *fig* [unburden]: **to ~ sthg on** OR **onto sb** descargar algo en alguien.

unlock [ˌʌn'lɒk] *vt* abrir (con llave).

unloved [ˌʌn'lʌvd] *adj*: **to be/feel** ~ no ser/ sentirse amado(da) por nadie.

unluckily [ʌn'lʌkɪlɪ] *adv* desgraciadamente.

unlucky [ʌn'lʌkɪ] (*compar* **-ier**, *superl* **-iest**) *adj* **-1.** [unfortunate] desgraciado(da). **-2.** [number, colour etc] de la mala suerte.

unmanageable [ʌn'mænɪdʒəbl] *adj* [vehicle, parcel] difícil de manejar; [situation] muy difícil, incontrolable.

unmanly [ˌʌn'mænlɪ] (*compar* **-ier**, *superl* **-iest**) *adj* cobarde.

unmanned [ˌʌn'mænd] *adj* no tripulado(da).

unmarked [ˌʌn'mɑːkt] *adj* **-1.** [uninjured] ileso(sa), sin un rasguño. **-2.** [unidentified - box, suitcase] sin marcar; ~ **police car** coche camuflado de la policía.

unmarried [ˌʌn'mærɪd] *adj* que no se ha casado.

unmask [ˌʌn'mɑːsk] *vt* [gen] desenmascarar; *fig* [truth etc] descubrir, exponer.

unmatched [ˌʌn'mætʃt] *adj* incomparable, sin par.

unmentionable [ʌn'menʃnəbl] *adj* que no se puede mencionar.

unmistakable [ˌʌnmɪ'steɪkəbl] *adj* inconfundible.

unmitigated [ʌn'mɪtɪgeɪtɪd] *adj* absoluto(ta).

unmoved [ˌʌn'muːvd] *adj*: **to be** ~ **by** permanecer impasible ante.

unnamed [ˌʌn'neɪmd] *adj* anónimo(ma).

unnatural [ʌn'nætʃrəl] *adj* **-1.** [unusual, strange] anormal. **-2.** [affected] afectado(da).

unnecessary [ʌn'nesəsərɪ] *adj* innecesario(ria).

unnerving [ˌʌn'nɜːvɪŋ] *adj* desconcertante.

unnoticed [ˌʌn'nəʊtɪst] *adj* inadvertido(da), desapercibido(da).

UNO (*abbr of* **United Nations Organization**) *n* ONU *f*.

unobserved [ˌʌnəb'zɜːvd] *adj* inadvertido(da), desapercibido(da).

unobtainable [ˌʌnəb'teɪnəbl] *adj* inasequible.

unobtrusive [ˌʌnəb'truːsɪv] *adj* discreto(ta).

unoccupied [ˌʌn'ɒkjʊpaɪd] *adj* **-1.** [place, seat] libre; [area] despoblado(da); [house] deshabitado(da). **-2.** [person] desocupado(da).

unofficial [ˌʌnə'fɪʃl] *adj* extraoficial, oficioso(sa).

unopened [ˌʌn'əʊpənd] *adj* sin abrir.

unorthodox [ˌʌn'ɔːθədɒks] *adj* poco convencional, poco ortodoxo(xa).

unpack [ˌʌn'pæk] ◇ *vt* **-1.** [box] desempaquetar, desembalar; [suitcases] deshacer. **-2.** [clothes] sacar (de la maleta). ◇ *vi* deshacer las maletas.

unpaid [ˌʌn'peɪd] *adj* **-1.** [person, job, leave] no retribuido(da). **-2.** [not yet paid] por pagar.

unpalatable [ʌn'pælətəbl] *adj* [food] incomible; [drink] imbebible; *fig* [difficult to accept] desagradable.

unparalleled [ʌn'pærəleld] *adj* incomparable, sin precedente.

unpatriotic ['ʌnˌpætrɪ'ɒtɪk] *adj* antipatriótico(ca).

unpick [ˌʌn'pɪk] *vt* descoser.

unpin [ˌʌn'pɪn] (*pt & pp* **-ned**, *cont* **-ning**) *vt* [sewing] quitar los alfileres de; [clothes] desabrochar; [hair] quitar las horquillas de.

unplanned [ˌʌn'plænd] *adj* imprevisto(ta).

unpleasant [ʌn'pleznt] *adj* **-1.** [disagreeable] desagradable. **-2.** [unfriendly, rude - person] antipático(ca); [- remark] mezquino(na).

unpleasantness [ʌn'plezntnɪs] *n* **-1.** [disagreeableness] lo desagradable. **-2.** [rudeness - of person] antipatía *f*; [- of remark] mezquindad *f*.

unplug [ʌn'plʌg] (*pt & pp* **-ged**, *cont* **-ging**) *vt* desenchufar, desconectar.

unpolished [ˌʌn'pɒlɪʃt] *adj* **-1.** [furniture] sin encerar; [shoes] sin lustrar. **-2.** [style etc] tosco(ca).

unpolluted [ˌʌnpə'luːtɪd] *adj* sin contaminar.

unpopular [ˌʌn'pɒpjʊlə'] *adj* impopular, poco popular.

unprecedented [ʌn'presɪdəntɪd] *adj* sin precedentes, inaudito(ta).

unpredictable [ˌʌnprɪ'dɪktəbl] *adj* imprevisible.

unprejudiced [ˌʌn'predʒʊdɪst] *adj* imparcial.

unprepared [ˌʌnprɪ'peəd] *adj*: **to be** ~ **(for)** no estar preparado(da) (para).

unprepossessing ['ʌnˌpriːpə'zesɪŋ] *adj* poco atractivo(va).

unpretentious [ˌʌnprɪ'tenʃəs] *adj* sin pretensiones, modesto(ta).

unprincipled [ʌn'prɪnsəpld] *adj* sin principios.

unprintable [ˌʌn'prɪntəbl] *adj fig* que no se puede repetir (en la prensa).

unproductive [ˌʌnprə'dʌktɪv] *adj* [land, work] improductivo(va); [discussion, meeting] infructuoso(sa).

unprofessional [ˌʌnprə'feʃənl] *adj* poco profesional.

unprofitable [ˌʌnˈprɒfɪtəbl] *adj* [company, product] no rentable.

unprompted [ˌʌnˈprɒmptɪd] *adj* espontáneo(a).

unpronounceable [ˌʌnprəˈnaʊnsəbl] *adj* impronunciable.

unprotected [ˌʌnprəˈtektɪd] *adj* sin protección, desprotegido(da).

unprovoked [ˌʌnprəˈvəʊkt] *adj* no provocado(da).

unpublished [ˌʌnˈpʌblɪʃt] *adj* inédito(ta), no publicado(da).

unpunished [ˌʌnˈpʌnɪʃt] *adj*: **to go ~** escapar sin castigo.

unqualified [ˌʌnˈkwɒlɪfaɪd] *adj* **-1.** [not qualified] sin título, no cualificado(da). **-2.** [total, complete] incondicional, completo(ta).

unquestionable [ʌnˈkwestʃənəbl] *adj* incuestionable, indiscutible.

unquestioning [ʌnˈkwestʃənɪŋ] *adj* incondicional.

unravel [ʌnˈrævl] (*Br pt & pp* **-led**, *cont* **-ling**, *Am pt & pp* **-ed**, *cont* **-ing**) *vt lit & fig* desenmarañar.

unreadable [ʌnˈriːdəbl] *adj* **-1.** [difficult, tedious to read] pesado(da) de leer. **-2.** [illegible] ilegible.

unreal [ˌʌnˈrɪəl] *adj* irreal.

unrealistic [ˌʌnrɪəˈlɪstɪk] *adj* [person] poco realista; [idea, plan] impracticable, fantástico(ca).

unreasonable [ʌnˈriːznəbl] *adj* **-1.** [person, behaviour, decision] poco razonable. **-2.** [demand, price] excesivo(va).

unrecognizable [ˌʌnˈrekəgnaɪzəbl] *adj* irreconocible.

unrecognized [ˌʌnˈrekəgnaɪzd] *adj* no reconocido(da).

unrecorded [ˌʌnrɪˈkɔːdɪd] *adj* no registrado(da).

unrefined [ˌʌnrɪˈfaɪnd] *adj* **-1.** [not processed] no refinado(da). **-2.** [vulgar - person] vulgar; [- manner] poco refinado(da).

unrehearsed [ˌʌnrɪˈhɜːst] *adj* improvisado(da).

unrelated [ˌʌnrɪˈleɪtɪd] *adj*: **to be ~ (to)** no tener conexión (con).

unrelenting [ˌʌnrɪˈlentɪŋ] *adj* implacable, inexorable.

unreliable [ˌʌnrɪˈlaɪəbl] *adj* que no es de fiar.

unrelieved [ˌʌnrɪˈliːvd] *adj* crónico(ca), constante.

unremarkable [ˌʌnrɪˈmɑːkəbl] *adj* ordinario(ria), corriente.

unremitting [ˌʌnrɪˈmɪtɪŋ] *adj* incesante, continuo(nua).

unrepeatable [ˌʌnrɪˈpiːtəbl] *adj* irrepetible.

unrepentant [ˌʌnrɪˈpentənt] *adj* impenitente.

unrepresentative [ˌʌnreprɪˈzentətɪv] *adj*: **~ (of)** poco representativo(va) (de).

unrequited [ˌʌnrɪˈkwaɪtɪd] *adj* no correspondido(da).

unreserved [ˌʌnrɪˈzɜːvd] *adj* **-1.** [wholehearted] incondicional, absoluto(ta). **-2.** [not reserved] libre, no reservado(da).

unresolved [ˌʌnrɪˈzɒlvd] *adj* sin resolver, pendiente.

unresponsive [ˌʌnrɪˈspɒnsɪv] *adj*: **to be ~** to ser insensible a.

unrest [ʌnˈrest] *n* (*U*) malestar *m*, inquietud *f*.

unrestrained [ˌʌnrɪˈstreɪnd] *adj* incontrolado(da), desenfrenado(da).

unrestricted [ˌʌnrɪˈstrɪktɪd] *adj* sin restricción.

unrewarding [ˌʌnrɪˈwɔːdɪŋ] *adj* que no ofrece satisfacción.

unripe [ˌʌnˈraɪp] *adj* verde, que no está maduro(ra).

unrivalled *Br*, **unrivaled** *Am* [ʌnˈraɪvld] *adj* incomparable, sin par.

unroll [ˌʌnˈrəʊl] *vt* desenrollar.

unruffled [ˌʌnˈrʌfld] *adj* [calm] imperturbable.

unruly [ʌnˈruːlɪ] (*compar* **-ier**, *superl* **-iest**) *adj* **-1.** [person, behaviour] revoltoso(sa). **-2.** [hair] rebelde.

unsafe [ˌʌnˈseɪf] *adj* [gen] inseguro(ra); [risky] arriesgado(da).

unsaid [ˌʌnˈsed] *adj*: **to leave sthg ~** dejar algo sin decir.

unsaleable, **unsalable** *Am* [ˌʌnˈseɪləbl] *adj* invendible.

unsatisfactory [ˈʌnˌsætɪsˈfæktərɪ] *adj* insatisfactorio(ria).

unsavoury, **unsavory** *Am* [ˌʌnˈseɪvərɪ] *adj* desagradable.

unscathed [ˌʌnˈskeɪðd] *adj* ileso(sa).

unscheduled [*Br* ˌʌnˈʃedjʊld, *Am* ˌʌnˈskedʒʊld] *adj* imprevisto(ta).

unscientific [ˈʌnˌsaɪənˈtɪfɪk] *adj* poco científico(ca).

unscrew [ˌʌnˈskruː] *vt* **-1.** [lid, top] abrir. **-2.** [sign, hinge] desatornillar.

unscripted [ˌʌnˈskrɪptɪd] *adj* sin guión, improvisado(da).

unscrupulous [ʌnˈskruːpjʊləs] *adj* desaprensivo(va), poco escrupuloso(sa).

unseat [,ʌn'siːt] *vt* **-1.** [rider] derribar, desarzonar. **-2.** *fig* [depose] deponer.

unseeded [,ʌn'siːdɪd] *adj* que no es cabeza de serie.

unseemly [ʌn'siːmlɪ] (*compar* **-ier,** *superl* **-iest**) *adj* impropio(pia), indecoroso(sa).

unseen [,ʌn'siːn] *adj* [person, escape] inadvertido(da).

unselfish [,ʌn'selfɪʃ] *adj* desinteresado(da), altruista.

unselfishly [,ʌn'selfɪʃlɪ] *adv* desinteresadamente, altruistamente.

unsettle [,ʌn'setl] *vt* perturbar, inquietar.

unsettled [,ʌn'setld] *adj* **-1.** [person] nervioso(sa), intranquilo(la). **-2.** [weather] variable, inestable. **-3.** [argument, matter, debt] pendiente. **-4.** [situation] inestable.

unsettling [,ʌn'setlɪŋ] *adj* inquietante, perturbador(ra).

unshak(e)able [ʌn'ʃeɪkəbl] *adj* inquebrantable.

unshaven [,ʌn'ʃeɪvn] *adj* sin afeitar.

unsheathe [,ʌn'ʃiːð] *vt* desenvainar.

unsightly [ʌn'saɪtlɪ] *adj* [building] feo (fea); [scar, bruise] desagradable.

unskilled [,ʌn'skɪld] *adj* [person] no cualificado(da); [work] no especializado(da).

unsociable [ʌn'səʊʃəbl] *adj* insociable, poco sociable.

unsocial [,ʌn'səʊʃl] *adj*: **to work ~ hours** trabajar a horas intempestivas.

unsold [,ʌn'səʊld] *adj* sin vender.

unsolicited [,ʌnsə'lɪsɪtɪd] *adj* no solicitado(da).

unsolved [,ʌn'sɒlvd] *adj* no resuelto(ta), sin resolver.

unsophisticated [,ʌnsə'fɪstɪkeɪtɪd] *adj* **-1.** [person] ingenuo(nua). **-2.** [method, device] rudimentario(ria).

unsound [,ʌn'saʊnd] *adj* **-1.** [conclusion, method] erróneo(a). **-2.** [building, structure] defectuoso(sa).

unspeakable [ʌn'spiːkəbl] *adj* [crime] incalificable; [pain] indecible.

unspeakably [ʌn'spiːkəblɪ] *adv* indescriptiblemente.

unspecified [,ʌn'spesɪfaɪd] *adj* sin especificar.

unspoiled [,ʌn'spɔɪld], **unspoilt** [,ʌn'spɔɪlt] *adj* sin estropear.

unspoken [,ʌn'spəʊkən] *adj* **-1.** [not expressed openly] no expresado(da). **-2.** [tacit] tácito(ta).

unsporting [,ʌn'spɔːtɪŋ] *adj* poco deportivo(va).

unstable [,ʌn'steɪbl] *adj* inestable.

unstated [,ʌn'steɪtɪd] *adj* no expresado(da).

unsteady [,ʌn'stedɪ] (*compar* **-ier,** *superl* **-iest**) *adj* [gen] inestable; [hands, voice] tembloroso(sa); [footsteps] vacilante.

unstinting [,ʌn'stɪntɪŋ] *adj* pródigo(ga).

unstoppable [,ʌn'stɒpəbl] *adj* irrefrenable, incontenible.

unstrap [,ʌn'stræp] (*pt & pp* **-ped,** *cont* **-ping**) *vt* desabrochar (las correas de).

unstructured [,ʌn'strʌktʃəd] *adj* poco organizado(da).

unstuck [,ʌn'stʌk] *adj*: **to come ~** [notice, stamp, label] despegarse, desprenderse; *fig* [plan, system, person] fracasar.

unsubstantiated [,ʌnsəb'stænʃɪeɪtɪd] *adj* no corroborado(da), sin probar.

unsuccessful [,ʌnsək'sesful] *adj* [person] fracasado(da); [attempt, meeting] infructuoso(sa).

unsuccessfully [,ʌnsək'sesfulɪ] *adv* sin éxito, en vano.

unsuitable [,ʌn'suːtəbl] *adj* inadecuado(da), inapropiado(da); **he is ~ for the job** no es la persona indicada para el trabajo; **I'm afraid 3 o'clock would be ~** lo siento, pero no me va bien a las 3.

unsuited [,ʌn'suːtɪd] *adj* **-1.** [not appropriate]: **to be ~ to** OR **for** ser inepto(ta) para. **-2.** [not compatible]: **to be ~ (to each other)** ser incompatibles (uno con el otro).

unsung [,ʌn'sʌŋ] *adj* no celebrado(da).

unsure [,ʌn'ʃɔːr] *adj* **-1.** [not confident]: **to be ~ of o.s.** sentirse inseguro(ra). **-2.** [not certain]: **to be ~ (about** OR **of)** no estar muy seguro (de).

unsurpassed [,ʌnsə'pɑːst] *adj* insuperado(da).

unsuspecting [,ʌnsə'spektɪŋ] *adj* desprevenido(da), confiado(da).

unsweetened [,ʌn'swiːtnd] *adj* sin azúcar.

unswerving [ʌn'swɜːvɪŋ] *adj* firme, inquebrantable.

unsympathetic ['ʌn,sɪmpə'θetɪk] *adj*: **~ to** indiferente a.

untamed [,ʌn'teɪmd] *adj* **-1.** [animal] indomado(da). **-2.** [place, land] sin cultivar. **-3.** [person] indómito(ta).

untangle [,ʌn'tæŋgl] *vt* desenmarañar.

untapped [,ʌn'tæpt] *adj* sin explotar.

untaxed [,ʌn'tækst] *adj* antes de impuestos.

untenable [,ʌn'tenəbl] *adj* insostenible.

unthinkable [ʌn'θɪŋkəbl] *adj* impensable, inconcebible.

unthinkingly [ʌn'θɪŋkɪŋlɪ] *adv* sin pensar, irreflexivamente.

untidy [ʌn'taɪdɪ] (*compar* **-ier,** *superl* **-iest**) *adj* [room, desk] desordenado(da); [person, appearance] desaliñado(da).

untie [ˌʌn'taɪ] (*cont* **untying**) *vt* desatar.

until [ən'tɪl] ◇ *prep* hasta; ~ **now/then** hasta ahora/entonces. ◇ *conj* **-1.** [gen] hasta que. **-2.** (*after negative*): **don't leave ~ you've finished** no te vayas hasta que no hayas terminado.

untimely [ʌn'taɪmlɪ] *adj* **-1.** [premature] prematuro(ra). **-2.** [inappropriate] inoportuno(na).

untiring [ʌn'taɪərɪŋ] *adj* incansable.

untold [ˌʌn'təʊld] *adj* [incalculable, vast] incalculable; [suffering, joy] indecible.

untouched [ˌʌn'tʌtʃt] *adj* **-1.** [scenery, place] no estropeado(da); [building etc] intacto(ta). **-2.** [food] sin probar.

untoward [ˌʌntə'wɔ:d] *adj* [event] adverso(sa); [behaviour] fuera de lugar.

untrained [ˌʌn'treɪnd] *adj* **-1.** [person, worker] no cualificado(da). **-2.** [voice, mind] no educado(da).

untrammelled *Br*, **untrammeled** *Am* [ʌn'træməld] *fml* **-1.** [unbounded - joy etc] sin límites. **-2.** [unrestricted] ~ **by** libre de.

untranslatable [ˌʌntræns'leɪtəbl] *adj* intraducible.

untreated [ˌʌn'tri:tɪd] *adj* **-1.** [illness, person] que no ha sido tratado(da). **-2.** [waste, effluent] sin tratar.

untried [ˌʌn'traɪd] *adj* no probado(da).

untroubled [ˌʌn'trʌbld] *adj*: **to be ~ by** no estar afectado(da) por.

untrue [ˌʌn'tru:] *adj* **-1.** [not true] falso(sa). **-2.** [unfaithful]: **to be ~ to** ser infiel OR desleal a.

untrustworthy [ˌʌn'trʌst,wɜ:ðɪ] *adj* indigno(na) de confianza.

untruth [ˌʌn'tru:θ] *n* mentira *f*.

untruthful [ˌʌn'tru:θfʊl] *adj* falso(sa), mentiroso(sa).

untutored [ˌʌn'tju:təd] *adj* no educado(da).

unusable [ˌʌn'ju:zəbl] *adj* inútil, inservible.

unused [*sense 1* ʌn'ju:zd, *sense 2* ʌn'ju:st] *adj* **-1.** [not previously used] nuevo(va), sin usar. **-2.** [unaccustomed]: **to be ~ to sthg/to doing sthg** no estar acostumbrado(da) a algo/a hacer algo.

unusual [ʌn'ju:ʒl] *adj* [rare] insólito(ta), poco común.

unusually [ʌn'ju:ʒəlɪ] *adv* **-1.** [exceptionally] extraordinariamente. **-2.** [surprisingly] sorprendentemente.

unvarnished [ʌn'vɑ:nɪʃt] *adj* *fig* [straightforward] sin adornos.

unveil [ˌʌn'veɪl] *vt* **-1.** [statue, plaque] descubrir. **-2.** *fig* [plans, policy] revelar.

unwaged [ˌʌn'weɪdʒd] *adj* *Br* desempleado(da).

unwanted [ˌʌn'wɒntɪd] *adj* [clothes, furniture] superfluo(flua); [child, pregnancy] no deseado(da).

unwarranted [ʌn'wɒrəntɪd] *adj* injustificado(da).

unwavering [ʌn'weɪvərɪŋ] *adj* [determination, feeling] firme, inquebrantable; [concentration] constante; [gaze] fijo(ja).

unwelcome [ʌn'welkəm] *adj* inoportuno(na).

unwell [ˌʌn'wel] *adj*: **to be/feel ~** estar/sentirse mal.

unwholesome [ˌʌn'həʊlsəm] *adj* **-1.** [unhealthy] insalubre. **-2.** [unpleasant, unnatural] malsano(na).

unwieldy [ʌn'wi:ldɪ] (*compar* **-ier,** *superl* **-iest**) *adj* **-1.** [object] abultado(da); [tool] poco manejable. **-2.** *fig* [system, organization] poco eficiente.

unwilling [ˌʌn'wɪlɪŋ] *adj* no dispuesto(ta); **to be ~ to do sthg** no estar dispuesto a hacer algo.

unwind [ˌʌn'waɪnd] (*pt* & *pp* **unwound**) ◇ *vt* desenrollar. ◇ *vi* *fig* [person] relajarse.

unwise [ˌʌn'waɪz] *adj* imprudente, poco aconsejable.

unwitting [ʌn'wɪtɪŋ] *adj* *fml* inconsciente.

unwittingly [ʌn'wɪtɪŋlɪ] *adv* *fml* inconscientemente, sin darse cuenta.

unworkable [ˌʌn'wɜ:kəbl] *adj* impracticable.

unworldly [ˌʌn'wɜ:ldlɪ] *adj* poco mundano(na).

unworthy [ʌn'wɜ:ðɪ] (*compar* **-ier,** *superl* **-iest**) *adj* [undeserving]: **to be ~ of** no ser digno(na) de.

unwound [ˌʌn'waʊnd] *pt* & *pp* → **unwind.**

unwrap [ˌʌn'ræp] (*pt* & *pp* **-ped,** *cont* **-ping**) *vt* [present] desenvolver; [parcel] desempaquetar.

unwritten law [ˌʌn'rɪtn-] *n* ley *f* no escrita.

unyielding [ʌn'ji:ldɪŋ] *adj* inflexible.

unzip [ˌʌn'zɪp] (*pt* & *pp* **-ped,** *cont* **-ping**) *vt* abrir la cremallera de.

up [ʌp] (*pt* & *pp* **-ped,** *cont* **-ping**) ◇ *adv* **-1.** [towards a higher position] hacia arriba; [in a higher position] arriba; **to throw sthg up** lanzar algo hacia arriba; **she's ~ in her room** está arriba en su cuarto; **pick it ~!** ¡cógelo!, ¡agárralo! *Amer*; **we walked ~ to the top** subimos hasta arriba del todo; **the sun came ~** el sol salió; **a house ~ in the mountains** una casa arriba en las monta-

ñas; **prices are going** ~ los precios están subiendo. **-2.** [into an upright position]: **to stand** ~ levantarse; **help me** ~ ayúdame a levantarme; ~ **you get!** ¡arriba! **-3.** [northwards]: **I'm going** ~ **to York next week** voy a subir a York la semana próxima; ~ **north** en el norte. **-4.** [along a road or river] adelante; **their house is 100 metres further** ~ su casa está 100 metros más adelante. **-5.** [close up, towards]: **to come** ~ **to sb** acercarse a alguien.
◇ *prep* **-1.** [towards a higher position]: **we went** ~ **the mountain** subimos por la montaña; **I went** ~ **the stairs** subí las escaleras. **-2.** [in a higher position] en lo alto de; ~ **a tree** en un árbol; **halfway** ~ **a mountain** en mitad de la subida a una montaña. **-3.** [at far end of] al final de; **they live** ~ **the road from us** viven al final de nuestra calle. **-4.** [against current of river]: ~ **the Amazon** Amazonas arriba.
◇ *adj* **-1.** [out of bed] levantado(da); **I was** ~ **at six today** hoy me levanté a las seis. **-2.** [at an end] terminado(da); **time's** ~ se acabó el tiempo. **-3.** [under repair]: **"road** ~" "carretera en obras". **-4.** *inf* [wrong]: **is something** ~? ¿pasa algo?, ¿algo va mal?; **what's** ~? ¿qué pasa?
◇ *n*: ~**s and downs** altibajos *mpl*.
◇ *vt inf* [price, cost] subir.
◆ **up against** *prep*: **we came** ~ **against a lot of opposition** nos enfrentamos con mucha oposición; **to be** ~ **against it** vérselas y deseárselas.
◆ **up and down** ◇ *adv*: **to jump** ~ **and down** saltar para arriba y para abajo; **to walk** ~ **and down** andar para un lado y para otro. ◇ *prep*: **she's** ~ **and down the stairs all day** lleva todo el día subiendo y bajando por las escaleras; **she looked** ~ **and down the ranks of soldiers** inspeccionó las filas de soldados de arriba a abajo; **we walked** ~ **and down the avenue** estuvimos caminando arriba y abajo de la avenida.
◆ **up to** *prep* **-1.** [indicating level] hasta; **it could take** ~ **to six weeks** podría tardar hasta seis semanas; **it's not** ~ **to standard** no tiene el nivel necesario. **-2.** [well or able enough for]: **to be** ~ **to doing sthg** sentirse con fuerzas (como) para hacer algo; **my French isn't** ~ **to much** mi francés no es gran cosa. **-3.** *inf* [secretly doing something]: **what are you** ~ **to?** ¿qué andas tramando? **-4.** [indicating responsibility]: **it's not** ~ **to me to decide** no depende de mí el decidir; **it's** ~ **to you** de tí depende.
◆ **up to, up until** *prep* hasta.
up-and-coming *adj* prometedor(ra), con futuro.

up-and-up *n*: **on the** ~ *Br* [improving] cada vez mejor; *Am* [honest] de confianza.
upbeat ['ʌpbiːt] *adj* optimista.
upbraid [ʌp'breɪd] *vt*: **to** ~ **sb (for)** reprender a alguien (por).
upbringing ['ʌp,brɪŋɪŋ] *n* educación *f*.
update [,ʌp'deɪt] *vt* actualizar.
upend [ʌp'end] *vt* volcar.
upfront [,ʌp'frʌnt] ◇ *adj*: **to be** ~ **(about)** ser franco(ca) (sobre). ◇ *adv* [in advance] por adelantado.
upgrade [,ʌp'greɪd] *vt* [job, status] ascender, subir de categoría; [facilities] implementar mejoras a ◇ *vi* implementar mejoras.
upheaval [ʌp'hiːvl] *n* trastorno *m*, agitación *f*.
upheld [ʌp'held] *pt & pp* → **uphold**.
uphill [,ʌp'hɪl] ◇ *adj* [rising] empinado(da), cuesta arriba; *fig* [difficult] arduo(dua), difícil. ◇ *adv* cuesta arriba.
uphold [ʌp'həʊld] (*pt & pp* **-held**) *vt* sostener, apoyar.
upholster [ʌp'həʊlstər] *vt* tapizar.
upholstery [ʌp'həʊlstəri] *n* tapicería *f*, tapizado *m*.
upkeep ['ʌpkiːp] *n* mantenimiento *m*.
upland ['ʌplənd] *adj* de la meseta.
◆ **uplands** *npl* tierras *fpl* altas.
uplift [ʌp'lɪft] *vt* inspirar.
uplifting [ʌp'lɪftɪŋ] *adj* inspirador(ra).
uplighter ['ʌplaɪtər] *n* lámpara o luz diseñada o colocada de manera que ilumina hacia arriba.
up-market *adj* de clase superior, de categoría.
upon [ə'pɒn] *prep fml* en, sobre; ~ **entering the room** al entrar en el cuarto; **question** ~ **question** pregunta tras pregunta; **summer is** ~ **us** ya tenemos el verano encima.
upper ['ʌpər] ◇ *adj* superior. ◇ *n* [of shoe] pala *f*.
upper class *n*: **the** ~ la clase alta.
◆ **upper-class** *adj* de clase alta.
uppercut ['ʌpəkʌt] *n* gancho *m*, uppercut *m*.
upper hand *n*: **to have/gain the** ~ **(in)** llevar/empezar a llevar la ventaja (en).
uppermost ['ʌpəməʊst] *adj* **-1.** [highest] más alto(ta). **-2.** [most important]: **to be** ~ **in one's mind** ser lo más importante para uno.
Upper Volta [-'vɒltə] *n* (el) Alto Volta.
uppity ['ʌpəti] *adj inf* engreído(da), arrogante.

upright [*adj senses 1 to 3 & adv* ‚ʌp'raɪt, *adj sense 4 & n* 'ʌpraɪt] ◇ *adj* **-1.** [erect - person] derecho(cha). **-2.** [standing vertically - object] vertical. **-3.** [chair] derecho(cha). **-4.** *fig* [honest] recto(ta), honrado(da). ◇ *adv* erguidamente. ◇ *n* poste *m*.

upright piano *n* piano *m* vertical.

uprising ['ʌp‚raɪzɪŋ] *n* sublevación *f*, alzamiento *m*.

uproar ['ʌprɔːʳ] *n* **-1.** (*U*) [commotion] alboroto *m*, guachafita *f Amer*. **-2.** [protest] escándalo *m*.

uproarious [ʌp'rɔːrɪəs] *adj* [noisy] estrepitoso(sa).

uproot [ʌp'ruːt] *vt* **-1.** [person] desplazar, mudar; **to ~ o.s.** mudarse. **-2.** BOT [plant] desarraigar.

upset [ʌp'set] (*pt & pp* **upset**, *cont* **-ting**) ◇ *adj* **-1.** [distressed] disgustado(da), afectado(da). **-2.** MED: **to have an ~ stomach** sentirse mal del estómago. ◇ *n*: **to have a stomach ~** sentirse mal del estómago. ◇ *vt* **-1.** [distress] disgustar, perturbar. **-2.** [mess up] dar al traste con, estropear. **-3.** [overturn, knock over] volcar.

upsetting [ʌp'setɪŋ] *adj* inquietante, perturbador(ra).

upshot ['ʌpʃɒt] *n* resultado *m*.

upside down [‚ʌpsaɪd-] ◇ *adj* al revés. ◇ *adv* al revés; **to turn sthg ~** revolver algo, desordenar algo.

upstage [‚ʌp'steɪdʒ] *vt* eclipsar a.

upstairs [‚ʌp'steəz] ◇ *adj* de arriba. ◇ *adv* arriba. ◇ *n* el piso de arriba.

upstanding [‚ʌp'stændɪŋ] *adj* ejemplar.

upstart ['ʌpstɑːt] *n* advenedizo *m*, -za *f*.

upstate ['ʌp'steɪt] *Am* ◇ *adj*: **~ New York** la parte norteña del Estado de Nueva York. ◇ *adv* en/hacia el norte del Estado.

upstream [‚ʌp'striːm] ◇ *adj*: **to be ~ (from)** estar río arriba (de). ◇ *adv* río arriba, corriente arriba.

upsurge ['ʌpsɜːdʒ] *n*: **~ of** OR **in** aumento *m* considerable de.

upswing ['ʌpswɪŋ] *n*: **~ (in)** mejora *f* notable OR alza *f* (en).

uptake ['ʌpteɪk] *n*: **to be quick on the ~** cogerlas al vuelo; **to be slow on the ~** ser un poco torpe.

uptight [ʌp'taɪt] *adj inf* tenso(sa), nervioso(sa).

up-to-date *adj* **-1.** [modern] moderno(na). **-2.** [most recent] actual, al día. **-3.** [informed]: **to keep ~ with** mantenerse al día de.

up-to-the-minute *adj* de última hora.

uptown [‚ʌp'taʊn] *Am* ◇ *adj* alejado(da)

del centro. ◇ *adv* [live, work] en las afueras; [go] a las afueras.

upturn ['ʌptɜːn] *n*: **~ (in)** mejora *f* (de).

upturned [ʌp'tɜːnd] *adj* **-1.** [nose] respingón(ona). **-2.** [upside down] volcado(da).

upward ['ʌpwəd] ◇ *adj* hacia arriba. ◇ *adv Am* = **upwards**.

upwardly-mobile ['ʌpwədlɪ-] *adj* con ganas de mejorar socialmente.

upwards ['ʌpwədz] *adv* hacia arriba.

◆ **upwards of** *prep* más de.

upwind [‚ʌp'wɪnd] *adj*: **to be ~** estar en el lado de donde sopla el viento.

URA (*abbr of* **Urban Renewal Administration**) *n organismo para la rehabilitación de zonas urbanas desfavorecidas*.

Urals ['jʊərəlz] *npl*: **the ~** los Urales.

uranium [jʊ'reɪnjəm] *n* uranio *m*.

Uranus ['jʊərənəs] *n* Urano *m*.

urban ['ɜːbən] *adj* urbano(na).

urbane [ɜː'beɪn] *adj* cortés, urbano(na).

urbanize, -ise ['ɜːbənaɪz] *vt* urbanizar.

urban renewal *n* renovación *f* urbana.

urchin ['ɜːtʃɪn] *n dated* pilluelo *m*, -la *f*, golfillo *m*, -lla *f*.

Urdu ['ʊəduː] *n* urdu *m*.

urge [ɜːdʒ] ◇ *n* impulso *m*, deseo *m*; **to have an ~ to do sthg** desear ardientemente hacer algo. ◇ *vt* **-1.** [try to persuade]: **to ~ sb to do sthg** instar a alguien a hacer algo. **-2.** [advocate] recomendar encarecidamente.

urgency ['ɜːdʒənsɪ] *n* (*U*) urgencia *f*.

urgent ['ɜːdʒənt] *adj* **-1.** [pressing] urgente. **-2.** [desperate] apremiante.

urgently ['ɜːdʒəntlɪ] *adv* **-1.** [as soon as possible] urgentemente. **-2.** [desperately] con insistencia.

urinal [‚jʊə'raɪnl] *n* [place] urinario *m*; [vessel] orinal *m*.

urinary ['jʊərɪnərɪ] *adj* urinario(ria).

urinate ['jʊərɪneɪt] *vi* orinar.

urination *n* micción *f*.

urine ['jʊərɪn] *n* orina *f*.

urn [ɜːn] *n* **-1.** [for ashes] urna *f*. **-2.** [for tea, coffee] *cilindro o barril con grifo para servir té o café en grandes cantidades*.

Uruguay ['jʊərəgwaɪ] *n* Uruguay.

Uruguayan [‚jʊərə'gwaɪən] ◇ *adj* uruguayo(ya). ◇ *n* uruguayo *m*, -ya *f*.

us [ʌs] *pers pron* **-1.** (*direct, indirect*) nos; **can you see/hear ~?** ¿puedes vernos/oírnos?; **it's ~** somos nosotros; **he sent ~ a letter** nos mandó una carta; **she gave it to ~** nos lo dio. **-2.** (*stressed, after prep, in comparisons etc*) nosotros *mpl*, -tras *fpl*; **you can't expect US to do it** no esperarás que lo hagamos

NOSOTROS; **with/without** ~ con/sin nosotros; **they are more wealthy than** ~ son más ricos que nosotros; **all of** ~ todos (nosotros); **some of** ~ algunos de nosotros.

US (*abbr of* United States) *n* EEUU *mpl.*

USA *n* **-1.** (*abbr of* United States of America) EEUU *mpl.* **-2.** (*abbr of* United States Army) *fuerzas armadas estadounidenses.*

usable ['ju:zəbl] *adj* utilizable, aprovechable.

USAF (*abbr of* United States Air Force) *n fuerzas aéreas estadounidenses.*

usage ['ju:zɪdʒ] *n* uso *m.*

USCG (*abbr of* United States Coast Guard) *n servicio de guardacostas en Estados Unidos.*

USDA (*abbr of* United States Department of Agriculture) *n ministerio estadounidense de agricultura.*

USDAW ['ʌzdɔː] (*abbr of* Union of Shop, Distributive and Allied Workers) *n sindicato británico de trabajadores del sector secundario.*

USDI (*abbr of* United States Department of the Interior) *n ministerio estadounidense del interior.*

use [*n & aux vb* ju:s, *vt* ju:z] ◇ *n* uso *m;* **to be in** ~ usarse; **to be out of** ~ no usarse; **"out of** ~**"** "no funciona"; **to make** ~ **of sthg** utilizar OR aprovechar algo; **he still has the** ~ **of his legs** todavía le funcionan las piernas; **to let sb have the** ~ **of sthg** dejar a alguien usar algo; **to be of/no** ~ ser útil/inútil; **what's the** ~ **(of doing sthg)?** ¿de qué sirve (hacer algo)?
◇ *aux vb* soler, acostumbrar; **he** ~**d to be fat** antes estaba gordo; **I** ~**d to go swimming** solía OR acostumbraba ir a nadar.
◇ *vt* **-1.** [utilize, employ] usar, emplear. **-2.** [exploit] usar, manejar.
◆ **use up** *vt sep* agotar.

used [*sense 1* ju:zd, *sense 2* ju:st] *adj* **-1.** [dirty, second-hand] usado(da). **-2.** [accustomed]: **to be** ~ **to** estar acostumbrado(da) a; **to get** ~ **to** acostumbrarse a.

useful ['ju:sfʊl] *adj* **-1.** [handy] útil, provechoso(sa); **to come in** ~ servir, ser útil. **-2.** [helpful - person] valioso(sa).

usefulness ['ju:sfʊlnɪs] *n* (*U*) utilidad *f,* valor *m.*

useless ['ju:slɪs] *adj* **-1.** [gen] inútil. **-2.** *inf* [hopeless] incompetente.

uselessness ['ju:slɪsnɪs] *n* (*U*) inutilidad *f.*

user ['ju:zə'] *n* usuario *m,* -ria *f.*

user-friendly *adj* [gen & COMPUT] fácil de utilizar.

USES (*abbr of* United States Employment Service) *n ministerio estadounidense de trabajo.*

usher ['ʌʃə'] ◇ *n* [at wedding] ujier *m;* [at theatre, concert] acomodador *m,* -ra *f.* ◇ *vt:* **to** ~ **sb in** hacer pasar a alguien; **to** ~ **sb out** acompañar a alguien hasta la puerta.

usherette [,ʌʃə'ret] *n* acomodadora *f.*

USIA (*abbr of* United States Information Agency) *n agencia estadounidense de noticias.*

USM *n* **-1.** (*abbr of* United States Mail) *servicio estadounidense de correos.* **-2.** (*abbr of* United States Mint) *organismo encargado de la fabricación de billetes y monedas en Estados Unidos,* ≃ Casa *f* de la Moneda.

USN (*abbr of* United States Navy) *n armada estadounidense.*

USPHS (*abbr of* United States Public Health Service) *n ministerio estadounidense de la seguridad social.*

USS (*abbr of* United States Ship) *buque de guerra estadounidense.*

USSR (*abbr of* Union of Soviet Socialist Republics) *n:* **the (former)** ~ la (antigua) URSS.

usu. *abbr of* usually.

usual ['ju:ʒəl] *adj* habitual; **as** ~ [as normal] como de costumbre; [as often happens] como siempre.

usually ['ju:ʒəlɪ] *adv* por regla general, normalmente; **more than** ~ más que de costumbre.

usurp [ju:'zɜ:p] *vt fml* usurpar.

usury ['ju:ʒʊrɪ] *n fml* usura *f.*

UT *abbr of* Utah.

Utah ['ju:tɑ:] *n* Utah.

utensil [ju:'tensl] *n* utensilio *m.*

uterus ['ju:tərəs] (*pl* **-ri** [-raɪ] OR **-ruses**) *n* útero *m.*

utilitarian [,ju:tɪlɪ'teərɪən] *adj* **-1.** [gen] utilitario(ria). **-2.** [functional] funcional.

utility [ju:'tɪlətɪ] (*pl* **-ies**) *n* **-1.** [gen & COMPUT] utilidad *f.* **-2.** [public service] servicio *m* público.

utility room *n* trascocina *f.*

utilize, -ise ['ju:təlaɪz] *vt* utilizar.

utmost ['ʌtməʊst] ◇ *adj* mayor, supremo(ma). ◇ *n:* **to do one's** ~ hacer lo imposible; **to the** ~ al máximo, a más no poder.

utopia [ju:'təʊpjə] *n* utopía *f.*

utter ['ʌtə'] ◇ *adj* puro(ra), completo(ta). ◇ *vt* [word] pronunciar; [sound, cry] emitir.

utterly ['ʌtəlɪ] *adv* completamente, totalmente.

U-turn *n lit* & *fig* giro *m* de 180°.

UV (*abbr of* ultra-violet) UV.

UV-A, UVA (*abbr of* ultra-violet-A) UVA.

UV-B, UVB (*abbr of* ultra-violet-B) UVB.

UWIST ['juːwɪst] (*abbr of* **University of Wales Institute of Science and Technology**) *n instituto de ciencia y tecnología de la Universidad de Gales.*

Uzbek ['ʊzbek] ◇ *adj* uzbeko(ka). ◇ *n* **-1.** [person] uzbeko *m*, -ka *f*. **-2.** [language] uzbeko *m*.

Uzbekistan [ʊz‚bekɪ'stɑːn] *n* (el) Uzbekistán.

v¹ (*pl* **v's** OR **vs**), **V** (*pl* **V's** OR **Vs**) [viː] *n* [letter] v *f*, V *f*.

v² **-1.** (*abbr of* **verse**) v. **-2.** (*abbr of* **volt**) v. **-3.** (*abbr of* **vide**) [cross-reference] v. **-4.** *abbr of* **versus**.

VA *abbr of* **Virginia**.

vac [væk] (*abbr of* **vacation**) *n Br inf* vacas *fpl*, vacaciones *fpl*.

vacancy ['veɪkənsɪ] (*pl* **-ies**) *n* **-1.** [job, position] vacante *f*. **-2.** [room available] habitación *f* libre; **"no vacancies"** "completo".

vacant ['veɪkənt] *adj* **-1.** [room, chair, toilet] libre. **-2.** [job, post] vacante. **-3.** [look, expression] distraído(da).

vacant lot *n* terreno *m* disponible.

vacantly ['veɪkəntlɪ] *adv* distraídamente.

vacate [və'keɪt] *vt* **-1.** [job, post] dejar vacante. **-2.** [room, seat, premises] desocupar.

vacation [və'keɪʃn] *n* vacaciones *fpl*.

vacationer [və'keɪʃənə˞] *n Am*: **summer ~** veraneante *m y f*.

vacation resort *n Am* colonia *f* veraniega.

vaccinate ['væksɪneɪt] *vt*: **to ~ sb (against sthg)** vacunar a alguien (de OR contra algo).

vaccination [‚væksɪ'neɪʃn] *n* vacunación *f*.

vaccine [*Br* 'væksiːn, *Am* væk'siːn] *n* vacuna *f*.

vacillate ['væsəleɪt] *vi*: **to ~ (between)** dudar OR vacilar (entre).

vacuum ['vækjʊəm] ◇ *n* **-1.** TECH & *fig* vacío *m*. **-2.** [cleaner] aspiradora *f*. ◇ *vt* pasar la aspiradora por.

vacuum cleaner *n* aspiradora *f*.

vacuum-packed *adj* envasado(da) al vacío.

vacuum pump *n* bomba *f* neumática.

vagabond ['vægəbɒnd] *n literary* vagabundo *m*, -da *f*.

vagaries ['veɪgərɪz] *npl fml* caprichos *mpl*.

vagina [və'dʒaɪnə] *n* vagina *f*.

vagrancy ['veɪgrənsɪ] *n* vagabundeo *m*.

vagrant ['veɪgrənt] *n* vagabundo *m*, -da *f*.

vague [veɪg] *adj* **-1.** [imprecise] vago(ga), impreciso(sa). **-2.** [person] poco claro(ra). **-3.** [feeling] leve. **-4.** [evasive] evasivo(va); **to be ~ about** ser impreciso respecto a. **-5.** [absent-minded] distraído(da). **-6.** [outline] borroso(sa).

vaguely ['veɪglɪ] *adv* **-1.** [imprecisely] vagamente. **-2.** [slightly, not very] levemente. **-3.** [indistinctly]: **I could ~ make out a ship** apenas distinguía un barco a lo lejos.

vain [veɪn] *adj* **-1.** *pej* [conceited] vanidoso(sa). **-2.** [futile] vano(na).
◆ **in vain** *adv* en vano.

vainly ['veɪnlɪ] *adv* vanamente.

valance ['væləns] *n* **-1.** [on bed] volante *m*. **-2.** *Am* [over window] galería *f* de cortina.

vale [veɪl] *n literary* valle *m*.

valedictory [‚vælɪ'dɪktərɪ] *adj fml* de despedida.

valentine card ['væləntaɪn-] *n* tarjeta *f* que se manda el Día de los Enamorados.

Valentine's Day ['væləntaɪnz-] *n*: **(St) ~** San Valentín *m*, Día *m* de los Enamorados.

valet ['væleɪ, 'vælɪt] *n* ayuda *m* de cámara.

valet parking *n aparcamiento del coche realizado por un mozo*.

valet service *n* **-1.** [for clothes] servicio *m* de lavandería. **-2.** [for cars] lavado *m* y limpieza.

Valetta, Valletta [və'letə] *n* Valleta.

valiant ['væljənt] *adj* valeroso(sa).

valid ['vælɪd] *adj* **-1.** [argument, explanation] válido(da). **-2.** [ticket, driving licence] valedero(ra).

validate ['vælɪdeɪt] *vt* validar, dar validez a.

validity [və'lɪdətɪ] *n* validez *f*.

Valium® ['vælɪəm] *n* valium® *m*.

Valletta = Valetta.

valley ['vælɪ] (*pl* **valleys**) *n* valle *m*.

valour *Br*, **valor** *Am* ['vælə˞] *n* (U) *fml* & *literary* valor *m*.

valuable ['væljʊəbl] *adj* valioso(sa).
◆ **valuables** *npl* objetos *mpl* de valor.

valuation [‚væljʊ'eɪʃn] *n* **-1.** [pricing, estimated price] evaluación *f*, valuación *f*. **-2.** [opinion, judging of worth] valoración *f*.

value ['væljuː] ◇ *n* valor *m*; **to place a high ~ on** conceder mucha importancia a; **to be good ~** estar muy bien de precio; **to be ~ for money** estar muy bien de precio; **to**

take sthg/sb at face ~ tomarse algo/a alguien en su sentido literal. ◇ vt **-1.** [estimate price of] valorar, tasar. **-2.** [cherish] apreciar.
◆ **values** npl [morals] valores mpl morales, principios mpl.

value-added tax [-'ædɪd-] n impuesto m sobre el valor añadido.

valued ['væljuːd] adj estimado(da), apreciado(da).

value judg(e)ment n juicio m de valor.

valuer ['væljuər] n tasador m, -ra f.

valve [vælv] n [in pipe, tube] válvula f.

vamoose [və'muːs] vi Am inf largarse.

vampire ['væmpaɪər] n vampiro m.

van [væn] n **-1.** AUT furgoneta f, camioneta f. **-2.** Br RAIL furgón m.

V and A (abbr of **Victoria and Albert Museum**) n gran museo londinense de artes decorativas.

vandal ['vændl] n vándalo m, gamberro m, -rra f.

vandalism ['vændəlɪzm] n vandalismo m, gamberrismo m.

vandalize, -ise ['vændəlaɪz] vt destruir, destrozar.

vanguard ['vængɑːd] n vanguardia f; in the ~ of a la vanguardia de.

vanilla [və'nɪlə] ◇ n vainilla f. ◇ comp de vainilla.

vanish ['vænɪʃ] vi desaparecer.

vanishing point ['vænɪʃɪŋ-] n punto m de fuga.

vanity ['vænətɪ] n pej vanidad f.

vanity unit n lavabo m empotrado.

vanquish ['væŋkwɪʃ] vt literary vencer.

vantagepoint ['vɑːntɪdʒ,pɔɪnt] n posición f ventajosa.

vapour Br, **vapor** Am ['veɪpər] n (U) vapor m.

vapour trail n estela f de humo.

variable ['veərɪəbl] ◇ adj variable. ◇ n variable f.

variance ['veərɪəns] n fml: at ~ (with) en desacuerdo (con).

variant ['veərɪənt] ◇ adj variante. ◇ n variante f.

variation [,veərɪ'eɪʃn] n: ~ (in/on) variación f (en/sobre).

varicose veins ['værɪkəus-] npl varices fpl.

varied ['veərɪd] adj variado(da).

variety [və'raɪətɪ] (pl **-ies**) n **-1.** [gen] variedad f; for a ~ of reasons por razones varias; a wide ~ of una gran diversidad de. **-2.** (U) THEATRE variedades fpl.

variety show n espectáculo m de variedades.

various ['veərɪəs] adj **-1.** [several] varios(rias). **-2.** [different] diversos(sas).

varnish ['vɑːnɪʃ] ◇ n barniz m. ◇ vt [with varnish] barnizar; [with nail varnish] pintar.

varnished ['vɑːnɪʃt] adj barnizado(da).

vary ['veərɪ] (pt & pt **-ied**) ◇ vt variar. ◇ vi: to ~ (in/with) variar (de/con).

varying ['veərɪɪŋ] adj variado(da), diverso(sa).

vascular ['væskjulər] adj MED vascular.

vase [Br vɑːz, Am veɪz] n florero m.

vasectomy [və'sektəmɪ] (pl **-ies**) n vasectomía f.

Vaseline® ['væsəliːn] n vaselina® f.

vast [vɑːst] adj enorme, inmenso(sa).

vastly ['vɑːstlɪ] adv enormemente.

vastness ['vɑːstnɪs] n inmensidad f.

vat [væt] n cuba f, tina f.

VAT [væt, viːeɪ'tiː] (abbr of **value added tax**) n IVA m.

Vatican ['vætɪkən] n: the ~ el Vaticano.

Vatican City n Ciudad del Vaticano.

vault [vɔːlt] ◇ n **-1.** [in bank] cámara f acorazada. **-2.** [in church] cripta f. **-3.** [roof] bóveda f. **-4.** [jump] salto m. ◇ vt saltar. ◇ vi: to ~ over sthg saltar por encima de algo.

vaulted ['vɔːltɪd] adj abovedado(da).

vaulting horse ['vɔːltɪŋ-] n potro m.

vaunted ['vɔːntɪd] adj fml: much ~ ensalzado(da).

VC n **-1.** (abbr of **vice-chairman**) vicepresidente. **-2.** (abbr of **Victoria Cross**) (titular de la) máxima distinción británica al valor.

VCR (abbr of **video cassette recorder**) n vídeo m.

VD (abbr of **venereal disease**) n ETS f.

VDU (abbr of **visual display unit**) n monitor m.

veal [viːl] n (U) ternera f.

veer [vɪər] vi virar.

veg [vedʒ] n inf **-1.** (abbr of **vegetable**): meat and two ~ carne y dos tipos de verdura. **-2.** (abbr of **vegetables**) verduras fpl.

vegan ['viːgən] n vegetariano que no consume ningún producto que provenga de un animal, como huevos, leche etc.

vegetable ['vedʒtəbl] ◇ n **-1.** BOT vegetal m. **-2.** [food] hortaliza f, legumbre f; ~s verduras fpl. ◇ adj vegetal.

vegetable garden n huerto m.

vegetable knife n cuchillo m de verdura.

vegetable oil n aceite m vegetal.

vegetarian [,vedʒɪ'teərɪən] ◇ *adj* vegetariano(na). ◇ *n* vegetariano *m*, -na *f*.

vegetarianism [,vedʒɪ'teərɪənɪzm] *n* vegetarianismo *m*.

vegetate ['vedʒɪteɪt] *vi pej* vegetar.

vegetation [,vedʒɪ'teɪʃn] *n* vegetación *f*.

veggie ['vedʒɪ] (*abbr of* **vegetarian**) *Br inf* ◇ *adj* vegetariano(na). ◇ *n* vegetariano *m*, -na *f*.

vehement ['viːəmənt] *adj* [person, denial] vehemente; [attack, gesture] violento(ta).

vehemently ['viːəməntlɪ] *adv* [deny, refuse] con vehemencia; [attack] violentamente.

vehicle ['viːəkl] *n* **-1.** [for transport] vehículo *m*. **-2.** *fig* [medium]: **a ~ for** un vehículo para.

vehicular [vɪ'hɪkjʊlər] *adj fml* rodado(da).

veil [veɪl] *n lit & fig* velo *m*.

veiled [veɪld] *adj* velado(da).

vein [veɪn] *n* **-1.** ANAT & BOT vena *f*. **-2.** [of mineral] filón *m*, veta *f*. **-3.** [style, mood] estilo *m*.

Velcro® ['velkrəʊ] *n* velcro® *m*.

vellum ['veləm] *n* vitela *f*.

velocity [vɪ'lɒsətɪ] (*pl* **-ies**) *n* velocidad *f*.

velour [və'lʊər] *n* veludillo *m*.

velvet ['velvɪt] ◇ *n* terciopelo *m*. ◇ *comp* de terciopelo.

vend [vend] *vt fml* vender.

vendetta [ven'detə] *n* enemistad *f* mortal.

vending machine ['vendɪŋ-] *n* máquina *f* de venta.

vendor ['vendɔːr] *n* vendedor *m*, -ra *f*.

veneer [və'nɪər] *n* [of wood] chapa *f*; *fig* [appearance] apariencia *f*.

venerable ['venərəbl] *adj fml* venerable.

venerate ['venəreɪt] *vt fml &* RELIG venerar.

venereal disease [vɪ'nɪərɪəl-] *n* enfermedad *f* venérea.

Venetian [vɪ'niːʃn] ◇ *adj* veneciano(na). ◇ *n* veneciano *m*, -na *f*.

venetian blind *n* persiana *f* veneciana.

Venezuela [,venɪz'weɪlə] *n* Venezuela.

Venezuelan [,venɪz'weɪlən] ◇ *adj* venezolano(na). ◇ *n* venezolano *m*, -na *f*.

vengeance ['vendʒəns] *n* venganza *f*; **with a ~** con creces.

vengeful ['vendʒfʊl] *adj literary* vengativo(va).

Venice ['venɪs] *n* Venecia.

venison ['venɪzn] *n* carne *f* de venado.

venom ['venəm] *n* [poison] veneno *m*; *fig* [spite] malevolencia *f*.

venomous ['venəməs] *adj* [poisonous] venenoso(sa); *fig* [spiteful] malvado(da).

vent [vent] ◇ *n* [opening] abertura *f* de escape; [grille] rejilla *f* de ventilación; **to give ~ to sthg** dar rienda suelta a algo. ◇ *vt*: **to ~ sthg (on)** desahogar algo (contra).

ventilate ['ventɪleɪt] *vt* ventilar.

ventilation [,ventɪ'leɪʃn] *n* ventilación *f*.

ventilator ['ventɪleɪtər] *n* ventilador *m*.

Ventimiglia [ventɪ'mɪljə] *n* Ventimiglia.

ventriloquist [ven'trɪləkwɪst] *n* ventrílocuo *m*, -cua *f*.

venture ['ventʃər] ◇ *n* empresa *f*; **business ~** empresa comercial. ◇ *vt* aventurar; **to ~ to do sthg** aventurarse a hacer algo. ◇ *vi* **-1.** [go somewhere dangerous]: **she ~d out**side se atrevió a salir. **-2.** [take a risk]: **to ~ into** lanzarse a.

venture capital *n* capital *m* de riesgo.

venturesome ['ventʃəsəm] *adj Am* **-1.** [person] arriesgado(da). **-2.** [action] peligroso(sa).

venue ['venjuː] *n* lugar *m* (*en que se celebra algo*).

Venus ['viːnəs] *n* [planet] Venus *m*.

veracity [və'ræsətɪ] *n fml* veracidad *f*.

veranda(h) [və'rændə] *n* veranda *f*.

verb [vɜːb] *n* verbo *m*.

verbal ['vɜːbl] *adj* verbal.

verbally ['vɜːbəlɪ] *adv* verbalmente.

verbatim [vɜː'beɪtɪm] ◇ *adj* literal. ◇ *adv* literalmente, palabra por palabra.

verbose [vɜː'bəʊs] *adj fml* [person] verboso(sa); [report] prolijo(ja).

verdict ['vɜːdɪkt] *n* **-1.** JUR veredicto *m*, fallo *m*. **-2.** [opinion]: **~ (on)** juicio *m* OR opinión *f* (sobre).

verge [vɜːdʒ] *n* **-1.** [edge, side] borde *m*. **-2.** [brink]: **on the ~ of sthg** al borde de algo; **on the ~ of doing sthg** a punto de hacer algo.

◆ **verge (up)on** *vt fus* rayar en.

verger ['vɜːdʒər] *n* sacristán *m*.

verification [,verɪfɪ'keɪʃn] *n* verificación *f*, comprobación *f*.

verify ['verɪfaɪ] (*pt & pp* **-ied**) *vt* **-1.** [check] verificar, comprobar. **-2.** [confirm] confirmar.

veritable ['verɪtəbl] *adj hum or fml* verdadero(ra).

vermilion [və'mɪljən] ◇ *adj* bermejo(ja). ◇ *n* bermellón *m*.

vermin ['vɜːmɪn] *npl* bichos *mpl*, sabandijas *fpl*.

Vermont [vɜː'mɒnt] *n* Vermont.

vermouth ['vɜːməθ] *n* vermut *m*.

vernacular [və'nækjʊlər] ◇ *adj* vernáculo(la). ◇ *n*: **the ~** la lengua vernácula.

verruca [vəˈruːkə] (*pl* **-cas** OR **-cae** [-kaɪ]) *n* verruga *f*.

versa → vice versa.

versatile [ˈvɜːsətaɪl] *adj* **-1.** [person] polifacético(ca). **-2.** [machine, tool] que tiene muchos usos.

versatility [ˌvɜːsəˈtɪlətɪ] *n* **-1.** [of person] carácter *m* polifacético. **-2.** [of machine, tool] diversidad *f* de usos.

verse [vɜːs] *n* **-1.** (*U*) [poetry] versos *mpl*, poesía *f*. **-2.** [stanza] estrofa *f*. **-3.** [in Bible] versículo *m*.

versed [vɜːst] *adj*: **well ~ in** versado(da) en.

version [ˈvɜːʃn] *n* versión *f*.

versus [ˈvɜːsəs] *prep* **-1.** SPORT contra. **-2.** [as opposed to] en oposición a.

vertebra [ˈvɜːtɪbrə] (*pl* **-brae** [-briː]) *n* vértebra *f*.

vertebrate [ˈvɜːtɪbreɪt] *n* vertebrado *m*.

vertical [ˈvɜːtɪkl] *adj* vertical.

vertical integration *n* FIN integración *f* vertical.

vertically [ˈvɜːtɪklɪ] *adv* verticalmente.

vertigo [ˈvɜːtɪɡəʊ] *n* vértigo *m*.

verve [vɜːv] *n* brío *m*, entusiasmo *m*.

very [ˈverɪ] *adv* **-1.** [as intensifier] muy; ~ **much** mucho. **-2.** [as euphemism]: **not ~** often OR **much** no mucho; **he's not ~ intelligent** no es muy inteligente; **is it good? - not ~** ¿es bueno? - no mucho. ◇ *adj* mismísimo(ma); **the ~ thing I was looking for** justo lo que estaba buscando; **the ~ thought makes me ill** sólo con pensarlo me pongo enfermo; **fighting for his ~ life** luchando por su propia vida; **the ~ best** el mejor (de todos); **at the ~ least** como muy poco; **a house of my ~ own** mi propia casa.

◆ **very well** *adv* muy bien; **you can't ~ well stop him now** es un poco tarde para impedírselo.

vespers [ˈvespəz] *n* (*U*) vísperas *fpl*.

vessel [ˈvesl] *n* *fml* **-1.** [boat] nave *f*. **-2.** [container] vasija *f*, recipiente *m*.

vest [vest] *n* **-1.** *Br* [undershirt] camiseta *f*. **-2.** *Am* [waistcoat] chaleco *m*.

vested interest [ˈvestɪd-] *n*: ~ **(in)** intereses *mpl* creados (en).

vestibule [ˈvestɪbjuːl] *n* **-1.** *fml* [entrance hall] vestíbulo *m*. **-2.** *Am* [on train] fuelle *m*.

vestige [ˈvestɪdʒ] *n* *fml* vestigio *m*.

vestry [ˈvestrɪ] (*pl* **-ies**) *n* sacristía *f*.

Vesuvius [vɪˈsuːvjəs] *n* Vesubio *m*.

vet [vet] (*pt* & *pp* **-ted**, *cont* **-ting**) ◇ *n* **-1.** *Br* (*abbr of* **veterinary surgeon**) veterinario *m*, -ria *f*. **-2.** *Am* (*abbr of* **veteran**) excomba-

tiente *m* y *f*. ◇ *vt* someter a una investigación.

veteran [ˈvetrən] ◇ *adj* veterano(na). ◇ *n* veterano *m*, -na *f*.

veteran car *n* *Br* coche *m* de época (*de antes de 1905*).

Veteran's Day *n* 11 de noviembre, día en que Norteamérica conmemora el final de las dos guerras mundiales.

veterinarian [ˌvetərɪˈneərɪən] *n* *Am* veterinario *m*, -ria *f*.

veterinary science [ˈvetərɪnrɪ-] *n* veterinaria *f*.

veterinary surgeon [ˈvetərɪnrɪ-] *n* *Br* *fml* veterinario *m*, -ria *f*.

veto [ˈviːtəʊ] (*pl* **-es**, *pt* & *pp* **-ed**, *cont* **-ing**) ◇ *n* veto *m*. ◇ *vt* vetar.

vetting [ˈvetɪŋ] *n* (*U*) investigación *f* (*del historial de una persona*).

vex [veks] *vt* *fml* molestar.

vexed question [vekst-] *n* manzana *f* de la discordia.

VFD (*abbr of* **voluntary fire department**) *n* cuerpo de bomberos voluntarios.

vg (*abbr of* **very good**) MB.

vgc (*abbr of* **very good condition**) m.b.e.

VHF (*abbr of* **very high frequency**) VHF.

VHS (*abbr of* **video home system**) *n* VHS.

VI *abbr of* **Virgin Islands**.

via [ˈvaɪə] *prep* **-1.** [travelling through] vía. **-2.** [by means of] a través de, por; ~ **satellite** por satélite.

viability [ˌvaɪəˈbɪlətɪ] *n* viabilidad *f*.

viable [ˈvaɪəbl] *adj* viable.

viaduct [ˈvaɪədʌkt] *n* viaducto *m*.

vibrant [ˈvaɪbrənt] *adj* **-1.** [colour, light] fuerte, vivo(va). **-2.** [voice] vibrante; [person] dinámico(ca); [city, atmosphere] animado(da).

vibrate [vaɪˈbreɪt] *vi* vibrar.

vibration [vaɪˈbreɪʃn] *n* vibración *f*.

vicar [ˈvɪkər] *n* [in Church of England] párroco *m*; [in Roman Catholic Church] vicario *m*.

vicarage [ˈvɪkərɪdʒ] *n* casa *f* del párroco.

vicarious [vɪˈkeərɪəs] *adj* indirecto(ta).

vice [vaɪs] *n* **-1.** [immorality, moral fault] vicio *m*. **-2.** [tool] torno *m* de banco.

vice- [vaɪs] *prefix* vice-.

vice-admiral *n* vicealmirante *m*.

vice-chairman *n* vicepresidente *m*.

vice-chancellor *n* UNIV rector *m*, -ra *f*.

vice-president *n* vicepresidente *m*, -ta *f*.

vice squad *n* brigada *f* antivicio.

vice versa [ˌvaɪsɪˈvɜːsə] *adv* viceversa.

vicinity [vɪˈsɪnətɪ] *n*: **in the ~ (of)** cerca (de).

vicious ['vɪʃəs] *adj* [dog] furioso(sa); [person, ruler] cruel, depravado(da); [criticism, attack] despiadado(da).

vicious circle *n* círculo *m* vicioso.

viciousness ['vɪʃəsnɪs] *n* [of dog] ferocidad *f*; [of person, system] crueldad *f*, perversidad *f*; [of crime] brutalidad *f*.

vicissitudes [vɪ'sɪsɪtjuːdz] *npl fml* vicisitudes *fpl*.

victim ['vɪktɪm] *n* víctima *f*.

victimize, -ise ['vɪktɪmaɪz] *vt* [retaliate against] tomar represalias contra; [pick on] mortificar.

victor ['vɪktər] *n literary* vencedor *m*, -ra *f*.

Victoria Cross [vɪk'tɔːrɪə-] *n condecoración militar británica.*

Victoria Falls [vɪk'tɔːrɪə-] *npl* las cataratas Victoria.

Victorian [vɪk'tɔːrɪən] *adj* victoriano(na).

Victoriana [ˌvɪktɔːrɪ'ɑːnə] *n* (U) antigüedades *fpl* victorianas.

victorious [vɪk'tɔːrɪəs] *adj* victorioso(sa).

victory ['vɪktərɪ] (*pl* -ies) *n*: ~ (over) victoria *f* (sobre).

video ['vɪdɪəʊ] (*pl* -s, *pt & pp* -ed, *cont* -ing) ◇ *n* -1. [recording, medium, machine] vídeo *m*. -2. [cassette] videocasete *m*. ◇ *comp* vídeo. ◇ *vt* -1. [using video recorder] grabar en vídeo. -2. [using camera] hacer un vídeo de.

video camera *n* videocámara *f*.

video cassette *n* videocasete *m*.

videodisc *Br*, **videodisk** *Am* ['vɪdɪəʊdɪsk] *n* videodisco *m*.

video game *n* videojuego *m*, juego *m* de vídeo.

video machine *n* vídeo *m*.

videophone ['vɪdɪəʊfəʊn] *n* videófono *m*, videoteléfono *m*.

video player, videorecorder ['vɪdɪəʊrɪˌkɔːdər] *n* vídeo *m*.

video recording *n* grabación *f* en vídeo.

video shop *n* tienda *f* de vídeos.

videotape ['vɪdɪəʊteɪp] *n* videocinta *f*.

vie [vaɪ] (*pt & pp* vied, *cont* vying) *vi*: to ~ (with sb for sthg/to do sthg) competir (con alguien por algo/para hacer algo).

Vienna [vɪ'enə] *n* Viena.

Viennese [ˌvɪə'niːz] ◇ *adj* vienés(esa). ◇ *n* vienés *m*, -esa *f*.

Vietnam [ˌvjet'næm] *n* (el) Vietnam.

Vietnamese [ˌvjetnə'miːz] ◇ *adj* vietnamita. ◇ *n* -1. [person] vietnamita *m y f*. -2. [language] vietnamita *m*.

view [vjuː] ◇ *n* -1. [opinion] parecer *m*, opinión *f*; what is your ~ on ...? ¿cuál es tu opinión sobre ...?; in my ~ en mi opinión; to take the ~ that pensar que. -2. [attitude]: ~ (of) actitud *f* (frente a). -3. [scene] vista *f*, panorama *m*. -4. [field of vision] vista *f*; to come into ~ aparecer. ◇ *vt* -1. [consider] ver, considerar. -2. *fml* [examine, look at - stars etc] observar; [- house, flat] visitar, ver.

◆ **in view of** *prep* en vista de.

◆ **with a view to** *conj* con miras OR vistas a.

viewdata ['vjuːˌdeɪtə] *n* videotexto *m*.

viewer ['vjuːər] *n* -1. [person] espectador *m*, -ra *f*. -2. [apparatus] visionador *m*.

viewfinder ['vjuːˌfaɪndər] *n* visor *m*.

viewpoint ['vjuːpɔɪnt] *n* -1. [opinion] punto *m* de vista. -2. [place] mirador *m*.

vigil ['vɪdʒɪl] *n* -1. [watch] vigilia *f*. -2. RELIG Vigilia *f*.

vigilance ['vɪdʒɪləns] *n* vigilancia *f*.

vigilant ['vɪdʒɪlənt] *adj* vigilante.

vigilante [ˌvɪdʒɪ'læntɪ] *n persona que extraoficialmente patrulla un área para protegerla, tomándose la justicia en sus manos.*

vigor *Am* = **vigour**.

vigorous ['vɪgərəs] *adj* enérgico(ca).

vigour *Br*, **vigor** *Am* ['vɪgər] *n* vigor *m*, energía *f*.

Viking ['vaɪkɪŋ] ◇ *adj* vikingo(ga). ◇ *n* vikingo *m*, -ga *f*.

vile [vaɪl] *adj* [person, act] vil, infame; [food, smell] repugnante; [mood] de perros.

vilify ['vɪlɪfaɪ] (*pt & pp* -ied) *vt fml* infamar.

villa ['vɪlə] *n* [in country] villa *f*; [in town] chalet *m*.

village ['vɪlɪdʒ] *n* aldea *f*, pueblecito *m*.

villager ['vɪlɪdʒər] *n* aldeano *m*, -na *f*.

villain ['vɪlən] *n* -1. [of film, book] malo *m*, -la *f*. -2. *dated* [criminal] canalla *m y f*, criminal *m y f*.

Vilnius ['vɪlnɪəs] *n* Vilna.

VIN (*abbr of* **vehicle identification number**) *n* NIV *m*.

vinaigrette [ˌvɪnɪ'gret] *n* vinagreta *f*.

vindicate ['vɪndɪkeɪt] *vt* justificar; his decision was ~d by the result el resultado dio la razón a su decisión.

vindication [ˌvɪndɪ'keɪʃn] *n* justificación *f*.

vindictive [vɪn'dɪktɪv] *adj* vindicativo(va).

vine [vaɪn] *n* [on ground] vid *f*; [climbing plant] parra *f*.

vinegar ['vɪnɪgər] *n* vinagre *m*.

vine leaf *n* hoja *f* de parra.

vineyard ['vɪnjəd] *n* viña *f*, viñedo *m*.

vintage ['vɪntɪdʒ] ◇ *adj* -1. [wine] añejo(ja). -2. [classic] clásico(ca). ◇ *n* cosecha *f* (*de vino*).

vintage car *n Br* coche *m* de época (*de entre 1919 y 1930*).

vintage wine *n* vino *m* añejo.

vintner ['vɪntnəʳ] *n* vinatero *m*, -ra *f*.

vinyl ['vaɪnɪl] ◇ *n* vinilo *m*. ◇ *comp* de vinilo.

viola [vɪ'əʊlə] *n* viola *f*.

violate ['vaɪəleɪt] *vt* **-1.** [law, treaty, rights] violar, infringir. **-2.** [peace, privacy] invadir. **-3.** [tomb, grave] profanar.

violation [,vaɪə'leɪʃn] *n* **-1.** [of law, treaty, rights] violación *f*. **-2.** [of peace, privacy] invasión *f*. **-3.** [of tomb, grave] profanación *f*.

violence ['vaɪələns] *n* violencia *f*.

violent ['vaɪələnt] *adj* **-1.** [gen] violento(ta). **-2.** [emotion, anger] intenso(sa). **-3.** [colour] chillón(ona). **-4.** [weather] borrascoso(sa).

violently ['vaɪələntlɪ] *adv* **-1.** [gen] violentamente. **-2.** [dislike] intensamente. **-3.** [swear, react] furiosamente.

violet ['vaɪələt] ◇ *adj* violeta, violado(da). ◇ *n* **-1.** [flower] violeta *f*. **-2.** [colour] violeta *m*.

violin [,vaɪə'lɪn] *n* violín *m*.

violinist [,vaɪə'lɪnɪst] *n* violinista *m y f*.

VIP (*abbr of* **very important person**) *n* celebridad *f*.

viper ['vaɪpəʳ] *n* víbora *f*.

viral ['vaɪrəl] *adj* vírico(ca).

virgin ['vɜːdʒɪn] ◇ *adj literary* [spotless] virgen. ◇ *n* virgen *m y f*.

Virginia [və'dʒɪnjə] *n* Virginia.

Virgin Islands *n*: **the ~** las islas Vírgenes.

virginity [və'dʒɪnətɪ] *n* virginidad *f*.

Virgo ['vɜːgəʊ] (*pl* **-s**) *n* Virgo *m*; **to be (a) ~** ser Virgo.

virile ['vɪraɪl] *adj* viril.

virility [vɪ'rɪlətɪ] *n* virilidad *f*.

virtual ['vɜːtʃʊəl] *adj*: **it's a ~ certainty** es casi seguro.

virtually ['vɜːtʃʊəlɪ] *adv* prácticamente, casi.

virtual memory *n* COMPUT memoria *f* virtual.

virtual reality *n* realidad *f* virtual.

virtue ['vɜːtjuː] *n* **-1.** [morality, good quality] virtud *f*. **-2.** [benefit] ventaja *f*; **there's no ~ in** no hay ninguna ventaja en.
 ♦ **by virtue of** *prep fml* en virtud de.

virtuoso [,vɜːtjʊ'əʊzəʊ] (*pl* **-sos** OR **-si** [-siː]) *n* virtuoso *m*, -sa *f*.

virtuous ['vɜːtjʊəs] *adj* virtuoso(sa).

virulent ['vɪrʊlənt] *adj lit* & *fig* virulento(ta).

virus ['vaɪrəs] *n* COMPUT & MED virus *m*.

visa ['viːzə] *n* visado *m*.

vis-à-vis [,viːzɑː'viː] *prep fml* con relación a.

viscose ['vɪskəʊs] *n* viscosa *f*.

viscosity [vɪ'skɒsətɪ] *n* CHEM viscosidad *f*.

viscount ['vaɪkaʊnt] *n* vizconde *m*.

viscous ['vɪskəs] *adj* CHEM viscoso(sa).

vise [vaɪs] *n Am* torno *m* de banco.

visibility [,vɪzɪ'bɪlətɪ] *n* visibilidad *f*.

visible ['vɪzəbl] *adj* visible.

visibly ['vɪzəblɪ] *adv* visiblemente.

vision ['vɪʒn] *n* **-1.** (*U*) [ability to see] visión *f*, vista *f*. **-2.** *fig* [foresight] clarividencia *f*. **-3.** [impression, dream] visión *f*. **-4.** (*U*) TV imagen *f*.

visionary ['vɪʒənrɪ] (*pl* **-ies**) ◇ *adj* con visión de futuro. ◇ *n* visionario *m*, -ria *f*.

visit ['vɪzɪt] ◇ *n* visita *f*; **on a ~** de visita. ◇ *vt* visitar.
 ♦ **visit with** *vt fus Am* **-1.** [talk with] hablar OR charlar con. **-2.** [go and see] visitar, ir a ver.

visiting card ['vɪzɪtɪŋ-] *n* tarjeta *f* de visita.

visiting hours ['vɪzɪtɪŋ-] *npl* horas *fpl* de visita.

visitor ['vɪzɪtəʳ] *n* **-1.** [to one's home, hospital] visita *f*. **-2.** [to museum, town etc] visitante *m y f*.

visitors' book *n* libro *m* de visitas.

visitor's passport *n Br* pasaporte *m* provisional.

visor ['vaɪzəʳ] *n* visera *f*.

vista ['vɪstə] *n* [view] vista *f*, perspectiva *f*; *fig* [wide range] perspectiva.

VISTA ['vɪstə] (*abbr of* **Volunteers in Service to America**) *n organización de voluntarios establecida por el gobierno estadounidense para ayudar a los pobres.*

visual ['vɪʒʊəl] *adj* [gen] visual; [of the eyes] ocular.

visual aids *npl* medios *mpl* visuales.

visual display unit *n* monitor *m*.

visualize, -ise ['vɪʒʊəlaɪz] *vt* visualizar; **to ~ (sb) doing sthg** imaginar (a alguien) haciendo algo.

visually ['vɪʒʊəlɪ] *adv* visualmente; **~ handicapped person** persona *f* con problemas visuales.

vital ['vaɪtl] *adj* **-1.** [essential] vital, esencial. **-2.** [full of life] enérgico(ca), lleno(na) de vida.

vitality [vaɪ'tælətɪ] *n* vitalidad *f*.

vitally ['vaɪtəlɪ] *adv* sumamente.

vital statistics *npl inf* medidas *fpl* (*del cuerpo de la mujer*).

vitamin [*Br* 'vɪtəmɪn, *Am* 'vaɪtəmɪn] *n* vitamina *f*.

vitriolic [ˌvɪtrɪˈɒlɪk] *adj fml* virulento(ta), mordaz.

viva [ˈviːvə] *n* = **viva voce**.

vivacious [vɪˈveɪʃəs] *adj* vivaz, animado(da).

vivacity [vɪˈvæsətɪ] *n* vivacidad *f*.

viva voce [ˌvaɪvəˈvəʊsɪ] *n* examen *m* oral.

vivid [ˈvɪvɪd] *adj* -1. [colour] vivo(va). -2. [description, memory] vívido(da).

vividly [ˈvɪvɪdlɪ] *adv* -1. [brightly] con colores muy vivos. -2. [clearly] vívidamente.

vivisection [ˌvɪvɪˈsekʃn] *n* vivisección *f*.

vixen [ˈvɪksn] *n* zorra *f*.

viz [vɪz] (*abbr of* **vide licet**) v. gr.

VLF (*abbr of* **very low frequency**) VLF.

V-neck *n* -1. [sweater, dress] jersey *m* con cuello de pico. -2. [neck] cuello *m* de pico.

VOA (*abbr of* **Voice of America**) *n emisora gubernamental estadounidense que promociona la cultura estadounidense en el mundo.*

vocabulary [vəˈkæbjʊlərɪ] (*pl* **-ies**) *n* vocabulario *m*.

vocal [ˈvəʊkl] *adj* -1. [outspoken] vociferante. -2. [of the voice] vocal.

◆ **vocals** *npl* cantante *m y f*; **on** ~ cantando.

vocal cords *npl* cuerdas *fpl* vocales.

vocalist [ˈvəʊkəlɪst] *n* [in orchestra] vocalista *m y f*; [in pop group] cantante *m y f*.

vocation [vəʊˈkeɪʃn] *n* vocación *f*; **to have a** ~ **for** tener vocación de.

vocational [vəʊˈkeɪʃənl] *adj* profesional.

vociferous [vəˈsɪfərəs] *adj fml* ruidoso(sa).

vodka [ˈvɒdkə] *n* [drink] vodka *m*.

vogue [vəʊg] ◇ *adj* de moda. ◇ *n* moda *f*; **in** ~ en boga, de moda.

voice [vɔɪs] ◇ *n* voz *f*; **to raise/lower one's** ~ elevar/bajar la voz; **to keep one's** ~ **down** no levantar la voz. ◇ *vt* [opinion, emotion] expresar.

voice box *n* caja *f* laríngea.

voice mail *n* COMPUT correo *m* de voz; **to send/receive** ~ mandar/recibir un mensaje de correo de voz.

voice-over *n* voz *f* en off.

void [vɔɪd] ◇ *adj* -1. [invalid] inválido(da); → **null**. -2. *fml* [empty]: ~ **of** falto(ta) de. ◇ *n literary* vacío *m*.

voile [vɔɪl] *n* (*U*) gasa *f*.

vol. (*abbr of* **volume**) vol.

volatile [*Br* ˈvɒlətaɪl, *Am* ˈvɒlətl] *adj* [situation] volátil; [person] voluble, inconstante.

vol-au-vent [ˈvɒləʊvɑ̃] *n* volován *m*.

volcanic [vɒlˈkænɪk] *adj* volcánico(ca).

volcano [vɒlˈkeɪnəʊ] (*pl* **-es** OR **-s**) *n* volcán *m*.

vole [vəʊl] *n* campañol *m*.

volition [vəˈlɪʃn] *n fml*: **of one's own** ~ por voluntad propia.

volley [ˈvɒlɪ] (*pl* **volleys**) ◇ *n* -1. [of gunfire] ráfaga *f*, descarga *f*. -2. *fig* [rapid succession] torrente *m*. -3. SPORT volea *f*. ◇ *vt* volear.

volleyball [ˈvɒlɪbɔːl] *n* balonvolea *m*, voleibol *m*.

volt [vəʊlt] *n* voltio *m*.

Volta [ˈvɒltə] *n*: **the** ~ el Volta.

voltage [ˈvəʊltɪdʒ] *n* voltaje *m*.

voluble [ˈvɒljʊbl] *adj fml* locuaz.

volume [ˈvɒljuːm] *n* [gen & COMPUT] volumen *m*.

volume control *n* botón *m* del volumen.

voluminous [vəˈluːmɪnəs] *adj fml* voluminoso(sa).

voluntarily [*Br* ˈvɒləntrɪlɪ, *Am* ˌvɒlənˈterəlɪ] *adv* voluntariamente.

voluntary [ˈvɒləntrɪ] *adj* voluntario(ria); ~ **organization** organización *f* benéfica.

voluntary liquidation *n* liquidación *f* voluntaria.

voluntary redundancy *n Br* despido *m* voluntario.

volunteer [ˌvɒlənˈtɪər] ◇ *n* [person who volunteers] voluntario *m*, -ria *f*. ◇ *v* -1. [offer of one's free will]: **to** ~ **to do sthg** ofrecerse para hacer algo. -2. [information, advice] dar, ofrecer. ◇ *vi* -1. [freely offer one's services]: **to** ~ **(for)** ofrecerse (para). -2. MIL alistarse.

voluptuous [vəˈlʌptjʊəs] *adj* voluptuoso(sa).

vomit [ˈvɒmɪt] ◇ *n* vómito *m*. ◇ *vi* vomitar.

voracious [vəˈreɪʃəs] *adj* [appetite, eater] voraz; [reader] ávido(da).

vortex [ˈvɔːteks] (*pl* **-texes** OR **-tices** [-tɪsiːz]) *n* -1. [whirlpool, whirlwind] vórtice *m*. -2. *fig* [of events] torbellino *m*.

vote [vəʊt] ◇ *n* -1. [gen] voto *m*; ~ **for/against** voto a favor de/en contra de. -2. [session, ballot, result] votación *f*; **to put sthg to the** ~ someter algo a votación. -3. [votes cast]: **the** ~ los votos. ◇ *vt* -1. [person, leader] elegir. -2. [choose]: **to** ~ **to do sthg** votar hacer algo. ◇ *vi*: **to** ~ **(for/against)** votar (a favor de/en contra de).

◆ **vote in** *vt sep* elegir.

◆ **vote out** *vt sep* rechazar.

vote of confidence (*pl* **votes of confidence**) *n* voto *m* de confianza.

vote of no confidence (*pl* **votes of no confidence**) *n* voto *m* de censura.

vote of thanks (*pl* **votes of thanks**) *n* palabras *fpl* de agradecimiento.

voter ['vəʊtə'] *n* votante *m y f.*

voting ['vəʊtɪŋ] *n* votación *f.*

vouch [vaʊtʃ]

◆ **vouch for** *vt fus* **-1.** [person] responder por. **-2.** [character, accuracy] dar fe de.

voucher ['vaʊtʃə'] *n* vale *m.*

vow [vaʊ] ◇ *n* RELIG voto *m;* [solemn promise] promesa *f* solemne. ◇ *vt:* **to ~ to do sthg** jurar hacer algo; **to ~ that** jurar que.

vowel ['vaʊəl] *n* vocal *f.*

voyage ['vɔɪɪdʒ] *n* viaje *m.*

voyeur [vwɑː'jɜːr] *n* mirón *m,* -ona *f,* voyeur *m y f.*

voyeurism [vwɑː'jɜːrɪzm] *n* voyeurismo *m.*

VP *n abbr of* **vice-president**.

vs *abbr of* **versus**.

VSO (*abbr of* **Voluntary Service Overseas**) *n* organización británica de voluntarios que ayuda a países en vías de desarrollo.

VSOP (*abbr of* **very special old pale**) *expresión que indica que un licor tiene de 20 a 25 años.*

VT *abbr of* **Vermont**.

VTOL ['viːtɒl] (*abbr of* **vertical takeoff and landing**) *n* aterrizaje y despegue verticales.

VTR (*abbr of* **video tape recorder**) *n* vídeo *m.*

vulgar ['vʌlgə'] *adj* **-1.** [in bad taste] ordinario(ria), vulgar. **-2.** [offensive] grosero(ra), guarango(ga) *Amer.*

vulgarity [vʌl'gærətɪ] *n* (*U*) **-1.** [poor taste] ordinariez *f,* vulgaridad *f.* **-2.** [offensiveness] grosería *f.*

vulnerability [,vʌlnərə'bɪlətɪ] *n* vulnerabilidad *f.*

vulnerable ['vʌlnərəbl] *adj:* **~ (to)** vulnerable (a).

vulture ['vʌltʃə'] *n lit & fig* buitre *m.*

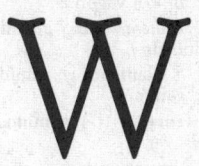

w (*pl* **w's** OR **ws**), **W** (*pl* **W's** OR **Ws**) ['dʌblju:] *n* [letter] w *f,* W *f.*

◆ **W -1.** (*abbr of* **west**) O. **-2.** (*abbr of* **watt**) w.

WA *abbr of* **Washington**.

wacky ['wækɪ] (*compar* **-ier**, *superl* **-iest**) *adj inf* estrafalario(ria).

wad [wɒd] *n* **-1.** [of paper] taco *m.* **-2.** [of banknotes, documents] fajo *m.* **-3.** [of cotton, cotton wool, tobacco] bola *f.*

wadding ['wɒdɪŋ] *n* relleno *m.*

waddle ['wɒdl] *vi* anadear.

wade [weɪd] *vi* caminar por el agua.

◆ **wade through** *vt fus fig:* **he was wading through the documents** le costaba mucho leer los documentos.

wadge [wɒdʒ] *n Br inf* [of food] tajada *f;* [of papers] fajo *m;* [of cotton wool] bola *f.*

wading pool ['weɪdɪŋ-] *n Am* piscina *f* para niños.

wafer ['weɪfə'] *n* [thin biscuit] barquillo *m.*

wafer-thin *adj* finísimo(ma), delgadísimo(ma).

waffle ['wɒfl] ◇ *n* **-1.** CULIN gofre *m.* **-2.** *Br inf* [vague talk] paja *f.* ◇ *vi* enrollarse.

waft [wɑːft, wɒft] *vi* flotar.

wag [wæg] (*pt & pp* **-ged**, *cont* **-ging**) ◇ *vt* menear. ◇ *vi* menearse.

wage [weɪdʒ] ◇ *n* [gen] salario *m;* [daily] jornal *m.* ◇ *vt:* **to ~ war** hacer la guerra.

◆ **wages** *npl* [gen] salario *m;* [daily] jornal *m.*

wage claim *n* reivindicación *f* salarial.

wage differential *n* diferencia *f* salarial.

wage earner *n* asalariado *m,* -da *f.*

wage freeze *n* congelación *f* salarial.

wage packet *n Br* **-1.** [envelope] sobre *m* de pago. **-2.** *fig* [pay] paga *f.*

wager ['weɪdʒə'] *n* apuesta *f.*

wage rise *n Br* aumento *m* de salario.

waggish ['wægɪʃ] *adj inf* [person, mood, behaviour] bromista; [remark] chistoso(sa).

waggle ['wægl] *inf* ◇ *vt* menear. ◇ *vi* menearse.

waggon ['wægən] *Br* = **wagon**.

wagon ['wægən] *n* **-1.** [horse-drawn vehicle] carro *m*. **-2.** *Br* RAIL vagón *m*.

waif [weɪf] *n literary* niño abandonado *m*, niña abandonada *f*.

wail [weɪl] ◇ *n* lamento *m*, gemido *m*. ◇ *vi* lamentarse, gemir.

wailing ['weɪlɪŋ] *n* (U) gemidos *mpl*, lamentos *mpl*.

waist [weɪst] *n* cintura *f*.

waistband ['weɪstbænd] *n* cinturilla *f*.

waistcoat ['weɪskəʊt] *n* chaleco *m*.

waistline ['weɪstlaɪn] *n* cintura *f*, talle *m*.

wait [weɪt] ◇ *n* espera *f*. ◇ *vi*: to ~ (for sthg/sb) esperar (algo/a alguien); to be unable to ~ to do sthg estar impaciente por hacer algo; (just) you ~! ¡me las pagarás!; to ~ and see esperar y ver lo que pasa; ~ a minute OR second OR moment [interrupting sb] ¡espera un minuto OR segundo OR momento!; [interrupting o.s.] ¡espera! ◇ *vt Am* [delay] retrasar.
◆ **wait about, wait around** *vi* esperar.
◆ **wait for** *vt fus* esperar.
◆ **wait on** *vt fus* [serve food to] servir.
◆ **wait up** *vi* quedarse despierto(ta) esperando.

waiter ['weɪtə'] *n* camarero *m*, mesero *m Amer*.

waiting game ['weɪtɪŋ-] *n*: to play a ~ esperar el momento oportuno.

waiting list ['weɪtɪŋ-] *n* lista *f* de espera.

waiting room ['weɪtɪŋ-] *n* sala *f* de espera.

waitress ['weɪtrɪs] *n* camarera *f*, mesera *f Amer*.

waive [weɪv] *vt fml* [rule] no aplicar.

waiver ['weɪvə'] *n* JUR renuncia *f*.

wake [weɪk] (*pt* woke OR **-d**, *pp* woken OR **-d**) ◇ *n* [of ship, boat] estela *f*; in its ~ *fig* tras de sí; in the ~ of *fig* tras. ◇ *vt* despertar. ◇ *vi* despertarse.
◆ **wake up** ◇ *vt sep* despertar. ◇ *vi* **-1.** [wake] despertarse. **-2.** *fig* [become aware]: to ~ up to darse cuenta de, tomar conciencia de.

waken ['weɪkən] *fml* ◇ *vt* despertar. ◇ *vi* despertarse.

waking hours ['weɪkɪŋ-] *npl* horas *fpl* de vigilia.

Wales [weɪlz] *n* Gales.

walk [wɔːk] ◇ *n* **-1.** [action of walking] andar *m*, paso *m*. **-2.** [journey on foot] paseo *m*; to go for a ~ dar un paseo; it's ten minutes' ~ away está a diez minutos andando. **-3.** [route for walking]: there are some nice ~s here se pueden hacer unas buenas caminatas por aquí.
◇ *vt* **-1.** [accompany on foot]: to ~ sb home acompañar a alguien a casa. **-2.** [dog] pasear. **-3.** [streets] andar por; [distance] recorrer, andar.
◇ *vi* **-1.** [move on foot] andar, caminar. **-2.** [for pleasure] pasear.
◆ **walk away with** *vt fus inf* llevarse.
◆ **walk in on** *vt fus* [meeting] interrumpir; [person] sorprender.
◆ **walk off** *vt sep* [headache, cramp] aliviar dando un paseo.
◆ **walk off with** *vt fus inf* llevarse.
◆ **walk out** *vi* **-1.** [leave suddenly] salirse. **-2.** [go on strike] declararse en huelga.
◆ **walk out on** *vt fus* dejar, abandonar.

walkabout ['wɔːkə,baʊt] *n Br* paseo *m* entre la gente; to go ~ [Queen, president etc] pasearse entre la gente.

walker ['wɔːkə'] *n* caminante *m y f*, paseante *m y f*.

walkie-talkie [,wɔːkɪ'tɔːkɪ] *n* walki-talki *m*.

walk-in *adj* **-1.** [cupboard] empotrado y suficientemente grande para entrar en él. **-2.** *Am* [easy] fácil.

walking ['wɔːkɪŋ] *n* (U) [for sport] marcha *f*; [for pleasure] andar *m*.

walking shoes *npl* zapatos *mpl* para caminar.

walking stick *n* bastón *m*.

Walkman® ['wɔːkmən] *n* walkman® *m*.

walk of life (*pl* walks of life) *n*: people from all walks of life gente de toda condición.

walk-on *adj* de figurante.

walkout ['wɔːkaʊt] *n* huelga *f*.

walkover ['wɔːk,əʊvə'] *n* victoria *f* fácil.

walkway ['wɔːkweɪ] *n* [on ship, oilrig, machine] pasarela *f*; [between buildings] paso *m*.

wall [wɔːl] *n* **-1.** [inside building, of cell, stomach] pared *f*. **-2.** [outside] muro *m*; to come up against a brick ~ llegar a un callejón sin salida; to drive sb up the ~ volverle loco a alguien.

wallaby ['wɒləbɪ] (*pl* **-ies**) *n* ualabí *m*.

wallchart ['wɔːltʃɑːt] *n* (gráfico) mural *m*.

wall cupboard *n* armario *m* de pared.

walled [wɔːld] *adj* amurallado(da).

wallet ['wɒlɪt] *n* cartera *f*, billetera *f*.

wallflower ['wɔːl,flaʊə'] *n* **-1.** [plant] alhelí *m*. **-2.** *inf fig* [person] *persona tímida que queda al margen de una fiesta*.

Walloon [wɒ'luːn] ◇ *adj* valón(ona). ◇ *n* **-1.** [person] valón *m*, -ona *f*. **-2.** [language] valón *m*.

wallop ['wɒləp] *inf* ◇ *n* [to person] torta *f*;

[to thing] golpazo *m.* ◇ *vt* [child] pegar una
torta a; [ball] golpear fuerte.

wallow ['wɒləʊ] *vi* **-1.** [in liquid] revolcarse.
-2. [in emotion]: **to ~ in self-pity** revolcarse
en la autocompasión.

wall painting *n* mural *m.*

wallpaper ['wɔːl,peɪpəʳ] ◇ *n* papel *m* de
pared OR de empapelar. ◇ *vt* empapelar.

Wall Street *n* Wall Street *f.*

WALL STREET:
Wall Street, en Nueva York, es el centro
financiero más importante de Estados Unidos; en esta calle se encuentra el edificio de
la Bolsa de Estados Unidos. Por extensión,
'Wall Street' se utiliza para referirse al mundo financiero estadounidense

wall-to-wall *adj*: **~ carpet** moqueta *f.*

wally ['wɒlɪ] (*pl* **-ies**) *n Br inf* majadero *m,*
-ra *f,* imbécil *m* y *f.*

walnut ['wɔːlnʌt] *n* **-1.** [nut] nuez *f.* **-2.**
[wood, tree] nogal *m.*

walrus ['wɔːlrəs] (*pl inv* OR **-es**) *n* morsa *f.*

waltz [wɔːls] ◇ *n* vals *m.* ◇ *vi* **-1.** [dance]
bailar el vals. **-2.** *inf dated* [walk confidently]:
to ~ in/out entrar/salir tan fresco(ca).

wan [wɒn] (*compar* **-ner**, *superl* **-nest**) *adj*
pálido(da).

wand [wɒnd] *n* varita *f* mágica.

wander ['wɒndəʳ] *vi* vagar; **my mind kept
~ing** se me iba la mente en otras cosas.

wanderer ['wɒndərəʳ] *n* errante *m* y *f.*

wandering ['wɒndərɪŋ] *adj* ambulante.

wanderlust ['wɒndəlʌst] *n* pasión *f* por viajar.

wane [weɪn] ◇ *n*: **on the ~** en el ocaso. ◇
vi [influence, interest] disminuir, decrecer.

wangle ['wæŋgl] *vt inf* agenciarse, conseguir.

wanna ['wɒnə] = want a, want to.

want [wɒnt] ◇ *n fml* **-1.** [need] necesidad *f.*
-2. [lack] falta *f*; **for ~ of** por OR a falta de.
-3. [deprivation] indigencia *f,* miseria *f.* ◇ *vt*
-1. [desire] querer; **to ~ to do sthg** querer
hacer algo; **to ~ sb to do sthg** querer que
alguien haga algo. **-2.** *inf* [need - subj: per-
son] tener que; [- subj: thing] necesitar, requerir; **you ~ to be more careful** tienes que
tener más cuidado; **the house ~s cleaning**
hace falta hacer limpieza en la casa.

want ad *n Am inf* anuncio *m* por palabras.

wanted ['wɒntɪd] *adj*: **to be ~ (by the police)** ser buscado(da) (por la policía).

wanting ['wɒntɪŋ] *adj fml* deficiente.

wanton ['wɒntən] *adj fml* gratuito(ta), sin
motivo.

war [wɔːʳ] (*pt* & *pp* **-red**, *cont* **-ring**) ◇ *n lit*
& *fig* guerra *f*; **to go to ~** entrar en guerra;
to have been in the ~s *Br* estar maltrecho.
◇ *vi* estar en guerra.

War., **Warks.** (*abbr of* **Warwickshire**) *condado inglés.*

warble ['wɔːbl] *vi literary* [bird] trinar, gorjear.

war crime *n* crimen *m* de guerra.

war criminal *n* criminal *m* y *f* de guerra.

war cry *n* [in battle] grito *m* de guerra.

ward [wɔːd] *n* **-1.** [in hospital] sala *f.* **-2.** *Br*
POL distrito *m* electoral. **-3.** JUR pupilo *m,* -la
f.
◆ **ward off** *vt fus* protegerse de.

war dance *n* danza *f* guerrera.

warden ['wɔːdn] *n* **-1.** [of park] guarda *m* y
f. **-2.** *Br* [of youth hostel, hall of residence] encargado *m,* -da *f.* **-3.** [of monument] guardián *m,* -ana *f.* **-4.** *Am* [prison governor] director *m,* -ra *f.*

warder ['wɔːdəʳ] *n* [in prison] carcelero *m,*
-ra *f.*

ward of court *n* menor *m* y *f* bajo tutela
judicial.

wardrobe ['wɔːdrəʊb] *n* **-1.** [piece of furni-
ture] armario *m,* guardarropa *m.* **-2.** [collec-
tion of clothes] guardarropa *m,* vestuario *m.*

wardrobe mistress *n Br* guardarropa *f.*

warehouse ['weəhaʊs, *pl* -haʊzɪz] *n* almacén *m.*

wares [weəz] *npl literary* mercancías *fpl.*

warfare ['wɔːfeəʳ] *n* (*U*) guerra *f.*

war game *n* **-1.** [military exercise] maniobras *fpl,* ejercicio *m* de maniobras. **-2.**
[game of strategy] juego *m* de estrategia militar.

warhead ['wɔːhed] *n* ojiva *f,* cabeza *f.*

warily ['weərəlɪ] *adv* con cautela, cautelo-
samente.

Warks. = War.

warlike ['wɔːlaɪk] *adj* belicoso(sa).

warm [wɔːm] ◇ *adj* **-1.** [pleasantly hot - gen]
caliente; [- weather, day] caluroso(sa); **it's/
I'm ~** hace/tengo calor; **are you ~ enough?**
no tendrás frío, ¿verdad?; [lukewarm] ti-
bio(bia), templado(da). **-2.** [clothes etc] que
abriga. **-3.** [colour, sound] cálido(da). **-4.**
[friendly - person, atmosphere, smile] afectuo-
so(sa); [- congratulations] efusivo(va). ◇ *vt*
calentar.
◆ **warm over** *vt sep Am* calentar; *fig* insistir en.
◆ **warm to** *vt fus* [person, place] tomar simpatía a; **we ~ed to the idea at once** en seguida nos hizo gracia la idea.

◆ **warm up** ◇ *vt sep* calentar. ◇ *vi* [gen] entrar en calor; [weather, room, engine] calentarse.

warm-blooded [-'blʌdɪd] *adj* de sangre caliente.

war memorial *n* monumento *m* a los caídos.

warm front *n* frente *m* cálido.

warm-hearted [-'hɑːtɪd] *adj* afectuoso(sa), cariñoso(sa).

warmly ['wɔːmlɪ] *adv* **-1.** [in warm clothes]: **to dress ~** vestirse con ropa de abrigo. **-2.** [in a friendly way] efusivamente, calurosamente.

warmness ['wɔːmnɪs] *n* [friendliness] cordialidad *f*, efusión *f*.

warmonger ['wɔːˌmʌŋgəʳ] *n* belicista *m y f*.

warmth [wɔːmθ] *n* **-1.** [heat] calor *m*. **-2.** [of clothes] abrigo *m*. **-3.** [friendliness] cordialidad *f*, efusión *f*.

warm-up *n* precalentamiento *m*.

warn [wɔːn] ◇ *vt* prevenir, advertir; **to ~ sb of sthg** prevenir a alguien algo; **to ~ sb not to do sthg** advertir a alguien que no haga algo. ◇ *vi*: **to ~ of sthg** prevenir contra algo.

warning ['wɔːnɪŋ] ◇ *adj* de aviso, de advertencia. ◇ *n* aviso *m*, advertencia *f*.

warning light *n* piloto *m*.

warning triangle *n* Br triángulo *m* de avería.

warp [wɔːp] ◇ *n* [of cloth] urdimbre *f*. ◇ *vt* **-1.** [wood] alabear, combar. **-2.** [personality] torcer, deformar. ◇ *vi* alabearse, combarse.

warpath ['wɔːpɑːθ] *n*: **to be** OR **go on the ~** *fig* estar buscando guerra.

warped [wɔːpt] *adj* **-1.** [wood] combado(da), alabeado(da). **-2.** [person] retorcido(da).

warrant ['wɒrənt] ◇ *n* orden *f* OR mandamiento *m* judicial. ◇ *vt fml* merecer.

warrant officer *n* grado intermedio entre suboficial y oficial.

warranty ['wɒrəntɪ] (*pl* **-ies**) *n* garantía *f*.

warren ['wɒrən] *n* zona *f* de conejos.

warring ['wɔːrɪŋ] *adj* contendiente.

warrior ['wɒrɪəʳ] *n literary* guerrero *m*, -ra *f*.

Warsaw ['wɔːsɔː] *n* Varsovia; **the ~ Pact** el Pacto de Varsovia.

warship ['wɔːʃɪp] *n* buque *m* de guerra.

wart [wɔːt] *n* verruga *f*.

wartime ['wɔːtaɪm] ◇ *adj* de la guerra. ◇ *n* tiempos *mpl* de guerra.

war widow *n* viuda *f* de guerra.

wary ['weərɪ] (*compar* **-ier**, *superl* **-iest**) *adj*: **~ (of)** receloso(sa) (de).

was [wɒz] *pt* → **be**.

wash [wɒʃ] ◇ *n* **-1.** [act of washing] lavado *m*, lavada *f*. **-2.** [things to wash] ropa *f* para lavar, ropa sucia. **-3.** [from boat] estela *f*. ◇ *vt* **-1.** [gen] lavar; [hands, face] lavarse. **-2.** [carry - subj: waves etc] arrastrar, llevarse. ◇ *vi* **-1.** [clean oneself] lavarse. **-2.** [waves, oil]: **to ~ over sthg** bañar algo.

◆ **wash away** *vt sep* [subj: water, waves] llevarse, barrer.

◆ **wash down** *vt sep* **-1.** [food] regar, rociar. **-2.** [clean] lavar.

◆ **wash out** *vt sep* **-1.** [stain, dye] quitar lavando. **-2.** [container] enjuagar.

◆ **wash up** ◇ *vt sep* **-1.** Br [dishes] lavar, fregar. **-2.** [subj: sea, river]: **to ~ up on the shore** arrojar a la playa. ◇ *vi* **-1.** Br [wash the dishes] fregar OR lavar los platos. **-2.** Am [wash o.s.] lavarse.

washable ['wɒʃəbl] *adj* lavable.

wash-and-wear *adj* de lava y pon.

washbasin Br ['wɒʃˌbeɪsn], **washbowl** Am ['wɒʃbəʊl] *n* lavabo *m*.

washcloth ['wɒʃˌklɒθ] *n* Am toallita *f* para lavarse la cara.

washed-out [wɒʃt-] *adj* **-1.** [pale] pálido(da), descolorido(da). **-2.** [exhausted] rendido(da).

washed-up [wɒʃt-] *adj inf* [person] acabado(da); [business, project] fracasado(da).

washer ['wɒʃəʳ] *n* **-1.** TECH arandela *f*. **-2.** [washing machine] lavadora *f*.

washer-dryer *n* lavadora-secadora *f*.

washing ['wɒʃɪŋ] *n* (*U*) **-1.** [operation] colada *f*. **-2.** [clothes - dirty] ropa *f* sucia OR para lavar; [- clean] colada *f*.

washing line *n* tendedero *m*.

washing machine *n* lavadora *f*.

washing powder *n* Br detergente *m*, jabón *m* en polvo.

Washington ['wɒʃɪŋtən] *n* **-1.** [state]: **~ State** Estado *m* de Washington. **-2.** [town]: **~ D.C.** ciudad *f* de Washington.

washing-up *n* **-1.** Br [crockery, pans etc] platos *mpl* para fregar. **-2.** [operation] fregado *m*; **to do the ~** fregar los platos.

washing-up liquid *n* Br detergente *m* para vajillas.

washout ['wɒʃaʊt] *n inf* desastre *m*, fracaso *m*.

washroom ['wɒʃrʊm] *n* Am lavabo *m*, aseos *mpl*.

wasn't [wɒznt] = **was not**.

wasp [wɒsp] *n* [insect] avispa *f*.

Wasp, WASP [wɒsp] (*abbr of* **White Anglo-Saxon Protestant**) *n inf* persona *de raza blanca, origen anglosajón y protestante*.

waspish ['wɒspɪʃ] *adj* mordaz, punzante.

wastage ['weɪstɪdʒ] *n* desperdicio *m*.

waste [weɪst] ◇ *adj* [land] yermo(ma); [material, fuel] de desecho. ◇ *n* **-1.** [misuse, incomplete use] desperdicio *m*, derroche *m*; **to go to ~ perderse; a ~ of time** una pérdida de tiempo. **-2.** (*U*) [refuse] desperdicios *mpl*; [chemical, toxic etc] residuos *mpl*. ◇ *vt* [time] perder; [money] malgastar, derrochar; [food, energy, opportunity] desperdiciar; **it would be ~d on me** no sabría aprovecharlo.
♦ **wastes** *npl literary* yermos *mpl*.

wastebasket *Am* = **wastepaper basket**.

waste disposal unit *n* triturador *m* de basuras.

wasteful ['weɪstful] *adj* derrochador(ra).

waste ground *n* (*U*) descampados *mpl*.

wasteland ['weɪst,lænd] *n* yermo *m*.

waste paper *n* papeles *mpl* viejos OR usados.

wastepaper basket [,weɪst'peɪpər-], **wastepaper bin** [,weɪst'peɪpər-], **wastebasket** *Am* ['weɪst,bɑːskɪt] *n* papelera *f*.

watch [wɒtʃ] ◇ *n* **-1.** [timepiece] reloj *m*. **-2.** [act of watching]: **to keep ~** estar de guardia; **to keep ~ on sthg/sb** vigilar algo/a alguien. **-3.** MIL [group of people] guardia *f*. ◇ *vt* **-1.** [look at - gen] mirar; [- sunset] contemplar; [- football match, TV] ver. **-2.** [spy on] vigilar. **-3.** [be careful about] tener cuidado con, vigilar; **~ it!** *inf* ¡cuidado!, ¡ojo! ◇ *vi* mirar, observar.
♦ **watch out** *vi* tener cuidado, estar atento(ta).
♦ **watch over** *vt fus* [look after] vigilar.

watchdog ['wɒtʃdɒg] *n* **-1.** [dog] perro *m* guardián. **-2.** *fig* [organization] comisión *f* de vigilancia.

watchful ['wɒtʃful] *adj* atento(ta).

watchmaker ['wɒtʃ,meɪkər] *n* relojero *m*, -ra *f*.

watchman ['wɒtʃmən] (*pl* **-men** [-mən]) *n* vigilante *m*, guarda *m*, rondín *m Amer*.

watchword ['wɒtʃwɜːd] *n* lema *m*.

water ['wɔːtər] ◇ *n* **-1.** [gen] agua *f*; **to pour** OR **throw cold ~ on** echar un jarro de agua fría sobre; **to tread ~** flotar haciendo la bicicleta; **that's ~ under the bridge** esto es agua pasada. **-2.** [urine]: **to pass ~** orinar. ◇ *vt* regar. ◇ *vi* **-1.** [eyes]: **my eyes are ~ing** me lloran los ojos. **-2.** [mouth]: **my mouth is ~ing** se me hace la boca agua.
♦ **waters** *npl* aguas *fpl*.
♦ **water down** *vt sep* **-1.** [dilute] diluir, aguar. **-2.** *usu pej* [moderate] moderar, suavizar.

water bed *n* cama *f* de agua.

water bird *n* ave *f* acuática.

water biscuit *n* tipo de galleta sin azúcar.

waterborne ['wɔːtəbɔːn] *adj* [disease] transmitido(da) a través del agua.

water bottle *n* cantimplora *f*.

water buffalo *n* búfalo *m* de agua.

water cannon *n* cañón *m* de agua.

water chestnut *n* tipo de tubérculo utilizado en la cocina china.

water closet *n* dated wáter *m*, retrete *m*.

watercolour ['wɔːtə,kʌlər] *n* acuarela *f*.

water-cooled [-,kuːld] *adj* refrigerado(da) por agua.

watercourse ['wɔːtəkɔːs] *n* cauce *m*.

watercress ['wɔːtəkres] *n* berro *m*.

watered-down [,wɔːtəd-] *adj usu pej* suavizado(da).

waterfall ['wɔːtəfɔːl] *n* cascada *f*, salto *m* de agua.

waterfront ['wɔːtəfrʌnt] *n* muelle *m*.

water heater *n* calentador *m* de agua.

waterhole ['wɔːtəhəʊl] *n* balsa *f* (donde acuden a beber los animales).

watering can ['wɔːtərɪŋ-] *n* regadera *f*.

water jump *n* ría *f* (*en carreras de caballos*).

water level *n* nivel *m* del agua.

water lily *n* nenúfar *m*.

waterline ['wɔːtəlaɪn] *n* NAUT línea *f* de flotación.

waterlogged ['wɔːtəlɒgd] *adj* inundado(da).

water main *n* cañería *f* principal.

watermark ['wɔːtəmɑːk] *n* **-1.** [in paper] filigrana *f*. **-2.** [showing water level] marca *f* del nivel del agua.

watermelon ['wɔːtə,melən] *n* sandía *f*.

water pipe *n* [in house, building] tubería *f* OR cañería *f* de agua.

water pistol *n* pistola *f* de agua.

water polo *n* water-polo *m*, polo *m* acuático.

waterproof ['wɔːtəpruːf] ◇ *adj* impermeable. ◇ *n* impermeable *m*. ◇ *vt* impermeabilizar.

water rates *npl Br* tarifa *f* del agua.

water-resistant *adj* resistente al agua.

watershed ['wɔːtəʃed] *n fig* momento *m* decisivo.

waterside ['wɔːtəsaɪd] ◇ *adj* ribereño(ña). ◇ *n*: **the ~** la orilla.

water skiing *n* esquí *m* acuático.

water softener *n* purificador *m* de agua.

water-soluble *adj* soluble en agua.

waterspout ['wɔːtəspaʊt] *n* tromba *f* marina.

water supply *n* reserva *f* de agua.

water table *n* nivel *m* del agua.

water tank *n* reserva *f* de agua.

watertight ['wɔːtətaɪt] *adj* **-1.** [waterproof] hermético(ca). **-2.** *fig* [agreement, plan] perfecto(ta); [argument, excuse] irrecusable, irrebatible.

water tower *n* arca *f* de agua.

waterway ['wɔːtəweɪ] *n* vía *f* navegable.

waterworks ['wɔːtəwɜːks] (*pl inv*) *n* [building] central *f* de agua.

watery ['wɔːtərɪ] *adj* **-1.** [food] soso(sa); [drink] aguado(da). **-2.** [pale] desvaído(da), pálido(da).

watt [wɒt] *n* vatio *m*.

wattage ['wɒtɪdʒ] *n* potencia *f* en vatios.

wave [weɪv] ◇ *n* **-1.** [of hand] ademán *m* OR señal *f* (con la mano). **-2.** [of water] ola *f*. **-3.** [of emotion, nausea, panic] arranque *m*; [of immigrants, crime etc] oleada *f*. **-4.** [of light, sound, heat] onda *f*. **-5.** [in hair] ondulación *f*.
◇ *vt* **-1.** [move about as signal] agitar. **-2.** [signal to] hacer señales OR señas a.
◇ *vi* **-1.** [with hand in greeting] saludar con la mano; [- to say goodbye] decir adiós con la mano; **to ~ at** OR **to sb** saludar a alguien con la mano. **-2.** [flag] ondear; [trees] agitarse.
◆ **wave aside** *vt sep fig* [dismiss] desechar.
◆ **wave down** *vt sep* hacer señas para que se pare.

wave band *n* banda *f* de frecuencias.

wavelength ['weɪvleŋθ] *n* longitud *f* de onda; **to be on the same ~** *fig* estar en la misma onda.

waver ['weɪvə'] *vi* **-1.** [falter - resolution, confidence] flaquear; [- person] vacilar, dudar; **to ~ (in)** flaquear (en). **-2.** [hesitate] dudar, vacilar. **-3.** [fluctuate] oscilar.

wavy ['weɪvɪ] (*compar* **-ier**, *superl* **-iest**) *adj* ondulado(da).

wax [wæks] ◇ *n* cera *f*. ◇ *vt* encerar. ◇ *vi dated* or *hum* [become] ponerse; **to ~ and wane** subir y bajar.

waxen ['wæksən] *adj* [pale] pálido(da).

wax paper *n Am* papel *m* de cera.

waxworks ['wækswɜːks] (*pl inv*) *n* museo *m* de cera.

way [weɪ] ◇ *n* **-1.** [manner, method] manera *f*, modo *m*; **~s and means** medios *mpl*; **in the same ~** del mismo modo, igualmente; **this/that ~** así; **in a ~** en cierto modo; **in a big/small ~** a gran/pequeña escala; **she has fallen for him in a big ~** está locamente enamorada de él; **to get** OR **have one's ~** salirse uno con la suya; **to have everything one's own ~** salirse siempre uno con la suya; **to have a ~ with people** tener don de gentes; **to have a ~ with words** tener un pico de oro; **to have a ~ of doing sthg** tener la costumbre de hacer algo. **-2.** [route, path] camino *m*; **to lose one's ~** perderse; **~ in** entrada *f*; **~ out** salida *f*; **it's out of my ~** no me pilla de camino; **it's out of the ~** [place] está algo aislado; **on the** OR **on one's ~** de camino; **I'm on my ~** voy de camino; **across** OR **over the ~** enfrente; **to be under ~** [ship] estar navegando; *fig* [meeting] estar en marcha; **to get under ~** [ship] zarpar; [meeting] ponerse en marcha; **to be in the ~** estar en medio; **to get sthg out of the ~** [task] quitarse algo de encima; **to go out of one's ~ to do sthg** tomarse muchas molestias para hacer algo; **to keep out of the ~** mantenerse alejado; **to make one's ~** to dirigirse hacia; **to make ~ for** dar paso a; **to stand in sb's ~** *fig* interponerse en el camino de alguien; **to work one's ~** to conseguir llegar a. **-3.** [direction] dirección *f*; **come this ~** ven por aquí; **go that ~** ve por ahí; **which ~ do we go?** ¿hacia dónde vamos?; **the wrong ~ up** OR **round** al revés; **the right ~ up** OR **round** del derecho. **-4.** [distance]: **all the ~** todo el camino OR trayecto; **we're with you all the ~** *fig* te apoyamos incondicionalmente; **most of the ~** casi todo el camino OR trayecto; **it's a long ~ away** está muy lejos; **we have a long ~ to go** queda mucho camino por recorrer; **to go a long ~ towards doing sthg** *fig* contribuir enormemente a hacer algo. **-5.** *phr:* **to give ~** [under weight, pressure] ceder; **"give ~"** *Br* "ceda el paso"; **no ~!** ¡ni hablar!
◇ *adv inf* [far] mucho; **it's ~ too big** es tela de grande.
◆ **ways** *npl* [customs, habits] costumbres *fpl*, hábitos *mpl*.
◆ **by the way** *adv* por cierto.
◆ **by way of** *prep* **-1.** [via] (pasando) por. **-2.** [as a sort of] a modo de, como.
◆ **in the way of** *prep:* **what do you have in the ~ of wine?** ¿qué clases de vino tiene?

waylay [ˌweɪˈleɪ] (*pt & pp* **-laid**) *vt* abordar.

way of life *n* modo *m* de vida.

way-out *adj inf dated* de lo más loco.

wayside ['weɪsaɪd] *n* [roadside] borde *m* del camino; **to fall by the ~** *fig* quedarse a mitad de camino.

wayward ['weɪwəd] *adj* [person, behaviour] incorregible.

WC (*abbr of* **water closet**) WC.

WCC (*abbr of* **World Council of Churches**) *n asamblea mundial de iglesias*.

we [wiː] *pers pron* nosotros *mpl*, -tras *fpl*; WE can't do it NOSOTROS no podemos hacerlo; as ~ say in France como decimos en Francia; ~ British nosotros los británicos.

weak [wiːk] *adj* -1. [gen] débil. -2. [material, structure] frágil. -3. [argument, tea etc] flojo(ja). -4. [lacking knowledge, skill]: to be ~ on sthg estar flojo(ja) en algo.

weaken ['wiːkn] ◇ *vt* debilitar. ◇ *vi* -1. [become less determined] ceder, flaquear. -2. [physically] debilitarse.

weak-kneed [-'niːd] *adj inf pej* pusilánime.

weakling ['wiːklɪŋ] *n pej* enclenque *m y f*.

weakly ['wiːklɪ] *adv* débilmente.

weak-minded [-'maɪndɪd] *adj* débil de carácter.

weakness ['wiːknɪs] *n* -1. [gen] debilidad *f*; to have a ~ for sthg tener debilidad por algo. -2. [imperfect point] defecto *m*.

weal [wiːl] *n* verdugón *m*.

wealth [welθ] *n* -1. [riches] riqueza *f*. -2. [abundance] profusión *f*, gran cantidad *f*.

wealth tax *n Br* impuesto *m* sobre el patrimonio.

wealthy ['welθɪ] (*compar* -ier, *superl* -iest) *adj* rico(ca), platudo(da) *Amer*.

wean [wiːn] *vt* -1. [from mother's milk] destetar. -2. [discourage]: to ~ sb from OR off sthg apartar gradualmente a alguien de algo.

weapon ['wepən] *n* arma *f*.

weaponry ['wepənrɪ] *n* (*U*) armamento *m*.

wear [weəʳ] (*pt* wore, *pp* worn) ◇ *n* (*U*) -1. [use] uso *m*; to be the worse for ~ [thing] estar deteriorado; [person] estar hecho un trapo. -2. [damage] desgaste *m*; ~ and tear desgaste. -3. [type of clothes] ropa *f*. ◇ *vt* -1. [clothes, hair] llevar; [shoes] calzar; to ~ red vestirse de rojo. -2. [damage] desgastar. ◇ *vi* -1. [deteriorate] desgastarse. -2. [last]: to ~ well/badly durar mucho/poco. -3. *phr*: to ~ thin [joke] dejar de ser gracioso.

◆ **wear away** ◇ *vt sep* desgastar. ◇ *vi* desgastarse.

◆ **wear down** ◇ *vt sep* -1. [reduce size of] desgastar. -2. [weaken] agotar. ◇ *vi* desgastarse.

◆ **wear off** *vi* desaparecer, disiparse.

◆ **wear on** *vi* transcurrir.

◆ **wear out** ◇ *vt sep* -1. [shoes, clothes] gastar. -2. [person] agotar. ◇ *vi* gastarse.

wearable ['weərəbl] *adj* que se puede llevar.

wearily ['wɪərɪlɪ] *adv* fatigosamente.

weariness ['wɪərɪnɪs] *n* fatiga *f*, cansancio *m*.

wearing ['weərɪŋ] *adj* [exhausting] fatigoso(sa).

weary ['wɪərɪ] (*compar* -ier, *superl* -iest) *adj* fatigado(da), cansado(da); to be ~ of sthg/ of doing sthg estar cansado de algo/de hacer algo.

weasel ['wiːzl] *n* comadreja *f*.

weather ['weðəʳ] ◇ *n* tiempo *m*; to make heavy ~ of sthg complicar algo innecesariamente; to be under the ~ no encontrarse muy bien. ◇ *vt* [crisis etc] superar. ◇ *vi*: to ~ well ser resistente.

weather-beaten *adj* [face, skin] curtido(da).

weathercock ['weðəkɒk] *n* veleta *f*.

weathered ['weðəd] *adj* deteriorado(da) (*por la intemperie*).

weather forecast *n* parte *m* meteorológico, pronóstico *m* del tiempo.

weatherman ['weðəmæn] (*pl* -men [-men]) *n* hombre *m* del tiempo.

weather map *n* mapa *m* del tiempo.

weatherproof ['weðəpruːf] *adj* [clothing] impermeable; [building] resistente a la intemperie.

weather report *n* [on radio, TV] parte *m* meteorológico; [in newspaper] información *f* meteorológica.

weather ship *n barco que informa sobre el estado del tiempo*.

weather vane [-veɪn] *n* veleta *f*.

weave [wiːv] (*pt* wove, *pp* woven) ◇ *n* tejido *m*. ◇ *vt* -1. [using loom] tejer. -2. [move along]: to ~ one's way (through) colarse (por entre). ◇ *vi* [move]: to ~ through colarse por entre.

weaver ['wiːvəʳ] *n* tejedor *m*, -ra *f*.

web [web] *n* -1. [cobweb] telaraña *f*. -2. *fig* [network] urdimbre *f*, entramado *m*.

webbed [webd] *adj* palmeado(da).

webbing ['webɪŋ] *n* (*U*) reps *m inv*.

web-footed [-'fʊtɪd] *adj* palmípedo(da).

Web site *n* COMPUT sitio *m* Web.

wed [wed] (*pt* & *pp* -ded OR wed) *literary* ◇ *vt* desposar. ◇ *vi* desposarse.

we'd [wiːd] = we had, we would.

Wed. (*abbr of* Wednesday) miérc.

wedded ['wedɪd] *adj* [committed]: ~ to sthg entregado(da) a algo.

wedding ['wedɪŋ] *n* boda *f*, casamiento *m*.

wedding anniversary *n* aniversario *m* de boda.

wedding cake *n* tarta *f* nupcial, pastel *m* de bodas.

wedding dress *n* traje *m* de novia.

wedding reception *n* fiesta *f* de bodas.

wedding ring *n* anillo *m* de boda, argolla *f* Amer.

wedge [wedʒ] ◇ *n* **-1.** [for steadying or splitting] cuña *f*; **to drive a ~ between** dividir a; **the thin end of the ~** la punta del iceberg. **-2.** [triangular slice] porción *f*, trozo *m*. ◇ *vt*: **to ~ sthg open/shut** dejar algo abierto/cerrado con una cuña.

wedlock ['wedlɒk] *n* (U) *literary* desposorio *m*.

Wednesday ['wenzdɪ] *n* miércoles *m* inv; see also **Saturday**.

wee [wiː] ◇ *adj Scot* pequeño(ña); **a ~ bit** un poquito. ◇ *n v inf* pipí *m*. ◇ *vi v inf* hacer pipí.

weed [wiːd] ◇ *n* **-1.** [wild plant] mala hierba *f*. **-2.** *Br inf* [feeble person] canijo *m*, -ja *f*. ◇ *vt* desherbar, escardar.
◆ **weed out** *vt sep* extirpar.

weeding ['wiːdɪŋ] *n* escarda *f*, limpieza *f* de malas hierbas.

weedkiller ['wiːd,kɪlər] *n* herbicida *m*.

weedy ['wiːdɪ] (*compar* -ier, *superl* -iest) *adj* **-1.** [overgrown with weeds] cubierto(ta) de malas hierbas. **-2.** *Br inf* [feeble] enclenque.

week [wiːk] *n* **-1.** [gen] semana *f*; **a ~ on Saturday, Saturday ~** del sábado en ocho días.

weekday ['wiːkdeɪ] *n* día *m* laborable.

weekend [,wiːk'end] *n* fin *m* de semana.

weekend bag *n* (bolsa *f* de) fin *m* de semana.

weekly ['wiːklɪ] ◇ *adj* semanal. ◇ *adv* semanalmente. ◇ *n* semanario *m*, periódico *m* semanal.

weeny ['wiːnɪ] *adj Br inf* chiquitín(ina); **a ~ bit** un poquitín.

weep ['wiːp] (*pt & pp* **wept**) ◇ *n*: **to have a ~** llorar. ◇ *vt* derramar. ◇ *vi* llorar.

weeping willow ['wiːpɪŋ-] *n* sauce *m* llorón.

weepy [wiːpɪ] (*compar* -ier, *superl* -iest) *adj* **-1.** [tearful] lloroso(sa). **-2.** [sad] triste.

wee-wee *n & vi* = **wee**.

weft [weft] *n* trama *f*.

weigh [weɪ] *vt* **-1.** [gen] pesar. **-2.** [consider carefully] sopesar.
◆ **weigh down** *vt sep* **-1.** [physically] sobrecargar. **-2.** [mentally]: **to be ~ed down by** OR **with** estar abrumado(da) de OR por.
◆ **weigh (up)on** *vt fus* abrumar.
◆ **weigh out** *vt sep* pesar.
◆ **weigh up** *vt sep* **-1.** [consider carefully] sopesar. **-2.** [size up] hacerse una idea de.

weighbridge ['weɪbrɪdʒ] *n Br* puente *m* basculante.

weighing machine ['weɪŋ-] *n* báscula *f*.

weight [weɪt] ◇ *n* **-1.** [gen] peso *m*; **to put on** OR **gain ~** engordar; **to lose ~** adelgazar; **to carry ~** tener peso; **it's a ~ off my mind** me ha quitado un peso de encima; **to pull one's ~** poner (uno) de su parte; **to take the ~ off one's feet** descansar; **to throw one's ~ about** comportarse de manera autoritaria. **-2.** [metal object] pesa *f*. ◇ *vt*: **to ~ sthg (down)** sujetar algo con un peso.

weighted ['weɪtɪd] *adj*: **to be ~ in favour/against** inclinarse a favor/en contra de.

weighting ['weɪtɪŋ] *n* prima por vivir en una ciudad con alto coste de vida.

weightlessness ['weɪtlɪsnɪs] *n* ingravidez *f*.

weightlifter ['weɪt,lɪftər] *n* levantador *m* de pesos.

weightlifting ['weɪt,lɪftɪŋ] *n* levantamiento *m* de pesos, halterofilia *f*.

weight training *n* levantamiento *m* de pesos.

weighty ['weɪtɪ] (*compar* -ier, *superl* -iest) *adj* [serious] de peso.

weir [wɪər] *n* presa *f*, dique *m*.

weird [wɪəd] *adj* raro(ra), extraño(ña).

weirdo ['wɪədəʊ] (*pl* -es) *n inf* bicho *m* raro.

welcome ['welkəm] ◇ *adj* **-1.** [guest] bienvenido(da); **to make sb ~** acoger bien a alguien. **-2.** [free]: **you're ~ to come** si quieres, puedes venir. **-3.** [appreciated]: **to be ~** ser de agradecer. **-4.** [in reply to thanks]: **you're ~** de nada. ◇ *n* bienvenida *f*. ◇ *vt* **-1.** [receive] dar la bienvenida a. **-2.** [approve, support] recibir bien. ◇ *excl* ¡bienvenido(da)!

welcoming ['welkəmɪŋ] *adj* cordial.

weld [weld] ◇ *n* soldadura *f*. ◇ *vt* soldar.

welder ['weldər] *n* soldador *m*, -ra *f*.

welfare ['welfeər] ◇ *adj* de asistencia social. ◇ *n* **-1.** [state of well-being] bienestar *m*. **-2.** *Am* [income support] subsidio *m* de la seguridad social.

welfare state *n*: **the ~** el Estado de bienestar.

well [wel] (*compar* **better**, *superl* **best**) ◇ *adj* bien; **to be ~** [healthy] estar bien (de salud); **all is ~** todo va bien; **(that's all) ~ and good** (eso está) muy bien; **(it's) just as ~** menos mal.
◇ *adv* **-1.** [satisfactorily, thoroughly] bien; **they were ~ beaten** fueron ampliamente derrotados; **to go ~** ir bien; **~ done!** ¡muy bien!; **~ and truly** completamente; **to be ~ in with sb** *inf* ser muy amiguete de alguien; **to be ~ out of sthg** *inf* tener la suerte de haberse salido de algo. **-2.** [definitely, certainly] claramente, definitivamente; **it was**

~ **worth it** sí que valió la pena. **-3.** [as emphasis]: **you know perfectly ~ (that)** sabes de sobra (que). **-4.** [very possibly]: **it could ~ rain** es muy posible que llueva.
◇ *n* pozo *m*.
◇ *excl* **-1.** [gen] bueno; **oh ~!** ¡en fin! **-2.** [in surprise] ¡vaya!
◆ **as well** *adv* **-1.** [in addition] también. **-2.** [with same result]: **you may** OR **might as ~ (do it)** ¿y por qué no (lo haces)?
◆ **as well as** *conj* además de.
◆ **well up** *vi* brotar.

we'll [wiːl] = **we shall, we will.**

well-adjusted *adj* muy integrado(da).

well-advised [-əd'vaɪzd] *adj* sensato(ta); **you would be ~ to do it** sería aconsejable que lo hicieras.

well-appointed [-ə'pɔɪntɪd] *adj* bien equipado(da).

well-balanced *adj* equilibrado(da).

well-behaved [-bɪ'heɪvd] *adj* formal, bien educado(da).

wellbeing [ˌwel'biːɪŋ] *n* bienestar *m*.

well-bred [-'bred] *adj* bien educado(da).

well-built *adj* fornido(da).

well-chosen *adj* atinado(da), acertado(da).

well-disposed *adj*: **to be ~ to sb/sthg, to be ~ towards sb/sthg** tener buena disposición hacia alguien/para algo.

well-done *adj* [thoroughly cooked] muy hecho(cha).

well-dressed [-'drest] *adj* bien vestido(da).

well-earned [-'ɜːnd] *adj* bien merecido(da).

well-established *adj* [custom, tradition] arraigado(da); [company] de sólida reputación.

well-fed *adj* bien alimentado(da).

well-groomed [-'gruːmd] *adj* bien arreglado(da).

wellhead ['welhed] *n* manantial *m*.

well-heeled [-'hiːld] *adj* *inf* ricachón(ona).

wellies [-'welɪz] *npl Br inf* botas *fpl* de agua.

well-informed *adj*: **to be ~ (about** OR **on)** estar bien informado(da) (sobre).

Wellington ['welɪŋtən] *n* Wellington.

wellington boots ['welɪŋtən-], **wellingtons** ['welɪŋtənz] *npl* botas *fpl* de agua.

well-intentioned [-ɪn'tenʃnd] *adj* bienintencionado(da).

well-kept *adj* **-1.** [neat, tidy] bien cuidado(da). **-2.** [not revealed] bien guardado(da).

well-known *adj* conocido(da).

well-mannered *adj* de buenos modales, educado(da).

well-meaning *adj* bienintencionado(da).

well-nigh *adv* casi.

well-off *adj* **-1.** [rich] acomodado(da), rico(ca). **-2.** [well-provided]: **to be ~ for sthg** tener bastante de algo; **not to know when one is ~** *inf* no saber uno la suerte que tiene.

well-paid *adj* bien pagado(da).

well-preserved *adj fig* bien conservado(da).

well-proportioned [-prə'pɔːʃnd] *adj* bien proporcionado(da).

well-read [-'red] *adj* instruido(da), culto(ta).

well-rounded [-'raʊndɪd] *adj* [varied] completo(ta).

well-spoken *adj* que tiene buen acento.

well-thought-of *adj* de buena reputación.

well-thought-out *adj* bien pensado(da).

well-timed *adj* oportuno(na).

well-to-do *adj* de dinero, adinerado(da).

wellwisher ['wel,wɪʃəʳ] *n* simpatizante *m* y *f* (que da muestras de apoyo).

well-woman clinic *n Br centro sanitario para mujeres o tiempo dedicado a la atención sanitaria a mujeres en ambulatorios.*

Welsh [welʃ] ◇ *adj* galés(esa). ◇ *n* [language] galés *m*. ◇ *npl*: **the ~** los galeses.

Welshman ['welʃmən] (*pl* **-men** [-mən]) *n* galés *m*.

Welsh rarebit [-'reəbɪt] *n tostada cubierta de queso fundido.*

Welshwoman ['welʃˌwʊmən] (*pl* **-women** [-ˌwɪmɪn]) *n* galesa *f*.

welter ['weltəʳ] *n* revoltijo *m*, batiburrillo *m*.

welterweight ['weltəweɪt] *n* peso *m* wélter.

wend [wend] *vt literary*: **to ~ one's way towards** encaminar (uno) sus pasos hacia.

wendy house ['wendɪ-] *n Br casita de juguete del tamaño de un niño.*

went [went] *pt* → **go.**

wept [wept] *pt & pp* → **weep.**

were [wɜːʳ] *pt* → **be.**

we're [wɪəʳ] = **we are.**

weren't [wɜːnt] = **were not.**

werewolf ['wɪəwʊlf] (*pl* **-wolves** [-wʊlvz]) *n* hombre *m* lobo.

west [west] ◇ *n* **-1.** [direction] oeste *m*. **-2.** [region]: **the West** el Oeste. ◇ *adj* del oeste. ◇ *adv*: ~ **(of)** al oeste (de).
◆ **West** *n* POL: **the West** Occidente.

West Bank *n*: **the ~** Cisjordania.

westbound ['westbaʊnd] *adj* con rumbo al oeste.

West Country n Br: **the ~** el sudoeste de Inglaterra.

West End n Br: **the ~** zona central de Londres, famosa por sus teatros, tiendas etc.

westerly ['westəlı] adj del oeste; **in a ~ direction** hacia el oeste.

western ['westən] ◇ adj occidental. ◇ n [book] novela f del oeste; [film] película f del oeste, western m.

Westerner ['westənər] n **-1.** POL occidental m y f. **-2.** [inhabitant of west of country] habitante m y f del oeste.

westernize, **-ise** ['westənaɪz] vt occidentalizar.

Western Samoa n Samoa Occidental.

West German ◇ adj de la Alemania Occidental. ◇ n [person] alemán m, -ana f occidental.

West Germany n: **(the former) ~** (la antigua) Alemania Occidental.

West Indian ◇ adj antillano(na). ◇ n [person] antillano m, -na f.

West Indies [-'ɪndiːz] npl Antillas.

Westminster ['westmɪnstər] n Westminster.

WESTMINSTER:
En este barrio londinense se encuentran el Parlamento británico y el palacio de Buckingham. El nombre 'Westminster' también se utiliza para referirse al parlamento

---

West Virginia n Virginia Occidental.

westward ['westwəd] ◇ adj hacia el oeste. ◇ adv = **westwards**.

westwards ['westwədz] adv hacia el oeste.

wet [wet] (compar **-ter**, superl **-test**, pt & pp **wet** OR **-ted**, cont **-ting**) ◇ adj **-1.** [soaked] mojado(da); [damp] húmedo(da). **-2.** [rainy] lluvioso(sa). **-3.** [paint, cement] fresco(ca). **-4.** [eyes] lleno(na) de lágrimas. **-5.** Br inf pej [weak, feeble] ñoño(ña). ◇ n inf POL político conservador moderado. ◇ vt **-1.** [soak] mojar; [dampen] humedecer. **-2.** [urinate in]: **to ~ the bed** orinarse en la cama; **to ~ o.s.** orinarse encima.

wet blanket n inf pej aguafiestas m y f.

wet-look adj brillante.

wetness ['wetnɪs] n **-1.** [dampness] humedad f. **-2.** Br inf pej [feebleness] ñoñez f.

wet nurse n nodriza f, ama f de cría.

wet rot n pudrimiento de la madera causado por la humedad.

wet suit n traje m de submarinista.

WEU (abbr of **Western European Union**) n UEO f.

we've [wiːv] = **we have**.

whack [wæk] inf ◇ n **-1.** [hit] castañazo m, cachetada f Amer. **-2.** [share] parte f. ◇ vt [person] pegar, zurrar; [object] dar un porrazo a.

whacked [wækt] adj Br inf [exhausted] molido(da), hecho(cha) polvo.

whacky ['wækı] = **wacky**.

whale [weɪl] n [animal] ballena f; **to have a ~ of a time** inf pasárselo bomba.

whaling ['weɪlɪŋ] n caza f de ballenas.

wham [wæm] excl inf ¡zas!

wharf [wɔːf] (pl **-s** OR **wharves** [wɔːvz]) n muelle m, embarcadero m.

what [wɒt] ◇ adj **-1.** (in direct, indirect questions) qué; **~ shape is it?** ¿qué forma tiene?; **he asked me ~ shape it was** me preguntó qué forma tenía; **~ colour is it?** ¿de qué color es? **-2.** (in exclamations) qué; **~ a surprise!** ¡qué sorpresa!; **~ a stupid idea!** ¡qué idea más tonta! ◇ pron **-1.** (interrogative) qué; **~ are they doing?** ¿qué hacen?; **~ are they talking about?** ¿de qué están hablando?; **~ is it called?** ¿cómo se llama?; **~ does it cost?** ¿cuánto cuesta?; **~ is it like?** ¿cómo es?; **~'s the Spanish for "book"?** ¿cómo se dice "book" en español?; **~ about another drink/going out for a meal?** ¿qué tal otra copa/si salimos a comer?; **~ about me?** ¿y yo qué?; **~ if nobody comes?** ¿y si no viene nadie, qué? **-2.** (relative) lo que; **I saw ~ happened/he did** yo vi lo que ocurrió/hizo; **I don't know ~ to do** no sé qué hacer. ◇ excl [expressing disbelief] ¿qué?; **~, no milk!** ¿cómo? ¿que no hay leche?

whatever [wɒt'evər] ◇ adj cualquier; **eat ~ food you find** come lo que encuentres; **no chance ~** ni la más remota posibilidad; **nothing ~** nada en absoluto. ◇ pron **-1.** [no matter what]: **~ they may offer** ofrezcan lo que ofrezcan; **~ you like** lo que (tú) quieras; **~ happens** pase lo que pase. **-2.** [indicating surprise]: **~ do you mean?** ¿qué diablos quieres decir? **-3.** [indicating ignorance]: **~ that is** OR **may be** sea lo que sea eso; **or ~** o lo que sea.

whatnot ['wɒtnɒt] n inf: **and ~** y cosas por el estilo.

whatsoever [,wɒtsəʊ'evər] adj: **nothing ~** nada en absoluto; **none ~** ni uno.

wheat [wiːt] n trigo m.

wheat germ n germen m de trigo.

wheatmeal ['wiːtmiːl] n harina f semiintegral.

wheedle ['wiːdl] vt decir con zalamería; **to ~ sb into doing sthg** camelar OR engatusar a alguien para que haga algo; **to ~ sthg out of sb** sonsacarle algo a alguien.

wheel [wiːl] ◇ n **-1.** [gen] rueda f. **-2.** [steering wheel] volante m. ◇ vt empujar (algo sobre ruedas). ◇ vi **-1.** [move in circle] dar vueltas. **-2.** [turn round]: **to ~ round** darse la vuelta.

wheelbarrow ['wiːl,bærəu] n carretilla f.

wheelbase ['wiːlbeɪs] n batalla f, distancia f entre ejes.

wheelchair [,wiːl'tʃeəʳ] n silla f de ruedas.

wheelclamp ['wiːlklæmp] n cepo m.

wheeler-dealer ['wiːlə-] n pej zorro m.

wheeling and dealing ['wiːlɪŋ-] n (U) pej tejemanejes mpl.

wheeze [wiːz] ◇ n [sound] resuello m. ◇ vi resollar.

wheezy ['wiːzɪ] (compar **-ier**, superl **-iest**) adj que resuella.

whelk [welk] n buccino m.

when [wen] ◇ adv (in direct, indirect question) cuándo; **~ does the plane arrive?** ¿cuándo llega el avión?; **he asked me ~ I would be in London** me preguntó cuándo estaría en Londres.
◇ conj cuando; **tell me ~ you've read it** avísame cuando lo hayas leído; **on the day ~ it happened** el día (en) que pasó; **you said it was black ~ it was actually white** dijiste que era negro cuando en realidad era blanco; **how can I buy it ~ I can't afford it?** ¿cómo voy a comprarlo si no tengo dinero?

whenever [wen'evəʳ] ◇ conj [no matter when] cuando; [every time] cada vez que; **~ you like** cuando quieras. ◇ adv cuando sea.

where [weəʳ] ◇ adv (in direct, indirect questions) dónde; **~ do you live?** ¿dónde vives?; **do you know ~ he lives?** ¿sabes dónde vive?; **~ are we going?** ¿adónde vamos?; **I don't know ~ to start** no sé por dónde empezar.
◇ conj **-1.** [referring to place, situation] donde; **this is ~ ...** es aquí donde ...; **go ~ you like** vete (a) donde quieras. **-2.** [whereas]: **children often understand ~ adults don't** los niños a menudo entienden en casos en los que los adultos no.

whereabouts [,weərə'bauts] ◇ adv (por) dónde. ◇ npl paradero m.

whereas [weər'æz] conj mientras que.

whereby [weə'baɪ] conj fml según el/la cual, por el/la cual.

wheresoever [,weəsəu'evəʳ] conj = wherever.

whereupon [,weərə'pɒn] conj fml tras OR con lo cual.

wherever [weər'evəʳ] ◇ conj [no matter where] dondequiera que; **~ you go** dondequiera que vayas; **sit ~ you like** siéntate donde quieras. ◇ adv **-1.** [no matter where] en cualquier parte. **-2.** [indicating surprise]: **~ did you hear that?** ¿dónde diablos habrás oído eso?

wherewithal ['weəwɪðɔːl] n fml: **to have the ~ to do sthg** disponer de los medios para hacer algo.

whet [wet] (pt & pp **-ted**, cont **-ting**) vt: **to ~ sb's appetite (for sthg)** despertar el interés de alguien (por algo).

whether ['weðəʳ] conj **-1.** [indicating choice, doubt] si; **I doubt ~ she'll do it** dudo que lo haga. **-2.** [no matter if]: **~ I want to or not** tanto si quiero como si no, quiera o no quiera.

whew [hwjuː] excl ¡buf!

whey [weɪ] n suero m.

which [wɪtʃ] ◇ adj **-1.** (in direct, indirect questions) qué; **~ house is yours?** ¿cuál es tu casa?, ¿qué casa es la tuya?; **~ one?** ¿cuál?; **~ ones?** ¿cuáles? **-2.** [to refer back to]: **in ~ case** en cuyo caso.
◇ pron **-1.** (in direct, indirect questions) cuál, cuáles (pl); **~ do you prefer?** ¿cuál prefieres?; **I can't decide ~ to have** no sé cuál coger. **-2.** (in relative clause replacing noun) que; **the table, ~ was made of wood, ...** la mesa, que OR la cual era de madera, ...; **the world in ~ we live** el mundo en que OR en el cual vivimos. **-3.** (to refer back to a clause) lo cual; **she denied it, ~ surprised me** lo negó, lo cual me sorprendió.

whichever [wɪtʃ'evəʳ] ◇ adj **-1.** [no matter which]: **~ route you take** vayas por donde vayas. **-2.** [the one which]: **~ colour you prefer** el color que prefieras. ◇ pron el que (f la que), los que (f las que) (pl); **take ~ you like** coge el que quieras.

whiff [wɪf] n **-1.** [smell] olorcillo m. **-2.** fig [sign] atisbo m.

while [waɪl] ◇ n rato m; **it's a long ~ since I did that** hace mucho que no hago eso; **for a ~** un rato; **after a ~** después de un rato; **in a ~** dentro de poco; **once in a ~** de vez en cuando; **to be worth one's ~** merecerle la pena a uno. ◇ conj **-1.** [during the time that] mientras. **-2.** [whereas] mientras que. **-3.** [although] aunque.
◆ **while away** vt sep pasar.

whilst [waɪlst] conj = while.

whim [wɪm] n capricho m.

whimper ['wɪmpəʳ] ◇ n gimoteo m, gemido m. ◇ vt & vi gimotear.

whimsical ['wɪmzɪkl] adj [idea, story] fanta-

sioso(sa); [remark] extravagante, poco usual;
[look] juguetón(ona).

whine [waɪn] ◇ *n* gemido *m*, lloriqueo *m*.
◇ *vi* **-1.** [child, dog] gemir; [siren] ulular. **-2.**
[complain]: **to ~ (about)** quejarse (de).

whinge [wɪndʒ] (*cont* **whingeing**) *vi Br*: **to
~ (about)** quejarse (de).

whip [wɪp] (*pt & pp* **-ped**, *cont* **-ping**) ◇ *n*
-1. [for hitting] látigo *m*, guasca *f Amer*; [for
horse] fusta *f*. **-2.** *Br* POL *miembro de un partido encargado de asegurar que otros miembros
voten en el parlamento.* ◇ *vt* **-1.** [gen] azotar.
-2. [take quickly]: **to ~ sthg out/off** sacar/
quitar algo rápidamente. **-3.** [whisk] batir.
◆ **whip up** *vt sep* [provoke] levantar.

whiplash injury ['wɪplæʃ-] *n* lesión *f* de
cervicales por efecto de la inercia.

whipped cream [wɪpt-] *n* nata *f* montada.

whippet ['wɪpɪt] *n tipo de galgo pequeño.*

whip-round *n Br inf*: **to have a ~** hacer
una colecta.

whirl [wɜːl] ◇ *n* **-1.** [rotating movement] remolino *m*; **to be in a ~** estar aturullado. **-2.**
fig [of activity, events] torbellino *m*. **-3.** *phr*:
let's give it a ~ *inf* lancémonos. ◇ *vt*: **to ~
sb/sthg round** hacer dar vueltas a alguien/
algo. ◇ *vi* **-1.** [move around] arremolinarse;
[dancers] girar vertiginosamente. **-2.** *fig*
[head, mind] dar vueltas.

whirlpool ['wɜːlpuːl] *n* remolino *m*.

whirlwind ['wɜːlwɪnd] ◇ *adj fig* vertigino-
so(sa). ◇ *n* torbellino *m*.

whirr [wɜːr] ◇ *n* zumbido *m*. ◇ *vi* zumbar.

whisk [wɪsk] ◇ *n* CULIN varilla *f*. ◇ *vt* **-1.**
[move quickly]: **to ~ sthg away/out**
llevarse/sacar algo rápidamente. **-2.** CULIN
batir.

whisker ['wɪskər] *n* (pelo *m* del) bigote *m*.
◆ **whiskers** *npl* [of person] patillas *fpl*; [of
cat] bigotes *mpl*.

whiskey ['wɪskɪ] (*pl* **whiskeys**) *n* whisky *m*
(*irlandés o americano*).

whisky ['wɪskɪ] (*pl* **-ies**) *n* whisky *m* (*escocés*).

whisper ['wɪspər] ◇ *n* [gen] susurro *m*; [of
voices] cuchicheo *m*. ◇ *vt* susurrar. ◇ *vi* cuchichear.

whispering ['wɪspərɪŋ] *n* (*U*) cuchicheos
mpl.

whist [wɪst] *n* whist *m*.

whistle ['wɪsl] ◇ *n* **-1.** [sound] silbido *m*,
pitido *m*. **-2.** [device] silbato *m*, pito *m*. ◇ *vt*
silbar. ◇ *vi* **-1.** [person] silbar, chiflar *Amer*;
[referee] pitar; [bird] piar. **-2.** [move quickly]:
to ~ past pasar como un rayo. **-3.** [kettle,
train] silbar, pitar.

whistle-stop tour *n recorrido rápido con
múltiples paradas.*

whit [wɪt] *n* ápice *m*, pizca *f*.

Whit [wɪt] *n Br* Pentecostés *m*.

white [waɪt] ◇ *adj* **-1.** [gen] blanco(ca); **to
go** OR **turn ~** ponerse blanco. **-2.** [coffee,
tea] con leche. ◇ *n* **-1.** [colour] blanco *m*.
-2. [person] blanco *m*, -ca *f*. **-3.** [of egg] clara
f. **-4.** [of eye] blanco *m*.
◆ **whites** *npl* ropa *f* blanca (*para tenis, críquet*).

white blood cell *n* glóbulo *m* blanco.

whiteboard ['waɪtbɔːd] *n* pizarra *f* blanca,
tablero *m* blanco (*para escribir con rotulado-
res*).

white Christmas *n* Navidad *f* con nieve.

white-collar *adj* de oficina; **~ worker** oficinista *m y f*.

white elephant *n fig* mamotreto *m* (*caro e
inútil*).

white goods *npl* **-1.** [household machines]
línea *f* blanca (de electrodomésticos). **-2.**
[linen] lencería *f*.

white-haired [-'heəd] *adj* canoso(sa), de
pelo blanco.

Whitehall ['waɪtɔːl] *n* Whitehall.

WHITEHALL:
En esta calle londinense se encuentran los
principales centros de la Administración británica. Por extensión, 'Whitehall' se utiliza
para referirse a la Administración británica

white horses *npl Br* cabrillas *fpl*.

white-hot *adj* candente, incandescente.

White House *n*: **the ~** la Casa Blanca.

white knight *n persona u organización que
invierte en una empresa para evitar que otra la
absorba.*

white lie *n* mentira *f* piadosa.

white light *n* (*U*) luz *f* blanca.

white magic *n* magia *f* blanca.

white meat *n* (*U*) carnes *fpl* blancas.

whiten ['waɪtn] ◇ *vt* blanquear. ◇ *vi* ponerse blanco(ca).

whitener ['waɪtnər] *n* blanqueador *m*.

whiteness ['waɪtnɪs] *n* blancura *f*.

white noise *n* (*U*) ruido *m* blanco.

whiteout ['waɪtaʊt] *n pérdida total de visibilidad a causa de la nieve.*

white paper *n* POL libro *m* blanco.

white sauce *n* (salsa *f*) bechamel *f*.

White Sea *n*: **the ~** el mar Blanco.

white spirit *n Br especie de aguarrás.*

white-tie *adj*: **~ dinner** cena *f* con traje de
etiqueta y pajarita blanca.

whitewash ['waɪtwɒʃ] ◇ *n* **-1.** (*U*) [paint] blanqueo *m*, lechada *f* (de cal). **-2.** *pej* [cover-up] encubrimiento *m*. ◇ *vt* **-1.** [paint] blanquear, encalar. **-2.** *pej* [cover up] encubrir.

whitewater rafting ['waɪt,wɔːtər-] *n* descenso *m* (de rápidos) en piragua.

white wedding *n* boda *f* de blanco.

white wine *n* vino *m* blanco.

whiting ['waɪtɪŋ] (*pl inv* OR **-s**) *n* pescadilla *f*.

Whit Monday *n* lunes *m* de Pentecostés.

Whitsun ['wɪtsn] *n* [day] Pentecostés *m*.

whittle ['wɪtl] *vt* [reduce]: **to ~ down** OR **away** reducir gradualmente.

whiz, **whizz** (*pt & pp* **-zed**, *cont* **-zing**), [wɪz] ◇ *n inf*: **to be a ~ at sthg** ser un genio OR prodigio en algo. ◇ *vi*: **to ~ past** OR **by** pasar muy rápido OR zumbando.

whiz(z) kid *n inf* genio *m*, prodigio *m*.

who [huː] *pron* **-1.** (*in direct, indirect questions*) quién, quiénes (*pl*); **~ are you?** ¿quién eres tú?; **~ did you see?** ¿a quién viste?; **I didn't know ~ she was** no sabía quién era. **-2.** (*in relative clauses*) que; **he's the doctor ~ treated me** es el médico que me atendió; **those ~ are in favour** los que están a favor.

WHO (*abbr of* **World Health Organization**) *n* OMS *f*.

who'd [huːd] = **who had**, **who would**.

whodu(n)nit [,huːˈdʌnɪt] *n inf* historia *f* policíaca de misterio.

whoever [huːˈevər] ◇ *pron* **-1.** [unknown person] quienquiera *m y f*, quienesquiera *mpl y fpl*; **~ finds it** quienquiera que lo encuentre; **tell ~ you like** díselo a quien quieras. **-2.** [indicating surprise, astonishment]: **~ can that be?** ¿quién podrá ser? **-3.** [no matter who]: **come in, ~ you are** pasa, seas quién seas.

whole [həʊl] ◇ *adj* **-1.** [entire, complete] entero(ra). **-2.** [for emphasis]: **a ~ lot of** muchísimos(mas); **a ~ lot taller** muchísimo más alto; **a ~ new idea** una idea totalmente nueva. ◇ *n* **-1.** [all]: **the ~ of the school/ summer** el colegio/verano entero. **-2.** [unit, complete thing] todo *m*.
◆ **as a whole** *adv* en conjunto, en su totalidad.
◆ **on the whole** *adv* en general.

wholefood ['həʊlfuːd] *n Br* comida *f* integral.

whole-hearted [-ˈhɑːtɪd] *adj* profundo(da).

wholemeal ['həʊlmiːl] *adj Br* integral.

wholemeal bread *n Br* pan *m* integral.

whole note *n Am* semibreve *f*.

wholesale ['həʊlseɪl] ◇ *adj* **-1.** COMM al por mayor. **-2.** *pej* [indiscriminate] indiscriminado(da). ◇ *adv* **-1.** COMM al por mayor. **-2.** *pej* [indiscriminately] indiscriminadamente.

wholesaler ['həʊl,seɪlər] *n* mayorista *m y f*.

wholesome ['həʊlsəm] *adj* sano(na), saludable.

whole wheat *Am* = **wholemeal**.

who'll [huːl] = **who will**.

wholly ['həʊlɪ] *adv* completamente, enteramente.

whom [huːm] *pron* **-1.** (*in direct, indirect questions*) *fml* quién, quiénes (*pl*); **from ~ did you receive it?** ¿de quién lo recibiste?; **for/of/to ~** por/de/a quién. **-2.** (*in relative clauses*) que; **the man ~ I saw** el hombre que vi; **the man to ~ I gave it** el hombre al que se lo di; **several people came, none of ~ I knew** vinieron varias personas, de las que no conocía a ninguna.

whoop [wuːp] ◇ *n* grito *m* alborozado. ◇ *vi* gritar alborozadamente.

whoopee [wʊˈpiː] *excl* ¡yupi!

whooping cough ['huːpɪŋ-] *n* tos *f* ferina.

whoops [wʊps] *excl* ¡uy!

whoosh [wʊʃ] *inf* ◇ *n* [of air] ráfaga *f*; [of water] chorro *m*. ◇ *vi* **-1.** [water]: **to ~ out** salir a chorro. **-2.** [car, train]: **to ~ past** pasar a toda pastilla.

whop [wɒp] *vt inf* ganar, derrotar.

whopper ['wɒpər] *n inf* **-1.** [big thing] bestialidad *f*. **-2.** [lie] bola *f*, trola *f*.

whopping ['wɒpɪŋ] *inf* ◇ *adj* enorme. ◇ *adv*: **a ~ great lorry/lie**, **a ~ big lorry/lie** un camión/una mentira enorme.

whore [hɔːr] *n pej* zorra *f*, puta *f*, cuero *m* *Amer*.

who're ['huːər] = **who are**.

whose [huːz] ◇ *pron* (*in direct, indirect questions*) de quién, de quiénes (*pl*); **~ is this?** ¿de quién es esto?; **I wonder ~ they are** me pregunto de quién serán. ◇ *adj* **-1.** (*in direct, indirect questions*) de quién; **~ car is that?** ¿de quién es ese coche? **-2.** (*in relative clauses*) cuyo(ya), cuyos(yas) (*pl*); **that's the boy ~ father's an MP** ese es el chico cuyo padre es diputado; **the woman ~ daughters are twins** la mujer cuyas hijas son gemelas.

whosoever [,huːsəʊˈevər] *pron dated* quienquiera que.

who's who [huːz-] *n* [book] Quién es Quién *m*.

who've [huːv] = **who have**.

why [waɪ] ◇ *adv* por qué; **~ did you lie to me?** ¿por qué me mentiste?; **~ don't you all come?** ¿por qué no venís todos?; **~ not?**

¿por qué no? ◇ *conj* por qué; **I don't know** ~ he said that no sé por qué dijo eso. ◇ *pron*: **there are several reasons** ~ he left hay varias razones por las que se marchó; **that's** ~ **she did it** por eso es por lo que lo hizo; **I don't know the reason** ~ no se por qué razón. ◇ *excl* ¡hombre!, ¡vaya!

◆ **why ever** *adv*: ~ **ever did you do that?** ¿por qué diablos has hecho eso?

WI ◇ *n abbr of* **Women's Institute**. ◇ **-1.** *abbr of* **West Indies**. **-2.** *abbr of* **Wisconsin**.

wick [wɪk] *n* mecha *f*; **to get on sb's** ~ *Br inf fig* sacar de quicio a alguien.

wicked ['wɪkɪd] *adj* **-1.** [evil] malvado(da). **-2.** [mischievous, devilish] travieso(sa). **-3.** *inf* [very good] molón(ona), chachi (*inv*).

wicker ['wɪkə'] *adj* de mimbre.

wickerwork ['wɪkəwɜːk] *n* (*U*) artículos *mpl* de mimbre.

wicket ['wɪkɪt] *n* CRICKET **-1.** [stumps] palos *mpl*. **-2.** [pitch] *parte del terreno de juego desde donde se lanza hasta donde se batea*.

wicket keeper *n* guardián *m* y *f* de los palos.

wide [waɪd] ◇ *adj* **-1.** [broad] ancho(cha); **it's 50 cm** ~ tiene 50 cm de ancho. **-2.** [range, choice etc] amplio(plia). **-3.** [gap, difference, implications] grande, considerable. **-4.** [eyes] muy abierto(ta). **-5.** [off-target] desviado(da). ◇ *adv* **-1.** [broadly]: **to open/spread sthg** ~ abrir/desplegar algo completamente. **-2.** [off target]: **to go** OR **be** ~ salir desviado.

wide-angle lens *n* gran angular *m*.

wide-awake *adj* completamente despierto(ta).

wide boy *n* *Br inf pej* pájaro *m* de cuenta.

wide-eyed [-'aɪd] *adj* **-1.** [surprised, frightened] con los ojos muy abiertos (*de miedo o sorpresa*). **-2.** [innocent, gullible] inocente, simple.

widely ['waɪdlɪ] *adv* **-1.** [smile, yawn] ampliamente. **-2.** [travel, read] extensamente. **-3.** [believed, known, loved] generalmente. **-4.** [differ, vary] mucho.

widen ['waɪdn] ◇ *vt* [gen] ampliar; [road, bridge] ensanchar. ◇ *vi* **-1.** [gen] ampliarse; [river, road] ensancharse. **-2.** [eyes] abrirse mucho.

wide open *adj* **-1.** [window, door] abierto(ta) de par en par. **-2.** [eyes] completamente abierto(ta). **-3.** [spaces] extenso(sa).

wide-ranging [-'reɪndʒɪŋ] *adj* [changes, survey, consequences] de gran alcance; [discussion, interests] de gran variedad; [selection] amplio(plia).

widespread ['waɪdspred] *adj* extendido(da), general.

widow ['wɪdəu] *n* [woman] viuda *f*.

widowed ['wɪdəud] *adj* viudo(da).

widower ['wɪdəuə'] *n* viudo *m*.

width [wɪdθ] *n* **-1.** [breadth] anchura *f*; **it's 50 cm in** ~ tiene 50 cm de ancho. **-2.** [in swimming pool] ancho *m*.

widthways ['wɪdθweɪz] *adv* a lo ancho.

wield [wiːld] *vt* **-1.** [weapon] esgrimir; [implement] manejar. **-2.** [power] ejercer.

wife [waɪf] (*pl* **wives**) *n* mujer *f*, esposa *f*.

wig [wɪg] *n* peluca *f*.

wiggle ['wɪgl] *inf* ◇ *n* **-1.** [movement] meneo *m*; [of hips etc] contoneo *m*. **-2.** [wavy line] línea *f* ondulada. ◇ *vt* menear; [hips etc] contonear. ◇ *vi* menearse; [hips etc] contonearse.

wiggly ['wɪglɪ] (*compar* **-ier**, *superl* **-iest**) *adj* *inf* **-1.** [line] ondulado(da). **-2.** [tooth, chair leg etc] suelto(ta).

wigwam ['wɪgwæm] *n* tienda *f* india (de campaña).

wild [waɪld] ◇ *adj* **-1.** [gen] salvaje; [plant, flower] silvestre; [bull] bravo(va), chúcaro(ra) *Amer*. **-2.** [landscape, scenery] agreste. **-3.** [weather, sea] borrascoso(sa). **-4.** [crowd, laughter, applause] frenético(ca); **to run** ~ descontrolarse. **-5.** [hair] alborotado(da). **-6.** [hope, idea, plan] descabellado(da). **-7.** [guess, exaggeration] extravagante. **-8.** *inf* [very enthusiastic]: **to be** ~ **about** estar loco por.

◇ *n*: **in the** ~ en libertad, en su habitat natural.

◆ **wilds** *npl*: **the** ~**s** las tierras remotas.

wild card *n* COMPUT comodín *m*.

wildcat ['waɪldkæt] *n* [animal] gato *m* montés.

wildcat strike *n* huelga *f* salvaje.

wildebeest ['wɪldɪbiːst] (*pl inv* OR **-s**) *n* ñu *m*.

wilderness ['wɪldənɪs] *n* **-1.** [barren land] yermo *m*, desierto *m*. **-2.** [overgrown land] jungla *f*. **-3.** *fig* [unimportant place]: **in the political** ~ en el anonimato político.

wildfire ['waɪld,faɪə'] *n*: **to spread like** ~ propagarse como un reguero de pólvora.

wild flower *n* flor *f* silvestre.

wild-goose chase *n* *inf* búsqueda *f* infructuosa.

wildlife ['waɪldlaɪf] *n* (*U*) fauna *f*.

wildly ['waɪldlɪ] *adv* **-1.** [enthusiastically] frenéticamente. **-2.** [without discipline, inaccurately] a lo loco. **-3.** [very] extremadamente. **-4.** [menacingly] salvajemente.

wild rice *n* arroz *m* silvestre.

wild west *n inf*: **the ~** el salvaje oeste.

wiles [waɪlz] *npl* artimañas *fpl*.

wilful *Br*, **willful** *Am* ['wɪlfʊl] *adj* **-1.** [stubborn] que siempre se tiene que salir con la suya. **-2.** [deliberate] deliberado(da), intencionado(da).

will¹ [wɪl] ◇ *n* **-1.** [gen] voluntad *f*; **against one's ~** contra la voluntad de uno; **at ~** a voluntad. **-2.** [document] testamento *m*. ◇ *vt*: **to ~ sthg to happen** desear mucho que ocurra algo; **to ~ sb to do sthg** desear mucho que alguien haga algo.

will² [wɪl] *modal vb* **-1.** [to express future tense]: **they say it ~ rain tomorrow** dicen que lloverá OR va a llover mañana; **I'll be arriving at six** llegaré a las seis; **when ~ we get paid?** ¿cuándo nos pagarán?; **~ they come? - yes, they ~** ¿vendrán? - sí. **-2.** [indicating willingness]: **~ you have some more tea?** ¿te apetece más té?; **I won't do it** no lo haré. **-3.** [in commands, requests]: **you ~ leave this house at once** vas a salir de esta casa ahora mismo; **close that window, ~ you?** cierra la ventana, ¿quieres?; **~ you be quiet!** ¿queréis hacer el favor de callaros? **-4.** [indicating possibility, what usually happens]: **the hall ~ hold up to 1,000 people** la sala tiene cabida para 1.000 personas; **this ~ stop any draughts** esto evitará las corrientes; **pensions ~ be paid monthly** las pensiones se abonarán mensualmente. **-5.** [expressing an assumption]: **that'll be your father** ese va a ser OR será tu padre; **as you'll have gathered, I'm not keen on the idea** como ya os imaginaréis, a mí no me hace gracia la idea. **-6.** [indicating irritation]: **well, if you ~ leave your toys everywhere** ... normal, si vais dejando los juguetes por todas partes ...; **she ~ keep phoning me** ¡y venga a llamarme!

willful *Am* = **wilful**.

willing ['wɪlɪŋ] *adj* **-1.** [prepared]: **to be ~ (to do sthg)** estar dispuesto(ta) (a hacer algo). **-2.** [eager] servicial.

willingly ['wɪlɪŋlɪ] *adv* de buena gana, gustosamente.

willingness ['wɪlɪŋnɪs] *n*: **~ (to do sthg)** disposición *f* (para hacer algo).

willow (tree) ['wɪləʊ-] *n* sauce *m*.

willowy ['wɪləʊɪ] *adj* esbelto(ta).

willpower ['wɪl,paʊəʳ] *n* fuerza *f* de voluntad.

willy ['wɪlɪ] (*pl* **-ies**) *n Br inf* pito *m*.

willy-nilly [,wɪlɪ'nɪlɪ] *adv* pase lo que pase.

wilt [wɪlt] *vi* [plant] marchitarse; [person] desfallecer, extenuarse.

Wilts [wɪlts] (*abbr of* **Wiltshire**) *condado inglés*.

wily ['waɪlɪ] (*compar* **-ier**, *superl* **-iest**) *adj* astuto(ta).

wimp [wɪmp] *n pej inf* blandengue *m y f*.

win [wɪn] (*pt & pp* **won**, *cont* **-ning**) ◇ *n* victoria *f*, triunfo *m*. ◇ *vt* ganar. ◇ *vi* ganar; **you/I** *etc* **can't ~** no hay manera.

◆ **win over, win round** *vt sep* convencer.

wince [wɪns] ◇ *vi* hacer una mueca de dolor; **to ~ at/with sthg** estremecerse ante/de algo. ◇ *n* mueca *f* de dolor.

winch [wɪntʃ] ◇ *n* torno *m*. ◇ *vt*: **to ~ sthg up/out** levantar/sacar algo con torno.

Winchester disk ['wɪntʃɪstəʳ-] *n*: COMPUT disquete *m* Winchester.

wind¹ [wɪnd] ◇ *n* **-1.** METEOR viento *m*. **-2.** [breath] aliento *m*, resuello *m*. **-3.** (*U*) [in stomach] gases *mpl*; **to break ~** *euphemism* ventosear. **-4.** [in orchestra]: **the ~** los instrumentos de viento. **-5.** *phr*: **to get ~ of sthg** *inf* enterarse de algo. ◇ *vt* **-1.** [knock breath out of] dejar sin aliento. **-2.** *Br* [baby] hacer que eructe.

wind² [waɪnd] (*pt & pp* **wound**) ◇ *vt* **-1.** [string, thread] enrollar; **to ~ sthg around sthg** enrollar algo alrededor de algo. **-2.** [clock, watch] dar cuerda a. **-3.** *phr*: **to ~ its way** serpentear. ◇ *vi* serpentear.

◆ **wind back** *vt sep* rebobinar.

◆ **wind down** ◇ *vt sep* **-1.** [car window] bajar. **-2.** [business] cerrar poco a poco. ◇ *vi* **-1.** [clock, watch] pararse. **-2.** [person] relajarse, descansar.

◆ **wind forward** *vt sep* pasar para adelante.

◆ **wind up** ◇ *vt sep* **-1.** [finish - activity] finalizar, concluir; [business] liquidar. **-2.** [clock, watch] dar cuerda a. **-3.** [car window] subir. **-4.** *Br inf* [annoy] vacilar, tomar el pelo a. ◇ *vi inf* [end up] terminar, acabar; **to ~ up doing sthg** acabar haciendo algo.

windbreak ['wɪndbreɪk] *n* protección *f* contra el viento.

windcheater *Br* ['wɪnd,tʃiːtəʳ], **windbreaker** *Am* ['wɪnd,breɪkəʳ] *n* cazadora *f*.

windchill ['wɪndtʃɪl] *n*: **~ factor** efecto por el cual el viento reduce la temperatura efectiva.

winded ['wɪndɪd] *adj* sin aliento.

windfall ['wɪndfɔːl] *n* **-1.** [fruit] fruta *f* caída. **-2.** [unexpected gift] dinero *m* llovido del cielo.

winding ['waɪndɪŋ] *adj* tortuoso(sa), sinuoso(da).

wind instrument [wɪnd-] *n* instrumento *m* de viento.

windmill ['wɪndmɪl] *n* [building] molino *m* de viento.

window ['wɪndəʊ] *n* **-1.** [gen & COMPUT] ventana *f.* **-2.** AUT ventanilla *f.* **-3.** [of shop] escaparate *m.*

window box *n* jardinera *f* (de ventana).

window cleaner *n* limpiacristales *m* y *f* *inv.*

window dressing *n* (U) **-1.** [in shop] escaparatismo *m.* **-2.** *fig* [non-essentials] pura fachada *f.*

window envelope *n* sobre *m* de ventanilla.

window frame *n* marco *m* de ventana.

window ledge *n* alféizar *m.*

window pane *n* cristal *m* (de la ventana).

window shade *n Am* persiana *f.*

window-shopping *n*: to go ~ ir de escaparates.

windowsill ['wɪndəʊsɪl] *n* alféizar *m.*

windpipe ['wɪndpaɪp] *n* tráquea *f.*

windscreen *Br* ['wɪndskriːn], **windshield** *Am* ['wɪndʃiːld] *n* parabrisas *m inv.*

windscreen washer *n* lavaparabrisas *m inv.*

windscreen wiper *n* limpiaparabrisas *m inv.*

windshield *Am* = **windscreen**.

windsock ['wɪndsɒk] *n* manga *f* de aire.

windsurfer ['wɪnd,sɜːfə'] *n* **-1.** [person] windsurfista *m* y *f.* **-2.** [board] tabla *f* de windsurf.

windsurfing ['wɪnd,sɜːfɪŋ] *n* windsurf *m.*

windswept ['wɪndswept] *adj* **-1.** [scenery] azotado(da) por el viento. **-2.** [person, hair] despeinado(da).

wind tunnel [wɪnd-] *n* túnel *m* aerodinámico.

Windward Islands ['wɪndwəd-] *n*: the ~ las islas de Barlovento.

windy ['wɪndɪ] (*compar* **-ier**, *superl* **-iest**) *adj* [day, weather] ventoso(sa), de mucho viento; [place] expuesto(ta) al viento; it's ~ hace viento.

wine [waɪn] ◇ *n* vino *m*; **red/white** ~ vino tinto/blanco. ◇ *vt*: to ~ and dine sb agasajar a alguien.

wine bar *n Br* bar *de cierta elegancia especializado en vinos que suele servir comidas.*

wine bottle *n* botella *f* de vino.

wine box *n especie de cartón de vino de unos tres litros con espita.*

wine cellar *n* bodega *f.*

wineglass ['waɪnglɑːs] *n* copa *f* OR vaso *m* (de vino).

wine list *n* lista *f* de vinos.

wine merchant *n Br* vinatero *m*, -ra *f.*

winepress ['waɪnpres] *n* lagar *m.*

wine tasting [-,teɪstɪŋ] *n* cata *f* de vinos.

wine waiter *n* sommelier *m.*

wing [wɪŋ] *n* **-1.** [gen] ala *f.* **-2.** AUT guardabarros *m inv.* **-3.** SPORT [side of pitch] banda *f*; [winger] extremo *m*, ala *m.*
◆ **wings** *npl* THEATRE: the ~s los bastidores.

wing commander *n Br* ≃ teniente *m* coronel de aviación.

winger ['wɪŋə'] *n* SPORT extremo *m*, ala *m.*

wing mirror *n* retrovisor *m.*

wing nut *n* palometa *f*, tuerca *f* de mariposa.

wingspan ['wɪŋspæn] *n* envergadura *f* (de alas).

wink [wɪŋk] ◇ *n* guiño *m*; **to have forty ~s** *inf* echarse un sueñecito; **not to sleep a ~**, **not to get a ~ of sleep** *inf* no pegar ojo. ◇ *vi* **-1.** [eye]: to ~ (at sb) guiñar (a alguien). **-2.** *literary* [lights] titilar, parpadear.

winkle ['wɪŋkl] *n* bígaro *m.*
◆ **winkle out** *vt sep* extraer.

winner ['wɪnə'] *n* ganador *m*, -ra *f.*

winning ['wɪnɪŋ] *adj* **-1.** [team, competitor] vencedor(ra), victorioso(sa); [goal, point] de la victoria; [ticket, number] premiado(da). **-2.** [smile, ways] atractivo(va).
◆ **winnings** *npl* ganancias *fpl.*

winning post *n* meta *f.*

Winnipeg ['wɪnɪ,peg] *n* Winnipeg.

winsome ['wɪnsəm] *adj literary* atractivo(va), encantador(ra).

winter ['wɪntə'] ◇ *n* (U) invierno *m*; **in** ~ en invierno. ◇ *comp* de invierno, invernal.

winter sports *npl* deportes *mpl* de invierno.

wintertime ['wɪntətaɪm] *n* (U) invierno *m*; **in** ~ en invierno.

wint(e)ry ['wɪntrɪ] *adj* [gen] de invierno, invernal; [showers] con nieve.

wipe ['waɪp] ◇ *n*: give the table a ~ pásale un trapo a la mesa. ◇ *vt* [rub to clean] limpiar, pasar un trapo a; [rub to dry] secar.
◆ **wipe away** *vt sep* [tears, sweat] enjugar.
◆ **wipe out** *vt sep* **-1.** [erase] borrar. **-2.** [eradicate] aniquilar.
◆ **wipe up** *vt sep* empapar, limpiar.

wiper ['waɪpə'] *n* [windscreen wiper] limpiaparabrisas *m inv.*

wire ['waɪə'] ◇ *n* **-1.** [gen] alambre *m*; ELEC cable *m.* **-2.** [telegram] telegrama *m.* ◇ *comp* de alambre. ◇ *vt* **-1.** [connect]: to ~ sthg to sthg conectar algo a algo. **-2.** [ELEC - house] poner la instalación eléctrica de; [- plug]

conectar el cable a. **-3.** [send telegram to] enviar un telegrama a.

wire brush *n* cepillo *m* de raíces.

wire cutters *npl* cortaalambres *m inv*.

wireless ['waɪəlɪs] *n dated* radio *f*.

wire netting *n* (U) tela *f* metálica.

wire-tapping [-ˌtæpɪŋ] *n* (U) intervención *f* telefónica.

wire wool *n Br* estropajo *m* metálico.

wiring ['waɪərɪŋ] *n* (U) instalación *f* eléctrica.

wiry ['waɪərɪ] (*compar* **-ier**, *superl* **-iest**) *adj* **-1.** [hair] estropajoso(sa). **-2.** [body, man] nervudo(da).

Wisconsin [wɪs'kɒnsɪn] *n* Wisconsin.

wisdom ['wɪzdəm] *n* **-1.** [learning] sabiduría *f*. **-2.** [good sense] sensatez *f*.

wisdom tooth *n* muela *f* del juicio.

wise [waɪz] *adj* **-1.** [learned] sabio(bia); **to get ~ to sthg** *inf* caer en la cuenta de algo; **she's no ~r** OR **none the ~r** sigue sin entender. **-2.** [sensible] prudente.
◆ **wise up** *vi* enterarse, ponerse al tanto.

wisecrack ['waɪzkræk] *n pej* broma *f*, chiste *m*.

wish [wɪʃ] ◇ *n*: **~ (for sthg/to do sthg)** deseo *m* (de algo/de hacer algo); **to make a ~** pedir un deseo. ◇ *vt*: **to ~ to do sthg** *fml* desear hacer algo; **to ~ sb sthg** desear a alguien algo; **I ~ (that) you had told me before!** ¡ojalá me lo hubieras dicho antes!; **I ~ (that) I were** OR **was rich** ojalá fuera rico; **I ~ (that) you would shut up** ¿por qué no te callas? ◇ *vi* [by magic]: **to ~ for sthg** pedir (como deseo) algo.
◆ **wishes** *npl*: **(with) best ~es** [in letter] muchos recuerdos.
◆ **wish on** *vt sep*: **to ~ sthg on sb** desearle algo a alguien.

wishbone ['wɪʃbəʊn] *n* espoleta *f*.

wishful thinking ['wɪʃful-] *n* (U): **it's just ~** no son más que (vanas) ilusiones.

wishy-washy ['wɪʃɪˌwɒʃɪ] *adj inf pej* soso(sa), insípido(da).

wisp [wɪsp] *n* **-1.** [of hair] mechón *m*; [of grass] brizna *f*. **-2.** [cloud] nubecilla *f*; [of smoke] voluta *f*.

wispy ['wɪspɪ] (*compar* **-ier**, *superl* **-iest**) *adj* [hair] ralo(la) y a mechones.

wistful ['wɪstful] *adj* triste, melancólico(ca).

wit [wɪt] *n* **-1.** [humour] ingenio *m*, agudeza *f*. **-2.** [funny person] chistoso *m*, -sa *f*. **-3.** [intelligence]: **to have the ~ to do sthg** tener el buen juicio de hacer algo.
◆ **wits** *npl*: **to have** OR **keep one's ~s about one** mantenerse alerta; **to be scared out of one's ~s** *inf* estar muerto de miedo;

to be at one's ~s end estar a punto de volverse loco.

witch [wɪtʃ] *n* bruja *f*.

witchcraft ['wɪtʃkrɑːft] *n* brujería *f*.

witchdoctor ['wɪtʃˌdɒktər] *n* hechicero *m*, -ra *f*.

witch-hazel *n* **-1.** [liquid] liquidámbar *m*. **-2.** [tree] ocozol *m*.

witch-hunt *n pej* caza *f* de brujas.

with [wɪð] *prep* **-1.** [in company of] con; **we stayed ~ them for a week** estuvimos con ellos una semana; **I play tennis ~ his wife** juego al tenis con su mujer; **~ me** conmigo; **~ you** contigo; **~ himself/herself** consigo. **-2.** [indicating opposition] con; **to argue ~ sb** discutir con alguien; **the war ~ Germany** la guerra con Alemania. **-3.** [indicating means, manner, feelings] con; **I washed it ~ detergent** lo lavé con detergente; **he filled it ~ wine** lo llenó de vino; **covered ~ mud** cubierto de barro; **she was trembling ~ fear** temblaba de miedo; **~ care** con cuidado; **"all right", she said ~ a smile** "vale", dijo con una sonrisa. **-4.** [having - gen] con; **a man ~ a beard** un hombre con barba; **the woman ~ the black hair/big dog** la señora del pelo negro/perro grande; **the computer comes ~ a printer** el ordenador viene con impresora. **-5.** [regarding] con; **he's very mean ~ money** es muy tacaño con el dinero; **what will you do ~ the house?** ¿qué haréis con la casa?; **the trouble ~ her is that ...** su problema es que .... **-6.** [indicating simultaneity]: **I can't do it ~ you watching me** no puedo hacerlo contigo ahí mirándome. **-7.** [because of] con; **the weather ~ as it is, we have decided to stay at home** con el tiempo como está hemos decidido quedarnos en casa; **~ my luck, I'll probably lose** con la suerte que tengo seguro que pierdo. **-8.** [indicating understanding]: **are you ~ me?** ¿me sigues?; **I'm sorry, I'm not ~ you** lo siento, me he perdido. **-9.** [indicating support] con; **I'm ~ Dad on this** en eso estoy con papá.

withdraw [wɪð'drɔː] (*pt* **-drew**, *pp* **-drawn**) ◇ *vt* **-1.** [gen]: **to ~ sthg (from)** retirar algo (de). **-2.** [money] sacar. ◇ *vi*: **to ~ (from/to)** retirarse (de/a).

withdrawal [wɪð'drɔːəl] *n* **-1.** [gen & MIL] retirada *f*. **-2.** [retraction] retractación *f*. **-3.** MED (síndrome *m* de) abstinencia *f*. **-4.** FIN reintegro *m*.

withdrawal symptoms *npl* síndrome *m* de abstinencia.

withdrawn [wɪð'drɔːn] ◇ *pp* → **withdraw**. ◇ *adj* [shy, quiet] reservado(da).

withdrew [wɪð'druː] *pt* → **withdraw**.

wither ['wɪðə'] ◇ vt marchitar. ◇ vi -1. [dry up] marchitarse. -2. [become weak] debilitarse, decaer.

withered ['wɪðəd] adj marchito(ta).

withering ['wɪðərɪŋ] adj [remark] mordaz; [look] fulminante.

withhold [wɪð'həʊld] (pt & pp -held) vt [gen] retener; [consent, permission] negar.

within [wɪ'ðɪn] ◇ prep -1. [gen] dentro de; ~ reach al alcance de la mano. -2. [less than - distance] a menos de; [- time] en menos de; it's ~ walking distance se puede ir andando; he was ~ five seconds of the leader estaba a cinco segundos del líder; ~ the next six months en los próximos seis meses; it arrived ~ a week llegó en una semana. ◇ adv dentro.

without [wɪð'aʊt] ◇ prep sin; ~ sthg/doing sthg sin algo/hacer algo; it happened ~ my realizing pasó sin que me diera cuenta. ◇ adv: to go OR do ~ sthg pasar sin algo.

withstand [wɪð'stænd] (pt & pp -stood) vt resistir, aguantar.

witness ['wɪtnɪs] ◇ n -1. [person] testigo m y f; to be ~ to sthg ser testigo de algo. -2. [testimony]: to bear ~ to sthg atestiguar algo, dar fe de algo. ◇ vt -1. [see] presenciar. -2. [countersign] firmar (como testigo).

witness box Br, **witness stand** Am n tribuna f (de los testigos).

witter ['wɪtə'] vi Br inf pej parlotear.

witticism ['wɪtɪsɪzm] n agudeza f, ocurrencia f.

witty ['wɪtɪ] (compar -ier, superl -iest) adj ingenioso(sa), ocurrente.

wives [waɪvz] pl → **wife**.

wizard ['wɪzəd] n -1. [magician] mago m (en cuentos). -2. [skilled person] genio m.

wizened ['wɪznd] adj marchito(ta).

wk (abbr of **week**) sem.

Wm. (abbr of **William**) Guillermo.

WO n abbr of **warrant officer**.

wobble ['wɒbl] vi [gen] tambalearse, bambolearse; [furniture] cojear; [legs] temblar.

wobbly ['wɒblɪ] (compar -ier, superl -iest) adj inf [jelly, flesh] bamboleante; [handwriting, legs] tembloroso(sa); [furniture] cojo(ja).

woe [wəʊ] n literary aflicción f, pesar m.
◆ **woes** npl literary or hum males mpl, penas fpl.

wok [wɒk] n sartén abombada y profunda con dos asas y sin mango.

woke [wəʊk] pt → **wake**.

woken ['wəʊkn] pp → **wake**.

wolf [wʊlf] (pl **wolves**) n ZOOL lobo m.

◆ **wolf down** vt sep inf zamparse, devorar.

wolf whistle n silbido m (piropo).

wolves ['wʊlvz] pl → **wolf**.

woman ['wʊmən] (pl **women**) ◇ n -1. [female] mujer f. -2. [womanhood] la mujer. ◇ comp: ~ doctor médica f; ~ prime minister primera ministra f.

womanhood ['wʊmənhʊd] n (U) -1. [adult life] edad f adulta (de mujer). -2. [all women] la mujer.

womanize, -ise ['wʊmənaɪz] vi pej ser un mujeriego.

womanly ['wʊmənlɪ] adj femenino(na).

womb [wuːm] n matriz f, útero m.

wombat ['wɒmbæt] n tipo de oso marsupial.

women ['wɪmɪn] pl → **woman**.

women's group n grupo m feminista.

Women's Institute n Br: the ~ organización cultural para mujeres.

women's liberation n liberación f de la mujer.

won [wʌn] pt & pp → **win**.

wonder ['wʌndə'] ◇ n -1. [amazement] asombro m, admiración f. -2. [cause for surprise]: it's a ~ (that) ... es un milagro que ...; no OR little OR small ~ ... no es de extrañar que .... -3. [amazing thing, person] maravilla f; to work OR do ~s hacer maravillas OR milagros.
◇ vt -1. [speculate]: to ~ (if OR whether) preguntarse (si). -2. [in polite requests]: I ~ if OR whether I could ask you a question? ¿le importaría que le hiciera una pregunta?
◇ vi -1. [speculate]: I was only ~ing (preguntaba) sólo por curiosidad; to ~ about sthg preguntarse por algo. -2. literary [be amazed]: to ~ at sthg quedarse maravillado ante algo.

wonderful ['wʌndəfʊl] adj maravilloso(sa), estupendo(da).

wonderfully ['wʌndəfʊlɪ] adv -1. [very well] estupendamente. -2. [very] extremadamente.

wonderland ['wʌndəlænd] n mundo m maravilloso.

wonky ['wɒŋkɪ] (compar -ier, superl -iest) adj Br inf [table, chair etc] cojo(ja); [picture, tie etc] torcido(da).

wont [wəʊnt] ◇ adj: to be ~ to do sthg ser dado(da) a hacer algo, soler hacer algo. ◇ n dated or literary: as is his/her etc ~ como de costumbre.

won't [wəʊnt] = will not.

woo [wuː] vt -1. literary [court] cortejar. -2. [try to win over] granjearse el apoyo de.

wood [wʊd] ◇ n **-1.** [timber] madera f; [for fire] leña f; **touch ~!** ¡toquemos madera! **-2.** [group of trees] bosque m; **I can't see the ~ for the trees** Br los árboles no me dejan ver el bosque. **-3.** GOLF (palo m de) madera f. ◇ comp de madera.

◆ **woods** npl bosque m.

wooded ['wʊdɪd] adj arbolado(da).

wooden ['wʊdn] adj **-1.** [of wood] de madera. **-2.** pej [actor] envarado(da).

wooden spoon n inf fig: **to win** OR **get the ~** quedar el último.

woodland ['wʊdlənd] n bosque m, arboleda f.

woodpecker ['wʊd,pekər] n pájaro m carpintero.

wood pigeon n paloma f torcaz.

woodshed ['wʊdʃed] n leñera f.

woodwind ['wʊdwɪnd] n: **the ~** los instrumentos de viento de madera.

woodwork ['wʊdwɜːk] n carpintería f.

woodworm ['wʊdwɜːm] n carcoma f.

woof [wuːf] n ladrido m; **~!** ¡guau!

wool [wʊl] n lana f; **to pull the ~ over sb's eyes** inf fig dar a alguien gato por liebre.

woollen Br, **woolen** Am ['wʊlən] adj de lana.

◆ **woollens** npl géneros mpl de lana.

woolly ['wʊlɪ] (compar **-ier**, superl **-iest**, pl **-ies**) ◇ adj **-1.** [woollen] de lana. **-2.** inf [fuzzy, unclear] confuso(sa). ◇ n inf prenda f de lana.

woolly-headed [-'hedɪd] adj inf pej de ideas confusas OR vagas.

woozy ['wuːzɪ] (compar **-ier**, superl **-iest**) adj inf mareado(da).

Worcester sauce ['wʊstər-] n (U) salsa f Perrins®.

Worcs (abbr of **Worcestershire**) antiguo condado inglés.

word [wɜːd] ◇ n **-1.** LING palabra f; **~ for ~** palabra por palabra; **in other ~s** en otras palabras; **in one's own ~s** (uno) con sus propias palabras; **not in so many ~s** no con esas palabras; **in a ~** en una palabra; **too ... for ~s** de lo más ...; **by ~ of mouth** de palabra; **to put in a (good) ~ for sb** hablar en favor de alguien; **just say the ~** no tienes más que decirlo; **she doesn't mince her ~s** no tiene pelos en la lengua; **to have a ~ with sb** hablar con alguien; **to have ~s with sb** inf tener unas palabritas con alguien; **to have the last ~** tener la última palabra; **to weigh one's ~s** medir (uno) sus palabras; **I couldn't get a ~ in edgeways** no pude meter baza. **-2.** (U) [news] noticia f. **-3.** [promise] palabra f; **to give sb one's ~** dar (uno) su palabra a alguien; **I give you my ~** te lo prometo; **to be as good as one's ~**, **to be true to one's ~** cumplir lo prometido. ◇ vt redactar, expresar.

word game n juego a base de palabras.

wording ['wɜːdɪŋ] n (U) términos mpl, forma f (de expresión).

word-perfect adj: **to be ~** saber perfectamente el papel.

wordplay ['wɜːdpleɪ] n (U) juegos mpl de palabras.

word processing n (U) proceso m de textos.

word processor n procesador m de textos.

wordwrap ['wɜːdræp] n COMPUT salto m de línea automático.

wordy ['wɜːdɪ] (compar **-ier**, superl **-iest**) adj pej prolijo(ja).

wore [wɔːr] pt → **wear**.

work [wɜːk] ◇ n **-1.** (U) [employment] trabajo m, empleo m; **to be in ~** tener trabajo; **to be out of ~** estar desempleado; **at ~** en el trabajo. **-2.** [activity, tasks] trabajo m; **at ~** trabajando; **to have one's ~ cut out doing sthg** OR **to do sthg** tenerlo muy difícil para hacer algo. **-3.** [of art, literature etc] obra f. **-4.** phr: **he's a nasty piece of ~** es un elemento de cuidado.

◇ vt **-1.** [employees, subordinates] hacer trabajar. **-2.** [machine] manejar, operar. **-3.** [wood, metal, land] trabajar. **-4.** [cause to become]: **to ~ o.s. into a frenzy** ponerse frenético. **-5.** [force]: **to ~ one's way through** [crowd etc] abrirse camino por; **to ~ one's way up** [in career] llegar a un (alto) puesto a fuerza de trabajo.

◇ vi **-1.** [person]: **to ~ (on sthg)** trabajar (en algo). **-2.** [machine, system, idea] funcionar. **-3.** [drug] surtir efecto. **-4.** [have effect]: **to ~ against sb/sthg** funcionar contra alguien/algo. **-5.** [become by movement]: **to ~ loose** soltarse; **to ~ free** desprenderse.

◆ **works** ◇ n [factory] fábrica f. ◇ npl **-1.** [mechanism] mecanismo m. **-2.** [digging, building] obras fpl. **-3.** inf [everything]: **the ~** todo completo.

◆ **work off** vt sep [anger, frustration] desahogar.

◆ **work on** vt fus **-1.** [pay attention to] trabajar en. **-2.** [take as basis] partir de.

◆ **work out** ◇ vt sep **-1.** [plan, schedule] elaborar. **-2.** [total, amount] calcular; [answer] dar con. ◇ vi **-1.** [figure etc]: **to ~ out at** salir a. **-2.** [turn out] resultar, resolverse. **-3.** [be successful] salir bien, resultar bien. **-4.** [train, exercise] entrenarse, hacer ejercicio.

◆ **work up** ◇ *vt sep* **-1.** [excite]: **to ~ o.s. up into a frenzy** ponerse frenético(ca). **-2.** [generate] despertar. ◇ *vi*: **to ~ up to sthg** mentalizarse para algo.

workable ['wɜːkəbl] *adj* factible, viable.

workaday ['wɜːkədeɪ] *adj pej* prosaico(ca), corriente.

workaholic [ˌwɜːkə'hɒlɪk] *n* adicto *m*, -ta *f* al trabajo.

workbasket ['wɜːkˌbɑːskɪt] *n* costurero *m*.

workbench ['wɜːkbentʃ] *n* banco *m* de trabajo.

workbook ['wɜːkbʊk] *n* libro *m* de ejercicios.

workday ['wɜːkdeɪ] *n* **-1.** [day's work] jornada *f* de trabajo. **-2.** [not weekend] día *m* laborable.

worked up [wɜːkt-] *adj* nervioso(sa).

worker ['wɜːkə'] *n* [person who works] trabajador *m*, -ra *f*; [manual worker] obrero *m*, -ra *f*; **a hard/fast ~** una persona que trabaja mucho/a prisa.

workforce ['wɜːkfɔːs] *n* mano *f* de obra.

workhouse ['wɜːkhaʊs] *n* **-1.** *Br* [poor house] *asilo para pobres en la época victoriana*. **-2.** *Am* [prison] correccional *m*.

working ['wɜːkɪŋ] *adj* **-1.** [in operation] funcionando. **-2.** [having employment] empleado(da). **-3.** [relating to work - gen] laboral; [- clothes] de trabajo; [- day] laborable. **-4.** [sufficient, adequate] suficiente.

◆ **workings** *npl* mecanismo *m*.

working capital *n* **-1.** [assets minus liabilities] capital *m* líquido. **-2.** [available money] capital *m* disponible.

working class *n*: **the ~** la clase obrera.

◆ **working-class** *adj* obrero(ra).

working day = workday.

working group *n* grupo *m* de trabajo, comisión *f* investigadora.

working knowledge *n* conocimientos *mpl* básicos.

working man *n* trabajador *m*.

working model *n* maqueta *f* operativa.

working order *n*: **to be in (good) ~** funcionar (bien).

working party *n* grupo *m* de trabajo, comisión *f* investigadora.

working week *n* semana *f* laboral.

work-in-progress *n* trabajo *m* en curso.

workload ['wɜːkləʊd] *n* cantidad *f* de trabajo.

workman ['wɜːkmən] (*pl* **-men** [-mən]) *n* obrero *m*.

workmanship ['wɜːkmənʃɪp] *n* artesanía *f*.

workmate ['wɜːkmeɪt] *n* compañero *m*, -ra *f* de trabajo, colega *m* y *f*.

work of art *n lit* & *fig* obra *f* de arte.

workout ['wɜːkaʊt] *n* ejercicios *mpl* físicos.

work permit [-ˌpɜːmɪt] *n* permiso *m* de trabajo.

workplace ['wɜːkpleɪs] *n* lugar *m* de trabajo.

workroom ['wɜːkrʊm] *n* taller *m*.

works council *n* ≈ comité *m* de empresa.

workshop ['wɜːkʃɒp] *n* taller *m*.

workshy ['wɜːkʃaɪ] *adj Br* vago(ga), gandul(la).

workstation ['wɜːkˌsteɪʃn] *n* COMPUT estación *f* de trabajo.

work surface *n* superficie *f* de trabajo.

worktable ['wɜːkˌteɪbl] *n* mesa *f* de trabajo.

worktop ['wɜːktɒp] *n Br* mármol *m*, encimera *f*.

work-to-rule *n Br* huelga *f* de celo.

world [wɜːld] ◇ *n* mundo *m*; **the best in the ~** el mejor del mundo; **what/where/why in the ~ ...?** ¿qué/dónde/por qué demonios ...?; **the ~ over** en todo el mundo; **to want the best of both ~s** querer estar en misa y repicando; **to think the ~ of sb** querer a alguien con locura; **to do sb the ~ of good** venirle de maravilla a alguien; **a ~ of difference** una diferencia enorme. ◇ *comp* mundial.

World Bank *n*: **the ~** el Banco Mundial.

world-class *adj* de primera categoría.

World Cup FTBL ◇ *n*: **the ~** los mundiales de fútbol. ◇ *comp* de la Copa del Mundo.

world-famous *adj* famoso(sa) en el mundo entero.

worldly ['wɜːldlɪ] *adj literary* mundano(na); **~ goods** bienes *mpl* materiales.

world music *n* música *f* étnica.

world power *n* potencia *f* mundial.

World Series *n*: **the ~** *la final de la liga estadounidense de béisbol*.

World War I *n* la Primera Guerra Mundial.

World War II *n* la Segunda Guerra Mundial.

world-weary *adj* hastiado(da), cansado(da) de la vida.

worldwide ['wɜːldwaɪd] ◇ *adj* mundial. ◇ *adv* en todo el mundo, a escala mundial.

World Wide Web *n*: **the ~** la (World Wide) Web.

worm [wɜːm] ◇ *n* [animal] gusano *m*; [earthworm] lombriz *f* (de tierra). ◇ *vt*: **to ~**

one's way into sthg [move] lograr colarse en algo; [wheedle] lograr atraer para sí algo.

◆ **worms** *npl* [parasites] lombrices *fpl*.

◆ **worm out** *vt sep*: **to ~ sthg out of sb** sonsacarle algo a alguien.

worn [wɔːn] ◇ *pp* → **wear**. ◇ *adj* **-1.** [threadbare] gastado(da). **-2.** [tired] ajado(da).

worn-out *adj* **-1.** [old, threadbare]: **to be ~** estar ya para tirar. **-2.** [tired] agotado(da).

worried ['wʌrɪd] *adj* preocupado(da); **to be ~ (sick) about** estar (muy) preocupado(da) por.

worrier ['wʌrɪə^r] *n*: **to be a ~** preocuparse por todo.

worry ['wʌrɪ] (*pl* **-ies**, *pt* & *pp* **-ied**) ◇ *n* preocupación *f*. ◇ *vt* [trouble] preocupar. ◇ *vi*: **to ~ (about)** preocuparse (por); **not to ~!** ¡no importa!

worrying ['wʌrɪɪŋ] *adj* preocupante.

worse [wɜːs] ◇ *adj* peor; **to get ~** empeorar. ◇ *adv* peor; **~ off** [gen] en peor situación; [financially] peor económicamente. ◇ *n*: **~ was to come** lo peor estaba aún por venir; **so much the ~** tanto peor; **for the ~** para peor.

worsen ['wɜːsn] *vt & vi* empeorar.

worsening ['wɜːsnɪŋ] *adj* cada vez peor.

worship ['wɜːʃɪp] (*Br pt & pp* **-ped**, *cont* **-ping**, *Am pt & pp* **-ed**, *cont* **-ing**) ◇ *vt lit & fig* adorar. ◇ *n lit & fig*: **~ (of)** culto *m* (a), adoración *f* (por).

◆ **Worship** *n*: **Your/Her/His Worship** su señoría; **his Worship the Mayor** el Excelentísimo Señor alcalde.

worshipper *Br*, **worshiper** *Am* ['wɜːʃɪpə^r] *n* RELIG & *fig* devoto *m*, -ta *f*.

worst [wɜːst] ◇ *adj* peor; **the ~ thing is ...** lo peor es que .... ◇ *adv* peor; **the ~ affected area** la región más afectada. ◇ *n*: **the ~** [thing] lo peor *m*; [person] el peor *m*, la peor *f*; **if the ~ comes to the ~** en último extremo.

◆ **at (the) worst** *adv* en el peor de los casos.

worsted ['wʊstɪd] *n* estambre *m*.

worth [wɜːθ] ◇ *prep* **-1.** [having the value of]: **it's ~ £50** vale 50 libras; **how much is it ~?** ¿cuánto vale? **-2.** [deserving of] digno(na) de, merecedor(ra) de; **the museum is ~ visiting** OR **a visit, it's ~ visiting the museum** el museo merece una visita. ◇ *n* **-1.** [amount]: **£50,000 ~ of antiques** antigüedades por valor de 50.000 libras; **a month's ~ of groceries** provisiones para un mes. **-2.** *fml* [value] valor *m*.

worthless ['wɜːθlɪs] *adj* **-1.** [object] sin valor. **-2.** [person] despreciable.

worthwhile [ˌwɜːθ'waɪl] *adj* que vale la pena; [cause] noble, digno(na).

worthy ['wɜːðɪ] (*compar* **-ier**, *superl* **-iest**) *adj* **-1.** [gen] digno(na). **-2.** [good but unexciting] encomiable.

would [wʊd] *modal vb* **-1.** (*in reported speech*): **she said she ~ come** dijo que vendría. **-2.** [indicating likelihood]: **what ~ you do?** ¿qué harías?; **he ~ have resigned** habría dimitido. **-3.** [indicating willingness]: **she ~n't go** no quiso/quería ir; **he ~ do anything for her** haría cualquier cosa por ella. **-4.** (*in polite questions*): **~ you like a drink?** ¿quieres beber algo?; **~ you mind closing the window?** ¿le importaría cerrar la ventana?; **help me shut this suitcase, ~ you?** ayúdame a cerrar esta maleta, ¿quieres? **-5.** [indicating inevitability]: **he WOULD say that, ~n't he?** hombre, era de esperar que dijera eso, ¿no? **-6.** [expressing opinions]: **I ~ have thought (that) it ~ be easy** hubiera pensado que sería fácil; **I ~ prefer ...** preferiría ...; **I ~ like ...** quisiera ..., quiero ... **-7.** [giving advice]: **I ~ report it if I were you** yo en tu lugar lo denunciaría.

would-be *adj*: **a ~ author** un aspirante a literato.

wouldn't ['wʊdnt] = **would not**.

would've ['wʊdəv] = **would have**.

wound[1] [wuːnd] ◇ *n* herida *f*; **to lick one's ~s** compadecerse de uno mismo tras la derrota. ◇ *vt lit & fig* herir.

wound[2] [waʊnd] *pt & pp* → **wind**.

wounded ['wuːndɪd] ◇ *adj* herido(da). ◇ *npl*: **the ~** los heridos.

wounding ['wuːndɪŋ] *adj* hiriente.

wove [wəʊv] *pt* → **weave**.

woven ['wəʊvn] *pp* → **weave**.

wow [waʊ] *excl inf* ¡anda!, ¡caramba!

WP -1. *abbr of* **word processing**. **-2.** *abbr of* **word processor**. **-3.** (*abbr of* **weather permitting**) *si el tiempo lo permite*.

WPC (*abbr of* **woman police constable**) *n* (*mujer del*) *rango más bajo de la policía británica*, ≈ agente *f*; **~ Roberts** agente Roberts.

wpm (*abbr of* **words per minute**) p.p.m.

WRAC [ræk] (*abbr of* **Women's Royal Army Corps**) *n sección femenina del ejército británico*.

WRAF [ræf] (*abbr of* **Women's Royal Air Force**) *n sección femenina de las fuerzas aéreas británicas*.

wrangle ['ræŋgl] ◇ *n* disputa *f*. ◇ *vi*: **to ~ (with sb over sthg)** discutir OR pelearse (con alguien por algo).

wrap [ræp] (*pt & pp* **-ped**, *cont* **-ping**) ◇ *vt* **-1.** [cover] envolver; **to ~ sthg in sthg** envolver algo en algo; **to ~ sthg around** OR **round sthg** liar algo alrededor de algo. **-2.** [encircle]: **he wrapped his hands around it** lo rodeó con sus manos. ◇ *n* [garment] echarpe *m*.

◆ **wrap up** ◇ *vt sep* **-1.** [cover] envolver. **-2.** *inf* [complete] cerrar, finiquitar. ◇ *vi* [put warm clothes on]: **~ up well** OR **warmly** abrígate bien.

wrapped up [ræpt-] *adj inf*: **to be ~ in sthg** estar absorto(ta) en algo; **to be ~ in sb** estar embelesado(da) con alguien.

wrapper ['ræpəʳ] *n* envoltorio *m*.

wrapping ['ræpɪŋ] *n* envoltorio *m*.

wrapping paper *n* (U) papel *m* de envolver.

wrath [rɒθ] *n literary* ira *f*, cólera *f*.

wreak [riːk] *vt* causar; **to ~ havoc** hacer estragos; **to ~ revenge** OR **vengeance** tomar la revancha.

wreath [riːθ] *n* corona *f* (de flores).

wreathe [riːð] *vt literary* cubrir, envolver.

wreck [rek] ◇ *n* **-1.** [of car, plane] restos *mpl* del siniestro; [of ship] restos del naufragio. **-2.** *inf* [person] guiñapo *m*; **to look a ~** estar hecho un trapo. ◇ *vt* **-1.** [destroy] destrozar. **-2.** NAUT hacer naufragar; **to be ~ed** naufragar. **-3.** [spoil] dar al traste con; [health] acabar con.

wreckage ['rekɪdʒ] *n* (U) [of plane, car] restos *mpl*; [of building] escombros *mpl*.

wrecker ['rekəʳ] *n Am* [vehicle] camión *m* grúa.

wren [ren] *n* chochín *m*.

wrench [rentʃ] ◇ *n* **-1.** [tool] llave *f* inglesa. **-2.** [injury] torcedura *f*. **-3.** [cause of suffering]: **it was a ~ to leave her** fue doloroso dejarla. ◇ *vt* **-1.** [pull violently]: **to ~ sthg (off)** arrancar algo; **to ~ sthg open** abrir algo de un tirón. **-2.** [twist and injure] torcer.

wrest [rest] *vt literary*: **to ~ sthg from sb** arrebatarle algo a alguien.

wrestle ['resl] ◇ *vt* luchar con OR contra. ◇ *vi lit* & *fig*: **to ~ (with)** luchar (con).

wrestler ['resləʳ] *n* luchador *m*, -ra *f*.

wrestling ['reslɪŋ] *n* lucha *f* libre.

wretch [retʃ] *n* desgraciado *m*, -da *f*, infeliz *m y f*.

wretched ['retʃɪd] *adj* **-1.** [miserable] miserable. **-2.** *inf* [damned] maldito(ta).

wriggle ['rɪgl] ◇ *vt* menear. ◇ *vi* **-1.** [move about] menearse. **-2.** [twist] escurrirse, deslizarse.

◆ **wriggle out of** *vt fus*: **to ~ out of sthg/doing sthg** escaquearse de algo/de hacer algo.

wring [rɪŋ] (*pt* & *pp* **wrung**) *vt* **-1.** [wet clothes etc] estrujar, escurrir. **-2.** *literary* [hands] retorcerse. **-3.** [neck] retorcer.

◆ **wring out** *vt sep* estrujar, escurrir.

wringing ['rɪŋɪŋ] *adj*: **~ (wet)** empapado(da).

wrinkle ['rɪŋkl] ◇ *n* arruga *f*. ◇ *vt* arrugar. ◇ *vi* arrugarse.

wrinkled ['rɪŋkld], **wrinkly** ['rɪŋklɪ] *adj* arrugado(da).

wrist [rɪst] *n* muñeca *f*.

wristband ['rɪstbænd] *n* [leather] correa *f*; [metal, plastic] brazalete *m*, pulsera *f*.

wristwatch ['rɪstwɒtʃ] *n* reloj *m* de pulsera.

writ [rɪt] *n* mandato *m* judicial.

write [raɪt] (*pt* **wrote**, *pp* **written**) ◇ *vt* **-1.** [gen & COMPUT] escribir; **to ~ sb a letter** escribirle una carta a alguien. **-2.** *Am* [person] escribir a. ◇ *vi* [gen & COMPUT] escribir; **to ~ to sb** *Br* escribir a alguien.

◆ **write back** *vt sep & vi* contestar.

◆ **write down** *vt sep* apuntar.

◆ **write in** *vi* escribir, mandar cartas.

◆ **write into** *vt sep* incluir en, insertar en.

◆ **write off** ◇ *vt sep* **-1.** [plan, hopes] abandonar. **-2.** [debt] cancelar, anular. **-3.** [person - as failure] considerar un fracaso. **-4.** *Br inf* [wreck] cargarse, destrozar. ◇ *vi*: **to ~ off (to sb)** escribir (a alguien); **to ~ off for sthg** escribir pidiendo algo.

◆ **write up** *vt sep* redactar.

write-off *n*: **the car was a ~** el coche quedó totalmente destrozado.

write-protect COMPUT ◇ *adj* de protección contra la copia. ◇ *vt* proteger contra la copia.

writer ['raɪtəʳ] *n* **-1.** [as profession] escritor *m*, -ra *f*. **-2.** [of letter, article, story] autor *m*, -ra *f*.

write-up *n inf* reseña *f*.

writhe [raɪð] *vi* retorcerse.

writing ['raɪtɪŋ] *n* **-1.** (U) [handwriting] letra *f*, caligrafía *f*. **-2.** [something written] escrito *m*; **in ~** por escrito. **-3.** [activity] escritura *f*.

◆ **writings** *npl* escritos *mpl*.

writing case *n Br* estuche con sobres y papel de carta.

writing desk *n* escritorio *m*.

writing paper *n* (U) papel *m* de carta.

written ['rɪtn] ◇ *pp* → **write**. ◇ *adj* **-1.** [not oral] escrito(ta). **-2.** [official] por escrito.

WRNS (*abbr of* **Women's Royal Naval Service**) *n* sección femenina de la armada británica.

wrong [rɒŋ] ◇ *adj* **-1.** [not normal, not satisfactory] malo(la); **the clock's ~** el reloj anda mal; **what's ~?** ¿qué pasa?, ¿qué va mal?; **there's nothing ~ with me** no me pasa

nada. **-2.** [not suitable, not correct] equivocado(da); [moment, time] inoportuno(na); **to be ~** equivocarse; **to be ~ to do sthg** cometer un error al hacer algo; **I got the ~ number** me equivoqué de número. **-3.** [morally bad] malo(la); **it's ~ to steal/lie** robar/mentir está mal; **what's ~ with being a communist?** ¿qué tiene de malo ser comunista?
◇ *adv* [incorrectly] mal; **to get sthg ~** entender mal algo; **to go ~** [make a mistake] cometer un error; [stop functioning] estropearse; **don't get me ~** *inf* no me malinterpretes.
◇ *n* **-1.** [evil] mal *m*; **to be in the ~** haber hecho mal; **he can do no ~** nada de lo que hace está mal. **-2.** [injustice] injusticia *f*.
◇ *vt* ser injusto(ta) con, agraviar.

wrong-foot *vt Br lit* & *fig* coger a contrapié a.

wrongful ['rɒŋfʊl] *adj* [dismissal] improcedente; [arrest, imprisonment] ilegal.

wrongly ['rɒŋlɪ] *adv* equivocadamente.

wrong number *n*: sorry, ~ lo siento, se ha equivocado de número.

wrote [rəʊt] *pt* → **write**.

wrought iron [rɔːt-] *n* hierro *m* forjado.

wrung [rʌŋ] *pt* & *pp* → **wring**.

WRVS (*abbr of* **Women's Royal Voluntary Service**) *n organización británica de mujeres que ayudan voluntariamente a los necesitados y en emergencias.*

wry [raɪ] *adj* **-1.** [amused] irónico(ca). **-2.** [displeased] de asco.

wt. *abbr of* **weight**.

WV *abbr of* **West Virginia**.

WW *abbr of* **world war**.

WWW (*abbr of* **World Wide Web**) *n* WWW *f*.

WY *abbr of* **Wyoming**.

Wyoming [waɪ'əʊmɪŋ] *n* Wyoming.

WYSIWYG ['wɪzɪwɪg] (*abbr of* **what you see is what you get**) *n* COMPUT lo que se ve en la pantalla es lo que aparece en la impresión.

x (*pl* **x's** OR **xs**), **X** (*pl* **X's** OR **Xs**) [eks] *n* **-1.** [letter] **x** *f inv*, **X** *f inv*. **-2.** [unknown quantity] equis *f inv*; **~ number of ...** un número equis de .... **-3.** [in algebra, to mark spot] **x** *f*. **-4.** [at end of letter]: **XXX** besos.
◆ **X** *n* [unknown name]: **Mr ~** el señor X.

xenophobia [ˌzenə'fəʊbjə] *n* xenofobia *f*.

Xerox® ['zɪərɒks] ◇ *n* **-1.** [machine] fotocopiadora *f*. **-2.** [copy] xerocopia *f*. ◇ *vt* xerocopiar.

Xmas ['eksməs] ◇ *n* Navidad *f*. ◇ *comp* de Navidad.

X-ray ◇ *n* **-1.** [ray] rayo *m* X. **-2.** [picture] radiografía *f*. ◇ *vt* examinar con rayos X, radiografiar.

xylophone ['zaɪləfəʊn] *n* xilofón *m*.

y (*pl* **y's** OR **ys**), **Y** (*pl* **Y's** OR **Ys**) [waɪ] *n* **-1.** [letter] **y** *f*, **Y** *f*. **-2.** [in algebra] **y** *f*.

yacht [jɒt] *n* yate *m*; [for racing] balandro *m*.

yachting ['jɒtɪŋ] *n* balandrismo *m*.

yachtsman ['jɒtsmən] (*pl* **-men** [-mən]) *n* balandrista *m*.

yachtswoman ['jɒts,wʊmən] (*pl* **-women** [-,wɪmɪn]) *n* balandrista *f*.

yahoo [jɑː'huː] *n* bruto *m*, patán *m*.

yak [jæk] *n* yak *m*.

Yale lock® [jeɪl-] *n* cerradura *f* de molinillo.

yam [jæm] *n* boniato *m*, batata *f*.

Yangtze ['jæŋtsɪ] *n*: **the ~** el Changjiang.

yank [jæŋk] *vt* dar un tirón a.

Yank [jæŋk] *n inf término peyorativo que designa a un estadounidense,* yanqui *m y f.*

Yankee ['jæŋkɪ] *n* **-1.** *Br inf* término peyorativo que designa a un estadounidense, yanqui *m* y *f*. **-2.** *Am* [citizen] yanqui *m* y *f*.

yap [jæp] (*pt* & *pp* **-ped**, *cont* **-ping**) *vi* **-1.** [dog] ladrar. **-2.** *pej* [person] parlotear, cotorrear.

yard [jɑːd] *n* **-1.** [unit of measurement] = *91,44 cm*, yarda *f*. **-2.** [walled area] patio *m*. **-3.** [shipyard] astillero *m*; **builder's/goods** ~ depósito *m* de materiales/de mercancías. **-4.** *Am* [attached to house] jardín *m*.

yardstick ['jɑːdstɪk] *n* criterio *m*, pauta *f*.

yarn [jɑːn] *n* **-1.** [thread] hilo *m*, hilaza *f*. **-2.** *inf* [story]: **to spin sb a** ~ contarle una batallita OR un cuento chino a alguien.

yashmak ['jæʃmæk] *n* velo *m* (*de musulmana*).

yawn [jɔːn] ◇ *n* **-1.** [when tired] bostezo *m*. **-2.** *Br inf* [boring event] rollo *m*. ◇ *vi* **-1.** [when tired] bostezar. **-2.** [gap] abrirse.

yd *abbr of* **yard**.

yeah [jeə] *adv inf* sí.

year [jɪəʳ] *n* **-1.** [gen] año *m*; ~ **in**, ~ **out** año tras año; **he's 25** ~**s old** tiene 25 años; **all (the)** ~ **round** todo el año. **-2.** SCH curso *m*; **he's in (his) first** ~ está en primero.

◆ **years** *npl* [ages] años *mpl*; **it's** ~**s since I last saw you** hace siglos que no te veo.

yearbook ['jɪəbʊk] *n* anuario *m*.

yearling ['jɪəlɪŋ] *n* potro *m* menor de dos años.

yearly ['jɪəlɪ] ◇ *adj* anual. ◇ *adv* **-1.** [once a year] una vez al año. **-2.** [every year] cada año.

yearn [jɜːn] *vi*: **to** ~ **for sthg/to do sthg** ansiar algo/hacer algo.

yearning ['jɜːnɪŋ] *n*: ~ **(for sb/sthg)** anhelo *m* (de alguien/algo).

yeast [jiːst] *n* levadura *f*.

yell [jel] ◇ *n* grito *m*, alarido *m*. ◇ *vt* & *vi* vociferar.

yellow ['jeləʊ] ◇ *adj* **-1.** [in colour] amarillo(lla). **-2.** [cowardly] cobarde. ◇ *n* amarillo *m*. ◇ *vi* ponerse amarillo(lla), amarillear.

yellow card *n* FTBL tarjeta *f* amarilla.

yellow fever *n* fiebre *f* amarilla.

yellow lines *n* líneas *fpl* amarillas (de tráfico).

YELLOW LINES:
En Gran Bretaña, una línea amarilla paralela a la acera denomina una zona de estacionamiento restringido. Dos líneas amarillas designan una zona donde se prohíbe aparcar

yellowness ['jeləʊnɪs] *n* amarillez *f*.

Yellow Pages® *n*: **the** ~ las páginas amarillas.

Yellow River *n*: **the** ~ el río Huang He.

Yellow Sea *n*: **the** ~ el mar Amarillo.

yelp [jelp] ◇ *n* aullido *m*. ◇ *vi* aullar.

Yemen ['jemən] *n* Yemen.

Yemeni ['jemənɪ] ◇ *adj* yemení. ◇ *n* yemení *m* y *f*.

yen [jen] (*pl sense 1 inv*) *n* **-1.** [Japanese currency] yen *m*. **-2.** [longing]: **to have a** ~ **for sthg/to do sthg** tener muchas ganas de algo/de hacer algo.

yeoman of the guard ['jəʊmən-] (*pl* **yeomen of the guard** ['jəʊmən-]) *n* alabardero de la Casa Real británica.

yep [jep] *adv inf* sí.

yes [jes] ◇ *adv* sí; ~, **please** sí, por favor; **to say** ~ decir que sí; **to say** ~ **to sthg** consentir algo. ◇ *n* sí *m*.

yes-man *n pej* pelotillero *m*.

yesterday ['jestədɪ] ◇ *n* ayer *m*. ◇ *adv* ayer; ~ **afternoon** ayer por la tarde; **the day before** ~ antes de ayer, anteayer.

yet [jet] ◇ *adv* **-1.** [gen] todavía, aún; **have you had lunch** ~? ¿has comido ya?; **their worst defeat** ~ la mayor derrota que han sufrido hasta la fecha; **as** ~ de momento, hasta ahora; **not** ~ todavía OR aún no. **-2.** [even]: ~ **another car** otro coche más; ~ **again** otra vez más; ~ **more** aún más. ◇ *conj* pero, sin embargo.

yeti ['jetɪ] *n* yeti *m*.

yew [juː] *n* tejo *m*.

Y-fronts *npl Br* eslip *m*.

YHA (*abbr of* **Youth Hostels Association**) *n* asociación internacional de albergues juveniles.

Yiddish ['jɪdɪʃ] ◇ *adj* yídish (*inv*). ◇ *n* yídish *m*.

yield [jiːld] ◇ *n* **-1.** AGR cosecha *f*. **-2.** FIN rédito *m*. ◇ *vt* **-1.** [gen] producir, dar. **-2.** [give up] ceder. ◇ *vi* **-1.** [shelf, lock etc] ceder. **-2.** *fml* [person, enemy] rendirse; **to** ~ **to sb/sthg** claudicar ante alguien/algo. **-3.** *Am* AUT [give way]: "~" "ceda el paso".

yippee [*Br* jɪ'piː, *Am* 'jɪpɪ] *excl* ¡yupi!

YMCA (*abbr of* **Young Men's Christian Association**) *n* asociación internacional de jóvenes cristianos.

yo [jəʊ] *excl Am inf* ¡hola!

yob(bo) ['jɒb(əʊ)] *n Br inf* gamberro *m*.

yodel ['jəʊdl] (*Br pt* & *pp* **-led**, *cont* **-ling**, *Am pt* & *pp* **-ed**, *cont* **-ing**) *vi* cantar a la tirolesa.

yoga ['jəʊgə] *n* yoga *m*.

yoghourt, **yoghurt**, **yogurt** [*Br* 'jɒgət, *Am* 'jəʊgərt] *n* yogur *m*.

yoke [jəʊk] *n lit* & *fig* yugo *m*.

yokel ['jəʊkl] *n pej* palurdo *m*, -da *f*, paleto *m*, -ta *f*.

yolk [jəʊk] *n* yema *f*.

yonder ['jɒndəʳ] *adv literary* acullá.

Yorks. [jɔːks] (*abbr of* **Yorkshire**) condado inglés.

Yorkshire pudding ['jɔːkʃə-] *n* masa horneada hecha de harina, huevos y leche que se sirve tradicionalmente con el rosbif.

Yorkshire terrier ['jɔːkʃəʳ-] *n* Yorkshire terrier *m*.

you [juː] *pers pron* **-1.** (*subject - sg*) tú, vos (+ *pl vb*) *Amer*, (- *formal use*) usted; (- *pl*) vosotros *mpl*, -tras *fpl*; (- *formal use*) ustedes (*pl*); ~'**re a good cook** eres/usted es un buen cocinero; **are** ~ **French?** ¿eres/es usted francés?; ~ **idiot!** ¡imbécil!; **if I were** OR **was** ~ si (yo) fuera tú/usted, yo en tu/su lugar; **excuse me, Madam, have** ~ **got the time?** perdone, señora, ¿tiene usted hora?; **there** ~ **are** [you've appeared] ¡ya estás/está usted aquí!; [have this] ahí tienes/tiene; **that jacket isn't really** ~ esa chaqueta no te/le pega. **-2.** (*direct object - unstressed - sg*) te; (- *pl*) os; (- *formal use*) le *m*, la *f*; (- *pl*) les *mpl*, las *fpl*; **I can see** ~ te/os veo; **yes, Madam, I understand** ~ sí, señora, la comprendo. **-3.** (*direct object - stressed*): **I don't expect** YOU **to do it** no te voy a pedir que TÚ lo hagas. **-4.** (*indirect object - sg*) te; (- *pl*) os; (- *formal use*) le; (- *pl*) les; **she gave it to** ~ te/os lo dio; **can I get** ~ **a chair, sir?** ¿le traigo una silla, señor? **-5.** (*after prep, in comparisons etc - sg*) ti; (- *pl*) vosotros *mpl*, -tras *fpl*; (- *formal use*) usted; (- *pl*) ustedes; **we shall go with/without** ~ iremos contigo/sin ti, iremos con/sin vosotros (*pl*); **I'm shorter than** ~ soy más bajo que tú/vosotros. **-6.** [anyone, one] uno; ~ **wouldn't have thought so** uno no lo habría pensado; **exercise is good for** ~ el ejercicio es bueno.

you'd [juːd] = **you had, you would**.

you'll [juːl] = **you will**.

young [jʌŋ] ◇ *adj* [not old] joven. ◇ *npl* **-1.** [young people]: **the** ~ los jóvenes. **-2.** [baby animals] crías *fpl*.

younger ['jʌŋgəʳ] *adj*: **Pitt the** ~ Pitt el joven, Pitt hijo.

youngish ['jʌŋɪʃ] *adj* bastante joven.

young man *n* joven *m*.

youngster ['jʌŋstəʳ] *n* joven *m y f*, chico *m*, -ca *f*.

young woman *n* (mujer *f*) joven *f*.

your [jɔːʳ] *poss adj* **-1.** (*everyday use - referring to one person*) tu; (- *referring to more than one person*) vuestro(tra); ~ **dog** tu/vuestro perro; ~ **children** tus niños; **what's** ~ **name?** ¿cómo te llamas?; **it wasn't** YOUR **fault** no fue culpa tuya/vuestra; **you didn't wash** ~ **hair** no te lavaste/os lavasteis el pelo. **-2.** (*formal use*) su; ~ **dog** su perro; **what are** ~ **names?** ¿cuáles son sus nombres? **-3.** (*impersonal - one's*): ~ **attitude changes as you get older** la actitud de uno cambia con la vejez; **it's good for** ~ **teeth/hair** es bueno para los dientes/el pelo; ~ **average Englishman** el inglés medio.

you're [jɔːʳ] = **you are**.

yours [jɔːz] *poss pron* **-1.** (*everyday use - referring to one person*) tuyo (tuya); (- *referring to more than one person*) vuestro (vuestra); **that money is** ~ ese dinero es tuyo/vuestro; **those keys are** ~ esas llaves son tuyas/vuestras; **my car hit** ~ mi coche chocó contra el tuyo/el vuestro; **it wasn't her fault, it was** YOURS no fue culpa de ella sino TUYA/VUESTRA; **a friend of** ~ un amigo tuyo/vuestro. **-2.** (*formal use*) suyo (suya).
◆ **Yours** *adv* [in letter] un saludo; *see also* **faithfully, sincerely** *etc*.

yourself [jɔːˈself] (*pl* **-selves** [-ˈselvz]) *pron* **-1.** (*as reflexive - sg*) te; (- *pl*) os; (- *formal use*) se; **did you hurt** ~? ¿te hiciste/se hizo daño? **-2.** (*after prep - sg*) ti mismo (ti misma); (- *pl*) vosotros mismos (vosotras mismas); (- *formal use*) usted mismo (usted misma); **with** ~ contigo mismo/misma. **-3.** (*for emphasis*): **you** ~ tú mismo (tú misma); (*formal use*) usted mismo (usted misma); **you yourselves** vosotros mismos (vosotras mismas); (*formal use*) ustedes mismos (ustedes mismas). **-4.** [without help] solo(la); **did you do it (by)** ~? ¿lo hiciste solo?

youth [juːθ] *n* **-1.** [gen] juventud *f*. **-2.** [boy, young man] joven *m*.

youth club *n* club *m* juvenil.

youthful ['juːθfʊl] *adj* juvenil.

youthfulness ['juːθfʊlnɪs] *n* juventud *f*.

youth hostel *n* albergue *m* juvenil.

youth hostelling [-ˈhɒstəlɪŋ] *n Br*: **to go** ~ ir de vacaciones durmiendo en albergues juveniles.

you've [juːv] = **you have**.

yowl [jaʊl] ◇ *n* aullido *m*. ◇ *vi* aullar.

yo-yo ['jəʊjəʊ] *n* yoyó *m*.

yr *abbr of* **year**.

YTS (*abbr of* **Youth Training Scheme**) *n* programa gubernamental de promoción del empleo juvenil en Gran Bretaña.

Yucatan [ˌjʌkəˈtɑːn] *n* Yucatán *m*.

yuck [jʌk] *excl inf* ¡puaj!

Yugoslav = **Yugoslavian**.

Yugoslavia [ˌjuːgəˈslɑːvjə] *n* Yugoslavia.

Yugoslavian [ˌjuːgəʊˈslɑːvɪən], **Yugoslav** [ˌjuːgəˈslɑːv] ◇ *adj* yugoslavo(va). ◇ *n* yugoslavo *m*, -va *f*.

yule log [juːl-] *n* **-1.** [piece of wood] *leño que se quema en Nochebuena.* **-2.** [cake] *pastel de Navidad en forma de leño.*

yuletide [ˈjuːltaɪd] *n* (U) *literary* Navidad *f*.

yummy [ˈjʌmɪ] (*compar* **-ier**, *superl* **-iest**) *adj inf* riquísimo(ma), para chuparse los dedos.

yuppie, yuppy [ˈjʌpɪ] (*pl* **-ies**) (*abbr of* **young urban professional**) *n* yuppy *m y f*.

YWCA (*abbr of* **Young Women's Christian Association**) *n* asociación internacional de jóvenes cristianas.

Z

z (*pl* **z's** OR **zs**), **Z** (*pl* **Z's** OR **Zs**) [*Br* zed, *Am* ziː] *n* [letter] z *f*, Z *f*.

Zagreb [ˈzɑːgreb] *n* Zagreb.

Zaïre [zɑːˈɪəʳ] *n* (el) Zaire.

Zaïrese [zɑːˈɪəriːz] *n* ◇ *adj* zaireño(ña). ◇ *n* zaireño *m*, -ña *f*.

Zambesi, Zambezi [zæmˈbiːzɪ] *n*: **the ~** el Zambeze.

Zambia [ˈzæmbɪə] *n* Zambia.

Zambian [ˈzæmbɪən] ◇ *adj* zambiano(na). ◇ *n* zambiano *m*, -na *f*.

zany [ˈzeɪnɪ] (*compar* **-ier**, *superl* **-iest**) *adj inf* [humour, trick] disparatado(da); [person] loco(ca).

Zanzibar [ˌzænzɪˈbɑː] *n* Zanzíbar.

zap [zæp] (*pt* & *pp* **-ped**, *cont* **-ping**) *inf* ◇ *vt* [kill] cargarse, matar. ◇ *vi*: **to ~ off (somewhere)** hacer una escapada (a algún sitio).

zeal [ziːl] *n fml* celo *m*.

zealot [ˈzelət] *n fml* fanático *m*, -ca *f*.

zealous [ˈzeləs] *adj fml* entusiasta, infatigable.

zebra [*Br* ˈzebrə, *Am* ˈziːbrə] (*pl inv* OR **-s**) *n* cebra *f*.

zebra crossing *n Br* paso *m* cebra.

zenith [*Br* ˈzenɪθ, *Am* ˈziːnəθ] *n* ASTRON & *fig* cenit *m*.

zeppelin [ˈzepəlɪn] *n* zepelín *m*.

zero [*Br* ˈzɪərəʊ, *Am* ˈziːrəʊ] (*pl inv* OR **-es**) ◇ *adj* cero (*inv*), nulo(la). ◇ *n* cero *m*; **below ~** bajo cero.

◆ **zero in on** *vt fus* **-1.** [subj: weapon] apuntar a. **-2.** [subj: person] centrarse en.

zero-rated [-ˌreɪtɪd] *adj Br* sin IVA.

zest [zest] *n* (U) **-1.** [excitement, eagerness] entusiasmo *m*. **-2.** [of orange, lemon] cáscara *f*.

zigzag [ˈzɪgzæg] (*pt* & *pp* **-ged**, *cont* **-ging**) ◇ *n* zigzag *m*. ◇ *vi* zigzaguear.

zilch [zɪltʃ] *n Am inf* **-1.** [zero] cerapio. **-2.** [nothing] na', nada.

Zimbabwe [zɪmˈbɑːbwɪ] *n* Zimbabue.

Zimbabwean [zɪmˈbɑːbwɪən] ◇ *adj* zimbabuense. ◇ *n* zimbabuense *m y f*.

Zimmer frame® [ˈzɪməʳ-] *n* andador *m* ortopédico.

zinc [zɪŋk] *n* cinc *m*, zinc *m*.

Zionism [ˈzaɪənɪzm] *n* sionismo *m*.

Zionist [ˈzaɪənɪst] ◇ *adj* sionista. ◇ *n* sionista *m y f*.

zip [zɪp] (*pt* & *pp* **-ped**, *cont* **-ping**) ◇ *n Br* [fastener] cremallera *f*, cierre *m* relámpago *Amer*. ◇ *vt* cerrar con cremallera. ◇ *vi*: **he zipped round the city in half an hour** dio la vuelta a la ciudad tan sólo en media hora.

◆ **zip up** *vt sep* cerrar la cremallera de.

zip code *n Am* código *m* postal.

zip fastener *n Br* = **zip**.

zipper [ˈzɪpəʳ] *n Am* = **zip**.

zit [zɪt] *n inf* grano *m*.

zither [ˈzɪðəʳ] *n* cítara *f*.

zodiac [ˈzəʊdɪæk] *n*: **the ~** el zodiaco; **sign of the ~** signo del zodiaco.

zombie [ˈzɒmbɪ] *n lit* & *fig* zombi *m y f*.

zone [zəʊn] *n* zona *f*.

zoo [zuː] *n* zoo *m*.

zoological [ˌzəʊəˈlɒdʒɪkl] *adj* zoológico(ca).

zoologist [zəʊˈɒlədʒɪst] *n* zoólogo *m*, -ga *f*.

zoology [zəʊˈɒlədʒɪ] *n* zoología *f*.

zoom [zuːm] *vi inf* **-1.** [move quickly]: **to ~ past** pasar zumbando. **-2.** [rise rapidly] dispararse.

◆ **zoom in** *vi*: **to ~ in (on)** enfocar en primer plano (a).

◆ **zoom off** *vi inf* salir zumbando.

zoom lens *n* zoom *m*.

zucchini [zuːˈkiːnɪ] (*pl inv*) *n Am* calabacín *m*.

Zulu [ˈzuːluː] ◇ *adj* zulú. ◇ *n* **-1.** [person] zulú *m y f*. **-2.** [language] zulú *m*.

Zürich [ˈzjʊərɪk] *n* Zúrich.

CUADRO DE CONJUGACIÓN

El cuadro de conjugación está integrado por ochenta y un modelos, uno para cada una de las tres conjugaciones regulares españolas, -ar, -er, -ir, los dos verbos auxiliares, ser y estar, setenta y dos modelos de conjugación irregular y cuatro modelos de verbos defectivos. A cada modelo le corresponde un número, sin embargo, en el cuerpo del diccionario, sólo los verbos que siguen un modelo de conjugación irregular llevarán el número correspondiente.

Modelos de conjugación regular y auxiliares
Para los modelos de las conjugaciones regulares y para los auxiliares damos todas las personas de los tiempos simples y las formas no personales.

Modelos de conjugación irregular
El orden de aparición de los modelos de conjugación irregular responde al tipo de irregularidad: cambios en la acentuación, cambios en la ortografía, diptongación, modificación de la vocal o la consonante de la raíz...; siempre que un tipo de irregularidad se presenta en las tres conjugaciones, hemos escogido un modelo para cada una de ellas, p. ej.: *acertar, mover, adquirir*.

Para los modelos de conjugación irregular, damos únicamente aquellos tiempos que contienen alguna forma irregular.

Si todas las personas de un tiempo son irregulares, hemos seleccionado la 1ª y 3ª del singular y la 1ª del plural, p. ej.: *cabré, cabrá, cabremos*; si la 1ª y la 3ª del singular coinciden, damos sólo la 1ª del singular y la 1ª del plural p. ej.: *condujera o condujese, condujéramos o condujésemos*.

Cuando en un mismo tiempo se alternan formas regulares y formas irregulares, hemos seleccionado la 1ª y 3ª del singular (generalmente irregulares) y la 1ª del plural (generalmente regular), p. ej.: *acierto, acierta, acertamos*; si la 1ª y la 3ª del singular coinciden, damos sólo la 1ª del singular y la 1ª del plural p. ej.: *acierte, acertemos*.

Cuando estas tres personas son todas irregulares (en algunos imperativos), hemos añadido la 2ª del plural para mostrar una forma regular, p. ej.: *duerme, duerma, durmamos, dormid*.

En algunos tiempos (pretérito perfecto simple) las únicas personas irregulares son la 3ª del singular y del plural, en esta ocasión hemos seleccionado dichas personas y la 1ª del plural, p. ej.: *pidió, pedimos, pidieron*.

Verbos defectivos
Para los verbos que sólo se conjugan en determinados tiempos y personas, hemos incluido los tiempos simples y las formas impersonales, indicando mediante una nota las formas que no se conjugan.

Conjugaciones regulares

a) verbos en -ar
Gerundio **-ando**,
terminaciones del presente de indicativo **-o, -as, -a, -amos, -áis, -an**

[1] amar

Presente indicativo
amo
amas
ama
amamos
amáis
aman

Imperfecto indicativo
amaba
amabas
amaba
amábamos
amabais
amaban

Pretérito perfecto simple
amé
amaste
amó
amamos
amasteis
amaron

Futuro
amaré
amarás
amará
amaremos
amaréis
amarán

Condicional
amaría
amarías
amaría
amaríamos
amaríais
amarían

Presente subjuntivo
ame
ames
ame
amemos
améis
amen

Imperfecto subjuntivo
amara o amase
amaras o amases
amara o amase
amáramos o amásemos
amarais o amaseis
amaran o amasen

Imperativo
ama (tú)
ame (él, ella)
amemos (nosotros)
amad (vosotros)
amen (ellos, ellas)

Gerundio
amando

Participio
amado, da

b) verbos en -er
Gerundio **-iendo**,
terminaciones del presente de indicativo **-o, -es, -e, -emos, -éis, -en**

[2] temer

Presente indicativo
temo
temes
teme
tememos
teméis
temen

Imperfecto indicativo
temía
temías
temía
temíamos
temíais
temían

Pretérito perfecto simple
temí
temiste
temió
temimos
temisteis
temieron

Futuro
temeré
temerás
temerá
temeremos
temeréis
temerán

Condicional
temería
temerías
temería
temeríamos
temeríais
temerían

Presente subjuntivo
tema
temas
tema
temamos
temáis
teman

Imperfecto subjuntivo
temiera o temiese
temieras o temieses
temiera o temiese
temiéramos o temiésemos
temierais o temieseis
temieran o temiesen

Imperativo
teme (tú)
tema (él, ella)
temamos (nosotros)
temed (vosotros)
teman (ellos, ellas)

Gerundio
temiendo

Participio
temido, da

c) verbos en -ir
Gerundio **-iendo**,
terminaciones del presente de indicativo **-o, -es, -e, -imos, -is, -en**

[3] partir

Presente indicativo
parto
partes
parte
partimos
partís
parten

Imperfecto indicativo
partía
partías
partía
partíamos
partíais
partían

Pretérito perfecto simple
partí
partiste
partió
partimos
partisteis
partieron

Futuro
partiré
partirás
partirá
partiremos
partiréis
partirán

Condicional
partiría
partirías
partiría
partiríamos
partiríais
partirían

Presente subjuntivo
parta
partas
parta
partamos
partáis
partan

Imperfecto subjuntivo
partiera o partiese
partieras o partieses
partiera o partiese
partiéramos o partiésemos
partierais o partieseis
partieran o partiesen

Imperativo
parte (tú)
parta (él, ella)
partamos (nosotros)
partid (vosotros)
partan (ellos, ellas)

Gerundio
partiendo

Participio
partido, da

Verbos auxiliares

[4] haber

Presente indicativo
he
has
ha
hemos
habéis
han

Imperfecto indicativo
había
habías
había
habíamos
habíais
habían

Pretérito perfecto simple
hube
hubiste
hubo
hubimos
hubisteis
hubieron

Futuro
habré
habrás
habrá
habremos
habréis
habrán

Condicional
habría
habrías
habría
habríamos
habríais
habrían

Presente subjuntivo
haya
hayas
haya
hayamos
hayáis
hayan

Imperfecto subjuntivo
hubiera o hubiese
hubieras o hubieses
hubiera o hubiese
hubiéramos o hubiésemos
hubierais o hubieseis
hubieran o hubiesen

Imperativo
he (tú)
haya (él, ella)
hayamos (nosotros)
habed (vosotros)
hayan (ellos, ellas)

Gerundio
habiendo

Participio
habido, da

[5] ser

Presente indicativo
soy
eres
es
somos
sois
son

Imperfecto indicativo
era
eras
era
éramos
erais
eran

Pretérito perfecto simple
fui
fuiste
fue
fuimos
fuisteis
fueron

Futuro
seré
serás
será
seremos
seréis
serán

Condicional
sería
serías
sería
seríamos
seríais
serían

Presente subjuntivo
sea
seas
sea
seamos
seáis
sean

Imperfecto subjuntivo
fuera o fuese
fueras o fueses
fuera o fuese
fuéramos o fuésemos
fuerais o fueseis
fueran o fuesen

Imperativo
sé (tú)
sea (él, ella)
seamos (nosotros)
sed (vosotros)
sean (ellos, ellas)

Gerundio
siendo

Participio
sido, da

Verbos irregulares

[6] actuar   actú- en sílaba tónica
actu- en sílaba átona

Presente indicativo	Presente subjuntivo	Imperativo
actúo	actúe	actúa (tú)
actúa	actuemos	actúe (él, ella)
actuamos		actuemos (nosotros)

[7] adecuar   adecu- en todas las personas y tiempos

Presente indicativo	Presente subjuntivo	Imperativo
adecuo	adecue	adecua (tú)
adecua	adecuemos	adecue (él, ella)
adecuamos		adecuemos (nosotros)

[8] cambiar   cambi- en todas las personas y tiempos

Presente indicativo	Presente subjuntivo	Imperativo
cambio	cambie	cambia (tú)
cambia	cambiemos	cambie (él, ella)
cambiamos		cambiemos (nosotros)

[9] guiar   guí- en sílaba tónica
gui- en sílaba átona

Presente indicativo	Presente subjuntivo	Imperativo
guío	guíe	guia (tú)
guía	guiemos	guíe (él, ella)
guiamos		guiemos (nosotros)

[10] sacar   sac- delante de -a, -á, -o, -ó
saqu- delante de -e, -é

Pretérito perfecto simple	Presente subjuntivo	Imperativo
saqué	saque	saca (tú)
sacó	saquemos	saque (él, ella)
sacamos		saquemos (nosotros)

[11] mecer   mec- delante de -e, -é, -i, -í
mez- delante de -a, -á, -o

Presente indicativo	Presente subjuntivo	Imperativo
mezo	meza	mece (tú)
mece	mezamos	meza (él, ella)
mecemos		mezamos (nosotros)
		meced (vosotros)

[12] zurcir   zurc- delante de -e, -i, -í
              zurz- delante de -a, -á, -o

Presente indicativo	**Presente subjuntivo**	**Imperativo**
zurzo	zurza	zurce (tú)
zurce	zurzamos	zurza (él, ella)
zurcimos		zurzamos (nosotros)

[13] cazar   caz- delante de -a, -á, -o, -ó
              cac- delante de -e, -é

Pretérito perfecto simple	**Presente subjuntivo**	**Imperativo**
cacé	cace	caza (tú)
cazó	cacemos	cace (él, ella)
cazamos		cacemos (nosotros)

[14] proteger   proteg- delante de -e, -é, -i, -í
                 protej- delante de -a, -á, -o

Presente indicativo	**Presente subjuntivo**	**Imperativo**
protejo	proteja	protege (tú)
protege	protejamos	proteja (él, ella)
protegemos		protejamos (nosotros)

[15] dirigir   dirig- delante de -e, -i, -í
             protej- delante de -a, -á, -o

Presente indicativo	**Presente subjuntivo**	**Imperativo**
dirijo	dirija	dirige (tú)
dirige	dirijamos	dirija (él, ella)
dirigimos		dirijamos (nosotros)

[16] llegar   lleg- delante de -a, -á, -o, -ó
              llegu- delante de -e, -é

Pretérito perfecto simple	**Presente subjuntivo**	**Imperativo**
llegué	llegue	llega (tú)
llegó	lleguemos	llegue (él, ella)
llegamos		lleguemos (nosotros)

[17] distinguir   distingu- delante de -e, -i, -í
                   disting- delante de -a, -á, -o

Presente indicativo	**Presente subjuntivo**	**Imperativo**
distingo	distinga	distingue (tú)
distingue	distingamos	distinga (él, ella)
distinguimos		distingamos (nosotros)

[18] delinquir   delinqu- delante de -e, -i, -í
                     delinc- delante de -a, -á, -o

Presente indicativo	Presente subjuntivo	Imperativo
delinco	delinca	delinque (tú)
delinque	delinca	delinca (él, ella)
delinquimos	delincamos	delincamos (nosotros)

[19] acertar   aciert- en sílaba tónica
                   acert- en sílaba átona

Presente indicativo	Presente subjuntivo	Imperativo
acierto	acierte	acierta (tú)
acierta	acertemos	acierte (él, ella)
acertamos		acertemos (nosotros)

[20] tender   tiend- en sílaba tónica
                  tend- en sílaba átona

Presente indicativo	Presente subjuntivo	Imperativo
tiendo	tienda	tiende (tú)
tiende	tendamos	tienda (él, ella)
tendemos		tendamos (nosotros)

[21] discernir   disciern- en sílaba tónica
                     discern- en sílaba átona

Presente indicativo	Presente subjuntivo	Imperativo
discierno	discierna	discierne (tú)
discierne	discernamos	discierna (él, ella)
discernimos		discernamos (nosotros)

[22] adquirir   adquier- en sílaba tónica
                    adquir- en sílaba átona

Presente indicativo	Presente subjuntivo	Imperativo
adquiero	adquiera	adquiere (tú)
adquiere	adquiramos	adquiera (él, ella)
adquirimos		adquiramos (nosotros)

[23] sonar   suen- en sílaba tónica
                 son- en sílaba átona

Presente indicativo	Presente subjuntivo	Imperativo
sueno	suene	suena (tú)
suena	sonemos	suene (él, ella)
sonamos		sonemos (nosotros)

[24] mover   muev- en sílaba tónica
                  mov- en sílaba átona

Presente indicativo	**Presente subjuntivo**	**Imperativo**
muevo	mueva	mueve (tú)
mueve	mueva	mueva (él, ella)
movemos	movamos	movamos (nosotros)

[25] dormir   duerm- en sílaba tónica
                   dorm-/durm- en sílaba átona

Presente indicativo	**Presente subjuntivo**	**Imperativo**
duermo	duerma	duerme (tú)
duerme	durmamos	duerma (él, ella)
dormimos		durmamos (nosotros)
	Imperfecto subjuntivo	dormid (vosotros)
Pretérito perfecto simple	durmiera o durmiese	
durmió	durmiéramos o durmiésemos	**Gerundio**
dormimos		durmiendo
durmieron		

[26] pedir   ped- / pid-

Presente indicativo	**Presente subjuntivo**	**Imperativo**
pido	pida	pide (tú)
pide	pidamos	pida (él, ella)
pedimos		pidamos (nosotros)
	Imperfecto subjuntivo	
Pretérito perfecto simple	pidiera o pidiese	**Gerundio**
pidió	pidiéramos o pidiésemos	pidiendo
pedimos		
pidieron		

[27] sentir   sent- / sient- / sint-

Presente indicativo	**Presente subjuntivo**	**Imperativo**
siento	sienta	siente (tú)
siente	sintamos	sienta (él, ella)
sentimos		sintamos (nosotros)
	Imperfecto subjuntivo	
Pretérito perfecto simple	sintiera o sintiese	**Gerundio**
sintió	sintiéramos o sintiésemos	sintiendo
sentimos		
sintieron		

[28] reír   re- / ri- / rí-

Presente indicativo
río
ríe
reímos

Pretérito perfecto simple
rió
reímos
rieron

Presente subjuntivo
ría
riamos

Imperfecto subjuntivo
riera o riese
riéramos o riésemos

Imperativo
ríe (tú)
ría (él, ella)
riamos (nosotros)
reíd (vosotros)

Gerundio
riendo

[29] nacer   nac- delante de -e, -é, -i, -í
                nazc- delante de -a, -á, -o

Presente indicativo
nazco
nace
nacemos

Presente subjuntivo
nazca
nazcamos

Imperativo
nace (tú)
nazca (él, ella)
nazcamos (nosotros)

[30] parecer   parec- delante de -e, -é, -i, -í
                  parezc- delante de -a, -á, -o

Presente indicativo
parezco
parece
parecemos

Presente subjuntivo
parezca
parezcamos

Imperativo
parece (tú)
parezca (él, ella)
parezcamos (nosotros)

[31] conocer   conoc- delante de -e, -é, -i, -í
                  conozc- delante de -a, -á, -o

Presente indicativo
conozco
conoce
conocemos

Presente subjuntivo
conozca
conozcamos

Imperativo
conoce (tú)
conozca (él, ella)
conozcamos (nosotros)

[32] lucir   luc- delante de -e, -i, -í
                luzc- delante de -a, -á, -o

Presente indicativo
luzco
luce
lucimos

Presente subjuntivo
luzca
luzcamos

Imperativo
luce (tú)
luzca (él, ella)
luzcamos (nosotros)

[33] conducir   conduc- delante de -e, -i, -í
conduzc- delante de -a, -á, -o
conduj- en el pretérito perfecto simple y en el imperfecto
de subjuntivo

Presente indicativo
conduzco
conduce
conducimos

Pretérito perfecto simple
conduje
condujo
condujimos

Presente subjuntivo
conduzca
conduzcamos

Imperfecto subjuntivo
condujera o condujese
condujéramos o condujésemos

Imperativo
conduce (tú)
conduzca (él, ella)
conduzcamos (nosotros)

[34] comenzar   comienz- en sílaba tónica y delante de -a, -o
comienc- en sílaba tónica y delante de -e
comenz- en sílaba átona y delante de -a, -á, -ó
comenc- en sílaba átona y delante de -e, -é

Presente indicativo
comienzo
comienza
comenzamos

Pretérito perfecto simple
comencé
comenzó
comenzamos

Presente subjuntivo
comience
comencemos

Imperativo
comienza (tú)
comience (él, ella)
comencemos (nosotros)

[35] negar   nieg- en sílaba tónica y delante de -a, -o
niegu- en sílaba tónica y delante de -e
neg- en sílaba átona y delante de -a, á, -ó
negu- en sílaba átona y delante de -e, -é

Presente indicativo
niego
niega
negamos

Pretérito perfecto simple
negué
negó
negamos

Presente subjuntivo
niegue
neguemos

Imperativo
niega (tú)
niegue (él, ella)
neguemos (nosotros)

[36] trocar   truec- en sílaba tónica y delante de -a, -o
                  truequ- en sílaba tónica y delante de -e
                  troc- en sílaba átona y delante de -a,-á, -ó
                  troqu- en sílaba átona y delante de -e, -é

Presente indicativo   **Presente subjuntivo**   **Imperativo**
trueco   trueque   trueca (tú)
trueca   troquemos   trueque (él, ella)
trocamos   troquemos (nosotros)
                                                                  trocad (vosotros)

Pretérito perfecto simple
troqué
trocó
trocamos

[37] forzar   fuerz- en sílaba tónica y delante de -a, -o
                  fuerc- en sílaba tónica y delante de -e
                  forz- en sílaba átona y delante de -a, -á, -ó
                  forc- en sílaba átona y delante de -e, -é

Presente indicativo   **Presente subjuntivo**   **Imperativo**
fuerzo   fuerce   fuerza (tú)
fuerza   forcemos   fuerce (él, ella)
forzamos   forcemos (nosotros)
                                                                  forzad (vosotros)

Pretérito perfecto simple
forcé
forzó
forzamos

[38] avergonzar   avergüenz- en sílaba tónica y delante de -a, -o
                      avergüenc- en sílaba tónica y delante de -e
                      avergonz- en sílaba átona y delante de -a, -á, -ó
                      avergonc- en sílaba átona y delante de -e, -é

Presente indicativo   **Presente subjuntivo**   **Imperativo**
avergüenzo   avergüence   avergüenza (tú)
avergüenza   avergoncemos   avergüence (él, ella)
avergonzamos   avergoncemos
                                                                  (nosotros)
Pretérito perfecto simple   avergonzad (vosotros)
avergoncé
avergonzó
avergonzamos

[39] colgar   cuelg- en sílaba tónica y delante de -a, -o
cuelgu- en sílaba tónica y delante de -e
colg- en sílaba átona y delante de -a, -á, -ó
colgu- en sílaba átona y delante de -e, -é

Presente indicativo
cuelgo
cuelga
colgamos

Presente subjuntivo
cuelgue
colguemos

Imperativo
cuelga (tú)
cuelgue (él, ella)
colguemos (nosotros)
colgad (vosotros)

Pretérito perfecto simple
colgué
colgó
colgamos

[40] jugar   jueg- en sílaba tónica y delante de -a, -o
juegu- en sílaba tónica y delante de -e
jug- en sílaba átona y delante de -a, á, -ó
jugu- en sílaba átona y delante de -e, -é

Presente indicativo
juego
juega
jugamos

Presente subjuntivo
juegue
juguemos

Imperativo
juega (tú)
juegue (él, ella)
juguemos (nosotros)
jugad (vosotros)

Pretérito perfecto simple
jugué
jugó
jugamos

[41] cocer   cuez- en sílaba tónica y delante de -a, -o
cuec- en sílaba tónica y delante de -e
coz- en sílaba átona y delante de -a, á
coc- en sílaba átona y delante de -e, -é, -i, -í

Presente indicativo
cuezo
cuece
cocemos

Presente subjuntivo
cueza
cozamos

Imperativo
cuece (tú)
cueza (él, ella)
cozamos (nosotros)
coced (vosotros)

[42] regir   reg- / rig- delante de -e, -i, -í
rij- delante de -a, -á, -o

Presente indicativo
rijo
rige
regimos

Presente subjuntivo
rija
rijamos

Imperfecto subjuntivo
rigiera o rigiese
rigiéramos o rigiésemos

Pretérito perfecto simple
rigió
regimos
rigieron

Imperativo
rige (tú)
rija (él, ella)
rijamos (nosotros)
regid (vosotros)

Gerundio
rigiendo

[43] seguir   segu- / sigu- delante de -e, -i, -í
                    sig- delante de -a, -á, -o

Presente indicativo   **Presente subjuntivo**   **Imperativo**
sigo   siga   sigue (tú)
sigue   sigamos   siga (él,ella)
seguimos   sigamos (nosotros)
                               Imperfecto subjuntivo   seguid (vosotros)
Pretérito perfecto simple siguiera o siguiese
siguió   siguiéramos o siguiésemos   **Gerundio**
seguimos   siguiendo
siguieron

[44] argüir   argü- delante de -i, -í
                    arguy- delante de -a, -á, -e, -o, -ó

Presente indicativo   **Presente subjuntivo**   **Imperativo**
arguyo   arguya   arguye (tú)
arguye   arguyamos   arguya (él, ella)
argüimos   arguyamos (nosotros)
                               Imperfecto subjuntivo   argüid (vosotros)
Pretérito perfecto simple arguyera o arguyese
arguyó   arguyéramos o arguyésemos   **Gerundio**
argüimos   arguyendo
arguyeron

[45] averiguar   averigu- delante de -a, -á, -o, -ó
                       averigü- delante de -e, -é

Pretérito perfecto simple **Presente subjuntivo**   **Imperativo**
averigüé   averigüe   averigua (tú)
averiguó   averigüemos   averigüe (él, ella)
averiguamos   averigüemos
                                                                  (nosotros)

[46] agorar   agüe- en sílaba tónica y delante de -e
                    agor- en sílaba átona y delante de -a, -á, -o

Presente indicativo   **Presente subjuntivo**   **Imperativo**
agüero   agüere   agüera (tú)
agüera   agoremos   agüere (él, ella)
agoramos   agoremos (nosotros)

[47] errar   yerr- en sílaba tónica
                   err- en sílaba átona

Presente indicativo   **Presente subjuntivo**   **Imperativo**
yerro   yerre   yerra (tú)
yerra   erremos   yerre (él, ella)
erramos   erremos (nosotros)

[48] desosar   deshues- en sílaba tónica
desos- en sílaba átona

Presente indicativo	**Presente subjuntivo**	**Imperativo**
deshueso	deshuese	deshuesa (tú)
deshuesa	desosemos	deshuese (él, ella)
desosamos		desosemos (nosotros)

[49] oler   huel- en sílaba tónica
ol- en sílaba átona

Presente indicativo	**Presente subjuntivo**	**Imperativo**
huelo	huela	huele (tú)
huele	olamos	huela (él, ella)
olemos		olamos (nosotros)

[50] leer   le- / ley-

Pretérito perfecto simple	**Imperfecto subjuntivo**	**Gerundio**
leyó	leyera o leyese	leyendo
leímos	leyéramos o leyésemos	
leyeron		

[51] huir   hui- / huy-

Presente indicativo	**Presente subjuntivo**	**Imperativo**
huyo	huya	huye (tú)
huye	huyamos	huya (él, ella)
huimos		huyamos (nosotros)
	Imperfecto subjuntivo	huid (vosotros)
Pretérito perfecto simple	huyera o huyese	
huyó	huyéramos o huyésemos	**Gerundio**
huimos		huyendo
huyeron		

[52] andar

Pretérito perfecto simple	**Imperfecto subjuntivo**
anduve	anduviera o anduviese
anduvo	anduviéramos o anduviésemos
anduvimos	

[53] asir   as- / asg-

Presente indicativo	**Presente subjuntivo**	**Imperativo**
asgo	asga	ase (tú)
ase	asgamos	asga (él, ella)
asimos		asgamos (nosotros)

[54] caber

Presente indicativo
quepo
cabe
cabemos

Pretérito perfecto simple
cupe
cupo
cupimos

Futuro
cabré
cabrá
cabremos

Condicional
cabría
cabríamos

Presente subjuntivo
quepa
quepamos

Imperfecto subjuntivo
cupiera o cupiese
cupiéramos o cupiésemos

Imperativo
cabe (tú)
quepa (él, ella)
quepamos (nosotros)

[55] caer

Presente indicativo
caigo
cae
caemos

Pretérito perfecto simple
cayó
caímos
cayeron

Presente subjuntivo
caiga
caigamos

Imperfecto subjuntivo
cayera o cayese
cayéramos o cayésemos

Imperativo
cae (tú)
caiga (él, ella)
caigamos (nosotros)

Gerundio
cayendo

[56] dar

Presente indicativo
doy
da
damos

Pretérito perfecto simple
di
dio
dimos

Presente subjuntivo
dé
demos

Imperfecto subjuntivo
diera o diese
diéramos o diésemos

Imperativo
da (tú)
dé (él, ella)
demos (nosotros)

[57] decir

Presente indicativo
digo
dice
decimos

Pretérito perfecto simple
dije
dijo
dijimos

Futuro
diré
dirá
diremos

Condicional
diría
diríamos

Presente subjuntivo
diga
digamos

Imperfecto subjuntivo
dijera o dijese
dijéramos o dijésemos

Imperativo
di (tú)
diga (él, ella)
digamos (nosotros)
decid (vosotros)

Gerundio
diciendo

Participio
dicho, cha

[58] erguir

Presente indicativo
irgo o yergo
irgue o yergue
erguimos

Pretérito perfecto simple
irguió
erguimos
irguieron

Presente subjuntivo
irga o yerga
irgamos

Imperfecto subjuntivo
irguiera o irguiese
irguiéramos o irguiésemos

Imperativo
irgue o yergue (tú)
irga o yerga (él, ella)
irgamos (nosotros)
erguid (vosotros)

Gerundio
irguiendo

[59] estar

Presente indicativo
estoy
está
estamos

Pretérito perfecto simple
estuve
estuvo
estuvimos

Presente subjuntivo
esté
estemos

Imperfecto subjuntivo
estuviera o estuviese
estuviéramos o estuviésemos

Imperativo
está (tú)
esté (él, ella)
estemos (nosotros)

[60] hacer

Presente indicativo
hago
hace
hacemos

Pretérito perfecto simple
hice
hizo
hicimos

Futuro
haré
hará
haremos

Condicional
haría
haríamos

Presente subjuntivo
haga
hagamos

Imperfecto subjuntivo
hiciera o hiciese
hiciéramos o hiciésemos

Imperativo
haz (tú)
haga (él, ella)
hagamos (nosotros)
haced (vosotros)

Participio
hecho, cha

[61] ir

Presente indicativo
voy
va
vamos

Pretérito perfecto simple
fui
fue
fuimos

Presente subjuntivo
vaya
vayamos

Imperfecto subjuntivo
fuera o fuese
fuéramos o fuésemos

Imperativo
ve (tú)
vaya (él, ella)
vayamos (nosotros)
id (vosotros)

Gerundio
yendo

[62] oír

Presente indicativo
oigo
oye
oímos

Pretérito perfecto simple
oyó
oímos
oyeron

Presente subjuntivo
oiga
oigamos

Imperfecto subjuntivo
oyera o oyese
oyéramos o oyésemos

Imperativo
oye (tú)
oiga (él, ella)
oigamos (nosotros)
oíd (vosotros)

Gerundio
oyendo

[63] placer

Presente indicativo
plazco
place
placemos

Pretérito perfecto simple
plació o plugo
placimos
placieron o pluguieron

Presente subjuntivo
plazca
plazca o plegue
plazcamos

Imperfecto subjuntivo
placiera o placiese
placiera, placiese, pluguiera o
pluguiese
placiéramos o placiésemos

Imperativo
place (tú)
plazca (él, ella)
plazcamos (nosotros)

[64] poder

Presente indicativo
puedo
puede
podemos

Pretérito perfecto simple
pude
pudo
pudimos

Futuro
podré
podrá
podremos

Condicional
podría
podríamos

Presente subjuntivo
pueda
podamos

Imperfecto subjuntivo
pudiera o pudiese
pudiéramos o pudiésemos

Imperativo
puede (tú)
pueda (él, ella)
podamos (nosotros)

Gerundio
pudiendo

[65] poner

Presente indicativo
pongo
pone
ponemos

Pretérito perfecto simple
puse
puso
pusimos

Futuro
pondré
pondrá
pondremos

Condicional
pondría
pondríamos

Presente subjuntivo
ponga
pongamos

Imperfecto subjuntivo
pusiera o pusiese
pusiéramos o pusiésemos

Imperativo
pon (tú)
ponga (él, ella)
pongamos (nosotros)
poned (vosotros)

Participio
puesto, ta

[66] predecir

Presente indicativo
predigo
predice
predecimos

Pretérito perfecto simple
predije
predijo
predijimos

Presente subjuntivo
prediga
predigamos

Imperfecto subjuntivo
predijera o predijese
predijéramos o predijésemos

Imperativo
predice (tú)
prediga (él, ella)
predigamos (nosotros)
predecid (vosotros)

Gerundio
prediciendo

[67] querer

Presente indicativo
quiero
quiere
queremos

Pretérito perfecto simple
quise
quiso
quisimos

Futuro
querré
querrá
querremos

Condicional
querría
querríamos

Presente subjuntivo
quiera
queramos

Imperfecto subjuntivo
quisiera o quisiese
quisiéramos o quisiésemos

Imperativo
quiere (tú)
quiera (él, ella)
queramos (nosotros)

[68] raer

Presente indicativo
rao, raigo o rayo
rae
raemos

Pretérito perfecto simple
rayó
raímos
rayeron

Presente subjuntivo
raiga o raya
raigamos o rayamos

Imperfecto subjuntivo
rayera o rayese
rayéramos o rayésemos

Imperativo
rae (tú)
raiga o raya (él, ella)
raigamos o rayamos
(nosotros)

Gerundio
rayendo

[69] roer

Presente indicativo
roo, roigo o royo
roe
roemos

Pretérito perfecto simple
royó
roímos
royeron

Presente subjuntivo
roa, roiga o roya
roamos, roigamos o royamos

Imperfecto subjuntivo
royera o royese
royéramos o royésemos

Imperativo
roe (tú)
roa, roiga o roya (él, ella)
roamos, roigamos o
royamos (nosotros)

Gerundio
royendo

[70] saber

Presente indicativo
sé
sabe
sabemos

Pretérito perfecto simple
supe
supo
supimos

Futuro
sabré
sabrá
sabremos

Condicional
sabría
sabríamos

Presente subjuntivo
sepas
sepamos

Imperfecto subjuntivo
supiera o supiese
supiéramos o supiésemos

Imperativo
sabe (tú)
sepa (él, ella)
sepamos (nosotros)

[71] salir

Presente indicativo
salgo
sale
salimos

Futuro
saldré
saldrá
saldremos

Condicional
saldría
saldríamos

Presente subjuntivo
salga
salgamos

Imperativo
sal (tú)
salga (él, ella)
salgamos (nosotros)
salid (vosotros)

[72] tener

Presente indicativo
tengo
tiene
tenemos

Pretérito perfecto simple
tuve
tuvo
tuvimos

Futuro
tendré
tendrá
tendremos

Condicional
tendría
tendríamos

Presente subjuntivo
tenga
tengamos

Imperfecto subjuntivo
tuviera o tuviese
tuviéramos o tuviésemos

Imperativo
ten (tú)
tenga (él, ella)
tengamos (nosotros)
tened (vosotros)

[73] traer

Presente indicativo
traigo
trae
traemos

Pretérito perfecto simple
traje
trajo
trajimos

Presente subjuntivo
traiga
traigamos

Imperfecto subjuntivo
trajera o trajese
trajéramos o trajésemos

Imperativo
trae (tú)
traiga (él, ella)
traigamos (nosotros)

Gerundio
trayendo

[74] valer

Presente indicativo
valgo
vale
valemos

Futuro
valdré
valdrá
valdremos

Condicional
valdría
valdríamos

Presente subjuntivo
valga
valgamos

Imperativo
vale (tú)
valga (él, ella)
valgamos (nosotros)

[75] venir

Presente indicativo
vengo
viene
venimos

Pretérito perfecto simple
vine
vino
vinimos

Futuro
vendré
vendrá
vendremos

Condicional
vendría
vendríamos

Presente subjuntivo
venga
vengamos

Imperfecto subjuntivo
viniera o viniese
viniéramos o viniésemos

Imperativo
ven (tú)
venga (él, ella)
vengamos (nosotros)
venid (vosotros)

Gerundio
viniendo

[76] ver

Presente indicativo
veo
ve
vemos

Pretérito perfecto simple
vi
vio
vimos

Imperfecto subjuntivo
viera o viese
viéramos o viésemos

Imperativo
ve (tú)
vea (él, ella)
veamos (nosotros)
ved (vosotros)

Gerundio
viendo

Participio
visto, ta

[77] yacer

Presente indicativo
yazco, yazgo o yago
yace
yacemos

Presente subjuntivo
yazca, yazga o yaga
yazcamos, yazgamos
o yagamos

Imperativo
yace o yaz (tú)
yazca, yazga
o yaga (él, ella)
yazcamos, yazgamos
o yagamos (nosotros)
yaced (vosotros)

Verbos defectivos

[78] abolir

Presente indicativo
(no se conjuga)
(no se conjuga)
(no se conjuga)
abolimos
abolís
(no se conjuga)

Futuro
aboliré
abolirás
abolirá
aboliremos
aboliréis
abolirán

Imperfecto subjuntivo
aboliera o aboliese
abolieras o abolieses
aboliera o aboliese
aboliéramos
o aboliésemos
abolierais o abolieseis
abolieran o aboliesen

Imperfecto indicativo
abolía
abolías
abolía
abolíamos
abolíais
abolían

Condicional
aboliría
abolirías
aboliría
aboliríamos
aboliríais
abolirían

Imperativo
(no se conjuga)
(no se conjuga)
abolid (vosotros)
(no se conjuga)

Pretérito perfecto simple
abolí
aboliste
abolió
abolimos
abolisteis
abolieron

Presente subjuntivo
(no se conjuga en ninguna
de sus personas)

Gerundio
aboliendo

Participio
abolido, da

Nota: verbo defectivo; se conjuga sólo en los tiempos cuya desinencia incluye la 'i'.

[79] balbucir

Presente indicativo
(no se conjuga)
balbuces
balbuce
balbucimos
balbucís
balbucen

Imperfecto indicativo
balbucía
balbucías
balbucía
balbucíamos
balbucíais
balbucían

Pretérito perfecto simple
balbucí
balbuciste
balbució
balbucimos
balbucisteis
balbucieron

Futuro
balbuciré
balbucirás
balbucirá
balbuciremos
balbuciréis
balbucirán

Condicional
balbuciría
balbucirías
balbuciría
balbuciríamos
balbuciríais
balbucirían

Presente subjuntivo
(no se conjuga en ninguna
de sus personas)

Imperfecto subjuntivo
balbuciera o balbuciese
balbucieras o balbucieses
balbuciera o balbuciese
balbuciéramos o
balbuciésemos
balbucierais o
balbucieseis
balbucieran o
balbuciesen

Imperativo
balbuce (tú)
(no se conjuga)
(no se conjuga)
balbucid (vosotros)
(no se conjuga)

Gerundio
balbuciendo

Participio
balbucido, da

Nota: verbo defectivo; las formas que no se conjugan se substituyen por las correspondientes del verbo balbucear.

[80] desolar

Nota: verbo defectivo; se usa solamente en infinitivo y como participio : desolado, da.

[81] soler

Presente indicativo
suelo
sueles
suele
solemos
soléis
suelen

Imperfecto indicativo
solía
solías
solía
solíamos
solíais
solían

Pretérito perfecto simple
solí
soliste
solió
solimos
solisteis
solieron

Futuro
(no se conjuga en ninguna
de sus personas)

Condicional
(no se conjuga en ninguna
de sus personas)

Presente subjuntivo
suela
suelas
suela
solamos
soláis
suelan

Imperfecto subjuntivo
soliera o solie
sesolieras o solieses
soliera o soliese
soliéramos o soliésemos
solierais o solieseis
solieran o soliesen

Gerundio
soliendo

Participio
solido, da

ENGLISH IRREGULAR VERBS

Infinitive	Past Tense	Past Participle
arise	arose	arisen
awake	awoke	awoken
be	was, were	been
bear	bore	born(e)
beat	beat	beaten
become	became	become
befall	befell	befallen
begin	began	begun
behold	beheld	beheld
bend	bent	bent
beseech	besought	besought
beset	beset	beset
bet	bet (also betted)	bet (also betted)
bid	bid (also bade)	bid (also bidden)
bind	bound	bound
bite	bit	bitten
bleed	bled	bled
blow	blew	blown
break	broke	broken
breed	bred	bred
bring	brought	brought
build	built	built
burn	burnt (also burned)	burnt (also burned)
burst	burst	burst
buy	bought	bought
can	could	-
cast	cast	cast
catch	caught	caught
choose	chose	chosen
cling	clung	clung
come	came	come
cost	cost	cost
creep	crept	crept
cut	cut	cut
deal	dealt	dealt
dig	dug	dug
do	did	done
draw	drew	drawn
dream	dreamed (also dreamt)	dreamed (also dreamt)
drink	drank	drunk
drive	drove	driven
dwell	dwelt	dwelt
eat	ate	eaten
fall	fell	fallen
feed	fed	fed
feel	felt	felt

Infinitive	Past Tense	Past Participle
fight	fought	fought
find	found	found
flee	fled	fled
fling	flung	flung
fly	flew	flown
forbid	forbade	forbidden
forecast	forecast	forecast
forego	forewent	foregone
foresee	foresaw	foreseen
foretell	foretold	foretold
forget	forgot	forgotten
forgive	forgave	forgiven
forsake	forsook	forsaken
freeze	froze	frozen
get	got	got (Am gotten)
give	gave	given
go	went	gone
grind	ground	ground
grow	grew	grown
hang	hung (also hanged)	hung (also hanged)
have	had	had
hear	heard	heard
hide	hid	hidden
hit	hit	hit
hold	held	held
hurt	hurt	hurt
keep	kept	kept
kneel	knelt (also kneeled)	knelt (also kneeled)
know	knew	known
lay	laid	laid
lead	led	led
lean	leant (also leaned)	leant (also leaned)
leap	leapt (also leaped)	leapt (also leaped)
learn	learnt (also learned)	learnt (also learned)
leave	left	left
lend	lent	lent
let	let	let
lie	lay	lain
light	lit (also lighted)	lit (also lighted)
lose	lost	lost
make	made	made
may	might	-
mean	meant	meant
meet	met	met
mistake	mistook	mistaken
mow	mowed	mown (also mowed)
pay	paid	paid
put	put	put
quit	quit (also quitted)	quit (also quitted)

Infinitive	Past Tense	Past Participle
read	read	read
rend	rent	rent
rid	rid	rid
ride	rode	ridden
ring	rang	rung
rise	rose	risen
run	ran	run
saw	sawed	sawn
say	said	said
see	saw	seen
seek	sought	sought
sell	sold	sold
send	sent	sent
set	set	set
shake	shook	shaken
shall	should	-
shear	sheared	shorn (also sheared)
shed	shed	shed
shine	shone	shone
shoot	shot	shot
show	showed	shown
shrink	shrank	shrunk
shut	shut	shut
sing	sang	sung
sink	sank	sunk
sit	sat	sat
slay	slew	slain
sleep	slept	slept
slide	slid	slid
sling	slung	slung
slit	slit	slit
smell	smelt (also smelled)	smelt (also smelled)
sow	sowed	sown (also sowed)
speak	spoke	spoken
speed	sped (also speeded)	sped (also speeded)
spell	spelt (also spelled)	spelt (also spelled)
spend	spent	spent
spill	spilt (also spilled)	spilt (also spilled)
spin	spun	spun
spit	spat	spat
split	split	split
spoil	spoiled (also spoilt)	spoiled (also spoilt)
spread	spread	spread
spring	sprang	sprung
stand	stood	stood
steal	stole	stolen
stick	stuck	stuck
sting	stung	stung
stink	stank	stunk

Infinitive	Past Tense	Past Participle
stride	strode	stridden
strike	struck	struck (also stricken)
strive	strove	striven
swear	swore	sworn
sweep	swept	swept
swell	swelled	swollen (also swelled)
swim	swam	swum
swing	swung	swung
take	took	taken
teach	taught	taught
tear	tore	torn
tell	told	told
think	thought	thought
throw	threw	thrown
thrust	thrust	thrust
tread	trod	trodden
wake	woke (also waked)	woken (also waked)
waylay	waylaid	waylaid
wear	wore	worn
weave	wove (also weaved)	woven (also weaved)
wed	wedded	wedded
weep	wept	wept
win	won	won
wind	wound	wound
withdraw	withdrew	withdrawn
withhold	withheld	withheld
withstand	withstood	withstood
wring	wrung	wrung
write	wrote	written

IMPRIMERIE MAURY-EUROLIVRES – 45300 MANCHECOURT
DÉPÔT LÉGAL : FÉVRIER 1994
IMPRIMÉ EN FRANCE *(Printed in France)* – 420402 – JANVIER 1998